# The Form Book ®

# FLAT ANNUAL FOR 2018

## THE OFFICIAL FORM BOOK

### ALL THE 2017 RETURNS

Complete record of Flat Racing
from 1 January to 31 December 2017

## Associated Raceform products

The Form Book is updated weekly. Subscribers receive a binder, together with all the early racing. Weekly sections and a new index are threaded into the binder to keep it up to date.

The data contained in *The Form Book Flat Annual for 2018* is available in paper form or on computer disk. The disk service Raceform Interactive, contains the same data as The Flat Form Book, and operates on any PC within a 'Windows' environment. The database is designed to allow access to the information in a number of different ways, and is extremely quick and easy to use.

Published in 2018 by Raceform Ltd
27 Kingfisher Court, Hambridge Road, Newbury, Berkshire RG14 5SJ



A catalogue record for this book is available from the British Library

ISBN 978-1-910497-56-2

Printed and bound by CPI Group (UK) Ltd, Croydon, CR0 4YY
Full details of all Raceform services and publications are available from:

Raceform Ltd, Sanders Road, Wellingborough, Northants NN8 4BX
Tel: 01933 304858 • Fax: 01933 304796
Email: shop@racingpost.com
www.racingpost.com

*Cover picture*: Wings Of Eagles winning the Derby.

# CONTENTS



Editor: Graham Dench

## • Racereaders

**Cathal Gahan**
**Walter Glynn**
**Keith McHugh**
**Richard Lowther**
**Lee McKenzie**
**Tim Mitchell**
**Jonathan Neesom**
**Darren Owen**
**Steve Payne**
**Colin Roberts**
**Joe Rowntree**
**Andrew Sheret**
**Richard Young**

# The Official Scale of Weight, Age & Distance (Flat)

The following scale should only be used in conjunction with the Official ratings published in this book. Use of any other scale will introduce errors into calculations. The allowances are expressed as the number of pounds that is deemed the average horse in each group falls short of maturity at different dates and distances.

| Dist | | Jan | | Feb | | Mar | | Apr | | May | | Jun | | Jul | | Aug | | Sep | | Oct | | Nov | | Dec | |
|---|---|---|---|---|---|---|---|---|---|---|---|---|---|---|---|---|---|---|---|---|---|---|---|---|---|
| (fur) | Age | 1-15 | 16-31 | 1-14 | 15-28 | 1-15 | 16-31 | 1-15 | 16-30 | 1-15 | 16-31 | 1-15 | 16-30 | 1-15 | 16-31 | 1-15 | 16-31 | 1-15 | 16-30 | 1-15 | 16-31 | 1-15 | 16-30 | 1-15 | 16-31 |
| 5 | 2 | - | - | - | - | - | 47 | 44 | 41 | 38 | 36 | 34 | 32 | 30 | 28 | 26 | 24 | 22 | 20 | 19 | 18 | 17 | 17 | 16 | 16 |
| | 3 | 15 | 15 | 14 | 14 | 13 | 12 | 11 | 10 | 9 | 8 | 7 | 6 | 5 | 4 | 3 | 2 | 1 | 1 | - | - | - | - | - | - |
| 6 | 2 | - | - | - | - | - | - | - | - | 44 | 41 | 38 | 36 | 33 | 31 | 28 | 26 | 24 | 22 | 21 | 20 | 19 | 18 | 17 | 17 |
| | 3 | 16 | 16 | 15 | 15 | 14 | 13 | 12 | 11 | 10 | 9 | 8 | 7 | 6 | 5 | 4 | 3 | 2 | 2 | 1 | 1 | - | - | - | - |
| 7 | 2 | - | - | - | - | - | - | - | - | - | - | - | - | 38 | 35 | 32 | 30 | 27 | 25 | 23 | 22 | 21 | 20 | 19 | 19 |
| | 3 | 18 | 18 | 17 | 17 | 16 | 15 | 14 | 13 | 12 | 11 | 10 | 9 | 8 | 7 | 6 | 5 | 4 | 3 | 2 | 2 | 1 | 1 | - | - |
| 8 | 2 | - | - | - | - | - | - | - | - | - | - | - | - | - | - | 37 | 34 | 31 | 28 | 26 | 24 | 23 | 22 | 21 | 20 |
| | 3 | 20 | 20 | 19 | 19 | 18 | 17 | 15 | 14 | 13 | 12 | 11 | 10 | 9 | 8 | 7 | 6 | 5 | 4 | 3 | 3 | 2 | 2 | 1 | 1 |
| 9 | 3 | 22 | 22 | 21 | 21 | 20 | 19 | 17 | 15 | 14 | 13 | 12 | 11 | 10 | 9 | 8 | 7 | 6 | 5 | 4 | 4 | 3 | 3 | 2 | 2 |
| | 4 | 1 | 1 | - | - | - | - | - | - | - | - | - | - | - | - | - | - | - | - | - | - | - | - | - | - |
| 10 | 3 | 23 | 23 | 22 | 22 | 21 | 20 | 19 | 17 | 15 | 14 | 13 | 12 | 10 | 9 | 8 | 7 | 6 | 5 | 4 | 4 | 3 | 3 | 2 | 2 |
| | 4 | 2 | 2 | 1 | 1 | - | - | - | - | - | - | - | - | - | - | - | - | - | - | - | - | - | - | - | - |
| 11 | 3 | 24 | 24 | 23 | 23 | 22 | 21 | 20 | 19 | 17 | 15 | 14 | 13 | 11 | 10 | 9 | 8 | 7 | 6 | 5 | 5 | 4 | 4 | 3 | 3 |
| 4 | 3 | 3 | 2 | 2 | 1 | 1 | - | - | - | - | - | - | - | - | - | - | - | - | - | - | - | - | - | - | - |
| 12 | 3 | 25 | 25 | 24 | 24 | 23 | 22 | 21 | 20 | 19 | 17 | 15 | 14 | 12 | 11 | 10 | 9 | 8 | 7 | 6 | 6 | 5 | 5 | 4 | 4 |
| | 4 | 4 | 4 | 3 | 3 | 2 | 2 | 1 | 1 | - | - | - | - | - | - | - | - | - | - | - | - | - | - | - | - |
| 13 | 3 | 26 | 26 | 25 | 25 | 24 | 23 | 22 | 21 | 20 | 19 | 17 | 15 | 13 | 11 | 10 | 9 | 8 | 7 | 6 | 6 | 5 | 5 | 4 | 4 |
| | 4 | 5 | 5 | 4 | 4 | 3 | 3 | 2 | 1 | - | - | - | - | - | - | - | - | - | - | - | - | - | - | - | - |
| 14 | 3 | 27 | 27 | 26 | 26 | 25 | 24 | 23 | 22 | 21 | 20 | 18 | 16 | 14 | 12 | 11 | 10 | 9 | 8 | 7 | 7 | 6 | 6 | 5 | 5 |
| | 4 | 6 | 6 | 5 | 5 | 4 | 4 | 3 | 2 | 1 | - | - | - | - | - | - | - | - | - | - | - | - | - | - | - |
| 15 | 3 | 28 | 28 | 27 | 27 | 26 | 25 | 24 | 23 | 22 | 21 | 19 | 17 | 15 | 13 | 12 | 11 | 10 | 8 | 8 | 7 | 6 | 6 | 5 | 5 |
| | 4 | 6 | 6 | 5 | 5 | 4 | 4 | 3 | 3 | 2 | 1 | - | - | - | - | - | - | - | - | - | - | - | - | - | - |
| 16 | 3 | 29 | 29 | 28 | 28 | 27 | 26 | 25 | 24 | 23 | 22 | 21 | 19 | 17 | 15 | 13 | 12 | 11 | 10 | 9 | 8 | 7 | 7 | 6 | 6 |
| | 4 | 7 | 7 | 6 | 6 | 5 | 5 | 4 | 4 | 3 | 2 | 1 | - | - | - | - | - | - | - | - | - | - | - | - | - |
| 18 | 3 | 31 | 31 | 30 | 30 | 29 | 28 | 27 | 26 | 25 | 24 | 23 | 21 | 19 | 17 | 15 | 13 | 12 | 11 | 10 | 9 | 8 | 7 | 6 | 6 |
| | 4 | 8 | 8 | 7 | 7 | 6 | 6 | 5 | 5 | 4 | 3 | 2 | 1 | - | - | - | - | - | - | - | - | - | - | - | - |
| 20 | 3 | 33 | 33 | 32 | 32 | 31 | 30 | 29 | 28 | 27 | 26 | 25 | 23 | 21 | 19 | 17 | 15 | 13 | 12 | 11 | 10 | 9 | 8 | 7 | 7 |
| | 4 | 9 | 9 | 8 | 8 | 7 | 7 | 6 | 6 | 5 | 4 | 3 | 2 | 1 | - | - | - | - | - | - | - | - | - | - | - |

# The Form Book

Welcome to the *The Form Book Flat Annual for 2018,* comprising the complete year's Flat results for 2017.

Race details contain Racing Post Ratings assessing the merit of each individual performance, speed figures for every horse that clocks a worthwhile time, weight-for-age allowances, stall positions for every race and the starting price percentage, in addition to the traditional features.

Race Focus comments are printed below most races, along with the results of stewards' enquiries.

## • The official record

**THE FORM BOOK** records comprehensive race details of every domestic race, every major European Group race and every foreign event in which a British-trained runner participated.

**MEETING BACK REFERENCE NUMBER** is the Raceform number of the last meeting run at the track and is shown to the left of the course name. Abandoned meetings are signified by a dagger.

**THE GOING**, The Official going, shown at the head of each meeting, is recorded as follows: Turf: Hard; Firm; Good to firm; Good; Good to soft; Soft; Heavy. All-Weather: Fast; Standard to fast; Standard; Standard to slow; Slow. There may be variations for non-British meetings

Where appropriate, a note is included indicating track bias and any differences to the official going indicated by race times.

**THE WEATHER** is shown below the date for selected meetings.

**THE WIND** is given as a strength and direction at the Winning Post, classified as follows:
Strength: gale; v.str; str; fresh; mod; slt; almost nil; nil.
Direction: (half) against; (half) bhd; (half) across from or towards stands.

**VISIBILITY** is good unless otherwise stated.

**RACE NUMBERS** for foreign races carry the suffix 'a' in the race header and in the index.

**RACE TITLE** is the name of the race as shown in the Racing Calendar.

**COMPETITIVE RACING CLASSIFICATIONS** are shown on a scale from Class 1 to Class 7. All Pattern races are Class 1.

**THE RACE DISTANCE** is given for all races, and is accompanied by (s) for races run on straight courses and (r) for courses where there is a round track of comparable distance. On All-Weather courses (F) for Fibresand or (P) for Polytrack indicates the nature of the artificial surface on which the race is run.

**OFFICIAL RACE TIME** as published in the Racing Calendar is followed in parentheses by the time when the race actually started. This is followed by the race class, age restrictions, handicap restrictions and the official rating of the top weight.

**PRIZE MONEY** shows penalty values down to sixth place (where applicable).

**THE POSITION OF THE STARTING STALLS** is shown against each race, in the form of: High (H), Centre (C) or Low (L). In keeping with all other major racing nations, stalls are now numbered from the inside rail. If the stalls are placed adjacent to the inside rail they are described as low, if against the outside rail they are described as high. Otherwise they are central.

**IN THE RACE RESULT**, the figures to the far left of each horse (under FORM) show the most recent form figures. The figure in bold is the finishing position in this race as detailed below.

**1...40** - finishing positions first to fortieth; **b** - brought down; **c** - carried out; **f** - fell; **p** - pulled up; **r** - refused; **ro** - ran out; **s** - slipped up; **u** - unseated rider; **v** - void race.

**THE OFFICIAL DISTANCES** between the horses are shown on the left-hand side immediately after their position at the finish.

**NUMBER OF DAYS SINCE PREVIOUS RUN** is the superscript figure immediately following the horse name and suffix.

**PREVIOUS RACEFORM RACE NUMBER** is the boxed figure to the right of the horse's name.

**THE HORSE'S AGE** is shown immediately before the weight carried.

**WEIGHTS** shown are actual weights carried.

**OFFICIAL RATING** is the figure in bold type directly after the horse's name in the race result. This figure indicates the Official BHA rating, at entry, after the following adjustments had been made:
(i) Overweight carried by the rider.
(ii) The number of pounds out of the handicap (if applicable).
(iii) Penalties incurred after the publication of the weights.
However, no adjustments have been made for:
(i) Weight-for-age.
(ii) Riders' claims.

**HEADGEAR** is shown immediately before the jockey's name and in parentheses and expressed as: **b** (blinkers); **v** (visor); **h** (hood); **e** (eyeshield); **c** (eyecover); **p** (sheepskin cheekpieces); **t** (tongue-tie).

**THE JOCKEY** is shown for every runner followed, in superscript, by apprentice allowances in parentheses.

**APPRENTICE ALLOWANCES** The holders of apprentice jockeys' licences under the provisions of Rule 60(iii) are permitted to claim the following allowances in Flat races:
7lb until they have won 20 Flat races run under the Rules of any recognised Turf Authority; thereafter 5lb until they have won 50 such Flat races; thereafter 3lb until they have won 95 such Flat races. These allowances can be claimed in the Flat races set out below, with the exception of races confined to apprentice jockeys:
(a) All handicaps other than those Rated stakes which are classified as listed races.
(b) All selling and claiming races.
(b) All weight-for-age races classified 3, 4, 5, 6 and 7.

**THE DRAW** for places at the start is shown after each jockey's name.

**RACING POST RATINGS**, which record the level of performance attained in this race for each horse, appear in the end column after each horse. These are the work of handicappers Simon Turner, Sam Walker and Paul Curtis, who head a dedicated team dealing with Flat races for Raceform and sister publication, the *Racing Post*.

**THE TRAINER** is shown for every runner.

**COMMENT-IN-RUNNING** is shown for each horse in an abbreviated form. Details of abbreviations appear later in this section.

**STARTING PRICES** appear below the jockey in the race result. The favourite indicator appears to the right of the Starting Price;
1 for the favourite, 2 for the second-favourite and 3 for third-favourite. Joint favourites share the same number.

**RACE TIMES** in Great Britain are official times which are electronically recorded and shown to 100th of a second. Figures in parentheses following the time show the number of seconds faster or slower than the Raceform Median Time for the course and distance.

**RACEFORM MEDIAN TIMES** are compiled from all races run over the course and distance in the preceding five years. Times equal to the median are shown as (0.00). Times under the median are preceded by minus, for instance, 1.8 seconds under the median would be shown (-1.8). Record times are displayed either referring to the juvenile record (2y crse rec) or to the overall record (course record).

**TRACK VARIANT** appears against each race to allow for changing conditions of the track and ground. It is shown to a hundredth of a second and indicates the adjustment per furlong against the median time. The going based on the going correction is shown in parentheses and is recorded in the following stages:
Turf: HD (Hard); F (Firm); GF (Good to firm); G (Good); GS (Good to soft); S (Soft); HVY (Heavy). All-Weather: FST (Fast); SF (Standard to fast); STD (Standard); SS (Standard to slow); SLW (Slow)

**WEIGHT-FOR-AGE** allowances are given where applicable for mixed-age races.

**STARTING PRICE PERCENTAGE** follows the going correction and weight-for-age details, and gives the total SP percentage of all runners that competed. It precedes the number of runners taking part in the race.

**SELLING DETAILS** (where applicable) and details of any claim are given. Friendly claims are not detailed.

**SPEED RATINGS** appear below the race time and going correction. They are the work of time expert Dave Bellingham and differ from conventional ratings systems in that they are an expression of a horse's ability in terms of lengths-per-mile, as opposed to pounds in weight. They are not directly comparable with BHA and Racing Post Ratings.

The ratings take no account of the effect of weight, either historically or on the day, and this component is left completely to the user's discretion. What is shown is a speed rating represented in its purest form, rather than one that has been altered for weight using a mathematical formula that treats all types of horses as if they were the same.

A comparison of the rating achieved with the 'par' figure for the grade of race - the rating that should be achievable by an average winner in that class of race - will both provide an at-a-glance indication of whether or not a race was truly run and also highlight the value of the form from a time perspective.

In theory, if a horse has a best speed figure five points superior to another and both run to their best form in a race over a mile, the first horse should beat the second by five lengths. In a race run over two miles, the margin should be ten lengths and so on.

Before the speed figures can be calculated, it is necessary to establish a set of standard or median times for every distance at every track, and this is done by averaging the times of all winners over a particular trip going back several years. No speed ratings are produced when insufficient races have been run over a distance for a reliable median time to be calculated.

Once a meeting has taken place, a raw unadjusted speed rating is calculated for each winner by calculating how many lengths per mile the winning time was faster or slower than the median for the trip. A difference of 0.2 of a second equals one length. The raw speed ratings of all winners on the card are then compared with the 'par' figure for the class of race. The difference between the 'raw' speed rating and the 'par' figure for each race is then noted, and both the fastest and slowest races are discarded before the rest are averaged to produce the going allowance or track variant. This figure gives an idea as to how much the elements, of which the going is one, have affected the final times of each race.

The figure representing the going allowance is then used to adjust the raw speed figures and produce the final ratings, which represent how fast the winners would have run on a perfectly good surface with no external influences, including the weather. The ratings for beaten horses are worked out by taking the number of lengths they were behind the winner, adjusting that to take into account the distance of the race, and deducting that figure from the winner's rating. The reader is left with a rating which provides an instant impression of the value of a time performance.

The speed 'pars' below act as benchmark with which to compare the speed figures earned by each horse in each race. A horse that has already exceeded the 'par' for the class he is about to run in is of special interest, especially if he has done it more than once, as are horses that have consistently earned higher figures than their rivals.

| | | |
|---|---|---|
| Class 1 Group One | | 117 |
| Class 1 Group Two | | 115 |
| Class 1 Group Three | 113 | |
| Class 1 Listed | 111 | |
| Class 2 | 109 | |
| Class 3 | 107 | |
| Class 4 | 105 | |
| Class 5 | 103 | |
| Class 6 | 101 | |
| Class 7 | 99 | |

Allowances need to be made for younger horses and for fillies. These allowances are as follows.

| MONTH | 2yo | 3yo |
|---|---|---|
| Jan / Feb | n/a | -6 |
| Mar / Apr | -11 | -5 |
| May / Jun | -10 | -4 |
| Jul / Aug | -9 | -3 |
| Sep / Oct | -8 | -2 |
| Nov / Dec | -7 | -1 |
| Races contested by fillies only | | -3 |

Allowances are cumulative. For example, using a combination of the above pars and allowances, the par figure for the Epsom Oaks would be 110. The Group One par is 117, then deduct 4 because the race is confined to three year olds and run in June, then subtract another 3 because the race is confined to fillies.

**TOTE** prices include £1 stake. Exacta dividends are shown in parentheses. The Computer Straight Forecast dividend is preceded by the letters CSF, Computer Tricast is preceded by CT and Trifecta dividend is preceded by the word Trifecta. Jackpot, Placepot and Quadpot details appear at the end of the meeting to which they refer.

**OWNER** is followed by the breeder's name and the trainer's location.

**STEWARDS' ENQUIRIES** are included with the result, and any suspensions and/or fines incurred. Objections by jockeys and officials are included, where relevant.

**HISTORICAL FOCUS** details occasional points of historical significance.

**FOCUS** The Focus section helps readers distinguish good races from bad races and reliable form from unreliable form, by drawing together the opinions of handicapper, time expert and paddock watcher and interpreting their views in a punter-friendly manner.

# Abbreviations and their meanings

## *Paddock comments*

gd sort - well made, above average on looks
attr - attractive, but not as impressive as good sort
gd bodied - good bodied, well put together
h.d.w - has done well, improved in looks
wl grwn - well grown, has filled to its frame
lengthy - longer than average for its height
tall - tall
rangy - lengthy and tall but in proportion.
cl cpld - close coupled
scope - scope for physical development
str - strong, powerful looking
w'like - workmanlike, ordinary in looks
lt-f - light-framed, not much substance
cmpt - compact
neat - smallish, well put together
leggy - long legs compared with body
angular - unfurnished behind the saddle, not filled to frame
unf - unfurnished in the midriff, not filled to frame
narrow - not as wide as side appearance would suggest
small - lacks any physical scope
nt grwn - not grown
lw - looked fit and well
bkwd - backward in condition
t - tubed
swtg - sweating
b (off fore or nr fore) - bandaged in front
b.hind (off or nr) - bandaged behind

## *At the start*

stdd s - jockey purposely reins back the horse
dwlt - missed the break and left for a short time
s.s - slow to start, left longer than a horse that dwelt
s.v.s - started very slowly
s.i.s - started on terms but took time to get going
ref to r - does not jump off, or travels a few yards then stops
rel to r - tries to pull itself up in mid-race
w.r.s - whipped round start

## *Position in the race*

led - in lead on its own
disp ld - upsides the leader
w ldr - almost upsides the leader

w ldrs - in a line of three or more disputing the lead
prom - on the heels of the leaders, in front third of the field
trckd ldr(s) - just in behind the leaders giving impression that it could lead if asked
chsd ldr - horse in second place
chsd clr ldrs - horse heads main body of field behind two clear leaders
chsd ldrs - horse is in the first four or five but making more of an effort to stay close to the pace than if it were tracking the leaders.
clsd - closed
in tch - close enough to have a chance
hdwy - making ground on the leader
gd hdwy - making ground quickly on the leader, could be a deliberate move
sme hdwy - making some ground but no real impact on the race
w.w - waited with
stdy hdwy - gradually making ground
ev ch - upsides the leaders when the race starts in earnest
rr - at the back of main group but not detached
bhd - detached from the main body of runners
hld up - restrained as a deliberate tactical move
nt rcvr - lost all chance after interference, mistake etc.
wknd - stride shortened as it began to tire
lost tch - had been in the main body but a gap appeared as it tired
lost pl - remains in main body of runners but lost several positions quickly

## Riding

effrt - short-lived effort
pushed along - received urgings with hands only, jockey not using legs
rdn - received urgings from saddle, including use of whip
hrd rdn - received maximum assistance from the saddle including use of whip
drvn - received forceful urgings, jockey putting in a lot of effort and using whip
hrd drvn - jockey very animated, plenty of kicking, pushing and reminders

## Finishing comments

jst failed - closing rapidly on the winner and probably would have led a stride after the line
r.o - jockey's efforts usually involved to produce an increase in pace without finding an appreciable turn of speed
r.o wl - jockey's efforts usually involved to produce an obvious increase in pace without finding an appreciable turn of speed
unable qckn - not visibly tiring but does not possess a sufficient change of pace
one pce - not tiring but does not find a turn of speed, from a position further out than unable qckn
nt r.o. - did not consent to respond to pressure
styd on - going on well towards the end, utilising stamina
nvr able to chal - unable to produce sufficient to reach a challenging position
nvr nr to chal - in the opinion of the racereader, the horse was never in a suitable position to challenge.
nrst fin - nearer to the winner in distance beaten than at any time since the race had begun in earnest
nvr nrr - nearer to the winner position-wise than at any time since the race had begun in earnest
rallied - responded to pressure to come back with a chance having lost its place
no ex - unable to sustain its run
bttr for r - likely to improve for the run and experience
rn green - inclined to wander and falter through inexperience
too much to do - left with too much leeway to make up

## Winning comments

v.easily - a great deal in hand
easily - plenty in hand
comf - something in hand, always holding the others
pushed out - kept up to its work with hands and heels without jockey resorting to whip or kicking along and wins fairly comfortably
rdn out - pushed and kicked out to the line, with the whip employed
drvn out - pushed and kicked out to the line, with considerable effort and the whip employed
all out - nothing to spare, could not have found any more
jst hld on - holding on to a rapidly diminishing lead, could not have found any more if passed
unchal - must either make all or a majority of the running and not be challenged from an early stage

# • Complete list of abbreviations

a - always
abt - about
a.p - always prominent
appr - approaching
awrdd - awarded
b.b.v - broke blood-vessel
b.d - brought down
bdly - badly
bef - before
bhd - behind
bk - back
blkd - baulked
blnd - blundered
bmpd - bumped
bnd - bend
btn- beaten
bttr - better
c - came
ch - chance
chal - challenged
chse - chase
chsd - chased
chsng - chasing
circ - circuit
cl - close
clr - clear
clsd - closed
comf - comfortably
cpld - coupled
crse - course
ct - caught
def - definite
dismntd - dismounted
disp - disputed
dist - distance
div - division
drvn - driven
dwlt - dwelt
edgd - edged
effrt - effort

ent - entering
ev ch - every chance
ex - extra
f - furlong
fin - finished
fnd - found
fnl - final
fr - from
gd - good
gng - going
gp - group
grad - gradually
grnd - ground
hd - head
hdd - headed
hdwy - headway
hld - held
hmpd - hampered
imp - impression
ins - inside
j.b - jumped badly
j.w - jumped well
jnd - joined
jst - just
kpt - kept
l - length
ld - lead
ldr - leader
lft - left
mod - moderate
m - mile
m.n.s - made no show
mde - made
mid div - mid division
mstke - mistake
n.d - never dangerous
n.g.t - not go through
n.m.r - not much room
nk - neck
no ex - no extra
nr - near
nrr - nearer
nrst fin - nearest finish
nt - not
nvr - never
one pce - one pace
out - from finish
outpcd - outpaced
p.u - pulled up
pce - pace
pckd - pecked
pl - place
plcd - placed
plld - pulled
press - pressure
prog - progress
prom - prominent
qckly - quickly
qckn - quicken
r - race
racd - raced
rch - reach
rcvr - recover
rdn - ridden
rdr - rider
reard - reared
ref - refused
rn - ran
rnd - round
r.o - ran on
rr - rear
rspnse - response
rt - right
s - start
sddle - saddle
shkn - shaken
slt - slight
sme - some
sn - soon
spd- speed
st - straight
stmbld - stumbled
stdd - steadied
stdy - steady
strly - strongly
styd - stayed
styng - staying
s. u - slipped up
swtchd - switched
swvd - swerved
tk - took
t.k.h - took keen hold
t.o - tailed off
tch - touch
thrght - throughout
trbld - troubled
trckd - tracked
u.p - under pressure
u.str.p- under strong pressure
w - with
w.r.s - whipped round start
wd - wide
whn - when
wknd - weakened
wl - well
wnr - winner
wnt - went
1/2-wy - halfway

# Racing Post Ratings

**Racing Post Ratings for each horse are shown in the right hand column, headed RPR, and indicate the actual level of performance attained in that race. The figure in the back index represents the BEST public form that Raceform's Handicappers still believe the horse capable of reproducing.**

To use the ratings constructively in determining those horses best-in in future events, the following procedure should be followed:

(i) In races where all runners are the same age and are set to carry the same weight, no calculations are necessary. The horse with the highest rating is best-in.

(ii) In races where all runners are the same age but are set to carry different weights, add one point to the Racing Post Rating for every pound less than 10 stone to be carried; deduct one point for every pound more than 10 stone.

For example,

| Horse | Age & wt | Adjustment from 10st | Base rating | Adjusted rating |
|---|---|---|---|---|
| Treclare | 3-10-1 | -1 | 78 | 77 |
| Buchan | 3-9-13 | +1 | 80 | 81 |
| Paper Money | 3-9-7 | +7 | 71 | 78 |
| Archaic | 3-8-11 | +17 | 60 | 77 |

**Therefore Buchan is top-rated (best-in)**

(iii) In races concerning horses of different ages the procedure in (ii) should again be followed, but reference must also be made to the Official Scale of Weight-For-Age.

For example,

12 furlongs, July 20th

| Horse | Age & wt | Adjustment from 10st | Base rating | Adjusted rating | W-F-A deduct | Final rating |
|---|---|---|---|---|---|---|
| Archaic | 5-10-0 | 0 | 90 | 90 | Nil | 90 |
| Orpheus | 4-9-9 | +5 | 88 | 93 | Nil | 93 |
| Lemonora | 3-9-4 | +10 | 85 | 95 | -12 | 83 |
| Tamar | 4-8-7 | +21 | 73 | 94 | Nil | 94 |

**Therefore Tamar is top-rated (best-in)**

(A 3-y-o is deemed 12lb less mature than a 4-y-o or older horse on 20th July over 12f. Therefore, the deduction of 12 points is necessary.)

The following symbols are used in conjunction with the ratings:

++: almost certain to prove better

+: likely to prove better

d: disappointing (has run well below best recently)

?: form hard to evaluate

t: tentative rating based on race-time rating may prove unreliable

**Weight adjusted ratings for every race are published daily in Raceform Private Handicap.**

**For subscription terms please contact the Subscription Department on 01933 304858.**

# Course descriptions

**(R.H.) denotes right-hand and (L.H.) left-hand courses.**

**ASCOT (R.H)**

Right-handed triangular track just under 1m 6f in length. The Round course descends from the 1m 4f start into Swinley Bottom, the lowest part of the track. It then turns right-handed and joins the Old Mile Course, which starts on a separate chute. The course then rises to the right-handed home turn over a new underpass to join the straight mile course. The run-in is about 3f, rising slightly to the winning post. The whole course is of a galloping nature with easy turns.

**AYR (L.H)**

A left-handed, galloping, flat oval track of 1m 4f with a 4f run-in. The straight 6f is essentially flat.

**BATH (L.H)**

Galloping, left-handed, level oval of 1m 4f 25y, with long, stiff run-in of about 4f which bends to the left. An extended chute provides for races over 5f 11y and 5f 161y.

**BEVERLEY (R.H)**

A right-handed oval of 1m 3f, generally galloping, with an uphill run-in of two and a half furlongs. The 5f course is very stiff.

**BRIGHTON (L.H)**

Left-handed, 1m 4f horseshoe with easy turns and a run-in of three and a half furlongs. Undulating and sharp, the track suits handy types.

**CARLISLE (R.H)**

Right-handed, 1m 4f pear-shaped track. Galloping and undulating with easy turns and a stiff uphill run-in of three and a half furlongs. 6f course begins on an extended chute.

**CATTERICK (L.H)**

A sharp, left-handed, undulating oval of 1m 180y with a downhill run-in of 3f.

**CHEPSTOW (L.H)**

A left-handed, undulating oval of about 2m, with easy turns, and a straight run-in of 5f. There is a straight track of 1m 14y.

**CHESTER (L.H)**

A level, sharp, left-handed, circular course of 1m 73y, with a short run-in of 230y. Chester is a specialists' track which generally suits the sharp-actioned horse.

**DONCASTER (L.H)**

A left-handed, flat, galloping course of 1m 7f 110y, with a long run-in which extends to a straight mile.

**EPSOM (L.H)**

Left-handed and undulating with easy turns, and a run-in of just under 4f. The straight 5f course is also undulating and downhill all the way, making it the fastest 5f in the world.

**FFOS LAS (L.H)**

The track is a 60m wide, basically flat, 1m4f oval with sweeping bends.

**GOODWOOD (R.H)**

A sharp, undulating, essentially right-handed track with a long run-in. There is also a straight 6f course.

**HAMILTON PARK (R.H)**

Sharp, undulating, right-handed course of 1m 5f with a five and a half furlong, uphill run-in. There is a straight track of 6f.

**HAYDOCK PARK (L.H)**

A galloping, almost flat, oval track, 1m 5f round, with a run-in of four and a half furlongs and a straight 6f course.

**KEMPTON PARK (R.H)**

A floodlit Polytrack circuit opened in March 2006. A 1m 2f outer track accommodates races over 6f, 7f, 1m, 1m 3f, 1m 4f and 2m. The 1m inner track caters for races over 5f and 1m 2f.

**LEICESTER (R.H)**

Stiff, galloping, right-handed oval of 1m 5f, with a 5f run-in. There is a straight course of 7f.

**LINGFIELD PARK (L.H)**

**Turf Course**: A sharp, undulating left-handed circuit, with a 7f 140y straight course.

**Polytrack course**: left-handed all-weather is 1m 2f round. It is a sharp, level track with a short run-in.

**MUSSELBURGH (R.H)**

A sharp, level, right-handed oval of 1m 2f, with a run-in of 4f. There is an additional 5f straight course.

**NEWBURY (L.H)**

Left-handed, oval track of about 1m 7f, with a slightly undulating straight mile. The round course is level and galloping with a four and a half furlong run-in. Races over the round mile and 7f 60y start on the adjoining chute.

**NEWCASTLE (L.H)**

Galloping, easy, left-handed oval of 1m 6f, with an uphill 4f run-in. There is a straight course of 1m 8y.

**NEWMARKET (R.H)**

**Rowley Mile Course**: There is a straight 1m2f course, which is wide and galloping. Races over 1m4f or more are right-handed. The Rowley course has a long run-in and a stiff finish.

**July Course**: Races up to a mile are run on the Bunbury course, which is straight. Races over 1m2f or more are right-handed, with a 7f run-in. Like the Rowley course, the July track is stiff.

**NOTTINGHAM (L.H)**

Left-handed, galloping, oval of about 1m 4f, and a run-in of four and a half furlongs. Flat with easy turns.

**PONTEFRACT (L.H)**

Left-handed oval, undulating course of 2m 133y, with a short run-in of 2f. It is a particularly stiff track with the last 3f uphill.

**REDCAR (L.H)**

Left-handed, level, galloping, oval course of 1m 6f with a straight run-in of 5f. There is also a straight 1m.

**RIPON (R.H)**

A sharp, undulating, right-handed oval of 1m 5f, with a 5f run-in. There is also a 6f straight course.

**SALISBURY (R.H)**

Right-handed and level, with a run-in of 4f. There is a straight 1m track. The last half mile is uphill, providing a stiff test of stamina.

**SANDOWN PARK (R.H)**

An easy right-handed oval course of 1m 5f with a stiff straight uphill run-in of 4f. Separate straight 5f track is also uphill. Galloping.

**SOUTHWELL (L.H)**

Left-handed oval, Fibresand course of 1m 2f with a 3f run-in. There is a straight 5f. Sharp and level, Southwell suits front-runners.

**THIRSK (L.H)**

Left-handed, oval of 1m 2f with sharp turns and an undulating run-in of 4f. There is a straight 6f track.

**WARWICK (L.H)**

Left-handed, sharp, level track of 1m 6f 32y in circumference, with a run-in of two and a half furlongs. There is also a 6f chute.

**WETHERBY (L.H)**

Left-handed, galloping track. Circuit 1m4f. 4f straight, slightly uphill.

**WINDSOR (Fig. 8)**

Figure eight track of 1m 4f 110y. The course is level and sharp with a long run-in. The 6f course is essentially straight.

**WOLVERHAMPTON (L.H)**

Left-handed oval, Tapeta course of 1m, with a run-in of 380y. A level track with sharp bends.

**YARMOUTH (L.H)**

Left-handed, level circuit of 1m 4f, with a run-in of 5f. The straight course is 1m long.

**YORK (L.H)**

Left-handed, level, galloping track, with a straight 6f. There is also an adjoining chute of 7f.

# SOUTHWELL (L-H)

Sunday, January 1

**OFFICIAL GOING: Fibresand: standard**

Wind: Moderate across Weather: Heavy cloud and rain

## 1 BETWAY MEDIAN AUCTION MAIDEN STKS 4f 214y(F)

**12:05** (12:05) (Class 6) 3-5-Y-O **£2,587** (£770; £384; £192) **Stalls** Centre

Form RPR

1 **Zandradee (IRE)** 3-8-8 0 AndrewMullen 5 61+
(David Barron) *dwlt: sn trcking ldrs: pushed along and hdwy 2f out: cl up and rdn over 1f out: led ins fnl f: styd on* **5/2**[2]

344- 2 ¾ **Heavenly Cry**[10] 8494 3-8-13 62 (v) JosephineGordon 2 60
(Phil McEntee) *cl up: effrt 2f out: rdn and ev ch ent fnl f: sn drvn and kpt on same pce* **9/2**[3]

/03- 3 1 ¼ **Private Donald**[12] 8472 4-9-11 59 (p) EoinWalsh(3) 6 62
(Robert Cowell) *t.k.h: cl up: led wl over 1f out: sn rdn: drvn and hdd ins fnl f: kpt on same pce* **6/1**

666- 4 nse **Cool Echo**[69] 7576 3-8-8 69 ConnorBeasley 1 50
(J R Jenkins) *chsd ldrs: rdn along and outpcd 1/2-way: hdwy wl over 1f out: kpt on fnl f* **2/1**[1]

00- 5 1 ½ **Defining Moment**[27] 8229 3-8-3 0 HollieDoyle(5) 8 45
(Rae Guest) *racd nr stands side: chsd ldrs: hdwy and cl up over 2f out: sn rdn: drvn appr fnl f: sn one pce* **8/1**

536- 6 6 **Allen's Folly**[228] 2372 4-9-9 48 LiamKeniry 4 29
(Peter Hiatt) *slt ld: pushed along 1/2-way: rdn and hdd wl over 1f out: sn drvn and grad wknd* **25/1**

7 shd **Frank's Legacy** 3-8-10 0 HectorCrouch(3) 7 28
(Ivan Furtado) *dwlt: a rr* **25/1**

00- 8 4 ½ **Garboesque (IRE)**[45] 7988 3-8-8 0 TomMarquand 3 7
(Shaun Harris) *sn rdn along in rr: sn outpcd and a bhd* **100/1**

59.72s (0.02) **Going Correction** +0.025s/f (Slow)
**WFA** 3 from 4yo 15lb 8 Ran SP% **114.2**
Speed ratings (Par 101): **100,98,96,96,94 84,84,77**
CSF £13.93 TOTE £3.20: £1.20, £1.80, £2.10; EX 12.20 Trifecta £49.90.
**Owner** Harrowgate Bloodstock Ltd **Bred** Mrs S C Barron **Trained** Maunby, N Yorks

**FOCUS**
A moderate maiden, but the winner has some potential. The second and third dictate the opening level.

## 2 32RED.COM H'CAP 6f 16y(F)

**12:35** (12:35) (Class 5) (0-70,70) 3-Y-O **£3,234** (£962; £481; £240) **Stalls** Low

Form RPR

532- 1 **Scotch Myst**[19] 8344 3-8-7 56 BarryMcHugh 5 59
(Richard Fahey) *cl up: rdn to ld wl over 1f out: drvn ins fnl f: kpt on wl towards fin* **9/4**[2]

032- 2 ¾ **Things Happen**[25] 8244 3-9-7 70 (v[1]) JFEgan 1 70
(David Evans) *dwlt and sn pushed along to trck ldng pair: rdn along 1/2-way: hdwy u.p on inner wl over 1f out: drvn to chal ins fnl f: ev ch tl no ex last 75 yds* **6/4**[1]

152- 3 3 ¼ **Pulsating (IRE)**[27] 8230 3-9-4 67 LiamKeniry 2 57
(Ali Stronge) *slt ld: pushed along 3f out: rdn over 2f out: hdd wl over 1f out: sn drvn and kpt on same pce* **4/1**[3]

340- 4 3 **Jet Setter (IRE)**[32] 8159 3-9-5 68 (b[1]) NickyMackay 3 48
(Brian Meehan) *trckd ldrs: pushed along 1/2-way: rdn over 2f out: sn wknd* **9/2**

1m 15.96s (-0.54) **Going Correction** -0.20s/f (Stan) 4 Ran SP% **109.0**
Speed ratings (Par 97): **95,94,89,85**
CSF £6.06 TOTE £3.40; EX 6.10 Trifecta £10.00.
**Owner** Mrs Camille Macdonald **Bred** New Hall Stud **Trained** Musley Bank, N Yorks

**FOCUS**
A modest sprint.

## 3 BETWAY BEST ODDS GUARANTEED PLUS CLAIMING STKS 1m 4f 14y(F)

**1:10** (1:10) (Class 6) 4-Y-O+ **£2,587** (£770; £384; £192) **Stalls** Low

Form RPR

321- 1 **Tatting**[19] 8348 8-9-1 76 ShaneKelly 7 83
(Lawrence Mullaney) *hld up in tch: hdwy 4f out: pushed along briefly 3f out: cl up on bridle 2f out: shkn up to ld jst ins fnl f: sn clr: eased nr fin* **6/4**[1]

012- 2 1 **Brigadoon**[19] 8348 10-8-13 72 RobertWinston 6 73
(Michael Appleby) *trckd ldrs: hdwy and cl up 4f out: chal wl over 2f out: rdn and slt advantage 11/2f out: sn drvn: hdd jst ins fnl f: kpt on* **8/1**

500- 3 nk **Luv U Whatever**[15] 8424 7-9-11 88 (v[1]) AndrewMullen 4 85
(Michael Attwater) *trckd ldng pair: hdwy and cl up 4f out: led over 3f out: rdn over 2f out: drvn and hdd 11/2f out: kpt on same pce* **11/2**[3]

510/ 4 2 ¼ **Entihaa**[386] 8210 9-8-10 90 HollieDoyle(5) 1 71
(Dai Burchell) *hld up in tch: hdwy over 3f out: chsd ldrs over 2f out: sn rdn and no imp appr fnl f* **16/1**

463- 5 11 **Obboorr**[85] 7139 8-9-5 74 (b[1]) TomEaves 5 58
(James Given) *dwlt and rr: in tch after 3f: trckd ;ldrs on outer 4f out: pushed along 3f out: rdn over 2f out: sn drvn and btn* **4/1**[2]

113- 6 4 ½ **An Fear Ciuin (IRE)**[78] 7357 6-8-8 80 (p) CallumRodriguez(7) 2 47
(Richard Ford) *led: pushed along 5f out: rdn along and hdd over 4f out: sn wknd* **13/2**

032- 7 ¾ **Edgar (GER)**[160] 1043 7-9-2 68 (p) RobHornby(3) 3 49
(David Bridgwater) *trckd ldr: cl up 6f out: slt ld over 4f out: rdn along and hdd over 3f out: sn drvn and wknd* **22/1**

2m 37.77s (-3.23) **Going Correction** -0.20s/f (Stan) 7 Ran SP% **110.1**
Speed ratings (Par 101): **102,101,101,99,92 89,88**
CSF £13.18 TOTE £2.10: £1.30, £3.90; EX 11.20 Trifecta £29.20.
**Owner** The Usual Suspects **Bred** Darley **Trained** Great Habton, N Yorks

**FOCUS**
This was a fair claimer. The runner-up helps pin the opening level.

## 4 BETWAY BEST ODDS GUARANTEED PLUS H'CAP 4f 214y(F)

**1:45** (1:46) (Class 3) (0-90,90) 4-Y-O+

**£9,337** (£2,796; £1,398; £699; £349; £175) **Stalls** Centre

Form RPR

034- 1 **Razin' Hell**[22] 8308 6-9-0 83 (v) AndrewMullen 11 91
(John Balding) *mde all: rdn wl over 1f out: drvn ins fnl f: hld on gamely* **12/1**

000- 2 ½ **Meadway**[22] 8308 6-9-7 90 (p) ConnorBeasley 9 96
(Bryan Smart) *trckd wnr: cl up 1/2-way: rdn wl over 1f out: drvn and ev ch ins fnl f: edgd lft and no ex towards fin* **8/1**[3]

405- 3 nse **Mappin Time (IRE)**[22] 8308 9-9-0 83 (be) JasonHart 4 89
(Tim Easterby) *sn rdn along towards rr: hmpd and squeezed out after 150 yds: sn bhd and swtchd rt towards stands side: hdwy 2f out: drvn over 1f out: fin strly* **8/1**[3]

560- 4 nk **Guishan**[30] 8192 7-9-5 88 RobertWinston 8 93
(Michael Appleby) *chsd ldrs: hdwy 2f out and sn rdn: drvn ent fnl f: kpt on same pce towards fin* **25/1**

601- 5 ¾ **Bring On A Spinner**[19] 8345 4-8-4 76 oh2 (be) AaronJones(3) 5 78
(Stuart Williams) *towards rr: rdn along 1/2-way: hdwy 2f out: swtchd lft and drvn over 1f out: kpt on fnl f* **11/4**[1]

003- 6 nk **Crosse Fire**[3] 8571 5-8-7 76 oh4 KieranO'Neill 6 77
(Scott Dixon) *midfield: pushed along 1/2-way: rdn 2f out: kpt on u.p fnl f* **12/1**

212- 7 ½ **Showdaisy**[22] 8308 4-9-0 88 (p) ShirleyTeasdale(5) 10 87
(Keith Dalgleish) *chsd ldrs: hdwy 2f out: rdn over 1f out: drvn and kpt on same pce fnl f* **6/1**[2]

414- 8 1 ¼ **Landing Night (IRE)**[16] 8403 5-8-10 79 (tp) PJMcDonald 3 74
(Rebecca Menzies) *dwlt and towards rr: hdwy towards far side 2f out: rdn to chse ldrs over 1f out: drvn and no imp fnl f* **8/1**[3]

050- 9 1 ¼ **Highland Acclaim (IRE)**[22] 8314 6-9-4 87 LiamKeniry 1 77
(David O'Meara) *chsd ldrs towards far side: rdn along over 2f out: sn wknd* **8/1**[3]

006- 10 ¾ **Normal Equilibrium**[12] 8463 7-8-11 80 RichardKingscote 7 68
(Robert Cowell) *racd towards far side: cl up: rdn over 2f out: sn wknd* **20/1**

001- 11 1 ½ **Oriental Relation (IRE)**[22] 8314 6-9-0 83 (v) TomEaves 12 65
(James Given) *racd towards stands side: chsd ldrs: rdn along 2f out: sn wknd* **20/1**

300- 12 1 ¼ **Borough Boy (IRE)**[75] 7443 7-8-4 76 (v) NoelGarbutt(3) 2 54
(Derek Shaw) *dwlt: a towards rr* **33/1**

58.92s (-0.78) **Going Correction** +0.025s/f (Slow) 12 Ran SP% **117.1**
Speed ratings (Par 107): **107,106,106,105,104 103,103,101,99,97 95,93**
CSF £97.90 CT £834.73 TOTE £16.20: £4.40, £2.10, £2.90; EX 175.80 Trifecta £1340.40.
**Owner** Timms, Timms & McCabe **Bred** Alan J McCabe **Trained** Scrooby, S Yorks

**FOCUS**
A competitive sprint on paper, but few actually got into it.

## 5 SUNBETS.CO.UK TOP PRICE ON ALL FAVOURITES H'CAP 7f 14y(F)

**2:20** (2:20) (Class 3) (0-95,91) 4-Y-O+

**£9,337** (£2,796; £1,398; £699; £349; £175) **Stalls** Low

Form RPR

211- 1 **Holiday Magic (IRE)**[13] 8455 6-8-13 86 NathanEvans(3) 11 102+
(Michael Easterby) *cl up: led 4f out: rdn clr wl over 1f out: kpt on strly: readily* **11/4**[1]

250- 2 3 ¼ **Boots And Spurs**[12] 8475 8-8-7 77 (v) KieranO'Neill 10 82
(Scott Dixon) *chsd ldrs: rdn along and hdwy wl over 2f out: drvn over 1f out: kpt on* **16/1**

002- 3 shd **Philba**[12] 8475 5-9-4 91 (tp) AlistairRawlinson(3) 3 96
(Michael Appleby) *cl up on inner: effrt over 2f out: sn rdn: drvn over 1f out: kpt on same pce fnl f* **9/2**[3]

160- 4 ¾ **Young John (IRE)**[12] 8475 4-9-1 85 TonyHamilton 7 88
(Richard Fahey) *slt ld: hdd after 3f: cl up: rdn along wl over 2f out: drvn wl over 1f out: kpt on same pce* **14/1**

013- 5 1 ¾ **Captain Revelation**[12] 8475 5-8-13 83 RichardKingscote 9 81
(Tom Dascombe) *trckd ldrs: hdwy over 2f out and sn rdn: drvn over 1f out: sn no imp* **3/1**[2]

400- 6 2 ¾ **Showboating (IRE)**[12] 8475 9-8-12 82 (p) ShaneGray 1 73
(John Balding) *dwlt and rr: sme hdwy over 2f out: sn rdn and nvr nr ldrs* **25/1**

604- 7 1 ½ **Zaeem**[12] 8475 8-8-9 82 (p) HectorCrouch(3) 2 69
(Ivan Furtado) *trckd ldrs: hdwy on inner 3f out: rdn over 2f out: drvn wl over 1f out and sn wknd* **14/1**

101- 8 1 **Al Khan (IRE)**[17] 8385 8-8-13 90 LewisEdmunds(7) 4 74
(Kevin Ryan) *hld up in tch: effrt wl over 2f out: sn rdn along and n.d* **8/1**

005- 9 5 **Lexington Times (IRE)**[17] 8385 5-8-11 81 JamesSullivan 5 52
(Ruth Carr) *dwlt: a rr* **12/1**

002- 10 1 **Shyron**[25] 8256 6-9-7 91 RyanPowell 6 59
(George Margarson) *dwlt: a rr* **12/1**

1m 26.48s (-3.82) **Going Correction** -0.20s/f (Stan) 10 Ran SP% **119.4**
Speed ratings (Par 107): **113,109,109,108,106 103,101,100,94,93**
CSF £49.45 CT £201.69 TOTE £3.40: £2.00, £5.10, £1.30; EX 57.40 Trifecta £535.10.
**Owner** A Saha **Bred** Mrs Ann Fortune **Trained** Sheriff Hutton, N Yorks

**FOCUS**
A pretty decent handicap and a good performance from the winner, who is currently on a roll.

## 6 SUNBETS.CO.UK H'CAP 1m 13y(F)

**2:55** (2:55) (Class 5) (0-75,75) 4-Y-O+ **£3,234** (£962; £481; £240) **Stalls** Low

Form RPR

003- 1 **House Of Commons (IRE)**[20] 8343 4-9-5 73 AndrewMullen 8 84
(Michael Appleby) *trckd ldng pair: hdwy 3f out: sn chsng ldr: rdn to ld 11/2f out: drvn ins fnl f: kpt on wl* **2/1**[1]

601- 2 2 ½ **Anton Chigurh**[26] 8240 8-9-6 74 RichardKingscote 11 79
(Tom Dascombe) *hld up: hdwy 3f out: chsd ldrs 2f out: sn rdn: kpt on wl u.p fnl f* **3/1**[2]

102- 3 1 **Pivotman**[37] 8100 9-9-2 73 (bt) NathanEvans(3) 10 76
(Michael Easterby) *cl up: led over 3f out: rdn over 2f out: hdd and drvn 11/2f out: kpt on same pce* **11/2**[3]

610- 4 1 **Stun Gun**[26] 8240 7-9-0 68 (v) TonyHamilton 1 68
(Derek Shaw) *towards rr: hdwy wl over 2f out: rdn wl over 1f out: kpt on appr fnl f: nrst fin* **20/1**

250- 5 4 ½ **So It's War (FR)**[44] 8011 6-9-3 71 (p) ConnorBeasley 5 61
(Keith Dalgleish) *in tch: hdwy 3f out: rdn to chse ldng pair 2f out: sn drvn and one pce* **14/1**

402- 6 11 **Gatillo**[26] 8240 4-9-2 70 TomEaves 4 35
(Philip McBride) *in tch: hdwy over 3f out: rdn along wl over 2f out: sn drvn and wknd* **9/1**

204- 7 nk **Greyfriarschorista**[13] 8455 10-9-5 73 JFEgan 13 37
(David Evans) *chsd ldrs: rdn along and outpcd over 3f out:* **11/1**

340- 8 shd **Gabrial The Terror (IRE)**[14] 8447 7-9-3 71 (p) StevieDonohoe 6 35
(Ian Williams) *dwlt: a towards rr* **40/1**

000- 9 10 **Rain In The Face**[54] 7857 4-8-13 67 (t[1]) ShaneGray 7 8
(Karen Tutty) *dwlt: a towards rr* **66/1**

004- **10** 1¼ **Ubla (IRE)**[30] 8191 4-9-1 **69**......(bt) TomMarquand 12 7
(Gay Kelleway) *in tch: rdn along over 3f out: sn wknd* **25/1**

040- **11** 7 **Yourartisonfire**[18] 8356 7-9-7 **75**......(p) LiamKeniry 3
(Lisa Williamson) *a towards rr* **66/1**

050- **12** ¾ **Starfield**[20] 8343 8-8-13 **70**......(b) RobHornby(3) 9
(Mandy Rowland) *led: rdn along and hdd over 2f out: drvn wl over 2f out: grad wknd* **12/1**

1m 42.02s (-1.68) **Going Correction** -0.20s/f (Stan) 12 Ran SP% **120.4**
Speed ratings (Par 103): **100,97,96,95,91 80,79,79,69,68 61,60**
CSF £7.49 CT £28.61 TOTE £3.00: £1.50, £1.20, £2.00; EX 9.50 Trifecta £25.90.
**Owner** C L Bacon **Bred** Sunderlans, Monceaux & Prodhomme **Trained** Oakham, Rutland

**FOCUS**
This looks solid handicap form for the grade.

## 7 SUNBETS.CO.UK DOWNLOAD THE APP H'CAP 1m 13y(F)
**3:30** (3:31) (Class 6) (0-60,61) 4-Y-O+ **£2,587** (£770; £384; £192) **Stalls** Low

Form RPR

001- **1** **Shearian**[12] 8471 7-9-0 **58**...... PhilDennis(5) 6 69
(Declan Carroll) *trckd ldrs: hdwy wl over 2f out: led wl over 1f: sn rdn: kpt on fnl f: comf* **2/1**[1]

622- **2** ½ **Playful Dude (USA)**[3] 8570 4-9-2 **55**......(h) JosephineGordon 5 63
(Phil McEntee) *slt ld: rdn along 2f out: hdd wl over 1f out and sn drvn: kpt on u.p fnl f* **11/4**[2]

361- **3** 1 **General Tufto**[12] 8470 12-8-13 **52**......(b) JoeyHaynes 1 57
(Charles Smith) *towards rr: hdwy on inner and in tch 1/2-way: rdn over 2f out: chsd ldrs over 1f out: sn drvn and kpt on wl fnl f* **10/1**

/40- **4** shd **Powered (IRE)**[13] 8457 4-9-1 **54**...... AndrewMullen 10 59
(David Evans) *dwlt and sn pushed along in rr: hdwy and in tch 1/2-way: effrt wl over 2f out: sn swtchd lft and drvn to chse ldrs over 1f out: kpt on* **7/1**[3]

026- **5** 3½ **Limerick Lord (IRE)**[26] 8241 5-8-12 **54**......(p) ShelleyBirkett(3) 12 51
(Julia Feilden) *cl up: rdn along over 2f out: drvn over 1f out: drvn and wknd fnl f* **15/2**

010- **6** 6 **Little Choosey**[52] 7890 7-9-0 **60**......(tp) KevinLundie(7) 2 42
(Roy Bowring) *in tch: hdwy wl over 2f out and sn rdn: drvn over 1f out: sn wknd* **25/1**

400- **7** 2½ **Gabrial The Thug (FR)**[13] 8458 7-9-3 **56**......(t) StevieDonohoe 13 32
(Ian Williams) *a towards rr* **16/1**

004- **8** 1¾ **Quadriga (IRE)**[12] 8471 7-8-8 **54**......(p[1]) PaulaMuir(7) 4 26
(Chris Grant) *chsd ldrs: rdn along over 3f out: wknd over 2f out* **33/1**

000- **9** 4 **Sayedaati Saadati (IRE)**[13] 8459 4-9-3 **56**......(be[1]) JFEgan 3 19
(John Butler) *cl up on inner: rdn along over 3f out: grad wknd* **25/1**

330- **10** 7 **The Dukkerer (IRE)**[120] 6137 6-9-8 **61**...... TomEaves 11 7
(James Given) *a rr* **16/1**

006- **11** 1¾ **Breathless**[22] 8307 5-9-4 **57**......(t) JamesSullivan 8
(Clive Mulhall) *in tch: rdn along over 3f out: sn wknd* **20/1**

060- **12** 5 **Moment To Dream**[10] 8499 5-8-7 **46** oh1...... RyanPowell 9
(Ken Wingrove) *a rr* **80/1**

1m 42.9s (-0.80) **Going Correction** -0.20s/f (Stan) 12 Ran SP% **121.8**
Speed ratings (Par 101): **96,95,94,94,90 84,82,80,76,69 67,62**
CSF £7.04 CT £46.37 TOTE £2.90: £1.50, £1.80, £2.30; EX 8.50 Trifecta £44.40.
**Owner** Mrs Sarah Bryan **Bred** Minehart Developments Ltd **Trained** Malton, N Yorks

**FOCUS**
An ordinary handicap, but the right horses came to the fore. The runner-up has been rated close to his recent maiden effort here.
T/Plt: £102.30 to a £1 stake. Pool: £48,217.52 - 343.96 winning units. T/Qpdt: £11.70 to a £1 stake. Pool: £4,173.12 - 262.77 winning units. **Joe Rowntree**

8 - 18a (Foreign Racing) - See Raceform Interactive

# [1]SOUTHWELL (L-H)
## Monday, January 2

**OFFICIAL GOING: Fibresand: standard**
Wind: Moderate behind Weather: Fine & dry

## 19 BETWAY AMATEUR RIDERS' H'CAP 2m 102y(F)
**12:10** (12:10) (Class 6) (0-65,64) 4-Y-O+ **£2,495** (£774; £386; £193) **Stalls** Low

Form RPR

/01- **1** **Canadian Diamond (IRE)**[19] 8359 10-10-10 **63**...... MrDavidTurner(3) 8 71
(Richard Rowe) *trckd ldng pair: cl up bef 1/2-way: led 7f out: pushed along over 3f out: rdn over 2f out: drvn appr fnl f: styd on* **6/4**[1]

614- **2** 1¼ **Chestnut Storm (IRE)**[23] 8309 4-9-9 **59**...... MitchellBastyan(7) 5 66
(Brian Barr) *hld up in tch: hdwy 6f out: trckd ldrs 4f out: hdwy to chse wnr over 2f out and sn rdn: drvn and edgd lft jst over 1f out: kpt on same pce* **13/2**

503- **3** 7 **Thackeray**[98] 6840 10-9-8 **47**...... MissBeckySmith(3) 7 45
(Chris Fairhurst) *hld up in tch: hdwy over 4f out: sn chsng ldng pair: chsd wnr 3f out: sn rdn and kpt on one pce* **20/1**

330- **4** 1¾ **Nafaath (IRE)**[44] 5726 11-10-5 **60**......(p) MissAMcCain(5) 1 46
(Donald McCain) *slt ld: hdd 1/2-way and sn pushed along: rdn along over 5f out: sn lost pl and bhd: fin 5th: plcd 4th* **12/1**

0/0- **5** 8 **Sabha (IRE)**[18] 8386 5-9-9 **48**...... ThomasGreatrex(3) 6 25
(K R Burke) *hld up in rr: hdwy on outer over 6f: in tch over 4f out: sn rdn along and outpcd over 3f out: fin 6th: plcd 5th* **20/1**

\- **6** 17 **Sinour (IRE)**[21] 2097 7-9-10 **53**......(t) MrMorganWinstone(7) 4 9
(Robert Stephens) *chsd ldrs: pushed along after 5f: rdn along 1/2-way: sn lost pl and bhd fnl 4f: fin 7th: plcd 6th* **50/1**

354- **7** 13 **Istimraar (IRE)**[14] 8459 6-10-9 **64**......(tp) JonjoO'Neill(5) 9 5
(Alexandra Dunn) *cl up: led 1/2-way: hdd 7f out: cl up and rdn along over 5f out: sn lost pl and bhd: fin 8th: plcd 7th* **7/2**[2]

600- **D** 8 **Our Little Sister (IRE)**[48] 7969 4-10-0 **57**...... MissSBrotherton 3 46
(Hughie Morrison) *trckd ldrs: pushed along and hdwy over 4f out: rdn along 3f out: sn drvn and wknd: fin 4th: later disqualified: prohibited substance fnd in sample* **5/1**[3]

3m 43.33s (-2.17) **Going Correction** -0.10s/f (Stan)
**WFA** 4 from 5yo+ 5lb 8 Ran SP% **111.4**
Speed ratings (Par 101): **101,100,96,92,88 79,73,92**
CSF £11.02 CT £129.39 TOTE £2.30: £1.10, £1.90, £4.60; EX 8.90 Trifecta £97.20.
**Owner** Nicholls Family **Bred** J S Bolger **Trained** Sullington, W Sussex

**FOCUS**
A modest staying handicap. The form might be worth being rated a shade better but there are the usual depth concerns at this level.

## 20 BETWAY H'CAP (DIV I) 6f 16y(F)
**12:40** (12:41) (Class 6) (0-60,60) 4-Y-O+ **£2,587** (£770; £384; £192) **Stalls** Low

Form RPR

364- **1** **Bonjour Steve**[13] 8474 6-9-6 **59**......(p) RichardKingscote 5 67
(Richard Price) *trckd ldrs: hdwy 2f out: swtchd rt and rdn over 1f out: drvn to chal ins fnl f: kpt on wl to ld last 50 yds* **4/1**[2]

4- **2** ¾ **Treaty Of Rome (USA)**[4] 8570 5-9-7 **60**......(v) TonyHamilton 6 66
(Derek Shaw) *cl up: rdn and slt ld over 1f out: drvn ins fnl f: hdd and no ex last 50 yds* **17/2**

560- **3** 1¼ **Pancake Day**[23] 8312 5-8-13 **52**...... StevieDonohoe 12 54
(David C Griffiths) *chsd ldrs on outer: wd st: rdn over 2f out: drvn wl over 1f out: kpt on wl fnl f* **18/1**

354- **4** nk **Letbygonesbeicons**[12] 8482 4-9-4 **57**...... RobertWinston 2 58
(John Balding) *trckd ldrs: pushed along wl over 2f out: rdn wl over 1f out: kpt on same pce fnl f* **15/2**

460- **5** shd **Wimboldsley**[24] 8288 6-8-7 **46** oh1...... KieranO'Neill 10 47
(Scott Dixon) *rr: hdwy over 2f out: rdn wl over 1f out: sn swtchd lft: drvn and kpt on wl fnl f: nrst fin* **20/1**

300- **6** nk **Spowarticus**[28] 8234 8-8-11 **57**......(b) NatalieHambling(7) 3 57
(Scott Dixon) *slt ld: rdn along 2f out: hdd over 1f out: sn drvn and kpt on same pce ins fnl f* **16/1**

450- **7** 1½ **Lucky Louie**[67] 7654 4-9-7 **60**...... TomMarquand 7 55+
(Roger Teal) *bhd and sn pushed along: rdn 1/2-way: styd on u.p fr over 1f out: nrst fin* **7/1**[3]

060- **8** 3¼ **Zebelini (IRE)**[4] 8572 5-8-2 **48**......(tp) RPWalsh(7) 1 34
(Roy Bowring) *chsd ldrs on inner: rdn along over 2f out: sn no imp* **20/1**

061- **9** shd **Tilsworth Micky**[18] 8383 5-9-3 **56**...... JoeFanning 9 41
(J R Jenkins) *dwlt and squeezed out s: sn swtchd rt to outer: racd wd and a rr* **11/1**

002- **10** nse **Arizona Snow**[18] 8383 5-8-12 **51**......(p) LukeMorris 11 36
(Ronald Harris) *a towards rr* **12/1**

300- **11** 1¼ **Culloden**[13] 8474 5-9-0 **58**...... CharlieBennett(5) 8 39
(Shaun Harris) *cl up: rdn along wl over 2f out: sn drvn and wknd* **50/1**

6- **12** ¾ **Not A Bad Oul Day (IRE)**[66] 7677 5-9-2 **55** ow1......(t[1]) DavidNolan 4 34
(John James Feane, Ire) *towards rr and sn pushed along: rdn bef 1/2-way: nvr a factor* **3/1**[1]

1m 16.1s (-0.40) **Going Correction** -0.10s/f (Stan) 12 Ran SP% **118.4**
Speed ratings (Par 101): **98,97,95,94,94 94,92,88,87,87 86,85**
CSF £37.08 CT £563.58 TOTE £4.60: £1.50, £2.80, £3.20; EX 34.00 Trifecta £222.20.
**Owner** Barry Veasey **Bred** The Pocock Family **Trained** Ullingswick, H'fords

**FOCUS**
A modest but competitive-looking sprint for the grade. The runner-up has been rated similar to his Irish form.

## 21 BETWAY H'CAP (DIV II) 6f 16y(F)
**1:10** (1:11) (Class 6) (0-60,60) 4-Y-O+ **£2,587** (£770; £384; £192) **Stalls** Low

Form RPR

050- **1** **Big Amigo (IRE)**[12] 8485 4-9-2 **58**...... EoinWalsh(3) 7 67
(Daniel Mark Loughnane) *in tch: pushed along over 3f out: hdwy 2f out: chsd ldrs and swtchd rt jst over 1f out: rdn to ld jst ins fnl f: sn edgd lft and kpt on strly* **7/2**[2]

355- **2** 2 **Hadley**[13] 8472 4-8-11 **50**...... JasonHart 8 53
(Tracy Waggott) *towards rr and sn pushed along: hdwy and wd st: rdn 2f out: styd on wl appr fnl f* **25/1**

346- **3** nk **Tavener**[35] 8137 5-9-5 **58**......(p) MartinDwyer 2 61+
(David C Griffiths) *hld up towards rr: hdwy 1/2-way: chsd ldrs 2f out: rdn over 1f out: drvn and kpt on fnl f* **9/1**[3]

000- **4** 1 **Pearl Noir**[13] 8474 7-9-4 **57**......(p) KieranO'Neill 1 56
(Scott Dixon) *cl up on inner: rdn along over 2f out: drvn over 1f out: kpt on same pce fnl f* **33/1**

054- **5** ¾ **Men United (FR)**[4] 8572 4-9-0 **53**...... AndrewMullen 3 50
(Garry Moss) *slt ld: rdn along 2f out: drvn over 1f out: hdd ins fnl f: grad wknd* **7/2**[2]

003- **6** ¾ **Fortinbrass (IRE)**[27] 8236 7-9-7 **60**...... RobertWinston 10 55
(John Balding) *prom: rdn along over 2f out: drvn over 1f out: hld whn n.m.r ent fnl f* **11/4**[1]

010- **7** ½ **Captain Scooby**[2] 8596 11-9-0 **56**......(b) GeorgeDowning(3) 4 49
(Richard Guest) *dwlt and towards rr: hdwy over 2f out: sn rdn and kpt on fnl f* **12/1**

011- **8** 1½ **Robbian**[69] 7596 6-8-5 **51**...... RPWalsh(7) 6 40
(Charles Smith) *chsd ldrs: rdn along 3f out: sn drvn and wknd* **20/1**

000- **9** 4½ **Anieres Boy**[31] 8188 5-9-0 **56**...... NathanEvans(3) 11 31
(Oliver Greenall) *cl up on outer: rdn along 3f out: sn drvn and wknd* **12/1**

000- **10** ¾ **Armelle (FR)**[27] 8236 6-8-7 **46** oh1......(p) LukeMorris 9 19
(Scott Dixon) *prom: rdn along wl over 2f out: sn drvn and wknd wl over 1f out* **80/1**

000- **P** **Speightowns Kid (USA)**[132] 5736 9-9-2 **60**......(be) AnnStokell(5) 5
(Ann Stokell) *towards rr: pushed along bef 1/2-way: edgd lft and hit rail home turn: sn rdn and bhd whn lost action and p.u jst over 1f out* **25/1**

1m 16.02s (-0.48) **Going Correction** -0.10s/f (Stan) 11 Ran SP% **113.1**
Speed ratings (Par 101): **99,96,95,94,93 92,91,89,83,82**
CSF £92.38 CT £734.51 TOTE £4.70: £1.60, £6.00, £2.80; EX 96.80 Trifecta £854.60.
**Owner** The Friday Morning Fourball **Bred** Kildaragh Stud **Trained** Rock, Worcs

**FOCUS**
The second division of a modest handicap and the time was similar to the first leg. The runner-up helps pin the opening level.

## 22 BETWAY BEST ODDS GUARANTEED PLUS H'CAP 4f 214y(F)
**1:40** (1:42) (Class 5) (0-70,72) 4-Y-O+ **£3,234** (£962; £481; £240) **Stalls** Centre

Form RPR

021- **1** **Lady Nayef**[18] 8390 4-9-4 **67**......(t) JFEgan 11 83
(John Butler) *cl up: led over 2f out: drvn ins fnl f: kpt on wl towards fin* **9/1**

112- **2** 1¼ **Piazon**[4] 8571 6-9-2 **72**......(be) JoshuaBryan(7) 6 84
(John Butler) *chsd ldrs: hdwy 2f out: rdn to chal ent fnl f: ev ch whn edgd lft last 100yds: no ex* **15/8**[1]

004- **3** 1¼ **Englishwoman**[19] 8358 4-9-1 **69**...... HollieDoyle(5) 2 76+
(David Evans) *in tch: hdwy 2f out: swtchd lft and rdn over 1f out: kpt on wl fnl f* **8/1**

001- **4** 2 **Richter Scale (IRE)**[6] 8535 4-9-8 **71** 6ex...... MartinDwyer 3 71+
(Iain Jardine) *chsd ldrs: rdn along 2f out: drvn and kpt on same pce fnl f* **5/1**[2]

200- **5** *hd* **You're Cool**[20] 8349 5-9-4 **67** RobertWinston 14 66
(John Balding) *slt ld: hdd over 2f out and sn rdn: drvn and edgd lft ins fnl f: kpt on same pce* **20/1**

002- **6** *nk* **Sarabi**[13] 8474 4-8-9 **65** (p) NatalieHambling(7) 1 63+
(Scott Dixon) *dwlt: sn chsng ldrs towards far rail: hdwy 2f out: sn rdn: drvn and kpt on same pce fnl f* **10/1**

605- **7** *hd* **Clubland (IRE)**[4] 8571 8-9-1 **67** RobHornby(3) 13 64
(Garry Moss) *dwlt and towards rr on stands side: rdn along and hdwy 2f out: edgd lft over 1f out: kpt on fnl f* **7/1**[3]

250- **8** *nk* **Socialites Red**[72] 7534 4-8-12 **61** (p) KieranO'Neill 7 57
(Scott Dixon) *towards rr centre: rdn along over 2f out: kpt on u.p fnl f* **40/1**

006- **9** *shd* **Fujin**[13] 8473 6-9-2 **65** (p) TomMarquand 9 61
(Shaun Harris) *chsd ldrs centre: rdn along over 2f out: sn drvn and no imp* **33/1**

160- **10** *shd* **Toni's A Star**[61] 7774 5-8-9 **63** GeorgiaCox(5) 5 58
(Tony Carroll) *towards rr: hdwy 2f out: sn swtchd lft to far rail and rdn: kpt on same pce fnl f* **66/1**

050- **11** *2* **Dusty Blue**[13] 8473 5-8-11 **63** GeorgeDowning(3) 4 51
(Tony Carroll) *racd towards far side: a towards rr* **25/1**

606- **12** *1 3/4* **Powerful Wind (IRE)**[20] 8349 8-9-7 **70** LukeMorris 10 52
(Charlie Wallis) *prom centre: rdn along over 2f out: sn wknd* **20/1**

063- **13** *4 1/2* **Archimedes (IRE)**[13] 8474 4-9-0 **63** (t) StevieDonohoe 12 29
(David C Griffiths) *rrd s: a rr* **25/1**

10/ **14** *7* **Ruby Looker**[504] 5439 6-8-11 **60** PaddyAspell 8
(J R Jenkins) *a towards rr* **66/1**

58.35s (-1.35) **Going Correction** -0.175s/f (Stan) **14** Ran SP% **119.7**
Speed ratings (Par 103): **103,101,99,95,95 95,94,94,94,93 90,87,80,69**
CSF £23.69 CT £151.08 TOTE £9.70: £2.50, £1.10, £2.40; EX 26.60 Trifecta £204.20.
**Owner** Greenstead Hall Racing Ltd **Bred** Greenstead Hall Racing Ltd **Trained** Newmarket, Suffolk

**FOCUS**
A competitive sprint for the grade and a 1-2 for trainer John Butler, albeit the market got it wrong. A length pb from the winner.

## 23 32RED.COM MAIDEN FILLIES' STKS 1m 3f 23y(F)
**2:10** (2:10) (Class 4) 4-Y-0+ **£5,175** (£1,540; £769; £384) **Stalls** Low

Form RPR

/02- **1** **Ominotago**[40] 8076 5-9-3 66 LukeMorris 5 71
(Michael Appleby) *trckd ldng pair on outer: hdwy over 3f out: rdn to ld wl and hung lft over 2f out: sn clr* **11/10**[1]

320- **2** *8* **Paper Faces (USA)**[14] 8459 4-9-0 63 (p) JackMitchell 1 57
(Roger Varian) *led: rdn along 3f out: sn hdd: n.m.r and swtchd rt wl over 2f out: sn drvn along and kpt on one pce* **9/2**[3]

**3** *9* **Planet Suite (FR)** 4-9-0 0 RichardKingscote 4 42
(Jonathan Portman) *hld up: hdwy over 3f out: rdn along over 2f out: kpt on one pce* **6/1**

6- **4** *6* **The Grey Hobbit**[38] 8096 4-9-0 0 ShaneGray 3 32
(Ed de Giles) *trckd ldrs: pushed along 4f out: rdn over 3f out: sn outpcd* **33/1**

33- **5** *6* **Vision Of Beauty (FR)**[30] 8212 4-9-0 0 ConnorBeasley 2 21
(Keith Dalgleish) *t.k.h: chsd ldr: rdn along over 3f out: sn wknd* **11/4**[2]

2m 25.5s (-2.50) **Going Correction** -0.10s/f (Stan)
**WFA** 4 from 5yo 2lb **5** Ran SP% **109.7**
Speed ratings (Par 102): **105,99,92,88,83**
CSF £6.42 TOTE £2.00: £1.40, £2.40; EX 5.20 Trifecta £12.10.
**Owner** I R Hatton **Bred** Howdale Bloodstock Ltd **Trained** Oakham, Rutland

**FOCUS**
An ordinary older maiden and they finished well strung out.

## 24 SUNBETS.CO.UK TOP PRICE ON ALL FAVOURITES CLAIMING STKS 1m 13y(F)
**2:40** (2:40) (Class 6) 4-Y-0+ **£2,587** (£770; £384; £192) **Stalls** Low

Form RPR

/50- **1** **Vivat Rex (IRE)**[97] 6863 6-9-4 78 (t[1]) DavidNolan 8 83
(John James Feane, Ire) *cl up on outer: wd st: rdn to chal 2f out: led 11/2f out: drvn and styd on wl fnl f* **11/2**[3]

110- **2** *1* **Marshgate Lane (USA)**[28] 8231 8-9-12 88 (p) LiamKeniry 9 89
(Neil Mulholland) *hld up in rr: smooth hdwy 3f out: cl up 2f out: sn rdn and ev ch: drvn ent fnl f: sn edgd rt and kpt on same pce* **1/1**[1]

613/ **3** *shd* **Regarde Moi**[59] 9-9-5 94 JacobMitchell(7) 4 89
(Marco Botti) *trckd ldr: cl up 1/2-way: rdn and led briefly 2f out: sn hdd and drvn: kpt on same pce fnl f* **7/1**

232- **4** *3 1/2* **Hail Clodius (IRE)**[166] 4532 5-9-8 87 TomMarquand 5 76
(Richard Hannon) *led: pushed along 3f out: rdn and hdd 2f out: sn drvn and one pce appr fnl f* **11/4**[2]

040- **5** *7* **Manolito**[38] 8100 5-8-13 72 (t) CharlieBennett(5) 2 56
(Hughie Morrison) *trckd ldrs on inner: pushed along 3f out: rdn 2f out: sn wknd* **16/1**

1m 42.31s (-1.39) **Going Correction** -0.10s/f (Stan) **5** Ran SP% **110.4**
Speed ratings (Par 101): **102,101,100,97,90**
CSF £11.67 TOTE £6.50: £2.40, £1.10; EX 15.50 Trifecta £70.20.The winner was claimed by Mr Conor Dore for £8,000.
**Owner** T E Hannigan **Bred** Western Bloodstock **Trained** Curragh, Co Kildare

**FOCUS**
A decent claimer in which the pace was ordinary, and it developed into a bit of a sprint.

## 25 SUNBETS.CO.UK H'CAP 7f 14y(F)
**3:10** (3:11) (Class 4) (0-80,82) 4-Y-0+ **£5,175** (£1,540; £769; £384) **Stalls** Low

Form RPR

421- **1** **Custard The Dragon**[20] 8351 4-8-9 **68** JoeFanning 6 76
(John Mackie) *in tch: hdwy 2f out: chal ins fnl f: sn rdn: led last 100 yds: drvn and edgd rt towards fin* **8/1**

623- **2** *3/4* **War Department (IRE)**[18] 8385 4-9-9 **82** (v) ConnorBeasley 13 88
(Keith Dalgleish) *towards rr: hdwy on outer and wd st: rdn 2f out: styd on and ev ch ins fnl f: kpt on* **5/1**[2]

022- **3** *shd* **Harwoods Star (IRE)**[13] 8473 7-8-13 **72** (be) JFEgan 9 78
(John Butler) *cl up: led 3f out: rdn along 2f out: drvn ent fnl f: hdd last 100 yds: n.m.r and no ex towards fin* **16/1**

621- **4** *1* **Sands Chorus**[21] 8343 5-9-6 **79** TomEaves 1 83
(James Given) *rdn along to ld on inner: pushed along and hdd 3f out: cl up and rdn 2f out: drvn over 1f out: hld whn n.m.r last 50 yds* **12/1**

003- **5** *1 1/2* **Among Angels**[17] 8402 5-9-0 **76** (b) NathanEvans(3) 3 75
(Daniel Mark Loughnane) *chsd ldrs on inner: hdwy over 2f out: sn rdn: drvn over 1f out: kpt on same pce* **50/1**

50-2 **6** *1/2* **Boots And Spurs**[1] 5 8-9-4 **77** (v) KieranO'Neill 11 75
(Scott Dixon) *cl up: rdn along over 2f out: drvn over 1f out: grad wknd* **6/1**[3]

120- **7** *2 1/4* **Rockley Point**[14] 8456 4-9-4 **77** ShaneKelly 5 69
(Paul D'Arcy) *trckd ldrs: hdwy 2f out: rdn over 1f out: sn drvn and one pce* **16/1**

260- **8** *1* **Red Touch (USA)**[221] 2620 5-9-4 **80** AlistairRawlinson(3) 8 69
(Michael Appleby) *rr: rdn along and hdwy over 2f out: kpt on fnl f* **10/1**

401- **9** *3 1/2* **Macho Mac**[20] 8350 4-8-13 **72** RobertHavlin 10 52+
(Hughie Morrison) *plld hrd early: trckd ldrs: hdwy 3f out: rdn along 2f out: sn drvn and btn* **15/8**[1]

506- **10** *2 1/4* **Lady Lydia (IRE)**[33] 8158 6-9-4 **80** NoelGarbutt(3) 7 54
(Gay Kelleway) *a rr* **33/1**

150- **11** *3/4* **Masarzain (IRE)**[14] 8456 4-9-5 **78** AndrewMullen 12 50
(James Given) *in tch: hdwy 3f out: rdn along 2f out: sn wknd* **16/1**

616- **12** *4 1/2* **Nag's Wag (IRE)**[11] 8493 4-9-1 **74** LiamKeniry 2 33
(George Baker) *midfield: rdn along over 3f out: sn wknd* **66/1**

000- **13** *2 1/4* **Showing Off (IRE)**[14] 8456 4-8-11 **70** RyanPowell 4 23
(Michael Wigham) *dwlt: a rr* **50/1**

1m 28.08s (-2.22) **Going Correction** -0.10s/f (Stan) **13** Ran SP% **119.6**
Speed ratings (Par 105): **108,107,107,105,104 103,101,99,95,93 92,87,84**
CSF £47.08 CT £657.20 TOTE £9.70: £2.60, £2.00, £4.50; EX 61.30 Trifecta £989.00.
**Owner** Derbyshire Racing **Bred** Mr & Mrs Kevan Watts **Trained** Church Broughton , Derbys

**FOCUS**
A useful handicap and the winner is progressive. The runner-up and fourth have been rated to form.

## 26 SUNBETS.CO.UK DOWNLOAD THE APP H'CAP 7f 14y(F)
**3:40** (3:42) (Class 6) (0-60,60) 4-Y-0+ **£2,587** (£770; £384; £192) **Stalls** Low

Form RPR

060- **1** **Essenaitch (IRE)**[21] 8343 4-9-7 **60** JFEgan 1 67
(David Evans) *led: rdn along wl over 1f out: drvn ins fnl f: hdd last 50 yds: rallied gamely to ld again nr line* **6/1**[3]

330- **2** *hd* **Prisom (IRE)**[34] 8145 4-9-5 **58** TomMarquand 3 64
(Gay Kelleway) *in tch on inner: hdwy wl over 2f out: chsd ldrs over 1f out: rdn to chal ins fnl f: sn drvn and kpt on to ld narrowly last 50 yds: hdd and no ex nr line* **9/1**

005- **3** *1/2* **Mustn't Grumble (IRE)**[13] 8474 4-8-11 **55** HollieDoyle(5) 4 60
(David Loughnane) *trckd ldrs: hdwy over 2f out: sn cl up: rdn and ev ch over 1f out: drvn ins fnl f: kpt on* **6/1**[3]

556- **4** *1/2* **Samphire Coast**[12] 8481 4-8-13 **55** (v[1]) NoelGarbutt(3) 6 59
(Derek Shaw) *towards rr: hdwy over 3f out: chsd ldrs and rdn over 1f out: kpt on wl fnl f* **12/1**

663- **5** *3/4* **Capital Gearing**[13] 8470 4-9-0 **53** (b) StevieDonohoe 14 55
(Henry Spiller) *cl up: chal on wd outside over 2f out: rdn and ev ch over 1f out: drvn and kpt on same pce ins fnl f* **4/1**[1]

000- **6** *3* **Basingstoke (IRE)**[23] 8306 8-9-5 **58** (p) LukeMorris 2 52
(Daniel Mark Loughnane) *chsd ldrs: rdn along 2f out: sn drvn and no imp* **7/1**

020- **7** *1/2* **Lmntrix**[30] 8207 5-8-13 **59** JaneElliott(7) 5 51
(George Margarson) *towards rr: hdwy over 2f out: kpt on: nvr nr ldrs* **11/2**[2]

000- **8** *2 3/4* **Dr Red Eye**[20] 8350 9-8-11 **50** (b[1]) KieranO'Neill 8 35
(Scott Dixon) *cl up: rdn along 3f out: drvn over 2f out and grad wknd* **20/1**

500- **9** *2* **Just Marion (IRE)**[18] 8383 5-8-7 **46** oh1 RyanPowell 7 25
(Clare Ellam) *.a towards rr* **33/1**

030- **10** *3 1/2* **De Lesseps (USA)**[254] 1632 9-9-7 **60** AndrewMullen 9 30
(John Murray) *nvr bttr than midfield* **33/1**

344- **11** *3/4* **Ershaad (IRE)**[13] 8470 5-8-10 **49** (p[1]) TomEaves 13 17
(Shaun Harris) *dwlt: a towards rr* **12/1**

000- **12** *1* **Doeadeer (IRE)**[66] 7663 4-9-6 **59** ConnorBeasley 10 24
(Keith Dalgleish) *chsd ldrs: rdn along over 2f out: sn drvn and wknd* **25/1**

0/0- **13** *9* **Mcelligott (IRE)**[209] 2999 4-8-7 **46** oh1 JoeFanning 11
(Richard Price) *dwlt: a rr* **50/1**

1m 29.43s (-0.87) **Going Correction** -0.10s/f (Stan) **13** Ran SP% **118.3**
Speed ratings (Par 101): **100,99,99,98,97 94,93,90,88,84 83,82,72**
CSF £54.80 CT £271.57 TOTE £7.40: £2.50, £2.90, £2.40; EX 70.10 Trifecta £361.10.
**Owner** Spiers & Hartwell Ltd **Bred** Charel Park Stud **Trained** Pandy, Monmouths

**FOCUS**
Just a modest handicap. The second to the fifth help set the standard.
T/Plt: £17.80 to a £1 stake. Pool: £85,439.25 - 3,493.58 winning units T/Qpdt: £9.10 to a £1 stake. Pool: £7,879.40 - 633.91 winning units **Joe Rowntree**

# NEWCASTLE (A.W) (L-H)
Tuesday, January 3

**OFFICIAL GOING: Tapeta: standard**
Wind: Strong against Weather: Heavy grey cloud

## 27 32RED CASINO MAIDEN STKS (PLUS 10 RACE) 6f (Tp)
**2:10** (2:12) (Class 4) 3-Y-0 **£5,175** (£1,540; £769; £384) **Stalls** Centre

Form RPR

62- **1** **Glorious Politics**[35] 8140 3-9-5 0 PhillipMakin 6 76+
(David Barron) *trckd ldng pair: cl up 1/2-way: led on bit wl over 1f out: sn pushed clr: easily* **2/9**[1]

0- **2** *3 3/4* **Life Won't Wait**[39] 8089 3-9-5 0 JasonHart 9 60+
(John Quinn) *trckd ldrs: pushed along and sltly outpcd over 2f out: rdn wl over 1f out: styd on fnl f* **25/1**

05- **3** *3/4* **Port Master**[17] 8425 3-9-0 0 RowanScott(5) 3 58
(Ann Duffield) *trckd ldrs: effrt 2f out and sn rdn: chsd wnr ent fnl f: sn drvn and kpt on same pce* **80/1**

05- **4** *2* **Bay Watch (IRE)**[27] 8243 3-9-5 0 DavidProbert 2 52
(Andrew Balding) *prom: pushed along over 2f out: rdn wl over 1f out: sn edgd lft and one pce* **9/2**[2]

00- **5** *5* **Ventura Jazz**[18] 8406 3-9-0 0 TonyHamilton 7 31
(Richard Fahey) *rr and sn pushed along: bhd fr 1/2-way* **50/1**

340- **6** *2* **Spinnaker Bay (IRE)**[49] 7966 3-9-0 70 JosephineGordon 4 24
(William Jarvis) *slt ld: pushed along 3f out: rdn 2f out: sn hdd & wknd* **12/1**[3]

1m 16.85s (4.35) **Going Correction** +0.55s/f (Slow) **6** Ran SP% **114.7**
Speed ratings (Par 99): **93,88,87,84,77 75**
CSF £11.20 TOTE £1.20: £1.10, £4.50; EX 7.60 Trifecta £148.30.
**Owner** Kangyu International Racing (HK) Limited **Bred** Trickledown Stud Limited **Trained** Maunby, N Yorks
■ Miss Montes was withdrawn. Price at time of withdrawal 25/1. Rule 4 does not apply.

**FOCUS**
An uncompetitive maiden. The winner did not need to improve to win.

## 28 BETWAY STAYERS H'CAP 2m 56y (Tp)
**2:40** (2:40) (Class 5) (0-70,72) 4-Y-0+ **£4,528** (£1,347; £673; £336) **Stalls** Low

Form RPR

625- **1** **Jan Smuts (IRE)**[24] 8309 9-8-12 **57**..............................(t) HollieDoyle(5) 7 63
(Wilf Storey) *hld up in rr: stdy hdwy 5f out: chsd ldrs 2f out: rdn over 1f out: styd on wl fnl f to ld nr fin* **12/1**

/14- **2** ½ **Medicine Hat**[5] 8565 6-10-4 **72**........................................ SamJames 9 77+
(Marjorie Fife) *hld up in midfield: hdwy 5f out: chsd ldr 3f out: rdn to ld 2f out: sn edgd lft: drvn ins fnl f: hdd and no ex nr fin* **2/1**[1]

110- **3** ¾ **Cavalieri (IRE)**[18] 8399 7-10-0 **68**.................................(tp) PhillipMakin 4 72
(Philip Kirby) *in tch: hdwy 5f out: chsd ldng pair over 2f out: rdn along: n.m.r and swtchd rt over 1f out: drvn and ev ch ins fnl f: kpt on* **12/1**

602- **4** *hd* **Hallstatt (IRE)**[31] 8211 11-9-9 **63**......................................(t) LukeMorris 6 67
(John Mackie) *hld up: hdwy over 5f out: chsd ldrs 3f out: rdn 2f out: drvn and ch ins fnl f: kpt on* **25/1**

322- **5** ¾ **Burnside (FR)**[16] 8445 4-9-4 **65**.................................(p) StevieDonohoe 2 69+
(Ian Williams) *trckd ldng pair: tk clsr order over 5f out: led over 3f out: rdn along and hdd 2f out: sn drvn and kpt on same pce fnl f* **2/1**[1]

125- **6** ¾ **Merriment**[19] 8387 4-9-1 **62**................................................(p) TomEaves 5 64
(Peter Niven) *hld up towards rr: hdwy over 4f out: effrt over 2f out and sn rdn: styd on appr fnl f: nrst fin* **8/1**[3]

202- **7** 9 **Maple Stirrup (IRE)**[24] 8309 5-8-10 **57**.............................. PaulaMuir(7) 1 48
(Patrick Holmes) *hld up: a towards rr* **12/1**

/00- **8** 60 **Rocky Two (IRE)**[21] 4971 7-8-9 **49** oh4...........................(p) JoeFanning 8
(Philip Kirby) *chsd clr ldr: pushed along 6f out: rdn over 4f out: sn wknd* **100/1**

063- **9** 3½ **Palindrome (USA)**[24] 8310 4-9-4 **65**................................ ShaneGray 10
(Ronald Thompson) *in tch: hdwy over 5f out: chsd ldng pair over 3f out: sn rdn and wknd* **10/1**

004- **10** 23 **Wordiness**[13] 8480 9-10-0 **68**........................................ AndrewMullen 3
(David Evans) *led: clr after 3f: pushed along 5f out: rdn along and hdd over 3f out: sn wknd* **7/1**[2]

3m 35.04s (-0.16) **Going Correction** +0.10s/f (Slow)
**WFA** 4 from 5yo+ 5lb **10** Ran SP% **127.3**
Speed ratings (Par 103): **104,103,103,103,102 102,98,68,66,54**
CSF £39.73 CT £322.41 TOTE £12.00: £2.30, £1.10, £3.60; EX 66.10 Trifecta £415.40.
**Owner** H S Hutchinson & W Storey **Bred** Tipper House Stud **Trained** Muggleswick, Co Durham

■ Stewards' Enquiry : Hollie Doyle four-day ban; used whip above the permitted level (17th-20th Jan)

**FOCUS**
Not a bad race for the grade. The winner has been rated to his recent best, with the third and fourth fitting.

## 29 BETWAY BEST ODDS GUARANTEED PLUS MAIDEN STKS 1m 2f 42y (Tp)
**3:10** (3:11) (Class 4) 4-Y-0+ **£5,175** (£1,540; £769; £384) **Stalls** High

Form RPR

04- **1** **Diamond Kut**[20] 8366 4-9-5 0.......................................... DavidProbert 5 73
(Andrew Balding) *set stdy pce: pushed along and qcknd 2f out: edgd rt and rdn over 1f out: edgd lft and drvn ins fnl f: hld on wl towards fin* **13/8**[2]

352- **2** *nk* **Fastnet Blast (IRE)**[14] 8462 4-9-5 67..........................(b) ThomasBrown 2 72
(Ed Walker) *t.k.h: hld up towards rr: smooth hdwy over 2f out: effrt to chal jst ins fnl f: sn rdn and ev ch tl drvn and kpt on same pce towards fin* **10/11**[1]

336- **3** 1½ **Ms Gillard**[132] 5763 4-9-0 62........................................ TomEaves 6 64
(David Simcock) *trckd ldrs: hdwy 3f out: swtchd lft and rdn over 1f out: drvn ins fnl f: kpt on same pce* **25/1**

006- **4** 5 **Page Of Wands**[18] 8400 4-9-0 54.........................................(v) LukeMorris 4 54
(Karen McLintock) *reminders s: trckd ldng pair: chsd wnr wnr: rdn along over 2f out: drvn and hld whn n.m.r and hmpd over 1f out: wknd* **12/1**

543- **5** 2 **Avoidable**[12] 8491 4-9-5 67.............................................. TonyHamilton 1 55
(David Simcock) *trckd wnr: pushed along 3f out: rdn over 2f out: sn wknd* **11/1**[3]

**6** 21 **Great Roar (USA)**[1362] 9-9-7 0............................................(t) ShaneGray 3 13
(Ronald Thompson) *a rr: rdn along 4f out: sn outpcd and bhd* **50/1**

2m 15.47s (5.07) **Going Correction** +0.10s/f (Slow)
**WFA** 4 from 9yo 1lb **6** Ran SP% **112.3**
Speed ratings (Par 105): **83,82,81,77,75 59**
CSF £3.41 TOTE £2.50: £1.40, £1.10; EX 3.90 Trifecta £16.70.
**Owner** John F Jarvis **Bred** Barry Walters Farms **Trained** Kingsclere, Hants

■ Stewards' Enquiry : Tom Eaves caution; careless riding.

**FOCUS**
Not a strong maiden run at a steady pace. The form makes sense rated around the second and third.

## 30 BETWAY H'CAP 1m 4f 98y (Tp)
**3:40** (3:40) (Class 5) (0-70,71) 4-Y-0+ **£4,528** (£1,347; £673; £336) **Stalls** High

Form RPR

111- **1** **Go George Go (IRE)**[13] 8480 4-9-2 **66**.............................. JoeFanning 5 75+
(Alan Swinbank) *set stdy pce: hdd 1/2-way: trckd ldr: led again over 2f out: rdn over 1f out: kpt on wl fnl f* **10/11**[1]

0F1- **2** ½ **Bamako Du Chatelet (FR)**[16] 8448 6-9-6 **66**.......(p) RichardKingscote 4 72
(Ian Williams) *prom: chsd wnr over 2f out: rdn to chal over 1f out: drvn ins fnl f: kpt on* **7/2**[2]

262- **3** 2 **Henpecked**[13] 8480 7-9-10 **70**..........................................(p) PJMcDonald 2 73
(Alistair Whillans) *t.k.h: hld up towards rr: hdwy over 3f out: chsd ldng pair wl over 1f out: drvn and kpt on same pce fnl f* **5/1**[3]

000/ **4** 8 **Rock A Doodle Doo (IRE)**[244] 1110 10-9-6 **69**.. RachelRichardson(3) 3 55
(Sean Regan) *hld up in rr: effrt 4f out: rdn along 3f out: sn outpcd* **66/1**

356- **D** 2¾ **Woodacre**[47] 7993 10-9-11 **71**........................................ PhillipMakin 6 69
(Richard Whitaker) *prom: hdwy to ld 1/2-way: rdn along and hdd over 2f out: sn drvn and wknd* **7/2**[2]

2m 46.75s (5.65) **Going Correction** +0.10s/f (Slow)
**WFA** 4 from 6yo+ 3lb **5** Ran SP% **115.0**
Speed ratings (Par 103): **85,84,83,76,81**
CSF £4.82 TOTE £1.80: £1.10, £2.30; EX 3.60 Trifecta £6.70.
**Owner** Lee Bond **Bred** Pat Grogan **Trained** Melsonby, N Yorks

**FOCUS**
A fair contest for the grade. The runner-up has been rated to form, with the third close to her recent C&D form.

## 31 32RED.COM H'CAP 7f 14y (Tp)
**4:10** (4:11) (Class 3) (0-95,92) 3-Y-O**£10,081** (£3,017; £1,508; £755; £376) **Stalls** Centre

Form RPR

225- **1** **Letmestopyouthere (IRE)**[8] 8525 3-9-0 **85**..................... AndrewMullen 5 89
(David Evans) *hld up in rr: hdwy over 2f out: chsd ldng pair and rdn over 1f out: swtchd rt ent fnl f and sn drvn to chal: kpt on wl to ld last 75 yds* **8/1**

411- **2** ½ **Dr Julius No**[18] 8405 3-9-4 **89**.................................... RichardKingscote 6 92+
(Ralph Beckett) *trckd ldrs: smooth hdwy 3f out: led over 2f out: rdn over 1f out: drvn ins fnl f: hdd last 75 yds: kpt on* **5/4**[1]

541- **3** ½ **Alkashaaf (USA)**[15] 8454 3-8-6 **77**..............................(tp) DavidProbert 3 78
(Archie Watson) *trckd ldrs: hdwy 3f out: sn chsng ldr: rdn over 1f out: drvn and kpt on fnl f* **9/2**[3]

532- **4** 8 **Atteq**[28] 8237 3-8-7 **78**............................................... BarryMcHugh 4 57
(Richard Fahey) *trckd ldrs: effrt 3f out: rdn along 2f out: sn drvn and btn over 1f out* **5/1**

265- **5** 2 **Monticello (IRE)**[78] 7409 3-9-7 **92**...................................... JoeFanning 1 66
(Mark Johnston) *led: rdn along 3f out: sn hdd & wknd 2f out* **7/2**[2]

134- **6** 1¾ **Whatsthemessage (IRE)**[91] 7042 3-8-7 **78**................. ConnorBeasley 2 47
(Keith Dalgleish) *cl up: rdn along 3f out: wknd over 2f out* **22/1**

1m 29.33s (3.13) **Going Correction** +0.55s/f (Slow) **6** Ran SP% **117.0**
Speed ratings (Par 101): **104,103,102,93,91 89**
CSF £19.59 TOTE £10.00: £3.60, £1.20; EX 24.30 Trifecta £81.70.
**Owner** J Abbey, C Heron & M Nolan **Bred** Mrs J A Dene **Trained** Pandy, Monmouths

**FOCUS**
The pace was steady for this competitive handicap with the front three finishing clear. The first two were closely matched on their Wolverhampton form, and have been rated to the better view of that.

## 32 SUNBETS.CO.UK H'CAP 7f 14y (Tp)
**4:40** (4:42) (Class 4) (0-80,84) 4-Y-0+ **£6,469** (£1,925; £962; £481) **Stalls** Centre

Form RPR

265- **1** **Dutch Art Dealer**[179] 4086 6-9-0 **80**.....................(v[1]) LewisEdmunds(7) 11 91
(Ivan Furtado) *hld up in rr: gd hdwy over 2f out: effrt: nt clr run and sltly hmpd jst over 1f out: rdn and qcknd ent fnl f: led last 100 yds: sn clr* **11/2**[3]

1- **2** 2¼ **Roller**[13] 8481 4-9-1 **77**...................................... NathanEvans(3) 9 82
(Michael Easterby) *cl up: led wl over 1f out: rdn ent fnl f: hdd and drvn last 100 yds: kpt on* **3/1**[2]

006- **3** ¾ **Jubilee Brig**[25] 8287 7-8-13 **72**........................................... JoeFanning 6 75
(Alan Swinbank) *trckd ldrs: hdwy wl over 1f out: rdn and n.m.r ent fnl f: kpt on* **33/1**

000- **4** *nk* **Merdon Castle (IRE)**[14] 8475 5-9-7 **80**......................(e) JamesSullivan 5 82
(Ruth Carr) *t.k.h: in tch: hdwy 2f out: nt clr run over 1f out: rdn and kpt on wl fnl f: nrst fin* **25/1**

213- **5** 1¾ **Inaam (IRE)**[12] 8487 4-9-2 **75**.............................................(h) DavidNolan 10 72
(Richard Fahey) *trckd ldrs: hdwy 3f out: rdn along over 2f out: drvn and kpt on same pce fnl f* **11/4**[1]

/22- **6** *shd* **Playtothewhistle**[123] 6095 6-8-11 **70**................................... LukeMorris 3 67
(Michael Appleby) *trckd ldrs: pushed along 3f out: rdn 2f out: sn drvn and kpt on same pce* **14/1**

161- **7** 1½ **Swiss Cross**[6] 8561 10-9-8 **84** 6ex....................(tp) CallumShepherd(3) 12 77
(Phil McEntee) *hld up towards rr: hdwy on outer wl over 2f out: chsd ldrs and rdn wl over 1f out: sn no imp* **7/1**

002- **8** ½ **Like No Other**[19] 8385 4-9-7 **80**.......................................... JasonHart 7 72
(Les Eyre) *set stdy pce: pushed along 3f out: rdn wl over 1f out: drvn and edgd rt jst over 1f out: sn edgd lft and wknd* **10/1**

000- **9** *nk* **Fingal's Cave (IRE)**[19] 8385 5-9-6 **79**.......................... PJMcDonald 8 70+
(Iain Jardine) *rrd s and lost several l: sn w field: pushed along 3f out: rdn wl over 2f out: sn wknd* **7/1**

000- **10** 6 **Extortion**[21] 8345 4-8-12 **71**........................................ ConnorBeasley 4 46
(Bryan Smart) *in tch: rdn along wl over 2f out: sn wknd* **50/1**

1m 29.08s (2.88) **Going Correction** +0.55s/f (Slow) **10** Ran SP% **116.6**
Speed ratings (Par 105): **105,102,101,101,99 99,97,96,96,89**
CSF £22.02 CT £512.16 TOTE £6.80: £2.00, £1.60, £7.20; EX 32.40 Trifecta £932.20.
**Owner** The Giggle Factor & Ubs Partners **Bred** Raymond Clive Tooth **Trained** Wiseton, Nottinghamshire

**FOCUS**
They went a steady pace for this open handicap. The level is a bit fluid.

## 33 BETWAY BEST ODDS GUARANTEED PLUS H'CAP 6f (Tp)
**5:10** (5:10) (Class 3) (0-95,96) 4-Y-0+ **£9,703** (£2,887; £1,443; £721) **Stalls** Centre

Form RPR

055- **1** **Tatlisu (IRE)**[4] 8583 7-8-12 **85**........................................ TonyHamilton 1 94
(Richard Fahey) *hld up in rr: smooth hdwy wl over 1f out: chal and carried lft ins fnl f: qcknd wl to ld last 75 yds* **8/1**

1- **2** 1¾ **Doc Sportello (IRE)**[18] 8402 5-9-3 **90**.........................(p) RobertWinston 6 93
(Michael Herrington) *hld up: smooth hdwy over 2f out: chal over 1f out: rdn to take slt ld ent fnl f: sn drvn and hung lft: hdd and nt qckn last 75 yds* **11/2**

662- **3** 1¾ **Poyle Vinnie**[4] 8583 7-9-7 **94**........................................... TomEaves 5 93
(Michael Appleby) *trckd ldrs: smooth hdwy over 2f out: cl up on bit wl over 1f out: shkn up to ld briefly 1f out: sn rdn and hdd ent fnl f: ev ch whn hmpd ins fnl f: kpt on same pce after* **2/1**[1]

256- **4** 3 **Intransigent**[47] 7984 8-9-6 **93**...........................................(h) DavidProbert 2 81
(Andrew Balding) *t.k.h: trckd ldrs on inner: pushed along and outpcd over 2f out: sn rdn: kpt on fnl f* **5/1**[3]

020- **5** 3¼ **Salvatore Fury (IRE)**[24] 8314 7-8-9 **82**.........................(p) AndrewMullen 3 59
(Keith Dalgleish) *trckd ldrs: rdn along 2f out: sn drvn and wknd* **50/1**

041- **6** 1½ **Luis Vaz De Torres (IRE)**[214] 2857 5-8-2 **82**......... NatalieHambling(7) 8 55
(Richard Fahey) *cl up: led 1/2-way: rdn along 2f out: drvn and hdd jst over 1f out: wknd fnl f* **33/1**

504- **7** 1¼ **Red Pike (IRE)**[47] 7990 6-9-6 **93**...................................... ConnorBeasley 4 62
(Bryan Smart) *slt ld: hdd 1/2-way: cl up tl rdn along over 2f out and sn wknd* **7/2**[2]

323- **8** 5 **Gentlemen**[8] 8530 6-9-9 **96**...........................................(h) JosephineGordon 7 49
(Phil McEntee) *chsd ldrs on outer: rdn along wl over 2f out: sn wknd* **7/2**[2]

1m 14.7s (2.20) **Going Correction** +0.55s/f (Slow) **8** Ran SP% **125.8**
Speed ratings (Par 107): **107,104,102,98,94 92,90,83**
CSF £56.53 CT £127.61 TOTE £9.10: £2.20, £2.00, £1.50; EX 68.50 Trifecta £358.70.
**Owner** Middleham Park Racing LIV **Bred** J C And Rocal Bloodstock **Trained** Musley Bank, N Yorks

**FOCUS**
A competitive handicap run at an honest pace. The winner is the key to the level.

T/Plt: £15.20 to a £1 stake. Pool: £95,881.11 - 4,602.68 winning units T/Qpdt: £4.90 to a £1 stake. Pool: £7,980.27 - 1,202.77 winning units **Joe Rowntree**

# LINGFIELD (L-H)

## Wednesday, January 4

**OFFICIAL GOING: Polytrack: standard**
Wind: light, half against Weather: light cloud

## 34 32RED.COM MAIDEN STKS — 7f 1y(P)

**1:10** (1:10) (Class 5) 3-Y-O — **£3,234** (£962; £481; £240) **Stalls** Low

Form — RPR

3- **1** **Dubai Art**[20] 8384 3-9-5 0 ... JackGarritty 1 — 75+
(Richard Fahey) *t.k.h: trckd ldrs: wnt 2nd and swtchd rt over 1f out: sn rdn: no imp tl styd on wl ins fnl f to ld last strides* — **9/4**[2]

52- **2** *hd* **La Guapita**[36] 8139 3-9-0 0 ... JosephineGordon 2 — 69
(Hugo Palmer) *broke wl and led: rdn and qckng 2f out: drvn ent fnl f: kpt on tl hdd and no ex last strides* — **4/1**[3]

**3** *¾* **Blaze Of Glory (FR)** 3-9-0 0 ... LucyKBarry(5) 9 — 72+
(Jamie Osborne) *awkward leaving stall: sn rcvrd to chse ldrs: effrt in 3rd ent fnl f: rn green and hung lft ins fnl f: kpt on* — **16/1**

00- **4** *1 ¾* **Revel**[56] 7867 3-9-5 0 ... (t) LiamKeniry 3 — 67+
(Stuart Williams) *hld up in tch in midfield: effrt on inner over 1f out: edgd rt and kpt on same pce ins fnl f* — **2/1**[1]

06- **5** *½* **Marwa**[21] 8362 3-9-0 0 ... TomMarquand 8 — 61
(Ed Dunlop) *hld up in tch in midfield: trying to switch rt and effrt over 1f out: kpt on same pce ins fnl f* — **20/1**

53- **6** *2 ½* **Parisian Chic (IRE)**[21] 8361 3-9-0 0 ... RobertWinston 6 — 54+
(Lee Carter) *t.k.h early: hld up in tch in midfield: effrt bnd wl over 1f out: no imp and kpt on same pce fnl f* — **16/1**

00- **7** *1* **Shiloh**[21] 8361 3-9-0 0 ... TimmyMurphy 5 — 51
(Simon Crisford) *chsd ldr tl over 1f out: sn outpcd and losing pl whn sltly hmpd ins fnl f: wknd fnl 100yds* — **66/1**

00- **8** *shd* **Jannia**[21] 8362 3-8-11 0 ... EdwardGreatrex(3) 7 — 51
(Eve Johnson Houghton) *s.i.s: hld up in rr: effrt over 1f out: swtchd rt and nt clr run 1f out: kpt on same pce ins fnl f* — **66/1**

0- **9** *½* **Hermeneutics (USA)**[39] 8119 3-9-5 0 ... GeorgeBaker 4 — 55+
(Ed Walker) *hld up in last pair: shkn up 2f out: no imp and wl hld whn eased wl ins fnl f* — **7/1**

1m 25.36s (0.56) **Going Correction** -0.05s/f (Stan) — **9** Ran SP% **116.1**
Speed ratings (Par 97): **94,93,92,90,90 87,86,86,85**
CSF £11.70 TOTE £3.40: £1.20, £1.90, £6.20; EX 11.10 Trifecta £95.20.
**Owner** Sheikh Rashid Dalmook Al Maktoum **Bred** Cheveley Park Stud Ltd **Trained** Musley Bank, N Yorks

**FOCUS**
This was quite steadily run and it proved hard to close from off the pace. It's been rated around the runner-up, with the fifth and eighth fitting.

## 35 BETWAY STAYERS H'CAP — 1m 7f 169y(P)

**1:45** (1:45) (Class 6) (0-60,61) 4-Y-O+ — **£2,587** (£770; £384; £192) **Stalls** Low

Form — RPR

064- **1** **Miss Dusky Diva (IRE)**[13] 8497 5-8-13 **49** ... MartinHarley 2 — 56
(David W Drinkwater) *taken down early: hld up in midfield: clsd and in tch 5f out: swtchd rt and hdwy over 2f out: chal and clr w ldr over 1f out: led 1f out: styd on and drew clr fnl 100yds* — **7/1**[3]

050- **2** *2 ½* **Grand Facile**[21] 8359 5-9-1 **51** ... (b) TimmyMurphy 9 — 55
(Gary Moore) *chsd ldr and clr of field tl 5f out: pushed into ld over 2f out: rdn and clr w wnr over 1f out: hdd 1f out: no ex and one pce ins fnl f* **25/1**

355- **3** *6* **Delagoa Bay (IRE)**[21] 8359 9-9-5 **60** ... MitchGodwin(5) 11 — 57
(Sylvester Kirk) *hld up off the pce in last trio: clsd 5f out: swtchd rt 3f out: effrt bnd 2f out: styd on ins fnl f: snatched 3rd last strides: no threat to ldng pair* — **12/1**

044- **4** *nk* **Lily Edge**[15] 8468 8-8-11 **47** ... (v) WilliamCarson 3 — 43
(John Bridger) *chsd clr ldng pair: clsd and in tch 5f out: rdn and unable qck over 2f out: kpt on same pce fnl 2f: lost 3rd last strides* — **14/1**

642- **5** *¾* **Ruby Wednesday**[16] 8459 4-9-4 **61** ... KierenFox 8 — 57
(John Best) *hld up off the pce in midfield: clsd and in tch 5f out: swtchd rt and effrt over 2f out: no imp u.p over 1f out: kpt on same pce fnl f* — **3/1**[1]

335- **6** *2 ¾* **Robben**[26] 1649 5-9-8 **58** ... (v) JosephineGordon 10 — 52
(Alexandra Dunn) *s.i.s: off the pce in last trio: clsd 5f out but nt on terms w ldrs: rdn over 2f out: sme hdwy over 1f out but nvr threatened ldrs* **16/1**

602- **7** *4 ½* **Par Three (IRE)**[13] 8497 6-8-11 **50** ... (p) GeorgeDowning(3) 1 — 37
(Tony Carroll) *led and sn clr w rival: c bk to field 5f out: rdn and hdd over 2f out: wknd over 1f out* — **9/2**[2]

026- **8** *4 ½* **Ali Bin Nayef**[20] 8386 5-9-4 **54** ... GeorgeBaker 6 — 35
(Michael Wigham) *chsd clr ldng pair: clsd and in tch 5f out: rdn and no imp over 2f out: wknd over 1f out* — **3/1**[1]

005- **9** *½* **Comedy House**[15] 8468 9-9-1 **51** ... LiamKeniry 7 — 32
(Michael Madgwick) *s.i.s: hld up off the pce in last trio: clsd but nt on terms w ldrs 5f out: effrt jst over 2f out: no imp and wknd over 1f out* **12/1**

656- **10** *6* **Movie Magic**[36] 724 6-8-10 **46** oh1 ... AdamBeschizza 5 — 20
(Mark Hoad) *off the pce in midfield: clsd and in tch 5f out: rdn over 3f out: lost pl and bhd 2f out: sn wknd* — **33/1**

050- **11** *3 ¼* **Divine Prince (GR)**[21] 8366 4-8-12 **55** ... (b[1]) ShaneKelly 4 — 25
(Amanda Perrett) *off the pce in midfield: clsd and in tch 5f out: rdn and lost pl over 2f out: bhd fnl f* — **14/1**

3m 21.12s (-4.58) **Going Correction** -0.05s/f (Stan)
**WFA** 4 from 5yo+ 5lb — **11** Ran SP% **122.1**
Speed ratings (Par 101): **109,107,104,104,104 102,100,98,98,95 93**
CSF £172.07 CT £2080.66 TOTE £7.90: £2.30, £7.80, £4.10; EX 239.00 Trifecta £3647.20.
**Owner** Advantage Chemicals Holdings Ltd **Bred** Advantage Chemicals Holdings Ltd **Trained** Hanley Castle, Worcs

**FOCUS**
A moderate staying race but it was run at a good gallop.

## 36 BETWAY H'CAP — 1m 2f (P)

**2:15** (2:15) (Class 4) (0-85,82) 4-Y-O+ — **£5,175** (£1,540; £769; £384) **Stalls** Low

Form — RPR

020- **1** **Elysian Prince**[118] 6267 6-9-4 **79** ... GeorgeBaker 1 — 86
(Neil King) *chsd ldr: clsd and upsides 3f out: rdn 2f out: led 1f out: hld on wl ins fnl f: all out* — **11/4**[2]

043- **2** *shd* **Dutch Uncle**[17] 8446 5-9-7 **82** ... MartinHarley 3 — 88
(Ed Dunlop) *in tch in midfield: wnt 3rd 2f out: sn swtchd lft and effrt over 1f out: hung lft 1f out: drvn and ev ch ins fnl f: kpt on but hld towards fin* — **11/8**[1]

466- **3** *½* **Exceeding Power**[13] 8487 6-8-11 **72** ... TomMarquand 7 — 77
(Martin Bosley) *hld up in midfield: effrt to chse ldrs over 1f out: swtchd rt whn bmpd and pushed lft 1f out: wnt 3rd and shifting lft ins fnl f: kpt on* — **16/1**

301- **4** *1 ½* **Believe It (IRE)**[15] 8469 5-8-1 **69** ... (b) NicolaCurrie(7) 5 — 71
(Richard Hughes) *led: pressed 3f out: rdn and hdd 1f out: edgd rt and no ex ins fnl f: wknd towards fin* — **6/1**

432- **5** *1 ½* **Starlit Cantata**[20] 8381 6-8-13 **77** ... (p) EdwardGreatrex(3) 6 — 76
(Eve Johnson Houghton) *in tch in midfield: swtchd rt and effrt over 1f out: sn drvn and styd on same pce ins fnl f* — **5/1**[3]

030- **6** *2 ½* **Icebuster**[137] 5650 9-9-7 **82** ... RyanTate 8 — 76
(Rod Millman) *hld up in last pair: effrt over 1f out: sn no imp: wl hld and kpt on same pce ins fnl f* — **33/1**

264- **7** *2 ¾* **The Gay Cavalier**[112] 6489 6-8-8 **76** ... (t) JonathanFisher(7) 2 — 64
(John Ryan) *s.i.s and sn rdn along: clsd onto bk of field 7f out: swtchd rt and effrt wd bnd 2f out: sn outpcd: wl hld fnl f* — **20/1**

500- **8** *8* **Genuine Approval (IRE)**[35] 8162 4-9-0 **77** ... LiamKeniry 4 — 49
(John Butler) *chsd ldrs: clsd to press ldrs 3f out: sn rdn and unable qck: lost pl wl over 1f out: sn bhd* — **33/1**

2m 4.33s (-2.27) **Going Correction** -0.05s/f (Stan)
**WFA** 4 from 5yo+ 1lb — **8** Ran SP% **116.3**
Speed ratings (Par 105): **107,106,106,105,104 102,99,93**
CSF £6.90 CT £45.50 TOTE £3.60: £1.30, £1.10, £4.80; EX 7.60 Trifecta £62.70.
**Owner** D S Lee **Bred** D S Lee **Trained** Barbury Castle, Wiltshire

**FOCUS**
There was a tight finish to this handicap. The second and third have been rated close to form.

## 37 SUNBETS.CO.UK MAIDEN STKS — 1m 1y(P)

**2:45** (2:45) (Class 5) 4-Y-O+ — **£3,234** (£962; £481; £240) **Stalls** High

Form — RPR

603- **1** **Rebel State (IRE)**[20] 8382 4-9-5 63 ... (p) GeorgeBaker 2 — 72
(Richard Spencer) *broke wl: sn stdd to trck ldrs: wnt 2nd 2f out: sn upsides ldr and hrd hld: led 1f out: nudged along and qcknd clr: easily* — **5/2**[2]

2/3- **2** *3 ¼* **Ribbing (USA)**[20] 8388 4-9-0 74 ... (h[1]) ShaneKelly 5 — 58
(David Simcock) *chsd ldr tl over 6f out: in tch in midfield after: effrt in 4th ent fnl 2f: kpt on same pce: wnt 2nd wl ins fnl f: no ch w wnr* — **9/4**[1]

64- **3** *2 ¼* **Tell A Story**[17] 8449 4-9-0 0 ... MartinHarley 3 — 53
(David Simcock) *flashed tail thrght: sn led: rdn and jnd over 1f out: hdd 1f out: sn btn: wknd and lost 2nd 50yds out* — **7/1**

**4** *1 ½* **Alhajjaj** 4-9-5 0 ... (h[1]) LiamKeniry 6 — 54
(Andrew Balding) *s.i.s: hdwy to chse ldr over 6f out tl 2f out: 3rd and unable qck over 1f out: wknd ins fnl f* — **11/4**[3]

**5** *5* **Marauder** 5-9-2 0 ... HectorCrouch(3) 4 — 42
(Henry Candy) *dwlt: rn green in rr: n.d* — **8/1**

0- **6** *¾* **Mount Vesuvius (IRE)**[7] 8559 9-9-2 0 ... (t) AaronJones(3) 1 — 40
(Paul Henderson) *in tch in midfield: 5th and rdn over 2f out: sn outpcd: bhd fnl f* — **50/1**

1m 37.24s (-0.96) **Going Correction** -0.05s/f (Stan) — **6** Ran SP% **111.6**
Speed ratings (Par 103): **102,98,96,95,90 89**
CSF £8.45 TOTE £3.70: £1.60, £1.70; EX 8.60 Trifecta £25.00.
**Owner** Rebel Racing III **Bred** B Kennedy **Trained** Newmarket, Suffolk

**FOCUS**
Just an ordinary maiden. The runner-up has been rated to her reappearance figure and the third close to her previous two starts.

## 38 BETWAY BEST ODDS GUARANTEED PLUS H'CAP — 1m 4f (P)

**3:15** (3:17) (Class 4) (0-85,84) 4-Y-O+ — **£5,175** (£1,540; £769; £384) **Stalls** Low

Form — RPR

011- **1** **Petite Jack**[35] 8162 4-9-3 **84** ... MartinHarley 5 — 95+
(Neil King) *hld up in tch in midfield: hdwy over 2f out: rdn and qcknd to ld on inner over 1f out: in command and r.o wl fnl f: readily* — **13/8**[1]

353- **2** *1 ½* **Dolphin Village (IRE)**[28] 8249 7-9-6 **83** ... (h) GeorgeBaker 6 — 88
(Jane Chapple-Hyam) *hld up in tch: hdwy to chse ldrs over 2f out: rdn 2f out: kpt on ins fnl f: wnt 2nd nr fin: no threat to wnr* — **5/1**[2]

214- **3** *nk* **Artful Rogue (IRE)**[17] 8447 6-9-0 **80** ... HectorCrouch(3) 7 — 85
(Amanda Perrett) *t.k.h: hld up in tch in midfield: effrt 2f out: nt clrest of runs and swtchd rt over 1f out: kpt on ins fnl f: wnt 3rd last strides: no threat to wnr* — **12/1**

021- **4** *nk* **Priors Brook**[35] 8161 6-9-0 **77** ... LiamKeniry 10 — 81
(Andrew Balding) *chsd ldrs tl wnt 2nd 9f out: rdn to chal 2f out tl outpcd by wnr over 1f out: kpt on same pce ins fnl f: lost 2 pls nr fin* — **12/1**

544- **5** *3 ½* **Daisy Boy (IRE)**[97] 6892 6-8-13 **79** ... (t) AaronJones(3) 9 — 77
(Stuart Williams) *sn led: rdn and jnd 2f out: hdd and unable qck over 1f out: wknd ins fnl f* — **12/1**

113- **6** *nk* **Cape Discovery**[17] 8447 5-9-7 **84** ... ShaneKelly 4 — 82
(Richard Hughes) *chsd ldr tl 9f out: styd chsng ldrs tl unable qck 2f out: sn outpcd: wknd ins fnl f* — **5/1**[2]

40- **7** *1 ¾* **Celestial Bay**[20] 8381 8-8-7 **75** ... MitchGodwin(5) 11 — 70
(Sylvester Kirk) *hld up in last pair: effrt over 2f out: no imp and one pced fr over 1f out* — **66/1**

562- **8** *½* **River Dart (IRE)**[28] 8254 5-8-11 **77** ... GeorgeDowning(3) 2 — 71
(Tony Carroll) *hld up in last pair: effrt over 1f out: no imp: n.d* — **10/1**

006- **9** *1* **The Twisler**[17] 8447 5-8-13 **83** ... RhiainIngram(7) 3 — 76
(Roger Ingram) *bustled along leaving stalls: hld up in last trio: rdn over 2f out: no imp: wl hld whn hmpd ins fnl f* — **33/1**

251/ **10** *½* **Included**[470] 6624 5-9-0 **77** ... TomMarquand 1 — 69
(David Dennis) *wl in tch in midfield: rdn over 2f out: little rspnse and sn outpcd: bhd ins fnl f* — **66/1**

31- **11** *71* **Snobbery (IRE)**[32] 8212 4-8-11 **78** ... RichardKingscote 8
(Roger Charlton) *wl in tch in midfield: rdn over 4f out: sn struggling and lost pl: bhd 3f out: t.o* — **6/1**[3]

2m 30.36s (-2.64) **Going Correction** -0.05s/f (Stan)
**WFA** 4 from 5yo+ 3lb — **11** Ran SP% **123.8**
Speed ratings (Par 105): **106,105,104,104,102 102,100,100,99,99 52**
CSF £10.29 CT £77.84 TOTE £2.80: £1.80, £2.10, £3.50; EX 12.40 Trifecta £84.40.
**Owner** W Burn **Bred** Mrs Liz Nelson Mbe **Trained** Barbury Castle, Wiltshire

**FOCUS**
A good handicap and the winner again showed his liking for this track. The third and fourth help set the standard.

## 39 BETWAY MIDDLE DISTANCE H'CAP 1m 4f (P)
3:45 (3:45) (Class 6) (0-65,66) 4-Y-0+ £2,587 (£770; £384; £192) Stalls Low

Form RPR
403- 1 **Karam Albaari (IRE)**[16] 8459 9-9-11 **66**........................(v) GeorgeBaker 7 74
(J R Jenkins) *hld up in last trio: clsd and travelling strly 2f out: upsides ldrs ins fnl f: shkn up to ld 100yds out: sn qcknd clr: easily* **6/1**
505- 2 3 ¼ **Macksville (IRE)**[25] 8318 4-9-4 **63**........................ RichardKingscote 8 66
(Jeremy Gask) *led tl 9f out: styd chsng ldrs: rdn and ev ch over 1f out: led 1f out tl hdd 100yds out: sn outpcd by wnr but kpt on to hold 2nd* **11/4**[1]
000- 3 ½ **Ruzeiz (USA)**[21] 8359 8-9-2 **57**........................ TomMarquand 5 59
(Peter Hedger) *hld up in last trio: effrt over 2f out: hdwy 1f out: styd on wl ins fnl f: wnt 3rd cl home: no threat to wnr* **25/1**
406- 4 nk **Chandon Elysees**[28] 8257 4-9-0 **62**........................ HectorCrouch(3) 3 64
(Gary Moore) *in tch in midfield: effrt on inner ent fnl 2f: drvn and ev ch 1f out: unable qck and one pce fnl 100yds* **4/1**[3]
135- 5 nk **Skylark Lady (IRE)**[50] 7309 4-9-1 **60**........................(b) NickyMackay 1 61
(Michael Wigham) *chsd ldrs: swtchd rt after 2f: hdwy to chse ldr over 8f out tl led 6f out: rdn over 3f out: hdd over 2f out: styd on same pce ins fnl f* **7/1**
000- 6 1 ¼ **Yul Finegold (IRE)**[21] 8364 7-9-9 **64**........................(b) MartinHarley 6 63
(Conor Dore) *stdd s: hld up in tch: hdwy into midfield 1/2-way: effrt 2f out: styd on same pce fr over 1f out* **25/1**
603- 7 1 **Combe Hay (FR)**[28] 8257 4-9-6 **65**........................(h) ShaneKelly 4 63
(Henry Spiller) *t.k.h: w ldrs tl led 9f out: hdd 6f out: chsd ldr tl led again over 2f out: rdn and hdd 1f out: no ex whn short of room ins fnl f: sn wknd* **7/2**[2]
634- 8 1 **Medicean Queen (IRE)**[7] 8554 6-9-0 **55**........................(t) WilliamCarson 2 53
(Phil McEntee) *chsd ldrs: rdn over 2f out: unable qck over 1f out: btn whn squeezed for room ins fnl f: no ch after* **7/1**
100- 9 6 **Fleetwood Poppy**[17] 8448 5-8-7 **51** oh4........................ EdwardGreatrex(3) 9 37
(Michael Attwater) *t.k.h: chsd ldrs tl dropped into midfield 9f out: rdn and no hdwy over 2f out: wknd fnl f* **33/1**

2m 32.46s (-0.54) **Going Correction** -0.05s/f (Stan)
**WFA** 4 from 5yo+ 3lb 9 Ran SP% **118.8**
Speed ratings (Par 101): **99,96,96,96,96 95,94,93,89**
CSF £23.14 CT £392.90 TOTE £6.90: £2.40, £1.30, £9.10; EX 23.20 Trifecta £855.90.
**Owner** Mark Goldstein **Bred** Morecool Stud **Trained** Royston, Herts

**FOCUS**
A modest affair, but a smooth performance from the winner.
T/Plt: £99.30 to a £1 stake. Pool: £73,064.37 - 536.66 winning units T/Qpdt: £4.90 to a £1 stake. Pool: £6,522.60 - 978.92 winning units **Steve Payne**

# 27 NEWCASTLE (A.W) (L-H)
Wednesday, January 4

**OFFICIAL GOING: Tapeta: standard**
Wind: Moderate against Weather: Cloudy

## 40 SUN BETS ON THE APP STORE MAIDEN STKS 1m 5y (Tp)
1:35 (1:35) (Class 5) 3-5-Y-0 £3,234 (£962; £481; £240) Stalls Centre

Form RPR
2- 1 **Dubaitwentytwenty**[21] 8355 3-8-3 0........................ LukeMorris 10 67
(Hugo Palmer) *cl up: rdn to ld over 1f out: drvn and hdd narrowly wl ins fnl f: styd on to ld again nr fin* **15/8**[1]
2 nk **Spiritofhayton (IRE)** 3-8-8 0........................ AndrewMullen 4 71
(David Barron) *in tch: hdwy over 2f out: rdn to chal ent fnl f: drvn to take narrow ld wl ins fnl f: hdd and no ex nr fin* **25/1**
3 1 ¼ **Touch Of Paradise (IRE)** 3-8-3 0........................ JoeFanning 6 63+
(Richard Fahey) *trckd ldrs: green and pushed along 3f out: rdn over 1f out: kpt on fnl f* **3/1**[3]
42- 4 1 ¾ **Oxford Thinking (IRE)**[25] 8305 3-8-8 0........................ RobertHavlin 3 64+
(John Gosden) *t.k.h: slt ld: pushed along 2f out: sn rdn and hdd over 1f out: drvn and edgd lft jst ins fnl f: kpt on same pce* **9/4**[2]
0- 5 hd **Cartavio (IRE)**[54] 7906 3-8-8 0........................ DavidProbert 2 63
(Andrew Balding) *trckd ldng pair: hdwy 3f out: rdn wl over 1f out: drvn and n.m.r jst ins fnl f: kpt on same pce* **6/1**
6 8 **Elite Icon** 3-8-8 0........................ MartinDwyer 9 44
(Iain Jardine) *green and rr: pushed along and sme hdwy wl over 1f out: n.d* **66/1**
60- 7 nse **Dreamofdiscovery (IRE)**[20] 8384 3-8-8 0........................ JoeDoyle 8 44
(Julie Camacho) *chsd ldrs: hdwy 3f out: rdn along 2f out: grad wknd* **80/1**
8 5 **Crindle Carr (IRE)** 3-8-8 0........................ SamJames 7 32
(David Barron) *in tch: pushed along 3f out: sn rdn and wknd* **40/1**
6- 9 ¾ **Scannermandango**[20] 8388 4-9-9 0........................ JamesSullivan 5 29
(Jim Goldie) *a rr* **100/1**
10 8 **What's Up Walter** 3-8-8 0........................ PJMcDonald 1 11
(Philip Kirby) *wnt lft s: a towards rr* **100/1**

1m 40.61s (2.01) **Going Correction** +0.30s/f (Slow)
**WFA** 3 from 4yo 20lb 10 Ran SP% **115.8**
Speed ratings (Par 103): **101,100,99,97,97 89,89,84,83,75**
CSF £50.90 TOTE £2.90: £1.20, £6.90, £1.70; EX 43.90 Trifecta £141.30.
**Owner** Rabbah Racing **Bred** Rabbah Bloodstock Limited **Trained** Newmarket, Suffolk

**FOCUS**
In contrast to the previous day the headwind had died right down. This probably wasn't a bad maiden for the time of year. It was run at a modest pace towards the stands' side. It's been rated around the pre-race modest standard.

## 41 32RED.COM H'CAP 5f (Tp)
2:05 (2:07) (Class 5) (0-75,75) 3-Y-0 £3,234 (£962; £481; £240) Stalls Centre

Form RPR
333- 1 **Erissimus Maximus (FR)**[16] 8453 3-9-6 **74**........................(p1) JoeFanning 3 79
(Chris Dwyer) *trckd ldrs on outer: cl up 1/2-way: led 2f out: rdn over 1f out: edgd rt ins fnl f: kpt on wl towards fin* **6/4**[1]
041- 2 ½ **Cajmere**[25] 8313 3-9-7 **75**........................ PJMcDonald 5 78
(Tom Dascombe) *trckd ldr: cl up 2f out: rdn to chal over 1f out: drvn and ev ch ins fnl f: kpt on* **5/2**[2]
443- 3 nk **White Royale (USA)**[5] 8582 3-9-6 **74**........................ ShaneGray 6 76
(Kevin Ryan) *cl up: pushed along and sltly outpcd 1/2-way: rdn wl over 1f out: styd on wl fnl f* **10/3**[3]
553- 4 1 **Royal Celebration**[26] 8285 3-8-0 **57** oh3 ow1........................ NathanEvans(3) 1 56
(Bryan Smart) *trckd ldr: hdwy and cl up 2f out: rdn and ev ch over 1f out: kpt on same pce ins fnl f* **7/1**
040- 5 nk **Oh So Dandy (IRE)**[26] 8285 3-8-1 **58**........................(v) NoelGarbutt(3) 2 55
(Derek Shaw) *dwlt and rr: pushed along over 2f out: rdn over 1f out: kpt on strly fnl f* **14/1**
140- 6 15 **Zig Zag Girl**[60] 7820 3-9-1 **69**........................(b) LukeMorris 4 12
(Scott Dixon) *led: pushed along 3f out: sn rdn and hdd 2f out: sn wknd* **40/1**

1m 0.41s (0.91) **Going Correction** +0.30s/f (Slow) 6 Ran SP% **113.3**
Speed ratings (Par 97): **104,103,102,101,100 76**
CSF £5.61 TOTE £2.20: £1.50, £1.40; EX 5.60 Trifecta £11.40.
**Owner** P Venner **Bred** Derek Clee **Trained** Newmarket, Suffolk

**FOCUS**
An ordinary 3yo sprint handicap that saw a bunched finish. A small pb from the winner, with the third close to form and fourth matching his C&D latest from out of the handicap.

## 42 BETWAY BEST ODDS GUARANTEED PLUS CLASSIFIED STKS 1m 2f 42y (Tp)
2:35 (2:35) (Class 5) 4-Y-0+ £2,911 (£866; £432; £216) Stalls High

Form RPR
023- 1 **L'Inganno Felice (FR)**[36] 8141 7-9-2 70........................(h) PJMcDonald 6 77
(Iain Jardine) *.trckd clr ldr: tk clsr order over 4f out: cl up 3f out: rdn to ld wl over 1f out: drvn and edgd rt ent fnl f: hld on wl towards fin* **4/1**[3]
435- 2 ½ **Siren's Cove**[19] 8399 5-9-2 73........................(b) JamesSullivan 5 76
(Kenneth Slack) *in tch: hdwy 4f out: chsd ldng pair 3f out: rdn to chse wnr over 1f out: swtchd lft and drvn jst ins fnl f: kpt on wl towards fin* **7/2**[2]
201- 3 hd **Bollihope**[36] 8141 5-9-2 72........................ ConnorBeasley 7 76+
(Richard Guest) *hld up in rr: hdwy over 3f out: trckd ldrs over 2f out: effrt and hanging lft wl over 1fr out: swtchd lft and rdn ent fnl f: styd on strly on inner: nt quite rch wnr* **2/1**[1]
205- 4 3 ¾ **Polar Forest**[5] 8584 7-8-13 74........................(e) NathanEvans(3) 2 68
(Richard Guest) *led and clr: pushed along and jnd 3f out: rdn 2f out: sn hdd and drvn: wknd appr fnl f* **7/1**
613- 5 ½ **Kicking The Can (IRE)**[20] 8387 6-9-2 64........................ BarryMcHugh 3 67
(David Thompson) *dwlt: sn trcking ldng pair: pushed along 3f out: rdn to chse ldrs over 2f out: drvn wl over 1f out: sn one pce* **14/1**
455- 6 1 **Storm King**[27] 8282 8-9-2 74........................(h) MartinDwyer 1 65
(David C Griffiths) *hld up: hdwy over 3f out: sn in tch: rdn along 2f out: sn drvn and no imp* **7/1**
520- 7 14 **All You (IRE)**[216] 2811 5-8-13 73........................ ShelleyBirkett(3) 4 37
(David O'Meara) *hld up: a rr: outpcd and bhd fr wl over 2f out* **12/1**

2m 11.83s (1.43) **Going Correction** +0.225s/f (Slow) 7 Ran SP% **114.9**
Speed ratings (Par 103): **103,102,102,99,99 98,87**
CSF £18.56 TOTE £5.00: £2.50, £2.10; EX 22.30 Trifecta £54.60.
**Owner** A Dawson & Mrs K Campbell **Bred** E A R L Elevage Des Loges **Trained** Carrutherstown, D'fries & G'way

**FOCUS**
A typically tight classified race on paper. There was no hanging around. The form makes sense at face value rated around the first three and fifth.

## 43 SUNBETS.CO.UK H'CAP 1m 5y (Tp)
3:05 (3:08) (Class 4) (0-85,87) 4-Y-0+ £4,851 (£1,443; £721; £360) Stalls Centre

Form RPR
131- 1 **Testa Rossa (IRE)**[26] 8286 7-8-10 **76**........................(b) NathanEvans(3) 5 85
(Jim Goldie) *hld up in rr: gd hdwy over 2f out: rdn to ld ent fnl f: sn drvn and kpt on wl towards fin* **11/2**[3]
322- 2 ½ **Constantino (IRE)**[14] 8478 4-9-9 **86**........................(p1) TonyHamilton 6 94
(Richard Fahey) *trckd ldrs. hdwy over 2f out: chal over 1f out: sn rdn and ev ch: drvn and edgd lft ins fnl f: kpt on* **15/8**[1]
233- 3 1 ¾ **Chevallier**[27] 8279 5-9-10 **87**........................ LukeMorris 1 91
(Archie Watson) *led: pushed along over 2f out: rdn wl over 1f out: hdd and drvn ent fnl f: kpt on same pce* **9/4**[2]
460- 4 1 ½ **Faithful Creek (IRE)**[8] 8539 5-9-7 **84**........................(p1) AndrewMullen 2 84
(Michael Appleby) *trckd ldrs: hdwy over 2f out: rdn over 1f out: drvn and no imp fnl f* **13/2**
062- 5 ¾ **Dusky Dawn**[22] 8347 5-9-1 **78**........................ JoeFanning 3 77
(Alan Swinbank) *trckd ldrs: hdwy 3f out and sn cl up: rdn 2f out: drvn and wknd appr fnl f* **16/1**
000- 6 hd **Mont Ras (IRE)**[14] 8478 10-9-3 **80**........................ ConnorBeasley 4 78
(Roger Fell) *trckd ldr: hdwy 3f out and cl up: rdn along 2f out: sn drvn and wknd appr fnl f* **33/1**
335- 7 1 ¾ **Jacbequick**[30] 8231 6-9-2 **86**........................(v) PatrickVaughan(7) 7 80
(David O'Meara) *t.k.h: trckd ldr: hdwy and cl up over 3f out: rdn along over 2f out: sn wknd* **9/1**

1m 41.23s (2.63) **Going Correction** +0.30s/f (Slow) 7 Ran SP% **113.1**
Speed ratings (Par 105): **98,97,95,94,93 93,91**
CSF £15.90 TOTE £5.20: £2.80, £1.40; EX 15.50 Trifecta £29.30.
**Owner** Mr & Mrs Gordon Grant **Bred** Hugo Merry And Khalid Al-Mudhaf **Trained** Uplawmoor, E Renfrews

**FOCUS**
This fair handicap was run at an uneven pace until 3f out. A small pb from the runnerup, with the third rated close to form.

## 44 SUNBETS.CO.UK H'CAP 1m 5y (Tp)
3:35 (3:38) (Class 6) (0-65,67) 4-Y-0+ £3,234 (£962; £481; £240) Stalls Centre

Form RPR
156- 1 **Rock Warbler (IRE)**[9] 8531 4-9-12 **67**........................(t) JamesSullivan 10 75
(Oliver Greenall) *hld up in rr: smooth hdwy wl over 2f out: trckd ldrs over 1f out: chal ent fnl f: sn rdn to ld and kpt on strly* **5/1**[3]
444- 2 2 **Orlando Rogue (IRE)**[13] 8499 5-8-13 **54**........................(v1) ConnorBeasley 13 58
(Keith Dalgleish) *trckd ldrs: hdwy over 2f out: rdn to ld over 1f out: jnd and drvn ent fnl f: sn hdd: kpt on* **10/1**
523- 3 1 **Dancin Alpha**[5] 8589 6-9-0 **55**........................ JoeFanning 5 56
(Alan Swinbank) *trckd ldrs: cl up 3f out: led 2f out: sn rdn and hdd over 1f out: drvn and kpt on same pce* **7/2**[2]
452- 4 ½ **Newmarket Warrior (IRE)**[5] 8588 6-9-4 **66**........................(p) JamieGormley(7) 7 66
(Iain Jardine) *t.k.h: hld up towards rr: hdwy over 2f out: rdn to chse ldrs over 1f out: kpt on fnl f: nrst fin* **11/4**[1]
034- 5 1 ¼ **Miss Goldsmith (IRE)**[13] 8493 4-9-7 **62**........................ TonyHamilton 12 60
(Richard Fahey) *prom: effrt over 2f out: rdn wl over 1f out: sn drvn and grad wknd* **14/1**
643- 6 shd **Cool Strutter (IRE)**[25] 8306 5-9-3 **58**........................(b) SamJames 6 55
(Karen Tutty) *hld up towards rr: hdwy over 2f out: rdn wl over 1f out: kpt on fnl f: nrst fin* **16/1**


The Form Book Flat, Raceform Ltd, Newbury, RG14 5SJ

525- **7** 3/4 **Hightime Girl**[19] 8400 4-9-4 **59**......(tp) PJMcDonald 1 55
(Roger Fell) *hld up towards rr: hdwy over 2f out: swtchd lft and rdn over 1f out: kpt on fnl f* **11/1**

006- **8** hd **Nelson's Bay**[36] 8142 8-8-4 **52**...... PaulaMuir(7) 9 47
(Wilf Storey) *dwlt: t.k.h in rr: hdwy 2f out: sn rdn and kpt on fnl f* **33/1**

044- **9** 1/2 **Wahaab (IRE)**[20] 8389 6-9-6 **66**......(p) ShirleyTeasdale(5) 8 60
(Iain Jardine) *t.k.h: in tch: hdwy to chse ldrs over 2f out: sn rdn: drvn and wknd over 1f out* **12/1**

030- **10** 1 1/2 **Life Of Fame**[14] 8483 4-9-1 **56**...... AndrewMullen 3 47
(Mark Walford) *led: pushed along 3f out: rdn and hdd 2f out: grad wknd* **66/1**

060- **11** 1 **Dark Forest**[48] 7995 4-9-4 **59**...... BarryMcHugh 11 48
(Marjorie Fife) *a towards rr* **20/1**

034- **12** 1/2 **Silver Duke (IRE)**[212] 2959 6-9-2 **60**...... NathanEvans(3) 4 48
(Jim Goldie) *a towards rr* **33/1**

103- **13** 6 **Attain**[21] 8364 8-9-11 **66**......(p) LukeMorris 14 40
(Archie Watson) *chsd ldrs on outer: rdn along over 3f out: sn wknd* **14/1**

300- **14** 5 **Let Right Be Done**[5] 8588 5-9-0 **55**...... ShaneGray 2 18
(Linda Perratt) *prom: rdn along wl over 2f out: sn wknd* **50/1**

1m 41.84s (3.24) **Going Correction** +0.30s/f (Slow) **14** Ran SP% **124.0**
Speed ratings (Par 101): **95,93,92,91,90 90,89,89,88,87 86,85,79,74**
CSF £53.61 CT £208.91 TOTE £6.00: £1.80, £3.10, £1.80; EX 52.30 Trifecta £232.80.
**Owner** R A Royle & S Evason **Bred** Sir E J Loder **Trained** Oldcastle Heath, Cheshire

**FOCUS**
A moderate handicap. They stuck to the centre throughout this time and the third sets the level.

## 45 BETWAY SPRINT H'CAP 5f (Tp)
**4:05** (4:08) (Class 5) (0-75,76) 4-Y-0+ **£3,234** (£962; £481; £240) **Stalls** Centre

Form RPR

06- **1** **Bahango (IRE)**[30] 8228 5-8-9 **68**......(p) LewisEdmunds(7) 4 75
(Patrick Morris) *in tch towards far side: hdwy wl over 1f out: rdn to chse ldrs ent fnl f: sn drvn and styd on strly to ld nr line* **25/1**

415- **2** nse **Poppy In The Wind**[19] 8403 5-9-3 **69**......(v) LukeMorris 2 76
(Alan Brown) *racd towards far side: trckd ldrs:. hdwy wl over 1f out: rdn to ld jst ins fnl f: sn drvn: hdd nr line* **6/1**[3]

225- **3** hd **Dark Side Dream**[20] 8389 5-9-6 **72**...... DavidProbert 7 78
(Chris Dwyer) *trckd ldrs centre: hdwy and cl up over 2f out: rdn to ld over 1f out: drvn and hdd ins fnl f: kpt on wl towards fin* **5/1**[2]

01-4 **4** 1 **Richter Scale (IRE)**[2] 22 4-8-12 **71** 6ex...... JamieGormley(7) 11 74
(Iain Jardine) *racd towards stands side: in tch: hdwy 2f out: chsd ldrs over 1f out: rdn and ch ins fnl f: kpt on same pce* **15/2**

030- **5** 1/2 **Fredricka**[19] 8403 6-9-7 **73**......(p) AndrewMullen 6 74
(David Barron) *hld up: hdwy wl over 1f out: effrt and n.m.r ent fnl f: sn rdn and styd on wl: nrst fin* **10/1**

366- **6** shd **Spirit Of Wedza (IRE)**[130] 5864 5-8-12 **64**...... JoeDoyle 8 65
(Julie Camacho) *led: rdn along over 2f out: drvn and hdd over 1f out: kpt on same pce fnl f* **20/1**

333- **7** 1 **Thorntoun Lady (USA)**[14] 8482 7-8-9 **61**...... JamesSullivan 12 58
(Jim Goldie) *hmpd and squeezed out s: bhd tl styd on wl fnl 2f: nrst fin* **20/1**

256- **8** 1/2 **Cruise Tothelimit (IRE)**[14] 8483 9-8-8 **63**...... NathanEvans(3) 3 58
(Patrick Morris) *prom: rdn along wl over 1f out: sn drvn and grad wknd* **40/1**

000- **9** hd **Something Lucky (IRE)**[19] 8403 5-9-4 **70**......(p) ShaneGray 1 64
(Kristin Stubbs) *dwlt and bhd tl sme late hdwy* **14/1**

060- **10** hd **Imperial Legend (IRE)**[19] 8403 8-8-13 **65**......(p) BarryMcHugh 14 59
(David Nicholls) *a towards rr* **33/1**

040- **11** 2 3/4 **Tailwind**[20] 8385 4-9-10 **76**...... JackMitchell 9 60
(Roger Varian) *trckd ldrs: hdwy and cl up over 2f out: rdn wl over 1f out: sn wknd* **15/8**[1]

030- **12** 3/4 **Elusivity (IRE)**[22] 8349 9-9-7 **73**......(p) DavidNolan 5 54
(Conor Dore) *prom: rdn along 2f out: sn wknd* **33/1**

054- **13** 3/4 **Lotara**[14] 8485 5-8-7 **59**...... ConnorBeasley 13 37
(Jim Goldie) *hmpd s: a rr* **11/1**

200- **14** 1 1/4 **Entertaining Ben**[98] 6879 4-9-5 **71**......(p) MartinDwyer 10 45
(Iain Jardine) *racd towards stands side: chsd ldr: rdn along bef 1/2-way: sn wknd* **28/1**

59.72s (0.22) **Going Correction** +0.30s/f (Slow) **14** Ran SP% **126.7**
Speed ratings (Par 103): **110,109,109,108,107 107,105,104,104,104 99,98,97,95**
CSF £166.61 CT £903.59 TOTE £38.80: £10.50, £2.80, £2.10; EX 297.60 Trifecta £1605.10.
**Owner** L P Richards **Bred** Corduff Stud Ltd **Trained** Prescot, Merseyside

**FOCUS**
An ordinary sprint handicap, run at a fair pace. The main action was far side. The third helps set the standard.
T/Plt: £86.60 to a £1 stake. Pool: £67,208.63 - 566.51 winning units T/Qpdt: £41.60 to a £1 stake. Pool: £4,870.77 - 86.64 winning units **Joe Rowntree**

# WOLVERHAMPTON (A.W) (L-H)
Wednesday, January 4

**OFFICIAL GOING: Tapeta: standard**
Wind: Light against Weather: Fine

## 46 BETWAY MIDDLE APPRENTICE H'CAP 1m 1f 104y (Tp)
**4:15** (4:15) (Class 6) (0-60,60) 4-Y-0+ **£2,587** (£770; £384; £192) **Stalls** Low

Form RPR

042- **1** **Nonchalant**[9] 8528 6-9-0 **60**......(b) AledBeech(7) 11 68
(Hugo Froud) *led over 8f out: clr 6f out: shkn up over 1f out: styd on* **11/2**[3]

443- **2** 1 1/4 **Frivolous Prince (IRE)**[9] 8528 4-7-13 **46**......(vt) KatherineGlenister(7) 7 52
(David Evans) *hld up: hdwy over 1f out: rdn and edgd lft ins fnl f: r.o* **6/1**

656- **3** shd **Dose**[20] 8382 4-8-12 **55**...... NatalieHambling(3) 10 60
(Richard Fahey) *sn led: hdd over 8f out: chsd ldr tl 5f out: remained handy: shkn up over 2f out: wnt 2nd again over 1f out: styd on* **5/1**[2]

350- **4** 2 1/4 **Dove Mountain (IRE)**[113] 6464 6-9-2 **60**......(tp) JoshuaBryan(5) 4 61
(Anabel K Murphy) *hld up: racd keenly: hdwy over 1f out: sn rdn: styd on* **28/1**

501- **5** 1 **Synodic (USA)**[34] 8179 5-9-6 **59**......(t) LouisSteward 2 58
(Seamus Durack) *hld up: swtchd rt 3f out: hdwy over 1f out: nt rch ldrs* **5/2**[1]

000- **6** 1 3/4 **Breakheart (IRE)**[28] 8258 10-8-8 **54**......(b) WilliamCox(7) 1 50
(Andrew Balding) *hld up: nt clr run over 2f out: hdwy over 1f out: no ex ins fnl f* **25/1**

444- **7** 1 3/4 **Qibtee (FR)**[53] 6840 7-8-13 **52**...... PhilDennis 6 45
(Les Eyre) *chsd ldrs: pushed along over 2f out: wknd over 1f out* **40/1**

000- **8** 1 3/4 **Thane Of Cawdor (IRE)**[23] 8337 8-9-6 **59**...... RobHornby 3 48
(Joseph Tuite) *hld up: rdn over 1f out: nvr on terms* **25/1**

640- **9** 2 3/4 **Mount Cheiron (USA)**[13] 8499 6-8-12 **54**......(b) CallumRodriguez(3) 8 38
(Richard Ford) *s.i.s: hdwy over 7f out: chsd ldr 5f out tl rdn and edgd lft over 1f out: wknd fnl f* **22/1**

231- **10** 3 1/2 **Ferryview Place**[9] 8528 8-8-9 **55** 6ex......(tp) LukeCatton(7) 13 32
(Ian Williams) *s.i.s: hdwy over 6f out: shkn up over 2f out: wknd over 1f out* **12/1**

336- **11** 1 1/4 **Les Gar Gan (IRE)**[230] 2397 6-8-11 **57**......(be) TobyEley(7) 12 32
(Daniel Mark Loughnane) *s.i.s: hld up: rdn over 2f out: sn wknd* **25/1**

051- **12** 10 **My Mistress (IRE)**[9] 8527 5-8-13 **52** 6ex......(p) CallumShepherd 5 18
(Phil McEntee) *chsd ldrs: rdn whn hmpd over 1f out: eased* **7/1**

2m 0.19s (-0.61) **Going Correction** -0.05s/f (Stan)
**WFA** 4 from 5yo+ 1lb **12** Ran SP% **116.9**
Speed ratings (Par 101): **100,98,98,96,95 94,92,91,88,85 84,75**
CSF £34.09 TOTE £5.60: £2.10, £2.30, £2.20; EX 36.00 Trifecta £182.20.
**Owner** Patrick Langdown **Bred** Stratford Place Stud **Trained** Bruton, Somerset

**FOCUS**
A moderate contest but it contained quite a few seemingly in-form types. The winner got the fractions spot on in front.

## 47 BETWAY H'CAP 1m 1f 104y (Tp)
**4:45** (4:46) (Class 5) (0-70,72) 4-Y-0+ **£3,881** (£1,155; £577; £288) **Stalls** Low

Form RPR

051- **1** **Kingthistle**[19] 8411 4-9-2 **66**...... StevieDonohoe 3 73
(Ian Williams) *trckd ldrs: rdn to ld 1f out: styd on* **7/2**[1]

005- **2** 3/4 **Cat Royale (IRE)**[15] 8462 4-9-1 **65**......(b[1]) DannyBrock 10 70
(Jane Chapple-Hyam) *led: rdn over 2f out: hdd 1f out: styd on* **13/2**[3]

314- **3** shd **Roman De Brut (IRE)**[36] 8141 5-8-13 **67**...... CharlieBennett(5) 4 72
(Daniel Mark Loughnane) *hld up in tch: rdn over 1f out: styd on* **7/1**

040- **4** 1 **Glenalmond (IRE)**[20] 8378 5-9-7 **70**...... JFEgan 2 73
(Daniel Steele) *hld up in tch: rdn and edgd lft over 1f out: styd on same pce wl ins fnl f* **14/1**

000- **5** 1 **Fantasy Gladiator**[34] 8178 11-9-4 **67**......(p) RobertWinston 1 68+
(Michael Appleby) *s.i.s: hld up: hdwy and nt clr run fr over 1f out tl swtchd rt wl ins fnl f: r.o* **14/1**

423- **6** nk **Mary Le Bow**[39] 8124 6-8-12 **64**......(t) CallumShepherd(3) 9 64
(Victor Dartnall) *hld up: rdn and r.o ins fnl f: nrst fin* **9/1**

01- **7** 3/4 **Raashdy (IRE)**[23] 8342 4-9-4 **68**...... AdamKirby 6 67
(Peter Hiatt) *chsd ldrs: rdn over 2f out: edgd lft and styd on same pce ins fnl f* **10/1**

**8** nk **Sevilla**[21] 7521 4-9-4 **68**...... KieranO'Neill 8 66
(Anabel K Murphy) *hld up: shkn up over 1f out: nt clr run ins fnl f: nt trble ldrs* **150/1**

505- **9** 1/2 **Bazooka (IRE)**[15] 8477 6-9-8 **71**...... GrahamLee 11 68
(David Flood) *s.i.s: hld up: rdn over 1f out: nt clr run ins fnl f: nvr trbld ldrs* **40/1**

000- **10** 2 1/2 **Dunquin (IRE)**[54] 7911 5-9-2 **65**...... DougieCostello 5 57
(John Mackie) *hld up in tch: rdn over 2f out: styd on same pce fr over 1f out* **11/2**[2]

321- **11** hd **Right Rebel**[82] 7327 5-9-6 **72**...... EoinWalsh(3) 12 63
(Alan Bailey) *sn w ldr: rdn and ev ch over 1f out: wknd ins fnl f* **13/2**[3]

046- **12** 2 1/2 **Idol Deputy (FR)**[23] 8343 11-9-2 **70**......(p) RachealKneller(5) 7 56
(James Bennett) *chsd ldrs: ridsden over 1f out: wknd fnl f* **25/1**

2m 0.05s (-0.75) **Going Correction** -0.05s/f (Stan)
**WFA** 4 from 5yo+ 1lb **12** Ran SP% **116.1**
Speed ratings (Par 103): **101,100,100,99,98 98,97,97,96,94 94,92**
CSF £24.89 CT £151.42 TOTE £4.60: £1.80, £3.10, £3.10; EX 30.70 Trifecta £184.30.
**Owner** E A Brook **Bred** R C Bond **Trained** Portway, Worcs

**FOCUS**
Some interesting types lined up for this modest contest. The runner-up has been rated in line with his form from the autumn.

## 48 32RED.COM MAIDEN AUCTION STKS 1m 142y (Tp)
**5:15** (5:16) (Class 5) 3-Y-0 **£3,881** (£1,155; £577; £288) **Stalls** Low

Form RPR

52- **1** **Multi Facets (IRE)**[13] 8486 3-9-5 0...... AdamKirby 8 74+
(David Simcock) *trckd ldrs: rdn to ld over 1f out: edgd lft ins fnl f: r.o* **4/11**[1]

42- **2** 2 **Special Relation (IRE)**[20] 8377 3-9-0 0...... CharlieBennett(5) 5 69+
(Hughie Morrison) *chsd ldrs: nt clr run over 2f out: rdn and edgd lft over 1f out: r.o to go 2nd wl ins fnl f* **11/4**[2]

02- **3** 2 1/4 **Do You Know (IRE)**[41] 8082 3-9-0 0...... DanielMuscutt 6 59
(Marco Botti) *led 1f: chsd ldr: led wl over 1f out: sn rdn and hdd: hung lft and no ex wl ins fnl f* **10/1**[3]

00- **4** 3/4 **Champagne Pink (FR)**[19] 8404 3-9-0 0......(h[1]) DougieCostello 1 57
(K R Burke) *prom: rdn over 2f out: edgd lft and styd on to go 4th nr fin* **50/1**

3- **5** hd **Lady Volante (IRE)**[29] 8237 3-9-0 65...... JFEgan 9 57
(David Evans) *led at stdy pce over 7f out: qcknd over 2f out: rdn and hdd wl over 1f out: no ex ins fnl f* **40/1**

6- **6** 1 1/2 **Baby Helmet**[81] 7355 3-9-5 0...... GrahamLee 3 58
(Mick Channon) *hld up: shkn up over 1f out: nvr on terms* **25/1**

**7** 1 3/4 **Whirlwind Romance (IRE)** 3-9-0 0...... JosephineGordon 7 49
(Hugo Palmer) *s.i.s: hld up: rdn over 2f out: wknd over 1f out* **22/1**

**8** 3 **Newton Heath (IRE)** 3-9-5 0...... StevieDonohoe 4 47
(Daniel Mark Loughnane) *s.i.s: hld up: rdn over 1f out: nvr on terms* **100/1**

04- **9** 2 **King Of Scotland (FR)**[18] 8423 3-9-5 0...... RobertWinston 2 43
(Hughie Morrison) *hld up: hung lft fr over 2f out: a in rr* **22/1**

1m 51.98s (1.88) **Going Correction** -0.05s/f (Stan) **9** Ran SP% **127.0**
Speed ratings (Par 97): **89,87,85,84,84 83,81,78,77**
CSF £1.82 TOTE £1.30: £1.10, £1.30, £1.80; EX 2.60 Trifecta £8.20.
**Owner** Jos & Mrs Jane Rodosthenous **Bred** Malih L Al Basti **Trained** Newmarket, Suffolk

**FOCUS**
The winner was heavily backed leading up to the off, and his form chance was obvious. A slight negative would be that this was run in a significantly slower time than the seller that followed it. The level is a bit fluid given the slow time and compressed field, but it's been rated around the fourth for now.

## 49 SUNBETS.CO.UK TOP PRICES ON ALL FAVOURITES (S) STKS 1m 142y (Tp)
**5:45** (5:48) (Class 6) 4-Y-0+ **£2,587** (£770; £384; £192) **Stalls** Low

Form RPR

003- **1** **Black Dave (IRE)**[23] 8337 7-9-1 72...... StevieDonohoe 1 70
(David Evans) *mde all: rdn over 1f out: styd on wl* **6/1**

506- **2** 1/2 **Pool House**[21] 8364 6-9-1 66...... RobertWinston 4 69
(Mike Murphy) *trckd ldrs: rdn over 1f out: r.o to go 2nd nr fin* **16/1**

616- **3** *nk* **Beautiful Stranger (IRE)**[13] 8498 6-9-7 72....................(p) PhillipMakin 5 74
(Keith Dalgleish) *s.i.s: hld up: hdwy over 1f out: sn rdn: r.o to go 3rd post* **7/2**[2]

264- **4** *nse* **With Pleasure**[20] 8379 4-9-0 74.................................... GrahamLee 2 68
(David O'Meara) *chsd ldrs: chsd wnr over 1f out: sn rdn: styd on same pce towards fin* **6/1**

043- **5** *nk* **Dana's Present**[28] 8252 8-9-7 72.................................... AdamKirby 9 74
(Tom Dascombe) *s.i.s: hld up: nt clr run wl over 1f out: rdn and r.o ins fnl f: nt rch ldrs* **5/2**[1]

030- **6** *1 ¼* **Dovil's Duel (IRE)**[9] 8528 6-8-12 60.................................. EoinWalsh(3) 3 65
(Tony Newcombe) *hld up: hdwy u.p over 1f out: hrd rdn ins fnl f: styd on same pce* **25/1**

004- **7** *1* **Cold Fusion (IRE)**[22] 8348 4-8-4 61..........................(p) HollieDoyle(5) 6 58
(David Flood) *chsd wnr: rdn over 2f out: lost 2nd over 1f out: no ex ins fnl f* **14/1**

/00- **8** *3 ¾* **Steady Major (IRE)**[13] 8498 5-8-10 68........................ CharlieBennett(5) 7 55
(Mark Brisbourne) *chsd ldrs: rdn over 2f out: wknd fnl f* **50/1**

014- **9** *½* **Jumbo Prado (USA)**[23] 8343 8-9-0 69............................(b) TobyEley(7) 10 60
(Daniel Mark Loughnane) *prom: rdn over 2f out: wknd over 1f out* **11/2**[3]

530- **10** *10* **Hannington**[15] 8469 6-8-8 65...................................(p) JordanUys(7) 8 33
(Barry Brennan) *hld up: rdn and wknd over 2f out* **150/1**

1m 48.45s (-1.65) **Going Correction** -0.05s/f (Stan)
**WFA** 4 from 5yo+ 1lb **10** Ran SP% **113.8**
Speed ratings (Par 101): **105,104,104,104,103 102,101,98,98,89**
CSF £92.13 TOTE £6.70: £2.00, £4.90, £1.50; EX 100.30 Trifecta £381.20.No bid for the winner. With Pleasure was claimed by Mr J. L. Flint for £6,000. Dana's Present was the subject of a friendly claim by Mr T. Dascombe for £6,000.
**Owner** Mrs E Evans & J Smith **Bred** Richard Frayne **Trained** Pandy, Monmouths

**FOCUS**
This seemed a competitive race of its type.

## 50 SUNBETS.CO.UK DOWNLOAD THE APP H'CAP — 7f 36y (Tp)
**6:15** (6:16) (Class 5) (0-70,71) 4-Y-0+ **£3,881** (£1,155; £577; £288) **Stalls** High

Form RPR

020- **1** **Gold Flash**[29] 8240 5-9-7 70..........................................(v[1]) PhillipMakin 3 78+
(Keith Dalgleish) *hld up: hdwy over 1f out: swtchd rt ins fnl f: r.o to ld post* **3/1**[2]

312- **2** *hd* **Cliff (IRE)**[14] 8482 7-9-4 67.................................... JosephineGordon 2 74
(Nigel Tinkler) *a.p: chsd ldr: 2f out: rdn to ld ins fnl f: hdd post* **5/1**[3]

522- **3** *1* **Rebel Lightning (IRE)**[20] 8378 4-9-8 71.........................(b) AdamKirby 9 76
(Richard Spencer) *chsd ldr: lft in ld 1/2-way: rdn over 1f out: hdd ins fnl f: styng on same pce whn n.m.r nr fin* **5/2**[1]

060- **4** *shd* **Dominium (USA)**[22] 8345 10-8-13 67.....................(b) DavidParkes(5) 5 71
(Jeremy Gask) *prom: rdn over 1f out: swtchd rt ins fnl f: r.o* **16/1**

450- **5** *1 ¾* **Siege Of Boston (IRE)**[87] 7194 4-8-13 62..............(t) TimmyMurphy 10 62
(Gordon Elliott, Ire) *prom: rdn over 1f out: styd on* **33/1**

134- **6** *3 ¾* **East Coast Lady (IRE)**[20] 8378 5-9-1 69........................ HollieDoyle(5) 1 59+
(William Stone) *awkward s: bhd: swtchd rt 6f out: hdwy over 5f out: chsd ldr over 3f out tl 2f out: sn rdn and hung lft: wknd ins fnl f* **15/2**

3- **7** *1* **Sheer Intensity (IRE)**[28] 8258 4-8-10 59.......................... JFEgan 11 46
(David Evans) *prom: rdn over 2f out: wknd over 1f out* **14/1**

023- **8** *1* **For Ayman**[42] 8067 6-9-5 68.......................................(t) GrahamLee 8 52
(Joseph Tuite) *s.i.s: hld up: nvr on terms* **20/1**

500- **9** *16* **Evanescent (IRE)**[15] 8473 8-9-0 63.............................. RobertWinston 4 4
(Tony Carroll) *led plld hrd and hung rt thrght: hdd 1/2-way: eased over 2f out* **8/1**

1m 27.98s (-0.82) **Going Correction** -0.05s/f (Stan) **9** Ran SP% **113.4**
Speed ratings (Par 103): **102,101,100,100,98 94,93,91,73**
CSF £18.08 CT £41.57 TOTE £4.60: £1.70, £1.60, £1.20; EX 20.40 Trifecta £71.70.
**Owner** Ronnie Docherty **Bred** C R Cawston Ltd **Trained** Carluke, S Lanarks

**FOCUS**
Two in-form horses plus a gambled-on winner fighting out the finish suggest this is fair form for the level. The runner-up has been rated to his best since October 2015, and the third close to his recent form.

## 51 SUNBETS.CO.UK H'CAP (DIV I) — 7f 36y (Tp)
**6:45** (6:46) (Class 6) (0-52,53) 4-Y-0+ **£2,587** (£770; £384; £192) **Stalls** High

Form RPR

01- **1** **Athassel**[8] 8542 8-9-6 51 6ex.................................... StevieDonohoe 7 57
(David Evans) *hld up in tch: lost pl over 4f out: hdwy over 2f out: rdn: edgd lft and r.o to ld nr fin* **10/11**[1]

660- **2** *nk* **Castlerea Tess**[13] 8500 4-8-12 46 oh1..........................(p[1]) JackDuern(3) 8 51
(Sarah Hollinshead) *led: rdn over 1f out: edgd lft ins fnl f: hdd nr fin* **33/1**

350- **3** *½* **Fossa**[8] 8542 7-8-10 46............................................ CharlieBennett(5) 3 50
(Mark Brisbourne) *chsd ldrs: rdn and swtchd lft over 1f out: r.o* **14/1**

105- **4** *1 ¼* **Kaaber (USA)**[8] 8541 6-9-8 53...................................... JackGarritty 9 54
(Roy Brotherton) *hld up: hdwy over 1f out: r.o* **14/1**

44-0 **5** *nk* **Ershaad (IRE)**[2] 26 5-9-4 49..............................(v[1]) JosephineGordon 5 49
(Shaun Harris) *sn pushed along to chse ldr: rdn over 1f out: styd on same pce ins fnl f* **14/1**

0/3- **6** *¾* **Rigid Rock (IRE)**[28] 8264 10-9-4 49...........................(b) JFEgan 10 47
(Adrian McGuinness, Ire) *plld hrd and prom: rdn over 1f out: styd on same pce ins fnl f* **10/1**

530- **7** *1* **Captain K (IRE)**[19] 8415 5-9-1 46.............................(h) DougieCostello 1 42
(Gordon Elliott, Ire) *hld up: nt clr run over 2f out: r.o ins fnl f: nvr nrr* **8/1**[3]

006- **8** *2 ¼* **Zed Candy Girl**[13] 8499 7-9-0 52..............................(p) TobyEley(7) 4 42
(Daniel Mark Loughnane) *hld up in tch: rdn over 2f out: edgd lft and wknd ins fnl f* **16/1**

0/5- **9** *8* **Birdie Must Fly**[28] 8247 5-8-10 46 oh1........................ HollieDoyle(5) 11 16
(Jimmy Fox) *hld up: plld hrd: wknd over 2f out* **66/1**

540- **10** *2* **Evident (IRE)**[271] 1319 7-9-7 52...................................... AdamKirby 2 17
(Tony Carroll) *mid-div: pushed along 1/2-way: hdwy u.p over 1f out: wknd ins fnl f* **13/2**[2]

600- **11** *½* **Firgrove Bridge (IRE)**[13] 8499 5-9-1 46 oh1.................(p) RyanPowell 6 10
(Kevin Frost) *s.i.s: hdwy 5f out: rdn over 2f out: sn wknd* **22/1**

400- **12** *4* **Minty Jones**[14] 8482 8-8-10 46 oh1..........................(v) PhilDennis(5) 12
(Michael Mullineaux) *hld up: racd keenly: hdwy over 4f out: rdn and wknd over 2f out* **80/1**

1m 28.48s (-0.32) **Going Correction** -0.05s/f (Stan) **12** Ran SP% **121.8**
Speed ratings (Par 101): **99,98,98,96,96 95,94,91,82,80 79,75**
CSF £50.26 CT £307.97 TOTE £1.70: £1.10, £9.60, £4.90; EX 46.40 Trifecta £320.90.
**Owner** Mrs E Evans **Bred** Moyns Park Estate And Stud Ltd **Trained** Pandy, Monmouths

**FOCUS**
The winner was well backed but only just got to the front in the dying strides.

## 52 SUNBETS.CO.UK H'CAP (DIV II) — 7f 36y (Tp)
**7:15** (7:16) (Class 6) (0-52,53) 4-Y-0+ **£2,587** (£770; £384; £192) **Stalls** High

Form RPR

04/- **1** **Oor Jock (IRE)**[19] 8417 9-9-5 50..............................(b) StevieDonohoe 3 57
(Adrian McGuinness, Ire) *hld up: hdwy over 2f out: rdn over 1f out: r.o to ld wl ins fnl f* **15/8**[1]

050- **2** *¾* **Prince Of Time**[78] 7427 5-8-8 46 oh1.................(p[1]) CallumRodriguez(7) 2 51
(Richard Ford) *hld up: hdwy 2f out: led over 1f out: rdn and hdd wl ins fnl f* **15/2**[3]

662- **3** *½* **Menelik (IRE)**[27] 8278 8-9-8 53.......................................(vt) AdamKirby 6 57
(Des Donovan, Ire) *hld up: hdwy over 1f out: r.o* **3/1**[2]

005- **4** *4* **Aye Aye Skipper (IRE)**[46] 8026 7-9-2 47......................(t) KieranO'Neill 10 41
(Ken Cunningham-Brown) *hld up: hdwy over 1f out: styd on: nt rch ldrs* **14/1**

000- **5** *shd* **Kodiac Lady (IRE)**[13] 8499 5-9-4 49.............................(be) JasonHart 1 44
(Simon West) *chsd ldrs: rdn over 1f out: no ex ins fnl f* **10/1**

606- **6** *3 ¾* **Tahiti One**[8] 8541 4-9-7 52..........................................(v[1]) WilliamCarson 8 36
(Tony Carroll) *led: rdn and hdd wl over 1f out: wknd ins fnl f* **10/1**

000- **7** *1* **Cytringan**[27] 8278 4-8-12 46 oh1................................ SimonPearce(3) 9 28
(Lydia Pearce) *chsd ldr tl rdn to ld and hung rt wl over 1f out: sn hdd: wknd ins fnl f* **40/1**

030- **8** *3 ½* **Bold Max**[27] 8278 6-9-1 46 oh1....................................(v) DougieCostello 7 19
(Zoe Davison) *hld up: effrt over 2f out: wknd over 1f out* **28/1**

000- **9** *½* **Wensara Dream**[41] 8079 4-8-12 46................................ RobHornby(3) 4 18
(Andrew Balding) *plld hrd and prom: rdn over 2f out: sn wknd* **18/1**

/06- **10** *5* **Club House (IRE)**[32] 8207 7-9-7 52..............................(p) RyanPowell 11 11
(Kevin Frost) *plld hrd and prom: rdn and wknd over 2f out* **12/1**

1m 27.81s (-0.99) **Going Correction** -0.05s/f (Stan) **10** Ran SP% **115.2**
Speed ratings (Par 101): **103,102,101,97,96 92,91,87,86,81**
CSF £16.40 CT £40.68 TOTE £3.00: £1.30, £2.40, £1.30; EX 17.20 Trifecta £75.80.
**Owner** D Daly **Bred** Thistle Bloodstock Ltd **Trained** Lusk, Co Dublin

**FOCUS**
A really moderate contest run at a fair gallop, and the three fancied runners in the betting came to the fore.
T/Plt: £27.00 to a £1 stake. Pool: £102,267.36 - 2,756.28 winning units T/Qpdt: £4.10 to a £1 stake. Pool: £12,935.01 - 2,282.90 winning units **Colin Roberts**

53 - 60a (Foreign Racing) - See Raceform Interactive

# CHELMSFORD (A.W) (L-H)
Thursday, January 5

**OFFICIAL GOING: Polytrack: standard**
Wind: Virtually nil Weather: Dry and cold

## 61 TOTEPLACEPOT RACING'S FAVOURITE BET H'CAP — 1m (P)
**5:45** (5:46) (Class 4) (0-85,87) 4-Y-0+ **£6,469** (£1,925; £962; £481) **Stalls** Low

Form RPR

606- **1** **Jimenez (IRE)**[76] 7506 4-9-1 79.....................................(p) MartinDwyer 6 86
(Brian Meehan) *sn chsng ldr tl led ent fnl 2f: rdn over 1f out: kpt on u.p and a doing enough ins fnl f: rdn out* **7/1**[3]

415- **2** *1 ¼* **Squire**[14] 8487 6-8-12 76...........................................(t) AdamBeschizza 4 80
(Michael Attwater) *stdd after s: hld up in tch in last trio: nt clr run jst over 2f out: rdn and hdwy over 1f out: styd on wl ins fnl f: wnt 2nd last strides: nvr getting to wnr* **7/1**[3]

051- **3** *shd* **Pendo**[21] 8378 6-8-11 75.............................................. KierenFox 2 79
(John Best) *taken down early: t.k.h early: in tch in midfield: lost pl over 2f out: hdwy u.p ent fnl f: styd on wl ins fnl f: snatched 3rd last stride: nvr getting to wnr* **7/2**[1]

410- **4** *hd* **Ice Royal (IRE)**[156] 4976 4-9-4 87................................ LucyKBarry(5) 7 90+
(Jamie Osborne) *s.i.s: hld up in tch in rr: effrt on inner and nt clrest of runs over 1f out: sn swtchd rt and again ins fnl f: kpt on wl fnl 75yds: snatched 4th last strides: nvr getting to wnr* **10/1**

006- **5** *nk* **Jack's Revenge (IRE)**[16] 8475 9-9-3 81........................(vt) SteveDrowne 1 84
(George Baker) *chsd ldr: rdn over 2f out: styd on to chse wnr ins fnl f: one pce and no imp and lost 3 pls cl home* **5/1**[2]

526- **6** *4* **Loyalty**[28] 8279 10-9-7 85............................................(v) TonyHamilton 5 78
(Derek Shaw) *sn led: hdd ent fnl 2f: rdn over 1f out: unable qck and lost 2nd ins fnl f: wknd and eased cl home* **7/2**[1]

320- **7** *2* **Russian Radiance**[36] 8158 5-9-6 84................................(h) LukeMorris 8 73
(Jonathan Portman) *in tch in midfield but stuck wd: rdn over 2f out: lost pl and bhd 1f out: wknd ins fnl f* **16/1**

005- **8** *2 ½* **One Pekan (IRE)**[203] 3324 7-9-4 82.............................. JackMitchell 3 65
(Roger Varian) *hld up in tch: c wd and effrt bnd wl over 1f out: sn u.p and no hdwy: bhd and wknd fnl f* **7/1**[3]

1m 38.24s (-1.66) **Going Correction** -0.075s/f (Stan) **8** Ran SP% **113.6**
Speed ratings (Par 105): **105,103,103,103,103 99,97,94**
CSF £53.87 CT £201.53 TOTE £8.50: £2.40, £2.60, £1.60; EX 60.40 Trifecta £344.40.
**Owner** Manton Thoroughbreds **Bred** Rathbarry Stud **Trained** Manton, Wilts

**FOCUS**
The early pace was fairly steady and it paid to race prominently. The winner has been rated as matching his turf form on his AW debut, and the standard is set by the second to the fifth.

## 62 TOTEPOOL RACECOURSE CASH BACK AVAILABLE H'CAP — 2m (P)
**6:15** (6:16) (Class 4) (0-85,83) 4-Y-0+ **£6,469** (£1,925; £962; £481) **Stalls** Low

Form RPR

223- **1** **Aldreth**[20] 8399 6-9-3 75......................................(p) NathanEvans(3) 4 83
(Michael Easterby) *chsd ldr tl 10f out: styd handy: n.m.r 2f out: rdn to ld 1f out: sn hdd but sustained effrt to ld again on post* **7/2**[2]

316- **2** *nse* **Bracken Brae**[29] 8250 5-9-0 69.................................. StevieDonohoe 2 76
(Mark H Tompkins) *hld up wl in tch in midfield: rdn to chal over 1f out: led ins fnl f: kpt on u.p: hdd on post* **8/1**

554- **3** *¾* **Percy Veer**[29] 8250 5-9-7 81........................................ MitchGodwin(5) 5 87
(Sylvester Kirk) *hld up in tch in midfield: rdn over 2f out: drvn and hdwy over 1f out: chsd ldrs ins fnl f: kpt on* **10/3**[1]

220- **4** *1 ¾* **Free Bounty**[28] 8084 4-7-13 66...................................(t) HollieDoyle(5) 8 70
(Philip McBride) *chsd ldrs: wnt 2nd 10f out tl rdn to ld over 1f out: hdd 1f out: styd on same pce ins fnl f* **20/1**

011- **5** *½* **Western Prince**[16] 8476 4-9-3 79...................................(h) LukeMorris 7 82
(Michael Appleby) *s.i.s: hld up in rr: swtchd rt and effrt u.p over 1f out: kpt on same pce ins fnl f* **10/3**[1]

206- **6** *hd* **Excellent Puck (IRE)**[36] 8161 7-9-8 **77** JoeFanning 3 80
(Shaun Lycett) *stdd s: t.k.h: hld up in last pair: nt clr run and swtchd rt over 1f out: swtchd bk lft and rdn ins fnl f: kpt on same pce fnl 100yds* **12/1**

454- **7** *1 1/2* **Cotton Club (IRE)**[8] 8558 6-10-0 **83** RyanTate 1 84
(Rod Millman) *in tch in midfield: unable qck u.p over 1f out: wknd ins fnl f* **5/1**[3]

360- **8** *12* **Modernism**[18] 8446 8-9-10 **79** (t[1]) RobertWinston 6 66
(Ian Williams) *sn led: rdn and hdd over 1f out: sn btn: bhd and eased ins fnl f* **12/1**

3m 31.26s (1.26) **Going Correction** -0.075s/f (Stan)
**WFA** 4 from 5yo+ 5lb 8 Ran SP% **116.3**
Speed ratings (Par 105): **93,92,92,91,91 91,90,84**
CSF £31.98 CT £101.25 TOTE £4.20: £1.50, £2.30, £1.60; EX 37.80 Trifecta £164.90.
**Owner** A Morse **Bred** Equine Breeding Limited **Trained** Sheriff Hutton, N Yorks

**FOCUS**
The pace steadied mid-race and then developed into a bit of a dash from the turn in. A small pb from the winner but in line with the better view of his form. The third has been rated to his recent form.

## 63 TOTEQUADPOT FOUR PLACES IN FOUR RACES H'CAP 5f (P)
**6:45** (6:45) (Class 2) (0-105,103) 4-Y-0+ **£12,291** (£3,657; £1,827; £913) **Stalls** Low

Form RPR

000- **1** **Lancelot Du Lac (ITY)**[187] 3909 7-9-7 **103** RobertWinston 3 115
(Dean Ivory) *trckd ldrs: effrt to chal over 1f out: rdn to ld 150yds out: r.o wl* **11/4**[2]

025- **2** *3/4* **Doctor Sardonicus**[45] 8050 6-8-12 **94** MartinHarley 6 102
(David Simcock) *chsd ldrs: rdn to chal over 1f out: led jst ins fnl f: sn hdd and styd on same pce fnl 150yds* **2/1**[1]

020- **3** *1 1/2* **Upavon**[20] 8407 7-8-6 **91** (bt[1]) AaronJones(3) 2 94
(Stuart Williams) *dwlt: hld up in tch in last pair: effrt over 1f out: sltly impeded and swtchd rt wl ins fnl f: styd on to go 3rd nr fin* **6/1**

020- **4** *1/2* **Bosham**[26] 8308 7-8-10 **95** (bt) NathanEvans(3) 4 96
(Michael Easterby) *taken down early: led: rdn and hrd pressed over 1f out: hdd jst ins fnl f: outpcd fnl 100yds* **8/1**

241- **5** *nk* **Distant Past**[15] 8484 6-8-10 **92** (v) ShaneGray 5 92
(Kevin Ryan) *in tch in midfield: effrt over 1f out: styd on same pce ins fnl f* **5/1**[3]

055- **6** *2* **Top Boy**[15] 8484 7-8-3 **85** (v) LukeMorris 1 78
(Derek Shaw) *t.k.h: hld up in tch in last pair: effrt over 1f out: drvn and no imp fnl f* **8/1**

58.64s (-1.56) **Going Correction** -0.075s/f (Stan) 6 Ran SP% **113.2**
Speed ratings (Par 109): **109,107,105,104,104 100**
CSF £8.84 TOTE £3.90: £1.90, £1.30; EX 6.80 Trifecta £28.70.
**Owner** Michael & Heather Yarrow **Bred** Elektra Di Fausto Martellozzo & C Sas **Trained** Radlett, Herts

**FOCUS**
A decent sprint and a good performance from the winner, who is classy at this level. The winner has been rated to his best, and the second as running as well as ever.

## 64 TOTEPOOLLIVEINFO.COM FOR RACING RESULTS H'CAP 5f (P)
**7:15** (7:18) (Class 6) (0-60,60) 4-Y-0+ **£3,234** (£962; £481; £240) **Stalls** Low

Form RPR

034- **1** **K'Gari Spirit**[143] 5470 4-9-4 **57** (t) NickyMackay 4 65
(Jeremy Gask) *in tch in midfield: effrt over 1f out: hdwy to chse ldr jst ins fnl f: styd on wl u.p to ld on post* **7/1**

654- **2** *nse* **Topsoil**[21] 8383 4-8-8 **47** (p) RyanPowell 2 55
(Ronald Harris) *taken down early: s.i.s and rdn along early: hdwy to ld over 3f out: rdn over 1f out: drvn ins fnl f: kpt on u.p: hdd on post* **9/2**[2]

611- **3** *3* **Secret Bird (IRE)**[20] 8408 5-9-1 **59** LuluStanford(5) 6 56+
(Dean Ivory) *taken down early: midfield but stuck wd thrght: rdn over 1f out: styd on ins fnl f to go 3rd towards fin: no threat to ldng pair* **5/6**[1]

550- **4** *1/2* **Name That Toon**[267] 1420 4-8-8 **47** (v) AdamBeschizza 5 42
(Derek Shaw) *s.i.s: outpcd in rr: hdwy u.p over 1f out: kpt on ins fnl f to go 4th towards fin: nvr trbld ldrs* **33/1**

006- **5** *nk* **Rojina (IRE)**[76] 7509 4-8-4 **46** oh1 (b[1]) NathanEvans(3) 1 40
(Lisa Williamson) *led: jinked rt 4f out: hdd over 3f out: rdn and unable qck over 1f out: wknd ins fnl f: lost 2 pls towards fin* **33/1**

560- **6** *2* **Justice Rock**[21] 8383 4-8-5 **47** (p) CallumShepherd(3) 8 34
(Phil McEntee) *chsd ldr tl pushed rt 4f out: chsd ldng pair after tl unable qck over 1f out: wknd ins fnl f* **16/1**

042- **7** *1* **Excellent Aim**[30] 8242 10-9-0 **60** JaneElliott(7) 7 44
(George Margarson) *s.i.s: outpcd in last pair: shkn up over 1f out: kpt on same pce ins fnl f: nvr trbld ldrs* **5/1**[3]

404- **8** *5* **Yisty**[294] 970 4-8-9 **48** (v) LukeMorris 3 14
(Derek Shaw) *midfield: hmpd 4f out: sn rdn and outpcd: no imp over 1f out: bhd and eased ins fnl f* **16/1**

59.95s (-0.25) **Going Correction** -0.075s/f (Stan) 8 Ran SP% **119.6**
Speed ratings (Par 101): **99,98,94,93,92 89,88,80**
CSF £40.27 CT £53.44 TOTE £8.30: £2.00, £1.60, £1.10; EX 44.90 Trifecta £105.40.
**Owner** Miss K M Dobb **Bred** Stuart Dobb & Miss Kate Dobb **Trained** Stockbridge, Hants

**FOCUS**
A low-grade sprint handicap.

## 65 @TOTEPOOLRACING WIN RACING TICKETS ON TWITTER MAIDEN STKS 1m 2f (P)
**7:45** (7:47) (Class 5) 3-4-Y-0 **£5,175** (£1,540; £769; £384) **Stalls** Low

Form RPR

03- **1** **Speedo Boy (FR)**[43] 8074 3-8-7 0 StevieDonohoe 4 79
(Ian Williams) *midfield: swtchd rt and rdn 3f out: chsd clr ldr wl over 1f out: styd on to ld ins fnl f: forged ahd towards fin* **6/1**[3]

323- **2** *1/2* **Draw Swords**[55] 7909 3-8-7 80 (b[1]) NickyMackay 7 78
(John Gosden) *racd freely: led and styd wd early: wl clr 6f out: reduced advantage over 2f out: rdn over 1f out: hdd 1f out: kpt on tl no ex and btn towards fin* **1/1**[1]

**3** *4 1/2* **Keswick** 3-8-7 0 (t[1]) DavidProbert 1 69
(John Gosden) *stdd s: hld up in midfield: effrt in 4th over 2f out: 3rd and styd on same pce fnl f* **11/4**[2]

460- **4** *3* **Upgrade**[16] 8466 3-8-7 71 JoeyHaynes 2 63
(K R Burke) *prom in main gp: chsd clr ldr 4f out tl over 1f out: sn drvn and unable qck: wknd ins fnl f* **9/1**

00- **5** *nse* **Mambo Dancer**[9] 8537 3-8-7 0 JoeFanning 6 63
(Mark Johnston) *bhd: sme hdwy over 2f out: swtchd rt over 1f out: hung lft and styd on ins fnl f: nvr trbld ldrs* **66/1**

**6** *3 3/4* **Star General** 3-8-7 0 DanielMuscutt 3 55
(Marco Botti) *hld up in last pair: effrt u.p over 2f out: no imp over 1f out* **14/1**

04- **7** *16* **Vrika Bay**[16] 8464 3-8-2 0 LukeMorris 5 18
(Robert Eddery) *chsd ldr tl 4f out: rdn and lost pl 3f out: bhd fnl f* **25/1**

2m 6.26s (-2.34) **Going Correction** -0.075s/f (Stan) 7 Ran SP% **113.0**
Speed ratings (Par 103): **106,105,102,99,99 96,83**
CSF £12.15 TOTE £6.70: £2.20, £1.30; EX 14.60 Trifecta £40.40.
**Owner** Paul Williams **Bred** E A R L Haras De Grandcamp Et Al **Trained** Portway, Worcs

**FOCUS**
A fair maiden. It's been rated at face value, with the second setting the standard and rated to his nursery latest.

## 66 TOTEPOOL BETTING ON ALL UK RACING H'CAP 7f (P)
**8:15** (8:16) (Class 4) (0-85,87) 4-Y-0+ **£6,469** (£1,925; £962; £481) **Stalls** Low

Form RPR

606- **1** **Hakam (USA)**[43] 8069 5-9-8 **86** LukeMorris 6 95
(Michael Appleby) *trckd ldrs: effrt to chal over 1f out: rdn to ld jst ins fnl f: styd on* **4/1**[3]

110- **2** *nk* **Firmdecisions (IRE)**[35] 8177 7-9-9 **87** RobertWinston 9 95
(Dean Ivory) *chsd ldr: rdn to ld over 1f out: hdd jst ins fnl f: kpt on wl u.p but a jst hld* **12/1**

4/0- **3** *1 1/4* **Miracle Ninetynine (IRE)**[48] 8015 5-8-12 **76** TomMarquand 7 81
(Ed Vaughan) *s.i.s: bhd: clsd and nt clrest of runs jst over 1f out: hdwy ins fnl f: r.o wl to go 3rd fnl 50yds: nt rch ldrs* **25/1**

000- **4** *3/4* **Strong Challenge (IRE)**[159] 4889 4-9-7 **85** DavidProbert 4 88
(Saeed bin Suroor) *t.k.h: hld up in tch in midfield: effrt in centre over 1f out: kpt on same pce ins fnl f* **3/1**[2]

221- **5** *1/2* **Ballylare**[17] 8456 4-9-3 **81** MartinHarley 1 83
(Lee Carter) *in tch in midfield: effrt to press ldrs over 1f out: styd on same pce u.p ins fnl f* **5/1**

013- **6** *1* **Out Of The Ashes**[17] 8456 4-8-11 **78** (t) EoinWalsh(3) 5 77
(Mohamed Moubarak) *hld up in tch in midfield: effrt 2f out: styd on same pce u.p fnl f* **16/1**

006- **7** *1/2* **Take The Helm**[29] 8251 4-9-5 **83** MartinDwyer 3 81
(Brian Meehan) *t.k.h: hld up in tch in last pair: hmpd over 3f out: shkn up and clsd jst over 1f out: nt clrest of runs and no real imp ins fnl f* **5/2**[1]

024- **8** *shd* **Shypen**[21] 8380 4-9-3 **81** TonyHamilton 2 78
(Richard Fahey) *t.k.h: led: sn hdd and trckd ldrs: effrt ent fnl f: unable qck and wknd ins fnl f* **7/1**

030- **9** *15* **Kingsley Klarion (IRE)**[26] 8311 4-9-8 **86** JoeFanning 8 43
(Mark Johnston) *dwlt: sn rcvrd to ld: rdn and hdd over 1f out: sn btn: bhd and eased ins fnl f* **33/1**

1m 25.67s (-1.53) **Going Correction** -0.075s/f (Stan) 9 Ran SP% **123.1**
Speed ratings (Par 105): **105,104,103,102,101 100,100,99,82**
CSF £54.44 CT £1091.53 TOTE £6.00: £1.70, £3.60, £5.40; EX 68.00 Trifecta £1375.60.
**Owner** The Horse Watchers **Bred** Jay W Bligh **Trained** Oakham, Rutland

**FOCUS**
Quite a competitive heat. They didn't go a strong gallop early.
T/Plt: £58.30 to a £1 stake. Pool: £109,469.39. 1,370.29 winning units. T/Qpdt: £14.90 to a £1 stake. Pool: £10,460.62. 518.40 winning units. **Steve Payne**

# [19]SOUTHWELL (L-H)
### Thursday, January 5

**OFFICIAL GOING: Fibresand: standard**
Wind: Virtually nil Weather: Fine & dry

## 67 SUNBETS.CO.UK TOP PRICE ON ALL FAVOURITES H'CAP 7f 14y(F)
**12:35** (12:40) (Class 6) (0-65,66) 4-Y-0+ **£2,587** (£770; £384; £192) **Stalls** Low

Form RPR

60-1 **1** **Essenaitch (IRE)**[3] 26 4-9-8 **66** 6ex DavidNolan 3 76+
(David Evans) *chsd ldrs: pushed along 1/2-way: rdn along wl over 2f out: hdwy wl over 1f out: sn chsng ldng pair: drvn and styd on wl fnl f to ld last 75 yds* **9/2**[1]

520- **2** *1 1/2* **Unnoticed**[15] 8482 5-9-6 **64** (t) RobertWinston 9 70
(Ollie Pears) *cl up: rdn to ld over 1f out: drvn ins fnl f: hdd and no ex last 75 yds* **9/2**[1]

006- **3** *1 1/2* **Secret Glance**[23] 8350 5-9-4 **62** AdamBeschizza 12 64
(Richard Rowe) *sn led and crossed to inner rail: pushed along over 2f out: rdn and hdd over 1f out: cl up and drvn ent fnl f: kpt on same pce* **5/1**[2]

340- **4** *3 1/2* **Call Out Loud**[30] 8241 5-9-5 **66** (tp) AlistairRawlinson(3) 5 59
(Michael Appleby) *t.k.h: n.m.r after s and sn swtchd lft: in tch: hdwy over 2f out: rdn wl over 1f out: kpt on fnl f* **20/1**

143- **5** *1* **Alpha Tauri (USA)**[23] 8350 11-9-7 **65** JoeyHaynes 4 58
(Charles Smith) *towards rr: pushed along 3f out: rdn and hdwy whn n.m.r and swtchd lft over 1f out: kpt on: nrst fin* **16/1**

261- **6** *1 1/2* **Justice Pleasing**[20] 8401 4-8-5 **56** (p) BenSanderson(7) 6 43
(Roger Fell) *towards rr: pushed along over 3f out: hdwy on outer 2f out: sn rdn and no imp* **14/1**

005- **7** *2* **Autumn Tonic (IRE)**[7] 8572 5-8-8 **52** (b) AndrewMullen 2 33
(David Barron) *chsd ldrs: rdn along over 2f out: drvn wl over 1f out: grad wknd* **14/1**

000- **8** *nk* **Kafeel (USA)**[14] 8498 6-9-5 **63** (p) LiamKeniry 13 44
(Linda Jewell) *cl up: rdn along 2f out: sn drvn and wknd over 1f out* **8/1**[3]

0/0- **9** *2 1/2* **Black Hambleton**[234] 2306 4-9-5 **63** ConnorBeasley 11 37
(Bryan Smart) *dwlt: a towards rr* **66/1**

3/1- **10** *3/4* **Mr Morse**[23] 8346 4-9-7 **65** DaleSwift 7 37
(Brian Ellison) *chsd ldrs: pushed along and outpcd after 3f: sn towards rr* **8/1**[3]

024- **11** *3* **Baileys Pursuit**[26] 8315 5-9-3 **61** (h) LukeMorris 8 25
(Gay Kelleway) *a towards rr* **12/1**

333- **12** *3/4* **Tasaaboq**[7] 8572 6-8-7 **54** (bt[1]) CallumShepherd(3) 10 16
(Phil McEntee) *chsd ldrs: hdwy 3f out: rdn along over 2f out: sn drvn and wknd* **12/1**

1m 30.48s (0.18) **Going Correction** +0.15s/f (Slow) 12 Ran SP% **116.1**
Speed ratings (Par 101): **104,102,100,96,95 93,91,91,88,87 83,83**
CSF £23.55 CT £106.65 TOTE £4.90: £1.70, £1.70, £2.00; EX 24.80 Trifecta £186.60.
**Owner** Spiers & Hartwell Ltd **Bred** Charel Park Stud **Trained** Pandy, Monmouths

**FOCUS**
A modest handicap and few ever got into it.

## 68 SUNBETS.CO.UK DOWNLOAD THE APP H'CAP (DIV I) 1m 13y(F)
**1:05** (1:10) (Class 6) (0-60,62) 4-Y-0+ **£2,587** (£770; £384; £192) **Stalls** Low

Form RPR
22-2 **1** **Playful Dude (USA)**[4] [7] 4-8-13 **55**...............(h) CallumShepherd[(3)] 10 63
(Phil McEntee) *cl up on outer: led wl over 2f out: sn rdn clr: edgd lft and kpt on fnl f* **5/4**[1]
000- **2** *2* **Swiftee (IRE)**[17] [8458] 4-9-7 **60**.......................................... DavidNolan 8 63
(Ivan Furtado) *chsd ldrs: rdn along and sltly outpcd over 3f out: wd st and hdwy over 2f out: rdn to chse wnr wl over 1f out: drvn and kpt on fnl f* **22/1**
61-3 **3** *nk* **General Tufto**[4] [7] 12-8-13 **52**..................................(b) JoeyHaynes 1 54
(Charles Smith) *sn rdn along and detached in rr: hdwy 3f out: rdn 2f out: styng on whn n.m.r and swtchd lft 1f out: sn drvn and kpt on* **6/1**[3]
020- **4** *2* **Catastrophe**[21] [8382] 4-9-8 **61**.......................................... JasonHart 3 59
(John Quinn) *chsd ldrs: rdn along and outpcd over 4f out: wd st and hdwy over 2f out: drvn to chse ldrs over 1f out: no imp* **12/1**
004- **5** *3* **Star Ascending (IRE)**[10] [8527] 5-9-4 **57**...................(v) JoeFanning 5 48
(Jennie Candlish) *slt ld: hdd 1/2-way: cl up and rdn along over 2f out: drvn wl over 1f out: grad wknd* **5/1**[2]
454- **6** *4* **Einstein**[14] [8491] 4-9-9 **62**..............................................(t) LukeMorris 9 44
(Mrs Ilka Gansera-Leveque) *cl up: led 1/2-way: rdn along and hdd wl over 2f out: drvn 2f out: sn wknd* **11/1**
505- **7** *1 1/4* **Hangman Jury**[19] [8428] 4-8-8 **54**.......................... StephenCummins[(7)] 4 33
(Richard Hughes) *chsd ldrs on inner: hdwy on far rail over 2f out: rdn wl over 1f out: sn wknd* **25/1**
000- **8** *69* **Desert Chief**[7] [8572] 5-8-7 **46** oh1..........................(be[1]) AndrewMullen 6
(Michael Appleby) *s.v.s and rel to r: a t.o* **7/1**

1m 46.25s (2.55) **Going Correction** +0.15s/f (Slow) **8** Ran SP% **112.1**
Speed ratings (Par 101): **93,91,90,88,85 81,80,11**
CSF £31.90 CT £124.44 TOTE £2.10: £1.10, £6.40, £1.60; EX 28.30 Trifecta £180.60.
**Owner** Mrs Rebecca McEntee **Bred** Jerry Jamgotchian **Trained** Newmarket, Suffolk

**FOCUS**
The first division of a moderate handicap. There was a disputed lead, but they didn't go very quick.

## 69 SUNBETS.CO.UK DOWNLOAD THE APP H'CAP (DIV II) 1m 13y(F)
**1:35** (1:40) (Class 6) (0-60,62) 4-Y-0+ **£2,587** (£770; £384; £192) **Stalls** Low

Form RPR
56-4 **1** **Samphire Coast**[3] [26] 4-9-2 **55**...................................(v) TonyHamilton 8 65
(Derek Shaw) *dwlt and towards rr: pushed along 1/2-way: hdwy over 3f out: wd st rdn to chse ldr over 1f out: strayed on strly to ld last 100 yds* **9/4**[2]
10-6 **2** *2 1/4* **Little Choosey**[4] [7] 7-9-0 **60**.................................(tp) KevinLundie[(7)] 5 64
(Roy Bowring) *cl up: led 3f out: rdn clr wl over 1f out: sn edgd lft: drvn ins fnl f: hdd and no ex last 100 yds* **25/1**
26-5 **3** *3 1/4* **Limerick Lord (IRE)**[4] [7] 5-8-12 **54**...................(p) ShelleyBirkett[(3)] 3 51
(Julia Feilden) *trckd ldng pair on inner: pushed along wl over 2f out: rdn wl over 1f out: kpt on same pce* **10/1**
054- **4** *3* **Arcane Dancer (IRE)**[23] [8347] 4-9-6 **62**....................(p) NathanEvans[(3)] 7 52
(Lawrence Mullaney) *chsd ldrs: rdn along 3f out: drvn and hung lft to inner 2f out: plugged on one pce* **4/1**[3]
40-4 **5** *2 1/4* **Powered (IRE)**[4] [7] 4-9-1 **54**.......................................... AndrewMullen 6 38
(David Evans) *chsd ldng pair: rdn along over 2f out: drvn wl over 1f out: sn btn* **7/4**[1]
000- **6** *9* **Zeteah**[70] [7642] 7-8-7 **46** oh1.................................................. JoeyHaynes 1 10
(Tony Carroll) *in tch on inner: rdn along bef 1/2-way: drvn over 3f out: sn outpcd* **100/1**
000- **7** *3 3/4* **Angel Of Light (IRE)**[93] [7052] 5-8-4 **50**..................... LauraCoughlan[(7)] 9 5
(Jo Hughes) *dwlt: in tch on wd outside: rdn along 1/2-way: sn outpcd and bhd* **25/1**
000- **8** *1 1/4* **Secret Interlude (IRE)**[6] [8589] 4-8-3 **49**.................... BenSanderson[(7)] 4 1
(Roger Fell) *sn rdn along in rr: bhd fr 1/2-way* **20/1**
000- **9** *5* **Spryt (IRE)**[23] [8351] 5-9-4 **57**................................................(b) JoeFanning 2
(Conor Dore) *slt ld: rdn along and hdd 3f out: drvn over 2f out and sn wknd* **25/1**

1m 45.36s (1.66) **Going Correction** +0.15s/f (Slow) **9** Ran SP% **113.5**
Speed ratings (Par 101): **97,94,91,88,86 77,73,72,67**
CSF £59.92 CT £473.44 TOTE £3.30: £1.30, £4.70, £2.30; EX 45.50 Trifecta £217.00.
**Owner** Paddy Barrett **Bred** P E Barrett **Trained** Sproxton, Leics

**FOCUS**
The winning time was 0.89sec faster than the first division.

## 70 BETWAY H'CAP 1m 4f 14y(F)
**2:10** (2:15) (Class 6) (0-60,66) 4-Y-0+ **£2,587** (£770; £384; £192) **Stalls** Low

Form RPR
041- **1** **Paladin (IRE)**[7] [8566] 8-9-11 **66** 6ex..........................(h) MitchGodwin[(5)] 8 74
(Michael Blake) *trckd ldrs: hdwy over 5f out: led 4f out: rdn 2f out: drvn ent fnl f: kpt on gamely* **3/1**[2]
004- **2** *nk* **Miss Macchiato (IRE)**[21] [8386] 4-8-6 **46** oh1................... JoeyHaynes 7 53
(Keith Dalgleish) *cl up: led over 7f out: hdd 4f out: cl up and sn pushed along: rdn 2f out: drvn over 1f out: styd on to chal ins fnl f: ev ch tl no ex nr fin* **20/1**
310- **3** *1 3/4* **Stonecoldsoba**[26] [8318] 4-9-7 **61**................................. AndrewMullen 10 65
(David Evans) *hld up in rr: stdy hdwy over 4f out: rdn along to chse ldrs 3f out: drvn wl over 1f out: kpt on: nrst fin* **6/1**
060- **4** *5* **Commissar**[26] [8318] 8-9-11 **61**....................................(tp) KieranO'Neill 11 57
(Mandy Rowland) *in tch: hdwy over 5f out and sn trcking ldrs: smooth effrt to chal 3f out: cl up and ev ch 2f out: sn rdn and wknd over 1f out* **20/1**
550- **5** *5* **Miss Tree**[26] [8309] 6-9-3 **53**................................................ JasonHart 9 41
(John Quinn) *hld up in rr: hdwy 1/2-way: chsd ldrs and wd st: sn rdn along and btn* **4/1**[3]
622- **6** *13* **Bridey's Lettuce (IRE)**[7] [8566] 5-9-11 **61**........................ DavidNolan 3 28
(Ivan Furtado) *trckd ldrs on inner: pushed along over 5f out: rdn over 4f out: sn outpcd* **5/2**[1]
062- **7** *2 1/4* **Port Lairge**[7] [8567] 7-9-3 **58**............................................. PhilDennis[(5)] 4 22
(Michael Chapman) *in tch: pushed along 5f: rdn 4f out: sn outpcd* **22/1**
406- **8** *10* **Nutzma**[7] [8567] 4-8-7 **47** oh1 ow1..............................(b[1]) ConnorBeasley 1
(Mike Murphy) *in tch on inner: rdn along and lost pl 6f out: sn bhd* **50/1**
060- **9** *16* **Chesham Rose (IRE)**[16] [8470] 4-8-7 **47** ow1.........(bt[1]) AdamBeschizza 5
(Dave Roberts) *chsd ldrs: rdn along 6f out: sn lost pl and bhd* **100/1**
554- **10** *22* **Mackiri (IRE)**[14] [8488] 4-8-7 **47**....................................(v[1]) LukeMorris 6
(Michael Appleby) *led: hdd over 7f out: rdn along over 5f out: sn wknd* **14/1**

2m 43.55s (2.55) **Going Correction** +0.15s/f (Slow)
**WFA** 4 from 5yo+ 3lb **10** Ran SP% **111.3**
Speed ratings (Par 101): **97,96,95,92,88 80,78,72,61,46**
CSF £63.51 CT £327.92 TOTE £3.90: £1.40, £4.20, £1.80; EX 58.40 Trifecta £463.60.
**Owner** The Moonlighters **Bred** Jim McCormack **Trained** Trowbridge, Wilts

■ Stewards' Enquiry : Mitch Godwin two-day ban (19-20 Jan): used whip above permitted level
David Nolan Stewards noted the trainer's explanation that the race had come too soon having raced seven days previously. The Veterinary Officer reported that a post-race examination failed to reveal any abnormalities.

**FOCUS**
A moderate middle-distance handicap. They didn't go quick early, but an injection of pace at halfway sorted them out and the front three had got away even before reaching the home straight.

## 71 BETWAY BEST ODDS GUARANTEED PLUS H'CAP 4f 214y(F)
**2:40** (2:45) (Class 4) (0-85,83) 4-Y-0+ **£5,175** (£1,540; £769; £384) **Stalls** Centre

Form RPR
551- **1** **The Big Lad**[19] [8430] 5-8-4 **72**.....................................(e) NicolaCurrie[(7)] 7 79
(Richard Hughes) *racd centre: cl up: rdn and edgd lft over 1f out: slt ld ins fnl f: hld on wl towards fin* **8/1**[3]
000- **2** *1/2* **Dungannon**[75] [7537] 10-9-0 **82**..................................(b) JoshuaBryan[(7)] 6 88
(Andrew Balding) *hld up: hdwy 2f out: cl up over 1f out: rdn to chal ent fnl f: sn drvn and ev ch tl nt qckn towards fin* **9/2**[2]
200- **3** *1/2* **I'll Be Good**[8] [8561] 8-9-5 **80**............................................... DaleSwift 2 84
(Brian Ellison) *racd towards far side: cl up: led 3f out: rdn wl over 1f out: drvn and hdd ins fnl f: kpt on* **8/1**[3]
03-6 **4** *3/4* **Crosse Fire**[4] [4] 5-8-11 **72**.........................................(p) KieranO'Neill 4 73
(Scott Dixon) *chsd ldrs: rdn along over 2f out: drvn over 1f out: kpt on wl fnl f* **9/2**[2]
025- **5** *1 3/4* **Archie Stevens**[19] [8429] 7-8-9 **70**................................ AndrewMullen 3 66
(David Evans) *racd centre: led 2f: cl up: rdn along wl over 1f out: drvn and hld whn n.m.r ent fnl f* **10/1**
311- **6** *4 1/2* **Captain Lars (SAF)**[7] [8571] 7-9-3 **83** 6ex......................(v) PhilDennis[(5)] 1 62
(Derek Shaw) *dwlt: racd towards far rail: trckd ldr: pushed along 2f out: rdn over 1f out: sn one pce* **5/4**[1]
005- **7** *19* **Krystallite**[14] [8495] 4-8-9 **70**.............................................. LukeMorris 5
(Scott Dixon) *racd centre: prom: rdn along 1/2-way: sn lost pl and bhd* **25/1**

1m 0.06s (0.36) **Going Correction** +0.20s/f (Slow) **7** Ran SP% **116.0**
Speed ratings (Par 105): **105,104,103,102,99 92,61**
CSF £44.59 TOTE £8.90: £4.10, £2.80; EX 47.30 Trifecta £304.20.
**Owner** Don Churston & Ray Greatorex **Bred** Lookout Partnership **Trained** Upper Lambourn, Berks

**FOCUS**
A fair sprint handicap and they certainly used the full width of the track. The third has been rated close to his turf form and the fourth close to his recent form.

## 72 BETWAY BEST ODDS GUARANTEED PLUS MEDIAN AUCTION MAIDEN STKS 6f 16y(F)
**3:10** (3:17) (Class 5) 3-5-Y-0 **£3,234** (£962; £481; £240) **Stalls** Low

Form RPR
42- **1** **Ascot Day (IRE)**[70] [7639] 3-8-12 0........................................ LiamKeniry 2 83+
(David Simcock) *trckd ldng pair: hdwy on outer over 2f out: led 11/2f out: sn qcknd clr: readily* **6/5**[1]
32-2 **2** *2 3/4* **Things Happen**[4] [2] 3-8-12 70........................................ AndrewMullen 4 70
(David Evans) *slt ld: hdd 1/2-way: cl up and rdn along over 2f out: rdn and edgd lft over 1f out: sn chsng wnr: no imp fnl f* **11/8**[2]
622- **3** *3* **Espresso Freddo (IRE)**[34] [8189] 3-8-12 75........................ LukeMorris 1 60
(Sir Mark Prescott Bt) *cl up: slt ld on inner 1/2-way: rdn over 2f out: hdd 11.2f out: sn drvn and kpt on same pce* **5/1**[3]
0- **4** *3/4* **Mimic's Memory**[49] [7988] 3-8-7 0.......................................... JoeyHaynes 3 53
(Ann Duffield) *in tch: green and pushed along after 2f: rdn along 1/2-way: kpt on appr fnl f* **50/1**

1m 16.41s (-0.09) **Going Correction** +0.15s/f (Slow) **4** Ran SP% **106.2**
Speed ratings (Par 103): **106,102,98,97**
CSF £3.04 TOTE £1.90; EX 2.80 Trifecta £3.20.
**Owner** Ahmed Jaber **Bred** Rabbah Bloodstock Limited **Trained** Newmarket, Suffolk

**FOCUS**
A modest 3yo maiden, though three of the four had finished runner-up last time out. The runner-up, who is key to the form, has been rated to his C&D handicap latest.

## 73 32RED.COM H'CAP 7f 14y(F)
**3:40** (3:45) (Class 6) (0-60,57) 3-Y-0 **£2,587** (£770; £384; £192) **Stalls** Low

Form RPR
003- **1** **Seaview**[121] [6208] 3-9-2 **55**.............................................. AaronJones[(3)] 6 69
(David Brown) *cl up on outer: led 4f out: rdn clr wl over 1f out: easily* **9/4**[1]
005- **2** *6* **Come On Percy**[31] [8230] 3-9-6 **56**.......................................... DavidNolan 3 53
(Richard Fahey) *.cl up: rdn along over 2f out: sn chsng wnr: drvn over 1f out: kpt on: no ch w wnr* **13/2**[3]
000- **3** *hd* **Log Off (IRE)**[56] [7885] 3-9-6 **56**........................................ KieranO'Neill 9 52
(David Evans) *towards rr: pushed along 1/2-way: rdn and hdwy over 2f out: drvn over 1f out: kpt on wl fnl f* **6/1**[2]
000- **4** *2 3/4* **Stag Party (IRE)**[30] [8235] 3-8-10 **53**...........................(b[1]) WilliamCox[(7)] 11 42
(Andrew Balding) *dwlt and rr: wd st: hdwy over 2f out: rdn wl over 1f out: kpt on fnl f: nrst fin* **6/1**[2]
004- **5** *1/2* **Fairy Lock (IRE)**[23] [8344] 3-9-5 **55**.................................. AndrewMullen 4 43
(David Barron) *trckd ldrs: hdwy 3f out rdn over 2f out: drvn wl over 1f out: sn one pce* **13/2**[3]
066- **6** *1 1/4* **Shaqoos (FR)**[30] [8237] 3-9-2 **52**.......................................... JoeyHaynes 5 37
(Jo Hughes) *in tch: hdwy 3f out: rdn over 2f out: n.d* **28/1**
000- **7** *3 1/4* **Bella Duchess (IRE)**[23] [8344] 3-8-10 **46** ow1.................. LiamKeniry 10 22
(David C Griffiths) *nvr bttr than midfield* **50/1**
003- **8** *2 3/4* **Magic Journey (IRE)**[65] [7749] 3-9-6 **56**............................(b) JasonHart 2 25
(John Quinn) *slt ld 3f: cl up: rdn wl over 2f out: sn drvn and wknd* **6/1**[2]
000- **9** *nk* **Chillililli**[43] [8071] 3-8-3 **46**................................................ RPWalsh[(7)] 8 14
(Michael Appleby) *a towards rr* **25/1**
000- **10** *5* **Copa Beech**[30] [8237] 3-8-6 **45**.................................(b) CallumShepherd[(3)] 7
(Olly Williams) *dwlt: a towards rr* **80/1**
450- **11** *3 1/2* **Elements Legacy**[116] [6388] 3-9-2 **57**.........................(v) JordanVaughan[(5)] 1 3
(K R Burke) *sn rdn along and outpcd: a bhd* **20/1**

1m 31.55s (1.25) **Going Correction** +0.15s/f (Slow) **11** Ran SP% **115.5**
Speed ratings (Par 95): **98,91,90,87,87 85,82,78,78,72 68**
CSF £15.72 CT £78.82 TOTE £3.40: £1.30, £2.30, £2.20; EX 17.10 Trifecta £86.80.
**Owner** Mrs Sandra Brown **Bred** Genesis Green Stud Ltd & John Troy **Trained** Averham Park, Notts

**FOCUS**
A moderate 3yo handicap contested by 11 maidens, but it proved one-way traffic.

T/Plt: £119.90 to a £1 stake. Pool: £84,189.16. 512.26 winning units. T/Qpdt: £43.30 to a £1 stake. Pool: £6,878.05. 117.45 winning units. **Joe Rowntree**

# [46]WOLVERHAMPTON (A.W) (L-H)

Thursday, January 5

**OFFICIAL GOING: Tapeta: standard**

Wind: Light, behind Weather: Fine

## 74 BETWAY MARATHON H'CAP 1m 5f 194y

2:00 (2:01) (Class 5) (0-75,75) 4-Y-O+ £3,072 (£914; £456; £228) Stalls Low

Form RPR

5/4- 1 **Pivot Bridge**[74] 7562 9-9-2 **65** AdamKirby 3 76
(Adrian McGuinness, Ire) *hld up: hdwy over 4f out: chsd ldr over 2f out: shkn up to ld over 1f out: edgd rt and rdn clr fnl f* **11/4**[2]

530/ 2 6 **Uncle Bernie (IRE)**[540] 1166 7-9-10 **73** JamesSullivan 10 76
(Sarah Hollinshead) *s.i.s: hld up: hdwy over 3f out: chsd wnr over 1f out: wknd ins fnl f* **50/1**

3 3 ½ **Remember The Man (IRE)**[67] 4-9-6 **75** (b[1]) JFEgan 8 73
(Ralph Beckett) *led over 12f out: clr over 10f out: shkn up over 2f out: hdd over 1f out: wknd fnl f* **11/4**[2]

000- 4 2 ¼ **Spiritoftomintoul**[16] 8476 8-9-7 **73** (t) GeorgeDowning(3) 5 68
(Tony Carroll) *s.i.s: hld up: hdwy over 1f out: nvr trbld ldrs* **6/1**[3]

330- 5 nk **Scrafton**[16] 8477 6-8-7 **63** AledBeech(7) 7 58
(Tony Carroll) *hld up: hmpd and stmbld over 12f out: styd on fr over 1f out: nt trble ldrs* **11/1**

51- 6 15 **Elusive Cowboy (USA)**[10] 8524 4-9-5 **74** 6ex StevieDonohoe 6 48
(Stuart Edmunds) *chsd ldrs: wnt 2nd 5f out tl rdn over 2f out: sn wknd* **9/4**[1]

400- 7 13 **English Summer**[16] 8477 10-9-10 **73** (t) GrahamLee 2 28
(Ian Williams) *chsd ldrs: nt clr run and lost pl over 4f out: hmpd over 3f out: n.d after* **33/1**

000- 8 10 **Amber Flush**[21] 5176 8-9-9 **72** PaddyAspell 1 13
(Clare Ellam) *hld up: wknd over 4f out* **100/1**

5/5- 9 60 **Skilled**[24] 8339 6-9-7 **70** (p[1]) GeorgeBaker 9
(Anabel K Murphy) *led: hdd over 12f out: chsd ldr who wnt clr over 10f out tl rdn 5f out: wknd over 3f out* **33/1**

2m 58.97s (-5.83) **Going Correction** -0.10s/f (Stan)
**WFA** 4 from 6yo+ 4lb 9 Ran SP% **115.6**
Speed ratings (Par 103): **112,108,106,105,105 96,89,83,49**
CSF £131.34 CT £414.49 TOTE £3.90: £1.70, £5.00, £1.30; EX 81.30 Trifecta £324.50.
**Owner** D Daly **Bred** Newsells Park Stud **Trained** Lusk, Co Dublin

**FOCUS**
It got down to -6C overnight and the track was harrowed to a depth of 3.5 inches and left open, before being returned to standard with a Gallop Master finish. They went a strong early gallop in this modest staying handicap. The winner has been rated back to his early 2016 level, with the runner-up close to his old form.

## 75 32RED.COM MAIDEN FILLIES' STKS (DIV I) 6f 20y (Tp)

2:30 (2:31) (Class 5) 3-Y-O+ £3,072 (£914; £456; £228) Stalls Low

Form RPR

44- 1 **Moonshine Dancer**[18] 8443 3-8-12 0 WilliamCarson 8 70+
(David Simcock) *chsd ldr 5f out: shkn up over 1f out: edgd rt and r.o to ld wl ins fnl f* **13/8**[1]

053- 2 nk **Hathfa (FR)**[17] 8454 3-8-12 68 (be) ShaneKelly 5 69
(Richard Hughes) *led early: chsd ldrs: rdn and ev ch whn edgd lft wl ins fnl f: r.o* **9/2**[3]

222- 3 nk **Bithynia (IRE)**[20] 8406 3-8-12 69 JFEgan 3 68
(David Evans) *sn led: rdn over 1f out: hdd wl ins fnl f* **4/1**[2]

5- 4 hd **Spinwheel**[8] 8557 3-8-12 0 PJMcDonald 7 67+
(Mark Johnston) *prom: pushed along and lost pl 5f out: rdn over 1f out: r.o wl ins fnl f* **15/2**

\- 5 1 ¼ **Exquisite Ruby** 3-8-12 0 DavidProbert 6 63
(Charles Hills) *prom: rdn over 1f out: styd on* **5/1**

50- 6 2 ¼ **Dashing Poet**[154] 5077 3-8-12 0 TomMarquand 1 56
(Jeremy Gask) *plld hrd and prom: rdn over 1f out: wknd wl ins fnl f* **28/1**

6- 7 1 ½ **Tink**[14] 8494 3-8-7 0 CharlieBennett(5) 9 51
(Mark Brisbourne) *s.i.s: hld up: swvd rt over 5f out: rdn over 1f out: nvr on terms* **100/1**

060- 8 hd **Just Over**[243] 2039 4-9-11 0 EoinWalsh(3) 2 55
(Robert Cowell) *hld up: rdn over 2f out: wknd fnl f* **150/1**

040- 9 2 ¼ **Satpura**[117] 6336 3-8-12 69 GrahamLee 4 44
(Mick Channon) *in rr and sn pushed along: rdn over 1f out: n.d* **16/1**

1m 14.33s (-0.17) **Going Correction** -0.10s/f (Stan)
**WFA** 3 from 4yo 16lb 9 Ran SP% **115.7**
Speed ratings (Par 100): **97,96,96,95,94 91,89,89,86**
CSF £9.17 TOTE £2.40: £1.20, £1.80, £1.40; EX 10.40 Trifecta £28.50.
**Owner** Walters Plant Hire & James & Jean Potter **Bred** Lady S K Marchwood **Trained** Newmarket, Suffolk

**FOCUS**
They finished in a heap in this fillies' maiden, which was slightly the slower of the two divisions. The form makes sense rated around the first three.

## 76 32RED.COM MAIDEN FILLIES' STKS (DIV II) 6f 20y (Tp)

3:00 (3:02) (Class 5) 3-Y-O+ £3,072 (£914; £456; £228) Stalls Low

Form RPR

1 **Garam (IRE)** 3-8-12 0 JosephineGordon 1 77+
(Hugo Palmer) *s.i.s: pushed along in rr: nt clr run over 2f out: swtchd rt and hdwy over 1f out: rdn: hung lft and r.o to ld wl ins fnl f* **9/4**[1]

3- 2 1 **Blue Bahia (IRE)**[8] 8556 3-8-12 80 PJMcDonald 7 70
(Mark Johnston) *chsd ldr tl led over 2f out: rdn over 1f out: edgd lft and hdd wl ins fnl f* **11/2**

325- 3 4 **Preobrajenska**[21] 8377 3-8-12 72 (h) SeanLevey 9 58
(Michael Bell) *prom: rdn and hung lft fr over 1f out: wknd wl ins fnl f* **4/1**[3]

3- 4 ½ **School Run (IRE)**[20] 8406 3-8-12 0 ShaneKelly 6 56
(David O'Meara) *hld up in tch: rdn over 1f out: hung lft and styd on same pce fnl f* **3/1**[2]

420- 5 1 **Prufrock (IRE)**[118] 6292 3-8-12 68 TomMarquand 8 53
(David Simcock) *hld up: rdn over 2f out: r.o ins fnl f: nvr nrr* **9/2**

0- 6 ¾ **Brean Flyer**[19] 8425 3-8-12 0 WilliamCarson 5 50
(Bill Turner) *plld hrd and prom: rdn and nt clr run over 1f out: hung lft and wknd ins fnl f* **200/1**

0- 7 nk **Celerity (IRE)**[36] 8151 3-8-12 64 JFEgan 3 49
(David Evans) *sn led: rdn and hdd over 2f out: wknd fnl f* **20/1**

00- 8 shd **Arya Stark**[43] 8065 3-8-9 0 GeorgeDowning(3) 4 49
(Tony Carroll) *s.i.s: effrt and nt clr run over 1f out: n.d* **200/1**

9 6 **Neptune Star** 3-8-7 0 DavidParkes(5) 2 30
(Jeremy Gask) *chsd ldrs: rdn over 2f out: hung lft and wknd over 1f out* **25/1**

1m 14.26s (-0.24) **Going Correction** -0.10s/f (Stan) 9 Ran SP% **118.9**
Speed ratings (Par 100): **97,95,90,89,88 87,86,86,78**
CSF £15.51 TOTE £3.60: £1.50, £1.60, £1.70; EX 14.40 Trifecta £45.90.
**Owner** Sheikh Mohamed Bin Maktoum Al Maktoum **Bred** C Farrell **Trained** Newmarket, Suffolk

**FOCUS**
Marginally the quicker of the two divisions. Those down the field had plenty to prove and potentially limit the form. It's been rated cautiously with that in mind.

## 77 32RED CASINO H'CAP 6f 20y (Tp)

3:30 (3:32) (Class 6) (0-60,60) 3-Y-O £2,587 (£770; £384; £192) Stalls Low

Form RPR

060- 1 **Magdalene Fox**[28] 8276 3-9-3 **56** (b) AdamKirby 9 65
(Ed Dunlop) *mde all: rdn over 1f out: hung rt wl ins fnl f: styd on* **9/1**

504- 2 ½ **In The Spotlight (IRE)**[119] 6252 3-9-6 **59** GeorgeBaker 8 67
(Henry Spiller) *hld up: hdwy over 1f out: rdn to chse wnr and hung lft ins fnl f: styd on* **3/1**[2]

404- 3 1 ¾ **Tranquil Daze (IRE)**[43] 8071 3-9-7 **60** PJMcDonald 3 62
(David Brown) *chsd wnr: rdn over 1f out: sn hung lft: styd on same pce ins fnl f* **9/4**[1]

040- 4 1 ¾ **Little Nosegay (IRE)**[41] 8097 3-9-3 **56** JFEgan 5 52
(David Evans) *hld up in tch: plld hrd: rdn over 1f out: kpt on* **6/1**

000- 5 1 **Vocalisation (IRE)**[102] 6807 3-8-12 **51** DavidProbert 2 44
(John Weymes) *chsd ldrs: rdn over 2f out: wknd ins fnl f* **33/1**

042- 6 1 **Red Mohican**[9] 8536 3-9-4 **57** (t) JosephineGordon 7 47
(Phil McEntee) *prom: rdn over 1f out: wknd ins fnl f* **11/2**[3]

630- 7 3 ¼ **Zaatar (IRE)**[16] 8467 3-9-1 **57** GeorgeDowning(3) 6 37
(Mick Channon) *s.i.s: in rr: rdn and hung lft over 1f out: n.d* **20/1**

004- 8 1 ¼ **Nuptials (USA)**[134] 5770 3-8-13 **55** EdwardGreatrex(3) 1 32
(Eve Johnson Houghton) *mid-div: pushed along over 3f out: rdn and wkng whn nt clr run over 1f out* **7/1**

060- 9 11 **Fully Focussed (IRE)**[106] 6682 3-9-0 **53** GrahamLee 4
(Ann Duffield) *s.i.s: in rr: pushed along 1/2-way: sn wknd* **25/1**

1m 13.64s (-0.86) **Going Correction** -0.10s/f (Stan) 9 Ran SP% **119.5**
Speed ratings (Par 95): **101,100,98,95,94 93,88,87,72**
CSF £36.75 CT £84.48 TOTE £10.50: £2.70, £1.60, £1.20; EX 50.60 Trifecta £219.60.
**Owner** R P Foden & Countess Of Wessex **Bred** Whitsbury Manor Stud **Trained** Newmarket, Suffolk

**FOCUS**
Not many got involved in this.

## 78 £10 FREE AT 32RED.COM H'CAP 7f 36y (Tp)

4:00 (4:00) (Class 5) (0-75,77) 3-Y-O £3,234 (£962; £481; £240) Stalls High

Form RPR

263- 1 **Dandy Flame (IRE)**[18] 8444 3-9-7 **75** AdamKirby 1 79
(William Haggas) *trckd ldrs: shkn up to chse ldr over 1f out: rdn to ld ins fnl f: styd on* **9/4**[1]

204- 2 ½ **Party Tiger**[29] 8244 3-9-6 **74** JackGarritty 2 76
(Richard Fahey) *led 1f: remained handy: rdn: carried hd high and hung lft fr over 1f out: r.o* **9/4**[1]

460- 3 ¾ **Shabeeh (IRE)**[22] 8353 3-9-3 **71** PJMcDonald 7 71
(Mark Johnston) *led at stdy pce 6f out: qcknd over 2f out: rdn over 1f out: hdd ins fnl f: styd on same pce* **13/2**[3]

660- 4 1 **Ode To Paris**[92] 7072 3-8-13 **67** DavidProbert 4 64
(Ed Dunlop) *hld up: rdn over 1f out: r.o towards fin: nt rch ldrs* **10/1**

204- 5 hd **Princess Way (IRE)**[43] 8072 3-8-6 **60** ow1 JFEgan 6 57
(David Evans) *prom: chsd ldr over 5f out: rdn over 2f out: lost 2nd over 1f out: no ex ins fnl f* **11/1**

004- 6 1 ¼ **Venetian Proposal (IRE)**[22] 8361 3-8-6 **60** (p) WilliamCarson 5 53
(Zoe Davison) *s.i.s: hld up: hdwy over 1f out: sn rdn: styd on same pce ins fnl f* **50/1**

150- 7 1 ½ **Monoshka (IRE)**[102] 6800 3-8-13 **74** LewisEdmunds(7) 3 63
(James Given) *pushed along in rr early: rdn over 2f out: nvr on terms* **9/2**[2]

1m 30.16s (1.36) **Going Correction** -0.10s/f (Stan) 7 Ran SP% **112.4**
Speed ratings (Par 97): **88,87,86,85,85 83,82**
CSF £6.95 CT £26.05 TOTE £3.10: £1.70, £1.50; EX 7.30 Trifecta £27.30.
**Owner** The Up In Flames Partnership **Bred** Limestone & Tara Studs **Trained** Newmarket, Suffolk

**FOCUS**
This was quite steadily run. The third has been rated close to his more recent maiden form.

## 79 BETWAY H'CAP 5f 21y (Tp)

4:30 (4:31) (Class 4) (0-85,85) 4-Y-O+ £4,851 (£1,443; £721; £360) Stalls Low

Form RPR

506- 1 **Zac Brown (IRE)**[20] 8407 6-9-7 **85** (t) WilliamCarson 1 94
(Charlie Wallis) *mde all: rdn and edgd lft ins fnl f: jst hld on* **12/1**

045- 2 nk **Steelriver (IRE)**[16] 8463 7-9-4 **82** GeorgeBaker 9 90+
(David Barron) *hld up: rdn: edgd lft and r.o wl ins fnl f: nt quite rch wnr* **5/1**[3]

01-0 3 1 ½ **Oriental Relation (IRE)**[4] 4 6-8-12 **83** (v) LewisEdmunds(7) 3 86
(James Given) *s.i.s: pushed along in rr early: hdwy over 1f out: r.o* **4/1**[2]

001- 4 shd **Silvanus (IRE)**[70] 7643 12-9-7 **85** DougieCostello 6 88
(Paul Midgley) *chsd wnr: rdn over 1f out: hung lft and styd on same pce ins fnl f* **20/1**

111- 5 ½ **Verne Castle**[105] 6699 4-9-3 **81** (h) DavidProbert 8 82
(Andrew Balding) *chsd ldrs: rdn over 1f out: edgd lft and styd on same pce ins fnl f* **13/2**

000- 6 ¾ **Invincible Ridge (IRE)**[7] 8571 9-8-11 **78** EoinWalsh(3) 2 77
(Eric Alston) *chsd ldrs: pushed along 1/2-way: styng on same pce whn n.m.r wl ins fnl f* **25/1**

002- 7 ¾ **Foxy Forever (IRE)**[20] 8403 7-9-3 **81** (t) AdamKirby 7 76
(Michael Wigham) *hld up: hdwy over 1f out: sn rdn: styd on same pce fnl f* **5/2**[1]

104- 8 ¾ **Seve**[16] 8463 5-9-7 **85** JosephineGordon 5 78
(Tom Dascombe) *hld up: rdn over 1f out: nvr on terms* **13/2**

230- 9 nk **King Of Swing**[75] 7540 4-9-0 **78** (h[1]) ShaneKelly 11 70
(Richard Hughes) *s.i.s: sn pushed along in rr: n.d* **16/1**

146- 10 ½ **Rosealee (IRE)**[160] 4831 4-8-11 **80** DavidParkes(5) 4 70
(Jeremy Gask) *prom: rdn over 1f out: wknd ins fnl f* **8/1**

1m 0.26s (-1.64) **Going Correction** -0.10s/f (Stan) 10 Ran SP% **125.2**
Speed ratings (Par 105): **109,108,106,105,105 103,102,101,101,100**
CSF £76.33 CT £299.73 TOTE £14.80: £3.40, £2.00, £2.10; EX 92.40 Trifecta £525.00.
**Owner** Dab Hand Racing **Bred** Tally-Ho Stud **Trained** Ardleigh, Essex

**FOCUS**
A decent sprint handicap. The winner has been rated to his best since winning here last spring.

## 80 BETWAY SPRINT H'CAP 6f 20y (Tp)
**5:00** (5:01) (Class 6) (0-60,64) 4-Y-0+ **£2,587** (£770; £384; £192) **Stalls** Low

Form | | | | RPR
001- **1** **Born To Finish (IRE)**[5] 8595 4-9-6 **64** 6ex................(p) DavidParkes(5) 9 74+
(Jeremy Gask) *s.i.s: hld up: hdwy over 1f out: swtchd rt ins fnl f: qcknd to ld nr fin* **15/8**[1]
0F0- **2** 1 ¼ **Disclosure**[26] 8306 6-9-4 **57**..............(h) AdamKirby 1 63
(Les Eyre) *trckd ldrs: rdn to ld ins fnl f: hdd nr fin* **8/1**[3]
502- **3** nk **Major Muscari (IRE)**[9] 8541 9-9-2 **55**...............(p) TomMarquand 2 60
(Shaun Harris) *chsd ldrs: rdn over 1f out: edgd lft ins fnl f: styd on* **12/1**
054- **4** shd **Harmonic Wave (IRE)**[21] 8390 4-9-7 **60**...............(p) PJMcDonald 4 65
(Rebecca Menzies) *hld up: hdwy over 1f out: r.o* **8/1**[3]
006- **5** 1 ¾ **Storm Trooper (IRE)**[21] 8390 6-9-6 **59**.............. PaddyAspell 12 58
(David Nicholls) *chsd ldr: rdn over 1f out: ev ch ins fnl f: styd on same pce: n.m.r nr fin* **28/1**
503- **6** ¾ **Emily Goldfinch**[17] 8457 4-9-5 **58**.............. JosephineGordon 11 55
(Phil McEntee) *sn led: rdn over 2f out: hdd and no ex ins fnl f* **20/1**
466- **7** ½ **Pushkin Museum (IRE)**[107] 6660 6-9-4 **57**.............. JackGarritty 13 52
(Patrick Morris) *led early: plld hrd: sn stdd and lost pl: hung lft and styd on ins fnl f* **28/1**
302- **8** 1 **Le Manege Enchante (IRE)**[15] 8483 4-9-2 **58**..........(p) NoelGarbutt(3) 8 50
(Derek Shaw) *s.i.s: hld up: hdwy over 1f out: styd on same pce ins fnl f* **16/1**
636- **9** nk **Kyllach Me (IRE)**[134] 5760 5-9-3 **56**..............(p) ConnorBeasley 6 47
(Bryan Smart) *plld hrd and prom: stdd and lost pl over 4f out: n.d after* **4/1**[2]
160- **10** 1 ¼ **Whipphound**[26] 8315 9-9-3 **56**..............(p) JamesSullivan 3 43
(Ruth Carr) *hld up: hdwy over 1f out: wknd ins fnl f* **20/1**
636- **11** ½ **Secret Millionaire (IRE)**[9] 8542 10-8-12 **54**..............(p) TimClark(3) 10 40
(Shaun Harris) *hld up: rdn and wknd over 1f out* **25/1**
505- **12** ½ **Generalyse**[26] 8316 8-9-0 **56**..............(b) GeorgeDowning(3) 7 40
(Anabel K Murphy) *chsd ldrs: rdn over 2f out: wknd over 1f out* **11/1**

1m 13.47s (-1.03) **Going Correction** -0.10s/f (Stan) **12** Ran SP% **119.2**
Speed ratings (Par 101): **102,100,99,99,97 96,95,94,94,92 91,91**
CSF £15.77 CT £144.53 TOTE £2.60: £1.30, £2.40, £2.00; EX 20.80 Trifecta £213.30.
**Owner** Crowd Racing Partnership **Bred** B Kennedy & Mrs Ann Marie Kennedy **Trained** Stockbridge, Hants

**FOCUS**
There was a decent pace on in this modest handicap.
T/Jkpt: Not won. T/Plt: £25.90 to a £1 stake. Pool: £92,977.63. 2,617.56 winning units. T/Qpdt: £10.90 to a £1 stake. Pool: £8,086.16. 547.78 winning units. **Colin Roberts**

# DEAUVILLE (R-H)
Thursday, January 5

**OFFICIAL GOING: Polytrack: standard**

## 81a PRIX DE SAINT-JAMES (CONDITIONS) (4YO+) (POLYTRACK) 6f 110y
**11:25** 4-Y-0+ **£8,974** (£3,589; £2,692; £1,794; £897)

RPR
**1** **Gamgoom**[76] 7525 6-9-2 0..............(b) EddyHardouin 1 87
(Mario Hofer, Germany) **18/5**[2]
**2** 2 **Wikita (FR)**[17] 6-9-3 0.............. TonyPiccone 2 82
(T Lemer, France) **19/10**[1]
**3** ½ **Comedia Eria (FR)**[10] 5-9-1 0.............. FabriceVeron 6 79
(P Monfort, France) **10/1**
**4** 1 **Desert Blanc**[68] 9-9-4 0.............. Pierre-CharlesBoudot 7 79
(C Baillet, France) **41/10**
**5** hd **Nine Ou Four (IRE)**[68] 6-9-0 0.............. TheoBachelot 5 75
(V Luka Jr, Czech Republic) **14/1**
**6** hd **Aguerooo (IRE)**[22] 8368 4-9-4 0..............(p) MaximeGuyon 8 78
(Richard Hannon) *trckd wnr: rdn and effrt into st: hung rt u.p and no ex fnl f: fdd* **19/5**[3]
**7** nk **Le Rebel (FR)**[76] 7525 5-9-6 0.............. Jean-BernardEyquem 3 79
(K Borgel, France) **89/10**
**8** 1 ¼ **Dakarus Fritz (GER)**[92] 4-9-8 0.............. AntoineHamelin 4 77
(M Figge, Germany) **17/1**
**9** 5 **Il Pittore (FR)**[523] 6-9-0 0.............. PierreBazire 9 55
(G Botti, France) **23/1**

WIN (incl. 1 euro stake): 4.60; PLACES: 1.90, 1.60, 3.10; DF: 11.90; SF: 21.90..
**Owner** Guido Werner Hermann Schmitt **Bred** Rabbah Bloodstock Limited **Trained** Germany

# MEYDAN (L-H)
Thursday, January 5

**OFFICIAL GOING: Dirt: fast; turf: good**

## 82a LONGINES LA GRANDE CLASSIQUE (H'CAP) (TURF) 1m 4f 11y
**3:05** (3:05) (95-105,105) 3-Y-0+
**£60,975** (£20,325; £10,162; £5,081; £3,048; £2,032)

RPR
**1** **Golden Wood (FR)**[40] 7-9-2 **101**..............(t) ChristopheSoumillon 8 107
(N Caullery, France) *settled in rr: smooth prog 3f out: rdn 1 1/2f out: r.o wl: led cl home* **20/1**
**2** shd **Carbon Dating (IRE)**[18] 8450 5-8-11 **97**.............. TadhgO'Shea 6 102
(S Seemar, UAE) *mid-div: smooth prog 3f out: led 2f out: hdd on line* **12/1**
**3** 2 ½ **Rio Tigre (IRE)**[308] 811 6-9-3 **102**.............. MickaelBarzalona 9 104
(S bin Ghadayer, UAE) *trckd ldr: ev ch 1 1/2f out: one pce fnl f* **12/1**
**4** ½ **Zamaam**[35] 8187 7-8-13 **98**..............(t) JimCrowley 2 99
(E Charpy, UAE) *broke awkwardly: nvr nr to chal: r.o fnl 2f* **10/1**
**5** hd **Good Trip (IRE)**[13] 8518 4-8-13 **101**..............(t) FernandoJara 5 103
(A R Al Rayhi, UAE) *settled in rr: r.o 2 1/2f out* **14/1**
**6** 1 ¾ **Emirates Flyer**[364] 94 6-9-3 **102**.............. ColmO'Donoghue 1 100
(Saeed bin Suroor) *trckd ldr: outpcd fnl 1 1/2f* **7/2**[2]
**7** 1 **Desert God (IND)**[103] 5-9-1 **100**.............. DavidAllan 10 96
(S Padmanabhan, India) *s.i.s: mid-div: chsd ldrs 3f out: wknd fnl 1 1/2f* **6/4**[1]
**8** 1 **Zambucca (SAF)**[32] 8214 8-8-11 **97**.............. RichardMullen 7 91
(S Seemar, UAE) *trckd ldrs: wknd fnl 2f* **12/1**
**9** 1 **Shamaal Nibras (USA)**[32] 8214 8-9-6 **105**.............. PatDobbs 4 98
(Doug Watson, UAE) *s.i.s: nvr nr to chal* **7/1**[3]
**10** 1 ¾ **Zain Eagle**[35] 8187 7-8-11 **97**.............. SamHitchcott 11 86
(Doug Watson, UAE) *sn led: hdd 2f out: sn btn* **28/1**
**11** 14 **Tempus Temporis (USA)**[13] 8518 5-9-1 **100**..............(bt) DaneO'Neill 3 68
(A R Al Rayhi, UAE) *Never bttr than mid-div* **50/1**

2m 30.73s
**WFA** 4 from 5yo+ 3lb **11** Ran SP% **123.7**
CSF: 248.30 TRICAST: 3,020.91.
**Owner** Mme Christian Wingtans **Bred** Jo Awouters **Trained** France

**FOCUS**
TRAKUS (metres covered compared to winner): 2nd -3, 3rd -5, 4th -16, 5th -7, 6th -19, 7th +2, 8th -11, 9th -11, 10th -11, 11th -17. The pace was steady, 26.99 (400m), 25.25 (800m), 24.94 (1200m), 25.25 (1600m), 24.9 (2000m), with the winner finishing in 23.21. The third and fourth help set the standard.

## 83a LONGINES PASSION IN EQUESTRIAN (H'CAP) (DIRT) 1m 1f 110y(D)
**3:40** (3:40) (95-115,113) 3-Y-0+
**£65,853** (£21,951; £10,975; £5,487; £3,292; £2,195)

RPR
**1** **Mizbah**[41] 8113 8-8-5 **95**.............. SamHitchcott 4 105+
(Doug Watson, UAE) *sn led: skipped clr 3 1/2f out: r.o wl: comf* **8/1**
**2** 7 ½ **Hunting Ground (USA)**[21] 8394 7-8-8 **102**.............. MickaelBarzalona 9 93+
(S bin Ghadayer, UAE) *settled in rr: r.o wl fnl 2f: nrst fin* **9/1**
**3** shd **Top Clearance (USA)**[21] 8394 5-8-10 **104**..............(t) ChrisHayes 5 94
(D Selvaratnam, UAE) *trckd ldr: rdn 4f out: r.o fnl 2 1/2f: no ch w wnr* **7/1**[3]
**4** ¾ **Trinity Force (IRE)**[21] 8394 6-8-5 **98**.............. TadhgO'Shea 3 88+
(A R Al Rayhi, UAE) *s.i.s: nvr bttr than mid-div* **14/1**
**5** 1 ½ **Sharpalo (FR)**[13] 8518 5-8-5 **95**..............(p) AntonioFresu 7 85
(A bin Harmash, UAE) *nvr nr to chal: r.o wl fnl 2f* **14/1**
**6** 2 ½ **Saltarin Dubai (ARG)**[194] 4-9-6 **113**.............. ChristopheSoumillon 6 95
(M F De Kock, South Africa) *trckd ldrs: rdn 3f out: wknd fnl 2f* **7/2**[2]
**7** shd **Storm Belt (USA)**[21] 8394 8-9-3 **110**.............. PatDobbs 1 91
(Doug Watson, UAE) *trckd ldrs: rdn 5f out: one pce fnl 3f* **5/4**[1]
**8** 10 **Prince Alzain (USA)**[307] 855 8-8-7 **95** ow2..............(h) FernandoJara 2 59
(Doug Watson, UAE) *slowly away: a in rr* **40/1**
**9** 20 **Jeeraan (USA)**[63] 7788 7-8-7 **99** ow2.............. DaneO'Neill 8 18
(Doug Watson, UAE) *nvr bttr than mid-div* **16/1**

1m 56.51s (-2.29)
**WFA** 4 from 5yo+ 1lb **9** Ran SP% **121.9**
CSF: 81.60 TRICAST: 539.80.
**Owner** EERC (Mngr: Mrs Rebecca Byrne) **Bred** Darley **Trained** United Arab Emirates

**FOCUS**
TRAKUS (metres covered compared to winner): 2nd +28, 3rd +11, 4th +12, 5th +7, 6th +21, 7th +6, 8th +14, 9th +23. The winner set a strong early pace (splits through opening 1600m were 26.31 from standing start, 23.23, 23.17, 24.5), but on a fast surface nothing could peg him back and the track record, previously set by Frosted in a Group 2 last year, was lowered by 0.16 sec. A pb from the winner.

## 84a LONGINES MASTER COLLECTION (H'CAP) (TURF) 5f
**4:15** (4:15) (95-116,116) 3-Y-0+
**£78,048** (£26,016; £13,008; £6,504; £3,902; £2,601)

RPR
**1** **Ertijaal (IRE)**[285] 1104 6-9-6 **116**.............. JimCrowley 6 122
(A R Al Rayhi, UAE) *sn led: rdn clr 1 1/2f out: r.o wl: comf* **8/11**[1]
**2** 1 ¾ **The Happy Prince (IRE)**[76] 7520 5-9-0 **110**..............(t) PatCosgrave 9 110
(James Moore, Macau) *trckd ldr: ev ch 1 1/2f out: r.o same pce fnl f* **16/1**
**3** shd **Caspian Prince (IRE)**[15] 8484 8-8-11 **108**..............(t) TomEaves 12 107
(Roger Fell) *trckd ldr: r.o fnl 2f: no ch w wnr* **13/2**[2]
**4** ¾ **Fityaan**[285] 1104 9-9-0 **110**..............(v) DaneO'Neill 14 107+
(M Al Mheiri, UAE) *nvr nr to chal: r.o wl fnl 2f* **16/1**
**5** nse **Line Of Reason (IRE)**[15] 8484 7-8-5 **102**.............. MartinLane 3 98
(Paul Midgley) *chsd ldr: r.o same pce fnl 1 1/2f* **14/1**
**6** ¾ **Saayerr**[315] 719 6-8-7 **104**.............. ChrisHayes 2 97
(D Selvaratnam, UAE) *mid-div: r.o fnl 2f: n.d* **20/1**
**7** nse **High On Life**[41] 8115 6-8-5 **96**..............(t) MickaelBarzalona 13 95
(S bin Ghadayer, UAE) *a mid-div* **33/1**
**8** hd **Sir Maximilian (IRE)**[31] 8232 8-8-7 **104**..............(p) TadhgO'Shea 5 96
(Ian Williams) *nvr nr to chal: r.o fnl 2f* **8/1**[3]
**9** 1 ½ **Taexali (IRE)**[86] 7250 4-8-5 **95**.............. SamHitchcott 8 89
(S Seemar, UAE) *s.i.s: nvr bttr than mid-div* **50/1**
**10** 1 **Moonraker**[124] 6112 5-8-5 **95**.............. MarcMonaghan 4 85
(Mick Channon) *nvr nr to chal* **33/1**
**11** ½ **Spirit Quartz (IRE)**[49] 7997 9-8-10 **110** ow3.......(p) JulianResimont(3) 10 88
(N Caullery, France) *nvr bttr than mid-div* **14/1**
**12** 1 **Mubtaghaa (IRE)**[69] 7683 5-8-6 **103** ow1.............. FernandoJara 7 80
(M Al Mheiri, UAE) *trckd ldr: outpcd fnl 2f* **25/1**
**13** hd **Roi De Vitesse (IRE)**[41] 8115 10-8-9 **106** ow1...........(v) AdriedeVries 15 82
(Ali Jan, Qatar) *nvr nr to chal* **20/1**
**14** ½ **Master Of War**[677] 741 7-8-5 **100**.............. PaoloSirigu 1 77
(D Selvaratnam, UAE) *nvr bttr than mid-div* **40/1**
**15** nk **Ahlan Emarati (IRE)**[41] 8115 5-8-5 **101**..............(b) RichardMullen 16 76
(S Seemar, UAE) *nvr bttr than mid-div* **66/1**
**16** 4 ½ **Fencing (USA)**[41] 8115 8-8-7 **104**.............. BrettDoyle 11 62
(R Bouresly, Kuwait) *slowly away: a in rr* **66/1**

57.79s **16** Ran SP% **134.1**
CSF: 15.36 TRICAST: 64.37.
**Owner** Hamdan Al Maktoum **Bred** Shadwell Estate Co Ltd **Trained** UAE

**FOCUS**
TRAKUS (metres covered compared to winner): 2nd -1, 3rd 0, 4th 0, 5th 0, 6th 0, 7th +1, 8th 0, 9th 0, 10th 0, 11th 0, 12th 0, 13th 0, 14th +1, 15th -1, 16th +1. The field split into two groups but there was good pace on both sides, it's just the winner was in a different league. A small pb from the winner, with the seventh helping to anchor the form.

## 85a AL MAKTOUM CHALLENGE R1 PRESENTED BY ELEGANCE IN EQUESTRIAN (GROUP 2) (DIRT) 1m (D)
4:50 (4:50) 3-Y-0+

£121,951 (£40,650; £20,325; £10,162; £6,097; £4,065)

RPR

1 **Le Bernardin (USA)**$^{21}$ 8396 8-9-0 110 (t) TadhgO'Shea 1 112
(A R Al Rayhi, UAE) *trckd ldrs: rdn 3f out: r.o wl fnl 1 1/2f: led 110yds out* 6/1

2 2 **Long River (USA)**$^{306}$ 842 7-9-0 102 (b) MickaelBarzalona 6 107
(S bin Ghadayer, UAE) *trckd ldrs: led 3f out: hdd fnl 110yds* 50/1

3 nk **Lindo Amor (ARG)**$^{249}$ 4-9-0 108 ChristopheSoumillon 3 107
(M F De Kock, South Africa) *s.i.s: mid-div: r.o fnl 2f: nrst fin* 20/1

4 1 **Gold City (IRE)**$^{21}$ 8394 8-9-0 106 (bt) RichardMullen 5 104
(S Seemar, UAE) *s.i.s: nvr nr to chal: r.o fnl 2f* 50/1

5 1 **Cool Cowboy (USA)**$^{21}$ 8396 6-9-0 112 (v) SamHitchcott 4 102
(Doug Watson, UAE) *trckd ldrs: ev ch 1f out: wknd fnl 110yds* 13/2

6 2½ **Emotionless (IRE)**$^{160}$ 4822 4-9-0 110 WilliamBuick 10 96
(Charlie Appleby) *nvr bttr than mid-div* 4/1$^{3}$

7 2¼ **Munaaser**$^{32}$ 8214 6-9-0 105 (t) JimCrowley 2 91
(A R Al Rayhi, UAE) *trckd ldrs: ev ch 2f out: wknd fnl f* 20/1

8 hd **Polar River (USA)**$^{49}$ 8004 4-8-9 112 PatDobbs 7 86
(Doug Watson, UAE) *s.i.s: nvr nr to chal* 5/2$^{1}$

9 6¾ **Fitzgerald (USA)**$^{21}$ 8396 5-9-0 108 (t) AntonioFresu 8 75
(A bin Harmash, UAE) *nvr bttr than mid-div* 11/4$^{2}$

10 7¼ **Frankyfourfingers (FR)**$^{21}$ 8396 7-9-0 108 ColmO'Donoghue 9 59
(S bin Ghadayer, UAE) *sn led: hdd 3f out: sn btn* 33/1

1m 36.67s (-0.83) **10 Ran SP% 119.2**
CSF: 276.15.
**Owner** Sheikh Ahmed bin Mohammed Al Maktoum **Bred** Mike G Rutherford **Trained** UAE

**FOCUS**
TRAKUS (metres covered compared to winner): 2nd +7, 3rd 0, 4th 0, 5th +11, 6th +10, 7th +3, 8th +3, 9th +11, 10th 0. There was a three-way battle up front and the pace was rapid early/slow late, 24.48 (allow about 2secs for standing start), 21.63, 24.36, with the winner home in 25.94. The winner and third set the standard.

## 86a SINGSPIEL STKS PRESENTED BY LONGINES PERFORMANCE IN EQUESTRIAN (LISTED RACE) (TURF) 1m 1f
5:25 (5:25) 3-Y-0+

£85,365 (£28,455; £14,227; £7,113; £4,268; £2,845)

RPR

1 **Light The Lights (SAF)**$^{341}$ 5-9-0 110 ChristopheSoumillon 2 112+
(M F De Kock, South Africa) *trckd ldrs: rdn 2 1/2f out: r.o wl to ld nr line* 10/1

2 nk **Championship (IRE)**$^{32}$ 8214 6-9-0 108 (t) ColmO'Donoghue 6 111
(A bin Harmash, UAE) *sn led: rdn clr 2f out: r.o but hdd cl home* 3/1$^{2}$

3 3 **Earnshaw (USA)**$^{21}$ 8396 6-9-0 107 (t) MickaelBarzalona 8 105+
(S bin Ghadayer, UAE) *nvr nr to chal* 14/1

4 2 **Sanshaawes (SAF)**$^{306}$ 843 7-9-0 109 BernardFayd'Herbe 11 101
(M F De Kock, South Africa) *trckd ldrs: ev ch 2f out: one pce fnl 1 1/2f* 20/1

5 ½ **Ertijaal (AUS)**$^{256}$ 1690 5-9-0 113 (b) JimCrowley 1 100
(M F De Kock, South Africa) *slowly away: mid-div: r.o fnl 2f: nvr nr to chal* 9/4$^{1}$

6 ½ **Silent Attack**$^{75}$ 7542 4-8-13 102 (p) PatCosgrave 3 99
(Saeed bin Suroor) *s.i.s: trckd ldrs: t.k.h: ev ch 2f out: wknd fnl 1 1/2f* 5/1$^{3}$

7 2 **Need To Know (SAF)**$^{21}$ 8396 8-9-0 96 (t) TadhgO'Shea 7 95
(A R Al Rayhi, UAE) *nvr bttr than mid-div* 40/1

8 1¾ **Dormello (IRE)**$^{21}$ 8396 9-9-0 109 ChrisHayes 5 91
(D Selvaratnam, UAE) *nvr bttr than mid-div* 14/1

9 shd **Gabrial (IRE)**$^{82}$ 7353 8-9-0 110 WilliamBuick 10 91
(Richard Fahey) *nvr nr to chal* 8/1

10 5¼ **Long Water (USA)**$^{21}$ 8396 6-9-0 90 (b) SamHitchcott 4 80
(H Al Alawi, UAE) *nvr nr to chal* 66/1

11 1¼ **Quel Avantage (IRE)**$^{343}$ 7-9-0 91 BrettDoyle 12 77
(R Bouresly, Kuwait) *trckd ldrs: wknd fnl 2 1/2f* 100/1

12 1¼ **Maftool (USA)**$^{21}$ 8396 5-9-0 112 DaneO'Neill 9 74
(M Al Mheiri, UAE) *nvr nr to chal* 10/1

1m 48.12s
**WFA** 4 from 5yo+ 1lb **12 Ran SP% 124.7**
CSF: 41.53.
**Owner** Sheikh Mohammed Bin Khalifa Al Maktoum **Bred** Hallmark Thoroughbreds **Trained** South Africa

**FOCUS**
TRAKUS (metres covered compared to winner): 2nd -6, 3rd +5, 4th +1, 5th -3, 6th -3, 7th +6, 8th 0, 9th 0, 10th -3, 11th +5, 12th -3. With nothing wanting to go on, the runner-up set a slow-fast pace (26.77, 23.42, 23.63, 22.57), racing a bit freely, and was paddling late as the winner finished in a slowing 11.62. The second and third, who have been rated to their recent best, help set the standard.

## 87a LONGINES DOLCE VITA (H'CAP) (TURF) 7f
6:00 (6:00) (100-113,112) 3-Y-0+

£65,853 (£21,951; £10,975; £5,487; £3,292; £2,195)

RPR

1 **Flash Fire (IRE)**$^{131}$ 5871 5-9-1 107 WilliamBuick 14 114+
(Charlie Appleby) *settled in rr: r.o wl fnl 2f: led fnl 110yds: comf* 11/2$^{2}$

2 2½ **Rene Mathis (GER)**$^{222}$ 2684 7-8-9 102 TomEaves 7 101
(Richard Fahey) *mid-div: r.o fnl 1 1/2f: no ch w wnr* 28/1

3 nk **Ghaamer (USA)**$^{21}$ 8395 7-9-6 112 (t) JimCrowley 6 111
(A R Al Rayhi, UAE) *sn led: rdn clr 2 1/2f out: wknd fnl 110yds* 14/1

4 shd **Mutawathea**$^{166}$ 4625 6-8-9 102 (p) MickaelBarzalona 8 100
(Simon Crisford) *mid-div: chsd ldrs: ev ch 1 1/2f out: r.o same pce fnl f* 20/1

5 nk **Elite Excalibur (AUS)**$^{46}$ 4-9-3 109 (b) MichaelRodd 10 107
(S Burridge, Singapore) *broke awkwardly: nvr bttr than mid-div* 10/1

6 shd **Banaadeer (AUS)**$^{308}$ 810 5-8-13 105 DaneO'Neill 1 103
(M F De Kock, South Africa) *mid-div: chsd ldrs 2f out: one pce fnl f* 16/1

7 ¾ **Anaerobio (ARG)**$^{314}$ 744 9-9-3 109 (t) BernardFayd'Herbe 5 105
(M F De Kock, South Africa) *nvr nr to chal: r.o wl fnl 1 1/2f* 16/1

8 nk **Mastermind (SAF)**$^{308}$ 810 5-9-0 106 PatCosgrave 12 101
(M F De Kock, South Africa) *trckd ldr: ev ch 1 1/2f out: one pce fnl f* 25/1

9 1 **Whistle Stop (SAF)**$^{350}$ 283 6-8-8 101 AntonioFresu 16 92
(M F De Kock, South Africa) *nvr nr to chal* 33/1

10 1¼ **Encipher (USA)**$^{278}$ 8-8-7 100 (t) TadhgO'Shea 13 88
(A R Al Rayhi, UAE) *nvr bttr than mid-div* 40/1

11 nse **Kanaf (IRE)**$^{41}$ 8113 10-8-7 103 ow2 (v) GeorgeBuckell$^{(3)}$ 11 89
(M Al Mheiri, UAE) *s.i.s: nvr nr to chal* 33/1

12 ½ **Fils Anges (IRE)**$^{308}$ 810 7-9-3 109 AdriedeVries 15 96
(Ali Jan, Qatar) *nvr nr to chal* 14/1

13 hd **Arcanada (IRE)**$^{113}$ 6482 4-9-0 106 RichardKingscote 9 93
(Tom Dascombe) *trckd ldrs: ev ch 2f out: wknd fnl f* 7/1$^{3}$

14 2¼ **American Hope (USA)**$^{308}$ 810 6-9-1 107 (h) ChristopheSoumillon 2 88
(Saeed bin Suroor) *trckd ldr: wknd fnl 2 1/2f* 11/8$^{1}$

15 1½ **Shaishee (USA)**$^{21}$ 8395 7-8-9 102 (v) FernandoJara 3 78
(M Al Mheiri, UAE) *s.i.s: nvr nr to chal* 33/1

16 14½ **Salateen**$^{103}$ 6788 5-8-10 103 PatDobbs 4 40
(David O'Meara) *nvr bttr than mid-div* 14/1

1m 23.01s **16 Ran SP% 134.2**
CSF: 168.41 TRICAST: 2,202.47. Placepot: £693.80 to a £1 stake. Pool of £7,128.25 - 7.5 winning units. Quadpot: £133.60 to a £1 stake. Pool of £740.30 - 4.1 winning units..
**Owner** Godolphin **Bred** Darley **Trained** Newmarket, Suffolk

**FOCUS**
TRAKUS (metres covered compared to winner): 2nd -4, 3rd -12, 4th -4, 5th -7, 6th -13, 7th -8, 8th -6, 9th -3, 10th -1, 11th +1, 12th -7, 13th -9, 14th -11, 15th -11, 16th -7. The third horse charged to the front to set a strong pace, 24.38 (from standing start), 22.94, 23.52, before the winner clocked 11.96 to the line.

# KEMPTON (A.W) (R-H)
Friday, January 6

**OFFICIAL GOING: Polytrack: standard to slow**
Wind: Almost nil Weather: Cloudy, rain from race 4

## 88 MATCHBOOK BETTING EXCHANGE H'CAP 6f (P)
2:00 (2:01) (Class 6) (0-55,58) 4-Y-0+ £2,264 (£673; £336; £168) Stalls Low

Form RPR

220- 1 **Multi Quest**$^{17}$ 8474 5-9-6 52 (b) RobertHavlin 12 57
(John E Long) *wl away fr wd draw and led after 1f: rdn and pressed for 2f out: jnd ins fnl f: hld on wl* 14/1

250- 2 shd **Krazy Paving**$^{27}$ 8315 5-9-3 49 (b) JosephineGordon 2 54
(Anabel K Murphy) *led 1f: styd prom: rdn over 2f out: wnt 2nd fnl f: str chal after: jst failed* 9/2$^{2}$

450- 3 1¼ **Great Expectations**$^{10}$ 8541 9-9-7 53 (vt) DougieCostello 5 54
(J R Jenkins) *hld up in rr: prog on inner over 2f out: rdn and kpt on to take 3rd ins fnl f* 6/1$^{3}$

322- 4 1 **Burauq**$^{32}$ 8234 5-9-7 53 (b) GeorgeBaker 9 51
(Milton Bradley) *t.k.h: trckd ldr after 2f: chal 2f out: fnd little whn rdn over 1f out: lost 2nd and fdd fnl f* 5/4$^{1}$

/06- 5 ¾ **Mistry**$^{15}$ 8496 4-9-4 50 LiamKeniry 1 46
(Mark Usher) *dwlt: sn chsd ldrs: outpcd 2f out: no ch after: plugged on* 16/1

000- 6 1½ **Nasri**$^{18}$ 8457 11-9-6 52 (v$^{1}$) StevieDonohoe 7 44
(Emma Owen) *t.k.h: chsd ldrs: outpcd and rdn over 2f out: no imp after* 6/1$^{3}$

050- 7 1¾ **Diamond Vine (IRE)**$^{101}$ 6852 9-9-2 48 (p) DavidProbert 10 34
(Ronald Harris) *towards rr: outpcd over 2f out: drvn and no hdwy after* 33/1

240- 8 ¾ **Nidnod**$^{44}$ 8070 4-9-2 48 WilliamCarson 11 32
(John Bridger) *hld up in last: outpcd fr 1/2-way: nvr on terms* 33/1

060- 9 5 **Zophilly (IRE)**$^{21}$ 8408 4-9-1 52 (t) DavidParkes$^{(5)}$ 8 21
(Jeremy Gask) *racd wd towards rr: lost grnd and last 1/2-way: sn bhd* 66/1

1m 13.53s (0.43) **Going Correction** +0.075s/f (Slow) **9 Ran SP% 111.1**
Speed ratings (Par 101): **100,99,98,96,95 93,91,90,83**
CSF £71.52 CT £414.86 TOTE £10.80: £2.10, £1.30, £1.80; EX 93.30 Trifecta £340.40.
**Owner** Martin J Gibbs **Bred** Mrs C Lloyd **Trained** Royston, Herts

**FOCUS**
A moderate sprint handicap in which few were seriously involved.

## 89 BETTER ODDS WITH MATCHBOOK BETTING EXCHANGE H'CAP 1m (P)
2:30 (2:30) (Class 6) (0-60,61) 3-Y-O £2,264 (£673; £336; £168) Stalls Low

Form RPR

046- 1 **Dangerous Ends**$^{46}$ 8046 3-8-11 50 (v$^{1}$) MartinDwyer 6 56
(Brett Johnson) *s.i.s: hld up in rr: drvn and prog on inner over 2f out: chsd ldr over 1f out: led ins fnl f: styd on wl* 20/1

024- 2 1½ **Still Waiting**$^{31}$ 8235 3-9-8 61 RobertHavlin 4 63
(William Jarvis) *trckd ldrs gng wl: led 2f out: hung lft over 1f out: hung rt and hdd ins fnl f: nt qckn* 7/4$^{1}$

660- 3 1¼ **Beauchamp Opal**$^{31}$ 8235 3-9-7 60 StevieDonohoe 7 59
(Charlie Fellowes) *hld up in rr: prog on inner wl over 1f out: styd on to take 3rd ins fnl f: unable to chal* 13/2$^{3}$

665- 4 nk **Too Many Shots**$^{53}$ 7954 3-9-6 59 KierenFox 3 57
(John Best) *trckd ldrs: rdn and no imp 2f out: kpt on fnl f: nvr able to threaten* 4/1$^{2}$

000- 5 2¾ **Chough**$^{17}$ 8467 3-9-0 58 CharlieBennett$^{(5)}$ 13 50
(Hughie Morrison) *hld up towards rr: pushed along over 3f out: rdn and kpt on one pce fr wl over 1f out to take 5th ins fnl f* 33/1

000- 6 1 **Av A Word**$^{118}$ 6319 3-9-7 60 (p$^{1}$) JosephineGordon 10 49
(Daniel Kubler) *t.k.h early: trckd ldrs: pushed along fr 1/2-way: outpcd 2f out: plugged on u.p* 14/1

440- 7 ¾ **Masquerade Bling (IRE)**$^{55}$ 7941 3-9-0 58 DavidParkes$^{(5)}$ 9 45
(Simon Hodgson) *hld up and sn in last: rdn over 2f out: modest late hdwy* 12/1

120- 8 hd **Viola Park**$^{8}$ 8568 3-8-12 51 RyanPowell 1 38
(Ronald Harris) *led to 2f out: hanging lft then carried lft over 1f out: wknd* 10/1

130- 9 ½ **Dragon Dream (IRE)**$^{55}$ 7941 3-9-8 61 MartinLane 14 47
(Roger Ingram) *forced to r wd: chsd ldrs: prog to take 2nd over 3f out: upsides over 2f out: carried lft and wknd over 1f out* 14/1

600- 10 shd **Ablaze**$^{135}$ 5764 3-9-2 55 LiamKeniry 5 41
(Laura Mongan) *hld up in midfield: shkn up and no prog 2f out: wknd fnl f* 40/1

060- 11 3 3/4 **Hollywood Style**[17] 8467 3-8-5 47 EdwardGreatrex(3) 12 24
(William Knight) *hld up wl in rr: brief effrt arnd rivals over 3f out: wknd 2f out* 50/1
000- 12 11 **Kingston Tasmania**[43] 8080 3-8-7 46 oh1 (b) DavidProbert 11
(Andrew Balding) *mostly pressed ldr to over 3f out: wknd rapidly over 2f out: t.o* 25/1
1m 39.95s (0.15) **Going Correction** +0.075s/f (Slow) 12 Ran SP% 115.8
Speed ratings (Par 95): **102,100,99,98,96 95,94,94,93,93 89,78**
CSF £51.92 CT £267.55 TOTE £26.30: £6.10, £1.30, £2.20; EX 82.20 Trifecta £627.50.
**Owner** Colin Westley **Bred** R S Cockerill (farms) Ltd **Trained** Epsom, Surrey

**FOCUS**
Another moderate handicap and the leaders looked to overdo it.

## 90 SMARTER BETS WITH MATCHBOOK BETTING EXCHANGE H'CAP 1m (P)
**3:00** (3:00) (Class 5) (0-70,71) 4-Y-0+ **£3,234** (£962; £481; £240) **Stalls** Low

Form RPR
412- 1 **Saleh (IRE)**[9] 8555 4-9-2 65 AdamKirby 2 76+
(Lee Carter) *trckd ldng pair after 2f: shkn up to ld wl over 1f out: styd on wl* 2/1[1]
443- 2 1 1/2 **Choral Clan (IRE)**[51] 7973 6-9-7 70 JackMitchell 8 76
(Philip Mitchell) *trckd ldr 2f: styd prom: rdn 2f out: styd on to take 2nd again ins fnl f: unable to threaten* 4/1[2]
10- 3 1/2 **Rightway (IRE)**[37] 8154 6-9-2 68 GeorgeDowning(3) 9 73
(Tony Carroll) *racd wd: chsd ldrs: rdn wl over 1f out: styd on to take 3rd ins fnl f* 40/1
300- 4 1 1/4 **Papou Tony**[116] 6416 4-9-4 67 LiamKeniry 11 69
(George Baker) *t.k.h: trckd ldr after 2f: chal 2f out but wnr sn wnt by: chsd him tl ins fnl f: fdd* 9/1
100- 5 1 1/4 **Check 'Em Tuesday (IRE)**[37] 8154 4-8-11 65 CharlieBennett(5) 5 64
(Daniel Mark Loughnane) *in tch in midfield: rdn 2f out: styd on same pce and nvr able to cl* 20/1
003- 6 nk **St Patrick's Day (IRE)**[31] 8241 5-9-3 66 (v) DougieCostello 6 64
(J R Jenkins) *t.k.h: hld up towards rr in slowly run r: rdn 2f out: styd on fnl f but no ch* 14/1
160- 7 hd **With Approval (IRE)**[50] 7985 5-8-13 65 (p) CallumShepherd(3) 3 63
(Laura Mongan) *led: set modest pce to 1/2-way: drvn over 2f out: hdd wl over 1f out: wknd* 25/1
604- 8 nk **Gracious George (IRE)**[17] 8469 7-9-6 69 TimmyMurphy 10 66+
(Jimmy Fox) *hld up in 10th and off the pce despite slow tempo: pushed along 2f out: reminder and kpt on fnl f: nvr involved* 20/1
260- 9 1 **Spiritual Star (IRE)**[36] 8178 8-9-2 70 PaddyBradley(5) 1 64
(Lee Carter) *t.k.h: hld up in midfield off slow pce: rdn 2f out: nt pce to make prog: fdd fnl f* 8/1[3]
552- 10 2 **Almanack**[22] 8382 7-8-12 64 NathanAlison(3) 12 54
(Mark Pattinson) *plld hrd early: racd on outer towards rr: wknd wl over 1f out* 12/1
005- 11 hd **Party Royal**[18] 8458 7-9-1 64 (e) MartinDwyer 7 53
(Nick Gifford) *c out of stall slowly: hld up in 11th and wl off the pce despite slow tempo: vigorously scrubbed along over 2f out: no hdwy and nvr involved* 33/1
305- 12 1 1/2 **Lucymai**[23] 8357 4-9-8 71 RobertWinston 4 57
(Dean Ivory) *v awkward s: mostly in last and wl off the pce: nvr involved* 14/1
1m 41.52s (1.72) **Going Correction** +0.075s/f (Slow) 12 Ran SP% 114.2
Speed ratings (Par 103): **94,92,92,90,89 89,89,88,87,85 85,84**
CSF £8.00 CT £235.13 TOTE £2.90: £1.70, £1.60, £8.10; EX 7.90 Trifecta £352.00.
**Owner** Only One Bid Partnership **Bred** Stowell Park Stud **Trained** Epsom, Surrey

**FOCUS**
A modest handicap and they didn't go that quick. The runner-up is a sound guide to the level.

## 91 WINNERS WELCOME AT MATCHBOOK EXCHANGE MEDIAN AUCTION MAIDEN STKS 1m 3f 219y(P)
**3:30** (3:30) (Class 5) 3-4-Y-0 **£3,234** (£962; £481; £240) **Stalls** Low

Form RPR
342- 1 **The Blues Master (IRE)**[32] 8227 3-8-7 74 PJMcDonald 2 70+
(Mark Johnston) *settled in 5th: pushed along at various times and others gng bttr: shkn up over 2f out: clsd qckly to ld over 1f out: styd on strly and clr fnl f* 4/9[1]
365- 2 3 **Condamine (IRE)**[23] 8366 4-10-0 73 MartinLane 6 66
(Jeremy Gask) *t.k.h: hld up in 4th: moved up to chal over 1f out: readily outpcd by wnr fnl f* 16/1
2- 3 1 **Burning Heat (IRE)**[29] 8281 4-10-0 72 RyanTate 5 65
(James Eustace) *led: stretched on over 3f out: hdd over 1f out: sn outpcd* 9/2[2]
00- 4 nse **Nothing Compares**[32] 8227 3-8-2 0 NickyMackay 4 59
(Mark Johnston) *trckd ldng pair: pushed along over 2f out: outpcd fnl f but kpt on steadily* 50/1
603- 5 1 3/4 **Gog Elles (IRE)**[43] 8080 3-8-2 45 (p[1]) RyanPowell 7 56?
(J S Moore) *t.k.h: sn trckd ldr: lost 2nd wl over 1f out: sn btn* 100/1
6 nk **Tambour**[27] 4-10-0 0 (t[1]) GeorgeBaker 1 62
(Roger Charlton) *s.s: hld up in last: effrt on inner and wl in tch over 1f out: wknd fnl f* 6/1[3]
00- 7 4 1/2 **Seaborn (IRE)**[9] 8557 3-8-7 0 DavidProbert 3 53
(Simon Hodgson) *hld up in 6th: rdn and dropped to last 2f out: wl btn after* 66/1
2m 36.27s (1.77) **Going Correction** +0.075s/f (Slow)
**WFA** 3 from 4yo 25lb 7 Ran SP% 112.0
Speed ratings (Par 103): **97,95,94,94,93 92,89**
CSF £9.31 TOTE £1.40: £1.20, £5.00; EX 9.80 Trifecta £19.30.
**Owner** Hjw Partnership **Bred** Mrs Helen Keaveney **Trained** Middleham Moor, N Yorks

**FOCUS**
A weak maiden run at a muddling-looking tempo. Muddling form.

## 92 MATCHBOOK TRADERS CONFERENCE H'CAP 1m 3f 219y(P)
**4:00** (4:01) (Class 5) (0-75,74) 4-Y-0+ **£3,234** (£962; £481; £240) **Stalls** Low

Form RPR
434- 1 **Dream Factory (IRE)**[167] 4636 4-9-1 69 (p[1]) TomMarquand 12 76
(Marco Botti) *trckd ldr to 1/2-way: styd cl up: rdn to go 2nd again 2f out: edgd lft but drvn ahd last 150yds: kpt on wl* 14/1
525- 2 1/2 **Santiburi Spring**[19] 8445 4-9-0 68 KierenFox 6 74
(John Best) *led: sent for home over 3f out and stretched field: drvn 2f out: hdd last 150yds: kpt on wl* 5/1[2]
560- 3 1 1/2 **Bridge Of Sighs**[30] 8251 5-9-7 74 TimClark(3) 3 79+
(Martin Smith) *hld up in midfield: gng bttr than most but only 8th whn sing to make prog jst over 2f out: wnt 3rd and cl enough over 1f out: nt qckn after* 20/1
653- 4 2 3/4 **Duck A L'Orange (IRE)**[37] 8162 4-9-5 73 (p) AdamKirby 4 72
(Michael Bell) *t.k.h early: trckd ldrs: rdn to dispute 2nd briefly 2f out: sn nt qckn: fdd ins fnl f* 3/1[1]
02P- 5 1 **Ayr Of Elegance**[150] 5262 5-9-9 73 (h[1]) GeorgeBaker 5 71
(Philip Hide) *hld up in 6th: shkn up 3f out: kpt on but nvr any imp on ldrs* 11/1
204- 6 1 1/2 **Saint Honore**[19] 8446 5-9-2 71 PaddyBradley(5) 8 66
(Pat Phelan) *hld up in rr: 9th whn pce lifted over 3f out: drvn and kpt on fnl 2f: no ch* 11/1
446- 7 1 **Mystikana**[30] 8253 4-8-7 68 (b) TylerSaunders(7) 11 62
(Marcus Tregoning) *t.k.h: trckd ldrs: prog to go 2nd 1/2-way to 2f out: steadily wknd* 9/1
0- 8 nk **Spin Point (IRE)**[19] 8446 5-9-9 73 (p[1]) StevieDonohoe 10 66
(Ian Williams) *t.k.h: hld up in last trio: rdn in last pl over 2f out: kpt on but no ch* 11/2[3]
055/ 9 1/2 **Monsieur Rieussec**[552] 3906 7-9-9 73 MartinLane 7 65
(Jonathan Portman) *stdd s: t.k.h briefly and restrained into last: nudged along over 2f out: sme late prog but nvr involved* 50/1
342/ 10 2 **Gone Viral (IRE)**[293] 7713 6-9-9 73 (t) LiamKeniry 9 62
(George Baker) *stdd s: t.k.h in last pair: pushed along and sme prog 2f out: wknd over 1f out* 66/1
353- 11 hd **Zephyros (GER)**[15] 8498 6-8-12 65 GeorgeDowning(3) 1 54
(David Bridgwater) *nvr bttr than midfield: rdn and dropped to rr 2f out* 8/1
003- 12 4 **Qortaaj**[21] 8411 4-8-13 67 DougieCostello 2 49
(David Loughnane) *chsd ldrs: rdn over 3f out: wknd over 2f out* 16/1
2m 33.65s (-0.85) **Going Correction** +0.075s/f (Slow)
**WFA** 4 from 5yo+ 3lb 12 Ran SP% 115.6
Speed ratings (Par 103): **105,104,103,101,101 100,99,99,98,97 97,94**
CSF £79.50 CT £1412.70 TOTE £18.10: £5.10, £1.80, £7.30; EX 108.90 Trifecta £3089.30.
**Owner** Mrs Roz Lloyd **Bred** Knockainey Stud **Trained** Newmarket, Suffolk

**FOCUS**
The front-running second got most of these on the stretch turning in, but not the winner, who was never worse than third. It's been rated around the runner-up.

## 93 MATCHBOOK BETTING PODCAST H'CAP (DIV I) 6f (P)
**4:30** (4:30) (Class 4) (0-85,87) 4-Y-0+ **£5,175** (£1,540; £769; £384) **Stalls** Low

Form RPR
124- 1 **Dutch Golden Age (IRE)**[36] 8176 5-9-0 78 TimmyMurphy 1 87
(Gary Moore) *mde all: shkn up 2f out: pressed ins fnl f: styd on wl* 8/1[3]
040- 2 nk **September Issue**[36] 8176 4-8-13 77 (p) TomMarquand 3 85
(Gay Kelleway) *t.k.h: hld up in midfield: prog 2f out to chse wnr over 1f out: chal ins fnl f: styd on but a hld* 16/1
45-2 3 1 1/4 **Steelriver (IRE)**[1] 79 7-9-4 82 GeorgeBaker 4 86
(David Barron) *stdd s: hld up in last trio: plenty to do whn prog over 1f out: r.o to take 3rd ins fnl f: no ch to chal* 2/1[1]
000- 4 1 1/2 **Mullionheir**[44] 8069 5-9-9 87 KierenFox 8 86
(John Best) *t.k.h early: hld up bhd ldrs: effrt over 1f out: kpt on to take 4th ins fnl f: no ch* 14/1
556- 5 1/2 **Florencio**[22] 8380 4-9-4 82 (h[1]) AdamKirby 2 80
(Marco Botti) *chsd ldrs: rdn to dispute 2nd briefly 2f out: one pce u.p after* 7/2[2]
041- 6 1 **Consulting**[22] 8389 4-9-2 80 (b) DavidProbert 9 74
(Martyn Meade) *t.k.h on outer: prog fr 1/2-way to chse wnr 2f out to over 1f out: wknd* 7/2[2]
050- 7 3/4 **Oeil De Tigre (FR)**[31] 8236 6-8-0 71 oh1 AledBeech(7) 7 63
(Tony Carroll) *hld up in midfield: shkn up over 2f out: hanging and no prog after: kpt on nr fin* 33/1
000- 8 2 1/2 **Fleckerl (IRE)**[27] 8314 7-9-1 79 (p) MartinLane 10 63
(Conor Dore) *slowly away: hld up in last trio: detached in 9th 2f out: fin w a flourish: nvr involved* 50/1
400- 9 3/4 **Illegally Blonde (IRE)**[27] 8314 4-9-2 85 LucyKBarry(5) 5 67
(Jamie Osborne) *t.k.h: chsd wnr to 2f out: wknd qckly over 1f out* 33/1
400- 10 3 **Masamah (IRE)**[17] 8463 11-8-10 74 (t[1]) StevieDonohoe 6 46
(Ian Williams) *s.s: a detached in last* 25/1
1m 13.15s (0.05) **Going Correction** +0.075s/f (Slow) 10 Ran SP% 113.1
Speed ratings (Par 105): **102,101,99,97,97 95,94,91,90,86**
CSF £115.30 CT £320.76 TOTE £8.90: £2.30, £3.40, £1.20; EX 81.10 Trifecta £409.70.
**Owner** R A Green **Bred** Denis Bergin **Trained** Lower Beeding, W Sussex

**FOCUS**
A fair sprint handicap but nothing could get to the front-running winner. A small pb from the winner, with the runner-up running as well as ever.

## 94 MATCHBOOK BETTING PODCAST H'CAP (DIV II) 6f (P)
**5:00** (5:01) (Class 4) (0-85,85) 4-Y-0+ **£5,175** (£1,540; £769; £384) **Stalls** Low

Form RPR
546- 1 **Eljaddaaf (IRE)**[27] 8319 6-8-13 77 (h) RobertWinston 8 92
(Dean Ivory) *stdd s: hld up in detached last pair off frntic gallop: smooth prog over 2f out: pushed into ld jst over 1f out: readily drew clr* 7/2[1]
001- 2 4 **Pretty Bubbles**[32] 8233 8-9-7 85 (v) GeorgeBaker 6 87
(J R Jenkins) *hld up off the pce in 2nd half of field: smooth prog 2f out: shkn up to chse wnr jst ins fnl f but readily lft bhd* 5/1[3]
125- 3 1 **Free Zone**[22] 8380 8-9-3 81 (v) AdamKirby 2 80
(Lee Carter) *led at furious pce but pressed: drvn 2f out: hdd jst over 1f out: kpt gng to hold 3rd and did best of those forcing the pce* 5/1[3]
041- 4 1 1/2 **Bridge Builder**[23] 8365 7-8-7 71 oh2 (p) TomMarquand 3 65
(Peter Hedger) *hld up off the pce in 2nd half of field: shkn up and hanging 2f out: kpt on fnl f to take 4th last strides* 9/1
652- 5 hd **Higher Court (USA)**[15] 8490 9-8-4 71 EdwardGreatrex(3) 7 64
(Emma Owen) *pressed ldng pair at str pce: wnt 2nd briefly jst over 2f out: fdd fnl f* 12/1
300- 6 1/2 **Equally Fast**[27] 8314 5-9-0 78 (h) LiamKeniry 9 70
(Peter Hiatt) *stdd s: hld up in detached last pair off frntic gallop: shkn up and no prog over 2f out: passed wkng rivals fnl f* 14/1
445- 7 1 1/4 **Gold Club**[36] 8176 6-8-12 76 (p) MartinDwyer 5 64
(Ed McMahon) *pushed up to chse ldrs: gng wl enough 2f out: sn rdn and fnd nil: wknd* 4/1[2]
146- 8 4 **Very Honest (IRE)**[152] 5205 4-9-5 83 StevieDonohoe 1 58
(Brett Johnson) *chsd ldrs at str pce: wnt 2nd 2f out to over 2f out: wknd rapidly* 20/1
140- 9 4 1/2 **Bouclier (IRE)**[17] 8475 7-9-1 82 GeorgeDowning(3) 4 43
(Tony Carroll) *tried to r promly but unable to do so: struggling in rr over 2f out: sn bhd* 16/1

033- **10** *1 ½* **Calypso Choir**[17] 8463 4-8-10 **79**................................ MitchGodwin(5) 10 35
(Sylvester Kirk) *t.k.h: spd fr wd draw to press ldr to over 2f out: wknd rapidly* **8/1**

1m 11.14s (-1.96) **Going Correction** +0.075s/f (Slow) **10** Ran SP% **121.7**
Speed ratings (Par 105): **116,110,109,107,107 106,104,99,93,91**
CSF £22.15 CT £92.34 TOTE £4.40: £1.50, £2.10, £2.10; EX 30.70 Trifecta £91.30.
**Owner** Wentdale Ltd & Mrs L A Ivory **Bred** Shadwell Estate Company Limited **Trained** Radlett, Herts

**FOCUS**
There was a rush for the early lead and the first two finishers came from well off the pace. The runner-up has been rated close to form.
T/Jkpt: Not won. T/Plt: £152.80 to a £1 stake. Pool: £83,469.02 - 398.56 winning tickets T/Qpdt: £18.30 to a £1 stake. Pool: £7,915.59 - 319.27 winning tickets **Jonathan Neesom**

# [74]WOLVERHAMPTON (A.W) (L-H)
## Friday, January 6

**OFFICIAL GOING: Tapeta: standard**
Wind: light, behind Weather: light rain

## 95 BETWAY H'CAP 5f 21y (Tp)
**5:45** (5:46) (Class 6) (0-65,66) 4-Y-O+ **£2,264** (£673; £336; £168) **Stalls** Low

Form RPR
642- **1** **Dreams Of Glory**[10] 8535 9-9-7 **65**...................................... LukeMorris 3 73
(Ron Hodges) *trckd ldrs tl wnt 2nd and swtchd rt wl over 1f out: sn rdn to chal: drvn to ld ins fnl f: hld on wl towards fin* **5/2**[1]
531- **2** *nk* **Temple Road (IRE)**[6] 8596 9-9-8 **66** 6ex........................(bt) JoeFanning 1 73
(Milton Bradley) *hld up in tch in midfield: shkn and up and clsd to press ldrs 1f out: rdn to chal ins fnl f: fnd little u.p and hld towards fin* **7/2**[3]
130- **3** *1 ¾* **David's Beauty (IRE)**[10] 8535 4-9-3 **61**.....................(p) ConnorBeasley 6 62
(Brian Baugh) *sn bustled up to ld: rdn and hrd pressed over 1f out: hdd ins fnl f: no ex and wknd towards fin* **18/1**
53/ **4** *2* **Tihana**[451] 7184 4-8-13 **57**................................................ AndrewMullen 5 50
(John Murray) *in tch in midfield: effrt over 1f out: keeping on same pce whn nt clrest of runs and swtchd rt ins fnl f: no imp on ldrs fnl 100yds* **22/1**
405- **5** *nse* **Noble Asset**[10] 8535 6-9-3 **64**...................................... HectorCrouch(3) 4 57
(Milton Bradley) *t.k.h: chsd ldr tl wl over 1f out: sn drvn and unable qck: wknd ins fnl f* **3/1**[2]
360- **6** *1 ¼* **Daydream (IRE)**[242] 2107 4-8-8 **57**................................ LuluStanford(5) 2 46
(Tony Newcombe) *hld up in last trio: effrt towards inner over 1f out: plugged on same pce fnl f: nvr trbld ldrs* **33/1**
266- **7** *4* **Whispering Soul (IRE)**[21] 8409 4-8-8 **52**......................(p) JoeyHaynes 7 26
(Brian Baugh) *chsd ldng trio tl lost pl u.p over 1f out: wknd fnl f* **16/1**
100- **8** *shd* **Silver Springs (IRE)**[69] 7693 4-8-8 **59**................ KatherineGlenister(7) 9 33
(David Evans) *a towards rr: n.d* **18/1**
004- **9** *2 ¾* **Spellmaker**[111] 6589 8-9-5 **66**........................................... EoinWalsh(3) 8 30
(Tony Newcombe) *hld up in last trio: wd and effrt wl over 1f out: sn rdn and btn: bhd fnl f* **6/1**

1m 1.43s (-0.47) **Going Correction** 0.0s/f (Stan) **9** Ran SP% **113.8**
Speed ratings (Par 101): **103,102,99,96,96 94,88,87,83**
CSF £11.19 CT £124.70 TOTE £3.00: £1.10, £1.30, £4.70; EX 11.50 Trifecta £95.30.
**Owner** P E Axon **Bred** P E Axon **Trained** Charlton Mackrell, Somerset

**FOCUS**
Not a strong handicap.

## 96 32REDSPORT.COM MAIDEN AUCTION FILLIES' STKS 7f 36y (Tp)
**6:15** (6:16) (Class 6) 3-Y-O **£2,264** (£673; £336; £168) **Stalls** High

Form RPR
005- **1** **Oberyn (IRE)**[10] 8536 3-9-0 0..................................... JosephineGordon 7 62
(Sylvester Kirk) *taken down early: chsd ldrs: effrt u.p over 1f out: hdwy to chse ldr ins fnl f: styd on wl u.p to ld last strides* **20/1**
552- **2** *hd* **Circulate**[19] 8443 3-9-0 70............................................ JoeFanning 6 62
(Tom Clover) *led: rdn over 1f out: kpt on u.p: hdd last strides* **4/5**[1]
56- **3** *1 ¼* **Camaradorie (IRE)**[29] 8277 3-8-11 0............................ SimonPearce(3) 8 59+
(Lydia Pearce) *swtchd lft after s: hld up in last trio: nt clr run 2f out: swtchd rt over 1f out: hdwy whn nt clr run and swtchd rt again ins fnl f: r.o wl fnl 100yds: clsng to go 3rd whn nt clrest of runs cl home* **100/1**
**4** *hd* **Never Folding (IRE)** 3-9-0 0........................................ JamesSullivan 4 58
(Seamus Durack) *hld up in tch in midfield: nt clr run ent fnl 2f: rdn and hdwy between horses wl over 1f out: styd on wl ins fnl: nt rchd ldrs* **7/2**[2]
0- **5** *½* **Implausible**[128] 6035 3-9-0 0................................................. LukeMorris 1 57
(Jonathan Portman) *in tch in midfield: nt clr run jst over 2f out: hdwy over 1f out and drvn to chse ldrs 1f out: styd on same pce ins fnl f* **14/1**
034- **6** *½* **Joyful Dream (IRE)**[32] 8230 3-8-9 54......................(p) LuluStanford(5) 11 56
(J S Moore) *chsd ldr after 1f out: jnd ldr 5f out tl unable qck and hung lft over 1f out: no ex and outpcd fnl 150yds* **10/1**
**7** *nk* **Bonnie Gals** 3-8-9 0............................................ ShirleyTeasdale(5) 10 55+
(Keith Dalgleish) *hld up in last trio: nt clr run jst over 2f out: shkn up and hdwy over 1f out: keeping on whn squeezed for room ins fnl f: no threat to ldrs but kpt on towards fin* **25/1**
0- **8** *2 ½* **Rockalater**[10] 8536 3-9-0 0.................................................. KieranO'Neill 5 49
(Sylvester Kirk) *chsd ldr for 1f: stdd bk to trck ldrs: rdn and unable qck over 1f out: wknd ins fnl f* **66/1**
00- **9** *½* **Lady Parker (IRE)**[23] 8361 3-8-9 0................................ HollieDoyle(5) 2 48
(J S Moore) *sn dropped to rr: effrt wd wl over 1f out: no imp and edgd lft over 1f out: nvr trbld ldrs* **100/1**
300- **10** *1 ¼* **Rita's Girl**[31] 8235 3-9-0 55..............................................(v[1]) JoeyHaynes 3 45
(K R Burke) *hld up in tch in midfield: u.p and wd bnd wl over 1f out: sn btn: wknd ins fnl f* **12/1**
**11** *11* **India Jane (FR)** 3-9-0 0......................................................... ShaneKelly 9 18
(Henry Spiller) *in tch in midfield: pushed along and lost pl 2f out: bhd ins fnl f* **15/2**[3]

1m 29.18s (0.38) **Going Correction** 0.0s/f (Stan) **11** Ran SP% **125.1**
Speed ratings (Par 92): **97,96,95,95,94 93,93,90,90,88 76**
CSF £38.23 TOTE £18.10: £3.60, £1.10, £21.60; EX 42.00 Trifecta £590.80.
**Owner** Mrs Barbara Facchino **Bred** Barouche Stud Ireland Ltd **Trained** Upper Lambourn, Berks

**FOCUS**
A modest maiden.

## 97 32RED.COM EBF FILLIES' H'CAP 1m 142y (Tp)
**6:45** (6:46) (Class 3) (0-95,91) 4-Y-O+ **£10,396** (£3,111; £1,555; £778; £387) **Stalls** Low

Form RPR
313- **1** **Gleaming Girl**[10] 8538 5-8-11 **78**................................ JosephineGordon 3 83+
(David Simcock) *s.i.s: hld up in rr: rdn 2f out: hdwy on inner over 1f out: chsd wnr jst ins fnl f: r.o wl to ld cl home* **7/2**[2]
515- **2** *nk* **Stosur (IRE)**[10] 8538 6-8-12 **79**.........................................(b) LukeMorris 5 83
(Gay Kelleway) *led: rdn and qcknd 2f out: drvn and kpt on fnl f: hdd cl home* **12/1**
131- **3** *1 ½* **Somethingthrilling**[20] 8426 5-9-3 **91**........................... JoshuaBryan(7) 1 92+
(David Elsworth) *restless in stalls: hld up in tch in last pair: nt clr run 2f out tl swtchd lft over 1f out: n.m.r 1f out: hdwy and edgd rt ins fnl f: kpt on* **4/6**[1]
550- **4** *nk* **Maggie Pink**[62] 7825 8-8-13 **83**.............................. AlistairRawlinson(3) 4 83
(Michael Appleby) *taken down early: chsd ldrs: effrt ent fnl 2f: kpt on same pce u.p ins fnl f* **25/1**
101- **5** *nk* **Threebagsue (IRE)**[22] 8379 4-8-1 **74**......................(b) LuluStanford(5) 7 73
(J S Moore) *in tch in midfield: effrt 2f out: kpt on same pce ins fnl f* **8/1**[3]
/21- **6** *¾* **Amber Mystique**[9] 8559 4-8-12 **80** 6ex.......................... TonyHamilton 6 77
(Kristin Stubbs) *chsd ldr: rdn 2f out: unable qck u.p ent fnl f: lost pl and btn whn short of room wl ins fnl f* **12/1**

1m 50.2s (0.10) **Going Correction** 0.0s/f (Stan)
**WFA** 4 from 5yo+ 1lb **6** Ran SP% **112.6**
Speed ratings (Par 104): **99,98,97,97,96 96**
CSF £40.86 TOTE £4.90: £1.60, £4.40; EX 25.50 Trifecta £66.00.
**Owner** Tick Tock Partnership **Bred** Rabbah Bloodstock Limited **Trained** Newmarket, Suffolk

**FOCUS**
The pace was honest for this fair handicap. The runner-up has been rated to the best of her form over the past year.

## 98 32RED ON THE APP STORE H'CAP 2m 120y (Tp)
**7:15** (7:16) (Class 6) (0-60,61) 4-Y-O+ **£2,264** (£673; £336; £168) **Stalls** Low

Form RPR
332- **1** **Yasir (USA)**[15] 8488 9-10-1 **61**............................................... JoeFanning 9 67
(Conor Dore) *stdd s: hld up in tch in rr: hdwy on outer 2f out: shkn up to chal 1f out: kpt on wl u.p to ld towards fin* **5/2**[1]
602- **2** *hd* **Lineman**[10] 8540 7-9-7 **56**................................................(b) JackDuern(3) 1 62
(Sarah Hollinshead) *hld up in tch in last trio: swtchd rt 4f out: rdn and hdwy over 2f out: led over 1f out: clr and battling w wnr fnl f: hdd and no ex cl home* **9/2**[3]
205- **3** *3 ½* **Dream Serenade**[48] 8039 4-8-11 **50**................................(h) LukeMorris 4 52
(Michael Appleby) *t.k.h: chsd ldr tl 13f out: styd chsng ldrs: effrt ent fnl 2f: 3rd and styd on same pce fnl f* **7/2**[2]
321/ **4** *2 ¾* **Azamesse (IRE)**[49] 8020 5-9-12 **58**..........................(vt[1]) TonyHamilton 5 56
(J R Jenkins) *t.k.h: hld up in tch into midfield: nt clr run over 2f out: rdn and hdwy wl over 1f out: no imp 1f out: plugged on* **11/1**
344- **5** *1 ¾* **Sakhra**[34] 8211 6-8-13 **45**............................................................. JFEgan 6 41
(Mark Brisbourne) *chsd ldrs: wnt 2nd 13f out tl led 1/2-way: rdn 3f out: hdd over 1f out: sn outpcd and wknd ins fnl f* **11/2**
006- **6** *2 ¼* **He's Magic**[91] 7106 6-8-13 **45**........................................... JamesSullivan 2 38
(Tim Fitzgerald) *in tch in midfield: swtchd rt 5f out: effrt ent fnl 2f: outpcd and btn whn pushed rt 1f out: wknd fnl f* **50/1**
000- **7** *6* **Mybrotherjohnny**[181] 4156 6-8-13 **45**..............................(t[1]) JoeyHaynes 7 31
(Fergal O'Brien) *t.k.h: hld up in tch in last trio: bmpd 5f out: hdwy over 4f out: rdn and ev ch over 2f out tl lost pl over 1f out: shifted rt 1f out: wknd fnl f* **6/1**
060- **8** *1 ½* **Major Franko**[10] 8540 5-9-2 **48**..................................(p[1]) KieranO'Neill 10 32
(Sarah-Jayne Davies) *chsd ldrs: drvn over 3f out: lost pl and bhd over 1f out* **100/1**
520- **9** *9* **Celestial Dancer (FR)**[233] 2370 5-9-2 **48**......................... ThomasBrown 8 22
(Nigel Twiston-Davies) *led tl 1/2-way: rdn and lost pl over 2f out: bhd over 1f out* **8/1**

3m 45.48s (1.78) **Going Correction** 0.0s/f (Stan)
**WFA** 4 from 5yo+ 5lb **9** Ran SP% **121.0**
Speed ratings (Par 101): **95,94,93,91,91 90,87,86,82**
CSF £14.88 CT £40.61 TOTE £3.50: £1.50, £1.70, £1.90; EX 16.20 Trifecta £51.80.
**Owner** Mrs Jennifer Marsh **Bred** Shadwell Farm LLC **Trained** Hubbert's Bridge, Lincs

**FOCUS**
They went a steady pace for this modest handicap.

## 99 32RED CASINO FILLIES' H'CAP 1m 1f 104y (Tp)
**7:45** (7:47) (Class 4) (0-80,84) 4-Y-O+ **£4,690** (£1,395; £697; £348) **Stalls** Low

Form RPR
0/2- **1** **Absolute Blast (IRE)**[28] 8286 5-9-9 **78**............................ PJMcDonald 2 93+
(Iain Jardine) *hld up in tch in midfield: clsd and travelling strly whn nt clr run jst over 1f out: swtchd rt jst ins fnl f: nudged along and sn qckند to ld and in command: v easily* **4/5**[1]
520- **2** *2* **Heartstone (IRE)**[69] 7691 4-8-13 **69**........................................... JFEgan 8 75
(David Evans) *chsd ldrs tl stdd into midfield 7f out: effrt 2f out: hdwy u.p to ld 1f out: hdd and outpcd by wnr ins fnl f: kpt on for clr 2nd* **18/1**
31- **3** *3 ¼* **Vogueatti (USA)**[15] 8491 4-9-5 **75**................................. DanielMuscutt 7 74
(Marco Botti) *stdd s: swtchd rt and hdwy to chse ldrs after 2f: rdn and ev ch 2f out tl no ex 1f out: outpcd fnl f* **5/1**[3]
231- **4** *½* **Favorite Girl (GER)**[9] 7775 9-8-12 **67**........................ AndrewMullen 5 65
(Michael Appleby) *led: rdn ent fnl 2f: hdd 1f out: sn outpcd* **12/1**
050- **5** *½* **Edge Of Heaven**[15] 8487 5-9-0 **69**..............................(p[1]) LukeMorris 4 66
(Jonathan Portman) *t.k.h: chsd ldrs: effrt 2f out: unable qck u.p over 1f out: outpcd fnl f* **20/1**
451- **6** *nse* **Daisy Bere (FR)**[10] 8538 4-10-0 **84** 6ex.........................(p) JoeyHaynes 3 81
(K R Burke) *hld up in rr: effrt 2f out: nt clr run ent fnl f: no ch w wnr and kpt on same pce fnl f* **3/1**[2]
165- **7** *1* **Sattelac**[24] 8347 4-8-7 **68**.....................................(p[1]) ShirleyTeasdale(5) 1 63
(Keith Dalgleish) *hld up in tch: effrt on inner to chse ldrs wl over 1f out: no ex 1f out: outpcd fnl f* **28/1**
340/ **8** *¾* **Langlauf (USA)**[206] 4-9-5 **75**............................................... RyanTate 6 68
(Rod Millman) *hld up in tch in last pair: effrt but stuck bhd a wall of horses over 1f out: switching rt but nvr fnd a gap fnl f: n.d* **33/1**

1m 58.84s (-1.96) **Going Correction** 0.0s/f (Stan)
**WFA** 4 from 5yo+ 1lb **8** Ran SP% **121.3**
Speed ratings (Par 102): **108,106,103,102,102 102,101,100**
CSF £20.24 CT £55.47 TOTE £1.60: £1.10, £4.70, £1.30; EX 18.50 Trifecta £78.00.
**Owner** Ibrahim Rachid **Bred** Mrs O M E McKeever **Trained** Carrutherstown, D'fries & G'way

**FOCUS**
A fair handicap won in decisive fashion. The winner has been rated in line with her French 3yo form, and the runner-up close to her turf best.

## 100 £10 FREE AT 32RED.COM H'CAP — 1m 1f 104y (Tp)
8:15 (8:15) (Class 5) (0-75,73) 3-Y-O — £2,911 (£866; £432; £216) Stalls Low

Form — RPR

626- **1** **Nastenka**[39] 8131 3-9-4 **70** ThomasBrown 1 — 72+
(Ed Walker) *hld up in midfield: rdn and hdwy over 1f out: edgd lft ins fnl f but r.o wl to ld fnl 50yds* **8/1**

163- **2** 3/4 **Bazwind (IRE)**[25] 8341 3-8-9 **61** JFEgan 6 — 61
(David Evans) *t.k.h: led for 2f: trckd ldrs after: effrt over 1f out: rdn to ld 1f out: hdd and no ex 50yds out* **8/1**

010- **3** 1/2 **Global Revival (IRE)**[162] 4802 3-9-7 **73** JosephineGordon 5 — 72+
(Ed Dunlop) *t.k.h: hld up in tch in midfield: rdn 3f out: hdwy over 1f out: nt clr run and swtchd rt ins fnl f: styd on wl towards fin* **9/2**[2]

005- **4** 1/2 **Broughtons Story**[17] 8466 3-8-9 **61** ConnorBeasley 2 — 59
(Henry Spiller) *hld up in tch in last pair: hdwy on inner over 1f out: rdn to chse ldrs 1f out: kpt on same pce ins fnl f* **11/2**

050- **5** hd **The Last Debutante**[25] 8340 3-9-0 **66** JoeFanning 3 — 64
(Mark Johnston) *t.k.h: stdd s: swtchd rt after 1f: rapid hdwy to chse ldrs 6f out: rdn and ev ch 2f out tl ins fnl f: styd on same pce fnl 100yds* **5/1**[3]

042- **6** 1 1/4 **Ocean Promise (USA)**[20] 8423 3-9-4 **70** ShaneKelly 8 — 65
(Richard Hughes) *t.k.h: hdwy to ld after 2f: rdn 2f out: hdd 1f out: no ex and wknd ins fnl f* **17/2**

020- **7** 3 1/4 **Areyoutheway (IRE)**[8] 8568 3-8-12 **64** (p) LukeMorris 7 — 52
(Michael Appleby) *rousted along leaving stalls: in tch: hdwy to chse ldr over 7f out tl over 2f out: lost pl u.p ent fnl f: wknd* **12/1**

345- **8** 1 1/2 **Lorikeet (USA)**[30] 8245 3-9-5 **71** AndrewMullen 4 — 56
(Mark Johnston) *midfield: rdn 4f out: wd and struggling bnd 2f out: sn bhd and bhd fnl f* **11/4**[1]

2m 1.21s (0.41) **Going Correction** 0.0s/f (Stan) 8 Ran SP% **117.3**
Speed ratings (Par 97): **98,97,96,96,96 95,92,90**
CSF £71.14 CT £326.52 TOTE £9.90: £2.80, £2.70, £1.70; EX 81.60 Trifecta £569.30.
**Owner** Miss K Rausing **Bred** Miss K Rausing **Trained** Upper Lambourn, Berks
■ Stewards' Enquiry : J F Egan caution; careless riding

**FOCUS**
An open handicap with plenty of unexposed types in the field. The fourth has been rated to his latest form.
T/Plt: £43.00 to a £1 stake. Pool: £85,714 - 1991.90 winning tickets T/Qpdt: £25.10 to a £1 stake. Pool: £5,865.00 - 233.41 winning tickets **Steve Payne**

101 - 113a (Foreign Racing) - See Raceform Interactive

# [34]LINGFIELD (L-H)
## Saturday, January 7

**OFFICIAL GOING: Polytrack: standard**
Wind: virtually nil Weather: overcast

## 114 32RED CASINO H'CAP — 1m 1y(P)
12:05 (12:05) (Class 4) (0-85,80) 3-Y-O — £4,690 (£1,395; £697) Stalls High

Form — RPR

022- **1** **Morning Suit (USA)**[40] 8132 3-9-7 **80** PJMcDonald 1 — 81
(Mark Johnston) *mde all: jnd over 2f out: shkn up over 1f out: rdn and qcknd clr jst ins fnl f: r.o strly* **5/4**[1]

433- **2** 1 1/4 **Envisaging (IRE)**[43] 8089 3-9-5 **78** DanielMuscutt 2 — 76
(James Fanshawe) *trckd ldr tl over 2f out: squeezed for room and swtchd rt ent fnl 2f: 3 l down over 1f out: rallied u.p ins fnl f: wnt 2nd wl ins fnl f: no threat to wnr* **9/5**[2]

005- **3** 1 1/4 **License To Thrill (USA)**[10] 8560 3-8-7 **66** oh1 JFEgan 3 — 61
(Simon Dow) *hld up in 3rd tl pushed up to join ldr over 2f out: rdn and ev ch over 1f out tl unable qck jst ins fnl f: lost 2nd and wknd wl ins fnl f* **11/4**[3]

1m 42.62s (4.42) **Going Correction** +0.075s/f (Slow) 3 Ran SP% **106.8**
Speed ratings (Par 99): **80,78,77**
CSF £3.68 TOTE £2.10; EX 2.40 Trifecta £2.60.
**Owner** Sheikh Hamdan bin Mohammed Al Maktoum **Bred** Darley **Trained** Middleham Moor, N Yorks

**FOCUS**
This was always going to be tactical with just the three runners. The winner has been rated to form.

## 115 32RED.COM MEDIAN AUCTION MAIDEN STKS — 1m 1y(P)
12:40 (12:41) (Class 6) 3-Y-O — £2,264 (£673; £336; £168) Stalls High

Form — RPR

**1** **Indian Dandy (IRE)** 3-9-5 0 JosephineGordon 6 — 76+
(Marco Botti) *s.i.s: hld up in tch in midfield: nt clr run ent fnl 2f: rdn and hdwy on inner over 1f out: chsd ldr 1f out: led wl ins fnl f: hld on u.p cl home* **7/1**

432- **2** shd **Pattie**[26] 8340 3-9-0 72 GrahamLee 8 — 70
(Mick Channon) *chsd ldr tl led 2f out: sn rdn: edgd rt and hdd ins fnl f: kpt on u.p but hld towards fin* **4/1**[2]

**3** 3/4 **Arsenio Lupin** 3-9-2 0 (t[1]) TimClark(3) 9 — 73+
(Denis Quinn) *s.i.s: hld up in rr: effrt and wd bnd 2f out: sn rdn: hdwy ins fnl f: styd on strly fnl 100yds: nt rch ldrs* **100/1**

0- **4** 3/4 **Salt Whistle Bay (IRE)**[71] 7664 3-9-5 0 DavidProbert 1 — 71
(Rae Guest) *chsd ldrs: effrt ent fnl 2f: styd on same pce u.p ins fnl f* **8/1**

5- **5** nk **Traveller (FR)**[58] 7883 3-9-5 0 (t) LukeMorris 3 — 71
(Charles Hills) *in tch in midfield: effrt ent fnl 2f: drvn over 1f out: kpt on same pce u.p ins fnl f* **5/1**[3]

65- **6** 4 1/2 **Critical Thinking (IRE)**[7] 8591 3-9-2 0 ShelleyBirkett(3) 10 — 60
(Julia Feilden) *in tch in midfield but stuck wd: hdwy to chse ldrs 3f out: rdn ent fnl 2f: sn lost pl and btn: wknd fnl f* **25/1**

**7** shd **Surfside** 3-8-11 0 GeorgeDowning(3) 2 — 55
(Mick Channon) *s.i.s: t.k.h: hld up towards rr: effrt ent fnl 2f: outpcd and btn over 1f out: wknd fnl f* **50/1**

**8** 1 3/4 **State Residence (IRE)** 3-9-5 0 DougieCostello 7 — 55
(David Simcock) *awkward leaving stalls and v.s.a: bhd: pushed along jst over 2f out: no imp whn nt clrest of runs over 1f out: nvr trbld ldrs* **12/1**

63- **9** shd **Naupaka**[22] 8397 3-9-0 0 TomEaves 4 — 50
(Brian Ellison) *led tl 2f out: sn rdn and unable qck: wknd fnl f* **6/1**

**10** 3 1/4 **Palermo (IRE)** 3-9-5 0 AdamKirby 5 — 47
(Michael Wigham) *hld up in midfield: reminder 2f out : sn btn: bhd and eased ins fnl f* **5/2**[1]

1m 37.63s (-0.57) **Going Correction** +0.075s/f (Slow) 10 Ran SP% **117.6**
Speed ratings (Par 95): **105,104,104,103,103 98,98,96,96,93**
CSF £35.18 TOTE £8.20: £2.80, £1.60, £18.40; EX 42.70 Trifecta £3168.80.
**Owner** Mubarak Al Naemi **Bred** Mubarak Al Naemi **Trained** Newmarket, Suffolk

**FOCUS**
A modest median auction maiden, but a couple of nice performances including from the winner.

## 116 SUNBETS ON THE APP STORE H'CAP — 7f 1y(P)
1:10 (1:10) (Class 5) (0-70,72) 4-Y-O+ — £2,911 (£866; £432; £216) Stalls Low

Form — RPR

050- **1** **Black Caesar (IRE)**[40] 7506 6-9-5 **67** GrahamLee 7 — 75
(Philip Hide) *chsd ldrs: effrt u.p over 1f out: hdwy to ld 150yds out: hld on wl u.p* **25/1**

362- **2** nk **Malaysian Boleh**[12] 8531 7-9-6 **68** (b) TomEaves 4 — 75
(Brian Ellison) *hld up in tch in midfield: effrt between horses to chal ent fnl f: edgd lft u.p and hld fnl 75yds* **7/2**[2]

103- **3** 2 1/4 **Billyoakes (IRE)**[16] 8490 5-9-8 **70** (p) LukeMorris 10 — 71
(Charlie Wallis) *chsd ldr: rdn to ld over 1f out: sn drvn and hdd 150yds out: outpcd fnl 100yds* **6/1**[3]

000- **4** 3/4 **Quintus Cerialis (IRE)**[23] 8382 5-8-9 **57** (tp) TomMarquand 1 — 56
(Karen George) *s.i.s: bhd: clsd 4f out: effrt wd bnd 2f out: styd on wl u.p ins fnl f: no threat to ldrs* **16/1**

000- **5** 1 1/4 **Noble Deed**[10] 8561 7-9-6 **68** JosephineGordon 6 — 64
(Michael Attwater) *taken down early: short of room leaving stalls: t.k.h in midfield: effrt over 1f out: styd on same pce ins fnl f* **20/1**

254- **6** hd **Tabla**[23] 8381 5-9-6 **68** KierenFox 3 — 63
(Lee Carter) *trckd ldrs: n.m.r on inner 2f out: effrt to press ldrs over 1f out: drvn and unable qck 1f out: wknd ins fnl f* **3/1**[1]

300- **7** 3/4 **Majestic Myles (IRE)**[31] 8258 9-9-1 **63** KieranO'Neill 8 — 56
(Lee Carter) *t.k.h: hld up in tch in midfield: effrt over 1f out: no imp and one pced fnl f: swtchd lft towards fin* **20/1**

150- **8** 1/2 **Gold Return (IRE)**[22] 8411 4-8-9 **62** LuluStanford(5) 5 — 54
(John Ryan) *hld up in tch towards rr: effrt and swtchd lft 1f out: no imp fnl f* **10/1**

00- **9** 2 3/4 **Falcao (IRE)**[32] 8239 5-9-10 **72** TimmyMurphy 9 — 56
(John Butler) *sn led: rdn over 1f out: sn hdd & wknd ins fnl f* **25/1**

060- **10** 3 1/4 **Star Of The Stage**[16] 8490 5-9-4 **66** AdamKirby 2 — 42
(John Butler) *bhd: clsd and in tch 4f out: wd and rdn bnd 2f out: sn btn: bhd fnl f* **3/1**[1]

1m 24.72s (-0.08) **Going Correction** +0.075s/f (Slow) 10 Ran SP% **118.7**
Speed ratings (Par 103): **103,102,100,99,97 97,96,96,93,89**
CSF £108.13 CT £622.72 TOTE £23.50: £6.10, £1.60, £1.80; EX 82.90 Trifecta £1500.10.
**Owner** The Long Furlong **Bred** Miss Hilary Mullen **Trained** Findon, W Sussex

**FOCUS**
An ordinary handicap, but a thrilling finish. The winner has been rated to last year's turf form.

## 117 BETWAY BEST ODDS GUARANTEED PLUS H'CAP — 1m 2f (P)
1:45 (1:45) (Class 3) (0-95,90) 4-Y-O — £7,246 (£2,168; £1,084; £542; £270) Stalls Low

Form — RPR

521- **1** **Coillte Cailin (IRE)**[11] 8539 7-9-7 **90** MartinHarley 4 — 97+
(David O'Meara) *hld up in tch towards rr: hdwy over 1f out: rdn to chal ins fnl f: r.o wl u.p to ld fnl 50yds* **3/1**[2]

311- **2** 1 **Van Huysen (IRE)**[20] 8446 5-9-1 **84** JFEgan 6 — 89
(Dominic Ffrench Davis) *chsd ldrs: effrt over 1f out: drvn to ld jst ins fnl f: hdd and no ex fnl 50yds* **5/2**[1]

053- **3** 3/4 **Mica Mika (IRE)**[11] 8539 9-8-8 **84** NatalieHambling(7) 2 — 87
(Richard Fahey) *chsd ldr tl 7f out: styd chsng ldrs: swtchd lft and effrt to press ldrs over 1f out: styd on same pce ins fnl f* **10/1**

005- **4** 1/2 **Fort Bastion (IRE)**[17] 8478 8-9-5 **88** TomEaves 8 — 90
(Brian Ellison) *stdd and dropped in bhd after s: hld up in tch: c wd and effrt over 1f out: hdwy 1f out: kpt on u.p ins fnl f: nt rch ldrs* **16/1**

10-2 **5** nk **Marshgate Lane (USA)**[5] 24 8-9-5 **88** (p) LiamKeniry 1 — 89
(Neil Mulholland) *dwlt and bustled along leaving stalls: hld up in tch: nt clr run over 2f out: swtchd rt and hmpd over 1f out: hdwy ins fnl f: kpt on: no threat to ldrs* **7/2**[3]

600- **6** 1 1/2 **Ready (IRE)**[12] 8529 7-9-4 **87** (p) SteveDrowne 3 — 85
(Clare Ellam) *led: rdn 2f out: hdd jst ins fnl f: no ex and wknd wl ins fnl f* **28/1**

300- **7** hd **Passing Star**[7] 8593 6-8-9 **81** CallumShepherd(3) 7 — 79
(Charles Hills) *hld up in tch in midfield: effrt over 1f out: unable qck and one pced ins fnl f* **10/1**

235- **8** 2 **Arrowzone**[87] 7287 6-8-10 **86** (b) LewisEdmunds(7) 5 — 80
(Ivan Furtado) *t.k.h: hld up in last pair: hdwy to chse ldr 7f out tl wl over 1f out: sn hanging lft and unable qck: wknd ins fnl f* **6/1**

2m 5.28s (-1.32) **Going Correction** +0.075s/f (Slow) 8 Ran SP% **117.6**
Speed ratings (Par 107): **108,107,106,105 104,104,103**
CSF £11.34 CT £66.01 TOTE £3.70: £1.70, £1.10, £2.50; EX 10.50 Trifecta £37.20.
**Owner** Peter J Moran **Bred** Whisperview Trading Ltd **Trained** Upper Helmsley, N Yorks

**FOCUS**
A decent handicap and a driving finish between two in-form horses, and the winner continues on the up.

## 118 SUNBETS.CO.UK CONDITIONS STKS — 1m 1y(P)
2:20 (2:20) (Class 2) 4-Y-O+
£11,827 (£3,541; £1,770; £885; £442; £222) Stalls High

Form — RPR

210- **1** **Alfred Hutchinson**[7] 8593 9-9-3 100 (p) AdamKirby 4 — 96
(David O'Meara) *stdd s: hld up in tch: effrt ent fnl 2f: hdwy u.p 1f out: r.o wl to ld towards fin* **11/4**[2]

001- **2** 3/4 **Realize**[16] 8489 7-9-3 105 (t) MartinHarley 2 — 94
(Stuart Williams) *trckd ldng pair: wnt 2nd 2f out: rdn to chal 1f out: drvn ins fnl f: kpt on to ld wl ins fnl f: sn hdd and no ex towards fin* **11/8**[1]

220- **3** nk **Dollar Reward**[147] 5403 4-9-3 82 AdamBeschizza 5 — 93
(Stuart Williams) *stdd s: hld up in tch in last trio: effrt on inner 2f out: drvn and ev ch ins fnl f: styd on same pce fnl 50yds* **25/1**

614- **4** hd **Kingston Kurrajong**[168] 4624 4-9-3 89 LiamKeniry 3 — 93
(Andrew Balding) *led: rdn and qcknd over 1f out: drvn and hrd pressed 1f out: hdd wl ins fnl f: styd on same pce towards fin* **10/1**[3]

200- **5** 1 1/2 **Captain Cat (IRE)**[56] 7933 8-9-3 100 GeorgeDowning 1 — 89
(Tony Carroll) *stdd s: hld up in tch in last pair: swtchd rt and effrt over 1f out: kpt on same pce ins fnl f: nvr threatened ldrs* **20/1**

002- **6** nk **You're Fired (IRE)**[52] 7978 6-9-3 107 DougieCostello 6 — 88
(K R Burke) *sn chsng ldr: rdn and lost 2nd 2f out: unable qck over 1f out: lost pl and one pced ins fnl f* **11/4**[2]

1m 36.27s (-1.93) **Going Correction** +0.075s/f (Slow) 6 Ran SP% **113.1**
Speed ratings (Par 109): **112,111,110,110,109 108**
CSF £7.06 TOTE £3.70: £2.00, £1.30; EX 7.50 Trifecta £50.10.
**Owner** R C Bond **Bred** R C Bond **Trained** Upper Helmsley, N Yorks


The Form Book Flat, Raceform Ltd, Newbury, RG14 5SJ

**FOCUS**
Two of the previous three winners of this conditions event, Grey Mirage and Captain Joy, went on to win the AW Mile Championship back here, albeit not in the same year. This was a thriller with four in a line around 50yds from home. The form is set around the 3rd/4th.

## 119 BETWAY SPRINT MAIDEN STKS 6f 1y(P)
2:55 (2:55) (Class 5) 3-Y-0+ £2,911 (£866; £432; £216) Stalls Low

Form RPR
1 **Jack Flash (FR)**[171] 4537 3-8-12 76 JasonHart 2 69
(Les Eyre) *mde all: rdn and fnd ex 2f out: hrd pressed 1f out: edgd rt and hld on wl u.p ins fnl f* **9/2**[3]
300- 2 *nk* **Dark Destroyer (IRE)**[120] 6288 3-8-12 80 JFEgan 7 68
(Joseph Tuite) *hld up in tch in midfield: clsd to trck ldrs 3f out: wnt 2nd wl over 1f out: rdn to chal 1f out: kpt on but a jst hld ins fnl f* **9/4**[2]
0- 3 *3 ½* **Roman Navigator (IRE)**[45] 8065 3-8-12 0 (t[1]) DanielMuscutt 4 57
(Marco Botti) *chsd ldr tl dropped bk to 3rd 4f out: effrt over 1f out: unable qck w ldng pair over 1f out: 3rd and kpt on same pce ins fnl f* **8/1**
0- 4 *nse* **Tai Hang Dragon (IRE)**[56] 7939 3-8-7 0 TomMarquand 8 52
(Richard Hannon) *stdd s and dropped in bhd after s: hld up in rr: swtchd rt over 1f out: hdwy between horses 1f out: kpt on but no threat to ldng pair* **16/1**
600- 5 *¾* **Pleadings (USA)**[9] 8572 4-10-0 40 (vt) AdamBeschizza 6 58?
(Charlie Wallis) *dwlt: in tch in last pair: effrt over 1f out: kpt on same pce u.p ins fnl f* **100/1**
6- 6 *¾* **Bo Selecta (IRE)**[24] 8353 3-8-12 0 LiamKeniry 1 52
(Richard Spencer) *in tch in midfield: effrt on inner but unable qck over 1f out: no threat to ldng pair and one pced fnl f* **9/2**[3]
222- 7 *2 ½* **Coral Sea**[12] 8526 3-8-7 72 (h) LukeMorris 5 39
(Charles Hills) *taken down early: jnd ldr after 2f tl rdn and unable qck 2f out: wknd fnl f* **2/1**[1]

1m 11.35s (-0.55) **Going Correction** +0.075s/f (Slow)
**WFA** 3 from 4yo 16lb 7 Ran SP% **118.4**
Speed ratings (Par 103): **106,105,100,100,99 98,95**
CSF £15.90 TOTE £4.90: £2.50, £1.80; EX 22.20 Trifecta £105.40.
**Owner** Billy Parker **Bred** S A R L De Chambure Haras D'Etreham **Trained** Catwick, N Yorks
**FOCUS**
A moderate maiden in which the first two finished well clear.

## 120 32REDSPORT.COM FILLIES' H'CAP 1m 2f (P)
3:30 (3:30) (Class 5) (0-70,73) 4-Y-0+ £2,911 (£866; £432; £216) Stalls Low

Form RPR
502- 1 **Heads You Win**[22] 8411 4-9-4 66 TimmyMurphy 6 73
(Jamie Osborne) *led after 1f and mde rest: rdn over 1f out: kpt on wl ins fnl f: rdn out* **16/1**
202- 2 *1* **Footlight**[7] 8590 4-9-4 73 NatalieHambling(7) 1 78
(Richard Fahey) *led for 1f: trckd ldrs after: effrt on inner over 1f out: chsd wnr 100yds out: kpt on but nvr getting to wnr* **3/1**[2]
330- 3 *½* **Mercy Me**[21] 8427 5-9-11 71 AdamKirby 8 75
(John Ryan) *hld up in midfield: hdwy on outer 4f out: rdn to chal over 2f out tl unable qck over 1f out: lost 2nd and one pced fnl 100yds* **3/1**[2]
033- 4 *1 ¼* **Celtic Ava (IRE)**[24] 8367 5-8-11 57 JFEgan 5 59
(Pat Phelan) *hld up in tch in midfield: effrt to chse ldng trio over 1f out: styd on same pce ins fnl f* **11/4**[1]
056- 5 *1 ¾* **Tommys Geal**[18] 8462 5-8-12 58 DanielMuscutt 9 56
(Michael Madgwick) *hld up in last pair: rdn over 1f out: hdwy into midfield over 1f out: kpt on same pce and no imp u.p ins fnl f* **10/1**
020- 6 *shd* **Go On Gal (IRE)**[36] 8194 4-8-6 57 ShelleyBirkett(3) 2 55
(Julia Feilden) *in tch in midfield: rdn over 2f out: no imp and kpt on same pce fnl f* **14/1**
610- 7 *nk* **Solveig's Song**[18] 8462 5-9-10 70 (p) JackMitchell 3 67
(Steve Woodman) *hld up in tch towards rr: swtchd rt and effrt wl over 1f out: kpt on same pce fnl f: nvr trbld ldrs* **9/1**[3]
145- 8 *1 ¾* **Owners Day**[20] 2996 7-9-6 66 LiamKeniry 7 60
(Neil Mulholland) *chsd ldr over 8f out tl over 2f out: sn rdn and unable qck: lost pl over 1f out: wknd fnl f* **12/1**
220- 9 *2 ¾* **Two In The Pink (IRE)**[20] 8448 7-9-3 63 DavidProbert 4 51
(Ralph J Smith) *hld up in tch: rdn over 2f out: sn struggling: bhd fnl f* **16/1**

2m 9.13s (2.53) **Going Correction** +0.075s/f (Slow)
**WFA** 4 from 5yo+ 1lb 9 Ran SP% **121.9**
Speed ratings (Par 100): **92,91,90,89,88 88,88,86,84**
CSF £67.40 CT £193.16 TOTE £13.10: £3.90, £1.80, £1.50; EX 56.50 Trifecta £146.20.
**Owner** Heads You Win Partnership **Bred** Park Farm Racing **Trained** Upper Lambourn, Berks
**FOCUS**
A modest fillies' handicap, run at an ordinary pace, in which not many got involved, but another pb from the winner.
T/Plt: £43.70 to a £1 stake. Pool: £40,453.63 - 674.52 winning units T/Qpdt: £7.60 to a £1 stake. Pool: £4,600.85 - 443.60 winning units **Steve Payne**

# 95 WOLVERHAMPTON (A.W) (L-H)
Saturday, January 7

**OFFICIAL GOING: Tapeta: standard**
Wind: Nil Weather: Overcast

## 121 BETWAY MIDDLE APPRENTICE H'CAP 1m 4f 51y (Tp)
5:45 (5:46) (Class 6) (0-55,55) 4-Y-0+ £2,425 (£721; £360; £180) Stalls Low

Form RPR
43-2 1 **Frivolous Prince (IRE)**[3] 46 4-8-3 46 (vt) KatherineGlenister(5) 12 54
(David Evans) *hld up: hdwy on outer over 2f out: rdn to ld over 1f out: hung lft wl ins fnl f: r.o* **3/1**[1]
040- 2 *1 ¾* **Cape Spirit (IRE)**[119] 6315 5-8-13 52 WilliamCox(5) 11 57
(Andrew Balding) *prom in main gp: tk clsr order 2f out: rdn and ev ch fr over 1f out tl edgd lft and styd on same pce wl ins fnl f* **22/1**
326- 3 *6* **Sund City (FR)**[18] 8468 4-8-10 51 JordanUys(3) 5 47
(Harry Dunlop) *plld hrd: led after 1f: wnt clr over 6f out: c bk to the field: 2f out: rdn and hdd over 1f out: wknd ins fnl f* **15/2**
360- 4 *1 ½* **Weardiditallgorong**[78] 7515 5-9-7 55 (b) DenisLinehan 7 48
(Des Donovan, Ire) *chsd clr ldrs: wnt 2nd 4f out tl rdn over 1f out: hung lft and wknd ins fnl f* **11/2**[3]
000- 5 *1* **Smoky Hill (IRE)**[18] 8468 8-9-1 54 (p[1]) AledBeech(5) 3 46
(Tony Carroll) *chsd ldrs: settled into mid-div after 2f: hdwy over 3f out: rdn over 1f out: wknd ins fnl f* **9/1**
604- 6 *1* **Spirit Of The Vale (IRE)**[16] 8492 4-8-5 46 (t) KieranSchofield(3) 9 36
(Oliver Greenall) *hld up: racd keenly: hdwy over 3f out: rdn and edgd lft over 1f out: wknd fnl f* **22/1**
230- 7 *2 ¼* **Moss Street**[21] 7888 7-9-6 54 (bt) CallumRodriguez 8 40
(Conor Dore) *s.i.s: hld up: rdn over 1f out: nvr on terms* **33/1**
4/6- 8 *nk* **Krafty One**[28] 8318 5-9-2 53 (p[1]) JoshQuinn(3) 10 39
(Michael Scudamore) *mid-div: hdwy over 4f out: rdn over 1f out: wknd fnl f* **28/1**
600- 9 *1 ½* **Doctor Kehoe**[47] 6424 5-9-2 53 (bt) JoshuaBryan(3) 1 37
(Tim Vaughan) *hld up: nvr on terms* **18/1**
0/0- 10 *14* **Bridge That Gap**[20] 8448 9-9-6 54 (p) RhiainIngram 6 15
(Roger Ingram) *hld up: rdn over 3f out: nvr on terms* **66/1**
224- 11 *7* **Just Fred (IRE)**[80] 7464 4-8-9 50 (p) JaneElliott(3) 2
(Neil Mulholland) *led 1f: plld hrd in 2nd: ldr wnt clr over 6f out: lost 2nd 5f out: wknd 3f out* **4/1**[2]
335- 12 *14* **Ryan The Giant**[11] 8540 4-8-3 48 (p) CharlotteMcFarland(7) 4 +
(Keith Dalgleish) *hld up: sddle slipped sn after s: bhd fnl 7f* **15/2**

2m 39.83s (-0.97) **Going Correction** -0.025s/f (Stan)
**WFA** 4 from 5yo+ 3lb 12 Ran SP% **115.8**
Speed ratings (Par 101): **102,100,96,95,95 94,93,92,91,82 77,68**
CSF £76.89 CT £456.88 TOTE £4.10: £1.80, £4.10, £1.80; EX 52.40 Trifecta £261.30.
**Owner** Mrs E Evans **Bred** Seamus Fox **Trained** Pandy, Monmouths
■ Stewards' Enquiry : Denis Linehan one-day ban; did not to keep straight from the stalls (21st Jan)
**FOCUS**
A moderate middle-distance handicap for apprentice riders.

## 122 BETWAY H'CAP 1m 1f 104y (Tp)
6:15 (6:16) (Class 5) (0-75,75) 4-Y-0+ £3,072 (£914; £456; £228) Stalls Low

Form RPR
535- 1 **Tan Arabiq**[43] 8100 4-8-11 66 LukeMorris 4 74
(Michael Appleby) *trckd ldrs: racd keenly: chsd ldr over 1f out: sn rdn: edgd rt ins fnl f: styd on u.p to ld post* **11/4**[1]
420- 2 *hd* **Ravenhoe (IRE)**[12] 8531 4-9-3 72 JoeFanning 8 79
(Mark Johnston) *led: rdn over 1f out: edgd rt ins fnl f: hdd post* **11/1**
46-0 3 *2 ½* **Idol Deputy (FR)**[3] 47 11-8-11 70 (p) RachealKneller(5) 6 72
(James Bennett) *hld up: hdwy over 1f out: styd on same pce wl ins fnl f* **40/1**
044- 4 *shd* **Dakota City**[12] 8524 6-9-5 73 (v) AdamBeschizza 7 75
(Julia Feilden) *dwlt: hld up: rdn over 1f out: r.o ins fnl f: nrst fin* **6/1**[3]
640- 5 *2* **Ban Shoof**[101] 6870 4-9-6 75 (v) TomMarquand 10 72
(Ismail Mohammed) *prom: rdn over 2f out: styd on* **4/1**[2]
026- 6 *½* **Green Howard**[60] 7857 9-9-6 74 TomEaves 1 70
(Rebecca Bastiman) *hld up in tch: rdn over 1f out: no ex ins fnl f* **16/1**
006- 7 *1 ½* **First Summer**[17] 8480 5-8-7 61 (p) JosephineGordon 3 54
(Shaun Harris) *chsd ldr tl rdn over 1f out: wknd ins fnl f* **40/1**
160- 8 *2 ½* **Cambodia (IRE)**[28] 8319 4-9-5 74 (h[1]) GeorgeBaker 9 62
(Chris Wall) *hld up: shkn up and sme hdwy over 2f out: wknd over 1f out* **11/4**[1]
300- 9 *6* **Freight Train (IRE)**[24] 8356 5-9-1 74 (p) HollieDoyle(5) 2 49
(Adrian Wintle) *rrd s: hld up: pushed along over 3f out: wknd over 2f out* **22/1**

2m 1.58s (0.78) **Going Correction** -0.025s/f (Stan)
**WFA** 4 from 5yo+ 1lb 9 Ran SP% **111.1**
Speed ratings (Par 103): **95,94,92,92,90 90,88,86,81**
CSF £32.30 CT £932.97 TOTE £4.10: £1.30, £2.90, £6.80; EX 32.70 Trifecta £532.10.
**Owner** Sarnian Racing **Bred** Michael Appleby **Trained** Oakham, Rutland
**FOCUS**
A fair handicap. They went a respectable gallop and the form makes sense.

## 123 BETWAY APP H'CAP (DIV I) 1m 1f 104y (Tp)
6:45 (6:45) (Class 6) (0-55,55) 4-Y-0+ £2,425 (£721; £360; £180) Stalls Low

Form RPR
020- 1 **Outlaw Torn (IRE)**[12] 8527 8-9-2 50 (e) JoeFanning 5 56
(Richard Guest) *trckd ldrs: wnt 2nd 7f out: rdn to ld ins fnl f: jst hld on* **14/1**
341- 2 *nk* **Deftera Lad (IRE)**[16] 8499 5-9-7 55 TimmyMurphy 7 60
(Natalie Lloyd-Beavis) *hld up in tch: rdn over 1f out: r.o u.p* **4/1**[2]
400- 3 *1* **Dukes Meadow**[18] 8462 6-8-13 54 RhiainIngram(7) 10 58
(Roger Ingram) *led 8f out: rdn and hdd ins fnl f: styd on same pce* **14/1**
31-0 4 *1 ¼* **Ferryview Place**[3] 46 8-9-4 52 (tp) StevieDonohoe 8 53
(Ian Williams) *s.i.s: pushed along in rr early: shkn up over 1f out: r.o wl ins fnl f: nt rch ldrs* **5/1**[3]
30-0 5 *shd* **Captain K (IRE)**[3] 51 5-8-12 46 (h) LiamKeniry 4 47
(Gordon Elliott, Ire) *hld up: plld hrd: hdwy and edgd lft over 1f out: r.o* **5/1**[3]
62-3 6 *nk* **Menelik (IRE)**[3] 52 8-8-12 53 (t[1]) DenisLinehan(7) 1 53
(Des Donovan, Ire) *plld hrd and prom: rdn over 2f out: styd on same pce ins fnl f* **11/4**[1]
605- 7 *1 ¼* **Dalavand (IRE)**[24] 8364 4-9-6 55 (t) GeorgeBaker 6 53
(Laura Mongan) *chsd ldrs: rdn over 1f out: styd on same pce fnl f* **8/1**
0/0- 8 *2 ¼* **Jordaura**[22] 8400 11-8-12 46 oh1 AndrewMullen 2 40
(John Murray) *hld up: sme hdwy over 1f out: no imp fnl f* **100/1**
000- 9 *9* **Silver Lining (IRE)**[18] 8468 5-9-0 48 RobertHavlin 3 25
(Mark Hoad) *hld up in tch: rdn over 2f out: wknd over 1f out* **28/1**
51-0 10 *6* **My Mistress (IRE)**[3] 46 5-9-2 50 (p) JosephineGordon 9 15
(Phil McEntee) *hld up: hdwy over 4f out: rdn over 2f out: sn wknd* **14/1**
000- 11 *nk* **Imperial Link**[19] 8457 5-9-5 53 LukeMorris 12 18
(John O'Shea) *hld up: plld hrd: rdn and wknd over 2f out* **66/1**

2m 0.43s (-0.37) **Going Correction** -0.025s/f (Stan)
**WFA** 4 from 5yo+ 1lb 11 Ran SP% **117.0**
Speed ratings (Par 101): **100,99,98,97,97 97,96,94,86,80 80**
CSF £68.66 CT £816.40 TOTE £14.60: £4.50, £1.70, £3.90; EX 59.20 Trifecta £1109.60.
**Owner** R C Guest **Bred** Derek Veitch & Rory O'Brien **Trained** Ingmanthorpe, W Yorks
■ Stewards' Enquiry : Timmy Murphy two-day ban; used whip above the permitted level (21st,23rd Jan)
**FOCUS**
The first division of a moderate handicap. The right horses came to the fore in an open race off a fair gallop.

## 124 BETWAY APP H'CAP (DIV II) 1m 1f 104y (Tp)
7:15 (7:17) (Class 6) (0-55,55) 4-Y-0+ £2,425 (£721; £360; £180) Stalls Low

Form RPR
123- 1 **Boychick (IRE)**[121] 6243 4-9-3 52 RichardKingscote 4 59+
(Ed Walker) *chsd ldrs: shkn up to ld ins fnl f: rdn out* **7/4**[1]
000- 2 *1 ¾* **Nouvelle Ere**[16] 8500 6-9-2 53 (t) GeorgeDowning(3) 5 57
(Tony Carroll) *led: rdn over 1f out: hdd ins fnl f: styd on same pce* **9/1**
506- 3 *nk* **Yasood (IRE)**[22] 8411 4-9-6 55 JosephineGordon 3 58
(Phil McEntee) *prom: rdn over 2f out: styd on* **13/2**[2]

654- **4** ¾ **Pivotal Dream (IRE)**[16] 8500 4-8-6 **46** CharlieBennett(5) 7 48
(Mark Brisbourne) *chsd ldr: rdn over 1f out: styd on same pce ins fnl f* **9/1**

000- **5** ¾ **Bassino (USA)**[26] 8342 4-9-1 **55** (h[1]) RachealKneller(5) 1 55
(James Bennett) *chsd ldrs: rdn over 2f out: no ex wl ins fnl f* **28/1**

006- **6** 1 ¼ **Foylesideview (IRE)**[12] 8528 5-8-12 **46** oh1 RobertHavlin 8 44
(Harry Chisman) *hld up: hdwy u.p over 1f out: nt trble ldrs* **11/1**

546- **7** 1 ¼ **Jazri**[16] 8500 6-9-4 **52** (b) LukeMorris 13 48
(Milton Bradley) *hld up: rdn over 1f out: nvr on terms* **7/1**[3]

56- **8** nk **Sarakova (IRE)**[18] 8471 4-9-1 **50** (v[1]) RyanPowell 10 45
(Kevin Frost) *hld up: rdn over 2f out: n.d* **20/1**

000- **9** 6 **Living Leader**[26] 7577 8-9-2 **50** (bt) StevieDonohoe 6 34
(Grace Harris) *pushed along in rr early: hld up: rdn and wknd over 1f out* **14/1**

500- **10** ¾ **Royal Acclaim (IRE)**[86] 7299 5-8-13 **47** TomEaves 2 29
(Rebecca Bastiman) *hld up in tch: racd keenly: rdn over 1f out: wknd fnl f* **33/1**

2m 1.94s (1.14) **Going Correction** -0.025s/f (Stan)
**WFA** 4 from 5yo+ 1lb **10** Ran SP% **108.3**
Speed ratings (Par 101): **93,91,91,90,89 88,87,87,82,81**
CSF £14.72 CT £62.19 TOTE £2.30: £1.10, £2.50, £2.00; EX 21.10 Trifecta £62.10.
**Owner** Laurence Bellman **Bred** Lynch Bages Ltd **Trained** Upper Lambourn, Berks
■ Tanzina was withdrawn. Price at time of withdrawal 17/2. Rule 4 applies to all bets - deduction 10p in the pound.

**FOCUS**
The second division of a moderate handicap. The winning time was 1.5 seconds slower, but that shouldn't mask an assured victory from a heavily backed winner.

## 125 32RED.COM CONDITIONS STKS (PLUS 10 RACE) 5f 21y (Tp)
**7:45** (7:45) (Class 2) 3-Y-O **£11,971** (£3,583; £1,791; £896; £446) **Stalls** Low

Form RPR

35- **1** **Visionary (IRE)**[35] 8209 3-9-0 91 LukeMorris 3 91
(Robert Cowell) *pushed along in 4th pl: hdwy over 1f out: rdn to ld and edgd lft wl ins fnl f* **7/2**[3]

413- **2** ¾ **Poet's Society**[74] 7600 3-9-0 89 AndrewMullen 2 88
(Mark Johnston) *led: rdn over 1f out: hdd wl ins fnl f* **13/8**[1]

111- **3** ½ **Dazacam**[19] 8453 3-8-9 79 RobertHavlin 5 81
(Michael Herrington) *hmpd s: hld up: hdwy over 1f out: rdn and ev ch ins fnl f: unable qck towards fin* **11/2**

15- **4** 2 **Chupalla**[226] 2624 3-8-9 93 JoeFanning 4 74
(Mark Johnston) *edgd rt s: racd keenly: prom: wnt 2nd over 3f out: shkn up over 1f out: no ex ins fnl f* **9/4**[2]

114- **5** hd **Gracious Tom (IRE)**[18] 8467 3-9-0 72 StevieDonohoe 1 78
(David Evans) *chsd ldr tl over 3f out: remained handy: rdn over 1f out: no ex ins fnl f* **18/1**

1m 0.8s (-1.10) **Going Correction** -0.025s/f (Stan) **5** Ran SP% **111.7**
Speed ratings (Par 103): **107,105,105,101,101**
CSF £9.82 TOTE £4.40: £1.90, £1.50; EX 10.80 Trifecta £30.60.
**Owner** Khalifa Dasmal **Bred** K A Dasmal **Trained** Six Mile Bottom, Cambs

**FOCUS**
A good conditions sprint for 3yos. They went a decent gallop and the form looks sound. The winner is improving, and this has been rated around the runner-up.

## 126 32RED CASINO H'CAP 6f 20y (Tp)
**8:15** (8:15) (Class 6) (0-55,55) 3-Y-O **£2,587** (£770; £384; £192) **Stalls** Low

Form RPR

055- **1** **Gentleman Giles (IRE)**[25] 8344 3-9-7 **55** TimmyMurphy 4 62+
(Jamie Osborne) *hld up: hdwy over 1f out: shkn up to ld ins fnl f: r.o* **7/2**[1]

640- **2** 1 **Mr Strutter (IRE)**[122] 6222 3-9-7 **55** JasonHart 10 58
(John Quinn) *chsd ldrs: rdn over 1f out: r.o to go 2nd wl ins fnl f* **7/2**[1]

430- **3** 1 ½ **Poppy May (IRE)**[25] 8344 3-9-5 **53** TomEaves 8 51
(James Given) *chsd ldrs: rdn over 1f out: styd on same pce ins fnl f* **10/1**[3]

00-5 **4** ¾ **Vocalisation (IRE)**[2] 77 3-8-12 **51** CharlieBennett(5) 2 47
(John Weymes) *led 1f: chsd ldr tl led again over 2f out: rdn over 1f out: hdd and unable qck ins fnl f* **7/1**[2]

6- **5** ½ **Tanksalot (IRE)**[21] 8425 3-9-5 **53** JosephineGordon 3 47
(Harry Dunlop) *led 5f out: rdn and hdd over 2f out: styd on same pce fnl f* **12/1**

366- **6** shd **Champagne Queen**[29] 8285 3-9-5 **53** LukeMorris 1 47
(Rae Guest) *prom: rdn over 1f out: no ex wl ins fnl f* **7/2**[1]

554- **7** 1 ¼ **Trust The Indian**[171] 4526 3-8-11 **50** JordanVaughan(5) 9 40
(Bill Turner) *prom: rdn over 2f out: no ex fnl f* **14/1**

660- **8** 2 ¾ **Aberdonian**[159] 4938 3-9-3 **51** NickyMackay 6 32
(Jeremy Gask) *s.i.s: hld up: sme hdwy over 1f out: eased ins fnl f* **14/1**

000- **9** 2 ½ **Raspberry Princess**[24] 8354 3-8-5 **46** oh1 (t) MillyNaseb(7) 7 19
(Stuart Williams) *s.i.s: hld up: pushed along over 2f out: nvr on terms* **20/1**

500- **10** 6 **Elmley Queen**[28] 8313 3-9-2 **50** TomMarquand 11 4
(Roy Brotherton) *hld up: rdn over 3f out: wknd over 2f out* **100/1**

1m 14.4s (-0.10) **Going Correction** -0.025s/f (Stan) **10** Ran SP% **115.0**
Speed ratings (Par 95): **99,97,95,94,94 93,92,88,85,77**
CSF £14.60 CT £112.34 TOTE £5.00: £1.60, £1.90, £2.60; EX 15.00 Trifecta £63.60.
**Owner** Dominic Christian **Bred** Tinnakill House & Fiona Craig **Trained** Upper Lambourn, Berks

**FOCUS**
A moderate 3yo sprint handicap. They went a decent gallop and two of the three co-favourites fought out the finish.

## 127 SUNBETS.CO.UK MAIDEN STKS 7f 36y (Tp)
**8:45** (8:47) (Class 5) 3-5-Y-O **£3,072** (£914; £456; £228) **Stalls** High

Form RPR

0- **1** **Fear The Fury (USA)**[23] 8384 3-8-5 0 JordanVaughan(5) 3 79+
(K R Burke) *a.p: racd keenly: rdn to ld ins fnl f: r.o* **13/2**

5- **2** 1 ¾ **Mountain Angel (IRE)**[23] 8384 3-8-10 0 JackMitchell 9 74
(Roger Varian) *led: rdn over 1f out: hdd and unable qck ins fnl f* **7/2**[2]

**3** 1 ¼ **Kencumin (FR)** 3-8-10 0 TomMarquand 4 71+
(Ralph Beckett) *hld up: plld hrd: hdwy and edgd lft over 1f out: styd on same pce ins fnl f* **2/1**[1]

4- **4** 5 **Champagne Freddie**[26] 8342 4-10-0 0 RobertHavlin 6 61
(John O'Shea) *prom: racd keenly: rdn and hung lft over 1f out: wknd fnl f* **50/1**

**5** ¾ **Invincible Man (IRE)** 3-8-10 0 LukeMorris 8 55+
(James Tate) *hld up: r.o ins fnl f: nvr nrr* **14/1**

**6** 2 ¼ **Alfolk (IRE)** 3-8-10 0 (h[1]) TomEaves 7 49+
(David Simcock) *s.i.s: hld up: r.o ins fnl f: nvr nrr* **10/1**

0- **7** nk **Life Of Luxury**[28] 8320 4-10-0 0 GeorgeBaker 12 52
(Mark Brisbourne) *prom: chsd ldr over 5f out: ev ch 2f out: wknd fnl f* **16/1**

0- **8** 1 ¾ **Spey Secret (IRE)**[269] 1421 4-10-0 0 RichardKingscote 1 47
(Tom Dascombe) *chsd ldrs: rdn over 2f out: wknd over 1f out* **40/1**

**9** nk **Dark Titan (IRE)** 3-8-10 0 ThomasBrown 11 43
(Ed Walker) *in rr: pushed along over 3f out: nvr on terms* **33/1**

**10** 2 ¾ **Basheer** 3-8-10 0 DanielMuscutt 10 35+
(Marco Botti) *s.s: plld hrd and hdwy over 4f out: ev ch over 2f out: wknd over 1f out* **6/1**[3]

/30- **11** 21 **Raise The Game (IRE)**[10] 8559 4-10-0 63 TimmyMurphy 2
(Bill Turner) *mid-div: pushed along 1/2-way: wknd over 2f out* **50/1**

1m 27.94s (-0.86) **Going Correction** -0.025s/f (Stan)
**WFA** 3 from 4yo 18lb **11** Ran SP% **114.1**
Speed ratings (Par 103): **103,101,99,93,93 90,90,88,87,84 60**
CSF £27.97 TOTE £8.10: £2.20, £1.50, £1.20; EX 33.50 Trifecta £143.00.
**Owner** Ftf Partnership **Bred** Sun Valley Farm & Darley **Trained** Middleham Moor, N Yorks

**FOCUS**
An ordinary maiden. They went a decent gallop and three of the more likely types came clear of the fourth horse home.
T/Plt: £57.10 to a £1 stake. Pool: £128,305.27 - 1,638.90 winning units T/Qpdt: £11.20 to a £1 stake. Pool: £10,341.55 - 677.68 winning units **Colin Roberts**

128 - 138a (Foreign Racing) - See Raceform Interactive

# [114]LINGFIELD (L-H)
Monday, January 9

**OFFICIAL GOING: Polytrack: standard**
Wind: Strong, half behind Weather: Overcast with rain

## 139 SUNBETS.CO.UK MAIDEN H'CAP 7f 1y(P)
**1:15** (1:17) (Class 6) (0-60,60) 3-Y-O+ **£2,587** (£770; £384; £192) **Stalls** Low

Form RPR

003- **1** **Ross Raith Rover**[40] 8156 4-9-12 **58** (p[1]) JackMitchell 10 65
(Robert Eddery) *trckd ldrs: wnt 2nd 2f out and sn lft in ld: shkn up and clr fnl f: readily* **9/2**[2]

502- **2** 2 **Zabdi**[21] 8457 4-9-8 **54** GeorgeBaker 12 56
(Lee Carter) *led: gng wl enough whn hung rt and wd bnd wl over 1f out: sn hdd: kpt on fnl f but no threat to wnr after* **9/2**[2]

044- **3** 1 **Metronomic (IRE)**[10] 8582 3-8-7 **57** (p[1]) KieranO'Neill 5 52
(Richard Hannon) *t.k.h: hld up towards rr: rchd midfield over 2f out gng bttr than most: rdn and nt qckn over 1f out: r.o fnl f to take 3rd last stride* **3/1**[1]

0/6- **4** nse **Frank Cool**[11] 8570 4-9-6 **55** GeorgeDowning(3) 1 54
(Tony Carroll) *trckd ldrs: rdn 2f out: chsd ldng pair fnl f: kpt on but lost 3rd last stride* **33/1**

340- **5** 2 **Wasseem (IRE)**[25] 8382 4-10-0 **60** (vt[1]) RobertHavlin 3 53
(Simon Crisford) *prom: chsd ldr 1/2-way to 2f out: urged along and wknd fnl f* **6/1**

504- **6** 1 ¼ **Bingo George (IRE)**[51] 8026 4-9-13 **59** (h) DavidProbert 7 49
(Andrew Balding) *hld up towards rr: shkn up 2f out: modest prog and nvr on terms* **5/1**[3]

065- **7** ½ **Annabella**[22] 8449 4-9-0 **46** RyanTate 2 35
(Tim McCarthy) *chsd ldrs: rdn on inner over 2f out: wknd jst over 1f out* **50/1**

630- **8** shd **Color Force (IRE)**[82] 7463 4-9-5 **51** (t[1]) LukeMorris 13 39
(Gay Kelleway) *s.i.s: hld up in last trio: rdn and v modest prog over 1f out: no ch* **10/1**

000- **9** 4 ½ **Dolly Dimples**[32] 8276 3-8-5 **55** JosephineGordon 8 27
(William Jarvis) *rdn in midfield after 2f: no prog 3f out: sn wknd* **25/1**

300- **10** 4 **Lily Fontana (IRE)**[14] 8526 3-8-1 **51** NickyMackay 6 12
(Richard Fahey) *a wl in rr: struggling fr 1/2-way* **25/1**

655- **11** 1 ½ **Aqshion Stations**[67] 7777 3-8-9 **59** ShaneKelly 14 16
(William Jarvis) *sn in last pair: no ch fnl 2f* **20/1**

000- **12** 12 **Miramonte Dancer (IRE)**[27] 8347 4-9-7 **53** (h[1]) MartinDwyer 11
(David C Griffiths) *rousted to chse ldr: lost 2nd 1/2-way and wknd qckly: t.o* **25/1**

1m 23.71s (-1.09) **Going Correction** -0.10s/f (Stan)
**WFA** 3 from 4yo 18lb **12** Ran SP% **122.6**
Speed ratings (Par 101): **102,99,98,98,96 94,94,94,88,84 82,68**
CSF £23.74 CT £73.45 TOTE £5.60: £1.60, £2.20, £1.60; EX 29.40 Trifecta £125.10.
**Owner** Mrs Pamela Aitken & Ian Anderson **Bred** Shadwell Estate Company Limited **Trained** Newmarket, Suffolk

**FOCUS**
An ordinary handicap in which the pace held up pretty well. The form looks pretty straightforward.

## 140 32REDSPORT.COM MAIDEN AUCTION STKS 6f 1y(P)
**1:45** (1:46) (Class 6) 3-Y-O **£2,587** (£770; £384; £192) **Stalls** Low

Form RPR

404- **1** **Just An Idea (IRE)**[65] 7819 3-9-5 82 (v[1]) LukeMorris 3 78+
(Harry Dunlop) *led 1f: led again 1/2-way: rdn clr wl over 1f out: in n.d after* **4/9**[1]

6- **2** 4 **Allegheny Bay (IRE)**[24] 8404 3-9-5 0 LiamKeniry 5 60
(J S Moore) *plld way into ld after 1f: hdd 1/2-way and sn in 3rd: rdn to chse wnr 2f out: one pce and no imp* **14/1**

0- **3** 3 ½ **Fiery Spice (IRE)**[24] 8406 3-9-5 0 JFEgan 2 49
(Robert Cowell) *t.k.h: hld up in last: shkn up and hanging bdly fr 1/2-way: kpt on to take modest 3rd ins fnl f* **12/1**[3]

636- **4** 1 **Atlanta Belle (IRE)**[44] 8118 3-9-0 74 ShaneKelly 4 41
(Chris Wall) *chsd wnr 1f: wnt 2nd again 1/2-way and tried to chal: sn rdn: wknd wl over 1f out* **3/1**[2]

1m 11.0s (-0.90) **Going Correction** -0.10s/f (Stan) **4** Ran SP% **108.6**
Speed ratings (Par 95): **102,96,92,90**
CSF £7.37 TOTE £1.20; EX 8.40 Trifecta £19.00.
**Owner** Love Lambourn **Bred** John T Heffernan **Trained** Lambourn, Berks

**FOCUS**
This proved very straightforward for the odds-on favourite.

## 141 BETWAY H'CAP 1m 7f 169y(P)
**2:15** (2:16) (Class 5) (0-70,69) 4-Y-O+ **£3,234** (£962; £481; £240) **Stalls** Low

Form RPR

061- **1** **Aurora Gray**[22] 8445 4-9-7 **69** GeorgeBaker 2 76+
(Hughie Morrison) *trckd ldrs: clsd on inner to ld over 1f out: styd on wl and in command fnl f* **5/4**[1]

302- **2** ¾ **Miss Tiger Lily**[26] 8363 7-9-13 **68** LukeMorris 4 73
(Harry Dunlop) *hld up in midfield: prog on outer 3f out: rdn to chal and upsides 2f out to over 1f out: chsd wnr after: styd on* **6/1**[3]

441- 3 nk **Dltripleseven (IRE)**[27] 8164 4-9-1 **63** ShaneKelly 7 67
(Richard Hughes) *hld up in last: smooth prog on inner over 2f out: hung fire whn clsng 1f out: drvn and styd on to duel for 2nd ins fnl f* **3/1**[2]

664- 4 3¾ **Shalimah (IRE)**[53] 7987 5-9-4 **66** (v) WilliamCox(7) 3 65
(Clive Cox) *hld up in midfield: cl up whn nt clr run 3f out: rdn and nt qckn 2f out: plugged on to take 4th nr fin* **14/1**

000- 5 1 **Night Generation (GER)**[46] 8084 5-9-9 **64** (p) LiamKeniry 9 62
(Chris Gordon) *cl up: chsd ldr 3f to 2f out: fdd over 1f out* **50/1**

243- 6 ½ **Lady Of Yue**[46] 8084 7-9-6 **61** (p) JosephineGordon 5 58
(Eugene Stanford) *led: rdn over 2f out and sn jnd: hdd & wknd over 1f out* **10/1**

500- 7 2 **Forced Family Fun**[12] 8554 7-9-10 **65** (h) SteveDrowne 6 60
(George Baker) *hld up in last trio: shkn up 4f out: no prog 3f out: sn btn* **25/1**

643- 8 2½ **Trust The Man (IRE)**[13] 8540 4-7-13 **50** AaronJones(3) 8 42
(Simon Dow) *chsd ldr to 3f out: steadily wknd* **10/1**

414/ 9 2 **Fennann**[754] 8193 6-9-9 **64** (b) JFEgan 1 54
(Natalie Lloyd-Beavis) *hld up in last trio: last whn nt clr run briefly over 2f out: wl btn after* **66/1**

3m 23.5s (-2.20) **Going Correction** -0.10s/f (Stan)
**WFA** 4 from 5yo+ 5lb 9 Ran SP% **115.9**
Speed ratings (Par 103): **101,100,100,98,98 97,96,95,94**
CSF £9.28 CT £19.15 TOTE £2.00: £1.30, £1.80, £1.40; EX 9.50 Trifecta £25.20.
**Owner** Wardley Bloodstock **Bred** Lakin Bloodstock/Wardley Bloodstock **Trained** East Ilsley, Berks

**FOCUS**
The field was fairly well bunched turning in and getting first run proved crucial. It's ben rated around the runner-up to her latest form.

## 142 32RED/EBF FILLIES' H'CAP 7f 1y(P)
**2:50** (2:50) (Class 3) (0-90,87) 4-Y-O+ **£10,396** (£3,111; £1,555; £778; £387) **Stalls** Low

Form RPR

032- 1 **Summer Icon**[23] 8426 4-9-7 **87** GeorgeBaker 6 96
(Mick Channon) *stdd s: hld up in last pair: prog on wd outside over 1f out: rdn to ld jst ins fnl f: r.o strly and sn clr* **3/1**[1]

20-0 2 2¼ **Russian Radiance**[4] 61 5-8-13 **84** (h) MitchGodwin(5) 2 87
(Jonathan Portman) *trckd ldrs: pushed along over 2f out: rdn and clsd on outer to chal jst over 1f out: r.o but outpcd by wnr ins fnl f* **7/1**

654- 3 2¾ **Bint Dandy (IRE)**[23] 8426 6-9-7 **87** (b) LukeMorris 5 83
(Chris Dwyer) *sn pressed ldng pair on outer: drvn into narrow ld 2f out: hdd jst ins fnl f and readily outpcd after* **7/1**

235- 4 1¾ **Rebel Surge (IRE)**[40] 8158 4-9-4 **84** (p) JosephineGordon 1 75
(Richard Spencer) *trckd ldrs: chal on inner over 1f out: sn wl outpcd* **5/1**

440- 5 ½ **Dutch Mist**[79] 7550 4-9-3 **83** ShaneKelly 7 72
(Kevin Ryan) *stdd s: hld up in last pair: lft bhd by rest 2f out and pushed along: no ch whn rdn fnl f: r.o nr fin* **10/1**

1- 6 hd **Notte Illuminata (IRE)**[25] 8388 4-8-8 **79** JordanVaughan(5) 3 68
(K R Burke) *t.k.h: mde most to 2f out: nt qckn over 1f out: wknd fnl f* **4/1**[3]

114- 7 2½ **Make Music**[184] 4139 4-9-0 **80** DavidProbert 4 62
(Andrew Balding) *t.k.h: pressed ldr: upsides jst over 2f out: wknd qckly jst over 1f out* **7/2**[2]

1m 23.21s (-1.59) **Going Correction** -0.10s/f (Stan) 7 Ran SP% **118.0**
Speed ratings (Par 104): **105,102,99,97,96 96,93**
CSF £25.50 CT £137.56 TOTE £3.60: £2.00, £4.90; EX 27.90 Trifecta £166.10.
**Owner** Allen, Porter, Voute Partnership 1 **Bred** New Hall Stud **Trained** West Ilsley, Berks

**FOCUS**
The pace became contested and eventually collapsed, the first two coming from behind out wide. The runner-up has been rated close to form.

## 143 BETWAY BEST ODDS GUARANTEED PLUS H'CAP 5f 6y(P)
**3:20** (3:20) (Class 7) (0-50,50) 3-Y-O+ **£2,264** (£673; £336; £168) **Stalls** High

Form RPR

603- 1 **Fabulous Flyer**[24] 8409 4-9-2 **47** DavidParkes(5) 8 53
(Jeremy Gask) *chsd ldrs in 5th: clsd towards outer over 1f out: nudged runner-up whn squeezing through to ld last 150yds: edgd rt but kpt on* **7/1**

004- 2 nk **Eland Ally**[24] 8409 9-9-10 **50** (b) GeorgeBaker 7 55
(Anabel K Murphy) *chsd ldng pair: chal on outer jst over 1f out: nudged by wnr sn after: drifted rt and nt qckn last 100yds* **9/2**[2]

260- 3 ¾ **Willow Spring**[24] 8408 5-9-6 **49** TimClark(3) 10 51
(Denis Quinn) *towards rr fr wdst draw: rdn and prog on wd outside over 1f out: styd on to take 3rd nr fin* **20/1**

362- 4 ¾ **Chandresh**[24] 8408 4-9-8 **48** (b) LukeMorris 5 48
(Robert Cowell) *trckd ldng pair: tried to chal on inner fnl f: nt pce of those racing wd after* **4/1**[1]

06-5 5 ¾ **Rojina (IRE)**[4] 64 4-9-5 **45** (b) JFEgan 4 42+
(Lisa Williamson) *led: drvn and hdd over 1f: upsides jst ins fnl f: fdd* **16/1**

60-6 6 ½ **Justice Rock**[4] 64 4-9-7 **47** (v) JosephineGordon 3 42
(Phil McEntee) *anticipated stall opening and missed break: wl in rr: r.o fnl f: nrst fin* **7/1**

334- 7 shd **Wattaboutsteve**[142] 5636 6-9-6 **46** DavidProbert 9 41+
(Ralph J Smith) *pressed ldr: rdn to ld over 1f out: hdd & wknd last 150yds* **9/2**[2]

240- 8 1 **Presto Boy**[24] 8408 5-9-2 **49** (e) StephenCummins(7) 6 40
(Richard Hughes) *awkward s and slowly away: bhd: swtchd lft towards inner fnl f: no real prog* **5/1**[3]

000- 9 1½ **Bubbly Bailey**[89] 7276 7-9-7 **50** (v) AlistairRawlinson(3) 1 36
(J R Jenkins) *chsd ldrs in 6th but sn pushed along: no prog 2f out: wknd* **12/1**

40-0 10 8 **Nidnod**[3] 88 4-9-1 **48** (p[1]) JaneElliott(7) 2 5+
(John Bridger) *s.v.s: a t.o* **20/1**

58.53s (-0.27) **Going Correction** -0.10s/f (Stan) 10 Ran SP% **121.1**
Speed ratings (Par 97): **98,97,96,95,93 93,92,91,88,76**
CSF £40.16 CT £471.91 TOTE £7.70: £1.70, £2.30, £6.10; EX 53.70 Trifecta £920.60.
**Owner** Gracelands Stud Partnership **Bred** Gracelands Stud **Trained** Stockbridge, Hants

**FOCUS**
A weak handicap run at a good gallop. A marginal pb from the winner.

## 144 32RED MAIDEN FILLIES' STKS 1m 2f (P)
**3:55** (3:55) (Class 5) 3-Y-O+ **£3,234** (£962; £481; £240) **Stalls** Low

Form RPR

1 **Ocean Drive (IRE)** 3-8-5 0 JFEgan 4 74+
(William Haggas) *dwlt: sn in midfield: prog to trck ldr 2f out: shkn up to ld jst over 1f out: rn green in front but a holding on* **9/2**[2]

00- 2 ½ **My Rosie (IRE)**[46] 8081 3-8-5 0 (b) LukeMorris 2 70
(John Gosden) *led: shkn up 4f out: drvn for home over 2f out: hdd jst over 1f out: styd on but a hld* **25/1**

3- 3 2 **Nurse Nightingale**[20] 8465 3-8-5 0 JosephineGordon 9 66+
(Hugo Palmer) *pushed up to go prom fr wd draw: rdn over 2f out: nt qckn on outer wl over 1f out: kpt on same pce fnl f* **6/5**[1]

4 2¾ **Utopian Dream** 3-8-5 0 NickyMackay 5 61+
(John Gosden) *dwlt: in rr tl rchd midfield 1/2-way: pushed along over 3f out: tried to make prog on outer over 2f out: rn green and outpcd fr wl over 1f out* **6/1**[3]

6- 5 1 **Tomorrow Mystery**[20] 8465 3-8-5 0 MartinDwyer 10 59+
(Jamie Osborne) *dwlt: hld up: detached in last over 4f out: wl bhd 3f out: shkn up and fin to sme effect fr over 1f out* **20/1**

0- 6 nk **Mayflair**[20] 8464 3-8-5 0 RyanTate 8 58
(Jonathan Portman) *in tch: dropped to rr over 3f out: detached fr ldng gp over 2f out: pushed along and kpt on fr over 1f out: nt disgracd* **66/1**

605- 7 hd **Lucrezia**[37] 8208 3-8-5 66 (v) DavidProbert 6 58
(Sir Michael Stoute) *in tch in midfield: cl up over 2f out: outpcd sn after and shkn up: kpt on last 150yds* **9/2**[2]

0/4- 8 3 **Shadele (IRE)**[25] 8388 4-9-12 0 GeorgeBaker 3 55
(Jeremy Noseda) *chsd ldr to 2f out: wknd* **12/1**

/24- 9 1¼ **Dizzey Heights (IRE)**[233] 2463 5-9-11 72 ShelleyBirkett(3) 1 52
(Stuart Kittow) *cl up on inner to 2f out: wknd over 1f out* **20/1**

P **Sirens Rock (IRE)** 4-9-12 0 ShaneKelly 7
(Eve Johnson Houghton) *slowly away: in tch in rr tl lost action over 3f out: sn p.u* **50/1**

2m 7.05s (0.45) **Going Correction** -0.10s/f (Stan)
**WFA** 3 from 4yo 23lb 4 from 5yo 1lb 10 Ran SP% **120.6**
Speed ratings (Par 100): **94,93,92,89,89 88,88,86,85,**
CSF £115.08 TOTE £5.30: £1.50, £6.90, £1.10; EX 92.20 Trifecta £393.60.
**Owner** M J Jooste **Bred** Mrs C Regalado-Gonzalez **Trained** Newmarket, Suffolk

**FOCUS**
An ordinary maiden, but one or two noteworthy performances. Muddling form.
T/Jkpt: £6,838.80 to a £1 stake. Pool: £47,871.93 - 7.0 winning units T/Plt: £23.80 to a £1 stake. Pool: £73,889.23 - 2,263.78 winning units T/Qpdt: £8.10 to a £1 stake. Pool: £6,399.39 - 583.80 winning units **Jonathan Neesom**

# 121 WOLVERHAMPTON (A.W) (L-H)
Monday, January 9

**OFFICIAL GOING: Tapeta: standard**
Wind: Blustery easing to light across after race 1 (1:55) Weather: Rain clearing after race 1

## 145 SUNBETS.CO.UK APPRENTICE H'CAP 7f 36y (Tp)
**1:55** (1:56) (Class 6) (0-65,67) 4-Y-O+ **£2,264** (£673; £336; £168) **Stalls** High

Form RPR

12-2 1 **Cliff (IRE)**[5] 50 7-9-6 **67** LewisEdmunds(3) 4 77
(Nigel Tinkler) *chsd ldrs: shkn up ins fnl f: r.o to ld nr fin* **5/6**[1]

511- 2 hd **Kenstone (FR)**[21] 8457 4-9-4 **62** (p) HollieDoyle 3 71
(Adrian Wintle) *led at stdy pce tl qcknd over 2f out: rdn ins fnl f: hdd nr fin* **7/2**[2]

300- 3 2 **Showtime Blues**[33] 8258 5-9-2 **60** (v[1]) CharlieBennett 2 64
(Jim Boyle) *chsd ldrs: rdn over 1f out: styd on same pce ins fnl f* **10/1**[3]

006- 4 1½ **Wink Oliver**[40] 8156 5-8-6 **57** (p) LauraCoughlan(7) 8 57
(Jo Hughes) *hld up: plld hrd: nt clr run and swtchd rt over 1f out: styd on to go 4th nr fin: nt trble ldrs* **10/1**[3]

462- 5 hd **George Baker (IRE)**[170] 4656 10-9-0 **65** AmeliaGlass(7) 6 65
(George Baker) *chsd ldr: shkn up over 1f out: hung lft and no ex ins fnl f* **20/1**

545- 6 2¾ **Binky Blue (IRE)**[18] 8493 5-8-13 **64** (h) TobyEley(7) 9 57
(Daniel Mark Loughnane) *hld up: hdwy over 1f out: edgd lft and wknd wl ins fnl f* **20/1**

020- 7 2¾ **Spice Mill (IRE)**[20] 8473 4-9-2 **65** (tp) BenRobinson(5) 1 51
(Michael Appleby) *dwlt: hld up: hdwy u.p over 1f out: nt clr run and wknd ins fnl f* **12/1**

605- 8 3 **Q Ten Girl (IRE)**[38] 8191 4-9-0 **61** (v) NatalieHambling(3) 7 40
(James Unett) *hld up in tch: rdn over 2f out: wknd over 1f out* **50/1**

666- 9 5 **Hercullian Prince**[312] 792 5-9-4 **65** (p) PatrickVaughan(3) 5 31+
(Conor Dore) *s.s: hld up: wknd over 2f out* **66/1**

1m 29.47s (0.67) **Going Correction** 0.0s/f (Stan) 9 Ran SP% **115.6**
Speed ratings (Par 101): **96,95,93,91,91 88,85,81,76**
CSF £3.58 CT £16.11 TOTE £1.80: £1.10, £1.10, £3.70; EX 4.40 Trifecta £19.80.
**Owner** W F Burton **Bred** John O'Connor **Trained** Langton, N Yorks

**FOCUS**
A modest handicap and the two in-form market leaders came to the fore. It's been rated as strong form for the grade.

## 146 BETWAY APP H'CAP 1m 4f 51y (Tp)
**2:30** (2:31) (Class 6) (0-55,54) 4-Y-O+ **£2,264** (£673; £336; £168) **Stalls** Low

Form RPR

533- 1 **Tred Softly (IRE)**[11] 8567 4-9-3 **54** (b) JasonHart 2 62
(John Quinn) *chsd ldrs: nt clr run and lost pl over 3f out: hdwy over 1f out: rdn and swtchd lft ins fnl f: r.o to ld nr fin* **9/2**[3]

021- 2 hd **My Renaissance**[18] 8497 7-9-7 **54** AdamKirby 10 62
(Sam England) *hld up: hdwy over 2f out: led over 1f out: rdn and edgd lft ins fnl f: hdd nr fin* **7/4**[1]

305- 3 1¼ **Rainbow Lad (IRE)**[24] 8410 4-9-2 **53** AndrewMullen 6 59
(Michael Appleby) *hld up in tch: racd keenly: led over 2f out: rdn and hdd over 1f out: styd on same pce wl ins fnl f* **7/1**

050- 4 2½ **Senor George (IRE)**[51] 8038 10-9-6 **53** (h) TomEaves 4 55
(Simon Hodgson) *hld up: hdwy 2f out: sn rdn: styd on same pce wl ins fnl f* **33/1**

640- 5 1¾ **Paddy's Rock (IRE)**[24] 8410 6-9-5 **52** PaddyAspell 1 51
(Lynn Siddall) *hld up in tch: nt clr run and lost pl over 3f out: r.o wl towards fin* **33/1**

330- 6 nk **Smiley Bagel (IRE)**[83] 7425 4-8-13 **50** RichardKingscote 12 49
(Ed Walker) *s.i.s: hld up: hdwy over 3f out: rdn over 1f out: wknd ins fnl f* **3/1**[2]

6/0- 7 hd **Sweeping Rock (IRE)**[24] 8410 7-9-3 **50** (tp) TomMarquand 7 48
(John Spearing) *chsd ldrs: rdn over 1f out: styd on same pce* **80/1**

445- 8 2 **Right Madam (IRE)**[18] 8497 5-8-10 **46** (b[1]) RobHornby(3) 3 41
(Sarah Hollinshead) *hld up: hdwy on outer over 3f out: hung rt wl over 1f out: wknd fnl f* **8/1**

404- 9 2¼ **Happy Jack (IRE)**[28] 8338 6-9-4 **51** (p) DougieCostello 5 43
(Dai Burchell) *sn led: hdd over 8f out: chsd ldrs: nt clr run over 2f out: rdn and wknd over 1f out* **20/1**

3- **10** *19* **All Dolled Up (IRE)**[28] 8338 5-9-3 **50**.......................... StevieDonohoe 8 11
(Sarah-Jayne Davies) *prom: jnd ldr over 5f out tl led over 3f out: rdn and hdd over 2f out: wknd over 1f out* **33/1**

30-0 **11** *5* **Moss Street**[2] 121 7-9-7 **54**.......................................(bt) MartinHarley 11 7
(Conor Dore) *dwlt: hdwy to ld over 8f out: pushed along and hdd over 3f out: wknd 2f out* **40/1**

2m 39.3s (-1.50) **Going Correction** 0.0s/f (Stan)
**WFA** 4 from 5yo+ 3lb **11** Ran SP% **120.4**
Speed ratings (Par 101): **105,104,104,102,101 101,100,99,98,85 82**
CSF £12.39 CT £56.19 TOTE £6.00: £1.70, £1.30, £2.00; EX 17.70 Trifecta £83.20.
**Owner** Ross Harmon **Bred** Mrs Eleanor Commins **Trained** Settrington, N Yorks

**FOCUS**
Just a moderate handicap.

## 147 BETWAY MIDDLE H'CAP — 1m 1f 104y (Tp)
**3:00** (3:00) (Class 6) (0-60,62) 4-Y-0+ **£2,264** (£673; £336; £168) **Stalls** Low

Form RPR

602- **1** **Seven Clans (IRE)**[38] 8190 5-9-7 **60**...............................(b) AdamKirby 1 70
(Neil Mulholland) *pushed along early then settled into mid-div: hdwy over 2f out: rdn to ld and hung lft ins fnl f: r.o wl* **7/2**[2]

041- **2** *3½* **L'Apogee**[110] 5921 4-9-4 **58**................................ TonyHamilton 12 61
(Richard Fahey) *sn pushed along and prom: chsd ldr over 5f out tl led over 1f out: rdn and hdd ins fnl f: styd on same pce* **12/1**

01-5 **3** *hd* **Synodic (USA)**[5] 46 5-9-6 **59**................................(t) RichardKingscote 8 62
(Seamus Durack) *trckd ldrs: shkn up over 1f out: styd on same pce ins fnl f* **5/2**[1]

543- **4** *2¼* **Caledonia Laird**[37] 8207 6-9-7 **60**.................................... JoeyHaynes 5 59
(Jo Hughes) *hld up: rdn over 1f out: r.o ins fnl f: nvr nrr* **6/1**[3]

410- **5** *nk* **Celtic Artisan (IRE)**[10] 8587 6-9-3 **56**...................(tp) DougieCostello 10 54
(Rebecca Menzies) *hld up: hdwy over 3f out: rdn over 2f out: styd on same pce fnl f* **18/1**

54-4 **6** *¾* **Pivotal Dream (IRE)**[2] 124 4-8-5 **48** ow2................. CharlieBennett(3) 6 45
(Mark Brisbourne) *chsd ldrs: nt clr run and lost pl over 2f out: rallied over 1f out: styd on same pce fnl f* **12/1**

06-0 **7** *½* **Breathless**[8] 7 5-9-4 **57**.......................................(t[1]) JamesSullivan 2 53
(Clive Mulhall) *hld up: sme hdwy over 1f out: sn rdn: no ex fnl f* **66/1**

632- **8** *2¼* **Dor's Law**[160] 4987 4-9-0 **59**.......................................... LuluStanford(5) 3 50
(Dean Ivory) *hld up: shkn up over 1f out: n.d* **7/1**

456- **9** *nk* **Limonata (IRE)**[23] 8428 4-9-8 **62**.......................................(p) MartinHarley 7 53
(Harry Whittington) *led: rdn and hdd over 1f out: wknd ins fnl f* **8/1**

000- **10** *1¾* **Pearly Queen**[21] 8457 4-8-9 **52**......................................(h) JackDuern(3) 11 40
(Dean Ivory) *chsd ldr 4f: remained handy: rdn over 2f out: wknd fnl f* **50/1**

00- **11** *15* **Tingo In The Tale (IRE)**[24] 8410 8-9-4 **57**.......................... TimmyMurphy 9 16
(Sophie Leech) *hld up: rdn 1/2-way: wknd over 3f out* **20/1**

1m 58.99s (-1.81) **Going Correction** 0.0s/f (Stan)
**WFA** 4 from 5yo+ 1lb **11** Ran SP% **117.6**
Speed ratings (Par 101): **108,104,104,102,102 101,101,99,99,97 84**
CSF £44.43 CT £123.74 TOTE £4.60: £1.80, £2.60, £1.20; EX 45.80 Trifecta £133.00.
**Owner** The Affordable (2) Partnership **Bred** Darley **Trained** Limpley Stoke, Wilts

**FOCUS**
A modest handicap and a decisive winner. The winner has been rated as running a pb, and the form stacks up okay in behind.

## 148 BETWAY CONDITIONS STKS — 1m 1f 104y (Tp)
**3:35** (3:35) (Class 2) 4-Y-0+ **£12,291** (£3,657; £1,827; £913) **Stalls** Low

Form RPR

200- **1** **Calling Out (FR)**[54] 7978 6-9-1 100.................................. JamieSpencer 2 103
(David Simcock) *trckd ldr 2f: remained handy: swtchd rt over 1f out: shkn up to ld wl ins fnl f: r.o: comf* **4/1**[3]

210- **2** *1¼* **Mythical Madness**[14] 8529 6-9-1 97.................................(p) AdamKirby 3 100
(David O'Meara) *chsd ldr over 7f out: rdn to ld over 1f out: hdd and unable qck wl ins fnl f* **6/4**[1]

141- **3** *½* **Forceful Appeal (USA)**[14] 8529 9-9-1 93.................. TomMarquand 4 99
(Simon Dow) *hld up: rdn over 1f out: r.o ins fnl f: nt trble ldrs* **4/1**[3]

004- **4** *1¾* **Our Channel (USA)**[14] 8529 6-9-4 103.......................... TimmyMurphy 1 98
(Jamie Osborne) *led: racd keenly: rdn and hdd over 1f out: edgd rt and no ex ins fnl f* **5/2**[2]

2m 0.55s (-0.25) **Going Correction** 0.0s/f (Stan) **4** Ran SP% **108.6**
Speed ratings (Par 109): **101,99,99,97**
CSF £10.40 TOTE £4.90; EX 12.20 Trifecta £33.70.
**Owner** Tick Tock Partnership **Bred** John Studd **Trained** Newmarket, Suffolk

**FOCUS**
Only four runners for this valuable conditions event and they went a steady pace, so the form needs treating with caution. Muddling form. The winner has been rated to last winter's AW form.

## 149 £10 FREE AT 32RED.COM H'CAP — 1m 1f 104y (Tp)
**4:05** (4:05) (Class 6) (0-60,61) 3-Y-0 **£2,264** (£673; £336; £168) **Stalls** Low

Form RPR

041- **1** **Babouska**[31] 8284 3-8-11 **53**.......................................... NathanEvans(3) 8 58
(Michael Easterby) *mde virtually all: rdn over 1f out: all out* **7/2**[2]

000- **2** *shd* **Serenade The Stars (IRE)**[35] 8227 3-9-7 **60**...............(v[1]) MartinHarley 4 65
(James Tate) *chsd ldrs: rdn to chse wnr fnl f: r.o u.p* **3/1**[1]

044- **3** *2¼* **Good Time Ahead (IRE)**[11] 8568 3-9-6 **59**...................... PaddyAspell 5 60
(Philip Kirby) *plld hrd and prom: wnt 2nd over 7f out: rdn and hung lft fr over 1f out: no ex ins fnl f* **12/1**

03-5 **4** *½* **Gog Elles (IRE)**[3] 91 3-8-2 **46** oh1...........................(p) HollieDoyle(5) 9 46
(J S Moore) *sn prom: rdn and hung lft fr over 1f out: styd on* **12/1**

506- **5** *hd* **Masterfilly (IRE)**[31] 8284 3-9-3 **56**.......................... RichardKingscote 11 56
(Ed Walker) *edgd lft s: mid-div: hdwy over 2f out: rdn and hung lft over 1f out: styd on* **6/1**

606- **6** *1¾* **Willie's Anne (IRE)**[86] 7366 3-9-2 **55**.............................. AndrewMullen 2 51
(Daniel Mark Loughnane) *chsd ldrs: rdn over 2f out: styd on same pce fnl f* **25/1**

062- **7** *1½* **La Vie En Rose**[56] 7954 3-9-8 **61**........................................ JoeFanning 1 54
(Mark Johnston) *hld up: rdn over 1f out: nvr on terms* **5/1**[3]

065- **8** *½* **Forest Steps (IRE)**[24] 8404 3-8-11 **50**............................. TomMarquand 6 43
(J S Moore) *mid-div: rdn and hung lft fr over 1f out: nvr trbld ldrs* **20/1**

000- **9** *2½* **Dragonite (IRE)**[47] 8074 3-8-13 **52**............................... StevieDonohoe 7 40
(Daniel Mark Loughnane) *hld up: nvr on terms* **33/1**

000- **10** *nk* **Secret Poet (IRE)**[26] 8353 3-8-5 **49**............................ LucyKBarry(5) 3 36
(Jamie Osborne) *hld up: rdn over 1f out: a in rr* **25/1**

036- **11** *2¼* **Our Boy John (IRE)**[11] 8568 3-9-0 **53**.......................... TonyHamilton 10 36
(Richard Fahey) *hmpd s: hld up: plld hrd: wknd 2f out* **17/2**

2m 0.44s (-0.36) **Going Correction** 0.0s/f (Stan) **11** Ran SP% **119.5**
Speed ratings (Par 95): **101,100,98,98,98 96,95,94,92,92 90**
CSF £13.93 CT £115.15 TOTE £4.50: £1.30, £1.60, £4.20; EX 18.80 Trifecta £171.40.
**Owner** A G Black & M Burrows **Bred** Alan Black And M W Easterby **Trained** Sheriff Hutton, N Yorks

■ Stewards' Enquiry : Nathan Evans ban: two-day. improper use of the whip (Jan 23 24)

**FOCUS**
A modest handicap in which it was beneficial to race prominently, with the first three home up there throughout.

## 150 32RED.COM MAIDEN AUCTION STKS — 7f 36y (Tp)
**4:35** (4:36) (Class 5) 3-Y-0 **£2,911** (£866; £432; £216) **Stalls** High

Form RPR

402- **1** **Peachey Carnehan**[9] 8591 3-9-5 70.................................(v) AdamKirby 6 67
(Michael Attwater) *chsd ldr tl shkn up to ld 2f out: edgd lft ins fnl f: drvn out* **4/6**[1]

P- **2** *2* **Crystal Stanza (IRE)**[32] 8277 3-9-5 0......................(v[1]) StevieDonohoe 7 61
(Charlie Fellowes) *led: rdn over 2f out: hdd over 1f out: styd on same pce ins fnl f* **11/1**

200- **3** *2½* **Bataka**[32] 8277 3-9-0 60.......................................... MartinHarley 4 49
(Harry Dunlop) *chsd ldrs: hung rt wl over 1f out: sn rdn: styd on same pce fnl f* **4/1**[2]

**4** *2¼* **Striking For Gold** 3-9-2 0................................................ JackDuern(3) 2 48
(Sarah Hollinshead) *hld up: pushed along over 2f out: styd on to go 4th over 1f out: nt trble ldrs* **33/1**

6- **5** *1½* **Midge Hall (IRE)**[168] 4699 3-9-0 0.......................................... JoeFanning 5 39+
(Bryan Smart) *chsd ldrs: rdn over 2f out: nt clr run and wknd over 1f out* **13/2**[3]

645- **6** *nk* **Oakley Pride (IRE)**[11] 8569 3-8-12 52................(bt[1]) GabrieleMalune(7) 1 43
(Gay Kelleway) *hld up: racd keenly: carried rt wl over 1f out: n.d* **16/1**

0 **7** *2¼* **What's Up Walter**[5] 40 3-9-5 0....................................... PaddyAspell 3 37
(Philip Kirby) *hld up: rdn over 2f out: sn outpcd* **125/1**

1m 32.16s (3.36) **Going Correction** 0.0s/f (Stan) **7** Ran SP% **111.3**
Speed ratings (Par 97): **80,77,74,72,70 70,67**
CSF £8.93 TOTE £1.50: £1.20, £3.80; EX 8.90 Trifecta £18.40.
**Owner** Jim Duggan & Scott Brown **Bred** J M Duggan & The Late T Duggan **Trained** Epsom, Surrey

**FOCUS**
An uncompetitive maiden and the favourite made no mistake. The winner has been rated to form for now.

## 151 32RED CASINO FILLIES' H'CAP — 7f 36y (Tp)
**5:05** (5:06) (Class 5) (0-75,75) 4-Y-0+ **£2,911** (£866; £432; £216) **Stalls** High

Form RPR

543- **1** **Bint Arcano (FR)**[119] 6426 4-9-5 **73**.............................. JamesSullivan 1 83+
(Julie Camacho) *chsd ldrs: shkn up to ld ins fnl f: r.o: comf* **3/1**[2]

041- **2** *2¼* **Arize (IRE)**[18] 8493 4-9-0 **68**........................................ TomEaves 3 71
(David Brown) *led: rdn and edgd rt wl over 1f out: hdd and unable qck ins fnl f* **11/2**

232- **3** *1½* **Palenville (IRE)**[26] 8357 4-9-4 **75**........................... CallumShepherd(3) 2 74
(Simon Crisford) *chsd ldr: rdn whn nt clr run wl over 1f out: no ex ins fnl f* **5/2**[1]

000- **4** *nk* **Veena (FR)**[168] 4708 4-9-5 **73**........................................ JamieSpencer 5 71
(David Simcock) *hld up: hdwy over 2f out: shkn up over 1f out: styd on same pce fnl f* **4/1**[3]

140- **5** *5* **Hyland Heather (IRE)**[12] 8561 4-9-5 **73**.....................(p) TonyHamilton 4 58
(Richard Fahey) *s.i.s: pushed along early in rr: hdwy over 1f out: wknd ins fnl f* **11/1**

303- **6** *6* **Wonderful Life (IRE)**[22] 8449 4-9-4 **72**............................... AdamKirby 7 40
(Richard Spencer) *hld up: rdn over 2f out: wknd over 1f out* **9/1**

620- **7** *1¼* **Loumarin (IRE)**[30] 8316 5-8-8 **62**.................................... AndrewMullen 6 27
(Michael Appleby) *plld hrd and prom: rdn over 2f out: sn wknd* **25/1**

1m 27.93s (-0.87) **Going Correction** 0.0s/f (Stan) **7** Ran SP% **111.1**
Speed ratings (Par 100): **104,101,99,99,93 86,85**
CSF £18.55 TOTE £4.50: £2.40, £3.50; EX 19.90 Trifecta £45.00.
**Owner** G B Turnbull Ltd **Bred** Rabbah Bloodstock Limited **Trained** Norton, N Yorks

**FOCUS**
A fair, competitive looking fillies' handicap and a tidy winner. It's been rated around the runner-up.
T/Plt: £30.00 to a £1 stake. Pool: £78,043.07 - 1,895.40 winning units T/Qpdt: £23.80 to a £1 stake. Pool: £4,489.82 - 139.18 winning units **Colin Roberts**

# [67]SOUTHWELL (L-H)
Tuesday, January 10

**OFFICIAL GOING: Fibresand: standard**
Wind: Fresh behind Weather: Cloudy

## 152 BETWAY SPRINT H'CAP (DIV I) — 6f 16y(F)
**12:15** (12:15) (Class 5) (0-75,77) 4-Y-0+ **£3,234** (£962; £481; £240) **Stalls** Low

Form RPR

04-3 **1** **Englishwoman**[8] 22 4-9-2 **69**................................................ JFEgan 2 80
(David Evans) *trckd ldrs: hdwy over 3f out: rdn to ld over 2f out: kpt on strly fnl f* **9/4**[1]

02-6 **2** *2¼* **Sarabi**[8] 22 4-8-12 **65**.....................................................(p) KieranO'Neill 6 69
(Scott Dixon) *cl up: rdn along over 2f out: drvn and edgd rt appr fnl f: kpt on* **14/1**

133- **3** *hd* **Vroom (IRE)**[21] 8473 4-8-11 **71**.................................(p) GabrieleMalune(7) 3 74
(Gay Kelleway) *trckd ldrs on inner: effrt over 2f out and sn pushed along rdn over 1f out: drvn and kpt on fnl f* **10/3**[2]

210- **4** *1½* **Ticks The Boxes (IRE)**[12] 8571 5-9-7 **77**....................(p) NathanEvans(3) 7 75
(Michael Herrington) *trckd ldng pair: wd st: rdn along 2f out: drvn over 1f out: kpt on same pce* **9/2**[3]

000- **5** *nk* **Bell Heather (IRE)**[15] 8531 4-8-13 **66**.............................. TonyHamilton 5 63
(Richard Fahey) *towards rr: wd st: hdwy over 2f out: rdn over 1f out: kpt on wl fnl f: nrst fin* **16/1**

023- **6** *shd* **Semana Santa**[126] 6216 4-9-7 **74**...................................... AndrewMullen 8 71
(David Barron) *chsd ldrs: wd st: rdn along over 2f out: drvn over 1f out: kpt on same pce* **11/2**

000- **7** *shd* **Satchville Flyer**[28] 8345 6-8-9 **62**................................ StevieDonohoe 9 59
(David Evans) *dwlt and bhd: sn swtchd to outer: pushed along and wd st: sn rdn: kpt on appr fnl f: nrst fin* **16/1**

310- **8** *3¾* **Desert Strike**[27] 8365 11-9-0 **67**....................................(p) ShaneGray 10 52
(Conor Dore) *slt ld: rdn along wl over 2f out: sn hdd: wknd wl over 1f out* **33/1**

066- **9** *7* **Bad Girl Caoimhe (IRE)**[164] 4861 4-9-0 **67**.................. BarryMcHugh 1 29
(Marjorie Fife) *a rr* **33/1**

000- **10** *hd* **Spiraea**[12] 8571 7-9-3 **70**................................................ LemosdeSouza 4 32
(Ivan Furtado) *a rr* **66/1**

1m 15.88s (-0.62) **Going Correction** -0.05s/f (Stan) **10** Ran SP% **113.2**
Speed ratings (Par 103): **102,99,98,96,96 96,96,91,81,81**
CSF £34.65 CT £102.94 TOTE £2.70: £1.70, £4.00, £1.10; EX 31.70 Trifecta £130.10.

**Owner** R Kent **Bred** Peter Winkworth **Trained** Pandy, Monmouths
**FOCUS**
They went a solid tempo in this modest sprint handicap. The runner-up has been rated to form, with the third close to his latest.

## 153 BETWAY SPRINT AWT "HANDS AND HEELS" SERIES APPRENTICE H'CAP (RACING EXCELLENCE INITIATIVE) 4f 214y(F)
**12:45** (12:49) (Class 6) (0-55,54) 4-Y-O+ **£2,587** (£770; £384; £192) **Stalls** Centre

Form RPR
60-3 **1** **Pancake Day**[8] 20 5-8-12 **52** ........ FinleyMarsh(7) 6 63
(David C Griffiths) *prom centre: cl up 1/2-way: led wl over1f out: sn rdn along and kpt on wl towards fin* **4/1**[1]
100- **2** *nk* **Very First Blade**[20] 8485 8-8-13 **51** ........(be) AledBeech(5) 1 61
(Michael Mullineaux) *racd towards far rail: chsd ldrs: hdwy over 2f out: rdn to chse wnr ins fnl f: ev ch til no ex towards fin* **8/1**
220- **3** *2 1/4* **Kodimoor (IRE)**[20] 8485 4-9-1 **53** ........(bt) GabrieleMalune(5) 12 55
(Christopher Kellett) *racd towards centre: chsd ldrs: cl up over 2f out: rdn over 1f out: kpt on same pce fnl f* **8/1**
006- **4** *1 3/4* **Charlie Lad**[10] 8596 5-9-0 **52** ........ TobyEley(5) 9 48
(Daniel Mark Loughnane) *chsd ldrs: pushed along and sltly outpcd 1/2-way: hdwy wl over 1f out: kpt on fnl f* **14/1**
000- **5** *2 1/2* **Bapak Bangsawan**[21] 8474 7-9-7 **54** ........(be) JaneElliott 2 41
(Ann Stokell) *racd towards far side: cl up: led 3f out: hdd 2f out: sn rdn and edgd lft: kpt on one pce* **9/1**
404- **6** *3/4* **Slim Chance (IRE)**[14] 8542 8-9-3 **53** ........(p) PaulaMuir(3) 14 37
(Simon West) *racd nr stands rail: towards rr: pushed along 1/2-way: kpt on wl fnl f:* **16/1**
333- **7** *3/4* **Swendab (IRE)**[14] 8542 9-9-5 **52** ........(b) JoshuaBryan 13 33
(John O'Shea) *chsd ldrs centre: rdn along 2f out: sn wknd* **6/1**[3]
54-5 **8** *nk* **Men United (FR)**[8] 21 4-9-6 **53** ........(p[1]) JoshQuinn 3 33
(Garry Moss) *cl up towards far side: led 2f out: sn rdn and hdd wl over 1f out: grad wknd* **11/2**[2]
11-0 **9** *1 1/2* **Robbian**[8] 21 6-9-4 **51** ........ BenRobinson 8 26
(Charles Smith) *towards rr: rdn along 1/2-way: n.d* **18/1**
060- **10** *2 1/2* **Pull The Pin (IRE)**[306] 895 8-8-12 **50** ........(bt) JonathanFisher(5) 4 16
(Mandy Rowland) *racd towards far side: slt ld 2f: cl up: rdn along 2f out: sn wknd* **25/1**
505- **11** *hd* **Lizzy's Dream**[152] 5335 9-8-13 **51** ........ BenSanderson(5) 5 16
(Rebecca Bastiman) *a towards rr* **50/1**
60-0 **12** *2 1/4* **Zebelini (IRE)**[8] 20 5-8-10 **48** ........(tp) WilliamCox(5) 7 5
(Roy Bowring) *a rr* **10/1**
36-6 **13** *3/4* **Allen's Folly**[9] 1 4-8-10 **48** ........ NicolaCurrie(5) 10
(Peter Hiatt) *chsd ldrs centre: rdn along 1/2-way: sn wknd* **33/1**
000- **14** *36* **Ciaras Cookie (IRE)**[14] 8541 5-8-11 **51** ........(h) JacobMitchell(7) 11
(Mandy Rowland) *bolted to s: dwlt: sn rdn along and detched in rr: t.o fr 1/2-way* **66/1**

59.38s (-0.32) **Going Correction** -0.05s/f (Stan) **14** Ran SP% **119.0**
Speed ratings (Par 101): **100,99,95,93,89 87,86,86,83,79 79,75,74,17**
CSF £34.18 CT £255.41 TOTE £4.60: £1.90, £2.80, £2.70; EX 36.10 Trifecta £392.80.
**Owner** Trojan Racing **Bred** Stuart Matheson **Trained** Bawtry, S Yorks
**FOCUS**
A weak 'hands and heels" sprint handicap and it was wide open. Straightforward form.

## 154 BETWAY H'CAP 1m 4f 14y(F)
**1:15** (1:15) (Class 5) (0-75,77) 4-Y-O+ **£3,234** (£962; £481; £240) **Stalls** Low

Form RPR
23-1 **1** **L'Inganno Felice (FR)**[6] 42 7-9-11 **76** 6ex........(h) PJMcDonald 8 90
(Iain Jardine) *trckd ldrs: cl up 1/2-way: led over 4f out: rdn over 2f out: clr appr fnl f: styd on strly* **11/4**[2]
621- **2** *7* **Come Back King (IRE)**[21] 8477 4-9-8 **77** ........(b) TomMarquand 6 81
(Michael Appleby) *trckd ldr: cl up 1/2-way: effrt to chal over 2f out: ev ch whn rdn and hung lft over 1f out: sn drvn and kpt on same pce* **11/10**[1]
/30- **3** *8* **Glorious Asset**[11] 8586 5-8-11 **62** ........ TomEaves 4 52
(Ivan Furtado) *led: pushed along and hdd over 4f out: rdn 3f out: drvn over 2f out: plugged on one pce* **25/1**
413- **4** *2 1/4* **Vercingetorix (IRE)**[13] 8348 6-9-10 **75** ........(p) TonyHamilton 5 61
(Harriet Bethell) *trckd ldrs: pushed along 4f out: rdn over 3f out: drvn wl over 2f out and plugged on one pce* **25/1**
400- **5** *11* **Cornelious (IRE)**[34] 8253 5-9-0 **65** ........(t[1]) AdamBeschizza 2 34
(Clifford Lines) *chsd ldng pair on inner: pushed along over 4f out: rdn over 3f out: sn wknd* **25/1**
300- **6** *5* **The Lock Master (IRE)**[21] 8477 10-9-8 **73** ........(p) AndrewMullen 7 34
(Michael Appleby) *dwlt and towards rr: hdwy on outer after 4f: chsd ldrs over 5f out: rdn along 4f out: sn wknd* **16/1**
00- **7** *43* **My Fantasea (IRE)**[14] 8539 4-9-4 **73** ........ JFEgan 1
(David Evans) *a: rr: bhd fr 1/2-way: t.o fnl 3f* **8/1**
03-1 **8** *34* **Karam Albaari (IRE)**[6] 39 9-9-7 **72** 6ex........(v) GeorgeBaker 3
(J R Jenkins) *dwlt: hld up in rr: pushed along over 4f out: sn outpcd and t.o whn eased fnl 2f* **15/2**[3]

2m 37.67s (-3.33) **Going Correction** -0.05s/f (Stan)
**WFA** 4 from 5yo+ 3lb **8** Ran SP% **114.6**
Speed ratings (Par 103): **109,104,99,97,90 86,58,35**
CSF £5.98 CT £52.53 TOTE £3.60: £1.10, £1.10, £4.80; EX 6.50 Trifecta £56.30.
**Owner** A Dawson & Mrs K Campbell **Bred** E A R L Elevage Des Loges **Trained** Carrutherstown, D'fries & G'way
**FOCUS**
This was run at an average pace and the two market leaders dominated the home straight. A clear pb from the winner, with the runner-up rated a bit below his latest form.

## 155 32RED.COM H'CAP 4f 214y(F)
**1:45** (1:45) (Class 4) (0-85,85) 3-Y-O **£5,175** (£1,540; £769; £384) **Stalls** Centre

Form RPR
14-5 **1** **Gracious Tom (IRE)**[3] 125 3-8-8 **72** ........ StevieDonohoe 3 82
(David Evans) *trckd ldrs: pushed along 2f out: rdn and gd hdwy over 1f out: drvn and qcknd ins fnl f: led last 100 yds* **7/2**[2]
153- **2** *1 1/2* **Major Jumbo**[133] 6010 3-8-4 **68** ........ ShaneGray 4 73
(Kevin Ryan) *slt ld: pushed along 2f out: rdn over 1f out: drvn ins fnl f: hdd last 100 yds* **8/1**
021- **3** *1 1/4* **Wick Powell**[101] 6954 3-9-7 **85** ........ AndrewMullen 1 86
(David Barron) *cl up: chal 2f out: rdn and ev ch over 1f out: drvn ent fnl f: kpt on same pce* **11/10**[1]
412- **4** *2 3/4* **Juan Horsepower**[11] 8582 3-8-13 **77** ........(b[1]) KieranO'Neill 2 69
(Richard Hannon) *rdn along s and cl up: rdn 2f out: drvn over 1f out: grad wknd* **5/1**[3]
301- **5** *3* **Nuzha**[12] 8569 3-8-5 **69** ........ JFEgan 5 52
(David Evans) *chsd ldrs: rdn along 2f out: sn drvn and wknd* **7/1**

58.63s (-1.07) **Going Correction** -0.05s/f (Stan) **5** Ran SP% **110.1**
Speed ratings (Par 99): **106,103,101,97,92**
CSF £27.95 TOTE £4.80: £1.90, £4.10; EX 30.80 Trifecta £73.60.
**Owner** Terry Reffell **Bred** Golden Vale Stud **Trained** Pandy, Monmouths
**FOCUS**
An interesting little 3yo sprint handicap, best rated around the second. The second and third have been rated pretty much to their Thirsk form in July.

## 156 SUNBETS.CO.UK H'CAP 1m 13y(F)
**2:20** (2:20) (Class 3) (0-95,87) 4-Y-O-**£7,561** (£2,263; £1,131; £566; £282) **Stalls** Low

Form RPR
301- **1** **Mithqaal (USA)**[21] 8475 4-9-7 **87** ........ AndrewMullen 6 97+
(Michael Appleby) *trckd ldrs: cl up 1/2-way: led over 3f out: rdn over 1f out: kpt on wl fnl f* **4/6**[1]
00-6 **2** *1 3/4* **Showboating (IRE)**[9] 5 9-8-9 **82** ........ LewisEdmunds(7) 2 87
(John Balding) *t.k.h early: hld up in rr: hdwy 2f out: rdn over 1f out: drvn to chse wnr ins fnl f: kpt on wl* **20/1**
50-1 **3** *2 3/4* **Vivat Rex (IRE)**[8] 24 6-9-4 **84** 6ex........(t) DavidNolan 7 83
(Conor Dore) *dwlt: hdwy to trck ldrs after 3f: effrt on outer over 2f out: rdn to chse wnr wl over 1f out: sn drvn and kpt on same pce* **10/1**
0-26 **4** *2 1/2* **Boots And Spurs**[8] 25 8-8-11 **77** ........(v) KieranO'Neill 3 70
(Scott Dixon) *slt ld 2f: prom: pushed along 3f out: rdn over 2f out: drvn wl over 1f out: kpt on same pce* **14/1**
026- **5** *hd* **Briardale (IRE)**[20] 8478 5-9-5 **85** ........ PJMcDonald 4 78
(James Bethell) *towards rr: hdwy 1/2-way: chsd ldrs 3f out: sn rdn: drvn 2f out: kpt on same pce* **8/1**[3]
13-5 **6** *3* **Captain Revelation**[9] 5 5-9-3 **83** ........(p) TomMarquand 5 69
(Tom Dascombe) *trckd ldrs: pushed along 4f out: sn lost pl and rdn along: n.d* **11/2**[2]
0/0- **7** *1 1/2* **Restive (IRE)**[14] 8539 4-8-9 **75** ........(p) MartinDwyer 8 57
(Iain Jardine) *cl up: led after 2f: rdn along and hdd over 3f out: drvn over 2f out: grad wknd* **20/1**
211- **8** *11* **Fort Jefferson**[194] 3816 4-8-11 **77** ........ DavidProbert 1 34
(Andrew Balding) *a towards rr: rdn along over 3f out: bhd whn eased fnl f* **10/1**

1m 41.9s (-1.80) **Going Correction** -0.05s/f (Stan) **8** Ran SP% **120.9**
Speed ratings (Par 107): **107,105,102,100,99 96,95,84**
CSF £19.60 CT £82.96 TOTE £1.50: £1.10, £5.20, £2.30; EX 17.60 Trifecta £129.90.
**Owner** The Horse Watchers **Bred** Extern Developments Ltd **Trained** Oakham, Rutland
**FOCUS**
The feature was run at a solid pace and the form makes some sense. The third has been rated to his claimer latest.

## 157 32RED CASINO (S) STKS 6f 16y(F)
**2:50** (2:50) (Class 5) 3-Y-O **£3,234** (£962; £481; £240) **Stalls** Low

Form RPR
240- **1** **Western Presence**[54] 7981 3-9-0 **63** ........ TonyHamilton 7 65
(Richard Fahey) *trckd ldng pair: smooth hdwy and cl up 2f out: led 11/2f out and sn rdn: edgd lft and drvn ins fnl f: kpt on* **3/1**[2]
52-3 **2** *1/2* **Pulsating (IRE)**[9] 2 3-8-8 **67** ........ JoshuaBryan(7) 5 65
(Ali Stronge) *trckd ldrs: hdwy on outer wl over 2f out: rdn to chse wnr over 1f out: drvn and kpt on fnl f* **13/8**[1]
40-4 **3** *2* **Jet Setter (IRE)**[9] 2 3-8-7 **68** ........(p[1]) JordanUys(7) 6 58
(Brian Meehan) *cl up: led wl over 2f out: sn rdn: drvn and hdd 11/2f out: kpt on same pce* **7/2**[3]
002- **4** *5* **Black Redstart**[107] 6808 3-8-9 **57** ........(h) DavidProbert 1 38
(Alan Bailey) *slt ld on inner: rdn along 3f out: sn hdd and grad wknd fnl 2f* **25/1**
0- **5** *7* **Joyroo (IRE)**[202] 3516 3-8-11 **0** ........ NathanEvans(3) 3 22
(Michael Easterby) *dwlt: green and sn rdn along: a rr* **10/1**
6- **6** *nse* **Doneraile (IRE)**[225] 2747 3-9-0 **0** ........(p[1]) JackMitchell 4 21
(Robert Eddery) *dwlt: a rr* **6/1**

1m 16.74s (0.24) **Going Correction** -0.05s/f (Stan) **6** Ran SP% **112.5**
Speed ratings (Par 97): **96,95,92,86,76 76**
.The winner was bought in for 7,500 guineas. Pulsating was claimed by Mr D. Steele for £5,000. Jet Setter was claimed by Mr A. W. Carroll for £5,000.\n\x\x
**Owner** Dan Gilbert **Bred** Dan Gilbert **Trained** Musley Bank, N Yorks
**FOCUS**
Straightforward enough plating form. The winner has been rated back to his best, with the runner-up pretty much to her best recent form.

## 158 DOWNLOAD THE BETWAY APP H'CAP 6f 16y(F)
**3:20** (3:21) (Class 6) (0-60,64) 4-Y-O+ **£2,587** (£770; £384; £192) **Stalls** Low

Form RPR
50-1 **1** **Big Amigo (IRE)**[8] 21 4-9-8 **64** 6ex........ EoinWalsh(3) 6 73
(Daniel Mark Loughnane) *trckd ldrs: effrt 2f out: swtchd lft and rdn wl over 1f out: drvn to ld ins fnl f: hld on wl towards fin* **9/4**[1]
4-2 **2** *nk* **Treaty Of Rome (USA)**[8] 20 5-9-3 **56** ........(v) TonyHamilton 5 64
(Derek Shaw) *dwlt and hld up towards rr: smooth hdwy over 2f out: chsd ldrs over 1f out: rdn to chal ent fnl f: sn drvn and ev ch: no ex towards fin* **3/1**[2]
05-3 **3** *nk* **Mustn't Grumble (IRE)**[8] 26 4-9-2 **55** ........(h[1]) PJMcDonald 4 62
(David Loughnane) *trckd ldr: cl up over 2f out: rdn wl over 1f out: sn ev ch: drvn ent fnl f and kpt on* **7/2**[3]
00-6 **4** *2 1/2* **Spowarticus**[8] 20 8-9-4 **57** ........(b) KieranO'Neill 1 57
(Scott Dixon) *led: rdn along 2f out: edgd rt and drvn over 1f out: hdd and no ex ins fnl f* **20/1**
46-3 **5** *4* **Tavener**[8] 21 5-9-5 **58** ........(p) MartinDwyer 9 46
(David C Griffiths) *chsd ldrs towards outer: wd st: rdn over 2f out: drvn over 1f out: kpt on one pce* **6/1**
000- **6** *nk* **Intense Starlet (IRE)**[26] 8390 6-9-7 **60** ........(p) SamJames 12 47
(Marjorie Fife) *rr: wd st: rdn and hdwy 2f out: styd on wl fnl f: nrst fin* **22/1**
55-2 **7** *nk* **Hadley**[8] 21 4-8-11 **50** ........ BarryMcHugh 7 36
(Tracy Waggott) *prom: rdn along over 2f out: drvn wl over 1f out: grad wknd* **14/1**
026- **8** *1 1/4* **Vivre La Reve**[12] 8572 5-8-13 **55** ........(h) CallumShepherd(3) 3 37
(James Unett) *chsd ldrs towards inner: cl up 1/2-way: rdn over 2f out: sn drvn and grad wknd* **33/1**
601- **9** *2 1/4* **Ocotillo (IRE)**[14] 8541 4-8-12 **51** ........ RyanPowell 8 26
(Kevin Frost) *prom: rdn along 1/2-way: sn wknd* **22/1**
600- **10** *1/2* **Outlaw Kate (IRE)**[130] 6106 5-8-2 **46** oh1........ PhilDennis(5) 2 20
(Michael Mullineaux) *chsd ldrs on inner: hdwy and cl up 1/2-way: rdn along wl over 2f out: drvn and wknd wl over 1f out* **100/1**

000- **11** 4 ½ **Or So (USA)**[25] 8408 5-8-5 **47**....................(v[1]) NoelGarbutt[(3)] 13 7
(Derek Shaw) *dwlt: a bhd* **66/1**

400- **12** 8 **Secret Clause**[12] 8571 4-9-8 **61**.................... TomMarquand 11
(Michael Appleby) *in tch on wd ouitsiode: pushed along and lost pl bef 1/2-way: wd st and sn bhd* **40/1**

1m 16.89s (0.39) **Going Correction** -0.05s/f (Stan) **12** Ran SP% **120.3**
Speed ratings (Par 101): **95,94,94,90,85 85,84,83,80,79 73,62**
CSF £8.43 CT £23.34 TOTE £3.30: £1.30, £1.50, £1.60; EX 11.50 Trifecta £34.70.
**Owner** The Friday Morning Fourball **Bred** Kildaragh Stud **Trained** Rock, Worcs

**FOCUS**
A moderate sprint handicap that saw a tight finish between the market leaders. Straightforward form, with the runner-up rated close to his recent form.

## 159 BETWAY SPRINT H'CAP (DIV II) 6f 16y(F)
**3:50** (3:50) (Class 5) (0-75,76) 4-Y-0+ **£3,234** (£962; £481; £240) **Stalls** Low

Form RPR

40-4 **1** **Call Out Loud**[5] 67 5-9-1 **66**....................(vt[1]) TomMarquand 8 71
(Michael Appleby) *sn led: rdn wl over 1f out: drvn ins fnl f: hdd last 75 yds: rallied gamely to ld again nr fin* **10/1**

03-5 **2** hd **Among Angels**[8] 25 5-9-8 **76**....................(b) NathanEvans[(3)] 7 80
(Daniel Mark Loughnane) *chsd ldrs on outer: wd st: rdn along on outer 2f out: drvn over 1f out: styd on wl towards fin* **7/2[1]**

041- **3** shd **Hold On Magnolia**[20] 8483 4-9-1 **66**.................... TonyHamilton 4 70
(Richard Fahey) *trckd ldrs: hdwy over 2f out: rdn over 1f out: drvn ins fnl f: led last 50 yds: edgd lft: hdd and no ex nr fin* **12/1**

203- **4** nk **Dodgy Bob**[32] 8287 4-9-5 **70**....................(p) KevinStott 9 73
(Kevin Ryan) *.cl up: rdn along wl over 1f out: drvn and ev ch ent fnl f tl no ex towards fin* **5/1[3]**

01-0 **5** ½ **Macho Mac**[8] 25 4-9-7 **72**....................(h[1]) PJMcDonald 2 73
(Hughie Morrison) *hld up in tch: hdwy over 2f out: rdn to chse ldrs over 1f out: sn drvn and kpt on fnl f* **4/1[2]**

3-64 **6** 1 ½ **Crosse Fire**[5] 71 5-9-6 **71**.................... KieranO'Neill 5 68
(Scott Dixon) *keen: chsd ldng pair on inner: rdn and along wl over 1f out: drvn and edgd lft ent fnl f: kpt on same pce* **11/2**

002- **7** 5 **Freddy With A Y (IRE)**[48] 8064 7-8-12 **63**.................... PaddyAspell 6 44
(J R Jenkins) *hld up: a rr* **25/1**

352- **8** 2 ¾ **Space War**[31] 8315 10-9-2 **67**....................(t) JamesSullivan 1 39
(Michael Easterby) *in tch: pushed along on inner 3f out: swtchd rt towards stands side 2f out: sn rdn along and wknd* **5/1[3]**

250- **9** 1 ¾ **Nora Batt (IRE)**[24] 8430 4-9-2 **67**.................... StevieDonohoe 3 33
(David Evans) *dwlt: a rr* **66/1**

1m 16.13s (-0.37) **Going Correction** -0.05s/f (Stan) **9** Ran SP% **113.1**
Speed ratings (Par 103): **100,99,99,99,98 96,89,86,83**
CSF £44.03 CT £429.15 TOTE £13.90: £3.60, £1.80, £2.80; EX 63.00 Trifecta £538.70.
**Owner** Kings Head Duffield Racing Partnership **Bred** Rabbah Bloodstock Limited **Trained** Oakham, Rutland

**FOCUS**
The second division of the modest 6f handicap saw a blanket finish. It was 0.25secs slower than the first. The winner has been rated to his best, but with the field bunched this is not one to be particularly confident about.
T/Jkpt: £5,000.00 to a £1 stake. Pool: £10,000.00 - 2.0 winning units T/Plt: £25.20 to a £1 stake. Pool: £63,890.67 - 1,847.83 winning units T/Qpdt: £7.80 to a £1 stake. Pool: £5,160.26 - 484.21 winning units **Joe Rowntree**

# [145]WOLVERHAMPTON (A.W) (L-H)
Tuesday, January 10

**OFFICIAL GOING: Tapeta: standard**
Wind: Light behind Weather: Overcast

## 160 32RED CASINO H'CAP 7f 36y (Tp)
**2:10** (2:11) (Class 5) (0-70,71) 3-Y-O **£2,911** (£866; £432; £216) **Stalls** High

Form RPR

404- **1** **Sky Ballerina**[147] 5524 3-9-6 **69**.................... RobertHavlin 6 72
(Simon Crisford) *hld up in tch: rdn over 1f out: r.o to ld wl ins fnl f* **8/1**

03-1 **2** 1 ¼ **Seaview**[5] 73 3-8-9 **61** 6ex.................... AaronJones[(3)] 2 60
(David Brown) *sn led: rdn and hung rt fr over 1f out: hdd wl ins fnl f* **5/2[1]**

131- **3** shd **Geraldine (GER)**[48] 8071 3-9-0 **63**.................... MartinHarley 8 63+
(Stuart Williams) *hld up: hdwy and nt clr run over 1f out: r.o* **7/1[3]**

60-3 **4** nse **Shabeeh (IRE)**[5] 78 3-9-8 **71**.................... JoeFanning 4 70
(Mark Johnston) *s.i.s: hld up: hdwy over 1f out: r.o* **8/1**

053- **5** nk **Hotfill**[25] 8398 3-9-4 **67**.................... PhillipMakin 3 65
(David Barron) *hld up: plld hrd: hdwy over 1f out: r.o* **4/1[2]**

400- **6** nk **Nicky Baby (IRE)**[137] 5848 3-9-0 **63**.................... RobertWinston 5 60
(Dean Ivory) *sn chsng ldr: pushed along and lost 2nd over 2f out: styd on* **16/1**

604- **7** 1 ¾ **Suffragette City (IRE)**[10] 8591 3-8-12 **66**....................(p[1]) HollieDoyle[(5)] 1 59
(Richard Hannon) *sn pushed along to chse ldrs: wnt 2nd over 2f out: rdn: hung rt and ev ch over 1f out: no ex wl ins fnl f* **10/1**

134- **8** 5 **Wentwell Yesterday (IRE)**[40] 8174 3-9-7 **70**.................... AdamKirby 7 49
(Jamie Osborne) *led early: chsd ldrs: rdn over 2f out: styd on same pce fr over 1f out* **7/1[3]**

1m 28.41s (-0.39) **Going Correction** -0.15s/f (Stan) **8** Ran SP% **110.8**
Speed ratings (Par 97): **96,94,94,94,94 93,91,86**
CSF £26.56 CT £141.48 TOTE £10.50: £2.70, £1.10, £2.50; EX 31.50 Trifecta £344.40.
**Owner** Saeed H Al Tayer **Bred** Qatar Bloodstock Ltd **Trained** Newmarket, Suffolk

**FOCUS**
Not a bad contest for the grade. A bunched finish and ordinary form. The runner-up has been rated below last week's Southwell romp, but the fourth has been rated to his C&D latest.

## 161 32RED.COM FILLIES' H'CAP 6f 20y (Tp)
**2:40** (2:43) (Class 5) (0-70,71) 4-Y-0+ **£2,911** (£866; £432; £216) **Stalls** Low

Form RPR

043- **1** **Beau Mistral (IRE)**[41] 8149 8-8-6 **55**....................(p) WilliamCarson 2 64
(Tony Carroll) *mde all: rdn over 1f out: r.o u.p: edgd lft towards fin* **16/1**

00-0 **2** 1 ½ **Doeadeer (IRE)**[8] 26 4-8-5 **59**....................(b[1]) ShirleyTeasdale[(5)] 3 63
(Keith Dalgleish) *hld up in tch: plld hrd: nt clr run over 5f out: chsd wnr fnl f: sn rdn and ev ch: no ex towards fin* **40/1**

011- **3** hd **Coquine**[31] 8315 4-9-2 **65**....................(p) AdamKirby 4 69
(David O'Meara) *chsd ldrs: rdn over 2f out: r.o* **13/8[1]**

104- **4** 2 **Nuala Tagula (IRE)**[14] 8535 4-8-13 **62**.................... JasonHart 1 59
(John Quinn) *trckd ldrs: racd keenly: rdn t chse wnr briefly over 1f out: styd on same pce fnl f* **5/1[3]**

202- **5** ½ **Lolita**[27] 8358 5-9-5 **71**.................... AlistairRawlinson[(3)] 6 67
(J R Jenkins) *s.i.s: pushed along early in rr: hdwy over 1f out: sn rdn: no imp ins fnl f* **12/1**

516- **6** 1 **Savannah Beau**[43] 8135 5-9-7 **70**.................... GrahamLee 5 62
(Iain Jardine) *hld up: plld hrd: rdn over 1f out: nvr on terms* **7/2[2]**

043- **7** 1 ¾ **Noble Act**[24] 8430 4-9-5 **68**....................(p[1]) MartinHarley 8 55
(Rae Guest) *racd keenly: w wnr 1f: racd in 2nd pl tl rdn and rdr dropped whip over 1f out: wknd ins fnl f* **13/2**

200- **8** 8 **Evening Starlight**[13] 8561 4-9-3 **66**.................... LukeMorris 7 27
(Ron Hodges) *chsd ldrs: lost pl over 3f out: rdn and wknd over 1f out* **16/1**

1m 13.65s (-0.85) **Going Correction** -0.15s/f (Stan) **8** Ran SP% **112.2**
Speed ratings (Par 100): **99,97,96,94,93 92,89,79**
CSF £439.04 CT £1596.72 TOTE £19.40: £3.80, £6.30, £1.10; EX 451.50 Trifecta £2149.70.
**Owner** A Mills **Bred** John McEnery **Trained** Cropthorne, Worcs

**FOCUS**
The pace was sound for this fair handicap. The winner has been rated to last year's turf form.

## 162 BETWAY MARATHON H'CAP 1m 5f 194y
**3:10** (3:10) (Class 5) (0-70,72) 4-Y-0+ **£2,911** (£866; £432; £216) **Stalls** Low

Form RPR

200- **1** **Start Seven**[186] 4082 5-9-11 **67**.................... AdamKirby 3 73
(Jamie Osborne) *broke wl: sn stdd and lost pl: racd keenly: rdn over 2f out: hdwy over 1f out: swtchd lft ins fnl f: r.o to ld nr fin* **8/1**

214- **2** ½ **Eurato (FR)**[208] 3302 7-9-13 **69**.................... MartinHarley 4 74
(Steve Gollings) *chsd ldrs: led 2f out: rdn over 1f out: hdd nr fin* **7/1**

011- **3** ¾ **Blue Top**[32] 3999 8-8-13 **60**....................(v) HollieDoyle[(5)] 1 64
(Dai Burchell) *s.i.s: hdwy on outer over 2f out: ev ch fr over 1f out: rdn ins fnl f: no ex towards fin* **33/1**

02-1 **4** 4 ½ **Ominotago**[8] 23 5-10-2 **72** 6ex.................... LukeMorris 8 70
(Michael Appleby) *hld up in tch: outpcd over 2f out: kpt on ins fnl f* **11/4[1]**

624- **5** 1 **Monna Valley**[25] 8410 5-9-1 **60**.................... AaronJones[(3)] 2 56
(Stuart Williams) *chsd ldrs: rdn over 1f out: wknd ins fnl f* **5/1[3]**

340- **6** hd **Mamoo**[23] 8445 4-8-10 **58**....................(p) ShaneKelly 5 54
(Mike Murphy) *sn led at stdy pce: qcknd 3f out: rdn and hdd 2f out: wknd ins fnl f* **7/1**

060/ **7** 4 ½ **Mahican (IRE)**[515] 5351 7-9-7 **63**.................... JoeFanning 7 53
(Jennie Candlish) *s.i.s: hld up: rdn over 2f out: wknd over 1f out* **10/1**

236- **8** 12 **Marshall Aid (IRE)**[13] 8558 4-9-4 **66**.................... LiamKeniry 6 39
(Mark Usher) *chsd ldr: ev ch over 2f out: sn rdn: wknd over 1f out* **4/1[2]**

3m 1.44s (-3.36) **Going Correction** -0.15s/f (Stan)
**WFA** 4 from 5yo+ 4lb **8** Ran SP% **111.5**
Speed ratings (Par 103): **103,102,102,99,99 99,96,89**
CSF £59.04 CT £1700.52 TOTE £9.00: £2.70, £1.90, £5.00; EX 60.80 Trifecta £458.00.
**Owner** Mehmet Kurt **Bred** Mehmet Kurt **Trained** Upper Lambourn, Berks
■ Stewards' Enquiry : Martin Harley two-day ban: used whip above permitted level. (Jan 24-25)

**FOCUS**
A steadily run handicap. A small pb from the winner, with the third running as well as ever on the Flat.

## 163 BETWAY H'CAP 1m 4f 51y (Tp)
**3:40** (3:40) (Class 4) (0-80,82) 4-Y-0+ **£4,722** (£1,405; £702; £351) **Stalls** Low

Form RPR

120- **1** **Ride The Lightning**[10] 8594 4-9-11 **81**.................... LukeMorris 5 86
(Archie Watson) *hld up: drvn along over 2f out: hung lft and r.o ins fnl f to ld nr fin* **5/1[2]**

310- **2** nk **Hermann**[23] 8447 4-9-11 **81**.................... SeanLevey 8 85
(Richard Hannon) *trckd ldrs: rdn over 1f out: led wl ins fnl f: hdd nr fin* **5/1[2]**

506- **3** hd **Ravens Quest**[27] 8363 4-9-2 **72**.................... DannyBrock 9 76
(John Ryan) *chsd ldr tl led 2f out: sn rdn: edgd lft and hdd wl ins fnl f* **66/1**

150- **4** ½ **Tangramm**[34] 8249 5-10-2 **82**....................(p) RobertWinston 7 85
(Dean Ivory) *s.i.s: hld up: rdn and hung lft fr over 1f out: r.o towards fin: nt rch ldrs* **8/1[3]**

60-4 **5** ½ **Faithful Creek (IRE)**[6] 43 5-9-13 **82**....................(p) AlistairRawlinson[(3)] 6 84
(Michael Appleby) *s.i.s: hld up: swtchd rt over 1f out: r.o ins fnl f: nvr nrr* **11/1**

034- **6** nk **Ardamir (FR)**[31] 8162 5-9-12 **78**.................... AdamKirby 3 85+
(Alan King) *hld up: shkn up and hdwy 2f out: nt clr run fr over 1f out: nvr able to chal* **15/8[1]**

036- **7** 1 ¼ **Giantstepsahead (IRE)**[55] 7980 8-10-2 **82**.................... DanielMuscutt 4 82
(Alan Bailey) *led at stdy pce: qcknd 3f out: hdd 2f out: rdn and edgd lft over 1f out: styd on same pce* **16/1**

001- **8** 1 ½ **Clovelly Bay (IRE)**[27] 8367 6-9-1 **74**.................... TylerSaunders[(7)] 1 73
(Marcus Tregoning) *hld up: hdwy wl over 1f out: cl up whn hmpd sn after: nt rcvr* **12/1**

322- **9** 9 **Threediamondrings**[15] 8524 4-8-6 **65**....................(t) EdwardGreatrex[(3)] 2 48+
(Brendan Powell) *chsd ldrs: rdn and cl up whn hmpd over 1f out: eased* **8/1[3]**

2m 36.8s (-4.00) **Going Correction** -0.15s/f (Stan)
**WFA** 4 from 5yo+ 3lb **9** Ran SP% **113.7**
Speed ratings (Par 105): **107,106,106,106,106 105,104,103,97**
CSF £29.70 CT £1446.95 TOTE £4.30: £1.20, £2.20, £11.30; EX 32.30 Trifecta £1794.90.
**Owner** The Ride The Lightning Partnership **Bred** Usk Valley Stud **Trained** Upper Lambourn, W Berks
■ Stewards' Enquiry : Tyler Saunders two-day ban: careless riding (Jan 24-25)

**FOCUS**
A competitive handicap. There were a number of hard-luck stories in behind. Messy form.

## 164 BETWAY MIDDLE DISTANCE H'CAP 1m 1f 104y (Tp)
**4:10** (4:10) (Class 6) (0-65,72) 4-Y-0+ **£2,264** (£673; £336; £168) **Stalls** Low

Form RPR

000- **1** **Trending (IRE)**[38] 8211 8-8-11 **61**....................(t) DavidParkes[(5)] 5 70
(Jeremy Gask) *rrd s: hld up: hdwy and nt clr run over 1f out: chsd ldr fnl f: edgd lft and r.o to ld nr fin* **14/1**

062- **2** hd **Captain Courageous (IRE)**[70] 7736 4-9-3 **63**.................... GeorgeBaker 2 72
(Ed Walker) *chsd ldrs: rdn to ld over 1f out: sn hung lft: hdd nr fin* **4/6[1]**

060/ **3** 4 ½ **Pour L'Amour (IRE)**[61] 3997 4-9-4 **64**.................... JoeFanning 1 64
(Daniel Mark Loughnane) *hld up: rdn over 1f out: styd on to go 3rd nr fin* **66/1**

400- **4** nk **Lord Of The Storm**[33] 8282 9-9-6 **65**.................... LukeMorris 3 65
(Michael Attwater) *hld up: drvn along 3f out: hdwy over 2f out: styd on same pce ins fnl f* **12/1**

600- **5** *shd* **King Oswald (USA)**[109] 6737 4-9-0 **63** RobHornby(3) 9 63
(James Unett) *hld up: hdwy on outer over 2f out: rdn over 1f out: edgd lft and styd on same pce ins fnl f* **16/1**

652- **6** *3 1/4* **May Mist**[29] 8342 5-9-3 **62** GrahamLee 7 56
(Trevor Wall) *prom: rdn over 2f out: wknd ins fnl f* **9/1**[3]

03-6 **7** *2* **St Patrick's Day (IRE)**[4] 90 5-9-7 **66** (v) DougieCostello 6 56
(J R Jenkins) *led 1f: led again over 6f out: rdn and hdd over 1f out: wknd ins fnl f* **9/2**[2]

005- **8** *1 1/4* **Petrucci (IRE)**[21] 8476 5-9-8 **67** (v[1]) MartinLane 4 54
(Derek Shaw) *pushed along to ld after 1f: hdd over 6f out: remained w ldr tl rdn over 2f out: wknd over 1f out* **14/1**

1m 58.39s (-2.41) **Going Correction** -0.15s/f (Stan)
**WFA** 4 from 5yo+ 1lb 8 Ran SP% **116.6**
Speed ratings (Par 101): **104,103,99,99,99 96,94,93**
CSF £24.45 CT £675.05 TOTE £18.30: £2.70, £1.30, £8.00; EX 36.60 Trifecta £1324.30.
**Owner** Crowd & The Twitterati **Bred** Thomas Hassett **Trained** Stockbridge, Hants
■ Stewards' Enquiry : Luke Morris two-day ban: used whip arm above shoulder height (Jan 24-25)

**FOCUS**
An uncompetitive handicap. The winner has been rated close to last year's best.

## 165 SUNBETS.CO.UK MAIDEN STKS 1m 142y (Tp)
4:40 (4:40) (Class 5) 4-Y-O+ £2,911 (£866; £432; £216) Stalls Low

Form RPR

346- **1** **Shah Of Armaan (IRE)**[32] 8286 4-9-5 72 TomEaves 4 75
(Kevin Ryan) *mde all: rdn over 2f out: styd on wl* **3/1**[2]

**2** *2 1/4* **Revolutionary War (USA)**[70] 4-9-5 85 AdamKirby 3 70
(Jamie Osborne) *prom: chsd wnr over 1f out: sn rdn and hung lft: styd on same pce fnl f* **4/11**[1]

3- **3** *3 1/4* **Belabour**[29] 8342 4-9-5 0 GeorgeBaker 1 62
(Mark Brisbourne) *hld up: hdwy to go 3rd 1f out: no imp ins fnl f* **14/1**[3]

44- **4** *6* **Gamrah (IRE)**[34] 8247 4-9-0 0 MartinHarley 2 44
(James Tate) *chsd wnr tl rdn and edgd rt over 1f out: wknd fnl f* **20/1**

**5** *3 3/4* **Bob Hopeful** 4-9-5 0 ShaneKelly 5 40
(Mike Murphy) *s.s: hdwy 1/2-way: rdn over 2f out: wknd over 1f out* **50/1**

1m 49.64s (-0.46) **Going Correction** -0.15s/f (Stan) 5 Ran SP% **111.7**
Speed ratings (Par 103): **96,94,91,85,82**
CSF £4.56 TOTE £3.40: £1.50, £1.10; EX 6.40 Trifecta £13.50.
**Owner** T A Rahman **Bred** Kilcarn Stud **Trained** Hambleton, N Yorks

**FOCUS**
A weak maiden. The winner made all to cause an upset. The winner has been rated to his form here two starts ago.

## 166 SUNBETS.CO.UK DOWNLOAD THE APP H'CAP 1m 142y (Tp)
5:10 (5:11) (Class 6) (0-65,69) 4-Y-O+ £2,264 (£673; £336; £168) Stalls Low

Form RPR

000- **1** **Gossiping**[38] 8206 5-9-7 **65** ShaneKelly 10 77
(Gary Moore) *hld up: hdwy over 2f out: led over 1f out: rdn out* **5/2**[2]

204- **2** *3 3/4* **What Usain**[11] 8587 5-9-2 **63** (h) AlistairRawlinson(3) 12 66
(Michael Appleby) *chsd ldrs: wnt 2nd 4f out: led over 2f out: rdn and hdd over 1f out: no ex ins fnl f* **12/1**

314- **3** *1 1/4* **Scribner Creek (IRE)**[25] 8411 4-9-3 **62** DaleSwift 6 62
(Daniel Mark Loughnane) *hld up: hdwy over 1f out: edgd lft: nt rch ldrs* **11/2**[3]

03-1 **4** *1* **Rebel State (IRE)**[6] 37 4-9-10 **69** 6ex (p) GeorgeBaker 8 67
(Richard Spencer) *hld up: hdwy over 1f out: sn rdn and hung lft: no ex wl ins fnl f* **9/4**[1]

655- **5** *1 1/4* **Spirit Of Gondree (IRE)**[59] 7944 9-8-12 **56** (b) LukeMorris 4 52
(Milton Bradley) *hld up in tch: racd keenly: rdn over 1f out: wknd ins fnl f* **33/1**

663- **6** *2 3/4* **Bazzat (IRE)**[22] 8458 4-9-0 **59** (p) DannyBrock 3 49
(John Ryan) *led: hdd 7f out: remained handy: rdn over 2f out: wknd over 1f out* **12/1**

010- **7** *1 1/2* **Siouxperhero (IRE)**[41] 8154 8-9-4 **62** (p) DougieCostello 2 49
(William Muir) *hld up in tch: pushed along over 4f out: nt clr run wl over 3f out: n.d after* **33/1**

240- **8** *1* **I Can't Stop**[31] 8320 4-9-0 **59** JoeFanning 9 44
(Milton Bradley) *stdd s: hld up: nvr on terms* **100/1**

121- **9** *1 1/4* **Admirable Art (IRE)**[89] 7298 7-9-4 **62** (p) AdamKirby 7 44
(Tony Carroll) *chsd ldr tl led 7f out: hdd over 5f out: rdn and wknd over 1f out* **11/1**

001- **10** *8* **The Magic Pencil (IRE)**[11] 8588 4-9-6 **65** (p) TomEaves 5 30
(Kevin Ryan) *sn prom: led over 5f out: rdn and hdd over 2f out: wknd over 1f out* **11/2**[3]

400- **11** *5* **Broughtons Fancy**[115] 6592 4-8-13 **58** TimmyMurphy 11 13
(Gary Moore) *chsd ldrs: rdn over 2f out: wknd over 1f out* **25/1**

1m 47.15s (-2.95) **Going Correction** -0.15s/f (Stan)
**WFA** 4 from 5yo+ 1lb 11 Ran SP% **124.5**
Speed ratings (Par 101): **107,103,102,101,100 98,96,95,94,87 83**
CSF £34.04 CT £164.82 TOTE £4.70: £1.80, £3.90, £2.10; EX 55.80 Trifecta £251.20.
**Owner** G L Moore & Partners **Bred** Darley **Trained** Lower Beeding, W Sussex

**FOCUS**
The pace was honest for this open handicap. Solid form, with a straightforward level set by the second and third.
T/Plt: £84.00 to a £1 stake. Pool: £74,977.47 - 650.97 winning units T/Qpdt: £37.10 to a £1 stake. Pool: £6,710.55 - 133.60 winning units **Colin Roberts**

# 88 KEMPTON (A.W) (R-H)
Wednesday, January 11

**OFFICIAL GOING: Polytrack: standard to slow**
Wind: light across Weather: Cloudy

## 167 OWEN FAMILY H'CAP 7f (P)
4:45 (4:45) (Class 7) (0-50,50) 4-Y-O+ £1,940 (£577; £288; £144) Stalls Low

Form RPR

650- **1** **Little Indian**[34] 8278 7-9-6 **49** AdamKirby 14 56
(J R Jenkins) *restrained leaving stalls and hld up in rr: shkn up 2f out and gd prog through pack gng wl: rdn over 1f out: kpt on wl to ld nr fin* **11/2**[2]

000- **2** *nk* **All Or Nothin (IRE)**[237] 2402 8-9-4 **50** CallumShepherd(3) 7 56
(Paddy Butler) *settled bhd ldr on inner: rdn over 2f out: kpt on wl fr over 1f out: led 100yds out: hdd cl home* **40/1**

500- **3** *nk* **Cuban Queen (USA)**[13] 8572 4-9-5 **48** AdamBeschizza 2 53
(Julia Feilden) *settled in mid-div on inner: shkn up over 2f out: sn rdn: kpt on wl on rail and led briefly 110yds out: sn hdd and dropped to 3rd* **7/1**

0- **4** *1 3/4* **Captain Kendall (IRE)**[62] 7896 8-9-5 **48** (p) SteveDrowne 11 49
(Harry Chisman) *sn led: rdn over 2f out: kpt on tl sed to weaken ent fnl f: hdd 110yds out: one pce after* **33/1**

/05- **5** *1/2* **Sir Jamie**[90] 7299 4-9-2 **45** JoeyHaynes 12 44
(Tony Carroll) *hld up in rr on outer: rdn over 2f out: kpt on fr over 1f out: nvr nrr* **11/2**[2]

046- **6** *nse* **Claude Greenwood**[22] 8470 7-8-11 **47** (b) AledBeech(7) 8 46
(Tony Carroll) *prom: rdn over 2f out: kpt on one pce fr over 1f out* **13/2**[3]

000- **7** *1 1/2* **Dalness Express**[49] 8070 4-9-1 **49** CiaranMckee(5) 10 44
(John O'Shea) *in rr-div: rdn over 2f out: no ex fnl f* **20/1**

040- **8** *1* **Welsh Inlet (IRE)**[71] 7736 9-9-3 **46** WilliamCarson 4 39
(John Bridger) *settled in mid-div on inner: shkn up over 2f out: nvr involved fnl f* **8/1**

4-05 **9** *1 1/2* **Ershaad (IRE)**[7] 51 5-9-6 **49** (vt) JosephineGordon 3 37
(Shaun Harris) *settled in mid-div: rdn 2f out: no imp whn n.m.r over 1f out: pushed out after* **10/3**[1]

/00- **10** *nk* **Gypsy Rider**[90] 7302 8-9-0 **46** EoinWalsh(3) 6 34
(Henry Tett) *chsd ldrs: rdn over 2f out: wknd fnl f* **25/1**

/45- **11** *1 1/2* **Twilight Angel**[20] 8491 9-9-6 **49** (p[1]) StevieDonohoe 1 33
(Emma Owen) *in rr: rdn along at 1/2-way: no imp fr 2f out* **25/1**

000- **12** *shd* **Chandrayaan**[34] 8278 10-9-3 **46** (v) RyanPowell 13 29
(John E Long) *mid-div: no ex fr over 1f out* **33/1**

000- **13** *1* **Chester Deelyte (IRE)**[34] 8278 9-9-2 **45** (v) TomMarquand 9 26
(Lisa Williamson) *settled bhd ldrs: rdn and began to lose pl fr 2f out: wknd fr over 1f out* **33/1**

060- **14** *nk* **Love In The Dark**[113] 6651 4-8-13 **47** (h) MitchGodwin(5) 5 27
(Nikki Evans) *pushed along early to hold pce: settled on outer of rr-div: pushed along bnd ent st: no ex fr 2f out* **50/1**

1m 27.31s (1.34) **Going Correction** +0.10s/f (Slow) 14 Ran SP% **116.5**
Speed ratings (Par 97): **96,95,95,93,92 92,90,89,88,87 86,85,84,84**
CSF £213.99 CT £1593.48 TOTE £5.30: £1.80, £6.40, £3.00; EX 138.30 Trifecta £1457.50.
**Owner** Two Little Indians **Bred** D R Tucker **Trained** Royston, Herts
■ Stewards' Enquiry : Joey Haynes caution: allowed mount to shift right-handed when not sufficiently clear

**FOCUS**
The description of the Polytrack was once again standard to slow. Low quality fare. Recent form was thin on the ground and it had a wide-open look to it.

## 168 32RED ON THE APP STORE MAIDEN FILLIES' STKS 7f (P)
5:15 (5:19) (Class 5) 3-Y-O+ £2,911 (£866; £432; £216) Stalls Low

Form RPR

**1** **Almoner**[40] 8201 5-10-0 70 RonanWhelan 6 80
(Tracey Collins, Ire) *sn led: shkn up over 2f out: clr ld whn rdn 2f out: kpt on strly ent fnl f: comf* **13/8**[1]

036- **2** *1* **Angel Of Darkness**[48] 8081 3-8-7 70 CallumShepherd(3) 3 73
(Charles Hills) *early spd: t.k.h bhd wnr: rdn to chse clr ldr 2f out: kpt on ins fnl f but n.d to wnr* **11/2**[3]

3- **3** *2 3/4* **Dreaming Of Paris**[24] 8443 3-8-10 0 WilliamCarson 2 66
(William Haggas) *settled in rr-div: shkn up and prog over 2f out: rdn 2f out: kpt on one pce after* **9/4**[2]

0- **4** *2 3/4* **Girl Squad**[24] 8443 3-8-10 0 DavidProbert 1 58
(William Jarvis) *settled in 5th on inner: rdn over 2f out: kpt on one pce fr over1f out* **50/1**

4- **5** *nk* **Tibibit**[47] 8093 4-9-11 0 EoinWalsh(3) 7 62
(Henry Tett) *wnt lft s: in rr: pushed along over 2f out w plenty to do: no imp tl kpt on nicely under hands and heels fnl f* **33/1**

**6** *3/4* **Finale** 3-8-10 0 LiamKeniry 4 56
(Hughie Morrison) *relucant to load: settled in 4th: rdn over 2f out: kpt on one pce* **33/1**

**7** *hd* **Faience** 3-8-5 0 GeorgiaCox(5) 8 55
(William Haggas) *s.s: in rr: rdn over 2f out: no imp fr over 1f out* **14/1**

6- **8** *1 1/4* **Aryeh (IRE)**[189] 4011 3-8-10 0 JosephineGordon 10 52
(Hugo Palmer) *in rr: niggled at 1/2-way: rdn and prog fr 2f out: nvr nrr* **6/1**

**9** *1 1/2* **Namirah** 3-8-10 0 StevieDonohoe 5 48
(Michael Bell) *broke wl: sn restrained and settled in mid-div on outer: niggled along ent st: pushed along after: nvr involved* **25/1**

0- **10** *6* **London Rebel (IRE)**[20] 8496 4-10-0 0 AdamKirby 11 35
(Richard Spencer) *chsd ldr: rdn over 2f out: sn wknd and eased fnl f* **50/1**

1m 26.67s (0.67) **Going Correction** +0.10s/f (Slow)
**WFA** 3 from 4yo+ 18lb 10 Ran SP% **118.9**
Speed ratings (Par 100): **100,98,95,92,92 91,91,89,88,81**
CSF £10.94 TOTE £2.50: £1.10, £1.90, £1.20; EX 11.90 Trifecta £32.50.
**Owner** Luca Somaini **Bred** Juddmonte Farms Ltd **Trained** The Curragh, Co Kildare
■ Pepita was withdrawn. Price at time of withdrawal 3/1. Rule 4 applies to bets struck prior to withdrawal - deduction 25p in the pound. New market formed.

**FOCUS**
This had the look of a fair fillies' maiden but the late withdrawal of Pepita weakened the value of the form somewhat. The winner has been rated similar to her Irish form, with the fourth and fith rated close to their initial marks.

## 169 32RED CASINO H'CAP 1m 2f 219y(P)
5:45 (5:47) (Class 5) (0-70,70) 4-Y-O+ £2,911 (£866; £432; £216) Stalls Low

Form RPR

644- **1** **Camakasi (IRE)**[28] 8367 6-9-2 **65** TomMarquand 6 77
(Ali Stronge) *hld up in rr-div: prog over 2f out: rdn in centre 2f out: kpt on wl and led 1f out: qcknd clr ins fnl f* **12/1**

033- **2** *4* **Thahab Ifraj (IRE)**[22] 8477 4-9-2 **68** LukeMorris 14 73
(Ismail Mohammed) *hld up in rr: c wd ent st: rdn w plenty to do over 2f out: kpt on wl fr over 1f out to take clr 2nd* **9/4**[1]

040- **3** *2* **Tyrsal (IRE)**[35] 8257 6-8-11 **60** AdamBeschizza 12 62
(Clifford Lines) *in rr-div: rdn along over 2f out: kpt on wl fr over 1f out: one pce fnl f* **16/1**

630- **4** *nk* **Rahmah (IRE)**[62] 7895 5-9-6 **69** JohnFahy 1 70
(Geoffrey Deacon) *t.k.h bhd ldrs on rail: rdn 2f out: ev ch ent fnl f: no ex sn after* **15/2**[2]

000- **5** *1* **Melabi (IRE)**[20] 8498 4-9-4 **70** GeorgeBaker 3 69
(Richard Ford) *in rr: gd run up inner over 2f out: sn rdn and ev ch jst over 1f out: one pce fnl f* **20/1**

000- **6** *3/4* **Marshal Dan Troop (IRE)**[36] 8241 4-8-5 **62** (b[1]) GeorgiaCox(5) 9 60
(Robyn Brisland) *settled bhd ldrs: committed for home ent st and sn led: kpt on wl fr over 1f out: hdd 1f out: no ex* **33/1**

001- **7** *hd* **Moojaned (IRE)**[13] 8567 6-8-0 **56** KatherineGlenister(7) 8 54
(David Evans) *pressed ldr: rdn over 2f out: kpt on one pce tl wknd ins fnl f* **11/1**

244- **8** *hd* **Tempuran**[98] 5208 8-9-2 **68** RobHornby(3) 7 65
(David Bridgwater) *mid-div on outer: rdn over 2f out: no ex fr over 1f out* **16/1**

515- **9** *3 1/4* **Jersey Bull (IRE)**[24] 8448 5-9-1 **64** (h) LiamKeniry 11 58
(Michael Madgwick) *hld up in rr: ct on heels over 2f out and lost ch: shuffled along fr over 1f out* **9/1**[3]

03-0 **10** *7* **Qortaaj**[5] 92 4-9-1 **67** ShaneKelly 4 47
(David Loughnane) *hld up in rr-div: rdn over 2f out: sn lft bhd and no ex fr over 1f out* **12/1**

00-0 **11** *1/2* **Thane Of Cawdor (IRE)**[7] 46 8-8-11 **60** ow1 (v[1]) RobertWinston 5 43
(Joseph Tuite) *settled in mid-div: rdn over 2f out: no imp fr over 1f out* **20/1**

3- **12** *2 1/4* **Wahiba (GER)**[14] 8559 4-9-2 **68** DanielMuscutt 10 43
(Marco Botti) *settled bhd ldrs: rdn and wknd fr 2f out* **9/1**[3]

0/- **13** *9* **Valantino Oyster (IRE)**[453] 5611 10-8-9 **65** (p) JoshuaBryan(7) 2 25
(Ali Stronge) *led on inner: hdd ent st: sn no ex and eased* **100/1**

200- **14** *20* **Speculator**[34] 8282 5-9-3 **66** (p) AdamKirby 13
(John Butler) *settled bhd ldr on outer: niggled along fr 1/2-way: no ex fr 2f out: wknd and eased fr over 1f out: t.o* **14/1**

2m 20.06s (-1.84) **Going Correction** +0.10s/f (Slow)
**WFA** 4 from 5yo+ 2lb **14** Ran SP% **118.1**
Speed ratings (Par 103): **110,107,105,105,104 104,104,103,101,96 96,94,87,73**
CSF £36.79 CT £452.12 TOTE £15.10: £3.80, £1.30, £5.00; EX 51.10 Trifecta £857.50.
**Owner** Shaw Racing 2 & Friends Of Castle Piece **Bred** Mrs Emily Henry **Trained** Eastbury, Berks

**FOCUS**
A fair pace for this modest handicap and it resulted in an easy winner. The runnerup has been rated to form, with the third and fourth close to their recent course form.

## 170 32RED CONDITIONS STKS 6f (P)
**6:15** (6:17) (Class 2) 4-Y-O+ **£11,827** (£3,541; £1,770; £885; £442) **Stalls** Low

Form RPR

205- **1** **Pretend (IRE)**[164] 4916 6-9-2 **111** AdamKirby 1 108+
(Charlie Appleby) *hld up in last: travelling smoothly on inner 2f out: swtchd to outer over 1f out: shkn up and gd prog to chse down ldrs: pushed along and led wl ins fnl f: easily* **11/10**[1]

23-0 **2** *1 1/2* **Gentlemen**[8] 33 6-9-2 **96** (h) CallumShepherd 2 101
(Phil McEntee) *settled in 4th on outer: prog wl over 1f out: led ent fnl f: hdd wl ins fnl f: kpt on one pce* **16/1**

021- **3** *1 1/2* **Spring Loaded (IRE)**[16] 8530 5-9-2 **105** ShaneKelly 3 96
(Paul D'Arcy) *settled in 3rd: travelling wl 2f out on inner: rdn under 1f out: no ex fnl f* **5/4**[2]

235- **4** *1* **Golden Amber (IRE)**[20] 8489 6-8-11 **95** RobertWinston 4 88
(Dean Ivory) *chsd ldr: shkn up over 2f out and pressed ldr fr over 1f out: no ex and wknd ins fnl f* **14/1**[3]

050- **5** *3/4* **Related**[12] 8583 7-9-2 **91** (v) MartinLane 5 91
(Paul Midgley) *sn led: shkn up over 1f out: hdd ent fnl f: no ex sn after and wknd* **40/1**

1m 13.08s (-0.02) **Going Correction** +0.10s/f (Slow) **5** Ran SP% **107.1**
Speed ratings (Par 109): **104,102,100,98,97**
CSF £16.33 TOTE £1.70: £1.20, £4.50; EX 18.00 Trifecta £27.20.
**Owner** Godolphin **Bred** Azienda Agricola Loreto Luciani **Trained** Newmarket, Suffolk

**FOCUS**
Despite the small field this looked a decent enough feature and this form could have a bearing on the AW Championship sprint final. The winner must have recorded some impressive fractions in the straight as he went away from his rivals. It's been rated around the runner-up.

## 171 32RED.COM H'CAP (DIV I) 6f (P)
**6:45** (6:47) (Class 6) (0-65,71) 4-Y-O+ **£2,264** (£673; £336; £168) **Stalls** Low

Form RPR

01-1 **1** **Born To Finish (IRE)**[6] 80 4-9-8 **71** 6ex (p) DavidParkes(5) 9 79+
(Jeremy Gask) *settled in rr-div: shkn up and gd prog fr over 1f out where briefly checked: sn angled to outer: rdn ent fnl f: qcknd up best and led 110yds out: kpt on wl* **7/4**[1]

003- **2** *1* **New Rich**[28] 8365 7-9-5 **63** (b) JohnFahy 6 67
(Eve Johnson Houghton) *hld up in rr-div: rdn over 2f out: kpt on strly fr over 1f out: tk 2nd cl home but no ch w wnr* **8/1**[3]

063- **3** *3/4* **Triple Dream**[11] 8595 12-9-3 **61** GeorgeBaker 7 63
(Milton Bradley) *sn led: pressed for ld fr over 2f out: hdd 110yds out: kpt on one pce and lost 2nd cl home* **12/1**

000- **4** *1/2* **Diamond Charlie (IRE)**[15] 8535 9-9-1 **62** HectorCrouch(3) 3 62
(Simon Dow) *mid-div: swtchd to inner 2f out: sn rdn: kpt on wl and ev ch jst over 1f out: one pce fnl f* **10/1**

100- **5** *nk* **Last Star Falling (IRE)**[28] 8365 4-9-6 **64** (b) StevieDonohoe 1 63
(Henry Spiller) *settled bhd ldr on inner: rdn over 2f out: kpt on one pce* **33/1**

654- **6** *1/2* **Ocean Legend (IRE)**[99] 7048 12-9-0 **58** LukeMorris 5 56
(Tony Carroll) *settled in mid-div: rdn over 2f out: kpt on one pce fr 1f out* **11/1**

041- **7** *1/2* **Major Valentine**[32] 8316 5-9-9 **67** AdamKirby 10 63
(John O'Shea) *settled bhd ldr on outer: disp ld over 2f out: sn rdn: no ex appr fnl f and wknd* **4/1**[2]

600- **8** *3/4* **Virile (IRE)**[14] 8555 6-8-11 **60** (b) MitchGodwin(5) 4 54
(Sylvester Kirk) *settled in mid-div on inner: rdn 2f out: one pce* **9/1**

320- **9** *3/4* **Only Ten Per Cent (IRE)**[49] 8064 9-9-2 **63** AlistairRawlinson(3) 8 55
(J R Jenkins) *half-rrd s: in rr: rdn over 2f out: no imp* **20/1**

064- **10** *3 1/2* **Flowing Clarets**[28] 8357 4-9-5 **63** WilliamCarson 2 44
(John Bridger) *tk fierce hold in 4th: rdn 2f out: sn hld and no ex fr over 1f out* **25/1**

1m 13.01s (-0.09) **Going Correction** +0.10s/f (Slow) **10** Ran SP% **114.1**
Speed ratings (Par 101): **104,102,101,101,100 99,99,98,97,92**
CSF £15.41 CT £128.01 TOTE £2.60: £1.20, £2.90, £2.50; EX 17.00 Trifecta £57.60.
**Owner** Crowd Racing Partnership **Bred** B Kennedy & Mrs Ann Marie Kennedy **Trained** Stockbridge, Hants
■ Stewards' Enquiry : David Parkes three-day ban: careless riding (Jan 25-27)

**FOCUS**
The first division of a run-of-the-mill sprint handicap.

## 172 32RED.COM H'CAP (DIV II) 6f (P)
**7:15** (7:20) (Class 6) (0-65,67) 4-Y-O+ **£2,264** (£673; £336; £168) **Stalls** Low

Form RPR

526- **1** **Compton Prince**[11] 8595 8-9-3 **61** (b) LukeMorris 7 67
(Milton Bradley) *racd in 4th: rdn over 1f out: kpt on wl between horses to ld 1f out: rdn out* **12/1**

00-6 **2** *nk* **Nasri**[5] 88 11-8-8 **52** (v) StevieDonohoe 3 57
(Emma Owen) *in rr: rdn over 2f out: kpt on wl fr over 1f out: nt get to wnr* **12/1**

503- **3** *1* **Tango Sky (IRE)**[21] 8483 8-9-5 **63** AdamKirby 5 65
(Paul Midgley) *settled in mid-div: rdn 2f out: kpt on one pce fnl f* **8/1**[3]

502- **4** *nk* **Rigolleto (IRE)**[57] 7964 9-9-9 **67** (p) GeorgeBaker 1 68
(Anabel K Murphy) *sn led: rdn over 1f out: kpt on wl tl hdd 1f out: wknd after* **11/4**[1]

01- **5** *1* **Monsieur Paddy**[33] 8290 4-9-5 **63** JoeyHaynes 2 61
(Tony Carroll) *racd in mid-div: rdn 2f out: kpt on wl fr over 1f out: no ex ins fnl f* **7/1**[2]

440- **6** *1/2* **Fleeting Glimpse**[32] 8320 4-8-8 **59** (t[1]) JoshuaBryan(7) 9 56
(Andrew Balding) *uns rdr on way to post: reluctant after and walked to s: t.k.h in rr: rdn 2f out: no imp on ldrs* **9/1**

105- **7** *nk* **Firesnake (IRE)**[28] 8365 4-8-10 **61** (p) JordanUys(7) 4 57
(Lisa Williamson) *settled bhd ldr: rdn 2f out: kpt on one pce* **10/1**

500- **8** *3/4* **Jack The Laird (IRE)**[15] 8535 4-9-5 **63** (bt) RobertWinston 8 57
(Dean Ivory) *settled bhd ldr on outer: rdn over 1f out: wknd after* **7/1**[2]

001- **9** *3/4* **Red Invader (IRE)**[149] 5470 7-9-7 **65** LiamKeniry 6 56
(John Butler) *a in rr: sme prog fnl f* **8/1**[3]

000- **10** *3/4* **Sehayli (IRE)**[14] 8555 4-8-13 **62** PaddyBradley(5) 10 51
(Lee Carter) *in rr: rdn along 2f out: no ex ent fnl f* **25/1**

1m 12.95s (-0.15) **Going Correction** +0.10s/f (Slow) **10** Ran SP% **112.2**
Speed ratings (Par 101): **105,104,103,102,101 100,100,99,98,97**
CSF £141.23 CT £1216.12 TOTE £10.60: £3.20, £3.90, £1.90; EX 139.70 Trifecta £1384.80.
**Owner** E A Hayward **Bred** Whitsbury Manor Stud **Trained** Sedbury, Gloucs
■ Stewards' Enquiry : Luke Morris two-day ban (26-27 Jan): used whip above shoulder height

**FOCUS**
The second division may have been marginally stronger and quicker, but it's still modest form. Straightforward form rated around the second, third and fourth.

## 173 100% PROFIT BOOST AT 32REDSPORT.COM AMATEUR RIDERS' H'CAP 1m 3f 219y(P)
**7:45** (7:47) (Class 4) (0-85,87) 4-Y-O+ **£4,523** (£1,402; £701; £350) **Stalls** Centre

Form RPR

254- **1** **Sennockian Star**[11] 8594 7-10-13 **84** MrAlexFerguson 9 90
(Mark Johnston) *racd in 3rd: tk clsr order over 3f out: upsides ldr and gng wl over 1f out: shkn up and sn led: kpt on wl ins fnl f: comf* **5/1**[3]

335- **2** *1 1/4* **Alcatraz (IRE)**[35] 8249 5-10-3 **77** (tp) MaxKendrick(3) 4 81
(George Baker) *t.k.h in rr: rdn over 2f out: kpt on wl on inner fr over 1f out: nvr nrr* **4/1**[2]

023- **3** *3/4* **Take Two**[42] 8161 8-9-7 **71** MrJBrace(7) 8 74
(Alex Hales) *s.s: sn in tch: rdn over 2f out: no imp tl kpt on wl ins fnl f* **12/1**

110- **4** *shd* **Ickymasho**[135] 5963 5-10-10 **84** MrJHarding(3) 7 87
(Jonathan Portman) *led after 2f: rdn wl over 1f out: sn hdd and kpt on one pce fnl f* **14/1**

240- **5** *1 1/2* **Golden Jubilee (USA)**[35] 8249 8-10-6 **77** (p) MrZBaker 1 77
(Nigel Twiston-Davies) *led early tl hdd after 2f: remained bhd ldr: rdn over 2f out: kpt on one pce after* **33/1**

656- **6** *shd* **Safira Menina**[22] 8476 5-9-11 **73** MrBJames(5) 2 73
(Martin Smith) *hld up in rr: rdn over 2f out: no imp on ldrs* **12/1**

046- **7** *3/4* **High Baroque (USA)**[16] 8529 5-11-0 **85** ThomasGreatrex 5 84
(Richard Fahey) *racd in 4th: rdn over 2f out: no ex fr over 1f out and wknd* **11/4**[1]

13-6 **8** *8* **Cape Discovery**[7] 38 5-10-8 **84** MrJamiePerrett(5) 3 70
(Richard Hughes) *a in rr: lost tch fr over 2f out: sn hld* **11/4**[1]

2m 35.56s (1.06) **Going Correction** +0.10s/f (Slow)
**WFA** 4 from 5yo+ 3lb **8** Ran SP% **115.0**
Speed ratings (Par 105): **100,99,98,98,97 97,97,91**
CSF £25.46 CT £226.96 TOTE £6.00: £1.50, £1.50, £2.50; EX 24.60 Trifecta £115.10.
**Owner** Kingsley Park 7 - Ready To Run **Bred** Cheveley Park Stud Ltd **Trained** Middleham Moor, N Yorks

**FOCUS**
An above average race in terms of amateur rider handicaps. It's been rated around the winner to his recent form.
T/Plt: £120.20 to a £1 stake. Pool: £83,840.47 - 508.76 winning units T/Qpdt: £45.80 to a £1 stake. Pool: £11,168.70 - 180.42 winning units **Cathal Gahan**

# [40]NEWCASTLE (A.W) (L-H)
Wednesday, January 11

**OFFICIAL GOING: Tapeta: standard**
Wind: Fairly strong, against Weather: Fine, dry

## 174 BETWAY AMATEUR RIDERS' H'CAP 1m 4f 98y (Tp)
**2:00** (2:01) (Class 6) (0-65,65) 4-Y-O+ **£2,183** (£677; £338; £169) **Stalls** High

Form RPR

004- **1** **Genres**[12] 8586 5-10-11 **62** MrSWalker 6 72+
(Alan Swinbank) *t.k.h: hld up: smooth hdwy on outside over 2f out: edgd lft and shkn up to ld appr fnl f: pushed clr: comf* **5/4**[1]

**2** *3 1/4* **Temasek Star (IRE)**[26] 8419 6-11-0 **65** (p) MrJCBarry 1 69
(Anthony McCann, Ire) *trckd ldrs: nt clr run and swtchd rt appr 2f out: effrt and chsd wnr 1f out: kpt on fnl f: nt pce to chal* **6/1**[2]

662- **3** *1/2* **Surround Sound**[214] 3154 7-10-5 **56** (t) MrWEasterby 5 59
(Tim Easterby) *dwlt: hld up: stdy hdwy over 2f out: shkn up over 1f out: kpt on ins fnl f: nrst fin* **18/1**

310- **4** *hd* **Glasgon**[55] 7992 7-9-11 **53** MissAMcCain(5) 3 56
(Ray Craggs) *prom: pushed along and outpcd 2f out: rallied fnl f: kpt on fin* **33/1**

50-5 **5** *2* **Miss Tree**[6] 70 6-9-13 **53** MrHHunt(3) 2 53
(John Quinn) *pressed ldr: led over 2f out to over 1f out: outpcd ins fnl f* **8/1**[3]

054- **6** *6* **Sennockian Song**[32] 8318 4-9-13 **59** MissEmmaBedford(5) 10 50+
(Mark Johnston) *led and sn crossed to ins rail: rdn and hdd over 2f out: rallied: wknd fnl f* **6/1**[2]

430- **7** *2 3/4* **Sherman McCoy**[44] 8134 11-10-8 **62** (p) MissBeckySmith(3) 11 49
(Marjorie Fife) *hld up in tch on outside: stdy hdwy to chse ldrs 1/2-way: rdn and outpcd 2f out: sn n.d* **66/1**

000- **8** *1 1/4* **Ralphy Lad (IRE)**[22] 8477 6-10-6 **60** RachaelMcDonald(3) 9 45
(Alan Swinbank) *dwlt: t.k.h in rr: shortlived effrt over 2f out: sn no imp: btn over 1f out* **11/1**

530- **9** *nk* **Swiss Lait**[12] 8586 6-9-11 **51** MissAWaugh(3) 7 36
(Patrick Holmes) *missed break: hld up: hdwy on outside and in tch over 3f out: rdn and wknd wl over 1f out* **33/1**

000- **10** *1 1/4* **Devious Spirit (IRE)**[12] 8586 5-10-2 **58** MrBLynn(5) 8 41
(Iain Jardine) *in tch: rdn and outpcd over 2f out: btn over 1f out* **10/1**

25-1 **11** *5* **Jan Smuts (IRE)**[8] 28 9-10-9 **63** 6ex....................(t) MissSMDoolan(3) 4 38
(Wilf Storey) *dwlt: t.k.h: in tch: rdn and outpcd over 2f out: sn btn* **16/1**

2m 44.12s (3.02) **Going Correction** +0.35s/f (Slow)
**WFA** 4 from 5yo+ 3lb **11** Ran SP% **120.1**
Speed ratings (Par 101): **103,100,100,100,99 95,93,92,92,91 88**
CSF £8.96 CT £96.26 TOTE £2.10: £1.30, £1.90, £3.80; EX 11.10 Trifecta £48.80.
**Owner** Brian Valentine **Bred** Millsec Limited **Trained** Melsonby, N Yorks

**FOCUS**
As was the case a week earlier there was a stiff headwind facing runners. Harrowing of the surface dictated it was likely to ride somewhat slower than standard too. This moderate handicap, confined to amateur riders, was run at a fair enough pace. Okay form for the level.

## 175 32RED.COM MAIDEN STKS 1m 2f 42y (Tp)
**2:30** (2:30) (Class 5) 3-4-Y-O **£3,234** (£962; £481; £240) **Stalls** High

Form RPR

223- **1** **Doctor Bartolo (IRE)**[30] 8340 3-8-7 **76**.............................. JoeFanning 6 81+
(Charles Hills) *hld up: smooth hdwy on outside to ld over 1f out: sn qcknd clr and drifted to far rail: easily* **9/4**[1]

3- **2** *3 ¼* **Bowban**[15] 8537 3-8-7 0.......................................................... TomEaves 3 72
(Brian Ellison) *in tch: effrt and rdn over 2f out: chsd (clr) wnr 1f out: kpt on fnl f: nt pce to chal* **5/2**[2]

**3** *1 ½* **Sugarloaf Mountain (IRE)**[84] 7479 4-10-0 0...................... DaleSwift 9 72
(Brian Ellison) *s.i.s: sn cl up: led 1/2-way: rdn and hdd over 1f out: kpt on same pce fnl f* **25/1**

220- **4** *1 ¾* **Vantage Point (IRE)**[60] 7940 3-8-7 **78**........................(p[1]) NickyMackay 7 66
(John Gosden) *t.k.h: chsd ldrs: wnt 2nd over 3f out: effrt and rdn wl over 1f out: outpcd fnl f* **7/2**[3]

4- **5** *½* **Mesophere**[47] 8089 3-8-7 0................................................ RobertHavlin 8 65
(John Gosden) *hld up midfield: rdn and outpcd 3f out: rallied and hung lft over 1f out: plugged on fnl f: no imp* **9/4**[1]

54- **6** *5* **Psychology**[21] 8481 4-10-0 0........................................ DougieCostello 10 58
(Kenny Johnson) *slowly away: hld up in last pl: smooth hdwy on outside over 1f out: shkn up briefly and hung lft ins fnl f: nvr nr to chal* **100/1**

50- **7** *6* **Rainbow Chimes (IRE)**[47] 8089 3-7-11 0..................... HollieDoyle(5) 1 38
(Ann Duffield) *trckd ldrs: rdn over 3f out: wknd over 2f out* **100/1**

**8** *3* **Archibelle** 3-8-0 0 ow1.................................................. NathanEvans(3) 2 33
(R Mike Smith) *hld up on ins: drvn along 3f out: struggling fnl 2f* **80/1**

05- **9** *4 ½* **Medici Moon**[36] 8237 3-8-7 0......................................... JamesSullivan 4 28
(Scott Dixon) *t.k.h: led to 1/2-way: cl up tl rdn and wknd over 2f out* **100/1**

060- **10** *3 ¼* **Mystic Maeve (IRE)**[47] 8087 3-8-2 **48**.......................(p) AndrewMullen 5 16
(Roger Fell) *hld up: rdn over 3f out: wknd over 2f out* **100/1**

2m 12.3s (1.90) **Going Correction** +0.35s/f (Slow)
**WFA** 3 from 4yo 23lb **10** Ran SP% **121.4**
Speed ratings (Par 103): **106,103,102,100,100 96,91,89,85,83**
CSF £8.68 TOTE £3.20: £1.10, £1.10, £6.90; EX 9.70 Trifecta £152.30.
**Owner** W Carson, C Corbett, M Gibbens, C Wright **Bred** Tally-Ho Stud **Trained** Lambourn, Berks

**FOCUS**
They went a sound early pace in this modest 3yo maiden. With the headwind it would have been quite a test. An improved effort from the winner and progress from the runner-up.

## 176 DOWNLOAD THE BETWAY APP H'CAP 1m 2f 42y (Tp)
**3:00** (3:03) (Class 7) (0-50,56) 4-Y-O+ **£1,704** (£503; £251) **Stalls** High

Form RPR

04-6 **1** **Spirit Of The Vale (IRE)**[4] 121 4-9-1 **46**......................(t[1]) KevinStott 14 55
(Oliver Greenall) *hld up in last pl: pushed along over 2f out: effrt and swtchd to outside over 1f out: led and drifted lft ins fnl f: kpt on wl* **5/1**[1]

040- **2** *2* **Highway Robber**[27] 8386 4-8-13 **49**............................... HollieDoyle(5) 9 54+
(Wilf Storey) *prom: wnt 2nd 4f out: led over 2f out to ins fnl f: kpt on same pce* **13/2**[3]

045- **3** *¾* **Lord Rob**[68] 7794 6-8-13 **45**.......................................... NathanEvans(3) 10 49
(David Thompson) *hld up: hdwy on outside to press ldr over 1f out: sn rdn and edgd lft: ch ins fnl f: one pce last 75yds* **6/1**[2]

006/ **4** *5* **Tenhoo**[435] 7687 11-8-10 **46**......................................... CallumRodriguez(7) 1 41
(Richard Ford) *prom: rdn and outpcd over 2f out: rallied fnl f: no ch w clr ldng trio* **10/1**

20-1 **5** *1 ½* **Outlaw Torn (IRE)**[4] 123 8-9-6 **56** 6ex................(e) LewisEdmunds(7) 2 48+
(Richard Guest) *t.k.h: led: clr after 4f: rdn and hdd over 2f out: wknd fnl f* **5/1**[1]

000- **6** *1* **Patron Of Explores (USA)**[32] 8306 6-9-2 **45**.............(t) JamesSullivan 3 36
(Patrick Holmes) *missed break: t.k.h in rr: effrt over 2f out: sn no imp* **33/1**

0/0- **7** *nk* **Southview Lady**[68] 7795 5-9-0 **46**......................... RachelRichardson(3) 4 36
(Sean Regan) *chsd ldrs: rdn over 2f out: sn outpcd: no imp fr over 1f out* **33/1**

045- **8** *1* **First Of Never (IRE)**[40] 7991 11-9-2 **45**........................... PaddyAspell 8 33
(Lynn Siddall) *hld up: stdy hdwy over 2f out: shkn up and edgd lft over 1f out: nvr able to chal* **33/1**

250- **9** *½* **Thatsthewaytodoit (IRE)**[22] 8471 4-9-5 **50**........................ DaleSwift 7 37
(Daniel Mark Loughnane) *hld up in tch: hdwy to press ldrs over 2f out: sn rdn and edgd lft: wknd appr fnl f* **7/1**

000- **10** *1 ¾* **Moccasin (FR)**[20] 8497 8-9-2 **45**.......................................(v) SamJames 5 29
(Geoffrey Harker) *hld up on ins: pushed along and outpcd 3f out: n.d after* **13/2**[3]

650- **11** *6* **The Big Day (IRE)**[12] 8589 4-9-5 **50**........................... AndrewMullen 13 23
(Nigel Tinkler) *hld up midfield: rdn along over 2f out: wknd wl over 1f out* **33/1**

006- **12** *hd* **Don't Tell Nik (IRE)**[224] 2804 4-8-7 **45**.................... BenSanderson(7) 11 18
(Roger Fell) *hld up: rdn along 3f out: btn fnl 2f* **50/1**

505- **13** *½* **Stanlow**[12] 8589 7-9-2 **45**...................................................(v) TomEaves 6 17
(Michael Mullineaux) *in tch: drvn and outpcd over 2f out: btn over 1f out* **16/1**

503- **14** *15* **Troy Boy**[90] 7300 7-8-11 **45**..........................................(b) RowanScott(5) 12
(Rebecca Bastiman) *chsd ldr to 4f out: rdn and wknd over 2f out: t.o* **25/1**

2m 13.8s (3.40) **Going Correction** +0.35s/f (Slow)
**WFA** 4 from 5yo+ 1lb **14** Ran SP% **119.3**
Speed ratings (Par 97): **100,98,97,93,92 91,91,90,90,88 84,84,83,71**
CSF £34.12 CT £202.72 TOTE £6.60: £2.10, £2.80, £2.30; EX 46.90 Trifecta £223.00.
**Owner** D B Salmon, Mrs L Salmon & M W Salmon **Bred** Tinnakill Bloodstock **Trained** Oldcastle Heath, Cheshire

**FOCUS**
A bottom-drawer handicap but it's not that bad form for the grade.

## 177 SUN BETS CONDITIONS STKS (PLUS 10 RACE) 1m 5y (Tp)
**3:30** (3:32) (Class 3) 3-Y-O **£7,762** (£2,310; £1,154; £577) **Stalls** Centre

Form RPR

1- **1** **Brittanic (IRE)**[27] 8384 3-9-2 0............................................ TomEaves 1 101+
(David Simcock) *stdd in tch: smooth hdwy over 1f out: led on bit ins fnl f: nudged along briefly and sn qcknd clr: promising* **2/1**[2]

1- **2** *1 ¾* **Ay Ay (IRE)**[14] 8556 3-9-2 **74**..................................... MartinHarley 4 92
(David Elsworth) *t.k.h early: trckd ldng pair: rdn: effrt and edgd lft over 1f out: wnt 2nd wl ins fnl f: kpt on: no ch w ready wnr* **3/1**[3]

552- **3** *½* **Mailshot (USA)**[16] 8525 3-9-2 **90**.................................. JoeFanning 2 91
(Mark Johnston) *led at ordinary gallop: rdn along over 1f out: hdd ins fnl f: sn one pce* **13/8**[1]

501- **4** *4 ½* **Mr Scaramanga**[25] 8423 3-9-2 **99**....................................... JFEgan 5 81
(Simon Dow) *t.k.h: pressed ldr: rdn over 2f out: lost 2nd over 1f out: wknd fnl f* **13/2**

1m 45.5s (6.90) **Going Correction** +0.35s/f (Slow) **4** Ran SP% **109.8**
Speed ratings (Par 101): **79,77,76,72**
CSF £8.16 TOTE £4.00; EX 11.60 Trifecta £23.10.
**Owner** Never Say Die Partnership **Bred** Fountain Syn & Flaxman Stables **Trained** Newmarket, Suffolk

**FOCUS**
An interesting little 3yo conditions event. It proved a sound test. The first two have been rated as improving from their debut wins.

## 178 32RED CASINO H'CAP 6f (Tp)
**4:00** (4:02) (Class 5) (0-75,76) 3-Y-O **£3,234** (£962; £481; £240) **Stalls** Centre

Form RPR

342- **1** **Golden Opportunity**[13] 8569 3-9-6 **70**........................... MartinHarley 5 77
(James Tate) *t.k.h early: in tch: smooth hdwy over 1f out: shkn up to ld ins fnl f: sn rdn: kpt on wl* **5/2**[1]

204- **2** *1* **Marquee Club**[23] 8453 3-9-12 **76**.................................. TimmyMurphy 2 80
(Jamie Osborne) *trckd ldrs: wnt 2nd gng wl over 2f out: shkn up and ev ch briefly ins fnl f: checked and kpt on same pce last 75yds* **3/1**[2]

260- **3** *3* **Ninety Years Young**[14] 8560 3-8-11 **66**.......................(b) HollieDoyle(5) 4 60
(David Elsworth) *led: rdn over 2f out: edgd lft and hdd ins fnl f: sn outpcd* **5/2**[1]

615- **4** *10* **Killermont Street (IRE)**[12] 8582 3-9-7 **71**......................... JoeFanning 3 33
(Mark Johnston) *dwlt: in tch: rdn and hung lft over 2f out: wknd wl over 1f out* **11/2**[3]

454- **5** *4 ½* **Skellig Michael**[77] 7615 3-8-8 **58**.................................. JamesSullivan 6 6
(Ben Haslam) *bhd: rdn and outpcd over 3f out: nvr on terms* **9/1**

50-0 **6** *¾* **Elements Legacy**[6] 73 3-8-4 **57**.........................(p[1]) JordanVaughan(3) 1
(K R Burke) *chsd ldr to over 2f out: sn rdn and wknd* **25/1**

1m 15.32s (2.82) **Going Correction** +0.35s/f (Slow) **6** Ran SP% **111.4**
Speed ratings (Par 97): **95,93,89,76,70 69**
CSF £10.12 TOTE £3.00: £1.40, £1.60; EX 11.60 Trifecta £19.10.
**Owner** Saeed Manana **Bred** R E Crutchley **Trained** Newmarket, Suffolk

**FOCUS**
An ordinary 3yo sprint handicap, run at a routine pace. The runner-up has been rated to form for now.

## 179 £10 FREE AT 32RED.COM H'CAP 5f (Tp)
**4:30** (4:30) (Class 6) (0-60,62) 3-Y-O **£2,264** (£673; £336; £168) **Stalls** Centre

Form RPR

53-4 **1** **Royal Celebration**[7] 41 3-8-11 **53**........................... NathanEvans(3) 7 59
(Bryan Smart) *prom: smooth hdwy to ld over 1f out: sn rdn: kpt on wl fnl f* **2/1**[2]

543- **2** *1* **Snuggy (IRE)**[22] 8467 3-9-2 **62**............................... LewisEdmunds(7) 2 64
(David Barron) *hld up: hdwy on far side of gp to chse wnr over 1f out: kpt on same pce ins fnl f* **11/8**[1]

020- **3** *1 ¼* **Local Artist (IRE)**[95] 7143 3-9-7 **60**................................. JasonHart 1 58
(John Quinn) *tk keen hold: hld up in tch: hdwy to chse ldrs over 1f out: kpt on same pce ins fnl f* **16/1**

000- **4** *1 ¼* **Little Kingdom (IRE)**[47] 8089 3-9-1 **54**.............................. DaleSwift 8 47
(Tracy Waggott) *hld up in tch: pushed along over 2f out: hdwy nr side of gp over 1f out: kpt on same pce ins fnl f* **14/1**

004- **5** *1 ¼* **Affordability**[15] 8536 3-9-5 **58**......................................... JoeFanning 3 47
(Daniel Mark Loughnane) *trckd ldrs: rdn and wnt 2nd over 2f out to over 1f out: wknd ins fnl f* **6/1**[3]

050- **6** *4 ½* **Cool Run Girl (IRE)**[79] 7579 3-9-0 **53**......................... PJMcDonald 5 25
(Iain Jardine) *pressed ldr to over 2f out: sn drvn: wknd over 1f out* **14/1**

004- **7** *1 ½* **Flying Hope (IRE)**[119] 6471 3-8-12 **51**............................. TomEaves 4 18
(Nigel Tinkler) *led to over 1f out: sn wknd* **25/1**

1m 2.45s (2.95) **Going Correction** +0.35s/f (Slow) **7** Ran SP% **112.8**
Speed ratings (Par 95): **90,88,86,84,82 75,72**
CSF £4.95 CT £28.25 TOTE £3.40: £1.70, £1.10; EX 4.90 Trifecta £27.30.
**Owner** The Smart Set **Bred** Alvediston Stud & Partners **Trained** Hambleton, N Yorks

**FOCUS**
A moderate 3yo sprint handicap, run at a fair pace.
T/Plt: £68.80 to a £1 stake. Pool: £68,328.78 - 724.13 winning units T/Qpdt: £16.80 to a £1 stake. Pool: £5,153.12 - 226.45 winning units **Richard Young**

180 - 187a (Foreign Racing) - See Raceform Interactive

# 61 CHELMSFORD (A.W) (L-H)
Thursday, January 12

**188 Meeting Abandoned - Snow**

# 174 NEWCASTLE (A.W) (L-H)
Thursday, January 12

**OFFICIAL GOING: Tapeta: standard**
Wind: Fresh, half against Weather: Overcast

## 194 BETWAY SPRINT H'CAP 5f (Tp)
**2:00** (2:00) (Class 4) (0-85,90) 4-Y-O+ **£5,822** (£1,732; £865; £432) **Stalls** Centre

Form RPR

146- **1** **Rich Again (IRE)**[13] 8583 8-9-2 **80**..................................(b) JoeFanning 3 89
(James Bethell) *s.i.s: hld up: hdwy on wd outside over 1f out: shkn up to ld ins fnl f: sn rdn: kpt on wl* **6/1**[3]

600- **2** ½ **Burning Thread (IRE)**[43] 8150 10-8-9 **73**.........................(b) ShaneKelly 2 80
(David Elsworth) *hld up in tch: effrt and hdwy over 1f out: chsd wnr ins fnl f: kpt on* **33/1**

55-1 **3** 2 **Tatlisu (IRE)**[9] 33 7-9-12 **90** 6ex.................................... TonyHamilton 5 90
(Richard Fahey) *hld up: pushed along and hdwy over 1f out: chsd ldng pair last 30yds: kpt on: nt pce to chal* **5/2**[1]

40-2 **4** ¾ **September Issue**[6] 93 4-8-13 **77**.................................(b[1]) LukeMorris 8 75
(Gay Kelleway) *prom: effrt and chsd ldr briefly 2f out: one pce whn nt carried rt and nt clr run ins fnl f: fin 5th: promoted to 4th* **11/4**[2]

25-5 **5** ½ **Archie Stevens**[7] 71 7-8-7 **71** oh1........................................... JFEgan 1 69
(David Evans) *t.k.h early: led: rdn over 1f out: drifted rt and hdd ins fnl f: no ex: fin 4th: plcd 5th* **18/1**

304- **6** ¾ **Red Stripes (USA)**[14] 8571 5-8-4 **71** oh2..............(b) JordanVaughan[(3)] 4 64
(Lisa Williamson) *chsd ldrs: rdn and edgd lft over 1f out: outpcd fnl f* **25/1**

30-5 **7** 1¼ **Fredricka**[8] 45 6-8-9 **73**................................................ AndrewMullen 6 64
(David Barron) *hld up: effrt and hdwy over 1f out: no imp whn nt clr run ins fnl f* **7/1**

240- **8** ½ **Gorokai (IRE)**[58] 7965 4-8-12 **76**............................................ TomEaves 9 62
(David Simcock) *chsd ldr to 2f out: sn rdn and wknd* **8/1**

320- **9** 3½ **Intibaah**[13] 8583 7-9-7 **85**..............................................(p) RobertWinston 7 59
(George Baker) *hld up: rdn along wl over 1f out: sn wknd* **12/1**

1m 0.5s (1.00) **Going Correction** +0.35s/f (Slow) 9 Ran SP% **112.9**
Speed ratings (Par 105): **106,105,102,100,101 98,96,96,90**
CSF £168.52 CT £615.26 TOTE £7.30: £2.40, £6.80, £1.10; EX 112.60 Trifecta £749.20.
**Owner** Richard T Vickers **Bred** Mrs Sandra Maye **Trained** Middleham Moor, N Yorks
■ Stewards' Enquiry : J F Egan jockey ban: three day ban (26-28th Jan) - guilty of careless riding

**FOCUS**
A useful sprint handicap and they went a good pace, with the winner coming from last to first. The winner has been rated back to his old best.

## 195 BETWAY MAIDEN STKS 1m 4f 98y (Tp)
**2:30** (2:31) (Class 5) 4-Y-O+ **£3,557** (£1,058; £529; £264) **Stalls** High

Form RPR

04- **1** **Persian Steel (IRE)**[13] 8585 5-9-2 0........................... BenRobinson[(7)] 4 75
(Brian Ellison) *hld up: shkn up and hdwy to ld over 2f out: pushed out fnl f* **66/1**

**2** 2½ **After Tonight (FR)**[30] 7-9-9 0...................................... ConnorBeasley 1 71
(Keith Reveley) *hld up: hdwy over 2f out: chsd wnr ins fnl f: kpt on: nt pce to chal* **14/1**

2- **3** 3 **Codeshare**[13] 8585 5-9-9 0................................................... JoeFanning 6 66
(Alan Swinbank) *t.k.h early: trckd ldrs: smooth hdwy and ev ch over 2f out: sn rdn: lost 2nd and no ex ins fnl f* **7/4**[1]

222- **4** 3 **Henry Croft**[33] 8310 4-9-5 81............................................... LukeMorris 7 61
(Tony Carroll) *t.k.h: led tl hdd and outpcd over 2f out: rallied fnl f: no imp* **7/4**[1]

**5** *shd* **Im Waiting (IRE)**[55] 8021 4-9-0 64..............................(p[1]) MartinHarley 2 56
(Anthony McCann, Ire) *hld up in tch on ins: pushed along and outpcd over 2f out: no imp fr over 1f out* **11/1**[3]

06-4 **6** 9 **Page Of Wands**[9] 29 4-9-0 54.........................................(v) TomEaves 3 42
(Karen McLintock) *prom: drvn along over 4f out: rallied: wknd fr over 1f out* **25/1**

303- **7** 2½ **Summer Collection (IRE)**[22] 8480 4-8-11 67......... JordanVaughan[(3)] 8 38
(K R Burke) *t.k.h: pressed ldr to over 2f out: sn rdn and wknd* **4/1**[2]

63-0 **8** *nk* **Palindrome (USA)**[9] 28 4-9-5 65..................................(b[1]) ShaneGray 5 42
(Ronald Thompson) *bmpd s: hld up: rdn along over 2f out: wknd wl over 1f out* **50/1**

2m 41.68s (0.58) **Going Correction** +0.35s/f (Slow)
**WFA** 4 from 5yo+ 3lb 8 Ran SP% **115.0**
Speed ratings (Par 103): **112,110,108,106,106 100,98,98**
CSF £771.17 TOTE £38.70: £9.80, £3.20, £1.30; EX 622.60 Trifecta £916.80.
**Owner** Mrs J A Martin **Bred** Mrs James Wigan & London TB Services Ltd **Trained** Norton, N Yorks

**FOCUS**
An ordinary maiden and a shock winner. The third has been rated close to his debut effort.

## 196 BETWAY MARATHON H'CAP 2m 56y (Tp)
**3:00** (3:00) (Class 4) (0-80,82) 4-Y-O+ **£5,822** (£1,732; £865; £432) **Stalls** Low

Form RPR

221- **1** **Isharah (USA)**[13] 8584 4-9-12 **82**........................................ JoeFanning 6 90
(Mark Johnston) *t.k.h early: trckd ldrs: smooth hdwy to ld over 2f out: hrd pressed and rdn over 1f out: styd on strly fnl f* **10/11**[1]

252- **2** 1¼ **Zakatal**[27] 8399 11-10-5 **82**........................................... DougieCostello 7 88
(Rebecca Menzies) *hld up in tch: smooth hdwy to press wnr over 2f out: effrt and ev ch over 1f out: sn rdn: kpt on same pce last 100yds* **12/1**

62-0 **3** 1¾ **River Dart (IRE)**[8] 38 5-10-0 **77**........................................ LukeMorris 2 81
(Tony Carroll) *hld up: hdwy to chse ldrs over 2f out: sn rdn: kpt on same pce ins fnl f* **10/1**[3]

000- **4** ¾ **Royal Flag**[13] 8586 7-8-12 **61**..................................................(p) TomEaves 9 64
(Brian Ellison) *hld up in last pl: rdn and hdwy on outside over 2f out: kpt on ins fnl f* **22/1**

616- **5** *hd* **Mister Bob (GER)**[27] 8399 8-9-13 **76**.........................(p) TonyHamilton 4 79
(James Bethell) *hld up: stdy hdwy over 2f out: rdn and hung lft over 1f out: sn one pce* **6/1**[2]

306/ **6** 2 **Wrap Star (IRE)**[20] 8514 6-9-7 **70**..................................(vt) MartinHarley 3 70
(Anthony McCann, Ire) *dwlt: hld up in tch: smooth hdwy to chse ldrs over 2f out: sn rdn: outpcd fnl f* **6/1**[2]

04-0 **7** 13 **Wordiness**[9] 28 9-9-5 **68**.............................................(p[1]) AndrewMullen 5 53
(David Evans) *pressed ldr tl edgd rt over 2f out: rdn and wknd fr 2f out* **14/1**

0/4- **8** 6 **Mister Fizz**[302] 838 9-9-11 **77**.................................(p) NathanEvans[(3)] 8 55
(Miss Imogen Pickard) *led to over 2f out: sn rdn and wknd* **40/1**

560- **9** 14 **Grand Meister**[27] 8399 6-9-6 **76**........................................ JoshQuinn[(7)] 1 37
(John Quinn) *t.k.h early: trckd ldrs: rdn and outpcd over 2f out: sn wknd* **40/1**

3m 39.13s (3.93) **Going Correction** +0.35s/f (Slow)
**WFA** 4 from 5yo+ 5lb 9 Ran SP% **113.6**
Speed ratings (Par 105): **104,103,102,102,102 101,94,91,84**
CSF £12.80 CT £67.37 TOTE £2.20: £1.20, £2.30, £3.00; EX 9.40 Trifecta £57.90.
**Owner** Abdulla Al Mansoori **Bred** M Buckley, M Buckley & K L Ramsey **Trained** Middleham Moor, N Yorks

**FOCUS**
A fair handicap run at an ordinary pace. Muddling form.

## 197 BETWAY H'CAP 1m 4f 98y (Tp)
**3:30** (3:30) (Class 2) (0-105,103) 4-Y-O+ **£12,938** (£3,850; £1,924; £962) **Stalls** High

Form RPR

123- **1** **Natural Scenery**[12] 8594 4-8-10 **91**........................ JosephineGordon 6 99+
(Saeed bin Suroor) *t.k.h early: trckd ldrs: shkn up and hdwy to ld 1f out: rdn out fnl f* **1/1**[1]

042- **2** ½ **Masterpaver**[13] 8584 6-8-10 **87**........................................ TonyHamilton 5 94
(Richard Fahey) *pressed ldr: rdn and led 2f out: hdd 1f out: rallied: hld nr fin* **7/1**[3]

021- **3** 2 **Watersmeet**[40] 8210 6-9-12 **103**.......................................... JoeFanning 3 107
(Mark Johnston) *led: rdn and hdd 2f out: rallied: kpt on same pce appr fnl f* **13/2**[2]

306- **4** *hd* **Royal Marskell**[12] 8594 8-8-11 **88**........................................ LukeMorris 8 91
(Gay Kelleway) *hld up: hdwy on outside over 2f out: sn rdn: kpt on same pce fnl f* **20/1**

052- **5** 3 **Barye**[26] 8424 6-9-11 **102**................................................... ShaneKelly 2 101
(Richard Hughes) *hld up in tch: effrt and pushed along over 2f out: no imp fr over 1f out* **7/1**[3]

500- **6** *nk* **Winterlude (IRE)**[17] 8529 7-9-5 **96**...................................... DavidNolan 4 94
(Jennie Candlish) *hld up in tch: pushed along over 2f out: sn no imp* **10/1**

210- **7** *hd* **Top Of The Glas (IRE)**[76] 5837 6-8-0 **84** oh3............ BenRobinson[(7)] 1 82
(Brian Ellison) *t.k.h early: trckd ldrs: rdn and outpcd over 2f out: n.d after* **14/1**

400- **8** *nse* **Castilo Del Diablo (IRE)**[17] 8529 8-8-11 **88**...................(p) TomEaves 7 86
(David Simcock) *hld up: rdn and outpcd over 2f out: rallied fnl f: nvr on terms* **22/1**

2m 39.54s (-1.56) **Going Correction** +0.35s/f (Slow)
**WFA** 4 from 6yo+ 3lb 8 Ran SP% **113.2**
Speed ratings (Par 109): **119,118,117,117,115 115,114,114**
CSF £8.29 CT £30.01 TOTE £1.90: £1.10, £2.20, £2.10; EX 11.00 Trifecta £35.80.
**Owner** Godolphin **Bred** Darley **Trained** Newmarket, Suffolk

**FOCUS**
A strong handicap, featuring several AW specialists, and smart form. The runner-up has been rated as running his best race since June 2015.

## 198 32RED.COM MAIDEN STKS 1m 5y (Tp)
**4:00** (4:00) (Class 5) 3-Y-O+ **£5,175** (£1,540; £769; £384) **Stalls** Centre

Form RPR

0- **1** **Moamar**[21] 8486 3-8-8 0............................................................ TomEaves 9 67+
(Ed Dunlop) *upset in stalls: hld up in tch: smooth hdwy over 2f out: shkn up to ld over 1f out: drvn and edgd lft ins fnl f: kpt on wl* **3/1**[2]

0 **2** ½ **Crindle Carr (IRE)**[8] 40 3-8-8 0......................................... AndrewMullen 8 66
(David Barron) *hld up in last pl: hdwy on nr side of gp to chse wnr appr fnl f: kpt on ins fnl f: hld towards fin* **33/1**

03- **3** ½ **Nick Vedder**[33] 8305 3-8-5 0........................................ JordanVaughan[(3)] 5 65
(K R Burke) *trckd ldrs: nt clr run over 2f out: effrt and hdwy over 1f out: edgd lft and kpt on ins fnl f: nt pce to chal* **9/2**[3]

**4** 2½ **Dance Dan Dan (IRE)** 3-8-8 0............................................ JoeFanning 4 59
(Mark Johnston) *cl up: led over 2f out to over 1f out: rdn and kpt on same pce* **9/1**

4- **5** 2 **Arctic Sea**[21] 8486 3-8-8 0.................................................... LukeMorris 7 54
(Paul Cole) *plld hrd: trckd ldrs: chal over 2f out to over 1f out: sn rdn and edgd lft: wknd ins fnl f* **1/1**[1]

0- **6** 1½ **Knightsbridge Liam (IRE)**[37] 8237 3-8-5 0............... NathanEvans[(3)] 2 51
(Michael Easterby) *t.k.h early: trckd ldrs: pushed along over 2f out: edgd lft and outpcd over 1f out: sn btn* **22/1**

640- **7** *hd* **Sandstream**[27] 8402 4-10-0 35.......................................(t[1]) JasonHart 3 54?
(Tracy Waggott) *stdd in tch: t.k.h: rdn and effrt over 2f out: wknd over 1f out* **100/1**

**8** 7 **Eye On You (IRE)** 4-9-9 0................................................... DavidNolan 1 32
(John Murray) *led to over 2f out: edgd lft and wknd over 1f out* **33/1**

1m 44.24s (5.64) **Going Correction** +0.35s/f (Slow)
**WFA** 3 from 4yo 20lb 8 Ran SP% **114.4**
Speed ratings (Par 103): **85,84,84,81,79 78,77,70**
CSF £90.86 TOTE £5.10: £1.40, £6.90, £1.70; EX 90.60 Trifecta £536.40.
**Owner** Abdullah Saeed Al Naboodah **Bred** Hascombe And Valiant Studs **Trained** Newmarket, Suffolk

**FOCUS**
Just a modest modest maiden. It was slowly run and, while the initial standard is set around the third, the likes of the seventh cast doubt on the level of the form.

## 199 SUNBETS.CO.UK H'CAP 7f 14y (Tp)
**4:30** (4:31) (Class 2) 4-Y-O+
**£28,012** (£8,388; £4,194; £2,097; £1,048; £526) **Stalls** Centre

Form RPR

001- **1** **Flaming Spear (IRE)**[22] 8478 5-9-2 **97**........................ RobertWinston 2 108+
(Kevin Ryan) *missed break: t.k.h: hld up in last pl in centre of gp: nt clr run fr over 2f out to ins fnl f: swtchd rt and qcknd smartly to ld nr fin* **3/1**[1]

05-4 **2** *nk* **Fort Bastion (IRE)**[5] 117 8-8-7 **88**....................................... TomEaves 14 94
(Brian Ellison) *slowly away: hld up: rdn and gd hdwy on nr side of gp over 1f out: led briefly last 25yds: jst hld* **20/1**

01-0 **3** *nk* **Al Khan (IRE)**[11] 5 8-8-9 **90**.............................................. KevinStott 5 95
(Kevin Ryan) *hld up: hdwy on far side of gp over 1f out: ev ch briefly last 25yds: jst hld* **33/1**

11-1 **4** ½ **Holiday Magic (IRE)**[11] 5 6-8-8 **92** 6ex.................. NathanEvans[(3)] 6 96+
(Michael Easterby) *t.k.h: in tch in centre of gp: hdwy to chal 1/2-way: rdn to ld over 1f out: hdd last 25yds: no ex* **4/1**[2]

000- **5** *nk* **Suzi's Connoisseur**[27] 8407 6-9-0 **95**..........................(vt) JoeFanning 7 98
(Stuart Williams) *hld up in centre of gp: hdwy whn nt clr run over 1f out: swtchd lft and kpt on ins fnl f: nrst fin* **20/1**

251- **6** *nk* **Nimr**[41] 8192 4-8-10 **91**...................................................... TonyHamilton 10 93+
(Richard Fahey) *plld hrd early: cl up in centre of gp: led and maintained slow gallop after 3f: rdn and hdd over 1f out: rallied: one pce ins fnl f* **9/2**[3]

02-0 **7** ¾ **Shyron**[11] 5 6-8-3 **91**........................................................ JaneElliott[(7)] 11 91
(George Margarson) *t.k.h: prom: effrt and rdn on nr side of gp over 1f out: ev ch briefly ins fnl f: one pce towards fin* **33/1**

300- **8** *nk* **Grey Mirage**[12] 8593 8-8-12 **93**...................................(b) LukeMorris 4 92
(Gay Kelleway) *t.k.h: hld up in tch in centre of pack: nt clr run fr over 2f out: shkn up over 1f out: n.m.r but kpt on steadily ins fnl f* **50/1**

122- **9** ½ **Qaffaal (USA)**[12] 8593 6-8-6 **87**.................................... JamesSullivan 13 85
(Michael Easterby) *led at slow pce for 3f on nr side of gp: prom: effrt and ch over 1f out: no ex ins fnl f* **6/1**

600- **10** *shd* **Horsted Keynes (FR)**[339] 503 7-8-10 **91**.......................... ShaneKelly 1 91+
(David Simcock) *hld up in centre of gp: nt clr run fr over 2f out: shkn up over 1f out: no imp whn n.m.r ins fnl f* **33/1**

514- **11** *1* **Pactolus (IRE)**[35] 8279 6-8-8 **92**................................(tp) AaronJones(3) 9 87
(Stuart Williams) *t.k.h: cl up towards far side of gp: rdn over 1f out: wknd ins fnl f* **14/1**

310- **12** *1 ¼* **Volunteer Point (IRE)**[15] 8563 5-9-0 **95**.......................... MartinHarley 3 87
(Mick Channon) *t.k.h: cl up on far side of gp: rdn over 2f out: wknd ins fnl f* **14/1**

131- **13** *shd* **Steel Train (FR)**[33] 8311 6-8-12 **100**...................... PatrickVaughan(7) 12 91
(David O'Meara) *hld up on nr side of gp: drvn along wl over 1f out: btn fnl f* **8/1**

1m 32.04s (5.84) **Going Correction** +0.35s/f (Slow) **13** Ran SP% **122.2**
Speed ratings (Par 109): **80,79,79,78,78 78,77,76,76,76 75,73,73**
CSF £72.57 CT £1760.22 TOTE £3.70: £1.60, £7.10, £8.40; EX 129.50 Trifecta £2771.60.
**Owner** Tony Bloom **Bred** Gerry Flannery Developments **Trained** Hambleton, N Yorks

**FOCUS**
A competitive, good-class sprint, but they went no pace and it developed into a two-furlong dash. The form has been rated around the second and third.

## 200 BETWAY CONDITIONS STKS (AN ARC ALL-WEATHER CHAMPIONSHIPS FAST-TRACK QUALIFIER) 5f (Tp)
**5:00** (5:02) (Class 2) 4-Y-O+ **£12,602** (£3,772; £1,886; £944; £470) **Stalls** Centre

Form RPR

1-2 **1** **Doc Sportello (IRE)**[9] 33 5-9-0 88.........................(p) RobertWinston 5 107
(Michael Herrington) *hld up in last pl: effrt and swtchd lft over 1f out: qcknd to ld ins fnl f: edgd rt: hld on wl cl home* **8/1**[3]

031- **2** *shd* **Justice Good (IRE)**[50] 8069 5-9-0 101.................................. ShaneKelly 9 106
(David Elsworth) *hld up: shkn up and gd hdwy on nr side of gp over 1f out: disp ld ins fnl f: rdn and kpt on: no ex nr fin* **7/1**[2]

135- **3** *1 ¼* **Dougan**[17] 8530 5-9-0 100................................................... AndrewMullen 6 103
(David Evans) *hld up towards rr in centre: rdn along over 2f out: hdwy over 1f out: keeping on whn checked cl home* **10/1**

412- **4** *¾* **Gracious John (IRE)**[22] 8484 4-9-0 110.................................. JFEgan 4 99
(David Evans) *t.k.h early: cl up in centre: rdn and led over 1f out to ins fnl f: kpt on same pce* **5/4**[1]

304- **5** *1* **Bowson Fred**[52] 8050 5-9-0 100........................................ NathanEvans 8 95
(Michael Easterby) *prom: hdwy on nr side of gp 1/2-way: rdn and ev ch over 1f out to ins fnl f: kpt on same pce* **9/1**

022- **6** *1* **Mythmaker**[17] 8530 5-9-0 104........................................ ConnorBeasley 7 92
(Bryan Smart) *early ldr: trckd ldr to 1/2-way: rdn and outpcd appr fnl f: rallied towards fin: no imp* **7/1**[2]

302- **7** *hd* **Royal Birth**[131] 6112 6-9-0 100...........................................(t) AaronJones 3 91
(Stuart Williams) *hld up on far side of gp: rdn and edgd lft over 1f out: sn no ex* **8/1**[3]

526- **8** *nse* **Lightscameraction (IRE)**[17] 8530 5-9-3 104..................(b) LukeMorris 2 94
(Gay Kelleway) *t.k.h: prom: rdn along over 1f out: outpcd ins fnl f* **16/1**

015- **9** *1 ¼* **Chiclet (IRE)**[27] 8418 6-8-9 97.............................................(h) GaryHalpin 1 81
(Tracey Collins, Ire) *dwlt: sn rcvrd and led on far side of gp: rdn and hdd over 1f out: sn wknd* **22/1**

59.45s (-0.05) **Going Correction** +0.35s/f (Slow) **9** Ran SP% **121.0**
Speed ratings (Par 109): **114,113,111,110,109 107,107,107,105**
CSF £65.75 TOTE £9.40: £2.50, £2.30, £3.40; EX 78.80 Trifecta £661.40.
**Owner** Mrs H Lloyd-Herrington **Bred** J Hutchinson **Trained** Cold Kirby, N Yorks
■ Stewards' Enquiry : Robert Winston caution: careless riding

**FOCUS**
A Fast-Track Qualifier run at a decent clip throughout, and it proved more competitive than the betting would suggest. The runner-up has been rated to form.
T/Plt: £434.80 to a £1 stake. Pool: £84,246.9 - 141.43 winning units T/Qpdt: £102.00 to a £1 stake. Pool: £6,148.55 - 44.58 winning units **Richard Young**

# [82]MEYDAN (L-H)
Thursday, January 12
**OFFICIAL GOING: Dirt: fast; turf: good**

## 201a NATIONAL INDUSTRIAL PARK (MAIDEN) (DIRT) 1m (D)
**2:30** (2:30) 3-Y-0
**£21,951** (£7,317; £3,658; £1,829; £1,097; £731)

RPR

**1** **Fawree (USA)**[14] 8574 3-9-0 0................................. BernardFayd'Herbe 3 97+
(M F De Kock, South Africa) *sn led: rdn clr 2f out: r.o wl: easily* **11/10**[1]

**2** *5* **Bee Jersey (USA)**[14] 8574 3-9-0 0.................................... PatDobbs 2 83
(Doug Watson, UAE) *trckd ldr: ev ch 1 1/2f out: one pce fnl f* **7/4**[2]

**3** *2 ¾* **Mazeed (USA)**[14] 8576 3-9-0 85......................... ChristopheSoumillon 9 77+
(M F De Kock, South Africa) *trckd ldng trio: r.o same pce fnl 2f: no ch w first two* **9/2**[3]

**4** *1 ¼* **Dawwass (USA)**[14] 8574 3-9-0 0.................................... RichardMullen 1 74
(S Seemar, UAE) *mid-div: r.o fnl 2f: nvr nr to chal* **40/1**

**5** *9 ¼* **Magical Forest (IRE)**[23] 8464 3-8-9 75................................ DaneO'Neill 7 48
(Marco Botti) *a in mid-div* **16/1**

**6** *1 ¾* **Forgivethenforget**[20] 8520 3-9-0 65............................(tp) AntonioFresu 5 49
(A bin Harmash, UAE) *trckd ldr: outpcd fnl 3f* **80/1**

**7** *nk* **Sboog (USA)**[70] 7784 3-9-0 0.............................................(t) JimCrowley 8 48
(A bin Harmash, UAE) *s.i.s: nvr bttr than mid-div* **33/1**

**8** *7 ¼* **Big Sigh (IRE)**[14] 8574 3-9-0 0.......................................(bt) AdriedeVries 6 31
(Ismail Mohammed) *nvr nr to chal* **100/1**

**9** *21* **Cape Of Eagles (USA)**[14] 8574 3-9-0 80................ ColmO'Donoghue 4
(Fawzi Abdulla Nass, Bahrain) *s.i.s: nvr nr to chal* **25/1**

1m 37.68s (0.18) **Going Correction** +0.025s/f (Slow) **9** Ran SP% **119.5**
Speed ratings: **100,95,92,91,81 80,79,72,51**
CSF: 3.28.
**Owner** Sheikh Mohammed Bin Khalifa Al Maktoum **Bred** John A Chandler, Jamm Ltd, C R McGaughey III & Mil **Trained** South Africa

**FOCUS**
TRAKUS (metres travelled compared to winner): 2nd -5, 3rd +7, 4th -3, 5th +5, 6th +4, 7th +12, 8th +4, 9th +12. This was run at a solid, gradually slowing pace, with the splits 25.28 (from standing start), 22.94, 24.24, before the winner finished in 25.22.

## 202a HAMDAN BIN MOHAMMED CRUISE TERMINAL (H'CAP) (TURF) 1m 6f 11y
**3:05** (3:05) (95-108,108) 3-Y-O+
**£78,048** (£26,016; £13,008; £6,504; £3,902; £2,601)

RPR

**1** **Red Galileo**[467] 6917 6-8-11 **100**........................... ChristopheSoumillon 4 101
(Saeed bin Suroor) *trckd ldr: led 8f out: hdd 2f out: r.o again to ld fnl 110yds* **9/2**[3]

**2** *nk* **Carbon Dating (IRE)**[7] 82 5-8-13 **101**......................... TadhgO'Shea 5 103
(S Seemar, UAE) *mid-div: chsd ldrs 3 1/2f out: r.o fnl 2f: nrst fin* **10/3**[2]

**3** *¾* **Rembrandt Van Rijn (IRE)**[28] 8394 6-9-3 **105**.....(b) MickaelBarzalona 7 106
(S bin Ghadayer, UAE) *settled in rr: chsd ldrs 8f out: led 2f out: hdd fnl 110yds* **10/1**

**4** *1 ½* **Warrior Of Light (IRE)**[390] 8308 6-8-10 **99**.................. RichardMullen 1 97
(Brendan Powell) *s.i.s: trckd ldr: ev ch 2f out: r.o same pce fnl f* **33/1**

**5** *5 ½* **Blue Rambler**[33] 7150 7-8-13 **101**................................ GeorgeDowning 3 92
(Ian Williams) *sn led: hdd 8f out: sn btn* **8/1**

**6** *nk* **Brass Ring**[656] 1092 7-8-11 **100**.......................................(v) AdriedeVries 6 90
(Ismail Mohammed) *nvr bttr than mid-div* **33/1**

**7** *nk* **Curbyourenthusiasm (IRE)**[50] 8068 6-9-6 **108**........... JamieSpencer 2 98
(David Simcock) *s.i.s: a in rr* **6/5**[1]

3m 0.12s (0.72) **Going Correction** +0.15s/f (Good) **7** Ran SP% **112.8**
Speed ratings: **103,102,102,101,98 98,98**
CSF: 19.28.
**Owner** Godolphin **Bred** T R G Vestey **Trained** Newmarket, Suffolk

**FOCUS**
Trakus (metres travelled compared to winner): 2nd +3, 3rd +6, 4th -3, 5th +2, 6th 0, 7th +2. This was a muddling race.

## 203a JAFZA (H'CAP) (TURF) 1m 2f
**3:40** (3:40) (78-94,93) 3-Y-O+
**£29,268** (£9,756; £4,878; £2,439; £1,463; £975)

RPR

**1** **Town's History (USA)**[20] 8517 4-8-8 **85**........................ RichardMullen 5 92+
(S Seemar, UAE) *trckd ldrs: rdn to ld 1f out: r.o wl: comf* **7/2**[1]

**2** *2 ½* **Alraased (USA)**[5] 128 8-8-5 **79**...................................(b) TadhgO'Shea 4 82
(A R Al Rayhi, UAE) *sn led: rdn 1 1/2f out: hdd fnl f: kpt on wl* **9/1**

**3** *1 ¼* **Hunters Creek (IRE)**[25] 8450 6-8-9 **84**......................... SamHitchcott 7 84
(S bin Ghadayer, UAE) *settled in rr: chsd ldrs 2 1/2f out: r.o same pce fnl 1 1/2f* **20/1**

**4** *1 ½* **Tried And True (USA)**[20] 8517 5-9-5 **93**.............................(v) PatDobbs 6 91+
(Doug Watson, UAE) *nvr nr to chal: r.o fnl 2f* **5/1**[2]

**5** *1* **Brabbham (USA)**[20] 8517 7-9-1 **89**.....................(t) ColmO'Donoghue 9 85
(A bin Harmash, UAE) *mid-div: r.o fnl 2f: n.d* **11/2**[3]

**6** *¾* **New Strategy (IRE)**[20] 8517 5-8-8 **83**......................(tp) AntonioFresu 1 76
(E Charpy, UAE) *trckd ldrs: ev ch 2 1/2f out: one pce fnl 2f* **25/1**

**7** *1* **Untold Secret**[14] 8580 5-8-9 **84**.............................(p) MickaelBarzalona 11 75
(S bin Ghadayer, UAE) *trckd ldr: ev ch 3f out: one pce fnl 2f* **16/1**

**8** *nk* **Prince Suhail (IRE)**[20] 8519 7-8-6 **81**..............................(t) ChrisHayes 8 71
(E Charpy, UAE) *nvr nr to chal* **8/1**

**9** *1 ¼* **Mutual Force (USA)**[19] 8522 9-8-5 **85** ow7...........(t) AdamMcLean(7) 12 75
(A R Al Rayhi, UAE) *nvr bttr than mid-div* **16/1**

**10** *1 ¼* **Maysoor (AUS)**[25] 8450 5-8-3 **85** ow3....................(b) CameronNoble(7) 2 70
(S Seemar, UAE) *nvr bttr than mid-div* **20/1**

**11** *1 ¼* **Emirates Airline**[20] 8517 5-8-10 **85**........................... MarcMonaghan 13 68
(E Charpy, UAE) *trckd ldr: wknd fnl 1 1/2f* **40/1**

**12** *4 ¾* **Ostaad (IRE)**[20] 8517 7-9-3 **91**.......................................(h) JimCrowley 10 65
(Doug Watson, UAE) *s.i.s: a in rr* **5/1**[2]

**13** *nk* **Layali Al Andalus**[25] 8450 10-9-1 **89**.........................(p) AdriedeVries 14 63
(S Seemar, UAE) *nvr nr to chal* **20/1**

**14** *34* **Ehtedaam (USA)**[14] 8579 8-9-1 **89**..................................(bt) DaneO'Neill 3
(A R Al Rayhi, UAE) *slowly away: nvr nr to chal* **33/1**

2m 2.77s (0.07) **Going Correction** +0.15s/f (Good)
**WFA** 4 from 5yo+ 1lb **14** Ran SP% **127.3**
Speed ratings: **105,103,102,100,100 99,98,98,97,96 95,91,91,64**
CSF: 34.31 TRICAST: 581.13.
**Owner** Amer Bin Asayan Almansouri **Bred** Darley **Trained** United Arab Emirates

**FOCUS**
TRAKUS (metres travelled compared to winner): 2nd +2, 3rd +2, 4th +3, 5th +5, 6th 0, 7th +5, 8th +10, 9th +10, 10th +1, 11th +6, 12th +7, 13th +8, 14th +9. A non-carnival handicap and a weak one at that. The runner-up set a fair pace - 25.72, 23.15, 24.1, 24.73, before the winner finished in 24.75 - but still not much got involved. The standard is set by the third, fourth , fifth and seventh.

## 204a MINA HAMRIYA (H'CAP) (DIRT) 1m (D)
**4:15** (4:15) (95-105,104) 3-Y-O+
**£60,975** (£20,325; £10,162; £5,081; £3,048; £2,032)

RPR

**1** **North America**[14] 8579 5-9-2 **100**.................................(t) RichardMullen 11 115
(S Seemar, UAE) *sn led: rdn 2f out: r.o wl* **11/4**[1]

**2** *1 ¼* **Heavy Metal**[14] 8578 7-9-0 **98**.......................... MickaelBarzalona 13 110
(S bin Ghadayer, UAE) *trckd ldr: ev ch 1 1/2f out: r.o wl* **9/1**

**3** *6 ¾* **Power Blade (KOR)**[25] 4-9-2 **100**..............................(e) PatCosgrave 10 97+
(Kim Young Kwan, Korea) *mid-div: r.o wl fnl 2f: no ch w front two* **13/2**[3]

**4** *3* **Pistol (SWE)**[74] 4-8-11 **96**............................................(tp) ElioneChaves 1 85+
(Patrick Wahl, Sweden) *nvr nr to chal* **20/1**

**5** *1 ¼* **First Selection (SPA)**[97] 7115 4-9-6 **104**........................ JimCrowley 6 91+
(Simon Crisford) *trckd ldrs: ev ch 3f out: r.o same pce fnl 2f* **8/1**

**6** *1 ¼* **Need To Know (SAF)**[7] 86 8-9-5 **103**.....................(bt) TadhgO'Shea 2 87+
(A R Al Rayhi, UAE) *nvr nr to chal* **16/1**

**7** *1 ½* **Diferent Dimension (USA)**[60] 5-9-0 **98**.......................(b) AdriedeVries 8 79+
(Peter Wolsley, Korea) *mid-div: r.o same pce fnl 2f* **16/1**

**8** *3* **Sea Of Flames**[61] 7933 4-8-13 **97**.......................................... DaneO'Neill 3 71+
(David Elsworth) *nvr nr to chal* **16/1**

**9** *3* **Beach Bar (IRE)**[80] 7573 6-8-13 **98** ow3....................(h) DanielTudhope 7 64+
(Brendan Powell) *a in rr* **33/1**

**10** *1 ½* **Pit Stop (IRE)**[42] 8187 6-8-10 **95**................................. FernandoJara 12 57+
(S bin Ghadayer, UAE) *a in rr* **20/1**

**11** *nk* **Wildcat Red (USA)**[341] 6-9-5 **103**........................................ PatDobbs 14 66+
(Doug Watson, UAE) *trckd ldrs: outpcd fnl 3f* **6/1**[2]

12 11 ½ **Sharpalo (FR)**[7] 83 5-8-10 **95**............................(h) ColmO'Donoghue 9 30+
(A bin Harmash, UAE) *s.i.s: a in rr* **12/1**

13 ¾ **Bluff (USA)**[20] 8517 5-9-1 **99**............................(vt) ChrisHayes 5 33+
(D Selvaratnam, UAE) *a in rr* **11/1**

14 8 ½ **Bear Faced**[223] 2870 4-8-11 **96**............................(t) AntonioFresu 4 +
(A bin Harmash, UAE) *nvr bttr than mid-div* **33/1**

15 21 **Redbrook (IRE)**[315] 810 6-8-13 **97**............................(v) SamHitchcott 15 +
(Doug Watson, UAE) *s.i.s: mid-div: virtually p.u 3f out* **33/1**

1m 35.65s (-1.85) **Going Correction** +0.025s/f (Slow) **15** Ran SP% **127.4**
Speed ratings: **110,108,102,99,97 96,95,92,89,87 87,75,74,66,45**
CSF: 27.07 TRICAST: 153.22.
**Owner** Imhamed M I Nagem **Bred** Qatar Bloodstock Ltd **Trained** United Arab Emirates

**FOCUS**
TRAKUS: 2nd +3, 3rd +6, 4th +1, 5th -2, 6th +6, 7th +2, 8th +5, 9th +13, 10th +16, 11th +9, 12th +15, 13th +7, 14th 0, 15th +14. The front two had this to themselves through splits of 24.79, 22.07, 24.27, 24.52, and the final time was fast.

## 205a MINA RASHID (H'CAP) (TURF) 1m
**4:50** (4:50) (95-105,105) 3-Y-O+

**£60,975** (£20,325; £10,162; £5,081; £3,048; £2,032)

RPR

1 **Fanciful Angel (IRE)**[21] 8489 5-9-4 **103**.................... DanielMuscutt 13 110
(Marco Botti) *s.i.s: settled in rr: rdn to chal 2 1/2f out: led fnl f out: r.o wl* **9/2**[1]

2 1 **Hors De Combat**[132] 6075 6-9-2 **101**............................ PatSmullen 6 106
(Denis Coakley) *trckd ldrs tl one pce fnl 2 1/2f* **12/1**

3 ¾ **Belgian Bill**[131] 6157 9-9-1 **100**............................ ColmO'Donoghue 3 103
(George Baker) *trckd ldr: ev ch 2f out: r.o same pce fnl f* **9/1**[3]

4 nk **Secret Brief (IRE)**[194] 3910 5-9-3 **102**............................ WilliamBuick 15 105+
(Charlie Appleby) *nvr nr to chal: r.o fnl 2f* **9/2**[1]

5 1 ½ **Art Wave (IRE)**[48] 8115 6-8-13 **98**............................(v) FernandoJara 9 97
(M Al Mheiri, UAE) *trckd ldr: led 2f out: hdd fnl f out: r.o same pce* **40/1**

6 ½ **Encipher (USA)**[7] 87 8-9-1 **100**............................(t) TadhgO'Shea 14 98
(A R Al Rayhi, UAE) *nvr nr to chal but r.o fnl 2f* **40/1**

7 ¾ **Tahanee (ARG)**[146] 4-9-6 **105**............................ ChristopheSoumillon 1 101
(M F De Kock, South Africa) *trckd ldrs: ev ch whn hmpd 1 1/2f out: nt rcvr* **11/2**[2]

8 shd **Cornwallville (IRE)**[33] 8311 5-8-13 **98**............................ DanielTudhope 2 99+
(Roger Fell) *nvr bttr than mid-div* **25/1**

9 1 ¼ **General Macarthur (USA)**[137] 5941 4-8-13 **98**........(t) JamieSpencer 12 91
(David Simcock) *settled in rr: styng on whn n.m.r 1 1/2f out: no rcvr* **20/1**

10 ¾ **Kanaf (IRE)**[7] 87 10-9-1 **100**............................(v) DaneO'Neill 5 91+
(M Al Mheiri, UAE) *slowly away: nvr nr to chal* **33/1**

11 3 ¾ **Limario (GER)**[315] 812 7-9-6 **105**............................(t) PatDobbs 10 88
(Doug Watson, UAE) *trckd ldr tl wknd fnl 2f* **16/1**

12 hd **Arabda**[123] 6-9-1 **100**............................(t) ElioneChaves 4 82
(Patrick Wahl, Sweden) *sn led: hdd 2f out: sn btn* **40/1**

13 nse **Queen's Parade (USA)**[188] 6-9-1 **100**............................ ChrisHayes 11 82
(D Selvaratnam, UAE) *nvr bttr than mid-div* **25/1**

14 1 **Mostaneer (IRE)**[34] 5-9-5 **104**............................ MickaelBarzalona 7 84
(N Bachalard, Saudi Arabia) *s.i.s: nvr nr to chal* **25/1**

15 ¾ **Silent Attack**[7] 86 4-9-3 **102**............................(p) PatCosgrave 8 80
(Saeed bin Suroor) *nvr bttr than mid-div* **9/2**[1]

16 4 ¾ **Prince Of All**[28] 8394 6-9-6 **105**............................(t) JimCrowley 16 72
(A R Al Rayhi, UAE) *nvr bttr than mid-div* **25/1**

1m 36.63s (-0.87) **Going Correction** +0.15s/f (Good) **16** Ran SP% **123.9**
Speed ratings: **110,109,108,107,106 105,105,105,103,103 99,99,99,98,97 92**
CSF: 53.00 TRICAST: 491.29.
**Owner** Touch Gold Racing (Fanciful) **Bred** Berjis Desai **Trained** Newmarket, Suffolk

**FOCUS**
TRAKUS (metres travelled compared to winner): 2nd -4, 3rd -8, 4th -4, 5th -9, 6th -2, 7th -8, 8th -11, 9th -8, 10th -7, 11th -3, 12th -12, 13th -4, 14th 0, 15th -7, 16th +1. A good handicap run at a strong early pace, 24.87 (from standing start), 22.85, 24.44, before the winner finished in 23.99. The second, fourth, fifth and seventh help set the standard.

## 206a DUBAWI STKS (LISTED RACE) (DIRT) 6f (D)
**5:25** (5:25) 3-Y-O+

**£85,365** (£28,455; £14,227; £7,113; £4,268; £2,845)

RPR

1 **Reynaldothewizard (USA)**[292] 1105 11-9-0 112.....(bt) RichardMullen 6 114
(S Seemar, UAE) *mid-div: hrd rdn 3f out: r.o wl: led cl home* **6/1**[3]

2 ½ **Muarrab**[28] 8395 8-9-0 115............................ JimCrowley 4 112+
(M Al Mheiri, UAE) *sn led: rdn clr 2 1/2f out: wknd and hdd fnl f* **13/8**[2]

3 4 ¼ **Wild Dude (USA)**[123] 6398 7-9-0 113............................(bt) PatSmullen 1 98
(M Halford, Ire) *mid-div: r.o fnl 2f: no ch w first two* **10/1**

4 5 ¼ **Desert Force**[14] 8578 5-9-0 108............................ PatDobbs 7 82
(Doug Watson, UAE) *trckd ldr: ev ch 2 1/2f out: one pce fnl 1 1/2f* **6/4**[1]

5 3 ½ **Moviesta (USA)**[83] 7520 7-9-0 107............................(b) WJLee 3 70
(Edward Lynam, Ire) *s.i.s: nvr nr to chal* **14/1**

6 12 **The Happy Prince (IRE)**[7] 84 5-9-2 110............................(tp) PatCosgrave 2 34
(James Moore, Macau) *s.i.s: a in rr* **25/1**

7 3 ¼ **Mubtaghaa (IRE)**[7] 84 5-9-0 99............................ DaneO'Neill 5 22
(M Al Mheiri, UAE) *a in rr* **66/1**

1m 10.66s (-0.94) **Going Correction** +0.025s/f (Slow) **7** Ran SP% **113.5**
Speed ratings: **107,106,100,93,89 73,68**
CSF: 15.97.
**Owner** Zabeel Racing International, Corp **Bred** Gibraltar Group Lp **Trained** United Arab Emirates

**FOCUS**
TRAKUS (metres travelled compared to winner): 2nd -5, 3rd -6, 4th -2, 5th 0, 6th -2, 7th +4. Only four of these really counted and the runner-up and was pressed by the fourth though strong fractions: 23.75, 22.54, with the winner home in a slowing 23.98. The winner has been rated as good as ever.

## 207a JEBEL ALI PORT (H'CAP) (TURF) 6f
**6:00** (6:00) (100-113,110) 3-Y-O+

**£65,853** (£21,951; £10,975; £5,487; £3,292; £2,195)

RPR

1 **Final Venture**[17] 8530 5-9-0 **104**............................(h) PatDobbs 11 112
(Paul Midgley) *sn led: hdd fnl f: r.o to ld again fnl strides* **7/1**[2]

2 nse **Steady Pace**[121] 6458 4-8-11 **102**............................ ChristopheSoumillon 7 109
(Saeed bin Suroor) *trckd ldrs: led fnl f: hdd cl home* **6/1**[1]

3 1 ¼ **Jamesie (IRE)**[104] 6931 9-8-11 **102**............................(t) ColmO'Donoghue 15 105+
(David Marnane, Ire) *mid-div: r.o fnl 1 1/2f: nrst fin* **12/1**

4 nk **Polybius**[103] 6943 6-8-11 **102**............................ JamieSpencer 9 104
(David Simcock) *s.i.s: nvr nr to chal* **12/1**

5 ¾ **Fityaan**[7] 84 9-9-6 **110**............................(v) JimCrowley 5 110
(M Al Mheiri, UAE) *nvr bttr than mid-div* **7/1**[2]

6 shd **Speed Hawk (USA)**[314] 852 6-8-11 **102**............................(t) ChrisHayes 13 101
(D Selvaratnam, UAE) *trckd ldrs: ev ch fnl f: one pce fnl 110yds* **20/1**

7 1 ¼ **Sole Power**[103] 6943 10-9-3 **107**............................ PatSmullen 14 103
(Edward Lynam, Ire) *settled in rr: r.o fnl 2f* **10/1**[3]

8 ½ **Roi De Vitesse (IRE)**[7] 84 10-8-13 **103**..........(v) MickaelBarzalona 10 98+
(Ali Jan, Qatar) *settled in rr: rdn 3f out: n.d* **33/1**

9 ¾ **Gordon Lord Byron (IRE)**[103] 6955 9-9-3 **107**............................ TadhgO'Shea 3 99
(T Hogan, Ire) *s.i.s: nvr bttr than mid-div* **16/1**

10 1 **Spirit Quartz (IRE)**[7] 84 9-9-0 **107**............................ JulianResimont[(3)] 12 96
(N Caullery, France) *trckd ldrs tl outpcd fnl 2f* **25/1**

11 4 **Eastern Impact (IRE)**[114] 6642 6-9-5 **109**............................ PatCosgrave 4 85
(Richard Fahey) *trckd ldrs tl outpcd fnl 1 1/2f* **7/1**[2]

12 1 ½ **Roicead (USA)**[329] 626 10-9-5 **109**............................(t) DaneO'Neill 6 80
(D Selvaratnam, UAE) *s.i.s: nvr nr to chal* **20/1**

13 2 ½ **Watchable**[103] 6942 7-8-13 **103**............................(b) DanielTudhope 8 66
(David O'Meara) *trckd ldrs tl outpcd fnl 1 1/2f* **7/1**[2]

14 3 **Hawkesbury**[383] 8356 5-9-1 **105**............................ RichardMullen 2 59
(S Seemar, UAE) *a in rr* **25/1**

15 17 **Naadirr (IRE)**[103] 6941 6-9-3 **107**............................(p) WilliamBuick 1 6
(Marco Botti) *nvr bttr than mid-div* **7/1**[2]

1m 10.92s (1.92) **Going Correction** +0.60s/f (Yiel) **15** Ran SP% **127.3**
Speed ratings: **111,110,109,108,107 107,106,105,104,103 97,95,92,88,65**
CSF: 47.46 TRICAST: 527.46.
**Owner** Taylor's Bloodstock Ltd **Bred** Newsells Park Stud **Trained** Westow, N Yorks

**FOCUS**
A competitive sprint handicap. The standard is set by the second and seventh.

## 208a MINA RASHID MARINA (H'CAP) (TURF) 1m 2f
**6:35** (6:35) (100-109,109) 3-Y-O+

**£85,365** (£28,455; £14,227; £7,113; £4,268; £2,845)

RPR

1 **Elhaame (IRE)**[357] 283 7-9-3 **106**............................ AdriedeVries 3 110
(Saeed bin Suroor) *trckd ldr: rdn to chal 1 1/2f out: led over 1f out: r.o wl* **11/2**[3]

2 ¾ **Good Trip (IRE)**[7] 82 4-8-9 **101**............................(t) TadhgO'Shea 2 103+
(A R Al Rayhi, UAE) *mid-div: chsd ldr 2 1/2f out: r.o fnl 1 1/2f: nrst fin* **10/1**

3 ¾ **Sanshaawes (SAF)**[7] 86 7-9-6 **109**............................ ChristopheSoumillon 13 110
(M F De Kock, South Africa) *trckd ldr: rdn to ld 1 1/2f out: hdd 1f out: r.o wl* **9/2**[2]

4 shd **Basateen (IRE)**[292] 1106 5-9-4 **107**............................ JimCrowley 5 108
(Doug Watson, UAE) *mid-div: chsd ldrs 2f out: r.o fnl 1 1/2f* **3/1**[1]

5 2 **Elleval (IRE)**[154] 5343 7-8-11 **101**............................(p) PatDobbs 12 97
(David Marnane, Ire) *nvr nr to chal* **8/1**

6 ¾ **Whistle Stop (SAF)**[7] 87 6-8-11 **101**............................ DaneO'Neill 10 95
(M F De Kock, South Africa) *nvr bttr than mid-div* **10/1**

7 nse **Master The World (IRE)**[43] 8160 6-9-5 **108**............................(p) SamHitchcott 9 103
(David Elsworth) *s.i.s: nvr nr to chal: r.o fnl 2 1/2f* **14/1**

8 1 ¼ **Hasanour (USA)**[123] 6389 7-8-10 **100**............................ PatSmullen 8 92
(M Halford, Ire) *mid-div: r.o sme pce fnl 2f* **14/1**

9 4 ¼ **Torchlighter (IRE)**[348] 408 6-8-11 **101**..............(vt) MickaelBarzalona 6 84
(S bin Ghadayer, UAE) *sn led: hdd & wknd 1 1/2f out* **16/1**

10 2 ¾ **Majeed**[117] 6600 7-9-1 **104**............................ JamieSpencer 7 83
(David Simcock) *s.i.s: a in rr* **8/1**

11 2 ¾ **Mawhub**[20] 8518 8-8-10 **100**............................(v) RichardMullen 1 72
(S Seemar, UAE) *slowly away: nvr nr to chal* **33/1**

12 3 ¼ **Maftool (USA)**[7] 86 5-9-6 **109**............................(v) FernandoJara 11 76
(M Al Mheiri, UAE) *trckd ldr tl wknd fnl 2 1/2f* **25/1**

2m 3.24s (0.54) **Going Correction** +0.15s/f (Good)
**WFA** 4 from 5yo+ 1lb **12** Ran SP% **125.0**
Speed ratings: **103,102,101,101,100 99,99,98,95,92 90,88**
CSF: 63.19 TRICAST: 276.99. Placepot. £34.90 to a £1 stake. Pool: £6,518.75 - 136.25 winning units. Quadpot £24.10 to a £1 stake. Pool: £485.60 - 14.90 winning units.
**Owner** Godolphin **Bred** W Maxwell Ervine **Trained** Newmarket, Suffolk

**FOCUS**
TRAKUS (metres travelled compared to winner): 2nd -1, 3rd +2, 4th +4, 5th +1, 6th +4, 7th +9, 8th 0, 9th 0, 10th +4, 11th -1, 12th +7. They went a modest pace, 26.66, 23.78, 24.76, 24.7, before the winner quickened up in 23.18. The third and fourth help set the standard.

# [139]LINGFIELD (L-H)
### Friday, January 13

**OFFICIAL GOING: Polytrack: standard to slow**
Wind: Fresh, half against towards stands Weather: Cold and cloudy

## 209 32RED.COM H'CAP (DIV I) 1m 1y(P)
**1:00** (1:05) (Class 6) (0-65,67) 3-Y-O **£2,911** (£866; £432; £216) **Stalls** High

Form RPR

620- 1 **Tisbutadream (IRE)**[16] 8557 3-9-9 **67**............................ ShaneKelly 10 77
(David Elsworth) *prom on outer: hrd rdn 3f out: wd st: styd on to ld 1f out: drvn out* **10/1**

003- 2 1 ½ **Ourmullion**[56] 8008 3-9-4 **62**............................ KierenFox 2 68
(John Best) *led for 1f: stdd to trck ldrs on inner: rdn over 2f out: wnt 2nd ins fnl f: a hld* **9/2**[2]

603- 3 2 ½ **No Not Again (IRE)**[24] 8466 3-9-6 **64**............................ SeanLevey 6 64
(Richard Hannon) *chsd ldrs: rdn over 2f out: one pce appr fnl f* **4/1**[1]

040- 4 hd **Presence Process**[16] 8560 3-9-1 **64**............................ PaddyBradley[(5)] 3 64
(Pat Phelan) *towards rr: rdn over 2f out: nrest at fin* **12/1**

501- 5 ½ **Wily Rumpus (IRE)**[81] 7571 3-9-7 **65**............................ ThomasBrown 1 63
(Ed Walker) *mid-div: hdwy over 1f out: no imp fnl f* **4/1**[1]

00-5 6 1 ¼ **Chough**[7] 89 3-8-9 **58**............................(b[1]) CharlieBennett[(5)] 7 53
(Hughie Morrison) *hdwy to ld after 1f: jnd over 2f out: hdd & wknd 1f out* **20/1**

000- 7 3 **Mac's Kyllachy**[58] 7975 3-9-4 **62**............................ DanielMuscutt 4 50
(James Fanshawe) *s.i.s and rdn along in rr early: nvr rchd ldrs* **8/1**[3]

60-4 8 1 ¼ **Ode To Paris**[8] 78 3-9-7 **65**............................ DavidProbert 9 50
(Ed Dunlop) *t.k.h: prom: jnd ldr over 2f out tl wknd 1f out* **4/1**[1]

555- 9 2 **Roman Legion (IRE)**[191] 4016 3-9-4 **62**............................ RobertWinston 8 42
(Dean Ivory) *a bhd* **8/1**[3]

020- 10 2 **Deleyll**[38] 8235 3-8-12 **56**............................ DannyBrock 5 32
(John Butler) *mid-div: outpcd 1/2-way: sn bhd* **25/1**

1m 38.18s (-0.02) **Going Correction** -0.05s/f (Stan) **10** Ran SP% **125.8**
Speed ratings (Par 95): **98,96,94,93,93 92,89,87,85,83**
CSF £59.10 CT £223.91 TOTE £9.20: £3.10, £1.70, £1.20; EX 56.00 Trifecta £453.30.
**Owner** Mrs Anne Coughlan & Ten Green Bottles **Bred** J F Tuthill **Trained** Newmarket, Suffolk

**FOCUS**
Following the snow, the surface was riding on the slow side. A modest handicap but quite an interesting one, and the first two look nicely ahead of their marks. A step forward from the winner and a pb from the runner-up.

## 210 32RED.COM H'CAP (DIV II) 1m 1y(P)
1:30 (1:35) (Class 6) (0-65,66) 3-Y-O £2,911 (£866; £432; £216) Stalls High

Form RPR
003- 1 **Elementary**[16] 8560 3-9-8 66 GeorgeBaker 7 71
(Michael Bell) *hld up towards rr: hdwy 2f out: led ins fnl f: edgd lft: drvn out* 9/4[1]
000- 2 hd **Sliceoflife**[24] 8467 3-9-4 62 JosephineGordon 3 67
(Marco Botti) *led for 1f: chsd ldr: led again over 1f out tl ins fnl f: kpt on wl* 20/1
24-2 3 1 3/4 **Still Waiting**[7] 89 3-9-3 61 (b[1]) RobertHavlin 10 61
(William Jarvis) *s.s: bhd: rdn and r.o fr over 1f out: nrest at fin* 3/1[2]
050- 4 3/4 **Tigerfish (IRE)**[36] 8276 3-7-11 46 oh1 (p) HollieDoyle(5) 1 45
(William Stone) *hld up in 4th: rdn to chse ldrs over 1f out: kpt on* 20/1
05-3 5 1 **License To Thrill (USA)**[6] 114 3-9-7 65 JFEgan 5 61
(Simon Dow) *chsd ldrs: rdn over 2f out: one pce appr fnl f* 5/1[3]
060- 6 1 1/2 **Poet's Charm (IRE)**[55] 8034 3-9-7 65 MartinLane 9 58
(Simon Crisford) *led after 1f tl wknd over 1f out* 7/1
600- 7 2 1/2 **Kyllachys Tale (IRE)**[78] 7647 3-9-6 64 TomMarquand 2 51
(Roger Teal) *mid-div tl outpcd and btn over 2f out* 50/1
660- 8 2 1/4 **Noble Ballad**[16] 8560 3-9-6 64 SeanLevey 4 45
(Ralph Beckett) *towards rr: stmbld after 1f: rdn and n.d fnl 2f* 6/1
044- 9 6 **Madam Prancealot (IRE)**[32] 8341 3-8-13 57 RobertWinston 8 24
(David Evans) *in tch on outer: drvn along 3f out: wd and wknd entered st* 14/1

1m 38.15s (-0.05) **Going Correction** -0.05s/f (Stan) 9 Ran SP% **117.4**
Speed ratings (Par 95): **98,97,96,95,94 92,90,88,82**
CSF £52.40 CT £141.62 TOTE £2.90: £1.10, £6.60, £1.20; EX 41.00 Trifecta £226.30.
**Owner** The Queen **Bred** The Queen **Trained** Newmarket, Suffolk

**FOCUS**
The winning time was very similar to the first division. The first two have been rated to their best.

## 211 BETWAY BEST ODDS GUARANTEED PLUS CLAIMING STKS 6f 1y(P)
2:00 (2:06) (Class 6) 4-Y-O+ £2,911 (£866; £432; £216) Stalls Low

Form RPR
210- 1 **Monumental Man**[15] 8571 8-9-4 76 (p) WilliamCarson 4 83
(Michael Attwater) *mde all: hrd rdn over 1f out: hld on wl* 10/1
25-3 2 1 1/4 **Free Zone**[7] 94 8-9-1 81 (v) RobertWinston 7 76
(Lee Carter) *chsd ldrs: rdn over 2f out: kpt on to take 2nd fnl 100yds* 15/8[1]
060- 3 1/2 **Flexible Flyer**[223] 2903 8-9-2 78 (h) JFEgan 3 76
(Chris Dwyer) *s.s: bhd: hdwy over 1f out: styd on to take 3rd nr fin* 6/1[3]
555- 4 1 **Yeeoow (IRE)**[28] 8402 8-9-2 77 (p) JoeyHaynes 2 73
(K R Burke) *chsd wnr: one pce ins fnl f: lost 2nd fnl 100yds* 7/2[2]
024- 5 1 **Doctor Parkes**[22] 8495 11-8-4 74 MillyNaseb(7) 6 65
(Stuart Williams) *s.s: bhd: rdn and sme hdwy over 1f out: styd on* 7/1
00-0 6 11 **Illegally Blonde (IRE)**[7] 93 4-9-3 85 (p[1]) GeorgeBaker 1 38
(Jamie Osborne) *in tch tl wknd wl over 1f out* 7/2[2]
060/ 7 3 1/4 **Catalyze**[843] 6631 9-8-11 46 (t) DannyBrock 5 22
(Paddy Butler) *sn outpcd: struggling in rr fr 1/2-way* 66/1

1m 11.36s (-0.54) **Going Correction** -0.05s/f (Stan) 7 Ran SP% **116.6**
Speed ratings (Par 101): **101,99,98,97,96 81,77**
CSF £30.24 TOTE £10.70: £4.10, £1.20; EX 38.50 Trifecta £155.00.
**Owner** Richard and Nicola Hunt **Bred** Christopher Chell **Trained** Epsom, Surrey

**FOCUS**
Not a bad claimer, but the winner was left alone in front and dominated throughout. The winner has been rated to form.

## 212 32RED.COM MAIDEN STKS 5f 6y(P)
2:30 (2:35) (Class 5) 3-Y-O £3,881 (£1,155; £577; £288) Stalls High

Form RPR
35- 1 **Monteamiata (IRE)**[26] 8443 3-9-0 0 ThomasBrown 3 69+
(Ed Walker) *dwlt: sn in tch: rdn into narrow ld ins fnl f: hld on wl* 4/1[3]
43- 2 nk **Speed Freak**[18] 8526 3-9-0 67 (b) JosephineGordon 6 68
(Ralph Beckett) *chsd ldr: drew level w wnr ins fnl f: r.o* 3/1[2]
22-3 3 2 1/4 **Bithynia (IRE)**[8] 75 3-9-0 69 JFEgan 4 60
(David Evans) *led tl ins fnl f: no ex* 5/2[1]
200- 4 1 1/4 **Snow Squaw**[24] 8464 3-9-0 72 ShaneKelly 2 55+
(David Elsworth) *in tch tl outpcd fnl 2f* 9/2
550- 5 1 1/4 **Rita's Man (IRE)**[16] 8560 3-9-5 66 TomMarquand 1 56
(Richard Hannon) *prom tl hrd rdn and btn over 1f out* 7/1
44-2 6 3 3/4 **Heavenly Cry**[12] 1 3-9-0 62 (v) HollieDoyle(5) 7 42
(Phil McEntee) *outpcd and bhd fr 1/2-way* 10/1
4- 7 1 1/4 **Jungle George**[15] 8569 3-9-5 0 (p) GeorgeBaker 5 38
(Scott Dixon) *dwlt: a bhd* 25/1

59.08s (0.28) **Going Correction** -0.05s/f (Stan) 7 Ran SP% **117.2**
Speed ratings (Par 97): **95,94,90,88,86 80,78**
CSF £17.12 TOTE £5.40: £2.80, £2.20; EX 20.10 Trifecta £74.60.
**Owner** Privee & Mrs Antoinette G Kavanagh **Bred** Kildaragh Stud **Trained** Upper Lambourn, Berks

**FOCUS**
Modest maiden form. It's been rated around the runner-up to her early form.

## 213 32RED FILLIES' H'CAP 1m 4f (P)
3:00 (3:05) (Class 5) (0-75,75) 4-Y-O+ £3,881 (£1,155; £577; £288) Stalls Low

Form RPR
451- 1 **Zain Arion (IRE)**[29] 8381 4-9-0 71 JFEgan 2 77
(John Butler) *trckd ldrs: nt clr run 2f out: fnd gap and led ins fnl f: rdn out* 6/4[1]
20-2 2 1 1/2 **Heartstone (IRE)**[7] 99 4-8-7 69 HollieDoyle(5) 6 73
(David Evans) *hld up in rr: effrt 2f out: r.o to take 2nd fnl 50yds* 3/1[3]
1- 3 1/2 **Dream Love**[30] 8366 4-9-4 75 RobertHavlin 4 78
(Simon Dow) *hld up in 4th: hdwy 2f out: kpt on same pce fnl f* 11/4[2]
0-0 4 1 1/4 **Celestial Bay**[9] 38 8-9-3 75 MitchGodwin(5) 5 76
(Sylvester Kirk) *chsd ldr: led over 2f out: hrd rdn over 1f out: hdd and no ex ins fnl f* 12/1
165- 5 17 **Princess Raihana**[29] 8381 4-9-0 71 (p) TomMarquand 1 45
(Marco Botti) *led tl wknd and n.m.r over 2f out: sn bhd* 7/1

2m 33.15s (0.15) **Going Correction** -0.05s/f (Stan)
**WFA** 4 from 5yo+ 3lb 5 Ran SP% **111.9**
Speed ratings (Par 100): **97,96,95,94,83**
CSF £6.43 TOTE £2.30: £1.20, £1.80; EX 6.80 Trifecta £16.40.
**Owner** Asaad Al Banwan **Bred** Lynch Bages & Camas Park Stud **Trained** Newmarket, Suffolk
■ Stewards' Enquiry : Tom Marquand caution; careless riding

**FOCUS**
This was steadily run and developed into a sprint.

## 214 SUNBETS.CO.UK H'CAP 1m 1y(P)
3:30 (3:37) (Class 6) (0-65,65) 4-Y-O+ £2,911 (£866; £432; £216) Stalls Low

Form RPR
200- 1 **Polymnia**[13] 8590 4-9-2 65 HollieDoyle(5) 11 73
(Richard Hannon) *sn w ldr: led 2f out and kicked 3 l clr: rdn out* 14/1
50-0 2 1 3/4 **Lucky Louie**[11] 20 4-9-2 60 JackMitchell 10 64
(Roger Teal) *dwlt: bhd: gd hdwy over 1f out: str run to take 2nd nr fin* 16/1
300- 3 hd **Athletic**[107] 6872 8-9-4 62 JFEgan 6 65
(David Evans) *hld up in 6th: hdwy to chse wnr 1f out: kpt on: eased and lost 2nd nr fin* 7/2[3]
466- 4 1 1/2 **Polar Kite (IRE)**[16] 8555 9-9-2 63 (h) RobHornby(3) 4 63
(Michael Attwater) *towards rr: hdwy over 1f out: nrest at fin* 12/1
60-0 5 1 1/2 **With Approval (IRE)**[7] 90 5-9-4 65 CallumShepherd(3) 3 61
(Laura Mongan) *towards rr: rdn over 2f out: sme late hdwy* 14/1
42-1 6 1/2 **Nonchalant**[9] 46 6-8-10 61 (b) AledBeech(7) 1 56
(Hugo Froud) *led tl 2f out: wknd over 1f out* 11/4[2]
400- 7 nk **Palace Moon**[140] 5832 12-8-10 54 (t) KierenFox 8 48
(Michael Attwater) *prom tl wknd wl over 1f out* 33/1
05-4 8 1 3/4 **Aye Aye Skipper (IRE)**[9] 52 7-8-7 51 oh4 (t[1]) WilliamCarson 7 41
(Ken Cunningham-Brown) *in tch: short of room and outpcd 2f out: hld whn nt clr run ins fnl f* 25/1
335- 9 2 1/2 **Bloodsweatandtears**[37] 8258 9-9-5 63 RobertHavlin 12 47
(William Knight) *hld up in rr: rdn over 2f out: nvr nr ldrs* 16/1
000- 10 1 1/4 **Etaad (USA)**[44] 8163 6-9-6 64 (b) GeorgeBaker 2 45
(Gary Moore) *a towards rr* 6/4[1]
66-0 11 2 **Hercullian Prince**[4] 145 5-9-0 65 (p) CallumRodriguez(7) 9 41
(Conor Dore) *chsd ldrs tl wknd over 2f out* 100/1

1m 36.47s (-1.73) **Going Correction** -0.05s/f (Stan) 11 Ran SP% **129.5**
Speed ratings (Par 101): **106,104,104,102,101 100,100,98,96,94 92**
CSF £233.94 CT £993.96 TOTE £16.60: £3.40, £5.00, £1.40; EX 183.60 Trifecta £2926.70.
**Owner** R Hannon **Bred** R G Percival **Trained** East Everleigh, Wilts
■ Stewards' Enquiry : J F Egan 10-day ban; not riding out (30th-4th Feb, 6th-9th Feb)

**FOCUS**
A modest handicap but it was well run and there were one or two noteworthy performances. The winner has been rated back to her best.

## 215 BETWAY APPRENTICE H'CAP 5f 6y(P)
4:00 (4:00) (Class 6) (0-65,73) 4-Y-O+ £2,911 (£866; £432; £216) Stalls High

Form RPR
21-1 1 **Lady Nayef**[11] 22 4-10-4 73 6ex (t) MillyNaseb 6 81
(John Butler) *led for over 2f: led again over 1f out: rdn out* 11/4[2]
31-2 2 3/4 **Temple Road (IRE)**[7] 95 9-9-3 65 (bt) FinleyMarsh(7) 4 70
(Milton Bradley) *hld up in midfield: smooth hdwy over 1f out: rdn and r.o to take 2nd nr fin* 6/4[1]
443- 3 1 1/4 **Pharoh Jake**[13] 8596 9-9-4 59 JaneElliott 2 60
(John Bridger) *plld hrd: prom on inner: chal over 1f out: one pce ins fnl f* 8/1
560- 4 3/4 **Misu Moneypenny**[181] 4378 4-9-10 65 (p) BenRobinson 3 63
(Scott Dixon) *dwlt: sn in midfield: effrt over 1f out: r.o fnl f* 33/1
604- 5 1/2 **Quality Art (USA)**[28] 8408 9-8-6 52 WilliamCox(5) 5 48
(Simon Hodgson) *sn cl up: rdn to press ldrs over 1f out: one pce* 14/1
064- 6 shd **Frank The Barber (IRE)**[13] 8596 5-8-12 56 (t) KatherineGlenister(3) 1 52
(Steph Hollinshead) *towards rr: rdn and dropped to last over 2f out: hdwy on inner over 1f out: no imp* 6/1[3]
205- 7 hd **Ask The Guru**[13] 8596 7-9-1 56 (p) KieranSchofield 7 51
(Michael Attwater) *chsd ldr: led over 2f out tl over 1f out: wknd fnl f* 20/1
42-0 8 3/4 **Excellent Aim**[8] 64 10-9-1 61 ow1 DarylMcLaughlin(5) 9 54
(George Margarson) *dropped in fr wd stall sn after s: nvr trbld ldrs* 16/1
040- 9 1 **Red Flute**[69] 7811 5-8-5 51 (v) JonathanFisher(5) 8 40+
(Denis Quinn) *rrd s and missed break: a bhd* 14/1

59.6s (0.80) **Going Correction** -0.05s/f (Stan) 9 Ran SP% **119.0**
Speed ratings (Par 101): **91,89,87,86,85 85,85,84,82**
CSF £7.50 CT £29.07 TOTE £3.60: £1.50, £1.30, £1.90; EX 8.20 Trifecta £30.40.
**Owner** Greenstead Hall Racing Ltd **Bred** Greenstead Hall Racing Ltd **Trained** Newmarket, Suffolk

**FOCUS**
An ordinary sprint run at a fairly steady early gallop, and two in-form horses came to the fore. The winner has been rated more or less to her Southwell form.
T/Jkpt: Not won. T/Plt: £126.80 to a £1 stake. Pool: £88,646.74 - 510.20 winning tickets T/Qpdt: £42.00 to a £1 stake. Pool: £6,997.96 - 123.10 winning tickets **Lee McKenzie**

# 160 WOLVERHAMPTON (A.W) (L-H)
Friday, January 13

**OFFICIAL GOING: Tapeta: standard**
Wind: Fresh across Weather: Fine

## 216 BETWAY SPRINT H'CAP (DIV I) 6f 20y (Tp)
5:45 (5:45) (Class 6) (0-60,61) 4-Y-O+ £2,749 (£818; £408; £204) Stalls Low

Form RPR
060- 1 **Top Of The Bank**[16] 8555 4-9-7 60 (p) TonyHamilton 8 68
(Kristin Stubbs) *mde all: rdn and edgd rt over 1f out: styd on* 8/1
54-4 2 1/2 **Harmonic Wave (IRE)**[8] 80 4-9-7 60 (p) PJMcDonald 10 66
(Rebecca Menzies) *hld up: hdwy over 1f out: r.o to go 2nd wl ins fnl f: nt quite rch wnr* 16/5[1]
36-0 3 3/4 **Kyllach Me (IRE)**[8] 80 5-9-0 56 (b) NathanEvans(3) 6 60
(Bryan Smart) *prom: rdn over 2f out: r.o* 7/2[2]
22-4 4 1 1/4 **Burauq**[7] 88 5-9-0 53 (b) LukeMorris 1 53
(Milton Bradley) *prom: rdn to chse wnr over 1f out: no ex wl ins fnl f* 8/1
50-0 5 nk **Socialites Red**[11] 22 4-9-8 61 (p) KieranO'Neill 3 60
(Scott Dixon) *chsd ldrs: rdn over 2f out: styd on same pce ins fnl f* 8/1
060- 6 1 3/4 **City Of Angkor Wat (IRE)**[13] 8595 7-9-6 59 (p) DavidNolan 7 53
(Conor Dore) *mid-div: pushed along and hdwy over 1f out: no ex ins fnl f* 5/1[3]
00-0 7 1/2 **Minty Jones**[9] 51 8-8-2 46 oh1 (v) PhilDennis(5) 2 38
(Michael Mullineaux) *plld hrd: trckd wnr tl rdn over 1f out: wknd ins fnl f* 100/1
600- 8 3/4 **Top Cop**[92] 7302 8-8-7 46 oh1 (p) DavidProbert 5 36
(Ronald Harris) *hld up: hdwy over 1f out: wknd ins fnl f* 14/1
3/4 9 1 **Tihana**[7] 95 4-9-4 57 AndrewMullen 9 44
(John Murray) *mid-div: pushed along over 2f out: wknd fnl f* 25/1
00-0 10 nk **Firgrove Bridge (IRE)**[9] 51 5-8-8 47 oh1 ow1 JohnFahy 4 33
(Kevin Frost) *s.i.s: shkn up over 1f out: nvr on terms* 33/1

300- **11** *9* **Smart Dj**[34] 8315 6-8-7 **49**................................ JackDuern(3) 11 8
(Sarah Hollinshead) *s.i.s: hld up: plld hrd: rdn over 2f out: sn wknd* **25/1**
1m 13.74s (-0.76) **Going Correction** -0.075s/f (Stan) **11** Ran SP% **114.3**
Speed ratings (Par 101): **102,101,100,98,98 95,95,94,92,92 80**
CSF £31.79 CT £106.63 TOTE £11.30: £3.00, £1.70, £1.70; EX 45.90 Trifecta £200.60.
**Owner** Paramount Racing I **Bred** D Carroll **Trained** Norton, N Yorks

**FOCUS**
This was lowly stuff and featured very few horses with recent place form. The winner was taking advantage of a career-low mark.

## 217 BETWAY SPRINT H'CAP (DIV II) — 6f 20y (Tp)
**6:15** (6:16) (Class 6) (0-60,61) 4-Y-0+ **£2,749** (£818; £408; £204) **Stalls** Low

Form RPR
465- **1** **Hamish McGonagain**[123] 6408 4-9-2 **60**..................(p) DavidParkes(5) 6 71+
(Jeremy Gask) *hld up in tch: shkn up over 1f out: rdn to ld and hung rt ins fnl f: r.o wl* **4/1**[3]
002- **2** *3 ¼* **Mr Chuckles (IRE)**[17] 8542 4-8-11 **50**......................(p) AndrewMullen 8 51
(Daniel Mark Loughnane) *prom: shkn up over 2f out: rdn and hmpd ins fnl f: styd on to go 2nd post* **2/1**[1]
040- **3** *shd* **Cee Jay**[22] 8496 4-9-5 **58**................................................(p) AdamKirby 7 59
(Robert Cowell) *sn pushed along to ld: rdn over 1f out: hdd and edgd rt ins fnl f: no ex* **7/2**[2]
30-0 **4** *¾* **Life Of Fame**[9] 44 4-9-3 **56**...................................... DougieCostello 1 55
(Mark Walford) *led early: chsd ldr to 1/2-way: rdn and ev ch over 1f out: no ex ins fnl f* **11/1**
50-0 **5** *¾* **Diamond Vine (IRE)**[7] 88 9-8-9 **48**.........................(p) DavidProbert 3 44
(Ronald Harris) *hld up: rdn over 2f out: nt trble ldrs* **25/1**
00-0 **6** *nk* **Cytringan**[9] 52 4-8-4 **46** oh1...................................... SimonPearce(3) 9 42
(Lydia Pearce) *hld up: hdwy over 1f out: no ex ins fnl f* **40/1**
24-0 **7** *hd* **Baileys Pursuit**[8] 67 5-9-8 **61**................................(v[1]) TonyHamilton 10 57
(Gay Kelleway) *chsd ldrs: wnt 2nd 1/2-way: rdn and ev ch over 1f out: hmpd ins fnl f: wknd towards fin* **11/2**
000- **8** *shd* **National Service (USA)**[17] 8542 6-9-0 **53**..........(p) TimmyMurphy 5 48
(Richard Ford) *hld up: effrt over 1f out: no ex ins fnl f* **14/1**
430- **9** *1* **Bushwise (IRE)**[17] 8542 4-8-7 **46** oh1...........................(p) LukeMorris 2 38
(Milton Bradley) *chsd ldrs: rdn over 2f out: wknd ins fnl f* **50/1**
1m 13.9s (-0.60) **Going Correction** -0.075s/f (Stan) **9** Ran SP% **114.2**
Speed ratings (Par 101): **101,96,96,95,94 94,93,93,92**
CSF £12.08 CT £29.67 TOTE £5.30: £1.50, £1.10, £1.90; EX 15.20 Trifecta £57.30.
**Owner** Hart Racing **Bred** Llety Farms **Trained** Stockbridge, Hants

**FOCUS**
This was every bit as weak as the first division and was run in a slower time. The winner landed some tidy bets. The race has been rated with feet on the ground.

## 218 BETWAY MARATHON H'CAP — 1m 5f 194y
**6:45** (6:45) (Class 6) (0-65,71) 4-Y-0+ **£2,749** (£818; £408; £204) **Stalls** Low

Form RPR
/4-1 **1** **Pivot Bridge**[8] 74 9-10-4 **71** 6ex...................................... AdamKirby 8 79
(Adrian McGuinness, Ire) *hld up: pushed along over 2f out: hdwy over 1f out: rdn to ld ins fnl f: styd on* **8/11**[1]
361- **2** *1 ¾* **Captain Swift (IRE)**[17] 8540 6-9-10 **63**..................(p) AndrewMullen 13 69
(John Mackie) *s.i.s: hld up: nt clr run over 2f out: hdwy over 1f out: rdn to chse wnr ins fnl f: styd on* **14/1**
10-3 **3** *1 ½* **Stonecoldsoba**[8] 70 4-9-2 **61**.............................. RobertWinston 7 64
(David Evans) *a.p: rdn over 2f out: styd on to go 3rd nr fin* **11/2**[2]
05-3 **4** *nk* **Dream Serenade**[7] 98 4-8-5 **50**..................................(h) LukeMorris 3 53
(Michael Appleby) *led 1f: chsd ldr tl led again over 2f out: rdn over 1f out: hdd ins fnl f: styd on same pce* **12/1**
05-2 **5** *1* **Macksville (IRE)**[9] 39 4-8-13 **63**............................... DavidParkes(5) 9 65
(Jeremy Gask) *hld up: hdwy over 1f out: sn rdn: no ex ins fnl f* **8/1**[3]
355- **6** *3 ¼* **Dynamo (IRE)**[135] 6022 6-9-5 **58**..........................................(t) ShaneKelly 6 55
(Richard Hughes) *hld up: hdwy over 2f out: rdn over 1f out: wknd ins fnl f* **33/1**
/60- **7** *1 ¾* **Gambol (FR)**[55] 7755 7-9-6 **62**..........................(p[1]) GeorgeDowning(3) 12 57
(Ian Williams) *led at stdy pce after 1f: qcknd over 3f out: rdn and hdd over 2f out: wknd ins fnl f* **14/1**
44-0 **8** *1 ¼* **Qibtee (FR)**[9] 46 7-8-8 **52**........................................... PhilDennis(5) 11 45
(Les Eyre) *hld up: rdn over 2f out: nvr on terms* **66/1**
00-6 **9** *nk* **Yul Finegold (IRE)**[9] 39 7-9-11 **64**..................................(b) DavidNolan 1 56
(Conor Dore) *dwlt: hld up: rdn over 3f out: a in rr* **66/1**
620- **10** *6* **Earthwindorfire**[65] 7870 6-9-8 **61**..............................(p) TimmyMurphy 10 45
(Geoffrey Deacon) *chsd ldrs tl rdn: hung rt and wknd over 2f out* **50/1**
535- **R** **Topaling**[22] 8488 6-9-6 **59**........................................ ThomasBrown 5
(Mark H Tompkins) *ref to r* **20/1**
3m 2.66s (-2.14) **Going Correction** -0.075s/f (Stan)
**WFA** 4 from 6yo+ 4lb **11** Ran SP% **118.1**
Speed ratings (Par 101): **103,102,101,100,100 98,97,96,96,93**
CSF £12.38 CT £37.82 TOTE £1.50: £1.10, £2.30, £2.20; EX 12.20 Trifecta £37.10.
**Owner** D Daly **Bred** Newsells Park Stud **Trained** Lusk, Co Dublin

**FOCUS**
This staying handicap revolved around last week's wide-margin winner Pivot Bridge, who produced a fine weight carrying performance to follow up under his penalty. Sound form for the grade.

## 219 BETWAY H'CAP — 6f 20y (Tp)
**7:15** (7:18) (Class 4) (0-85,87) 4-Y-0+ **£5,175** (£1,540; £769; £384) **Stalls** Low

Form RPR
040- **1** **Fast Track**[111] 6792 6-9-7 **85**........................................ PhillipMakin 5 93
(David Barron) *trckd ldrs: wnt 2nd over 2f out: rdn to ld ins fnl f: r.o* **11/4**[1]
1-03 **2** *nk* **Oriental Relation (IRE)**[8] 79 6-9-5 **83**..........................(v) TomEaves 7 90
(James Given) *chsd ldr tl led over 3f out: rdn over 1f out: edgd rt and hdd ins fnl f: r.o* **20/1**
014- **3** *nk* **Captain Dion**[14] 8583 4-9-7 **85**..........................................(p[1]) KevinStott 4 91
(Kevin Ryan) *sn led: hdd over 3f out: chsd ldr: rdn and ev ch fr over 1f out: r.o* **7/2**[2]
064- **4** *½* **Fairway To Heaven (IRE)**[28] 8402 8-9-2 **80**..................... AdamKirby 2 84
(Michael Wigham) *chsd ldrs: rdn over 1f out: styd on* **25/1**
333- **5** *nk* **Sophisticated Heir (IRE)**[16] 8561 7-8-9 **80**.........(b) LewisEdmunds(7) 8 83
(Michael Herrington) *hld up in tch: plld hrd: pushed along and swtchd lft over 1f out: unable qck towards fin* **9/2**[3]
14-0 **6** *2 ¼* **Landing Night (IRE)**[12] 4 5-9-1 **79**........................(tp) PJMcDonald 13 75
(Rebecca Menzies) *s.i.s: hld up: rdn over 1f out: r.o towards fin: nvr nrr* **40/1**
000- **7** *½* **Picture Dealer**[29] 8380 8-8-10 **77**..............................(t) SimonPearce(3) 3 72
(Lydia Pearce) *s.i.s: hld up: hdwy over 1f out: no imp ins fnl f* **66/1**
342- **8** *½* **Plucky Dip**[29] 8380 6-9-5 **83**............................................. DannyBrock 12 76
(John Ryan) *chsd ldrs: rdn over 2f out: hung lft and no ex fnl f* **16/1**

30-0 **9** *¾* **King Of Swing**[8] 79 4-9-0 **78**........................................(h) ShaneKelly 1 69
(Richard Hughes) *in rr whn pushed along 4f out: nvr on terms* **100/1**
340- **10** *½* **Welease Bwian (IRE)**[43] 8176 8-8-7 **74**....................... AaronJones(3) 9 63
(Stuart Williams) *in rr and rdn 1/2-way: nvr on terms* **150/1**
1m 12.66s (-1.84) **Going Correction** -0.075s/f (Stan) **10** Ran SP% **87.1**
Speed ratings (Par 105): **109,108,108,107,107 104,103,102,101,101**
CSF £32.35 CT £68.83 TOTE £2.60: £1.20, £2.90, £1.50; EX 25.10 Trifecta £70.10.
**Owner** Mrs Christine Barron **Bred** Jnp Bloodstock Ltd **Trained** Maunby, N Yorks
■ Eljaddaaf was withdrawn. Price at time of withdrawal 5/2f. Rule 4 applies to all bets - deduction 25p in the pound.

**FOCUS**
This feature handicap was robbed of much of its interest following the late withdrawal of last week's easy Kempton winner Eljaddaaf. It still took plenty of winning, though and served up a good finish. It's been rated around the runner-up.

## 220 BETWAY MIDDLE DISTANCE H'CAP — 1m 4f 51y (Tp)
**7:45** (7:45) (Class 5) (0-75,72) 4-Y-0+ **£3,234** (£962; £481; £240) **Stalls** Low

Form RPR
F1-2 **1** **Bamako Du Chatelet (FR)**[10] 30 6-9-4 **66**.......(p) RichardKingscote 6 73
(Ian Williams) *chsd ldrs: rdn over 1f out: r.o to ld nr fin* **7/4**[1]
461- **2** *hd* **Zabeel Star (IRE)**[24] 8462 5-9-10 **72**............................ RobertWinston 4 78
(Graeme McPherson) *hld up: racd keenly: hdwy 2f out: shkn up to ld 1f out: sn rdn: hdd nr fin* **15/8**[2]
220- **3** *3 ½* **Handsome Dan (IRE)**[111] 1067 11-9-6 **71**...................... JackDuern(3) 3 71
(Sarah Hollinshead) *hld up: hdwy 1/2-way: rdn over 2f out: styd on same pce ins fnl f* **16/1**
320- **4** *nk* **Chantecler**[42] 6365 6-9-10 **72**..........................................(t) LiamKeniry 7 72
(Neil Mulholland) *plld hrd in 2nd: tl rdn to ld over 1f out: sn hdd: no ex ins fnl f* **9/1**
062- **5** *2* **Maroc**[30] 8364 4-9-1 **67**..............................................(p) LukeMorris 1 64
(Nikki Evans) *racd keenly: led at stdy pce tl qckd over 2f out: rdn and hdd over 1f out: wknd wl ins fnl f* **50/1**
006- **6** *7* **Cottesloe (IRE)**[18] 8524 8-9-6 **68**.......................................(h) AdamKirby 2 54
(Neil Mulholland) *hld up: pushed along over 3f out: outpcd fr over 2f out* **4/1**[3]
2m 39.4s (-1.40) **Going Correction** -0.075s/f (Stan)
**WFA** 4 from 5yo+ 3lb **6** Ran SP% **109.0**
Speed ratings (Par 103): **101,100,98,98,97 92**
CSF £4.98 TOTE £2.10: £1.80, £1.40; EX 4.80 Trifecta £33.00.
**Owner** Macable Partnership **Bred** S N C Ecurie Jouenne Gerard **Trained** Portway, Worcs

**FOCUS**
This was fought out by two in-form horses and rates as solid form for the level. Muddling form rated around the first two.

## 221 SUNBETS.CO.UK MEDIAN AUCTION MAIDEN STKS — 7f 36y (Tp)
**8:15** (8:17) (Class 6) 3-4-Y-0 **£2,749** (£818; £408; £204) **Stalls** High

Form RPR
22-3 **1** **Espresso Freddo (IRE)**[8] 72 3-8-10 75....................(p[1]) LukeMorris 8 76
(Sir Mark Prescott Bt) *hld up in tch: plld hrd: shkn up over 1f out: led ins fnl f: r.o* **5/1**[3]
432- **2** *1 ½* **Sidewinder (IRE)**[16] 8556 3-8-10 72........................ RichardKingscote 9 72
(Tom Dascombe) *edgd rt s: chsd ldr tl led over 1f out: rdn and hdd ins fnl f: styd on same pce* **3/1**[2]
3- **3** *1 ¼* **Hart Stopper**[238] 2437 3-8-10 0....................................... TomMarquand 10 69+
(Michael Bell) *hmpd s: hld up: hdwy over 1f out: r.o* **15/2**
0 **4** *3 ¾* **State Residence (IRE)**[6] 115 3-8-10 0.............................. ShaneKelly 3 60+
(David Simcock) *hld up: rdn over 2f out: r.o ins fnl f: nvr nrr* **9/1**
2-22 **5** *nk* **Things Happen**[8] 72 3-8-10 70...................................... RobertWinston 7 59
(David Evans) *wnt lft s: chsd ldrs: rdn over 2f out: edgd lft and wknd ins fnl f* **5/2**[1]
0- **6** *1 ¾* **Jai Hanuman (IRE)**[30] 8352 3-8-10 0..................................(t) LiamKeniry 2 55
(Seamus Durack) *chsd ldrs: rdn over 2f out: wknd fnl f* **50/1**
4-4 **7** *¾* **Champagne Freddie**[6] 127 4-9-9 0............................. CiaranMckee(5) 4 57
(John O'Shea) *sn led: rdn and hdd over 1f out: wknd ins fnl f* **50/1**
**8** *1 ½* **Sanches** 3-8-10 0................................................................ MartinLane 1 50
(Simon Crisford) *mid-div: sn pushed along: effrt over 2f out: wknd fnl f* **8/1**
**9** *12* **Mister Raffles** 3-8-7 0..................................................(t[1]) EoinWalsh(3) 12 20
(Mohamed Moubarak) *dwlt: outpcd* **66/1**
3- **10** *1* **Joys Delight**[42] 8189 3-8-5 0........................................... AndrewMullen 6 13
(Daniel Mark Loughnane) *hmpd s: hung rt almost thrght: hdwy over 4f out: eased fnl 2f* **22/1**
00- **11** *2 ½* **Pipe Dreamer**[57] 7988 3-8-10 0........................................ TomEaves 5 12
(Kevin Ryan) *sn outpcd* **50/1**
1m 28.33s (-0.47) **Going Correction** -0.075s/f (Stan)
**WFA** 3 from 4yo 18lb **11** Ran SP% **114.8**
Speed ratings (Par 101): **99,97,95,91,91 89,88,86,72,71 68**
CSF £19.21 TOTE £5.90: £2.10, £1.60, £2.30; EX 22.60 Trifecta £128.50.
**Owner** Middleham Park Racing LII **Bred** Knocklong House Stud **Trained** Newmarket, Suffolk

**FOCUS**
A fair maiden and positives to take from the first four home.

## 222 SUNBETS.CO.UK DOWNLOAD THE APP H'CAP — 7f 36y (Tp)
**8:45** (8:47) (Class 6) (0-60,60) 4-Y-0+ **£2,749** (£818; £408; £204) **Stalls** High

Form RPR
00-0 **1** **Dr Red Eye**[11] 26 9-8-11 **50**...........................................(p) KieranO'Neill 4 56
(Scott Dixon) *led: rdn and hdd over 1f out: rallied to ld post* **33/1**
30-2 **2** *shd* **Prisom (IRE)**[11] 26 4-9-5 **58**....................................(p[1]) TomMarquand 3 64
(Gay Kelleway) *chsd ldrs: rdn to ld over 1f out: hdd post* **7/2**[1]
50-3 **3** *½* **Fossa**[9] 51 7-8-2 **46** oh1........................................ CharlieBennett(5) 2 51
(Mark Brisbourne) *hld up: hmpd 2f out: swtchd rt and hdwy over 1f out: rdn and hung lft ins fnl f: r.o* **8/1**
132- **4** *hd* **Keene's Pointe**[87] 7444 7-9-7 **60**................................... AdamBeschizza 1 64
(Steph Hollinshead) *hld up: hdwy and nt clr run over 2f out: rdn over 1f out: unable qck towards fin* **25/1**
0-05 **5** *1 ¼* **Captain K (IRE)**[6] 123 5-8-7 **46**..........................................(h) JohnFahy 5 47
(Gordon Elliott, Ire) *chsd ldr 3f: remained handy: nt clr run over 1f out: styd on same pce ins fnl f* **4/1**[2]
343- **6** *1 ½* **Forest Lakes (IRE)**[95] 7230 4-9-5 **58**.................................. ShaneKelly 9 56
(Paul D'Arcy) *hld up: r.o ins fnl f: nvr nrr* **17/2**
405- **7** *nk* **Misu Pete**[22] 8490 5-9-1 **54**.......................................... SteveDrowne 7 51
(Mark Usher) *hld up in tch: plld hrd: rdn over 1f out: styd on same pce fnl f* **8/1**
00-6 **8** *shd* **Basingstoke (IRE)**[11] 26 8-9-5 **58**................................(b) LukeMorris 10 55
(Daniel Mark Loughnane) *sn prom: chsd ldr 4f out tl rdn over 1f out: edgd lft and no ex ins fnl f* **11/1**


The Form Book Flat, Raceform Ltd, Newbury, RG14 5SJ

F0-2 **9** 1/2 **Disclosure**[8] 80 6-9-4 **57**....(h) JasonHart 6 52
(Les Eyre) *hld up: racd keenly: nt clr run 2f out: hdwy over 1f out: sn rdn: no ex ins fnl f* **9/2**[3]

000- **10** 13 **Eddy Mercs**[113] 6703 5-8-0 **46** oh1....(t[1]) RPWalsh(7) 12 9
(Michael Appleby) *dwlt: hdwy 1/2-way: rdn and wknd over 2f out* **66/1**

600- **11** 3 1/4 **Never To Be (USA)**[22] 8500 6-8-12 **54**....(vt) CallumShepherd(3) 8 10
(Nikki Evans) *hld up: hdwy over 4f out: rdn and wknd over 1f out* **22/1**

1m 29.36s (0.56) **Going Correction** -0.075s/f (Stan) **11** Ran SP% **114.1**
Speed ratings (Par 101): **93,92,92,92,90 88,88,88,87,73 69**
CSF £138.32 CT £814.13 TOTE £31.60: £6.50, £1.70, £2.80; EX 148.80 Trifecta £998.40.
**Owner** P J Dixon & Partners **Bred** G E Amey **Trained** Babworth, Notts

**FOCUS**
An ordinary handicap, though no shortage of drama as veteran Dr Red Eye battled back for a surprise win. The runner-up helps set the opening level.
T/Plt: £3.70 to a £1 stake. Pool: £126,654.09 - 24,410.96 winning tickets T/Qpdt: £2.20 to a £1 stake. Pool: £10,015.83 - 3,321.82 winning tickets **Colin Roberts**

223 - 226a (Foreign Racing) - See Raceform Interactive

## 101 DUNDALK (A.W) (L-H)
Friday, January 13
**OFFICIAL GOING: Polytrack: standard**

### 227a VODATRADE.IE - DIGITAL MARKETING AND WEBSITE DESIGN SERVICES H'CAP 2m (P)
**7:00** (7:00) 4-Y-0+ **£12,615** (£3,897; £1,846; £820; £307)

RPR

1 **Winter Lion (IRE)**[42] 8202 7-8-11 **79**....(bt) WayneLordan 5 91+
(Matthew J Smith, Ire) *mde all: over 1 l clr at 1/2-way: stl gng wl appr st: drvn clr over 1f out and sn in command: styd on wl: comf* **3/1**[2]

2 5 1/2 **Venezia (IRE)**[42] 8202 6-8-6 **74**....(bt) ConorHoban 2 78
(M Halford, Ire) *dwlt and pushed along in rr early: disp 6th at 1/2-way: sme hdwy on outer over 1f out: rdn into mod 2nd ins fnl f and no imp on easy wnr: kpt on same pce* **9/2**

3 3/4 **Mandatario**[63] 7916 6-9-10 **92**....(t) KevinManning 1 95
(J S Bolger, Ire) *chsd ldrs in 3rd early: 5th 1/2-way: 4th appr st: rdn and no imp on wnr 2f out: kpt on one pce in mod 3rd wl ins fnl f* **10/3**[3]

4 1/2 **Sharjah (IRE)**[21] 8516 7-7-13 **72**.... KillianLeonard(5) 7 75+
(Andrew Slattery, Ire) *cl up early tl sn settled bhd ldrs: disp 6th at 1/2-way: rdn in 6th 2f out and no imp over 1f out: kpt on u.p into mod 4th wl ins fnl f* **12/1**

5 2 3/4 **Guard of Honour (IRE)**[23] 8479 6-9-8 **90**....(b) ColinKeane 6 90
(George Baker) *hld up bhd ldrs tl tk clsr order in 2nd after 3f: rdn in 2nd appr st and sn no imp on easy wnr: one pce after and wknd into mod 5th ins fnl f* **5/2**[1]

6 1 1/2 **Black Label**[7] 105 6-7-11 **72** oh3....(b) DannySheehy(7) 3 70
(Adrian McGuinness, Ire) *hld up bhd ldrs: 3rd 1/2-way: rdn 2f out and no imp on wnr: wknd 1f out* **10/1**

7 25 **Rathmuck Native (IRE)**[21] 8514 9-7-11 **72** oh5.... SeanDavis(7) 4 42
(Peter Fahey, Ire) *cl up early: 4th 1/2-way: pushed along disputing 5th 4f out and no ex appr st where dropped to rr: wknd* **33/1**

3m 32.9s (3.30) **Going Correction** +0.35s/f (Slow) **7** Ran SP% **114.6**
Speed ratings: **105,102,101,101,100 99,87**
CSF £16.95 TOTE £4.10: £3.20, £1.90; DF 14.30 Trifecta £56.20.
**Owner** B J Hooper **Bred** Abergwaun Farms **Trained** Kilmessan, Co. Meath

**FOCUS**
A very straightforward success for the winner, taking advantage of the soft lead he was offered. A pb from the winner, with the runner-up offering a guide to the level.

228 - 231a (Foreign Racing) - See Raceform Interactive

## 209 LINGFIELD (L-H)
Saturday, January 14
**OFFICIAL GOING: Polytrack: standard**
Wind: Half against, moderate becoming almost nil Weather: Cloudy, raining race 3

### 232 32RED.COM FILLIES' H'CAP 1m 1y(P)
**12:15** (12:15) (Class 5) (0-75,76) 4-Y-0+ **£2,911** (£866; £432; £216) **Stalls** High

Form RPR

012- **1** **Skidby Mill (IRE)**[26] 8458 7-9-3 **71**.... GeorgeBaker 5 78
(Laura Mongan) *mde all: booted clr wl over 1f out: ld dwindled fnl f but a in command* **11/4**[2]

200- **2** 1/2 **Remember Me**[23] 8490 4-9-0 **68**.... RobertHavlin 3 74
(Hughie Morrison) *hld up in 5th: prog on outer over 2f out: rdn to chse clr wnr over 1f out: clsd fnl f but nvr gng to get there* **11/2**

103- **3** 4 **First Experience**[23] 8493 6-9-8 **76**....(v) AdamKirby 6 72
(Lee Carter) *cl up: rdn on outer 3f out: prog to chse wnr over 2f out to over 1f out: one pce* **9/4**[1]

506- **4** 1 3/4 **Minminwin (IRE)**[23] 8490 4-8-9 **63**....(t) TomMarquand 1 55
(Gay Kelleway) *dwlt: mostly in last: rdn 3f out and no prog: kpt on one pce fr over 1f out* **11/1**

300- **5** 3 **Italian Beauty (IRE)**[18] 8538 5-9-1 **69**....(p) WilliamCarson 8 54
(John Wainwright) *s.i.s: rousted to chse wnr: lost 2nd over 2f out: steadily wknd* **50/1**

025- **6** 3 **Jacquotte Delahaye**[36] 8287 6-9-6 **74**.... TomEaves 2 52
(David Brown) *hld up in rr: rdn and no prog over 2f out: sltly impeded sn after: no ch* **6/1**

226- **7** 13 **Indigo Princess**[30] 8381 4-8-10 **64**.... LukeMorris 7 10
(Michael Appleby) *chsd ldrs: rdn in 5th and hld whn stmbld bdly 2f out: nt rcvr and eased* **5/1**[3]

1m 37.35s (-0.85) **Going Correction** -0.05s/f (Stan) **7** Ran SP% **114.1**
Speed ratings (Par 100): **102,101,97,95,92 89,76**
CSF £18.09 CT £38.32 TOTE £2.90: £1.50, £4.20; EX 18.60 Trifecta £59.50.
**Owner** Charlie's Starrs **Bred** Michael O'Mahony **Trained** Epsom, Surrey

**FOCUS**
The going was given as standard, in contrast to the previous day's standard to slow. A modest fillies' race dominated by a course specialist. A small pb from the winner.

### 233 BETWAY CLASSIFIED (S) STKS 1m 4f (P)
**12:50** (12:50) (Class 6) 4-6-Y-0 **£2,264** (£673; £336; £168) **Stalls** Low

Form RPR

525- **1** **Fast Play (IRE)**[31] 8363 5-9-13 **67**....(b) ShaneKelly 7 71
(Richard Hughes) *hld up: prog on outer 3f out: tk 2nd 2f out: shkn up and upsides over 1f out: drvn to ld last 150yds: styd on* **5/2**[1]

00-6 **2** 1 1/4 **Marshal Dan Troop (IRE)**[3] 169 4-9-3 **62**....(b) GeorgeBaker 2 63
(Robyn Brisland) *dwlt: hld up in 4th: prog to trck ldng pair 2f out gng easily: shkn up to chal on inner over 1f out and upsides: fnd little and one pce last 150yds* **5/2**[1]

200- **3** 1/2 **Firestorm (GER)**[25] 8477 6-9-7 **69**....(e) AdamKirby 4 62
(Michael Attwater) *trckd ldng pair: wnt 2nd 3f out and rdn to ld jst over 2f out: jnd on both sides over 1f out: hdd and one pce last 150yds* **5/2**[1]

05-0 **4** 11 **Dalavand (IRE)**[7] 123 4-8-10 **53**.... OllieJago(7) 5 45
(Laura Mongan) *hld up in rr: rdn and no prog 3f out: wl btn after: tk modest 4th nr fin* **20/1**

04-0 **5** 1/2 **Cold Fusion (IRE)**[10] 49 4-9-9 **58**....(b) JamieSpencer 6 50
(David Flood) *hld up in rr: rdn and no prog 3f out: wl btn after* **16/1**

660- **6** 4 **Kissy Suzuki**[85] 7507 5-9-2 **55**.... CharlieBennett(5) 3 37
(Hughie Morrison) *chsd clr ldr to 3f out: wknd* **8/1**[2]

366- **7** 2 **Heavensfield**[16] 8565 4-9-3 **60**....(b[1]) StevieDonohoe 1 34
(Mark H Tompkins) *racd freely: led and clr: hdd & wknd qckly jst over 2f out* **14/1**[3]

2m 35.19s (2.19) **Going Correction** -0.05s/f (Stan)
**WFA** 4 from 5yo+ 3lb **7** Ran SP% **114.1**
Speed ratings: **90,89,88,81,81 78,77**
CSF £8.63 TOTE £3.50: £1.90, £1.60; EX 10.10 Trifecta £24.20.There was no bid for the winner.
**Owner** Boyd Mortimer Terry Wellard Partners **Bred** Fintan Walsh **Trained** Upper Lambourn, Berks

**FOCUS**
With the first-time blinkered Heavensfield setting a good gallop and the field racing more or less in single file, this was set up for the closers. It's possible the form is better than rated but it's against the grain to take chances at this level.

### 234 BETWAY BEST ODDS GUARANTEED PLUS H'CAP 6f 1y(P)
**1:25** (1:26) (Class 3) (0-95,96) 4-Y-0+ **£7,246** (£2,168; £1,084; £542; £270) **Stalls** Low

Form RPR

061- **1** **Jordan Sport**[29] 8407 4-9-2 **87**....(h) WilliamCarson 8 99
(David Simcock) *mde all: rdn over 1f out: styd on strly and clr fnl f* **9/2**[3]

030- **2** 2 **Kasbah (IRE)**[29] 8407 5-9-7 **92**.... JackMitchell 7 97
(Amanda Perrett) *s.i.s: t.k.h: hld up in last trio: prog on inner wl over 1f out: rdn and styd on to take 2nd last 50yds* **8/1**

000- **3** nk **Sign Of The Kodiac (IRE)**[24] 8484 4-9-11 **96**.... TomEaves 4 100
(James Given) *cl up on inner: rdn to chse wnr over 1f out: kpt on but no imp: lost 2nd last 50yds* **16/1**

152- **4** shd **Boomerang Bob (IRE)**[35] 8314 8-9-6 **91**....(p[1]) GeorgeBaker 1 95
(Jamie Osborne) *sn in midfield: rdn wl over 1f out: styd on to press for a pl fnl f: no threat to wnr* **15/8**[1]

013- **5** nk **Memories Galore (IRE)**[35] 8308 5-9-4 **89**.... LukeMorris 6 92
(Harry Dunlop) *t.k.h: hld up in midfield: prog over 1f out: kpt on to press for a pl ins fnl f* **7/2**[2]

50-0 **6** 1 3/4 **Highland Acclaim (IRE)**[13] 4 6-9-0 **85**.... SeanLevey 5 82
(David O'Meara) *t.k.h: hld up in tch: effrt over 2f out but wdst of all bnd sn after and lost grnd: kpt on one pce after* **12/1**

050- **7** 2 1/4 **Quatrieme Ami**[54] 8050 4-9-5 **90**....(t) DavidProbert 9 80
(Philip McBride) *hld up in last trio: rdn 2f out: brief effrt over 1f out: sn no prog* **8/1**

30-0 **8** 1 **Kingsley Klarion (IRE)**[9] 66 4-8-12 **83**.... JoeFanning 2 70
(Mark Johnston) *hld up in last trio: detached in last wl over 1f out: no ch* **20/1**

160- **9** nse **Ballesteros**[29] 8407 8-8-11 **82**.... TonyHamilton 10 69
(Richard Fahey) *t.k.h: chsd wnr to over 1f out: wknd qckly* **40/1**

400- **10** 4 **Sandfrankskipsgo**[25] 8463 8-8-12 **83**.... ShaneKelly 3 57
(Peter Crate) *plld hrd and sn pressed ldrs: wknd rapidly wl over 1f out* **50/1**

1m 10.56s (-1.34) **Going Correction** -0.05s/f (Stan) **10** Ran SP% **120.1**
Speed ratings (Par 107): **106,103,102,102,102 100,97,95,95,90**
CSF £40.90 CT £538.80 TOTE £5.60: £1.80, £2.60, £4.30; EX 46.50 Trifecta £675.00.
**Owner** M Khan X2 Pip Walter Harry Wigan **Bred** Rabbah Bloodstock Limited **Trained** Newmarket, Suffolk

**FOCUS**
A fast break from the winner soon saw him in the lead, and he was able to steady things once in control. The second to the fifth have been rated close to form.

### 235 SUNBETS.CO.UK H'CAP 1m 1y(P)
**2:00** (2:01) (Class 2) (0-105,98) 4-Y-0+ **£11,971** (£3,583; £1,791; £896; £446) **Stalls** Low

Form RPR

001- **1** **My Target (IRE)**[14] 8593 6-9-0 **91**.... DavidProbert 3 102+
(Michael Wigham) *hld up in rr: smooth prog fr 2f out: clsd on ldrs 1f: cajoled along to ld last 120yds: comf* **4/1**[3]

033- **2** 1 1/4 **Mr Bossy Boots (IRE)**[14] 8593 6-9-0 **94**....(t) KieranShoemark(3) 5 101
(Amanda Perrett) *rrd bdly s: hld up in rr: rdn over 2f out: prog on outer jst over 1f out: r.o to take 2nd nr fin: no ch to chal* **6/1**

654- **3** 1 **Bold Prediction (IRE)**[14] 8593 7-8-12 **89**.... LukeMorris 2 94
(Ed Walker) *led 2f: chsd ldr: rdn to take narrow ld over 1f out: hdd and outpcd last 120yds: lost 2nd nr fin* **5/1**

505- **4** nk **Third Time Lucky (IRE)**[14] 8593 5-9-7 **98**.... TonyHamilton 6 102
(Richard Fahey) *hld up in rr: shkn up and effrt 2f out: kpt on fr over 1f out but nvr pce to chal* **11/4**[1]

340- **5** 1 1/2 **Supersta**[37] 8279 6-9-2 **93**....(p) GeorgeBaker 8 94
(Michael Appleby) *t.k.h: hld up tl plld way through to ld after 2f: narrowly hdd over 1f out: wknd last 150yds* **8/1**

303- **6** 1/2 **Hawatif (IRE)**[111] 6810 4-8-2 **84** ow1.... MitchGodwin(5) 4 83
(Anthony Carson) *chsd ldrs: rdn over 2f out: no imp and wknd fr over 1f out* **66/1**

311- **7** 3 1/4 **Chester Street**[37] 8279 4-8-10 **87**....(h) JosephineGordon 1 79
(Roger Charlton) *broke out of stall bef r: t.k.h: chsd ldr 2f: rdn over 2f out: wknd over 1f out* **3/1**[2]

420- **8** 4 **Cricklewood Green (USA)**[18] 8539 6-7-13 **79**.... NoelGarbutt(3) 7 62
(Sylvester Kirk) *t.k.h early and hld up in last: rdn and struggling 1/2-way: sn bhd* **66/1**

1m 36.59s (-1.61) **Going Correction** -0.05s/f (Stan) **8** Ran SP% **116.7**
Speed ratings (Par 109): **106,104,103,103,101 101,98,94**
CSF £28.78 CT £121.86 TOTE £4.90: £1.80, £1.70, £2.20; EX 30.30 Trifecta £108.10.
**Owner** G Linder, M Wigham & J Williams **Bred** Darley **Trained** Newmarket, Suffolk

**FOCUS**
A good handicap, and an impressive performance from the winner, who at the age of six has never been better. The second has been rated as running as well as ever, and the third close to form.

## 236 32RED.COM MAIDEN STKS (DIV I) 1m 1y(P)
**2:35** (2:36) (Class 5) 3-Y-O £2,911 (£866; £432; £216) **Stalls** High

Form RPR
3 **1** **Blaze Of Glory (FR)**[10] 34 3-9-5 0 AdamKirby 9 85+
(Jamie Osborne) *mde virtually all at decent pce: drew clr over 2f out: in n.d over 1f out: pushed out* **9/4**[2]
**2** *1 ¼* **Fashion Business** 3-9-5 0 GeorgeBaker 6 78
(Roger Charlton) *sn in 4th: pushed along over 2f out: shkn up and prog over 1f out: tk 2nd jst ins fnl f: styd on wl and clsd on wnr but no ch* **9/2**[3]
**3** *1 ½* **Whosyourhousemate** 3-9-5 0 StevieDonohoe 11 74
(Ed Vaughan) *s.i.s: wl in rr: prog on outer over 2f out but stl long way off the pce: rdn and styd on wl to take 3rd ins fnl f: nrst fin* **50/1**
5- **4** *3 ¾* **Rock N Roll Global (IRE)**[31] 8353 3-9-5 0 ShaneKelly 8 65
(Richard Hughes) *sn chsd wnr: rdn fr 1/2-way: lost 2nd over 1f out: fdd* **6/1**
0- **5** *¾* **Sandy Shores**[31] 8361 3-9-0 0 JoeFanning 7 58
(Brian Meehan) *mostly in 6th: outpcd over 2f out: kpt on one pce fnl f* **20/1**
022- **6** *hd* **Ettu**[31] 8362 3-9-0 73 JamieSpencer 1 58
(Jeremy Noseda) *trckd ldng pair: drvn and no rspnse 2f out: wnt 2nd over 1f out to jst ins fnl f: wknd* **7/4**[1]
0- **7** *3 ¼* **Everdina**[73] 7762 3-9-0 0 ThomasBrown 10 50
(Ed Walker) *s.s: a wl in rr and wl off the pce* **50/1**
50- **8** *nk* **Greyjoy (IRE)**[17] 8557 3-9-0 0 MitchGodwin(5) 5 54
(Sylvester Kirk) *chsd ldrs in 5th: rdn over 2f out: wknd over 1f out* **100/1**
0- **9** *1 ½* **Bessemer Lady**[38] 8246 3-9-0 0 TomMarquand 4 46
(Ralph Beckett) *mostly in last pair and a bhd* **14/1**
0- **10** *nk* **Trautmann (IRE)**[29] 8404 3-8-12 0 TobyEley(7) 3 50
(Daniel Mark Loughnane) *a in rr: nvr a factor: wknd fnl f* **100/1**
1m 36.24s (-1.96) **Going Correction** -0.05s/f (Stan) **10** Ran SP% **116.9**
Speed ratings (Par 97): **107,105,104,100,99 99,96,96,94,94**
CSF £12.54 TOTE £4.00: £1.10, £2.00, £5.20; EX 13.70 Trifecta £221.70.
**Owner** Melbourne 10 Racing **Bred** Ecurie Des Monceaux **Trained** Upper Lambourn, Berks
**FOCUS**
This looked a fair maiden and the winner was impressive. The time was 1.02sec faster than the second division. The time and those with form back rating the race at this sort of level, but the fourth, seventh, eighth and ninth suggest the race could be rated a bit higher at face value.

## 237 32RED.COM MAIDEN STKS (DIV II) 1m 1y(P)
**3:10** (3:12) (Class 5) 3-Y-O £2,911 (£866; £432; £216) **Stalls** High

Form RPR
2- **1** **Opinionate**[38] 8245 3-9-5 0 RobertHavlin 6 79+
(Amanda Perrett) *trckd ldng pair: chal on outer 2f out: sltly green but drvn to ld 1f out: sn asserted and styd on wl* **15/8**[1]
42-2 **2** *1 ½* **Special Relation (IRE)**[10] 48 3-9-5 76 LiamKeniry 5 74
(Hughie Morrison) *trckd ldng trio: shkn up 2f out: nt qckn and outpcd by ldng trio: styd on fr over 1f out to take 2nd last 75yds* **2/1**[2]
6- **3** *1 ¼* **Cloud Dragon (IRE)**[30] 8384 3-9-5 0 JosephineGordon 2 71
(Hugo Palmer) *led: rdn 2f out and jnd: hdd and outpcd 1f out: lost 2nd last 75yds* **10/3**[3]
5-4 **4** *2* **Spinwheel**[9] 75 3-9-0 0 JoeFanning 8 61
(Mark Johnston) *trckd ldr: chal and upsides fr 2f out to jst over 1f out: fdd ins fnl f* **10/1**
**5** *½* **Trade Route (IRE)** 3-9-5 0 ShaneKelly 7 65
(David Elsworth) *in tch in midfield: pushed along and outpcd over 2f out: shkn up over 1f out: styd on ins fnl f and shaped w promise* **14/1**
**6** *hd* **Abaad (IRE)** 3-9-2 0 (b[1]) KieranShoemark(3) 9 64
(Roger Charlton) *s.i.s: mostly in last pair tl shkn up over 2f out: hanging and green over 1f out: styd on fnl f: nrst fin* **20/1**
**7** *2* **Damo** 3-9-5 0 JFEgan 3 60
(Simon Dow) *wl in tch: steadily lost pl fr 1/2-way and dropped to last trio 2f out: shkn up over 1f out: one pce after* **50/1**
- **8** *2* **Willwams (IRE)** 3-9-5 0 SeanLevey 10 55
(Richard Hannon) *in tch on outer: rdn 3f out: sn outpcd: nvr on terms after* **25/1**
0- **9** *2* **Lyrica's Lion (IRE)**[31] 8355 3-9-5 0 AdamBeschizza 4 50
(Mark Hoad) *a in last pair: nvr a factor* **150/1**
0- **10** *4 ½* **Dawn Goddess**[14] 8591 3-8-11 0 HectorCrouch(3) 1 34
(Gary Moore) *chsd ldrs: steadily wknd on inner fr over 2f out* **66/1**
1m 37.26s (-0.94) **Going Correction** -0.05s/f (Stan) **10** Ran SP% **119.7**
Speed ratings (Par 97): **102,100,99,97,96 96,94,92,90,86**
CSF £5.86 TOTE £2.90: £1.10, £1.40, £1.30; EX 6.60 Trifecta £15.10.
**Owner** K Abdullah **Bred** Millsec Limited **Trained** Pulborough, W Sussex
**FOCUS**
The slower of the two divisions by 1.02sec, and the first two both look the types to improve for a step up to 1m2f plus. The fourth could back the form being rated a bit better, but the ordinary time/pace and those behind ultimately determine the level.

## 238 BETWAY H'CAP 1m 2f (P)
**3:40** (3:46) (Class 6) (0-60,60) 4-Y-O+ £2,264 (£673; £336; £168) **Stalls** Low

Form RPR
134- **1** **Maverik**[74] 7754 9-9-7 60 (tp) AdamKirby 7 67
(Neil Mulholland) *trckd ldr: led 3f out and committed for home: drvn and pressed fr 2f out: kpt on and a jst holding off rivals* **11/4**[1]
544- **2** *½* **Dark Amber**[45] 8155 7-9-3 56 (tp) JosephineGordon 14 62
(Brendan Powell) *slowly away: wl in rr: gd prog between rivals over 1f out: drvn and styd on to take 2nd last 75yds: a jst hld* **8/1**
003- **3** *nk* **Suitsus**[74] 7736 6-9-5 58 (t[1]) TimmyMurphy 11 63
(Geoffrey Deacon) *slowly away: hld up wl in rr: effrt on outer whn v wd bnd 2f out: gd hdwy over 1f out: styd on ins fnl f: nvr quite able to chal* **25/1**
200- **4** *½* **Shining Romeo**[25] 8477 5-9-7 60 RobertHavlin 8 65
(Denis Quinn) *dwlt: sn in midfield: rdn and prog to chse wnr over 2f out: tried to chal over 1f out: nt qckn and hld after: lost 2 pls last 75yds* **8/1**
200- **5** *nk* **Runaiocht (IRE)**[25] 8462 7-9-2 60 (b) DavidParkes(5) 10 64
(Paul Burgoyne) *slowly away: hld up in last pair: gd prog and clr run on inner over 1f out: styd on fnl f: nrst fin* **15/2**
010- **6** *1* **Sunshineandbubbles**[19] 8524 4-9-1 59 (p) GeorgeDowning(3) 1 61
(Daniel Mark Loughnane) *in tch: effrt over 2f out: nt qckn and no imp ldrs over 1f out: one pce* **10/1**
103- **7** *½* **Kristal Hart**[19] 8527 8-9-5 58 (p) LiamKeniry 6 59
(Neil Mulholland) *chsd ldrs: rdn 3f out: one pce and no prog fr 2f out* **6/1**[3]
200- **8** *¾* **Hydrant**[15] 8586 11-9-6 59 JFEgan 13 59
(Richard Guest) *led: rdn and hdd 3f out: stl in 3rd 1f out: wknd* **33/1**
020- **9** *1 ¼* **Sexy Secret**[45] 8155 6-8-13 55 (p) SimonPearce(3) 2 52
(Lydia Pearce) *cl up on inner: rdn wl over 2f out: wknd over 1f out* **16/1**
356- **10** *2* **Gunner Moyne**[128] 6243 5-9-6 59 GeorgeBaker 5 53
(Gary Moore) *a towards rr: struggling over 2f out: sn no ch* **4/1**[2]
000- **11** *2 ¾* **Bookmaker**[17] 8555 7-9-2 55 (b) WilliamCarson 3 43
(John Bridger) *nvr bttr than midfield: u.p 4f out: wl btn over 2f out* **33/1**
000- **12** *15* **Daleelak (IRE)**[19] 8527 4-9-4 59 JoeFanning 12 19
(Mark Johnston) *prom tl wknd rapidly over 2f out: eased and t.o* **16/1**
2m 6.42s (-0.18) **Going Correction** -0.05s/f (Stan)
**WFA** 4 from 5yo+ 1lb **12** Ran SP% **125.5**
Speed ratings (Par 101): **98,97,97,96,96 95,95,94,93,92 90,78**
CSF £26.67 CT £474.10 TOTE £3.50: £2.30, £1.90, £8.70; EX 21.60 Trifecta £434.10.
**Owner** Star Contractors Limited **Bred** J G Davis & Star Pointe Ltd **Trained** Limpley Stoke, Wilts
■ Rianna Star was withdrawn. Price at time of withdrawal 8/1. Rule 4 applies to bets placed prior to withdrawal, but not to SP bets - dedcuction 10p in the pound. New market formed.
**FOCUS**
A moderate handicap. Straightforward form.
T/Plt: £57.10 to a £1 stake. Pool: £69,198.66 - 883.39 winning units T/Qpdt: £11.20 to a £1 stake. Pool: £6,074.89 - 398.80 winning units **Jonathan Neesom**

# 216 WOLVERHAMPTON (A.W) (L-H)
Saturday, January 14

**OFFICIAL GOING: Tapeta: standard**
Wind: light across Weather: Fine

## 239 SUNBETS.CO.UK DOWNLOAD THE APP APPRENTICE H'CAP 1m 142y (Tp)
**5:45** (5:45) (Class 6) (0-60,61) 4-Y-O+ £2,587 (£770; £384; £192) **Stalls** Low

Form RPR
/00- **1** **Sir Lancelott**[15] 8588 5-9-4 60 (p) PatrickVaughan(3) 7 66
(David O'Meara) *trckd ldrs: rdn to ld over 1f out: pushed out fnl 75yds: reduced advantage nr fin but nvr in danger* **16/1**
50-4 **2** *nk* **Dove Mountain (IRE)**[10] 46 6-9-2 60 (tp) JoshuaBryan(5) 11 65+
(Anabel K Murphy) *hld up in rr: rdn and briefly tight for room over 1f out: r.o wl fnl f: wnt 2nd post* **9/1**
40-0 **3** *shd* **Mount Cheiron (USA)**[10] 46 6-8-9 51 (v) CallumRodriguez(3) 13 56+
(Richard Ford) *dwlt: hld up: rdn over 1f out: kpt on wl fnl f* **14/1**
344- **4** *shd* **John Caesar (IRE)**[92] 7336 6-9-4 60 (t) RowanScott(3) 2 65
(Rebecca Bastiman) *midfield: rdn 2f out: kpt on* **7/2**[1]
030- **5** *hd* **Amor Invicto (IRE)**[33] 8342 4-9-7 61 (b) RobHornby 4 65
(Daniel Kubler) *prom: led over 3f out: rdn over 2f out: hdd over 1f out: kpt on same pce: lost 3 pls nr fin* **11/2**[3]
30-0 **6** *1 ½* **The Dukkerer (IRE)**[13] 7 6-9-4 60 LewisEdmunds(3) 1 61
(James Given) *dwlt: midfield on inner: swtchd rt 2f out: rdn over 1f out: one pce* **6/1**
003- **7** *1* **Rocket Ronnie (IRE)**[43] 8191 7-9-7 60 (t[1]) AlistairRawlinson 3 59
(Brian Barr) *racd keenly: trckd ldrs: rdn 2f out: no ex fnl f* **12/1**
3-0 **8** *hd* **Sheer Intensity (IRE)**[10] 50 4-8-12 59 KatherineGlenister(7) 6 57
(David Evans) *trckd ldrs: rdn and lost pl 2f out: no threat after* **15/2**
230- **9** *½* **Poor Duke (IRE)**[15] 8588 7-9-3 56 PhilDennis 10 53
(Michael Mullineaux) *midfield: rdn and hdwy to chse ldrs over 1f out: wknd ins fnl f* **50/1**
1-04 **10** *¾* **Ferryview Place**[7] 123 8-8-6 52 (p) LukeCatton(7) 8 48
(Ian Williams) *s.i.s: hld up: rdn 2f out: nvr threatened* **5/1**[2]
/0-0 **11** *12* **Mcelligott (IRE)**[12] 26 4-8-6 46 oh1 HollieDoyle 5 17
(Richard Price) *led: hdd over 3f out: sn wknd* **100/1**
1m 52.49s (2.39) **Going Correction** -0.075s/f (Stan)
**WFA** 4 from 5yo+ 1lb **11** Ran SP% **113.5**
Speed ratings (Par 101): **86,85,85,85,85 84,83,82,82,81 71**
CSF £147.49 CT £2060.09 TOTE £8.70: £3.00, £2.70, £4.10; EX 57.90 Trifecta £846.60.
**Owner** G Brogan **Bred** P Balding **Trained** Upper Helmsley, N Yorks
**FOCUS**
The pace was steady and they finished in a heap. Muddling form.

## 240 SUNBETS.CO.UK H'CAP 1m 142y (Tp)
**6:15** (6:15) (Class 4) (0-85,87) 4-Y-O+ £5,498 (£1,636; £817; £408) **Stalls** Low

Form RPR
21-4 **1** **Sands Chorus**[12] 25 5-9-3 79 TomEaves 1 85
(James Given) *chsd ldr: rdn over 2f out: led over 1f out: strly ins fnl f: hld on wl* **4/1**[2]
061- **2** *hd* **Byres Road**[14] 8590 4-9-4 81 PJMcDonald 2 86
(Mark Johnston) *in tch: rdn over 3f out: chsd ldrs over 1f out: chal strly ins fnl f: hit across face by winning rdr's whip 75yds out: kpt on* **9/4**[1]
10-4 **3** *hd* **Ice Royal (IRE)**[9] 61 4-9-5 87 LucyKBarry(5) 5 92
(Jamie Osborne) *midfield: rdn over 2f out: hdwy to chse ldrs over 1f out: kpt on* **5/1**[3]
443- **4** *1* **Magic City (IRE)**[42] 8205 8-8-8 73 NathanEvans(3) 3 76
(Michael Easterby) *s.i.s: sn midfield: rdn over 2f out: hdwy to chse ldrs over 1f out: one pce towards fin* **4/1**[2]
300- **5** *4 ½* **It Must Be Faith**[146] 5679 7-8-11 73 TomMarquand 6 65
(Michael Appleby) *led: racd keenly and sn 4 l clr: rdn and reduced advantage over 2f out: hdd over 1f out: wknd ins fnl f* **25/1**
06-5 **6** *nk* **Jack's Revenge (IRE)**[9] 61 9-8-11 80 (v) AmeliaGlass(7) 4 72
(George Baker) *hld up: pushed along over 1f out: nvr threatened* **9/1**
000- **7** *6* **Jack Of Diamonds (IRE)**[25] 8475 8-9-5 84 RobHornby(3) 8 62
(Roger Teal) *hld up: rdn over 1f out: sn wknd* **12/1**
30-6 **8** *nk* **Icebuster**[10] 36 9-9-3 79 RichardKingscote 7 56
(Rod Millman) *dwlt: a towards rr* **25/1**
1m 46.97s (-3.13) **Going Correction** -0.075s/f (Stan)
**WFA** 4 from 5yo+ 1lb **8** Ran SP% **112.8**
Speed ratings (Par 105): **110,109,109,108,104 104,99,98**
CSF £13.04 CT £44.20 TOTE £4.00: £1.40, £1.30, £1.90; EX 15.10 Trifecta £51.80.
**Owner** The Cool Silk Partnership **Bred** Worksop Manor Stud **Trained** Willoughton, Lincs
■ Stewards' Enquiry : Lucy K Barry two-day ban: used whip above permitted level (Jan 28 & 30)
**FOCUS**
A fair handicap.

## 241 BETWAY MARATHON H'CAP 2m 120y (Tp)
**6:45** (6:45) (Class 6) (0-60,64) 4-Y-O+ £2,587 (£770; £384; £192) **Stalls** Low

Form RPR
64-1 **1** **Miss Dusky Diva (IRE)**[10] 35 5-9-7 55 WilliamCarson 5 62+
(David W Drinkwater) *hld up: gd hdwy on outer 3f out: pushed along to ld appr fnl f: styd on wl* **6/4**[1]

44-5 **2** 2 1/2 **Sakhra**[8] 98 6-8-7 **46** oh1 HollieDoyle(5) 2 48
(Mark Brisbourne) *trckd ldrs: rdn 3f out: led over 1f out: hdd appr fnl f: one pce and sn no ch w wnr* **11/1**
55-3 **3** *nk* **Delagoa Bay (IRE)**[10] 35 9-9-6 **59** MitchGodwin(5) 9 61
(Sylvester Kirk) *prom: lost pl over 7f out: rdn 3f out: plugged on: wnt 3rd ins fnl f* **8/1**
32-1 **4** *1* **Yasir (USA)**[8] 98 9-10-2 **64** MartinLane 7 64
(Conor Dore) *dwlt: hld up in rr: stl plenty to do whn pushed along 2f out: kpt on ins fnl f: nrst fin* **11/2**[3]
036- **5** *3/4* **Oyster Card**[31] 8359 4-8-7 **48** TomMarquand 4 48
(Michael Appleby) *midfield: lost pl and towards rr 7f out: rdn over 2f out: kpt on* **4/1**[2]
14-2 **6** *2 3/4* **Chestnut Storm (IRE)**[12] 19 4-9-5 **60** TomEaves 6 56
(Brian Barr) *hld up in midfield: hdwy to ld 1/2-way: rdn over 3f out: hdd over 1f out: wknd ins fnl f* **7/1**
000/ **7** *2 1/2* **Anton Dolin (IRE)**[19] 6062 9-9-0 **53** (be[1]) PhilDennis(5) 3 46
(Michael Mullineaux) *in tch: rdn over 3f out: wknd over 1f out* **66/1**
00-4 **D** *8* **Our Little Sister (IRE)**[12] 19 4-8-9 **55** CharlieBennett(5) 1 39
(Hughie Morrison) *led at stdy pce: hdd 1/2-way: trckd ldr: rdn 5f out: wknd over 1f out: fin 8th: later disqualified; prohibited substance fnd in sample* **12/1**

3m 42.79s (-0.91) **Going Correction** -0.075s/f (Stan)
**WFA** 4 from 5yo+ 5lb 8 Ran SP% **116.5**
Speed ratings (Par 101): **99,97,97,97,96 95,94,90**
CSF £20.61 CT £103.72 TOTE £2.50: £1.10, £2.90, £2.10; EX 17.90 Trifecta £122.80.
**Owner** Advantage Chemicals Holdings Ltd **Bred** Advantage Chemicals Holdings Ltd **Trained** Hanley Castle, Worcs

**FOCUS**
A moderate staying handicap. The second and third help set the opening level.

## 242 BETWAY H'CAP — 6f 20y (Tp)
7:15 (7:17) (Class 5) (0-70,71) 4-Y-0+ £3,234 (£962; £481; £240) Stalls Low

Form RPR
532- **1** **Dream Farr (IRE)**[28] 8429 4-9-7 **70** (t) ThomasBrown 2 79+
(Ed Walker) *midfield on inner: pushed along and gd hdwy over 1f out: rdn to ld ins fnl f: edgd rt: kpt on* **5/2**[1]
454- **2** *1* **Indian Affair**[14] 8595 7-9-2 **65** (bt) DougieCostello 6 70
(Milton Bradley) *chsd ldrs: rdn over 2f out: kpt on: wnt 2nd towards fin* **15/2**
506- **3** *1/2* **Ebony N Ivory**[64] 7899 4-9-8 **71** (p[1]) LukeMorris 7 74
(Archie Watson) *prom: rdn to ld wl over 1f out: hdd ins fnl f: no ex and lost 2nd towards fin* **11/2**[3]
064- **4** *1 1/2* **Burtonwood**[122] 6475 5-8-8 **64** KieranSchofield(7) 1 62
(Julie Camacho) *midfield: rdn 2f out: kpt on fnl f* **16/1**
022- **5** *shd* **Colourbearer (IRE)**[14] 8595 10-9-4 **67** (t) AdamBeschizza 3 65
(Charlie Wallis) *prom: rdn over 2f out: no ex ins fnl f* **9/1**
60-4 **6** *1/2* **Dominium (USA)**[10] 50 10-8-13 **67** (b) DavidParkes(5) 9 63
(Jeremy Gask) *hld up: sn pushed along: kpt on ins fnl f: nvr threatened* **4/1**[2]
135- **7** *3/4* **Divine Call**[35] 8315 10-8-13 **62** (b) RichardKingscote 12 56
(Milton Bradley) *dwlt: hld up: nvr threatened* **16/1**
404- **8** *nk* **See Vermont**[111] 6813 9-8-9 **63** RowanScott(5) 5 56
(Rebecca Bastiman) *dwlt: hld up: rdn 2f out: nvr threatened* **66/1**
140- **9** *1 1/4* **Head Space (IRE)**[19] 8531 9-9-4 **67** AndrewMullen 11 56
(David Evans) *midfield on outside: rdn over 2f out: wknd over 1f out* **25/1**
500- **10** *2 3/4* **Sir Theodore (IRE)**[32] 8349 4-9-7 **70** TomMarquand 4 50
(Richard Spencer) *led: rdn whn hdd wl over 1f out: wknd appr fnl f* **33/1**
000- **11** *6* **Point North (IRE)**[30] 8389 10-9-7 **70** (b) RobertWinston 8 31
(John Balding) *chsd ldrs: rdn 2f out: wknd fnl f and eased* **14/1**

1m 13.65s (-0.85) **Going Correction** -0.075s/f (Stan) 11 Ran SP% **112.4**
Speed ratings (Par 103): **102,100,100,98,97 97,96,95,94,90 82**
CSF £20.10 CT £94.10 TOTE £3.30: £1.20, £2.00, £2.30; EX 17.70 Trifecta £90.20.
**Owner** Mrs T Walker **Bred** Jim McCormack **Trained** Upper Lambourn, Berks

**FOCUS**
A modest sprint handicap.

## 243 SUNBETS.CO.UK H'CAP — 5f 21y (Tp)
7:45 (7:45) (Class 4) (0-85,82) 3-Y-O £5,498 (£1,636; £817; £408) Stalls Low

Form RPR
11-3 **1** **Dazacam**[7] 125 3-9-7 **82** RobertWinston 4 85+
(Michael Herrington) *hld up in tch: pushed along over 1f out: qcknd to ld ins fnl f: kpt on: shade cosily* **11/8**[1]
4-51 **2** *1/2* **Gracious Tom (IRE)**[4] 155 3-9-3 **78** 6ex StevieDonohoe 1 79
(David Evans) *chsd ldr towards inner: rdn over 1f out: ev ch 1f out: kpt on* **2/1**[2]
01- **3** *1 1/2* **Imdancinwithurwife (IRE)**[280] 1342 3-8-12 **73** RichardKingscote 3 68
(Tom Dascombe) *chsd ldr: rdn over 1f out: no ex fnl 110yds* **15/2**
501- **4** *nk* **Street Jazz**[19] 8526 3-8-7 **68** AndrewMullen 2 62
(James Given) *led: rdn wl over 1f out: hdd ins fnl f: no ex* **10/3**[3]

1m 2.19s (0.29) **Going Correction** -0.075s/f (Stan) 4 Ran SP% **110.3**
Speed ratings (Par 99): **94,93,90,90**
CSF £4.52 TOTE £2.50; EX 4.30 Trifecta £8.80.
**Owner** Darren & Annaley Yates **Bred** Mr & Mrs D Yates **Trained** Cold Kirby, N Yorks

**FOCUS**
Only four runners, but a fair race.

## 244 32RED.COM MAIDEN STKS — 6f 20y (Tp)
8:15 (8:15) (Class 5) 3-Y-O+ £3,557 (£1,058; £529; £264) Stalls Low

Form RPR
33- **1** **Boost**[226] 2817 3-8-7 0 LukeMorris 4 74+
(Sir Mark Prescott Bt) *w ldr: led over 3f out: pushed along over 2f out: rdn over 1f out: kpt on to draw clr ins fnl f* **4/9**[1]
043- **2** *3 3/4* **Alfonso Manana (IRE)**[18] 8536 3-8-12 69 (p[1]) RichardKingscote 6 67
(James Given) *led narrowly: hdd over 3f out: remained cl up: rdn over 2f out: one pce and no ch w wnr ins fnl f* **11/4**[2]
05- **3** *2 1/4* **Deeley's Double (FR)**[35] 8320 4-9-11 0 GeorgeDowning(3) 1 64
(Tony Carroll) *dwlt: hld up: pushed along over 2f out: kpt on fr over 1f out: wnt modest 3rd ins fnl f* **12/1**[3]
06- **4** *1/2* **Mister Freeze (IRE)**[31] 8354 3-8-12 0 (t) JohnFahy 7 58
(Clive Cox) *chsd ldrs towards outer: rdn over 2f out: grad wknd over 1f out* **14/1**
0- **5** *5* **Fast Tack (IRE)**[19] 8526 3-8-12 0 JasonHart 2 42
(John Quinn) *trckd ldrs: rdn over 2f out: wknd over 1f out* **33/1**
0-0 **6** *3/4* **Rockalater**[8] 96 3-8-2 0 MitchGodwin(5) 5 35
(Sylvester Kirk) *hld up: pushed along over 2f out: nvr threatened* **33/1**
**7** *3 1/4* **Clanvellyn** 3-8-7 0 JoeyHaynes 3 24
(K R Burke) *chsd ldrs: rdn over 2f out: wknd over 1f out* **12/1**[3]
6-0 **8** *nk* **Tink**[9] 75 3-8-7 0 JFEgan 8 23
(Mark Brisbourne) *s.i.s: hld up: sme hdwy on outside over 2f out: wknd over 1f out* **50/1**

1m 13.2s (-1.30) **Going Correction** -0.075s/f (Stan)
**WFA** 3 from 4yo 16lb 8 Ran SP% **125.8**
Speed ratings (Par 103): **105,100,97,96,89 88,84,83**
CSF £2.31 TOTE £1.30: £1.10, £1.10, £2.90; EX 2.30 Trifecta £8.30.
**Owner** Cheveley Park Stud **Bred** Cheveley Park Stud Ltd **Trained** Newmarket, Suffolk

**FOCUS**
An uncompetitive sprint maiden.

## 245 32RED CASINO H'CAP — 7f 36y (Tp)
8:45 (8:46) (Class 6) (0-60,63) 3-Y-O £2,911 (£866; £432; £216) Stalls High

Form RPR
000- **1** **Mia Cara**[77] 7688 3-9-7 **60** AndrewMullen 5 65
(David Evans) *chsd ldrs: rdn over 2f out: led over 1f out: drvn and kpt on* **8/1**
060- **2** *1 1/4* **Sentinel**[38] 8243 3-9-7 **60** StevieDonohoe 2 62+
(Charlie Fellowes) *rrd s and s.i.s: hld up: pushed along over 2f out: hdwy over 1f out and angled towards outer: kpt on wl fnl f* **6/4**[1]
03-0 **3** *1/2* **Magic Journey (IRE)**[9] 73 3-9-2 **55** (b) JasonHart 7 56
(John Quinn) *midfield: pushed along over 2f out: rdn and hdwy to chse ldr appr fnl f: kpt on* **7/1**
000- **4** *1 1/2* **Tranquil Tracy**[32] 8344 3-8-9 **48** AdamBeschizza 4 45
(John Norton) *chsd ldrs: rdn over 2f out: one pce* **80/1**
54-0 **5** *1/2* **Trust The Indian**[7] 126 3-8-10 **49** LukeMorris 10 45
(Bill Turner) *in tch towards outer: rdn over 2f out: hung lft over 1f out: one pce fnl f* **33/1**
05-1 **6** *2* **Oberyn (IRE)**[8] 96 3-9-5 **63** MitchGodwin(5) 3 54
(Sylvester Kirk) *pressed ldr: rdn over 2f out: wknd ins fnl f* **2/1**[2]
052- **7** *1 3/4* **Warba (IRE)**[28] 8425 3-9-9 **62** JFEgan 1 49
(Mohamed Moubarak) *led narrowly: rdn over 2f out: hdd over 1f out: wknd fnl f* **11/2**[3]
000- **8** *9* **Quintessential**[19] 8526 3-8-7 **46** oh1 BarryMcHugh 8 11
(Richard Fahey) *dwlt: hld up: rdn over 3f out: wknd fnl 2f* **50/1**
000- **9** *5* **Young Officer (IRE)**[38] 8243 3-8-9 **55** (p[1]) JordanUys(7) 9 7
(Brian Meehan) *s.i.s: hld up: rdn over 3f out: sn wknd and bhd* **14/1**

1m 28.38s (-0.42) **Going Correction** -0.075s/f (Stan) 9 Ran SP% **125.1**
Speed ratings (Par 95): **99,97,97,95,94 92,90,80,74**
CSF £22.21 CT £97.63 TOTE £9.70: £2.40, £1.20, £1.60; EX 27.50 Trifecta £146.70.
**Owner** Countess Lonsdale & Richard Kent **Bred** Richard Kent & Lady Lonsdale **Trained** Pandy, Monmouths

■ Stewards' Enquiry : Adam Beschizza two-day ban: improper use of the whip (Jan 28 & 30)

**FOCUS**
A moderate handicap in which a slow start seemed to cost the well-backed favourite. The fourth and fifth help pin the opening level.
T/Plt: £51.10 to a £1 stake. Pool: £118,350.05 - 1,690.71 winning units T/Qpdt: £5.20 to a £1 stake. Pool: £11,107.67 - 1,572.77 winning units **Andrew Sheret**

246 - 249a (Foreign Racing) - See Raceform Interactive

# 201 MEYDAN (L-H)
Saturday, January 14

**OFFICIAL GOING: Dirt: fast; turf: good**

## 250a AL NABOODAH TRAVEL TROPHY (H'CAP) (TURF) — 6f
2:20 (2:20) (80-94,92) 3-Y-O+ £23,127 (£7,709; £4,240; £2,312; £1,156)

RPR
**1** **Acolyte (IRE)**[469] 6942 5-9-3 **91** HarryBentley 2 102+
(Saeed bin Suroor) *mid-division, rdn to ld 2 1/2f out, ran on wl, comfortably* **7/2**[1]
**2** *1 1/2* **Salvadori (IRE)**[8] 111 6-8-10 **85** ow2 BReis 4 89+
(R Bouresly, Kuwait) *settled rear, ran on wl fnl 1 1/2f, nrst finish* **14/1**
**3** *1 1/2* **Almargo (IRE)**[30] 8395 6-9-2 **90** (v) ColmO'Donoghue 8 90
(A bin Harmash, UAE) *tracked leaders, ev ch 1 1/2f out, one pace fnl 1f* **16/1**
**4** *1/2* **Time Flies**[72] 7789 5-9-2 **90** AntonioFresu 16 89
(S bin Ghadayer, UAE) *soon led, hdd 2 1/2f out, ran on same pace fnl 1 1/2f* **20/1**
**5** *1 1/4* **Roossey (IRE)**[72] 7789 5-9-3 **91** (t) ChrisHayes 9 86
(D Selvaratnam, UAE) *tracked leaders, ev ch 2f out, one pace fnl 1 1/2f* **9/1**
**6** *1/2* **Mushaakis (IRE)**[36] 8301 7-9-4 **92** (t) PaoloSirigu 11 85
(A R Al Rayhi, UAE) *tracked leaders til outpcd fnl 1 1/2f* **14/1**
**7** *shd* **Akeed Champion**[34] 8324 5-8-13 **87** (t) RichardMullen 12 80
(S Seemar, UAE) *mid-division, chsd leaders 2f out, ran on same pace fnl 1 1/2f* **5/1**[3]
**8** *1 1/2* **Well Acquainted (IRE)**[350] 410 7-9-0 **88** (t) AdriedeVries 10 76
(Ismail Mohammed) *never nr to challenge* **25/1**
**9** *hd* **Special Boy (IRE)**[8] 112 8-8-10 **85** JRosales 13 71
(M Al Mheiri, UAE) *slowly into strd, nv nr to challenge* **33/1**
**10** *1/2* **Lytham St Annes (IRE)**[36] 8301 4-9-0 **88** PatDobbs 1 74
(Doug Watson, UAE) *slowly into strd, stlld rear, nvr able to challenge* **4/1**[2]
**11** *1* **Beachy Head (IRE)**[22] 8518 6-9-2 **90** (t) TadhgO'Shea 7 72
(A R Al Rayhi, UAE) *slowly into strd, nvr nr to challenge* **16/1**
**12** *1/2* **Dairam (USA)**[8] 110 7-8-6 **81** ow1 (bt) FernandoJara 15 61
(M Al Mheiri, UAE) *never better than mid-division* **25/1**
**13** *4 1/4* **General Marshall (USA)**[408] 8101 5-8-8 **83** ow1 PatCosgrave 5 49
(M F De Kock, South Africa) *never better than mid-division* **10/1**
**14** *4 1/2* **Ajraam (USA)**[16] 8578 7-9-3 **91** DaneO'Neill 6 44
(M Al Mheiri, UAE) *tracked leaders, wknd fnl 2f* **14/1**
**15** *1* **Zalzilah**[16] 8577 6-8-4 **85** (t) CameronNoble(6) 3 34
(S Seemar, UAE) *slowly into strd, trkd leaders til wknd fnl 2 1/2f* **20/1**
**16** *18* **English Deer (IRE)**[16] 8578 7-8-8 **88** (bt) IKoyuncu(6) 14
(A R Al Rayhi, UAE) *never better than mid-division* **40/1**

1m 11.46s 16 Ran SP% **132.3**
CSF: 53.68; TRICAST: 743.68.
**Owner** Godolphin **Bred** Drumlin Bloodstock **Trained** Newmarket, Suffolk

251 - 263a (Foreign Racing) - See Raceform Interactive

# [239]WOLVERHAMPTON (A.W) (L-H)

Monday, January 16

**OFFICIAL GOING: Tapeta: standard**

Wind: Light across Weather: Light rain

## 264 32RED CASINO H'CAP 6f 20y (Tp)

**1:50** (1:51) (Class 6) (0-65,67) 3-Y-O **£2,619** (£779; £389; £194) **Stalls** Low

Form RPR

502- **1** **Cappananty Con**[25] 8494 3-9-9 **67**................................ RobertWinston 7 75+
(Dean Ivory) *broke wl sn stdd and lost pl: swtchd lft and hdwy over 1f out: r.o to ld nr fin* **5/1**[3]

60-1 **2** ¾ **Magdalene Fox**[11] 77 3-9-3 **61**......................................(b) AdamKirby 4 67
(Ed Dunlop) *sn pushed along to ld: rdn over 2f out: edgd rt ins fnl f: hdd nr fin* **10/3**[1]

130- **3** 3 **Bismarck The Flyer (IRE)**[101] 7110 3-9-5 **63**................ PJMcDonald 1 60
(Ollie Pears) *mid-div: rdn over 2f out: hdwy over 1f out: styd on* **16/1**

353- **4** *nk* **Oh Geno**[34] 8344 3-9-6 **64**............................................. JamieSpencer 5 60
(Richard Spencer) *chsd ldrs: shkn up over 1f out: styd on same pce ins fnl f* **4/1**[2]

32-1 **5** ½ **Scotch Myst**[15] 2 3-9-0 **58**......................................... TonyHamilton 6 52
(Richard Fahey) *in rr: sme hdwy over 1f out: nt trble ldrs* **11/2**

55-1 **6** ½ **Gentleman Giles (IRE)**[9] 126 3-9-3 **61**..................... TimmyMurphy 9 54
(Jamie Osborne) *chsd ldrs: nt clr run and lost pl over 4f out: hung rt over 2f out: styd on ins fnl f* **8/1**

40-2 **7** ½ **Mr Strutter (IRE)**[9] 126 3-8-13 **57**................................ JasonHart 8 48
(John Quinn) *hld up in tch: rdn over 2f out: styd on same pce fnl f* **6/1**

230- **8** 1 ¾ **Fethiye Boy**[62] 7966 3-9-7 **65**............................................. LukeMorris 3 51
(Ronald Harris) *chsd ldr: rdn over 2f out: wknd ins fnl f* **20/1**

0-0 **9** 3 ½ **Celerity (IRE)**[11] 76 3-9-2 **60**................................. AndrewMullen 2 36
(David Evans) *s.i.s: sn chsng ldrs: rdn over 1f out: sn wknd* **100/1**

505- **10** 21 **Poppy Pivot (IRE)**[203] 3707 3-9-0 **65**..................... LewisEdmunds(7) 10
(Michael Appleby) *sn pushed along towards rr: rdn and wknd over 2f out* **66/1**

1m 13.88s (-0.62) **Going Correction** -0.175s/f (Stan) **10** Ran SP% **113.7**
Speed ratings (Par 95): **97,96,92,91,90 90,89,87,82,54**
CSF £21.17 CT £251.84 TOTE £6.50: £2.20, £1.70, £4.20; EX 26.10 Trifecta £490.30.
**Owner** Jim Biggane, John Waterfall & Dean Ivory **Bred** Miss H Botterill & Mr D R Botterill **Trained** Radlett, Herts

■ Stewards' Enquiry : Luke Morris two-day ban: used whip above shoulder height (Jan 30-31)

**FOCUS**
Three recent winners in this modest 3yo sprint handicap, but they were eclipsed by the strong-finishing top weight who took a definite small step forward.

## 265 32RED.COM MAIDEN STKS 1m 1f 104y (Tp)

**2:20** (2:20) (Class 5) 3-Y-O **£3,234** (£962; £481; £240) **Stalls** Low

Form RPR

422- **1** **Pete So High (GER)**[20] 8537 3-9-5 74..........................(p[1]) SeanLevey 1 75
(Richard Hannon) *led: pushed along and hdd 2f out: rdn and hung rt over 1f out: hmpd wl ins fnl f: styd on u.p to ld towards fin* **11/8**[2]

**2** *shd* **Bush House (IRE)** 3-9-5 0..................................(b[1]) JosephineGordon 2 74
(Hugo Palmer) *chsd wnr: led 2f out: hmpd over 1f out: rdn and hung lft wl ins fnl f: hdd towards fin* **12/1**

00- **3** 3 ¾ **Dream Magic (IRE)**[35] 8340 3-9-5 0................................ LukeMorris 10 66
(Daniel Mark Loughnane) *hld up: pushed along hdwy over 2f out: rdn over 1f out: hung lft ins fnl f: styd on same pce* **100/1**

**4** 3 ½ **Born To Reason (IRE)** 3-9-5 0..................................... TimmyMurphy 4 59+
(Jamie Osborne) *s.i.s and stmbld sn after s: hld up: r.o ins fnl f: nrst fin* **33/1**

23-2 **5** 1 **Draw Swords**[11] 65 3-9-5 80......................................(t[1]) RobertHavlin 3 57
(John Gosden) *trckd ldrs: plld hrd: shkn up over 2f out: wknd fnl f* **10/11**[1]

0- **6** 8 **Brother In Arms (IRE)**[33] 8354 3-9-5 0........................ JamieSpencer 8 40
(Jamie Osborne) *hld up: shkn up over 2f out: nvr nrr* **11/1**[3]

0- **7** 1 **Costa Percy**[20] 8537 3-9-5 0........................................ DougieCostello 7 38
(K R Burke) *hld up: pushed along 1/2-way: nvr on terms* **33/1**

0- **8** 3 ½ **Born Legend (IRE)**[20] 8537 3-9-2 0...................... CallumShepherd(3) 9 30
(Charles Hills) *s.i.s: hdwy over 7f out: rdn over 3f out: wknd over 2f out* **100/1**

0- **9** 11 **Major Tom**[20] 8537 3-9-2 0...................................... AlistairRawlinson(3) 6 7
(Michael Appleby) *chsd ldrs: rdn over 3f out: wknd 2f out* **100/1**

0-0 **10** 14 **Hermeneutics (USA)**[12] 34 3-9-5 0.............................. GeorgeBaker 5
(Ed Walker) *mid-div: drvn along 1/2-way: wknd wl over 2f out* **40/1**

1m 59.14s (-1.66) **Going Correction** -0.175s/f (Stan) **10** Ran SP% **121.8**
Speed ratings (Par 97): **100,99,96,93,92 85,84,81,71,59**
CSF £18.27 TOTE £2.70: £1.10, £2.20, £4.00; EX 17.60 Trifecta £349.40.
**Owner** Middleham Park Racing VII & K Sohi **Bred** Stiftung Gestut Fahrhof **Trained** East Everleigh, Wilts

**FOCUS**
An interesting maiden with those at the head of the market setting a decent standard, although it appeared to be a match according to the market. However, that was not how it worked out though the winner has been rated close to form.

## 266 SUNBETS.CO.UK H'CAP 1m 142y (Tp)

**2:55** (2:55) (Class 3) (0-95,97) 4-Y-O- **£8,506** (£2,546; £1,273; £637; £317) **Stalls** Low

Form RPR

10-2 **1** **Mythical Madness**[7] 148 6-9-11 **97**.........................(p) DanielTudhope 4 106+
(David O'Meara) *hld up: hdwy and nt clr run over 1f out: shkn up to ld ins fnl f: r.o* **9/2**[3]

40-5 **2** 1 **Supersta**[2] 235 6-9-7 **93**...............................................(p) GeorgeBaker 3 99
(Michael Appleby) *hld up: shkn up over 1f out: rdn: hung lft and r.o ins fnl f: wnt 2nd nr fin* **4/1**[2]

052- **3** ½ **Perfect Cracker**[21] 8529 9-9-4 **90**.................................... AdamKirby 6 95
(Clive Cox) *hld up in tch: rdn to chse ldr over 1f out: ev ch ins fnl f: styd on same pce towards fin* **7/1**

61-2 **4** ½ **Byres Road**[2] 240 4-8-8 **81**............................................ JoeFanning 7 85
(Mark Johnston) *sn w ldr: led over 5f out: rdn and hdd ins fnl f: no ex towards fin* **3/1**[1]

400- **5** 1 **Trendsetter (IRE)**[37] 8317 6-8-13 **88**......................(p) AaronJones(3) 1 90
(Micky Hammond) *hld up: rdn over 1f out: r.o ins fnl f: nt rch ldrs* **28/1**

43-2 **6** ½ **Dutch Uncle**[12] 36 5-8-12 **84**.....................................(v[1]) MartinHarley 5 84
(Ed Dunlop) *trckd ldrs: rdn over 1f out: sn hung lft: styd on same pce ins fnl f* **4/1**[2]

554- **7** *nk* **Lacan (IRE)**[317] 833 6-9-2 **88**............................................ SeanLevey 9 88
(Ralph Beckett) *hld up: hdwy over 1f out: hung lft and styd on same pce ins fnl f* **9/1**

00-6 **8** 3 ½ **Ready (IRE)**[9] 117 7-8-13 **85**...................................(p) SteveDrowne 8 77
(Clare Ellam) *chsd ldrs: wnt 2nd over 4f out: rdn over 2f out: lost 2nd over 1f out: wknd ins fnl f* **50/1**

54- **9** ¾ **London (FR)**[66] 7903 4-8-10 **83**.......................(t) JosephineGordon 2 73
(Phil McEntee) *racd keenly: led 3f: remained handy: rdn over 1f out: wknd fnl f* **20/1**

1m 46.99s (-3.11) **Going Correction** -0.175s/f (Stan)
**WFA** 4 from 5yo+ 1lb **9** Ran SP% **115.9**
Speed ratings (Par 107): **106,105,104,104,103 102,102,99,98**
CSF £22.46 CT £124.30 TOTE £5.10: £2.10, £1.80, £2.20; EX 22.50 Trifecta £59.30.
**Owner** J C G Chua **Bred** Highbank Stud Llp **Trained** Upper Helmsley, N Yorks

**FOCUS**
A good-class mile handicap won in comfortable style by the top weight. They may have gone too hard in front as the first two came from off the pace. The form looks sound set around those behind the winner.

## 267 SUNBETS.CO.UK DOWNLOAD THE APP CLASSIFIED CLAIMING STKS 7f 36y (Tp)

**3:25** (3:26) (Class 6) 4-Y-O+ **£2,587** (£770; £384; £192) **Stalls** High

Form RPR

20-1 **1** **Gold Flash**[12] 50 5-9-2 75..........................................(v) PhillipMakin 1 80
(Keith Dalgleish) *hld up: hdwy over 1f out: nt clr run ent fnl f: r.o to ld wl ins fnl f* **7/2**[2]

463- **2** 1 ½ **Mehdi (IRE)**[47] 8150 8-9-0 74.................................(t) TonyHamilton 3 74
(Richard Fahey) *a.p: rdn over 1f out: r.o* **6/1**[3]

02-3 **3** *hd* **Pivotman**[15] 6 9-8-9 72.........................................(bt) NathanEvans(3) 7 72
(Michael Easterby) *led 6f out tl over 4f out: remained handy: rdn over 1f out: ev ch ins fnl f: styd on* **2/1**[1]

03-1 **4** *shd* **Black Dave (IRE)**[12] 49 7-9-0 72.......................... StevieDonohoe 6 74
(David Evans) *led 1f: led again over 4f out: rdn over 1f out: hdd wl ins fnl f* **10/1**

43-5 **5** *nk* **Dana's Present**[12] 49 8-9-0 72......................................... LiamKeniry 8 73
(Tom Dascombe) *chsd ldrs: rdn over 1f out: styd on* **12/1**

051- **6** *nse* **Chelwood Gate (IRE)**[40] 8252 7-8-11 72...............(v) HectorCrouch(3) 9 74
(Patrick Chamings) *s.i.s: hld up: nt clr run and swtchd rt 1f out: r.o wl ins fnl f* **16/1**

436- **7** 1 ¼ **Corporal Maddox**[32] 8378 10-9-2 75...........................(p) LukeMorris 2 72
(Ronald Harris) *mid-div: swtchd rt and hdwy over 1f out: sn rdn: styd on same pce ins fnl f* **25/1**

005- **8** ¾ **Smokethatthunders (IRE)**[21] 8531 7-9-1 73............ DanielMuscutt 10 69
(James Unett) *hld up: hdwy 1/2-way: rdn over 1f out: styd on same pce* **12/1**

22-3 **9** 4 ½ **Rebel Lightning (IRE)**[12] 50 4-9-2 71..................(b) JamieSpencer 11 71
(Richard Spencer) *chsd ldrs: wnt 2nd 1/2-way tl rdn over 1f out: edgd lft and wknd fnl f* **6/1**[3]

000- **10** 3 ½ **Layla's Hero (IRE)**[27] 8473 10-8-11 69.................... JosephineGordon 4 45
(Roger Teal) *mid-div: pushed along 1/2-way: wknd over 2f out* **50/1**

040- **11** 1 ¾ **Hijran (IRE)**[34] 8347 4-9-2 65..................................(p) AndrewMullen 5 46
(Michael Appleby) *hld up: rdn 1/2-way: wknd over 2f out* **50/1**

1m 27.96s (-0.84) **Going Correction** -0.175s/f (Stan) **11** Ran SP% **122.3**
Speed ratings (Par 101): **97,95,95,94,94 94,93,92,87,83 81**
CSF £25.76 TOTE £4.30: £1.70, £2.10, £1.20; EX 32.70 Trifecta £95.90.No bid for the winner.
**Owner** Ronnie Docherty **Bred** C R Cawston Ltd **Trained** Carluke, S Lanarks

**FOCUS**
A very competitive claimer on paper, with the majority rated within a few pounds of each other. There were plenty in with a chance halfway up the straight, but the winner scored a shade cosily.

## 268 BETWAY (FAST TRACK QUALIFIER) CONDITIONS STKS 2m 120y (Tp)

**4:00** (4:00) (Class 2) 4-Y-O+
**£12,450** (£3,728; £1,864; £932; £466; £234) **Stalls** Low

Form RPR

410- **1** **Antiquarium (IRE)**[149] 5655 5-9-3 105................................ AdamKirby 4 112
(Charlie Appleby) *hld up in tch: chsd ldr over 4f out: rdn to ld over 1f out: edgd lft ins fnl f: styd on* **6/4**[2]

3/3- **2** 1 ¾ **Famous Kid (USA)**[347] 453 6-9-3 110.................... JosephineGordon 2 109
(Saeed bin Suroor) *w ldr tl led at stdy pce over 14f out: qcknd over 3f out: rdn and hdd over 1f out: styd on same pce ins fnl f* **6/5**[1]

523- **3** 4 ½ **Steve Rogers (IRE)**[26] 8479 6-9-3 98................................ JackMitchell 3 104
(Roger Varian) *led: hdd over 14f out: chsd ldr tl over 12f out: remained handy: rdn over 2f out: no ex fnl f* **13/2**[3]

000- **4** 1 **Sandro Botticelli (IRE)**[65] 7946 5-9-6 107.................(p) MartinHarley 1 106
(John Ryan) *hld up in tch: rdn over 2f out: styd on same pce fr over 1f out* **16/1**

050- **5** 8 **Gang Warfare**[26] 8479 6-9-3 98.......................................(b[1]) GeorgeBaker 8 93
(Jamie Osborne) *hld up: rdn over 1f out: nvr trbld ldrs* **10/1**

130- **6** 5 **Intense Tango**[96] 7271 6-8-12 99...............................(t) DougieCostello 5 82
(K R Burke) *chsd ldrs: wnt 2nd over 10f out tl over 5f out: rdn over 3f out: wknd over 2f out* **33/1**

0/3- **7** 2 **Old Town Boy**[288] 1219 6-9-3 89..................................... PaddyBradley 6 85
(Philip McBride) *hld up: rdn and wknd over 2f out* **100/1**

3m 34.39s (-9.31) **Going Correction** -0.175s/f (Stan) **7** Ran SP% **117.7**
Speed ratings (Par 109): **114,113,111,110,106 104,103**
CSF £3.84 TOTE £2.70: £1.40, £1.40; EX 4.60 Trifecta £12.10.
**Owner** Godolphin **Bred** Darley **Trained** Newmarket, Suffolk

**FOCUS**
The feature race and a high-class conditions race for stayers bordering on Listed class. The early pace was ordinary and it was dominated by the Godolphin runners, who headed the market, but the form makes sense around the third and fourth.

## 269 BETWAY MIDDLE H'CAP 1m 4f 51y (Tp)

**4:30** (4:30) (Class 3) (0-90,90) 4-Y-O- **£8,506** (£2,546; £1,273; £637; £317) **Stalls** Low

Form RPR

6/5- **1** **Hot Beat (IRE)**[51] 8123 5-9-11 **90**.................................... MartinHarley 5 98+
(David Simcock) *hld up: hdwy over 1f out: rdn to ld and hung lft wl ins fnl f: r.o* **7/2**[2]

431- **2** ¾ **Plutocracy (IRE)**[29] 8447 7-9-9 **88**.................................(p) AdamKirby 6 95
(Gary Moore) *sn led:: clr 8f out: rdn over 1f out: hdd and unable qck wl ins fnl f* **5/1**

562- **3** 1 ½ **Alinstante**[16] 8594 4-9-7 **90**......................................(p) LukeMorris 4 96+
(Sir Mark Prescott Bt) *hld up: racd keenly: hdwy over 3f out: chsd ldr over 1f out: rdn and hung lft whn hmpd ins fnl f: kpt on* **11/8**[1]

452- 4 ½ **Persun**80 7669 5-9-0 **79** GrahamLee 7 83
(Mick Channon) *chsd ldrs: rdn over 1f out: styd on same pce ins fnl f* **11/1**

460- 5 2 **Energia Fox (BRZ)**40 8249 6-9-0 **79** TonyHamilton 1 80
(Richard Fahey) *hld up: hmpd over 2f out: styd on ins fnl f: nvr nrr* **28/1**

405- 6 1 **Midtech Star (IRE)**19 8558 5-9-2 **81** (v) StevieDonohoe 8 80
(Ian Williams) *chsd ldrs: rdn over 2f out: no ex fnl f* **28/1**

400- 7 ½ **Silver Quay (IRE)**16 8594 5-9-11 **90** GeorgeBaker 3 88
(Jamie Osborne) *s.i.s: hld up: sme hdwy over 1f out: sn rdn: wknd ins fnl f* **9/2**3

00-3 8 1 **Luv U Whatever**15 3 7-9-7 **86** AndrewMullen 2 83
(Michael Attwater) *chsd ldr over 6f: remained handy: wnt 2nd again over 2f out tl rdn over 1f out: wknd ins fnl f* **33/1**

0/ 9 18 **Red Turtle (FR)**96 6-9-4 **83** JamieSpencer 9 51
(Rune Haugen) *hld up: hdwy over 5f out: chsd ldr over 4f out tl rdn over 2f out: sn wknd* **25/1**

2m 36.55s (-4.25) **Going Correction** -0.175s/f (Stan)
**WFA** 4 from 5yo+ 3lb 9 Ran SP% **121.2**
Speed ratings (Par 107): **107,106,105,105,103 103,102,102,90**
CSF £21.56 CT £35.56 TOTE £4.70: £1.60, £1.90, £1.10; EX 28.20 Trifecta £58.90.
**Owner** Charles Wentworth **Bred** Ammerland Verwaltung Gmbh & Co Kg **Trained** Newmarket, Suffolk

**FOCUS**
Another decent handicap, this time over 1m4f. The pace was dictated by the runner-up, but the ex-German winner produced a decent turn of foot to score and there could be more to come.

## 270 BETWAY SPRINT H'CAP (DIV I) 5f 21y (Tp)
**5:00** (5:00) (Class 6) (0-55,55) 3-Y-0+ **£2,587** (£770; £384; £192) **Stalls** Low

Form RPR

020- 1 **Lady Bacchus**18 8572 4-9-6 **51** (b) RobertWinston 6 60
(Richard Guest) *hld up: hdwy over 1f out: rdn to ld and edgd rt wl ins fnl f* **9/2**3

/00- 2 1½ **Teepee Time**162 5197 4-8-10 **46** PhilDennis(5) 7 50
(Michael Mullineaux) *chsd ldr: rdn to ld wl ins fnl f: sn hdd and unable qck* **66/1**

302- 3 ¾ **Tribesman**18 8572 4-9-8 **53** (t) BarryMcHugh 1 54
(Marjorie Fife) *hld up: hdwy over 1f out: sn rdn: styd on* **11/2**

006- 4 nse **Fuel Injection**26 8485 6-9-8 **53** (p) JackGarritty 10 54
(Paul Midgley) *sn led: rdn over 1f out: hung rt and hdd wl ins fnl f* **15/2**

62-4 5 1 **Chandresh**7 143 4-9-3 **48** (p) LukeMorris 2 45
(Robert Cowell) *chsd ldrs: carried rt wl over 1f out: sn rdn: styd on same pce ins fnl f* **4/1**2

000- 6 nk **Ambitious Boy**37 8315 8-9-0 **50** CiaranMckee(5) 11 46
(John O'Shea) *s.s: r.o ins fnl f: nvr nrr* **14/1**

36-0 7 ¾ **Secret Millionaire (IRE)**11 80 10-9-7 **52** TomMarquand 5 45
(Shaun Harris) *hld up: rdn over 1f out: nvr on terms* **8/1**

140- 8 3 **Bilash**37 8316 10-8-12 **46** JackDuern(3) 8 31
(Sarah Hollinshead) *hld up: nt clr run wl over 1f out: n.d* **33/1**

550- 9 ¾ **Master Pekan**128 6317 4-8-10 **46** oh1 (h¹) MitchGodwin(5) 3 26
(Roy Brotherton) *chsd ldrs: pushed along 1/2-way: edgd rt wl over 1f out: wknd ins fnl f* **33/1**

04-2 10 1¼ **Eland Ally**7 143 9-9-5 **50** (b) GeorgeBaker 4 25
(Anabel K Murphy) *chsd ldrs: hung rt 1/2-way: sn wknd* **11/4**1

1m 1.42s (-0.48) **Going Correction** -0.175s/f (Stan) 10 Ran SP% **117.2**
Speed ratings (Par 101): **96,93,92,92,90 90,89,84,83,81**
CSF £268.91 CT £1713.22 TOTE £4.90: £1.70, £9.20, £1.60; EX 235.70 Trifecta £2122.20.
**Owner** Brooklands Racing **Bred** G Tomkins & J Luck **Trained** Ingmanthorpe, W Yorks

**FOCUS**
The first division of this low-grade sprint and again the winner came from off the pace in a race run at a decent tempo.

## 271 BETWAY SPRINT H'CAP (DIV II) 5f 21y (Tp)
**5:30** (5:32) (Class 6) (0-55,55) 3-Y-0+ **£2,587** (£770; £384; £192) **Stalls** Low

Form RPR

54-2 1 **Topsoil**11 64 4-9-5 **50** (p) RyanPowell 8 58
(Ronald Harris) *sn pushed along to ld: rdn and hung lft over 1f out: styd on* **7/1**

435- 2 ½ **Dandilion (IRE)**25 8496 4-9-5 **53** (t) CallumShepherd(3) 4 62+
(Alex Hales) *hld up: hdwy wl over 1f out: nt clr run and hmpd 1f out: r.o wl* **8/1**

552- 3 ¾ **Roy's Legacy**16 8596 8-9-5 **55** CharlieBennett(5) 1 58
(Shaun Harris) *chsd wnr 2f: rdn to go 2nd again and edgd rt over 1f out: styd on u.p* **7/2**2

020- 4 ¾ **Gettin' Lucky**18 8572 4-9-1 **46** AndrewMullen 2 47
(John Balding) *chsd ldrs: rdn over 1f out: styd on* **2/1**1

66-0 5 3 **Whispering Soul (IRE)**10 95 4-9-5 **50** (p) DougieCostello 9 40
(Brian Baugh) *chsd ldrs: wnt 2nd 3f out tl rdn over 1f out: wknd wl ins fnl f* **50/1**

302- 6 ¾ **Whispering Wolf**26 8485 4-9-1 **46** oh1 BarryMcHugh 5 33
(Suzzanne France) *sn outpcd: r.o towards fin* **9/1**

020- 7 hd **Warm Order**317 837 6-9-0 **48** GeorgeDowning(3) 3 34
(Tony Carroll) *mid-div: pushed along 1/2-way: hdwy over 1f out: wknd ins fnl f* **40/1**

33-0 8 ½ **Swendab (IRE)**6 153 9-9-2 **52** (b) MitchGodwin(5) 10 37
(John O'Shea) *hdwy over 3f out: rdn 1/2-way: hung lft and wknd ins fnl f* **5/1**3

600- 9 ¾ **Imjin River (IRE)**32 8383 10-8-11 **47** (tp) HollieDoyle(5) 7 29
(William Stone) *chsd ldrs: hmpd 4f out: sn lost pl: nvr on terms after* **33/1**

530- 10 12 **Edith Weston**38 8288 4-9-1 **46** oh1 (p) LukeMorris 6
(Robert Cowell) *s.s: a bhd* **12/1**

1m 1.47s (-0.43) **Going Correction** -0.175s/f (Stan) 10 Ran SP% **120.9**
Speed ratings (Par 101): **96,95,94,92,88 86,86,85,84,65**
CSF £63.28 CT £238.19 TOTE £7.50: £2.10, £2.40, £2.00; EX 51.10 Trifecta £381.00.
**Owner** Robert & Nina Bailey **Bred** Christopher & Annabelle Mason **Trained** Earlswood, Monmouths
■ Stewards' Enquiry : Charlie Bennett two-day ban (30-31 Jan): careless riding

**FOCUS**
The second leg of this sprint handicap was run fractionally slower than the first, and the winner, taking a slight step up, made virtually all the running.
T/Jkpt: £7,299.90 to a £1 stake. Pool: £10,949.97 - 1.50 winning units T/Plt: £18.80 to a £1 stake. Pool: £104,764.88 - 4,057.79 winning units T/Qpdt: £3.50 to a £1 stake. Pool: £8,846.29 - 1,818.62 winning units **Colin Roberts**

# CHANTILLY (R-H)
Monday, January 16
**OFFICIAL GOING: Polytrack: standard**

## 272a PRIX PRINCELINE (CONDITIONS) (3YO) (POLYTRACK) 7f 110y
**12:25** 3-Y-0
**£17,675** (£7,145; £5,264; £3,384; £2,068; £1,316)

RPR

1 **Ecrin Des Bieffes (FR)**66 7928 3-8-13 0 IoritzMendizabal 5 93
(J A Remolina Diez, France) **15/1**

2 1½ **Phoceen (FR)**155 5450 3-8-13 0 ChristopheSoumillon 7 89
(F Chappet, France) **11/1**

3 1¼ **Jeannajonh (FR)** 3-8-9 0 Francois-XavierBertras 3 82
(W Walton, France) **40/1**

4 nk **Admiralty Arch**62 7971 3-8-13 0 (p) MaximeGuyon 4 85
(Richard Hughes) *keen: chsd ldrs: cl 4th between horses 1 1/2f out: sn rdn and styd on fnl f: nt pce to get on terms* **4/1**2

5 1 **Spotlight Dream (IRE)**33 3-8-13 0 AlexandreRoussel 6 83
(Louis Baudron, France) **7/1**3

6 ¾ **Pastichop (FR)**197 3-8-13 0 MickaelForest 8 81
(A Chopard, France) **9/1**

7 hd **Frosty Bay (FR)**33 3-9-0 0 ow1 Pierre-CharlesBoudot 2 81
(H-F Devin, France) **17/2**

8 13 **Joycetick (FR)**55 3-8-13 0 GregoryBenoist 1 48
(P Sogorb, France) **1/1**1

9 3½ **Whip My Love (FR)**21 8532 3-8-9 0 CristianDemuro 9 35
(Y Barberot, France) **55/1**

PARI-MUTUEL (all including 1 euro stake): WIN 16.00; PLACE 4.30, 3.90, 10.70; DF 41.70; SF 106.00.
**Owner** Jose Alberto Remolina Diez **Bred** M Bridoux **Trained** France

# 167 KEMPTON (A.W) (R-H)
Tuesday, January 17
**OFFICIAL GOING: Polytrack: standard to slow**
Wind: Nil Weather: Fine, crisp

## 273 MATCHBOOK BETTING EXCHANGE H'CAP 6f (P)
**1:55** (1:58) (Class 6) (0-55,55) 4-Y-0+ **£2,587** (£770; £384; £192) **Stalls** Low

Form RPR

61-0 1 **Tilsworth Micky**15 20 5-9-5 **55** GeorgeBaker 11 64
(J R Jenkins) *dropped in fr wd draw: hld up in midfield: stdy prog on inner over 2f out: rdn to ld 1f out but sn hrd pressed: edgd lft nr fin but hld on wl* **8/1**

544- 2 ½ **Tidal's Baby**214 3349 8-9-0 **53** GeorgeDowning(3) 3 61
(Tony Carroll) *in tch: clsd on ldrs fr 2f out: chal 1f out and pressed wnr after: jst hld whn sltly impeded nr fin* **5/1**2

455- 3 3½ **Wedgewood Estates**112 6853 6-9-5 **55** DavidProbert 2 52
(Tony Carroll) *hld up in rr: rdn and prog fr 2f out: styd on fnl f to take 3rd last strides* **7/1**

000- 4 nk **Royal Normandy**46 8188 5-9-1 **54** (b) RobHornby(3) 10 50+
(Grace Harris) *w ldr: led 1/2-way: rdn over 2f out: hdd 1f out: wknd nr fin* **12/1**

0-31 5 2 **Pancake Day**7 153 5-8-9 **52** FinleyMarsh(7) 6 42+
(David C Griffiths) *chsd ldng pair: rdn 2f out: fdd fnl f* **3/1**1

20-1 6 3½ **Multi Quest**11 88 5-9-5 **55** (b) RobertHavlin 7 35
(John E Long) *led to 1/2-way: wknd fr over 1f out* **7/1**

000- 7 3 **Indus Valley (IRE)**17 8595 10-9-2 **52** KieranO'Neill 9 23
(Lee Carter) *awkward s then stdd: sn wl off the pce in last and pushed along: nvr in it* **25/1**

03-6 8 nk **Emily Goldfinch**12 80 4-9-2 **55** CallumShepherd(3) 8 25
(Phil McEntee) *t.k.h: chsd ldng pair: rdn 1/2-way: hanging lft and wknd jst over 2f out* **10/1**

620- 9 ½ **Just Fab (IRE)**49 8146 4-8-12 **53** PaddyBradley(5) 1 21
(Lee Carter) *sn pushed along and struggling in last pair: nvr a factor* **11/2**3

60-6 10 1 **Daydream (IRE)**11 95 4-9-2 **55** EoinWalsh(3) 5 20
(Tony Newcombe) *sltly awkward s: t.k.h: hld up in rr: struggling fr 1/2-way* **25/1**

1m 13.05s (-0.05) **Going Correction** +0.125s/f (Slow) 10 Ran SP% **117.6**
Speed ratings (Par 101): **105,104,99,99,96 91,87,87,86,85**
CSF £48.22 CT £302.27 TOTE £8.10: £2.80, £1.90, £2.30; EX 69.90 Trifecta £404.40.
**Owner** M Ng **Bred** Michael Ng **Trained** Royston, Herts

**FOCUS**
A weak sprint handicap to start, but they went a fair pace. The winner's effort was in line with his Chelmsford win and earlier form.

## 274 RACING UK HD H'CAP 7f (P)
**2:30** (2:30) (Class 6) (0-52,52) 4-Y-0+ **£2,587** (£770; £384; £192) **Stalls** Low

Form RPR

500- 1 **Whaleweigh Station**26 8492 6-9-3 **48** (v) GeorgeBaker 9 55
(J R Jenkins) *pressed ldr: led 2f out gng strly: clr fnl f: rdn out* **7/2**2

050- 2 2¼ **Afkar (IRE)**74 7794 9-9-7 **52** (p) DavidNolan 7 53
(Ivan Furtado) *led: rdn and hdd 2f out: kpt on same pce after* **10/3**1

00- 3 1 **Pick Of Any (IRE)**28 8474 4-9-3 **51** EoinWalsh(3) 13 49+
(Tony Carroll) *dropped in fr wd draw and hld up towards rr: hrd rdn and no rspnse over 2f out: styd on fr over 1f out to take 3rd last strides* **5/1**3

500- 4 nk **Mowhoob**40 8278 7-8-10 **48** JoshuaBryan(7) 14 45
(Brian Barr) *chsd ldrs: rdn over 2f out: kpt on to dispute 3rd fnl f: unable to threaten* **25/1**

00-0 5 shd **Chandrayaan**6 167 10-9-1 **46** (v) RobertHavlin 3 43
(John E Long) *chsd ldng pair: rdn over 2f out: hanging after but stl in 3rd ins fnl f: one pce* **25/1**

363- 6 1 **Altaira**134 6188 6-9-4 **52** GeorgeDowning(3) 8 46
(Tony Carroll) *chsd ldrs: rdn over 2f out: one pce and nvr able to threaten* **13/2**

06-5 7 hd **Mistry**11 88 4-9-2 **47** LiamKeniry 5 41
(Mark Usher) *chsd ldrs: rdn over 2f out: effrt to dispute 3rd briefly 1f out: wknd* **14/1**

660- **8** 2½ **Seamoor Secret**[26] 8499 5-9-1 **46** oh1..........................(t) LukeMorris 11 33
(Alex Hales) *towards rr: rdn over 2f out: no imp ldrs and nvr any ch* **25/1**

624- **9** *nk* **The Reel Way (GR)**[96] 7302 6-9-1 **46**.......................... DanielMuscutt 4 34
(Patrick Chamings) *chsd ldrs: rdn and no prog over 2f out: eased whn no ch last 100yds* **8/1**

000- **10** ¾ **Abertillery**[44] 6891 5-9-1 **46** oh1.......................... DavidProbert 12 30
(Michael Blanshard) *sn in last: urged along and no prog 3f out: kpt on fnl 150yds* **25/1**

/5-0 **11** *hd* **Birdie Must Fly**[13] 51 5-9-1 **46** oh1.......................... TomMarquand 2 30
(Jimmy Fox) *dwlt: a in rr: nvr a factor* **66/1**

400/ **12** 2 **Deftera Fantutte (IRE)**[656] 1156 6-9-7 **52**.................... TimmyMurphy 1 30
(Natalie Lloyd-Beavis) *nvr beyond midfield: wknd 2f out* **66/1**

006- **13** 7 **Let It Go**[26] 8491 5-8-8 **46** oh1.......................... AledBeech(7) 6 5
(Tony Carroll) *t.k.h: hld up in midfield and racd wd: wknd over 2f out: t.o* **66/1**

000- **14** ¾ **Blanco (USA)**[90] 7459 4-9-6 **51**..........................(t) SteveDrowne 10 8
(George Baker) *a wl in rr: rdn 1/2-way: nvr a factor: t.o* **20/1**

1m 26.98s (0.98) **Going Correction** +0.125s/f (Slow) **14** Ran SP% **117.7**
Speed ratings (Par 101): **99,96,95,94,94 93,93,90,90,89 89,86,78,78**
CSF £13.60 CT £58.89 TOTE £4.50: £1.90, £1.90, £2.40; EX 19.00 Trifecta £123.40.

**Owner** J Melo **Bred** A Black **Trained** Royston, Herts

**FOCUS**
This was even worse than the opener, effectively a 32-52 handicap. Few ever got into it with the two market leaders up there throughout. The winner was well treated on last summer's form.

## 275 BETTER ODDS WITH MATCHBOOK BETTING EXCHANGE H'CAP 7f (P)
**3:05** (3:05) (Class 3) (0-90,90) 4-Y-0+
**£7,470** (£2,236; £1,118; £419; £419; £140) **Stalls** Low

Form RPR

56-4 **1** **Intransigent**[14] 33 8-9-4 **90**.......................... RobHornby(3) 9 98
(Andrew Balding) *t.k.h early: trckd ldrs: pushed along to cl over 1f out: rdn to ld last 75yds: styd on wl: eased last strides* **9/1**

054- **2** ½ **Joey's Destiny (IRE)**[41] 8256 7-9-4 **87**.......................... LiamKeniry 13 93
(George Baker) *hld up in rr: prog on inner fr 2f out: clsd on ldrs fnl f: styd on to take 2nd last strides* **20/1**

000- **3** *hd* **Fiftyshadesofgrey (IRE)**[174] 4758 6-9-7 **90**.................. SteveDrowne 1 95
(George Baker) *slowly away: sn in midfield: prog towards inner fr 2f out: styd on u.p fnl f to take 3rd last stride* **16/1**

000- **4** *hd* **Quixote (GER)**[27] 8478 7-9-4 **90**.......................... GeorgeDowning(3) 14 95
(Tony Carroll) *racd wd early: led after 2f: shkn up over 1f out: kpt on but hdd last 75yds and lost pls nr fin* **14/1**

400- **4** *dht* **Valbchek (IRE)**[26] 8489 8-9-7 **90**..........................(p) GeorgeBaker 2 95
(Jane Chapple-Hyam) *t.k.h early: trckd ldrs: wnt 2nd over 2f out: chal fr over 1f out: stl pressing ins fnl f: one pce last strides* **8/1**[3]

10-2 **6** 2 **Firmdecisions (IRE)**[12] 66 7-9-7 **90**.......................... RobertWinston 12 88
(Dean Ivory) *prom: chsd ldr 1/2-way to over 2f out: sn rdn and nt qckn: kpt on same pce after* **10/1**

23-2 **7** *nk* **War Department (IRE)**[15] 25 4-9-0 **83**..........................(b) PhillipMakin 5 80
(Keith Dalgleish) *hld up in rr: pushed along 2f out: sme prog and shkn up 1f out: kpt on but nvr really involved* **6/1**[2]

010- **8** ½ **Outer Space**[164] 5174 6-9-6 **89**.......................... JamieSpencer 8 85+
(Jamie Osborne) *hld up in last of main gp: swtchd to wd outside over 2f out: limited prog tl reminders fnl f: nvr on terms* **8/1**[3]

33-6 **9** *nk* **Aguerooo (IRE)**[12] 81 4-9-7 **90**..........................(b) SeanLevey 11 85
(Richard Hannon) *hld up wl in rr: shkn up over 2f out: kpt on but nvr pce to threaten* **20/1**

00-4 **10** *nse* **Mullionheir**[11] 93 5-9-3 **86**.......................... KierenFox 3 81
(John Best) *fast away: led 2f: styd prom: rdn 2f out: wknd jst ins fnl f* **14/1**

60-4 **11** 3¾ **Young John (IRE)**[16] 5 4-9-1 **84**.......................... TonyHamilton 6 67
(Richard Fahey) *t.k.h: hld up bhd ldrs: wknd 2f out* **14/1**

430- **12** 1½ **Bahamian Dollar**[122] 6583 4-8-11 **80**.......................... AndrewMullen 7 58
(David Evans) *racd wd in midfield: dropped to rr over 2f out: wl btn after* **14/1**

65-1 **13** 13 **Dutch Art Dealer**[14] 32 6-8-10 **86**..........................(v) LewisEdmunds(7) 4 22
(Ivan Furtado) *rel to r and lft 150yds: drvn and tried to make sme grnd but nvr able to cl* **4/1**[1]

1m 26.36s (0.36) **Going Correction** +0.125s/f (Slow) **13** Ran SP% **117.7**
Speed ratings (Par 107): **102,101,101,100,100 98,98,97,97,97 93,91,76**
CSF £173.43 CT £2879.59 TOTE £12.30: £3.40, £8.10, £6.20; EX 197.70 Trifecta £3684.80.

**Owner** Kingsclere Racing Club **Bred** Kingsclere Stud **Trained** Kingsclere, Hants

**FOCUS**
This was more like it, a decent handicap and a thrilling finish. The winner has been rated close to his best in the past year.

## 276 SMARTER BETS WITH MATCHBOOK BETTING EXCHANGE CONDITIONS STKS (PLUS 10 RACE) (AW CHAMPS' QUALIFIER) 6f (P)
**3:40** (3:40) (Class 2) 3-Y-O **£11,827** (£3,541; £1,770; £885; £442) **Stalls** Low

Form RPR

21- **1** **Second Thought (IRE)**[32] 8406 3-9-2 83.................... RobertWinston 1 104
(William Haggas) *trckd ldrs on inner: pushed along to cl fr over 1f out: tk 2nd fnl f: rdn and sustained effrt to ld last 50yds* **3/1**[2]

023- **2** *nk* **Sutter County**[45] 8209 3-9-2 103.......................... PJMcDonald 6 103
(Mark Johnston) *disp ld: pushed into narrow advantage 2f out: drvn and styd on wl fnl f but hdd last 50yds* **9/4**[1]

432- **3** 5 **Tomily (IRE)**[87] 7536 3-9-2 99.......................... SeanLevey 3 87
(Richard Hannon) *disp ld: narrowly hdd and shkn up 2f out: lost 2nd fnl f and steadily wknd* **3/1**[2]

25-1 **4** 3¾ **Letmestopyouthere (IRE)**[14] 31 3-9-2 87.......................... AndrewMullen 2 75
(David Evans) *cl up bhd ldrs: rdn over 2f out: hanging and sn btn: wknd over 1f out* **8/1**

011- **5** 2¾ **Turin Redstar**[30] 8444 3-9-2 84.......................... AdamKirby 5 66
(Ralph Beckett) *cl up on outer: rdn over 2f out and sn btn: wknd over 1f out* **5/1**[3]

1m 12.13s (-0.97) **Going Correction** +0.125s/f (Slow) **5** Ran SP% **108.5**
Speed ratings (Par 103): **111,110,103,98,95**
CSF £9.82 TOTE £5.00: £1.50, £2.10; EX 11.10 Trifecta £39.60.

**Owner** Liam Sheridan **Bred** Tally-Ho Stud **Trained** Newmarket, Suffolk

**FOCUS**
An interesting race, despite the small field, and a qualifier for the 3yo Championship over this trip on Finals Day. There was a disputed lead and the quintet finished well spread out. The race has been rated around the runner-up.

## 277 WINNERS WELCOME AT MATCHBOOK EXCHANGE H'CAP 1m (P)
**4:10** (4:10) (Class 4) (0-80,80) 4-Y-0+ **£5,175** (£1,540; £769; £384) **Stalls** Low

Form RPR

000- **1** **In The Red (IRE)**[30] 8446 4-9-6 **79**..........................(b) TimmyMurphy 11 92
(Richard Hannon) *trckd ldr: pushed into the ld over 1f out: rdn and styd on strly fnl f* **25/1**

51-3 **2** 2¾ **Pendo**[12] 61 6-9-2 **75**.......................... GeorgeBaker 3 81
(John Best) *hld up in midfield: prog on inner over 2f out: tried to chal over 1f out: sn no ch w wnr but kpt on* **7/1**[3]

41- **3** 1¼ **Noble Star (IRE)**[64] 7960 4-9-4 **77**.......................... DanielMuscutt 1 80
(James Fanshawe) *trckd ldng pair: rdn over 2f out: tried to cl jst over 1f out but kpt on same pce after* **13/8**[1]

15-2 **4** ½ **Squire**[12] 61 6-9-3 **76**..........................(t) LukeMorris 10 78
(Michael Attwater) *trckd ldrs: rdn over 2f out: kpt on but nvr pce to chal* **14/1**

231- **5** *nk* **Rio's Cliffs**[34] 8357 4-9-7 **80**..........................(b) DavidProbert 6 81
(Martyn Meade) *towards rr: latched on to ldng gp over 2f out: rdn and kpt on but nvr able to threaten* **9/1**

504- **6** ½ **Starboard**[26] 8487 8-9-3 **76**..........................(be[1]) JamieSpencer 8 76
(David Simcock) *hld up in midfield on outer: rdn over 2f out: kpt on same pce fr over 1f out* **9/1**

223- **7** ¾ **Berrahri (IRE)**[192] 4138 6-9-2 **75**.......................... KierenFox 5 73
(John Best) *trckd ldrs in 5th: checked after 1f: rdn over 2f out: no imp over 1f out: fdd ins fnl f* **33/1**

212- **8** 2½ **Baltic Prince (IRE)**[28] 8469 7-8-11 **73**.................... GeorgeDowning(3) 7 65
(Tony Carroll) *led at gd pce: drvn and hdd over 1f out: wknd* **16/1**

/0-3 **9** 1½ **Miracle Ninetynine (IRE)**[12] 66 5-9-4 **77**..............(h) TomMarquand 9 66
(Ed Vaughan) *hld up and sn in last pair: lost tch w ldng gp over 2f out: taken out wd and no prog* **6/1**[2]

200- **10** 1 **Major Crispies**[34] 8356 6-9-1 **79**..........................(t) DavidParkes(5) 4 66
(Jeremy Gask) *a wl in rr: lost tch w ldng gp over 2f out: no ch after* **33/1**

000- **11** 2 **Ocean Tempest**[21] 8539 8-9-5 **78**..........................(p) AdamKirby 2 60
(John Ryan) *hld up wl in rr: lost tch w ldng gp over 2f out: rdn and fnd nil after* **40/1**

054- **12** *hd* **Torment**[17] 8590 4-8-13 **72**.......................... SeanLevey 12 54
(Richard Hannon) *hld up wl in rr: rdn and lost tch w ldng gp over 2f out: fnd nil after* **14/1**

1m 38.57s (-1.23) **Going Correction** +0.125s/f (Slow) **12** Ran SP% **116.3**
Speed ratings (Par 105): **111,108,107,106,106 105,104,102,100,99 97,97**
CSF £183.25 CT £458.60 TOTE £40.80: £8.00, £2.40, £1.30; EX 415.80 Trifecta £2800.30.

**Owner** Noodles Racing **Bred** Airlie Stud **Trained** East Everleigh, Wilts

**FOCUS**
A fair handicap, but it paid to be handy with the winner, third and fourth always up there. The winner has been rated back to his best.

## 278 MATCHBOOK TRADERS CONFERENCE H'CAP (DIV I) 1m 3f 219y(P)
**4:40** (4:41) (Class 6) (0-55,60) 4-Y-0+ **£2,587** (£770; £384; £192) **Stalls** Centre

Form RPR

324- **1** **Lobster Cocktail (IRE)**[19] 8566 4-9-5 **56**..........................(t) LukeMorris 14 63
(Ed Walker) *swtchd sharply after s fr wdst draw to inner: hld up in midfield: prog over 2f out: swtchd rt wl over 1f out: sn clsd to ld and drvn clr* **11/2**[2]

550- **2** 3 **Barnacle**[160] 5303 8-8-12 **45**..........................(bt) StevieDonohoe 8 47+
(Emma Owen) *s.s: wl off the pce in last pair: prog on inner over 2f out: styd on fnl f to take 2nd last strides* **40/1**

003- **3** *nse* **Sir Jack**[19] 8566 4-8-13 **53**.......................... GeorgeDowning(3) 2 55
(Tony Carroll) *in tch on outer: urged along over 4f out: responded and drvn to dispute 2nd fr over 1f out tl nr fin* **10/1**[3]

34-0 **4** *nk* **Medicean Queen (IRE)**[13] 39 6-9-4 **54**...........(t) CallumShepherd(3) 6 56
(Phil McEntee) *trckd ldrs in 5th: clsd over 2f out: drvn to chal wl over 1f out: one pce ins fnl f* **20/1**

026- **5** 2¼ **Galuppi**[90] 7464 6-9-7 **54**..........................(v) GeorgeBaker 11 52
(J R Jenkins) *hld up wl in rr: gng strly wl over 2f out: sn rdn and v limited rspnse: kpt on fr over 1f out: nrst fin* **12/1**

44-4 **6** *hd* **Lily Edge**[13] 35 8-8-13 **46**..........................(v) WilliamCarson 1 44
(John Bridger) *hld up in midfield on inner: prog over 2f out: chal on inner wl over 1f out: wknd ins fnl f* **16/1**

504- **7** 1½ **Rianna Star**[47] 8179 4-9-3 **57**.......................... HectorCrouch(3) 10 52
(Gary Moore) *wl in rr: urged along over 3f out: sme prog over 2f out: nt rch ldrs over 1f out: fdd last 150yds* **10/1**[3]

000- **8** ½ **Street Art (IRE)**[21] 8540 5-8-13 **46** ow1...................(bt[1]) RobertWinston 3 41
(Mike Murphy) *s.v.s: wl off the pce in last: jst in tch and gng wl enough 3f out: rdn and racd awkwardly over 2f out: modest prog over 1f out: nvr a factor* **33/1**

33-1 **9** 1¾ **Tred Softly (IRE)**[8] 146 4-9-9 **60** 6ex..........................(b) JasonHart 7 52+
(John Quinn) *trckd ldng trio at str pce: clsd to ld over 2f out: immediately fnd nil in front: hdd over 1f out and sn btn* **11/8**[1]

000- **10** *nk* **Tractive Effort**[28] 8468 4-8-10 **47**.......................... KierenFox 13 38+
(Michael Attwater) *trckd ldr: led over 3f out and committed for home: hdd over 2f out: stl upsides wl over 1f out: sn wknd* **25/1**

000- **11** *nk* **Fishergate**[96] 7310 4-8-9 **53**.......................... GabrieleMalune(7) 4 44
(Richard Rowe) *t.k.h: hld up in rr: urged along 4f out: no hdwy* **50/1**

00-0 **12** 10 **Sayedaati Saadati (IRE)**[16] 7 4-9-2 **53**.......................... AdamKirby 5 28+
(John Butler) *chsd ldng pair tl wknd qckly over 3f out* **20/1**

250- **13** 10 **Dancing Rainbow (GR)**[30] 8445 4-8-8 **45**..............(b) TomMarquand 12 4+
(Amanda Perrett) *racd freely: led at str pce: hdd over 3f out: wknd rapidly over 2f out: t.o* **16/1**

2m 36.26s (1.76) **Going Correction** +0.125s/f (Slow)
**WFA** 4 from 5yo+ 3lb **13** Ran SP% **115.8**
Speed ratings (Par 101): **99,97,96,96,95 95,94,93,92,92 92,85,78**
CSF £219.44 CT £2130.64 TOTE £4.30: £1.90, £10.30, £3.70; EX 213.70 Trifecta £2383.20.

**Owner** Mrs T Walker **Bred** Glending Bloodstock **Trained** Upper Lambourn, Berks

■ Stewards' Enquiry : Callum Shepherd two-day ban: used whip above permitted level (Jan 31 - Feb 1)

**FOCUS**
The first division of a moderate middle-distance handicap, but a decisive winner.

## 279 MATCHBOOK TRADERS CONFERENCE H'CAP (DIV II) 1m 3f 219y(P)
**5:10** (5:11) (Class 6) (0-55,55) 4-Y-0+ **£2,587** (£770; £384; £192) **Stalls** Centre

Form RPR
036- **1** **Staplehurst (IRE)**[21] 8540 4-9-0 **52**............................(t) TimmyMurphy 7 58
(Geoffrey Deacon) *hld up in midfield: clsd on ldrs gng strly over 2f out: shkn up to chal over 1f out: led ins fnl f: rdn out* **6/1**[2]
005- **2** *1* **Awesome Rock (IRE)**[103] 7104 8-8-12 **46** oh1............... RobertHavlin 5 50
(Roger Ingram) *tk fierce hold early and hld up in last trio: prog on inner over 2f out: rdn to ld jst over 1f out tl ins fnl f: kpt on* **20/1**
26-0 **3** *1* **Ali Bin Nayef**[13] 35 5-9-5 **53**.......................................... AdamKirby 11 55
(Michael Wigham) *hld up in rr: rdn wl over 2f out and limited prog: styd on fr over 1f out to take 3rd nr fin* **6/1**[2]
00-5 **4** *1 1/2* **Smoky Hill (IRE)**[10] 121 8-9-2 **53**......................(p) GeorgeDowning(3) 10 53+
(Tony Carroll) *pushed up to chse ldr: rdn to ld over 2f out: hdd jst over 1f out: no ex and lost 3rd nr fin* **12/1**
050- **5** *1* **Sixties Idol**[94] 7367 4-8-7 **48**......................................... NathanAlison(3) 9 46
(Sheena West) *hld up in last trio: pushed along on inner over 2f out and prog into midfield: no ch whn light reminders fnl f: kpt on but nvr involved* **25/1**
P62- **6** *hd* **Graceful Lady**[19] 8468 4-9-3 **55**......................................... JackMitchell 3 56
(Robert Eddery) *trckd ldng pair: cl up whn short of room over 2f out and lost pl: n.m.r wl over 1f out: kpt on same pce after* **10/3**[1]
50-0 **7** *1/2* **Divine Prince (GR)**[13] 35 4-8-12 **53**..................(b) HectorCrouch(3) 12 50
(Amanda Perrett) *trckd ldrs: rdn over 2f out: nt qckn wl over 1f out: one pce after* **33/1**
600- **8** *4* **Mulled Wine**[33] 8382 4-9-1 **53**................................................ KierenFox 4 44
(John Best) *hld up towards rr: clsd fr 3f out: rdn over 2f out and no hdwy after: wknd jst over 1f out* **7/1**[3]
00U- **9** *8* **Salient**[67] 7905 13-8-13 **50**....................................... EdwardGreatrex(3) 6 28
(Michael Attwater) *nvr bttr than midfield: rdn wl over 3f out: wl btn over 2f out* **16/1**
**10** *1/2* **Cornelius (FR)**[508] 4712 5-9-0 **55**.................................... JordanUys(7) 8 32
(Jonathan Geake) *trckd ldng pair tl wknd qckly over 2f out* **33/1**
00-0 **11** *8* **Mybrotherjohnny**[11] 98 6-8-12 **46** oh1........................(t) JoeyHaynes 1 10+
(Fergal O'Brien) *won battle for ld at str pce: tried to stdy it after 4f: hdd over 2f out: wknd rapidly wl over 1f out* **12/1**
600- **12** *14* **Lions Charge (USA)**[22] 8155 10-8-13 **54**........(v) LamornaBardwell(7) 13
(Seamus Mullins) *s.v.s: rapid prog on outer to chse ldrs 1/2-way: wknd as rapidly over 4f out: t.o* **25/1**
000- **R** **Katalan (GER)**[269] 1653 4-8-10 **48** oh1 ow2........................ LiamKeniry 2
(John Butler) *ref to r: tk no part* **8/1**
2m 37.21s (2.71) **Going Correction** +0.125s/f (Slow)
**WFA** 4 from 5yo+ 3lb **13** Ran SP% **114.9**
Speed ratings (Par 101): **95,94,93,92,92 91,91,88,83,83 77,68,**
CSF £124.13 CT £742.89 TOTE £5.30: £2.00, £4.30, £1.80; EX 89.30 Trifecta £665.80.
**Owner** Compton Racing Club **Bred** Stuart McPhee Bloodstock Ltd **Trained** Compton, Berks

**FOCUS**
The winning time was nearly a second slower than the first division. A slight step forward from the winner.

## 280 MATCHBOOK BETTING PODCAST H'CAP 1m 7f 218y(P)
**5:40** (5:40) (Class 5) (0-75,77) 4-Y-0+ **£3,234** (£962; £481; £240) **Stalls** Low

Form RPR
61-1 **1** **Aurora Gray**[8] 141 4-9-2 **75** 6ex....................................... GeorgeBaker 5 84+
(Hughie Morrison) *hld up bhd ldrs: smoothly clsd to chal 2f out: rdn to chse new ldr over 1f out: kpt on wl to ld last strides* **6/5**[1]
013- **2** *nk* **El Campeon**[20] 8558 5-9-6 **75**...................................... HectorCrouch(3) 2 82
(Simon Dow) *stdd s: t.k.h: hld up in last: clsd smoothly over 2f out: led over 1f out: sn rdn and edgd lft fnl f: kpt on but hdd last strides* **11/2**[3]
02-2 **3** *3 3/4* **Miss Tiger Lily**[8] 141 7-9-2 **68**........................................... LukeMorris 3 71
(Harry Dunlop) *led 6f: trckd ldr: led again over 2f out: sn rdn: hdd and one pce over 1f out* **10/3**[2]
4-00 **4** *1 1/2* **Wordiness**[5] 196 9-9-2 **68**............................................... AndrewMullen 6 69
(David Evans) *t.k.h: hld up: in tch whn drvn wl over 2f out: one pce over 1f out* **16/1**
220- **5** *3/4* **Saborido (USA)**[20] 8558 11-9-11 **77**...........................(v[1]) RobertHavlin 1 77
(Amanda Perrett) *chsd ldr 5f: in tch: rdn wl over 2f out: one pce over 1f out* **14/1**
304- **6** *26* **Winter Spice (IRE)**[34] 8363 6-9-9 **75**..............................(b) AdamKirby 4 44
(Clive Cox) *s.s: hld up in last: t.k.h and plld way through to ld after 6f: sn clr: hdd & wknd over 2f out: eased and t.o* **9/1**
3m 32.7s (2.60) **Going Correction** +0.125s/f (Slow)
**WFA** 4 from 5yo+ 5lb **6** Ran SP% **106.5**
Speed ratings (Par 103): **98,97,95,95,94 81**
CSF £7.19 TOTE £2.10: £1.30, £2.40; EX 8.10 Trifecta £19.20.
**Owner** Wardley Bloodstock **Bred** Lakin Bloodstock/Wardley Bloodstock **Trained** East Ilsley, Berks

**FOCUS**
An ordinary staying handicap in which the pace suddenly picked up with under a circuit left and it became more of a test. The winner remains on the upgrade.
T/Jkpt: Not Won. T/Plt: £460.50 to a £1 stake. Pool: £79,300.86 - 125.71 winning units T/Qpdt: £139.40 to a £1 stake. Pool: £6,944.04 - 36.84 winning units **Jonathan Neesom**

# [273]KEMPTON (A.W) (R-H)
Wednesday, January 18

**OFFICIAL GOING: Polytrack: standard to slow**
Wind: nil Weather: Clear, cold

## 281 RACING UK ANYWHERE H'CAP 1m 2f 219y(P)
**4:20** (4:21) (Class 7) (0-50,52) 4-Y-0+ **£1,940** (£577; £288; £144) **Stalls** Low

Form RPR
606- **1** **Rail Dancer**[20] 8566 5-9-7 **50**....................................(v[1]) RobertWinston 12 57
(Richard Rowe) *sn led and mde all: rdn over 2f out: clr advantage over 1f out: kpt on wl ins fnl f* **14/1**
3-21 **2** *1 1/4* **Frivolous Prince (IRE)**[11] 121 4-9-4 **50**.................(vt) StevieDonohoe 2 55
(David Evans) *hld up in rr: tk clsr order over 3f out: rdn w plenty to do over 2f out: kpt on wl fr over 1f out: nvr nrr* **4/1**[2]
000- **3** *1 3/4* **Rezwaan**[214] 3401 10-9-6 **49**......................................(b) ShaneKelly 13 51
(Murty McGrath) *settled in mid-div: tk clsr order 3f out: rdn on outer over 2f out: kpt on wl ins fnl f* **7/1**
4-61 **4** *nk* **Spirit Of The Vale (IRE)**[7] 176 4-9-6 **52** 6ex...................(t) KevinStott 6 54
(Oliver Greenall) *hld up in rr: c wd bnd: rdn over 2f out: kpt one pce fr over 1f out* **9/1**
062- **5** *3 1/4* **Brooke's Point**[153] 5572 4-9-2 **48**....................................(p[1]) LiamKeniry 3 45
(Neil Mulholland) *chsd ldr: rdn over 2f out: one pce fr over 1f out* **15/8**[1]
050- **6** *3/4* **Whip Up A Frenzy (IRE)**[27] 8497 5-8-9 **45**............. GabrieleMalune(7) 9 40
(Richard Rowe) *settled bhd ldr: rdn over 2f out: sn no ex and one pce fr over 1f out* **20/1**
5/0- **7** *4* **Cappielow Park**[21] 1547 8-9-6 **49**.............................(tp) TomMarquand 11 38
(Ali Stronge) *chsd ldrs: rdn over 2f out: no ex fr over 1f out* **50/1**
640- **8** *1 1/4* **Haaffa Sovereign**[27] 8497 6-9-4 **47**...............................(b) MartinHarley 1 34
(Kevin Morgan) *settled in mid-divsion: rdn over 2f out: sn hld* **10/1**
200- **9** *2* **White Dog (IRE)**[22] 8540 5-9-5 **48**..............................(t) DougieCostello 10 32
(Sarah Humphrey) *tk fierce hold in mid-div: nudged along over 2f out: no ex fr over 1f out* **40/1**
00-0 **10** *6* **Silver Lining (IRE)**[11] 123 5-9-2 **45**.........................(b[1]) TimmyMurphy 4 19
(Mark Hoad) *in rr: rdn over 2f out: one pce fr over 1f out* **66/1**
006- **11** *6* **Race Time (USA)**[49] 8157 4-9-2 **48**........................(b[1]) FergusSweeney 7 13
(Seamus Durack) *in rr-div: rdn over 2f out: wknd over 1f out* **33/1**
000- **12** *18* **Storming Ambition**[34] 8382 4-8-13 **48**......................(b) NoelGarbutt(3) 14
(Conrad Allen) *in rr-divsion on outer: pushed along over 2f out: wknd fr 2f out: eased fnl f: t.o* **200/1**
451- **13** *12* **Master Of Heaven**[27] 8492 4-9-4 **50**...........................(tp) AdamKirby 8
(Jim Boyle) *t.k.h: settled on outer: losing over 3f out: no ex fr over 2f out: heavily eased fr over 1f out: t.o* **6/1**[3]
2m 21.7s (-0.20) **Going Correction** +0.05s/f (Slow)
**WFA** 4 from 5yo+ 2lb **13** Ran SP% **121.4**
Speed ratings (Par 97): **102,101,99,99,97 96,93,92,91,87 82,69,60**
CSF £68.01 CT £441.71 TOTE £17.30: £4.20, £1.70, £2.70; EX 95.30 Trifecta £959.60.
**Owner** Mark Cashmore **Bred** Scuderia Blueberry SRL **Trained** Sullington, W Sussex

**FOCUS**
A low-grade handicap dominated from the front by the winner, while the runner-up helps pin the level.

## 282 100% PROFIT BOOST AT 32REDSPORT.COM H'CAP 1m (P)
**4:50** (4:50) (Class 6) (0-55,56) 4-Y-0+ **£2,264** (£673; £336; £168) **Stalls** Low

Form RPR
060- **1** **Magic Mirror**[27] 8492 4-8-12 **46** oh1.........................(v[1]) TomMarquand 6 56
(Mark Rimell) *mde all: shkn up in centre over 2f out: sn rdn: kpt on wl ins fnl f: hld on wl* **50/1**
01-1 **2** *1* **Athassel**[14] 51 8-9-5 **53**........................................................ AdamKirby 4 60
(David Evans) *hld up in rr-div: tk clsr order on inner over 2f out: sn rdn: gd prog fr over 1f out: clsng nr fin: nvr nrr* **5/4**[1]
622- **3** *2 3/4* **Henry Grace (IRE)**[56] 8070 6-9-5 **53**...........................(b) KieranO'Neill 1 54
(Jimmy Fox) *mid-div on outer: rdn over 2f out: kpt on wl ent fnl f: tk 3rd post* **5/1**[3]
000- **4** *1/2* **Los Cerritos (SWI)**[19] 8586 5-9-7 **55**................................(b) KevinStott 3 55
(Oliver Greenall) *chsd ldrs on inner: rdn over 2f out: kpt on fr over 1f out: one pce nr fin and lost 3rd post* **8/1**
054/ **5** *2 1/4* **Monsieur Royale**[665] 1026 7-9-7 **55**................................ JackMitchell 14 50
(Clive Drew) *hld up in last: tk clsr order on inner fr 2f out: prog fr over 1f out: nvr nrr* **50/1**
500- **6** *2* **West Leake (IRE)**[92] 7427 11-9-3 **51**.................................. LiamKeniry 5 41
(Paul Burgoyne) *mid-div on rail: rdn over 2f out: no ex and one pce fr over 1f out* **20/1**
355- **7** *3/4* **Ertidaad (IRE)**[29] 8470 5-9-1 **49**...................................(b) LukeMorris 12 37
(Emma Owen) *cl up w ldr: rdn over 2f out: losing tch fr 2f out: sn hld* **14/1**
453- **8** *6* **Jessica Jo (IRE)**[29] 8471 4-9-3 **51**................................(b) PJMcDonald 7 26
(Mark Johnston) *settled in mid-div: rdn along fr over 3f out: wknd fr over 1f out* **4/1**[2]
00-6 **9** *1 1/4* **Zeteah**[13] 69 7-8-12 **46** oh1.........................................(p[1]) DavidProbert 9 18
(Tony Carroll) *in rr-div: effrt over 2f out: sn lft bhd* **50/1**
36-0 **10** *1/2* **Les Gar Gan (IRE)**[14] 46 6-9-7 **55**......................(be) StevieDonohoe 11 28
(Daniel Mark Loughnane) *in rr-div: nt clrest of runs over 2f out: pushed along after* **20/1**
005- **11** *1 3/4* **Caius College Girl (IRE)**[23] 8528 5-9-8 **56**...............(b) TimmyMurphy 8 23
(Natalie Lloyd-Beavis) *t.k.h and sn settled on outer of ldr: disp ld 3f out: sn rdn: wknd fr over 1f out* **20/1**
000- **12** *6* **Magical Peak**[99] 7240 5-8-7 **46** oh1............................... MitchGodwin(5) 10
(John O'Shea) *mid-div on outer: rdn over 3f out to hold pl: wknd fr over 1f out: eased* **100/1**
1m 39.77s (-0.03) **Going Correction** +0.05s/f (Slow) **12** Ran SP% **120.0**
Speed ratings (Par 101): **102,101,98,97,95 93,92,86,85,85 83,77**
CSF £110.51 CT £414.96 TOTE £57.60: £12.80, £1.10, £1.80; EX 330.40 Trifecta £2815.20.
**Owner** William Wood **Bred** Hesmonds Stud Ltd **Trained** Leafield, Oxon

**FOCUS**
Another moderate heat and once again the leader wasn't for catching.

## 283 32RED ON THE APP STORE MAIDEN FILLIES' STKS 1m (P)
**5:20** (5:24) (Class 5) 3-Y-0+ **£2,911** (£866; £432; £216) **Stalls** Low

Form RPR
3-3 **1** **Dreaming Of Paris**[7] 168 3-8-12 0................................... JoeFanning 10 76+
(William Haggas) *settled bhd ldr: upsides ldr gng wl fr 2f out: shkn up ent fnl f and sn led: styd on wl* **5/4**[1]
0- **2** *1 3/4* **Driver's Girl (USA)**[232] 2764 3-8-12 0......................... DanielMuscutt 13 71
(Marco Botti) *sn led: pressed by wnr fr 2f out: sn rdn: hdd ent fnl f: kpt on after* **33/1**
0-6 **3** *1 1/2* **Mayflair**[9] 144 3-8-7 0.............................................. MitchGodwin(5) 4 67
(Jonathan Portman) *chsd ldr: rdn over 2f out: rn green over 1f out: sn stened up: pushed along and kpt on again ins fnl f* **50/1**
**4** *1 1/4* **Persistence (IRE)** 3-8-12 0........................................ DavidProbert 6 64+
(Ralph Beckett) *s.s: rn green in rr tl prog fr 3f out: kpt on nicely fr over 1f out into nvr nrr 4th: improver* **15/8**[2]
55- **5** *nk* **Summer Falls (IRE)**[21] 8559 4-9-11 0............................ AaronJones(3) 8 64
(Rae Guest) *reluctant to load: chsd ldrs: rdn over 2f out: kpt on fr over 1f out* **25/1**
**6** *hd* **Melodine** 3-8-12 0........................................................... LukeMorris 7 63+
(Sir Mark Prescott Bt) *settled in mid-div: rn green most of way: prog fr over 2f out: picking up fr over 1f out: nvr nrr* **14/1**
**7** *2 1/2* **Raweeya** 3-8-12 0.......................................................... TomMarquand 1 57
(Marco Botti) *pushed along early in rr-div on inner: rdn over 2f out: kpt on one pce fr over 1f out* **16/1**
**8** *3 1/4* **Seeking Attention (USA)** 3-8-12 0................................ RobertHavlin 9 49
(George Scott) *settled bhd ldrs: rdn over 2f out: one pce and wknd fr over 1f out* **25/1**

9 ½ **Penny Poet (IRE)** 4-10-0 0 LiamKeniry 3 49
(Neil Mulholland) *s.s: in rr: rdn over 2f out: kpt on* **100/1**
10 1¼ **Feisty One U R** 3-8-12 0 MartinDwyer 11 45
(George Baker) *mid-div on outer: pushed along over 3f out: no ex fr over 1f out and pushed out after* **66/1**
4- 11 ¾ **Sublime**[21] 8556 3-8-12 0 RyanTate 5 43
(Rod Millman) *settled bhd ldrs on rail: shkn up over 2f out: wknd fr over 1f out* **33/1**
12 hd **L'Ami De Rouge** 4-9-11 0 (h[1]) HectorCrouch(3) 12 44
(Ralph J Smith) *s.s: a in rr* **150/1**
00/ 13 2½ **Swinford Lass**[436] 7774 5-9-11 0 GeorgeDowning(3) 14 38
(Tony Carroll) *in rr-div: pushed along 3f out: sn hld* **200/1**
14 nse **Satin Ribbon** 3-8-12 0 ShaneKelly 2 36
(David Elsworth) *s.s: rn green and pushed along most of way: a in rr* **15/2**[3]

1m 40.69s (0.89) **Going Correction** +0.05s/f (Slow)
**WFA** 3 from 4yo+ 20lb **14** Ran SP% **122.7**
Speed ratings (Par 100): **97,95,93,92,92 92,89,86,85,84 83,83,81,81**
CSF £61.36 TOTE £2.40: £1.20, £6.70, £13.00; EX 48.00 Trifecta £964.20.
**Owner** Qatar Racing Limited **Bred** Faisal Meshrf Alqahtani **Trained** Newmarket, Suffolk

**FOCUS**
Not a particularly strong maiden and once again the pace held up well. The winner has been rated in line with her debut form.

## 284 32RED.COM H'CAP (LONDON MILE SERIES QUALIFIER) 1m (P)
**5:50** (5:53) (Class 5) (0-70,70) 3-Y-O **£2,911** (£866; £432; £216) **Stalls** Low

Form RPR
00-4 1 **Revel**[14] 34 3-9-7 **70** (t) AdamKirby 8 76+
(Stuart Williams) *settled bhd ldrs: shkn up and led 2f out: sn in command and shuffled along ins fnl f: cosily* **13/8**[1]
560- 2 1½ **Pobbles**[29] 8466 3-9-5 **68** (p[1]) GeorgeBaker 1 69
(Roger Charlton) *settled in rr: shkn up 2f out w plenty to do: smooth prog on inner fr over 1f out: sn rdn and kpt on wl ins fnl f* **9/2**[2]
033- 3 1¼ **Settle Petal**[18] 8591 3-8-11 **65** PaddyBradley(5) 2 63
(Pat Phelan) *hld up in mid-div on inner: hld together over 2f out waiting for cutaway: sn rdn: kpt on one pce* **16/1**
241- 4 ¾ **Booshbash (IRE)**[58] 8046 3-9-1 **64** MartinHarley 7 60
(Ed Dunlop) *sson led: rdn over 2f: hdd 2f out: no ex and wknd* **5/1**[3]
5-35 5 1¾ **License To Thrill (USA)**[5] 210 3-9-1 **64** TomMarquand 4 56
(Simon Dow) *covered up in mid-divsion: rdn over 2f out: sn hld* **7/1**
42-6 6 ½ **Ocean Promise (USA)**[12] 100 3-9-5 **68** ShaneKelly 5 59
(Richard Hughes) *broke wl and sn restrained into rr-div: t.k.h: shuffled along 2f out: nt clrest run ent fnl f: nvr involved* **11/1**
040- 7 1½ **Conkering Hero (IRE)**[112] 6881 3-9-4 **67** JFEgan 3 55
(Joseph Tuite) *settled bhd ldrs on inner: rdn over 2f out: no ex and wknd fr over 1f out* **16/1**
500- 8 2¾ **My Lady Marie**[35] 8355 3-9-7 **70** RobertHavlin 6 51
(Amanda Perrett) *t.k.h in mid-div on outer: rdn over 2f out: no ex and kpt on one pce after* **14/1**

1m 40.43s (0.63) **Going Correction** +0.05s/f (Slow) **8** Ran SP% **112.2**
Speed ratings (Par 97): **98,96,95,94,92 92,90,88**
CSF £8.49 CT £81.31 TOTE £2.70: £1.20, £1.60, £3.60; EX 10.90 Trifecta £86.00.
**Owner** Stuart C Williams **Bred** Limestone And Tara Studs **Trained** Newmarket, Suffolk

**FOCUS**
A modest handicap and yet again it paid to race on the pace. The race has been rated around the placed horses.

## 285 32RED/EBF STALLIONS BREEDING FILLIES' H'CAP 1m (P)
**6:20** (6:20) (Class 3) (0-95,90) 4-Y-O+
**£9,648** (£2,889; £1,444; £722; £361; £181) **Stalls** Low

Form RPR
/2-1 1 **Absolute Blast (IRE)**[12] 99 5-9-7 **90** PJMcDonald 4 101+
(Iain Jardine) *hld up in 7th: full of running on heels of ldrs over 1f out: shkn up and smooth prog ent fnl f: sn rdn and led wl ins fnl f: qcknd clr: easily* **8/11**[1]
54-3 2 1½ **Bint Dandy (IRE)**[9] 142 6-9-4 **87** (p) DavidProbert 1 91
(Chris Dwyer) *hld up in 6th on rail: rdn over 2f out and sn ev ch: kpt on wl ins fnl f* **7/1**[3]
35-4 3 nk **Rebel Surge (IRE)**[9] 142 4-9-1 **84** (p) StevieDonohoe 7 87
(Richard Spencer) *in rr: swtchd to outer over 2f out: in last but in tch over 1f out: sn rdn and kpt on wl ins fnl f* **14/1**
0-02 4 nk **Russian Radiance**[9] 142 5-8-8 **82** (h) MitchGodwin(5) 6 85
(Jonathan Portman) *racd in 3rd: rdn over 2f out: upsides 2f out: led over 1f out: hdd wl ins fnl f: no ex last 100yds* **10/1**
06-0 5 ¾ **Lady Lydia (IRE)**[16] 25 6-8-7 **79** NoelGarbutt(3) 5 80
(Martin Smith) *racd keenly on rail bhd ldrs: swtchd off rail over 4f out: nt clr run fr over 1f out: rdn between horses ent fnl f: no ex fnl 110yds* **25/1**
13-1 6 shd **Gleaming Girl**[12] 97 5-8-8 **80** AaronJones(3) 2 81
(David Simcock) *in rr: rdn over 2f out on outer: nt qckn tl styd on ins fnl f* **11/2**[2]
50-4 7 2 **Maggie Pink**[12] 97 8-8-9 **81** AlistairRawlinson(3) 3 77
(Michael Appleby) *led for 2f: settled bhd ldr on rail after: rdn 2f out: wknd fnl f* **20/1**
15-2 8 1½ **Stosur (IRE)**[12] 97 6-8-10 **79** (b) LukeMorris 8 71
(Gay Kelleway) *led after 2f: rdn 2f out: hdd & wknd fr over 1f out* **16/1**

1m 39.86s (0.06) **Going Correction** +0.05s/f (Slow) **8** Ran SP% **117.0**
Speed ratings (Par 104): **101,99,99,98,98 98,96,94**
CSF £6.71 CT £37.89 TOTE £1.60: £1.10, £2.30, £3.10; EX 7.20 Trifecta £41.10.
**Owner** Ibrahim Rachid **Bred** Mrs O M E McKeever **Trained** Carrutherstown, D'fries & G'way

**FOCUS**
A good handicap and the winner proved to be in a different league.

## 286 32RED CASINO H'CAP 1m 3f 219y(P)
**6:50** (6:51) (Class 5) (0-70,72) 4-Y-O+ **£2,911** (£866; £432; £216) **Stalls** Centre

Form RPR
43-2 1 **Choral Clan (IRE)**[12] 90 6-9-7 **70** JackMitchell 12 78
(Philip Mitchell) *hld up in rr: shkn up over 3f out: clr run up rail over 2f: sn rdn: led under 1f out on inner: kpt on wl* **11/1**
363- 2 ¾ **On Fire**[19] 8585 4-8-7 **60** LukeMorris 9 66
(James Bethell) *mid-div on outer: rdn over 2f out w plenty to do: prog over 1f out on outer: keeping on strly nr fin: nvr nrr* **16/1**
33-2 3 1½ **Thahab Ifraj (IRE)**[7] 169 4-8-12 **68** LouisSteward(3) 3 72
(Ismail Mohammed) *chsd ldr: rdn over 2f out: led over 1f out: hdd ent fnl f: kpt on* **9/4**[1]
15-0 4 1 **Jersey Bull (IRE)**[7] 169 5-9-1 **64** (h) LiamKeniry 6 66
(Michael Madgwick) *racd bhd ldrs: rdn over 2f out: kpt on one pce fr over 1f out* **25/1**
44-1 5 nse **Camakasi (IRE)**[7] 169 6-9-8 **71** 6ex TomMarquand 5 73
(Ali Stronge) *settled in mid-div on inner: rdn over 2f out: one pce fr over 1f out* **7/2**[2]
206- 6 2¼ **Sandy Cove**[127] 6457 6-9-7 **70** RyanTate 4 69
(James Eustace) *s.s and pushed along to get bk on terms after 2f: in rr: rdn over 2f out: kpt on past btn horses fr over 1f out: nvr nrr* **25/1**
06-3 7 ¾ **Ravens Quest**[8] 163 4-9-5 **72** DannyBrock 7 70
(John Ryan) *sn led: rdn over 2f out where pressed: hdd over 1f out: wknd fnl f* **10/1**
231- 8 ¾ **Fast And Hot (IRE)**[84] 7613 4-9-2 **69** (b) KieranO'Neill 2 65
(Richard Hannon) *settled bhd ldrs: rdn over 2f out: wknd over 1f out* **7/1**[3]
2- 9 ½ **My Matador (IRE)**[31] 8448 6-9-4 **67** (tp) GeorgeBaker 11 63
(Victor Dartnall) *hld up in rr: effrt over 2f out: nt qckn and kpt on one pce* **8/1**
140- 10 2 **Pivotal Flame (IRE)**[111] 6901 4-9-3 **70** ShaneKelly 10 62
(Pat Phelan) *in rr-div: rdn over 2f out: sn hld* **66/1**
41-1 11 2¾ **Paladin (IRE)**[13] 70 8-9-2 **70** (h) MitchGodwin(5) 8 58
(Michael Blake) *settled bhd ldrs on outer: rdn over 2f out: no ex and wknd* **12/1**
10-0 12 2 **Solveig's Song**[11] 120 5-9-6 **69** (p) AdamKirby 1 54
(Steve Woodman) *settled bhd ldr on inner: rdn over 2f out: wknd qckly fr 1f out and sn eased* **25/1**

2m 33.32s (-1.18) **Going Correction** +0.05s/f (Slow)
**WFA** 4 from 5yo+ 3lb **12** Ran SP% **120.6**
Speed ratings (Par 103): **105,104,103,102,102 101,100,100,99,98 96,95**
CSF £169.17 CT £543.35 TOTE £13.00: £3.50, £4.90, £1.40; EX 251.70 Trifecta £805.50.
**Owner** Bob Harris & Patricia Mitchell **Bred** L Queally **Trained** Kingston Lisle, Oxfordshire
■ Stewards' Enquiry : Danny Brock four-day ban; used whip with his arm above shoulder height (9th-11th, 13th Feb)

**FOCUS**
A modest handicap in which those held up had more of a say than in the earlier races.
T/Jkpt: Not Won. T/Plt: £30.20 to a £1 stake. Pool: £87,542.36 - 2,109.43 winning units T/Qpdt: £6.40 to a £1 stake. Pool: £10,403.02 - 1,192.14 winning units **Cathal Gahan**

# 232 LINGFIELD (L-H)
## Wednesday, January 18

**OFFICIAL GOING: Polytrack: standard**
Wind: virtually nil Weather: bright, chilly

## 287 SUN BETS BET £10 GET £20 FREE H'CAP 7f 1y(P)
**12:50** (12:50) (Class 4) (0-85,85) 4-Y-O+ **£4,690** (£1,395; £697; £348) **Stalls** Low

Form RPR
14-0 1 **Make Music**[9] 142 4-9-2 **80** DavidProbert 1 89+
(Andrew Balding) *wl in tch in midfield: nt clr run and swtchd rt over 1f out: rdn and hdwy 1f out: r.o wl to ld 50yds out* **14/1**
06-0 2 ½ **Take The Helm**[13] 66 4-9-4 **82** (p[1]) PaulMulrennan 13 88
(Brian Meehan) *hld up in tch in midfield: effrt bnd 2f out: hdwy to chse ldrs 1f out: kpt on wl u.p fnl 100yds: wnt 2nd cl home* **5/1**[2]
055- 3 nk **Honiara**[144] 5878 4-9-7 **85** (t) LukeMorris 11 90
(Paul Cole) *s.i.s: hld up in tch in last quartet: hdwy over 3f out: drvn to chse ldrs 1f out: kpt on u.p fnl 100yds: wnt 3rd last strides* **25/1**
141- 4 hd **Evening Attire**[23] 8531 6-9-2 **80** TomMarquand 10 84
(William Stone) *led: rdn over 1f out: drvn ins fnl f: hdd 50yds: no ex and lost 2 pls cl home* **10/1**[3]
05-0 5 nk **Lexington Times (IRE)**[17] 5 5-9-1 **79** JamesSullivan 4 85+
(Ruth Carr) *hld up in tch in last quartet: nt clr run over 1f out: hdwy and swtchd lft 1f out: chsng ldrs but nvr enough room ins fnl f: swtchd lft towards fin* **12/1**
61-0 6 ½ **Swiss Cross**[15] 32 10-8-13 **80** (tp) CallumShepherd(3) 3 82
(Phil McEntee) *in tch in midfield: effrt on inner whn nt clr run over 1f out: swtchd rt 1f out: hdwy ins fnl f: kpt on u.p fnl 100yds* **14/1**
24-1 7 ½ **Dutch Golden Age (IRE)**[12] 93 5-9-5 **83** GeorgeBaker 6 84
(Gary Moore) *trckd ldrs: effrt and swtchd lft over 1f out: chsd wnr 1f out tl ins fnl f: styd on same pce towards fin* **5/1**[2]
143- 8 ¾ **Mr Christopher (IRE)**[23] 8531 5-8-13 **77** (p[1]) LiamKeniry 12 76
(Tom Dascombe) *chsd ldr: rdn over 1f out: unable qck and lost 2nd 1f out: no ex and btn ins fnl f: eased towards fin* **14/1**
50-1 9 ¾ **Black Caesar (IRE)**[11] 116 6-8-8 **72** oh1 ow1 TomEaves 7 69
(Philip Hide) *wl in tch in midfield: effrt 2f out: struggling to qckn and squeezed for room over 1f out: no imp and one pced fnl f* **16/1**
500- 10 2 **Flying Fantasy**[30] 8456 5-8-6 **73** AaronJones(3) 2 65
(Stuart Williams) *s.i.s: hld up in tch in rr: effrt over 1f out: nt clr run 1f out swtchd rt 1f out: no threat to ldrs* **25/1**
04-0 11 1¼ **Greyfriarschorista**[17] 6 10-8-7 **71** oh1 JFEgan 5 59
(David Evans) *hld up in last trio: effrt over 1f out: no imp: n.d* **50/1**
663- 12 1½ **Mezzotint (IRE)**[30] 8455 8-9-0 **78** RobertWinston 8 69+
(Lee Carter) *wl in tch in midfield: effrt whn hmpd and snatched up over 1f out: nt rcvr: bhd and eased wl ins fnl f* **12/1**
00-4 13 1½ **Strong Challenge (IRE)**[13] 66 4-9-6 **84** AdamKirby 9 64
(Saeed bin Suroor) *chsd ldrs: effrt u.p in 3rd 2f out: unable qck and losing pl whn squeezed for room over 1f out: bhd ins fnl f* **15/8**[1]

1m 23.2s (-1.60) **Going Correction** +0.10s/f (Slow) **13** Ran SP% **128.1**
Speed ratings (Par 105): **113,112,112,111,111 110,110,109,108,106 104,103,101**
CSF £87.30 CT £1851.81 TOTE £20.40: £5.30, £2.40, £7.70; EX 138.70 Trifecta £2267.10.
**Owner** Mrs I A Balding **Bred** Brook Stud Bloodstock Ltd **Trained** Kingsclere, Hants

**FOCUS**
A fair handicap, but they finished in a bit of a heap. A clear personal best from the winner with the runner-up helping set the standard.

## 288 32RED.COM MAIDEN FILLIES' STKS 5f 6y(P)
**1:25** (1:26) (Class 5) 3-Y-O+ **£2,911** (£866; £432; £108; £108) **Stalls** High

Form RPR
53-2 1 **Hathfa (FR)**[13] 75 3-8-13 69 (be) ShaneKelly 3 71
(Richard Hughes) *mde all: hung rt wl over 1f out: sn pushed clr and in command 1f out: pushed out* **7/2**[3]
2 1¼ **Berryessa (IRE)** 3-8-13 0 DavidProbert 7 66
(Rae Guest) *s.i.s: in tch in rr: nt clr run and swtchd rt over 1f out: hdwy 1f out: chsd clr wnr wl ins fnl f: styd on wl but nvr gng to rch wnr* **33/1**
43- 3 2¼ **Mitigate**[35] 8362 3-8-13 0 SeanLevey 4 57+
(David Elsworth) *in tch in midfield: nt clr run over 1f out: swtchd lft 1f out: kpt on u.p ins fnl f: wnt 3rd last strides: no threat to wnr* **3/1**[2]

560- 4 hd **Bellevarde (IRE)**[68] 7898 3-8-13 69 DanielMuscutt 10 57
(James Fanshawe) *in tch in midfield: effrt over 1f out: kpt on same pce u.p ins fnl f* **2/1**[1]

2-33 4 dht **Bithynia (IRE)**[5] 212 3-8-13 68 JFEgan 6 57
(David Evans) *t.k.h: chsd ldrs: effrt over 1f out: chsd wnr u.p 1f out: no imp and lost 2nd wl ins fnl f* **6/1**

6 2 ½ **Scala Regia (FR)** 3-8-13 0 LukeMorris 9 48+
(Sir Mark Prescott Bt) *s.i.s: sn pushed along in last pair: kpt on ins fnl f: nvr trbld ldrs* **20/1**

0-6 7 1 ½ **Brean Flyer**[13] 76 3-8-13 0 WilliamCarson 8 42
(Bill Turner) *in tch towards rr: rdn and outpcd wl over 1f out: wl hld and one pced fnl f* **100/1**

0 8 ½ **Neptune Star**[13] 76 3-8-8 0 (h[1]) MitchGodwin(5) 5 40
(Jeremy Gask) *sn chsng wnr: rdn over 1f out: lost 2nd and hung lft 1f out: sn wknd* **66/1**

450- 9 1 **Ginger Truffle**[49] 8152 3-8-13 51 MartinDwyer 1 37+
(Brett Johnson) *t.k.h: hld up in tch in midfield: effrt over 1f out: squeezed for room and hmpd jst ins fnl f: nt rcvr* **66/1**

0- 10 nse **Cherry Leyf**[49] 8152 3-8-10 0 AaronJones(3) 2 37+
(Stuart Williams) *hld up in tch in rr: effrt on inner over 1f out: squeezed for room and hmpd jst ins fnl f: nt rcvr* **6/1**

59.65s (0.85) **Going Correction** +0.10s/f (Slow) **10** Ran SP% **120.8**
Speed ratings (Par 100): **97,95,91,91,91 87,84,83,82,82**
CSF £116.65 TOTE £5.10: £1.70, £12.20, £1.10; EX 135.10 Trifecta £340.30.
**Owner** Al Shaqab Racing **Bred** East Bloodstock, Henri Bozo Et Al **Trained** Upper Lambourn, Berks

**FOCUS**
A modest fillies' maiden, but a clear winner, who set the standard, and an eye-catching second.

## 289 BETWAY MEDIAN AUCTION MAIDEN STKS 1m 4f (P)
**2:00** (2:00) (Class 6) 4-6-Y-O **£2,264** (£673; £336; £168) **Stalls** Low

Form RPR
2P-5 1 **Ayr Of Elegance**[12] 92 5-9-4 72 GeorgeBaker 1 61+
(Philip Hide) *trckd ldrs: shkn up over 1f out: rdn and hdwy to ld ins fnl f: kpt on: rdn out* **1/2**[1]

2 1 ¼ **Treble Strike (USA)**[39] 4-9-5 0 RobertWinston 3 62
(Dean Ivory) *chsd ldr tl 5f out: effrt and ev ch 2f out: chsd wnr and one pced ins fnl f* **10/1**[3]

0/0- 3 hd **Darebin (GER)**[23] 603 5-9-6 75 (b) HectorCrouch(3) 5 66+
(Gary Moore) *hld up in tch: effrt to chse ldrs 1f out: nt clr run and swtchd rt 100yds out: kpt on towards fin* **9/4**[2]

5 4 2 ½ **Marauder**[14] 37 5-9-9 0 FergusSweeney 4 58
(Henry Candy) *led tl 5f out: rdn to ld again jst over 2f out: hdd and no ex jst ins fnl f: wknd fnl 100yds* **16/1**

U/ 5 10 **Worthy Spirit (GER)**[654] 7019 6-9-9 0 DougieCostello 6 42
(Adrian Wintle) *awkward leaving stalls and s.i.s: t.k.h: trckd ldrs after 2f tl over 3f out: outpcd and rdn over 2f out: wknd over 1f out* **66/1**

000- 6 5 **Respectability**[197] 3987 5-9-4 37 (h[1]) DavidProbert 2 29
(David C Griffiths) *stdd s: t.k.h: hld up in tch in rr: swtchd rt 6f out: hdwy to ld 5f out tl rdn and hdd jst over 2f out: wknd over 1f out* **66/1**

2m 38.98s (5.98) **Going Correction** +0.10s/f (Slow)
**WFA** 4 from 5yo+ 3lb **6** Ran SP% **115.4**
Speed ratings: **84,83,83,81,74 71**
CSF £7.61 TOTE £1.40: £1.10, £3.40; EX 5.90 Trifecta £9.70.
**Owner** W F Davis **Bred** W F Davis **Trained** Findon, W Sussex

**FOCUS**
A moderate older-horse maiden in which they went a dawdle until halfway and the form is weak.

## 290 BETWAY BEST ODDS GUARANTEED PLUS H'CAP 1m 5f (P)
**2:30** (2:30) (Class 6) (0-65,73) 4-Y-O+ **£2,264** (£673; £336; £168) **Stalls** Low

Form RPR
400- 1 **Pinwood (IRE)**[109] 6965 4-9-5 65 (t) JFEgan 4 74+
(Adam West) *t.k.h: hld up in tch in midfield: hdwy over 6f out to join ldr 5f out: led over 2f out: rdn and asserted over 1f out: in command and r.o wl fnl f* **25/1**

614- 2 3 **Major Ben**[32] 8428 4-9-5 65 AdamKirby 10 70
(David Evans) *chsd ldr: rdn to press wnr over 2f out: swtchd lft and unable qck over 1f out: styd on same pce fnl f* **5/2**[1]

242- 3 ¾ **Thomas Blossom (IRE)**[29] 6825 7-9-9 64 (t) DavidProbert 5 67
(Ali Stronge) *stdd s: hld up in rr: clsd 3f out: hdwy between horses wl over 1f out: styd on same pce ins fnl f: wnt 3rd on post* **7/2**[2]

40-2 4 nse **Cape Spirit (IRE)**[11] 121 5-8-5 53 WilliamCox(7) 1 56
(Andrew Balding) *chsd ldrs: effrt in 3rd 2f out: unable qck and no imp over 1f out: kpt on same pce ins fnl f: lost 3rd on post* **4/1**[3]

010- 5 hd **Multigifted**[35] 8359 4-8-13 59 (h) LiamKeniry 8 62
(Michael Madgwick) *stdd s: t.k.h: hld up in rr: hdwy on outer 4f out: rdn and styd on same pce fr over 1f out* **7/1**

600- 6 8 **Epsom Day (IRE)**[35] 8367 4-9-5 65 GeorgeBaker 2 57
(Laura Mongan) *stdd s: hld up in tch in midfield: nt clrest of runs 2f out: effrt over 1f out: sn rdn and btn: wknd ins fnl f* **6/1**

00-3 7 ¾ **Ruzeiz (USA)**[14] 39 8-9-2 57 TomMarquand 9 47
(Peter Hedger) *hld up in tch in last trio: effrt over 2f out: no imp u.p and btn over 1f out: wknd fnl f* **20/1**

000- 8 4 ½ **Loving Your Work**[29] 8462 6-9-4 62 (p) HectorCrouch(3) 3 45
(Ken Cunningham-Brown) *chsd ldrs: rdn and lost pl ent fnl 2f out: wknd u.p over 1f out* **14/1**

000- 9 2 ¼ **Norse Castle**[31] 8448 4-8-12 58 RobertHavlin 6 38
(Martin Bosley) *led tl rdn and hdd over 2f out: lost pl 2f out: wknd over 1f out* **14/1**

2m 45.24s (-0.76) **Going Correction** +0.10s/f (Slow)
**WFA** 4 from 5yo+ 3lb **9** Ran SP% **119.5**
Speed ratings (Par 101): **106,104,103,103,103 98,98,95,94**
CSF £90.35 CT £288.56 TOTE £32.20: £7.90, £1.10, £1.50; EX 130.60 Trifecta £943.40.
**Owner** David Phelan **Bred** Knocklong House Stud **Trained** Epsom, Surrey

**FOCUS**
A moderate staying handicap in which they went steady until halfway, at which point the winner made a significant move. He was very well treated on his 2016 Irish form.

## 291 32RED.COM H'CAP 5f 6y(P)
**3:05** (3:05) (Class 2) (0-105,93) 3-Y-**£11,971** (£3,583; £1,791; £896; £446) **Stalls** High

Form RPR
42-1 1 **Ascot Day (IRE)**[13] 72 3-8-10 82 JamieSpencer 1 90+
(David Simcock) *trckd ldrs: wnt 2nd over 1f out: shkn up to chal 1f out: led 100yds out: r.o* **1/1**[1]

214- 2 ¾ **Monte Cinq (IRE)**[46] 8209 3-8-13 85 TomEaves 2 87
(Jason Ward) *led: rdn over 1f out: drvn 1f out: hdd and one pced fnl 100yds* **8/1**

-512 3 1 **Gracious Tom (IRE)**[4] 243 3-8-7 79 7ex JFEgan 4 77
(David Evans) *in tch in rr: effrt over 1f out: kpt on u.p ins fnl f: no threat to wnr* **11/4**[2]

04-1 4 1 ¾ **Just An Idea (IRE)**[9] 140 3-9-3 89 7ex (v) LukeMorris 6 81
(Harry Dunlop) *chsd ldrs on outer: effrt and drifted rt bnd 2f out: unable qck over 1f out: styd on same pce fnl f* **7/1**[3]

15-4 5 10 **Chupalla**[11] 125 3-9-7 93 JoeFanning 3 49
(Mark Johnston) *t.k.h: chsd ldr tl lost pl over 1f out: bhd and hung lft 1f out: eased ins fnl f* **8/1**

58.41s (-0.39) **Going Correction** +0.10s/f (Slow) **5** Ran SP% **111.4**
Speed ratings (Par 103): **107,105,104,101,85**
CSF £9.78 TOTE £1.90: £1.30, £2.60; EX 10.20 Trifecta £17.50.
**Owner** Ahmed Jaber **Bred** Rabbah Bloodstock Limited **Trained** Newmarket, Suffolk

**FOCUS**
A decent 3yo sprint handicap and the form should work out, with the race rated around the runner-up.

## 292 BETWAY MIDDLE DISTANCE H'CAP 1m 2f (P)
**3:35** (3:35) (Class 5) (0-75,76) 3-Y-O **£2,911** (£866; £432; £216) **Stalls** Low

Form RPR
513- 1 **Poetic Force (IRE)**[23] 8525 3-9-4 73 (t) GeorgeDowning(3) 2 75
(Tony Carroll) *hld up in wl in tch in 4th: effrt wl over 1f out: hdwy u.p to chal ins fnl f: r.o wl to ld towards fin* **5/4**[1]

10-3 2 ½ **Global Revival (IRE)**[12] 100 3-9-7 73 GeorgeBaker 5 74
(Ed Dunlop) *chsd ldr: rdn and ev ch wl over 1f out: led u.p jst ins fnl f: hdd and one pced towards fin* **5/4**[1]

63-2 3 1 ½ **Bazwind (IRE)**[12] 100 3-8-11 63 JFEgan 4 61
(David Evans) *led: rdn and drifted rt wl over 1f out: drvn and hdd jst ins fnl f: no ex and outpcd fnl 75yds* **4/1**[2]

4 2 ¼ **Olympic Legend (IRE)**[119] 6691 3-9-7 73 RobertHavlin 1 67
(Martin Bosley) *stdd s: trckd ldrs: effrt on inner over 1f out: no imp and hung rt ins fnl f* **12/1**[3]

2m 9.5s (2.90) **Going Correction** +0.10s/f (Slow) **4** Ran SP% **116.6**
Speed ratings (Par 97): **92,91,90,88**
CSF £3.40 TOTE £2.20; EX 4.20 Trifecta £5.40.
**Owner** W McLuskey & S Barton **Bred** S J Macdonald **Trained** Cropthorne, Worcs

**FOCUS**
An ordinary and muddling 3yo handicap, weakened by the late withdrawal of the fancied Hochfeld. The remaining quartet only went a steady pace and it became a 3f sprint.

## 293 SUNBETS.CO.UK APPRENTICE H'CAP 7f 1y(P)
**4:05** (4:06) (Class 6) (0-60,62) 4-Y-O+ **£2,264** (£673; £336; £168) **Stalls** Low

Form RPR
000- 1 **Harry Holland**[23] 8531 5-9-6 62 (h) MillyNaseb(3) 4 67
(Tom Dascombe) *t.k.h: w ldr tl led 2f out: rdn over 1f out: kpt on u.p ins fnl f: jst hld on* **10/3**[2]

02-3 2 shd **Major Muscari (IRE)**[13] 80 9-9-4 57 (p) KevinLundie 6 62
(Shaun Harris) *hld up in tch in last trio: clsd to chse ldrs and hung lft 1f out: swtchd rt ins fnl f: shkn up and r.o wl fnl 100yds: jst failed* **14/1**

02-2 3 nk **Zabdi**[9] 139 4-9-1 54 PaddyBradley 2 58
(Lee Carter) *in tch in midfield: effrt to chse wnr over 1f out: ev ch fnl f: kpt on but a jst hld* **11/4**[1]

06-4 4 1 ½ **Wink Oliver**[9] 145 5-8-11 57 (p) LauraCoughlan(7) 9 58
(Jo Hughes) *stdd s and slowly away: dropped in bhd: t.k.h: in tch towards rr: hdwy on inner 2f out: rdn to chse ldrs 1f out: kpt on same pce ins fnl f* **10/1**

60-6 5 ¾ **City Of Angkor Wat (IRE)**[5] 216 7-9-6 59 (p) CallumRodriguez 5 57
(Conor Dore) *in tch in midfield: effrt over 1f out: unable qck and styd on same pce ins fnl f* **12/1**

5-40 6 ½ **Aye Aye Skipper (IRE)**[5] 214 7-8-7 46 oh1 (t) LuluStanford 8 44
(Ken Cunningham-Brown) *t.k.h: hld up in tch: carried rt bnd 4f out: dropped in over 3f out: swtchd rt over 1f out: kpt on ins fnl f: nvr trbld ldrs* **8/1**

063- 7 1 ¼ **Encapsulated**[21] 8555 7-9-4 57 RhiainIngram 1 50
(Roger Ingram) *taken down early and led rdrless to post: t.k.h: hld up in tch in midfield: swtchd rt 4f out: rdn and no imp over 1f out: one pced fnl f* **6/1**[3]

024- 8 ¾ **Arcanista (IRE)**[49] 8156 4-9-2 60 (b) NicolaCurrie(5) 7 51
(Richard Hughes) *chsd ldrs: rdn and unable qck over 1f out: wknd ins fnl f* **7/1**

40-6 9 1 ¼ **Fleeting Glimpse**[7] 172 4-9-3 59 (t) JoshuaBryan(3) 3 47
(Andrew Balding) *taken down early: led tl 2f out: rdn and lost pl over 1f out: bhd ins fnl f* **10/1**

1m 25.19s (0.39) **Going Correction** +0.10s/f (Slow) **9** Ran SP% **120.2**
Speed ratings (Par 101): **101,100,100,98,97 97,95,95,93**
CSF £51.04 CT £148.88 TOTE £4.00: £1.60, £2.50, £1.20; EX 61.80 Trifecta £236.80.
**Owner** Manor House Racing Club **Bred** Mrs F M Gordon **Trained** Malpas, Cheshire

**FOCUS**
A moderate apprentice handicap, but a thrilling finish. The form looks straightforward rated around the placed horses.
T/Plt: £47.90 to a £1 stake. Pool: £65,062.28 - 991.29 winning units T/Qpdt: £4.60 to a £1 stake. Pool: £6,373.58 - 1,018.12 winning units **Steve Payne**

294 - 301a (Foreign Racing) - See Raceform Interactive

# [61]CHELMSFORD (A.W) (L-H)
Thursday, January 19

**OFFICIAL GOING: Polytrack: standard**
Wind: virtually nil Weather: fine

## 302 BET TOTEPLACEPOT AT BETFRED.COM H'CAP (DIV I) 6f (P)
**5:20** (5:20) (Class 6) (0-65,67) 4-Y-O+ **£3,234** (£962; £481; £240) **Stalls** Centre

Form RPR
22-5 1 **Colourbearer (IRE)**[5] 242 10-9-9 67 (t) WilliamCarson 1 73
(Charlie Wallis) *early to post: led: hdd over 4f out: chsd ldr: rdn to chal strly over 1f out: edgd ahd ins fnl f: all out* **5/1**[3]

66-6 2 shd **Spirit Of Wedza (IRE)**[15] 45 5-9-5 63 JoeDoyle 7 69
(Julie Camacho) *prom: led over 4f out: rdn whn strly pressed over 1f out: hdd narrowly ins fnl f: kpt on: jst failed* **9/2**[2]

0-05 3 ¾ **Socialites Red**[6] 216 4-9-1 59 (p) DaleSwift 2 62
(Scott Dixon) *chsd ldrs: rdn over 2f out: kpt on* **8/1**

441- 4 hd **Commanche**[41] 8288 8-9-2 65 (b) GeorgiaCox(5) 6 68
(Chris Dwyer) *hld up: rdn over 3f out: kpt on ins fnl f: nrst fin* **6/1**

54-2 5 nk **Indian Affair**[5] 242 7-9-7 65 (bt) DougieCostello 9 67
(Milton Bradley) *hld up in tch: rdn over 2f out: kpt on ins fnl f* **5/1**[3]

004- 6 ½ **Humour (IRE)**[31] 8457 6-8-12 **56** (b) RobertHavlin 4 56
(Christine Dunnett) *dwlt: hld up in tch: rdn and hdwy to chse ldrs over 1f out: no ex fnl 110yds* **6/1**

03-2 7 1¼ **New Rich**[8] 171 7-9-5 **63** (b) JohnFahy 5 61
(Eve Johnson Houghton) *sn pushed along in rr: minor late hdwy: nvr threatened* **4/1**[1]

300- 8 7 **Mighty Zip (USA)**[23] 8535 5-8-10 **59** (b) CharlieBennett(5) 8 35
(Lisa Williamson) *chsd ldrs: rdn over 2f out: wknd over 1f out* **20/1**

1m 12.17s (-1.53) **Going Correction** -0.175s/f (Stan) **8** Ran SP% **116.0**
Speed ratings (Par 101): **103,102,101,101,101 100,98,89**
CSF £28.15 CT £179.24 TOTE £5.80: £1.70, £1.50, £2.80; EX 26.10 Trifecta £228.10.
**Owner** Roalco Limited **Bred** Corduff Stud & J Corcorcan **Trained** Ardleigh, Essex
■ Quiet Warrior was withdrawn. Price at time of withdrawal 5/2f. Rule 4 applies to all bets - deduction 25p in the pound.

**FOCUS**
This looked a competitive heat beforehand and indeed they finished in a bit of a heap.

## 303 BET TOTEPLACEPOT AT BETFRED.COM H'CAP (DIV II) 6f (P)
**5:50** (5:50) (Class 6) (0-65,67) 4-Y-O+ **£3,234** (£962; £481; £240) **Stalls** Centre

Form RPR

06-0 1 **Fujin**[17] 22 6-9-0 **63** (p) CharlieBennett(5) 7 69
(Shaun Harris) *prom: rdn over 2f out: led narrowly ins fnl f: kpt on* **10/1**

11-3 2 hd **Secret Bird (IRE)**[14] 64 5-8-10 **59** LuluStanford(5) 3 64
(Dean Ivory) *led: rdn over 2f out: hdd ins fnl f: kpt on but a jst hld* **11/4**[2]

266- 3 1¾ **Camdora (IRE)**[36] 8358 5-9-2 **60** (t) TimmyMurphy 5 60
(Jamie Osborne) *midfield inner: rdn and sme hdwy over 1f out: wnt 3rd 110yds out: kpt on but no threat ldng pair* **5/1**[3]

/54- 4 ¾ **Lightsome**[43] 8248 4-8-12 **56** DavidProbert 1 54
(Harry Dunlop) *chsd ldrs: rdn over 2f out: lost 3rd 110yds out: no ex* **9/4**[1]

05-0 5 ¾ **Firesnake (IRE)**[8] 172 4-9-3 **61** (p) AdamKirby 8 57
(Lisa Williamson) *midfield: rdn and sme hdwy over 1f out: one pce fnl f: nvr threatened* **16/1**

35-0 6 3 **Divine Call**[5] 242 10-9-4 **62** (b) WilliamCarson 4 49
(Milton Bradley) *hld up: rdn and outpcd in rr bef 1/2-way: nvr threatened* **10/1**

33-0 7 1 **Tasaaboq**[14] 67 6-8-5 **52** (t) CallumShepherd(3) 6 36
(Phil McEntee) *midfield: rdn over 2f out: wknd fnl f* **16/1**

23-0 8 ¾ **For Ayman**[15] 50 6-9-2 **67** (t) SophieScardifield(7) 2 48
(Joseph Tuite) *stdd s: hld up in rr: pushed along over 2f out: nvr threatened* **8/1**

2-62 9 4½ **Sarabi**[9] 152 4-9-7 **65** (p) DaleSwift 9 33
(Scott Dixon) *chsd ldrs: rdn over 2f out: wknd over 1f out* **14/1**

1m 12.23s (-1.47) **Going Correction** -0.175s/f (Stan) **9** Ran SP% **121.8**
Speed ratings (Par 101): **102,101,99,98,97 93,92,91,85**
CSF £39.90 CT £162.56 TOTE £12.60: £3.10, £1.20, £2.10; EX 51.60 Trifecta £336.30.
**Owner** Mrs S L Robinson **Bred** Juddmonte Farms Ltd **Trained** Carburton, Notts

**FOCUS**
Few got into this, the winner and second racing in the first two places throughout. The winner enjoyed a good trip and a step forward from the second.

## 304 BET TOTETRIFECTA AT BETFRED.COM CLAIMING STKS 1m (P)
**6:25** (6:26) (Class 6) 4-Y-O+ **£3,234** (£962; £481; £240) **Stalls** Low

Form RPR

01-5 1 **Threebagsue (IRE)**[13] 97 4-8-6 72 (b) LuluStanford(5) 1 76
(J S Moore) *mde all: rdn over 2f out: strly pressed fr over 1f out: hld on gamely* **5/1**[3]

000- 2 shd **Lunar Deity**[19] 8593 8-9-7 90 SeanLevey 8 86
(Stuart Williams) *trckd ldrs: rdn over 2f out: chal strly over 1f out: kpt on* **4/1**[2]

13/3 3 1¾ **Regarde Moi**[17] 24 9-8-12 90 JacobMitchell(7) 4 80
(Marco Botti) *trckd ldrs: rdn over 2f out: kpt on same pce: hld in 3rd whn bit short of room on towards fin* **5/1**[3]

0/3- 4 2 **Gramercy (IRE)**[144] 5915 10-8-12 89 (p) StevieDonohoe 6 68
(Ian Williams) *midfield: rdn over 2f out: hdwy to dispute 3rd appr fnl f: no ex fnl 110yds* **20/1**

0-25 5 2½ **Marshgate Lane (USA)**[12] 117 8-9-7 87 (p) LiamKeniry 2 71
(Neil Mulholland) *s.i.s: sn midfield: rdn over 2f out: hung lft over 1f out: no imp* **7/4**[1]

50-0 6 3¼ **Gold Return (IRE)**[12] 116 4-8-3 62 NoelGarbutt(3) 5 48
(John Ryan) *dwlt: hld up: rdn over 2f out: nvr threatened* **40/1**

654- 7 1¼ **Aqua Libre**[167] 5123 4-8-9 82 DavidProbert 7 48
(Philip McBride) *hld up: rdn over 2f out: nvr threatened* **6/1**

/03- 8 45 **Big Whiskey (IRE)**[120] 6683 7-9-4 92 SteveDrowne 3
(Clare Ellam) *w ldr: rdn wl over 2f out: wknd qckly: eased and t.o* **20/1**

1m 38.41s (-1.49) **Going Correction** -0.175s/f (Stan) **8** Ran SP% **115.9**
Speed ratings (Par 101): **100,99,98,96,93 90,89,44**
CSF £24.95 TOTE £7.50: £1.90, £1.50, £1.90; EX 26.60 Trifecta £133.00.
**Owner** The Well Fleeced Partnership **Bred** S Couldrige **Trained** Upper Lambourn, Berks

**FOCUS**
A decent claimer, but again it proved hard to come from off the pace and the winner enjoyed the run of things.

## 305 BET TOTEQUADPOT AT BETFRED.COM H'CAP 1m 2f (P)
**7:00** (7:02) (Class 6) (0-60,62) 3-Y-O **£3,234** (£962; £481; £240) **Stalls** Low

Form RPR

00-2 1 **Serenade The Stars (IRE)**[10] 149 3-9-7 **60** (v) MartinHarley 4 68+
(James Tate) *prom: rdn to ld over 1f out: kpt on wl to draw clr* **11/10**[1]

62-0 2 4 **La Vie En Rose**[10] 149 3-9-8 **61** JoeFanning 2 61
(Mark Johnston) *chsd ldrs: rdn over 2f out: one pce* **10/1**

523- 3 ½ **Aventus (IRE)**[21] 8568 3-8-13 **52** (b) DannyBrock 11 51
(Jane Chapple-Hyam) *led: rdn over 2f out: hdd over 1f out: kpt on but no ch w wnr* **7/1**[2]

00-6 4 1¾ **Av A Word**[13] 89 3-9-5 **58** (p) AdamKirby 1 56+
(Daniel Kubler) *midfield on inner: rdn and outpcd on over 3f out: kpt on wl fr over 1f out* **10/1**

00- 5 2 **Whatelseaboutyou (IRE)**[35] 8384 3-9-7 **60** TonyHamilton 8 52
(Richard Fahey) *hld up in midfield: rdn over 3f out: plugged on fr over 1f out: nvr threatened ldrs* **7/1**[2]

000- 6 shd **Master Billie (IRE)**[85] 7622 3-9-0 **53** DanielMuscutt 3 45
(William Muir) *chsd ldrs: rdn and outpcd over 2f out: plugged on fr over 1f out* **12/1**

062- 7 1 **Lulu The Rocket**[41] 8284 3-9-0 **58** GeorgiaCox(5) 12 48
(Peter Chapple-Hyam) *dwlt: swtchd lft after s: hld up in rr: stl lot to do whn bit short of room over 2f out: sme late hdwy: n.d* **8/1**[3]

20-0 8 2 **Areyoutheway (IRE)**[13] 100 3-9-9 **62** (b[1]) LukeMorris 10 49
(Michael Appleby) *trckd ldrs: rdn 3f out: wknd fnl f* **16/1**

00-0 9 3½ **Ablaze**[13] 89 3-8-12 **51** LiamKeniry 6 31
(Laura Mongan) *midfield: rdn 3f out: wknd over 1f out* **50/1**

66-6 10 7 **Shaqoos (FR)**[14] 73 3-8-10 **49** JoeyHaynes 7 17
(Jo Hughes) *dwlt: a towards rr* **100/1**

000- 11 4 **Lady Rowena**[23] 8536 3-8-7 **46** JasonHart 5 7
(Mark Johnston) *a in rr* **40/1**

65-0 12 2¼ **Forest Steps (IRE)**[10] 149 3-8-6 **50** (h[1]) LuluStanford(5) 9 7
(J S Moore) *hld up in midfield: lost pl over 3f out and sn bhd* **40/1**

2m 7.44s (-1.16) **Going Correction** -0.175s/f (Stan) **12** Ran SP% **123.3**
Speed ratings (Par 95): **97,93,93,92,90 90,89,87,85,79 76,74**
CSF £13.98 CT £61.26 TOTE £1.90: £1.20, £2.90, £2.80; EX 11.50 Trifecta £61.70.
**Owner** Saeed Manana **Bred** Summerville Bloodstock **Trained** Newmarket, Suffolk

**FOCUS**
Following the pattern set by the previous races on the card, very few got into this, the pace holding up well. The race has been rated through the placed horses.

## 306 BET TOTEEXACTA AT BETFRED.COM H'CAP 1m 2f (P)
**7:30** (7:31) (Class 4) (0-85,86) 4-Y-O+ **£6,469** (£1,925; £962; £481) **Stalls** Low

Form RPR

55/0 1 **Monsieur Rieussec**[13] 92 7-8-7 **71** DavidProbert 9 81
(Jonathan Portman) *chsd ldr: led 2f out: sn rdn: kpt on: hld on all out* **16/1**

042- 2 nse **Bunbury**[32] 8446 5-9-8 **86** ShaneKelly 1 96+
(Richard Hughes) *midfield: pushed along and hdwy over 1f out: drvn to chse ldr jst ins fnl f: kpt on wl: jst failed* **11/4**[1]

054- 3 3¼ **Berlusca (IRE)**[23] 8539 8-9-1 **79** DanielTudhope 8 82
(David O'Meara) *hld up in midfield: rdn and hdwy over 1f out: wnt 3rd ins fnl f: one pce* **7/1**

66-3 4 1 **Exceeding Power**[15] 36 6-8-9 **73** TomMarquand 6 74
(Martin Bosley) *midfield: rdn over 2f out: hdwy to chse ldr over 1f out: no ex fnl f* **10/1**

03-1 5 shd **House Of Commons (IRE)**[18] 6 4-8-13 **79** LukeMorris 5 80
(Michael Appleby) *hld up in midfield: rdn over 2f out: hung lft over 1f out: kpt on ins fnl f: nvr threatened ldrs* **3/1**[2]

30-3 6 1½ **Mercy Me**[12] 120 5-8-7 **71** RyanPowell 2 69
(John Ryan) *midfield: rdn over 2f out: wknd ins fnl f* **16/1**

005- 7 2½ **Zamperini (IRE)**[32] 8447 5-9-7 **85** (b) RobertWinston 7 78
(Mike Murphy) *dwlt: hld up: nvr threatened* **14/1**

20-2 8 2½ **Ravenhoe (IRE)**[12] 122 4-8-9 **75** JoeFanning 4 63
(Mark Johnston) *chsd ldr: rdn 3f out: wknd over 1f out* **10/1**

160- 9 5 **Iberica Road (USA)**[49] 8177 4-8-6 **75** (bt[1]) RobHornby(3) 3 53
(Andrew Balding) *led: racd keenly and sn 4 l clr: reduced advantage over 3f out: hdd 2f out: wknd* **9/2**[3]

0-13 10 9 **Vivat Rex (IRE)**[9] 156 6-9-4 **82** (bt) PaulMulrennan 10 42
(Conor Dore) *hld up in rr: rdn over 3f out: edgd rt over 1f out and wknd* **33/1**

2m 4.58s (-4.02) **Going Correction** -0.175s/f (Stan)
**WFA** 4 from 5yo+ 1lb **10** Ran SP% **121.9**
Speed ratings (Par 105): **109,108,106,105,105 104,102,100,96,89**
CSF £62.71 CT £355.30 TOTE £17.60: £6.30, £2.40, £1.60; EX 96.40 Trifecta £776.90.
**Owner** J T Habershon-Butcher **Bred** Mrs James Wigan **Trained** Upper Lambourn, Berks

**FOCUS**
A fair handicap. Once again it paid to be up there.

## 307 TOTEPOOL BETTING AT BETFRED.COM MEDIAN AUCTION MAIDEN STKS 6f (P)
**8:00** (8:03) (Class 5) 3-5-Y-O **£5,175** (£1,540; £769; £384) **Stalls** Centre

Form RPR

0-3 1 **Roman Navigator (IRE)**[12] 119 3-8-12 0 (t) DanielMuscutt 7 75
(Marco Botti) *mde all: rdn over 1f out: strly pressed appr fnl f: kpt on wl* **20/1**

3- 2 ½ **Al Sail (FR)**[36] 8353 3-8-12 0 SeanLevey 8 73
(Richard Hannon) *racd keenly: trckd ldr: rdn to chal strly appr fnl f: one pce fnl 50yds* **15/8**[2]

422- 3 ¾ **Arzaak (IRE)**[31] 8454 3-8-12 76 DavidProbert 2 71
(Chris Dwyer) *trckd ldr: rdn 2f out: one pce* **6/4**[1]

40- 4 hd **Zilza (IRE)**[19] 8591 3-8-4 0 (t[1]) NoelGarbutt(3) 5 65+
(Conrad Allen) *hld up: pushed along 2f out: r.o fnl f: nrst fin* **28/1**

3- 5 1¼ **Porto Ferro (IRE)**[50] 8152 3-8-7 0 LukeMorris 1 61
(Dr Jon Scargill) *dwlt: hld up: rdn 2f out: one pce and nvr threatened* **7/2**[3]

20-5 6 2½ **Prufrock (IRE)**[14] 76 3-8-7 65 WilliamCarson 3 53
(David Simcock) *midfield: rdn over 2f out: wknd ins fnl f* **12/1**

7 3 **Clean Cut** 3-8-7 0 JoeyHaynes 6 43
(Ivan Furtado) *dwlt: sn in tch on outer: rdn over 2f out: wknd over 1f out* **40/1**

1m 12.84s (-0.86) **Going Correction** -0.175s/f (Stan) **7** Ran SP% **115.3**
Speed ratings (Par 103): **98,97,96,96,94 91,87**
CSF £58.25 TOTE £15.80: £5.60, £2.00; EX 57.10 Trifecta £184.70.
**Owner** Mubarak Al Naemi **Bred** Mubarak Al Naemi **Trained** Newmarket, Suffolk
■ Fille The Force was withdrawn. Price at time of withdrawal 50/1. Rule 4 does not apply.

**FOCUS**
An ordinary maiden and again the place to be was on the front end.

## 308 COLLECT TOTEPOOL WINNINGS AT BETFRED SHOPS FILLIES' H'CAP 6f (P)
**8:30** (8:30) (Class 5) (0-70,70) 4-Y-O+ **£5,175** (£1,540; £769; £384) **Stalls** Centre

Form RPR

43-1 1 **Beau Mistral (IRE)**[9] 161 8-8-12 **61** 6ex WilliamCarson 3 65
(Tony Carroll) *led narrowly: rdn 2f out: hdd ins fnl f: kpt on: led again towards fin* **4/1**[3]

021- 2 hd **Assertive Agent**[120] 6677 7-8-10 **62** GeorgeDowning(3) 1 65
(Tony Carroll) *chsd ldrs: rdn over 2f out: kpt on fnl f: wnt 2nd nr fin* **7/1**

64-3 3 hd **Tell A Story**[15] 37 4-8-13 **62** MartinHarley 4 64
(David Simcock) *dwlt sltly: sn trckd ldrs: pushed along to chal over 1f out: rdn to ld ins fnl f: flashed tail and edgd lft: hdd towards fin* **2/1**[1]

060- 4 1¾ **Penny Dreadful**[21] 8571 5-9-2 **65** (p) DaleSwift 6 62
(Scott Dixon) *sn w ldr: rdn over 2f out: no ex fnl 110yds* **10/1**

320- 5 7 **Be Royale**[36] 8358 7-9-7 **70** (t) RobertWinston 5 44
(Michael Appleby) *in tch towards outer: rdn 3f out: sn outpcd: wknd ins fnl f* **7/2**[2]

00-5 6 2½ **Last Star Falling (IRE)**[8] 171 4-9-1 **64** (b) StevieDonohoe 2 30
(Henry Spiller) *chsd ldrs: rdn over 2f out: wknd over 1f out* **5/1**

1m 12.69s (-1.01) **Going Correction** -0.175s/f (Stan) **6** Ran SP% **113.8**
Speed ratings (Par 100): **99,98,98,96,86 83**
CSF £31.22 TOTE £4.80: £1.10, £4.70; EX 17.20 Trifecta £47.20.
**Owner** A Mills **Bred** John McEnery **Trained** Cropthorne, Worcs


The Form Book Flat, Raceform Ltd, Newbury, RG14 5SJ

**FOCUS**
A tight finish to this fillies' handicap.

## 309 GOING RACING? STAY AT CHANNELS CHANNELSLODGE.CO.UK H'CAP 7f (P)
**9:00** (9:00) (Class 7) (0-50,50) 4-Y-O+ **£2,587** (£770; £384; £192) **Stalls** Low

Form RPR
00-2 **1** **All Or Nothin (IRE)**[8] 167 8-9-4 **50**........................ CallumShepherd(3) 3 56
(Paddy Butler) *led for 1f: hld up in tch: pushed along and hdwy over 1f out: rdn to ld ins fnl f: kpt on* **6/1**[3]
050- **2** ½ **Moving Robe (IRE)**[28] 8492 4-9-2 **45**............................(t) RobertHavlin 4 50
(Conrad Allen) *chsd ldrs towards inner: rdn 2f out: swtchd rt over 1f out: kpt on* **12/1**
000- **3** ½ **Moayadd (USA)**[157] 5486 5-9-2 **45**.............................. FergusSweeney 9 48
(Neil Mulholland) *dwlt: hld up in tch: rdn and hdwy over 1f out: sn chsd ldr: kpt on same pce* **5/2**[2]
50-2 **4** 1 ¼ **Prince Of Time**[15] 52 5-8-11 **47**......................(p) CallumRodriguez(7) 7 47
(Richard Ford) *led narrowly after 1f: rdn over 2f out: hdd ins fnl f: no ex* **2/1**[1]
000- **5** 2 **Sober Up**[30] 8470 5-9-7 **50**.................................................. TomEaves 8 45
(Ivan Furtado) *pressed ldr: rdn over 2f out: wknd ins fnl f* **8/1**
506- **6** ½ **Kingfisher Girl**[35] 8383 4-9-2 **45**......................................(p) LukeMorris 2 39
(Michael Appleby) *chsd ldrs: rdn over 2f out: wknd ins fnl f* **14/1**
004- **7** 9 **Louis Vee (IRE)**[23] 8541 9-9-0 **48**..............................(p) CiaranMckee(5) 1 18
(John O'Shea) *dwlt: a rr* **11/1**
40-0 **8** 9 **Evident (IRE)**[15] 51 7-9-7 **50**........................................... AdamKirby 10
(Tony Carroll) *chsd ldrs on outer: rdn over 2f out: sn wknd* **10/1**
000- **P** **Alberto**[23] 8541 7-8-9 **45**...............................................(b) JordanUys(7) 5
(Lisa Williamson) *hld up: wnt wrong and p.u 6f out* **50/1**

1m 26.71s (-0.49) **Going Correction** -0.175s/f (Stan) 9 Ran SP% **121.0**
Speed ratings (Par 97): **95,94,93,92,90 89,79,69,**
CSF £78.34 CT £231.02 TOTE £5.20: £1.80, £3.60, £1.70; EX 80.70 Trifecta £702.70.
**Owner** Miss M P Bryant, David & Eileen Bryant **Bred** Ballyhane Stud **Trained** East Chiltington, E Sussex

**FOCUS**
An ordinary 0-50 and there was plenty of competition for the lead this time. That set things up for a closer.
T/Jkpt: Not won. T/Plt: £87.30 to a £1 stake. Pool: £108,417.69 - 906.36 winning units. T/Qpdt: £12.70 to a £1 stake. Pool: £15,311.27 - 885.84 winning units. **Andrew Sheret**

# 152 SOUTHWELL (L-H)
Thursday, January 19

**OFFICIAL GOING: Fibresand: standard**
Wind: Virtually nil Weather: Heavy low cloud

## 310 32REDSPORT.COM MAIDEN AUCTION STKS 1m 13y(F)
**12:55** (12:57) (Class 6) 3-Y-O **£2,587** (£770; £384; £192) **Stalls** Low

Form RPR
00-3 **1** **Log Off (IRE)**[14] 73 3-8-9 55.................................. AndrewMullen 6 57
(David Evans) *trckd ldrs on outer: pushed along over 3f out: rdn over 2f out: drvn to chal over 1f out: kpt on wl u.p to ld last 75 yds* **6/1**
0 **2** ½ **Bonnie Gals**[13] 96 3-8-4 0.................................... ShirleyTeasdale(5) 4 55
(Keith Dalgleish) *cl up: led wl over 1f out: jnd and rdn over 1f out: sn drvn and hung lft ent fnl f: hdd and no ex last 75 yds* **10/1**
03- **3** 3 ¼ **Miss Osier**[56] 8082 3-8-9 0.............................................. LukeMorris 3 48
(Rae Guest) *slt ld: rdn along 3f out: hdd wl over 1f out and sn drvn: hld whn n.m.r and swtchd rt jst ins fnl f: kpt on same pce* **4/1**[3]
0- **4** nse **Mirimar (IRE)**[28] 8486 3-9-0 0........................................ TomMarquand 7 53
(Ed Vaughan) *dwlt: trckd ldrs on outer: wd st and rdn along wl over 2f out: drvn wl over 1f out: kpt on one pce* **7/4**[1]
6 **5** ¾ **Alfolk (IRE)**[12] 127 3-9-0 0................................................(h) TomEaves 5 51
(David Simcock) *hld up: smooth hdwy over 2f out: shkn up wl over 1f out: sn rdn and swtchd rt ins fnl f: one pce* **9/4**[2]
00-4 **6** nk **Stag Party (IRE)**[14] 73 3-8-7 51...............................(b) WilliamCox(7) 1 50
(Andrew Balding) *trckd ldrs on inner: pushed along 3f out: rdn over 2f out: sn drvn and one pce* **33/1**

1m 43.66s (-0.04) **Going Correction** -0.075s/f (Stan) 6 Ran SP% **113.5**
Speed ratings (Par 95): **97,96,93,93,92 92**
CSF £59.69 TOTE £5.50: £2.70, £9.50; EX 47.40 Trifecta £101.30.
**Owner** Mrs E Evans **Bred** M A Doyle **Trained** Pandy, Monmouths

**FOCUS**
A very weak maiden in which the front pair pulled well clear.

## 311 BETWAY BEST ODDS GUARANTEED H'CAP 6f 16y(F)
**1:30** (1:31) (Class 7) (0-50,50) 3-Y-O+ **£2,385** (£704; £352) **Stalls** Low

Form RPR
60-5 **1** **Wimboldsley**[17] 20 6-9-5 **45**.......................................... KieranO'Neill 5 50
(Scott Dixon) *mde all: rdn clr wl over 1f out: drvn and edgd persistently lft ins fnl f: kpt on wl towards fin* **9/2**[2]
05-0 **2** nk **Autumn Tonic (IRE)**[14] 67 5-9-10 **50**.......................(b) AndrewMullen 6 54
(David Barron) *midfield: hdwy 3f out: chsd wnr wl over 1f out and sn rdn: drvn and ev ch ins fnl f: kpt on* **7/2**[1]
5-20 **3** 1 ¾ **Hadley**[9] 158 4-9-10 **50**..................................................... JasonHart 14 49
(Tracy Waggott) *swtchd lft s and hld up in rr: wd st: hdwy over 2f out: rdn wl over 1f out: styd on wl fnl f* **8/1**
066- **4** 1 ½ **Cadeaux Pearl**[84] 7645 9-8-13 **46**.................................. RPWalsh(7) 2 40
(Scott Dixon) *rr: wd st: hdwy over 2f out: rdn wl over 1f out: kpt on wl fnl f* **12/1**
60- **5** 1 ¼ **Kopassus (IRE)**[51] 8146 5-9-6 **46**..............................(p) PaulMulrennan 1 37
(Lawrence Mullaney) *bhd: rdn along wl over 2f out: sn swtchd rt: hdwy and swtchd lft over 1f out: drvn and kpt on wl fnl f* **14/1**
300- **6** 2 ¼ **Bedazzling Lady (IRE)**[54] 8120 4-9-7 **47**......................... JackMitchell 3 31
(Robert Eddery) *chsd ldrs on inner: rdn along wl over 2f out: drvn wl over 1f out: sn no imp* **16/1**
0-00 **7** nk **Zebelini (IRE)**[9] 153 5-9-8 **48**.............................(vt[1]) RobertWinston 12 31
(Roy Bowring) *chsd ldrs: rdn along and wd st: drvn 2f out: sn wknd* **16/1**
000- **8** 1 **Lily Cliff**[57] 8065 3-8-3 **45**............................................... LukeMorris 4 21
(Paul D'Arcy) *midfield: hdwy over 2f out: rdn wl over 1f out: sn drvn and kpt on same pce* **14/1**
00-0 **9** ½ **Desert Chief**[14] 68 5-9-2 **45**.............................. AlistairRawlinson(3) 8 23
(Michael Appleby) *v.s.a and rel to r: t.o: rdn along over 3f out: styd on u.p on inner fnl 2f* **15/2**[3]
000- **10** nk **Archipentura**[149] 5753 5-9-10 **50**.................................. TonyHamilton 9 28
(J R Jenkins) *sn pushed along to chse ldrs: rdn along 3f out: drvn over 2f out and sn wknd* **11/1**
045- **11** 1 ¾ **Cerulean Silk**[124] 6586 7-9-2 **45**.............................. GeorgeDowning(3) 7 17
(Tony Carroll) *midfield: hdwy over 2f out: sn rdn and btn* **16/1**
60-0 **12** ¾ **Pull The Pin (IRE)**[9] 153 8-9-7 **50**........................(bt) RobHornby(3) 11 20
(Mandy Rowland) *cl up: rdn along 3f out: drvn 2f out: sn wknd* **14/1**
064- **13** 4 ½ **Saxony**[37] 8346 6-9-0 **45**......................................... LucyKBarry(5) 10 2
(Matthew Salaman) *cl up: rdn along over 3f out: sn wknd* **33/1**

1m 16.7s (0.20) **Going Correction** -0.075s/f (Stan)
**WFA** 3 from 4yo+ 16lb 13 Ran SP% **119.9**
Speed ratings (Par 97): **95,94,92,90,88 85,85,83,83,82 80,79,73**
CSF £20.63 CT £129.65 TOTE £4.90: £1.60, £1.80, £2.40; EX 20.60 Trifecta £189.70.
**Owner** Paul J Dixon And The Chrystal Maze Ptn **Bred** Paul Dixon & Crystal Maze Partnership **Trained** Babworth, Notts

**FOCUS**
A basement handicap and a minefield for punters with few coming into the race in any sort of form. The market leaders dominated.

## 312 BETWAY H'CAP 6f 16y(F)
**2:00** (2:00) (Class 4) (0-80,80) 3-Y-O+ **£5,040** (£1,508; £754; £377; £188) **Stalls** Low

Form RPR
01-5 **1** **Bring On A Spinner**[18] 4 4-9-5 **74**........................(be) AaronJones(3) 1 84
(Stuart Williams) *slt ld on inner: hdd 1/2-way and cl up: led again 2f out: sn rdn and edgd rt over 1f out: drvn and hung rt ent fnl f: kpt on wl u.p towards fin* **3/1**[2]
33-5 **2** 1 ¼ **Sophisticated Heir (IRE)**[6] 219 7-10-0 **80**............(b) RobertWinston 5 86
(Michael Herrington) *trckd ldrs: hdwy over 2f out: sn n.m.r and swtchd rt: rdn to chal over 1f out: drvn and ev ch ins fnl f: no ex towards fin* **2/1**[1]
-646 **3** ½ **Crosse Fire**[9] 159 5-9-5 **71**.............................................(p) KieranO'Neill 3 75
(Scott Dixon) *prom: cl up 1/2-way: chal 2f out: ev ch whn n.m.r and swtchd lft ent fnl f: sn drvn and kpt on* **16/1**
4-31 **4** 2 **Englishwoman**[9] 152 4-9-9 **75** 6ex.................................. AndrewMullen 2 73+
(David Evans) *trckd ldrs: effrt and nt clr run wl over 1f out: sn swtchd rt and rdn: no imp* **8/1**
345- **5** 6 **Boater (IRE)**[52] 8136 3-8-10 **78**.......................................... PJMcDonald 11 53
(Mark Johnston) *cl up on outer: slt ld 1/2-way: rdn and hdd 2f out: sn drvn and grad wknd* **12/1**
0-41 **6** hd **Call Out Loud**[9] 159 5-9-1 **70** 6ex.....................(vt) AlistairRawlinson(3) 9 48
(Michael Appleby) *cl up: rdn over 2f out: drvn wl over 1f out: grad wknd* **12/1**
3-52 **7** 2 ¼ **Among Angels**[9] 159 5-9-8 **74**............................................(b) DaleSwift 10 45
(Daniel Mark Loughnane) *rr: pushed along and wd st: rdn and sme hdwy 2f out: n.d* **6/1**[3]
223- **8** nk **Jacob's Pillow**[78] 7774 6-8-11 **68**................................... RowanScott(5) 8 38
(Rebecca Bastiman) *in tch: rdn along wl over 2f out: sn wknd* **16/1**
400- **9** 1 **Miracle Garden**[30] 8463 5-9-11 **77**......................................(p) TomEaves 6 44
(Roy Brotherton) *a towards rr* **50/1**
004/ **10** 3 ½ **Baron Run**[574] 3544 7-8-13 **72**..................................... RussellHarris(7) 4 28
(K R Burke) *a rr* **50/1**
00-0 **11** ½ **Borough Boy (IRE)**[18] 4 7-9-6 **72**.............................(v) TonyHamilton 7 26
(Derek Shaw) *a rr* **20/1**

1m 15.36s (-1.14) **Going Correction** -0.075s/f (Stan)
**WFA** 3 from 4yo+ 16lb 11 Ran SP% **119.6**
Speed ratings (Par 105): **104,102,101,99,91 90,87,87,86,81 80**
CSF £9.40 TOTE £3.70: £1.50, £1.50, £4.60; EX 12.10 Trifecta £135.50.
**Owner** J W Parry **Bred** J W Parry **Trained** Newmarket, Suffolk
■ Stewards' Enquiry : Dale Swift trainer could offer no explanation for the gelding's performance
Kieran O'Neill caution; careless riding

**FOCUS**
Not a bad sprint handicap and another race where the winner did well to score after getting involved in a three-way battle for the early lead.

## 313 32RED.COM H'CAP 4f 214y(F)
**2:35** (2:35) (Class 5) (0-75,73) 3-Y-O **£3,234** (£962; £481; £240) **Stalls** Centre

Form RPR
500- **1** **Wild Approach (IRE)**[132] 6295 3-8-9 **61**............................ JoeFanning 1 65
(Robert Cowell) *racd towards far side: cl up: rdn over 1f out: chal ins fnl f: led last 75 yds* **7/2**[2]
43-3 **2** hd **White Royale (USA)**[15] 41 3-9-0 **73**.................(p[1]) LewisEdmunds(7) 2 76
(Kevin Ryan) *slt ld: rdn ent fnl f: drvn and hung rt ins fnl f: hdd last 75 yds: kpt on* **8/11**[1]
01-5 **3** 6 **Nuzha**[9] 155 3-9-3 **69**....................................................... AndrewMullen 6 50
(David Evans) *racd towards stands side: chsd ldrs: rdn over 2f out: drvn wl over 1f out: kpt on same pce* **15/2**[3]
100- **4** ¾ **Mesmeric Moment**[151] 5675 3-7-12 **57**.............................. RPWalsh(7) 5 36
(Shaun Harris) *cl up centre: rdn along wl over 1f out: sn drvn and kpt on one pce* **50/1**
5- **5** 6 **De Vegas Kid (IRE)**[24] 8526 3-8-12 **67**................... GeorgeDowning(3) 4 24
(Tony Carroll) *dwlt: in tch: rdn along 1/2-way: sn outpcd and bhd* **16/1**
316- **6** hd **Dixie's Double**[150] 5707 3-9-3 **69**....................................... LukeMorris 3 25
(Daniel Kubler) *cl up: rdn along 1/2-way: sn outpcd and hung lft to far rail: sn bhd* **8/1**

58.86s (-0.84) **Going Correction** -0.225s/f (Stan) 6 Ran SP% **110.8**
Speed ratings (Par 97): **97,96,87,85,75 76**
CSF £6.26 TOTE £5.50: £1.80, £1.10; EX 8.50 Trifecta £26.40.
**Owner** T Morley & G Johnson **Bred** Mike's Wildcat Partnership **Trained** Six Mile Bottom, Cambs

**FOCUS**
An ordinary 3yo sprint handicap and the market leaders had it to themselves from some way out, but the result could have been different.

## 314 SUNBETS.CO.UK MAIDEN H'CAP 1m 13y(F)
**3:10** (3:10) (Class 5) (0-70,72) 3-Y-O+ **£3,234** (£962; £481; £240) **Stalls** Low

Form RPR
0/0- **1** **Zoravan (USA)**[64] 7973 4-9-12 **68**..................................(v) PhillipMakin 6 81
(Keith Dalgleish) *trckd ldrs: hdwy 3f out: sn chsng ldr: rdn to ld wl over 1f out: edgd lft ent fnl f: drvn clr* **11/2**[3]
000- **2** 4 **Ramblow**[21] 8566 4-9-3 **59**............................................(t[1]) BenCurtis 1 63
(Michael Appleby) *led: rdn over 2f out: hdd wl over 1f out: sn drvn swtchd rt ent fnl f: kpt on same pce* **25/1**
544- **3** ¾ **Sun Angel (IRE)**[22] 8560 3-8-8 **70**...............................(p[1]) LukeMorris 8 67
(Henry Candy) *trckd ldng pair on outer: pushed along 3f out: rdn over 2f out swtchd lft and drvn over 1f out: kpt on fnl f* **5/1**[2]
552- **4** 4 ½ **Warm Words**[44] 8235 3-8-9 **71**....................................... TomMarquand 5 58
(Ralph Beckett) *stmbld sn after s and lost pl: rr and sn swtchd rt to outer: sn rdn along: drvn and wd st: kpt on u.p fnl 2f: n.d* **11/10**[1]

23-3 **5** *1 ½* **Dancin Alpha**[15] 44 6-9-0 56 oh1 (b¹) JoeFanning 7 44
(Alan Swinbank) *trckd ldrs: pushed along 3f out: rdn along on inner 2f out: sn outpcd* **6/1**
000- **6** *2* **Tynecastle Park**[119] 6702 4-9-6 62 JackMitchell 2 46
(Robert Eddery) *dwlt and outpcd in rr: bhd 1/2-way: plugged on u.p fnl 2f: nvr a factor* **25/1**
/00- **7** *1 ¼* **Pacommand**[216] 3357 4-9-13 69 AndrewMullen 4 50
(David Barron) *a towards rr* **8/1**
03-6 **8** *8* **Wonderful Life (IRE)**[10] 151 4-9-9 72 (h¹) PatrickVaughan(7) 3 35
(Richard Spencer) *chsd ldr: rdn along 3f out: sn drvn and wknd over 2f out* **66/1**

1m 42.13s (-1.57) **Going Correction** -0.075s/f (Stan)
**WFA** 3 from 4yo+ 20lb **8** Ran SP% **114.3**
Speed ratings (Par 103): **104,100,99,94,93 91,90,82**
CSF £121.23 CT £737.77 TOTE £7.00: £1.90, £1.70, £1.90; EX 135.80 Trifecta £1238.50.
**Owner** Prestige Thoroughbred Racing **Bred** His Highness The Aga Khan Studs S C **Trained** Carluke, S Lanarks

**FOCUS**
A maiden handicap in which the eight runners had a combined record of 0-52. Few ever got into it and the form looks weak behind the winner.

## 315 BETWAY AMATEUR RIDERS' H'CAP 1m 6f 21y(F)
**3:45** (3:46) (Class 5) (0-70,67) 4-Y-0+ **£3,293** (£1,013; £506) **Stalls** Low

Form RPR
20-4 **1** **Free Bounty**[14] 62 4-10-6 65 (t) MissSBrotherton 7 74
(Philip McBride) *trckd ldrs: hdwy over 3f out: cl up over 2f out: sn swtchd rt and rdn to ld jst over 1f out: styd on strly* **3/1²**
/30- **2** *3 ¼* **Noguchi (IRE)**[38] 8337 12-10-7 67 (p) MissEBushe(7) 10 71
(Chris Dwyer) *cl up: led after 2f: pushed along and jnd over 3f out: rdn over 2f out: drvn and hdd jst over 1f out: kpt on same pce* **10/1**
03-3 **3** *1 ½* **Thackeray**[17] 19 10-9-6 48 oh2 MissBeckySmith(3) 9 50
(Chris Fairhurst) *bhd: hdwy into midfield 1/2-way: chsd ldrs 3f out: rdn 2f out: styd on fnl f: tk 3rd nr line* **12/1**
00-0 **4** *hd* **Ralphy Lad (IRE)**[8] 174 6-10-7 60 (b¹) MrSWalker 8 62
(Alan Swinbank) *t.k.h: led 2f: trckd ldng pair: hdwy and cl up on inner over 3f out: effrt to chal over 2f out and sn rdn: drvn and ev ch over 1f out: grad wknd: lost 3rd nr line* **2/1¹**
2/0- **5** *13* **Idle Talker (IRE)**[43] 8257 5-10-9 62 (p) MrDHDunsdon 6 46
(Nick Gifford) *hld up in tch: hdwy on outer 1/2-way: rdn along 4f out: sn outpcd* **16/1**
45-0 **6** *8* **Twilight Angel**[8] 167 9-9-4 50 ow1 (vt) MrMichaelPalmer(7) 5 22
(Emma Owen) *a towards rr* **66/1**
650- **7** *hd* **Thou Swell (IRE)**[23] 8540 5-10-4 57 MrsCBartley 3 29
(Shaun Harris) *a towards rr* **16/1**
21/4 **8** *3 ½* **Azamesse (IRE)**[13] 98 5-9-11 57 (vt) MrSSayers(7) 2 24
(J R Jenkins) *trckd ldrs on inner: pushed along 1/2-way: sn rdn: lost pl and bhd* **20/1**
25-6 **9** *hd* **Merriment**[16] 28 4-10-0 62 (p) MrHHunt(3) 4 29
(Peter Niven) *trckd ldrs: rdn along over 3f out: sn wknd* **4/1³**
62-0 **10** *27* **Port Lairge**[14] 70 7-9-12 58 (b) MrCAJones(7) 1
(Michael Chapman) *prom: cl up 1/2-way: rdn along over 4f out: sn lost pl and bhd* **33/1**

3m 8.25s (-0.05) **Going Correction** -0.075s/f (Stan)
**WFA** 4 from 5yo+ 4lb **10** Ran SP% **116.1**
Speed ratings (Par 103): **97,95,94,94,86 82,82,80,79,64**
CSF £32.27 CT £316.62 TOTE £4.30: £2.00, £3.10, £2.90; EX 29.90 Trifecta £149.00.
**Owner** Four Winds Racing & Serafino Agodino **Bred** Wood Farm Stud (Waresley) **Trained** Newmarket, Suffolk

**FOCUS**
An ordinary amateur riders' staying handicap and quite a test with stamina at a premium.
T/Plt: £250.40 to a £1 stake. Pool: £61,969.35 - 180.60 winning units T/Qpdt: £13.90 to a £1 stake. Pool: £6,518.36 - 344.90 winning units **Joe Rowntree**

# 246 MEYDAN (L-H)
Thursday, January 19

**OFFICIAL GOING: Dirt: fast; turf: good**

## 316a DISTRICT ONE TROPHY (H'CAP) (DIRT) 1m (D)
**2:30** (2:30) (76-92,92) 3-Y-0+
**£29,268** (£9,756; £4,878; £2,439; £1,463; £975)

RPR
**1** **Nathr (USA)**[27] 8518 6-9-4 92 (v) JimCrowley 10 101
(Doug Watson, UAE) *trckd ldrs: led 2 1/2f out: r.o wl: easily* **5/1²**
**2** *4* **Muhtaram**[21] 8579 7-8-13 87 (v) FernandoJara 1 87
(M Al Mheiri, UAE) *trckd ldrs: ev ch 2f out: r.o same pce fnl 1 1/2f* **9/4¹**
**3** *¾* **Bannock (IRE)**[21] 8579 8-8-5 79 (t) PaoloSirigu 4 77+
(A bin Harmash, UAE) *s.i.s: nvr nr to chal but r.o wl fnl 1 1/2f* **12/1**
**4** *2 ¾* **Active Spirit (IRE)**[21] 8579 6-8-11 86 (vt) PatDobbs 7 77
(Doug Watson, UAE) *sn led: hdd 2f out: r.o same pce* **5/1²**
**5** *2 ½* **Secret Ambition**[13] 109 4-8-5 78 (t) RichardMullen 6 65
(S Seemar, UAE) *mid-div: r.o same pce fnl 2f: n.d* **7/1³**
**6** *hd* **Always Welcome (USA)**[13] 110 4-8-5 79 (t) TadhgO'Shea 11 65
(A R Al Rayhi, UAE) *mid-div: r.o same pce fnl 2f: n.d* **16/1**
**7** *2 ¼* **Emirates Airline**[7] 203 5-8-7 82 (p) AntonioFresu 3 61
(E Charpy, UAE) *s.i.s: nvr nr to chal* **40/1**
**8** *shd* **Long Water (USA)**[14] 86 6-9-2 90 (v) PatCosgrave 9 70
(H Al Alawi, UAE) *nvr nr to chal* **14/1**
**9** *¾* **Druids Ridge**[319] 5-8-10 85 AdriedeVries 8 62
(M Al Mheiri, UAE) *trckd ldrs: led 3f out: hdd 2 1/2f out: wknd fnl 2f* **20/1**
**10** *5 ¼* **Alareef (SAF)**[21] 8578 6-9-1 89 (b) DaneO'Neill 2 55
(M F De Kock, South Africa) *s.i.s: nvr able to chal* **12/1**
**11** *5* **Not A Given (USA)**[5] 251 8-8-9 84 (t) ChrisHayes 5 38
(A R Al Rayhi, UAE) *nvr bttr than mid-div* **20/1**
**12** *4 ½* **Pit Stop (IRE)**[7] 204 6-9-2 90 MickaelBarzalona 12 34
(S bin Ghadayer, UAE) *nvr nr to chal* **16/1**
**13** *7 ½* **Dragon Falls (IRE)**[700] 614 8-9-3 91 BReis 13 18
(R Bouresly, Kuwait) *nvr nr to chal* **50/1**

1m 37.51s (0.01) **Going Correction** +0.25s/f (Slow) **13** Ran SP% **124.3**
Speed ratings: **109,105,104,101,99 98,96,96,95,90 85,80,73**
CSF: 16.60; TRICAST: 140.08.
**Owner** Hamdan Al Maktoum **Bred** Courtlandt Farm **Trained** United Arab Emirates

**FOCUS**
TRAKUS (metres travelled compared to winner): 2nd -10, 3rd -6, 4th -4, 5th 0, 6th +2, 7th 0, 8th +11, 9th -5, 10th -7, 11th +2, 12th +9, 13th +7. Not many got competitive in this non-carnival handicap, with the pace fast but not too frantic by dirt standards: 24.95, 22.76, 24.72, 25.08. The second and third have been rated to their recent form.

## 317a UAE 1000 GUINEAS TRIAL SPONSORED BY DISTRICT ONE VILLAS (CONDITIONS) (FILLIES) (DIRT) 7f (D)
**3:05** (3:05) 3-Y-0
**£48,780** (£16,260; £8,130; £4,065; £2,439; £1,626)

RPR
**1** **Really Special**[82] 7698 3-8-11 96 ChristopheSoumillon 3 100+
(Saeed bin Suroor) *trckd ldrs: rdn to ld 1f out: r.o wl* **5/6¹**
**2** *3 ¼* **Complimenti (USA)**[21] 8575 3-8-11 0 PatDobbs 13 90
(Doug Watson, UAE) *trckd ldng pair: ev ch 1 1/2f out: nt qckn fnl 110yds* **8/1³**
**3** *1 ¾* **Rajar**[65] 7972 3-8-11 89 RichardMullen 4 85
(Richard Fahey) *sn led: r.o wl but hdd 1f out* **20/1**
**4** *1* **Sasha Waltz (IRE)**[81] 3-8-11 80 FernandoJara 8 83
(Fredrik Reuterskiold, Sweden) *mid-div: r.o fnl 2f: but nvr nr to chal* **40/1**
**5** *½* **Calare (IRE)**[102] 7193 3-8-11 102 WilliamBuick 11 81
(Charlie Appleby) *trckd ldng pair: ev ch 3f out: one pce fnl 2f* **3/1²**
**6** *7 ¼* **Mabrouka**[49] 8182 3-8-11 79 SamHitchcott 12 62
(Doug Watson, UAE) *Always mid-div* **33/1**
**7** *1 ¼* **Nomorerichblondes (USA)**[21] 8575 3-8-11 84 (t) AntonioFresu 7 58
(A bin Harmash, UAE) *nvr bttr than mid-div* **33/1**
**8** *1 ¾* **Island Vision (IRE)**[82] 7698 3-8-11 90 JamieSpencer 1 54
(David Simcock) *s.i.s: nvr nr to chal* **10/1**
**9** *¾* **Midnight Chica (USA)**[21] 8577 3-8-11 83 (t) ChrisHayes 5 52
(D Selvaratnam, UAE) *nvr bttr than mid-div* **66/1**
**10** *¾* **Voice Of Truth (IRE)**[98] 7307 3-8-11 84 ColmO'Donoghue 14 50
(Saeed bin Suroor) *trckd ldrs tl wknd fnl 3f* **14/1**
**11** *3 ½* **French Pass**[170] 4981 3-8-11 0 JacobButterfield 6 40
(E Jeanne, UAE) *s.i.s: a in rr* **100/1**
**12** *4 ¾* **Spanish Moon (RUS)**[193] 3-8-11 85 (b) DaneO'Neill 10 27
(Doug Watson, UAE) *slowly away: nvr nr to chal* **25/1**
**13** *¾* **Don't Lie Kitten (USA)**[49] 8186 3-8-11 80 JimCrowley 2 25
(A bin Harmash, UAE) *a in rr* **28/1**
**14** *27* **Decruz (IRE)**[5] 246 3-8-11 0 BReis 9
(R Bouresly, Kuwait) *a in rr* **200/1**

1m 25.89s (0.79) **Going Correction** +0.25s/f (Slow) **14** Ran SP% **129.8**
Speed ratings: **105,101,99,98,97 89,87,85,85,84 80,74,73,43**
CSF: 8.85.
**Owner** Godolphin **Bred** Darley **Trained** Newmarket, Suffolk

**FOCUS**
TRAKUS (metres travelled compared to winner): 2nd +9, 3rd 0, 4th +13, 5th +7, 6th +12, 7th +5, 8th +17, 9th +7, 10th +6, 11th +10, 12th +17, 13th +8, 14th +5. This was run at a strong, gradually slowing pace: 24.71 (standing start), 23.49, 24.81, 12.88. The standard hangs on the first four.

## 318a MEYDAN SOBHA TROPHY (H'CAP) (TURF) 5f (T)
**3:40** (3:40) (95-105,105) 3-Y-0+
**£60,975** (£15,243; £15,243; £5,081; £3,048; £2,032)

RPR
**1** **Medicean Man**[68] 7932 11-9-1 105 (tp) DavidParkes(5) 12 108+
(Jeremy Gask) *broke awkwardly: settled in rr: chsd ldrs 2 1/2f out: led 1f out: r.o wl* **7/1**
**2** *1 ½* **Sir Maximilian (IRE)**[14] 84 8-9-5 104 (p) PatDobbs 9 102
(Ian Williams) *mid-div: r.o same pce fnl 1 1/2f* **7/2²**
**2** *dht* **Harry Hurricane**[109] 6990 5-9-0 99 (b) PatCosgrave 13 97
(George Baker) *settled in rr: chsd ldrs 2f out: ev ch 1f out: r.o same pce fnl 110yds* **8/1**
**4** *hd* **Line Of Reason (IRE)**[14] 84 7-9-3 102 MartinLane 10 99
(Paul Midgley) *mid-div: chsd ldrs 2f out: one pce fnl f* **11/4¹**
**5** *hd* **Saayerr**[14] 84 6-9-5 104 ChrisHayes 2 100
(D Selvaratnam, UAE) *trckd ldng pair: ev ch 2f out: nt qckn fnl f* **14/1**
**6** *nk* **Maljaa**[163] 5268 5-9-4 103 (b) JimCrowley 8 98
(M Al Mheiri, UAE) *trckd ldng pair: rdn to ld 2f out: hdd 1f out: wknd fnl 110yds* **6/1³**
**7** *1 ¼* **Moonraker**[14] 84 5-8-9 95 MarcMonaghan 1 85
(Mick Channon) *nvr nr to chal but r.o fnl 2f* **25/1**
**8** *hd* **Midlander (IRE)**[35] 8395 5-8-9 95 RichardMullen 7 84
(S Seemar, UAE) *trckd ldrs: rdn and ev ch 2f out: wknd fnl f* **20/1**
**9** *1* **High On Life**[14] 84 6-8-10 96 (t) MickaelBarzalona 3 81
(S bin Ghadayer, UAE) *trckd ldng pair tl outpcd fnl 1 1/2f* **8/1**
**10** *½* **Wonder Of Qatar (IRE)**[645] 5-8-10 95 ow1 BReis 6 79
(R Bouresly, Kuwait) *sn led: hdd 2f out: one pce fnl f* **50/1**
**11** *1* **Krypton Factor**[307] 999 9-9-3 102 (b) AdriedeVries 11 83
(Fawzi Abdulla Nass, Bahrain) *s.i.s: a in rr* **25/1**
**12** *nse* **Master Of War**[14] 84 7-9-1 100 TadhgO'Shea 4 81
(D Selvaratnam, UAE) *a in rr* **33/1**
**13** *1* **Dream Dubai**[110] 6942 4-9-1 100 BernardFayd'Herbe 5 77
(M F De Kock, South Africa) *nvr nr to chal* **16/1**

57.5s (0.40) **Going Correction** +0.35s/f (Good) **13** Ran SP% **127.8**
Speed ratings: **110,107,107,107,106 106,104,104,102,101 100,100,98**
CSF: MM/SM 16.07, MM/HH 31.33 ; TRICAST: MM/SM 91.87, MM/HH 102.85.
**Owner** Stuart Dobb & Miss Kate Dobb **Bred** Barry Taylor **Trained** Stockbridge, Hants

**FOCUS**
The first four were drawn 12, 9, 13, 10 and nothing could live with the winner.

## 319a MEYDAN SOBHA (H'CAP) (DIRT) 1m 2f (D)
**4:15** (4:15) (95-108,105) 3-Y-0+
**£60,975** (£20,325; £10,162; £5,081; £3,048; £2,032)

RPR
**1** **Hunting Ground (USA)**[14] 83 7-9-1 100 MickaelBarzalona 5 105+
(S bin Ghadayer, UAE) *sn led: skipped clr 3f out: r.o wl* **7/2¹**
**2** *½* **Triple Nine (KOR)**[32] 5-9-6 105 (e) PatCosgrave 4 108+
(Kim Young Kwan, Korea) *mid-div: r.o wl fnl 1 1/2f: nrst fin* **9/2²**
**3** *3 ¼* **Los Barbados (IRE)**[35] 8394 5-8-11 97 (b) AdriedeVries 8 93
(Fawzi Abdulla Nass, Bahrain) *settled in rr: chsd ldrs 3 1/2f out: r.o same pce fnl 2 1/2f* **16/1**
**4** *2 ½* **Grand Argentier (FR)**[27] 8518 5-8-9 95 (v) PatDobbs 7 86
(Doug Watson, UAE) *trckd ldng pair: ev ch 2 1/2f out: one pce fnl 2f* **11/1**
**5** *hd* **Etijaah (USA)**[35] 8394 7-9-4 103 (h) DaneO'Neill 2 94
(Doug Watson, UAE) *settled in rr: r.o fnl 2 1/2f: nvr able to chal* **7/1**

6 2 1/4 **Beach Bar (IRE)**[7] 204 6-8-9 **95**....(h) TadhgO'Shea 9 81
(Brendan Powell) *nvr nr to chal: but r.o fnl 2f* **33/1**
7 hd **Munaaser**[14] 85 6-9-6 **105**....(t) JimCrowley 6 91
(A R Al Rayhi, UAE) *trckd ldng pair: ev ch 3f out: wknd fnl 1 1/2f* **11/2**[3]
8 5 3/4 **Top Clearance (USA)**[14] 83 5-9-3 **102**....(vt) ChrisHayes 11 77
(D Selvaratnam, UAE) *trckd ldrs tl wknd 4 1/2f out* **9/1**
9 16 **Toolain (IRE)**[684] 825 9-9-2 **101**....(b) RichardMullen 3 44
(S Seemar, UAE) *a in rr* **16/1**
10 shd **Fog Of War**[494] 6365 6-8-13 **98**.... ChristopheSoumillon 1 41
(Saeed bin Suroor) *mid-div: rdn 6f out: sn btn* **9/2**[2]
11 8 3/4 **Hard Divorce (USA)**[26] 6-8-11 **97**....(bt) FernandoJara 10 21
(M Al Balushi, Oman) *s.i.s: a in rr* **40/1**

2m 4.69s (-0.01) **Going Correction** +0.25s/f (Slow) 11 Ran SP% **121.9**
Speed ratings: **110,109,107,105,104 103,102,98,85,85 78**
CSF: 19.74; TRICAST: 229.88.
**Owner** Sheikh Hamdan bin Mohammed Al Maktoum **Bred** Darley **Trained** United Arab Emirates

**FOCUS**
TRAKUS (metres travelled compared to winner): 2nd +10, 3rd +20, 4th +21, 5th +7, 6th +16, 7th +11, 8th +6, 9th +12, 10th +2, 11th +14. The winner made all through strong, gradually slowing fractions: 25.25 (standing start), 23.78, 24.38, 25.25, 26.03. The race has been rated around the balance of the first three.

## 320a AL FAHIDI FORT SPONSORED BY MOHAMMED BIN RASHID AL MAKTOUM - DISTRICT ONE (GROUP 2) (TURF) 7f
**4:50** (4:50) 3-Y-0+
**£121,951** (£40,650; £20,325; £10,162; £6,097; £4,065)

RPR
1 **Championship (IRE)**[14] 86 6-9-0 110....(t) ColmO'Donoghue 1 116+
(A bin Harmash, UAE) *sn led: rdn clr 3f out: r.o wl* **5/2**[2]
2 3 1/2 **Flash Fire (IRE)**[14] 87 5-9-0 112.... WilliamBuick 7 107+
(Charlie Appleby) *trckd ldng pair: rdn 3f out: r.o fnl 1 1/2f but no ch w wnr* **5/4**[1]
3 3/4 **Noah From Goa (SAF)**[376] 4-9-0 114.... ChristopheSoumillon 5 105
(M F De Kock, South Africa) *mid-div: nvr able to chal but r.o fnl 2f* **5/1**[3]
4 2 1/2 **Anaerobio (ARG)**[14] 87 9-9-0 109....(t) PatCosgrave 2 98
(M F De Kock, South Africa) *trckd ldng pair: ev ch 3f out: one pce fnl 1 1/2f* **12/1**
5 4 **Dark Emerald (IRE)**[140] 6056 7-9-0 108....(vt) RichardMullen 6 87
(Brendan Powell) *s.i.s: nvr bttr than mid-div* **18/1**
6 1 3/4 **Dragon Mall (USA)**[28] 8489 4-9-0 104.... JamieSpencer 4 82
(David Simcock) *s.i.s: nvr nr to chal* **7/1**
7 18 **Graystorm (TUR)**[117] 4-9-0 104.... AhmetCelik 8 34
(Mehmet Cucel, Turkey) *trckd ldrs: rdn 4f out: sn btn* **40/1**
8 hd **Nabbaash**[321] 852 6-9-0 100.... BReis 3 33
(R Bouresly, Kuwait) *s.i.s: a in rr* **100/1**

1m 22.82s (-1.28) **Going Correction** +0.225s/f (Good) 8 Ran SP% **118.6**
Speed ratings: **116,112,111,108,103 101,81,80**
CSF: 6.25.
**Owner** Sheikh Mansoor bin Mohammed al Maktoum **Bred** Ms Natalie Cleary **Trained** United Arab Emirates

**FOCUS**
TRAKUS (metres travelled compared to winner): 2nd +6, 3rd +5, 4th +2, 5th +9, 6th +7, 7th +7, 8th 0. The winner made all under a well-judged ride, with Colm O'Donoghue gradually increasing the pace - 25.77, 22.97, 22.39, before finishing in 11.84 - and no horse took a shorter route. This was a personal best from him.

## 321a DISTRICT ONE (H'CAP) (DIRT) 6f (D)
**5:25** (5:25) (95-108,105) 3-Y-0+
**£60,975** (£20,325; £10,162; £5,081; £3,048; £2,032)

RPR
1 **Main Stay (KOR)**[39] 4-8-9 **95**....(e) PatCosgrave 4 98+
(Kim Young Kwan, Korea) *s.i.s but sn led: rdn 3f out: qcknd 1 1/2f out: r.o wl* **4/1**[1]
2 2 3/4 **Mashaaref**[69] 7923 9-9-6 **105**.... BernardFayd'Herbe 1 100
(M Al Mheiri, UAE) *mid-div: r.o wl 1 1/2f out: nrst fin* **20/1**
3 nk **Shaishee (USA)**[14] 87 7-9-3 **102**....(v) DaneO'Neill 5 96
(M Al Mheiri, UAE) *mid-div: r.o fnl 2f: nrst fin* **8/1**
4 hd **Seoul Bullet (KOR)**[39] 6-8-10 **96**....(e) TadhgO'Shea 6 89+
(Kim Young Kwan, Korea) *nvr nr to chal but r.o fnl 2f* **9/2**[2]
5 1 1/4 **The Taj (USA)**[307] 999 7-9-1 **100**.... JimCrowley 3 90
(Doug Watson, UAE) *trckd ldr: ev ch 1f out: wknd fnl 110yds* **7/1**[3]
6 1 **Spirit Quartz (IRE)**[7] 207 9-9-2 **104**.... JulianResimont(3) 9 90
(N Caullery, France) *trckd ldr tl outpcd fnl f* **25/1**
7 3/4 **Indianapolis (USA)**[35] 8395 6-8-11 **97**....(bt) RichardMullen 8 80
(S Seemar, UAE) *nvr nr to chal but r.o fnl 2f* **16/1**
8 2 3/4 **Calder Prince (IRE)**[101] 7213 4-8-11 **97**.... RichardKingscote 7 71
(Tom Dascombe) *s.i.s: nvr bttr than mid-div* **7/1**[3]
9 8 **United Color (USA)**[35] 8395 8-9-3 **102**....(t) ChrisHayes 10 52
(D Selvaratnam, UAE) *nvr bttr than mid-div* **8/1**
P **Giftorm (USA)**[130] 7-9-1 **100**.... FernandoJara 2
(Fredrik Reuterskiold, Sweden) *p.u 55yds out* **4/1**[1]

1m 11.63s (0.03) **Going Correction** +0.25s/f (Slow) 10 Ran SP% **119.9**
Speed ratings: **109,105,104,104,103 101,100,97,86,**
CSF: 87.12; TRICAST: 623.11.
**Owner** Baek Su-Hyeon **Bred** Nokwon Farm **Trained** Korea

**FOCUS**
TRAKUS (metres travelled compared to winner): 2nd -4, 3rd -1, 4th -1, 5th -5, 6th +3, 7th +8, 8th +4, 9th +10. The winner made just about all through solid fractions: 24.43, 22.83, 24.37.

## 322a DISTRICT ONE MANSIONS (H'CAP) (TURF) 1m 2f
**6:00** (6:00) (95-105,105) 3-Y-0+
**£60,975** (£20,325; £10,162; £5,081; £3,048; £2,032)

RPR
1 **Artigiano (USA)**[322] 812 7-9-1 **100**.... WilliamBuick 12 106
(Charlie Appleby) *sn led: rdn clr 2f out: r.o wl* **8/1**
2 1 3/4 **Folkswood**[144] 5932 4-9-2 **102**....(p) ColmO'Donoghue 2 105
(Charlie Appleby) *trckd ldrs: ev ch 1 1/2f out: r.o wl* **4/1**[2]
3 4 3/4 **Brex Drago (ITY)**[58] 5-9-5 **104**.... AntonioFresu 1 97+
(Marco Botti) *mid-div: r.o fnl 2f: nrst fin* **20/1**
4 1/2 **Moonlight Dash**[424] 9-8-13 **98**.... RichardMullen 10 90+
(S Seemar, UAE) *mid-div: r.o fnl 2f but nvr nr to chal* **33/1**
5 3 1/4 **Huge Future**[89] 7538 4-8-13 **99**.... AdriedeVries 4 85
(Saeed bin Suroor) *trckd ldrs: ev ch 2f out: wknd fnl 1 1/2f* **9/4**[1]
6 1 3/4 **Busker (USA)**[399] 8275 9-9-3 **102**....(t) PaoloSirigu 5 84+
(A bin Harmash, UAE) *a in rr* **40/1**
7 1 **Mutasayyid**[46] 8214 5-8-13 **98**.... JimCrowley 8 78
(Doug Watson, UAE) *trckd ldrs: ev ch 3 1/2f out: r.o same pce fnl 2f* **12/1**
8 nse **Oasis Fantasy (IRE)**[103] 7154 6-9-1 **100**.... JamieSpencer 9 79
(David Simcock) *nvr nr to chal* **12/1**
9 3 1/4 **Whistle Stop (SAF)**[7] 208 6-9-2 **101**.... DaneO'Neill 7 74
(M F De Kock, South Africa) *s.i.s: nvr nr to chal* **12/1**
10 2 **Rio Tigre (IRE)**[14] 82 6-9-3 **102**.... MickaelBarzalona 14 71
(S bin Ghadayer, UAE) *nvr bttr than mid-div* **10/1**
11 2 1/2 **Hasanour (USA)**[7] 208 7-9-1 **100**....(p) TadhgO'Shea 13 64
(M Halford, Ire) *nvr nr to chal* **20/1**
12 2 1/4 **Tannaaf (IRE)**[327] 757 5-9-6 **105**.... ChristopheSoumillon 6 64
(M F De Kock, South Africa) *a in rr* **6/1**[3]
13 2 **Night Run (FR)**[322] 812 5-8-7 **99**.... AdamMcLean(7) 3 54
(Y Al Blooshi, UAE) *a in rr* **66/1**
14 nse **Jalapeno (IRE)**[42] 4-9-1 **101**....(t) CarloFiocchi 11 57
(Agostino Affe', Italy) *trckd ldrs tl wknd 3 1/2f out* **20/1**

2m 2.27s (-0.43) **Going Correction** +0.225s/f (Good)
**WFA** 4 from 5yo+ 1lb 14 Ran SP% **129.5**
Speed ratings: **110,108,104,104,101 100,99,99,96,95 93,91,89,89**
CSF: 39.93; TRICAST: 654.34; Placepot: £24.90 to a £1 stake. Pool of £4,557.00 - 182.65 winning units; Quadpot: £10.80 to a £1 stake. Pool of £358 - 33 winning units..
**Owner** Godolphin **Bred** Darley **Trained** Newmarket, Suffolk

**FOCUS**
TRAKUS (metres travelled compared to winner): 2nd -3, 3rd 0, 4th +3, 5th +2, 6th +4, 7th +3, 8th +1, 9th +7, 10th +11, 11th +13, 12th +7, 13th 0, 14th +7. They went steady and quickened up in the closing stages - 26.18, 23.99, 25.00, 23.72, 23.38 - and the forwardly ridden first pair pulled clear of a field that lacked depth, with the favourite below form. The second, third and fourth help with setting the standard.

# [287]LINGFIELD (L-H)
Friday, January 20

**OFFICIAL GOING: Polytrack: standard**
Wind: Light, across Weather: Sunny, crisp

## 323 32REDSPORT.COM H'CAP 7f 1y(P)
**1:00** (1:01) (Class 6) (0-65,66) 3-Y-O **£2,264** (£673; £336; £168) **Stalls** Low

Form RPR
254- 1 **Sea Tea Dea**[43] 8277 3-9-7 **65**.... WilliamCarson 8 68
(Anthony Carson) *hld up in rr: shkn up over 2f out: prog on outer over 1f out: r.o wl fnl f to ld nr fin* **16/1**
31-3 2 nk **Geraldine (GER)**[10] 160 3-9-5 **63**.... MartinHarley 4 65
(Stuart Williams) *s.i.s: sn in 5th: prog to chse ldr wl over 1f out: rdn and nt qckn sn after: nt clr run and swtchd lft fnl f: r.o nr fin but wnr already gone past* **6/4**[1]
025- 3 nk **Seprani**[50] 8174 3-9-3 **61**....(h) DanielMuscutt 3 62
(Marco Botti) *chsd ldr and clr of rest early: led 2f out: drvn fnl f: hdd nr fin* **10/1**
616- 4 3/4 **Bruny Island (IRE)**[35] 8398 3-8-10 **54**....(h[1]) StevieDonohoe 9 53
(Charlie Fellowes) *t.k.h: hld up in last pair: stl there 2f out: nt clr run over 1f out tl ins fnl f: r.o nr fin* **6/1**[3]
621- 5 1/2 **Lord Cooper**[31] 8467 3-9-8 **66**....(tp) RenatoSouza 2 64
(Jose Santos) *chsd ldng pair: short of room on inner 2f out: rdn and tried to cl fr over 1f out: kpt on same pce* **11/4**[2]
326- 6 1/2 **Imperial City (USA)**[65] 7974 3-9-7 **65**.... DavidProbert 6 61
(Charles Hills) *chsd ldrs: rdn over 2f out: stl in w ch 1f out: one pce* **10/1**
040- 7 4 **Sixties Habana**[44] 8244 3-8-11 **60**.... PaddyBradley(5) 7 46
(Pat Phelan) *racd on outer in midfield: rdn over 2f out: wknd over 1f out* **16/1**
000- 8 7 **Oceanus (IRE)**[23] 8560 3-9-7 **65**....(b) TomEaves 1 32
(Ed Dunlop) *racd freely: led at str pce: hdd & wknd rapidly 2f out* **20/1**
00-5 9 5 **Ventura Jazz**[17] 27 3-8-8 **52**.... BarryMcHugh 5 5
(Richard Fahey) *s.i.s: a in last pair: bhd over 2f out: t.o* **33/1**

1m 24.0s (-0.80) **Going Correction** -0.075s/f (Stan) 9 Ran SP% **118.6**
Speed ratings (Par 95): **101,100,100,99,98 98,93,85,80**
CSF £41.62 CT £274.16 TOTE £14.00: £2.80, £1.10, £3.10; EX 47.90 Trifecta £237.40.
**Owner** Clive Dennett **Bred** Clive Dennett **Trained** Newmarket, Suffolk

**FOCUS**
A moderate handicap in which the second, fourth and fifth had interrupted trips. A small step forward from the winner, while the third helps set the opening level.

## 324 32RED CASINO H'CAP 5f 6y(P)
**1:30** (1:30) (Class 6) (0-65,65) 3-Y-O **£2,264** (£673; £336; £168) **Stalls** High

Form RPR
005- 1 **Popsilca**[95] 7414 3-8-6 **50**.... WilliamCarson 5 54
(Mick Quinn) *t.k.h: chsd ldr: rdn over 1f out: clsd u.p to ld last 100yds: kpt on* **33/1**
016- 2 1/2 **Little Miss Daisy**[32] 8453 3-9-4 **62**.... MartinHarley 7 64
(William Muir) *in tch in midfield: rdn over 1f out: r.o fnl f to take 2nd nr fin* **9/2**[2]
43-2 3 shd **Snuggy (IRE)**[9] 179 3-9-4 **62**.... PhillipMakin 4 64
(David Barron) *chsd ldrs pushed along fr 1/2-way: drvn over 1f out: styd on fnl f to take 3rd nr fin* **9/2**[2]
2-32 4 1/2 **Pulsating (IRE)**[10] 157 3-9-0 **65**....(b[1]) MillyNaseb(7) 6 65
(Daniel Steele) *hld up in 7th: nt clr run over 1f out and swtchd rt: r.o wl fnl f: nrst fin* **10/1**
031- 5 hd **Spin Top**[34] 8425 3-9-5 **63**....(v) LiamKeniry 2 62
(Joseph Tuite) *racd freely: led: drvn over 1f out: hdd last 100yds: lost pls on inner nr fin* **5/1**[3]
340- 6 nk **Goodwood Crusader (IRE)**[129] 6440 3-8-12 **63**.... FinleyMarsh(7) 1 61
(Richard Hughes) *chsd ldng pair: rdn over 1f out: racd on inner and lost pls ins fnl f* **7/1**
666- 7 3/4 **Dream Reversion**[31] 8467 3-9-4 **62**.... PJMcDonald 3 57
(Tom Dascombe) *nvr bttr than midfield: rdn 2f out: kpt on but no threat* **5/1**[3]
50-6 8 1 1/2 **Dashing Poet**[15] 75 3-9-1 **59**....(h[1]) TimmyMurphy 8 49
(Jeremy Gask) *slowly away: t.k.h: hld up in last pair: brought wd in st: no real prog* **20/1**
615- 9 nse **Roundabout Magic (IRE)**[33] 8444 3-9-3 **64**.... HectorCrouch(3) 9 54
(Simon Dow) *slowly away: t.k.h: hld up in last: pushed along on inner over 1f out: no prog and nvr involved* **4/1**[1]

59.35s (0.55) **Going Correction** -0.075s/f (Stan) 9 Ran SP% **119.0**
Speed ratings (Par 95): **92,91,91,90,89 89,88,85,85**
CSF £180.86 CT £822.31 TOTE £33.80: £8.80, £1.70, £1.50; EX 332.10 Trifecta £988.70.
**Owner** John Quorn **Bred** Mickley Stud & Mr W T Whittle **Trained** Newmarket, Suffolk

**FOCUS**
A moderate sprint handicap. The field was compressed at the finish and the form has been rated as very ordinary.

## 325 BETWAY CLASSIFIED CLAIMING STKS — 1m 5f (P)
**2:00** (2:00) (Class 5) 4-Y-O+ — **£2,911** (£866; £432) **Stalls** Low

Form — RPR

430- **1** **Oratorio's Joy (IRE)**[25] 8524 7-9-8 75........................(p) TimmyMurphy 2 — 73
(Jamie Osborne) *mde all: rdn 2f out: kpt away fr inner in st: kpt on wl* **5/4**[1]

00-0 **2** 2 ¼ **English Summer**[15] 74 10-9-0 70........................(t) StevieDonohoe 3 — 63
(Ian Williams) *hld up in last: chsd wnr over 2f out and chal wl over 1f out: fnd little and readily hld fnl f* **2/1**[2]

13-4 **3** 6 **Vercingetorix (IRE)**[10] 154 6-9-2 75........................(p) DougieCostello 4 — 54
(Harriet Bethell) *trckd wnr: urged along fr 5f out and nt keen: dropped to last over 2f out and sn btn* **5/2**[3]

2m 45.89s (-0.11) **Going Correction** -0.075s/f (Stan) — **3** Ran SP% **106.3**
Speed ratings (Par 103): **97,95,91**
CSF £3.85 TOTE £2.00; EX 3.90 Trifecta £3.80.There was no bid for the winner
**Owner** A F Tait **Bred** R Mahon & J Reilly **Trained** Upper Lambourn, Berks

**FOCUS**
An uncompetitive, steadily run claimer with doubts over all three. The winner has been rated to her latter 2016 form.

## 326 BETWAY H'CAP — 6f 1y(P)
**2:35** (2:35) (Class 2) (0-105,99) 4-Y-O+
**£11,827** (£3,541; £1,770; £885; £442; £222) **Stalls** Low

Form — RPR

30-2 **1** **Kasbah (IRE)**[6] 234 5-9-0 92........................ JackMitchell 1 — 101
(Amanda Perrett) *mostly trckd ldng pair: clsd between them over 1f out to ld jst ins fnl f: sn in command: rdn out* **7/2**[1]

302- **2** 1 **Big Time (IRE)**[91] 7523 6-9-7 99........................(v) MartinHarley 8 — 106+
(Kevin Ryan) *hld up in rr: prog whn checked 1f out: r.o to take 2nd last 75yds: no ch to chal* **5/1**[3]

06-1 **3** ¾ **Zac Brown (IRE)**[15] 79 6-8-10 88........................(t) WilliamCarson 5 — 91
(Charlie Wallis) *pressed ldr: rdn to chal fr 2f out: outpcd ins fnl f: kpt on* **8/1**

600- **4** ½ **Dhahmaan (IRE)**[29] 8489 4-9-5 97........................(v[1]) DanielTudhope 4 — 99
(David O'Meara) *in tch in midfield: rdn over 1f out: styd on ins fnl f but nvr pce to threaten* **9/2**[2]

3-60 **5** nk **Aguerooo (IRE)**[3] 275 4-8-12 90........................(p) SeanLevey 2 — 91
(Richard Hannon) *hld up in rr: pushed along on inner fr over 1f out: styng on but no ch whn reminders nr fin* **7/1**

20-4 **6** hd **Bosham**[15] 63 7-8-13 94........................(bt) NathanEvans(3) 3 — 94
(Michael Easterby) *led: rdn 2f out: hdd jst ins fnl f: fdd and lost pls last 75yds* **20/1**

010- **7** nk **Robot Boy (IRE)**[90] 7537 7-9-4 96........................ PhillipMakin 9 — 95
(David Barron) *in tch in midfield: hanging whn rdn wl over 1f out: styd on ins fnl f: nrst fin but n.d* **14/1**

20-3 **8** ¾ **Upavon**[15] 63 7-8-9 90........................(bt) AaronJones(3) 7 — 87
(Stuart Williams) *dwlt: mostly in last pair: rdn over 2f out: kpt on fnl f but no ch* **10/1**

3-02 **9** 1 ¼ **Gentlemen**[9] 170 6-9-1 96........................(h) CallumShepherd(3) 10 — 89
(Phil McEntee) *towards rr: prog on outer 1/2-way: wd bnd 2f out and forfeited grnd: nvr on terms after* **10/1**

00-3 **10** 1 ¼ **Sign Of The Kodiac (IRE)**[6] 234 4-9-4 96........................ TomEaves 6 — 85
(James Given) *prom: rdn to chse ldng pair briefly over 2f out: wknd over 1f out* **8/1**

1m 9.87s (-2.03) **Going Correction** -0.075s/f (Stan) — **10** Ran SP% **121.4**
Speed ratings (Par 109): **110,108,107,107,106 106,105,104,103,101**
CSF £21.83 CT £137.63 TOTE £4.30: £1.80, £1.70, £3.40; EX 23.90 Trifecta £180.10.
**Owner** Coombelands Racing Syndicate **Bred** Castlemartin Sky & Skymarc Farm **Trained** Pulborough, W Sussex

**FOCUS**
A decent sprint handicap. The winner was building on his recent C&D run and has been rated back to his best.

## 327 BETWAY BEST ODDS GUARANTEED PLUS H'CAP — 5f 6y(P)
**3:10** (3:11) (Class 6) (0-60,66) 4-Y-O+ — **£2,587** (£770; £384; £192) **Stalls** High

Form — RPR

65-1 **1** **Hamish McGonagain**[7] 217 4-9-8 66 6ex........................(p) DavidParkes(5) 8 — 77+
(Jeremy Gask) *dwlt: wl in rr: wdst of all bnd 2f out and plenty to do: gd prog over 1f out: str run to ld last 50yds: won gng away* **15/8**[1]

000- **2** 1 ¼ **Annie Salts**[34] 8429 4-9-7 60........................(h) JoeFanning 1 — 66
(Chris Dwyer) *dwlt: rcvrd to join ldr over 3f out: rdn 2f out: narrow ld over 1f out tl hdd and outpcd last 50yds* **16/1**

52-3 **3** ½ **Roy's Legacy**[4] 271 8-8-11 55........................ CharlieBennett(5) 5 — 59
(Shaun Harris) *led: jnd over 3f out: narrowly hdd over 1f out: outpcd last 50yds* **4/1**[3]

43-3 **4** ¾ **Pharoh Jake**[7] 215 9-9-6 59........................ WilliamCarson 9 — 61
(John Bridger) *chsd ldrs: urged along fr 2f out: nt qckn over 1f out: hld whn tight for room briefly ins fnl f* **10/1**

06-4 **5** nk **Charlie Lad**[10] 153 5-8-13 52........................ StevieDonohoe 3 — 52
(Daniel Mark Loughnane) *chsd ldrs: rdn 2f out: kpt on same pce fr over 1f out and nvr able to chal* **8/1**

030- **6** 1 **Costa Filey**[50] 8181 6-9-7 60........................ MartinHarley 7 — 57
(Ed Vaughan) *in tch: rdn 2f out: hld whn tightened up jst ins fnl f: one pce after* **7/2**[2]

060- **7** nse **Molly Jones**[125] 6586 8-8-12 51........................ JohnFahy 4 — 48
(Matthew Salaman) *stdd after s: hld up and sn detached in last: pushed along over 1f out: r.o ins fnl f: far too late* **66/1**

05-0 **8** 1 **Ask The Guru**[7] 215 7-9-3 56........................(p) RobertHavlin 6 — 49
(Michael Attwater) *dwlt: racd on inner and a towards rr: no prog over 1f out* **10/1**

030- **9** 1 ¾ **Equinette (IRE)**[37] 8358 4-8-13 55........................(b[1]) KieranShoemark(3) 10 — 42
(Amanda Perrett) *dwlt: rcvrd fr wdst draw to press ldrs: u.p over 2f out: lost pl wl over 1f out* **25/1**

58.75s (-0.05) **Going Correction** -0.075s/f (Stan) — **9** Ran SP% **117.5**
Speed ratings (Par 101): **97,95,94,93,92 90,90,89,86**
CSF £36.59 CT £113.30 TOTE £2.80: £1.20, £5.00, £1.50; EX 36.70 Trifecta £220.00.
**Owner** Hart Racing **Bred** Llety Farms **Trained** Stockbridge, Hants
■ Stewards' Enquiry : John Fahy £140.00 fine; failing to report that the mare did not handle coming down the hill.

**FOCUS**
A moderate sprint handicap, but a fair performance form the improving winner.

## 328 32RED.COM MAIDEN STKS — 1m 2f (P)
**3:40** (3:40) (Class 5) 3-Y-O — **£2,911** (£866; £432; £216) **Stalls** Low

Form — RPR

3 **1** **Keswick**[15] 65 3-9-5 0........................(t) RobertHavlin 5 — 76+
(John Gosden) *hld up disputing 5th: shkn up 3f out: prog 2f out to chse ldr fnl f: drvn and clsd to ld last 75yds: r.o wl* **2/1**[1]

6-5 **2** 1 ¼ **Tomorrow Mystery**[11] 144 3-9-0 0........................ TimmyMurphy 7 — 68
(Jamie Osborne) *t.k.h: trckd ldr 2f and again over 5f out: led over 2f out and committed for home: styd on fnl f but hdd and outpcd last 75yds* **20/1**

**3** 3 ¾ **Fearsome** 3-9-5 0........................ SeanLevey 8 — 65
(Ralph Beckett) *prog to trck ldr after 2f to over 5f out: styd cl up: rdn to chse ldr 2f out: no imp over 1f out: lost 2nd fnl f and fin weakly* **9/4**[2]

**4** ½ **Turnpike Trip** 3-9-2 0........................ HectorCrouch(3) 1 — 64+
(Henry Candy) *dwlt: rn green in last: stl last over 1f out: picked up wl fnl f: gng on at fin* **25/1**

4 **5** 1 ½ **Dance Dan Dan (IRE)**[8] 198 3-9-5 0........................ JoeFanning 4 — 61
(Mark Johnston) *hld up disputing 5th: rdn over 2f out: no prog and btn over 1f out* **20/1**

04- **6** hd **Caracas**[24] 8537 3-9-2 0........................ KieranShoemark(3) 6 — 61
(Roger Charlton) *hld up in last pair: shkn up 3f out: no prog 2f out: wl hld after: one pce* **8/1**

0- **7** 1 ¼ **Marettimo (IRE)**[66] 7962 3-9-5 0........................ DanielTudhope 2 — 58
(Charles Hills) *led to over 2f out: wknd over 1f out* **11/4**[3]

0 **8** 2 ¼ **Whirlwind Romance (IRE)**[16] 48 3-8-11 0........................(b[1]) NoelGarbutt(3) 3 — 49
(Hugo Palmer) *cl up: rdn over 2f out: hanging and wknd qckly over 1f out* **33/1**

2m 5.54s (-1.06) **Going Correction** -0.075s/f (Stan) — **8** Ran SP% **118.2**
Speed ratings (Par 97): **101,100,97,96,95 95,94,92**
CSF £45.65 TOTE £2.70: £1.20, £4.80, £1.30; EX 22.80 Trifecta £188.30.
**Owner** Lady Rothschild **Bred** Carwell Equities Ltd **Trained** Newmarket, Suffolk

**FOCUS**
They went a muddling pace in this ordinary maiden, but some of these may well improve.
T/Plt: £19.20 to a £1 stake. Pool: £64,988.20 - 2464.65 winning units T/Qpdt: £6.40 to a £1 stake. Pool: £5,994.44, 692.20 winning units **Jonathan Neesom**

# 264 WOLVERHAMPTON (A.W) (L-H)
Friday, January 20

**OFFICIAL GOING: Tapeta: standard**
Wind: light, against Weather: dry, chilly

## 329 32RED.COM H'CAP — 7f 36y (Tp)
**5:45** (5:45) (Class 4) (0-80,78) 3-Y-O — **£5,175** (£1,540; £769; £384) **Stalls** High

Form — RPR

011- **1** **Vatican Hill (IRE)**[23] 8560 3-9-2 78........................ LucyKBarry(5) 3 — 83
(Jamie Osborne) *chsd ldr for 1f: trckd ldrs after: effrt over 1f out: str run to ld 75yds out: r.o wl and gng away at fin* **9/2**[3]

032- **2** 1 **Tailor's Row (USA)**[20] 8592 3-9-6 77........................ PJMcDonald 2 — 79
(Mark Johnston) *led: rdn 2f out: hung lft over 1f out: hdd and one pced fnl 75yds* **3/1**[2]

41-3 **3** nk **Alkashaaf (USA)**[17] 31 3-9-6 77........................(tp) DavidProbert 6 — 78
(Archie Watson) *chsd ldr after 1f out: effrt over 1f out: ev ch ins fnl f: styd on same pce fnl 75yds* **7/4**[1]

32-4 **4** 2 ½ **Atteq**[17] 31 3-9-5 76........................ TonyHamilton 1 — 70
(Richard Fahey) *trckd ldrs: swtchd rt and effrt over 1f out: unable qck 1f out and nt clrest of runs jst ins fnl f: wknd wl ins fnl f* **7/1**

450- **5** 1 ¾ **Ladofash**[95] 7406 3-8-10 67........................ JoeyHaynes 5 — 57
(K R Burke) *in tch in last pair: rdn over 2f out: unable qck and outpcd over 1f out: wl hld and one pced fnl f* **22/1**

254- **6** nk **Sans Souci Bay**[20] 8592 3-8-13 77........................ TinaSmith(7) 4 — 66
(Richard Hannon) *dwlt and hmpd leaving stalls: hld up in last pair: swtchd rt and effrt bnd wl over 1f out: no imp u.p over 1f out: nvr trbld ldrs* **7/1**

1m 27.24s (-1.56) **Going Correction** -0.10s/f (Stan) — **6** Ran SP% **108.9**
Speed ratings (Par 99): **104,102,102,99,97 97**
CSF £17.15 TOTE £3.90: £2.70, £2.00; EX 10.90 Trifecta £30.00.
**Owner** J A Osborne **Bred** Mrs Gillian McCalmont **Trained** Upper Lambourn, Berks

**FOCUS**
A fair 3yo handicap and they went a solid pace. Straightforward form rated around the runner-up.

## 330 BETWAY H'CAP — 5f 21y (Tp)
**6:15** (6:19) (Class 5) (0-70,70) 4-Y-O+ — **£3,396** (£1,010; £505; £252) **Stalls** Low

Form — RPR

00-5 **1** **You're Cool**[18] 22 5-8-9 65........................ LewisEdmunds(7) 6 — 73
(John Balding) *chsd ldr: swtchd rt and clsd over 1f out: rdn to ld ins fnl f: kpt on: rdn out* **4/1**[1]

016- **2** ¾ **Fly True**[34] 8430 4-9-4 67........................(h) DavidProbert 5 — 72+
(Jeremy Gask) *s.i.s: off the pce in rr: swtchd rt over 1f out: hdwy ins fnl f: r.o strly to go 2nd nr fin: nvr quite getting to wnr* **5/1**[2]

5-54 **3** ½ **Archie Stevens**[8] 194 7-9-6 69........................ AndrewMullen 4 — 72
(David Evans) *chsd ldng pair: effrt 2f out: clsd and drvn to chse wnr ins fnl f: kpt on same pce fnl 100yds: lost 2nd nr fin* **11/2**[3]

05-5 **4** hd **Noble Asset**[14] 95 6-8-13 62........................ RobertWinston 9 — 65
(Milton Bradley) *led rdrless to post: t.k.h: off the pce towards rr: rdn and hdwy over 1f out: r.o wl ins fnl f: nvr quite getting to ldrs* **12/1**

1-22 **5** ½ **Temple Road (IRE)**[7] 215 9-9-5 68........................(bt) AdamKirby 8 — 69
(Milton Bradley) *s.i.s: off the pce in rr: hdwy over 1f out: rdn and styd on wl ins fnl f: nt rch ldrs* **4/1**[1]

04-6 **6** nk **Red Stripes (USA)**[8] 194 5-9-6 69........................ KevinStott 1 — 69
(Lisa Williamson) *off the pce in midfield: hmpd over 3f out: rdn and hdwy over 1f out: chsd ldrs ins fnl f: kpt on* **11/1**

030- **7** hd **Aragon Knight**[34] 8430 4-9-6 69........................ TomMarquand 10 — 68
(Heather Main) *chsd ldng trio: rdn and drifted lft over 1f out: kpt on same pce ins fnl f* **14/1**

30-0 **8** ¾ **Elusivity (IRE)**[16] 45 9-9-7 70........................(p) PaulMulrennan 11 — 66
(Conor Dore) *off the pce in midfield: hung lft u.p over 1f out: one pce and no imp ins fnl f* **25/1**

120- **9** 2 **Noah Amor (IRE)**[36] 8390 4-8-9 65........................ DanielleMooney(7) 3 — 54
(David Nicholls) *off the pce in midfield: effrt on inner over 1f out: no imp fnl f* **9/1**

410- **10** 1 ½ **Mambo Spirit (IRE)**[41] 8315 13-8-13 65........................ EoinWalsh(3) 7 — 49
(Tony Newcombe) *v.s.a: nvr rcvrd and n.d* **50/1**

06-0 11 *nk* **Powerful Wind (IRE)**[18] 22 8-9-4 **67**................................(t) BenCurtis 2 50
(Charlie Wallis) *taken down early: led and set fast gallop: rdn and drifted rt over 1f out: hdd ins fnl f: sn btn and fdd fnl 100yds* **14/1**

1m 0.92s (-0.98) **Going Correction** -0.10s/f (Stan) 11 Ran SP% **117.2**
Speed ratings (Par 103): **103,102,101,101,100 99,99,98,95,92 92**
CSF £23.49 CT £111.10 TOTE £5.50: £2.40, £2.00, £1.50; EX 26.30 Trifecta £111.10.
**Owner** D Bichan & J Roberts **Bred** Tirnaskea Stud **Trained** Scrooby, S Yorks
■ Stewards' Enquiry : Andrew Mullen caution; entered the wrong stall.

**FOCUS**
A fair handicap run at a good pace, but it still paid to race prominently. The winner has been rated close to his best.

## 331 SUNBETS.CO.UK DOWNLOAD THE APP MAIDEN STKS 7f 36y (Tp)
**6:45** (6:47) (Class 5) 3-Y-O+ **£3,396** (£1,010; £505; £252) **Stalls** High

Form RPR
1 **Mystique Moon** 3-8-10 0.................................................. MartinLane 6 82
(Charlie Appleby) *chsd ldr: effrt to press wnr and rn green over 1f out: rdn to ld ins fnl f: r.o wl* **2/1**[2]

0- 2 *3/4* **Fast Landing**[76] 7812 3-8-10 0............................................. KevinStott 8 79
(Saeed bin Suroor) *chsd ldrs: effrt in 3rd and rn green over 1f out: drvn to chse wnr ins fnl f: kpt on u.p* **10/11**[1]

0-4 3 *1 3/4* **Tai Hang Dragon (IRE)**[13] 119 3-8-5 0......................... KieranO'Neill 9 69
(Richard Hannon) *led: rdn over 1f out: hdd ins fnl f: no ex and outpcd fnl 100yds* **13/2**[3]

4 *6* **Arabella Rose** 3-8-5 0...................................................... JoeyHaynes 7 53
(Ivan Furtado) *dwlt: t.k.h: hld up towards rr: hdwy 4f out: chsd ldrs 3f out: rdn and unable qck over 1f out: sn outpcd and btn 1f out* **50/1**

00- 5 *1 1/4* **Rebel Flame**[104] 7142 3-8-10 0....................................... TomMarquand 2 55
(Garry Moss) *chsd ldrs: 4th and unable qck over 1f out: sn btn: wknd fnl f* **66/1**

6 *5* **Dibloam (USA)** 4-10-0 0............................................... AndrewMullen 3 46
(David Evans) *hld up in last quartet: swtchd rt and pushed along over 1f out: no threat to ldrs but kpt on steadily ins fnl f* **33/1**

0- 7 *hd* **Street Jester**[23] 8556 3-8-7 0........................................ RobHornby(3) 11 41
(Robert Stephens) *midfield: 7th and rdn over 2f out: sn outpcd and wknd over 1f out* **100/1**

0 8 *nse* **Newton Heath (IRE)**[16] 48 3-8-10 0................................. BenCurtis 4 41
(Daniel Mark Loughnane) *midfield: outpcd and rdn over 2f out: wknd over 1f out* **100/1**

9 *1/2* **Way Up High**[30] 5-9-2 0............................................. JoshuaBryan(7) 12 39
(Steve Flook) *dwlt: sn rcvrd and in tch in midfield: clsd to chse ldrs 4f out: outpcd 2f out: hung lft and wknd over 1f out* **100/1**

10 *6* **River Warrior** 3-8-10 0............................................... TonyHamilton 1 23
(Richard Fahey) *midfield: rdn and outpcd over 2f out: sn btn and wknd over 1f out* **12/1**

11 *1 3/4* **Easy Wind** 3-8-5 0.................................................... RyanPowell 5 13
(Sir Mark Prescott Bt) *hld up in rr: struggling over 2f out: bhd whn swtchd lft over 1f out* **20/1**

6- 12 *3 1/2* **House Of Frauds (IRE)**[48] 8212 9-9-11 0.................... EoinWalsh(3) 10 14
(Tony Newcombe) *stdd s: t.k.h: hld up in tch in rr: rdn over 2f out: sn struggling and bhd over 1f out* **100/1**

1m 28.67s (-0.13) **Going Correction** -0.10s/f (Stan)
**WFA** 3 from 4yo+ 18lb 12 Ran SP% **121.9**
Speed ratings (Par 103): **96,95,93,86,84 79,78,78,78,71 69,65**
CSF £4.13 TOTE £2.70: £1.20, £1.10, £1.80; EX 4.70 Trifecta £14.40.
**Owner** Godolphin **Bred** Meon Valley Stud **Trained** Newmarket, Suffolk

**FOCUS**
An ordinary maiden lacking depth and a 1-2 for Godolphin.

## 332 SUNBETS.CO.UK H'CAP 7f 36y (Tp)
**7:15** (7:18) (Class 6) (0-60,60) 4-Y-O+ **£2,587** (£770; £384; £192) **Stalls** High

Form RPR
1-12 1 **Athassel**[2] 282 8-9-0 **53**................................................ StevieDonohoe 6 64+
(David Evans) *stdd bk into midfield after 1f: t.k.h: effrt over 1f out: chal 1f out: led ins fnl f: styd on: rdn out* **10/11**[1]

55-5 2 *1 3/4* **Spirit Of Gondree (IRE)**[10] 166 9-9-3 **56**.................(b) RobertWinston 9 63
(Milton Bradley) *t.k.h: chsd ldr tl rdn to ld over 1f out: hdd ins fnl f: no ex and outpcd fnl 100yds* **11/1**

32-4 3 *3/4* **Keene's Pointe**[7] 222 7-9-4 **60**.......................................... RobHornby(3) 7 65
(Steph Hollinshead) *hld up in tch in last quartet: effrt and hdwy over 1f out: 3rd and kpt on same pce u.p ins fnl f* **16/1**

00-0 4 *4 1/2* **Kafeel (USA)**[15] 67 6-9-7 **60**...........................................(t[1]) LiamKeniry 11 54
(Linda Jewell) *stdd s: hld up in last pair: hdwy over 2f out: rdn over 1f out: styd on same pce and no threat to ldrs ins fnl f: wnt 4th cl home* **20/1**

00-3 5 *1/2* **Showtime Blues**[11] 145 5-9-7 **60**......................................(v) AdamKirby 4 53
(Jim Boyle) *trckd ldrs: effrt on inner over 1f out: drvn and little rspnse 1f out: fdd ins fnl f* **5/1**[2]

260- 6 *2 1/2* **Ada Misobel (IRE)**[41] 8307 4-9-1 **54**...........................(p) AndrewMullen 3 41
(Garry Moss) *led: rdn and hdd over 1f out: sn btn: fdd ins fnl f* **16/1**

000- 7 *1 3/4* **Zorlu (IRE)**[49] 7937 4-8-11 **55**.......................................(v[1]) CiaranMckee(5) 1 38
(John O'Shea) *hld up towards rr: rdn ent fnl 2f: sn struggling: wknd over 1f out* **100/1**

653- 8 *2 1/2* **Oak Bluffs (IRE)**[21] 8588 6-9-6 **59**................................ TonyHamilton 8 35
(Richard Fahey) *dwlt: sn rcvrd to chse ldrs and t.k.h: chsd ldrs after 1f: rdn and lost pl over 2f out: bhd fnl f* **7/1**[3]

05-4 9 *1 1/4* **Kaaber (USA)**[16] 51 6-9-0 **53**..........................................(b) TomMarquand 5 26
(Roy Brotherton) *hld up in last pair: reminder 4f out: rdn over 2f out: sn btn: bhd fnl f* **12/1**

1m 27.97s (-0.83) **Going Correction** -0.10s/f (Stan) 9 Ran SP% **115.1**
Speed ratings (Par 101): **100,98,97,92,91 88,86,83,82**
CSF £12.41 CT £100.23 TOTE £1.60: £1.10, £3.60, £3.30; EX 12.30 Trifecta £125.10.
**Owner** Mrs E Evans **Bred** Moyns Park Estate And Stud Ltd **Trained** Pandy, Monmouths

**FOCUS**
Only a moderate handicap with the first three clear and the odds-on favourite made no mistake.

## 333 BETWAY MIDDLE H'CAP 1m 4f 51y (Tp)
**7:45** (7:45) (Class 6) (0-65,67) 4-Y-O+ **£2,587** (£770; £384; £192) **Stalls** Low

Form RPR
020- 1 **Sebastian's Wish (IRE)**[64] 7992 4-8-3 **53**.............. ShirleyTeasdale(5) 9 59
(Keith Dalgleish) *taken down early: t.k.h: chsd ldr tl 5f out: styd trcking ldrs: nt clr run over 2f out: effrt to chal on inner 1f out: led ins fnl f: kpt on u.p* **9/1**

00-1 2 *nk* **Trending (IRE)**[10] 164 8-9-7 **67** 6ex...........................(t) DavidParkes(5) 1 73
(Jeremy Gask) *hld up in tch in midfield: rdn and clsd to chse ldrs 2f out: hdwy to ld 1f out: hdd ins fnl f: kpt on wl but hld towards fin* **11/2**[3]

050- 3 *1 1/4* **Askari**[223] 3160 4-9-6 **65**.............................................................. AdamKirby 12 69
(Tom Clover) *dropped in after s: hld up in rr: hdwy on outer 3f out: rdn over 1f out: kpt on ins fnl f: wnt 3rd nr fin* **7/1**

20-2 4 *1/2* **Paper Faces (USA)**[18] 23 4-9-3 **62**..............................(h[1]) JackMitchell 2 65
(Roger Varian) *chsd ldrs: effrt over 1f out: rdn to chse ldng pair ins fnl f: kpt on same pce fnl 100yds: lost 3rd nr fin* **11/2**[3]

512- 5 *1 1/4* **Kay Sera**[25] 8527 9-9-0 **58**................................................... EoinWalsh(3) 7 59
(Tony Newcombe) *t.k.h: hld up towards rr: hdwy 3f out: nt clr run over 1f out: swtchd rt 1f out: styd on ins fnl f: no threat to ldrs* **9/2**[2]

60-0 6 *3/4* **Gambol (FR)**[7] 218 7-9-7 **62**........................................(b[1]) StevieDonohoe 4 62
(Ian Williams) *led to post: stdd s: hld up in rr: hdwy over 2f out: nt clr run jst over 1f out: swtchd rt ins fnl f: kpt on ins fnl f: nvr threatened ldrs* **10/1**

7 *hd* **Walkabout (IRE)**[14] 107 5-8-13 **54**....................................... LiamKeniry 8 53
(Gordon Elliott, Ire) *wl in tch in midfield: hdwy to join ldr over 2f out: rdn over 1f out: unable qck and wknd ins fnl f* **3/1**[1]

600- 8 *1 1/4* **Henryhudsonbridge (USA)**[177] 4763 5-9-5 **60**........(b) DanielMuscutt 5 57
(John Flint) *chsd ldrs: wnt 2nd 5f out: rdn and ev ch 2f out: unable qck 1f out: hung lft and wknd ins fnl f* **40/1**

210- 9 *3 1/4* **Turnbury**[18] 4057 6-9-6 **64**....................................(p) EdwardGreatrex(3) 10 56
(Nikki Evans) *led: rdn wl over 1f out: drvn and hdd 1f out: sn btn: hung lft and wknd ins fnl f* **40/1**

00-0 10 *2 1/2* **Steady Major (IRE)**[16] 49 5-9-3 **63**.......................... CharlieBennett(5) 3 51
(Mark Brisbourne) *hld up in midfield: nt clr run over 1f out: swtchd rt and then bk lft jst ins fnl f: nt clr run on inner ins fnl f: eased off fnl 100yds* **50/1**

000- 11 *16* **Officer In Command (USA)**[49] 8190 11-8-10 **51** oh6.(tp) JoeyHaynes 6 13
(Alan Bailey) *rn in snatches: in tch but a towards rr: dropped to last and struggling u.p over 1f out: bhd ins fnl f* **80/1**

2m 39.55s (-1.25) **Going Correction** -0.10s/f (Stan)
**WFA** 4 from 5yo+ 3lb 11 Ran SP% **113.6**
Speed ratings (Par 101): **100,99,98,98,97 97,97,96,94,92 81**
CSF £54.96 CT £367.76 TOTE £8.60: £3.00, £1.70, £2.70; EX 56.70 Trifecta £641.80.
**Owner** Two Goldfish & A Balloon **Bred** Gestut Schlenderhan **Trained** Carluke, S Lanarks
■ Stewards' Enquiry : Shirley Teasdale two-day ban; used whip in the incorrect place (3rd-4th Feb)

**FOCUS**
A modest handicap and straightforward form.

## 334 BETWAY APP H'CAP 1m 1f 104y (Tp)
**8:15** (8:15) (Class 7) (0-50,50) 4-Y-O+ **£2,264** (£673; £336; £168) **Stalls** Low

Form RPR
6/5- 1 **Royal Blessing**[14] 108 5-9-5 **49**.......................................(b) AdamKirby 8 57
(Peter Fahey, Ire) *stdd after s and dropped in bhd: swtchd rt and hdwy over 1f out: chsd clr ldr 1f out: str run to ld wl ins fnl f: sn clr and gng away at fin* **6/4**[1]

-055 2 *2 1/4* **Captain K (IRE)**[7] 222 5-9-2 **46**.................................(h) TimmyMurphy 1 50
(Gordon Elliott, Ire) *chsd ldr tl led and rdn to qckn clr 2f out: stl 3 l ahd 1f out: drvn ins fnl f: hdd wl ins fnl f: sn outpcd* **9/2**[2]

350- 3 *3 1/4* **Cahar Fad (IRE)**[25] 8527 5-9-4 **48**..............................(bt) RobertWinston 9 46
(Steph Hollinshead) *t.k.h: hld up in last trio: effrt u.p over 1f out: wnt 3rd 100yds out: styd on but no threat to ldrs* **9/2**[2]

001- 4 *1 1/2* **Pipers Piping (IRE)**[29] 8500 11-9-2 **49**......................... RobHornby(3) 2 44
(Mandy Rowland) *hld up in midfield: effrt u.p over 1f out: styd on same pce and no threat to ldrs ins fnl f* **12/1**

56-0 5 *1/2* **Sarakova (IRE)**[13] 124 4-9-2 **47**..................................(v) RyanPowell 13 41
(Kevin Frost) *wnt rt s: hdwy to chse ldrs after 2f: rdn to chse ldr but ldr clr 2f out: no imp: lost 2nd 1f out: wknd and lost 2nd ins fnl f* **16/1**

24-0 6 *3 1/2* **Just Fred (IRE)**[13] 121 4-9-5 **50**........................................(t[1]) LiamKeniry 4 37
(Neil Mulholland) *t.k.h: hld up in last trio: effrt over 1f out: no imp and wknd fnl f* **8/1**[3]

536- 7 *nk* **Never Say (IRE)**[239] 2608 4-9-0 **50**................................ DavidParkes(5) 6 37
(Jason Ward) *t.k.h: hld up in midfield: nt clrest of runs over 2f out: effrt and no imp over 1f out: sn wknd* **25/1**

46-6 8 *3 3/4* **Claude Greenwood**[9] 167 7-9-0 **47**...................(b) GeorgeDowning(3) 5 27
(Tony Carroll) *led: rdn and hdd 2f out: sn outpcd and lost pl over 1f out: bhd fnl f* **11/1**

540- 9 *7* **Farrah's Choice**[36] 8383 5-9-5 **49**................................. TomMarquand 12 15
(James Grassick) *chsd ldr tl 3f out: sn u.p and lost pl: bhd fnl f* **66/1**

1m 59.93s (-0.87) **Going Correction** -0.10s/f (Stan)
**WFA** 4 from 5yo+ 1lb 9 Ran SP% **114.7**
Speed ratings (Par 97): **99,97,94,92,92 89,88,85,79**
CSF £8.13 CT £24.27 TOTE £2.30: £1.20, £1.50, £1.80; EX 8.70 Trifecta £29.40.
**Owner** Madhatters On Tour Syndicate **Bred** Highbury Stud Ltd **Trained** Monasterevln, Co. Kildare

**FOCUS**
A low-grade handicap which was dominated by a couple of Irish raiders and not many positives behind them.
T/Plt: £17.20 to a £1 stake. Pool: £112,323.71 - 4,765.94 winning tickets T/Qpdt: £4.50 to a £1 stake. Pool: £9,689.83 - 1,564.42 winning tickets **Steve Payne**

335 - 348a (Foreign Racing) - See Raceform Interactive

# [323]LINGFIELD (L-H)
## Saturday, January 21

**OFFICIAL GOING: Polytrack: standard**
Wind: light, across Weather: bright, chilly

## 349 SUNBETS.CO.UK H'CAP 1m 1y(P)
**12:50** (12:52) (Class 4) (0-85,87) 4-Y-O+ **£4,690** (£1,395; £697; £348) **Stalls** High

Form RPR
002- 1 **Franco's Secret**[38] 8356 6-9-5 **81**...............................(v) TomMarquand 8 88
(Peter Hedger) *stdd s: hld up in tch in rr: effrt 2f out: hdwy and swtchd rt 1f out: str run u.p fnl 100yds to ld last strides* **7/1**

33-3 2 *nk* **Chevallier**[17] 43 5-9-11 **87**................................................ LukeMorris 3 93
(Archie Watson) *trckd ldng pair: effrt and trying to switch rt over 1f out: drvn to chal jst ins fnl f: hrd drvn to ld wl ins fnl f: hdd last strides* **7/4**[1]

000- 3 *1/2* **Dutiful Son (IRE)**[38] 8356 7-9-4 **80**................................ AdamKirby 1 85
(Simon Dow) *hld up in tch in last pair: effrt over 1f out: hdwy u.p to chse ldrs jst ins fnl f: kpt on: wnt 3rd nr fin* **11/2**[3]

26-6 4 *1/2* **Loyalty**[16] 61 10-9-7 **83**...............................................(v) MartinLane 7 87
(Derek Shaw) *led: rdn and qcknd 2f out: drvn and hrd pressed jst ins fnl f: hdd and no ex wl ins fnl f* **12/1**

1-24 5 *3 1/4* **Byres Road**[5] 266 4-9-5 **81**................................................ JoeFanning 5 78
(Mark Johnston) *chsd ldr: rdn 2f out: ev ch tl no ex and btn jst ins fnl f: wknd fnl 150yds* **9/4**[2]

63-0 **6** *1* **Mezzotint (IRE)**[3] 287 8-8-11 **78** PaddyBradley(5) 2 72
(Lee Carter) *hld up in tch in midfield: effrt but unable qck over 1f out: wl hld and one pced fnl f* **20/1**

006- **7** *3 ¾* **Best Example (USA)**[34] 8446 5-8-13 **78** (h) ShelleyBirkett(3) 4 64
(Julia Feilden) *in tch in midfield: rdn 2f out: sn lost pl: bhd fnl f* **22/1**

1m 36.18s (-2.02) **Going Correction** -0.125s/f (Stan) 7 Ran SP% **111.8**
Speed ratings (Par 105): **105,104,104,103,100 99,95**
CSF £18.84 CT £71.15 TOTE £7.80: £3.20, £1.60; EX 15.70 Trifecta £84.10.
**Owner** P C F Racing Ltd **Bred** J J Whelan **Trained** Hook, Hampshire

**FOCUS**
Not a bad handicap to start, but the pace was ordinary. The winner has been rated back to his best.

## 350 32RED CASINO H'CAP 1m 1y(P)
**1:25** (1:30) (Class 3) (0-95,90) 3-Y-O **£7,246** (£2,168; £1,084) **Stalls** High

Form RPR

52-3 **1** **Mailshot (USA)**[10] 177 3-9-7 **90** JoeFanning 3 94
(Mark Johnston) *mde all: rdn and qcknd wl over 1f out: in command and r.o wl fnl f: readily* **4/9**[1]

03-1 **2** *2 ½* **Elementary**[8] 210 3-7-13 **71** AaronJones(3) 1 69
(Michael Bell) *t.k.h: trckd wnr tl 5f out: styd handy: wnt 2nd again wl over 1f out: shkn up and little rspnse over 1f out: one pced fnl f* **2/1**[2]

060- **3** *11* **Bee Case**[21] 8592 3-8-8 **77** TomMarquand 2 50
(Simon Dow) *trckd rivals tl wnt 2nd 5f out: rdn over 2f out: dropped to last wl over 1f out: sn btn: wknd and hung lft 1f out* **10/1**[3]

1m 37.22s (-0.98) **Going Correction** -0.125s/f (Stan) 3 Ran SP% **111.7**
Speed ratings (Par 101): **99,96,85**
CSF £1.77 TOTE £1.40; EX 1.80 Trifecta £1.90.
**Owner** Sheikh Hamdan bin Mohammed Al Maktoum **Bred** Darley **Trained** Middleham Moor, N Yorks

■ Indian Dandy was withdrawn. Price at the time of withdrawal 13-8. Rule 4 applies to bets struck prior to withdrawal but not to SP bets. Deduction 35p in the pound. New market formed.

**FOCUS**
The complexion of this race was changed completely when Indian Dandy was withdrawn after getting rid of Luke Morris at the start and then running loose. That seemed to set off Mailshot and Elementary, who also both then gave trouble. The form probably doesn't add up to much.

## 351 BETWAY MIDDLE DISTANCE H'CAP 1m 2f (P)
**2:00** (2:00) (Class 6) (0-65,67) 4-Y-O+ **£2,264** (£673; £336; £168) **Stalls** Low

Form RPR

00-0 **1** **Etaad (USA)**[8] 214 6-9-4 **62** (b) GeorgeBaker 7 69
(Gary Moore) *chsd ldng trio: effrt over 1f out: rdn 1f out: chsd wnr ins fnl f: styd on wl to ld last stride* **14/1**

02-1 **2** *shd* **Seven Clans (IRE)**[12] 147 5-9-9 **67** (b) AdamKirby 8 74+
(Neil Mulholland) *hld up in tch in last quartet: swtchd rt: rdn and gd hdwy over 2f out: led over 1f out: drvn to forge ahd 1f out: kpt on: hdd last stride* **1/1**[1]

00-5 **3** *1 ½* **Runaiocht (IRE)**[7] 238 7-8-11 **60** (b) DavidParkes(5) 9 64
(Paul Burgoyne) *taken down early: t.k.h: chsd ldrs: effrt over 1f out: kpt on same pce u.p ins fnl f* **10/1**[3]

03-0 **4** *1 ¼* **Attain**[17] 44 8-9-7 **65** LukeMorris 4 67+
(Archie Watson) *hld up in tch in midfield: effrt ent fnl 2f: outpcd wl over 1f out: rallied and kpt on u.p ins fnl f* **12/1**

23-6 **5** *1 ½* **Mary Le Bow**[17] 47 6-9-2 **63** (t) CallumShepherd(3) 5 62+
(Victor Dartnall) *hld up in midfield on outer: hdwy to chse ldrs 5f out: effrt in cl 3rd 2f out: unable qck 1f out: wknd ins fnl f* **11/1**

10-6 **6** *nk* **Sunshineandbubbles**[7] 238 4-8-11 **57** (p) DavidProbert 10 55
(Daniel Mark Loughnane) *led: pressed and rdn 2f out: hdd over 1f out: no ex 1f out: wknd ins fnl f* **16/1**

621- **7** *1 ¼* **Candesta (USA)**[33] 8458 7-9-4 **65** ShelleyBirkett(3) 3 61
(Julia Feilden) *chsd ldrs: nt clr run and shuffled bk 2f out: tried to rally 1f out: sn no imp and wknd ins fnl f* **14/1**

01-0 **8** *2 ¼* **Raashdy (IRE)**[17] 47 4-9-7 **67** RobertWinston 2 59
(Peter Hiatt) *in tch in midfield: pushed along on inner over 1f out: no imp and swtchd rt ins fnl f* **11/1**

005- **9** *1 ¼* **Barren Brook**[24] 8554 10-9-4 **62** (h) LiamKeniry 11 51
(Laura Mongan) *dwlt: sn rcvrd to chse ldr: rdn whn short of room and lost pl ent fnl 2f: wknd over 1f out* **66/1**

300- **10** *¾* **Pc Dixon**[21] 8590 4-9-4 **64** ShaneKelly 1 52
(Mick Channon) *in tch towards rr: effrt ent fnl 2f: sn outpcd: bhd ins fnl f* **9/1**[2]

3-00 **11** *3 ¼* **Sheer Intensity (IRE)**[7] 239 4-8-12 **58** StevieDonohoe 6 40
(David Evans) *hld up in rr: effrt on outer over 2f out: sn btn: bhd fnl f* **33/1**

2m 4.25s (-2.35) **Going Correction** -0.125s/f (Stan)
**WFA** 4 from 5yo+ 1lb 11 Ran SP% **117.1**
Speed ratings (Par 101): **104,103,102,101,100 100,99,97,96,95 93**
CSF £28.18 CT £160.54 TOTE £13.50: £3.70, £1.10, £3.50; EX 37.70 Trifecta £215.00.
**Owner** Ian J Herbert **Bred** Shadwell Farm LLC **Trained** Lower Beeding, W Sussex

**FOCUS**
A modest handicap in which they didn't go a great pace.

## 352 BETWAY H'CAP 1m 4f (P)
**2:35** (2:35) (Class 2) (0-105,102) 4-Y-O+
**£11,827** (£3,541; £1,770; £885; £442; £222) **Stalls** Low

Form RPR

351- **1** **Pinzolo**[35] 8424 6-9-11 **102** SeanLevey 3 110
(Ismail Mohammed) *mde all: rdn wl over 1f out: sustained duel w rival fnl f: hld on wl u.p: all out* **5/2**[1]

212- **2** *½* **Rock Steady (IRE)**[49] 8210 4-9-0 **98** KieranShoemark(3) 2 105
(Roger Charlton) *taken down early: trckd ldrs: effrt 2f out: rdn and ev ch over 1f out: sustained duel w wnr fnl f: unable qck and hld towards fin* **3/1**[3]

54-1 **3** *nse* **Sennockian Star**[10] 173 7-8-9 **86** JoeFanning 5 93
(Mark Johnston) *hld up in tch in last pair: nt clr run and swtchd lft jst over 2f out: shkn up over 1f out: hdwy 1f out: rdn and styd on strly ins fnl f: nvr quite getting to ldrs* **7/1**

65- **4** *1 ¼* **Cohesion**[126] 6597 4-9-3 **101** RobHornby(3) 8 106
(David Bridgwater) *stdd s: hld up in tch in rr: effrt and hdwy into midfield 2f out: chsng ldrs and rdn 1f out: nvr enough room ins fnl f: kpt on to snatch 4th last stride* **33/1**

035- **5** *shd* **Blue Surf**[36] 6089 8-9-1 **92** JackMitchell 6 97
(Amanda Perrett) *chsd wnr tl over 1f out: stl pressing ldrs but unable qck u.p 1f out: kpt on same pce ins fnl f* **16/1**

423- **6** *4 ½* **John Reel (FR)**[14] 8529 8-9-6 **97** AdamKirby 4 95
(David Evans) *in tch in midfield: rdn 3f out: drvn and no hdwy ent fnl 2f: wknd over 1f out* **15/2**

430- **7** *20* **Erhaaf (USA)**[49] 8210 5-8-9 **86** StevieDonohoe 7 52
(Charlie Fellowes) *dwlt and bustled along leaving stalls: hdwy into midfield after 2f: rdn over 2f out: sn struggling and lost pl: bhd 1f out* **11/4**[2]

2m 26.99s (-6.01) **Going Correction** -0.125s/f (Stan) course record
**WFA** 4 from 5yo+ 3lb 7 Ran SP% **113.3**
Speed ratings (Par 109): **115,114,114,113,113 110,97**
CSF £10.13 CT £44.16 TOTE £3.20: £1.30, £2.10; EX 9.50 Trifecta £22.60.
**Owner** Sultan Ali **Bred** Fittocks Stud **Trained** Newmarket, Suffolk

**FOCUS**
A decent handicap, but despite the gallop looking a solid one rather than strong, they set a new course record. The race has been rated around the placed horses.

## 353 BETWAY BEST ODDS GUARANTEED PLUS MAIDEN STKS 1m 4f (P)
**3:10** (3:10) (Class 5) 4-Y-O+ **£2,911** (£866; £432; £216) **Stalls** Low

Form RPR

405- **1** **Enmeshing**[71] 7911 4-9-3 73 DanielMuscutt 3 80
(James Fanshawe) *hld up in tch in midfield: effrt to chse ldng pair 2f out: chalng and hung lft 1f out: led 150yds out: stl edging lft but kpt on fnl 100yds* **5/1**[3]

30- **2** *nk* **Ceyhan**[204] 3845 5-9-7 0 GeorgeBaker 6 79
(Jamie Osborne) *led: rdn ent fnl 2f: hdd and nudged lft 150yds out: kpt on but a jst hld fnl 100yds* **22/1**

34-6 **3** *6* **Ardamir (FR)**[11] 163 5-9-7 78 AdamKirby 2 75
(Alan King) *chsd ldrs tl wnt 2nd 9f out: effrt u.p over 2f out: 3rd and struggling to qckn whn squeezed for room 1f out: sn hung lft and wknd* **10/11**[1]

/3-2 **4** *2 ½* **Ribbing (USA)**[17] 37 4-8-12 68 JamieSpencer 5 60
(David Simcock) *stdd after s: hld up in last pair: shkn up ent fnl 2f: hung lft and no imp over 1f out: nvr trbld ldrs* **12/1**

**5** *hd* **Green Or Black (IRE)**[108] 7084 5-9-2 79 LiamKeniry 1 60
(Neil Mulholland) *t.k.h: chsd ldr tl 9f out: styd chsng ldrs tl 4th and outpcd 2f out: sn btn and wknd over 1f out* **4/1**[2]

**6** *1 ½* **Holly Bush Henry (IRE)**[56] 6-9-7 0 (t) RobertWinston 7 62
(Graeme McPherson) *s.i.s: hld up in last pair: effrt but no imp whn drifted wd bnd 2f out: sn wknd* **10/1**

3- **7** *10* **Demographic (USA)**[22] 728 8-9-7 0 (v) DavidProbert 4 46
(Emma Lavelle) *dwlt and hmpd leaving stalls: sn rcvrd and in midfield: rdn 4f out: sn struggling and dropped to rr: bhd 2f out* **50/1**

2m 31.03s (-1.97) **Going Correction** -0.125s/f (Stan)
**WFA** 4 from 5yo+ 3lb 7 Ran SP% **112.1**
Speed ratings (Par 103): **101,100,96,95,95 94,87**
CSF £92.01 TOTE £6.20: £2.40, £7.10; EX 97.90 Trifecta £432.80.
**Owner** Ben CM Wong **Bred** Compagnia Generale Srl **Trained** Newmarket, Suffolk

■ Stewards' Enquiry : Daniel Muscutt caution; careless riding

**FOCUS**
Probably a more interesting race than most older-horse maidens at this time of year.

## 354 SUN BETS BET £10 GET £20 FREE MAIDEN STKS 1m 1y(P)
**3:45** (3:47) (Class 5) 3-Y-O+ **£2,911** (£866; £432; £216) **Stalls** High

Form RPR

2 **1** **Revolutionary War (USA)**[11] 165 4-10-0 80 AdamKirby 6 84
(Jamie Osborne) *sn led: rdn 2f out: clr w chalr over 1f out: hdd ins fnl f: rallied u.p to ld again last strides* **7/4**[2]

02- **2** *hd* **Al Yarmouk**[57] 8089 3-8-8 0 (p[1]) RobertHavlin 2 78
(John Gosden) *chsd wnr: shkn up and wnt clr of field over 1f out: chalng 1f out: rdn to ld ins fnl f: hdd last strides* **11/8**[1]

0 **3** *4 ½* **Dark Titan (IRE)**[14] 127 3-8-8 0 ThomasBrown 3 67
(Ed Walker) *chsd ldrs: rdn ent fnl 2f: sn outpcd by ldng pair: 3rd and kpt on same pce ins fnl f* **33/1**

00- **4** *hd* **Mikey Ready (USA)**[25] 8537 3-8-8 0 (t) NickyMackay 4 67
(Ed Walker) *hld up in tch in midfield: effrt and wd bnd 2f out: sn outpcd by ldng pair: battling for 3rd but no threat to ldrs fnl f: kpt on* **16/1**

24- **5** *4* **Tifl**[24] 8559 4-10-0 0 JackMitchell 9 63
(Heather Main) *t.k.h: hld up in tch in last trio: effrt ent fnl 2f: sn outpcd and no threat to ldrs over 1f out: plugged on* **16/1**

6- **6** *nk* **Dragons Voice**[24] 8557 3-8-8 0 JoeFanning 1 57
(Philip Hide) *chsd ldrs tl rdn: outpcd and lost pl ent fnl 2f: 5th and wl hld over 1f out: wknd fnl f* **12/1**

00- **7** *¾* **Seeing Things (IRE)**[38] 8353 3-8-8 0 JohnFahy 5 55
(Philip McBride) *s.i.s: hld up in rr: stl bhd whn rdn and nt clr run over 1f out: n.d* **100/1**

0 **8** *nk* **Surfside**[14] 115 3-8-3 0 LukeMorris 8 49
(Mick Channon) *in tch in last trio: rdn over 2f out: sn struggling and outpcd 2f out: no ch over 1f out* **28/1**

22- **9** *¾* **Galinthias**[24] 8559 5-9-11 0 HectorCrouch(3) 7 58
(Simon Dow) *in tch in midfield: rdn over 2f out: sn lost pl: no ch over 1f out* **8/1**[3]

1m 37.64s (-0.56) **Going Correction** -0.125s/f (Stan)
**WFA** 3 from 4yo+ 20lb 9 Ran SP% **116.4**
Speed ratings (Par 103): **97,96,92,92,88 87,87,86,86**
CSF £4.48 TOTE £2.60: £1.10, £1.10, £6.30; EX 4.60 Trifecta £73.50.
**Owner** Sabah Mubarak Al Sabah **Bred** Joseph Allen **Trained** Upper Lambourn, Berks

**FOCUS**
An ordinary maiden dominated by the big two in the market from the off.

## 355 BETWAY BEST ODDS GUARANTEED PLUS H'CAP 6f 1y(P)
**4:15** (4:17) (Class 5) (0-70,72) 4-Y-O+ **£2,911** (£866; £432; £216) **Stalls** Low

Form RPR

41-4 **1** **Bridge Builder**[15] 94 7-9-6 **69** (p) TomMarquand 6 77
(Peter Hedger) *chsd ldr: effrt wl over 1f out: rdn to ld 1f out: kpt on wl: rdn out* **9/2**[2]

40-0 **2** *1 ¼* **Head Space (IRE)**[7] 242 9-9-2 **65** AdamKirby 9 69+
(David Evans) *dwlt and dropped in bhd after s: hld up in last pair: shkn up and swtchd rt 1f out: r.o strly fnl 100yds: snatched 2nd on post* **10/1**

106- **3** *nse* **Geoff Potts (IRE)**[138] 6190 4-9-4 **72** (h) DavidParkes(5) 3 76
(Jeremy Gask) *taken down early: t.k.h: trckd ldrs: shkn up over 1f out: rdn ins fnl f: kpt on fnl 100yds: snatched 3rd on post* **4/1**[1]

03-3 **4** *nse* **Billyoakes (IRE)**[14] 116 5-9-7 **70** (p) ShaneKelly 2 74
(Charlie Wallis) *chsd ldng pair: effrt 2f out: swtchd lft and over 1f out: drvn and chsd wnr ins fnl f: kpt on same pce: lost 2 pls last stride* **9/2**[2]

00-0 **5** *nk* **Masamah (IRE)**[15] 93 11-9-7 **70** (p) StevieDonohoe 5 73
(Ian Williams) *in tch in midfield: rdn 2f out: hdwy jst ins fnl f: r.o wl fnl 100yds: nvr gng to rch wnr* **16/1**

516- **6** *hd* **False Id**[184] 4563 4-9-5 **68**................ JackMitchell 7 70+
(Robert Eddery) *swtchd lft sn after s: hld up in tch in midfield: nt clr run ent fnl 2f: hdwy on inner 1f out: kpt on ins fnl f: nt rch ldrs* **9/1**

26-1 **7** *1* **Compton Prince**[10] 172 8-9-1 **64**................(b) LukeMorris 10 63
(Milton Bradley) *t.k.h: hld up in midfield: effrt 2f out: hdwy ent fnl f: kpt on u.p fnl 150yds: nvr trbld ldrs* **18/1**

020- **8** *nk* **Bush Warrior (IRE)**[30] 8495 6-9-8 **71**................(v) GeorgeBaker 4 69
(Anabel K Murphy) *led: rdn over 1f out: hdd 1f out: no ex: lost 2nd ins fnl f: wknd towards fin* **13/2**[3]

02-4 **9** *1 3/4* **Rigolleto (IRE)**[10] 172 9-8-11 **67**................(p) JoshuaBryan[(7)] 8 59
(Anabel K Murphy) *in tch in midfield: effrt and unable qck over 1f out: wknd ins fnl f* **16/1**

50-0 **10** *1* **Nora Batt (IRE)**[11] 159 4-8-11 **60**................ DanielMuscutt 1 49
(David Evans) *in tch in midfield: effrt towards inner over 1f out: unable qck and wknd ins fnl f* **50/1**

00-5 **11** *10* **Noble Deed**[14] 116 7-9-3 **66**................ JoeFanning 11 23
(Michael Attwater) *taken down early: wd and a rr: lost tch and eased over 1f out* **14/1**

1m 10.96s (-0.94) **Going Correction** -0.125s/f (Stan) **11** Ran SP% **114.4**
Speed ratings (Par 103): **101,99,99,99,98 98,97,96,94,93 79**
CSF £47.64 CT £197.26 TOTE £6.20: £1.70, £3.30, £2.10; EX 62.20 Trifecta £423.80.
**Owner** P C F Racing Ltd **Bred** D J And Mrs Deer **Trained** Hook, Hampshire

**FOCUS**
An ordinary sprint handicap and they finished in a heap behind the winner, who took another step forward. The first, third and fourth were always up there. The form is set around the runner-up and fourth.
T/Plt: £70.30 to a £1 stake. Pool: £91,027.20 - 944.81 winning units. T/Qpdt: £26.10 to a £1 stake. Pool: £6,924.62 - 196.05 winning units. **Steve Payne**

# [194]NEWCASTLE (A.W) (L-H)
Saturday, January 21

**OFFICIAL GOING: Tapeta: standard**
Wind: Almost nil

## 356 32RED.COM H'CAP 6f (Tp)
**5:45** (5:45) (Class 5) (0-75,77) 3-Y-O **£3,881** (£1,155; £577; £288) **Stalls** Centre

Form RPR

04-2 **1** **Marquee Club**[10] 178 3-9-9 **77**................ DougieCostello 5 80
(Jamie Osborne) *chsd ldng pair: pushed along and wnt 2nd over 2f out: clsd over 1f out: rdn and led ent fnl f: edgd lft: kpt on wl* **6/1**[3]

106- **2** *nk* **Red Gunner**[21] 8592 3-9-2 **75**................(p) GeorgiaCox[(5)] 1 77
(William Haggas) *hld up in last pl: pushed along over 2f out: edgd lft and hdwy over 1f out: chsd wnr ins fnl f: kpt on: hld nr fin* **6/1**[3]

42-1 **3** *1/2* **Golden Opportunity**[10] 178 3-9-7 **75**................ MartinHarley 3 75
(James Tate) *stdd in tch: t.k.h: smooth hdwy over 1f out: rdn and chsd wnr briefly ins fnl f: no ex towards fin* **11/10**[1]

400- **4** *nk* **Mama Africa (IRE)**[119] 6787 3-8-13 **67**................ AndrewMullen 4 66
(David Barron) *in tch: rdn and outpcd over 2f out: rallied fnl f: keeping on at fin: nt pce to chal* **8/1**

32-2 **5** *nk* **Sidewinder (IRE)**[8] 221 3-9-4 **72**................(v[1]) PaulMulrennan 6 71
(Tom Dascombe) *t.k.h: led: clr over 4f out to over 1f out: rdn and hdd ent fnl f: edgd lft and sn one pce* **7/2**[2]

50-0 **6** *2 1/2* **Monoshka (IRE)**[16] 78 3-9-3 **71**................ TomEaves 2 62
(James Given) *chsd clr ldr to over 2f out: sn rdn and outpcd: wknd ins fnl f* **28/1**

1m 13.04s (0.54) **Going Correction** +0.10s/f (Slow) **6** Ran SP% **113.0**
Speed ratings (Par 97): **100,99,98,98,98 94**
CSF £40.52 TOTE £5.50: £2.20, £2.90; EX 41.30 Trifecta £80.00.
**Owner** Melbourne 10 Racing **Bred** Norman Court Stud, P Taplin & McB Ltd **Trained** Upper Lambourn, Berks

**FOCUS**
An ordinary 3yo sprint handicap.

## 357 BETWAY BEST ODDS GUARANTEED PLUS MAIDEN STKS 5f (Tp)
**6:15** (6:16) (Class 5) 3-5-Y-O **£3,557** (£1,058; £529; £264) **Stalls** Centre

Form RPR

50- **1** **Scuzeme**[197] 4110 3-8-13 0................ PhillipMakin 6 75+
(David Barron) *t.k.h: hld up in tch: cruised through over 1f out: led on bit ent fnl f: shkn up briefly and qcknd clr last 100yds: readily* **7/4**[1]

3-4 **2** *3* **School Run (IRE)**[16] 76 3-8-8 0................ TomEaves 3 55
(David O'Meara) *pressed ldr: rdn to ld wl over 1f out: hdd ent fnl f: kpt on: no ch w ready wnr* **7/2**[2]

544- **3** *nk* **Absolutely Awesome**[26] 8526 3-8-13 64................ PaulMulrennan 5 59
(Scott Dixon) *prom: effrt and drvn along 2f out: kpt on same pce fnl f* **5/1**[3]

5- **4** *1 1/4* **Highly Focussed (IRE)**[36] 8406 3-8-13 0................ GrahamLee 2 55
(Ann Duffield) *t.k.h: trckd ldrs: shkn up over 1f out: outpcd ins fnl f* **15/2**

520- **5** *1* **Nefetari**[22] 8589 4-9-9 47................(b) BenCurtis 1 52
(Alan Brown) *led tl rdn and hdd wl over 1f out: sn outpcd* **33/1**

20-3 **6** *2 1/2* **Local Artist (IRE)**[10] 179 3-8-5 59................ NathanEvans[(3)] 7 37
(John Quinn) *hld up: pushed along over 2f out: drifted lft and wknd fnl f* **7/2**[2]

**7** *7* **Catskill** 3-8-3 0................ HollieDoyle[(5)] 4 12
(Wilf Storey) *s.i.s: rn green in rr: struggling after 2f: nvr on terms* **33/1**

59.18s (-0.32) **Going Correction** +0.10s/f (Slow)
**WFA** 3 from 4yo 15lb **7** Ran SP% **115.1**
Speed ratings (Par 103): **106,101,100,98,97 93,81**
CSF £8.26 TOTE £2.50: £1.80, £1.60; EX 10.10 Trifecta £48.20.
**Owner** Laurence O'Kane **Bred** R S Hoskins & Hermes Services **Trained** Maunby, N Yorks

**FOCUS**
A modest sprint maiden.

## 358 BETWAY BEST ODDS GUARANTEED PLUS H'CAP 5f (Tp)
**6:45** (6:45) (Class 4) (0-85,85) 4-Y-O+ **£5,175** (£1,540; £769; £384) **Stalls** Centre

Form RPR

15-2 **1** **Poppy In The Wind**[17] 45 5-8-2 **71** oh1................(v) HollieDoyle[(5)] 8 79
(Alan Brown) *cl up: carried rt over 3f out: sn tacked over bk to centre: led and rdn over 1f out: hld on wl towards fin* **11/4**[1]

0-50 **2** *hd* **Fredricka**[9] 194 6-8-7 **71**................ AndrewMullen 4 78
(David Barron) *hld up: pushed along and hdwy over 1f out: wnt 2nd wl ins fnl f: kpt on wl: jst hld* **8/1**

02-0 **3** *3/4* **Foxy Forever (IRE)**[16] 79 7-9-2 **80**................(t) ConnorBeasley 1 84
(Michael Wigham) *t.k.h: hld up: hdwy to trck ldrs over 1f out: sn rdn: wnt 2nd briefly ins fnl f: edgd lft: no ex nr fin* **10/3**[2]

414- **4** *3/4* **Dynamo Walt (IRE)**[31] 8484 6-9-3 **84**................(v) NoelGarbutt[(3)] 5 86
(Derek Shaw) *t.k.h: trckd ldrs: effrt and rdn over 1f out: kpt on same pce ins fnl f* **9/2**[3]

616- **5** *1/2* **Bold**[23] 8571 5-8-9 **73**................(vt) BenCurtis 2 73
(Stuart Williams) *pressed ldr: ev ch over 2f out to over 1f out: drvn and no ex ins fnl f* **9/2**[3]

60-0 **6** *1 1/4* **Ballesteros**[7] 234 8-9-1 **79**................ TonyHamilton 3 74
(Richard Fahey) *led at ordinary gallop: rdn and hdd over 1f out: outpcd ins fnl f* **16/1**

20-5 **7** *shd* **Salvatore Fury (IRE)**[18] 33 7-9-3 **81**................(p) PhillipMakin 7 76
(Keith Dalgleish) *lost nr-side cheekpiece leaving stalls: hld up in tch: pushed along and effrt over 1f out: no imp fnl f* **16/1**

01-4 **8** *1 3/4* **Silvanus (IRE)**[16] 79 12-9-7 **85**................ DougieCostello 6 74
(Paul Midgley) *taken early to post: t.k.h: swtchd to stands' rail over 3f out: effrt and drvn over 2f out: edgd lft and wknd over 1f out* **16/1**

59.65s (0.15) **Going Correction** +0.10s/f (Slow) **8** Ran SP% **114.9**
Speed ratings (Par 105): **102,101,100,99,98 96,96,93**
CSF £25.55 CT £75.91 TOTE £3.90: £1.60, £2.50, £1.60; EX 31.40 Trifecta £131.90.
**Owner** Mrs M Doherty & Mrs W A D Craven **Bred** P Balding **Trained** Yedingham, N Yorks
■ Stewards' Enquiry : Hollie Doyle caution; careless riding

**FOCUS**
They didn't look to go that quick early and some of these raced keenly.

## 359 SUNBETS.CO.UK H'CAP 1m 5y (Tp)
**7:15** (7:16) (Class 4) (0-80,82) 4-Y-O+ **£5,175** (£1,540; £769; £384) **Stalls** Centre

Form RPR

156- **1** **Eastern Dragon (IRE)**[57] 8092 7-8-10 **76**................(p) CallumRodriguez[(7)] 12 84
(Iain Jardine) *dwlt: hld up: hdwy nr side of gp over 2f out: led wl ins fnl f: kpt on wl* **16/1**

56-1 **2** *3/4* **Rock Warbler (IRE)**[17] 44 4-9-0 **73**................(t) KevinStott 5 79+
(Oliver Greenall) *stdd s: hld up: hdwy to ld over 1f out: sn rdn: hdd wl ins fnl f: kpt on* **4/1**[1]

620- **3** *1* **Warfare**[147] 5883 8-9-2 **75**................ BarryMcHugh 10 79
(Tim Fitzgerald) *hld up: angled to nr side of gp and gd hdwy over 1f out: kpt on wl fnl f: nrst fin* **40/1**

31-1 **4** *nk* **Testa Rossa (IRE)**[17] 43 7-9-4 **80**................(b) GeorgeDowning[(3)] 8 83
(Jim Goldie) *hld up: hdwy whn n.m.r over 2f out: swtchd lft and n.m.r over 1f out: kpt on wl fnl f: nvr nrr* **5/1**[2]

50-5 **5** *shd* **So It's War (FR)**[20] 6 6-8-5 **69**................(v[1]) ShirleyTeasdale[(5)] 13 72
(Keith Dalgleish) *t.k.h: hld up: hdwy on nr side of gp and led briefly over 1f out: sn rdn and edgd lft: no ex ins fnl f* **16/1**

1-2 **6** *1* **Roller**[18] 32 4-9-2 **78**................ NathanEvans[(3)] 9 79+
(Michael Easterby) *t.k.h: cl up: hdwy to ld over 2f out: hdd over 1f out: rdn and outpcd ins fnl f* **4/1**[1]

05-4 **7** *1/2* **Polar Forest**[17] 42 7-8-13 **72**................(e) DougieCostello 7 72
(Richard Guest) *hld up in tch: effrt and drvn over 2f out: kpt on same pce fr over 1f out* **33/1**

222- **8** *3/4* **Cadeau Magnifique**[30] 8498 5-9-1 **74**................(p) TonyHamilton 14 72
(Richard Fahey) *hld up in tch on nr side of gp: rdn over 2f out: edgd lft and no imp over 1f out* **5/1**[2]

360- **9** *1/2* **Ansaab**[34] 8446 9-9-6 **79**................(tp) BenCurtis 3 76
(Marjorie Fife) *hld up on far side of gp: rdn and effrt over 2f out: no imp fr over 1f out* **25/1**

065- **10** *1/2* **Zain Emperor (IRE)**[34] 8446 4-9-4 **77**................ GrahamLee 11 73
(John Butler) *hld up towards rr: pushed along fr over 2f out: no imp over 1f out* **7/1**[3]

526- **11** *shd* **Eurystheus (IRE)**[45] 8249 8-9-1 **77**................(tp) AlistairRawlinson[(3)] 2 72
(Michael Appleby) *trckd ldrs on far side of gp: rdn over 2f out: wknd over 1f out* **16/1**

0-62 **12** *1 1/4* **Showboating (IRE)**[11] 156 9-9-2 **82**................ LewisEdmunds[(7)] 6 74
(John Balding) *prom: rdn over 2f out: wknd wl over 1f out* **11/1**

000- **13** *2* **Kiwi Bay**[43] 8286 12-8-10 **69**................ ConnorBeasley 4 57
(Michael Dods) *led to over 2f out: sn rdn and lost pl* **66/1**

/30- **14** *99* **Like A Diamond (IRE)**[18] 5033 7-9-0 **80**................(b) BenRobinson[(7)] 1
(Brian Ellison) *t.k.h: trckd ldr to over 2f out: sn lost pl qckly: btn and eased fr over 1f out: b.b.v* **50/1**

1m 38.73s (0.13) **Going Correction** +0.10s/f (Slow) **14** Ran SP% **124.5**
Speed ratings (Par 105): **103,102,101,100,100 99,99,98,98,97 97,96,94,**
CSF £79.31 CT £2668.59 TOTE £20.40: £4.90, £1.90, £11.50; EX 114.40 Trifecta £6923.10.
**Owner** George Brian Davidson **Bred** James Mahon **Trained** Carrutherstown, D'fries & G'way

**FOCUS**
A fair and competitive handicap.

## 360 SUN BETS ON THE APP STORE H'CAP (DIV I) 1m 5y (Tp)
**7:45** (7:45) (Class 6) (0-65,67) 4-Y-O+ **£2,587** (£770; £384; £192) **Stalls** Centre

Form RPR

44-2 **1** **Orlando Rogue (IRE)**[17] 44 5-8-12 **56**................(v) ConnorBeasley 2 65
(Keith Dalgleish) *cl up: led over 3f out: shkn up and led over 1f out: pressed ins fnl f: edgd rt: hld on wl towards fin* **13/2**[3]

321- **2** *1/2* **Swansway**[22] 8587 4-9-0 **61**................ NathanEvans[(3)] 11 69+
(Michael Easterby) *hld up in last pl: pushed along over 2f out: hdwy and angled rt over 1f out: chsd wnr ins fnl f: kpt on same pce towards fin* **6/4**[1]

001- **3** *3/4* **Star Of Spring (IRE)**[42] 8306 5-9-9 **67**................(h) PJMcDonald 8 73
(Iain Jardine) *hld up: rdn and hdwy over 1f out: kpt on ins fnl f* **9/2**[2]

144- **4** *2* **Mr Potter**[22] 8589 4-8-10 **54**................(e) AndrewMullen 6 56
(Richard Guest) *t.k.h: stdd in tch: rdn along and effrt 2f out: kpt on same pce ins fnl f* **12/1**

01-0 **5** *nse* **The Magic Pencil (IRE)**[11] 166 4-9-7 **65**................(p) TomEaves 5 67
(Kevin Ryan) *led at ordinary gallop: rdn and hdd over 1f out: edgd lft and one pce ins fnl f* **12/1**

06-2 **6** *1/2* **Pool House**[17] 49 6-9-8 **66**................ GrahamLee 10 67
(Mike Murphy) *hld up in tch on nr side of gp: rdn and effrt over 2f out: outpcd fnl f* **20/1**

00-5 **7** *3/4* **Bell Heather (IRE)**[11] 152 4-9-6 **64**................ TonyHamilton 1 63
(Richard Fahey) *t.k.h early: prom on outside: rdn and edgd lft over 1f out: sn outpcd* **8/1**

340- **8** *3/4* **Dominannie (IRE)**[22] 8587 4-9-4 **62**................ BenCurtis 3 59
(Alan Swinbank) *t.k.h: hld up in tch: effrt and pushed along 2f out: wknd fnl f* **33/1**

402- **9** *1* **Bromance**[22] 8587 4-8-11 **55**................(p) JamesSullivan 9 50
(Peter Niven) *t.k.h: hld up: rdn over 2f out: wknd over 1f out* **9/2**[2]

00-0 **10** *6* **Royal Acclaim (IRE)**[14] 124 5-7-9 **46** oh1................ RPWalsh[(7)] 7 28
(Rebecca Bastiman) *chsd ldr to over 3f out: rdn and wknd over 2f out* **80/1**

1m 40.11s (1.51) **Going Correction** +0.10s/f (Slow) **10** Ran SP% **125.1**
Speed ratings (Par 101): **96,95,94,92,92 92,91,90,89,83**
CSF £17.72 CT £53.77 TOTE £7.00: £1.90, £1.50, £1.80; EX 25.70 Trifecta £93.30.

**Owner** Equus I **Bred** Barbara Prendergast **Trained** Carluke, S Lanarks

**FOCUS**

The first leg of a modest handicap. The winner has been rated near the best of his 2016 form, and the second and third have been rated a bit higher in line with expectations.

## 361 SUN BETS ON THE APP STORE H'CAP (DIV II) 1m 5y (Tp)

**8:15** (8:15) (Class 6) (0-65,66) 4-Y-0+ **£2,587** (£770; £384; £192) **Stalls** Centre

Form RPR

602- **1** **Pickett's Charge**[22] 8586 4-9-8 **66** ........ DanielTudhope 1 75
(Richard Guest) *prom: smooth hdwy over 2f out: rdn to ld ins fnl f: kpt on strly* **3/1**[1]

550- **2** 2 ¾ **Broctune Papa Gio**[22] 8587 10-8-7 **58** ........ (b[1]) LewisEdmunds[(7)] 5 61
(Keith Reveley) *trckd ldrs: rdn and outpcd wl over 1f out: rallied and chsd wnr wl ins fnl f: kpt on* **13/2**

560- **3** hd **Chiswick Bey (IRE)**[26] 8531 9-9-7 **65** ........ TonyHamilton 10 68
(Richard Fahey) *hld up: pushed along over 2f out: gd hdwy over 1f out: kpt on fnl f: nrst fin* **11/2**

003- **4** ¾ **Foolaad**[22] 8587 6-8-13 **64** ........ (t) KevinLundie[(7)] 8 65
(Roy Bowring) *taken early to post: led: rdn over 2f out: hdd ins fnl f: no ex and lost two pls last 50yds* **10/3**[2]

000- **5** 4 **Tsarglas**[194] 4214 6-8-2 **46** oh1 ........ (t) JamesSullivan 6 38
(Christopher Wilson) *in tch: drvn along over 2f out: no imp fr over 1f out* **66/1**

125- **6** nk **Lozah**[22] 8588 4-8-13 **64** ........ BenSanderson[(7)] 7 55
(Roger Fell) *dwlt: hld up and bhd: pushed along over 2f out: hdwy over 1f out: no imp fnl f* **4/1**[3]

20-4 **7** 6 **Catastrophe**[16] 68 4-9-2 **60** ........ JasonHart 2 38
(John Quinn) *in tch: pushed along over 2f out: wknd fr over 1f out* **10/1**

10-5 **8** ½ **Celtic Artisan (IRE)**[12] 147 6-8-11 **55** ........ (bt) DougieCostello 3 32
(Rebecca Menzies) *pressed ldr to over 2f out: rdn and wknd over 1f out* **14/1**

540/ **9** 3 ¼ **Pixie Cut (IRE)**[509] 5686 7-8-5 **54** ........ RowanScott[(5)] 4 24
(Alistair Whillans) *hld up towards rr: pushed along over 3f out: wknd fr 2f out* **40/1**

326- **10** 13 **Who's Shirl**[22] 8588 11-8-11 **55** ........ TomEaves 9
(Chris Fairhurst) *dwlt: hld up: rdn and struggling over 3f out: sn btn* **28/1**

1m 38.96s (0.36) **Going Correction** +0.10s/f (Slow) 10 Ran SP% **119.9**
Speed ratings (Par 101): **102,99,99,98,94 94,88,87,84,71**
CSF £23.58 CT £106.93 TOTE £4.20: £1.40, £2.50, £2.30; EX 26.70 Trifecta £154.40.
**Owner** Cool Racing 2 **Bred** Stratford Place Stud **Trained** Ingmanthorpe, W Yorks

**FOCUS**

Few got seriously involved in this second division. A minor pb from the winner, with the runner-up rated close to his very recent best.

## 362 BETWAY H'CAP 6f (Tp)

**8:45** (8:48) (Class 6) (0-60,61) 4-Y-0+ **£2,587** (£770; £384; £192) **Stalls** Centre

Form RPR

022- **1** **First Excel**[165] 5270 5-8-9 **55** ........ (b) KevinLundie[(7)] 14 65
(Roy Bowring) *hld up on nr side of gp: hdwy to ld 2f out: rdn and r.o wl fnl f* **7/1**

565- **2** 1 **Spirit Of Zebedee (IRE)**[75] 7852 4-9-6 **59** ........ (p) JasonHart 13 66
(John Quinn) *in tch on nr side of gp: rdn and chsd wnr wl over 1f out: kpt on ins fnl f* **11/2**[3]

66-0 **3** 2 ¼ **Pushkin Museum (IRE)**[16] 80 6-9-2 **55** ........ GrahamLee 8 55
(Patrick Morris) *in tch: smooth hdwy over 2f out: effrt and rdn over 1f out: one pce fnl f* **9/1**

440- **4** ½ **Diamond Indulgence**[23] 8570 4-8-8 **50** ........ (h) NoelGarbutt[(3)] 7 49
(Derek Shaw) *hld up: rdn over 2f out: gd hdwy over 1f out: r.o wl: nrst fin* **33/1**

33-0 **5** 1 ½ **Thorntoun Lady (USA)**[17] 45 7-9-7 **60** ........ JamesSullivan 6 54
(Jim Goldie) *s.i.s: bhd: struggling over 3f out: styd on wl fnl f: nrst fin* **8/1**

600/ **6** nse **Beau Amadeus (IRE)**[453] 7514 8-9-2 **55** ........ JoeyHaynes 3 49
(Susan Corbett) *cl up: rdn over 2f out: outpcd over 1f out* **50/1**

043- **7** 4 ½ **Windforpower (IRE)**[31] 8485 7-9-3 **56** ........ (p) DaleSwift 12 37
(Tracy Waggott) *t.k.h: towards rr: pushed along and edgd lft over 2f out: sn no imp* **20/1**

4-50 **8** 1 ¾ **Men United (FR)**[11] 153 4-8-11 **50** ........ (be) AndrewMullen 4 25
(Garry Moss) *trckd ldrs: rdn and wknd over 1f out* **20/1**

00-6 **9** ½ **Intense Starlet (IRE)**[11] 158 6-9-5 **58** ........ (p) SamJames 11 32
(Marjorie Fife) *towards rr: rdn over 2f out: sn no imp* **14/1**

130- **10** shd **Mr Conundrum**[25] 8542 4-8-12 **51** ........ PaddyAspell 2 25
(Lynn Siddall) *bhd on far side of gp: outpcd over 2f out: n.d after* **33/1**

54-4 **11** nk **Letbygonesbeicons**[19] 20 4-8-10 **56** ........ LewisEdmunds[(7)] 1 29
(John Balding) *led on far side of gp to 2f out: sn wknd* **5/1**[2]

4-42 **12** 3 ¼ **Harmonic Wave (IRE)**[8] 216 4-9-8 **61** ........ (p) PJMcDonald 10 24
(Rebecca Menzies) *prom: drvn along over 2f out: wknd wl over 1f out* **7/2**[1]

000- **13** 3 ¼ **Misu Mac**[68] 7961 7-8-9 **55** ........ BenRobinson[(7)] 5 8
(Neville Bycroft) *sn pushed along towards rr: struggling over 2f out: sn btn* **6/1**

1m 12.6s (0.10) **Going Correction** +0.10s/f (Slow) 13 Ran SP% **126.2**
Speed ratings (Par 101): **103,101,98,98,96 95,89,87,86,86 86,82,77**
CSF £45.24 CT £364.40 TOTE £8.60: £2.30, £2.30, £3.40; EX 54.20 Trifecta £540.00.
**Owner** S R Bowring **Bred** S R Bowring **Trained** Edwinstowe, Notts

**FOCUS**

A moderate sprint handicap. The top two stalls produced the first two finishers. It's possible the form is a bit better than rated.

## 363 SUN BETS BET £10 GET £20 FREE APPRENTICE H'CAP 7f 14y (Tp)

**9:15** (9:16) (Class 5) (0-75,75) 4-Y-0+ **£2,911** (£866; £432; £216) **Stalls** Centre

Form RPR

1U5- **1** **Safe Voyage (IRE)**[118] 6810 4-9-2 **75** ........ JoshQuinn[(5)] 10 86
(John Quinn) *hld up nr side of gp: hdwy over 2f out: rdn to ld ins fnl f: edgd lft last 100yds: kpt on wl* **11/2**[2]

10-4 **2** 2 **Ticks The Boxes (IRE)**[11] 152 5-9-7 **75** ........ (p) JordanVaughan 11 80
(Michael Herrington) *taken early to post: prom on nr side of gp: hdwy to ld over 2f out: hdd ins fnl f: kpt on same pce* **8/1**[3]

210- **3** 1 ¼ **Curzon Line**[30] 8487 8-9-7 **75** ........ NathanEvans 12 77
(Michael Easterby) *cl up in centre: effrt and chal over 2f out to over 1f out: edgd lft and one pce ins fnl f* **7/2**[1]

44-0 **4** 1 **Wahaab (IRE)**[17] 44 6-8-8 **65** ........ (p) CallumRodriguez[(3)] 5 64
(Iain Jardine) *hld up on far side of gp: rdn over 2f out: hdwy over 1f out: kpt on same pce ins fnl f* **11/2**[2]

410- **5** ½ **Win Lose Draw (IRE)**[49] 8207 5-8-12 **66** ........ (p) AlistairRawlinson 8 64
(Michael Appleby) *trckd ldrs in centre: drvn along over 2f out: edgd lft and one pce fr over 1f out* **9/1**

06-3 **6** nk **Jubilee Brig**[18] 32 7-9-0 **71** ........ PatrickVaughan[(3)] 6 68
(Alan Swinbank) *hld up on nr side of gp: rdn and outpcd over 2f out: rallied fnl f: nt pce to chal* **8/1**[3]

/0-0 **7** ¾ **Restive (IRE)**[11] 156 4-8-11 **72** ........ JamieGormley[(7)] 1 67
(Iain Jardine) *hld up on far side of gp: outpcd over 2f out: hdwy fnl f: nrst fin* **9/1**

152- **8** ¾ **The Tichborne (IRE)**[50] 8191 9-8-13 **67** ........ (v) JoshDoyle 2 60
(Patrick Morris) *t.k.h early: in tch on far side of gp: rdn and effrt over 2f out: wknd appr fnl f* **14/1**

660- **9** ¾ **Argaki (IRE)**[43] 8286 7-8-7 **68** ........ CharlotteMcFarland[(7)] 3 59
(Keith Dalgleish) *led in centre to over 2f out: wknd appr fnl f* **16/1**

26-6 **10** ½ **Green Howard**[14] 122 9-9-1 **72** ........ RowanScott[(3)] 4 61
(Rebecca Bastiman) *hld up towards rr in centre: hdwy over 2f out: wknd fnl f* **9/1**

050- **11** ½ **Jess**[37] 8389 4-8-6 **63** ........ (p) LewisEdmunds[(3)] 7 51
(Kevin Ryan) *towards rr in centre: drvn along over 2f out: edgd lft and wknd over 1f out* **25/1**

506- **12** 7 **Order Of Service**[164] 5291 7-9-4 **72** ........ (t) CharlieBennett 13 41
(Shaun Harris) *taken early to post: missed break: bhd: struggling 1/2-way: sn btn* **20/1**

1m 26.61s (0.41) **Going Correction** +0.10s/f (Slow) 12 Ran SP% **126.4**
Speed ratings (Par 103): **101,98,97,96,95 95,94,93,92,92 91,83**
CSF £52.73 CT £163.23 TOTE £6.70: £3.10, £3.50, £1.20; EX 62.90 Trifecta £254.50.
**Owner** Ross Harmon **Bred** Schneider Adolf **Trained** Settrington, N Yorks
■ Stewards' Enquiry : Alistair Rawlinson two-day ban; used whip over the permitted level (4th,6th Feb)

**FOCUS**

Like in the preceding race, the main action unfolded near side - the first three were drawn 10, 11, 12.

T/Plt: £140.10 to a £1 stake. Pool: £111,358.11 - 579.92 winning units. T/Qpdt: £15.80 to a £1 stake. Pool: £12,576.39 - 585.39 winning units. **Richard Young**

# CAGNES-SUR-MER

Saturday, January 21

**OFFICIAL GOING: Polytrack: standard**

## 364a PRIX DE LA GAUDE (H'CAP) (5YO+) (POLYTRACK) 1m 4f

**3:30** 5-Y-0+ **£7,264** (£2,905; £2,179; £1,452; £726)

RPR

**1** **Varing (FR)**[16] 7-9-5 **0** ........ (p) Pierre-CharlesBoudot 11 62
(M Cesandri, France) **13/5**[1]

**2** ¾ **Grand Gala (FR)**[291] 6-9-4 **0** ........ (b) FranckBlondel 7 60
(S Labate, France) **11/2**[2]

**3** ½ **Desert Dune (FR)**[294] 5-9-1 **0** ........ (p) EddyHardouin 8 56
(Y Fertillet, France) **137/10**

**4** hd **Arizona Run (FR)**[624] 2063 9-9-3 **0** ........ (p) TheoBachelot 12 58
(C Scandella, France) **119/10**

**5** nk **Monika Jem (FR)**[16] 6-9-2 **0** ........ (p) AntoineHamelin 3 56
(S Jesus, France) **29/1**

**6** 1 **Veneziano (FR)**[53] 8-9-1 **0** ........ RonanThomas 5 54
(Robert Collet, France) **182/10**

**7** shd **Stracciatella (IRE)**[369] 7-8-7 **0** ........ MickaelForest 6 45
(P Nador, France) **49/1**

**8** hd **Le Grand Voyage (FR)**[384] 8-9-2 **0** ........ Roberto-CarlosMontenegro 15 54
(E Daure, France) **185/10**

**9** 3 **Devil's Eye (IRE)**[99] 5-9-6 **0** ........ GabrieleCongiu 4 53
(Mlle L-L Rohn-Pelvin, France) **11/2**[2]

**10** 4 **Uphold**[36] 8421 10-9-4 **0** ........ (b) MaximeGuyon 10 45
(Gay Kelleway) *trckd ldr outside rival: jnd ldr 3f out: led wl over 2f out: rdn and hdd over 1 1/2f out: hld whn eased ins fnl f* **11/1**

**11** 1 ¼ **Slon He**[19] 5-9-5 **0** ........ (p) TonyPiccone 14 44
(E Dell'Ova, France) **49/1**

**12** 2 ½ **Zafora (IRE)** 9-9-5 **0** ........ (p) Jean-BernardEyquem 1 40
(S Labate, France) **87/1**

**13** shd **White Light (FR)**[417] 6-9-4 **0** ........ RaphaelMarchelli 2 39
(J-M Capitte, France) **52/1**

**14** 1 **Boker Mazal (FR)**[283] 6-9-4 **0** ........ (p) FranckForesi 9 37
(F Foresi, France) **79/1**

**15** 4 **Crescendo Forte (FR)**[265] 8-9-6 **0** ........ (p) FabriceVeron 16 33
(F Foresi, France) **178/10**

**16** dist **Trois Points (FR)**[36] 8422 5-9-2 **0** ........ ThomasHuet 13
(Gay Kelleway) *settled in midfield on outer early: rapid prog to chse ldng trio after 2f: 4th and pushed along 2 1/2f out: sn rdn and btn: eased ins fnl 1 1/2f: t.o* **102/10**[3]

PARI-MUTUEL (all including 1 euro stake): WIN 3.60; PLACE 1.70, 2.10, 3.70; DF 9.00; SF 12.80.
**Owner** M Bouly, A Hebbali & Mme H Manier **Bred** C Baudouin, J Baudouin, MME J Cygler **Trained** France

365 - 375a (Foreign Racing) - See Raceform Interactive

# 329 WOLVERHAMPTON (A.W) (L-H)

Monday, January 23

**OFFICIAL GOING: Tapeta: standard**

Wind: light, behind Weather: light cloud, dry

## 376 £10 FREE AT 32RED.COM H'CAP (DIV I) 7f 36y (Tp)

**2:00** (2:01) (Class 6) (0-55,57) 3-Y-O **£2,264** (£673; £336; £168) **Stalls** High

Form RPR

000- **1** **American Patrol (IRE)**[46] 8276 3-9-7 **55** ........ AdamKirby 5 63+
(Neil Mulholland) *trckd ldrs. swtchd rt and effrt in 3rd 2f out: rdn to ld ent fnl f: styd on and gng away towards fin* **11/10**[1]

005- **2** 2 **Hazell Berry (IRE)**[74] 7881 3-8-12 **46** oh1 ........ (b[1]) AndrewMullen 2 47
(David Evans) *broke fast: sn hdd and chsd ldrs: rdn to chal 2f out: led over 1f out: sn hdd and styd on same pce ins fnl f* **20/1**

44-3 **3** 1 **Metronomic (IRE)**[14] 139 3-9-9 **57** ........ (p) KieranO'Neill 3 56
(Richard Hannon) *t.k.h: hld up in tch in midfield: effrt over 2f out: chsd ldng pair ent fnl f: styd on same pce u.p ins fnl f* **5/2**[2]

04-5 **4** 3 **Fairy Lock (IRE)**[18] 73 3-9-4 **52** ........ PJMcDonald 9 46+
(David Barron) *short of room leaving stalls and sn swtchd rt: hld up towards rr: hdwy and hung lft over 1f out: swtchd rt 1f out: styd on but no threat to ldrs* **7/1**[3]

00-0 **5** 3/4 **Arya Stark**[18] 76 3-9-4 **55**........ GeorgeDowning(3) 7 44
(Tony Carroll) *hld up in midfield: rdn 3f out: sme hdwy on inner over 1f out: kpt on ins fnl f: no threat to ldrs* **50/1**

00-4 **6** 3/4 **Tranquil Tracy**[9] 245 3-8-13 **47**........ PaddyAspell 11 35
(John Norton) *taken down early: in tch in midfield: effrt over 2f out: unable qck and outpcd 2f out: wknd fnl f* **33/1**

6-5 **7** 1 **Tanksalot (IRE)**[16] 126 3-9-2 **50**........(v1) MartinHarley 6 35
(Harry Dunlop) *sn bustled along to ld: rdn and hrd pressed 2f out: hdd over 1f out: 4th and btn 1f out: wknd fnl f* **11/1**

000- **8** 3 3/4 **Valley Lodge**[25] 8568 3-9-1 **52**........(p) ShelleyBirkett(3) 4 28
(Julia Feilden) *sn dropped to rr: rdn over 3f out: drifted rt and kpt on ins fnl f: n.d* **25/1**

600- **9** 1/2 **Son Castello (IRE)**[138] 6236 3-8-12 **46** oh1........ ShaneKelly 1 21
(Gary Moore) *a towards rr: rdn and struggling over 2f out: wl hld and drifted rt fnl f* **25/1**

30-0 **10** 3 **Zaatar (IRE)**[18] 77 3-9-6 **54**........ GeorgeBaker 10 21
(Mick Channon) *chsd ldr 6f out tl over 2f out: sn btn: wknd over 1f out* **40/1**

000- **11** 7 **Paco Dawn**[69] 7963 3-9-0 **48**........ TomEaves 8
(Philip Hide) *a towards rr: wd and struggling u.p over 2f out: bhd over 1f out* **100/1**

1m 27.47s (-1.33) **Going Correction** -0.10s/f (Stan) 11 Ran SP% **117.8**
Speed ratings (Par 95): **103,100,99,96,95 94,93,89,88,85 77**
CSF £30.94 CT £51.07 TOTE £1.90: £1.10, £3.90, £1.20; EX 24.60 Trifecta £79.20.
**Owner** American Patrol Partnership **Bred** Con Marnane **Trained** Limpley Stoke, Wilts

**FOCUS**
The track was harrowed and left open after the fixture on the 20th, then reinstated with a Gallop Master finish. Adam Kirby said of the surface after the first: "It's not great out there as it seems to get quicker in the cold weather." Effectively this was just a maiden handicap, notable for the gamble landed by the winner, from whom there is more to come at a low level. It was the quicker division by nearly a second.

## 377 £10 FREE AT 32RED.COM H'CAP (DIV II) 7f 36y (Tp)
**2:30** (2:31) (Class 6) (0-55,56) 3-Y-O **£2,264** (£673; £336; £168) **Stalls** High

Form RPR

502- **1** **Beepeecee**[65] 8025 3-9-4 **52**........(p) ShaneKelly 1 58
(Richard Hughes) *hld up in tch in midfield: pushed along to cl 2f out: led 1f out: hung rt but drew clr fnl f: readily* **7/2**[2]

053- **2** 3 1/2 **Auric Goldfinger (IRE)**[46] 8276 3-9-3 **56**........(b) HollieDoyle(5) 6 53
(Richard Hannon) *t.k.h: hld up wl in tch in midfield: clsd to trck ldrs over 2f out: effrt over 1f out: styd on same pce ins fnl f: wnt 2nd towards fin* **10/3**[1]

600- **3** 1/2 **Bartholomew J (IRE)**[149] 5876 3-8-9 **46**........(v1) SimonPearce(3) 10 42
(Lydia Pearce) *stdd after s: t.k.h: hld up in last pair: effrt over 1f out: hdwy and swtchd rt ins fnl f: styd on wl to snatch 3rd cl home: no threat to wnr* **50/1**

20-0 **4** 1/2 **Viola Park**[17] 89 3-9-2 **50**........(p1) RyanPowell 5 45
(Ronald Harris) *led: hung rt bnd over 2f out: hung rt again over 1f out: hdd 1f out: styd on same pce after: lost 2 pls towards fin* **13/2**

50-4 **5** nk **Tigerfish (IRE)**[10] 210 3-8-12 **46** oh1........(p) KieranO'Neill 4 40
(William Stone) *dropped to rr sn after s: hld up in last pair: effrt and hung lft over 1f out: hdwy u.p 1f out: styd on: no threat to wnr* **15/2**

650- **6** 1 1/2 **Everkyllachy (IRE)**[45] 8284 3-9-2 **55**........(b) LuluStanford(5) 8 45
(J S Moore) *racd keenly: pressed ldr: carried rt over 2f out: rdn and ev ch 2f out tl unable qck 1f out: wknd ins fnl f* **14/1**

36-0 **7** 1/2 **Our Boy John (IRE)**[14] 149 3-9-4 **52**........ TonyHamilton 11 41
(Richard Fahey) *in tch in midfield: rdn over 2f out and sn outpcd: rallied 1f out: kpt on ins fnl f: no threat to ldrs* **12/1**

406- **8** 2 **Panther In Pink (IRE)**[38] 8406 3-9-2 **55**........ RowanScott(5) 3 39
(Ann Duffield) *in tch towards rr: effrt on inner over 2f out: no imp over 1f out: wknd ins fnl f* **25/1**

4-05 **9** 1 1/2 **Trust The Indian**[9] 245 3-8-10 **47**........(v1) JordanVaughan(3) 7 27
(Bill Turner) *chsd ldr: rdn over 2f out: sn struggling: wknd over 1f out* **12/1**

30-3 **10** 3 **Poppy May (IRE)**[16] 126 3-9-3 **51**........ TomEaves 2 24
(James Given) *chsd ldrs tl over 2f out: sn lost pl: bhd ins fnl f* **6/1**[3]

000- **11** 1/2 **Demi's Quest**[117] 6867 3-8-9 **46** oh1........ GeorgeDowning(3) 9 18
(Tony Carroll) *hld up in last trio: effrt whn carried lft and hmpd over 1f out: bhd fnl f* **100/1**

1m 28.41s (-0.39) **Going Correction** -0.10s/f (Stan) 11 Ran SP% **113.5**
Speed ratings (Par 95): **98,94,93,92,92 90,90,87,86,82 82**
CSF £14.78 CT £490.02 TOTE £3.70: £1.70, £1.60, £8.90; EX 12.40 Trifecta £679.90.
**Owner** BPC Partnership **Bred** Equine Origin Ltd **Trained** Upper Lambourn, Berks

**FOCUS**
The slower division by just under a second, but possibly a bit more to come from the winner.

## 378 32RED CASINO MAIDEN AUCTION STKS 1m 1f 104y (Tp)
**3:00** (3:03) (Class 5) 3-Y-O **£2,911** (£866; £432; £216) **Stalls** Low

Form RPR

44-3 **1** **Good Time Ahead (IRE)**[14] 149 3-9-5 59........ PaddyAspell 6 67
(Philip Kirby) *chsd ldr tl rdn to ld jst over 2f out: kpt on wl ins fnl f: rdn out* **9/1**

50-5 **2** 2 1/4 **The Last Debutante**[17] 100 3-9-0 65........ PJMcDonald 3 57
(Mark Johnston) *rousted along leaving stalls: chsd ldrs: rdn to chse wnr 2f out: unable qck u.p 1f out and one pced fnl f* **11/10**[1]

6-6 **3** 1 3/4 **Baby Helmet**[19] 48 3-9-5 0........ GeorgeBaker 2 59
(Mick Channon) *t.k.h: hld up in tch: clsd and swtchd rt over 1f out: 3rd and kpt on same pce ins fnl f* **6/1**

0 **4** 4 1/2 **Damo**[9] 237 3-9-5 0........ AdamKirby 4 49
(Simon Dow) *chsd lading trio: rdn ent fnl 2f: outpcd and btn over 1f out: wknd fnl f* **5/1**[3]

445- **5** 3 **Charlie Rascal (FR)**[25] 8568 3-9-5 62........ RichardKingscote 1 43
(Peter Chapple-Hyam) *led: hdd and rdn jst over 2f out: wknd over 1f out* **7/2**[2]

00 **6** 13 **What's Up Walter**[14] 150 3-9-5 0........ DougieCostello 7 16
(Philip Kirby) *in tch: rdn over 3f out: struggling over 2f out: lost tch over 1f out* **200/1**

4- **7** 60 **Rupertcambellblack (IRE)**[150] 5828 3-9-5 0........ RyanPowell 5
(Ronald Harris) *uns rdr bef s: s.i.s: rn green in rr: lost tch 5f out: t.o* **66/1**

2m 0.24s (-0.56) **Going Correction** -0.10s/f (Stan) 7 Ran SP% **112.8**
Speed ratings (Par 97): **98,96,94,90,87 76,22**
CSF £18.93 TOTE £7.50: £2.90, £1.40; EX 18.90 Trifecta £67.20.
**Owner** P Kirby **Bred** Mrs M Dowdall Blake **Trained** East Appleton, N Yorks

**FOCUS**
Modest maiden form and hard to be confident over its value.

## 379 32RED.COM H'CAP 5f 21y (Tp)
**3:30** (3:31) (Class 4) (0-85,86) 3-Y-O **£4,690** (£1,395; £697) **Stalls** Low

Form RPR

41-2 **1** **Cajmere**[19] 41 3-9-7 **75**........ RichardKingscote 1 78
(Tom Dascombe) *mde all: shkn up over 1f out: rdn 1f out: asserted ins fnl f: styd on: rdn out* **4/7**[1]

01-4 **2** 1 **Street Jazz**[9] 243 3-8-12 **66**........(b) TomEaves 2 65
(James Given) *chsd wnr tl dropped to 3rd and pushed along over 3f out: rdn 2f out: kpt on u.p ins fnl f: wnt 2nd nr fin: nvr threatening wnr* **9/2**[3]

15-0 **3** 1/2 **Roundabout Magic (IRE)**[3] 324 3-8-5 **64**........ HollieDoyle(5) 4 61
(Simon Dow) *stdd s: t.k.h: dashed up to join ldr over 3f out: rdn ent fnl f: no ex u.p and btn 100yds out: kpt on same pce after: lost 2nd nr fin* **3/1**[2]

1m 2.1s (0.20) **Going Correction** -0.10s/f (Stan) **3** Ran SP% **106.8**
Speed ratings (Par 99): **94,92,91**
CSF £3.28 TOTE £1.80; EX 2.80 Trifecta £2.30.
**Owner** John Dance **Bred** A H And C E Robinson Partnership **Trained** Malpas, Cheshire

**FOCUS**
A modest small-field handicap and the form looks shaky.

## 380 BETWAY MARATHON H'CAP 1m 5f 194y
**4:00** (4:01) (Class 5) (0-75,75) 4-Y-O+ **£2,911** (£866; £432; £216) **Stalls** Low

Form RPR

00-1 **1** **Start Seven**[13] 162 5-9-5 **70**........ AdamKirby 5 83+
(Jamie Osborne) *trckd ldr and travelled strly: lost 2nd 5f out but stl travelled wl: trckd ldr again 3f out: shkn up to ld 1f out: sn clr: easily* **1/1**[1]

14-2 **2** 3 1/2 **Eurato (FR)**[13] 162 7-9-5 **70**........ MartinHarley 6 75
(Steve Gollings) *led and set stdy gallop: drvn over 1f out: hdd 1f out: sn outpcd by wnr but kpt on for clr 2nd* **9/2**[3]

40-0 **3** 2 1/2 **Gabrial The Terror (IRE)**[22] 6 7-9-6 **71**........(p) StevieDonohoe 7 73
(Ian Williams) *s.i.s: t.k.h: hld up in rr: hdwy over 2f out: wnt 3rd 1f out: kpt on same pce u.p fianl f* **25/1**

30/2 **4** 1/2 **Uncle Bernie (IRE)**[18] 74 7-9-9 **74**........ JamesSullivan 3 75
(Sarah Hollinshead) *t.k.h: hld up in tch in rr: nt clr run and swtchd rt over 2f out: sme hdwy over 1f out: swtchd rt ins fnl f: pushed along and kpt on fnl 150yds: nvr trbld ldrs* **9/1**

63-5 **5** 1 1/4 **Obboorr**[22] 3 8-9-7 **72**........ TomEaves 4 71
(James Given) *chsd ldrs for 4f out: styd wl in tch in midfield: rdn and unable qck over 2f out: outpcd and wl hld over 1f out: plugged on* **10/1**

40-5 **6** 3/4 **Ban Shoof**[16] 122 4-8-13 **73**........(h1) LouisSteward(3) 2 71
(Ismail Mohammed) *t.k.h: hld up in tch in midfield: effrt and hung bdly rt over 2f out: no ch over 1f out: eased wl ins fnl f* **3/1**[2]

2/0- **7** 3 1/4 **Perspicace**[68] 3639 6-9-10 **75**........(p) DougieCostello 1 69
(David Pipe) *dwlt and reminder sn after s: hld up in last pair: swtchd rt and hdwy after 2f: chsd ldrs 10f out tl wnt 2nd 5f out: rdn and lost 2nd 2f out: wknd over 1f out* **33/1**

3m 2.93s (-1.87) **Going Correction** -0.10s/f (Stan)
**WFA** 4 from 5yo+ 4lb 7 Ran SP% **119.1**
Speed ratings (Par 103): **101,99,97,97,96 96,94**
CSF £6.48 TOTE £2.50: £1.40, £1.80; EX 7.30 Trifecta £74.50.
**Owner** Melbourne 10 Racing **Bred** Mehmet Kurt **Trained** Upper Lambourn, Berks

**FOCUS**
This was steadily run, the pace only winding up in the last half-mile or so. The winner confirmed recent form with the runner-up and still looks capable of better.

## 381 BETWAY H'CAP 1m 4f 51y (Tp)
**4:30** (4:30) (Class 4) (0-80,82) 4-Y-O+ **£4,690** (£1,395; £697; £348) **Stalls** Low

Form RPR

60-0 **1** **Modernism**[18] 62 8-9-5 **77**........ StevieDonohoe 8 84
(Ian Williams) *chsd ldng trio: gd hdwy to ld 3f out: hld on wl u.p ins fnl f: rdn out* **20/1**

01-0 **2** 1 **Clovelly Bay (IRE)**[13] 163 6-8-9 **74**........ TylerSaunders(7) 7 79
(Marcus Tregoning) *hld up in tch in midfield: effrt on inner over 1f out: chsd ldng pair ins fnl f: kpt on to snatch 2nd last stride* **8/1**

34-1 **3** shd **Dream Factory (IRE)**[17] 92 4-8-11 **73**........(p) TomMarquand 1 79+
(Marco Botti) *chsd ldr for 2f: styd chsng ldrs: swtchd rt and effrt to chse wnr ent fnl 2f: kpt on same pce u.p ins fnl f: lost 2nd last stride: p.u qckly and dismntd after fin* **9/4**[1]

31-0 **4** 1 **Snobbery (IRE)**[19] 38 4-9-2 **78**........(t1) GeorgeBaker 3 81
(Roger Charlton) *stdd s: hld up in last pair: shkn up and hdwy over 1f out: rdn 1f out: kpt on ins fnl f* **5/1**[3]

50-4 **5** 1 3/4 **Tangramm**[13] 163 5-9-10 **82**........(p) RobertWinston 4 82
(Dean Ivory) *hld up in midfield: clsd over 2f out: rdn to chse ldrs 1f out: sn no ex and outpcd ins fnl f* **5/2**[2]

024- **6** 3 1/4 **Be My Sea (IRE)**[106] 7183 6-9-4 **79**........ GeorgeDowning(3) 9 74
(Tony Carroll) *s.i.s: hdwy to chse ldr after 2f: lost 2nd and rdn 3f out: lost pl and btn over 1f out: wknd ins fnl f* **11/1**

060- **7** hd **Spes Nostra**[45] 8283 9-9-6 **78**........(b) PJMcDonald 2 73
(Iain Jardine) *led: hdd and rdn 3f out: no ex over 1f out: wknd ins fnl f* **12/1**

613/ **8** 1 1/2 **Rowlestone Lass**[500] 6266 7-9-5 **77**........ RichardKingscote 6 70
(Richard Price) *hld up in tch in midfield: pushed along and no hdwy over 1f out: wknd fnl f* **50/1**

424- **9** 9 **With Hindsight (IRE)**[253] 772 9-8-12 **70**........ TomEaves 5 48
(Steve Gollings) *hld up in last pair: rdn over 2f out: sn struggling: bhd fnl f* **50/1**

2m 37.33s (-3.47) **Going Correction** -0.10s/f (Stan)
**WFA** 4 from 5yo+ 3lb 9 Ran SP% **111.8**
Speed ratings (Par 105): **107,106,106,105,104 102,102,101,95**
CSF £163.01 CT £501.47 TOTE £25.70: £5.40, £2.40, £1.30; EX 209.90 Trifecta £752.60.
**Owner** Dr Marwan Koukash **Bred** Darley **Trained** Portway, Worcs

**FOCUS**
A fair handicap, run at a modest gallop, with the winner back to form off a good mark.

## 382 BETWAY MIDDLE H'CAP 1m 1f 104y (Tp)
**5:00** (5:00) (Class 5) (0-75,77) 4-Y-O+ **£2,911** (£866; £432; £216) **Stalls** Low

Form RPR

2-33 **1** **Pivotman**[7] 267 9-8-13 **72**........(bt) LewisEdmunds(7) 8 81
(Michael Easterby) *t.k.h: pressed ldr tl led 2f out: sn rdn and qcknd clr: r.o wl: comf* **4/1**[3]

14-3 **2** 4 1/2 **Roman De Brut (IRE)**[19] 47 5-8-11 **68**........ CharlieBennett(5) 7 68
(Daniel Mark Loughnane) *chsd ldrs: effrt 2f out: chsd clr wnr over 1f out: no imp on wnr but battled on wl to hold 2nd ins fnl f* **10/1**

100- 3 nse **Hard To Handel**[24] 8584 5-9-7 73........ PaddyAspell 5 73
(Clare Ellam) *tk keen hols: chsd ldrs: effrt 2f out: battling for 2nd but wnr clr 1f out: kpt on u.p but no imp on wnr* **100/1**

52-2 4 nk **Fastnet Blast (IRE)**[20] 29 4-9-2 69........(b) GeorgeBaker 4 68
(Ed Walker) *t.k.h: hld up in tch in midfield: effrt over 1f out: 4th and u.p 1f out: kpt on but no imp on wnr* **9/4**[2]

00-1 5 nk **Gossiping**[13] 166 5-9-7 73........ ShaneKelly 12 72+
(Gary Moore) *t.k.h: hld up in tch in midfield: effrt over 1f out: hung lft 1f out: kpt on ins fnl f: no threat to wnr* **6/4**[1]

20-0 6 1 1/4 **All You (IRE)**[19] 42 5-9-5 71........(v) DanielTudhope 13 68
(David O'Meara) *hld up in tch in midfield: nt clr run and hmpd jst over 2f out: hdwy whn nt clrest of runs and swtchd lft 1f out: kpt on: no threat to wnr* **33/1**

113/ 7 2 3/4 **Instill**[488] 6657 5-9-3 72........ RobHornby(3) 2 62
(Mandy Rowland) *in tch in midfield: rdn over 1f out: unable qck: wknd ins fnl f* **25/1**

6-03 8 3/4 **Idol Deputy (FR)**[16] 122 11-8-12 69........(p) RachealKneller(5) 1 58
(James Bennett) *in tch in midfield: shuffled bk on inner over 1f out: rdn and tried to rally over 1f out: no imp fnl f* **50/1**

000- 9 1 **Silver Alliance**[82] 7775 9-9-0 69........(p) ShelleyBirkett(3) 11 56
(Julia Feilden) *stdd after s: hld up in tch in last trio: effrt over 1f out: no imp: wl hld fnl f* **100/1**

16-3 10 hd **Beautiful Stranger (IRE)**[19] 49 6-9-6 72........(p) ConnorBeasley 10 58
(Keith Dalgleish) *t.k.h: hld up in tch in midfield: shkn up and unable qck over 1f out: sn btn and wknd fnl f* **14/1**

0/ 11 hd **Melanna (IRE)**[96] 7478 6-9-4 77........ CallumRodriguez(7) 3 63
(Richard Ford) *sn dropped to rr and niggled along: clsd onto bk of field and travelling bttr 1/2-way: swtchd rt and effrt over 1f out: no imp: swtchd rt 1f out: wl hld fnl f* **40/1**

42/0 12 1 3/4 **Gone Viral (IRE)**[17] 92 6-9-5 71........(p1) LiamKeniry 6 53
(George Baker) *sn led: hdd and rdn 2f out: sn outpcd and btn: wknd 1f out* **33/1**

1m 59.69s (-1.11) **Going Correction** -0.10s/f (Stan)
**WFA** 4 from 5yo+ 1lb **12 Ran SP% 122.6**
Speed ratings (Par 103): **100,96,95,95,95 94,91,91,90,90 89,88**
CSF £42.83 CT £3475.46 TOTE £4.30: £1.70, £3.00, £15.10; EX 31.60 Trifecta £1654.90.
**Owner** K Wreglesworth **Bred** Cheveley Park Stud Ltd **Trained** Sheriff Hutton, N Yorks

**FOCUS**
This was steadily run and the first three were always towards the fore. The winner put up his best effort since 2015.

## 383 SUNBETS.CO.UK H'CAP 1m 142y (Tp)
**5:30** (5:32) (Class 6) (0-55,55) 4-Y-O+ **£2,264** (£673; £336; £168) **Stalls** Low

Form RPR

00-0 1 **Gabrial The Thug (FR)**[22] 7 7-9-4 52........(t) AdamKirby 6 58
(Ian Williams) *trckd ldrs: swtchd lft and effrt on inner over 1f out: rdn to ld 1f out: styd on: rdn out* **5/2**[1]

00-5 2 1 **Bassino (USA)**[16] 124 4-8-13 53........(h) RachealKneller(5) 12 57
(James Bennett) *sn chsng ldr: effrt 2f out: rdn to ld over 1f out: hdd 1f out: kpt on same pce ins fnl f* **16/1**

4-46 3 1/2 **Pivotal Dream (IRE)**[14] 147 4-8-6 46........ CharlieBennett(5) 3 49
(Mark Brisbourne) *in tch in midfield: effrt 2f out: hdwy 1f out: kpt on u.p ins fnl f: wnt 3rd towards fin* **16/1**

545- 4 3/4 **Hold Firm**[32] 8500 5-9-7 55........ StevieDonohoe 5 56
(Mark H Tompkins) *chsd ldrs: effrt 2f out: styd on same pce u.p ins fnl f: lost 3rd towards fin* **13/2**

4-05 5 1/2 **Cold Fusion (IRE)**[9] 233 4-9-1 55........ HollieDoyle(5) 4 55
(David Flood) *hld up in tch towards rr: swtchd rt and effrt over 1f out: nt clrest of runs 1f out: rdn and kpt on fnl 100yds* **14/1**

00-3 6 1 **Dukes Meadow**[16] 123 6-8-13 54........ RhiainIngram(7) 9 52
(Roger Ingram) *dwlt and rousted along early: in tch in midfield on outer: effrt 2f out: unable qck over 1f out: wknd wl ins fnl f* **6/1**[3]

00-0 7 1 **Tingo In The Tale (IRE)**[14] 147 8-9-6 54........(p) TomMarquand 11 50
(Sophie Leech) *swtchd lft after 1f: in tch in rr: rdn 3f out: one pced and nvr threatened ldrs* **50/1**

6/3- 8 hd **Hymn For The Dudes**[237] 2784 4-9-3 52........(t) MartinHarley 8 48
(John Berry) *hld up in tch towards rr: c wd and effrt bnd 2f out: no imp u.p over 1f out: wknd ins fnl f* **10/3**[2]

00-0 9 hd **Broughtons Fancy**[13] 166 4-9-6 55........ GeorgeBaker 7 50
(Gary Moore) *taken down early: led: rdn and hdd over 1f out: no ex u.p: wknd ins fnl f* **10/1**

00-0 P **Devious Spirit (IRE)**[12] 174 5-9-7 55........ PJMcDonald 10
(Iain Jardine) *virtually ref to r and v.s.a: p.u 7f out* **8/1**

1m 49.55s (-0.55) **Going Correction** -0.10s/f (Stan)
**WFA** 4 from 5yo+ 1lb **10 Ran SP% 119.9**
Speed ratings (Par 101): **98,97,96,96,95 94,93,93,93,**
CSF £46.91 CT £561.11 TOTE £3.50: £1.70, £4.90, £3.40; EX 77.30 Trifecta £1036.40.
**Owner** Dr Marwan Koukash **Bred** Alain Plainfosse **Trained** Portway, Worcs

**FOCUS**
A very modest event. The winner looks on the way back for his new stable and every chance of defying a small rise.
T/Plt: £11.20 to a £1 stake. Pool: £83,151.50 - 5,380.87 winning units T/Qpdt: £5.90 to a £1 stake. Pool: £5,225.98 - 652.79 winning units **Steve Payne**

# 364 CAGNES-SUR-MER
Monday, January 23
**OFFICIAL GOING: Polytrack: standard**

## 384a PRIX DU SERPOLET (CLAIMER) (4YO+) (POLYTRACK) 6f 110y
**2:55** 4-Y-O+ **£7,264** (£2,905; £2,179; £1,452; £726)

RPR

1 **Giogiobbo**[191] 4-9-2 0........(p) Pierre-CharlesBoudot 7 89
(Francesco Santella, Italy) **49/10**[3]

2 4 1/2 **Pensierieparole**[246] 2518 5-9-2 0........ DarioVargiu 2 76
(Il Cavallo In Testa, Italy) **18/1**

3 3/4 **Surewecan**[159] 5538 5-9-2 0........ FranckBlondel 5 74
(F Rossi, France) **15/1**

4 nse **Roman Spectrum**[92] 4-9-6 0........ CristianDemuro 1 78
(Il Cavallo In Testa, Italy) **24/1**

5 nk **Rockyl (IRE)**[69] 5-9-6 0........(b) NicolasPerret 3 77
(F Rossi, France) **5/2**[1]

6 nse **Lisnavagh (FR)**[292] 5-8-13 0........ MaximeGuyon 9 70
(Jane Soubagne, France) **14/1**

7 1 **Grey Mirage**[11] 199 8-8-11 0........(b) IoritzMendizabal 8 65
(Gay Kelleway) *tk a t.k.h: hld up in fnl trio: drvn and effrt wl over 1 1/2f out but no real imp: kpt on at same pce fnl f* **5/1**

8 1 1/2 **Chanche The Life (IRE)**[67] 7998 4-8-13 0........ EddyHardouin 4 62
(K Borgel, France) **13/2**

9 6 **La Houssay (FR)**[35] 5-9-7 0........ ChristopheSoumillon 10 53
(C Escuder, France) **48/10**[2]

10 1 **Turflady (GER)**[456] 4-8-8 0........(b) FabriceVeron 6 37
(Frau C Barsig, Germany) **39/1**

PARI-MUTUEL (all including 1 euro stake): WIN 5.90; PLACE 2.70, 6.00, 5.20; DF 31.80; SF 75.60.
**Owner** Marco Bozzi **Bred** Orbit Performance **Trained** Italy

# 310 SOUTHWELL (L-H)
Tuesday, January 24
**OFFICIAL GOING: Fibresand: standard**
Wind: Light across Weather: Fine and dry

## 385 32RED MAIDEN H'CAP 1m 13y(F)
**1:40** (1:40) (Class 6) (0-65,67) 3-Y-O **£2,911** (£866; £432; £216) **Stalls** Low

Form RPR

002- 1 **Daily Trader**[26] 8568 3-9-0 57........ AndrewMullen 4 69
(David Evans) *in tch: pushed along and hdwy over 3f out: rdn to chse clr ldr wl over 1f out: sn drvn and styd on strly fnl f: led last 75 yds* **11/4**[1]

420- 2 2 **Elegantly Bound (IRE)**[48] 8244 3-9-10 67........(b) TomEaves 1 74
(James Given) *led: pushed clr over 2f out: rdn over 1f out: sn hung lft and drvn: hdd and no ex last 75 yds* **7/1**

05-0 3 8 **Medici Moon**[13] 175 3-8-11 54........(p1) KieranO'Neill 7 45
(Scott Dixon) *dwlt: bhd and sn rdn along: swtchd rt to outer and wd st: drvn wl wl over 1f out: kpt on wl u.p fnl f* **11/1**

000- 4 7 **Mungo Madness**[27] 8560 3-9-2 62........ ShelleyBirkett(3) 5 35
(Julia Feilden) *cl up: rdn along over 3f out: drvn over 2f out: grad wknd* **16/1**

300- 5 1 3/4 **Baileys Apprentice**[35] 8466 3-9-7 64........ JoeFanning 9 32
(Mark Johnston) *prom: pushed along 1/2-way: rdn over 3f out: sn lost pl* **12/1**

046- 6 1/2 **Greengairs**[131] 6499 3-9-10 67........(p1) ConnorBeasley 3 34
(Keith Dalgleish) *trckd ldrs: hdwy to chse ldr 3f out: sn rdn: drvn along 2f out and grad wknd* **8/1**

036- 7 1 3/4 **Georgio (GER)**[180] 4802 3-9-5 62........(h1) DavidProbert 8 25
(Andrew Balding) *dwlt: rr and wd st: nvr a factor* **4/1**[2]

05-2 8 nk **Come On Percy**[19] 73 3-8-13 56........ TonyHamilton 6 19
(Richard Fahey) *cl up: rdn along 3f out: drvn over 2f out: sn wknd* **5/1**[3]

00-0 9 1 1/2 **Chillililli**[19] 73 3-8-0 50 oh5........ RPWalsh(7) 10 9
(Michael Appleby) *chsd ldrs on outer: rdn along over 3f out: sn wknd* **100/1**

000- 10 8 **Shadow Of Hercules (IRE)**[71] 7954 3-8-7 50 oh5....(be) MartinDwyer 2
(Michael Mullineaux) *chsd ldrs: pushed along bef 1/2-way: sn lost pl and bhd* **100/1**

1m 42.99s (-0.71) **Going Correction** -0.05s/f (Stan) **10 Ran SP% 110.8**
Speed ratings (Par 95): **106,104,96,89,87 86,85,84,83,75**
CSF £20.97 CT £175.35 TOTE £3.30: £1.30, £2.30, £3.60; EX 19.00 Trifecta £148.50.
**Owner** Shropshire Wolves **Bred** Cheveley Park Stud Ltd **Trained** Pandy, Monmouths

**FOCUS**
They finished well strung out in this maiden handicap and an improved effort from the winner.

## 386 BETWAY SPRINT H'CAP 6f 16y(F)
**2:10** (2:12) (Class 6) (0-60,61) 4-Y-O+ **£2,911** (£866; £432; £216) **Stalls** Low

Form RPR

03-6 1 **Fortinbrass (IRE)**[22] 21 7-9-0 60........ LewisEdmunds(7) 6 66
(John Balding) *cl up: slt ld 11/2f out: sn rdn: drvn ins fnl f: hld on wl towards fin* **8/1**[3]

66-4 2 nk **Cadeaux Pearl**[5] 311 9-8-0 46........(b) RPWalsh(7) 2 51
(Scott Dixon) *slt ld: rdn along 2f out and sn hdd: drvn and renewed effrt ins fnl f: ev ch tl no ex cl home* **20/1**

0-51 3 3/4 **Wimboldsley**[5] 311 6-8-12 51 6ex........ KieranO'Neill 5 54
(Scott Dixon) *trckd ldrs: cl up over 2f out: rdn to chal over 1f out: ev ch whn drvn and edgd lft ins fnl f: kpt on same pce* **8/1**[3]

4-22 4 nk **Treaty Of Rome (USA)**[14] 158 5-9-7 60........(p1) TonyHamilton 12 62
(Derek Shaw) *trckd ldrs: hdwy over 2f out: swtchd markedly rt to outer over 1f out: sn rdn and kpt on* **3/1**[1]

605- 5 2 1/4 **Upper Lambourn (IRE)**[40] 8383 9-8-2 46 oh1........(t) LuluStanford(5) 1 41
(John Holt) *chsd ldrs on inner: hdwy 3f out: rdn along 2f out: drvn and kpt on same pce fnl f* **20/1**

00-0 6 nse **Satchville Flyer**[14] 152 6-9-7 60........ StevieDonohoe 11 56+
(David Evans) *towards rr: pushed along over 3f out: rdn and hdwy over 2f out: kpt on u.p fnl f: nrst fin* **9/2**[2]

0-04 7 nse **Life Of Fame**[11] 217 4-9-2 55........ DougieCostello 10 50
(Mark Walford) *cl up: rdn along wl over 2f out: grad wknd* **25/1**

0-64 8 2 1/2 **Spowarticus**[14] 158 8-9-1 54........(v) DaleSwift 14 41
(Scott Dixon) *racd wd: in tch: rdn along and wd st: kpt on u.p fnl 2f* **9/1**

20-0 9 1 1/2 **Loumarin (IRE)**[15] 151 5-9-8 61........ AndrewMullen 8 44
(Michael Appleby) *a towards rr* **25/1**

5-33 10 1/2 **Mustn't Grumble (IRE)**[14] 158 4-8-11 57........(h) GerO'Neill(7) 4 38
(David Loughnane) *a towards rr* **3/1**[1]

000- 11 9 **Barnsdale**[28] 8541 4-8-0 46 oh1........ MeganEllingworth(7) 3
(John Holt) *a towards rr* **200/1**

600- 12 6 **Pyroclastic (IRE)**[105] 7260 5-8-7 51........(p) DavidParkes(5) 9
(Nick Kent) *chsd ldrs: rdn along 3f out: sn wknd* **66/1**

00-0 13 24 **Outlaw Kate (IRE)**[14] 158 5-8-7 46 oh1........(be1) MartinDwyer 7
(Michael Mullineaux) *a rr* **200/1**

1m 16.23s (-0.27) **Going Correction** -0.05s/f (Stan) **13 Ran SP% 120.1**
Speed ratings (Par 101): **99,98,97,97,94 94,94,90,88,88 76,68,36**
CSF £159.15 CT £1329.98 TOTE £10.40: £3.70, £5.60, £2.70; EX 167.80 Trifecta £817.90.
**Owner** Billy Herring **Bred** Tom Wallace **Trained** Scrooby, S Yorks
■ Stewards' Enquiry : R P Walsh seven-day ban: used whip above permitted level. (Feb 7-14)


The Form Book Flat, Raceform Ltd, Newbury, RG14 5SJ

**FOCUS**
A moderate handicap in which the pace held up. The winner was on a fair mark.

## 387 BETWAY BEST ODDS GUARANTEED PLUS (S) STKS 4f 214y(F)
**2:40** (2:40) (Class 6) 4-Y-0+ **£2,587** (£770; £384; £192) **Stalls** Centre

| Form | | | | RPR |
|---|---|---|---|---|
| 00-2 | 1 | | **Dungannon**[19] 71 10-8-13 82.....(b) JoshuaBryan(7) 3 | 83+ |
| | | | (Andrew Balding) *trckd ldrs: hdwy on bit over 1f out: sn cl up: shkn up to ld ins fnl f: sn clr* **1/2**[1] | |
| -543 | 2 | 2 ¾ | **Archie Stevens**[4] 330 7-9-0 69..... AndrewMullen 6 | 64+ |
| | | | (David Evans) *slt ld: rdn over 1f out: drvn and hdd ins fnl f: kpt on* **5/1**[3] | |
| 00-0 | 3 | 3 | **Imjin River (IRE)**[8] 271 10-8-9 47.....(tp) HollieDoyle(5) 1 | 53 |
| | | | (William Stone) *cl up: rdn along wl over 1f out: kpt on same pce* **100/1** | |
| 0/1- | 4 | ½ | **Moondyne Joe (IRE)**[232] 2982 4-9-6 82..... BenCurtis 7 | 57 |
| | | | (K R Burke) *cl up: rdn along 2f out: kpt on same pce* **4/1**[2] | |
| 24-5 | 5 | nk | **Doctor Parkes**[11] 211 11-9-3 73..... MillyNaseb(7) 8 | 60 |
| | | | (Stuart Williams) *cl up: rdn along wl over 1f out: sn drvn and kpt on same pce* **20/1** | |
| 450- | 6 | 26 | **Desirable**[174] 5013 4-8-10 63 ow1.....(v[1]) StevieDonohoe 2 | |
| | | | (Brian Barr) *dwlt: sn rdn along and outpcd in rr: t.o fr 1/2-way* **200/1** | |

58.82s (-0.88) **Going Correction** -0.125s/f (Stan) **6** Ran SP% **109.6**
Speed ratings (Par 101): **102,97,92,92,91 49**
CSF £3.24 TOTE £1.50: £1.20, £1.60; EX 3.70 Trifecta £32.80.The winner was bought in for 4,750gns.
**Owner** Dr E Harris **Bred** J A E Hobby **Trained** Kingsclere, Hants

**FOCUS**
Not a bad seller, with the winner well capable of holding his own in handicaps off his current mark in the low 80s. The race has been rated through the third.

## 388 BETWAY BEST ODDS GUARANTEED PLUS H'CAP 4f 214y(F)
**3:10** (3:10) (Class 2) (0-105,102) 4-Y-0+
**£12,450** (£3,728; £1,864; £932; £466; £234) **Stalls** Centre

| Form | | | | RPR |
|---|---|---|---|---|
| 62-3 | 1 | | **Poyle Vinnie**[21] 33 7-8-13 97.....(p) AlistairRawlinson(3) 2 | 106 |
| | | | (Michael Appleby) *chsd ldrs: pushed along 1/2-way: hdwy 2f out: rdn to chal ent fnl f: led last 100 yds* **5/1**[2] | |
| 34-1 | 2 | 2 ½ | **Razin' Hell**[23] 4 6-8-4 85.....(v) AndrewMullen 9 | 85+ |
| | | | (John Balding) *slt ld centre: rdn over 1f out: drvn and edgd lft ins fnl f: hdd and no ex last 100 yds* **17/2** | |
| 04-5 | 3 | hd | **Bowson Fred**[12] 200 5-9-4 99..... JamesSullivan 8 | 98 |
| | | | (Michael Easterby) *racd towards stands side: in tch: rdn along over 2f out: hdwy over 1f out: drvn and styd on wl fnl f* **12/1** | |
| 1-11 | 4 | shd | **Lady Nayef**[11] 215 4-7-11 83 oh4.....(t) HollieDoyle(5) 10 | 82 |
| | | | (John Butler) *racd nr stands rail: towards rr: rdn along and hdwy over 2f out: drvn over 1f out: edgd lft and styd on wl fnl f* **10/1** | |
| 41-5 | 5 | 1 | **Distant Past**[19] 63 6-8-11 92.....(v) JoeDoyle 6 | 87 |
| | | | (Kevin Ryan) *racd centre: cl up: chal 2f out and sn rdn: drvn appr fnl f: kpt on same pce* **7/1**[3] | |
| 12-0 | 6 | 1 ¼ | **Showdaisy**[23] 4 4-8-7 88.....(p) JasonHart 7 | 79+ |
| | | | (Keith Dalgleish) *towards rr: hdwy over 2f out: sn rdn and kpt on fnl f* **8/1** | |
| 55-6 | 7 | 1 ½ | **Top Boy**[19] 63 7-8-2 83 oh1.....(v) KieranO'Neill 5 | 68 |
| | | | (Derek Shaw) *rr: rdn along 1/2-way: kpt on fnl f* **33/1** | |
| 014- | 8 | ½ | **Encore D'Or**[50] 8232 5-9-6 101..... JoeFanning 1 | 85+ |
| | | | (Robert Cowell) *racd towards far side: chsd ldrs on outer: effrt 2f out: sn rdn and wknd appr fnl f* **7/2**[1] | |
| 00-2 | 9 | shd | **Meadway**[23] 4 6-8-9 90.....(p) ConnorBeasley 4 | 73 |
| | | | (Bryan Smart) *racd centre: cl up: rdn along over 2f out: sn wknd* **5/1**[2] | |
| 26-0 | 10 | 2 ¼ | **Lightscameraction (IRE)**[12] 200 5-9-7 102.....(b) TonyHamilton 3 | 77 |
| | | | (Gay Kelleway) *cl up centre: rdn along wl over 1f out: sn drvn and wknd* **14/1** | |

58.09s (-1.61) **Going Correction** -0.125s/f (Stan) **10** Ran SP% **116.1**
Speed ratings (Par 109): **107,103,102,102,100 98,96,95,95,91**
CSF £46.85 CT £494.71 TOTE £5.10: £2.20, £2.50, £4.50; EX 51.40 Trifecta £494.90.
**Owner** C L Bacon **Bred** Cecil And Miss Alison Wiggins **Trained** Oakham, Rutland

**FOCUS**
A good handicap, and a four-way go up front helped set things up for a closer. The winner has been rated to last year's best.

## 389 BETWAY H'CAP 1m 4f 14y(F)
**3:40** (3:40) (Class 3) (0-90,90) 4-Y-0-**£7,561** (£2,263; £1,131; £566; £282) **Stalls** Low

| Form | | | | RPR |
|---|---|---|---|---|
| 21-1 | 1 | | **Isharah (USA)**[12] 196 4-9-3 87..... JoeFanning 2 | 95+ |
| | | | (Mark Johnston) *trckd ldrs on inner: hdwy and cl up 2f out: rdn to take narrow ld jst ins fnl f: sn drvn and hld on wl towards fin* **5/1**[3] | |
| 3-11 | 2 | shd | **L'Inganno Felice (FR)**[14] 154 7-9-3 83.....(h) PJMcDonald 3 | 90+ |
| | | | (Iain Jardine) *trckd ldrs: hdwy 2f out: effrt and n.m.r over 1f out: sn squeezed through and rdn to chal jst ins fnl f: sn drvn and ev ch: kpt on wl towards fin: jst hld* **15/8**[1] | |
| 0-30 | 3 | 2 ¾ | **Luv U Whatever**[8] 269 7-9-6 86..... AndrewMullen 6 | 89 |
| | | | (Michael Attwater) *led: pushed along 3f out: rdn 2f out: drvn over 1f out: hdd jst ins fnl f: kpt on same pce* **20/1** | |
| 11-5 | 4 | 1 | **Western Prince**[19] 62 4-8-9 79.....(h) BenCurtis 5 | 80 |
| | | | (Michael Appleby) *t.k.h early: hld up in rr: hdwy on outer 1/2-way: chsd ldrs 3f out: rdn and cl up 2f out: drvn over 1f out: kpt on same pce* **7/2**[2] | |
| 06-4 | 5 | shd | **Royal Marskell**[12] 197 8-9-7 87..... TomEaves 1 | 88 |
| | | | (Gay Kelleway) *trckd ldrs: hdwy over 3f out: rdn along over 2f out: sn swtchd rt and drvn over 1f out: kpt on u.p fnl f* **14/1** | |
| 500- | 6 | 1 ¾ | **Tommy Docc (IRE)**[213] 3658 5-9-10 90..... PhillipMakin 4 | 88 |
| | | | (Keith Dalgleish) *trckd ldr: cl up 4f out: rdn along wl over 2f out: sn drvn and grad wknd* **7/1** | |
| 21-1 | 7 | 2 ¼ | **Tatting**[23] 3 8-8-12 78..... PaulMulrennan 7 | 72 |
| | | | (Lawrence Mullaney) *hld up: pushed along 5f out: outpcd and bhd 4f out: rdn along and wd st: styd on u.p fnl 2f* **7/1** | |

2m 38.69s (-2.31) **Going Correction** -0.05s/f (Stan)
**WFA** 4 from 5yo+ 3lb **7** Ran SP% **110.1**
Speed ratings (Par 107): **105,104,103,102,102 101,99**
CSF £13.69 TOTE £4.40: £2.10, £1.50; EX 14.90 Trifecta £156.90.
**Owner** Abdulla Al Mansoori **Bred** M Buckley, M Buckley & K L Ramsey **Trained** Middleham Moor, N Yorks

**FOCUS**
The early gallop wasn't that strong and the race developed into a bit of a dash from the turn in. The form isn't that fluid, but another step up from the winner.

## 390 SUNBETS.CO.UK H'CAP 1m 13y(F)
**4:10** (4:12) (Class 6) (0-60,60) 4-Y-0+ **£2,911** (£866; £432; £216) **Stalls** Low

| Form | | | | RPR |
|---|---|---|---|---|
| 56-3 | 1 | | **Dose**[20] 46 4-9-3 56..... JackGarritty 6 | 65 |
| | | | (Richard Fahey) *led 1f: trckd ldrs: hdwy on inner wl over 2f out: rdn to ld over 1f out: drvn ins fnl f: hld on wl towards fin* **6/1**[3] | |
| 2-21 | 2 | shd | **Playful Dude (USA)**[19] 68 4-9-3 59.....(h) CallumShepherd(3) 5 | 68 |
| | | | (Phil McEntee) *midfield: hdwy over 3f out: effrt on outer and cl up 2f out: rdn to chal over 1f out: drvn and ev ch ins fnl f: no ex towards fin* **5/1**[2] | |
| 6-41 | 3 | 3 ¼ | **Samphire Coast**[19] 69 4-9-7 60.....(v) TonyHamilton 8 | 62 |
| | | | (Derek Shaw) *prom: trckd ldng pair 1/2-way: effrt 2f out and sn rdn: swtchd markedly rt over 1f out: sn drvn and kpt on fnl f* **2/1**[1] | |
| 54-6 | 4 | ¾ | **Einstein**[19] 68 4-9-0 60.....(t) MillyNaseb(7) 12 | 60 |
| | | | (Mrs Ilka Gansera-Leveque) *cl up: led after 1f: rdn along 2f out: drvn and hdd over 1f out: kpt on same pce* **16/1** | |
| 1-33 | 5 | 1 ¾ | **General Tufto**[19] 68 12-8-13 52.....(b) MartinLane 13 | 48 |
| | | | (Charles Smith) *trckd ldrs: hdwy to dispute ld 2f out and sn rdn: drvn and one pce fr over 1f out* **10/1** | |
| 03-0 | 6 | 3 ¾ | **Rocket Ronnie (IRE)**[10] 239 7-8-13 57.....(t) RachealKneller(5) 3 | 44 |
| | | | (Brian Barr) *hld up towards rr:. hdwy wl over 2f out: rdn wl over 1f out: sn no imp* **28/1** | |
| 055- | 7 | 2 | **Albert Boy (IRE)**[26] 8566 4-8-13 52.....(b[1]) KieranO'Neill 2 | 34 |
| | | | (Scott Dixon) *chsd ldrs on inner and sn pushed along: rdn along over 3f out: drvn 2f out: no imp* **25/1** | |
| 0-45 | 8 | 2 ½ | **Powered (IRE)**[19] 69 4-9-1 54.....(b) StevieDonohoe 11 | 31+ |
| | | | (David Evans) *v.s.a and lost 10 l s: rr: hdwy 3f out: sn rdn along and n.d* **7/1** | |
| 500- | 9 | 1 ¾ | **Trust Me Boy**[27] 8555 9-9-6 59..... PaddyAspell 4 | 32 |
| | | | (John E Long) *rr: wd st and sn rdn along: nvr a factor* **50/1** | |
| 0-06 | 10 | 1 | **The Dukkerer (IRE)**[10] 239 6-9-5 58..... AndrewMullen 1 | 28 |
| | | | (James Given) *a rr* **40/1** | |
| 0-62 | 11 | hd | **Little Choosey**[19] 69 7-9-0 60.....(bt) KevinLundie(7) 10 | 32 |
| | | | (Roy Bowring) *prom: cl up 1/2-way: rdn along wl over 2f out: sn drvn and wknd* **10/1** | |
| 360- | 12 | 1 ½ | **Falcon's Reign (FR)**[10] 1047 8-8-11 53.....(p) AlistairRawlinson(3) 7 | 19 |
| | | | (Michael Appleby) *chsd ldrs: rdn along 3f out: sn drvn and wknd* **16/1** | |

1m 42.77s (-0.93) **Going Correction** -0.05s/f (Stan) **12** Ran SP% **118.4**
Speed ratings (Par 101): **102,101,98,97,96 92,90,87,86,85 84,83**
CSF £34.88 CT £81.82 TOTE £6.90: £2.10, £1.80, £1.50; EX 39.70 Trifecta £114.40.
**Owner** Richard Fahey Ebor Racing Club Ltd **Bred** Cheveley Park Stud Ltd **Trained** Musley Bank, N Yorks

**FOCUS**
A moderate heat, but the right horses came to the fore and the form looks sound enough for the level. The winner has been rated back to her form of this time last year.
T/Jkpt: Not won. T/Plt: £55.90 to a £1 stake. Pool: £69,240.32 - 902.78 winning units T/Qpdt: £4.60 to a £1 stake. Pool: £7,241.50 - 1,142.90 winning units **Joe Rowntree**

# 384 CAGNES-SUR-MER
Tuesday, January 24
**OFFICIAL GOING: Polytrack: standard**

## 391a PRIX DES OLIVIERS (CLAIMER) (4YO) (POLYTRACK) 1m (P)
**2:55** 4-Y-0 **£6,410** (£2,564; £1,923; £1,282; £641)

| | | | RPR |
|---|---|---|---|
| 1 | | **Going Viral (IRE)**[68] 7999 4-9-4 0.....(b) AntoineHamelin 4 | 69 |
| | | (Matthieu Palussiere, France) **135/10** | |
| 2 | nk | **Nadeem Alward (FR)**[82] 4-9-8 0..... ChristopheSoumillon 3 | 72 |
| | | (F Vermeulen, France) **10/1** | |
| 3 | 3 | **Alfieri (FR)**[27] 4-9-4 0..... GregoryBenoist 6 | 61 |
| | | (N Caullery, France) **43/10**[2] | |
| 4 | snk | **Paques Island (FR)**[137] 6310 4-9-0 0.....(p) KyllanBarbaud(5) 9 | 62 |
| | | (J Phelippon, France) **14/1** | |
| 5 | hd | **Dark Road (IRE)**[22] 4-9-3 0..... JeromeMoutard(5) 8 | 65 |
| | | (P Monfort, France) **8/1**[3] | |
| 6 | ½ | **Star Of Paris (IRE)**[22] 4-9-5 0.....(p) Pierre-CharlesBoudot 5 | 60 |
| | | (F-X Belvisi, France) **33/10**[1] | |
| 7 | 1 | **My Sweet Meera (FR)**[39] 4-8-11 0..... MickaelForest 14 | 50 |
| | | (J-M Lefebvre, France) **37/1** | |
| 8 | nk | **Romasparita (IRE)**[135] 4-9-8 0..... CristianDemuro 7 | 60 |
| | | (Endo Botti, Italy) **17/1** | |
| 9 | ¾ | **Ever Desdemone (FR)**[22] 4-8-11 0.....(p) MaximeGuyon 13 | 48 |
| | | (T Castanheira, France) **18/1** | |
| 10 | nse | **Lisala (FR)**[22] 4-8-11 0..... FabriceVeron 15 | 48 |
| | | (Mlle M Henry, France) **43/1** | |
| 11 | 1 ½ | **Sterling Lines**[22] 4-9-4 0..... TheoBachelot 1 | 51 |
| | | (P Monfort, France) **35/1** | |
| 12 | 2 | **Iron Born (FR)**[17] 4-8-11 0..... ThibaultSpeicher(4) 10 | 44 |
| | | (Mme G Rarick, France) **118/1** | |
| 13 | snk | **Prisom (IRE)**[11] 222 4-8-11 0..... IoritzMendizabal 16 | 39 |
| | | (Gay Kelleway) **17/2** | |
| 14 | 5 ½ | **Minminwin (IRE)**[10] 232 4-8-13 0.....(b) ThomasHuet 2 | 29 |
| | | (Gay Kelleway) **9/1** | |
| 15 | 2 ½ | **Lady Wulfruna**[116] 4-8-8 0.....(b) RemiFradet 12 | 18 |
| | | (P Marion, France) **130/1** | |
| 16 | 4 | **Pas La Pas La Bas** 4-9-1 0..... FranckBlondel 11 | 16 |
| | | (Gerard Martin, Austria) **58/1** | |

1m 36.82s **16** Ran SP% **118.2**
PARI-MUTUEL (all including 1 euro stake): WIN 14.50; PLACE 4.60, 4.20, 2.20; DF 80.80; SF 184.10.
**Owner** Mrs Theresa Marnane **Bred** Ken Lynch **Trained** France

# $^{349}$LINGFIELD (L-H)

## Wednesday, January 25

**OFFICIAL GOING: Polytrack: standard**

Wind: Light, across Weather: Misty, cold

### 392 32RED.COM FILLIES' H'CAP — 1m 1y(P)

**1:05** (1:06) (Class 5) (0-75,75) 3-Y-O — **£2,911** (£866; £432; £216) **Stalls** High

Form — RPR

20-1 **1** **Tisbutadream (IRE)**$^{12}$ [209] 3-9-6 **74**.................. ShaneKelly 6 79+
(David Elsworth) *led after 2f: mde rest: kicked for home 2f out: 2 l ahd fnl f: ld dwindled nr fin but a holding on* **9/2$^{2}$**

04-1 **2** ½ **Sky Ballerina**$^{15}$ [160] 3-9-4 **72**.................. MartinLane 7 74
(Simon Crisford) *led 2f: chsd wnr: rdn 2f out: clsd fnl f but a hld* **5/1$^{3}$**

144- **3** 1 ¼ **African Beat (IRE)**$^{36}$ [8466] 3-9-7 **75**.................. RobertTart 3 74+
(John Gosden) *racd wd: hld up in midfield: rdn 2f out: styd on fr over 1f out to take 3rd last 100yds: no threat to wnr* **7/4$^{1}$**

02-3 **4** 1 ½ **Do You Know (IRE)**$^{21}$ [48] 3-8-12 **66**.................. DanielMuscutt 2 61
(Marco Botti) *trckd ldrs: rdn to dispute 2nd towards inner over 1f out: one pce after* **20/1**

315- **5** 1 **Chica De La Noche**$^{25}$ [8592] 3-9-6 **74**.................. TomMarquand 8 67
(Simon Dow) *dropped in fr wd draw and hld up in last: prog on inner 2f out: shkn up over 1f out: no hdwy after* **25/1**

60-2 **6** ½ **Pobbles**$^{7}$ [284] 3-8-11 **68**.................. (p) KieranShoemark$^{(3)}$ 5 59
(Roger Charlton) *s.i.s and early reminder: mostly in 7th: rdn over 2f out: plugged on* **7/1**

541- **7** 3 ¼ **Washington Blue**$^{36}$ [8466] 3-9-4 **72**.................. (b$^{1}$) AdamKirby 1 56
(Clive Cox) *rousted along early to get gng: rdn in midfield 2f out: wknd jst over 1f out* **9/2$^{2}$**

061- **8** 2 **Touch Me (IRE)**$^{25}$ [8591] 3-8-10 **67**.................. (h) JordanVaughan$^{(3)}$ 4 46
(K R Burke) *plld hrd: trckd ldrs to 2f out: wknd qckly fnl f* **16/1**

1m 38.52s (0.32) **Going Correction** +0.125s/f (Slow) **8** Ran SP% **116.4**
Speed ratings (Par 94): **103,102,101,99,98 98,95,93**
CSF £27.75 CT £53.89 TOTE £5.20: £1.60, £1.80, £1.10; EX 24.90 Trifecta £69.00.

**Owner** Mrs Anne Coughlan & Ten Green Bottles **Bred** J F Tuthill **Trained** Newmarket, Suffolk

**FOCUS**

A fair race of its type with half the eight-strong field having won their most recent starts, but not many got into it with the first two up there throughout.

### 393 £10 FREE AT 32RED.COM MAIDEN AUCTION STKS — 7f 1y(P)

**1:35** (1:35) (Class 6) 3-Y-O — **£2,264** (£673; £336; £168) **Stalls** Low

Form — RPR

0-5 **1** **Implausible**$^{19}$ [96] 3-8-11 0.................. RichardKingscote 5 69+
(Jonathan Portman) *led 2f: trckd ldr: led again wl over 1f out: shkn up and sn clr: pushed out* **5/1$^{3}$**

6-2 **2** 4 ½ **Allegheny Bay (IRE)**$^{16}$ [140] 3-9-2 0.................. LiamKeniry 4 60
(J S Moore) *hld up but plld way through to ld after 2f: rdn and hdd wl over 1f out: no ch w wnr but hld on for 2nd* **7/2$^{2}$**

0- **3** ½ **Flying Fynn (IRE)**$^{29}$ [8536] 3-9-2 0.................. (p$^{1}$) RenatoSouza 1 59
(Jose Santos) *chsd ldrs: outpcd fr 2f out: tk 3rd over 1f out: kpt on* **25/1**

00- **4** 1 ½ **African Girl**$^{42}$ [8352] 3-8-8 0.................. SimonPearce$^{(3)}$ 7 50
(Lydia Pearce) *hld up in last: pushed along over 2f out: sme prog on inner 1f out: rdn last 100yds: nvr involved but kpt on* **100/1**

52-2 **5** ½ **Circulate**$^{19}$ [96] 3-8-11 70.................. JoeFanning 6 48
(Tom Clover) *hld up and sn in 5th: pushed along and no prog 2f out: rdn and nt qckn over 1f out: no ch after* **4/5$^{1}$**

**6** ½ **Fun Raiser (IRE)** 3-8-11 0.................. LukeMorris 8 47
(Harry Dunlop) *rn green in last pair: outpcd 2f out: hanging over 1f out: kpt on nr fin* **14/1**

5- **7** 2 ¼ **Circuit**$^{48}$ [8277] 3-8-6 0.................. CharlieBennett$^{(5)}$ 9 41
(Mick Quinn) *chsd ldng pair: rdn over 2f out: wknd over 1f out* **16/1**

1m 26.08s (1.28) **Going Correction** +0.125s/f (Slow) **7** Ran SP% **111.8**
Speed ratings (Par 95): **97,91,91,89,89 88,85**
CSF £21.73 TOTE £5.90: £2.80, £2.90; EX 24.30 Trifecta £205.40.

**Owner** Portlee Bloodstock **Bred** Mrs D O Joly **Trained** Upper Lambourn, Berks

**FOCUS**

A moderate maiden lacking depth, especially with the hot favourite running a shocker, but a clear-cut winner.

### 394 32RED FILLIES' H'CAP — 7f 1y(P)

**2:05** (2:05) (Class 5) (0-70,68) 4-Y-O+ — **£2,911** (£866; £432; £216) **Stalls** Low

Form — RPR

212- **1** **Simply Me**$^{86}$ [7725] 4-9-5 **66**.................. (p) RichardKingscote 3 72+
(Tom Dascombe) *trckd ldrs: rdn and prog over 1f out: chsd ldr ins fnl f: drvn and r.o to ld last 75yds* **2/1$^{1}$**

040- **2** ½ **So Much Fun (IRE)**$^{76}$ [7887] 4-9-5 **66**.................. SeanLevey 4 70
(Ismail Mohammed) *trckd ldr: rdn to ld 2f out: kpt on u.p but hdd and hld last 75yds* **6/1**

412- **3** 2 ¼ **Garter (IRE)**$^{49}$ [8248] 4-9-3 **67**.................. CallumShepherd$^{(3)}$ 6 70+
(Charles Hills) *hld up in last pair: rdn and prog wl over 1f out: trying to cl but hld whn nt clr run 75yds out and eased* **11/4$^{2}$**

41-2 **4** 3 ¾ **Arize (IRE)**$^{16}$ [151] 4-9-7 **68**.................. AdamKirby 2 56
(David Brown) *led: tried to kick on over 2f out but sn hdd: lost 2nd and short of room 150yds out: eased* **4/1$^{3}$**

4-33 **5** 1 **Tell A Story**$^{6}$ [308] 4-9-1 **62**.................. JamieSpencer 5 47
(David Simcock) *stdd s: t.k.h: hld up in last pair: tail swishing fr 4f out: lost tch w rest 2f out: rdn to pass one wkng rival ins fnl f* **6/1**

44-4 **6** 3 ½ **Gamrah (IRE)**$^{15}$ [165] 4-9-2 **63**.................. MartinHarley 1 39
(James Tate) *t.k.h: trckd ldng pair: rdn 2f out: lost pl and hanging bdly lft over 1f out: wknd* **25/1**

1m 25.84s (1.04) **Going Correction** +0.125s/f (Slow) **6** Ran SP% **112.4**
Speed ratings (Par 100): **99,98,95,91,90 86**
CSF £14.47 TOTE £2.90: £1.40, £3.20; EX 16.90 Trifecta £35.80.

**Owner** Laurence Bellman **Bred** Highclere Stud **Trained** Malpas, Cheshire

■ Stewards' Enquiry : Callum Shepherd caution: careless riding

**FOCUS**

An ordinary race, though the majority of these fillies came into the contest in decent form and it produced a driving finish.

### 395 BETWAY H'CAP — 1m 7f 169y(P)

**2:40** (2:40) (Class 6) (0-60,62) 4-Y-O+ — **£2,264** (£673; £336; £168) **Stalls** Low

Form — RPR

114- **1** **Shan Dun na nGall (IRE)**$^{29}$ [8540] 6-9-6 **56**.................. (vt) GeorgeBaker 4 64
(Amy Murphy) *stdd s: hld up in last pair: waiting for room over 2f out but plenty available whn prog to ld over 1f out: shkn up and sn clr* **6/5$^{1}$**

055- **2** 2 ¾ **Le Tissier**$^{37}$ [8459] 4-8-8 **54**.................. (p) RobHornby$^{(3)}$ 2 61
(Michael Attwater) *trckd ldrs: gng bttr than most over 2f out: trapped bhd rivals over 1f out as wnr assumed command: shkn up and styd on to take 2nd last 75yds: no ch to threaten* **6/1$^{3}$**

00-5 **3** 1 ½ **Night Generation (GER)**$^{16}$ [141] 5-9-12 **62**.................. (p) AdamKirby 7 65
(Chris Gordon) *trckd ldr: rdn 3f out: chal over 2f out: one pce u.p over 1f out* **5/1$^{2}$**

60/0 **4** 1 ¾ **Mahican (IRE)**$^{15}$ [162] 7-9-10 **60**.................. (p) JoeFanning 5 61
(Jennie Candlish) *led: rdn and pressed over 2f out: hdd and fdd over 1f out* **5/1$^{2}$**

50-2 **5** 2 ½ **Barnacle**$^{8}$ [278] 8-8-10 **46** oh1.................. (vt) StevieDonohoe 3 44
(Emma Owen) *s.s: hld up in last pair: pushed along and prog 3f out: chsd ldng pair 2f out: wknd over 1f out* **10/1**

50-0 **6** 2 ¼ **Thou Swell (IRE)**$^{6}$ [315] 5-9-2 **57**.................. CharlieBennett$^{(5)}$ 6 52
(Shaun Harris) *chsd ldrs: urged along fr 5f out: lost pl and btn over 2f out* **25/1**

0/0- **7** 9 **Byron Blue (IRE)**$^{56}$ [6022] 8-8-7 **46** oh1.................. (t) EdwardGreatrex$^{(3)}$ 8 31
(Brian Barr) *s.s: t.k.h: hld up in rr: prog on outer to trck ldrs 5f out: wknd 3f out: sn bhd* **12/1**

3m 28.55s (2.85) **Going Correction** +0.125s/f (Slow)
**WFA** 4 from 5yo+ 5lb **7** Ran SP% **113.7**
Speed ratings (Par 101): **97,95,94,94,92 91,87**
CSF £8.83 CT £26.32 TOTE £1.80: £1.10, £3.10; EX 8.00 Trifecta £32.70.

**Owner** J Melo **Bred** Donal Mac A Bhaird **Trained** Newmarket, Suffolk

**FOCUS**

A moderate staying handicap and the pace wasn't strong. The winner is in great order and the runner-up sets the level.

### 396 BETWAY BEST ODDS GUARANTEED PLUS H'CAP — 1m 2f (P)

**3:15** (3:15) (Class 2) (0-105,108) 4-Y£01,971 (£3,583; £1,791; £896; £446) **Stalls** Low

Form — RPR

00-6 **1** **Winterlude (IRE)**$^{13}$ [197] 7-9-0 **95**.................. JoeFanning 7 100
(Jennie Candlish) *awkward s: sn rcvrd and led after 2f: jnd over 2f out: kicked on wl over 1f out: drvn out and hld on* **4/1$^{3}$**

**2** hd **Kyllachy Gala**$^{52}$ 4-9-8 **105**.................. DanielMuscutt 5 109
(Marco Botti) *t.k.h: trckd ldrs: rdn over 1f out: styd on to take 2nd nr fin and cl on wnr last strides* **20/1**

2/ **3** ½ **Eddystone Rock (IRE)**$^{153}$ [5818] 5-9-5 **100**.................. KierenFox 2 103
(John Best) *led at modest pce for 2f: trckd wnr: chal and upsides over 2f out: nt qckn over 1f out: styd on same pce and lost 2nd nr fin* **4/1$^{3}$**

11-2 **4** ¾ **Van Huysen (IRE)**$^{18}$ [117] 5-8-5 **86**.................. JosephineGordon 3 88
(Dominic Ffrench Davis) *t.k.h: hld up in last pair: shkn up and tried to cl towards inner over 1f out: kpt on but nt qckn and nvr able to chal* **3/1$^{2}$**

21-1 **5** ½ **Coillte Cailin (IRE)**$^{18}$ [117] 7-8-13 **94**.................. MartinHarley 1 95
(David O'Meara) *t.k.h: hld up in last pair: pushed along on inner over 1f out and briefly threatened to cl: nt qckn fnl f and dropped to last nr fin* **6/4$^{1}$**

2m 8.93s (2.33) **Going Correction** +0.125s/f (Slow)
**WFA** 4 from 5yo+ 1lb **5** Ran SP% **109.8**
Speed ratings (Par 109): **95,94,94,93,93**
CSF £56.37 TOTE £4.50: £2.10, £3.70; EX 33.80 Trifecta £92.40.

**Owner** Brian Verinder & Alan Baxter **Bred** Darley **Trained** Basford Green, Staffs

**FOCUS**

A warm handicap, but because of the small field they went no pace which was of benefit to the winner, but not to the market leaders. The form looks dubious.

### 397 32RED.COM MAIDEN STKS — 6f 1y(P)

**3:50** (3:50) (Class 5) 3-Y-O — **£2,911** (£866; £432; £216) **Stalls** Low

Form — RPR

24- **1** **Winning Ways (IRE)**$^{209}$ [3805] 3-9-5 0.................. (t$^{1}$) AdamKirby 5 77
(Jeremy Noseda) *trckd ldrs: shkn up 2f out and quite wd on bnd: rdn and clsd to ld jst ins fnl f: sn clr* **1/3$^{1}$**

53- **2** 5 **Edged In Blue**$^{177}$ [4943] 3-8-11 0.................. JordanVaughan$^{(3)}$ 2 56
(K R Burke) *trckd ldrs: shkn up to ld over 1f out: hdd and easily outpcd jst ins fnl f* **5/1$^{2}$**

6 **3** 1 **Scala Regia (FR)**$^{7}$ [288] 3-9-0 0.................. LukeMorris 7 55+
(Sir Mark Prescott Bt) *settled in rr: bmpd along fr over 2f out: sme prog on inner over 1f out: nt clr run 100yds out but sn tk 3rd* **14/1$^{3}$**

00- **4** hd **Malt Teaser (FR)**$^{25}$ [8591] 3-9-5 0.................. KierenFox 1 57+
(John Best) *mostly in last pair: shkn up wl over 1f out: kpt on quite encouragingly ins fnl f* **16/1**

50-0 **5** 1 **Ginger Truffle**$^{7}$ [288] 3-9-0 51.................. StevieDonohoe 3 49
(Brett Johnson) *tk fierce hold: led to over 1f out: wknd* **100/1**

0- **6** 1 ½ **Vivian Ward**$^{42}$ [8362] 3-9-0 0.................. RobertTart 8 44
(John Gosden) *t.k.h: pressed ldr to wl over 1f out: wknd qckly* **14/1$^{3}$**

**7** 13 **Akuna Mattatta (IRE)** 3-9-2 0.................. HectorCrouch$^{(3)}$ 6 8
(Ralph J Smith) *s.v.s: a last: jst in tch 3f out: hanging rt and c v wd bnd 2f out: ended up against nr side rail and t.o* **50/1**

1m 13.19s (1.29) **Going Correction** +0.125s/f (Slow) **7** Ran SP% **113.9**
Speed ratings (Par 97): **96,89,88,87,86 84,67**
CSF £2.44 TOTE £1.20: £1.10, £1.60; EX 2.60 Trifecta £8.20.

**Owner** P Makin **Bred** Swordlestown Stud **Trained** Newmarket, Suffolk

**FOCUS**

An uncompetitive 3yo maiden and very much as the market expected.

### 398 SUNBETS.CO.UK APPRENTICE H'CAP — 7f 1y(P)

**4:20** (4:21) (Class 6) (0-55,57) 4-Y-O+ — **£2,264** (£673; £336; £168) **Stalls** Low

Form — RPR

00-0 **1** **Bookmaker**$^{11}$ [238] 7-9-7 **52**.................. (p$^{1}$) JaneElliott 9 57
(John Bridger) *hld up in 7th: prog on outer over 1f out: shkn up to ld last 75yds: jst hld on* **14/1**

6-44 **2** nse **Wink Oliver**$^{7}$ [293] 5-9-5 **57**.................. (p) LauraCoughlan$^{(7)}$ 11 62
(Jo Hughes) *s.i.s: hld up in last trio: gd prog on outer over 1f out: pushed along and r.o to take 2nd wl ins fnl f: jst failed* **8/1**

2-32 **3** ½ **Major Muscari (IRE)**[7] [293] 9-9-7 **57**............................(p) TobyEley(5) 8 61
(Shaun Harris) *trckd ldrs in 5th: clsd to ld 1f out: hdd and jst outpcd last 75yds* **9/2**[2]

40-0 **4** ¾ **Welsh Inlet (IRE)**[14] [167] 9-8-10 **46** oh1................. SophieRalston(5) 12 48
(John Bridger) *dwlt: wl in rr: prog and weaved through fr jst over 1f out: styd on but unable to chal* **25/1**

2-23 **5** 1 **Zabdi**[7] [293] 4-9-10 **55**........................................................ JoshuaBryan 3 54
(Lee Carter) *t.k.h: trckd ldng pair: led briefly jst over 1f out: one pce ins fnl f* **9/4**[1]

00-4 **6** ½ **Quintus Cerialis (IRE)**[18] [116] 5-9-10 **55**.....................(tp) JordanUys 2 52+
(Karen George) *s.s: mostly in last: stl there over 1f out: styd on ins fnl f: nrst fin* **5/1**[3]

00-3 **7** 1 **Cuban Queen (USA)**[14] [167] 4-8-13 **49**...................(p) FinleyMarsh(5) 6 44
(Julia Feilden) *hld up in 6th: effrt whn nt clr run on inner wl over 1f out: one pce whn in the clr fnl f* **7/1**

0-62 **8** 3½ **Nasri**[14] [172] 11-9-9 **54**.....................................................(p) BenRobinson 1 39
(Emma Owen) *chsd ldng trio: wknd jst over 1f out: eased* **14/1**

050- **9** ½ **Justice (IRE)**[29] [8542] 4-8-12 **46** oh1..................(p) ManuelFernandes(3) 7 30
(Jose Santos) *led 1f: rdn to ld again jst over 2f out: hdd & wknd qckly jst over 1f out* **66/1**

000- **10** 3¾ **No Refund (IRE)**[47] [8288] 6-9-6 **51**.......................................(p) GerO'Neill 4 25
(David Loughnane) *s.i.s: a wl in rr* **16/1**

00-4 **11** 11 **Royal Normandy**[8] [273] 5-9-9 **54**.....................................(b) JoshQuinn 5 +
(Grace Harris) *sddle slipped s: plld way through to ld after 1f: hdd jst over 2f out and wknd qckly* **16/1**

1m 24.62s (-0.18) **Going Correction** +0.125s/f (Slow) **11** Ran SP% **119.7**
Speed ratings (Par 101): **106,105,105,104,103 102,101,97,97,92 80**
CSF £123.63 CT £463.78 TOTE £17.90: £4.80, £3.20, £2.00; EX 100.20 Trifecta £1177.30.
**Owner** T Wallace & J J Bridger **Bred** Benjamin Newton And Graycroft Farm **Trained** Liphook, Hants

**FOCUS**
A moderate apprentice handicap and a rather messy race with a tight finish. The form looks straightforward.
T/Plt: £95.80 to a £1 stake. Pool: £57,375.90 - 436.87 winning units T/Qpdt: £17.60 to a £1 stake. Pool: £4,404.72 - 184.77 winning units **Jonathan Neesom**

# 356 NEWCASTLE (A.W) (L-H)
## Wednesday, January 25

**OFFICIAL GOING: Tapeta: standard**
Wind: Almost nil

### 399 BETWAY H'CAP 2m 56y (Tp)
**4:15** (4:16) (Class 5) (0-75,74) 4-Y-O+ **£3,234** (£962; £481; £240) **Stalls** Low

Form RPR
00-4 **1** **Royal Flag**[13] [196] 7-9-1 **61**........................................................ TomEaves 4 68
(Brian Ellison) *t.k.h: chsd ldr: led over 5f out: rdn and hrd pressed over 1f out: hld on gamely fnl f* **9/2**[3]

0/6- **2** nk **Lac Leman (GER)**[26] [8584] 6-10-0 **74**..............................(h[1]) GrahamLee 2 80
(Pauline Robson) *t.k.h: chsd ldrs: stdy hdwy over 2f out: rdn to chal over 1f out to ins fnl f: kpt on same pce last 50yds* **9/2**[3]

10-3 **3** 3¾ **Cavalieri (IRE)**[22] [28] 7-9-8 **68**.........................................(tp) KevinStott 1 70
(Philip Kirby) *led at v slow gallop: hdd over 5f out: pressed wnr to 2f out: sn no ex* **11/4**[2]

00-4 **4** ¾ **Spiritoftomintoul**[20] [74] 8-9-8 **71**........................ GeorgeDowning(3) 3 72
(Tony Carroll) *hld up in last pl: pushed along 3f out: hdwy over 1f out: nvr rchd ldrs* **2/1**[1]

5-10 **5** 6 **Jan Smuts (IRE)**[14] [174] 9-8-8 **59**.....................................(t) HollieDoyle(5) 5 52
(Wilf Storey) *t.k.h: hld up in tch: hdwy over 6f out: outpcd and hung lft over 2f out: btn over 1f out* **6/1**

4m 12.67s (37.47) **Going Correction** +0.225s/f (Slow) **5** Ran SP% **110.6**
Speed ratings (Par 103): **15,14,12,12,9**
CSF £23.81 TOTE £3.50: £1.70, £2.10; EX 27.10 Trifecta £48.20.
**Owner** Dean Woodhouse & Brian Ellison **Bred** Darley **Trained** Norton, N Yorks

**FOCUS**
A run-of-the-mill staying handicap in which they raised barely a gallop until past halfway. The time was very slow and as a result the form can be taken with a pinch of salt, with the principals previously unproven at the trip.

### 400 SUNBETS.CO.UK APPRENTICE H'CAP 1m 5y (Tp)
**4:45** (4:47) (Class 6) (0-55,55) 4-Y-O+ **£2,264** (£673; £336; £168) **Stalls** Centre

Form RPR
6-3 **1** **Yasood (IRE)**[18] [124] 4-9-4 **55**.................................... LuluStanford(3) 10 60
(Phil McEntee) *t.k.h early: cl up: led over 1f out: styd on wl fnl f* **6/1**[2]

320- **2** ¾ **Canford Belle**[26] [8589] 4-9-2 **53**...................................... PatrickVaughan(3) 4 56
(Grant Tuer) *stdd s: hld up: swtchd rt over 3f out: effrt and gd hdwy nr side of gp over 1f out: chsd wnr last 100yds: no ex nr fin* **16/1**

50-2 **3** ½ **Afkar (IRE)**[8] [274] 9-9-1 **52**....................................(p) LewisEdmunds(3) 11 54
(Ivan Furtado) *t.k.h: led at stdy pce:l rdn and hdd over 1f out: chsd wnr to last 100yds: kpt on same pce* **7/1**

360- **4** 1 **A Boy Named Sue**[156] [5732] 4-9-1 **49**..............................(p) JoshDoyle 5 49
(Peter Niven) *t.k.h: prom: pushed along over 2f out: hdwy over 1f out: kpt on ins fnl f* **16/1**

0-0P **5** nk **Devious Spirit (IRE)**[2] [383] 5-9-7 **55**.................................. EoinWalsh 7 54
(Iain Jardine) *missed break: hld up: stdy hdwy on far side of gp 1/2-way: effrt and rdn 2f out: kpt on same pce fnl f* **13/2**[3]

536- **6** shd **Mr Sundowner (USA)**[26] [8589] 5-9-4 **52**.........................(t) HollieDoyle 3 53
(Wilf Storey) *trckd ldrs: pushed along over 2f out: outpcd whn n.m.r and checked over 1f out: rallied: one pce fnl f* **9/2**[1]

400- **7** 1½ **Haymarket**[46] [8309] 8-9-3 **51**.............................................. GeorgeDowning 6 46
(R Mike Smith) *t.k.h: hld up: pushed along and outpcd over 2f out: rallied over 1f out: kpt on fnl f: nt pce to chal* **14/1**

61-6 **8** 1 **Justice Pleasing**[20] [67] 4-9-0 **55**..........................(p) BenSanderson(7) 2 48
(Roger Fell) *t.k.h: cl up: ev ch over 2f out to over 1f out: rdn and wknd fnl f* **7/1**

000/ **9** 2¼ **Frontline Phantom (IRE)**[453] [7602] 10-8-11 **52**.......... RussellHarris(7) 8 39
(K R Burke) *t.k.h: trckd ldrs: pushed along over 2f out: wknd over 1f out* **66/1**

0-03 **10** hd **Mount Cheiron (USA)**[11] [239] 6-9-0 **51**............(v) CallumRodriguez(3) 9 38+
(Richard Ford) *t.k.h: hld up on nr side of gp: drvn and outpcd over 2f out: sn n.d: btn over 1f out* **9/2**[1]

6-00 **11** ¾ **Breathless**[16] [147] 5-8-11 **52**........................................(tp) RossTurner(7) 12 37
(Clive Mulhall) *dwlt: hld up: pushed along and outpcd over 2f out: sn btn* **16/1**

00-6 **12** ½ **Patron Of Explores (USA)**[14] [176] 6-8-9 **46** oh1.....(t) RowanScott(3) 1 30
(Patrick Holmes) *chsd ldrs on far side of gp: rdn over 2f out: sn wknd* **33/1**

1m 41.16s (2.56) **Going Correction** +0.225s/f (Slow) **12** Ran SP% **117.7**
Speed ratings (Par 101): **96,95,94,93,93 93,91,90,88,88 87,87**
CSF £97.33 CT £699.23 TOTE £6.30: £2.00, £4.00, £2.80; EX 85.70 Trifecta £356.90.
**Owner** Miss Robin Blaze McEntee **Bred** Epona Bloodstock Ltd **Trained** Newmarket, Suffolk
■ Stewards' Enquiry : Patrick Vaughan four-day ban: used whip above permitted level (Feb 8-11)

**FOCUS**
This low-grade but competitive-looking apprentice handicap had plenty with chances entering the last furlong. It paid to race towards the far side, but the early pace was slow so probably not form to be relied on.

### 401 32RED.COM H'CAP 7f 14y (Tp)
**5:15** (5:16) (Class 5) (0-70,70) 3-Y-O **£2,911** (£866; £432; £216) **Stalls** Centre

Form RPR
5-44 **1** **Spinwheel**[11] [237] 3-9-4 **67**................................................. PJMcDonald 4 73+
(Mark Johnston) *mde all at ordinary gallop: rdn and qcknd over 1f out: kpt on wl fnl f: eased cl home* **9/1**

53-5 **2** 1¾ **Hotfill**[15] [160] 3-9-4 **67**.......................................................... SamJames 6 68
(David Barron) *hld up in tch: hdwy nr side of gp and chsd wnr 1f out: kpt on ins fnl f: nt pce to chal* **3/1**[2]

300- **3** nk **Bloomin Lovely (IRE)**[109] [7140] 3-9-7 **70**.............................. JasonHart 5 70
(John Quinn) *fractious in stalls: trckd ldrs: rdn and effrt wl over 1f out: kpt on same pce ins fnl f* **10/1**

000- **4** shd **Out Of Order (IRE)**[69] [7988] 3-9-1 **64**.........................(t[1]) JamesSullivan 7 64+
(Tim Easterby) *s.i.s: hld up: hdwy whn nt clr run appr fnl f: rdn and kpt on fnl f: nrst fin* **20/1**

100- **5** ½ **Galahad**[28] [8560] 3-9-4 **67**................................................. TonyHamilton 8 65
(Richard Fahey) *pressed wnr to appr fnl f: drvn and sn one pce* **15/8**[1]

320- **6** 1¾ **Dusty Bin**[27] [8568] 3-9-2 **65**..........................................(p[1]) AndrewMullen 2 59
(Garry Moss) *t.k.h: cl up: effrt and rdn over 1f out: outpcd ins fnl f* **4/1**[3]

0-40 **7** 2¾ **Ode To Paris**[12] [209] 3-9-1 **64**........................................... DavidProbert 3 50
(Ed Dunlop) *in tch: effrt on far side of gp over 2f out: edgd lft over 1f out: wknd fnl f* **8/1**

424- **8** 4½ **Sheila's Return**[85] [7750] 3-8-7 **56**........................................ TomEaves 1 30
(John Balding) *hld up: drvn and outpcd over 2f out: btn over 1f out* **25/1**

1m 28.6s (2.40) **Going Correction** +0.225s/f (Slow) **8** Ran SP% **118.6**
Speed ratings (Par 97): **95,93,92,92,91 89,86,81**
CSF £37.65 CT £283.69 TOTE £8.10: £2.20, £1.50, £4.10; EX 28.20 Trifecta £359.20.
**Owner** Sheikh Hamdan bin Mohammed Al Maktoum **Bred** Darley **Trained** Middleham Moor, N Yorks

**FOCUS**
A tight little 3yo handicap, but a good winner who made all.

### 402 SUN BETS ON THE APP STORE MAIDEN STKS 1m 5y (Tp)
**5:45** (5:45) (Class 5) 3-5-Y-O **£2,911** (£866; £432; £216) **Stalls** Centre

Form RPR
0- **1** **Shamrokh (IRE)**[34] [8486] 3-8-8 0..................................(tp) NickyMackay 2 76+
(John Gosden) *mde all: drvn clr appr fnl f* **8/13**[1]

0-34 **2** 5 **Shabeeh (IRE)**[15] [160] 3-8-8 71........................................... PJMcDonald 5 64
(Mark Johnston) *dwlt: hld up in tch: rdn and hdwy to chse wnr over 1f out: no imp fnl f* **5/2**[2]

0-2 **3** 3 **Life Won't Wait**[22] [27] 3-8-8 0................................................ JasonHart 7 57
(John Quinn) *dwlt: hld up: pushed along and outpcd over 2f out: rallied over 1f out: no imp fnl f* **8/1**[3]

5- **4** ½ **The Bard's Advice**[145] [6099] 3-7-12 0...................... ShirleyTeasdale(5) 3 51
(Keith Dalgleish) *t.k.h: prom: rdn and edgd lft over 1f out: btn fnl f* **12/1**

**5** ¾ **Billys Connoisseur (IRE)** 4-10-0 0................................ DuranFentiman 6 59
(Tim Easterby) *dwlt: t.k.h and sn trcking wnr: rdn along wl over 1f out: wknd ins fnl f* **66/1**

6-0 **6** 1½ **Scannermandango**[21] [40] 4-9-9 0.................................. JamesSullivan 4 51
(Jim Goldie) *t.k.h: hld up: rdn and outpcd over 2f out: sn n.d* **100/1**

6- **7** 5 **Night Shadow**[255] [2265] 3-8-3 0........................................... PhilDennis(5) 1 39
(Alan Brown) *plld hrd: cl up tl edgd lft and wknd over 1f out* **80/1**

1m 42.6s (4.00) **Going Correction** +0.225s/f (Slow)
**WFA** 3 from 4yo 20lb **7** Ran SP% **113.0**
Speed ratings (Par 103): **89,84,81,80,79 78,73**
CSF £2.30 TOTE £1.50: £1.10, £1.50; EX 2.50 Trifecta £5.50.
**Owner** Al Shaqab Racing **Bred** Diomed Blds Ltd & Herbertstown Hse Stud **Trained** Newmarket, Suffolk

**FOCUS**
The time of this fair-looking maiden was 1.34 sec slower than the earlier apprentice handicap after they dawdled early on. The race worked out as the market suggested.

### 403 BETWAY BEST ODDS GUARANTEED PLUS H'CAP 6f (Tp)
**6:15** (6:15) (Class 4) (0-85,86) 4-Y-O+ **£5,040** (£1,508; £754; £377; £188) **Stalls** Centre

Form RPR
14-3 **1** **Captain Dion**[12] [219] 4-9-7 **85**..........................................(v[1]) KevinStott 4 94
(Kevin Ryan) *trckd ldrs: effrt and wnt 2nd 1f out: kpt on fnl f: nt rch wnr* **11/8**[1]

25-3 **2** 1½ **Dark Side Dream**[21] [45] 5-8-9 **73**.................................... DavidProbert 5 77
(Chris Dwyer) *mde all at ordinary gallop: rdn over 1f out: edgd rt ins fnl f: kpt on wl* **9/2**[2]

050- **3** nk **Pearl Spectre (USA)**[36] [8475] 6-9-3 **86**.......................... LuluStanford(5) 3 89
(Phil McEntee) *t.k.h: trckd ldrs: effrt and drvn along over 1f out: kpt on ins fnl f* **13/2**

0-50 **4** nk **Salvatore Fury (IRE)**[4] [358] 7-9-3 **81**.........................(b[1]) PhillipMakin 6 83
(Keith Dalgleish) *t.k.h: hld up in tch: shkn up and effrt over 1f out: kpt on ins fnl f: nvr able to chal* **16/1**

502- **5** 1¾ **Buccaneers Vault (IRE)**[99] [7434] 5-9-2 **80**..............(p) PaulMulrennan 7 76
(Paul Midgley) *t.k.h: trckd wnr to 1f out: drvn and wknd last 75yds* **6/1**[3]

00-4 **6** hd **Merdon Castle (IRE)**[22] [32] 5-9-0 **78**.......................(e) JamesSullivan 1 74
(Ruth Carr) *hld up in last pl: pushed along over 1f out: kpt on fnl f: no imp* **7/1**

41-6 **7** 2¼ **Luis Vaz De Torres (IRE)**[22] [33] 5-9-2 **80**................ TonyHamilton 2 69
(Richard Fahey) *t.k.h: stdd in tch: effrt and rdn 2f out: wknd ins fnl f* **20/1**

1m 12.81s (0.31) **Going Correction** +0.225s/f (Slow) **7** Ran SP% **111.1**
Speed ratings (Par 105): **106,104,103,103,100 100,97**
CSF £7.20 TOTE £2.10: £1.30, £2.60; EX 6.60 Trifecta £26.00.
**Owner** T A Rahman **Bred** Miss R J Dobson **Trained** Hambleton, N Yorks

**FOCUS**
The feature race and a decent sprint handicap. The favourite made all and fought off several challenges with a little in hand.

## 404 32REDSPORT.COM H'CAP 5f (Tp)
6:45 (6:45) (Class 5) (0-75,76) 3-Y-O **£2,911** (£866; £432; £216) **Stalls** Centre

Form RPR
53-2 **1** **Major Jumbo**[15] 155 3-9-4 **69** ShaneGray 2 83
(Kevin Ryan) *mde all: rdn over 1f out: clr ins fnl f: r.o wl* **7/2**[3]
33-1 **2** 2 ¼ **Erissimus Maximus (FR)**[21] 41 3-9-11 **76** (p) DavidProbert 1 82
(Chris Dwyer) *hld up in tch: effrt and edgd lft over 2f out: chsd (clr) wnr ins fnl f: r.o* **15/8**[1]
0-12 **3** 1 ¼ **Magdalene Fox**[9] 264 3-8-10 **61** (b) PJMcDonald 4 63
(Ed Dunlop) *pressed wnr: rdn along over 2f out: edgd lft and outpcd ins fnl f* **5/2**[2]
600- **4** 4 ½ **Lady Cristal (IRE)**[124] 6743 3-9-5 **70** DougieCostello 5 55
(K R Burke) *in tch: drvn along 1/2-way: no imp over 1f out: sn btn* **12/1**
666- **5** hd **Brother McGonagall**[46] 8313 3-8-13 **64** DuranFentiman 7 49
(Tim Easterby) *hld up: rdn along 1/2-way: sme hdwy over 1f out: nvr able to chal* **10/1**
01-3 **6** 19 **Imdancinwithurwife (IRE)**[11] 243 3-9-7 **72** PaulMulrennan 6
(Tom Dascombe) *hld up in tch: drvn along over 2f out: wknd wl over 1f out* **12/1**
05-0 **7** 2 ¼ **Poppy Pivot (IRE)**[9] 264 3-9-0 **65** (vt[1]) BenCurtis 3
(Michael Appleby) *s.i.s: bhd: struggling over 2f out: sn btn* **100/1**

58.87s (-0.63) **Going Correction** -0.075s/f (Stan) 7 Ran SP% **111.0**
Speed ratings (Par 97): **102,98,96,89,88 58,54**
CSF £9.85 TOTE £4.80: £2.50, £1.50; EX 9.40 Trifecta £27.00.
**Owner** T A Rahman **Bred** D R Botterill **Trained** Hambleton, N Yorks

**FOCUS**
A fair 3yo sprint over the minimum trip and a fourth winner from four races on the straight track to make all. Few got into it and the first three were clear.
T/Plt: £39.30 to a £1 stake. Pool: £70,301.75 - 1,303.38 winning units T/Qpdt: £6.20 to a £1 stake. Pool: £10,888.96 - 1,292.09 winning units **Richard Young**

405 - 413a (Foreign Racing) - See Raceform Interactive

# [385] SOUTHWELL (L-H)
Thursday, January 26

**OFFICIAL GOING: Fibresand: standard**
Wind: Moderate against Weather: Heavy cloud

## 414 BETWAY H'CAP 1m 4f 14y(F)
1:05 (1:11) (Class 6) (0-55,57) 4-Y-O+ **£2,587** (£770; £384; £192) **Stalls** Low

Form RPR
21-2 **1** **My Renaissance**[17] 146 7-9-7 **57** JaneElliott[(7)] 3 64
(Sam England) *trckd ldrs: cl up on outer 4f out: led 3f out: rdn clr wl over 1f out: kpt on wl fnl f* **6/1**[3]
20-6 **2** 1 ¾ **Go On Gal (IRE)**[19] 120 4-9-6 **56** ShelleyBirkett[(3)] 4 60
(Julia Feilden) *trckd ldrs: hdwy 3f out: rdn 2f out: chsd wnr over 1f out: drvn ins fnl f: kpt on same pce* **20/1**
40-5 **3** ¾ **Paddy's Rock (IRE)**[17] 146 6-9-8 **51** PaddyAspell 1 54
(Lynn Siddall) *trckd ldng pair on inner: pushed along 3f out: rdn 2f out: drvn over 1f out: kpt on* **20/1**
000- **4** 1 ½ **Crakehall Lad (IRE)**[25] 8309 6-9-2 **45** (b) NeilFarley 8 46
(Andrew Crook) *hld up towards rr: hdwy over 4f out: rdn along wl over 2f out: styd on appr fnl f: nrst fin* **20/1**
04-2 **5** 2 **Miss Macchiato (IRE)**[21] 70 4-9-2 **49** ConnorBeasley 7 46
(Keith Dalgleish) *trckd ldr: cl up bef 1/2-way: pushed along over 3f out and sn rdn: drvn 2f out and grad wknd* **9/4**[1]
06/4 **6** ½ **Tenhoo**[15] 176 11-8-9 **45** CallumRodriguez[(7)] 6 42
(Richard Ford) *chsd ldrs: rdn along wl over 3f out: drvn over 2f out: sn no imp* **14/1**
04-0 **7** 1 ¼ **Quadriga (IRE)**[25] 7 7-9-9 **52** (be[1]) TonyHamilton 13 47
(Chris Grant) *trckd ldrs: hdwy over 4f out: rdn along over 3f out: drvn over 2f out and grad wknd* **50/1**
01-0 **8** 2 ¾ **Moojaned (IRE)**[15] 169 6-9-13 **56** AndrewMullen 2 29
(David Evans) *led: pushed along over 4f out: sn rdn: hdd 3f out: sn drvn and wknd: lame: fin 9th: plcd 8th* **4/1**[2]
50-4 **9** 5 **Senor George (IRE)**[17] 146 10-9-9 **52** TomEaves 14 17
(Simon Hodgson) *a in rr: bhd fnl 3f: fin 10th: plcd 9th* **16/1**
040- **10** 5 **Ambitious Rosie**[344] 602 6-8-13 **45** GeorgeDowning[(3)] 12 2
(Tony Carroll) *a in rr: bhd fnl 3f: fin 11th: plcd 10th* **125/1**
6/6- **11** 14 **Hollywood All Star (IRE)**[14] 701 8-9-2 **45** LiamKeniry 11
(Graeme McPherson) *a bhd: fin 12th: plcd 11th* **11/1**
000- **12** 22 **Last Summer**[86] 7739 6-9-7 **50** LukeMorris 5
(Grace Harris) *a bhd: fin 13th: plcd 12th* **12/1**
0-40 **D** 11 **Our Little Sister (IRE)**[12] 241 4-8-12 **52** TheodoreLadd[(7)] 10 29
(Hughie Morrison) *chsd ldrs: rdn along over 3f out: sn wknd: fin 8th: later disqualified; prohibited substance fnd in sample* **22/1**

2m 46.67s (5.67) **Going Correction** +0.25s/f (Slow)
**WFA** 4 from 6yo+ 3lb 13 Ran SP% **115.0**
Speed ratings (Par 101): **91,89,89,88,87 86,85,76,73,70 60,46,78**
CSF £124.70 CT £2232.88 TOTE £5.10: £2.00, £5.40, £6.60; EX 94.30 Trifecta £1154.10.
**Owner** Panther Racing Ltd **Bred** Aston House Stud **Trained** Guiseley, West Yorkshire

**FOCUS**
A weak yet competitive middle-distance handicap rated around the second and fourth. The pace was steady and the first three were all making their Fibresand debuts. The form is rated around the second and fourth.

## 415 BETWAY BEST ODDS GUARANTEED PLUS MAIDEN STKS 4f 214y(F)
1:35 (1:40) (Class 5) 3-Y-O+ **£3,234** (£962; £481; £240) **Stalls** Centre

Form RPR
0-3 **1** **Fiery Spice (IRE)**[17] 140 3-8-13 0 LukeMorris 12 63
(Robert Cowell) *racd nr stands side: cl up: effrt and green over 1f out: rdn to ld ent fnl f: sn edgd lft: kpt on* **16/1**
002- **2** 1 **Luv U Always**[48] 8285 3-8-8 51 PJMcDonald 9 54
(Iain Jardine) *racd towards stands side: slt ld: rdn 1 1/2f out: hdd ent fnl f: sn drvn and kpt on* **9/2**[2]
6-6 **3** 1 **Bo Selecta (IRE)**[19] 119 3-8-13 0 StevieDonohoe 3 55+
(Richard Spencer) *towards rr: hdwy 2f out: swtchd rt and rdn over 1f out: styd on strly fnl f: nrst fin* **9/1**
43-2 **4** ½ **Speed Freak**[13] 212 3-8-3 68 (b) PatrickO'Donnell[(5)] 5 49
(Ralph Beckett) *racd towards centre: cl up rdn along 2f out and ev ch: drvn ent fnl f: kpt on same pce* **8/11**[1]
5 **5** ¾ **Ebitda** 3-8-1 0 RPWalsh[(7)] 7 46+
(Scott Dixon) *dwlt and towards rr: hdwy 2f out: rdn over 1f out: kpt on wl fnl f: nrst fin* **25/1**
0-5 **6** hd **Joyroo (IRE)**[16] 157 3-8-8 0 MeganNicholls[(5)] 6 50
(Michael Easterby) *chsd ldrs centre: rdn along over 2f out: sn drvn and kpt on one pce* **66/1**
5-4 **7** 1 **Highly Focussed (IRE)**[5] 357 3-8-13 0 GrahamLee 1 47
(Ann Duffield) *chsd ldrs: rdn along 2f out: kpt on one pce appr fnl f* **8/1**[3]
0-6 **8** 1 ¼ **Jai Hanuman (IRE)**[13] 221 3-8-13 0 (t) LiamKeniry 11 42
(Seamus Durack) *rr: rdn along 2f out: swtchd lft and drvn over 1f out: no imp* **25/1**
50-0 **9** hd **Master Pekan**[10] 270 4-9-9 45 (b[1]) MitchGodwin[(5)] 2 47
(Roy Brotherton) *prom centre: rdn along over 2f out: drvn wl over 1f out: sn wknd* **50/1**
4-0 **10** ¾ **Jungle George**[13] 212 3-8-13 0 (b[1]) KieranO'Neill 8 39
(Scott Dixon) *dwlt and rr: swtchd lft 1/2-way: racd towards far side and a bhd* **25/1**
0-0 **11** 8 **London Rebel (IRE)**[15] 168 4-9-9 0 TomMarquand 10 11
(Richard Spencer) *racd nr stands rail: rdn along and outpcd bef 1/2-way: sn bhd* **80/1**

1m 3.22s (3.52) **Going Correction** +0.60s/f (Slow)
**WFA** 3 from 4yo 15lb 11 Ran SP% **119.3**
Speed ratings (Par 103): **95,93,91,91,89 89,87,85,85,84 71**
CSF £83.13 TOTE £12.30: £2.90, £1.40, £2.80; EX 71.00 Trifecta £560.60.
**Owner** Khalifa Dasmal **Bred** K A Dasmal **Trained** Six Mile Bottom, Cambs

**FOCUS**
A moderate and uncompetitive sprint maiden. Few got into it and the runner-up sets the standard.

## 416 BETWAY BEST ODDS GUARANTEED PLUS H'CAP 4f 214y(F)
2:10 (2:12) (Class 5) (0-75,75) 4-Y-O+ **£3,234** (£962; £481; £240) **Stalls** Centre

Form RPR
63-0 **1** **Archimedes (IRE)**[24] 22 4-8-7 **61** (t[1]) JosephineGordon 1 73
(David C Griffiths) *cl up centre: slt ld 3f out: rdn wl over 1f out: kpt on strly fnl f* **20/1**
-314 **2** 2 ½ **Englishwoman**[7] 312 4-9-7 **75** StevieDonohoe 7 78
(David Evans) *towards rr: pushed along 1/2-way: rdn wl over 1f out: drvn and styd on wl fnl f* **15/2**[3]
150- **3** shd **Mysterious Look**[44] 8349 4-9-3 **74** RobHornby[(3)] 5 77
(Ed McMahon) *trckd ldrs: hdwy 1/2-way: chsd wnr over 1f out and sn rdn: drvn ins fnl f: kpt on same pce* **11/1**
006- **4** 1 **Brockholes**[41] 8403 4-9-2 **70** PaulMulrennan 3 69
(Bryan Smart) *cl up centre: rdn along wl over 1f out: drvn fnl f and grad wknd* **10/1**
/13- **5** nk **Berlios (IRE)**[44] 8349 4-9-5 **73** AndrewMullen 6 71
(David Barron) *in tch centre: pushed along over 2f out: swtchd lft and rdn over 1f out: sn drvn and no imp ins fnl f* **5/2**[1]
4-66 **6** ¾ **Red Stripes (USA)**[6] 330 5-9-0 **68** KevinStott 9 63
(Lisa Williamson) *cl up: pushed along and sltly outpcd 1/2-way: rdn wl over 1f out: kpt on fnl f* **12/1**
60-4 **7** 2 **Misu Moneypenny**[13] 215 4-8-10 **64** (p) LukeMorris 2 52
(Scott Dixon) *prom: rdn along 2f out: drvn and edgd lft over 1f out: sn wknd* **25/1**
166- **8** 3 ½ **Waneen (IRE)**[49] 8280 4-9-6 **74** RobertWinston 8 49
(John Butler) *slt ld 1f: prom: rdn along 1/2-way: sn wknd* **16/1**
6463 **9** 1 **Crosse Fire**[7] 312 5-9-2 **70** (p) DaleSwift 4 42
(Scott Dixon) *s.i.s and bhd: swtchd lft to far rail and rdn along bef 1/2-way: nvr a factor* **4/1**[2]
000- **10** 8 **King Crimson**[28] 8571 5-9-6 **74** TimmyMurphy 11 17
(John Butler) *racd towards stands side: t.k.h and in tch: pushed along bef 1/2-way: sn outpcd and bhd* **100/1**
/0- **11** ¾ **Rocking Rudolph (USA)**[111] 7112 4-9-6 **74** RichardKingscote 12 14
(Robert Cowell) *racd nr stands rail: chsd ldrs: sn rdn along and outpcd: bhd fr 1/2-way* **12/1**

1m 1.36s (1.66) **Going Correction** +0.60s/f (Slow) 11 Ran SP% **108.6**
Speed ratings (Par 103): **110,106,105,104,103 102,99,93,92,79 78**
CSF £126.26 CT £1128.31 TOTE £21.50: £5.00, £1.70, £2.90; EX 185.60 Trifecta £1550.80.
**Owner** Ladies And The Tramps **Bred** Paddy Twomey & Irish National Stud **Trained** Bawtry, S Yorks
■ Piazon was withdrawn. Price at time of withdrawal 5-1. Rule 4 applies to all bets - deduction 15p in the pound.

**FOCUS**
An ordinary sprint handicap weakened slightly when Piazon was withdrawn after getting upset in the stalls. Six of the 11 remaining runners were C&D winners and the winner has been rated to his best since his debut.

## 417 32RED.COM H'CAP 1m 13y(F)
2:45 (2:45) (Class 4) (0-80,75) 3-Y-O **£5,175** (£1,540; £769; £384) **Stalls** Low

Form RPR
60-4 **1** **Upgrade**[21] 65 3-9-1 **69** DougieCostello 5 75
(K R Burke) *mde all: qcknd clr wl over 2f out: kpt on strly* **6/1**[3]
001- **2** 3 **Haraka (IRE)**[28] 8568 3-9-1 **69** (b) RichardKingscote 3 68
(Ralph Beckett) *dwlt: hld up in tch: wd st: hdwy 2f out: rdn to chse wnr wl over 1f out: drvn and no imp fnl f* **5/4**[1]
00-1 **3** 3 ½ **Mia Cara**[12] 245 3-8-10 **64** AndrewMullen 4 55
(David Evans) *trckd ldng pair: hdwy over 3f out: rdn over 2f out: drvn wl over 1f out: kpt on same pce* **7/1**
34-6 **4** 1 ¼ **Whatsthemessage (IRE)**[23] 31 3-9-7 **75** PhillipMakin 1 63
(Keith Dalgleish) *chsd wnr: rdn along wl over 2f out: drvn wl over 1f out: kpt on one pce* **11/1**
411- **5** 25 **Dream Team**[51] 8235 3-9-3 **71** (p) PaulMulrennan 2 2
(Michael Dods) *trckd ldrs: pushed along 1/2-way: rdn over 3f out: sn outpcd and bhd* **5/2**[2]

1m 45.44s (1.74) **Going Correction** +0.25s/f (Slow) 5 Ran SP% **108.1**
Speed ratings (Par 99): **101,98,94,93,68**
CSF £13.61 TOTE £9.70: £3.10, £1.10; EX 18.10 Trifecta £52.60.
**Owner** Mrs Melba Bryce **Bred** Laundry Cottage Stud Farm **Trained** Middleham Moor, N Yorks

**FOCUS**
Not a bad 3yo handicap despite the small field with three of the five runners successful last time out, but a finely judged ride from the winning jockey. The winner has been rated back to his best.

## 418 32RED.COM H'CAP 6f 16y(F)
3:20 (3:23) (Class 6) (0-65,66) 3-Y-O **£2,587** (£770; £384; £192) **Stalls** Low

Form RPR
06-4 **1** **Mister Freeze (IRE)**[12] 244 3-9-5 **63** (t) LukeMorris 6 76
(Clive Cox) *sn led: rdn wl over 1f out: clr appr fnl f: kpt on strly* **6/1**



The Form Book Flat, Raceform Ltd, Newbury, RG14 5SJ

030- **2** *3 ¾* **Moondust (IRE)**[102] [7380] 3-9-8 **66**.................................. NickyMackay 3 68
(John Gosden) *rr and pushed along early: sn in tch towards rr: hdwy 1/2-way: effrt to chse ldrs wl over 1f out: sn rdn and chsd wnr ent fnl f: sn drvn and no imp* **10/3**[2]

04-0 **3** *1 ¼* **Suffragette City (IRE)**[16] [160] 3-9-5 **63**....................(b) TomMarquand 7 61
(Richard Hannon) *dwlt: sn cl up: rdn along 2f out: drvn over 1f out: kpt on same pce* **4/1**[3]

40-0 **4** *¾* **Masquerade Bling (IRE)**[20] [89] 3-8-12 **56**....................... TomEaves 2 52
(Simon Hodgson) *hld up: hdwy on inner over 2f out: swtchd rt and rdn over 1f out: kpt on u.p fnl f* **16/1**

66-4 **5** *¾* **Cool Echo**[25] [1] 3-9-2 **60**........................................... ConnorBeasley 5 54
(J R Jenkins) *dwlt: in tch on outer: pushed along 2f out: rdn over 2f out: sn drvn and kpt on one pce* **13/2**

3-5 **6** *nk* **Lady Volante (IRE)**[22] [48] 3-9-6 **64**............................ AndrewMullen 4 57
(David Evans) *chsd ldrs: rdn along wl over 2f out: sn drvn and kpt on one pce* **10/1**

40-1 **7** *¾* **Western Presence**[16] [157] 3-9-7 **65**.............................. TonyHamilton 1 56
(Richard Fahey) *trckd ldng pair: smooth hdwy on inner and cl up 2f out: rdn to chal over 1f out and ev ch: sn drvn and wknd fnl f* **3/1**[1]

1m 19.03s (2.53) **Going Correction** +0.25s/f (Slow) **7** Ran SP% **110.7**
Speed ratings (Par 95): **93,88,86,85,84 83,82**
CSF £24.50 TOTE £7.80: £3.00, £1.80; EX 27.30 Trifecta £174.40.
**Owner** Ken Lock Racing **Bred** Malachy M Harney **Trained** Lambourn, Berks

**FOCUS**
A moderate 3yo sprint handicap, with only one previous winner in the field, but the first two were making their handicap debuts. Another powerful front-running performance on the card.

## 419 SUNBETS.CO.UK H'CAP 1m 13y(F)
**3:55** (3:56) (Class 5) (0-75,75) 4-Y-0+ **£3,557** (£1,058; £529; £264) **Stalls** Low

Form RPR

43-5 **1** **Alpha Tauri (USA)**[21] [67] 11-8-4 **65**....................... BenRobinson(7) 12 79
(Charles Smith) *cl up: led wl over 2f out: rdn clr wl over 1f out: styd on strly* **33/1**

244- **2** *10* **Royal Holiday (IRE)**[37] [8477] 10-9-1 **69**.........................(p) TomEaves 10 60
(Marjorie Fife) *led: rdn along and hdd wl over 2f out: drvn wl over 1f out: kpt on: no ch w wnr* **16/1**

10-4 **3** *nk* **Stun Gun**[25] [6] 7-8-13 **67**..........................................(p) TonyHamilton 6 57
(Derek Shaw) *towards rr: wd st and hdwy over 2f out: sn rdn and styd on wl appr fnl f* **14/1**

01-2 **4** *1* **Anton Chigurh**[25] [6] 8-9-7 **75**................................ RichardKingscote 9 63
(Tom Dascombe) *hld up: hdwy wl over 2f out: sn chsng ldrs: rdn wl over 1f out: kpt on same pce* **4/1**[2]

04-2 **5** *1* **What Usain**[16] [166] 5-8-9 **63**............................................... LukeMorris 14 49
(Michael Appleby) *rr and sn pushed along: rdn wl over 3f out: hdwy over 2f out: swtchd rt and drvn over 1f out: kpt on: nrst fin* **9/1**

0-11 **6** *1 ¾* **Essenaitch (IRE)**[21] [67] 4-9-4 **72**.......................... AndrewMullen 3 54
(David Evans) *trckd ldrs towards inner: hdwy over 3f out: rdn along wl over 2f out: drvn wl over 1f out: one pce* **8/1**[3]

/0-1 **7** *3* **Zoravan (USA)**[7] [314] 4-9-6 **74** 6ex...............................(v) PhillipMakin 4 49
(Keith Dalgleish) *trckd ldrs: hdwy over 3f out: chsd ldng pair over 2f out: sn rdn: drvn wl over 1f out: grad wknd* **6/4**[1]

52-0 **8** *1* **Space War**[16] [159] 10-8-8 **67**....................................(t) MeganNicholls(5) 8 39
(Michael Easterby) *dwlt and towards rr: wd st and sme hdwy over 2f out: sn rdn and edgd lft: n.d* **33/1**

006- **9** *nk* **St Andrews (IRE)**[217] [3579] 4-8-13 **67**.........................(t) StevieDonohoe 7 39
(Ian Williams) *dwlt and bhd tl sme late hdwy* **33/1**

000- **10** *6* **Cosmic Ray**[148] [6028] 5-9-1 **69**..........................................(h) JasonHart 11 27
(Les Eyre) *cl up: rdn along 3f out: drvn over 2f out and sn wknd* **66/1**

1-05 **11** *nse* **Macho Mac**[16] [159] 4-8-11 **70**.................................(h) CharlieBennett(5) 5 28
(Hughie Morrison) *t.k.h: hld up towards rr: effrt and sme hdwy 3f out: rdn over 2f out and n.d* **10/1**

0/0- **12** *¾* **One Man Army**[236] [2918] 5-8-3 **62**.................................. PhilDennis(5) 13 18
(Julia Brooke) *chsd ldrs on outer: rdn along and wd st: drvn 2f out and sn wknd* **100/1**

34-5 **13** *4* **Miss Goldsmith (IRE)**[22] [44] 4-8-7 **61**........................ BarryMcHugh 2 8
(Richard Fahey) *chsd ldrs on inner: rdn along over 3f out: sn wknd* **33/1**

00-0 **14** *18* **Showing Off (IRE)**[24] [25] 4-8-13 **67**.............................. RyanPowell 1
(Michael Wigham) *a rr: bhd fr 1/2-way* **150/1**

1m 44.47s (0.77) **Going Correction** +0.25s/f (Slow) **14** Ran SP% **117.7**
Speed ratings (Par 103): **106,96,95,94,93 91,88,87,87,81 81,80,76,58**
CSF £468.36 CT £7711.46 TOTE £40.50: £8.60, £5.00, £3.90; EX 467.80 Trifecta £8584.10.
**Owner** J R Theaker **Bred** Flaxman Holdings Ltd **Trained** Temple Bruer, Lincs

**FOCUS**
An ordinary handicap, but an incredible performance by another Charles Smith-trained veteran at this track.
T/Plt: £12,993.20 to a £1 stake. Pool: £70,305.85 - 3.95 winning units T/Qpdt: £947.30 to a £1 stake. Pool: £8,321.71 - 6.50 winning units **Joe Rowntree**

# [376]WOLVERHAMPTON (A.W) (L-H)
Thursday, January 26

**OFFICIAL GOING: Tapeta: standard**
Wind: medium half against Weather: cold

## 420 BETWAY MIDDLE APPRENTICE H'CAP (DIV I) 1m 1f 104y (Tp)
**5:50** (5:51) (Class 6) (0-60,60) 4-Y-0+ **£2,749** (£818; £408; £204) **Stalls** Low

Form RPR

400- **1** **Black Hole Sun**[68] [8038] 5-8-11 **50**............................ JosephineGordon 2 56
(Ian Williams) *trckd ldr: rdn over 2f out: led over 1f out: edgd lft ins fnl f: drvn out* **8/1**

10-0 **2** *2* **Siouxperhero (IRE)**[16] [166] 8-9-7 **60**..........................(p) LouisSteward 3 62
(William Muir) *trckd ldng pair: rdn over 2f out: kpt on to take 2nd 75yds out but hld by wnr* **5/1**[2]

33-5 **3** *½* **Vision Of Beauty (FR)**[24] [23] 4-9-4 **61**................. ShirleyTeasdale(3) 4 62
(Keith Dalgleish) *wnt to post early: t.k.h: led: rdn 2f out: hdd over 1f out: unable qck: lost 2nd 75yds out* **7/1**

0-06 **4** *½* **Gold Return (IRE)**[7] [304] 4-9-1 **62**.......................... JonathanFisher(7) 1 62
(John Ryan) *s.i.s: in rr: rdn over 2f out: styd on fnl f: wnt 4th post* **10/1**

00-1 **5** *hd* **Sir Lancelott**[12] [239] 5-9-4 **62**..................................(p) PatrickVaughan(5) 9 64
(David O'Meara) *midfield: hdwy 2f out: sn rdn: styng on whn hmpd on ins and lost momentum 100yds out: one pce after* **4/1**[1]

0-42 **6** *1 ¾* **Dove Mountain (IRE)**[12] [239] 6-9-0 **60**.........................(tp) JoshuaBryan(7) 8 57
(Anabel K Murphy) *hld up: rdn over 2f out: kpt on same pce and nvr able to chal* **5/1**[2]

32-0 **7** *5* **Dor's Law**[17] [147] 4-9-4 **58**......................................................... JackDuern 6 45
(Dean Ivory) *s.s: hld up: hdwy 4f out: rdn 2f out: wkng whn hmpd over 1f out* **11/2**[3]

30-5 **8** *hd* **Amor Invicto (IRE)**[12] [239] 4-9-7 **61**.....................(b) GeorgeDowning 10 48
(Daniel Kubler) *hld up: rdn over 3f out: wknd over 1f out* **15/2**

-000 **U** **Sheer Intensity (IRE)**[5] [351] 4-8-11 **58**..........(b1) KatherineGlenister(7) 7
(David Evans) *pushed along fr stalls to chse ldrs: stmbld ins first f and sddle slipped: eased bk through field 4f out: wl bhd whn uns rdr wl over 1f out* **16/1**

2m 1.81s (1.01) **Going Correction** +0.075s/f (Slow)
**WFA** 4 from 5yo+ 1lb **9** Ran SP% **119.1**
Speed ratings (Par 101): **98,96,95,95,95 93,89,88,**
CSF £49.24 CT £299.95 TOTE £9.60: £2.50, £2.20, £2.00; EX 54.50 Trifecta £500.80.
**Owner** The Ferandlin Peaches **Bred** Shully Liebermann **Trained** Portway, Worcs
■ Stewards' Enquiry : Shirley Teasdale three-day ban; allowed her horse to drift left-handed, away from the whip, without timely correction. (9th-11th Feb)

**FOCUS**
The first division of a modest handicap, in which it paid to race close to the pace.

## 421 BETWAY MIDDLE APPRENTICE H'CAP (DIV II) 1m 1f 104y (Tp)
**6:25** (6:25) (Class 6) (0-60,62) 4-Y-0+ **£2,749** (£818; £408; £204) **Stalls** Low

Form RPR

23-1 **1** **Boychick (IRE)**[19] [124] 4-9-2 **56**...................................... HectorCrouch 1 66+
(Ed Walker) *hld up: hdwy over 2f out: wnt 3rd over 1f out: r.o to ld ins fnl f: drvn out* **5/2**[1]

00-5 **2** *nk* **King Oswald (USA)**[16] [164] 4-9-7 **61**......................... GeorgeDowning 7 70
(James Unett) *hld up in rr: hdwy over 2f out: sn drvn: chsd ldr over 1f out: kpt on and ev ch ins fnl f: jst hld* **15/2**[3]

0-24 **3** *1 ½* **Paper Faces (USA)**[6] [333] 4-9-8 **62**......................... JosephineGordon 3 68
(Roger Varian) *led 1f: cl up: ld again over 2f out: rdn to go 4 l up over 1f out: hdd and no ex ins fnl f* **4/1**[2]

-040 **4** *7* **Ferryview Place**[12] [239] 8-8-5 **51**..............................(vt) LukeCatton(7) 10 44
(Ian Williams) *s.s and bhd: sn pushed along: in tch after 4f: stl last over 1f out where drvn: styd on fnl f* **20/1**

60-4 **5** *1* **Commissar**[21] [70] 8-9-7 **60**...........................................(tp) RobHornby 4 51
(Mandy Rowland) *midfield: drvn over 1f out: nt qckn* **12/1**

540- **6** *4 ½* **General Brook (IRE)**[56] [8179] 7-8-12 **51**..............(p1) AlistairRawlinson 6 33
(John O'Shea) *prom: led after 1f tl rdn and hdd over 2f out: lost 2nd over 1f out: wknd* **16/1**

30-3 **7** *2 ¼* **Glorious Asset**[16] [154] 5-9-2 **60**......................... LewisEdmunds(5) 8 38
(Ivan Furtado) *chsd ldrs: rdn over 2f out: wknd over 1f out* **5/2**[1]

254- **8** *2 ¾* **Ifan (IRE)**[170] [5264] 9-9-4 **60**........................................(p) MitchGodwin(3) 2 33
(Tim Vaughan) *midfield: rdn over 3f out: wknd over 2f out* **20/1**

000- **9** *6* **Just For Show (IRE)**[41] [8411] 4-9-4 **58**...................... CallumShepherd 5 20
(Shaun Lycett) *chsd ldrs: rdn and hung rt 4f out: wknd over 2f out* **100/1**

2m 0.28s (-0.52) **Going Correction** +0.075s/f (Slow)
**WFA** 4 from 5yo+ 1lb **9** Ran SP% **113.0**
Speed ratings (Par 101): **105,104,103,97,96 92,90,87,82**
CSF £21.20 CT £71.45 TOTE £3.30: £1.10, £2.10, £2.10; EX 22.80 Trifecta £72.40.
**Owner** Laurence Bellman **Bred** Lynch Bages Ltd **Trained** Upper Lambourn, Berks

**FOCUS**
The time was marginally quicker than the first leg, with the front three pulling clear. There should be even better to come from the winner.

## 422 BETWAY H'CAP 2m 120y (Tp)
**7:00** (7:02) (Class 4) (0-85,84) 4-Y-0+ **£5,175** (£1,540; £769; £384) **Stalls** Low

Form RPR

54-0 **1** **Cotton Club (IRE)**[21] [62] 6-9-12 **82**.................................... RyanTate 6 89
(Rod Millman) *hld up in last pair: rdn and hdwy 2f out: drifted sltly rt home turn over 1f out: styd on to ld fnl 100 yds* **18/1**

52-2 **2** *¾* **Zakatal**[14] [196] 11-10-0 **84**................................................ PJMcDonald 2 90
(Rebecca Menzies) *trckd ldrs: hdwy to press ldr after 7f: led over 2f out: sn drvn: hdd and unable qck fnl 100 yds* **10/1**[3]

54-3 **3** *nk* **Percy Veer**[21] [62] 5-9-11 **81**.......................................... GeorgeBaker 9 86
(Sylvester Kirk) *led 1f: styd prom: rdn 3f out: styd on to chal ins fnl f: unable qck towards fin* **11/4**[2]

012- **4** *1* **Charismatic Man (IRE)**[29] [8558] 4-9-0 **82**............. PatrickO'Donnell(5) 3 86
(Ralph Beckett) *hld up bhd ldrs: rdn 3f out: carried sltly wd home turn over 1f out: styd on and ch early ins fnl f: nt qckn fnl 100 yds* **4/5**[1]

/00- **5** *5* **Esteaming**[113] [7077] 7-9-10 **80**.......................................(p1) ConnorBeasley 7 78
(Keith Dalgleish) *hld up in last pair: drvn 3f out: styd on one pce and no threat fnl 2f* **25/1**

06-6 **6** *2* **Excellent Puck (IRE)**[21] [62] 7-9-6 **76**....................... FergusSweeney 5 72
(Shaun Lycett) *prom tl led after 1f: set stdy gallop tl jnd and qcknd pce after 7f: rdn 3f out: sn hdd: wknd over 1f out* **16/1**

20-3 **7** *4* **Handsome Dan (IRE)**[13] [220] 11-8-11 **70**...................... JackDuern(3) 8 61
(Sarah Hollinshead) *hld up bhd ldrs: rdn over 3f out: wknd 2f out* **28/1**

3m 44.31s (0.61) **Going Correction** +0.075s/f (Slow)
**WFA** 4 from 5yo+ 5lb **7** Ran SP% **109.8**
Speed ratings (Par 105): **101,100,100,100,97 96,94**
CSF £162.99 CT £609.02 TOTE £16.70: £4.80, £2.60; EX 82.80 Trifecta £120.00.
**Owner** The Links Partnership **Bred** Patrick Gleeson **Trained** Kentisbeare, Devon
■ Stewards' Enquiry : Ryan Tate caution; careless riding

**FOCUS**
They went a steady early pace in this useful staying handicap, with the tempo lifting when heading out onto the final circuit.

## 423 BETWAY APP CLASSIFIED CLAIMING STKS 1m 5f 194y
**7:30** (7:31) (Class 5) 4-Y-0+ **£3,234** (£962; £481; £240) **Stalls** Low

Form RPR

02-4 **1** **Hallstatt (IRE)**[23] [28] 11-9-0 63.................................(t) LukeMorris 3 67
(John Mackie) *chsd ldr: rdn 3f out: led 2f out: strly pressed fnl f: jst hld on* **8/1**[3]

22-5 **2** *shd* **Burnside (FR)**[23] [28] 4-8-9 65.............................(p) GeorgeDowning(3) 2 71
(Ian Williams) *hld up bhd ldrs: hdwy over 2f out: sn drvn: ev ch ins fnl f: jst hld* **6/4**[1]

61-2 **3** *2 ½* **Captain Swift (IRE)**[13] [218] 6-9-4 65.........................(p) GrahamLee 6 68
(John Mackie) *hld up in last pair: hdwy 2f out: drvn to go 3rd 1f out: no further imp* **11/4**[2]

0-62 **4** *10* **Marshal Dan Troop (IRE)**[12] [233] 4-8-3 60.............(b) GeorgiaCox(5) 7 50
(Robyn Brisland) *s.s: t.k.h in rr: hdwy to ld after 6f: drvn over 2f out: sn hdd: wknd fnl f* **8/1**[3]

00/0 **5** *2* **Anton Dolin (IRE)**[12] [241] 9-9-1 50...........................(be) PhilDennis(5) 5 53
(Michael Mullineaux) *led tl hdd after 6f and dropped bk to 3rd: drvn 4f out: wknd over 2f out* **200/1**

0-02 **6** *16* **English Summer**[6] 325 10-9-0 70..............................(t[1]) StevieDonohoe 1 24
(Ian Williams) *chsd ldrs: rdn and little rspnse over 2f out: sn wknd* **14/1**

3m 6.2s (1.40) **Going Correction** +0.075s/f (Slow)
**WFA** 4 from 6yo+ 4lb **6 Ran SP% 96.1**
Speed ratings (Par 103): **99,98,97,91,90 81**
CSF £14.83 TOTE £3.70: £2.20, £1.90; EX 15.50 Trifecta £29.60.There was no bid for winner.
**Owner** NSU Leisure & Mrs Carolyn Seymour **Bred** Darley **Trained** Church Broughton , Derbys
■ Street Outlaw was withdrawn. Price at time of withdrawal 15/2. Rule 4 applies to all bets - deduction 10p in the pound.

**FOCUS**
Only a modest claimer and a muddling race with the winner enjoying a good trip.

## 424 32RED.COM MAIDEN FILLIES' STKS 1m 142y (Tp)
**8:00** (8:02) (Class 5) 3-Y-O+ **£3,234** (£962; £481; £240) **Stalls** Low

Form RPR
262- **1** **Mums The Word**[41] 8397 3-8-6 80.................................. BarryMcHugh 5 63
(Richard Fahey) *racd keenly: mde all: rdn clr over 1f out: r.o wl* **13/2[3]**

**2** *5* **Wedding Breakfast (IRE)** 3-8-6 0.......................... JosephineGordon 2 51
(Hugo Palmer) *hooded in paddock: upset in stalls: s.i.s: in rr: last whn swtchd ins over 1f out: styd on u.p to go 2nd 75 yds out but no threat to wnr: improve* **3/1[2]**

- **3** *1 ¼* **Night Poetry (IRE)** 3-8-6 0.................................... MartinLane 1 49+
(Charlie Appleby) *s.i.s: sn trcking ldrs: rdn 3f out: wnt 2nd over 1f out: qckly outpcd by wnr: lost 2nd fnl 75 yds* **1/1[1]**

6-0 **4** *1 ¼* **Aryeh (IRE)**[15] 168 3-8-6 0.................................... TomMarquand 4 46
(Hugo Palmer) *t.k.h bhd ldrs: rdn over 1f out: kpt on same pce and nvr able to chal* **25/1**

356- **5** *¾* **Kerry Icon**[41] 8410 4-9-13 41.............................(h) PJMcDonald 3 49?
(Iain Jardine) *hld up: rdn 2f out: clsd to press for modest 2nd early ins fnl f: sn no ex* **80/1**

**6** *1* **Zehrah (IRE)** 3-8-6 0.................................................. RyanPowell 7 42
(Simon Crisford) *s.i.s: sn chsng ldrs: rdn over 2f out: one pce* **8/1**

**7** *2 ¼* **Haddeya** 3-8-6 0...................................................... LukeMorris 6 37
(Ed Walker) *trckd wnr: rdn over 2f out: lost 2nd over 1f out: weakeneing whn n.m.r jst ins fnl f* **16/1**

1m 52.27s (2.17) **Going Correction** +0.075s/f (Slow)
**WFA** 3 from 4yo 22lb **7 Ran SP% 110.4**
Speed ratings (Par 100): **93,88,87,86,85 84,82**
CSF £24.43 TOTE £5.80: £2.20, £2.40; EX 25.60 Trifecta £55.50.
**Owner** Nb & M&m Racing **Bred** Brook Stud Bloodstock Ltd **Trained** Musley Bank, N Yorks

**FOCUS**
A fair maiden and the winner made all the running to make the most of an easy lead/task, but there was some promise in behind from a couple of newcomers.

## 425 SUN BETS ON THE APP STORE H'CAP 1m 142y (Tp)
**8:30** (8:31) (Class 7) (0-50,49) 4-Y-O+ **£2,264** (£673; £336; £168) **Stalls** High

Form RPR
-463 **1** **Pivotal Dream (IRE)**[3] 383 4-8-12 46...................... CharlieBennett(5) 4 52
(Mark Brisbourne) *chsd ldr: relegated to 3rd and rdn 3f out: led ins fnl f: r.o* **9/2[2]**

066- **2** *1 ¼* **Lutine Charlie (IRE)**[35] 8492 10-9-3 45..................(p) StevieDonohoe 6 48
(Emma Owen) *t.k.h bhd ldrs: hdwy to ld narrowly 3f out: drvn over 1f out: hdd and unable qck ins fnl f* **14/1**

05-5 **3** *¾* **Sir Jamie**[15] 167 4-8-13 45.................................... GeorgeDowning(3) 10 47
(Tony Carroll) *chsd ldrs: rdn over 2f out: hung lft and r.o ins fnl f: tk 3rd nr fin* **4/1[1]**

00-5 **4** *½* **Kodiac Lady (IRE)**[22] 52 5-9-0 47.............................(e) HollieDoyle(5) 1 48
(Simon West) *led: hdd 3f out but styd cl up: ev ch u.p ins fnl f: no ex fnl 100 yds: lost 3rd nr fin* **9/1[3]**

00-4 **5** *¾* **Mowhoob**[9] 274 7-9-6 48.............................................. LukeMorris 3 47
(Brian Barr) *chsd ldrs: rdn 3f out: kpt on tl hld ins fnl f* **11/1**

065- **6** *1 ¼* **Castanea**[191] 4482 5-8-12 45.................................... CiaranMckee(5) 13 42
(Ronald Harris) *s.i.s: hld up in rr: rdn 2f out: styd on fnl f: nrst fin* **66/1**

6-05 **7** *1 ½* **Sarakova (IRE)**[6] 334 4-9-4 47..................................(v) RyanPowell 8 40
(Kevin Frost) *chsd along fr stalls: sn in midfield: drvn 3f out: no imp on ldrs fnl f* **11/1**

06-0 **8** *3 ¼* **Zed Candy Girl**[22] 51 7-9-7 49..................................(p) AndrewMullen 7 36
(Daniel Mark Loughnane) *towards rr: rdn over 1f out: no real imp* **14/1**

/00- **9** *3 ¼* **Boboli Gardens**[93] 7602 7-9-5 47.............................. PJMcDonald 11 27+
(Iain Jardine) *s.i.s: towards rr: effrt 2f out: no hdwy* **4/1[1]**

06-6 **10** *3 ¾* **Foylesideview (IRE)**[19] 124 5-9-3 45........................ SteveDrowne 12 17
(Harry Chisman) *midfield: rdn over 2f out: sn wknd* **16/1**

05-0 **11** *1* **Stanlow**[15] 176 7-8-12 45......................................(be) PhilDennis(5) 9 15
(Michael Mullineaux) *in rr: effrt over 2f out: sn wknd* **33/1**

630- **12** *31* **King Julien (IRE)**[13] 7230 4-9-5 48...........................(t[1]) RobertWinston 5
(John Ryan) *sltly hmpd leaving stalls: sn midfield: rdn and lost pl 4f out: bhd fnl 3f: t.o* **9/1[3]**

1m 50.55s (0.45) **Going Correction** +0.075s/f (Slow)
**WFA** 4 from 5yo+ 1lb **12 Ran SP% 118.5**
Speed ratings (Par 97): **101,99,99,98,98 97,95,92,89,86 85,58**
CSF £66.23 CT £278.76 TOTE £4.90: £1.60, £4.00, £2.60; EX 57.70 Trifecta £595.20.
**Owner** The Bourne Connection **Bred** Old Carhue & Graeng Bloodstock **Trained** Great Ness, Shropshire

**FOCUS**
A low-grade handicap that went to a long-standing maiden. It paid to race prominently and the winner deserved this breakthrough win.

## 426 SUNBETS.CO.UK H'CAP 7f 36y (Tp)
**9:00** (9:01) (Class 6) (0-65,65) 4-Y-O+ **£2,749** (£818; £408; £204) **Stalls** High

Form RPR
111- **1** **Fire Diamond**[29] 8555 4-9-7 65..............................(p) RichardKingscote 9 74
(Tom Dascombe) *hld up: clsd 3f out: rdn to ld ins fnl f: r.o wl* **7/2[2]**

00-3 **2** *2* **Athletic**[13] 214 8-9-4 62........................................ SteveDonohoe 6 66
(David Evans) *hld up: rdn over 1f out: r.o wl down outer to take 2nd wl ins fnl f: unable to chal wnr* **11/4[1]**

320- **3** *¾* **Top Offer**[174] 5114 8-9-7 65........................................ GrahamLee 8 67
(Patrick Morris) *hld up: hdwy 4f out: rdn to ld on ins jst over 1f out: hdd and one pce ins fnl f* **40/1**

5-52 **4** *nk* **Spirit Of Gondree (IRE)**[6] 332 9-8-10 54...............(b) FrannyNorton 11 57
(Milton Bradley) *t.k.h: chsd ldrs: nt clr run briefly over 1f out: r.o fnl f* **11/1**

20-2 **5** *4* **Unnoticed**[21] 67 5-9-7 65........................................(t[1]) RobertWinston 2 57
(Ollie Pears) *trckd ldrs: rdn appr fnl f: sn one pce* **4/1[3]**

62-5 **6** *½* **George Baker (IRE)**[17] 145 10-8-13 64.................. AmeliaGlass(7) 3 55
(George Baker) *midfield tl lost pl 3f out: shkn up and styd on fnl f* **33/1**

021- **7** *1 ½* **Napoleon Solo**[28] 8570 5-9-5 63.............................. AndrewMullen 4 50
(David Barron) *led: rdn 2f out: hdd jst over 1f out: wknd* **5/1**

05-3 **8** *nk* **Deeley's Double (FR)**[12] 244 4-9-3 64................. GeorgeDowning(3) 7 50
(Tony Carroll) *midfield tl dropped towards rr 4f out: drvn 3f out: modest late prog* **6/1**

45-6 **9** *nse* **Binky Blue (IRE)**[17] 145 5-9-3 61.................................. LukeMorris 1 47
(Daniel Mark Loughnane) *cl up: rdn 2f out: ch appr fnl f: sn wknd* **25/1**

00-0 **10** *2 ½* **Virile (IRE)**[15] 171 6-8-9 58.....................................(bt) MitchGodwin(5) 5 38
(Sylvester Kirk) *s.s: drvn 3f out: a towards rr* **40/1**

40-0 **11** *2* **I Can't Stop**[16] 166 4-8-12 56...................................(b[1]) DougieCostello 12 35
(Milton Bradley) *cl up: drvn to chal 3f out: wkng whn bmpd appr fnl f* **150/1**

1m 27.91s (-0.89) **Going Correction** +0.075s/f (Slow) **11 Ran SP% 120.5**
Speed ratings (Par 101): **108,105,104,104,99 99,97,97,97,94 92**
CSF £13.48 CT £334.96 TOTE £3.30: £1.20, £1.70, £6.50; EX 13.20 Trifecta £439.10.
**Owner** John Brown **Bred** John Brown **Trained** Malpas, Cheshire

**FOCUS**
A modest handicap and solid form for the grade. There's a definite chance of more to come from the winner.
T/Jkpt: Not Won. T/Plt: £583.30 to a £1 stake. Pool: £111,748.87 - 139.84 winning units T/Qpdt: £72.00 to a £1 stake. Pool: £10,974.21 - 112.70 winning units **Richard Lowther**

# [391] CAGNES-SUR-MER
Thursday, January 26
**OFFICIAL GOING: Polytrack: standard**

## 427a PRIX DES ARUMS (CLAIMER) (3YO) (POLYTRACK) 1m (P)
**11:55** 3-Y-O **£7,264** (£2,905; £2,179; £1,452; £726)

RPR
**1** **Admiralty Arch**[10] 272 3-9-6 0...................................(p) MaximeGuyon 11 87
(Richard Hughes) **7/10[1]**

**2** *5 ½* **Charlie The Lad (FR)** 3-9-6 0...................................(b) FabriceVeron 8 74
(Matthieu Palussiere, France) **28/1**

**3** *1 ½* **Desaguadero (FR)** 3-9-6 0........................................ EddyHardouin 1 71
(Matthieu Palussiere, France) **32/1**

**4** *1* **Numeration (FR)**[20] 3-9-3 0........................................ TonyPiccone 9 66
(C Escuder, France) **31/5[3]**

**5** *¼* **Alfa Manifesto (FR)**[149] 6015 3-9-6 0......................(p) AntoineHamelin 4 68
(Matthieu Palussiere, France) **30/1**

**6** *2* **Narellan (FR)** 3-8-8 0.......................................... Francois-XavierBertras 3 51
(F Rohaut, France) **242/10**

**7** *1* **Fankairos Ranger (USA)**[174] 5141 3-8-13 0........(p) MarvinGrandin(7) 7 61
(Cedric Rossi, France) **152/10**

**8** *3 ½* **Mathonville (FR)**[168] 3-8-13 0.................................... CristianDemuro 10 46
(J-C Rouget, France) **83/10**

**9** *5* **Golden Sage (FR)** 3-9-3 0...............................(b) Pierre-CharlesBoudot 6 39
(J Phelippon, France) **59/10[2]**

**10** *5* **Tanis (FR)** 3-8-13 0................................................ FranckBlondel 5 23
(R Martens, France) **90/1**

**11** *17* **Parissa (IRE)** 3-8-8 0...........................................(p) AntoineCoutier 2
(Carina Fey, France) **71/1**

1m 38.85s **11 Ran SP% 120.3**
PARI-MUTUEL (all including 1 euro stake): WIN 1.70; PLACE 1.20, 5.20, 5.10; DF 25.60; SF 32.00.
**Owner** The Queens & Partner **Bred** G B Partnership **Trained** Upper Lambourn, Berks

# [316] MEYDAN (L-H)
Thursday, January 26
**OFFICIAL GOING: Dirt: fast; turf: good**

## 428a AABAR PROPERTIES, AN IPIC GROUP COMPANY (H'CAP) (TURF) 1m 4f 11y(T)
**3:05** (3:05) (100-113,113) 3-Y-O+
**£85,365** (£28,455; £14,227; £7,113; £4,268; £2,845)

RPR
**1** **Gold Trail (IRE)**[138] 6333 6-9-3 107.................................. AdamKirby 9 111
(Charlie Appleby) *trckd ldrs: led 2 1/2f out: r.o wl* **15/8[2]**

**2** *1* **Prize Money**[82] 7824 4-9-6 113..........................(h) ChristopheSoumillon 8 116
(Saeed bin Suroor) *mid-div: chsd ldrs 3 1/2f out: ev ch 1 1/2f out: one pce fnl 110yds* **7/4[1]**

**3** *2 ¼* **Rembrandt Van Rijn (IRE)**[14] 202 6-9-1 105.....(b) MickaelBarzalona 2 103
(S bin Ghadayer, UAE) *s.i.s: nvr nr to chal but r.o fnl 3f* **12/1**

**4** *½* **Majeed**[14] 208 7-8-11 102............................................ AndreaAtzeni 7 99
(David Simcock) *s.i.s: nvr nr to chal but r.o fnl 2f* **25/1**

**5** *¾* **Busker (USA)**[7] 322 9-8-11 102.....................................(t) PatCosgrave 1 97
(A bin Harmash, UAE) *mid-div: chsd ldrs 3f out: wknd fnl f* **50/1**

**6** *1 ¼* **Good Trip (IRE)**[14] 208 4-8-8 102...............................(t) AdriedeVries 4 96
(A R Al Rayhi, UAE) *nvr bttr than mid-div* **15/2[3]**

**7** *1 ¼* **Desert God (IND)**[21] 82 5-8-9 100.............................. ChrisHayes 3 91
(S Padmanabhan, India) *sn led: racd keenly: rdn 4f out: hdd 3f out: sn btn* **8/1**

**8** *½* **Khusoosy (USA)**[312] 1020 5-9-2 106.............................(t) JimCrowley 6 98
(A R Al Rayhi, UAE) *mid-div: chsd ldrs 4f out: wknd fnl 2f* **18/1**

**9** *1* **Elleval (IRE)**[14] 208 7-8-10 101...................................(p) PatDobbs 5 90
(David Marnane, Ire) *s.i.s: a in rr* **18/1**

2m 33.52s (1.72) **Going Correction** +0.375s/f (Good)
**WFA** 4 from 5yo+ 3lb **9 Ran SP% 118.0**
Speed ratings: **109,108,106,106,106 105,104,104,103**
CSF: 5.70; TRICAST: 28.80.
**Owner** Godolphin **Bred** Mrs Sm Rogers & Sir Thomas Pilkington **Trained** Newmarket, Suffolk

**FOCUS**
TRAKUS (metres travelled compared to winner): 2nd +1, 3rd -6, 4th +1, 5th -7, 6th 0, 7th -7, 8th 0, 9th -6. This was slowly run and turned into a sprint - 27.6, 27.5, 26.2, 25.97, 23.62, 22.63 - and the winner had the best run round. The first two have been rated in line with their Doncaster wins.

## 429a AL RASHIDIYA EMPOWERED BY IPIC (GROUP 2) (TURF) 1m 1f (T)
**3:40** (3:40) 3-Y-O+

**£97,560** (£32,520; £16,260; £8,130; £4,878; £3,252)

RPR
1 **Promising Run (USA)**[103] 7351 4-8-8 105.....................(p) JimCrowley 3 108+
(Saeed bin Suroor) *mid-div: smooth prog 3f out: rdn to ld fnl half f* **4/1**[2]
2 ½ **Light The Lights (SAF)**[21] 86 5-9-0 111.......... ChristopheSoumillon 7 112
(M F De Kock, South Africa) *wl away: sn led: rdn 2f out: r.o but hdd cl home* **8/11**[1]
3 nk **Earnshaw (USA)**[21] 86 6-9-0 107.......................(t) MickaelBarzalona 6 111+
(S bin Ghadayer, UAE) *settled rr: r.o fnl 2f: nrst fin* **16/1**
4 2 **Elite Excalibur (AUS)**[21] 87 4-9-0 109............(b) BernardFaydʼHerbe 4 107
(S Burridge, Singapore) *trckd ldrs: ev ch 3f out: one pce fnl 2f* **8/1**
5 1 **Gabrial (IRE)**[21] 86 8-9-0 110........................................ AndreaAtzeni 1 105
(Richard Fahey) *nvr nr to chal* **25/1**
6 ¾ **Farrier (USA)**[42] 8396 9-9-0 111.................................... RichardMullen 2 103
(S Seemar, UAE) *nvr bttr than mid-div* **20/1**
7 2 **Mr Owen (USA)**[57] 8165 5-9-0 109.................................(t) OisinMurphy 5 99
(F Rohaut, France) *trckd ldr tl wknd fnl 2f* **6/1**[3]

1m 49.43s (0.33) **Going Correction** +0.375s/f (Good)
**WFA** 4 from 5yo+ 1lb 7 Ran SP% **117.8**
Speed ratings: **113,112,112,110,109 108,107**
CSF: 7.64.
**Owner** Godolphin **Bred** Darley **Trained** Newmarket, Suffolk

**FOCUS**
TRAKUS (metres travelled compared to winner): 2nd -3, 3rd +2, 4th -3, 5th, 6th -2, 7th -4, 8th 0. Not a strong field for this Group 2 and a muddling race. The runner-up took them through the first 1600m in 26.61, 23.66, 24.97, 22.91, before the winner finished in 11.26. The race has been rated around the balance of the first four.

## 430a UAE 2000 GUINEAS TRIAL EMPOWERED BY NOVA, AN IPIC GROUP COMPANY (CONDITIONS) (DIRT) 7f (D)
**4:15** (4:15) 3-Y-O

**£48,780** (£16,260; £8,130; £4,065; £2,439; £1,626)

RPR
1 **Fly At Dawn (USA)**[28] 8575 3-8-8 98.......................(t) MickaelBarzalona 3 105
(Charlie Appleby) *s.i.s: mid-div: chsd ldr 2f out: r.o wl to ld fnl half f* **13/2**
2 1 **Cosmo Charlie (USA)**[42] 8391 3-8-8 99.............................. PatDobbs 8 102
(Doug Watson, UAE) *sn led: skipped clr 2 1/2f out but hdd fnl half f* **5/2**[1]
3 6 ¼ **Top Score**[99] 7469 3-8-8 94.............................................. AdriedeVries 12 85
(Saeed bin Suroor) *s.i.s: mid-div: r.o fnl 2f but no ch w first two* **12/1**
4 1 ¼ **Best Solution (IRE)**[88] 7722 3-8-10 111........................ AndreaAtzeni 14 84
(Saeed bin Suroor) *trckd ldr: ev ch 2 1/2f out: r.o same pce fnl 2f* **11/4**[2]
5 ½ **Van Der Decken**[28] 8575 3-8-9 104 ow1............................ DaneOʼNeill 6 82
(Charlie Appleby) *mid-div: r.o same pce fnl 2f* **9/2**[3]
6 5 ¼ **Silent Assassin (IRE)**[133] 6525 3-8-8 78...................... SamHitchcott 10 67
(S Seemar, UAE) *trckd ldr: r.o same pce fnl 2 1/2f* **40/1**
7 ¾ **Victor Kalejs (USA)**[57] 3-8-8 90........................(t) Per-AndersGraberg 11 65
(Roy Arne Kvisla, Sweden) *a in rr* **50/1**
8 1 ½ **Kahrab (IRE)**[12] 246 3-8-10 84 ow2............................................ BReis 1 62
(R Bouresly, Kuwait) *nvr bttr than mid-div* **66/1**
9 nse **Mufeed (USA)**[28] 8575 3-8-8 82.................................(bt) RichardMullen 5 60
(S Seemar, UAE) *trckd ldr: one pce fnl 3f* **40/1**
10 8 ¼ **Mazeed (USA)**[14] 201 3-8-8 83....................................(b) PatCosgrave 2 38
(M F De Kock, South Africa) *nvr bttr than mid-div* **33/1**
11 1 ½ **Masham Star (IRE)**[29] 8564 3-8-8 101....................... RoystonFfrench 13 34
(Mark Johnston) *nvr bttr than mid-div* **20/1**
12 ½ **Good Omen**[75] 7930 3-8-8 93.............................................. OisinMurphy 7 33
(David Simcock) *s.i.s: a in rr* **25/1**
13 3 ½ **French Pass**[7] 317 3-8-5 0.................................................. ChrisHayes 4 20
(E Jeanne, UAE) *a in rr* **250/1**
14 13 ½ **Megnaas (ARG)**[382] 3-9-4 90............................... ChristopheSoumillon 9
(M F De Kock, South Africa) *a in rr* **10/1**

1m 24.48s (-0.62) **Going Correction** +0.30s/f (Slow) 14 Ran SP% **123.8**
Speed ratings: **115,113,106,105,104 98,97,96,96,86 84,84,80,64**
CSF: 22.41.
**Owner** Godolphin **Bred** Darley **Trained** Newmarket, Suffolk

**FOCUS**
TRAKUS (metres travelled compared to winner): 2nd -5, 3rd +11, 4th +9, 5th +4, 6th +4, 7th +3, 8th -4, 9th -2, 10th -4, 11th +7, 12th +9, 13th +4, 14th +10. The runner-up set a sensible pace, 24.81, 23.49, 23.96, before the winner finished in 12.11. The winner scored with a bit to spare and a personal best from the second.

## 431a CAPE VERDI EMPOWERED BY CEPSA, AN IPIC GROUP COMPANY (GROUP 2) (F&M) (TURF) 1m
**4:50** (4:50) 3-Y-O+

**£97,560** (£32,520; £16,260; £8,130; £4,878; £3,252)

RPR
1 **Very Special (IRE)**[202] 4107 5-9-0 113..........................(h) JimCrowley 1 109
(Saeed bin Suroor) *trckd ldr: rdn 2f out: r.o wl to ld fnl half f* **5/6**[1]
2 ½ **Opal Tiara (IRE)**[111] 7115 4-9-0 109................................ OisinMurphy 2 108+
(Mick Channon) *mid-div: r.o wl fnl 1 1/2f: nrst fin* **20/1**
3 nk **Muffri'Ha (IRE)**[91] 7650 5-9-0 109................................... PatCosgrave 7 107
(William Haggas) *trckd ldr: led 1 1/2f out: hdd fnl half f* **11/2**
4 nk **Silver Step (FR)**[123] 6824 4-9-0 103.................(h) MickaelBarzalona 6 107+
(Mme Pia Brandt, France) *settled in rr: r.o wl fnl 2f: nrst fin* **40/1**
5 1 ½ **Tahanee (ARG)**[14] 205 4-9-0 105........................ ChristopheSoumillon 10 103
(M F De Kock, South Africa) *wl away: sn led: hdd 1 1/2f out: r.o same pce* **5/1**[3]
6 ¾ **Via Firenze (IRE)**[29] 8563 4-9-0 98.........................(t) RichardMullen 4 101
(Mme Pia Brandt, France) *slowly away: nvr nr to chal* **40/1**
7 1 ¼ **Realtra (IRE)**[29] 8563 5-9-0 109........................................ AndreaAtzeni 3 99
(Roger Varian) *nvr bttr than mid-div* **7/2**[2]
8 1 **Queen's Parade (USA)**[14] 205 6-9-0 100............................. ChrisHayes 9 96
(D Selvaratnam, UAE) *a in rr* **100/1**
9 2 **Anahita (FR)**[683] 927 6-9-0 99.............................(p) RoystonFfrench 8 92
(S bin Ghadayer, UAE) *nvr nr to chal* **50/1**
10 8 ½ **Arabda**[14] 205 6-9-0 100.......................................(t) Per-AndersGraberg 5 72
(Patrick Wahl, Sweden) *nvr bttr than mid-div* **100/1**

1m 37.21s (-0.29) **Going Correction** +0.375s/f (Good) 10 Ran SP% **122.4**
Speed ratings: **116,115,115,114,113 112,111,110,108,99**
CSF: 26.07.
**Owner** Godolphin **Bred** Ballylinch Stud **Trained** Newmarket, Suffolk

**FOCUS**
TRAKUS (metres travelled compared to winner): 2nd 0, 3rd +4, 4th +6, 5th +1, 6th +1, 7th +5, 8th +6, 9th +2, 10th +6. They went a sensible pace early, 25.87 (400m from standing start), 23.92 (800m), before slowing up on the bend, 24.82 (1200m), and the winner quickened up to finish in 22.38.

## 432a ADCOP, AN IPIC INVESTMENT (H'CAP) (DIRT) 1m (D)
**5:25** (5:25) (100-115,104) 3-Y-O+

**£65,853** (£21,951; £10,975; £5,487; £3,292; £2,195)

RPR
1 **Heavy Metal**[14] 204 7-9-2 **100**.................................. MickaelBarzalona 6 110+
(S bin Ghadayer, UAE) *mid-div: smooth prog 2 1/2f out: rdn to ld fnl f* **5/2**[2]
2 2 **Frankyfourfingers (FR)**[21] 85 7-9-4 **102**................ RoystonFfrench 2 107+
(S bin Ghadayer, UAE) *sn led: skipped clr 3 1/2f out: wknd 1 1/2f out: hdd fnl f* **16/1**
3 3 **Alabaster (USA)**[385] 94 5-9-2 **100**..............................(b) OisinMurphy 5 98+
(Saeed bin Suroor) *slowly away: mid-div: r.o same pce fnl 2f* **16/1**
4 shd **Stunned**[48] 8301 6-9-2 **100**.......................................................(v) PatDobbs 7 98+
(Doug Watson, UAE) *nvr nr to chal but r.o fnl 2f* **12/1**
5 1 ¼ **Ross (IRE)**[40] 8431 5-9-6 **104**...................................... AdriedeVries 10 99
(P Schiergen, Germany) *a in rr* **11/1**[3]
6 1 ¼ **Tumbaga (USA)**[509] 6128 6-9-4 **102**......................... ChristopheSoumillon 1 94
(Saeed bin Suroor) *trckd ldr tl outpcd fnl 3f* **6/5**[1]
7 ¾ **Need To Know (SAF)**[14] 204 8-9-3 **101**.................(bt) RichardMullen 8 91
(A R Al Rayhi, UAE) *nvr nr to chal* **33/1**
8 2 **Munaaser**[7] 319 6-9-4 **102**.......................................................(t) JimCrowley 4 88
(A R Al Rayhi, UAE) *nvr bttr than mid-div* **14/1**
9 6 **Mutawathea**[21] 87 6-9-4 **102**.............................................(p) DaneOʼNeill 9 74
(Simon Crisford) *a in rr* **14/1**
10 dist **Wildcat Red (USA)**[14] 204 6-9-5 **103**............................ SamHitchcott 3
(Doug Watson, UAE) *nvr bttr than mid-div* **33/1**

1m 37.84s (0.34) **Going Correction** +0.30s/f (Slow) 10 Ran SP% **121.0**
Speed ratings: **110,108,105,104,103 102,101,99,93,**
CSF: 44.43; TRICAST: 541.92.
**Owner** Sheikh Hamdan bin Mohammed Al Maktoum **Bred** Darley **Trained** United Arab Emirates

**FOCUS**
TRAKUS (metres travelled compared to winner): 2nd -11, 3rd -10, 4th -1, 5th +2, 6th -8, 7th -1, 8th -1, 9th +4, 10th -1. The runner-up set a rapid pace - 24.84 (400m from standing start), 22.59 (800m), 23.98 (1200m) - but only his stablemate could get to him, finishing in 25.95.

## 433a BOREALIS, AN IPIC GROUP COMPANY (H'CAP) (TURF) 6f
**6:00** (6:00) (100-109,109) 3-Y-O+

**£85,365** (£28,455; £14,227; £7,113; £4,268; £2,845)

RPR
1 **Baccarat (IRE)**[135] 6458 8-9-4 **107**.......................................... AdamKirby 9 114+
(Charlie Appleby) *broke awkwardly: settled rr: smooth prog 3f out: rdn to ld fnl f r.o wl* **9/2**[2]
2 nk **Jungle Cat (IRE)**[181] 4824 5-9-6 **109**.....................(p) MickaelBarzalona 7 115
(Charlie Appleby) *trckd ldrs: led briefly 1 1/2f out: hdd 1f out: r.o wl* **4/1**[1]
3 1 ¼ **Final Venture**[14] 207 5-9-5 **108**...............................................(h) PatDobbs 2 110
(Paul Midgley) *sn led: hdd 1 1/2f out but r.o wl* **9/2**[2]
4 nk **Steady Pace**[14] 207 4-9-2 **105**.............................. ChristopheSoumillon 1 106
(Saeed bin Suroor) *trckd ldrs: ev ch 1 1/2f out: r.o same pce fnl f* **9/2**[2]
5 ½ **Mastermind (SAF)**[4] 365 5-9-2 **105**.................(bt) BernardFaydʼHerbe 5 104
(M F De Kock, South Africa) *trckd ldrs: ev ch 2f out: r.o same pce fnl 2f* **25/1**
6 ¾ **Jamesie (IRE)**[14] 207 9-8-13 **102**...................................(t) SamHitchcott 6 99
(David Marnane, Ire) *nvr bttr than mid-div* **9/1**[3]
7 ¾ **Watchable**[14] 207 7-9-0 **103**.........................................(p) AdriedeVries 4 98
(David O'Meara) *bmpd at s: nvr nr to chal* **16/1**
8 2 ¼ **Eastern Impact (IRE)**[14] 207 6-8-13 **108**............. CameronNoble[(6)] 10 95
(Richard Fahey) *trckd ldrs tl outpcd fnl 1 1/2f* **16/1**
9 nk **Gordon Lord Byron (IRE)**[14] 207 9-9-3 **106**................ OisinMurphy 8 92
(T Hogan, Ire) *trckd ldrs tl outpcd fnl 1 1/2f* **20/1**
10 1 ½ **Majestic Mount**[336] 723 7-8-11 **101**.........................(t) RichardMullen 11 82
(S Seemar, UAE) *a in rr* **33/1**
11 2 ½ **Fityaan**[14] 207 9-9-6 **109**................................................(v) JimCrowley 14 83
(M Al Mheiri, UAE) *a in rr* **12/1**
12 9 ¾ **Muwaary (AUS)**[299] 4-8-13 **102**............................................ PatCosgrave 3 44
(M F De Kock, South Africa) *bmpd at s: a in rr* **25/1**
13 2 **Roicead (USA)**[14] 207 10-9-5 **108**..................................(t) ChrisHayes 13 44
(D Selvaratnam, UAE) *a in rr* **33/1**
14 22 **Banaadeer (AUS)**[21] 87 5-9-2 **105**................................(b) DaneOʼNeill 12
(M F De Kock, South Africa) *a in rr* **14/1**

1m 9.48s (0.48) **Going Correction** +0.375s/f (Good) 14 Ran SP% **129.0**
Speed ratings: **111,110,108,108,107 106,105,102,102,100 97,84,81,52**
CSF: 23.07; TRICAST: 92.69; PLACEPOT: £110.00 to a £1 stake. Pool: £5,277.83 - 35.0 winning units; QUADPOT: £6.00 to a £1 stake. Pool: £668.50 - 81.90 winning units..
**Owner** Godolphin **Bred** Twelve Oaks Stud **Trained** Newmarket, Suffolk

**FOCUS**
Strong form, with a couple of horses who had won first-time up over C&D last year filling the first two places, while the third and fourth had finished 1-2 in a similar event two weeks ago.

# [392]LINGFIELD (L-H)
Friday, January 27

**OFFICIAL GOING: Polytrack: standard**
Wind: Light, half behind Weather: Fine but cloudy

## 434 32RED.COM H'CAP 1m 1y(P)
**1:10** (1:10) (Class 6) (0-65,67) 3-Y-O **£2,716** (£808; £404; £202) **Stalls** High

Form RPR
5-16 1 **Oberyn (IRE)**[13] 245 3-9-0 **63**...................................... MitchGodwin[(5)] 10 69
(Sylvester Kirk) *chsd ldr to 1/2-way: styd cl up: rdn and clsd on outer over 1f out: led last 100yds: styd on* **20/1**
00-2 2 nk **Sliceoflife**[14] 210 3-9-8 **66**........................................ JosephineGordon 2 71
(Marco Botti) *hld up in midfield on inner: prog on inner wl over 1f out: taken off rail and clsd to chal fnl f: upsides 100yds out: jst outpcd* **6/1**[3]

15-4 **3** 3/4 **Killermont Street (IRE)**[16] 178 3-9-9 **67**.......................... JoeFanning 9 70
(Mark Johnston) *t.k.h: prom on outer: trckd ldr 1/2-way: rdn to ld wl over 1f out: hdd last 100yds: kpt on* **16/1**
41-1 **4** 3 1/2 **Babouska**[18] 149 3-9-0 **58**.......................... JamieSpencer 8 53
(Michael Easterby) *led: rdn and hdd wl over 1f out: fdd fnl f* **5/2**[1]
01-5 **5** hd **Wily Rumpus (IRE)**[14] 209 3-9-7 **65**.......................... ThomasBrown 1 60
(Ed Walker) *trckd ldrs on inner: rdn and fnd little over 1f out: wl hld after* **7/2**[2]
03-3 **6** 1 1/2 **No Not Again (IRE)**[14] 209 3-9-6 **64**..........................(p[1]) SeanLevey 4 55
(Richard Hannon) *t.k.h: hld up bhd ldrs: rdn over 1f out: hanging and fnd nil* **7/2**[2]
06-5 **7** 2 3/4 **Marwa**[23] 34 3-9-6 **64**.......................... AdamKirby 5 49
(Ed Dunlop) *towards rr: prog on outer to chse ldrs over 3f out: rdn over 2f out: sn btn* **6/1**[3]
53-6 **8** nk **Parisian Chic (IRE)**[23] 34 3-9-6 **64**.......................... RobertWinston 3 48
(Lee Carter) *stdd sn after s: hld up in last pair: pushed along on inner 2f out: one reminder 1f: no prog and nvr involved* **16/1**
000- **9** 1 **Hi There Silver (IRE)**[79] 7866 3-8-7 **51** oh6.......................... RyanPowell 6 33
(Michael Madgwick) *towards rr: rdn and struggling over 3f out* **100/1**
40-0 **10** 3/4 **Satpura**[22] 75 3-9-4 **65**.......................... GeorgeDowning[(3)] 7 45
(Mick Channon) *s.i.s: urged along in last pair by 1/2-way: nvr a factor* **50/1**

1m 38.77s (0.57) **Going Correction** +0.025s/f (Slow) **10** Ran SP% **121.1**
Speed ratings (Par 95): **98,97,96,93,93 91,89,88,87,86**
CSF £139.29 CT £2040.17 TOTE £29.60: £5.90, £1.90, £4.00; EX 207.10 Trifecta £3159.10.
**Owner** Mrs Barbara Facchino **Bred** Barouche Stud Ireland Ltd **Trained** Upper Lambourn, Berks

**FOCUS**
A modest 3yo handicap and something of a surprise result. It's rated tentatively around the third.

## 435 32REDSPORT.COM CLAIMING STKS 7f 1y(P)
**1:40** (1:43) (Class 6) 3-Y-O **£2,716** (£808; £404; £202) **Stalls** Low

Form RPR
63-1 **1** **Dandy Flame (IRE)**[22] 78 3-9-10 78.......................... AdamKirby 3 74
(William Haggas) *in tch in midfield: prog over 2f out: drvn to take 2nd 1f out: clsd to ld last 100yds: kpt on* **10/11**[1]
65-6 **2** 1 **Critical Thinking (IRE)**[20] 115 3-8-9 63.......................... FinleyMarsh[(7)] 2 64
(Julia Feilden) *hld up in rr: plenty to do whn prog on inner 2f out: swtchd rt jst over 1f out: shkn up and r.o to take 2nd nr fin: too late to threaten wnr* **12/1**
02-1 **3** 1/2 **Peachey Carnehan**[18] 150 3-9-10 70..........................(v) WilliamCarson 7 70
(Michael Attwater) *led: sent for home and 3 l clr 2f out: drvn over 1f out: hdd and fdd last 100yds* **10/1**
34-6 **4** 1/2 **Joyful Dream (IRE)**[21] 96 3-8-4 54..........................(p) LuluStanford[(5)] 8 54
(J S Moore) *t.k.h: hld up in midfield on outer: stl gng wl whn r unfolded over 2f out: shkn up over 1f out and hanging: styd on ins fnl f: too late to threaten* **14/1**
0-6 **5** 2 **Brother In Arms (IRE)**[11] 265 3-9-2 0.......................... JamieSpencer 5 56
(Jamie Osborne) *slowly away: hld up in last: long way off the pce whn pushed along over 2f out: shkn up over 1f out: styd on ins fnl f: nvr involved* **6/1**[3]
44-0 **6** hd **Madam Prancealot (IRE)**[14] 210 3-8-9 55.......................... AdamBeschizza 4 48
(David Evans) *prom: disp 2nd fr 3f out to 1f out: wknd* **33/1**
110- **7** 1/2 **Drop Kick Murphi (IRE)**[83] 7820 3-9-6 78.......................... SteveDrowne 9 58
(George Baker) *prom: chsd ldr 4f out to 1f out: wknd* **5/1**[2]
006- **8** 2 1/4 **Love And Be Loved**[31] 8536 3-8-5 60..........................(h[1]) HollieDoyle[(5)] 6 42
(Peter Chapple-Hyam) *t.k.h: chsd ldr 3f: wknd over 1f out* **25/1**
04-5 **9** 2 3/4 **Princess Way (IRE)**[22] 78 3-8-11 59.......................... StevieDonohoe 1 35
(David Evans) *drvn in rr by 1/2-way: sn no ch* **14/1**

1m 25.3s (0.50) **Going Correction** +0.025s/f (Slow) **9** Ran SP% **120.2**
Speed ratings (Par 95): **98,96,96,95,93 93,92,90,86**
CSF £14.77 TOTE £1.90: £1.10, £3.70, £2.70; EX 15.30 Trifecta £79.60.The winner was subject of a friendly claim. Joyful Dream was subject of a friendly claim. Brother In Arms was claimed by Mr A W Carroll for £6000. Drop Kick Murphi was claimed by Mrs Christine Dunnett for £8000.
**Owner** The Up In Flames Partnership **Bred** Limestone & Tara Studs **Trained** Newmarket, Suffolk

**FOCUS**
Few could be seriously fancied in this 3yo claimer and the favourite got the job done. He's rated a bit below his best.

## 436 BETWAY BEST ODDS GUARANTEED PLUS (S) H'CAP 1m 7f 169y(P)
**2:10** (2:11) (Class 6) (0-60,62) 4-Y-0+ **£2,587** (£770; £384; £192) **Stalls** Low

Form RPR
501- **1** **King Olav (UAE)**[36] 8488 12-10-0 **61**.......................... GeorgeDowning[(3)] 9 72
(Tony Carroll) *trckd ldrs: led over 3f out: rdn and kpt on wl to draw clr fr over 1f out* **8/1**
35-0 **2** 6 **Ryan The Giant**[20] 121 4-8-11 **48**..........................(v) JamieSpencer 3 52
(Keith Dalgleish) *trckd ldrs: wnt 2nd over 2f out: sn rdn: one pce and lft bhd by wnr fr over 1f out* **7/2**[2]
400- **3** 1 **Newtown Cross (IRE)**[44] 8359 7-9-4 **48**.......................... TomMarquand 10 51
(Jimmy Fox) *hld up in last pair: urged along and reminders 7f out: gng bttr whn prog 4f out: drvn to take 3rd over 1f out: one pce after* **7/1**
56-0 **4** 10 **Movie Magic**[11] 35 6-8-8 **45**..........................(b[1]) JoshuaBryan[(7)] 6 36
(Mark Hoad) *hld up in tch: outpcd by ldrs fr 3f out: tk v modest 4th over 1f out* **50/1**
4-04 **5** 5 **Medicean Queen (IRE)**[10] 278 6-9-10 **54**..........(t) JosephineGordon 5 39+
(Phil McEntee) *trckd ldr: led 4f out gng wl: hdd and rdn over 3f out: immediately btn: wknd 2f out* **8/1**
0-60 **6** 3 1/2 **Yul Finegold (IRE)**[14] 218 7-10-4 **62**..........................(b) JoeFanning 8 43
(Conor Dore) *hld up towards rr: pushed along over 4f out: lft bhd by ldrs fr over 3f out: sn no ch* **16/1**
000- **7** 1/2 **Lorelei**[39] 8459 5-9-9 **53**..........................(p) MartinDwyer 4 33
(William Muir) *mostly in last: urged along 5f out: no prog and wl btn 3f out* **6/1**[3]
50-2 **8** 1 **Grand Facile**[23] 35 5-9-10 **54**..........................(b) TimmyMurphy 1 33
(Gary Moore) *led to 4f out: sn wknd and bhd* **2/1**[1]
5-06 **9** 1 1/2 **Twilight Angel**[8] 315 9-9-2 **46**..........................(v) StevieDonohoe 7 23
(Emma Owen) *a towards rr: urged along 5f out: sn struggling* **50/1**
000- **10** 22 **Murraqib (USA)**[29] 8566 4-8-5 **47**.......................... HollieDoyle[(5)] 2
(Brett Johnson) *in tch in midfield but nvr gng wl: wknd rapidly 3f out: t.o* **12/1**

3m 23.34s (-2.36) **Going Correction** +0.025s/f (Slow)
**WFA** 4 from 5yo+ 5lb **10** Ran SP% **122.1**
Speed ratings (Par 101): **106,103,102,97,95 93,93,92,91,80**
CSF £37.96 CT £212.25 TOTE £5.50: £1.70, £1.60, £2.70; EX 36.30 Trifecta £303.70.No bid for the winner.
**Owner** Cover Point Racing **Bred** Darley **Trained** Cropthorne, Worcs

**FOCUS**
A moderate staying selling handicap and they finished spread out all over Surrey. The winner's best figure since 2014.

## 437 32RED CASINO MAIDEN STKS 1m 2f (P)
**2:40** (2:44) (Class 5) 3-Y-O **£3,234** (£962; £481; £240) **Stalls** Low

Form RPR
2 **1** **Fashion Business**[13] 236 3-9-5 0.......................... GeorgeBaker 3 69+
(Roger Charlton) *trckd ldr to 4f out: styd cl up: shkn up 2f out: no imp and looked hld 1f out: styd on last 150yds to ld fnl strides* **4/7**[1]
362- **2** nk **American History (USA)**[65] 8073 3-9-5 72..........................(b[1]) RyanMoore 9 68
(John Gosden) *sn led: rdn and hrd pressed 2f out: edgd rt and nudged rival jst ins fnl f: hung rt and bmpd rival 75yds out: hdd last 75yds* **3/1**[2]
0-0 **3** hd **Born Legend (IRE)**[11] 265 3-9-5 0..........................(b[1]) MichaelJMMurphy 4 68
(Charles Hills) *cl up: trckd ldr 4f out: chal 2f out: upsides whn nudged by rival jst ins fnl f: stl upsides whn bmpd 75yds out: nt rcvr and dropped to 3rd last strides* **66/1**
6 **4** 1 1/4 **Abaad (IRE)**[13] 237 3-9-2 0.......................... KieranShoemark[(3)] 6 65
(Roger Charlton) *hld up in tch on outer: rdn whn wdst of all bnd 2f out: tried to cl over 1f out: kpt on same pce* **8/1**
0-5 **5** 3/4 **Cartavio (IRE)**[23] 40 3-9-5 0.......................... DavidProbert 5 64
(Andrew Balding) *chsd ldrs: drvn over 2f out: tried to cl over 1f out: kpt on same pce fnl f* **6/1**[3]
**6** nk **Gee Sixty Six** 3-9-5 0.......................... TimmyMurphy 2 63
(Mark H Tompkins) *awkward to load into stall: dwlt: t.k.h and sn in midfield: gng strly over 2f out: shkn up briefly on inner 1f out: kpt on same pce: shaped w promise* **100/1**
45 **7** 1 1/2 **Dance Dan Dan (IRE)**[7] 328 3-9-5 0..........................(b[1]) JoeFanning 1 60
(Mark Johnston) *hld up in rr: rdn over 2f out: tried to cl on ldrs over 1f out: one pce* **20/1**
**8** 6 **Astrostorm** 3-9-5 0.......................... StevieDonohoe 8 48
(Mark H Tompkins) *dwlt: rn green in last: lost tch over 3f out: urged along after: fin w a flourish last 100yds* **66/1**
0-0 **9** 2 1/2 **Bessemer Lady**[13] 236 3-9-0 0.......................... RichardKingscote 7 38
(Ralph Beckett) *dwlt: a in rr: lost tch 3f out: bhd after* **20/1**

2m 7.46s (0.86) **Going Correction** +0.025s/f (Slow) **9** Ran SP% **127.5**
Speed ratings (Par 97): **97,96,96,95,95 94,93,88,86**
CSF £2.92 TOTE £1.50: £1.10, £1.40, £16.50; EX 3.30 Trifecta £115.60.
**Owner** Andrew Rosen **Bred** Andrew Rosen **Trained** Beckhampton, Wilts

**FOCUS**
An uncompetitive 3yo maiden and a driving finish between the first three. The form is rated around the runner-up.

## 438 BETWAY BEST ODDS GUARANTEED PLUS H'CAP 6f 1y(P)
**3:10** (3:13) (Class 6) (0-52,52) 4-Y-0+ **£2,716** (£808; £404; £202) **Stalls** Low

Form RPR
50-2 **1** **Krazy Paving**[21] 88 5-9-6 **51**..........................(b) AdamKirby 4 57
(Anabel K Murphy) *cl up: rdn to chse ldr 2f out: clsd u.p fnl f: led last 75yds* **3/1**[1]
0-66 **2** nk **Justice Rock**[18] 143 4-9-1 **46** oh1.......................... JosephineGordon 2 51
(Phil McEntee) *led: sent for home 2f out: drvn fnl f: hdd last 75yds: kpt on* **14/1**
00-5 **3** 1 1/4 **Pleadings (USA)**[20] 119 4-9-5 **50**..........................(vt) ShaneKelly 1 51
(Charlie Wallis) *hld up bhd ldrs: shkn up and nt qckn over 1f out: styd on to take 3rd ins fnl f but too late to chal* **5/1**[3]
50-3 **4** hd **Great Expectations**[21] 88 9-7 **52**..........................(vt) GeorgeBaker 7 53
(J R Jenkins) *tk fierce hold: hld up in last: prog 2f out but towards inner: disp 3rd ins fnl f: nt qckn after* **3/1**[1]
0-00 **5** 1 3/4 **Nidnod**[18] 143 4-8-8 **46** oh1.......................... JaneElliott[(7)] 10 42
(John Bridger) *chsd ldrs: rdn 2f out: nt qckn over 1f out: one pce after* **33/1**
00-0 **6** nk **National Service (USA)**[14] 217 6-9-5 **50**..........................(p) TimmyMurphy 6 45
(Richard Ford) *t.k.h: hld up in rr: prog 2f out but on inner and effrt flattened out fnl f* **8/1**
0-05 **7** nk **Diamond Vine (IRE)**[14] 217 9-9-1 **46**..........................(p) DavidProbert 3 40
(Ronald Harris) *hld up in rr: rdn over 1f out: kpt on fnl f: nvr nr enough to threaten* **14/1**
2-44 **8** 2 1/2 **Burauq**[14] 216 5-9-5 **50**..........................(b) RobertWinston 9 40
(Milton Bradley) *t.k.h early: hld up on outer: snatched up after 1f: wd bnd 2f out: shuffled along and steadily lost grnd* **9/2**[2]
00-6 **9** 2 1/2 **Bedazzling Lady (IRE)**[8] 311 4-8-11 **47**..........................(v[1]) GeorgiaCox[(5)] 12 26
(Robert Eddery) *gd spd fr wdst draw: chsd ldr to 2f out: wknd* **20/1**
60/0 **10** 2 3/4 **Catalyze**[14] 211 9-9-1 **46**..........................(t) DannyBrock 8 16
(Paddy Butler) *t.k.h early: hld up and racd wdst of all: rdn over 2f out: sn wknd* **66/1**

1m 13.68s (1.78) **Going Correction** +0.025s/f (Slow) **10** Ran SP% **118.5**
Speed ratings (Par 101): **89,88,86,86,84 83,83,80,76,73**
CSF £48.28 CT £186.14 TOTE £3.70: £1.20, £3.80, £1.80; EX 51.60 Trifecta £333.40.
**Owner** All The Kings Horses & Aiden Murphy **Bred** Trebles Holford Farm Thoroughbreds **Trained** Wilmcote, Warwicks

■ Stewards' Enquiry : Jane Elliott two-day ban; careless riding (10th-11th Feb)

**FOCUS**
A poor sprint handicap and not many got into it. The winner was close to his best 2016 form.

## 439 £10 FREE AT 32RED.COM H'CAP 1m 2f (P)
**3:40** (3:40) (Class 5) (0-75,75) 3-Y-O **£3,557** (£1,058; £529; £264) **Stalls** Low

Form RPR
101- **1** **Emenem**[32] 8525 3-9-6 **74**.......................... AdamKirby 1 77
(Simon Dow) *trckd ldrs: rdn 2f out: styd on inner but clsd fnl f: drvn ahd last 100yds: kpt on wl* **7/2**[2]
1 **2** 1/2 **Ocean Drive (IRE)**[18] 144 3-9-7 **75**.......................... RyanMoore 2 77
(William Haggas) *pressed ldr: chal 2f out: rdn over 1f out: led jst ins fnl f: hdd and hld last 100yds* **8/11**[1]
632- **3** 3/4 **Quothquan (FR)**[38] 8466 3-9-5 **73**.......................... LiamKeniry 6 73
(Michael Madgwick) *t.k.h: hld up in last pair: prog on outer 3f out: rdn 2f out: kpt on fnl f to take 3rd nr fin but nvr able to chal* **8/1**[3]
41-4 **4** 1 **Booshbash (IRE)**[9] 284 3-8-10 **64**.......................... JosephineGordon 3 62
(Ed Dunlop) *led at mod pce: kicked on over 2f out: hdd and fdd jst ins fnl f* **20/1**
26-1 **5** 1/2 **Nastenka**[21] 100 3-9-5 **73**.......................... ThomasBrown 4 70
(Ed Walker) *hld up in last: poorly plcd whn kick for home sed over 2f out: rdn over 1f out: kpt on but nvr pce to threaten* **8/1**[3]



The Form Book Flat, Raceform Ltd, Newbury, RG14 5SJ

610- **6** 1 1/4 **Sadhbh (IRE)**[51] 8244 3-8-8 **67** HollieDoyle(5) 5 62
(Richard Hannon) *chsd ldrs: rdn and lost pl over 2f out: one pce and no ch fnl f* **16/1**

2m 10.9s (4.30) **Going Correction** +0.025s/f (Slow) **6** Ran SP% **113.0**
Speed ratings (Par 97): **83,82,82,81,80 79**
CSF £6.54 TOTE £4.00: £1.90, £1.10; EX 6.90 Trifecta £27.20.
**Owner** Robert Moss and Christopher Brennan **Bred** D R Tucker **Trained** Ashtead, Surrey
■ Stewards' Enquiry : Adam Kirby two-day ban; used whip above the permitted level.
Ryan Moore two-day ban; used whip above the permitted level.

**FOCUS**
Probably not a bad little contest of its type with all six having won at least once previously, but the pace was moderate. The fourth is the key.

## 440 BETWAY AMATEUR RIDERS' H'CAP 1m 4f (P)
4:10 (4:10) (Class 5) (0-75,75) 4-Y-O+ **£3,119** (£967; £483; £242) **Stalls** Low

Form RPR

3-04 **1** **Attain**[6] 351 8-10-4 **65** MrSWalker 5 74
(Archie Watson) *s.i.s: hld up in midfield: clsd on ldrs 3f out: squeezed through to chse ldr 1f out: drvn and styd on wl to ld last strides* **5/1**

124- **2** 1/2 **General Hazard (IRE)**[36] 8498 4-10-4 **74** (p[1]) MrBJames(5) 4 82
(Michael Bell) *trckd ldrs: cl up fr 3f out: led on inner over 1f out and sent for home: urged along fnl f: hdd last strides* **11/4[1]**

0-60 **3** 3 1/2 **Icebuster**[13] 240 9-11-0 **75** MrPMillman 11 77
(Rod Millman) *hld up in rr: effrt on wd outside 3f out: rdn 2f out: styd on fr over 1f out to take 3rd last 75yds* **20/1**

1-21 **4** 1 1/4 **Bamako Du Chatelet (FR)**[14] 220 6-10-8 **69** (v[1]) MissSBrotherton 8 69
(Ian Williams) *cl up: prog to go 2nd over 3f out: jnd ldr 2f out: sn rdn: outpcd fr over 1f out* **3/1[2]**

143- **5** 2 1/4 **Heart Locket**[32] 8524 5-10-9 **70** MissJoannaMason 7 67
(Michael Easterby) *trckd ldr 4f: styd cl up: lost pl 3f out: rdn and struggling 2f out: plugged on* **4/1[3]**

23-3 **6** 2 1/2 **Take Two**[16] 173 8-10-3 **71** MrJBrace(7) 9 64
(Alex Hales) *prog to join ldr after 4f: led 4f out: hdd over 1f out: wknd qckly* **8/1**

44-0 **7** nk **Tempuran**[16] 169 8-10-1 **67** PoppyBridgwater(5) 1 59
(David Bridgwater) *towards rr: pushed along and struggling fr 3f out* **16/1**

630- **8** 1/2 **My Lord**[167] 5406 9-10-1 **67** MissMBryant(5) 2 59
(Paddy Butler) *slowly away: t.k.h: hld up towards rr: no prog over 2f out: wl btn after* **66/1**

64-0 **9** 3/4 **The Gay Cavalier**[23] 36 6-10-7 **75** (t) MissHVKnowles(7) 10 65
(John Ryan) *dwlt: hld up in last and detached early: nudged along and passed rivals fr 3f out: nvr a threat and fdd fnl f* **33/1**

30-2 **10** 7 **Noguchi (IRE)**[8] 315 12-9-13 **67** (p) MissEBushe(7) 6 46
(Chris Dwyer) *led to 4f out: wknd rapidly over 2f out* **14/1**

050- **11** 13 **Athenian Garden (USA)**[283] 1547 10-9-7 **61** oh16... MissJMOlliver(7) 3 19
(Paddy Butler) *stdd s: a in rr: wknd 3f out: t.o* **100/1**

2m 31.1s (-1.90) **Going Correction** +0.025s/f (Slow)
**WFA** 4 from 5yo+ 3lb **11** Ran SP% **122.2**
Speed ratings (Par 103): **107,106,104,103,102 100,100,99,99,94 85**
CSF £19.53 CT £263.07 TOTE £5.80: £2.00, £1.30, £6.00; EX 23.80 Trifecta £355.60.
**Owner** Boadicea Bloodstock **Bred** Millsec Limited **Trained** Upper Lambourn, W Berks

**FOCUS**
An ordinary amateur riders' middle-distance handicap in which they seemed to go an even pace. The winner is rated back to his old best.
T/Plt: £52.60 to a £1 stake. Pool: £75,730.02 - 1049.02 winning units T/Qpdt: £6.00 to a £1 stake. Pool: £7,738.76 - 950.62 winning units **Jonathan Neesom**

# 399 NEWCASTLE (A.W) (L-H)
Friday, January 27

**OFFICIAL GOING: Tapeta: standard**
Wind: Almost nil

## 441 SUNBETS.CO.UK H'CAP 7f 14y (Tp)
5:45 (5:46) (Class 4) (0-80,81) 4-Y-O+ **£4,851** (£1,443; £721; £360) **Stalls** Centre

Form RPR

U5-1 **1** **Safe Voyage (IRE)**[6] 363 4-9-3 **75** JasonHart 5 86+
(John Quinn) *t.k.h: mde all at stdy pce: rdn and hrd pressed over 1f out: asserted fnl 100yds: pushed out* **11/8[1]**

5-05 **2** 1 1/2 **Lexington Times (IRE)**[9] 287 5-9-7 **79** JackGarritty 4 85
(Ruth Carr) *prom: hdwy to chal over 1f out to last 100yds: edgd lft and kpt on same pce* **9/2[3]**

21-1 **3** 1 3/4 **Custard The Dragon**[25] 25 4-8-13 **71** AndrewMullen 2 72
(John Mackie) *prom: effrt and rdn 2f out: kpt on fnl f: nt pce to chal* **11/4[2]**

200- **4** 1 1/2 **Mime Dance**[143] 6220 6-8-9 **70** (p) ShelleyBirkett(3) 7 67
(David O'Meara) *t.k.h: chsd wnr to 2f out: drvn and sn one pce* **33/1**

60-0 **5** 1 1/4 **Red Touch (USA)**[25] 25 5-9-3 **78** AlistairRawlinson(3) 3 72
(Michael Appleby) *trckd ldrs: rdn and outpcd wl over 1f out: sn btn* **12/1**

0-55 **6** 1/2 **So It's War (FR)**[6] 359 6-8-6 **69** (v) ShirleyTeasdale(5) 1 62
(Keith Dalgleish) *s.i.s: plld hrd in tch: rdn and outpcd over 2f out: edgd lft and btn over 1f out* **6/1**

1m 28.76s (2.56) **Going Correction** +0.175s/f (Slow) **6** Ran SP% **111.9**
Speed ratings (Par 105): **92,90,88,86,85 84**
CSF £7.95 TOTE £2.10: £1.50, £2.10; EX 7.00 Trifecta £16.10.
**Owner** Ross Harmon **Bred** Schneider Adolf **Trained** Settrington, N Yorks

**FOCUS**
The two at the head of the market arrived here at the top of their game. It was steadily run and was dominated throughout by the front-running favourite who was fully entitled to win this.

## 442 BETWAY BEST ODDS GUARANTEED PLUS MAIDEN STKS 6f (Tp)
6:15 (6:15) (Class 5) 3-5-Y-O **£2,911** (£866; £432; £216) **Stalls** Centre

Form RPR

22-6 **1** **Ettu**[13] 236 3-8-5 73 FrannyNorton 4 72
(Jeremy Noseda) *pressed ldr: hdwy to ld over 2f out: shkn up and qcknd clr over 1f out: pushed out: readily* **11/8[2]**

**2** 4 1/2 **Van Velde (IRE)** 3-8-10 0 JasonHart 7 63+
(John Quinn) *trckd ldrs: outpcd and green over 2f out: rallied fnl f: tk 2nd nr fin: no ch w ready wnr* **5/4[1]**

0-4 **3** nse **Mimic's Memory**[22] 72 3-8-5 0 ShaneGray 5 57+
(Ann Duffield) *t.k.h: in tch: shkn up and hdwy over 1f out: chsd (clr) wnr ins fnl f: no imp: lost 2nd cl home* **25/1**

**4** 1 3/4 **Scealtara (IRE)** 3-8-2 0 ShelleyBirkett(3) 2 52
(David O'Meara) *prom: pushed along and hdwy to chse (clr) wnr over 1f out to ins fnl f: sn btn* **20/1**

0- **5** 3/4 **Magical Molly Joe**[70] 8009 3-8-5 0 AndrewMullen 3 49
(David Barron) *t.k.h: hld up: pushed along over 2f out: hdwy over 1f out: nvr able to chal* **33/1**

**6** 1/2 **Boogie Babe** 3-8-5 0 BarryMcHugh 6 48
(Richard Fahey) *t.k.h: led to over 2f out: lost 2nd over 1f out: sn outpcd: btn ins fnl f* **13/2[3]**

**7** 2 **Spike's Princess (IRE)** 3-8-5 0 PaulQuinn 1 41
(David Nicholls) *hld up: pushed along over 3f out: wknd over 2f out* **50/1**

1m 13.4s (0.90) **Going Correction** +0.175s/f (Slow) **7** Ran SP% **113.4**
Speed ratings (Par 103): **101,95,94,92,91 90,88**
CSF £3.28 TOTE £2.10: £1.40, £1.10; EX 4.30 Trifecta £27.10.
**Owner** Marc Keller **Bred** Widden Stud Australia Pty Ltd **Trained** Newmarket, Suffolk

**FOCUS**
A moderate maiden and an easy winner who probably didn't need to match her previous form.

## 443 BETWAY H'CAP 5f (Tp)
6:45 (6:45) (Class 4) (0-85,84) 4-Y-O+ **£4,851** (£1,443; £721; £360) **Stalls** Centre

Form RPR

46-1 **1** **Rich Again (IRE)**[15] 194 8-9-7 **84** (b) PJMcDonald 2 93
(James Bethell) *stdd in last pl: pushed along wl over 1f out: gd hdwy to ld wl ins fnl f: comf* **11/4[2]**

2-03 **2** 1 **Foxy Forever (IRE)**[6] 358 7-9-3 **80** (bt) ConnorBeasley 6 85
(Michael Wigham) *t.k.h: led on nr side of gp: rdn over 1f out: hdd wl ins fnl f: one pce* **5/2[1]**

-502 **3** 1/2 **Fredricka**[6] 358 6-8-8 **71** AndrewMullen 1 74
(David Barron) *hld up: pushed along 1/2-way: hdwy to chse ldr over 1f out to ins fnl f: kpt on same pce* **4/1[3]**

06-1 **4** 1 1/4 **Bahango (IRE)**[23] 45 5-8-4 **70** (p) NathanEvans(3) 4 69
(Patrick Morris) *t.k.h early: prom: effrt and rdn over 1f out: nt qckn ins fnl f* **7/1**

141- **5** shd **One Boy (IRE)**[100] 7474 6-9-1 **78** JackGarritty 8 76
(Paul Midgley) *t.k.h early: in tch on nr side of gp: effrt and rdn over 1f out: outpcd last 100yds* **16/1**

000- **6** 1 **Willbeme**[101] 7433 9-8-3 **73** BenRobinson(3) 3 68
(Neville Bycroft) *cl up on outside of gp: rdn along over 2f out: outpcd fnl f* **66/1**

06-0 **7** nse **Normal Equilibrium**[26] 4 7-9-1 **78** TomEaves 5 73
(Ivan Furtado) *t.k.h early: prom: stdy hdwy over 2f out: rdn over 1f out: outpcd ins fnl f* **12/1**

141- **8** 4 **Aprovado (IRE)**[119] 6927 5-9-3 **80** (p) PaulMulrennan 7 60
(Michael Dods) *cl up: rdn over 2f out: wknd over 1f out* **17/2**

59.09s (-0.41) **Going Correction** +0.175s/f (Slow) **8** Ran SP% **113.3**
Speed ratings (Par 105): **110,108,107,105,105 103,103,97**
CSF £9.87 CT £25.87 TOTE £3.20: £1.50, £1.30, £1.50; EX 10.30 Trifecta £33.20.
**Owner** Richard T Vickers **Bred** Mrs Sandra Maye **Trained** Middleham Moor, N Yorks

**FOCUS**
A good quality sprint handicap, in which four of the runners had won last time out. They went fast early and the race was set up perfectly for the patiently ridden Rich Again. He posted a length pb.

## 444 SUN BETS ON THE APP STORE H'CAP 1m 5y (Tp)
7:15 (7:15) (Class 6) (0-65,67) 4-Y-O+ **£2,264** (£673; £336; £168) **Stalls** Centre

Form RPR

200- **1** **Barwah (USA)**[120] 6908 6-9-7 **65** AndrewMullen 9 72
(Peter Niven) *dwlt: t.k.h and sn prom: rdn to ld on nr side of gp over 1f out: hld on wl fnl f* **14/1**

13-5 **2** 3/4 **Kicking The Can (IRE)**[23] 42 6-9-1 **64** LewisEdmunds(5) 7 69
(David Thompson) *t.k.h early: cl up: effrt and chsd wnr over 1f out: kpt on ins fnl f* **3/1[2]**

241- **3** 1/2 **Leonard Thomas**[48] 8307 7-9-2 **63** (p) EoinWalsh(3) 6 67
(Tony Carroll) *hld up: effrt and hdwy over 1f out: kpt on ins fnl f: nt pce to chal* **4/1[3]**

25-6 **4** 3/4 **Lozah**[6] 361 4-9-6 **64** JackGarritty 3 67
(Roger Fell) *t.k.h: hld up in last pl: rdn and hdwy over 1f out: kpt on fnl f: no imp* **5/1**

01-3 **5** hd **Star Of Spring (IRE)**[6] 360 5-9-2 **67** (h) CallumRodriguez(7) 2 69
(Iain Jardine) *dwlt: t.k.h: hld up: rdn along and effrt wl over 1f out: no imp fnl f* **5/2[1]**

26-0 **6** 1 3/4 **Indigo Princess**[13] 232 4-9-3 **64** AlistairRawlinson(3) 8 62
(Michael Appleby) *t.k.h: led: rdn over 2f out: hdd over 1f out: sn outpcd* **11/1**

66-0 **7** 3/4 **Bad Girl Caoimhe (IRE)**[17] 152 4-9-4 **62** BarryMcHugh 5 59
(Marjorie Fife) *in tch: rdn over 2f out: wknd over 1f out* **33/1**

425- **8** 4 1/2 **Gladys Cooper (IRE)**[106] 7300 4-8-12 **56** TonyHamilton 1 43
(Richard Fahey) *t.k.h: cl up on outside tl rdn and wknd wl over 1f out* **8/1**

1m 41.23s (2.63) **Going Correction** +0.175s/f (Slow) **8** Ran SP% **119.3**
Speed ratings (Par 101): **93,92,91,91,90 89,88,83**
CSF £58.41 CT £207.90 TOTE £16.90: £3.70, £1.50, £1.50; EX 26.50 Trifecta £369.30.
**Owner** Keep The Faith Partnership **Bred** Shadwell Farm LLC **Trained** Barton-le-Street, N Yorks

**FOCUS**
A typically competitive handicap for the level but the pace was slow. Straightforward form.

## 445 SUNBETS H'CAP 7f 14y (Tp)
7:45 (7:47) (Class 6) (0-60,62) 4-Y-O+ **£2,264** (£673; £336; £168) **Stalls** Centre

Form RPR

/0-0 **1** **Black Hambleton**[22] 67 4-9-6 **58** PaulMulrennan 6 65
(Bryan Smart) *prom: drvn along over 2f out: edgd lft and rallied to ld 1f out: styd on wl* **25/1**

1-60 **2** 1 3/4 **Justice Pleasing**[2] 400 4-8-10 **55** (p) BenSanderson(7) 2 58
(Roger Fell) *t.k.h early: cl up: led over 2f out to 1f out: kpt on same pce ins fnl f* **10/1**

40-0 **3** nse **Sandstream**[15] 198 4-8-7 **45** (t) JasonHart 10 48
(Tracy Waggott) *taken early to post: dwlt: t.k.h in rr: rdn 3f out: hdwy on nr side of gp over 1f out: kpt on fin* **33/1**

44-4 **4** 2 1/2 **Mr Potter**[6] 360 4-9-2 **54** (e) DanielTudhope 11 52
(Richard Guest) *hld up in tch: smooth hdwy and cl up over 1f out: rdn: edgd rt and no ex ins fnl f* **7/4[1]**

43-6 **5** 4 **Cool Strutter (IRE)**[23] 44 5-9-0 **57** (b) GemmaTutty(5) 8 43
(Karen Tutty) *taken early to post: plld hrd in rr: effrt and pushed along over 2f out: outpcd over 1f out* **11/2[3]**

054- **6** 1/2 **George Bailey (IRE)**[42] 8401 5-8-7 **48** NathanEvans(3) 7 33
(Suzzanne France) *in tch on nr side of gp: drvn along over 2f out: wknd over 1f out* **16/1**

004- **7** 3 1/4 **Jessie Allan (IRE)**[28] 8588 6-8-9 **47** JoeDoyle 12 24
(Jim Goldie) *t.k.h: hld up nr side of gp: rdn over 2f out: sn wknd* **25/1**

53-0 **8** *nse* **Oak Bluffs (IRE)**[7] 332 6-9-7 **59** ........ TonyHamilton 1 36
(Richard Fahey) *midfield on far side of gp: drvn and struggling wl over 2f out: sn btn* **15/2**

00-1 **9** *3 ¾* **Harry Holland**[9] 293 5-9-3 **62** ........ (h) MillyNaseb(7) 3 29
(Tom Dascombe) *s.i.s: bhd on far side of gp: struggling over 2f out: sn btn* **5/2**[2]

000- **10** *3 ½* **Miss Uppity**[38] 8471 4-8-10 **48** ........ TomEaves 4 7
(Ivan Furtado) *led to over 2f out: rdn and wknd over 1f out* **66/1**

1m 26.29s (0.09) **Going Correction** +0.175s/f (Slow) **10** Ran SP% **119.2**
Speed ratings (Par 101): **106,104,103,101,96 95,92,92,87,83**
CSF £251.31 CT £8177.52 TOTE £20.10: £3.70, £2.90, £11.10; EX 223.10 Trifecta £3157.40 Part Won..
**Owner** The Smart Duena Partnership **Bred** M E Wates **Trained** Hambleton, N Yorks

**FOCUS**
A weak race and not many got involved. The winner is rated near his earlier form.

## 446 BETWAY BEST ODDS GUARANTEED PLUS H'CAP 5f (Tp)
**8:15** (8:16) (Class 6) (0-60,60) 4-Y-O+ **£2,264** (£673; £336; £168) **Stalls** Centre

Form RPR

43-0 **1** **Windforpower (IRE)**[6] 362 7-9-3 **56** ........ (v) BenCurtis 11 62
(Tracy Waggott) *t.k.h: hld up midfield: hdwy over 1f out: rdn to ld wl ins fnl f: r.o* **8/1**

323- **2** *nk* **Sugar Town**[126] 6745 7-9-1 **57** ........ NathanEvans(3) 8 62
(Peter Niven) *led: rdn along over 1f out: hdd wl ins fnl f: kpt on fin* **13/2**

040- **3** *1 ¼* **Sea Of Green**[28] 8589 5-8-7 **46** ........ JoeDoyle 7 46
(Jim Goldie) *hld up towards rr: rdn and hdwy on far side of gp over 1f out: kpt on ins fnl f: nt rch first two* **18/1**

300- **4** *hd* **Roaring Rory**[43] 8390 4-9-2 **60** ........ (p) LewisEdmunds(5) 13 60
(Ollie Pears) *hld up on nr side of gp: rdn over 2f out: hdwy over 1f out: kpt on ins fnl f* **11/1**

04-0 **5** *hd* **See Vermont**[13] 242 9-9-5 **58** ........ (p) DanielTudhope 12 57
(Rebecca Bastiman) *hld up: rdn along and hdwy over 1f out: kpt on ins fnl f: nrst fin* **5/1**[1]

06-4 **6** *nse* **Fuel Injection**[11] 270 6-9-0 **53** ........ (p) JackGarritty 5 52
(Paul Midgley) *t.k.h: trckd ldrs: effrt and rdn wl over 1f out: no ex ins fnl f* **16/1**

02-6 **7** *½* **Whispering Wolf**[11] 271 4-8-7 **46** oh1 ........ BarryMcHugh 4 43
(Suzzanne France) *w ldr to 1/2-way: cl up tl rdn and no ex ins fnl f* **33/1**

211- **8** *shd* **Novabridge**[37] 8485 9-9-1 **59** ........ (b) GemmaTutty(5) 9 56
(Karen Tutty) *dwlt: puled hrd in rr and sn angled to far side of gp: rdn along 2f out: no imp fnl f* **6/1**[3]

04-4 **9** *½* **Nuala Tagula (IRE)**[17] 161 4-9-0 **60** ........ JoshQuinn(7) 2 55
(John Quinn) *t.k.h: trckd ldrs: rdn along 2f out: no ex ins fnl f* **7/1**

20-1 **10** *1 ½* **Lady Bacchus**[11] 270 4-9-4 **57** 6ex ........ (b) ConnorBeasley 1 46
(Richard Guest) *t.k.h: hld up on far side of gp: rdn along 1/2-way: no imp over 1f out* **11/2**[2]

20-4 **11** *1 ½* **Gettin' Lucky**[11] 271 4-8-7 **46** ........ AndrewMullen 3 30
(John Balding) *plld hrd in midfield: rdn wl over 1f out: wknd fnl f* **6/1**[3]

142- **12** *7* **Insolenceofoffice (IRE)**[254] 2360 9-8-11 **57** ...(p) CallumRodriguez(7) 10 16
(Richard Ford) *dwlt: sn drvn along in rr: struggling 1/2-way: nvr on terms* **33/1**

59.72s (0.22) **Going Correction** +0.175s/f (Slow) **12** Ran SP% **122.9**
Speed ratings (Par 101): **105,104,102,102,101 101,101,100,100,97 95,84**
CSF £61.57 CT £922.79 TOTE £11.40: £3.20, £2.50, £6.20; EX 82.20 Trifecta £1989.00 Part Won..
**Owner** David Tate **Bred** Tally-Ho Stud **Trained** Spennymoor, Co Durham

**FOCUS**
A competitive, though moderate sprint handicap. A compressed finish, typical of 5f here.
T/Plt: £466.60 to a £1 stake. Pool: £104,483.57 - 163.45 winning units T/Qpdt: £295.00 to a £1 stake. Pool: £9,530.51 - 23.9 winning units **Richard Young**

447 - 454a (Foreign Racing) - See Raceform Interactive

# 281 KEMPTON (A.W) (R-H)
Saturday, January 28

**OFFICIAL GOING: Polytrack: standard**
Wind: Almost nil Weather: Partial cloud

## 455 RACING UK H'CAP 6f (P)
**5:45** (5:45) (Class 7) (0-50,52) 4-Y-O+ **£1,940** (£577; £288; £144) **Stalls** Low

Form RPR

00-1 **1** **Whaleweigh Station**[11] 274 6-9-9 **52** ........ (v) GeorgeBaker 7 66
(J R Jenkins) *mde all: qcknd clr over 1f out: comf* **7/4**[1]

6-50 **2** *4 ½* **Mistry**[11] 274 4-8-11 **45** ........ (v[1]) RachealKneller(5) 3 45
(Mark Usher) *chsd wnr: rdn 2f out: unable qck* **14/1**

02-2 **3** *1 ¼* **Mr Chuckles (IRE)**[15] 217 4-9-7 **50** ........ (p) AndrewMullen 8 46
(Daniel Mark Loughnane) *in tch: drvn into 3rd over 1f out: one pce* **4/1**[2]

40-4 **4** *½* **Diamond Indulgence**[7] 362 4-9-6 **49** ........ (h) DougieCostello 2 44
(Derek Shaw) *dwlt: sn in midfield: hmpd over 4f out: rdn and styd on fnl 2f* **8/1**

0-33 **5** *1 ¼* **Fossa**[15] 222 7-8-13 **47** ........ CharlieBennett(5) 9 38
(Mark Brisbourne) *dwlt: towards rr whn bdly hmpd over 4f out: sme hdwy over 1f out: nvr rchd ldrs* **15/2**[3]

00-0 **6** *1 ¼* **Storming Ambition**[10] 281 4-9-3 **46** ........ (t[1]) StevieDonohoe 1 33
(Conrad Allen) *chsd ldrs: bdly hmpd and lost pl over 4f out: nvr rcvrd* **80/1**

0-06 **7** *½* **National Service (USA)**[1] 438 6-9-7 **50** ........ (p) TimmyMurphy 4 36
(Richard Ford) *in tch: squeezed for room over 4f out: wknd over 1f out* **15/2**[3]

60-0 **8** *3 ¾* **Just Over**[23] 75 4-9-4 **50** ........ EoinWalsh(3) 6 25
(Robert Cowell) *prom tl wknd 2f out* **50/1**

00-2 **9** *½* **Teepee Time**[12] 270 4-8-13 **47** ........ PhilDennis(5) 12 20
(Michael Mullineaux) *chsd ldrs on outer tl wknd over 2f out* **33/1**

060- **10** *2 ¾* **Camino**[102] 7427 4-9-7 **50** ........ (h) MartinLane 10 15
(Andi Brown) *a bhd* **20/1**

02-0 **11** *1 ¼* **Arizona Snow**[26] 20 5-9-7 **50** ........ (p) LukeMorris 11 11
(Ronald Harris) *a towards rr: no ch fnl 2f* **20/1**

1m 12.83s (-0.27) **Going Correction** -0.05s/f (Stan) **11** Ran SP% **113.3**
Speed ratings (Par 97): **99,93,91,90,89 87,86,81,81,77 75**
CSF £25.85 CT £86.87 TOTE £3.00: £1.30, £4.70, £1.50; EX 31.30 Trifecta £175.40.
**Owner** J Melo **Bred** A Black **Trained** Royston, Herts

**FOCUS**
A moderate sprint handicap. The strong favourite made all at a decent tempo, but there was trouble in behind approaching the turn for home. He's rated near his best 2016 form.

## 456 32RED CASINO H'CAP 6f (P)
**6:15** (6:15) (Class 6) (0-60,62) 3-Y-O **£2,264** (£673; £336; £168) **Stalls** Low

Form RPR

04-2 **1** **In The Spotlight (IRE)**[23] 77 3-9-9 **62** ........ GeorgeBaker 7 73+
(Henry Spiller) *hld up towards rr: smooth hdwy 2f out: led 1f out: rdn clr* **11/10**[1]

0-60 **2** *3 ¼* **Dashing Poet**[8] 324 3-9-4 **57** ........ (h) MartinLane 2 56
(Jeremy Gask) *hld up in midfield: hdwy to ld briefly over 1f out: sn outpcd by wnr* **16/1**

66-6 **3** *2* **Champagne Queen**[21] 126 3-8-11 **50** ........ (t) LukeMorris 4 43
(Rae Guest) *chsd ldrs: rdn over 2f out: one pce appr fnl f* **10/1**[3]

000- **4** *nk* **Mezyan (IRE)**[138] 6421 3-9-3 **56** ........ AdamKirby 10 48
(John Butler) *stdd s: hld up in rr: sme hdwy and rdn over 1f out: styd on same pce* **25/1**

5-16 **5** *½* **Gentleman Giles (IRE)**[12] 264 3-9-8 **61** ........ TimmyMurphy 3 52
(Jamie Osborne) *dwlt: hld up in rr: sme hdwy and rdn over 1f out: nvr able to chal* **5/2**[2]

6-50 **6** *1 ¾* **Tanksalot (IRE)**[5] 376 3-8-11 **50** ........ (v) TomMarquand 6 36
(Harry Dunlop) *chsd ldr tl outpcd 2f out* **16/1**

40-4 **7** *3 ½* **Little Nosegay (IRE)**[23] 77 3-9-2 **55** ........ AndrewMullen 8 30+
(David Evans) *led: 4 l clr 1/2-way: hdd & wknd over 1f out* **10/1**[3]

04-0 **8** *nk* **Nuptials (USA)**[23] 77 3-9-1 **54** ........ (b[1]) RobertWinston 9 28
(Eve Johnson Houghton) *in tch tl wknd 2f out* **25/1**

6-00 **9** *39* **Tink**[14] 244 3-8-6 **50** ........ CharlieBennett(5) 11
(Mark Brisbourne) *swvd lft s and hung lft thrght: sn prom: rn wd and wknd 3f out* **66/1**

1m 12.64s (-0.46) **Going Correction** -0.05s/f (Stan) **9** Ran SP% **115.3**
Speed ratings (Par 95): **101,96,94,93,92 90,85,85,33**
CSF £21.50 CT £124.67 TOTE £2.50: £1.10, £3.30, £1.60; EX 18.30 Trifecta £124.80.
**Owner** Dethrone Racing **Bred** Ms Patricia Walsh **Trained** Newmarket, Suffolk

**FOCUS**
A modest 3yo handicap, but an improving filly at the head of the weights outclassed this field from off a solid gallop. The winner has improved.

## 457 32RED ON THE APP STORE MAIDEN STKS 1m 3f 219y(P)
**6:45** (6:46) (Class 5) 4-Y-O+ **£3,234** (£962; £481; £240) **Stalls** Centre

Form RPR

3-3 **1** **Belabour**[18] 165 4-9-5 0 ........ JamieSpencer 6 79
(Mark Brisbourne) *hld up in midfield: hdwy 3f out: chsd ldr 2f out: led ins fnl f: drvn out* **5/1**[3]

625- **2** *1 ½* **Lord Napier (IRE)**[68] 8051 4-9-5 80 ........ (p) AdamKirby 5 77
(John Ryan) *chsd ldrs: wnt 2nd after 4f: led and kicked on over 3f out: hdd ins fnl f: kpt on* **5/2**[2]

30-2 **3** *5* **Ceyhan**[7] 353 5-9-9 79 ........ GeorgeBaker 3 69
(Jamie Osborne) *led for 1f: prom: chsd ldr 3f out tl 2f out: one pce* **4/11**[1]

0- **4** *15* **Mamnoon (IRE)**[77] 7942 4-9-5 0 ........ TomMarquand 1 45
(Roy Brotherton) *bhd: hrd rdn and wnt modest 4th over 2f out: n.d* **100/1**

40- **5** *1 ½* **Hannah Just Hannah**[32] 5623 8-8-13 0 ........ (t) LucyKBarry(5) 7 38
(Matthew Salaman) *s.i.s: towards rr: last and struggling 3f out: no ch after* **14/1**

/00- **6** *4 ½* **Mr Standfast**[249] 2553 4-9-5 51 ........ TimmyMurphy 2 35
(Alan Phillips) *mid-div: lost pl 1/2-way: n.d fnl 3f* **50/1**

000- **7** *27* **Selena Rose**[304] 1141 4-8-9 38 ........ CiaranMckee(5) 4
(Ronald Harris) *chsd ldrs tl wknd over 3f out* **125/1**

4- **8** *20* **Feisty Girl**[53] 5353 7-8-13 0 ........ (b[1]) PhilDennis(5) 8
(Michael Mullineaux) *led after 1f tl over 3f out: wknd qckly* **66/1**

2m 32.98s (-1.52) **Going Correction** -0.05s/f (Stan)
**WFA** 4 from 5yo+ 3lb **8** Ran SP% **130.5**
Speed ratings (Par 103): **103,102,98,88,87 84,66,53**
CSF £20.79 TOTE £11.10: £1.50, £1.10, £1.10; EX 38.10 Trifecta £43.50.
**Owner** Zen Racing **Bred** Darley **Trained** Great Ness, Shropshire

**FOCUS**
A fair middle-distance maiden and they went a respectable gallop. The favourite bounced on his second run after a break and the winner improved upped in trip to take full advantage.

## 458 32RED.COM H'CAP 6f (P)
**7:15** (7:16) (Class 4) (0-85,80) 3-Y-O **£4,690** (£1,395; £697; £348) **Stalls** Low

Form RPR

4-21 **1** **Marquee Club**[7] 356 3-9-7 **80** ........ GeorgeBaker 10 88
(Jamie Osborne) *mde all: hrd rdn over 1f out: hld on wl* **11/2**[3]

006- **2** *2* **Kamra (USA)**[41] 8444 3-9-4 **77** ........ AdamKirby 2 79
(Jeremy Noseda) *chsd wnr: kpt on u.p fnl 2f: a hld* **16/1**

2-13 **3** *nse* **Golden Opportunity**[7] 356 3-9-2 **75** ........ (p[1]) MartinHarley 1 77
(James Tate) *hld up in 5th: hdwy 2f out: disp 2nd ins fnl f: kpt on* **9/2**[2]

1-33 **4** *2 ¼* **Alkashaaf (USA)**[8] 329 3-9-4 **77** ........ (tp) DavidProbert 9 72
(Archie Watson) *hld up in 7th: sme hdwy into 4th over 1f out: styd on same pce* **7/2**[1]

60-3 **5** *1 ½* **Ninety Years Young**[17] 178 3-8-1 **65** ........ (b) HollieDoyle(5) 3 55
(David Elsworth) *bhd: drvn along 3f out: sme late hdwy* **7/1**

5123 **6** *nk* **Gracious Tom (IRE)**[10] 291 3-9-6 **79** ........ AndrewMullen 4 68
(David Evans) *chsd ldrs: rdn over 2f out: one pce* **8/1**

-324 **7** *nse* **Pulsating (IRE)**[8] 324 3-7-13 **65** ........ (v[1]) KieranSchofield(7) 8 54
(Daniel Steele) *t.k.h in 6th on outer: rdn and no hdwy fnl 2f* **33/1**

3-32 **8** *3 ¾* **White Royale (USA)**[9] 313 3-9-2 **75** ........ (p) KevinStott 5 52
(Kevin Ryan) *a towards rr* **12/1**

1 **9** *1 ¼* **Garam (IRE)**[23] 76 3-9-5 **78** ........ JosephineGordon 7 51
(Hugo Palmer) *sn outpcd towards rr* **7/2**[1]

60-3 **10** *1* **Bee Case**[7] 350 3-8-13 **72** ........ TomMarquand 6 42
(Simon Dow) *prom: hrd rdn 2f out: sn wknd* **50/1**

1m 11.98s (-1.12) **Going Correction** -0.05s/f (Stan) **10** Ran SP% **120.1**
Speed ratings (Par 99): **105,102,102,99,97 96,96,91,90,88**
CSF £91.75 CT £442.58 TOTE £6.50: £2.30, £3.60, £2.00; EX 89.90 Trifecta £709.00.
**Owner** Melbourne 10 Racing **Bred** Norman Court Stud, P Taplin & McB Ltd **Trained** Upper Lambourn, Berks

**FOCUS**
A fair 3yo sprint handicap. It hadn't been easy to come from off the pace on this card and the in-form winner came over to get on the lead from a wide draw and picked up well when asked to assert over a furlong out.

## 459 32RED H'CAP 7f (P)
7:45 (7:45) (Class 3) (0-95,96) 4-Y-0+
£7,158 (£2,143; £1,071; £535; £267; £134) Stalls Low

Form RPR
414- 1 **Keystroke**[38] 8478 5-9-7 95 AdamKirby 6 108+
(Jeremy Noseda) *hld up in 6th: hdwy 2f out: led over 1f out: rdn out* **11/8**[1]
6-41 2 2½ **Intransigent**[11] 275 8-9-1 92 RobHornby(3) 3 97
(Andrew Balding) *t.k.h: cl up: rdn to press ldrs over 1f out: kpt on to take 2nd ins fnl f* **6/1**[3]
0-26 3 ½ **Firmdecisions (IRE)**[11] 275 7-9-2 90 RobertWinston 10 94
(Dean Ivory) *t.k.h: pressed ldr on outer: slt ld 2f out tl over 1f out: one pce* **20/1**
00-4 4 nk **Valbchek (IRE)**[11] 275 8-9-2 90 (p) StevieDonohoe 4 93
(Jane Chapple-Hyam) *mid-div tl rdn and styd on fnl 2f* **16/1**
060/ 5 2½ **Professor**[469] 7282 7-9-7 95 LukeMorris 2 91
(Michael Attwater) *in tch: rdn over 2f out: one pce appr fnl f* **40/1**
1-03 6 hd **Al Khan (IRE)**[16] 199 8-9-4 92 KevinStott 14 88
(Kevin Ryan) *stdd s and dropped in: hld up in rr: rdn 2f out: nrest at fin* **25/1**
000- 7 1 **Majestic Moon (IRE)**[28] 8593 7-9-3 91 AdamBeschizza 7 84
(Julia Feilden) *led tl 2f out: wknd over 1f out* **33/1**
42-0 8 nk **Plucky Dip**[15] 219 6-8-1 82 DarraghKeenan(7) 9 74
(John Ryan) *towards rr: rdn over 2f out: nvr able to chal* **25/1**
006- 9 nse **Georgian Bay (IRE)**[28] 8593 7-8-13 90 (v) JordanVaughan(3) 5 82
(K R Burke) *prom tl hrd rdn and wknd wl over 1f out* **9/2**[2]
010- 10 1¼ **Presumido (IRE)**[28] 8593 7-8-13 87 TomMarquand 8 76
(Simon Dow) *dwlt: bhd: sme hdwy in midfield whn nt clr run on inner over 1f out: n.d* **20/1**
40-5 11 hd **Dutch Mist**[19] 142 4-8-8 82 (v) ShaneGray 1 70
(Kevin Ryan) *mid-div: effrt over 2f out: wknd over 1f out* **33/1**
10-0 12 3¼ **Outer Space**[11] 275 6-9-0 88 JamieSpencer 13 67
(Jamie Osborne) *stdd s: a bhd* **12/1**
026- 13 nk **Intrude**[133] 6580 5-9-6 94 GeorgeBaker 11 72
(Stuart Williams) *a towards rr* **20/1**
1m 25.04s (-0.96) **Going Correction** -0.05s/f (Stan) **13** Ran SP% **118.4**
Speed ratings (Par 107): **103,100,99,99,96 96,95,94,94,93 92,89,88**
CSF £7.75 CT £122.40 TOTE £2.40: £1.30, £1.80, £4.10; EX 11.60 Trifecta £85.50.
**Owner** Front Runner Racing III **Bred** Cheveley Park Stud Ltd **Trained** Newmarket, Suffolk

**FOCUS**
The feature contest was a good handicap. A strong move in the betting for a horse reportedly working really well in Newmarket proved entirely accurate. The right horses were in behind off a solid gallop.

## 460 32RED ON THE APP STORE H'CAP 1m (P)
8:15 (8:15) (Class 4) (0-80,82) 4-Y-0+ £4,690 (£1,395; £697; £348) Stalls Low

Form RPR
0-15 1 **Gossiping**[5] 382 5-9-0 73 ShaneKelly 4 83+
(Gary Moore) *hld up in midfield: hdwy on inner 2f out: qcknd to ld jst ins fnl f: rdn out* **7/2**[2]
65-0 2 1½ **Zain Emperor (IRE)**[7] 359 4-9-3 76 JosephineGordon 11 82
(John Butler) *towards rr: rdn over 2f out: late hdwy to take 2nd nr fin* **12/1**
432- 3 nk **Mariee**[225] 3364 4-9-7 80 JoeFanning 5 85
(Mark Johnston) *prom on inner: chal 2f out: one pce fnl f* **9/2**[3]
006- 4 1¼ **Tee It Up Tommo (IRE)**[47] 7817 8-8-0 66 oh8 KieranSchofield(7) 6 68
(Daniel Steele) *bhd: rdn over 2f out: gd late hdwy* **80/1**
21 5 shd **Revolutionary War (USA)**[7] 354 4-9-7 80 AdamKirby 2 82
(Jamie Osborne) *led tl 2f out: w ldrs tl no ex ins fnl f* **5/2**[1]
21-0 6 1½ **Right Rebel**[24] 47 5-8-10 72 EoinWalsh(3) 9 70
(Alan Bailey) *t.k.h: trckd ldr: slt ld 2f out tl wknd jst ins fnl f* **33/1**
1-32 7 nse **Pendo**[11] 277 6-9-4 77 KierenFox 12 75
(John Best) *chsd ldrs: hrd rdn 2f out: btn over 1f out* **8/1**
5-40 8 1 **Polar Forest**[7] 359 7-8-12 71 (e) ConnorBeasley 8 67
(Richard Guest) *in tch tl outpcd fnl 2f* **20/1**
13-6 9 1¼ **Out Of The Ashes**[23] 66 4-9-5 78 (t) TomEaves 3 71
(Mohamed Moubarak) *s.i.s: sn rdn to chse ldrs: wknd wl over 1f out* **33/1**
4-00 10 3½ **Greyfriarschorista**[10] 287 10-8-9 68 AndrewMullen 1 53
(David Evans) *a towards rr* **66/1**
00-3 11 1¾ **Dutiful Son (IRE)**[7] 349 7-9-7 80 JamieSpencer 7 61
(Simon Dow) *a bhd* **6/1**
00-0 12 1 **Jack Of Diamonds (IRE)**[14] 240 8-9-7 80 RobertWinston 10 59
(Roger Teal) *in tch tl wknd over 2f out* **16/1**
1m 39.01s (-0.79) **Going Correction** -0.05s/f (Stan) **12** Ran SP% **121.3**
Speed ratings (Par 105): **101,99,99,97,97 96,96,95,94,90 88,87**
CSF £43.99 CT £200.43 TOTE £5.00: £1.90, £3.40, £1.80; EX 74.30 Trifecta £792.00.
**Owner** G L Moore & Partners **Bred** Darley **Trained** Lower Beeding, W Sussex

**FOCUS**
A fair handicap. The winner bounced back to form off a stronger gallop than last time.

## 461 100% PROFIT BOOST AT 32REDSPORT.COM H'CAP (DIV I) 1m 3f 219y(P)
8:45 (8:47) (Class 6) (0-60,61) 4-Y-0+ £2,264 (£673; £336; £168) Stalls Centre

Form RPR
00-4 1 **Shining Romeo**[14] 238 5-9-10 60 (v) LukeMorris 8 66
(Denis Quinn) *hld up in midfield: hdwy 2f out: led ins fnl f: rdn out* **15/2**
433- 2 1½ **Santadelacruze**[37] 8500 8-9-1 51 ShaneKelly 3 55
(Mark Hoad) *towards rr: rdn over 2f out: late hdwy to take 2nd fnl strides* **16/1**
06-1 3 nk **Rail Dancer**[10] 281 5-9-5 55 (v) RobertWinston 7 58
(Richard Rowe) *plld hrd: chsd ldr: led over 2f out tl ins fnl f: one pce* **2/1**[1]
0-33 4 nse **Stonecoldsoba**[15] 218 4-9-7 61 AdamKirby 11 64
(David Evans) *chsd ldrs: drvn along over 2f out: styd on fnl f* **3/1**[2]
26-5 5 3½ **Galuppi**[11] 278 6-9-3 53 (v) GeorgeBaker 6 50
(J R Jenkins) *bhd: rdn 2f out: nrest at fin* **14/1**
450- 6 nk **Kilim**[57] 8194 4-9-4 58 (t) TomMarquand 10 55
(John Berry) *mid-div: outpcd over 2f out: styng on at fin* **25/1**
40-3 7 1 **Tyrsal (IRE)**[17] 169 6-9-9 59 AdamBeschizza 2 54
(Clifford Lines) *prom tl wknd over 1f out* **8/1**
36-1 8 5 **Staplehurst (IRE)**[11] 279 4-9-2 56 (t) TimmyMurphy 9 43
(Geoffrey Deacon) *t.k.h in midfield on outer: rdn over 2f out: sn wknd* **7/2**[3]
500- 9 4½ **Heart Of An Angel**[131] 6631 4-9-6 60 (b[1]) StevieDonohoe 4 40
(Henry Spiller) *plld hrd in rr: sme hdwy 2f out: sn wknd* **50/1**
/00- 10 7 **Stimulator**[96] 7572 4-8-6 46 oh1 (h) AndrewMullen 5 15
(Andi Brown) *led: 5 l clr after 3f tl 6f out: hdd & wknd over 2f out* **66/1**
2m 35.46s (0.96) **Going Correction** -0.05s/f (Stan)
**WFA** 4 from 5yo+ 3lb **10** Ran SP% **123.3**
Speed ratings (Par 101): **94,93,92,92,90 90,89,86,83,78**
CSF £123.19 CT £335.59 TOTE £7.70: £2.40, £3.90, £1.40; EX 88.70 Trifecta £549.60.
**Owner** John Mangan **Bred** Newsells Park Stud **Trained** Newmarket, Suffolk

**FOCUS**
The first division of a modest middle-distance handicap. The winning time was slow and the favourite raced a tad too freely into the lead in the straight before fading back to third. Straightforward form.

## 462 100% PROFIT BOOST AT 32REDSPORT.COM H'CAP (DIV II) 1m 3f 219y(P)
9:15 (9:16) (Class 6) (0-60,61) 4-Y-0+ £2,264 (£673; £336; £168) Stalls Centre

Form RPR
014- 1 **Stand Guard**[30] 8567 13-9-8 58 LiamKeniry 6 66
(John Butler) *mid-div: hdwy over 2f out: led wl over 1f out: sn in command* **8/1**
6-03 2 2 **Ali Bin Nayef**[11] 279 5-9-3 53 AdamKirby 11 59
(Michael Wigham) *mid-div: hdwy and swtchd lft 2f out: chsd wnr fnl f: kpt on* **7/2**[2]
14- 3 1¼ **Tasty Ginger (IRE)**[49] 6367 4-9-7 61 GeorgeBaker 10 64
(J R Jenkins) *towards rr: hdwy over 1f out: nrest at fin* **7/4**[1]
035/ 4 2¼ **Money Talks**[235] 3579 7-9-10 60 DanielMuscutt 2 59
(Michael Madgwick) *chsd ldrs: briefly wnt 2nd over 1f out: no ex fnl f* **16/1**
50-5 5 2¼ **Sixties Idol**[11] 279 4-8-5 48 NathanAlison(3) 8 44
(Sheena West) *towards rr: effrt and in tch 2f out: no imp over 1f out* **16/1**
00-0 6 2¼ **Hydrant**[14] 238 11-9-6 56 ConnorBeasley 5 48
(Richard Guest) *in tch tl outpcd 2f out* **12/1**
600- 7 1¾ **Hint Of Grey (IRE)**[30] 8567 4-9-3 57 JoeFanning 7 46
(Don Cantillon) *bhd tl sme late hdwy* **15/2**[3]
0 8 6 **Cornelius (FR)**[11] 279 5-8-9 52 (v[1]) JordanUys(7) 1 32
(Jonathan Geake) *led tl wknd wl over 1f out* **50/1**
0-00 9 nk **Divine Prince (GR)**[11] 279 4-8-8 51 (b) KieranShoemark(3) 9 30
(Amanda Perrett) *chsd ldrs tl wknd 2f out* **14/1**
466- 10 3 **Demand Respect**[40] 8459 4-8-6 46 oh1 (b[1]) KieranO'Neill 4 21
(Henry Spiller) *dwlt: hdwy to press ldr after 1f: wknd over 2f out* **20/1**
2m 34.38s (-0.12) **Going Correction** -0.05s/f (Stan)
**WFA** 4 from 5yo+ 3lb **10** Ran SP% **114.3**
Speed ratings (Par 101): **98,96,95,94,92 91,90,86,85,83**
CSF £35.39 CT £71.22 TOTE £9.10: £2.30, £1.50, £1.40; EX 27.30 Trifecta £77.50.
**Owner** Miss Alice Haynes **Bred** Juddmonte Farms Ltd **Trained** Newmarket, Suffolk

**FOCUS**
The second division of a modest middle-distance handicap. The winning time was over a second quicker, but off another ordinary gallop. Stand Guard may not have stopped winning yet.
T/Plt: £31.40 to a £1 stake. Pool: £98,500.29 - 2,288.74 winning units T/Qpdt: £11.50 to a £1 stake. Pool: £9,493.00 - 609.46 winning units **Lee McKenzie**

# [434] LINGFIELD (L-H)
Saturday, January 28

**OFFICIAL GOING: Polytrack: standard**
Wind: light, half behind Weather: mainly cloudy, brighter spells

## 463 32RED H'CAP 7f 1y(P)
1:20 (1:20) (Class 6) (0-60,62) 3-Y-0 £2,587 (£770; £384; £192) Stalls Low

Form RPR
53-2 1 **Auric Goldfinger (IRE)**[5] 377 3-8-12 56 (b) HollieDoyle(5) 7 67+
(Richard Hannon) *hld up in last pair: pushed along briefly 5f out: effrt over 1f out: gd hdwy to ld ins fnl f: r.o strly and stormed clr: readily* **7/2**[2]
66-0 2 4½ **Dream Reversion**[8] 324 3-9-7 60 RichardKingscote 4 61
(Tom Dascombe) *s.i.s: hld up in rr: clsd and nt clr run over 1f out: gap opened and effrt 1f out: no match for wnr but kpt on to snatch 2nd last stride* **5/1**[3]
0-45 3 shd **Tigerfish (IRE)**[5] 377 3-8-7 46 oh1 (p) AdamBeschizza 3 45
(William Stone) *hld up in tch: clsd and nt clr run over 1f out: swtchd rt ent fnl f: squeezing between rivals and battling for placings ins fnl f: kpt on but no ch w wnr* **10/1**
00-6 4 nse **Nicky Baby (IRE)**[18] 160 3-9-9 62 RobertWinston 1 61
(Dean Ivory) *led: drvn and forged ahd over 1f out: hdd and totally outpcd by wnr ins fnl f: kpt on same pce and lost 2 pls last strides* **3/1**[1]
4-33 5 shd **Metronomic (IRE)**[5] 376 3-9-4 57 (p) KieranO'Neill 6 55
(Richard Hannon) *t.k.h: trckd ldrs: sltly impeded and dropped to midfield 3f out: sn rdn: clsd to chse ldrs but awkward hd carriage 1f out: kpt on same pce ins fnl f* **3/1**[1]
05-2 6 2½ **Hazell Berry (IRE)**[5] 376 3-8-7 46 oh1 (b) AndrewMullen 5 38
(David Evans) *pressed ldr: unable qck u.p over 1f out: btn and losing pl whn squeezed for room ins fnl f: wknd* **7/1**
00-0 7 1½ **Rita's Girl**[22] 96 3-8-11 50 (v) BenCurtis 8 38
(K R Burke) *in tch in midfield on outer: clsd and edgd lft 3f out: pressing ldng pair and drvn 2f out: unable qck and losing pl whn hmpd over 1f out: wknd* **33/1**
00-0 8 ½ **Lily Cliff**[9] 311 3-8-7 46 oh1 (t[1]) LukeMorris 2 32
(Paul D'Arcy) *in tch in midfield: effrt u.p on inner 2f out: no ex 1f out: wknd qckly ins fnl f* **33/1**
1m 24.79s (-0.01) **Going Correction** 0.0s/f (Stan) **8** Ran SP% **116.4**
Speed ratings (Par 95): **100,94,94,94,94 91,90,89**
CSF £21.81 CT £157.95 TOTE £4.10: £1.30, £2.10, £2.50; EX 25.60 Trifecta £133.90.
**Owner** R Hannon **Bred** Hyde Park Stud **Trained** East Everleigh, Wilts

**FOCUS**
Breezy but mildish conditions for this six-race card. The eight runners in this poor opener entered the race with a combined record of 0-62. The winner is waited a bit better than the bare form.

## 464 SUN BETS ON THE APP STORE MAIDEN STKS 7f 1y(P)
1:50 (1:52) (Class 5) 3-Y-0+ £3,234 (£962; £481; £240) Stalls Low

Form RPR
60- 1 **Abatement**[147] 6108 3-8-10 0 JosephineGordon 6 79+
(Roger Charlton) *t.k.h: trckd ldrs: effrt over 1f out: chsd ldr 1f out: led ins fnl f: r.o strly and sn clr: eased towards fin: readily* **5/1**
- 2 2¼ **Saxon Flames (GER)** 3-8-10 0 MartinDwyer 3 72
(William Muir) *trckd ldrs: lft pressing ldr 2f out: rdn to ld jst over 1f out: hdd ins fnl f: no ex and outpcd fnl 75yds* **4/1**[2]

32- **3** *nk* **Arnarson**[44] 8384 3-8-10 0 DavidProbert 8 71
(Ed Dunlop) *in tch in midfield: nt clrest of runs briefly wl over 1f out: swtchd rt and hdwy over 1f out: chsd ldng pair ins fnl f: styd on to press for 2nd nr fin: no ch w wnr* **11/10**[1]

03- **4** *4* **Thetrioandme (IRE)**[31] 8557 3-8-10 0 KierenFox 1 60
(John Best) *led: rdn wl over 1f out: hdd jst over 1f out: no ex: lost 3rd and wknd ins fnl f* **8/1**

42-4 **5** *2* **Oxford Thinking (IRE)**[24] 40 3-8-10 70 NickyMackay 9 55
(John Gosden) *trckd ldrs on outer: pushed along over 2f out: carried rt and wd bnd 2f out: lost pl and no threat to ldrs after: kpt on same pce* **9/2**[3]

0/0- **6** *1 1/4* **Irvine Lady (IRE)**[49] 8320 4-9-2 0 SophieScardifield(7) 4 51?
(Gay Kelleway) *pressed ldr tl rdn: hung rt and lost pl bnd 2f out: sn lost pl: wknd over 1f out* **100/1**

**7** *3/4* **Tilly's Bridge** 4-9-9 0 JackMitchell 10 49
(Steve Woodman) *s.i.s: swtchd lft after s: rn green and outpcd in last pair: sme hdwy ent fnl 2f: no imp over 1f out: nvr trbld ldrs* **66/1**

0-0 **8** *8* **Street Jester**[8] 331 3-8-7 0 RobHornby(3) 5 28
(Robert Stephens) *dropped to last trio and outpcd after 1f out: nvr on terms after* **100/1**

00- **9** *1 1/4* **Dervish**[37] 8486 3-8-10 0 AdamBeschizza 7 24
(John Berry) *in tch in midfield tl dropped to last quartet and outpcd after 2f: nvr on terms after* **100/1**

**10** *1 3/4* **Zerafino (BEL)** 4-10-0 0 KieranO'Neill 2 25
(Jimmy Fox) *s.i.s: r.o in rr thrght: nvr on terms* **100/1**

1m 24.85s (0.05) **Going Correction** 0.0s/f (Stan)
**WFA** 3 from 4yo 18lb **10 Ran SP% 119.0**
Speed ratings (Par 103): **99,96,96,91,89 87,86,77,76,74**
CSF £26.01 TOTE £7.00: £1.90, £1.40, £1.10; EX 36.90 Trifecta £72.10.
**Owner** Highclere T'Bred Racing- Rudyard Kipling **Bred** Exors Of The Late J Ellis **Trained** Beckhampton, Wilts

**FOCUS**
A routine winter maiden, and a winning time almost identical to that of the opening 0-60 handicap, albeit the winner was eased.

## 465 SUN BETS ON THE APP STORE H'CAP 1m 1y(P)
**2:25** (2:25) (Class 3) (0-95,97) 4-Y-O **£7,246** (£2,168; £1,084; £542; £270) **Stalls** High

Form RPR

3-32 **1** **Chevallier**[7] 349 5-9-0 87 LukeMorris 4 95
(Archie Watson) *trckd ldrs: effrt 2f out: hdwy u.p to ld 100yds out: styd on and a doing enough after: rdn out* **7/2**[1]

**2** *nk* **Cherbourg (FR)**[104] 5-8-4 82 PatrickO'Donnell(5) 9 89
(Ralph Beckett) *in tch in midfield: nt clr run wl over 1f out: swtchd rt over 1f out: hdwy 1f out: str run u.p ins fnl f: wnt 2nd and clsng on wnr qckly towards fin: nvr quite getting up* **10/1**

00-0 **3** *1/2* **Horsted Keynes (FR)**[16] 199 7-9-2 89 JamieSpencer 8 95
(David Simcock) *hld up in last pair: hdwy ent fnl 2f: chsd ldrs 1f out: kpt on wl ins fnl f* **10/1**

54-3 **4** *3/4* **Bold Prediction (IRE)**[14] 235 7-9-2 89 ThomasBrown 3 93
(Ed Walker) *led: rdn and hdd ent fnl 2f: outpcd u.p over 1f out: rallied ins fnl f: kpt on u.p fnl 100yds* **9/2**[2]

00-5 **5** *hd* **Captain Cat (IRE)**[21] 118 8-9-7 97 GeorgeDowning(3) 7 101
(Tony Carroll) *stdd s: hld up in rr: effrt over 1f out: hdwy jst ins fnl f: kpt on wl fnl 100yds: nt rch ldrs* **20/1**

14-4 **6** *shd* **Kingston Kurrajong**[21] 118 4-9-2 89 LiamKeniry 6 92
(Andrew Balding) *t.k.h: chsd ldr: rdn and wnt on w new ldr ent fnl 2f: ev ch tl no ex u.p ins fnl f: outpcd towards fin* **7/1**[3]

055- **7** *hd* **Special Season**[58] 8177 4-9-2 89 AdamKirby 10 92
(Jamie Osborne) *in tch in midfield: hdwy on outer 3f out: rdn to ld ent fnl 2f: drvn over 1f out: hdd ins fnl f: no ex and outpcd towards fin* **9/2**[2]

31-3 **8** *hd* **Somethingthrilling**[22] 97 5-9-4 91 ShaneKelly 2 93
(David Elsworth) *trckd ldrs: nt clr run and shuffled bk ent fnl 2f: swtchd rt ent fnl f: rallied u.p and kpt on fnl 100yds: nvr getting to ldrs* **7/2**[1]

1m 37.73s (-0.47) **Going Correction** 0.0s/f (Stan) **8 Ran SP% 116.3**
Speed ratings (Par 107): **102,101,101,100,100 100,99,99**
CSF £39.93 CT £323.03 TOTE £4.30: £1.50, £3.10, £3.70; EX 45.90 Trifecta £708.50.
**Owner** The Chevallier Partnership **Bred** Kincorth Investments Inc **Trained** Upper Lambourn, W Berks

**FOCUS**
A good 0-95 handicap run at a searching pace, and the complexion of the contest changed utterly inside the final 100 yards.

## 466 SUNBETS.CO.UK MEDIAN AUCTION MAIDEN STKS 1m 1y(P)
**3:00** (3:02) (Class 6) 3-5-Y-O **£2,587** (£770; £384; £192) **Stalls** High

Form RPR

**1** **Cyrus Dallin** 3-8-8 0 NickyMackay 2 77+
(John Gosden) *trckd ldng pair: pushed along 3f out: rdn and clsng on ldng pair whn hmpd ins fnl f: rallied wl ins fnl f and str run to ld last strides* **11/2**[3]

5- **2** *hd* **He's A Lad (IRE)**[208] 3954 3-8-8 0 DavidProbert 3 76
(Andrew Balding) *t.k.h: chsd ldr: rdn to chal and qcknd 2f out: pushed rt and hmpd ins fnl f: stl ev ch and kpt on wl after: lost 2nd cl home: fin 3rd plcd 2nd* **5/2**[2]

202- **3** *hd* **Pepita (IRE)**[227] 3275 3-8-3 88 KieranO'Neill 4 71
(Richard Hannon) *broke fast: led and set stdy gallop: rdn and qcknd w chalr 2f out: hung bdly rt u.p ins fnl f: kpt on: hdd last strides: fin 2nd: disqualified and plcd 3rd* **15/8**[1]

3 **4** *1* **Arsenio Lupin**[21] 115 3-8-5 0 (t) TimClark(3) 6 73
(Denis Quinn) *hld up in tch in midfield: effrt ent fnl 2f: clsd and cl 4th whn hmpd ins fnl f: kpt on same pce fnl 100yds* **6/1**

**5** *1 3/4* **Alabaster** 3-8-8 0 LukeMorris 5 69
(Sir Mark Prescott Bt) *in tch in 5th: pushed along and unable qck ent fnl 2f: kpt on ins fnl f wout threatening ldrs* **7/1**

6- **6** *6* **Beatisa**[28] 8591 3-8-3 0 JosephineGordon 7 50
(Ed Walker) *s.i.s: in tch in rr: rdn ent fnl 2f: unable qck and sn outpcd: wknd fnl f* **20/1**

1m 38.8s (0.60) **Going Correction** 0.0s/f (Stan) **6 Ran SP% 110.3**
Speed ratings (Par 101): **97,96,96,95,93 87**
CSF £18.90 TOTE £6.50: £2.50, £2.20; EX 21.60 Trifecta £81.30.
**Owner** Ms Rachel D S Hood **Bred** J A And Mrs Duffy **Trained** Newmarket, Suffolk
■ Stewards' Enquiry : Kieran O'Neill four-day ban; careless riding (11th, 13th-15th Feb)

**FOCUS**
A messy finale to this median auction maiden, which was run at a crawl, but the best horse on the day still won. The for has been given a token rating through the fourth.

## 467 BETWAY H'CAP 1m 4f (P)
**3:35** (3:35) (Class 3) (0-95,95) 4-Y-O **£7,246** (£2,168; £1,084; £542; £270) **Stalls** Low

Form RPR

4-13 **1** **Sennockian Star**[7] 352 7-9-0 87 JoeFanning 2 98
(Mark Johnston) *chsd ldrs tl wnt 2nd over 3f out: led over 2f out: rdn wl over 1f out: forged ahd 1f out: styd on: rdn out* **5/2**[1]

535- **2** *3/4* **Rydan (IRE)**[28] 8594 6-9-2 89 (v) ShaneKelly 9 98
(Gary Moore) *hld up in tch in midfield: hdwy to join wnr over 2f out: rdn over 1f out: drvn and kpt on same pce ins fnl f* **6/1**

000- **3** *1/2* **Afonso De Sousa (USA)**[49] 8317 7-8-11 87 AlistairRawlinson(3) 8 95
(Michael Appleby) *hld up in last trio: hdwy 4f out: effrt to chse ldrs and edgd lft 2f out: drvn 1f out: kpt on u.p ins fnl f* **28/1**

00-0 **4** *9* **Silver Quay (IRE)**[12] 269 5-9-1 88 AdamKirby 3 82
(Jamie Osborne) *dwlt and bustled along early: sn rcvrd and in tch in midfield: rdn whn squeezed for room and hmpd bnd 2f out: wl hld 4th and no imp u.p after* **10/3**[3]

500- **5** *1 3/4* **Archangel Raphael (IRE)**[33] 6919 5-8-11 87 (p) KieranShoemark(3) 4 78
(Amanda Perrett) *in tch in midfield: effrt whn squeezed for room and hmpd bnd 2f out: no ch after: plugged on* **16/1**

10/4 **6** *nk* **Entihaa**[27] 3 9-8-9 87 HollieDoyle(5) 5 77
(Dai Burchell) *off the pce in last pair: rdn 4f out: passed btn rivals over 1f out: nvr trbld ldrs* **28/1**

20-1 **7** *3 3/4* **Elysian Prince**[24] 36 6-8-8 81 JackMitchell 6 65
(Neil King) *led for 3f: chsd ldr tl over 3f out: nt clr run on inner and shuffled bk jst over 2f out: hmpd 2f out: nt rcvr and wl hld over 1f out* **3/1**[2]

244/ **8** *3* **Aussie Andre**[469] 7295 6-8-5 85 RhiainIngram(7) 10 65
(Roger Ingram) *s.i.s: off the pce in last pair: nvr on terms* **50/1**

340/ **9** *1/2* **Nexius (IRE)**[28] 8-9-8 95 TimmyMurphy 1 74
(Emma Lavelle) *midfield tl dropped to last trio: rdn and no rspnse over 3f out: no ch after* **50/1**

/05- **10** *3 1/4* **Novis Adventus (IRE)**[42] 8424 5-9-7 94 (b[1]) JamieSpencer 7 68
(Jeremy Noseda) *t.k.h: hld up in tch in midfield: hdwy to ld 9f out and sn clr: hdd over 2f out: edgd rt and lost pl 2f out: bhd and eased ins fnl f* **10/1**

2m 28.16s (-4.84) **Going Correction** 0.0s/f (Stan) **10 Ran SP% 116.7**
Speed ratings (Par 107): **116,115,115,109,108 107,105,103,102,100**
CSF £17.57 CT £333.96 TOTE £3.00: £1.10, £2.00, £8.00; EX 18.20 Trifecta £271.40.
**Owner** Kingsley Park 7 - Ready To Run **Bred** Cheveley Park Stud Ltd **Trained** Middleham Moor, N Yorks

**FOCUS**
A generous pace to this decent middle-distance handicap.

## 468 BETWAY BEST ODDS GUARANTEED PLUS H'CAP 6f 1y(P)
**4:10** (4:10) (Class 6) (0-65,67) 4-Y-O+ **£2,587** (£770; £384; £192) **Stalls** Low

Form RPR

6-01 **1** **Fujin**[9] 303 6-9-4 67 (v) CharlieBennett(5) 7 75
(Shaun Harris) *chsd ldrs: wnt 2nd 1/2-way tl led over 1f out: rdn and wnt clr 1f out: in command and r.o wl after: rdn out* **11/2**[2]

0-02 **2** *1 1/4* **Head Space (IRE)**[7] 355 9-9-8 66 AdamKirby 1 70
(David Evans) *hld up in midfield: effrt over 1f out: hdwy u.p ins fnl f: chsd clr wnr wl ins fnl f: r.o but nvr getting on terms* **7/4**[1]

-420 **3** *1* **Harmonic Wave (IRE)**[7] 362 4-8-12 61 (p) HollieDoyle(5) 11 63
(Rebecca Menzies) *dwlt and short of room leaving stalls: hld up in rr: effrt over 1f out: hung lft and swtchd rt jst ins fnl f: r.o strly fnl 100yds: snatched 3rd last strides: no threat to wnr* **9/1**

00-0 **4** *hd* **Jack The Laird (IRE)**[17] 172 4-9-2 60 (b) RobertWinston 5 61
(Dean Ivory) *hld up in midfield: hmpd and snatched up after 1f: effrt jst over 1f out: rdn 1f out: kpt on to go 3rd wl ins fnl f: no threat to ldrs and lost 3rd last strides* **8/1**

6-10 **5** *3/4* **Compton Prince**[7] 355 8-9-6 64 (b) LukeMorris 8 62
(Milton Bradley) *t.k.h: trckd ldrs: effrt over 1f out: wnt 2nd and hrd drvn jst ins fnl f: no imp: lost 3 pls wl ins fnl f* **11/1**

3-00 **6** *1* **For Ayman**[9] 303 6-9-7 65 (t) JosephineGordon 6 60
(Joseph Tuite) *stdd and swtchd lft after s: hld up off the pce in last trio: rdn and hdwy 2f out: swtchd rt 1f out: kpt on same pce ins fnl f* **15/2**[3]

64-0 **7** *hd* **Flowing Clarets**[17] 171 4-8-9 60 JaneElliott(7) 4 55
(John Bridger) *t.k.h: hld up in tch in midfield: effrt over 1f out: styd on same pce ins fnl f* **33/1**

000- **8** *1* **Blackthorn Stick (IRE)**[59] 8156 8-8-9 58 DavidParkes(5) 9 50
(Paul Burgoyne) *taken down early: hld up in last quartet: effrt wl over 1f out: no imp and styd on same pce after* **16/1**

10-0 **9** *3/4* **Desert Strike**[18] 152 11-9-7 65 (p) PaulMulrennan 12 55+
(Conor Dore) *taken down early: bustled along and led fr wd draw: rdn and hdd over 1f out: lost 2nd jst ins fnl f: sn wknd* **14/1**

01-0 **10** *1 1/4* **Red Invader (IRE)**[17] 172 7-9-6 64 LiamKeniry 3 50
(John Butler) *broke wl: sn stdd and hld up wl in tch in midfield: shkn up over 1f out: unable qck u.p 1f out: n.m.r and wknd ins fnl f* **16/1**

0-00 **11** *1* **Nora Batt (IRE)**[7] 355 4-8-13 57 TomMarquand 10 40
(David Evans) *a towards rr: n.d* **66/1**

00-0 **12** *1 1/4* **Silver Springs (IRE)**[22] 95 4-8-11 58 PhilipPrince(3) 2 37
(David Evans) *chsd ldr tl 1/2-way: rdn jst over 2f out: lost pl u.p over 1f out: wknd fnl f* **20/1**

1m 11.36s (-0.54) **Going Correction** 0.0s/f (Stan) **12 Ran SP% 120.6**
Speed ratings (Par 101): **103,101,100,99,98 97,97,95,94,93 91,90**
CSF £15.44 CT £90.28 TOTE £5.60: £1.90, £1.10, £3.60; EX 18.20 Trifecta £193.90.
**Owner** Mrs S L Robinson **Bred** Juddmonte Farms Ltd **Trained** Carburton, Notts
■ Stewards' Enquiry : Paul Mulrennan two-day ban; careless riding (11th,13th Feb)

**FOCUS**
A moderate but competitive sprint handicap, and another race in which it paid to race handy. The winner is rated back to his best.

T/Plt: £82.20 to a £1 stake. Pool: £74,251.11 - 658.83 winning units T/Qpdt: £19.80 to a £1 stake. Pool: £4,595.65 - 171.0 winning units **Steve Payne**

# GULFSTREAM PARK (L-H)

Saturday, January 28

**OFFICIAL GOING: Dirt: fast; turf: firm**

## 469a PEGASUS WORLD CUP INVITATIONAL STKS (GRADE 1) (4YO+) (DIRT) 1m 1f (D)

10:40 4-Y-0+

**£5,691,056** (£1,422,764; £813,008; £203,252; £203,252; £203,252)

RPR

1 **Arrogate (USA)**[83] 7838 4-8-12 0 MikeESmith 1 130+
(Bob Baffert, U.S.A) **9/10**[1]

2 4 ¾ **Shaman Ghost (CAN)**[64] 8110 5-8-12 0 JoseLOrtiz 7 118
(James Jerkens, U.S.A) **198/10**

3 3 ½ **Neolithic (USA)**[45] 4-8-12 0 (b) JohnRVelazquez 3 112
(Todd Pletcher, U.S.A) **234/10**

4 2 ¾ **Keen Ice (USA)**[42] 5-8-12 0 JavierCastellano 9 105
(Todd Pletcher, U.S.A) **163/10**[3]

5 2 ¼ **War Story (USA)**[42] 5-8-12 0 AntonioAGallardo 5 100
(Jorge Navarro, U.S.A) **49/1**

6 1 **Noble Bird (USA)**[64] 8110 6-8-12 0 JulienRLeparoux 4 98
(Mark Casse, Canada) **30/1**

7 9 **Semper Fortis (USA)**[33] 8534 4-8-12 0 TylerGaffalione 8 80
(Doug O'Neill, U.S.A) **160/1**

8 3 ¼ **Breaking Lucky (CAN)**[64] 8110 5-8-12 0 LuisContreras 10 72
(Reade Baker, Canada) **75/1**

9 3 **California Chrome (USA)**[41] 8452 6-8-12 0 (b) VictorEspinoza 12 66+
(Art Sherman, U.S.A) **6/5**[2]

10 4 ¼ **Prayer For Relief (USA)**[64] 8110 9-8-12 0 (b) FlorentGeroux 2 57
(Dale Romans, U.S.A) **138/1**

11 10 ½ **War Envoy (USA)**[63] 5-8-12 0 (b) LuisSaez 6 35
(Mick Ruis, U.S.A) **188/1**

12 dist **Eragon (ARG)**[77] 5-8-7 0 EdgarSPrado 11
(Laura Wohlers, U.S.A) **82/1**

1m 46.83s (-2.34)
**WFA** 4 from 5yo+ 1lb 12 Ran SP% **122.4**
PARI-MUTUEL (all including 2 usd stake): WIN 3.80; PLACE (1-2) 2.80, 8.60; SHOW (1-2-3) 2.20, 5.80, 6.00; SF 33.80.
**Owner** Juddmonte Farms Inc **Bred** Clearsky Farms **Trained** USA

**FOCUS**
The inaugural running of the Pegasus World Cup, which has replaced the Donn Handicap in the calendar, and with 12 sets of connections each paying a 1,000,000USD entry fee it was the richest race in thoroughbred history. It was billed as a rematch between the previous year's Breeders' Cup Classic one-two, Arrogate and California Chrome, but only one of those ran their race and in doing so he was way too good for the others. The pace was fast: 23.46, 22.68, 23.66, 24.10, 13.71.

470 - 476a (Foreign Racing) - See Raceform Interactive

# 414 SOUTHWELL (L-H)

Monday, January 30

**OFFICIAL GOING: Fibresand: standard**
Wind: Virtually nil Weather: Heavy grey cloud

## 477 BETWAY BEST ODDS GUARANTEED PLUS H'CAP 1m 6f 21y(F)

1:30 (1:31) (Class 5) (0-70,76) 4-Y-0+ £3,881 (£1,155; £577; £288) Stalls Low

Form RPR

0-11 1 **Start Seven**[7] 380 5-10-3 **76** 6ex AdamKirby 1 91+
(Jamie Osborne) *mde all: pushed clr over 2f out: eased towards fin* **4/5**[1]

12-2 2 8 **Brigadoon**[29] 3 10-9-13 **72** RobertWinston 5 73
(Michael Appleby) *trckd wnr: pushed along 3f out: rdn over 2f out: drvn wl over 1f out: kpt on: no ch w wnr* **14/1**[3]

30-5 3 1 ¾ **Scrafton**[25] 74 6-8-13 **61** GeorgeDowning(3) 2 60
(Tony Carroll) *hld up in rr: hdwy over 3f out: rdn to chse ldrs 2f out: sn drvn and kpt on same pce* **16/1**

0-41 4 3 **Free Bounty**[11] 315 4-9-0 **70** (t) HollieDoyle(5) 3 64
(Philip McBride) *trckd ldng pair on inner: pushed along over 4f out: rdn 3f out: drvn and one pce fnl 2f* **15/8**[2]

135- 5 8 **Moonshine Ridge (IRE)**[202] 4239 6-9-11 **70** NeilFarley 4 53
(Alan Swinbank) *trckd ldrs: pushed along over 3f out: rdn wl over 2f out: sn wknd* **16/1**

3m 9.65s (1.35) **Going Correction** -0.05s/f (Stan)
**WFA** 4 from 5yo+ 4lb 5 Ran SP% **108.8**
Speed ratings (Par 103): **94,89,88,86,82**
CSF £12.46 TOTE £1.70: £1.20, £3.50; EX 10.10 Trifecta £43.40.
**Owner** Melbourne 10 Racing **Bred** Mehmet Kurt **Trained** Upper Lambourn, Berks

**FOCUS**
What looked a match on paper turned into a facile win for the improving favourite. The race has been rated at face value around the runner-up to his recent claimer form.

## 478 SUNBETS.CO.UK DOWNLOAD THE APP CLAIMING STKS 1m 13y(F)

2:00 (2:00) (Class 6) 4-Y-0+ £2,587 (£770; £384; £192) Stalls Low

Form RPR

3/33 1 **Regarde Moi**[11] 304 9-8-12 87 JacobMitchell(7) 4 86
(Marco Botti) *t.k.h early: trckd ldrs: hdwy over 2f out: cl up 11/2f out: sn chal: rdn to ld ins fnl f: kpt on wl* **10/3**[2]

050- 2 nk **Pearl Nation (USA)**[289] 1478 8-9-12 97 (h) AndrewMullen 5 92
(Michael Appleby) *trckd ldr: cl up 3f out: led wl over 1f out: sn rdn: drvn and hdd ins fnl f: kpt on wl towards fin* **7/2**[3]

-130 3 2 ¾ **Vivat Rex (IRE)**[11] 306 6-9-0 80 (t) PaulMulrennan 2 74
(Conor Dore) *trckd ldrs on inner: hdwy 3f out: cl up over 2f out: rdn along wl over 1f out: drvn and kpt on same pce fnl f* **9/2**

05-0 4 nk **Smokethatthunders (IRE)**[14] 267 7-9-5 71 DanielMuscutt 3 78
(James Unett) *led: pushed along 3f out: rdn over 2f out: hdd wl over 1f out: sn drvn and kpt on same pce* **16/1**

20/- 5 2 ¼ **Retrieve (AUS)**[729] 7689 9-9-12 105 AdamKirby 6 80
(Jamie Osborne) *trckd ldrs on outer: pushed along over 3f out: rdn wl over 2f out: sn wknd* **6/4**[1]

1m 42.62s (-1.08) **Going Correction** -0.05s/f (Stan) 5 Ran SP% **109.4**
Speed ratings (Par 101): **103,102,99,99,97**
CSF £14.78 TOTE £5.40: £1.60, £1.70; EX 14.20 Trifecta £30.80.There was no bid for the winner.
**Owner** Mrs Lucie Botti **Bred** Soc Finanza Locale Consulting Srl **Trained** Newmarket, Suffolk
■ Jacon Mitchell's first winner.

**FOCUS**
A competitive little claimer. The winner has been rated close to his better figures.

## 479 SUNBETS.CO.UK MAIDEN STKS 1m 13y(F)

2:30 (2:31) (Class 5) 3-Y-0+ £3,557 (£1,058; £529; £264) Stalls Low

Form RPR

20-4 1 **Vantage Point (IRE)**[19] 175 3-8-8 77 (p) NickyMackay 6 78
(John Gosden) *prom on outer: slt ld 1/2-way: rdn 2f out: drvn and kpt on wl fnl f* **7/4**[2]

6 2 2 **Finale**[19] 168 3-8-3 0 FrannyNorton 9 68
(Hughie Morrison) *trckd ldrs: hdwy over 2f out: rdn to chal over 1f out: drvn and edgd rt ent fnl f: kpt on* **12/1**

52-4 3 2 ¼ **Warm Words**[11] 314 3-8-3 71 (b[1]) JoeFanning 10 63
(Ralph Beckett) *cl up: slt ld after 3f: hdd 1/2-way: cl up: rdn along over 2f out: sltly outpcd over 1f out: swtchd rt ins fnl f: kpt on same pce* **6/4**[1]

04 4 3 ¼ **State Residence (IRE)**[17] 221 3-8-8 0 TomEaves 7 61
(David Simcock) *in tch: hdwy to chse ldrs over 3f out: rdn along wl over 2f out: kpt on same pce* **6/1**[3]

4 5 2 ¾ **Alhajjaj**[26] 37 4-10-0 0 (h) LiamKeniry 3 59
(Andrew Balding) *chsd ldrs: rdn along wl over 2f out: sn one pce* **10/1**

0-6 6 6 **Knightsbridge Liam (IRE)**[18] 198 3-8-5 0 NathanEvans(3) 5 41
(Michael Easterby) *in tch: rdn along wl over 3f out: sn drvn and outpcd* **66/1**

0-0 7 7 **Spey Secret (IRE)**[23] 127 4-10-0 0 RichardKingscote 8 30
(Tom Dascombe) *slt ld 3f: rdn along 1/2-way: sn lost pl and bhd* **25/1**

0 8 2 ¾ **Way Up High**[10] 331 5-9-2 0 JoshuaBryan(7) 4 18
(Steve Flook) *a rr* **250/1**

0- 9 12 **Barbary Prince**[32] 8570 5-9-9 0 CharlieBennett(5) 2
(Shaun Harris) *a bhd* **250/1**

0- 10 8 **Duxbury**[33] 8556 3-8-8 0 BarryMcHugh 1
(Richard Fahey) *sn rdn along on inner: a rr: bhd fr 1/2-way* **33/1**

1m 42.46s (-1.24) **Going Correction** -0.05s/f (Stan)
**WFA** 3 from 4yo+ 20lb 10 Ran SP% **116.5**
Speed ratings (Par 103): **104,102,99,96,93 87,80,78,66,58**
CSF £22.25 TOTE £3.00: £1.20, £2.80, £1.20; EX 24.00 Trifecta £53.10.
**Owner** Mrs F Hay,Mrs J Magnier,M Tabor,D Smith **Bred** Smithfield Inc **Trained** Newmarket, Suffolk

**FOCUS**
An ordinary maiden. The winner has been rated close to his maiden best, with the fourth and fifth close to their early maiden figures.

## 480 BETWAY H'CAP 6f 16y(F)

3:05 (3:06) (Class 5) (0-70,73) 4-Y-0+ £3,881 (£1,155; £577; £288) Stalls Low

Form RPR

0-00 1 **Elusivity (IRE)**[10] 330 9-9-5 **68** (p) PaulMulrennan 2 76
(Conor Dore) *slt ld: rdn along over 1f out: narrowly hdd over 1f out: : sn drvn to ld again and edgd sltly rt: jst hld on* **20/1**

-011 2 nse **Fujin**[2] 468 6-9-5 **73** 6ex (v) CharlieBennett(5) 8 80
(Shaun Harris) *cl up: rdn to take slt ld over 1f out: drvn and hdd ins fnl f: kpt on wl u.p towards fin* **4/1**[1]

41-3 3 1 ¾ **Hold On Magnolia**[20] 159 4-9-3 **66** TonyHamilton 9 67
(Richard Fahey) *trckd ldng pair: effrt on outer over 2f out: rdn wl over 1f out: drvn and kpt on same pce fnl f* **9/2**[2]

4630 4 1 ¾ **Crosse Fire**[4] 416 5-9-7 **70** (p) KieranO'Neill 1 66
(Scott Dixon) *dwlt and towards rr: rdn along 1/2-way: hdwy wl over 1f out: kpt on u.p fnl f: nrst fin* **13/2**

0-11 5 1 ¾ **Big Amigo (IRE)**[20] 158 4-9-2 **68** (p[1]) EoinWalsh(3) 3 58+
(Daniel Mark Loughnane) *chsd ldrs on inner whn n.m.r: hmpd and lost pl bnd 4f out: rr and sn rdn: hdwy over 2f out: swtchd rt ent fnl f: kpt on wl: nrst fin* **5/1**[3]

0-00 6 ¾ **Borough Boy (IRE)**[11] 312 7-9-5 **68** (v) MartinLane 5 56
(Derek Shaw) *chsd ldrs on inner: rdn along over 2f out: drvn wl over 1f out: grad wknd* **16/1**

02-0 7 ½ **Freddy With A Y (IRE)**[20] 159 7-9-0 **63** PaddyAspell 7 49
(J R Jenkins) *dwlt and rr: wd st: nvr a factor* **33/1**

00-5 8 1 ½ **It Must Be Faith**[16] 240 7-9-7 **70** AdamKirby 10 51
(Michael Appleby) *in tch: hdwy to chse ldrs 3f out: rdn along on outer 2f out: sn drvn and btn* **9/2**[2]

0-40 9 1 ¾ **Misu Moneypenny**[4] 416 4-9-1 **64** BenCurtis 4 40
(Scott Dixon) *chsd ldrs on inner: rdn along 1/2-way: sn wknd* **20/1**

2-51 10 shd **Colourbearer (IRE)**[11] 302 10-9-6 **69** (t) WilliamCarson 6 44
(Charlie Wallis) *chsd ldrs: rdn wl over 2f out: sn wknd* **12/1**

1m 15.68s (-0.82) **Going Correction** -0.05s/f (Stan) 10 Ran SP% **112.4**
Speed ratings (Par 103): **103,102,100,98,95 94,94,92,89,89**
CSF £93.01 CT £439.45 TOTE £23.70: £4.30, £1.70, £1.80; EX 138.20 Trifecta £1497.40.
**Owner** Mrs Louise Marsh **Bred** J Costello **Trained** Hubbert's Bridge, Lincs

**FOCUS**
A competitive handicap for the grade and it paid to race up with the pace, with the first three home being prominent throughout. The winner has been rated close to his autumn form, with the second running a pb.

## 481 SUNBETS.CO.UK TOP PRICE ON ALL FAVOURITES H'CAP 7f 14y(F)

3:40 (3:41) (Class 6) (0-60,62) 4-Y-0+ £2,587 (£770; £384; £192) Stalls Low

Form RPR

60-0 1 **Dark Forest**[26] 44 4-9-3 **56** BarryMcHugh 6 66
(Marjorie Fife) *chsd ldng pair: rdn along over 2f out: chsd clr ldr over 1f out: sn drvn and styd on strly to ld last 100 yds* **9/1**[3]

06-3 2 1 ¾ **Secret Glance**[25] 67 5-9-9 **62** (v[1]) RobertWinston 4 67
(Richard Rowe) *cl up: led 3f out: rdn clr wl over 1f out: drvn ent fnl f: sn edgd lft: hdd and no ex last 100 yds* **9/4**[1]

0-06 3 3 ½ **Satchville Flyer**[6] 386 6-9-7 **60** StevieDonohoe 5 56
(David Evans) *dwlt and rr: rdn along bef 1/2-way: hdwy 2f out: styd on wl u.p appr fnl f: nrst fin* **7/1**[2]

00-0 4 1 ¼ **Trust Me Boy**[6] 390 9-9-6 **59** FrannyNorton 13 51+
(John E Long) *chsd ldrs: rdn along and outpcd over 3f out: wd st: drvn 2f out: styd on: nrst fin* **20/1**

6-42 5 1 ½ **Cadeaux Pearl**[6] 386 9-8-0 **46** oh1 (b) RPWalsh(7) 1 34
(Scott Dixon) *chsd ldrs on inner: rdn along over 2f out: sn drvn and kpt on same pce* **12/1**

-330 6 ¾ **Mustn't Grumble (IRE)**[6] 386 4-9-4 **57** (p[1]) AndrewMullen 10 43
(David Loughnane) *t.k.h: trckd ldrs: pushed along and wd st: sn rdn and no imp* **10/1**

4-64 7 3 ½ **Einstein**[6] 390 4-9-0 **60** (t) MillyNaseb(7) 12 37
(Mrs Ilka Gansera-Leveque) *in tch: rdn along and v wd st: sn drvn and n.d* **7/1**[2]

6-53 **8** ½ **Limerick Lord (IRE)**[25] 69 5-8-10 **52**..................(p) ShelleyBirkett(3) 2 28
(Julia Feilden) *in tch on inner: pushed along and lost pl 4f out: rdn wl over 2f out: no hdwy* **16/1**

6-35 **9** nk **Tavener**[20] 158 5-9-4 **57**..........................................(vt[1]) AdamKirby 3 32
(David C Griffiths) *slt ld on inner: rdn along and hdd 3f out: drvn along 2f out: grad wknd* **10/1**

340- **10** ½ **Keiba (IRE)**[118] 7038 4-9-5 **58**.......................................... LiamKeniry 9 31
(Murty McGrath) *dwlt: a rr* **66/1**

60-5 **11** 6 **Kopassus (IRE)**[11] 311 5-8-7 **46** oh1...........................(p) ShaneGray 8 3
(Lawrence Mullaney) *a rr* **25/1**

601- **12** 3 **Clever Divya**[32] 8572 4-9-2 **55**.......................................... TonyHamilton 7 4
(J R Jenkins) *a rr* **20/1**

24-0 **13** 5 **Arcanista (IRE)**[12] 293 4-9-6 **59**...................................(b) ShaneKelly 11
(Richard Hughes) *t.k.h: chsd ldrs: rdn along over 3f out: sn wknd* **14/1**

1m 29.61s (-0.69) **Going Correction** -0.05s/f (Stan) 13 Ran SP% **119.1**
Speed ratings (Par 101): **101,99,95,93,91 91,87,86,86,85 78,75,69**
CSF £27.99 CT £156.52 TOTE £10.00: £3.40, £1.40, £2.60; EX 43.50 Trifecta £281.60.
**Owner** David Haddrell **Bred** Genesis Green Stud Ltd **Trained** Stillington, N Yorks

**FOCUS**
A modest handicap and again not much got into it from off the pace. Sound form for the grade.

## 482 SUNBETS.CO.UK H'CAP 1m 13y(F)
**4:15** (4:16) (Class 6) (0-60,62) 4-Y-O+ **£2,587** (£770; £384; £192) **Stalls** Low

Form RPR

552- **1** **Schottische**[41] 8471 7-8-9 **53**..................................(b) DavidParkes(5) 2 61+
(Alan Bailey) *trckd ldrs: hdwy over 2f out: swtchd rt and rdn to chal 11/2f out: sn led: clr ins fnl f: kpt on strly* **20/1**

-335 **2** 3¼ **General Tufto**[6] 390 12-8-13 **52**...................................(b) MartinLane 6 53
(Charles Smith) *sn rdn along: outpcd and detached in rr: gd hdwy over 3f out: styd on wl u.p fr over 1f out: nrst fin* **14/1**

-121 **3** ¾ **Athassel**[10] 332 8-9-5 **58**.......................................... StevieDonohoe 3 57
(David Evans) *towards rr: hdwy over 2f out: sn swtchd rt and rdn: styd on u.p appr fnl f: nrst fin* **9/1**[3]

-212 **4** nk **Playful Dude (USA)**[6] 390 4-9-6 **59**...............................(h) AdamKirby 8 57
(Phil McEntee) *trckd ldrs: cl up on outer 3f out: led over 2f out: rdn wl over 1f out: sn drvn and hdd over 1f out: wknd fnl f* **11/10**[1]

0-66 **5** 2¾ **Sunshineandbubbles**[9] 351 4-9-0 **56**...............(p) GeorgeDowning(3) 4 48
(Daniel Mark Loughnane) *rr: hdwy and wd st: carried rt 2f out: sn rdn and kpt on wl fnl f: nrst fin* **28/1**

-055 **6** 2¼ **Cold Fusion (IRE)**[7] 383 4-8-11 **55**............................ HollieDoyle(5) 7 42
(David Flood) *chsd ldrs: rdn along bef 1/2-way: sn lost pl and towards rr: hdwy 2f out: swtchd lft to inner rail and rdn over 1f out: kpt on: n.d* **25/1**

0-02 **7** 1¼ **Lucky Louie**[17] 214 4-9-7 **60**...................................... JackMitchell 10 44
(Roger Teal) *led 2f: cl up on inner: rdn along over 2f out: sn drvn and grad wknd* **8/1**[2]

00-2 **8** 2¾ **Swiftee (IRE)**[25] 68 4-9-3 **61**.............................. LewisEdmunds(5) 9 38
(Ivan Furtado) *dwlt: sn in tch: rdn along 1/2-way: sn lost pl and towards rr whn drvn and hmpd 2f out* **8/1**[2]

41-2 **9** 1¼ **L'Apogee**[21] 147 4-9-6 **59**.......................................... TonyHamilton 11 34
(Richard Fahey) *cl up: rdn along over 3f out: drvn 2f out: sn wknd* **12/1**

00-2 **10** ¾ **Ramblow**[11] 314 4-9-6 **59**.......................................(tp) BenCurtis 12 32
(Michael Appleby) *cl up: led after 2f: rdn along over 3f out: hdd over 2f out and sn wknd* **12/1**

0-65 **11** 2¾ **City Of Angkor Wat (IRE)**[12] 293 7-9-3 **56**............(p) PaulMulrennan 5 22
(Conor Dore) *chsd ldrs on outer: rdn along 3f out: wknd over 2f out* **20/1**

20-0 **12** 12 **Two In The Pink (IRE)**[23] 120 7-9-9 **62**........................ AndrewMullen 1 1
(Ralph J Smith) *sn outpcd in rr: wl bhd fr over 3f out* **66/1**

1m 43.15s (-0.55) **Going Correction** -0.05s/f (Stan) 12 Ran SP% **120.2**
Speed ratings (Par 101): **100,96,96,95,92 90,89,86,85,84 81,69**
CSF £261.82 CT £2701.06 TOTE £23.20: £4.80, £4.10, £2.60; EX 222.60 Trifecta £2932.50.
**Owner** AB Racing Limited **Bred** Mrs M L Parry & P M Steele-Mortimer **Trained** Newmarket, Suffolk

**FOCUS**
A modest handicap and a big-priced winner. The form has a straightforward feel about it.
T/Jkpt: Partly Won. T/Plt: £106.50 to a £1 stake. Pool: £81,838.79 - 560.54 winning units T/Qpdt: £36.60 to a £1 stake. Pool: £8,211.77 - 165.99 winning units **Joe Rowntree**

483 - 493a (Foreign Racing) - See Raceform Interactive

# 420 WOLVERHAMPTON (A.W) (L-H)
Tuesday, January 31

**OFFICIAL GOING: Tapeta: standard**
Wind: Light behind Weather: Light rain clearing

## 494 SUNBETS.CO.UK DOWNLOAD THE APP AMATEUR RIDERS' H'CAP (DIV I) 6f 20y (Tp)
**2:10** (2:10) (Class 6) (0-55,55) 4-Y-O+ **£2,651** (£822; £410; £205) **Stalls** Low

Form RPR

60-2 **1** **Castlerea Tess**[27] 51 4-10-6 **47**.......................................(p) MrSWalker 6 58
(Sarah Hollinshead) *chsd ldr: hung lft fr over 1f out: led ins fnl f: r.o: comf* **4/1**[2]

3-00 **2** 1½ **Swendab (IRE)**[15] 271 9-10-9 **50**...................(b) MissBrodieHampson 8 56
(John O'Shea) *sn pushed along to ld: rdn over 1f out: hdd ins fnl f: styd on same pce* **20/1**

2-36 **3** 2½ **Menelik (IRE)**[24] 123 8-10-7 **53**........................(bt) PoppyBridgwater(5) 4 52+
(Des Donovan, Ire) *s.i.s and pushed along in rr early: hdwy over 1f out: styd on: nt trble ldrs* **4/1**[2]

05-0 **4** 1½ **Misu Pete**[18] 222 5-10-11 **52**.......................................... MrPMillman 3 46
(Mark Usher) *chsd ldrs: lost pl after 1f: rdn over 2f out: styd on ins fnl f* **9/2**[3]

00-2 **5** 2 **Very First Blade**[21] 153 8-10-8 **54**.......................(be) MrLewisStones(5) 1 42
(Michael Mullineaux) *chsd ldrs: rdn over 1f out: wknd fnl f* **16/1**

0-60 **6** 1 **Intense Starlet (IRE)**[10] 362 6-11-0 **55**.............(p) MissJoannaMason 9 40
(Marjorie Fife) *hld up: pushed along over 2f out: n.d* **10/1**

5-02 **7** nk **Autumn Tonic (IRE)**[12] 311 5-10-12 **53**...............(b) MissSBrotherton 2 37
(David Barron) *hld up: hdwy over 2f out: rdn and wknd over 1f out* **11/4**[1]

002/ **8** 3¾ **Pillar**[18] 228 4-10-7 **48**..........................................(b) MrLJMcGuinness 5 21
(Adrian McGuinness, Ire) *s.i.s: hld up: racd keenly: rdn over 2f out: nvr on terms* **7/1**

005- **9** 10 **Portrush Storm**[142] 6381 12-9-12 **46** oh1................. MissSPeacock(7) 7
(Ray Peacock) *hdwy to chse ldrs 5f out: pushed along and hung rt over 2f out: sn wknd* **100/1**

1m 14.91s (0.41) **Going Correction** +0.025s/f (Slow) 9 Ran SP% **118.1**
Speed ratings (Par 101): **98,96,92,90,88 86,86,81,67**
CSF £80.35 CT £346.72 TOTE £4.20: £1.60, £5.20, £1.50; EX 69.70 Trifecta £387.50.
**Owner** Graham Brothers Racing Partnership **Bred** Graham Brothers Racing Partnership **Trained** Upper Longdon, Staffs

**FOCUS**
The pace held up in this amateur riders' event, and very few got involved. The third has been rated as running a few lengths below this year's 7f form.

## 495 SUNBETS.CO.UK DOWNLOAD THE APP AMATEUR RIDERS' H'CAP (DIV II) 6f 20y (Tp)
**2:45** (2:45) (Class 6) (0-55,54) 4-Y-O+ **£2,651** (£822; £410; £205) **Stalls** Low

Form RPR

6-03 **1** **Pushkin Museum (IRE)**[10] 362 6-11-0 **54**........................ MrSWalker 5 71
(Patrick Morris) *s.i.s: hld up: hdwy over 3f out: led over 1f out: r.o wl* **11/4**[2]

4/-1 **2** 3 **Oor Jock (IRE)**[18] 229 9-10-13 **53**.......................(b) MrLJMcGuinness 7 61
(Adrian McGuinness, Ire) *hld up: hdwy over 1f out: chsd wnr fnl f: styd on same pce* **2/1**[1]

54-4 **3** 4 **Lightsome**[12] 303 4-10-11 **54**...................................(v[1]) MissPFuller(3) 1 50
(Harry Dunlop) *s.i.s: hdwy 5f out: rdn over 1f out: styd on same pce* **8/1**

02-3 **4** hd **Tribesman**[15] 270 4-10-10 **53**...........................(bt) MissBeckySmith(3) 3 48
(Marjorie Fife) *w ldrs: led 2f out: rdn: edgd lft and hdd over 1f out: wknd ins fnl f* **10/1**

-335 **5** 1¼ **Fossa**[3] 455 7-10-4 **47**...................................... MissBeckyBrisbourne(3) 4 41
(Mark Brisbourne) *chsd ldrs: pushed along and lost pl over 3f out: effrt and nt clr run over 1f out: styd on same pce* **7/1**

00-0 **6** nk **Gypsy Rider**[20] 167 8-9-12 **45**.............................. MrCAJones(7) 8 36
(Henry Tett) *broke wl: sn lost pl: sme hdwy over 1f out: wknd ins fnl f* **66/1**

04-0 **7** 2¾ **Louis Vee (IRE)**[12] 309 9-10-6 **46**...................... MissBrodieHampson 2 29
(John O'Shea) *sn led: rdn and hdd 2f out: wknd fnl f* **25/1**

2-23 **8** 2¾ **Mr Chuckles (IRE)**[3] 455 4-10-5 **50**.......................(p) JonjoO'Neill(5) 6 24
(Daniel Mark Loughnane) *led early: chsd ldrs: rdn over 2f out: wknd over 1f out* **4/1**[3]

1m 14.87s (0.37) **Going Correction** +0.025s/f (Slow) 8 Ran SP% **118.0**
Speed ratings (Par 101): **98,94,88,88,86 86,82,79**
CSF £9.02 CT £38.88 TOTE £3.60: £1.30, £1.10, £2.70; EX 11.00 Trifecta £66.10.
**Owner** Dr Marwan Koukash **Bred** Miss Nicola Cullen **Trained** Prescot, Merseyside

**FOCUS**
There was good competition for the lead and that played into the hands of those ridden with a bit of patience. Simon Walker, who is on a different level in these events, completed a double after riding Castelrea Tess to victory in the first division. The time was very similar to the first leg.

## 496 £10 FREE AT 32RED.COM CLAIMING STKS 6f 20y (Tp)
**3:20** (3:20) (Class 6) 3-Y-O **£2,749** (£818; £408; £204) **Stalls** Low

Form RPR

3-11 **1** **Dandy Flame (IRE)**[4] 435 3-9-11 78.................................. AdamKirby 7 81+
(William Haggas) *hld up: hdwy 2f out: shkn up to ld and hung lft fr over 1f out: rdn out* **1/3**[1]

34-0 **2** 3¼ **Wentwell Yesterday (IRE)**[21] 160 3-9-2 69............... LucyKBarry(5) 2 67
(Jamie Osborne) *led: rdn over 2f out: hdd over 1f out: styd on same pce ins fnl f* **13/2**[2]

0-00 **3** 1½ **Celerity (IRE)**[15] 264 3-8-2 55....................................... AndrewMullen 4 44
(David Evans) *sn chsng ldrs: rdn over 1f out: styd on same pce fnl f* **33/1**

3240 **4** ½ **Pulsating (IRE)**[3] 458 3-8-13 65............................ KieranSchofield(7) 5 60+
(Daniel Steele) *s.s: hdwy over 2f out: rdn and edgd rt over 1f out: styd on same pce fnl f* **11/1**[3]

333- **5** 9 **Billy's Boots**[225] 3472 3-9-4 66...................................(h[1]) LuluStanford(5) 6 36+
(Dean Ivory) *racd keenly in 2nd pl: jnd ldr after 1f: rdn over 2f out: wknd over 1f out* **25/1**

0-56 **6** 1½ **Prufrock (IRE)**[12] 307 3-8-10 62................................ JosephineGordon 1 19
(David Simcock) *chsd ldrs: rdn over 3f out: wknd over 2f out* **12/1**

1m 14.2s (-0.30) **Going Correction** +0.025s/f (Slow) 6 Ran SP% **111.2**
Speed ratings (Par 95): **103,98,96,96,84 82**
CSF £2.97 TOTE £1.30: £1.10, £2.60; EX 3.30 Trifecta £36.70.The winner was claimed by Mr D. Nicholls for £12000
**Owner** The Up In Flames Partnership **Bred** Limestone & Tara Studs **Trained** Newmarket, Suffolk

**FOCUS**
There was a good gallop on here and that played into the hands of the well-backed favourite, who was dropping back in distance. The form makes sense rated around the second, third and fourth.

## 497 32REDSPORT.COM FILLIES' H'CAP 1m 4f 51y (Tp)
**3:50** (3:50) (Class 5) (0-75,75) 4-Y-O+ **£3,752** (£1,116; £557; £278) **Stalls** Low

Form RPR

31-4 **1** **Favorite Girl (GER)**[25] 99 9-9-0 **66**.................... AlistairRawlinson(3) 5 72
(Michael Appleby) *sn led: clr over 9f out tl over 6f out: rdn over 1f out: hdd ins fnl f: rallied to ld nr fin* **11/1**

231- **2** nk **High On Light**[47] 8387 4-9-5 **72**........................................ SamJames 7 77
(David Barron) *chsd ldrs: wnt 2nd 7f out tl over 5f out: remained handy: wnt 2nd again over 2f out: rdn to ld and hung lft ins fnl f: hdd nr fin* **2/1**[1]

25-1 **3** hd **Fast Play (IRE)**[17] 233 5-9-5 **68**..................................(b) ShaneKelly 2 73
(Richard Hughes) *hld up in tch: rdn over 1f out: edgd lft ins fnl f: r.o* **5/1**[2]

0-22 **4** 2¼ **Heartstone (IRE)**[18] 213 4-9-5 **72**.............................. AndrewMullen 9 73
(David Evans) *hld up in tch: rdn over 1f out: styd on: nt trble ldrs* **6/1**[3]

51/0 **5** 1¾ **Included**[27] 38 5-9-12 **75**.......................................... DanielTudhope 8 74
(David Dennis) *chsd wnr 5f: remained handy: rdn and hung lft ins fnl f: styd on same pce* **16/1**

30-1 **6** 2¾ **Oratorio's Joy (IRE)**[11] 325 7-9-12 **75**.....................(p) TimmyMurphy 6 69
(Jamie Osborne) *dwlt: hdwy over 9f out: chsd wnr over 5f out: rdn over 3f out: lost 2nd over 2f out: wknd ins fnl f* **12/1**

44-2 **7** 1 **Dark Amber**[17] 238 7-8-8 **57**................................(tp) JosephineGordon 4 50
(Brendan Powell) *hld up: rdn over 3f out: nvr on terms* **7/1**

035- **8** ½ **Shadow Spirit**[36] 8524 4-9-3 **70**........................................ PJMcDonald 1 62
(Iain Jardine) *hld up: rdn over 2f out: wknd ins fnl f* **10/1**

0-04 **9** 8 **Celestial Bay**[18] 213 8-9-10 **73**.......................................... AdamKirby 3 61
(Sylvester Kirk) *hld up: shkn up over 2f out: rdn and hung lft over 1f out: sn wknd* **15/2**

2m 38.67s (-2.13) **Going Correction** +0.025s/f (Slow)
**WFA** 4 from 5yo+ 3lb 9 Ran SP% **119.5**
Speed ratings (Par 100): **108,107,107,106,105 103,102,102,96**
CSF £34.60 CT £130.86 TOTE £12.80: £3.60, £1.10, £2.20; EX 43.10 Trifecta £293.30.
**Owner** Terry Pryke **Bred** Gestut Gorlsdorf **Trained** Oakham, Rutland

**FOCUS**
A fair fillies' handicap. Ordinary form rated around the second and third to their marks.

## 498 32RED CASINO H'CAP 1m 142y (Tp)
**4:20** (4:21) (Class 5) (0-75,75) 3-Y-O **£3,881** (£1,155; £577; £288) **Stalls** Low

Form RPR

13-1 **1** **Poetic Force (IRE)**[13] 292 3-9-7 **75**.......................(t) GeorgeDowning 2 79
(Tony Carroll) *chsd ldrs: rdn to ld 1f out: edgd lft: jst hld on* **11/4**[3]

432- **2** nk **Enfolding (IRE)**[34] 8557 3-9-4 **72** DanielMuscutt 1 75
(James Fanshawe) *hld up in tch: rdn and swtchd rt 1f out: r.o* **9/4**[1]

0-1 **3** nse **Moamar**[19] 198 3-9-2 **70** AdamKirby 4 73
(Ed Dunlop) *hld up: rn green at times: shkn up over 3f out: rdn and r.o wl ins fnl f* **5/2**[2]

-342 **4** 2 **Shabeeh (IRE)**[6] 402 3-9-3 **71** JoeFanning 5 69
(Mark Johnston) *racd keenly: jnd ldr after 1f tl settled into 2nd 6f out: shkn up led ld wl over 1f out: hdd 1f out: styd on same pce ins fnl f* **7/1**

04-2 **5** ½ **Party Tiger**[26] 78 3-9-7 **75** TonyHamilton 3 72
(Richard Fahey) *led: rdn and hdd wl over 1f out: no ex ins fnl f* **7/1**

1m 50.85s (0.75) **Going Correction** +0.025s/f (Slow) 5 Ran SP% **111.0**
Speed ratings (Par 97): **97,96,96,94,94**
CSF £9.42 TOTE £2.50: £1.20, £2.10; EX 8.60 Trifecta £21.10.
**Owner** W McLuskey & S Barton **Bred** S J Macdonald **Trained** Cropthorne, Worcs

**FOCUS**
An interesting handicap for 3yos, and a tight finish between the first three. The second and third have been rated as improving on their maiden form, with the fourth close to form.

## 499 32RED.COM EBF FILLIES' H'CAP 1m 142y (Tp)
**4:50** (4:51) (Class 2) (0-105,98) 4-Y-0+
**£16,807** (£5,032; £2,516; £1,258; £629; £315) **Stalls** Low

Form RPR
132- **1** **Carolinae**[35] 8538 5-8-11 **85** (h) StevieDonohoe 7 89+
(Charlie Fellowes) *hld up: plld hrd: hdwy 2f out: racd wd fr over 1f out: rdn and r.o to ld nr fin* **4/1**[2]

2-11 **2** ½ **Absolute Blast (IRE)**[13] 285 5-9-10 **98** PJMcDonald 1 101+
(Iain Jardine) *reluctant to s and gave many l away: latched on to the rr of the field 7f out: hdwy over 1f out: rdn and r.o wl ins fnl f: wnt 2nd nr fin* **4/6**[1]

32-1 **3** nse **Summer Icon**[22] 142 4-9-4 **93** GrahamLee 6 96
(Mick Channon) *led at stdy pce over 7f out: qcknd 2f out: rdn ins fnl f: hdd nr fin* **7/1**[3]

3-16 **4** 1¼ **Gleaming Girl**[13] 285 5-8-6 **80** JosephineGordon 5 80
(David Simcock) *chsd ldrs: rdn over 1f out: no ex wl ins fnl f* **15/2**

03-6 **5** nk **Hawatif (IRE)**[17] 235 4-8-2 **82** MitchGodwin(5) 3 81
(Anthony Carson) *led at stdy pce 1f: trckd ldr: shkn up over 1f out: styd on same pce ins fnl f* **20/1**

6-05 **6** 3½ **Lady Lydia (IRE)**[13] 285 6-8-2 **79** oh1 NoelGarbutt(3) 2 70
(Martin Smith) *hld up: plld hrd: nt clr run over 2f out: rdn over 1f out: no ex ins fnl f* **33/1**

1m 55.38s (5.28) **Going Correction** +0.025s/f (Slow)
**WFA** 4 from 5yo+ 1lb 6 Ran SP% **112.0**
Speed ratings (Par 96): **77,76,76,75,75 72**
CSF £7.04 TOTE £4.20: £1.90, £1.10; EX 8.30 Trifecta £18.40.
**Owner** The Dalmunzie Devils Partnership **Bred** Meon Valley Stud **Trained** Newmarket, Suffolk

**FOCUS**
A messy race, with the favourite giving them all a big head start, and the race turning into a sprint after a dawdling early gallop. The third has been rated to her Lingfield latest, with the fourth and fifth close to form.

## 500 SUNBETS.CO.UK MAIDEN STKS 7f 36y (Tp)
**5:20** (5:22) (Class 5) 3-Y-0+ **£3,752** (£1,116; £557; £278) **Stalls** High

Form RPR
0-2 **1** **Fast Landing**[11] 331 3-8-10 0 (p[1]) KevinStott 6 77
(Saeed bin Suroor) *mde all: racd keenly: shkn up over 1f out: r.o wl* **11/10**[1]

**2** 2¾ **Naab (FR)** 3-8-11 0 ow1 (h[1]) RobertTart 1 70
(John Gosden) *s.i.s: hld up: racd keenly: hdwy over 1f out: chsd wnr fnl f: styd on same pce* **7/1**

**3** 1 **The Eagle's Nest (IRE)** 3-8-10 0 TonyHamilton 5 66
(Richard Fahey) *hld up: shkn up and hdwy over 1f out: hung lft and styd on same pce ins fnl f* **12/1**

22- **4** 1¾ **Havelock (IRE)**[248] 2682 3-8-10 0 JoeFanning 4 61
(Mark Johnston) *sn chsng wnr: shkn up over 2f out: lost 2nd over 1f out: edgd lft and wknd ins fnl f* **7/2**[2]

**5** nk **Dreaming Time** 3-8-5 0 JosephineGordon 3 55
(Hugo Palmer) *chsd ldrs: shkn up over 2f out: wknd ins fnl f* **4/1**[3]

1m 28.47s (-0.33) **Going Correction** +0.025s/f (Slow) 5 Ran SP% **110.0**
Speed ratings (Par 103): **102,98,97,95,95**
CSF £9.31 TOTE £2.00: £1.40, £2.30; EX 8.30 Trifecta £53.80.
**Owner** Godolphin **Bred** Darley **Trained** Newmarket, Suffolk

**FOCUS**
A fair maiden. The level is fluid. It's been rated around the winner's latest effort for now.

## 501 SUNBETS.CO.UK TOP PRICES ON ALL FAVOURITES H'CAP 7f 36y (Tp)
**5:50** (5:51) (Class 5) (0-70,72) 4-Y-0+ **£3,752** (£1,116; £557; £278) **Stalls** High

Form RPR
0-05 **1** **Masamah (IRE)**[10] 355 11-9-6 **69** (h) StevieDonohoe 7 75
(Ian Williams) *hld up in tch: rdn and swtchd rt ins fnl f: r.o to ld nr fin* **20/1**

2-30 **2** nk **Rebel Lightning (IRE)**[15] 267 4-9-8 **71** (b) AdamKirby 12 76
(Richard Spencer) *hld up: shkn up over 1f out: hmpd ins fnl f: rdn and r.o wl to go 2nd nr fin: nt quite get there* **11/1**

500- **3** nk **Captain Bob (IRE)**[102] 7506 6-9-3 **66** JoeFanning 1 70
(Robert Cowell) *led: rdn over 1f out: hdd nr fin* **13/2**[3]

366- **4** nk **Langham**[162] 5725 4-9-1 **67** AlistairRawlinson(3) 8 70
(Michael Appleby) *hld up: hdwy over 1f out: rdn and edgd lft ins fnl f: r.o wl* **50/1**

3-34 **5** ½ **Billyoakes (IRE)**[10] 355 5-9-7 **70** (p) ShaneKelly 4 72
(Charlie Wallis) *chsd ldr: rdn over 2f out: styd on* **25/1**

2-21 **6** 1 **Cliff (IRE)**[22] 145 7-9-4 **72** LewisEdmunds(5) 10 71
(Nigel Tinkler) *hld up: hdwy over 1f out: sn hung lft: nt clr run ins fnl f: styd on* **8/1**

0-32 **7** shd **Athletic**[5] 426 8-8-13 **62** (v) AndrewMullen 5 65+
(David Evans) *chsd ldrs: wnt 2nd over 1f out: denied clr run thrght fnl f: eased towards fin* **5/2**[1]

10-5 **8** ½ **Win Lose Draw (IRE)**[10] 363 5-9-1 **64** (v[1]) BenCurtis 3 62
(Michael Appleby) *chsd ldrs: rdn over 2f out: edgd rt and hmpd ins fnl f: styd on same pce* **7/1**

0-46 **9** ¾ **Dominium (USA)**[17] 242 10-8-13 **67** (b) DavidParkes(5) 9 63
(Jeremy Gask) *hld up: effrt over 1f out: eased whn hld wl ins fnl f* **16/1**

00-4 **10** hd **Papou Tony**[25] 90 4-9-3 **66** LiamKeniry 2 61+
(George Baker) *hld up: nt clr run over 1f out: nvr on terms* **9/1**

011- **11** 7 **Dark Confidant (IRE)**[91] 7751 4-9-0 **63** PaulHanagan 6 39
(Richard Fahey) *mid-div: pushed along over 2f out: rdn and edgd lft over 1f out: wknd and eased fnl f* **7/2**[2]

1m 28.12s (-0.68) **Going Correction** +0.025s/f (Slow) 11 Ran SP% **122.5**
Speed ratings (Par 103): **104,103,103,102,102 101,101,100,99,99 91**
CSF £228.72 CT £1644.58 TOTE £14.90: £6.10, £3.30, £2.60; EX 306.00 Trifecta £4642.00.
**Owner** Dr Marwan Koukash **Bred** Stanley Estate & Stud Co & Mount Coote Stud **Trained** Portway, Worcs

**FOCUS**
There was a bunched finish to this modest handicap. The runner-up has been rated close to his best and helps set the standard.
T/Plt: £12.10 to a £1 stake. Pool: £80,580.19 - 4,838.38 winning units T/Qpdt: £3.50 to a £1 stake. Pool: £6,647.84 - 1,375.39 winning units **Colin Roberts**

# 455 KEMPTON (A.W) (R-H)
### Wednesday, February 1

**OFFICIAL GOING: Polytrack: standard**
Wind: nil Weather: white cloud

## 502 MATCHBOOK BETTING EXCHANGE H'CAP 1m (P)
**2:20** (2:22) (Class 6) (0-60,61) 3-Y-O **£2,264** (£673; £336; £168) **Stalls** Low

Form RPR
46-1 **1** **Dangerous Ends**[26] 89 3-9-2 **55** (v) MartinDwyer 13 62+
(Brett Johnson) *settled in rr-div: shkn up and tk clsr order fr 3f out: rdn over 1f out and gd prog through pack: kpt on wl to ld wl ins fnl f* **9/1**

00-0 **2** 1¾ **Mac's Kyllachy**[19] 209 3-9-7 **60** (v[1]) DanielMuscutt 2 62
(James Fanshawe) *settled bhd ldr on inner: rdn over 2f out: almost upsides and ev ch ent fnl f: kpt on* **16/1**

60-3 **3** ¾ **Beauchamp Opal**[26] 89 3-9-7 **60** StevieDonohoe 14 60
(Charlie Fellowes) *in rr: rdn and prog fr over 2f out: kpt on strly fr over 1f out: nvr nrr* **8/1**[3]

65-4 **4** ½ **Too Many Shots**[26] 89 3-9-5 **58** KierenFox 1 57
(John Best) *disp ld tl led over 5f out: rdn over 2f out: kpt on wl tl hdd & wknd wl ins fnl f* **6/1**[2]

0-31 **5** ½ **Log Off (IRE)**[13] 310 3-9-6 **59** AdamBeschizza 4 57
(David Evans) *settled bhd ldrs: rdn over 2f out: kpt on one pce fr over 1f out* **20/1**

00-0 **6** 1¼ **Kyllachys Tale (IRE)**[19] 210 3-9-7 **60** OisinMurphy 9 55
(Roger Teal) *broke wl and sn led: hdd over 5f out but remained pressing ldr: rdn over 2f out: kpt on one pce ent fnl f* **50/1**

00-1 **7** 1½ **American Patrol (IRE)**[9] 376 3-9-8 **61** 6ex AdamKirby 6 53
(Neil Mulholland) *settled on outer in rr-div: shkn up to make sme prog over 3f out: rdn over 2f out: shuffled along fr over 1f out on outer: nvr involved* **4/6**[1]

060- **8** ½ **Mr Mac**[49] 8354 3-9-6 **59** TomMarquand 11 49
(Peter Hedger) *settled bhd ldrs rdn over 2f out: no ex ent fnl f* **12/1**

006- **9** ½ **Ede's E Rider**[35] 8556 3-9-6 **59** KieranO'Neill 12 48
(Pat Phelan) *in rr: rdn over 2f out: no imp on ldr* **66/1**

00-0 **10** ¾ **Young Officer (IRE)**[18] 245 3-8-4 **50** (v[1]) JordanUys(7) 8 38
(Brian Meehan) *hld up in mid-div: shkn up and prog on inner fr over 2f out: sn rdn and ev ch ent fnl f: sn wknd qckly and lost numerous pls* **150/1**

04-0 **11** 2¾ **Vrika Bay**[27] 65 3-9-2 **60** GeorgiaCox(5) 5 41
(Robert Eddery) *pushed along early to hold pl in mid-div: rdn over 3f out: one pce st* **33/1**

450- **12** nk **London Grammar (IRE)**[110] 7330 3-9-7 **60** RyanTate 10 41
(Ralph J Smith) *in rr: rdn over 2f out: hld fr wl over 1f out* **100/1**

00-0 **13** 10 **Paco Dawn**[9] 376 3-8-9 **48** (b[1]) ShaneKelly 7 6
(Philip Hide) *t.k.h bhd ldrs: rdn ent st: lost tch fr over 1f out* **100/1**

00-0 **14** 2½ **Shiloh**[28] 34 3-9-2 **55** MartinLane 3 7
(Simon Crisford) *t.k.h bhd ldrs: pushed along over 4f out: losing tch 3f out: no ex fr over 1f out: t.o* **33/1**

1m 40.26s (0.46) **Going Correction** 0.0s/f (Stan) 14 Ran SP% **125.7**
Speed ratings (Par 95): **97,95,94,94,93 92,90,90,89,89 86,85,75,73**
CSF £141.32 CT £1260.50 TOTE £10.70: £2.40, £4.20, £2.10; EX 207.10 Trifecta £1360.80.
**Owner** Colin Westley **Bred** R S Cockerill (farms) Ltd **Trained** Epsom, Surrey

**FOCUS**
Modest fare, but competitive enough with several potential improvers making their handicap debuts. The 1-3-4 here filled exactly the same positions over C&D a month ago. Another step forward from the winner, and a minor one from the second.

## 503 BETTER ODDS WITH MATCHBOOK BETTING EXCHANGE MAIDEN STKS (DIV I) 1m (P)
**2:50** (2:53) (Class 5) 3-Y-0+ **£2,911** (£866; £432; £216) **Stalls** Low

Form RPR
**1** **Broad Appeal** 3-8-4 0 MitchGodwin(5) 11 67+
(Jonathan Portman) *hld up in rr: rdn 2f out: ev ch over 1f out: kpt on tl qcknd up best ent fnl f: led fnl stride* **25/1**

4-5 **2** shd **Tibibit**[21] 168 4-9-9 0 GeorgeBaker 1 67
(Henry Tett) *led tl hdd after 2f: stl prom and rdn 2f out: kpt on wl and led ent fnl f: hdd last stride* **14/1**

**3** nk **Excel Again** 3-8-9 0 OisinMurphy 5 66+
(James Tate) *settled bhd ldrs: rn green bnd and pushed along: rdn 2f out: swtchd out wd over 1f out and gd prog ins fnl f: improver* **9/2**[3]

0- **4** nk **Alexander M (IRE)**[205] 4188 3-8-9 0 FrannyNorton 4 65
(Mark Johnston) *settled bhd ldrs early: rdn 2f out: kpt on and ev ch ent fnl f: no imp cl home* **5/1**

5 **5** hd **Trade Route (IRE)**[18] 237 3-8-9 0 ShaneKelly 7 65
(David Elsworth) *settled bhd ldrs: rdn over 2f out: swtchd wd and gd prog fr over 1f out: styd on wl nr fin: nvr nrr* **7/4**[1]

06- **6** 1½ **My Brother Mike (IRE)**[53] 8305 3-8-9 0 StevieDonohoe 3 61
(Daniel Mark Loughnane) *settled in mid-div on inner: rdn jst over 2f out: ev ch on heels of ldrs jst over 1f out where nt clrest run: fdd ins fnl f* **33/1**

**7** ½ **Drumochter** 3-8-4 0 WilliamCarson 2 55
(Charles Hills) *hld up in mid-divson on inner: rdn over 2f out: kpt on wl and ev ch ent fnl f: no ex sn after* **16/1**

**8** hd **William Sayle** 3-8-9 0 NickyMackay 10 59+
(John Gosden) *hmpd s: kpt out wd and mde up grnd to sit bhd ldr bef bnd: rdn over 2f out: ev ch ent fnl f: fdd sn after* **4/1**[2]

0 **9** nk **Feisty One U R**[14] 283 3-8-4 0 MartinDwyer 6 54
(George Baker) *s.s: in rr: hanging bdly lft in st: prog and ev ch on inner over 1f out w jockey only able to nurse filly along: unable to go through w effrt: eased wl ins fnl f* **66/1**

4-0 **10** *26* **Sublime**[14] 283 3-8-4 0 ........ RyanTate 9
(Rod Millman) *settled bhd ldrs out wd: nt handled and c v wd st: sn btn and eased: t.o* **100/1**

U/5 **U** **Worthy Spirit (GER)**[14] 289 6-10-0 0 ........ DougieCostello 8
(Adrian Wintle) *wnt bdly lft and hmpd rival: ref to r and uns rdr* **200/1**

1m 40.84s (1.04) **Going Correction** 0.0s/f (Stan)
**WFA** 3 from 4yo+ 19lb **11** Ran SP% **113.5**
Speed ratings (Par 103): **94,93,93,93,93 91,91,90,90,64**
CSF £316.66 TOTE £28.80: £6.60, £2.80, £1.90; EX 272.80 Trifecta £3850.90.
**Owner** Berkeley Racing **Bred** S Dibb & J Repard **Trained** Upper Lambourn, Berks

**FOCUS**
The first division of a modest maiden with little solid form from those to have run. Barely a length separated the front five at the line. Muddling form, but it's been rated at face value around the fifth and sixth for now.

## 504 BETTER ODDS WITH MATCHBOOK BETTING EXCHANGE MAIDEN STKS (DIV II) 1m (P)
**3:20** (3:23) (Class 5) 3-Y-O+ **£2,911** (£866; £432; £216) **Stalls** Low

Form RPR

25- **1** **Bois de Boulogne (USA)**[41] 8486 3-8-9 0 ........(b[1]) NickyMackay 9 83+
(John Gosden) *mid-div on outer: nt handle bnd and niggled along: shkn up and prog to chse ldrs over 2f out: sn rdn on rail and kpt on strly fr over 1f out: led fnl strides* **6/5[1]**

2- **2** *nk* **Flight Of Fantasy**[43] 8465 3-8-4 0 ........ KieranO'Neill 5 77
(Harry Dunlop) *settled bhd ldr: shkn up and led gng wl 2f out: kpt on wl fr over 1f out: wore down fnl strides* **9/2[3]**

5 **3** *5* **Invincible Man (IRE)**[25] 127 3-8-9 0 ........ OisinMurphy 8 71
(James Tate) *broke wl: sn settled bhd ldrs: rdn over 2f out: swtchd rt and chsd ldr fr over 1f out: stl ev ch ent fnl f: wknd qckly after* **7/1**

33-2 **4** *3¼* **Envisaging (IRE)**[25] 114 3-8-9 77 ........ DanielMuscutt 6 63
(James Fanshawe) *settled bhd ldrs on outer: rdn over 2f out: ev ch ent fnl f: wknd after* **11/4[2]**

0-0 **5** *2¼* **Everdina**[18] 236 3-7-13 0 ........ HollieDoyle(5) 10 53+
(Ed Walker) *in rr-div on outer: nt handle bnd and niggled along: rdn ent st: kpt on nicely under hands and heels fr over 1f out* **33/1**

0 **6** *2¼* **Penny Poet (IRE)**[14] 283 4-9-9 0 ........ LiamKeniry 4 53
(Neil Mulholland) *in rr on inner: rdn over 2f out: lft bhd fr over 1f out* **66/1**

**7** *¾* **Incredible Dream (IRE)** 4-10-0 0 ........ RobertWinston 1 56
(Dean Ivory) *s.s and in rr: rdn over 2f out: no ex sn after* **33/1**

0 **8** *¾* **L'Ami De Rouge**[14] 283 4-9-9 0 ........(h) TimmyMurphy 3 49
(Ralph J Smith) *in rr-div on inner: rdn over 2f out: sn lft bhd* **150/1**

00 **9** *3¼* **Whirlwind Romance (IRE)**[12] 328 3-8-1 0 ........(b) NoelGarbutt(3) 2 37
(Hugo Palmer) *sn led and set str pce taking a t.k.h: rdn over 2f out: hdd 2f out: wknd after* **66/1**

1m 38.87s (-0.93) **Going Correction** 0.0s/f (Stan)
**WFA** 3 from 4yo 19lb **9** Ran SP% **112.3**
Speed ratings (Par 103): **104,103,98,95,93 90,90,89,86**
CSF £6.63 TOTE £2.20: £1.10, £1.50, £1.70; EX 7.90 Trifecta £25.50.
**Owner** Godolphin **Bred** Darley **Trained** Newmarket, Suffolk

**FOCUS**
This looked the stronger division on paper and the winning time was almost two seconds faster than the first division. It's been rated around the well-placed runner-up.

## 505 SMARTER BETS WITH MATCHBOOK BETTING EXCHANGE FILLIES' H'CAP 7f (P)
**3:50** (3:51) (Class 5) (0-70,72) 4-Y-O+ **£2,911** (£866; £432; £216) **Stalls** Low

Form RPR

25-6 **1** **Jacquotte Delahaye**[18] 232 6-9-11 72 ........(b) PaulMulrennan 2 84
(David Brown) *mde all: rdn over 2f out: kpt on wl: in command wl ins fnl f: rdn out* **7/1[3]**

05-0 **2** *3¾* **Lucymai**[26] 90 4-9-6 67 ........ RobertWinston 1 69
(Dean Ivory) *hld up bhd ldrs on inner: rdn over 2f out: kpt on tl no ex ent fnl f* **9/2[2]**

12-3 **3** *3¼* **Garter (IRE)**[7] 394 4-9-3 67 ........ CallumShepherd(3) 7 60
(Charles Hills) *settled bhd ldr: rdn over 2f out: no imp on wnr and no ex ent fnl f* **6/4[1]**

0-00 **4** *1* **I Can't Stop**[6] 426 4-8-9 56 ........(b) FrannyNorton 8 47
(Milton Bradley) *in rr on inner: rdn over 2f out: sn lft bhd* **33/1**

035- **5** *4½* **Musical Taste**[32] 8595 4-8-12 59 ........ KieranO'Neill 3 37
(Pat Phelan) *in rr: rdn over 2f out: sn hld* **16/1**

34-6 **6** *½* **East Coast Lady (IRE)**[28] 50 5-9-2 68 ........ HollieDoyle(5) 4 45
(William Stone) *s.s: in rr: rdn over 2f out: nvr involved* **9/2[2]**

1m 25.73s (-0.27) **Going Correction** 0.0s/f (Stan) **6** Ran SP% **97.7**
Speed ratings (Par 100): **101,96,93,91,86 86**
CSF £27.69 CT £43.15 TOTE £5.60: £3.30, £2.50; EX 29.40 Trifecta £66.90.
**Owner** Mrs F Denniff **Bred** A S Denniff **Trained** Averham Park, Notts
■ Lolita was withdrawn. Price at time of withdrawal 15/2. Rule 4 applies to all bets - deduction 10p in the pound.

**FOCUS**
An ordinary fillies' handicap in which they went no pace and that was to the advantage of the winner. She's been rated to her best figure since winning over the C&D back in August 2015.

## 506 WINNERS WELCOME AT MATCHBOOK EXCHANGE H'CAP 7f (P)
**4:20** (4:20) (Class 4) (0-85,86) 4-Y-O+ **£4,690** (£1,395; £697; £348) **Stalls** Low

Form RPR

402- **1** **Twin Point**[82] 7902 6-9-1 78 ........(t) StevieDonohoe 6 87
(Charlie Fellowes) *mde all: rdn over 2f out: hrd pressed over 1f out: kpt on wl ins fnl f: rdn out* **11/2[3]**

-052 **2** *½* **Lexington Times (IRE)**[5] 441 5-9-2 79 ........ JackGarritty 10 86
(Ruth Carr) *hld up in rr: shkn up 2f out: cruising on heels ent fnl f: sn rdn: kpt on cl home but nvr getting to wnr* **6/1**

050- **3** *1½* **Childesplay**[193] 4627 6-9-0 77 ........ TomMarquand 8 80
(Heather Main) *settled bhd ldr on rail: rdn over 2f out: kpt on and ev ch ent fnl f: no ex nr fin* **14/1**

50-3 **4** *nk* **Pearl Spectre (USA)**[7] 403 6-9-9 86 ........ AdamKirby 4 88
(Phil McEntee) *chsd ldr: rdn over 2f out: kpt on wl and ev ch ent fnl f: no ex wl ins fnl f* **4/1[2]**

315- **5** *1¼* **Red Trooper (FR)**[56] 8251 4-9-1 78 ........ SteveDrowne 2 77
(George Baker) *mid-div on rail: rdn over 2f out: kpt on one pce fr over 1f out* **4/1[2]**

314- **6** *2* **Mystical Spirit (FR)**[307] 1161 5-9-7 84 ........ PaulMulrennan 1 77
(Martyn Meade) *t.k.h in rr: rdn over 2f out: no ex fr jst over 1f out* **7/2[1]**

565- **7** *shd* **Anonymous John (IRE)**[35] 8561 5-8-13 76 ........ LiamKeniry 3 69
(Dominic Ffrench Davis) *mid-div: rdn over 2f out: ev ch over 1f out: wknd ent fnl f* **14/1**

0-30 **8** *4* **Dutiful Son (IRE)**[4] 460 7-8-12 80 ........ HollieDoyle(5) 9 62
(Simon Dow) *awkward s and tk false step: in rr: effrt over 2f out: nvr involved* **8/1**

1m 25.55s (-0.45) **Going Correction** 0.0s/f (Stan) **8** Ran SP% **116.3**
Speed ratings (Par 105): **102,101,99,99,97 95,95,90**
CSF £38.92 CT £440.42 TOTE £5.60: £2.10, £1.90, £4.30; EX 40.90 Trifecta £413.70.
**Owner** F J Perry **Bred** V I Araci **Trained** Newmarket, Suffolk
■ Stewards' Enquiry : Adam Kirby two-day ban: used whip in the incorrect place (Feb 15-17)

**FOCUS**
A fair handicap, but not many got into it. A length pb from the winner.

## 507 MATCHBOOK TRADERS CONFERENCE H'CAP (LONDON MIDDLE DISTANCE QUALIFIER) 1m 2f 219y(P)
**4:50** (4:51) (Class 4) (0-80,81) 4-Y-O+ **£4,690** (£1,395; £697; £348) **Stalls** Low

Form RPR

52-4 **1** **Persun**[16] 269 5-9-7 79 ........ GrahamLee 2 88
(Mick Channon) *cl up bhd ldrs: rdn over 2f out: swtchd wd sn after: sltly hmpd over 1f out: str run ent fnl f: got up post* **9/1**

35-2 **2** *hd* **Alcatraz (IRE)**[21] 173 5-9-5 77 ........(tp) AdamKirby 12 85
(George Baker) *sluggish s: in rr in detached quartet: tk clsr order over 3f out: rdn over 2f out: kpt on wl and led 1f out: hdd post* **9/2[2]**

40/0 **3** *1¼* **Langlauf (USA)**[26] 99 4-8-10 75 ........(p) LuluStanford(5) 10 81
(Rod Millman) *settled in mid-div: shkn up and tk clsr order on outer fr over 2f out: shuffled along over 1f out: kpt on wl ent fnl f: nvr involved* **22/1**

61-2 **4** *½* **Zabeel Star (IRE)**[19] 220 5-9-2 74 ........ LiamKeniry 6 79
(Graeme McPherson) *settled in mid-div on rail: rdn over 2f out: led over 1f out: hdd 1f out: no ex cl home and wknd* **5/1[3]**

44-4 **5** *½* **Dakota City**[25] 122 6-9-0 72 ........(p) AdamBeschizza 11 76
(Julia Feilden) *in rr in detached quartet: tk clsr order over 2f out: sn rdn: ev ch between horses ent fnl f: wknd sn after* **14/1**

44-5 **6** *½* **Daisy Boy (IRE)**[28] 38 6-9-3 78 ........(t) AaronJones(3) 1 81
(Stuart Williams) *chsd ldrs: rdn over 2f out: kpt on tl wknd ent fnl f* **7/1**

4-15 **7** *3¼* **Camakasi (IRE)**[14] 286 6-9-0 72 ........ TomMarquand 5 70
(Ali Stronge) *in rr in detached quartet: rdn over 2f out: kpt on one pce* **10/1**

3-14 **8** *1* **Black Dave (IRE)**[16] 267 7-9-0 72 ........ SteveDrowne 3 68
(David Evans) *settled bhd ldrs: rdn over 2f out: no ex fr over 1f out* **33/1**

5/01 **9** *nk* **Monsieur Rieussec**[13] 306 7-9-4 76 ........ RichardKingscote 4 72
(Jonathan Portman) *chsd ldr: led over 2f out: hung lft and hdd over 1f out where hmpd rival: wknd fnl f* **4/1[1]**

36-0 **10** *1¼* **Giantstepsahead (IRE)**[22] 163 8-9-9 81 ........ DanielMuscutt 9 74
(Alan Bailey) *sn led and set str gallop: hdd over 2f out: wknd after* **12/1**

00-3 **11** *7* **Hard To Handel**[9] 382 5-9-1 73 ........ PaddyAspell 13 55
(Clare Ellam) *in rr in detached quartet: no ex ebtering st* **66/1**

51-6 **12** *16* **Elusive Cowboy (USA)**[27] 74 4-8-13 73 ........(p[1]) StevieDonohoe 8 27
(Stuart Edmunds) *chsd ldrs and t.k.h: btn st* **16/1**

2m 18.56s (-3.34) **Going Correction** 0.0s/f (Stan)
**WFA** 4 from 5yo+ 1lb **12** Ran SP% **115.5**
Speed ratings (Par 105): **112,111,110,110,110 109,107,106,106,105 100,88**
CSF £47.14 CT £870.27 TOTE £10.20: £2.90, £1.70, £8.30; EX 33.70 Trifecta £553.10.
**Owner** J Mitchell **Bred** Mrs Joan Tice **Trained** West Ilsley, Berks

**FOCUS**
A fair middle-distance handicap, but the leaders looked to go off too quick. The runner-up has been rated to the balance of his form, with the fourth fitting and fifth close to his recent form.

## 508 MATCHBOOK BETTING PODCAST H'CAP 1m 7f 218y(P)
**5:20** (5:20) (Class 6) (0-65,66) 4-Y-O+ **£2,264** (£673; £336; £168) **Stalls** Low

Form RPR

01-1 **1** **Canadian Diamond (IRE)**[30] 19 10-10-2 66 ........ AdamBeschizza 7 73
(Richard Rowe) *settled bhd ldrs: tk clsr order wl over 3f out w front pair roughly 8 l clr: almost upsides jst over 2f out: sn rdn and led: wnt hd to hd w runner-up fr 2f out: on top wl ins fnl f: pushed out* **5/2[1]**

42-3 **2** *¾* **Thomas Blossom (IRE)**[14] 290 7-10-0 64 ........(t) AdamKirby 8 70
(Ali Stronge) *hld up in mid-div: tk clsr order over 3f out on outer: rdn wl over 2f and sn upsides: wnt hd to hd w wnr fr 2f: kpt on wl tl no ex wl ins fnl f* **4/1[2]**

300- **3** *7* **Vedani (IRE)**[32] 7039 8-9-2 52 ........(p) GeorgeDowning 5 50
(Tony Carroll) *chsd ldrs: rdn wl over 2f out: kpt on one pce* **20/1**

/0-0 **4** *1¾* **Cappielow Park**[14] 281 8-8-11 47 ........(tp) TomMarquand 6 43
(Ali Stronge) *in rr off the pce: rdn over 2f out: no ex* **33/1**

36-5 **5** *9* **Oyster Card**[18] 241 4-8-5 47 ........(p[1]) MartinDwyer 3 32
(Michael Appleby) *racd in 2nd tl pressed ldr over 7f out and wnt on clr of pack: rdn over 3f out: wkng qckly over 2f out: sn hld* **4/1[2]**

20-0 **6** *8* **Celestial Dancer (FR)**[26] 98 5-8-6 47 ........ HollieDoyle(5) 2 22
(Nigel Twiston-Davies) *sn led: pressed fr over 7f out and increased pce w rival to go clr of gp: rdn over 3f out: wkng qckly whn hdd jst over 2f out: sn no ex* **20/1**

00-6 **7** *hd* **Tynecastle Park**[13] 314 4-9-1 57 ........ JackMitchell 1 32
(Robert Eddery) *awkward s: settled in 3rd on inner: lost pl ent st and sn hld* **4/1[2]**

2-14 **8** *dist* **Yasir (USA)**[18] 241 9-10-0 64 ........ PaulMulrennan 4
(Conor Dore) *in rr-div: losing tch fr wl over 3f out: heavily eased st: t.o* **10/1[3]**

3m 30.16s (0.06) **Going Correction** 0.0s/f (Stan)
**WFA** 4 from 5yo+ 4lb **8** Ran SP% **110.1**
Speed ratings (Par 101): **99,98,95,94,89 85,85,**
CSF £11.45 CT £144.56 TOTE £3.30: £1.10, £1.70, £4.60; EX 11.60 Trifecta £144.30.
**Owner** Nicholls Family **Bred** J S Bolger **Trained** Sullington, W Sussex

**FOCUS**
A moderate staying handicap, but a decent test of stamina with the two leaders taking each other on a long way out. That set it up for the closers with the front pair having the race to themselves once the pace-setters fell in a hole. Straightforward form.

T/Jkpt: Not Won. T/Plt: £1,688.30 to a £1 stake. Pool: £62,562.76 - 27.05 winning units T/Qpdt: £45.50 to a £1 stake. Pool: £7,335.69 - 119.10 winning units **Cathal Gahan**

# 441 NEWCASTLE (A.W) (L-H)

Wednesday, February 1

**OFFICIAL GOING: Tapeta: standard**

Wind: Breezy, half behind

## 509 BETWAY H'CAP 1m 4f 98y (Tp)

**4:25** (4:27) (Class 5) (0-75,75) 4-Y-0+ **£3,234** (£962; £481; £240) **Stalls** High

Form RPR

123- **1** **Taopix**[33] 8586 5-8-12 **66**........ LukeMorris 9 74
(Karen McLintock) *t.k.h: hld up in tch: effrt and pushed along over 2f out: hdwy over 1f out: led and edgd lft ins fnl f: r.o wl* **3/1**[3]

200/ **2** *1 1/4* **Magistral**[431] 7481 7-9-3 **71**........(p) PJMcDonald 5 77
(Iain Jardine) *prom: shkn up and hdwy to ld over 1f out: hdd ins fnl f: kpt on* **16/1**

11-1 **3** *1 1/2* **Go George Go (IRE)**[29] 30 4-9-0 **71**........ JoeFanning 4 76
(Alan Swinbank) *trckd ldrs: hdwy to ld after 4f: hdd 1/2-way: regained ld and gng wl over 2f out: hdd over 1f out: rallied: one pce wl ins fnl f* **7/4**[1]

14-2 **4** *1/2* **Medicine Hat**[29] 28 6-9-5 **73**........(p[1]) SamJames 2 77
(Marjorie Fife) *cl up: hdwy to ld 1/2-way: hdd over 2f out: rallied: keeping on u.p whn n.m.r ins fnl f: no ex* **11/4**[2]

026- **5** *3* **Highwayman**[33] 8585 4-8-4 **61**........ AndrewMullen 3 59
(David Thompson) *t.k.h: hld up in tch: pushed along over 2f out: no imp fr over 1f out* **50/1**

050/ **6** *8* **Thorntoun Care**[514] 6131 6-8-6 **67**........ JamieGormley[(7)] 6 52
(Iain Jardine) *hld up in last pl: rdn and outpcd over 2f out: n.d after* **16/1**

560- **7** *6* **Card High (IRE)**[54] 8283 7-9-4 **75**........(t) NathanEvans[(3)] 1 51
(Wilf Storey) *t.k.h: led 4f: cl up tl rdn and wknd fr over 2f out* **25/1**

56-4 **U** **Woodacre**[29] 30 10-9-2 **70**........ GeorgeChaloner 7
(Richard Whitaker) *fractious in stalls: hld up: hdwy over 2f out: rdn and outpcd whn broke down and uns rdr over 1f out: fatally injured* **12/1**

2m 43.94s (2.84) **Going Correction** +0.325s/f (Slow)
**WFA** 4 from 5yo+ 2lb **8** Ran SP% **113.3**
Speed ratings (Par 103): **103,102,101,100,98 93,89,**
CSF £47.58 CT £105.98 TOTE £3.90: £1.10, £3.70, £1.10; EX 51.60 Trifecta £144.00.
**Owner** Roger Stockdale **Bred** Lady Jennifer Green **Trained** Ingoe, Northumberland

■ Maulesden May was withdrawn. Price at time of withdrawal 20-1. Rule 4 does not apply.

**FOCUS**
There were several lead changes and that helped set things up for something to close from off the pace. The third and fourth have been rated to form.

## 510 SUNBETS.CO.UK MAIDEN FILLIES' STKS 7f 14y (Tp)

**5:00** (5:09) (Class 5) 3-5-Y-0 **£2,911** (£866; £432; £216) **Stalls** Centre

Form RPR

5- **1** **Elusive Olivia (USA)**[92] 7733 3-8-11 0........(t) PaulHanagan 7 70
(Joseph Tuite) *t.k.h early: in tch: hdwy and pushed along 2f out: sn edgd lft: led last 40yds: styd on wl* **2/1**[1]

00-3 **2** *nk* **Bloomin Lovely (IRE)**[7] 401 3-8-11 70........ JasonHart 9 69
(John Quinn) *cl up: rdn to ld 2f out: sn edgd rt: hdd last 40yds: kpt on* **5/2**[2]

**3** *1 1/4* **Voi** 3-8-11 0........ JosephineGordon 2 65+
(Hugo Palmer) *wore hood in paddock: hld up in tch: pushed along and green over 2f out: sn outpcd: rallied fnl f: kpt on: nt rch first two* **6/1**[3]

00-4 **4** *nse* **Mama Africa (IRE)**[11] 356 3-8-12 67 ow1........ PhillipMakin 4 68+
(David Barron) *trckd ldrs: effrt and cl up whn n.m.r briefly over 1f out: outpcd ins fnl f: rallied towards fin* **5/2**[2]

5-4 **5** *nk* **The Bard's Advice**[7] 402 3-8-11 0........ ConnorBeasley 5 64
(Keith Dalgleish) *led to 2f out: sn pushed along and rallied: outpcd last 100yds* **12/1**

00/- **6** *9* **Ivy Matilda**[474] 7252 4-9-9 25........ MeganNicholls[(5)] 8 45?
(Colin Teague) *s.i.s: t.k.h and sn prom: drvn and outpcd over 2f out: n.d after* **100/1**

**7** *5* **Six Of The Best** 5-10-0 0........ PJMcDonald 3 31
(Ollie Pears) *s.i.s: hld up: rdn and struggling over 2f out: sn btn* **66/1**

060- **8** *4* **Bellamay**[247] 2739 3-8-11 45........ LukeMorris 1 16
(John Weymes) *s.i.s: hld up: rdn and outpcd over 2f out: sn btn* **100/1**

1m 28.16s (1.96) **Going Correction** +0.075s/f (Slow)
**WFA** 3 from 4yo+ 17lb **8** Ran SP% **115.9**
Speed ratings (Par 100): **91,90,89,89,88 78,72,68**
CSF £7.46 TOTE £2.80: £1.10, £1.30, £1.80; EX 7.90 Trifecta £33.80.
**Owner** A A Byrne & Partner **Bred** Hidden Brook Farm, K Latta Et Al **Trained** Lambourn, Berks

■ Thornton Mary was withdrawn. Price at time of withdrawal 100-1. Rule 4 does not apply.

**FOCUS**
A modest maiden and they finished in a heap, but the winner landed a bit of a punt. The level is set around the runner-up and fourth.

## 511 32RED.COM H'CAP 5f (Tp)

**5:30** (5:35) (Class 6) (0-60,62) 3-Y-0 **£2,264** (£673; £336; £168) **Stalls** Centre

Form RPR

00-4 **1** **Little Kingdom (IRE)**[21] 179 3-9-0 **53**........ BenCurtis 8 58
(Tracy Waggott) *prom: effrt and rdn over 1f out: edgd lft: led last 50yds: kpt on* **12/1**

04-0 **2** *1* **Flying Hope (IRE)**[21] 179 3-8-9 **48**........(t) JosephineGordon 9 49
(Nigel Tinkler) *t.k.h: led: rdn over 1f out: edgd rt and hdd last 50yds: one pce* **25/1**

3-41 **3** *3/4* **Royal Celebration**[21] 179 3-9-1 **57**........ NathanEvans[(3)] 1 55
(Bryan Smart) *prom on outside: effrt and rdn over 1f out: kpt on same pce ins fnl f* **5/2**[1]

31-5 **4** *shd* **Spin Top**[12] 324 3-9-9 **62**........(v) PaulHanagan 5 60
(Joseph Tuite) *in tch: rdn and outpcd 2f out: rallied ins fnl f: kpt on: nt pce to chal* **11/2**[3]

30-3 **5** *1* **Bismarck The Flyer (IRE)**[16] 264 3-9-9 **62**........ PJMcDonald 2 56
(Ollie Pears) *hld up bhd ldng gp on outside: rdn and outpcd over 2f out: rallied over 1f out: kpt on fnl f: no imp* **7/1**

1 **6** *3/4* **Zandradee (IRE)**[31] 1 3-9-7 **60**........ AndrewMullen 4 52
(David Barron) *stdd s: t.k.h early in rr: effrt and angled to nr side of gp 1/2-way: rdn over 1f out: sn no imp* **11/4**[2]

0-54 **7** *2* **Vocalisation (IRE)**[25] 126 3-8-8 **47**........ LukeMorris 7 31
(John Weymes) *t.k.h early: chsd ldr to over 1f out: sn rdn and wknd* **14/1**

0-36 **8** *3/4* **Local Artist (IRE)**[11] 357 3-9-4 **57**........ JasonHart 3 39
(John Quinn) *trckd ldrs: drvn and outpcd over 2f out: n.d after* **16/1**

05-3 **9** *1 1/2* **Port Master**[29] 27 3-9-2 **60**........ RowanScott[(5)] 6 36
(Ann Duffield) *s.i.s: hld up: rdn whn carried sltly rt and rdn over 2f out: wknd over 1f out* **14/1**

59.96s (0.46) **Going Correction** +0.075s/f (Slow) **9** Ran SP% **113.9**
Speed ratings (Par 95): **99,97,96,96,94 93,90,88,86**
CSF £259.29 CT £995.04 TOTE £14.60: £3.60, £5.70, £1.40; EX 253.70 Trifecta £1286.50.
**Owner** Steve Sawley **Bred** Rabbah Bloodstock Limited **Trained** Spennymoor, Co Durham

**FOCUS**
An ordinary sprint, and the pace was towards the stands' side. Few got seriously involved. A step forward from the winner, with the runner-up to her mark.

## 512 32RED CASINO H'CAP 7f 14y (Tp)

**6:00** (6:02) (Class 4) (0-80,82) 3-Y-O **£4,725** (£1,414; £707; £354; £176) **Stalls** Centre

Form RPR

2-31 **1** **Espresso Freddo (IRE)**[19] 221 3-9-4 **75**........(p) LukeMorris 1 80
(Sir Mark Prescott Bt) *hld up: hdwy nr side of gp and led over 1f out: sn hrd pressed: drvn and hld on wl fnl f* **5/1**

32-2 **2** *1/2* **Tailor's Row (USA)**[12] 329 3-9-7 **78**........ JoeFanning 4 81
(Mark Johnston) *early ldr: trckd ldrs: effrt and ev ch briefly on far side of gp over 1f out: edgd rt: kpt on fnl f: hld nr fin* **7/2**[3]

4-12 **3** *3 1/4* **Sky Ballerina**[7] 392 3-9-1 **72**........ PaulHanagan 5 66
(Simon Crisford) *t.k.h: trckd ldrs: effrt and led over 2f out to over 1f out: kpt on same pce ins fnl f* **2/1**[1]

204- **4** *1* **Re Run (IRE)**[35] 8557 3-9-6 **77**........ TonyHamilton 2 69
(Richard Fahey) *hld up in tch: drvn and outpcd over 2f out: rallied over 1f out: kpt on fnl f: nt pce to chal* **11/1**

11-1 **5** *1 3/4* **Vatican Hill (IRE)**[12] 329 3-9-6 **82**........ LucyKBarry[(5)] 6 69
(Jamie Osborne) *prom: rdn along over 2f out: outpcd over 1f out: edgd lft and sn no imp* **11/4**[2]

400- **6** *4 1/2* **Man About Town (IRE)**[167] 5583 3-8-9 **69**........ JordanVaughan[(3)] 3 44
(K R Burke) *dwlt: t.k.h and sn led: hdd over 2f out: rdn and wknd over 1f out* **16/1**

1m 25.73s (-0.47) **Going Correction** +0.075s/f (Slow) **6** Ran SP% **113.1**
Speed ratings (Par 99): **105,104,100,99,97 92**
CSF £22.91 TOTE £6.40: £2.50, £2.30; EX 21.40 Trifecta £79.50.
**Owner** Middleham Park Racing LII **Bred** Knocklong House Stud **Trained** Newmarket, Suffolk

**FOCUS**
A fair handicap. The runner-up has been rated close to the possible level of his early form.

## 513 SUN BETS ON THE APP STORE CLASSIFIED STKS 7f 14y (Tp)

**6:30** (6:30) (Class 5) 4-Y-0+ **£3,234** (£962; £481; £240) **Stalls** Centre

Form RPR

63-2 **1** **Mehdi (IRE)**[16] 267 8-9-2 74........(t) PaulHanagan 6 78
(Richard Fahey) *trckd ldrs: rdn to ld over 1f out: sn hrd pressed: drvn and styd on wl fnl f* **9/2**[3]

6-12 **2** *3/4* **Rock Warbler (IRE)**[11] 359 4-9-2 75........(t) KevinStott 5 76
(Oliver Greenall) *dwlt: hld up in last pl: niggled along over 2f out: hdwy and pressed wnr over 1f out: sn rdn: kpt on fnl f: no ex last 50yds* **10/11**[1]

6-36 **3** *1 3/4* **Jubilee Brig**[11] 363 7-9-2 70........ JoeFanning 1 71
(Alan Swinbank) *t.k.h: in tch: rdn and outpcd over 2f out: rallied fnl f: nt rch first two* **14/1**

00-4 **4** *nk* **Mime Dance**[5] 441 6-9-2 70........(v[1]) DanielTudhope 3 70
(David O'Meara) *t.k.h and racd wd of centre gp: led and sn clr: rdn and hdd over 1f out: outpcd ins fnl f* **12/1**

214- **5** *3/4* **Capolavoro (FR)**[37] 8531 6-8-13 74........ EoinWalsh[(3)] 4 68
(Robert Cowell) *restless in stalls: chsd clr ldr: rdn and ev ch briefly over 1f out: no ex ins fnl f* **3/1**[2]

1m 26.79s (0.59) **Going Correction** +0.075s/f (Slow) **5** Ran SP% **109.9**
Speed ratings (Par 103): **99,98,96,95,94**
CSF £9.12 TOTE £3.60: £2.20, £1.30; EX 9.40 Trifecta £45.00.
**Owner** Dr Marwan Koukash **Bred** Douglas Taylor **Trained** Musley Bank, N Yorks

**FOCUS**
There was a good gallop on here and that set things up for the closers. The fourth has been rated similar to his C&D latest.

## 514 BETWAY BEST ODDS GUARANTEED PLUS APPRENTICE H'CAP 6f (Tp)

**7:00** (7:00) (Class 5) (0-75,75) 4-Y-0+ **£2,911** (£866; £432; £216) **Stalls** Centre

Form RPR

64-4 **1** **Burtonwood**[18] 242 5-8-6 **63**........ KieranSchofield[(3)] 6 70
(Julie Camacho) *in tch: rdn to ld 2f out: edgd lft ins fnl f: kpt on strly* **14/1**

32-3 **2** *3/4* **Palenville (IRE)**[23] 151 4-9-6 **74**........ CharlieBennett 5 79
(Simon Crisford) *cl up: pushed along 2f out: edgd rt appr fnl f: kpt on* **3/1**[2]

430- **3** *hd* **Art Obsession (IRE)**[99] 7590 6-9-7 **75**........ JoshDoyle 3 80+
(Paul Midgley) *hld up: rdn over 2f out: hdwy and chsng ldrs whn short of room briefly appr fnl f: kpt on* **7/1**[3]

/1-0 **4** *1 1/4* **Mr Morse**[27] 67 4-8-8 **65**........ BenRobinson[(3)] 8 65
(Brian Ellison) *prom on nr side of gp: rdn over 2f out: edgd lft over 1f out: kpt on ins fnl f* **8/1**

16-6 **5** *3/4* **Savannah Beau**[22] 161 5-9-2 **70**........ CallumRodriguez 9 68
(Iain Jardine) *stdd s: hld up: smooth hdwy over 2f out: chsng ldrs and rdn over 1f out: no ex ins fnl f* **8/1**

03-4 **6** *hd* **Dodgy Bob**[22] 159 4-9-2 **70**........(p) LewisEdmunds 1 66
(Kevin Ryan) *t.k.h: cl up: rdn along over 2f out: outpcd ins fnl f: fin seventh: plcd sixth* **2/1**[1]

050- **7** *2 1/4* **Silhuette (IRE)**[92] 7743 4-9-4 **72**........ MeganNicholls 2 61
(Colin Teague) *hld up on far side of gp: drvn and outpcd over 2f out: btn over 1f out: fin eighth: plcd seventh* **66/1**

04/0 **8** *3 3/4* **Baron Run**[13] 312 7-8-9 **68**........ RussellHarris[(5)] 7 45
(K R Burke) *led tl rdn and hdd 2f out: sn lost pl: btn fnl f: fin ninth: plcd eighth* **25/1**

23-6 **D** *1/2* **Semana Santa**[22] 152 4-9-5 **73**........ RowanScott 4 69
(David Barron) *plld hrd: hld up bhd ldng gp and sddle sn slipped forward: pushed along over 2f out: kpt on ins fnl f: fin sixth: disqualified and plcd last* **8/1**

1m 12.79s (0.29) **Going Correction** +0.075s/f (Slow) **9** Ran SP% **116.2**
Speed ratings (Par 103): **101,100,99,98,97 96,93,88,96**
CSF £56.31 CT £328.73 TOTE £15.30: £3.60, £1.40, £2.30; EX 65.60 Trifecta £457.20.
**Owner** Judy & Richard Peck & Partner **Bred** Brightwalton Stud **Trained** Norton, N Yorks

**FOCUS**
A competitive sprint handicap. The runner-up has been rated to form.

T/Plt: £27.80 to a £1 stake. Pool: £77,488.48. 2,034.07 winning units. T/Qpdt: £16.50 to a £1 stake. Pool: £8,889.72. 397.59 winning units. **Richard Young**

## 427 CAGNES-SUR-MER
Wednesday, February 1

**OFFICIAL GOING: Polytrack: standard**

### 515a PRIX DES HORTENSIAS (CLAIMER) (4YO+) (POLYTRACK) 1m 2f (P)
3:55 4-Y-0+ £6,410 (£2,564; £1,923; £1,282; £641)

RPR
1 **Butte Montmartre (FR)**[26] 6-9-8 0 JeffersonSmith(4) 15 59
(R Le Gal, France) **16/5**[1]
2 snk **Avenue Du Monde (FR)**[601] 3086 5-8-7 0 AntonioOrani(6) 2 46
(Laura Grizzetti, Italy) **30/1**
3 2 1/2 **Special Request (FR)**[35] 10-8-13 0 KyllanBarbaud(7) 10 48
(N Caullery, France) **53/10**
4 3/4 **Becquarius (FR)**[93] 7-9-2 0 AntoineHamelin 5 42
(Eric Saint-Martin, France) **6/1**
5 shd **One Deal (FR)** 6-8-10 0 DimitriIbouth(6) 7 42
(J-L Dubord, France) **28/1**
6 snk **Tartaros (FR)**[55] 4-9-2 0 HakimTabet 8 43
(M Rulec, Germany) **98/1**
7 1 **Kashani (IRE)** 4-9-2 0 (b[1]) TheoBachelot 4 41
(Frau C Barsig, Germany) **217/10**
8 nse **Great Dora (FR)**[65] 4-8-7 0 (p) JeromeMoutard(6) 6 38
(T Castanheira, France) **5/1**[2]
9 snk **Fantastic Way (FR)**[25] 8-8-4 0 (b) JeremieMonteiro(7) 3 34
(Mme C Barande-Barbe, France) **188/10**
10 nse **Crystal Gazing (FR)**[470] 5-9-3 0 (b) ChristopheSoumillon 9 40
(C Escuder, France) **51/10**[3]
11 1 **Vesper (GER)**[35] 7-8-11 0 MlleIsisMagnin(6) 12 38
(J-M Lefebvre, France) **37/1**
12 11 **King Wood (TUR)**[465] 7-8-6 0 MlleElauraCieslik(5) 11 10
(F Foresi, France) **83/1**
13 6 **Stella D'Oroux (FR)**[840] 7270 6-9-3 0 EddyHardouin 13 4
(Y Fertillet, France) **36/1**
14 nk **Turf Express (AUS)**[257] 10-8-8 0 FabienMasse(3) 14
(Christophe Mosse, France) **97/1**
15 6 **Trois Points (FR)**[11] 364 5-8-11 0 (p) IoritzMendizabal 1
(Gay Kelleway) *a little slow to stride: sn settled towards rr: pushed along wl over 3f out but no imp: wknd 2f out: bhd whn eased fr 1 1/2f out* **151/10**

2m 5.93s **15 Ran SP% 117.9**
PARI-MUTUEL (all including 1 euro stake): WIN 4.20PLACE 1.90, 6.40, 1.90DF 46.70SF 75.90.
**Owner** Romain Le Gal **Bred** A Capozzi **Trained** France

## 302 CHELMSFORD (A.W) (L-H)
Thursday, February 2

**OFFICIAL GOING: Polytrack: standard**
Wind: medium, behind Weather: dry

### 516 TOTEPLACEPOT SIX PLACES IN SIX RACES APPRENTICE H'CAP 1m (P)
5:50 (5:50) (Class 5) (0-75,76) 4-Y-0+ £5,175 (£1,540; £769; £384) Stalls Low

Form RPR
04-6 1 **Starboard**[16] 277 8-9-7 75 (b) AaronJones 4 86
(David Simcock) *taken down early: hld up in midfield: pushed along and clsd on outer over 2f out: rdn to chal over 1f out: led 1f out: styd on strly and drew clr fnl f: readily* **7/1**[3]
2 2 3/4 **Zorba The Greek**[111] 7341 5-9-2 70 CallumShepherd 12 75+
(Ed Vaughan) *hld up in midfield: clsd and nt clr run over 2f out: rdn and hdwy whn nt clr run and swtchd rt 1f out: styd on u.p to go 2nd wl ins fnl f: no threat to wnr* **10/1**
43-4 3 shd **Magic City (IRE)**[19] 240 8-9-4 72 NathanEvans 8 76
(Michael Easterby) *s.i.s: towards rr: clsd and nt clr run over 2f out: swtchd rt and effrt ent fnl 2f: hdwy over 1f out: styd on strly ins fnl f: wnt 3rd towards fin: no threat to wnr* **9/2**[2]
-31 4 3/4 **Yasood (IRE)**[8] 400 4-8-2 61 6ex LuluStanford(5) 11 64
(Phil McEntee) *stdd after s: hld up towards rr: effrt wd bnd 2f out: hdwy over 1f out: styd on wl ins fnl f to go 4th towards fin: no threat to wnr* **20/1**
12-0 5 1 **Baltic Prince (IRE)**[16] 277 7-8-12 73 AledBeech(7) 6 73
(Tony Carroll) *led: rdn over 1f out: hdd and unable qck 1f out: no ex and lost 2nd wl ins fnl f: wknd towards fin* **16/1**
21-0 6 hd **Candesta (USA)**[12] 351 7-8-4 65 FinleyMarsh(7) 2 65
(Julia Feilden) *chsd ldr: rdn and ev ch over 1f out tl unable qck 1f out: wknd wl ins fnl f* **9/1**
5-24 7 1 1/4 **Squire**[16] 277 6-9-3 76 (t) PaddyBradley(5) 1 73
(Michael Attwater) *chsd ldrs: rdn and unable qck over 1f out: wknd ins fnl f* **7/2**[1]
00-0 8 3/4 **Fleckerl (IRE)**[27] 93 7-9-6 74 (p) LouisSteward 7 69
(Conor Dore) *s.i.s: hld up in rr: hdwy on inner over 1f out: styd on same pce and no imp ins fnl f* **14/1**
100- 9 2 1/4 **Russian Reward (IRE)**[50] 8356 5-9-7 75 KieranShoemark 5 65
(Amanda Perrett) *in tch in midfield: rdn over 2f out: unable qck and lost pl over 1f out: wknd ins fnl f* **7/1**[3]
053- 10 2 1/4 **Rivers Of Asia**[33] 8590 4-9-1 72 (t) HollieDoyle(3) 13 57
(Philip McBride) *midfield but nvr on terms w ldrs: effrt over 1f out: swtchd rt 1f out: no imp: n.d* **16/1**
3-14 11 1 1/4 **Rebel State (IRE)**[23] 166 4-8-9 68 (b[1]) PatrickVaughan(5) 3 50
(Richard Spencer) *wl in tch in midfield: rdn over 1f out: no rspnse and sn lost pl: wknd fnl f* **12/1**
01-4 12 4 1/2 **Believe It (IRE)**[29] 36 5-8-8 69 (b) StephenCummins(7) 10 41
(Richard Hughes) *t.k.h: midfield but v wd: hdwy to chse ldrs after 2f tl lost pl qckly ent fnl 2f: bhd 1f out: fin lame* **10/1**
600- 13 19 **Torch**[45] 8455 4-9-6 74 HectorCrouch 9
(John Butler) *wl in tch in midfield: rdn 3f out: sn dropped out: wl bhd over 1f out: t.o* **33/1**

1m 39.09s (-0.81) **Going Correction** -0.075s/f (Stan) **13 Ran SP% 127.4**
Speed ratings (Par 103): **101,98,98,97,96 96,94,94,91,89 88,83,64**
CSF £80.63 CT £372.96 TOTE £8.80: £2.80, £2.80, £2.10; EX 82.70 Trifecta £542.30.
**Owner** Khalifa Dasmal & Partners **Bred** Juddmonte Farms Ltd **Trained** Newmarket, Suffolk

**FOCUS**
They went a good pace and that set things up for a closer.

### 517 @TOTEPOOLRACING WIN TICKETS ON TWITTER H'CAP 1m 2f (P)
6:25 (6:26) (Class 5) (0-70,78) 4-Y-0+ £5,175 (£1,540; £769; £384) Stalls Low

Form RPR
3-11 1 **Boychick (IRE)**[7] 421 4-8-7 56 LukeMorris 7 67+
(Ed Walker) *midfield: hdwy over 3f out: rdn to chse ldr and clr of field wl over 1f out: led 1f out: styd on strly and drew clr ins fnl f: readily* **7/2**[1]
40-4 2 3 1/4 **Glenalmond (IRE)**[29] 47 5-9-7 69 (p) OisinMurphy 4 74+
(Daniel Steele) *hld up off the pce towards rr: clsd but stl plenty to do whn nt clr run and swtchd rt over 1f out: styd on wl ins fnl f: wnt 2nd last strides: no ch w wnr* **8/1**
51-1 3 nk **Kingthistle**[29] 47 4-9-6 69 StevieDonohoe 6 73
(Ian Williams) *t.k.h: hld up off the pce in midfield: effrt and n.m.r over 2f out: hdwy u.p over 1f out: chsd clr wnr ins fnl f: kpt on but nvr threatening wnr: lost 2nd last strides* **5/1**[2]
-331 4 2 1/4 **Pivotman**[10] 382 9-9-13 78 6ex (bt) NathanEvans(3) 10 78
(Michael Easterby) *chsd ldr tl 6f out: styd chsng ldrs tl led over 2f out: rdn 2f out: clr w wnr over 1f out: hdd 1f out: no ex: wknd ins fnl f and lost 2 pls fnl 75yds* **7/1**
0-12 5 1 3/4 **Trending (IRE)**[13] 333 8-9-7 69 (t) GeorgeBaker 13 65
(Jeremy Gask) *stdd and dropped in bhd after s: hld up off the pce in rr: hdwy on outer 3f out: nt on terms w wnr whn nudged rt over 1f out: no imp fnl f* **16/1**
603- 6 4 1/2 **Boycie**[44] 8462 4-9-6 69 KieranO'Neill 11 56
(Richard Hannon) *dropped in bhd after s and niggled along early: swtchd rt and effrt over 2f out: plugged on to pass btn horses but nvr on terms w ldrs* **14/1**
02-1 7 1/2 **Heads You Win**[26] 120 4-9-6 69 TimmyMurphy 12 55
(Jamie Osborne) *wl in tch in midfield: rdn and unable qck wl over 1f out: btn whn edgd lft 1f out: wknd fnl f* **20/1**
6-30 8 2 1/4 **Ravens Quest**[15] 286 4-9-9 72 AdamKirby 2 54
(John Ryan) *midfield but nvr on terms w ldrs: pushed along 4f out: rdn over 2f out: no prog and wl btn over 1f out* **6/1**[3]
34-1 9 1 **Maverik**[19] 238 9-8-9 62 (tp) LucyKBarry(5) 9 42
(Neil Mulholland) *chsd ldrs tl wnt 2nd 6f out: led 4f out tl hdd and rdn over 2f out: sn outpcd and wknd over 1f out: collapsed after r (fatally injured)* **12/1**
00-5 10 8 **Cornelious (IRE)**[23] 154 5-9-2 64 (v) AdamBeschizza 5 28
(Clifford Lines) *chsd ldrs: rdn and unable qck over 2f out: wknd over 1f out* **14/1**
00-3 11 30 **Firestorm (GER)**[19] 233 6-9-3 65 (e) WilliamCarson 1
(Michael Attwater) *led tl 4f out: short of room and lost pl qckly 3f out: sn wl bhd: t.o* **16/1**
00-5 P **Fantasy Gladiator**[29] 47 11-9-5 67 (p) RobertWinston 3
(Michael Appleby) *rrd as stalls opened and rdr unable to remove hood: v.s.a and lost any ch: p.u sn after s* **12/1**
340- P **Power Up**[49] 8381 6-8-11 59 MartinLane 8
(Roger Ingram) *a towards rr and nvr on terms: rdn over 3f out: lost tch and eased over 2f out: p.u 1f out: burst blood vessel* **50/1**

2m 5.98s (-2.62) **Going Correction** -0.075s/f (Stan) **13 Ran SP% 124.0**
Speed ratings (Par 103): **107,104,104,102,100 97,96,95,94,87 63, ,**
CSF £32.70 CT £145.75 TOTE £4.40: £1.70, £3.40, £2.00; EX 43.20 Trifecta £230.00.
**Owner** Laurence Bellman **Bred** Lynch Bages Ltd **Trained** Upper Lambourn, Berks

**FOCUS**
A modest handicap run at a good gallop.

### 518 TOTEQUADPOT FOUR PLACES IN FOUR RACES H'CAP 5f (P)
7:00 (7:00) (Class 5) (0-75,74) 4-Y-0+ £5,175 (£1,540; £769; £384) Stalls Low

Form RPR
100- 1 **Zipedeedodah (IRE)**[42] 8495 5-9-7 74 (t) OisinMurphy 1 83
(Joseph Tuite) *pressed ldr tl rdn to ld over 1f out: r.o wl and in command 100yds out: eased towards fin* **11/1**
0-51 2 3/4 **You're Cool**[13] 330 5-8-11 69 LewisEdmunds(5) 4 74
(John Balding) *t.k.h: led tl rdn and hdd over 1f out: kpt on same pce ins fnl f* **9/2**[2]
32-1 3 1/2 **Dream Farr (IRE)**[19] 242 4-9-7 74 (t) ThomasBrown 2 78
(Ed Walker) *t.k.h: hld up in tch in midfield: effrt over 1f out: chsd ldng pair 1f out: kpt on same pce ins fnl f: eased cl home* **9/4**[1]
4-55 4 1/2 **Doctor Parkes**[9] 387 11-8-13 73 MillyNaseb(7) 7 75
(Stuart Williams) *wnt rt s: chsd ldrs: effrt over 1f out: kpt on same pce and no imp ins fnl f* **16/1**
34-1 5 1 1/4 **K'Gari Spirit**[28] 64 4-8-9 62 (t) NickyMackay 5 59
(Jeremy Gask) *dwlt and swtchd lft after s: hld up in tch in rr of main gp: effrt on inner over 1f out: kpt on same pce and no imp ins fnl f* **14/1**
51-1 6 1/2 **The Big Lad**[28] 71 5-9-7 74 (e) ShaneKelly 8 69+
(Richard Hughes) *pushed rt s: t.k.h: hld up in tch in rr of main gp: effrt over 2f out: pushed rt over 1f out: no imp and one pced ins fnl f* **5/1**[3]
40-0 7 4 **Welease Bwian (IRE)**[20] 219 8-9-0 70 AaronJones(3) 9 51
(Stuart Williams) *rrd as stalls opened ad slowly away: a rr* **12/1**
06-3 8 3/4 **Ebony N Ivory**[19] 242 4-9-3 70 (p) LukeMorris 3 48
(Archie Watson) *dwlt and bustled along leaving stalls: nt clr run and swtchd lft over 1f out: sme no imp: wl hld and eased ins fnl f* **9/2**[2]
00-0 9 1 **Sir Theodore (IRE)**[19] 242 4-8-7 67 PatrickVaughan(7) 11 42
(Richard Spencer) *sn chsng ldrs: rdn 2f out: outpcd and edgd rt over 1f out: sn btn and wknd fnl f* **33/1**

59.24s (-0.96) **Going Correction** -0.075s/f (Stan) **9 Ran SP% 115.3**
Speed ratings (Par 103): **104,102,102,101,99 98,92,90,89**
CSF £59.83 CT £153.17 TOTE £12.90: £3.50, £1.40, £1.10; EX 78.70 Trifecta £371.20.
**Owner** D M Synergy & Mark Wellbelove **Bred** Tally-Ho Stud **Trained** Lambourn, Berks

**FOCUS**
Few got involved, with the pace holding up well.

### 519 TOTEPOOL RACECOURSE CASH BACK AVAILABLE H'CAP 1m 6f (P)
7:30 (7:30) (Class 4) (0-85,84) 4-Y-0+ £7,762 (£2,310; £1,154; £577) Stalls Low

Form RPR
05-6 1 **Midtech Star (IRE)**[17] 269 5-9-9 79 (v) AdamKirby 1 86
(Ian Williams) *chsd ldrs: effrt 2f out: drvn and styd on to chal ins fnl f: led 75yds out: styd on and gng away at fin* **4/1**[2]
20-1 2 1 **Ride The Lightning**[23] 163 4-9-7 82 LukeMorris 7 87
(Archie Watson) *chsd ldr: rdn ent fnl 2f: drvn to ld 1f out: hdd 75yds out: no ex and one pced after* **7/2**[1]
/10- 3 1 1/4 **Tetradrachm**[251] 2638 4-9-7 82 OisinMurphy 8 85
(David Simcock) *t.k.h: dropped in after s: hld up in tch: effrt and swtchd rt 2f out: drvn over 1f out: hung lft ins fnl f: kpt on to go 3rd towards fin* **5/1**[3]

-303 **4** 1/2 **Luv U Whatever**[9] 389 7-10-0 **84** WilliamCarson 3 86
(Michael Attwater) *led and set stdy gallop: rdn and qcknd ent fnl 2f: drvn and hdd 1f out: no ex and one pced ins fnl f* **12/1**

13-2 **5** nse **El Campeon**[16] 280 5-9-5 **78** HectorCrouch(3) 2 80
(Simon Dow) *t.k.h: hld up in tch in midfield: effrt on inner to chse ldrs and rdn over 1f out: styd on same pce ins fnl f* **5/1**[3]

514- **6** 2 **Paris Magic**[34] 8584 4-9-6 **81** (b) JosephineGordon 4 80
(Hugo Palmer) *t.k.h: hld up in tch in last pair: effrt u.p over 1f out: kpt on ins fnl f: nvr enough pce to get on terms* **7/2**[1]

0-33 **7** 4 1/2 **Cavalieri (IRE)**[8] 399 7-8-12 **68** (tp) KevinStott 5 61
(Philip Kirby) *stdd s: hld up in tch in rr: pushed along over 3f out: no imp u.p over 1f out: n.d* **12/1**

06-0 **8** 3 1/2 **The Twisler**[29] 38 5-9-11 **81** MartinLane 6 69
(Roger Ingram) *wl in tch in midfield: swtchd rt and clsd to press ldrs 4f out: rdn and struggling to qckn whn pushed rt 2f out: wknd over 1f out* **16/1**

3m 7.53s (4.33) **Going Correction** -0.075s/f (Stan)
**WFA** 4 from 5yo+ 3lb **8** Ran SP% **119.0**
Speed ratings (Par 105): **84,83,82,82,82 81,78,76**
CSF £19.31 CT £72.47 TOTE £4.80: £1.70, £1.70, £2.20; EX 17.70 Trifecta £99.00.
**Owner** Midtech **Bred** Denis McDonnell **Trained** Portway, Worcs

**FOCUS**
They went steady early but the pace really picked up leaving the back straight.

## 520 TOTEPOOLLIVEINFO.COM FOR RACING RESULTS MAIDEN FILLIES' STKS 6f (P)
**8:00** (8:02) (Class 5) 3-Y-0+ **£5,175** (£1,540; £769; £384) **Stalls** Centre

Form RPR

**1** **Bastia** 3-8-13 0 DavidProbert 3 68+
(Martyn Meade) *dwlt: rn green in rr early: clsd on outer to chse ldrs over 2f out: pushed along to chal over 1f out: sustained chal to ld wl ins fnl f: r.o* **2/1**[2]

40-4 **2** 1/2 **Zilza (IRE)**[14] 307 3-8-13 0 (t) MartinDwyer 6 66
(Conrad Allen) *chsd ldng pair: j. path 4f out: clsd to go 2nd and pressing ldr over 2f out: rdn to ld over 1f out: sn hrd pressed: hdd and one pced wl ins fnl f* **11/4**[3]

2-25 **3** 3 **Circulate**[8] 393 3-8-13 70 JackMitchell 1 56
(Tom Clover) *chsd ldr: clsd whn nt clr run and lost 2nd over 2f out: swtchd lft over 1f out: 3rd and no imp u.p fnl f* **7/4**[1]

**4** 2 1/4 **Sarrab (IRE)** 3-8-10 0 (h[1]) NoelGarbutt(3) 4 49
(Conrad Allen) *dwlt: t.k.h: hld up in 4th: pushed along to cl 3f out: nt clr run over 2f out: hmpd over 1f out: 4th and no imp fnl f* **20/1**

3-60 **5** 12 **Wonderful Life (IRE)**[14] 314 4-10-0 67 (b[1]) AdamKirby 2 14
(Richard Spencer) *sn led: wnt clr 4f out tl hdd and rdn 2f out: hung lft over 1f out: sn lost pl: bhd fnl f* **7/1**

1m 13.75s (0.05) **Going Correction** -0.075s/f (Stan)
**WFA** 3 from 4yo 15lb **5** Ran SP% **113.6**
Speed ratings (Par 100): **96,95,91,88,72**
CSF £8.20 TOTE £3.10: £1.30, £3.10; EX 9.60 Trifecta £15.80.
**Owner** Snailwell Stud **Bred** R W Russell **Trained** Newmarket, Suffolk
■ Stewards' Enquiry : Jack Mitchell two-day ban: careless riding (Feb 16-17)

**FOCUS**
A modest maiden, but it was run at a good pace.

## 521 COLLECT ANY TOTEPOOL WINNINGS AT BETFRED SHOPS H'CAP 6f (P)
**8:30** (8:30) (Class 6) (0-60,62) 4-Y-0+ **£3,234** (£962; £481; £240) **Stalls** Centre

Form RPR

63-0 **1** **Encapsulated**[15] 293 7-8-11 **56** RhiainIngram(7) 2 61
(Roger Ingram) *taken down early and led to s: chsd ldr tl led 1/2-way: sn clr: rdn 1f out: jst hld on: all out* **8/1**

-620 **2** shd **Nasri**[8] 398 11-9-2 **54** (v) ShaneKelly 7 59
(Emma Owen) *chsd ldrs: wnt 3rd 2f out: effrt u.p over 1f out: drvn to chse clr wnr jst ins fnl f: clsd and ev ch wl ins fnl f: jst hld* **20/1**

0-11 **3** hd **Whaleweigh Station**[5] 455 6-9-6 **58** 6ex (v) GeorgeBaker 8 62
(J R Jenkins) *off the pce in midfield: effrt and wd wl over 1f out: hdwy 1f out: chsd ldrs ins fnl f: r.o strly towards fin: nt quite rch ldng pair* **7/4**[1]

66-3 **4** 1 1/4 **Camdora (IRE)**[14] 303 5-9-7 **59** (t) TimmyMurphy 5 59
(Jamie Osborne) *stdd after s: wl off the pce in last pair: effrt on inner over 1f out: hdwy 1f out: kpt on ins fnl f: nt rch ldrs* **4/1**[2]

0-16 **5** 3/4 **Multi Quest**[16] 273 5-9-3 **55** (b) FrannyNorton 4 53
(John E Long) *chsd ldng pair tl 2f out: kpt on same pce u.p fr over 1f out* **14/1**

3-60 **6** 1/2 **Emily Goldfinch**[16] 273 4-9-0 **52** JosephineGordon 3 49
(Phil McEntee) *sn led: hdd 1/2-way: sn rdn and nt matching pce of wnr: lost 2nd jst ins fnl f: wknd wl ins fnl f* **16/1**

110- **7** 2 **Suni Dancer**[37] 8542 6-8-8 **53** AledBeech(7) 9 45
(Tony Carroll) *wl off the pce in rr: clsd whn nt clr run and swtchd rt 1f out: kpt on: nvr threatened ldrs* **25/1**

322- **8** 1 1/4 **La Fortuna**[44] 8472 4-9-5 **57** LukeMorris 11 44
(Charlie Wallis) *off the pce in midfield: shkn up over 1f out: no imp and wl hld fnl f* **5/1**[3]

04-6 **9** 1 3/4 **Humour (IRE)**[14] 302 6-9-0 **55** (b) EoinWalsh(3) 1 37
(Christine Dunnett) *off the pce in midfield: effrt over 1f out: no imp: wknd ins fnl f* **5/1**[3]

1m 12.75s (-0.95) **Going Correction** -0.075s/f (Stan) **9** Ran SP% **122.0**
Speed ratings (Par 101): **103,102,102,100,99 96,96,94,92**
CSF £158.27 CT £411.97 TOTE £8.20: £2.60, £4.90, £1.40; EX 141.10 Trifecta £579.50.
**Owner** Mrs E N Nield **Bred** Juddmonte Farms Ltd **Trained** Epsom, Surrey

**FOCUS**
An ordinary sprint, but a good ride on the winner.

## 522 BOOK TICKETS AT CHELMSFORDCITYRACECOURSE.COM H'CAP 7f (P)
**9:00** (9:00) (Class 6) (0-60,68) 3-Y-0 **£3,234** (£962; £481; £240) **Stalls** Low

Form RPR

000- **1** **Toy Theatre**[101] 7571 3-9-7 **59** AdamKirby 1 68+
(Michael Appleby) *trckd ldr after 1f: rdn to chal over 2f out: led over 1f out: drifted rt 1f out: styd on and a doing enough ins fnl f* **5/1**[3]

600- **2** 2 **Delfie Lane**[63] 8174 3-9-9 **61** ShaneKelly 5 65
(Richard Hughes) *t.k.h: chsd ldr for 1f out: trckd ldng pair after: effrt and hung lft over 1f out: chsd wnr 1f out: kpt on same pce ins fnl f* **7/2**[2]

4-21 **3** 1 1/4 **In The Spotlight (IRE)**[5] 456 3-9-13 **68** 6ex LouisSteward(3) 7 69
(Henry Spiller) *v.s.a: clsd onto bk of field and t.k.h after 1f: swtchd rt and shkn up over 1f out: 3rd and styd on same pce ins fnl f* **5/6**[1]

45-6 **4** 6 **Oakley Pride (IRE)**[24] 150 3-9-0 **52** (b) LukeMorris 3 37
(Gay Kelleway) *led: jnd and rdn over 2f out: hdd over 1f out: lost 2nd 1f out: sn wknd* **20/1**

00-4 **5** 3 3/4 **Mezyan (IRE)**[5] 456 3-9-4 **56** GeorgeBaker 6 30
(John Butler) *t.k.h: hld up in tch in 4th: shkn up over 1f out: sn btn and bhd fnl f* **6/1**

1m 26.61s (-0.59) **Going Correction** -0.075s/f (Stan) **5** Ran SP% **112.5**
Speed ratings (Par 95): **100,97,96,89,85**
CSF £22.55 TOTE £6.40: £2.90, £2.20; EX 28.70 Trifecta £40.20.
**Owner** L J Vaessen **Bred** Darley **Trained** Oakham, Rutland
■ Stewards' Enquiry : Louis Steward jockey said filly ran flat
George Baker jockey said filly lost its action; vet reported filly to be stiff all round

**FOCUS**
An ordinary handicap.
T/Jkpt: £177,318.30 to a £1 stake. Pool: £443,296 - 2.50 winning units. T/Plt: £25.40 to a £1 stake. Pool: £114,060.98 - 3277.11 winning units. T/Qpdt: £6.20 to a £1 stake. Pool: £12,087.33 - 1430.81 winning units. **Steve Payne**

# [477]SOUTHWELL (L-H)
Thursday, February 2

**OFFICIAL GOING: Fibresand: standard**
Wind: Strong against Weather: Overcast

## 523 BETWAY SPRINT H'CAP 4f 214y(F)
**1:45** (1:45) (Class 6) (0-65,67) 4-Y-0+ **£2,587** (£770; £384; £192) **Stalls** Centre

Form RPR

-224 **1** **Treaty Of Rome (USA)**[9] 386 5-9-2 **60** (v) TonyHamilton 8 70
(Derek Shaw) *sn swtchd lft to trck ldrs centre: hdwy 1/2-way and sn cl up: led over 1f out: sn rdn and kpt on wl* **3/1**[2]

00-0 **2** 1 1/4 **Spiraea**[23] 152 7-9-7 **65** PaulMulrennan 7 71+
(Ivan Furtado) *swtchd markedly lft towards far side sn after s: in tch: hdwy on outer and prom 2f out: sn rdn: drvn to chse wnr ins fnl f: kpt on* **40/1**

00-4 **3** 1 1/4 **Pearl Noir**[31] 21 7-8-4 **55** (b) RPWalsh(7) 2 56
(Scott Dixon) *dwlt: sn trcking ldrs centre: cl up 1/2-way: rdn and ev ch over 1f out: drvn and kpt on same pce fnl f* **12/1**

23-0 **4** 3/4 **Jacob's Pillow**[14] 312 6-9-7 **65** DanielTudhope 6 63+
(Rebecca Bastiman) *prom centre: rdn along and sltly outpcd over 2f out: swtchd rt towards stands rail and drvn wl over 1f out: kpt on fnl f* **3/1**[2]

2-33 **5** shd **Roy's Legacy**[13] 327 8-8-6 **55** CharlieBennett(5) 12 53
(Shaun Harris) *prom centre: rdn along 2f out: sn drvn and grad wknd* **16/1**

3-01 **6** 1 1/4 **Archimedes (IRE)**[7] 416 4-9-9 **67** 6ex (tp) JosephineGordon 11 60
(David C Griffiths) *racd cl to stands rail: in tch: rdn along and sltly outpcd 2f out: kpt on fnl f* **11/4**[1]

6-45 **7** 3/4 **Charlie Lad**[13] 327 5-8-7 **51** oh1 LukeMorris 5 42
(Daniel Mark Loughnane) *chsd ldrs: rdn along and lost pl bef 1/2-way: rr and swtchd lft towards far rail 2f out: no prog* **9/1**[3]

0-03 **8** nk **Imjin River (IRE)**[9] 387 10-8-2 **51** oh6 (tp) HollieDoyle(5) 3 41
(William Stone) *slt ld centre: rdn along 2f out: hdd and drvn over 1f out: sn wknd* **10/1**

020- **9** 6 **Harpers Ruby**[48] 8409 7-8-10 **54** PaddyAspell 4 22
(Lynn Siddall) *chsd ldrs centre: rdn along over 2f out: sn drvn and wknd* **33/1**

000- **10** 5 **Emerald Bay**[48] 8408 4-8-8 **52** (p[1]) AndrewMullen 9 2
(Ronald Thompson) *n.m.r after s: racd nr stands rail and sn pushed along in rr: rdn and outpcd bef 1/2-way: sn bhd* **100/1**

1m 0.53s (0.83) **Going Correction** +0.20s/f (Slow) **10** Ran SP% **115.7**
Speed ratings (Par 101): **101,99,97,95,95 93,92,91,82,74**
CSF £116.76 CT £1299.17 TOTE £3.90: £1.40, £8.40, £3.70; EX 107.50 Trifecta £1183.50.
**Owner** John R Saville **Bred** Fred W Hertrich III & John D Fielding **Trained** Sproxton, Leics

**FOCUS**
A moderate sprint handicap with the action unfolding up the centre of the track. The third helps set the level.

## 524 BETWAY H'CAP 1m 3f 23y(F)
**2:20** (2:20) (Class 5) (0-75,75) 4-Y-0+ **£3,234** (£962; £481; £240) **Stalls** Low

Form RPR

02-2 **1** **Footlight**[26] 120 4-9-4 **74** PaulHanagan 3 84+
(Richard Fahey) *trckd ldr: led wl over 2f out: rdn over 1f out: drvn and edgd lft fnl f: kpt on wl* **9/2**[3]

55-6 **2** 1 **Storm King**[29] 42 8-9-4 **72** JosephineGordon 6 79
(David C Griffiths) *sn led: pushed along and hdd wl over 2f out: chsd wnr and sn rdn: drvn and kpt on wl fnl f* **10/3**[2]

00-6 **3** 3 3/4 **The Lock Master (IRE)**[23] 154 10-9-2 **70** (p) AndrewMullen 4 71
(Michael Appleby) *trckd ldrs: pushed along 3f out: rdn to chse ldng pair 2f out: drvn over 1f out: kpt on same pce* **8/1**

-413 **4** 1/2 **Samphire Coast**[9] 390 4-8-2 **61** oh1 (v) NoelGarbutt(3) 5 62
(Derek Shaw) *hld up in tch: racd wd bk st: hdwy over 3f out: rdn to chse ldng pair wl over 1f out: sn drvn and kpt on one pce* **2/1**[1]

60-0 **5** 12 **Ansaab**[12] 359 9-9-7 **75** (tp) BenCurtis 2 56
(Marjorie Fife) *hld up in tch: hdwy over 3f out: rdn to chse ldrs on outer over 2f out: drvn and wknd wl over 1f out* **9/2**[3]

0-3 **6** 33 **Rightway (IRE)**[27] 90 6-9-0 **68** LukeMorris 1
(Tony Carroll) *t.k.h: chsd ldrs: rdn along 5f out: sn lost pl and bhd fnl 3f* **11/1**

2m 25.61s (-2.39) **Going Correction** -0.075s/f (Stan)
**WFA** 4 from 6yo+ 1lb **6** Ran SP% **112.2**
Speed ratings (Par 103): **105,104,101,101,92 68**
CSF £19.68 TOTE £4.00: £1.80, £1.90; EX 18.90 Trifecta £78.10.
**Owner** Mrs P B E P Farr **Bred** Worksop Manor Stud **Trained** Musley Bank, N Yorks

**FOCUS**
A modest handicap with little depth, rated around the runner-up.

## 525 BETWAY BEST ODDS GUARANTEED PLUS H'CAP 1m 4f 14y(F)
**2:55** (2:55) (Class 6) (0-65,65) 4-Y-0+ **£2,587** (£770; £384; £192) **Stalls** Low

Form RPR

1-21 **1** **My Renaissance**[7] 414 7-9-1 **63** 6ex JaneElliott(7) 3 71
(Sam England) *trckd ldrs: smooth hdwy over 3f out: led wl over 2f out: rdn over 1f out: kpt on wl towards fin* **15/8**[1]

22-6 **2** nk **Bridey's Lettuce (IRE)**[28] 70 5-9-10 **65** TonyHamilton 2 72
(Ivan Furtado) *trckd ldr: hdwy over 4f out and sn cl up: disp ld 3f out: sn rdn: chsd wnr and drvn over 1f out: kpt on wl u.p towards fin* **13/2**[3]

4-25 **3** 19 **What Usain**[7] 419 5-9-5 **63** (h) AlistairRawlinson(3) 7 40
(Michael Appleby) *led: pushed along 4f out: rdn over 3f out: sn jnd and hdd wl over 2f out: drvn and kpt on one pce fnl 2f* **11/4**[2]

03-3 **4** *8* **Sir Jack**[16] 278 4-8-9 **53**...........................(p[1]) AndrewMullen 5 17
(Tony Carroll) *in tch: hdwy over 4f out: rdn along to chse ldng trio over 3f out: drvn along wl over 2f out and sn outpcd* **7/1**

064- **5** *3 ¾* **Mcvicar**[153] 6103 8-9-3 **58**...........................(p) DanielTudhope 4 16
(John Davies) *in tch: pushed along over 4f out: rdn over 3f out: sn outpcd and bhd* **10/1**

556- **6** *2 ¾* **Shulammite Man (IRE)**[204] 4255 4-8-6 **50**........................... NeilFarley 6 3
(Alan Swinbank) *a rr* **16/1**

53-0 **7** *4 ½* **Jessica Jo (IRE)**[15] 282 4-8-5 **49**...........................(b) JoeFanning 1
(Mark Johnston) *trckd ldr on inner: pushed along over 4f out: sn rdn: lost pl and bhd fr over 3f out* **10/1**

2m 39.12s (-1.88) **Going Correction** -0.075s/f (Stan)
**WFA** 4 from 5yo+ 2lb **7** Ran SP% **111.3**
Speed ratings (Par 101): **103,102,90,84,82 80,77**
CSF £13.78 TOTE £2.30: £1.50, £2.50; EX 12.80 Trifecta £38.70.
**Owner** Panther Racing Ltd **Bred** Aston House Stud **Trained** Guiseley, West Yorkshire

**FOCUS**
An ordinary handicap and not many got into it. The pace was sound and they finished spread out all over Nottinghamshire. It's hard to believe the form is all that it seems.

## 526 BETWAY MIDDLE DISTANCE H'CAP 1m 4f 14y(F)
**3:30** (3:30) (Class 4) (0-80,81) 4-Y-0+ **£5,175** (£1,540; £769; £384) **Stalls** Low

Form RPR

0-45 **1** **Faithful Creek (IRE)**[23] 163 5-9-5 **81**...........................(p) AlistairRawlinson(3) 2 88
(Michael Appleby) *trckd ldrs on outer: cl up 4f out: chal wl over 2f out: rdn 2f out and sn led: jnd and drvn ins fnl f: hld on wl towards fin* **6/4**[1]

5/4- **2** *hd* **Serenity Now (IRE)**[44] 8476 9-8-5 **71**........................... BenRobinson(7) 4 77
(Brian Ellison) *hld up in rr: racd wd bk st and pushed along over 4f out: hdwy and cl up on outer whn rdn and edgd lft over 2f out: hdwy to chal over 1f out: ev ch ins fnl f: kpt on* **9/4**[2]

00-5 **3** *¾* **Esteaming**[7] 422 7-9-7 **80**...........................(p) ConnorBeasley 3 84
(Keith Dalgleish) *trckd ldng pair: hdwy and cl up over 4f out: chal 3f out: rdn 2f out and ev ch tl drvn and kpt on same pce ins fnl f* **9/2**[3]

24-0 **4** *5* **Dizzey Heights (IRE)**[24] 144 5-8-8 **70**........................... ShelleyBirkett(3) 5 66
(Stuart Kittow) *sn trcking ldr: cl up 4f out: rdn along to dispute ld 3f out: sn slt advantage: hdd wl over 1f out: sn drvn and grad wknd* **14/1**

3-55 **5** *¾* **Obboorr**[10] 380 8-8-13 **72**........................... AndrewMullen 1 67
(James Given) *led: jnd 4f out: rdn along over 3f out: hdd wl over 2f out: sn drvn and wknd over 1f out* **6/1**

2m 43.0s (2.00) **Going Correction** -0.075s/f (Stan) **5** Ran SP% **109.9**
Speed ratings (Par 105): **90,89,89,86,85**
CSF £5.11 TOTE £2.20: £1.10, £1.60; EX 5.10 Trifecta £12.80.
**Owner** C L Bacon **Bred** Tally-Ho Stud **Trained** Oakham, Rutland

**FOCUS**
A fair handicap, but they went no pace and the time was 3.88sec slower than the preceding race. There were still four in a line turning in with only the runner-up detached. The winner is rated close to recent form.

## 527 SUNBETS.CO.UK H'CAP 1m 13y(F)
**4:05** (4:07) (Class 5) (0-70,71) 4-Y-0+ **£3,234** (£962; £481; £240) **Stalls** Low

Form RPR

01-1 **1** **Shearian**[32] 7 7-8-10 **64**........................... PhilDennis(5) 7 77+
(Declan Carroll) *trckd ldrs: smooth hdwy over 3f out: cl up on bit 2f out: led 1 1/2f out: pushed clr ent fnl f: eased towards fin: readily* **5/2**[1]

3-51 **2** *2* **Alpha Tauri (USA)**[7] 419 11-9-1 **71** 6ex........................... BenRobinson(7) 1 76
(Charles Smith) *slt ld on inner: rdn along 3f out: sn hdd narrowly: cl up and drvn wl over 1f out: kpt on fnl f: no ch w wnr* **4/1**[2]

22-6 **3** *3 ½* **Playtothewhistle**[30] 32 6-9-4 **70**...........................(v) AlistairRawlinson(3) 3 67
(Michael Appleby) *cl up: slt ld wl over 2f out and sn rdn: drvn and hdd 1 1/2f out: kpt on same pce* **5/2**[1]

0-43 **4** *3 ¼* **Stun Gun**[7] 419 7-9-4 **67**...........................(p) TonyHamilton 8 57
(Derek Shaw) *prom on outer: cl up over 3f out: rdn along wl over 2f out: sn drvn and one pce* **9/2**[3]

3-00 **5** *1* **Palindrome (USA)**[21] 195 4-8-12 **61**...........................(p) AndrewMullen 6 49
(Ronald Thompson) *cl up: rdn along 3f out: drvn over 2f out: sn wknd* **25/1**

1-00 **6** *11* **Raashdy (IRE)**[12] 351 4-8-11 **65**........................... CharlieBennett(5) 2 27
(Peter Hiatt) *chsd ldrs: rdn along 1/2-way: sn outpcd and bhd* **16/1**

050- **7** *2* **Cabal**[142] 6453 10-9-6 **69**...........................(v) SamJames 4 27
(Geoffrey Harker) *dwlt: a towards rr* **50/1**

00-0 **8** *20* **Speculator**[22] 169 5-9-1 **64**...........................(p) DannyBrock 5
(John Butler) *a rr: bhd fr over 2f out* **25/1**

1m 42.38s (-1.32) **Going Correction** -0.075s/f (Stan) **8** Ran SP% **110.9**
Speed ratings (Par 103): **103,101,97,94,93 82,80,60**
CSF £11.85 CT £24.85 TOTE £3.10: £1.80, £1.80, £1.10; EX 10.80 Trifecta £26.90.
**Owner** Mrs Sarah Bryan **Bred** Minehart Developments Ltd **Trained** Malton, N Yorks

**FOCUS**
A modest handicap, though featuring a few course specialists and there was a four-way battle for the lead. A clear pb from the winner.

## 528 SUNBETS.CO.UK DOWNLOAD THE APP APPRENTICE H'CAP 7f 14y(F)
**4:35** (4:35) (Class 5) (0-75,76) 4-Y-0+ **£3,234** (£962; £481; £240) **Stalls** Low

Form RPR

33-3 **1** **Vroom (IRE)**[23] 152 4-9-1 **70**...........................(p) RhiainIngram(5) 2 78
(Gay Kelleway) *led 1f: cl up on inner: slt ld over 2f out and sn rdn: drvn ent fnl f: kpt on wl* **8/1**

200- **2** *¾* **Aqua Ardens (GER)**[84] 7886 9-9-7 **71**...........................(tp) RobHornby 3 77
(George Baker) *chsd ldrs early: sn pushed along: lost pl and bhd: hdwy on outer 2f out: sn rdn and edgd lft over 1f out: drvn: carried hd awkwardly and kpt on fnl f* **9/2**[3]

-416 **3** *2 ¾* **Call Out Loud**[14] 312 5-9-3 **67**...........................(vt) AlistairRawlinson 6 66
(Michael Appleby) *cl up: slt ld after 1f: pushed along and hdd over 2f out: sn rdn: drvn and hld whn swtchd lft ent fnl f: kpt on same pce* **5/1**

-264 **4** *3* **Boots And Spurs**[23] 156 8-9-5 **76**...........................(vt) BenRobinson(7) 5 66
(Scott Dixon) *chsd ldrs: sn pushed along and lost pl after 2f: bhd and swtchd wd home turn: hdwy wl over 1f out: drvn and kpt on fnl f* **3/1**[1]

22-3 **5** *2* **Harwoods Star (IRE)**[31] 25 7-9-3 **74**...........................(be) JoshuaBryan(7) 8 59
(John Butler) *dwlt: sn prom on wd outside: cl 1/2-way: rdn along 3f out: drvn 2f out: sn wknd* **7/2**[2]

00-0 **6** *1 ¼* **Falcao (IRE)**[26] 116 5-8-11 **68**........................... DarraghKeenan(7) 1 50
(John Butler) *a towards rr* **25/1**

000- **7** *1* **Monsieur Jimmy**[69] 8094 5-8-9 **62**........................... PhilDennis(3) 9 41
(Declan Carroll) *cl up towards outer: rdn along 3f out: wknd over 2f out* **8/1**

-640 **8** *3 ¼* **Spowarticus**[9] 386 8-8-10 **60** oh6...........................(v) TimClark 7 30
(Scott Dixon) *prom towards outer: cl up 1/2-way: rdn along 3f out: drvn over 2f out: sn wknd* **20/1**

1m 29.87s (-0.43) **Going Correction** -0.075s/f (Stan) **8** Ran SP% **112.9**
Speed ratings (Par 103): **99,98,95,91,89 87,86,83**
CSF £42.62 CT £198.16 TOTE £5.60: £1.60, £1.90, £2.00; EX 37.50 Trifecta £220.20.
**Owner** Buy,Clarke,Whatley & Panther Racing **Bred** Paul & T J Monaghan **Trained** Exning, Suffolk

**FOCUS**
A modest apprentice handicap and three of these did their chances little good by racing very wide into the first bend. The winner is rated to form.
T/Plt: £31.50 to a £1 stake. Pool: £64,275.02 - 1,489.25 winning units T/Qpdt: £6.10 to a £1 stake. Pool: £5,278.31 - 637.49 winning units **Joe Rowntree**

529 - 536a (Foreign Racing) - See Raceform Interactive

# [470]MEYDAN (L-H)
Thursday, February 2

**OFFICIAL GOING: Dirt: fast; turf: good**

## 537a EGA BILLETS TROPHY (H'CAP) (DIRT) 1m 1f 110y(D)
**2:30** (2:30) (80-94,94) 3-Y-0+

**£29,268** (£9,756; £4,878; £2,439; £1,463; £975)

RPR

**1** **Grand Argentier (FR)**[14] 319 5-9-6 **94**...........................(v) SamHitchcott 1 102
(Doug Watson, UAE) *wl away: sn led: rdn clr 2 1/2f out: r.o wl* **5/1**[3]

**2** *2 ½* **Galvanize (USA)**[144] 6372 4-8-9 **85**........................... DaneO'Neill 8 87+
(Doug Watson, UAE) *mid-div: r.o fnl 2 1/2f: nrst fin* **14/1**

**3** *¾* **Vivernus (USA)**[19] 248 4-8-6 **82**........................... FernandoJara 7 82
(M Al Mheiri, UAE) *trckd ldr: rdn 4f out: ev ch 2 1/2f out: one pce fnl 2f* **11/2**

**4** *2 ¼* **Groor**[5] 474 5-9-1 **89**........................... AdriedeVries 6 86
(Ali Jan, Qatar) *a mid-div* **16/1**

**5** *shd* **Ormindo (USA)**[19] 247 7-8-9 **84**...........................(tp) PaoloSirigu 9 80+
(A bin Harmash, UAE) *mid-div: r.o same pce fnl 2 1/2f* **6/1**

**6** *3 ½* **Winslow (USA)**[35] 8578 5-9-3 **91**........................... PatDobbs 3 80
(Doug Watson, UAE) *nvr nr to chal* **3/1**[2]

**7** *2 ¼* **Pit Stop (IRE)**[14] 316 6-8-8 **83**........................... RoystonFfrench 5 67
(S bin Ghadayer, UAE) *trckd ldr: rdn 4f out: wknd fnl 3f* **16/1**

**8** *29* **Brabbham (USA)**[13] 343 7-9-4 **92**...........................(t) ColmO'Donoghue 2 17
(A bin Harmash, UAE) *nvr bttr than mid-div* **5/2**[1]

**9** *40* **Night Run (FR)**[14] 322 5-9-0 **94**........................... AdamMcLean(6) 4
(Y Al Blooshi, UAE) *a in rr* **100/1**

1m 58.15s (-0.65) **Going Correction** +0.15s/f (Slow) **9** Ran SP% **119.3**
Speed ratings: **108,106,105,103,103 100,98,75,43**
CSF: 74.01; TRICAST: 404.22.
**Owner** EERC (Mngr: Mrs Rebecca Byrne) **Bred** Claude Lambert **Trained** United Arab Emirates

**FOCUS**
TRAKUS (metres travelled compared to winner): 2nd +17, 3rd +8, 4th +8, 5th +22, 6th +8, 7th +4, 8th +10, 9th +16. The winner was allowed an uncontested lead and covered less ground than any of his rivals through the following fractions: 26.14 (400m from standing start), 23.15 (800m), 24.01 (1200m), 25.25 (1600m), 19.6 (line). The placed horses have been rated close to form, and the winner back to his best.

## 538a EGA POTLINES TROPHY (H'CAP) (TURF) 1m
**3:05** (3:05) (100-113,108) 3-Y-0+

**£65,853** (£21,951; £10,975; £5,487; £3,292; £2,195)

RPR

**1** **Cymric (USA)**[188] 4822 4-9-5 **107**........................... WilliamBuick 1 109
(Charlie Appleby) *trckd ldr: led 1 1/2f out: r.o wl* **15/8**[1]

**2** *½* **Elite Excalibur (AUS)**[7] 429 4-9-6 **108**...........................(p) BernardFayd'Herbe 2 109+
(S Burridge, Singapore) *trckd ldng pair: ev ch 2 1/2f out: r.o fnl 1 1/2f* **13/2**

**3** *1* **American Hope (USA)**[28] 87 6-9-5 **107**........................... AdriedeVries 8 106
(Saeed bin Suroor) *sn led: hdd 1 1/2f out: lost 2nd fnl 110yds* **6/1**[3]

**4** *1* **Arcanada (IRE)**[28] 87 4-9-4 **106**........................... RichardKingscote 4 102+
(Tom Dascombe) *mid-div: r.o fnl 2f: nrst fin* **11/1**

**5** *1 ¼* **Limario (GER)**[21] 205 7-9-0 **102**...........................(t) PatDobbs 5 96+
(Doug Watson, UAE) *nvr bttr than mid-div* **40/1**

**6** *1 ½* **Fanciful Angel (IRE)**[21] 205 5-9-6 **108**........................... DanielMuscutt 6 98+
(Marco Botti) *slowly away: nvr nr to chal* **2/1**[2]

**7** *1 ½* **Muwaary (AUS)**[7] 433 4-9-0 **102**........................... JimCrowley 7 89+
(M F De Kock, South Africa) *a in rr* **66/1**

**8** *½* **Dark Emerald (IRE)**[14] 320 7-9-6 **108**...........................(vt) RichardMullen 3 93+
(Brendan Powell) *s.i.s: trckd ldng pair: one pce fnl 2f* **10/1**

1m 37.49s (-0.01) **Going Correction** +0.25s/f (Good) **8** Ran SP% **117.1**
Speed ratings: **110,109,108,107,106 104,103,102**
CSF: 15.29, TRICAST: 62.67.
**Owner** Godolphin **Bred** Jamm Ltd **Trained** Newmarket, Suffolk

**FOCUS**
TRAKUS (metres travelled compared to winner): 2nd +3, 3rd -3, 4th +2, 5th -2, 6th +1, 7th -4, 8th -2. The third-placed finisher set a fairly even pace - 25.45 (from standing start), 23.69, 24.27 - before the winner finished in 23.93. The runner-up has been rated to his best, with the winner and third just off their peaks.

## 539a AL SHINDAGHA SPRINT SPONSORED BY EMIRATES GLOBAL ALUMINIUM (GROUP 3) (DIRT) 6f (D)
**3:40** (3:40) 3-Y-0+

**£97,560** (£32,520; £16,260; £8,130; £4,878; £3,252)

RPR

**1** **Cool Cowboy (USA)**[28] 85 6-9-0 110........................... PatDobbs 5 115
(Doug Watson, UAE) *mid-div: smooth prog 2 1/2f out: rdn to ld 110yds out: r.o wl* **4/1**[2]

**2** *nk* **Muarrab**[21] 206 8-9-0 112........................... JimCrowley 4 114
(M Al Mheiri, UAE) *trckd ldrs: smooth prog to ld 2 1/2f out: hdd fnl 110yds* **4/11**[1]

**3** *4 ¾* **Wild Dude (USA)**[21] 206 7-9-0 112...........................(bt) PatSmullen 2 99
(M Halford, Ire) *a in mid-div* **8/1**[3]

**4** *1* **Stunned**[7] 432 6-9-0 100...........................(v) SamHitchcott 6 96
(Doug Watson, UAE) *nvr nr to chal: r.o same pce fnl 2f* **50/1**

**5** *5 ¼* **Shaishee (USA)**[14] 321 7-9-0 102...........................(v) DaneO'Neill 3 79
(M Al Mheiri, UAE) *s.i.s: rdn to trck ldrs tl wknd fnl 2f* **33/1**



The Form Book Flat, Raceform Ltd, Newbury, RG14 5SJ

6 19 1/2 **Moviesta (USA)**[21] 206 7-9-0 107 (b) WJLee 1 16
(Edward Lynam, Ire) *sn led: hdd 2 1/2f out: sn btn* **25/1**

1m 11.49s (-0.11) **Going Correction** +0.15s/f (Slow) 6 Ran SP% **113.2**
Speed ratings: **106,105,99,97,90 64**
CSF: 5.95.
**Owner** Zaur Sekrekov **Bred** Columbiana Farm **Trained** United Arab Emirates

**FOCUS**
TRAKUS (metres travelled compared to winner): 2nd +3, 3rd -5, 4th +5, 5th -2, 6th -5. It rained ahead of this race. The pace was ordinary by dirt standards: 24.21 (400m), 23.43 (800m), before the winner finished in 23.76. A pb from the winner, with the second, third and fourth in line with their more recent efforts.

## 540a EGA CASTHOUSE TROPHY (H'CAP) (TURF) 2m
**4:15** (4:15) (95-108,108) 3-Y-O+

**£78,048** (£26,016; £13,008; £6,504; £3,902; £2,601)

RPR

1 **Zamaam**[5] 474 7-8-9 **98** (t) JimCrowley 1 101
(E Charpy, UAE) *settled in rr: rdn 3f out: r.o wl to ld fnl f* **9/1**

2 1 1/4 **Los Barbados (IRE)**[14] 319 5-8-8 **97** (b) AdriedeVries 6 99
(Fawzi Abdulla Nass, Bahrain) *trckd ldr: led main gp: smooth prog to ld 5f out: rdn clr 2 1/2f out: hdd fnl f* **16/1**

3 1 1/2 **Red Galileo**[21] 202 6-9-1 **103** ChristopheSoumillon 8 104
(Saeed bin Suroor) *mid-div: rdn 3f out: r.o fnl 2f: nrst fin* **2/1**[1]

4 1 1/4 **Carbon Dating (IRE)**[21] 202 5-9-0 **102** TadhgO'Shea 7 102
(S Seemar, UAE) *settled in rr: r.o fnl 3f: hmpd 2f out: nrst fin* **10/3**[2]

5 8 1/2 **Rio Tigre (IRE)**[14] 322 6-8-13 **101** MickaelBarzalona 5 91
(S bin Ghadayer, UAE) *nvr nr to chal* **10/1**

6 1 **Warrior Of Light (IRE)**[21] 202 6-8-10 **99** (h) RichardMullen 3 87
(Brendan Powell) *nvr bttr than mid-div* **12/1**

7 4 1/4 **Blue Rambler**[21] 202 7-8-13 **101** GeorgeDowning 9 85
(Ian Williams) *nvr bttr than mid-div* **16/1**

8 7 1/2 **Curbyourenthusiasm (IRE)**[21] 202 6-9-6 **108** JamieSpencer 4 84
(David Simcock) *slowly away: a in rr* **7/2**[3]

9 13 1/2 **Beach Bar (IRE)**[14] 319 6-8-6 **95** (h) SamHitchcott 2 55
(Brendan Powell) *sn led: clr 11f out: hdd 5f out: sn btn* **66/1**

3m 23.95s (-0.55) **Going Correction** +0.25s/f (Good) 9 Ran SP% **118.7**
Speed ratings: **111,110,109,109,104 104,102,98,91**
CSF: 143.49, TRICAST 403.95.
**Owner** Hamdan Al Maktoum **Bred** Shadwell Estate Co Ltd **Trained** United Arab Emirates

**FOCUS**
TRAKUS (metres travelled compared to winner): 2nd -6, 3rd -1, 4th +2, 5th +4, 6th -7, 7th 0, 8th -2, 9th -7. The seemingly non-staying Beach Bar gradually opened up a clear lead whilst setting a modest pace. It's been rated around the balance of the first four.

## 541a AL MAKTOUM CHALLENGE R2 SPONSORED BY EMIRATES GLOBAL ALUMINIUM (GROUP 2) (DIRT) 1m 1f 110y(D)
**4:50** (4:50) 3-Y-O+

**£121,951** (£40,650; £20,325; £10,162; £6,097; £4,065)

RPR

1 **Furia Cruzada (CHI)**[102] 7568 5-8-9 108 AntonioFresu 1 107
(E Charpy, UAE) *mid-div: rdn to ld 1 1/2f out: jst hld on* **18/1**

2 nse **Second Summer (USA)**[221] 3703 5-9-0 110 (t) PatDobbs 3 112+
(Doug Watson, UAE) *settled in rr: smooth prog 3f out: r.o wl fnl 1 1/2f: jst failed* **13/2**

3 5 **Power Blade (KOR)**[21] 204 4-8-13 100 (e) PatCosgrave 6 102
(Kim Young Kwan, Korea) *trckd ldng pair: rdn 6f out: wknd fnl 1 1/2f* **14/1**

4 nk **Le Bernardin (USA)**[28] 85 8-9-0 113 (t) TadhgO'Shea 9 101
(A R Al Rayhi, UAE) *mid-div: chsd ldrs 2f out: r.o same pce fnl 1 1/2f* **11/4**[1]

5 1/2 **Gold City (IRE)**[28] 85 8-9-0 106 (bt) RichardMullen 4 100
(S Seemar, UAE) *s.i.s: nvr nr to chal but r.o fnl 2f* **14/1**

6 4 3/4 **Fitzgerald (USA)**[28] 85 5-9-0 108 (t) ColmO'Donoghue 2 90
(A bin Harmash, UAE) *trckd ldrs: led 3f out: hdd 1 1/2f out: one pce fnl f* **11/2**[3]

7 10 3/4 **Lindo Amor (ARG)**[28] 85 4-9-0 108 ChristopheSoumillon 7 68
(M F De Kock, South Africa) *mid-div: chsd ldrs 3 1/2f out: wknd fnl 2 1/2f* **3/1**[2]

8 26 **Long River (USA)**[28] 85 7-9-0 109 (b) MickaelBarzalona 5 15
(S bin Ghadayer, UAE) *sn led: hdd 3f out: sn btn* **11/2**[3]

9 1 **Storm Belt (USA)**[28] 83 8-9-0 110 SamHitchcott 8 13
(Doug Watson, UAE) *trckd ldng pair: wknd fnl 4f* **20/1**

1m 58.85s (0.05) **Going Correction** +0.15s/f (Slow) 9 Ran SP% **119.1**
Speed ratings: **105,104,100,100,100 96,87,67,66**
CSF: 133.77.
**Owner** F Fantini **Bred** Haras Dadinco **Trained** United Arab Emirates

**FOCUS**
TRAKUS (metres travelled compared to winner): 2nd 0, 3rd +17, 4th +18, 5th +11, 6th +8, 7th +21, 8th +5, 9th +32. A messy race - they didn't go that quick (25.74, 23.9, 24.55, 25.74, 18.92) by dirt standards or compared to the earlier non-carnival handicap, and the final time 0.70sec slower than that race. The winner has been rated back to form, with the second and third as running personal bests.

## 542a EGA JEBEL ALI TROPHY (H'CAP) (TURF) 1m 2f
**5:25** (5:25) (100-110,110) 3-Y-O+

**£85,365** (£28,455; £14,227; £7,113; £4,268; £2,845)

RPR

1 **Sanshaawes (SAF)**[21] 208 7-9-5 **109** ChristopheSoumillon 3 113
(M F De Kock, South Africa) *mid-div: smooth prog 3f out: rdn to ld fnl 110yds* **9/4**[1]

2 1 1/4 **Dylan Mouth (IRE)**[109] 7402 6-9-6 **110** AndreaAtzeni 4 112+
(Marco Botti) *s.i.s: settled in rr: r.o wl fnl 2f: nrst fin* **4/1**[2]

3 shd **Belgian Bill**[21] 205 9-8-9 **100** PatCosgrave 5 100
(George Baker) *trckd ldr: led 2f out: hdd fnl 110yds* **4/1**[2]

4 5 1/4 **Master The World (IRE)**[21] 208 6-9-4 **108** (p) PatDobbs 7 99
(David Elsworth) *s.i.s: nvr nr to chal: r.o fnl 2f* **11/2**[3]

5 1 1/2 **Oasis Fantasy (IRE)**[14] 322 6-8-9 **100** JamieSpencer 6 87
(David Simcock) *a mid-div* **12/1**

6 shd **Dormello (IRE)**[28] 86 9-9-5 **109** ChrisHayes 9 97
(D Selvaratnam, UAE) *s.i.s: nvr nr to chal* **28/1**

7 3 1/2 **Saltarin Dubai (ARG)**[13] 345 4-9-4 **108** (t) BernardFayd'Herbe 8 89
(M F De Kock, South Africa) *trckd ldr: rdn 3 1/2f out: sn btn* **16/1**

8 4 3/4 **Khusoosy (USA)**[7] 428 5-9-2 **106** (t) JimCrowley 2 77
(A R Al Rayhi, UAE) *nvr bttr than mid-div* **14/1**

9 9 1/4 **Epsom Icon**[124] 6949 4-9-0 **105** PatSmullen 10 58
(Mick Channon) *nvr bttr than mid-div* **20/1**

10 1 1/2 **Munaaser**[7] 432 6-9-1 **105** DaneO'Neill 1 55
(A R Al Rayhi, UAE) *sn led: hdd 2f out: sn btn* **20/1**

2m 3.17s (0.47) **Going Correction** +0.325s/f (Good) 10 Ran SP% **119.4**
Speed ratings: **111,110,109,105,104 104,101,97,90,89**
CSF: 11.04, TRICAST: 34.65.
**Owner** Sh Ahmed bin Mohd bin Khalifa Al Maktoum **Bred** Oldlands Stud **Trained** South Africa

**FOCUS**
TRAKUS (metres travelled compared to winner): 2nd +6, 3rd +2, 4th +6, 5th +6, 6th +1, 7th +6, 8th +1, 9th +6, 10th 0. It was raining quite heavily before and during this race. The pace slowed a bit in the mid-section but it was a fair enough-run race: 25.49, 23.4, 25.05, 24.79, before the winner finished in 24.26. The winner has been rated back to his best.

## 543a EGA AL TAWEELAH TROPHY (H'CAP) (TURF) 5f (T)
**6:00** (6:00) (95-109,109) 3-Y-O+

**£78,048** (£26,016; £13,008; £6,504; £3,902; £2,601)

RPR

1 **Speed Hawk (USA)**[21] 207 6-8-13 **102** (t) ChrisHayes 8 103
(D Selvaratnam, UAE) *settled in rr: rdn 3f out: r.o wl fnl 2f: led on line* **20/1**

2 nse **Medicean Man**[14] 318 11-9-1 **109** (tp) DavidParkes(5) 1 110
(Jeremy Gask) *trckd ldrs: led 2f out: r.o wl: hdd on line* **8/1**

3 nk **Fityaan**[7] 433 9-9-4 **107** (v) DaneO'Neill 4 106
(M Al Mheiri, UAE) *settled in rr: r.o wl fnl 2f: jst failed* **20/1**

4 1/2 **Sole Power**[21] 207 10-9-4 **107** PatSmullen 3 105
(Edward Lynam, Ire) *settled in rr: r.o wl fnl 2f: nrst fin* **7/1**[3]

5 hd **Caspian Prince (IRE)**[28] 84 8-9-5 **108** (t) TomEaves 9 105
(Roger Fell) *sn led: hdd 2f out: one pce fnl 1 1/2f* **7/1**[3]

6 nk **Line Of Reason (IRE)**[14] 318 7-8-13 **102** RichardMullen 12 99
(Paul Midgley) *nvr nr to chal but r.o fnl 1 1/2f* **9/1**

7 hd **Taexali (IRE)**[28] 84 4-8-5 **95** SamHitchcott 14 84
(S Seemar, UAE) *mid-div: r.o fnl 1 1/2f: nrst fin* **40/1**

8 1 3/4 **Magnus Maximus**[152] 6112 6-9-3 **106** MartinHarley 13 95
(Robyn Brisland) *chsd ldrs tl outpcd fnl 1 1/2f* **11/1**

9 1 **Wonder Of Qatar (IRE)**[14] 318 5-8-6 **95** ow1 AntonioFresu 6 81
(R Bouresly, Kuwait) *chsd ldrs tl outpcd fnl 2f* **80/1**

10 3/4 **Moonraker**[14] 318 5-8-5 **95** MarcMonaghan 5 77
(Mick Channon) *nvr nr to chal* **33/1**

11 hd **Sir Maximilian (IRE)**[14] 318 8-9-1 **104** (p) PatDobbs 7 86
(Ian Williams) *nvr nr to chal* **5/1**[1]

12 1/2 **Polybius**[21] 207 6-8-13 **102** JamieSpencer 10 82
(David Simcock) *nvr nr to chal* **11/2**[2]

13 shd **Maljaa**[14] 318 5-9-0 **103** (b) JimCrowley 11 83
(M Al Mheiri, UAE) *nvr bttr than mid-div* **7/1**[3]

14 8 1/4 **Harry Hurricane**[14] 318 5-8-9 **99** (b) PatCosgrave 2 48
(George Baker) *trckd ldrs tl outpcd fnl 2f* **9/1**

58.41s (1.31) **Going Correction** +0.55s/f (Yiel) 14 Ran SP% **125.1**
Speed ratings: **111,110,110,109,109 108,108,105,104,102 102,101,101,88**
CSF 171.72, TC 3356.89; Placepot: 153.70; Quadpot: 34.00.
**Owner** Khalifa Dasmal **Bred** Santa Rosa Partners **Trained** United Arab Emirates

**FOCUS**
TRAKUS (metres travelled compared to winner): 2nd +1, 3rd +1, 4th +1, 5th +1, 6th +1, 7th +2, 8th 0, 9th +1, 10th +1, 11th 0, 12th +2, 13th 0, 14th +2. The rain continued, and the pace was sensible for a sprint, with not many making up significant ground. The first six have all been rated roughly in line with their recent form.

# 502 KEMPTON (A.W) (R-H)
Friday, February 3

**OFFICIAL GOING: Polytrack: standard**
Wind: Very strong, across (away from stands) Weather: Raining

## 544 RASHER FRITH MEMORIAL H'CAP 7f (P)
**5:45** (5:46) (Class 7) (0-50,50) 4-Y-O+ **£1,940** (£577; £288; £144) **Stalls** Low

Form RPR

0-04 1 **Welsh Inlet (IRE)**[9] 398 9-8-9 **45** JaneElliott(7) 1 57
(John Bridger) *trckd ldrs: prog to ld jst over 2f out: rdn and pressed over 1f out: kpt on wl and gng away at fin* **8/1**

0-24 2 1 3/4 **Prince Of Time**[15] 309 5-8-10 **46** (t[1]) CallumRodriguez(7) 5 53
(Richard Ford) *s.s: last early and stl wl in rr 3f out: gd prog and weaved through over 2f out: chsd wnr over 1f out and cl enough: hung lft and no ex last 150yds* **5/1**[1]

00-6 3 5 **West Leake (IRE)**[16] 282 11-9-5 **48** LiamKeniry 3 42
(Paul Burgoyne) *hld up in rr: prog on inner fr 3f out: disp 2nd briefly over 1f out: sn outpcd by ldng pair* **7/1**[3]

0-05 4 1 1/2 **Chandrayaan**[17] 274 10-9-2 **45** (v) FrannyNorton 8 35
(John E Long) *urged along early then t.k.h: wl in rr: hanging whn rdn over 2f out: styd on fr over 1f out: nrst fin* **20/1**

63-6 5 nk **Altaira**[17] 274 6-9-7 **50** WilliamCarson 2 39
(Tony Carroll) *trckd ldrs: rdn and little rspnse jst over 2f out: one pce after* **8/1**

66-2 6 nse **Lutine Charlie (IRE)**[8] 425 10-8-11 **45** (p) HollieDoyle(5) 7 34
(Emma Owen) *w ldr: stl upsides over 2f out: fnd little and sn btn* **13/2**[2]

0-4 7 2 **Captain Kendall (IRE)**[23] 167 8-9-5 **48** (p) SteveDrowne 13 31
(Harry Chisman) *trckd ldng pair: rdn over 2f out: steadily wknd over 1f out* **25/1**

0/00 8 3/4 **Catalyze**[7] 438 9-9-3 **46** (t) DannyBrock 6 27
(Paddy Butler) *mde most to jst over 2f out: wknd* **100/1**

0-53 9 3 3/4 **Pleadings (USA)**[7] 438 4-9-7 **50** (vt) ShaneKelly 12 21
(Charlie Wallis) *trapped out wd: nvr bttr than midfield: struggling towards rr over 2f out: n.d after* **7/1**[3]

0-30 10 3/4 **Cuban Queen (USA)**[9] 398 4-9-6 **49** (p) AdamBeschizza 4 18
(Julia Feilden) *chsd ldrs: rdn over 3f out: wknd u.p 2f out* **8/1**

55-0 11 1/2 **Ertidaad (IRE)**[16] 282 5-8-13 **47** (t[1]) DavidParkes(5) 9 15
(Emma Owen) *nvr on terms w ldrs: u.p and wl btn over 2f out* **9/1**

00-0 12 4 1/2 **Dalness Express**[23] 167 4-8-13 **47** CiaranMckee(5) 10
(John O'Shea) *t.k.h early: hld up: wknd over 2f out* **33/1**

666- 13 29 **Man Of La Mancha (IRE)**[154] 6105 4-9-3 **46** (p) RobertWinston 11
(Ben Haslam) *dropped to last after 3f: sn bhd: t.o* **14/1**

1m 25.93s (-0.07) **Going Correction** +0.025s/f (Slow) 13 Ran SP% **117.5**
Speed ratings (Par 97): **101,99,93,91,91 91,88,88,83,82 82,77,44**
CSF £45.24 CT £241.88 TOTE £9.90: £3.10, £2.00, £3.10; EX 54.10 Trifecta £591.30.
**Owner** J J Bridger **Bred** Patrick Gleeson **Trained** Liphook, Hants

**FOCUS**
An ordinary contest. The front pair were clear, but it was typically limited form in behind

## 545 32RED ON THE APP STORE MAIDEN STKS 7f (P)
6:15 (6:16) (Class 5) 3-Y-O+ £3,234 (£962; £481; £240) Stalls Low

Form RPR

00-2 1 **Dark Destroyer (IRE)**[27] 119 3-8-11 75 LiamKeniry 9 76+
(Joseph Tuite) *t.k.h: pressed ldr: led over 2f out gng wl and sn pressed on: wandered sltly but in command fnl f* 5/2[1]

2 1 1/4 **Tricorn (IRE)** 3-8-11 0 NickyMackay 10 72+
(John Gosden) *dwlt: rcvrd on outer to chse ldrs: rdn: lost pl and struggling over 2f out: styd on again over 1f out to take 2nd last 75yds: nrst fin but unable to chal* 5/2[1]

5-4 3 1/2 **Rock N Roll Global (IRE)**[20] 236 3-8-11 0 ShaneKelly 2 70
(Richard Hughes) *cl up: nt qckn and outpcd whn ldng pair kicked on 2f out: styd on again fnl f: tk 3rd last strides* 4/1[3]

0 4 1/2 **Basheer**[27] 127 3-8-11 0 (h[1]) LukeMorris 3 69
(Marco Botti) *t.k.h: hld up bhd ldrs: quick prog to take 2nd 2f out and tried to chal: no imp wnr over 1f out: one pce and lost 2 pls last 75yds* 3/1[2]

0-0 5 6 **Trautmann (IRE)**[20] 236 3-8-11 0 JosephineGordon 6 53+
(Daniel Mark Loughnane) *hld up wl in rr: pushed along and prog fr 2f out: tk modest 5th last 100yds: nt disgracd* 150/1

6 1 **Swilly Bay (IRE)** 3-8-11 0 MichaelJMMurphy 8 50+
(Charles Hills) *s.i.s: rn green and wl in rr: pushed along firmly over 2f out: kpt on same pce fr over 1f out* 14/1

00- 7 1 3/4 **Secret Willow**[50] 8377 3-8-11 0 FrannyNorton 1 45
(John E Long) *led to over 2f out: sn btn: wknd qckly fnl f* 150/1

030- 8 nk **Major Assault**[121] 7076 4-10-0 70 JohnFahy 13 49
(Matthew Salaman) *hld up in rr and racd wd: shkn up and brief effrt 2f out: sn no prog* 66/1

04 9 shd **Damo**[11] 378 3-8-8 0 HectorCrouch(3) 11 44
(Simon Dow) *hld up towards rr: shkn up over 2f out and outpcd: no ch after* 25/1

10 1 3/4 **Navajo Star (IRE)** 3-7-13 0 RPWalsh(7) 5 34
(Michael Appleby) *slowly away and swvd s: detached in last and stl same 1f out: passed two rivals late on* 66/1

0- 11 2 3/4 **Maarit (IRE)**[34] 8591 3-8-7 0 ow1 (t[1]) TomMarquand 4 28
(Denis Coakley) *t.k.h: chsd ldrs over 4f: wknd* 50/1

60- 12 1/2 **Golden Harbour (FR)**[51] 8352 3-8-6 0 (t) MitchGodwin(5) 7 31
(Brian Barr) *nvr bttr than midfield: wknd on inner 2f out* 100/1

1m 27.27s (1.27) **Going Correction** +0.025s/f (Slow)
**WFA** 3 from 4yo 17lb 12 Ran SP% **119.9**
Speed ratings (Par 103): **93,91,91,90,83 82,80,80,79,77 74,74**
CSF £8.91 TOTE £3.60: £1.20, £1.40, £1.40; EX 12.00 Trifecta £34.70.
**Owner** P Gleeson & Goldrush Thoroughbreds **Bred** Castle Estates **Trained** Lambourn, Berks

**FOCUS**
A fair maiden.

## 546 32RED CASINO H'CAP 6f (P)
6:45 (6:45) (Class 6) (0-55,55) 3-Y-O £2,587 (£770; £384; £192) Stalls Low

Form RPR

54-5 1 **Skellig Michael**[23] 178 3-9-7 55 (p[1]) AdamKirby 2 61
(Ben Haslam) *chsd ldr: rdn and no imp over 2f out: hrd drvn over 1f out: responded wl and styd on to ld last 100yds* 5/2[2]

05-1 2 3/4 **Popsilca**[14] 324 3-9-4 52 WilliamCarson 5 56
(Mick Quinn) *racd freely: led: looked in command 2f out: shkn up over 1f out: pressed and rdn fnl f: hdd last 100yds* 13/8[1]

0-05 3 6 **Arya Stark**[11] 376 3-9-6 54 (p[1]) DavidProbert 6 40
(Tony Carroll) *chsd ldng pair: rdn wl over 2f out: sn outpcd and dropped to rr: kpt on to take remote 3rd last 100yds* 9/1

00-0 4 1 3/4 **Raspberry Princess**[27] 126 3-8-9 46 oh1 (t) AaronJones(3) 1 27
(Stuart Williams) *chsd ldrs: rdn over 2f out and nt qckn: easily outpcd by ldng pair after: lost remote 3rd last 100yds* 16/1

000- 5 2 1/2 **Sallee**[84] 7906 3-8-11 50 HollieDoyle(5) 3 23
(Adrian Wintle) *hld up in last: shkn up over 2f out: outpcd and nvr a factor after* 10/1

060- 6 3/4 **Secret Icon**[174] 5395 3-9-1 49 TimmyMurphy 4 20
(Jamie Osborne) *t.k.h: hld up in 5th: outpcd and shkn up over 2f out: no prog* 5/1[3]

1m 13.65s (0.55) **Going Correction** +0.025s/f (Slow) 6 Ran SP% **108.3**
Speed ratings (Par 95): **97,96,88,85,82 81**
CSF £6.43 TOTE £3.50: £1.40, £2.50; EX 6.50 Trifecta £22.50.
**Owner** James Pak Racing,Trojan Horse,Wellingham **Bred** Mrs Sally Hicks **Trained** Middleham Moor, N Yorks

**FOCUS**
The first two had this between them from some way out. There are doubts about the depth of this.

## 547 32RED.COM H'CAP 6f (P)
7:15 (7:16) (Class 4) (0-85,84) 4-Y-O+ £4,690 (£1,395; £697; £348) Stalls Low

Form RPR

4-10 1 **Dutch Golden Age (IRE)**[16] 287 5-9-6 83 GeorgeBaker 4 94
(Gary Moore) *trckd ldng pair: led wl over 1f out gng strly: sn 2 l clr: rdn out and kpt on wl* 7/2[1]

64-4 2 2 1/2 **Fairway To Heaven (IRE)**[21] 219 8-9-2 79 AdamKirby 5 82
(Michael Wigham) *dwlt: towards rr: prog over 2f out: drvn and styd on to take 2nd last 100yds: no threat to wnr* 8/1

1-11 3 hd **Born To Finish (IRE)**[23] 171 4-8-8 76 (p) DavidParkes(5) 12 78+
(Jeremy Gask) *dwlt: dropped in fr wd draw and wl in rr: prog fr 2f out: styd on wl fnl f to press for 2nd nr fin* 6/1[2]

0-25 4 1/2 **September Issue**[22] 194 4-9-3 80 (p) LukeMorris 1 81
(Gay Kelleway) *trckd ldrs: hrd rdn fr 2f out: disp 2nd briefly ins fnl f: one pce nr fin* 7/1

-032 5 nk **Oriental Relation (IRE)**[21] 219 6-9-7 84 (v) PaulMulrennan 11 84
(James Given) *urged along fr wd draw and gd spd to ld: hdd wl over 1f out: one pce and lost pls last 100yds* 14/1

-504 6 1/2 **Salvatore Fury (IRE)**[9] 403 7-9-2 79 (b) ConnorBeasley 8 77
(Keith Dalgleish) *t.k.h: hld up wl in rr: prog over 2f out: tried to cl on ldrs 1f out: kpt on but nvr pce to threaten* 20/1

441- 7 1 3/4 **Under Siege (IRE)**[139] 6583 5-9-5 82 (t) OisinMurphy 2 75+
(Stuart Williams) *hld up in midfield: effrt over 2f out: drvn to cl on ldrs over 1f out: wl hld ins fnl f: eased nr fin* 7/2[1]

114- 8 3 **Darma (IRE)**[185] 4984 5-8-13 81 HollieDoyle(5) 6 64
(Martyn Meade) *chsd ldrs: rdn sn after 1/2-way: wknd 2f out* 12/1

46-0 9 1/2 **Very Honest (IRE)**[28] 94 4-9-2 79 MartinDwyer 10 60
(Brett Johnson) *chsd ldr to over 2f out: wknd* 25/1

0-00 10 3 3/4 **King Of Swing**[21] 219 4-8-12 75 (h) ShaneKelly 9 44
(Richard Hughes) *detached in last and urged along: nvr a factor* 50/1

0-06 11 3 3/4 **Highland Acclaim (IRE)**[20] 234 6-9-6 83 DanielTudhope 7 40+
(David O'Meara) *t.k.h: hld up in midfield and trapped wd: shkn up and hanging over 2f out: wknd and heavily eased* 13/2[3]

1m 10.75s (-2.35) **Going Correction** +0.025s/f (Slow) 11 Ran SP% **120.6**
Speed ratings (Par 105): **116,112,112,111,111 110,108,104,103,98 93**
CSF £32.56 CT £169.77 TOTE £4.40: £1.60, £2.90, £3.00; EX 36.70 Trifecta £208.30.
**Owner** R A Green **Bred** Denis Bergin **Trained** Lower Beeding, W Sussex

**FOCUS**
This looked a competitive sprint but the winner beat the rest comfortably.

## 548 32RED H'CAP (LONDON MILE SERIES QUALIFIER) 1m (P)
7:45 (7:45) (Class 4) (0-85,87) 4-Y-O+ £4,690 (£1,395; £697; £348) Stalls Low

Form RPR

02-1 1 **Franco's Secret**[13] 349 6-9-4 82 (v) TomMarquand 8 90
(Peter Hedger) *dwlt: hld up in last: prog towards inner jst over 2f out: rdn to join ld fnl f: narrow advantage last 75yds: hld on wl* 8/1

0-43 2 hd **Ice Royal (IRE)**[20] 240 4-9-9 87 TimmyMurphy 3 94
(Jamie Osborne) *trckd ldng trio: clsd to ld wl over 1f out: drvn and jnd fnl f: narrowly hdd last 75yds: jst hld* 7/1[3]

310- 3 1 **Winners Follow Me (GER)**[44] 8478 4-9-8 86 LukeMorris 1 90
(James Tate) *hld up in 6th: shkn up and nt qckn over 2f out: drvn over 1f out: r.o fnl f to take 3rd nr fin* 5/1[2]

263- 4 1/2 **Mister Music**[98] 7671 8-9-2 80 AdamKirby 5 83
(Tony Carroll) *hld up in 7th: gng strly over 2f out: swtchd ins and bmpd along to cl wl over 1f out: reminder fnl f: styd on but nvr cl enough to chal* 5/1[2]

55-3 5 1/2 **Honiara**[16] 287 4-9-4 85 (t) CallumShepherd(3) 2 87
(Paul Cole) *t.k.h: hld up in 8th: prog over 2f out: rdn to chal over 1f out: nt qckn and one pce fnl f* 9/2[1]

54-0 6 3 **Lacan (IRE)**[18] 266 6-9-8 86 SeanLevey 6 81
(Ralph Beckett) *t.k.h: trckd ldng pair: wnt 2nd 3f out and led briefly 2f out: sn rdn: fdd over 1f out* 5/1[2]

1-41 7 nk **Sands Chorus**[20] 240 5-9-2 80 PaulMulrennan 9 74
(James Given) *t.k.h: pressed ldr: led 1/2-way: hdd 2f out: sn btn and fdd* 10/1

1- 8 6 **Blue Revelation**[65] 8157 4-9-3 81 GeorgeBaker 4 62
(Paul Webber) *hld up in 5th: rdn over 2f out: no prog and wknd over 1f out* 12/1

00-0 9 28 **Freight Train (IRE)**[27] 122 5-8-2 71 oh1 (p) HollieDoyle(5) 7
(Adrian Wintle) *drvn to ld: hdd 1/2-way: wknd rapidly 3f out: t.o* 150/1

1m 38.21s (-1.59) **Going Correction** +0.025s/f (Slow) 9 Ran SP% **109.2**
Speed ratings (Par 105): **108,107,106,106,105 102,102,96,68**
CSF £57.19 CT £283.93 TOTE £6.40: £2.60, £2.50, £2.00; EX 56.40 Trifecta £377.10.
**Owner** P C F Racing Ltd **Bred** J J Whelan **Trained** Hook, Hampshire

**FOCUS**
There was a tight finish to this handicap.

## 549 100% PROFIT BOOST AT 32REDSPORT.COM H'CAP 1m 3f 219y(P)
8:15 (8:16) (Class 6) (0-65,67) 4-Y-O+ £2,264 (£673; £336; £168) Stalls Centre

Form RPR

42-5 1 **Ruby Wednesday**[30] 35 4-9-0 61 KierenFox 2 66
(John Best) *cl up: wnt 2nd over 2f out and rdn to ld wl over 1f out: hrd pressed last 150yds: hld on wl* 7/1

06- 2 nk **Light Of Air (FR)**[27] 7223 4-9-3 67 HectorCrouch(3) 3 72
(Gary Moore) *trckd ldr to over 2f out where briefly short of pce and room: rallied to go 2nd jst over 1f out: str chal last 150yds: nt qckn and hld nr fin* 16/1

00-1 3 2 3/4 **Black Hole Sun**[8] 420 5-8-7 51 oh1 JosephineGordon 4 51
(Ian Williams) *led after nthing else would: set v modest pce: tried to qckn wl over 2f out but w only mod success and hdd wl over 1f out: kpt on same pce in 3rd fnl f* 9/4[1]

0-53 4 3/4 **Runaiocht (IRE)**[13] 351 7-8-11 60 (b) DavidParkes(5) 9 59
(Paul Burgoyne) *hld up in last pair: shkn up and tried to make prog fr over 2f out: styd on but nvr pce to threaten ldrs* 10/1

46-0 5 2 1/4 **Mystikana**[28] 92 4-8-13 67 (b) TylerSaunders(7) 7 62
(Marcus Tregoning) *t.k.h: hld up in last pair: bdly outpcd whn pce lifted over 2f out: r.o fnl f: no ch* 9/2[3]

562- 6 1 **The Ginger Berry**[86] 7870 7-9-7 65 (h) AdamKirby 5 59
(Dr Jon Scargill) *hld up in tch: looked poised to chal fr 2f out but hanging and fnd nil after: wknd qckly fnl f* 6/1

064- 7 1 3/4 **Golden Muscade (USA)**[154] 6073 4-8-10 62 RachealKneller(5) 6 53
(Brian Barr) *prom: trckd ldr 5f out to over 2f out: sn lost pl and btn* 40/1

/24- 8 1/2 **Goodby Inheritence**[47] 8448 5-9-7 65 (t) GeorgeBaker 1 55
(Seamus Durack) *hld up in tch: outpcd whn r fnlly sed in earnest over 2f out: nvr on terms after* 7/2[2]

2m 39.87s (5.37) **Going Correction** +0.025s/f (Slow)
**WFA** 4 from 5yo+ 2lb 8 Ran SP% **115.4**
Speed ratings (Par 101): **83,82,80,80,78 78,77,76**
CSF £108.39 CT £330.95 TOTE £7.90: £2.10, £4.40, £1.10; EX 95.30 Trifecta £387.70.
**Owner** Harris, Beckett & Millen **Bred** Best Breeding **Trained** Oad Street, Kent

**FOCUS**
This was a steadily run affair and turned into a sprint up the straight. Routine form for the grade.
T/Jkpt: Not won. T/Plt: £27.50 to a £1 stake. Pool: £112,430.61 - 2,978.94 winning tickets
T/Qpdt: £9.60 to a £1 stake. Pool: £8,136.05 - 622.58 winning tickets **Jonathan Neesom**

# [463] LINGFIELD (L-H)
Friday, February 3

**OFFICIAL GOING: Polytrack: standard**
Wind: medium, half behind Weather: light cloud, rain from race 4

## 550 32RED.COM FILLIES' H'CAP 1m 1y(P)
2:00 (2:00) (Class 5) (0-75,75) 4-Y-O+ £3,234 (£962; £481; £240) Stalls High

Form RPR

00-2 1 **Remember Me**[20] 232 4-9-2 70 RyanMoore 2 77
(Hughie Morrison) *trckd ldr for 1f: chsd ldng pair after: rdn over 2f out: hdwy u.p to press ldr over 1f out: led ins fnl f: styd on: rdn out* 6/5[1]

12-1 2 1 1/2 **Skidby Mill (IRE)**[20] 232 7-9-7 75 GeorgeBaker 3 78
(Laura Mongan) *led: shkn up over 1f out: rdn 1f out: hdd and styd on same pce ins fnl f* 7/4[2]

54-6 3 3/4 **Tabla**[27] 116 5-8-13 67 KierenFox 4 69
(Lee Carter) *chsd ldr after 1f tl dropped to 3rd and unable qck over 1f out: kpt on same pce ins fnl f* 9/2[3]


The Form Book Flat, Raceform Ltd, Newbury, RG14 5SJ

-064 **4** *11* **Gold Return (IRE)**[8] [420] 4-8-1 **62**.......................... DarraghKeenan(7) 1 37
(John Ryan) *s.i.s: rdn along: clsd onto bk of field over 6f out: rdn 4f out: outpcd over 2f out: wl btn fnl 2f* **14/1**

1m 38.69s (0.49) **Going Correction** +0.125s/f (Slow) **4** Ran SP% **106.7**
Speed ratings (Par 100): **102,100,99,88**
CSF £3.48 TOTE £1.60; EX 3.10 Trifecta £4.40.
**Owner** Harry & Julie Parkes **Bred** Aiden Murphy **Trained** East Ilsley, Berks

**FOCUS**
An uncompetitive, small-field fillies' handicap with the tactics very much as predicted. The first two met over C&D 20 days ago and the form was reversed.

## 551 SUN BETS ON THE APP STORE CLAIMING STKS 7f 1y(P)
**2:30** (2:30) (Class 6) 4-Y-O+ **£2,587** (£770; £384; £192) **Stalls** Low

Form RPR

015- **1** **Flowers On Venus (IRE)**[125] [6962] 5-9-10 **87**......... RichardKingscote 4 85
(Tom Dascombe) *chsd ldr tl 4f out: styd trcking ldrs: lft 2nd again bnd 2f out: rdn to chal ent fnl f: led ins fnl f: hld on wl towards fin: rdn out* **6/4**[1]

60-3 **2** *shd* **Flexible Flyer**[21] [211] 8-9-10 **77**..................................(h) DavidProbert 5 85
(Chris Dwyer) *hld up in tch in midfield: rdn and hdwy over 1f out: str chal ins fnl f: r.o wl but hld towards fin* **16/1**

3-52 **3** *1 ½* **Sophisticated Heir (IRE)**[15] [312] 7-9-12 **80**...........(b) RobertWinston 8 83
(Michael Herrington) *hld up in last pair: rdn and hdwy over 1f out: chsd ldrs ins fnl f: kpt on to go 3rd last strides* **7/2**[2]

5-32 **4** *nk* **Free Zone**[21] [211] 8-9-6 **79**..........................................(v) AdamKirby 10 76
(Lee Carter) *led: rdn and qckng ent fnl 2f: drvn and hdd ins fnl f: no ex: wknd cl home and lost 3rd last strides* **8/1**

36-0 **5** *hd* **Corporal Maddox**[18] [267] 10-9-6 **72**..............................(p) LukeMorris 6 75
(Ronald Harris) *hld up in tch in midfield: effrt over 1f out: drvn and kpt on ins fnl f* **25/1**

516- **6** *1 ½* **Seek The Fair Land**[45] [8469] 11-8-7 **66**........................(b) JaneElliott(7) 1 65
(Lee Carter) *hld up in tch in midfield: effrt on inner over 1f out: no ex 1f out: wknd ins fnl f* **25/1**

/3-4 **7** *½* **Gramercy (IRE)**[15] [304] 10-9-0 **87**..............................(p) MartinDwyer 9 64
(Ian Williams) *hld up in tch: effrt over 1f out: nudged rt ins fnl f: styd on fnl 100yds: nvr trbld ldrs* **6/1**[3]

0-42 **8** *1 ¾* **Ticks The Boxes (IRE)**[13] [363] 5-9-5 **77**...........(p) JordanVaughan(3) 2 67
(Michael Herrington) *taken down early: chsd ldrs tl lost pl u.p over 1f out: squeezed for room: swtchd rt and nudged rival ins fnl f: wknd fnl 100yds* **10/1**

54-0 **9** *7* **Aqua Libre**[15] [304] 4-8-12 **82**.................................... JohnFahy 3 38
(Philip McBride) *dwlt: hld up in rr: swtchd rt and wd over 3f out: lost pl bnd 2f out: n.d after* **20/1**

006- **10** *30* **Balliol**[101] [7596] 5-9-2 **57**...................................................(b) ShaneKelly 7
(Ronald Harris) *stdd s and s.i.s: t.k.h: sn rcvrd and in midfield: hdwy to join ldr 4f out tl hung bdly rt and lost pl bnd 2f out: wl bhd and eased after: t.o* **100/1**

1m 25.29s (0.49) **Going Correction** +0.125s/f (Slow) **10** Ran SP% **116.0**
Speed ratings (Par 101): **102,101,100,99,99 97,97,95,87,53**
CSF £27.55 TOTE £2.50: £1.20, £3.70, £1.50; EX 26.00 Trifecta £90.90.Free Zone was claimed by Claes Bjorling for £8,000.
**Owner** Owen Promotions Limited **Bred** Mrs A J Donnelly **Trained** Malpas, Cheshire

**FOCUS**
Not a bad little claimer, with seven of the ten runners rated between 77 and 87. The runner-up is probably the key.

## 552 32REDSPORT.COM MEDIAN AUCTION MAIDEN STKS 1m 2f (P)
**3:00** (3:02) (Class 6) 3-Y-O **£2,587** (£770; £384; £192) **Stalls** Low

Form RPR

55- **1** **Earthly (USA)**[123] [7013] 3-9-5 0........................................ RyanMoore 6 71
(Ralph Beckett) *dwlt: sn rcvrd to chse ldrs: wnt 2nd 5f out: rdn over 2f out: drvn to chal 1f out: led ins fnl f: styd on and forged clr fnl 75yds* **4/5**[1]

00-3 **2** *2 ½* **Dream Magic (IRE)**[18] [265] 3-9-5 67.............................. LukeMorris 5 66
(Daniel Mark Loughnane) *chsd ldr tl led 8f out: rdn 3f out: drvn and hrd pressed 1f out: hdd ins fnl f: sn btn and wknd towards fin* **5/1**[3]

**3** *nk* **Abel Tasman** 3-9-5 0.................................................. ThomasBrown 3 66+
(Ed Walker) *dwlt and bustled along leaving stalls: in tch in midfield: effrt over 2f out: styd on ins fnl f: no threat to wnr* **10/3**[2]

5-62 **4** *½* **Critical Thinking (IRE)**[7] [435] 3-9-2 63.................... ShelleyBirkett(3) 4 65
(Julia Feilden) *hld up in tch: nt clr run over 2f out: swtchd rt and effrt wl over 1f out: kpt on ins fnl f: no threat to wnr* **12/1**

6 **5** *¾* **Gee Sixty Six**[7] [437] 3-9-5 0...................................... TimmyMurphy 2 63
(Mark H Tompkins) *broke wl: t.k.h: led for 2f: chsd ldr tl 8f out: rdn 2f out: swtchd rt 1f out: kpt on same pce ins fnl f* **16/1**

00- **6** *7* **Life Happens**[45] [8465] 3-9-0 0............................................. RyanTate 1 45
(Jonathan Portman) *niggled along in rr: in tch tl outpcd u.p over 2f out: bhd over 1f out* **66/1**

00 **7** *11* **Surfside**[13] [354] 3-9-0 0.................................................. ShaneKelly 7 24
(Mick Channon) *in tch: rdn 4f out: lost pl and bhd 2f out* **100/1**

2m 6.81s (0.21) **Going Correction** +0.125s/f (Slow) **7** Ran SP% **111.4**
Speed ratings (Par 95): **104,102,101,101,100 95,86**
CSF £4.98 TOTE £1.70: £1.30, £1.90; EX 5.40 Trifecta £12.60.
**Owner** K Abdullah **Bred** Juddmonte Farms Inc **Trained** Kimpton, Hants

**FOCUS**
An uncompetitive 3yo maiden. The winner didn't need to improve to win.

## 553 SUNBETS.CO.UK APPRENTICE H'CAP 7f 1y(P)
**3:35** (3:35) (Class 3) (0-95,94) 3-Y-O **£7,246** (£2,168; £1,084) **Stalls** Low

Form RPR

034- **1** **Spirit Of Sarwan (IRE)**[171] [5506] 3-8-2 **75** oh2.............. ShelleyBirkett 2 76
(Julia Feilden) *awkward leaving stalls and slowly away: in tch in rr: effrt on inner over 1f out: chal 1f out: r.o wl to ld last strides* **11/1**[3]

2-31 **2** *nk* **Mailshot (USA)**[13] [350] 3-9-4 **94**..................... RichardOliver(3) 6 94
(Mark Johnston) *led: rdn and rdr dropped whip wl over 1f out: kpt on wl tl hdd last strides* **9/4**[2]

31 **3** *nse* **Blaze Of Glory (FR)**[20] [236] 3-9-0 **87**........................ KieranShoemark 5 87
(Jamie Osborne) *t.k.h: chsd ldr: upsides 3f out: rdn 2f out: unable qck u.p wl ins fnl f* **4/9**[1]

1m 26.95s (2.15) **Going Correction** +0.125s/f (Slow) **3** Ran SP% **108.4**
Speed ratings (Par 101): **92,91,91**
CSF £29.10 TOTE £6.20; EX 12.20 Trifecta £15.60.
**Owner** Mr & Mrs George Bhatti **Bred** John Fallon **Trained** Exning, Suffolk

**FOCUS**
A decimated field for this Class 3 handicap with only half of those declared at the 48-hour stage going to post, but the remaining trio produced a thriller. The big two in the market had both made all here in their most recent starts, so something had to give.

## 554 BETWAY BEST ODDS GUARANTEED PLUS MAIDEN STKS 5f 6y(P)
**4:10** (4:11) (Class 5) 3-Y-O+ **£3,234** (£962; £481; £240) **Stalls** High

Form RPR

030- **1** **Hot Stuff**[56] [8290] 4-10-0 58................................................ DavidProbert 4 61
(Tony Carroll) *broke wl: led for 1f: styd upsides ldr: rdn over 1f out: led ins fnl f: kpt on and won on the nod* **5/1**[2]

64- **2** *nse* **Gnaad (IRE)**[84] [7900] 3-9-0 0........................................ LukeMorris 3 55
(Robert Cowell) *t.k.h: trckd ldrs: swtchd lft and effrt over 1f out: drvn and ev ch 1f out: kpt on: lost on the nod* **4/5**[1]

060- **3** *¾* **Deer Song**[34] [8596] 4-9-7 54........................................... JaneElliott(7) 2 58
(John Bridger) *w ldr tl led after 1f: edgd rt u.p over 1f out: hdd ins fnl f: no ex and styd on same pce wl ins fnl f* **8/1**

00 **4** *2* **Neptune Star**[16] [288] 3-8-6 0 ow2................................(h) DavidParkes(5) 1 42
(Jeremy Gask) *sn dropped towards rr: rdn and hdwy on inner over 1f out: kpt on same pce ins fnl f* **20/1**

406- **5** *2 ¼* **Glam'Selle**[72] [8071] 3-8-9 49............................................ TomMarquand 6 32
(Ronald Harris) *in tch in midfield: effrt over 1f out: sn hung lft and no imp 1f out: wl hld and kpt on same pce ins fnl f* **10/1**

/60- **6** *2 ¼* **Oddsocks (IRE)**[56] [8288] 5-9-9 39.................................... WilliamCarson 5 30
(Tony Carroll) *in tch towards rr: squeezed for room bnd 2f out: effrt over 1f out: no imp u.p 1f out: wknd ins fnl f* **50/1**

4 **7** *2* **Scealtara (IRE)**[7] [442] 3-8-6 0.................................... ShelleyBirkett(3) 7 17
(David O'Meara) *sn dropped to rr: effrt over 1f out: no imp: n.d* **6/1**[3]

59.91s (1.11) **Going Correction** +0.125s/f (Slow)
**WFA** 3 from 4yo+ 14lb **7** Ran SP% **113.4**
Speed ratings (Par 103): **96,95,94,91,87 84,81**
CSF £9.25 TOTE £5.30: £2.10, £1.20; EX 11.70 Trifecta £36.00.
**Owner** Lady Whent **Bred** Lady Whent **Trained** Cropthorne, Worcs

**FOCUS**
A poor sprint maiden. The winner finished second in this race last year which says plenty about the quality of this contest. The winner and third help with the level.

## 555 BETWAY BEST ODDS GUARANTEED PLUS H'CAP 1m 5f (P)
**4:40** (4:40) (Class 6) (0-65,70) 4-Y-O+ **£2,587** (£770; £384; £192) **Stalls** Low

Form RPR

2-52 **1** **Burnside (FR)**[8] [423] 4-9-3 **65**.............................................(v) AdamKirby 3 73
(Ian Williams) *chsd ldr tl 10f out: styd chsng ldrs: wnt 2nd again 4f out: rdn to ld 2f out: forged ahd u.p 1f out: styd on and in command ins fnl f* **11/10**[1]

36-0 **2** *2 ¾* **Marshall Aid (IRE)**[24] [162] 4-9-3 **65**............................... KieranO'Neill 1 69
(Mark Usher) *hld up in tch: clsd to trck ldrs 3f out: effrt in 3rd 2f out: hung lft ins fnl f: no threat to wnr but kpt on to go 2nd wl ins fnl f* **14/1**

405- **3** *1 ¼* **Halling's Wish**[51] [8367] 7-9-7 **65**...............................(b) GeorgeBaker 7 67
(Gary Moore) *led: hdd 2f out: shkn up and unable qck over 1f out: rdn and btn 1f out: plugged on same pce and lost 2nd wl ins fnl f* **8/1**[3]

-041 **4** *3 ¼* **Attain**[7] [440] 8-9-12 **70** 6ex............................................... LukeMorris 2 69
(Archie Watson) *hld up in tch in rr: effrt in 5th over 2f out: sn outpcd and struggling: 4th and kpt on same pce ins fnl f: eased towards fin* **2/1**[2]

40-6 **5** *1 ¾* **Mamoo**[24] [162] 4-8-9 **57**..........................................(p) JosephineGordon 4 52
(Mike Murphy) *hld up in tch: hdwy on outer 5f out: rdn and outpcd over 2f out: wknd over 1f out* **8/1**[3]

0U-0 **6** *10* **Salient**[17] [279] 13-8-7 **51** oh2.............................................. KierenFox 8 31
(Michael Attwater) *chsd ldrs tl 10f out: styd wl in tch in midfield: struggling u.p and lost pl 3f out: no ch fnl 2f* **50/1**

00-6 **7** *45* **Epsom Day (IRE)**[16] [290] 4-8-12 **63**...................(b) CallumShepherd(3) 6
(Laura Mongan) *v keen to post: squeezed for room s: in rr tl hdwy to chse ldr 10f out: rdn and lost pl 4f out: wl bhd and eased 2f out: t.o* **25/1**

2m 44.82s (-1.18) **Going Correction** +0.125s/f (Slow)
**WFA** 4 from 7yo+ 2lb **7** Ran SP% **115.6**
Speed ratings (Par 101): **108,106,105,103,102 96,68**
CSF £19.28 CT £88.47 TOTE £2.40: £1.40, £6.80; EX 18.60 Trifecta £83.60.
**Owner** Ian Williams Racing Club **Bred** Guy Pariente Holding Sprl **Trained** Portway, Worcs

**FOCUS**
A modest staying handicap in which they went an even pace. Fair form for the grade.
T/Plt: £131.60 to a £1 stake. Pool: £76,364.40 - 423.31 winning tickets T/Qpdt: £51.40 to a £1 stake. Pool: £4,933.78 - 71.00 winning tickets **Steve Payne**

556 - 569a (Foreign Racing) - See Raceform Interactive

# 550 LINGFIELD (L-H)
### Saturday, February 4

**OFFICIAL GOING: Polytrack: standard**
Wind: light, across Weather: dry, light cloud

## 570 SUNBETS ON THE APP STORE H'CAP 7f 1y(P)
**12:50** (12:51) (Class 5) (0-70,72) 4-Y-O+ **£2,911** (£866; £432; £216) **Stalls** Low

Form RPR

66-4 **1** **Polar Kite (IRE)**[22] [214] 9-8-10 **62**..................................(h) RobHornby(3) 2 68
(Michael Attwater) *hld up in midfield: clsd on inner over 1f out: rdn to chse ldrs and swtchd rt ins fnl f: chsd clr ldr 100yds out: r.o strly to ld cl home* **12/1**

0-01 **2** *shd* **Bookmaker**[10] [398] 7-7-13 **55**.......................................(p) JaneElliott(7) 6 61
(John Bridger) *chsd ldrs tl shuffled bk into midfield 3f out: rdn and hdwy over 1f out: wnt 3rd 100yds: r.o strly and ev ch towards fin: jst hld* **14/1**

0-10 **3** *½* **Black Caesar (IRE)**[17] [287] 6-9-7 **70**............................ GeorgeBaker 8 75
(Philip Hide) *led: rdn and kicked clr over 1f out: stl clr 100yds: wknd towards fin and hdd cl home* **6/1**[3]

11-1 **4** *1 ½* **Fire Diamond**[9] [426] 4-9-9 **72**...............................(p) RichardKingscote 3 73
(Tom Dascombe) *dwlt: hld up in tch in last pair: effrt but stl plenty to do over 1f out: styd on u.p ins fnl f: nvr threatened ldrs* **13/8**[1]

1-41 **5** *nse* **Bridge Builder**[14] [355] 7-9-9 **72**................................(p) TomMarquand 7 72
(Peter Hedger) *nt that wl away: styd wd early and midfield tl hdwy to chse ldr over 5f out: rdn and unable qck over 1f out: lost 2nd 100yds out: wknd towards fin* **6/1**[3]

56-0 **6** *2 ¾* **Gunner Moyne**[21] [238] 5-8-5 **57**.................................(b[1]) NoelGarbutt(3) 9 50
(Gary Moore) *stdd s: hld up in tch in rr: effrt and rdn wl over 1f out: styd on ins fnl f: nvr trbld ldrs* **33/1**

03-1 **7** *shd* **Ross Raith Rover**[26] [139] 4-9-0 **63**...............................(p) JackMitchell 1 56
(Robert Eddery) *chsd ldr tl over 5f out: styd chsng ldrs tl unable qck u.p over 1f out: wknd ins fnl f* **7/2**[2]

04-0 **8** *1* **Ubla (IRE)**[34] 6 4-9-4 **67**..........(t[1]) LukeMorris 5 57
(Gay Kelleway) *hld up in tch: hdwy on outer to chse ldrs over 2f out: sn rdn: outpcd and lost pl over 1f out: wl hld ins fnl f* **25/1**

60-0 **9** *2 ½* **Star Of The Stage**[28] 116 5-9-3 **66**.......... DannyBrock 4 49
(John Butler) *in tch in midfield: rdn over 2f out: sn struggling: bhd ins fnl f* **33/1**

1m 23.87s (-0.93) **Going Correction** -0.075s/f (Stan) **9** Ran SP% **113.0**
Speed ratings (Par 103): **102,101,101,99,99 96,96,95,92**
CSF £155.41 CT £1107.43 TOTE £12.40: £3.00, £4.10, £1.90; EX 134.20 Trifecta £2072.70.
**Owner** Christian Main **Bred** Holborn Trust Co **Trained** Epsom, Surrey

**FOCUS**
This was run at a decent gallop and the first two finished well to collar the third.

## 571 BETWAY STAYERS H'CAP 1m 7f 169y(P)
**1:25** (1:25) (Class 5) (0-75,77) 4-Y-O+ **£2,911** (£866; £432; £216) **Stalls** Low

Form RPR

14- **1** **Byron Flyer**[63] 6804 6-10-2 **77**.......... AdamKirby 5 87+
(Ian Williams) *hld up in tch: trckd ldrs 3f out: rdn to ld on inner over 1f out: sn in command and r.o strly: readily* **1/2**[1]

2-23 **2** *4* **Miss Tiger Lily**[18] 280 7-9-9 **70**.......... LukeMorris 4 75
(Harry Dunlop) *led: rdn ent fnl 2f: hdd over 1f out: sn brushed aside by wnr: kpt on for clr 2nd* **6/1**[3]

2-03 **3** *2 ¾* **River Dart (IRE)**[23] 196 5-10-2 **77**.......... GeorgeDowning 3 79
(Tony Carroll) *hld up in tch in last pair: effrt and stl plenty to do wl over 1f out: rdn ent fnl f: kpt on to go 3rd cl home: no ch w ldrs* **11/2**[2]

-004 **4** *nk* **Wordiness**[18] 280 9-9-5 **66**.......... StevieDonohoe 7 68
(David Evans) *hld up in last pair: hdwy on outer over 3f out: rdn to go 2nd and edgd lft ent fnl 2f: lost 2nd and outpcd over 1f out: wl hld and one pced fnl f: lost 3rd cl home* **12/1**

20-5 **5** *¾* **Saborido (USA)**[18] 280 11-9-11 **75**.......... KieranShoemark(3) 1 76
(Amanda Perrett) *chsd ldrs: lost pl and rdn 3f out: outpcd 2f out: wl hld and kpt on same pce after* **10/1**

40-0 **6** *15* **Pivotal Flame (IRE)**[17] 286 4-9-1 **68**.......... ShaneKelly 6 51
(Pat Phelan) *sn chsng ldr: rdn and lost 2nd whn hmpd bnd ent fnl f: sn dropped to rr and bhd* **40/1**

3m 24.7s (-1.00) **Going Correction** -0.075s/f (Stan)
**WFA** 4 from 5yo+ 4lb **6** Ran SP% **115.6**
Speed ratings (Par 103): **99,97,95,95,95 87**
CSF £4.42 CT £8.65 TOTE £1.50: £1.20, £2.00; EX 4.20 Trifecta £7.70.
**Owner** Anchor Men **Bred** Barton Stud **Trained** Portway, Worcs

**FOCUS**
This proved straightforward for the odds-on favourite.

## 572 BETWAY BEST ODDS GUARANTEED PLUS CLEVES STKS (LISTED RACE) 6f 1y(P)
**2:00** (2:00) (Class 1) 4-Y-O+
**£25,519** (£9,675; £4,842; £2,412; £1,210; £607) **Stalls** Low

Form RPR

00-1 **1** **Lancelot Du Lac (ITY)**[30] 63 7-9-0 107.......... RobertWinston 5 111
(Dean Ivory) *t.k.h: hld up in tch in midfield: effrt over 1f out: drvn to press ldrs 1f out: r.o wl u.p: edgd lft wl ins fnl f: led last stride* **11/2**[2]

22-6 **2** *nse* **Mythmaker**[23] 200 5-9-0 102.......... PaulMulrennan 7 111
(Bryan Smart) *sn led: rdn wl over 1f out: hrd pressed 1f out: battled on gamely u.p: hdd last stride* **16/1**

166- **3** *nk* **Boom The Groom (IRE)**[116] 7242 6-9-0 107.......... AndreaAtzeni 2 110
(Tony Carroll) *taken down early: hld up in tch in last pair: rdn and gd hdwy on inner over 1f out: ev ch 1f out: r.o: unable qck towards fin* **20/1**

12-4 **4** *nk* **Gracious John (IRE)**[23] 200 4-9-0 109.......... AdamKirby 8 109
(David Evans) *t.k.h: chsd ldr after 1f: rdn wl over 1f out: kpt on wl u.p: unable qck and hld whn sltly impeded towards fin* **8/1**[3]

05-1 **5** *nk* **Pretend (IRE)**[24] 170 6-9-0 111.......... WilliamBuick 1 109+
(Charlie Appleby) *t.k.h: chsd ldrs: short of room and hmpd after 1f: styd chsng ldrs: effrt over 1f out: styd pressing ldrs: kpt on: unable qck ins fnl f: hld whn squeezed for room and eased nr fin* **4/5**[1]

31-2 **6** *1 ¼* **Justice Good (IRE)**[23] 200 5-9-0 103.......... ShaneKelly 3 104
(David Elsworth) *chsd ldr tl pushed lft and hmpd after 1f: in tch in midfield after: effrt and swtchd rt wl over 1f out: no imp and one pce fnl f* **8/1**[3]

341- **7** *¾* **Amazour (IRE)**[36] 8583 5-9-0 100.......... SeanLevey 6 102
(Ismail Mohammed) *dwlt: in tch in last pair: effrt on outer bnd wl over 1f out: no imp u.p: one pce fnl f* **9/1**

1m 10.12s (-1.78) **Going Correction** -0.075s/f (Stan) **7** Ran SP% **113.8**
Speed ratings (Par 111): **108,107,107,107,106 105,104**
CSF £81.16 TOTE £5.20: £2.30, £6.70; EX 81.10 Trifecta £888.40.
**Owner** Michael & Heather Yarrow **Bred** Elektra Di Fausto Martellozzo & C Sas **Trained** Radlett, Herts

**FOCUS**
A good Listed sprint, but the early pace wasn't that strong and they finished in a heap.

## 573 BETWAY BEST ODDS GUARANTEED PLUS H'CAP 5f 6y(P)
**2:30** (2:31) (Class 4) (0-85,81) 4-Y-O+ **£4,690** (£1,395; £697; £348) **Stalls** High

Form RPR

11-5 **1** **Verne Castle**[30] 79 4-9-7 **81**..........(h) DavidProbert 3 90
(Andrew Balding) *led: sn hdd and chsd ldr after tl rdn to ld again 1f out: r.o wl* **9/4**[1]

424- **2** *1* **Vimy Ridge**[38] 8561 5-9-0 **74**.......... JosephineGordon 4 79
(Alan Bailey) *in tch in midfield: effrt over 1f out: hdwy u.p to chse wnr 100yds out: kpt on but nvr enough pce to chal* **9/2**[2]

00-2 **3** *¾* **Burning Thread (IRE)**[23] 194 10-9-2 **76**..........(b) ShaneKelly 7 78
(David Elsworth) *in tch in last trio: swtchd rt and nt clr run over 1f out: hdwy jst ins fnl f: r.o wl fnl 100yds: wnt 3rd cl home: no threat to wnr* **12/1**

002- **4** *½* **Mossgo (IRE)**[49] 8430 7-8-7 **67**..........(t) KierenFox 2 67
(John Best) *chsd ldrs: rdn over 1f out: unable qck and kpt on same pce ins fnl f: lost 3rd cl home* **10/1**

520- **5** *¾* **Taajub (IRE)**[71] 8099 10-8-12 **72**.......... JamieSpencer 8 69
(Peter Crate) *chsd ldng trio: hung rt bnd 2f out: shkn up over 1f out: unable qck and kpt on same pce ins fnl f: eased towards fin* **7/1**

46-0 **6** *shd* **Rosealee (IRE)**[30] 79 4-8-13 **78**.......... DavidParkes(5) 9 75
(Jeremy Gask) *in tch in last trio: effrt over 1f out: kpt on ins fnl f: nvr threatened ldrs* **12/1**

16-2 **7** *½* **Fly True**[15] 330 4-8-8 **68**..........(h) AdamBeschizza 5 63
(Jeremy Gask) *s.i.s: in tch in rr: effrt on inner over 1f out: kpt on same pce ins fnl f: nvr trbld ldrs* **7/1**

002- **8** *hd* **Come On Dave (IRE)**[46] 8463 8-9-5 **79**..........(v) LiamKeniry 1 73
(John Butler) *taken down early: sn bustled up to ld: rdn over 1f out: hdd 1f out: lost 2nd and wknd ins fnl f* **6/1**[3]

340- **9** *½* **Secret Asset (IRE)**[168] 5648 12-9-5 **79**..........(p) LukeMorris 6 72
(Lisa Williamson) *in tch in midfield: effrt 2f out: unable qck over 1f out: bhd and kpt on same pce ins fnl f* **33/1**

57.85s (-0.95) **Going Correction** -0.075s/f (Stan) **9** Ran SP% **115.7**
Speed ratings (Par 105): **104,102,101,100,99 99,98,97,97**
CSF £12.16 CT £98.84 TOTE £3.10: £1.40, £1.80, £2.90; EX 14.30 Trifecta £98.10.
**Owner** J C Smith **Bred** Littleton Stud **Trained** Kingsclere, Hants

**FOCUS**
The two for money came first and second and the form looks pretty solid.

## 574 BETWAY WINTER DERBY TRIAL STKS (LISTED RACE) (ALL-WEATHER CHAMPIONSHIPS FAST-TRACK QUALIFIER) 1m 2f (P)
**3:05** (3:08) (Class 1) 4-Y-O+
**£25,519** (£9,675; £4,842; £2,412; £1,210; £607) **Stalls** Low

Form RPR

121- **1** **Decorated Knight**[205] 4326 5-9-5 112.......... AndreaAtzeni 1 116
(Roger Charlton) *chsd ldrs: effrt and qcknd to chal 1f out: led 100yds out: r.o wl and a jst holding runner-up after* **9/2**

124- **2** *shd* **Arab Spring (IRE)**[111] 7402 7-9-5 113.......... RyanMoore 3 115
(Sir Michael Stoute) *chsd ldng pair: wnt 2nd 3f out tl rdn to ld wl over 1f out: drvn and hrd pressed 1f out: hdd 100yds out: r.o wl but a jst hld* **9/4**[1]

211- **3** *1 ¼* **Battalion (IRE)**[49] 8427 7-9-3 106.......... GeorgeBaker 4 110
(Jamie Osborne) *s.i.s: hld up in tch in rr: clsd and nt clr run ent fnl 2f: hdwy over 1f out: rdn to chse ldrs and hung lft ins fnl f: kpt on* **5/2**[2]

143- **4** *shd* **Grendisar (IRE)**[49] 8427 7-9-0 110..........(p) AdamKirby 2 107
(Marco Botti) *hld up in tch in midfield: effrt over 1f out: hdwy and drvn to chse ldrs ins fnl f: kpt on same pce wl ins fnl f* **3/1**[3]

0-21 **5** *1 ½* **Mythical Madness**[19] 266 6-9-0 101..........(v) DanielTudhope 5 104
(David O'Meara) *in tch in midfield: swtchd rt and clsd over 2f out: rdn to chse ldr over 1f out: sn dropped to 3rd and unable qck 1f out: lost 2 pls ins fnl f: eased towards fin* **20/1**

640- **6** *½* **Solar Deity (IRE)**[40] 8529 8-9-0 100..........(p) StevieDonohoe 8 103
(Jane Chapple-Hyam) *s.i.s: hld up in tch: effrt on outer over 2f out: no imp 1f out: kpt on same pce ins fnl f* **50/1**

41-3 **7** *7* **Forceful Appeal (USA)**[26] 148 9-9-0 93.......... TomMarquand 6 89
(Simon Dow) *led for 2f: chsd ldr tl 3f out: nt clr run on inner and shuffled bk 2f out: lost any ch and wl hld over 1f out* **50/1**

04-4 **8** *6* **Our Channel (USA)**[26] 148 6-9-0 102..........(p) JamieSpencer 7 77
(Jamie Osborne) *pressed ldrs on outer tl led after 2f: rdn 3f out: hdd wl over 1f out: sn btn and dropped out: bhd fnl f* **50/1**

2m 1.55s (-5.05) **Going Correction** -0.075s/f (Stan) **8** Ran SP% **113.2**
Speed ratings (Par 111): **117,116,115,115,114 114,108,103**
CSF £14.54 TOTE £5.00: £1.30, £1.40, £1.40; EX 15.50 Trifecta £42.90.
**Owner** Saleh Al Homaizi & Imad Al Sagar **Bred** Saleh Al Homaizi & Imad Al Sagar **Trained** Beckhampton, Wilts

**FOCUS**
A good, competitive Listed race, and the two carrying Group 3 penalties fought out the finish.

## 575 BETWAY SPRINT H'CAP 6f 1y(P)
**3:40** (3:43) (Class 5) (0-75,76) 4-Y-O+ **£2,911** (£866; £432; £216) **Stalls** Low

Form RPR

056- **1** **Varsovian**[38] 8561 7-9-6 **74**.......... RobertWinston 2 83
(Dean Ivory) *chsd ldng trio: effrt to chse ldr 1f out: r.o and rdn to ld wl ins fnl f: pushed out towards fin* **7/4**[1]

20-0 **2** *¾* **Rockley Point**[33] 25 4-9-7 **75**..........(p[1]) ShaneKelly 8 81
(Paul D'Arcy) *hld up in tch in midfield: swtchd rt and effrt over 1f out: styd on wl u.p ins fnl f: snatched 2nd last strides* **11/2**[2]

30-0 **3** *nk* **Aragon Knight**[15] 330 4-8-11 **68**.......... HectorCrouch(3) 11 73
(Heather Main) *led: edgd lft bnd 2f out: rdn over 1f out: hdd and no ex wl ins fnl f: lost 2nd last strides* **16/1**

5-11 **4** *¾* **Hamish McGonagain**[15] 327 4-8-13 **72**..........(p) DavidParkes(5) 9 75+
(Jeremy Gask) *off the pce in last pair: effrt over 1f out: hdwy ins fnl f: r.o strly fnl 100yds: nt rch ldrs* **6/1**[3]

42-1 **5** *nse* **Dreams Of Glory**[29] 95 9-9-0 **68**.......... LukeMorris 10 71
(Ron Hodges) *chsd ldrs: effrt over 1f out: unable qck u.p and styd on same pce ins fnl f* **25/1**

-022 **6** *nk* **Head Space (IRE)**[7] 468 9-8-13 **67**.......... StevieDonohoe 1 69
(David Evans) *hld up in midfield: effrt on inner over 1f out: kpt on but no imp ins fnl f* **8/1**

16-0 **7** *hd* **Nag's Wag (IRE)**[33] 25 4-9-6 **74**.......... LiamKeniry 6 75
(George Baker) *hld up in midfield: pushed along and effrt over 1f out: drvn ins fnl f: kpt on wout ever threatening wnr* **33/1**

00-0 **8** *2* **Picture Dealer**[22] 219 8-9-3 **74**..........(t) SimonPearce(3) 7 69
(Lydia Pearce) *squeezed for room leaving stalls and s.i.s: off the pce in last pair: effrt on inner over 1f out: kpt on: nvr trbld ldrs* **14/1**

000- **9** *2* **Bertie Blu Boy**[38] 8561 9-9-7 **75**..........(b) TomMarquand 3 63
(Lisa Williamson) *chsd ldr: squeezed for room and impeded bnd 2f out: rdn and unable qck over 1f out: lost 2nd 1f out: wknd qckly ins fnl f* **14/1**

021- **10** *½* **Gabrielle**[113] 7335 4-9-6 **74**.......... AdamKirby 5 61
(Dr Jon Scargill) *hld up in midfield: rdn and unable qck over 1f out: wknd ins fnl f* **16/1**

50-0 **11** *3 ¾* **Masarzain (IRE)**[33] 25 4-9-8 **76**.......... PaulMulrennan 4 51
(James Given) *sn in rr: a bhd* **10/1**

1m 10.75s (-1.15) **Going Correction** -0.075s/f (Stan) **11** Ran SP% **118.1**
Speed ratings (Par 103): **104,103,102,101,101 101,100,98,95,94 89**
CSF £10.98 CT £119.71 TOTE £2.80: £1.40, £2.30, £4.60; EX 13.90 Trifecta £134.60.
**Owner** Radlett Racing **Bred** Darley **Trained** Radlett, Herts

**FOCUS**
The money was a decent guide in this sprint handicap, the first two attracting good support.

## 576 BETWAY BEST ODDS GUARANTEED PLUS MAIDEN STKS 1m 4f (P)
**4:15** (4:15) (Class 5) 4-Y-O+ **£2,911** (£866; £432; £216) **Stalls** Low

Form RPR

/0-3 **1** **Darebin (GER)**[17] 289 5-9-8 75..........(b) GeorgeBaker 4 81
(Gary Moore) *hld up in last pair: hdwy to chse ldng pair over 3f out: clsd to trck ldrs 2f out: effrt to chal and bmpd 1f out: rdn and fnd enough ins fnl f to ld nr fin* **11/2**

3 **2** *nk* **Remember The Man (IRE)**[30] 74 4-9-5 74.......... RyanMoore 3 80
(Ralph Beckett) *led: rdn and edgd rt 2f out: edgd rt again 1f out: drvn and kpt on same pce ins fnl f: hdd nr fin* **7/4**[1]

**3** *8* **Appy Days (IRE)**[15] 7-9-3 0.......... AdamKirby 1 62
(Ian Williams) *chsd ldrs: rdn and lost 3rd over 3f out: stl cl enough in 4th 2f out: sn outpcd and wl hld 1f out: plugged on to go 3rd towards fin* **2/1**[2]

253- 4 ¾ **Casablanca (IRE)**[101] 7607 4-9-0 74................................ DavidProbert 5 61
(Andrew Balding) *chsd ldr: rdn and ev ch whn bmpd 2f out: dropped to 3rd and btn over 1f out: wknd fnl f: lost 3rd towards fin* **9/2**[3]
0- 5 16 **Montycristo**[346] 691 4-9-5 0.......................................... JamieSpencer 6 40
(Philip Hide) *in tch: 5th and rdn 3f out: sn btn: wl bhd over 1f out* **33/1**
2 6 92 **Treble Strike (USA)**[17] 289 4-9-5 0............................ RobertWinston 2
(Dean Ivory) *wl in tch in midfield: pushed along 8f out: reminder 7f out: rdn and dropped to last 3f out: sn lost tch and eased: t.o* **16/1**
2m 29.76s (-3.24) **Going Correction** -0.075s/f (Stan)
**WFA** 4 from 5yo+ 2lb **6** Ran SP% **112.1**
Speed ratings (Par 103): **107,106,101,100,90 28**
CSF £15.57 TOTE £7.90: £2.90, £1.30; EX 21.10 Trifecta £52.20.
**Owner** Chris Stedman & Mark Albon **Bred** Stall 5-Stars **Trained** Lower Beeding, W Sussex
**FOCUS**
An ordinary maiden. The first two had this between them from a furlong out.
T/Plt: £296.40 to a £1 stake. Pool: £76,825.26 - 189.19 winning units T/Qpdt: £36.10 to a £1 stake. Pool: £6,664.41 - 136.38 winning units **Steve Payne**

## 509 NEWCASTLE (A.W) (L-H)
### Saturday, February 4

**OFFICIAL GOING: Tapeta: standard**
Wind: Virtually nil Weather: Cloudy

### 577 32RED.COM H'CAP 1m 5y (Tp)
**5:45** (5:46) (Class 4) (0-80,78) 3-Y-O **£5,355** (£1,603; £801; £401) **Stalls** Centre

Form RPR
1 1 **Mystique Moon**[15] 331 3-9-7 78........................................ MartinLane 1 83+
(Charlie Appleby) *wnt lft s: trckd ldng pair: pushed along 2f out: rdn to chal jst over 1f out: qckd to ld ins fnl f: kpt on wl* **10/11**[1]
1 2 ¾ **Indian Dandy (IRE)**[28] 115 3-9-6 77........................(h[1]) DanielMuscutt 2 80
(Marco Botti) *trckd ldr: cl up 3f out: rdn to chal over 1f out: drvn and ev ch ent fnl f: kpt on* **3/1**[2]
505- 3 ¾ **Portledge (IRE)**[50] 8405 3-9-1 72....................................... PaulHanagan 4 73
(James Bethell) *set stdy pce: shkn up and qcknd over 2f out: rdn over 1f out: sn drvn: hdd ins fnl f: kpt on same pce* **4/1**[3]
011- 4 1 ¼ **Ronnie The Rooster**[88] 7854 3-8-10 67....................... ConnorBeasley 3 65
(David Barron) *trckd ldng pair: hdwy on outer and cl up 1/2-way: rdn over 1f out: ev ch tl drvn and kpt on same pce ins fnl f* **9/1**
1m 43.47s (4.87) **Going Correction** +0.20s/f (Slow) **4** Ran SP% **107.4**
Speed ratings (Par 99): **83,82,81,80**
CSF £3.82 TOTE £1.70; EX 3.90 Trifecta £7.50.
**Owner** Godolphin **Bred** Meon Valley Stud **Trained** Newmarket, Suffolk
**FOCUS**
A fair 3yo handicap which turned into a sprint for home from over 2f out off a slow gallop on standard Tapeta.

### 578 32RED CASINO H'CAP 6f (Tp)
**6:15** (6:16) (Class 5) (0-75,77) 3-Y-O **£3,557** (£1,058; £529; £264) **Stalls** Centre

Form RPR
-334 1 **Alkashaaf (USA)**[7] 458 3-9-9 77..................................(tp) OisinMurphy 3 82
(Archie Watson) *trckd ldrs: hdwy on inner over 2f out: rdn to chal jst over 1f out: drvn ins fnl f: kpt on to ld last 100 yds* **9/4**[1]
1 2 ¾ **Jack Flash (FR)**[28] 119 3-9-3 76.............................. LewisEdmunds(5) 1 78
(Les Eyre) *led: pushed along over 2f out: rdn over 1f out: drvn ent fnl f: hdd and kpt on same pce fnl 100 yds* **7/2**[2]
22-3 3 1 ¼ **Arzaak (IRE)**[16] 307 3-9-7 75............................................ JoeFanning 6 73
(Chris Dwyer) *trckd ldr: hdwy and cl up 2f out: rdn over 1f out and ev ch: drvn and kpt on same pce fnl f* **7/1**
0-20 4 hd **Mr Strutter (IRE)**[19] 264 3-8-1 58 ow2...................(h[1]) NathanEvans(3) 5 55
(John Quinn) *trckd ldrs: hdwy over 2f out: rdn along and sltly outpcd wl over 1f out: kpt on fnl f* **11/1**
-225 5 1 **Things Happen**[22] 221 3-9-2 70........................................ ConnorBeasley 7 64
(David Evans) *cl up on outer: pushed along 1/2-way: rdn over 2f out: wknd over 1f out* **7/1**
3-52 6 ½ **Hotfill**[10] 401 3-8-13 67......................................................... PhillipMakin 4 60
(David Barron) *hld up: hdwy wl over 2f out: rdn along wl over 1f out: sn no imp* **4/1**[3]
126- 7 4 ½ **Trick Of The Lyte (IRE)**[138] 6614 3-8-13 67........................ JasonHart 2 45
(John Quinn) *dwlt: a rr* **12/1**
1m 12.97s (0.47) **Going Correction** +0.20s/f (Slow) **7** Ran SP% **114.0**
Speed ratings (Par 97): **104,103,101,101,99 99,93**
CSF £10.19 TOTE £3.20: £1.90, £1.90; EX 12.50 Trifecta £32.40.
**Owner** The Keg Partnership **Bred** Shadwell Farm LLC **Trained** Upper Lambourn, W Berks
**FOCUS**
A fair 3yo sprint handicap. They went a respectable gallop and it is sound form.

### 579 SUN BETS ON THE APP STORE APPRENTICE H'CAP 7f 14y (Tp)
**6:45** (6:46) (Class 6) (0-60,58) 4-Y-O+ **£2,264** (£673; £336; £168) **Stalls** Centre

Form RPR
322- 1 **Table Manners**[36] 8589 5-9-3 54.......................................... HollieDoyle 3 61
(Wilf Storey) *trckd ldrs: pushed along and hdwy over 2f out: led jst over 1f out: sn rdn and kpt on* **11/2**[2]
-602 2 nk **Justice Pleasing**[8] 445 4-8-13 55.....................(p) BenSanderson(5) 5 61
(Roger Fell) *cl up: led wl over 2f out: rdn and ev ch whn bmpd jst over 1f out: sn drvn and kpt on wl towards fin* **6/1**[3]
0-20 3 1 ¾ **Disclosure**[22] 222 6-9-7 58.......................................(h) PhilDennis 12 60
(Les Eyre) *hld up in rr: smooth hdwy on outer over 2f out: chal over 1f out: sn rdn and hung bdly lft: kpt on ins fnl f* **20/1**
20-2 4 shd **Canford Belle**[10] 400 4-9-3 54................................... PatrickVaughan 1 56
(Grant Tuer) *hld up in tch: hdwy over 2f out: chsd ldrs over 1f out: sn rdn and kpt on same pce* **12/1**
-323 5 nk **Major Muscari (IRE)**[10] 398 9-9-7 58..................(v[1]) CharlieBennett 10 59
(Shaun Harris) *t.k.h: hld up towards rr: hdwy over 2f out: chsd ldrs over 1f out: sn rdn and kpt on same pce* **7/1**
3-65 6 ½ **Cool Strutter (IRE)**[8] 445 5-9-6 57..............................(b) GemmaTutty 9 57
(Karen Tutty) *t.k.h: hld up in rr: hdwy over 2f out: rdn over 1f out: kpt on fnl f: nrst fin* **14/1**
000- 7 3 ¼ **Tom's Anna (IRE)**[56] 8307 7-8-3 45.................................. PaulaMuir(5) 11 37
(Sean Regan) *chsd ldrs: pushed along over 2f out: sn rdn and grad wknd* **100/1**
60-4 8 ¾ **A Boy Named Sue**[10] 400 4-8-11 48..............................(p) JoshDoyle 2 38
(Peter Niven) *midfield: hdwy on inner and in tch 1/2-way: rdn along over 2f out: n.d* **9/1**
04-0 9 1 ½ **Jessie Allan (IRE)**[8] 445 6-8-8 45.................................... RowanScott 6 31
(Jim Goldie) *trckd ldrs: rdn along 2f out: grad wknd* **66/1**
-0P5 10 2 **Devious Spirit (IRE)**[10] 400 5-9-3 54.......................... CallumRodriguez 7 35
(Iain Jardine) *s.i.s and lost several l s: bhd tl hdwy 1/2-way: rdn and in tch on inner 2f out: sn drvn and wknd* **7/1**
004- 11 3 ½ **Centre Haafhd**[57] 8289 6-8-8 45.................................... LewisEdmunds 8 17
(Kenneth Slack) *trckd ldng pair: pushed along wl over 2f out: sn rdn and wknd* **7/2**[1]
00-0 12 2 ¼ **Daleelak (IRE)**[21] 238 4-9-4 55........................................ RichardOliver 4 22
(Mark Johnston) *slt ld: pushed along 3f out: sn rdn: hdd & wknd* **25/1**
00-0 13 nk **Boboli Gardens**[9] 425 7-8-4 46.............................. JamieGormley(5) 13 12
(Iain Jardine) *midfield: hdwy on outer and in tch 21/2f out: sn rdn and wknd* **14/1**
1m 27.26s (1.06) **Going Correction** +0.20s/f (Slow) **13** Ran SP% **119.0**
Speed ratings (Par 101): **101,100,98,98,98 97,93,93,91,89 85,82,82**
CSF £37.19 CT £644.37 TOTE £6.20: £2.20, £2.20, £6.40; EX 40.30 Trifecta £650.10.
**Owner** Geegeez.co.uk 1 **Bred** Raymond Clive Tooth **Trained** Muggleswick, Co Durham
**FOCUS**
A moderate apprentice riders' handicap, but they went a sound gallop and generally the right horses came to the fore. The winner found a fraction on previous form.

### 580 SUN BETS MAIDEN STKS 1m 5y (Tp)
**7:15** (7:15) (Class 5) 3-5-Y-O **£3,234** (£962; £481; £240) **Stalls** Centre

Form RPR
1 **Garrick** 3-8-9 0........................................................................ NickyMackay 9 81+
(John Gosden) *in tch: hdwy over 3f out: pushed along over 2f out: rdn to chse ldr over 1f out: swtchd lft ent fnl f: styd on wl u.p to ld last 100 yds* **1/1**[1]
0- 2 1 ¼ **War At Sea (IRE)**[85] 7908 3-8-9 0.................................. OisinMurphy 11 78+
(David Simcock) *prom: cl up over 4f out: led 3f out: rdn clr wl over 1f out: drvn and edgd rt ent fnl f: hdd and no ex last 100 yds* **11/4**[2]
63-0 3 6 **Naupaka**[28] 115 3-8-4 71.......................................................... BenCurtis 2 59
(Brian Ellison) *t.k.h early: hld up: hdwy 3f out: rdn along 2f out: styd on u.p appr fnl f* **16/1**
02 4 ½ **Crindle Carr (IRE)**[23] 198 3-8-9 0................................ ConnorBeasley 6 63
(David Barron) *hld up and bhd: swtchd rt and hdwy 3f out: sn pushed along: rdn 2f out: styd on u.p fnl f* **16/1**
0-0 5 1 **Costa Percy**[19] 265 3-8-9 0............................................ JoeyHaynes 12 61
(K R Burke) *cl up: rdn along wl over 2f out: sn drvn and grad wknd* **50/1**
6 6 6 **Dibloam (USA)**[15] 331 4-10-0 0.................................... PhillipMakin 7 52
(David Evans) *chsd ldrs: rdn along 3f out: sn outpcd* **100/1**
54-6 7 3 ½ **Psychology**[24] 175 4-10-0 0...................................... DougieCostello 10 44
(Kenny Johnson) *dwlt and hld up in rr: hdwy 3f out: rdn along over 2f out: sn wknd* **80/1**
000- 8 3 ½ **Diamond Eagle (IRE)**[36] 8585 5-9-9 0.................... CharlieBennett(5) 4 36
(Shaun Harris) *slt ld: rdn along and hdd 3f out: sn wknd* **200/1**
0 9 1 ½ **River Warrior**[15] 331 3-8-9 0........................................ TonyHamilton 8 28
(Richard Fahey) *a towards rr* **100/1**
3 10 5 **Touch Of Paradise (IRE)**[31] 40 3-8-4 0..................... PaulHanagan 5 11
(Richard Fahey) *trckd ldrs: pushed along over 3f out: rdn wl over 2f out and sn wknd* **3/1**[3]
0/- 11 nk **Roundabout Time (IRE)**[476] 7283 4-10-0 0.................... GrahamLee 3 20
(Ann Duffield) *a towards rr* **100/1**
5 12 8 **Billys Connoisseur (IRE)**[10] 402 4-10-0 0............... DuranFentiman 1
(Tim Easterby) *prom on inner: pushed along over 3f out:. sn rdn and wknd* **100/1**
1m 39.78s (1.18) **Going Correction** +0.20s/f (Slow)
**WFA** 3 from 4yo+ 19lb **12** Ran SP% **121.1**
Speed ratings (Par 103): **102,100,94,94,93 87,83,80,78,73 73,65**
CSF £4.07 TOTE £2.50: £1.20, £1.10, £3.10; EX 5.30 Trifecta £32.70.
**Owner** Denford Stud **Bred** Denford Stud Ltd **Trained** Newmarket, Suffolk
**FOCUS**
An ordinary maiden in terms of prior form, but the front two came well clear of a 71-rated horse in third who reproduced her best C&D display.

### 581 SUNBETS.CO.UK H'CAP 7f 14y (Tp)
**7:45** (7:45) (Class 4) (0-85,83) 4-Y-O+ **£5,498** (£1,636; £817; £408) **Stalls** Centre

Form RPR
003- 1 **Free Code (IRE)**[56] 8319 6-9-2 78.................................. PhillipMakin 11 87
(David Barron) *prom: cl up 1/2-way: rdn to chse ldr over 1f out: drvn ins fnl f: kpt on wl to ld nr fin* **12/1**
10-3 2 nk **Curzon Line**[14] 363 8-8-9 74...................................... NathanEvans(3) 2 82
(Michael Easterby) *set stdy pce: pushed along and qcknd 2f out: rdn over 1f out:. drvn ins fnl f: hdd and no ex nr fin* **14/1**
24-0 3 1 ½ **Shypen**[30] 66 4-9-4 80.......................................................... PaulHagan 4 84
(Richard Fahey) *trckd ldrs: hdwy over 2f out: rdn over 1f out: drvn and kpt on same pce fnl f* **8/1**[3]
3-20 4 nk **War Department (IRE)**[18] 275 4-9-7 83................(v) ConnorBeasley 13 86
(Keith Dalgleish) *trckd ldrs: pushed along over 2f out: rdn over 1f out: kpt on fnl f: nrst fin* **5/1**[2]
1-14 5 nk **Testa Rossa (IRE)**[14] 359 7-8-13 80.................(b) LewisEdmunds(5) 10 82+
(Jim Goldie) *hld up in rr: hdwy wl over 1f out: rdn and nt clr run jst ins fnl f: sn swtchd rt and styd on wl towards fin* **4/1**[1]
43-1 6 ½ **Bint Arcano (FR)**[26] 151 4-9-3 79........................................ JoeDoyle 5 80
(Julie Camacho) *cl up: rdn along 2f out: drvn over 1f out: wknd fnl f* **8/1**[3]
215 7 nse **Revolutionary War (USA)**[7] 460 4-9-3 79................... DougieCostello 6 80
(Jamie Osborne) *midfield: rdn along over 2f out: n.d* **10/1**
0-46 8 nk **Merdon Castle (IRE)**[10] 403 5-9-1 77..........................(e) JackGarritty 9 77
(Ruth Carr) *hld up towards rr: hdwy 2f out: rdn to chse ldrs ent fnl f: sn drvn and kpt on same pce* **16/1**
0-40 9 ½ **Young John (IRE)**[18] 275 4-9-6 82................................. TonyHamilton 1 80
(Richard Fahey) *t.k.h: chsd ldrs: rdn along over 2f out: sn drvn and wknd* **14/1**
5-11 10 1 **Safe Voyage (IRE)**[8] 441 4-9-7 83...................................... JasonHart 7 79
(John Quinn) *in tch: pushed along 3f out: rdn along over 2f out: sn wknd* **5/1**[2]
02-0 11 1 ½ **Like No Other**[32] 32 4-8-12 79..................................(p[1]) PhilDennis(5) 12 71
(Les Eyre) *a towards rr* **20/1**
550- 12 ¾ **Shamaheart (IRE)**[92] 7796 7-9-7 83..........................(p) JoeFanning 8 73
(Geoffrey Harker) *dwlt: a rr* **33/1**
1m 27.39s (1.19) **Going Correction** +0.20s/f (Slow) **12** Ran SP% **119.3**
Speed ratings (Par 105): **101,100,98,98,98 97,97,97,96,95 93,93**
CSF £170.10 CT £1452.54 TOTE £16.40: £3.60, £4.40, £2.90; EX 184.30 Trifecta £2510.20.
**Owner** Ron Hull & Laurence O'Kane **Bred** Rory O'Brien **Trained** Maunby, N Yorks

**FOCUS**
The feature contest was a decent handicap, but they went a modest gallop and it paid to race prominently.

## 582 BETWAY FILLIES' H'CAP 6f (Tp)
8:15 (8:15) (Class 5) (0-75,75) 4-Y-0+ **£3,234** (£962; £481; £240) **Stalls Centre**

| Form | | | | RPR |
|---|---|---|---|---|
| 00-4 | 1 | | **Veena (FR)**[26] 151 4-9-3 **71** ... OisinMurphy 2 (David Simcock) *trckd ldng pair: cl up 2f out: sn chal: rdn to ld ins fnl f: drvn out* **5/2**[1] | 80 |
| 5-21 | 2 | *hd* | **Poppy In The Wind**[14] 358 5-9-0 **73** ...(v) HollieDoyle(5) 5 (Alan Brown) *trckd ldrs: hdwy over 1f out: rdn ent fnl f: sn chal and ev ch: rdr dropped reins last 50 yds: hld towards fin* **5/2**[1] | 81 |
| 3142 | 3 | *1 ¾* | **Englishwoman**[9] 416 4-9-2 **75** ... LewisEdmunds(5) 4 (David Evans) *trckd ldr: cl up 2f out: rdn to ld over 1f out: drvn and hdd ins fnl f: kpt on same pce* **3/1**[2] | 78 |
| 23-2 | 4 | *2* | **Sugar Town**[8] 446 7-8-3 **60** ... NathanEvans(3) 1 (Peter Niven) *led: jnd and rdn 2f out: sn hdd & wknd appr fnl f* **9/2**[3] | 56 |
| 3-05 | 5 | *1* | **Thorntoun Lady (USA)**[14] 362 7-8-4 **58** ... NickyMackay 3 (Jim Goldie) *hld up: hdwy to chse ldrs on inner 2f out: sn rdn and wknd* **9/1** | 51 |

1m 13.66s (1.16) **Going Correction** +0.20s/f (Slow) **5** Ran SP% **110.3**
Speed ratings (Par 100): **100,99,97,94,93**
CSF £9.04 TOTE £3.60: £1.90, £1.20; EX 10.00 Trifecta £21.00.
**Owner** Chola Dynasty **Bred** Ecurie Haras De Beauvoir **Trained** Newmarket, Suffolk

**FOCUS**
A fair fillies' handicap. They went a respectable gallop and the form makes sense.

## 583 BETWAY H'CAP 6f (Tp)
8:45 (8:49) (Class 6) (0-65,65) 4-Y-0+ **£2,587** (£770; £384; £192) **Stalls Centre**

| Form | | | | RPR |
|---|---|---|---|---|
| 65-2 | 1 | | **Spirit Of Zebedee (IRE)**[14] 362 4-9-3 **61** ...(p) JasonHart 5 (John Quinn) *cl up: rdn to ld over 1f out: drvn ins fnl f: kpt on wl towards fin* **10/3**[1] | 67 |
| 41-4 | 2 | *¾* | **Commanche**[16] 302 8-9-7 **65** ...(b) JoeFanning 4 (Chris Dwyer) *prom: effrt to chal over 1f out: sn rdn and ev ch: drvn ins fnl f: no ex towards fin* **6/1**[3] | 69 |
| -203 | 3 | *nk* | **Hadley**[16] 311 4-8-6 **50** ... BenCurtis 6 (Tracy Waggott) *hld up: hdwy over 2f out: rdn to chse ldrs over 1f out: drvn and kpt on fnl f* **12/1** | 53 |
| 033- | 4 | *hd* | **Ki Ki**[95] 7747 5-9-2 **60** ... ConnorBeasley 8 (Bryan Smart) *chsd ldrs:. hdwy 2f out: rdn over 1f out: drvn and kpt on fnl f* **6/1**[3] | 62 |
| 40-3 | 5 | *1 ¼* | **Sea Of Green**[8] 446 5-8-2 **46** ... NickyMackay 3 (Jim Goldie) *towards rr: hdwy 2f out: sn rdn and kpt on fnl f* **25/1** | 45 |
| 6-62 | 6 | *½* | **Spirit Of Wedza (IRE)**[16] 302 5-9-6 **64** ... JoeDoyle 7 (Julie Camacho) *slt ld: rdn along 2f out: sn hdd and drvn: wknd fnl f* **4/1**[2] | 61 |
| 03-3 | 7 | *nk* | **Tango Sky (IRE)**[24] 172 8-9-4 **62** ... GrahamLee 1 (Paul Midgley) *in tch: hdwy to chse ldrs 2f out: rdn over 1f out: sn one pce* **16/1** | 58 |
| 42-0 | 8 | *6* | **Insolenceofoffice (IRE)**[8] 446 9-8-11 **55** ...(p) JackGarritty 10 (Richard Ford) *towards rr: rdn along and outpcd fr 1/2-way* **50/1** | 33 |
| 00/6 | 9 | *nse* | **Beau Amadeus (IRE)**[14] 362 8-8-9 **53** ... JoeyHaynes 2 (Susan Corbett) *chsd ldrs on inner: rdn along over 2f out: sn wknd* **16/1** | 31 |
| 21-0 | 10 | *3 ½* | **Napoleon Solo**[9] 426 5-9-5 **63** ... PhillipMakin 9 (David Barron) *midfield: rdn along over 2f out:. sn wknd* **4/1**[2] | 30 |

1m 12.25s (-0.25) **Going Correction** +0.20s/f (Slow) **10** Ran SP% **116.9**
Speed ratings (Par 101): **109,108,107,107,105 105,104,96,96,91**
CSF £23.70 CT £215.19 TOTE £4.10: £1.60, £1.80, £3.00; EX 25.80 Trifecta £264.60.
**Owner** Malcolm Walker **Bred** N Hartery **Trained** Settrington, N Yorks
■ Stewards' Enquiry : Jason Hart jockey ban: two day ban (18 & 20 February) - used whip in the incorrect place
Connor Beasley jockey said the mare hung left in the closing stages

**FOCUS**
A modest handicap, but they went a solid gallop, and the form should hold up to scrutiny despite a bunched finish. The second looks the best guide.
T/Plt: £183.40 to a £1 stake. Pool: £105,836.36 - 421.24 winning units T/Qpdt: £79.20 to a £1 stake. Pool: £9,481.59 - 88.57 winning units **Joe Rowntree**

# 515 CAGNES-SUR-MER
Saturday, February 4
**OFFICIAL GOING: Polytrack: standard**

## 584a PRIX DU QUARTIER SAINT-JEAN (MAIDEN) (3YO) (POLYTRACK) 1m (P)
1:50 3-Y-0 **£10,256** (£4,102; £3,076; £2,051; £1,025)

| | | | RPR |
|---|---|---|---|
| 1 | | **Sixty Sixty (FR)** 3-9-2 0 ... HugoJourniac 5 (J-C Rouget, France) **11/10**[1] | |
| 2 | *2* | **Naadheer (IRE)** 3-9-2 0 ... Francois-XavierBertras 4 (F Rohaut, France) **68/10**[3] | |
| 3 | *¾* | **Dibazari (FR)** 3-9-2 0 ... PierreBazire 6 (G Botti, France) **99/10** | |
| 4 | *1 ½* | **Tilo (IRE)** 3-9-2 0 ... FranckBlondel 11 (Simone Brogi, France) **142/10** | |
| 5 | *shd* | **Cima Da Conegliano (FR)** 3-9-2 0 ...(p) CristianDemuro 2 (M Arienti, Italy) **187/10** | |
| 6 | *1 ½* | **Espoir Bere (FR)** 3-9-2 0 ... Pierre-CharlesBoudot 3 (D Prod'Homme, France) **84/10** | |
| 7 | *1 ¼* | **Different Views (USA)**[176] 5377 3-9-2 0 ... MickaelForest 10 (Gay Kelleway) *chsd ldrs: drvn to chal over 1 1/2f out: sn rdn and nt qckn: wknd ins fnl f* **55/1** | |
| 8 | *1 ¼* | **Best Vision (FR)** 3-9-2 0 ... RaphaelMarchelli 1 (J-M Capitte, France) **38/1** | |
| 9 | *4* | **O'Goshi (FR)**[49] 3-9-2 0 ... RonanThomas 8 (J Phelippon, France) **11/2**[2] | |
| 10 | *7* | **Iteratif** 3-9-2 0 ... TonyPiccone 7 (K Borgel, France) **134/10** | |

1m 37.81s **10** Ran SP% **118.6**
PARI-MUTUEL (all including 1 euro stake): WIN: 2.10; PLACE: 1.10, 1.90, 2.00; DF: 7.10; SF: 9.10.
**Owner** Sarl Ecurie J L Tepper **Bred** Mme G Forien & G Forien **Trained** Pau, France

585 - 597a (Foreign Racing) - See Raceform Interactive

# 494 WOLVERHAMPTON (A.W) (L-H)
Monday, February 6
**OFFICIAL GOING: Tapeta: standard**
Wind: Light across Weather: Overcast with the odd shower

## 598 SUN BETS ON THE APP STORE H'CAP 7f 36y (Tp)
2:20 (2:20) (Class 3) (0-95,95) 4-Y-0 **£7,246** (£2,168; £1,084; £542; £270) **Stalls High**

| Form | | | | RPR |
|---|---|---|---|---|
| 51-6 | 1 | | **Nimr**[25] 199 4-9-2 **90** ... TonyHamilton 2 (Richard Fahey) *a.p: chsd ldr over 2f out: rdn to ld wl ins fnl f: r.o* **3/1**[2] | 100 |
| 633- | 2 | *½* | **Russian Soul (IRE)**[45] 8513 9-9-5 **93** ...(p) AdamKirby 9 (Jamie Osborne) *s.i.s: hld up: hdwy over 1f out: rdn and edgd lft ins fnl f: r.o wl* **9/2**[3] | 101+ |
| 4-31 | 3 | *¾* | **Captain Dion**[12] 403 4-9-1 **89** ...(v) KevinStott 7 (Kevin Ryan) *led: rdn over 1f out: hung lft: hdd and unable qck wl ins fnl f* **11/4**[1] | 95 |
| 54-2 | 4 | *2* | **Joey's Destiny (IRE)**[20] 275 7-8-13 **87** ... LiamKeniry 8 (George Baker) *hld up: rdn over 1f out: hung lft and r.o ins fnl f* **6/1** | 88 |
| 2-00 | 5 | *5* | **Shyron**[25] 199 6-8-9 **90** ... JaneElliott(7) 1 (George Margarson) *hld up: effrt and nt clr run over 1f out: styd on same pce* **10/1** | 77 |
| 120- | 6 | *shd* | **George Cinq**[184] 5146 7-9-7 **95** ... OisinMurphy 5 (George Scott) *prom: rdn over 1f out: wknd ins fnl f* **14/1** | 82 |
| 1-06 | 7 | *nk* | **Swiss Cross**[19] 287 10-8-7 **81** oh1 ...(tp) JosephineGordon 4 (Phil McEntee) *hld up: pushed along and hdwy over 2f out: rdn over 1f out: wknd fnl f* **22/1** | 67 |
| 245- | 8 | *1 ½* | **Alejandro (IRE)**[95] 7781 8-8-9 **83** ... PJMcDonald 6 (David Loughnane) *chsd ldrs: rdn over 2f out: wknd over 1f out* **20/1** | 65 |
| 400- | 9 | *4 ½* | **Suqoor**[128] 6962 4-9-4 **92** ... JoeFanning 3 (Chris Dwyer) *chsd ldr tl rdn over 2f out: wknd over 1f out* **25/1** | 62 |

1m 26.4s (-2.40) **Going Correction** 0.0s/f (Stan) **9** Ran SP% **112.8**
Speed ratings (Par 107): **113,112,111,109,103 103,103,101,96**
CSF £15.93 CT £39.77 TOTE £3.70: £1.40, £1.60, £1.40; EX 18.00 Trifecta £50.90.
**Owner** Al Shaqab Racing **Bred** Mr & Mrs G Middlebrook **Trained** Musley Bank, N Yorks

**FOCUS**
A useful handicap, it paid to race handy and the runner-up, therefore, needs his effort upgrading. The winner is still improving.

## 599 BETWAY H'CAP 1m 1f 104y (Tp)
2:50 (2:50) (Class 4) (0-85,87) 4-Y-0+ **£5,498** (£1,636; £817; £408) **Stalls Low**

| Form | | | | RPR |
|---|---|---|---|---|
| 200- | 1 | | **Count Montecristo (FR)**[163] 5886 5-9-2 **77** ... TomEaves 6 (Kevin Ryan) *mde all: pushed clr wl over 1f out: styd on wl: eased nr fin* **12/1** | 88 |
| 301- | 2 | *2 ¼* | **Hairdryer**[77] 8048 4-9-0 **75** ... OisinMurphy 7 (Andrew Balding) *trckd ldrs: racd keenly: shkn up to chse wnr over 1f out: rdn and edgd lft ins fnl f: styd on same pce* **7/2**[2] | 80 |
| 0-45 | 3 | *¾* | **Tangramm**[14] 381 5-9-7 **82** ...(p) RobertWinston 8 (Dean Ivory) *hld up: rdn and hung lft over 1f out: r.o ins fnl f: wnt 3rd post: nt rch ldrs* **7/1** | 85 |
| 0- | 4 | *shd* | **A L'Anglaise**[83] 4-9-5 **80** ... LukeMorris 10 (Rae Guest) *hld up in tch: rdn over 1f out: edgd lft and styd on same pce ins fnl f* **25/1** | 83 |
| 541/ | 5 | *½* | **Every Chance (IRE)**[420] 8225 4-9-12 **87** ... AdamKirby 5 (Jamie Osborne) *s.i.s: hld up: nt clr run over 1f out: r.o ins fnl f: nt rch ldrs* **11/4**[1] | 89+ |
| 0-01 | 6 | *½* | **Modernism**[14] 381 8-9-5 **80** ... StevieDonohoe 4 (Ian Williams) *chsd ldrs: rdn over 2f out: no ex ins fnl f* **15/2** | 81 |
| 042- | 7 | *1 ¼* | **Craftsmanship (FR)**[93] 7816 6-9-5 **80** ... JackMitchell 2 (Robert Eddery) *prom: rdn over 1f out: no ex fnl f* **15/2** | 78 |
| 54-3 | 8 | *hd* | **Berlusca (IRE)**[18] 306 8-8-13 **79** ... JoshDoyle(5) 1 (David O'Meara) *hld up: rdn and hung lft fr over 1f out: nvr trbld ldrs* **11/2**[3] | 77 |
| 0- | 9 | *hd* | **Takbeer (IRE)**[131] 6870 5-9-5 **80** ...(p) DavidProbert 3 (Nikki Evans) *hld up: rdn over 1f out: nvr on terms* **100/1** | 77 |
| 0-30 | 10 | *1 ½* | **Hard To Handel**[5] 507 5-8-12 **73** ... PaddyAspell 9 (Clare Ellam) *chsd wnr: rdn over 2f out: lost 2nd over 1f out: wknd fnl f* **66/1** | 67 |

1m 58.57s (-2.23) **Going Correction** 0.0s/f (Stan) **10** Ran SP% **114.3**
Speed ratings (Par 105): **109,107,106,106,105 105,104,104,103,102**
CSF £52.43 CT £321.92 TOTE £15.20: £3.60, £2.20, £1.80; EX 76.80 Trifecta £575.20.
**Owner** Middleham Park Racing XLVI **Bred** Jean-Pierre Deroubaix **Trained** Hambleton, N Yorks

**FOCUS**
A decent handicap, it again paid to race handily. There were a few performances of note and the race should produce winners, with the winner rated to his best.

## 600 BETWAY MEDIAN AUCTION MAIDEN STKS 6f 20y (Tp)
3:20 (3:22) (Class 6) 3-5-Y-0 **£2,587** (£770; £384; £192) **Stalls Low**

| Form | | | | RPR |
|---|---|---|---|---|
| 045- | 1 | | **Right Action**[163] 5884 3-8-13 73 ... TonyHamilton 3 (Richard Fahey) *a.p: rdn to ld ins fnl f: styd on* **5/2**[2] | 68 |
| 262- | 2 | *½* | **Poetic Queen (IRE)**[59] 8290 4-9-9 55 ... AdamKirby 2 (Eric Alston) *chsd ldrs: wnt 2nd over 2f out: rdn over 1f out: ev ch ins fnl f: kpt on* **11/1** | 65 |
| | 3 | *1 ½* | **Harlequin Storm (IRE)** 3-8-13 0 ... RobertWinston 1 (Dean Ivory) *mid-div: hdwy over 1f out: styd on* **25/1** | 62+ |
| 3-2 | 4 | *¾* | **Blue Bahia (IRE)**[32] 76 3-8-8 73 ... PJMcDonald 8 (Mark Johnston) *led: shkn up over 1f out: rdn: hdd and no ex ins fnl f* **6/5**[1] | 54 |
| 4 | 5 | *nk* | **Arabella Rose**[17] 331 3-8-8 0 ... JoeyHaynes 6 (Ivan Furtado) *prom: racd keenly: rdn and hung lft fr over 1f out: styd on same pce* **8/1**[3] | 53 |
| 5- | 6 | *3 ¾* | **Trotter**[213] 4083 3-8-13 0 ... OisinMurphy 9 (Stuart Kittow) *chsd ldr tl rdn over 2f out: wknd ins fnl f* **16/1** | 47 |
| 5 | 7 | *1 ½* | **Ebitda**[11] 415 3-8-8 0 ... LukeMorris 7 (Scott Dixon) *mid-div: rdn over 2f out: wknd over 1f out* **20/1** | 40 |
| 0- | 8 | *1* | **Captain Sedgwick (IRE)**[54] 8352 3-8-8 0 ... TomMarquand 4 (John Spearing) *hld up: racd keenly: rdn over 2f out: nvr on terms* **200/1** | 35 |
| | 9 | *6* | **Groundskeeperwilly** 3-8-13 0 ... AndrewMullen 10 (David Evans) *s.i.s: a in rr* **16/1** | 22 |
| | 10 | *6* | **Gerry** 4-9-9 0 ... JohnFahy 5 (Matthew Salaman) *s.s: rdn over 2f out: a in rr* **200/1** | |


The Form Book Flat, Raceform Ltd, Newbury, RG14 5SJ

0/ **11** ½ **Inspire**[938] 4269 5-9-9 0 StevieDonohoe 11
(Matthew Salaman) *s.i.s: sn outpcd* **100/1**

1m 14.96s (0.46) **Going Correction** 0.0s/f (Stan)
**WFA** 3 from 4yo+ 15lb **11** Ran SP% **115.8**
Speed ratings (Par 101): **96,95,93,92,91 86,84,83,75,67 66**
CSF £28.47 TOTE £4.10: £1.40, £2.50, £5.20; EX 27.50 Trifecta £329.40.
**Owner** Middleham Park Racing LVII & Partner **Bred** Aunty Ifl **Trained** Musley Bank, N Yorks

**FOCUS**
A pretty modest maiden, with the runner-up rated just 55 and the favourite disappointing. The winner remains well below his standout 2yo effort.

## 601 BETWAY SPRINT H'CAP (DIV I) 6f 20y (Tp)
**3:50** (3:50) (Class 6) (0-60,60) 4-Y-0+ **£2,587** (£770; £384; £192) **Stalls** Low

Form RPR

-031 **1** **Pushkin Museum (IRE)**[6] 495 6-9-7 **60** 6ex GrahamLee 8 68+
(Patrick Morris) *hld up: racd keenly: hdwy over 1f out: r.o to ld wl ins fnl f* **6/4**[1]

6-03 **2** ½ **Kyllach Me (IRE)**[24] 216 5-8-13 **55** (b) NathanEvans(3) 1 61
(Bryan Smart) *a.p: rdn over 2f out: chsd wnr over 1f out: ev ch ins fnl f: r.o* **9/2**[2]

0-00 **3** 1¼ **Loumarin (IRE)**[13] 386 5-9-5 **58** (p¹) BenCurtis 2 60
(Michael Appleby) *sn w ldr: led over 3f out: rdn and hdd wl ins fnl f: styd on same pce* **16/1**

-662 **4** 5 **Justice Rock**[10] 438 4-8-9 **48** JosephineGordon 7 35
(Phil McEntee) *led: hdd over 3f out: rdn over 2f out: wknd ins fnl f* **20/1**

0-00 **5** ½ **Silver Springs (IRE)**[9] 468 4-8-10 **56** KatherineGlenister(7) 3 42
(David Evans) *sn pushed along to chse ldrs: rdn over 2f out: wknd over 1f out* **33/1**

0-00 **6** ½ **Virile (IRE)**[11] 426 6-8-12 **56** (b) MitchGodwin(5) 12 40
(Sylvester Kirk) *s.i.s: sn pushed along in rr: r.o ins fnl f: nvr nrr* **14/1**

-053 **7** ½ **Socialites Red**[18] 302 4-9-6 **59** (p) LukeMorris 13 42
(Scott Dixon) *w ldr early: remained handy: rdn over 2f out: wknd over 1f out* **14/1**

55-3 **8** 2¾ **Wedgewood Estates**[20] 273 6-9-1 **54** GeorgeDowning 5 29
(Tony Carroll) *mid-div: hdwy over 2f out: rdn over 1f out: wknd fnl f* **12/1**

4-00 **9** 3½ **Baileys Pursuit**[24] 217 5-9-6 **59** (v) TonyHamilton 4 23
(Gay Kelleway) *s.i.s and hmpd s: nvr on terms* **12/1**

00-0 **10** 5 **Barnsdale**[13] 386 4-8-0 **46** oh1 MeganEllingworth(7) 6
(John Holt) *chsd ldrs tl wknd wl over 1f out* **150/1**

64-0 **11** 33 **Saxony**[18] 311 6-8-10 **49** oh1 ow3 JohnFahy 10
(Matthew Salaman) *mid-div on outer: lost pl 4f out: wknd wl over 2f out* **200/1**

1-01 **P** **Tilsworth Micky**[20] 273 5-9-7 **60** GeorgeBaker 9
(J R Jenkins) *hld up: a in rr: eased over 1f out: p.u and dismntd ins fnl f: b.b.v* **5/1**[3]

1m 14.35s (-0.15) **Going Correction** 0.0s/f (Stan) **12** Ran SP% **118.3**
Speed ratings (Par 101): **101,100,98,92,91 90,90,86,81,75 31,**
CSF £7.64 CT £79.87 TOTE £2.50: £1.20, £1.50, £4.30; EX 9.40 Trifecta £95.40.
**Owner** Dr Marwan Koukash **Bred** Miss Nicola Cullen **Trained** Prescot, Merseyside

**FOCUS**
The two market leaders came to the fore and it's reasonable form for the level, with the race rated around the placed horses.

## 602 BETWAY SPRINT H'CAP (DIV II) 6f 20y (Tp)
**4:20** (4:21) (Class 6) (0-60,60) 4-Y-0+ **£2,587** (£770; £384; £192) **Stalls** Low

Form RPR

553- **1** **Strictly Carter**[175] 5470 4-9-2 **55** DavidProbert 7 61
(Alan Bailey) *hld up: hdwy over 1f out: rdn and edgd lft wl ins fnl f: r.o u.p to ld post* **9/1**[3]

636- **2** shd **Indian Pursuit (IRE)**[84] 7961 4-9-6 **59** JasonHart 5 65
(John Quinn) *led 1f: chsd ldrs tl led again over 2f out: rdn and hdd ins fnl f: rallied to ld again sn after: hdd post* **10/3**[2]

0-04 **3** ½ **Jack The Laird (IRE)**[9] 468 4-9-7 **60** (b) RobertWinston 4 64
(Dean Ivory) *racd keenly: w ldrs tl settled and remained handy after 1f: rdn to ld ins fnl f: sn hdd: nt qckn towards fin* **5/2**[1]

2-00 **4** ½ **Excellent Aim**[24] 215 10-8-12 **58** JaneElliott(7) 2 61
(George Margarson) *hld up: hdwy 2f out: shkn up over 1f out: r.o* **12/1**

500- **5** 1¼ **Kingstreet Lady**[208] 4262 4-8-10 **49** TomMarquand 9 48
(Richard Price) *prom: hmpd and lost pl after 1f: r.o ins fnl f: nt rch ldrs* **25/1**

56-0 **6** hd **Cruise Tothelimit (IRE)**[33] 45 9-9-7 **60** (vt¹) GrahamLee 11 58
(Patrick Morris) *plld hrd and sn prom: rdn over 1f out: styd on* **9/1**[3]

5-60 **7** hd **Binky Blue (IRE)**[11] 426 5-9-0 **60** TobyEley(7) 10 64+
(Daniel Mark Loughnane) *hld up: nt clr run: swtchd lft and r.o ins fnl f: nvr nr to chal* **10/1**

-050 **8** 1¼ **Diamond Vine (IRE)**[10] 438 9-8-7 **46** oh1 (p) LukeMorris 3 40
(Ronald Harris) *hld up: hdwy over 1f out: sn rdn: styd on same pce fnl f* **20/1**

00-0 **9** nse **Mighty Zip (USA)**[18] 302 5-8-10 **56** (p) JordanUys(7) 8 50
(Lisa Williamson) *led 5f out: hdd over 2f out: rdn and ev ch 1f out: no ex ins fnl f* **25/1**

000- **10** 4 **Angelito**[58] 8316 8-9-1 **57** EoinWalsh(3) 1 39
(Tony Newcombe) *s.i.s: in rr: shkn up 1/2-way: nt clr run over 2f out: nt clr run and swtchd lft over 1f out: r.o ins fnl f: eased sn after* **11/1**

000- **11** 1¼ **Hellarious**[126] 7011 4-8-7 **46** oh1 (t¹) JosephineGordon 12 24
(Geoffrey Deacon) *prom: rdn 1/2-way: wknd over 1f out* **18/1**

000- **12** 6 **Rubheira**[51] 8430 5-8-0 **46** oh1 (b) RPWalsh(7) 6 6
(Paul Burgoyne) *jnd ldr after 1f tl over 2f out: wknd over 1f out* **150/1**

1m 15.3s (0.80) **Going Correction** 0.0s/f (Stan) **12** Ran SP% **115.1**
Speed ratings (Par 101): **94,93,93,92,90 90,90,88,88,83 81,73**
CSF £36.44 CT £98.68 TOTE £9.70: £3.00, £1.70, £1.30; EX 37.40 Trifecta £169.90.
**Owner** A Bailey **Bred** Mickley Stud & Mr D Mossop **Trained** Newmarket, Suffolk
■ Stewards' Enquiry : David Probert two-day ban (20-21 Feb): used whip without giving mount sufficient time to respond

**FOCUS**
As in the first division the right horses came to the fore and sound enough form, with the runner-up pinning the level.

## 603 BETWAY MARATHON H'CAP 1m 5f 194y
**4:50** (4:52) (Class 5) (0-75,77) 4-Y-0+ **£3,557** (£1,058; £529; £264) **Stalls** Low

Form RPR

624- **1** **Tartan Bute**[185] 5111 4-9-6 **74** (p) JoeFanning 3 81+
(Mark Johnston) *chsd ldrs: led over 2f out: shkn up over 1f out: styd on: comf* **10/3**[2]

0-03 **2** 2¼ **Gabrial The Terror (IRE)**[14] 380 7-9-7 **70** (p) StevieDonohoe 2 73
(Ian Williams) *hld up: racd keenly: hdwy over 2f out: hung lft fr over 1f out: kpt on to go 2nd wl ins fnl f* **13/2**

21-2 **3** ½ **Come Back King (IRE)**[27] 154 4-9-9 **77** BenCurtis 4 79
(Michael Appleby) *led at stdy pce over 7f: chsd ldr: rdn and ev ch over 2f out: no ex ins fnl f* **5/6**[1]

11-3 **4** 7 **Blue Top**[27] 162 8-8-6 **60** (v) HollieDoyle(5) 5 53
(Dai Burchell) *s.i.s: hld up: hdwy to chse ldr over 9f out: led over 6f out: rdn and hdd over 2f out: wknd ins fnl f* **11/2**[3]

/4-0 **5** 6 **Mister Fizz**[25] 196 9-9-7 **75** DavidParkes(5) 6 59
(Miss Imogen Pickard) *chsd ldrs: rdn over 4f out: wknd over 2f out* **25/1**

3m 5.15s (0.35) **Going Correction** 0.0s/f (Stan)
**WFA** 4 from 7yo+ 3lb **5** Ran SP% **110.2**
Speed ratings (Par 103): **99,97,97,93,90**
CSF £23.13 TOTE £3.80: £1.50, £2.40; EX 19.80 Trifecta £31.90.
**Owner** Frank Bird **Bred** Newsells Park Stud **Trained** Middleham Moor, N Yorks

**FOCUS**
No great gallop on here, but a good winner who was off a fair mark and is the type to do better this year.

## 604 BETWAY APP H'CAP 5f 21y (Tp)
**5:20** (5:20) (Class 6) (0-65,67) 4-Y-0+ **£2,587** (£770; £384; £192) **Stalls** Low

Form RPR

00-2 **1** **Annie Salts**[17] 327 4-9-4 **61** (h) JoeFanning 2 67
(Chris Dwyer) *led: hdd over 3f out: remained w ldr tl led again 2f out: shkn up ins fnl f: r.o* **10/1**[3]

0-43 **2** 1¼ **Pearl Noir**[4] 523 7-8-5 **55** (b) RPWalsh(7) 5 57
(Scott Dixon) *chsd ldrs: rdn to chse wnr over 1f out: hung lft ins fnl f: styd on same pce* **10/1**[3]

5-54 **3** 1 **Noble Asset**[17] 330 6-9-5 **62** LukeMorris 4 62
(Milton Bradley) *plld hrd and prom: lost pl after 1f: nt clr run 1/2-way: hdwy over 1f out: styd on to go 3rd post* **9/2**[2]

530- **4** hd **Powerful Dream (IRE)**[51] 8429 4-9-10 **67** (p¹) OisinMurphy 7 64
(Ronald Harris) *hld up: hdwy over 1f out: rdn and edgd lft ins fnl f: styd on same pce* **9/2**[2]

40-3 **5** 1¼ **Cee Jay**[24] 217 4-9-0 **57** (p) TomEaves 10 50
(Robert Cowell) *sn pushed along to chse ldrs: led over 3f out: hdd 2f out: sn rdn: no ex ins fnl f* **10/1**[3]

10-0 **6** 1¼ **Mambo Spirit (IRE)**[17] 330 13-9-4 **64** EoinWalsh(3) 6 52
(Tony Newcombe) *s.i.s: in rr and pushed along 1/2-way: nvr nrr* **40/1**

1-32 **7** nk **Secret Bird (IRE)**[18] 303 5-9-0 **62** LuluStanford(5) 3 49
(Dean Ivory) *hld up in tch: pushed along 1/2-way: no ex fnl f* **11/8**[1]

-000 **8** 2 **Nora Batt (IRE)**[9] 468 4-8-10 **53** AndrewMullen 1 33
(David Evans) *sn pushed along to chse ldrs: rdn over 1f out: wknd ins fnl f* **22/1**

1m 1.5s (-0.40) **Going Correction** 0.0s/f (Stan) **8** Ran SP% **112.5**
Speed ratings (Par 101): **103,101,99,99,97 95,94,91**
CSF £99.86 CT £511.89 TOTE £9.80: £3.30, £3.30, £2.00; EX 76.90 Trifecta £297.80.
**Owner** Mrs Shelley Dwyer **Bred** D R Botterill **Trained** Newmarket, Suffolk

**FOCUS**
A moderate sprint, with the favourite disappointing, and rated around the first two.

## 605 SUNBETS.CO.UK H'CAP 1m 142y (Tp)
**5:50** (5:51) (Class 6) (0-55,59) 4-Y-0+ **£2,587** (£770; £384; £192) **Stalls** Low

Form RPR

0-50 **1** **Celtic Artisan (IRE)**[16] 361 6-9-6 **54** (bt) OisinMurphy 2 63
(Rebecca Menzies) *led: hdd 7f out: chsd ldr tl led again and edgd lft wl over 1f out: rdn out* **6/1**[3]

002- **2** 2½ **Simply Clever**[46] 8499 4-9-7 **55** TomEaves 11 59
(David Brown) *sn pushed along to chse ldrs: led 7f out: rdn and hdd whn hmpd wl over 1f out: styd on same pce ins fnl f* **14/1**

/3-0 **3** ½ **Hymn For The Dudes**[14] 383 4-9-3 **51** (t¹) AdamKirby 4 54
(John Berry) *hld up in tch: rdn over 1f out: styd on same pce ins fnl f* **4/1**[1]

52-1 **4** 2 **Schottische**[7] 482 7-9-6 **59** 6ex (b) DavidParkes(5) 1 58
(Alan Bailey) *hld up: hdwy over 1f out: nt trble ldrs* **11/2**[2]

05-0 **5** shd **Caius College Girl (IRE)**[19] 282 5-9-5 **53** TimmyMurphy 3 52
(Natalie Lloyd-Beavis) *chsd ldrs: rdn over 1f out: no ex ins fnl f* **20/1**

0-52 **6** 1¼ **Bassino (USA)**[14] 383 4-9-2 **55** (h) RachealKneller(5) 8 51
(James Bennett) *chsd ldrs: rdn over 1f out: styd on same pce fnl f* **13/2**

600- **7** ½ **Rising Sunshine (IRE)**[212] 4159 4-9-5 **53** (b¹) LukeMorris 9 48
(Milton Bradley) *hld up: hdwy u.p over 1f out: no ex ins fnl f* **33/1**

0-24 **8** hd **Canford Belle**[2] 579 4-8-13 **54** PatrickVaughan(7) 6 48
(Grant Tuer) *s.s: in rr tl styd on ins fnl f* **13/2**

0556 **9** shd **Cold Fusion (IRE)**[7] 482 4-9-1 **54** HollieDoyle(5) 5 49
(David Flood) *prom: lost pl 7f out: nt clr run over 1f out: styd on ins fnl f* **16/1**

060- **10** 1¾ **Fire Empress**[42] 8528 4-9-2 **50** (h) RyanPowell 12 41
(James Unett) *s.i.s: nvr on terms* **200/1**

4631 **11** nse **Pivotal Dream (IRE)**[11] 425 4-8-11 **50** CharlieBennett(5) 7 40
(Mark Brisbourne) *.hld up: rdn over 3f out: hdwy over 2f out: wknd over 1f out* **8/1**

6-00 **12** 2 **Les Gar Gan (IRE)**[19] 282 6-9-4 **52** (be) JosephineGordon 10 38
(Daniel Mark Loughnane) *hld up: hdwy u.p over 1f out: wknd fnl f* **20/1**

000- **13** 3 **Frap**[37] 8595 4-9-7 **55** StevieDonohoe 13 35
(Ian Williams) *unruly in stalls: sn prom: rdn over 2f out: wknd over 1f out* **10/1**

1m 49.21s (-0.89) **Going Correction** 0.0s/f (Stan) **13** Ran SP% **122.1**
Speed ratings (Par 101): **103,100,100,98,98 97,96,96,96,95 95,93,90**
CSF £85.52 CT £396.41 TOTE £6.90: £2.40, £3.80, £2.20; EX 89.50 Trifecta £303.30.
**Owner** EPDS Racing Partnership 11 **Bred** Fortbarrington Stud **Trained** Mordon, Durham

**FOCUS**
A lowly handicap and it very much paid to race up with the pace. The winner may be value for more.

T/Jkpt: Not won. T/Plt: £47.50 to a £1 stake. Pool: £117,443.38 - 1801.42 winning units T/Qpdt: £16.10 to a £1 stake. Pool: £11,285.76 - 517.54 winning units **Colin Roberts**

# MARSEILLE PONT-DE-VIVAUX
Monday, February 6
**OFFICIAL GOING: Polytrack: standard**

## 606a PRIX DE LA GARRIGUE (CONDITIONS) (4YO) (POLYTRACK) 7f 110y
7:10 4-Y-0 £7,692 (£3,076; £2,307; £1,538; £769)

RPR
1 **Enjoy The Silence (FR)**[35] 4-9-6 0........... Roberto-CarlosMontenegro 1 80
(C Boutin, France) **4/1**[3]
2 *shd* **He's A Dreamer (IRE)**[33] 4-9-2 0.................................. JulianResimont 10 76
(F Sanchez, France) **8/5**[1]
3 *2* **Zalamea (IRE)**[33] 4-8-13 0.............................................. AndyLustiere(7) 2 75
(K Borgel, France) **14/5**[2]
4 *hd* **Bibione (FR)**[86] 4-9-1 0...........................................(p) StephaneLaurent 7 69
(J Parize, France) **194/10**
5 *shd* **Issauroma (FR)**[143] 4-8-7 0..................................(p) NathanKasztelan(6) 6 67
(C Escuder, France) **35/1**
6 *snk* **Randulina (FR)**[129] 4-9-3 0.............................................. TonyPiccone 5 71
(K Borgel, France) **142/10**
7 *shd* **Yosemite**[33] 4-8-3 0.................................................. BrunoPanicucci(7) 8 63
(J Reynier, France) **89/10**
8 *5* **Prisom (IRE)**[13] 391 4-8-10 0.......................................(p) MickaelForest 3 51
(Gay Kelleway) **26/1**
9 *6* **Petite Slickly (FR)**[555] 4897 4-8-10 0..........................(p) FranckBlondel 4 36
(S Labate, France) **181/10**

PARI-MUTUEL (all including 1 euro stake): WIN: 5.00; PLACE: 1.40, 1.20, 1.30; DF: 5.50; SF: 13.00.
**Owner** Benoit Cambier **Bred** C Laffon-Parias & Stilvi Compania Financiera Sa **Trained** France

# 577 NEWCASTLE (A.W) (L-H)
Tuesday, February 7
**OFFICIAL GOING: Tapeta: standard**
Wind: Light across Weather: Fine and dry

## 607 BETWAY BEST ODDS GUARANTEED PLUS APPRENTICE H'CAP (DIV I) 1m 2f 42y (Tp)
1:30 (1:30) (Class 6) (0-60,61) 4-Y-0+ £2,264 (£673; £336; £168) Stalls High

Form RPR
400- 1 **Exclusive Waters (IRE)**[71] 8134 7-9-3 51.................... LewisEdmunds 2 62+
(Garry Moss) *dwlt and towards rr: hdwy on outer to trck ldrs over 5f out: chsd ldng pair over 2f out: rdn to chal ent fnl f: sn led: kpt on strly* **4/1**[3]
40-2 2 *4* **Highway Robber**[27] 176 4-9-1 50.......................................... HollieDoyle 9 54
(Wilf Storey) *sn led at stdy pce: qcknd over 3f out: jnd and rdn 2f out: drvn ent fnl f: sn hdd and kpt on same pce* **9/2**
440- 3 *1 3/4* **Percy Verence**[54] 8387 4-9-6 55......................................(t) CliffordLee 5 56
(K R Burke) *hld up in rr: hdwy 4f out: chsd ldrs 3f out: rdn along 2f out: kpt on same pce u.p fnl f* **3/1**[1]
45-3 4 *3/4* **Lord Rob**[27] 176 6-8-11 45..................................... CallumRodriguez 8 44
(David Thompson) *trckd ldr: hdwy over 3f out: effrt and cl up over 2f out: sn rdn and ev ch: drvn and wknd over 1f out* **7/2**[2]
36-0 5 *8* **Never Say (IRE)**[18] 334 4-8-12 47...................................... DavidParkes 4 32
(Jason Ward) *trckd ldrs: pushed along over 3f out: rdn wl over 2f out: sn one pce* **33/1**
0-15 6 *2* **Outlaw Torn (IRE)**[27] 176 8-9-5 53.........................(e) JordanVaughan 3 34
(Richard Guest) *t.k.h: trckd ldrs: pushed along over 3f out: rdn wl over 2f out: sn btn* **12/1**
0-20 7 *3* **Swiftee (IRE)**[8] 482 4-9-12 61.............................................. JoshDoyle 1 37
(Ivan Furtado) *trckd ldrs on inner: pushed along over 3f out: sn rdn and wknd* **16/1**
0-60 8 *1* **Patron Of Explores (USA)**[13] 400 6-8-11 45..............(t) RowanScott 6 19
(Patrick Holmes) *t.k.h: hld up: a rr* **80/1**
025- 9 *11* **Wayside Magic**[124] 7096 4-8-12 50...........................(p) BenRobinson(3) 7
(Neville Bycroft) *trckd ldrs: pushed along bef 1/2-way: rdn 4f out: sn lost pl and bhd* **11/1**

2m 10.35s (-0.05) **Going Correction** +0.175s/f (Slow) 9 Ran SP% **111.5**
Speed ratings (Par 101): **107,103,102,101,95 93,91,90,81**
CSF £21.21 CT £58.53 TOTE £3.40: £1.40, £1.80, £1.40; EX 20.80 Trifecta £98.30.
**Owner** Ms Sara Hattersley **Bred** M M Sammon **Trained** Wynyard, Stockton-On-Tees

**FOCUS**
The going was standard. Race distances as advertised. A modest apprentice handicap won under a good ride from Lewis Edmunds. The winner was back to some better form for his new trainer.

## 608 BETWAY BEST ODDS GUARANTEED PLUS APPRENTICE H'CAP (DIV II) 1m 2f 42y (Tp)
2:00 (2:06) (Class 6) (0-60,56) 4-Y-0+ £2,264 (£673; £336; £168) Stalls High

Form RPR
00-3 1 **Moayadd (USA)**[19] 309 5-8-10 45......................................... HollieDoyle 3 56+
(Neil Mulholland) *hld up in tch: pushed along and hdwy 3f out: chsd clr ldr wl over 1f out: rdn to ld ins fnl f: kpt on strly* **8/11**[1]
56-5 2 *4* **Kerry Icon**[12] 424 4-8-9 45...........................................(h) CliffordLee 8 48
(Iain Jardine) *trckd ldrs: hdwy over 3f out: rdn along 2f out: styd ion fnl f* **9/1**[2]
-030 3 *nk* **Mount Cheiron (USA)**[13] 400 6-9-2 51................(b) CallumRodriguez 1 53
(Richard Ford) *dwlt and rr: hdwy on inner 4f out: swtchd rt to outer 3f out and sn chsng ldrs: rdn 2f out: kpt on wl fnl f: nrst fin* **10/1**[3]
006- 4 *1 1/4* **Stamp Duty (IRE)**[43] 8527 9-8-10 45.............................. JordanVaughan 4 45
(Suzzanne France) *trckd ldr: led 6f out: pushed clr over 3f out: rdn over 1f out: hdd & wknd ins fnl f* **10/1**[3]
30-0 5 *1/2* **Swiss Lait**[27] 174 6-8-8 48................................................ PaulaMuir(5) 5 47
(Patrick Holmes) *hld up in rr: hdwy on outer 3f out: rdn along 2f out: kpt on fnl f: nrst fin* **12/1**
000U 6 *nk* **Sheer Intensity (IRE)**[12] 420 4-9-1 56.............. KatherineGlenister(5) 6 55
(David Evans) *chsd ldrs: pushed along on outer over 3f out: rdn wl over 2f out: sn drvn and btn* **25/1**
000- 7 *2* **Wright Patterson (IRE)**[165] 5835 4-8-11 50.................... JoshQuinn(3) 2 45
(John Quinn) *trckd ldng pair on inner: pushed along 4f out: rdn over 3f out: sn wknd* **11/1**
0-06 8 *12* **Hydrant**[10] 462 11-9-5 54................................................... MeganNicholls 7 26
(Richard Guest) *led: hdd 6f out: chsd ldr: rdn along over 3f out: sn wknd* **9/1**[2]

2m 10.71s (0.31) **Going Correction** +0.175s/f (Slow) 8 Ran SP% **116.0**
Speed ratings (Par 101): **105,101,101,100,100 99,98,88**
CSF £8.38 CT £39.42 TOTE £1.70: £1.10, £1.90, £1.80; EX 7.80 Trifecta £36.60.
**Owner** P & Mrs K E Malcolm **Bred** Darley **Trained** Limpley Stoke, Wilts

**FOCUS**
The second division of the apprentice handicap looked less competitive than the first, especially after the second-favourite was withdrawn, and it was won with something to spare. The race has been rated around the next three behind the winner.

## 609 32RED.COM FILLIES' H'CAP 1m 2f 42y (Tp)
2:30 (2:30) (Class 5) (0-75,77) 4-Y-0+ £2,911 (£866; £432; £216) Stalls High

Form RPR
60-5 1 **Energia Fox (BRZ)**[22] 269 6-9-10 77............................. PaulHanagan 6 84
(Richard Fahey) *trckd ldrs: hdwy over 3f out: rdn to ld jst over 1f out: drvn and kpt on wl fnl f* **5/2**[1]
36-3 2 *1* **Ms Gillard**[35] 29 4-8-8 62................................................... TomEaves 4 67
(David Simcock) *hld up in tch: hdwy on outer 3f out: rdn to chal ent fnl f: sn drvn and ev ch: kpt on same pce towards fin* **12/1**
445- 3 *1 1/4* **Victoria Pollard**[227] 3659 5-9-10 77........................... PaulMulrennan 5 80+
(Andrew Balding) *trckd ldrs: hdwy and cl up on bit wl over 1f out: shkn up ins fnl f: sn rdn and kpt on same pce* **9/2**[2]
45- 4 *2 1/2* **Tenerezza (IRE)**[108] 7531 4-8-10 64.................................... JoeFanning 7 62
(Iain Jardine) *prom: trckd ldr after 2f: clsd up 3f out: rdn to take slt ld wl over 1f out: drvn and hdd appr fnl f: kpt on one pce* **6/1**
5-64 5 *1 3/4* **Lozah**[11] 444 4-8-10 64 ow1.............................................. JackGarritty 2 58
(Roger Fell) *hld up in rr: hdwy over 3f out: rdn 2f out: sn drvn and no imp* **9/1**
5 6 *2 1/4* **Green Or Black (IRE)**[17] 353 5-9-10 77........................... LiamKeniry 3 67
(Neil Mulholland) *trckd ldrs: effrt over 3f out and sn pushed along: rdn over 2f out and sn wknd* **5/1**[3]
-224 7 *4* **Heartstone (IRE)**[7] 497 4-9-4 72................................... AndrewMullen 9 54
(David Evans) *sn led at stdy pce: pushed along 3f out: jnd and rdn 2f out: sn hdd & wknd* **5/1**[3]
0/0 8 *4 1/2* **Melanna (IRE)**[15] 382 6-9-7 74.......................................... GrahamLee 1 47
(Richard Ford) *towards rr: rdn along over 3f out: sn outpcd and bhd* **50/1**

2m 13.37s (2.97) **Going Correction** +0.175s/f (Slow) 8 Ran SP% **114.0**
Speed ratings (Par 100): **95,94,93,91,89 88,84,81**
CSF £34.28 CT £127.85 TOTE £2.90: £1.60, £3.20, £1.80; EX 35.20 Trifecta £230.60.
**Owner** Dr Marwan Koukash **Bred** Haras Estrela Energia **Trained** Musley Bank, N Yorks

**FOCUS**
A decent Class 5 fillies' handicap with some fairly interesting sorts. It was run at a decent pace and punters got it right. The winner has been rated in line with her 2016 form.

## 610 BETWAY H'CAP 2m 56y (Tp)
3:05 (3:05) (Class 6) (0-60,62) 4-Y-0+ £2,587 (£770; £384; £192) Stalls Low

Form RPR
5-02 1 **Ryan The Giant**[11] 436 4-8-7 48................................(v) ConnorBeasley 6 53
(Keith Dalgleish) *trckd ldrs: hdwy over 3f out: led wl over 2f out: rdn and wandered over 1f out: drvn out* **85/40**[2]
-105 2 *1* **Jan Smuts (IRE)**[13] 399 9-9-5 59.............................(tp) HollieDoyle(5) 8 63
(Wilf Storey) *hld up and bhd: hdwy 3f out: rdn to chse ldrs over 1f out: drvn and kpt on fnl f* **6/1**[3]
215- 3 *1* **Pass The Time**[101] 592 8-9-13 62.......................................(p) LiamKeniry 7 65
(Neil Mulholland) *trckd ldng pair: hdwy 3f out: rdn along and ev ch wl over 1f out: sn drvn and kpt on same pce* **15/8**[1]
550- 4 *5* **Yorkshireman (IRE)**[158] 6102 7-8-10 45........................(b) PaddyAspell 1 42
(Lynn Siddall) *trckd ldng pair: hdwy on inner over 3f out: rdn along wl over 2f out: drvn wl over 1f out: sn one pce* **16/1**
300- 5 *3 1/4* **Adrakhan (FR)**[26] 8309 6-8-7 47.................................. MeganNicholls(5) 4 40
(Wilf Storey) *trckd ldr: led after 6f: hdd 5f out: cl up and led again over 3f out: sn rdn and hdd wl over 2f out: sn drvn and wknd* **20/1**
-000 6 *1 1/4* **Breathless**[13] 400 5-9-1 50......................................(tp) PaulMulrennan 5 41
(Clive Mulhall) *trckd ldrs: hdwy 4f out: rdn along wl over 2f out: sn drvn and wknd* **33/1**
/00- 7 *3 1/2* **Strikemaster (IRE)**[225] 3704 11-8-10 45...........................(t) GrahamLee 2 32
(Lee James) *hld up towards rr: effrt and sme hdwy over 4f out: rdn along wl over 3f out: n.d* **50/1**
3-33 8 *nse* **Thackeray**[19] 315 10-8-4 46............................................ PaulaMuir(7) 9 33
(Chris Fairhurst) *hld up: a bhd* **15/2**
06-6 9 *17* **He's Magic**[32] 98 6-8-10 45.............................................(p[1]) BarryMcHugh 3 12
(Tim Fitzgerald) *led 6f: cl up: led again 5f out: rdn along 4f out: sn hdd & wknd* **20/1**

3m 37.18s (1.98) **Going Correction** +0.175s/f (Slow)
**WFA** 4 from 5yo+ 4lb 9 Ran SP% **113.1**
Speed ratings (Par 101): **102,101,101,98,96 96,94,94,85**
CSF £14.08 CT £26.65 TOTE £2.90: £1.20, £1.80, £1.10; EX 13.30 Trifecta £35.40.
**Owner** Middleham Park Racing LXXIX **Bred** Newsells Park Stud **Trained** Carluke, S Lanarks

**FOCUS**
A two-horse race as far as punters were concerned and the winner got off the mark at the 25th attempt.

## 611 SUNBETS.CO.UK H'CAP 1m 5y (Tp)
3:40 (3:40) (Class 4) (0-80,82) 4-Y-0+ £4,787 (£1,424; £711; £355) Stalls Centre

Form RPR
440- 1 **Worlds His Oyster**[136] 6778 4-9-9 82................................... JasonHart 7 91
(John Quinn) *trckd ldrs: hdwy over 2f out: rdn to chal over 1f out: led ins fnl f: kpt on strly* **5/1**[3]
32-3 2 *2 1/4* **Mariee**[10] 460 4-9-7 80.................................................... JoeFanning 6 84
(Mark Johnston) *trckd ldrs: hdwy and cl up over 3f out: led wl over 2f out: rdn wl over 1f out and sn jnd: drvn and hdd ins fnl f: kpt on same pce* **5/2**[1]
62-5 3 *2 1/4* **Dusky Dawn**[34] 43 5-9-4 77.............................................. NeilFarley 1 76
(Alan Swinbank) *prom: hdwy and cl up over 3f out: rdn along over 2f out: drvn over 1f out: kpt on same pce fnl f* **25/1**
606- 4 *nk* **King Of Dreams**[164] 5875 4-9-4 77...................................... TomEaves 5 75
(David Simcock) *trckd ldrs: hdwy over 2f out: rdn over 1f out: drvn and kpt on one pce fnl f* **5/1**[3]
56-1 5 *3/4* **Eastern Dragon (IRE)**[17] 359 7-9-0 80............(p) CallumRodriguez(7) 8 76
(Iain Jardine) *dwlt and towards rr: hdwy over 2f out: sn rdn along: kpt on u.p fnl f* **3/1**[2]
000- 6 *1 1/2* **Weather Front (USA)**[74] 8092 4-8-11 70............................ LukeMorris 3 63
(Karen McLintock) *dwlt and rr: pushed along wl over 2f out: rdn wl over 1f out: kpt on towards fin* **7/1**

0-20 **7** ½ **Ravenhoe (IRE)**[19] 306 4-9-2 **75** PJMcDonald 4 67
(Mark Johnston) *trckd ldr: cl up 3f out: rdn along over 2f out: drvn wl over 1f out: sn wknd* **12/1**

00-0 **8** ½ **Kiwi Bay**[17] 359 12-8-7 **66** oh1 ConnorBeasley 2 57
(Michael Dods) *led: pushed along over 3f out: rdn and hdd wl over 2f out: sn wknd* **33/1**

1m 38.63s (0.03) **Going Correction** +0.175s/f (Slow) 8 Ran SP% **113.9**
Speed ratings (Par 105): **106,103,101,101,100 98,98,97**
CSF £17.77 CT £283.15 TOTE £5.90: £1.80, £1.20, £5.00; EX 18.30 Trifecta £230.70.
**Owner** Ross Harmon **Bred** Cheveley Park Stud Ltd **Trained** Settrington, N Yorks

**FOCUS**
An open-looking 1m Class 4 handicap where nothing got into it from off the pace. The race has been rated around the second.

## 612 32RED CASINO MAIDEN FILLIES' STKS 6f (Tp)
**4:10** (4:10) (Class 5) 3-Y-O+ **£2,911** (£866; £432; £216) **Stalls** Centre

Form RPR

00-4 **1** **Lady Cristal (IRE)**[13] 404 3-8-11 68 BenCurtis 2 66
(K R Burke) *t.k.h: mde all: rdn over 1f out: drvn and edgd lft ins fnl f: jst hld on* **2/1**[1]

0-5 **2** *nse* **Magical Molly Joe**[11] 442 3-8-11 0 AndrewMullen 1 65
(David Barron) *hld up and bhd: swtchd rt 1/2-way: hdwy wl over 1f out: rdn ent fnl f: sn chsng wnr: styd on strly: jst failed* **50/1**

63 **3** 1 ¾ **Scala Regia (FR)**[13] 397 3-8-11 0 LukeMorris 4 59
(Sir Mark Prescott Bt) *prom: cl up 1/2-way: rdn and ev ch over 1f out: drvn ent fnl f: kpt on same pce* **7/2**[2]

4- **4** *hd* **Deep Dream**[363] 516 4-9-12 0 OisinMurphy 7 63
(Andrew Balding) *trckd ldrs on outer: hdwy and cl up over 2f out: rdn over 1f out: kpt on same pce fnl f* **2/1**[1]

**5** ½ **Appreciating** 3-8-11 0 ShaneGray 5 57
(Kevin Ryan) *trckd ldrs: pushed along over 2f out: rdn over 1f out: grad wknd* **12/1**

**6** 3 ½ **Angelou** 3-8-11 0 PhillipMakin 6 46
(David O'Meara) *prom: effrt and cl up 2f out: rdn over 1f out: wknd fnl f* **5/1**[3]

0 **7** ¾ **Clean Cut**[19] 307 3-8-11 0 JoeyHaynes 3 43
(Ivan Furtado) *chsd ldrs on inner: pushed along over 2f out: sn rdn and wknd* **66/1**

1m 13.16s (0.66) **Going Correction** +0.175s/f (Slow)
**WFA** 3 from 4yo 15lb 7 Ran SP% **116.7**
Speed ratings (Par 100): **102,101,99,99,98 94,93**
CSF £93.63 TOTE £2.90: £2.40, £11.70; EX 59.80 Trifecta £248.10.
**Owner** Champagne Charlies Club & Mrs E Burke **Bred** Knocktoran Stud And Carrigbeg Stud **Trained** Middleham Moor, N Yorks

**FOCUS**
A modest fillies' maiden that almost resulted in a shock thanks to the slightly wayward finishing effort of the winner. The form is taken at face value around the winner, but the next three are all improving.

## 613 BETWAY BEST ODDS GUARANTEED PLUS H'CAP 1m 4f 98y (Tp)
**4:40** (4:41) (Class 4) (0-80,80) 4-Y-O+ **£4,690** (£1,395; £697; £348) **Stalls** High

Form RPR

/6-2 **1** **Lac Leman (GER)**[13] 399 6-9-2 **75** (h) GrahamLee 6 82
(Pauline Robson) *hld up in tch: hdwy over 2f out: swtchd rt and rdn to chal ent fnl f: sn drvn: styd on wl nr fin to ld on line* **11/2**

31-2 **2** *shd* **High On Light**[7] 497 4-8-10 **72** SamJames 2 78
(David Barron) *set stdy pce: qcknd over 3f out: jnd and rdn 2f out: drvn ent fnl f: kpt on wl: ct on line* **9/4**[2]

04-1 **3** ¾ **Genres**[27] 174 5-8-9 **68** JoeFanning 4 73
(Alan Swinbank) *trckd ldr: hdwy over 2f out: sn chal: rdn over 1f out: disp ld ent fnl f: sn drvn and ev ch tl no ex towards fin* **5/4**[1]

310- **4** 1 ½ **Major Rowan**[154] 6219 6-9-0 **73** PhillipMakin 1 75
(John Davies) *rrd and lost 3 l s: hld up in rr: hdwy on outer 3f out: chsd ldrs 2f out: rdn to chal over 1f out: ev ch tl drvn ins fnl f and kpt on same pce* **16/1**

04-1 **5** 1 ½ **Persian Steel (IRE)**[26] 195 5-8-10 **76** BenRobinson(7) 3 76
(Brian Ellison) *plld hrd early: trckd ldng pair: hdwy over 3f out: rdn along over 2f out: drvn over 1f out and kpt on one pce* **5/1**[3]

2m 51.5s (10.40) **Going Correction** +0.175s/f (Slow)
**WFA** 4 from 5yo+ 2lb 5 Ran SP% **113.1**
Speed ratings (Par 105): **72,71,71,70,69**
CSF £18.67 TOTE £7.00: £2.40, £2.10; EX 18.90 Trifecta £35.90.
**Owner** D&D Armstrong Ltd **Bred** Gestut Auenquelle **Trained** Kirkharle, Northumberland

**FOCUS**
A small field, but a competitive Class 4 middle-distance handicap with potential upside to all five runners. They went a steady pace and everything had a chance with 2f to run.
T/Jkpt: £6,666.60 to a £1 stake. Pool of £10,000 - 1.5 winning units T/Plt: £20.80 to a £1 stake. Pool: £89,174.13 - 3,119.41 winning units T/Qpdt: £10.60 to a £1 stake. Pool: £7,153.52 - 495.78 winning units **Joe Rowntree**

# 516 CHELMSFORD (A.W) (L-H)
Wednesday, February 8

**OFFICIAL GOING: Polytrack: standard**
Wind: light, half against Weather: overcast, chilly wind

## 614 BOOK TICKETS AT CHELMSFORDCITYRACECOURSE.COM H'CAP 1m (P)
**2:00** (2:01) (Class 7) (0-50,52) 4-Y-O+ **£2,587** (£770; £384; £192) **Stalls** Low

Form RPR

0-45 **1** *nse* **Mowhoob**[13] 425 7-9-3 **46** LukeMorris 8 51
(Brian Barr) *hld up in midfield: effrt to chse ldrs and bmpd over 1f out: drvn and ev ch ent fnl f: led ins fnl f: r.o wl u.p: hdd on post: fin 2nd: awrdd the r* **14/1**

/20- **2** **Randall's Alannah (IRE)**[74] 8121 7-8-13 **47** ConorMcGovern(5) 4 52+
(Seamus Fahey, Ire) *hld up in tch: clsd to chse ldrs and nt clr run over 1f out: sn swtchd rt and bmpd rival: squeezing between rivals and chal jst ins fnl f: r.o wl to ld on post: fin 1st disqualified: plcd 2nd* **7/1**

000- **3** 2 ¾ **Kristoff (IRE)**[39] 8590 4-8-9 **45** RhiainIngram(7) 9 44
(Jim Boyle) *chsd ldrs: effrt to chal over 1f out: rdn to ld 1f out: hdd ins fnl f: no ex and wknd wl ins fnl f* **25/1**

0552 **4** ¾ **Captain K (IRE)**[19] 334 5-9-5 **48** (h) TimmyMurphy 5 45
(Gordon Elliott, Ire) *t.k.h: chsd ldr: rdn to ld over 1f out: hdd and unable qck 1f out: kpt on same pce u.p ins fnl f* **4/1**[2]

-530 **5** *nk* **Limerick Lord (IRE)**[9] 481 5-9-6 **52** (p) ShelleyBirkett(3) 10 48
(Julia Feilden) *hld up in tch in midfield: effrt on outer over 2f out: unable qck over 1f out: kpt on same pce ins fnl f* **14/1**

0-23 **6** *nk* **Afkar (IRE)**[14] 400 9-9-4 **52** LewisEdmunds(5) 6 47
(Ivan Furtado) *chsd ldrs: pushed rt and nt clr run wl over 1f out: sn swtchd rt and rdn: unable qck and kpt on same pce ins fnl f* **5/1**[3]

000- **7** *shd* **Mr Turner**[172] 5636 4-9-2 **45** StevieDonohoe 2 40
(Mark H Tompkins) *t.k.h: hld up towards rr: effrt u.p over 1f out: styd on ins fnl f: nvr trbld ldrs* **20/1**

50-2 **8** ¾ **Moving Robe (IRE)**[20] 309 4-9-3 **46** (t) NickyMackay 1 40
(Conrad Allen) *hld up in tch towards rr: nt clr run over 1f out tl ins fnl f: lost any ch and kpt on same pce after* **7/1**

5-00 **9** ½ **Ertidaad (IRE)**[5] 544 5-8-13 **47** (b) DavidParkes(5) 13 39
(Emma Owen) *in rr: effrt over 1f out: edgd lft u.p and kpt on ins fnl f: nvr trbld ldrs* **16/1**

-004 **10** *nse* **I Can't Stop**[7] 505 4-9-7 **50** (b) FrannyNorton 7 42
(Milton Bradley) *in rr: sme hdwy 1f out: swtchd rt ins fnl f: kpt on: nvr trbld ldrs* **10/1**

500/ **11** 2 **Mobley Chaos**[1052] 1081 7-9-2 **45** (p[1]) DanielMuscutt 15 33
(John Flint) *dwlt and swtchd lft after s: t.k.h and hdwy to chse ldrs after 2f: rdn over 1f out: unable qck and edgd rt 1f out: wknd ins fnl f* **80/1**

000- **12** ½ **Lord Murphy (IRE)**[278] 2008 4-9-3 **46** AdamKirby 12 32
(Daniel Mark Loughnane) *midfield: hdwy to chse ldrs after 2f: effrt and hung lft wl over 1f out: sn lost pl and btn* **7/2**[1]

00-0 **13** 1 **Just Marion (IRE)**[37] 26 5-9-2 **45** PaddyAspell 11 29
(Clare Ellam) *a towards rr: n.d* **66/1**

500- **14** ½ **Cyflymder (IRE)**[60] 8306 11-9-6 **49** OisinMurphy 3 32
(David C Griffiths) *led: rdn and hdd over 1f out: wknd fnl f* **20/1**

0-00 **R** **Desert Chief**[20] 311 5-8-13 **45** (h[1]) AlistairRawlinson(3) 14
(Michael Appleby) *walked out of stalls and ref to r* **33/1**

1m 39.94s (0.04) **Going Correction** -0.10s/f (Stan) 15 Ran SP% **131.2**
Speed ratings (Par 97): **94,95,92,91,91 90,90,90,89,89 87,86,85,85,**
CSF £110.73 CT £2494.84 TOTE £14.30: £4.30, £2.90, £11.60; EX 202.10 Trifecta £3869.90.
**Owner** Brian Barr Racing Club **Bred** Scuderia Archi Romani **Trained** Longburton, Dorset

**FOCUS**
A decent turnout out for this Class 7 event, but it was a trappy affair with the pace collapsing and some hard luck stories in behind. The placings were reversed in the stewards' room and the promoted winner sets the level.

## 615 WINNER.CO.UK BEATEN BY A LENGTH FREE BET MAIDEN AUCTION STKS 1m (P)
**2:30** (2:33) (Class 5) 3-Y-O **£5,175** (£1,540; £769; £384) **Stalls** Low

Form RPR

0-2 **1** **Driver's Girl (USA)**[21] 283 3-8-13 0 (h[1]) DanielMuscutt 4 72
(Marco Botti) *mde all: shkn up and qcknd clr over 1f out: r.o wl fnl f: v easily* **4/5**[1]

**2** 9 **Miami Sunset** 3-8-9 0 DavidProbert 2 47
(Philip McBride) *dwlt: sn rcvrd to chse ldrs: nt clr run over 2f out: swtchd rt and rdn to go 2nd but wnr gng clr over 1f out: no ch w wnr but kpt on steadily fnl f* **16/1**

0-3 **3** 2 ½ **Flying Fynn (IRE)**[14] 393 3-8-6 0 (p) RhiainIngram(7) 6 46
(Jose Santos) *chsd wnr: rdn over 2f out: outpcd and lost 2nd over 1f out: 3rd and wl hld fnl f* **10/1**[2]

**4** 1 **Mystery Of War (IRE)** 3-9-4 0 OisinMurphy 5 48
(George Scott) *dwlt: t.k.h: hld up wl in tch: effrt in cl 5th 2f out: outpcd over 1f out: no ch fnl f* **14/1**[3]

5-0 **5** *nse* **Circuit**[14] 393 3-8-8 0 WilliamCarson 7 38
(Mick Quinn) *t.k.h: hld up wl in tch in midfield: rdn over 2f out: unable qck and btn over 1f out: no ch fnl f* **66/1**

**6** 8 **Touch Of Faith (IRE)** 3-8-11 0 AlistairRawlinson(3) 3 26
(Michael Appleby) *dwlt: in tch in rr: rdn over 3f out: sn struggling: bhd whn hung lft over 1f out* **40/1**

1m 39.93s (0.03) **Going Correction** -0.10s/f (Stan) 6 Ran SP% **81.1**
Speed ratings (Par 97): **95,86,83,82,82 74**
CSF £5.33 TOTE £1.20: £1.10, £5.40; EX 6.50 Trifecta £20.10.
**Owner** Gute Freunde Partnership **Bred** W S Farish **Trained** Newmarket, Suffolk

**FOCUS**
This race was significantly weakened following the withdrawal of Never Folding who got on her toes beforehand and then tried to duck under the starting stalls. That left the one horse who had already shown ability to win as she liked and the form has no depth.

## 616 WINNER.CO.UK BET & WATCH H'CAP 2m (P)
**3:00** (3:02) (Class 5) (0-70,71) 4-Y-O+ **£5,175** (£1,540; £769; £384) **Stalls** Low

Form RPR

16-2 **1** **Bracken Brae**[34] 62 5-10-0 **70** StevieDonohoe 6 77+
(Mark H Tompkins) *in tch in midfield: swtchd rt and effrt to chse ldr 2f out: led jst ins fnl f: styd on: rdn out* **13/8**[1]

14-3 **2** 1 **Tasty Ginger (IRE)**[11] 462 4-8-13 **61** OisinMurphy 7 66
(J R Jenkins) *hld up in tch in rr: rdn 3f out: hdwy and hanging lft 1f out: kpt onto go 2nd last strides: nvr getting to wnr* **5/1**[3]

00-1 **3** *nk* **Pinwood (IRE)**[21] 290 4-9-9 **71** (t) LukeMorris 3 75
(Adam West) *led: rdn and drifted rt wl over 1f out: drvn and hdd jst ins fnl f: styd on same pce after: lost 2nd last strides* **9/2**[2]

1-23 **4** 2 ¼ **Captain Swift (IRE)**[13] 423 6-9-9 **65** (p) AndrewMullen 4 66
(John Mackie) *wl in tch in midfield: effrt over 1f out: styd on same pce and no imp fnl f* **8/1**

/50- **5** 1 ¾ **Hazariban (IRE)**[41] 6308 8-8-13 **60** (t) ConorMcGovern(5) 5 59
(Seamus Fahey, Ire) *hld up in tch in last pair: effrt 2f out: no imp u.p over 1f out: kpt on same pce ins fnl f* **16/1**

2-3 **6** ½ **Burning Heat (IRE)**[33] 91 4-9-9 **71** RyanTate 1 70
(James Eustace) *chsd ldrs: effrt on inner 2f out: swtchd lft over 1f out: unable qck 1f out: wknd ins fnl f* **9/2**[2]

/0-0 **7** 3 ¾ **Perspicace**[16] 380 6-10-0 **70** (p) DougieCostello 2 64
(David Pipe) *dwlt: hdwy to chse ldr after 2f: rdn 3f out: lost 2nd 2f out and sn struggling: wknd fnl f* **28/1**

3m 30.2s (0.20) **Going Correction** -0.10s/f (Stan)
**WFA** 4 from 5yo+ 4lb 7 Ran SP% **111.6**
Speed ratings (Par 103): **95,94,94,93,92 92,90**
CSF £9.51 TOTE £2.20: £1.20, £3.30; EX 9.70 Trifecta £21.20.
**Owner** David P Noblett **Bred** Dullingham Park Stud & Mr D Noblett **Trained** Newmarket, Suffolk

**FOCUS**
Modest form and this was good opportunity for the favourite to record another victory around here.

## 617 WINNER.CO.UK MOBILE LOYALTY FREE BETS FILLIES' CONDITIONS STKS (AW FAST-TRACK QUALIFIER) 7f (P)
**3:30** (3:33) (Class 2) 4-Y-0+ **£12,938** (£3,850; £1,924; £962) **Stalls** Low

Form RPR
650- 1 **Ashadihan**138 6746 4-9-5 105 (p) KevinStott 2 108+
(Kevin Ryan) *chsd ldng pair: shkn up and qcknd to ld ent fnl f: rdn and r.o wl ins fnl f: eased towards fin* **11/4**2
10-0 2 1 ½ **Volunteer Point (IRE)**27 199 5-9-0 93 GrahamLee 6 98
(Mick Channon) *t.k.h: hld up in tch in last pair: effrt and swtchd lft over 1f out: hdwy to chse clr wnr 100yds out: kpt on but no threat to wnr* **14/1**
230- 3 ½ **Mise En Rose (USA)**104 7650 4-9-0 105 (p) WilliamBuick 4 97
(Charlie Appleby) *hld up in tch: effrt on outer over 1f out: drvn and kpt on ins fnl f: wnt 3rd 75yds out: no threat to wnr* **11/8**1
35-4 4 1 ¼ **Golden Amber (IRE)**28 170 6-9-0 95 RobertWinston 1 93
(Dean Ivory) *broke wl: led: rdn and drifted rt wl over 1f out: hdd and unable qck w wnr ent fnl f: lost 2nd 100yds out: wknd towards fin* **14/1**
260- 5 1 **Bahaarah (IRE)**144 6557 4-9-0 97 SeanLevey 7 91
(Richard Hannon) *dropped in bhd after s: swtchd rt and effrt over 1f out: keeping on but no threat to wnr whn swtchd lft ins fnl f* **16/1**
22- 6 1 ½ **Buying Trouble (USA)**165 5880 4-9-0 105 AdamKirby 5 87
(David Evans) *in tch in midfield: rdn over 2f out: unable qck u.p over 1f out: wknd ins fnl f* **9/2**3
4-01 7 nse **Make Music**21 287 4-9-0 83 DavidProbert 3 86
(Andrew Balding) *pressed ldr: rdn over 1f out: sn lost 2nd and unable qck: wknd ins fnl f* **14/1**
1m 24.26s (-2.94) **Going Correction** -0.10s/f (Stan) **7** Ran SP% **112.8**
Speed ratings (Par 96): **112,110,109,108,107 105,105**
CSF £37.70 TOTE £3.20: £1.80, £6.80; EX 44.00 Trifecta £105.80.
**Owner** T A Rahman **Bred** Highbank Stud Llp **Trained** Hambleton, N Yorks

**FOCUS**
A fast-track qualifier for the AW Championships fillies & mares race and a taking performance from the winner, who put up a performance in line with her better 3yo form. The race has been rated around the runner-up.

## 618 WINNER.CO.UK ACCA CLUB H'CAP 5f (P)
**4:05** (4:06) (Class 4) (0-85,84) 4-Y-0+ **£6,469** (£1,925; £962; £481) **Stalls** Low

Form RPR
5-60 1 **Top Boy**15 388 7-9-3 80 (v) MartinLane 2 88
(Derek Shaw) *bustled along leaving stalls: in tch in midfield: hdwy u.p over 1f out: led 1f out: r.o wl: rdn out* **3/1**2
14-4 2 1 **Dynamo Walt (IRE)**18 358 6-9-4 84 (v) NoelGarbutt(3) 5 88
(Derek Shaw) *in tch in last pair: effrt over 1f out: hdwy and switching lft 1f out: stl edging lft but wnt 2nd wl ins fnl f: styd on wout threatening wnr* **5/1**3
0325 3 ½ **Oriental Relation (IRE)**5 547 6-9-7 84 (v) PaulMulrennan 4 86
(James Given) *pressed ldng pair: rdn 2f out: unable qck u.p 1f out: kpt on same pce ins fnl f* **9/4**1
10-1 4 hd **Monumental Man**26 211 8-9-6 83 (p) WilliamCarson 1 84
(Michael Attwater) *t.k.h: pressed ldr on inner tl led and hung rt 3f out: rdn over 1f out: hdd 1f out: styd on same pce ins fnl f* **5/1**3
00-0 5 shd **Sandfrankskipsgo**25 234 8-9-3 80 GeorgeBaker 7 81
(Peter Crate) *hld up wl in tch in midfield: swtchd rt wl over 1f out: shkn up and effrt ent fnl f: rdn and styd on same pce fnl 150yds* **10/1**
1-40 6 2 ¼ **Silvanus (IRE)**18 358 12-9-7 84 PaulHanagan 3 77
(Paul Midgley) *taken down early: led tl 1/2-way: styd w ldrs tl rdn and unable qck over 1f out: lost pl and nt clrest run jst ins fnl f: wknd* **7/1**
646- 7 1 ¼ **Saved My Bacon (IRE)**189 5040 6-9-2 79 (h) DavidProbert 6 67
(Chris Dwyer) *stdd and wnt rt s: sn swtchd lft and in tch in last pair: effrt over 1f out: no imp: wknd ins fnl f* **20/1**
59.27s (-0.93) **Going Correction** -0.10s/f (Stan) **7** Ran SP% **115.5**
Speed ratings (Par 105): **103,101,100,100,100 96,94**
CSF £18.71 TOTE £3.70: £2.10, £2.30; EX 20.30 Trifecta £60.10.
**Owner** Brian Johnson (Northamptonshire) **Bred** Mrs C R Philipson & Mrs H G Lascelles **Trained** Sproxton, Leics

**FOCUS**
A typical sprint handicap where they went a true pace. The runner-up sets the standard.

## 619 BLUE AT LADIES DAY H'CAP 1m 5f 66y(P)
**4:40** (4:40) (Class 5) (0-75,75) 4-Y-0+ **£5,175** (£1,540; £769; £384) **Stalls** Low

Form RPR
061- 1 **Lost The Moon**51 8459 4-9-2 71 StevieDonohoe 2 79+
(Mark H Tompkins) *t.k.h: trckd ldrs: swtchd rt ent fnl 2f: rdn to chal over 1f out: led 1f out: edging lft u.p but styd on wl and drew clr ins fnl f* **2/1**1
4-22 2 2 ¼ **Eurato (FR)**16 380 7-9-6 71 (p) AdamKirby 7 75
(Steve Gollings) *trckd ldrs on outer: rdn over 2f out: chal u.p over 1f out: chsd wnr and styd on same pce ins fnl f: eased towards fin* **5/1**3
-603 3 ¾ **Icebuster**12 440 9-9-10 75 OisinMurphy 5 78
(Rod Millman) *t.k.h: hld up in tch: effrt and swtchd lft over 1f out: kpt on ins fnl furlon* **8/1**
06-6 4 ¾ **Sandy Cove**21 286 6-9-5 70 RyanTate 1 72
(James Eustace) *dwlt: in tch: rdn over 2f out: clsd to chse ldrs and nt clr run over 1f out: swtchd rt and kpt on ins fnl f* **10/1**
53-4 5 1 ¾ **Duck A L'Orange (IRE)**33 92 4-9-1 73 (v1) LouisSteward(3) 3 72
(Michael Bell) *led: rdn and qcknd ent fnl 2f: drvn and hdd 1f out: sn outpcd: wknd ins fnl f* **4/1**2
1-02 6 2 ½ **Clovelly Bay (IRE)**16 381 6-9-3 75 TylerSaunders(7) 6 71
(Marcus Tregoning) *t.k.h: w ldr: rdn over 2f out: unable qck 1f out: sn lost pl and wknd ins fnl f* **5/1**3
3-10 7 4 **Karam Albaari (IRE)**29 154 9-9-6 71 (v) GeorgeBaker 4 61
(J R Jenkins) *stdd after s: hld up in tch in rr: shkn up over 1f out: rdn and no hdwy 1f out: wl hld and eased towards fin* **14/1**
2m 50.43s (-3.17) **Going Correction** -0.10s/f (Stan)
**WFA** 4 from 6yo+ 2lb **7** Ran SP% **113.5**
Speed ratings (Par 103): **105,103,103,102,101 100,97**
CSF £12.10 TOTE £2.90: £1.70, £2.20; EX 9.40 Trifecta £37.00.
**Owner** AEDOS & Tompkins **Bred** John Brenchley & Dullingham Park **Trained** Newmarket, Suffolk

**FOCUS**
No more than fair form with the runner-up setting the standard, but a winner who's progressing.

## 620 UB40 HERE IN AUGUST H'CAP 7f (P)
**5:10** (5:12) (Class 6) (0-60,62) 4-Y-0+ **£3,234** (£962; £481; £240) **Stalls** Low

Form RPR
50-5 1 **Siege Of Boston (IRE)**35 50 4-9-7 60 (t) AdamKirby 8 66
(John Butler) *v.s.i.s: hld up in last trio: swtchd rt and hdwy over 1f out: rdn to ld jst ins fnl f: styd on wl* **7/2**2
026- 2 1 **Hidden Gem**52 8449 4-9-2 58 (vt1) AaronJones(3) 1 62
(Stuart Williams) *chsd ldrs: nt clr run on inner over 1f out: swtchd rt and hdwy ins fnl f: styd on to go 2nd towards fin* **8/1**3
-350 3 nk **Tavener**9 481 5-9-4 57 (p) DavidProbert 6 59
(David C Griffiths) *t.k.h: trckd ldrs: effrt to press ldrs ent fnl f: kpt on same pce u.p ins fnl f* **12/1**
6202 4 nse **Nasri**6 521 11-9-1 54 (v) StevieDonohoe 2 56
(Emma Owen) *t.k.h: led: rdn over 1f out: drvn and hdd ins fnl f: styd on same pce u.p after: lost 2 pls cl home* **8/1**3
-442 5 2 **Wink Oliver**14 398 5-8-12 58 (p) LauraCoughlan(7) 7 55
(Jo Hughes) *v.s.a: hld up in tch in rr on outer: effrt 2f out: edgd lft and kpt on same pce ins fnl f* **8/1**3
-113 6 shd **Whaleweigh Station**6 521 6-9-9 62 (v) OisinMurphy 9 59
(J R Jenkins) *t.k.h: chsd ldr: rdn over 1f out: unable qck 1f out: wknd wl ins fnl f* **7/2**2
355- 7 ½ **Hipz (IRE)**42 8555 6-9-6 59 (p) GeorgeBaker 4 54
(Laura Mongan) *hld up wl in tch in midfield: effrt over 1f out: chsd ldrs and rdn 1f out: unable qck and outpcd wl ins fnl f* **3/1**1
0-21 8 8 **All Or Nothin (IRE)**20 309 8-8-10 52 CallumShepherd(3) 5 26
(Paddy Butler) *in tch in last trio: effrt over 1f out: no imp u.p and btn 1f out: sn wknd* **12/1**
1m 26.06s (-1.14) **Going Correction** -0.10s/f (Stan) **8** Ran SP% **118.2**
Speed ratings (Par 101): **102,100,100,100,98 98,97,88**
CSF £32.57 CT £307.66 TOTE £5.60: £1.70, £2.70, £3.80; EX 43.70 Trifecta £419.90.
**Owner** Mark McKay **Bred** Willie McKay **Trained** Newmarket, Suffolk

**FOCUS**
A typically moderate 0-60 handicap, but a few of these did come into the race in good form. The winner made most of the class drop and the runner-up sets the level.
T/Plt: £110.80 to a £1 stake. Pool: £66,356.42 - 436.93 winning units T/Qpdt: £12.70 to a £1 stake. Pool: £6,914.28 - 402.10 winning units **Steve Payne**

# 544 KEMPTON (A.W) (R-H)
## Wednesday, February 8

**OFFICIAL GOING: Polytrack: standard**
Wind: Light, across Weather: Overcast, cold

## 621 RACING UK ANYWHERE H'CAP 1m 1f 219y(P)
**5:20** (5:20) (Class 7) (0-50,50) 4-Y-0+ **£1,940** (£577; £288; £144) **Stalls** Low

Form RPR
30-6 1 **Smiley Bagel (IRE)**30 146 4-9-5 49 RichardKingscote 11 54
(Ed Walker) *hld up in midfield: prog on inner fr 2f out: rdn to ld jst over 1f out: hdd last 110 yds: kpt on to pass idling ldr fnl strides* **9/4**1
46-0 2 hd **Jazri**32 124 6-9-6 49 (b) FrannyNorton 7 53
(Milton Bradley) *heavily restrained s: hld up wl in rr: gd prog on wd outside fr 2f out: clsd to ld 110yds out: fnd nil in front and hdd last strides* **6/1**3
/00- 3 1 ¼ **Frankie**77 8070 6-9-2 45 KieranO'Neill 5 47
(Jimmy Fox) *hld up wl in rr: rdn over 3f out: trying to make prog whn nt clr run 2f out to over 1f out: styd on wl fnl f on outer: tk 3rd nr fin* **66/1**
65-6 4 ¾ **Castanea**13 425 5-9-2 45 RyanPowell 12 46
(Ronald Harris) *s.s: hld up in last: stl last 2f: rapid prog on outer over 1f out: styd on to take 4th nr fin: no ch* **33/1**
05-2 5 2 **Awesome Rock (IRE)**22 279 8-9-4 47 LiamKeniry 14 44
(Roger Ingram) *hld up wl in rr: prog on wd outside over 2f out: rdn to chal jst over 1f out: fnd nil and outpcd fnl f* **16/1**
50-6 6 1 ¾ **Whip Up A Frenzy (IRE)**21 281 5-8-9 45 GabrieleMalune(7) 6 39+
(Richard Rowe) *prom: rdn to chse ldr wl over 2f out to over 1f out: wknd* **8/1**
0-55 7 shd **Sixties Idol**11 462 4-8-13 46 NathanAlison(3) 1 40
(Sheena West) *trckd ldrs but off the pce by 1/2-way: cl up 3f out: trapped bhd wkng rival on inner and lost grnd over 2f out: nudged along and prog over 1f out: outpcd fnl f* **20/1**
45- 8 ½ **No No Cardinal (IRE)**28 6405 8-9-6 49 TimmyMurphy 9 42
(Mark Gillard) *hld up off the pce: clsd gng strly 3f out: shkn up and no rspnse over 1f out: fin weakly* **33/1**
/30- 9 1 **Goldmadchen (GER)**327 981 9-9-5 48 TomEaves 2 39+
(James Given) *chsd ldr 2f: styd prom: urged along over 4f out: wknd fnl f* **25/1**
065- 10 ½ **Understory (USA)**48 8492 10-9-6 49 LukeMorris 3 41
(Tim McCarthy) *led 4f: led again 3f out to jst over 1f out: wknd* **10/1**
0-00 11 1 ¾ **Silver Lining (IRE)**21 281 5-9-2 45 (t) AdamBeschizza 13 34
(Mark Hoad) *off the pce towards rr: clsd fr 3f out: lost grnd bhd wkng rival over 2f out: drvn and prog over 1f out: keeping on but no ch whn hmpd ins fnl f and eased* **66/1**
5-53 12 8 **Sir Jamie**13 425 4-9-1 45 GeorgeDowning 8 18+
(Tony Carroll) *chsd ldrs: u.p bef 1/2-way: sing to lost pl whn hmpd jst over 1f out: wknd* **10/3**2
000- 13 7 **Ledbury (IRE)**168 5777 5-9-7 50 (b) KierenFox 10 10
(Lee Carter) *v awkward s: t.k.h and sn rcvrd to chse ldrs: led after 4f out to 3f out: wknd rapidly: t.o* **20/1**
2m 7.46s (-0.54) **Going Correction** -0.175s/f (Stan) **13** Ran SP% **116.5**
Speed ratings (Par 97): **95,94,93,93,91 90,90,89,88,88 87,80,75**
CSF £13.95 CT £677.22 TOTE £3.30: £1.30, £2.00, £11.80; EX 16.30 Trifecta £1203.90.
**Owner** Laurence Bellman **Bred** Max Morris **Trained** Upper Lambourn, Berks

**FOCUS**
This was run at a good gallop and was set up for the closers. The winner didn't need to match the best of last year's best figures.

## 622 RACING UK HD H'CAP 5f (P)
**5:50** (5:50) (Class 7) (0-50,50) 4-Y-0+ **£1,940** (£577; £288; £144) **Stalls** Low

Form RPR
-002 1 **Swendab (IRE)**8 494 9-9-5 50 (b) TimmyMurphy 2 58
(John O'Shea) *pressed ldr: rdn to ld 1f out: clr ins fnl f: kpt on* **9/2**2

03-1 **2** *1 ½* **Fabulous Flyer**[30] 143 4-9-0 **50**.................................... DavidParkes(5) 4 53
(Jeremy Gask) *s.i.s: sn in 6th: rdn over 1f out: styd on fnl f to take 2nd last 50yds* **9/4**[1]

6624 **3** *½* **Justice Rock**[2] 601 4-9-3 **48**.................................... JosephineGordon 3 49
(Phil McEntee) *chsd ldrs in 5th: rdn over 1f out: kpt on fnl f to take 3rd last strides* **7/1**

40-0 **4** *shd* **Presto Boy**[30] 143 5-8-9 **47**..........................................(e) NicolaCurrie(7) 6 47
(Richard Hughes) *awkward s: sn in 7th: effrt on outer over 1f out: styd on fnl f: nrst fin* **16/1**

05-0 **5** *nk* **Lizzy's Dream**[29] 153 9-9-3 **48**.......................................... LukeMorris 8 47
(Rebecca Bastiman) *sn in 8th: rdn and kpt on fnl f: nrst fin but no ch* **6/1**[3]

40-0 **6** *nk* **Red Flute**[26] 215 5-9-1 **49**..................................................(v) TimClark(3) 1 47
(Denis Quinn) *urged along to ld fr ins draw and then t.k.h: rdn and hdd 1f out: fdd and lost pls last 50yds* **15/2**

004- **7** *1 ¼* **Give Us A Belle (IRE)**[91] 7863 8-9-2 **47**..................(vt) AdamBeschizza 7 41
(Christine Dunnett) *chsd ldng trio: drvn over 1f out: fdd ins fnl f* **25/1**

650- **8** *hd* **Leith Bridge**[54] 8409 5-9-5 **50**.............................................. LiamKeniry 9 43
(Mark Usher) *dwlt and dropped in fr wd draw: effrt on inner over 1f out: kpt on but nt pce to threaten* **10/1**

000- **9** *1 ¾* **Burnt Cream**[181] 5335 10-9-4 **49**.................................(t) TomMarquand 10 36
(Martin Bosley) *dwlt: dropped in fr wdst draw and hld up in last: nvr on terms* **66/1**

60-3 **10** *2 ¼* **Willow Spring**[30] 143 5-9-4 **49**.......................................... SeanLevey 5 28
(Denis Quinn) *chsd ldng pair to jst over 1f out: wknd rapidly* **7/1**

59.8s (-0.70) **Going Correction** -0.175s/f (Stan) 10 Ran SP% **120.3**
Speed ratings (Par 97): **98,95,94,94,94 93,91,91,88,84**
CSF £15.55 CT £71.99 TOTE £4.80: £1.90, £1.60, £2.60; EX 18.30 Trifecta £71.50.
**Owner** E&G Racing: Swendab **Bred** P Brady **Trained** Elton, Gloucs

**FOCUS**
A low-grade sprint with the winner up a fraction on his recent best.

## 623 32RED.COM H'CAP 5f (P)
**6:20** (6:22) (Class 5) (0-75,76) 3-Y-O **£2,911** (£866; £432; £216) **Stalls** Low

Form RPR

16-2 **1** **Little Miss Daisy**[19] 324 3-8-11 **62**.................................. MartinDwyer 6 68
(William Muir) *hld up in 5th: shkn up over 1f out: clsd qckly to ld last 100yds: readily* **9/2**[3]

12-4 **2** *1 ¼* **Juan Horsepower**[29] 155 3-9-11 **76**...........................(p) KieranO'Neill 1 77
(Richard Hannon) *urged along to ld: rdn 2f out: kpt on but hdd and outpcd last 100yds* **15/8**[1]

300- **3** *½* **Endeavour (IRE)**[70] 8159 3-9-0 **65**.............................. TomMarquand 3 64
(Richard Hannon) *mostly chsd ldr: rdn and nt qckn over 1f out: one pce fnl f* **7/1**

5-03 **4** *¾* **Roundabout Magic (IRE)**[16] 379 3-8-6 **62**................. HollieDoyle(5) 7 59
(Simon Dow) *tk fierce hold: chsd ldrs on outer: rdn over 1f out: nt qckn and hld after* **10/1**

3-21 **5** *½* **Hathfa (FR)**[21] 288 3-9-7 **72**..........................................(be) ShaneKelly 2 69
(Richard Hughes) *chsd ldng pair: chalng on inner whn short of room jst over 1f out and lost momentum: nt rcvr* **9/4**[2]

350- **6** *½* **Who Told Jo Jo (IRE)**[113] 7440 3-9-7 **72**........................ LiamKeniry 5 65
(Joseph Tuite) *hld up in last: detached 1/2-way: reminders fnl f: kpt on but nvr in it* **16/1**

59.49s (-1.01) **Going Correction** -0.175s/f (Stan) 6 Ran SP% **111.2**
Speed ratings (Par 97): **101,99,98,97,96 95**
CSF £13.14 TOTE £4.10: £2.50, £1.70; EX 14.20 Trifecta £101.80.
**Owner** Mrs J M Muir **Bred** Hungerford Park Stud **Trained** Lambourn, Berks

**FOCUS**
This was run at a good gallop. A length personal best from the winner, who continus to progress, with the race rated around the runner-up.

## 624 32RED ON THE APP STORE MAIDEN FILLIES' STKS 7f (P)
**6:50** (6:59) (Class 5) 3-Y-O+ **£2,911** (£866; £432; £216) **Stalls** Low

Form RPR

02-2 **1** **Pepita (IRE)**[11] 466 3-8-11 84.............................................. SeanLevey 9 71+
(Richard Hannon) *reluctant to enter stall: mde all: looked wl in command whn shkn up over 1f out: wandered after and rdr lost an iron ins fnl f: hld on* **4/7**[1]

4-52 **2** *nk* **Tibibit**[7] 503 4-10-0 0................................................ RichardKingscote 12 70
(Henry Tett) *chsd wnr: rdn and no imp 2f out: kpt on as wnr faltered ins fnl f: a hld* **7/2**[2]

0-5 **3** *2 ¾* **Sandy Shores**[25] 236 3-8-4 0..................................... JordanUys(7) 6 58+
(Brian Meehan) *chsd ldrs in 5th: rdn and outpcd 2f out: kpt on to take 3rd ins fnl f: no threat to ldng pair* **7/1**[3]

6 **4** *1 ½* **Fun Raiser (IRE)**[14] 393 3-8-11 0.................................. LukeMorris 1 54
(Harry Dunlop) *chsd ldng pair: rdn over 2f out: sn outpcd: lost 3rd ins fnl f* **16/1**

36- **5** *nk* **Andanotherone (IRE)**[90] 7894 4-9-11 0............................ TimClark(3) 8 58
(Denis Quinn) *chsd ldng trio: rdn over 2f out: sn outpcd and btn* **33/1**

**6** *1 ½* **Miss M (IRE)** 3-8-11 0.......................................................... MartinDwyer 4 49
(William Muir) *dwlt: hld up in last pair: pushed along and prog wl over 1f out: n.d but kpt on* **12/1**

0-0 **7** *3 ¾* **Cherry Leyf**[21] 288 3-8-11 0...................................... AdamBeschizza 10 39
(Stuart Williams) *s.s: t.k.h and hld up in rr: outpcd fr 2f out: wknd fnl f* **33/1**

**8** *½* **Rocksette** 3-8-11 0.................................................................. LiamKeniry 7 37
(Philip Hide) *dwlt: nvr bttr than midfield: shkn up over 2f out: wknd over 1f out* **66/1**

**9** *3* **Secret Sands (IRE)** 3-8-11 0................................ MichaelJMMurphy 5 29
(Pat Phelan) *a towards rr: wknd wl over 1f out* **33/1**

**10** *4 ½* **Our Ruth** 4-10-0 0...................................................................... KieranO'Neill 3 22
(Jimmy Fox) *dwlt: a in last pair and rn green: wl bhd fnl 2f* **150/1**

1m 26.76s (0.76) **Going Correction** -0.175s/f (Stan)
**WFA** 3 from 4yo 17lb 10 Ran SP% **122.9**
Speed ratings (Par 100): **88,87,84,82,82 80,76,75,72,67**
CSF £2.96 TOTE £1.60: £1.10, £1.20, £1.70; EX 3.40 Trifecta £9.50.
**Owner** Rockcliffe Stud **Bred** R O'Callaghan And D Veitch **Trained** East Everleigh, Wilts

**FOCUS**
An ordinary fillies' maiden and late drama.

## 625 32RED CASINO H'CAP 7f (P)
**7:20** (7:25) (Class 5) (0-75,77) 3-Y-O **£2,911** (£866; £432; £216) **Stalls** Low

Form RPR

0-43 **1** **Tai Hang Dragon (IRE)**[19] 331 3-8-12 **66**......................... SeanLevey 5 70
(Richard Hannon) *hld up in rr: shkn up and effrt whn impeded 2f out: clsd to chal 1f out: gd battle w runner-up and led last 50yds* **7/1**[3]

333- **2** *nk* **Jumping Jack (IRE)**[132] 6898 3-9-6 **74**............................ ShaneKelly 7 77
(Richard Hughes) *hld up in last: gd prog on inner over 2f out but sn hung bdly lft: led 1f out: hrd pressed after: styd on but hdd last 50yds* **7/1**[3]

21- **3** *3* **Marzouq (USA)**[150] 6369 3-9-7 **75**.................................... LukeMorris 6 70
(Jeremy Noseda) *racd on outer: in tch: rdn and no prog over 2f out: styd on fr over 1f out to take 3rd last 50yds* **11/4**[2]

200- **4** *nk* **Baby Gal**[65] 8230 3-8-10 **69**......................................... CharlieBennett(5) 3 63
(Jim Boyle) *hld up in tch: effrt and rdn 2f out: styd on to chse ldng pair ins fnl f: no threat to ldng pair and lost 3rd last 50yds* **66/1**

323- **5** *2 ¼* **Rapid Rise (IRE)**[71] 8140 3-9-6 **77**......................... KieranShoemark(3) 8 65
(David Brown) *led after 1f: hung bdly lft fr jst over 2f out: hdd & wknd 1f out* **11/1**

130- **6** *8* **Lord Clenaghcastle (IRE)**[70] 8153 3-9-3 **71**.................. GeorgeBaker 1 37
(Gary Moore) *led 1f: racd in 2nd to 5f out and again 3f out to 2f out: wknd qckly* **5/2**[1]

005- **7** *3 ½* **Mister Sunshine (IRE)**[136] 6800 3-9-7 **75**........................ AdamKirby 4 32
(Clive Cox) *t.k.h: pressed ldrs: rdn and no rspnse over 2f out: wknd u.p over 1f out* **17/2**

52-2 **8** *6* **La Guapita**[35] 34 3-9-4 **72**........................................ JosephineGordon 2 13
(Hugo Palmer) *plld hrd: pressed ldrs: hanging whn rdn over 2f out and sn gave up: virtually p.u ins fnl f* **7/1**[3]

1m 24.79s (-1.21) **Going Correction** -0.175s/f (Stan) 8 Ran SP% **113.1**
Speed ratings (Par 97): **99,98,95,94,92 83,79,72**
CSF £53.40 CT £166.20 TOTE £7.90: £1.80, £2.30, £1.40; EX 45.70 Trifecta £202.60.
**Owner** Rockcliffe Stud **Bred** Lynn Lodge Stud **Trained** East Everleigh, Wilts

**FOCUS**
A competitive race. The pace was pretty decent and it ended up being fought out by a couple of the hold-up horses.

## 626 32RED H'CAP (LONDON MILE SERIES QUALIFIER) 1m (P)
**7:50** (7:50) (Class 3) (0-95,90) 3-Y-O
**£7,158** (£2,143; £1,071; £535; £267; £134) **Stalls** Low

Form RPR

0-11 **1** **Tisbutadream (IRE)**[14] 392 3-8-5 **79**........................... HollieDoyle(5) 4 87
(David Elsworth) *mde all: stretched on fr 3f out: rdn and jnd 1f out: fnd ex and kpt on wl fnl f* **11/2**

51- **2** *½* **Makaarim**[43] 8537 3-8-11 **80**.......................................... DanielMuscutt 1 87
(Marco Botti) *t.k.h in 3rd: trckd wnr over 3f out: rdn to chal and upsides 1f out: nt qckn sn after and hld last 150yds* **7/4**[1]

142- **3** *2* **Hajaj (IRE)**[56] 8360 3-8-7 **76**..................................... StevieDonohoe 7 78
(Charlie Fellowes) *hld up in last: hanging lft bnd over 3f out: rdn over 2f out: kpt on fr over 1f out to take 3rd ins fnl f* **9/2**[3]

1-2 **4** *½* **Ay Ay (IRE)**[28] 177 3-9-7 **90**.............................................. ShaneKelly 6 91
(David Elsworth) *hld up in 4th: prog on inner and cl up 2f out: sn rdn and nt qckn: one pce over 1f out* **8/1**

5-14 **5** *¾* **Letmestopyouthere (IRE)**[22] 276 3-9-4 **87**............... AndrewMullen 2 86
(David Evans) *hld up in 5th: rdn over 2f out: one pce and no imp on ldrs after* **20/1**

2-22 **6** *2 ½* **Tailor's Row (USA)**[7] 512 3-8-9 **78**............................... PJMcDonald 5 71
(Mark Johnston) *chsd wnr to over 3f out: dropped to last over 2f out and wl btn after* **3/1**[2]

1m 38.64s (-1.16) **Going Correction** -0.175s/f (Stan) 6 Ran SP% **110.8**
Speed ratings (Par 101): **98,97,95,95,94 91**
CSF £15.20 TOTE £6.20: £2.30, £1.30; EX 18.40 Trifecta £61.80.
**Owner** Mrs Anne Coughlan & Ten Green Bottles **Bred** J F Tuthill **Trained** Newmarket, Suffolk

**FOCUS**
Quite an interesting handicap, and the form looks pretty sound despite the winner dominating from the front. The race has been rated around the third and fourth.

## 627 100% PROFIT BOOST AT 32REDSPORT.COM H'CAP 1m 3f 219y(P)
**8:20** (8:20) (Class 6) (0-65,67) 3-Y-O **£2,264** (£673; £336; £168) **Stalls** Centre

Form RPR

0-21 **1** **Serenade The Stars (IRE)**[20] 305 3-9-9 **67**...............(v) LukeMorris 5 76+
(James Tate) *hld up in tch: shkn up and prog over 2f out: rdn to ld over 1f out: styd on wl and clr fnl f* **8/11**[1]

0-52 **2** *4* **The Last Debutante**[16] 378 3-9-6 **64**.............................. PJMcDonald 1 65
(Mark Johnston) *trckd ldrs: quick move to ld over 2f out: sn rdn: hdd over 1f out: kpt on same pce and no ch w wnr* **13/2**[3]

000- **3** *¾* **Hot Lick**[58] 8340 3-8-12 **56**..................................................(h) LiamKeniry 9 56+
(Andrew Balding) *awkward s: in tch: shuffled bk over 3f out: hanging and outpcd over 2f out: rdn and prog to 4th over 1f out: styd on after to take 3rd nr fin* **33/1**

00-0 **4** *½* **Hi There Silver (IRE)**[12] 434 3-8-2 **46** oh1.................. KieranO'Neill 10 45
(Michael Madgwick) *hld up in rr: quick prog arnd rivals over 3f out to chal over 2f out: sn rdn: battled for 2nd fr over 1f out tl nr fin* **80/1**

3-54 **5** *7* **Gog Elles (IRE)**[30] 149 3-7-13 **48**................................(p) HollieDoyle(5) 6 36
(J S Moore) *chsd ldrs: rdn over 4f out: effrt on outer over 3f out: wknd over 2f out* **12/1**

600- **6** *1 ¼* **Affair**[41] 8568 3-8-6 **57**.................................................... TheodoreLadd(7) 7 43
(Hughie Morrison) *dropped out in detached last: tried to make prog over 2f out but too late to be a factor* **50/1**

506- **7** *12* **Dusty Berry**[187] 5120 3-9-7 **65**...........................................(p[1]) JohnFahy 3 32
(Eve Johnson Houghton) *mostly in last pair: rdn and struggling 1/2-way: sn no ch* **50/1**

00-0 **8** *¾* **Shadow Of Hercules (IRE)**[15] 385 3-7-9 **46** oh1....(v[1]) AledBeech(7) 2 11
(Michael Mullineaux) *led to 4f out: wknd wl over 2f out: sn bhd* **125/1**

06-5 **9** *9* **Masterfilly (IRE)**[30] 149 3-8-12 **56**......................... RichardKingscote 4 7
(Ed Walker) *pressed ldr: led 4f out to over 2f out: wknd v rapidly: t.o* **7/2**[2]

00-6 **10** *3 ¼* **Master Billie (IRE)**[20] 305 3-8-7 **51**................................. MartinDwyer 8
(William Muir) *chsd ldrs on outer: rdn over 4f out: sn wknd rapidly: t.o* **12/1**

2m 33.69s (-0.81) **Going Correction** -0.175s/f (Stan) 10 Ran SP% **117.7**
Speed ratings (Par 95): **95,92,91,91,86 86,78,77,71,69**
CSF £6.17 CT £88.40 TOTE £1.90: £1.10, £1.80, £6.70; EX 6.20 Trifecta £93.80.
**Owner** Saeed Manana **Bred** Summerville Bloodstock **Trained** Newmarket, Suffolk

**FOCUS**
A bit of a messy race pace-wise, but the winner continues on an upward curve.

T/Jkpt: Not won. T/Plt: £18.90 to a £1 stake. Pool: £95,181.52 - 3,660.18 winning units T/Qpdt: £5.90 to a £1 stake. Pool: £9,669.66 - 1,196.42 winning units **Jonathan Neesom**

628 - 635a (Foreign Racing) - See Raceform Interactive

# [614]CHELMSFORD (A.W) (L-H)

Thursday, February 9

**OFFICIAL GOING: Polytrack: standard**

Wind: Light against Weather: Misty

## 636 BET TOTEPLACEPOT AT BETFRED.COM APPRENTICE H'CAP 1m 2f (P)

**5:50** (5:51) (Class 6) (0-55,60) 4-Y-O+ **£3,234** (£962; £481; £240) **Stalls** Low

Form RPR

-501 **1** **Celtic Artisan (IRE)**[3] 605 6-9-7 **60** 6ex....................(bt) PaulaMuir(5) 4 69
(Rebecca Menzies) *mde all: clr 4f out: rdn and edgd rt over 1f out: styd on wl* **11/8**[1]

45-4 **2** *3 1/4* **Hold Firm**[17] 383 5-9-1 **54**.............................. GabrieleMalune(5) 12 57
(Mark H Tompkins) *edgd lft s: sn w wnr tl 8f out: remained handy: rdn to chse wnr over 1f out: no imp ins fnl f* **11/1**

006/ **3** *1 1/4* **Flying Author (IRE)**[680] 1128 6-8-13 **47**......................(tp) JaneElliott 7 48
(Phil McEntee) *hld up: hdwy over 2f out: rdn over 1f out: styd on* **33/1**

-060 **4** *1/2* **The Dukkerer (IRE)**[16] 390 6-9-7 **55**.................... LewisEdmunds 10 55
(James Given) *hmpd s: mid-div: hdwy over 1f out: nt rch ldrs* **10/1**

-060 **5** *nk* **Hydrant**[2] 608 11-9-1 **54**.................................... BenSanderson(5) 11 53
(Richard Guest) *hmpd s: sn prom: outpcd over 3f out: styd on fnl f* **20/1**

51-0 **6** *1* **Master Of Heaven**[22] 281 4-9-1 **50**.......................(p) PaddyBradley 13 47
(Jim Boyle) *prom: chsd wnr 8f out: rdn over 3f out: lost 2nd over 1f out: wknd ins fnl f* **16/1**

3352 **7** *1/2* **General Tufto**[10] 482 12-9-1 **52**............................(b) BenRobinson(3) 3 48
(Charles Smith) *s.i.s: in rr: pushed along and hdwy over 2f out: nt trble ldrs* **9/1**

00-2 **8** *1* **Nouvelle Ere**[33] 124 6-9-1 **54**..............................(t) AledBeech(5) 8 48
(Tony Carroll) *prom: outpcd over 3f out: n.d after* **8/1**[3]

00-6 **9** *nk* **Breakheart (IRE)**[36] 46 10-8-13 **52**.......................(b) WilliamCox(5) 14 46
(Andrew Balding) *hld up in tch: rdn over 2f out: nt clr run and edgd lft over 1f out: wknd fnl f* **25/1**

0-30 **10** *1 1/4* **Tyrsal (IRE)**[12] 461 6-9-9 **57**.................................. KevinLundie 9 48
(Clifford Lines) *a in rr: rdn over 2f out: nvr on terms* **6/1**[2]

/0-0 **11** *nse* **Bridge That Gap**[33] 121 9-9-3 **51**..........................(p) RhiainIngram 5 42
(Roger Ingram) *hld up: n.d* **50/1**

2-00 **12** *nk* **Dor's Law**[14] 420 4-9-8 **57**.................................... LuluStanford 6 48
(Dean Ivory) *prom: lost pl over 7f out: n.d after* **12/1**

00-6 **13** *5* **Mr Standfast**[12] 457 4-9-2 **51**................................ MeganNicholls 1 32
(Alan Phillips) *prom: lost pl over 8f out: n.d after* **50/1**

2m 6.18s (-2.42) **Going Correction** -0.20s/f (Stan) **13** Ran SP% **124.0**
Speed ratings (Par 101): **101,98,97,97,96 95,95,94,94,93 93,93,89**
CSF £17.68 CT £371.79 TOTE £2.10: £1.40, £3.40, £12.40; EX 19.80 Trifecta £987.10.
**Owner** EPDS Racing Partnership 11 **Bred** Fortbarrington Stud **Trained** Mordon, Durham

**FOCUS**
An open handicap run at an honest pace. A significant personal best from the winner and a sensible standard rated around the balance of those in behind.

## 637 BET TOTEEXACTA AT BETFRED.COM H'CAP 1m 2f (P)

**6:25** (6:25) (Class 6) (0-60,61) 3-Y-O **£3,234** (£962; £481; £240) **Stalls** Low

Form RPR

00-0 **1** **Seaborn (IRE)**[34] 91 3-9-0 **56**.................................. RobHornby(3) 8 62
(Simon Hodgson) *led after 1f: rdn over 3f out: styd on* **16/1**

05-4 **2** *2* **Broughtons Story**[34] 100 3-9-7 **60**............................ GeorgeBaker 6 62
(Henry Spiller) *hld up: hdwy over 1f out: rdn to chse wnr ins fnl f: swvd rt wl ins fnl f: styd on same pce* **15/8**[1]

0-56 **3** *2 1/2* **Chough**[27] 209 3-8-10 **54**...................................... CharlieBennett(5) 11 51
(Hughie Morrison) *chsd ldrs: rdn over 2f out: styd on same pce ins fnl f* **12/1**

2-02 **4** *hd* **La Vie En Rose**[21] 305 3-9-8 **61**................................ JoeFanning 9 58
(Mark Johnston) *chsd ldr after 1f: rdn over 2f out: no ex ins fnl f* **7/2**[3]

0-64 **5** *4* **Av A Word**[21] 305 3-9-4 **57**...................................(b[1]) AdamKirby 5 46
(Daniel Kubler) *sn drvn along to go prom: swtchd rt after 1f: rdn over 3f out: wknd ins fnl f* **5/2**[2]

00-0 **6** *10* **Son Castello (IRE)**[17] 376 3-8-4 **46** oh1..................(b) NoelGarbutt(3) 3 16
(Gary Moore) *sn led: hdd after 1f: remained handy tl rdn and wknd over 1f out* **33/1**

5-00 **7** *1* **Forest Steps (IRE)**[21] 305 3-8-0 **46**...................... GeorgiaDobie(7) 2 14
(J S Moore) *hld up: racd keenly: rdn and wknd over 2f out* **50/1**

00-0 **8** *nk* **Lady Parker (IRE)**[34] 96 3-8-7 **51**.......................... HollieDoyle(5) 7 19
(J S Moore) *s.i.s: a in rr: wknd over 2f out* **50/1**

004- **9** *1 1/2* **Girlofinkandstars (IRE)**[189] 5052 3-9-3 **56**............... AdamBeschizza 1 21
(Rae Guest) *sn pushed along and prom: lost pl over 7f out: rdn over 4f out: wknd over 3f out* **8/1**

2m 7.63s (-0.97) **Going Correction** -0.20s/f (Stan) **9** Ran SP% **117.1**
Speed ratings (Par 95): **95,93,91,91,88 80,79,79,77**
CSF £46.87 CT £389.52 TOTE £15.40: £4.30, £1.10, £3.30; EX 70.10 Trifecta £694.60.
**Owner** Ms Debbie Grey **Bred** Michael Fennessy **Trained** Queen Camel, Somerset

**FOCUS**
The pace was steady for this moderate handicap with the winner taking a modest step forward.

## 638 BET TOTEQUADPOT AT BETFRED.COM MAIDEN STKS 5f (P)

**7:00** (7:02) (Class 4) 3-4-Y-O **£6,469** (£1,925; £962; £481) **Stalls** Low

Form RPR

30-0 **1** **Fethiye Boy**[24] 264 3-9-0 62.................................... ShaneKelly 3 71
(Ronald Harris) *mde all: rdn ins fnl f: all out* **8/1**[3]

224- **2** *hd* **Red Alert**[120] 7269 3-9-0 74.................................... LiamKeniry 4 70
(Joseph Tuite) *chsd wnr: rdn and hung lft fr over 1f out: r.o* **1/1**[1]

02- **3** *3/4* **Fantasy Keeper**[66] 8229 3-9-0 0.............................. AndrewMullen 1 68
(Michael Appleby) *s.i.s: pushed along and hdwy over 3f out: rdn over 1f out: r.o* **6/4**[2]

4-26 **4** *3 3/4* **Heavenly Cry**[27] 212 3-9-0 62..........................(v) JosephineGordon 2 54
(Phil McEntee) *chsd ldrs: pushed along 1/2-way: rdn and hung rt over 1f out: styd on same pce* **12/1**

**5** *nk* **Seneca Chief** 3-9-0 0.......................................... GeorgeDowning 7 53
(Daniel Kubler) *s.i.s: sn pushed along in rr: nvr on terms* **33/1**

59.71s (-0.49) **Going Correction** -0.20s/f (Stan) **5** Ran SP% **111.7**
Speed ratings (Par 105): **95,94,93,87,87**
CSF £12.88 TOTE £10.00: £3.40, £1.30; EX 17.90 Trifecta £39.10.
**Owner** Mrs Ruth M Serrell **Bred** Longdon Stud Ltd **Trained** Earlswood, Monmouths

**FOCUS**
A modest maiden which was weakened further prior to the off as the well-backed favourite bolted to post and had to be withdrawn. Another all-the-way winner rated close to his standout turf run.

## 639 BET TOTETRIFECTA AT BETFRED.COM H'CAP 6f (P)

**7:30** (7:30) (Class 3) (0-95,95) 4-Y-O+ **£9,703** (£2,887; £1,443; £721) **Stalls** Centre

Form RPR

52-4 **1** **Boomerang Bob (IRE)**[26] 234 8-9-3 **91**........................(p) AdamKirby 2 99
(Jamie Osborne) *a.p: rdn to ld wl ins fnl f: styd on* **9/4**[1]

6-13 **2** *nk* **Zac Brown (IRE)**[20] 326 6-8-9 **88**.......................(t) LewisEdmunds(5) 1 95
(Charlie Wallis) *trckd ldrs: plld hrd: rdn to ld over 1f out: hdd wl ins fnl f: r.o* **5/1**[2]

46-1 **3** *nk* **Eljaddaaf (IRE)**[34] 94 6-9-1 **89**.............................(h) RobertWinston 10 95+
(Dean Ivory) *s.i.s: hld up: swtchd lft over 4f out: rdn over 1f out: swtchd lft and r.o ins fnl f: nt rch ldrs* **6/1**[3]

-020 **4** *1 3/4* **Gentlemen**[20] 326 6-9-7 **95**...........................(h) JosephineGordon 4 95
(Phil McEntee) *sn chsng ldr: rdn over 1f out: styd on same pce fnl f* **8/1**

051- **5** *1 1/4* **Shamshon (IRE)**[131] 6944 6-9-5 **93**..........................(t) SeanLevey 5 89
(Stuart Williams) *hld up: rdn over 1f out: r.o ins fnl f* **5/1**[2]

60-4 **6** *3/4* **Guishan**[39] 4 7-8-11 **88**...................................... TimClark(3) 7 82
(Michael Appleby) *led: rdn and hdd over 1f out: no ex ins fnl f* **33/1**

540- **7** *2 1/4* **King Robert**[41] 8583 4-9-3 **91**.................................. PaulMulrennan 9 78
(Bryan Smart) *prom: rdn over 2f out: wknd fnl f* **8/1**

113- **8** *nse* **Outrage**[41] 8583 5-9-7 **95**......................................(b) GeorgeBaker 8 82
(Daniel Kubler) *hld up: rn wd turning for home: nvr on terms* **10/1**

50-0 **9** *1 1/4* **Quatrieme Ami**[26] 234 4-9-0 **88**...............................(t) DavidProbert 6 71
(Philip McBride) *pushed along in rr early: rdn over 2f out: wknd fnl f* **14/1**

1m 11.02s (-2.68) **Going Correction** -0.20s/f (Stan) **9** Ran SP% **119.3**
Speed ratings (Par 107): **109,108,108,105,104 103,100,100,98**
CSF £13.99 CT £61.23 TOTE £3.30: £1.40, £1.40, £2.20; EX 13.20 Trifecta £67.60.
**Owner** Melbourne 10 Racing **Bred** Dr Dean Harron & Ederidge Ltd **Trained** Upper Lambourn, Berks

**FOCUS**
They went a sound pace for this competitive handicap. It paid to race handy with the first two always well placed.

## 640 TOTEPOOL BETTING AT BETFRED.COM H'CAP 6f (P)

**8:00** (8:00) (Class 6) (0-52,54) 4-Y-O+ **£3,234** (£962; £481; £240) **Stalls** Centre

Form RPR

-363 **1** **Menelik (IRE)**[9] 494 8-9-8 **53**............................(bt) DavidProbert 7 62
(Des Donovan, Ire) *s.i.s: sn chsng ldrs: led 4f out: rdn out* **20/1**

0-21 **2** *2 1/2* **Krazy Paving**[13] 438 5-9-9 **54**..............................(b) AdamKirby 4 55
(Anabel K Murphy) *led 1f: chsd ldrs: chsd wnr over 2f out: rdn over 1f out: styd on same pce ins fnl f* **9/2**[2]

05-5 **3** *1* **Upper Lambourn (IRE)**[16] 386 9-8-8 **46** oh1...........(t) KevinLundie(7) 5 44
(John Holt) *mid-div: hdwy u.p over 1f out: r.o to go 3rd nr fin* **33/1**

0-00 **4** *1/2* **Broughtons Fancy**[17] 383 4-9-7 **52**.......................... GeorgeBaker 3 49+
(Gary Moore) *hld up in tch: rdn over 1f out: styd on same pce ins fnl f* **11/10**[1]

4-44 **5** *1* **Mr Potter**[13] 445 4-9-8 **53**.................................(v[1]) ConnorBeasley 13 47+
(Richard Guest) *s.i.s: in rr: swtchd lft over 1f out: r.o ins fnl f: nrst fin* **7/1**

3-00 **6** *nk* **Tasaaboq**[21] 303 6-9-5 **50**.............................(t) JosephineGordon 9 43+
(Phil McEntee) *hld up: pushed along 1/2-way: rdn and hdwy over 1f out: nt trble ldrs* **14/1**

01-0 **7** *2 1/2* **Ocotillo (IRE)**[30] 158 4-9-6 **51**................................ RyanPowell 2 36+
(Kevin Frost) *hld up: hdwy over 1f out: nvr nrr* **20/1**

10-0 **8** *2* **Suni Dancer**[7] 521 6-9-8 **53**................................. GeorgeDowning 10 32+
(Tony Carroll) *s.i.s: nt clr run over 1f out: styd on: nvr on terms* **16/1**

0-40 **9** *2* **Royal Normandy**[15] 398 5-9-7 **52**.........................(b) TomMarquand 12 25+
(Grace Harris) *hld up: rdn over 2f out: n.d* **33/1**

24-0 **10** *1 1/2* **The Reel Way (GR)**[23] 274 6-9-1 **46** oh1.................. DanielMuscutt 6 15
(Patrick Chamings) *prom: rdn over 2f out: wknd over 1f out* **25/1**

06-6 **11** *2 1/4* **Tahiti One**[36] 52 4-9-4 **49**.................................(h[1]) WilliamCarson 14 11
(Tony Carroll) *chsd ldrs: rdn over 2f out: sn wknd* **33/1**

60-6 **12** *1* **Oddsocks (IRE)**[6] 554 5-9-1 **46** oh1.......................... TimmyMurphy 1 5
(Tony Carroll) *prom: lost pl over 4f out: bhd fr 1/2-way* **50/1**

2-00 **13** *2* **Arizona Snow**[12] 455 5-9-3 **48**.............................(p) LukeMorris 8 1
(Ronald Harris) *chsd ldrs: led 5f out: hdd 4f out: chsd wnr tl rdn over 2f out: wknd over 1f out* **33/1**

60-0 **14** *2 3/4* **Camino**[12] 455 4-9-1 **46** oh1.................................(h) MartinLane 11
(Andi Brown) *chsd ldrs: rdn over 2f out: wknd wl over 1f out* **50/1**

1m 11.91s (-1.79) **Going Correction** -0.20s/f (Stan) **14** Ran SP% **129.4**
Speed ratings (Par 101): **103,99,98,97,96 95,92,89,87,85 82,80,78,74**
CSF £33.09 CT £862.81 TOTE £4.80: £2.20, £1.80, £6.60; EX 37.30 Trifecta £631.90.
**Owner** D Donovan **Bred** Irish National Stud **Trained** Dualla, Co Tipperary

**FOCUS**
A modest contest run at a decent pace. The impressive winner again made all and he has been rated to his best form of recent years.

## 641 COLLECT TOTEPOOL WINNINGS AT BETFRED SHOPS H'CAP 1m (P)

**8:30** (8:31) (Class 5) (0-70,70) 4-Y-O+ **£5,175** (£1,540; £769; £384) **Stalls** Low

Form RPR

62-2 **1** **Captain Courageous (IRE)**[30] 164 4-9-7 **70**.............. GeorgeBaker 3 80
(Ed Walker) *hld up in tch: rdn to ld ins fnl f: r.o* **5/2**[2]

11-2 **2** *3/4* **Kenstone (FR)**[31] 145 4-8-12 **66**..........................(p) HollieDoyle(5) 11 74
(Adrian Wintle) *hld up: plld hrd: hdwy over 2f out: rdn to chse wnr ins fnl f: sn ev ch: unable qck nr fin* **16/1**

5-02 **3** *2 1/4* **Lucymai**[8] 505 4-9-4 **67**........................................ RobertWinston 8 70
(Dean Ivory) *sn chsng ldrs: led over 2f out: rdn over 1f out: hdd and no ex ins fnl f* **10/1**

14-0 **4** *nk* **Jumbo Prado (USA)**[36] 49 8-9-2 **68**.......................(b) EoinWalsh(3) 6 70
(Daniel Mark Loughnane) *prom: lost pl over 6f out: pushed along 1/2-way: hdwy u.p over 1f out: r.o* **33/1**

2 **5** *hd* **Zorba The Greek**[7] 516 5-9-4 **70**........................ CallumShepherd(3) 4 72
(Ed Vaughan) *hld up: hdwy over 1f out: sn rdn: styd on same pce ins fnl f* **2/1**[1]

160- **6** *nk* **Foie Gras**[70] 8178 7-9-2 **65**..................................(p) DavidProbert 9 66
(Chris Dwyer) *hld up: hdwy over 1f out: nt trble ldrs* **33/1**

60-0 **7** *1 1/2* **Spiritual Star (IRE)**[34] 90 8-8-13 **67**.................. PaddyBradley(5) 7 65
(Lee Carter) *hld up: rdn over 1f out: n.d* **25/1**

043- **8** *3/4* **Air Of York (IRE)**[61] 8316 5-9-1 **64**........................(p) DanielMuscutt 10 60
(John Flint) *chsd ldrs: rdn over 2f out: wknd ins fnl f* **25/1**

145- **9** *1/2* **Ebbisham (IRE)**[40] 8590 4-8-12 **66**.....................(p[1]) CharlieBennett(5) 2 61
(Jim Boyle) *led: rdn and hdd over 2f out: wknd fnl f* **9/2**[3]

0-5P **10** *nk* **Fantasy Gladiator**[7] 517 11-9-4 **67**........................(p) AndrewMullen 12 61
(Michael Appleby) *s.i.s: sn pushed along in rr: nvr on terms* **25/1**

00-4 **11** *10* **Lord Of The Storm**[30] 164 9-9-0 **63** ... LukeMorris 1 34
(Michael Attwater) *prom: rdn over 2f out: wknd over 1f out: eased* **12/1**
1m 37.99s (-1.91) **Going Correction** -0.20s/f (Stan) **11** Ran SP% **120.2**
Speed ratings (Par 103): **101,100,98,97,97 97,95,94,94,94 84**
CSF £39.24 CT £354.37 TOTE £3.90: £1.20, £2.80, £3.80; EX 35.30 Trifecta £256.00.
**Owner** Laurence Bellman **Bred** Edgeridge & Glenvale **Trained** Upper Lambourn, Berks
**FOCUS**
The pace was steady for this open handicap, but the winner found a bit more improvement and saw it out well.
T/Jkpt: Not won. T/Plt: £49.00 to a £1 stake. Pool: £120307.20 - 1791.84 winning units. T/Qpdt: £9.00 to a £1 stake. Pool: £11,894.26 - 977.26 winning units. **Colin Roberts**

## 570 LINGFIELD (L-H)
### Thursday, February 9

**OFFICIAL GOING: Polytrack: standard**
Wind: light, half against Weather: overcast, cold

## 642 32RED.COM MAIDEN AUCTION STKS 1m 2f (P)
**1:35** (1:36) (Class 6) 3-Y-O **£2,911** (£866; £432; £216) **Stalls** Low

Form RPR
**1** **Lunch (IRE)** 3-9-5 0 ... TimmyMurphy 6 71+
(Jamie Osborne) *stdd after s: hld up in rr: effrt over 1f out: gd hdwy u.p 1f out: led ins fnl f: r.o wl* **20/1**
**2** *nk* **Fulham (IRE)** 3-9-5 0 ... TomMarquand 7 70+
(Robyn Brisland) *wnt rt and stmbld leaving stalls: rn green and niggled along in midfield: rdn over 3f out: gd hdwy 1f out: ev ch ins fnl f: r.o wl but a jst hld* **20/1**
**3** *2 ¼* **Bishops Cannings (IRE)** 3-9-0 0 ... ShaneKelly 5 61
(David Elsworth) *dwlt and bustled along leaving stalls: in tch in last pair: hdwy on outer to press ldrs over 3f out: nudged into ld 1f out: rn green in front and rdn: hdd and outpcd fnl 100yds* **10/1**
**4** *1 ½* **Pinnata (IRE)** 3-9-2 0 ... (t[1]) AaronJones(3) 2 63
(Stuart Williams) *in tch in midfield: nt clr run 2f out: hdwy ent fnl f: no imp and one pced ins fnl f* **9/2**[3]
6-22 **5** *1 ¾* **Allegheny Bay (IRE)**[15] 393 3-9-5 65 ... LiamKeniry 4 60
(J S Moore) *taken down early: sn led: rdn 2f out: hdd 1f out: sn btn and wknd ins fnl f* **8/1**
202- **6** *1* **Masonic (IRE)**[119] 7304 3-9-5 72 ... LukeMorris 3 58
(Robyn Brisland) *chsd ldrs: wnt 2nd 8f out: rdn and ev ch over 2f out: unable qck over 1f out: wknd and swtchd rt ins fnl f* **6/4**[1]
65 **7** *1 ½* **Alfolk (IRE)**[21] 310 3-9-5 0 ... (h) GeorgeBaker 1 55
(David Simcock) *t.k.h: led: sn hdd and chsd ldr tl 8f out: trckd ldrs after: effrt over 1f out: little rspnse and sn btn: wknd ins fnl f* **5/2**[2]
2m 5.65s (-0.95) **Going Correction** +0.125s/f (Slow) **7** Ran SP% **116.5**
Speed ratings (Par 95): **108,107,105,104,103 102,101**
CSF £330.62 TOTE £18.20: £7.40, £8.20; EX 346.10 Trifecta £1486.30.
**Owner** J A Osborne **Bred** Celbridge Estates Ltd **Trained** Upper Lambourn, Berks
**FOCUS**
An uncompetitive maiden, but a complete placepot-buster with all four newcomers finishing ahead of the trio with experience.

## 643 32RED.COM CONDITIONS STKS (PLUS 10 RACE) 6f 1y(P)
**2:05** (2:05) (Class 3) 3-Y-O **£7,561** (£2,263; £1,131; £566; £282) **Stalls** Low

Form RPR
32-3 **1** **Tomily (IRE)**[23] 276 3-9-0 99 ... SeanLevey 5 88+
(Richard Hannon) *racd keenly: pressed ldr: rdn and ev ch over 1f out: led ins fnl f: r.o wl: rdn out* **5/1**[2]
23-2 **2** *½* **Sutter County**[23] 276 3-9-0 103 ... PJMcDonald 3 86+
(Mark Johnston) *led: rdn over 1f out: drifted rt 1f out: hdd ins fnl f: kpt on wl but a hld* **4/6**[1]
5-1 **3** *2 ¼* **Visionary (IRE)**[33] 125 3-9-0 94 ... LukeMorris 2 79+
(Robert Cowell) *t.k.h: wl in tch in 4th: rdn 2f out: rdr dropped rein 1f out: no threat to ldng pair but kpt on u.p to go 3rd cl home* **5/1**[2]
24-1 **4** *hd* **Winning Ways (IRE)**[15] 397 3-9-0 80 ... (t) ShaneKelly 4 79
(Jeremy Noseda) *stdd s: hld up in tch in rr: effrt on inner whn nt clr run and swtchd rt over 1f out: kpt on same pce ins fnl f* **8/1**[3]
501- **5** *nk* **Ferocity (IRE)**[44] 8536 3-9-0 76 ... RobertWinston 1 78?
(Robyn Brisland) *t.k.h: trckd ldng pair: rdn: unable qck and edgd lft over 1f out: kpt on same pce ins fnl f: lost 2 pls cl home* **14/1**
1m 14.08s (2.18) **Going Correction** +0.125s/f (Slow) **5** Ran SP% **111.1**
Speed ratings (Par 101): **90,89,86,86,85**
CSF £9.02 TOTE £5.30: £2.30, £1.10; EX 9.90 Trifecta £30.80.
**Owner** Des Anderson **Bred** D J Anderson **Trained** East Everleigh, Wilts
**FOCUS**
A warm 3yo conditions event, but a steady pace and only the two old rivals were ever really in it.

## 644 SUNBETS.CO.UK H'CAP 7f 1y(P)
**2:40** (2:42) (Class 7) (0-50,51) 3-Y-O+ **£2,264** (£673; £336; £168) **Stalls** Low

Form RPR
453 **1** **Tigerfish (IRE)**[12] 463 3-8-1 45 ... (p) HollieDoyle(5) 8 46
(William Stone) *t.k.h: chsd ldrs tl upsides ldr 4f out: rdn to ld 2f out: kpt on u.p ins fnl f: jst hld on* **4/1**[2]
-041 **2** *shd* **Welsh Inlet (IRE)**[6] 544 9-9-8 51 6ex ... JaneElliott(7) 3 57
(John Bridger) *hld up in tch in midfield: clsd to chse ldrs 2f out: swtchd rt and effrt over 1f out: chsd wnr wl ins fnl f: r.o wl: jst hld* **9/2**[3]
30-0 **3** *1 ¼* **Bold Max**[36] 52 6-9-9 45 ... (v) LiamKeniry 6 48
(Zoe Davison) *t.k.h: hld up in tch: swtchd rt and effrt over 1f out: r.o wl ins fnl f: wnt 3rd cl home* **33/1**
0-06 **4** *½* **Rockalater**[26] 244 3-8-4 48 ... MitchGodwin(5) 9 44
(Sylvester Kirk) *led for 2f: lft in ld again 4f out: rdn and hdd 2f out: styd on same pce ins fnl f: lost 2 pls wl ins fnl f* **20/1**
5524 **5** *hd* **Captain K (IRE)**[1] 614 5-9-12 48 ... (h) TimmyMurphy 5 49
(Gordon Elliott, Ire) *t.k.h: wl in tch in midfield: clsd to chse ldrs 2f out: sn rdn and unable qck over 1f out: kpt on same pce ins fnl f* **9/2**[3]
00-3 **6** *½* **Bartholomew J (IRE)**[17] 377 3-8-4 46 ... (v) SimonPearce(3) 7 40
(Lydia Pearce) *dwlt and bustled along leaving stalls: in rr: effrt over 1f out: hdwy 1f out: kpt on u.p ins fnl f* **6/1**
-054 **7** *2 ¼* **Chandrayaan**[6] 544 10-9-2 45 ... (v) GinaMangan(7) 14 38
(John E Long) *chsd ldrs: carried wd and dropped to midfield 4f out: rdn and unable qck over 1f out: kpt on same pce ins fnl f* **25/1**
65-0 **8** *nk* **Annabella**[31] 139 4-9-9 45 ... RyanTate 2 38
(Tim McCarthy) *s.i.s: a towards rr: effrt and drvn over 1f out: kpt on same pce ins fnl f* **33/1**

/000 **9** *7* **Catalyze**[6] 544 9-9-6 45 ... (t) CallumShepherd(3) 13 19
(Paddy Butler) *kicked by rival at s: t.k.h: stdd after s: hld up in tch towards rr: rdn over 2f out: sn btn* **66/1**
60-0 **10** *10* **Love In The Dark**[29] 167 4-9-9 45 ... (h) DavidProbert 10
(Nikki Evans) *w ldr tl led after 2f: hung bdly rt bnd and hdd 4f out: rcvrd and chsng ldrs again whn hung bdly rt again bnd 2f out: wl bhd after* **66/1**
**R** **Goodluck Joey**[104] 7674 3-8-6 45 ... LukeMorris 4
(Emmet Michael Butterly, Ire) *ref to r* **10/1**
-242 **R** **Prince Of Time**[6] 544 5-9-3 46 ... (vt[1]) CallumRodriguez(7) 12
(Richard Ford) *ref to r* **3/1**[1]
1m 26.93s (2.13) **Going Correction** +0.125s/f (Slow)
**WFA** 3 from 4yo+ 17lb **12** Ran SP% **122.2**
Speed ratings (Par 97): **92,91,90,89,89 89,86,86,78,66**
CSF £21.65 CT £539.37 TOTE £4.70: £1.90, £2.00, £6.70; EX 31.40 Trifecta £646.40.
**Owner** Miss Caroline Scott **Bred** Swordlestown Little **Trained** West Wickham, Cambs
**FOCUS**
This is about as weak as it gets and an eventful race with the favourite and Goodluck Joey both refusing to come out of the stalls.

## 645 BETWAY BEST ODDS GUARANTEED PLUS H'CAP (DIV I) 1m 5f (P)
**3:10** (3:11) (Class 6) (0-55,57) 4-Y-O+ **£2,911** (£866; £432; £216) **Stalls** Low

Form RPR
000- **1** **Willyegolassiego**[38] 3769 4-8-8 46 oh1 ... LiamKeniry 7 54+
(Neil Mulholland) *stdd s: hld up in tch in last trio: hdwy on outer over 3f out: chsd ldrs 2f out: shkn up to ld 1f out: rdn and drew clr fnl f: readily* **5/1**[3]
55-2 **2** *3 ½* **Le Tissier**[15] 395 4-9-1 56 ... (p) RobHornby(3) 2 59
(Michael Attwater) *hld up in tch in midfield: shuffled bk over 3f out: hdwy into midfield and nt clr run jst over 2f out tl 1f out: r.o wl ins fnl f to go 2nd towards fin: no threat to wnr* **9/4**[1]
62-6 **3** *½* **Graceful Lady**[23] 279 4-9-3 55 ... LukeMorris 3 56
(Robert Eddery) *t.k.h: hld up in tch in midfield: hdwy over 3f out: pressing ldrs and rdn ent fnl 2f: drvn to ld jst over 1f out: sn hdd and one pced ins fnl f: lost 2nd towards fin* **8/1**
/0-0 **4** *1 ¼* **Sweeping Rock (IRE)**[31] 146 7-8-12 49 ... (tp) EdwardGreatrex(3) 1 48
(John Spearing) *rn wout declared tongue strap: in tch in midfield: squeezed for room and hmpd bnd after 1f: nt clr run 2f out: swtchd rt ins fnl f: kpt on wl: no threat to wnr* **20/1**
6-55 **5** *½* **Galuppi**[12] 461 6-9-1 52 ... (v) AlistairRawlinson(3) 4 51
(J R Jenkins) *stdd after s: hld up in tch in last trio: effrt and switching rt over 1f out: kpt on ins fnl f: no threat to wnr* **16/1**
1/0- **6** *½* **Giant Sequoia (USA)**[100] 7739 13-8-13 47 ... (t) DavidProbert 9 45
(Des Donovan, Ire) *hld up in tch in midfield: hdwy into midfield 4f out: chsd ldrs and nt clr run 2f out: swtchd rt over 1f out: kpt on same pce ins fnl f* **3/1**[2]
6/46 **7** *1 ¼* **Tenhoo**[14] 414 11-8-12 46 oh1 ... PJMcDonald 11 42
(Richard Ford) *led: rdn ent fnl 2f: hdd over 1f out: sn btn and wknd ins fnl f* **16/1**
/00- **8** *nse* **New Tarabela**[49] 8499 6-9-0 48 ... (p) GeorgeDowning 6 44
(Tony Carroll) *in tch in midfield: hdwy to chse ldr 10f out: rdn over 3f out: led over 1f out: sn hdd and no ex: wknd qckly ins fnl f* **33/1**
024- **9** *6* **Sudden Wish (IRE)**[16] 2326 8-9-7 55 ... (p) GeorgeBaker 5 42
(Gary Moore) *chsd ldr tl 10f out: in tch in midfield after: effrt over 1f out: little rspnse and sn btn: eased ins fnl f* **6/1**
660/ **10** *6* **Blake Dean**[32] 7212 9-9-9 57 ... (bt) TomMarquand 8 35
(Chris Gordon) *wl in tch in midfield: lost pl and u.p over 3f out: bhd over 1f out* **50/1**
50-6 **11** *8* **Kilim**[12] 461 4-9-4 56 ... (t) JosephineGordon 10 22
(John Berry) *t.k.h: in tch in midfield: hdwy to chse ldrs 8f out: rdn and lost pl 3f out: bhd over 1f out: eased ins fnl f* **8/1**
2m 46.78s (0.78) **Going Correction** +0.125s/f (Slow)
**WFA** 4 from 6yo+ 2lb **11** Ran SP% **130.4**
Speed ratings (Par 101): **102,99,99,98,98 98,97,97,93,89 85**
CSF £18.36 CT £97.34 TOTE £6.40: £2.10, £1.50, £1.90; EX 24.50 Trifecta £151.90.
**Owner** John Hobbs **Bred** Southcourt Stud **Trained** Limpley Stoke, Wilts
**FOCUS**
The first division of a moderate staying handicap, but probably more to come from the winner.

## 646 BETWAY BEST ODDS GUARANTEED PLUS H'CAP (DIV II) 1m 5f (P)
**3:40** (3:43) (Class 6) (0-55,55) 4-Y-O+ **£2,911** (£866; £432; £216) **Stalls** Low

Form RPR
0-20 **1** **Grand Facile**[13] 436 5-9-6 54 ... (b) TimmyMurphy 1 59
(Gary Moore) *chsd ldr tl 10f out: styd chsng ldrs: rdn to ld and kicked clr 2f out: kpt on wl and in command after* **10/1**
04-0 **2** *2 ¾* **Rianna Star**[23] 278 4-9-3 55 ... GeorgeBaker 10 56
(Gary Moore) *led: cocked jaw and reminder 9f out: hdd 7f out: chsd ldr tl 5f out: styd handy: rdn and outpcd 2f out: rallied 1f out: styd on to snatch 2nd last stride: no threat to wnr* **8/1**[3]
33-2 **3** *shd* **Santadelacruze**[12] 461 8-9-4 52 ... ShaneKelly 4 53
(Mark Hoad) *hld up in tch in last trio: hdwy 1/2-way: chsd ldrs 3f out: rdn to chse clr wnr 2f out: no imp and kpt on same pce after: lost 2nd last stride* **8/1**[3]
5-04 **4** *nk* **Dalavand (IRE)**[26] 233 4-8-8 53 ... OllieJago(7) 9 53
(Laura Mongan) *stdd after s and dropped in bhd: hld up in rr: rdn and hdwy on inner over 1f out: no threat to wnr but battling for placings ins fnl f: kpt on* **25/1**
62-5 **5** *nk* **Brooke's Point**[22] 281 4-8-10 48 ... (p) LiamKeniry 3 48
(Neil Mulholland) *hld up in tch in midfield: clsd to chse ldrs and rdn 2f out: no imp and edging lft 1f out: battling for placings and styd on same pce ins fnl f* **4/5**[1]
/33- **6** *1 ¼* **Helium (FR)**[39] 7039 12-9-4 52 ... JosephineGordon 6 50
(Alexandra Dunn) *in tch in midfield: n.m.r over 2f out: rdn over 1f out: kpt on same pce ins fnl f* **16/1**
02-0 **7** *¾* **Par Three (IRE)**[36] 35 6-9-2 50 ... (p) GeorgeDowning 2 47
(Tony Carroll) *in tch in last trio: sme hdwy over 2f out: no imp u.p over 1f out: kpt on same pce fnl f* **10/1**
000- **8** *1* **Briac (FR)**[55] 8410 6-8-9 46 oh1 ... NathanAlison(3) 5 41
(Mark Pattinson) *t.k.h: hld up in tch in midfield: hdwy on outer 3f out: rdn and unable qck over 1f out: sn outpcd and wl hld fnl f* **6/1**[2]
1/40 **9** *1 ½* **Azamesse (IRE)**[21] 315 5-9-0 55 ... GinaMangan(7) 7 48
(J R Jenkins) *hld up in tch towards rr: dropped to last 5f out: nvr threatened ldrs* **33/1**

00-0 **10** *2 ½* **Fleetwood Poppy**[36] 39 5-8-10 **47**....................... EdwardGreatrex(3) 8 36
(Michael Attwater) *t.k.h: hld up in midfield on outer: hdwy to chse ldr 10f out tl led 7f out: rdn and hdd whn hmpd 2f out: sn lost pl: bhd ins fnl f* **33/1**

2m 48.41s (2.41) **Going Correction** +0.125s/f (Slow)
**WFA** 4 from 5yo+ 2lb **10** Ran SP% **125.9**
Speed ratings (Par 101): **97,95,95,95,94 94,93,93,92,90**
CSF £92.44 CT £687.32 TOTE £14.30: £3.10, £2.40, £1.80; EX 101.70 Trifecta £548.50.
**Owner** Patterson Hinds & Curwen **Bred** Lofts Hall Stud **Trained** Lower Beeding, W Sussex

**FOCUS**
The winning time was 1.63sec slower than the first division. It resulted in a 1-2 for trainer Gary Moore.

## 647 32RED CASINO H'CAP 1m 2f (P)
**4:15** (4:15) (Class 5) (0-75,76) 3-Y-O **£3,234** (£962; £481; £240) **Stalls** Low

Form RPR
0-32 **1** **Global Revival (IRE)**[22] 292 3-9-6 **74**.................... JosephineGordon 6 77
(Ed Dunlop) *pressed ldr: rdn jst over 1f out: led ins fnl f: r.o wl and a doing enough after: rdn out* **5/1**[3]
003- **2** *½* **Mullarkey**[40] 8592 3-9-0 **68**....................................... KierenFox 5 70
(John Best) *wl in tch in 4th: effrt over 1f out: r.o wl u.p ins fnl f: wnt 2nd last stride* **7/1**
44-3 **3** *shd* **African Beat (IRE)**[15] 392 3-9-7 **75**........................... RobertTart 3 77
(John Gosden) *trckd ldng pair: effrt over 1f out: hdwy and drvn to chal ins fnl f: kpt on same pce towards fin: lost 2nd last stride* **1/1**[1]
214- **4** *½* **Hochfeld (IRE)**[45] 8525 3-9-8 **76**...................................... PJMcDonald 2 77
(Mark Johnston) *dwlt and bustled along leaving stalls: in tch in last pair: effrt on outer bnd wl over 1f out: kpt on wl ins fnl f* **3/1**[2]
4 **5** *1 ¾* **Olympic Legend (IRE)**[22] 292 3-9-3 **71**...................... TomMarquand 1 68
(Martin Bosley) *stdd after s: t.k.h: hld up in tch in last pair: effrt and swtchd rt over 1f out: kpt on same pce ins fnl f* **50/1**
-161 **6** *½* **Oberyn (IRE)**[13] 434 3-8-7 **66**................................ MitchGodwin(5) 4 62
(Sylvester Kirk) *led: shkn up 2f out: rdn over 1f out: hdd ins fnl f: no ex: lost pl and wl hld whn wnt rt towards fin* **12/1**

2m 7.77s (1.17) **Going Correction** +0.125s/f (Slow) **6** Ran SP% **113.8**
Speed ratings (Par 97): **100,99,99,99,97 97**
CSF £38.55 TOTE £6.80: £2.20, £3.20; EX 45.10 Trifecta £83.10.
**Owner** Dr Johnny Hon **Bred** John Cullinan **Trained** Newmarket, Suffolk

**FOCUS**
An ordinary 3yo handicap and they didn't go a great pace for the first mile.

## 648 BETWAY H'CAP (FOR LADY AMATEUR RIDERS) 1m 2f (P)
**4:50** (4:50) (Class 5) (0-75,75) 4-Y-O+ **£3,119** (£967; £483; £242) **Stalls** Low

Form RPR
0-05 **1** **Ansaab**[7] 524 9-10-4 **75**.......................................(t) MissBeckySmith(3) 3 83
(Marjorie Fife) *hld up towards rr: gd hdwy over 3f out: jnd ldr and kicked clr 2f out: led over 1f out: forged ahd ins fnl f: styd on: rdn out* **8/1**[2]
4-61 **2** *1 ¼* **Starboard**[7] 516 8-10-7 **75**.......................................(b) MissSBrotherton 5 81
(David Simcock) *taken down early: hld up in tch in midfield: effrt to chse clr ldng pair 2f out: styd on ins fnl f: wnt 2nd towards fin: nvr getting on terms w wnr* **8/15**[1]
-140 **3** *¾* **Black Dave (IRE)**[8] 507 7-9-11 **72**.................... MissEMacKenzie(7) 1 76
(David Evans) *t.k.h: led: rdn and kicked clr w wnr 2f out: hdd over 1f out: kpt on same pce ins fnl f: lost 2nd towards fin* **12/1**[3]
53-0 **4** *2 ¼* **Zephyros (GER)**[34] 92 6-9-3 **64**...................... PoppyBridgwater(7) 9 64+
(David Bridgwater) *hld up towards rr: effrt but stl plenty to do over 1f out: r.o wl ins fnl f: nvr getting to ldrs: eased towards fin* **14/1**
502- **5** *1* **Gaelic Silver (FR)**[43] 8554 11-10-0 **75**..............(p) MissBeckyButler(7) 10 73
(Gary Moore) *s.i.s: hld up in last trio: hdwy on outer over 2f out: 4th 1f out: kpt on wout ever threatening ldrs* **20/1**
20-3 **6** *1* **Warfare**[19] 359 8-10-2 **75**................................................ MissHDukes(5) 7 71
(Tim Fitzgerald) *s.i.s: t.k.h: hld up in rr: effrt and stl plenty to do over 1f out: hdwy 1f out: kpt on: nvr trbld ldrs* **12/1**[3]
64-4 **7** *2* **With Pleasure**[36] 49 4-9-11 **71**.....................(p[1]) MissNatalieParker(5) 12 63
(John Flint) *t.k.h: chsd ldrs: rdn and unable qck 2f out: wknd ins fnl f* **25/1**
10-0 **8** *1* **Turnbury**[20] 333 6-9-1 **62**..........................................(p) EmmaTaff(7) 4 52
(Nikki Evans) *t.k.h: hld up in tch in midfield: n.m.r and shuffled bk over 2f out: effrt over 1f out: no real imp* **33/1**
00-0 **9** *nk* **Genuine Approval (IRE)**[36] 36 4-10-1 **73**......... MissAliceHaynes(3) 6 62
(John Butler) *chsd ldrs tl shuffled bk and nt clr run over 2f out: wknd over 1f out* **20/1**
30-0 **10** *1* **My Lord**[13] 440 9-9-6 **65**.................................................. MissMBryant(5) 2 52
(Paddy Butler) *chsd ldrs tl shuffled bk and n.m.r over 2f out: wknd over 1f out* **66/1**
623- **11** *nse* **Taurian**[53] 7274 6-9-11 **65**.................................................(p) MissADeniel 11 52
(Ian Williams) *stdd after s: t.k.h: hld up in rr: hdwy on outer over 3f out: rdn 2f out: sn struggling and wknd over 1f out* **16/1**
2-16 **12** *9* **Nonchalant**[27] 214 6-9-3 **64**............................................ MissHHeal(7) 8 33
(Hugo Froud) *t.k.h: chsd ldr tl over 2f out: sltly hmpd and lost pl bnd 2f out: bhd ins fnl f* **14/1**

2m 6.53s (-0.07) **Going Correction** +0.125s/f (Slow) **12** Ran SP% **128.7**
Speed ratings (Par 103): **105,104,103,101,100 100,98,97,97,96 96,89**
CSF £12.98 CT £66.72 TOTE £9.40: £1.80, £1.10, £3.60; EX 21.30 Trifecta £134.30.
**Owner** Craig Buckingham **Bred** Castlemartin Stud And Skymarc Farm **Trained** Stillington, N Yorks

**FOCUS**
A modest lady amateur riders' handicap with the red-hot favourite turned over, but a well-handicapped winner.
T/Plt: £2,764.80 to a £1 stake. Pool: £64,385.94 - 17.00 winning units. T/Qpdt: £27.10 to a £1 stake. Pool: £8,815.55 - 240.26 wining units. **Steve Payne**

# 537 MEYDAN (L-H)
Thursday, February 9
**OFFICIAL GOING: Turf: good; dirt: fast**

## 649a MEYDAN CLASSIC TRIAL SPONSORED BY JAGUAR XF (CONDITIONS) (TURF) 7f
**3:05** (3:05) 3-Y-O
**£48,780** (£16,260; £8,130; £4,065; £2,439; £1,626)

RPR
**1** **Top Score**[14] 430 3-8-9 94............................................. AdriedeVries 1 84
(Saeed bin Suroor) *trckd ldr: smooth prog to ld 2 1/2f out: hdd briefly a f out: r.o again to ld cl home* **6/4**[1]
**2** *nse* **Nobelium (USA)** 3-8-11 0 ow2............................................. BReis 5 86
(R Bouresly, Kuwait) *mid-div: rdn to chal 2 1/2f out: briefly led a f out but hdd cl home* **66/1**
**3** *2 ¼* **Daqeeq (AUS)**[268] 3-9-4 90..........................................(t) JimCrowley 6 80
(M F De Kock, South Africa) *mid-div: r.o wl fnl 1 1/2f: nrst fin* **9/2**[2]
**4** *1 ¼* **Souls In The Wind (IRE)**[26] 246 3-8-5 75.................... AntonioFresu 2 70
(S Seemar, UAE) *trckd ldr: ev ch 1 1/2f out: one pce fnl f* **33/1**
**5** *nk* **Grey Britain**[145] 6572 3-8-9 98.......................................(v) MartinHarley 8 74
(John Ryan) *settled in rr: chsd ldr 2 1/2f out: one pce fnl f* **8/1**
**6** *shd* **Masham Star (IRE)**[14] 430 3-8-9 101............................ OisinMurphy 11 73
(Mark Johnston) *mid-div: chsd ldrs and ev ch 2 1/2f out: one pce fnl f* **10/1**
**7** *½* **Island Vision (IRE)**[21] 317 3-8-5 90........................... SamHitchcott 12 68
(David Simcock) *s.i.s: nvr nr to chal but r.o fnl 2f* **10/1**
**8** *7* **Arborist (IRE)**[13] 3-8-9 78..........................................(b) TadhgO'Shea 14 53
(A R Al Rayhi, UAE) *sn ld: hdd 2 1/2f out: sn btn* **66/1**
**9** *2 ½* **Almizhar (IRE)**[12] 470 3-8-9 0.................................... GoranMesetovic 4 46
(R Bouresly, Kuwait) *s.i.s: nvr nr to chal* **100/1**
**10** *6 ¼* **Mirdif**[192] 4957 3-8-9 102............................................... PatSmullen 10 34
(M D O'Callaghan, Ire) *nvr bttr than mid-div* **6/1**[3]
**11** *1* **Megnaas (ARG)**[14] 430 3-9-4 90..................... ChristopheSoumillon 13 24
(M F De Kock, South Africa) *nvr nr to chal* **9/1**
**12** *2 ¾* **General Line (USA)**[26] 246 3-8-5 0.............................. RichardMullen 7 15
(Doug Watson, UAE) *nvr nr to chal* **40/1**

1m 24.45s (0.35) **Going Correction** +0.25s/f (Good) **12** Ran SP% **121.1**
Speed ratings: **108,107,105,103,103 103,102,94,92,84 83,80**
CSF: 155.74.
**Owner** Godolphin **Bred** Darley **Trained** Newmarket, Suffolk

**FOCUS**
Rail on turf track out 12 metres. TRAKUS (metres travelled compared to winner): 2nd -1, 3rd +1, 4th +3, 5th +2, 6th +3, 7th +2, 8th 0, 9th -1, 10th +7, 11th +8, 12th +4. This was run at quite an even pace: 25.19 (400m from standing start), 23.72 (800m), 23.45 (1200m), 12.09 (line), but it did not look a good race with an unlikely type in a close second and the fourth holding the form down.

## 650a RANGE ROVER SPORT (H'CAP) (DIRT) 1m 2f (D)
**3:40** (3:40) (95-108,108) 3-Y-O+
**£60,975** (£15,243; £15,243; £5,081; £3,048; £2,032)

RPR
**1** **Alabaster (USA)**[14] 432 5-8-13 **100**...............................(b) OisinMurphy 5 103
(Saeed bin Suroor) *trckd ldng pair: led 3 1/2f out: hdd a f out but r.o to ld cl home* **9/1**
**2** *nk* **Etijaah (USA)**[21] 319 7-9-0 **101**........................................(h) JimCrowley 6 103
(Doug Watson, UAE) *wl away: trckd ldng pair: rdn to ld a f out but hdd cl home* **14/1**
**2** *dht* **Emotionless (IRE)**[35] 85 4-9-6 **108**............................... WilliamBuick 4 110+
(Charlie Appleby) *settled in rr: r.o wl fnl 2f: nrst fin* **10/3**[2]
**4** *3 ¼* **Triple Nine (KOR)**[21] 319 5-9-5 **106**..............................(e) PatCosgrave 9 102
(Kim Young Kwan, Korea) *trckd ldr: led briefly 4f out: hdd 3 1/2f out: r.o same pce fnl 2 1/2f* **11/4**[1]
**5** *hd* **Layl (USA)**[341] 842 7-9-6 **107**............................................... PatDobbs 1 102+
(Doug Watson, UAE) *mid-div: r.o same pce fnl 2f* **5/1**
**6** *6 ½* **Mizbah**[35] 83 8-9-3 **104**................................................ SamHitchcott 8 86
(Doug Watson, UAE) *sn led: hdd 4f out: sn btn* **4/1**[3]
**7** *3 ¼* **Top Clearance (USA)**[21] 319 5-8-10 **98**.........................(t) ChrisHayes 3 73
(D Selvaratnam, UAE) *nvr bttr than mid-div* **16/1**
**8** *2* **Toolain (IRE)**[21] 319 9-9-0 **101**...................................(b) RichardMullen 2 73
(S Seemar, UAE) *nvr nr to chal* **40/1**
**9** *7 ¾* **Trinity Force (IRE)**[12] 474 6-8-8 **96**...........................(t) TadhgO'Shea 11 51
(A R Al Rayhi, UAE) *nvr bttr than mid-div* **33/1**
**10** *2* **Interpret (USA)**[56] 8394 9-8-10 **98**..................................(v) AdriedeVries 7 49
(M Al Mheiri, UAE) *nvr nr to chal* **33/1**
**11** *3 ¼* **Sea Of Flames**[28] 204 4-8-8 **97**................................ MickaelBarzalona 10 42
(David Elsworth) *nvr bttr than mid-div* **33/1**

2m 4.25s (-0.45) **Going Correction** +0.25s/f (Slow) **11** Ran SP% **120.2**
Speed ratings: **111,110,110,108,108 102,100,98,92,90 88**
CSF: 7-1 £19.50 7-5 £62.38; TRICAST: 7-1-5 £215.61 7-5-1 £256.13.
**Owner** Godolphin **Bred** Darley **Trained** Newmarket, Suffolk

**FOCUS**
TRAKUS (metres travelled compared to winner): 2nd (Emotionless) +6, 2nd (Etijaah) -7, 4th -2, 5th -9, 6th -11, 7th -2, 8th -12, 9th +10, 10th +11, 11th +9. An ordinary-looking race of its type run at a solid, gradually slowing pace: 25.74 (from standing start), 23.46, 24.23, 24.72, 26.1.

## 651a JAGUAR F-PACE (H'CAP) (TURF) 6f
**4:15** (4:15) (95-105,105) 3-Y-O+
**£60,975** (£20,325; £10,162; £5,081; £3,048; £2,032)

RPR
**1** **Krypton Factor**[21] 318 9-9-1 **100**...................................(b) AdriedeVries 8 107
(Fawzi Abdulla Nass, Bahrain) *trckd ldrs: led 1 1/2f out: r.o wl* **25/1**
**2** *1 ½* **Jamesie (IRE)**[14] 433 9-9-2 **101**..................................(t) SamHitchcott 5 103+
(David Marnane, Ire) *mid-div: r.o fnl 2f: nrst fin* **10/1**
**3** *nse* **Sir Maximilian (IRE)**[7] 543 8-9-4 **103**.................................(p) PatDobbs 7 105+
(Ian Williams) *mid-div: r.o fnl 2f: nrst fin* **7/1**[3]
**4** *½* **Watchable**[14] 433 7-8-9 **101**.................................(p) CameronNoble(7) 6 101
(David O'Meara) *sn led: hdd 1 1/2f out: but r.o* **12/1**
**5** *nk* **Line Of Reason (IRE)**[7] 543 7-9-2 **101**....................... RichardMullen 11 99
(Paul Midgley) *settled in rr: r.o fnl 2f: but nvr able to chal* **13/2**[2]
**6** *¾* **Naadirr (IRE)**[28] 207 6-9-6 **105**......................(p) ChristopheSoumillon 13 104
(Marco Botti) *mid-div: r.o same pce fnl 2f* **11/2**[1]
**7** *¾* **Roi De Vitesse (IRE)**[28] 207 10-9-2 **101**............(v) MickaelBarzalona 14 97
(Ali Jan, Qatar) *nvr nr to chal but r.o fnl 2f* **16/1**
**8** *hd* **Fannaan (USA)**[110] 7542 5-9-6 **105**..................................... JimCrowley 9 100
(M Al Mheiri, UAE) *s.i.s: nvr nr to chal* **11/2**[1]
**9** *1* **Roicead (USA)**[14] 433 10-9-5 **104**....................................(t) OisinMurphy 3 96
(D Selvaratnam, UAE) *s.i.s: settled in rr: r.o same pce fnl 2f* **40/1**
**10** *¾* **Mastermind (SAF)**[14] 433 5-9-6 **105**................(bt) BernardFayd'Herbe 10 95
(M F De Kock, South Africa) *nvr bttr than mid-div* **9/1**
**11** *3 ½* **Solar Flair**[111] 7497 5-9-1 **100**.......................................... MartinHarley 4 78
(William Knight) *nvr bttr than mid-div* **10/1**
**12** *½* **Scrutineer (IRE)**[136] 6837 4-9-1 **100**.................................. PatSmullen 1 77
(Mick Channon) *nvr bttr than mid-div* **16/1**
**13** *1 ¼* **Saayerr**[21] 318 6-9-5 **104**.................................................. ChrisHayes 2 77
(D Selvaratnam, UAE) *trckd ldr tl outpcd fnl 2 1/2f* **12/1**

14 *2* **Eastern Impact (IRE)**[14] 433 6-9-6 **105**............... ColmO'Donoghue 12 71
(Richard Fahey) *trckd ldr tl outpcd 2 1/2f out* **8/1**
1m 10.69s (1.69) **Going Correction** +0.55s/f (Yiel) **14** Ran SP% **129.3**
Speed ratings: **110,108,107,107,106 106,105,105,103,102 98,97,95,93**
CSF: £275.52; TRICAST: £1,977.37.
**Owner** Fawzi Abdulla Nass **Bred** Lady Fairhaven **Trained** Bahrain
**FOCUS**
Rail on turf track out 12 metres. Not a strong race of its type.

## 652a UAE 1000 GUINEAS SPONSORED BY AL TAYER MOTORS (LISTED RACE) (FILLIES) (DIRT) 1m (D)
**4:50** (4:50) 3-Y-O

**£121,951** (£40,650; £20,325; £10,162; £6,097; £4,065)

RPR
1 **Nashmiah (KSA)**[19] 3-8-9 85.................................... MickaelBarzalona 4 96
(N Bachalard, Saudi Arabia) *trckd ldr: led 4 1/2f out: r.o wl: jst hld on* **40/1**
2 *hd* **Nomorerichblondes (USA)**[21] 317 3-8-9 80...........(tp) AntonioFresu 3 96
(A bin Harmash, UAE) *mid-div: r.o wl fnl 2 1/2f: jst failed* **66/1**
3 *1 1/4* **Rajar**[21] 317 3-8-9 89....................................................(h) RichardMullen 2 93
(Richard Fahey) *trckd ldr: ev ch 2 1/2f out: r.o fnl 2f* **33/1**
4 *nk* **Complimenti (USA)**[21] 317 3-8-9 93................................ PatDobbs 11 92
(Doug Watson, UAE) *mid-div: chsd ldrs 3f out: r.o same pce fnl 2f* **9/1**
5 *2 3/4* **Really Special**[21] 317 3-8-9 103........................................ JimCrowley 9 86
(Saeed bin Suroor) *bmpd at s: mid-div: r.o same pce fnl 2 1/2f* **1/2**[1]
6 *2* **Sasha Waltz (IRE)**[21] 317 3-8-9 87.............................. FernandoJara 5 81
(Fredrik Reuterskiold, Sweden) *nvr nr to chal* **33/1**
7 *6 3/4* **Calare (IRE)**[21] 317 3-8-9 102..........................................(p) WilliamBuick 8 66
(Charlie Appleby) *sn led: hdd 4 1/2f out: wknd fnl 3f* **11/2**[2]
8 *6* **Spanish Moon (RUS)**[21] 317 3-8-9 85........................... ZKashirgov 10 52
(Doug Watson, UAE) *s.i.s: a in rr* **66/1**
9 *12* **Melesina (IRE)**[113] 7480 3-8-9 102..................................... PatSmullen 7 24
(Richard Fahey) *trckd ldrs tl wknd 4f out* **14/1**
10 *28* **Voice Of Truth (IRE)**[21] 317 3-8-9 84..................... ColmO'Donoghue 1
(Saeed bin Suroor) *nvr nr to chal* **50/1**
11 *32* **Fursa (AUS)**[250] 3-9-5 104.................................... ChristopheSoumillon 6
(M F De Kock, South Africa) *s.i.s: nvr nr to chal* **13/2**[3]
1m 40.75s (3.25) **Going Correction** +0.25s/f (Slow) **11** Ran SP% **125.3**
Speed ratings: **93,92,91,91,88 86,79,73,61,33 1**
CSF: £1,547.57.
**Owner** Sons Of The Late King Abdulla Bin A'Aziz **Bred** King Abdullah Bin Abdulaziz Sons **Trained** Saudi Arabia
**FOCUS**
TRAKUS (metres travelled compared to winner): 2nd +3, 3rd -2, 4th +9, 5th +10, 6th 0, 7th +10, 8th +15, 9th +6, 10th +2, 11th +8. A really weak running of the UAE 1000 Guineas and they went hard early and finished desperately slowly: 25.01 (from standing start), 23.06, 25.6, 27.24.

## 653a RANGE ROVER (H'CAP) (TURF) 7f
**5:25** (5:25) (100-112,112) 3-Y-0+

**£85,365** (£28,455; £14,227; £7,113; £4,268; £2,845)

RPR
1 **Salateen**[35] 87 5-8-10 **103**............................................... AdriedeVries 9 102
(David O'Meara) *trckd ldr: led 2f out: r.o wl: hld on gamely* **33/1**
2 *nse* **Flash Fire (IRE)**[21] 320 5-9-6 **112**............................. WilliamBuick 3 112+
(Charlie Appleby) *settled in rr: r.o fnl 1 1/2f: nrst fin* **1/1**[1]
3 *shd* **Oh This Is Us (IRE)**[96] 7821 4-8-13 **105**.......................... PatDobbs 10 105+
(Richard Hannon) *settled in rr: smooth prog 3f out: r.o wl: jst failed* **7/1**[3]
4 *hd* **Tahanee (ARG)**[14] 431 4-9-0 **106** ow1................ ChristopheSoumillon 4 105
(M F De Kock, South Africa) *mid-div: rdn 2 1/2f out and chsd ldrs: ev ch a f out: nt qckn fnl 110yds* **3/1**[2]
5 *1 1/2* **First Selection (SPA)**[28] 204 4-8-11 **104**......................... PatSmullen 1 98
(Simon Crisford) *sn led: hdd 400m out: wknd fnl f* **11/1**
6 *2 1/2* **Anaerobio (ARG)**[21] 320 9-9-2 **108**.............................(t) PatCosgrave 2 96
(M F De Kock, South Africa) *trckd ldrs: ev ch 2f out: one pce fnl 1 1/2f out* **20/1**
7 *2 1/4* **Johann Strauss**[341] 845 6-9-1 **107**......................(t) BernardFayd'Herbe 6 89
(M F De Kock, South Africa) *slowly away: nvr nr to chal* **33/1**
8 *shd* **Encipher (USA)**[28] 205 8-8-7 **100**...............................(t) TadhgO'Shea 8 81
(A R Al Rayhi, UAE) *a in rr* **25/1**
9 *3/4* **Rene Mathis (GER)**[35] 87 7-8-9 **102**......................... RichardMullen 7 81
(Richard Fahey) *nvr bttr than mid-div* **10/1**
10 *1 1/2* **Sahaafy (USA)**[328] 999 5-8-11 **104**............................... JimCrowley 5 79
(M Al Mheiri, UAE) *trckd ldrs tl wknd fnl 2f* **20/1**
1m 23.72s (-0.38) **Going Correction** +0.25s/f (Good) **10** Ran SP% **124.2**
Speed ratings: **112,111,111,111,109 107,104,104,103,101**
CSF: £67.94; TRICAST: £304.70.
**Owner** Sheikh Abdullah Almalek Alsabah **Bred** Mrs Janis Macpherson **Trained** Upper Helmsley, N Yorks
**FOCUS**
Rail on turf track out 12 metres. TRAKUS (metres travelled compared to winner): 2nd -2, 3rd -1, 4th -3, 5th -4, 6th -3, 7th +1, 8th +1, 9th +2, 10th +1. This was run at a solid pace and the form is strong with a well-treated winner.

## 654a JAGUAR F-TYPE (H'CAP) (TURF) 1m 1f (T)
**6:00** (6:00) (95-105,105) 3-Y-0+

**£60,975** (£20,325; £10,162; £5,081; £3,048; £2,032)

RPR
1 **Folkswood**[21] 322 4-9-5 **104**...............................(p) ColmO'Donoghue 10 112
(Charlie Appleby) *trckd ldrs: rdn to ld 2 1/2f out: r.o wl* **4/1**[3]
2 *2* **Elleval (IRE)**[14] 428 7-9-1 **100**.......................................(p) SamHitchcott 9 104+
(David Marnane, Ire) *settled in rr: hmpd after 2f: r.o wl fnl 2f: nrst fin* **16/1**
3 *1 3/4* **Hors De Combat**[28] 205 6-9-4 **103**............................... PatSmullen 1 103
(Denis Coakley) *trckd ldr: ev ch 2f out: r.o tl wknd fnl 110yds* **7/1**
4 *hd* **Secret Brief (IRE)**[28] 205 5-9-3 **102**........................... WilliamBuick 11 102+
(Charlie Appleby) *mid-div: r.o fnl 2f: nrst fin* **7/2**[2]
5 *2 3/4* **Moonlight Dash**[21] 322 9-8-13 **98**......................... RichardMullen 6 92
(S Seemar, UAE) *trckd ldr: ev ch 3f out: r.o same pce fnl 2f* **25/1**
6 *2* **Brex Drago (ITY)**[21] 322 5-9-5 **104**............................. AntonioFresu 7 94
(Marco Botti) *sn led: but stdy pce: hdd 2 1/2f out: r.o same pce fnl 1 1/2f* **20/1**
7 *1 1/2* **Limario (GER)**[7] 538 7-9-1 **100**...............................................(t) PatDobbs 8 87
(Doug Watson, UAE) *mid-div: r.o same pce fnl 2f* **20/1**
8 *hd* **Whistle Stop (SAF)**[21] 322 6-8-13 **98**..............................(e) JimCrowley 4 84
(M F De Kock, South Africa) *nvr nr to chal* **20/1**
9 *3/4* **Jalapeno (IRE)**[21] 322 4-9-1 **100**.....................................(t) CarloFiocchi 2 85
(Agostino Affe', Italy) *nvr nr to chal. but r.o fnl 2f* **33/1**
10 *1 3/4* **Good Trip (IRE)**[14] 428 4-9-3 **102**..............................(t) TadhgO'Shea 14 83
(A R Al Rayhi, UAE) *nvr bttr than mid-div* **16/1**
11 *nk* **Start Right**[313] 10-9-0 **99**...............................................(p) PatCosgrave 13 79
(S Seemar, UAE) *s.i.s: nvr bttr than mid-div* **40/1**
12 *13* **Kyllachy Gala**[15] 396 4-9-6 **105**........................ ChristopheSoumillon 5 58
(Marco Botti) *a in rr* **14/1**
13 *1* **Classic Collection**[12] 474 5-9-1 **100**............................ AdriedeVries 12 51
(Saeed bin Suroor) *trckd ldr tl wknd fnl 3 1/2f* **10/1**
P **Best Of Times**[198] 4731 5-9-6 **105**..................................... OisinMurphy 3
(Saeed bin Suroor) *s.i.s: p.u 4 1/2f out* **10/3**[1]
1m 49.52s (0.42) **Going Correction** +0.25s/f (Good) **14** Ran SP% **128.8**
Speed ratings: **108,106,104,104,102 100,98,98,98,96 96,84,83,**
CSF: £64.09; TRICAST: £467.31; Placepot: £3,295.10 to a £1 stake. Pool: £4,513.87 - 0.20 winning units. Quadpot: £292.00 to a £1 stake. Pool: £394.70 - 0.30 winning units.
**Owner** Godolphin **Bred** Hascombe & Valiant Studs **Trained** Newmarket, Suffolk
**FOCUS**
Rail on turf track out 12 metres. TRAKUS (metres travelled compared to winner): 2nd -4, 3rd -5, 4th +1, 5th -1, 6th -4, 7th -2, 8th 0, 9th -3, 10th +7, 11th +4, 12th +6, 13th +5. The splits were 25.54, 23.31, 24.42, 23.55, 12.69.

# 607 NEWCASTLE (A.W) (L-H)
Friday, February 10

**OFFICIAL GOING: Tapeta: standard**
Wind: Almost nil

## 655 SUNBETS.CO.UK H'CAP 1m 5y (Tp)
**5:45** (5:47) (Class 6) (0-65,67) 4-Y-0+ **£2,911** (£866; £432; £216) **Stalls** Centre

Form RPR
60-3 **1** **Chiswick Bey (IRE)**[20] 361 9-9-0 **65**.................... NatalieHambling(7) 7 73
(Richard Fahey) *prom: pushed along over 2f out: hdwy to ld over 1f out: rdn and r.o wl fnl f* **5/2**[1]
0-40 **2** *3/4* **A Boy Named Sue**[6] 579 4-8-1 **48**.........................(v[1]) NathanEvans(3) 5 54
(Peter Niven) *cl up: led over 2f out to over 1f out: kpt on ins fnl f* **11/2**
52-4 **3** *2 3/4* **Newmarket Warrior (IRE)**[37] 44 6-9-1 **66**.........(p) JamieGormley(7) 6 66
(Iain Jardine) *hld up: swtchd rt and stdy hdwy over 2f out: effrt and pushed along over 1f out: edgd lft and no ex ins fnl f* **7/2**[2]
00-5 **4** *3 1/2* **Check 'Em Tuesday (IRE)**[35] 90 4-9-5 **63**...................... DaleSwift 1 55
(Daniel Mark Loughnane) *prom: rdn over 2f out: edgd lft over 1f out: sn outpcd* **10/1**
2-00 **5** *2 1/4* **Space War**[15] 419 10-9-0 **65**........................................(t) RyanTimby(7) 8 52
(Michael Easterby) *led to over 2f out: rdn and wknd over 1f out* **7/1**
6-06 **6** *9* **Scannermandango**[16] 402 4-8-6 **55**...................... LewisEdmunds(5) 2 23
(Jim Goldie) *dwlt: hld up: drvn and outpcd over 2f out: sn wknd* **33/1**
0/-6 **7** *7* **Ivy Matilda**[9] 510 4-8-3 **47** oh1 ow1.................................. JoeyHaynes 9
(Colin Teague) *s.i.s: hld up: rdn and hung lft over 2f out: sn wknd* **100/1**
2-0 **8** *21* **My Matador (IRE)**[23] 286 6-9-9 **67**...............................(t) PaulHanagan 4
(Victor Dartnall) *cl up: lost pl over 3f out: struggling fnl 2f: t.o* **4/1**[3]
1m 39.38s (0.78) **Going Correction** +0.225s/f (Slow) **8** Ran SP% **111.7**
Speed ratings (Par 101): **105,104,101,98,95 86,79,58**
CSF £15.87 CT £45.83 TOTE £3.80: £1.30, £1.80, £1.30; EX 16.30 Trifecta £47.00.
**Owner** M J Macleod **Bred** Mrs Kay Egan **Trained** Musley Bank, N Yorks
**FOCUS**
A modest handicap and it was competitive for the grade. This winner has been rated to the best of his recent figures.

## 656 32RED.COM MAIDEN AUCTION STKS 5f (Tp)
**6:15** (6:16) (Class 6) 3-Y-O **£2,264** (£673; £336; £168) **Stalls** Centre

Form RPR
- **1** **Intense Romance (IRE)** 3-9-0 0................................. ConnorBeasley 1 65+
(Michael Dods) *pressed ldr: ev ch and rdn over 1f out: sn carried lft: bmpd wl ins fnl f: led cl home* **11/2**[2]
43-2 **2** *shd* **Alfonso Manana (IRE)**[27] 244 3-9-5 69...................(p) PaulHanagan 3 69
(James Given) *t.k.h: led: hrd pressed and rdn over 1f out: sn drifted lft: bmpd wnr wl ins fnl f: hdd cl home* **2/9**[1]
**3** *4 1/2* **Mia Wallace (IRE)** 3-8-11 0.................................... ShelleyBirkett(3) 4 49+
(David O'Meara) *trckd ldrs tl rdn and outpcd fr over 1f out* **12/1**[3]
0 **4** *3 3/4* **Spike's Princess (IRE)**[14] 442 3-9-0 0................................. PaulQuinn 2 34
(David Nicholls) *dwlt: sn prom: rdn and hung lft over 2f out: sn wknd* **18/1**
1m 2.6s (3.10) **Going Correction** +0.125s/f (Slow) **4** Ran SP% **110.2**
Speed ratings (Par 95): **80,79,72,66**
CSF £7.63 TOTE £7.50; EX 8.40 Trifecta £8.60.
**Owner** Hugh Malcolm Linsley **Bred** John O'Connor **Trained** Denton, Co Durham
**FOCUS**
There was a turn-up in this ordinary maiden.

## 657 32RED CASINO H'CAP 5f (Tp)
**6:45** (6:45) (Class 4) (0-85,78) 3-Y-O **£4,690** (£1,395; £697; £348) **Stalls** Centre

Form RPR
00-1 **1** **Wild Approach (IRE)**[22] 313 3-8-7 **64**............................. LukeMorris 5 72
(Robert Cowell) *pressed ldr: rdn and hung bdly lft 1/2-way: rallied against far rail to ld wl ins fnl f: jst hld on* **9/2**[2]
3-21 **2** *shd* **Major Jumbo**[16] 404 3-9-6 **77**............................................ ShaneGray 4 84
(Kevin Ryan) *t.k.h: led: rdn over 1f out: sn hung lft: hdd wl ins fnl f: rallied: jst hld* **8/11**[1]
2-44 **3** *8* **Atteq**[21] 329 3-9-3 **74**........................................................... PaulHanagan 3 52
(Richard Fahey) *sn bdly outpcd in last pl: hdwy over 1f out: chsd clr ldng pair ins fnl f: no imp* **9/2**[2]
1-21 **4** *1 3/4* **Cajmere**[18] 379 3-9-7 **78**...............................................(p) PJMcDonald 2 50
(Tom Dascombe) *cl up: rdn and edgd lft over 2f out: outpcd whn edgd rt over 1f out: btn and lost modest 3rd pl ins fnl f* **6/1**[3]
100- **5** *3 1/2* **Bay Station**[108] 7600 3-9-0 **71**............................................ PaulQuinn 1 30
(David Nicholls) *dwlt: sn outpcd and drvn along: struggling bef 1/2-way: nvr on terms* **50/1**
58.48s (-1.02) **Going Correction** +0.125s/f (Slow) **5** Ran SP% **110.5**
Speed ratings (Par 99): **113,112,100,97,91**
CSF £8.36 TOTE £4.30: £2.10, £1.10; EX 11.10 Trifecta £21.80.
**Owner** T Morley & G Johnson **Bred** Mike's Wildcat Partnership **Trained** Six Mile Bottom, Cambs

**FOCUS**
Not the strongest 3yo handicap for the grade, but the two principals pulled well clear. The level is a bit fluid.

## 658 £10 FREE AT 32RED.COM MAIDEN FILLIES' STKS 1m 5y (Tp)
7:15 (7:17) (Class 5) 3-Y-0+ £2,911 (£866; £432; £216) Stalls Centre

Form RPR
1 **Signe (IRE)** 4-9-12 0 PaulHanagan 2 77+
(William Haggas) *stdd in tch: smooth hdwy to ld over 2f out: rdn and hrd pressed over 1f out to ins fnl f: asserted last 75yds: pushed out* 4/9[1]

2 ½ **Hot Natured (IRE)** 3-8-7 0 PJMcDonald 5 71
(K R Burke) *dwlt: hld up in tch: smooth hdwy to chal over 1f out: sn rdn: kpt on: hld last 75yds* 12/1

3 4½ **Dalavida (FR)** 3-8-7 0 (h[1]) TomEaves 6 61
(David Simcock) *hld up in last pl: stdy hdwy over 2f out: pushed along and effrt over 1f out: no imp fnl f* 7/1[3]

6 4 1¼ **Melodine**[23] 283 3-8-7 0 LukeMorris 4 58
(Sir Mark Prescott Bt) *t.k.h: in tch: drvn and outpcd wl over 1f out: sn no imp* 4/1[2]

0- 5 ½ **Stretewise (IRE)**[125] 7142 3-8-7 0 ShaneGray 3 57
(Jason Ward) *led at ordinary gallop: rdn and hdd over 2f out: rallied: wknd over 1f out* 100/1

0 6 12 **Archibelle**[30] 175 3-8-4 0 NathanEvans(3) 1 29
(R Mike Smith) *cl up: rdn along over 3f out: hung lft and wknd over 2f out* 100/1

1m 41.23s (2.63) **Going Correction** +0.225s/f (Slow)
**WFA** 3 from 4yo 19lb 6 Ran SP% **111.4**
Speed ratings (Par 100): **95,94,90,88,88 76**
CSF £7.25 TOTE £1.30: £1.10, £5.30; EX 7.30 Trifecta £22.60.

**Owner** Fiona and Ian Carmichael-Jennings **Bred** Vimal And Gillian Khosla **Trained** Newmarket, Suffolk

**FOCUS**
Another ordinary maiden for older horses, taken by a well-backed and expensive 4yo. The level of the form is open to question with the fifth not beaten far.

## 659 32RED.COM APPRENTICE H'CAP 1m 5y (Tp)
7:45 (7:45) (Class 5) (0-75,71) 3-Y-0 £2,911 (£866; £432; £216) Stalls Centre

Form RPR
5-43 1 **Killermont Street (IRE)**[14] 434 3-9-0 67 RichardOliver(3) 1 70
(Mark Johnston) *mde all: set mod gallop: rdn and edgd both ways fr over 1f out: hld on wl fnl f* 8/1

00-4 2 ½ **Out Of Order (IRE)**[16] 401 3-8-13 63 (t) NathanEvans 5 65
(Tim Easterby) *t.k.h: hld up in tch: rdn and outpcd over 2f out: rallied over 1f out: chsd wnr ins fnl f: kpt on: hld nr fin* 7/4[1]

342- 3 hd **Major Cornwallis (IRE)**[134] 6903 3-9-0 69 NatalieHambling(5) 2 70
(Richard Fahey) *trckd ldr: rdn over 2f out: rallied and edgd lft over 1f out: lost 2nd ins fnl f: kpt on: hld towards fin* 11/4[2]

50-5 4 2¼ **Ladofash**[21] 329 3-8-11 64 (v[1]) JordanVaughan(3) 4 60
(K R Burke) *t.k.h: trckd ldrs: rdn and outpcd wl over 1f out: rallied ins fnl f: no imp* 9/2[3]

3-03 5 ¾ **Naupaka**[6] 580 3-9-0 71 KieranSchofield(7) 3 65
(Brian Ellison) *hld up in tch: outpcd and edgd lft over 2f out: rallied over 1f out: sn no imp* 9/2[3]

1m 41.74s (3.14) **Going Correction** +0.225s/f (Slow) 5 Ran SP% **110.5**
Speed ratings (Par 97): **93,92,92,90,89**
CSF £22.57 TOTE £5.00: £2.50, £1.60; EX 13.40 Trifecta £41.20.

**Owner** Douglas Livingston **Bred** Ballylinch Stud **Trained** Middleham Moor, N Yorks

**FOCUS**
A fair 3yo handicap and the winner made all. The winner has been rated back to the level of her maiden win.

## 660 BETWAY SPRINT H'CAP 6f (Tp)
8:15 (8:16) (Class 4) (0-85,85) 4-Y-0+ £4,690 (£1,395; £697; £348) Stalls Centre

Form RPR
003- 1 **Slingsby**[57] 8389 6-8-4 71 oh1 (p) NathanEvans(3) 7 78
(Michael Easterby) *cl up on nr side of gp: rdn over 2f out: led over 1f out: edgd lft ins fnl f: kpt on wl* 5/2[1]

01-2 2 1¼ **Pretty Bubbles**[35] 94 8-9-4 85 (v) AlistairRawlinson(3) 6 88
(J R Jenkins) *dwlt: hld up: pushed along 1/2-way: hdwy over 1f out: chsd wnr ins fnl f: kpt on* 7/1

41-0 3 nk **Aprovado (IRE)**[14] 443 5-9-2 80 (p) ConnorBeasley 3 82
(Michael Dods) *led: rdn over 2f out: hdd over 1f out: rallied: kpt on same pce ins fnl f* 12/1

000- 4 nk **Elysian Flyer (IRE)**[174] 5648 5-9-2 80 GrahamLee 1 81
(Paul Midgley) *cl up on outside of gp: pushed along over 2f out: kpt on same pce ins fnl f* 10/1

-520 5 ½ **Among Angels**[22] 312 5-8-12 76 (b) LukeMorris 8 75
(Daniel Mark Loughnane) *hld up in tch on nr side of gp: drvn and outpcd over 2f out: kpt on ins fnl f: nt pce to chal* 6/1[3]

600- 6 1¾ **Tarboosh**[141] 6699 4-9-0 78 PaulHanagan 4 72
(Paul Midgley) *t.k.h: hld up in tch: smooth hdwy to chal over 1f out: sn rdn: wknd ins fnl f* 6/1[3]

50-0 7 6 **Silhuette (IRE)**[9] 514 4-8-8 72 (p[1]) PJMcDonald 5 47
(Colin Teague) *hld up: drvn and struggling over 2f out: edgd lft and sn wknd* 50/1

106- 8 12 **Foresight (FR)**[108] 7593 4-8-13 77 TomEaves 2 13
(Kevin Ryan) *cl up: rdn over 2f out: wknd qckly wl over 1f out* 3/1[2]

1m 12.39s (-0.11) **Going Correction** +0.225s/f (Slow) 8 Ran SP% **113.4**
Speed ratings (Par 105): **109,107,106,106,105 103,95,79**
CSF £20.20 CT £174.41 TOTE £3.20: £1.30, £1.90, £2.30; EX 5.70.

**Owner** S Hull, B Hoggarth & Mrs C Mason **Bred** R H Mason **Trained** Sheriff Hutton, N Yorks

**FOCUS**
A well-contested sprint handicap, run at an ordinary pace. The winner has been rated around his best form at this track in 2016.

T/Plt: £51.10 to a £1 stake. Pool: £80,089.94 - 1,142.37 winning tickets T/Qpdt: £4.10 to a £1 stake. Pool: £6,989.19 - 1,243.32 winning tickets **Richard Young**

# [523] SOUTHWELL (L-H)
Friday, February 10

**OFFICIAL GOING: Fibresand: standard**
Wind: Light across Weather: Overcast

## 661 BETWAY (S) H'CAP 1m 4f 14y(F)
1:30 (1:30) (Class 6) (0-60,61) 4-Y-0+ £2,587 (£770; £384; £192) Stalls Low

Form RPR
0-06 1 **Thou Swell (IRE)**[16] 395 5-8-9 53 (v[1]) CharlieBennett(5) 2 60
(Shaun Harris) *pushed along s and sn led: rdn clr 3f out: drvn over 1f out: kpt on wl u.p fnl f* 25/1

0-04 2 1¾ **Ralphy Lad (IRE)**[22] 315 6-9-5 58 JoeFanning 5 63
(Alan Swinbank) *trckd ldrs: pushed along over 3f out: chsd wnr wl over 2f out and sn rdn drvn over 1f out: kpt on u.p fnl f* 6/4[1]

-334 3 ¾ **Stonecoldsoba**[13] 461 4-9-5 61 AndrewMullen 7 64
(David Evans) *in tch: niggled along on outer 7f out: rdn over 4f out: chsd ldng pair and swtchd lft wl over 1f out: sn drvn and kpt on* 6/4[1]

4-00 4 14 **Quadriga (IRE)**[15] 414 7-8-11 50 TonyHamilton 3 30
(Chris Grant) *trckd ldng pair: pushed along and wd st: sn rdn and btn 2f out* 20/1

0-45 5 ¾ **Commissar**[15] 421 8-9-1 57 (tp) RobHornby(3) 4 36
(Mandy Rowland) *hld up: a rr* 13/2[2]

-606 6 1¾ **Yul Finegold (IRE)**[14] 436 7-9-7 60 (v) PaulMulrennan 1 36
(Conor Dore) *chsd wnr: pushed along over 5f out: rdn 4f out: sn ndrvn and wknd* 16/1[3]

2m 39.72s (-1.28) **Going Correction** -0.175s/f (Stan)
**WFA** 4 from 5yo+ 2lb 6 Ran SP% **107.8**
Speed ratings (Par 101): **97,95,95,86,85 84**
CSF £58.62 TOTE £23.00: £5.00, £1.10; EX 64.30 Trifecta £193.60.There was no bid for the winner. Stonecoldsoba was claimed by Mr Denis Quinn £5,500.
**Owner** All Weather Bloodstock **Bred** My Meadowview Llc **Trained** Carburton, Notts

**FOCUS**
A moderate selling handicap, but they went a good pace and plenty of credit goes to the winning rider. The first three pulled miles clear of the rest and the winner has been rated within 8lb of last year's best.

## 662 SUNBETS.CO.UK DOWNLOAD THE APP MAIDEN STKS 7f 14y(F)
2:00 (2:01) (Class 5) 3-Y-0+ £2,911 (£866; £432; £216) Stalls Low

Form RPR
3 1 **Kencumin (FR)**[34] 127 3-8-11 0 GrahamLee 9 79+
(Ralph Beckett) *dwlt: sn trcking ldrs on outer: wd st: hdwy to chse ldr wl over 1f out: swtchd lft and rdn jst over 1f out: chal ins fnl f: kpt on wl to ld last 50 yds* 13/8[1]

20-2 2 ½ **Elegantly Bound (IRE)**[17] 385 3-8-11 71 (b) AndrewMullen 10 77
(James Given) *sn led: rdn along wl over 1f out: edgd rt jst over 1f out: jnd and drvn ins fnl f: sn edgd lft: hdd and no ex last 50 yds* 3/1[2]

22-4 3 4½ **Havelock (IRE)**[10] 500 3-8-11 0 JoeFanning 6 65
(Mark Johnston) *cl up: rdn along 2f out: drvn over 1f out: kpt on same pce* 12/1

4 1½ **Trenchard (USA)** 3-8-11 0 NickyMackay 5 61+
(John Gosden) *dwlt: green and sn pushed along towards rr: gd hdwy and trckd ldrs after 2f: rdn along over 2f out: kpt on same pce* 4/1[3]

5-3 5 nk **He's A Lad (IRE)**[13] 466 3-8-11 0 DavidProbert 4 60
(Andrew Balding) *chsd ldrs: pushed along and sltly outpcd 1/2-way: rdn and hdwy over 2f out: drvn over 1f out: kpt on* 3/1[2]

0-0 6 6 **Major Tom**[25] 265 3-8-11 0 TomMarquand 3 44
(Michael Appleby) *trckd ldrs: pushed along over 3f out: rdn over 2f out: sn outpcd* 200/1

3-56 7 2¾ **Lady Volante (IRE)**[15] 418 3-8-6 62 FrannyNorton 7 31
(David Evans) *prom: rdn along over 3f out: swtchd rt and drvn over 2f out: sn wknd* 66/1

4 8 ½ **Striking For Gold**[32] 150 3-8-11 0 MichaelJMMurphy 1 35
(Sarah Hollinshead) *in tch on inner on inner: rdn along 1/2-way: sn outpcd* 100/1

00 9 14 **Newton Heath (IRE)**[21] 331 3-8-11 0 DougieCostello 8
(Daniel Mark Loughnane) *dwlt: a rr: bhd fr 1/2-way* 200/1

10 5 **Delphyne**[56] 5-9-4 0 CharlieBennett(5) 2
(Shaun Harris) *sn outpcd and a bhd* 200/1

1m 28.0s (-2.30) **Going Correction** -0.175s/f (Stan)
**WFA** 3 from 5yo 17lb 10 Ran SP% **119.8**
Speed ratings (Par 103): **106,105,100,98,98 91,88,87,71,65**
CSF £7.18 TOTE £2.80: £1.10, £1.30, £3.00; EX 8.70 Trifecta £47.20.
**Owner** The Anagram Partnership **Bred** Marcello Randelli & Sonja Banziger **Trained** Kimpton, Hants

**FOCUS**
Not a bad maiden for the track with a few having shown ability plus a fascinating newcomer. The first two pulled clear and the form has some depth to it.

## 663 SUNBETS.CO.UK H'CAP 7f 14y(F)
2:30 (2:30) (Class 5) (0-70,71) 4-Y-0+ £2,911 (£866; £432; £216) Stalls Low

Form RPR
1-13 1 **Custard The Dragon**[14] 441 4-9-8 71 (p[1]) JoeFanning 6 80+
(John Mackie) *hld up: hdwy over 2f out: rdn to chal ins fnl f: led last 100 yds* 2/1[1]

0-25 2 1¼ **Unnoticed**[15] 426 5-9-2 65 (t) RobertWinston 4 70
(Ollie Pears) *trckd ldrs: smooth hdwy and cl up over 2f out: led over 1f out: sn rdn: hdd and no ex last 100 yds* 13/2

0-01 3 ½ **Dark Forest**[11] 481 4-8-13 62 6ex (p) BarryMcHugh 1 66
(Marjorie Fife) *trckd ldrs on inner: hdwy over 2f out: cl up and rdn over 1f out: drvn and ev ch ins fnl f: kpt on* 11/2[3]

63-5 4 ½ **Capital Gearing**[39] 26 4-8-7 56 oh3 (b) TomMarquand 3 58
(Henry Spiller) *towards rr: hdwy on inner over 2f out: rdn to chse ldrs over 1f out: drvn and ch ent fnl f: kpt on same pce* 12/1

3-61 5 nk **Fortinbrass (IRE)**[17] 386 7-8-13 62 JoeDoyle 8 63
(John Balding) *cl up: rdn to take narrow ld 2f out: hdd and drvn jst over 1f out: kpt on same pce* 20/1

0112 6 ½ **Fujin**[11] 480 6-9-3 71 (v) CharlieBennett(5) 7 71
(Shaun Harris) *cl up: rdn 2f out and ev ch tl drvn appr fnl f and kpt on same pce* 8/1

2-63 7 1 **Playtothewhistle**[8] 527 6-9-4 70 (v) AlistairRawlinson(3) 9 67
(Michael Appleby) *towards rr: rdn along and wd st: kpt on u.p fnl 2f* 5/1[2]

/0-0 8 nk **One Man Army**[15] 419 5-8-4 58 RowanScott(5) 10 55
(Julia Brooke) *dwlt: a towards rr* 66/1

-000 **9** *nk* **Greyfriarschorista**[13] 460 10-9-2 **65**........................ AndrewMullen 11 61
(David Evans) *chsd ldrs: rdn along 3f out: sn wknd* **20/1**

055- **10** *1/2* **Llewellyn**[59] 8350 9-8-6 **60**........................ PhilDennis(5) 2 54
(Declan Carroll) *slt ld on inner: rdn along 3f out: hdd 2f out and grad wknd* **20/1**

0-00 **11** *21* **Showing Off (IRE)**[15] 419 4-9-0 **63**........................ DavidProbert 5
(Michael Wigham) *dwlt: a bhd* **66/1**

1m 28.59s (-1.71) **Going Correction** -0.175s/f (Stan) **11** Ran SP% **114.8**
Speed ratings (Par 103): **102,100,100,99,99 98,97,97,96,96 72**
CSF £13.54 CT £61.98 TOTE £3.00: £1.50, £2.20, £1.80; EX 17.10 Trifecta £43.40.
**Owner** Derbyshire Racing **Bred** Mr & Mrs Kevan Watts **Trained** Church Broughton , Derbys

**FOCUS**
An ordinary handicap, but no shortage of pace on with a three-way battle for the early lead and that suited the winner. The form looks straightforward rated around the placed horses.

## 664 BETWAY BEST ODDS GUARANTEED PLUS H'CAP 4f 214y(F)
**3:00** (3:00) (Class 3) (0-95,91) 4-Y-0+ **£7,439** (£2,213; £1,106; £553) **Stalls** Centre

Form RPR

500- **1** **Sir Billy Wright (IRE)**[70] 8192 6-8-7 **82**........................ CliffordLee(5) 1 91
(David Evans) *racd towards far side: chsd ldrs: hdwy over 2f out: rdn to ld jst over 1f out: kpt on strly fnl f* **14/1**

1-55 **2** *3/4* **Distant Past**[17] 388 6-9-7 **91**........................(v) KevinStott 10 96
(Kevin Ryan) *racd towards stands side: prom: chal over 1f out: sn rdn and hung lft ins fnl f: kpt on* **12/1**

-114 **3** *nk* **Lady Nayef**[17] 388 4-8-12 **82**........................(t) JFEgan 3 86
(John Butler) *racd towards far side: prom: hdwy to chal 2f out: rdn and ev ch over 1f out: drvn and edgd rt ins fnl f: kpt on* **8/1**

0-21 **4** *nk* **Dungannon**[17] 387 10-8-5 **82**........................(b) JoshuaBryan(7) 11 85
(Andrew Balding) *racd towards stands side: in tch on outer: hdwy wl over 1f out: rdn ent fnl f: kpt on wl towards fin* **15/2**[3]

0-20 **5** *1 1/2* **Meadway**[17] 388 6-9-6 **90**........................(p) PaulMulrennan 6 88
(Bryan Smart) *racd centre: cl up: slt ld 2f out: sn rdn and hdd over 1f out: hld whn n.m.r and sltly hmpd ins fnl f* **8/1**

1-51 **6** *1 3/4* **Bring On A Spinner**[22] 312 4-8-4 **77**........................(be) AaronJones(3) 5 68
(Stuart Williams) *chsd ldrs: rdn along wl over 1f out: kpt on same pce* **5/2**[1]

200- **7** *1* **Seamster**[156] 6234 10-8-7 **84**........................(t) GerO'Neill(7) 7 72
(David Loughnane) *towards rr: rdn along and hdwy wl over 1f out: n.d* **80/1**

020- **8** *1* **Orient Class**[100] 7773 6-9-0 **84**........................ JackGarritty 2 68
(Paul Midgley) *racd towards far side: prom: rdn along 2f out: sn wknd* **50/1**

04-0 **9** *1 3/4* **Seve**[36] 79 5-9-1 **85**........................ FrannyNorton 4 63
(Tom Dascombe) *in tch centre: rdn along 2f out: n.d* **16/1**

2-06 **10** *4* **Showdaisy**[17] 388 4-9-3 **87**........................(p) PhillipMakin 9 51+
(Keith Dalgleish) *s.i.s: a bhd* **9/1**

4-12 **11** *hd* **Razin' Hell**[17] 388 6-9-1 **85**........................(v) AndrewMullen 8 48
(John Balding) *racd centre: slt ld: rdn along 1/2-way: sn hdd & wknd* **9/2**[2]

58.43s (-1.27) **Going Correction** -0.10s/f (Stan) **11** Ran SP% **114.2**
Speed ratings (Par 107): **106,104,104,103,101 98,97,95,92,86 85**
CSF £166.25 CT £1464.39 TOTE £15.70: £4.90, £2.90, £2.20; EX 200.80 Trifecta £3572.40.
**Owner** Shropshire Wolves **Bred** Grangecon Stud **Trained** Pandy, Monmouths

**FOCUS**
A decent sprint handicap and five of these met over C&D 17 days ago. Typically they went hard and it seemed to be an advantage to be drawn low. The winner has been rated to his best.

## 665 BETWAY BEST ODDS GUARANTEED PLUS CLASSIFIED CLAIMING STKS 4f 214y(F)
**3:35** (3:35) (Class 6) 4-Y-0+ **£2,587** (£770; £384; £192) **Stalls** Centre

Form RPR

12-2 **1** **Piazon**[39] 22 6-8-12 75........................(be) JoshuaBryan(7) 1 78
(John Butler) *dwlt: sn cl up towards far side: rdn to chal wl over 1f out: drvn to ld ins fnl f* **1/1**[1]

5432 **2** *1/2* **Archie Stevens**[17] 387 7-8-5 69........................ KatherineGlenister(7) 5 70
(David Evans) *cl up centre: slt ld over 2f out: rdn wl over 1f out: drvn and hdd ins fnl f: kpt on* **9/2**[3]

-001 **3** *nse* **Elusivity (IRE)**[11] 480 9-9-4 68........................(p) PaulMulrennan 4 75
(Conor Dore) *slt ld centre: hdd over 2f out: cl up and rdn over 1f out: drvn and ev ch ent fnl f: kpt on* **5/1**

2-35 **4** *5* **Harwoods Star (IRE)**[8] 528 7-9-4 74........................(be) JFEgan 3 57
(John Butler) *s.i.s: a bhd* **7/2**[2]

000- **5** *4* **Touch The Clouds**[106] 7646 6-8-10 42........................(p) HollieDoyle(5) 2 40
(William Stone) *chsd ldng pair centre: rdn along bef 1/2-way: sn outpcd and bhd* **100/1**

59.02s (-0.68) **Going Correction** -0.10s/f (Stan) **5** Ran SP% **108.1**
Speed ratings (Par 101): **101,100,100,92,85**
CSF £5.65 TOTE £1.90: £1.10, £2.50; EX 5.90 Trifecta £13.10.Archie Stevens was claimed by Mr Matt Watkinson for £3,000.
**Owner** Royale Racing Syndicate **Bred** Peter Baldwin **Trained** Newmarket, Suffolk
■ Stewards' Enquiry : Joshua Bryan two-day ban; used whip above the permitted level (Feb 24-25)

**FOCUS**
A reasonable claimer despite the small field with a few coming into it in form. The front three had a right battle from before halfway and there was little between them at the line.

## 666 BETWAY H'CAP 2m 102y(F)
**4:05** (4:07) (Class 4) (0-80,85) 4-Y-0+ **£4,851** (£1,443; £721; £360) **Stalls** Low

Form RPR

651- **1** **Fern Owl**[43] 8565 5-9-13 **80**........................(b) RobertWinston 5 89
(Hughie Morrison) *hld up in tch: hdwy 4f out: trckd ldrs 3f out: chsd ldng pair 2f out: sn rdn: drvn to chal ent fnl f: styd on wl to ld towards fin* **4/5**[1]

-111 **2** *3/4* **Start Seven**[11] 477 5-10-4 **85** 6ex........................ GeorgeBaker 2 93+
(Jamie Osborne) *trckd ldrs: cl up over 3f out: led 2f out and sn rdn: drvn ent fnl f: hdd and no ex towards fin* **13/8**[2]

032- **3** *2 1/4* **Katie Gale**[43] 8565 7-9-6 **73**........................(p[1]) AndrewMullen 6 78
(Michael Appleby) *prom: slt ld 7f out: rdn along 3f out: hdd and drvn 2f out: ev ch ent fnl f: grad wknd* **8/1**[3]

164- **4** *8* **Virnon**[33] 864 6-9-6 **73**........................ JoeFanning 8 68
(Alan Swinbank) *hld up in tch: hdwy to chse ldrs over 4f out: rdn along over 3f out: drvn over 2f out and plugged on one pce* **20/1**

641/ **5** *1/2* **La Estrella (USA)**[409] 8383 14-9-5 **72**........................ GrahamLee 1 67
(Don Cantillon) *hld up in tch: hdwy over 4f out: rdn along 3f out: kpt on one pce fnl 2f* **12/1**

13-6 **6** *4 1/2* **An Fear Ciuin (IRE)**[40] 3 6-9-4 **78**........................(v) CallumRodriguez(7) 4 67
(Richard Ford) *trckd ldr: led after 6f: pushed along and hdd 7f out: sn rdn and cl up on inner 4f out: drvn over 3f out and sn wknd* **20/1**

24-0 **7** *34* **With Hindsight (IRE)**[18] 381 9-8-11 **67**........................ KieranShoemark(3) 3 16
(Steve Gollings) *led 6f: chsd ldrs: rdn along over 5f out: sn lost pl and bhd* **50/1**

00-0 **8** *4 1/2* **Amber Flush**[17] 74 8-9-0 **67**........................(t[1]) PaddyAspell 7 10
(Clare Ellam) *sn rdn along in rr: outpcd and detached after 5f: bhd fr 1/2-way* **100/1**

3m 40.16s (-5.34) **Going Correction** -0.175s/f (Stan) **8** Ran SP% **124.9**
Speed ratings (Par 105): **106,105,104,100,100 98,81,78**
CSF £2.55 CT £5.91 TOTE £1.60: £1.10, £1.30, £1.60; EX 2.50 Trifecta £7.40.
**Owner** Sir Thomas Pilkington **Bred** Sir Thomas Pilkington **Trained** East Ilsley, Berks

**FOCUS**
A decent race of its type featuring a couple of impressive recent course winners, another course specialist and a local legend. It produced a thrilling finish between the big two.

## 667 32RED.COM H'CAP 6f 16y(F)
**4:40** (4:43) (Class 6) (0-60,60) 3-Y-O **£2,587** (£770; £384; £192) **Stalls** Low

Form RPR

04-3 **1** **Tranquil Daze (IRE)**[36] 77 3-9-4 **60**........................ KieranShoemark(3) 3 71+
(David Brown) *trckd ldrs: smooth hdwy on inner wl over 1f out: rdn to ld ins fnl f: sn clr* **7/4**[1]

565- **2** *2 3/4* **Not Now Nadia (IRE)**[109] 7579 3-9-2 **55**........................ PaulMulrennan 9 56
(Michael Dods) *trckd ldrs: hdwy over 2f out: rdn to ld 1 1/2f out: drvn ent fnl f: sn hdd and kpt on same pce* **9/2**[3]

02-2 **3** *1 3/4* **Luv U Always**[15] 415 3-9-0 **53**........................ JoeFanning 1 49
(Iain Jardine) *led: rdn along over 2f out: hdd 1 1/2f out: sn drvn and kpt on same pce* **11/4**[2]

000- **4** *hd* **Harvest Ranger**[83] 8034 3-8-7 **49**........................ EoinWalsh(3) 7 44
(Michael Appleby) *dwlt and rr: hdwy on outer 3f out: wd st and sn rdn: drvn over 1f out: kpt on: nrst fin* **7/1**

24-0 **5** *3/4* **Sheila's Return**[16] 401 3-9-2 **55**........................ AndrewMullen 4 48
(John Balding) *cl up: rdn along wl over 2f out: drvn wl over 1f out: sn one pce* **12/1**

656- **6** *2* **Red Shanghai (IRE)**[43] 8569 3-8-4 **46** oh1........................ NoelGarbutt(3) 6 33
(Charles Smith) *a towards rr* **66/1**

00-4 **7** *1 1/2* **Mesmeric Moment**[22] 313 3-8-8 **54**........................ JoshuaBryan(7) 8 36
(Shaun Harris) *cl up: rdn along wl over 2f out: sn drvn and wknd* **12/1**

1m 16.56s (0.06) **Going Correction** -0.175s/f (Stan) **7** Ran SP% **110.6**
Speed ratings (Par 95): **92,88,86,85,84 82,80**
CSF £9.29 CT £18.57 TOTE £2.60: £1.30, £2.20; EX 10.30 Trifecta £26.30.
**Owner** J C Fretwell **Bred** John Malone **Trained** Averham Park, Notts

**FOCUS**
A moderate 3yo handicap with only one of these having scored before. The winner looks better than this level.
T/Jkpt: £18,652.60 to a £1 stake. Pool: £18,653.00 - 1 winning ticket. T/Plt: £32.70 to a £1 stake. Pool: £84,441.16 - 1,880.03 winning tickets T/Qpdt: £9.70 to a £1 stake. Pool: £7,425.49 - 565.59 winning tickets **Joe Rowntree**

668 - 676a (Foreign Racing) - See Raceform Interactive

# [642]LINGFIELD (L-H)
Saturday, February 11

**OFFICIAL GOING: Polytrack: standard**
Wind: light, half against Weather: snow flurries clearing, cold

## 677 32RED.COM FILLIES' H'CAP 1m 1y(P)
**1:25** (1:27) (Class 5) (0-75,76) 4-Y-0+ **£2,911** (£866; £432; £216) **Stalls** High

Form RPR

12-1 **1** **Simply Me**[17] 394 4-9-2 **70**........................(p) RichardKingscote 4 77+
(Tom Dascombe) *hld up in tch in midfield: effrt over 1f out: str run u.p ins fnl f to ld 50yds out: r.o wl* **5/4**[1]

03-3 **2** *3/4* **First Experience**[28] 232 6-9-8 **76**........................(p) AdamKirby 8 80
(Lee Carter) *stdd after s: hld up in tch in rr: clsd and nt clr run whn swtchd rt over 1f out: r.o strly u.p ins fnl f: wnt 2nd towards fin: nvr getting to wnr* **6/1**[3]

032- **3** *1/2* **Pacolita (IRE)**[156] 6266 5-9-2 **75**........................ MitchGodwin(5) 2 78
(Sylvester Kirk) *stdd after s: hld up in tch in last trio: nt clr run ent fnl 2f: hdwy and swtchd rt jst over 1f out: kpt on wl ins fnl f* **8/1**

2-12 **4** *shd* **Skidby Mill (IRE)**[8] 550 7-9-7 **75**........................ GeorgeBaker 1 78
(Laura Mongan) *led: rdn and fnd ex over 1f out: rdn ins fnl f: hdd and no ex 50yds out: lost 2 pls towards fin* **7/2**[2]

040- **5** *nse* **Lemon Thyme**[291] 1755 4-8-6 **60**........................(h) MartinDwyer 6 63
(Mike Murphy) *stdd after s: t.k.h: hld up in tch in last pair: effrt over 1f out: r.o wl u.p ins fnl f: nvr getting to wnr* **66/1**

005- **6** *3/4* **Golly Miss Molly**[184] 5319 6-8-10 **64**........................(b) MartinLane 9 65
(Jeremy Gask) *dwlt: steadily rcvrd to press ldr over 6f out: rdn ent fnl 2f: unable qck over 1f out: kpt on same pce ins fnl f* **25/1**

00-5 **7** *4 1/2* **Italian Beauty (IRE)**[28] 232 5-8-13 **67**........................(p) WilliamCarson 5 57
(John Wainwright) *chsd ldr tl over 6f out: styd chsng ldrs tl unable qck u.p over 1f out: wknd ins fnl f* **40/1**

4-63 **8** *nse* **Tabla**[8] 550 5-8-5 **66**........................ JaneElliott(7) 3 56
(Lee Carter) *wl in tch in midfield: chsd ldng pair 5f out tl unable qck over 1f out: wknd ins fnl f: b.b.v* **6/1**[3]

1m 37.12s (-1.08) **Going Correction** -0.05s/f (Stan) **8** Ran SP% **114.1**
Speed ratings (Par 100): **103,102,101,101,101 100,96,96**
CSF £9.23 CT £42.48 TOTE £1.90: £1.10, £2.50, £2.50; EX 8.70 Trifecta £37.30.
**Owner** Laurence Bellman **Bred** Highclere Stud **Trained** Malpas, Cheshire

**FOCUS**
An ordinary fillies' handicap in which they went an even pace and finished in a bit of a heap. The winner is progressive, though. It's been rated around the runner-up and third.

## 678 32RED CASINO H'CAP 6f 1y(P)
**2:00** (2:00) (Class 3) (0-95,88) 3-Y-O **£7,246** (£2,168; £1,084; £542; £270) **Stalls** Low

Form RPR

11-5 **1** **Turin Redstar**[25] 276 3-9-3 **84**........................(p[1]) AdamKirby 4 87
(Ralph Beckett) *hld up in tch in 4th: wnt 3rd 1/2-way: effrt on inner over 1f out: rdn to chse ldr 1f out: r.o wl to ld 50yds out: gng away at fin* **15/8**[2]

-211 **2** *1/2* **Marquee Club**[14] 458 3-9-6 **87**........................ GeorgeBaker 3 88
(Jamie Osborne) *led: shkn up and wnt clr wl over 1f out: rdn ins fnl f: hdd and no ex 50yds out* **11/8**[1]

1-31 **3** *1 1/4* **Dazacam**[28] 243 3-9-5 **86**........................ RobertWinston 1 83
(Michael Herrington) *taken down early: stdd after s: hld up in rr: clsd on inner and swtchd lft ent fnl f: r.o to go 3rd and swtchd rt wl ins fnl f: no threat to ldrs* **9/2**[3]

62-1 **4** *1/2* **Mums The Word**[16] 424 3-8-13 **80**........................ TonyHamilton 5 75
(Richard Fahey) *chsd ldng pair tl 1/2-way: rdn 2f out: kpt on same pce u.p ins fnl f* **8/1**

5-45 **5** 2 **Chupalla**[24] 291 3-9-7 88 FrannyNorton 2 77
(Mark Johnston) *racd keenly early: chsd ldr: shkn up 2f out: edgd lft and unable qck u.p over 1f out: wknd ins fnl f* **20/1**

1m 11.24s (-0.66) **Going Correction** -0.05s/f (Stan) **5** Ran SP% **110.9**
Speed ratings (Par 101): **102,101,99,99,96**
CSF £4.90 TOTE £2.80: £1.50, £1.20; EX 4.50 Trifecta £8.40.
**Owner** The Hon R J Arculli **Bred** K Snell **Trained** Kimpton, Hants

**FOCUS**
A decent 3yo sprint handicap with three of the five successful last time out. It produced a stirring finish between the big two in the market. The third has been rated close to her recent 5f form.

## 679 32RED MEDIAN AUCTION MAIDEN STKS 5f 6y(P)
**2:35** (2:36) (Class 6) 3-Y-O **£2,264** (£673; £336; £168) **Stalls** High

Form RPR
2 **1** **Berryessa (IRE)**[24] 288 3-9-0 0 DavidProbert 7 65+
(Rae Guest) *trckd ldrs: clsd to chse ldr wl over 1f out: rdn to chal 1f out: drvn to ld and edgd lft ins fnl f: kpt on and pushed out towards fin* **5/4**[1]

502- **2** ½ **Mercers**[117] 7414 3-9-0 62 ShaneKelly 8 63
(Peter Crate) *taken down early: trckd ldrs: effrt 2f out: hdwy u.p on inner over 1f out: ev ch ins fnl f: styd on same pce wl ins fnl f* **8/1**

534- **3** ¾ **Sheila's Palace**[84] 8027 3-8-9 59 HollieDoyle(5) 2 60
(J S Moore) *sn led: rdn over 1f out: hdd and no ex ins fnl f: 3rd and keeping on same pce whn n.m.r wl ins fnl f* **7/1**[3]

**4** 1 ¾ **Jack The Truth (IRE)** 3-9-5 0 AdamKirby 4 59
(George Scott) *chsd ldr tl wl over 1f out: 4th and kpt on same pce ins fnl f* **15/8**[2]

0 **5** 9 **Akuna Mattatta (IRE)**[17] 397 3-9-5 0 TimmyMurphy 3 27
(Ralph J Smith) *s.i.s: a off the pce in rr* **66/1**

040- **6** hd **Snoozy Sioux (IRE)**[93] 7881 3-8-11 59 (h[1]) TimClark(3) 1 24
(Martin Smith) *rrd as stalls opened and slowly away: sn pushed into 5th but nvr really on terms: wknd fnl f* **16/1**

58.94s (0.14) **Going Correction** -0.05s/f (Stan) **6** Ran SP% **110.2**
Speed ratings (Par 95): **96,95,94,91,76 76**
CSF £11.57 TOTE £2.10: £1.10, £3.20; EX 8.60 Trifecta £18.20.
**Owner** RGRL Syndicate 2 **Bred** Samuel William Ormsby **Trained** Newmarket, Suffolk

**FOCUS**
A weak 3yo sprint maiden. The winner did not need to build on her debut level to take this. Ordinary form rated around the second and third.

## 680 SUNBETS.CO.UK H'CAP 1m 1y(P)
**3:10** (3:10) (Class 2) (0-105,100) 4-Y-0+
**£11,827** (£3,541; £1,770; £885; £442; £222) **Stalls** High

Form RPR
01-1 **1** **My Target (IRE)**[28] 235 6-9-4 97 ConnorBeasley 2 105+
(Michael Wigham) *stdd after s: hld up in 5th: effrt on outer wl over 1f out: rdn and hdwy 1f out: qcknd to ld ins fnl f: r.o wl: readily* **11/8**[1]

-412 **2** 1 ¼ **Intransigent**[14] 459 8-8-11 93 RobHornby(3) 4 98
(Andrew Balding) *broke wl: stdd to trck ldrs and t.k.h: nt clr run ent fnl 2f: effrt on inner over 1f out: rdn and ev ch jst ins fnl f: chsd wnr and kpt on same pce fnl 100yds* **5/1**[3]

10-1 **3** ¾ **Alfred Hutchinson**[35] 118 9-9-7 100 (p) AdamKirby 5 103
(David O'Meara) *led and set stdy gallop: rdn and qcknd 2f out: drvn and hdd ins fnl f: no ex and one pced after: eased nr fin* **11/4**[2]

10-0 **4** 1 **Presumido (IRE)**[14] 459 7-8-7 86 JFEgan 1 87
(Simon Dow) *stdd after s: hld up in tch in rr: effrt on inner over 1f out: chsd ldrs: edgd rt and kpt on same pce ins fnl f* **12/1**

00-2 **5** ¾ **Lunar Deity**[23] 304 8-8-1 87 MillyNaseb(7) 6 86
(Stuart Williams) *sn w ldr: rdn 2f out: unable qck and outpcd over 1f out: kpt on same pce ins fnl f* **11/1**

0-55 **6** 2 ½ **Captain Cat (IRE)**[14] 465 8-9-4 97 GeorgeDowning 3 91
(Tony Carroll) *s.i.s: sn rcvrd and in tch in 4th: swtchd rt and clsd to press ldrs 2f out: sn rdn and unable qck over 1f out: wknd ins fnl f* **9/1**

1m 37.99s (-0.21) **Going Correction** -0.05s/f (Stan) **6** Ran SP% **111.5**
Speed ratings (Par 109): **99,97,97,96,95 92**
CSF £8.56 TOTE £2.00: £1.80, £1.80; EX 8.20 Trifecta £16.40.
**Owner** G Linder, M Wigham & J Williams **Bred** Darley **Trained** Newmarket, Suffolk

**FOCUS**
A warm handicap despite the small field and a race for the old guard, with the six runners aged between six and nine. They didn't go a great pace, though, which makes the winner's performance all the more impressive. Muddling form rated around the second and third.

## 681 32RED.COM MAIDEN STKS 1m 1y(P)
**3:45** (3:48) (Class 5) 3-Y-O **£2,911** (£866; £432; £216) **Stalls** High

Form RPR
6-3 **1** **Cloud Dragon (IRE)**[28] 237 3-9-5 0 JosephineGordon 1 73
(Hugo Palmer) *t.k.h: mde all: shkn up over 1f out: clr 1f out: pushed along and a doing enough ins fnl f* **6/4**[2]

**2** nk **Long John Silver (IRE)** 3-9-5 0 AdamKirby 3 72+
(Jamie Osborne) *rn green: trckd ldrs tl wnt 2nd over 2f out: rdn and unable qck over 1f out: rn green: edgd lft but rallied ins fnl f: kpt on wl towards fin* **7/2**[3]

**3** 1 ½ **Royalistic (IRE)** 3-9-5 0 NickyMackay 7 71+
(John Gosden) *in tch in midfield: pushed along over 2f out: rn green and wnt wd bnd 2f out: looked wl hld in 4th 1f out: rallied ins fnl f: kpt on wl fnl 100yds: wnt 3rd last strides* **1/1**[1]

**4** nk **Accomplice** 3-9-0 0 DavidProbert 2 63
(Michael Blanshard) *s.i.s: rn green and pushed along early: clsd and wl in tch in 5th over 4f out: effrt in 3rd 2f out: kpt on same pce ins fnl f: lost 3rd last strides* **40/1**

**5** 11 **Mount Cleshar** 3-9-5 0 JackMitchell 5 43
(John Butler) *v.s.a: off the pce in last pair: wnt 6th over 3f out: lft modest 5th wl over 1f out: no imp* **25/1**

060- **6** 2 ¾ **Just Heather (IRE)**[203] 4663 3-9-0 37 WilliamCarson 8 32
(John Wainwright) *chsd wnr tl hung rt and lost 2nd over 2f out: hung rt and lost pl qckly bnd 2f out: sn wl btn* **50/1**

**7** 1 ¼ **Khaleefa Bay** 3-8-11 0 TimClark(3) 6 29
(Martin Smith) *in tch in midfield tl lost pl and rdn over 4f out: nvr on terms after: no ch fnl 2f* **50/1**

**8** ½ **Lady Maritime (IRE)** 3-8-11 0 AlistairRawlinson(3) 4 28
(Brett Johnson) *v.s.a: a bhd* **25/1**

1m 37.91s (-0.29) **Going Correction** -0.05s/f (Stan) **8** Ran SP% **126.3**
Speed ratings (Par 97): **99,98,97,96,85 83,81,81**
CSF £7.86 TOTE £2.60: £1.10, £1.40, £1.10; EX 8.30 Trifecta £12.20.
**Owner** Sun Bloodstock Sarl **Bred** Prostock Ltd **Trained** Newmarket, Suffolk

**FOCUS**
An uncompetitive 3yo maiden, but featuring a couple of interesting newcomers. Experience counted for plenty, however. It's been rated around the winner.

## 682 BETWAY BEST ODDS GUARANTEED PLUS H'CAP 6f 1y(P)
**4:20** (4:20) (Class 5) (0-75,77) 4-Y-0+ **£2,911** (£866; £432; £216) **Stalls** Low

Form RPR
-113 **1** **Born To Finish (IRE)**[8] 547 4-9-10 76 (p) MartinLane 1 80+
(Jeremy Gask) *dwlt: off the pce in 7th: effrt but stl plenty to do in 5th 2f out: gd hdwy to chse ldrs and swtchd lft ins fnl f: rdn to ld 75yds out: r.o wl* **4/5**[1]

00-0 **2** ¾ **Bertie Blu Boy**[7] 575 9-9-6 72 (b) JFEgan 6 73
(Lisa Williamson) *pressed ldr: kicked clr w ldr 2f out: rdn over 1f out: chsd wnr and kpt on u.p wl ins fnl f* **14/1**

0-06 **3** nk **Ballesteros**[21] 358 8-9-11 77 PaulHanagan 4 77
(Richard Fahey) *chsd ldrs: outpcd ent fnl 2f: swtchd rt and rallied over 1f out: chal u.p ins fnl f: kpt on same pce towards fin* **7/1**[3]

66-0 **4** 1 ¼ **Waneen (IRE)**[16] 416 4-8-13 72 DarraghKeenan(7) 5 68
(John Butler) *chsd ldng trio: outpcd ent fnl 2f: rallied 1f out: keeping on but nt threat to wnr whn n.m.r and swtchd rt wl ins fnl f* **25/1**

300- **5** hd **Panther Patrol (IRE)**[72] 8176 7-9-4 73 (b) EdwardGreatrex(3) 9 70+
(Eve Johnson Houghton) *off the pce towards rr of main gp: effrt and plenty to do 2f out: hdwy u.p jst over 1f out: keeping on but no threat to wnr whn nt clr run towards fin* **13/2**[2]

-510 **6** shd **Colourbearer (IRE)**[12] 480 10-9-3 69 (t) WilliamCarson 7 64
(Charlie Wallis) *taken down early: led: rdn and kicked clr w chalr 2f out: drvn over 1f out: hdd 75yds out: no ex and wknd towards fin* **20/1**

-000 **7** ¾ **King Of Swing**[8] 547 4-9-4 70 (h) ShaneKelly 2 63
(Richard Hughes) *t.k.h: midfield: hung rt and lost pl bnd 2f out: rallied ins fnl f: kpt on but no threat to ldrs* **7/1**[3]

00-0 **8** 8 **Something Lucky (IRE)**[38] 45 5-9-2 68 NickyMackay 3 35
(Daniel Steele) *sn dropped to last and detached: n.d* **16/1**

1m 11.86s (-0.04) **Going Correction** -0.05s/f (Stan) **8** Ran SP% **115.0**
Speed ratings (Par 103): **98,97,96,94,94 94,93,82**
CSF £14.33 CT £51.67 TOTE £1.70: £1.10, £3.50, £2.20; EX 12.90 Trifecta £50.80.
**Owner** Crowd Racing Partnership **Bred** B Kennedy & Mrs Ann Marie Kennedy **Trained** Stockbridge, Hants

**FOCUS**
An ordinary sprint handicap, but a decent pace and two held a clear advantage turning in before being run down. The third has been rated to his AW best.

## 683 BETWAY H'CAP 1m 4f (P)
**4:50** (4:50) (Class 4) (0-85,87) 4-Y-0+ **£4,690** (£1,395; £697; £348) **Stalls** Low

Form RPR
00-3 **1** **Afonso De Sousa (USA)**[14] 467 7-9-6 87 AlistairRawlinson(3) 6 95
(Michael Appleby) *hld up off the pce: clsd over 2f out: rdn to ld ent fnl f: styd on wl: rdn out* **11/4**[2]

0-04 **2** 1 ¼ **Silver Quay (IRE)**[14] 467 5-9-8 86 (p[1]) AdamKirby 1 92
(Jamie Osborne) *t.k.h: hld up off the pce: clsd over 2f out: swtchd rt and effrt over 1f out: hung lft but styd on ins fnl f: wnt 2nd towards fin: no threat to wnr* **9/4**[1]

53-3 **3** 1 **Mica Mika (IRE)**[35] 117 9-9-6 84 PaulHanagan 8 88
(Richard Fahey) *chsd clr ldng pair: clsd over 2f out: rdn and chal ent fnl f: chsd wnr and kpt on same pce ins fnl f: lost 2nd towards fin* **10/1**

5-62 **4** 1 ½ **Storm King**[9] 524 8-8-10 74 JosephineGordon 3 76
(David C Griffiths) *w ldr and sn clr: shkn up wl over 1f out: sn rdn and unable qck: kpt on same pce ins fnl f* **11/1**

10-4 **5** 6 **Ickymasho**[31] 173 5-9-0 83 MitchGodwin(5) 2 75
(Jonathan Portman) *t.k.h: led and clr w rival: rdn 2f out: hdd ent fnl f: sn btn and eased wl ins fnl f* **7/1**

6-45 **R** **Royal Marskell**[18] 389 8-9-7 85 ShaneKelly 5
(Gay Kelleway) *ref to r* **5/1**[3]

4/2- **P** **Injun Sands**[322] 1092 6-9-2 80 (h[1]) NickyMackay 7
(Jane Chapple-Hyam) *s.i.s: off the pce in rr: u.p and lost tch 7f out: p.u and dismntd 5f out* **10/1**

44/0 **P** **Aussie Andre**[14] 467 6-8-11 82 RhiainIngram(7) 4
(Roger Ingram) *chsd clr ldrs: rdn over 3f out: dropped to last and struggling 2f out: bhd whn p.u and dismntd ins fnl f* **40/1**

2m 29.2s (-3.80) **Going Correction** -0.05s/f (Stan) **8** Ran SP% **115.6**
Speed ratings (Par 105): **110,109,108,107,103 , ,**
CSF £9.50 CT £51.86 TOTE £3.90: £1.60, £1.50, £1.70; EX 11.40 Trifecta £53.70.
**Owner** Mick Appleby Racing **Bred** Monticule **Trained** Oakham, Rutland

**FOCUS**
A fair middle-distance handicap, but a strange race with one refusing to race and two being pulled up. Two soon went a long way clear and set it up for the closers. The third has been rated to his AW best.
T/Plt: £3.90 to a £1 stake. Pool: £66,261.90 - 1,2167.35 winning units T/Qpdt: £2.10 to a £1 stake. Pool: £3,614.52 - 1,258.93 winning units **Steve Payne**

# 598 WOLVERHAMPTON (A.W) (L-H)
Saturday, February 11

**OFFICIAL GOING: Tapeta: standard**
Wind: Light breeze Weather: Light mist, very cold

## 684 SUNBETS.CO.UK AMATEUR RIDERS' H'CAP 1m 142y (Tp)
**5:45** (5:46) (Class 6) (0-60,60) 4-Y-0+ **£2,651** (£822; £410; £205) **Stalls** Low

Form RPR
0-01 **1** **Gabrial The Thug (FR)**[19] 383 7-10-10 56 (t) MrSWalker 8 65
(Ian Williams) *trckd ldrs: hdwy 2f out: led fnl f: comf* **2/1**[1]

1213 **2** ¾ **Athassel**[12] 482 8-10-7 58 MrJFlook(5) 3 64
(David Evans) *mid-div: hdwy ent st: r.o wl ins fnl f* **9/4**[2]

604- **3** nse **Munaawib**[61] 8337 9-10-5 58 (bt) MissSPeacock(7) 7 64
(Ray Peacock) *keen: prom: led 4f out: hdd fnl f: rdn and no ex* **66/1**

4-00 **4** ¾ **Arcanista (IRE)**[12] 481 4-10-4 57 MrMSHarris(7) 9 62
(Richard Hughes) *hld up: hdwy 2f out: styd on wl ins fnl f* **25/1**

2-14 **5** 1 ¼ **Schottische**[5] 605 7-10-8 59 (b) MissJCooley(5) 1 62
(Alan Bailey) *mid div on inner: effrt 2f out: styd on one pce* **8/1**[3]

-450 **6** 1 **Powered (IRE)**[18] 390 4-10-3 54 MissEMacKenzie(5) 5 54
(David Evans) *hld up: rdn 2f out: styd on* **11/1**

120- **7** 2 **Blue Jacket (USA)**[245] 3153 6-11-0 60 MissEmmaSayer 4 56
(Dianne Sayer) *led 4f: remain prom tl wknd ent fnl f* **25/1**

046- **8** 1 ¼ **The Special One (IRE)**[152] 6408 4-10-8 57 (h[1]) MrJoshuaNewman(3) 10 50
(Ali Stronge) *hld up: u.p 2f out: nom imp* **33/1**


The Form Book Flat, Raceform Ltd, Newbury, RG14 5SJ

0-00 **9** *nk* **Steady Major (IRE)**[22] 333 5-10-11 **60**....... MissBeckyBrisbourne(3) 12 53
(Mark Brisbourne) *racd wd in rr: rdn and no hdwy fnl 2f* **22/1**

6-00 **10** *hd* **Bad Girl Caoimhe (IRE)**[15] 444 4-10-10 **59**...... MissBeckySmith(3) 11 51
(Marjorie Fife) *trckd ldrs: effrt st: one pce* **33/1**

300- **11** *½* **Sublimation (IRE)**[172] 5753 7-10-7 **60**...................... MissSATrotter(7) 13 51
(Steve Gollings) *racd wd: in rr: rdn 2f out and no hdwy* **33/1**

4-40 **12** *2¾* **Champagne Freddie**[29] 221 4-10-12 **58**........... MissBrodieHampson 2 43
(John O'Shea) *keen: prom: 3rd ent st: sn rdn and wknd* **8/1**[3]

00-0 **13** *48* **Heart Of An Angel**[14] 461 4-10-4 **55**..............(b) MrRomainClavreul(5) 6
(Henry Spiller) *v.s.a: rel to r: a wl bhd* **66/1**

1m 52.04s (1.94) **Going Correction** +0.075s/f (Slow) **13** Ran SP% **118.5**
Speed ratings (Par 101): **94,93,93,92,91 90,88,87,87,87 86,84,41**
CSF £5.78 CT £211.13 TOTE £2.80: £1.30, £1.30, £7.20; EX 7.90 Trifecta £275.40.
**Owner** Dr Marwan Koukash **Bred** Alain Plainfosse **Trained** Portway, Worcs

**FOCUS**
The track was cultivated to a depth of 3.5 inches, then reinstated with a Gallop Master finish. A moderate amateur riders' handicap in which it paid to race prominently. The runner-up has been rated to form.

## 685 SUNBETS.CO.UK H'CAP 7f 36y (Tp)
**6:15** (6:16) (Class 5) (0-75,76) 4-Y-0+ **£3,881** (£1,155; £577; £288) **Stalls** High

Form RPR

200- **1** **Tripartite (IRE)**[113] 7506 4-9-3 **71**....................................... LukeMorris 6 79+
(Jeremy Gask) *trckd ldr: led over 1f out: rdn and hld on wl* **11/2**[2]

3-43 **2** *½* **Magic City (IRE)**[9] 516 8-9-1 **72**.............................(p[1]) NathanEvans(3) 3 78
(Michael Easterby) *racd in 3rd: u.p and chsd wnr over 1f out: r.o wl ins fnl f* **5/2**[1]

3-21 **3** *nk* **Mehdi (IRE)**[10] 513 8-9-8 **76**...............................................(t) DavidNolan 1 81
(Richard Fahey) *mid-div: 5th st: sn pushed along and r.o wl ins fnl f* **13/2**

004- **4** *1½* **Clement (IRE)**[54] 8456 7-9-7 **75**.......................................... TimmyMurphy 4 76
(John O'Shea) *trckd ldrs: effrt and rdn 2f out: one pce fnl f* **18/1**

-114 **5** *nk* **Hamish McGonagain**[7] 575 4-8-13 **72**....................(p) DavidParkes(5) 9 72
(Jeremy Gask) *mid-div: rdn ent st: r.o ins fnl f* **10/1**

310- **6** *1* **Veeraya**[45] 8555 7-8-11 **65**.............................................(t) AdamBeschizza 2 63
(Julia Feilden) *mid-div: rdn over 1f out: styd on one pce* **16/1**

-320 **7** *½* **Athletic**[11] 501 8-8-8 **62**..................................................(v) AndrewMullen 10 58+
(David Evans) *in rr: rdn 2f out: sme late hdwy* **7/1**

-556 **8** *hd* **So It's War (FR)**[15] 441 6-9-1 **69**..........................(b[1]) ConnorBeasley 7 65
(Keith Dalgleish) *in rr on inner: rdn 2f out: no imp* **12/1**

00-6 **9** *hd* **Equally Fast**[36] 94 5-9-7 **75**.........................................(h) LiamKeniry 11 70
(Peter Hiatt) *led tl hdd over 1f out: rdn and wknd* **40/1**

06-0 **10** *1¾* **St Andrews (IRE)**[16] 419 4-8-9 **63**...........................(t) GeorgeDowning 8 53
(Ian Williams) *hld up: pushed along 2f out: nvr a factor* **40/1**

0-00 **11** *1¼* **Fleckerl (IRE)**[9] 516 7-9-4 **72**...................................(p) DougieCostello 12 59
(Conor Dore) *racd wd in rr: rdn and no hdwy st* **40/1**

-051 **12** *¾* **Masamah (IRE)**[11] 501 11-9-3 **71**...................................(h) GeorgeBaker 5 56
(Ian Williams) *prom tl lost pl 2f out: wknd* **6/1**[3]

1m 29.04s (0.24) **Going Correction** +0.075s/f (Slow) **12** Ran SP% **119.3**
Speed ratings (Par 103): **101,100,100,98,98 96,96,96,95,93 92,91**
CSF £19.47 CT £92.17 TOTE £6.50: £2.30, £1.50, £2.30; EX 20.70 Trifecta £125.50.
**Owner** The Salt House Syndicate **Bred** Tally-Ho Stud **Trained** Stockbridge, Hants

**FOCUS**
A modest handicap in which the each-way support for Tripartite proved accurate. It again proved hard to come from behind. The runner-up helps set the standard.

## 686 32RED.COM (S) STKS 7f 36y (Tp)
**6:45** (6:46) (Class 6) 3-Y-O **£2,749** (£818; £408; £204) **Stalls** High

Form RPR

5-64 **1** **Oakley Pride (IRE)**[9] 522 3-8-7 50...........................(vt[1]) CliffordLee(5) 2 66
(Gay Kelleway) *hld up in rr: hdwy ent st: pushed along and slipped through on ins to chal over 1f out: led fnl f: r.o wl u.p: comf* **33/1**

-560 **2** *3* **Lady Volante (IRE)**[1] 662 3-8-7 62................................... AndrewMullen 5 54
(David Evans) *trckd ldr: pushed along ent st: rdn and kpt on ins fnl fjurlong* **11/2**[3]

2-13 **3** *¾* **Peachey Carnehan**[15] 435 3-9-4 72..............................(v) LukeMorris 1 63
(Michael Attwater) *keen in mid-div: hdwy ent st: rdn and kpt on fnl f* **1/1**[1]

4-64 **4** *1¼* **Joyful Dream (IRE)**[15] 435 3-8-2 57..........................(p) HollieDoyle(5) 6 49
(J S Moore) *led tl rdn and hdd fnl f: one pce* **3/1**[2]

4-06 **5** *3¼* **Madam Prancealot (IRE)**[15] 435 3-8-7 55.............. AdamBeschizza 7 41
(David Evans) *in rr: hdwy u.p over 1f out: sn wknd* **14/1**

00-0 **6** *2¾* **Valley Lodge**[19] 376 3-8-9 50...............................(p) ShelleyBirkett(3) 3 39
(Julia Feilden) *trckd ldrs: pushed along 3f out: fdd* **50/1**

4-50 **7** *½* **Princess Way (IRE)**[15] 435 3-8-7 58......................... ConnorBeasley 4 33
(David Evans) *in rr: rdn along 3f out: no imp* **8/1**

1m 29.54s (0.74) **Going Correction** +0.075s/f (Slow) **7** Ran SP% **113.1**
Speed ratings (Par 95): **98,94,93,92,88 85,84**
.There was no bid for the winner. Peachey Carnehan was the subject of a friendly claim by Mr M. J. Attwater for £6,000.\n\x\x
**Owner** Brian C Oakley **Bred** Peter McCutcheon **Trained** Exning, Suffolk

**FOCUS**
A weak seller in which the favourite was entitled to win at the weights, but there was a shock winner. A much improved effort from the winner, but the form has been rated cautiously.

## 687 BETWAY MAIDEN STKS 1m 4f 51y (Tp)
**7:15** (7:15) (Class 5) 4-Y-O+ **£3,396** (£1,010; £505; £252) **Stalls** Low

Form RPR

**1** **Big Country (IRE)**[115] 7479 4-9-5 75................................. LukeMorris 1 81+
(Michael Appleby) *mid-div: smooth hdwy 3f out: wnt 2nd over 2f out: sn led: rdn clr: eased wl ins fnl f: easily* **4/5**[1]

0-23 **2** *7* **Ceyhan**[14] 457 5-9-8 79.................................................... GeorgeBaker 5 65
(Jamie Osborne) *led 5f: remained prom: 3rd st: rdn and styd on to take 2nd wl ins fnl f* **7/4**[2]

433- **3** *½* **Red Hot Chilly (IRE)**[91] 5895 4-9-5 72.......................... DavidProbert 3 64
(Dai Burchell) *chsd ldr: keen and racd awkwardly bef led after 5f: rdn and hdd over 2f out: one pce and lost 2nd cl home* **7/1**[3]

- **4** *½* **Lucky Gal**[10] 7-8-12 0..................................................(h) AliceMills(5) 2 58
(Martin Hill) *in rr: pushed along to go 4th ent st: rdn and styd on fnl 2f* **50/1**

**5** *4½* **Paris Bound**[24] 4-8-12 0............................................ JoshuaBryan(7) 4 56
(Andrew Balding) *hld up: rdn tl hdwy to go prom after 5f: pushed along 1/2-way: u.p 3f out: no rspnse* **25/1**

6 **6** *38* **Great Roar (USA)**[39] 29 9-9-8 0.................................(t) AndrewMullen 6
(Ronald Thompson) *4th early: lost pl and struggling 4f out: pushed along and grad lost tch* **100/1**

2m 38.29s (-2.51) **Going Correction** +0.075s/f (Slow)
**WFA** 4 from 5yo+ 2lb **6** Ran SP% **111.2**
Speed ratings (Par 103): **111,106,106,105,102 77**
CSF £2.36 TOTE £1.80: £1.30, £1.20; EX 2.90 Trifecta £4.50.
**Owner** The Horse Watchers **Bred** Mrs Jacqueline O'Brien **Trained** Oakham, Rutland

**FOCUS**
An uncompetitive maiden in which the favourite made easy work of it. There's some doubt the second and third ran to their marks.

## 688 BETWAY H'CAP 1m 4f 51y (Tp)
**7:45** (7:45) (Class 5) (0-75,72) 4-Y-O+ **£3,881** (£1,155; £577; £288) **Stalls** Low

Form RPR

5-13 **1** **Fast Play (IRE)**[11] 497 5-9-3 **69**................................(b) DougieCostello 9 79+
(Conor Dore) *hld up: hdwy over 2f out: led over 1f out: rdn and r.o strly: comf* **12/1**

/50- **2** *3* **Paddys Runner**[23] 1760 5-9-5 **71**......................................... LukeMorris 7 76
(Alan King) *trckd ldrs: rdn 2f out: chsd wnr fnl f: styd on* **2/1**[1]

-555 **3** *2¼* **Obboorr**[9] 526 8-9-3 **69**................................................... AndrewMullen 3 69
(James Given) *in rr: pushed along 4f out: rdn st: r.o wl ins fnl f* **15/2**

43-5 **4** *1* **Heart Locket**[15] 440 5-8-10 **69**...................................... HarrisonShaw(7) 2 68
(Michael Easterby) *mid-div: hdwy ent st: rdn 1f out: one pce* **7/2**[2]

13/0 **5** *3¼* **Instill**[19] 382 5-9-1 **70**........................................................ RobHornby(3) 1 64
(Mandy Rowland) *trckd ldrs: led over 2f out: hdd over 1f out: fdd* **12/1**

0-63 **6** *½* **The Lock Master (IRE)**[9] 524 10-8-11 **68**...............(p) DavidParkes(5) 6 61
(Michael Appleby) *trckd ldrs: pushed along over 2f out: sn rdn and wknd* **17/2**

0/0- **7** *2¾* **Mazaaher**[248] 3030 7-9-6 **72**.............................................. ConnorBeasley 5 60
(David Evans) *in rr: rdn st: nvr a factor* **66/1**

0-30 **8** *3¾* **Handsome Dan (IRE)**[16] 422 11-8-13 **68**...................... JackDuern(3) 8 50
(Sarah Hollinshead) *led: hdd and rdn over 2 out: wknd* **12/1**

642- **9** *8* **Dovils Date**[100] 5131 8-9-4 **70**........................................... DavidProbert 4 40
(Tim Vaughan) *hld up in rr: rdn 3f out: no imp* **7/1**[3]

2m 43.8s (3.00) **Going Correction** +0.075s/f (Slow) **9** Ran SP% **114.9**
Speed ratings (Par 103): **93,91,89,88,86 86,84,82,76**
CSF £36.19 CT £198.76 TOTE £9.60: £3.00, £1.20, £2.70; EX 44.30 Trifecta £210.40.
**Owner** Mrs Jennifer Marsh & Mrs Louise Marsh **Bred** Fintan Walsh **Trained** Hubbert's Bridge, Lincs

**FOCUS**
A moderate handicap in which they went only a steady gallop before it quickened in the back straight. Muddling form, but it's been rated at face value around the second and third.

## 689 BETWAY MIDDLE H'CAP (DIV I) 1m 1f 104y (Tp)
**8:15** (8:16) (Class 6) (0-60,62) 4-Y-O+ **£2,749** (£818; £408; £204) **Stalls** Low

Form RPR

-156 **1** **Outlaw Torn (IRE)**[4] 607 8-9-0 **53**............................(e) DougieCostello 7 58
(Richard Guest) *mde all: rdn ent fnl f: jst hld on u.p* **14/1**

100- **2** *hd* **Tulip Dress**[45] 8555 4-9-7 **60**........................................... WilliamCarson 4 65
(Anthony Carson) *hld up: hdwy 2f out: str run ins fnl f: jst hld* **22/1**

03-3 **3** *nk* **Suitsus**[28] 238 6-9-5 **58**................................................(t) TimmyMurphy 2 62
(Geoffrey Deacon) *mid-div: smooth hdwy over 2f out: rdn ins fnl f: r.o* **9/4**[1]

00-0 **4** *½* **Frap**[5] 605 4-9-2 **55**...................................................(h[1]) GeorgeDowning 12 58
(Ian Williams) *in rr: pushed along over 1f out: sn rdn and r.o* **20/1**

-640 **5** *nse* **Einstein**[12] 481 4-8-13 **57**............................................(t) DavidParkes(5) 5 60
(Mrs Ilka Gansera-Leveque) *mid-div: hdwy 2f out: rdn and no ex* **8/1**

06-0 **6** *1* **First Summer**[35] 122 5-9-1 **59**...............................(p) CharlieBennett(5) 13 60
(Shaun Harris) *hld up: pushed along ent st: kpt on* **20/1**

50-3 **7** *nk* **Cahar Fad (IRE)**[22] 334 5-8-9 **48**...........................(bt) AdamBeschizza 8 49
(Steph Hollinshead) *mid-div: rdn over 1f out: r.o but n.d* **6/1**

0-15 **8** *1¾* **Sir Lancelott**[16] 420 5-9-9 **62**.....................................(p) DanielTudhope 10 59
(David O'Meara) *hld up: hdwy 2f out: sn rdn and no ex* **4/1**[2]

3-53 **9** *1¼* **Vision Of Beauty (FR)**[16] 420 4-9-7 **60**.................(p[1]) ConnorBeasley 1 55
(Keith Dalgleish) *prom tl rdn and wknd st* **5/1**[3]

-005 **10** *1* **Palindrome (USA)**[9] 527 4-9-4 **57**.............................(p) AndrewMullen 11 50
(Ronald Thompson) *in rr: rdn sraight: no imp* **40/1**

600- **11** *¾* **Somepink (IRE)**[71] 8194 4-8-2 **46** oh1.............................. HollieDoyle(5) 3 38
(Daniel Mark Loughnane) *chsd wnr 2f: sn rdn and wknd* **100/1**

000- **12** *23* **Marmalad (IRE)**[215] 4200 5-9-7 **60**..................................... LukeMorris 6 8
(Shaun Lycett) *in rr: rdn 3f out: nvr a threat* **14/1**

0/-0 **13** *4½* **Valantino Oyster (IRE)**[31] 169 10-9-7 **60**.......................(p) LiamKeniry 9
(Ali Stronge) *trckd ldrs tl struggling 3f out: lost tch* **66/1**

2m 0.75s (-0.05) **Going Correction** +0.075s/f (Slow) **13** Ran SP% **125.0**
Speed ratings (Par 101): **103,102,102,102,102 101,100,99,98,97 96,76,72**
CSF £299.86 CT £963.99 TOTE £6.50: £3.30, £5.90, £1.50; EX 202.30 Trifecta £4056.30.
**Owner** R C Guest **Bred** Derek Veitch & Rory O'Brien **Trained** Ingmanthorpe, W Yorks

**FOCUS**
A moderate handicap in which the winner made all the running to hold on in a tight finish. Straightforward low-grade form, with the runner-up rated to her mark.

## 690 BETWAY MIDDLE H'CAP (DIV II) 1m 1f 104y (Tp)
**8:45** (8:45) (Class 6) (0-60,60) 4-Y-O+ **£2,749** (£818; £408; £204) **Stalls** Low

Form RPR

-534 **1** **Runaiocht (IRE)**[8] 549 7-9-2 **60**...............................(b) DavidParkes(5) 3 66
(Paul Burgoyne) *hld up: stl plenty to do 3f out: hdwy on ins 2f out: chal and hrd rdn 1f out: led cl home* **7/1**

120- **2** *nk* **Pensax Lady (IRE)**[47] 8527 4-9-1 **54**.................................. LukeMorris 2 59
(Daniel Mark Loughnane) *mid-div: hdwy into 3rd over 2f out: rdn and led over 1f out: ct cl home* **11/1**

0-30 **3** *2¼* **Glorious Asset**[16] 421 5-9-0 **58**................................ LewisEdmunds(5) 5 59
(Ivan Furtado) *hld up: pushed along and hdwy over 2f out: hrd drvn and styd on one pce* **13/2**[3]

30-6 **4** *1½* **Dovil's Duel (IRE)**[38] 49 6-9-3 **59**...................................... EoinWalsh(3) 4 59
(Tony Newcombe) *hld up last: pushed along and rn wd ent st: rdn and r.o wl fnl 2f* **16/1**

0404 **5** *2¼* **Ferryview Place**[16] 421 8-8-11 **50**.......................(vt) GeorgeDowning 7 44
(Ian Williams) *hld up: pushed along 3f out swtchd wd 2f out: styd on* **10/1**

30-0 **6** *1¼* **Hannington**[38] 49 6-9-7 **60**............................................ AndrewMullen 1 52
(Michael Appleby) *trckd ldrs: hdwy and pushed along to go 2nd ent st: rdn over 2f out: one pce* **16/1**

/5-1 **7** *4½* **Royal Blessing**[22] 334 5-9-4 **57**.......................................(b) LiamKeniry 8 40
(Peter Fahey, Ire) *mid-div: rdn over 1f out: no imp* **6/4**[1]

24-5 **8** *1½* **Monna Valley**[32] 162 5-9-4 **60**.......................................... AaronJones(3) 6 40
(Stuart Williams) *chsd ldrs: rdn st: btn over 1f out* **9/2**[2]

6-26 **9** 1 1/4 **Lutine Charlie (IRE)**[8] 544 10-8-1 47 (p) JordanUys(7) 9 25
(Emma Owen) *in tch: rdn over 2f out: wknd* **33/1**
00U6 **10** 1/2 **Sheer Intensity (IRE)**[4] 608 4-9-3 56 (v) ConnorBeasley 11 33+
(David Evans) *pushed along into early ld: 2 l clr ent st: rdn and hdd over 1f out: wknd qckly* **25/1**
6-00 **11** 7 **Herculian Prince**[29] 214 5-9-7 60 (p) DougieCostello 12 24
(Conor Dore) *s.i.s: a in rr* **100/1**
54-0 **12** 16 **Ifan (IRE)**[16] 421 9-9-5 58 (p) DavidProbert 10
(Tim Vaughan) *prom tl lost pl and wknd qckly 2f out* **33/1**
2m 0.19s (-0.61) **Going Correction** +0.075s/f (Slow) **12** Ran SP% **123.9**
Speed ratings (Par 101): **105,104,102,101,99 98,94,92,91,91 85,70**
CSF £82.90 CT £537.24 TOTE £8.30: £2.20, £3.40, £2.50; EX 88.60 Trifecta £588.50.
**Owner** Knowle Rock Racing **Bred** J S Bolger **Trained** Shepton Montague, Somerset

**FOCUS**
The second division of this handicap in which they went a quicker gallop, resulting in a faster time. The winner has been rated in keeping with his best previous form, with the runner-up to her mark.
T/Plt: £87.00 to a £1 stake. Pool: £104,106.01 - 873.32 winning units T/Qpdt: £44.00 to a £1 stake. Pool: £8,024.94 - 134.80 winning units **Keith McHugh**

# [584] CAGNES-SUR-MER
Saturday, February 11

**OFFICIAL GOING: Polytrack: standard**

## 691a PRIX GROUPE CAVALLARI KIA (PRIX CHARLES DU BREIL) (CLAIMER) (4YO+) (GENTLEMEN RIDERS) (POLYTRACK) 1m 4f
**1:50** 4-Y-0+ **£6,410** (£2,564; £1,923; £1,282; £641)

RPR
**1** **Polo (GER)**[291] 7-10-12 0 (b) MrHugoBoutin 2 63
(R Chotard, France) **5/2**[1]
**2** shd **Special Request (FR)**[10] 515 10-11-0 0 MrFlorentGuy 12 65
(N Caullery, France) **7/2**[2]
**3** 3 **Uphold**[21] 364 10-10-11 0 (b) MrRBirkett 6 57
(Gay Kelleway) *wl away: disp ld early: settled 2nd: dropped to 4th 6f out: remained handy: pushed along over 2f out: drvn and styd on one pce fnl f* **77/1**
**4** snk **Solmen (FR)**[229] 3733 9-10-8 0 MrKevinBraye 7 54
(M Krebs, France) **75/1**
**5** nk **Fantastic Love (FR)**[277] 8-11-0 0 (b) MrGuilainBertrand 8 59
(J-M Capitte, France) **114/10**
**6** 6 1/2 **Gondaro (GER)** 4-11-3 0 (p) MrDamienArtu 1 55
(Frau C Barsig, Germany) **77/10**
**7** 1/2 **Ston (IRE)**[482] 7327 5-10-11 0 MrAlexandreLemarie 5 45
(Simone Brogi, France) **22/5**[3]
**8** 3/4 **Attention Baileys (FR)**[475] 7-10-11 0 MrEMonfort 9 44
(P Monfort, France) **168/10**
**9** 1 1/2 **Jadala (FR)**[36] 4-10-13 0 MrRubensSeror 10 47
(K Borgel, France) **25/1**
**10** nk **Kashani (IRE)**[10] 515 4-10-9 0 MrJonathanPlassard 11 42
(Frau C Barsig, Germany) **77/1**
**11** 6 **Raphaelus (FR)**[1711] 10-10-8 0 (p) MrSylvainMaussion 3 28
(P Khozian, France) **34/1**
**F** **Vesper (GER)**[10] 515 7-10-4 0 MrJean-PhilippeBoisgontier 4
(J-M Lefebvre, France) **13/2**

PARI-MUTUEL (all including 1 euro stake): WIN 3.50; PLACE 1.60, 1.70, 9.90; DF 7.80; SF 15.90.
**Owner** Mme Caroline Petit **Bred** Gestut Etzean **Trained** France

692 - 693a (Foreign Racing) - See Raceform Interactive

# [649] MEYDAN (L-H)
Saturday, February 11

**OFFICIAL GOING: Turf: good; dirt: fast**

## 694a THE TRACK MEYDAN GOLF (H'CAP) (DIRT) 6f (D)
**3:05** (3:05) (95-108,108) 3-Y-0+ **£60,975** (£20,325; £10,162; £5,081; £3,048; £2,032)

RPR
**1** **Comicas (USA)**[44] 8578 4-8-9 98 (b) WilliamBuick 3 102
(Charlie Appleby) *sn led: rdn clr 3f out: r.o wl* **11/2**
**2** 1 **Dundonnell (USA)**[24] 296 7-9-6 108 (h) ChristopheSoumillon 5 110
(C Fownes, Hong Kong) *trckd ldrs: ev ch 2f out: r.o same pce fnl f* **6/1**
**3** 4 1/2 **Shaishee (USA)**[9] 539 7-8-11 100 (v) JimCrowley 1 86
(M Al Mheiri, UAE) *chsd ldrs: r.o same pce fnl 2f* **8/1**
**4** 1/2 **Main Stay (KOR)**[23] 321 4-8-13 101 (e) PatCosgrave 6 87
(Kim Young Kwan, Korea) *slowly away: nvr nr to chal but r.o fnl 2f* **11/4**[1]
**5** 3/4 **Indianapolis (USA)**[23] 321 6-8-6 95 (bt) RichardMullen 9 77
(S Seemar, UAE) *nvr bttr than mid-div* **20/1**
**6** nk **Beachy Head (IRE)**[22] 345 6-8-10 99 (t) TadhgO'Shea 7 80
(A R Al Rayhi, UAE) *nvr bttr than mid-div* **33/1**
**7** 1/2 **Acolyte (IRE)**[28] 250 5-8-6 95 HarryBentley 2 75
(Saeed bin Suroor) *nvr bttr than mid-div* **5/1**[3]
**8** 6 1/4 **Breakdancer (FR)**[104] 4-8-7 96 FernandoJara 10 56
(Fredrik Reuterskiold, Sweden) *nvr nr to chal* **25/1**
**9** nse **Fabulous One (NZ)**[24] 296 5-9-3 105 (t) OisinMurphy 4 66
(W Y So, Hong Kong) *trckd ldr tl outpcd fnl 2 1/2f* **3/1**[2]
**10** shd **Saving Kenny (IRE)**[90] 7-8-6 95 (t) Per-AndersGraberg 8 54
(Roy Arne Kvisla, Sweden) *nvr nr to chal* **25/1**
1m 11.78s (0.18) **Going Correction** +0.325s/f (Slow) **10** Ran SP% **124.5**
Speed ratings: **111,109,103,103,102 101,100,92,92,92**
CSF: 39.22; TRICAST: 273.06.
**Owner** Godolphin **Bred** Darley **Trained** Newmarket, Suffolk

**FOCUS**
TRAKUS (metres travelled compared to winner): 2nd +8, 3rd -4, 4th +11, 5th 0, 6th +7, 7th +2, 8th +11, 9th +5, 10th +7. The winner made just about all through sensible fractions: 24.51, 23.46, 23.81. The runner-up helps set the standard.

## 695a FIREBREAK STKS SPONSORED BY MEYDAN ONE MALL (GROUP 3) (DIRT) 1m (D)
**3:40** (3:40) 3-Y-0+ **£97,560** (£32,520; £16,260; £8,130; £4,878; £3,252)

RPR
**1** **North America**[30] 204 5-9-0 106 (t) RichardMullen 2 115+
(S Seemar, UAE) *trckd ldr: led 4f out: r.o wl: easily* **9/4**[2]
**2** 7 **Ennobled Friend (USA)**[22] 345 7-9-0 100 (bt) ColmO'Donoghue 3 99
(A bin Harmash, UAE) *settled in rr: smooth prog to chse ldr 2 1/2f out: r.o fnl 2f but no ch w wnr* **40/1**
**3** 3 1/4 **Lindo Amor (ARG)**[9] 541 4-9-0 106 ChristopheSoumillon 1 92
(M F De Kock, South Africa) *a mid-div* **10/1**
**4** 1 1/2 **Heavy Metal**[16] 432 7-9-0 104 MickaelBarzalona 4 88
(S bin Ghadayer, UAE) *mid-div: chsd ldr 2 1/2f out: wknd fnl f* **8/1**
**5** 8 3/4 **Desert Force**[30] 206 5-9-0 108 PatDobbs 8 68
(Doug Watson, UAE) *sn led: hdd 4f out: sn btn* **4/1**[3]
**6** 11 **Surfer (USA)**[401] 92 8-9-0 112 (t) PatCosgrave 6 43
(S Seemar, UAE) *nvr nr to chal* **11/1**
**7** 26 **Nabbaash**[23] 320 6-9-0 97 BReis 5
(R Bouresly, Kuwait) *s.i.s: a in rr* **150/1**
**8** 13 **Confrontation (USA)**[322] 1105 7-9-0 113 (t) JimCrowley 7
(Saeed bin Suroor) *trckd ldng pair tl wknd 3 1/2f out* **7/4**[1]
1m 36.51s (-0.99) **Going Correction** +0.325s/f (Slow) **8** Ran SP% **118.8**
Speed ratings: **117,110,106,105,96 85,59,46**
CSF: 82.10.
**Owner** Imhamed M I Nagem **Bred** Qatar Bloodstock Ltd **Trained** United Arab Emirates

**FOCUS**
TRAKUS (metres travelled compared to winner): 2nd +12, 3rd +1, 4th +7, 5th +6, 6th +14, 7th +5, 8th +12. They went a proper pace early on but nothing could live with the winner, who sustained his challenge to record a smart time: 24.71, 22.93, 24.97, 24.36. The level is a bit fluid and hangs on the winner.

## 696a BAB AL SHAMS DESERT RESORT AND SPA (H'CAP) (TURF) 6f
**4:15** (4:15) (100-110,110) 3-Y-0+ **£85,365** (£28,455; £14,227; £7,113; £4,268; £2,845)

RPR
**1** **Final Venture**[16] 433 5-9-4 108 (h) PatDobbs 1 112
(Paul Midgley) *chsd ldr: led 2f out: r.o wl* **4/1**[2]
**2** 3/4 **Fityaan**[9] 543 9-9-3 107 (v) JimCrowley 3 109
(M Al Mheiri, UAE) *mid-div: r.o wl fnl 2f: nrst fin* **12/1**
**3** 2 1/2 **Polybius**[9] 543 6-8-11 102 OisinMurphy 8 95
(David Simcock) *nvr bttr than mid-div* **10/1**
**4** shd **Steady Pace**[16] 433 4-9-1 105 (p) HarryBentley 6 99
(Saeed bin Suroor) *s.i.s: mid-div: r.o same pce fnl 2f* **4/1**[2]
**5** 1/2 **Naadirr (IRE)**[2] 651 6-9-1 105 (p) ColmO'Donoghue 9 97
(Marco Botti) *nvr able to chal* **14/1**
**6** 1 **Log Out Island (IRE)**[224] 3909 4-9-5 109 WilliamBuick 5 98
(Charlie Appleby) *sn led: hdd 2f out: r.o same pce* **7/2**[1]
**7** 1 1/2 **Magnus Maximus**[9] 543 6-9-2 106 MartinHarley 2 90
(Robyn Brisland) *trckd ldr tl outpcd fnl 2 1/2f* **8/1**
**8** nk **Dream Dubai**[23] 318 4-8-10 101 ow1 PatCosgrave 7 83
(M F De Kock, South Africa) *nvr nr to chal* **25/1**
**9** 8 1/4 **The Happy Prince (IRE)**[30] 206 5-9-6 110 (t) ChristopheSoumillon 4 67
(James Moore, Macau) *chsd ldrs: wknd rapidly 2f out* **5/1**[3]
1m 9.62s (0.62) **Going Correction** +0.40s/f (Good) **9** Ran SP% **117.3**
Speed ratings: **111,110,106,106,105 104,102,102,91**
CSF: 51.62; TRICAST: 456.01.
**Owner** Taylor's Bloodstock Ltd **Bred** Newsells Park Stud **Trained** Westow, N Yorks

**FOCUS**
Rail on turf track out 12 metres. A good sprint handicap in which the main action unfolded far side. The first two help set the standard.

## 697a UAE 2000 GUINEAS SPONSORED BY DISTRICT ONE MOHAMMED BIN RASHID AL MAKTOUM CITY (GROUP 3) (DIRT) 1m (D)
**4:50** (4:50) 3-Y-0 **£121,951** (£40,650; £20,325; £10,162; £6,097; £4,065)

RPR
**1** **Thunder Snow (IRE)**[104] 7721 3-9-0 116 ChristopheSoumillon 5 115+
(Saeed bin Suroor) *trckd ldr: led 4f out: r.o wl: easily* **6/4**[1]
**2** 5 3/4 **Bee Jersey (USA)**[30] 201 3-9-0 87 (t) SamHitchcott 9 100
(Doug Watson, UAE) *mid-div: chsd wnr 3f out: r.o same pce fnl 1 1/2f* **20/1**
**3** 3 3/4 **Capezzano (USA)**[44] 8574 3-9-0 93 WilliamBuick 6 91
(Charlie Appleby) *sn led: hdd 4f out: r.o same pce fnl 2 1/2f* **10/3**[3]
**4** 1 1/2 **Qatar Man (IRE)**[87] 7977 3-9-0 80 (b) HarryBentley 7 88
(Marco Botti) *nvr bttr than mid-div* **33/1**
**5** 1 **Han Sense (USA)**[35] 3-9-0 96 FernandoJara 2 85
(M Al Mheiri, UAE) *nvr bttr than mid-div* **33/1**
**6** 4 1/4 **Cosmo Charlie (USA)**[16] 430 3-9-0 107 PatDobbs 4 76
(Doug Watson, UAE) *nvr bttr than mid-div* **5/2**[2]
**7** 2 3/4 **Victor Kalejs (USA)**[16] 430 3-9-0 90 (t) Per-AndersGraberg 3 69
(Roy Arne Kvisla, Sweden) *nvr nr to chal* **100/1**
**8** 19 **Best Solution (IRE)**[16] 430 3-9-0 111 AdriedeVries 8 26
(Saeed bin Suroor) *nvr bttr than mid-div* **7/1**
**9** 5 **Silent Assassin (IRE)**[16] 430 3-9-0 82 RichardMullen 1 14
(S Seemar, UAE) *nvr nr to chal* **50/1**
1m 38.48s (0.98) **Going Correction** +0.325s/f (Slow) **9** Ran SP% **117.7**
Speed ratings: **108,102,98,97,96 91,89,70,65**
CSF: 36.86.
**Owner** Godolphin **Bred** Darley **Trained** Newmarket, Suffolk

**FOCUS**
TRAKUS (metres travelled compared to winner): 2nd +10, 3rd +5, 4th 0, 5th 0, 6th +3, 7th 0, 8th +7, 9th -2. The front-running winner covered the first 800m in a time 0.28sec faster than North America in the earlier older-horse Group 3, which was unsustainable, so a fast-slow pace scenario: 24.76, 22.6, 25.1, 26.02.

## 698a ZABEEL FEEDMILL (H'CAP) (TURF) 1m
**5:25** (5:25) (95-105,105) 3-Y-0+

**£60,975** (£20,325; £10,162; £5,081; £3,048; £2,032)

RPR

1 **Bravo Zolo (IRE)**[122] 7292 5-9-5 **104** WilliamBuick 11 107
(Charlie Appleby) *trckd ldr: led 2 1/2f out: r.o wl: comf* **6/4**[1]

2 1 1/2 **Suyoof (AUS)**[315] 4-9-5 **104** JimCrowley 13 104+
(M F De Kock, South Africa) *s.i.s: settled in rr: r.o wl fnl 2f: nrst fin* **14/1**

3 nk **Diferent Dimension (USA)**[30] 204 5-8-13 **98** (b) AdriedeVries 5 97
(Peter Wolsley, Korea) *trckd ldng pair tl wknd fnl 3f* **33/1**

4 shd **Belgian Bill**[9] 542 9-9-1 **100** PatCosgrave 9 99
(George Baker) *trckd ldng pair: ev ch 1 1/2f out: r.o same pce fnl f* **5/1**[2]

5 nk **Dragon Mall (USA)**[23] 320 4-9-5 **104** (h) MartinHarley 12 102
(David Simcock) *settled in rr: nvr able to chal but r.o wl fnl 1 1/2f* **7/1**[3]

6 1 3/4 **Ijmaaly (IRE)**[14] 474 5-8-13 **98** (p) DaneO'Neill 6 92
(A R Al Rayhi, UAE) *s.i.s: nvr able to chal* **33/1**

7 shd **General Macarthur (USA)**[30] 205 4-8-13 **98** SamHitchcott 1 92
(David Simcock) *nvr bttr than mid-div* **25/1**

8 nk **Hasanour (USA)**[23] 322 7-8-11 **97** (tp) TadhgO'Shea 2 89
(M Halford, Ire) *mid-div: chsd ldrs 3f out: one pce fnl 2f* **33/1**

9 2 **Tupi (IRE)**[161] 6117 5-9-6 **105** PatDobbs 8 94
(Richard Hannon) *nvr bttr than mid-div* **5/1**[2]

10 shd **Tumbaga (USA)**[16] 432 6-9-1 **100** HarryBentley 4 89
(Saeed bin Suroor) *trckd ldng pair tl wknd fnl 2 1/2f* **14/1**

11 1 **Muwaary (AUS)**[9] 538 4-8-13 **98** AntonioFresu 3 84
(M F De Kock, South Africa) *nvr bttr than mid-div* **33/1**

12 3/4 **Epsom Icon**[9] 542 4-9-6 **105** OisinMurphy 7 90
(Mick Channon) *nvr nr to chal* **40/1**

13 3/4 **Silent Attack**[30] 205 4-9-1 **100** (p) ColmO'Donoghue 14 83
(Saeed bin Suroor) *sn led: hdd 2 1/2f out: sn btn* **14/1**

14 2 3/4 **Cornwallville (IRE)**[30] 205 5-8-13 **98** BenCurtis 10 75
(Roger Fell) *nvr bttr than mid-div* **20/1**

1m 36.47s (-1.03) **Going Correction** +0.125s/f (Good) **14** Ran SP% **128.6**
Speed ratings: **110,108,108,108,107 106,105,105,103,103 102,101,101,98**
CSF: 27.52; TRICAST: 586.65.
**Owner** Godolphin **Bred** Tipper House Stud **Trained** Newmarket, Suffolk

**FOCUS**
Rail on turf track out 12 metres. TRAKUS (metres travelled compared to winner): 2nd +2, 3rd -1, 4th +4, 5th -2, 6th 0, 7th -5, 8th 0, 9th +3, 10th -5, 11th -4, 12th +4, 13th -4, 14th +6. You won't get a much more evenly run race than this: 25.23 (standing start), 23.63, 23.63, 23.98.

## 699a THE MEYDAN HOTEL (H'CAP) (TURF) 1m 4f 38y(T)
**6:00** (6:00) (95-114,114) 3-Y-0+

**£78,048** (£26,016; £13,008; £6,504; £3,902; £2,601)

RPR

1 **Prize Money**[16] 428 4-9-6 **114** (h) AdriedeVries 14 117
(Saeed bin Suroor) *settled in rr: smooth prog 3f out: rdn to ld fnl f: styd on* **7/2**[3]

2 nk **Rembrandt Van Rijn (IRE)**[16] 428 6-8-13 **105** (b) MickaelBarzalona 13 107
(S bin Ghadayer, UAE) *settled in rr: nvr nr to chal but r.o fnl 1 1/2f: nrst fin* **12/1**

3 hd **Dylan Mouth (IRE)**[9] 542 6-9-4 **110** AntonioFresu 3 112
(Marco Botti) *trckd ldr: led 3f out: hdd fnl f but r.o* **3/1**[2]

4 1 1/4 **Kidmenever (IRE)**[161] 6153 4-8-9 **104** ow2 ColmO'Donoghue 4 104
(Charlie Appleby) *mid-div: r.o same pce fnl 2f: nrst fin* **14/1**

5 shd **Carbon Dating (IRE)**[9] 540 5-8-8 **101** TadhgO'Shea 10 100
(S Seemar, UAE) *mid-div: r.o fnl 2f: nrst fin* **18/1**

6 3/4 **Los Barbados (IRE)**[9] 540 5-8-8 **101** ow2 (b) GeraldAvranche 1 98
(Fawzi Abdulla Nass, Bahrain) *sn led: hdd 2f out: wknd fnl f* **16/1**

7 hd **Basateen (IRE)**[30] 208 5-9-1 **107** JimCrowley 11 105
(Doug Watson, UAE) *nvr nr to chal: r.o fnl 2f* **8/1**

8 nk **Majeed**[16] 428 7-8-10 **103** ow1 MartinHarley 9 100
(David Simcock) *nvr nr to chal but r.o fnl 2f* **14/1**

9 1/2 **Busker (USA)**[16] 428 9-8-10 **103** ow1 (t) PatCosgrave 7 99
(A bin Harmash, UAE) *nvr bttr than mid-div* **50/1**

10 1 1/2 **Dormello (IRE)**[9] 542 9-9-0 **106** ChrisHayes 2 100
(D Selvaratnam, UAE) *nvr nr to chal* **40/1**

11 7 1/4 **Viren's Army (IRE)**[281] 1994 4-8-9 **104** WilliamBuick 6 87
(Charlie Appleby) *nvr bttr than mid-div* **5/2**[1]

12 4 **Fog Of War**[23] 319 6-8-5 **98** HarryBentley 8 73
(Saeed bin Suroor) *nvr bttr than mid-div* **12/1**

13 10 1/2 **Nolohay (IRE)**[22] 345 6-8-6 **98** ow1 (v) FernandoJara 12 58
(M Al Mheiri, UAE) *nvr bttr than mid-div* **40/1**

14 34 **Saltarin Dubai (ARG)**[9] 542 4-9-0 **106** ow1...(b) ChristopheSoumillon 5 11
(M F De Kock, South Africa) *s.i.s: a in rr* **40/1**

2m 31.32s (-0.48) **Going Correction** +0.125s/f (Good)
**WFA** 4 from 5yo+ 2lb **14** Ran SP% **136.0**
Speed ratings: **106,105,105,104,104 104,104,103,103,102 97,95,88,65**
CSF: 51.50; TRICAST: 152.63; PLACEPOT: 253.50. Pool of 6044.70 - 27.80 winning units. QUADPOT: 26.40. Pool of 503.50 - 21.80 winning units.
**Owner** Godolphin **Bred** Darley **Trained** Newmarket, Suffolk

**FOCUS**
Rail on turf track out 12 metres. TRAKUS (metres travelled compared to winner): 2nd -9, 3rd -13, 4th -14, 5th -5, 6th -16, 7th -2, 8th -6, 9th -17, 10th -13, 11th -5, 12th +4, 13th +13, 14th +2. The pace really picked up in the penultimate section, 26.18 (400m), 24.82 (800m), 25.16 (1200m), 25.11 (1600m), 23.82 (2000m), before the winner finished in 25.85.

700 - 712a (Foreign Racing) - See Raceform Interactive

# 691 CAGNES-SUR-MER
Sunday, February 12

**OFFICIAL GOING: Polytrack: standard**

## 713a PRIX DES CAGNOIS (H'CAP) (4YO+) (POLYTRACK) 6f 110y
**3:20** 4-Y-0+ **£7,264** (£2,905; £2,179; £1,452; £726)

RPR

1 **Daring Storm (GER)**[58] 7-9-1 **0** (b) MlleAlisonMassin(3) 4 63
(P Hern, France) **76/10**

2 1/2 **Qaboos (FR)**[16] 4-9-5 **0** (b) ChristopheSoumillon 8 63
(F Chappet, France) **83/10**

3 1 **Bernina Range (FR)**[36] 5-9-2 **0** Pierre-CharlesBoudot 2 57
(J-M Lefebvre, France) **7/5**[1]

4 nk **My Approach (IRE)**[36] 7-9-6 **0** (p) TonyPiccone 6 60
(Robert Collet, France) **99/10**

5 hd **Montalban (FR)**[74] 10-8-11 **0** (b) RaphaelMarchelli 5 51
(D De Waele, France) **59/10**[2]

6 2 **Tiberio (SPA)**[48] 7-8-10 **0** (p) StephanePasquier 10 44
(F-X Belvisi, France) **28/1**

7 3/4 **Majik Charly (FR)**[55] 5-9-2 **0** (b) JeromeMoutard(3) 13 51
(T Castanheira, France) **67/10**[3]

8 nse **Onirique (IRE)**[48] 6-9-3 **0** (b) MrHugoBoutin 12 49
(M Boutin, France) **81/1**

9 1 **Magic Mc Henry (IRE)**[36] 4-8-13 **0** (b) PierreBazire 7 42
(Mme G Rarick, France) **33/1**

10 1 1/4 **Minminwin (IRE)**[19] 391 4-9-6 **0** (b) IoritzMendizabal 1 45
(Gay Kelleway) *dwlt: sn racing in midfield: drvn and no imp 2f out: one pce fnl f: wl hld whn eased late on* **51/1**

11 2 1/2 **Adona (FR)**[96] 4-9-5 **0** AntoineHamelin 11 37
(J Parize, France) **269/10**

12 4 **Dobby First (FR)**[41] 4-8-10 **0** (p) MaximeGuyon 3 16
(Mlle V Dissaux, France) **187/10**

PARI-MUTUEL (all including 1 euro stake): WIN 8.60; PLACE 2.60, 2.50, 1.50; DF 40.70; SF 112.90.
**Owner** Ecurie Villebadin **Bred** Gestut Auenquelle **Trained** France

# ST MORITZ (R-H)
Sunday, February 12

**OFFICIAL GOING: Snow: frozen**

## 714a PREIS WHITE TURF JOCKEY CLUB ST MORITZ (CONDITIONS) (4YO+) (SNOW) 1m
**10:30** 4-Y-0+

**£3,333** (£1,666; £1,190; £793; £396; £238)

RPR

1 **Eric (GER)**[140] 6-9-8 0 AlexanderPietsch 3
(C Von Der Recke, Germany) **33/10**[1]

2 1 3/4 **Oriental Ghost (GER)** 5-8-11 0 TimBurgin(5) 5
(Dagmar Geissmann, Switzerland)

3 3 **Kontrast (IRE)** 4-9-11 0 VaclavJanacek 2
(M Weiss, Switzerland)

4 1/2 **Zyrjann (IRE)**[238] 5-8-0 0 NadiaBurger(7) 8
(Meret Kaderli, Switzerland)

5 5 **Berrahri (IRE)**[26] 277 6-10-3 0 KierenFox 4
(John Best) *led: drvn whn pressed 1/2-way: hdd 3f out: grad dropped away*

6 1 1/4 **Dancing Diamond (GER)** 5-9-3 0 RaphaelLingg 1
(P Schaerer, Switzerland)

7 3 **Ajasam**[966] 3512 6-9-11 0 DennisSchiergen 6
(M Weiss, Switzerland)

8 10 **Zryw (POL)** 5-9-0 0 BauyrzhanMurzabayev 7
(Robert Swiatek, Poland)

1m 53.54s **8** Ran SP% **23.3**

**Owner** Frau Gabriele Inge Gaul **Bred** Frau Gabriele Inge Gaul **Trained** Weilerswist, Germany

## 715a GROSSER PREIS WROCLAWSKI TOR WYSCIGOW KONNYCH (CONDITIONS) (4YO+) (SNOW) 6f 110y
**11:00** 4-Y-0+

**£6,000** (£3,000; £2,142; £1,428; £714; £428)

RPR

1 **Filou (SWI)**[518] 6-9-4 0 RaphaelLingg 4
(P Schaerer, Switzerland) **9/5**[1]

2 1 3/4 **Footprintinthesand (IRE)**[357] 663 7-9-0 0 (p) VaclavJanacek 2
(M Weiss, Switzerland)

3 6 **Holidayend (IRE)** 5-9-4 0 DennisSchiergen 3
(M Weiss, Switzerland)

4 9 **Ferro Sensation (GER)**[638] 11-9-4 0 SonjaDaroszewski 5
(C Von Der Recke, Germany)

5 1 1/4 **Zarras (GER)**[357] 663 8-9-6 0 DanielePorcu 1
(P Schaerer, Switzerland)

6 8 **Gung Ho Jack**[46] 8561 8-9-0 0 KierenFox 6
(John Best) *racd in fnl trio: drvn 1/2-way but no imp: wl hld fnl f*

7 4 **Uczitelka Tanca (POL)** 6-9-1 0 BauyrzhanMurzabayev 7
(M Borkowski, Poland)

**Owner** R & M Gunthardt **Bred** Fritz Von Ballmoos **Trained** Switzerland

## 716a GROSSER PREIS LONGINES (CONDITIONS) (4YO+) (SNOW) 1m 1f
**1:15** 4-Y-0+

**£6,666** (£3,333; £2,380; £1,587; £793; £476)

RPR

1 **Soundtrack (IRE)**[140] 6-9-8 0 DanielePorcu 2
(P Schaerer, Switzerland) **13/2**[1]

2 5 **Fabrino (IRE)**[272] 2318 9-9-2 0 DennisSchiergen 1
(M Weiss, Switzerland)

3 nk **Los Cerritos (SWI)**[25] 282 5-9-0 0 AlexanderPietsch 3
(Oliver Greenall) *chsd ldrs: clsd into 3rd 1/2-way: drvn to ld over 2f out: rdn and hdd ent fnl f: kpt on gamely: fin 2nd: plcd 3rd*

4 3 1/2 **Eddystone Rock (IRE)**[18] 396 5-9-6 0 KierenFox 8
(John Best) *led: scrubbed along and hdd over 2f out: plugged on at one pce*

5 nk **Red Hot Calypso (IRE)**[161] 6-9-2 0 MichaelCadeddu 4
(Dr A Bolte, Germany)

6 3 **Erato (GER)**[678] 6-9-2 0 MaximPecheur 6
(Karin Suter-Weber, Switzerland)

7 nk **Sing With Bess (IRE)**[272] 2318 6-9-3 0 VaclavJanacek 5
(M Weiss, Switzerland)
8 5 **Sleeping Giant (GER)**[721] 660 7-9-0 0 RaphaelLingg 7
(P Schaerer, Switzerland)
2m 13.28s 8 Ran SP% 13.3
**Owner** Stall Engelberg **Bred** Wardley Bloodstock **Trained** Switzerland

# 684 WOLVERHAMPTON (A.W) (L-H)
Monday, February 13

**OFFICIAL GOING: Tapeta: standard**
Wind: Fresh half-against Weather: Fine

## 717 32RED CASINO MAIDEN FILLIES' STKS 1m 142y (Tp)
**2:20** (2:21) (Class 5) 3-Y-0+ **£2,911** (£866; £432; £216) **Stalls** Low

Form RPR
5- 1 **Flood Warning**[61] 8361 3-8-5 0 LukeMorris 2 76
(Clive Cox) *mde all: set stdy pce tl qcknd over 2f out: shkn up and edgd lft over 1f out: r.o wl* **11/8**[1]
2 2 **Shankara (IRE)** 3-8-5 0 JosephineGordon 6 71
(David Simcock) *a.p: chsd wnr over 1f out: sn swtchd rt: styd on* **13/8**[2]
22- 3 4 **Sea Dweller**[53] 8491 4-9-12 0 WilliamCarson 7 67
(Anthony Carson) *chsd wnr: rdn over 2f out: hung lft and lost 2nd over 1f out: styd on same pce* **7/2**[3]
0 4 6 **Navajo Star (IRE)**[10] 545 3-8-5 0 AndrewMullen 4 48
(Michael Appleby) *chsd ldrs: rdn over 2f out: wknd over 1f out* **50/1**
06 5 2 **Penny Poet (IRE)**[12] 504 4-9-12 0 LiamKeniry 5 49
(Neil Mulholland) *s.i.s: hld up: rdn: edgd lft and wknd wl over 1f out* **40/1**
6 17 **Toolatetodelegate** 3-8-2 0 EdwardGreatrex(3) 1 5
(Brian Barr) *s.i.s: a in rr: bhd fr 1/2-way* **150/1**
1m 53.97s (3.87) **Going Correction** +0.025s/f (Slow)
**WFA** 3 from 4yo 21lb 6 Ran SP% 107.5
Speed ratings (Par 100): **83,81,77,72,70 55**
CSF £3.51 TOTE £2.30: £1.40, £1.40; EX 4.50 Trifecta £6.90.
**Owner** Cheveley Park Stud **Bred** New England Myriad Stanley & Cheveley Pk **Trained** Lambourn, Berks

**FOCUS**
An uncompetitive fillies' maiden but fair enough form. The third has been rated close to form.

## 718 32RED.COM H'CAP 1m 1f 104y (Tp)
**2:50** (2:52) (Class 5) (0-70,70) 3-Y-0 **£2,911** (£866; £432; £216) **Stalls** Low

Form RPR
2255 1 **Things Happen**[9] 578 3-9-5 68 (v) AdamKirby 1 71
(David Evans) *prom: lost pl after 1f: hdwy u.p over 2f out: nt clr run sn after: led over 1f out: drvn out* **6/1**
0-66 2 ¾ **Knightsbridge Liam (IRE)**[14] 479 3-8-4 56 oh2 NathanEvans(3) 7 57
(Michael Easterby) *hld up: hdwy over 1f out: r.o* **33/1**
0-63 3 1½ **Mayflair**[26] 283 3-8-13 67 MitchGodwin(5) 3 65
(Jonathan Portman) *chsd ldrs: led over 2f out: rdn and hdd over 1f out: styd on same pce ins fnl f* **16/1**
01-2 4 hd **Haraka (IRE)**[18] 417 3-9-6 69 (b) RichardKingscote 6 67
(Ralph Beckett) *chsd ldrs: rdn and ev ch over 1f out: styd on same pce ins fnl f* **9/4**[1]
255- 5 ¾ **Scarlet Thrush (IRE)**[55] 8465 3-9-1 69 (h[1]) DavidParkes(5) 8 65
(Marco Botti) *hld up in tch: rdn and lost pl over 3f out: hdwy over 1f out: styd on same pce fnl f* **11/1**
00-4 6 2 **Mikey Ready (USA)**[23] 354 3-9-6 69 (t) ThomasBrown 4 62+
(Ed Walker) *hld up: racd keenly: hdwy over 1f out: no ex ins fnl f* **7/2**[2]
00-2 7 1¼ **My Rosie (IRE)**[35] 144 3-9-7 70 (b) LukeMorris 5 59
(John Gosden) *jnd ldr after 1f tl settled into 2nd pl over 6f out: rdn and ev ch over 1f out: wknd ins fnl f* **4/1**[3]
046- 8 34 **Shee's Lucky**[48] 8537 3-9-5 68 JoeFanning 2
(Mark Johnston) *sn led: hdd over 2f out: sn wknd and eased* **8/1**
2m 1.01s (0.21) **Going Correction** +0.025s/f (Slow) 8 Ran SP% 115.5
Speed ratings (Par 97): **100,99,98,97,97 95,94,64**
CSF £165.19 CT £2975.62 TOTE £7.50: £1.90, £5.30, £3.30; EX 224.80 Trifecta £1827.80.
**Owner** Paul & Clare Rooney **Bred** R Kent & D Evans **Trained** Pandy, Monmouths

**FOCUS**
A modest handicap. A small pb from the winner, with the third rated close to her maiden form.

## 719 BETWAY MIDDLE H'CAP 1m 1f 104y (Tp)
**3:20** (3:20) (Class 4) (0-85,87) 4-Y-0+ **£4,690** (£1,395; £697; £348) **Stalls** Low

Form RPR
3-26 1 **Dutch Uncle**[28] 266 5-9-7 83 GeorgeBaker 2 91
(Ed Dunlop) *led 1f: chsd ldrs: nt clr run over 2f out: swtchd rt over 1f out: led ins fnl f: sn rdn and edgd lft: r.o* **3/1**[1]
123- 2 1½ **Final**[181] 5520 5-9-7 83 JoeFanning 3 88
(Mark Johnston) *hld up: hdwy and nt clr run over 1f out: sn swtchd rt: r.o to go 2nd nr fin* **13/2**
442- 3 hd **Toga Tiger (IRE)**[48] 8539 10-9-4 80 RichardKingscote 1 84
(Daniel Mark Loughnane) *hld up: hdwy over 1f out: sn rdn styd on same pce wl ins fnl f* **15/2**
60-0 4 2½ **Spes Nostra**[21] 381 9-8-13 75 (b) PJMcDonald 5 74
(Iain Jardine) *led over 8f out: rdn and hdd wl over 1f out: no ex ins fnl f* **11/1**
3-15 5 ¾ **House Of Commons (IRE)**[25] 306 4-9-0 79 AlistairRawlinson(3) 4 77
(Michael Appleby) *chsd ldrs: rdn over 2f out: nt clr run over 1f out: hmpd sn after: styd on same pce* **4/1**[2]
-255 6 hd **Marshgate Lane (USA)**[25] 304 8-9-11 87 (p) AdamKirby 7 84
(Neil Mulholland) *prom: chsd ldr over 6f out tl rdn to ld wl over 1f out: hdd ins fnl f: wknd towards fin* **6/1**
3314 7 1 **Pivotman**[11] 517 9-8-13 78 (bt) NathanEvans(3) 8 73
(Michael Easterby) *hld up: rdn over 1f out: wknd ins fnl f* **5/1**[3]
040- 8 6 **Freud (FR)**[197] 4927 7-9-3 79 (t[1]) GeorgeDowning 6 61
(Ian Williams) *hld up: rdn and wknd over 1f out* **50/1**
1m 59.86s (-0.94) **Going Correction** +0.025s/f (Slow) 8 Ran SP% 111.3
Speed ratings (Par 105): **105,103,103,101,100 100,99,94**
CSF £21.59 CT £127.35 TOTE £4.40: £2.50, £2.00, £2.10; EX 19.50 Trifecta £105.20.
**Owner** The Hon R J Arculli **Bred** Cheveley Park Stud Ltd **Trained** Newmarket, Suffolk
■ Stewards' Enquiry : Joe Fanning caution: careless riding

**FOCUS**
A fair handicap. The winner has been rated to his best and the third close to form.

## 720 BETWAY H'CAP 1m 1f 104y (Tp)
**3:50** (3:50) (Class 2) (0-105,97) 4-Y-0+
**£11,827** (£3,541; £1,770; £885; £442; £222) **Stalls** Low

Form RPR
14-0 1 **Pactolus (IRE)**[32] 199 6-8-13 92 (t) AaronJones(3) 3 98
(Stuart Williams) *hld up: hdwy over 1f out: rdn and hung lft ins fnl f: r.o to ld nr fin* **11/2**[3]
0-61 2 ½ **Winterlude (IRE)**[19] 396 7-9-7 97 DavidNolan 4 102
(Jennie Candlish) *chsd ldrs: n.m.r over 1f out: rdn to ld and edgd lft ins fnl f: hdd nr fin* **6/1**
1-15 3 shd **Coillte Cailin (IRE)**[19] 396 7-9-4 94 DanielTudhope 2 99
(David O'Meara) *sn prom: rdn and ev ch ins fnl f: r.o: carried lft towards fin* **4/1**[2]
-131 4 ½ **Sennockian Star**[16] 467 7-9-0 90 JoeFanning 8 94
(Mark Johnston) *chsd ldr over 7f out: led wl over 1f out: sn edgd lft: rdn and hdd ins fnl f: styd on* **3/1**[1]
5 1 **Vettori Rules**[106] 4-9-6 96 LukeMorris 7 98
(Gay Kelleway) *s.i.s: hld up: rdn over 2f out: swtchd lft over 1f out: hdwy sn after: nt rch ldrs* **16/1**
52-3 6 ½ **Perfect Cracker**[28] 266 9-9-0 90 AdamKirby 1 91
(Clive Cox) *plld hrd and prom: shkn up over 1f out: styd on same pce wl ins fnl f* **4/1**[2]
23-6 7 shd **John Reel (FR)**[23] 352 8-8-13 96 KatherineGlenister(7) 6 96
(David Evans) *sn led: hdd wl over 1f out: styd on same pce ins fnl f* **10/1**
50-2 8 10 **Pearl Nation (USA)**[14] 478 8-9-4 94 (h) AndrewMullen 5 73
(Michael Appleby) *hld up: wknd over 1f out* **25/1**
2m 0.31s (-0.49) **Going Correction** +0.025s/f (Slow) 8 Ran SP% 113.5
Speed ratings (Par 109): **103,102,102,102,101 100,100,91**
CSF £37.58 CT £145.18 TOTE £7.30: £2.10, £1.90, £1.50; EX 46.00 Trifecta £206.40.
**Owner** T W Morley & Mrs J Morley **Bred** Tom McDonald **Trained** Newmarket, Suffolk

**FOCUS**
A decent handicap, although lacking in unexposed types. Muddling form. The winner has been rated as running a pb and the runner-up to form.

## 721 BETWAY MARATHON H'CAP 2m 120y (Tp)
**4:20** (4:20) (Class 6) (0-60,61) 4-Y-0+ **£2,264** (£673; £336; £168) **Stalls** Low

Form RPR
5-34 1 **Dream Serenade**[31] 218 4-8-8 49 (h) LukeMorris 7 54
(Michael Appleby) *sn chsng ldr: led over 3f out: rdn clr over 1f out: styd on* **6/1**
5-33 2 1¼ **Delagoa Bay (IRE)**[30] 241 9-9-5 59 MitchGodwin(5) 5 63
(Sylvester Kirk) *hld up: hdwy over 1f out: styd on to go 2nd wl ins fnl f* **11/1**
060/ 3 nk **Ascendant**[15] 7866 11-9-8 57 LiamKeniry 3 60
(Johnny Farrelly) *hld up: swtchd rt over 4f out: rdn over 3f out: hdwy over 2f out: hung lft ins fnl f: styd on* **11/4**[2]
0/05 4 2 **Anton Dolin (IRE)**[18] 423 9-8-10 50 (be) PhilDennis(5) 1 51
(Michael Mullineaux) *led: hdd over 3f out: sn rdn: styd on same pce ins fnl f* **66/1**
02-2 5 nk **Lineman**[38] 98 7-9-6 58 (b) JackDuern(3) 4 58
(Sarah Hollinshead) *hld up: rdn over 3f out: styd on fr over 1f out: edgd lft ins fnl f: nt trble ldrs* **11/2**[3]
50-4 6 1¾ **Yorkshireman (IRE)**[6] 610 7-8-10 45 (b) PaddyAspell 6 43
(Lynn Siddall) *chsd ldrs: rdn over 3f out: n.m.r and no ex ins fnl f* **14/1**
4-11 7 5 **Miss Dusky Diva (IRE)**[30] 241 5-9-12 61 MartinHarley 8 53
(David W Drinkwater) *hld up: hdwy to join ldr over 3f out tl rdn over 2f out: wknd ins fnl f* **6/4**[1]
14/0 8 17 **Fennann**[14] 141 6-9-12 61 (b) TimmyMurphy 2 33
(Natalie Lloyd-Beavis) *chsd ldrs tl wknd over 3f out* **100/1**
3m 42.36s (-1.34) **Going Correction** +0.025s/f (Slow)
**WFA** 4 from 5yo+ 4lb 8 Ran SP% 113.8
Speed ratings (Par 101): **104,103,103,102,102 101,99,91**
CSF £67.62 CT £220.56 TOTE £6.80: £1.70, £2.20, £1.50; EX 55.40 Trifecta £197.30.
**Owner** Tykes And Terriers Racing Club **Bred** Judith Jones **Trained** Oakham, Rutland
■ Stewards' Enquiry : Martin Harley jockey said mare ran too free; vert reported a routine examination failed to reveal any abnormalities

**FOCUS**
A moderate staying handicap. A little step up from the winner, with the runner-up rated to form.

## 722 BETWAY SPRINT H'CAP (DIV I) 5f 21y (Tp)
**4:50** (4:52) (Class 6) (0-55,56) 4-Y-0+ **£2,264** (£673; £336; £168) **Stalls** Low

Form RPR
0/4- 1 **Times In Anatefka (IRE)**[17] 447 7-8-12 46 oh1 (tp) MartinHarley 1 54
(Adrian Brendan Joyce, Ire) *trckd ldrs: rdn to ld wl ins fnl f: r.o* **11/4**[2]
04-0 2 ¾ **Give Us A Belle (IRE)**[5] 622 8-8-13 47 (vt) AdamBeschizza 4 52
(Christine Dunnett) *led: rdn: edgd rt and hdd wl ins fnl f: styd on same pce* **12/1**
35-2 3 nk **Dandilion (IRE)**[28] 271 4-9-7 55 (t) AdamKirby 8 59+
(Alex Hales) *hld up: shkn up over 1f out: r.o ins fnl f: nt rch ldrs* **9/4**[1]
2-45 4 2¼ **Chandresh**[28] 270 4-8-12 46 (v) LukeMorris 9 42
(Robert Cowell) *chsd ldr: rdn over 1f out: edgd rt and no ex ins fnl f* **16/1**
0-00 5 ½ **Pull The Pin (IRE)**[25] 311 8-8-9 46 (t) RobHornby(3) 3 40
(Mandy Rowland) *prom: rdn over 1f out: styd on same pce fnl f* **33/1**
20-3 6 1 **Kodimoor (IRE)**[34] 153 4-8-13 52 (bt) DavidParkes(5) 11 43
(Christopher Kellett) *hld up: sme hdwy over 1f out: edgd lft ins fnl f: nt trble ldrs* **8/1**
/0-6 7 ½ **Irvine Lady (IRE)**[16] 464 4-9-1 54 CliffordLee(5) 2 43
(Gay Kelleway) *mid-div: pushed along 1/2-way: rdn over 1f out: no ex ins fnl f* **12/1**
60-0 8 1¾ **Molly Jones**[24] 327 8-9-3 51 JohnFahy 6 34
(Matthew Salaman) *hld up: shkn up over 1f out: edgd lft fnl f: nvr trbld ldrs* **40/1**
0021 9 ¾ **Swendab (IRE)**[5] 622 9-9-8 56 6ex (b) TimmyMurphy 7 36
(John O'Shea) *half-rrd s: hld up: sme hdwy over 1f out: wknd ins fnl f* **4/1**[3]
0-00 10 ¾ **Just Over**[16] 455 4-8-9 46 oh1 (p[1]) EoinWalsh(3) 5 23
(Robert Cowell) *s.i.s: sn pushed along to chse ldrs: rdn over 1f out: wknd fnl f* **100/1**
1m 2.11s (0.21) **Going Correction** +0.025s/f (Slow) 10 Ran SP% 116.2
Speed ratings (Par 101): **99,97,97,93,92 91,90,87,86,85**
CSF £35.19 CT £87.34 TOTE £3.60: £1.50, £3.30, £1.30; EX 35.70 Trifecta £129.80.
**Owner** Thomas M Kelly **Bred** John Griffin **Trained** Athlone, Co Roscommon

**FOCUS**
The first division of a moderate sprint handicap. The third has been rated a bit below her recent form.

## 723 BETWAY SPRINT H'CAP (DIV II) 5f 21y (Tp)
**5:20** (5:21) (Class 6) (0-55,55) 4-Y-0+ **£2,264** (£673; £336; £168) **Stalls** Low

Form RPR
0-20 **1** **Teepee Time**[16] 455 4-8-7 **46**........................ PhilDennis(5) 4 53
(Michael Mullineaux) *chsd ldr: shkn up over 1f out: led ins fnl f: jst hld on* **16/1**
64-6 **2** *hd* **Frank The Barber (IRE)**[31] 215 5-9-6 **54**..............(t) AdamBeschizza 3 60
(Steph Hollinshead) *trckd ldrs: rdn to chse wnr wl ins fnl f: r.o* **7/2**[2]
355- **3** *¾* **Dream Ally (IRE)**[48] 8542 7-9-3 **51**....................(be) LukeMorris 5 54
(John Weymes) *hld up: hdwy and nt clr run fr over 1f out tl wl ins fnl f: r.o wl* **5/2**[1]
0-10 **4** *hd* **Lady Bacchus**[17] 446 4-9-7 **55**......................(b) ConnorBeasley 9 58
(Richard Guest) *s.s: hld up: hdwy over 1f out: sn rdn: r.o* **4/1**[3]
5-05 **5** *½* **Lizzy's Dream**[5] 622 9-9-0 **48**........................ PJMcDonald 2 49
(Rebecca Bastiman) *chsd ldrs: swtchd rt over 1f out: sn rdn: styd on* **9/2**
2-60 **6** *2 ¼* **Whispering Wolf**[17] 446 4-8-12 **46** oh1.................... TomEaves 1 39
(Suzzanne France) *led: rdn over 1f out: hdd and no ex ins fnl f* **17/2**
20-0 **7** *3 ¼* **Warm Order**[28] 271 6-8-12 **46** oh1.................... GeorgeDowning 7 27
(Tony Carroll) *chsd ldrs: rdn and edgd rt 1/2-way: wknd ins fnl f* **22/1**
065- **8** *1 ¼* **Rat Catcher (IRE)**[255] 2856 7-8-6 **47**................(p) JordanUys(7) 8 23
(Lisa Williamson) *s.s: nvr on terms* **28/1**
30-0 **9** *4 ½* **Edith Weston**[28] 271 4-8-12 **46** oh1..............(p) JosephineGordon 6 6
(Robert Cowell) *s.s: a bhd* **20/1**

1m 2.21s (0.31) **Going Correction** +0.025s/f (Slow) **9** Ran SP% **117.9**
Speed ratings (Par 101): **98,97,96,96,95 91,86,84,77**
CSF £71.22 CT £193.66 TOTE £21.50: £5.40, £1.60, £1.90; EX 82.70 Trifecta £448.00.
**Owner** G Cornes **Bred** Brook Stud Bloodstock Ltd **Trained** Alpraham, Cheshire

**FOCUS**
The second leg of a moderate sprint. Straightforward form rated around the principals.

## 724 SUNBETS.CO.UK H'CAP 7f 36y (Tp)
**5:50** (5:52) (Class 6) (0-60,66) 4-Y-0+ **£2,264** (£673; £336; £168) **Stalls** High

Form RPR
/23- **1** **Bounty Pursuit**[250] 3009 5-9-0 **56**..............(h) AlistairRawlinson(3) 5 64
(Michael Appleby) *chsd ldr tl led over 1f out: edgd lft ins fnl f: rdn out* **13/2**[2]
0-51 **2** *1* **Siege Of Boston (IRE)**[5] 620 4-9-13 **66** 6ex..............(t) AdamKirby 9 72
(John Butler) *hld up: hdwy over 1f out: rdn to chse wnr ins fnl f: r.o* **4/6**[1]
30-0 **3** *2* **Raise The Game (IRE)**[37] 127 4-9-1 **59**.................. RyanWhile(5) 8 60
(Bill Turner) *hld up: rdn over 2f out: r.o ins fnl f: nt rch ldrs* **66/1**
00-0 **4** *2* **Blackthorn Stick (IRE)**[16] 468 8-8-13 **57**..........(p) DavidParkes(5) 6 53
(Paul Burgoyne) *hld up in tch: rdn over 2f out: edgd lft and styd on same pce ins fnl f* **14/1**
4425 **5** *nk* **Wink Oliver**[5] 620 5-8-12 **58**....................(p) LauraCoughlan(7) 11 53
(Jo Hughes) *s.s: hld up: r.o ins fnl f: nrst fin* **8/1**
2-43 **6** *¾* **Keene's Pointe**[24] 332 7-9-7 **60**...................... AdamBeschizza 7 53
(Steph Hollinshead) *hld up: edgd lft and styd on fr over 1f out: nvr trbld ldrs* **14/1**
0-02 **7** *½* **Doeadeer (IRE)**[34] 161 4-9-6 **59**.....................(b) ConnorBeasley 3 51
(Keith Dalgleish) *hld up: racd keenly: hdwy u.p over 1f out: nt trble ldrs* **14/1**
000- **8** *nk* **El Tel**[174] 435 5-9-2 **60**.......................... HollieDoyle(5) 2 51
(Shaun Harris) *hld up: rdn over 2f out: nvr on terms* **80/1**
/20- **9** *1 ½* **Declamation (IRE)**[65] 8316 7-9-4 **57**.................. RobertWinston 1 45
(Alistair Whillans) *led: hdd over 1f out: edgd rt and wknd ins fnl f* **15/2**[3]
00-0 **10** *1 ¼* **Rising Sunshine (IRE)**[7] 605 4-9-0 **53**..............(b) LukeMorris 12 45
(Milton Bradley) *chsd ldrs: rdn over 2f out: hmpd ins fnl f: eased* **33/1**
320- **11** *2* **Cooperess**[111] 7602 4-9-3 **56**...................... TimmyMurphy 4 36
(John O'Shea) *chsd ldrs tl wknd over 1f out* **33/1**
4-60 **12** *1* **Humour (IRE)**[11] 521 6-9-0 **53**....................(v[1]) LiamKeniry 10 30
(Christine Dunnett) *hld up: nvr on terms* **33/1**

1m 27.83s (-0.97) **Going Correction** +0.025s/f (Slow) **12** Ran SP% **127.7**
Speed ratings (Par 101): **106,104,102,100,99 99,98,98,96,95 92,91**
CSF £11.80 CT £319.28 TOTE £8.50: £2.30, £1.10, £14.70; EX 17.20 Trifecta £739.30.
**Owner** C L Bacon **Bred** Cecil And Miss Alison Wiggins **Trained** Oakham, Rutland

**FOCUS**
Another moderate handicap but a good race for the level. The runner-up has been rated near his better figures.
T/Jkpt: Not Won. T/Plt: £762.00 to a £1 stake. Pool: £91,035.82 - 87.21 winning units T/Qpdt: £45.30 to a £1 stake. Pool: £9,898.56 - 161.55 winning units **Colin Roberts**

725 - (Foreign Racing) - See Raceform Interactive

# 655 NEWCASTLE (A.W) (L-H)
Tuesday, February 14

**OFFICIAL GOING: Tapeta: standard**
Wind: Moderate behind Weather: Grey cloud

## 726 BETWAY APPRENTICE H'CAP 1m 4f 98y (Tp)
**2:10** (2:10) (Class 6) (0-65,65) 4-Y-0+ **£3,234** (£962; £481; £240) **Stalls** High

Form RPR
600- **1** **Life Knowledge (IRE)**[42] 8400 5-8-6 **52**.................. PaulaMuir(7) 1 60
(Patrick Holmes) *hld up in rr: stdy hdwy 4f out: cl up on inner over 2f out: led wl over 1f out: sn rdn and kpt on strly* **4/1**[3]
60/3 **2** *3 ¼* **Pour L'Amour (IRE)**[35] 164 4-9-0 **63**.................. TobyEley(7) 8 66
(Daniel Mark Loughnane) *in tch: hdwy over 4f out: cl up over 3f out: chal on outer over 2f out and ev ch: rdn wl over 1f out: drvn and kpt on same pce fnl f* **7/1**
014- **3** *6* **Lady Turpin (IRE)**[209] 4522 4-8-6 **53**.............. NatalieHambling(5) 3 47
(Richard Fahey) *chsd clr ldr: clsd up over 4f out: led over 3f out: jnd and rdn over 2f out: hdd wl over 1f out: sn drvn and kpt on one pce* **9/2**
0-53 **4** *½* **Paddy's Rock (IRE)**[19] 414 6-8-9 **51**.................. JoshDoyle(3) 6 44
(Lynn Siddall) *t.k.h: hld up in rr: hdwy over 4f out: chsd ldrs 3f out: rdn along over 2f out: sn drvn and no imp* **5/2**[1]
400- **5** *14* **Prairie Impulse**[16] 4314 4-8-10 **57**.................. RowanScott(5) 4 29
(Rebecca Menzies) *trckd ldng pair: hdwy over 4f out: cl up over 3f out: rdn along wl over 2f out: sn wknd* **14/1**
50/6 **6** *37* **Thorntoun Care**[13] 509 6-9-9 **65**.................. CliffordLee(3) 2 +
(Iain Jardine) *rdn along s: sn led and clr: pushed along over 4f out: sn jnd and rdn: hdd over 3f out: sn lost pl and bhd* **3/1**[2]

2m 40.38s (-0.72) **Going Correction** +0.225s/f (Slow)
**WFA** 4 from 5yo+ 2lb **6** Ran SP% **110.9**
Speed ratings (Par 101): **111,108,104,104,95 70**
CSF £29.81 CT £123.79 TOTE £5.40: £3.00, £3.80; EX 33.80 Trifecta £133.80.
**Owner** Mrs C M Clarke, Foulrice Park Racing Ltd **Bred** Patrick Ryan **Trained** Middleham, N Yorks

**FOCUS**
The leader went off miles too fast and it was set up for one of the closers. The winner has been rated to his best.

## 727 BETWAY BEST ODDS GUARANTEED PLUS CLASSIFIED STKS 1m 2f 42y (Tp)
**2:40** (2:40) (Class 5) 4-Y-0+ **£5,175** (£1,540; £769; £384) **Stalls** High

Form RPR
415- **1** **Thello**[46] 8586 5-8-11 63.................. LewisEdmunds(5) 7 75
(Garry Moss) *prom: hdwy on outer 3f out: led wl over 1f out and sn rdn: drvn ins fnl f: edgd lft and hld on gamely towards fin* **7/2**[2]
0-00 **2** *nk* **Restive (IRE)**[24] 363 4-9-1 70.................. (h[1]) TomEaves 11 74
(Iain Jardine) *hld up: hdwy 3f out: rdn to chal over 1f out: drvn and ev ch ins fnl f: no ex nr fin* **10/1**
23-1 **3** *nse* **Taopix**[13] 509 5-9-2 70.................. LukeMorris 8 74+
(Karen McLintock) *hld up in tch: hdwy 3f out: chsd ldrs 2f out: rdn and n.m.r over 1f out: swtchd lft and drvn ins fnl f: n.m.r on inner: kpt on wl towards fin* **3/1**[1]
00-5 **4** *2 ¾* **Melabi (IRE)**[34] 169 4-9-1 68.................. PaulMulrennan 13 69
(Richard Ford) *hld up towards rr: hdwy 3f out: chsd ldrs 2f out: sn rdn and swtchd rt jst over 1f out: drvn and kpt on fnl f* **20/1**
4-32 **5** *¾* **Roman De Brut (IRE)**[22] 382 5-8-11 68.................. CharlieBennett(5) 10 67
(Daniel Mark Loughnane) *trckd ldrs: hdwy and cl up 3f out: rdn along 2f out: drvn jst over 1f out: grad wknd* **8/1**
35-0 **6** *1 ¼* **Shadow Spirit**[14] 497 4-8-8 68.................. JamieGormley(7) 1 65
(Iain Jardine) *hld up towards rr: hdwy over 3f out: swtchd lft to inner and effrt over 2f out: n.m.r and swtchd rt over 1f out: kpt on fnl f* **20/1**
004- **7** *1* **Muqarred (USA)**[67] 8286 5-9-2 66.................. ConnorBeasley 2 63
(Roger Fell) *hld up towards rr: hdwy over 3f out: swtchd lft to inner and rdn along 2f out: sn no imp* **12/1**
062- **8** *shd* **Optima Petamus**[9] 8142 5-8-9 68.................. (p) PaulaMuir(7) 3 62
(Patrick Holmes) *hld up in rr: sme hdwy on outer over 2f out: sn rdn and nvr nr ldrs* **33/1**
0605 **9** *1* **Hydrant**[5] 636 11-8-9 54.................. BenSanderson(7) 6 60
(Richard Guest) *led: rdn along and jnd over 3f out: hdd 2f out: sn drvn and grad wknd* **125/1**
-032 **10** *1 ¾* **Gabrial The Terror (IRE)**[8] 603 7-9-2 70..............(v[1]) PaulHanagan 9 57
(Ian Williams) *dwlt: a rr* **9/1**
24-5 **11** *½* **Tifl**[24] 354 4-9-1 69.................. OisinMurphy 4 56
(Heather Main) *prom: trckd ldr 1/2-way: cl up 3f out: rdn to ld briefly 2f out: sn hdd and drvn: wknd appr fnl f: eased* **20/1**
4-13 **P** **Genres**[7] 613 5-9-2 68.................. JoeFanning 12
(Alan Swinbank) *trckd ldrs: hdwy over 3f out: rdn along over 2f out: sn wknd and eased: p.u and dismntd ins fnl f* **4/1**[3]

2m 11.86s (1.46) **Going Correction** +0.225s/f (Slow) **12** Ran SP% **123.1**
Speed ratings (Par 103): **103,102,102,100,99 98,98,98,97,95 95,**
CSF £37.21 TOTE £5.30: £1.70, £4.70, £1.60; EX 68.70 Trifecta £364.20.
**Owner** James Gaffney **Bred** Mickley Stud & Mr W T Whittle **Trained** Wynyard, Stockton-On-Tees
■ Polar Forest was withdrawn. Price at time of withdrawal 6/1. Rule 4 applies to bets struck prior to withdrawal but not to SP bets - deduction 10p in the pound. New market formed.

**FOCUS**
There was a tight finish to this classified race. It's been rated around the third.

## 728 BETWAY H'CAP 2m 56y (Tp)
**3:10** (3:11) (Class 3) (0-95,95) 4-Y-0+ **£16,172** (£4,812; £2,405; £1,202) **Stalls** Low

Form RPR
23-1 **1** **Natural Scenery**[33] 197 4-9-6 **95**.................. JosephineGordon 8 106+
(Saeed bin Suroor) *trckd ldr: cl up 3f out: led jst over 2f out: shkn up and qcknd clr over 1f out: rdn and kpt on strly fnl f* **7/4**[1]
211- **2** *2 ½* **London Prize**[10] 7624 6-8-13 **82**.................. LukeMorris 9 88
(Ian Williams) *t.k.h: hld up in rr: hdwy over 3f out: rdn to chse ldrs 2f out: drvn and chsd wnr over 1f out: no imp ins fnl f* **11/4**[2]
/5-1 **3** *nk* **Hot Beat (IRE)**[29] 269 5-9-12 **95**.................. MartinHarley 7 100
(David Simcock) *hld up and bhd: hdwy 3f out: nt clr run and swtchd rt to outer 1 1/2f out: sn rdn to chse ldng pair: drvn and kpt on fnl f* **10/3**[3]
42-2 **4** *2 ¼* **Masterpaver**[33] 197 6-9-6 **89**.................. PaulHanagan 6 92
(Richard Fahey) *trckd ldrs: hdwy 3f out: rdn along 2f out: sn drvn and kpt on same pce* **6/1**
100- **5** *1 ¼* **Time Of My Life (GER)**[33] 6561 6-9-2 **85**..............(p) DanielTudhope 4 86
(Patrick Holmes) *hld up: hdwy and in tch 5f out: rdn along to chse ldrs over 2f out: sn drvn and no imp* **33/1**
2-22 **6** *1 ½* **Zakatal**[19] 422 11-9-2 **85**.................. PJMcDonald 1 84
(Rebecca Menzies) *trckd ldng pair: effrt 3f out: rdn along over 2f out: sn drvn and kpt on same pce* **20/1**
200- **7** *1 ¼* **Havana Beat (IRE)**[45] 8594 7-9-9 **92**.................. GeorgeDowning 3 90
(Tony Carroll) *trckd ldrs: pushed along 3f out: rdn along 2f out: sn drvn and no hdwy* **40/1**
0-53 **8** *1* **Esteaming**[12] 526 7-8-12 **81** oh2..............(p) ConnorBeasley 2 78
(Keith Dalgleish) *set stdy pce: pushed along and qcknd over 3f out: sn rdn: drvn over 2f out: sn hdd & wknd* **50/1**
633- **9** *10* **Highland Castle**[33] 6293 9-9-2 **88**.................. RachelRichardson(3) 5 73
(Lucinda Egerton) *t.k.h: hld up towards rr: effrt and sme hdwy over 3f out: rdn along wl over 2f out: sn btn* **125/1**

3m 41.97s (6.77) **Going Correction** +0.225s/f (Slow)
**WFA** 4 from 5yo+ 4lb **9** Ran SP% **113.3**
Speed ratings (Par 107): **92,90,90,89,88 88,87,86,81**
CSF £6.28 CT £13.46 TOTE £2.50: £1.10, £1.60, £1.60; EX 7.20 Trifecta £19.20.
**Owner** Godolphin **Bred** Darley **Trained** Newmarket, Suffolk

**FOCUS**
This was quite steadily run and although the winner was surely the best horse in the race, she was also the best placed of the principals. The fifth has been rated to his best form in Britain.

## 729 32RED CASINO FILLIES' H'CAP 7f 14y (Tp)
**3:40** (3:40) (Class 5) (0-75,74) 3-Y-0+ **£5,175** (£1,540; £769; £384) **Stalls** Centre

Form RPR
-441 **1** **Spinwheel**[20] 401 3-8-9 **72**.................. PJMcDonald 1 76
(Mark Johnston) *led: hdd over 4f out: cl up: led again over 2f out: rdn ent fnl f: kpt on wl towards fin* **6/4**[1]

00-1 **2** *nk* **Barwah (USA)**[18] 444 6-9-8 **68** ................................... AndrewMullen 6 76
(Peter Niven) *hld up in rr: hdwy 2f out: chsd wnr ent fnl f: sn rdn to chal and ev ch: drvn and no ex towards fin* **9/2**[3]

0-50 **3** *2 3/4* **Bell Heather (IRE)**[24] 360 4-9-2 **62** ................................ PaulHanagan 4 63
(Richard Fahey) *trckd ldrs: hdwy 2f out: rdn over 1f out: drvn and kpt on same pce fnl f* **4/1**[2]

2-32 **4** *1 1/2* **Palenville (IRE)**[13] 514 4-9-7 **74** ............................ PatrickVaughan(7) 5 71
(Grant Tuer) *prom: effrt over 2f out and sn rdn: drvn over 1f out: sn one pce* **4/1**[2]

66-4 **5** *3/4* **Langham**[14] 501 4-9-3 **66** ............................ AlistairRawlinson(3) 7 61
(Michael Appleby) *trckd ldng pair on outer: pushed along 3f out: rdn over 2f out: sn drvn and wknd* **7/1**

50-0 **6** *3 3/4* **Cabal**[12] 527 10-9-7 **67** .......................................(v) SamJames 3 51
(Geoffrey Harker) *dwlt and rr: hdwy after 1f and sn cl up: led over 4f out: rdn along and hdd over 2f out: sn wknd* **33/1**

1m 26.62s (0.42) **Going Correction** +0.025s/f (Slow)
**WFA** 3 from 4yo+ 17lb **6** Ran SP% **113.6**
Speed ratings (Par 100): **98,97,94,92,91 87**
CSF £8.86 TOTE £2.30: £1.30, £2.40; EX 9.20 Trifecta £25.70.
**Owner** Sheikh Hamdan bin Mohammed Al Maktoum **Bred** Darley **Trained** Middleham Moor, N Yorks

**FOCUS**
A good effort from the winner, who unlike last time did not have things all her own way. A pb from the second.

## 730 SUNBETS.CO.UK H'CAP 7f 14y (Tp)
**4:10** (4:12) (Class 2) 4-Y-O+
**£32,463** (£9,720; £4,860; £2,430; £1,215; £610) **Stalls** Centre

Form RPR

00-5 **1** **Suzi's Connoisseur**[33] 199 6-9-0 **95** ..........................(vt) OisinMurphy 1 104
(Stuart Williams) *trckd ldrs: hdwy on inner over 1f out: rdn to chal ins fnl f: led last 75 yds: kpt on* **9/1**

1-14 **2** *hd* **Holiday Magic (IRE)**[33] 199 6-8-10 **94** ..................... NathanEvans(3) 8 102
(Michael Easterby) *set stdy pce: qcknd over 2rf out: rdn over 1f out: jnd and drvn ins fnl f: hdd last 75 yds: no ex nr fin* **7/2**[1]

0-03 **3** *1/2* **Horsted Keynes (FR)**[17] 465 7-8-8 **89** ............................ TomEaves 9 96
(David Simcock) *t.k.h: in tch: hdwy 2f out: rdn over 1f out: drvn ins fnl f: kpt on wl towards fin* **14/1**

33-2 **4** *1* **Russian Soul (IRE)**[8] 598 9-8-12 **93** .......................(p) TimmyMurphy 4 97+
(Jamie Osborne) *t.k.h: cl up: pushed along 2f out: sn chsng ldr and rdn over 1f out: drvn and kpt on same pce fnl f* **9/2**[2]

-036 **5** *1/2* **Al Khan (IRE)**[17] 459 8-8-11 **92** .......................................... KevinStott 5 95
(Kevin Ryan) *t.k.h: trckd ldrs:. rdn along over 2f out: drvn over 1f out: kpt on same pce fnl f* **16/1**

03-1 **6** *shd* **Free Code (IRE)**[10] 581 6-7-11 **83** ........................ HollieDoyle(5) 13 85
(David Barron) *prom on outer: rdn along 2f out: drvn over 1f out: kpt on same pce fnl f* **9/1**

01-2 **7** *nk* **Realize**[38] 118 7-9-10 **105** .................................................(t) SeanLevey 2 107+
(Stuart Williams) *t.k.h: cl up on inner: effrt 2f out and sn rdn along: drvn ent fnl f: grad wknd* **10/1**

0-52 **8** *3/4* **Supersta**[18] 450 6-8-13 **94** ..........................................(p) AndrewMullen 6 93
(Michael Appleby) *dwlt and t.k.h in rr: hdwy 2f out: rdn over 1f out: kpt on fnl f* **20/1**

000- **9** *nk* **Angelic Lord (IRE)**[60] 8407 5-9-2 **97** ............................ MartinHarley 12 98+
(Tom Dascombe) *hld up in rr: effrt and sme hdwy wl over 1f out: sn rdn and n.d* **14/1**

31-0 **10** *hd* **Steel Train (FR)**[33] 199 6-9-5 **100** ............................... DanielTudhope 3 102+
(David O'Meara) *t.k.h: hld up towards rr: hdwy over 2f out: chsd ldrs and rdn wl over 1f out sn btn* **8/1**[3]

5-13 **11** *1 1/2* **Tatlisu (IRE)**[33] 194 7-8-9 **90** ..................................... TonyHamilton 7 84
(Richard Fahey) *hld up: a towards rr* **14/1**

-145 **12** *2 3/4* **Testa Rossa (IRE)**[10] 581 7-8-0 **81** oh1 ..................(b) JamesSullivan 11 68
(Jim Goldie) *a rr* **14/1**

104/ **13** *33* **Fast And Furious (IRE)**[449] 7956 4-8-4 **85** ................... PaulHanagan 10
(James Bethell) *keern hold: chsd ldrs: pushed along wl over 2f out: sn rdn and wknd* **100/1**

1m 26.76s (0.56) **Going Correction** +0.025s/f (Slow) **13** Ran SP% **118.9**
Speed ratings (Par 109): **97,96,96,95,94 94,94,93,92,92 90,87,50**
CSF £40.18 CT £465.06 TOTE £9.00: £3.20, £2.00, £4.40; EX 52.00 Trifecta £692.70.
**Owner** The Connoisseurs **Bred** Greenstead Hall Racing Ltd **Trained** Newmarket, Suffolk

**FOCUS**
The early gallop wasn't strong and it didn't pay to be held up too far back. The winner has been rated close to his turf best, with the third, fifth and sixth close to their recent marks.

## 731 32RED.COM MAIDEN STKS 6f (Tp)
**4:40** (4:42) (Class 5) 3-Y-O
**£5,175** (£1,540; £769; £384) **Stalls** Centre

Form RPR

**1** **Batten The Hatches** 3-9-5 0 ............................................ PhillipMakin 3 76+
(David Barron) *t.k.h early: trckd ldrs: smooth hdwy and cl up 2f out: led over 1f out: rdn: green and edgd lft ins fnl f: kpt on strly* **7/2**[2]

**2** *2* **Hitchcock** 3-9-5 0 ............................................................ TomEaves 4 69+
(Kevin Ryan) *trckd ldrs on outer: cl up over 2f out: rdn to chse wnr ent fnl f: sn drvn and edgd lft: no imp* **10/11**[1]

0-32 **3** *1 3/4* **Bloomin Lovely (IRE)**[13] 510 3-9-0 69 ............................ JasonHart 5 59
(John Quinn) *trckd ldr: cl up over 2f out: rdn and ev ch over 1f out: drvn and kpt on same pce fnl f* **7/2**[2]

6-0 **4** *1 3/4* **Night Shadow**[20] 402 3-9-0 0 .................................... PhilDennis(5) 6 58
(Alan Brown) *led: rdn along 2f out: hdd over 1f out: kpt on same pce* **40/1**

**5** *4* **Channel Packet** 3-9-2 0 ................................ AlistairRawlinson(3) 1 45
(Michael Appleby) *dwlt: sn in tch: pushed along over 2f out: sn rdn: green and one pce* **20/1**[3]

6 **6** *5* **Boogie Babe**[18] 442 3-9-0 0 ........................................ TonyHamilton 2 24
(Richard Fahey) *t.k.h early: chsd ldrs: rdn along 1/2-way: sn outpcd and bhd* **20/1**[3]

1m 12.17s (-0.33) **Going Correction** +0.025s/f (Slow) **6** Ran SP% **108.8**
Speed ratings (Par 97): **103,100,98,95,90 83**
CSF £6.66 TOTE £4.60: £2.20, £1.20; EX 8.90 Trifecta £17.70.
**Owner** Harrowgate Bloodstock Ltd & Partner **Bred** Whitsbury Manor Stud **Trained** Maunby, N Yorks

**FOCUS**
With Bloomin Lovely fairly exposed now, this looked open to a newcomer, and the first two were both well supported in opposition to her. The standard is set by the third.

## 732 BETWAY BEST ODDS GUARANTEED PLUS H'CAP 5f (Tp)
**5:10** (5:10) (Class 6) (0-65,65) 3-Y-O+
**£3,234** (£962; £481; £240) **Stalls** Centre

Form RPR

36-2 **1** **Indian Pursuit (IRE)**[8] 602 4-9-5 **59** ................................ JasonHart 10 68
(John Quinn) *trckd ldrs on outer: hdwy and cl up 2f out: rdn to ld ent fnl f: sn drvn and edgd lft: kpt on wl* **7/1**[3]

0-02 **2** *hd* **Spiraea**[12] 523 7-9-11 **65** ................................................ TomEaves 1 73
(Ivan Furtado) *cl up on inner: effrt 2f out: rdn to chal ins fnl f: sn drvn and kpt on* **22/1**

20-0 **3** *1 1/4* **Noah Amor (IRE)**[25] 330 4-9-1 **62** ........................ DanielleMooney(7) 11 66
(David Nicholls) *cl up: led over 3f out: rdn 2f out: hdd ent fnl f: sn drvn and kpt on* **16/1**

11-0 **4** *shd* **Novabridge**[18] 446 9-9-0 **59** ......................................(b) GemmaTutty(5) 9 62
(Karen Tutty) *hld up towards rr: hdwy 2f out: sn rdn: kpt on fnl f: nrst fin* **14/1**

4-41 **5** *1/2* **Burtonwood**[13] 514 5-9-4 **65** ................................ KieranSchofield(7) 2 67
(Julie Camacho) *dwlt: sn in tch: hdwy 2f out: rdn wl over 1f out: kpt on fnl f: nrst fin* **5/1**[2]

3-01 **6** *nk* **Windforpower (IRE)**[18] 446 7-9-6 **60** ............................(v) BenCurtis 4 61
(Tracy Waggott) *chsd ldrs: rdn along 2f out: drvn over 1f out: kpt on u.p fnl f* **14/1**

**7** *1/2* **Ken's Sam's (IRE)**[18] 447 4-9-9 **63** ..........................(tp) MartinHarley 8 62
(Adrian Brendan Joyce, Ire) *trckd ldrs: hdwy over 2f out: rdn to chse ldng trio over 1f out: sn drvn and wknd ins fnl f* **9/4**[1]

3-04 **8** *1* **Jacob's Pillow**[12] 523 6-9-10 **64** ................................ DanielTudhope 6 59
(Rebecca Bastiman) *slt ld: hdd over 3f out: cl up: rdn along over 2f out: grad wknd* **8/1**

-055 **9** *hd* **Thorntoun Lady (USA)**[10] 582 7-9-2 **56** ..................... JamesSullivan 7 50
(Jim Goldie) *a towards rr* **20/1**

01-5 **10** *1/2* **Monsieur Paddy**[34] 172 4-9-9 **63** ................................ GeorgeDowning 3 56
(Tony Carroll) *towards rr: hdwy on inner over 2f out: chsd ldrs over 1f out: drvn and btn fnl f: wknd* **10/1**

50-0 **11** *4 1/2* **Jess**[24] 363 4-9-1 **60** ..................................................(p) LewisEdmunds(5) 5 36
(Kevin Ryan) *sn rdn along and in tch: lost pl bef 1/2-way: sn bhd* **12/1**

58.91s (-0.59) **Going Correction** +0.025s/f (Slow) **11** Ran SP% **116.2**
Speed ratings (Par 101): **105,104,102,102,101 101,100,98,98,97 90**
CSF £146.89 CT £2397.09 TOTE £6.80: £2.10, £5.70, £4.70; EX 88.00 Trifecta £1197.60.
**Owner** Malcolm Walker **Bred** Sean Gorman **Trained** Settrington, N Yorks

**FOCUS**
A modest sprint. Straightforward form rated around the winner to last year's level and the second matching his Southwell run.
T/Jkpt: Not won. T/Plt: £44.60 to a £1 stake. Pool: £88,837.00 - 1,453.95 winning units T/Qpdt: £6.60 to a £1 stake. Pool: £8,503.56 - 947.90 winning units **Joe Rowntree**

# 621 KEMPTON (A.W) (R-H)
## Wednesday, February 15
**OFFICIAL GOING: Polytrack: standard**
Wind: Nil Weather: Mild

## 733 RACING UK APPRENTICE H'CAP 1m 2f 219y(P)
**5:20** (5:21) (Class 7) (0-50,51) 4-Y-O+
**£1,940** (£577; £288; £144) **Stalls** Low

Form RPR

0-31 **1** **Moayadd (USA)**[8] 608 5-9-8 **51** 6ex ................................ HollieDoyle 5 64+
(Neil Mulholland) *settled bhd ldrs on rail: travelling wl over 2f out where ct on heels: swtchd to inner and rdn 2f out: plenty to do over 1f out and chsd clr ldr: styd on strly ent fnl f: led wl ins fnl f: cosily* **1/4**[1]

00-0 **2** *1 1/2* **Street Art (IRE)**[29] 278 5-8-13 **45** ..........................(bt) KevinLundie(3) 12 52
(Mike Murphy) *pressed ldr and t.k.h: led ent st: rdn over 2f out: clr ldr over 1f out: began to wknd 1f out: no ex and hdd wl ins fnl f* **25/1**

00-3 **3** *6* **Rezwaan**[28] 281 10-9-6 **49** ..............................................(b) DavidParkes 2 46
(Murty McGrath) *broke wl and sn restrained bhd ldrs: rdn over 2f out: kpt on one pce but no imp on ldng pair* **5/1**[2]

00-R **4** *2 1/4* **Katalan (GER)**[29] 279 4-8-7 **45** ..........................(h[1]) DarraghKeenan(7) 13 39
(John Butler) *settled bhd ldrs on outer: rdn over 2f out: kpt on one pce* **50/1**

30-0 **5** *hd* **Color Force (IRE)**[37] 139 4-9-1 **49** ............................ RhiainIngram(3) 9 42
(Gay Kelleway) *in rr-div: rdn over 2f out: sn n.m.r: no imp after* **20/1**

4045 **6** *1/2* **Ferryview Place**[4] 690 8-9-0 **50** ....................................(p) LukeCatton(7) 3 43
(Ian Williams) *settled in mid-div on outer: rdn over 2f out: hung rt over 1f out: sn hld* **10/1**[3]

0-60 **7** *2* **Zeteah**[28] 282 7-9-2 **45** .............................................. JordanVaughan 14 34
(Tony Carroll) *in rr: rdn over 2f out: sn lft bhd* **100/1**

0-04 **8** *hd* **Cappielow Park**[14] 508 8-8-10 **46** ..............................(bt) WilliamCox(7) 6 35
(Ali Stronge) *settled in mid-div: rdn over 2f out: no imp* **16/1**

330/ **9** *shd* **Gamesters Lad**[521] 6350 5-9-7 **50** ...................................(p[1]) JoshDoyle 4 39
(Oliver Greenall) *led as slow pce: hdd ent st: rdn over 2f out: wknd after* **25/1**

0-05 **10** *nk* **Swiss Lait**[8] 608 6-9-0 **48** ........................................... PaulaMuir(5) 7 37
(Patrick Holmes) *prom early: lost pl over 5f out: niggled along on bnd: rdn over 3f out: no ex st* **25/1**

00/0 **11** *1* **Frontline Phantom (IRE)**[21] 400 10-9-0 **50** ............. RussellHarris(7) 1 39
(K R Burke) *in rr-div: snatched up and lost pl after 4f: rdn over 2f out: no imp* **50/1**

40-0 **12** *7* **Ambitious Rosie**[20] 414 6-8-9 **45** ................................ AledBeech(7) 11 21
(Tony Carroll) *in rr: rdn over 2f out: no imp* **150/1**

50-0 **13** *5* **Athenian Garden (USA)**[19] 440 10-8-9 **45** .................. GinaMangan(7) 10 13
(Paddy Butler) *in rr and racd wd: t.k.h: prog at 1/2-way to sit bhd ldrs: rdn over 2f out: sn wknd* **66/1**

2m 25.68s (3.78) **Going Correction** +0.225s/f (Slow)
**WFA** 4 from 5yo+ 1lb **13** Ran SP% **135.0**
Speed ratings (Par 97): **95,93,89,87,87 87,85,85,85,85 84,79,76**
CSF £21.01 CT £30.11 TOTE £1.30: £1.10, £6.20, £1.70; EX 27.40 Trifecta £91.10.
**Owner** P & Mrs K E Malcolm **Bred** Darley **Trained** Limpley Stoke, Wilts


The Form Book Flat, Raceform Ltd, Newbury, RG14 5SJ

**FOCUS**
They only wanted to know about one horse in the betting, and the favourite did land the odds, but not without giving his backers a fright. The runner-up is the key to the level.

## 734 100% PROFIT BOOST AT 32REDSPORT.COM H'CAP 7f (P)
**5:50** (5:51) (Class 6) (0-65,66) 4-Y-0+ **£2,264** (£673; £336; £168) **Stalls** Low

Form RPR

000- **1** **Murdanova (IRE)**[68] 8287 4-9-4 **62** ........ TomEaves 7 69
(Daniel Mark Loughnane) *settled bhd ldrs: rdn to chse clr ldr 2f out: led wl ins fnl f: kpt on wl* **33/1**

000- **2** 1 1/2 **Muthraab Aldaar (IRE)**[83] 8086 4-9-2 **60** ........ JackMitchell 5 63
(Jim Boyle) *sluggish s: hld up in rr: rdn over 2f out on rail w plenty to do: kpt on strly fr over 1f out: nvr nrr* **14/1**

506/ **3** shd **Talksalot (IRE)**[576] 4456 6-9-4 **62** ........(h[1]) DougieCostello 8 65
(Mark Bradstock) *t.k.h in mid-div: rdn in centre 2f out: kpt on wl fr over 1f out* **50/1**

0-46 **4** 1/2 **Quintus Cerialis (IRE)**[21] 398 5-8-4 **53**........(tp) PatrickO'Donnell[(5)] 2 55
(Karen George) *t.k.h in rr-div: almost last ent st: shkn up and gd prog up rail: rdn 2f out: kpt on wl tl no ex nr fin* **4/1**[2]

-460 **5** 1 **Dominium (USA)**[15] 501 10-9-3 **66**........(p) DavidParkes[(5)] 4 67
(Jeremy Gask) *in rr: c wd st: hemmed in fr 2f out: rdn ent fnl f: nvr nrr* **7/2**[1]

4-25 **6** 3/4 **Indian Affair**[27] 302 7-9-7 **65**........(bt) FrannyNorton 1 62
(Milton Bradley) *settled bhd ldrs: rdn over 2f out: lft bhd fr over 1f out: kpt on one pce* **5/1**[3]

-012 **7** nk **Bookmaker**[11] 570 7-8-5 **56**........(p) JaneElliott[(7)] 10 52
(John Bridger) *settled in mid-div: rdn over 2f out: sn one pce* **4/1**[2]

20-0 **8** hd **Only Ten Per Cent (IRE)**[35] 171 9-9-5 **63**........ ShaneKelly 9 59
(J R Jenkins) *hld up in rr: rdn over 2f out wd: kpt on one pce* **25/1**

/53- **9** 1 1/4 **Forever Yours (IRE)**[155] 6459 4-9-4 **65**........ JackDuern[(3)] 3 57+
(Dean Ivory) *led as str pce: clr ld and booted for home ent st: stl clr over 1f out: no ex ent fnl f w pack clsng rapidly: hdd wl ins fnl f: wknd qckly after* **25/1**

0-06 **10** 2 **Falcao (IRE)**[13] 528 5-9-6 **64**........ DannyBrock 6 51+
(John Butler) *chsd ldr: rdn over 2f out: losing pl fr over 1f out: wknd after* **8/1**

0-10 **11** 6 **Harry Holland**[19] 445 5-9-6 **64**........(h) JosephineGordon 11 36
(Tom Dascombe) *reluctant to load: cl up bhd ldrs: rdn over 2f out: sn wknd* **8/1**

00-0 **12** 1 **Layla's Hero (IRE)**[30] 267 10-9-7 **65**........(p) TomMarquand 12 34
(Roger Teal) *s.s: in rr on outer: struggling over 3f out: no ex st* **33/1**

1m 26.56s (0.56) **Going Correction** +0.225s/f (Slow) 12 Ran SP% **123.3**
Speed ratings (Par 101): **105,103,103,102,101 100,100,100,98,96 89,88**
CSF £432.54 CT £20703.32 TOTE £37.00: £8.00, £4.90, £11.90; EX 580.60 Trifecta £10109.00.
**Owner** Phil Slater **Bred** John Lyons **Trained** Rock, Worcs

**FOCUS**
This was run at a strong pace and the closers had their day. The level is a bit fluid but it'll be a surprise if this is far out.

## 735 32RED ON THE APP STORE FILLIES' H'CAP 6f (P)
**6:20** (6:20) (Class 5) (0-70,65) 4-Y-0+ **£2,911** (£866; £432; £216) **Stalls** Low

Form RPR

21-2 **1** **Assertive Agent**[27] 308 7-9-4 **62**........ DavidProbert 2 71
(Tony Carroll) *hld up bhd ldrs: shkn up and smooth prog in centre wl over 1f out: rdn ent fnl f: wnt hd to hd w runner-up ins fnl f: led 100yds out: kpt on wl* **3/1**[2]

-022 **2** nk **Spiraea**[1] 732 7-9-7 **65**........ TomEaves 5 73
(Ivan Furtado) *s.s and in rr: prog on rail over 2f out: rdn 2f out: kpt on wl and led ent fnl f: hrd pressed by wnr tl hdd 100yds out: kpt on* **2/1**[1]

60-4 **3** 6 **Penny Dreadful**[27] 308 5-9-5 **63**........(p) DaleSwift 8 53
(Scott Dixon) *led: rdn over 2f out: kpt on wl tl hdd ent fnl f: wknd after* **15/2**

01-0 **4** 1/2 **Clever Divya**[16] 481 4-8-3 **54**........ GinaMangan[(7)] 7 43
(J R Jenkins) *in rr: rdn over 2f out: nt much imp tl kpt on under hands and heels ent fnl f* **16/1**

550/ **5** 3 **Lily Ash (IRE)**[453] 7921 4-9-5 **63**........ ShaneKelly 1 43
(Mike Murphy) *cl up bhd ldr on rail: rdn over 2f out: wknd fr over 1f out* **12/1**

4-00 **6** 1 3/4 **Flowing Clarets**[18] 468 4-8-7 **58**........ JaneElliott[(7)] 6 32
(John Bridger) *racd wd bhd ldrs: c wd ent st and dropped to rr over 2f out: no imp after* **8/1**

3-11 **7** 3/4 **Beau Mistral (IRE)**[27] 308 8-9-4 **62**........(p) GeorgeDowning 4 34
(Tony Carroll) *racd bhd ldrs: rdn over 2f out: outpcd sn after: kpt on one pce* **5/1**[3]

230- **8** 1 **Royal Rettie**[133] 7069 5-9-2 **60**........(h) DannyBrock 3 29
(Paddy Butler) *chsd ldr: rdn over 2f out: lft bhd sn after and wknd fr over 1f out* **25/1**

1m 13.4s (0.30) **Going Correction** +0.225s/f (Slow) 8 Ran SP% **115.3**
Speed ratings (Par 100): **107,106,98,97,93 91,90,89**
CSF £9.52 CT £39.93 TOTE £3.70: £1.70, £1.10, £2.20; EX 11.70 Trifecta £54.20.
**Owner** Wedgewood Estates **Bred** Miss Liza Judd **Trained** Cropthorne, Worcs

**FOCUS**
This developed into a duel between the first two inside the final furlong. The winner's penultimate run could be rated nearly this good and perhaps this could be rated a little higher.

## 736 32RED H'CAP (LONDON MILE QUALIFIER) 1m (P)
**6:50** (6:52) (Class 4) (0-85,84) 4-Y-0+ **£4,690** (£1,395; £697; £348) **Stalls** Low

Form RPR

45-0 **1** **Alejandro (IRE)**[9] 598 8-9-6 **83**........ JosephineGordon 8 92
(David Loughnane) *reluctant to load: t.k.h bhd ldr: rdn over 2f out where almost upsides: led under 2f out out: wnt hd to hd w runner-up fr over 1f out: kpt on wl cl home* **25/1**

2-11 **2** hd **Franco's Secret**[12] 548 6-9-7 **84**........(v) TomMarquand 5 92
(Peter Hedger) *hld up on rail bhd ldrs: rdn over 2f out: wnt hd to hd w wnr fr over 1f out: jst failed* **3/1**[2]

63-4 **3** 2 1/2 **Mister Music**[12] 548 8-9-2 **79**........ ShaneKelly 4 81
(Tony Carroll) *settled in rr-div: shkn up on heels of ldrs over 1f out: sn rdn and kpt on wl: nvr involved* **11/2**[3]

1-14 **4** 1/2 **Fire Diamond**[11] 570 4-8-9 **72**........(p) FrannyNorton 9 73
(Tom Dascombe) *racd in 3rd: rdn over 2f out: no ex sn after and kpt on one pce* **8/1**

052- **5** hd **Beleave**[230] 3816 4-8-12 **75**........(h) DanielMuscutt 3 75
(Luke Dace) *walked to post: rrd in stalls: in rr-div: shkn up and swtchd wd over 2f out: sn rdn and kpt on one pce* **16/1**

2 **6** nse **Cherbourg (FR)**[18] 465 5-9-6 **83**........ GeorgeBaker 10 83
(Ralph Beckett) *led: hld together over 2f out: sn rdn and hdd under 2f out: kpt on one pce tl wknd ins fnl f* **1/1**[1]

512/ **7** 2 3/4 **Matravers**[877] 6609 6-8-9 **75**........ KieranShoemark[(3)] 6 69
(Mary Hambro) *in rr-div: rdn over 2f out: kpt on one pce* **33/1**

04-0 **8** 6 **Zaeem**[45] 5 8-9-4 **81**........(t[1]) TomEaves 2 61
(Ivan Furtado) *taken bk leaving stalls and in rr: rdn over 2f out: nvr involved* **20/1**

1m 41.34s (1.54) **Going Correction** +0.225s/f (Slow) 8 Ran SP% **118.9**
Speed ratings (Par 105): **101,100,98,97,97 97,94,88**
CSF £100.99 CT £494.56 TOTE £24.00: £6.00, £1.60, £1.90; EX 97.00 Trifecta £469.40.
**Owner** Lydonford Ltd **Bred** Yeomanstown Stud **Trained** Market Drayton, Shropshire

**FOCUS**
There was a turn-up here. The winner has been rated back to the level of his second start for his current stable.

## 737 32RED.COM MAIDEN STKS 1m 3f 219y(P)
**7:20** (7:23) (Class 5) 3-4-Y-0 **£3,234** (£962; £481; £240) **Stalls** Centre

Form RPR

626- **1** **Peaceful Passage (USA)**[72] 8227 3-8-2 73........ NickyMackay 7 77
(John Gosden) *settled bhd ldrs: travelling best wl over 2f out: shkn up over 1f out swtchd to inner: led ent fnl f: pushed out: easily* **11/8**[1]

6-52 **2** 3 1/4 **Tomorrow Mystery**[26] 328 3-7-11 69........ HollieDoyle[(5)] 4 72
(Jamie Osborne) *led: rdn over 2f out: kpt on wl tl hdd ent fnl f: no ex* **7/2**[2]

22-4 **3** 9 **Henry Croft**[34] 195 4-10-0 76........ GeorgeDowning 5 66
(Tony Carroll) *hld up in mid-div: rdn over 2f out: kpt on one pce but shaped w sme promise* **25/1**

0-4 **4** 1 1/4 **Alexander M (IRE)**[14] 503 3-8-7 0........ FrannyNorton 9 61
(Mark Johnston) *t.k.h bhd ldr: rdn over 2f out: sn lft bhd by ldng pair: one pce after* **10/1**

0-4 **5** hd **Salt Whistle Bay (IRE)**[39] 115 3-8-7 0........ MartinDwyer 10 60
(Rae Guest) *cl up out wd: rdn along ent st: no imp fr 2f out* **9/1**

26 **6** 3 3/4 **Treble Strike (USA)**[11] 576 4-9-11 0........(p[1]) JackDuern[(3)] 6 57
(Dean Ivory) *in rr-div: rdn over 2f out: lft bhd by front pair fr over 1f out: kpt on one pce* **66/1**

**7** 6 **Swallow Dancer** 3-7-11 0 ow2........ RhiainIngram[(7)] 2 42
(Harry Dunlop) *in rr: rdn over 2f out: nvr a factor* **33/1**

0-55 **8** 7 **Cartavio (IRE)**[19] 437 3-8-7 69........ DavidProbert 1 33
(Andrew Balding) *chsd ldrs: rdn over 2f out: no ex and wknd fr over 1f out and wknd* **7/1**[3]

**9** 1 3/4 **Kyneton (IRE)** 3-8-7 0........(b[1]) TomMarquand 3 31
(John Gosden) *in rr wl off the pce and pushed along to hold tch: no ch fr over 3f out* **10/1**

**10** 2 1/2 **Shine Through (IRE)** 3-8-2 0........ JosephineGordon 8 22
(Hugo Palmer) *settled bhd ldrs on rail: pushed along to hold pl at 1/2-way: lft bhd st and wknd* **20/1**

2m 33.61s (-0.89) **Going Correction** +0.225s/f (Slow)
**WFA** 3 from 4yo 24lb 10 Ran SP% **118.1**
Speed ratings (Par 103): **111,108,102,102,101 99,95,90,89,87**
CSF £5.82 TOTE £2.30: £1.10, £1.70, £3.30; EX 7.90 Trifecta £60.60.
**Owner** Mrs Emory A Hamilton **Bred** Emory A Hamilton **Trained** Newmarket, Suffolk

**FOCUS**
An ordinary maiden in which the first two in the market drew clear. Little depth to the form and the level is a bit fluid.

## 738 RACING UK HD H'CAP 1m 3f 219y(P)
**7:50** (7:52) (Class 6) (0-60,62) 4-Y-0+ **£2,264** (£673; £336; £168) **Stalls** Centre

Form RPR

00-0 **1** **Tractive Effort**[29] 278 4-8-4 **46**........ JosephineGordon 4 51
(Michael Attwater) *broke wl and restrained bhd ldrs under a t.k.h: rdn wl over 1f out: kpt on between horses wl ent fnl f: led wl ins fnl f: rdn out* **33/1**

63-2 **2** nk **On Fire**[28] 286 4-9-6 **62**........ LukeMorris 7 67
(James Bethell) *settled on outer bhd ldrs: rdn under 2f out: kpt on wl on outside ins fnl f* **13/8**[1]

600- **3** 3/4 **Iona Island**[59] 8448 4-9-0 **59**........ EoinWalsh[(3)] 5 63
(Peter Hiatt) *settled bhd ldrs: rdn 2f out: led ent fnl f: kpt on tl hdd wl ins fnl f* **25/1**

4-32 **4** nk **Tasty Ginger (IRE)**[7] 616 4-9-5 **61**........(v) ShaneKelly 6 64
(J R Jenkins) *s.s: rushed up to chse ldrs by 1/2-way: rdn 2f out: kpt on wl fr over 1f out: hld nr fin* **11/2**[2]

600- **5** 3/4 **Jackblack**[83] 8085 5-9-2 **60**........(h[1]) DavidParkes[(5)] 1 62
(Brett Johnson) *in rr-div: rdn 2f out: kpt on one pce wl ins fnl f* **66/1**

-032 **6** 1 **Ali Bin Nayef**[18] 462 5-9-1 **54**........ DavidProbert 2 55
(Michael Wigham) *settled in mid-div on rail: rdn over 2f out: kpt on one pce* **8/1**

14-1 **7** nse **Stand Guard**[18] 462 13-9-9 **62**........ LiamKeniry 3 62
(John Butler) *mid-div: shkn up over 2f out: rdn 2f out: kpt on one pce* **8/1**

06-4 **8** shd **Chandon Elysees**[42] 39 4-9-4 **60**........ GeorgeBaker 10 60
(Gary Moore) *sn led at mod pce: rdn over 2f out: kpt on tl hdd ent fnl f: n.m.r sn after and eased* **6/1**[3]

6-13 **9** 2 1/2 **Rail Dancer**[18] 461 5-9-2 **55**........(p) AdamBeschizza 9 51
(Richard Rowe) *t.k.h in mid-divsion: rdn over 2f out: lft bhd sn after* **7/1**

001- **10** 2 **Munsarim (IRE)**[119] 7464 10-9-0 **58**........(b) PaddyBradley[(5)] 8 51+
(Lee Carter) *s.s: nvr involved* **33/1**

2m 40.58s (6.08) **Going Correction** +0.225s/f (Slow)
**WFA** 4 from 5yo+ 2lb 10 Ran SP% **113.7**
Speed ratings (Par 101): **88,87,87,87,86 85,85,85,84,82**
CSF £83.53 CT £1437.55 TOTE £33.00: £6.40, £1.20, £5.90; EX 118.30 Trifecta £4092.80.
**Owner** Canisbay Bloodstock **Bred** Canisbay Bloodstock Ltd **Trained** Epsom, Surrey

**FOCUS**
This was steadily run and turned into a sprint up the straight. The second and third help set a very ordinary level.

## 739 32RED CASINO H'CAP (DIV I) 1m (P)
**8:20** (8:21) (Class 6) (0-55,55) 4-Y-0+ **£2,264** (£673; £336; £168) **Stalls** Low

Form RPR

-235 **1** **Zabdi**[21] 398 4-9-7 **55**........ JosephineGordon 3 65
(Lee Carter) *led: shkn up over 3f out and stole a gd ld: rdn over 2f out: clr ld over 1f out: in command and pushed out* **4/1**[2]

0-36 **2** 3 **Dukes Meadow**[23] 383 6-8-12 **53**........ RhiainIngram[(7)] 7 56+
(Roger Ingram) *hld up in rr: rdn and plenty to do over 2f out: kpt on wl fr over 1f out: nvr nrr* **11/2**[3]

00- **3** nk **Ixelles Diamond (IRE)**[148] 6662 6-8-13 **52**........(h) PaddyBradley[(5)] 2 54
(Lee Carter) *mid-div on rail: rdn over 2f out: kpt on one pce* **8/1**

45-0 **4** 2 1/2 **No No Cardinal (IRE)**[7] 621 8-8-10 **49**........ HollieDoyle[(5)] 1 46
(Mark Gillard) *in rr-div: rdn over 2f out: no ex* **16/1**

50-1 **5** 3/4 **Little Indian**[35] 167 7-9-4 **52**........ GeorgeBaker 9 47
(J R Jenkins) *hld up in rr: plenty to do whn rdn 2f out: kpt on wl* **4/1**[2]

54/5 **6** ½ **Monsieur Royale**$^{28}$ [282] 7-9-6 **54** .......... JackMitchell 10 48
(Clive Drew) *settled bhd ldr: rdn over 2f out: one pce and no ex fr over 1f out* **10/1**

-005 **7** ½ **Nidnod**$^{19}$ [438] 4-8-5 **46** oh1 .......... JaneElliott$^{(7)}$ 4 39
(John Bridger) *t.k.h in mid-div: rdn over 2f out: no ex* **25/1**

060- **8** 2 **Les Darcy**$^{128}$ [7200] 6-8-12 **46** oh1 .......... (h$^{1}$) ShaneKelly 5 34
(Ken Cunningham-Brown) *in rr-div: rdn over 2f out: nvr involved* **50/1**

-600 **9** nk **Patron Of Explores (USA)**$^{8}$ [607] 6-8-12 **46** oh1 .......... TomEaves 11 33
(Patrick Holmes) *dropped to rr on leaving stalls: a in rr* **33/1**

-524 **10** 1 ¾ **Spirit Of Gondree (IRE)**$^{20}$ [426] 9-9-7 **55** .......... (b) LukeMorris 6 38
(Milton Bradley) *t.k.h in mid-divsion: effrt over 2f out: no imp and eased* **9/4$^{1}$**

00/0 **11** 46 **Deftera Fantutte (IRE)**$^{29}$ [274] 6-8-13 **50** .......... PhilipPrince$^{(3)}$ 8
(Natalie Lloyd-Beavis) *cl up on outer: rdn and lost pl over 3f out: wknd and eased fr over 1f out: eased after: t.o* **66/1**

1m 40.67s (0.87) **Going Correction** +0.225s/f (Slow) **11 Ran SP% 122.5**
Speed ratings (Par 101): **104,101,100,98,97 96,96,94,94,92 46**
CSF £26.91 CT £177.37 TOTE £5.00: £1.50, £2.30, £2.70; EX 29.20 Trifecta £202.50.
**Owner** Mrs S A Pearson **Bred** Theakston Stud **Trained** Epsom, Surrey

**FOCUS**
Another winner for Josephine Gordon, who made every yard on a horse who had previously proved hard to win with. The fourth helps offer some perspective to the level of the form.

## 740 32RED CASINO H'CAP (DIV II) 1m (P)
**8:50** (8:51) (Class 6) (0-55,55) 4-Y-0+ **£2,264** (£673; £336; £168) **Stalls** Low

Form RPR

22-3 **1** **Henry Grace (IRE)**$^{28}$ [282] 6-9-0 **53** .......... (b) HollieDoyle$^{(5)}$ 7 59
(Jimmy Fox) *hld up in mid-div: prom in pack 4f out but stl plenty to do: shkn up over 2f out: gd prog to chsd down ldng pair over 1f out on outer: styd on strly and led fnl 100yds* **6/4$^{1}$**

00-0 **2** ¾ **Mulled Wine**$^{29}$ [279] 4-9-4 **52** .......... KierenFox 6 56
(John Best) *pushed up and settled bhd clr ldr: clsd gap wl over 3f out but stl 7 l to find w 5 l bk to the remainder: rdn over 2f out: kpt on wl and tk 2nd nr fin* **8/1$^{3}$**

0540 **3** nk **Chandrayaan**$^{6}$ [644] 10-8-5 **46** oh1 .......... (v) GinaMangan$^{(7)}$ 9 50
(John E Long) *led after 2f and sn set str pce clr of gp: over 7 l clr of nrest pursuer over 3f out: sn kicked for home: stl clr over 1f out: wkng ent fnl f: hdd last 100yds: lost 2nd nr fin* **33/1**

0-63 **4** ¾ **West Leake (IRE)**$^{12}$ [544] 11-8-12 **46** .......... LiamKeniry 4 48
(Paul Burgoyne) *t.k.h most of way: stl in rr w plenty to do whn shuffled along over 2f out: kpt on wl fr over 1f out: clsng on ldrs fnl 110yds: nvr involved* **8/1$^{3}$**

3-06 **5** 1 ¾ **Rocket Ronnie (IRE)**$^{22}$ [390] 7-9-7 **55** .......... LukeMorris 3 53
(Brian Barr) *hld up in rr on inner: rdn over 2f out: kpt on wl fr over 1f out* **12/1**

00-0 **6** hd **Palace Moon**$^{33}$ [214] 12-9-4 **52** .......... (t) GeorgeBaker 5 49
(Michael Attwater) *led for 2f tl settled in mid-divsion: rdn over 2f out: kpt on one pce* **8/1$^{3}$**

-526 **7** 1 ¼ **Bassino (USA)**$^{9}$ [605] 4-9-2 **55** .......... (h) RachealKneller$^{(5)}$ 8 50
(James Bennett) *in rr-div on outer: rdn over 2 out: kpt on but no imp on ldrs* **6/1$^{2}$**

0040 **8** 2 ¼ **I Can't Stop**$^{7}$ [614] 4-9-2 **50** .......... (b) FrannyNorton 1 39
(Milton Bradley) *in rr-div on outer: rdn over 2f out: no imp* **8/1$^{3}$**

60-0 **9** ¾ **Seamoor Secret**$^{29}$ [274] 5-8-12 **46** oh1 .......... (t) TomMarquand 2 34
(Alex Hales) *in rr: c wd st: sn rdn and no imp* **33/1**

20-0 **10** 14 **Just Fab (IRE)**$^{29}$ [273] 4-8-12 **51** .......... PaddyBradley$^{(5)}$ 10 6
(Lee Carter) *in rr: nvr involved: t.o* **20/1**

1m 42.6s (2.80) **Going Correction** +0.225s/f (Slow) **10 Ran SP% 117.1**
Speed ratings (Par 101): **95,94,93,93,91 91,90,87,87,73**
CSF £13.80 CT £274.12 TOTE £2.20: £1.30, £2.40, £6.90; EX 16.00 Trifecta £333.80.
**Owner** Barbara Fuller & Claire Underwood **Bred** D Fuller **Trained** Collingbourne Ducis, Wilts

**FOCUS**
The early pace wasn't that fast but things soon picked up once Chandrayaan was allowed to stride on, and that eventually played into the hands of the winner. The winner has been rated just off his best.
T/Jkpt: Not Won. T/Plt: £958.40 to a £1 stake. Pool: £93,979.05 - 71.58 winning units T/Qpdt: £10.00 to a £1 stake. Pool: £11,476.52 - 841.28 winning units **Cathal Gahan**

# 717 WOLVERHAMPTON (A.W) (L-H)
Wednesday, February 15

**OFFICIAL GOING: Tapeta: standard**
Wind: Light behind Weather: Showers

## 741 BETWAY MARATHON ALL WEATHER "HANDS AND HEELS" SERIES APPRENTICE H'CAP (RACING EXCELLENCE) 1m 5f 194y
**2:00** (2:00) (Class 6) (0-60,60) 4-Y-0+ **£2,264** (£673; £336; £168) **Stalls** Low

Form RPR

0-53 **1** **Scrafton**$^{16}$ [477] 6-9-4 **59** .......... AledBeech$^{(5)}$ 3 65+
(Tony Carroll) *hld up: racd keenly: hdwy to ld over 1f out: pushed along and edgd lft ins fnl f: styd on* **2/1$^{2}$**

0-24 **2** shd **Cape Spirit (IRE)**$^{28}$ [290] 5-8-12 **53** .......... (p) WilliamCox$^{(5)}$ 7 59
(Andrew Balding) *s.i.s: sn prom: pushed along and ev ch fr over 1f out: carried lft ins fnl f: styd on* **7/4$^{1}$**

0-00 **3** 4 **Tingo In The Tale (IRE)**$^{23}$ [383] 8-9-2 **52** .......... (p) JordanUys 2 52
(Sophie Leech) *hld up: swtchd rt over 1f out: edgd lft and r.o to go 3rd wl ins fnl f* **10/1**

4-26 **4** 4 **Chestnut Storm (IRE)**$^{32}$ [241] 4-9-5 **60** .......... JoshuaBryan 4 55
(Brian Barr) *chsd ldrs: pushed along over 2f out: ev ch over 1f out: wknd ins fnl f* **13/2$^{3}$**

0-25 **5** 2 **Barnacle**$^{21}$ [395] 8-8-10 **46** .......... (vt) PatrickVaughan 1 38
(Emma Owen) *s.i.s: hld up: hdwy over 1f out: wknd ins fnl f* **16/1**

0-06 **6** shd **Celestial Dancer (FR)**$^{14}$ [508] 5-8-10 **46** .......... JoshQuinn 5 38
(Nigel Twiston-Davies) *led at stdy pce tl qcknd over 3f out: pushed along and hdd over 1f out: wknd ins fnl f* **20/1**

446/ **7** nse **Mighty Missile (IRE)**$^{10}$ [6980] 6-9-10 **60** .......... (vt) JaneElliott 9 52
(Brian Barr) *chsd ldrs: pushed along over 3f out: wknd over 1f out* **16/1**

400- **8** 1 ¾ **Hyperlink (IRE)**$^{274}$ [2338] 8-9-10 **60** .......... PaulaMuir 8 49
(Clare Ellam) *chsd ldr: pushed along over 2f out: wknd fnl f* **66/1**

260/ **9** 22 **Fire In Babylon (IRE)**$^{508}$ [6735] 9-8-7 **50** .......... (b) GeorgiaDobie$^{(7)}$ 6 8
(Giles Bravery) *hld up: pushed along and hmpd over 2f out: sn wknd* **33/1**

3m 6.44s (1.64) **Going Correction** -0.025s/f (Stan)
**WFA** 4 from 5yo+ 3lb **9 Ran SP% 113.1**
Speed ratings (Par 101): **94,93,91,89,88 88,88,87,74**
CSF £5.58 CT £24.55 TOTE £2.80: £1.10, £1.10, £2.80; EX 7.30 Trifecta £37.80.
**Owner** Mrs P Clark **Bred** Bearstone Stud Ltd **Trained** Cropthorne, Worcs

**FOCUS**
A low-grade staying handicap of which Tony Carroll had trained the winner three times in the previous five years and made it four here. The pace was ordinary but the principals came clear. The runner-up has been rated roughly to form.

## 742 BETWAY SPRINT H'CAP (DIV I) 5f 21y (Tp)
**2:30** (2:32) (Class 6) (0-60,62) 4-Y-0+ **£2,264** (£673; £336; £168) **Stalls** Low

Form RPR

/4-1 **1** **Times In Anatefka (IRE)**$^{2}$ [722] 7-8-13 **52** 6ex ow1 .. (tp) MartinHarley 1 66
(Adrian Brendan Joyce, Ire) *trckd ldrs: nt clr run and swtchd rt over 1f out: rdn to ld ins fnl f: r.o: hung lft towards fin* **13/8$^{1}$**

20-0 **2** 2 **Harpers Ruby**$^{13}$ [523] 7-8-13 **52** .......... PaddyAspell 3 58
(Lynn Siddall) *led: rdn and hung rt fr over 1f out: hdd ins fnl f: styd on same pce* **28/1**

4-05 **3** ½ **See Vermont**$^{19}$ [446] 9-9-4 **57** .......... (p) DanielTudhope 6 61
(Rebecca Bastiman) *s.i.s: hld up: hdwy over 1f out: r.o* **13/2**

250- **4** ¾ **Blistering Dancer (IRE)**$^{179}$ [5628] 7-8-7 **46** oh1 .......... WilliamCarson 2 48
(Tony Carroll) *hld up: hdwy 1/2-way: rdn over 1f out: styd on* **25/1**

4-62 **5** 1 ¼ **Frank The Barber (IRE)**$^{2}$ [723] 5-9-1 **54** .......... (t) AdamBeschizza 8 51
(Steph Hollinshead) *chsd ldr tl hmpd over 1f out: sn rdn: no ex ins fnl f* **8/1**

0530 **6** nk **Socialites Red**$^{9}$ [601] 4-8-13 **59** .......... (p) RPWalsh$^{(7)}$ 4 55
(Scott Dixon) *hld up: rdn 1/2-way: nt trble ldrs* **16/1**

-043 **7** hd **Jack The Laird (IRE)**$^{9}$ [602] 4-9-7 **60** .......... (v) RobertWinston 10 55
(Dean Ivory) *hld up: rdn over 1f out: nvr on terms* **5/1$^{3}$**

0-00 **8** 2 **Mighty Zip (USA)**$^{9}$ [602] 5-8-10 **56** .......... (p) JordanUys$^{(7)}$ 7 44
(Lisa Williamson) *chsd ldrs: rdn 1/2-way: wknd ins fnl f* **50/1**

4-21 **9** 5 **Topsoil**$^{30}$ [271] 4-9-1 **54** .......... (p) OisinMurphy 5 24
(Ronald Harris) *s.i.s: plld hrd: hdwy over 3f out: rdn 1/2-way: wknd over 1f out: eased* **4/1$^{2}$**

1m 1.4s (-0.50) **Going Correction** -0.025s/f (Stan) **9 Ran SP% 114.3**
Speed ratings (Par 101): **103,99,99,97,95 95,95,91,83**
CSF £57.55 CT £243.69 TOTE £2.10: £1.10, £8.80, £2.80; EX 67.40 Trifecta £332.50.
**Owner** Thomas M Kelly **Bred** John Griffin **Trained** Athlone, Co Roscommon

**FOCUS**
The first division of a moderate sprint handicap and a cosy win for the well-backed favourite. The runner-up has been rated back to form.

## 743 BETWAY SPRINT H'CAP (DIV II) 5f 21y (Tp)
**3:00** (3:00) (Class 6) (0-60,60) 4-Y-0+ **£2,264** (£673; £336; £168) **Stalls** Low

Form RPR

00-4 **1** **Roaring Rory**$^{19}$ [446] 4-9-2 **60** .......... (p) LewisEdmunds$^{(5)}$ 2 69
(Ollie Pears) *s.i.s: sn pushed along in rr: hdwy travelling wl 1/2-way: rdn to ld and edgd lft wl ins fnl f: r.o* **9/2$^{2}$**

3-12 **2** 1 ¾ **Fabulous Flyer**$^{7}$ [622] 4-8-11 **50** .......... MartinLane 3 53
(Jeremy Gask) *chsd ldrs: led over 1f out: rdn: hdd and unable qck wl ins fnl f* **5/1$^{3}$**

06-5 **3** 1 ¾ **Storm Trooper (IRE)**$^{41}$ [80] 6-9-3 **56** .......... BarryMcHugh 9 52
(David Nicholls) *chsd ldrs: rdn and nt clr run over 1f out: styd on same pce ins fnl f* **3/1$^{1}$**

**4** 1 ¾ **Mr Michael (IRE)**$^{12}$ [563] 4-9-4 **57** .......... (tp) MartinHarley 7 47
(Adrian Brendan Joyce, Ire) *chsd ldrs: rdn and nt clr run 1f out: styd on same pce* **9/2$^{2}$**

30-3 **5** nk **David's Beauty (IRE)**$^{40}$ [95] 4-9-5 **58** .......... (p) ConnorBeasley 4 47+
(Brian Baugh) *disp ld tl rdn over 1f out: wknd wl ins fnl f* **12/1**

-432 **6** shd **Pearl Noir**$^{9}$ [604] 7-8-8 **54** .......... (b) RPWalsh$^{(7)}$ 6 43+
(Scott Dixon) *disp ld tl rdn over 1f out: styd on same pce fnl f* **9/1**

60-0 **7** 1 **Toni's A Star**$^{44}$ [22] 5-9-2 **60** .......... GeorgiaCox$^{(5)}$ 5 45
(Tony Carroll) *s.i.s: sn outpcd: hdwy over 1f out: wknd ins fnl f* **8/1**

6-55 **8** 1 ¾ **Rojina (IRE)**$^{37}$ [143] 4-8-8 **47** oh1 ow1 .......... (b) JFEgan 8 30+
(Lisa Williamson) *disp ld tl rdn 1/2-way: eased whn btn ins fnl f* **66/1**

2-00 **9** 5 **Insolenceofoffice (IRE)**$^{11}$ [583] 9-8-13 **52** .......... (p) GrahamLee 1 13
(Richard Ford) *sn outpcd* **28/1**

1m 1.69s (-0.21) **Going Correction** -0.025s/f (Stan) **9 Ran SP% 111.8**
Speed ratings (Par 101): **100,97,94,91,91 90,89,86,78**
CSF £26.01 CT £75.97 TOTE £5.70: £1.90, £1.30, £1.50; EX 30.00 Trifecta £122.00.
**Owner** Ownaracehorse Ltd (ownaracehorse.co.uk) **Bred** R S Hoskins & Hermes Services **Trained** Norton, N Yorks

**FOCUS**
The second leg of this moderate sprint handicap was run 0.29 secs slower than the first despite what looked a frantic early pace. The race changed complexion late. The winner has been rated to his best.

## 744 SUNBETS.CO.UK CONDITIONS STKS 1m 142y (Tp)
**3:30** (3:30) (Class 2) 4-Y-0+ **£11,827** (£3,541; £1,770; £885; £442) **Stalls** Low

Form RPR

05-4 **1** **Third Time Lucky (IRE)**$^{32}$ [235] 5-9-0 97 .......... PaulHanagan 5 103
(Richard Fahey) *trckd ldr: racd keenly: led 1/2-way: qckmd 2f out: rdn ins fnl f: edgd rt towards fin: styd on* **15/8$^{2}$**

-215 **2** nk **Mythical Madness**$^{11}$ [574] 6-9-0 101 .......... (v) DanielTudhope 2 102+
(David O'Meara) *hld up: shkn up over 1f out: hdwy to chse wnr ins fnl f: sn rdn: r.o* **13/8$^{1}$**

000- **3** 1 ½ **Bancnuanaheireann (IRE)**$^{77}$ [8160] 10-9-0 101 ...... AlistairRawlinson 3 99
(Michael Appleby) *chsd ldrs: wnt 2nd over 3f out: rdn over 1f out: styd on same pce ins fnl f* **20/1**

1/ **4** 1 ¾ **Andastra (GER)**$^{504}$ [6857] 4-8-9 87 .......... OisinMurphy 4 90+
(Ralph Beckett) *led to 1/2-way: remained handy: rdn over 1f out: no ex ins fnl f* **2/1$^{3}$**

100/ **5** 6 **Lanceur (FR)**$^{369}$ [4165] 8-9-0 92 .......... MartinLane 6 81?
(William Stone) *hld up: pushed along 1/2-way: nvr on terms* **200/1**

1m 48.55s (-1.55) **Going Correction** -0.025s/f (Stan) **5 Ran SP% 111.5**
Speed ratings (Par 109): **105,104,103,101,96**
CSF £5.42 TOTE £3.10: £2.00, £1.10; EX 4.70 Trifecta £16.90.
**Owner** The Musley Bank Partnership & Partner **Bred** Oghill House Stud **Trained** Musley Bank, N Yorks

**FOCUS**
One of the feature races; a good class conditions race despite the smallish field and a good tactical ride on the winner. The winner has been rated to his recent form, with the third to last year's best.

## 745 SUNBETS.CO.UK DOWNLOAD THE APP CLASSIFIED (S) STKS 7f 36y (Tp)
**4:00** (4:00) (Class 6) 3-Y-0+ **£2,264** (£673; £336; £168) **Stalls** High

Form RPR

4163 **1** **Call Out Loud**$^{13}$ [528] 5-9-2 67 .......... (vt) AlistairRawlinson$^{(3)}$ 9 73
(Michael Appleby) *mde all: rdn over 1f out: styd on* **9/1**

62-2 **2** 1 ¼ **Malaysian Boleh**$^{39}$ [116] 7-9-5 70 .......... (b) BenCurtis 8 70
(Brian Ellison) *hld up: hdwy over 1f out: r.o to go 2nd nr fin: nt rch ldr* **9/4$^{1}$**

460- **3** ½ **Light From Mars**[88] 8037 12-9-5 69.................................(p) LukeMorris 2 69
(Ronald Harris) *trckd ldrs: racd keenly: rdn to chse wnr and hung lft fr over 1f out: styd on same pce* 11/1

3-40 **4** 1 ½ **Dodgy Bob**[14] 514 4-9-5 69.................................... KevinStott 1 65
(Kevin Ryan) *chsd wnr: rdn and hung rt over 2f out: lost 2nd over 1f out: no ex ins fnl f* 9/2[2]

06-0 **5** nse **Order Of Service**[14] 363 7-9-5 70.................................. PaddyAspell 6 65
(Shaun Harris) *s.i.s: pushed along in rr early: rdn over 1f out: r.o towards fin* 33/1

0-44 **6** shd **Mime Dance**[14] 513 6-9-5 68.................................(v) DanielTudhope 3 65
(David O'Meara) *chsd ldrs: rdn over 2f out: edgd lft and styd on same pce fnl f* 13/2

50-0 **7** hd **Oeil De Tigre (FR)**[40] 93 6-9-5 68.............................. WilliamCarson 4 64
(Tony Carroll) *hld up in tch: racd keenly: rdn over 1f out: no ex ins fnl f* 20/1

20-3 **8** 2 ½ **Top Offer**[20] 426 8-9-5 64.................................... GrahamLee 7 58
(Patrick Morris) *hld up: rdn over 1f out: nvr on terms* 6/1[3]

6-26 **9** nk **Pool House**[25] 360 6-9-5 64.................................... RobertWinston 5 57
(Mike Murphy) *hld up: rdn over 1f out: n.d* 17/2

1m 28.25s (-0.55) **Going Correction** -0.025s/f (Stan) 9 Ran SP% **113.1**
Speed ratings (Par 101): **102,100,100,98,98 98,97,95,94**
CSF £28.96 TOTE £9.20: £2.50, £1.10, £3.20; EX 32.60 Trifecta £272.60.Dodgy Bob was bought by Mr Michael Mullineaux for £6000. Mime Dance was bought by Miss Alice Haynes for £6000.
**Owner** Kings Head Duffield Racing Partnership **Bred** Rabbah Bloodstock Limited **Trained** Oakham, Rutland

**FOCUS**
A competitive seller on paper and the form looks reasonable for the grade. A minor career best from the winner, with the runner-up just off his recent figures.

## 746 BETWAY H'CAP 2m 120y (Tp)
**4:30** (4:30) (Class 2) (0-105,96) 4-Y-0+
**£11,827** (£3,541; £1,770; £885; £442; £222) **Stalls** Low

Form RPR

604- **1** **Haines**[102] 7814 6-9-3 **90**.................................... RobHornby(3) 9 98
(Andrew Balding) *hld up: hdwy over 2f out: rdn to ld over 1f out: hung lft ins fnl f: styd on* 16/1

14-1 **2** nk **Byron Flyer**[11] 571 6-9-0 **84**.................................... LukeMorris 4 92+
(Ian Williams) *chsd ldrs: nt clr run wl over 1f out: rdn and ev ch sn after: hung lft ins fnl f: styd on* 7/2[2]

1-11 **3** 1 ¼ **Isharah (USA)**[22] 389 4-9-2 **92**.................................... JoeFanning 8 99
(Mark Johnston) *s.i.s: rcvrd to go prom after 1f: chsd ldr 2f out: rdn and ev ch over 1f out: styd on same pce ins fnl f* 4/1[3]

000- **4** nk **Gavlar**[60] 8424 6-9-3 **90**.................................(v) CallumShepherd(3) 3 96
(William Knight) *hld up in tch: racd keenly: rdn over 1f out: styd on same pce ins fnl f* 40/1

/61- **5** 1 **Calvinist**[131] 7123 4-9-0 **90**.................................(t) OisinMurphy 11 95+
(Archie Watson) *prom: nt clr run over 1f out: rdn and hung lft ins fnl f: styd on same pce* 9/4[1]

0/46 **6** 3 ½ **Entihaa**[18] 467 9-8-12 **85**.................................... NoelGarbutt(3) 2 86
(Dai Burchell) *s.i.s: hld up: rdn over 2f out: styd on ins fnl f: nvr nrr* 66/1

4-33 **7** hd **Percy Veer**[20] 422 5-8-6 **81**.................................(b[1]) MitchGodwin(5) 10 82
(Sylvester Kirk) *chsd ldr tl rdn 2f out: hmpd wl over 1f out: wknd ins fnl f* 14/1

00-0 **8** nk **Castilo Del Diablo (IRE)**[34] 197 8-9-2 **86**.................................... PaulHanagan 1 86
(David Simcock) *hld up: pushed along and hdwy on outer over 2f out: hung lft and wknd ins fnl f* 12/1

310- **9** nk **Oceane (FR)**[151] 6582 5-9-8 **92**.................................(p) MartinHarley 5 92
(Alan King) *led at stdy pce tl qcknd over 3f out: rdn and hdd over 1f out: wknd ins fnl f* 6/1

5/0- **10** 11 **Treasure The Ridge (IRE)**[377] 440 8-8-5 **80**.................... AliceMills(5) 7 67
(Martin Hill) *mid-div: hdwy 12f out: rdn whn hmpd over 2f out: sn wknd* 100/1

50-5 **11** 2 **Gang Warfare**[30] 268 6-9-12 **96**.................................(h) TimmyMurphy 6 80
(Jamie Osborne) *hld up: a in rr: wknd over 2f out* 16/1

3m 38.53s (-5.17) **Going Correction** -0.025s/f (Stan)
**WFA** 4 from 5yo+ 4lb 11 Ran SP% **118.3**
Speed ratings (Par 109): **111,110,110,110,109 108,107,107,107,102 101**
CSF £71.79 CT £276.88 TOTE £14.90: £3.90, £1.60, £1.30; EX 102.60 Trifecta £577.30.
**Owner** Bow River Racing **Bred** Spring Bloodstock Ltd **Trained** Kingsclere, Hants

**FOCUS**
The other feature contest and a strong, competitive handicap for stayers despite the top weight being rated 9lb below the race ceiling.They didn't appear to go that quick but three progressive stayers made the frame, so the form might prove sound. A small pb from the winner, with the fourth helping to set the standard.

## 747 BETWAY MIDDLE MAIDEN STKS 1m 1f 104y (Tp)
**5:00** (5:01) (Class 5) 4-Y-0+ **£2,911** (£866; £432; £216) **Stalls** Low

Form RPR

45 **1** **Alhajjaj**[16] 479 4-9-5 0.................................(h) OisinMurphy 1 72
(Andrew Balding) *plld hrd and prom: chsd ldr over 2f out: rdn to ld over 1f out: styd on* 11/4[2]

6-32 **2** 2 **Ms Gillard**[8] 609 4-9-0 62.................................... MartinHarley 2 62
(David Simcock) *hld up in tch: pushed along over 2f out: rdn to chse wnr and hung lft fr over 1f out: styd on same pce wl ins fnl f* 11/10[1]

22-3 **3** 2 ¼ **Sea Dweller**[2] 717 4-9-0 0.................................... WilliamCarson 10 58
(Anthony Carson) *chsd ldrs: rdn over 2f out: hung lft fr over 1f out: no ex ins fnl f* 7/2[3]

5 **4** nk **Bob Hopeful**[36] 165 4-9-5 0.................................(h[1]) GrahamLee 7 62
(Mike Murphy) *hld up: hdwy 2f out: rdn over 1f out: no ex ins fnl f* 33/1

00- **5** 3 ½ **One For Jodie (IRE)**[293] 1800 6-9-2 0.................... AlistairRawlinson(3) 9 55
(Michael Appleby) *hld up: r.o ins fnl f: nvr nrr* 80/1

64-0 **6** ½ **Golden Muscade (USA)**[12] 549 4-8-7 58.................... JoshuaBryan(7) 4 49
(Brian Barr) *chsd ldr: led over 7f out: rdn over 2f out: hdd over 1f out: wknd ins fnl f* 20/1

-060 **7** ¾ **Twilight Angel**[19] 436 9-9-0 45.................................(vt) JFEgan 6 47
(Emma Owen) *sn led: hdd over 7f out: chsd ldr: rdn over 2f out: lost 2nd over 1f out: wknd fnl f* 150/1

00 **8** 6 **Way Up High**[16] 479 5-9-0 0.................................... MartinLane 8 34
(Steve Flook) *hld up in tch: rdn over 3f out: wknd wl over 1f out* 200/1

0-0 **9** 23 **Barbary Prince**[16] 479 5-9-5 0.................................... PaddyAspell 3
(Shaun Harris) *hld up: rdn and wknd 1/2-way* 200/1

0 **10** 12 **Incredible Dream (IRE)**[14] 504 4-9-5 0.................... RobertWinston 11
(Dean Ivory) *s.s: a in rr: rdn: hung lft and wknd over 2f out* 10/1

1m 59.86s (-0.94) **Going Correction** -0.025s/f (Stan) 10 Ran SP% **116.2**
Speed ratings (Par 103): **103,101,99,98,95 95,94,89,68,58**
CSF £6.04 TOTE £3.60: £1.60, £1.10, £1.40; EX 6.90 Trifecta £14.00.
**Owner** Salem Rashid **Bred** Newsells Park Stud **Trained** Kingsclere, Hants

**FOCUS**
A very ordinary looking older horse maiden in which those at the head of the market held sway, but the form looks moderate. The runner-up has been rated just off the balance of her form.
T/Plt: £9.60 to a £1 stake. Pool: £85,347.36 - 6,437.55 winning units T/Qpdt: £4.60 to a £1 stake. Pool: £5,906.29 - 941.91 winning units **Colin Roberts**

# 711 CAGNES-SUR-MER
Wednesday, February 15
**OFFICIAL GOING: Polytrack: standard**

## 748a PRIX DES CROCUS (CLAIMER) (3YO COLTS & GELDINGS) (POLYTRACK) 1m (P)
**2:20** (2:20) 3-Y-0 **£6,837** (£2,735; £2,051; £1,367; £683)

RPR

**1** **Fankairos Ranger (USA)**[20] 427 3-9-2 0......(p) ChristopheSoumillon 7 78
(Cedric Rossi, France) 7/2[3]

**2** 1 ½ **Stormberg (IRE)**[51] 3-8-8 0.................................... KyllanBarbaud(8) 5 75
(N Caullery, France) 2/1[1]

**3** 1 **Alfa Manifesto (FR)**[20] 427 3-8-11 0.....................(b) AntoineHamelin 9 68
(Matthieu Palussiere, France) 53/10

**4** nse **Different Views (USA)**[11] 584 3-9-2 0............. Pierre-CharlesBoudot 8 73
(Gay Kelleway) *sn hld up in fnl trio: pushed along 3f out but no imp: hdwy on outer 2f out: rdn to chse ldng pair over 1f out: one pce fnl f* 96/10

**5** 2 ½ **Mind Juggler (ITY)** 3-8-11 0.....................................(p) FranckBlondel 1 62
(Simone Brogi, France) 31/10[2]

**6** nk **Papa Winner (FR)**[51] 3-8-11 0.....................................(p) TonyPiccone 6 61
(S Jesus, France) 25/1

**7** 3 **Alexis Des Fosses (FR)**[107] 3-9-2 0.........................(p) RonanThomas 4 59
(J Phelippon, France) 146/10

**8** hd **Star On Sunday (FR)** 3-8-6 0...........................(b) ErwannLebreton(5) 3 54
(A Lopez, France) 59/1

**9** 5 ½ **Mesa Arch (FR)**[58] 3-8-6 0.................................... JeromeMoutard(5) 2 41
(Mlle V Dissaux, France) 71/1

1m 37.34s 9 Ran SP% **118.6**
PARI-MUTUEL (all including 1 euro stake): WIN 4.50; PLACE 1.50, 1.30, 1.60; DF 7.50; SF 16.40.
**Owner** Dream With Me Stable Inc **Bred** Lisa Reynolds **Trained** France

749 - 756a (Foreign Racing) - See Raceform Interactive

# 636 CHELMSFORD (A.W) (L-H)
Thursday, February 16
**OFFICIAL GOING: Polytrack: standard**
Wind: light, half behind Weather: dry

## 757 TOTEPLACEPOT RACING'S FAVOURITE BET AMATEUR RIDERS' H'CAP 1m (P)
**5:50** (5:51) (Class 6) (0-65,65) 4-Y-0+ **£3,119** (£967; £483; £242) **Stalls** Low

Form RPR

000- **1** **Hernando Torres**[48] 8588 9-10-12 **63**.................(tp) MissJoannaMason 3 73
(Michael Easterby) *chsd clr ldr after 1f: clsd over 2f out: rdn to ld over 1f out: sn clr and in n.d fnl f: eased towards fin* 4/1[2]

650- **2** 5 **Strictly Art (IRE)**[8] 8490 4-9-12 **54**.............................(p) MissJCooley(5) 2 53
(Alan Bailey) *broke wl: sn hdd and off the pce in 3rd after 1f: pushed along 1/2-way: rdn to chse clr wnr over 1f out: clr 2nd but no imp fnl f: eased towards fin* 8/1[3]

0-00 **3** 8 **My Lord**[7] 648 9-10-9 **65**.................................... MissMBryant(5) 5 46
(Paddy Butler) *off the pce in last trio: modest 4th 2f out: sn rdn: plugged on to go 3rd ins fnl f: n.d* 50/1

5011 **4** 1 ¾ **Celtic Artisan (IRE)**[7] 636 6-10-4 **60** 6ex.....................(bt) MrBLynn(5) 7 38+
(Rebecca Menzies) *sn led and pushed wl clr: rdn wl over 2f out: hdd over 1f out: sn btn: fdd fnl f* 4/11[1]

0-00 **5** 11 **Heart Of An Angel**[5] 684 4-9-13 **55**................(b) MrRomainClavreul(5) 6 8
(Henry Spiller) *s.i.s: a in rr: nvr on terms* 100/1

-050 **6** 4 **Swiss Lait**[1] 733 6-10-0 **51** oh3.................................(p) MissAWaugh 4
(Patrick Holmes) *off the pce in last trio: u.p and no hdwy 3f out: nvr on terms* 22/1

1m 40.11s (0.21) **Going Correction** 0.0s/f (Stan) 6 Ran SP% **111.7**
Speed ratings (Par 101): **98,93,85,83,72 68**
CSF £31.34 TOTE £5.90: £2.30, £5.50; EX 26.00 Trifecta £224.90.
**Owner** Clive Sigsworth **Bred** Mrs J A Chapman & Mrs Shelley Dwyer **Trained** Sheriff Hutton, N Yorks

**FOCUS**
An unusually uncompetitive amateur riders' handicap and, with the long odds-on favourite going off too quickly and burning himself out in front, it proved plain sailing for the well treated Hernando Torres.

## 758 TOTEPOOLLIVEINFO.COM FOR RACING RESULTS MEDIAN AUCTION MAIDEN STKS 1m (P)
**6:25** (6:25) (Class 5) 3-5-Y-0 **£5,175** (£1,540; £769; £384) **Stalls** Low

Form RPR

0 **1** **Faience**[36] 168 3-8-4 0.................................... BenCurtis 6 68
(William Haggas) *w ldr: drvn over 1f out: edgd lft u.p 1f out: sustained effrt to ld wl ins fnl f: kpt on* 8/1

**2** nk **Dubai Waves** 3-8-4 0.................................... JosephineGordon 7 67+
(Hugo Palmer) *trckd ldrs: shkn up to chse ldng pair 2f out: rdn ent fnl f: no imp tl styd on wl towards fin: wnt 2nd last strides* 11/1

5-5 **3** hd **Traveller (FR)**[40] 115 3-8-9 0.................................(t) MichaelJMMurphy 4 72
(Charles Hills) *led: rdn 2f out: drvn ent fnl f: hdd and one pced wl ins fnl f: lost 2nd last strides* 5/1[3]

5 **4** 1 ¾ **Alabaster**[19] 466 3-8-9 0.................................... LukeMorris 2 68+
(Sir Mark Prescott Bt) *awkward leaving stalls and s.i.s: in tch in rr of main gp: shkn up over 1f out: rdn 1f out: edging lft but kpt on fnl 100yds: nvr getting on terms w ldrs* 6/5[1]

**5** 1 **Specialist (IRE)** 3-8-9 0.................................... FrannyNorton 3 66
(Mark Johnston) *rn green: in tch in rr of main gp: effrt on inner over 1f out: kpt on same pce ins fnl f: eased towards fin* 12/1

3- **6** 1 **Ahead Of Time**[253] 3032 3-8-9 0.................................... TomEaves 1 63
(David Simcock) *t.k.h: trckd ldrs: shkn up and swtchd rt over 1f out: unable qck and lost pl 1f out: kpt on same pce after* 7/2[2]

7 2 1/2 **Indian Red** 3-8-2 0 ........ GabrieleMalune(7) 8 58
(Mark H Tompkins) *restless in stalls: rdr struggled to remove hood and v.s.a: rn green and sn pushed along in detached last: clsd 1/2-way and in tch: rdn and kpt on same pce fr over 1f out* **50/1**

1m 39.09s (-0.81) **Going Correction** 0.0s/f (Stan) 7 Ran SP% **113.4**
Speed ratings (Par 103): **104,103,103,101,100 99,97**
CSF £85.85 TOTE £9.90: £3.40, £3.30; EX 76.00 Trifecta £316.70.
**Owner** Cheveley Park Stud **Bred** Cheveley Park Stud Ltd **Trained** Newmarket, Suffolk

**FOCUS**
An informative, though probably only moderate maiden. The first three finished in a heap. The third helps set the standard.

## 759 TOTEQUADPOT FOUR PLACES IN FOUR RACES H'CAP — 2m (P)

**7:00** (7:00) (Class 4) (0-85,86) 4-Y-0+ **£6,469** (£1,925; £962; £481) **Stalls** Low

Form RPR

0/3- 1 **Duke Street (IRE)**[91] [619] 5-9-12 **83** ........ LukeMorris 11 91
(Dr Richard Newland) *pressed ldr: rdn over 2f out: led u.p over 1f out: forged ahd ins fnl f: hrd pressed and hld on wl towards fin* **9/1**

23-1 2 hd **Aldreth**[42] [62] 6-9-3 **77** ........(p) NathanEvans(3) 8 84
(Michael Easterby) *trckd ldrs: effrt over 1f out: drvn to chse wnr jst ins fnl f: kpt on and str chal towards fin: hld cl home* **10/3[2]**

5-61 3 2 1/4 **Midtech Star (IRE)**[14] [519] 5-9-11 **82** ........(v) BenCurtis 5 86
(Ian Williams) *chsd ldrs: cl 3rd and rdn ent fnl 2f: ev ch u.p over 1f out: 3rd and no ex 150yds out: sn outpcd* **7/2[3]**

4-01 4 1 1/2 **Cotton Club (IRE)**[21] [422] 6-10-0 **85** ........ RyanTate 10 88
(Rod Millman) *hld up in last pair: pushed along and hdwy over 3f out: rdn over 2f out: kpt on ins fnl f: nvr enough pce to threaten ldrs* **14/1**

-042 5 nk **Silver Quay (IRE)**[5] [683] 5-10-1 **86** ........(p) GeorgeBaker 3 88
(Jamie Osborne) *t.k.h: hld up in last trio: clsd and swtchd rt wl over 1f out: sn wanting to hang lft: hdwy 1f out: kpt on ins fnl f: nvr threatened ldrs* **7/4[1]**

-330 6 nk **Cavalieri (IRE)**[14] [519] 7-8-10 **67** ........(tp) KevinStott 9 69
(Philip Kirby) *hld up in tch in midfield: effrt over 2f out: kpt on same pce u.p fnl f* **22/1**

3034 7 2 1/2 **Luv U Whatever**[14] [519] 7-9-13 **84** ........ AndrewMullen 2 83
(Michael Attwater) *led: rdn and qcknd over 1f out: hdd and no ex u.p over 1f out: wknd ins fnl f* **16/1**

000- 8 3/4 **Glan Y Gors (IRE)**[158] [6379] 5-9-11 **82** ........(h) TomEaves 4 80
(David Simcock) *stdd and dropped in bhd after s: t.k.h: hld up in rr: effrt on inner wl over 1f out: no imp: nvr trbld ldrs* **16/1**

020- 9 7 **Chartbreaker (FR)**[75] [8051] 6-9-4 **80** ........(p) MeganNicholls(5) 1 69
(Chris Gordon) *in tch in midfield: rdn 3f out: sn dropped to rr: bhd over 1f out* **20/1**

3m 31.97s (1.97) **Going Correction** 0.0s/f (Stan) 9 Ran SP% **119.2**
Speed ratings (Par 105): **95,94,93,93,92 92,91,91,87**
CSF £40.46 CT £129.02 TOTE £10.10: £2.30, £1.30, £2.10; EX 40.00 Trifecta £120.90.
**Owner** Chris Stedman & Mark Albon **Bred** Mrs Joan Keaney **Trained** Claines, Worcs

**FOCUS**
This was run at pedestrian early pace and developed into an unsatisfactory dash up the home straight. The first three home were always in the first four. Muddling form. A small pb from the winner, with the third and fourth rated close to their best.

## 760 @TOTEPOOLRACING WIN TICKETS ON TWITTER H'CAP — 7f (P)

**7:30** (7:32) (Class 4) (0-85,86) 4-Y-0+ **£6,469** (£1,925; £962; £481) **Stalls** Low

Form RPR

0-00 1 **Outer Space**[19] [459] 6-9-8 **86** ........ GeorgeBaker 4 95+
(Jamie Osborne) *hld up in tch in rr: clsd and nt clr run over 1f out: shkn up: edgd lft and qcknd to ld 1f out: rdn ins fnl f: a doing enough after: rdn out* **7/2[1]**

6-64 2 1/2 **Loyalty**[26] [349] 10-9-4 **82** ........(v) FrannyNorton 5 89
(Derek Shaw) *hld up in tch in midfield: nt clr run over 1f out: sltly hmpd 1f out: hdwy u.p to chse wnr ins fnl f: r.o wl to press wnr towards fin but a hld* **8/1**

050- 3 3 1/2 **Until Midnight (IRE)**[152] [6579] 7-8-11 **80** ........ LuluStanford(5) 8 78
(Eugene Stanford) *wl in tch in midfield: effrt u.p over 1f out: no threat to ldng pair and kpt on same pce ins fnl f: wnt 3rd last strides* **20/1**

2-00 4 hd **Plucky Dip**[19] [459] 6-9-2 **80** ........ DannyBrock 6 77
(John Ryan) *hld up in tch in midfield: nt clr run over 1f out tl hdwy u.p ins fnl f: chsd clr ldng pair 100yds out: no imp and lost 3rd last strides* **5/1[2]**

41-4 5 1/2 **Evening Attire**[29] [287] 6-8-11 **80** ........ HollieDoyle(5) 7 76
(William Stone) *dwlt: hld up in tch in rr: effrt on outer over 1f out: kpt on same pce ins fnl f: no threat to ldrs* **5/1[2]**

0-11 6 1 **Gold Flash**[31] [267] 5-9-0 **78** ........(v) PhillipMakin 1 71+
(Keith Dalgleish) *hld up in tch towards rr: nt clr run over 1f out: gap opened eventually ins fnl f but no ch: pushed along and kpt on same pce after* **6/1[3]**

0-32 7 3/4 **Curzon Line**[12] [581] 8-8-6 **77** ........ HarrisonShaw(7) 9 68
(Michael Easterby) *sn led: rdn over 1f out: hdd 1f out: sn outpcd and wknd ins fnl f* **10/1**

0-34 8 1 **Pearl Spectre (USA)**[15] [506] 6-9-4 **85** ........ CallumShepherd(3) 3 73
(Phil McEntee) *chsd ldrs: rdn over 1f out: unable qck u.p and losing pl whn jostled 1f out: wknd ins fnl f* **8/1**

600- 9 1 1/2 **Welliesinthewater (IRE)**[72] [8239] 7-8-12 **76** ........(v) MartinLane 2 60
(Derek Shaw) *chsd ldr tl unable qck u.p over 1f out: wknd ins fnl f* **12/1**

200- 10 1 1/4 **Thaqaffa (IRE)**[141] [6877] 4-9-2 **80** ........ LemosdeSouza 11 61
(Amy Murphy) *t.k.h: chsd ldrs: rdn and unable qck over 1f out: btn whn squeezed for room ent fnl f: sn wknd* **20/1**

00-0 11 12 **Flying Fantasy**[29] [287] 5-8-5 **72** ........ AaronJones(3) 10 20
(Stuart Williams) *s.i.s: racd wd and a in rr* **25/1**

1m 24.42s (-2.78) **Going Correction** 0.0s/f (Stan) 11 Ran SP% **122.2**
Speed ratings (Par 105): **115,114,110,110,109 108,107,106,104,103 89**
CSF £32.42 CT £504.99 TOTE £4.70: £1.80, £2.60, £5.80; EX 36.10 Trifecta £1047.50.
**Owner** Tony Taylor & Patrick Gage **Bred** Catridge Farm Stud & B & H Jellett **Trained** Upper Lambourn, Berks

**FOCUS**
They went a good clip in this handicap, setting the race up perfectly for the gambled-on winner. The winner has been rated as good as ever.

## 761 TOTEPOOL RACECOURSE DEBIT CARD BETTING AVAILABLE H'CAP — 7f (P)

**8:00** (8:02) (Class 6) (0-52,54) 4-Y-0+ **£3,234** (£962; £481; £240) **Stalls** Low

Form RPR

-445 1 **Mr Potter**[7] [640] 4-9-8 **53** ........(v) ConnorBeasley 3 58
(Richard Guest) *taken down early: stdd s: t.k.h: hld up in last trio: swtchd rt and effrt 2f out: hdwy u.p 1f out: wnt 3rd and hung bdly lft ins fnl f: stened and r.o strly towards fin to ld on post* **3/1[1]**

60- 2 nse **Home Again**[82] [8121] 4-9-5 **50** ........ MartinHarley 8 55
(Lee Carter) *chsd ldr: rdn and ev ch over 1f out: forged ahd u.p wl ins fnl f: kpt on wl: hdd on post* **8/1[3]**

140- 3 3/4 **Rosie Crowe (IRE)**[48] [8589] 5-9-5 **50** ........(v) JosephineGordon 7 53
(Shaun Harris) *led: rdn over 1f out: hdd ins fnl f: no ex and one pced wl ins fnl f* **7/1[2]**

5305 4 1 3/4 **Limerick Lord (IRE)**[8] [614] 5-9-1 **49** ........(p) ShelleyBirkett(3) 6 47
(Julia Feilden) *wl in tch: effrt u.p 2f out: kpt on ins fnl f: nvr quite enough pce to get on terms* **7/1[2]**

5-53 5 hd **Upper Lambourn (IRE)**[7] [640] 9-8-8 **46** oh1 ........(t) KevinLundie(7) 2 44
(John Holt) *hld up in tch in midfield: effrt u.p over 1f out: styd on ins fnl f: nvr threatened ldrs* **10/1**

0-20 6 1 1/2 **Moving Robe (IRE)**[8] [614] 4-9-1 **46** ........(t) WilliamCarson 5 40
(Conrad Allen) *wl in tch in midfield: effrt to chse ldrs 2f out: no imp and one pced fr over 1f out: lost 3 pls ins fnl f* **10/1**

00-0 7 3/4 **Archipentura**[28] [311] 5-8-8 **46** ........ GinaMangan(7) 12 38
(J R Jenkins) *t.k.h: hld up in tch in midfield: effrt over 1f out: kpt on ins fnl f wout threatening ldrs* **50/1**

640- 8 shd **Free To Roam (IRE)**[118] [7515] 4-9-6 **51** ........(p[1]) LukeMorris 13 43
(Luke McJannet) *chsd ldrs: 4th and drvn 2f out: unable qck and kpt on same pce fr over 1f out* **12/1**

00-0 9 3 **Mr Turner**[8] [614] 4-8-8 **46** oh1 ........ GabrieleMalune(7) 11 30
(Mark H Tompkins) *short of room leaving stalls: in tch in midfield: pushed rt after 1f: effrt 2f out: no imp over 1f out: wl hld and one pced fnl f* **16/1**

001- 10 1 1/2 **Turaathy (IRE)**[70] [8278] 4-9-6 **54** ........ EoinWalsh(3) 14 34
(Tony Newcombe) *hld up in tch in midfield: effrt u.p 2f out: unable qck and btn over 1f out: wknd ins fnl f* **9/1**

0-44 11 1 1/4 **Diamond Indulgence**[19] [455] 4-9-3 **48** ........(h) MartinLane 1 25
(Derek Shaw) *t.k.h: hld up towards rr: rdn over 3f out: no rspnse and btn 2f out: wl hld over 1f out* **7/1[2]**

6000 12 1 1/4 **Patron Of Explores (USA)**[1] [739] 6-9-1 **46** oh1 ........ TomEaves 4 20
(Patrick Holmes) *stdd s: t.k.h: hld up in last trio: swtchd rt and effrt on outer over 2f out: pushed wd and lost pl 2f out: sn wknd* **25/1**

4/6- 13 4 **Bella's Boy (IRE)**[185] [5474] 4-9-7 **52** ........ AdamKirby 9 15
(John Ryan) *s.i.s: hld up in tch in rr: rdn 2f out: no rspnse and sn bhd* **20/1**

0-00 14 7 **London Rebel (IRE)**[21] [415] 4-9-1 **46** oh1 ........(p[1]) TomMarquand 10 7
(Richard Spencer) *wnt rt s: in tch in midfield: wnt rt again 6f out: rdn and lost pl over 2f out: sn dropped to rr and drvn: bhd fnl f* **50/1**

1m 26.11s (-1.09) **Going Correction** 0.0s/f (Stan) 14 Ran SP% **127.9**
Speed ratings (Par 101): **106,105,105,103,102 101,100,100,96,95 93,92,87,86**
CSF £27.61 CT £164.54 TOTE £4.20: £1.50, £2.90, £2.20; EX 39.60 Trifecta £243.40.
**Owner** A Turton, J Blackburn & Partner **Bred** P Balding **Trained** Ingmanthorpe, W Yorks

**FOCUS**
What this handicap lacked in terms of class it more than made up for in drama as Mr Potter rocketed home for an unlikely success. The third has been rated to the pick of her recent form.

## 762 EAT-DRINK-CELEBRATE AT CHANNELS ESTATE CHANNELSESTATE.CO.UK H'CAP — 1m 5f 66y(P)

**8:30** (8:30) (Class 6) (0-60,60) 4-Y-0+ **£3,234** (£962; £481; £240) **Stalls** Low

Form RPR

12-5 1 **Kay Sera**[27] [333] 9-9-2 **58** ........ EoinWalsh(3) 1 64
(Tony Newcombe) *stdd s: t.k.h: in rr: effrt to chse clr ldng pair 3f out: steadily clsd u.p over 1f out: chal ins fnl f: kpt on wl u.p to ld towards fin* **9/2[3]**

00-1 2 nk **Willyegolassiego**[7] [645] 4-8-8 **51** 6ex ........ LiamKeniry 5 57
(Neil Mulholland) *trckd ldr: rdn and kicked clr w ldr over 3f out: led 2f out: rn green and edgd lft u.p ins fnl f: hdd and no ex towards fin* **4/7[1]**

6-55 3 2 1/4 **Oyster Card**[15] [508] 4-8-3 **46** ........(p) LukeMorris 3 49
(Michael Appleby) *led: rdn and qcknd clr w rival over 3f out: hdd 2f out: stl ev ch tl no ex u.p ins fnl f: wknd towards fin* **4/1[2]**

054- 4 1/2 **Topalova**[114] [7592] 4-7-13 **49** ........ GabrieleMalune(7) 4 51
(Mark H Tompkins) *hld up in 4th: rdn and outpcd over 3f out: kpt on steadily fr over 1f out: nvr enough pce to threaten ldrs* **10/1**

/400 5 7 **Azamesse (IRE)**[7] [646] 5-8-9 **55** ........(v) GinaMangan(7) 6 47
(J R Jenkins) *stdd after s: chsd ldrs: rdn and outpcd over 3f out: dropped to last over 2f out: no ch after* **33/1**

2m 54.84s (1.24) **Going Correction** 0.0s/f (Stan)
**WFA** 4 from 5yo+ 2lb 5 Ran SP% **113.9**
Speed ratings (Par 101): **96,95,94,94,89**
CSF £7.91 TOTE £5.10: £2.10, £1.02; EX 9.70 Trifecta £23.20.
**Owner** Nigel Hardy **Bred** Nigel Hardy **Trained** Yarnscombe, Devon

**FOCUS**
This was strongly run and placed plenty of emphasis on stamina.
T/Jkpt: Not won. T/Plt: £543.70 to a £1 stake. Pool: £95,169.47. 127.76 winning units. T/Qpdt: £12.80 to a £1 stake. Pool: £15,041.93. 863.85 winning units. **Steve Payne**

# 677 LINGFIELD (L-H)

## Thursday, February 16

**OFFICIAL GOING: Polytrack: standard**
Wind: Moderate, half behind Weather: Fine

## 763 32RED CASINO H'CAP — 7f 1y(P)

**1:45** (1:46) (Class 6) (0-65,67) 3-Y-O **£2,264** (£673; £336; £168) **Stalls** Low

Form RPR

0-13 1 **Mia Cara**[21] [417] 3-9-6 **64** ........(v) AdamKirby 12 69
(David Evans) *pressed ldr: led 3f out and mde most after: rdn over 2f out: drvn a l ahd fnl f: kpt on* **9/1**

333- 2 1 **Moneyoryourlife**[99] [7866] 3-8-5 **56** ........ TinaSmith(7) 7 58
(Richard Hannon) *hld up towards rr: nudged along and prog fr wl over 1f out: tk 2nd wl ins fnl f: too late to threaten wnr* **10/1**

25-3 3 1/2 **Seprani**[27] [323] 3-9-3 **61** ........(h) LukeMorris 9 62
(Marco Botti) *t.k.h: pressed ldng pair: rdn 2f out: nt qckn jst over 1f out: styd on same pce last 150yds* **6/1[3]**

3-21 4 shd **Auric Goldfinger (IRE)**[19] [463] 3-9-1 **64** ........(b) HollieDoyle(5) 4 64+
(Richard Hannon) *hld up in last pair: pushed along and prog on outer over 1f out: r.o fnl f: gaining at fin but too much to do* **9/4[1]**

00-4 5 nk **Malt Teaser (FR)**[22] [397] 3-9-7 **65** ........ KierenFox 13 65+
(John Best) *dwlt: sn in midfield: pushed along and outpcd over 2f out: styd on fr over 1f out: gng on at fin* **12/1**

56-3 6 shd **Camaradorie (IRE)**[41] [96] 3-8-13 **60** ........ SimonPearce(3) 2 59
(Lydia Pearce) *pressed ldrs: rdn over 2f out: styd on inner in st: one pce and lost pls wl ins fnl f* **20/1**

30-0 **7** 1/2 **Dragon Dream (IRE)**41 89 3-9-2 **60** MartinLane 1 58
(Roger Ingram) *led to 3f out: sn rdn: led again briefly 2f out: pressed wnr tl ins fnl f: fdd and lost pls nr fin* **20/1**

54-1 **8** 2 1/2 **Sea Tea Dea**27 323 3-9-9 **67** WilliamCarson 5 58
(Anthony Carson) *hld up in rr: wl off the pce over 2f out: shuffled along and sme prog on outer over 1f out: no hdwy fnl f and eased* **5/1**2

05-4 **9** 2 **Bay Watch (IRE)**44 27 3-9-4 **65** (p1) RobHornby(3) 8 51
(Andrew Balding) *hld up in last: pushed along and passed a few fnl f: nvr in it* **7/1**

155- **10** 1/2 **Ivor's Magic (IRE)**162 6236 3-8-11 **62** RhiainIngram(7) 3 46
(David Elsworth) *hld up towards rr: off the pce over 2f out: pushed along on inner and no real prog* **20/1**

544- **11** nk **Hold Me Tight (IRE)**69 8284 3-8-11 **55** (b1) LiamKeniry 10 39
(J S Moore) *t.k.h: pressed ldrs: rdn over 2f out: wknd qckly over 1f out* **33/1**

20-0 **12** nk **Deleyll**34 209 3-8-10 **54** DannyBrock 6 37
(John Butler) *a towards rr: u.p fr 1/2-way and no prog* **66/1**

1m 24.95s (0.15) **Going Correction** -0.05s/f (Stan) 12 Ran SP% **119.7**
Speed ratings (Par 95): **97,95,95,95,94 94,94,91,89,88 88,87**
CSF £89.29 CT £591.64 TOTE £8.70: £3.20, £3.20, £2.00; EX 95.70 Trifecta £693.90.
**Owner** Countess Lonsdale & Richard Kent **Bred** Richard Kent & Lady Lonsdale **Trained** Pandy, Monmouths

**FOCUS**
A moderate 3yo handicap and not many ever got into it. The winner has been rated back to her best, with the third fitting.

## 764 £10 FREE AT 32RED.COM MEDIAN AUCTION MAIDEN FILLIES' STKS 6f 1y(P)
2:15 (2:20) (Class 6) 3-5-Y-O £2,264 (£673; £336; £168) Stalls Low

Form RPR

3-5 **1** **Porto Ferro (IRE)**28 307 3-8-9 72 (p1) LukeMorris 2 52
(Dr Jon Scargill) *trckd ldrs: waiting for room on inner 2f out: shkn up to ld 1f out: sn hrd rdn: kpt on* **2/5**1

-502 **2** 1 1/2 **Mistry**19 455 4-9-5 45 (v) RachealKneller(5) 5 51
(Mark Usher) *pressed ldr: rdn to chal over 1f out: hanging and nt qckn after: chsd wnr ins fnl f: no imp* **12/1**3

0- **3** 1/2 **Sparkling Cossack**78 8151 3-8-9 0 MartinLane 3 45
(Jeremy Gask) *reluctant to enter stall: dwlt: hld up in last: shkn up and green over 2f out: clsd and nt clr run briefly over 1f out: kpt on to take 3rd nr fin* **12/1**3

0-0 **4** shd **Captain Sedgwick (IRE)**10 600 3-8-9 0 TomMarquand 6 45
(John Spearing) *led: rdn 2f out: hdd 1f out: fdd last 100yds* **50/1**

00- **5** nk **Cloud Nine (FR)**280 2177 4-9-10 60 GeorgeDowning 4 48
(Tony Carroll) *hld up in last pair: shkn up over 2f out: kpt on same pce fr over 1f out: nvr able to chal* **20/1**

6-45 **6** 1 1/2 **Cool Echo**21 418 3-8-2 57 (v1) GinaMangan(7) 7 39
(J R Jenkins) *v reluctant to enter stall: s.i.s: wl in tch on outer: rdn 2f out: wknd over 1f out* **5/1**2

1m 13.52s (1.62) **Going Correction** -0.05s/f (Stan)
**WFA** 3 from 4yo 15lb 6 Ran SP% **110.2**
Speed ratings (Par 98): **87,85,84,84,83 81**
CSF £6.18 TOTE £1.20: £1.10, £3.90; EX 4.60 Trifecta £19.70.
**Owner** D Tunmore **Bred** Roundhill Stud & Gleadhill House Stud Ltd **Trained** Newmarket, Suffolk

**FOCUS**
A weak and uncompetitive maiden.

## 765 32RED.COM H'CAP 6f 1y(P)
2:45 (2:45) (Class 4) (0-80,80) 3-Y-O £4,690 (£1,395; £697; £348) Stalls Low

Form RPR

12 **1** **Jack Flash (FR)**12 578 3-9-4 **77** JasonHart 4 79
(Les Eyre) *pressed ldr: shkn up to ld jst over 2f out: drvn over 1f out: all out to hang on nr fin* **2/1**1

02-1 **2** nk **Cappananty Con**31 264 3-9-0 **73** RobertWinston 2 74+
(Dean Ivory) *t.k.h: hld up in last pair: gng best 2f out but stl same pl: cajoled along and prog over 1f out: reminders fnl f: styd on to take 2nd nr fin but got there too late* **5/2**2

2-42 **3** shd **Juan Horsepower**8 623 3-9-3 **76** (p) KieranO'Neill 5 77
(Richard Hannon) *pushed along to dispute 3rd: rdn over 2f out: styd on to chse wnr ins fnl f: clsd but lost 2nd nr fin* **5/1**

2-33 **4** 2 1/4 **Arzaak (IRE)**12 578 3-9-1 **74** DavidProbert 6 68
(Chris Dwyer) *hld up in last pair: rdn over 2f out: no prog tl kpt on to take 4th ins fnl f* **4/1**3

010- **5** 2 **Giennah (IRE)**147 6697 3-9-7 **80** (h) LukeMorris 3 67
(Daniel Mark Loughnane) *chsd ldng pair: rdn over 2f out: wknd fnl f* **14/1**

10-0 **6** 2 **Drop Kick Murphi (IRE)**20 435 3-9-5 **78** AdamKirby 1 59
(Christine Dunnett) *led narrowly: rdn and hdd jst over 2f out: lost 2nd and wknd ins fnl f* **28/1**

1m 11.1s (-0.80) **Going Correction** -0.05s/f (Stan) 6 Ran SP% **108.7**
Speed ratings (Par 99): **103,102,102,99,96 94**
CSF £6.73 TOTE £3.10: £1.90, £1.60; EX 7.90 Trifecta £24.20.
**Owner** Billy Parker **Bred** S A R L De Chambure Haras D'Etreham **Trained** Catwick, N Yorks

**FOCUS**
A fair 3yo sprint handicap and a tight finish between the first three. The third helps set the standard.

## 766 32RED CASINO CLAIMING STKS 1m 2f (P)
3:20 (3:20) (Class 6) 3-Y-O £2,264 (£673; £336; £168) Stalls Low

Form RPR

-624 **1** **Critical Thinking (IRE)**13 552 3-8-6 65 FinleyMarsh(7) 4 67
(Julia Feilden) *n.m.r s and hld up in last: wnt 4th over 2f out gng strly: rdn to cl whn nowhere to go on inner over 1f out: renewed effrt fnl f: styd on to ld nr fin* **5/2**2

4-31 **2** hd **Good Time Ahead (IRE)**24 378 3-9-3 67 PaddyAspell 6 68
(Philip Kirby) *pressed ldr: led 6f out: rdn 2f out: kpt on but hdd nr fin* **3/1**3

3-23 **3** 1 1/4 **Bazwind (IRE)**29 292 3-8-12 63 SeanLevey 1 60
(David Evans) *led to 6f out: chsd ldr to over 2f out: drvn to go 2nd again over 1f out to ins fnl f: one pce* **9/4**1

-545 **4** 1 1/2 **Gog Elles (IRE)**8 627 3-8-1 48 (b1) HollieDoyle(5) 3 51
(J S Moore) *hld up in 5th: prog to chse ldr over 2f out: rdn and no rspnse wl over 1f out: fdd* **12/1**

00-6 **5** 12 **Affair**8 627 3-7-11 57 TheodoreLadd(7) 5 27
(Hughie Morrison) *sn racd wd: chsd ldrs: dropped away fr 3f out* **14/1**

0-23 **6** 2 **Life Won't Wait**22 402 3-9-2 65 JasonHart 2 35
(John Quinn) *chsd ldrs: urged along sn after 1/2-way: wknd fr 3f out* **8/1**

2m 5.95s (-0.65) **Going Correction** -0.05s/f (Stan) 6 Ran SP% **109.8**
Speed ratings (Par 95): **100,99,98,97,88 86**
CSF £9.92 TOTE £3.50: £2.60, £1.50; EX 9.20 Trifecta £23.50.The winner was claimed by Mr Kevin Frost for £7,000.
**Owner** Newmarket Equine Tours Racing Club **Bred** Rolyon Stud **Trained** Exning, Suffolk

**FOCUS**
A modest 3yo claimer with nothing rated above 67, but five of the six runners were within just 4lb of each other on these terms.

## 767 BETWAY CONDITIONS STKS 1m 4f (P)
3:55 (3:56) (Class 2) 4-Y-O+ £11,971 (£3,583; £1,791; £896; £223) Stalls Low

Form RPR

21-3 **1** **Watersmeet**35 197 6-9-2 103 JoeFanning 4 100+
(Mark Johnston) *mde all: shkn up and stretched away fr 2f out: in n.d after: eased nr fin* **2/1**1

00-1 **2** 2 **Calling Out (FR)**38 148 6-9-2 102 SeanLevey 1 94
(David Simcock) *trckd ldrs: rdn to go 2nd wl over 1f out: no imp on clr wnr but kpt on* **5/1**

65-4 **3** nk **Cohesion**26 352 4-8-13 101 RobHornby 6 94
(David Bridgwater) *trckd ldrs: rdn on outer 2f out: pressed for 2nd fnl f but no ch w wnr* **3/1**3

0/-5 **4** 1 **Retrieve (AUS)**17 478 9-9-2 100 (t) TimmyMurphy 5 92
(Jamie Osborne) *hld up in last: effrt 2f out: rdn and kpt on fnl f on inner: n.d* **33/1**

/50- **5** nse **Dashing Star**103 7824 7-9-2 98 ShaneKelly 3 92
(David Elsworth) *chsd wnr: urged along 3f out: lost 2nd and nt qckn wl over 1f out: one pce after* **14/1**

12-2 **5** dht **Rock Steady (IRE)**26 352 4-8-13 99 KieranShoemark 2 92
(Roger Charlton) *taken down early: hld up in 5th: rdn over 2f out: trying to press for a pl whn n.m.r fr over 1f out: one pce* **5/2**2

2m 30.53s (-2.47) **Going Correction** -0.05s/f (Stan)
**WFA** 4 from 6yo+ 2lb 6 Ran SP% **113.2**
Speed ratings (Par 109): **106,104,104,103,103 103**
CSF £12.68 TOTE £2.70: £1.40, £2.80; EX 13.00 Trifecta £33.80.
**Owner** J Barson **Bred** Stetchworth & Middle Park Studs **Trained** Middleham Moor, N Yorks

**FOCUS**
A decent conditions event with the six runners rated between 98 and 103, but the winner was allowed to dictate and his rivals played right into his hands. They finished in official ratings order. The form is far from solid.

## 768 BETWAY BEST ODDS GUARANTEED PLUS H'CAP 6f 1y(P)
4:30 (4:30) (Class 6) (0-65,65) 4-Y-O+ £2,264 (£673; £336; £168) Stalls Low

Form RPR

5-21 **1** **Spirit Of Zebedee (IRE)**12 583 4-9-6 **64** (p) JasonHart 5 70
(John Quinn) *chsd ldr: drvn over 1f out: clsd to dispute ld jst ins fnl f: gained upper hand last 75yds* **11/4**1

44-2 **2** nk **Tidal's Baby**30 273 8-8-12 **56** GeorgeDowning 3 61
(Tony Carroll) *in tch in midfield: rdn wl over 1f out: styd on wl fnl f to take 2nd last stride* **7/2**2

-105 **3** hd **Compton Prince**19 468 8-9-5 **63** (b) JoeFanning 2 67
(Milton Bradley) *trckd ldr: shkn up over 1f out: clsd to dispute ld jst ins fnl f: nt qckn last 100yds: lost 2nd post* **8/1**

3503 **4** 1/2 **Tavener**8 620 5-8-12 **56** (p) DavidProbert 7 59
(David C Griffiths) *chsd ldrs: rdn and nt qckn wl over 1f out: styd on ins fnl f but a safely hld* **6/1**3

-203 **5** 1/2 **Disclosure**12 579 6-8-9 **58** PhilDennis(5) 8 59
(Les Eyre) *t.k.h: hld up in last pair: prog over 1f out: swtchd ins and styd on fnl f: nrst fin* **10/1**

1-00 **6** 1/2 **Red Invader (IRE)**19 468 7-9-4 **62** LiamKeniry 6 62
(John Butler) *dwlt: hld up towards rr: effrt on wd outside 2f out: styd on fnl f but nvr pce to rch ldrs* **25/1**

061- **7** 1 1/2 **Picansort**61 8429 10-9-7 **65** (b) ShaneKelly 10 60
(Peter Crate) *sn chsd ldrs: rdn and nt qckn over 1f out: wknd ins fnl f* **20/1**

3-01 **8** 3 3/4 **Encapsulated**14 521 7-8-7 **58** RhiainIngram(7) 1 42
(Roger Ingram) *t.k.h: hld up in rr: last 2f out: nudged along and no great prog after* **10/1**

-530 **9** 1 1/2 **Pleadings (USA)**13 544 4-8-7 **51** oh2 (vt) WilliamCarson 4 31
(Charlie Wallis) *dwlt: a in rr: shkn up and no prog over 2f out* **14/1**

2-40 **10** 2 1/4 **Rigolleto (IRE)**26 355 9-9-7 **65** (p) GeorgeBaker 9 38
(Anabel K Murphy) *led: stretched on over 2f out: jnd whn lost action jst ins fnl f and virtually p.u* **8/1**

500- **R** **Ghost Train (IRE)**73 8234 8-9-1 **59** (b1) MartinLane 12
(Tim McCarthy) *ref to r: tk no part* **40/1**

1m 11.38s (-0.52) **Going Correction** -0.05s/f (Stan) 11 Ran SP% **121.3**
Speed ratings (Par 101): **101,100,100,99,99 98,96,91,89,86**
CSF £12.27 CT £70.71 TOTE £3.60: £1.50, £1.90, £2.20; EX 14.40 Trifecta £102.50.
**Owner** Malcolm Walker **Bred** N Hartery **Trained** Settrington, N Yorks

**FOCUS**
A moderate sprint handicap. Straightforward form rated around the placed horses.

## 769 BETWAY H'CAP 1m 2f (P)
5:00 (5:00) (Class 5) (0-75,74) 4-Y-O+ £2,911 (£866; £432; £216) Stalls Low

Form RPR

6-34 **1** **Exceeding Power**28 306 6-9-5 **72** TomMarquand 7 80
(Martin Bosley) *trckd ldr 2f: wnt 2nd again 4f out: rdn to ld 2f out: hrd pressed fr over 1f out: kpt finding and hld on wl* **5/1**2

0-36 **2** hd **Mercy Me**28 306 5-9-3 **70** AdamKirby 5 77
(John Ryan) *wl in tch bhd ldrs: prog to to take 2nd wl over 1f out and sn upsides wnr: sustained chal fnl f but jst hld* **6/1**3

1-24 **3** 1 1/2 **Zabeel Star (IRE)**15 507 5-9-7 **74** LiamKeniry 4 78+
(Graeme McPherson) *hld up in midfield: rdn over 2f out: effrt on outer over 1f out: styd on fnl f to snatch 3rd last stride* **3/1**1

1403 **4** nse **Black Dave (IRE)**7 648 7-9-2 **72** KieranShoemark(3) 6 76
(David Evans) *t.k.h: trckd ldrs: rdn over 2f out: chsd ldng pair jst over 1f out: no imp and lost 3rd last stride* **8/1**

3-04 **5** 1/2 **Zephyros (GER)**7 648 6-8-8 **64** RobHornby(3) 9 67
(David Bridgwater) *dwlt: hld up in rr: rdn over 2f out: prog over 1f out to press for 3rd fnl f: kpt on* **5/1**2

00-0 **6** 3 1/4 **Russian Reward (IRE)**14 516 5-9-6 **73** JackMitchell 8 69
(Amanda Perrett) *led 4f: chsd ldr to 4f out: rdn over 2f out: wknd jst over 1f out* **8/1**

455- **7** 1 **Al Khafji**166 6138 4-9-1 **74** DavidParkes(5) 1 68
(Jeremy Gask) *hld up wl in rr: shkn up over 3f out: struggling in last pair over 2f out: no ch after: kpt on fnl 100yds* **8/1**

0-02 **8** 1/2 **Siouxperhero (IRE)**21 420 8-8-7 **60** (p) MartinDwyer 2 53
(William Muir) *towards rr: urged along over 3f out: brief effrt on inner over 1f out: sn no prog* **25/1**

/04- **9** 6 **Gold Merlion (IRE)**198 4967 4-9-2 **70** JoeFanning 10 51
(Mark Johnston) *trckd ldr after 2f: led after 4f: hdd 2f out: wknd rapidly jst over 1f out* **33/1**

00-0 **10** *17* **Torch**[14] 516 4-9-2 **70** ..................................................... TimmyMurphy 3 17
(John Butler) *stdd s: hld up: a last: lost tch 4f out: t.o* **66/1**

2m 6.4s (-0.20) **Going Correction** -0.05s/f (Stan) **10** Ran SP% **114.2**
Speed ratings (Par 103): **98,97,96,96,96 93,92,92,87,74**
CSF £33.74 CT £104.58 TOTE £6.30: £2.30, £2.00, £1.60; EX 30.30 Trifecta £92.00.
**Owner** The Chalfonts **Bred** Rabbah Bloodstock Limited **Trained** Chalfont St Giles, Bucks

**FOCUS**

An ordinary handicap. Muddling form. The winner has been rated close to his best, with the runner-up to form.

T/Plt: £36.90 to a £1 stake. Pool: £66,607.84. 1,316.30 winning units. T/Qpdt: £6.10 to a £1 stake. Pool: £5,644.52. 673.83 winning units. **Jonathan Neesom**

770 - (Foreign Racing) - See Raceform Interactive

# 693 MEYDAN (L-H)

Thursday, February 16

**OFFICIAL GOING: Dirt: fast; turf: good**

## 771a BALANCHINE SPONSORED BY CITIZEN K (GROUP 2) (F&M) (TURF) 1m 1f (T)

**3:05** (3:05) 3-Y-O+

**£97,560** (£32,520; £16,260; £8,130; £4,878; £3,252)

RPR

1 **Opal Tiara (IRE)**[21] 431 4-9-0 109 ..................................... OisinMurphy 2 109
(Mick Channon) *mid-div: rdn 3f out: led 1f out: r.o wl* **15/2**[3]

2 *nk* **Via Firenze (IRE)**[21] 431 4-9-0 102 ..................(t) MaximeGuyon 6 108+
(Mme Pia Brandt, France) *settled in rr: r.o fnl 2 1/2f: nrst fin* **20/1**

3 *1 1/4* **Muffri'Ha (IRE)**[21] 431 5-9-0 109 ..................................... PatCosgrave 3 105
(William Haggas) *sn led: rdn 2 1/2f out: hdd 1f out: lost 2nd fnl 110yds* **11/4**[2]

4 *1/2* **Silver Step (FR)**[21] 431 4-9-0 107 ..........................(h) MickaelBarzalona 1 104+
(Mme Pia Brandt, France) *settled in rr: r.o fnl 2f but nvr able to chal* **10/1**

5 *nse* **Very Special (IRE)**[21] 431 5-9-3 113 ..........................(h) JimCrowley 4 107
(Saeed bin Suroor) *trckd ldr: ev ch 2f out: one pce fnl f* **5/6**[1]

6 *9 3/4* **Realtra (IRE)**[21] 431 5-9-0 109 ..................................... AndreaAtzeni 5 84
(Roger Varian) *Mid-div: rdn 4 1/2f out: sn btn* **16/1**

1m 49.72s (0.62) **Going Correction** +0.10s/f (Good) **6** Ran SP% **112.7**
Speed ratings: **101,100,99,99,99 90**
CSF: 118.87.
**Owner** The Filly Folly & Sweet Partnership **Bred** Mike Channon Bloodstock Ltd & Mrs G H Hedley **Trained** West Ilsley, Berks

**FOCUS**

TRAKUS: 2nd -1, 3rd -3, 4th -3, 5th 0, 6th -4. This doesn't look strong form. The pace soon picked up to be too fast, with the front pair in the betting taking each other on for the lead, and the first five finishers were covered by only around 2l at the line. Here are the splits: 26.57, 23.17, 23.23, 23.81, 12.94. It's been rated around the balance of the winner, third and fourth.

## 772a WATCH TIME (H'CAP) (DIRT) 7f (D)

**3:40** (3:40) (98-108,108) 3-Y-O+

**£78,048** (£26,016; £13,008; £6,504; £3,902; £2,601)

RPR

1 **Stunned**[14] 539 6-8-11 100 ..........................................(v) PatDobbs 4 103
(Doug Watson, UAE) *mid-div: smooth prog to ld 2 1/2f out: r.o wl* **11/4**[1]

2 *1 1/2* **Ross (IRE)**[21] 432 5-9-1 103 ..................................... AdriedeVries 7 103+
(P Schiergen, Germany) *settled in rr: r.o fnl 2f: nrst fin* **13/2**

3 *1/2* **Encipher (USA)**[7] 653 8-8-9 98 ..................................(t) TadhgO'Shea 3 96
(A R Al Rayhi, UAE) *s.i.s: chsd ldr 3f out: one pce fnl 1 1/2f* **10/1**

4 *1* **Shaishee (USA)**[5] 694 7-8-10 99 ..................................(v) JimCrowley 8 94
(M Al Mheiri, UAE) *mid-div: chsd ldr 2 1/2f out: r.o same pce fnl 2f* **7/1**

5 *5* **Fannaan (USA)**[7] 651 5-9-3 105 ..................................... DaneO'Neill 2 87
(M Al Mheiri, UAE) *s.i.s: nvr nr to chal* **4/1**[3]

6 *1/2* **Raafid**[172] 5944 4-8-10 99 ..................................... SamHitchcott 1 79
(A R Al Rayhi, UAE) *mid-div tl wknd fnl 3f* **14/1**

7 *3* **Wild Dude (USA)**[14] 539 7-9-6 108 ..............................(bt) PatSmullen 6 81
(M Halford, Ire) *nvr bttr than mid-div* **3/1**[2]

8 *4* **Sahaafy (USA)**[7] 653 5-9-2 104 ..................................(v) FernandoJara 5 66
(M Al Mheiri, UAE) *sn led: clr 4 1/2f out: hdd 2 1/2f out: wknd qckly* **16/1**

1m 24.71s (-0.39) **Going Correction** +0.225s/f (Slow) **8** Ran SP% **119.1**
Speed ratings: **111,109,108,107,101 101,97,93**
CSF: 22.21; TRICAST: 160.56.
**Owner** Mohd Khalifa Al Basti **Bred** Whitsbury Manor Stud & Pigeon House Stud **Trained** United Arab Emirates

**FOCUS**

TRAKUS: 2nd +5, 3rd +2, 4th +8, 5th +3, 6th -2, 7th +6, 8th -1. Not strong form. The splits were 24.43, 22.89, 24.57, 12.82 for a final time slightly slower than the earlier non-carnival handicap.

## 773a MEYDAN SPRINT SPONSORED BY FRIDAY (GROUP 3) (TURF) 5f (T)

**4:15** (4:15) 3-Y-O+

**£85,365** (£28,455; £14,227; £7,113; £4,268; £2,845)

RPR

1 **Ertijaal (IRE)**[42] 84 6-9-0 118 ..................................... JimCrowley 8 123
(A R Al Rayhi, UAE) *trckd ldr: led 2 1/2f out: r.o wl: easily* **4/7**[1]

2 *2 3/4* **Jungle Cat (IRE)**[21] 433 5-9-0 112 ..............................(p) WilliamBuick 1 113
(Charlie Appleby) *mid-div: r.o wl fnl 2f but no ch w wnr* **10/3**[2]

3 *4 1/4* **Caspian Prince (IRE)**[14] 543 8-9-0 107 ..............................(t) PatDobbs 7 98
(Roger Fell) *trckd ldr: ev ch 3f out: r.o same pce fnl 2f* **25/1**

4 *1* **Speed Hawk (USA)**[14] 543 6-9-0 104 ..............................(t) ChrisHayes 6 94
(D Selvaratnam, UAE) *mid-div: r.o same pce fnl 2f* **33/1**

5 *shd* **Watchable**[7] 651 7-9-0 101 ..............................(p) ColmO'Donoghue 9 94
(David O'Meara) *mid-div: r.o same pce fnl 2f* **40/1**

6 *3/4* **Sole Power**[14] 543 10-9-0 107 ..................................... PatSmullen 3 91
(Edward Lynam, Ire) *s.i.s: nvr nr to chal but r.o fnl 2f* **13/2**[3]

7 *2* **Harry Hurricane**[14] 543 5-9-0 99 ..............................(b) PatCosgrave 10 84
(George Baker) *nvr bttr than mid-div* **66/1**

8 *3/4* **Line Of Reason (IRE)**[7] 651 7-9-0 100 ..................... RichardMullen 5 81
(Paul Midgley) *s.i.s: nvr nr to chal* **25/1**

9 *3 3/4* **Moviesta (USA)**[14] 539 7-9-0 107 ..................................(p) WJLee 2 68
(Edward Lynam, Ire) *nvr nr to chal* **25/1**

10 *2 3/4* **Dragon Falls (IRE)**[4] 710 8-9-0 97 ..................................... BReis 4 58
(R Bouresly, Kuwait) *s.i.s: a in rr* **100/1**

11 *6 1/2* **The Happy Prince (IRE)**[5] 696 5-9-2 110 ..................(bt) AdriedeVries 11 36
(James Moore, Macau) *sn led: hdd & wknd 2 1/2f out* **40/1**

55.9s (-1.20) **Going Correction** +0.20s/f (Good) **11** Ran SP% **121.9**
Speed ratings: **117,112,105,104,104 102,99,98,92,88 77**
CSF: 2.50.
**Owner** Hamdan Al Maktoum **Bred** Shadwell Estate Co Ltd **Trained** UAE

**FOCUS**

Some changes to the sprint programme for 2017 saw this race moved from its usual slot on Super Saturday, so no longer a direct stepping stone to the Al Quoz Sprint, with the distance of that Group 1 event going from 5f to 6f. A high-class performance from the winner.

## 774a ZABEEL MILE SPONSORED BY GULF NEWS (GROUP 2) (TURF) 1m

**4:50** (4:50) 3-Y-O+

**£121,951** (£40,650; £20,325; £10,162; £6,097; £4,065)

RPR

1 **Championship (IRE)**[28] 320 6-9-3 114 ..................(t) ColmO'Donoghue 2 118
(A bin Harmash, UAE) *mid-div: smooth prog to ld 1 1/2f out: r.o wl* **11/4**[2]

2 *2 3/4* **Noah From Goa (SAF)**[28] 320 4-9-0 114 ......... ChristopheSoumillon 6 109
(M F De Kock, South Africa) *mid-div: rdn 2 1/2f out: r.o fnl 1 1/2f but no ch w wnr* **9/4**[1]

3 *hd* **Cymric (USA)**[14] 538 4-9-0 111 ..................................... MickaelBarzalona 1 109
(Charlie Appleby) *settled in rr: chsd ldr 2f out: 2nd 1 1/2f out: lost 2nd cl home* **13/2**

4 *2 1/2* **Gifted Master (IRE)**[132] 7115 4-9-0 110 ..................................... PatSmullen 3 103
(Hugo Palmer) *sn led: hdd 1 1/2f out: wknd fnl f* **12/1**

5 *1 1/2* **Light The Lights (SAF)**[21] 429 5-9-0 111 .............. BernardFayd'Herbe 5 99
(M F De Kock, South Africa) *trckd ldr tl outpcd fnl 2f* **8/1**

6 *6 1/4* **Fanciful Angel (IRE)**[14] 538 5-9-0 108 ..................................... DanielMuscutt 4 85
(Marco Botti) *s.i.s: nvr bttr than mid-div* **20/1**

7 *14 1/2* **Flash Fire (IRE)**[7] 653 5-9-0 112 ..................................... WilliamBuick 7 52
(Charlie Appleby) *s.i.s: nvr nr to chal* **9/2**[3]

1m 35.19s (-2.31) **Going Correction** +0.10s/f (Good) **7** Ran SP% **112.5**
Speed ratings: **115,112,112,109,108 101,87**
CSF: 9.05.
**Owner** Sheikh Mansoor bin Mohammed al Maktoum **Bred** Ms Natalie Cleary **Trained** United Arab Emirates

**FOCUS**

TRAKUS: 2nd +2, 3rd -2, 4th 0, 5th 0, 6th +4, 7th +4. The pace gradually picked up: 25.83, 23.35, 23.29, 22.56.

## 775a INSIDEOUT (H'CAP) (DIRT) 1m (D)

**5:25** (5:25) (95-105,105) 3-Y-O+

**£60,975** (£20,325; £10,162; £5,081; £3,048; £2,032)

RPR

1 **Heavy Metal**[5] 695 7-9-5 **104** ..................................... MickaelBarzalona 2 114
(S bin Ghadayer, UAE) *sn led: rdn clr 2f out: r.o wl: easily* **7/2**[3]

2 *3 3/4* **Nathr (USA)**[28] 316 6-9-1 **100** ..................................(v) JimCrowley 3 101
(Doug Watson, UAE) *trckd ldr: ev ch 2f out: r.o same pce fnl 1 1/2f* **6/4**[1]

3 *1 1/4* **Brex Drago (ITY)**[7] 654 5-9-3 **102** ..................................... AntonioFresu 7 100
(Marco Botti) *mid-div: r.o same pce fnl 2f* **20/1**

4 *1 1/4* **Footbridge (USA)**[63] 8396 7-9-6 **105** ..............................(b) WilliamBuick 10 100
(Charlie Appleby) *settled in rr: r.o fnl 2f but nvr able to chal* **15/2**

5 *1 1/2* **American Hope (USA)**[14] 538 6-9-3 **102** ..................................... AdriedeVries 4 94
(Saeed bin Suroor) *mid-div: wknd fnl 2f* **3/1**[2]

6 *nk* **Calder Prince (IRE)**[28] 321 4-8-9 **95** ..................... RichardKingscote 1 85
(Tom Dascombe) *nvr bttr than mid-div* **25/1**

7 *4 3/4* **Diferent Dimension (USA)**[5] 698 5-8-13 **98** ..........(b) RichardMullen 9 78
(Peter Wolsley, Korea) *trckd ldr tl wknd fnl 2 1/2f* **14/1**

8 *16 1/2* **Cornwallville (IRE)**[5] 698 5-8-10 **96** ..............................(bt) OisinMurphy 8 37
(Roger Fell) *s.i.s: racd in rr: virtually p.u 3 1/2f out* **33/1**

P **Beachy Head (IRE)**[5] 694 6-8-10 **96** ..............................(t) TadhgO'Shea 6
(A R Al Rayhi, UAE) *broke awkwardly: racd in rr: p.u 4f out* **40/1**

1m 37.65s (0.15) **Going Correction** +0.225s/f (Slow) **9** Ran SP% **119.6**
Speed ratings: **108,104,103,101,100 99,95,78,**
CSF: 9.16.
**Owner** Sheikh Hamdan bin Mohammed Al Maktoum **Bred** Darley **Trained** United Arab Emirates

■ Need To Know was withdrawn. Price at time of withdrawal 40/1. Rule 4 does not apply.

**FOCUS**

TRAKUS: 2nd +5, 3rd +12, 4th +13, 5th +7, 6th +2, 7th +11, 8th +7. The winner made just about all in strong, gradually slowing fractions - 25.02 (from standing start, as always), 23.08, 24.21, 25.31 - and the final time was nothing out of the ordinary.

## 776a DUBAI MILLENNIUM STKS SPONSORED BY WHEELS (GROUP 3) (TURF) 1m 2f

**6:00** (6:00) 3-Y-O+

**£97,560** (£32,520; £16,260; £8,130; £4,878; £3,252)

RPR

1 **Zarak (FR)**[138] 6973 4-8-13 116 ..................... ChristopheSoumillon 4 116+
(A De Royer-Dupre, France) *trckd ldrs: smooth prog to ld 1 1/2f out: r.o wl* **10/11**[1]

2 *1 3/4* **Earnshaw (USA)**[21] 429 6-9-0 110 ..........................(t) MickaelBarzalona 5 111
(S bin Ghadayer, UAE) *settled in rr: r.o fnl 2f but no ch w wnr* **8/1**

3 *1 1/2* **Promising Run (USA)**[21] 429 4-8-11 108 ..................(p) OisinMurphy 10 106
(Saeed bin Suroor) *sn led: t.k.h: hdd 1 1/2f out: r.o same pce* **9/2**[2]

4 *1* **Sanshaawes (SAF)**[14] 542 7-9-0 111 ..................................... PatCosgrave 1 106
(M F De Kock, South Africa) *mid-div: r.o same pce fnl 2 1/2f* **5/1**[3]

5 *2 3/4* **Master The World (IRE)**[14] 542 6-9-0 106 ..................(p) DaneO'Neill 8 101
(David Elsworth) *nvr nr to chal but r.o fnl 2f* **22/1**

6 *nk* **Elite Excalibur (AUS)**[14] 538 4-9-0 109 ..................(p) MichaelRodd 6 100
(S Burridge, Singapore) *trckd ldrs tl outpcd fnl 2f* **20/1**

7 *1 1/2* **Manson**[78] 8160 4-8-13 95 ..................................... PatDobbs 3 97
(Dominic Ffrench Davis) *s.i.s: nvr nr to chal* **50/1**

8 *1* **Fauvism (USA)**[55] 8517 8-9-0 95 ..................................... BReis 7 95
(R Bouresly, Kuwait) *nvr bttr than mid-div* **100/1**

9 *1 1/4* **Khusoosy (USA)**[14] 542 5-9-0 105 ..............................(bt) JimCrowley 9 92
(A R Al Rayhi, UAE) *trckd ldr: ev ch 2 1/2f out: wknd fnl 1 1/2f* **33/1**

10 *2 1/2* **Elliptique (IRE)**[67] 8333 6-9-5 115 ..................................... RichardMullen 2 92
(S Seemar, UAE) *nvr bttr than mid-div* **10/1**

2m 3.73s (1.03) **Going Correction** +0.10s/f (Good) **10** Ran SP% **122.4**
Speed ratings: **99,97,96,95,93 93,91,91,90,88**
CSF: 9.35; Placepot: £125.00 to a £1 stake. Pool of £5,687.30 - 33.20 winning units; Quadpot: £7.40 to a £1 stake. Pool of £519.30 - 51.90 winning units..
**Owner** H H Aga Khan **Bred** Sa Aga Khan **Trained** Chantilly, France

**FOCUS**
TRAKUS: 2nd 0, 3rd -4, 4th -3, 5th +3, 6th -7, 7th -3, 8th +3, 9th 0, 10th -9. A steady early pace - 27.71, 24.9, 25.08, 23.52 - before the promising winner quickened to the line in 22.44.

# [726]NEWCASTLE (A.W) (L-H)

Friday, February 17

**OFFICIAL GOING: Tapeta: standard**
Wind: Breezy, half against Weather: Overcast

## 777 32RED CASINO MAIDEN STKS (PLUS 10 RACE) 1m 5y (Tp)
**2:20** (2:23) (Class 4) 3-Y-O **£6,301** (£1,886; £943; £472; £235) **Stalls** Centre

Form RPR
3 **1** **Excel Again**[16] 503 3-9-5 0 MartinHarley 5 76
(James Tate) *pressed ldr: led over 2f out: rdn over 1f out: edgd rt ins fnl f: kpt on strly* **4/1**[3]
3-2 **2** *1 ³/₄* **Bowban**[37] 175 3-9-5 0 TomEaves 7 71
(Brian Ellison) *led tl rdn and hdd over 2f out: rallied: kpt on ins fnl f: nt pce of wnr* **9/4**[1]
2 **3** *7* **Spiritofhayton (IRE)**[44] 40 3-9-5 0 PhillipMakin 1 54
(David Barron) *plld hrd: hld up on outside: rdn over 2f out: hdwy over 1f out: sn one pce: hld whn lft 3rd last 100yds* **9/4**[1]
0- **4** *6* **Redarna**[287] 2014 3-9-5 0 JamesSullivan 3 40
(Dianne Sayer) *prom: drvn over 2f out: wknd fr over 1f out: lft modest 4th last 100yds* **200/1**
**5** *2 ¹/₄* **Coral Princess (IRE)** 3-8-9 0 ShirleyTeasdale(5) 6 29
(Keith Dalgleish) *missed break: hld up: rdn over 2f out: sn no imp* **66/1**
6 **6** *3 ¹/₄* **Elite Icon**[44] 40 3-9-5 0 DougieCostello 4 27
(Iain Jardine) *plld hrd early: in tch: outpcd 3f out: sn struggling* **66/1**
00 **7** *19* **River Warrior**[13] 580 3-8-12 0 SebastianWoods(7) 8
(Richard Fahey) *in tch tl rdn and wknd over 2f out: eased whn btn fnl f* **200/1**
-2 **U** **Saxon Flames (GER)**[20] 464 3-9-5 0 MartinDwyer 2
(William Muir) *reluctant to enter stalls: t.k.h in rr: rdn over 2f out: hdwy over 1f out: disputing 2nd pl and keeping on whn broke down and uns rdr last 100yds: fatally injured* **5/2**[2]

1m 41.29s (2.69) **Going Correction** +0.075s/f (Slow) **8** Ran SP% **114.1**
Speed ratings (Par 99): **89,87,80,74,72 68,49,**
CSF £13.40 TOTE £5.70: £1.60, £1.10, £1.10; EX 17.00 Trifecta £34.20.
**Owner** Sheikh Rashid Dalmook Al Maktoum **Bred** Darley **Trained** Newmarket, Suffolk

**FOCUS**
An interesting 3yo maiden with a few of these having already shown promise, but a sad conclusion. The form is rated around the runner-up.

## 778 32RED CASINO CONDITIONS STKS (PLUS 10 RACE) 5f (Tp)
**2:50** (2:50) (Class 3) 3-Y-O **£7,470** (£2,236; £1,118; £559) **Stalls** Centre

Form RPR
3-22 **1** **Sutter County**[8] 643 3-9-0 103 JoeFanning 1 100
(Mark Johnston) *trckd ldr: shkn up to ld over 1f out: rdn clr ins fnl f: comf* **4/7**[1]
-313 **2** *2 ¹/₄* **Dazacam**[6] 678 3-8-9 86 PaulHanagan 4 87
(Michael Herrington) *sn niggled along in tch: effrt and hdwy over 1f out: chsd (clr) wnr ins fnl f: kpt on* **4/1**[2]
211- **3** *1 ³/₄* **Merry Banter**[147] 6734 3-8-9 85 OisinMurphy 3 81
(Paul Midgley) *plld hrd: led tl rdn and hdd over 1f out: no ex and lost 2nd ins fnl f* **13/2**[3]
2112 **4** *1* **Marquee Club**[6] 678 3-9-0 87 DougieCostello 2 82
(Jamie Osborne) *trckd ldrs: drvn along 1/2-way: outpcd fr over 1f out* **8/1**

58.8s (-0.70) **Going Correction** +0.075s/f (Slow) **4** Ran SP% **108.1**
Speed ratings (Par 101): **108,104,101,100**
CSF £3.15 TOTE £1.20; EX 3.10 Trifecta £7.10.
**Owner** Sheikh Hamdan bin Mohammed Al Maktoum **Bred** Darley **Trained** Middleham Moor, N Yorks

**FOCUS**
An interesting little conditions event, but easy for the hot favourite, who was entitled to win this well.

## 779 BETWAY H'CAP 1m 4f 98y (Tp)
**3:25** (3:25) (Class 3) (0-95,96) 4-Y-O+ **£6,752** (£4,715; £2,357; £1,180; £587) **Stalls** High

Form RPR
604- **1** **Hamelin (IRE)**[62] 8424 7-9-7 95 OisinMurphy 10 102
(George Scott) *t.k.h: hld up: pushed along over 2f out: hdwy over 1f out: led last 100yds: styd on wl* **11/1**
11-1 **2** *³/₄* **Petite Jack**[44] 38 4-8-13 90 MartinHarley 9 95
(Neil King) *prom: effrt and pushed along over 2f out: edgd lft fr over 1f out: disp ld briefly last 100yds: kpt on: hld nr fin* **2/1**[1]
1314 **3** *³/₄* **Sennockian Star**[4] 720 7-9-2 90 JoeFanning 8 94
(Mark Johnston) *trckd ldr to 2f out: sn rdn and rallied: keeping on whn n.m.r wl ins fnl f: styd on cl home* **11/4**[2]
204- **4** *hd* **Cape Of Glory (IRE)**[66] 6142 4-8-9 86 (v) ConnorBeasley 7 89
(Keith Dalgleish) *t.k.h: hld up in tch: effrt on outside over 2f out: drvn and kpt on ins fnl f: nt pce to chal* **16/1**
630- **5** *nk* **Fattsota**[18] 7824 9-9-2 90 PhillipMakin 6 93
(David O'Meara) *dwlt: sn in tch: drvn and outpcd over 2f out: rallied over 1f out: kpt on ins fnl f* **16/1**
006- **6** *nse* **Mistiroc**[104] 7824 6-9-7 95 (v) DougieCostello 3 98
(John Quinn) *led: rdn and qcknd over 2f out: hdd last 100yds: kpt on same pce* **20/1**
3-60 **7** *1* **John Reel (FR)**[4] 720 8-9-3 96 CliffordLee(5) 4 97
(David Evans) *t.k.h: trckd ldrs: drvn along over 2f out: rallied: one pce fr over 1f out* **8/1**
/00- **8** *9* **Buthelezi (USA)**[58] 8479 9-8-11 85 BenCurtis 1 72
(Brian Ellison) *t.k.h: hld up: rdn and outpcd 3f out: btn fnl 2f* **50/1**
106- **9** *3 ³/₄* **Euchen Glen**[167] 6110 4-8-7 84 JFEgan 2 65
(Jim Goldie) *t.k.h: hld up: rdn and hung lft over 2f out: wknd wl over 1f out* **7/1**[3]

2m 40.87s (-0.23) **Going Correction** +0.15s/f (Slow) **9** Ran SP% **110.4**
**WFA** 4 from 6yo+ 2lb
Speed ratings (Par 107): **106,105,105,104,104 104,103,97,95**
CSF £31.12 CT £74.49 TOTE £8.20: £3.20, £1.50, £1.20; EX 36.70 Trifecta £90.00.
**Owner** Lordship Stud **Bred** Lordship Stud **Trained** Newmarket, Suffolk

**FOCUS**
A quality handicap, but they only went an even pace and the first seven finished in a heap. The form is rated cautiously.

## 780 BETWAY BEST ODDS GUARANTEED PLUS MAIDEN STKS 1m 4f 98y (Tp)
**3:55** (3:55) (Class 5) 4-Y-O+ **£5,175** (£1,540; £769; £384) **Stalls** High

Form RPR
2-3 **1** **Codeshare**[36] 195 5-9-8 0 JoeFanning 3 79
(Alan Swinbank) *t.k.h: hld up on ins: smooth hdwy to ld over 2f out: pushed clr fnl f: eased nr fin* **6/1**
53-4 **2** *3* **Casablanca (IRE)**[13] 576 4-9-0 72 OisinMurphy 6 68
(Andrew Balding) *prom: hdwy and chal over 2f out to over 1f out: sn edgd lft: kpt on same pce fnl f* **5/1**[3]
2 **3** *1 ¹/₄* **After Toniight (FR)**[36] 195 7-9-8 0 ConnorBeasley 5 71
(Gillian Boanas) *t.k.h: hld up: hdwy to chse ldng pair wl over 1f out: edgd rt and kpt on fnl f: nrst fin* **7/1**
3 **4** *1 ¹/₂* **Sugarloaf Mountain (IRE)**[37] 175 4-9-5 72 DaleSwift 4 69+
(Brian Ellison) *chsd ldrs: effrt and pushed along over 2f out: hung lft: kpt on same pce fnl f* **5/4**[1]
**5** *7* **Clondaw Banker (IRE)**[41] 8-9-8 0 MartinHarley 1 57
(Nicky Henderson) *led to 1/2-way: pressed ldr: regained ld over 3f out: hdd over 2f out: sn wknd* **9/2**[2]
435- **6** *3 ¹/₄* **Rasasee (IRE)**[169] 6049 4-9-5 75 PaulHanagan 2 52
(Tim Vaughan) *t.k.h: prom: hdwy to ld 1/2-way: hdd over 3f out: wknd fr 2f out* **18/1**
**7** *1 ¹/₄* **Ibreeq (IRE)**[42] 4-9-5 0 JackGarritty 7 50
(Roger Fell) *t.k.h: hld up: rdn and outpcd over 3f out: btn fnl 2f* **100/1**

2m 41.85s (0.75) **Going Correction** +0.15s/f (Slow)
**WFA** 4 from 5yo+ 2lb **7** Ran SP% **112.3**
Speed ratings (Par 103): **103,101,100,99,94 92,91**
CSF £34.30 TOTE £6.20: £2.70, £2.20; EX 30.20 Trifecta £82.40.
**Owner** Elsa Crankshaw & G Allan **Bred** Juddmonte Farms Ltd **Trained** Melsonby, N Yorks

**FOCUS**
An ordinary older-horse maiden and they finished well spread out. The winner improved latest form with the third.

## 781 £10 FREE AT 32RED.COM FILLIES' H'CAP 1m 2f 42y (Tp)
**4:25** (4:27) (Class 4) (0-85,80) 4-Y-O+ **£6,301** (£1,886; £943; £472; £235) **Stalls** High

Form RPR
31-3 **1** **Vogueatti (USA)**[42] 99 4-9-0 74 DanielMuscutt 4 82
(Marco Botti) *hld up in tch: hdwy over 2f out: edgd rt and led appr fnl f: rdn out* **4/1**
2-32 **2** *2* **Mariee**[10] 611 4-9-6 80 JoeFanning 1 83
(Mark Johnston) *t.k.h early: trckd ldrs: lost pl but in tch 1/2-way: pushed along and edgd lft over 2f out: hdwy over 1f out: kpt on to take 2nd cl home: no ch w wnr* **9/4**[1]
2-21 **3** *shd* **Footlight**[15] 524 4-9-4 78 PaulHanagan 5 81
(Richard Fahey) *led 4f: cl up: effrt and rdn over 2f out: kpt on ins fnl f: nt pce to chal* **7/1**
45-3 **4** *nk* **Victoria Pollard**[10] 609 5-9-4 77 (p) OisinMurphy 3 79
(Andrew Balding) *cl up led gng wl over 2f out: rdn and hdd appr fnl f: no ex and lost two pls nr fin* **7/2**[3]
1-22 **5** *10* **High On Light**[10] 613 4-8-13 73 PhillipMakin 2 55
(David Barron) *t.k.h: prom: hdwy to ld after 4f: hdd over 2f out: rdn and wknd over 1f out* **10/3**[2]

2m 9.1s (-1.30) **Going Correction** +0.15s/f (Slow) **5** Ran SP% **108.6**
Speed ratings (Par 102): **111,109,109,109,101**
CSF £12.96 TOTE £4.30: £2.20, £1.50; EX 14.60 Trifecta £56.90.
**Owner** Khalid Bin Ali Al Khalifa **Bred** Haymarket Farm Llc **Trained** Newmarket, Suffolk

**FOCUS**
A fair little fillies' handicap and a nice performance from the winner, but a bit of a messy race.

## 782 SUNBETS.CO.UK H'CAP 1m 5y (Tp)
**4:55** (4:57) (Class 4) (0-85,88) 4-Y-O+ **£6,301** (£1,886; £943; £472; £235) **Stalls** Centre

Form RPR
13-5 **1** **Inaam (IRE)**[45] 32 4-8-11 75 (h) PaulHanagan 2 83+
(Richard Fahey) *hld up on far side of gp: rdn and hdwy over 1f out: led wl ins fnl f: pushed out* **10/1**
-245 **2** *nk* **Byres Road**[27] 349 4-9-3 81 JoeFanning 6 88
(Mark Johnston) *cl up: rdn over 2f out: led over 1f out to wl ins fnl f: kpt on: hld cl home* **13/2**[3]
46-1 **3** *1 ¹/₄* **Shah Of Armaan (IRE)**[38] 165 4-8-9 73 TomEaves 10 77
(Kevin Ryan) *cl up: led over 2f out to over 1f out: sn rdn: kpt on same pce ins fnl f* **8/1**
066- **4** *1* **Swift Emperor (IRE)**[202] 4858 5-9-9 87 PhillipMakin 4 88
(David Barron) *t.k.h: in tch: effrt and pushed along 2f out: kpt on steadily ins fnl f* **7/1**
6-15 **5** *³/₄* **Eastern Dragon (IRE)**[10] 611 7-8-9 80 (p) CallumRodriguez(7) 5 79
(Iain Jardine) *s.i.s: hld up: rdn and effrt over 2f out: kpt on fnl f: nt pce to chal* **16/1**
40-1 **6** *³/₄* **Worlds His Oyster**[10] 611 4-9-10 88 6ex JasonHart 1 85
(John Quinn) *t.k.h: prom on outside of gp: rdn over 2f out: edgd lft and outpcd fr over 1f out* **3/1**[1]
0-36 **7** *shd* **Warfare**[8] 648 8-8-11 75 BarryMcHugh 8 72
(Tim Fitzgerald) *t.k.h: in tch on nr side of gp: effrt and rdn 2f out: kpt on same pce fnl f* **22/1**
02-1 **8** *1* **Pickett's Charge**[27] 361 4-8-7 71 ConnorBeasley 9 65
(Richard Guest) *plld hrd: prom: rdn over 2f out: outpcd fr over 1f out* **4/1**[2]
050- **9** *¹/₂* **Nicholas T**[155] 6500 5-8-12 76 JFEgan 7 69
(Jim Goldie) *stdd s: t.k.h: hld up on nr side of gp: rdn over 1f out: no imp* **14/1**
32-4 **10** *3* **Hail Clodius (IRE)**[46] 24 5-9-7 85 JackGarritty 11 70
(Roger Fell) *led on nr side of gp: rdn and hdd over 2f out: wknd over 1f out* **16/1**
**11** *10* **Main Fact (USA)**[153] 4-8-13 77 JamesSullivan 3 35
(Dianne Sayer) *hld up: rdn and struggling over 2f out: sn wknd* **125/1**

1m 39.23s (0.63) **Going Correction** +0.075s/f (Slow) **11** Ran SP% **114.6**
Speed ratings (Par 105): **99,98,97,96,95 94,94,93,93,90 80**
CSF £71.72 CT £557.70 TOTE £13.00: £2.70, £2.40, £2.30; EX 44.00 Trifecta £446.40.
**Owner** Yorkshire Connections Ltd **Bred** John Doyle **Trained** Musley Bank, N Yorks

**FOCUS**
A competitive handicap but rated as ordinary form.

## 783 BETWAY BEST ODDS GUARANTEED PLUS H'CAP 6f (Tp)
5:25 (5:27) (Class 4) (0-85,82) 4-Y-O+ **£6,301** (£1,886; £943; £472; £235) **Stalls** Centre

Form RPR
660- **1** **Handsome Dude**[49] 8583 5-9-7 **82**....................(b) PhillipMakin 9 93
(David Barron) *mde all: rdn over 1f out: kpt on wl fnl f* **9/2**[3]
30-0 **2** *2* **Bahamian Dollar**[31] 275 4-8-12 **78**.................... CliffordLee(5) 8 83
(David Evans) *prom: rdn and outpcd over 2f out: rallied to chse wnr ins fnl f: kpt on: nt pce to chal* **15/2**
5-32 **3** *2* **Dark Side Dream**[23] 403 5-8-12 **73**.................... JoeFanning 2 71
(Chris Dwyer) *cl up: drvn over 2f out: kpt on same pce ins fnl f* **4/1**[2]
-460 **4** *½* **Merdon Castle (IRE)**[13] 581 5-9-0 **75**....................(e) JamesSullivan 5 72
(Ruth Carr) *hld up: rdn along 2f out: kpt on fnl f: nvr able to chal* **8/1**
1126 **5** *shd* **Fujin**[7] 663 6-8-11 **77**....................(v) CharlieBennett(5) 10 73
(Shaun Harris) *cl up: rdn over 2f out: outpcd ins fnl f* **12/1**
02-5 **6** *2¼* **Buccaneers Vault (IRE)**[23] 403 5-9-5 **80**....................(p) PaulHanagan 4 69
(Paul Midgley) *dwlt: hld up: pushed along 2f out: no imp fnl f* **8/1**
4-42 **7** *1* **Fairway To Heaven (IRE)**[14] 547 8-9-4 **79**.................... ConnorBeasley 6 65
(Michael Wigham) *hld up in tch: rdn over 2f out: wknd fr over 1f out* **7/2**[1]
300- **8** *2¾* **Newstead Abbey**[115] 7593 7-9-7 **82**.................... TomEaves 3 59
(Michael Herrington) *hld up: rdn over 2f out: nvr rchd ldrs* **14/1**
3-40 **9** *1* **Gramercy (IRE)**[14] 551 10-9-5 **80**.................... JackGarritty 1 54
(Patrick Morris) *t.k.h: hld up on far side of gp: struggling over 2f out: btn over 1f out* **25/1**
020- **10** *2¼* **Extrasolar**[180] 5669 7-9-6 **81**.................... SamJames 7 48
(Geoffrey Harker) *prom tl rdn and wknd fr 2f out* **125/1**

1m 11.35s (-1.15) **Going Correction** +0.075s/f (Slow) 10 Ran SP% **113.4**
Speed ratings (Par 105): **110,107,104,104,103 100,99,95,94,91**
CSF £37.07 CT £148.26 TOTE £5.80: £2.20, £2.50, £1.80; EX 41.70 Trifecta £191.60.
**Owner** W D & Mrs D A Glover **Bred** Fifehead Farms M C Denning **Trained** Maunby, N Yorks
**FOCUS**
A fair sprint handicap, but all the action unfolded towards the nearside and those drawn low were up against it. The winner is rated close to his 2016 best.
T/Jkpt: £40,907.70 to a £1 stake. Pool: £122,723.15 - 3.0 winning units T/Plt: £55.20 to a £1 stake. Pool: £68,561.19 - 905.70 winning units T/Qpdt: £23.60 to a £1 stake. Pool: £4,414.79 - 138.0 winning units **Richard Young**

# 741 WOLVERHAMPTON (A.W) (L-H)
Friday, February 17

**OFFICIAL GOING: Tapeta: standard**
Wind: Fresh behind Weather: Cloudy

## 784 SUNBETS.CO.UK DOWNLOAD THE APP APPRENTICE H'CAP 7f 36y (Tp)
5:45 (5:46) (Class 6) (0-60,62) 4-Y-O+ **£2,425** (£721; £360; £180) **Stalls** High

Form RPR
4255 **1** **Wink Oliver**[4] 724 5-8-12 **58**....................(p[1]) LauraCoughlan(7) 5 67
(Jo Hughes) *chsd ldrs: swtchd lft over 2f out: nt clr run sn after: led over 1f out: r.o wl* **7/2**[2]
26-0 **2** *6* **Vivre La Reve**[38] 158 5-8-13 **52**....................(h) GeorgeDowning 4 48
(James Unett) *chsd ldrs: rdn and nt clr run over 1f out: sn hung lft: styd on same pce: wnt 2nd nr fin* **25/1**
3355 **3** *nk* **Fossa**[17] 495 7-8-7 **46**.................... JordanVaughan 9 40
(Mark Brisbourne) *trckd ldr: rdn and ev ch over 1f out: sn hung lft: no ex ins fnl f* **10/1**
5-04 **4** *nk* **Misu Pete**[17] 494 5-8-8 **50**....................(v) LuluStanford(3) 11 45
(Mark Usher) *s.i.s: hld up: rdn whn hmpd wl over 1f out: r.o ins fnl f* **11/2**[3]
0-01 **5** *2* **Dr Red Eye**[35] 222 9-8-13 **52**....................(vp) DavidParkes 10 40
(Scott Dixon) *led: rdn over 2f out: hdd over 1f out: wknd ins fnl f (wore a visor instead of declared hood)* **14/1**
00-5 **6** *nk* **Kingstreet Lady**[11] 602 4-8-10 **49**.................... HollieDoyle 2 40
(Richard Price) *mid-div: hdwy and hmpd over 2f out: hmpd again wl over 1f out: sn rdn: nt trble ldrs* **12/1**
05-0 **7** *2½* **Portrush Storm**[17] 494 12-8-7 **46** oh1.................... CallumShepherd 1 31
(Ray Peacock) *hld up: nt clr run over 2f out: hmpd wl over 1f out: n.d* **200/1**
26-2 **8** *2½* **Hidden Gem**[9] 620 4-9-5 **58**....................(vt) AaronJones 3 33
(Stuart Williams) *s.i.s: pushed along in rr early: drvn along 1/2-way: hmpd wl over 1f out: nvr on terms* **5/2**[1]
600- **U** **Secret Lightning (FR)**[66] 8351 5-8-11 **50**.................... EoinWalsh 12
(Michael Appleby) *mid-div: rdn over 2f out: disputing 3 l 5th whn hmpd and uns rdr wl over 1f out* **16/1**
00/0 **F** **Mobley Chaos**[9] 614 7-8-0 **46** oh1....................(p) WilliamCox(7) 8 +
(John Flint) *trckd ldrs: racd keenly: disputing cl 3rd whn clipped heels and fell wl over 1f out* **40/1**
-600 **B** **Binky Blue (IRE)**[11] 602 5-9-0 **60**.................... TobyEley(7) 7 +
(Daniel Mark Loughnane) *hld up: nt clr run over 2f out: b.d wl over 1f out* **6/1**

1m 28.27s (-0.53) **Going Correction** 0.0s/f (Stan) 11 Ran SP% **116.6**
Speed ratings (Par 101): **103,96,95,95,93 92,89,87, ,**
CSF £88.77 CT £806.09 TOTE £4.30: £1.60, £5.80, £3.20; EX 84.90 Trifecta £700.80.
**Owner** P & L Partners **Bred** Norman Court Stud **Trained** Lambourn, Berks
■ Laura Coughlan's first winner.
**FOCUS**
They bunched up on the home turn and there was a nasty incident when Mobley Chaos clipped heels and came down, in turn unseating Secret Lightning and bringing down Binky Blue. The winner could be worth a few lengths more.

## 785 SUNBETS.CO.UK MAIDEN STKS 7f 36y (Tp)
6:15 (7:49) (Class 5) 3-Y-O+ **£3,072** (£914; £456; £228) **Stalls** High

Form RPR
2 **1** **Tricorn (IRE)**[14] 545 3-8-11 0.................... NickyMackay 4 76+
(John Gosden) *mde all: qcknd over 2f out: pushed out* **1/4**[1]
53 **2** *1¼* **Invincible Man (IRE)**[16] 504 3-8-11 0.................... LukeMorris 3 71
(James Tate) *trckd wnr: rdn over 2f out: ev ch wl over 1f out: sn hung lft: styd on same pce ins fnl f* **10/3**[2]
**3** *8* **Slaying The Dragon (IRE)**[13] 4-9-9 0.................... LewisEdmunds(5) 5 55
(Nigel Tinkler) *s.s: hdwy 1/2-way: rdn over 2f out: wknd over 1f out* **66/1**[3]
0 **4** *8* **Groundskeeperwilly**[11] 600 3-8-11 0.................... AndrewMullen 1 28
(David Evans) *plld hrd and prom: lost pl 1/2-way: rdn over 2f out: wknd wl over 1f out* **66/1**[3]

1m 32.6s (3.80) **Going Correction** 0.0s/f (Stan)
**WFA** 3 from 4yo+ 17lb 4 Ran SP% **106.1**
Speed ratings (Par 103): **78,76,67,58**
CSF £1.28 TOTE £1.10; EX 1.40 Trifecta £3.90.
**Owner** HRH Princess Haya Of Jordan **Bred** N Hartery **Trained** Newmarket, Suffolk
**FOCUS**
This proved a straightforward task for the hot favourite. It was slowly run and the form is rated around the runner-up.

## 786 BETWAY H'CAP 1m 5f 194y
6:45 (8:05) (Class 5) (0-75,75) 4-Y-O+ **£3,234** (£962; £481; £240) **Stalls** Low

Form RPR
14/- **1** **Vosne Romanee**[281] 610 6-9-11 **72**....................(tp) GrahamLee 3 78+
(Dr Richard Newland) *a.p: chsd ldr over 1f out: rdn to ld ins fnl f: styd on* **15/8**[1]
6-02 **2** *1* **Marshall Aid (IRE)**[14] 555 4-8-13 **65**....................(p[1]) KieranO'Neill 1 69
(Mark Usher) *chsd ldrs: nt clr run wl over 1f out: sn rdn: r.o* **4/1**[3]
-140 **3** *1* **Yasir (USA)**[16] 508 9-8-12 **64**.................... LewisEdmunds(5) 8 67
(Conor Dore) *s.i.s: hld up: rdn over 1f out: r.o ins fnl f: wnt 3rd post: nt rch ldrs* **14/1**
/12- **4** *hd* **Consortium (IRE)**[320] 786 5-9-7 **68**....................(p) StevieDonohoe 5 70
(Miss Imogen Pickard) *led 1f: chsd ldr who wnt clr 9f out: tk clsr order 5f out: rdn to ld over 1f out: hdd ins fnl f: styd on same pce* **20/1**
0-16 **5** *½* **Oratorio's Joy (IRE)**[17] 497 7-9-12 **73**....................(p) TimmyMurphy 2 75
(Jamie Osborne) *s.i.s: hld up: hdwy whn nt clr run fr over 1f out tl wl ins fnl f: r.o: nvr able to chal* **9/1**
0-44 **6** *4½* **Spiritoftomintoul**[23] 399 8-9-10 **71**....................(t) GeorgeDowning 6 66
(Tony Carroll) *s.i.s: rcvrd to ld after 1f: wnt clr 9f out tl c bk to the field 5f out: rdn and hdd over 2f out: wknd ins fnl f* **7/1**
-131 **7** *16* **Fast Play (IRE)**[6] 688 5-10-0 **75** 6ex....................(b) PaulMulrennan 4 48
(Conor Dore) *hld up: hdwy on outer over 3f out: sn rdn: wknd over 1f out* **3/1**[2]

3m 6.41s (1.61) **Going Correction** 0.0s/f (Stan)
**WFA** 4 from 5yo+ 3lb 7 Ran SP% **113.7**
Speed ratings (Par 103): **95,94,93,93,93 90,81**
CSF £9.55 CT £77.55 TOTE £2.70: £1.80, £2.30; EX 14.30 Trifecta £72.10.
**Owner** Foxtrot NH Racing Partnership VI **Bred** Mrs L M G Walsh **Trained** Claines, Worcs
**FOCUS**
They went a decent enough gallop here. The winner is entitled to rate higher.

## 787 £10 FREE AT 32RED.COM H'CAP 5f 21y (Tp)
7:15 (8:27) (Class 6) (0-60,68) 3-Y-O **£2,749** (£818; £408; £204) **Stalls** Low

Form RPR
3-42 **1** **School Run (IRE)**[27] 357 3-9-9 **62**.................... AdamKirby 4 67
(David O'Meara) *sn led: hdd over 3f out: chsd ldr tl rdn to ld again over 1f out: drvn out* **7/2**[1]
06-5 **2** *1* **Glam'Selle**[14] 554 3-8-8 **47**.................... LukeMorris 2 48
(Ronald Harris) *prom: nt clr run and lost pl 4f out: hdwy and nt clr run over 1f out: sn rdn: r.o* **33/1**
-413 **3** *shd* **Royal Celebration**[16] 511 3-9-1 **57**.................... NathanEvans(3) 1 59
(Bryan Smart) *chsd ldrs: lost pl over 3f out: hdwy wl over 1f out: nt clr run sn after: rdn to chse wnr ins fnl f: r.o* **7/2**[1]
-003 **4** *1¼* **Celerity (IRE)**[17] 496 3-8-10 **52**....................(v[1]) PhilipPrince(3) 3 49
(David Evans) *mid-div: pushed along 1/2-way: hdwy over 1f out: r.o* **22/1**
65-2 **5** *1* **Not Now Nadia (IRE)**[7] 667 3-9-2 **55**.................... PaulMulrennan 6 48
(Michael Dods) *chsd ldrs: rdn over 1f out: styd on same pce fnl f* **9/1**
000- **6** *nk* **Backinanger**[156] 6477 3-9-7 **60**.................... JoeDoyle 5 55+
(Kevin Ryan) *s.i.s: outpcd: r.o ins fnl f: nvr nrr* **4/1**[2]
5-40 **7** *¾* **Highly Focussed (IRE)**[22] 415 3-9-6 **59**.................... GrahamLee 9 48+
(Ann Duffield) *hld up: effrt and nt clr run 1f out: nvr trbld ldrs* **22/1**
4-02 **8** *2¼* **Flying Hope (IRE)**[16] 511 3-8-6 **50**.................... LewisEdmunds(5) 7 31
(Nigel Tinkler) *pushed along to chse ldrs: led over 3f out: rdn and hdd over 1f out: wknd ins fnl f* **6/1**[3]
16 **9** *hd* **Zandradee (IRE)**[16] 511 3-9-6 **59**.................... AndrewMullen 8 39
(David Barron) *w ldrs: hung rt over 3f out: rdn over 1f out: wknd ins fnl f* **7/1**
0-40 **10** *3¼* **Little Nosegay (IRE)**[20] 456 3-9-0 **53**.................... StevieDonohoe 10 22
(David Evans) *chsd ldrs tl rdn and wknd over 1f out* **16/1**

1m 2.13s (0.23) **Going Correction** 0.0s/f (Stan) 10 Ran SP% **118.7**
Speed ratings (Par 95): **98,96,96,94,92 92,90,87,87,81**
CSF £127.77 CT £390.38 TOTE £3.90: £1.60, £4.10, £1.40; EX 52.00 Trifecta £290.10.
**Owner** Clipper Logistics **Bred** Southacre Bloodstock **Trained** Upper Helmsley, N Yorks
**FOCUS**
An ordinary sprint handicap, rated round the winner.

## 788 32RED.COM H'CAP 7f 36y (Tp)
7:45 (8:47) (Class 4) (0-85,87) 3-Y-O **£4,851** (£1,443; £721; £360) **Stalls** High

Form RPR
33-1 **1** **Boost**[34] 244 3-9-7 **77**.................... LukeMorris 2 83+
(Sir Mark Prescott Bt) *prom: racd keenly: hmpd over 6f out: chsd ldr 1/2-way: shkn up to ld over 1f out: edgd lft ins fnl f: rdn out* **7/2**[3]
-431 **2** *½* **Killermont Street (IRE)**[7] 659 3-8-11 **67**.................... PJMcDonald 5 71
(Mark Johnston) *s.s: hld up: hdwy 1/2-way: rdn over 2f out: chsd wnr ins fnl f: styd on* **12/1**
313 **3** *1½* **Blaze Of Glory (FR)**[14] 553 3-10-3 **87**.................... AdamKirby 3 87
(Jamie Osborne) *led: qcknd over 2f out: rdn and hdd over 1f out: no ex wl ins fnl f* **9/4**[2]
4-25 **4** *1¼* **Party Tiger**[17] 498 3-9-5 **75**....................(p[1]) PaulMulrennan 1 72
(Richard Fahey) *prom: hmpd over 6f out: lost pl 1/2-way: rdn over 2f out: styd on same pce fnl f* **18/1**
0-1 **5** *2¼* **Fear The Fury (USA)**[41] 127 3-9-6 **76**.................... JamieSpencer 4 67+
(K R Burke) *plld hrd and prom: wnt 2nd 6f out: lost 2nd 1/2-way: rdn over 1f out: wknd ins fnl f* **11/8**[1]

1m 28.5s (-0.30) **Going Correction** 0.0s/f (Stan) 5 Ran SP% **108.1**
Speed ratings (Par 99): **101,100,98,97,94**
CSF £35.50 TOTE £4.30: £1.80, £4.30; EX 23.30 Trifecta £46.40.
**Owner** Cheveley Park Stud **Bred** Cheveley Park Stud Ltd **Trained** Newmarket, Suffolk

**FOCUS**
A bit of a tactical affair.

## 789 32RED CASINO FILLIES' H'CAP 1m 4f 51y (Tp)
8:15 (9:05) (Class 5) (0-75,74) 4-Y-O+ £3,148 (£990; £533) Stalls Low

Form RPR
1-41 **1** **Favorite Girl (GER)**[17] 497 9-9-1 **68**.................... AlistairRawlinson(3) 1 72
(Michael Appleby) *sn led: rdn and hdd over 1f out: rallied to ld nr fin* **15/8**[2]
2240 **2** *nk* **Heartstone (IRE)**[10] 609 4-9-4 **71**.................................. AdamKirby 3 74
(David Evans) *chsd wnr: rdn to ld over 1f out: sn edgd lft: hdd nr fin* **7/4**[1]
23-0 **3** *8* **Taurian**[8] 648 6-9-1 **65**...................................................(p) StevieDonohoe 4 55
(Ian Williams) *hld up: hdwy to go 3rd 5f out: clsd on ldrs over 3f out: rdn over 2f out: sn outpcd* **7/1**
13/0 **P** **Rowlestone Lass**[25] 381 7-9-10 **74**.................................. GeorgeBaker 2
(Richard Price) *racd in 3rd pl but sn off the pce: lost 3rd 5f out: tk clsr order over 3f out: eased over 2f out: p.u and dismntd over 1f out* **3/1**[3]

2m 38.78s (-2.02) **Going Correction** 0.0s/f (Stan)
**WFA** 4 from 5yo+ 2lb 4 Ran SP% **108.6**
Speed ratings (Par 100): **106,105,100,**
CSF £5.53 TOTE £3.10; EX 6.60 Trifecta £11.00.
**Owner** Terry Pryke **Bred** Gestut Gorlsdorf **Trained** Oakham, Rutland

**FOCUS**
A dramatic finish to this minor fillies' event. The first two are rated similar to their C&D form last month.
T/Plt: £183.00 to a £1 stake. Pool: £63,996.24 - 255.21 winning units T/Qpdt: £17.20 to a £1 stake. Pool: £8,014.83 - 343.50 winning units **Colin Roberts**

790 - 794a (Foreign Racing) - See Raceform Interactive

# 668 DUNDALK (A.W) (L-H)
Friday, February 17

**OFFICIAL GOING: Polytrack: standard**

## 795a GAIN H'CAP 6f (P)
8:00 (8:00) 4-Y-O+ £12,615 (£3,897; £1,846; £820; £307)

RPR
**1** **Togoville (IRE)**[56] 8513 7-9-8 **92**............................(b) DeclanMcDonogh 9 101
(Georgios Pakidis, Ire) *mde all: pushed along early: 1 l clr 3f out: gng wl into st: rdn over 1f out and kpt on wl ins fnl f where edgd rt u.p: all out* **20/1**
**2** *1 1/4* **Shepherd's Purse**[14] 561 5-9-2 **86**.................................... GaryCarroll 6 91
(Joseph G Murphy, Ire) *hld up in tch: 6th 3f out: rdn 2f out and sme hdwy u.p bhd ldrs over 1f out: wnt 2nd wl ins fnl f and kpt on same pce: nt trble wnr* **6/1**[3]
**3** *1/2* **Oneoveryou (IRE)**[42] 101 6-8-12 **82**..............................(t) ConorHoban 4 85
(S J Mahon, Ire) *settled in 2nd: rdn under 2f out and no imp on wnr u.p in 2nd ent fnl f: sltly impeded and swtchd lft wl ins fnl f: no ex in 3rd clsng stages* **7/1**
**4** *1 3/4* **Gentlemen**[8] 639 6-9-10 **94**....................................(h) JosephineGordon 5 91
(Phil McEntee) *hld up towards rr: 8th 3f out: rdn into st and no imp in rr under 2f out: r.o wl ins fnl f to snatch 4th fnl strides: nrst fin* **9/2**[2]
**5** *nk* **Split The Atom (IRE)**[14] 561 5-8-3 **78**..................(b) KillianLeonard(5) 1 74
(David Marnane, Ire) *dwlt sltly and pushed along towards rr early: short of room on inner after 1f where checked and dropped to rr: sme hdwy far side under 2f out to chse ldrs in 4th: no imp on wnr clsng stages: denied 4th fnl strides* **6/1**[3]
**6** *1 3/4* **Northern Surprise (IRE)**[21] 450 6-9-0 **84**.............................. WJLee 3 75
(Timothy Doyle, Ire) *dwlt sltly and pushed along in rr early: 7th 3f out: tk clsr order bhd ldrs over 2f out: sn rdn and no ex in 6th ins fnl f : one pce clsng stages* **8/1**
**7** *shd* **Rapid Applause**[350] 825 5-8-8 **81**................................ ShaneBKelly(3) 2 72
(M D O'Callaghan, Ire) *chsd ldrs: 4th 3f out: disp 2nd 2f out: sn rdn and no ex over 1f out: wknd* **25/1**
**8** *4 1/4* **Patrick (IRE)**[14] 561 5-9-4 **88**............................................ PatSmullen 7 65
(Richard John O'Brien, Ire) *sltly awkward s: chsd ldrs: 5th 3f out: rdn bhd ldrs and no ex 2f out: sn wknd* **9/4**[1]
**9** *3* **Grey Danube (IRE)**[28] 340 8-9-3 **94**........................(t) DamienMelia(7) 8 61
(D J Bunyan, Ire) *towards rr early tl tk clsr order on outer bef 1/2-way: 3rd 3f out: rdn and wknd 2f out* **12/1**

1m 11.66s (-0.74) **Going Correction** +0.225s/f (Slow) 9 Ran SP% **117.4**
Speed ratings: **113,111,110,108,107 105,105,99,95**
CSF £137.13 CT £947.54 TOTE £18.90: £3.50, £1.80, £1.70; DF 146.80 Trifecta £799.40.
**Owner** Patrick Joseph McCann **Bred** Steven Nolan **Trained** Kilmore, Co. Armagh

**FOCUS**
A big return to form from the winner, a real stalwart around here, and under forcing tactics he couldn't be caught. The race has been rated around the balance of the first three.

796 - 797a (Foreign Racing) - See Raceform Interactive

# 837 CHANTILLY (R-H)
Friday, February 17

**OFFICIAL GOING: Polytrack: standard**

## 798a PRIX DE CHAUVRY (CONDITIONS) (4YO+) (POLYTRACK) 1m 2f 110y
1:05 4-Y-O+ £8,974 (£3,589; £2,692; £1,794; £897)

RPR
**1** **Zemindari (FR)**[46] 5-9-2 0............................................ ThomasMessina 2 90
(H-F Devin, France) **4/5**[1]
**2** *3 1/2* **Kapstadt (FR)**[41] 3219 7-9-2 0.......................................... SylvainRuis 8 83
(Ian Williams) *chsd ldr (pair 5l clr of rest): drvn to chal 2f out: sn led: hdd wl over 1f out: one pce fnl f* **7/1**[3]
**3** *3* **Speed Of Thought (FR)**[87] 7-9-2 0............................ YohannBourgois 3 77
(J-V Toux, France) **115/10**
**4** *2 1/2* **Hit The Jackpot (IRE)**[21] 8-9-4 0...................................... AndreBest 4 74
(Caroline Fuchs, Germany) **40/1**
**5** *1 1/4* **Girl's Hope (IRE)**[46] 4-9-3 0.......................................... DavidMichaux 7 73
(D De Watrigant, France) **3/1**[2]
**6** *1* **Syndromos (FR)**[78] 5-9-0 0.......................................... FrankPanicucci 5 66
(J Bertran De Balanda, France) **28/1**
**7** *3/4* **Miss Steff (IRE)**[43] 4-9-3 0............................................ CyrilleStefan 6 69
(B Lefevre, France) **114/10**
**8** *1 3/4* **Amiga Intima (FR)**[42] 7-9-3 0.......................................... AntonioPolli 1 64
(C Plisson, France) **269/10**
**9** *20* **Sainte Tempete (FR)**[43] 4-8-10 0............................. MlleLauraGrosso 9 20
(Heike Dorothea Altevogt, Switzerland) **78/1**

PARI-MUTUEL (all including 1 euro stake): WIN 1.80; PLACE 1.10, 1.60, 1.70; DF 5.60; SF 7.20.
**Owner** Mme B Ashbrooke & Mme H Devin **Bred** Mme H Devin & Mme B Ashbrooke **Trained** France

## 799a PRIX DU CASTEL (CONDITIONS) (3YO) (POLYTRACK) 1m 1f
1:35 3-Y-O
£17,675 (£7,145; £5,264; £3,384; £2,068; £1,316)

RPR
**1** **Phoceen (FR)**[32] 272 3-8-13 0............................ ChristopheSoumillon 1 89
(F Chappet, France) **21/10**[1]
**2** *3/4* **Speedo Boy (FR)**[43] 65 3-8-13 0............................ AurelienLemaitre 10 87
(Ian Williams) *broke wl fr wd draw: a cl up on outer: disp ld 2f out: drvn and styd on to ld ent fnl f: hdd cl home: no ex* **32/1**
**3** *3/4* **Domfront (IRE)**[116] 7586 3-9-3 0............................ StephanePasquier 9 89
(N Clement, France) **54/10**[3]
**4** *shd* **Lilly Kafeine (FR)** 3-8-9 0............................................ MaximeGuyon 5 81
(J C Napoli, France) **19/2**
**5** *nk* **Gris D'Argent (FR)** 3-8-13 0.......................................... IoritzMendizabal 4 85
(D De Watrigant, France) **5/1**[2]
**6** *snk* **Kick And Rush (GER)**[51] 8562 3-9-5 0............................ StephenHellyn 3 90
(Mario Hofer, Germany) **68/10**
**7** *1* **Rhenius (FR)**[32] 3-8-13 0............................................ TheoBachelot 8 82
(M Nigge, France) **73/10**
**8** *3* **Blue Hills (FR)**[21] 3-8-9 0............................................ GregoryBenoist 2 72
(Y Barberot, France) **27/1**
**9** *2 1/2* **Husani (IRE)**[51] 3-8-13 0............................................ CristianDemuro 6 71
(C Lerner, France) **14/1**
**10** *1 1/2* **Tulipa Rosa (IRE)** 3-8-9 0............................................ HugoJourniac 7 63
(J Boisnard, France) **158/10**

PARI-MUTUEL (all including 1 euro stake): WIN 3.10; PLACE 1.70, 6.30, 2.30; DF 51.90; SF 64.10.
**Owner** Le Haras De La Gousserie **Bred** Scea Haras Du Ma **Trained** France

800 - 805a (Foreign Racing) - See Raceform Interactive

# 733 KEMPTON (A.W) (R-H)
Saturday, February 18

**OFFICIAL GOING: Polytrack: standard**
Wind: Almost nil Weather: Cloudy

## 806 32RED CASINO H'CAP 1m 2f 219y(P)
5:45 (5:45) (Class 6) (0-65,67) 4-Y-O+ £2,264 (£673; £336; £168) Stalls Low

Form RPR
-253 **1** **What Usain**[16] 525 5-9-2 **63**..............................(p[1]) AlistairRawlinson(3) 4 73
(Michael Appleby) *prom: led 2f out: drvn out* **10/1**
-111 **2** *hd* **Boychick (IRE)**[16] 517 4-9-4 **64**.......................................... LukeMorris 7 74
(Ed Walker) *in tch: rdn 3f out: effrt and wnt 2nd over 1f out: grad clsd on wnr: a jst hld* **11/10**[1]
3- **3** *1 1/2* **Pillard (FR)**[24] 1830 5-9-7 **65**..........................................(t[1]) GeorgeBaker 5 72
(Jonjo O'Neill) *towards rr: hrd rdn and hdwy wl over 1f out: styd on fnl f* **9/2**[2]
6/1- **4** *1 3/4* **Hallings Comet**[98] 7936 8-9-1 **62**............................ KieranShoemark(3) 1 66
(Shaun Lycett) *chsd ldr tl over 2f out: one pce appr fnl f* **12/1**
5-04 **5** *1 1/4* **Jersey Bull (IRE)**[31] 286 5-9-5 **63**.................................(h) LiamKeniry 2 65
(Michael Madgwick) *mid-div: hdwy on inner 2f out: no ex over 1f out* **8/1**[3]
254- **6** *3/4* **Innoko (FR)**[25] 5102 7-9-3 **61**....................................(h) GeorgeDowning 11 62
(Tony Carroll) *mid-div: rdn over 2f out: styng on at fin* **25/1**
0-06 **7** *nse* **Pivotal Flame (IRE)**[14] 571 4-9-0 **65**........................ PaddyBradley(5) 6 66
(Pat Phelan) *chsd ldrs: hrd rdn 2f out: sn outpcd* **25/1**
00-0 **8** *5* **Silver Alliance**[26] 382 9-9-2 **67**............................(p) FinleyMarsh(7) 3 59
(Julia Feilden) *chsd ldrs tl wknd wl over 1f out* **50/1**
00-2 **9** *1 1/2* **Tulip Dress**[7] 689 4-9-1 **61**............................................ WilliamCarson 12 50
(Anthony Carson) *a towards rr* **16/1**
061- **10** *3/4* **Mr Frankie**[126] 7369 6-8-13 **57**........................................ MartinHarley 10 45
(John Spearing) *sn led fr wd stall: hdd & wknd 2f out* **16/1**
500- **11** *23* **Bushel (USA)**[72] 8282 7-9-7 **65**............................................ RyanPowell 9 14
(Tony Newcombe) *a bhd: rdn 1/2-way: no ch fnl 3f* **50/1**
600/ **12** *30* **Well Painted (IRE)**[82] 7909 8-9-5 **63**..........................(t) StevieDonohoe 8
(Daniel Steele) *s.s: a wl bhd* **66/1**

2m 20.46s (-1.44) **Going Correction** -0.05s/f (Stan)
**WFA** 4 from 5yo+ 1lb 12 Ran SP% **118.6**
Speed ratings (Par 101): **103,102,101,100,99 99,99,95,94,93 77,55**
CSF £20.63 CT £61.19 TOTE £13.20: £3.20, £1.10, £2.10; EX 31.00 Trifecta £137.60.
**Owner** Michael Appleby **Bred** Bond Thoroughbred Corporation **Trained** Oakham, Rutland

**FOCUS**
A modest handicap in which the well-backed favourite was just denied.

## 807 32RED ON THE APP STORE MAIDEN STKS 6f (P)
6:15 (6:16) (Class 5) 3-Y-O+ £2,911 (£866; £432; £216) Stalls Low

Form RPR
4- **1** **Artscape**[163] 6247 5-10-0 0.......................................(h) RobertWinston 12 75+
(Dean Ivory) *w ldr: sltly outpcd over 1f out: rallied and str chal ins fnl f: got up on line* **14/1**
3-2 **2** *nse* **Al Sail (FR)**[30] 307 3-8-13 0............................................ SeanLevey 7 71
(Richard Hannon) *led and gng wl: rdn over 1f out: drvn along and kpt on fnl f: hdd on line* **4/6**[1]
34- **3** *2 1/2* **Dance Rebel**[70] 8320 4-9-9 0.......................................... MitchGodwin(5) 4 67
(Dr Jon Scargill) *chsd ldng pair: kpt on same pce fnl 2f* **20/1**
**4** *1 1/2* **Cold Fire (IRE)** 4-9-9 0............................................ DavidParkes(5) 2 62
(Jeremy Gask) *mid-div: hdwy into 4th 2f out: one pce* **50/1**
**5** *3/4* **Hungarian Rhapsody** 3-8-13 0.......................................... JamieSpencer 9 56
(Jamie Osborne) *chsd ldrs tl outpcd fnl 2f* **3/1**[2]
**6** *1 3/4* **Tojosimbre** 3-8-13 0............................................ ShaneKelly 1 50+
(Richard Hughes) *t.k.h in midfield on inner: outpcd fnl 2f* **40/1**
**7** *1 3/4* **Spare Parts (IRE)** 3-8-13 0.......................................... MichaelJMMurphy 11 45
(Charles Hills) *in tch tl rdn and btn 2f out* **25/1**
4-4 **8** *2* **Deep Dream**[11] 612 4-9-9 0............................................ OisinMurphy 10 37+
(Andrew Balding) *dwlt: plld hrd towards rr: pushed along 2f out: nvr in chalng position* **8/1**[3]

30- **9** ½ **Hurricane Rock**[115] 7616 4-10-0 0 TomMarquand 5 41
(Simon Dow) *dwlt: plld hrd towards rr: rdn over 2f out: nvr trbld ldrs* **25/1**
0 **10** 4 **Zerafino (BEL)**[21] 464 4-10-0 0 KieranO'Neill 3 28
(Jimmy Fox) *dwlt: a towards rr* **150/1**
05- **11** hd **Waggle (IRE)**[51] 8570 4-10-0 0 AdamKirby 8 27
(Michael Wigham) *dwlt: a towards rr* **40/1**
0 **12** 51 **Mister Raffles**[36] 221 3-8-13 0 (bt¹) JFEgan 6
(Mohamed Moubarak) *sn outpcd and wl bhd* **100/1**

1m 13.67s (0.57) **Going Correction** -0.05s/f (Stan)
**WFA** 3 from 4yo+ 15lb **12** Ran SP% **123.7**
Speed ratings (Par 103): **94,93,90,88,87 85,82,80,79,74 74,6**
CSF £23.92 TOTE £18.00: £3.30, £1.10, £3.80; EX 37.60 Trifecta £281.20.
**Owner** Harlequin Direct Ltd & D Bloy **Bred** Darley **Trained** Radlett, Herts

**FOCUS**
Few got involved here, the first three racing in those positions throughout.

## 808 100% PROFIT BOOST AT 32REDSPORT.COM H'CAP 6f (P)
**6:45** (6:47) (Class 5) (0-75,75) 4-Y-O+ **£2,911** (£866; £432; £216) **Stalls** Low

Form RPR
2-13 **1** **Dream Farr (IRE)**[16] 518 4-9-6 **74** (t) ThomasBrown 5 81
(Ed Walker) *mid-div: hdwy over 1f out: r.o to ld fnl 50yds* **3/1**¹
06-3 **2** hd **Geoff Potts (IRE)**[28] 355 4-8-13 **72** (h) DavidParkes(5) 8 78
(Jeremy Gask) *in tch: clsd on ldrs over 1f out: ev ch nr fin: r.o* **17/2**
52-5 **3** hd **Higher Court (USA)**[43] 94 9-9-2 **70** (t¹) StevieDonohoe 1 75
(Emma Owen) *s.i.s: bhd: gd hdwy on inner over 1f out: fin wl* **13/2**
65-0 **4** nk **Anonymous John (IRE)**[17] 506 5-9-6 **74** GeorgeBaker 2 78
(Dominic Ffrench Davis) *towards rr: hdwy over 1f out: styd on wl fnl f* **4/1**²
24-2 **5** ¾ **Vimy Ridge**[14] 573 5-9-7 **75** JosephineGordon 3 77
(Alan Bailey) *prom: led wl over 1f out: hrd rdn fnl f: hdd and no ex fnl 50yds* **5/1**³
-415 **6** 1 ¾ **Bridge Builder**[14] 570 7-9-4 **72** (p) TomMarquand 4 68+
(Peter Hedger) *led: hrd rdn and hdd wl over 1f out: no ex* **7/1**
6-00 **7** 1 ½ **Nag's Wag (IRE)**[14] 575 4-9-5 **73** LiamKeniry 7 64
(George Baker) *towards rr: rdn over 2f out: no imp* **25/1**
/01- **8** 1 ¼ **Kashtan**[126] 7364 4-9-7 **75** MichaelJMMurphy 11 62
(J S Moore) *chsd ldrs tl outpcd 2f out* **50/1**
453- **9** ½ **Q Cee**[58] 8496 4-8-6 **65** LuluStanford(5) 12 51
(Eugene Stanford) *chsd ldr: hung rt and lost 2nd over 2f out: sn wknd* **25/1**
200- **10** nk **Picket Line**[109] 7738 5-9-6 **74** TimmyMurphy 9 59
(Geoffrey Deacon) *in tch tl rdn and btn over 2f out* **16/1**
0-00 **11** 3 ½ **Something Lucky (IRE)**[7] 682 5-8-12 **66** (h¹) JFEgan 6 39
(Daniel Steele) *rrd s: a bhd* **50/1**
501- **12** 2 ¾ **Nezar (IRE)**[247] 3322 6-9-7 **75** (h¹) RobertWinston 10 40
(Dean Ivory) *dwlt: a bhd* **20/1**

1m 11.38s (-1.72) **Going Correction** -0.05s/f (Stan) **12** Ran SP% **120.3**
Speed ratings (Par 103): **109,108,108,108,107 104,102,101,100,100 95,91**
CSF £27.98 CT £159.35 TOTE £4.50: £1.60, £3.10, £2.50; EX 29.60 Trifecta £233.00.
**Owner** Mrs T Walker **Bred** Jim McCormack **Trained** Upper Lambourn, Berks

**FOCUS**
This was run at a good gallop and it set up for a closer.

## 809 32RED.COM H'CAP (LONDON MIDDLE DISTANCE QUALIFIER) 1m 2f 219y(P)
**7:15** (7:15) (Class 4) (0-85,87) 4-Y-O+ **£4,690** (£1,395; £697; £348) **Stalls** Low

Form RPR
1-13 **1** **Kingthistle**[16] 517 4-8-5 **69** LukeMorris 3 76
(Ian Williams) *t.k.h in 4th: hrd rdn over 2f out: styd on wl fnl f: led on line* **9/2**
41/5 **2** nse **Every Chance (IRE)**[12] 599 4-9-9 **87** AdamKirby 2 94
(Jamie Osborne) *trckd ldng pair: chal over 1f out: slt ld 75yds out: kpt on: hdd on line* **9/4**¹
01-2 **3** nk **Hairdryer**[12] 599 4-8-11 **75** OisinMurphy 6 81
(Andrew Balding) *dwlt: t.k.h: sn trcking ldr: led and hung rt 3f out: narrowly hdd 75yds out: kpt on* **3/1**²
5-22 **4** 5 **Alcatraz (IRE)**[17] 507 5-9-3 **79** (vt¹) LiamKeniry 1 77
(George Baker) *stdd s: t.k.h in rr: wnt 4th over 2f out: nvr able to chal* **4/1**³
221/ **5** 8 **Sky Cape**[500] 7035 5-9-11 **87** TomMarquand 5 71
(Heather Main) *dwlt: t.k.h in 5th: wknd over 2f out* **9/1**
00-5 **6** 5 **Archangel Raphael (IRE)**[21] 467 5-9-7 **83** (p) JackMitchell 4 58
(Amanda Perrett) *led tl 3f out: sn wknd* **14/1**

2m 20.41s (-1.49) **Going Correction** -0.05s/f (Stan)
**WFA** 4 from 5yo 1lb **6** Ran SP% **110.6**
Speed ratings (Par 105): **103,102,102,99,93 89**
CSF £14.59 TOTE £5.30: £2.00, £1.90; EX 14.50 Trifecta £46.80.
**Owner** E A Brook **Bred** R C Bond **Trained** Portway, Worcs

**FOCUS**
No great pace on early and it developed into a bit of a dash from the turn in.

## 810 32RED/EBF STALLIONS BREEDING FILLIES' H'CAP 7f (P)
**7:45** (7:47) (Class 3) (0-95,95) 4-Y-O+
**£9,648** (£2,889; £1,444; £722; £361; £181) **Stalls** Low

Form RPR
-61 **1** **Jacquotte Delahaye**[17] 505 6-8-6 **79** (b) JosephineGordon 6 86
(David Brown) *mde all: rdn over 2f out: hld on wl* **10/1**
1-51 **2** ½ **Threebagsue (IRE)**[30] 304 4-7-13 **77** (b) HollieDoyle(5) 5 82
(J S Moore) *chsd ldrs: wnt cl 2nd 3f out: chal fnl f: r.o* **25/1**
2-13 **3** nk **Summer Icon**[18] 499 4-9-7 **94** GeorgeBaker 7 98+
(Mick Channon) *dwlt: towards rr: hdwy 2f out: styd on to take 3rd fnl 50yds* **5/1**³
5-43 **4** ¾ **Rebel Surge (IRE)**[31] 285 4-8-10 **83** (p) StevieDonohoe 1 85
(Richard Spencer) *mid-div on inner: hdwy over 1f out: styd on* **12/1**
-010 **5** 1 ½ **Make Music**[10] 617 4-8-10 **83** OisinMurphy 10 81
(Andrew Balding) *chsd ldrs: one pce fnl 2f* **12/1**
50-3 **6** ¾ **Childesplay**[17] 506 6-8-3 **76** LukeMorris 3 72
(Heather Main) *in tch: effrt on inner 2f out: no ex 1f out* **8/1**
5-44 **7** nse **Golden Amber (IRE)**[10] 617 6-9-6 **93** RobertWinston 11 89+
(Dean Ivory) *bhd tl rdn and styd on fnl 2f* **16/1**
0- **8** ½ **Ibazz**[66] 4-9-1 **88** JackMitchell 9 82+
(Archie Watson) *bhd: rdn and sme hdwy over 1f out: nvr rchd ldrs* **4/1**²
3-65 **9** 1 ¼ **Hawatif (IRE)**[18] 499 4-8-3 **81** MitchGodwin(5) 4 72
(Anthony Carson) *in tch tl outpcd fnl 2f* **25/1**
413- **10** ¾ **Bargain Buy**[63] 8426 4-8-9 **87** GeorgiaCox(5) 14 76+
(William Haggas) *rrd s: bhd: sme hdwy on inner over 1f out: no further prog* **7/2**¹
0-40 **11** 2 ¼ **Maggie Pink**[31] 285 8-8-6 **79** BenCurtis 13 62
(Michael Appleby) *chsd wnr tl 3f out: wknd 2f out* **50/1**
110- **12** 1 ¼ **Staintondale Lass (IRE)**[169] 6072 4-8-13 **86** MartinHarley 8 65
(Ed Vaughan) *mid-div: rdn over 2f out: sn btn* **20/1**
4-32 **13** 12 **Bint Dandy (IRE)**[31] 285 6-9-0 **87** (p) DavidProbert 2 34
(Chris Dwyer) *a towards rr: rdn and n.d fnl 2f* **9/1**

1m 24.35s (-1.65) **Going Correction** -0.05s/f (Stan) **13** Ran SP% **124.8**
Speed ratings (Par 104): **107,106,106,105,103 102,102,102,100,99 97,95,82**
CSF £249.96 CT £1416.40 TOTE £11.30: £3.50, £6.40, £2.10; EX 234.80 Trifecta £2176.10.
**Owner** Mrs F Denniff **Bred** A S Denniff **Trained** Averham Park, Notts

**FOCUS**
The pace seemed honest but the first two were prominent throughout.

## 811 FOLLOW @RACING_UK ON TWITTER H'CAP (DIV I) 1m (P)
**8:15** (8:16) (Class 6) (0-65,71) 4-Y-O+ **£2,264** (£673; £336; £168) **Stalls** Low

Form RPR
06-4 **1** **Tee It Up Tommo (IRE)**[21] 460 8-9-5 **63** StevieDonohoe 3 73
(Daniel Steele) *hld up in rr: smooth hdwy over 1f out: led ins fnl f: pushed out* **11/2**³
-004 **2** 2 **Arcanista (IRE)**[7] 684 4-8-13 **57** (be¹) ShaneKelly 1 62
(Richard Hughes) *hld up in 5th: hdwy 2f out: led 1f out tl ins fnl f: one pce* **13/2**
35-0 **3** 1 ¼ **Bloodsweatandtears**[36] 214 9-9-3 **61** GeorgeBaker 7 64
(William Knight) *reversed into front of stalls: hld up in rr: rdn over 2f out: nrest at fin* **7/1**
024- **4** nk **Swot**[52] 8555 5-9-2 **60** (p) RobertWinston 8 62
(Roger Teal) *chsd ldrs: rdn over 2f out: styd on same pce* **5/2**¹
165- **5** nk **Adventure Zone (IRE)**[138] 7014 4-9-6 **64** (p) MartinHarley 4 65
(Lee Carter) *sn led at gd pce: drvn along over 3f out: hdd & wknd 1f out* **16/1**
00-0 **6** 1 ¼ **Cosmic Ray**[23] 419 5-9-7 **65** (h) OisinMurphy 9 63
(Les Eyre) *broke wl: chsd ldr tl ins fnl 2f: 4th and hld whn short of room over 1f out* **12/1**
000- **7** 2 ½ **Haabis (USA)**[58] 8498 4-9-1 **59** (vt) LukeMorris 5 52
(George Peckham) *modest 6th tl rdn and btn 2f out* **16/1**
-522 **8** 7 **Tibibit**[10] 624 4-9-13 **71** RichardKingscote 2 47
(Henry Tett) *chsd ldng pair tl wknd 2f out* **10/3**²

1m 39.32s (-0.48) **Going Correction** -0.05s/f (Stan) **8** Ran SP% **112.3**
Speed ratings (Par 101): **100,98,96,96,96 94,92,85**
CSF £39.25 CT £251.35 TOTE £6.10: £2.10, £1.90, £2.20; EX 35.00 Trifecta £253.00.
**Owner** Vectis Racing **Bred** Oghill House Stud **Trained** Henfield, W Sussex

**FOCUS**
This was run at a strong gallop.

## 812 FOLLOW @RACING_UK ON TWITTER H'CAP (DIV II) 1m (P)
**8:45** (8:45) (Class 6) (0-65,67) 4-Y-O+ **£2,264** (£673; £336; £168) **Stalls** Low

Form RPR
0-40 **1** **Papou Tony**[18] 501 4-9-6 **64** LiamKeniry 1 72
(George Baker) *hld up in 5th: smooth hdwy to dispute ld whn edgd lft 1f out: drvn ahd ins fnl f* **7/2**¹
2-00 **2** 1 **Freddy With A Y (IRE)**[19] 480 7-9-5 **63** PaddyAspell 4 69
(J R Jenkins) *chsd ldrs: effrt and disp ld whn edgd rt 1f out: jst outpcd by wnr ins fnl f* **6/1**
200- **3** 1 ¾ **Betsalottie**[123] 7425 4-8-5 **56** JaneElliott(7) 3 58
(John Bridger) *t.k.h: a.p: one pce appr fnl f* **8/1**
160- **4** 2 **Embankment**[151] 6662 8-9-0 **58** LukeMorris 2 55
(Michael Attwater) *towards rr: rdn over 2f out: styd on fnl f* **16/1**
04-0 **5** ½ **Gracious George (IRE)**[43] 90 7-9-4 **67** HollieDoyle(5) 5 63
(Jimmy Fox) *in tch: outpcd 2f out: styd on fnl f* **4/1**²
14-3 **6** ½ **Scribner Creek (IRE)**[39] 166 4-9-3 **61** DaleSwift 7 56
(Daniel Mark Loughnane) *hld up in rr: rdn over 2f out: nvr rchd ldrs* **5/1**³
4134 **7** nse **Samphire Coast**[16] 524 4-9-1 **59** (v) DougieCostello 6 54
(Derek Shaw) *restless in stalls and missed break: bhd: effrt on inner over 2f out: sn wknd* **6/1**
130- **8** 4 **Rustique**[157] 6485 5-9-7 **65** ThomasBrown 8 50
(Ed Walker) *chsd ldr tl wknd 2f out* **8/1**
220- **9** 1 ¾ **Mossy's Lodge**[93] 7985 4-9-7 **65** WilliamCarson 9 68+
(Anthony Carson) *led tl hdd and bdly squeezed 1f out: snatched up and eased* **20/1**

1m 39.95s (0.15) **Going Correction** -0.05s/f (Stan) **9** Ran SP% **120.3**
Speed ratings (Par 101): **97,96,94,92,91 91,91,87,85**
CSF £26.00 CT £160.92 TOTE £4.50: £1.50, £2.90, £2.80; EX 39.80 Trifecta £368.20.
**Owner** PJL, Clark & Moore **Bred** Litex Commerce **Trained** Manton, Wilts

**FOCUS**
The early pace wasn't particularly strong here.

## 813 RACINGUK.COM/HD H'CAP 6f (P)
**9:15** (9:17) (Class 6) (0-65,68) 3-Y-O **£2,264** (£673; £336; £168) **Stalls** Low

Form RPR
21-5 **1** **Lord Cooper**[29] 323 3-9-8 **66** (tp) RenatoSouza 4 73
(Jose Santos) *dwlt: towards rr: gd hdwy on inner 2f out: led ins fnl f: rdn out* **9/4**¹
40-6 **2** ½ **Goodwood Crusader (IRE)**[29] 324 3-9-4 **62** ShaneKelly 6 67
(Richard Hughes) *hld up towards rr: gd hdwy over 1f out: fin wl: jst snatched 2nd* **8/1**
4-31 **3** nse **Tranquil Daze (IRE)**[8] 667 3-9-7 **68** KieranShoemark(3) 7 73
(David Brown) *led: rdn over 2f out: hdd ins fnl f: kpt on* **9/2**²
0-43 **4** 1 ¾ **Jet Setter (IRE)**[39] 157 3-9-5 **63** (h) GeorgeDowning 1 62
(Tony Carroll) *chsd ldrs: one pce appr fnl f* **8/1**
2404 **5** ½ **Pulsating (IRE)**[18] 496 3-9-4 **62** (b) StevieDonohoe 2 60
(Daniel Steele) *chsd ldr tl over 1f out: no ex fnl f* **15/2**³
060- **6** 1 ½ **Harbour Town**[131] 7209 3-9-6 **64** LukeMorris 10 57
(Harry Dunlop) *prom: rdn over 2f out: btn over 1f out* **16/1**
33-5 **7** 1 **Billy's Boots**[18] 496 3-9-0 **63** (h) LuluStanford(5) 3 53
(Dean Ivory) *mid-div: effrt 2f out: btn over 1f out* **33/1**
-602 **8** 1 ¼ **Dashing Poet**[21] 456 3-8-13 **57** (h) MartinLane 11 43
(Jeremy Gask) *plld hrd in rr: rdn over 2f out: n.d* **16/1**
52-0 **9** ½ **Warba (IRE)**[35] 245 3-9-2 **60** (t¹) JFEgan 8 44
(Mohamed Moubarak) *mid-div: trapped wd on home turn: sn struggling* **16/1**
1-54 **10** 1 **Spin Top**[17] 511 3-9-4 **62** OisinMurphy 12 43
(Joseph Tuite) *in tch tl outpcd 2f out* **14/1**
00-6 **11** nk **Man About Town (IRE)**[17] 512 3-9-6 **64** DougieCostello 5 44
(K R Burke) *a in rr* **12/1**

1m 12.99s (-0.11) **Going Correction** -0.05s/f (Stan) **11** Ran SP% **117.9**
Speed ratings (Par 95): **98,97,97,94,94 92,90,89,88,87 86**
CSF £20.66 CT £76.63 TOTE £3.30: £1.70, £1.70, £2.70; EX 23.30 Trifecta £127.00.
**Owner** R Cooper Racing Ltd **Bred** Miss K Rausing **Trained** Upper Lambourn, Berks

■ Stewards' Enquiry : J F Egan The Stewards held an enquiry following a report from the Starter that the filly had entered the wrong stall. Having heard his evidence and viewed recordings of the start they found him in breach of Rule (D)44.2 and cautioned him as to his future conduct in races.

**FOCUS**

This was run at a good gallop.

T/Plt: £61.30 to a £1 stake. Pool: £104,383.08 - 1,242.76 winning units T/Qpdt: £38.00 to a £1 stake. Pool: £8,981.92 - 174.47 winning units **Lee McKenzie**

# 763 LINGFIELD (L-H)

## Saturday, February 18

**OFFICIAL GOING: Polytrack: standard**

Wind: light, half behind Weather: light cloud, bright spells

## 814 32RED MAIDEN FILLIES' STKS (PLUS 10 RACE) — 1m 1y(P)

**1:10** (1:10) (Class 5) 3-Y-O — **£2,911** (£866; £432; £216) **Stalls** High

Form — RPR

5 **1** **Dreaming Time**[18] 500 3-9-0 0 JackMitchell 3 — 73
(Hugo Palmer) *mde all: rdn over 1f out: styd on wl and a doing enough ins fnl f: rdn out* **5/1**[3]

**2** ½ **First Moon** 3-9-0 0 (t[1]) JosephineGordon 4 — 72
(Hugo Palmer) *t.k.h: trckd ldrs: effrt to chse wnr and swtchd rt over 1f out: chalng and rdn ins fnl f: kpt on but a hld* **9/2**[2]

2-2 **3** ½ **Flight Of Fantasy**[17] 504 3-9-0 0 LukeMorris 2 — 70
(Harry Dunlop) *dwlt and bustled along leaving stalls: sn rcvrd and in midfield: hdwy to chse ldrs 4f out: rdn 3f out: unable qck over 1f out: rallied to chse ldrs 1f out: kpt on towards fin* **10/11**[1]

50- **4** 3¼ **Prize Diva**[120] 7494 3-9-0 0 ShaneKelly 7 — 63
(David Elsworth) *sn w ldr: rdn 2f out: outpcd and drifted rt 1f out: pushed along in 4th and kpt on same pce ins fnl f* **6/1**

6-6 **5** 1 **Beatisa**[21] 466 3-9-0 0 RichardKingscote 6 — 61
(Ed Walker) *hld up in tch in last pair: effrt and sme hdwy on inner 2f out: no imp 1f out: wknd ins fnl f* **33/1**

05- **6** ½ **Zenovia (IRE)**[64] 8397 3-9-0 0 (h) MartinHarley 5 — 60+
(David Simcock) *stdd after s: hld up in last pair: pushed along and sme hdwy over 1f out: no imp ins fnl f* **8/1**

00- **7** 3¼ **Follow Me (IRE)**[134] 7125 3-9-0 0 KieranO'Neill 8 — 52
(Lee Carter) *hld up in tch in last trio: rdn and wd bnd 2f out: n.d after* **80/1**

6- **8** 1¾ **Diamante (IRE)**[122] 7466 3-9-0 0 GeorgeDowning 1 — 48
(Daniel Kubler) *chsd ldrs tl 4f out: lost pl and pushed along over 3f out: bhd over 1f out* **50/1**

1m 38.42s (0.22) **Going Correction** -0.05s/f (Stan) — 8 Ran SP% **118.8**
Speed ratings (Par 94): **96,95,95,91,90 90,87,85**
CSF £28.56 TOTE £5.80: £1.90, £2.00, £1.02; EX 41.40 Trifecta £78.10.
**Owner** Saeed Manana **Bred** Rabbah Bloodstock Limited **Trained** Newmarket, Suffolk

**FOCUS**

An uncompetitive fillies' maiden to start and it resulted in a 1-2 for trainer Hugo Palmer. The first three pulled clear.

## 815 BETWAY SPRINT H'CAP — 6f 1y(P)

**1:45** (1:45) (Class 6) (0-65,67) 4-Y-O+ — **£2,264** (£673; £336; £168) **Stalls** Low

Form — RPR

-005 **1** **Space War**[8] 655 10-9-2 63 (t) NathanEvans(3) 6 — 71
(Michael Easterby) *in tch in midfield: effrt to chse ldrs over 1f out: wnt between rivals and r.o strly ins fnl f to ld towards fin* **10/3**[2]

3-34 **2** ¾ **Pharoh Jake**[29] 327 9-8-7 58 JaneElliott(7) 7 — 63
(John Bridger) *chsd ldrs: effrt over 1f out: kpt on u.p ins fnl f: wnt 2nd last strides* **14/1**

0-50 **3** hd **Noble Deed**[28] 355 7-9-5 63 LukeMorris 2 — 67
(Michael Attwater) *chsd ldrs: effrt to chse ldr 2f out: styd on and drvn to chal 1f out: led wl ins fnl f: hdd and no ex towards fin: lost 2nd last strides* **10/1**

3-20 **4** ½ **New Rich**[30] 302 7-9-5 63 (b) JohnFahy 10 — 66+
(Eve Johnson Houghton) *hld up in midfield: effrt over 1f out: styd on strly u.p ins fnl f: nt rch ldrs* **17/2**

0226 **5** hd **Head Space (IRE)**[14] 575 9-9-9 67 (t) AdamKirby 4 — 69+
(David Evans) *hld up in midfield: pushed along over 2f out: swtchd rt ent fnl f: styd on wl u.p ins fnl f: nt rch ldrs* **11/4**[1]

1136 **6** 1¾ **Whaleweigh Station**[10] 620 6-9-2 60 (v) TomEaves 1 — 57
(J R Jenkins) *led: rdn over 1f out: hdd wl ins fnl f: fdd towards fin* **11/2**[3]

-006 **7** 2¼ **Borough Boy (IRE)**[19] 480 7-9-7 65 (v) DougieCostello 3 — 54+
(Derek Shaw) *dwlt: hld up in tch in last trio: effrt on inner over 1f out: nt clr run ins fnl f: nvr threatened ldrs* **7/1**

4/4- **8** 1½ **Jeanie's Place**[383] 419 4-9-8 66 BenCurtis 5 — 51
(Charlie Wallis) *chsd ldr tl 2f out: no ex u.p and lost pl over 1f out: wknd ins fnl f* **25/1**

-006 **9** 1 **For Ayman**[21] 468 6-9-5 63 (t) OisinMurphy 9 — 54
(Joseph Tuite) *hld up in tch in last trio: effrt ent fnl f: no imp ins fnl f: lost action nr fin* **8/1**

00-0 **10** 10 **Rubheira**[12] 602 5-8-4 51 oh6 (b) NoelGarbutt(3) 8
(Paul Burgoyne) *taken down early and led to post: t.k.h: hld up in tch in last trio: effrt 2f out: sn btn: bhd ins fnl f* **100/1**

1m 11.6s (-0.30) **Going Correction** -0.05s/f (Stan) — 10 Ran SP% **119.9**
Speed ratings (Par 101): **100,99,98,98,97 95,92,90,89,75**
CSF £50.95 CT £443.12 TOTE £4.10: £1.60, £3.90, £3.20; EX 46.90 Trifecta £1139.30.
**Owner** M W Easterby **Bred** Shutford Stud And O F Waller **Trained** Sheriff Hutton, N Yorks

**FOCUS**

A modest sprint handicap and a bunch finish, though the pace looked solid.

## 816 BETWAY DASH H'CAP — 5f 6y(P)

**2:20** (2:21) (Class 4) (0-85,85) 4-Y-O+ — **£4,690** (£1,395; £697; £348) **Stalls** High

Form — RPR

1-51 **1** **Verne Castle**[14] 573 4-9-7 85 (h) DavidProbert 8 — 93+
(Andrew Balding) *t.k.h: trckd ldr: rdn to ld ent fnl f: in command and r.o wl ins fnl f: rdn out* **15/8**[1]

0-14 **2** ¾ **Monumental Man**[10] 618 8-9-5 83 (p) WilliamCarson 3 — 87
(Michael Attwater) *led: rdn over 1f out: hdd ent fnl f: kpt on u.p but a hld* **10/1**

00-0 **3** ½ **Seamster**[8] 664 10-8-11 82 (t) GerO'Neill(7) 4 — 84
(David Loughnane) *hld up in tch: effrt over 1f out: hdwy u.p 1f out: wnt 3rd wl ins fnl f: nvr gng to rch wnr: eased last strides* **16/1**

02-0 **4** ¾ **Come On Dave (IRE)**[14] 573 8-9-0 78 (v) LiamKeniry 10 — 78
(John Butler) *stdd and dropped in bhd after s: hld up in last pair: rdn and hdwy on inner over 1f out: kpt on ins fnl f: no threat to wnr* **25/1**

335- **5** ½ **Just Us Two (IRE)**[80] 8150 5-9-4 82 LukeMorris 1 — 80
(Robert Cowell) *chsd ldng pair: effrt 2f out: kpt on same pce u.p ins fnl f* **6/1**[2]

00-1 **6** hd **Zipedeedodah (IRE)**[16] 518 5-9-0 78 (t) OisinMurphy 2 — 75
(Joseph Tuite) *s.i.s: sn rcvrd to r in midfield on inner: effrt to chse ldrs 1f out: no ex ins fnl f: wknd wl ins fnl f* **6/1**[2]

4-42 **7** ¾ **Dynamo Walt (IRE)**[10] 618 6-9-7 85 (v) DougieCostello 7 — 79+
(Derek Shaw) *hld up in tch: effrt and wd bnd 2f out: kpt on but no threat to ldrs ins fnl f* **8/1**

0-05 **8** 2½ **Sandfrankskipsgo**[10] 618 8-8-12 79 KieranShoemark(3) 9 — 64
(Peter Crate) *in tch in midfield: lost pl bnd 2f out: no imp u.p over 1f out: wl hld fnl f* **14/1**

330- **9** 2 **Gwendolyn (GER)**[180] 5730 4-9-7 85 AdamKirby 6 — 63
(Amy Murphy) *chsd ldrs: rdn 2f out: unable qck and lost pl over 1f out: wknd fnl f* **7/1**[3]

504/ **10** 15 **Dr Doro (IRE)**[498] 7094 4-9-1 79 (h) RobertWinston 5 — 3
(Ian Williams) *squeezed for room and dropped to rr sn after s: sn outpcd and detached in last* **28/1**

57.67s (-1.13) **Going Correction** -0.05s/f (Stan) — 10 Ran SP% **115.9**
Speed ratings (Par 105): **107,105,105,103,103 102,101,97,94,70**
CSF £21.80 CT £238.39 TOTE £2.60: £1.20, £3.50, £5.00; EX 20.40 Trifecta £249.70.
**Owner** J C Smith **Bred** Littleton Stud **Trained** Kingsclere, Hants

**FOCUS**

Not a bad sprint handicap, but few got into it.

## 817 BETWAY MIDDLE DISTANCE H'CAP — 1m 2f (P)

**2:55** (2:55) (Class 3) (0-95,96) 4-Y-O **£7,246** (£2,168; £1,084; £542; £270) **Stalls** Low

Form — RPR

23-2 **1** **Final**[5] 719 5-8-10 83 JoeFanning 5 — 92
(Mark Johnston) *trckd ldr: rdn to ld over 1f out: kpt on wl ins fnl f: rdn out* **5/2**[2]

22-0 **2** 1½ **Qaffaal (USA)**[37] 199 6-8-11 87 NathanEvans(3) 6 — 93
(Michael Easterby) *stdd s: hld up in tch in last pair: clsd and nt clrest of runs wl over 1f out: effrt over 1f out: drvn 1f out: chsd wnr ins fnl f: kpt on but a hld* **11/8**[1]

1-24 **3** 1¾ **Van Huysen (IRE)**[24] 396 5-8-13 86 SeanLevey 1 — 89
(Dominic Ffrench Davis) *t.k.h: trckd ldrs: rdn jst over 2f out: kpt on same pce u.p fnl f* **9/2**[3]

006- **4** 1 **Black Night (IRE)**[7] 7765 5-8-4 80 PhilipPrince(3) 4 — 81?
(J Moon, Jersey) *led: rdn and qcknd over 2f out: hdd and no ex over 1f out: lost 2nd and wknd ins fnl f* **20/1**

1-30 **5** ½ **Forceful Appeal (USA)**[14] 574 9-9-1 93 HollieDoyle(5) 2 — 93
(Simon Dow) *stdd s: hld up in last pair: pushed along and unable qck over 2f out: kpt on same pce ins fnl f* **5/1**

2m 8.07s (1.47) **Going Correction** -0.05s/f (Stan) — 5 Ran SP% **110.3**
Speed ratings (Par 107): **92,90,89,88,88**
CSF £6.38 TOTE £2.80: £1.20, £1.80; EX 6.40 Trifecta £16.10.
**Owner** C H Greensit & W A Greensit **Bred** C H And W A Greensit **Trained** Middleham Moor, N Yorks

**FOCUS**

Not as competitive a handicap as it should be for the money, especially with the non-runners, and not surprisingly it proved tactical. The winner was always well placed.

## 818 BETWAY BEST ODDS GUARANTEED PLUS H'CAP — 6f 1y(P)

**3:30** (3:31) (Class 2) (0-105,103) 4-Y£01,971 (£3,583; £1,791; £896; £446) **Stalls** Low

Form — RPR

-132 **1** **Zac Brown (IRE)**[9] 639 6-8-8 90 (t) WilliamCarson 3 — 97
(Charlie Wallis) *mde all: rdn and qcknd over 1f out: 2 l clr and drvn 1f out: jst hld on* **10/1**

0-21 **2** nse **Kasbah (IRE)**[29] 326 5-9-1 97 JackMitchell 6 — 104+
(Amanda Perrett) *t.k.h: trckd ldrs: effrt over 1f out: chsd clr wnr 1f out: styd on strly u.p fnl 100yds: jst failed* **3/1**[2]

00-0 **3** 1¼ **Suqoor**[12] 598 4-8-7 89 (p[1]) JoeFanning 1 — 92
(Chris Dwyer) *stdd after s: hld up in last pair: rdn and hdwy on inner over 1f out: chsd ldrs and hung rt ins fnl f: kpt on same pce fnl 100yds* **22/1**

40-1 **4** ¾ **Fast Track**[36] 219 6-8-5 87 JosephineGordon 2 — 88
(David Barron) *chsd ldr: rdn over 1f out: lost 2nd 1f out and sn swtchd rt: kpt on same pce ins fnl f* **9/4**[1]

2-31 **5** nk **Poyle Vinnie**[25] 388 7-9-4 103 (p) AlistairRawlinson(3) 9 — 103
(Michael Appleby) *taken down early: t.k.h: hld up in tch in midfield: hdwy to chse ldrs on outer 1/2-way: lost pl bnd 2f out: kpt on ins fnl f* **12/1**

165- **6** 1¾ **Kadrizzi (FR)**[141] 6916 4-9-6 102 RobertWinston 5 — 98+
(Dean Ivory) *in rr: hdwy ent fnl f: keeping on whn nt clr run and swtchd lft ins fnl f: no imp after* **6/1**

25-2 **7** ¾ **Doctor Sardonicus**[44] 63 6-8-13 95 MartinHarley 7 — 87
(David Simcock) *chsd ldrs: rdn and unable to over 1f out: wknd ins fnl f* **4/1**[3]

1m 9.91s (-1.99) **Going Correction** -0.05s/f (Stan) — 7 Ran SP% **111.2**
Speed ratings (Par 109): **111,110,109,108,107 105,104**
CSF £37.83 CT £628.94 TOTE £9.40: £3.80, £2.10; EX 39.10 Trifecta £355.40.
**Owner** Dab Hand Racing **Bred** Tally-Ho Stud **Trained** Ardleigh, Essex

**FOCUS**

A warm sprint handicap, but reduced by one when Swiss Cross was withdrawn after arriving at the start minus the declared cheekpieces.

## 819 BETWAY BEST ODDS GUARANTEED PLUS MAIDEN STKS — 5f 6y(P)

**4:05** (4:05) (Class 5) 3-Y-O+ — **£2,911** (£866; £432; £216) **Stalls** High

Form — RPR

02-2 **1** **Mercers**[7] 679 3-8-5 62 NickyMackay 5 — 68
(Peter Crate) *taken down early: hld up in tch in midfield: nt clr run briefly 2f out: sn lft in ld on inner: rdn clr ins fnl f: r.o wl* **9/4**[1]

**2** 1½ **Midnightly** 3-8-5 0 AdamBeschizza 1 — 63
(Rae Guest) *pushed along in midfield: hdwy on inner over 1f out: styd on to chse wnr wl ins fnl f: kpt on but nvr threatened wnr* **7/1**

6- **3** 1¼ **Jashma (IRE)**[250] 3231 3-8-10 0 ShaneKelly 8 — 63
(Richard Hughes) *sn in tch in midfield: clsd to trck ldrs 1/2-way: wnt between rivals and squeezed for room briefly 2f out: sn rdn and ev ch: no ex ins fnl f: lost 2nd and wknd wl ins fnl f* **6/1**[3]

**4** hd **Miss Mirabeau** 3-8-5 0 LukeMorris 6 — 57+
(Sir Mark Prescott Bt) *off the pce in last trio: shkn up and hdwy over 1f out: styd on strly ins fnl f: nt rch ldrs* **11/1**

00-3 **5** hd **Endeavour (IRE)**[10] 623 3-8-10 64 SeanLevey 10 — 62
(Richard Hannon) *taken down early: chsd ldrs: effrt and hung rt bnd 2f out: kpt on same pce ins fnl f* **5/2**[2]

0- **6** 2 ¾ **Beach Dancer (IRE)**[87] 8065 3-8-7 0........................ EdwardGreatrex(3) 2 52+
(William Knight) *taken down early: stdd s: hld up off the pce in last pair: effrt over 1f out: swtchd rt jst ins fnl f: stl shifting rt and kpt on ins fnl f: nvr trbld ldrs* **10/1**

-264 **7** 2 ¼ **Heavenly Cry**[9] 638 3-8-10 60...............................(b) JosephineGordon 4 44
(Phil McEntee) *chsd ldrs: rdn and ev ch ent fnl 2f: lost pl u.p over 1f out: wknd ins fnl f* **12/1**

00 **8** ½ **Clean Cut**[11] 612 3-8-5 0........................................ KieranO'Neill 9 37
(Ivan Furtado) *midfield but nvr on terms: rdn over 2f out: no imp* **66/1**

0 **9** *hd* **Frank's Legacy**[48] 1 3-8-10 0......................................... TomEaves 3 41
(Ivan Furtado) *stdd s: hld up in rr: rdn and no hdwy 2f out: n.d* **33/1**

500- **10** 3 ½ **Hurricane Alert**[64] 8409 5-9-3 44...............................(v) JoshuaBryan(7) 7 35
(Mark Hoad) *taken down early: led: rdn and drifted rt bnd 2f out: sn hdd and lost pl: fdd ins fnl f* **100/1**

58.53s (-0.27) **Going Correction** -0.05s/f (Stan)
**WFA** 3 from 5yo 14lb **10** Ran SP% **116.7**
Speed ratings (Par 103): **100,97,95,95,94 90,86,86,85,80**
CSF £18.65 TOTE £2.90: £1.10, £2.50, £2.10; EX 20.10 Trifecta £123.70.
**Owner** Peter Crate **Bred** Peter Crate **Trained** Newdigate, Surrey

**FOCUS**
A moderate sprint maiden, but a couple of eye-catching performances.

## 820 BETWAY H'CAP — 1m 4f (P)
**4:40** (4:40) (Class 6) (0-55,59) 4-Y-0+ **£2,264** (£673; £336; £168) Stalls Low

Form RPR

0-61 **1** **Smiley Bagel (IRE)**[10] 621 4-9-0 **51**........................ RichardKingscote 8 59+
(Ed Walker) *hld up in tch in midfield: clsng and switching rt over 2f out: rdn and hdwy bnd 2f out: led 1f out: r.o wl: rdn out* **9/4**[1]

-212 **2** 1 ¼ **Frivolous Prince (IRE)**[31] 281 4-9-1 **52**.....................(vt) AdamKirby 11 57
(David Evans) *t.k.h: hld up in midfield: hdwy 3f out: rdn and ev ch 2f out tl unable qck ins fnl f: styd on same pce fnl 100yds* **5/2**[2]

000- **3** *hd* **The Detainee**[192] 5303 4-8-13 **55**................................ DavidParkes(5) 5 59
(Jeremy Gask) *hld up in tch in midfield: nt clr run over 2f out: hdwy u.p over 1f out: styd on strly ins fnl f: nt rch wnr* **16/1**

/41- **4** *nk* **Hawaiian Freeze**[7] 8-8-10 **47**.......................................... PhilipPrince(3) 9 51
(J Moon, Jersey) *squeezed for room sn after s: hld up in last trio: hdwy u.p on outer bnd 2f out: styd on strly ins fnl f: nt rch wnr* **66/1**

3-23 **5** ¾ **Santadelacruze**[9] 646 8-8-10 **51**.................................. JoshuaBryan(7) 4 54
(Mark Hoad) *wl in tch in midfield: effrt to chse ldrs 2f out: 4th and drvn 1f out: kpt on same pce ins fnl f* **11/1**

0-30 **6** ½ **Cahar Fad (IRE)**[7] 689 5-8-13 **47**..........................(bt) AdamBeschizza 6 49
(Steph Hollinshead) *t.k.h: chsd ldrs: hdwy to ld 5f out: rdn and hrd pressed ent fnl 2f: hdd 1f out: no ex and outpcd fnl 150yds* **14/1**

6/0- **7** 1 ½ **Soundbyte**[145] 6825 12-8-6 **47**..................................(v) RhiainIngram(7) 1 47
(John Gallagher) *s.i.s: hld up in rr: stuck bhd a wall of horses over 2f out: sme hdwy 1f out: kpt on ins fnl f: nvr trbld ldrs* **66/1**

-201 **8** *nk* **Grand Facile**[9] 646 5-9-11 **59**.................................(b) TimmyMurphy 12 58
(Gary Moore) *hld up in rr early: hdwy into midfield on outer 8f out: clsd to chse ldrs 3f out: rdn and pressing ldrs 2f out: unable qck over 1f out: wknd ins fnl f* **7/1**[3]

-555 **9** ¾ **Galuppi**[9] 645 6-8-10 **51**...............................................(v) GinaMangan(7) 3 49
(J R Jenkins) *t.k.h early: stdd bk to last trio after 1f: hld up: nt clr run and swtchd rt jst over 2f out: sme hdwy 1f out: kpt on ins fnl f: nvr trbld ldrs* **25/1**

65-0 **10** 4 **Understory (USA)**[10] 621 10-8-12 **46**.............................. MartinLane 10 38
(Tim McCarthy) *chsd ldrs: jnd ldr after 2f tl 6f out: styd chsng ldrs tl lost pl u.p 2f out: wknd fnl f* **33/1**

U-06 **11** 6 **Salient**[15] 555 13-9-0 **48**..........................................(t[1]) JosephineGordon 2 30
(Michael Attwater) *led for 2f: styd chsng ldrs tl lost pl over 2f out: wknd u.p over 1f out* **20/1**

5-6 **12** 16 **Dynamo (IRE)**[36] 218 6-9-9 **57**......................................(t) ShaneKelly 7 13
(Richard Hughes) *led after 2f tl 5f out:chsd ldr after tl lost pl on inner and impeded over 2f out: eased over 1f out* **7/1**[3]

2m 32.34s (-0.66) **Going Correction** -0.05s/f (Stan)
**WFA** 4 from 5yo+ 2lb **12** Ran SP% **119.8**
Speed ratings (Par 101): **100,99,99,98,98 98,97,96,96,93 89,78**
CSF £7.56 CT £71.27 TOTE £3.00: £1.20, £1.70, £5.60; EX 10.00 Trifecta £171.60.
**Owner** Laurence Bellman **Bred** Max Morris **Trained** Upper Lambourn, Berks

**FOCUS**
A moderate middle-distance handicap. Only two mattered according to the market and they fought out the finish.
T/Plt: £55.90 to a £1 stake. Pool: £72,119.65 - 941.46 winning units. T/Qpdt: £14.00 to a £1 stake. Pool: £5,160.22 - 272.05 winning units. **Steve Payne**

821 - (Foreign Racing) - See Raceform Interactive

# 748 CAGNES-SUR-MER
Saturday, February 18
**OFFICIAL GOING: Polytrack: standard**

## 822a PRIX DE JUAN-LES-PINS (H'CAP) (4YO+) (POLYTRACK) — 1m 4f
**4:15** 4-Y-0+
**£10,444** (£4,222; £3,111; £2,000; £1,222; £777)

RPR

**1** **Volzapone (FR)**[193] 5281 7-9-2 **0**.......................... ChristopheSoumillon 9 70
(Y Fertillet, France) **41/10**[2]

**2** ½ **Big Bear (FR)**[47] 5-8-11 **0**.......................................(b) GregoryBenoist 3 64
(N Caullery, France) **13/5**[1]

**3** ¾ **Monika Jem (FR)**[28] 364 6-8-7 **0**.................................(p) AntoineHamelin 6 59
(S Jesus, France) **165/10**

**4** 1 ½ **Nostromo (FR)**[220] 5-8-7 **0**.......................................(p) SebastienMaillot 7 57
(M Boutin, France) **78/10**

**5** *nk* **Special Request (FR)**[7] 691 10-9-1 **0**........................ KyllanBarbaud(5) 1 69
(N Caullery, France) **11/2**[3]

**6** *nse* **Bonsai (FR)**[66] 5-8-10 **0**............................................(p) RonanThomas 5 59
(Robert Collet, France) **197/10**

**7** *hd* **Attention Baileys (FR)**[7] 691 7-9-2 **0**............................ FabriceVeron 8 65
(P Monfort, France) **34/1**

**8** 1 ¼ **Ty Cobb (IRE)**[928] 4998 6-9-3 **0**...................................... FranckForesi 11 64
(F Foresi, France) **269/10**

**9** *nk* **Kant Excell (FR)**[47] 5-9-4 **0**.......................................... AurelienLemaitre 2 64
(N Caullery, France) **31/1**

**10** 1 ¼ **Varing (FR)**[28] 364 7-9-0 **0** ow1.......................(p) Pierre-CharlesBoudot 4 58
(M Cesandri, France) **56/10**

**11** 2 ½ **Uphold**[7] 691 10-8-4 **0**...........................................(b) MickaelForest 10 44
(Gay Kelleway) *dwlt: in rr early: tk clsr order and gd hdwy over 3f out: pushed along 2f out: sn btn and eased fnl f* **106/10**

PARI-MUTUEL (all including 1 euro stake): WIN: 5.10; PLACE: 1.90, 1.50, 3.40; DF: 10.20; SF: 21.50.
**Owner** Thierry Lenique **Bred** D Cosse & G Tomasino **Trained** France

823 - 833a (Foreign Racing) - See Raceform Interactive

# 714 ST MORITZ (R-H)
Sunday, February 19
**OFFICIAL GOING: Snow: frozen**

## 834a GROSSER PREIS CHRISTOFFEL BAU TROPHY (CONDITIONS) (4YO+) (SNOW) — 6f 110y
**11:00** 4-Y-0+
**£6,000** (£3,000; £2,142; £1,428; £714; £428)

RPR

**1** **Holidayend (IRE)**[7] 715 5-9-4 0.................................. DennisSchiergen 7
(M Weiss, Switzerland) **49/10**[1]

**2** 1 ¾ **Footprintinthesand (IRE)**[7] 715 7-9-0 0.................(p) MilanZatloukal 3
(M Weiss, Switzerland)

**3** *nk* **Filou (SWI)**[7] 715 6-9-4 0........................................... RaphaelLingg 6
(P Schaerer, Switzerland)

**4** 7 **Zarras (GER)**[7] 715 8-8-11 0........................................... TimBurgin(5) 4
(P Schaerer, Switzerland)

**5** 3 **Gung Ho Jack**[7] 715 8-9-0 0................................................ KierenFox 2
(John Best)

**6** 2 **Ferro Sensation (GER)**[7] 715 11-9-4 0................ SonjaDaroszewski 5
(C Von Der Recke, Germany)

**7** *nk* **Lunardo (SWI)** 7-9-4 0........................................... NicolasGuilbert 1
(J Stadelmann, Switzerland)

**Owner** Stall Tell **Bred** Epona Bloodstock Ltd **Trained** Switzerland

## 835a GROSSER PREIS LONGINES (CONDITIONS) (4YO+) (SNOW) — 1m 1f
**1:15** 4-Y-0+
**£6,000** (£3,000; £2,142; £1,428; £714; £428)

RPR

**1** **Renny Storm (CZE)**[364] 663 7-9-2 0........................ AlexanderPietsch 3
(C Von Der Recke, Germany) **11/2**[1]

**2** 3 **Take A Guess (FR)**[565] 5-9-6 0.......................................... MaximeGuyon 2
(Claudia Erni, Switzerland)

**3** 6 **Sleeping Giant (GER)**[7] 716 7-9-0 0.........................(b) RaphaelLingg 5
(P Schaerer, Switzerland)

**4** *nk* **Berrahri (IRE)**[7] 714 6-9-6 0...................................... DennisSchiergen 6
(John Best)

**5** 3 ½ **Cominols (SWI)**[1148] 6-9-2 0..................................... ClementL'Heureux 1
(A Schaerer, Switzerland)

**6** 1 **Archi Pink** 5-9-2 0.......................................................... MilanZatloukal 4
(M Weiss, Switzerland)

**7** 5 **Eddystone Rock (IRE)**[7] 716 5-9-6 0.................................. KierenFox 7
(John Best)

1m 58.03s **7** Ran SP% **15.4**

**Owner** Stall Chevalex **Bred** Hrebcin Napajedla **Trained** Weilerswist, Germany

836 - (Foreign Racing) - See Raceform Interactive

# 272 CHANTILLY (R-H)
Tuesday, February 14
**OFFICIAL GOING: Polytrack: standard**

## 837a PRIX DU LAY DU PRIEURE (CLAIMER) (4YO) (POLYTRACK) — 1m 5f 110y
**1:35** 4-Y-0 **£6,837** (£2,735; £2,051; £1,367; £683)

RPR

**1** **Burnside (FR)**[11] 555 4-9-2 0..................................(b) ThibaultSpeicher 8 79
(Daniel Mark Loughnane) *trckd clr ldr: clsd 1/2-way and sn disputing on outer: led into st: rdn 2f out: styd on and in n.d after: comf* **11/5**[2]

**2** 6 **Anse Marcel (FR)**[39] 4-8-13 0.......................................... GabrieleCongiu 1 67
(J-P Gauvin, France) **9/5**[1]

**3** 7 **Mondelino (FR)**[114] 4-8-11 0......................................(b) FlavienMasse 6 55
(Mme C Head-Maarek, France) **6/1**[3]

**4** ½ **Ernestine (FR)**[106] 4-8-11 0....................................... YohannBourgois 4 54
(J-M Lefebvre, France) **13/1**

**5** 2 **War Again (FR)**[90] 4-9-1 0............................................ SylvainRuis 10 55
(C Martinon, France) **12/1**

**6** 2 **Rebecamille (FR)**[12] 4-8-8 0............................................ AntonioPolli 5 45
(N Branchu, France) **44/5**

**7** 1 ¼ **Waki Delight (FR)**[38] 4-8-8 0......................................(b) StephaneBreux 2 43
(F Alloncle, France) **47/1**

**8** ½ **Titfortat Succes (FR)**[128] 4-8-8 0............................(p) JimmyTastayre 9 42
(Miss V Haigh, France) **106/1**

**9** 2 ½ **Zuckerprinz (FR)**[68] 4-9-4 0.................................. JeremyCrocquevieille 3 48
(Frau Erika Mader, Germany) **15/1**

**10** 20 **Fancify**[277] 4-8-8 0........................................................... MlleLauraGrosso 7 8
(F Caenepeel-Legrand, Belgium) **72/1**

PARI-MUTUEL (all including 1 euro stake): WIN 3.20; PLACE 1.30, 1.30, 1.70; DF 4.00; SF 5.90.
**Owner** B Dunn **Bred** Guy Pariente Holding Sprl **Trained** Rock, Worcs

## 838a PRIX DU LAYON GASPARD (CLAIMER) (3YO) (POLYTRACK) — 7f 110y
**2:40** 3-Y-0 **£7,264** (£2,905; £2,179; £1,452; £726)

RPR

**1** **Melissa Jane**[48] 8560 3-9-5 0................................ ChristopheSoumillon 8 72
(Henry Spiller) *midfield: rdn 2f out: kpt on fnl f and jst up to ld post* **3/1**[1]



The Form Book Flat, Raceform Ltd, Newbury, RG14 5SJ

2 shd **La Dame En Rouge (FR)**[5] 3-9-1 0 Pierre-CharlesBoudot 16 68
(J Phelippon, France) 3/1[1]
3 4 1/2 **Killing Joke (FR)**[50] 3-9-5 0 (b) GregoryBenoist 7 61
(M Boutin, France) 9/1[3]
4 1/2 **Black Dream (IRE)**[18] 3-8-9 0 AdrienMoreau(6) 1 56
(Mlle B Renk, France) 11/2[2]
5 1/2 **Makhzen (FR)**[50] 3-8-9 0 JeromeMoutard(6) 11 54
(M Boutin, France) 56/1
6 nse **Wedding Song (IRE)**[105] 3-8-10 0 MlleJuliaZambudioPerez(8) 2 57
(M Delcher Sanchez, France) 74/1
7 3/4 **Ilovetoboogie (FR)**[57] 3-8-8 0 TheoBachelot 6 45
(P Monfort, France) 10/1
8 1/2 **Atnaga (FR)**[5] 3-8-7 0 TomLefranc(8) 4 51
(C Boutin, France) 88/1
9 3/4 **Tu Te Calmes (FR)**[199] 3-9-1 0 (b) AntoineCoutier 10 49
(F Chappet, France) 11/1
10 1 1/4 **Etta (FR)**[50] 3-8-6 0 MlleAlisonMassin(5) 13 42
(M Boutin, France) 15/1
11 snk **Jantine (FR)**[39] 3-8-8 0 (p) SylvainRuis 9 39
(E Wianny, France) 49/1
12 3 1/2 **Zahiria (FR)**[50] 3-8-11 0 LudovicBoisseau(4) 5 37
(P Adda, France) 16/1
13 9 **Venexiana (FR)** 3-8-11 0 MlleZoePfeil(4) 15 14
(G Collet, France) 113/1
14 1/2 **Petit Poulain (FR)** 3-8-11 0 StephenHellyn 3
(Mme D De Wulf, Belgium) 76/1
15 1 **Wishful Thinking (FR)**[78] 3-8-8 0 AntonioPolli 12
(J-V Toux, France) 113/1
16 15 **Battle Of Wits (IRE)**[136] 6961 3-9-5 0 FabianXavierWeissmeier 14
(Frau R Weissmeier, Germany) 16/1

PARI-MUTUEL (all including 1 euro stake): WIN 4.00; PLACE 1.80, 1.70, 2.80; DF 6.60; SF 13.50.
**Owner** J Gill/ H Spiller/ G Waterhouse **Bred** Whitsbury Manor Stud **Trained** Newmarket, Suffolk

# 784 WOLVERHAMPTON (A.W) (L-H)

## Monday, February 20

**OFFICIAL GOING: Tapeta: standard**
Wind: Fresh behind Weather: Cloudy

### 839 BETWAY APP AMATEUR RIDERS' H'CAP 1m 4f 51y (Tp)
**2:10** (2:10) (Class 6) (0-52,52) 4-Y-0+ **£2,745** (£851; £425; £212) **Stalls** Low

Form RPR
2122 1 **Frivolous Prince (IRE)**[2] 820 4-10-8 **52** (vt) MissEMacKenzie(5) 2 59
(David Evans) *prom: lost pl over 7f out: hdwy and nt clr run over 2f out: rdn to ld wl ins fnl f: styd on* 11/8[1]
/054 2 hd **Anton Dolin (IRE)**[7] 721 9-10-9 **50** (be) MrLewisStones(5) 5 56
(Michael Mullineaux) *hld up in tch: shkn up over 2f out: rdn to ld and hung lft over 1f out: hdd wl ins fnl f: styd on* 16/1
405- 3 2 1/2 **Ted's Brother (IRE)**[125] 7426 9-10-5 **48** (h) MissAPeck(7) 12 50+
(Laura Morgan) *hld up: pushed along 5f out: r.o ins fnl f: nt rch ldrs* 50/1
/0-6 4 1 1/2 **Giant Sequoia (USA)**[11] 645 13-10-11 **47** (t) MissSBrotherton 9 47
(Des Donovan, Ire) *hld up: hdwy over 6f out: rdn over 2f out: styd on same pce fnl f* 15/2[3]
4-25 5 1 1/4 **Miss Macchiato (IRE)**[25] 414 4-10-10 **49** (p) MissCWalton 11 47
(Keith Dalgleish) *led: rdn and hdd over 1f out: wknd wl ins fnl f* 15/2[3]
06-0 6 1 1/2 **Race Time (USA)**[33] 281 4-10-2 **46** (p) JonjoO'Neill(5) 10 41
(Seamus Durack) *hld up: hdwy u.p over 1f out: wknd ins fnl f* 66/1
0-40 7 1 1/2 **Senor George (IRE)**[25] 414 10-11-0 **50** (t[1]) MrAlexFerguson 3 44
(Simon Hodgson) *chsd ldrs: rdn over 2f out: nt clr run and swtchd rt over 1f out: hmpd and wknd ins fnl f* 10/1
30-0 8 1 1/4 **Goldmadchen (GER)**[12] 621 9-10-10 **46** MrSWalker 4 38
(James Given) *chsd ldr: rdn and ev ch wl over 1f out: hmpd sn after: wknd ins fnl f* 7/1[2]
000- 9 2 3/4 **Rainford Glory (IRE)**[60] 8497 7-10-4 **45** MissHDukes(5) 7 31
(Tim Fitzgerald) *hld up: hdwy over 7f out: rdn over 2f out: wknd fnl f* 28/1
/40- 10 3 **Akinspirit (IRE)**[364] 674 13-10-3 **46** (t) MrsDScott(7) 1 28
(Nikki Evans) *s.s: hld up: plld hrd: nvr on terms* 66/1
0006 11 3 3/4 **Breathless**[13] 610 5-11-0 **50** (tp) MrJohnDawson 8 26
(Clive Mulhall) *hld up: wknd over 2f out* 33/1
0-04 12 17 **Sweeping Rock (IRE)**[11] 645 7-10-13 **49** (p) ThomasGreatrex 6
(John Spearing) *prom: rdn over 2f out: wknd and eased over 1f out* 15/2[3]

2m 42.99s (2.19) **Going Correction** 0.0s/f (Stan)
**WFA** 4 from 5yo+ 2lb 12 Ran SP% **116.2**
Speed ratings (Par 101): **92,91,90,89,88 87,86,85,83,81 79,67**
CSF £25.32 CT £756.27 TOTE £2.40: £1.20, £3.60, £9.70; EX 23.80 Trifecta £485.00.
**Owner** Mrs E Evans **Bred** Seamus Fox **Trained** Pandy, Monmouths

**FOCUS**
A moderate amateur riders' handicap. The winner stood out on recent form.

### 840 BETWAY MAIDEN STKS 1m 1f 104y (Tp)
**2:40** (2:41) (Class 5) 3-Y-0+ **£3,557** (£1,058; £529; £264) **Stalls** Low

Form RPR
2 1 **Bush House (IRE)**[35] 265 3-8-7 0 (b) JosephineGordon 3 76+
(Hugo Palmer) *led at stdy pce tl qcknd over 2f out: rdn and hdd wl over 1f out: rallied to ld wl ins fnl f: r.o* 4/5[1]
0-2 2 nk **War At Sea (IRE)**[16] 580 3-8-7 0 OisinMurphy 6 75+
(David Simcock) *chsd wnr tl led wl over 1f out: sn edgd lft: rdn and hdd wl ins fnl f* 6/5[2]
3 3 1/2 **Waterville Dancer (IRE)** 3-8-9 0 ow2 ShaneKelly 2 70
(Richard Hughes) *prom: shkn up over 2f out: styd on* 33/1
4 4 3 1/2 **Born To Reason (IRE)**[35] 265 3-8-7 0 RyanPowell 1 60
(Kevin Frost) *trckd ldrs: plld hrd: rdn over 2f out: wknd fnl f* 20/1[3]
000- 5 50 **Millady Percy**[89] 8075 4-9-9 37 (h) TomEaves 4
(Roy Brotherton) *stdd s: hld up: wknd over 1/2-way* 200/1

2m 4.08s (3.28) **Going Correction** 0.0s/f (Stan)
**WFA** 3 from 4yo 21lb 5 Ran SP% **109.2**
Speed ratings (Par 103): **85,84,81,78,34**
CSF £1.96 TOTE £1.70: £1.10, £1.10; EX 2.10 Trifecta £5.50.
**Owner** W J and T C O Gredley **Bred** Camas Park, Lynch Bages & Summerhill **Trained** Newmarket, Suffolk

**FOCUS**
A maiden with little depth and the two market leaders were dominant. It was slowly run and the level of the form is hard to pin down.

### 841 BETWAY MIDDLE H'CAP 1m 1f 104y (Tp)
**3:10** (3:10) (Class 6) (0-65,66) 4-Y-0+ **£2,911** (£866; £432; £216) **Stalls** Low

Form RPR
00-0 1 **Dunquin (IRE)**[47] 47 5-9-4 **62** LukeMorris 6 69
(John Mackie) *chsd ldrs: led at stdy pce over 7f out: qcknd over 2f out: drvn out* 5/1[2]
45-4 2 1/2 **Tenerezza (IRE)**[13] 609 4-9-5 **63** JoeFanning 1 69+
(Iain Jardine) *a.p: rdn to chse wnr wl ins fnl f: r.o* 7/1
3-52 3 1/2 **Kicking The Can (IRE)**[24] 444 6-9-7 **65** DavidNolan 10 70
(David Thompson) *led after 1f: hdd over 7f out: chsd ldrs: rdn to chse wnr over 1f out tl wl ins fnl f: styd on* 11/1
2132 4 nk **Athassel**[9] 684 8-9-2 **60** StevieDonohoe 4 64
(David Evans) *hld up in tch: rdn over 2f out: r.o* 11/2[3]
0-52 5 nk **King Oswald (USA)**[25] 421 4-9-6 **64** AdamKirby 5 68+
(James Unett) *hld up: hdwy u.p over 1f out: nt rch ldrs* 5/2[1]
04-0 6 1 1/2 **Muqarred (USA)**[6] 727 5-9-8 **66** (p) JackGarritty 3 67
(Roger Fell) *led 1f: chsd ldrs: rdn over 1f out: styd on same pce fnl f* 10/1
41-3 7 nk **Leonard Thomas**[24] 444 7-9-5 **63** (p) GeorgeDowning 9 63
(Tony Carroll) *hld up: rdn over 1f out: r.o ins fnl f: nvr nrr* 14/1
0-06 8 nse **Hannington**[9] 690 6-8-11 **58** (vt[1]) AlistairRawlinson(3) 2 58
(Michael Appleby) *hld up: styd on fr over 1f out: nt trble ldrs* 16/1
60-0 9 3 1/4 **Argaki (IRE)**[30] 363 7-9-6 **64** ConnorBeasley 13 57
(Keith Dalgleish) *prom: chsd wnr over 7f out tl rdn over 1f out: wknd ins fnl f* 18/1
44-4 10 2 3/4 **John Caesar (IRE)**[37] 239 6-8-11 **60** (t) RowanScott(5) 11 47
(Rebecca Bastiman) *hld up: rdn over 1f out: nvr on terms* 25/1
000- 11 7 **Shamlan (IRE)**[128] 7368 5-9-2 **63** (tp) NoelGarbutt(3) 12 36
(Johnny Farrelly) *sn outpcd: drvn along and wknd over 3f out* 100/1

2m 0.99s (0.19) **Going Correction** 0.0s/f (Stan) 11 Ran SP% **113.2**
Speed ratings (Par 101): **99,98,98,97,97 96,95,95,93,90 84**
CSF £38.32 CT £364.12 TOTE £4.50: £1.80, £3.00, £3.30; EX 42.20 Trifecta £288.50.
**Owner** Mrs Carolyn Seymour **Bred** Darley **Trained** Church Broughton , Derbys

**FOCUS**
A modest handicap run at an ordinary pace, and the first four were always prominent. The third helps with the standard.

### 842 BETWAY H'CAP 5f 21y (Tp)
**3:45** (3:47) (Class 2) 4-Y-0+
**£28,635** (£8,574; £4,287; £2,143; £1,071; £538) **Stalls** Low

Form RPR
10-0 1 **Robot Boy (IRE)**[31] 326 7-8-12 **95** PhillipMakin 4 105
(David Barron) *led: hdd wl over 3f out: hmpd sn after: remained handy: shkn up 1/2-way: rdn to ld ins fnl f: r.o* 10/1
4-53 2 1 1/4 **Bowson Fred**[27] 388 5-8-13 **99** NathanEvans(3) 3 105
(Michael Easterby) *prom: chsd ldr over 3f out: rdn and ev ch ins fnl f: edgd lft: styd on same pce* 5/1[2]
02-0 3 1 **Royal Birth**[39] 200 6-8-13 **99** (t) AaronJones(3) 5 101
(Stuart Williams) *mid-div: hmpd over 4f out: hdwy 2f out: rdn over 1f out: r.o: nt rch ldrs* 7/1[3]
61-1 4 1 1/4 **Jordan Sport**[37] 234 4-8-10 **93** (h) WilliamCarson 11 90
(David Simcock) *crossed over fr wd draw sn after s: led wl over 3f out: sn edgd lft: rdn and edgd rt over 1f out: hdd ins fnl f: styd on same pce* 7/1[3]
14-0 5 1/2 **Encore D'Or**[27] 388 5-9-3 **100** LukeMorris 10 96+
(Robert Cowell) *hld up: rdn over 1f out: r.o ins fnl f: nvr nrr* 12/1
66-3 6 1 **Boom The Groom (IRE)**[16] 572 6-9-10 **107** AndreaAtzeni 1 99+
(Tony Carroll) *chsd ldrs: hmpd and lost pl wl over 3f out: hdwy 2f out: no ex ins fnl f* 3/1[1]
103- 7 hd **Judicial (IRE)**[149] 6779 5-9-3 **100** (e) JoeDoyle 7 91
(Julie Camacho) *hmpd wl over 4f out: sn chsng ldrs: rdn over 1f out: wknd wl ins fnl f* 12/1
51-5 8 3/4 **Shamshon (IRE)**[11] 639 6-8-10 **93** (t) SeanLevey 9 82+
(Stuart Williams) *hld up: shkn up over 1f out: nvr on terms* 14/1
0-30 9 shd **Sign Of The Kodiac (IRE)**[31] 326 4-8-12 **95** (p[1]) AndrewMullen 6 83
(James Given) *mid-div: hmpd wl over 4f out: rdn and hung lft fr over 1f out: n.d* 25/1
1-21 10 6 **Doc Sportello (IRE)**[39] 200 5-9-7 **104** (p) RobertWinston 8 71+
(Michael Herrington) *in rr whn hmpd over 3f out: nvr on terms* 5/1[2]
000- 11 hd **Red Baron (IRE)**[170] 6119 8-8-3 **91** HollieDoyle(5) 2 57
(Eric Alston) *hld up: nvr on terms* 33/1

59.89s (-2.01) **Going Correction** 0.0s/f (Stan) 11 Ran SP% **121.3**
Speed ratings (Par 109): **116,114,112,110,109 108,107,106,106,96 96**
CSF £61.33 CT £384.06 TOTE £11.50: £3.20, £1.80, £3.00; EX 66.40 Trifecta £410.70.
**Owner** Laurence O'Kane & Paul Murphy **Bred** Corduff Stud Ltd **Trained** Maunby, N Yorks
■ Stewards' Enquiry : William Carson jockey ban: three days (6-8th March) - guilty of careless riding

**FOCUS**
A competitive, good-quality sprint and smart form, although quite a messy race. The winner is rated to the best view of his 2016 form.

### 843 BETWAY SPRINT H'CAP (DIV I) 6f 20y (Tp)
**4:20** (4:21) (Class 5) (0-70,72) 4-Y-0+ **£3,557** (£1,058; £529; £264) **Stalls** Low

Form RPR
1-42 1 **Commanche**[16] 583 8-9-2 **65** (p) JoeFanning 10 72
(Chris Dwyer) *a.p: chsd ldr over 4f out: shkn up over 1f out: rdn and r.o to ld wl ins fnl f* 14/1
13-5 2 hd **Berlios (IRE)**[25] 416 4-9-9 **72** PhillipMakin 4 78+
(David Barron) *hld up: hdwy: nt clr run and swtchd rt over 1f out: r.o* 7/2[2]
0311 3 hd **Pushkin Museum (IRE)**[14] 601 6-9-2 **65** AdamKirby 1 70+
(Patrick Morris) *hld up in tch: nt clr run over 1f out: sn rdn: r.o* 2/1[1]
6-30 4 3/4 **Ebony N Ivory**[18] 518 4-9-2 **70** (p) HollieDoyle(5) 11 73
(Archie Watson) *led: rdn over 1f out: hdd and unable qck wl ins fnl f* 11/1
242- 5 nk **Inshaa**[175] 5972 5-9-3 **66** TomEaves 3 68
(Michael Herrington) *trckd ldrs: racd keenly: shkn up over 1f out: styd on same pce towards fin* 8/1
5106 6 1 1/2 **Colourbearer (IRE)**[9] 682 10-9-5 **68** (t) BenCurtis 5 65
(Charlie Wallis) *chsd ldr tl over 4f out: remained handy: rdn over 1f out: styd on same pce ins fnl f* 20/1
-020 7 hd **Doeadeer (IRE)**[7] 724 4-8-10 **59** (v[1]) ConnorBeasley 6 56
(Keith Dalgleish) *hld up: racd keenly: nt clr run over 1f out: r.o towards fin: nvr nrr* 20/1

/10- 8 ½ **Tadaawol**[73] 8287 4-9-7 70...(p[1]) PJMcDonald 7 65
(Roger Fell) *hld up: rdn over 2f out: edgd lft and styd on same pce fnl f* 5/1[3]

2265 9 ¾ **Head Space (IRE)**[2] 815 9-8-11 67...(t) KatherineGlenister(7) 8 60
(David Evans) *broke wl: sn lost pl: n.d after* 16/1

5-06 10 3 **Divine Call**[32] 303 10-8-11 60...(b) FrannyNorton 2 43
(Milton Bradley) *hld up: rdn over 1f out: wknd ins fnl f* 20/1

1m 13.96s (-0.54) **Going Correction** 0.0s/f (Stan) **10** Ran SP% **118.5**
Speed ratings (Par 103): **103,102,102,101,101 99,98,98,97,93**
CSF £61.86 CT £143.82 TOTE £9.20: £2.60, £1.80, £1.20; EX 65.30 Trifecta £175.70.
**Owner** M M Foulger **Bred** Paramount Bloodstock **Trained** Newmarket, Suffolk

**FOCUS**
The first division of a fair handicap and they finished in a bit of a heap. The slower division by 1.10sec, with the winner showing his best form since mid-2015.

## 844 BETWAY SPRINT H'CAP (DIV II) 6f 20y (Tp)
**4:55** (4:55) (Class 5) (0-70,70) 4-Y-O+ **£3,557** (£1,058; £529; £264) **Stalls** Low

Form RPR

-626 1 **Spirit Of Wedza (IRE)**[16] 583 5-9-0 63... JoeDoyle 10 73
(Julie Camacho) *led over 4f: rallied to ld ins fnl f: r.o* 7/1

0-50 2 ¾ **It Must Be Faith**[21] 480 7-9-4 67... AdamKirby 6 75
(Michael Appleby) *a.p: chsd wnr over 3f out: led over 1f out: sn rdn and edgd lft: hdd ins fnl f: styd on* 11/4[1]

-000 3 ¾ **Fleckerl (IRE)**[9] 685 7-9-7 70...(p) PaulMulrennan 9 75+
(Conor Dore) *dwlt: outpcd: rdn over 2f out: r.o ins fnl f: nt rch ldrs* 11/1

41-0 4 1 **Major Valentine**[40] 171 5-9-4 67... TimmyMurphy 3 69
(John O'Shea) *hld up in tch: rdn over 1f out: styd on same pce ins fnl f* 10/1

140- 5 1 **Vale Of Flight (IRE)**[130] 7303 4-9-3 66...(b[1]) LukeMorris 7 65
(Luke McJannet) *hld up: hdwy over 1f out: sn rdn: styd on same pce ins fnl f* 40/1

-345 6 3½ **Billyoakes (IRE)**[20] 501 5-9-6 69...(p) BenCurtis 1 57
(Charlie Wallis) *s.i.s: hld up: rdn over 1f out: nvr on terms* 6/1[3]

-554 7 shd **Doctor Parkes**[18] 518 11-9-0 70... MillyNaseb(7) 2 57
(Stuart Williams) *prom: nt clr run over 2f out: sn lost pl* 7/1

3-24 8 5 **Sugar Town**[16] 582 7-8-8 60... NathanEvans(3) 4 31
(Peter Niven) *chsd wnr over 2f: remained handy: rdn over 2f out: wknd over 1f out* 14/1

-256 9 2¼ **Indian Affair**[5] 734 7-9-2 65...(bt) FrannyNorton 5 29
(Milton Bradley) *hld up: rdn over 2f out: sn wknd* 7/2[2]

1m 12.86s (-1.64) **Going Correction** 0.0s/f (Stan) **9** Ran SP% **114.7**
Speed ratings (Par 103): **110,109,108,106,105 100,100,93,90**
CSF £26.39 CT £211.09 TOTE £9.30: £2.20, £1.30, £3.30; EX 39.30 Trifecta £296.80.
**Owner** Owners Group 005 **Bred** N Hartery **Trained** Norton, N Yorks

**FOCUS**
The second division of a fair handicap and not many got into it, with the first two being up there throughout. The time was 1.1 sec quicker than the first leg. The winner's best form since he was a 2yo.

## 845 32RED.COM MAIDEN FILLIES' STKS 7f 36y (Tp)
**5:25** (5:25) (Class 5) 3-Y-O+ **£3,557** (£1,058; £529; £264) **Stalls** High

Form RPR

3-24 1 **Blue Bahia (IRE)**[14] 600 3-8-9 71... PJMcDonald 1 72
(Mark Johnston) *chsd ldrs: wnt 2nd over 2f out: rdn to ld ins fnl f: styd on wl* 9/2[3]

042- 2 2 **Rutherford (IRE)**[139] 7055 3-8-9 77... ShaneGray 4 66
(Kevin Ryan) *led: shkn up over 2f out: rdn and hdd ins fnl f: styd on same pce* 5/6[1]

06- 3 2½ **Lady Hester (USA)**[68] 8361 3-8-9 0... NickyMackay 2 59
(John Gosden) *hld up: hdwy to go 3rd over 1f out: no imp fnl f* 4/1[2]

4 1½ **Dusky Maid (IRE)** 3-8-9 0... AndrewMullen 5 55
(James Given) *rn green towards rr: drvn along 1/2-way: no ex fnl f* 10/1

5 20 **Play With Me** 3-8-9 0... ConnorBeasley 6
(Keith Dalgleish) *chsd ldr: hung rt fr over 3f out: lost 2nd over 2f out: sn wknd* 11/1

1m 29.23s (0.43) **Going Correction** 0.0s/f (Stan) **5** Ran SP% **110.2**
Speed ratings (Par 100): **97,94,91,90,67**
CSF £8.82 TOTE £5.10: £3.00, £1.10; EX 8.70 Trifecta £14.50.
**Owner** Lady O'Reilly **Bred** Castlemartin Sky & Skymarc Farm **Trained** Middleham Moor, N Yorks

**FOCUS**
A modest fillies' maiden, the winner rated to her British form.

## 846 32RED CASINO H'CAP 1m 142y (Tp)
**5:55** (5:57) (Class 5) (0-75,77) 3-Y-O **£3,557** (£1,058; £529; £264) **Stalls** Low

Form RPR

-233 1 **Bazwind (IRE)**[4] 766 3-8-12 63...(p[1]) SeanLevey 1 67
(David Evans) *mde all: rdn over 1f out: jst hld on* 7/1[3]

14-4 2 nk **Hochfeld (IRE)**[11] 647 3-9-11 76... PJMcDonald 4 79+
(Mark Johnston) *chsd ldrs: rdn over 1f out: r.o* 3/1[2]

4312 3 2 **Killermont Street (IRE)**[3] 788 3-9-4 69... JoeFanning 5 67+
(Mark Johnston) *s.i.s: hld up: hdwy to chse wnr over 1f out: sn rdn and hung lft: no ex wl ins fnl f* 15/8[1]

33-2 4 3 **Jumping Jack (IRE)**[12] 625 3-9-12 77... ShaneKelly 6 69
(Richard Hughes) *hld up: rdn over 2f out: styd on to go 4th ins fnl f: nvr trbld ldrs* 3/1[2]

45 5 1 **Olympic Legend (IRE)**[11] 647 3-9-4 69... TomMarquand 7 58
(Martin Bosley) *chsd wnr: rdn over 2f out: lost 2nd over 1f out: wknd ins fnl f* 25/1

4-64 6 2 **Whatsthemessage (IRE)**[25] 417 3-9-7 72... PhillipMakin 2 57
(Keith Dalgleish) *chsd ldrs: rdn over 3f out: wknd fnl f* 10/1

5-5 7 2½ **De Vegas Kid (IRE)**[32] 313 3-8-12 63... GeorgeDowning 3 42
(Tony Carroll) *s.i.s: hld up: pushed along 1/2-way: wknd over 2f out* 25/1

1m 49.34s (-0.76) **Going Correction** 0.0s/f (Stan) **7** Ran SP% **114.1**
Speed ratings (Par 97): **103,102,100,98,97 95,93**
CSF £28.10 TOTE £7.70: £3.00, £2.30; EX 23.70 Trifecta £68.40.
**Owner** B McCabe, L Cullimore, A Cooke **Bred** Paul McCarthy & Julie Carlton **Trained** Pandy, Monmouths

**FOCUS**
A fair, open-looking 3yo handicap. The winner's best form since early last year.
T/Jkpt: Not won. T/Plt: £40.30 to a £1 stake. Pool: £87,208.32 - 1,577.48 winning units T/Qpdt: £25.40 to a £1 stake. Pool: £7,367.78 - 213.83 winning units **Colin Roberts**

# 821 CAGNES-SUR-MER
Monday, February 20

**OFFICIAL GOING: Turf: soft**

## 847a PRIX DU FORT CARRE (MAIDEN) (3YO COLTS & GELDINGS) (TURF) 7f 110y
**11:55** 3-Y-O **£10,256** (£4,102; £3,076; £2,051; £1,025)

RPR

1 **Raaghib** 3-9-2 0... ChristopheSoumillon 7
(J-C Rouget, France) 2/5[1]

2 1 **Deimos (FR)**[114] 7717 3-9-2 0... EddyHardouin 6
(K Borgel, France) 59/10[2]

3 2 **Buzet (FR)** 3-8-11 0... FranckForesi 2
(F Foresi, France) 52/1

4 ½ **Cool (FR)** 3-8-11 0... NicolasPerret 5
(F Rossi, France) 91/10

5 2 **Espoir Bere (FR)**[16] 584 3-9-2 0... Pierre-CharlesBoudot 1
(D Prod'Homme, France) 79/10[3]

6 1 **Saphirblue (FR)** 3-8-11 0... AntoineHamelin 9
(J Parize, France) 217/10

7 4 **Different Views (USA)**[5] 748 3-9-2 0...(b[1]) MickaelForest 8
(Gay Kelleway) *qckly into stride: settled bhd ldr: pushed along over 2f out: drvn over 1f out and sn btn: eased ins fnl f* 245/10

8 ½ **Namran (FR)** 3-8-11 0... SebastienMaillot 4
(P Decouz, France) 52/1

1m 37.8s **8** Ran SP% **119.2**
PARI-MUTUEL (all including 1 euro stake): WIN: 1.40; PLACE: 1.10, 1.10, 1.10; DF: 3.60; SF: 3.70.
**Owner** Hamdan Al Maktoum **Bred** Bobble Barn Stud **Trained** Pau, France

# 661 SOUTHWELL (L-H)
Tuesday, February 21

**OFFICIAL GOING: Fibresand: standard**
Wind: Moderate across Weather: Cloudy

## 848 32RED H'CAP 1m 13y(F)
**2:10** (2:11) (Class 6) (0-60,62) 3-Y-O **£2,587** (£770; £384; £192) **Stalls** Low

Form RPR

0-06 1 **Kyllachys Tale (IRE)**[20] 502 3-9-6 58... JackMitchell 6 71+
(Roger Teal) *cl up: led 2f out: sn rdn clr: edgd lft appr fnl f: kpt on strly: readily* 9/1

5-03 2 7 **Medici Moon**[28] 385 3-9-0 52...(p) DaleSwift 1 47
(Scott Dixon) *t.k.h: sn led: pushed along and hdd 2f out: sn rdn: drvn and no imp fnl f* 14/1

06-0 3 2¼ **Panther In Pink (IRE)**[29] 377 3-8-12 50... FrannyNorton 13 40
(Ann Duffield) *chsd ldrs: pushed along 3f out: rdn over 2f out: drvn wl over 1f out: kpt on same pce* 25/1

0-46 4 nk **Stag Party (IRE)**[33] 310 3-8-8 51...(t[1]) RowanScott(5) 2 40
(Julia Brooke) *in tch: hdwy on inner 3f out: rdn to chse ldrs 2f out: sn drvn and kpt on same pce* 40/1

-315 5 4 **Log Off (IRE)**[20] 502 3-9-7 59... AndrewMullen 8 39+
(David Evans) *n.m.r and stmbld sn after s: sn bhd and pushed along: rdn and hdwy 3f out: kpt on u.p fnl 2f* 10/3[1]

5-26 6 1 **Hazell Berry (IRE)**[24] 463 3-8-5 46...(v) PhilipPrince(3) 11 24
(David Evans) *towards rr: hdwy on outer and wd st: sn rdn and kpt on: n.d* 11/1

5-44 7 nse **Too Many Shots**[20] 502 3-9-6 58... KierenFox 3 36
(John Best) *rr: rdn along and hdwy over 2f out: drvn wl over 1f out: kpt on fnl f* 7/2[2]

4-00 8 ¾ **Sublime**[20] 503 3-8-10 48... OisinMurphy 7 24
(Rod Millman) *prom: rdn along 3f out: drvn 2f out: grad wknd* 25/1

6-63 9 2¼ **Bo Selecta (IRE)**[26] 415 3-9-10 62... StevieDonohoe 12 33
(Richard Spencer) *towards rr and wd st: nvr a factor* 6/1[3]

404- 10 12 **Our Lois (IRE)**[180] 5799 3-9-3 55... PhillipMakin 5
(Keith Dalgleish) *a towards rr* 16/1

550- 11 2½ **Albizu Campos**[161] 6446 3-9-5 57... JasonHart 4
(Lawrence Mullaney) *chsd ldng pair on inner: rdn along wl over 2f out: sn drvn and wknd* 66/1

00-4 12 1¼ **Mungo Madness**[28] 385 3-9-3 58... ShelleyBirkett(3) 9
(Julia Feilden) *a towards rr* 7/1

000- 13 2 **Diamond Princess**[70] 8344 3-8-7 45...(h) LukeMorris 10
(Michael Appleby) *chsd ldrs on outer: rdn along over 3f out: sn wknd* 33/1

1m 41.6s (-2.10) **Going Correction** -0.175s/f (Stan) **13** Ran SP% **117.5**
Speed ratings (Par 95): **103,96,93,93,89 88,88,87,85,73 70,69,67**
CSF £119.23 CT £3123.24 TOTE £10.60: £3.50, £4.30, £7.30; EX 173.80 Trifecta £6207.90.
**Owner** Barry Kitcherside **Bred** Old Carhue Stud **Trained** Great Shefford, Berks

**FOCUS**
A moderate affair, but an easy winner. The form isn't the most solid.

## 849 SUNBETS.CO.UK MAIDEN STKS 1m 13y(F)
**2:40** (2:41) (Class 5) 3-Y-O+ **£3,234** (£962; £481; £240) **Stalls** Low

Form RPR

022- 1 **Native Prospect**[137] 7125 3-8-9 76... OisinMurphy 5 82+
(Andrew Balding) *dwlt: sn chsng ldrs on outer: cl up after 3f: led 1/2-way: jnd and rdn 2f out: drvn and hung rt jst over 1f out: drvn out* 10/11[1]

0-22 2 4½ **Elegantly Bound (IRE)**[11] 662 3-8-9 74...(b) AndrewMullen 7 71
(James Given) *prom: hdwy to chal 2f out: rdn and ev ch whn swtchd lft over 1f out: sn drvn and kpt on same pce* 9/4[2]

62 3 6 **Finale**[22] 479 3-8-4 0... FrannyNorton 2 52
(Hughie Morrison) *led: hdd 1/2-way: cl up on inner: rdn along over 2f out: sn drvn and grad wknd* 13/2[3]

4- 4 2¼ **Tewafeedj**[120] 7580 3-8-9 0... KevinStott 1 52
(Kevin Ryan) *chsd ldrs on inner: rdn along over 3f out: sn one pce* 8/1

66 5 9 **Dibloam (USA)**[17] 580 4-9-11 0... PhilipPrince(3) 4 37
(David Evans) *prom: rdn along over 3f out: sn drvn and outpcd* 40/1


The Form Book Flat, Raceform Ltd, Newbury, RG14 5SJ

6 **6** *28* **Touch Of Faith (IRE)**13 615 3-8-9 0 BenCurtis 3
(Michael Appleby) *a rr: rdn along 1/2-way: sn outpcd and bhd* **66/1**

1m 41.11s (-2.59) **Going Correction** -0.175s/f (Stan)
**WFA** 3 from 4yo 19lb 6 Ran SP% **111.5**
Speed ratings (Par 103): **105,100,94,92,83 55**
CSF £3.10 TOTE £1.90: £1.20, £1.30; EX 3.50 Trifecta £6.90.
**Owner** Mick and Janice Mariscotti **Bred** Overbury Stallions Ltd & Dukes Stud **Trained** Kingsclere, Hants

**FOCUS**
A fair maiden and they finished stretched out, but the time was ordinary.

## 850 SUNBETS.CO.UK H'CAP 7f 14y(F)
**3:10** (3:11) (Class 5) (0-75,77) 4-Y-0+ **£3,234** (£962; £481; £240) **Stalls** Low

Form RPR
5205 **1** **Among Angels**11 660 5-9-7 **75** (b) DaleSwift 13 83
(Daniel Mark Loughnane) *pushed along s and sn cl up: rdn along 3f out: chal wl over 1f out: drvn to ld ins fnl f: kpt on wl* **20/1**

3-31 **2** *1* **Vroom (IRE)**19 528 4-9-1 **74** (p) CliffordLee(5) 3 79
(Gay Kelleway) *led: jnd and rdn along 2f out: drvn over 1f out: hdd ins fnl f: kpt on* **11/2**2

-512 **3** *nk* **Alpha Tauri (USA)**19 527 11-8-13 **74** BenRobinson(7) 2 78
(Charles Smith) *chsd ldrs on inner: rdn along over 2f out: drvn over 1f out: kpt on wl fnl f* **16/1**

-131 **4** *½* **Custard The Dragon**11 663 4-9-7 **75** (p) JoeFanning 7 78+
(John Mackie) *hld up towards rr: hdwy wl over 2f out: chsd ldrs and swtchd rt jst over 1f out: sn rdn and kpt on* **5/2**1

2-53 **5** *½* **Dusky Dawn**14 611 5-9-8 **76** BenCurtis 4 77
(Alan Swinbank) *cl up: chal over 2f out and sn rdn: drvn over 1f out: kpt on same pce* **10/1**

0/5- **6** *shd* **Pullman Brown (USA)**39 226 5-9-0 **68** PaddyAspell 10 69+
(Philip Kirby) *towards rr: hdwy over 2f out: rdn wl over 1f out: kpt on wl fnl f: nrst fin* **10/1**

-252 **7** *hd* **Unnoticed**11 663 5-8-11 **65** (t) FrannyNorton 8 66
(Ollie Pears) *hld up in midfield: hdwy over 2f out: chsd ldrs over 1f out: no imp fnl f* **7/1**3

2644 **8** *3 ½* **Boots And Spurs**19 528 8-9-6 **74** LukeMorris 9 65
(Scott Dixon) *chsd ldrs: rdn along over 2f out: sn drvn and grad wknd* **10/1**

-116 **9** *nse* **Essenaitch (IRE)**26 419 4-9-4 **72** AndrewMullen 12 63
(David Evans) *in tch: rdn along wl over 2f out: sn drvn and one pce* **10/1**

-434 **10** *2 ½* **Stun Gun**19 527 7-8-11 **65** (p) TonyHamilton 11 49
(Derek Shaw) *towards rr: wd st: n.d* **20/1**

-354 **11** *3* **Harwoods Star (IRE)**11 665 7-8-12 **73** (be) JoshuaBryan(7) 6 49
(John Butler) *midfield: rdn along wl over 2f out: no hdwy* **25/1**

-420 **12** *1 ¼* **Ticks The Boxes (IRE)**18 551 5-9-9 **77** (p) RobertWinston 1 50
(Michael Herrington) *in tch on inner: rdn along over 2f out: sn wknd* **25/1**

-000 **13** *6* **Showing Off (IRE)**11 663 4-8-7 **61** oh1 RyanPowell 5 18
(Michael Wigham) *dwlt and sn swiched rt to outer in rr: wd st: a bhd* **100/1**

1m 28.81s (-1.49) **Going Correction** -0.175s/f (Stan) 13 Ran SP% **116.9**
Speed ratings (Par 103): **101,99,99,98,98 98,98,94,93,91 87,86,79**
CSF £117.93 CT £1895.82 TOTE £27.40: £6.30, £2.00, £3.90; EX 176.30 Trifecta £3081.70.
**Owner** Phil Slater **Bred** The Pineapple Stud Ltd **Trained** Rock, Worcs

**FOCUS**
The pace held up here, the first three racing in the first four most of the way. The closers were gradually edging nearer at the line and they finished in a bit of a heap. The winner is up a length on recent form.

## 851 BETWAY BEST ODDS GUARANTEED PLUS H'CAP 4f 214y(F)
**3:40** (3:41) (Class 3) (0-90,88) 4-Y-0+ **£7,439** (£2,213; £1,106; £553) **Stalls** Centre

Form RPR
005- **1** **Escalating**103 7892 5-8-6 **78** (t) LewisEdmunds(5) 2 89
(Michael Appleby) *trckd ldrs: hdwy 2f out: swtchd lft and effrt ent fnl f: sn rdn: qcknd to ld last 75 yds* **2/1**1

6304 **2** *1* **Crosse Fire**22 480 5-8-2 **69** KieranO'Neill 4 76
(Scott Dixon) *cl up centre: chal 2f out: rdn over 1f out: slt ld ent fnl f: sn drvn: hdd and no ex last 75 yds* **9/1**

1143 **3** *1 ½* **Lady Nayef**11 664 4-9-1 **82** (t) RobertWinston 3 85
(John Butler) *slt ld centre: hdd 3f out: cl up: led again 2f out: sn rdn: drvn and hdd ent fnl f: kpt on same pce* **7/2**2

11-6 **4** *2 ¼* **Captain Lars (SAF)**47 71 7-9-0 **81** (v) TonyHamilton 6 75
(Derek Shaw) *chsd ldrs: rdn along wl over 1f out: drvn and kpt on same pce fnl f* **12/1**

-016 **5** *½* **Archimedes (IRE)**19 523 4-8-2 **69** oh1 (vt) JosephineGordon 1 61
(David C Griffiths) *sn cl up: led 3f out: rdn along and hdd 2f out: cl up tl drvn over 1f out and grad wknd* **10/1**

-214 **6** *¾* **Dungannon**11 664 10-8-8 **82** (b) JoshuaBryan(7) 8 71
(Andrew Balding) *hld up: hdwy wl over 1f out: sn rdn: kpt on fnl f* **9/2**3

/01- **7** *2* **Wentworth Falls**111 7772 5-9-7 **88** PhillipMakin 7 70
(Geoffrey Harker) *in tch: rdn along 2f out: sn outpcd* **12/1**

20-0 **8** *½* **Orient Class**11 664 6-8-13 **80** JackGarritty 5 60
(Paul Midgley) *in tch: rdn along 2f out: sn outpcd* **25/1**

57.97s (-1.73) **Going Correction** -0.15s/f (Stan) 8 Ran SP% **112.1**
Speed ratings (Par 107): **107,105,103,99,98 97,94,93**
CSF £20.15 CT £58.16 TOTE £2.90: £1.20, £2.60, £2.40; EX 23.30 Trifecta £115.30.
**Owner** The Horse Watchers **Bred** Juddmonte Farms Ltd **Trained** Oakham, Rutland

**FOCUS**
A good performance from the winner, who looks improved for a gelding operation. He's rated to his best.

## 852 BETWAY SPRINT H'CAP 6f 16y(F)
**4:10** (4:10) (Class 6) (0-55,62) 4-Y-0+ **£2,587** (£770; £384; £192) **Stalls** Low

Form RPR
23-1 **1** **Bounty Pursuit**8 724 5-9-12 **62** 6ex (h) AlistairRawlinson(3) 7 73+
(Michael Appleby) *n.m.r after s and sn towards rr: pushed along and wd st: hdwy 2f out: rdn to chse clr ldr over 1f out: swtchd lft and drvn ins fnl f: led last 75 yds: kpt on strly* **10/11**1

0-40 **2** *½* **Gettin' Lucky**25 446 4-8-12 **45** (p1) BenCurtis 5 54
(John Balding) *led: rdn clr 2f out: drvn and edgd rt ins fnl f: hdd and no ex last 75 yds* **18/1**

242R **3** *1 ½* **Prince Of Time**12 644 5-8-8 **48** CallumRodriguez(7) 6 52
(Richard Ford) *dwlt and bhd: hdwy wl over 1f out: sn swtchd rt: styd on wl fnl f: nrst fin* **14/1**

-425 **4** *1 ¾* **Cadeaux Pearl**22 481 9-8-6 **46** (b) RPWalsh(7) 10 45
(Scott Dixon) *in tch: hdwy over 2f out: rdn to chse ldrs wl over 1f out: drvn and kpt on fnl f* **20/1**

-020 **5** *½* **Autumn Tonic (IRE)**21 494 5-9-6 **53** (b) PhillipMakin 1 50
(David Barron) *in tch: hdwy to chse ldrs 3f out: rdn along 2f out: drvn and kpt on same pce fnl f* **10/1**3

6-02 **6** *hd* **Vivre La Reve**4 784 5-9-5 **52** (h) GeorgeDowning 11 48
(James Unett) *towards rr: hdwy over 2f out: sn rdn and kpt on fnl f* **25/1**

-165 **7** *¾* **Multi Quest**19 521 5-9-7 **54** (b) FrannyNorton 4 48
(John E Long) *plld hrd: chsd ldrs: rdn along 2f out: sn drvn and grad wknd* **16/1**

50-4 **8** *1* **Name That Toon**47 64 4-8-13 **46** (v) AdamBeschizza 9 37
(Derek Shaw) *prom: rdn along wl over 2f out: grad wknd* **66/1**

55-0 **9** *hd* **Llewellyn**11 663 9-9-5 **57** (v1) PhilDennis(5) 8 47
(Declan Carroll) *cl up: rdn along 3f out: wknd fnl 2f* **10/1**3

00-0 **10** *1 ½* **Culloden**50 20 5-9-5 **57** CharlieBennett(5) 3 42
(Shaun Harris) *chsd ldrs on inner: hdwy 3f out: rdn 2f out: sn drvn and wknd over 1f out* **66/1**

0-25 **11** *¾* **Very First Blade**21 494 8-8-13 **53** (be) AledBeech(7) 2 36
(Michael Mullineaux) *a towards rr* **14/1**

-032 **12** *1 ¾* **Kyllach Me (IRE)**15 601 5-9-7 **57** (b) NathanEvans(3) 12 34
(Bryan Smart) *dwlt and rr: wd st: sn rdn and a bhd* **6/1**2

1m 16.75s (0.25) **Going Correction** -0.175s/f (Stan) 12 Ran SP% **120.9**
Speed ratings (Par 101): **91,90,88,86,85 85,84,82,82,80 79,77**
CSF £20.67 CT £157.95 TOTE £1.80: £1.10, £6.00, £4.10; EX 29.30 Trifecta £234.10.
**Owner** C L Bacon **Bred** Cecil And Miss Alison Wiggins **Trained** Oakham, Rutland

**FOCUS**
A moderate affair and the hot favourite made hard work of it. There are some positives over the second and third.

## 853 BETWAY H'CAP 1m 4f 14y(F)
**4:40** (4:40) (Class 6) (0-65,67) 4-Y-0+ **£2,587** (£770; £288; £288) **Stalls** Low

Form RPR
-636 **1** **The Lock Master (IRE)**10 688 10-9-12 **66** (v1) AlistairRawlinson(3) 6 73
(Michael Appleby) *trckd ldrs: hdwy 5f out: cl up 4f out: led 3f out: rdn wl over 1f out: drvn and kpt on strly fnl f* **7/1**3

0-20 **2** *2 ½* **Noguchi (IRE)**25 440 12-10-1 **66** (p) JosephineGordon 9 69
(Chris Dwyer) *hld up in tch: swtchd rt to outer 1/2-way: hdwy 3f out: rdn 2f out and sn chsng ldrs: drvn and kpt on wl fnl f* **9/1**

65-0 **3** *shd* **Sattelac**46 99 4-9-12 **66** PhillipMakin 2 69
(Keith Dalgleish) *prom: hdwy 4f out and sn chsng ldng pair: rdn along over 2f out: drvn wl over 1f out: kpt on u.p fnl f* **16/1**

0-62 **3** *dht* **Go On Gal (IRE)**26 414 4-9-0 **57** ShelleyBirkett(3) 5 60
(Julia Feilden) *prom: pushed along 3f out: rdn to chse wnr 2f out: sn drvn: kpt on u.p fnl f* **8/1**

-211 **5** *5* **My Renaissance**19 525 7-9-8 **66** JaneElliott(7) 8 61
(Sam England) *t.k.h: trckd ldrs: hdwy and cl up after 4f: led over 4f out: hdd 3f out and sn rdn along: drvn wl over 1f out: sn wknd* **7/4**1

034- **6** *4* **Horseguardsparade**44 3746 6-10-2 **67** (p) ThomasBrown 7 55
(Nigel Twiston-Davies) *v s.i.s and detached: tk clsr order over 5 out: rdn along over 3f out: drvn and plugged on fnl 2f* **8/1**

-042 **7** *¾* **Ralphy Lad (IRE)**11 661 6-9-7 **58** BenCurtis 3 45
(Alan Swinbank) *trckd ldrs: rdn along over 3f out: sn wknd* **9/2**2

625- **8** *19* **Indulgent**15 5921 4-8-7 **50** NathanEvans(3) 10 7
(Mike Sowersby) *towards rr: hdwy to take slt ld after 3f: rdn along 5f out: sn hdd & wknd* **100/1**

2-00 **9** *6* **Port Lairge**6 315 7-9-0 **56** PhilDennis(5) 4 3
(Michael Chapman) *a rr: bhd fnl 4f* **100/1**

54-6 **10** *1 ¼* **Sennockian Song**41 174 4-9-4 **58** JoeFanning 1 3
(Mark Johnston) *led 3f: prom on inner: pushed along 5f out: rdn 4f out: sn wknd* **10/1**

2m 39.18s (-1.82) **Going Correction** -0.175s/f (Stan)
**WFA** 4 from 6yo+ 2lb 10 Ran SP% **116.2**
Speed ratings (Par 101): **99,97,97,97,93 91,90,78,74,73**
WIN: 11.50; PL: 2.60 TLM, 2.50 SL, 1.50 GOG, 2.50 NG; EX: 78.40; CSF: 68.12; TC: TLM/NG/SL 485.80, TLM/NG/GOG 257.74; TF: TLM/NG/SL 560.80, TLM/NG/GOG 196.90.
**Owner** K G Kitchen **Bred** Patrick F Kelly **Trained** Oakham, Rutland

**FOCUS**
An ordinary race but the winner handed his trainer Michael Appleby a quick-fire treble on the card. The form is rated around the dead-heaters for third.
T/Plt: £1,681.80 to a £1 stake. Pool: £76,674.47 - 33.28 winning units T/Qpdt: £56.50 to a £1 stake. Pool: £10,791.64 - 141.19 winning units **Joe Rowntree**

# 806 KEMPTON (A.W) (R-H)
## Wednesday, February 22

**OFFICIAL GOING: Polytrack: standard**
Wind: Across (away from stands), strong becoming moderate Weather: Overcast, rain from race 3 onwards

## 854 RACING UK ALL WEATHER "HANDS AND HEELS" SERIES APPRENTICE H'CAP 1m (P)
**5:45** (5:45) (Class 7) (0-50,50) 4-Y-0+ **£1,940** (£577; £288; £144) **Stalls** Low

Form RPR
00-0 **1** **Living Leader**46 124 8-9-4 **47** BenRobinson 7 54
(Grace Harris) *trckd ldr: led 2f out: pushed along and kpt on wl fnl f* **25/1**

0-60 **2** *1 ¼* **Breakheart (IRE)**13 636 10-8-11 **50** (b) JasonWatson(10) 8 54
(Andrew Balding) *s.i.s: hld up in last: gd prog on inner over 2f out: kpt on to take 2nd ins fnl f: no imp on wnr nr fin* **8/1**

603- **3** *¾* **Rafaaf (IRE)**130 7369 9-9-7 **50** KieranSchofield 4 52
(Peter Hiatt) *hld up in midfield: prog to chal 2f out: chsd wnr to ins fnl f: kpt on same pce* **10/1**

-260 **4** *2 ½* **Lutine Charlie (IRE)**11 690 10-8-12 **46** (p) DarraghKeenan(5) 6 42
(Emma Owen) *hld up in rr: pushed along over 2f out: kpt on to take 4th fnl f: nt pce to threaten* **12/1**

055- **5** *1 ¾* **Gavarnie Encore**113 7736 5-9-1 **49** LauraCoughlan(5) 11 41
(Michael Blanshard) *hld up in last pair fr wd draw: pushed along over 2f out: kpt on one pce fr over 1f out: n.d* **9/2**1

-300 **6** *½* **Cuban Queen (USA)**19 544 4-9-0 **48** FinleyMarsh(5) 10 39
(Julia Feilden) *hld up in rr: effrt over 2f out: no great prog* **16/1**

3553 **7** *1* **Fossa**5 784 7-8-12 **46** (h1) GabrieleMalune(5) 9 36
(Mark Brisbourne) *t.k.h: racd wd: towards rr: one pce and no imp ldrs fr 2f out* **9/1**

00-3 **8** *½* **Kristoff (IRE)**14 614 4-8-6 **45** IsobelFrancis(10) 1 33
(Jim Boyle) *trckd ldng pair: on terms jst over 2f out: steadily wknd over 1f out* **7/1**3

5403 **9** ¾ **Chandrayaan**[7] 740 10-8-11 **45**................................(v) GinaMangan(5) 14 31
(John E Long) *trapped out wd but sn chsd ldrs: fnd nil over 2f out: sn btn* **16/1**

000- **10** ½ **Tallulah Fleur**[238] 3777 4-8-13 **45**..............................(p) GerO'Neill(3) 2 30
(David Loughnane) *t.k.h: led to 2f out: wknd* **33/1**

-452 **11** 1¼ **Mowhoob**[14] 614 7-9-7 **50**.......................................... JoshuaBryan 5 32
(Brian Barr) *chsd ldrs: urged along over 3f out: wknd over 2f out* **8/1**

-400 **12** nk **Royal Normandy**[13] 640 5-9-6 **49**..............................(p) JaneElliott 12 30
(Grace Harris) *chsd ldrs: urged along 3f out: sn wknd* **25/1**

3-65 **13** ½ **Altaira**[19] 544 6-8-12 **47**..............................................(p[1]) AledBeech(6) 3 27
(Tony Carroll) *t.k.h: hld up in tch: wknd over 2f out* **11/2**[2]

1m 40.83s (1.03) **Going Correction** +0.175s/f (Slow) **13** Ran SP% **117.5**
Speed ratings (Par 97): **101,99,99,96,94 94,93,92,92,91 90,89,89**
CSF £207.13 CT £2150.88 TOTE £20.80: £7.30, £3.00, £3.30; EX 351.70 Trifecta £6223.40.
**Owner** Ms Michelle Harris **Bred** D J And Mrs Deer **Trained** Shirenewton, Monmouthshire

**FOCUS**
A really weak race and something of a turn-up.

## 855 32RED ON THE APP STORE MAIDEN STKS 1m 2f 219y(P)
**6:15** (6:16) (Class 5) 3-4-Y-O **£2,911** (£866; £432; £216) **Stalls** Low

Form RPR

54 **1** **Alabaster**[6] 758 3-8-7 0.............................................. LukeMorris 6 69+
(Sir Mark Prescott Bt) *trckd ldr: shkn up over 2f out and carried hd quite high: rdn to press new ldr jst over 1f out: drvn ahd last 100yds: kpt on* **6/4**[1]

**2** nk **Here And Now** 3-8-7 0.............................................. OisinMurphy 2 68+
(Ralph Beckett) *trckd ldng pair: pushed up to ld 2f out: pressed and shkn up jst over 1f out: hdd 100yds out: kpt on but jst hld aft* **6/1**[3]

43- **3** nk **Balashakh (USA)**[155] 6655 3-8-8 0 ow1........................ JamieSpencer 8 68+
(David Simcock) *hld up in last pair early: prog and prom 1/2-way: rdn jst over 2f out: clsd to chal 1f out: nt qckn and a hld after* **13/8**[2]

**4** 5 **Eggesford** 3-8-7 0.............................................. DavidProbert 4 59
(Martyn Meade) *in tch in midfield: outpcd and shkn up 2f out: no imp ldrs after but tk 4th last strides* **10/1**

0-4 **5** hd **Mamnoon (IRE)**[25] 457 4-10-0 0................................ TomMarquand 3 63?
(Roy Brotherton) *led: set mod pce to 4f out: rdn and hdd 2f out: wknd fnl f* **100/1**

0 **6** 7 **Astrostorm**[26] 437 3-8-0 0........................................ GabrieleMalune(7) 5 47
(Mark H Tompkins) *in tch: taken wd bnd 4f out to 3f out: sn lft bhd by ldrs* **50/1**

0 **7** 9 **Secret Sands (IRE)**[14] 624 3-8-2 0................................ KieranO'Neill 7 26
(Pat Phelan) *t.k.h: hld up bhd ldrs: wknd over 2f out: sn bhd* **100/1**

**8** 2½ **Sun Or Shade (IRE)** 3-8-7 0........................................(b[1]) NickyMackay 1 27
(John Gosden) *slowly away: rn green and a last: lost tch over 2f out* **7/1**

2m 25.95s (4.05) **Going Correction** +0.175s/f (Slow)
**WFA** 3 from 4yo 23lb **8** Ran SP% **117.9**
Speed ratings (Par 103): **92,91,91,87,87 82,76,74**
CSF £11.77 TOTE £2.60: £1.30, £1.80, £1.10; EX 14.60 Trifecta £25.40.
**Owner** Charles C Walker - Osborne House **Bred** Miss K Rausing **Trained** Newmarket, Suffolk

**FOCUS**
Some interesting debutants here, but it was two with experience who dominated the betting. They went a steady early gallop before sprinting up the straight. There are some doubts over the bare form.

## 856 100% PROFIT BOOST AT 32REDSPORT.COM H'CAP 1m 3f 219y(P)
**6:45** (6:46) (Class 5) (0-75,75) 4-Y-O+ **£2,911** (£866; £432; £216) **Stalls** Centre

Form RPR

0/03 **1** **Langlauf (USA)**[21] 507 4-8-13 **75**................................(p) LuluStanford(5) 8 82
(Rod Millman) *t.k.h: trckd ldr after 3f: shkn up to ld over 1f out: hrd pressed fnl f: hld on wl* **4/1**[2]

0-31 **2** hd **Darebin (GER)**[18] 576 5-9-7 **75**..................................(b) GeorgeBaker 6 81
(Gary Moore) *hld up in midfield: shkn up 2f out: rdn to chal jst over 1f out: nt qckn and a jst hld last 150yds* **9/4**[1]

56-6 **3** 1½ **Safira Menina**[42] 173 5-8-11 **72**................................ MillyNaseb(7) 3 76
(Martin Smith) *hld up in rr: shkn up 2f out: prog jst over 1f out: styd on wl and pushed along to take 3rd nr fin* **11/1**

3-36 **4** ½ **Take Two**[26] 440 8-9-2 **70**........................................ LukeMorris 1 73
(Alex Hales) *trckd ldrs: clsd 3f out: drvn to ld briefly wl over 1f out: one pce fnl f* **8/1**[3]

1/05 **5** 1¼ **Included**[22] 497 5-9-5 **73**........................................(t[1]) OisinMurphy 4 74
(David Dennis) *led at mod gallop: tried to commit for home over 2f out: hdd wl over 1f out: fdd fnl f* **12/1**

6-64 **6** 1 **Sandy Cove**[14] 619 6-9-1 **69**........................................ RyanTate 7 69
(James Eustace) *s.s: hld up in last: stl there over 2f out: shkn up and kpt on one pce after: nvr in it* **12/1**

50-3 **7** 2½ **Askari**[33] 333 4-8-8 **65**............................................ JamieSpencer 2 61
(Tom Clover) *t.k.h early: trckd ldr 3f: styd prom: rdn over 2f out: sn lost pl and btn* **4/1**[2]

5553 **8** 7 **Obboorr**[11] 688 8-9-0 **68**........................................ PaulMulrennan 5 52
(James Given) *s.i.s: mostly in last pair: rdn 3f out: sn btn* **12/1**

2m 34.85s (0.35) **Going Correction** +0.175s/f (Slow)
**WFA** 4 from 5yo+ 2lb **8** Ran SP% **113.3**
Speed ratings (Par 103): **105,104,103,103,102 102,100,95**
CSF £13.16 CT £88.59 TOTE £4.50: £1.50, £1.40, £2.10; EX 15.00 Trifecta £130.70.
**Owner** Tony Bloom **Bred** Darley **Trained** Kentisbeare, Devon

**FOCUS**
A modest race, with most of these having questions to answer in some respect. The third and fourth look the best guides to the form.

## 857 32RED.COM H'CAP 6f (P)
**7:15** (7:15) (Class 4) (0-85,84) 4-Y-O+ **£4,690** (£1,395; £697; £348) **Stalls** Low

Form RPR

56-5 **1** **Florencio**[47] 93 4-8-12 **80**........................................(t[1]) GeorgeWood(5) 2 88
(Marco Botti) *trckd ldrs: poised to chal 2f out gng strly: led over 1f out: rdn out and a on top fnl f* **5/1**[2]

41-0 **2** ¾ **Under Siege (IRE)**[19] 547 5-9-5 **82**..........................(t) OisinMurphy 9 88
(Stuart Williams) *hld up bhd ldrs: prog fr 2f out: rdn to press wnr ins fnl f: styd on but readily hld* **7/1**

-004 **3** ½ **Plucky Dip**[6] 760 6-9-3 **80**........................................(p) AdamKirby 11 84
(John Ryan) *hld up towards rr: prog fr 2f out: rdn and tried to chal ins fnl f: styd on* **6/1**

520- **4** 1¾ **Parkour (IRE)**[69] 8380 4-9-3 **80**..................................(b) LukeMorris 7 78
(Marco Botti) *pressed ldr: chal 2f out: rdn and nt qckn over 1f out: fdd steadily last 150yds* **12/1**

5-23 **5** shd **Steelriver (IRE)**[47] 93 7-9-7 **84**................................ JamieSpencer 5 82
(David Barron) *s.s: hld up in last pair: stl there and pushed along 2f out: prog fnl f: styd on and nrly snatched 4th but nvr in it* **3/1**[1]

600- **6** ¾ **Excellent George**[90] 8083 5-9-0 **80**..........................(t) AaronJones(3) 1 76
(Stuart Williams) *hld up in midfield: prog on inner to chal over 1f out: fdd ins fnl f* **8/1**

5046 **7** ½ **Salvatore Fury (IRE)**[19] 547 7-9-2 **79**......................(v) DougieCostello 10 73
(Keith Dalgleish) *stdd s and dropped in fr wd draw: t.k.h towards rr: tried to cl on ldrs over 1f out: no hdwy fnl f* **33/1**

403- **8** ½ **He's My Cracker**[78] 8239 4-8-10 **76**........................ HectorCrouch(3) 3 68
(Clive Cox) *pressed ldrs: rdn over 2f out: lost pl and fdd over 1f out* **11/2**[3]

3253 **9** shd **Oriental Relation (IRE)**[14] 618 6-9-7 **84**..................(v) PaulMulrennan 8 76
(James Given) *spd fr wd draw to ld: rdn and hdd over 1f out: wknd fnl f* **8/1**

00-0 **10** ¾ **Major Crispies**[36] 277 6-8-9 **77**..............................(b) DavidParkes(5) 6 67
(Jeremy Gask) *awkward s: t.k.h: hld up in last pair: shkn up and no prog 2f out* **16/1**

1m 12.29s (-0.81) **Going Correction** +0.175s/f (Slow) **10** Ran SP% **122.6**
Speed ratings (Par 105): **112,111,110,108,107 106,106,105,105,104**
CSF £42.21 CT £224.84 TOTE £7.20: £2.40, £2.30, £2.20; EX 49.60 Trifecta £448.00.
**Owner** Excel Racing **Bred** Newsells Park Stud **Trained** Newmarket, Suffolk

**FOCUS**
A fair sprint handicap, which looked competitive enough for the grade. The winner is rated to his best.

## 858 32RED CONDITIONS STKS (ALL-WEATHER CHAMPIONSHIP FAST-TRACK QUALIFIER) 1m 7f 218y(P)
**7:45** (7:45) (Class 2) 4-Y-O+ **£11,827** (£3,541; £1,770; £885; £442) **Stalls** Low

Form RPR

-612 **1** **Winterlude (IRE)**[9] 720 7-9-2 97.................................. JoeFanning 4 106
(Jennie Candlish) *hld up in 4th: prog on inner to ld wl over 1f out: decisive move and in command after: cajoled along and styd on* **9/2**[3]

5 **2** 1¾ **Vettori Rules**[9] 720 4-8-10 96...................................... LukeMorris 2 103
(Gay Kelleway) *mostly trckd ldr: t.k.h 6f out: rdn to chal whn wnr sailed by 2f out: drvn to take 2nd again over 1f out: kpt on one pce* **13/2**

602- **3** nk **First Mohican**[63] 8479 9-9-2 101..................................(h) HollieDoyle 5 103
(Alan King) *hld up in last: sweeping move on outer bnd over 3f out: rdn over 2f out: fnd little after but pressed for 2nd ins fnl f* **3/1**[2]

30-6 **4** 1½ **Intense Tango**[25] 268 6-8-11 98................................(t) CliffordLee 1 96
(K R Burke) *led: sent for home over 3f out: hdd wl over 1f out: steadily fdd* **8/1**

00-4 **5** 4 **Sandro Botticelli (IRE)**[37] 268 5-9-5 106....................(p) AdamKirby 3 99
(John Ryan) *trckd ldng pair: clsd 6f out: wnt 2nd 5f out to 3f out: sn rdn and nt qckn: wl hld after* **6/4**[1]

3m 31.39s (1.29) **Going Correction** +0.175s/f (Slow)
**WFA** 4 from 5yo+ 4lb **5** Ran SP% **107.6**
Speed ratings (Par 109): **103,102,101,101,99**
CSF £29.24 TOTE £5.10: £1.70, £2.60; EX 17.70 Trifecta £66.00.
**Owner** Brian Verinder & Alan Baxter **Bred** Darley **Trained** Basford Green, Staffs

**FOCUS**
The feature race on the card and a fast-track qualifier for the marathon race on finals day. Despite the small field they went an even enough gallop.

## 859 32RED CASINO H'CAP 1m 7f 218y(P)
**8:15** (8:15) (Class 6) (0-60,61) 4-Y-O+ **£2,264** (£673; £336; £168) **Stalls** Low

Form RPR

60/3 **1** **Ascendant**[9] 721 11-9-7 **57**........................................ StevieDonohoe 4 63
(Johnny Farrelly) *sn cl up on inner: drvn through to ld wl over 1f out: sn pressed: hld on wl last 100yds* **11/2**[3]

0-53 **2** shd **Night Generation (GER)**[28] 395 5-9-11 **61**................(tp) LukeMorris 5 66
(Chris Gordon) *hld up in midfield: nt clr run briefly over 2f out: prog sn after to press wnr over 1f out: str chal fnl f: jst denied* **12/1**

5/4- **3** 1¼ **Shalianzi (IRE)**[24] 4637 7-9-10 **60**................................(b) GeorgeBaker 6 64
(Chris Gordon) *hld up in last: stl there over 2f out: prog and rdn wl over 1f out: styd on to take 3rd nr fin: too late to chal* **33/1**

35/4 **4** ½ **Money Talks**[25] 462 7-9-8 **58**.................................... DanielMuscutt 7 61
(Michael Madgwick) *led at modest pce for 3f: styd prom: drvn to chal 2f out: one pce over 1f out: lost 3rd nr fin* **15/2**

00-3 **5** hd **Newtown Cross (IRE)**[26] 436 7-8-12 **48**........................ TomMarquand 11 51
(Jimmy Fox) *towards rr: rdn and no prog over 2f out: swtchd lft over 1f out: styd on after to press for a pl nr fin* **11/1**

-332 **6** ¾ **Delagoa Bay (IRE)**[9] 721 9-9-9 **59**................................ AdamKirby 3 61
(Sylvester Kirk) *hld up in last trio: rdn over 2f out: kpt on fr over 1f out on outer but nvr pce to threaten* **9/2**[2]

403- **7** 1¾ **Tarakkom (FR)**[55] 8565 5-9-0 **55**................................ DavidParkes(5) 1 55
(Peter Hiatt) *hld up in midfield: dropped to rr 1/2-way: trapped bhd rivals over 2f out: sme prog over 1f out: no hdwy fnl f* **20/1**

5-22 **8** ¾ **Le Tissier**[13] 645 4-9-0 **56**........................................(p) RobHornby 9 55
(Michael Attwater) *trckd ldrs: rdn and stl cl up over 2f out: steadily fdd over 1f out* **11/2**[3]

14-1 **9** nk **Shan Dun na nGall (IRE)**[28] 395 6-9-10 **60**..........(vt) LemosdeSouza 8 59
(Amy Murphy) *hld up towards rr: rdn over 2f out: tried to cl over 1f out but only kpt on at one pce* **7/4**[1]

00-0 **10** 19 **Last Summer**[27] 414 6-8-9 **48**..................................(p[1]) HectorCrouch(3) 2 24
(Grace Harris) *hld up in last pair: rapid prog to press ldr after 6f: lost 2nd and wknd qckly over 2f out: t.o* **50/1**

-255 **11** nk **Barnacle**[7] 741 8-8-10 **46**........................................(vt) JoeFanning 10 21
(Emma Owen) *led after 3f but nt at str pce: hdd & wknd qckly wl over 1f out: t.o* **33/1**

3m 33.42s (3.32) **Going Correction** +0.175s/f (Slow)
**WFA** 4 from 5yo+ 4lb **11** Ran SP% **125.7**
Speed ratings (Par 101): **98,97,97,97,96 96,95,95,95,85 85**
CSF £71.39 CT £2037.63 TOTE £6.60: £2.20, £3.80, £6.60; EX 75.70 Trifecta £901.20.
**Owner** F A Clegg **Bred** Cheveley Park Stud Ltd **Trained** Enmore, Somerset

**FOCUS**
Just a moderate handicap, but a few of these came into the race in fair form with the majority of the runners having placed on their most recent start. They went a stop/start gallop and it was more akin to a cycling peloton in the early stages than a horse race. The messy nature of the race was in evidence in the straight too with a number suffering with the lack of a clear run. The veteran winner was off a good mark.

T/Jkpt: Not won. T/Plt: £1,035.50 to a £1 stake. Pool: £86,245.21. 60.80 winning units. T/Qpdt: £115.50 to a £1 stake. Pool: £10,466.87. 67.06 winning units. **Jonathan Neesom**

# [814]LINGFIELD (L-H)

## Wednesday, February 22

**OFFICIAL GOING: Polytrack: standard**
Wind: medium, across Weather: overcast, blustery

## 860 SUNBETS.CO.UK H'CAP 7f 1y(P)
2:20 (2:20) (Class 6) (0-60,60) 4-Y-0+ £2,911 (£649; £216) Stalls Low

Form RPR
-020 1 **Lucky Louie**[23] 482 4-9-7 **60**..........................................(p) JackMitchell 1 67
(Roger Teal) *stdd s: hld up in tch in rr: rdn and hdwy on inner over 1f out: 5th and swtchd rt jst ins fnl f: r.o strly fnl 100yds to ld last strides* **4/1**[1]
3631 2 hd **Menelik (IRE)**[13] 640 8-9-6 **59**....................................(bt) DavidProbert 9 65
(Des Donovan, Ire) *sn led: wnt clr 1/2-way: 5 l clr and drifted rt bnd wl over 1f out: sn rdn: stl 2 l clr 100yds out: tired towards fin: hdd last stride* **9/2**[2]
55-0 2 dht **Hipz (IRE)**[14] 620 6-9-5 **58**............................................(p) GeorgeBaker 3 64
(Laura Mongan) *trckd ldrs: effrt wl over 1f out: chsd ldr and 2 l to find 100yds out: steadily clsd and ev ch nr fin: kpt on* **7/1**[3]
4-50 4 ½ **Miss Goldsmith (IRE)**[27] 419 4-9-4 **60**............... AdamMcNamara(3) 4 65
(Richard Fahey) *hld in midfield: effrt wl over 1f out: hdwy u.p jst over 1f out: r.o strly ins fnl f: nt rch ldrs* **10/1**
0-04 5 ½ **Blackthorn Stick (IRE)**[9] 724 8-8-13 **57**.................(p) DavidParkes(5) 2 60
(Paul Burgoyne) *taken down early: hld up in tch in midfield: rdn and hdwy on inner over 1f out: 4th and clsng 1f out: kpt on but nvr quite getting to ldrs* **8/1**
0-03 6 1½ **Bold Max**[13] 644 6-8-7 **46** oh1..........................................(v) LukeMorris 5 45
(Zoe Davison) *hld up in tch in rr: effrt over 1f out: kpt on wl u.p ins fnl f: nt rch ldrs* **20/1**
3235 7 nse **Major Muscari (IRE)**[18] 579 9-9-5 **58**........................(p) OisinMurphy 14 57
(Shaun Harris) *t.k.h: hld up in tch in midfield: effrt over 1f out: styd on wl ins fnl f: nt rch ldrs* **8/1**
0-03 8 nse **Raise The Game (IRE)**[9] 724 4-9-1 **59**....................... RyanWhile(5) 13 58
(Bill Turner) *chsd ldr: 5 l down and rdn 2f out: drvn over 1f out: kpt on wout ever getting on terms w ldr: lost 2nd ins fnl f: wknd towards fin* **14/1**
00-0 9 hd **Majestic Myles (IRE)**[46] 116 9-9-7 **60**............................ KieranO'Neill 11 58
(Lee Carter) *hld up in tch in midfield: effrt over 2f out: nt clr run over 1f out: hdwy ins fnl f: kpt on wout threatening ldrs* **14/1**
0050 10 ¾ **Nidnod**[7] 739 4-8-0 **46** oh1.................................... SophieRalston(7) 10 42
(John Bridger) *dwlt: hld up in rr: rdn and sme hdwy jst over 1f out: kpt on wout threatening ldrs* **66/1**
0412 11 1 **Welsh Inlet (IRE)**[13] 644 9-8-6 **52**............................. JaneElliott(7) 8 46
(John Bridger) *wl in tch in midfield: rdn and unable qck over 1f out: wknd ins fnl f* **11/1**
00-0 12 ½ **Sehayli (IRE)**[42] 172 4-9-2 **60**.................................. PaddyBradley(5) 6 52
(Lee Carter) *s.i.s: hld up in tch in midfield: rdn over 1f out: no prog: n.d* **33/1**
0-40 13 1½ **Captain Kendall (IRE)**[19] 544 8-8-7 **46**..................(b[1]) NickyMackay 12 34
(Harry Chisman) *chsd ldrs: rdn 2f out: unable qck over 1f out: wknd fnl f* **40/1**
-005 14 ½ **Silver Springs (IRE)**[16] 601 4-9-1 **54** ow1....................... AdamKirby 7 41
(David Evans) *in tch in midfield: rdn and lost pl over 1f out: sn btn and wknd fnl f* **14/1**

1m 24.35s (-0.45) **Going Correction** +0.05s/f (Slow) **14** Ran SP% **122.0**
Speed ratings (Par 101): **104,103,103,103,102 100,100,100,100,99 98,98,96,95**
WIN: 4.50; PL: LL 1.70, M 1.40, H 3.00; EX: LL-M 12.60, LL-H 20.10; CSF: LL-M 10.47, LL-H 15.56; TC: LL-M-H 64.75, LL-H-M 69.14; TF: LL-M-H 54.70, LL-H-M 71.20.
**Owner** Great Shefford Racing **Bred** Whatton Manor Stud **Trained** Great Shefford, Berks

**FOCUS**
A moderate handicap to start, but as dramatic a race as it gets. It was run at a good pace and the winner is rated to his best.

## 861 BETWAY BEST ODDS GUARANTEED PLUS H'CAP 1m 7f 169y(P)
2:55 (2:55) (Class 5) (0-75,74) 4-Y-0+ £3,557 (£1,058; £529; £264) Stalls Low

Form RPR
32 1 **Remember The Man (IRE)**[18] 576 4-9-6 **74**................. OisinMurphy 5 82+
(Ralph Beckett) *chsd ldr: clsd and upsides 3f out tl led ent fnl 2f: rdn 1f out: r.o wl and in command fnl f: quite comf* **1/1**[1]
-214 2 2 **Bamako Du Chatelet (FR)**[26] 440 6-9-7 **69**.................(p) AdamKirby 4 74
(Ian Williams) *trckd ldng pair: effrt to chse wnr over 1f out: kpt on for clr 2nd but a hld by wnr ins fnl f* **3/1**[2]
4-00 3 5 **Tempuran**[26] 440 8-9-3 **65**.................................................. RobHornby 1 64
(David Bridgwater) *led: jnd and rdn 3f out: hdd ent fnl 2f out: 3rd and outpcd over 1f out: plugged on same pce fnl f* **10/1**
4-45 4 hd **Dakota City**[21] 507 6-9-9 **71**.........................................(p) AdamBeschizza 3 70
(Julia Feilden) *hld up off the pce in rr: clsd and in tch 7f out: effrt over 2f out: outpcd by ldng pair over 1f out: plugged on same pce ins fnl f* **7/1**[3]
04-6 5 2½ **Saint Honore**[47] 92 5-9-3 **70**..............................(p[1]) PaddyBradley(5) 2 66
(Pat Phelan) *hld up off the pce in 5th: clsd and in tch 7f out: pushed along 2f out: outpcd and rdn ent fnl f: wl hld and plugged on same pce after* **8/1**
26/- 6 2 **Jolly Roger (IRE)**[25] 5548 10-8-11 **59**............................... DavidProbert 6 52
(Dai Burchell) *hld up off the pce in midfield: clsd and in tch 7f out: rdn 3f out: outpcd 2f out: bhd over 1f out* **20/1**

3m 21.74s (-3.96) **Going Correction** +0.05s/f (Slow)
**WFA** 4 from 5yo+ 4lb **6** Ran SP% **112.5**
Speed ratings (Par 103): **111,110,107,107,106 105**
CSF £4.18 TOTE £1.70: £1.10, £1.90; EX 3.80 Trifecta £24.70.
**Owner** S Hanson **Bred** Fair Salinia Ltd **Trained** Kimpton, Hants

**FOCUS**
A modest staying handicap run at a moderate pace, but still dominated by the market leaders. The form is rated around the fourth.

## 862 32RED.COM MAIDEN FILLIES' STKS (PLUS 10 RACE) 1m 2f (P)
3:25 (3:26) (Class 5) 3-Y-O £3,557 (£1,058; £529; £264) Stalls Low

Form RPR
1 **Falcon Cliffs (IRE)** 3-9-0 0.............................................. OisinMurphy 4 73
(Joseph Tuite) *hld up in tch in last pair: effrt and qcknd between rivals to chal ent fnl f: rn green: edging lft but led ins fnl f: r.o wl: pushed out* **22/1**
3 2 ½ **Bishops Cannings (IRE)**[13] 642 3-9-0 0.............................. ShaneKelly 2 72
(David Elsworth) *squeezed for room sn after s and hmpd over 8f out: in tch in 4th: hdwy on outer to join ldr 4f out: pushed into ld over 1f out: sn hdd and carried lft jst ins fnl f: kpt on* **3/1**[2]
2 3 ½ **Shankara (IRE)**[9] 717 3-9-0 0.......................................... JamieSpencer 3 71
(David Simcock) *trckd ldrs: short of room 4f out: sn swtchd rt: effrt and rdn to ld over 1f out: edgd lft 1f out: hdd and one pced ins fnl f* **13/8**[1]
4 4 7 **Utopian Dream**[44] 144 3-9-0 0......................................... NickyMackay 5 57
(John Gosden) *pressed ldr tl rdn 4f out: styd chsng ldrs tl unable qck ent fnl f: sn wknd* **7/2**[3]
2 5 7 **Wedding Breakfast (IRE)**[27] 424 3-9-0 0.............. JosephineGordon 1 43
(Hugo Palmer) *led: rdn and hdd over 1f out: sn btn and fdd fnl f* **7/2**[3]
6 5 **Dashanti** 3-9-0 0........................................................................ RyanTate 6 33
(Jonathan Portman) *s.i.s: niggled along and rn green in rr: rdn over 2f out: bhd over 1f out* **50/1**

2m 7.33s (0.73) **Going Correction** +0.05s/f (Slow) **6** Ran SP% **113.8**
Speed ratings (Par 94): **99,98,98,92,87 83**
CSF £87.93 TOTE £17.70: £6.20, £1.40; EX 87.20 Trifecta £306.50.
**Owner** A A Byrne & Mark Wellbelove **Bred** Gerry Smith **Trained** Lambourn, Berks

**FOCUS**
The four to have run before had all shown ability on their debuts, but this went to one of the two newcomers. The favourite was close to her debut figure.

## 863 SUN BETS ON THE APP STORE MAIDEN STKS 7f 1y(P)
3:55 (3:55) (Class 5) 3-Y-O+ £3,557 (£1,058; £529; £264) Stalls Low

Form RPR
43-3 1 **Mitigate**[35] 288 3-7-13 69.............................................. HollieDoyle(5) 10 75
(David Elsworth) *chsd ldr: shkn up and qcknd to ld 1f out: r.o strly and drew wl clr fnl f: easily* **9/2**[3]
2-43 2 4 **Havelock (IRE)**[12] 662 3-8-9 72.......................................... JoeFanning 4 69
(Mark Johnston) *led: rdn over 1f out: hdd 1f out: immediately outpcd by wnr: kpt on same pce and a holding 2nd ins fnl f* **2/1**[1]
4-5 3 1¼ **Arctic Sea**[41] 198 3-8-9 0.................................................. PJMcDonald 5 66
(Paul Cole) *trckd ldng pair: outpcd u.p over 1f out: no ch w wnr and kpt on same pce ins fnl f* **9/2**[3]
05- 4 1 **Road To Dubai (IRE)**[88] 8119 3-8-9 0.............................. OisinMurphy 9 63
(George Scott) *trckd ldng trio: rdn and outpcd over 1f out: wl hld and kpt on same pce ins fnl f* **9/4**[2]
6 5 4½ **Swilly Bay (IRE)**[19] 545 3-8-6 0............................ CallumShepherd(3) 6 51+
(Charles Hills) *hld up in rr: shkn up briefly over 4f out: pushed along over 1f out: kpt on to pass bhd horses ins fnl f: nvr trbld ldrs* **12/1**
0- 6 ¾ **King Otto**[109] 7812 3-8-9 0.................................................... LukeMorris 1 49
(Phil McEntee) *t.k.h: hld up in midfield: outpcd and shkn up over 1f out: wl btn after* **33/1**
0- 7 2 **Noreena**[147] 6874 3-8-4 0...................................................... JoeyHaynes 3 39
(Paul D'Arcy) *t.k.h: hld up in last trio: shkn up over 1f out: sn btn* **100/1**
0 8 ½ **Tilly's Bridge**[25] 464 4-9-7 0............................................ JackMitchell 8 43
(Steve Woodman) *t.k.h: hld up in tch in midfield: rdn over 2f out: sn struggling: bhd over 1f out* **40/1**
05 9 1¼ **Akuna Mattatta (IRE)**[11] 679 3-8-9 0.............................. DavidProbert 7 39
(Ralph J Smith) *t.k.h: hld up in last trio: effrt and wd bnd 2f out: sn bhd* **100/1**

1m 25.37s (0.57) **Going Correction** +0.05s/f (Slow)
**WFA** 3 from 4yo 17lb **9** Ran SP% **115.5**
Speed ratings (Par 103): **98,93,92,90,85 84,82,82,80**
CSF £13.84 TOTE £6.10: £1.50, £1.20, £1.50; EX 16.00 Trifecta £48.00.
**Owner** G B Partnership **Bred** Shutford Stud **Trained** Newmarket, Suffolk

**FOCUS**
An uncompetitive maiden with all of these having previous experience. The order didn't change much and few got into it, but the winner could hardly have been more impressive and showed improved form.

## 864 32RED CASINO APPRENTICE H'CAP 1m 2f (P)
4:30 (4:30) (Class 6) (0-65,62) 3-Y-O £2,911 (£866; £432; £216) Stalls Low

Form RPR
006- 1 **Maori Bob (IRE)**[69] 8377 3-9-8 **61**.................................. LuluStanford(5) 4 64
(Michael Bell) *t.k.h: led and set stdy gallop: rdn and qcknd over 1f out: distracted and wnt rt ins fnl f: hld on towards fin* **7/2**[2]
33-2 2 shd **Moneyoryourlife**[6] 763 3-9-1 **56**........................................ TinaSmith(7) 1 58
(Richard Hannon) *hld up in tch: effrt to chse wnr over 1f out: kpt on u.p and ev ch wl ins fnl f: jst hld* **9/4**[1]
6-11 3 ½ **Dangerous Ends**[21] 502 3-10-0 **62**........................(v) AlistairRawlinson 2 63+
(Brett Johnson) *hld up in rr: effrt over 1f out: hdwy u.p 1f out: chsd ldng pair 100yds out: r.o wl: nt quite rch ldrs* **9/4**[1]
00-5 4 1¼ **Whatelseaboutyou (IRE)**[34] 305 3-9-11 **59**........... AdamMcNamara 5 58
(Richard Fahey) *t.k.h: chsd wnr tl unable qck over 1f out: kpt on same pce u.p ins fnl f* **9/2**[3]
06-6 5 ¾ **My Brother Mike (IRE)**[21] 503 3-9-7 **62**.............................. TobyEley(7) 3 59
(Daniel Mark Loughnane) *hld up in tch: effrt over 1f out: kpt on same pce ins fnl f* **7/1**
0-00 6 7 **Young Officer (IRE)**[21] 502 3-8-6 **47**...........................(v) JordanUys(7) 7 30
(Brian Meehan) *dwlt: sn chsd ldng pair: rdn: wd and lost pl bnd 2f out: bhd fnl f* **40/1**

2m 10.55s (3.95) **Going Correction** +0.05s/f (Slow) **6** Ran SP% **115.5**
Speed ratings (Par 95): **86,85,85,84,83 78**
CSF £12.30 TOTE £4.00: £2.60, £1.10; EX 13.10 Trifecta £36.10.
**Owner** P Philipps, C Philipps, T Redman **Bred** Peter Molony **Trained** Newmarket, Suffolk

**FOCUS**
An uncompetitive 3yo apprentice handicap and the pace was steady, which somewhat played into the hands of the winner. The form is rated around the runner-up.

## 865 BETWAY AMATEUR RIDERS' H'CAP 1m 2f (P)
5:05 (5:05) (Class 6) (0-60,60) 4-Y-O+ £2,807 (£870; £435; £217) Stalls Low

Form RPR
1-53 1 **Synodic (USA)**[44] 147 5-10-9 **60**................................(t) JonjoO'Neill(5) 4 67+
(Seamus Durack) *hld up in tch in midfield: clsd to trck ldrs over 2f out: shkn up and qcknd to ld ins fnl f: sn in command and edgd rt: r.o* **7/2**[1]
-665 2 1 **Sunshineandbubbles**[23] 482 4-10-7 **54**...............(p) MissSBrotherton 7 59
(Daniel Mark Loughnane) *chsd ldrs: wnt 2nd 3f out: rdn and ev ch over 1f out: chsd wnr and kpt on same pce ins fnl f* **5/1**[3]
0/00 3 1¼ **Frontline Phantom (IRE)**[7] 733 10-9-13 **50**...... MissCAGreenway(5) 8 53
(K R Burke) *in tch in midfield: nt clr run over 2f out: effrt and swtchd lft over 1f out: chsd ldng trio 1f out: kpt on to snatch 3rd last strides* **40/1**
1561 4 hd **Outlaw Torn (IRE)**[11] 689 8-10-10 **56**................(e) MissJoannaMason 1 58
(Richard Guest) *taken down early: led tl 7f out: chsd ldr tl led again 4f out: rdn wl over 1f out: hdd ins fnl f: no ex and wknd towards fin: lost 3rd last strides* **9/1**
00-0 5 hd **Ledbury (IRE)**[14] 621 5-9-10 **47**................................ SeanHoulihan(5) 11 49
(Lee Carter) *hld up in tch in midfield: effrt and drifted rt u.p over 1f out: kpt on ins fnl f* **33/1**

50-2 **6** 1½ **Strictly Art (IRE)**[6] 757 4-10-2 **54**...............(p) MissJCooley(5) 6 53
(Alan Bailey) *chsd ldr tl over 7f out: styd handy: rdn 2f out: unable qck over 1f out: kpt on same pce ins fnl f* **6/1**

4506 **7** hd **Powered (IRE)**[11] 684 4-10-1 **53**............... MissEMacKenzie(5) 2 51+
(David Evans) *hld up in last pair: effrt over 1f out: hdwy 1f out: kpt on wl ins fnl f: nvr trbld ldrs* **8/1**

2-31 **8** ½ **Henry Grace (IRE)**[7] 740 6-10-6 **59** 6ex...............(b) MrJRPatterson(7) 5 56+
(Jimmy Fox) *hld up in last trio: stuck bhd a wall of horses over 2f out: swtchd rt and pushed along ent fnl f: kpt on wl: nvr trbld ldrs* **9/2**[2]

-000 **9** 1 **Steady Major (IRE)**[11] 684 5-10-6 **55**........ MissBeckyBrisbourne(3) 10 50
(Mark Brisbourne) *t.k.h: hld up in tch in midfield: nt clr run over 2f out: swtchd rt and lost pl wl over 1f out: kpt on u.p ins fnl f: no threat to ldrs* **10/1**

0-00 **10** ¾ **Two In The Pink (IRE)**[23] 482 7-10-13 **59**............ ThomasGreatrex 13 53
(Ralph J Smith) *stdd and dropped in bhd after s: hld up in rr: hdwy u.p on inner over 1f out: no imp jst ins fnl f: wknd fnl 100yds* **25/1**

0-00 **11** 3½ **Bridge That Gap**[13] 636 9-9-8 **47**...............(p[1]) MrNathanMcCann(7) 3 34
(Roger Ingram) *dwlt: hld up in rr: hdwy on outer over 3f out: lost pl bnd 2f out: n.d after* **33/1**

04-0 **12** ¾ **Happy Jack (IRE)**[44] 146 6-10-1 **50**...............(p) MissJodieHughes(3) 9 35
(Dai Burchell) *chsd ldrs: 4th and rdn 2f out: sn lost pl and wknd over 1f out* **12/1**

00-0 **13** 16 **Imperial Link**[46] 123 5-10-3 **49**............... MissBrodieHampson 14 2
(John O'Shea) *s.i.s: hdwy on outer to ld 7f out: hdd 4f out: rdn and lost pl over 2f out: bhd over 1f out* **33/1**

2m 7.22s (0.62) **Going Correction** +0.05s/f (Slow) **13 Ran SP% 124.4**
Speed ratings (Par 101): **99,98,97,97,96 95,95,95,94,93 90,90,77**
CSF £20.52 CT £623.25 TOTE £4.30: £1.90, £2.00, £12.40; EX 19.80 Trifecta £941.20.
**Owner** A M Gibbons **Bred** Flaxman Holdings Limited **Trained** Upper Lambourn, Berkshire

**FOCUS**
A moderate amateur riders' handicap. The runner-up is a fair guide to this form.
T/Plt: £81.20 to a £1 stake. Pool: £72,683.63. 652.80 winning units. T/Qpdt: £31.00 to a £1 stake. Pool: £4,998.10. 119.10 winning units. **Steve Payne**

866 - 873a (Foreign Racing) - See Raceform Interactive

## 757 CHELMSFORD (A.W) (L-H)
Thursday, February 23

**OFFICIAL GOING: Polytrack: standard**
Wind: very strong, half behind Weather: very windy, showers

### 874 GOING RACING? STAY AT CHANNELS CHANNELS.CO.UK APPRENTICE H'CAP 5f (P)
**1:50** (1:53) (Class 6) (0-60,58) 4-Y-0+ **£3,234** (£962; £481; £240) **Stalls** Low

Form RPR

-000 **1** **Mighty Zip (USA)**[8] 742 5-9-0 **53**...............(p) JordanUys(2) 3 59
(Lisa Williamson) *bmpd s: in tch in last trio: effrt over 1f out: str run u.p wl ins fnl f led on post* **6/1**

-004 **2** nse **Excellent Aim**[17] 602 10-9-7 **58**............... JaneElliott 8 64
(George Margarson) *pressed ldr: pushed into ld ins fnl f: kpt on: hdd on post* **6/1**

0-00 **3** 1¼ **Barnsdale**[17] 601 4-8-2 **45**...............(p) MeganEllingworth(6) 6 46
(John Holt) *led: pushed along over 1f out: kpt on tl hdd ins fnl f: kpt on same pce towards fin* **50/1**

4326 **4** nse **Pearl Noir**[8] 743 7-9-0 **55**...............(b) TobyEley(4) 2 56
(Scott Dixon) *bmpd s: chsd ldrs: rdn over 1f out: n.m.r ins fnl f: kpt on towards fin* **11/4**[1]

5022 **5** 1¼ **Mistry**[7] 764 4-8-8 **45**...............(v) LuluStanford 5 41
(Mark Usher) *wnt lft s: in tch in last trio: effrt over 1f out: kpt on same pce ins fnl f* **7/2**[3]

00-0 **6** nk **Hurricane Alert**[5] 819 5-8-6 **45**...............(t[1]) JoshuaBryan(2) 7 40
(Mark Hoad) *taken down early: dwlt and tongue tie c adrift leaving stalls: in tch in rr: effrt over 1f out: drvn 1f out: no imp ins fnl f* **20/1**

04-0 **7** 1¼ **Yisty**[49] 64 4-8-8 **47**...............(v) BenRobinson(2) 1 38
(Derek Shaw) *chsd ldrs: rdn over 1f out: no ex ins fnl f: wknd fnl 100yds* **16/1**

-210 **8** nk **Topsoil**[8] 742 4-9-3 **54**...............(p) PaddyBradley 4 44
(Ronald Harris) *dwlt and hmpd leaving stalls: rcvrd to chse ldrs over 3f out: unable qck over 1f out: wknd ins fnl f* **3/1**[2]

1m 0.37s (0.17) **Going Correction** -0.025s/f (Stan) **8 Ran SP% 115.1**
Speed ratings (Par 101): **97,96,94,94,92 92,90,89**
CSF £41.83 CT £1652.22 TOTE £7.10: £1.80, £1.70, £11.80; EX 48.90 Trifecta £2975.70.
**Owner** Heath House Racing **Bred** Dr Catherine Wills **Trained** Saighton, Cheshire

**FOCUS**
A moderate apprentice sprint handicap for which the conditions did not look pleasant. Weak form.

### 875 UB40 HERE ON AUGUST 12TH H'CAP 7f (P)
**2:20** (2:24) (Class 6) (0-65,66) 3-Y-0 **£3,234** (£962; £481; £240) **Stalls** Low

Form RPR

0-04 **1** **Viola Park**[31] 377 3-8-6 **50**............... RyanPowell 3 53
(Ronald Harris) *led: rdn over 1f out: hdd ins fnl f: kpt on u.p and led again wl ins fnl f: hld on cl home* **10/1**

00-1 **2** nk **Toy Theatre**[21] 522 3-9-3 **64**............... AlistairRawlinson(3) 7 66+
(Michael Appleby) *in tch in midfield on outer: effrt to chal u.p over 1f out: led ins fnl f: sn edging lft and hdd wl ins fnl f: kpt on same pce cl home* **11/4**[1]

005- **3** hd **Whatalove**[203] 5072 3-7-9 **46** oh1............... RhiainIngram(7) 10 47
(Martin Keighley) *chsd ldrs: rdn and ev ch 2f out: kpt on wl tl unable qck wl ins fnl f* **20/1**

600- **4** shd **It's How We Roll (IRE)**[99] 7975 3-9-7 **65**.........(b[1]) MichaelJMMurphy 12 66
(Charles Hills) *s.i.s: in rr: hdwy into midfield: 4f out: effrt over 1f out: ev ch ins fnl f: kpt on* **14/1**

0-64 **5** 2 **Nicky Baby (IRE)**[26] 463 3-9-3 **61**............... RobertWinston 1 57
(Dean Ivory) *chsd ldrs: rdn and ev ch over 1f out tl no ex 1f out: wknd and wnt rt wl ins fnl f* **11/4**[1]

53-2 **6** hd **Edged In Blue**[29] 397 3-9-1 **62**............... JordanVaughan(3) 2 57
(K R Burke) *t.k.h: wl in tch in midfield: rdn and unable qck over 1f out: kpt on same pce ins fnl f* **7/1**[3]

060- **7** 14 **Sunovarebel**[71] 8354 3-9-5 **63**............... JoeyHaynes 9 20+
(Alan Bailey) *rrd as stalls opened: slowly away: a bhd: lost tch over 1f out* **25/1**

20-6 **8** 2½ **Dusty Bin**[29] 401 3-9-5 **63**............... KevinStott 4 14
(Scott Dixon) *s.i.s: a rr: lost tch over 1f out* **6/1**[2]

0-33 **9** 5 **Flying Fynn (IRE)**[15] 615 3-9-5 **63**...............(p) OscarPereira 6
(Jose Santos) *in tch in midfield tl and lost pl 3f out: lost tch over 1f out* **20/1**

30-2 **10** 2¼ **Moondust (IRE)**[28] 418 3-9-8 **66**...............(p[1]) NickyMackay 8
(John Gosden) *chsd wnr: rdn over 3f out: lost pl over 2f out: bhd and eased fnl f* **8/1**

1m 26.96s (-0.24) **Going Correction** -0.025s/f (Stan) **10 Ran SP% 120.4**
Speed ratings (Par 95): **100,99,99,99,97 96,80,77,72,69**
CSF £37.96 CT £575.11 TOTE £11.40: £3.10, £1.40, £7.00; EX 55.50 Trifecta £379.20.
**Owner** John & Margaret Hatherell & RHS Ltd **Bred** Limestone Stud **Trained** Earlswood, Monmouths

**FOCUS**
A modest 3yo contest, though half the field were making their handicap debuts. There was little between the first four at the line.

### 876 WINNER.CO.UK BEATEN BY A LENGTH FREE BET H'CAP 1m (P)
**2:55** (3:18) (Class 4) (0-85,85) 4-Y-0+ **£6,469** (£1,925; £962; £481) **Stalls** Low

Form RPR

-642 **1** **Loyalty**[7] 760 10-9-4 **82**...............(v) MartinLane 6 93
(Derek Shaw) *hld up in tch: clsd to trck ldrs 2f out: rdn and qcknd to ld jst over 1f out: sn clr and pushed out ins fnl f: easily* **85/40**[2]

06-4 **2** 7 **King Of Dreams**[16] 611 4-8-13 **77**...............(p) JamieSpencer 7 72
(David Simcock) *stdd s: hld up in tch in rr: effrt over 1f out: hdwy u.p to chse clr wnr 150yds: no imp and one pced after* **7/1**

-340 **3** ½ **Pearl Spectre (USA)**[7] 760 6-9-7 **85**............... JosephineGordon 8 79
(Phil McEntee) *hld up in tch: effrt and edging lft over 1f out: wnt 2nd but wnr gone clr: lost 2nd and kpt on same pce ins fnl f* **14/1**

-200 **4** 1½ **Ravenhoe (IRE)**[16] 611 4-8-4 **73**............... RichardOliver(5) 3 63
(Mark Johnston) *trckd ldrs: rdn over 1f out: unable qck: wl hld and kpt on same pce ins fnl f* **20/1**

2452 **5** 1 **Byres Road**[6] 782 4-9-3 **81**............... FrannyNorton 1 69
(Mark Johnston) *w ldr on inner: led 3f out: rdn wl over 1f out: hdd jst over 1f out: sn outpcd* **15/8**[1]

54-0 **6** ¾ **London (FR)**[38] 266 4-9-3 **81**...............(t[1]) DavidProbert 5 67
(Phil McEntee) *chsd ldrs on outer: wnt 2nd over 2f out: rdn and unable qck over 1f out: sn btn* **16/1**

-410 **7** 8 **Sands Chorus**[20] 548 5-9-2 **80**............... PaulMulrennan 4 48
(James Given) *led tl 3f out: sn u.p and lost pl: bhd 1f out* **5/1**[3]

1m 38.58s (-1.32) **Going Correction** -0.025s/f (Stan) **7 Ran SP% 113.3**
Speed ratings (Par 105): **105,98,97,96,95 94,86**
CSF £16.99 CT £163.26 TOTE £2.90: £1.60, £3.10; EX 18.30 Trifecta £173.40.
**Owner** Brian Johnson (Northamptonshire) **Bred** Ecoutila Partnership **Trained** Sproxton, Leics

**FOCUS**
Not a bad handicap, but it proved one-sided. There was a contested pace which set it up for the winner.

### 877 WINNER.CO.UK BET & WATCH H'CAP 6f (P)
**3:30** (3:46) (Class 4) (0-85,82) 3-Y-0 **£6,469** (£1,925; £962; £481) **Stalls** Centre

Form RPR

0- **V** 5 **Grecian Divine (IRE)**[125] 7519 3-9-0 **82**............... SophieScardifield(7) 5 46
(Joseph Tuite) *hld up in rr: n.d* **50/1**

3-12 **V** 4½ **Erissimus Maximus (FR)**[29] 404 3-9-2 **77**...............(p) StevieDonohoe 3 57
(Chris Dwyer) *t.k.h: w ldrs tl dropped into 3rd over 4f out: rdn and struggling 2f out: wknd over 1f out* **9/2**[3]

45-1 **V** 1½ **Right Action**[17] 600 3-8-12 **73**............... TonyHamilton 6 73
(Richard Fahey) *chsd wnr: rdn and unable qck w wnr over 1f out: kpt on same pce ins fnl f* **16/1**

421- **V** 1 **Zamjar**[55] 8582 3-9-7 **82**...............(b) JosephineGordon 7 76+
(Ed Dunlop) *hld up in tch in last trio: effrt u.p over 1f out: kpt on same pce ins fnl f* **9/2**[3]

2-12 **V** ½ **Cappananty Con**[7] 765 3-8-12 **73**............... RobertWinston 2 71+
(Dean Ivory) *t.k.h: hld up in tch: effrt over 1f out: styd on u.p and swtchd rt ins fnl f: wnt 3rd last strides: no threat to wnr* **5/2**[1]

3341 **V** nk **Alkashaaf (USA)**[19] 578 3-9-5 **80**...............(tp) DavidProbert 4 77
(Archie Watson) *chsd ldrs: effrt in 3rd and unable qck over 1f out: kpt on same pce ins fnl f* **5/1**

100- **V** **Nautical Haven**[153] 6734 3-9-2 **82**............... LewisEdmunds(5) 1 88
(Kevin Ryan) *mde all: rdn and qcknd over 1f out: in command and kpt fnl f: rdn out* **3/1**[2]

.

**FOCUS**
Quite a decent 3yo sprint handicap and a nice performance from the 'winner', but the race was subsequently voided by the stewards after the advanced flag operator momentarily and mistakenly raised the yellow recall flag after the start. The jockeys were unaware that the flag had been raised.

### 878 WINNER.CO.UK MOBILE LOYALTY FREE BETS MAIDEN STKS 6f (P)
**4:05** (4:21) (Class 4) 3-4-Y-0 **£6,469** (£1,925; £962; £481) **Stalls** Centre

Form RPR

24-2 **1** **Red Alert**[14] 638 3-8-13 67............... FrannyNorton 2 72
(Joseph Tuite) *mde all: rdn over 1f out: kpt on ins fnl f: rdn out* **5/2**[2]

**2** 1¼ **Calypso Jo** 3-8-13 0............... KevinStott 1 68
(Kevin Ryan) *chsd ldrs and clr in ldng quartet: effrt: rn green and hung lft over 1f out: chsd wnr jst ins fnl f: kpt on* **10/1**

3-22 **3** hd **Alfonso Manana (IRE)**[13] 656 3-8-13 69...........(p) JosephineGordon 5 67
(James Given) *chsd ldrs and clr in ldng quartet: effrt over 2f out: hung lft 1f out: kpt on u.p ins fnl f* **5/1**[3]

**4** 2 **Captain Bond** 3-8-10 0............... ShelleyBirkett(3) 6 61+
(David O'Meara) *wnt rt s: midfield: outpcd in 5th 4f out: rdn 3f out: hdwy 1f out: kpt on wl ins fnl f: nvr trbld ldrs* **20/1**

**5** 1 **Essential** 3-8-13 0............... JamieSpencer 4 57+
(George Scott) *stdd and swtchd lft s: hld up off the pce in 7th: swtchd rt and rdn over 2f out: clsd and swtchd lft ins fnl f: eased towards fin: nvr trbld ldrs* **11/1**

04 **6** 14 **Basheer**[20] 545 3-8-13 0...............(h) DanielMuscutt 3 13
(Marco Botti) *t.k.h: w ldr: rdn jst over 1f out: no rspnse: stopped to nthing ins fnl f: virtually p.u fnl 75yds: burst blood vessel* **6/5**[1]

**7** ½ **Slipalongtrevaskis** 4-9-7 0............... GinaMangan(7) 8 15
(J R Jenkins) *pushed rt s: rn green: off the pce in 6th: rdn 3f out: no ch after* **50/1**

0-04 **8** 25 **Raspberry Princess**[20] 546 3-8-3 38...............(b[1]) LuluStanford(5) 7
(Phil McEntee) *pushed rt s: a bhd: t.o 1/2-way* **66/1**

1m 13.32s (-0.38) **Going Correction** -0.025s/f (Stan)
**WFA** 3 from 4yo 15lb **8 Ran SP% 116.3**
Speed ratings (Par 105): **101,99,99,96,95 76,75,42**
CSF £27.20 TOTE £3.70: £1.40, £2.60, £1.60; EX 34.00 Trifecta £98.90.
**Owner** A A Byrne **Bred** Miss Jacqueline Goodearl **Trained** Lambourn, Berks


The Form Book Flat, Raceform Ltd, Newbury, RG14 5SJ

**FOCUS**
A valuable maiden, but not many got into it. Hard to be confident about this form.

## 879 WINNER.CO.UK ACCA CLUB FILLIES' H'CAP 6f (P)
**4:40** (4:55) (Class 5) (0-75,77) 4-Y-0+ **£5,175** (£1,540; £769; £384) **Stalls** Centre

Form RPR
0-41 **1** **Veena (FR)**[19] 582 4-9-7 **75** JamieSpencer 5 83
(David Simcock) *wnt rt s: hld up in tch: squeezed for room after 1f: effrt to chal and awkward hd carriage over 1f out: rdn to ld jst ins fnl f: rdn out hands and heels and a jst doing enough after* **11/8**[1]

-110 **2** *hd* **Beau Mistral (IRE)**[8] 735 8-8-8 **62** WilliamCarson 1 69
(Tony Carroll) *chsd ldr tl over 2f out: styd handy: drvn to chal over 1f out: led 1f out: sn hdd: kpt on u.p but a jst hld after* **5/1**[3]

0-43 **3** *4* **Penny Dreadful**[8] 735 5-8-9 **63** (p) KieranO'Neill 7 57
(Scott Dixon) *led: rdn over 1f out: hdd 1f out: wknd ins fnl f* **7/1**

01-0 **4** *3 ¾* **Kashtan**[5] 808 4-9-7 **75** MichaelJMMurphy 2 57
(J S Moore) *chsd ldrs: wnt rt after 1f: chsd ldr 4f out tl over 2f out: wknd u.p over 1f out* **7/1**

-056 **5** *7* **Lady Lydia (IRE)**[23] 499 6-9-3 **76** CliffordLee(5) 8 36
(Gay Kelleway) *chsd ldrs: rdn over 2f out: wd and struggling bnd 2f out: sn wknd* **11/4**[2]

000- **6** *5* **Ms Arsenal**[217] 4565 5-7-13 **60** JaneElliott(7) 6 4
(Giles Bravery) *wnt rt s: a detached in last: n.d* **25/1**

1m 12.14s (-1.56) **Going Correction** -0.025s/f (Stan) **6** Ran SP% **114.3**
Speed ratings (Par 100): **109,108,103,98,89 82**
CSF £9.06 CT £34.97 TOTE £2.30: £1.20, £3.00; EX 9.70 Trifecta £33.40.
**Owner** Chola Dynasty **Bred** Ecurie Haras De Beauvoir **Trained** Newmarket, Suffolk

**FOCUS**
An ordinary fillies' sprint handicap, but a tight finish. Pretty weak form for the grade.

## 880 CHELMSFORDCITYRACECOURSE.COM H'CAP 1m 2f (P)
**5:15** (5:31) (Class 6) (0-55,57) 4-Y-0+ **£3,234** (£962; £481; £240) **Stalls** Low

Form RPR
0-20 **1** **Nouvelle Ere**[14] 636 6-9-6 **54** (t) GeorgeDowning 5 65
(Tony Carroll) *pushed and led for 1f: chsd ldrs after: 3rd and rdn over 3f out: hdwy u.p to ld over 2f out: clr over 1f out: styd on wl* **10/1**

-000 **2** *4* **Ertidaad (IRE)**[15] 614 5-8-7 **46** oh1 (b) DavidParkes(5) 2 49
(Emma Owen) *wl in tch in midfield: effrt in 4th 2f out: chsd clr wnr ent fnl f: kpt on but no imp* **25/1**

40-3 **3** *nk* **Percy Verence**[16] 607 4-9-1 **55** (t) CliffordLee(5) 4 57
(K R Burke) *hld up in midfield: effrt ent fnl 2f: hdwy u.p over 1f out: battling for 2nd but no imp on wnr ins fnl f: kpt on* **3/1**[1]

6-02 **4** *½* **Jazri**[15] 621 6-9-2 **50** (b) FrannyNorton 1 51
(Milton Bradley) *hld up in midfield: effrt over 1f out: hdwy 1f out: kpt on u.p ins fnl f: no threat to wnr* **9/2**[2]

5-64 **5** *1* **Castanea**[15] 621 5-8-12 **46** oh1 WilliamCarson 3 45
(Ronald Harris) *stdd after s: t.k.h: hld up towards rr: clsd and nt clr run over 2f out: hdwy over 1f out: kpt on same pce u.p ins fnl f* **9/1**

0-65 **6** *3* **Mamoo**[20] 555 4-9-6 **55** (b[1]) ShaneKelly 8 48
(Mike Murphy) *in tch in midfield: hdwy to ld over 7f out: rdn over 2f out: sn hdd and unable qck over 1f out: lost 2nd 1f out: wknd ins fnl f* **5/1**[3]

25-0 **7** *2* **Gladys Cooper (IRE)**[27] 444 4-9-6 **55** TonyHamilton 7 44
(Richard Fahey) *pushed along leaving stalls: midfield: rdn ent fnl 2f: swtchd lft over 1f out: kpt on ins fnl f: nvr trbld ldrs* **12/1**

0604 **8** *hd* **The Dukkerer (IRE)**[14] 636 6-9-6 **54** PaulMulrennan 11 43
(James Given) *in tch in midfield: effrt in 6th over 2f out: no imp over 1f out: wknd fnl f* **14/1**

1-06 **9** *¾* **Master Of Heaven**[14] 636 4-9-1 **50** (p) JackMitchell 15 38
(Jim Boyle) *pushed along leaving stalls: midfield: effrt on inner over 1f out: no imp: wl hld fnl f* **14/1**

0-66 **10** *2 ¾* **Whip Up A Frenzy (IRE)**[15] 621 5-8-12 **46** oh1..(v[1]) DougieCostello 10 28
(Richard Rowe) *led after 1f tl over 7f out: rdn over 3f out: wknd over 1f out* **33/1**

06/3 **11** *shd* **Flying Author (IRE)**[14] 636 6-8-6 **47** (tp) JaneElliott(7) 14 29
(Phil McEntee) *stdd s: hld up in rr: nvr on terms* **20/1**

5-25 **12** *4 ½* **Awesome Rock (IRE)**[15] 621 8-8-12 **46** MartinLane 16 19
(Roger Ingram) *hld up in midfield: effrt over 2f out: sn struggling: wknd over 1f out* **25/1**

20-0 **13** *2 ¼* **Sexy Secret**[40] 238 6-9-3 **54** (p) SimonPearce(3) 12 22
(Lydia Pearce) *rousted along leaving stalls: chsd ldrs: rdn over 3f out: wknd over 1f out* **16/1**

0-00 **14** *22* **Ambitious Rosie**[8] 733 6-8-12 **46** oh1 (b[1]) LuluStanford 9
(Tony Carroll) *hld up in rr: lost tch 2f out: bhd and eased ins fnl f* **50/1**

2m 8.12s (-0.48) **Going Correction** -0.025s/f (Stan) **14** Ran SP% **123.2**
Speed ratings (Par 101): **100,96,96,96,95 92,91,91,90,88 88,84,82,65**
CSF £250.09 CT £944.51 TOTE £12.90: £3.70, £9.00, £1.70; EX 456.40 Trifecta £2880.80.
**Owner** Martyn C Palmer **Bred** Lady Jennifer Green **Trained** Cropthorne, Worcs

**FOCUS**
A moderate handicap and not form to dwell on.
T/Jkpt: Not won. T/Plt: £37.70 to a £1 stake. Pool: £52,773.25 - 1,020.22 winning units. T/Qpdt: £4.00 to a £1 stake. Pool: £7,897.43 - 1,452.65 winning units. **Steve Payne**

# [839]WOLVERHAMPTON (A.W) (L-H)
Thursday, February 23

**OFFICIAL GOING: Tapeta: standard**
Wind: Strong across Weather: Cloudy with the odd shower

## 881 32RED CASINO H'CAP 1m 4f 51y (Tp)
**5:50** (5:50) (Class 6) (0-65,63) 3-Y-0 **£2,425** (£721; £360; £180) **Stalls** Low

Form RPR
0-00 **1** **Bessemer Lady**[27] 437 3-8-13 **55** (b[1]) RichardKingscote 10 61
(Ralph Beckett) *s.i.s: rcvrd to chse ldr after 1f: led wl over 2f out: rdn clr over 1f out: hld on* **15/2**[3]

**2** *½* **Baltic Eagle (GER)**[144] 3-9-7 **63** AdamBeschizza 4 68+
(Rune Haugen) *mid-div: hdwy over 3f out: swtchd rt over 2f out: rdn to chse wnr over 1f out: sn hung lft: styd on* **16/1**

060- **3** *1 ½* **Spirit Of Rome (IRE)**[87] 8130 3-9-1 **57** PJMcDonald 6 60
(James Bethell) *hld up: hdwy over 2f out: sn rdn: hung lft fnl f: styd on* **11/1**

-563 **4** *5* **Chough**[14] 637 3-8-6 **53** CharlieBennett(5) 7 48
(Hughie Morrison) *chsd ldrs: wnt 2nd over 2f out tl rdn over 1f out: wknd ins fnl f* **11/2**[1]

06-6 **5** *8* **Willie's Anne (IRE)**[45] 149 3-8-11 **53** LukeMorris 2 35
(Daniel Mark Loughnane) *chsd ldrs: rdn over 3f out: wknd over 2f out* **9/1**

00-4 **6** *½* **Nothing Compares**[48] 91 3-9-5 **61** AdamKirby 3 42
(Mark Johnston) *stmbld s: sn pushed along in last pl: reminders over 9f out: drvn along and hung rt 5f out: nvr nrr* **6/1**[2]

0-05 **7** *1* **Everdina**[22] 504 3-9-4 **60** ThomasBrown 1 40
(Ed Walker) *mid-div: rdn whn nt clr run over 2f out: sn wknd* **6/1**[2]

00-5 **8** *½* **Baileys Apprentice**[30] 385 3-9-4 **60** JoeFanning 9 39
(Mark Johnston) *led: rdn and hdd wl over 2f out: son wknd and eased* **8/1**

00-3 **9** *1 ¼* **Hot Lick**[15] 627 3-9-0 **56** (h) LiamKeniry 5 33
(Andrew Balding) *hld up: rdn over 3f out: wknd over 2f out* **6/1**[2]

0-60 **10** *37* **Master Billie (IRE)**[15] 627 3-8-1 **48** (b[1]) GeorgeWood(5) 8
(William Muir) *sn prom: rdn and wknd over 3f out* **16/1**

2m 41.56s (0.76) **Going Correction** 0.0s/f (Stan) **10** Ran SP% **111.2**
Speed ratings (Par 95): **97,96,95,92,87 86,86,85,84,60**
CSF £113.54 CT £1270.36 TOTE £7.70: £2.90, £4.50, £5.10; EX 141.10 Trifecta £1536.40.
**Owner** Chasemore Farm **Bred** Chasemore Farm **Trained** Kimpton, Hants

**FOCUS**
With Storm Doris battering most of the country, this was run in gusty, difficult conditions. This was weak and the first three home, all of which were making their handicap debuts, pulled clear.

## 882 32RED.COM MAIDEN STKS 1m 142y (Tp)
**6:25** (6:25) (Class 5) 3-Y-0 **£3,072** (£914; £456; £228) **Stalls** Low

Form RPR
03 **1** **Dark Titan (IRE)**[33] 354 3-9-5 0 ThomasBrown 7 69
(Ed Walker) *w ldr tl led over 7f out: rdn over 2f out: styd on wl* **11/2**

**2** *hd* **Solajan (IRE)** 3-9-5 0 (h[1]) AdamKirby 4 68
(Ed Dunlop) *a.p: chsd wnr over 7f out: rdn over 1f out: ev ch ins fnl f: styd on* **3/1**[2]

**3** *¾* **Secret Salvage (IRE)** 3-9-0 0 FergusSweeney 8 62+
(Jamie Osborne) *hld up: rdn over 2f out: hdwy over 1f out: r.o* **33/1**

56- **4** *nk* **Forest Angel (IRE)**[181] 5846 3-9-0 0 LukeMorris 1 61
(James Tate) *chsd ldrs: rdn over 1f out: edgd lft ins fnl f: styd on* **13/2**

-0 **5** *hd* **Willwams (IRE)**[40] 237 3-9-5 0 TomMarquand 3 66
(Richard Hannon) *led 1f: chsd ldrs: rdn over 1f out: kpt on* **14/1**

**6** *4 ½* **Magic Pass** 3-9-5 0 (h[1]) LiamKeniry 6 55
(Andrew Balding) *hld up: hdwy over 1f out: swtchd rt and no ex ins fnl f* **9/2**[3]

**7** *1 ½* **Oxford Don** 3-9-2 0 AaronJones(3) 2 52
(David Simcock) *s.i.s: hld up: rdn over 2f out: nvr on terms* **16/1**

**8** *5* **Chippenham (IRE)** 3-9-5 0 RobertTart 5 40
(John Gosden) *s.s: sn pushed along and rn green in rr: rdn and wknd over 2f out* **11/4**[1]

1m 52.52s (2.42) **Going Correction** 0.0s/f (Stan) **8** Ran SP% **114.1**
Speed ratings (Par 97): **89,88,88,87,87 83,82,77**
CSF £22.26 TOTE £7.30: £1.50, £1.20, £7.00; EX 27.70 Trifecta £352.20.
**Owner** Chi Un Fred Ma **Bred** Airlie Stud **Trained** Upper Lambourn, Berks

**FOCUS**
An informative maiden, in which experience proved key. A rather muddling race with a bunch finish. The winner set only a modest level coming into this.

## 883 SUNBETS.CO.UK FILLIES' H'CAP 1m 142y (Tp)
**7:00** (7:02) (Class 5) (0-70,70) 4-Y-0+ **£3,072** (£914; £456; £228) **Stalls** Low

Form RPR
5-42 **1** **Tenerezza (IRE)**[3] 841 4-9-0 **63** JoeFanning 7 70
(Iain Jardine) *trckd ldrs: racd keenly: led over 1f out: sn hung lft: rdn out* **13/8**[1]

6-31 **2** *shd* **Dose**[30] 390 4-8-12 **61** TomEaves 4 67
(Richard Fahey) *hld up: hdwy 2f out: chsd wnr and n.m.r ins fnl f: r.o* **10/3**[3]

4-66 **3** *4* **East Coast Lady (IRE)**[22] 505 5-8-13 **67** HollieDoyle(5) 1 64
(William Stone) *led: stdd pce over 5f out: qcknd over 2f out: rdn and hdd over 1f out: nt clr run sn after: no ex ins fnl f* **10/1**

/30- **4** *nk* **Little Kipling**[267] 2795 4-9-3 **66** RichardKingscote 2 62
(Stuart Williams) *chsd ldrs: rdn over 1f out: nt clr run and no ex ins fnl f* **5/2**[2]

36-5 **5** *3 ¼* **Andanotherone (IRE)**[15] 624 4-8-13 **62** DannyBrock 8 50
(Denis Quinn) *w ldr: pushed along and ev ch over 2f out: wknd fnl f* **28/1**

50- **6** *6* **Any Joy (IRE)**[90] 8093 4-8-7 **56** oh2 LukeMorris 3 31
(Ben Haslam) *s.i.s: hld up: rdn and wknd over 2f out* **50/1**

1m 49.4s (-0.70) **Going Correction** 0.0s/f (Stan) **6** Ran SP% **104.2**
Speed ratings (Par 100): **103,102,99,99,96 90**
CSF £6.16 CT £26.45 TOTE £2.30: £1.10, £2.50; EX 6.40 Trifecta £17.80.
**Owner** Compas Racing **Bred** Bjorn Nielsen **Trained** Carrutherstown, D'fries & G'way

**FOCUS**
Few could be seriously fancied in this fillies-only handicap and the market got it right. The form's only modest.

## 884 BETWAY MIDDLE CLAIMING STKS 1m 1f 104y (Tp)
**7:30** (7:30) (Class 5) 4-Y-0+ **£3,072** (£914; £456; £228) **Stalls** Low

Form RPR
/-54 **1** **Retrieve (AUS)**[7] 767 9-9-8 **100** (t) AdamKirby 1 92
(Jamie Osborne) *chsd ldr 1f: remained handy: shkn up over 3f out: rdn over 1f out: styd on u.p to ld wl ins fnl f* **6/4**[1]

2556 **2** *1 ¼* **Marshgate Lane (USA)**[10] 719 8-9-5 **87** (p) LiamKeniry 5 86
(Neil Mulholland) *chsd ldr over 8f out: rdn to ld over 1f out: edgd lft: hdd and unable qck wl ins fnl f* **3/1**[2]

-016 **3** *hd* **Modernism**[17] 599 8-9-1 **80** (p) LukeMorris 6 81
(Ian Williams) *led: qcknd over 3f out: rdn and hdd over 1f out: ev ch ins fnl f: unable qck towards fin* **7/2**[3]

/331 **4** *2 ¼* **Regarde Moi**[24] 478 9-9-0 **87** JacobMitchell(7) 3 82
(Marco Botti) *chsd ldrs: shkn up over 2f out: hung lft fr over 1f out: styd on same pce* **7/2**[3]

-000 **5** *19* **Les Gar Gan (IRE)**[17] 605 6-8-6 **49** JoeFanning 2 27
(Daniel Mark Loughnane) *s.i.s: hld up: wknd over 2f out* **125/1**

2m 1.09s (0.29) **Going Correction** 0.0s/f (Stan) **5** Ran SP% **110.2**
Speed ratings (Par 103): **98,96,96,94,77**
CSF £6.35 TOTE £2.40: £1.50, £1.70; EX 6.70 Trifecta £14.00.Marshgate Lane was claimed by Mr Claes Bjorling for £12,000
**Owner** Melbourne 10 Racing **Bred** Darley **Trained** Upper Lambourn, Berks

**FOCUS**
A good-quality claimer that revolved around the favourably treated market leader. The second and third are the best guides to the form.

## 885 BETWAY H'CAP — 1m 1f 104y (Tp)
**8:00** (8:00) (Class 4) (0-85,86) 4-Y-0+ **£4,690** (£1,395; £697; £348) **Stalls** Low

Form RPR
10-3 **1** **Winners Follow Me (GER)**[20] 548 4-9-8 **86**.................... LukeMorris 5 97
(James Tate) *trckd ldr: rdn over 1f out: led wl ins fnl f: edgd lft: r.o* **5/2**[2]
00-1 **2** *2 1/4* **Count Montecristo (FR)**[17] 599 5-9-4 **82**.................... TomEaves 8 88
(Kevin Ryan) *led: rdn over 1f out: hdd and unable qck wl ins fnl f* **9/4**[1]
210- **3** *nse* **Nonios (IRE)**[75] 8317 5-9-3 **84**....................(h) AaronJones(3) 3 90+
(David Simcock) *hld up: hdwy 2f out: sn rdn: r.o* **9/2**[3]
42-3 **4** *2 1/4* **Toga Tiger (IRE)**[10] 719 10-9-2 **80**.................... RichardKingscote 7 81
(Daniel Mark Loughnane) *hld up: rdn over 1f out: r.o ins fnl f: nt trble ldrs* **11/2**
215- **5** *1 3/4* **Auntie Barber (IRE)**[287] 2181 4-8-9 **73**.................... AdamBeschizza 2 70
(Stuart Williams) *hld up: hdwy 3f out: rdn over 1f out: styd on same pce* **22/1**
4-30 **6** *1* **Berlusca (IRE)**[17] 599 8-9-0 **78**.................... JoeFanning 4 73
(David O'Meara) *trckd ldrs: plld hrd: shkn up over 2f out: wknd ins fnl f* **8/1**
35-0 **7** *5* **Arrowzone**[47] 117 6-9-7 **85**.................... RyanPowell 1 70
(Kevin Frost) *prom: racd keenly: pushed along and lost pl over 3f out: wknd over 2f out* **50/1**
012/ **8** *32* **Masterful Act (USA)**[419] 6 10-9-0 **78**.................... BenCurtis 6
(John Balding) *s.i.s: hld up: wknd over 3f out* **66/1**

1m 59.02s (-1.78) **Going Correction** 0.0s/f (Stan) 8 Ran SP% **111.8**
Speed ratings (Par 105): **107,105,104,102,101 100,96,67**
CSF £8.09 CT £21.75 TOTE £3.10: £1.10, £1.40, £1.70; EX 8.70 Trifecta £29.10.
**Owner** Sheikh Juma Dalmook Al Maktoum **Bred** Gestut Ammerland **Trained** Newmarket, Suffolk

**FOCUS**
This feature handicap was dominated by the market principals. Improved form from the winner.

## 886 BETWAY SPRINT H'CAP — 5f 21y (Tp)
**8:30** (8:30) (Class 5) (0-75,75) 4-Y-0+ **£3,072** (£914; £456; £228) **Stalls** Low

Form RPR
-512 **1** **You're Cool**[21] 518 5-8-10 **69**.................... LewisEdmunds(5) 4 76
(John Balding) *plld hrd and prom: nt clr run and lost pl over 3f out: hdwy over 1f out: r.o to ld last strides* **3/1**[1]
00-6 **2** *nk* **Invincible Ridge (IRE)**[49] 79 9-9-7 **75**.................... JasonHart 7 81
(Eric Alston) *prom: rdn 1/2-way: r.o to ld nr fin: hdd last strides* **9/1**
4322 **3** *3/4* **Archie Stevens**[13] 665 7-9-0 **68**.................... PaddyAspell 9 71
(Clare Ellam) *prom: chsd ldr over 3f out: rdn to ld wl ins fnl f: hdd nr fin* **28/1**
-225 **4** *3/4* **Temple Road (IRE)**[34] 330 9-9-0 **68**....................(bt) JoeFanning 5 69
(Milton Bradley) *hld up: shkn up and nt clr run over 1f out: r.o ins fnl f: nt rch ldrs* **14/1**
6-00 **5** *hd* **Normal Equilibrium**[27] 443 7-9-2 **75**.................... HollieDoyle(5) 8 75
(Ivan Furtado) *led: rdn over 1f out: hdd and unable qck wl ins fnl f* **11/2**[3]
512- **6** *1* **Compton River**[63] 8495 5-9-4 **72**.................... BenCurtis 2 68
(Bryan Smart) *hmpd s: hld up: hdwy over 1f out: sn rdn and edgd lft: styd on same pce wl ins fnl f* **9/2**[2]
2-15 **7** *1* **Dreams Of Glory**[19] 575 9-9-0 **68**.................... LukeMorris 1 61
(Ron Hodges) *wnt rt s: sn prom: rdn over 1f out: styd on same pce ins fnl f* **15/2**
00-0 **8** *hd* **Miracle Garden**[35] 312 5-9-6 **74**....................(p) TomEaves 3 74+
(Roy Brotherton) *hmpd s: hld up: running on whn nowhere to go and hmpd ins fnl f: nvr able to chal* **10/1**
00-0 **9** *nse* **Entertaining Ben**[50] 45 4-9-0 **68**.................... TomMarquand 6 60
(Iain Jardine) *chsd ldrs: rdn over 1f out: styd on same pce fnl f* **22/1**
00-0 **10** *9* **King Crimson**[28] 416 5-9-4 **72**.................... AdamKirby 10 31
(John Butler) *s.i.s: hld up: pushed along 1/2-way: wknd over 1f out* **10/1**
6-04 **11** *7* **Waneen (IRE)**[12] 682 4-9-2 **70**.................... LiamKeniry 11 4
(John Butler) *chsd ldrs to 1/2-way* **12/1**

1m 0.98s (-0.92) **Going Correction** 0.0s/f (Stan) 11 Ran SP% **120.7**
Speed ratings (Par 103): **107,106,105,104,103 102,100,100,100,85 74**
CSF £31.75 CT £660.28 TOTE £4.00: £1.50, £3.30, £5.20; EX 30.20 Trifecta £1020.90.
**Owner** D Bichan & J Roberts **Bred** Tirnaskea Stud **Trained** Scrooby, S Yorks

**FOCUS**
This was strongly run and looks reliable form for the level. The winner is rated to his best.
T/Plt: £229.70 to a £1 stake. Pool: £65,956.73 - 209.56 winning units. T/Qpdt: £4.90 to a £1 stake. Pool: £12,693.91 - 1,904.69 winning units. **Colin Roberts**

# 770 MEYDAN (L-H)
Thursday, February 23

**OFFICIAL GOING: Turf: good; dirt: fast**

## 887a MEYDAN CLASSIC SPONSORED BY AL NABOODAH GOODYEAR (LISTED RACE) (TURF) — 7f
**3:05** (3:05) 3-Y-O
**£73,170** (£24,390; £12,195; £6,097; £3,658; £2,439)

RPR
**1** **Top Score**[14] 649 3-9-0 98.................... AdriedeVries 7 107
(Saeed bin Suroor) *s.i.s: mid-div: smooth prog 2 1/2f out: rdn to ld fnl 110yds* **9/1**[3]
**2** *1/2* **Fly At Dawn (USA)**[28] 430 3-9-0 109....................(t) WilliamBuick 4 106
(Charlie Appleby) *sn led: kicked clr 2 1/2f out: hdd 110yds out: r.o* **7/4**[2]
**3** *hd* **Really Special**[14] 652 3-8-9 103.................... OisinMurphy 1 100
(Saeed bin Suroor) *trckd ldng pair: ev ch 1 1/2f out: r.o fnl f: nrst fin* **11/8**[1]
**4** *2 1/2* **Masham Star (IRE)**[14] 649 3-9-0 98.................... PatDobbs 2 98
(Mark Johnston) *mid-div: r.o same pce fnl 2f* **16/1**
**5** *1/2* **Nobelium (USA)**[14] 649 3-9-0 99.................... ChristopheSoumillon 10 97
(R Bouresly, Kuwait) *settled in rr: n.m.r 3f out: r.o same pce fnl 2f* **9/1**[3]
**6** *1* **Grey Britain**[14] 649 3-9-0 98....................(v) JimCrowley 11 94
(John Ryan) *trckd ldrs: one pce fnl 2f* **16/1**
**7** *3 1/4* **Mufeed (USA)**[28] 430 3-9-0 82....................(t) ColmO'Donoghue 8 86
(S Seemar, UAE) *s.i.s: a in rr* **66/1**
**8** *shd* **Good Omen**[28] 430 3-9-0 93.................... PatCosgrave 9 85
(David Simcock) *trckd ldng pair tl outpcd fnl 2 1/2f* **20/1**
**9** *2 1/2* **Souls In The Wind (IRE)**[14] 649 3-8-9 84.................... TadhgO'Shea 6 74
(S Seemar, UAE) *s.i.s: trckd ldr tl wknd fnl 2 1/2f* **40/1**
**10** *9 1/2* **Island Vision (IRE)**[14] 649 3-8-9 90.................... SamHitchcott 3 48
(David Simcock) *nvr bttr than mid-div* **25/1**
**11** *2 1/4* **Silent Assassin (IRE)**[12] 697 3-9-0 80.................... RichardMullen 5 47
(S Seemar, UAE) *nvr bttr than mid-div* **66/1**

1m 24.61s (0.51) **Going Correction** +0.275s/f (Good) 11 Ran SP% **124.3**
Speed ratings: **108,107,107,104,103 102,98,98,95,85 82**
CSF: 25.76.
**Owner** Godolphin **Bred** Darley **Trained** Newmarket, Suffolk

**FOCUS**
TRAKUS (metres travelled compared to winner): 2nd -1, 3rd -1, 4th +3, 5th +5, 6th +7, 7th +1, 8th +5, 9th +2, 10th +7, 11th +10. The rail was out 12 metres on the turf course. The runner-up set sensible fractions of 25.77, 23.95, 22.8, before the winner finished in 11.88. The winner has been rated as stepping up on his decent juvenile form.

## 888a AL NABOODAH HARLEY-DAVIDSON TROPHY (H'CAP) (TURF) — 1m 2f
**3:40** (3:40) (95-108,108) 3-Y-O+
**£60,975** (£20,325; £10,162; £5,081; £3,048; £2,032)

RPR
**1** **Viren's Army (IRE)**[12] 699 4-9-1 **104**....................(p) ColmO'Donoghue 5 109+
(Charlie Appleby) *sn led: hdd 7f out: led again 3f out: r.o wl* **5/1**[3]
**2** *1 1/2* **Kidmenever (IRE)**[12] 699 4-8-13 **102**.................... WilliamBuick 4 104+
(Charlie Appleby) *mid-div: n.m.r 3f out: r.o wl: nrst fin* **15/8**[1]
**3** *2* **Huge Future**[35] 322 4-8-9 **99**....................(p) AdriedeVries 7 96+
(Saeed bin Suroor) *mid-div: r.o fnl 2f: nrst fin* **7/2**[2]
**4** *1 1/2* **Hasanour (USA)**[12] 698 7-8-8 **97**....................(t) MarcMonaghan 1 91
(M Halford, Ire) *mid-div: r.o fnl 2f but nvr nr to chal* **40/1**
**5** *1 1/4* **Limario (GER)**[14] 654 7-8-9 **98**....................(t) PatDobbs 3 90
(Doug Watson, UAE) *nvr nr to chal but r.o fnl 2f* **33/1**
**6** *nk* **Classic Collection**[14] 654 5-8-11 **100**.................... OisinMurphy 12 91
(Saeed bin Suroor) *nvr bttr than mid-div* **12/1**
**7** *1* **Dragon Mall (USA)**[12] 698 4-9-1 **104**....................(h) JimCrowley 13 94
(David Simcock) *s.i.s: nvr nr to chal* **8/1**
**8** *shd* **Elleval (IRE)**[14] 654 7-8-13 **101**....................(p) SamHitchcott 14 91
(David Marnane, Ire) *nvr nr to chal* **10/1**
**9** *1* **Start Right**[14] 654 10-8-10 **99**....................(p) RichardMullen 6 86
(S Seemar, UAE) *s.i.s: nvr nr to chal* **50/1**
**10** *nk* **First Selection (SPA)**[14] 653 4-8-13 **102**....................(h) DaneO'Neill 9 89
(Simon Crisford) *trckd ldr: led 7f out: hdd 3f out: one pce fnl 2 1/2f* **20/1**
**11** *1/2* **Busker (USA)**[12] 699 9-8-11 **100**....................(t) PatCosgrave 10 85
(A bin Harmash, UAE) *s.i.s: nvr nr to chal* **40/1**
**12** *1/2* **Kyllachy Gala**[14] 654 4-9-2 **105**.................... TadhgO'Shea 2 90
(Marco Botti) *trckd ldrs: rdn 4f out: sn btn* **33/1**
**13** *3/4* **Queen's Parade (USA)**[28] 431 6-8-11 **100**....................(p) ChrisHayes 8 83
(D Selvaratnam, UAE) *trckd ldrs tl wknd fnl 3f* **33/1**
**14** *2 1/4* **Elite Excalibur (AUS)**[7] 776 4-9-6 **108**............(p) BernardFayd'Herbe 11 87
(S Burridge, Singapore) *trckd ldr: rdn 4f out: sn btn* **18/1**

2m 3.48s (0.78) **Going Correction** +0.275s/f (Good) 14 Ran SP% **127.3**
Speed ratings: **107,105,104,103,102 101,100,100,100,99 99,99,98,96**
CSF: 14.69; TRICAST: 40.18.
**Owner** Godolphin **Bred** Ruskerne Ltd **Trained** Newmarket, Suffolk

**FOCUS**
TRAKUS: 2nd +3, 3rd +7, 4th -3, 5th -2, 6th +8, 7th +5, 8th -2, 9th +2, 10th -1, 11th +8, 12th -1, 13th +3, 14th +4. The rail was out 12 metres. They went a muddling pace: 26.61, 23.74, 25.02, 24.13, 23.98. As in the preceding race, a 1-2-3 for Godolphin.

## 889a UAE OAKS SPONSORED BY AL NABOODAH - ASHOK LEYLAND (FILLIES) (GROUP 3) (DIRT) — 1m 1f 110y(D)
**4:15** (4:15) 3-Y-O
**£121,951** (£40,650; £20,325; £10,162; £6,097; £4,065)

RPR
**1** **Nomorerichblondes (USA)**[14] 652 3-9-0 96...........(tp) AntonioFresu 6 97
(A bin Harmash, UAE) *trckd ldr: led 3f out: r.o wl: comf* **7/2**[2]
**2** *1 1/2* **Midnight Chica (USA)**[35] 317 3-9-0 76....................(t) ChrisHayes 8 94+
(D Selvaratnam, UAE) *mid-div: rdn to chse ldrs 5f out: r.o fnl 1 1/2f: nrst fin* **66/1**
**3** *3/4* **Complimenti (USA)**[14] 652 3-9-0 93.................... PatDobbs 2 92
(Doug Watson, UAE) *trckd ldng pair: rdn 3f out: ev ch 1f out: wknd fnl 110yds* **5/4**[1]
**4** *3/4* **Melesina (IRE)**[14] 652 3-9-0 102.................... OisinMurphy 7 91
(Richard Fahey) *nvr nr to chal but r.o fnl 2 1/2f* **12/1**
**5** *nk* **Calare (IRE)**[14] 652 3-9-0 92....................(p) WilliamBuick 5 90
(Charlie Appleby) *trckd ldng trio: ev ch 3 1/2f out: one pce fnl 2f* **4/1**[3]
**6** *1 3/4* **Rajar**[14] 652 3-9-0 93....................(h) RichardMullen 1 87
(Richard Fahey) *wl away: sn led: hdd 3f out: sn btn* **6/1**
**7** *5 3/4* **Magical Forest (IRE)**[42] 201 3-9-0 75....................(b) ColmO'Donoghue 3 75
(Marco Botti) *s.i.s: nvr bttr than mid-div* **40/1**
**8** *9 1/2* **Don't Lie Kitten (USA)**[35] 317 3-9-0 75....................(bt) JimCrowley 4 55
(A bin Harmash, UAE) *nvr nr to chal* **20/1**

2m 1.85s (3.05) **Going Correction** +0.25s/f (Slow) 8 Ran SP% **117.3**
Speed ratings: **97,95,95,94,94 92,88,80**
CSF: 204.37.
**Owner** Buti Bintooq Almarri **Bred** Blue Devil Racing Llc **Trained** United Arab Emirates

**FOCUS**
TRAKUS: 2nd +12, 3rd -7, 4th +4, 5th +2, 6th -11, 7th -6, 8th +1. The 2016 running of the UAE Oaks saw the smart Polar River defeat Vale Dori, who has since won multiple Graded races in the US, but there's rarely much depth to the division - it was a three-runner race 12 months ago - and it was desperately weak stuff this year, with there not even a standout filly amongst them. Nashmiah, a narrow winner of the UAE 1000 Guineas a fortnight earlier, was scratched and this was the slowest of 29 dirt races to date over 9.5f at Meydan. The winner, third and fifth help set the standard.

## 890a NAD AL SHEBA TROPHY SPONSORED BY AL NABOODAH - VDL BUSES (GROUP 3) (TURF) — 1m 6f 11y
**4:50** (4:50) 3-Y-O+
**£97,560** (£32,520; £16,260; £8,130; £4,878; £3,252)

RPR
**1** **Beautiful Romance**[103] 7948 5-8-9 110.................... OisinMurphy 6 110
(Saeed bin Suroor) *mid-div: rdn to ld 3f out: r.o wl* **9/2**[3]
**2** *1 1/2* **Vazirabad (FR)**[123] 7569 5-9-0 117.................... ChristopheSoumillon 4 113+
(A De Royer-Dupre, France) *settled in rr: smooth prog to trck ldrs 2 1/2f out: ev ch 1 1/2f out: one pce fnl f* **4/5**[1]
**3** *3 1/4* **Sheikhzayedroad**[131] 7349 8-9-0 118....................(h) RichardMullen 5 108
(David Simcock) *trckd ldrs: ev ch 2f out: one pce fnl 1 1/2f* **9/4**[2]

4 1 1/4 **Basateen (IRE)**[12] 699 5-9-0 107 ........ DaneO'Neill 1 107+
(Doug Watson, UAE) *mid-div: r.o fnl 2f but nvr able to chal* **33/1**

5 1 **Los Barbados (IRE)**[12] 699 5-9-0 99 ........ (b) ColmO'Donoghue 8 105
(Fawzi Abdulla Nass, Bahrain) *sn led: hdd 3f out: r.o same pce fnl 2f* **50/1**

6 2 3/4 **Zamaam**[21] 540 7-9-0 102 ........ (t) JimCrowley 3 101
(E Charpy, UAE) *nvr nr to chal* **33/1**

7 2 1/2 **Red Galileo**[21] 540 6-9-0 103 ........ AdriedeVries 2 98
(Saeed bin Suroor) *nvr bttr than mid-div* **20/1**

8 1 1/2 **Carbon Dating (IRE)**[12] 699 5-9-0 101 ........ TadhgO'Shea 7 96
(S Seemar, UAE) *trckd ldng pair tl wknd fnl 3f* **50/1**

9 18 1/4 **Rio Tigre (IRE)**[21] 540 6-9-0 100 ........ MickaelBarzalona 9 70
(S bin Ghadayer, UAE) *s.i.s: settled in rr: smooth prog 8f out: wknd 4f out* **66/1**

2m 58.44s (-0.96) **Going Correction** +0.275s/f (Good) **9** Ran SP% **120.6**
Speed ratings: **113,112,110,109,109 107,106,105,94**
CSF: 8.70.
**Owner** Godolphin **Bred** Rabbah Bloodstock Limited **Trained** Newmarket, Suffolk

**FOCUS**
TRAKUS: 2nd 0, 3rd -7, 4th -9, 5th -4, 6th +7, 7th -8, 8th 0, 9th +3. The rail was out 12 metres. This race is something of a trial for the Group 2 Dubai Gold Cup, which is run on World Cup day (March 25 this year). It was steadily run - they were 1.59sec slower through the first mile than in last year's race, when the rail was out by the same distance - but it was a high-quality contest, with three really good stayers filling the first three places. The fourth and sixth help set the standard.

## 891a CURLIN H'CAP SPONSORED BY AL NABOODAH SUNWIN BUSES (LISTED HANDICAP) (DIRT) 1m 2f (D)

**5:25** (5:25) (95-117,117) 3-Y-0+

**£78,048** (£26,016; £13,008; £6,504; £3,902; £2,601)

RPR

1 **Etijaah (USA)**[14] 650 7-8-5 **102** ........ (h) SamHitchcott 6 107+
(Doug Watson, UAE) *mid-div: smooth prog 2 1/2f out: led 1 1/2f out: r.o wl* **7/1**[3]

2 2 1/2 **Mubtaahij (IRE)**[138] 7178 5-9-6 **117** ........ ChristopheSoumillon 3 117
(M F De Kock, South Africa) *mid-div: smooth prog 3f out: ev ch 1 1/2f out: one pce fnl 110yds* **2/1**[1]

3 4 1/2 **Alabaster (USA)**[14] 650 5-8-5 **102** ........ (b) OisinMurphy 4 93
(Saeed bin Suroor) *trckd ldr: led 6f out: rdn clr 3 1/2f out: hdd 1 1/2f out: r.o same pce* **2/1**[1]

4 2 3/4 **Sharpalo (FR)**[6] 803 5-8-5 **98** ........ (b) AntonioFresu 5 88
(A bin Harmash, UAE) *mid-div: r.o same pce fnl 2 1/2f* **40/1**

5 4 1/2 **Layl (USA)**[14] 650 7-8-9 **107** ........ (v) PatDobbs 9 83
(Doug Watson, UAE) *s.i.s: nvr nr to chal* **11/2**[2]

6 2 1/4 **Storm Belt (USA)**[21] 541 8-8-7 **105** ........ FernandoJara 2 76
(Doug Watson, UAE) *trckd ldr: wknd fnl 3f* **20/1**

7 3/4 **Gold City (IRE)**[21] 541 8-8-5 **103** ........ (bt) RichardMullen 7 73
(S Seemar, UAE) *slowly away: nvr nr to chal* **12/1**

9 31 **Memorial Day (IRE)**[124] 7545 6-8-11 **109** ........ AdriedeVries 1 17
(Saeed bin Suroor) *sn led: hdd 6f out: sn btn* **9/1**

10 10 1/2 **Beach Bar (IRE)**[21] 540 6-8-5 **95** ........ (h) TadhgO'Shea 8
(Brendan Powell) *nvr bttr than mid-div* **100/1**

2m 3.95s (-0.75) **Going Correction** +0.25s/f (Slow) **10** Ran SP% **120.4**
Speed ratings: **113,111,107,105,101 99,99,74,66**
CSF: 22.18; TRICAST: 39.97.
**Owner** Hamdan Al Maktoum **Bred** Shadwell Farm LLC **Trained** United Arab Emirates

**FOCUS**
TRAKUS: 2nd -3, 3rd +10, 4th +9, 5th +1, 6th +8, 7th +3, 8th -4, 9th +19. Listed status for the first time and a new title for a race won by the brilliant Curlin ahead of his 2008 Dubai World Cup triumph, and also by California Chrome in 2016 ahead of his DWC success. They went solid fractions: 25.19, 23.63, 23.87, 25.4, 25.37. The runner-up helps set the standard.

## 892a AL NABOODAH KAESER COMPRESSOR TROPHY (H'CAP) (TURF) 7f

**6:00** (6:00) (100-111,111) 3-Y-0+

**£65,853** (£21,951; £10,975; £5,487; £3,292; £2,195)

RPR

1 **Suyoof (AUS)**[12] 698 4-9-0 **105** ........ JimCrowley 7 106+
(M F De Kock, South Africa) *s.i.s: settled in rr: rdn 3f out: r.o wl: led cl home* **8/1**

2 nk **Bravo Zolo (IRE)**[12] 698 5-9-4 **109** ........ WilliamBuick 6 109+
(Charlie Appleby) *mid-div: chsd ldrs 2f out: r.o fnl 1 1/2f: led briefly ins fnl f: r.o* **7/4**[1]

3 shd **Tahanee (ARG)**[14] 653 4-9-0 **105** ........ ChristopheSoumillon 2 105+
(M F De Kock, South Africa) *mid-div: rdn 3f out: r.o fnl 1 1/2f: jst failed* **7/1**[3]

4 1 1/4 **Steady Pace**[12] 696 4-8-13 **104** ........ AdriedeVries 13 100
(Saeed bin Suroor) *trckd ldr: led 2f out: hdd ins fnl f: wknd fnl 55yds* **14/1**

5 1 1/2 **Oh This Is Us (IRE)**[14] 653 4-9-0 **105** ........ PatDobbs 1 97
(Richard Hannon) *settled in rr: r.o fnl 2f: nrst fin* **3/1**[2]

6 shd **Mutawathea**[28] 432 6-8-10 **102** ........ (p) MickaelBarzalona 5 93
(Simon Crisford) *trckd ldr: ev ch 1 1/2f out: one pce fnl f* **25/1**

7 4 **Mr Owen (USA)**[28] 429 5-9-4 **109** ........ (t) OisinMurphy 8 90
(F Rohaut, France) *nvr nr to chal* **33/1**

8 2 1/2 **Dark Emerald (IRE)**[21] 538 7-9-0 **105** ........ (vt) TadhgO'Shea 12 79
(Brendan Powell) *s.i.s: a in rr* **33/1**

9 1 **Akeed Champion**[11] 710 5-8-10 **102** ........ (t) RichardMullen 10 73
(S Seemar, UAE) *nvr bttr than mid-div* **12/1**

10 1 1/4 **Ghaamer (USA)**[32] 365 7-9-6 **111** ........ (t) DaneO'Neill 9 79
(A R Al Rayhi, UAE) *sn led: hdd & wknd 2f out* **33/1**

11 1 1/4 **Haalick (IRE)**[11] 710 4-8-13 **104** ........ ChrisHayes 4 69
(D Selvaratnam, UAE) *s.i.s: nvr bttr than mid-div* **12/1**

12 1 1/2 **Johann Strauss**[14] 653 6-9-0 **105** ........ (t) BernardFayd'Herbe 14 66
(M F De Kock, South Africa) *a in rr* **33/1**

13 2 3/4 **Mastermind (SAF)**[14] 651 5-8-11 **103** ........ PatCosgrave 11 56
(M F De Kock, South Africa) *a in rr* **50/1**

14 5 3/4 **Salateen**[14] 653 5-8-13 **104** ........ ColmO'Donoghue 3 42
(David O'Meara) *nvr bttr than mid-div* **25/1**

1m 24.06s (-0.04) **Going Correction** +0.275s/f (Good) **14** Ran SP% **128.4**
Speed ratings: **111,110,110,109,107 107,102,99,98,97 95,94,91,84**
CSF: 22.44; TRICAST: 113.97; PLACEPOT: £3.30 to a £1 stake. Pool: £5,659.61 - 1,227.18 winning units. QUADPOT: £2.40 to a £1 stake. Pool: £551.90 - 163.80 winning units..
**Owner** Hamdan Al Maktoum **Bred** Yarraman Park Stud Pty Ltd **Trained** South Africa

**FOCUS**
TRAKUS: 2nd -1, 3rd -4, 4th +1, 5th -6, 6th -6, 7th -1, 8th -3, 9th +4, 10th -3, 11th +1, 12th +3, 13th +3, 14th -5. The rail was out 12 metres. The final handicap of the 2017 carnival was a good, competitive one and it was evenly run - 25.53, 23.32, 23.1, with the winner home in 11.69. The second and third help set the level.

# 860 LINGFIELD (L-H)

Friday, February 24

**OFFICIAL GOING: Polytrack: standard**
Wind: light, half against Weather: light cloud, bright spells

## 893 BETWAY BEST ODDS GUARANTEED PLUS H'CAP 1m 4f (P)

**2:20** (2:20) (Class 6) (0-65,66) 4-Y-0+ **£2,264** (£673; £336; £168) **Stalls** Low

Form RPR

6-05 **1** **Mystikana**[21] 549 4-8-12 **66** ........ (bt) TylerSaunders(7) 5 75
(Marcus Tregoning) *hld up in last pair: clsd over 2f out: swtchd rt over 1f out: str run 1f out to ld ins fnl f: r.o strly: readily* **11/4**[1]

62-6 **2** 3 **The Ginger Berry**[21] 549 7-9-7 **65** ........ (h) RobertWinston 6 69
(Dr Jon Scargill) *hld up in midfield: clsd over 2f out: shkn up ent fnl f: rdn 1f out: chsd wnr and kpt on same pce fnl 100yds* **11/2**

-045 **3** 3/4 **Jersey Bull (IRE)**[6] 806 5-9-5 **63** ........ (h) LiamKeniry 2 66
(Michael Madgwick) *t.k.h early: midfield: clsd over 2f out: rdn to ld on inner over 1f out: hdd ins fnl f: kpt on same pce after* **17/5**[3]

0-R4 **4** 5 **Katalan (GER)**[9] 733 4-7-11 **51** oh6 ........ (h) DarraghKeenan(7) 8 46
(John Butler) *wnt rt leaving stalls and slowly away: hld up in last pair: effrt and urged along wl over 1f out: no ch w ldrs but plugged on to go 4th wl ins fnl f* **22/1**

24-0 **5** 1 1/4 **Goodby Inheritence**[21] 549 5-9-6 **64** ........ (t) GeorgeBaker 4 57
(Seamus Durack) *prom in main gp: clsd over 2f out: rdn and ev ch over 1f out: sn unable qck and wknd ins fnl f* **3/1**[2]

0-30 **6** 6 **Firestorm (GER)**[22] 517 6-9-1 **62** ........ (e) KieranShoemark(3) 3 45
(Michael Attwater) *led and sn wl clr: rdn 2f out: hdd over 1f out: sn btn and fdd fnl f* **15/2**

-003 **7** 4 1/2 **My Lord**[8] 757 9-9-4 **62** ........ DannyBrock 7 38
(Paddy Butler) *chsd clr ldr: drvn over 2f out: sn lost pl: bhd fnl f* **22/1**

2m 32.5s (-0.50) **Going Correction** 0.0s/f (Stan)
**WFA** 4 from 5yo+ 2lb **7** Ran SP% **110.2**
Speed ratings (Par 101): **101,99,98,95,94 90,87**
CSF £16.82 CT £47.95 TOTE £3.50: £2.00, £3.30; EX 15.10 Trifecta £72.20.
**Owner** Mrs Victoria Brown **Bred** Chasemore Farm **Trained** Whitsbury, Hants

**FOCUS**
A moderate handicap with recent winning form thin on the ground. The bulk of the field ignored the tearaway leader. A minor pb from the winner, with the runner-up rated a fraction below.

## 894 BETWAY BEST ODDS GUARANTEED PLUS MAIDEN STKS 1m 4f (P)

**2:55** (2:55) (Class 5) 4-Y-0+ **£2,911** (£866; £432; £216) **Stalls** Low

Form RPR

3-42 **1** **Casablanca (IRE)**[7] 780 4-9-0 72 ........ DavidProbert 2 68+
(Andrew Balding) *trckd ldrs: wnt 2nd jst over 2f out: upsides ldr and travelling strly over 1f out: led ins fnl f: rdn and asserted fnl 100yds: styd on* **2/1**[2]

3 **2** 3/4 **Appy Days (IRE)**[20] 576 7-9-3 0 ........ AdamKirby 1 66
(Ian Williams) *led: rdn ent fnl 2f: jnd over 1f out: hdd and styd on same pce ins fnl f* **9/5**[1]

**3** 7 **The Blue Bomber**[16] 5-9-8 0 ........ GeorgeBaker 5 60
(Mick Channon) *hld up in 5th: clsd jst over 2f out: effrt in 3rd wl over 1f out: no imp: wl hld and plugged on same pce fnl f* **9/4**[3]

00 **4** 1 1/4 **L'Ami De Rouge**[23] 504 4-9-0 0 ........ (h) LiamKeniry 6 53
(Ralph J Smith) *stdd s: hld up in rr: nt clr run 2f out: shkn up on inner wl over 1f out: wl hld 4th and no imp ins fnl f* **250/1**

5 **5** 1 1/4 **Paris Bound**[13] 687 4-9-5 0 ........ RobHornby 3 56
(Andrew Balding) *s.i.s: sn rcvrd to chse ldr: led 10f out tl cocked jaw and hung bdly rt to paddock exit 9f out: pressing ldr again 8f out tl rdn and unable qck over 2f out: wknd over 1f out* **12/1**

54 **6** 2 3/4 **Marauder**[37] 289 5-9-8 0 ........ FergusSweeney 4 51
(Henry Candy) *t.k.h: in tch: rdn 3f out: struggling and outpcd 2f out: wknd over 1f out* **25/1**

2m 34.78s (1.78) **Going Correction** 0.0s/f (Stan)
**WFA** 4 from 5yo+ 2lb **6** Ran SP% **111.8**
Speed ratings (Par 103): **94,93,88,88,87 85**
CSF £5.95 TOTE £2.50: £1.20, £1.40; EX 6.60 Trifecta £12.00.
**Owner** A M Balding **Bred** Ballyreddin Stud **Trained** Kingsclere, Hants

**FOCUS**
An uncompetitive older-horse maiden, but a couple of these were quite interesting for different reasons. The pace was ordinary, but the first two still pulled well clear. Muddling form.

## 895 32RED.COM H'CAP 1m 1y(P)

**3:25** (3:26) (Class 6) (0-65,66) 3-Y-0 **£2,264** (£673; £336; £168) **Stalls** High

Form RPR

03-2 **1** **Ourmullion**[42] 209 3-9-7 **65** ........ KierenFox 5 69
(John Best) *led tl over 5f out: styd trcking ldrs: effrt u.p on inner over 1f out: drvn to ld ins fnl f: styd on: drvn out* **4/1**[2]

00-2 **2** nk **Delfie Lane**[22] 522 3-9-4 **62** ........ ShaneKelly 1 65
(Richard Hughes) *broke wl: stdd and wl in tch in midfield: swtchd rt and effrt wl over 1f out: awkward hd carriage and unable qck ent fnl f: drvn ins fnl f: hdwy to chse wnr wl ins fnl f: styd on* **8/1**

-214 **3** 1 **Auric Goldfinger (IRE)**[8] 763 3-9-6 **64** ........ (b) TomMarquand 9 65
(Richard Hannon) *in tch: hdwy to chse ldr 5f out: rdn and ev ch over 1f out tl unable qck ins fnl f: edgd lft in 3rd and styd on same pce wl ins fnl f* **7/4**[1]

0-33 **4** nk **Beauchamp Opal**[23] 502 3-9-2 **60** ........ StevieDonohoe 11 60+
(Charlie Fellowes) *stdd after s: hld up in last trio: effrt ent fnl 2f: hdwy jst over 1f out: swtchd lft kpt on wl ins fnl f* **11/2**[3]

0-53 **5** 1 1/4 **Sandy Shores**[16] 624 3-9-0 **65** ........ JordanUys(7) 2 62+
(Brian Meehan) *hld up in tch in midfield: effrt u.p over 1f out: hdwy 1f out: chsng ldrs but keeping on same pce whn sltly squeezed for room towards fin* **16/1**

044 **6** 1/2 **State Residence (IRE)**[25] 479 3-9-5 **63** ........ AdamKirby 10 59
(David O'Meara) *stdd s: hld up in tch in rr: swtchd lft and effrt on inner over 1f out: hdwy u.p 1f out: edgd lft and kpt on ins fnl f* **8/1**

50-0 **7** hd **London Grammar (IRE)**[23] 502 3-8-13 **57** ........ RyanTate 3 53
(Ralph J Smith) *in tch in midfield: rdn over 2f out: wd and lost pl bnd 2f out: no threat to ldrs but kpt on again ins fnl f* **100/1**

-641 **8** 1 1/4 **Oakley Pride (IRE)**[13] 686 3-9-3 **66** ........ (vt) CliffordLee(5) 6 60
(Gay Kelleway) *stdd s: hld up in tch in last pair: hdwy u.p on inner over 1f out: keeping on same pce and hld whn nt clr run wl ins fnl f* **25/1**

6-63 **9** 3/4 **Baby Helmet**[32] 378 3-9-6 **64** ........ GeorgeBaker 8 55
(Mick Channon) *chsd ldr tl led 6f out: rdn and hdd over 1f out: no ex 1f out: wknd ins fnl f* **8/1**

50-0 **10** 1 ¾ **Greyjoy (IRE)**[41] 236 3-9-4 **65**.............................. KieranShoemark(3) 7 52
(Sylvester Kirk) *in tch in midfield: shuffled bk to rr and nt clrest of runs over 1f out: n.d after* **25/1**

36-0 **11** ½ **Georgio (GER)**[31] 385 3-9-1 **59**.............................. RobHornby 4 45
(Andrew Balding) *broke wl: sn stdd and t.k.h: chsd ldrs: pushed along over 1f out: no rspnse and sn btn: wknd ins fnl f* **14/1**

1m 38.78s (0.58) **Going Correction** 0.0s/f (Stan) **11** Ran SP% **126.3**
Speed ratings (Par 95): **97,96,95,95,94 93,93,92,91,89 89**
CSF £38.59 CT £79.64 TOTE £4.30: £1.50, £3.20, £1.50; EX 40.80 Trifecta £140.40.
**Owner** David & Elaine Long **Bred** Best Breeding **Trained** Oad Street, Kent

**FOCUS**
A modest 3yo handicap and it paid to be handy. The fourth has been rated to form.

## 896 SUNBETS.CO.UK H'CAP 7f 1y(P)
4:00 (4:01) (Class 3) (0-90,90) 4-Y-O **£7,246** (£2,168; £1,084; £542; £270) **Stalls** Low

Form RPR

6-02 **1** **Take The Helm**[37] 287 4-9-0 **83**.............................. KierenFox 6 91
(Brian Meehan) *w ldr and travelled strly: rdn to ld over 1f out: drvn and hrd pressed jst ins fnl f: kpt on wl and won on the nod* **9/2**[1]

5-35 **2** shd **Honiara**[21] 548 4-9-2 **85**..............................(b[1]) PJMcDonald 2 92
(Paul Cole) *trckd ldrs: effrt between horses ent fnl f: drvn and chal jst ins fnl f: kpt on u.p: lost on the nod* **6/1**[2]

445- **3** nk **The Warrior (IRE)**[212] 4758 5-8-12 **84**.................. KieranShoemark(3) 4 90
(Amanda Perrett) *hld up wl in tch in midfield: effrt over 1f out: hdwy and kpt on wl u.p fnl 100yds* **8/1**[3]

00-3 **4** 1 ¾ **Fiftyshadesofgrey (IRE)**[38] 275 6-9-7 **90**.................. SteveDrowne 9 91
(George Baker) *t.k.h: hld up wl in tch in midfield: effrt over 1f out: kpt on u.p ins fnl f* **12/1**

-263 **5** hd **Firmdecisions (IRE)**[27] 459 7-9-7 **90**.............................. RobertWinston 13 91
(Dean Ivory) *t.k.h: chsd ldrs on outer: rdn and ev ch 2f out tl unable qck 1f out: wknd wl ins fnl f* **14/1**

4-03 **6** ½ **Shypen**[20] 581 4-8-11 **80**.............................. JackGarritty 11 80+
(Richard Fahey) *t.k.h: hld up in tch in rr: effrt over 1f out: swtchd lft and hdwy jst ins fnl f: kpt on wl: nt rch ldrs* **16/1**

-005 **7** ¾ **Shyron**[18] 598 6-9-5 **88**.............................. AdamKirby 7 86+
(George Margarson) *in tch in rr of main gp: effrt u.p on inner over 1f out: hdwy 1f out: kpt on same pce fnl 100yds* **6/1**[2]

02-1 **8** nk **Twin Point**[23] 506 6-8-13 **82**..............................(t) StevieDonohoe 1 79
(Charlie Fellowes) *taken down early: led: rdn 2f out: hdd over 1f out: no ex and wknd ins fnl f* **6/1**[2]

0522 **9** nse **Lexington Times (IRE)**[23] 506 5-8-12 **81**.................. JamesSullivan 10 78
(Ruth Carr) *t.k.h: hld up in tch in midfield: effrt over 1f out: kpt on same pce and no imp ins fnl f* **16/1**

-144 **10** ¾ **Fire Diamond**[9] 736 4-8-7 **76** oh4..............................(p) DavidProbert 12 71+
(Tom Dascombe) *stdd and dropped in bhd after s: hld up in tch in rr: effrt over 1f out: kpt on but no real imp ins fnl f* **20/1**

4-24 **11** hd **Joey's Destiny (IRE)**[18] 598 7-9-4 **87**.............................. LiamKeniry 5 81
(George Baker) *t.k.h: hld up in tch: effrt over 1f out: keeping on same pce whn bmpd ins fnl f: wl hld after* **8/1**[3]

0-44 **12** 15 **Valbchek (IRE)**[27] 459 8-9-7 **90**..............................(p) GeorgeBaker 8 44
(Jane Chapple-Hyam) *dwlt: sn reluctant and detached in last: nvr a factor* **8/1**[3]

1m 23.76s (-1.04) **Going Correction** 0.0s/f (Stan) **12** Ran SP% **125.3**
Speed ratings (Par 107): **105,104,104,102,102 101,100,100,100,99 99,82**
CSF £32.59 CT £219.23 TOTE £3.80: £1.60, £2.70, £4.10; EX 39.40 Trifecta £434.90.
**Owner** J S Threadwell **Bred** Wilsdon & Habton **Trained** Manton, Wilts
■ Stewards' Enquiry : Jack Garritty £290.00 fine; using mobile phone outside the designated area.

**FOCUS**
A warm handicap and a thrilling finish, but another race where you had to be handy. The first two have been rated around their January C&D form.

## 897 32REDSPORT.COM H'CAP 7f 1y(P)
4:35 (4:35) (Class 6) (0-55,56) 3-Y-O **£2,264** (£673; £336; £168) **Stalls** Low

Form RPR

531 **1** **Tigerfish (IRE)**[15] 644 3-8-8 **47**..............................(p) HollieDoyle(5) 1 52+
(William Stone) *lunged forward jst bef stalls opened and dwlt: sn rcvrd and in tch in midfield: clsd to chse ldrs 2f out: rdn to ld 1f out: r.o strly: readily* **11/4**[2]

0-04 **2** 2 ¼ **Masquerade Bling (IRE)**[29] 418 3-9-6 **54**.............................. RobHornby 10 53
(Simon Hodgson) *hld up in tch in last trio: effrt on outer bnd 2f out: hdwy 1f out: styd on strly ins fnl f: wnt 2nd on post: no threat to ldrs* **9/1**

44-0 **3** nse **Hold Me Tight (IRE)**[8] 763 3-9-7 **55**..............................(b) LiamKeniry 5 54
(J S Moore) *w ldr: rdn and ev ch whn drifted rt over 1f out: styd on same pce ins fnl f* **14/1**

-204 **4** nse **Mr Strutter (IRE)**[20] 578 3-9-8 **56**..............................(h) JackGarritty 3 55
(John Quinn) *taken down early: led: rdn over 1f out: hdd 1f out: outpcd by wnr and kpt on same pce after: lost 2 pls last stride* **9/4**[1]

-644 **5** ¾ **Joyful Dream (IRE)**[13] 686 3-9-7 **55**.................. MichaelJMMurphy 2 52
(J S Moore) *trckd ldrs: effrt over 1f out: no ch w wnr and kpt on same pce u.p ins fnl f* **7/1**[3]

0-06 **6** 4 ½ **Valley Lodge**[13] 686 3-8-6 **47**..............................(p) FinleyMarsh(7) 7 32
(Julia Feilden) *hld up in tch in last pair: effrt on inner over 1f out: sn no imp: wknd ins fnl f* **50/1**

-053 **7** nk **Arya Stark**[21] 546 3-9-2 **50**..............................(p) DavidProbert 6 34
(Tony Carroll) *chsd ldrs: effrt and unable qck over 1f out: sn lost pl and wknd fnl f* **25/1**

0-36 **8** 1 ¾ **Bartholomew J (IRE)**[15] 644 3-8-9 **46**..................(v) SimonPearce(3) 9 25
(Lydia Pearce) *dwlt and bustled along early: hld up in rr: effrt over 1f out: no imp u.p fnl f* **7/1**[3]

-064 **9** 2 **Rockalater**[15] 644 3-8-10 **47**.............................. KieranShoemark(3) 4 21
(Sylvester Kirk) *in tch in midfield: rdn ent fnl 2f: lost pl over 1f out: wknd fnl f* **9/1**

1m 25.41s (0.61) **Going Correction** 0.0s/f (Stan) **9** Ran SP% **114.9**
Speed ratings (Par 95): **96,93,93,93,92 87,86,84,82**
CSF £27.67 CT £295.23 TOTE £3.20: £1.10, £2.70, £4.40; EX 30.90 Trifecta £284.10.
**Owner** Miss Caroline Scott **Bred** Swordlestown Little **Trained** West Wickham, Cambs

**FOCUS**
A weak 3yo handicap with only one winner in the field and that was still the case afterwards. A small step forward from the winner.

## 898 32RED CASINO H'CAP 5f 6y(P)
5:05 (5:07) (Class 5) (0-70,70) 3-Y-O **£2,911** (£866; £432; £216) **Stalls** High

Form RPR

-034 **1** **Roundabout Magic (IRE)**[16] 623 3-8-11 **60**.................. NickyMackay 3 67
(Simon Dow) *stdd s: t.k.h: trckd ldrs: effrt on inner over 1f out: rdn to ld 1f out: clr ins fnl f: jst hld on* **4/1**

050- **2** shd **Met By Moonlight**[246] 3556 3-8-10 **59**.............................. DavidProbert 4 65+
(Ron Hodges) *in tch in rr: effrt and wd bnd 2f out: stl last jst ins fnl f: hdwy to chse clr wnr 75yds out: styd on strly: jst failed* **16/1**

50-6 **3** 2 ¼ **Who Told Jo Jo (IRE)**[16] 623 3-9-7 **70**.............................. LiamKeniry 1 68
(Joseph Tuite) *led: rdn and hrd pressed over 1f out: hdd 1f out: sn outpcd and wknd fnl 100yds* **7/2**[3]

5-12 **4** ¾ **Popsilca**[21] 546 3-8-7 **56** oh1.............................. WilliamCarson 2 51
(Mick Quinn) *chsd ldr: effrt and ev ch over 1f out: sn rdn and unable qck: wknd fnl 100yds* **9/4**[2]

1-42 **5** ½ **Street Jazz**[32] 379 3-9-2 **65**..............................(b) AdamKirby 5 58
(James Given) *chsd ldrs: rdn and drifted rt bnd 2f out: sn struggling to qckn: wknd ins fnl f* **2/1**[1]

59.27s (0.47) **Going Correction** 0.0s/f (Stan) **5** Ran SP% **112.2**
Speed ratings (Par 97): **96,95,92,91,90**
CSF £50.46 TOTE £5.20: £2.30, £4.80; EX 46.00 Trifecta £237.70.
**Owner** Six Mile Hill Racing **Bred** T F Lacy **Trained** Ashtead, Surrey

**FOCUS**
An ordinary 3yo sprint handicap and the leaders may have gone off too quick, as the first two came from behind. The winner has been rated to form.
T/Jkpt: £30,216.30 to a £1 stake. Pool: £30,216.39 - 1.0 winning unit T/Plt: £225.40 to a £1 stake. Pool: £81,974.18 - 265.46 winning units T/Qpdt: £68.30 to a £1 stake. Pool: £5,958.92 - 64.50 winning units **Steve Payne**

# 881 WOLVERHAMPTON (A.W) (L-H)
Friday, February 24

**OFFICIAL GOING: Tapeta: standard**
Wind: Light behind Weather: Cloudy

## 899 BETWAY SPRINT APPRENTICE H'CAP 6f 20y (Tp)
5:45 (5:47) (Class 7) (0-50,50) 3-Y-O+ **£2,264** (£673; £336; £168) **Stalls** Low

Form RPR

00-3 **1** **Pick Of Any (IRE)**[38] 274 4-9-12 **50**..............................(h) GeorgeWood 11 57
(Michael Appleby) *s.i.s: hld up: hdwy over 2f out: rdn and hung lft over 1f out: styd on u.p to ld nr fin* **2/1**[1]

-230 **2** ½ **Mr Chuckles (IRE)**[24] 495 4-9-10 **48**.............................. CharlieBennett 10 54
(Daniel Mark Loughnane) *sn chsng ldr: led over 2f out: rdn over 1f out: hdd nr fin* **7/1**[3]

-060 **3** hd **National Service (USA)**[27] 455 6-9-9 **47**............(tp) CallumRodriguez 3 52
(Richard Ford) *s.s: bhd: hdwy: nt clr run and swtchd rt ins fnl f: r.o wl* **9/1**

1-00 **4** shd **Ocotillo (IRE)**[15] 640 4-9-9 **50**..............................(p[1]) GerO'Neill(3) 8 55
(Kevin Frost) *a.p: chsd ldr 2f out: rdn and hung lft over 1f out: r.o* **7/1**[3]

-055 **5** 1 **Lizzy's Dream**[11] 723 9-9-9 **47**.............................. RowanScott 6 49
(Rebecca Bastiman) *hld up: hdwy u.p over 1f out: r.o* **14/1**

00-6 **6** shd **Ambitious Boy**[39] 270 8-9-10 **48**.............................. MitchGodwin 1 49
(John O'Shea) *s.i.s: in rr: hdwy over 1f out: sn rdn: r.o* **9/2**[2]

6-05 **7** ¾ **Whispering Soul (IRE)**[39] 271 4-9-5 **48**..................(p) TobyEley(5) 7 47
(Brian Baugh) *hld up: hdwy over 1f out: nt trble ldrs* **33/1**

0-04 **8** ½ **Presto Boy**[16] 622 5-9-3 **46**..............................(be[1]) StephenCummins(5) 9 44
(Richard Hughes) *chsd ldrs: rdn over 1f out: no ex wl ins fnl f* **11/1**

65-0 **9** 1 ¼ **Rat Catcher (IRE)**[11] 723 7-9-9 **47**..............................(b) DavidParkes 5 41
(Lisa Williamson) *prom: rdn over 1f out: styd on same pce fnl f* **33/1**

20-5 **10** 8 **Nefetari**[34] 357 4-9-9 **47**..............................(b) JoshDoyle 4 17
(Alan Brown) *sn led: hdd over 2f out: rdn: edgd lft and wknd over 1f out* **14/1**

-005 **11** 1 **Pull The Pin (IRE)**[11] 722 8-9-8 **46**..............................(t) MeganNicholls 12 13
(Mandy Rowland) *led early: chsd ldrs: pushed along over 2f out: sn wknd* **66/1**

1m 14.39s (-0.11) **Going Correction** -0.175s/f (Stan) **11** Ran SP% **115.6**
Speed ratings (Par 97): **93,92,92,91,90 90,89,88,87,76 75**
CSF £15.61 CT £104.60 TOTE £3.50: £2.20, £1.90, £2.90; EX 16.70 Trifecta £140.90.
**Owner** Michael Appleby **Bred** D Maher **Trained** Oakham, Rutland

**FOCUS**
An ordinary sprint handicap. The second and third help set the modest opening level.

## 900 BETWAY MARATHON H'CAP 1m 5f 194y
6:15 (6:17) (Class 6) (0-60,59) 4-Y-O+ **£2,587** (£770; £384; £192) **Stalls** Low

Form RPR

00-3 **1** **Iona Island**[9] 738 4-9-0 **59**.............................. DavidParkes(5) 8 65
(Peter Hiatt) *chsd ldrs: pushed along over 3f out: rdn and edgd rt fr over 1f out: led ins fnl f: styd on* **18/1**

-003 **2** nk **Tingo In The Tale (IRE)**[9] 741 8-9-3 **52**..................(t[1]) JamieSpencer 4 58
(Sophie Leech) *hld up: swtchd rt and hdwy over 1f out: sn rdn: carried rt ins fnl f: styd on* **9/1**

003- **3** 2 ½ **Asian Wing (IRE)**[14] 674 8-9-10 **59**..............................(tp) DavidNolan 9 61+
(John James Feane, Ire) *hld up: hdwy over 6f out: chsd ldr 4f out: led over 1f out: sn rdn and edgd rt: hdd ins fnl f: styd on same pce* **11/2**

3-10 **4** ½ **Tred Softly (IRE)**[38] 278 4-9-4 **58**..............................(b) JasonHart 7 59
(John Quinn) *hld up: plld hrd: hdwy over 3f out: rdn over 2f out: styd on same pce fnl f* **11/4**[1]

-341 **5** 3 **Dream Serenade**[11] 721 4-9-1 **55** 6ex..............................(h) LukeMorris 6 52
(Michael Appleby) *prom: chsd ldr 12f out tl led 4f out: rdn and hdd over 1f out: wknd wl ins fnl f* **9/2**[3]

-531 **6** 3 **Scrafton**[9] 741 6-9-3 **59**.............................. AledBeech(7) 3 52
(Tony Carroll) *hld up: racd keenly: hdwy over 5f out: rdn and wknd over 1f out* **3/1**[2]

2-25 **7** 1 ¼ **Lineman**[11] 721 7-9-6 **58**..............................(b) JackDuern(3) 2 49
(Sarah Hollinshead) *hld up: hdwy over 5f out: pushed along and lost pl over 4f out: n.d after* **8/1**

030/ **8** 11 **Musical Moon**[23] 7419 7-9-8 **57**..............................(p) MartinLane 1 33
(Steve Flook) *s.i.s: sn drvn along to ld: hdd 4f out: wknd over 2f out* **150/1**

00-0 **9** 12 **Somepink (IRE)**[13] 689 4-8-5 **45**..............................(p[1]) FrannyNorton 5 4
(Daniel Mark Loughnane) *led early: chsd ldrs: lost pl over 6f out: wknd over 4f out* **100/1**

3m 3.07s (-1.73) **Going Correction** -0.175s/f (Stan)
**WFA** 4 from 6yo+ 3lb **9** Ran SP% **113.3**
Speed ratings (Par 101): **97,96,95,95,93 91,90,84,77**
CSF £165.86 CT £1014.64 TOTE £19.10: £3.30, £2.90, £2.10; EX 155.80 Trifecta £841.60.
**Owner** P W Hiatt **Bred** Laundry Cottage Stud Farm **Trained** Hook Norton, Oxon
■ Stewards' Enquiry : David Parkes caution; careless riding

**FOCUS**
They went fairly steady early and then the pace picked up heading down the back the final time. Ordinary form.

## 901 BETWAY H'CAP — 5f 21y (Tp)
**6:45** (6:46) (Class 6) (0-65,67) 4-Y-0+ — **£2,587** (£770; £384; £192) **Stalls** Low

Form — RPR

5-23 **1** **Dandilion (IRE)**[11] 722 4-8-13 **55**.....................(t) CallumShepherd(3) 5 — 63
(Alex Hales) *hld up: pushed along and hdwy over 1f out: nt clr run and swtchd rt ins fnl f: rdn and r.o to ld post* **7/2**[2]

6-06 **2** *shd* **Cruise Tothelimit (IRE)**[18] 602 9-9-6 **59**..................(v) FrannyNorton 9 — 66
(Patrick Morris) *led: rdn over 1f out: hdd post* **16/1**

0430 **3** *½* **Jack The Laird (IRE)**[9] 742 4-9-4 **60**........................(v) JackDuern(3) 4 — 65
(Dean Ivory) *trckd ldrs: shkn up over 1f out: r.o* **11/1**

0-35 **4** *1* **David's Beauty (IRE)**[9] 743 4-9-5 **58**....................(v1) ConnorBeasley 3 — 60
(Brian Baugh) *chsd ldrs: rdn 1/2-way: styd on* **22/1**

55-3 **5** *¾* **Dream Ally (IRE)**[11] 723 7-8-12 **51**.............................(be) LukeMorris 6 — 50
(John Weymes) *sn pushed along in rr: hdwy over 1f out: rdn and edgd lft ins fnl f: styd on* **11/1**

0-41 **6** *2* **Roaring Rory**[9] 743 4-9-8 **66** 6ex.........................(p) LewisEdmunds(5) 8 — 58
(Ollie Pears) *dwlt: r.o ins fnl f: nvr nrr* **9/2**[3]

-502 **7** *½* **It Must Be Faith**[4] 844 7-9-11 **67**.......................(p) AlistairRawlinson(3) 1 — 57
(Michael Appleby) *chsd ldr: chal 2f out: rdn over 1f out: hung lft and wknd wl ins fnl f* **11/8**[1]

40-0 **8** *10* **Bilash**[39] 270 10-8-7 **46** oh1.............................................. KieranO'Neill 2
(Sarah Hollinshead) *prom: pushed along and lost pl over 3f out: rdn and wknd over 1f out* **150/1**

4-02 **9** *15* **Give Us A Belle (IRE)**[11] 722 8-8-7 **46**................(vt) AdamBeschizza 7
(Christine Dunnett) *s.i.s: outpcd* **18/1**

1m 0.82s (-1.08) **Going Correction** -0.175s/f (Stan) — **9** Ran SP% **115.3**
Speed ratings (Par 101): **101,100,100,98,97 94,93,77,53**
CSF £57.18 CT £562.58 TOTE £5.50: £1.90, £5.20, £2.70; EX 69.00 Trifecta £490.70.
**Owner** The Golden Horse Racing Club **Bred** Ballyhane Stud **Trained** Edgcote, Northamptonshire
■ Stewards' Enquiry : Jack Duern caution; entered the wrong stall.

**FOCUS**
This was run at a strong gallop and the winner came from a long way back. The runner-up has been rated close to his best of recent times.

## 902 32RED.COM H'CAP — 7f 36y (Tp)
**7:15** (7:16) (Class 4) (0-85,86) 3-Y-O — **£5,175** (£1,540; £769; £384) **Stalls** High

Form — RPR

01- **1** **Gilgamesh**[206] 4981 3-9-6 **79**............................................ JamieSpencer 3 — 84+
(George Scott) *hld up: pushed along over 2f out: hdwy wl over 1f out: led and hung lft 1f out: r.o* **11/10**[1]

-226 **2** *1* **Tailor's Row (USA)**[16] 626 3-9-7 **80**............................. FrannyNorton 4 — 82
(Mark Johnston) *chsd ldrs who wnt clr over 5f out: tk clsr order turning for home: rdn and ev ch 1f out: styd on same pce towards fin* **7/2**[2]

2-14 **3** *¾* **Mums The Word**[13] 678 3-9-6 **79**................................. TonyHamilton 2 — 79
(Richard Fahey) *chsd ldr: rdn and ev ch over 1f out: hung lft and styd on same pce wl ins fnl f* **9/1**

-225 **4** *1½* **Allegheny Bay (IRE)**[15] 642 3-8-5 **64**............................ LukeMorris 1 — 60
(J S Moore) *led at gd pce: rdn and hdd 1f out: no ex ins fnl f* **16/1**

34-1 **5** *1¾* **Spirit Of Sarwan (IRE)**[21] 553 3-9-3 **76**.................... AdamBeschizza 6 — 67
(Julia Feilden) *dwlt: hld up: rdn over 2f out: nvr on terms* **12/1**

-145 **6** *1¾* **Letmestopyouthere (IRE)**[16] 626 3-9-13 **86**............ PaulMulrennan 5 — 73
(David Evans) *hld up: rdn over 2f out: n.d* **11/2**[3]

1m 27.27s (-1.53) **Going Correction** -0.175s/f (Stan) — **6** Ran SP% **108.8**
Speed ratings (Par 99): **101,99,99,97,95 93**
CSF £4.71 TOTE £2.00: £1.30, £1.80; EX 5.20 Trifecta £21.60.
**Owner** Niarchos Family **Bred** Niarchos Family **Trained** Newmarket, Suffolk

**FOCUS**
This was run at a good gallop. The runner-up has been rated to form.

## 903 £10 FREE AT 32RED.COM H'CAP — 6f 20y (Tp)
**7:45** (7:45) (Class 6) (0-65,72) 3-Y-O — **£2,587** (£770; £384; £192) **Stalls** Low

Form — RPR

1-51 **1** **Lord Cooper**[6] 813 3-9-10 **72** 6ex..............................(tp) DavidParkes(5) 5 — 75
(Jose Santos) *trckd ldrs: rdn to ld and edgd lft wl ins fnl f: r.o* **5/4**[1]

-434 **2** *½* **Jet Setter (IRE)**[6] 813 3-9-6 **63**................................ GeorgeDowning 4 — 64
(Tony Carroll) *led: qcknd over 2f out: rdn over 1f out: hdd wl ins fnl f* **9/2**[3]

060- **3** *¾* **Vaux (IRE)**[139] 7143 3-9-3 **60**........................................... LukeMorris 6 — 59
(Ben Haslam) *hld up: rdn over 1f out: r.o ins fnl f: nt rch ldrs* **9/1**

2-15 **4** *½* **Scotch Myst**[39] 264 3-9-1 **58**.......................................... TonyHamilton 7 — 55
(Richard Fahey) *chsd ldr: rdn over 1f out: edgd lft ins fnl f: styd on same pce* **9/2**[3]

0-35 **5** *¾* **Bismarck The Flyer (IRE)**[23] 511 3-8-12 **60**......... LewisEdmunds(5) 3 — 55
(Ollie Pears) *awkward s: sn chsng ldrs: shkn up over 2f out: no ex ins fnl f* **3/1**[2]

1m 14.79s (0.29) **Going Correction** -0.175s/f (Stan) — **5** Ran SP% **115.8**
Speed ratings (Par 95): **91,90,89,88,87**
CSF £7.83 TOTE £2.10: £1.30, £1.90; EX 6.70 Trifecta £19.50.
**Owner** R Cooper Racing Ltd **Bred** Miss K Rausing **Trained** Upper Lambourn, Berks

**FOCUS**
A modest sprint for 3yos, but won by an improving sort. The third has been rated as running close to his more recent form.

## 904 32RED.COM CASINO MAIDEN STKS — 5f 21y (Tp)
**8:15** (8:16) (Class 5) 3-Y-O — **£4,204** (£1,251; £625; £312) **Stalls** Low

Form — RPR

400- **1** **Logi (IRE)**[134] 7305 3-9-5 75..............................................(b) PhillipMakin 5 — 77
(David Barron) *mde all: rdn over 1f out: styd on wl* **5/2**[1]

4 **2** *3½* **Jack The Truth (IRE)**[13] 679 3-9-5 0............................. JamieSpencer 2 — 64
(George Scott) *chsd ldrs: wnt 2nd 1/2-way: rdn over 1f out: no imp fnl f* **7/2**[3]

6- **3** *5* **Lostock**[295] 1976 3-9-5 0.................................................. PaulMulrennan 6 — 51
(Michael Dods) *sn pushed along in 4th pl: rdn 1/2-way: wnt 3rd wl ins fnl f: nvr trbld ldrs* **5/2**[1]

40- **4** *1¾* **Jack Blane**[162] 6515 3-9-5 0........................................ GeorgeDowning 3 — 40
(Daniel Kubler) *sn outpcd: nvr nrr* **22/1**

64- **5** *nk* **Zavikon**[158] 6622 3-9-5 0.................................................... ShaneKelly 4 — 39
(Richard Hughes) *racd keenly in 2nd pl to 1/2-way: rdn over 1f out: wknd fnl f* **3/1**[2]

50 **6** *1½* **Ebitda**[18] 600 3-9-0 0........................................................ DaleSwift 1 — 29
(Scott Dixon) *s.i.s: outpcd* **50/1**

1m 0.81s (-1.09) **Going Correction** -0.175s/f (Stan) — **6** Ran SP% **110.7**
Speed ratings (Par 97): **101,95,87,84,84 81**
CSF £11.27 TOTE £3.80: £1.70, £1.40; EX 11.50 Trifecta £30.10.
**Owner** Let's Be Lucky Racing 11 **Bred** S Couldrige **Trained** Maunby, N Yorks

**FOCUS**
They finished strung out in this maiden, the winner returning to something like his best. There was no great depth to the race.
T/Plt: £46.60 to a £1 stake. Pool: £100,258.37 - 1,568.10 winning units T/Qpdt: £8.80 to a £1 stake. Pool: £8,907.43 - 748.86 winning units **Colin Roberts**

905 - 913a (Foreign Racing) - See Raceform Interactive

# DOHA
Friday, February 24

**OFFICIAL GOING: Turf: good**

## 914a IRISH THOROUGHBRED MARKETING CUP (LOCAL GROUP 2) (3YO+) (TURF) — 1m
**4:45** 3-Y-0+ — **£92,682** (£35,772; £17,886; £9,756; £6,504)

RPR

**1** **Sovereign Debt (IRE)**[69] 8431 8-9-2 0.......................... AndrewMullen 3 — 112
(David Nicholls) *chsd ldng gp: drvn and clsd 1 1/2f out: chsd ldrs into fnl f: styd on wl to ld 75yds out: hld on gamely*

**2** *½* **Cougar Mountain (IRE)**[75] 8332 6-9-2 0..........(tp) DonnachaO'Brien 15 — 111
(A P O'Brien, Ire) *w.w in rr wl off the pce: hdwy on outer 2f out: r.o fnl f: nvr quite on terms*

**3** *½* **Roman Legend (IRE)**[36] 6-9-2 0..................................(t) HarryBentley 5 — 110
(Jassim Mohammed Ghazali, Qatar)

**4** *1* **Diplomat (GER)**[110] 7841 6-9-2 0.................................. AdriedeVries 14 — 107
(Mario Hofer, Germany)

**5** *hd* **Extremis (IRE)**[323] 5-9-2 0...........................................(b) FrankieDettori 2 — 107
(Jassim Mohammed Ghazali, Qatar)

**6** *1¼* **Barwod**[57] 8573 4-9-2 0................................................ MarcoMonteriso 9 — 104
(J Smart, Qatar)

**7** *1½* **Moheet (IRE)**[36] 5-9-2 0.............................................. FalehBughanaim 8 — 101
(Jassim Mohammed Ghazali, Qatar)

**8** *2* **Baltic Knight (IRE)**[364] 744 7-9-2 0.............................. DuranFentiman 4 — 96
(Husain Aldailami, Bahrain)

**9** *shd* **Chilworth Icon**[22] 7-9-2 0............................................... TomLukasek 1 — 96
(Debbie Mountain, Qatar)

**10** *¾* **Itorio (IRE)**[36] 5-9-2 0..............................................(b) GeraldAvranche 12 — 94
(Mohammed Jassim Ghazali, Qatar)

**11** *¾* **Bretherton**[364] 744 6-9-2 0........................................(p) MarvinSuerland 11 — 92
(Mohammed Jassim Ghazali, Qatar)

**12** *½* **Zman Awal (IRE)**[65] 6-8-11 0......................................... AlbertoSanna 7 — 86
(H Al Ramzani, Qatar)

**13** *3½* **Felix Leiter**[22] 5-9-2 0.................................................. J-PGuillambert 16 — 83
(Jassim Mohammed Ghazali, Qatar)

**14** *2* **Crescent (IRE)**[43] 5-9-2 0..........................................(p) SaleemGolam 10 — 79
(Ahmed Kobeissi, Qatar)

**15** *nk* **Tupi (IRE)**[13] 698 5-9-2 0.................................................. SeanLevey 6 — 78
(Richard Hannon) *pressed ldr: cl up and ev ch wl over 1 1/2f out: sn rdn and nt qckn: wknd fnl f*

**16** *12* **Mind Of Madness (IRE)**[70] 5-9-2 0.......................... EduardoPedroza 13 — 50
(Ibrahim Al Malki, Qatar)

1m 35.28s — **16** Ran

**Owner** Lady O'Reilly **Bred** Yeomanstown Stud **Trained** Sessay, N Yorks

# 834 ST MORITZ (R-H)
Friday, February 24

**OFFICIAL GOING: Snow: frozen**

## 915a GRAND PRIX LONGINES (CONDITIONS) (4YO+) (SNOW) — 1m
**3:30** 4-Y-0+ — **£5,000** (£2,500; £1,785; £1,190; £595)

RPR

**1** **Berrahri (IRE)**[5] 835 6-10-3 0........................................ RaphaelLingg 5
(John Best) *mde all: broke wl and led: kicked 2 l clr under 1 1/2f out: drvn and styd on fnl f: readily* **17/5**[1]

**2** *2½* **Kontrast (IRE)**[12] 714 4-9-11 0..................................... MilanZatloukal 4
(M Weiss, Switzerland)

**3** *2* **Eyecatsher (IRE)** 9-8-8 0......................................(p) CherylSchoch(6) 3
(M Weiss, Switzerland)

**4** *1¼* **Semilla (FR)**[369] 665 6-8-3 0.......................... MlleMichaelaCasanova(7) 1
(A Schaerer, Switzerland)

**5** *1¾* **Erato (GER)**[12] 716 6-9-11 0....................................... DennisSchiergen 2
(Karin Suter-Weber, Switzerland)

1m 40.07s — **5** Ran SP% **22.7**

**Owner** White Turf Racing Uk **Bred** Kilnamoragh Stud **Trained** Oad Street, Kent

# 893 LINGFIELD (L-H)
Saturday, February 25

**OFFICIAL GOING: Polytrack: standard**
Wind: strong, half behind Weather: overcast, breezy

## 916 SUNBETS.CO.UK MAIDEN STKS — 1m 1y(P)
**1:30** (1:34) (Class 5) 3-Y-0+ — **£2,911** (£866; £432; £216) **Stalls** High

Form — RPR

**1** **Mori Yoshinari (IRE)** 3-8-9 0......................................... TomMarquand 3 — 73+
(Richard Hannon) *s.i.s: clsd and in tch in midfield after 3f: effrt bnd 2f out: rdn and hdwy to chal jst ins fnl f: kpt on wl to ld wl ins fnl f: rdn out* **7/1**

03- **2** *½* **Oud Metha Bridge (IRE)**[135] 7307 3-8-9 0..................... AndreaAtzeni 5 — 72
(Ed Dunlop) *trckd ldrs: effrt to ld over 1f out: sn drvn: hdd and one pced wl ins fnl f* **5/4**[1]

55 **3** *1* **Trade Route (IRE)**[24] 503 3-8-9 0...............................(p1) ShaneKelly 4 — 70
(David Elsworth) *chsd ldrs: reminders over 3f out: nt clr run 2f out: swtchd lft and rdn to chse ldng pair 1f out: kpt on same pce ins fnl f* **9/2**[3]

4 3 1/4 **Many Waters (USA)** 3-8-4 0........................................ RobHornby 2 58+
(Andrew Balding) *s.i.s and rn green early: clsd and in tch after 3f: rdn wl over 1f out: no threat to ldrs but plugged on to go 4th ins fnl f* **11/4$^{2}$**

5 6 **Badenscoth** 3-8-6 0........................................ JackDuern(3) 9 49
(Dean Ivory) *t.k.h: led tl rdn and hdd over 1f out: sn btn and fdd ins fnl f* **66/1**

6 1 1/2 **Hajaam (IRE)** 3-8-9 0........................................ StevieDonohoe 6 45
(Charlie Fellowes) *s.i.s: a rr: clsd and in tch 5f out: struggling and rdn over 2f out: wl btn over 1f out* **10/1**

7 7 **Pocket Warrior**$^{837}$ 6-10-0 0........................................ GeorgeBaker 8 35
(Martin Bosley) *w ldr: rdn wl over 1f out: sn btn and fdd fnl f* **100/1**

8 dist **Cheapo** 4-9-9 0........................................ DavidParkes(5) 1
(Brett Johnson) *broke okay: rn green and sn dropped to rr: lost tch over 3f out: t.o and virtually p.u fnl 2f* **100/1**

1m 37.53s (-0.67) **Going Correction** -0.05s/f (Stan)
**WFA** 3 from 4yo+ 19lb **8** Ran SP% **114.4**
Speed ratings (Par 103): **101,100,99,96,90 88,81,**
CSF £16.28 TOTE £8.00: £2.20, £1.10, £1.60; EX 18.20 Trifecta £47.30.

**Owner** Myerscough, Cox & Anastasiou **Bred** Eyrefield Lodge Stud **Trained** East Everleigh, Wilts

**FOCUS**
An ordinary maiden. The level is a bit fluid. The runner-up has been rated below form.

## 917 BETWAY HEVER SPRINT STKS (LISTED RACE) (ALL-WEATHER CHAMPIONSHIP FAST-TRACK QUALIFIER) 5f 6y(P)

**2:05** (2:10) (Class 1) 4-Y-0+

**£25,519** (£9,675; £4,842; £2,412; £1,210; £607) **Stalls** High

Form RPR

2-03 1 **Royal Birth**$^{5}$ [842] 6-9-0 99........................................(t) AaronJones 2 105
(Stuart Williams) *hld up in tch in midfield: clsd to trck ldrs 2f out: nt clrest of runs jst ins fnl f: str run 100yds out to go between rivals and ld towards fin: rdn out* **8/1**

0-11 2 1/2 **Lancelot Du Lac (ITY)**$^{21}$ [572] 7-9-3 108.................... RobertWinston 6 106
(Dean Ivory) *pressed ldrs: rdn and ev ch over 1f out: led 1f out: kpt on u.p: hdd and no ex towards fin* **4/1$^{2}$**

-511 3 hd **Verne Castle**$^{7}$ [816] 4-9-0 90........................................(h) DavidProbert 1 102
(Andrew Balding) *w ldrs tl led on inner 3f out: rdn over 1f out: hdd 1f out: stl ev ch: kpt on same pce towards fin* **12/1**

6-36 4 nse **Boom The Groom (IRE)**$^{5}$ [842] 6-9-0 107.................... AndreaAtzeni 7 102
(Tony Carroll) *taken down early: led tl 3f out: styd chsng ldrs: effrt 2f out: ev ch ins fnl f: kpt on same pce towards fin* **8/1**

5-15 5 1 **Pretend (IRE)**$^{21}$ [572] 6-9-0 109........................................ AdamKirby 3 99
(Charlie Appleby) *stdd s: hld up in last pair: effrt wd over 1f out: hdwy ins fnl f: styd on fnl 100yds: nvr threatened ldrs* **5/4$^{1}$**

-300 6 3/4 **Sign Of The Kodiac (IRE)**$^{5}$ [842] 4-9-0 95.................... LukeMorris 9 96
(James Given) *rousted along leaving stalls: chsd ldrs: hung lft u.p over 1f out: kpt on same pce ins fnl f* **66/1**

22-6 7 1/2 **Buying Trouble (USA)**$^{17}$ [617] 4-8-9 99.................... StevieDonohoe 5 89
(David Evans) *dwlt: in tch in last pair: effrt over 1f out: kpt on ins fnl f: nvr trbld ldrs* **25/1**

/30- 8 1/2 **Ride Like The Wind (IRE)**$^{165}$ 5-9-0 105.................... JamieSpencer 4 92
(Kevin Ryan) *hld up in tch: effrt on inner over 1f out: no imp ins fnl f: eased towards fin* **7/1$^{3}$**

56.77s (-2.03) **Going Correction** -0.05s/f (Stan) **8** Ran SP% **112.2**
Speed ratings (Par 111): **114,113,112,112,111 110,109,108**
CSF £38.43 TOTE £7.80: £2.20, £2.30, £2.60; EX 38.30 Trifecta £219.50.

**Owner** The Morley Family **Bred** Old Mill Stud & S Williams & J Parry **Trained** Newmarket, Suffolk

■ Stewards' Enquiry : Jamie Spencer caution; failing to take all reasonable and permissible measures to obtain the best possible placing

**FOCUS**
A good, competitive Listed sprint, and there was a contested lead, but they didn't go that quick and it proved hard to make up significant ground, with the first four finishers in the front four positions from the turn into the straight. The sixth has been rated close to his winter best.

## 918 SUN BETS ON THE APP STORE H'CAP 1m 1y(P)

**2:40** (2:40) (Class 3) (0-95,91) 4-Y-0- **£7,246** (£2,168; £1,084; £542; £270) **Stalls** High

Form RPR

-321 1 **Chevallier**$^{28}$ [465] 5-9-5 **89**........................................ LukeMorris 1 96
(Archie Watson) *trckd ldrs: effrt on inner over 1f out and sn chalng: drvn to ld ins fnl f: r.o wl* **9/2$^{2}$**

22-2 2 1/2 **Constantino (IRE)**$^{52}$ [43] 4-9-4 **88**........................(b$^{1}$) JamieSpencer 8 94
(Richard Fahey) *niggled along in midfield: hdwy to chse ldrs and t.k.h after 2f: rdn ent fnl 2f: pressing ldrs and edging lft jst ins fnl f: styd on same pce fnl 100yds* **9/2$^{2}$**

-432 3 1 **Ice Royal (IRE)**$^{22}$ [548] 4-9-4 **88**........................................ AdamKirby 4 92
(Jamie Osborne) *in tch in midfield: rdn over 3f out: kpt on wl ins fnl f: nvr enough pce to threaten ldrs* **3/1$^{1}$**

105- 4 shd **Haaf A Sixpence**$^{67}$ [8475] 8-8-13 **88**.................... PatrickO'Donnell(5) 2 91
(Ralph Beckett) *chsd ldr: rdn to ld jst over 1f out: hdd ins fnl f: no ex and wknd towards fin* **13/2$^{3}$**

0-04 5 hd **Presumido (IRE)**$^{14}$ [680] 7-9-1 **85**........................................ JimCrowley 6 88
(Simon Dow) *stdd s: hld up in rr: swtchd rt and effrt over 1f out: hdwy ins fnl f: kpt on wl towards fin: nt rch ldrs* **20/1**

26-0 6 1/2 **Intrude**$^{28}$ [459] 5-9-7 **91**........................................ OisinMurphy 5 94+
(Stuart Williams) *in tch in midfield: effrt over 1f out: chsng ldrs whn squeezed for room and edgd lft ins fnl f: kpt on same pce after* **20/1**

11-0 7 3 1/4 **Chester Street**$^{42}$ [235] 4-9-0 **87**........................(h) KieranShoemark(3) 7 81
(Roger Charlton) *stdd after s: hld up in tch in last trio: effrt 2f out: no imp u.p over 1f out: nvr trbld ldrs* **7/1**

4-46 8 1 1/4 **Kingston Kurrajong**$^{28}$ [465] 4-9-5 **89**.................... GeorgeBaker 9 80
(Michael Attwater) *led: rdn over 1f out: sn hdd: struggling to qckn whn squeezed for room and nudged ins fnl f: no ch after* **14/1**

-112 9 1/2 **Franco's Secret**$^{10}$ [736] 6-9-3 **87**........................(v) TomMarquand 3 77+
(Peter Hedger) *stdd s: hld up in tch in last trio: effrt on inner over 1f out: squeezed for room and bdly hmpd jst ins fnl f: no ch after* **9/1**

1m 36.92s (-1.28) **Going Correction** -0.05s/f (Stan) **9** Ran SP% **113.4**
Speed ratings (Par 107): **104,103,102,102,102 101,98,97,96**
CSF £24.57 CT £68.82 TOTE £5.50: £1.90, £2.30, £1.10; EX 19.80 Trifecta £39.10.

**Owner** The Chevallier Partnership **Bred** Kincorth Investments Inc **Trained** Upper Lambourn, W Berks

**FOCUS**
A useful handicap. Another small pb from the winner, with the fifth to his Lingfield best.

## 919 BETWAY WINTER DERBY STKS (GROUP 3) (ALL-WEATHER CHAMPIONSHIP FAST-TRACK QUALIFIER) 1m 2f (P)

**3:15** (3:15) (Class 1) 4-Y-0+

**£56,710** (£21,500; £10,760; £5,360; £2,690; £1,350) **Stalls** Low

Form RPR

235- 1 **Convey**$^{147}$ [6955] 5-9-0 111........................................ AndreaAtzeni 10 110
(Sir Michael Stoute) *hld up in tch in midfield: effrt over 1f out: rdn to chal 1f out: r.o wl u.p to ld towards fin* **11/2$^{3}$**

51-1 2 nk **Pinzolo**$^{35}$ [352] 6-9-0 105........................................(p) TomMarquand 9 109
(Ismail Mohammed) *led: rdn and qcknd 2f out: hrd pressed and drvn 1f out: hdd ins fnl f: kpt on: no ex cl home* **17/2**

-112 3 hd **Absolute Blast (IRE)**$^{25}$ [499] 5-8-11 100.................... OisinMurphy 5 106
(Archie Watson) *trckd ldng pair: effrt to chal over 1f out: edgd rt 1f out: led ins fnl f: kpt on u.p tl hdd and no ex towards fin* **9/1**

550- 4 nk **Zhui Feng (IRE)**$^{133}$ [7354] 4-8-13 102........................ JimCrowley 8 108
(Amanda Perrett) *chsd ldr: rdn and ev ch over 1f out: kpt on wl u.p tl no ex cl home* **11/1**

43-4 5 nk **Grendisar (IRE)**$^{21}$ [574] 7-9-0 108........................(b$^{1}$) AdamKirby 2 107
(Marco Botti) *hld up in tch in midfield: effrt over 1f out: swtchd lft 1f out: kpt on u.p ins fnl f: nvr quite getting to ldrs* **11/4$^{2}$**

11-3 6 3 1/2 **Battalion (IRE)**$^{21}$ [574] 7-9-0 108........................ GeorgeBaker 1 100
(Jamie Osborne) *s.i.s: hld up in rr: swtchd rt and nt clr run ent fnl 2f: swtchd bk lft and effrt on inner but stl plenty to do over 1f out: no real imp fnl f: nvr trbld ldrs* **7/4$^{1}$**

02-6 7 2 **You're Fired (IRE)**$^{49}$ [118] 6-9-0 107........................ DougieCostello 6 96
(K R Burke) *stdd s: hld up in last trio: rdn and effrt over 2f out: struggling 2f out: sn wknd* **50/1**

2152 8 22 **Mythical Madness**$^{10}$ [744] 6-9-0 101........................(p) JamieSpencer 3 52
(David O'Meara) *awkward as stalls opened: awkward and hld up in last trio: rdn over 2f out: no imp: wknd over 1f out: eased ins fnl f* **20/1**

40-6 P **Solar Deity (IRE)**$^{21}$ [574] 8-9-0 100........................(p) StevieDonohoe 4
(Jane Chapple-Hyam) *in tch in midfield tl lost action, p.u and dismntd 8f out: fatally injured* **40/1**

2m 4.68s (-1.92) **Going Correction** -0.05s/f (Stan) **9** Ran SP% **116.4**
Speed ratings (Par 113): **105,104,104,104,104 101,99,82,**
CSF £50.41 TOTE £8.00: £2.00, £2.80, £2.50; EX 53.60 Trifecta £458.40.

**Owner** Robert Ng **Bred** Juddmonte Farms Ltd **Trained** Newmarket, Suffolk

**FOCUS**
In the absence of Mutakayyef, who would have been a warm favourite, this was an ordinary Winter Derby and the first five finished in a bunch. The level is set by the runner-up and fourth.

## 920 32RED MAIDEN AUCTION STKS 5f 6y(P)

**3:50** (3:51) (Class 5) 3-Y-0 **£2,911** (£866; £432; £216) **Stalls** High

Form RPR

1 **Family Fortunes** 3-9-5 0........................................ TomMarquand 3 79+
(Sylvester Kirk) *dwlt and niggled along in 3rd early: clsd to trck ldrs 1/2-way: effrt and rdn to chal over 1f out: led ins fnl f: r.o strly and sn clr: readily* **25/1**

232- 2 3 1/4 **Rag Tatter**$^{133}$ [7355] 3-9-5 75........................................ KevinStott 4 67
(Kevin Ryan) *led: shkn up ent fnl f: little rspnse and sn rdn and hdd ins fnl f: sn outpcd by wnr and one pced* **8/13$^{1}$**

-223 3 shd **Alfonso Manana (IRE)**$^{2}$ [878] 3-9-5 69..............(p) RichardKingscote 2 67
(James Given) *sn pressing ldr on inner: rdn 2f out: stl ev ch tl outpcd by wnr ins fnl f: one pced after* **15/8$^{2}$**

4 3 1/2 **Ivor's Fantasy (IRE)** 3-9-0 0........................................ ShaneKelly 1 49
(David Elsworth) *s.i.s: detached in last: pushed along and sme prog 1/2-way: struggling again over 1f out: wknd ins fnl f* **10/1$^{3}$**

57.87s (-0.93) **Going Correction** -0.05s/f (Stan) **4** Ran SP% **109.6**
Speed ratings (Par 97): **105,99,99,94**
CSF £43.24 TOTE £15.70; EX 40.70 Trifecta £50.00.

**Owner** R Hannon & Sylvester Kirk **Bred** A Parrish & Mrs L Sadler **Trained** Upper Lambourn, Berks

**FOCUS**
A weak sprint maiden, but an impressive enough winner. It's been rated at face value around the third, with the runner-up 10lb off his 2yo 6f form.

## 921 BETWAY BEST ODDS GUARANTEED PLUS H'CAP 1m 4f (P)

**4:25** (4:25) (Class 3) (0-95,91) 4-Y-0- **£7,246** (£2,168; £1,084; £542; £270) **Stalls** Low

Form RPR

3143 1 **Sennockian Star**$^{8}$ [779] 7-9-6 **90**........................................ JoeFanning 6 99
(Mark Johnston) *w ldr tl led 10f out: hdd 9f out: chsd ldr after tl pushed into ld again over 2f out: drvn and pressed 1f out: lft in command ins fnl f: styd on* **3/1$^{2}$**

35-5 2 2 **Blue Surf**$^{35}$ [352] 8-9-7 **91**........................................ JimCrowley 7 98
(Amanda Perrett) *in tch in midfield: effrt to chse wnr 2f out: styd on and chalng 1f out: lost action 100yds out and btn towards fin: dismntd after fin* **9/2$^{3}$**

35-2 3 1 3/4 **Rydan (IRE)**$^{28}$ [467] 6-9-6 **90**........................................(v) GeorgeBaker 5 93
(Gary Moore) *hld up in lat pair: clsd and wl in tch 3f out: effrt to chse ldng pair over 1f out: kpt on same pce ins fnl f* **11/8$^{1}$**

25-2 4 1 1/4 **Lord Napier (IRE)**$^{28}$ [457] 4-8-7 **80**........................(p) DavidProbert 2 81
(John Ryan) *hld up in tch in last pair: clsd 3f out: effrt u.p over 1f out: no imp and kpt on same pce ins fnl f* **20/1**

2-24 5 1 **Masterpaver**$^{11}$ [728] 6-9-5 **89**........................................ TonyHamilton 1 89+
(Richard Fahey) *led for 2f: chsd ldrs after: short of room and shuffled bk to rr jst over 2f out: no threat to ldrs after and one pced fnl f* **13/2**

30-5 6 5 **Fattsota**$^{8}$ [779] 9-9-6 **90**........................................(v$^{1}$) JamieSpencer 3 82
(David O'Meara) *in tch: hdwy to ld 9f out: rdn and hdd over 2f out: racd awkwardly and lost 2nd 2f out: sn lost pl: bhd ins fnl f* **11/1**

456- P **Precision Five**$^{155}$ [1092] 8-8-10 **83**........................ KieranShoemark(3) 4
(Nick Lampard) *in tch in midfield tl dropped to last 7f out: sn lost tch: t.o whn p.u and dismntd over 4f out* **50/1**

2m 29.95s (-3.05) **Going Correction** -0.05s/f (Stan)
**WFA** 4 from 6yo+ 2lb **7** Ran SP% **113.7**
Speed ratings (Par 107): **108,106,105,104,104 100,**
CSF £16.66 TOTE £3.60: £2.00, £2.40; EX 15.50 Trifecta £42.20.

**Owner** Kingsley Park 7 - Ready To Run **Bred** Cheveley Park Stud Ltd **Trained** Middleham Moor, N Yorks

**FOCUS**
Few got into this Class 3 handicap. The winner has been rated to his best form since mid-2015, with the runner-up close to his late-2016 form.

## 922 BETWAY H'CAP 1m 2f (P)
**5:00** (5:02) (Class 5) (0-70,72) 4-Y-0+ **£2,911** (£866; £432; £216) **Stalls** Low

Form RPR

236- **1** **Music Major**[56] 8590 4-9-2 **66** AdamBeschizza 10 74
(Michael Attwater) *stdd s: hld up in tch towards rr: clsd to chse ldrs ent fnl 2f: n.m.r and swtchd lft over 1f out: hrd drvn to ld 100yds out: r.o wl* **14/1**

0-01 **2** *nk* **Etaad (USA)**[35] 351 6-9-4 **67** (b) GeorgeBaker 3 74
(Gary Moore) *led: sn hdd and trckd ldrs after 8f out: rdn to ld again ent fnl f: hdd 100yds out: kpt on u.p but hld towards fin* **9/2**[2]

**3** *1 1/4* **Fire Tree (IRE)**[222] 4466 4-9-6 **70** (t) StevieDonohoe 1 75
(Charlie Fellowes) *wl in tch in midfield: effrt and carried sltly lft over 1f out: swtchd lft and rdn to chse ldrs 1f out: kpt on same pce ins fnl f* **13/8**[1]

640- **4** *nk* **Estibdaad (IRE)**[67] 8462 7-8-12 **61** (t) DannyBrock 11 65
(Paddy Butler) *led after 1f: rdn wl over 2f out: hdd ent fnl f: kpt on same pce u.p ins fnl f* **25/1**

-362 **5** *3/4* **Mercy Me**[9] 769 5-9-9 **72** RyanPowell 7 74+
(John Ryan) *dwlt: hld up in tch in rr: effrt over 1f out: hdwy u.p: kpt on ins fnl f: no threat to ldrs* **8/1**

5341 **6** *1 1/2* **Runaiocht (IRE)**[14] 690 7-8-11 **65** (b) DavidParkes(5) 2 64
(Paul Burgoyne) *taken down early: hld up in tch in midfield: rdn and unable qck over 1f out: one pced ins fnl f* **10/1**

56-5 **7** *3/4* **Tommys Geal**[49] 120 5-8-8 **57** DanielMuscutt 8 55
(Michael Madgwick) *chsd ldrs: effrt ent fnl 2f out: drvn to press ldrs over 1f out: no ex 1f out: wknd ins fnl f* **18/1**

0-00 **8** *3/4* **Solveig's Song**[38] 286 5-9-5 **68** (p) JackMitchell 9 64
(Steve Woodman) *dropped to last pair after 2f: in tch effrt over 1f out: kpt on same pce and no imp ins fnl f* **33/1**

31-0 **9** *1* **Fast And Hot (IRE)**[38] 286 4-9-4 **68** (b) KieranO'Neill 4 62
(Richard Hannon) *dwlt: t.k.h: hld up in tch in midfield: effrt u.p but unable qck ent fnl f: wknd and wnt rt fnl 150yds* **6/1**[3]

234- **10** *6* **Red Cossack (CAN)**[67] 8462 6-9-7 **70** (t) WilliamCarson 6 52
(Paul Webber) *taken down early: t.k.h: chsd ldr 8f out tl lost pl and squeezed for room over 1f out: bhd and eased wl ins fnl f* **12/1**

0-05 **11** *hd* **With Approval (IRE)**[43] 214 5-8-11 **63** CallumShepherd(3) 5 45
(Laura Mongan) *in tch in last quartet: effrt on outer over 2f out: dropped to rr bnd 2f out: no ch after* **22/1**

2m 5.89s (-0.71) **Going Correction** -0.05s/f (Stan) 11 Ran SP% **121.5**
Speed ratings (Par 103): **100,99,98,98,97 96,96,95,94,89 89**
CSF £77.00 CT £162.75 TOTE £15.60: £3.80, £2.20, £1.10; EX 97.10 Trifecta £539.00.
**Owner** The Attwater Partnership & J Daniels **Bred** Kevin Daniel Crabb **Trained** Epsom, Surrey

**FOCUS**
A moderate but competitive handicap. The fourth has been rated close to his winter form, while the runner-up helps set the standard.
T/Plt: £1,218.00 to a £1 stake. Pool: £88,651.82 - 53.13 winning units T/Qpdt: £177.20 to a £1 stake. Pool: £4,719.30 - 19.7 winning units **Steve Payne**

# 899 WOLVERHAMPTON (A.W) (L-H)
Saturday, February 25

**OFFICIAL GOING: Tapeta: standard**
Wind: Light behind turning fresh behind after race 2 Weather: Raining

## 923 BETWAY SPRINT CLASSIFIED (S) STKS 6f 20y (Tp)
**5:45** (5:46) (Class 5) 3-Y-O+ **£3,234** (£962; £481; £240) **Stalls** Low

Form RPR

4045 **1** **Pulsating (IRE)**[7] 813 3-8-4 60 (b) HollieDoyle(5) 4 67
(Daniel Steele) *hld up: hdwy: nt clr run and swtchd rt over 1f out: rdn to ld ins fnl f: r.o wl* **9/2**[2]

0-62 **2** *2* **Invincible Ridge (IRE)**[2] 886 9-9-4 75 JasonHart 9 59
(Eric Alston) *trckd ldrs: shkn up to ld over 1f out: rdn and hdd ins fnl f: styd on same pce* **13/8**[1]

622- **3** *3* **Summerinthecity (IRE)**[350] 919 10-8-13 68 LewisEdmunds(5) 5 49
(Patrick Morris) *hld up: hdwy and nt clr run over 1f out: styd on same pce ins fnl f: wnt 3rd post* **12/1**

0013 **4** *nse* **Elusivity (IRE)**[15] 665 9-9-10 74 (p) PaulMulrennan 1 55
(Conor Dore) *led: rdn: edgd rt and hdd over 1f out: wknd wl ins fnl f* **13/2**[3]

20-0 **5** *2 1/2* **Spice Mill (IRE)**[47] 145 4-9-1 63 (vt[1]) AlistairRawlinson(3) 7 41
(Michael Appleby) *s.i.s: pushed along and hdwy over 4f out: rdn and hung lft fr over 1f out: wknd ins fnl f* **14/1**

0510 **6** *nse* **Masamah (IRE)**[14] 685 11-9-10 71 (h) LukeMorris 3 47
(Ian Williams) *prom: drvn along 1/2-way: wknd ins fnl f* **13/2**[3]

0-00 **7** *1 1/4* **Masarzain (IRE)**[21] 575 4-9-1 72 NathanEvans(3) 6 37
(James Given) *s.i.s: hld up: hdwy u.p over 2f out: wknd fnl f* **10/1**

220- **8** *3 1/2* **Viva Verglas (IRE)**[165] 6451 6-8-13 62 PaddyBradley(5) 2 25
(Daniel Mark Loughnane) *chsd ldr: rdn whn hmpd over 1f out: wknd ins fnl f* **16/1**

6-60 **9** *11* **Allen's Folly**[46] 153 4-8-11 45 KieranSchofield(7) 8
(Peter Hiatt) *hld up: rdn over 3f out: wknd wl over 2f out* **100/1**

1m 13.74s (-0.76) **Going Correction** -0.125s/f (Stan)
**WFA** 3 from 4yo+ 15lb 9 Ran SP% **113.3**
Speed ratings (Par 103): **100,97,93,93,89 89,88,83,68**
CSF £11.91 TOTE £4.90: £1.60, £1.20, £3.00; EX 15.30 Trifecta £150.90.winner was brought in for 5,000 gns
**Owner** D Steele **Bred** Mrs Margaret Sinanan **Trained** Henfield, W Sussex

**FOCUS**
A fair seller. They went a respectable gallop and a previous C&D winner landed a gamble by taking her form to a new level from off the pace with a ready victory. It's been rated cautiously around the winner's better winter form.

## 924 BETWAY H'CAP 1m 4f 51y (Tp)
**6:15** (6:16) (Class 6) (0-60,60) 4-Y-0+ **£2,587** (£770; £384; £192) **Stalls** Low

Form RPR

**1** **Carvelas (IRE)**[15] 675 8-8-12 **56** LewisEdmunds(5) 3 64
(P J F Murphy, Ire) *hld up: hdwy and nt clr run over 1f out: r.o to ld towards fin* **5/2**[1]

534- **2** *3/4* **Forecast**[45] 2397 5-9-5 **58** (t) LiamKeniry 9 64
(Martin Keighley) *racd keenly and wnt 2nd after 1f: shkn up to ld over 2f out: rdn ins fnl f: hdd towards fin* **9/2**[2]

3343 **3** *nse* **Stonecoldsoba**[15] 661 4-9-4 **60** (v[1]) LukeMorris 4 66
(Denis Quinn) *chsd ldrs: rdn and hung lft fr over 1f out: ev ch wl ins fnl f: styd on* **11/2**[3]

0-60 **4** *3/4* **Kilim**[16] 645 4-8-12 **54** (t) FrannyNorton 2 59
(John Berry) *hld up: rdn over 1f out: r.o ins fnl f: nt rch ldrs* **28/1**

0-06 **5** *1 1/4* **Gambol (FR)**[16] 333 7-9-6 **59** (b) GeorgeDowning 6 62
(Ian Williams) *hld up: racd keenly: rdn over 1f out: r.o ins fnl f: nvr nrr* **7/1**

-060 **6** *hd* **Hannington**[5] 841 6-9-2 **58** (vt) AlistairRawlinson(3) 7 60
(Michael Appleby) *chsd ldrs: rdn over 2f out: edgd lft ins fnl f: styd on same pce* **6/1**

000- **7** *1 1/2* **Grams And Ounces**[68] 7628 10-8-9 **55** (t) BenRobinson(7) 1 55
(Grace Harris) *s.i.s: hld up: rdn over 2f out: nt trble ldrs* **40/1**

0326 **8** *nk* **Ali Bin Nayef**[10] 738 5-9-1 **54** PJMcDonald 5 53
(Michael Wigham) *prom: rdn over 3f out: no ex fnl f* **8/1**

6405 **9** *1 1/2* **Einstein**[14] 689 4-8-8 **57** (t) MillyNaseb(7) 8 54
(Mrs Ilka Gansera-Leveque) *led: hdd over 2f out: rdn and ev ch over 1f out: wknd ins fnl f* **9/1**

2m 39.43s (-1.37) **Going Correction** -0.125s/f (Stan)
**WFA** 4 from 5yo+ 2lb 9 Ran SP% **115.9**
Speed ratings (Par 101): **99,98,98,97,97 97,96,95,94**
CSF £13.68 CT £56.25 TOTE £3.30: £1.60, £1.80, £1.30; EX 14.70 Trifecta £78.40.
**Owner** The Last Chance Saloon Partnership **Bred** George Grothier **Trained** Castlecomer, Co Kilkenny

**FOCUS**
A moderate middle-distance handicap. They went a modest gallop. The favourite did well to come through to win from off the pace. The runner-up has been rated as matching his earlier form.

## 925 £10 FREE AT 32RED.COM MAIDEN AUCTION STKS 1m 4f 51y (Tp)
**6:45** (6:45) (Class 5) 3-Y-O **£3,557** (£1,058; £529; £264) **Stalls** Low

Form RPR

2 **1** **Fulham (IRE)**[16] 642 3-9-5 0 TomMarquand 3 77
(Robyn Brisland) *hld up: hdwy 8f out: chsd ldr over 1f out: rdn to ld and hmpd ins fnl f: styd on* **11/8**[1]

5 **2** *1 3/4* **Specialist (IRE)**[9] 758 3-9-5 0 FrannyNorton 1 73
(Mark Johnston) *led over 4f: chsd ldr tl shkn up to ld wl over 1f out: sn hung lft: rdn: hung rt and hdd ins fnl f: styd on same pce: swvd lft towards fin* **2/1**[2]

024 **3** *11* **Crindle Carr (IRE)**[21] 580 3-9-5 67 PhillipMakin 5 56
(David Barron) *in rr and pushed along early: hdwy 8f out: rdn over 3f out: wknd over 1f out: wnt 3rd nr fin* **9/1**

4 **4** *3/4* **Pinnata (IRE)**[16] 642 3-9-2 0 (t) AaronJones(3) 2 54
(Stuart Williams) *plld hrd: trckd ldrs: wnt 2nd 9f out: led over 7f out: rdn and hdd wl over 1f out: wknd fnl f* **7/2**[3]

66 **5** *44* **Touch Of Faith (IRE)**[4] 849 3-9-2 0 AlistairRawlinson(3) 4
(Michael Appleby) *chsd ldr 3f: remained handy tl rdn over 4f out: sn wknd* **100/1**

2m 39.24s (-1.56) **Going Correction** -0.125s/f (Stan) 5 Ran SP% **108.7**
Speed ratings (Par 97): **100,98,91,91,61**
CSF £4.27 TOTE £2.00: £1.10, £1.50; EX 4.10 Trifecta £11.70.
**Owner** Franconson Partners **Bred** C J Foy **Trained** Newmarket, Suffolk

**FOCUS**
A modest 3yo middle-distance maiden. They went a modest gallop and the horse with the best form from limited evidence beforehand readily justified favouritism moving up in trip. The level is a bit fluid, with the third below form up in trip and the fourth too keen.

## 926 32RED.COM H'CAP 5f 21y (Tp)
**7:15** (7:15) (Class 4) (0-85,87) 3-Y-O **£5,175** (£1,540; £769; £384) **Stalls** Low

Form RPR

-212 **1** **Major Jumbo**[15] 657 3-9-2 **82** LewisEdmunds(5) 3 91+
(Kevin Ryan) *plld hrd and prom: shkn up and n.m.r over 1f out: r.o to ld wl ins fnl f: readily* **7/5**[1]

**2** *1 1/4* **Blitz**[113] 7799 3-9-5 **80** AdamKirby 5 84+
(Clive Cox) *led: rdn over 1f out: hdd and unable qck wl ins fnl f* **3/1**[2]

3132 **3** *2 3/4* **Dazacam**[8] 778 3-9-11 **86** RobertWinston 4 80
(Michael Herrington) *hld up: hdwy over 1f out: sn rdn: styd on same pce ins fnl f* **10/1**

0-11 **4** *shd* **Wild Approach (IRE)**[15] 657 3-8-9 **70** LukeMorris 2 64
(Robert Cowell) *plld hrd in 2nd pl to 1/2-way: rdn over 1f out: edgd lft and no ex ins fnl f* **4/1**[3]

14-2 **5** *2* **Monte Cinq (IRE)**[38] 291 3-9-7 **87** CliffordLee(5) 6 74
(Jason Ward) *plld hrd and prom: wnt 2nd 1/2-way: rdn over 1f out: wknd ins fnl f* **15/2**

01-5 **6** *2 1/4* **Ferocity (IRE)**[16] 643 3-9-1 **76** TomMarquand 1 54
(Robyn Brisland) *hld up: rdn and wknd over 1f out* **8/1**

1m 0.66s (-1.24) **Going Correction** -0.125s/f (Stan) 6 Ran SP% **118.6**
Speed ratings (Par 99): **104,102,97,97,94 90**
CSF £6.35 TOTE £2.30: £1.40, £2.50; EX 7.80 Trifecta £38.20.
**Owner** T A Rahman **Bred** D R Botterill **Trained** Hambleton, N Yorks

**FOCUS**
A decent 3yo sprint handicap. They went a proper gallop and a horse who was backed as if defeat was out of the question overcame a troubled passage to win going away. The race has been rated slightly positively.

## 927 32RED CASINO H'CAP 1m 142y (Tp)
**7:45** (7:45) (Class 4) (0-85,82) 3-Y-O **£5,498** (£1,636; £817; £408) **Stalls** Low

Form RPR

3-11 **1** **Poetic Force (IRE)**[25] 498 3-9-3 **78** (t) GeorgeDowning 3 84
(Tony Carroll) *hld up: hdwy over 2f out: shkn up to ld ins fnl f: sn rdn and edgd lft: r.o* **11/4**[2]

0-1 **2** *hd* **Shamrokh (IRE)**[31] 402 3-9-7 **82** (tp) NickyMackay 4 87
(John Gosden) *racd keenly in 2nd tl led over 2f out: rdn over 1f out: hdd ins fnl f: running on whn hmpd nr fin* **11/8**[1]

4411 **3** *7* **Spinwheel**[11] 729 3-9-2 **77** PJMcDonald 2 65
(Mark Johnston) *led: qcknd over 2f out: sn hdd: wknd ins fnl f* **5/1**

1 **4** *1 1/2* **Cyrus Dallin**[28] 466 3-9-4 **79** AdamKirby 1 64
(William Muir) *trckd ldrs: plld hrd: outpcd over 2f out: wknd over 1f out* **10/3**[3]

1m 49.66s (-0.44) **Going Correction** -0.125s/f (Stan) 4 Ran SP% **108.5**
Speed ratings (Par 99): **96,95,89,88**
CSF £6.97 TOTE £2.90; EX 7.80 Trifecta £13.40.
**Owner** W McLuskey & S Barton **Bred** S J Macdonald **Trained** Cropthorne, Worcs
■ Stewards' Enquiry : George Downing caution; careless riding

**FOCUS**
A decent little 3yo handicap. They went a steady gallop, but the right two horses fought out a thrilling battle for supremacy in the straight. The level is a bit fluid.

## 928 SUNBETS.CO.UK H'CAP — 1m 142y (Tp)
8:15 (8:18) (Class 5) (0-70,71) 4-Y-0+ £3,234 (£962; £481; £240) Stalls Low

Form / RPR

-030 **1** **Idol Deputy (FR)**[33] 382 11-9-0 **68**......................(p) RachealKneller(5) 2 — 77
(James Bennett) *chsd ldrs: hmpd over 7f out: led over 1f out: sn hung lft: rdn out* **22/1**

-011 **2** 2 1/4 **Gabrial The Thug (FR)**[14] 684 7-8-12 **61**...............(t) StevieDonohoe 4 — 65
(Ian Williams) *chsd ldrs: hmpd over 7f out: rdn over 2f out: styd on to go 2nd wl ins fnl f* **6/1**[3]

0-42 **3** nk **Glenalmond (IRE)**[23] 517 5-9-7 **70**.................................(p) AdamKirby 6 — 73
(Daniel Steele) *a.p: rdn over 1f out: styd on same pce ins fnl f* **3/1**[1]

2531 **4** 3/4 **What Usain**[7] 806 5-9-2 **68**................................(h) AlistairRawlinson(3) 9 — 69+
(Michael Appleby) *prom: hmpd and lost pl over 7f out: hdwy u.p over 1f out: edgd lft and styd on ins fnl f* **9/2**[2]

-325 **5** 1/2 **Roman De Brut (IRE)**[11] 727 5-9-4 **67**.............................. DaleSwift 8 — 67
(Daniel Mark Loughnane) *pushed along in rr early: hdwy u.p over 1f out: kpt on* **8/1**

-300 **6** 2 3/4 **Hard To Handel**[19] 599 5-9-7 **70**................................... PaddyAspell 12 — 64
(Clare Ellam) *s.i.s: hld up: rdn over 1f out: nvr nrr* **28/1**

-150 **7** 3/4 **Sir Lancelott**[14] 689 5-8-12 **61**..................................(p) PaulMulrennan 5 — 53
(David O'Meara) *chsd ldrs: rdn over 2f out: wknd ins fnl f* **22/1**

4-04 **8** nk **Jumbo Prado (USA)**[16] 641 8-9-4 **67**.........................(b) LukeMorris 10 — 59
(Daniel Mark Loughnane) *led 1f: sn edgd rt and lost pl: rdn whn nt clr run wl over 1f out: n.d after* **12/1**

0-06 **9** 3/4 **All You (IRE)**[33] 382 5-9-7 **70**.........................................(v) PhillipMakin 7 — 60
(David O'Meara) *s.i.s: hld up: sme hdwy over 1f out: wknd ins fnl f* **10/1**

-125 **10** 2 3/4 **Trending (IRE)**[23] 517 8-9-6 **69**.........................(t) RichardKingscote 1 — 52
(Jeremy Gask) *led over 7f out: rdn and hdd over 1f out: wknd ins fnl f* **6/1**[3]

53-0 **11** 2 **Rivers Of Asia**[23] 516 4-9-3 **71**...............................(t) PaddyBradley(5) 3 — 50
(Philip McBride) *sn pushed along and prom: hmpd over 7f out: chsd ldr over 6f out: rdn over 2f out: wknd fnl f* **16/1**

/0-0 **12** 12 **Mazaaher**[14] 688 7-9-4 **70**.......................................... PhilipPrince(3) 11 — 21
(David Evans) *s.i.s: hld up: rdn over 3f out: wknd over 2f out* **50/1**

1m 48.07s (-2.03) **Going Correction** -0.125s/f (Stan) **12** Ran SP% **119.6**
Speed ratings (Par 103): **104,102,101,101,100 98,97,97,96,94 92,81**
CSF £145.63 CT £522.89 TOTE £25.80: £6.50, £2.30, £1.60; EX 227.40 Trifecta £2938.70.
**Owner** Miss J C Blackwell **Bred** Sheikh Sultan Bin Khalifa Al Nayan **Trained** Letcombe Bassett, Oxon

**FOCUS**
A modest handicap. They went a proper gallop and a veteran course-specialist won readily from just off the pace. The winner has been rated to the better view of his winter form.

## 929 SUNBETS.CO.UK DOWNLOAD THE APP H'CAP — 7f 36y (Tp)
8:45 (8:48) (Class 6) (0-65,66) 4-Y-0+ £2,587 (£770; £384; £192) Stalls High

Form / RPR

00-1 **1** **Murdanova (IRE)**[10] 734 4-9-7 **65**..................................... DaleSwift 12 — 74
(Daniel Mark Loughnane) *hld up: hdwy u.p over 1f out: hung lft and r.o to ld wl ins fnl f:* **16/1**

5034 **2** 1 1/4 **Tavener**[9] 768 5-8-5 **56**...............................................(p) FinleyMarsh(7) 2 — 62
(David C Griffiths) *chsd ldr tl led over 2f out: rdn over 1f out: hdd wl ins fnl f* **14/1**

00-3 **3** 3/4 **Captain Bob (IRE)**[25] 501 6-9-8 **66**.......................... AdamBeschizza 3 — 70
(Robert Cowell) *chsd ldrs: wnt 2nd over 1f out: sn rdn: styd on same pce wl ins fnl f* **3/1**[1]

2551 **4** 1/2 **Wink Oliver**[8] 784 5-9-0 **65**......................................(p) LauraCoughlan(7) 8 — 68
(Jo Hughes) *hld up: hdwy over 1f out: edgd lft: styd on* **9/1**

0-30 **5** 1/2 **Top Offer**[10] 745 8-9-0 **63**......................................(p) LewisEdmunds(5) 11 — 65
(Patrick Morris) *hld up: rdn: hung lft and r.o ins fnl f: nt rch ldrs* **14/1**

11-3 **6** hd **Coquine**[46] 161 4-9-7 **65**...........................................(p) AdamKirby 10 — 66
(David O'Meara) *hld up: rdn over 1f out: styd on: nt rch ldrs* **8/1**

-013 **7** 1/2 **Dark Forest**[15] 663 4-9-3 **61**.....................................(p) PaulMulrennan 9 — 61
(Marjorie Fife) *chsd ldrs: rdn over 2f out: no ex ins fnl f* **7/1**[3]

3200 **8** 1/2 **Athletic**[14] 685 8-9-2 **60**...........................................(v) StevieDonohoe 4 — 59
(David Evans) *s.i.s: hdwy over 5f out: rdn over 1f out: no ex ins fnl f* **4/1**[2]

305- **9** 1 **Ducissa**[147] 6960 4-9-5 **63**.........................................(h) RichardKingscote 7 — 60
(Daniel Kubler) *hld up: shkn up over 1f out: nvr on terms* **20/1**

006- **10** nk **Magic Moments**[59] 8559 4-9-1 **59**.................................. LukeMorris 5 — 55
(Alan King) *slowly in to stride: hld up: rdn over 2f out: sme hdwy over 1f out: no ex fnl f* **20/1**

43-0 **11** 3 **Air Of York (IRE)**[16] 641 5-9-6 **64**...........................(p) DanielMuscutt 1 — 53
(John Flint) *led: racd keenly: hdd over 2f out: wknd ins fnl f* **14/1**

11-0 **12** 1 **Dark Confidant (IRE)**[25] 501 4-9-5 **63**......................(b) JackGarritty 6 — 50
(Richard Fahey) *hld up in tch: plld hrd: rdn over 2f out: wknd fnl f* **18/1**

1m 28.09s (-0.71) **Going Correction** -0.125s/f (Stan) **12** Ran SP% **119.3**
Speed ratings (Par 101): **99,97,96,96,95 95,94,94,93,92 89,88**
CSF £223.73 CT £868.17 TOTE £14.00: £3.30, £5.10, £1.80; EX 312.50 Trifecta £3184.80.
**Owner** Phil Slater **Bred** John Lyons **Trained** Rock, Worcs

**FOCUS**
A modest handicap. They went a proper gallop and the winner did well to overcome a poor draw to follow up his recent C&D victory. Straightforward form. A small step up from the winner, with the runner-up fitting.
T/Plt: £36.80 to a £1 stake. Pool: £90,511.88 - 1793.94 winning units T/Qpdt: £21.70 to a £1 stake. Pool: £6,231.27 - 211.84 winning units **Colin Roberts**

# 847 CAGNES-SUR-MER
### Saturday, February 25
**OFFICIAL GOING: Turf: good; polytrack: standard**

## 930a PRIX DU LAUTARET (H'CAP) (4YO+) (POLYTRACK) — 6f 110y
3:15 4-Y-0+ £7,264 (£2,905; £2,179; £1,452; £726)

RPR

**1** **Split Step**[49] 6-8-0 **0**.................................................(b) EddyHardouin 5 — 41
(C Boutin, France) **21/1**

**2** 1/2 **Passior (FR)**[79] 8-9-1 **0**...........................................(b) MaximeGuyon 13 — 55
(D De Waele, France) **41/10**[2]

**3** 1 1/2 **Boltcity (FR)**[49] 10-8-7 **0**...........................................(p) MrHugoBoutin 8 — 43
(M Boutin, France) **11/2**

**4** 1 **Majik Charly (FR)**[13] 713 5-9-6 **0**...............................(b) TheoBachelot 11 — 53
(T Castanheira, France) **19/2**

**5** nk **Prince Gris (FR)**[214] 12-8-5 **0**...................................(b) FabriceVeron 12 — 37
(F Foresi, France) **40/1**

**6** hd **Bernina Range (FR)**[13] 713 5-9-4 **0**................ Pierre-CharlesBoudot 9 — 49
(J-M Lefebvre, France) **21/10**[1]

**7** 1 1/4 **Be On The Bell**[131] 7-8-0 **0**........................................ MlleSarahCallac 14 — 28
(C Biancheri, France) **61/1**

**8** nk **Silver Treasure (FR)**[51] 6-8-13 **0** ow2.............. ChristopheSoumillon 4 — 40
(J-M Capitte, France) **22/5**[3]

**9** 2 **Minminwin (IRE)**[13] 713 4-9-2 **0**..................................(p) KyllanBarbaud(3) 6 — 40
(Gay Kelleway) *hld up in midfield: rdn and no imp fr 2 1/2f out* **85/1**

**10** 1 **Adona (FR)**[13] 713 4-9-6 **0**............................................ ValentinSeguy 7 — 38
(J Parize, France) **41/1**

**11** 1 3/4 **Fuchias De Cerisy (FR)**[134] 4-8-8 **0**.............................(b) DavidBreux 2 — 21
(M Planard, France) **50/1**

**12** 1 1/2 **Tenorio (FR)**[54] 4-8-11 **0**.........................................(p) AurelienLemaitre 10 — 20
(Mlle V Dissaux, France) **162/10**

**13** 1 1/2 **Dobby First (FR)**[13] 713 4-8-13 **0**...............(p) Francois-XavierBertras 1 — 17
(Mlle V Dissaux, France) **31/1**

PARI-MUTUEL (all including 1 euro stake): WIN 22.00 PLACE 4.40, 2.30, 2.70 DF 66.30 SF 216.10.
**Owner** Cedric Boutin **Bred** G B Partnership **Trained** France

931 - (Foreign Racing) - See Raceform Interactive

# 914 DOHA
### Saturday, February 25
**OFFICIAL GOING: Turf: good**

## 932a DUKHAN SPRINT (LOCAL GROUP 3) (3YO+) (TURF) — 6f
11:05 3-Y-0+ £115,853 (£44,715; £22,357; £12,195; £8,130)

RPR

**1** **Izzthatright (IRE)**[23] 5-9-2 0.......................................... HarryBentley 10 — 107
(Jassim Mohammed Ghazali, Qatar)

**2** nk **Black Granite (IRE)**[31] 5-9-2 0.................................(b) FrankieDettori 11 — 106+
(Jassim Mohammed Ghazali, Qatar)

**3** hd **Caspian Prince (IRE)**[9] 773 8-9-2 0................................(t) TomEaves 8 — 105
(Roger Fell) *broke wl and led: set str gallop: drvn wl over 1f out: hdd fnl 125yds: no ex*

**4** 1/2 **Gracious John (IRE)**[21] 572 4-9-2 0...................................... JFEgan 12 — 104
(David Evans) *nudged along to chse ldng quartet: styd on fr over 1f out: nt pce to chal*

**5** 1 1/4 **Risk Adjusted (IRE)**[23] 4-9-2 0.................................. GeraldAvranche 1 — 100+
(Mohammed Hussain, Qatar)

**6** 1/2 **Beach Samba (IRE)**[37] 5-9-2 0.....................................(bt) SaleemGolam 4 — 98
(Ibrahim Al Malki, Qatar)

**7** 1/2 **Lupie (IRE)**[31] 5-9-2 0.................................................(b) RichardMullen 9 — 97
(Mohammed Jassim Ghazali, Qatar)

**8** hd **Medicean Man**[23] 543 11-9-2 0......................................(tp) AdriedeVries 2 — 96
(Jeremy Gask) *w.w in fnl trio: hdwy over 1 1/2f out: styd on ins fnl f: nvr on terms*

**9** 2 **Victory Laurel (IRE)**[23] 7-9-2 0..................................(t) EduardoPedroza 6 — 90
(Ibrahim Al Malki, Qatar)

**10** hd **French Encore**[52] 4-9-2 0............................................... AlanMunro 13 — 89
(Debbie Mountain, Qatar)

**11** 2 1/2 **Malik (FR)**[16] 4-9-2 0..................................................... OlivierPeslier 3 — 81
(A De Mieulle, Qatar)

**12** 1/2 **Qatar Light (IRE)**[23] 5-9-2 0....................................(bt) DarrenWilliams 7 — 79
(Majed Seifeddine, Qatar)

**13** 1 1/2 **Sandbetweenourtoes (IRE)**[23] 8-9-2 0......................(b) J-PGuillambert 5 — 75
(Mubarak Al Khayarin, Qatar)

1m 9.4s **13** Ran

**Owner** Injaaz Stud **Bred** Patrick Cummins **Trained** Qatar

## 933a AL BIDDAH MILE (LOCAL GROUP 2) (3YO) (TURF) — 1m
11:35 3-Y-0 £115,853 (£44,715; £22,357; £12,195; £8,130)

RPR

**1** **Mr Scaramanga**[45] 177 3-9-2 0....................................... AdriedeVries 2 — 97
(Simon Dow) *racd v freely towards rr: plld way to chse ldrs bef 1/2-way: drvn 2f out and styd on to ld appr fnl f: rdn out*

**2** 3/4 **Pazeer (FR)**[23] 3-9-2 0............................................... EduardoPedroza 11 — 95
(Ibrahim Al Malki, Qatar)

**3** hd **Notalot (IRE)**[16] 3-9-2 0............................................. GeraldAvranche 5 — 95
(Tariq Issa, Qatar)

**4** nk **Sea Fox (IRE)**[126] 7544 3-9-2 0............................................... JFEgan 1 — 94
(David Evans) *a cl up: led appr 1/2-way: hrd pressed and drvn 2f out: hdd appr fnl f: kpt on gamely u.p*

**5** 2 1/2 **Perfect Storm (IRE)**[16] 3-9-2 0..................................... SaleemGolam 12 — 88
(Ibrahim Al Malki, Qatar)

**6** nk **Pleaseletmewin (IRE)**[16] 3-9-2 0.................................. HarryBentley 14 — 88
(Jassim Mohammed Ghazali, Qatar)

**7** 1 1/2 **Moi Moi Moi (IRE)**[16] 3-9-2 0.......................................... TomLukasek 4 — 84
(Ibrahim Al Malki, Qatar)

**8** shd **Trouble Of Course (FR)**[59] 8564 3-9-2 0..........(t) Per-AndersGraberg 8 — 84
(Niels Petersen, Norway)

**9** 1/2 **What A Surprise (IRE)**[16] 3-9-2 0.................................. AlbertoSanna 9 — 83
(Ibrahim Al Malki, Qatar)

**10** 1/2 **Catch A Wave (IRE)**[23] 3-9-2 0........................................ AlanMunro 6 — 82
(Debbie Mountain, Qatar)

**11** shd **Ghayyar (IRE)**[129] 7471 3-9-2 0...................................... FrankieDettori 7 — 81
(Richard Hannon) *chsd ldrs: drvn to hold pl 3f out: grad dropped away ins fnl 1 1/2f*

**12** 1 1/2 **Third Order (IRE)**[23] 3-9-2 0............................ PierantonioConvertino 15 — 78
(Jassim Mohammed Ghazali, Qatar)

**13** hd **Incandescent**[23] 3-8-11 0........................................ FalehBughanaim 13 — 73
(H Al Ramzani, Qatar)

**14** 11 **Prince Of Cool**[123] 7600 3-9-2 0...................................... MarvinSuerland 10 — 52
(H Aashoor, Qatar)

1m 34.85s **14** Ran

**Owner** Robert Moss and Christopher Brennan **Bred** Lordship Stud **Trained** Ashtead, Surrey


The Form Book Flat, Raceform Ltd, Newbury, RG14 5SJ

## 934a H.H THE EMIRS TROPHY (LOCAL GROUP 1) (3YO+) (TURF) 1m 4f
1:15 3-Y-O+ £126,666 (£48,888; £24,444; £13,333; £8,888)

RPR
1 Chopin (GER)[22] 7-9-2 0 AlbertoSanna 6 110
(Abdulla Kuwaiti, Bahrain)
2 4 Noor Al Hawa (FR)[58] 8573 4-8-13 0 AdriedeVries 4 104
(A Wohler, Germany)
3 3/4 Fundamental (USA)[30] 5-9-2 0 (b) RichardMullen 1 102
(J Smart, Qatar)
4 hd Vitally Important (IRE)[44] 7-9-2 0 DarrenWilliams 11 102
(Majed Seifeddine, Qatar)
5 1/2 Migwar (IRE)[66] 5-9-2 0 OlivierPeslier 2 101
(A De Mieulle, Qatar)
6 1 1/4 Duke Of Dundee (FR)[23] 5-9-2 0 (b) CristianDemuro 3 99
(A De Mieulle, Qatar)
7 1/2 Mango Tango (FR)[44] 4-8-8 0 EduardoPedroza 5 93
(Ibrahim Al Malki, Qatar)
8 shd Now We Can[132] 7396 8-9-2 0 StephanePasquier 8 98
(N Clement, France)
9 2 The Blue Eye[23] 5-9-2 0 HarryBentley 15 95
(Jassim Mohammed Ghazali, Qatar)
10 shd Arab Spring (IRE)[21] 574 7-9-2 0 FrankieDettori 10 95
(Sir Michael Stoute) *trckd ldrs: rdn along 3 1/2f out: chsd clr ldr over 2f out: wknd qckly 1f out*
11 1/2 Gabrial (IRE)[30] 429 8-9-2 0 PaulHanagan 9 94
(Richard Fahey) *t.k.h: a towards rr*
12 shd Royal Albert Hall[53] 5-9-2 0 (t) AlanGarcia 7 94
(Doug O'Neill, U.S.A)
13 hd Fort Moville (FR)[44] 5-9-2 0 (p) FalehBughanaim 12 94
(Ahmed Kobeissi, Qatar)
14 1/2 Ponfeigh (IRE)[23] 6-9-2 0 (p) AlanMunro 13 93
(Debbie Mountain, Qatar)
15 7 Dubawi Flame[23] 4-8-13 0 GeraldAvranche 16 82
(H Al Ramzani, Qatar)
16 dist Ningara[30] 7-9-2 0 PierantonioConvertino 14
(Mohammed Jassim Ghazali, Qatar)

2m 26.5s
WFA 4 from 5yo+ 2lb 16 Ran

**Owner** Maher Ebrahim Lutfalla **Bred** Gestut Graditz **Trained** Bahrain

**FOCUS**
The form's rated around the third to sixth in line with their recent best.

935 - 952a (Foreign Racing) - See Raceform Interactive

# 915 ST MORITZ (R-H)
Sunday, February 26

**OFFICIAL GOING: Snow: frozen (racing abandoned after race 1 due to unsafe track)**

## 953a GRAND PRIX MOYGLARE STUD (CONDITIONS) (4YO+) (SNOW) 6f 110y
10:00 4-Y-O+
£10,000 (£5,000; £3,571; £2,380; £1,190; £714)

RPR
1 Footprintinthesand (IRE)[7] 834 7-9-2 0 ow2(p) ChristopheSoumillon 3
(M Weiss, Switzerland) 14/5[1]
2 nk Special Season[29] 465 4-9-4 0 FergusSweeney 1
(Jamie Osborne) *disp ld tl hdd and chsd ldr after 2f: 3rd and styng on u.p whn lft 2nd ins fnl f: kpt on wl u.p*
3 3 Filou (SWI)[7] 834 6-9-4 0 RaphaelLingg 6
(P Schaerer, Switzerland)
4 nk Gung Ho Jack[7] 834 8-9-0 0 KierenFox 7
(John Best) *w.w towards rr: 6th and styng on whn slipped and nrly fell ins fnl f: rcvrd and kpt on gamely*
5 4 Uczitelka Tanca (POL)[14] 715 6-9-1 0 BauyrzhanMurzabayev 4
(M Borkowski, Poland)
6 dist Mai O'Higgins (IRE)[37] 342 4-9-1 0 DougieCostello 8
(Tracey Collins, Ire) *towards rr: rn v wd first bnd: nvr able to get in contention*
F Zarras (GER)[7] 834 8-9-6 0 TimBurgin 5
(P Schaerer, Switzerland)
F Holidayend (IRE)[7] 834 5-9-4 0 MilanZatloukal 2
(M Weiss, Switzerland)
F Boomerang Bob (IRE)[17] 639 8-9-11 0 GeorgeBaker 9
(Jamie Osborne) *w.w in rr: drvn and no immediate imp 3f out: began to stay on over 1 1/2f out: disputing 4th and clsng whn fell ins fnl f: fatally injured*

**Owner** Appapays Racing Club **Bred** Moygaddy Stud **Trained** Switzerland

# 923 WOLVERHAMPTON (A.W) (L-H)
Monday, February 27

**OFFICIAL GOING: Tapeta: standard**
Wind: Fresh behind Weather: Showers

## 954 BETWAY MIDDLE DISTANCE H'CAP 1m 1f 104y (Tp)
2:20 (2:21) (Class 6) (0-65,67) 4-Y-O+ £2,264 (£673; £336; £168) Stalls Low

Form RPR
21-0 1 Admirable Art (IRE)[48] 166 7-9-4 62 AdamKirby 1 69
(Tony Carroll) *mde all: qcknd over 2f out: rdn over 1f out: styd on* 16/1
-020 2 1 1/2 Siouxperhero (IRE)[11] 769 8-9-2 60 (p) TomMarquand 10 64
(William Muir) *chsd wnr after 1f: rdn over 2f out: edgd lft ins fnl f: styd on* 33/1
0112 3 3/4 Gabrial The Thug (FR)[2] 928 7-9-3 61 (t) StevieDonohoe 4 64
(Ian Williams) *chsd ldrs: rdn over 2f out: styd on* 3/1[2]
0/32 4 3/4 Pour L'Amour (IRE)[13] 726 4-9-5 63 LukeMorris 2 64
(Daniel Mark Loughnane) *hld up in tch: rdn over 2f out: styd on u.p: nt rch ldrs* 13/2
-525 5 1 1/4 King Oswald (USA)[7] 841 4-9-6 64 GeorgeDowning 7 63
(James Unett) *hld up: hdwy over 1f out: sn rdn and edgd rt: no imp ins fnl f* 11/4[1]
5-06 6 3/4 Shadow Spirit[13] 727 4-9-4 67 LewisEdmunds[(5)] 6 65
(Iain Jardine) *s.i.s: hld up: rdn over 1f out: nvr nrr* 11/2[3]
05-2 7 shd Cat Royale (IRE)[54] 47 4-9-1 66 (p) DarraghKeenan[(7)] 5 63
(John Butler) *sn pushed along to chse ldrs: rdn over 2f out: no ex fnl f* 11/2[3]
52-6 8 3 3/4 May Mist[48] 164 5-9-3 61 GrahamLee 9 51
(Trevor Wall) *hld up: rdn over 2f out: nvr on terms* 22/1
40-5 9 5 Lemon Thyme[16] 677 4-9-2 60 (h) ShaneKelly 8 41
(Mike Murphy) *prom: pushed along 1/2-way: rdn and wknd over 2f out* 18/1

1m 59.91s (-0.89) **Going Correction** -0.125s/f (Stan) 9 Ran SP% 114.2
Speed ratings (Par 101): **98,96,96,95,94 93,93,90,85**
CSF £416.31 CT £2007.16 TOTE £10.80: £3.50, £6.30, £1.60; EX 197.00 Trifecta £874.00.
**Owner** D Morgan **Bred** Longview Stud & Bloodstock Ltd **Trained** Cropthorne, Worcs

**FOCUS**
It proved hard to make up ground, with the 1-2-3 racing 1-2-4 for most of the way. The winner has been rated back to his best, with the second, third and fourth close to their recent levels.

## 955 BETWAY SPRINT DISTANCE H'CAP 5f 21y (Tp)
2:55 (2:55) (Class 5) (0-75,76) 4-Y-O+ £2,911 (£866; £432; £216) Stalls Low

Form RPR
30-4 1 Powerful Dream (IRE)[21] 604 4-8-11 65 (p) OisinMurphy 11 73
(Ronald Harris) *hld up: n.m.r 2f out: hdwy and nt clr run over 1f out: rdn and r.o to ld wl ins fnl f* 8/1
6-14 2 1/2 Bahango (IRE)[31] 443 5-8-13 70 (p) NathanEvans[(3)] 1 76
(Patrick Morris) *edgd rt s: chsd ldrs: rdn to ld over 1f out: edgd rt and hdd wl ins fnl f* 11/2[3]
0-00 3 nse Miracle Garden[4] 886 5-9-6 74 (p) TomEaves 3 82+
(Roy Brotherton) *hld up in tch: racd keenly: nt clr run 2f out: shkn up over 1f out: nt clr run and swtchd rt ins fnl f: r.o wl* 3/1[1]
2254 4 1 1/4 Temple Road (IRE)[4] 886 9-9-0 68 (bt) JoeFanning 10 69
(Milton Bradley) *hld up: nt clr run over 1f out: swtchd rt and r.o ins fnl f: nt rch ldrs* 13/2
006- 5 nk Emjayem[67] 8495 7-9-2 70 (p[1]) AdamKirby 7 70
(John Holt) *led to 1/2-way: rdn over 1f out: hung lft ins fnl f: styd on same pce* 12/1
3223 6 1 1/4 Archie Stevens[4] 886 7-9-0 68 PaddyAspell 5 64
(Clare Ellam) *w ldr tl led 1/2-way: rdn and hdd over 1f out: no ex wl ins fnl f* 13/2
-304 7 2 1/2 Ebony N Ivory[7] 843 4-8-13 70 (b[1]) HollieDoyle[(3)] 9 57
(Archie Watson) *chsd ldrs: rdn 1/2-way: no ex fnl f* 7/2[2]
-666 8 2 3/4 Red Stripes (USA)[32] 416 5-8-13 67 (v) KevinStott 4 44
(Lisa Williamson) *in rr and rdn 1/2-way: nvr on terms* 10/1

1m 0.97s (-0.93) **Going Correction** -0.125s/f (Stan) 8 Ran SP% 117.2
Speed ratings (Par 103): **102,101,101,99,98 96,92,88**
CSF £52.54 CT £164.66 TOTE £10.50: £3.10, £2.10, £1.70; EX 55.40 Trifecta £443.40.
**Owner** Ridge House Stables Ltd **Bred** Ballyhane Stud **Trained** Earlswood, Monmouths
■ Stewards' Enquiry : Nathan Evans jockey ban: two days (13-14 March) - used whip with arm above shoulder height

**FOCUS**
There was a contested pace and this set up for the closers. The winner has been rated back to her best, while the second helps set the standard.

## 956 BETWAY MAIDEN STKS 6f 20y (Tp)
3:25 (3:27) (Class 5) 3-Y-O+ £2,911 (£866; £432; £216) Stalls Low

Form RPR
62-2 1 Poetic Queen (IRE)[21] 600 4-9-8 60 AdamKirby 3 66
(Eric Alston) *chsd ldrs: rdn over 1f out: edgd rt and r.o to ld wl ins fnl f* 5/2[2]
5-6 2 shd Trotter[21] 600 3-8-12 0 OisinMurphy 8 66
(Stuart Kittow) *w ldrs: shkn up over 1f out: rdn and ev ch ins fnl f: edgd lft nr fin: r.o* 18/1
265- 3 1/2 Prazeres[137] 7296 3-8-12 72 JasonHart 4 64
(Les Eyre) *led: rdn and edgd rt over 1f out: hdd wl ins fnl f* 6/1
3 4 1 1/2 Harlequin Storm (IRE)[21] 600 3-8-12 0 RobertWinston 2 60
(Dean Ivory) *hld up in tch: rdn over 1f out: styd on same pce wl ins fnl f* 9/4[1]
6-3 5 hd Jashma (IRE)[9] 819 3-8-12 0 ShaneKelly 9 59
(Richard Hughes) *hld up in tch: racd keenly: shkn up and edgd lft over 2f out: styd on same pce wl ins fnl f* 7/2[3]
6 2 Eddiebet 3-8-9 0 ShelleyBirkett[(3)] 7 53+
(David O'Meara) *s.i.s: hdwy over 1f out: nt trble ldrs* 14/1
6- 7 12 Elemento[287] 2295 3-8-12 0 LukeMorris 5 14
(Phil McEntee) *plld hrd and prom: lost pl 4f out: rdn over 2f out: sn wknd* 50/1
0 8 3/4 Six Of The Best[26] 510 5-9-8 0 TomEaves 6 11
(Ollie Pears) *hld up: wknd over 2f out* 100/1
04 9 3/4 Groundskeeperwilly[10] 785 3-8-12 0 StevieDonohoe 1 9
(David Evans) *in rr: pushed along over 3f out: wknd over 2f out* 66/1

1m 14.16s (-0.34) **Going Correction** -0.125s/f (Stan)
**WFA** 3 from 4yo+ 15lb 9 Ran SP% 112.2
Speed ratings (Par 103): **97,96,96,94,93 91,75,74,73**
CSF £43.43 TOTE £3.50: £1.70, £4.00, £2.30; EX 40.10 Trifecta £211.10.
**Owner** Mr & Mrs G Middlebrook **Bred** Mr & Mrs G Middlebrook **Trained** Longton, Lancs

**FOCUS**
The 1-2-3 raced 3-2-1 for much of the way in this modest sprint maiden. The winner has been rated to form, with the runner-up a big improver.

## 957 BETWAY H'CAP 6f 20y (Tp)
3:55 (3:56) (Class 2) (0-105,95) 4-Y-O£11,971 (£3,583; £1,791; £896; £446) Stalls Low

Form RPR
40-0 1 King Robert[18] 639 4-9-1 89 (v[1]) BenCurtis 10 98
(Bryan Smart) *a.p: rdn and edgd lft over 1f out: r.o to ld nr fin* 14/1
0-30 2 nk Upavon[38] 326 7-8-11 88 (bt) AaronJones[(3)] 4 96
(Stuart Williams) *hld up in tch: rdn to ld and edgd lft wl ins fnl f: hdd nr fin* 12/1
0-14 3 hd Fast Track[9] 818 6-8-13 87 PhillipMakin 7 94
(David Barron) *hld up in tch: rdn over 2f out: r.o* 9/2[1]
000- 4 nk Go Far[198] 5418 7-9-7 95 DavidProbert 5 101
(Alan Bailey) *chsd ldrs: rdn to ld 1f out: hdd wl ins fnl f* 50/1

306- **5** ½ **Ninjago**[129] 7497 7-9-1 **89**....(p) PaulMulrennan 3 94+
(Paul Midgley) *hld up: nt clr run over 1f out: rdn: edgd lft and r.o wl ins fnl f* **11/2**[3]

3-24 **6** *nk* **Russian Soul (IRE)**[13] 730 9-9-6 **94**....(p) AdamKirby 12 98+
(Jamie Osborne) *s.i.s: hld up: rdn over 1f out: r.o ins fnl f: nt clr run towards fin: nt rch ldrs* **5/1**[2]

2044 **7** ½ **Gentlemen**[10] 795 6-9-5 **93**....(b) JosephineGordon 6 95
(Phil McEntee) *hld up: rdn over 2f out: r.o ins fnl f: nvr nrr* **8/1**

6-13 **8** ¾ **Eljaddaaf (IRE)**[18] 639 6-9-2 **90**.... RobertWinston 13 90+
(Dean Ivory) *hld up: shkn up over 1f out: nvr on terms* **8/1**

-235 **9** *nk* **Steelriver (IRE)**[5] 857 7-8-10 **84**.... OisinMurphy 8 83
(David Barron) *s.i.s: hld up: rdn over 1f out: nvr trbld ldrs* **8/1**

6-11 **10** 1 ¼ **Rich Again (IRE)**[31] 443 8-9-0 **88**....(b) PJMcDonald 1 83
(James Bethell) *hld up: hdwy over 1f out: n.m.r and styd on same pce ins fnl f* **14/1**

0-46 **11** *nse* **Bosham**[38] 326 7-9-1 **92**....(bt) NathanEvans[(3)] 2 87
(Michael Easterby) *led: rdn and hdd 1f out: wknd towards fin* **8/1**

123- **12** 3 ½ **Mishaal (IRE)**[178] 6082 7-9-2 **90**.... TomEaves 9 74
(Michael Herrington) *chsd ldr tl rdn over 1f out: wknd ins fnl f* **40/1**

1m 12.7s (-1.80) **Going Correction** -0.125s/f (Stan) **12** Ran SP% **120.1**
Speed ratings (Par 109): **107,106,106,105,105 104,104,103,102,101 101,96**
CSF £173.92 CT £900.66 TOTE £21.70: £5.50, £3.70, £1.80; EX 258.00 Trifecta £2208.20.
**Owner** Ceffyl Racing **Bred** Mrs P A Clark **Trained** Hambleton, N Yorks
■ Stewards' Enquiry : Ben Curtis two-day ban: used whip above the permitted level (Mar 13-14)

**FOCUS**
A decent, competitive sprint handicap. It's been rated around the first two to their C&D December form.

## 958 BETWAY APP H'CAP — 1m 4f 51y (Tp)
**4:25** (4:25) (Class 5) (0-75,75) 4-Y-0+ **£2,911** (£866; £432; £216) **Stalls** Low

Form RPR

-300 **1** **Ravens Quest**[25] 517 4-8-13 **70**.... DannyBrock 3 78
(John Ryan) *led: hdd over 10f out: chsd ldrs: led again over 2f out: rdn out* **13/2**[3]

3-54 **2** 2 ½ **Heart Locket**[16] 688 5-8-7 **68**.... HarrisonShaw[(7)] 2 72
(Michael Easterby) *hld up: hdwy over 3f out: pushed along to chse wnr over 1f out: edgd lft: styd on* **8/1**

2-22 **3** 1 ¾ **Brigadoon**[28] 477 10-9-4 **72**.... RobertWinston 7 73
(Michael Appleby) *mid-div: hdwy over 3f out: rdn over 1f out: styd on same pce ins fnl f* **20/1**

4-00 **4** 2 ½ **The Gay Cavalier**[31] 440 6-9-7 **75**....(t) AdamKirby 8 72
(John Ryan) *hld up: hdwy u.p over 2f out: styd on same pce fnl f* **10/1**

1310 **5** 1 **Fast Play (IRE)**[10] 786 5-9-7 **75**....(b) PaulMulrennan 4 71
(Conor Dore) *hld up: rdn over 1f out: hung lft and styd on ins fnl f: nt trble ldrs* **16/1**

60-0 **6** 2 ¼ **Grand Meister**[46] 196 6-9-5 **73**....(p) JasonHart 6 65
(John Quinn) *hld up: rdn over 2f out: nvr trbld ldrs* **11/1**

-026 **7** *nk* **English Summer**[32] 423 10-9-0 **68**....(tp) StevieDonohoe 5 60
(Ian Williams) *mid-div: hdwy over 3f out: rdn over 1f out: wknd fnl f* **40/1**

0-04 **8** *nk* **Spes Nostra**[14] 719 9-8-13 **72**....(b) LewisEdmunds[(5)] 1 63+
(Iain Jardine) *chsd ldrs: nt clr run and lost pl 4f out: wknd over 1f out* **5/2**[1]

4-24 **9** 3 ¾ **Medicine Hat**[26] 509 6-9-5 **73**....(p) PhillipMakin 11 58
(Marjorie Fife) *sn pushed along and prom: chsd ldr over 10f out: led over 4f out: rdn and hdd over 2f out: wknd over 1f out* **3/1**[2]

4-00 **10** 4 ½ **With Hindsight (IRE)**[17] 666 9-8-10 **64**.... TomEaves 9 42
(Steve Gollings) *hld up: bhd fnl 4f* **80/1**

40-0 **11** 52 **Freud (FR)**[14] 719 7-9-7 **75**....(vt[1]) GeorgeDowning 10
(Ian Williams) *s.i.s and sn pushed along: hdwy to ld over 10f out: rdn and hdd over 4f out: wknd over 3f out* **40/1**

2m 36.73s (-4.07) **Going Correction** -0.125s/f (Stan)
**WFA** 4 from 5yo+ 2lb **11** Ran SP% **112.2**
Speed ratings (Par 103): **108,106,105,103,102 101,101,100,98,95 60**
CSF £52.91 CT £972.97 TOTE £6.60: £2.70, £2.50, £3.70; EX 63.40 Trifecta £843.60.
**Owner** John Stocker **Bred** Deepwood Farm Stud **Trained** Newmarket, Suffolk

**FOCUS**
A modest handicap. The form is set around the second and third.

## 959 32RED.COM MAIDEN STKS — 1m 1f 104y (Tp)
**4:55** (4:56) (Class 5) 3-Y-O **£2,911** (£866; £432; £216) **Stalls** Low

Form RPR

63- **1** **Atkinson Grimshaw (FR)**[154] 6828 3-9-5 0.... OisinMurphy 8 77
(Andrew Balding) *racd keenly in 2nd pl tl led over 1f out: drvn out* **5/4**[1]

4- **2** ¾ **Blushing Red (FR)**[140] 7225 3-9-5 0.... AdamKirby 5 74
(Ed Dunlop) *trckd ldrs: shkn up over 2f out: rdn to chse wnr and hung lft over 1f out: kpt on* **6/4**[2]

254- **3** 5 **Avantgardist (GER)**[79] 8305 3-9-5 72.... JoeFanning 2 63
(Mark Johnston) *led: rdn and hdd over 1f out: no ex ins fnl f* **9/2**[3]

44 **4** 2 **Born To Reason (IRE)**[7] 840 3-9-5 0.... RyanPowell 7 59
(Kevin Frost) *hld up: shkn up over 2f out: sn outpcd* **20/1**

0 **5** ¾ **Swallow Dancer**[12] 737 3-8-7 0.... RhiainIngram[(7)] 6 52
(Harry Dunlop) *hld up: pushed along over 3f out: outpcd fnl 2f* **50/1**

5 **6** 14 **Mount Cleshar**[16] 681 3-9-5 0.... StevieDonohoe 3 28
(John Butler) *sn outpcd* **50/1**

1m 59.37s (-1.43) **Going Correction** -0.125s/f (Stan) **6** Ran SP% **111.3**
Speed ratings (Par 97): **101,100,95,94,93 81**
CSF £3.32 TOTE £2.10: £1.60, £1.30; EX 4.00 Trifecta £5.90.
**Owner** David Brownlow **Bred** Ali Alqama **Trained** Kingsclere, Hants

**FOCUS**
A weak 3yo maiden. The fourth has been rated close to his previous C&D runs.

## 960 32RED CASINO H'CAP — 5f 21y (Tp)
**5:25** (5:26) (Class 6) (0-60,60) 3-Y-O **£2,264** (£673; £336; £168) **Stalls** Low

Form RPR

-400 **1** **Little Nosegay (IRE)**[10] 787 3-8-8 **50**.... PhilipPrince[(3)] 1 56
(David Evans) *hld up: hdwy 1/2-way: rdn over 1f out: hung lft and r.o to ld wl ins fnl f* **8/1**

0034 **2** 1 ¼ **Celerity (IRE)**[10] 787 3-8-12 **51**.... StevieDonohoe 3 52
(David Evans) *chsd ldrs: rdn to ld ins fnl f: sn hdd: styd on same pce* **13/2**[3]

64-2 **3** *nk* **Gnaad (IRE)**[24] 554 3-9-5 **58**....(p[1]) LukeMorris 7 60+
(Robert Cowell) *dwlt: hdwy over 1f out: nt clr run ins fnl f: sn rdn and hung lft: r.o* **7/4**[1]

6-04 **4** ½ **Night Shadow**[13] 731 3-9-7 **60**.... DaleSwift 11 58
(Alan Brown) *hld up: nt clr run: swtchd rt and r.o wl ins fnl f: nt rch ldrs* **10/1**

-020 **5** *nk* **Flying Hope (IRE)**[10] 787 3-8-6 **50**....(v[1]) LewisEdmunds[(5)] 4 47
(Nigel Tinkler) *hld up: plld hrd: hdwy over 1f out: rdn ins fnl f: styd on* **8/1**

6-52 **6** ½ **Glam'Selle**[10] 787 3-8-9 **48**....(p[1]) ShaneKelly 9 44
(Ronald Harris) *chsd ldrs: rdn and ev ch over 1f out: styng on same pce whn hmpd towards fin* **11/2**[2]

-540 **7** *nse* **Vocalisation (IRE)**[26] 511 3-8-2 **46** oh1....(p[1]) CharlieBennett[(5)] 2 41
(John Weymes) *led: rdn over 1f out: hdd ins fnl f: styd on same pce* **14/1**

3-50 **8** 1 ½ **Billy's Boots**[9] 813 3-9-7 **60**.... RobertWinston 6 54
(Dean Ivory) *hld up: hmpd over 3f out: shkn up over 1f out: running on whn nt clr run wl ins fnl f: eased* **8/1**

4-05 **9** 2 ¼ **Sheila's Return**[17] 667 3-9-0 **53**.... AndrewMullen 10 35
(John Balding) *chsd ldrs: rdn: hung rt and wknd over 1f out* **14/1**

00-0 **10** 3 **Elmley Queen**[51] 126 3-8-7 **46** oh1.... TomMarquand 5 17
(Roy Brotherton) *w ldr tl hung rt over 3f out: wknd 2f out* **125/1**

1m 1.9s **Going Correction** -0.125s/f (Stan) **10** Ran SP% **121.6**
Speed ratings (Par 95): **95,93,92,91,91 90,90,87,84,79**
CSF £61.85 CT £137.01 TOTE £9.90: £2.80, £2.30, £1.40; EX 66.20 Trifecta £276.10.
**Owner** David Berry **Bred** Mrs Amanda McCreery **Trained** Pandy, Monmouths

**FOCUS**
Low-grade stuff, but it was eventful enough. The runner-up has been rated to her best.
T/Jkpt: Not won. T/Plt: £325.60 to a £1 stake. Pool: £100,384.28 - 225.01 winning units. T/Qpdt: £42.40 to a £1 stake. Pool: £7,626.07 - 132.83 winning units. **Colin Roberts**

# [916] LINGFIELD (L-H)
### Tuesday, February 28

**OFFICIAL GOING: Polytrack: standard**
Wind: medium to strong, across Weather: overcast, breezy

## 961 BETWAY SPRINT H'CAP — 5f 6y(P)
**2:00** (2:03) (Class 6) (0-65,66) 4-Y-0+ **£2,264** (£673; £336; £168) **Stalls** High

Form RPR

02-4 **1** **Mossgo (IRE)**[24] 573 7-9-8 **66**....(t) KierenFox 5 74
(John Best) *mde all: rdn and drifted rt over 1f out: kpt on wl ins fnl f: rdn out* **3/1**[1]

61-0 **2** 1 **Picansort**[12] 768 10-9-7 **65**....(b) ShaneKelly 3 69
(Peter Crate) *dwlt: hld up in last pair: effrt and hdwy ent fnl f: styd on wl fnl 100yds: wnt 2nd last strides: nvr threatening wnr* **7/2**[2]

30-1 **3** *hd* **Hot Stuff**[25] 554 4-9-0 **58**.... DavidProbert 4 62
(Tony Carroll) *uns rdr on way to post but sn ct: in tch in midfield: effrt over 1f out: kpt on to chse wnr wl ins fnl f: nvr getting to wnr and lost 2nd last strides* **5/1**[3]

-342 **4** *hd* **Pharoh Jake**[10] 815 9-9-0 **58**.... LiamKeniry 8 61
(John Bridger) *hld up in last trio: effrt over 1f out: hdwy u.p 1f out: styd on wl fnl 100yds: nvr threatening wnr* **8/1**

0-21 **5** ½ **Annie Salts**[22] 604 4-9-7 **65**....(h) JoeFanning 9 66
(Chris Dwyer) *taken down early: dwlt: sn rcvrd to chse ldrs: effrt over 1f out: rdn to chse wnr jst ins fnl f: no imp: lost 2nd wl ins fnl f: wknd towards fin* **6/1**

0-06 **6** 1 ¼ **Red Flute**[20] 622 5-8-7 **51** oh3....(v) LukeMorris 10 48
(Denis Quinn) *chsd ldr: rdn wl over 1f out: drvn and unable qck ent fnl f: wknd ins fnl f* **20/1**

0-00 **7** 5 **Desert Strike**[31] 468 11-9-5 **63**....(p) PaulMulrennan 2 42
(Conor Dore) *taken down early: chsd ldrs tl pushed along and lost pl over 1f out: sn wknd and bhd fnl f: fin lame* **6/1**

0-00 **8** 9 **Rubheira**[10] 815 5-8-4 **51** oh6....(h[1]) NoelGarbutt[(3)] 1
(Paul Burgoyne) *taken down early: sn dropped to rr: outpcd 3f out: no ch fnl 2f* **100/1**

58.4s (-0.40) **Going Correction** -0.025s/f (Stan) **8** Ran SP% **109.3**
Speed ratings (Par 101): **102,100,100,99,98 96,88,74**
CSF £12.42 CT £42.09 TOTE £4.10: £1.60, £1.30, £2.00; EX 14.20 Trifecta £63.10.
**Owner** Hucking Horses V **Bred** Louis Robinson **Trained** Oad Street, Kent
■ Powerful Dream was withdrawn. Price at time of withdrawal 12-1. Rule 4 applies to all bets - deduction 5p in the pound.

**FOCUS**
Modest sprinting form, the winner made every yard. The winner has been rated near the best of last year's form.

## 962 32RED CASINO MAIDEN STKS — 7f 1y(P)
**2:30** (2:30) (Class 5) 3-Y-O **£2,911** (£866; £432; £216) **Stalls** Low

Form RPR

5-53 **1** **Traveller (FR)**[12] 758 3-9-5 74....(t) SilvestreDeSousa 2 71
(Charles Hills) *mde all: rdn ent fnl 2f: forged ahd u.p over 1f out: styd on: eased towards fin* **1/3**[1]

4 **2** 2 ¼ **Never Folding (IRE)**[53] 96 3-9-0 0.... RobertWinston 5 58
(Seamus Durack) *wnt rt s: chsd wnr: rdn and pressing wnr ent fnl 2f: unable qck over 1f out: kpt on same pce ins fnl f* **11/4**[2]

**3** 1 ½ **Island Brave (IRE)** 3-9-5 0.... LiamKeniry 1 59
(J S Moore) *chsd ldng pair: pushed along wl over 1f out: kpt on ins fnl f: no threat to wnr* **14/1**[3]

6 **4** 1 ½ **Toolatetodelegate**[15] 717 3-8-11 0.... EdwardGreatrex[(3)] 3 50
(Brian Barr) *rn green and rdn along off the pce in last pair: sme hdwy jst over 1f out: wnt 4th and kpt on ins fnl f: nvr trbld ldrs* **100/1**

0 **5** 5 **Rocksette**[20] 624 3-9-0 0.... ShaneKelly 7 36
(Philip Hide) *dwlt: sn in tch in midfield: rdn and outpcd ent fnl 2f: wknd fnl f* **66/1**

**6** 9 **Taurean Gold** 3-8-12 0.... JaneElliott[(7)] 6 17
(John Bridger) *s.i.s and bustled along early: a off the pce in last pair: lost tch wl over 1f out* **100/1**

1m 25.32s (0.52) **Going Correction** -0.025s/f (Stan) **6** Ran SP% **111.8**
Speed ratings (Par 97): **96,93,91,90,84 74**
CSF £1.54 TOTE £1.20: £1.10, £1.30; EX 1.70 Trifecta £3.20.
**Owner** Isa Salman **Bred** Eric Puerari **Trained** Lambourn, Berks

**FOCUS**
No depth to this maiden and the 74-rated favourite ran out a workmanlike winner. The runner-up has been rated to her debut effort.

## 963 BETWAY BEST ODDS GUARANTEED PLUS H'CAP — 1m 2f (P)
**3:00** (3:00) (Class 3) (0-95,96) 4-Y-O **£7,246** (£2,168; £1,084; £542; £270) **Stalls** Low

Form RPR

621- **1** **Banditry (IRE)**[87] 7608 5-8-12 **86**....(h) StevieDonohoe 4 93
(Ian Williams) *stdd s: hld up in tch in rr: swtchd rt and hdwy to join ldrs 3f out: wnt clr w runner up and sustained duel fr 2f out: forged ahd u.p wl ins fnl f: styd on* **11/4**[2]

-261 **2** ½ **Dutch Uncle**[15] 719 5-8-13 **87** SilvestreDeSousa 5 93
(Ed Dunlop) *chsd ldng pair tl wnt 2nd and t.k.h over 6f out: led wl over 2f out and kicked clr w wnr 2f out: sustained duel after tl hdd and no ex wl ins fnl f* **11/4**[2]

-243 **3** 3¾ **Van Huysen (IRE)**[10] 817 5-8-12 **86** JFEgan 1 85
(Dominic Ffrench Davis) *chsd ldr tl swtchd rt and lost 2nd over 6f out: styd trcking ldrs tl rdn and unable qck over 2f out: one pced and no imp fr over 1f out* **8/1**

153 **4** 1¾ **Coillte Cailin (IRE)**[15] 720 7-9-7 **95** MartinHarley 3 90
(David O'Meara) *stdd s: hld up in tch in 4th: rdn and outpcd jst over 2f out: no imp u.p over 1f out* **6/1**[3]

1431 **5** ½ **Sennockian Star**[3] 921 7-9-8 **96** 6ex JoeFanning 2 90
(Mark Johnston) *led: stdd gallop over 6f out: hdd and rdn wl over 2f out: sn outpcd and dropped to last 2f out: n.d after* **9/4**[1]

2m 4.02s (-2.58) **Going Correction** -0.025s/f (Stan) **5** Ran SP% **109.5**
Speed ratings (Par 107): **109,108,105,104,103**
CSF £10.49 TOTE £3.50: £1.40, £1.70; EX 10.20 Trifecta £42.70.
**Owner** Buxted Partnership **Bred** Darley **Trained** Portway, Worcs

**FOCUS**
A good handicap, two were left to fight it out in the straight and the form looks solid. The pace steadied after 4f. The runner-up has been rated to the best view of his form, with the winner running a small pb.

## 964 BRITISH STALLION STUDS/32RED EBF FILLIES' CONDITIONS STKS 1m 1y(P)
3:30 (3:30) (Class 2) 4-Y-0+ **£16,807** (£5,032; £2,516; £1,258) **Stalls** High

Form RPR

32-1 **1** **Carolinae**[28] 499 5-9-0 88 (h) StevieDonohoe 3 77+
(Charlie Fellowes) *stdd and dropped into last after s: hld up in rr: wnt 2nd and clsd on clr ldr over 2f out: led on bridle over 1f out: nudged out ins fnl f: easily* **1/6**[1]

3-32 **2** 2 **First Experience**[17] 677 6-9-0 76 (p) MartinHarley 5 72+
(Lee Carter) *stdd after s: hld up in 3rd: rdn and clsd on clr ldr over 2f out: wnt 2nd jst over 1f out: swtchd rt and kpt on same pce ins fnl f* **9/2**[2]

6-55 **3** 7 **Andanotherone (IRE)**[5] 883 4-9-0 62 LukeMorris 1 55
(Denis Quinn) *chsd clr ldr: rdn and dropped to last over 2f out: n.d: plugged on into modest 3rd ins fnl f* **40/1**[3]

000 **4** 3½ **Way Up High**[13] 747 5-9-0 42 JoshuaBryan 4 47?
(Steve Flook) *led and sn wl clr: rdn jst over 2f out: hdd over 1f out: sn btn and wknd fnl f* **100/1**

1m 38.32s (0.12) **Going Correction** -0.025s/f (Stan) **4** Ran SP% **107.3**
Speed ratings (Par 96): **98,96,89,85**
CSF £1.25 TOTE £1.10; EX 1.40 Trifecta £1.70.
**Owner** The Dalmunzie Devils Partnership **Bred** Meon Valley Stud **Trained** Newmarket, Suffolk

**FOCUS**
No Miss En Rose, who would have been a very short price favourite, but we ended up with another at long odds on and she won readily. The form has been rated cautiously with the first two below their best in a messy race.

## 965 BETWAY H'CAP 1m 5f (P)
4:00 (4:00) (Class 5) (0-70,71) 4-Y-0+ **£2,911** (£866; £432; £216) **Stalls** Low

Form RPR

/36- **1** **Amanto (GER)**[34] 882 7-9-8 **68** (t) TomMarquand 2 77
(Ali Stronge) *in tch in midfield: effrt to chse ldng pair over 1f out: rdn ins fnl f: styd on wl to ld fnl 50yds: gng away at fin* **40/1**

0-13 **2** 1¼ **Pinwood (IRE)**[20] 616 4-9-7 **71** (t) JFEgan 5 78
(Adam West) *led: rdn and qcknd over 2f out: clr 2f out: drvn 1f out: hdd and no ex 50yds out* **11/4**[2]

06-2 **3** ½ **Light Of Air (FR)**[25] 549 4-9-3 **70** HectorCrouch(3) 1 76
(Gary Moore) *chsd ldrs: effrt to chse ldr 2f out: hanging lft and swtchd rt 1f out: kpt on same pce ins fnl f* **7/1**

2142 **4** 3¼ **Bamako Du Chatelet (FR)**[6] 861 6-9-9 **69** (v) AdamKirby 7 70
(Ian Williams) *hld up in tch in midfield: effrt over 2f out: nt clrest of runs and swtchd lft wl over 1f out: no imp and kpt on same pce after* **9/5**[1]

0414 **5** 1 **Attain**[25] 555 8-9-9 **69** JackMitchell 3 69
(Archie Watson) *bustled along leaving stalls: sn rcvrd and wl in tch in midfield: effrt over 2f out: outpcd u.p and btn over 1f out: wl hld and plugged same pce after* **7/2**[3]

0-41 **6** 5 **Shining Romeo**[31] 461 5-9-2 **62** (v) LukeMorris 8 54
(Denis Quinn) *sn chsng ldr: rdn over 2f out: lost 2nd and struggling 2f out: wknd over 1f out* **9/1**

-60 **7** 3¼ **Dynamo (IRE)**[10] 820 6-8-4 **57** (t) NicolaCurrie(7) 10 44
(Richard Hughes) *t.k.h: hld up in tch in last trio: outpcd and pushed along 3f out: n.d after* **40/1**

01-0 **8** 3 **Munsarim (IRE)**[13] 738 10-8-12 **58** (b) RobHornby 6 41
(Lee Carter) *s.i.s: hld up in tch in last trio: rdn over 2f out: sn struggling: wknd over 1f out* **50/1**

40-5 **9** 45 **Hannah Just Hannah**[31] 457 8-9-0 **67** (t[1]) JordanUys(7) 4
(Matthew Salaman) *t.k.h: hld up in tch in last trio: rdn and struggling over 4f out: t.o fnl 2f* **66/1**

2m 44.42s (-1.58) **Going Correction** -0.025s/f (Stan)
**WFA** 4 from 5yo+ 2lb **9** Ran SP% **115.4**
Speed ratings (Par 103): **103,102,101,99,99 96,94,92,64**
CSF £147.18 CT £897.45 TOTE £40.40: £8.00, £1.20, £2.10; EX 165.20 Trifecta £1130.10.
**Owner** Shaw Racing Partnership 2 **Bred** Gestut Hof Ittlingen **Trained** Eastbury, Berks

**FOCUS**
No great gallop on for this modest handicap and there was a bit of a shock result. The third has been rated to the best view of his form.

## 966 SUNBETS.CO.UK APPRENTICE H'CAP 1m 1y(P)
4:30 (4:31) (Class 6) (0-55,56) 4-Y-0+ **£2,264** (£673; £336; £168) **Stalls** High

Form RPR

5-42 **1** **Hold Firm**[19] 636 5-9-7 **54** GabrieleMalune(5) 8 60
(Mark H Tompkins) *hld up in tch in midfield: effrt in 4th 2f out: rdn and str run ins fnl f to ld 75yds out: hld on wl towards fin* **11/2**[3]

0120 **2** nk **Bookmaker**[13] 734 7-9-11 **56** (p) JaneElliott(3) 11 61
(John Bridger) *stdd after s and hld up in midfield: effrt 2f out: hdwy u.p jst over 1f out: ev ch ins fnl f: kpt on but hld towards fin* **9/2**[2]

-036 **3** 2 **Bold Max**[6] 860 6-9-3 **45** (v) RobHornby 4 45
(Zoe Davison) *stdd after s: hld up in tch in last trio: effrt ent fnl 2f: hdwy towards inner over 1f out: wnt 3rd wl ins fnl f: kpt on* **8/1**

00-3 **4** nk **Betsalottie**[10] 812 4-10-0 **56** MitchGodwin 3 56
(John Bridger) *chsd ldrs: rdn and outpcd jst over 2f out: rallied u.p 1f out: kpt on* **4/1**[1]

00-0 **5** 1¼ **Indus Valley (IRE)**[42] 273 10-9-3 **48** (v) PaddyBradley(3) 5 45
(Lee Carter) *hld up in tch: effrt and swtchd rt wl over 1f out: kpt on u.p ins fnl f* **16/1**

5-04 **6** 1 **No No Cardinal (IRE)**[13] 739 8-8-13 **46** JordanUys(5) 2 40
(Mark Gillard) *chsd ldr: rdn: ev ch and kicked clr w ldr 2f out: no ex jst ins fnl f: wknd qckly fnl 100yds* **12/1**

000- **7** ½ **Locommotion**[77] 8350 5-9-3 **45** (t[1]) CallumShepherd 10 39
(Matthew Salaman) *led: rdn and kicked clr w a rival 2f out: drvn over 1f out: hdd ins fnl f: sn wknd* **16/1**

0U60 **8** 1¼ **Sheer Intensity (IRE)**[17] 690 4-9-4 **53** KeelanBaker(7) 7 43
(David Evans) *sn dropped to rr of main gp: rdn and wd bnd 2f out: hung lft and kpt on same pce ins fnl f* **20/1**

-362 **9** 1¼ **Dukes Meadow**[13] 739 6-9-8 **53** RhiainIngram(3) 1 40
(Roger Ingram) *bustled along leaving stalls: chsd ldrs: hmpd after 1f: hmpd again and dropped to rr 4f out: effrt over 1f out: no imp: wl hld fnl f* **9/2**[2]

-602 **10** 2¼ **Breakheart (IRE)**[6] 854 10-9-1 **50** (b) MichaelColes(7) 6 32
(Andrew Balding) *slowly away stride: a detached in last* **7/1**

1m 38.16s (-0.04) **Going Correction** -0.025s/f (Stan) **10** Ran SP% **119.6**
Speed ratings (Par 101): **99,98,96,96,95 94,93,92,91,88**
CSF £31.35 CT £205.50 TOTE £5.70: £2.10, £2.20, £2.50; EX 33.50 Trifecta £228.50.
**Owner** Raceworld **Bred** Richard W Farleigh **Trained** Newmarket, Suffolk

**FOCUS**
An open race to finish, the front pair sat a little bit off the pace early. It's been rated around the winner to his mark.
T/Jkpt: Part won. £9,320.78 to a £1 stake - 0.5 winning units. T/Plt: £23.90 to a £1 stake. Pool: £89,574.11 - 2,731.84 winning units. T/Qpdt: £15.80 to a £1 stake. Pool: £4,656.61 - 217.45 winning units. **Steve Payne**

# 777 NEWCASTLE (A.W) (L-H)
Wednesday, March 1

**OFFICIAL GOING: Tapeta: standard**
Wind: Light against Weather: Cloudy

## 967 32REDSPORT.COM H'CAP 1m 2f 42y (Tp)
5:30 (5:32) (Class 5) (0-70,70) 3-Y-O **£3,234** (£962; £481; £240) **Stalls** High

Form RPR

02-1 **1** **Daily Trader**[36] 385 3-9-2 **65** AndrewMullen 7 69
(David Evans) *trckd ldrs: hdwy to chse ldr wl over 1f out and sn rdn: swtchd rt and drvn to chal ins fnl f: styd on gamely to ld on line* **10/3**[1]

-312 **2** nse **Good Time Ahead (IRE)**[13] 766 3-9-4 **67** PaddyAspell 9 70
(Philip Kirby) *trckd ldrs: hdwy to chse ldng pair over 2f out and sn cl up: rdn to ld wl over 1f out: drvn ins fnl f: kpt on: hdd on line* **11/2**

0-54 **3** ¾ **Whatelseaboutyou (IRE)**[7] 864 3-8-10 **59** (p[1]) PaulHanagan 3 60
(Richard Fahey) *hld up: hdwy 4f out: pushed along 3f out: rdn to chse ldrs wl over 1f out: drvn to chal and ev ch ins fnl f: kpt on same pce towards fin* **5/1**

0-42 **4** ¾ **Out Of Order (IRE)**[19] 659 3-9-0 **63** (t) JamesSullivan 2 63
(Tim Easterby) *dwlt and rr: hdwy over 3f out: effrt to chse ldrs wl over 1f out: rdn and styd on to chal jst ins fnl f: sn drvn and kpt on same pce* **9/2**[3]

06-1 **5** 1 **Maori Bob (IRE)**[7] 864 3-8-7 **61** LuluStanford(5) 4 59
(Michael Bell) *led: hdd over 7f out: trckd ldrs on inner: swtchd rt and hdwy over 2f out: rdn over 1f out: drvn and kpt on same pce fnl f* **7/2**[2]

0-54 **6** 2¾ **Ladofash**[19] 659 3-8-11 **60** (v) PJMcDonald 5 52
(K R Burke) *in tch: hdwy 3f out: rdn along 2f out: sn drvn and no imp* **14/1**

04-0 **7** 3½ **Our Lois (IRE)**[8] 848 3-8-6 **55** (v[1]) ConnorBeasley 6 40
(Keith Dalgleish) *prom: cl up 1/2-way: rdn along to take slt ld over 2f out: sn drvn and hdd wl over 1f out: sn wknd* **50/1**

0-20 **8** 12 **My Rosie (IRE)**[16] 718 3-9-7 **70** (b) NickyMackay 8 31
(John Gosden) *prom: led over 7f out: pushed along and jnd over 3f out: rdn and hdd over 2f out: sn wknd* **10/1**

034- **9** 4 **Ok By Me (IRE)**[171] 6366 3-9-4 **67** JFEgan 1 20
(David Evans) *a rr* **20/1**

2m 11.82s (1.42) **Going Correction** +0.25s/f (Slow) **9** Ran SP% **118.0**
Speed ratings (Par 98): **104,103,103,102,101 99,96,87,84**
CSF £22.62 CT £91.62 TOTE £4.10: £1.50, £1.90, £2.00; EX 20.70 Trifecta £102.60.
**Owner** Shropshire Wolves **Bred** Cheveley Park Stud Ltd **Trained** Pandy, Monmouths
■ Stewards' Enquiry : Lulu Stanford jockey said gelding was denied a cler run
Connor Beasley jockey said filly hung left in closing stages
Andrew Mullen four-day ban (15-18 Mar): used whip above permitted level

**FOCUS**
A modest 3yo handicap. They went a muddling gallop on standard Tapeta, but the winner proved his stamina for the 2f longer trip by narrowly following up his 1m Southwell victory in January. The winner has been rated in line with his Southwell win, and the runner-up close to his early best.

## 968 SUNBETS.CO.UK H'CAP 1m 5y (Tp)
6:00 (6:01) (Class 5) (0-70,71) 4-Y-0+ **£3,234** (£962; £481; £240) **Stalls** Centre

Form RPR

0-00 **1** **Kiwi Bay**[22] 611 12-8-6 **62** CallumRodriguez(7) 9 69
(Michael Dods) *set stdy pce: shkn up and qcknd jst over 2f out: rdn ins fnl f: kpt on wl* **25/1**

60-6 **2** ¾ **Foie Gras**[20] 641 7-9-1 **64** (p) SilvestreDeSousa 12 69
(Chris Dwyer) *hld up in rr: hdwy 2f out: chsd ldrs over 1f out: rdn and styd on wl fnl f* **15/2**

-363 **3** ¾ **Jubilee Brig**[28] 513 7-9-7 **70** JoeFanning 8 73
(Alan Swinbank) *t.k.h early: trckd ldrs: hdwy to chse wnr 2f out: rdn over 1f out: drvn and kpt on same pce fnl f* **12/1**

0-06 **4** shd **Cabal**[15] 729 10-9-2 **65** (v) SamJames 5 68
(Geoffrey Harker) *hld up in rr: hdwy over 2f out: chsd ldrs ent fnl f: sn rdn and kpt on* **50/1**

22-1 **5** 1¾ **Table Manners**[25] 579 5-8-6 **58** HollieDoyle(3) 4 57
(Wilf Storey) *trckd wnr: pushed along over 2f out: rdn wl over 1f out: kpt on same pce fnl f* **13/2**[3]

6-60 **6** 1¼ **Green Howard**[39] 363 9-9-6 **69** DanielTudhope 10 65
(Rebecca Bastiman) *trckd ldrs: smooth hdwy over 2f out: rdn and ev ch over 1f out: wknd fnl f* **8/1**

465- **7** nk **Archipeligo**[269] 2811 6-9-8 **71** DavidNolan 2 66
(Iain Jardine) *trckd ldrs: pushed along over 2f out: rdn wl over 1f out: sn drvn and kpt on same pce* **11/1**

2-10 **8** ½ **Pickett's Charge**[12] 782 4-9-8 **71** ConnorBeasley 3 65
(Richard Guest) *hld up: hdwy on inner 1/2-way: chsd ldrs 2f out: rdn along wl over 1f out: sn drvn and one pce* **4/1**[1]

0-31 **9** 1 1/2 **Chiswick Bey (IRE)**[19] 655 9-9-6 **69**........................ PaulHanagan 11 60
(Richard Fahey) *trckd ldrs: pushed along over 3f out: rdn wl over 2f out: sn wknd* **9/2**[2]

00-0 **10** 3/4 **Pacommand**[41] 314 4-9-2 **65**........................ PhillipMakin 7 54
(David Barron) *midfield: pushed along wl over 2f out: sn rdn and n.d* **18/1**

140- **11** 4 **Yulong Xiongba (IRE)**[138] 7334 5-9-3 **66**........................(h) JoeDoyle 13 46
(Julie Camacho) *racd wd: in tch on outer: rdn along 3f out: sn wknd* **7/1**

1m 42.65s (4.05) **Going Correction** +0.25s/f (Slow) **11** Ran SP% **114.0**
Speed ratings (Par 103): **89,88,87,87,85 84,84,83,82,81 77**
CSF £196.26 CT £2370.12 TOTE £25.10: £6.20, £2.50, £3.30; EX 174.10 Trifecta £3838.70.
**Owner** Kiwi Racing **Bred** Templeton Stud **Trained** Denton, Co Durham

**FOCUS**
A modest handicap. They went a sedate gallop until about 2f out where the leader kicked on and stole the race under a canny front-running ride. Muddling form. The runner-up has been rated close to his best.

## 969 SUNBETS ON THE APP STORE H'CAP 7f 14y (Tp)
**6:30** (6:30) (Class 6) (0-60,61) 4-Y-0+ **£2,587** (£770; £384; £192) **Stalls** Centre

Form RPR

000- **1** **Symbolic Star (IRE)**[61] 8589 5-8-4 **50**................(p[1]) ConnorMurtagh(7) 5 59
(Barry Murtagh) *hld up towards rr: hdwy over 2f out: chsd ldrs over 1f out: rdn to chal ins fnl f: kpt on wl to ld towards fin* **25/1**

6022 **2** 1/2 **Justice Pleasing**[25] 579 4-8-12 **58**................(p) BenSanderson(7) 6 65
(Roger Fell) *trckd ldr: led 4f out: rdn wl over 1f out: drvn ins fnl f: hdd and no ex towards fin* **11/2**[3]

42R3 **3** 1 3/4 **Prince Of Time**[8] 852 5-8-9 **48**........................ PJMcDonald 3 51
(Richard Ford) *hld up in midfield: hdwy 2f out: chsd ldr jst ins fnl f: sn no imp* **8/1**

4-00 **4** 1 3/4 **Jessie Allan (IRE)**[25] 579 6-8-7 **46** oh1........................ SamJames 10 45
(Jim Goldie) *in tch: hdwy on outer 3f out: chse ldrs wl over 1f out: sn rdn and kpt on same pce* **66/1**

-656 **5** nk **Cool Strutter (IRE)**[25] 579 5-8-12 **56**................(p[1]) GemmaTutty(5) 8 54
(Karen Tutty) *hld up: hdwy 2f out: rdn over 1f out: kpt on fnl f: nrst fin* **12/1**

2000 **6** 1 **Athletic**[4] 929 8-9-7 **60**........................ JFEgan 9 55
(David Evans) *trckd ldrs: hdwy wl over 2f out: effrt to chse wnr wl over 1f out and sn rdn: drvn and wknd ent fnl f* **10/3**[1]

6-05 **7** 1 **Never Say (IRE)**[22] 607 4-8-7 **46** oh1........................ LukeMorris 14 39
(Jason Ward) *hld up: hdwy on outer 2f out: sn rdn and n.d* **22/1**

0-03 **8** 1/2 **Sandstream**[33] 445 4-8-7 **46**........................(t) BenCurtis 13 38
(Tracy Waggott) *hld up towards rr: sme hdwy 2f out: sn rdn and n.d* **5/1**[2]

-063 **9** 3 3/4 **Satchville Flyer**[30] 481 6-9-5 **58**........................ AndrewMullen 4 40
(David Evans) *t.k.h: chsd ldng pair: pushed along over 2f out: sn rdn and wknd* **7/1**

410- **10** 2 **Adventureman**[261] 3220 5-9-8 **61**........................ JamesSullivan 1 39
(Ruth Carr) *prom: pushed along over 2f out: sn rdn and wknd wl over 1f out* **18/1**

00-0 **11** 2 1/4 **El Tel**[16] 724 5-9-0 **58**........................ CharlieBennett(5) 11 30
(Shaun Harris) *chsd ldrs: rdn along over 2f out: sn wknd* **33/1**

06-0 **12** 1 1/4 **Nelson's Bay**[56] 44 8-8-10 **52**........................ HollieDoyle(3) 7 21
(Wilf Storey) *chsd ldrs: rdn along wl over 2f out: sn wknd* **11/1**

4-60 **13** 1 3/4 **Psychology**[25] 580 4-9-7 **60**........................ DougieCostello 2 24
(Kenny Johnson) *dwlt: a rr* **33/1**

1m 28.01s (1.81) **Going Correction** +0.25s/f (Slow) **13** Ran SP% **115.6**
Speed ratings (Par 101): **99,98,96,94,94 92,91,91,86,84 82,80,78**
CSF £147.03 CT £1219.41 TOTE £29.70: £8.30, £2.40, £3.00; EX 208.20 Trifecta £2312.30.
**Owner** Murtagh, O'Rourke & Trinders **Bred** Darley **Trained** Low Braithwaite, Cumbria

**FOCUS**
A moderate handicap. They went a respectable gallop and it produced a shock winner off a small break at 25-1, but the close second is a reliable yardstick. The third helps set the level.

## 970 32RED.COM MAIDEN STKS 1m 5y (Tp)
**7:00** (7:04) (Class 5) 3-Y-O **£3,234** (£962; £481; £240) **Stalls** Centre

Form RPR

**1** **Harlow** 3-9-5 0........................(h[1]) JosephineGordon 3 82+
(Hugo Palmer) *dwlt: sn trcking ldrs: hdwy to chse ldng pair over 1f out: rdn to ld ent fnl f: kpt on strly* **9/2**[3]

4 **2** 5 **Trenchard (USA)**[19] 662 3-9-5 0........................ NickyMackay 4 67
(John Gosden) *cl up: led 5f out: pushed along over 2f out: rdn and hung bdly lft jst over 1f out: hdd and drvn ent fnl f: kpt on same pce* **3/1**[2]

50- **3** nk **Cray (IRE)**[96] 8088 3-9-5 0........................ PJMcDonald 8 66
(James Bethell) *hld up towards rr: hdwy over 2f out: rdn over 1f out: styd on wl fnl f* **16/1**

23 **4** hd **Spiritofhayton (IRE)**[12] 777 3-9-5 0........................ PhillipMakin 5 65
(David Barron) *hld up: hdwy 2f out: rdn over 1f out: kpt on fnl f* **9/2**[3]

**5** 1 1/2 **Temir Kazyk** 3-9-5 0........................ TomEaves 7 62
(David Simcock) *dwlt and rr: hdwy wl over 1f out: styd on fnl f: nrst fin* **20/1**

33- **6** nk **Armandihan (IRE)**[138] 7329 3-9-5 0........................ KevinStott 1 61
(Kevin Ryan) *slt ld 3f: cl up: chal over 2f out: rdn and ev ch whn carried lft jst over 1f out: n.m.r and swtchd rt jst ins fnl f: one pce* **5/4**[1]

0-5 **7** 1/2 **Stretewise (IRE)**[19] 658 3-9-0 0........................ ShaneGray 2 55
(Jason Ward) *chsd ldrs: rdn along 3f out: sn wknd* **66/1**

5 **8** 4 **Coral Princess (IRE)**[12] 777 3-9-0 0........................ ConnorBeasley 6 45
(Keith Dalgleish) *chsd ldrs: rdn along 3f out: sn wknd* **50/1**

0-06 **9** 1/2 **Elements Legacy**[49] 178 3-9-5 50........................(h[1]) DaleSwift 9 49
(Tracy Waggott) *trckd ldng pair: pushed along over 3f out: sn rdn and wknd over 2f out* **28/1**

1m 42.83s (4.23) **Going Correction** +0.25s/f (Slow) **9** Ran SP% **123.4**
Speed ratings (Par 98): **88,83,82,82,81 80,80,76,75**
CSF £19.29 TOTE £6.30: £1.80, £1.40, £3.80; EX 28.20 Trifecta £185.10.
**Owner** C I Racing/Newsells Park Stud **Bred** Newsells Park Stud **Trained** Newmarket, Suffolk

**FOCUS**
A fair 3yo maiden. They went a respectable gallop, at best, but a well-touted newcomer ran out a decisive winner. It's been rated around the second and third.

## 971 BETWAY H'CAP 6f (Tp)
**7:30** (7:33) (Class 5) (0-75,77) 4-Y-O+ **£3,234** (£962; £481; £240) **Stalls** Centre

Form RPR

03-4 **1** **Foolaad**[39] 361 6-8-10 **64**........................(t) JFEgan 2 75+
(Roy Bowring) *prom: cl up 1/2-way: led over 2f out: rdn appr fnl f: kpt on wl* **15/2**[3]

30-3 **2** 1 3/4 **Art Obsession (IRE)**[28] 514 6-9-7 **75**........................ PaulMulrennan 4 80
(Paul Midgley) *trckd ldrs: hdwy to chse wnr over 1f out and sn rdn: drvn and kpt on same pce fnl f* **10/1**

000- **3** nk **Meshardal (GER)**[158] 6769 7-8-13 **67**........................ JamesSullivan 9 71+
(Ruth Carr) *hld up: swtchd rt towards stands rail over 2f out: hdwy wl over 1f out: rdn ent fnl f: kpt on same pce* **18/1**

10-0 **4** hd **Tadaawol**[9] 843 4-9-2 **70**........................(p) PJMcDonald 7 73+
(Roger Fell) *towards rr: hdwy wl over 1f out: sn rdn and styd on strly fnl f* **14/1**

03-1 **5** 1 1/4 **Slingsby**[19] 660 6-9-3 **74**........................(p) NathanEvans(3) 6 73
(Michael Easterby) *prom: cl up 1/2-way: rdn along wl over 1f out: sn drvn and kpt on same pce* **4/1**[2]

4200 **6** 1 1/4 **Ticks The Boxes (IRE)**[8] 850 5-9-6 **77**..........(b[1]) JordanVaughan(3) 12 72
(Michael Herrington) *racd wd towards stands rail: t.k.h: cl up: led after 2f: pushed along and hdd over 2f out: sn rdn and grad wknd fr over 1f out* **28/1**

3-52 **7** 1/2 **Berlios (IRE)**[9] 843 4-9-4 **72**........................ PhillipMakin 10 66
(David Barron) *hld up towards rr: hdwy 2f out: rdn over 1f out: drvn and no imp fnl f* **10/3**[1]

-115 **8** 1 3/4 **Big Amigo (IRE)**[30] 480 4-8-9 **68**........................(p) CliffordLee(5) 1 56
(Daniel Mark Loughnane) *hld up effrt and sme hdwy on outer 1/2-way: sn rdn along and n.d* **22/1**

-415 **9** 1 3/4 **Burtonwood**[15] 732 5-8-4 **65**........................ KieranSchofield(7) 3 48
(Julie Camacho) *dwlt: sn chsng ldrs: rdn along 2f out: sn wknd* **11/1**

054- **10** 2 **The Hooded Claw (IRE)**[107] 7959 6-9-3 **71**........................ JasonHart 5 47
(Tim Easterby) *led 2f: prom: rdn along wl over 2f out: sn drvn and wknd* **8/1**

510- **11** 6 **Be Bold**[117] 7797 5-9-1 **69**........................ TomEaves 8 26
(Rebecca Bastiman) *a towards rr* **80/1**

-063 **12** 1 3/4 **Ballesteros**[18] 682 8-9-9 **77**........................ PaulHanagan 11 28
(Richard Fahey) *chsd ldrs: rdn along over 2f out: sn wknd* **18/1**

1-04 **13** 2 **Mr Morse**[28] 514 4-8-9 **63**........................(p[1]) BenCurtis 13 8
(Brian Ellison) *a towards rr* **16/1**

1m 12.5s **Going Correction** +0.25s/f (Slow) **13** Ran SP% **115.5**
Speed ratings (Par 103): **110,107,107,107,105 103,103,100,98,95 87,85,82**
CSF £76.28 CT £1342.73 TOTE £8.60: £2.60, £3.70, £5.20; EX 75.70 Trifecta £1074.30.
**Owner** K Nicholls **Bred** Darley **Trained** Edwinstowe, Notts

**FOCUS**
A fair handicap. They went a proper gallop and the winner justified sustained each-way support back in trip. Sound form rated around the winner to something like his early form, and the runner-up to his C&D form.

## 972 32RED CASINO H'CAP 5f (Tp)
**8:00** (8:00) (Class 5) (0-75,77) 3-Y-O **£3,881** (£1,155; £577; £288) **Stalls** Centre

Form RPR

0-31 **1** **Fiery Spice (IRE)**[34] 415 3-8-10 **62**........................ LukeMorris 2 67
(Robert Cowell) *dwlt: sn cl up: chal over 2f out: rdn to ld over 1f out: drvn and edgd lft ins fnl f: kpt on wl towards fin* **4/1**[3]

-334 **2** 3/4 **Arzaak (IRE)**[13] 765 3-9-7 **73**........................(p[1]) SilvestreDeSousa 1 75
(Chris Dwyer) *cl up: effrt 2f out: sn rdn: drvn to chal ins fnl f: kpt on same pce towards fin* **13/8**[1]

0-41 **3** 1 3/4 **Lady Cristal (IRE)**[22] 612 3-9-2 **68**........................(p[1]) BenCurtis 3 64
(K R Burke) *slt ld: rdn along 2f out: hdd and drvn over 1f out: kpt on same pce* **4/1**[3]

51- **4** 2 1/2 **El Hombre**[144] 7142 3-9-11 **77**........................ ConnorBeasley 4 64
(Keith Dalgleish) *chsd ldrs: rdn along 2f out: drvn and ch on outer over 1f out: wknd fnl f* **15/8**[2]

1m 0.17s (0.67) **Going Correction** +0.25s/f (Slow) **4** Ran SP% **112.9**
Speed ratings (Par 98): **104,102,100,96**
CSF £11.28 TOTE £5.50; EX 7.30 Trifecta £23.20.
**Owner** Khalifa Dasmal **Bred** K A Dasmal **Trained** Six Mile Bottom, Cambs

**FOCUS**
The feature contest was a fair little 3yo sprint handicap. They went a decent gallop and an unexposed horse at the right end of the handicap delivered a game victory. The runner-up has been rated to form.
T/Jkpt: Not won. T/Plt: £1,670.70 to a £1 winning stake. Pool: £121,025.93 - 52.88 winning units T/Qpdt: £114.70 to a £1 winning stake. Pool: £12,156.01 - 78.40 winning units **Joe Rowntree**

973 - 980a (Foreign Racing) - See Raceform Interactive

874
# CHELMSFORD (A.W) (L-H)
Thursday, March 2

**OFFICIAL GOING: Polytrack: standard**
Wind: light, across Weather: dry

## 981 TOTEPLACEPOT RACING'S FAVOURITE BET H'CAP (DIV I) 6f (P)
**5:20** (5:24) (Class 6) (0-52,54) 4-Y-O+ **£3,234** (£962; £481; £240) **Stalls** Centre

Form RPR

5-35 **1** **Dream Ally (IRE)**[6] 901 7-9-6 **51**........................(be) LukeMorris 2 57
(John Weymes) *in tch in midfield: effrt over 1f out: rdn to chal 1f out: led 100yds out: styd on wl* **9/4**[1]

6243 **2** 1 1/2 **Justice Rock**[22] 622 4-9-2 **47**........................ JosephineGordon 9 49
(Phil McEntee) *taken down early: w ldr: rdn ent fnl 2f: chsd wnr and kpt on same pce fnl 75yds* **12/1**

-006 **3** 1 **Virile (IRE)**[24] 601 6-9-4 **54**........................(b) MitchGodwin(5) 6 53
(Sylvester Kirk) *dwlt and rdn along leaving stalls: in tch in midfield on outer: effrt u.p over 1f out: kpt on ins fnl f: wnt 3rd last strides* **7/2**[2]

0050 **4** hd **Silver Springs (IRE)**[8] 860 4-9-5 **53**........................ PhilipPrince(3) 8 52
(David Evans) *led: rdn ent fnl 2f: drvn over 1f out: hdd 100yds out and rdr mistk winning post and stood up: pushed along and one pce fnl 75yds: lost 3rd last strides* **8/1**[3]

4-00 **5** 1 1/4 **Louis Vee (IRE)**[30] 495 9-8-10 **46** oh1................(p) PatrickO'Donnell(5) 7 40
(John O'Shea) *chsd ldrs: rdn 2f out: unable qck over 1f out: hld and kpt on same pce ins fnl f* **14/1**

0-60 **6** 1 **Irvine Lady (IRE)**[17] 722 4-9-2 **52**................(p[1]) CliffordLee(5) 3 43
(Gay Kelleway) *dwlt: t.k.h: hld up in tch in last pair: effrt u.p over 1f out: no imp* **8/1**[3]

00-0 **7** 1 1/2 **Emerald Bay**[28] 523 4-9-3 **48**........................(p) RobertWinston 4 35
(Ronald Thompson) *trckd ldrs: effrt and unable qck over 1f out: wknd ins fnl f* **33/1**

-000 **8** 1 3/4 **Insolenceofoffice (IRE)**[15] 743 9-9-4 **49**................(p) PaddyAspell 5 30
(Richard Ford) *hld up in last pair: effrt over 1f out: no imp* **25/1**

5-30 **P** **Wedgewood Estates**[24] 601 6-9-7 **52**........................ GeorgeDowning 1
(Tony Carroll) *in tch in midfield tl lost pl qckly and p.u 4f out: (dismntd): hit by horse shoe* **7/2**[2]

1m 12.66s (-1.04) **Going Correction** -0.15s/f (Stan) **9** Ran SP% **118.6**
Speed ratings (Par 101): **100,98,96,96,94 93,91,89,**
CSF £32.57 CT £95.55 TOTE £3.40: £1.50, £2.20, £1.70; EX 13.20 Trifecta £101.80.
**Owner** High Moor Racing 4 **Bred** Noel & Roger O'Callaghan **Trained** Middleham Moor, N Yorks


The Form Book Flat, Raceform Ltd, Newbury, RG14 5SJ

■ Stewards' Enquiry : Philip Prince ten day ban: (16-18,20-25,27 March) - guilty of failing to ride out on a horse

**FOCUS**
A low-grade sprint handicap. The runner-up has been rated near his recent best.

## 982 TOTEPLACEPOT RACING'S FAVOURITE BET H'CAP (DIV II) 6f (P)
**5:55** (5:55) (Class 6) (0-52,54) 4-Y-0+ **£3,234** (£962; £481; £240) **Stalls** Centre

Form RPR

-212 **1** **Krazy Paving**[21] 640 5-9-8 **53**........(b) AdamKirby 9 60
(Anabel K Murphy) *trckd ldrs: nudged and effrt wl over 1f out: drvn and ev ch ent fnl f: led ins fnl f: edgd sltly lft but styd on wl fnl 100yds* **7/2**[2]

0001 **2** ½ **Mighty Zip (USA)**[7] 874 5-9-0 **52**........(p) JordanUys[(7)] 7 58
(Lisa Williamson) *led: rdn over 1f out: hdd ins fnl f: kpt on same pce towards fin* **8/1**

60-2 **3** 1 **Home Again**[14] 761 4-9-7 **52**........ MartinHarley 1 55
(Lee Carter) *trckd ldrs: swtchd rt and clsd wl over 1f out: sn ev ch and rdn: no ex and hld whn sltly squeezed for room wl ins fnl f* **9/4**[1]

-006 **4** 1 ¼ **Tasaaboq**[21] 640 6-9-3 **48**........(t) JosephineGordon 2 47
(Phil McEntee) *hld up in tch in midfield: nt clr run over 2f out: swtchd rt and effrt to chse ldrs whn nt clrest of runs 1f out: edgd lft and one pced ins fnl f* **6/1**[3]

1650 **5** 1 **Multi Quest**[9] 852 5-9-9 **54**........(b) RyanPowell 8 50
(John E Long) *in tch in midfield on outer: effrt over 1f out: no imp and kpt on same pce ins fnl f* **20/1**

005- **6** 3 ¾ **Zebedee's Girl (IRE)**[135] 7444 4-9-2 **47**........ JFEgan 4 32
(David Evans) *in tch: rdn over 2f out: lost pl over 1f out: wl hld fnl f* **8/1**

50-4 **7** 1 **Blistering Dancer (IRE)**[15] 742 7-9-1 **46** oh1........ WilliamCarson 3 28
(Tony Carroll) *t.k.h: w ldr: rdn over 1f out: no ex ent fnl f: wknd ins fnl f* **10/1**

0603 **8** 1 ½ **National Service (USA)**[6] 899 6-9-2 **47**........(tp) PaddyAspell 6 24
(Richard Ford) *v.s.a: grad rcvrd and clsd onto bk of field over 3f out: rdn over 1f out: sn btn* **7/1**

/6-0 **9** ½ **Bella's Boy (IRE)**[14] 761 4-9-5 **50**........(p[1]) DannyBrock 5 26
(John Ryan) *in tch in rr of main gp: rdn over 2f out: sn struggling and lost pl over 1f out: bhd fnl f* **50/1**

1m 12.4s (-1.30) **Going Correction** -0.15s/f (Stan) 9 Ran SP% **117.8**
Speed ratings (Par 101): **102,101,100,98,97 92,90,88,88**
CSF £32.37 CT £76.85 TOTE £4.20: £2.70, £2.60, £1.20; EX 23.40 Trifecta £73.80.
**Owner** All The Kings Horses & Aiden Murphy **Bred** Trebles Holford Farm Thoroughbreds **Trained** Wilmcote, Warwicks

**FOCUS**
The quicker of the two divisions by 0.26sec. The second and third have been rated close to their recent form.

## 983 TOTEPOOL RACECOURSE DEBIT CARD BETTING AVAILABLE MAIDEN FILLIES' STKS 6f (P)
**6:25** (6:26) (Class 5) 3-Y-0+ **£5,175** (£1,540; £769; £384) **Stalls** Centre

Form RPR

434- **1** **Atalante**[211] 5009 4-10-0 66........(h) RyanMoore 5 72
(Jeremy Noseda) *t.k.h: chsd ldr: pushed along to ld ent fnl f: rdn clr ins fnl f: easily* **8/11**[1]

50/5 **2** 4 **Lily Ash (IRE)**[15] 735 4-10-0 60........ ShaneKelly 1 59
(Mike Murphy) *led: rdn 2f out: hdd ent fnl f: outpcd and no ch w wnr fnl f: battled on u.p to hold 2nd* **8/1**[3]

40 **3** nse **Scealtara (IRE)**[27] 554 3-8-11 0........ ShelleyBirkett[(3)] 4 55
(David O'Meara) *broke wl: sn stdd to trck ldng pair: effrt on inner over 1f out: no ch w wnr but battling for 2nd fnl f: kpt on* **25/1**

6- **4** 2 ¼ **Huddersfilly Town**[118] 7792 3-9-0 0........ LemosdeSouza 3 48
(Ivan Furtado) *dwlt: rn green: in tch in rr: rdn and unable qck over 1f out: wl hld and kpt on same pce ins fnl f* **10/1**

**5** ½ **From A Distance (IRE)** 3-9-0 0........ MartinHarley 2 46
(David Simcock) *dwlt: in tch in 4th: effrt and rn green over 1f out: wl hld and kpt on same pce ins fnl f* **2/1**[2]

1m 12.83s (-0.87) **Going Correction** -0.15s/f (Stan)
**WFA** 3 from 4yo 14lb 5 Ran SP% **115.3**
Speed ratings (Par 100): **99,93,93,90,89**
CSF £8.08 TOTE £1.60: £1.10, £3.50; EX 6.00 Trifecta £33.30.
**Owner** M Swinburn & Exors Late Walter Swinburn **Bred** Rockwell Bloodstock **Trained** Newmarket, Suffolk

**FOCUS**
A weak fillies' maiden. The winner has been rated to form.

## 984 TOTEQUADPOT INSURE YOUR PLACEPOT LAST FOUR H'CAP 7f (P)
**6:55** (6:55) (Class 5) (0-75,77) 4-Y-0+ **£5,175** (£1,540; £769; £384) **Stalls** Low

Form RPR

00-0 **1** **Welliesinthewater (IRE)**[14] 760 7-9-7 **75**........(v) MartinLane 8 84+
(Derek Shaw) *dwlt: hld up in rr of main gp: rdn 2f out: clsng and swtchd rt over 1f out: nt clr run and bdly hmpd jst ins fnl f: sn swtchd lft and r.o strly fnl 100yds to ld towards fin* **10/1**

460- **2** ½ **Intensical (IRE)**[85] 8251 6-9-7 **75**........(p) DavidNolan 1 81
(Ivan Furtado) *trckd ldrs: effrt on inner over 1f out: drvn to ld ins fnl f: kpt on tl hdd and no ex towards fin* **10/1**

0-02 **3** ½ **Rockley Point**[26] 575 4-9-4 **77**........(p) CliffordLee[(5)] 6 82
(Paul D'Arcy) *trckd ldrs: effrt over 1f out: drvn and pressing ldrs 1f out: kpt on towards fin: nvr quite getting to ldrs* **4/1**[2]

43-0 **4** ½ **Noble Act**[51] 161 4-8-13 **67**........ JosephineGordon 3 70
(Phil McEntee) *chsd ldr: rdn to ld over 1f out: hdd and no ex u.p ins fnl f: kpt on same pce fnl 100yds* **33/1**

00-1 **5** 1 **Tripartite (IRE)**[19] 685 4-9-6 **74**........ LukeMorris 11 75+
(Jeremy Gask) *hld up in tch towards rr: shkn up and effrt over 1f out: hdwy ins fnl f: styd on wl fnl 100yds: nvr trbld ldrs* **9/2**[3]

-516 **6** shd **Bring On A Spinner**[20] 664 4-9-6 **77**........(be) AaronJones[(3)] 9 77
(Stuart Williams) *sn led: rdn over 1f out: hdd and hung lft ins fnl f: wknd wl ins fnl f* **5/1**

16-6 **7** ¾ **False Id**[40] 355 4-9-0 **68**........ WilliamCarson 2 66
(Robert Eddery) *hld up in tch in midfield: effrt and edgd rt jst over 1f out: kpt on same pce u.p ins fnl f* **14/1**

-432 **8** 2 ¾ **Magic City (IRE)**[19] 685 8-9-2 **73**........(b[1]) NathanEvans[(3)] 7 64
(Michael Easterby) *taken down early: t.k.h: sn chsng ldrs: rdn ent fnl f: sn struggling to qckn and lost pl over 1f out: wknd ins fnl f* **11/4**[1]

00- **9** 3 **The Happy Hammer (IRE)**[140] 7310 11-8-5 **64**........ LuluStanford[(5)] 10 47
(Eugene Stanford) *s.i.s: sn detached in last: sme prog over 3f out: rdn over 1f out: sn btn and wknd fnl f* **25/1**

04-4 **10** 3 ¼ **Clement (IRE)**[19] 685 7-9-5 **73**........ FergusSweeney 4 47
(John O'Shea) *in tch in midfield on outer: rdn 3f out: lost pl over 1f out: bhd and wknd fnl f* **14/1**

1m 25.07s (-2.13) **Going Correction** -0.15s/f (Stan) 10 Ran SP% **119.8**
Speed ratings (Par 103): **106,105,104,104,103 103,102,99,95,91**
CSF £108.37 CT £487.21 TOTE £11.80: £3.20, £3.30, £2.10; EX 138.70 Trifecta £953.20.
**Owner** Shawthing Racing Partnership **Bred** Brendan Ryan **Trained** Sproxton, Leics

**FOCUS**
They went a decent enough gallop here. The winner was value for a bit further.

## 985 TOTEPOOLLIVEINFO.COM VISIT FOR RACING RESULTS CONDITIONS STKS (AW CHAMPIONSHIP FAST-TRACK QUAL.) 2m (P)
**7:25** (7:28) (Class 2) 4-Y-0+ **£12,938** (£3,850; £1,924; £962) **Stalls** Low

Form RPR

1-31 **1** **Watersmeet**[14] 767 6-9-3 104........ JoeFanning 1 105+
(Mark Johnston) *led for 1f: trckd ldrs after: swtchd rt 3f out: sn chsng ldr: rdn to ld and hung lft over 1f out: rdn clr and r.o strly ins fnl f: eased towards fin: comf* **5/2**[2]

361- **2** 3 **Winning Story**[71] 8479 4-8-12 104........ OisinMurphy 5 101+
(Saeed bin Suroor) *t.k.h: w ldr tl led over 3f out: rdn ent fnl 2f: hdd over 1f out: sn pushed lft: hmpd and swtchd rt 1f out: no ch w wnr and kpt on same pce after: eased towards f* **6/4**[1]

1/0- **3** 2 ¼ **Pique Sous (FR)**[13] 797 10-9-3 96........(t) RyanMoore 2 98
(W P Mullins, Ire) *hld up in tch in 5th: rdn over 3f out: chsd clr ldng pair wl over 1f out: kpt on ins fnl f: nvr threatened ldrs* **9/2**

-541 **4** hd **Retrieve (AUS)**[7] 884 9-9-3 100........(t) AdamKirby 4 97
(Jamie Osborne) *stdd s: hld up in tch in rr: rdn over 3f out: wnt 4th over 1f out: battling for 3rd and kpt on u.p ins fnl f: nvr threatened ldrs* **16/1**

61-5 **5** 11 **Calvinist**[15] 746 4-8-12 90........(t) DavidProbert 3 84
(Archie Watson) *led after 1f: rdn and qcknd 4f out: struggling whn lost 2nd over 2f out: 5th and wknd over 1f out* **7/2**[3]

630- **6** 7 **Pearl Castle (IRE)**[293] 2222 7-9-3 94........ CliffordLee 6 76
(K R Burke) *hld up in tch: rdn over 3f out: sn struggling and outpcd over 2f out: bhd over 1f out* **50/1**

3m 25.55s (-4.45) **Going Correction** -0.15s/f (Stan)
**WFA** 4 from 6yo+ 3lb 6 Ran SP% **116.8**
Speed ratings (Par 109): **105,103,102,102,96 93**
CSF £7.06 TOTE £3.40: £1.50, £1.50; EX 6.80 Trifecta £25.40.
**Owner** J Barson **Bred** Stetchworth & Middle Park Studs **Trained** Middleham Moor, N Yorks

**FOCUS**
A decent race and a comfortable victory for the winner, who got the longer trip well. The 1-2 were the form pair.

## 986 @TOTEPOOLRACING FOR RACING NEWS H'CAP 1m (P)
**7:55** (7:57) (Class 5) (0-70,70) 4-Y-0+ **£5,175** (£1,540; £769; £384) **Stalls** Low

Form RPR

1-22 **1** **Kenstone (FR)**[21] 641 4-9-3 **69**........(p) HollieDoyle[(3)] 3 78
(Adrian Wintle) *restless in stalls: hld up in tch: clsd to press ldrs and travelling strly 2f out: rdn to ld jst over 1f out: asserted ins fnl f: r.o wl* **7/2**[2]

6-41 **2** ¾ **Tee It Up Tommo (IRE)**[12] 811 8-9-5 **68**........ StevieDonohoe 7 75
(Daniel Steele) *stdd and dropped in bhd after s: swtchd rt and effrt over 1f out: hdwy 1f out: styd on u.p to chse wnr wl ins fnl f: kpt on* **7/1**[3]

12-1 **3** 1 ¼ **Saleh (IRE)**[55] 90 4-9-7 **70**........ AdamKirby 8 74
(Lee Carter) *hld up in tch in last trio: effrt over 1f out: rdn and kpt on ins fnl f: wnt 3rd cl home: no threat to wnr* **2/1**[1]

4- **4** nk **World Of Good**[34] 448 4-9-5 **68**........(b) JosephineGordon 1 71
(Anabel K Murphy) *trckd ldng trio: effrt on inner to chal over 1f out: sn drvn: no ex and btn ins fnl f: lost 2 pls wl ins fnl f* **8/1**

4-05 **5** 2 ¾ **Gracious George (IRE)**[12] 812 7-9-4 **67**........ KieranO'Neill 2 64
(Jimmy Fox) *in tch in midfield: rdn over 3f out: nt clr run 2f out: effrt on inner over 1f out: styd on same pce u.p ins fnl f* **7/1**[3]

3-0 **6** hd **Wahiba (GER)**[50] 169 4-9-0 **63**........ DanielMuscutt 5 60
(Marco Botti) *t.k.h: led: rdn and hdd over 1f out: wnadered u.p 1f out: sn wknd* **10/1**

-446 **7** 2 **Mime Dance**[15] 745 6-9-5 **68**........(p) DannyBrock 4 60
(John Butler) *hld up in tch in last pair: nt clr run and swtchd rt over 1f out: no imp 1f out: wl hld and kpt on same pce ins fnl f* **25/1**

02-6 **8** 4 ½ **Gatillo**[60] 6 4-9-7 **70**........ AdamBeschizza 9 52
(Julia Feilden) *pressed ldrs tl rdn and lost pl over 1f out: sn btn and wknd over 1f out* **18/1**

4-50 **9** 12 **Tifl**[16] 727 4-9-3 **66**........ OisinMurphy 10 20
(Heather Main) *pressed ldr tl wl over 1f out: sn lost pl: bhd and eased ins fnl f* **16/1**

1m 37.69s (-2.21) **Going Correction** -0.15s/f (Stan) 9 Ran SP% **115.7**
Speed ratings (Par 103): **105,104,103,102,99 99,97,93,81**
CSF £28.34 CT £61.32 TOTE £5.20: £1.50, £2.10, £1.40; EX 31.70 Trifecta £83.50.
**Owner** Glyn Byard **Bred** Guy Pariente Holding Sprl **Trained** Westbury-On-Severn, Gloucs

**FOCUS**
An ordinary handicap, but the first two are bang in form and it rates a fair race for the grade. The winner contunues to progress.

## 987 COLLECT TOTEPOOL WINNINGS AT BETFRED SHOPS H'CAP 1m (P)
**8:25** (8:28) (Class 6) (0-60,62) 3-Y-0 **£3,234** (£962; £481; £240) **Stalls** Low

Form RPR

0-22 **1** **Delfie Lane**[6] 895 3-9-3 **62**........(p[1]) FinleyMarsh[(7)] 8 69
(Richard Hughes) *trckd ldr for 2f: styd trcking ldrs: swtchd rt and effrt over 1f out: rdn to ld and hung lft ins fnl f: sn in command and r.o wl: comf* **9/4**[1]

3-36 **2** 2 ½ **No Not Again (IRE)**[34] 434 3-9-10 **62**........ TomMarquand 5 63
(Richard Hannon) *led: rdn over 1f out: hdd ins fnl f: no ex and outpcd by wnr fnl 100yds* **9/2**[2]

-266 **3** ¾ **Hazell Berry (IRE)**[9] 848 3-8-8 **46**........(b) JFEgan 1 46
(David Evans) *hld up in tch in midfield: effrt and switching rt over 1f out: kpt on same pce ins fnl f: snatched 3rd last strides* **8/1**

**4** nk **Lady Morel (IRE)**[130] 7560 3-9-7 **59**........ OisinMurphy 3 58
(Joseph Tuite) *chsd ldrs: wnt 2nd 6f out: rdn and ev ch over 1f out: no ex jst ins fnl f: wknd towards fin and lost 3rd last strides* **6/1**[3]

05-3 **5** 1 ¾ **Whatalove**[7] 875 3-8-0 **45**........ RhiainIngram[(7)] 2 40
(Martin Keighley) *dwlt and bustled along in midfield: sn hmpd and t.k.h in midfield: switching rt and effrt bnd 2f out: kpt on ins fnl f wout threatening ldrs* **9/4**[1]

-360 **6** 1 ½ **Bartholomew J (IRE)**[6] 897 3-8-5 **46**........(p[1]) SimonPearce[(3)] 4 37
(Lydia Pearce) *s.i.s: hld up in last pair: effrt on inner over 1f out: styd on same pce ins fnl f* **16/1**

4-00 **7** *5* **Vrika Bay**[29] 502 3-9-3 **55**........(p[1]) WilliamCarson 10 35
(Robert Eddery) *dwlt: sn rcvrd to chse ldrs: rdn in 4th ent fnl 2f: no ex u.p over 1f out: wknd 1f out and hung lft ins fnl f* **28/1**

00-5 **8** *hd* **Sallee**[27] 546 3-8-4 **45**........ HollieDoyle(3) 6 24
(Adrian Wintle) *t.k.h: hld up in tch: dropped to last pair 4f out: nt clr run and swtchd lft wl over 1f out: sn rdn and btn: wknd* **33/1**

00-0 **9** *5* **Demi's Quest**[38] 377 3-8-7 **45**........(p[1]) GeorgeDowning 7 13
(Tony Carroll) *t.k.h: hld up in last pair: rdn over 1f out: sn wknd* **50/1**

1m 39.61s (-0.29) **Going Correction** -0.15s/f (Stan) **9** Ran SP% **119.3**
Speed ratings (Par 96): **95,92,91,91,89 88,83,83,78**
CSF £13.12 CT £70.68 TOTE £3.30: £1.20, £1.80, £2.40; EX 12.90 Trifecta £60.00.
**Owner** Richard Hughes **Bred** Catridge Farm Stud **Trained** Upper Lambourn, Berks
■ Stewards' Enquiry : Finley Marsh jockey ban: one day (breach of rules), two days (17-18 March) - guily of careless riding

**FOCUS**
A moderate contest but the comfortable winner looks capable of going in again. The second and third set a very limited standard.

## 988 UB40 HERE ON 12TH AUGUST H'CAP 1m 5f 66y(P)
**8:55** (8:55) (Class 6) (0-52,52) 4-Y-0+ **£3,234** (£962; £481; £240) **Stalls** Low

Form RPR

2-00 **1** **Par Three (IRE)**[21] 646 6-9-4 **49**........(p) AdamKirby 7 54
(Tony Carroll) *s.i.s and rousted along early: hld up in last trio: swtchd rt and effrt 2f out: hdwy u.p 1f out: styd on wl to ld towards fin* **4/1**[1]

5560 **2** *¾* **Cold Fusion (IRE)**[24] 605 4-9-1 **52**........ HollieDoyle(3) 6 56
(David Flood) *led for 2f: mostly chsd ldr after: rdn and ev ch over 1f out: led and veered rt ins fnl f: kpt on tl hdd and no ex towards fin* **8/1**

54-4 **3** *1* **Topalova**[14] 762 4-8-7 **48**........ GabrieleMalune(7) 2 51
(Mark H Tompkins) *hld up in tch in midfield: swtchd rt and hdwy on outer 4f out: rdn and ev ch 2f out tl no ex and one pced ins fnl f* **5/1**[2]

/0-0 **4** *1* **Soundbyte**[12] 820 12-8-9 **47**........(v) RhiainIngram(7) 10 48
(John Gallagher) *hld up in last quartet: rdn 3f out: hdwy and switching lft jst over 1f out: squeezed for room ins fnl f: styd on wl fnl 100yds: nt rch ldrs* **16/1**

/0-0 **5** *½* **Byron Blue (IRE)**[25] 395 8-8-8 **46** oh1........(t) JoshuaBryan(7) 13 47
(Brian Barr) *hdwy on outer to ld after 2f: rdn 2f out: kpt on u.p tl hdd ins fnl f: no ex and one pced fnl 150yds* **25/1**

0-05 **6** *1½* **Color Force (IRE)**[15] 733 4-9-0 **48**........(t) LukeMorris 3 46
(Gay Kelleway) *hld up in tch in midfield: nt clrest of runs over 2f out: edging lft and sme hdwy u.p over 1f out: kpt on same pce ins fnl f* **6/1**[3]

6/30 **7** *nk* **Flying Author (IRE)**[7] 880 6-9-2 **47**........(tp) JosephineGordon 4 45
(Phil McEntee) *t.k.h: chsd ldrs: rdn and unable qck over 1f out: wknd ins fnl f* **12/1**

0050 **8** *1¼* **Palindrome (USA)**[19] 689 4-9-4 **52**........(p) StevieDonohoe 11 48
(Ronald Thompson) *t.k.h: hld up in toouch in midfield: swtchd rt over 3f out: drvn and unable qck over 1f out: wknd ins fnl f* **16/1**

00-3 **9** *1¼* **Vedani (IRE)**[29] 508 8-9-6 **51**........ GeorgeDowning 5 45
(Tony Carroll) *chsd ldrs: rdn over 3f out: and unable qck and btn over 1f out: wknd ins fnl f* **5/1**[2]

040- **10** *2½* **Pension Madness (IRE)**[19] 7767 4-8-13 **52**......(v[1]) RachealKneller(5) 12 43
(Mark Usher) *hld up in tch towards rr: rdn 3f out: no imp over 1f out: nvr trbld ldrs* **16/1**

60/0 **11** *1¼* **Fire In Babylon (IRE)**[15] 741 9-9-3 **48**........(b) AdamBeschizza 1 42
(Giles Bravery) *in tch in midfield: clsd to chse ldrs and rdn ent fnl 2f: unable qck over 1f out: keeping on same pce and hld whn squeezed for room and hmpd ins fnl f: eased after* **25/1**

-044 **12** *2* **Dalavand (IRE)**[21] 646 4-8-11 **52**........ OllieJago(7) 14 38
(Laura Mongan) *stdd and dropped in bhd after s: t.k.h: hld up in rr: effrt and swtchd rt over 1f out: no prog: n.d* **10/1**

00 **13** *11* **Cornelius (FR)**[33] 462 5-8-9 **47**........ JordanUys(7) 9 18
(Jonathan Geake) *t.k.h: hld up in midfield on outer: dropped to rr and u.p 3f out: bhd over 1f out* **33/1**

0-00 **14** *42* **Sayedaati Saadati (IRE)**[44] 278 4-9-2 **50**........(t) RobertWinston 8
(John Butler) *t.k.h: chsd ldrs tl lost pl over 3f out: bhd and eased over 1f out: t.o* **14/1**

2m 51.12s (-2.48) **Going Correction** -0.15s/f (Stan)
**WFA** 4 from 5yo+ 1lb **14** Ran SP% **130.5**
Speed ratings (Par 101): **101,100,99,99,99 98,97,97,96,94 94,92,86,60**
CSF £38.56 CT £173.97 TOTE £5.90: £2.00, £3.30, £2.60; EX 47.20 Trifecta £361.90.
**Owner** Property Players Partnership **Bred** Mrs Vanessa Hutch **Trained** Cropthorne, Worcs
■ Stewards' Enquiry : Joshua Bryan jockey ban: two days (16-17 March) - used whip above the permitted level

**FOCUS**
A moderate handicap in which they got racing plenty soon enough. The winner has been rated as finding only a fraction on his recent best.
T/Plt: £11.10 to a £1 stake. Pool: £80,177.32 - 5,260.86 winning units T/Qpdt: £5.60 to a £1 stake. Pool: £9,669.41 - 1,270.04 winning units **Steve Payne**

# 967 NEWCASTLE (A.W) (L-H)
Thursday, March 2

**OFFICIAL GOING: Tapeta: standard**
Wind: Fresh against Weather: Fine

## 989 SUNBETS.CO.UK H'CAP 7f 14y (Tp)
**2:10** (2:12) (Class 4) (0-85,86) 4-Y-0+ **£7,762** (£2,310; £1,154; £577) **Stalls** Centre

Form RPR

-204 **1** **War Department (IRE)**[26] 581 4-9-6 **82**........(v) ConnorBeasley 8 94+
(Keith Dalgleish) *a.p: chsd ldr over 2f out: led over 1f out: rdn clr fnl f: eased nr fin* **7/2**[1]

-110 **2** *1¼* **Safe Voyage (IRE)**[26] 581 4-9-7 **83**........ JasonHart 7 88
(John Quinn) *chsd ldrs: rdn over 2f out: wnt 2nd ins fnl f: kpt on* **5/1**[3]

40-0 **3** *1* **Bouclier (IRE)**[55] 94 7-8-13 **78**........ AlistairRawlinson(3) 6 80
(Michael Appleby) *hld up: r.o ins fnl f: wnt 3rd nr fin: nt rch ldrs* **10/1**

5-10 **4** *hd* **Dutch Art Dealer**[44] 275 6-9-10 **86**........(v) SilvestreDeSousa 4 88
(Ivan Furtado) *s.i.s: hld up: hdwy u.p over 1f out: styd on same pce ins fnl f* **4/1**[2]

50-0 **5** *1½* **Shamaheart (IRE)**[26] 581 7-9-2 **78**........(p) SamJames 5 76
(Geoffrey Harker) *s.i.s: hld up: rdn over 1f out: r.o ins fnl f: nvr trbld ldrs* **25/1**

3-16 **6** *1¾* **Free Code (IRE)**[16] 730 6-9-6 **82**........ PhillipMakin 1 75
(David Barron) *led 1f: chsd ldr tl rdn over 2f out: styd on same pce fr over 1f out* **4/1**[2]

0-60 **7** *½* **Equally Fast**[19] 685 5-8-13 **75**........ LiamKeniry 9 67
(Peter Hiatt) *w ldr tl led 6f out: rdn and hdd over 1f out: wknd ins fnl f* **16/1**

4604 **8** *3½* **Merdon Castle (IRE)**[13] 783 5-8-11 **73**........(e) JamesSullivan 2 55
(Ruth Carr) *prom: lost pl over 5f out: rdn over 2f out: wknd over 1f out* **8/1**

00-0 **9** *3¼* **Newstead Abbey**[13] 783 7-9-3 **79**........ TomEaves 3 52
(Michael Herrington) *hld up in tch: rdn and wknd over 1f out* **25/1**

1m 28.64s (2.44) **Going Correction** +0.375s/f (Slow) **9** Ran SP% **112.7**
Speed ratings (Par 105): **101,99,98,98,96 94,93,89,86**
CSF £20.49 CT £155.33 TOTE £4.40: £1.40, £2.00, £2.50; EX 25.60 Trifecta £296.40.
**Owner** Weldspec Glasgow Limited **Bred** Tom McDonald **Trained** Carluke, S Lanarks
■ Stewards' Enquiry : Sam James jockey fine: £140 - failure to report at scales

**FOCUS**
A decent handicap. They went a respectable gallop on standard Tapeta and there is a headwind in the straight. The form has been rated close to face value around the runner-up.

## 990 BETWAY STAYERS H'CAP 2m 56y (Tp)
**2:40** (2:41) (Class 6) (0-65,67) 4-Y-0+ **£3,234** (£962; £481; £240) **Stalls** Low

Form RPR

035- **1** **Stoneham**[25] 7251 6-9-9 **67**........(h) LewisEdmunds(5) 6 76
(Iain Jardine) *hld up: hdwy over 2f out: rdn to ld 1f out: styd on* **11/2**[3]

0-41 **2** *nk* **Royal Flag**[36] 399 7-9-11 **64**........ TomEaves 8 72
(Brian Ellison) *hld up: racd keenly: hdwy over 7f out: rdn over 2f out: ev ch fr over 1f out: styd on* **3/1**[2]

-021 **3** *2¼* **Ryan The Giant**[23] 610 4-8-6 **50**........(v) ConnorBeasley 4 55
(Keith Dalgleish) *prom: chsd clr ldr over 12f out: tk clsr order over 4f out: rdn to ld over 2f out: edgd lft and hdd 1f out: no ex wl ins fnl f* **2/1**[1]

1052 **4** *5* **Jan Smuts (IRE)**[23] 610 9-9-1 **59**........(t) MeganNicholls(5) 9 58
(Wilf Storey) *hld up: hdwy over 4f out: hung lft wl over 3f out: sn rdn: edgd lft over 1f out: no ex* **9/1**

6-60 **5** *8* **He's Magic**[23] 610 6-8-7 **46** oh1........(p) JamesSullivan 5 36
(Tim Fitzgerald) *hld up: rdn over 3f out: wknd over 2f out* **80/1**

0/66 **6** *½* **Thornton Care**[16] 726 6-9-5 **65**........ JamieGormley(7) 1 54
(Iain Jardine) *led: clr after 2f tl c bk to the field over 4f out: rdn and hdd over 2f out: wknd over 1f out* **28/1**

060- **7** *8* **Bilko's Back (IRE)**[146] 7105 5-8-10 **49**........(t) JoeyHaynes 2 29
(Susan Corbett) *chsd ldrs: lost pl 5f out: rdn and wknd over 2f out* **200/1**

362- **8** *5* **Cosmic Tigress**[138] 7367 6-9-5 **58**........ JasonHart 7 32
(John Quinn) *chsd ldr who wnt clr after 2f: lost 2nd over 12f out: remained handy: rdn over 3f out: wknd over 2f out* **11/2**[3]

1403 **9** *71* **Yasir (USA)**[13] 786 9-9-10 **63**........ PaulMulrennan 3
(Conor Dore) *hld up: a in rr: rdn 4f out: sn wknd* **14/1**

3m 38.98s (3.78) **Going Correction** +0.375s/f (Slow)
**WFA** 4 from 5yo+ 3lb **9** Ran SP% **110.9**
Speed ratings (Par 101): **105,104,103,101,97 96,92,90,54**
CSF £20.98 CT £41.54 TOTE £6.50: £1.80, £1.30, £1.40; EX 22.70 Trifecta £68.00.
**Owner** The Dregs Of Humanity & Partner **Bred** Norman Court Stud **Trained** Carrutherstown, D'fries & G'way

**FOCUS**
A modest staying handicap. They went a respectable gallop and it was hard work for these horses into the headwind on the climb to the line. Sound form but it lacks depth.

## 991 BETWAY FREE BET CLUB H'CAP 1m 4f 98y (Tp)
**3:10** (3:12) (Class 4) (0-85,87) 4-Y-0 **£7,561** (£2,263; £1,131; £566; £282) **Stalls** High

Form RPR

2-31 **1** **Codeshare**[13] 780 5-9-3 **79**........ SilvestreDeSousa 9 88
(Alan Swinbank) *hld up: hdwy over 3f out: led over 1f out: sn rdn: jst hld on* **9/4**[1]

6-21 **2** *shd* **Lac Leman (GER)**[23] 613 6-9-1 **77**........(h) GrahamLee 8 85
(Pauline Robson) *hld up: swtchd rt over 3f out: hdwy over 2f out: rdn to chse wnr ins fnl f: r.o* **15/2**[2]

-451 **3** *1½* **Faithful Creek (IRE)**[28] 526 5-9-4 **83**........(p) AlistairRawlinson(3) 5 88
(Michael Appleby) *hld up in tch: chsd ldr over 2f out: rdn and ev ch over 1f out: styd on same pce ins fnl f* **15/2**[2]

00-5 **4** *nk* **Time Of My Life (GER)**[16] 728 6-9-7 **83**........(p) DanielTudhope 10 88
(Patrick Holmes) *hld up: hdwy over 2f out: rdn over 1f out: styd on same pce ins fnl f* **8/1**[3]

425- **5** *8* **Craggaknock**[40] 2163 6-9-6 **82**........ DougieCostello 6 74
(Mark Walford) *chsd ldrs: rdn over 3f out: wknd fnl f* **9/1**

404- **6** *½* **Great Fighter**[26] 6540 7-8-13 **75**........(p) SamJames 4 66
(Jim Goldie) *s.i.s: hld up: rdn over 2f out: nvr nrr* **12/1**

10-4 **7** *2* **Major Rowan**[23] 613 6-8-11 **73**........ ConnorBeasley 2 61
(John Davies) *hld up: rdn over 2f out: nvr on terms* **25/1**

531/ **8** *3* **Bank Bonus**[33] 1472 8-8-6 **75**........(h) BenRobinson(7) 11 58
(Brian Ellison) *s.i.s: hld up: pushed along over 5f out: n.d* **80/1**

-112 **9** *1¼* **L'Inganno Felice (FR)**[37] 389 7-9-11 **87**........(h) PJMcDonald 1 68
(Iain Jardine) *plld hrd: trckd ldr: rdn over 2f out: wknd over 1f out* **8/1**[3]

155- **10** *1½* **Be Perfect (USA)**[145] 7139 8-9-4 **80**........(p) JamesSullivan 7 59
(Ruth Carr) *led: rdn over 2f out: hdd & wknd over 1f out* **18/1**

3-33 **11** *5* **Mica Mika (IRE)**[19] 683 9-9-7 **83**........ PaulHanagan 3 54
(Richard Fahey) *chsd ldrs: rdn over 3f out: wknd over 2f out* **11/1**

2m 40.36s (-0.74) **Going Correction** +0.375s/f (Slow) **11** Ran SP% **112.9**
Speed ratings (Par 105): **117,116,115,115,110 110,108,106,105,104 101**
CSF £17.93 CT £106.42 TOTE £3.30: £1.40, £2.10, £2.80; EX 20.50 Trifecta £107.70.
**Owner** Elsa Crankshaw & G Allan **Bred** Juddmonte Farms Ltd **Trained** Melsonby, N Yorks

**FOCUS**
A decent middle-distance handicap. They went a proper gallop and the favourite, an improving 5yo, narrowly won a real thriller. The fourth helps set the standard.

## 992 BETWAY H'CAP 1m 2f 42y (Tp)
**3:45** (3:47) (Class 4) (0-80,80) 4-Y-0+ **£7,762** (£2,310; £1,154; £577) **Stalls** High

Form RPR

24-2 **1** **General Hazard (IRE)**[34] 440 4-9-4 **77**........ BenCurtis 11 87+
(Archie Watson) *hld up: hdwy over 2f out: led over 1f out: rdn and edgd lft ins fnl f: styd on* **5/2**[1]

22-0 **2** *½* **Cadeau Magnifique**[40] 359 5-9-0 **73**........(p) PaulHanagan 10 82
(Richard Fahey) *chsd ldrs: rdn and ev ch over 1f out: styd on* **7/1**[2]

-040 **3** *1* **Spes Nostra**[3] 958 9-8-8 **72**........(b) LewisEdmunds(5) 5 79
(Iain Jardine) *hld up: nt clr run over 2f out: hdwy over 1f out: r.o* **11/1**

-364 **4** *3* **Take Two**[8] 856 8-8-8 **70**........ CallumShepherd(3) 1 71
(Alex Hales) *hld up: hdwy over 2f out: rdn and edgd rt over 1f out: styd on same pce ins fnl f* **16/1**

-5P0 **5** *nk* **Fantasy Gladiator**[21] 641 11-8-7 **66** oh2........(p) AndrewMullen 7 66
(Michael Appleby) *hld up: rdn over 2f out: nt clr run over 1f out: r.o ins fnl f: nvr nrr* **80/1**

-624 **6** *2½* **Storm King**[19] 683 8-9-1 **74**........ FrannyNorton 12 69
(David C Griffiths) *led: rdn and edgd rt over 2f out: hdd over 1f out: no ex ins fnl f* **14/1**

000- 7 hd **Framley Garth (IRE)**[49] 7359 5-8-6 72 PaulaMuir(7) 14 67
(Patrick Holmes) *hld up in tch: racd keenly: rdn over 2f out: nt clr run over 1f out: styd on same pce* 125/1

-002 8 1 **Restive (IRE)**[16] 727 4-8-11 70 (h) TomEaves 8 63
(Iain Jardine) *hld up: rdn over 2f out: wknd ins fnl f* 12/1

0/00 9 2 3/4 **Melanna (IRE)**[23] 609 6-8-10 69 GrahamLee 9 57
(Richard Ford) *hld up: hdwy over 2f out: sn rdn: wknd fnl f* 200/1

00/2 10 1 3/4 **Magistral**[29] 509 7-8-13 72 (p) PJMcDonald 3 56
(Iain Jardine) *prom: rdn over 2f out: nt clr run over 1f out: sn wknd* 17/2

-243 11 1 1/2 **Zabeel Star (IRE)**[14] 769 5-9-1 74 LiamKeniry 6 55
(Graeme McPherson) *s.i.s and sn pushed along in rr: rdn over 2f out: wknd over 1f out* 8/1[3]

0-4 12 7 **A L'Anglaise**[24] 599 4-9-7 80 SilvestreDeSousa 13 47
(Rae Guest) *chsd ldr: nt clr run and swtchd lft over 2f out: hmpd over 1f out: eased* 7/1[2]

3140 13 73 **Pivotman**[17] 719 9-8-10 76 (bt) HarrisonShaw(7) 2
(Michael Easterby) *trckd ldrs: plld hrd: wknd wl over 2f out: eased* 20/1

2m 11.65s (1.25) **Going Correction** +0.375s/f (Slow) 13 Ran SP% 111.1
Speed ratings (Par 105): **110,109,108,106,106 104,104,103,101,99 98,92,34**
CSF £17.21 CT £153.33 TOTE £3.10: £1.50, £2.20, £3.30; EX 15.70 Trifecta £163.60.
**Owner** Boadicea Bloodstock **Bred** London Thoroughbred Services Ltd **Trained** Upper Lambourn, W Berks
■ Stewards' Enquiry : Callum Shepherd jockey ban: three days (16-18 March) - guilty of careless riding

**FOCUS**
A fair handicap. They went a respectable gallop and the in-form favourite won well from an awkward draw back in trip. The form has been rated slightly positively through the runner-up to his 3yo form.

## 993 BETWAY MAIDEN STKS 1m 2f 42y (Tp)
**4:20** (4:21) (Class 5) 4-Y-O+ **£3,881** (£1,155; £577; £288) **Stalls** High

Form RPR

3-22 1 **On Fire**[15] 738 4-9-5 63 (p1) PJMcDonald 2 75
(James Bethell) *chsd ldr: led over 2f out: rdn out* 2/1[2]

-322 2 4 1/2 **Ms Gillard**[15] 747 4-9-0 67 TomEaves 3 61
(David Simcock) *hld up in tch: rdn over 3f out: chsd wnr over 1f out: styd on same pce ins fnl f* 3/1[3]

2-62 3 1 **Bridey's Lettuce (IRE)**[28] 525 5-9-5 67 SilvestreDeSousa 1 64
(Ivan Furtado) *led: rdn and hdd over 2f out: no ex ins fnl f* 13/8[1]

4 4 1/2 **Dan's Hopeforglory** 5-9-0 0 AndrewMullen 8 50
(Peter Niven) *prom: rdn over 2f out: styd on same pce fr over 1f out* 33/1

5 2 3/4 **Absolute Angel**[520] 6-9-0 0 JamesSullivan 5 45
(Peter Niven) *s.i.s: hld up: rdn over 3f out: n.d* 20/1

3 6 3/4 **Slaying The Dragon (IRE)**[13] 785 4-9-0 0 LewisEdmunds(5) 4 48
(Nigel Tinkler) *hld up: rdn over 3f out: nvr on terms* 28/1

6 7 2 **Tambour**[55] 91 4-9-5 0 ConnorBeasley 6 44
(Keith Dalgleish) *chsd ldr: rdn and ev ch over 2f out: wknd fnl f* 10/1

8 3 **Heavenly Gait**[70] 5-9-0 0 ShaneGray 7 33
(Jason Ward) *s.s: hld up: a in rr* 100/1

2m 16.44s (6.04) **Going Correction** +0.375s/f (Slow) 8 Ran SP% 117.7
Speed ratings (Par 103): **90,86,85,82,79 79,77,75**
CSF £8.46 TOTE £3.10: £1.20, £1.50, £1.10; EX 10.50 Trifecta £15.40.
**Owner** The Hon Mrs C M Holliday **Bred** Cleaboy Farms Co **Trained** Middleham Moor, N Yorks

**FOCUS**
A modest maiden. They went a steady gallop and it proved an insufficient test for the front-running favourite. A pb from the winner, but the level is a bit fluid.

## 994 32RED CASINO FILLIES' H'CAP 7f 14y (Tp)
**4:55** (4:56) (Class 3) (0-95,95) 4-Y-O+
**£15,562** (£4,660; £2,330; £1,165; £582; £292) **Stalls** Centre

Form RPR

3-16 1 **Bint Arcano (FR)**[26] 581 4-8-5 79 JoeDoyle 7 87
(Julie Camacho) *sn prom: racd keenly: led over 1f out: rdn out* 9/2[3]

32-3 2 1 1/2 **Pacolita (IRE)**[19] 677 5-8-2 76 oh1 FrannyNorton 4 80
(Sylvester Kirk) *hld up in tch: lost pl over 3f out: rallied over 1f out: rdn and edgd lft ins fnl f: kpt on* 8/1

13-0 3 nk **Bargain Buy**[12] 810 4-8-7 86 GeorgiaCox(5) 1 89+
(William Haggas) *awkward s: hld up: pushed along and hdwy over 1f out: edgd lft ins fnl f: styd on same pce towards fin* 11/4[1]

-535 4 1 1/2 **Dusky Dawn**[9] 850 5-8-2 76 NeilFarley 6 75
(Alan Swinbank) *trckd ldr: plld hrd: led over 2f out: rdn: edgd lft and hdd over 1f out: no ex ins fnl f* 9/1

0-0 5 6 **Ibazz**[12] 810 4-8-12 86 BenCurtis 2 69
(Archie Watson) *hld up: hdwy over 3f out: rdn over 2f out: outpcd fr over 1f out* 4/1[2]

0-02 6 shd **Volunteer Point (IRE)**[22] 617 5-9-7 95 GrahamLee 3 78
(Mick Channon) *trckd ldrs: rdn over 2f out: wknd fnl f* 9/2[3]

150- 7 6 **Nouvelli Dancer (IRE)**[119] 7781 4-8-9 83 PaulHanagan 5 49
(David C Griffiths) *led: qcknd 1/2-way: hdd over 2f out: wknd over 1f out* 20/1

1m 29.53s (3.33) **Going Correction** +0.375s/f (Slow) 7 Ran SP% 108.9
Speed ratings (Par 104): **95,93,92,91,84 84,77**
CSF £35.35 TOTE £5.80: £2.60, £3.40; EX 31.00 Trifecta £138.60.
**Owner** G B Turnbull Ltd **Bred** Rabbah Bloodstock Limited **Trained** Norton, N Yorks

**FOCUS**
The feature contest was a good fillies' handicap. The favourite blew the start again, but they didn't go a hectic pace, and she was able to latch onto the back of the pack. A muddling race, but the runner-up has been rated to her best for now.

## 995 BETWAY SPRINT H'CAP 5f (Tp)
**5:25** (5:26) (Class 4) (0-85,80) 3-Y-O+ **£7,762** (£2,310; £1,154; £577) **Stalls** Centre

Form RPR

35-5 1 **Just Us Two (IRE)**[12] 816 5-9-5 80 (p) LewisEdmunds(5) 3 89
(Robert Cowell) *trckd ldrs: plld hrd: led 2f out: rdn out* 10/3[2]

1-03 2 1 **Aprovado (IRE)**[20] 660 5-9-10 80 (p) PaulMulrennan 4 85
(Michael Dods) *led 3f: sn rdn: styd on* 12/1

4-25 3 1/2 **Vimy Ridge**[12] 808 5-9-1 74 (p) CallumShepherd(3) 1 77
(Alan Bailey) *hld up: pushed along and hdwy over 1f out: styd on* 8/1

331- 4 hd **Royal Brave (IRE)**[104] 8010 6-9-3 73 PJMcDonald 9 75
(Rebecca Bastiman) *s.i.s: hld up: r.o ins fnl f: nt trble ldrs* 9/1

-323 5 1/2 **Dark Side Dream**[13] 783 5-9-2 72 SilvestreDeSousa 2 73
(Chris Dwyer) *chsd ldrs: rdn 1/2-way: styd on same pce ins fnl f* 5/2[1]

00-6 6 1/2 **Tarboosh**[20] 660 4-9-7 77 PaulHanagan 6 76
(Paul Midgley) *hld up: plld hrd: hdwy over 1f out: rdn and no ex wl ins fnl f* 10/1

106- 7 3/4 **New Road Side**[112] 7892 4-9-8 78 ConnorBeasley 5 74
(Richard Guest) *chsd ldr tl rdn 1/2-way: no ex ins fnl f* 6/1[3]

41-5 8 1/2 **One Boy (IRE)**[34] 443 6-9-7 77 GrahamLee 8 71
(Paul Midgley) *prom: racd keenly: rdn over 1f out: no ex ins fnl f* 14/1

40-0 9 6 **Secret Asset (IRE)**[26] 573 12-9-7 77 (b) TomEaves 7 50
(Lisa Williamson) *hld up: a in rr: wknd over 1f out* 40/1

1m 0.33s (0.83) **Going Correction** +0.375s/f (Slow) 9 Ran SP% 112.9
Speed ratings (Par 105): **108,106,105,105,104 103,102,101,92**
CSF £41.60 CT £293.19 TOTE £4.90: £1.90, £5.50, £2.70; EX 35.90 Trifecta £284.70.
**Owner** T W Morley **Bred** Andy Macdonald & Sarah Wigley **Trained** Six Mile Bottom, Cambs

**FOCUS**
A fair sprint handicap, and a competitive contest on paper, but the top-weight proved far too good for this field. Straightforward form rated around the runner-up.
T/Jkpt: £6,666.60 to a £1 stake. Pool: £10,000.00 - 1.50 winning units T/Plt: £40.50 to a £1 stake. Pool: £82,806.60 - 1,490.31 winning units T/Qpdt: £14.70 to a £1 stake. Pool: £6,770.78 - 339.69 winning units **Colin Roberts**

# 961 LINGFIELD (L-H)
Friday, March 3

**OFFICIAL GOING: Polytrack: standard**
Wind: Moderate, behind Weather: Cloudy

## 996 32RED.COM FILLIES' H'CAP 1m 1y(P)
**2:00** (2:00) (Class 5) (0-75,76) 4-Y-O+ **£2,911** (£866; £432; £216) **Stalls** High

Form RPR

2-11 1 **Simply Me**[20] 677 4-9-6 74 (p) RichardKingscote 6 85+
(Tom Dascombe) *hld up in last pair: gng wl fr 3 out: shkn up over 1f out: clsd and squeezed between rivals to ld last 100yds: sn clr: comf* 1/1[1]

-322 2 1 1/2 **First Experience**[3] 964 6-9-8 76 (p) AdamKirby 4 80
(Lee Carter) *trckd ldng pair: rdn over 2f out: clsd to take 2nd over 1f out and sn chalng: upsides ins fnl f: sn outpcd* 10/3[2]

0-21 3 shd **Remember Me**[28] 550 4-9-0 73 (p1) CharlieBennett(5) 1 77
(Hughie Morrison) *pressed ldr: led over 2f out: sn drvn: hdd and outpcd last 100yds* 4/1[3]

-124 4 2 1/2 **Skidby Mill (IRE)**[20] 677 7-9-4 75 CallumShepherd(3) 3 73
(Laura Mongan) *racd freely: led: hdd and rdn over 2f out: tried to rally on inner over 1f out: fdd ins fnl f* 10/1

30-0 5 hd **Rustique**[13] 812 5-8-11 65 ThomasBrown 2 62
(Ed Walker) *trckd ldng pair: rdn over 2f out: hanging and nt qckn over 1f out: sn btn* 12/1

660- 6 3 1/4 **Smart Mover (IRE)**[37] 7272 4-8-11 65 LukeMorris 5 54
(Nikki Evans) *hld up in last pair: rdn over 2f out: hanging over 1f out and sn wknd* 50/1

1m 37.81s (-0.39) **Going Correction** -0.025s/f (Stan) 6 Ran SP% 111.8
Speed ratings (Par 100): **100,98,98,95,95 92**
CSF £4.54 TOTE £1.90: £1.20, £1.60; EX 4.80 Trifecta £12.10.
**Owner** Laurence Bellman **Bred** Highclere Stud **Trained** Malpas, Cheshire

**FOCUS**
They didn't go a great pace early on and the favourite wasn't ideally positioned from the turn in, but she had too much in hand and won easily anyway. The form is rated around the second and third.

## 997 £10 FREE AT 32RED.COM MAIDEN STKS 7f 1y(P)
**2:30** (2:30) (Class 5) 3-Y-O **£2,911** (£866; £432; £216) **Stalls** Low

Form RPR

523- 1 **Millie's Kiss**[102] 8047 3-9-0 73 SilvestreDeSousa 3 74
(Philip McBride) *chsd ldr: pushed along 3f out: rdn 2f out: clsd to ld 1f out: styd on and sn clr* 15/8[2]

-432 2 3 **Havelock (IRE)**[9] 863 3-9-5 72 JoeFanning 1 71
(Mark Johnston) *led at gd pce: tried to stretched on 2f out: rdn and hdd 1f out: fnd nil and immediately btn* 11/10[1]

3-6 3 1 1/4 **Ahead Of Time**[15] 758 3-9-5 0 JamieSpencer 6 68
(David Simcock) *hld up bhd ldng pair: pushed along and no imp 2f out: reminder fnl f and kpt on: nvr posed a threat* 3/1[3]

00 4 18 **Secret Sands (IRE)**[9] 855 3-9-0 0 MichaelJMMurphy 5 14
(Pat Phelan) *stdd s: hld up in last pair: pushed along and jst in tch 3f out: sn wknd* 100/1

5 39 **Watar Day** 3-9-0 0 LiamKeniry 4
(Linda Jewell) *stdd s: rn green and sn bhd: t.o 3f out* 100/1

1m 25.01s (0.21) **Going Correction** -0.025s/f (Stan) 5 Ran SP% 109.4
Speed ratings (Par 98): **97,93,92,71,27**
CSF £4.24 TOTE £3.20: £1.50, £1.10; EX 4.00 Trifecta £5.30.
**Owner** Four Winds Racing Partnership **Bred** Wood Farm Stud (Waresley) **Trained** Newmarket, Suffolk

**FOCUS**
An ordinary maiden run at a fair clip. THe winner was close to form with the second close to his C&D latest.

## 998 BETWAY CLASSIFIED CLAIMING STKS 1m 2f (P)
**3:05** (3:05) (Class 5) 4-Y-O+ **£2,911** (£866; £432; £216) **Stalls** Low

Form RPR

0-06 1 **Russian Reward (IRE)**[15] 769 5-9-6 71 (p) SilvestreDeSousa 5 75
(Amanda Perrett) *led to 6f out: led again 4f out: booted for home over 2f out: 3 l clr over 1f out: drvn out and styd on* 3/1[3]

02-5 2 2 1/2 **Gaelic Silver (FR)**[22] 648 11-8-7 72 (p) HectorCrouch(3) 1 60
(Gary Moore) *hld up in last: waiting for room on inner 2f out: prog over 1f out but wnr already gone: styd on to take 2nd last 50yds* 11/4[2]

-050 3 nk **With Approval (IRE)**[6] 922 5-9-0 63 LiamKeniry 2 63
(Laura Mongan) *trckd ldrs: rdn to chse wnr wl over 1f out: no imp and lost 2nd last 50yds* 25/1

-004 4 1 1/4 **The Gay Cavalier**[4] 958 6-9-8 75 (t) StevieDonohoe 6 69
(John Ryan) *s.s and rousted early: hld up in last pair: shkn up over 2f out: styd on fnl f to take 4th nr fin: no ch* 5/1

4034 5 1/2 **Black Dave (IRE)**[15] 769 7-9-1 72 AdamKirby 3 61
(David Evans) *t.k.h: trckd ldng pair: reminder over 3f out: rdn and nt qckn wl over 1f out: n.d after* 7/4[1]

005- 6 10 **Thrtypointstothree (IRE)**[71] 8499 6-8-10 42 (bt) LukeMorris 4 36
(Nikki Evans) *t.k.h: pressed wnr: led 6f out to 4f out: lost 2nd and wknd rapidly wl over 1f out* 100/1

2m 6.48s (-0.12) **Going Correction** -0.025s/f (Stan) 6 Ran SP% 109.5
Speed ratings (Par 103): **99,97,96,95,95 87**
CSF £11.05 TOTE £4.10: £2.10, £1.80; EX 11.50 Trifecta £95.20.
**Owner** A D Spence **Bred** Times Of Wigan Ltd **Trained** Pulborough, W Sussex

**FOCUS**
They went steady early on and the winner was always well placed on a day pace held up. The form is rated cautiously.

## 999 SUNBETS.CO.UK H'CAP 7f 1y(P)
3:40 (3:40) (Class 2) (0-105,101) 4-Y-0+

£11,827 (£3,541; £1,770; £885; £442; £222) Stalls Low

Form RPR

3403 1 **Pearl Spectre (USA)**[8] 876 6-8-5 **85**........ JosephineGordon 5 92
(Phil McEntee) *mde all: committed for home wl over 2f out: rdn 4 l clr wl over 1f out: ld dwindled nr fin but nvr gng to be ct* **10/1**

0050 2 1 **Shyron**[7] 896 6-8-1 **88**........(v[1]) JaneElliott(7) 2 92+
(George Margarson) *hld up in last trio: rdn and prog on outer over 1f out: styd on to take 2nd last strides: nvr able to chal* **11/2**[3]

-033 3 hd **Horsted Keynes (FR)**[17] 730 7-8-10 **90**........ JamieSpencer 6 93
(David Simcock) *trckd ldrs: rdn over 2f out: prog over 1f out: styd on to take 2nd briefly nr fin: nvr able to chal* **9/2**[1]

0-03 4 1 **Suqoor**[13] 818 4-8-9 **89**........(p) SilvestreDeSousa 9 90
(Chris Dwyer) *chsd wnr after 1f: rdn and outpcd over 2f out: styd on to cl the gap ins fnl f but lost 2 pls nr fin* **11/2**[3]

4122 5 ½ **Intransigent**[20] 680 8-8-13 **93**........ RobHornby 4 92
(Andrew Balding) *t.k.h: hld up in midfield: encouraged along fr 2f out: nt qckn over 1f out: kpt on ins fnl f: no ch* **5/1**[2]

00-0 6 ¾ **Angelic Lord (IRE)**[17] 730 5-9-1 **95**........ RichardKingscote 7 92
(Tom Dascombe) *chsd wnr 1f: rdn in 3rd pl over 2f out: lost pl over 1f out* **9/2**[1]

500- 7 nk **Baraweez (IRE)**[167] 6558 7-9-6 **100**........ DaleSwift 8 97+
(Brian Ellison) *broke wl but restrained into last: stl last and pushed along over 1f out: fin w a flourish but nvr involved* **20/1**

-060 8 nk **Swiss Cross**[25] 598 10-7-13 **82** oh3........(tp) HollieDoyle(3) 1 78
(Phil McEntee) *hld up in rr: pushed along in last pair 2f out: no prog and nvr a factor* **33/1**

65-6 9 ¾ **Kadrizzi (FR)**[13] 818 4-9-7 **101**........ RobertWinston 3 95
(Dean Ivory) *trckd ldrs: short of room briefly on inner 2f out: shkn up and no prog over 1f out: fdd* **15/2**

1m 22.95s (-1.85) **Going Correction** -0.025s/f (Stan) 9 Ran SP% **112.4**
Speed ratings (Par 109): **109,107,107,106,105 105,104,104,103**
CSF £61.88 CT £284.39 TOTE £11.20: £3.00, £2.10, £2.00; EX 78.60 Trifecta £344.00.
**Owner** Steve Jakes **Bred** Estate Of Edward P Evans **Trained** Newmarket, Suffolk

**FOCUS**
Not a bad handicap. Another front-running winner, but not form to be confident about.

## 1000 32REDSPORT.COM H'CAP 7f 1y(P)
4:10 (4:10) (Class 5) (0-75,75) 3-Y-O £2,911 (£866; £432; £108; £108) Stalls Low

Form RPR

45-5 1 **Boater (IRE)**[43] 312 3-9-7 **75**........ JoeFanning 5 79
(Mark Johnston) *mde all: rdn over 1f out: styd on and a fending off rivals* **15/2**

61-0 2 ¾ **Touch Me (IRE)**[37] 392 3-8-10 **67**........(h) JordanVaughan(3) 2 68
(K R Burke) *hld up in tch: prog 2f out: racing awkwardly but chsd wnr fnl f: nt qckn and a hld* **20/1**

03-2 3 shd **Mullarkey**[22] 647 3-9-0 **68**........ KierenFox 1 69
(John Best) *trckd ldrs: rdn on inner to try to chal 1f out: kpt on but a hld* **9/4**[1]

404- 4 1¼ **El Torito (IRE)**[169] 6525 3-9-7 **75**........ AdamKirby 7 72+
(Jim Boyle) *hld up in last: nudged along on inner fr over 1f out: kpt on fnl f: nrst fin: can do bttr* **11/4**[2]

500- 4 dht **Plato's Kode (IRE)**[122] 7750 3-8-9 **63**........(bt[1]) OisinMurphy 8 60
(Seamus Durack) *t.k.h: trckd wnr: rdn over 1f out: one pce and lost 2nd fnl f* **5/1**[3]

23-5 6 ½ **Rapid Rise (IRE)**[23] 625 3-9-4 **75**........ KieranShoemark(3) 3 71
(David Brown) *hld up: rdn and no prog over 2f out: no ch after: kpt on nr fin* **6/1**

3-60 7 ¾ **Parisian Chic (IRE)**[35] 434 3-8-7 **61**........ KieranO'Neill 4 55
(Lee Carter) *hld up in rr: shkn up fr 3f out: no prog* **33/1**

0-00 8 1 **Dragon Dream (IRE)**[15] 763 3-8-5 **59**........ LukeMorris 6 50
(Roger Ingram) *hld up in rr: rdn over 2f out: no prog and wl btn over 1f out* **12/1**

1m 24.13s (-0.67) **Going Correction** -0.025s/f (Stan) 8 Ran SP% **115.5**
Speed ratings (Par 98): **102,101,101,99,99 99,98,97**
CSF £138.41 CT £447.69 TOTE £7.90: £2.40, £3.10, £1.10; EX 65.80 Trifecta £255.40.
**Owner** Sheikh Hamdan bin Mohammed Al Maktoum **Bred** Darley **Trained** Middleham Moor, N Yorks

**FOCUS**
The pace held up again here and the winner is rated close to his 2yo form.

## 1001 32RED CASINO MAIDEN STKS 1m 4f (P)
4:45 (4:46) (Class 5) 3-Y-O £2,911 (£866; £432; £216) Stalls Low

Form RPR

645- 1 **Addicted To You (IRE)**[88] 8227 3-9-5 72........ JoeFanning 4 73+
(Mark Johnston) *mde all: pressed over 2f out: rdn to assert over 1f out: kpt on fnl f and jst clung on* **4/5**[1]

2 nk **Ulysses (GER)** 3-9-5 0........ FranBerry 1 71+
(Ralph Beckett) *in tch in last: reminder 5f out: outpcd and shkn up over 3f out: tk 3rd sn after: kpt on to take 2nd ins fnl f: clsd on wnr nr fin* **6/1**[3]

32 3 1 **Bishops Cannings (IRE)**[9] 862 3-9-0 0........ ShaneKelly 3 65
(David Elsworth) *trckd wnr after 2f: rdn to chal over 2f out: nt qckn over 1f out: lost 2nd ins fnl f: one pce* **15/8**[2]

0 4 3½ **Indian Red**[15] 758 3-9-5 0........ StevieDonohoe 2 64
(Mark H Tompkins) *t.k.h early: trckd wnr 2f: rdn and outpcd over 3f out: sn in last: one pce and no threat after* **20/1**

2m 30.5s (-2.50) **Going Correction** -0.025s/f (Stan) 4 Ran SP% **109.4**
Speed ratings (Par 98): **107,106,106,103**
CSF £6.04 TOTE £1.70; EX 5.30 Trifecta £7.90.
**Owner** Markus Graff **Bred** M W Graff **Trained** Middleham Moor, N Yorks

**FOCUS**
An ordinary maiden for 3yos which Mark Johnston has made a habit of winning. The fourth consecutive winner to make all.

T/Plt: £49.40 to a £1 stake. Pool: £70,556.98 - 1,042.52 winning tickets T/Qpdt: £23.00 to a £1 stake. Pool: £4,463.85 - 143.42 winning tickets **Jonathan Neesom**

# 989 NEWCASTLE (A.W) (L-H)
Friday, March 3

**OFFICIAL GOING: Tapeta: standard**
Wind: Almost nil Weather: Overcast, raining

## 1002 BETWAY STAYERS H'CAP 2m 56y (Tp)
5:15 (5:15) (Class 4) (0-85,84) 4-Y-O+ £4,851 (£1,443; £721; £360) Stalls Low

Form RPR

-226 1 **Zakatal**[17] 728 11-9-12 **84**........ DougieCostello 3 91
(Rebecca Menzies) *hld up: smooth hdwy on outside to ld over 2f out: rdn and hrd pressed fr over 1f out: drvn and hld on wl fnl f* **12/1**

000/ 2 nk **Fair Loch**[26] 5051 9-8-0 **65** oh6........ KieranSchofield(7) 5 71
(Brian Ellison) *s.i.s: sn niggled in rr: gd hdwy on outside to press wnr over 2f out: sn rdn: kpt on fnl f: hld nr fin* **33/1**

3-12 3 nk **Aldreth**[15] 759 6-9-5 **80**........(p) NathanEvans(3) 1 85
(Michael Easterby) *prom: effrt and rdn 2f out: kpt on fnl f: no ex towards fin* **11/4**[1]

16-5 4 1¾ **Mister Bob (GER)**[50] 196 8-9-4 **76**........(p) TedDurcan 4 79
(James Bethell) *dwlt: hld up: effrt and pushed along 2f out: kpt on fnl f: nvr able to chal* **13/2**[3]

2-41 5 4½ **Persun**[30] 507 5-9-10 **82**........ GrahamLee 6 80
(Mick Channon) *t.k.h early: prom: drvn along over 2f out: wknd fr over 1f out* **11/4**[1]

/06- 6 11 **Mere Anarchy (IRE)**[172] 6415 6-8-11 **69**........(t[1]) PaulMulrennan 7 53
(Robert Stephens) *chsd clr ldr: clsd over 3f out: rdn and wknd fr over 2f out* **10/1**

10-3 7 2 **Tetradrachm**[29] 519 4-9-5 **82**........ TomEaves 2 64
(David Simcock) *hld up in tch on ins: drvn and outpcd 3f out: btn fnl 2f* **7/2**[2]

00-0 8 10 **Buthelezi (USA)**[14] 779 9-9-8 **80**........ BenCurtis 8 50
(Brian Ellison) *led and sn clr: hdd over 2f out: sn lost pl and struggling* **33/1**

3m 32.43s (-2.77) **Going Correction** -0.075s/f (Stan)
**WFA** 4 from 5yo+ 3lb 8 Ran SP% **111.6**
Speed ratings (Par 105): **103,102,102,101,99 94,93,88**
CSF £294.95 CT £1372.48 TOTE £14.10: £2.70, £4.50, £1.10; EX 122.50 Trifecta £845.20.
**Owner** David Furman & John Sugarman **Bred** H H The Aga Khan's Studs Sc **Trained** Mordon, Durham

**FOCUS**
A filthy wet evening at Gosforth Park, but a fair stayers' handicap for the grade to start with. The pacesetter was ignored until around half a mile out. A small pb from the winner.

## 1003 32RED.COM MAIDEN FILLIES' STKS (PLUS 10 RACE) 1m 5y (Tp)
5:45 (5:48) (Class 5) 3-Y-O £3,072 (£914; £456; £228) Stalls Centre

Form RPR

1 **Eyes On Asha (IRE)** 3-9-2 0........ KevinStott 4 76+
(Kevin Ryan) *dwlt: hld up: pushed along and rn green over 2f out: rallied to ld 1f out: edgd lft and pushed clr: readily* **3/1**[2]

020- 2 2½ **Sulafah (IRE)**[115] 7855 3-9-2 72........(p[1]) JasonHart 3 68
(Simon West) *led at ordinary gallop: qcknd 2f out: hdd 1f out: kpt on fnl f: nt pce of wnr* **28/1**

- 3 ½ **Fiendish (USA)** 3-9-2 0........ FrannyNorton 5 66+
(Mark Johnston) *in tch: pushed along over 2f out: effrt and edgd lft over 1f out: kpt on fnl f: nt pce to chal* **7/2**[3]

06-3 4 1 **Lady Hester (USA)**[11] 845 3-9-2 0........ TedDurcan 7 64
(John Gosden) *trckd ldrs: drvn along over 2f out: kpt on same pce fnl f* **10/1**

2 5 2 **Hot Natured (IRE)**[21] 658 3-9-2 0........ PJMcDonald 6 59+
(K R Burke) *trckd ldrs: rdn along over 2f out: effrt and edgd lft over 1f out: wknd fnl f* **1/1**[1]

6 1 **Magic Approach** 3-9-2 0........ TomEaves 8 57
(David Simcock) *missed break: hld up: shkn up and swtchd lft over 2f out: no imp fr over 1f out* **33/1**

60- 7 3¾ **Rosemay (FR)**[113] 7882 3-9-2 0........ JamesSullivan 1 48
(Iain Jardine) *t.k.h: cl up tl rdn and wknd over 2f out* **16/1**

8 1 **R U Mine (IRE)** 3-9-2 0........ ConnorBeasley 2 45
(Keith Dalgleish) *slowly away: bhd: drvn and struggling over 2f out: sn wknd* **33/1**

1m 39.92s (1.32) **Going Correction** -0.075s/f (Stan) 8 Ran SP% **121.5**
Speed ratings (Par 95): **90,87,87,86,84 83,79,78**
CSF £83.36 TOTE £4.60: £1.70, £5.90, £1.70; EX 71.30 Trifecta £389.80.
**Owner** T A Rahman **Bred** Haras Du Mont Dit Mont **Trained** Hambleton, N Yorks

**FOCUS**
A passable 3yo fillies' maiden for the time of year, and a very taking winner. The runner-up is rated close to form.

## 1004 32RED CASINO MAIDEN STKS 5f (Tp)
6:15 (6:16) (Class 5) 3-Y-O £2,911 (£866; £432; £216) Stalls Centre

Form RPR

1 **Rock Of America (USA)** 3-9-5 0........ DanielTudhope 4 78+
(David O'Meara) *dwlt: t.k.h on in tch: prom: effrt over 1f out: gng clr w runner up whn shkn up to ld ins fnl f: pushed out: comf* **11/10**[1]

- 2 ½ **Poet's Reward** 3-9-5 0........ PhillipMakin 6 76+
(David Barron) *trckd ldrs: led over 1f out: gng clr w wnr whn rdn and hdd ins fnl f: kpt on: hld nr fin* **10/3**[3]

545- 3 5 **Kodicat (IRE)**[147] 7122 3-9-0 67........ TomEaves 5 53
(Kevin Ryan) *prom: rdn over 2f out: outpcd appr fnl f: kpt on to take 3rd pl last 25yds: nt rch first two* **9/4**[2]

6- 4 1 **Wishing Time (IRE)**[67] 8526 3-9-0 0........ SamJames 8 49
(David O'Meara) *led: rdn over 2f out: hdd over 1f out: edgd lft and outpcd fnl f* **12/1**

500- 5 ½ **Violet Mist (IRE)**[138] 7381 3-9-0 0........(t[1]) GrahamLee 3 48
(Ben Haslam) *trckd ldrs: rdn over 2f out: wknd fnl f* **100/1**

00 6 ¾ **Frank's Legacy**[13] 819 3-9-5 0........ DavidNolan 1 50
(Ivan Furtado) *t.k.h: hld up in tch: rdn over 2f out: wknd over 1f out* **66/1**

0-5 7 ½ **Fast Tack (IRE)**[48] 244 3-9-5 0........ JasonHart 2 48
(John Quinn) *s.i.s: sn pushed along in rr: nvr on terms* **33/1**

45 8 nk **Arabella Rose**[25] 600 3-9-0 0........ TonyHamilton 7 42
(Ivan Furtado) *s.i.s: bhd and outpcd: struggling fr 1/2-way* **20/1**

59.04s (-0.46) **Going Correction** -0.075s/f (Stan) 8 Ran SP% **119.3**
Speed ratings (Par 98): **100,99,91,89,88 87,86,86**
CSF £5.39 TOTE £2.00: £1.10, £1.60, £1.10; EX 7.10 Trifecta £16.30.
**Owner** West Coast Haulage Limited **Bred** Northwest Farms Llc **Trained** Upper Helmsley, N Yorks

**FOCUS**
Two potentially decent newcomers finished a mile clear in this sprint maiden. The level of the form is fluid.

## 1005 32RED.COM H'CAP 6f (Tp)
6:45 (6:45) (Class 5) (0-70,69) 3-Y-O £3,072 (£914; £456; £228) Stalls Centre

Form RPR
-1 1 **Intense Romance (IRE)**[21] 656 3-9-3 **65**.................. ConnorBeasley 9 72+
(Michael Dods) *t.k.h: prom: hdwy to ld 2f out: rdn and kpt on wl fnl f* **8/1**
4-51 2 1 3/4 **Skellig Michael**[28] 546 3-8-12 **60**..................(p) GrahamLee 4 61
(Ben Haslam) *t.k.h early: pressed ldr: rdn and ev ch briefly 2f out: kpt on same pce ins fnl f* **16/1**
00-6 3 1/2 **Backinanger**[14] 787 3-8-10 **58**.................................................. JoeDoyle 1 57
(Kevin Ryan) *led tl rdn and hdd 2f out: rallied: edgd lft and kpt on same pce fnl f* **15/2**[3]
-313 4 shd **Tranquil Daze (IRE)**[13] 813 3-9-7 **69**.................................. TedDurcan 3 68
(David Brown) *prom: effrt and rdn 2f out: edgd lft: kpt on same pce ins fnl f* **2/1**[2]
1 5 8 **Bastia**[29] 520 3-9-7 **69**........................................................ DavidProbert 5 42
(Martyn Meade) *t.k.h: hld up in tch: drvn and outpcd over 2f out: btn over 1f out* **13/8**[1]
26-0 6 6 **Trick Of The Lyte (IRE)**[27] 578 3-9-4 **66**........................... JasonHart 2 20
(John Quinn) *s.i.s: plld hrd: hld up in tch: drvn and struggling 1/2-way: btn fnl f* **12/1**

1m 12.16s (-0.34) **Going Correction** -0.075s/f (Stan) 6 Ran SP% **107.9**
Speed ratings (Par 98): **99,96,96,95,85 77**
CSF £100.45 CT £875.21 TOTE £6.80: £3.10, £5.20; EX 38.60 Trifecta £259.60.
**Owner** Hugh Malcolm Linsley **Bred** John O'Connor **Trained** Denton, Co Durham

**FOCUS**
One of the two winning debutants followed up in this sprint handicap, but not the one the market most expected. The winner impressed from her maiden win.

## 1006 BETWAY SPRINT H'CAP 5f (Tp)
7:15 (7:19) (Class 6) (0-55,55) 3-Y-O+ £2,425 (£721; £360; £180) Stalls Centre

Form RPR
323- 1 **Kinloch Pride**[197] 5582 5-9-5 **50**......................................(p) GrahamLee 8 59
(Noel Wilson) *trckd ldrs: smooth hdwy to ld over 1f out: shkn up and kpt on strly fnl f: comf* **11/1**
3264 2 2 1/4 **Pearl Noir**[8] 874 7-9-2 **54**..........................................(b) RPWalsh[(7)] 4 55
(Scott Dixon) *led to over 1f out: rallied: kpt on fnl f: nt pce to chal* **14/1**
2033 3 2 1/2 **Hadley**[27] 583 4-9-5 **50**..........................................................(p[1]) BenCurtis 2 42
(Tracy Waggott) *trckd ldrs: drvn over 2f out: edgd rt and kpt on fnl f: nt pce to chal* **5/1**[1]
0000 4 3/4 **Nora Batt (IRE)**[25] 604 4-9-2 **50**.................................. PhilipPrince[(3)] 11 39
(David Evans) *midfield: rdn and hdwy over 1f out: kpt on fnl f: no imp* **28/1**
0-35 5 1/2 **Sea Of Green**[27] 583 5-9-1 **46**.................................................. SamJames 12 33
(Jim Goldie) *hld up: pushed along and hdwy over 1f out: kpt on fnl f: no imp* **9/1**[3]
-104 6 nk **Lady Bacchus**[18] 723 4-9-10 **55**.................................(b) FrannyNorton 13 41
(Richard Guest) *hld up: rdn and effrt wll over 1f out: no imp fnl f* **5/1**[1]
0-34 7 nk **Great Expectations**[35] 438 9-9-6 **51**..............................(vt) TomEaves 5 36
(J R Jenkins) *hld up on far side of gp: drvn and outpcd wl over 1f out: kpt on fnl f: no imp* **10/1**
0-40 8 2 **Name That Toon**[10] 852 4-9-1 **46**......................................(v) JasonHart 3 24
(Derek Shaw) *trckd ldrs: drvn over 2f out: wknd appr fnl f* **25/1**
230- 9 nk **Bogsnog (IRE)**[182] 6100 7-9-9 **54**....................................... JamesSullivan 7 35
(Ruth Carr) *in tch: rdn over 2f out: no room fr over 1f out to ins fnl f: sn hmpd: nt rcvr* **9/1**[3]
000- 10 1/2 **Gowanless**[153] 6959 4-9-7 **52**........................................(p) PaulMulrennan 1 27
(Michael Dods) *hld up in tch on far side of gp: drvn along and effrt 2f out: outpcd fnl f* **8/1**[2]
4-00 11 hd **Yisty**[8] 874 4-9-2 **47**..................................................................(v) TonyHamilton 9 21
(Derek Shaw) *midfield: drvn and outpcd over 2f out: n.d after* **80/1**
-003 12 nk **Barnsdale**[8] 874 4-8-8 **46** oh1..........................(p) MeganEllingworth[(7)] 14 19
(John Holt) *towards rr on nr side of gp: struggling over 2f out: sn btn* **40/1**
606- 13 1 **Little Belter (IRE)**[223] 4647 5-9-7 **52**................................(v) PhillipMakin 6 30+
(Keith Dalgleish) *hld up midfield: n.m.r 1/2-way and over 1f out: sn rdn: btn fnl f* **10/1**
640- 14 hd **A J Cook (IRE)**[72] 8485 7-9-3 **48**.................................... AndrewMullen 10 17
(Ron Barr) *dwlt: bhd and sn rdn along: struggling fr 1/2-way* **16/1**

58.76s (-0.74) **Going Correction** -0.075s/f (Stan) 14 Ran SP% **114.5**
Speed ratings (Par 101): **102,98,94,93,92 91,91,88,87,86 86,86,84,84**
CSF £143.98 CT £889.10 TOTE £11.00: £3.30, £3.30, £2.00; EX 103.60 Trifecta £716.50.
**Owner** G J Paver **Bred** Mrs C K Paver **Trained** Marwood, Co Durham

**FOCUS**
A big field for this very moderate handicap, but precious few got involved. It rates a minor pb from the winner.

## 1007 SUNBETS.CO.UK APPRENTICE H'CAP 7f 14y (Tp)
7:45 (7:45) (Class 5) (0-75,77) 4-Y-O+ £3,072 (£914; £456; £228) Stalls Centre

Form RPR
00-0 1 **Fingal's Cave (IRE)**[59] 32 5-9-4 **76**.......................... JamieGormley[(7)] 8 86
(Iain Jardine) *prom: hdwy to ld appr fnl f: rdn clr* **6/1**[2]
3-60 2 4 1/2 **Out Of The Ashes**[34] 460 4-9-4 **76**..................(vt[1]) DarraghKeenan[(7)] 2 74
(Mohamed Moubarak) *chsd ldr on nr side of gro: led over 2f out: hdd appr fnl f: kpt on: nt pce of wnr* **9/1**
-312 3 1 3/4 **Dose**[8] 883 4-8-3 **61**............................................. ConnorMurtagh[(7)] 5 54
(Richard Fahey) *towards rr: outpcd 1/2-way: rallied over 1f out: kpt on to take 3rd pl wl ins fnl f: no ch w first two* **2/1**[1]
2006 4 1/2 **Ticks The Boxes (IRE)**[2] 971 5-9-12 **77**.......................(b) CliffordLee 3 69
(Michael Herrington) *hld up: rdn over 2f out: hdwy wl over 1f out: no imp fnl f* **17/2**
1-05 5 hd **The Magic Pencil (IRE)**[41] 360 4-8-6 **64**.............(p) SeamusCronin[(7)] 1 55
(Kevin Ryan) *led at decent gallop: hdd over 2f out: rallied: wknd ins fnl f* **7/1**[3]
1160 6 2 1/2 **Essenaitch (IRE)**[10] 850 4-9-7 **72**.......................................... PhilipPrince 9 56
(David Evans) *in tch: drvn and outpcd over 3f out: n.d after* **9/1**
513- 7 1 1/4 **London Glory**[284] 2545 4-9-6 **71**.............................................. JoshDoyle 7 52
(David Thompson) *hld up: pushed along 1/2-way: hdwy wl over 1f out: sn no imp* **12/1**
00-1 8 7 **Hernando Torres**[15] 757 9-8-12 **70**.............................(tp) RyanTimby[(7)] 4 32
(Michael Easterby) *s.i.s: hld up on far side of gp: rdn over 2f out: sn no imp: btn over 1f out* **8/1**
056- 9 18 **Mr Andros**[289] 2375 4-9-7 **72**........................................ EdwardGreatrex 6
(Brendan Powell) *hld up: rdn and outpcd over 2f out: sn wknd: t.o* **16/1**

1m 25.5s (-0.70) **Going Correction** -0.075s/f (Stan) 9 Ran SP% **115.3**
Speed ratings (Par 103): **101,95,93,93,93 90,88,80,60**
CSF £58.44 CT £146.27 TOTE £6.00: £2.20, £2.70, £1.40; EX 77.70 Trifecta £401.60. **Owner** S Middleton **Bred** Rathasker Stud **Trained** Carrutherstown, D'fries & G'way

**FOCUS**
As with the preceding contest, few took much of a hand. The winner is rated back to something like his best.
T/Plt: £235.50 to a £1 stake. Pool: £913,16.09 - 282.95 winning tickets T/Qpdt: £32.60 to a £1 stake. Pool: £11,479.77 - 260.50 winning tickets **Richard Young**

1008 - 1011a (Foreign Racing) - See Raceform Interactive

# 905 DUNDALK (A.W) (L-H)
Friday, March 3

**OFFICIAL GOING: Polytrack: standard**

## 1012a 32RED.COM RACE 7f (P)
7:30 (7:30) 3-Y-O £13,141 (£4,059; £1,923; £854)

RPR
1 **Visionary (IRE)**[22] 643 3-9-10 94................................. PatSmullen 3 94+
(Robert Cowell) *settled bhd ldr: pushed along into st: rdn to ld narrowly gng best ins fnl f and kpt on wl to assert clsng stages* **4/1**[3]
2 1 1/4 **Rock In Peace (IRE)**[35] 449 3-9-4 82................................ GaryCarroll 4 85
(G M Lyons, Ire) *led: stl gng wl into st: pushed along 2f out and pressed clly u.p over 1f out: hdd narrowly ins fnl f and no imp on wnr clsng stages* **4/1**[3]
3 nk **Tuff Love (IRE)**[28] 560 3-9-4 0........................................... ColinKeane 2 84
(G M Lyons, Ire) *hld up bhd ldr: 4th at 1/2-way: rdn and sme hdwy far side fr 2f out: almost on terms ent fnl f: no imp on wnr wl ins fnl f: kpt on same pce in 3rd clsng stages* **11/8**[1]
4 1 3/4 **Remember The Days (IRE)**[14] 791 3-9-1 82..... DonnachaO'Brien[(3)] 1 79
(Joseph Patrick O'Brien, Ire) *w.w in rr: clsr in 3rd at 1/2-way: rdn 2f out and sn no ex u.p in rr: kpt on one pce ins fnl f* **9/4**[2]

1m 26.77s (1.67) **Going Correction** +0.225s/f (Slow) 4 Ran SP% **112.9**
Speed ratings: **99,97,97,95**
CSF £18.75 TOTE £3.80; DF 11.00 Trifecta £29.30.
**Owner** Khalifa Dasmal **Bred** K A Dasmal **Trained** Six Mile Bottom, Cambs

**FOCUS**
A good professional performance from the winner, and the champion jockey was impressed.

1013a - (Foreign Racing) - See Raceform Interactive

## 1014a FOLLOW DUNDALK STADIUM ON TWITTER H'CAP 1m 2f 150y(P)
8:30 (8:34) 4-Y-O+ £5,256 (£1,623; £555; £555; £128)

RPR
1 **King Christophe (IRE)**[7] 912 5-8-9 **58**..................(b) ShaneBKelly[(3)] 12 64+
(Miss Nicole McKenna, Ire) *unruly bef s: hld up in rr of mid-div: hdwy fr over 1f out: sltly hmpd ins fnl f and r.o wl to ld cl home where edgd sltly lft* **16/1**
2 3/4 **Ligeti (IRE)**[7] 911 4-9-12 **72**...........................................(t) ConnorKing 14 78
(Joseph Patrick O'Brien, Ire) *mid-div: gng wl tl tk clsr order after 1f: disp 6th 3f out: rdn 2f out and clsd u.p ins fnl f where edgd sltly rt: r.o clsng stages where sltly impeded between horses* **6/4**[1]
3 hd **Settle For Red (IRE)**[21] 671 7-8-9 **60**........................ TomMadden[(5)] 6 65
(David Marnane, Ire) *sn chsd ldrs: 4th 3f out: rdn bhd ldrs 2f out and ev ch between horses wl ins fnl f: no ex clsng stages and jnd for 3rd* **14/1**
3 dht **Tenerezza (IRE)**[8] 883 4-9-4 **67**.............................. RobbieDowney[(3)] 4 73
(Iain Jardine) *hld up bhd ldr: t.k.h between horses in 5th 3f out: rdn to ld over 1f out: all out wl ins fnl f and no ex clsng stages where hdd and dropped to dead heat for 3rd* **7/1**[3]
5 nk **Ineffable (IRE)**[28] 556 4-9-2 **67**...........................(tp) DylanRobinson[(5)] 2 72
(Rodger Sweeney, Ire) *chsd ldrs: 3rd 3f out: impr to ld briefly under 2f out: hdd u.p over 1f out: no ex wl ins fnl f and dropped to 5th cl home* **12/1**
6 1 1/4 **Dark Amber**[31] 497 7-8-4 **57**............................................(t) SeanDavis[(7)] 5 59
(Damian Joseph English, Ire) *hld up in rr of mid-div: tk clsr order over 2f out: sn rdn and no imp on ldrs wl ins fnl f: kpt on one pce* **18/1**
7 nk **So Sensible (IRE)**[91] 8200 6-9-9 **69**.............................. MichaelHussey 1 70
(Tracey Collins, Ire) *mid-div: disp 6th 3f out: prog far side 2f out to chal over 1f out: sn no ex and wknd wl ins fnl f* **6/1**[2]
8 hd **Manorov**[14] 792 7-8-13 **62**..........................................(vt) RossCoakley[(3)] 10 63
(T G McCourt, Ire) *mid-div: hdwy nr side over 1f out: hmpd between horses ins fnl f and no imp on ldrs: one pce in 8th clsng stages* **16/1**
9 1 3/4 **I Will Excel (IRE)**[181] 6146 5-9-4 **71**...................................(t) ETDaly[(7)] 13 68
(John James Feane, Ire) *dwlt: hld up in rr early: gng wl towards rr into st: nt clr run fr 2f out: rdn bhd horses over 1f out and no imp in 9th ins fnl f: kpt on one pce* **14/1**
10 3 3/4 **Hello Humpfrey (IRE)**[7] 912 8-7-9 **51**................ ScottMcCullagh[(10)] 8 41
(Peter Casey, Ire) *dwlt sltly: towards rr: rdn on outer into st and sn no ex: one pce fnl 2f* **7/1**[3]
11 3 **Pyla (IRE)**[21] 673 5-9-9 **69**..................................................... RobsonAguiar 3 53
(Luke Comer, Ire) *in rr of mid-div for most: rdn and no imp 2f out: one pce* **33/1**
12 1 **Mulzamm (IRE)**[7] 905 5-9-5 **70**..............................(t) DonaghO'Connor[(5)] 7 52
(James McAuley, Ire) *sn led: rdn and hdd under 2f out: wknd* **40/1**
13 3 1/2 **Spirit Of The Law (IRE)**[274] 2842 8-7-13 **52**..........(t) AndrewBreslin[(7)] 9 27
(James McAuley, Ire) *cl up: pushed along briefly in 2nd over 4f out: rdn over 2f out and sn wknd* **50/1**
14 31 **King Of Country**[33] 3226 5-9-7 **72**....................(b[1]) ConorMcGovern[(5)] 11
(M Halford, Ire) *chsd ldrs: rdn and wknd under 4f out: eased st* **8/1**

2m 17.02s (1.52) **Going Correction** +0.225s/f (Slow) 14 Ran SP% **135.8**
Speed ratings: **103,102,102,102,102 101,100,100,99,96 94,93,91,68**
PL: 1.20 Tenerezza, 1.70 Settle For Red; TC: 201.57, 107.59; TF: 11&2&8: 616.90, 11&2&10: 1,289.90 CSF £44.93 TOTE £20.00: £5.50, £1.30; DF 73.20.
**Owner** Patrick J McKenna **Bred** Canning Downs & Dermot Farington **Trained** Dugannon, Co Tyrone
■ Stewards' Enquiry : Robson Aguiar jockey ban: two day ban - use of whip

**FOCUS**
The finish of the night, the winner pouncing late and fast. It's been rated around the balance of the first five.

1013 - 1021a (Foreign Racing) - See Raceform Interactive

# 996 LINGFIELD (L-H)

Saturday, March 4

**OFFICIAL GOING: Polytrack: standard**

Wind: quite strong, behind Weather: cloudy

## 1022 BETWAY SPRINT H'CAP 5f 6y(P)

**2:00** (2:00) (Class 6) (0-55,55) 4-Y-O+ **£2,264** (£673; £336; £168) **Stalls** High

Form RPR

-625 **1** **Frank The Barber (IRE)**17 [742] 5-9-7 **55**......................(t) AdamKirby 7 65
(Steph Hollinshead) *trckd ldr: drvn to ld over 1f out: drifted lft and flashed tail but r.o strly fnl f: rdn out* **7/2[2]**

-122 **2** *2* **Fabulous Flyer**17 [743] 4-8-11 **50**.......................... DavidParkes(5) 2 53
(Jeremy Gask) *chsd ldrs: rdn 2f out: kpt on to chse wnr fnl 120yds: a being hld* **5/2[1]**

-066 **3** *1 1/4* **Red Flute**4 [961] 5-9-0 **48**.......................................(b[1]) DannyBrock 4 46
(Denis Quinn) *led: rdn and hdd over 1f out: sn hld: no ex fnl 120yds* **11/2[3]**

-335 **4** *nk* **Roy's Legacy**30 [523] 8-9-1 **54**........................ CharlieBennett(5) 8 51
(Shaun Harris) *trckd ldrs: rdn wl over 1f out: kpt on ins fnl f* **13/2**

5-00 **5** *1/2* **Ask The Guru**43 [327] 7-9-6 **54**..................................(p) LukeMorris 10 49
(Michael Attwater) *mid-div: c wd ent st: sn rdn: kpt on ins fnl f but nt quite pce to get on terms* **14/1**

533- **6** *nse* **The Wee Chief (IRE)**224 [4658] 11-9-6 **54**..................... KieranO'Neill 6 49
(Jimmy Fox) *stdd s: hdwy over 1f out: sn drvn: nvr threatened: no ex fnl 120yds* **12/1**

0-00 **7** *nk* **Molly Jones**19 [722] 8-9-0 **48**...................................... JohnFahy 1 42
(Matthew Salaman) *rrd leaving stalls: bhd: kpt on fnl f: nvr trbld ldrs* **40/1**

60-3 **8** *1 1/2* **Deer Song**29 [554] 4-8-13 **54**.............................. JaneElliott(7) 5 43
(John Bridger) *sn pushed along in last trio: nvr gng pce to get involved* **7/1**

0-30 **9** *3 3/4* **Willow Spring**24 [622] 5-8-11 **48**................................ TimClark(3) 3 23
(Denis Quinn) *s.i.s: sn mid-div: rdn over 1f out: wknd fnl f* **16/1**

58.01s (-0.79) **Going Correction** 0.0s/f (Stan) **9** Ran SP% **114.7**
Speed ratings (Par 101): **106,102,100,100,99 99,98,96,90**
CSF £12.57 CT £46.23 TOTE £4.30: £1.80, £1.40, £2.20; EX 14.90 Trifecta £79.20.
**Owner** Debbie Hodson **Bred** Tally-Ho Stud **Trained** Upper Longdon, Staffs

**FOCUS**
A moderate sprint handicap. They went a decent gallop on standard Polytrack. This rates a fractional pb from the winner.

## 1023 SUNBETS.CO.UK H'CAP 1m 1y(P)

**2:35** (2:36) (Class 2) (0-105,102) 4-Y-O+ **£11,971** (£3,583; £1,791; £896; £446) **Stalls** High

Form RPR

1-11 **1** **My Target (IRE)**21 [680] 6-9-7 **102**........................... ConnorBeasley 5 111+
(Michael Wigham) *hld up: hdwy 2f out: shkn up for str run ent fnl f: led fnl 70yds: readily* **11/4[1]**

1120 **2** *1/2* **Franco's Secret**7 [918] 6-8-6 **87**...............................(v) TomMarquand 4 94
(Peter Hedger) *s.i.s: last pair: rdn and hdwy over 1f out: r.o strly fnl f: wnt 2nd cl home* **16/1**

5-41 **3** *1* **Third Time Lucky (IRE)**17 [744] 5-9-6 **101**.................... PaulHanagan 2 106
(Richard Fahey) *trckd ldr: led 3f out: edgd lft whn rdn over 1f out: no ex whn hdd fnl 70yds: lost 2nd cl home* **5/1[3]**

6421 **4** *3/4* **Loyalty**9 [876] 10-8-9 **90**..................................................(v) MartinLane 1 93
(Derek Shaw) *trckd ldrs: rdn whn swtchd rt to chse ldr over 1f out: kpt on same pce fnl f* **14/1**

000- **5** *1 1/4* **Mutarakez (IRE)**112 [7933] 5-8-12 **93**......................... DougieCostello 9 93
(Brian Meehan) *trckd ldrs: rdn 2f out: kpt on same pce ins fnl f* **33/1**

0-13 **6** *hd* **Alfred Hutchinson**21 [680] 9-9-4 **99**...........................(p) AdamKirby 11 99
(David O'Meara) *mid-div: sme hdwy over 1f out: kpt on same pce fnl f: nt pce to threaten* **11/1**

42-2 **7** *1/2* **Bunbury**44 [306] 5-8-9 **90**.............................................. ShaneKelly 10 88
(Richard Hughes) *trckd ldrs: rdn over 2f out: wknd ins fnl f* **8/1**

6-00 **8** *1 1/2* **Sea Of Flames**23 [650] 4-9-1 **96**........................ SilvestreDeSousa 7 91
(David Elsworth) *mid-div: pushed wdst ent st: nvr threatened* **5/1[3]**

3211 **9** *shd* **Chevallier**7 [918] 5-8-12 **93**........................................ LukeMorris 6 88+
(Archie Watson) *dwlt bdly: a towards rr* **9/2[2]**

234/ **10** *32* **Mansfield**458 [8080] 4-8-6 **87**............................. JosephineGordon 3 8
(Michael Wigham) *led tl 3f out: sn rdn: wknd 2f out* **50/1**

1m 36.05s (-2.15) **Going Correction** 0.0s/f (Stan) **10** Ran SP% **115.1**
Speed ratings (Par 109): **110,109,108,107,106 106,105,104,104,72**
CSF £50.02 CT £210.60 TOTE £3.30: £1.30, £4.60, £1.50; EX 45.30 Trifecta £323.30.
**Owner** G Linder,M Wigham,J Williams,A Dearden **Bred** Darley **Trained** Newmarket, Suffolk
■ Stewards' Enquiry : Silvestre De Sousa caution; entered wrong stall
Shane Kelly caution; entered wrong stall

**FOCUS**
A good handicap. They went a respectable gallop and the favourite continued his excellent run of form over this C&D from another course specialist in second.

## 1024 BETWAY MAIDEN STKS 6f 1y(P)

**3:10** (3:12) (Class 5) 3-Y-O+ **£2,911** (£866; £432; £216) **Stalls** Low

Form RPR

604- **1** **Daring Guest (IRE)**164 [6670] 3-8-3 62........................... JaneElliott(7) 4 67
(George Margarson) *trckd ldr: led over 1f out: qcknd clr: readily* **4/1[2]**

2254 **2** *1 1/2* **Allegheny Bay (IRE)**8 [902] 3-8-10 63............................. LiamKeniry 2 61
(J S Moore) *led: rdn and hdd over 1f out: kpt on but nt pce of wnr* **11/2[3]**

4 **3** *1/2* **Miss Mirabeau**14 [819] 3-8-5 0....................................... LukeMorris 5 54+
(Sir Mark Prescott Bt) *trckd ldr: chal 3f out tl sltly outpcd 2f out: kpt on ins fnl f but nvr any threat to wnr* **6/4[1]**

0-3 **4** *2 3/4* **Sparkling Cossack**16 [764] 3-8-5 0....................... AdamBeschizza 3 46
(Jeremy Gask) *in tch: rdn over 2f out: kpt on same pce* **25/1**

0- **5** *1* **Shouldertoshoulder**80 [8353] 3-8-7 0......................... AaronJones(3) 7 47
(Stuart Williams) *hld up in last trio: rdn and sme prog wl over 1f out but nt pce to get on terms* **14/1**

0 **6** *nk* **Pocket Warrior**7 [916] 6-9-10 0................................. TomMarquand 9 50
(Martin Bosley) *sn chsng ldrs: rdn 2f out: sn one pce* **80/1**

0-6 **7** *3 3/4* **Beach Dancer (IRE)**14 [819] 3-8-10 0.................(h[1]) SilvestreDeSousa 1 34
(William Knight) *racd keenly: in tch: rdn over 2f out: wknd fnl f* **6/1**

**8** *2* **Amber Mischief** 3-8-5 0.............................................. JimmyQuinn 8 23
(Adam West) *s.i.s: a towards rr* **40/1**

4 **9** *60* **Cold Fire (IRE)**14 [807] 4-9-5 0.................................... DavidParkes(5) 6
(Jeremy Gask) *s.i.s: sn pushed along in last pair: wknd over 2f out: eased* **15/2**

1m 11.73s (-0.17) **Going Correction** 0.0s/f (Stan)
**WFA** 3 from 4yo+ 14lb **9** Ran SP% **115.6**
Speed ratings (Par 103): **101,99,98,94,93 92,87,85,5**
CSF £25.93 TOTE £5.30: £2.00, £1.70, £1.10; EX 28.40 Trifecta £67.30.
**Owner** John Guest Racing **Bred** Ringfort Stud **Trained** Newmarket, Suffolk

**FOCUS**
A modest maiden. They went a respectable gallop, at best, and the favourite failed to find the anticipated progression from her promising debut.

## 1025 BETWAY H'CAP 5f 6y(P)

**3:45** (3:45) (Class 2) (0-105,101) 4-Y-O+ **£11,971** (£3,583; £1,791; £896; £446) **Stalls** High

Form RPR

4-05 **1** **Encore D'Or**12 [842] 5-9-5 **99**..................................... LukeMorris 1 107
(Robert Cowell) *trckd ldrs: rdn over 1f out: edgd lft but r.o ins fnl f: led fnl stride* **5/2[1]**

1321 **2** *hd* **Zac Brown (IRE)**14 [818] 6-8-7 **94**.............................(t) JoshuaBryan(7) 7 101
(Charlie Wallis) *pressed ldr: rdn into narrow advantage 2 out: strly pressed and kpt on fnl f: hdd fnl stride* **7/1[3]**

0-01 **3** *1/2* **Robot Boy (IRE)**12 [842] 7-9-7 **101**........................... PhillipMakin 2 106
(David Barron) *led: rdn and narrowly hdd wl over 1f out: kpt on w ev ch: hld fnl 100yds* **5/2[1]**

-212 **4** *3 3/4* **Kasbah (IRE)**14 [818] 5-9-5 **99**................................... JoeFanning 3 91
(Amanda Perrett) *trckd ldrs: rdn 2f out: kpt on same pce* **11/4[2]**

-420 **5** *shd* **Dynamo Walt (IRE)**14 [816] 6-8-5 **85**......................(v) PaulHanagan 6 76
(Derek Shaw) *last but in tch: rdn 2f out: little imp* **16/1**

-142 **6** *2* **Monumental Man**14 [816] 8-8-4 **84**.........................(p) WilliamCarson 5 68
(Michael Attwater) *hmpd s: sn pushed along to chse ldrs: wknd over 1f out* **7/1[3]**

56.8s (-2.00) **Going Correction** 0.0s/f (Stan) **6** Ran SP% **114.7**
Speed ratings (Par 109): **116,115,114,108,108 105**
CSF £20.64 TOTE £3.30: £2.00, £2.70; EX 25.60 Trifecta £127.10.
**Owner** Mrs Morley,G Johnson,Newsells Park Stud **Bred** Newsells Park Stud **Trained** Six Mile Bottom, Cambs
■ Stewards' Enquiry : Joshua Bryan two-day ban; careless riding (18th,20th Mar)

**FOCUS**
A good sprint handicap. The winning time wasn't far off the course record.

## 1026 32RED SPRING CUP STKS (LISTED RACE) 7f 1y(P)

**4:20** (4:20) (Class 1) 3-Y-O

**£25,519** (£9,675; £4,842; £2,412; £1,210; £607) **Stalls** Low

Form RPR

21-1 **1** **Second Thought (IRE)**46 [276] 3-9-1 104.................. RobertWinston 3 105+
(William Haggas) *in tch: pushed along to take clsr order 2f out: shkn up and r.o wl fnl f: led towards fin* **13/8[1]**

-221 **2** *3/4* **Sutter County**15 [778] 3-9-1 103................................... JoeFanning 1 103
(Mark Johnston) *trckd ldr: led over 1f out: sn rdn: kpt on: hdd towards fin* **4/1[2]**

61- **3** *2 1/4* **Volatile**114 [7882] 3-9-1 89.......................................... MartinHarley 7 96
(James Tate) *led: rdn and hdd over 1f out: kpt on but no ex ins fnl f* **4/1[2]**

4-56 **4** *2 1/2* **Grey Britain**9 [887] 3-9-1 98...........................................(p[1]) AdamKirby 8 90
(John Ryan) *chsd ldrs: rdn over 2f out: kpt on but sn outpcd by front three* **10/1**

031- **5** *1 1/4* **High Acclaim (USA)**152 [7004] 3-9-1 86.................. SilvestreDeSousa 2 86
(Roger Teal) *trckd ldrs: rdn 2f out: sn one pce* **16/1**

1124 **6** *1/2* **Marquee Club**15 [778] 3-9-1 89.............................. DougieCostello 5 85
(Jamie Osborne) *hld up: rdn 2f out: kpt on same pce* **50/1**

11-2 **7** *1* **Dr Julius No**60 [31] 3-9-1 90.......................................... FranBerry 6 82
(Ralph Beckett) *hld up last: rdn over 2f out: nvr any imp* **8/1[3]**

-111 **8** *shd* **Tisbutadream (IRE)**24 [626] 3-8-10 85............................ ShaneKelly 4 77
(David Elsworth) *s.i.s: last pair: rdn 2f out: no imp* **14/1**

41- **9** *3/4* **Annie Fior (IRE)**100 [8081] 3-8-10 80..........................(h) PaulHanagan 9 75
(Denis Coakley) *hld up towards rr: rdn 2f out: no imp* **33/1**

1m 22.1s (-2.70) **Going Correction** 0.0s/f (Stan) **9** Ran SP% **115.7**
Speed ratings (Par 106): **115,114,111,108,107 106,105,105,104**
CSF £8.07 TOTE £2.10: £1.10, £1.30, £2.20; EX 8.60 Trifecta £24.80.
**Owner** Liam Sheridan **Bred** Tally-Ho Stud **Trained** Newmarket, Suffolk

**FOCUS**
The feature contest was a good quality 3yo Listed race which was won by the very smart sprinter Ertijaal in 2014 and 2,000 Guineas runner-up Dubawi Gold in 2011. The winning time was once again not far off a course record and the three most interesting horses at the head of the betting were clear of the fourth.

## 1027 BETWAY APPRENTICE H'CAP (PART OF THE RACING EXCELLENCE INITIATIVE) 1m 7f 169y(P)

**4:55** (4:55) (Class 4) (0-85,85) 4-Y-O+ **£6,301** (£1,886; £943; £472; £235) **Stalls** Low

Form RPR

24-1 **1** **Tartan Bute**26 [603] 4-9-3 **79**.......................................(p) JaneElliott 5 84+
(Mark Johnston) *led tl over 7f out: trckd ldr: pushed along over 2f out: led ent fnl f: kpt on wl: pushed out* **7/2[2]**

61-1 **2** *nk* **Lost The Moon**24 [619] 4-8-12 **77**......................... GabrieleMalune(3) 1 81+
(Mark H Tompkins) *trckd ldrs: rdn over 1f out: kpt on ins fnl f: wnt 2nd cl home* **13/8[1]**

-45R **3** *1/2* **Royal Marskell**21 [683] 8-9-9 **85**.............................(h[1]) JacobMitchell(5) 3 88
(Gay Kelleway) *awkwardly away: racd keenly trcking ldrs: hdwy to ld over 7f out: rdn and hdd ent fnl f: kpt on: lost 2nd cl home* **8/1**

5-34 **4** *1/2* **Victoria Pollard**15 [781] 5-9-6 **77**..............................(p) JoshuaBryan 6 80
(Andrew Balding) *hld up in tch: rdn into 4th over 1f out: kpt on same pce fnl f* **7/1**

0-00 **5** *1/2* **Castilo Del Diablo (IRE)**17 [746] 8-9-8 **84**............ DarylMcLaughlin(5) 2 86
(David Simcock) *trckd ldrs: rdn 2f out: kpt on but nt pce to get on terms* **4/1[3]**

505- **6** *hd* **Aumerle**299 [2105] 5-8-6 **68**............................................ NicolaCurrie(5) 4 70
(Shaun Lycett) *racd keenly trcking ldrs: rdn 2f out: kpt on but nt pce to get involved* **40/1**

5316 **7** *1 1/4* **Scrafton**8 [900] 6-8-6 **66** oh4........................................ AledBeech(3) 7 66?
(Tony Carroll) *hld up bhd last but in tch: rdn 2f out: little imp* **20/1**

3m 27.85s (2.15) **Going Correction** 0.0s/f (Stan)
**WFA** 4 from 5yo+ 3lb **7** Ran SP% **111.1**
Speed ratings (Par 105): **94,93,93,93,93 93,92**
CSF £9.03 TOTE £3.70: £1.90, £1.10; EX 10.70 Trifecta £35.30.
**Owner** Frank Bird **Bred** Newsells Park Stud **Trained** Middleham Moor, N Yorks

**FOCUS**
A decent staying handicap for apprentice riders and part of the All-Weather Hands and Heels series. The winner kept on well in the straight to win the riding series outright for his jockey Jane Elliott. It was a slightly fortunate success, though, off a sedate gallop.

## 1028 BETWAY FREE BET CLUB H'CAP — 1m 4f (P)
**5:30** (5:30) (Class 5) (0-70,70) 4-Y-0+ — **£2,911** (£866; £432; £216) **Stalls** Low

Form — RPR

-531 **1** **Synodic (USA)**[10] 865 5-9-2 **65**.....(t) JoeFanning 7 — 73+
(Seamus Durack) *cl up: shkn up to chse ldr over 1f out: r.o to ld fnl 90yds: readily* **7/4**[1]

4145 **2** ¾ **Attain**[4] 965 8-9-3 **69**..... EdwardGreatrex(3) 4 — 75
(Archie Watson) *racd keenly: trckd ldr: led over 1f out: rdn and no ex whn hdd fnl 90yds* **15/8**[2]

1-30 **3** 1¾ **Leonard Thomas**[12] 841 7-9-0 **63**.....(p) GeorgeDowning 3 — 66
(Tony Carroll) *cl up: rdn 2f out: kpt on but nt pce of front pair ins fnl f* **7/1**[3]

05-0 **4** ½ **Party Royal**[57] 90 7-8-12 **61**.....(p) MartinLane 5 — 63
(Nick Gifford) *hld up: rdn over 2f out: styd on to go hld 4th ins fnl f* **25/1**

-100 **5** hd **Karam Albaari (IRE)**[24] 619 9-9-7 **70**.....(v) AdamKirby 8 — 72
(J R Jenkins) *hld up: rdn over 2f out: styd on to chal for hld 4th ins fnl f* **10/1**

001- **6** 3½ **Juste Pour Nous**[80] 8364 4-9-4 **69**.....(t[1]) DougieCostello 2 — 65
(David Pipe) *trckd ldrs: rdn over 1f out: wknd fnl f* **8/1**

0-00 **7** ½ **Genuine Approval (IRE)**[23] 648 4-9-5 **70**..... RobertWinston 6 — 66
(John Butler) *led: rdn and hdd over 1f out: wknd fnl f* **16/1**

/60- **8** 2½ **Art History (IRE)**[194] 5724 9-8-13 **62**.....(t[1]) LiamKeniry 1 — 54
(Zoe Davison) *rrd and stmbld leaving stalls: last: rdn over 2f out: nvr any imp* **66/1**

2m 39.83s (6.83) **Going Correction** 0.0s/f (Stan)
**WFA** 4 from 5yo+ 1lb — **8 Ran SP% 115.1**
Speed ratings (Par 103): **77,76,75,75,74 72,72,70**
CSF £5.32 CT £16.51 TOTE £2.30: £1.10, £1.50, £2.10; EX 5.30 Trifecta £18.60.
**Owner** A M Gibbons **Bred** Flaxman Holdings Limited **Trained** Upper Lambourn, Berkshire
■ Stewards' Enquiry : Edward Greatrex two-day ban; used his whip without allowing sufficient time for his mount to respond (18th,20th Mar)

**FOCUS**
A modest middle-distance handicap. They went a sedate gallop once again, but the improving favourite followed up in smooth fashion up in trip.
T/Plt: £8.50 to a £1 stake. Pool: £86,287.76 - 7370.53 winning units. T/Qpdt: £4.50 to a £1 stake. Pool: £4,872.02 - 789.95 winning units. **Tim Mitchell**

# 1002 NEWCASTLE (A.W) (L-H)
## Saturday, March 4

**OFFICIAL GOING: Tapeta: standard**
Wind: Virtually nil Weather: Cloudy

## 1029 32RED.COM H'CAP — 1m 5y (Tp)
**5:45** (5:45) (Class 5) (0-75,75) 3-Y-O — **£3,881** (£1,155; £577; £288) **Stalls** Centre

Form — RPR

21 **1** **Tricorn (IRE)**[15] 785 3-9-7 **75**..... NickyMackay 1 — 90+
(John Gosden) *trckd ldrs: hdwy on inner 3f out: sn cl up: led wl over 1f out: rdn appr fnl f: sn clr: readily* **9/4**[2]

21-3 **2** 4 **Marzouq (USA)**[24] 625 3-9-5 **73**..... JFEgan 6 — 79
(Jeremy Noseda) *trckd ldrs: pushed along over 2f out: rdn wl over 1f out: kpt on u.p fnl f: no imp* **2/1**[1]

11-4 **3** 1½ **Ronnie The Rooster**[28] 577 3-8-12 **66**..... AndrewMullen 4 — 69
(David Barron) *trckd ldrs on outer: cl up 1/2-way: effrt to chal over 2f out: rdn and ev ch over 1f out: sn drvn and kpt on same pce* **10/1**

11-5 **4** 8 **Dream Team**[37] 417 3-9-3 **71**.....(p) PaulMulrennan 3 — 55
(Michael Dods) *t.k.h: trckd ldrs: pushed along wl over 2f out: sn rdn and outpcd 2f out* **22/1**

01 **5** nk **Faience**[16] 758 3-9-2 **70**..... BenCurtis 2 — 53
(William Haggas) *slt ld: pushed along 3f out: rdn over 2f out: hdd wl over 1f out and sn wknd* **9/2**[3]

-035 **6** 2¾ **Naupaka**[22] 659 3-8-13 **67**..... TomEaves 7 — 44
(Brian Ellison) *hld up: a towards rr* **25/1**

42-3 **7** 6 **Major Cornwallis (IRE)**[22] 659 3-9-1 **69**..... TonyHamilton 5 — 32
(Richard Fahey) *cl up: pushed along 3f out: rdn over 2f out: sn wknd* **8/1**

1m 37.96s (-0.64) **Going Correction** +0.125s/f (Slow) — **7 Ran SP% 110.7**
Speed ratings (Par 98): **108,104,102,94,94 91,85**
CSF £6.66 TOTE £3.00: £2.00, £1.30; EX 6.80 Trifecta £42.00.
**Owner** HRH Princess Haya Of Jordan **Bred** N Hartery **Trained** Newmarket, Suffolk

**FOCUS**
A fairly competitive looking 3yo handicap on paper but a clear cut winner who looks quite useful.

## 1030 £10 FREE BET AT 32RED.COM FILLIES' H'CAP — 6f (Tp)
**6:15** (6:17) (Class 5) (0-75,78) 4-Y-0+ — **£3,881** (£1,155; £577; £288) **Stalls** Centre

Form — RPR

33-4 **1** **Ki Ki**[28] 583 5-8-6 **60**..... BenCurtis 4 — 68
(Bryan Smart) *trckd ldrs: hdwy on inner over 2f out: chal over 1f out: rdn to ld ent fnl f: sn edgd rt: drvn out* **5/2**[1]

5023 **2** ½ **Fredricka**[36] 443 6-9-4 **72**.....(v[1]) RenatoSouza 7 — 78
(Jose Santos) *cl up: led 2f out: rdn over 1f out: hdd ent fnl f: sn drvn and n.m.r: kpt on gamely* **13/2**

-212 **3** nk **Poppy In The Wind**[28] 582 5-9-3 **76**.....(v) JoshDoyle(5) 8 — 81
(Alan Brown) *trckd ldrs: hdwy wl over 1f out: rdn and cl up ent fnl f: sn drvn and kpt on* **7/2**[3]

-411 **4** ½ **Veena (FR)**[9] 879 4-9-10 **78**..... TomEaves 3 — 81
(David Simcock) *hld up in rr: swtchd rt to outer and hdwy 2f out: rdn to chse ldrs over 1f out: drvn and kpt on same pce fnl f* **11/4**[2]

3-66 **5** 2 **Semana Santa**[31] 514 4-9-5 **73**..... SamJames 6 — 70
(David Barron) *hld up in tch: pushed along over 2f out: rdn wl over 1f out: sn no imp* **7/1**

0-00 **6** 3½ **Jess**[18] 732 4-8-3 **57**.....(p) JoeDoyle 1 — 43
(Kevin Ryan) *slt ld 2f: cl up: rdn along over 2f out: wknd wl over 1f out* **20/1**

0-00 **7** ½ **Silhuette (IRE)**[22] 660 4-8-8 **67**.....(v[1]) MeganNicholls(5) 5 — 51
(Colin Teague) *awkward s and rr: sn swtchd rt and hdwy to ld after 2f: rdn along over 2f out: sn hdd & wknd* **100/1**

1m 12.58s (0.08) **Going Correction** +0.125s/f (Slow) — **7 Ran SP% 109.0**
Speed ratings (Par 100): **104,103,102,102,99 94,94**
CSF £17.27 CT £49.53 TOTE £3.00: £1.90, £2.80; EX 16.50 Trifecta £38.30.
**Owner** B Smart **Bred** Mrs P A Clark **Trained** Hambleton, N Yorks

**FOCUS**
A run of the mill sprint for older fillies and mares, but the four market leaders all had a chance entering the final furlong.

## 1031 BETWAY H'CAP — 5f (Tp)
**6:45** (6:45) (Class 5) (0-70,72) 4-Y-0+ — **£3,234** (£962; £481; £240) **Stalls** Centre

Form — RPR

544- **1** **Ambitious Icarus**[105] 8031 8-8-13 **62**.....(e) JFEgan 4 — 69
(Richard Guest) *trckd ldrs: effrt and n.m.r over 1f out: swtchd rt and hdwy ent fnl f: rdn and qcknd to ld last 75 yds: kpt on* **9/2**[3]

432- **2** nk **Horsforth**[79] 8390 5-9-2 **65**.....(b) PaulMulrennan 2 — 71
(Richard Guest) *hld up in rr: swtchd rt and gd hdwy over 1f out: rdn to chal ins fnl f and ev ch: sn drvn and kpt on* **11/4**[1]

0-00 **3** ½ **Entertaining Ben**[9] 886 4-9-2 **65**..... TomEaves 6 — 69
(Iain Jardine) *slt ld: jnd and rdn along 2f out: drvn ent fnl f: hdd and no ex last 75 yds* **11/1**

-016 **4** 1½ **Windforpower (IRE)**[18] 732 7-8-11 **60**.....(v) BenCurtis 1 — 59
(Tracy Waggott) *in tch: rdn along and sltly outpcd over 2f out: styd on u.p fnl f* **7/1**

5306 **5** hd **Socialites Red**[17] 742 4-8-1 **57**.....(p) RPWalsh(7) 8 — 55
(Scott Dixon) *towards rr: pushed along on outer 1/2-way: rdn 2f out: kpt on u.p fnl f* **14/1**

12-6 **6** ½ **Compton River**[9] 886 5-9-2 **72**..... CallumRodriguez(7) 5 — 68
(Bryan Smart) *prom: cl up 1/2-way: disp ld 2f out: rdn and ev ch over 1f out: drvn and wknd fnl f* **3/1**[2]

60-1 **7** 1¼ **Top Of The Bank**[50] 216 4-9-0 **63**.....(p) TonyHamilton 3 — 55
(Kristin Stubbs) *prom: rdn along 2f out: sn wknd* **11/2**

58.85s (-0.65) **Going Correction** +0.125s/f (Slow) — **7 Ran SP% 112.7**
Speed ratings (Par 103): **110,109,108,106,106 105,103**
CSF £16.78 CT £124.95 TOTE £6.00: £2.50, £1.50; EX 19.50 Trifecta £235.90.
**Owner** ABS Metals & Waste **Bred** L T Roberts **Trained** Ingmanthorpe, W Yorks

**FOCUS**
This modest sprint handicap and another good finish, with a one-two for trainer Richard Guest.

## 1032 SUNBETS.CO.UK H'CAP — 1m 5y (Tp)
**7:15** (7:17) (Class 4) (0-85,88) 4-Y-0+ — **£5,822** (£1,732; £865; £432) **Stalls** Centre

Form — RPR

66-4 **1** **Swift Emperor (IRE)**[15] 782 5-9-10 **86**..... BenCurtis 4 — 95
(David Barron) *cl up: led 6f out at stdy clip: qcknd over 2f out: rdn over 1f out: styd on strly* **9/4**[1]

21-6 **2** 1¾ **Amber Mystique**[57] 97 4-8-12 **74**..... TonyHamilton 9 — 79
(Richard Fahey) *trckd ldrs: pushed along over 2f out: hdwy wl over 1f out: sn rdn: drvn and kpt on wl fnl f* **14/1**

1450 **3** ¾ **Testa Rossa (IRE)**[18] 730 7-9-3 **79**.....(b) SamJames 5 — 82
(Jim Goldie) *hld up: hdwy over 2f out: rdn over 1f out: chsd wnr ent fnl f: sn drvn and kpt on same pce* **11/2**[3]

4525 **4** 2¾ **Byres Road**[9] 876 4-9-7 **83**..... JasonHart 8 — 80
(Mark Johnston) *slt ld at stdy pce: hdd over 6f out: cl up: rdn along 2f out: drvn appr fnl f: kpt on same pce* **3/1**[2]

040- **5** ½ **Trinity Star (IRE)**[129] 7623 6-8-12 **74**..... PaulMulrennan 3 — 70
(Michael Dods) *hld up in rr: pushed along and hung lft 2f out: rdn over 1f out: styd on fnl f* **12/1**

-155 **6** 1¼ **Eastern Dragon (IRE)**[15] 782 7-8-10 **79**.....(p) CallumRodriguez(7) 2 — 72
(Iain Jardine) *dwlt and towards rr: hdwy on inner to trck ldrs 5f out: cl up over 3f out: rdn along 2f out: grad wknd* **7/1**

0-12 **7** hd **Barwah (USA)**[18] 729 6-8-10 **72**..... AndrewMullen 1 — 64
(Peter Niven) *hld up: hdwy to trck ldrs over 3f out: rdn along 2f out: drvn and wknd fnl f* **6/1**

000- **8** 6 **Billy Roberts (IRE)**[126] 7702 4-9-0 **76**..... JFEgan 6 — 54
(Richard Guest) *t.k.h: cl up: pushed along 3f out: rdn over 2f out: sn wknd* **18/1**

1m 39.28s (0.68) **Going Correction** +0.125s/f (Slow) — **8 Ran SP% 117.6**
Speed ratings (Par 105): **101,99,98,95,95 94,93,87**
CSF £36.41 CT £161.03 TOTE £3.40: £1.30, £3.30, £1.60; EX 38.00 Trifecta £199.80.
**Owner** DC Racing Partnership **Bred** John Davison **Trained** Maunby, N Yorks

**FOCUS**
The feature race and a decent handicap run 1.32 secs slower than the opening contest but a ready winner who made all.

## 1033 32RED.COM MAIDEN STKS (PLUS 10 RACE) — 7f 14y (Tp)
**7:45** (7:46) (Class 4) 3-Y-O — **£5,822** (£1,732; £865) **Stalls** Centre

Form — RPR

252- **1** **Ray's The Money (IRE)**[164] 6682 3-9-2 79.....(v) LouisSteward(3) 4 — 73+
(Michael Bell) *trckd ldr: hdwy wl over 1f out: chal ent fnl f: sn rdn and qcknd to ld 150 yds out: styd on* **8/13**[1]

02 **2** 2½ **Bonnie Gals**[44] 310 3-8-9 0..... ShirleyTeasdale(5) 3 — 61
(Keith Dalgleish) *set v stdy pce: pushed along and qcknd jst over 2f out: rdn over 1f out: jnd ent fnl f: sn hdd and kpt on same pce* **14/1**[3]

424- **3** 1½ **Glorious Artist (IRE)**[157] 6869 3-9-5 76..... MichaelJMMurphy 1 — 62
(Charles Hills) *t.k.h: hld up in rr: hdwy 2f out: sn rdn and no imp fnl f* **7/4**[2]

1m 38.1s (11.90) **Going Correction** +0.125s/f (Slow) — **3 Ran SP% 104.9**
Speed ratings (Par 100): **37,34,32**
CSF £6.48 TOTE £1.50; EX 6.60 Trifecta £5.00.
**Owner** Mr & Mrs Ray Jenner **Bred** Ballybrennan Stud Ltd **Trained** Newmarket, Suffolk

**FOCUS**
A small field for this 3yo maiden and it was run at a very steady pace before turning into a 2f dash. The favourite produced the best change of pace.

## 1034 32REDSPORT.COM APPRENTICE H'CAP — 7f 14y (Tp)
**8:15** (8:15) (Class 6) (0-60,57) 3-Y-O — **£3,234** (£962; £481; £240) **Stalls** Centre

Form — RPR

650- **1** **African Grey**[231] 4405 3-9-4 **57**..... BenRobinson(3) 2 — 62+
(David Barron) *dwlt and towards rr: hdwy to trck ldrs 4f out: cl up 2f out: rdn to ld over 1f out: kpt on wl fnl f* **4/1**[2]

006- **2** 2 **Kazanan (IRE)**[249] 3749 3-9-0 **50**..... CallumRodriguez 3 — 51
(Michael Dods) *t.k.h: hld up towards rr: hdwy wl over 1f out: rdn and styd on wl fnl f* **16/1**

50-0 **3** ½ **Albizu Campos**[11] 848 3-8-9 **50**..... BenSanderson(5) 4 — 48
(Lawrence Mullaney) *t.k.h: trckd ldrs: hdwy over 2f out: rdn to chse wnr ent fnl f: kpt on same pce* **16/1**

000- **4** 1¼ **Rey Loopy (IRE)**[79] 8384 3-9-5 **55**..... MeganNicholls 6 — 50
(Ben Haslam) *hld up: hdwy 2f out: rdn over 1f out: no imp fnl f* **6/1**

6-03 **5** 3¾ **Panther In Pink (IRE)**[11] 848 3-8-9 **48**..... GerO'Neill(3) 5 — 34
(Ann Duffield) *chsd ldrs: rdn along over 2f out: sn btn: fin 6th, plcd 5th* **9/2**[3]

650 6 8 **Alfolk (IRE)**[23] 642 3-9-4 57 .......................... JordanUys(3) 1 23
(David Simcock) *plld hrd: trckd ldr: pushed along wl over 2f out: sn rdn and wknd: fin 7th, plcd 6th* 2/1[1]
654- D 1/2 **Hollywood Harry (IRE)**[190] 5840 3-9-3 56 ..................(p) PaulaMuir(3) 7 44
(Keith Dalgleish) *led: rdn along 2f out: drvn and hdd over 1f out: wknd fnl f: fin 5th: disq: weighed in 5lb light* 4/1[2]

1m 28.69s (2.49) **Going Correction** +0.125s/f (Slow) **7** Ran SP% **117.6**
Speed ratings (Par 96): **90,87,87,85,80 71,85**
CSF £63.43 CT £931.44 TOTE £5.20: £2.60, £5.00; EX 49.40 Trifecta £575.50.
**Owner** M Rozenbroek **Bred** David Brocklehurst **Trained** Maunby, N Yorks

**FOCUS**
This low-grade apprentice handicap for 3yos featured several from shrewd yards making their handicap debuts. It was run steadily early but was still 9.41 secs slower than the preceding maiden, which was run at a crawl.
T/Plt: £127.70 to a £1 stake. Pool: £84,902.00 - 485.29 winning units. T/Qpdt: £40.90 to a £1 stake. Pool: £6,538.91 - 118.12 winning units. **Joe Rowntree**

1035 - 1039a (Foreign Racing) - See Raceform Interactive

# [935]MEYDAN (L-H)

Saturday, March 4

**OFFICIAL GOING: Dirt: fast; turf: good**

## 1040a AL BASTAKIYA SPONSORED BY EMIRATES SKYWARDS (LISTED RACE) (DIRT) 1m 1f 110y(D)

12:00 3-Y-O

**£121,951** (£40,650; £20,325; £10,162; £6,097; £4,065)

RPR

1 **Cosmo Charlie (USA)**[21] 697 3-9-0 107 ..................(v) PatDobbs 5 104
(Doug Watson, UAE) *sn led: rdn clr 2 1/2f out: r.o wl* 7/1
2 1 **Qatar Man (IRE)**[21] 697 3-9-0 96 ..................(b) RyanMoore 2 102
(Marco Botti) *trckd ldr: r.o wl fnl 3f but nt rch wnr* 16/1
3 5 **Capezzano (USA)**[21] 697 3-9-0 98 .................. WilliamBuick 11 92
(Charlie Appleby) *trckd ldrs: ev ch 3f out: one pce fnl 2f* 6/1[3]
4 3/4 **Nobelium (USA)**[9] 887 3-9-2 100 ow2 .................. OlivierPeslier 4 92+
(R Bouresly, Kuwait) *settled in rr: r.o fnl 2 1/2f: nrst fin* 11/1
5 3/4 **Somerset House (USA)**[65] 8576 3-9-0 92 ..........(b) ColmO'Donoghue 6 89
(Charlie Appleby) *trckd ldr: rdn 3 1/2f out: one pce fnl 2 1/2f* 8/1
6 4 3/4 **Dawwass (USA)**[51] 201 3-9-0 80 .................. RichardMullen 1 79
(S Seemar, UAE) *nvr bttr than mid-div* 40/1
7 11 **Victor Kalejs (USA)**[21] 697 3-9-0 87 ..................(t) AntonioFresu 9 56
(Roy Arne Kvisla, Sweden) *nvr bttr than mid-div* 100/1
8 4 1/4 **Al Barez (USA)**[43] 344 3-9-0 80 ..................(vt) JimCrowley 8 48
(A bin Harmash, UAE) *a in rr* 100/1
9 5 1/4 **Thegreatcollection (USA)**[154] 3-9-0 95 ..................(bt) SamHitchcott 10 37
(Doug Watson, UAE) *nvr bttr than mid-div* 20/1
10 16 **Zumurudee (USA)**[101] 8073 3-9-0 90 .................. ChristopheSoumillon 7 4
(Marco Botti) *a in rr* 7/2[2]
11 2 3/4 **Han Sense (USA)**[21] 697 3-9-0 96 ..................(b) FernandoJara 3
(Maria Ritchie, UAE) *a in rr* 33/1
U **Fawree (USA)**[51] 201 3-9-0 98 .................. BernardFayd'Herbe 12
(M F De Kock, South Africa) *uns rdr at s* 13/8[1]

1m 58.87s (0.07) **12** Ran SP% **124.6**
CSF: 112.58; TRICAST: 725.99.
**Owner** Kildare Stud - Frankie O'Connor **Bred** Roger S Braugh Jr **Trained** United Arab Emirates

**FOCUS**
Rail on turf track out 4 metres. TRAKUS (metres travelled compared to winner): 2nd +5, 3rd +18, 4th +9, 5th +14, 6th +1, 7th +13, 8th +14, 9th +26, 10th +20, 11th +3. The winner made all through strong, gradually slowing fractions: 25.28 (400m from standing start), 23.52 (800m), 24.76 (1200m), 25.48 (1600m). The form is rated at the lower end of the race averages.

## 1041a MAHAB AL SHIMAAL SPONSORED BY EMIRATES SKYWARDS (GROUP 3) (DIRT) 6f (D)

12:35 (12:35) 3-Y-0+

**£97,560** (£32,520; £16,260; £8,130; £4,878; £3,252)

RPR

1 **Morawij**[15] 802 7-9-5 105 .................. ChrisHayes 6 115
(D Selvaratnam, UAE) *sn led: rdn clr 2 1/2f out: r.o: jst hld on* 12/1
2 hd **Cool Cowboy (USA)**[30] 539 6-9-5 112 .................. PatDobbs 3 114+
(Doug Watson, UAE) *mid-div: rdn 3f out: r.o wl: jst failed* 15/8[2]
3 1 1/4 **Dundonnell (USA)**[21] 694 7-9-5 110 ..............(h) ChristopheSoumillon 2 110
(C Fownes, Hong Kong) *trckd ldr: ev ch 2 1/2f out: r.o same pce fnl 2f* 5/1[3]
4 2 3/4 **Comicas (USA)**[21] 694 4-9-5 104 ..................(b) WilliamBuick 7 101+
(Charlie Appleby) *mid-div: r.o fnl 2f but nvr able to chal* 15/2
5 1/2 **Wild Dude (USA)**[16] 772 7-9-5 104 ..................(bt) ShaneFoley 1 100
(M Halford, Ire) *nvr nr to chal but r.o same pce fnl 2f* 33/1
6 4 3/4 **Muarrab**[30] 539 8-9-5 111 .................. JimCrowley 8 84
(Maria Ritchie, UAE) *nvr bttr than mid-div* 7/4[1]
7 3 3/4 **Dios Corrida (JPN)**[70] 3-8-9 105 ..................(h) AndreaAtzeni 9 72
(Yoshitada Takahashi, Japan) *trckd ldr tl wknd 3 1/2f out* 16/1
8 nk **Raafid**[16] 772 4-9-5 99 .................. DaneO'Neill 5 71
(A R Al Rayhi, UAE) *slowly away: a in rr* 50/1
9 1 1/2 **High On Life**[15] 802 6-9-5 98 ..................(t) RoystonFfrench 4 67
(S bin Ghadayer, UAE) *s.i.s: trckd ldrs tl outpcd 3f out* 40/1

1m 11.23s (-0.37)
**WFA** 3 from 4yo+ 14lb **9** Ran SP% **120.5**
CSF: 36.26; TRICAST: 136.09.
**Owner** Sheikh Ahmed Al Maktoum **Bred** Dunchurch Lodge Stud Co **Trained** United Arab Emirates

**FOCUS**
TRAKUS (metres travelled compared to winner): 2nd -2, 3rd -5, 4th +4, 5th -4, 6th +8, 7th +5, 8th +3, 9th -1. The winner got away with setting sensible enough fractions: 24.04, 22.8, 24.39. HE posted a pb with the next three in line with recent C&D figures.

## 1042a DUBAI CITY OF GOLD SPONSORED BY EMIRATES SKYCARGO (GROUP 2) (TURF) 1m 4f 11y(T)

1:10 (1:10) 3-Y-0+

**£121,951** (£40,650; £20,325; £10,162; £6,097; £4,065)

RPR

1 **Prize Money**[21] 699 4-8-11 115 ..................(h) AdriedeVries 4 113
(Saeed bin Suroor) *settled in rr: smooth prog 3f out: rdn to ld 165yds out: r.o wl* 4/1[2]





2 nk **Postponed (IRE)**[153] 6989 6-9-0 124 .................. AndreaAtzeni 10 113+
(Roger Varian) *mid-div: rdn 3f out: r.o wl fnl 1 1/2f: jst failed* 2/5[1]
3 3/4 **Emotionless (IRE)**[23] 650 4-8-11 109 .................. WilliamBuick 7 111
(Charlie Appleby) *mid-div: chsd ldrs 3f out: led 1 1/2f out: hdd 165yds out: one pce fnl 110yds* 12/1[3]
4 1 1/4 **Rembrandt Van Rijn (IRE)**[21] 699 6-9-0 105 .....(b) MickaelBarzalona 1 110
(S bin Ghadayer, UAE) *slowly away: nvr nr to chal but r.o fnl 2f* 25/1
5 2 1/4 **Dylan Mouth (IRE)**[21] 699 6-9-0 110 .................. FrankieDettori 6 107
(Marco Botti) *trckd ldr: led 3 1/2f out: hdd 1 1/2f out: n.m.r 1f out: wknd* 12/1[3]
6 3 1/4 **Memorial Day (IRE)**[9] 891 6-9-0 109 .................. JimCrowley 3 101
(Saeed bin Suroor) *trckd ldr: ev ch 3f out: one pce fnl 2f* 40/1
7 2 1/2 **Famous Kid (USA)**[47] 268 6-9-0 108 .................. OisinMurphy 2 97
(Saeed bin Suroor) *nvr bttr than mid-div* 33/1
8 3 1/4 **Cooptado (ARG)**[34] 6-9-0 101 .................. RichardMullen 8 92
(P Schiergen, Germany) *mid-div tl wknd 4f out* 100/1
9 2 **King Bolete (IRE)**[199] 5558 5-9-0 102 .................. JackMitchell 5 89
(Roger Varian) *sn led: hdd 3 1/2f out: sn btn* 66/1
10 5 3/4 **Good Trip (IRE)**[15] 803 4-8-11 101 ..................(t) SaeedAlMazrooei 9 79
(A R Al Rayhi, UAE) *nvr nr to chal* 100/1

2m 29.33s (-2.47)
**WFA** 4 from 5yo+ 1lb **10** Ran SP% **119.5**
CSF: 5.99; TRICAST: 17.29.
**Owner** Godolphin **Bred** Darley **Trained** Newmarket, Suffolk

**FOCUS**
The pace steadied a little at halfway but overall the favourite's pacemaker King Bolete took them along at a good gallop. They went 25.52 (400m), 24.30 (800m), 24.62 (1200m), 25.02 (1600m) and 24.26 (2000m), before the winner finished in 24.61. TRAKUS (metres travelled compared to winner): 2nd +4, 3rd +4, 4th +2, 5th +2, 6th -1, 7th -6, 8th +8, 9th -5, 10th +12. Prize Money is rated to his previous handiap form.

## 1043a BURJ NAHAAR SPONSORED BY EMIRATES HOLIDAYS (GROUP 3) (DIRT) 1m (D)

1:45 (1:45) 3-Y-0+

**£97,560** (£32,520; £16,260; £8,130; £4,878; £3,252)

RPR

1 **Heavy Metal**[16] 775 7-9-0 109 .................. MickaelBarzalona 5 119+
(S bin Ghadayer, UAE) *sn led: skipped clr 3f out: r.o wl: easily* 7/4[1]
2 6 1/2 **Ross (IRE)**[16] 772 5-9-0 104 .................. AndreaAtzeni 4 104
(P Schiergen, Germany) *settled in rr: nvr able to chal but r.o fnl 2f* 20/1
3 1/2 **Alabaster (USA)**[9] 891 5-9-0 102 ..................(b) OisinMurphy 8 103
(Saeed bin Suroor) *s.i.s: settled in rr: nvr nr to chal but r.o wl fnl 2f* 8/1
4 1 1/2 **Stormardal (IRE)**[93] 8185 6-9-0 104 ..................(p) AdriedeVries 1 100
(Ismail Mohammed) *trckd ldrs: ev ch 3f out: wknd fnl 1 1/2f* 4/1[2]
5 1 1/4 **Power Blade (KOR)**[30] 541 4-9-0 103 ..................(e) PatCosgrave 2 97
(Kim Young Kwan, Korea) *s.i.s: settled in rr: rdn to chse ldrs 3f out: wknd fnl f* 16/1
6 1 1/4 **Shamaal Nibras (USA)**[15] 803 8-9-0 103 .................. DaneO'Neill 13 94
(Doug Watson, UAE) *nvr nr to chal but r.o same pce fnl 3f* 33/1
7 3/4 **Stunned**[16] 772 6-9-0 104 ..................(v) PatDobbs 3 92
(Doug Watson, UAE) *nvr nr to chal* 16/1
8 2 1/2 **Le Bernardin (USA)**[30] 541 8-9-0 112 ..................(t) TadhgO'Shea 10 86
(A R Al Rayhi, UAE) *chsd ldrs: rdn 4f out: one pce fnl 3f* 6/1[3]
9 5 **Ennobled Friend (USA)**[21] 695 7-9-0 100 .......(bt) ColmO'Donoghue 12 75
(A bin Harmash, UAE) *a in rr* 33/1
10 3 3/4 **Lindo Amor (ARG)**[21] 695 4-9-0 105 ..............(b) ChristopheSoumillon 6 66
(M F De Kock, South Africa) *s.i.s: trckd ldrs tl wknd fnl 3f* 16/1
11 2 1/2 **Nathr (USA)**[16] 775 6-9-0 100 ..................(v) JimCrowley 11 60
(Doug Watson, UAE) *s.i.s: nvr bttr than mid-div* 16/1
12 1 **Brex Drago (ITY)**[16] 775 5-9-0 102 .................. AntonioFresu 7 58
(Marco Botti) *chsd ldrs tl wknd 3 1/2f out* 40/1
13 5 1/4 **Polar River (USA)**[58] 85 4-8-9 110 .................. SamHitchcott 9 41
(Doug Watson, UAE) *s.i.s: nvr nr to chal* 10/1

1m 37.19s (-0.31) **13** Ran SP% **127.5**
CSF: 48.94; TRICAST: 251.38.
**Owner** Sheikh Hamdan bin Mohammed Al Maktoum **Bred** Darley **Trained** United Arab Emirates

**FOCUS**
TRAKUS (metres travelled compared to winner): 2nd +5, 3rd +11, 4th -2, 5th -4, 6th +16, 7th +1, 8th +6, 9th +12, 10th +6, 11th +11, 12th +3, 13th +13. The winner set a good pace and saw it out well: 24.87, 23.03, 24.59, 24.7. Another pb from Heavy Metal.

## 1044a NAD AL SHEBA TURF SPRINT SPONSORED BY ARABIAN ADVENTURES (CONDITIONS) (TURF) 6f

2:20 (2:20) 3-Y-0+

**£97,560** (£32,520; £16,260; £8,130; £4,878; £3,252)

RPR

1 **Jungle Cat (IRE)**[16] 773 5-9-0 112 ..................(p) WilliamBuick 6 116
(Charlie Appleby) *settled in rr: smooth prog 2 1/2f out: led 1f out: r.o wl* 6/4[1]
2 2 **Baccarat (IRE)**[37] 433 8-9-0 111 .................. ColmO'Donoghue 16 110
(Charlie Appleby) *settled in rr: r.o wl fnl 1 1/2f: nrst fin* 4/1[2]
3 1 3/4 **The Right Man**[123] 7758 5-9-0 113 .................. Francois-XavierBertras 14 104
(D Guillemin, France) *mid-div: r.o fnl 2f but no ch w wnr* 7/1
4 2 1/4 **Tupi (IRE)**[8] 914 5-9-0 101 ..................(b) MickaelBarzalona 2 97
(Richard Hannon) *s.i.s: settled in rr: r.o fnl 2f: nrst fin* 33/1
5 nk **Final Venture**[21] 696 5-9-0 111 ..................(h) PatDobbs 7 96
(Paul Midgley) *trckd ldrs: ev ch 2f out: r.o same pce fnl f* 11/2[3]
6 1 1/4 **Mustallib (IRE)**[15] 802 4-9-0 96 .................. DaneO'Neill 11 92
(A R Al Rayhi, UAE) *mid-div: r.o fnl 2f: n.d* 50/1
7 1/2 **Caspian Prince (IRE)**[7] 932 8-9-0 107 ..................(t) FrankieDettori 4 90
(Roger Fell) *sn led: hdd 2f out: r.o same pce fnl 1 1/2f* 25/1
8 nk **Speed Hawk (USA)**[16] 773 6-9-0 104 ..................(t) ChrisHayes 9 89
(D Selvaratnam, UAE) *nvr bttr than mid-div* 40/1
9 3/4 **Roicead (USA)**[23] 651 10-9-0 100 ..................(t) RichardMullen 8 87
(D Selvaratnam, UAE) *nvr bttr than mid-div* 66/1
10 1/2 **Fabulous One (NZ)**[21] 694 5-9-0 105 ..................(t) OisinMurphy 5 85
(W Y So, Hong Kong) *trckd ldr: led briefly 2f out: sn hdd & wknd* 20/1
11 2 1/4 **Tahanee (ARG)**[9] 892 4-8-9 106 ..................(p) PatCosgrave 1 73
(M F De Kock, South Africa) *nvr nr to chal* 11/1
12 nk **Magnus Maximus**[21] 696 6-9-0 104 .................. TadhgO'Shea 3 77
(Robyn Brisland) *trckd ldr tl outpcd 2 1/2f out* 40/1
13 4 1/2 **Solar Flair**[23] 651 5-9-0 100 .................. AndreaAtzeni 13 63
(William Knight) *nvr bttr than mid-div* 40/1
14 shd **Krypton Factor**[15] 802 9-9-0 104 ..................(b) SamHitchcott 15 62
(Fawzi Abdulla Nass, Bahrain) *nvr bttr than mid-div* 50/1

15 1 ¼ **Watchable**16 773 7-9-0 101 (p) AdriedeVries 10 58
(David O'Meara) *nvr nr to chal* **40/1**
16 3 **Ghaamer (USA)**9 892 7-9-0 109 (t) JimCrowley 12 49
(A R Al Rayhi, UAE) *slowly away: a in rr* **33/1**
1m 9.21s (0.21) **16** Ran SP% **125.9**
CSF: 6.43; TRICAST: 36.97.
**Owner** Godolphin **Bred** Darley **Trained** Newmarket, Suffolk
**FOCUS**
This went pretty much to form, four of the top five rated horses finishing in the first four places. The gallop was a good one, which set things up for the closers. Caspian Prince took them along in 23.69 (400m) and 21.52 (800m) before the winner closed in 24.00. TRAKUS (metres travelled compared to winner): 2nd -1, 3rd -1, 4th 0, 5th 0, 6th 0, 7th -1, 8th -1, 9th 0, 10th 0, 11th -1, 12th 0, 13th 0, 14th +1, 15th 0, 16th +1

## 1045a AL MAKTOUM CHALLENGE R3 SPONSORED BY EMIRATES AIRLINE (GROUP 1) (DIRT) 1m 2f (D)
**2:55** (2:55) 3-Y-O+
**£195,121** (£65,040; £32,520; £16,260; £9,756; £6,504)

RPR
1 **Long River (USA)**30 541 7-9-0 106 (b) MickaelBarzalona 2 112
(S bin Ghadayer, UAE) *sn led: rdn 3f out: r.o wl: hld on gamely* **25/1**
2 1 ¼ **Special Fighter (IRE)**343 1108 6-9-0 115 FernandoJara 5 110+
(Maria Ritchie, UAE) *trckd ldr: ev ch 1 1/2f out: one pce fnl f* **5/1**3
3 1 ¼ **Furia Cruzada (CHI)**30 541 5-8-9 108 AntonioFresu 4 102+
(E Charpy, UAE) *mid-div: r.o fnl 3f but nvr able to chal* **6/1**
4 ¾ **Move Up**154 6940 4-9-0 115 AdriedeVries 3 106+
(Saeed bin Suroor) *mid-div: r.o same pce fnl 2 1/2f but nvr able to chal* **7/2**2
5 6 ¼ **Triple Nine (KOR)**23 650 5-9-0 105 (e) PatCosgrave 1 93
(Kim Young Kwan, Korea) *nvr nr to chal* **14/1**
6 6 ½ **Lani (USA)**90 8215 4-9-0 113 RyanMoore 8 80
(Mikio Matsunaga, Japan) *a in rr* **11/2**
7 ½ **Second Summer (USA)**30 541 5-9-0 111 (t) PatDobbs 6 79
(Doug Watson, UAE) *settled in rr: nvr able to chal* **15/8**1
8 14 ½ **Mizbah**15 803 8-9-0 102 SamHitchcott 7 50
(Doug Watson, UAE) *trckd ldr: rdn 6f out: sn btn* **25/1**
2m 4.2s (-0.50) **8** Ran SP% **117.7**
CSF: 148.59; TRICAST: 862.07.
**Owner** Sheikh Hamdan bin Mohammed Al Maktoum **Bred** Darley **Trained** United Arab Emirates
**FOCUS**
TRAKUS (metres travelled compared to winner): 2nd +9, 3rd +15, 4th +2, 5th +3, 6th +16, 7th +13, 8th +20. The winner got a sensible, well-judged ride, setting the following fractions to become the fourth front-running winner from as many dirt races on the card: 25.74, 24.09, 24.39, 24.73, 25.25. Long River is rated back to the pick of his 2014 form.

## 1046a JEBEL HATTA SPONSORED BY EMIRATES AIRLINE (GROUP 1) (TURF) 1m 1f (T)
**3:30** (3:30) 3-Y-O+
**£146,341** (£48,780; £24,390; £12,195; £7,317; £4,878)

RPR
1 **Decorated Knight**28 574 5-9-0 113 AndreaAtzeni 1 114+
(Roger Charlton) *mid-div: n.m.r 2 1/2f out: r.o wl once clr: led cl home* **2/1**1
2 nk **Folkswood**23 654 4-9-0 110 (p) WilliamBuick 12 113
(Charlie Appleby) *sn led: rdn clr 2 1/2f out: r.o but hdd cl home* **5/1**2
3 nk **Muffri'Ha (IRE)**16 771 5-8-9 109 PatCosgrave 3 108+
(William Haggas) *mid-div: r.o wl fnl 2f: nrst fin* **6/1**3
4 nk **Sanshaawes (SAF)**16 776 7-9-0 110 BernardFayd'Herbe 11 112
(M F De Kock, South Africa) *trckd ldrs: ev ch 1 1/2f out: one pce fnl 110yds* **16/1**
5 ½ **Earnshaw (USA)**16 776 6-9-0 110 (t) MickaelBarzalona 4 111+
(S bin Ghadayer, UAE) *settled in rr: r.o fnl 2 1/2f but nvr able to chal* **9/1**
6 1 ¼ **Light The Lights (SAF)**16 774 5-9-0 111 ChristopheSoumillon 5 108
(M F De Kock, South Africa) *mid-div: r.o same pce fnl 2f* **14/1**
7 ½ **Promising Run (USA)**16 776 4-8-9 108 (p) RyanMoore 8 102
(Saeed bin Suroor) *trckd ldr: ev ch 2f out: wknd fnl f* **7/1**
8 2 ¾ **Epsom Icon**21 698 4-8-9 100 MarcMonaghan 6 97
(Mick Channon) *nvr bttr than mid-div* **66/1**
9 nk **Elliptique (IRE)**16 776 6-9-0 115 RichardMullen 2 101
(S Seemar, UAE) *s.i.s: nvr nr to chal* **25/1**
10 1 ¾ **Elleval (IRE)**9 888 7-9-0 101 (p) SamHitchcott 7 97
(David Marnane, Ire) *mid-div: wd: outpcd fnl 3f* **50/1**
11 7 **Roi De Vitesse (IRE)**23 651 10-9-0 100 DaneO'Neill 9 83
(Ali Jan, Qatar) *nvr nr to chal* **100/1**
P **Ertijaal (AUS)**58 86 5-9-0 113 JimCrowley 10
(M F De Kock, South Africa) *s.i.s: p.u 8f out* **7/1**
1m 49.95s (0.85) **12** Ran SP% **120.1**
CSF: 11.53; TRICAST: 53.69; PLACEPOT: £55.00 to a £1 stake. Pool: £4,946.40 - 65.65 winning tickets; QUADPOT: £11.80 to a £1 stake. Pool: £671.00 - 41.90 winning tickets..
**Owner** Saleh Al Homaizi & Imad Al Sagar **Bred** Saleh Al Homaizi & Imad Al Sagar **Trained** Beckhampton, Wilts
**FOCUS**
A weak Group 1. They didn't go a strong early pace and they finished in a bit of a heap, the winner doing well to cut down the runner-up close home. Folkswood took them along in 26.47 (400m), 24.56 (800m), 24.38 (1200m) and 22.72 (1600m) before the winner finished in 11.83. TRAKUS (metres travelled compared to winner): 2nd +1, 3rd +1, 4th -1, 5th +4, 6th +4, 7th +5, 8th +6, 9th +2, 10th +7, 11th +5. The second, fourth and fifth help with the standard.

1047 - 1061a (Foreign Racing) - See Raceform Interactive

# 954WOLVERHAMPTON (A.W) (L-H)
Monday, March 6
**OFFICIAL GOING: Tapeta: standard**
Wind: Fresh across Weather: Cloudy with sunny spells

## 1062 BETWAY SPRINT H'CAP (DIV I) 6f 20y (Tp)
**2:10** (2:11) (Class 5) (0-70,72) 4-Y-O+ **£3,234** (£962; £481; £240) **Stalls** Low

Form RPR
-15 1 **K'Gari Spirit**32 518 4-8-13 62 (t) NickyMackay 2 73
(Jeremy Gask) *hld up: hdwy 1/2-way: led 1f out: rdn out* **14/1**
6261 2 2 ¼ **Spirit Of Wedza (IRE)**14 844 5-9-3 66 JoeDoyle 8 70
(Julie Camacho) *chsd ldr tl led over 3f out: rdn and hdd 1f out: styd on same pce* **3/1**1
0-21 3 ¾ **Castlerea Tess**34 494 4-8-7 56 oh4 (p) JamesSullivan 3 57
(Sarah Hollinshead) *sn pushed along and prom: outpcd over 3f out: hdwy over 1f out: rdn and edgd lft ins fnl f: styd on* **16/1**
2-22 4 shd **Malaysian Boleh**19 745 7-9-7 70 (b) BenCurtis 9 71
(Brian Ellison) *s.i.s: outpcd: r.o ins fnl f: nt trble ldrs* **9/2**2
00-5 5 2 **Panther Patrol (IRE)**23 682 7-9-6 72 (v) EdwardGreatrex(3) 10 67
(Eve Johnson Houghton) *s.i.s: outpcd: hdwy over 1f out: styd on same pce ins fnl f* **8/1**
01-0 6 ½ **Nezar (IRE)**16 808 6-9-9 72 (h) RobertWinston 5 65
(Dean Ivory) *prom: rdn over 1f out: edgd lft and no ex ins fnl f* **10/1**
0-03 7 1 ½ **Aragon Knight**30 575 4-9-6 69 OisinMurphy 1 57
(Heather Main) *chsd ldrs: rdn over 1f out: wknd wl ins fnl f* **7/1**
062 8 4 ½ **Cruise Tothelimit (IRE)**10 901 9-8-11 60 (v) FrannyNorton 6 34
(Patrick Morris) *led: hdd over 3f out: chsd ldr tl rdn over 1f out: wknd fnl f* **8/1**
460- 9 6 **Moi Aussie**125 7751 4-8-7 56 SilvestreDeSousa 7 11
(Michael Appleby) *prom: lost pl over 4f out: pushed along 1/2-way: wknd over 1f out: eased fnl f* **6/1**3
1m 13.67s (-0.83) **Going Correction** -0.05s/f (Stan) **9** Ran SP% **113.8**
Speed ratings (Par 103): **103,100,99,98,96 95,93,87,79**
CSF £55.15 CT £695.10 TOTE £20.40: £5.10, £1.50, £3.20; EX 77.70 Trifecta £908.00.
**Owner** Miss K M Dobb **Bred** Stuart Dobb & Miss Kate Dobb **Trained** Stockbridge, Hants
**FOCUS**
They went a good gallop up front and that set things up for a closer. A clear pb from the winner, with the runner-up rated a bit below his C&D latest.

## 1063 BETWAY SPRINT H'CAP (DIV II) 6f 20y (Tp)
**2:40** (2:41) (Class 5) (0-70,72) 4-Y-O+ **£3,234** (£962; £481; £240) **Stalls** Low

Form RPR
1324 1 **Athassel**14 841 8-8-4 60 KatherineGlenister(7) 3 69
(David Evans) *s.i.s: hld up: hdwy and swtchd rt over 1f out: rdn to ld wl ins fnl f: edgd lft: r.o* **13/2**
0003 2 1 **Fleckerl (IRE)**14 844 7-9-7 70 (p) PaulMulrennan 2 76
(Conor Dore) *s.s: hld up: rdn and r.o ins fnl f: wnt 2nd towards fin* **3/1**2
-003 3 ½ **Loumarin (IRE)**28 601 5-8-9 58 (p) SilvestreDeSousa 5 62
(Michael Appleby) *sn led: rdn and edgd rt over 1f out: hdd wl ins fnl f: styd on same pce* **6/1**
2560 4 ¾ **Indian Affair**14 844 7-8-13 62 (bt) LukeMorris 6 64
(Milton Bradley) *led early: chsd ldr: rdn over 1f out: styd on same pce ins fnl f* **14/1**
3113 5 ¾ **Pushkin Museum (IRE)**14 843 6-9-3 66 AdamKirby 1 67
(Patrick Morris) *chsd ldrs: nt clr run fr over 1f out tl swtchd lft ins fnl f: styd on same pce* **11/4**1
00-0 6 ½ **Picket Line**16 808 5-9-9 72 JosephineGordon 8 70
(Geoffrey Deacon) *prom: plld hrd tl drvn along over 3f out: hung lft and styd on same pce fnl f* **8/1**
0222 7 4 ½ **Spiraea**19 735 7-9-5 68 TomEaves 7 52
(Ivan Furtado) *chsd ldrs: rdn over 1f out: wknd fnl f* **11/2**3
1m 14.2s (-0.30) **Going Correction** -0.05s/f (Stan) **7** Ran SP% **112.4**
Speed ratings (Par 103): **100,98,98,97,96 95,89**
CSF £25.38 CT £121.96 TOTE £7.60: £3.00, £2.20; EX 27.00 Trifecta £178.40.
**Owner** Mrs E Evans **Bred** Moyns Park Estate And Stud Ltd **Trained** Pandy, Monmouths
**FOCUS**
Run in a time 0.53sec slower than the first division, this was a messy race pace-wise, and luck in running played a part in the result. It's been rated around the third.

## 1064 BETWAY SPRINT MAIDEN STKS 6f 20y (Tp)
**3:10** (3:11) (Class 5) 3-Y-O+ **£3,234** (£962; £481; £240) **Stalls** Low

Form RPR
0- 1 **Derek Duval (USA)**205 5395 3-8-9 0 (t) AaronJones(3) 3 71
(Stuart Williams) *hld up in tch: shkn up over 1f out: edgd rt ins fnl f: r.o to ld nr fin* **3/1**2
5-62 2 nk **Trotter**7 956 3-8-12 0 OisinMurphy 5 70
(Stuart Kittow) *chsd ldrs: led over 1f out: rdn and edgd rt ins fnl f: hdd nr fin* **9/4**1
65-3 3 1 ¾ **Prazeres**7 956 3-8-12 72 JasonHart 6 64
(Les Eyre) *led early: chsd ldr: rdn and ev ch over 1f out: styd on same pce ins fnl f* **7/2**3
6-3 4 6 **Lostock**10 904 3-8-12 0 PaulMulrennan 1 47
(Michael Dods) *dwlt: hld up: rdn over 2f out: wnt 4th wl ins fnl f: nvr on terms* **9/2**
5 5 ½ **Seneca Chief**25 638 3-8-12 0 GeorgeDowning 4 43
(Daniel Kubler) *sn led: rdn and hdd over 1f out: wknd ins fnl f* **20/1**
66 6 ½ **Boogie Babe**20 731 3-8-4 0 (h1) SammyJoBell(3) 8 37
(Richard Fahey) *sn outpcd* **28/1**
- 7 ½ **Anna Medici** 3-8-7 0 LukeMorris 2 35
(Sir Mark Prescott Bt) *s.i.s: rn green: outpcd* **14/1**
0 8 23 **Gerry**28 600 4-9-7 0 JohnFahy 7
(Matthew Salaman) *hld up: rdn and wknd 1/2-way* **150/1**
1m 13.95s (-0.55) **Going Correction** -0.05s/f (Stan)
**WFA** 3 from 4yo 14lb **8** Ran SP% **111.7**
Speed ratings (Par 103): **101,100,98,90,89 88,88,57**
CSF £9.62 TOTE £4.50: £1.60, £1.30, £1.20; EX 14.80 Trifecta £32.60.
**Owner** G & J Racing **Bred** SF Bloodstock LLC **Trained** Newmarket, Suffolk
**FOCUS**
A modest maiden but the winner landed a bit of a gamble. It's been rated around the second and third.

## 1065 SUNBETS.CO.UK CLAIMING STKS 1m 142y (Tp)
**3:40** (3:40) (Class 6) 4-Y-O+ **£2,587** (£770; £384; £192) **Stalls** Low

Form RPR
4-06 1 **Lacan (IRE)**31 548 6-9-10 83 FranBerry 3 84
(Ralph Beckett) *plld hrd: w ldr tl settled to trck ldrs after 1f: swtchd rt and wnt 2nd over 2f out: shkn up to ld over 1f out: sn hung rt: rdn and hung lft wl ins fnl f: styd on* **11/8**1
-116 2 1 **Gold Flash**18 760 5-9-10 78 (v) PhillipMakin 1 82
(Keith Dalgleish) *hld up: nt clr run over 2f out: rdn over 1f out: r.o* **11/2**3
-306 3 1 ½ **Berlusca (IRE)**11 885 8-9-4 78 DanielTudhope 7 75
(David O'Meara) *hld up: hdwy over 1f out: sn rdn: styd on same pce wl ins fnl f* **7/2**2
045- 4 1 ½ **Mr Red Clubs (IRE)**222 4774 8-8-3 72 (p) JaneElliott(7) 8 62
(Michael Appleby) *sn prom: led over 6f out: rdn and hdd over 1f out: styd on same pce ins fnl f* **11/1**
3-55 5 1 ½ **Dana's Present**49 267 8-8-12 71 LiamKeniry 5 60
(Tom Dascombe) *hld up in tch: rdn over 1f out: hung lft and styd on same pce fnl f* **17/2**

3006 **6** ½ **Hard To Handel**[9] [928] 5-9-0 69 ........ PaddyAspell 2 61
(Clare Ellam) *prom: rdn over 2f out: no ex fnl f* **33/1**

-260 **7** 6 **Pool House**[19] [745] 6-8-6 63 ........ JosephineGordon 6 41
(Mike Murphy) *chsd ldrs: rdn 3f out: wknd over 1f out* **20/1**

-040 **8** 10 **Jumbo Prado (USA)**[9] [928] 8-9-0 66 ........(b) LukeMorris 4 28
(Daniel Mark Loughnane) *sn led: hdd over 6f out: chsd ldr tl rdn over 2f out: wknd over 1f out* **12/1**

1m 48.55s (-1.55) **Going Correction** -0.05s/f (Stan) **8** Ran SP% **114.0**
Speed ratings (Par 101): **104,103,101,100,99 98,93,84**
CSF £9.24 TOTE £2.30: £1.20, £1.70, £1.40; EX 10.20 Trifecta £28.50.Lacan was claimed by Mr B. R. Johnson for £12,000.
**Owner** China Horse Club International Limited **Bred** Sheikh Sultan Bin Khalifa Al Nahyan **Trained** Kimpton, Hants

**FOCUS**
A fair claimer. It's been rated around the runner-up to his recent form.

## 1066 32RED.COM FILLIES' H'CAP 7f 36y (Tp)
**4:10** (4:10) (Class 5) (0-75,80) 4-Y-O+ **£3,234** (£962; £481; £240) **Stalls** High

Form RPR

0565 **1** **Lady Lydia (IRE)**[11] [879] 6-9-6 74 ........(t[1]) DanielMuscutt 6 81
(Gay Kelleway) *s.i.s: hld up: hdwy: nt clr run and swtchd rt over 1f out: rdn: edgd lft and r.o to ld wl ins fnl f* **20/1**

-663 **2** 1 **East Coast Lady (IRE)**[11] [883] 5-8-9 66 ........ CallumShepherd(3) 2 70
(William Stone) *chsd ldr who wnt clr over 5f out: tk clsr order over 2f out: led over 1f out: sn rdn and edgd lft: hdd wl ins fnl f* **16/1**

-111 **3** 1 **Simply Me**[3] [996] 4-9-12 80 6ex ........(p) RichardKingscote 1 83+
(Tom Dascombe) *chsd ldrs: effrt and nt clr run over 1f out: sn rdn: styd on same pce wl ins fnl f* **10/11**[1]

0-36 **4** ¾ **Childesplay**[16] [810] 6-9-0 75 ........ CallumRodriguez(7) 3 76+
(Heather Main) *hld up: rdn over 2f out: hdwy and nt clr run over 1f out: r.o: nt rch ldrs* **10/3**[2]

**5** hd **The Yellow Bus**[208] [5314] 4-9-5 73 ........ AdamKirby 5 72
(Michael Wigham) *chsd ldrs: rdn over 1f out: no ex wl ins fnl f* **8/1**

1102 **6** 2 ¼ **Beau Mistral (IRE)**[11] [879] 8-8-10 64 ........ GeorgeDowning 7 57
(Tony Carroll) *led: clr over 5f out tl c bk to the field over 2f out: rdn and hdd over 1f out: nt clr run and wknd ins fnl f* **20/1**

21-0 **7** 7 **Gabrielle**[30] [575] 4-9-3 71 ........ LukeMorris 4 45
(Dr Jon Scargill) *pushed along in rr: rdn 1/2-way: wknd over 1f out* **33/1**

-504 **8** nk **Miss Goldsmith (IRE)**[12] [860] 4-8-3 60 ........ SammyJoBell(3) 8 33
(Richard Fahey) *hld up: a in rr: wknd over 1f out* **7/1**[3]

1m 27.68s (-1.12) **Going Correction** -0.05s/f (Stan) **8** Ran SP% **117.4**
Speed ratings (Par 100): **104,102,101,100,100 98,90,89**
CSF £289.36 CT £598.51 TOTE £27.00: £5.30, £4.10, £1.10; EX 223.30 Trifecta £2012.30.
**Owner** Vince Smith & Partner **Bred** Albert Conneally **Trained** Exning, Suffolk

**FOCUS**
Beau Mistral set a good pace out in front but as she came back to the field she caused the favourite to be held up in her run, and there was a surprise result. The winner has been rated in line with this year's handicap best.

## 1067 BETWAY FREE BET CLUB H'CAP 1m 1f 104y (Tp)
**4:40** (4:40) (Class 6) (0-60,60) 4-Y-O+ **£2,587** (£770; £384; £192) **Stalls** Low

Form RPR

0202 **1** **Siouxperhero (IRE)**[7] [954] 8-9-7 60 ........(p) TomMarquand 2 67
(William Muir) *led: hdd over 7f out: chsd ldrs: rdn over 1f out: r.o to ld towards fin* **8/1**

-303 **2** ½ **Glorious Asset**[23] [690] 5-9-5 58 ........ DavidNolan 3 64
(Ivan Furtado) *a.p: racd keenly: wnt 2nd over 6f out tl led over 1f out: rdn over 1f out: edgd lft ins fnl f: hdd towards fin* **9/2**[1]

600- **3** ¾ **Filament Of Gold (USA)**[69] [8540] 6-9-1 54 ........(p) JosephineGordon 6 59
(Roy Brotherton) *prom: lost pl over 6f out: rdn and hdwy over 2f out: r.o* **8/1**

20-2 **4** 1 ½ **Pensax Lady (IRE)**[23] [690] 4-9-4 57 ........ LukeMorris 4 59
(Daniel Mark Loughnane) *hld up in tch: nt clr run over 2f out: rdn to chse wnr over 1f out: n.m.r ins fnl f: styd on same pce* **5/1**[2]

5060 **5** ½ **Powered (IRE)**[12] [865] 4-8-13 52 ........ SilvestreDeSousa 10 53
(David Evans) *hld up: nt clr run over 2f out: r.o ins fnl f: nvr nrr* **11/2**[3]

0-00 **6** nk **Turnbury**[25] [648] 6-9-4 60 ........(p) EdwardGreatrex(3) 8 60
(Nikki Evans) *hld up: hdwy 2f out: sn rdn: styd on same pce ins fnl f* **33/1**

500- **7** nk **Victor's Bet (SPA)**[153] [7037] 8-9-7 60 ........ DougieCostello 5 60
(Ralph J Smith) *s.i.s: hld up: rdn and r.o ins fnl f: nrst fin* **20/1**

-201 **8** nk **Nouvelle Ere**[11] [880] 6-9-7 60 ........(t) GeorgeDowning 7 59
(Tony Carroll) *hld up: rdn over 1f out: r.o ins fnl f: nvr on terms* **8/1**

-145 **9** 2 ¼ **Schottische**[23] [684] 7-9-1 59 ........(b) DavidParkes(5) 9 54
(Alan Bailey) *s.i.s: hld up: nvr nrr* **14/1**

0-50 **10** 1 ¾ **Lemon Thyme**[7] [954] 4-9-7 60 ........ ShaneKelly 1 52
(Mike Murphy) *prom: nt clr run and lost pl over 2f out: n.d after* **25/1**

3-33 **11** 6 **Suitsus**[23] [689] 6-9-5 58 ........(t) TimmyMurphy 11 38
(Geoffrey Deacon) *wnt prom over 6f out: chsd ldr briefly 2f out: sn rdn: wknd fnl f* **7/1**

0-00 **12** 7 **Speculator**[32] [527] 5-9-7 60 ........(p) AdamKirby 13 27
(John Butler) *sn chsng ldr: led over 7f out: rdn and hdd over 2f out: wknd wl over 1f out* **14/1**

2m 0.92s (0.12) **Going Correction** -0.05s/f (Stan) **12** Ran SP% **120.9**
Speed ratings (Par 101): **97,96,95,94,94 93,93,93,91,89 84,78**
CSF £43.79 CT £306.21 TOTE £9.40: £2.60, £2.20, £2.70; EX 52.50 Trifecta £494.30.
**Owner** Muir Racing Partnership - Bath **Bred** J & J Waldron **Trained** Lambourn, Berks

**FOCUS**
They went an ordinary pace and it paid to race handily. The runner-up has been rated close to the balance of his form.

## 1068 BETWAY H'CAP 1m 4f 51y (Tp)
**5:10** (5:11) (Class 2) (0-105,104) 4-Y-O+ **£11,971** (£3,583; £1,791; £896; £446) **Stalls** Low

Form RPR

5-43 **1** **Cohesion**[18] [767] 4-9-5 101 ........ OisinMurphy 1 109
(David Bridgwater) *sn pushed along: wnt prom over 10f out: rdn over 2f out: styd on u.p to ld wl ins fnl f* **6/1**[2]

6121 **2** 1 ¼ **Winterlude (IRE)**[12] [858] 7-9-10 104 ........ JoeFanning 10 110
(Jennie Candlish) *hld up: hdwy over 2f out: rdn and edgd lft ins fnl f: styd on* **7/1**[3]

301- **3** nk **Fabricate**[153] [7058] 5-9-7 101 ........(p) AdamKirby 5 107
(Michael Bell) *hld up in tch: rdn over 2f out: hung lft over 1f out: styd on* **2/1**[1]

06-6 **4** ¾ **Mistiroc**[17] [779] 6-9-1 95 ........(v) DougieCostello 2 99
(John Quinn) *w ldr 2f: remained handy: chsd ldr over 4f out: led over 2f out: rdn and hdd wl ins fnl f: styd on same pce* **6/1**[2]

52-5 **5** 2 **Barye**[53] [197] 6-9-7 101 ........ ShaneKelly 7 102
(Richard Hughes) *hld up: rdn over 2f out: hung lft and styd on ins fnl f: nvr nrr* **9/1**

04-1 **6** 1 **Haines**[19] [746] 6-9-0 94 ........ RobHornby 3 94
(Andrew Balding) *hld up: rdn over 2f out: hdwy over 1f out: nt trble ldrs* **8/1**

-600 **7** 2 ½ **John Reel (FR)**[17] [779] 8-9-1 95 ........ SilvestreDeSousa 6 91
(David Evans) *prom: chsd ldr over 8f out: led over 5f out: rdn and hdd over 2f out: wknd fnl f* **11/1**

435/ **8** 3 ¾ **Red Tornado (FR)**[163] [7027] 5-8-9 92 ........ EdwardGreatrex(3) 11 82
(Dan Skelton) *hld up: rdn over 2f out: a in rr* **33/1**

31-2 **P** **Plutocracy (IRE)**[49] [269] 7-8-7 90 ........(p) HectorCrouch(3) 4
(Gary Moore) *led: hdd over 5f out: sn rdn: wknd over 3f out: bhd whn p.u and dismntd ins fnl f* **6/1**[2]

2m 35.19s (-5.61) **Going Correction** -0.05s/f (Stan)
**WFA** 4 from 5yo+ 1lb **9** Ran SP% **121.1**
Speed ratings (Par 109): **116,115,114,114,113 112,110,108,**
CSF £49.89 CT £115.36 TOTE £6.50: £2.90, £2.10, £1.20; EX 44.70 Trifecta £142.90.
**Owner** Andrew Duffield **Bred** Millsec Limited **Trained** Icomb, Gloucs

**FOCUS**
A good handicap run at a decent gallop, the lead changing hands several times. It's been rated around the fourth.

## 1069 BETWAY MAIDEN STKS 1m 1f 104y (Tp)
**5:40** (5:42) (Class 5) 3-Y-O+ **£3,234** (£962; £481; £240) **Stalls** Low

Form RPR

32-2 **1** **Enfolding (IRE)**[34] [498] 3-8-7 74 ........ SilvestreDeSousa 2 71+
(James Fanshawe) *chsd ldr 5f: wnt 2nd again over 3f out: led over 1f out: drvn out* **1/2**[1]

52 **2** hd **Specialist (IRE)**[9] [925] 3-8-7 0 ........ FrannyNorton 1 70+
(Mark Johnston) *led: hdd over 4f out: chsd ldr tl over 3f out: swtchd rt over 1f out: rdn and ev ch ins fnl f: r.o* **2/1**[2]

**3** 3 **Bosphorus Prince (IRE)**[939] [5215] 5-9-13 0 ........ JohnFahy 8 70
(Matthew Salaman) *chsd ldrs: rdn over 3f out: hung lft ins fnl f: styd on same pce* **20/1**

0 **4** 1 **Delphyne**[24] [662] 5-9-1 0 ........ AidenBlakemore(7) 7 63
(Shaun Harris) *hld up: rdn over 2f out: styd on ins fnl f: nt trble ldrs* **100/1**

**5** 1 ½ **Amitie Waltz (FR)**[265] 5-9-13 0 ........ ShaneKelly 6 65
(Richard Hughes) *trckd ldrs: racd keenly: qcknd to ld over 4f out: rdn and hdd over 1f out: no ex ins fnl f* **8/1**[3]

05 **6** 1 ¾ **Swallow Dancer**[7] [959] 3-7-9 0 ........ RhiainIngram(7) 5 50
(Harry Dunlop) *s.i.s: hld up: rdn over 2f out: nvr on terms* **20/1**

00 **7** 99 **Mister Raffles**[16] [807] 3-8-10 0 ow3 ........ TomEaves 3
(Mohamed Moubarak) *hld up: wknd 1/2-way* **50/1**

2m 2.87s (2.07) **Going Correction** -0.05s/f (Stan)
**WFA** 3 from 5yo+ 20lb **7** Ran SP% **123.6**
Speed ratings (Par 103): **88,87,85,84,82 81,**
CSF £1.99 TOTE £1.30: £1.70, £1.10; EX 1.70 Trifecta £11.50.
**Owner** Ben CM Wong **Bred** Kenilworth Partnership **Trained** Newmarket, Suffolk
■ Running Squaw was withdrawn. Price at time of withdrawal 150-1. Rule 4 does not apply.

**FOCUS**
An ordinary maiden in which the front two in the market came through to fight out the finish. The first two have been rated below their pre-race marks.
T/Jkpt: Not won. T/Plt: £41.50 to a £1 stake. Pool: £104,417.53 - 1,834.12 winning tickets
T/Qpdt: £4.60 to a £1 stake. Pool: £9,243.99 - 1,482.79 winning tickets **Colin Roberts**

# GHLIN
Monday, March 6
**OFFICIAL GOING: Fibresand: standard**

## 1070a PRIX EUROTIERCE - DE CORK (H'CAP) (4YO ) (FIBRESAND) 7f 110y
**5:30** 4-Y-O
**£4,273** (£1,282; £641; £427; £106; £106)

RPR

**1** **Barbados Bob (USA)**[20] 7-10-0 0 ........(b) MlleZoePfeil 10
(Ecurie Fievez, Belgium) **108/10**

**2** ¾ **Comparative**[270] [3069] 5-8-11 0 ........ AlexanderPietsch 2
(C Von Der Recke, Germany) **131/10**

**3** 1 **Jordan's Tiger (FR)** 6-8-9 0 ........(b) JozefBojko 12
(Jolanda Van Wesel, Belgium) **6/1**[3]

**4** ½ **Inkerman (IRE)**[396] 7-9-8 0 ........ ClementCadel 11
(Leo Braem, Belgium) **81/10**

**5** 1 ¾ **Fergand (FR)**[691] 8-9-2 0 ........ StephenHellyn 9
(F Sergeant, France) **16/5**[1]

**5** dht **Capital Gearing**[24] [663] 4-9-1 0 ........(b) FilipMinarik 13
(Henry Spiller) *a cl up on outer: drvn to chse ldrs appr fnl f: one pce u.p: jnd post for 5th* **66/10**

**7** 2 ½ **S Grillo**[60] 9-8-10 0 ........(b) FabienLefebvre 4
(G Bernaud, Belgium) **26/5**[2]

**8** nk **Gentle Jaime (IRE)**[25] 4-8-5 0 ow1 ........ MlleAnnaVanDenTroost 8
(Leo Braem, Belgium) **173/10**

**9** snk **Viennoise (FR)**[356] 7-8-7 0 ........ MlleAliceBertiaux 5
(Mme V Botte, Belgium) **53/1**

**10** 2 ½ **Alandil (FR)**[928] [5618] 5-9-3 0 ........(p) MarioWaterschoot 7
(T de Vlaminck, Belgium) **155/10**

**11** 1 ¾ **Ozz**[1031] [2174] 8-9-2 0 ........(b) DanielePorcu 3
(Frank Sheridan, Italy) **136/10**

**12** snk **Makin (IRE)**[1022] 7-8-3 0 ........(b) MmeZoeVandeVelde 14
(T de Vlaminck, Belgium) **44/1**

**13** 8 **Zamuja**[246] 6-10-0 0 ........ TimDevos 6
(M Rosseel, France) **78/1**

PARI-MUTUEL (all including 1 euro stake): WIN 11.80 PLACE 4.00, 4.90, 3.40 DF 89.80 SF 207.90.
**Owner** Ecurie Fievez **Bred** Merrydale Farm Partners 2003 Llc **Trained** Belgium



The Form Book Flat, Raceform Ltd, Newbury, RG14 5SJ

# [848]SOUTHWELL (L-H)

Tuesday, March 7

**OFFICIAL GOING: Fibresand: standard**

Wind: Moderate across Weather: Cloudy with sunny periods

## 1071 BETWAY SPRINT H'CAP 4f 214y(F)

**2:00** (2:00) (Class 5) (0-70,70) 4-Y-O+ **£3,234** (£962; £481; £240) **Stalls** Centre

Form RPR

50-0 **1** **Dusty Blue**[64] 22 5-8-11 **60** SilvestreDeSousa 8 70
(Michael Appleby) *racd towards stands side: prom: effrt 2f out: rdn to chal jst over 1f out: drvn ins fnl f: led last 100 yds* **11/2**

2241 **2** *hd* **Treaty Of Rome (USA)**[33] 523 5-9-2 **65** (v) TonyHamilton 11 74
(Derek Shaw) *racd towards stands side: prom: rdn over 1f out: drvn and styd on wl fnl f* **9/2**[2]

3042 **3** *½* **Crosse Fire**[14] 851 5-9-7 **70** KieranO'Neill 6 77
(Scott Dixon) *cl up centre: rdn along wl over 1f out: swtchd lft and drvn to chal ent fnl f: ev ch: edgd lft and no ex towards fin* **9/4**[1]

6-00 **4** *¾* **Powerful Wind (IRE)**[46] 330 8-9-2 **65** (t) BenCurtis 2 70
(Charlie Wallis) *racd centre: led: rdn wl over 1f out: drvn ent fnl f: hdd and one pce last 100 yds* **5/1**[3]

200- **5** *nk* **Ryedale Rio (IRE)**[230] 4512 4-8-12 **64** RachelRichardson(3) 9 67
(Tim Easterby) *racd centre: trckd ldrs: rdn along wl over 1f out: swtchd lft and drvn ent fnl f: kpt on wl towards fin* **66/1**

6660 **6** *hd* **Red Stripes (USA)**[8] 955 5-8-11 **67** (v) JordanUys(7) 5 70
(Lisa Williamson) *chsd ldrs centre: rdn along wl over 1f out: drvn and edgd lft appr fnl f: kpt on* **11/1**

-400 **7** *4* **Misu Moneypenny**[36] 480 4-8-5 **61** (p) RPWalsh(7) 4 49
(Scott Dixon) *racd towards far side: chsd ldrs: rdn over 2f out: sn drvn and no imp* **25/1**

-006 **8** *3¾* **Red Invader (IRE)**[19] 768 7-8-13 **62** LiamKeniry 7 37
(John Butler) *a towards rr* **16/1**

0-00 **9** *1¼* **King Crimson**[12] 886 5-9-6 **69** AdamKirby 3 39
(John Butler) *dwlt: a towards rr* **20/1**

-040 **9** *dht* **Waneen (IRE)**[12] 886 4-9-5 **68** JFEgan 1 38
(John Butler) *chsd ldrs: rdn along bef 1/2-way: sn lost pl and bhd* **12/1**

00-0 **11** *4* **Evanescent (IRE)**[62] 50 8-9-0 **63** RobertWinston 10 19
(Tony Carroll) *a towards rr* **25/1**

58.26s (-1.44) **Going Correction** -0.225s/f (Stan) 11 Ran SP% **116.9**

Speed ratings (Par 103): **102,101,100,99,99 98,92,86,84,84 78**

CSF £28.94 CT £73.37 TOTE £7.00: £2.10, £1.50, £1.40; EX 32.30 Trifecta £96.30.

**Owner** M Chung **Bred** Denford Stud Ltd **Trained** Oakham, Rutland

**FOCUS**

An ordinary sprint handicap in which the main action unfolded nearside. The third has been rated close to his winter best.

## 1072 BETWAY FREE BET CLUB H'CAP 1m 4f 14y(F)

**2:30** (2:30) (Class 6) (0-65,67) 4-Y-O+ **£2,587** (£770; £384; £192) **Stalls** Low

Form RPR

054- **1** **Deep Resolve (IRE)**[59] 8238 6-9-7 **65** (b[1]) JoeFanning 4 71
(Alan Swinbank) *trckd ldrs: hdwy 4f out: sn cl up: led wl over 2f out: rdn clr and edgd lft to far rail over 1f out: drvn and kpt on fnl f* **5/1**[3]

5-03 **2** *1* **Sattelac**[14] 853 4-9-6 **66** ConnorBeasley 6 70
(Keith Dalgleish) *cl up: led over 3f out: sn jnd: rdn and hdd wl over 2f out: swtchd rt and drvn over 1f out: kpt on u.p fnl f* **11/4**[1]

-623 **3** *6* **Bridey's Lettuce (IRE)**[5] 993 5-9-9 **67** TomEaves 2 62
(Ivan Furtado) *trckd ldrs: hdwy 4f out: chsd ldng pair 3f out: rdn along over 2f out: sn drvn and kpt on same pce* **7/2**[2]

-324 **4** *11* **Tasty Ginger (IRE)**[20] 738 4-9-1 **61** OisinMurphy 5 38
(J R Jenkins) *dwlt and sn swtch to outer: in tch: hdwy 4f out: rdn along 3f out: sn drvn and one pce* **7/2**[2]

060- **5** *1* **Brahma**[204] 5486 4-8-9 **60** CharlieBennett(5) 7 36
(Hughie Morrison) *towards rr: pushed along 1/2-way: rdn 5f out: sn outpcd and bhd* **11/2**

30/0 **6** *nse* **Gamesters Lad**[20] 733 5-8-7 **51** oh4 (p) JamesSullivan 3 27
(Oliver Greenall) *cl up: led over 4f out: rdn along and hdd over 3f out: sn drvn and wknd* **33/1**

0-20 **7** *51* **Ramblow**[36] 482 4-8-13 **59** (tp) BenCurtis 1
(Michael Appleby) *led: rdn along 5f out: sn hdd & wknd bhd fnl 3f* **20/1**

2m 37.19s (-3.81) **Going Correction** -0.225s/f (Stan)

**WFA** 4 from 5yo+ 1lb 7 Ran SP% **110.9**

Speed ratings (Par 101): **103,102,98,91,90 90,56**

CSF £17.93 TOTE £6.30: £2.30, £1.80; EX 20.10 Trifecta £68.40.

**Owner** Panther Racing Ltd **Bred** Dermot & Catherine Dwan **Trained** Melsonby, N Yorks

**FOCUS**

A moderate handicap in which the early pace was steady, but they still finished well strung out. It's been rated around the front pair.

## 1073 BETWAY STAYERS H'CAP 1m 6f 21y(F)

**3:00** (3:01) (Class 5) (0-75,73) 4-Y-O+ **£3,234** (£962; £481; £240) **Stalls** Low

Form RPR

5/2- **1** **Samtu (IRE)**[206] 5406 6-9-12 **73** BarryMcHugh 1 84
(Marjorie Fife) *mde most: rdn wl over 2f out: drvn over 1f out: kpt on wl fnl f* **20/1**

32-3 **2** *4* **Katie Gale**[25] 666 7-9-12 **73** (p) AndrewMullen 4 78
(Michael Appleby) *trckd ldrs on outer: hdwy 4f out: chsd wnr 3f out and sn rdn: drvn and ev ch over 1f out: kpt on same pce fnl f* **3/1**[2]

-222 **3** *1½* **Eurato (FR)**[27] 619 7-9-11 **72** (p) AdamKirby 3 75
(Steve Gollings) *trckd ldrs: hdwy 4f out: chsd ldng pair over 2f out: swtchd lft and rdn over 1f out: sn ev ch: drvn and kpt on same pce fnl f* **6/1**

-003 **4** *3* **Tempuran**[13] 861 8-9-2 **63** OisinMurphy 7 62
(David Bridgwater) *cl up: rdn along over 3f out: drvn over 2f out: grad wknd* **17/2**

-132 **5** *9* **Pinwood (IRE)**[7] 965 4-9-6 **71** (t) JFEgan 6 57
(Adam West) *t.k.h early: trckd ldrs: hdwy 4f out: rdn along over 3f out: sn drvn and wknd* **2/1**[1]

-202 **6** *11* **Noguchi (IRE)**[14] 853 12-9-5 **66** (p) SilvestreDeSousa 2 37
(Chris Dwyer) *trckd ldng pair on inner: pushed along over 5f out: rdn over 4f out: sn lost pl and bhd* **5/1**[3]

-446 **7** *2¼* **Spiritoftomintoul**[18] 786 8-9-8 **69** (t) GeorgeDowning 5 37
(Tony Carroll) *dwlt: a rr: drvn along wl over 3f out: sn outpcd* **12/1**

3m 3.87s (-4.43) **Going Correction** -0.225s/f (Stan)

**WFA** 4 from 6yo+ 2lb 7 Ran SP% **112.3**

Speed ratings (Par 103): **103,100,99,98,93 86,85**

CSF £76.33 TOTE £13.60: £4.80, £1.90; EX 51.70 Trifecta £113.70.

**Owner** Martin Lawrence **Bred** Rabbah Bloodstock Limited **Trained** Stillington, N Yorks

**FOCUS**

An ordinary staying handicap, but a game effort from the winner. The winner has been rated close to his old best, and the seocnd and third close to their recent form.

## 1074 SUNBETS.CO.UK H'CAP 1m 13y(F)

**3:30** (3:32) (Class 4) (0-80,82) 4-Y-O+ **£5,822** (£1,732; £865; £432) **Stalls** Low

Form RPR

-620 **1** **Showboating (IRE)**[45] 359 9-9-7 **80** DanielTudhope 13 91
(John Balding) *hld up in rr: wd st: hdwy 2f out: rdn over 1f out: styd on strly fnl f: led last 75 yds* **7/1**[2]

0-10 **2** *1¼* **Zoravan (USA)**[40] 419 4-9-4 **77** (v) PhillipMakin 9 85
(Keith Dalgleish) *trckd ldrs: hdwy over 2f out: swtchd rt and rdn to ld jst over 1f out: drvn ins fnl f: hdd last 75 yds: no ex* **15/2**[3]

3-56 **3** *1* **Captain Revelation**[56] 156 5-9-9 **82** BenCurtis 7 88
(Tom Dascombe) *towards rr: hdwy 3f out: rdn along over 2f out: chsd ldrs over 1f out: sn drvn and kpt on* **17/2**

6440 **4** *¾* **Boots And Spurs**[14] 850 8-8-12 **71** (v) LukeMorris 14 75
(Scott Dixon) *cl up on outer: rdn to ld wl over 1f out: drvn and hdd appr fnl f: kpt on same pce* **22/1**

0-05 **5** *1¼* **Red Touch (USA)**[39] 441 5-9-2 **70** (h[1]) AlistairRawlinson(3) 11 79
(Michael Appleby) *t.k.h early: in tch: hdwy on outer wl over 2f out: swtchd lft to inner and rdn to chse ldrs over 1f out: swtchd rt and drvn ins fnl f: kpt on: nrst fin* **12/1**

4-06 **6** *1* **London (FR)**[12] 876 4-9-6 **79** (h[1]) AdamKirby 2 78
(Phil McEntee) *sn led on inner: rdn over 2f out: hdd wl over 1f out: sn drvn and grad wknd* **16/1**

00-2 **7** *nk* **Aqua Ardens (GER)**[33] 528 9-8-13 **72** (tp) PatCosgrave 3 70
(George Baker) *in tch on inner: hdwy 1/2-way: chsd ldrs 3f out: rdn 2f out: drvn and edgd lft ent fnl f: kpt on same pce* **10/1**

-630 **8** *½* **Playtothewhistle**[25] 663 6-8-7 **66** (v) SilvestreDeSousa 10 63
(Michael Appleby) *rr: hdwy over 2f out: sn rdn and kpt on fnl f: n.d* **11/2**[1]

1-11 **9** *1¼* **Shearian**[33] 527 7-8-9 **73** PhilDennis(5) 12 67
(Declan Carroll) *trckd ldrs on outer: effrt over 2f out: rdn along wl over 1f out: grad wknd* **8/1**

2051 **10** *2¾* **Among Angels**[14] 850 5-9-5 **78** (b) DaleSwift 6 66
(Daniel Mark Loughnane) *cl up: rdn along over 2f out: drvn wl over 1f out: grad wknd* **12/1**

1-24 **11** *3¼* **Anton Chigurh**[40] 419 8-9-2 **75** FrannyNorton 5 56
(Tom Dascombe) *dwlt: a towards rr* **14/1**

6-13 **12** *3¼* **Shah Of Armaan (IRE)**[18] 782 4-9-0 **73** TomEaves 4 46
(Kevin Ryan) *in tch on inner: rdn along wl over 3f out: sn outpcd* **15/2**[3]

1m 40.62s (-3.08) **Going Correction** -0.225s/f (Stan) 12 Ran SP% **114.4**

Speed ratings (Par 105): **106,104,103,103,101 100,100,99,98,95 92,89**

CSF £56.56 CT £459.50 TOTE £8.90: £3.10, £3.10, £2.90; EX 71.20 Trifecta £565.50.

**Owner** M & Mrs L Cooke & A McCabe **Bred** Crone Stud Farms Ltd **Trained** Scrooby, S Yorks

**FOCUS**

A fair and competitive handicap. They went a good pace and that helped the winner. The third helps set the standard.

## 1075 SUN BETS ON THE APP STORE H'CAP 7f 14y(F)

**4:00** (4:03) (Class 6) (0-52,52) 4-Y-O+ **£2,587** (£770; £384; £192) **Stalls** Low

Form RPR

5530 **1** **Fossa**[13] 854 7-8-10 **46** oh1 (h) CharlieBennett(5) 14 52
(Mark Brisbourne) *midfield: hdwy wl over 2f out: chsd ldrs and edgd lft wl over 1f out: sn rdn on outer: styd on strly to ld ins fnl f* **8/1**

3520 **2** *1¾* **General Tufto**[26] 636 12-9-6 **51** (b) JoeyHaynes 11 52
(Charles Smith) *in tch and sn rdn along: hdwy wl over 2f out: chsd ldrs on inner over 1f out: drvn and led briefly ins fnl f: sn hdd and kpt on same pce* **5/1**[3]

000- **3** *nk* **Rupert Boy (IRE)**[77] 8470 4-9-5 **50** (b) DaleSwift 9 50
(Scott Dixon) *cl up: rdn along 3f out: led briefly 2f out:. sn edgd lft and hdd: drvn and kpt on fnl f* **14/1**

0064 **4** *1¼* **Tasaaboq**[5] 982 6-9-3 **48** (t) AdamKirby 5 45
(Phil McEntee) *chsd ldrs: hdwy 3f out: cl up 2f out: sn rdn and led wl over 1f out: drvn and hdd ins fnl: kpt on same pce* **3/1**[1]

3054 **5** *½* **Limerick Lord (IRE)**[19] 761 5-9-0 **48** (p) ShelleyBirkett(3) 6 46
(Julia Feilden) *trckd ldrs: hdwy whn n.m.r wl over 1f out: sn rdn and kpt on one pce* **7/2**[2]

-210 **6** *2¼* **All Or Nothin (IRE)**[27] 620 8-9-7 **52** DannyBrock 2 42
(Paddy Butler) *slt ld on inner: rdn along 3f out: hdd 2f out: sn drvn and grad wknd* **20/1**

560- **7** *6* **Bold Grove**[169] 6636 5-9-1 **46** oh1 RobHornby 13 19
(Edward Bevan) *midfield: rdn along over 2f out: n.d* **12/1**

00-5 **8** *7* **Sober Up**[47] 309 5-9-2 **47** (v[1]) TomEaves 7 2
(Ivan Furtado) *a towards rr* **16/1**

60-0 **9** *1½* **Les Darcy**[20] 739 6-9-1 **46** oh1 (t[1]) LiamKeniry 3
(Ken Cunningham-Brown) *dwlt: a rr* **33/1**

05-6 **10** *½* **Thrtypointstothree (IRE)**[4] 998 6-9-1 **46** oh1 (bt) LukeMorris 4
(Nikki Evans) *a towards rr* **22/1**

00-0 **11** *1½* **Tallulah Fleur**[13] 854 4-8-8 **46** oh1 (p) GerO'Neill(7) 12
(David Loughnane) *chsd ldrs: rdn along 1/2-way: sn wknd* **33/1**

400- **12** *13* **Madam Mai Tai**[152] 7097 5-9-3 **48** DanielTudhope 10
(Rebecca Bastiman) *a towards rr* **16/1**

/00- **13** *16* **Dramatic Voice**[236] 4290 4-9-1 **46** oh1 (t[1]) KieranO'Neill 1
(Ken Cunningham-Brown) *dwlt: hdwy into midfield 4f out: rdn along on inner wl over 3f out: sn wknd* **100/1**

1m 29.55s (-0.75) **Going Correction** -0.225s/f (Stan) 13 Ran SP% **117.1**

Speed ratings (Par 101): **95,93,92,91,90 88,81,73,71,70 69,54,36**

CSF £44.12 CT £557.95 TOTE £7.90: £2.20, £2.10, £4.60; EX 48.70 Trifecta £682.00.

**Owner** D Slingsby **Bred** G B Turnbull Ltd **Trained** Great Ness, Shropshire

■ Stewards' Enquiry : Joey Haynes four-day ban: used whip above permitted level (Mar 21-24)

**FOCUS**
A poor 46-52 handicap. The second and fourth help set the level.

## 1076 BETWAY H'CAP — 6f 16y(F)
4:30 (4:31) (Class 6) (0-60,62) 4-Y-O+ — £2,587 (£770; £384; £192) Stalls Low

Form — RPR

20-0 **1** **Viva Verglas (IRE)**[10] 923 6-9-7 **60** LukeMorris 2 67
(Daniel Mark Loughnane) *trckd ldrs: hdwy and cl up over 2f out: led wl over 1f out and sn rdn: drvn and kpt on wl fnl f* **9/1**

00-0 **2** *1* **Monsieur Jimmy**[33] 528 5-9-6 **59** DanielTudhope 13 63
(Declan Carroll) *towards rr: wd st: hdwy on outer over 2f out: rdn to chse ldrs over 1f out: drvn and kpt on wl fnl f* **9/2**[1]

-615 **3** *nk* **Fortinbrass (IRE)**[25] 663 7-9-2 **62** JoshuaBryan(7) 6 65
(John Balding) *prom: cl up over 2f out: rdn wl over 1f out and ev ch: drvn fnl f: kpt on* **15/2**

0060 **4** *½* **Borough Boy (IRE)**[17] 815 7-9-9 **62** (v) TonyHamilton 8 64
(Derek Shaw) *hld up in tch: smooth hdwy over 2f out: rdn to chal over 1f out: ev ch tl drvn ins fnl f and kpt on same pce* **5/1**[2]

0-05 **5** *1 ½* **Spice Mill (IRE)**[10] 923 4-9-4 **60** (vt) AlistairRawlinson(3) 3 57
(Michael Appleby) *dwlt and sn swtchd rt towards outer: bhd: hdwy over 2f out: rdn to chse ldrs on inner over 1f out: drvn and kpt on same pce fnl f* **13/2**[3]

0042 **6** *1 ¼* **Excellent Aim**[12] 874 10-8-12 **58** JaneElliott(7) 12 51
(George Margarson) *in tch towards outer: hdwy 2f out: rdn to chse ldrs over 1f out: sn drvn and no imp* **10/1**

4254 **7** *1 ½* **Cadeaux Pearl**[14] 852 9-8-0 **46** oh1 (b) RPWalsh(7) 10 35
(Scott Dixon) *cl up: led over 3f out: rdn over 2f out and sn hdd: drvn and grad wknd fr over 1f out* **16/1**

2350 **8** *1* **Major Muscari (IRE)**[13] 860 9-8-13 **57** (p) CharlieBennett(5) 1 43
(Shaun Harris) *towards rr: hdwy on inner over 2f out: in tch and rdn over 1f out: sn drvn and one pce* **12/1**

6400 **9** *2* **Spowarticus**[33] 528 8-9-0 **53** (v) DaleSwift 9 33
(Scott Dixon) *slt ld: hdd over 3f out and sn rdn along: drvn 2f out and grad wknd* **12/1**

1366 **10** *4 ½* **Whaleweigh Station**[17] 815 6-9-6 **59** (v) TomEaves 7 25
(J R Jenkins) *chsd ldrs: rdn along wl over 2f out: sn drvn and wknd* **16/1**

0200 **11** *4* **Doeadeer (IRE)**[15] 843 4-9-4 **57** (p[1]) ConnorBeasley 5 11
(Keith Dalgleish) *towards rr: sme hdwy and wd st: sn rdn and wknd* **14/1**

1m 15.59s (-0.91) **Going Correction** -0.225s/f (Stan) 11 Ran SP% **112.9**
Speed ratings (Par 101): **97,95,95,94,92 90,88,87,84,78 73**
CSF £47.17 CT £325.34 TOTE £10.20: £3.80, £1.90, £2.40; EX 59.80 Trifecta £300.80.
**Owner** Mrs C Loughnane **Bred** Mrs Mary Coonan **Trained** Rock, Worcs

**FOCUS**
A moderate sprint handicap to end, but the pace was generous thanks to a disputed lead between the two Scott Dixon horses. The third helps set the level.
T/Jkpt: Not won. T/Plt: £140.80 to a £1 stake. Pool: £101,542.04 - 526.26 winning units. T/Qpdt: £54.10 to a £1 stake. Pool: £7,666.21 - 104.85 winning units. **Joe Rowntree**

1077 - (Foreign Racing) - See Raceform Interactive

# [81]DEAUVILLE (R-H)
Tuesday, March 7
**OFFICIAL GOING: Polytrack: standard**

## 1078a PRIX DE LESSARD LE CHENE (CLAIMER) (4YO) (POLYTRACK) — 7f 110y
1:20 4-Y-O — £8,119 (£3,247; £2,435; £1,623; £811)

RPR

**1** **Zalamea (IRE)**[29] 606 4-9-6 0 TonyPiccone 2 76
(K Borgel, France) **43/10**[2]

**2** *hd* **Going Viral (IRE)**[18] 4-8-11 0 (b) ChristopheSoumillon 10 66
(G Botti, France) **23/5**[3]

**3** *snk* **Little Ghetto Boy**[99] 4-8-9 0 JeffersonSmith(6) 6 70
(J-C Rouget, France) **84/10**

**4** *hd* **Sir Ottoman (FR)**[23] 4-9-5 0 (p) MaximeGuyon 7 73
(C Ferland, France) **6/5**[1]

**5** *½* **Olsztyn (FR)**[64] 4-8-9 0 MlleAlisonMassin(10) 9 68
(M Boutin, France) **30/1**

**6** *1 ¾* **See Your Starr (FR)**[18] 4-8-11 0 EddyHardouin 5 60
(P Lenogue, France) **221/10**

**7** *shd* **Kashtan**[12] 879 4-8-8 0 (p) IoritzMendizabal 8 56
(J S Moore) *in tch: rdn and effrt 2f out: short of room over 1f out: nt rcvr and fdd fnl f* **66/10**

**8** *2* **Ciel Russe (FR)**[18] 4-8-11 0 StephaneBreux 3 54
(Edouard Thueux, France) **167/1**

**9** *¾* **All To The Red (FR)**[424] 4-9-1 0 AlexisBadel 1 56
(R Le Dren Doleuze, France) **39/1**

**10** *4* **El Mansour (FR)**[61] 4-8-11 0 EmmanuelEtienne(4) 4 46
(D Retif, France) **154/1**

**11** *2* **Lila Mahyana (FR)**[273] 3007 4-8-7 0 TomLefranc(8) 11 41
(C Boutin, France) **106/1**

PARI-MUTUEL (all including 1 euro stake): WIN 5.30 PLACE 1.80, 2.10, 2.90 DF 10.00 SF 23.10.
**Owner** Michel Delaunay **Bred** S F Bloodstock LLC **Trained** France

# [854]KEMPTON (A.W) (R-H)
Wednesday, March 8
**OFFICIAL GOING: Polytrack: standard to slow**
Wind: nil Weather: cloudy, mild

## 1079 32RED H'CAP — 1m 1f 219y(P)
5:45 (5:45) (Class 2) (0-105,101) 4-Y-O+
£11,827 (£3,541; £1,770; £885; £442; £222) Stalls Low

Form — RPR

040- **1** **Abareeq**[107] 8049 4-8-8 **88** JoeFanning 1 97
(Mark Johnston) *settled in 3rd on rail: swtchd out at 1/2-way: shkn up 2f out: pushed along over 1f out on outside: rdn ins fnl f: qcknd up and led nr fin: easily* **5/1**[3]

**2** *1 ½* **Getback In Paris (IRE)**[29] 4-8-5 **85** JimmyQuinn 5 91
(Richard Hughes) *settled bhd ldr: shkn up over 2f out: rdn between horses and led ent fnl f: kpt on tl hdd nr fin* **12/1**

24-0 **3** *3* **Manson**[20] 776 4-9-1 **95** OisinMurphy 3 95
(Dominic Ffrench Davis) *racd in 4th: shkn up over 2f out: sn rdn: hung lft ent fnl f: no ex: jst hld 3rd* **11/10**[1]

-556 **4** *hd* **Captain Cat (IRE)**[25] 680 8-9-0 **94** GeorgeDowning 6 94
(Tony Carroll) *s.s: in last: shkn up 2f out: shuffled along over 1f out: last: kpt on nicely fnl f: jst failed for 3rd* **8/1**

4-40 **5** *2 ¾* **Our Channel (USA)**[32] 574 6-9-7 **101** AdamKirby 4 95
(Jamie Osborne) *sn led: rdn over 2f out: hdd ent fnl f: wknd qckly fnl f* **4/1**[2]

160/ **6** *¾* **Allumage**[496] 7587 5-8-8 **88** TomMarquand 2 81
(Sylvester Kirk) *racd in 5th: rdn wl over 2f out: ev ch bhd ldrs ent fnl f: sn wknd* **14/1**

2m 4.02s (-3.98) **Going Correction** -0.05s/f (Stan) 6 Ran SP% **109.8**
Speed ratings (Par 109): **113,111,109,109,107 106**
CSF £54.18 TOTE £6.10: £2.30, £4.20; EX 77.30 Trifecta £264.60.
**Owner** A D Spence & M B Spence **Bred** Shadwell Estate Company Limited **Trained** Middleham Moor, N Yorks

**FOCUS**
Clerk of the course Ed Gretton reported that the track had been ameliorated to a depth of 100mm and compacted back to replicate standard going, but that the surface may ride standard to slow. Not a bad handicap, and there were a few in with a chance approaching the last.

## 1080 32RED CASINO H'CAP — 6f (P)
6:15 (6:17) (Class 6) (0-65,66) 4-Y-O+ — £2,264 (£673; £336; £168) Stalls Low

Form — RPR

3241 **1** **Athassel**[2] 1063 8-9-1 **66** 6ex KatherineGlenister(7) 3 75
(David Evans) *hld up in rr on rail: prog over 2f out: rdn over 1f out w clr run up rail: led ins fnl f: pushed out* **7/2**[1]

241- **2** *nk* **El Principe**[224] 4771 4-9-6 **64** (h) JasonHart 1 72
(Les Eyre) *chsd ldr on inner and t.k.h: rdn over 1f out and sn led: hdd ins fnl f: kpt on wl* **4/1**[2]

/6-4 **3** *1 ¼* **Frank Cool**[58] 139 4-8-10 **54** GeorgeDowning 7 58
(Tony Carroll) *mid-div: prog to sit bhd ldrs fr 2f out: kpt on but no threat to ldng pair* **16/1**

1053 **4** *2 ½* **Compton Prince**[20] 768 8-9-6 **64** (b) JoeFanning 4 61
(Milton Bradley) *broke wl and chsd ldrs: rdn ent fnl f: kpt on wl* **12/1**

0-00 **5** *½* **Only Ten Per Cent (IRE)**[21] 734 9-9-0 **61** AlistairRawlinson(3) 6 56
(J R Jenkins) *hld up in rr: rdn 2f out: kpt on fr over 1f out: nvr nrr* **20/1**

-503 **6** *¾* **Noble Deed**[18] 815 7-9-5 **63** LukeMorris 8 56
(Michael Attwater) *loaded wout jockey: mid-div: nudged along 2f out: rdn over 1f out: kpt on one pce* **12/1**

0-30 **7** *1* **Deer Song**[4] 1022 4-8-3 **54** JaneElliott(7) 2 44
(John Bridger) *led and set gd gallop: rdn over 2f out: hdd over 1f out: wknd after* **14/1**

-204 **8** *1 ¼* **New Rich**[18] 815 7-9-4 **62** (b) JohnFahy 11 48
(Eve Johnson Houghton) *in rr: rdn on wd outside 2f out: kpt on tl one pce ent fnl f* **8/1**

4605 **9** *¾* **Dominium (USA)**[21] 734 10-9-7 **65** (b) AdamBeschizza 5 49
(Jeremy Gask) *in rr: rdn over 2f out: lft bhd fr over 1f out* **5/1**[3]

40-5 **10** *5* **Vale Of Flight (IRE)**[16] 844 4-9-0 **65** BenRobinson(7) 12 34
(Luke McJannet) *wnt lft ss: in rr-div: rdn along out wd fr wl over 3f out: wdst st: no imp and wknd fr over 1f out* **20/1**

500- **11** *3 ¾* **Nocturn**[81] 8430 8-9-7 **65** (p) OisinMurphy 9 23
(Ronald Harris) *settled bhd ldr: shkn up wl over 1f out: wknd sn after* **20/1**

-400 **12** *1 ½* **Rigolleto (IRE)**[20] 768 9-9-7 **65** (p) AdamKirby 10 18+
(Anabel K Murphy) *rdn leaving stalls to sit bhd ldrs: rdn out wd over 2f out: sn hld* **16/1**

1m 11.85s (-1.25) **Going Correction** -0.05s/f (Stan) 12 Ran SP% **118.1**
Speed ratings (Par 101): **106,105,103,100,99 98,97,95,94,88 83,81**
CSF £16.38 CT £193.37 TOTE £4.80: £1.10, £2.20, £5.00; EX 22.60 Trifecta £339.20.
**Owner** Mrs E Evans **Bred** Moyns Park Estate And Stud Ltd **Trained** Pandy, Monmouths

**FOCUS**
A modest contest but won by an in-form sprinter. Another step forward from the winner, with the third to the balance of his form.

## 1081 32RED ON THE APP STORE H'CAP (DIV I) — 1m 3f 219y(P)
6:45 (6:47) (Class 6) (0-55,55) 4-Y-O+ — £2,264 (£673; £336; £168) Stalls Centre

Form — RPR

00-0 **1** **Briac (FR)**[27] 646 6-8-12 **46** oh1 DanielMuscutt 9 52
(Mark Pattinson) *s.s: settled in mid-div: rdn 2f out: kpt on wl ent fnl f: clsng on ldr wl ins fnl f: led nr fin* **10/1**

0605 **2** *nk* **Powered (IRE)**[2] 1067 4-9-2 **52** AdamKirby 12 58
(David Evans) *mid-div on outer: rdn over 2f out: led over 1f out: kpt on wl tl hdd nr fin* **7/2**[1]

-130 **3** *2 ¾* **Rail Dancer**[21] 738 5-9-6 **54** (v) AdamBeschizza 5 55
(Richard Rowe) *in rr: plenty to do over 2f out: sn rdn and kpt on strly out wd fr over 1f out: snatched 3rd post: nvr nrr* **6/1**

205/ **4** *shd* **Hong Kong Joe**[510] 7230 7-9-1 **49** (e) SteveDrowne 13 50
(Lydia Richards) *dropped out s: in rr: shkn up over 2f out: clsr over 1f out and rdn: kpt on wl: lost 3rd post* **40/1**

05-3 **5** *1 ½* **Ted's Brother (IRE)**[16] 839 9-9-0 **48** (h) ShaneKelly 6 50
(Laura Morgan) *settled in mid-div on rail: gng wl whn nt clr run over 2f out: lost pl: rdn over 1f out: kpt on wl: nvr involved* **5/1**[3]

3260 **6** *1 ½* **Ali Bin Nayef**[11] 924 5-9-4 **52** SilvestreDeSousa 8 48
(Michael Wigham) *chsd ldrs: rdn over 2f out: kpt on one pce* **9/2**[2]

-455 **7** *1 ½* **Commissar**[26] 661 8-9-7 **55** (vt[1]) RobHornby 7 49
(Mandy Rowland) *hld up bhd ldrs: rdn over 2f out: kpt on one pce* **14/1**

-250 **8** *shd* **Awesome Rock (IRE)**[13] 880 8-8-12 **46** oh1 OisinMurphy 2 41
(Roger Ingram) *settled in rr-div on rail: n.m.r and rdn on inner jst over 2f out: no imp over 1f out* **14/1**

-600 **9** *¾* **Zeteah**[21] 733 7-8-12 **46** oh1 GeorgeDowning 3 38
(Tony Carroll) *mid-div on rail: rdn 2f out: no imp sn after* **66/1**

6-04 **10** *1* **Movie Magic**[9] 436 6-8-9 **46** oh1 (b) AaronJones(3) 10 37
(Mark Hoad) *sn led: slowed pce over 4f out: rdn over 2f out: hdd over 1f out: wknd* **66/1**

2550 **11** *hd* **Barnacle**[14] 859 8-8-12 **46** oh1 (bt) StevieDonohoe 1 36
(Emma Owen) *in rr: rdn over 2f out: no imp* **25/1**

336- **12** *¾* **Cranwell**[160] 6890 5-9-5 **53** FergusSweeney 4 42
(George Baker) *led for 1f: settled in mid-div: rdn over 2f out: ev ch on inner over 1f out: wknd qckly fnl f* **16/1**

060- **13** *5* **Rebel Woods (FR)**[169] 6650 4-8-12 **48** JosephineGordon 11 29
(Geoffrey Deacon) *chsd ldr: bmpd along to hold pl most of r: rdn wl over 3f out: wknd qckly 2f out* **10/1**

2m 34.59s (0.09) **Going Correction** -0.05s/f (Stan)
**WFA** 4 from 5yo+ 1lb 13 Ran SP% **118.0**
Speed ratings (Par 101): **97,96,94,94,93 92,91,91,91,90 90,90,86**
CSF £43.49 CT £233.43 TOTE £14.10: £4.00, £1.80, £2.20; EX 69.00 Trifecta £420.30.



The Form Book Flat, Raceform Ltd, Newbury, RG14 5SJ

**Owner** O S Harris **Bred** P J Loivel & R Dugardin **Trained** Epsom, Surrey

**FOCUS**

A low-grade handicap. Routine form for the grade.

## 1082 32RED ON THE APP STORE H'CAP (DIV II) 1m 3f 219y(P)

**7:15** (7:16) (Class 6) (0-55,57) 4-Y-O+ **£2,264** (£673; £336; £168) **Stalls** Centre

Form RPR

-611 **1** **Smiley Bagel (IRE)**[18] 820 4-9-7 **57**........................ RichardKingscote 8 66+
(Ed Walker) *sat handy bhd ldrs on inner: shkn up to take clsr order over 3f out: rdn 2f out: led over 1f out: kpt on wl* **5/4**[1]

2-63 **2** *1* **Graceful Lady**[27] 645 4-9-5 **55**.......................................... LukeMorris 3 61
(Robert Eddery) *settled in rr-div: rdn on inner over 2f out: kpt on wl but no imp on wnr* **10/1**[2]

-235 **3** *3 ¼* **Santadelacruze**[18] 820 8-9-2 **50**................................ AdamBeschizza 1 51
(Mark Hoad) *chsd ldrs on rail: rdn over 2f out: kpt on one pce ins fnl f* **11/1**[3]

0-33 **4** *1 ¼* **Rezwaan**[21] 733 10-9-0 **48**...............................................(b) ShaneKelly 9 47
(Murty McGrath) *bhd ldrs tl led 7f out: increased pce wl over 3f out: rdn over 2f out: hdd over 1f out: wknd* **11/1**[3]

00-3 **5** *½* **Frankie**[28] 621 6-8-12 **46** oh1.......................................... KieranO'Neill 14 44
(Jimmy Fox) *in rr: rdn over 2f out on inner: kpt on wl past horse fr over 1f out: nvr nrr* **20/1**

0-00 **6** *nse* **Athenian Garden (USA)**[21] 733 10-8-12 **46** oh1.......... DannyBrock 12 44
(Paddy Butler) *in rr: rdn on inner over 2f out: prog over 1f out: kpt on* **100/1**

5602 **7** *hd* **Cold Fusion (IRE)**[6] 988 4-8-9 **52**.............................. RossaRyan(7) 10 50
(David Flood) *settled bhd ldrs: rdn over 2f out: no imp on ldrs ent fnl f: one pce after* **14/1**

0-02 **8** *½* **Street Art (IRE)**[21] 733 5-8-13 **47**...........................(bt) RobertWinston 13 44
(Mike Murphy) *prom bhd ldrs and t.k.h: upsides gng wl over 1f out out where hld together: sn rdn: fnd nil and one pce fnl f* **12/1**

3-34 **9** *½* **Sir Jack**[34] 525 4-9-3 **53**...............................................(p) GeorgeDowning 7 49
(Tony Carroll) *mid-div: c wd st: rdn over 2f out: kpt on one pce* **12/1**

00-0 **10** *½* **Abertillery**[50] 274 5-8-12 **46** oh1...................................... DavidProbert 4 41
(Michael Blanshard) *in rr: rdn over 2f out: kpt on one pce* **33/1**

-645 **11** *¾* **Castanea**[13] 880 5-8-12 **46** oh1........................................ OisinMurphy 6 41
(Ronald Harris) *midi-div on outer and t.k.h: lost pl ent st: rdn over 2f out where n.m.r: one pce after* **12/1**

-550 **12** *nse* **Sixties Idol**[28] 621 4-8-7 **46** oh1.................................. NathanAlison(3) 2 40
(Sheena West) *mid-div on outer: rdn over 2f out: no imp* **33/1**

40-0 **13** *1 ¾* **Akinspirit (IRE)**[16] 839 13-8-12 **46** oh1....................(t) TomMarquand 11 37
(Nikki Evans) *in rr: rdn over 2f out: no imp* **100/1**

03-0 **14** *3 ½* **Tarakkom (FR)**[14] 859 5-9-5 **53**....................................... LiamKeniry 5 39
(Peter Hiatt) *led tl hdd 7f out: remained prom: hung lft on bnd over 3f out: wknd sn after* **20/1**

2m 34.82s (0.32) **Going Correction** -0.05s/f (Stan)
**WFA** 4 from 5yo+ 1lb **14** Ran SP% **117.3**
Speed ratings (Par 101): **96,95,93,92,92 91,91,91,91,90 90,90,89,86**
CSF £12.20 CT £99.06 TOTE £1.90: £1.10, £2.30, £3.30; EX 12.00 Trifecta £93.80.
**Owner** Laurence Bellman **Bred** Max Morris **Trained** Upper Lambourn, Berks

**FOCUS**

The slower of the two divisions by 0.23sec. Another step forward from the winner.

## 1083 100% PROFIT BOOST AT 32REDSPORT.COM MAIDEN STKS 1m (P)

**7:45** (7:52) (Class 5) 3-Y-O **£2,911** (£866; £432; £216) **Stalls** Low

Form RPR

6- **1** **Surrey Hope (USA)**[138] 7501 3-9-5 0.............................. OisinMurphy 5 84+
(Joseph Tuite) *settled bhd ldrs and t.k.h early: travelling best wl over 1f out: upsides over 1f out: shkn up and sprinted clr ent fnl f: in n.d and pushed out cl home: impressive* **7/2**[2]

**2** *4* **Hold Sway (IRE)** 3-9-5 0...................................................... AdamKirby 1 73+
(Charlie Appleby) *settled in mid-div on outer: shkn up 2f out and rn green: rdn and picked up wl ent fnl f: kpt on to take 2nd 100yds out: improver* **7/4**[1]

6-6 **3** *1* **Dragons Voice**[46] 354 3-9-5 0................................ RichardKingscote 13 71
(Philip Hide) *pressed ldr: ev ch between horses over 1f out: sn rdn and lft bhd by wnr: kpt on tl lost 2nd 100yds out* **20/1**

**4** *hd* **Wonderfillo (IRE)** 3-9-2 0.......................................... CallumShepherd(3) 6 70+
(Paul Cole) *mid-div on outer: stl travelling whn nt clr run over 2f out and lost pl: pushed along after: rdn ent fnl f and styd on strly: shaped w promise* **20/1**

**5** *2 ¼* **The Raven Master (IRE)** 3-9-5 0...............................(h[1]) PatCosgrave 11 65
(Michael Bell) *in rr-div on outer: rdn over 2f out: kpt on wl fnl f* **33/1**

**6** *nk* **Entangling (IRE)** 3-9-5 0........................................... SilvestreDeSousa 3 64+
(Chris Wall) *s.s and detached in rr: clsr by 1/2-way: shuffled along fr over 2f out: nvr nrr: likely improver* **4/1**[3]

4 **7** *shd* **Accomplice**[25] 681 3-9-0 0.............................................. DavidProbert 10 59
(Michael Blanshard) *led: rdn over 2f out: hdd ent fnl f: wknd qckly after* **14/1**

6 **8** *1 ½* **Hajaam (IRE)**[11] 916 3-9-5 0.......................................... StevieDonohoe 2 61
(Charlie Fellowes) *chsd ldrs on inner: rdn over 2f out: kpt on tl wknd fnl f* **10/1**

**9** *4* **Harbour Quay** 3-9-0 0................................................... DavidParkes(5) 8 51
(Jeremy Gask) *in rr-div: shkn up over 2f out where rn green: picked up strly fr over 1f out: nvr nrr: can do bttr* **50/1**

0-6 **10** *1 ½* **King Otto**[14] 863 3-9-5 0...................................................... LukeMorris 4 48
(Phil McEntee) *in rr-div: on inner: rdn over 2f out: no imp* **66/1**

64 **11** *6* **Fun Raiser (IRE)**[28] 624 3-9-0 0.................................. TomMarquand 12 29
(Harry Dunlop) *chsd ldrs: rdn out wd over 2f out: no imp sn after and wknd* **50/1**

**12** *32* **Poet's Quest** 3-9-0 0..................................................... RobertWinston 7
(Dean Ivory) *taken bk leaving stalls: in rr: rdn over 2f out: eased fr over 1f out* **40/1**

1m 38.99s (-0.81) **Going Correction** -0.05s/f (Stan) **12** Ran SP% **114.7**
Speed ratings (Par 98): **102,98,97,96,94 94,94,92,88,87 81,49**
CSF £8.90 TOTE £4.40: £1.60, £1.20, £6.10; EX 13.90 Trifecta £130.80.
**Owner** Surrey Racing Limited **Bred** Nancy Mazzoni **Trained** Lambourn, Berks

■ Zoffany Bay was withdrawn. Price at time of withdrawal 33-1. Rule 4 does not apply.

**FOCUS**

Just a fair maiden, but a good performance from the winner. It's been rated around the third.

## 1084 RACING UK HD H'CAP 1m (P)

**8:15** (8:18) (Class 7) (0-50,50) 4-Y-O+ **£1,940** (£577; £288; £144) **Stalls** Low

Form RPR

00-U **1** **Secret Lightning (FR)**[19] 784 5-9-7 **50**...............(p) SilvestreDeSousa 7 56
(Michael Appleby) *mid-div: rdn 2f out: kpt on wl and led over 1f out: pressed fnl f: kpt on wl cl home* **4/1**[2]

40-0 **2** *nk* **Free To Roam (IRE)**[20] 761 4-8-13 **49**........................ BenRobinson(7) 2 54
(Luke McJannet) *chsd ldrs: rdn over 2f out: kpt on wl to press wnr nr fin: no ex fin* **6/1**[3]

55-5 **3** *shd* **Gavarnie Encore**[14] 854 5-9-5 **48**................................ DavidProbert 11 53
(Michael Blanshard) *hld up in rr: rdn out wd over 2f out: kpt on wl w plenty to do ent fnl f: nrst fin* **7/2**[1]

05-6 **4** *¾* **Zebedee's Girl (IRE)**[6] 982 4-9-4 **47**........................................ JFEgan 9 50
(David Evans) *in rr-div: rdn over 2f out: kpt on ent fnl f* **16/1**

0-00 **5** *½* **Rising Sunshine (IRE)**[23] 724 4-9-7 **50**....................(bt) LukeMorris 12 52
(Milton Bradley) *in rr: rdn over 2f out: picked up wl ent fnl f: nvr nrr* **14/1**

00-0 **6** *shd* **Never To Be (USA)**[54] 222 6-9-1 **49**........................(bt) LuluStanford(5) 1 51
(Nikki Evans) *mid-div and t.k.h: rdn on rail over 2f out: kpt on wl and ev ch ent fnl f: pressed wnr tl no ex and lost numerous pls cl home* **14/1**

-400 **7** *2* **Senor George (IRE)**[16] 839 10-9-5 **48**..........................(p) KieranO'Neill 8 45
(Simon Hodgson) *cl up: rdn over 2f out: kpt on one pce* **10/1**

006- **8** *½* **Zebedee's Son (IRE)**[185] 5830 4-8-12 **48**...............(p) RhiainIngram(7) 4 44
(Roger Ingram) *chsd ldrs: wdst in st over 2f out: kpt on one pce* **25/1**

0-00 **9** *3 ½* **Just Fab (IRE)**[21] 740 4-9-6 **49**.....................................(b) AdamKirby 14 36
(Lee Carter) *led: rdn over 2f out: hrd pressed and stuck on wl tl hdd over 1f out: wknd after* **20/1**

4030 **10** *1* **Chandrayaan**[14] 854 10-8-10 **46**...............................(v) GinaMangan(7) 10 31
(John E Long) *a in rr* **25/1**

0/0- **11** *1* **Xclusive**[117] 7910 7-9-2 **45**...................................................... ShaneKelly 6 28
(Ronald Harris) *chsd ldr on inner: rdn over 2f out: wknd fr over 1f out* **9/1**

01-4 **12** *1 ½* **Pipers Piping (IRE)**[47] 334 11-9-6 **49**.............................. RobHornby 5 28
(Mandy Rowland) *racd wd w no cover in mid-div: rdn over 2f out: wknd sn after* **12/1**

1m 40.78s (0.98) **Going Correction** -0.05s/f (Stan) **12** Ran SP% **115.0**
Speed ratings (Par 97): **93,92,92,91,91 91,89,88,85,84 83,81**
CSF £26.49 CT £91.10 TOTE £5.00: £1.70, £2.30, £1.70; EX 25.40 Trifecta £70.40.
**Owner** Mick Appleby Racing **Bred** Jeffrey Colin Smith **Trained** Oakham, Rutland

**FOCUS**

A weak race run at a messy pace. It's been rated as routine form around the principals.

## 1085 32RED APPRENTICE H'CAP (LONDON MILE SERIES QUALIFIER) 1m (P)

**8:45** (8:46) (Class 5) (0-75,75) 4-Y-O+ **£2,911** (£866; £432; £216) **Stalls** Low

Form RPR

1-40 **1** **Believe It (IRE)**[34] 516 5-8-10 **69**...................(b) StephenCummins(5) 12 78
(Richard Hughes) *mde all: rdn over 2f out and hrd pressed by runner-up fr wl over 1f out to wl ins fnl f: on top fnl 100yds* **20/1**

2-13 **2** *1 ¼* **Saleh (IRE)**[6] 986 4-8-13 **70**......................................... PaddyBradley(3) 2 76
(Lee Carter) *cl up bhd wnr on inner: upsides and rdn 2f out: kpt on wl to press wnr fr wl over 1f out tl wknd fnl 100yds* **2/1**[1]

6-42 **3** *1 ½* **King Of Dreams**[13] 876 4-9-4 **75**.............................. SophieKilloran(3) 11 78+
(David Simcock) *in rr: plenty to do over 2f out: rdn 2f out: prog and kpt on strly ent fnl f to snatch 3rd post: nvr nrr* **11/2**[2]

5-30 **4** *nk* **Deeley's Double (FR)**[41] 426 4-8-9 **63**.............................. CliffordLee 4 65
(Tony Carroll) *in rr-div on inner: rdn 2f out: kpt on wl ent fnl f: jst lost 3rd* **12/1**

2004 **5** *½* **Ravenhoe (IRE)**[13] 876 4-8-10 **71**......................... SharnaArmstrong(7) 6 72
(Mark Johnston) *covered up in mid-div: swtchd wdst over 2f out: shuffled along fr over 1f out: nvr involved* **16/1**

55-0 **6** *1* **Al Khafji**[20] 769 4-9-4 **72**..................................................(b[1]) DavidParkes 7 70
(Jeremy Gask) *mid-divison: rdn over 2f out: kpt on one pce* **12/1**

0-00 **7** *½* **Jack Of Diamonds (IRE)**[39] 460 8-9-7 **75**.................. GeorgeWood 8 72
(Roger Teal) *in rr-divsion on outer: rdn on outer over 2f out: briefly threatened to get involved ent fnl f: fdd sn after* **10/1**

540- **8** *½* **Bluff Crag**[154] 7076 4-8-9 **68**...................................... FinleyMarsh(5) 5 64
(Richard Hughes) *missed beak: in rr: rdn over 2f out: no imp* **10/1**

34-0 **9** *1 ¾* **Red Cossack (CAN)**[11] 922 6-9-1 **69**..........................(t) GeorgiaCox 9 61
(Paul Webber) *sn cl up w ldr: rdn over 2f out: wknd ent fnl f* **12/1**

52-5 **10** *1* **Beleave**[21] 736 4-9-5 **73**...........................................(h) PatrickO'Donnell 1 63
(Luke Dace) *rrd up leaving stalls and completely missed break: latched onto bk of pack after 3f: prog travelling wl over 2f out: rdn over 1f out and wknd* **6/1**[3]

60-3 **11** *½* **Light From Mars**[21] 745 12-8-12 **69**..................(p) CameronNoble(3) 10 58
(Ronald Harris) *settled bhd ldr: rdn over 2f out: wknd sn after* **25/1**

0-00 **12** *6* **Freight Train (IRE)**[33] 548 5-8-6 **65**.................... KieranSchofield(5) 3 40
(Adrian Wintle) *mid-div on inner: shkn up over 3f out: began to lose pl sn after: wknd* **100/1**

1m 38.72s (-1.08) **Going Correction** -0.05s/f (Stan) **12** Ran SP% **119.7**
Speed ratings (Par 103): **103,101,100,99,99 98,97,97,95,94 94,88**
CSF £59.76 CT £271.12 TOTE £19.40: £4.00, £1.70, £2.10; EX 67.70 Trifecta £522.60.
**Owner** Richard Hughes **Bred** The Kathryn Stud **Trained** Upper Lambourn, Berks

**FOCUS**

Few got into this, the pace holding up.

T/Jkpt: Not won. T/Plt: £60.70 to a £1 stake. Pool: £93,354.84. 1,121.89 winning units. T/Qpdt: £4.40 to a £1 stake. Pool: £12,271.24. 2,051.33 winning units. **Cathal Gahan**

# 1022 LINGFIELD (L-H)

Wednesday, March 8

**OFFICIAL GOING: Polytrack: standard**

Wind: Fresh, across (towards stands) Weather: Overcast

## 1086 SUNBETS.CO.UK H'CAP 1m 1y(P)

**2:00** (2:05) (Class 6) (0-65,65) 4-Y-O+ **£2,264** (£673; £336; £168) **Stalls** High

Form RPR

5514 **1** **Wink Oliver**[11] 929 5-9-7 **65**................................................(p) JFEgan 2 72
(Jo Hughes) *hld up in midfield: prog 3f out to trck ldrs: rdn to ld over 1f out: hdd last 100yds: kpt on wl to ld again post* **11/2**[3]

6-41 **2** *shd* **Polar Kite (IRE)**[32] 570 9-9-6 **64**......................................(h) RobHornby 1 71
(Michael Attwater) *hld up in rr: stl plenty to do over 2f out: gd prog to cl on ldrs over 1f out: drvn to ld last 100yds: kpt on but hdd post* **11/2**[3]

0-00 **3** *shd* **Spiritual Star (IRE)**[27] 641 8-9-2 **65**........................ PaddyBradley(5) 10 72
(Lee Carter) *hld up towards rr: prog on wd outside fr 3f out: clsng whn hmpd wl over 1f out: rallied fnl f: r.o nr fin: jst failed* **5/1**[2]

0000 **4** *2 1/4* **Greyfriarschorista**[26] 663 10-9-5 **63**............................(v) AdamKirby 12 64
(David Evans) *drvn fr wd draw and chsd ldng pair: clr of rest 1/2-way: rdn to chal and upsides over 1f out: nt qckn jst ins fnl f: wknd nr fin* **10/1**

-002 **5** *1/2* **Freddy With A Y (IRE)**[18] 812 7-9-5 **63**......................... PaddyAspell 6 63
(J R Jenkins) *hld up wl off the pce in last pair: pushed along 2f out: styd on steadily fr over 1f out: nvr involved* **8/1**

0-06 **6** *1* **Cosmic Ray**[18] 811 5-9-3 **61**...............................................(h) JasonHart 9 59
(Les Eyre) *hld up wl in rr: rdn over 3f out and no prog: styd on fr over 1f out: nrst fin but n.d* **11/1**

2-56 **7** *1 1/4* **George Baker (IRE)**[41] 426 10-9-4 **62**......................... SteveDrowne 5 57
(George Baker) *chsd clr ldrs: lost pl on inner over 2f out: clsd over 1f out: no prog fnl f* **20/1**

500- **8** *3/4* **Shifting Star (IRE)**[78] 8462 12-8-9 **60**...........................(vt) JaneElliott(7) 7 53
(John Bridger) *t.k.h: led at str pce: hdd 3f out but stl on terms over 1f out: wknd fnl f* **9/1**

0-00 **9** *1 1/4* **Majestic Myles (IRE)**[14] 860 9-9-1 **59**........................... KieranO'Neill 8 49
(Lee Carter) *urged along early to press ldr: led 3f out: hdd over 1f out and squeezed out sn after: wknd* **16/1**

555- **10** *9* **Stormbound (IRE)**[78] 8469 8-9-7 **65**...............................(b) LukeMorris 3 33
(Paul Cole) *restless stalls: chsd ldrs: rdn 3f out: sn wknd and bhd* **9/2**[1]

**11** *11* **Tsundoku (IRE)**[24] 7494 6-9-1 **62**............................. LouisSteward(3) 11 4
(Alexandra Dunn) *s.i.s: a struggling in last: t.o* **33/1**

1m 36.63s (-1.57) **Going Correction** 0.0s/f (Stan) **11** Ran SP% **117.7**
Speed ratings (Par 101): **107,106,106,104,104 103,101,101,99,90 79**
CSF £35.90 CT £165.30 TOTE £6.10: £2.20, £1.90, £2.30; EX 33.20 Trifecta £202.30.
**Owner** P & L Partners **Bred** Norman Court Stud **Trained** Lambourn, Berks

**FOCUS**
A moderate handicap, but a thrilling finish between the front three. It's been rated around the principals to their recent form.

## 1087 BETWAY CLAIMING STKS 6f 1y(P)
**2:30** (2:35) (Class 6) 4-Y-0+ **£2,264** (£673; £336; £168) **Stalls** Low

Form RPR

15-1 **1** **Flowers On Venus (IRE)**[33] 551 5-9-9 87............ RichardKingscote 2 86
(Tom Dascombe) *mde all: skipped 2 l clr over 1f out: shkn up and styd on fnl f: unchal* **8/13**[1]

-420 **2** *1 1/2* **Fairway To Heaven (IRE)**[19] 783 8-9-7 77...................... AdamKirby 1 80
(Michael Wigham) *trckd ldng pair: shkn up to go 2nd over 1f out: kpt on but no imp on wnr* **5/2**[2]

20-0 **3** *3/4* **Bush Warrior (IRE)**[46] 355 6-9-4 69....................(v) JosephineGordon 3 74
(Anabel K Murphy) *t.k.h: trckd wnr: rdn over 2f out: lost 2nd over 1f out: one pce after* **18/1**

2650 **4** *1 3/4* **Head Space (IRE)**[16] 843 9-9-3 65.......................................... JFEgan 5 68
(David Evans) *hld up in last: shkn up and outpcd wl over 1f out: one pce after: tk 4th last stride* **20/1**

0-23 **5** *nse* **Burning Thread (IRE)**[32] 573 10-9-12 76.....................(b) ShaneKelly 6 77
(David Elsworth) *hld up in 4th: shkn up and outpcd wl over 1f out: no imp after* **12/1**[3]

1m 12.04s (0.14) **Going Correction** 0.0s/f (Stan) **5** Ran SP% **108.2**
Speed ratings (Par 101): **99,97,96,93,93**
CSF £2.24 TOTE £1.30: £1.10, £1.90; EX 2.70 Trifecta £9.80.
**Owner** Owen Promotions Limited **Bred** Mrs A J Donnelly **Trained** Malpas, Cheshire

**FOCUS**
An uncompetitive claimer and they finished very much as adjusted official ratings suggested they should. The third and fourth are key to the level.

## 1088 32RED H'CAP 5f 6y(P)
**3:00** (3:05) (Class 6) (0-65,65) 3-Y-O **£2,264** (£673; £336; £168) **Stalls** High

Form RPR

0341 **1** **Roundabout Magic (IRE)**[12] 898 3-9-4 **64**.................. NickyMackay 8 69
(Simon Dow) *sltly impeded s: hld up towards rr: rdn and prog on outer over 1f out: r.o wl fnl f to ld last strides* **8/1**

0-62 **2** *1/2* **Goodwood Crusader (IRE)**[18] 813 3-9-4 **64**.................. ShaneKelly 4 67
(Richard Hughes) *pressed ldr on inner: chal and upsides fr 2f out tl drvn ahd ins fnl f: hdd and outpcd last strides* **7/2**[2]

2-21 **3** *1/2* **Mercers**[18] 819 3-9-4 **64**.................................................... TomQueally 5 66
(Peter Crate) *taken down early: awkward s: sn pressed ldr on outer: led over 2f out but then jnd: hdd and one pce ins fnl f* **3/1**[1]

005- **4** *1 1/4* **Coping Stone**[89] 8285 3-9-2 **62**........................................ SeanLevey 3 59
(David Brown) *chsd ldrs: rdn and no imp over 1f out: kpt on ins fnl f* **11/2**

16-6 **5** *nse* **Dixie's Double**[48] 313 3-9-5 **65**......................................... LukeMorris 7 62
(Daniel Kubler) *sltly impeded s: chsd ldrs: rdn and no imp wl over 1f out: styd on ins fnl f* **33/1**

05- **6** *nk* **Canberra Cliffs (IRE)**[79] 8454 3-9-3 **63**............................ LiamKeniry 2 63+
(Don Cantillon) *stdd s: hld up in 8th: stl there over 1f out then rn into trble: swtchd rt and rdn fnl f: fin wl* **11/1**

010- **7** *1 1/4* **Prancelina (IRE)**[148] 7258 3-9-3 **63**.......................... JosephineGordon 6 54
(Phil McEntee) *wnt rt s: led to over 2f out: wknd fnl f* **33/1**

0-65 **8** *1/2* **Brother In Arms (IRE)**[40] 435 3-9-2 **62**.................. GeorgeDowning 10 51
(Tony Carroll) *s.i.s: outpcd and bhd in last: r.o fnl 150yds: nrst fin* **20/1**

50-2 **9** *nk* **Met By Moonlight**[12] 898 3-9-2 **62**............................ DavidProbert 1 50+
(Ron Hodges) *no room on inner after 100yds and snatched up: nvr able to rcvr* **4/1**[3]

58.7s (-0.10) **Going Correction** 0.0s/f (Stan) **9** Ran SP% **112.7**
Speed ratings (Par 96): **100,99,98,96,96 95,93,93,92**
CSF £34.49 CT £103.27 TOTE £9.70: £2.80, £1.40, £1.10; EX 42.00 Trifecta £99.40.
**Owner** Six Mile Hill Racing **Bred** T F Lacy **Trained** Ashtead, Surrey

**FOCUS**
A modest 3yo sprint handicap, but they went a good pace. Another step forward from the winner.

## 1089 32RED CASINO MAIDEN STKS 1m 2f (P)
**3:30** (3:35) (Class 5) 3-Y-O **£2,911** (£866; £432; £216) **Stalls** Low

Form RPR

-2 **1** **Solajan (IRE)**[13] 882 3-9-5 0...........................................(h) AdamKirby 1 77+
(Ed Dunlop) *plld hrd bhd ldrs: gap opened 6f out and sn led: settled bttr in front: drvn 2f out: wandered sltly but kpt on wl fnl f* **9/4**[1]

3 **2** *1/2* **Waterville Dancer (IRE)**[16] 840 3-9-5 0.......................... ShaneKelly 5 74
(Richard Hughes) *slowly away: hld up in tch: prog over 4f out: chsd wnr over 3f out where bmpd rival and slipped sltly: drvn 2f out: kpt on but a hld* **5/1**[3]

34 **3** *4* **Arsenio Lupin**[39] 466 3-9-5 0.........................................(t) LukeMorris 4 66
(Denis Quinn) *t.k.h early: cl up on outer: dropped to last and urged along 1/2-way: rn in snatches after: tk 3rd over 3f out: no imp ldng pair over 1f out: wknd ins fnl f* **11/4**[2]

00- **4** *4 1/2* **Padrinho (IRE)**[186] 6108 3-9-5 0........................................ KierenFox 3 57
(John Best) *pressed ldr 4f: lost pl but in tch: shkn up over 2f out: no prog* **9/4**[1]

**5** *3/4* **Cookie's Star** 3-9-0 0........................................ SilvestreDeSousa 6 51
(Philip McBride) *s.s: in tch in last pair: outpcd fr over 2f out* **20/1**

-330 **6** *10* **Flying Fynn (IRE)**[13] 875 3-9-5 60...............................(p) OscarPereira 2 36
(Jose Santos) *led to wl over 5f out: bmpd and squeezed out over 3f out: sn wknd and bhd* **66/1**

2m 8.16s (1.56) **Going Correction** 0.0s/f (Stan) **6** Ran SP% **111.1**
Speed ratings (Par 98): **93,92,89,85,85 77**
CSF £13.64 TOTE £3.20: £1.60, £2.50; EX 13.60 Trifecta £24.70.
**Owner** Saeed Jaber **Bred** G Devlin **Trained** Newmarket, Suffolk

■ Stewards' Enquiry : Oscar Pereira jockey ban: five days (22-25,27 March) - used whip when out of contention

**FOCUS**
A modest maiden though a couple had already shown ability. They went no pace early. Muddling form.

## 1090 32RED H'CAP 5f 6y(P)
**4:00** (4:06) (Class 3) (0-95,85) 3-Y-O **£7,246** (£2,168; £1,084; £542; £270) **Stalls** High

Form RPR

-423 **1** **Juan Horsepower**[20] 765 3-8-12 **76**...........................(p) KieranO'Neill 3 80
(Richard Hannon) *wl away: mde all: kicked on wl over 1f out and sn at least 2 l clr: in n.d after* **6/4**[1]

11-3 **2** *1 3/4* **Merry Banter**[19] 778 3-9-2 **85**.................................... DavidParkes(5) 5 83
(Paul Midgley) *t.k.h: w wnr but hanging rt: pushed along and nt qckn over 1f out: rdn and one pce fnl f* **3/1**[3]

4-25 **3** *1/2* **Monte Cinq (IRE)**[11] 926 3-9-7 **85**...................................... TomEaves 1 81
(Jason Ward) *plld v hrd bhd ldng pair: stl keen 2f out: nthing lft whn asked for effrt over 1f out* **5/2**[2]

0-0 **4** *2 1/4* **Grecian Divine (IRE)**[13] 877 3-8-11 **82**.............. SophieScardifield(7) 2 70
(Joseph Tuite) *awkward s: hld up in last but in tch: outpcd 2f out: nvr on terms after* **25/1**

0451 **5** *hd* **Pulsating (IRE)**[11] 923 3-8-0 **71** oh4..............................(b) JaneElliott(7) 6 58
(Daniel Steele) *s.i.s: cl up on outer: outpcd 2f out: nvr on terms after* **6/1**

58.42s (-0.38) **Going Correction** 0.0s/f (Stan) **5** Ran SP% **111.7**
Speed ratings (Par 102): **103,100,99,95,95**
CSF £6.46 TOTE £2.30: £1.50, £1.70; EX 7.30 Trifecta £12.80.
**Owner** Middleham Park Racing LXXXIII **Bred** Max Weston **Trained** East Everleigh, Wilts

**FOCUS**
A valuable sprint handicap, but the top weight was 10lb below the race ceiling. The race lost much of its interest with the absence of the unexposed Scuzeme and, despite only being 3yos, the remaining five runners had already run 66 times between them. The order didn't change much. The winner has been rated to the better view of his form, with the runner-up close to form.

## 1091 BETWAY H'CAP 6f 1y(P)
**4:30** (4:35) (Class 4) (0-85,85) 4-Y-O+ **£4,690** (£1,395; £697; £348) **Stalls** Low

Form RPR

0105 **1** **Make Music**[18] 810 4-9-5 **83**.............................................. DavidProbert 1 91
(Andrew Balding) *mde most: rdn over 1f out: taken wd in st: hdd briefly ins fnl f: styd on and a holding on nr fin* **11/4**[2]

6-06 **2** *nk* **Rosealee (IRE)**[32] 573 4-8-7 **76**................................... DavidParkes(5) 4 83
(Jeremy Gask) *w wnr to 2f out: stl nrly upsides over 1f out on outer: styd on but a jst hld* **8/1**

0-03 **3** *1/2* **Seamster**[18] 816 10-8-11 **82**............................................(t) GerO'Neill(7) 2 87
(David Loughnane) *pressed ldng pair: chal on inner over 1f out: narrow ld briefly ins fnl f: nt qckn last 100yds* **7/1**[3]

56-1 **4** *1* **Varsovian**[32] 575 7-9-1 **79**............................................ RobertWinston 5 81
(Dean Ivory) *t.k.h early: trckd ldrs: shkn up over 2f out: nt qckn over 1f out: one pce after* **5/2**[1]

2-56 **5** *shd* **Buccaneers Vault (IRE)**[19] 783 5-9-0 **78**.................. PaulMulrennan 3 80
(Paul Midgley) *settled in last trio: effrt on inner over 1f out: kpt on but nvr pce to chal* **14/1**

0460 **6** *nse* **Salvatore Fury (IRE)**[14] 857 7-8-13 **77**...........................(v) PhillipMakin 6 79+
(Keith Dalgleish) *hld up in last: asked for effrt over 1f out but hanging and then nt clr run: styd on ins fnl f: nvr a threat* **8/1**

0600 **7** *3/4* **Swiss Cross**[5] 999 10-8-12 **79**.........................(tp) CallumShepherd(3) 11 78
(Phil McEntee) *pressed ldrs on outer: rdn over 2f out: steadily fdd over 1f out* **10/1**

10-0 **8** *3/4* **Staintondale Lass (IRE)**[18] 810 4-9-7 **85**..................... OisinMurphy 9 82
(Ed Vaughan) *in tch in last trio: shkn up over 2f out: no prog over 1f out: one pce* **12/1**

1m 10.92s (-0.98) **Going Correction** 0.0s/f (Stan) **8** Ran SP% **113.4**
Speed ratings (Par 105): **106,105,104,103,103 103,102,101**
CSF £24.51 CT £137.66 TOTE £4.10: £1.60, £2.40, £2.20; EX 28.70 Trifecta £130.30.
**Owner** Mrs I A Balding **Bred** Brook Stud Bloodstock Ltd **Trained** Kingsclere, Hants

**FOCUS**
A fair sprint handicap, but not many got into it. It's been rated around the second and third.

## 1092 BETWAY STAYERS H'CAP 1m 7f 169y(P)
**5:00** (5:06) (Class 5) (0-75,77) 4-Y-O+ **£2,911** (£866; £432; £216) **Stalls** Low

Form RPR

P-51 **1** **Ayr Of Elegance**[49] 289 5-9-9 **72**............................ RichardKingscote 2 77
(Philip Hide) *hld up bhd ldrs: shkn up 2f out: prog on outer to go 2nd ins fnl f: rdn and steadily clsd to ld last 2 strides* **5/2**[2]

6033 **2** *nk* **Icebuster**[28] 619 9-9-12 **75**............................................... RyanTate 7 79
(Rod Millman) *stdd s: hld up in last and t.k.h after 4f: prog to press ldng pair 5f out: chal on outer fr 3f out: drvn to ld over 1f out: kpt on but hdd last strides* **7/2**[3]

266 **3** *1* **Treble Strike (USA)**[21] 737 4-8-8 **65**..............................(p) JackDuern(3) 4 68
(Dean Ivory) *trckd ldr 3f: styd in tch: effrt on inner 2f out: rdn and kpt on to take 3rd ins fnl f: nt pce to chal* **9/1**

-414 **4** *2 3/4* **Free Bounty**[37] 477 4-9-1 **69**.................................(t) SilvestreDeSousa 5 69
(Philip McBride) *trckd ldr after 3f: chal over 3f out: rdn to ld over 2f out: hdd over 1f out: fdd fnl f* **15/8**[1]

134- **5** *1* **Wynford (IRE)**[20] 7320 4-9-8 **76**.............................. JosephineGordon 9 74
(David Loughnane) *led: drvn 3f out: hdd over 2f out but styd on terms: wknd fnl f* **13/2**



The Form Book Flat, Raceform Ltd, Newbury, RG14 5SJ

131/ 6 3 3/4 **Rocky Elsom (USA)**[14] 2835 10-9-1 64......................(t[1]) TimmyMurphy 6 58
(Sophie Leech) *hld up: last 5f out: gng wl enough but nt on terms after: nudged along and no prog fnl 2f* **25/1**

3m 28.46s (2.76) **Going Correction** 0.0s/f (Stan)
**WFA** 4 from 5yo+ 3lb 6 Ran SP% **112.8**
Speed ratings (Par 103): **93,92,92,90,90 88**
CSF £11.76 CT £64.61 TOTE £3.40: £2.20, £2.30; EX 11.80 Trifecta £52.50.
**Owner** W F Davis **Bred** W F Davis **Trained** Findon, W Sussex

**FOCUS**
This ordinary staying handicap was hit by non-runners and they went a steady pace. The winner has been rated to form, with the runner-up close to his recent form.
T/Plt: £23.50 to a £1 stake. Pool: £99,394.46. 3,086.42 winning units. T/Qpdt: £7.10 to a £1 stake. Pool: £7,329.92. 757.80 winning units. **Jonathan Neesom**

1093 - 1100a (Foreign Racing) - See Raceform Interactive

## [1029]NEWCASTLE (A.W) (L-H)
Thursday, March 9

**OFFICIAL GOING: Tapeta: standard**
Wind: light against Weather: Fine

### 1101 BETWAY H'CAP 1m 2f 42y (Tp)
**5:45** (5:48) (Class 6) (0-60,61) 4-Y-0+ **£2,264** (£673; £336; £168) **Stalls** High

Form RPR
-614 1 **Spirit Of The Vale (IRE)**[50] 281 4-8-12 51......................(t) KevinStott 6 59
(Oliver Greenall) *hld up: hdwy on bit 2f out: rdn appr fnl f: r.o wl: led 110yds out* **7/2**[2]
6-52 2 2 **Kerry Icon**[30] 608 4-8-0 46 oh1..............................(h) JamieGormley(7) 4 49
(Iain Jardine) *in tch: hdwy to chal over 2f out: rdn to ld appr fnl f: hdd 110yds out: one pce* **9/1**
60-4 3 1 **Embankment**[19] 812 8-9-5 58.............................. LukeMorris 8 60
(Michael Attwater) *s.i.s: hld up in midfield: rdn and hdwy over 2f out: kpt on same pce: wnt 3rd towards fin* **8/1**
3-35 4 1/2 **Dancin Alpha**[49] 314 6-9-1 54.............................. JoeFanning 7 55
(Alan Swinbank) *chsd ldr: led over 2f out: sn rdn: hdd appr fnl f: no ex* **10/3**[1]
100- 5 5 **Bogardus (IRE)**[158] 6684 6-9-8 61.............................. DanielTudhope 3 53
(Patrick Holmes) *in tch: rdn over 2f out: wknd over 1f out* **13/2**
540- 6 6 **Patent**[112] 7993 4-9-7 60.............................. JamesSullivan 2 41
(Peter Niven) *midfield: rdn over 2f out: sn wknd* **17/2**
54-6 7 1/2 **Innoko (FR)**[19] 806 7-9-6 59..............................(h) GeorgeDowning 1 39
(Tony Carroll) *hld up: reminder 5f out: rdn 3f out: sn btn* **5/1**[3]
000- 8 27 **Frightened Rabbit (USA)**[65] 5227 5-9-2 55.................(bt) PhillipMakin 5
(Susan Corbett) *led: rdn whn hdd over 2f out: wknd and eased* **20/1**

2m 10.9s (0.50) **Going Correction** +0.075s/f (Slow) 8 Ran SP% **111.7**
Speed ratings (Par 101): **101,99,98,98,94 89,89,67**
CSF £32.88 CT £228.80 TOTE £3.70: £1.30, £2.10, £1.90; EX 17.20 Trifecta £147.10.
**Owner** D B Salmon, Mrs L Salmon & M W Salmon **Bred** Tinnakill Bloodstock **Trained** Oldcastle Heath, Cheshire

**FOCUS**
This was run at a good gallop and the winner came from last place. Straightforward form set around the runner-up to her recent level.

### 1102 32RED.COM MAIDEN FILLIES' STKS (PLUS 10 RACE) 7f 14y (Tp)
**6:15** (6:15) (Class 5) 3-Y-0 **£2,911** (£866; £432; £216) **Stalls** Centre

Form RPR
42-2 1 **Rutherford (IRE)**[17] 845 3-9-2 75.............................. ShaneGray 4 69
(Kevin Ryan) *mde all: pushed along 2f out: rdn ins fnl f: kpt on* **8/11**[1]
4 2 2 **Dusky Maid (IRE)**[17] 845 3-9-2 0.............................. AndrewMullen 2 63
(James Given) *trckd ldr: rdn over 2f out: kpt on same pce and a hld* **7/1**[3]
3 2 1/2 **Harbour Siren** 3-9-2 0.............................. OisinMurphy 5 56
(David Brown) *dwlt: sn trckd ldr: pushed along over 2f out: no ex ins fnl f* **5/2**[2]
50 4 6 **Coral Princess (IRE)**[8] 970 3-9-2 0.............................. PhillipMakin 3 40
(Keith Dalgleish) *hld up in tch: rdn over 2f out: wknd fnl f* **33/1**
0 5 7 **R U Mine (IRE)**[6] 1003 3-9-2 0.............................. ConnorBeasley 1 21
(Keith Dalgleish) *sn pushed along: a rr* **16/1**

1m 28.66s (2.46) **Going Correction** +0.20s/f (Slow) 5 Ran SP% **107.8**
Speed ratings (Par 95): **93,90,87,81,73**
CSF £6.18 TOTE £1.60: £1.10, £2.30; EX 6.00 Trifecta £7.70.
**Owner** Mrs Angie Bailey **Bred** Eimear Mulhern & Abbeville Stud **Trained** Hambleton, N Yorks

**FOCUS**
An ordinary maiden and a straightforward win for the favourite. The level is fluid.

### 1103 BETWAY SPRINT H'CAP 6f (Tp)
**6:45** (6:46) (Class 3) (0-95,95) 3-Y-0+ **£7,439** (£2,213; £1,106; £553) **Stalls** Centre

Form RPR
130- 1 **Jaywalker (IRE)**[112] 7990 6-9-3 84.............................. PJMcDonald 2 93
(Rebecca Bastiman) *mde most: rdn over 1f out: kpt on* **8/1**[3]
-313 2 1/2 **Captain Dion**[31] 598 4-9-8 89..............................(v) KevinStott 6 96
(Kevin Ryan) *prom: rdn and ev ch over 1f out: edgd rt and one pce fnl 110yds* **7/4**[1]
-130 3 1 **Tatlisu (IRE)**[23] 730 7-9-2 90.............................. SebastianWoods(7) 11 94+
(Richard Fahey) *dwlt: hld up in rr: pushed along 2f out: r.o fnl f: wnt 3rd post* **10/1**
000- 4 shd **Intense Style (IRE)**[134] 7610 5-9-7 88.............................. ConnorBeasley 5 92
(Les Eyre) *trckd ldrs: rdn 2f out: ev ch appr fnl f: no ex fnl 110yds: lost 3rd post* **14/1**
206- 5 1/2 **God Willing**[103] 8122 6-9-9 90.............................. DanielTudhope 12 92
(Declan Carroll) *hld up in tch: pushed along 2f out: rdn appr fnl f: kpt on same pce* **9/2**[2]
-605 6 1 1/2 **Aguerooo (IRE)**[48] 326 4-9-8 89.............................. AndrewMullen 1 86
(Ollie Pears) *s.i.s: hld up: pushed along over 2f out: nvr threatened* **20/1**
1-60 7 hd **Luis Vaz De Torres (IRE)**[43] 403 5-8-11 78...........(h[1]) PaulHanagan 3 75
(Richard Fahey) *in tch: rdn 2f out: no ex ins fnl f* **20/1**
101- 8 1 1/2 **Giant Spark**[141] 7475 5-10-0 95.............................. PaulMulrennan 10 87
(Paul Midgley) *hld up: pushed along 1/2-way: nvr threatened* **14/1**
60/5 9 nk **Professor**[40] 459 7-9-11 92.............................. LukeMorris 8 83
(Michael Attwater) *in tch: rdn along and outpcd 1/2-way: no threat after* **11/1**
00-4 10 2 **Elysian Flyer (IRE)**[27] 660 5-8-12 79.............................. GrahamLee 4 63
(Paul Midgley) *prom: rdn over 2f out: wknd fnl f* **14/1**

1m 11.99s (-0.51) **Going Correction** +0.20s/f (Slow)
**WFA** 3 from 4yo+ 14lb 10 Ran SP% **112.6**
Speed ratings (Par 107): **111,110,109,108,108 106,105,103,103,100**
CSF £21.50 CT £145.54 TOTE £9.80: £2.10, £1.50, £2.60; EX 25.80 Trifecta £182.20.
**Owner** Ms M Austerfield **Bred** Kilfrush Stud **Trained** Cowthorpe, N Yorks

**FOCUS**
A decent sprint handicap, but few got involved with the speed holding up well. The winner has been rated as finding a bit on his late-2016 form.

### 1104 32RED CASINO FILLIES' H'CAP 1m 5y (Tp)
**7:15** (7:15) (Class 4) (0-80,77) 4-Y-0+ **£4,690** (£1,395; £697; £348) **Stalls** Centre

Form RPR
5354 1 **Dusky Dawn**[7] 994 5-9-5 75.............................. JoeFanning 1 82
(Alan Swinbank) *hld up in tch: hdwy to ld over 2f out: pushed along over 1f out: sn clr: edgd lft fnl 75yds* **5/1**[2]
-120 2 3 1/2 **Barwah (USA)**[5] 1032 6-9-2 72.............................. AndrewMullen 2 71
(Peter Niven) *trckd ldr: pushed along 2f out: rdn over 1f out: one pce and sn no ch wnr* **9/1**[3]
500- 3 1 3/4 **Forever A Lady (IRE)**[128] 7743 4-9-3 73.............................. ConnorBeasley 3 68
(Keith Dalgleish) *trckd ldr: rdn over 2f out: no ex fnl f* **25/1**
455- 4 nk **Livella Fella (IRE)**[104] 8090 4-9-3 73.............................. PhillipMakin 4 67
(Keith Dalgleish) *led: rdn whn hdd over 2f out: sn outpcd and btn* **16/1**
1/ 5 79 **Mandrell (USA)**[450] 8233 4-9-7 77.............................. AdamKirby 5
(Charlie Appleby) *dwlt: sn trckd ldr racing keenly: pushed along and wknd rapidly over 2f out: eased and virtually p.u* **1/3**[1]

1m 40.24s (1.64) **Going Correction** +0.20s/f (Slow) 5 Ran SP% **111.4**
Speed ratings (Par 102): **99,95,93,93,14**
CSF £42.57 TOTE £7.20: £4.50, £2.60; EX 23.10 Trifecta £77.60.
**Owner** Ray Parsons **Bred** Countrywide Classics Ltd **Trained** Melsonby, N Yorks

**FOCUS**
The race lost much of its interest with the disappointing run of the odds-on favourite, but the winner came through strongly from off the pace to take it. Pretty weak form which has been rated cautiously.

### 1105 SUNBETS.CO.UK H'CAP 7f 14y (Tp)
**7:45** (7:45) (Class 4) (0-85,88) 4-Y-0+ **£4,690** (£1,395; £697; £348) **Stalls** Centre

Form RPR
/31- 1 **Via Via (IRE)**[131] 7702 5-9-7 85.............................. LukeMorris 2 95+
(James Tate) *hld up: hdwy over 2f out: rdn along to chal over 1f out: led 110yds out: kpt on wl* **11/10**[1]
2041 2 1/2 **War Department (IRE)**[7] 989 4-9-10 88 6ex...........(v) ConnorBeasley 6 96
(Keith Dalgleish) *dwlt: hld up: pushed along and gd hdwy 2f out: drvn to chal over 1f out: kpt on wl* **7/2**[2]
023- 3 nk **Twin Appeal (IRE)**[124] 7825 6-9-9 87..............................(b) PhillipMakin 9 94
(David Barron) *hld up: gd hdwy over 2f out: rdn to ld over 1f out: hdd 110yds out: one pce* **7/2**[2]
120- 4 7 **Enjoy Life (IRE)**[99] 8158 4-8-12 76..............................(p) TomEaves 7 64
(Kevin Ryan) *led: rdn 2f out: hdd over 1f out: wknd fnl f* **12/1**[3]
2-40 5 5 **Hail Clodius (IRE)**[20] 782 5-9-5 83.............................. DanielTudhope 10 58
(Roger Fell) *chsd ldr: rdn over 2f out: wknd over 1f out* **14/1**
2-05 6 nk **Baltic Prince (IRE)**[35] 516 7-8-8 72.............................. GeorgeDowning 1 46
(Tony Carroll) *chsd ldr: rdn 3f out: wknd over 1f out* **20/1**
601- 7 hd **Glorious Poet**[136] 7583 4-8-13 77.............................. AndrewMullen 8 50
(Tony Carroll) *dwlt: hld up: pushed along over 2f out: nvr threatened* **25/1**
400- 8 18 **Shootingsta (IRE)**[142] 7433 5-8-12 76..............................(p) PaulMulrennan 5
(Bryan Smart) *trckd ldrs: plld hrd: rdn over 2f out: wknd and eased* **33/1**

1m 25.51s (-0.69) **Going Correction** +0.20s/f (Slow) 8 Ran SP% **118.0**
Speed ratings (Par 105): **111,110,110,102,96 96,95,75**
CSF £5.21 CT £10.42 TOTE £2.10: £1.10, £1.30, £1.50; EX 5.70 Trifecta £12.20.
**Owner** Saeed Manana **Bred** Kenilworth House Stud **Trained** Newmarket, Suffolk

**FOCUS**
The big three in the market pulled clear here. The third has been rated to his best.

### 1106 SUN BETS ON THE APP H'CAP 7f 14y (Tp)
**8:15** (8:15) (Class 6) (0-60,62) 4-Y-0+ **£2,264** (£673; £336; £168) **Stalls** Centre

Form RPR
0222 1 **Justice Pleasing**[8] 969 4-8-12 58..............................(p) BenSanderson(7) 5 63
(Roger Fell) *prom: pushed along to ld 2f out: rdn over 1f out: hld on all out* **2/1**[2]
661- 2 nse **Ad Vitam (IRE)**[78] 8482 9-9-9 62..............................(bt) TomEaves 2 67
(Suzzanne France) *stdd s: hld up: pushed along and hdwy over 2f out: rdn over 1f out: kpt on fnl f: jst failed* **14/1**
404- 3 3/4 **Make On Madam (IRE)**[170] 6644 5-9-8 61.............................. JasonHart 10 64
(Les Eyre) *trckd ldrs: rdn over 2f out: bit outpcd over 1f out: kpt on ins fnl f* **14/1**
4451 4 nk **Mr Potter**[21] 761 4-9-4 57..............................(v) PaulMulrennan 6 59
(Richard Guest) *dwlt: hld up in rr: racd keenly: stl on bit over 1f out: swtchd lft appr fnl f: rdn and kpt on ins fnl f* **5/1**[3]
4-21 5 1 1/4 **Orlando Rogue (IRE)**[47] 360 5-9-7 60..............................(v) ConnorBeasley 4 59
(Keith Dalgleish) *trckd ldrs: rdn and ev ch appr fnl f: wknd fnl 75yds* **7/4**[1]
000- 6 6 **Harbour Patrol (IRE)**[169] 6685 5-9-2 55.............................. DanielTudhope 7 39
(Rebecca Bastiman) *led: rdn whn hdd 2f out: sn wknd* **8/1**
04-0 7 3 1/4 **Centre Haafhd**[33] 579 6-8-7 46 oh1.............................. JamesSullivan 1 22
(Kenneth Slack) *trckd ldrs: racd quite keenly: rdn over 2f out: sn wknd* **12/1**

1m 27.51s (1.31) **Going Correction** +0.20s/f (Slow) 7 Ran SP% **118.5**
Speed ratings (Par 101): **100,99,99,98,97 90,86**
CSF £30.76 CT £321.00 TOTE £3.10: £1.90, £5.40; EX 21.70 Trifecta £161.30.
**Owner** R G Fell **Bred** D R Botterill **Trained** Nawton, N Yorks

**FOCUS**
A moderate handicap and they finished in a heap. The runner-up has been rated to his mark.
T/Plt: £27.10 to a £1 stake. Pool: £90,653.41 - 2,434.67 winning units. T/Qpdt: £9.40 to a £1 stake. Pool: £8,872.04 - 693.37 winning units. **Andrew Sheret**

## [1071]SOUTHWELL (L-H)
Thursday, March 9

**OFFICIAL GOING: Fibresand: standard**
Wind: Strong behind Weather: Fine, dry and windy

### 1107 32RED H'CAP 1m 13y(F)
**2:10** (2:10) (Class 6) (0-55,55) 3-Y-0 **£2,587** (£770; £384; £192) **Stalls** Low

Form RPR
654- 1 **Padleyourowncanoe**[182] 6253 3-9-4 52.............................. AndrewMullen 10 59+
(Daniel Mark Loughnane) *chsd ldrs: pushed along 1/2-way: rdn along 3f out: hdwy to chse clr ldr wl over 1f out: rdn and hung bdly lft to far rail jst over 1f out: drvn and styd on strly to ld last 100 yds* **9/2**[2]
-645 2 2 1/2 **Av A Word**[28] 637 3-9-7 55..............................(p) JosephineGordon 7 56
(Daniel Kubler) *cl up: pushed along and lost pl after 3f: sn in rr: rdn along over 3f out: hdwy 2f out: styd on wl appr fnl f: tk 2nd nr line* **6/1**

063- **3** *nk* **Topmeup**[128] 7734 3-9-5 **53**........................ JFEgan 1 53
(David Evans) *trckd ldrs: hdwy over 3f out: led over 2f out: rdn clr wl over 1f out: drvn ins fnl f: hdd last 100 yds: kpt on same pce* **8/1**

-041 **4** *6* **Viola Park**[14] 875 3-9-3 **51**........................(p) RyanPowell 11 37
(Ronald Harris) *prom on outer: cl up 1/2-way: led over 3f out: sn rdn and hdd over 2f out: sn drvn and kpt on one pce* **11/2**[3]

4-03 **5** *1* **Hold Me Tight (IRE)**[13] 897 3-9-7 **55**........................(b) LiamKeniry 2 38
(J S Moore) *trckd ldrs on inner: pushed along bef 1/2-way: hdwy 3f out: rdn over 2f out: sn drvn and no imp* **10/1**

000- **6** *2* **Chamasay**[112] 7981 3-9-0 **51**........................ PhilipPrince(3) 9 30
(David Evans) *towards rr: hdwy 3f out: rdn over 2f out: kpt on u.p fnl f* **25/1**

0-06 **7** *3 1/4* **Major Tom**[27] 662 3-9-5 **53**........................ SilvestreDeSousa 3 24
(Michael Appleby) *a towards rr* **7/2**[1]

56-6 **8** *1 3/4* **Red Shanghai (IRE)**[27] 667 3-8-9 **46** oh1........................ NoelGarbutt(3) 6 13
(Charles Smith) *in tch on inner: rdn along over 3f out: sn outpcd and bhd* **100/1**

-600 **9** *4 1/2* **Master Billie (IRE)**[14] 881 3-8-12 **46**........................(p[1]) DanielMuscutt 5 2
(Roger Teal) *racd wd: a bhd* **25/1**

000- **10** *7* **Millybond**[152] 7142 3-8-12 **46** oh1........................ TomEaves 4
(David Brown) *slt ld: rdn along and hdd over 3f out: sn wknd and beind* **33/1**

6-00 **11** *11* **Georgio (GER)**[13] 895 3-9-7 **55**........................(h) DavidProbert 8
(Andrew Balding) *t.k.h: cl up: rdn along over 3f out: sn wknd and bhd* **6/1**

1m 43.31s (-0.39) **Going Correction** -0.175s/f (Stan) **11** Ran SP% **116.2**
Speed ratings (Par 96): **94,91,91,85,84 82,78,77,72,65 54**
CSF £30.17 CT £213.51 TOTE £7.10: £2.40, £2.20, £2.60; EX 37.30 Trifecta £188.50.
**Owner** The Batham Boys **Bred** Lianne Barrett & Ferdiant Stud **Trained** Rock, Worcs

**FOCUS**
A moderate 3yo handicap run at a good clip, with the first two home coming from off the pace. It's been rated around the second and third.

## 1108 BETWAY (S) STKS — 1m 4f 14y(F)
**2:45** (2:45) (Class 6) 4-Y-0+ **£2,587** (£770; £384; £192) **Stalls** Low

Form RPR

0340 **1** **Luv U Whatever**[21] 759 7-8-13 83........................ AndrewMullen 6 80
(Michael Attwater) *cl up: led over 6f out: pushed clr over 3f out: unchal* **4/11**[1]

55 **2** *8* **Paris Bound**[13] 894 4-8-11 0........................ DavidProbert 3 59
(Andrew Balding) *cl up on inner: disp ld after 3f: pushed along on inner over 7 out: sn lost pl and swtchd rt: rdn along and hdwy to chse ldng pair 4f out: drvn wl over 2f out: plugged on one pce* **12/1**

400- **3** *8* **Monzino (USA)**[98] 8180 9-8-8 47........................ PhilDennis(5) 7 46
(Michael Chapman) *trckd ldrs: hdwy and cl up over 4f out: rdn along over 3f out: drvn wl over 2f out: sn one pce* **200/1**

160- **4** *25* **Brassbound (USA)**[317] 1760 9-9-5 79........................ ShaneKelly 5 12
(Michael Appleby) *slt ld: pushed along and hdd over 6f out: sn rdn and outpcd fr over 4f out* **5/1**[2]

6/0- **5** *12* **Stomachion (IRE)**[236] 4399 7-8-10 92........................ HectorCrouch(3) 4
(John Butler) *trckd ldrs: pushed along 5f out: rdn over 4f out: sn outpcd and bhd* **8/1**[3]

2m 37.99s (-3.01) **Going Correction** -0.175s/f (Stan)
**WFA** 4 from 7yo+ 1lb **5** Ran SP% **109.3**
Speed ratings (Par 101): **103,97,92,75,67**
CSF £5.81 TOTE £1.30: £1.10, £3.20; EX 5.60 Trifecta £67.40.There was no bids for the winner.
**Owner** Richard and Nicola Hunt **Bred** Richard Hunt **Trained** Epsom, Surrey
■ Stewards' Enquiry : Shane Kelly caution: careless riding

**FOCUS**
An uncompetitive seller and the odds-on favourite was in a different league. A token rating has been given.

## 1109 SUNBETS.CO.UK H'CAP — 7f 14y(F)
**3:20** (3:20) (Class 5) (0-70,72) 4-Y-0+ **£3,234** (£962; £481; £240) **Stalls** Low

Form RPR

000- **1** **Hammer Gun (USA)**[112] 7985 4-8-10 **58**........................(v) FrannyNorton 2 67
(Derek Shaw) *chsd ldrs on inner: hdwy and cl up 3f out: chal 2f out: rdn over 1f out: led ins fnl f: drvn out* **100/1**

414/ **2** *1 1/4* **Dark Profit (IRE)**[506] 7356 5-9-0 **67**........................(p) ShirleyTeasdale(5) 7 72
(Keith Dalgleish) *t.k.h early: cl up: led wl over 2f out: jnd and rdn wl over 1f out: hdd and drvn ins fnl f: kpt on same pce* **16/1**

4404 **3** *1 1/2* **Boots And Spurs**[2] 1074 8-9-9 **71**........................(v) DaleSwift 4 72
(Scott Dixon) *prom on outer: rdn along wl over 2f out: drvn over 1f out: kpt on same pce* **7/2**[2]

0004 **4** *nse* **Greyfriarschorista**[1] 1086 10-8-12 **63**........................(v) PhilipPrince(3) 5 64
(David Evans) *chsd ldrs: hdwy over 2f out: rdn and ev ch wl over 1f out: sn drvn and kpt on same pce* **11/1**

3540 **5** *5* **Harwoods Star (IRE)**[16] 850 7-9-9 **71**........................(be) JFEgan 6 59
(John Butler) *in tch: rdn along 3f out: sn no imp* **25/1**

-050 **6** *3/4* **Macho Mac**[42] 419 4-9-7 **69**........................(h) FranBerry 9 54
(Hughie Morrison) *chsd ldrs: rdn along 3f out: sn drvn and btn* **4/1**[3]

014/ **7** *shd* **Swilly Sunset**[482] 7823 4-9-1 **63**........................ WilliamCarson 8 48
(Anthony Carson) *a towards rr* **20/1**

1-00 **8** *4 1/2* **Napoleon Solo**[33] 583 5-9-1 **63**........................ RobHornby 10 36
(David Barron) *a towards rr* **8/1**

3-11 **9** *3* **Bounty Pursuit**[16] 852 5-9-1 **66**........................(h) AlistairRawlinson(3) 3 31
(Michael Appleby) *s.i.s and lost 5 l s: a bhd* **15/8**[1]

0134 **10** *2* **Elusivity (IRE)**[12] 923 9-9-10 **72**........................(p) PaulMulrennan 1 32
(Conor Dore) *led: rdn along 3f out: sn hdd & wknd 2f out* **33/1**

1m 28.36s (-1.94) **Going Correction** -0.175s/f (Stan) **10** Ran SP% **114.9**
Speed ratings (Par 103): **104,102,100,100,95 94,94,88,85,83**
CSF £1196.98 CT £7120.98 TOTE £55.60: £21.70, £4.70, £1.30; EX 1605.50 Trifecta £6875.20.
**Owner** A Flint **Bred** Her Majesty The Queen **Trained** Sproxton, Leics

**FOCUS**
A fair handicap and a surprise winner. The third has been rated similar to his run here two days earlier, and the fourth close to his run at Lingfield the previous day.

## 1110 BETWAY H'CAP — 4f 214y(F)
**3:55** (3:55) (Class 4) (0-85,87) 4-Y-0+ **£5,822** (£1,732; £865; £432) **Stalls** Centre

Form RPR

2146 **1** **Dungannon**[16] 851 10-8-12 **81**........................(b) JoshuaBryan(7) 1 93
(Andrew Balding) *racd towards far rail: cl up: led 2f out: rdn over 1f out: styd on strly* **7/2**[2]

06-0 **2** *2 1/4* **New Road Side**[7] 995 4-9-2 **78**........................ FrannyNorton 3 82
(Richard Guest) *racd centre: prom: rdn to chse wnr over 1f out: drvn and kpt on fnl f* **6/1**

00-1 **3** *1/2* **Sir Billy Wright (IRE)**[27] 664 6-9-5 **86**........................ CliffordLee(5) 5 88
(David Evans) *chsd ldrs centre: rdn along and sltly outpcd 1/2-way: hdwy and rdn over 1f out: kpt on same pce ins fnl f* **5/2**[1]

1-16 **4** *3/4* **The Big Lad**[35] 518 5-8-5 **74**........................(e) NicolaCurrie(7) 8 74
(Richard Hughes) *racd towards stands side: outpcd and towards rr: rdn along 1/2-way: styd on wl appr fnl f* **8/1**

1433 **5** *1 1/4* **Lady Nayef**[16] 851 4-9-6 **82**........................(t) JFEgan 2 77
(John Butler) *racd towards far side: chsd ldrs: rdn 2f out: drvn appr fnl f: kpt on one pce* **4/1**[3]

46-0 **6** *2 1/2* **Saved My Bacon (IRE)**[29] 618 6-9-1 **77**........................(h) SilvestreDeSousa 4 63
(Chris Dwyer) *racd towards far side: in tch: rdn along 2f out: sn no imp* **16/1**

20-0 **7** *nk* **Extrasolar**[20] 783 7-9-2 **78**........................ SamJames 7 63
(Geoffrey Harker) *chsd ldrs centre: rdn along over 2f out: sn wknd* **66/1**

50-3 **8** *3 1/4* **Mysterious Look**[42] 416 4-8-12 **74**........................ RobHornby 9 47
(Sarah Hollinshead) *racd towards stands side: sn outpcd and a rr* **20/1**

00-0 **9** *2 1/4* **Red Baron (IRE)**[17] 842 8-9-11 **87**........................(b) JasonHart 6 52
(Eric Alston) *racd centre: sn led: rdn along and hdd 2f out: sn drvn and wknd* **25/1**

57.63s (-2.07) **Going Correction** -0.275s/f (Stan) **9** Ran SP% **112.2**
Speed ratings (Par 105): **105,101,100,99,97 93,92,87,84**
CSF £23.38 CT £60.00 TOTE £4.50: £1.60, £2.20, £1.20; EX 29.20 Trifecta £100.60.
**Owner** Dr E Harris **Bred** J A E Hobby **Trained** Kingsclere, Hants

**FOCUS**
A useful, open-looking sprint, in which it paid to race handily. The runner-up has been rated to her penultimate C&D form.

## 1111 SUNBETS.CO.UK MEDIAN AUCTION MAIDEN STKS — 1m 13y(F)
**4:30** (4:31) (Class 5) 3-5-Y-0 **£3,234** (£962; £481; £240) **Stalls** Low

Form RPR

5-35 **1** **He's A Lad (IRE)**[27] 662 3-8-10 76........................ DavidProbert 8 76
(Andrew Balding) *cl up on outer: hdwy 2f out: rdn to ld and hung lft over 1f out: sn clr: kpt on strly* **5/4**[1]

**2** *5* **Clock Chimes** 3-8-10 0........................ TedDurcan 1 64
(David Brown) *trckd ldrs: hdwy over 2f out: rdn and green over 1f out: kpt on fnl f* **6/1**[3]

3 **3** *1 1/4* **Secret Salvage (IRE)**[14] 882 3-8-5 0........................ JosephineGordon 4 56
(Jamie Osborne) *cl up: led wl over 2f out and sn rdn: green and hdd over 1f out: kpt on same pce* **3/1**[2]

**4** *10* **Last Chance Paddy (USA)** 3-8-10 0........................ NeilFarley 6 37
(Alan Swinbank) *dwlt: sn chsng ldrs on outer: hdwy over 3f out: rdn along wl over 2f out: sn outpcd* **7/1**

60-0 **5** *1/2* **Sunovarebel**[14] 875 3-8-10 60........................ JoeyHaynes 7 36
(Alan Bailey) *trckd ldrs: hdwy over 3f out: rdn along wl over 2f out: sn wknd* **25/1**

**6** *1/2* **Stragar** 3-8-10 0........................ SilvestreDeSousa 5 35
(Michael Appleby) *trckd ldrs: pushed along over 3f out: rdn along wl over 2f out: sn wknd* **10/1**

0- **7** *17* **Melo Magic**[220] 4951 3-7-12 0........................ GinaMangan(7) 2
(J R Jenkins) *slt ld: rdn along over 3f out: sn hdd & wknd* **66/1**

1m 41.69s (-2.01) **Going Correction** -0.175s/f (Stan) **7** Ran SP% **110.7**
Speed ratings (Par 103): **103,98,96,86,86 85,68**
CSF £8.71 TOTE £2.20: £1.50, £3.20; EX 8.70 Trifecta £23.40.
**Owner** Sheikh Juma Dalmook Al Maktoum **Bred** Rathbarry Stud **Trained** Kingsclere, Hants

**FOCUS**
An ordinary maiden. The winner has been rated to his Lingfield form.

## 1112 BETWAY SPRINT H'CAP — 6f 16y(F)
**5:05** (5:06) (Class 6) (0-52,54) 4-Y-0+ **£2,587** (£770; £384; £192) **Stalls** Low

Form RPR

0205 **1** **Autumn Tonic (IRE)**[16] 852 5-9-7 **52**........................(b) RobHornby 7 59
(David Barron) *trckd ldrs: hdwy over 2f out: swtchd rt to outer and effrt 2f out: rdn to ld jst over 1f out: sn edgd rt to stands rail: clr ins fnl f* **4/1**[2]

4000 **2** *2 1/2* **Spowarticus**[2] 1076 8-9-8 **53**........................(v) DaleSwift 5 51
(Scott Dixon) *chsd ldng pair: hdwy over 2f out: rdn along wl over 1f out and ev ch: drvn and kpt on fnl f* **11/2**[3]

000- **3** *hd* **Oscars Journey**[79] 8474 7-9-9 **54**........................(v) TomQueally 2 51
(J R Jenkins) *slt ld: rdn 2f out: drvn and hdd jst over 1f out: kpt on same pce* **9/1**

0-31 **4** *2 1/4* **Pick Of Any (IRE)**[13] 899 4-9-8 **53**........................(h) SilvestreDeSousa 1 43+
(Michael Appleby) *in tch on inner: hdwy 3f out: rdn along wl over 1f out: drvn and kpt on same pce fnl f* **6/4**[1]

**5** *2 3/4* **Kanade (IRE)**[55] 229 4-8-12 **46** oh1........................ AlistairRawlinson(3) 10 28
(Emmet Mullins, Ire) *chsd ldrs: rdn along wl over 2f out: plugged on one pce* **8/1**

-000 **6** *1* **Arizona Snow**[28] 640 5-9-1 **46**........................(b[1]) JFEgan 6 25
(Ronald Harris) *cl up: rdn along wl over 2f out: sn wknd* **11/1**

/60- **7** *nk* **Wotabond**[135] 7602 4-9-1 **46** oh1........................ PaulQuinn 4 24
(Richard Whitaker) *s.i.s: a rr* **28/1**

006- **8** *6* **Ormering**[163] 6857 4-9-1 **46** oh1........................(p) TomMarquand 11 6
(Roger Teal) *a rr* **20/1**

-600 **9** *1/2* **Allen's Folly**[12] 923 4-8-8 **46** oh1........................ MollyKing(7) 8 5
(Peter Hiatt) *chsd ldrs: rdn along 1/2-way: sn wknd* **40/1**

1m 16.02s (-0.48) **Going Correction** -0.175s/f (Stan) **9** Ran SP% **115.5**
Speed ratings (Par 101): **96,92,92,89,85 84,84,76,75**
CSF £25.62 CT £187.47 TOTE £5.10: £1.80, £1.90, £2.40; EX 25.90 Trifecta £148.90.
**Owner** Let's Be Lucky Racing 8 **Bred** Yeomanstown Stud **Trained** Maunby, N Yorks

**FOCUS**
Only a moderate handicap. The winner has been rated to his best form of recent times, with the third to his recent standard.

## 1113 BETWAY APPRENTICE H'CAP — 1m 3f 23y(F)
**5:35** (5:35) (Class 5) (0-75,77) 4-Y-0+ **£3,234** (£962; £481; £240) **Stalls** Low

Form RPR

6246 **1** **Storm King**[7] 992 8-9-1 **74**........................ FinleyMarsh(7) 5 79
(David C Griffiths) *trckd ldrs: hdwy and wd st: cl up over 2f out: chal wl over 1f out: rdn to ld appr fnl f: kpt on wl* **5/2**[2]

21-4 **2** *1* **Priors Brook**[64] 38 6-9-6 **77**........................ JoshuaBryan(5) 2 80
(Andrew Balding) *cl up: rdn to chal over 2f out: slt ld briefly over 1f out: sn hdd and drvn: kpt on fnl f* **9/4**[1]

6361 **3** *nk* **The Lock Master (IRE)**[16] 853 10-9-4 **70**........................(v) AlistairRawlinson 1 72
(Michael Appleby) *led: rdn along over 2f out: drvn and hdd over 1f out: kpt on wl u.p fnl f* **11/2**[3]

1-13 **4** *10* **Go George Go (IRE)**[36] 509 4-9-4 **71**........................ CallumShepherd 6 56
(Alan Swinbank) *hld up: hdwy 3f out: rdn along wl over 2f out: sn drvn and btn* **5/2**[2]



The Form Book Flat, Raceform Ltd, Newbury, RG14 5SJ

300- **5** *7* **Falcon's Fire (IRE)**[149] 7251 4-9-7 **74**........................ ShirleyTeasdale 3 48
(Keith Dalgleish) *trckd ldng pair: hdwy over 4f out: rdn along 3f out: drvn over 2f out and sn wknd* **25/1**

2m 25.7s (-2.30) **Going Correction** -0.175s/f (Stan) **5** Ran SP% **107.1**
Speed ratings (Par 103): **101,100,100,92,87**
CSF £8.01 TOTE £3.00: £1.50, £1.50; EX 8.40 Trifecta £21.20.
**Owner** Eros Bloodstock **Bred** Norcroft Park Stud And D Laidlaw **Trained** Bawtry, S Yorks
■ Stewards' Enquiry : Callum Shepherd caution: careless riding

**FOCUS**
A fair handicap and the pace was ordinary. It's been rated around the first three close to their recent marks.
T/Jkpt: Not won. T/Plt: £44.90 to a £1 stake. Pool: £77,683.82 - 1,262.62 winning units. T/Qpdt: £14.30 to a £1 stake. Pool: £6,891.99 - 356.40 winning units. **Joe Rowntree**

# FONTAINEBLEAU
Thursday, March 9

**OFFICIAL GOING: Turf: very soft**

## 1114a PRIX MAURICE CAILLAULT (LISTED RACE) (3YO) (TURF) 1m 1f
2:55 3-Y-O **£23,504** (£9,401; £7,051; £4,700; £2,350)

RPR
**1** **Speedo Boy (FR)**[20] 799 3-8-13 0........................ AurelienLemaitre 3 104
(Ian Williams) *hld up wl in tch: rdn 2f out: chal over 1f out: styd on and led towards fin* **23/5**[3]
**2** *½* **Phoceen (FR)**[20] 799 3-8-13 0........................ ChristopheSoumillon 1 103
(F Chappet, France) **13/10**[1]
**3** *2* **Saglawy (FR)**[92] 3-8-13 0........................ StephanePasquier 5 99
(N Clement, France) **2/1**[2]
**4** *½* **Just A Formality (FR)**[12] 3-8-13 0........................(b) MaximeGuyon 4 98
(C Escuder, France) **15/1**
**5** *¾* **Fox Tin (FR)** 3-8-13 0........................ JulienAuge 6 96
(C Ferland, France) **48/10**

PARI-MUTUEL (all including 1 euro stake): WIN 5.80; PLACE 2.40, 1.60; SF 10.80.
**Owner** Paul Williams **Bred** E A R L Haras De Grandcamp Et Al **Trained** Portway, Worcs

1115 - 1121a (Foreign Racing) - See Raceform Interactive

# [1101]NEWCASTLE (A.W) (L-H)
Friday, March 10

**OFFICIAL GOING: Tapeta: standard**
Wind: Light half against Weather: Overcast

## 1122 BETWAY MAIDEN STKS 1m 4f 98y (Tp)
5:45 (5:46) (Class 5) 3-4-Y-O **£3,234** (£962; £481; £240) **Stalls** High

Form RPR
4-2 **1** **Blushing Red (FR)**[11] 959 3-8-7 0........................ JosephineGordon 1 64+
(Ed Dunlop) *t.k.h: trckd ldng pair on inner: hdwy and nt clr run 2f out: swtchd rt and rdn over 1f out: qcknd wl to chal ins fnl f: led last 100 yds* **4/7**[1]
34 **2** *½* **Sugarloaf Mountain (IRE)**[21] 780 4-10-0 72........................(t[1]) BenCurtis 2 66
(Brian Ellison) *hld up towards rr: hdwy over 2f out: rdn and hung lft wl over 1f out: swtchd rt and drvn ins fnl f: kpt on wl towards fin* **9/4**[2]
06 **3** *½* **Archibelle**[28] 658 3-8-1 0 ow2........................ NathanEvans(3) 6 59
(R Mike Smith) *trckd ldrs: hdwy 3f out: chal 2f out: sn rdn and disp ld tl led briefly ins fnl f: drvn: hdd and kpt on same pce last 100 yds* **200/1**
4-4 **4** *1 ¼* **Tewafeedj**[17] 849 3-8-7 0........................ ShaneGray 4 61
(Kevin Ryan) *trckd ldr: hdwy to ld wl over 2f out: sn jnd and rdn: drvn ent fnl f: sn hdd and kpt on same pce* **5/1**[3]
26-5 **5** *3* **Highwayman**[37] 509 4-10-0 59........................ DavidNolan 7 58
(David Thompson) *hld: a rr* **20/1**
0 **6** *5* **Ibreeq (IRE)**[21] 780 4-10-0 0........................ JackGarritty 3 50
(Roger Fell) *led: pushed along over 3f out: rdn and hdd wl over 2f out: sn wknd* **100/1**

2m 47.87s (6.77) **Going Correction** +0.025s/f (Slow) **6** Ran SP% **117.3**
**WFA** 3 from 4yo 23lb
Speed ratings (Par 103): **78,77,77,76,74 71**
CSF £2.34 TOTE £1.60: £1.10, £1.50; EX 3.00 Trifecta £38.40.
**Owner** The Hon R J Arculli **Bred** Robert Brard & Jean Dupont Cariot **Trained** Newmarket, Suffolk

**FOCUS**
A weak, steadily run maiden.

## 1123 32RED.COM H'CAP 7f 14y (Tp)
6:15 (6:16) (Class 6) (0-60,62) 3-Y-O **£3,234** (£962; £481; £240) **Stalls** Centre

Form RPR
633 **1** **Scala Regia (FR)**[31] 612 3-9-7 **60**........................ LukeMorris 7 66+
(Sir Mark Prescott Bt) *trckd ldrs: hdwy over 2f out: rdn over 1f out: chal ins fnl f: drvn and kpt on wl to ld last 50 yds* **8/1**[3]
54-5 **2** *1* **Hollywood Harry (IRE)**[6] 1034 3-9-3 **56**........................(p) ConnorBeasley 12 57
(Keith Dalgleish) *cl up: led 3f out: jnd and rdn 2f out: drvn ent fnl f: hdd and no ex last 50 yds* **14/1**
5-50 **3** *nk* **De Vegas Kid (IRE)**[18] 846 3-9-5 **58**........................(p) GeorgeDowning 4 59
(Tony Carroll) *towards rr: hdwy over 2f out: rdn to chse ldrs whn n.m.r and swtchd lft jst over 1f out: drvn whn nt clr run and swtchd rt ins fnl f: n.m.r and swtchd lft last 100 yds: kpt on wl nr fin* **22/1**
50-1 **4** *½* **African Grey**[6] 1034 3-8-11 **57**........................ BenRobinson(7) 10 56
(David Barron) *rrd and lost several l s: bhd tl tk clsr order 1/2-way: hdwy and chal 2f out: sn rdn: drvn and carried hd high appr fnl f: kpt on same pce* **6/4**[1]
3-03 **5** *1 ¾* **Magic Journey (IRE)**[55] 245 3-9-2 **55**........................(b) JasonHart 8 50
(John Quinn) *t.k.h early and towards rr: pushed along 1/2-way: rdn along to chse ldrs over 2f out: drvn over 1f out: kpt on one pce* **8/1**[3]
0-46 **6** *shd* **Tranquil Tracy**[46] 376 3-8-0 **46** oh1........................ AledBeech(7) 3 41
(John Norton) *towards rr: hdwy on inner 2f out: rdn over 1f out: n.m.r ins fnl f: kpt on: nrst fin* **40/1**
56-4 **7** *½* **Forest Angel (IRE)**[15] 882 3-9-9 **62**........................ DanielTudhope 2 55
(James Tate) *trckd ldrs on inner: hdwy 3f out: rdn along 2f out: drvn over 1f out: sn wknd* **11/4**[2]
066- **8** *¾* **Born To Boogie**[237] 4404 3-8-13 **52**........................ TonyHamilton 9 43
(Chris Grant) *towards rr: hdwy wl over 1f out: sn rdn and kpt on fnl f: nrst fin* **100/1**
5602 **9** *1 ¾* **Lady Volante (IRE)**[27] 686 3-9-4 **60**........................ PhilipPrince(3) 11 47
(David Evans) *led: rdn along and hdd 3f out: sn drvn and wknd* **22/1**
-500 **10** *2* **Princess Way (IRE)**[27] 686 3-9-5 **58**........................ JFEgan 5 40
(David Evans) *midfield: rdn along 3f out: sn outpcd* **40/1**
006- **11** *1 ¼* **I Don't Believe It**[127] 7777 3-8-13 **52**........................(p[1]) GrahamLee 6 31
(Micky Hammond) *cl up: rdn along 3f out: sn wknd* **33/1**
600- **12** *8* **La Haule Lady**[154] 7109 3-9-6 **59**........................ PaulMulrennan 1 18
(Paul Midgley) *prom: ridden along over 3f out: sn wknd* **33/1**

1m 27.44s (1.24) **Going Correction** +0.025s/f (Slow) **12** Ran SP% **116.0**
Speed ratings (Par 96): **93,91,91,90,88 88,88,87,85,83 81,72**
CSF £101.07 CT £2379.34 TOTE £7.50: £1.60, £2.90, £5.60; EX 89.70 Trifecta £3428.80.
**Owner** Cyril Humphris **Bred** Cyril Humphris **Trained** Newmarket, Suffolk

**FOCUS**
A fair-looking race for the grade and the favourite ran much better than his finishing position suggests.

## 1124 32RED CASINO H'CAP 6f (Tp)
6:45 (6:45) (Class 4) (0-85,87) 3-Y-O **£4,851** (£1,443; £721; £360) **Stalls** Centre

Form RPR
21-3 **1** **Wick Powell**[59] 155 3-9-7 **85**........................ AndrewMullen 2 96
(David Barron) *mde all: rdn clr ent fnl f: kpt on strly* **5/1**[2]
510- **2** *3 ¾* **Hemingway (IRE)**[204] 5583 3-9-2 **80**........................ TomEaves 1 78
(Kevin Ryan) *cl up: pushed along over 2f out: rdn wl over 1f out: kpt on u.p fnl f* **6/1**[3]
21-5 **3** *½* **Zamjar**[15] 877 3-9-4 **82**........................(b) JosephineGordon 8 78
(Ed Dunlop) *racd towards stands side: in tch: hdwy to chse ldrs 2f out: sn rdn and kpt on fnl f* **9/2**[1]
1323 **4** *nk* **Dazacam**[13] 926 3-9-2 **85**........................ CliffordLee(5) 5 80+
(Michael Herrington) *hld up: hdwy over 2f out: rdn to chse wnr jst ins fnl f: sn drvn and edgd rt: wknd last 100 yds* **14/1**
-646 **5** *3 ¼* **Whatsthemessage (IRE)**[18] 846 3-8-0 **69**........... ShirleyTeasdale(5) 4 54
(Keith Dalgleish) *towards rr: pushed along and sme hdwy 2f out: sn rdn and n.d* **40/1**
06-2 **6** *¾* **Kamra (USA)**[41] 458 3-9-0 **78**........................ JFEgan 7 60
(Jeremy Noseda) *chsd ldrs: prom 1/2-way: rdn along jst over 2f out: sn drvn and wknd* **9/1**
-126 **7** *4* **Erissimus Maximus (FR)**[15] 877 3-8-13 **77**........................(p) JoeFanning 9 46
(Chris Dwyer) *hld up towards stands side: pushed along over 2f out: sn rdn and nvr a factor* **8/1**
-241 **8** *1* **Blue Bahia (IRE)**[18] 845 3-8-7 **71**........................ PJMcDonald 6 37
(Mark Johnston) *chsd ldrs: rdn along wl over 2f out: sn wknd* **16/1**
3414 **9** *½* **Alkashaaf (USA)**[15] 877 3-9-3 **81**........................(tp) OisinMurphy 3 46
(Archie Watson) *a towards rr* **9/2**[1]
01- **10** *14* **Royal Opera House (IRE)**[92] 8277 3-9-9 **87**........... DougieCostello 10 7
(Jamie Osborne) *racd towards stands side: a towards rr* **15/2**

1m 11.45s (-1.05) **Going Correction** +0.025s/f (Slow) **10** Ran SP% **115.2**
Speed ratings (Par 100): **108,103,102,101,97 96,91,89,89,70**
CSF £34.64 CT £147.21 TOTE £5.40: £1.70, £2.30, £1.50; EX 32.30 Trifecta £142.30.
**Owner** Miss N J Barron **Bred** Usk Valley Stud, Mr Martin Graham **Trained** Maunby, N Yorks

**FOCUS**
A fair 3yo sprint handicap and a winner who is evidently better than this level.

## 1125 SUNBETS ON THE APP STORE H'CAP 1m 5y (Tp)
7:15 (7:16) (Class 6) (0-60,68) 4-Y-O+ **£3,234** (£962; £481; £240) **Stalls** Centre

Form RPR
6-00 **1** **Nelson's Bay**[9] 969 8-8-6 **52**........................ PaulaMuir(7) 9 59
(Wilf Storey) *sltly hmpd s and hld up in rr: swtchd rt and smooth hdwy nr strnds rails 2f out: led appr fnl f: kpt on strly: readily* **33/1**
U600 **2** *2 ½* **Sheer Intensity (IRE)**[10] 966 4-9-0 **53**........................ JFEgan 10 55
(David Evans) *hld up in rr: hdwy 3f out: pushed along to chse ldrs 2f out: rdn to chal over 1f out and ev ch: drvn and kpt on same pce fnl f* **12/1**
-402 **3** *2 ½* **A Boy Named Sue**[28] 655 4-8-8 **50**........................(v) NathanEvans(3) 7 46
(Peter Niven) *in tch: hdwy to chse ldrs over 2f out: rdn wl over 1f out: drvn and kpt on one pce fnl f* **9/4**[1]
-001 **4** *½* **Kiwi Bay**[9] 968 12-9-8 **68** 6ex........................ CallumRodriguez(7) 6 63
(Michael Dods) *trckd ldrs: hdwy and cl up 1/2-way: led 3f out: rdn along 2f out: drvn: edgd lft and hdd over 1f out: sn wknd* **4/1**[2]
4-40 **5** *nk* **John Caesar (IRE)**[18] 841 6-9-5 **58**........................(tp) DanielTudhope 3 52
(Rebecca Bastiman) *in tch: hdwy to chse ldrs over 2f out: rdn along wl over 1f out: sn drvn and no imp* **7/1**
36-6 **6** *2 ¼* **Mr Sundowner (USA)**[44] 400 5-8-7 **51**........................(t) MeganNicholls(5) 2 40
(Wilf Storey) *trckd ldrs: pushed along 3f out: rdn wl over 2f out: sn wknd* **5/1**[3]
560- **7** *1 ½* **Luath**[184] 6238 4-9-7 **60**........................ NickyMackay 8 46
(Suzzanne France) *nvr nr ldrs* **20/1**
-004 **8** *4* **Jessie Allan (IRE)**[9] 969 6-8-7 **46** oh1........................(h[1]) SamJames 5 23
(Jim Goldie) *led: pushed along and hdd 3f out: cl up tl rdn 2f out and sn wknd* **20/1**
300- **9** *¾* **New Abbey Angel (IRE)**[155] 7096 4-9-1 **59**........(p) ShirleyTeasdale(5) 1 37
(Keith Dalgleish) *plld hrd: cl up: rdn along over 3f out: sn wknd* **7/1**

1m 39.24s (0.64) **Going Correction** +0.025s/f (Slow) **9** Ran SP% **112.6**
Speed ratings (Par 101): **97,94,92,91,91 88,87,83,82**
CSF £361.87 CT £1261.17 TOTE £36.50: £7.20, £3.10, £1.20; EX 396.60 Trifecta £1337.00.
**Owner** The Durham Company & W Storey **Bred** Raymond Clive Tooth **Trained** Muggleswick, Co Durham

**FOCUS**
A moderate contest.

## 1126 BETWAY H'CAP 5f (Tp)
7:45 (7:47) (Class 6) (0-60,60) 4-Y-O+ **£2,425** (£721; £360; £180) **Stalls** Centre

Form RPR
-355 **1** **Sea Of Green**[7] 1006 5-8-7 **46**........................(p[1]) SamJames 8 52
(Jim Goldie) *dwlt and rr: hdwy over 2f out: chsd ldrs over 1f out: rdn to chal ins fnl f: kpt on wl to ld nr fin* **14/1**
0164 **2** *hd* **Windforpower (IRE)**[6] 1031 7-9-7 **60**........................(p) BenCurtis 7 65
(Tracy Waggott) *trckd ldrs: hdwy and cl up 2f out: rdn to ld briefly ins fnl f: sn drvn: hdd and no ex nr fin* **15/2**[3]
000- **3** *½* **Lackaday**[137] 7584 5-9-4 **57**........................(p) GrahamLee 6 60
(Noel Wilson) *slt ld: rdn along 2f out: drvn and hdd ins fnl f: kpt on* **14/1**
-053 **4** *1* **See Vermont**[23] 742 9-9-4 **57**........................(p) DanielTudhope 14 56
(Rebecca Bastiman) *hld up towards rr: hdwy towards stands rail wl over 1f out: sn rdn and kpt on wl fnl f: nrst fin* **7/1**[2]
1-04 **5** *nk* **Novabridge**[24] 732 9-9-1 **59**........................(b) GemmaTutty(5) 10 58
(Karen Tutty) *hld up towards rr: hdwy wl over 1f out: rdn and kpt on fnl f: nrst fin* **8/1**

-354 **6** *hd* **David's Beauty (IRE)**[14] 901 4-9-4 **57**..................(v) DougieCostello 13 55
(Brian Baugh) *cl up: disp ld 1/2-way: rdn wl over 1f out and ev ch tl drvn ins fnl f and kpt on same pce* **20/1**

-231 **7** *½* **Dandilion (IRE)**[14] 901 4-9-1 **57**..........................(t) CallumShepherd(3) 4 53
(Alex Hales) *hld up in midfield: hdwy 2f out: rdn over 1f out: kpt on same pce u.p fnl f* **7/4**[1]

06-0 **8** *½* **Little Belter (IRE)**[7] 1006 5-8-13 **52**..........................(p) ConnorBeasley 3 46
(Keith Dalgleish) *chsd ldrs: rdn along over 2f out: sn drvn and grad wknd* **20/1**

0630 **9** *4* **Satchville Flyer**[9] 969 6-9-2 **58**.................................. PhilipPrince(3) 11 38
(David Evans) *rr: swtchd lft towards far rail bef 1/2-way: sn rdn along and nvr a factor* **8/1**

260- **10** *2 ¾* **The Burnham Mare (IRE)**[7] 1009 4-9-6 **59**..........(p) JosephineGordon 9 29
(Barry John Murphy, Ire) *cl up: rdn along over 2f out: sn drvn and wknd* **12/1**

-606 **11** *½* **Whispering Wolf**[25] 723 4-8-4 **46** oh1................. JordanVaughan(3) 12 14
(Suzzanne France) *racd towards stands rail: chsd ldrs: rdn along 2f out: sn wknd* **20/1**

0004 **12** *3* **Nora Batt (IRE)**[7] 1006 4-8-11 **50**............................................... JFEgan 2 7
(David Evans) *chsd ldrs on inner: rdn along over 2f out: sn wknd* **20/1**

59.26s (-0.24) **Going Correction** +0.025s/f (Slow) **12** Ran SP% **122.9**
Speed ratings (Par 101): **102,101,100,99,98 98,97,96,90,86 85,80**
CSF £112.21 CT £1492.92 TOTE £16.20: £4.80, £2.40, £5.90; EX 123.00 Trifecta £4341.90 Part won..
**Owner** James Callow **Bred** Frank Brady **Trained** Uplawmoor, E Renfrews
■ Stewards' Enquiry : Josephine Gordon caution; careless riding

**FOCUS**
The front pair dictate a modest level.

## 1127 £10 FREE AT 32RED.COM APPRENTICE H'CAP 6f (Tp)
**8:15** (8:15) (Class 6) (0-65,65) 3-Y-O **£2,425** (£721; £360; £180) **Stalls** Centre

Form RPR

0-60 **1** **Man About Town (IRE)**[20] 813 3-9-3 **59**........................ CliffordLee(3) 7 68
(K R Burke) *mde all: rdn clr appr fnl f: kpt on strly* **6/1**

0342 **2** *2 ½* **Celerity (IRE)**[11] 960 3-8-12 **51**.......................................(b) PhilipPrince 3 52
(David Evans) *trckd ldrs: hdwy to chse wnr wl over 1f out: sn rdn and edgd lft: kpt on same pce* **10/1**

0-63 **3** *3 ¼* **Backinanger**[7] 1005 3-8-12 **58**................................... SeamusCronin(7) 2 49
(Kevin Ryan) *t.k.h: trckd ldrs on inner: pushed along over 2f out: rdn wl over 1f out: sn drvn and one pce fnl f* **11/4**[1]

400- **4** *1 ¼* **Fast Kar (IRE)**[21] 790 3-8-9 **53**................................ PatrickVaughan(5) 6 41
(Barry John Murphy, Ire) *dwlt and rr: hdwy 2f out: sn rdn and kpt on fnl f: nvr nr ldrs* **16/1**

5-45 **5** *1 ¼* **The Bard's Advice**[37] 510 3-9-9 **65**..................(p1) ShirleyTeasdale(3) 5 49
(Keith Dalgleish) *prom: rdn along 2f: drvn and n.m.r over 1f out: sn wknd* **16/1**

2044 **6** *hd* **Mr Strutter (IRE)**[14] 897 3-9-3 **56**...........................(h) AdamMcNamara 1 39
(John Quinn) *dwlt: a towards rr* **10/3**[2]

4342 **7** *1 ¾* **Jet Setter (IRE)**[14] 903 3-9-11 **64**................................. GeorgeDowning 8 42
(Tony Carroll) *in tch: hdwy to chse ldrs 1/2-way: sn rdn and wknd* **5/1**[3]

5-25 **8** *5* **Not Now Nadia (IRE)**[21] 787 3-8-11 **55**...........(p) CallumRodriguez(5) 4 18
(Michael Dods) *in tch: hdwy to chse ldrs over 2f out: sn rdn and wknd* **17/2**

1m 12.78s (0.28) **Going Correction** +0.025s/f (Slow) **8** Ran SP% **112.1**
Speed ratings (Par 96): **99,95,91,89,88 87,85,78**
CSF £60.57 CT £200.31 TOTE £7.30: £2.00, £2.60, £1.70; EX 73.20 Trifecta £365.10.
**Owner** Clipper Logistics **Bred** Ballyhane Stud Ltd **Trained** Middleham Moor, N Yorks
■ Stewards' Enquiry : Philip Prince caution; careless riding

**FOCUS**
Not much depth to this apprentices' handicap. The winner has been rated back to his best from the previous year.
T/Jkpt: Not won. T/Plt: £375.50 to a £1 stake. Pool: £77,791.00 - 207.12 winning units. T/Qpdt: £61.10 to a £1 stake. Pool: £8,156.00 - 133.49 winning units. **Joe Rowntree**

1128 - 1138a (Foreign Racing) - See Raceform Interactive

# 981 CHELMSFORD (A.W) (L-H)
Saturday, March 11

**OFFICIAL GOING: Polytrack: standard**
Wind: light, half behind Weather: dry

## 1139 GOING RACING? STAY AT CHANNELS CHANNELSLODGE.CO.UK APPRENTICE H'CAP 1m (P)
**5:45** (5:45) (Class 6) (0-55,57) 4-Y-O+ **£3,234** (£962; £481; £240) **Stalls** Low

Form RPR

-421 **1** **Hold Firm**[11] 966 5-9-4 **57**........................................ GabrieleMalune(5) 6 62
(Mark H Tompkins) *chsd ldrs: effrt to chal u.p over 1f out: led jst ins fnl f: hrd pressed towards fin: hld on wl: all out* **5/2**[1]

4520 **2** *shd* **Mowhoob**[17] 854 7-8-11 **50**........................................ JoshuaBryan(5) 9 55
(Brian Barr) *hld up in tch in last quartet: rdn and hdwy over 1f out: chsd wnr 100yds out: styd on and str chal wl ins fnl f: hld cl home* **14/1**

46-0 **3** *1* **The Special One (IRE)**[28] 684 4-9-7 **55**..................(h) GeorgeWood 8 57
(Ali Stronge) *in tch in midfield: hdwy over 1f out: chsd ldrs 1f out: styd on same pce u.p fnl 100yds* **7/1**

100- **4** *1 ½* **Makhfar (IRE)**[75] 8528 6-9-7 **55**...................................(v) MitchGodwin 4 54
(Mark Usher) *stdd after s: hld up in rr: rdn and hdwy over 1f out: swtchd rt ent fnl f: sn lugging lft: kpt on ins fnl f: nvr threatening ldrs* **6/1**

-045 **5** *¾* **Blackthorn Stick (IRE)**[17] 860 8-9-8 **56**..................(p) DavidParkes 10 53
(Paul Burgoyne) *taken down early: chsd ldr tl led over 2f out: rdn over 1f out: hdd jst ins fnl f: no ex and wknd fnl 75yds* **8/1**

20-1 **6** *1* **Randall's Alannah (IRE)**[31] 614 7-9-1 **52**........... ConorMcGovern(3) 7 47
(Seamus Fahey, Ire) *racd in last pair: rdn over 2f out: hdwy u.p over 1f out: styd on ins fnl f: nvr trbld ldrs* **9/2**[2]

5240 **7** *¾* **Spirit Of Gondree (IRE)**[24] 739 9-9-6 **54**...............(b) CharlieBennett 2 47
(Milton Bradley) *t.k.h early: chsd ldrs: unable qck over 1f out: wknd ins fnl f* **5/1**[3]

0-30 **8** *5* **Kristoff (IRE)**[17] 854 4-8-5 **46** oh1.................................. IsobelFrancis(7) 5 27
(Jim Boyle) *t.k.h: hld up in tch in last quartet: nt clr run and bdly hmpd wl over 1f out: no ch after* **11/1**

6-00 **9** *hd* **Bella's Boy (IRE)**[9] 982 4-8-7 **46** oh1..................... DarraghKeenan(5) 3 26
(John Ryan) *dwlt and bustled along leaving stalls: in tch in midfield: lost pl u.p over 1f out: wknd fnl f* **33/1**

00-6 **10** *18* **Ms Arsenal**[16] 879 5-9-2 **53**........................................ LuluStanford(3) 1
(Giles Bravery) *t.k.h: sn led: hdd over 2f out: sn dropped out: swtchd rt over 1f out: wl bhd fnl f* **20/1**

1m 38.7s (-1.20) **Going Correction** -0.225s/f (Stan) **10** Ran SP% **124.0**
Speed ratings (Par 101): **97,96,95,94,93 92,91,86,86,68**
CSF £44.31 CT £231.19 TOTE £3.20: £1.20, £4.70, £2.60; EX 47.30 Trifecta £208.80.
**Owner** Raceworld **Bred** Richard W Farleigh **Trained** Newmarket, Suffolk

**FOCUS**
A moderate contest.

## 1140 WATCH CHELTENHAM FESTIVAL LIVE ON WINNER.CO.UK H'CAP 6f (P)
**6:15** (6:15) (Class 5) (0-75,75) 4-Y-O+ **£5,175** (£1,540; £769; £384) **Stalls** Centre

Form RPR

1265 **1** **Fujin**[22] 783 6-9-2 **75**..................................................(v) CharlieBennett(5) 1 83
(Shaun Harris) *led after 1f: mde rest: rdn ent fnl 2f: 2 l clr and in command 1f out: styd on wl: rdn out* **6/1**

0232 **2** *2* **Fredricka**[7] 1030 6-9-6 **74**................................................(v) RenatoSouza 7 76
(Jose Santos) *chsd ldrs: effrt over 1f out: chsd clr wnr jst ins fnl f: no imp and hung lft u.p wl ins fnl f* **5/1**[3]

45-0 **3** *nse* **Gold Club**[64] 94 6-9-7 **75**............................................... PatCosgrave 6 76
(Tom Clover) *hld up in tch in midfield: effrt towards inner over 1f out: hdwy u.p to battle for 2nd jst ins fnl f: kpt on but no imp on wnr* **4/1**[1]

106- **4** *½* **Himalayan Queen**[96] 8233 4-8-7 **66**........................ SophieKilloran(5) 4 66
(William Jarvis) *dwlt: hld up in tch in rr of main gp: pushed along along and hdwy over 1f out: pressing for 2nd ins fnl f: edgd lft and kpt on same pce fnl 100yds* **16/1**

1066 **5** *1* **Colourbearer (IRE)**[19] 843 10-8-13 **67**.....................(t) WilliamCarson 3 64
(Charlie Wallis) *led for 1f: chsd wnr after: rdn: unable qck and hung lft over 1f out: lost 2nd jst ins fnl f: wknd wl ins fnl f* **16/1**

430- **6** *2* **Chetan**[135] 7644 5-9-6 **74**.............................................(tp) AdamBeschizza 5 64
(Charlie Wallis) *bustled along early: in tch in rr of main gp: rdn over 2f out: swtchd rt and drvn over 1f out: no imp ins fnl f* **8/1**

0-02 **7** *2 ½* **Bertie Blu Boy**[28] 682 9-9-4 **72**......................................(b) LiamKeniry 2 54
(Lisa Williamson) *t.k.h: chsd ldng trio: rdn and unable qck over 1f out: wknd ins fnl f* **8/1**

0032 **8** *½* **Fleckerl (IRE)**[5] 1063 7-9-2 **70**...................................(p) PaulMulrennan 9 51+
(Conor Dore) *v.s.a: detached in last pair: clsd onto bk of field 3f out: rdn over 1f out: sn wknd* **9/2**[2]

2-53 **9** *8* **Higher Court (USA)**[21] 808 9-9-2 **70**.....................(t) StevieDonohoe 10 25+
(Emma Owen) *v.s.a and wnt rt s: swtchd lft and t.k.h in detached last pair: clsd onto bk of field 3f out: hung lft and wknd over 1f out* **5/1**[3]

1m 11.99s (-1.71) **Going Correction** -0.225s/f (Stan) **9** Ran SP% **119.8**
Speed ratings (Par 103): **102,99,99,98,97 94,91,90,79**
CSF £37.50 CT £137.79 TOTE £6.70: £2.20, £2.40, £1.40; EX 46.70 Trifecta £273.70.
**Owner** Mrs S L Robinson **Bred** Juddmonte Farms Ltd **Trained** Carburton, Notts

**FOCUS**
Two of the market leaders were slowly away and effectively out of the race early on, which meant this was less competitive than expected. The pace held up.

## 1141 WINNER.CO.UK CHELTENHAM MOBILE PRICE BOOST MAIDEN STKS 7f (P)
**6:45** (6:46) (Class 5) 3-4-Y-O **£5,175** (£1,540; £769; £384) **Stalls** Low

Form RPR

034- **1** **Lualiwa**[140] 7541 3-8-12 **78**.................................................. KevinStott 7 75
(Kevin Ryan) *t.k.h: mde all: nudged along and asserted over 1f out: eased towards fin: easily* **11/8**[2]

52- **2** *2 ¾* **Muqaatil (USA)**[116] 7963 3-8-12 **0**........................................ SeanLevey 2 66
(Richard Hannon) *chsd wnr: rdn over 2f out: unable qck and btn over 1f out: styd on same pce after* **1/1**[1]

64 **3** *3 ½* **Toolatetodelegate**[11] 962 3-8-7 **0**.................................. NickyMackay 1 51
(Brian Barr) *t.k.h: chsd ldng pair: rdn over 1f out: wl hld 3rd and kpt on same pce fnl f* **50/1**

5 **4** *½* **Badenscoth**[14] 916 3-8-12 **0**............................................... LiamKeniry 3 55
(Dean Ivory) *stdd s: hld up in tch: pushed along 3f out: swtchd rt wl over 1f out: rn green and wnt rt 1f out: no ch but kpt on ins fnl f* **33/1**

0-0 **5** *¾* **Noreena**[17] 863 3-8-7 **0**...................................................... JoeyHaynes 4 48
(Paul D'Arcy) *in tch in midfield: 4th and rdn over 2f out: outpcd over 1f out: wl hld and one pced after* **66/1**

**6** *14* **Bobbio (IRE)** 3-8-12 **0**................................................... DanielMuscutt 5 15
(Marco Botti) *s.i.s: rn v green and a rr: lost tch over 1f out* **6/1**[3]

**7** *12* **Tilsworth Lukey** 4-9-7 **0**................................................ GinaMangan(7) 6
(J R Jenkins) *s.i.s and rn green: hdwy into midfield and tk keen t.k.h after 1f: struggling over 2f out: lost qckly tch over 1f out* **50/1**

1m 25.2s (-2.00) **Going Correction** -0.225s/f (Stan)
**WFA** 3 from 4yo 16lb **7** Ran SP% **114.7**
Speed ratings (Par 103): **102,98,94,94,93 77,63**
CSF £3.10 TOTE £2.70: £1.70, £1.10; EX 3.60 Trifecta £29.60.
**Owner** Mrs Rosie Richer **Bred** M E Broughton **Trained** Hambleton, N Yorks

**FOCUS**
The market leaders dominated in this maiden, but the result went against the flow of money.

## 1142 WINNER.CO.UK CHELTENHAM FREE BETS FOR FALLERS H'CAP 1m (P)
**7:15** (7:16) (Class 3) (0-95,95) 3-Y-O **£9,703** (£2,887; £1,443; £721) **Stalls** Low

Form RPR

-312 **1** **Mailshot (USA)**[36] 553 3-9-6 **94**..................................... FrannyNorton 3 100
(Mark Johnston) *broke okay but sn dropped to rr and niggled along: rdn over 3f out: hdwy to chal over 1f out: led 1f out: sn clr and r.o wl* **8/1**

631- **2** *2 ¼* **Mutawatheb (IRE)**[141] 7493 3-9-7 **95**.................................. SeanLevey 4 97+
(Richard Hannon) *led for 1f: styd trcking ldrs: effrt on inner whn nt clr run and hmpd over 1f out: swtchd rt and effrt u.p 1f out: kpt on but no ch w wnr: wnt 2nd towards fin* **9/4**[1]

-111 **3** *nk* **Poetic Force (IRE)**[14] 927 3-8-10 **84**......................(t) GeorgeDowning 1 84
(Tony Carroll) *t.k.h: hld up in tch: swtchd rt and hdwy over 1f out: hung lft and chsd clr wnr jst ins fnl f: no imp and lost 2nd towards fin* **6/1**

0-12 **4** *3 ¼* **Shamrokh (IRE)**[14] 927 3-8-13 **87**..........................(bt1) FrankieDettori 6 80
(John Gosden) *dwlt and roustead along leaving stalls: hdwy to ld after 1f and t.k.h: rdn and edgd lft over 1f out: hdd 1f out: sn btn and lost 2nd: wknd fnl 100yds* **5/2**[2]

51 **5** *2* **Dreaming Time**[21] 814 3-8-3 **77**................................. JosephineGordon 2 65
(Hugo Palmer) *t.k.h: hld up in tch: effrt over 1f out: swtchd rt and nt clr run ent fnl f: sn wknd* **10/1**

51-2 **6** *shd* **Makaarim**[31] 626 3-8-10 **84**.............................................. TomMarquand 5 72
(Marco Botti) *t.k.h: trckd ldrs tl wnt 2nd 5f out: rdn and ev ch over 2f out tl unable qck over 1f out: wknd ins fnl f* **4/1**[3]

1m 36.8s (-3.10) **Going Correction** -0.225s/f (Stan) **6** Ran SP% **113.8**
Speed ratings (Par 102): **106,103,103,100,98 98**
CSF £26.94 TOTE £7.40: £3.80, £1.50; EX 25.60 Trifecta £98.40.

**Owner** Sheikh Hamdan bin Mohammed Al Maktoum **Bred** Darley **Trained** Middleham Moor, N Yorks

**FOCUS**

With Shamrokh not settling in front and setting a good gallop, the pace collapsed from the turn in.

## 1143 WINNER.CO.UK CHELTENHAM EXTRA PLACES EVERY DAY MAIDEN FILLIES' STKS — 1m 2f (P)

**7:45** (7:47) (Class 4) 3-4-Y-0 — **£6,469** (£1,925; £962; £481) Stalls Low

| Form | Pos | Dist | Horse / Comment | Jockey | RPR |
|---|---|---|---|---|---|
| | 1 | | **Rosa Damascena (FR)**[98] 4-10-0 0 (Alan King) *restless in stalls: hld up in last pair: hdwy on outer over 2f out: rdn to chse ldr jst over 1f out: flashed tail u.p but styd on to ld towards fin* **9/1** | MartinHarley 5 | 79 |
| 6 | 2 | ¾ | **Zehrah (IRE)**[44] 424 3-8-7 0 (Simon Crisford) *t.k.h: chsd ldr tl lft in ld after 1f tl 8f out: hmpd 7f out and trckd ldrs after: rdn to ld over 1f out: clr w wnr ins fnl f: hdd towards fin and hld whn rdr dropped whip cl home* **5/1**[3] | SilvestreDeSousa 4 | 72 |
| 3 | 3 | 7 | **Dalavida (FR)**[29] 658 3-8-7 0 (David Simcock) *hld up in last piar: swtchd rt: effrt and racd awkwardly over 1f out: no ch w ldrs: kpt on to go wl hld 3rd 75yds out* **7/1** | (h) OisinMurphy 7 | 58 |
| | 4 | 1¾ | **Becuna (USA)** 3-8-0 0 (Michael Bell) *urged along in midfield: t.k.h and hdwy to join ldrs 7f out: pushed along and unable qck jst over 2f out: outpcd and btn over 1f out: plugged on same pce ins fnl f* **25/1** | TristanPrice(7) 3 | 55 |
| 2 | 5 | ¾ | **Dubai Waves**[23] 758 3-8-7 0 (Hugo Palmer) *t.k.h: led tl rn green and hdd after 1f: chsd ldrs tl swtchd rt and jnd ldr 7f out: ev ch and rdn over 1f out: sn outpcd and btn 3rd 1f out: hung lft and wknd ins fnl f: fin lame* **5/6**[1] | JosephineGordon 2 | 53 |
| 04 | 6 | 2¾ | **Navajo Star (IRE)**[26] 717 3-8-7 0 (Michael Appleby) *in tch in midfield: swtchd rt and hdwy 7f out: lost pl and pushed along over 4f out: wknd over 1f out* **66/1** | TomMarquand 8 | 48 |
| 0 | 7 | 6 | **Shine Through (IRE)**[24] 737 3-8-4 0 (Hugo Palmer) *in tch in midfield: rdn 4f out: wknd over 1f out* **50/1** | NoelGarbutt(3) 1 | 36 |
| -3 | 8 | 4 | **Night Poetry (IRE)**[44] 424 3-8-7 0 (Charlie Appleby) *dwlt: swtchd rt sn after s and rdn along: hdwy to ld 8f out: rdn and hdd over 1f out: sn btn and eased ins fnl f* **7/2**[2] | MartinLane 6 | 28 |

2m 5.66s (-2.94) **Going Correction** -0.225s/f (Stan)
**WFA** 3 from 4yo 21lb — 8 Ran SP% **123.2**
Speed ratings (Par 102): **102,101,95,94,93 91,86,83**
CSF £56.55 TOTE £12.90: £3.00, £2.20, £1.90; EX 78.60 Trifecta £292.50.
**Owner** McNeill Family **Bred** E A R L Elevage Des Loges **Trained** Barbury Castle, Wilts

**FOCUS**

A messy race from a pace perspective, with several getting involved in a stop-start gallop up front early on.

## 1144 GATES FORD H'CAP — 1m 2f (P)

**8:15** (8:15) (Class 5) (0-75,81) 4-Y-0+ — **£5,175** (£1,540; £769; £384) Stalls Low

| Form | Pos | Dist | Horse / Comment | Jockey | RPR |
|---|---|---|---|---|---|
| 4-21 | 1 | | **General Hazard (IRE)**[9] 992 4-10-2 **81** (Archie Watson) *in tch in last pair: effrt to chse ldrs 2f out: hdwy u.p to chse ldr 100yds out: styd on wl to ld on post* **7/4**[1] | BenCurtis 4 | 89 |
| -061 | 2 | nse | **Russian Reward (IRE)**[8] 998 5-9-7 **72** (Amanda Perrett) *led: rdn and fnd ex over 1f out: drvn ins fnl f: kpt on: hdd on post* **6/1**[3] | (p) JackMitchell 3 | 79 |
| 1-23 | 3 | 1¼ | **Hairdryer**[21] 809 4-9-12 **77** (Andrew Balding) *t.k.h: trckd ldrs: effrt to chse ldr over 2f out: unable qck over 1f out: styd on same pce ins fnl f* **7/4**[1] | OisinMurphy 2 | 81 |
| 3625 | 4 | 2 | **Mercy Me**[14] 922 5-9-7 **72** (John Ryan) *trckd ldrs: swtchd rt and effrt over 1f out: no ex u.p 1f out: wknd fnl 100yds* **7/1** | JosephineGordon 1 | 72 |
| 36-1 | 5 | 16 | **Music Major**[14] 922 4-9-5 **70** (Michael Attwater) *stdd s: hld up in tch in last pair: effrt 2f out: unable qck and outpcd over 1f out: wknd and eased ins fnl f* **7/2**[2] | AdamBeschizza 5 | 38 |
| 06/ | 6 | 16 | **Summer Dove (USA)**[414] 310 4-9-0 **65** (George Peckham) *chsd ldr tl rdn and lost pl over 2f out: bhd and eased fnl f* **33/1** | LukeMorris 6 | |

2m 5.92s (-2.68) **Going Correction** -0.225s/f (Stan) — 6 Ran SP% **124.7**
Speed ratings (Par 103): **101,100,99,98,85 72**
CSF £15.17 TOTE £2.60: £1.50, £2.50; EX 13.00 Trifecta £26.10.
**Owner** Boadicea Bloodstock **Bred** London Thoroughbred Services Ltd **Trained** Upper Lambourn, W Berks

**FOCUS**

This was steadily run and the winner did well to take it from off the pace.

## 1145 ROA/RACING POST OWNERS' JACKPOT H'CAP (DIV I) — 1m 2f (P)

**8:45** (8:46) (Class 6) (0-55,57) 4-Y-0+ — **£3,234** (£962; £481; £240) Stalls Low

| Form | Pos | Dist | Horse / Comment | Jockey | RPR |
|---|---|---|---|---|---|
| 0606 | 1 | | **Hannington**[14] 924 6-9-7 **55** (Michael Appleby) *chsd ldrs tl wnt 2nd 3f out: led 2f out: sn drvn: kpt on u.p and a doing enough ins fnl f* **3/1**[1] | (t) SilvestreDeSousa 4 | 63 |
| -306 | 2 | 1½ | **Cahar Fad (IRE)**[21] 820 5-8-12 **46** (Steph Hollinshead) *chsd ldr tl 3f out: nt clr run over 2f out: swtchd rt and drvn to chse wnr over 1f out: kpt on but a hld ins fnl f* **9/2** | (bt) AdamBeschizza 3 | 50 |
| -024 | 3 | 3¼ | **Jazri**[16] 880 6-9-2 **50** (Milton Bradley) *hld up in last trio: clsd 3f out: effrt over 1f out: chsd clr ldng pair 1f out: no imp* **7/2**[2] | (b) FrannyNorton 1 | 48 |
| -065 | 4 | 5 | **Rocket Ronnie (IRE)**[24] 740 7-9-5 **53** (Brian Barr) *hld up on last trio: clsd on outer over 2f out: outpcd and rdn over 1f out: sn btn: wknd fnl f* **6/1** | LukeMorris 2 | 41 |
| 614 | 5 | 1¾ | **Outlaw Torn (IRE)**[17] 865 8-9-8 **56** (Richard Guest) *taken down early: sn led and clr: hdd 2f out: lost pl over 1f out: sn wknd* **8/1** | (e) DougieCostello 9 | 41 |
| 2604 | 6 | 7 | **Lutine Charlie (IRE)**[17] 854 10-8-12 **46** oh1 (Emma Owen) *midfield: clsd 3f out: rdn wl over 1f out: sn btn and bhd fnl f* **25/1** | (p) StevieDonohoe 7 | 18 |
| 3-03 | 7 | nk | **Hymn For The Dudes**[33] 605 4-9-3 **51** (John Berry) *midfield: clsd and swtchd rt over 2f out: rdn: outpcd and drifted rt over 1f out: sn wknd* **4/1**[3] | (tp) MartinHarley 6 | 22 |
| /-00 | 8 | 2¾ | **Valantino Oyster (IRE)**[28] 689 10-9-7 **55** (Ali Stronge) *a rr: reminders 7f out: nvr travelling wl or involved after* **20/1** | (t[1]) TomMarquand 5 | 21 |

2m 5.84s (-2.76) **Going Correction** -0.225s/f (Stan) — 8 Ran SP% **119.4**
Speed ratings (Par 101): **102,100,98,94,92 87,86,84**
CSF £17.73 CT £49.96 TOTE £3.60: £1.30, £1.80, £1.60; EX 17.10 Trifecta £60.70.
**Owner** From The Front Racing **Bred** Bearstone Stud Ltd **Trained** Oakham, Rutland

**FOCUS**

The runner-up pins an ordinary level for the bare form but the winner was previously capable of rating higher and is back on the right track.

## 1146 ROA/RACING POST OWNERS' JACKPOT H'CAP (DIV II) — 1m 2f (P)

**9:15** (9:16) (Class 6) (0-55,57) 4-Y-0+ — **£3,234** (£962; £481; £240) Stalls Low

| Form | Pos | Dist | Horse / Comment | Jockey | RPR |
|---|---|---|---|---|---|
| -060 | 1 | | **Master Of Heaven**[16] 880 4-9-1 **49** (Jim Boyle) *chsd ldrs: wnt 2nd 7f out tl rdn to ld over 1f out: hld on u.p ins fnl f: all out* **4/1**[1] | (p) PatCosgrave 2 | 55 |
| 033- | 2 | ½ | **Muzaahim (IRE)**[81] 8469 6-9-8 **56** (Laura Morgan) *trckd ldrs: effrt wl over 1f out: rdn and ev ch 1f out: drvn ins fnl f: kpt on same pce and hld towards fin* **4/1**[1] | (h[1]) ShaneKelly 3 | 61 |
| 00-0 | 3 | 4½ | **Sublimation (IRE)**[28] 684 7-9-6 **57** (Steve Gollings) *in tch in midfield: rdn 3f out: kpt on same pce u.p and no imp ins fnl f: snatched 3rd last stride* **12/1** | KieranShoemark(3) 7 | 54 |
| 00-0 | 4 | nk | **Spryt (IRE)**[65] 69 5-9-5 **53** (John Butler) *t.k.h: led 8f out tl rdn and hdd over 1f out: 3rd and unable qck 1f out: wknd ins fnl f: lost 3rd last strides* **7/1** | (h[1]) LiamKeniry 9 | 49 |
| /16- | 5 | 1¾ | **Fast On (IRE)**[78] 8515 8-8-12 **51** (Seamus Fahey, Ire) *dwlt: racd in last pair: rdn over 2f out: no ch w ldrs but kpt on u.p ins fnl f* **5/1**[2] | (p) ConorMcGovern(5) 5 | 44 |
| 0002 | 6 | nk | **Ertidaad (IRE)**[16] 880 5-8-7 **46** oh1 (Emma Owen) *in tch in midfield rdn over 2f out: swtchd rt wl over 1f out: sn outpcd: wl hld and kpt on same pce fnl f* **7/1** | (b) DavidParkes(5) 6 | 38 |
| 0-00 | 7 | 1¼ | **Mr Turner**[23] 761 4-8-12 **46** oh1 (Mark H Tompkins) *stdd s: hld up in last pair: swtchd lft and effrt u.p over 1f out: no imp: wknd ins fnl f* **10/1** | StevieDonohoe 8 | 37 |
| 00-0 | 8 | 2¼ | **Haabis (USA)**[21] 811 4-9-7 **55** (George Peckham) *t.k.h: hld up in tch in midfield: effrt u.p in 4th 2f out: sn struggling: wknd fnl f* **10/1** | (t[1]) LukeMorris 4 | 40 |
| 6050 | P | | **Hydrant**[25] 727 11-9-4 **52** (Richard Guest) *led for 2f: chsd ldrs tl lost pl over 3f out: bhd and eased 2f out: p.u ins fnl f: lame* **6/1**[3] | JFEgan 1 | |

2m 6.31s (-2.29) **Going Correction** -0.225s/f (Stan) — 9 Ran SP% **121.8**
Speed ratings (Par 101): **100,99,96,95,94 94,93,91,**
CSF £21.04 CT £182.33 TOTE £4.30: £2.00, £1.70, £3.50; EX 22.40 Trifecta £325.70.
**Owner** Maid In Heaven Partnership **Bred** Qatar Bloodstock Ltd **Trained** Epsom, Surrey

**FOCUS**

The market proved correct, with the two backed late coming clear and this form may prove up to 2l better than rated. It was the slower of the two divisions by 0.47sec.
T/Plt: £200.30 to a £1 stake. Pool: £92,055.96 - 335.40 winning units T/Qpdt: £52.40 to a £1 stake. Pool: £10,198.60 - 143.86 winning units **Steve Payne**

# 1062 WOLVERHAMPTON (A.W) (L-H)

Saturday, March 11

**OFFICIAL GOING: Tapeta: standard**

Wind: Light behind Weather: Overcast

## 1147 BETWAY CLASSIFIED CLAIMING STKS — 5f 21y (Tp)

**1:30** (1:31) (Class 5) 4-Y-0+ — **£3,234** (£962; £481; £240) Stalls Low

| Form | Pos | Dist | Horse / Comment | Jockey | RPR |
|---|---|---|---|---|---|
| -224 | 1 | | **Malaysian Boleh**[5] 1062 7-8-2 70 (Brian Ellison) *pushed along to chse ldrs: led over 1f out: rdn out* **2/1**[1] | (v[1]) BenRobinson(7) 1 | 71 |
| 00-0 | 2 | 1½ | **Point North (IRE)**[56] 242 10-9-5 68 (John Balding) *hld up: hdwy over 1f out: chsd wnr ins fnl f: styd on* **11/1** | (b) DanielTudhope 8 | 76 |
| 1150 | 3 | 2¼ | **Big Amigo (IRE)**[10] 971 4-9-4 67 (Daniel Mark Loughnane) *pushed along in rr early: hung lft and nt clr run over 1f out: r.o to go 3rd wl ins fnl f* **6/1**[3] | SilvestreDeSousa 6 | 67+ |
| 06-5 | 4 | nk | **Emjayem**[12] 955 7-9-9 69 (John Holt) *plld hrd and prom: rdn over 1f out: styd on same pce ins fnl f* **9/1** | (p) AdamKirby 4 | 71 |
| 2236 | 5 | ½ | **Archie Stevens**[12] 955 7-8-8 66 (Clare Ellam) *led 1f: remained w ldr tl led again wl over 1f out: sn rdn and hdd: no ex ins fnl f* **13/2** | PaddyPilley(5) 3 | 59 |
| 5540 | 6 | 1¾ | **Doctor Parkes**[19] 844 11-7-10 68 (Stuart Williams) *sn chsng ldrs: rdn over 1f out: wknd fnl f* **7/2**[2] | MillyNaseb(7) 7 | 43 |
| 22-3 | 7 | ¾ | **Summerinthecity (IRE)**[14] 923 10-8-10 67 (Patrick Morris) *hld up in tch: rdn 1/2-way: wknd over 1f out* **11/1** | (p) PaulHanagan 5 | 47 |
| 0-00 | 8 | ¾ | **Master Pekan**[44] 415 4-8-11 43 (Roy Brotherton) *w ldr tl led 4f out: hung rt 1/2-way: rdn and hdd wl over 1f out: wknd ins fnl f* **100/1** | (b) TomMarquand 2 | 45 |

1m 1.74s (-0.16) **Going Correction** -0.025s/f (Stan) — 8 Ran SP% **110.8**
Speed ratings (Par 103): **100,97,94,93,92 89,88,87**
CSF £23.83 TOTE £2.60: £1.10, £3.50, £2.50; EX 27.20 Trifecta £182.60.Malaysian Boleh was claimed by Mr P. S. McEntee for £5,000.
**Owner** D Gilbert, M Lawrence, A Bruce, G Wllls **Bred** John & Sue Davis **Trained** Norton, N Yorks

**FOCUS**

A modest 0-70 classified claimer.

## 1148 SUNBETS.CO.UK LINCOLN TRIAL H'CAP — 1m 142y (Tp)

**2:05** (2:05) (Class 2) (0-105,105) 4-Y-0+
**£31,125** (£9,320; £4,660; £2,330; £1,165; £585) Stalls Low

| Form | Pos | Dist | Horse / Comment | Jockey | RPR |
|---|---|---|---|---|---|
| 1-61 | 1 | | **Nimr**[33] 598 4-8-13 **94** (Richard Fahey) *trckd ldrs: racd keenly: shkn up to ld ins fnl f: r.o* **3/1**[1] | TonyHamilton 8 | 103+ |
| -305 | 2 | 1¾ | **Forceful Appeal (USA)**[21] 817 9-8-10 **91** (Simon Dow) *chsd ldrs: rdn to ld over 1f out: edgd lft and hdd ins fnl f: sn hung rt: styd on same pce* **22/1** | LukeMorris 6 | 95 |
| -142 | 3 | hd | **Holiday Magic (IRE)**[25] 730 6-8-12 **96** (Michael Easterby) *hld up in tch: rdn over 1f out: styd on* **15/2** | NathanEvans(3) 2 | 100 |
| 035- | 4 | ½ | **Examiner (IRE)**[75] 8529 6-8-11 **92** (Stuart Williams) *hld up: carried wd wl over 1f out: rdn: hung lft and r.o ins fnl f: nt rch ldrs* **13/2**[3] | OisinMurphy 5 | 94+ |
| 00-0 | 5 | nk | **Baraweez (IRE)**[8] 999 7-9-3 **98** (Brian Ellison) *hld up: swtchd rt and hdwy over 1f out: rdn and edgd lft ins fnl f: r.o* **8/1** | DaleSwift 3 | 100 |
| -520 | 6 | ½ | **Supersta**[25] 730 6-8-12 **93** (Michael Appleby) *s.i.s and hmpd s: hld up: racd keenly: shkn up and hdwy over 1f out: sn rdn: r.o* **11/2**[2] | (p) SilvestreDeSousa 4 | 94+ |
| 40-1 | 7 | ½ | **Abareeq**[3] 1079 4-8-13 **94** 6ex (Mark Johnston) *chsd ldr: rdn: edgd lft and ev ch over 1f out: styng on same pce whn hmpd towards fin* **10/1** | JoeFanning 11 | 93 |

530- **8** 3/4 **Dream Walker (FR)**[147] 7354 8-9-6 **101**..............................(t) BenCurtis 7 99
(Brian Ellison) *led: rdn and hdd over 1f out: no ex ins fnl f* **66/1**

500- **9** 1/2 **Emell**[122] 7868 7-9-0 **95**..................................................(b) KieranO'Neill 10 92
(Richard Hannon) *hld up: hdwy on outer over 2f out: rdn over 1f out: hung lft and no ex ins fnl f* **22/1**

002- **10** *hd* **Top Notch Tonto (IRE)**[228] 4747 7-9-3 **105**............... BenRobinson(7) 9 101
(Brian Ellison) *hld up: shkn up over 1f out: nvr on terms* **25/1**

6/0- **11** *nk* **Parish Boy**[54] 5941 5-9-0 **95**.................................... JosephineGordon 13 90
(David Loughnane) *s.i.s: hld up: nvr on terms* **80/1**

1-00 **12** *nk* **Steel Train (FR)**[25] 730 6-9-5 **100**.................................. DanielTudhope 1 98+
(David O'Meara) *s.i.s: hld up: effrt over 1f out: hmpd ins fnl f: n.d* **11/1**

4-01 **13** 1 1/2 **Pactolus (IRE)**[26] 720 6-8-11 **95**..............................(t) AaronJones(3) 12 86
(Stuart Williams) *hdwy to go prom 7f out: rdn over 1f out: n.m.r sn after: wknd ins fnl f* **16/1**

1m 47.89s (-2.21) **Going Correction** -0.025s/f (Stan) **13** Ran SP% **115.2**
Speed ratings (Par 109): **108,106,106,105,105 105,104,104,103,103 103,102,101**
CSF £78.26 CT £470.95 TOTE £3.90: £1.80, £6.30, £2.20; EX 76.10 Trifecta £239.00.
**Owner** Al Shaqab Racing **Bred** Mr & Mrs G Middlebrook **Trained** Musley Bank, N Yorks

**FOCUS**
A typically competitive renewal of this contest. Seven of these are entered for the Doncaster showpiece, including the winner.

## 1149 32RED.COM H'CAP 7f 36y (Tp)
**2:40** (2:41) (Class 4) (0-85,86) 3-Y-O £5,175 (£1,540; £769; £384) **Stalls** High

Form RPR

01-1 **1** **Gilgamesh**[15] 902 3-9-7 **83**........................................... JamieSpencer 5 91+
(George Scott) *hld up in tch: racd keenly: rdn to ld and hung lft ins fnl f: styd on* **7/4**[1]

332- **2** *shd* **Tafaakhor (IRE)**[141] 7496 3-9-6 **82**.................................... RyanMoore 3 89
(Richard Hannon) *racd keenly: trckd ldrs: rdn and hung lft fr over 1f out: carried lft ins fnl f: styd on* **5/2**[2]

2-25 **3** 1 1/4 **Sidewinder (IRE)**[49] 356 3-8-10 **72**........................ RichardKingscote 1 76
(Tom Dascombe) *chsd ldrs: rdn over 1f out: sn ev ch: styd on same pce towards fin* **16/1**

3-11 **4** *hd* **Boost**[22] 788 3-9-5 **81**........................................................ LukeMorris 7 84
(Sir Mark Prescott Bt) *chsd ldr 6f out tl rdn to ld over 1f out: sn hung lft: hdd ins fnl f: styd on same pce* **9/2**[3]

311 **5** 2 1/4 **Espresso Freddo (IRE)**[38] 512 3-9-3 **79**.................(p) OisinMurphy 11 76
(Robert Stephens) *hld up: hdwy over 1f out: styd on same pce ins fnl f* **16/1**

150- **6** 1/2 **Heir Of Excitement (IRE)**[205] 5583 3-9-0 **76**.................... ShaneGray 2 72
(Kevin Ryan) *sn led: rdn and hdd over 1f out: hmpd sn after: no ex ins fnl f* **33/1**

54-6 **7** 3/4 **Sans Souci Bay**[50] 329 3-8-13 **75**................................ TomMarquand 6 69
(Richard Hannon) *hld up: rdn over 1f out: nvr trbld ldrs* **22/1**

1456 **8** *nk* **Letmestopyouthere (IRE)**[15] 902 3-9-10 **86**........................ JFEgan 9 79
(David Evans) *hld up: rdn over 2f out: nvr on terms* **33/1**

4113 **9** 3/4 **Spinwheel**[14] 927 3-9-0 **76**............................................ PJMcDonald 4 67
(Mark Johnston) *prom: rdn over 2f out: wknd fnl f* **25/1**

1-15 **10** 5 **Vatican Hill (IRE)**[38] 512 3-9-6 **82**...................................... AdamKirby 10 59
(Jamie Osborne) *broke wl: plld hrd: sn stdd and lost pl: nvr on terms after: eased fnl f* **14/1**

410- **11** 2 3/4 **Tor**[117] 7956 3-9-4 **80**........................................................ TomEaves 8 50
(Iain Jardine) *hld up: rdn 1/2-way: wknd over 2f out* **66/1**

1m 28.2s (-0.60) **Going Correction** -0.025s/f (Stan) **11** Ran SP% **117.1**
Speed ratings (Par 100): **102,101,100,100,97 97,96,95,95,89 86**
CSF £5.63 CT £50.26 TOTE £2.80: £1.40, £1.20, £4.20; EX 7.90 Trifecta £80.10.
**Owner** Niarchos Family **Bred** Niarchos Family **Trained** Newmarket, Suffolk

**FOCUS**
A decent 3yo handicap with a few of these coming into it in top form, but not many got into it. Things got tight between the front pair late on, but the stewards allowed the result to stand.

## 1150 SUNBETS.CO.UK LADY WULFRUNA STKS (LISTED RACE) (ALL-WEATHER CHAMPIONSHIPS FAST-TRACK QUALIFIER) 7f 36y (Tp)
**3:15** (3:16) (Class 1) 4-Y-O+ £28,355 (£10,750; £5,380; £2,680; £1,3415; £Form) **Stalls** High

-010 **1** **Salateen**[16] 892 5-9-3 104........................................ PhillipMakin 12 109
(David O'Meara) *mde virtually all: qcknd clr over 2f out: rdn over 1f out: hung lft ins fnl f all out* **25/1**

14-1 **2** *nse* **Keystroke**[42] 459 5-9-3 103............................................ AdamKirby 7 109+
(Jeremy Noseda) *hld up: hdwy over 1f out: rdn to chse wnr ins fnl f: r.o wl* **7/4**[1]

041- **3** *shd* **Yuften**[147] 7354 6-9-3 105.............................................. AndreaAtzeni 9 108+
(Roger Charlton) *hld up: shkn up over 1f out: rdn and hung lft ins fnl f: fin wl* **9/2**[2]

41-0 **4** 1 1/4 **Amazour (IRE)**[35] 572 5-9-3 100................................... TomMarquand 3 104
(Ismail Mohammed) *s.i.s: hld up: hdwy over 2f out: rdn over 1f out: r.o* **16/1**

4-20 **5** 1 3/4 **Rene Mathis (GER)**[30] 653 7-9-3 103............................. PaulHanagan 1 99
(Richard Fahey) *chsd ldrs: rdn over 2f out: styd on same pce ins fnl f* **28/1**

-111 **6** *nk* **My Target (IRE)**[7] 1023 6-9-3 107.............................. ConnorBeasley 11 99
(Michael Wigham) *hmpd s: hld up: rdn over 1f out: r.o towards fin: nt trble ldrs* **7/1**

1-20 **7** *nse* **Realize**[25] 730 7-9-3 105..................................................(t) OisinMurphy 4 99
(Stuart Williams) *sn chsng wnr: rdn over 2f out: no ex and lost 2nd ins fnl f* **10/1**

-065 **8** *hd* **Naadirr (IRE)**[28] 696 6-9-3 103.........................................(p) RyanMoore 2 98
(Marco Botti) *prom: rdn over 1f out: styd on same pce* **13/2**[3]

-133 **9** 3/4 **Summer Icon**[21] 810 4-8-12 95........................................... ShaneKelly 5 91
(Mick Channon) *hld up: rdn over 1f out: nvr on terms* **25/1**

134/ **10** 2 1/2 **Eltezam (IRE)**[611] 4071 4-9-3 100........................................ SeanLevey 6 89
(Richard Hannon) *plld hrd and prom: rdn over 1f out: wknd fnl f* **18/1**

011- **11** 4 1/2 **Swift Approval (IRE)**[159] 7027 5-9-6 101...........................(p) FranBerry 8 80
(Stuart Williams) *hld up: pushed along and hdwy over 2f out: wknd over 1f out* **40/1**

1m 26.75s (-2.05) **Going Correction** -0.025s/f (Stan) **11** Ran SP% **114.2**
Speed ratings (Par 111): **110,109,109,108,106 106,106,105,104,102 96**
CSF £65.15 TOTE £27.10: £7.10, £1.10, £1.80; EX 105.20 Trifecta £645.10.
**Owner** Sheikh Abdullah Almalek Alsabah **Bred** Mrs Janis Macpherson **Trained** Upper Helmsley, N Yorks

**FOCUS**
A fascinating Listed event, but probably won and lost in the first furlong.

## 1151 32RED CASINO MAIDEN FILLIES' STKS 1m 142y (Tp)
**3:50** (3:50) (Class 5) 3-Y-O+ £3,234 (£962; £481; £240) **Stalls** Low

Form RPR

**1** **Ice Dancing (IRE)** 3-8-7 0.............................................. LukeMorris 7 71+
(Michael Bell) *uns rdr on the way to post: chsd ldrs: rdn over 1f out: edgd lft and r.o to ld wl ins fnl f* **16/1**

2402 **2** 2 1/4 **Heartstone (IRE)**[22] 789 4-9-13 71.................................... AdamKirby 8 72
(David Evans) *chsd ldr tl led over 6f out: qcknd over 2f out: rdn and edgd rt over 1f out: hdd wl ins fnl f* **9/2**[2]

6 **3** 2 3/4 **Miss M (IRE)**[31] 624 3-8-7 0........................................... MartinDwyer 2 60
(William Muir) *hld up: rn green in rr: shkn up over 1f out: hung lft and styd on to go 3rd nr fin* **11/1**[3]

2 **4** *nk* **First Moon**[21] 814 3-8-7 0.................................................(t) JackMitchell 1 59
(Hugo Palmer) *racd keenly: led: hdd over 6f out: chsd ldr: rdn over 2f out: hung lft over 1f out: no ex wl ins fnl f* **2/5**[1]

5 **5** *shd* **Appreciating**[32] 612 3-8-7 0............................................... ShaneGray 4 59
(Kevin Ryan) *chsd ldrs: rdn over 2f out: styd on same pce fr over 1f out* **25/1**

**6** 3 **California Cliffs (IRE)** 3-8-7 0.......................................... DavidProbert 3 52
(Rae Guest) *hld up: rdn over 2f out: n.d* **33/1**

1m 50.27s (0.17) **Going Correction** -0.025s/f (Stan)
**WFA** 3 from 4yo 20lb **6** Ran SP% **110.6**
Speed ratings (Par 100): **98,96,93,93,93 90**
CSF £81.47 TOTE £11.20: £4.40, £2.00; EX 35.60 Trifecta £151.40.
**Owner** Sheikh Marwan Al Maktoum **Bred** Darley **Trained** Newmarket, Suffolk
■ Stewards' Enquiry : Jack Mitchell three-day ban: weighed in heavy having had a drink after weighing out (Mar 25, 27-28)

**FOCUS**
An uncompetitive fillies' maiden, but a shock result.

## 1152 BETWAY SPRINT H'CAP 6f 20y (Tp)
**4:25** (4:26) (Class 2) (0-105,102) 4-Y-O+
£15,562 (£4,660; £2,330; £1,165; £582; £292) **Stalls** Low

Form RPR

00-4 **1** **Go Far**[12] 957 7-9-0 **95**...................................................(v) DavidProbert 9 104
(Alan Bailey) *led early: settled in 2nd sn after: rdn to ld ins fnl f: edgd lft: r.o* **14/1**

-302 **2** 3/4 **Upavon**[12] 957 7-8-5 **89**.............................................(bt) AaronJones(3) 2 96
(Stuart Williams) *prom: nt clr run and lost pl after 1f: hdwy over 1f out: rdn and ev ch ins fnl f: styd on* **8/1**

-000 **3** 1 **Eastern Impact (IRE)**[30] 651 6-9-7 **102**........................ PaulHanagan 1 105
(Richard Fahey) *chsd ldrs: rdn whn hmpd 1f out: styd on* **15/2**

-246 **4** *nk* **Russian Soul (IRE)**[12] 957 9-8-13 **94**.......................(p) OisinMurphy 8 96
(Jamie Osborne) *hld up: rdn over 1f out: r.o ins fnl f: nt rch ldrs* **7/2**[1]

-532 **5** 1/2 **Bowson Fred**[19] 842 5-9-2 **100**................................... NathanEvans(3) 3 101
(Michael Easterby) *sn led: rdn and hdd ins fnl f: styd on same pce* **9/2**[2]

03-0 **6** 1/2 **Judicial (IRE)**[19] 842 5-9-4 **99**.........................................(e) JoeDoyle 5 98+
(Julie Camacho) *hld up: plld hrd: rdn over 1f out: r.o ins fnl f: nt trble ldrs* **7/1**

1-50 **7** *hd* **Shamshon (IRE)**[19] 842 6-8-11 **92**..............................(t) AndreaAtzeni 4 91
(Stuart Williams) *s.i.s: hld up: hmpd over 4f out: hdwy over 1f out: sn rdn: styd on same pce ins fnl f* **13/2**

0440 **8** 2 1/4 **Gentlemen**[12] 957 6-8-11 **92**...................................(h) SilvestreDeSousa 7 83
(Phil McEntee) *hld up: plld hrd: pushed along and hdwy on outer over 2f out: wknd fnl f* **6/1**[3]

**9** 8 **Old Fashioned (CHI)**[160] 4-9-5 **100**.......................................(t[1]) JFEgan 6 66
(Rune Haugen) *plld hrd and prom: rdn over 2f out: wknd over 1f out* **33/1**

1m 13.04s (-1.46) **Going Correction** -0.025s/f (Stan) **9** Ran SP% **113.0**
Speed ratings (Par 109): **108,107,105,105,104 103,103,100,90**
CSF £117.87 CT £910.88 TOTE £10.20: £3.30, £2.50, £2.80; EX 36.70 Trifecta £604.70.
**Owner** R West **Bred** Michael Turner **Trained** Newmarket, Suffolk

**FOCUS**
A warm sprint handicap in which four of the nine runners met over C&D 12 days ago, including the first two here.

## 1153 BETWAY H'CAP 1m 5f 194y
**5:00** (5:00) (Class 4) (0-85,86) 4-Y-O+ £5,175 (£1,540; £769; £384) **Stalls** Low

Form RPR

-613 **1** **Midtech Star (IRE)**[23] 759 5-9-10 **82**..................(v) RichardKingscote 4 92
(Ian Williams) *hld up: hdwy over 2f out: edgd lft and r.o u.p to ld post* **5/1**[2]

4-63 **2** *nk* **Ardamir (FR)**[49] 353 5-9-6 **78**...................................... FergusSweeney 3 87
(Alan King) *a.p: racd keenly: chsd ldr over 2f out: led and hung lft over 1f out: sn rdn: hdd post* **11/2**[3]

4-11 **3** 3 3/4 **Tartan Bute**[7] 1027 4-9-5 **81**...............................................(p) JoeFanning 2 84
(Mark Johnston) *chsd ldrs: shkn up over 2f out: styd on same pce fnl f* **9/4**[1]

3001 **4** *hd* **Ravens Quest**[12] 958 4-8-13 **75**........................................ DannyBrock 9 78
(John Ryan) *racd keenly in 2nd pl: jnd ldr over 5f out: led over 3f out: rdn and hdd over 1f out: hung lft and no ex fnl f* **6/1**

3-25 **5** 1 3/4 **El Campeon**[37] 519 5-9-6 **78**............................................. JFEgan 8 79
(Simon Dow) *hld up: hdwy and hung lft fr over 1f out: nvr trbld ldrs* **11/1**

0/24 **6** 1 **Uncle Bernie (IRE)**[47] 380 7-9-1 **73**............................. JamesSullivan 6 72
(Sarah Hollinshead) *stdd s: hld up: rdn over 1f out: r.o ins fnl f: nt trble ldrs* **20/1**

0425 **7** 1 3/4 **Silver Quay (IRE)**[23] 759 5-10-0 **86**.................................. AdamKirby 1 83
(Jamie Osborne) *hld up: hdwy over 2f out: rdn over 1f out: wknd fnl f* **5/1**[2]

110- **8** 4 1/2 **Bertie Moon**[154] 7158 7-9-7 **84**.....................................(t[1]) CliffordLee(5) 5 74
(Lydia Pearce) *led: hdd over 3f out: rdn and wknd over 1f out* **40/1**

42-0 **9** 1/2 **Dovils Date**[28] 688 8-8-11 **69**......................................... DavidProbert 7 59
(Tim Vaughan) *hld up: rdn and wknd over 2f out* **66/1**

/466 **10** 16 **Entihaa**[24] 746 9-9-9 **84**.................................................(v[1]) PhilipPrince(3) 10 51
(Dai Burchell) *chsd ldrs: rdn over 3f out: wknd over 2f out* **25/1**

3m 1.57s (-3.23) **Going Correction** -0.025s/f (Stan)
**WFA** 4 from 5yo+ 2lb **10** Ran SP% **114.6**
Speed ratings (Par 105): **108,107,105,105,104 104,103,100,100,91**
CSF £30.73 CT £78.02 TOTE £6.50: £2.50, £2.10, £1.50; EX 36.50 Trifecta £132.20.
**Owner** Midtech **Bred** Denis McDonnell **Trained** Portway, Worcs

**FOCUS**
A fair staying handicap, but they didn't go much of a pace so not the greatest test of stamina.
T/Plt: £119.60 to a £1 stake. Pool: £96,968.93 - 591.61 winning units T/Qpdt: £29.50 to a £1 stake. Pool: £6,522.52 - 163.28 winning units **Colin Roberts**


The Form Book Flat, Raceform Ltd, Newbury, RG14 5SJ

1154 - 1158a (Foreign Racing) - See Raceform Interactive

# SAINT-CLOUD (L-H)

Saturday, March 11

**OFFICIAL GOING: Turf: heavy**

## 1159a PRIX ALTIPAN (LISTED RACE) (4YO+) (TURF) 1m

3:15 4-Y-O+ £22,222 (£8,888; £6,666; £4,444; £2,222)

RPR
1 **Kourkan (FR)**[132] [7723] 4-9-3 0 ChristopheSoumillon 7 109+
(J-M Beguigne, France) 9/5[1]
2 3/4 **Djiguite (FR)**[106] [8117] 5-9-3 0 GregoryBenoist 6 107
(D Smaga, France) 2/1[2]
3 nse **Dream Dy (FR)**[103] 4-9-0 0 Pierre-CharlesBoudot 3 104
(C Ferland, France) 8/1
4 1 1/2 **Dhevanafushi**[133] [7711] 4-9-0 0 MickaelBarzalona 5 101
(H-A Pantall, France) 91/10
5 4 **Cersei**[21] [821] 4-8-10 0 StephanePasquier 2 88
(F Rohaut, France) 89/10
6 2 1/2 **Czabo**[267] [3339] 4-9-0 0 AlexisBadel 4 86
(Mick Channon) 79/10[3]
7 nk **Kahouanne (FR)**[22] 5-9-0 0 AntoineHamelin 1 85
(G Botti, France) 134/10

1m 44.36s (-3.14) 7 Ran SP% 118.3
PARI-MUTUEL (all including 1 euro stake): WIN 2.80; PLACE 1.60, 1.60; SF 6.90.
**Owner** Suc. Henri De La Chauvelais **Bred** Mme H De La Chauvelais **Trained** France

1160 - 1174a (Foreign Racing) - See Raceform Interactive

# 1139 CHELMSFORD (A.W) (L-H)

Monday, March 13

**OFFICIAL GOING: Polytrack: standard**
Wind: Light across Weather: Overcast

## 1175 GOING RACING? STAY AT CHANNELS CHANNELSLODGE.CO.UK APPRENTICE FILLIES' H'CAP 1m 5f 66y(P)

5:50 (5:50) (Class 5) (0-75,74) 4-Y-O+ £5,175 (£1,540; £769; £384) Stalls Low

Form RPR
3/0P 1 **Rowlestone Lass**[24] [789] 7-9-11 74 CliffordLee(3) 6 81
(Richard Price) *a.p: chsd ldr and edgd lft over 1f out: rdn to ld ins fnl f: styd on* 16/1
-051 2 1 **Mystikana**[17] [893] 4-9-2 72 (bt) TylerSaunders(7) 5 77+
(Marcus Tregoning) *hld up: hdwy over 1f out: sn rdn: r.o* 5/1[3]
-421 3 nk **Casablanca (IRE)**[17] [894] 4-9-2 72 JoshuaBryan(7) 1 76
(Andrew Balding) *led at stdy pce: racd keenly: qcknd over 3f out: rdn over 1f out: hdd ins fnl f: styd on same pce* 3/1[2]
-165 4 2 **Oratorio's Joy (IRE)**[24] [786] 7-9-10 73 (p) LucyKBarry(3) 2 74
(Jamie Osborne) *hld up in tch: hmpd and lost pl after 1f: rdn over 2f out: styd on fr over 1f out: nt rch ldrs* 5/1[3]
0644 5 1 1/2 **Gold Return (IRE)**[38] [550] 4-8-4 60 (t[1]) DarraghKeenan(7) 3 59
(John Ryan) *s.s: hld up: hdwy over 1f out: nt trble ldrs* 20/1
6-21 6 hd **Bracken Brae**[33] [616] 5-9-5 72 GabrieleMalune(7) 7 71
(Mark H Tompkins) *chsd ldr: rdn over 2f out: lost 2nd over 1f out: no ex fnl f* 9/4[1]
-542 7 1 1/4 **Heart Locket**[14] [958] 5-9-2 69 HarrisonShaw(7) 8 66
(Michael Easterby) *chsd ldrs: rdn over 2f out: wknd over 1f out:* 7/1
3105 8 5 **Fast Play (IRE)**[14] [958] 5-10-0 74 (b) AdamMcNamara 4 63
(Conor Dore) *prom: racd keenly: rdn over 3f out: wknd over 1f out* 20/1

2m 54.93s (1.33) **Going Correction** -0.225s/f (Stan)
**WFA** 4 from 5yo+ 1lb 8 Ran SP% 117.0
Speed ratings (Par 100): **86,85,85,83,83 82,82,79**
CSF £95.64 CT £308.64 TOTE £16.90: £3.70, £1.70, £1.70; EX 96.70 Trifecta £1102.90.
**Owner** Ocean's Five **Bred** G E Amey **Trained** Ullingswick, H'fords

**FOCUS**
This was steadily run and turned into a bit of a dash up the straight. The winner was not far off her old best, with the third setting the standard.

## 1176 WINNER.CO.UK CHELTENHAM MOBILE PRICE BOOST H'CAP 1m (P)

6:20 (6:20) (Class 4) (0-85,84) 3-Y-O £6,469 (£1,925; £962; £481) Stalls Low

Form RPR
12 1 **Indian Dandy (IRE)**[37] [577] 3-9-2 79 (h) DanielMuscutt 2 83+
(Marco Botti) *racd keenly: wnt 2nd 7f out: rdn to ld over 1f out: edgd lft: styd on* 7/4[1]
3-21 2 1/2 **Ourmullion**[17] [895] 3-8-7 70 KierenFox 1 72+
(John Best) *chsd ldr 1f: remained handy tl drvn and outpcd over 2f out: rallied and swtchd rt over 1f out: r.o* 2/1[2]
143 3 1 **Mums The Word**[17] [902] 3-9-1 78 PaulHanagan 5 78
(Richard Fahey) *led at stdy pce tl qcknd 3f out: rdn and hdd over 1f out: styd on same pce ins fnl f* 11/4[3]
04-4 4 1 1/4 **El Torito (IRE)**[10] [1000] 3-8-12 75 PatCosgrave 7 72
(Jim Boyle) *hld up: rdn over 2f out: nt trble ldrs* 4/1

1m 39.18s (-0.72) **Going Correction** -0.225s/f (Stan) 4 Ran SP% 116.4
Speed ratings (Par 100): **94,93,92,91**
CSF £6.08 TOTE £2.20; EX 4.70 Trifecta £9.20.
**Owner** Mubarak Al Naemi **Bred** Mubarak Al Naemi **Trained** Newmarket, Suffolk

**FOCUS**
A competitive little handicap. They went fairly steady early on and the unexposed winner progressed again.

## 1177 WINNER.CO.UK CHELTENHAM FREE BETS FOR FALLERS H'CAP 1m (P)

6:50 (6:53) (Class 3) (0-95,93) 4-Y-O+ £9,703 (£2,887; £1,443; £721) Stalls Low

Form RPR
2-02 1 **Qaffaal (USA)**[23] [817] 6-9-2 88 RyanMoore 9 96
(Michael Easterby) *hld up: hdwy over 1f out: nt clr run and swtchd rt ins fnl f: r.o to ld post* 9/4[1]
-021 2 hd **Take The Helm**[17] [896] 4-8-13 85 KierenFox 2 92
(Brian Meehan) *plld hrd and a.p: rdn to ld ins fnl f: hdd post* 4/1[2]
4-34 3 3/4 **Bold Prediction (IRE)**[44] [465] 7-9-2 88 ThomasBrown 1 93
(Ed Walker) *led: rdn over 1f out: hdd ins fnl f: styd on* 6/1[3]
4323 4 nk **Ice Royal (IRE)**[16] [918] 4-9-2 88 (p[1]) JoeFanning 8 92
(Jamie Osborne) *a.p: chsd ldr over 4f out: rdn and ev ch fr over 1f out: kpt on* 7/1
4214 5 nk **Loyalty**[9] [1023] 10-9-4 90 (v) MartinLane 7 93
(Derek Shaw) *s.i.s: hld up: hdwy over 1f out: sn rdn: styd on* 12/1
3314 6 1 3/4 **Regarde Moi**[18] [884] 9-8-10 87 GeorgeWood(5) 6 86
(Marco Botti) *chsd ldr over 3f: remained handy: rdn over 1f out: styd on same pce fnl f* 25/1
0333 7 1 1/4 **Horsted Keynes (FR)**[10] [999] 7-9-5 91 JamieSpencer 3 87
(David Simcock) *hld up in tch: plld hrd: rdn over 2f out: hung lft fr over 1f out: no ex fnl f* 6/1[3]
2110 8 2 1/4 **Chevallier**[9] [1023] 5-9-7 93 LukeMorris 4 84
(Archie Watson) *hld up in tch: rdn over 2f out: wknd ins fnl f: b.b.v* 7/1

1m 38.0s (-1.90) **Going Correction** -0.225s/f (Stan) 8 Ran SP% 115.9
Speed ratings (Par 107): **100,99,99,98,98 96,95,93**
CSF £11.42 CT £47.14 TOTE £3.40: £1.30, £1.60, £2.20; EX 15.70 Trifecta £91.80.
**Owner** Michael Burrows, Calam & Holdsworth **Bred** Shadwell Farm LLC **Trained** Sheriff Hutton, N Yorks

**FOCUS**
A decent handicap and another win for the ever improving Qaffaal, who loves it round here. The placed horses set the standard.

## 1178 WINNER.CO.UK CHELTENHAM EXTRA PLACES EVERY DAY H'CAP 1m 2f (P)

7:20 (7:21) (Class 4) (0-85,87) 4-Y-O+ £6,469 (£1,925; £962; £481) Stalls Low

Form RPR
0-45 1 **Ickymasho**[30] [683] 5-9-6 82 RichardKingscote 1 94
(Jonathan Portman) *chsd ldrs: led over 1f out: sn rdn and hung lft: styd on* 6/1[3]
3-21 2 2 **Final**[23] [817] 5-9-11 87 JoeFanning 2 95
(Mark Johnston) *prom: pushed along over 3f out: rdn and ev ch over 1f out: styd on same pce ins fnl f* 15/8[1]
-213 3 2 **Footlight**[24] [781] 4-9-2 78 PaulHanagan 4 82
(Richard Fahey) *prom: rdn over 2f out: hung lft ins fnl f: kpt on* 7/1
12/0 4 1/2 **Matravers**[26] [736] 6-8-10 72 JackMitchell 11 75+
(Mary Hambro) *s.i.s: hld up: hdwy u.p on outer over 1f out: edgd lft ins fnl f: r.o: nt rch ldrs* 25/1
42-0 5 3/4 **Craftsmanship (FR)**[35] [599] 6-9-3 79 AndreaAtzeni 6 81
(Robert Eddery) *hld up: hdwy u.p over 1f out: styd on same pce ins fnl f* 5/1[2]
0541 6 1/2 **Berrahri (IRE)**[17] [915] 6-8-12 74 KierenFox 9 75
(John Best) *disp ld tl rdn and hdd over 1f out: no ex ins fnl f* 14/1
5-00 7 1 1/4 **Arrowzone**[18] [885] 6-9-7 83 RyanPowell 3 81
(Kevin Frost) *hld up: hdwy u.p over 1f out: wknd ins fnl f* 33/1
610- 8 1/2 **Inniscastle Lad**[96] [8249] 5-9-5 81 (v[1]) PatCosgrave 8 78
(Stuart Williams) *disp ld tl rdn and hdd over 1f out: wknd ins fnl f* 8/1
00/5 9 1 3/4 **Lanceur (FR)**[26] [744] 8-9-8 87 CallumShepherd(3) 10 81
(William Stone) *hld up: rdn over 2f out: n.d* 16/1
0-05 10 3 1/2 **Ibazz**[11] [994] 4-9-1 82 CliffordLee(5) 7 69
(Archie Watson) *hld up: rdn over 3f out: nvr on terms* 8/1

2m 3.27s (-5.33) **Going Correction** -0.225s/f (Stan) 10 Ran SP% 119.8
Speed ratings (Par 105): **112,110,108,108,107 107,106,106,104,101**
CSF £18.13 CT £83.70 TOTE £6.50: £1.80, £1.80, £2.00; EX 18.80 Trifecta £119.60.
**Owner** C R Lambourne, M Forbes, D Losse **Bred** Allseasons Bloodstock **Trained** Upper Lambourn, Berks

**FOCUS**
This was a well-run race, Berrahri and the first-time-visored Inniscastle Lad taking each other on in front. The winner was back to form and the race has been rated around the third.

## 1179 WATCH CHELTENHAM FESTIVAL LIVE ON WINNER.CO.UK MEDIAN AUCTION MAIDEN STKS 6f (P)

7:50 (7:51) (Class 5) 3-5-Y-O £5,175 (£1,540; £769; £384) Stalls Centre

Form RPR
20- 1 **Cinque Port**[159] [7064] 3-9-0 0 ShaneKelly 6 81
(Richard Hughes) *chsd ldrs: shkn up over 2f out: led ins fnl f: pushed out* 4/1[3]
32-2 2 1 3/4 **Rag Tatter**[16] [920] 3-9-0 75 KevinStott 7 75
(Kevin Ryan) *sn pushed along to ld: rdn and hung rt over 1f out: hdd ins fnl f: styd on same pce* 7/2[2]
6- 3 6 **Kassandra (IRE)**[145] [7465] 3-8-9 0 AndreaAtzeni 5 51
(Richard Hannon) *s.i.s: sn pushed along to prom 5f out: rdn 1/2-way: styng on same pce whn hung lft fnl f* 3/1[1]
34 4 1/2 **Harlequin Storm (IRE)**[14] [956] 3-9-0 0 RobertWinston 10 54
(Dean Ivory) *chsd ldrs: rdn and hung rt over 1f out: styd on same pce* 14/1
6 5 3/4 **Eddiebet**[14] [956] 3-8-11 0 ShelleyBirkett(3) 9 52+
(David O'Meara) *s.i.s: hld up: shkn up and hung lft over 1f out: nvr on terms* 20/1
-0 6 2 1/2 **Anna Medici**[7] [1064] 3-8-9 0 LukeMorris 1 39+
(Sir Mark Prescott Bt) *sn outpcd: styd on ins fnl f: nvr nrr* 33/1
4322 7 3/4 **Havelock (IRE)**[10] [997] 3-9-0 72 JoeFanning 8 41
(Mark Johnston) *sn chsng ldr: rdn and hung rt over 1f out: wknd fnl f* 4/1[3]
- 8 nk **Sawlaat (IRE)** 3-9-0 0 SeanLevey 3 40+
(Richard Hannon) *s.i.s: hld up: effrt and hmpd over 1f out: n.d* 7/1
0 9 6 **Slipalongtrevaskis**[18] [878] 4-9-7 0 GinaMangan(7) 4 25
(J R Jenkins) *hld up in tch: plld hrd: rdn and hung lft over 1f out: sn wknd* 100/1

1m 11.4s (-2.30) **Going Correction** -0.225s/f (Stan)
**WFA** 3 from 4yo 14lb 9 Ran SP% 115.1
Speed ratings (Par 103): **106,103,95,95,94 90,89,89,81**
CSF £18.05 TOTE £5.10: £1.70, £1.50, £1.50; EX 16.90 Trifecta £62.70.
**Owner** M H Dixon **Bred** M H Dixon **Trained** Upper Lambourn, Berks

**FOCUS**
The first two pulled nicely clear in this maiden and the race has been rated around the runner-up.

## 1180 DOWNLOAD BOOKEE IN THE APP STORE H'CAP 6f (P)

8:20 (8:20) (Class 6) (0-60,62) 4-Y-O+ £3,234 (£962; £481; £240) Stalls Centre

Form RPR
6312 1 **Menelik (IRE)**[19] [860] 8-9-7 60 (bt) DavidProbert 12 75
(Des Donovan, Ire) *chsd ldrs: led over 1f out: sn hung lft: r.o wl* 7/2[1]
0-06 2 2 1/2 **Mambo Spirit (IRE)**[35] [604] 13-9-9 62 MartinDwyer 4 69
(Tony Newcombe) *hld up: hdwy over 1f out: nt clr run and swtchd rt ent fnl f: r.o to go 2nd nr fin* 8/1
0012 3 1/2 **Mighty Zip (USA)**[11] [982] 5-8-8 54 (p) JordanUys(7) 3 59
(Lisa Williamson) *chsd ldrs: rdn and ev ch over 1f out: no ex ins fnl f* 6/1[2]
2024 4 3/4 **Nasri**[33] [620] 11-9-1 54 (v) LukeMorris 6 57
(Emma Owen) *prom: rdn and hung lft over 1f out: styd on same pce fnl f* 7/1[3]

/00- **5** *1 1/2* **Caledonian Gold**[146] 7442 4-9-6 **59**.................................... JoeyHaynes 5 57
(Paul D'Arcy) *hld up: hdwy u.p over 1f out: nt trble ldrs* **16/1**

-433 **6** *3 1/4* **Penny Dreadful**[18] 879 5-9-7 **60**..........................................(p) DaleSwift 7 49
(Scott Dixon) *led: rdn and hdd over 1f out: wknd ins fnl f* **7/1**[3]

0-56 **7** *1 1/4* **Kingstreet Lady**[24] 784 4-8-8 **47**.................................... JoeFanning 9 32
(Richard Price) *hld up: rdn over 1f out: nvr on terms* **14/1**

-01P **8** *1* **Tilsworth Micky**[35] 601 5-9-7 **60**.................................... TomQueally 8 42
(J R Jenkins) *s.i.s: outpcd* **10/1**

05-0 **9** *2 3/4* **Ducissa**[16] 929 4-9-7 **60**.................................... RichardKingscote 2 34
(Daniel Kubler) *trckd ldrs: rdn over 1f out: wknd fnl f* **7/2**[1]

/4-0 **10** *5* **Jeanie's Place**[23] 815 4-9-9 **62**..............................(t[1]) WilliamCarson 10 21
(Charlie Wallis) *plld hrd and prom: rdn and wknd over 1f out* **33/1**

1m 11.15s (-2.55) **Going Correction** -0.225s/f (Stan) **10** Ran SP% **119.4**
Speed ratings (Par 101): **108,104,104,103,101 96,95,93,90,83**
CSF £33.21 CT £169.92 TOTE £3.90: £1.60, £2.40, £2.00; EX 31.40 Trifecta £132.50.
**Owner** D Donovan **Bred** Irish National Stud **Trained** Dualla, Co Tipperary

**FOCUS**
A moderate affair, but taken in style by the in-form winner, who is moving closer to his older form.
T/Jkpt: Not won. T/Plt: £43.60 to a £1 stake. Pool: £105,110.83 - 1756.33 winning units. T/Qpdt: £5.00 to a £1 stake. Pool: £1,3267.78 - 1926.38 winning units. **Colin Roberts**

# COMPIEGNE (L-H)
## Monday, March 13

**OFFICIAL GOING: Turf: heavy**

## 1181a PRIX DE L'AILETTE (CLAIMER) (4YO) (TURF) 1m 2f
**3:55** 4-Y-O **£6,837** (£2,735; £2,051; £1,367; £683)

RPR

**1** **Falcao Negro**[96] 4-9-8 **0**.................................... ChristopheSoumillon 2 73
(M Delzangles, France) **11/10**[1]

**2** *4* **Noble Agrippina (GER)** 4-9-1 **0**.................................... CristianDemuro 5 58
(E Lyon, France) **87/10**

**3** *1/2* **War Again (FR)**[27] 837 4-8-4 **0**..............................(p) MlleLauraGrosso[(7)] 3 49
(C Martinon, France) **148/10**

**4** *3* **Chief's App (FR)**[224] 4-9-1 **0**.................................... AdrienFouassier 10 51
(Y Barberot, France) **78/10**[3]

**5** *snk* **Obiwan (FR)**[176] 4-8-0 **0**.................................... TomLefranc[(8)] 1 44
(C Boutin, France) **39/1**

**6** *2* **Damasia (FR)**[173] 4-8-11 **0**.................................... ErwannLebreton[(8)] 9 51
(F Vermeulen, France) **23/5**[2]

**7** *1 3/4* **Celeste Mogador (FR)**[103] 4-8-2 **0**.................................... MlleSophieChuette[(6)] 4 32
(T Castanheira, France) **79/10**

**8** *10* **Masqueraded (USA)**[24] 4-8-7 **0**................(b) EstherRuthWeissmeier[(4)] 7 15
(Frau R Weissmeier, Germany) **29/1**

**9** *1* **Man Whipp (FR)**[67] 4-9-1 **0**..............................(p) MorganDelalande 11 21
(W Delalande, France) **53/1**

**10** *8* **Fishergate**[42] 278 4-8-11 **0**..............................(b) LouisBeuzelin 6 1
(Richard Rowe) **178/10**

2m 17.77s **10** Ran SP% **117.7**
PARI-MUTUEL (all including 1 euro stake): WIN 2.10 PLACE 1.50, 2.30, 2.50 DF 10.10 SF 12.40.
**Owner** Haras Bonne Chance **Bred** G Sayao Da Silva & P-F Carvalho De Oliveira **Trained** France

# 1107 SOUTHWELL (L-H)
## Tuesday, March 14

**OFFICIAL GOING: Fibresand: standard**
Wind: Moderate across Weather: Cloudy

## 1182 BET ON THE FESTIVAL WITH BETWAY H'CAP 1m 4f 14y(F)
**1:10** (1:10) (Class 5) (0-75,79) 4-Y-O+ **£3,234** (£962; £481; £240) **Stalls** Low

Form RPR

/2-1 **1** **Samtu (IRE)**[7] 1073 6-9-12 **79** 6ex.................................... BarryMcHugh 5 87
(Marjorie Fife) *pushed along s and sn led: rdn along over 2f out: drvn over 1f out: edgd lft ins fnl f: styd on* **7/4**[1]

400- **2** *1 1/2* **Busy Street**[150] 7359 5-9-7 **74**.................................... JoeFanning 2 81
(Alan Swinbank) *trckd ldrs: hdwy 3f out: chsd wnr wl over 1f out: rdn and styng on on inner and ev ch whn nt clr run ins fnl f: swtchd rt and kpt on* **2/1**[2]

2461 **3** *1 1/4* **Storm King**[5] 1113 8-8-12 **72**.................................... FinleyMarsh[(7)] 4 76
(David C Griffiths) *trckd wnr on outer: hdwy and cl up 3f out: rdn along wl over 1f out and ev ch: kpt on same pce fnl f* **2/1**[2]

320/ **4** *17* **Rathealy (IRE)**[15] 2642 6-8-12 **65**..............................(p) LukeMorris 3 42
(Christine Dunnett) *prom on inner: pushed along over 4f out: rdn over 3f out: sn outpcd* **100/1**

003- **5** *shd* **Alshan Fajer**[280] 2995 7-8-13 **73**.................................... GinaMangan[(7)] 1 50
(J R Jenkins) *rr: pushed along and tk clsr over over 5f out: rdn wl over 3f out: sn outpcd* **40/1**[3]

2m 36.99s (-4.01) **Going Correction** -0.15s/f (Stan) **5** Ran SP% **106.5**
Speed ratings (Par 103): **107,106,105,93,93**
CSF £5.19 TOTE £2.70: £1.20, £1.50; EX 5.90 Trifecta £6.90.
**Owner** Martin Lawrence **Bred** Rabbah Bloodstock Limited **Trained** Stillington, N Yorks

**FOCUS**
A modest handicap, but featuring a couple of recent course winners. A small personal best from Samtu.

## 1183 32RED.COM MAIDEN STKS 4f 214y(F)
**1:45** (1:46) (Class 5) 3-Y-O **£3,234** (£962; £481; £240) **Stalls** Centre

Form RPR

4-23 **1** **Gnaad (IRE)**[15] 960 3-9-5 **58**..............................(p) LukeMorris 7 62
(Robert Cowell) *racd towards stands side: cl up: led after 1f: rdn clr 2f out: drvn and edgd lft ent fnl f: kpt on strly* **11/4**[2]

5 **2** *1 3/4* **Hungarian Rhapsody**[24] 807 3-9-5 **0**.................................... JamieSpencer 3 56
(Jamie Osborne) *racd centre: trckd ldrs: hdwy 1/2-way: rdn along to chse wnr 2f out: drvn over 1f out: hung lft ent fnl f: kpt on same pce* **5/6**[1]

0- **3** *2 1/4* **Darvie**[235] 4601 3-9-5 **0**.................................... PhillipMakin 2 48
(David Barron) *dwlt: sn chsng ldrs on outer: hdwy 1/2-way: rdn and chsd ldng pair wl over 1f out: kpt on same* **4/1**[3]

5- **4** *1/2* **Stopdworldnletmeof**[216] 5283 3-8-12 **0**.................................... RossaRyan[(7)] 6 46
(David Flood) *sn rdn along and outpcd in rr: hdwy wl over 1f out: kpt on fnl f* **33/1**

6-0 **5** *10* **Elemento**[15] 956 3-9-5 **0**.................................... JosephineGordon 1 10
(Phil McEntee) *slt ld centre 1f: cl up: rdn along 1/2-way: drvn and edgd rt 2f out: sn wknd* **66/1**

05- **6** *1* **Joysunny**[251] 4000 3-8-7 **0**.................................... HarrisonShaw[(7)] 5
(Michael Easterby) *racd centre: cl up: rdn along after 2f: sn outpcd* **66/1**

58.79s (-0.91) **Going Correction** -0.15s/f (Stan) **6** Ran SP% **107.1**
Speed ratings (Par 98): **101,98,94,93,77 76**
CSF £4.92 TOTE £3.50: £1.40, £1.20; EX 5.40 Trifecta £8.10.
**Owner** Ahmed Jaber **Bred** Rabbah Bloodstock Limited **Trained** Six Mile Bottom, Cambs

**FOCUS**
An uncompetitive maiden with the two favourites dominating. The race has been rated around the winner.

## 1184 MONEY BACK AT CHELTENHAM WITH BETWAY H'CAP 4f 214y(F)
**2:25** (2:28) (Class 6) (0-60,62) 4-Y-O+ **£2,587** (£770; £384; £192) **Stalls** Centre

Form RPR

-040 **1** **Jacob's Pillow**[28] 732 6-9-12 **62**.................................... DanielTudhope 1 70
(Rebecca Bastiman) *prom centre: cl up 1/2-way: led wl over 1f out: sn rdn and edgd rt ent fnl f: sn drvn and kpt on wl* **9/4**[1]

0604 **2** *1* **Borough Boy (IRE)**[7] 1076 7-9-12 **62**..............................(v) TonyHamilton 8 67
(Derek Shaw) *trckd ldrs centre: hdwy 2f out: rdn over 1f out: kpt on u.p fnl f* **11/4**[2]

0663 **3** *1* **Red Flute**[10] 1022 5-8-8 **47**..............................(v) TimClark[(3)] 6 48
(Denis Quinn) *slt ld centre: rdn along 2f out and sn hdd: cl up and drvn whn n.m.r ent fnl f: kpt on same pce* **14/1**

-030 **4** *1/2* **Imjin River (IRE)**[40] 523 10-8-8 **47**..............................(tp) HollieDoyle[(3)] 2 46
(William Stone) *chsd ldrs centre: rdn along 2f out: n.m.r and swtchd lft ent fnl f: sn drvn and kpt on same pce* **14/1**

6300 **5** *hd* **Satchville Flyer**[4] 1126 6-9-7 **57**.................................... JamieSpencer 7 55+
(David Evans) *dwlt and towards rr nr stands side: rdn along and hdwy over 1f out: n.m.r and swtchd lft ins fnl f: kpt on wl towards fin* **6/1**

00-3 **6** *nk* **Oscars Journey**[5] 1112 7-9-4 **54**..............................(v) TomQueally 9 51
(J R Jenkins) *racd towards stands side: cl up: disp ld 1/2-way: rdn along wl over 1f out: grad wknd* **12/1**

-005 **7** *3* **Only Ten Per Cent (IRE)**[6] 1080 9-9-8 **61**..........(v) AlistairRawlinson[(3)] 3 48
(J R Jenkins) *racd towards far side: in tch: hdwy and prom 2f out: sn rdn and wknd over 1f out* **5/1**[3]

-020 **8** *5* **Give Us A Belle (IRE)**[18] 901 8-8-12 **48**..............................(vt) JFEgan 5 17
(Christine Dunnett) *chsd ldrs centre: rdn along over 2f out: sn wknd* **50/1**

250 **9** *1/2* **Very First Blade**[21] 852 8-8-10 **51**..............................(be) PhilDennis[(5)] 4 18
(Michael Mullineaux) *a rr: bhd fr 1/2-way* **16/1**

59.1s (-0.60) **Going Correction** -0.15s/f (Stan) **9** Ran SP% **117.3**
Speed ratings (Par 101): **98,96,94,94,93 93,88,80,79**
CSF £8.66 CT £68.94 TOTE £3.30: £1.40, £1.40, £3.30; EX 11.00 Trifecta £68.50.
**Owner** Miss Rebecca Bastiman **Bred** Lael Stables **Trained** Cowthorpe, N Yorks

**FOCUS**
A moderate sprint handicap with the main action unfolding up the middle of the track. The race has been rated around the winner's best form of recent times.

## 1185 CHELTENHAM OFFERS AT BETWAY H'CAP 6f 16y(F)
**3:05** (3:06) (Class 4) (0-85,87) 4-Y-O+ **£5,175** (£1,540; £769; £384) **Stalls** Low

Form RPR

0423 **1** **Crosse Fire**[7] 1071 5-8-8 **70**.................................... KieranO'Neill 1 80
(Scott Dixon) *qckly away: mde all: rdn clr wl over 1f out: drvn and hung bdly lft to far rail appr fnl: kpt on strly* **10/1**

05-1 **2** *2 1/4* **Escalating**[21] 851 5-9-7 **83**..............................(t) SilvestreDeSousa 5 86+
(Michael Appleby) *midfield whn n.m.r and lost pl after 1f: rr and wd st: hdwy on outer 2f out: sn rdn: drvn and edgd lft ent fnl f: styd on* **2/1**[1]

-254 **3** *3/4* **September Issue**[39] 547 4-8-10 **79**..............................(p) DavidEgan[(7)] 2 79
(Gay Kelleway) *trckd ldrs on inner: hdwy 2f out: rdn to chse wnr over 1f out: drvn and kpt on fnl f* **8/1**[3]

-312 **4** *1 1/2* **Vroom (IRE)**[21] 850 4-8-6 **75**..............................(p) RhiainIngram[(7)] 4 71
(Gay Kelleway) *cl up: rdn along wl over 2f out: drvn wl over 1f out: kpt on same pce* **10/1**

1-64 **5** *hd* **Captain Lars (SAF)**[21] 851 7-9-5 **81**..............................(v) TonyHamilton 7 76
(Derek Shaw) *in tch: hdwy on outer 3f out: rdn along over 2f out: drvn wl over 1f out: kpt on fnl f* **20/1**

250- **6** *4* **Vallarta (IRE)**[158] 7126 7-8-12 **74**.................................... JamesSullivan 6 56
(Ruth Carr) *chsd ldrs: n.m.r and hmpd after 1f: in tch: rdn along and hdwy over 2f out: drvn wl over 1f out: no imp* **20/1**

0510 **7** *2* **Among Angels**[7] 1074 5-9-2 **78**..............................(b) DaleSwift 9 54
(Daniel Mark Loughnane) *dwlt: a towards rr* **16/1**

5166 **8** *1 3/4* **Bring On A Spinner**[12] 984 4-8-12 **77**..................(be) AaronJones[(3)] 10 47
(Stuart Williams) *cl up on outer: rdn along over 2f out: drvn wl over 1f out: grad wknd* **7/2**[2]

650- **9** *1 1/2* **Valley Of Fire**[129] 7825 5-9-11 **87**.................................... JasonHart 3 52
(Les Eyre) *a towards rr* **20/1**

0-02 **10** *4 1/2* **Bahamian Dollar**[25] 783 4-8-12 **79**..............................(t[1]) CliffordLee[(5)] 8 30
(David Evans) *cl up: pushed along 3f out: rdn over 2f out: sn wknd* **8/1**[3]

1m 15.27s (-1.23) **Going Correction** -0.15s/f (Stan) **10** Ran SP% **116.1**
Speed ratings (Par 105): **102,99,98,96,95 90,87,85,83,77**
CSF £29.29 CT £169.44 TOTE £10.80: £2.70, £1.20, £2.80; EX 39.30 Trifecta £429.30.
**Owner** Paul J Dixon & Darren Lucas **Bred** Dr A Gillespie **Trained** Babworth, Notts

**FOCUS**
A fair sprint handicap which may have been won at the start. Not many got into it. The winner stepped up on this winter's form, but still 10lb below last winter.

## 1186 SUN BETS ON THE APP STORE CLASSIFIED CLAIMING STKS 1m 13y(F)
**3:45** (3:45) (Class 6) 4-Y-O+ **£2,587** (£770; £384; £192) **Stalls** Low

Form RPR

4-06 **1** **Muqarred (USA)**[22] 841 5-9-6 **63**..............................(p) DanielTudhope 8 76+
(Roger Fell) *trckd ldrs: hdwy 3f out: led 2f out: rdn clr appr fnl f: kpt on strly* **3/1**[1]

2600 **2** *4* **Pool House**[8] 1065 6-8-4 **63**.................................... KieranO'Neill 5 50
(Mike Murphy) *in tch on inner: hdwy over 2f out: rdn wl over 1f out: sn chsng wnr: drvn and no imp fnl f* **18/1**

0044 **3** *1 3/4* **Greyfriarschorista**[5] 1109 10-8-8 **63**..............................(vt) JFEgan 4 50
(David Evans) *cl up: led over 3f out: rdn along and hdd 2f out: drvn over 1f out: kpt on same pce* **7/2**[2]

52-0 **4** *1 1/2* **Almanack**[67] 90 7-8-12 **64**.................................... LukeMorris 3 50
(Mark Pattinson) *prom: cl up 3f out: rdn along over 2f out: drvn wl over 1f out: grad wknd* **12/1**

3123 **5** *3/4* **Dose**[11] 1007 4-8-11 **63**.................................... SebastianWoods[(7)] 9 55
(Richard Fahey) *in tch on outer: pushed along and lost pl 1/2-way: wd st: hdwy 2f out: swtchd lft and rdn over 1f out: styd on fnl f* **7/2**[2]

50-0 6 1 1/2 **Starfield**[72] 6 8-9-8 65....(t[1]) RobHornby 10 55
(Mandy Rowland) *half rrd and slowly away: bhd: hdwy over 3f out: rdn to chse ldrs 2f out: sn drvn and wknd* 25/1
4340 7 4 1/2 **Stun Gun**[21] 850 7-9-2 64....(p) TonyHamilton 6 39
(Derek Shaw) *sn rdn along in rr: a outpcd and bhd* 7/1[3]
10-6 8 11 **Veeraya**[31] 685 7-8-10 65....(t) AdamBeschizza 7 8
(Julia Feilden) *prom on outer: rdn along over 3f out: sn wknd* 8/1
65-5 9 1/2 **Adventure Zone (IRE)**[24] 811 4-9-0 62....(p) JosephineGordon 1 10
(Lee Carter) *slt ld on inner: pushed along 1/2-way: sn hdd and rdn: drvn over 2f out: sn wknd* 25/1
6-06 10 14 **Race Time (USA)**[22] 839 4-8-2 45....(p) FrannyNorton 2
(Seamus Durack) *cl up: rdn along over 3f out: sn wknd* 50/1
1m 42.86s (-0.84) **Going Correction** -0.15s/f (Stan) 10 Ran SP% **115.7**
Speed ratings (Par 101): **98,94,92,90,90 88,84,73,72,58**
CSF £56.72 TOTE £3.90: £1.40, £5.80, £1.40; EX 59.90 Trifecta £221.60.
**Owner** R G Fell **Bred** Shadwell Farm LLC **Trained** Nawton, N Yorks
**FOCUS**
A modest 0-65 classified claimer and the winner outclassed them. He was rated 78 last year.

## 1187 SUNBETS.CO.UK H'CAP 7f 14y(F)
4:25 (4:26) (Class 6) (0-60,64) 4-Y-O+ £2,587 (£770; £384; £192) Stalls Low

Form RPR
00-1 1 **Hammer Gun (USA)**[5] 1109 4-9-11 64 6ex....(v) FrannyNorton 4 72
(Derek Shaw) *cl up: led over 3f out: rdn clr wl over 1f out: readily* 6/4[1]
5202 2 1 1/4 **General Tufto**[7] 1075 12-8-12 51....(b) JoeyHaynes 3 54
(Charles Smith) *towards rr and sn pushed along: rdn and hdwy wl over 2f out: styd on u.p appr fnl f* 10/1
0130 3 1 1/4 **Dark Forest**[17] 929 4-9-8 61....(p) BarryMcHugh 8 60
(Marjorie Fife) *cl up on outer: hdwy to chse wnr wl over 1f out: sn drvn and kpt on same pce* 9/4[2]
0545 4 3 **Limerick Lord (IRE)**[7] 1075 5-8-6 48....(p) ShelleyBirkett(3) 7 39
(Julia Feilden) *chsd ldrs: rdn along wl over 2f out: sn drvn and one pce* 10/1
00-3 5 3 1/4 **Rupert Boy (IRE)**[7] 1075 4-8-4 50....(b) RPWalsh(7) 5 32
(Scott Dixon) *slt ld: rdn along and hdd wl over 3f out: sn wknd* 16/1
60-0 6 shd **Wotabond**[5] 1112 4-8-2 46 oh1.... PhilDennis(5) 6 28
(Richard Whitaker) *chsd ldrs: hdwy 3f out: rdn over 2f out: sn one pce* 50/1
200- 7 3 1/4 **Balducci**[74] 8586 10-9-2 62....(b) BenSanderson(7) 1 35
(Roger Fell) *a bhd* 20/1
-055 8 15 **Spice Mill (IRE)**[7] 1076 4-9-7 60....(vt) SilvestreDeSousa 2
(Michael Appleby) *cl up on inner: rdn along over 3f out: wknd qckly wl over 2f out* 8/1[3]
1m 29.08s (-1.22) **Going Correction** -0.15s/f (Stan) 8 Ran SP% **112.7**
Speed ratings (Par 101): **100,98,97,93,90 89,86,69**
CSF £17.30 CT £32.90 TOTE £2.50: £1.30, £2.30, £1.20; EX 15.50 Trifecta £38.70.
**Owner** A Flint **Bred** Her Majesty The Queen **Trained** Sproxton, Leics
**FOCUS**
A moderate handicap, but the winner is better than this grade.

## 1188 BETWAY APPRENTICE H'CAP 1m 4f 14y(F)
5:00 (5:00) (Class 6) (0-60,58) 4-Y-O+ £2,587 (£770; £384; £192) Stalls Low

Form RPR
14-3 1 **Lady Turpin (IRE)**[28] 726 4-8-12 53.... ConnorMurtagh(5) 3 61+
(Richard Fahey) *trckd ldrs: hdwy and cl up over 4f out: led wl over 2f out: rdn clr over 1f out: kpt on* 8/1
-623 2 2 1/4 **Go On Gal (IRE)**[21] 853 4-9-2 57.... FinleyMarsh(5) 2 61
(Julia Feilden) *trckd ldrs: hdwy over 3f out: rdn over 2f out: drvn to chse wnr over 1f out: kpt on* 9/4[1]
-061 3 11 **Thou Swell (IRE)**[32] 661 5-9-5 58....(b) AidenBlakemore(5) 1 44
(Shaun Harris) *cl up. led after 1 1/2f: sn clr: pushed along over 3f out: rdn and hdd over 2f out: plugged on u.p fr over 1f out* 7/1[3]
6052 4 1 1/4 **Powered (IRE)**[6] 1081 4-8-13 52....(p) KatherineGlenister(3) 5 36
(David Evans) *hld up in tch: hdwy 4f out: chsd ldrs 3f out: rdn over 2f out: sn drvn and no imp* 14/1
0/00 5 3 1/4 **Fire In Babylon (IRE)**[12] 988 9-8-7 46....(b) DarraghKeenan(5) 8 25
(Giles Bravery) *towards rr: rdn along over 3f out: plodded on fnl 2f* 25/1
00-4 6 1/2 **Crakehall Lad (IRE)**[38] 414 6-8-11 45....(b) JaneElliott 4 23
(Andrew Crook) *sn rdn along in rr: detached after 2f: a bhd* 7/1[3]
25-0 7 nk **Wayside Magic**[35] 607 4-8-9 48....(t[1]) BenRobinson(3) 6 26
(Neville Bycroft) *led 1 1/2f: chsd clr ldr: tk clsr order over 4f out: rdn along over 3f out: sn wknd* 20/1
244- 8 5 **Toboggan's Gift**[228] 4260 5-9-3 51.... MeganNicholls 7 21
(Ann Duffield) *trckd ldrs on outer: pushed along 4f out: rdn 3f out: sn wknd* 8/1
2m 39.27s (-1.73) **Going Correction** -0.15s/f (Stan)
**WFA** 4 from 5yo+ 1lb 8 Ran SP% **113.3**
Speed ratings (Par 101): **99,97,90,89,87 86,86,83**
CSF £25.90 CT £132.96 TOTE £8.00: £2.10, £1.20, £2.20; EX 23.90 Trifecta £121.50.
**Owner** UK Racing Syndicate **Bred** Michael Kelly **Trained** Musley Bank, N Yorks
**FOCUS**
A moderate middle-distance apprentice handicap with the first two pulling miles clear. A personal best from the winner.
T/Plt: £8.00 to a £1 stake. Pool: £54,850.62 - 5,000.55 winning units. T/Qpdt: £4.10 to a £1 stake. Pool: £4,390.09 - 788.90 winning units. **Joe Rowntree**

# 1147 WOLVERHAMPTON (A.W) (L-H)
Tuesday, March 14

**OFFICIAL GOING: Tapeta: standard**
Wind: Light behind Weather: Fine

## 1189 SUNBETS.CO.UK APPRENTICE H'CAP 7f 36y (Tp)
5:45 (5:50) (Class 5) (0-75,75) 4-Y-O+ £3,072 (£914; £456; £228) Stalls High

Form RPR
1631 1 **Call Out Loud**[27] 745 5-9-6 71....(vt) AlistairRawlinson 6 78
(Michael Appleby) *mde all: shkn up and qcknd over 2f out: rdn over 1f out: styd on* 7/2[3]
-302 2 nk **Rebel Lightning (IRE)**[42] 501 4-9-7 72....(b) HectorCrouch 4 78
(Richard Spencer) *a.p: chsd wnr 3f out: rdn over 1f out: r.o* 5/2[2]
-056 3 2 **Baltic Prince (IRE)**[5] 1105 7-9-0 72.... AledBeech(7) 2 73
(Tony Carroll) *chsd wnr 4f: rdn over 1f out: styd on same pce wl ins fnl f* 15/2
0-10 4 3 1/2 **Hernando Torres**[11] 1007 9-8-12 70....(p) RyanTimby(7) 5 61+
(Michael Easterby) *s.s: hld up: styd on ins fnl f: nvr nrr* 12/1

5106 5 1 1/4 **Masamah (IRE)**[17] 923 11-9-5 70....(t[1]) GeorgeDowning 1 58
(Ian Williams) *prom: rdn and hung lft over 1f out: wknd fnl f* 16/1
0-11 6 9 **Murdanova (IRE)**[17] 929 4-9-6 71.... CharlieBennett 7 34
(Daniel Mark Loughnane) *hld up: rdn and hung rt over 2f out: wknd wl over 1f out* 7/4[1]
1m 28.04s (-0.76) **Going Correction** -0.05s/f (Stan) 6 Ran SP% **112.5**
Speed ratings (Par 103): **102,101,99,95,93 83**
CSF £12.73 CT £58.92 TOTE £4.30: £1.70, £2.40; EX 14.10 Trifecta £49.90.
**Owner** Kings Head Duffield Racing Partnership **Bred** Rabbah Bloodstock Limited **Trained** Oakham, Rutland
■ Stewards' Enquiry : Hector Crouch two-day ban: used whip above permitted level (28-29 march)
**FOCUS**
The winner put on a show of front-running here and this was a small step up from him.

## 1190 MONEY BACK AT CHELTENHAM WITH BETWAY MAIDEN STKS 1f 104y (Tp)
6:15 (6:16) (Class 5) 3-Y-O+ £3,072 (£914; £456; £228) Stalls Low

Form RPR
2 1 **Long John Silver (IRE)**[31] 681 3-8-10 0 ow2.... JamieSpencer 3 86+
(Jamie Osborne) *trckd ldrs: led on bit and edgd lft ins fnl f: r.o: comf* 2/5[1]
0 2 2 3/4 **Oxford Don**[19] 882 3-8-5 0.... AaronJones(3) 5 71
(David Simcock) *s.i.s: hld up: hdwy and nt clr run over 1f out: rdn: hung lft and r.o ins fnl f: wnt 2nd post* 16/1
0 3 shd **Chippenham (IRE)**[19] 882 3-8-8 0....(b[1]) NickyMackay 1 71
(John Gosden) *pushed along to chse ldrs: led 8f out: hdd 7f out: remained handy: shkn up over 2f out: rdn and ev ch ins fnl f: styd on same pce* 9/1[3]
323- 4 1 1/4 **Laureate**[210] 5518 3-8-3 71.... JoeFanning 4 63
(Mark Johnston) *led: hdd 8f out: chsd ldr over 6f out tl led again over 2f out: rdn over 1f out: hung lft and hdd ins fnl f: wknd towards fin* 4/1[2]
5 5 **Hazamar (IRE)**[122] 2709 4-10-0 75....(t) LukeMorris 7 64
(Sophie Leech) *chsd ldrs: led 7f out: rdn and hdd over 2f out: wknd fnl f* 18/1
6 9 **Mr Magill (FR)**[276] 5-10-0 0.... TimmyMurphy 2 45
(Karen George) *s.s: a in rr: hung rt over 6f out: lost tch fr over 3f out* 100/1
2m 1.48s (0.68) **Going Correction** -0.05s/f (Stan)
**WFA** 3 from 4yo+ 20lb 6 Ran SP% **113.6**
Speed ratings (Par 103): **94,91,91,90,85 77**
CSF £9.33 TOTE £1.30: £1.10, £5.50; EX 14.10 Trifecta £31.20.
**Owner** Michael Buckley & T Hyde **Bred** George Kent **Trained** Upper Lambourn, Berks
**FOCUS**
This was a modest maiden, but the improving winner has plenty more to offer.

## 1191 BET ON THE FESTIVAL WITH BETWAY H'CAP 1m 5f 194y
6:45 (6:46) (Class 6) (0-60,63) 4-Y-O+ £2,264 (£673; £336; £168) Stalls Low

Form RPR
655- 1 **Monjeni**[162] 7006 4-9-6 60....(p) JosephineGordon 3 69+
(Ian Williams) *chsd ldr 1f: remained handy: led over 1f out: rdn out* 7/1[3]
62-3 2 2 **Surround Sound**[62] 174 7-9-3 56....(t) RachelRichardson(3) 2 60
(Tim Easterby) *s.s: hld up: hdwy over 1f out: r.o to go 2nd wl ins fnl f: nt rch wnr* 9/1
0032 3 1 1/2 **Tingo In The Tale (IRE)**[18] 900 8-9-5 55....(t[1]) JamieSpencer 12 57
(Sophie Leech) *hld up: hdwy 2f out: rdn and nt clr run over 1f out: styd on* 12/1
-553 4 1 1/4 **Oyster Card**[26] 762 4-8-6 46....(p) LukeMorris 10 46
(Michael Appleby) *chsd ldr after 1f: rdn over 2f out: lost 2nd over 1f out: styd on same pce ins fnl f* 9/1
1 5 1/2 **Carvelas (IRE)**[17] 924 8-9-5 60.... DavidParkes(5) 1 60
(P J F Murphy, Ire) *hld up in tch: rdn over 2f out: styd on same pce fnl f* 7/2[2]
020- 6 nse **Hier Encore (FR)**[101] 8211 5-9-4 57.... HectorCrouch(3) 8 57
(David Menuisier) *sn led: qcknd over 3f out: rdn: edgd lft and hdd over 1f out: no ex ins fnl f* 16/1
4-43 7 3/4 **Topalova**[12] 988 4-8-1 48.... GabrieleMalune(7) 9 47
(Mark H Tompkins) *chsd ldrs: rdn over 2f out: no ex fnl f* 14/1
054- 8 hd **The Lampo Genie**[208] 5573 5-9-10 60....(b) StevieDonohoe 4 58
(Johnny Farrelly) *hld up: rdn over 2f out: hdwy over 1f out: no ex ins fnl f* 18/1
-242 9 1/2 **Cape Spirit (IRE)**[27] 741 5-9-5 55....(p) OisinMurphy 5 53
(Andrew Balding) *hld up: rdn over 2f out: hdwy and nt clr run over 1f out: no ex ins fnl f* 11/4[1]
-306 10 1 **Firestorm (GER)**[18] 893 6-9-10 60....(e) AdamKirby 11 56
(Michael Attwater) *s.i.s: hld up: rdn over 1f out: nvr on terms* 12/1
00-0 11 4 1/2 **New Tarabela**[33] 645 6-8-10 46....(p) GeorgeDowning 7 36
(Tony Carroll) *hld up in tch: rdn over 2f out: wknd over 1f out* 50/1
3m 3.63s (-1.17) **Going Correction** -0.05s/f (Stan)
**WFA** 4 from 5yo+ 2lb 11 Ran SP% **116.5**
Speed ratings (Par 101): **101,99,99,98,98 97,97,97,97,96 94**
CSF £67.93 CT £746.80 TOTE £7.00: £2.30, £3.50, £3.00; EX 80.40 Trifecta £552.20.
**Owner** Ian Williams **Bred** The Kathryn Stud **Trained** Portway, Worcs
**FOCUS**
An ordinary handicap, but the winner could be one to keep on side at this level. The race has been rated around the first and third.

## 1192 32REDSPORT.COM MEDIAN AUCTION MAIDEN FILLIES' STKS 6f 20y (Tp)
7:15 (7:17) (Class 6) 3-5-Y-O £2,264 (£673; £336; £168) Stalls Low

Form RPR
6 1 **Magic Approach**[11] 1003 3-9-0 0.... JamieSpencer 6 63
(David Simcock) *hld up in tch: rdn over 1f out: r.o to ld nr fin* 11/2[3]
2 hd **Royal Request (IRE)** 3-9-0 0.... LukeMorris 5 62
(James Tate) *s.i.s: hdwy over 2f out: rdn over 1f out: r.o* 3/1[2]
36-4 3 shd **Atlanta Belle (IRE)**[64] 140 3-9-0 70.... TedDurcan 4 62
(Chris Wall) *plld hrd and prom: rdn to ld 1f out: hdd nr fin* 3/1[2]
2-20 4 1 1/2 **La Guapita**[34] 625 3-9-0 71.... JosephineGordon 2 45
(Hugo Palmer) *prom: racd keenly: rdn and ev ch 1f out: wknd wl ins fnl f: fin 5th: plcd 4th* 15/8[1]
6000 5 2 **Allen's Folly**[5] 1112 4-9-7 45.... MollyKing(7) 8 42
(Peter Hiatt) *led: rdn over 2f out: hdd over 1f out: wknd ins fnl f: fin 6th: plcd 5th* 125/1
6 3 **Tooty Fruitti** 3-9-0 0.... JFEgan 7 3
(Jo Hughes) *s.i.s: sn prom: chsd ldr over 4f out: edgd rt over 2f out: led over 1f out: sn rdn and hdd: wknd ins fnl f: fin 7th: plcd 6th* 20/1
3 7 8 **Mia Wallace (IRE)**[32] 656 3-8-11 0.... ShelleyBirkett(3) 3 3
(David O'Meara) *s.i.s: outpcd: fin 8th: plcd 7th* 20/1
00- 8 26 **Precious Equity (FR)**[118] 7977 3-8-11 0.... HectorCrouch(3) 1
(David Menuisier) *in tch: lost pl after 1f: in rr and pushed along 1/2-way: sn lost tch: eased over 1f out: fin 9th: plcd 8th* 66/1

0-04 **D** 3¾ **Captain Sedgwick (IRE)**[26] 764 3-9-0 47.................. TomMarquand 9 50
(John Spearing) *prom: lost pl over 3f out: sn outpcd: styd on ins fnl f: fin 4th: disqualified rdr failed to weigh in* **50/1**
1m 14.81s (0.31) **Going Correction** -0.05s/f (Stan)
**WFA** 3 from 4yo 14lb 9 Ran SP% **113.9**
Speed ratings (Par 98): **95,94,94,87,84 80,70,35,89**
CSF £21.07 TOTE £6.30: £1.70, £1.30, £1.40; EX 27.80 Trifecta £83.50.
**Owner** The Athens Wood Partnership **Bred** Mrs Y E Mullin & B McGarrigle **Trained** Newmarket, Suffolk
■ Stewards' Enquiry : Tom Marquand three-day ban: rider failed to weigh-in (Mar 28-30)

**FOCUS**
A modest maiden but a good finish.

## 1193 £10 FREE AT 32RED.COM H'CAP — 6f 20y (Tp)
**7:45** (7:46) (Class 6) (0-60,60) 3-Y-O **£2,264** (£673; £336; £168) **Stalls** Low

Form RPR
-044 **1** **Night Shadow**[15] 960 3-9-7 **60**.............................. DaleSwift 5 63
(Alan Brown) *chsd ldr: rdn over 1f out: styd on to ld post* **6/1**
600- **2** *hd* **Blastofmagic**[153] 7275 3-9-1 **54**..............................(p[1]) OisinMurphy 1 56
(David Dennis) *chsd ldrs: rdn over 1f out: led wl ins fnl f: hdd post* **14/1**
34-3 **3** *nk* **Sheila's Palace**[31] 679 3-9-6 **59**.............................. JosephineGordon 2 60
(J S Moore) *chsd ldrs: rdn over 1f out: r.o* **5/1**[3]
5400 **4** 1¼ **Vocalisation (IRE)**[15] 960 3-8-7 **46** oh1.......................... DavidProbert 3 43
(John Weymes) *led: rdn over 1f out: hdd wl ins fnl f: styd on same pce* **12/1**
6-63 **5** 1¾ **Champagne Queen**[45] 456 3-8-8 **47**..............................(t) LukeMorris 6 38+
(Rae Guest) *hld up: pushed along 1/2-way: swtchd rt and hdwy over 1f out: rdn and hung lft ins fnl f: nt rch ldrs* **11/2**
-000 **6** ½ **Tink**[45] 456 3-8-5 **49** ow3..............................(p[1]) CharlieBennett[(5)] 4 39+
(Mark Brisbourne) *hld up: hdwy over 1f out: sn rdn: styd on same pce ins fnl f* **50/1**
0-43 **7** *shd* **Mimic's Memory**[46] 442 3-9-7 **60**.............................. ShaneGray 8 50+
(Ann Duffield) *s.i.s: hld up: racd keenly: rdn over 1f out: nvr on terms* **16/1**
6500 **8** 1¾ **Alfolk (IRE)**[10] 1034 3-9-2 **55**..............................(h) JamieSpencer 7 39+
(David Simcock) *s.i.s: hld up: shkn up over 1f out: n.d* **9/2**[2]
60-3 **9** 3¼ **Vaux (IRE)**[18] 903 3-9-7 **60**.............................. AdamKirby 9 34+
(Ben Haslam) *hld up in tch: racd keenly: rdn over 2f out: wknd over 1f out* **3/1**[1]
1m 14.33s (-0.17) **Going Correction** -0.05s/f (Stan) 9 Ran SP% **111.7**
Speed ratings (Par 96): **99,98,98,96,94 93,93,91,86**
CSF £81.27 CT £444.73 TOTE £7.10: £1.90, £3.10, £1.90; EX 98.90 Trifecta £657.30.
**Owner** G Morrill **Bred** Mrs Yvette Dixon **Trained** Yedingham, N Yorks
■ Stewards' Enquiry : Oisin Murphy two-day ban: used whip with excessive force (28-30 march)

**FOCUS**
They didn't go that quick early and the first four raced in the first four positions throughout, just switching places between themselves in the closing stages. The third and fourth help set the level.

## 1194 32RED CASINO CLASSIFIED STKS — 6f 20y (Tp)
**8:15** (8:15) (Class 5) 3-Y-O **£3,234** (£962; £481; £240) **Stalls** Low

Form RPR
-133 **1** **Peachey Carnehan**[31] 686 3-9-0 70..............................(v) WilliamCarson 3 73
(Michael Attwater) *mde all: pushed clr over 2f out: rdn out* **2/1**[2]
15 **2** 3 **Bastia**[11] 1005 3-9-0 69.............................. DavidProbert 5 63
(Martyn Meade) *chsd wnr: rdn over 2f out: styng on same pce whn hung lft ins fnl f* **7/2**[3]
100- **3** *shd* **Hidden Stash**[174] 6664 3-9-0 70.............................. OisinMurphy 4 63+
(Andrew Balding) *chsd ldrs: rdn over 2f out: styd on towards fin* **7/4**[1]
0-06 **4** 9 **Monoshka (IRE)**[52] 356 3-9-0 68.............................. AndrewMullen 6 34
(James Given) *s.i.s: sn pushed along in rr: outpcd fr over 2f out* **8/1**
1m 14.18s (-0.32) **Going Correction** -0.05s/f (Stan) 4 Ran SP% **103.0**
Speed ratings (Par 98): **100,96,95,83**
CSF £8.02 TOTE £2.20; EX 6.10 Trifecta £7.60.
**Owner** Jim Duggan & Scott Brown **Bred** J M Duggan & The Late T Duggan **Trained** Epsom, Surrey

**FOCUS**
A tight race on the ratings, but the winner dominated from the off.

## 1195 32RED.COM H'CAP — 1m 1f 104y (Tp)
**8:45** (8:45) (Class 5) (0-75,76) 3-Y-O **£3,234** (£962; £481; £240) **Stalls** Low

Form RPR
5-1 **1** **Flood Warning**[29] 717 3-9-13 **76**.............................. AdamKirby 4 84+
(Clive Cox) *hld up: hdwy over 2f out: shkn up to ld over 1f out: edgd lft: rdn out* **5/2**[2]
031 **2** ¾ **Dark Titan (IRE)**[19] 882 3-9-6 **69**.............................. ThomasBrown 6 74
(Ed Walker) *hld up: hdwy and nt clr run over 1f out: sn rdn: r.o to go 2nd wl ins fnl f: nt rch wnr* **11/2**
6241 **3** 2 **Critical Thinking (IRE)**[26] 766 3-8-10 **66**.................... FinleyMarsh[(7)] 3 67
(Kevin Frost) *hld up: nt clr run over 2f out: swtchd rt and hdwy over 1f out: sn rdn and hung lft: styd on same pce ins fnl f* **9/1**
231- **4** 2 **Plead**[99] 8227 3-9-12 **75**.............................. JackMitchell 2 72+
(Archie Watson) *led: hdd 8f out: chsd ldr tl led again over 3f out: rdn and hdd over 1f out: no ex ins fnl f* **2/1**[1]
3122 **5** 1½ **Good Time Ahead (IRE)**[13] 967 3-9-6 **69**.............................. PaddyAspell 7 63
(Philip Kirby) *chsd ldr tl led 8f out: hdd over 3f out: sn rdn: wknd wl ins fnl f* **5/1**[3]
444 **6** 2 **Born To Reason (IRE)**[15] 959 3-8-13 **62**.............................. RyanPowell 1 51
(Kevin Frost) *chsd ldrs: rdn over 2f out: wknd fnl f* **33/1**
55-5 **7** 2 **Scarlet Thrush (IRE)**[29] 718 3-8-13 **67**..................(h) GeorgeWood[(5)] 5 52
(Marco Botti) *chsd ldrs: rdn over 3f out: wknd over 2f out* **17/2**
1m 58.94s (-1.86) **Going Correction** -0.05s/f (Stan) 7 Ran SP% **117.4**
Speed ratings (Par 98): **106,105,103,101,100 98,96**
CSF £17.42 TOTE £2.80: £2.30, £2.40; EX 22.70 Trifecta £158.60.
**Owner** Cheveley Park Stud **Bred** New England Myriad Stanley & Cheveley Pk **Trained** Lambourn, Berks

**FOCUS**
The lead was disputed and the first three raced in the last three positions for much of the race.
T/Plt: £84.60 to a £1 stake. Pool: £77,962.59 - 672.63 winning units. T/Qpdt: £52.70 to a £1 stake. Pool: £7,926.96 - 111.26 winning units. **Colin Roberts**

# DORTMUND (R-H)
Tuesday, March 14
**OFFICIAL GOING: Sand: standard**

## 1196a FRUHLINGSPREIS (H'CAP) (4YO+) (SAND) — 1m 1f 165y
**5:10** 4-Y-0+ **£2,564** (£1,025; £769; £512; £256)

RPR
**1** **Meerwind (GER)** 5-9-6 **0**.............................. NicolaSechi[(11)] 8
(L W J Van Der Meulen, Holland) **61/10**
**2** *hd* **Barocca (GER)** 5-9-2 **0**.............................. DanielePorcu 7
(S Smrczek, Germany) **8/1**
**3** ½ **Khala (POL)**[632] 5-8-10 **0**.............................. NormanRichter 3
(Frau Marion Rotering, Germany) **10/1**
**4** ½ **Los Cerritos (SWI)**[13] 5-9-8 **0**..............................(b) AlexanderPietsch 5
(Oliver Greenall) **8/5**[1]
**5** 3 **Rock Of Tiger (GER)** 5-9-0 **0**..............................(b) FilipMinarik 4
(T Potters, Germany) **37/10**[2]
**6** 1¾ **Zaphiras Adventure** 6-8-9 **0**.............................. MaximPecheur 6
(S Richter, Germany) **144/10**
**7** *hd* **Emiglia (GER)** 8-9-2 **0** ow1.............................. AlexanderWeis 2
(Frau S Weis, Germany) **29/1**
**8** 1¼ **Schirkan (GER)** 5-9-4 **0**.............................. EstherRuthWeissmeier 1
(R Werning, Germany) **48/10**[3]
**9** 1¾ **Venture Capital (FR)**[77] 5-8-10 **0**.............................. MichaelCadeddu 9
(U Schwinn, Germany) **42/1**
**10** 8 **American Day (GER)** 6-9-3 **0**.............................. IanFerguson 10
(A Kleinkorres, Germany) **125/10**

**Owner** The Dutch Master Stables **Bred** Gestut Gorlsdorf **Trained** Holland

# 1122 NEWCASTLE (A.W) (L-H)
Wednesday, March 15
**OFFICIAL GOING: Tapeta: standard**
Wind: Almost nil

## 1197 BET ON THE FESTIVAL WITH BETWAY H'CAP — 2m 56y (Tp)
**5:50** (5:50) (Class 6) (0-60,62) 4-Y-0+ **£2,264** (£673; £336; £168) **Stalls** Low

Form RPR
6/4- **1** **Up Ten Down Two (IRE)**[159] 7105 8-9-7 **58**...(t) RachelRichardson[(3)] 10 63
(Michael Easterby) *t.k.h: cl up: ev ch over 2f out: rdn whn checked 1f out: kpt on wl to ld last stride* **5/4**[1]
0213 **2** *nse* **Ryan The Giant**[13] 990 4-8-11 **50**..............................(v) ConnorBeasley 6 55
(Keith Dalgleish) *prom: smooth hdwy to ld over 2f out: sn rdn: hung bdly lft to far rail appr fnl f: kpt on fnl f: hdd last stride* **11/4**[2]
/00- **3** 1¾ **Mr Globetrotter (USA)**[9] 8411 4-9-4 **62**.............................. CliffordLee[(5)] 3 65
(Iain Jardine) *hld up: pushed along 4f out: hdwy to chse ldrs 2f out: sn rdn: kpt on same pce ins fnl f* **7/1**[3]
-600 **4** 1½ **Psychology**[14] 969 4-9-2 **55**.............................. DougieCostello 7 56
(Kenny Johnson) *missed break: hld up: smooth hdwy and in tch over 1f out: rdn and kpt on same pce ins fnl f* **50/1**
56-6 **5** ¾ **Shulammite Man (IRE)**[41] 525 4-8-9 **48**.............................. NeilFarley 8 48
(Alan Swinbank) *hld up in tch: n.m.r briefly over 2f out: sn rdn: kpt on same pce fr over 1f out* **14/1**
202- **6** 1¾ **Feeltherhythm (IRE)**[31] 5155 6-9-0 **48**..............................(v) SamJames 9 46
(Chris Grant) *hld up in tch: rdn along over 2f out: sn no imp* **33/1**
260- **7** 3 **Next Edition (IRE)**[22] 7138 9-9-8 **61**..............................(p) PhilDennis[(5)] 1 56
(Philip Kirby) *t.k.h: hld up: hdwy on outside over 3f out: rdn and edgd lft over 2f out: sn outpcd* **25/1**
02-0 **8** *hd* **Maple Stirrup (IRE)**[38] 28 5-9-9 **57**..............................(p[1]) TomEaves 4 51
(Patrick Holmes) *trckd ldrs: drvn along over 2f out: wknd wl over 1f out* **12/1**
00-5 **9** ¾ **Adrakhan (FR)**[36] 610 6-8-12 **46**.............................. CamHardie 2 44
(Wilf Storey) *led at modest gallop: rdn and hdd over 2f out: wknd wl over 1f out* **28/1**
00-0 **10** 16 **Strikemaster (IRE)**[36] 610 11-8-4 **45**.................(t) KieranSchofield[(7)] 11 19
(Lee James) *s.i.s: hld up: rdn along over 3f out: wknd over 2f out* **125/1**
3m 45.16s (9.96) **Going Correction** +0.075s/f (Slow)
**WFA** 4 from 5yo+ 3lb 10 Ran SP% **111.0**
Speed ratings (Par 101): **78,77,77,76,75 75,73,73,73,65**
CSF £4.02 CT £14.13 TOTE £2.10: £1.10, £1.30, £2.40; EX 6.20 Trifecta £25.60.
**Owner** A Chandler, L Westwood & Mrs C Daurge **Bred** Ammerland Verwaltung Gmbh **Trained** Sheriff Hutton, N Yorks
■ Stewards' Enquiry : Connor Beasley caution: guilty of careless riding

**FOCUS**
This was steadily run and developed into a sprint. The winner was rated in the 70s some time ago.

## 1198 32RED.COM MAIDEN STKS — 1m 5y (Tp)
**6:20** (6:20) (Class 5) 3-Y-O **£2,911** (£866; £432; £216) **Stalls** Centre

Form RPR
03-2 **1** **Oud Metha Bridge (IRE)**[18] 916 3-9-5 76.............................. JosephineGordon 1 81
(Ed Dunlop) *t.k.h: pressed ldr: led over 2f out: rdn clr fr over 1f out* **6/5**[1]
5- **2** 6 **Prancing Oscar (IRE)**[200] 5885 3-9-5 0.............................. CamHardie 3 67
(Ben Haslam) *hld up in tch: stdy hdwy over 3f out: rdn and chsd (clr) wnr over 1f out: no imp fnl f* **33/1**
4- **3** 3½ **The Grey Warrior (IRE)**[152] 7329 3-9-5 0.............................. TomEaves 5 59
(Kevin Ryan) *led: drvn and hdd over 2f out: outpcd fr over 1f out* **5/4**[2]
5 **4** 5 **Play With Me**[23] 845 3-9-0 0.............................. ConnorBeasley 6 43
(Keith Dalgleish) *t.k.h: hld up in tch: stdy hdwy over 3f out: rdn over 2f out: sn wknd* **50/1**
0- **5** ½ **Zacchetto (USA)**[207] 5637 3-9-5 0.............................. PJMcDonald 4 47
(Mark Johnston) *t.k.h: chsd ldrs: outpcd 1/2-way: wknd over 2f out* **6/1**[3]
05 **6** 18 **R U Mine (IRE)**[6] 1102 3-8-7 0.............................. CharlotteMcFarland[(7)] 2
(Keith Dalgleish) *missed break: bhd: struggling over 3f out: sn lost tch* **100/1**
1m 39.51s (0.91) **Going Correction** +0.075s/f (Slow) 6 Ran SP% **110.1**
Speed ratings (Par 98): **98,92,88,83,83 65**
CSF £30.60 TOTE £1.90: £1.10, £11.40; EX 20.50 Trifecta £41.60.
**Owner** Mohammed Jaber **Bred** Rabbah Bloodstock Limited **Trained** Newmarket, Suffolk

**FOCUS**
Just an ordinary maiden, but run at a sound pace and they finished well strung out.

## 1199 32RED CASINO MAIDEN AUCTION FILLIES' STKS (PLUS 10 RACE) 7f 14y (Tp)
**6:50** (6:50) (Class 5) 3-Y-O **£2,911** (£866; £432; £216) **Stalls** Centre

Form RPR
1 **Aquamarina** 3-9-0 0 TomMarquand 3 76
(Robyn Brisland) *dwlt: sn trcking ldrs: led gng wl over 1f out: edgd rt and pushed out fnl f: comf* **7/2[2]**

2 2 3/4 **Acadian Angel (IRE)** 3-9-0 0 JasonHart 2 69
(John Quinn) *missed break: hld up in tch: pushed along and hdwy over 1f out: chsd wnr ins fnl f: kpt on: nt pce to chal* **8/1**

20-2 3 3 **Sulafah (IRE)**[12] 1003 3-8-11 72 (p) HollieDoyle(3) 5 60
(Simon West) *t.k.h: trckd ldr: effrt and ev ch over 1f out: outpcd ins fnl f* **7/2[2]**

0-44 4 shd **Mama Africa (IRE)**[42] 510 3-9-0 67 PhillipMakin 4 60
(David Barron) *led: rdn and hdd over 1f out: drvn and outpcd fnl f* **7/4[1]**

63- 5 1 1/2 **Eponina (IRE)**[117] 8009 3-9-0 0 GrahamLee 1 56
(Ben Haslam) *hld up in tch: rdn and outpcd over 2f out: sn btn* **13/2[3]**

1m 27.25s (1.05) **Going Correction** +0.075s/f (Slow) 5 Ran SP% **105.3**
Speed ratings (Par 95): **97,93,90,90,88**
CSF £25.56 TOTE £4.20: £2.20, £3.50; EX 23.00 Trifecta £122.60.
**Owner** Franconson Partners **Bred** Broughton Bloodstock **Trained** Newmarket, Suffolk

**FOCUS**
The two newcomers came to the fore here.

## 1200 MONEY BACK AT CHELTENHAM WITH BETWAY H'CAP 5f (Tp)
**7:20** (7:23) (Class 6) (0-65,65) 3-Y-O+ **£2,264** (£673; £336; £168) **Stalls** Centre

Form RPR
1642 1 **Windforpower (IRE)**[5] 1126 7-9-6 59 (p) BenCurtis 8 66
(Tracy Waggott) *hld up: rdn along 1/2-way: hdwy over 1f out: kpt on wl fnl f to ld cl home* **4/1[2]**

6-21 2 hd **Indian Pursuit (IRE)**[29] 732 4-9-10 63 JasonHart 5 69
(John Quinn) *chsd ldr: hdwy to ld over 1f out: sn rdn: kpt on fnl f: hdd cl home* **9/2[3]**

32-2 3 3/4 **Horsforth**[11] 1031 5-9-12 65 (b) ConnorBeasley 6 69
(Richard Guest) *hld up in tch: smooth hdwy over 2f out: shkn up and ev ch over 1f out to ins fnl f: one pce nr fin* **3/1[1]**

3065 4 nk **Socialites Red**[11] 1031 4-8-9 55 (p) RPWalsh(7) 2 58
(Scott Dixon) *trckd ldrs: effrt and drvn along 2f out: kpt on same pce fnl f* **20/1**

-003 5 1 1/2 **Entertaining Ben**[11] 1031 4-9-12 65 (p) TomEaves 3 62
(Iain Jardine) *led at decent gallop: rdn and hdd over 1f out: outpcd ins fnl f* **7/1**

510- 6 nk **Groundworker (IRE)**[107] 8137 6-9-10 63 (t) PaulMulrennan 1 59
(Paul Midgley) *plld hrd: hld up: shkn up and hdwy over 1f out: no imp fnl f* **12/1**

2-21 7 1 1/4 **Poetic Queen (IRE)**[16] 956 4-9-11 64 PhillipMakin 7 56
(Eric Alston) *hld up in tch: effrt and drvn wl over 1f out: sn no imp: btn fnl f* **6/1**

630/ 8 5 **Tabikat Elle (IRE)**[512] 7361 4-9-12 65 PaulHanagan 9 39
(Ollie Pears) *bhd: drvn and outpcd over 2f out: sn btn* **33/1**

006 9 1 1/4 **Jess**[11] 1030 4-8-9 55 (v[1]) SeamusCronin(7) 4 24
(Kevin Ryan) *hld up: drvn and struggling over 2f out: btn over 1f out* **25/1**

59.23s (-0.27) **Going Correction** +0.075s/f (Slow) 9 Ran SP% **109.2**
Speed ratings (Par 101): **105,104,103,103,100 100,98,90,88**
CSF £20.05 CT £54.17 TOTE £4.90: £1.90, £1.70, £1.20; EX 22.60 Trifecta £71.60.
**Owner** David Tate **Bred** Tally-Ho Stud **Trained** Spennymoor, Co Durham

**FOCUS**
A tight finish to this sprint handicap. The winner ran near the form of his recent start here.

## 1201 SUN BETS ON THE APP H'CAP 1m 5y (Tp)
**7:50** (7:50) (Class 5) (0-75,74) 4-Y-O+ **£2,911** (£866; £432; £216) **Stalls** Centre

Form RPR
4320 1 **Magic City (IRE)**[13] 984 8-9-2 72 (p) NathanEvans(3) 5 83
(Michael Easterby) *stdd in tch: effrt and pushed along over 2f out: led over 1f out: rdn clr fnl f* **15/8[1]**

-360 2 4 1/2 **Warfare**[26] 782 8-9-7 74 BarryMcHugh 4 75
(Tim Fitzgerald) *hld up: effrt and pushed along whn n.m.r briefly over 2f out: angled lft and hdwy over 1f out: chsd (clr) wnr wl ins fnl f: r.o* **15/2**

5560 3 hd **So It's War (FR)**[32] 685 6-8-13 66 (p) ConnorBeasley 2 66
(Keith Dalgleish) *t.k.h: cl up: led over 2f out to over 1f out: sn one pce: lost 2nd wl ins fnl f* **9/2[2]**

200- 4 3/4 **Thecornishbarron (IRE)**[138] 7671 5-9-6 73 StevieDonohoe 6 71
(John Ryan) *trckd ldrs: effrt and drvn along over 2f out: kpt on same pce fnl f* **12/1**

320- 5 9 **Al Hawraa**[180] 6541 4-8-12 65 KevinStott 3 43
(Kevin Ryan) *led at ordinary gallop: rdn and hdd over 2f out: wknd over 1f out* **7/1**

40-5 6 2 **Trinity Star (IRE)**[11] 1032 6-9-6 73 PaulMulrennan 1 46
(Michael Dods) *wnt lft s: tacked over to r on outside of gp after 2f: prom: rdn over 3f out: wknd over 2f out* **11/2[3]**

65-0 7 1 1/4 **Archipeligo**[14] 968 6-9-3 70 TomEaves 7 40
(Iain Jardine) *hld up: stdy hdwy over 3f out: rdn over 2f out: wknd over 1f out* **10/1**

1m 38.78s (0.18) **Going Correction** +0.075s/f (Slow) 7 Ran SP% **109.4**
Speed ratings (Par 103): **102,97,97,96,87 85,84**
CSF £14.97 TOTE £2.40: £1.70, £3.90; EX 15.30 Trifecta £49.00.
**Owner** A Turton, J Blackburn & Mrs L Folwell **Bred** Miss Annmarie Burke **Trained** Sheriff Hutton, N Yorks

**FOCUS**
A fair handicap and the winner brought to an end a lengthy barren spell. He has been rated back to last year's best.

## 1202 SUNBETS.CO.UK H'CAP 7f 14y (Tp)
**8:20** (8:20) (Class 4) (0-80,82) 4-Y-O+ **£4,690** (£1,395; £697; £348) **Stalls** Centre

Form RPR
3-51 1 **Inaam (IRE)**[26] 782 4-9-6 79 PaulHanagan 7 84
(Richard Fahey) *t.k.h: hld up in tch: rdn and hdwy over 1f out: led ins fnl f: kpt on wl* **7/2[2]**

124- 2 1/2 **Mutamid**[239] 4474 5-9-9 82 SeanLevey 3 86
(Ismail Mohammed) *cl up in chsng gp: effrt and edgd lft over 1f out: disp ld briefly ins fnl f: kpt on: hld nr fin* **5/2[1]**

-166 3 shd **Free Code (IRE)**[13] 989 6-9-9 82 PhillipMakin 1 86
(David Barron) *cl up in chsng gp: drvn and outpcd wl over 1f out: rallied ins fnl f: kpt on fin* **8/1**

103- 4 nk **Lawyer (IRE)**[131] 7796 6-9-8 81 BenCurtis 6 84
(David Barron) *hld up: stdy hdwy over 2f out: rdn and effrt over 1f out: kpt on ins fnl f* **8/1**

0-04 5 nk **Tadaawol**[14] 971 4-8-10 69 (p) PJMcDonald 4 71
(Roger Fell) *hld up: effrt and drvn along over 1f out: kpt on ins fnl f: nvr able to chal* **11/2[3]**

0043 6 1/2 **Plucky Dip**[21] 857 6-9-7 80 StevieDonohoe 5 81
(John Ryan) *hld up: effrt on far side of gp over 2f out: sn rdn: kpt on same pce fnl f* **6/1**

0-05 7 nk **Shamaheart (IRE)**[13] 989 7-9-5 78 (p) SamJames 8 78
(Geoffrey Harker) *dwlt: hld up: rdn and hdwy over 1f out: no imp fnl f* **12/1**

06-0 8 2 1/2 **Foresight (FR)**[33] 660 4-9-2 75 TomEaves 2 68
(Kevin Ryan) *t.k.h: led and sn clr: rdn over 1f out: hdd ins fnl f: sn wknd* **66/1**

1m 26.17s (-0.03) **Going Correction** +0.075s/f (Slow) **8** Ran SP% **111.9**
Speed ratings (Par 105): **103,102,102,101,101 101,100,97**
CSF £12.09 CT £62.30 TOTE £3.90: £1.60, £1.20, £2.50; EX 13.20 Trifecta £58.70.
**Owner** Yorkshire Connections Ltd **Bred** John Doyle **Trained** Musley Bank, N Yorks

**FOCUS**
This was run at a good gallop, Foresight soon having them well strung out, but they closed him down with a furlong to run and the rest of the field finished in a heap. Ordinary form.

## 1203 CHELTENHAM OFFERS AT BETWAY H'CAP 6f (Tp)
**8:50** (8:51) (Class 6) (0-65,67) 3-Y-O+ **£2,264** (£673; £336; £168) **Stalls** Centre

Form RPR
323- 1 **Epeius (IRE)**[92] 8346 4-9-12 62 GrahamLee 9 68
(Ben Haslam) *hld up: hdwy on nr side of gp to ld appr fnl f: rdn out* **8/1**

-211 2 1/2 **Spirit Of Zebedee (IRE)**[27] 768 4-10-2 66 (p) JasonHart 10 71
(John Quinn) *led on nr side of gp: rdn and hdd appr fnl f: rallied: kpt on: hld nr fin* **4/1[1]**

42-5 3 3/4 **Inshaa**[23] 843 5-9-11 66 CliffordLee(5) 4 68
(Michael Herrington) *taken early to post: prom on far side of gp: effrt and rdn wl over 1f out: kpt on ins fnl f* **5/1[3]**

44-1 4 shd **Ambitious Icarus**[11] 1031 8-10-0 64 (e) JFEgan 8 66
(Richard Guest) *taken early to post: t.k.h: hld up bhd ldng gp: rdn and effrt over 1f out: kpt on fnl f: nrst fin* **8/1**

3-41 5 hd **Ki Ki**[11] 1030 5-9-13 63 BenCurtis 7 64
(Bryan Smart) *w ldr: rdn over 1f out: no ex ins fnl f* **9/2[2]**

-413 6 3 1/2 **Lady Cristal (IRE)**[14] 972 3-9-3 67 (p) DougieCostello 6 54
(K R Burke) *cl up: drvn and ch over 1f out: wknd ins fnl f* **16/1**

2-15 7 3/4 **Table Manners**[14] 968 5-9-5 58 HollieDoyle(3) 3 47
(Wilf Storey) *taken early to post: bhd: outpcd 1/2-way: sme late hdwy: nvr rchd ldrs* **10/1**

525- 8 1 3/4 **Grecian King**[370] 885 4-9-13 63 (h[1]) PhillipMakin 2 46
(David Barron) *hld up: shkn up wl over 1f out: nvr rchd ldrs* **10/1**

00-0 9 1/2 **Gowanless**[12] 1006 4-9-0 50 (b) PaulMulrennan 5 32
(Michael Dods) *dwlt: hld up bhd ldng gp: stdy hdwy 2f out: rdn and wknd fnl f* **33/1**

2035 10 2 3/4 **Disclosure**[27] 768 6-9-8 58 ConnorBeasley 1 32
(Les Eyre) *wore hood in paddock: t.k.h: cl up on far side of gp tl rdn and wknd over 1f out* **8/1**

1m 12.75s (0.25) **Going Correction** +0.075s/f (Slow)
**WFA** 3 from 4yo+ 14lb **10** Ran SP% **115.2**
Speed ratings (Par 101): **101,100,99,99,98 94,93,90,90,86**
CSF £39.53 CT £181.18 TOTE £9.30: £3.10, £1.40, £2.40; EX 43.80 Trifecta £236.70.
**Owner** Trojan Horse Partnership/Carol Aldridge **Bred** Mrs Dolores Gleeson **Trained** Middleham Moor, N Yorks

**FOCUS**
A wide-open sprint handicap and straighforward form.
T/Plt: £27.10 to a £1 stake. Pool: £79,108.50 - 2,130.44 winning units T/Qpdt: £14.60 to a £1 stake. Pool: £7,626.45 - 384.81 winning units **Richard Young**

# 1182 SOUTHWELL (L-H)
Wednesday, March 15

**OFFICIAL GOING: Fibresand: standard**
Wind: Light across Weather: Fine & dry

## 1204 32RED.COM H'CAP 4f 214y(F)
**1:20** (1:21) (Class 6) (0-65,65) 3-Y-O **£2,587** (£770; £384; £192) **Stalls** Centre

Form RPR
-311 1 **Fiery Spice (IRE)**[14] 972 3-9-7 65 LukeMorris 4 73
(Robert Cowell) *cl up centre: slt ld over 3f out: rdn and edgd lft 1f out: drvn and hung lft to far rail ins fnl f: kpt on strly* **11/8[1]**

-154 2 2 **Scotch Myst**[19] 903 3-8-13 57 TonyHamilton 3 58
(Richard Fahey) *towards rr: sn rdn along and outpcd: hdwy 2f out: styd on strly fnl f: tk 2nd nr fin* **7/2[3]**

160 3 nk **Zandradee (IRE)**[26] 787 3-8-13 57 SilvestreDeSousa 1 58
(David Barron) *cl up: effrt to dispute ld 2f out and sn rdn: drvn whn carried sltly lft and swtchd rt ins fnl f: kpt on same pce* **11/4[2]**

4001 4 5 **Little Nosegay (IRE)**[16] 960 3-8-10 54 JFEgan 5 36
(David Evans) *racd towards stands side: cl up: rdn along wl over 2f out: sn drvn and wkng whn n.m.r and swtchd lft over 1f out* **12/1**

-400 5 2 **Highly Focussed (IRE)**[26] 787 3-8-13 57 GrahamLee 2 32
(Ann Duffield) *towards rr: rdn along 1/2-way: n.d* **12/1**

330- 6 1 1/2 **Lady Molly (IRE)**[134] 7748 3-9-7 65 ConnorBeasley 7 34
(Keith Dalgleish) *slt ld: hdd over 3f out: rdn along 1/2-way: wknd fnl 2f* **16/1**

0-40 7 nk **Mesmeric Moment**[33] 667 3-7-13 50 (v[1]) RPWalsh(7) 6 18
(Shaun Harris) *dwlt and wnt rt s: hdwy towards stands rail and sn cl up: rdn along over 2f out: sn drvn: edgd lft and wknd* **50/1**

58.72s (-0.98) **Going Correction** -0.05s/f (Stan) 7 Ran SP% **114.2**
Speed ratings (Par 96): **105,101,101,93,90 87,87**
CSF £6.49 TOTE £1.90: £1.10, £2.00; EX 5.80 Trifecta £16.70.
**Owner** Khalifa Dasmal **Bred** K A Dasmal **Trained** Six Mile Bottom, Cambs

**FOCUS**
A moderate 3yo sprint handicap, but another step forward from the improving winner.

## 1205 SUNBETS.CO.UK MAIDEN STKS — 7f 14y(F)
1:55 (1:56) (Class 5) 3-Y-O+ £3,234 (£962; £481; £240) Stalls Low

Form RPR
2 **1** **Clock Chimes**[6] 1111 3-8-12 0 ........ TedDurcan 8 73
(David Brown) *cl up: led wl over 2f out: rdn over 1f out: styd on strly fnl f* 7/4[1]
532 **2** 2 ¼ **Invincible Man (IRE)**[26] 785 3-8-12 71 ........ LukeMorris 2 67
(James Tate) *trckd ldrs on inner: hdwy 3f out: chsd wnr 2f out: sn rdn to chal and ev ch tl drvn and kpt on same pce fnl f* 5/2[2]
00-4 **3** ½ **It's How We Roll (IRE)**[20] 875 3-8-12 65 ........(b) GrahamLee 4 66
(Charles Hills) *hmpd after 150 yds: trckd ldrs: hdwy over 2f out: rdn to chse ldng pair over 1f out: sn drvn and kpt on* 4/1[3]
**4** 2 ½ **Deep Challenger (IRE)**[317] 1942 5-10-0 0 ........ FergusSweeney 6 65
(Jamie Osborne) *in tch: hdwy over 2f out: rdn to chse ldrs and n.m.r whn swtchd lft jst over 1f out : sn drvn and kpt on* 11/2
0 **5** 1 ½ **Seeking Attention (USA)**[56] 283 3-8-7 0 ........ OisinMurphy 9 50
(George Scott) *dwlt: sn in tch on outer: pushed along and green 1/2-way: hdwy over 2f out: sn rdn and no imp* 18/1
660- **6** 2 **Ejabah (IRE)**[105] 8159 3-8-7 63 ........ JoeyHaynes 11 45
(Charles Smith) *prom: rdn along over 2f out: sn drvn and grad wknd* 50/1
6-4 **7** 5 **Huddersfilly Town**[13] 983 3-8-7 0 ........ SilvestreDeSousa 7 31
(Ivan Furtado) *led and wnt lft sn after s: pushed along over 3f out: rdn and hdd wl over 2f out: sn drvn and wknd over 1f out* 33/1
00- **8** 23 **Momentori**[285] 2861 4-9-9 0 ........ KieranO'Neill 3
(Scott Dixon) *hmpd after 150 yds: sn outpcd and bhd* 100/1
56 **9** 1 **Mount Cleshar**[16] 959 3-8-12 0 ........ StevieDonohoe 1
(John Butler) *sn outpcd and a bhd* 100/1
6-0 **10** 1 ¼ **House Of Frauds (IRE)**[54] 331 9-9-11 0 ........ TimClark(3) 5
(Tony Newcombe) *dwlt: a outpcd and bhd* 150/1

1m 29.35s (-0.95) **Going Correction** -0.05s/f (Stan)
**WFA** 3 from 4yo+ 16lb **10** Ran SP% **113.1**
Speed ratings (Par 103): **103,100,99,97,95 93,87,61,59,58**
CSF £5.96 TOTE £2.40: £1.10, £1.30, £1.80; EX 6.30 Trifecta £15.10.
**Owner** J C Fretwell **Bred** Whitsbury Manor Stud & A W M Christie-Miller **Trained** Averham Park, Notts
■ Stewards' Enquiry : Silvestre De Sousa two day ban (29-30 March) - guilty of careless riding

**FOCUS**
Not as competitive as the numbers would suggest, but a couple of interesting types and the market principals dominated. The winner stepped up from his recent debut.

## 1206 MONEY BACK AT CHELTENHAM WITH BETWAY (S) STKS — 4f 214y(F)
2:35 (2:35) (Class 6) 3-Y-O+ £2,587 (£770; £384) Stalls Centre

Form RPR
2-21 **1** **Piazon**[33] 665 6-9-7 77 ........(be) JoshuaBryan(7) 2 66+
(John Butler) *trckd ldr: smooth hdwy to ld 11/2f out: pushed clr and edgd lft ins fnl f: easily* 1/4[1]
6633 **2** 1 ¼ **Red Flute**[1] 1184 5-9-8 47 ........(v) TimClark(3) 1 52
(Denis Quinn) *led: rdn along and hdd 112/2f out: drvn and kpt on fnl f: no ch w wnr* 20/1[3]
6504 **3** 6 **Head Space (IRE)**[7] 1087 9-9-8 65 ........ RobertWinston 3 27+
(David Evans) *rr and sn pushed along: rdn along and outpcd over 3f out: a bhd* 7/2[2]

59.74s (0.04) **Going Correction** -0.05s/f (Stan) **3** Ran SP% **107.0**
Speed ratings (Par 101): **97,95,85**
CSF £5.29 TOTE £1.20; EX 4.00 Trifecta £4.10.The winner was bought-in for 6,250 guineas.
**Owner** Royale Racing Syndicate **Bred** Peter Baldwin **Trained** Newmarket, Suffolk

**FOCUS**
A most uncompetitive three-runner seller and straightforward for the hot favourite.

## 1207 BET ON THE FESTIVAL WITH BETWAY H'CAP — 1m 6f 21y(F)
3:15 (3:18) (Class 5) (0-70,71) 4-Y-O+ £3,234 (£962; £481; £240) Stalls Low

Form RPR
-223 **1** **Brigadoon**[16] 958 10-9-13 71 ........ SilvestreDeSousa 3 83+
(Michael Appleby) *trckd ldr: led after 3f: rdn clr over 2f out: unchal* 6/1
313- **2** 10 **Denmead**[176] 6659 4-9-7 69 ........ RobertWinston 7 64
(John Butler) *hld up: hdwy over 6f out: trckd ldrs 4f out: rdn along 3f out: chsd wnr over 1f out: no imp* 11/4[2]
64-4 **3** 3 **Virnon**[9] 666 6-9-13 71 ........ JoeFanning 4 62
(Alan Swinbank) *trckd ldrs: effrt over 3f out: rdn wl over 2f out: sn drvn and plugged on same pce* 8/1
-330 **4** 1 **Thackeray**[36] 610 10-8-0 51 oh5 ........ PaulaMuir(7) 8 40
(Chris Fairhurst) *dwlt and rr: hdwy on inner wl over 3f out: sn chsd ldrs and rdn: drvn and plugged on same pce fnl 2f* 33/1
00-0 **5** 1 ¼ **Bushel (USA)**[25] 806 7-9-2 60 ........ MartinDwyer 5 48
(Tony Newcombe) *prom: chsd wnr after 3f: rdn along 3f out: drvn 2f out: grad wknd* 18/1
41/5 **6** 5 **La Estrella (USA)**[33] 666 14-9-12 70 ........ GrahamLee 10 51
(Don Cantillon) *hld up in tch: pushed along over 4f out: rdn over 3f out: sn outpcd* 5/1[3]
00-3 **7** ½ **Monzino (USA)**[6] 1108 9-8-4 51 oh4 ........ NoelGarbutt(3) 6 31
(Michael Chapman) *chsd ldrs: pushed along 1/2-way: sn lost pl and bhd* 80/1
5500 **8** 12 **Barnacle**[7] 1081 8-8-0 51 oh6 ........(bt) RPWalsh(7) 9 14
(Emma Owen) *dwlt: a rr: bhd fnl 4f* 50/1
**9** 17 **Bibliotheca (JPN)**[171] 6818 4-9-6 68 ........ JFEgan 2 7
(W P Browne, Ire) *prom on inner: pushed along over 5f out: rdn along over 4f out: sn lost pl and bhd whn eased wl over 2f out* 2/1[1]

3m 6.58s (-1.72) **Going Correction** -0.05s/f (Stan)
**WFA** 4 from 6yo+ 2lb **9** Ran SP% **113.5**
Speed ratings (Par 103): **102,96,94,94,93 90,90,83,73**
CSF £22.30 CT £131.92 TOTE £6.80: £1.70, £1.70, £2.10; EX 23.20 Trifecta £98.20.
**Owner** Nick Hoare **Bred** Biddestone Stud **Trained** Oakham, Rutland

**FOCUS**
An ordinary staying handicap and not a convincing field, but the winner took it apart.

## 1208 SUN BETS ON THE APP STORE H'CAP — 7f 14y(F)
3:55 (3:55) (Class 3) (0-95,92) 4-Y-O+
£7,470 (£2,236; £1,118; £559; £279; £140) Stalls Low

Form RPR
20-6 **1** **George Cinq**[37] 598 7-9-5 90 ........ OisinMurphy 1 99
(George Scott) *qckly away: mde all: rdn over 1f out: kpt on strly towards fin* 8/1
-001 **2** 1 ½ **Outer Space**[27] 760 6-9-7 92 ........ TimmyMurphy 4 97
(Jamie Osborne) *trckd ldrs: hdwy 2f out: rdn to chse wnr ins fnl f: sn drvn: no imp towards fin* 15/2
6201 **3** nse **Showboating (IRE)**[8] 1074 9-9-1 86 6ex ........ DanielTudhope 3 91
(John Balding) *hld up: hdwy over 2f out: chsd ldrs and swtchd rt to outer over 1f out: sn rdn and kpt on wl fnl f* 3/1[1]
5-02 **4** 1 ¾ **Special Season**[17] 953 4-9-3 88 ........ FergusSweeney 8 88
(Jamie Osborne) *cl up: rdn to chal over 2f out: drvn over 1f out: kpt on same pce* 9/2[2]
-460 **5** 1 ¼ **Kingston Kurrajong**[18] 918 4-9-3 88 ........ AdamBeschizza 2 85
(Michael Attwater) *trckd ldng pair on inner: hdwy 3f out: rdn along over 2f out: sn drvn and wknd over 1f out* 16/1
310- **6** 7 **Bahama Moon (IRE)**[141] 7594 5-9-3 88 ........ SilvestreDeSousa 7 66
(David Barron) *chsd ldrs: rdn along over 3f out: outpcd fnl 2f* 3/1[1]
612- **7** ½ **Bertiewhittle**[130] 7821 9-9-3 88 ........ JoeFanning 5 64
(David Barron) *a towards rr: rdn along 3f out: sn outpcd* 6/1[3]

1m 28.16s (-2.14) **Going Correction** -0.05s/f (Stan) **7** Ran SP% **111.2**
Speed ratings (Par 107): **110,108,108,106,104 96,96**
CSF £61.05 CT £214.13 TOTE £7.70: £4.10, £3.50; EX 26.70 Trifecta £191.80.
**Owner** Breen, Humphreys & Randle **Bred** Oakhill Stud **Trained** Newmarket, Suffolk

**FOCUS**
A decent handicap, though five of the seven runners were making their Fibresand debut including the first two. This looks solid form.

## 1209 CHELTENHAM OFFERS AT BETWAY H'CAP — 6f 16y(F)
4:35 (4:36) (Class 6) (0-60,66) 4-Y-O+ £2,587 (£770; £384; £192) Stalls Low

Form RPR
0-01 **1** **Viva Verglas (IRE)**[8] 1076 6-9-13 66 6ex ........ LukeMorris 4 73
(Daniel Mark Loughnane) *trckd ldrs: hdwy wl over 2f out: rdn over 1f out: led jst ins fnl f: drvn out* 9/4[1]
2540 **2** 1 **Cadeaux Pearl**[8] 1076 9-8-7 46 oh1 ........(b) KieranO'Neill 3 50
(Scott Dixon) *slt ld: rdn along 2f out: drvn over 1f out: hdd ins fnl f: kpt on* 9/1
6153 **3** nk **Fortinbrass (IRE)**[8] 1076 7-9-2 62 ........ JoshuaBryan(7) 6 65
(John Balding) *cl up towards outer: wd st: rdn 2f out: drvn and kpt on fnl f* 11/4[2]
005- **4** 2 ¼ **Clergyman**[167] 6910 5-9-1 54 ........ DanielTudhope 7 50
(Rebecca Bastiman) *in tch: hdwy on outer and wd st: cl up 2f out: sn rdn and kpt on one pce fnl f* 10/3[3]
0002 **5** 1 **Spowarticus**[6] 1112 8-9-0 53 ........(v) DaleSwift 5 46
(Scott Dixon) *cl up: disp ld over 2f out and sn rdn: drvn over 1f out: wknd appr fnl f* 8/1
4000 **6** 2 ½ **Misu Moneypenny**[8] 1071 4-9-8 61 ........ NickyMackay 1 47
(Scott Dixon) *trckd ldrs on inner: hdwy and cl up over 2f out: sn rdn: drvn and wknd over 1f out* 16/1
360- **7** 1 **Hab Reeh**[160] 7092 9-8-13 52 ........(p) JamesSullivan 2 35
(Ruth Carr) *a rr* 28/1

1m 16.5s **Going Correction** -0.05s/f (Stan) **7** Ran SP% **111.0**
Speed ratings (Par 101): **98,96,96,93,91 88,87**
CSF £21.61 CT £54.16 TOTE £3.00: £1.60, £4.20; EX 20.30 Trifecta £84.00.
**Owner** Mrs C Loughnane **Bred** Mrs Mary Coonan **Trained** Rock, Worcs

**FOCUS**
A moderate sprint handicap in which four of the seven runners met over C&D eight days earlier including the first three here. The whole field were in a line across the track coming to the last furlong. Straightforward form rated around the places horses.

## 1210 SUNBETS.CO.UK H'CAP — 1m 13y(F)
5:15 (5:15) (Class 5) (0-70,70) 4-Y-O+ £3,234 (£962; £481; £240) Stalls Low

Form RPR
3032 **1** **Glorious Asset**[9] 1067 5-8-9 58 ........ SilvestreDeSousa 2 66
(Ivan Furtado) *slt ld: rdn over 2f out: drvn and hdd over 1f out: rallied u.p ins fnl f to ld again last 75 yds* 2/1[1]
6-05 **2** nk **Order Of Service**[28] 745 7-8-13 68 ow1 ........(e[1]) AidenBlakemore(7) 1 76
(Shaun Harris) *in tch: hdwy over 3f out: chsd ldrs 2f out: sn chal: rdn to ld over 1f out: hdd and no ex last 75 yds* 20/1
44-2 **3** 6 **Royal Holiday (IRE)**[48] 419 10-9-6 69 ........(p) RobertWinston 3 62
(Marjorie Fife) *cl up: rdn along over 2f out: drvn wl over 1f out and kpt on same pce* 7/2[3]
3633 **4** 3 **Jubilee Brig**[14] 968 7-9-7 70 ........ JoeFanning 4 56
(Alan Swinbank) *prom: rdn along 3f out: sn drvn and outpcd* 9/2
5314 **5** ½ **What Usain**[18] 928 5-9-2 68 ........(p) AlistairRawlinson(3) 8 53
(Michael Appleby) *s.i.s and lost several l s: bhd and rdn along 1/2-way: hdwy over 2f out: styd on: n.d* 5/2[2]
-000 **6** 1 **Silhuette (IRE)**[11] 1030 4-8-11 60 ........(p) JamesSullivan 5 43
(Colin Teague) *trckd ldng pair on inner: pushed along 3f out: rdn over 2f out: sn wknd* 100/1
0-00 **7** 30 **Torch**[27] 769 4-9-2 65 ........ TimmyMurphy 6
(John Butler) *dwlt: a bhd* 33/1

1m 42.55s (-1.18) **Going Correction** -0.05s/f (Stan) **7** Ran SP% **111.0**
Speed ratings (Par 103): **103,102,96,93,93 92,62**
CSF £37.27 CT £126.80 TOTE £2.70: £1.50, £7.70; EX 26.30 Trifecta £218.70.
**Owner** The Giggle Factor Partnership **Bred** Minehart Developments Ltd **Trained** Wiseton, Nottinghamshire

**FOCUS**
An ordinary handicap, but the pace was solid. A small step up from the winner on recent form.
T/Plt: £19.70 to a £1 stake. Pool: £52,643.70 - 1,949.30 winning units T/Qpdt: £11.10 to a £1 stake. Pool: £2,785.49 - 185.40 winning units **Joe Rowntree**

1211 - 1218a (Foreign Racing) - See Raceform Interactive

# [1175] CHELMSFORD (A.W) (L-H)
Thursday, March 16

**OFFICIAL GOING: Polytrack: standard**
Wind: light, half against Weather: dry

## 1219 TOTEPOOL PLACE YOUR BETS AT CHELTENHAM AMATEUR RIDERS' H'CAP — 6f (P)
5:45 (5:49) (Class 5) (0-75,72) 4-Y-O+ £4,991 (£1,548; £773; £387) Stalls Centre

Form RPR
2411 **1** **Athassel**[8] 1080 8-10-13 72 12ex ........ MrJFlook(5) 6 78
(David Evans) *midfield: rdn over 2f out: hdwy u.p ins fnl f: styd on wl u.p ins fnl f: led last strides* 7/2[2]
1026 **2** hd **Beau Mistral (IRE)**[10] 1066 8-10-3 64 ........ MrGGilbertson(7) 4 69
(Tony Carroll) *chsd ldng pair: nudged along and clsd jst over 1f out: chal 100yds out: stl nudged along and led towards fin: hdd last strides* 5/1


The Form Book Flat, Raceform Ltd, Newbury, RG14 5SJ

0051 **3** *hd* **Space War**[26] 815 10-10-12 **66**.............................(t) MissJoannaMason 1 70
(Michael Easterby) *midfield: rdn and hdwy over 1f out: styd on to ld 75yds: sn hdd and no ex cl home* **2/1**[1]

000- **4** *¾* **Knight Of The Air**[135] 7732 5-10-4 **65**......................... MrsCPownall(7) 9 67
(Joseph Tuite) *chsd ldr: pushed along over 1f out: clsd 1f out: ev ch 100yds out: no ex and out pced towards fin* **20/1**

3040 **5** *nk* **Ebony N Ivory**[17] 955 4-11-0 **68**.......................................(p) MrSWalker 8 69
(Archie Watson) *led: wnt clr 1/2-way: rdn over 1f out: drvn and tired ins fnl f: hdd 75yds out: wknd towards fin* **4/1**[3]

-421 **6** *2¼* **Commanche**[24] 843 8-10-6 **67**...................................(p) MissEBushe(7) 7 62
(Chris Dwyer) *midfield: wd and rdn 2f out: kpt on same pce ins fnl f* **5/1**

100- **7** *1½* **Frangarry (IRE)**[134] 7774 5-9-12 **57**.............................(b) MissJCooley(5) 5 47
(Alan Bailey) *s.i.s: off the pce in lat pair: effrt and edgd lft over 1f out: no imp and kpt on same pce ins fnl f* **16/1**

0000 **8** *4½* **Catalyze**[35] 644 9-9-12 **57** oh9 ow3.............................. MissMBryant(5) 3 34
(Paddy Butler) *rdr struggling to remover hood and slowly away: a bhd* **66/1**

1m 12.41s (-1.29) **Going Correction** -0.15s/f (Stan) **8** Ran SP% **121.0**
Speed ratings (Par 103): **102,101,101,100,100 97,95,89**
CSF £22.84 CT £45.13 TOTE £3.60: £1.30, £1.90, £1.40; EX 19.70 Trifecta £72.40.
**Owner** Mrs E Evans **Bred** Moyns Park Estate And Stud Ltd **Trained** Pandy, Monmouths

**FOCUS**
Ebony N Ivory went off a bit too quick and didn't quite get home. Four of the closers had their chance with half a furlong to run and there was a blanket finish. The winner just keeps finding more.

## 1220 TOTEPOOL BETTING ON ALL UK RACING H'CAP (DIV I) 5f (P)
**6:15** (6:17) (Class 6) (0-55,57) 3-Y-O+ **£3,234** (£962; £481; £240) **Stalls** Low

Form RPR

0-00 **1** *1½* **Culloden**[23] 852 5-9-1 **54**........................................... CharlieBennett(5) 4 60
(Shaun Harris) *chsd ldng trio: effrt ent fnl 2f: rdn to chse clr wnr 1f out: kpt on but nvr getting to wnr: fin 2nd: plcd 1st* **8/1**

0-06 **2** *1* **Hurricane Alert**[21] 874 5-8-12 **46** oh1......................... AdamBeschizza 9 43
(Mark Hoad) *taken down early: dwlt and short of room leaving stalls: hdwy u.p over 1f out: kpt on to go 3rd wl ins fnl f: no threat to wnr: fin 3rd plcd 2nd* **40/1**

1222 **3** *nk* **Fabulous Flyer**[12] 1022 4-8-11 **50**.............................. DavidParkes(5) 10 46
(Jeremy Gask) *hld up in midfield on outer: clsng whn nt clr run and swtchd rt over 1f out: kpt on u.p ins fnl f: no threat to wnr: fin 4th plcd 3rd* **9/2**[3]

-000 **4** *nk* **Zebelini (IRE)**[56] 311 5-8-12 **46** oh1..............................(p) MartinLane 3 41
(Roy Bowring) *chsd ldrs: rdn ent fnl 2f: styd on same pce ins fnl f: fin 5th plcd 4th* **14/1**

300- **5** *¾* **Andalusite**[125] 7913 4-9-7 **55**............................................... LukeMorris 8 47
(John Gallagher) *rousted along early: t.k.h after 1f and hld up in tch in midfield: shkn up over 1f out: rdn and kpt on same pce ins fnl f: fin 6th plcd 5th* **14/1**

0-06 **6** *1¾* **Cytringan**[62] 217 4-8-9 **46** oh1...................................... SimonPearce(3) 1 32
(Lydia Pearce) *unruly and eventually led rdrless to post: wnt rt s: in tch in midfield: effrt u.p over 1f out: no imp ins fnl f: fin 7th plcd 6th* **20/1**

2-00 **7** *1* **Warba (IRE)**[26] 813 3-8-4 **57**..........................................(t) DavidEgan(7) 5 34
(Mohamed Moubarak) *bustled along leaving stalls: midfield: hung rt 3f out: outpcd u.p over 1f out: wl hld and kpt on same pce ins fnl f: fin 8th plcd 7th* **5/1**

-000 **8** *2¼* **Yisty**[13] 1006 4-8-12 **46** oh1.............................................(v) TonyHamilton 2 20
(Derek Shaw) *s.i.s: a bhd: fin 9th plcd 8th* **25/1**

0014 **9** *1* **Little Nosegay (IRE)**[1] 1204 3-8-8 **54**.................................. JFEgan 6 27
(David Evans) *sn bustled along to ld: rdn and hdd over 1f out: lost 2nd 1f out: sn btn and eased ins fnl f: fin 10th plcd 9th* **7/2**[2]

0123 **D** **Mighty Zip (USA)**[3] 1180 5-8-7 **54**................................(p) JordanUys(7) 7 53
(Lisa Williamson) *chsd ldr: rdn to ld over 1f out: clr 1f out: edgd lft and kpt on ins fnl f: rdn out: fin 1st: disqualified - rdr weighed in 6lb light* **5/2**[1]

59.2s (-1.00) **Going Correction** -0.15s/f (Stan)
**WFA** 3 from 4yo+ 12lb **10** Ran SP% **121.1**
Speed ratings (Par 101): **99,98,97,97,95 93,91,87,86,102**
CSF £296.93 CT £1667.90 TOTE £10.90: £2.60, £7.80, £1.90; EX 437.80 Trifecta £2990.60.
**Owner** Burflex (Scaffolding) Ltd **Bred** Burton Agnes Stud Co Ltd **Trained** Carburton, Notts

**FOCUS**
The first division of an ordinary sprint handicap, but a controversial outcome.

## 1221 TOTEPOOL BETTING ON ALL UK RACING H'CAP (DIV II) 5f (P)
**6:45** (6:54) (Class 6) (0-55,56) 3-Y-O+ **£3,234** (£962; £481; £240) **Stalls** Low

Form RPR

6020 **1** **Dashing Poet**[26] 813 3-8-10 **56**.......................................(h) MartinLane 1 62
(Jeremy Gask) *hld up wl in tch in midfield: effrt on inner over 1f out: rdn to ld 1f out: sn pushed clr and r.o wl: comf* **11/4**[2]

00-0 **2** *2½* **Bubbly Bailey**[66] 143 7-8-12 **46**............................(v) SilvestreDeSousa 4 48
(J R Jenkins) *chsd ldr tl led over 1f out: sn hung rt and hdd: kpt on same pce u.p ins fnl f* **12/1**

1046 **3** *nse* **Lady Bacchus**[13] 1006 4-9-6 **54**.......................................(b) ShaneKelly 2 57
(Richard Guest) *taken down early: in tch: clsd to chse ldrs whn squeezed for room and hmpd over 1f out: kpt on u.p ins fnl f and pressing for 2nd towards fin: no ch w wnr* **9/2**[3]

0210 **4** *1¼* **Swendab (IRE)**[31] 722 9-9-7 **55**................................(b) TimmyMurphy 6 52
(John O'Shea) *rousted along leaving stalls: sn prom: rdn over 1f out: unable qck: wl hld and kpt on same pce ins fnl f* **9/2**[3]

0-00 **5** *3½* **Warm Order**[31] 723 6-8-12 **46** oh1..........................(b) GeorgeDowning 3 31
(Tony Carroll) *hld up in rr of main gp: swtchd lft and effrt over 1f out: sn no imp: wknd ins fnl f* **20/1**

3422 **6** *1¾* **Celerity (IRE)**[6] 1127 3-8-5 **51**................................................(b) JFEgan 9 24
(David Evans) *wd in midfield: rdn 1/2-way: outpcd wl over 1f out: n.d after* **5/2**[1]

5-00 **7** *1¼* **Rat Catcher (IRE)**[20] 899 7-8-5 **46** oh1.......................(b) JordanUys(7) 7 20
(Lisa Williamson) *half rrd as stalls opened and slowly away: a bhd* **20/1**

-400 **8** *nse* **Name That Toon**[13] 1006 4-8-12 **46** oh1.......................(v) TonyHamilton 5 21
(Derek Shaw) *led tl hdd over 1f out: losing pl whn hmpd jst over 1f out: bhd after* **14/1**

-550 **9** *½* **Rojina (IRE)**[29] 743 4-8-5 **46** oh1..................................(b) DavidEgan(7) 8 18
(Lisa Williamson) *sn rousted along: chsd ldrs tl 1/2-way: lost pl 2f out: wknd over 1f out* **25/1**

58.77s (-1.43) **Going Correction** -0.15s/f (Stan)
**WFA** 3 from 4yo+ 12lb **9** Ran SP% **119.3**
Speed ratings (Par 101): **105,101,100,98,93 90,88,88,87**
CSF £35.38 CT £148.18 TOTE £4.40: £1.70, £2.60, £1.60; EX 44.50 Trifecta £244.10.
**Owner** The Dashing Poets **Bred** Qatar Bloodstock Ltd **Trained** Stockbridge, Hants

**FOCUS**
This was run in a time 0.43sec faster than that taken by the disqualified winner of the first division. The race has been rated around the placed horses.

## 1222 @TOTEPOOLRACING WIN TICKETS ON TWITTER H'CAP 5f (P)
**7:15** (7:20) (Class 3) (0-95,94) 4-Y-O+ **£9,703** (£2,887; £1,443; £721) **Stalls** Low

Form RPR

5-20 **1** **Doctor Sardonicus**[26] 818 6-9-7 **94**................................ MartinHarley 8 102
(David Simcock) *chsd ldrs: effrt over 1f out: rdn to ld ins fnl f: sn in command and r.o wl: comf* **4/1**[2]

000- **2** *1½* **Stepper Point**[178] 6633 8-9-0 **87**...................................(p) MartinDwyer 11 90
(William Muir) *hld up in midfield: swtchd rt and effrt over 1f out: hdwy u.p 1f out: styd on wl to go 2nd and edgd lft cl home: nvr getting to wnr* **14/1**

5-51 **3** *½* **Just Us Two (IRE)**[14] 995 5-8-11 **84**..............................(p) LukeMorris 2 85
(Robert Cowell) *chsd ldrs: swtchd rt over 1f out: drvn to chse clr wnr 100yds out: kpt on same pce after: lost 2nd cl home* **5/1**[3]

1426 **4** *½* **Monumental Man**[12] 1025 8-8-11 **84**..........................(p) WilliamCarson 9 83
(Michael Attwater) *in tch in midfield: effrt over 1f out: drvn and kpt on ins fnl f: nvr enough pce to threaten wnr* **25/1**

4205 **5** *nse* **Dynamo Walt (IRE)**[12] 1025 6-8-11 **84**.......................(v) TonyHamilton 7 83
(Derek Shaw) *hld up in tch in last trio: swtchd rt and effrt over 1f out: hdwy ins fnl f: styd on wl towards fin: nvr trbld ldrs* **12/1**

460 **6** *1* **Bosham**[17] 957 7-9-0 **90**.........................................(bt) NathanEvans(3) 6 85
(Michael Easterby) *taken down early: w ldr: rdn over 1f out: unable qck w wnr ins fnl f: wknd towards fin* **5/1**[3]

-406 **7** *½* **Silvanus (IRE)**[36] 618 12-8-9 **82**......................................... CamHardie 3 75
(Paul Midgley) *led: rdn over 1f out: hdd and no ex ins fnl f: wknd wl ins fnl f* **50/1**

-601 **8** *1¼* **Top Boy**[36] 618 7-8-11 **84**..................................................(v) MartinLane 5 73
(Derek Shaw) *t.k.h: hld up in tch in midfield: effrt over 1f out: unable qck u.p and wknd ins fnl f* **10/1**

3022 **9** *½* **Upavon**[5] 1152 7-8-13 **89**.............................................(bt) AaronJones(3) 4 76
(Stuart Williams) *rrd as stalls opened and s.i.s: in tch in last pair: effrt on inner over 1f out: no real imp: nvr trbld ldrs* **10/3**[1]

-032 **10** *3¼* **Foxy Forever (IRE)**[48] 443 7-8-8 **81**...........................(t) RyanPowell 10 56
(Michael Wigham) *s.i.s: a bhd* **20/1**

000- **11** *hd* **Brother Tiger**[115] 8050 8-9-0 **87**................................................ JFEgan 1 62
(David C Griffiths) *taken down early: hld up in tch in midfield: effrt over 1f out: no imp and sn btn: eased ins fnl f* **8/1**

58.08s (-2.12) **Going Correction** -0.15s/f (Stan) **11** Ran SP% **121.5**
Speed ratings (Par 107): **110,107,106,106,105 104,103,101,100,95 95**
CSF £59.50 CT £298.02 TOTE £5.00: £1.90, £4.40, £2.20; EX 77.00 Trifecta £547.70.
**Owner** Charles Wentworth **Bred** D M James **Trained** Newmarket, Suffolk

**FOCUS**
A decent sprint handicap with the winner rated to his recent best.

## 1223 TOTEPOOL RACECOURSE DEBIT CARD BETTING AVAILABLE H'CAP 2m (P)
**7:45** (7:49) (Class 4) (0-85,80) 4-Y-O+ **£6,469** (£1,925; £962; £481) **Stalls** Low

Form RPR

-123 **1** **Aldreth**[13] 1002 6-9-7 **80**................................................(p) NathanEvans(3) 2 88
(Michael Easterby) *chsd ldr: clsd and trcking ldng pair 6f out: nt clr run jst over 2f out: swtchd lft and effrt jst over 1f out: rdn and qcknd to ld ins fnl f: r.o wl and gng away at fin* **6/4**[1]

-216 **2** *2* **Bracken Brae**[3] 1175 5-9-2 **72**......................................... StevieDonohoe 3 77
(Mark H Tompkins) *chsd ldrs tl clsd to press ldr 6f out: rdn to ld 2f out: drvn ent fnl f: hdd ins fnl f: kpt on same pce after* **5/2**[2]

00-0 **3** *1¾* **Glan Y Gors (IRE)**[28] 759 5-9-10 **80**.............................(h) MartinHarley 7 83
(David Simcock) *stdd s: hld up in rr: clsd and wl in tch 4f out: rdn to chse ldr over 1f out: 3rd and styd on same pce fnl f* **4/1**[3]

145- **4** *5* **Ruler Of The Nile**[13] 1296 5-9-4 **74**................................(t[1]) LukeMorris 5 71
(Robert Stephens) *midfield: rdn over 3f out: outpcd u.p over 1f out: wl hld and plugged on same pce fnl f* **14/1**

2-32 **5** *nk* **Katie Gale**[9] 1073 7-9-3 **73**................................................ ShaneKelly 6 69
(Michael Appleby) *led: rdn and hdd 2f out: sn outpcd: wknd and edgd rt ins fnl f* **7/1**

04-6 **6** *½* **Winter Spice (IRE)**[58] 280 6-9-5 **75**.............................(h[1]) PatCosgrave 1 71
(Sam Thomas) *hld up in last pair: rdn 3f out: sn struggling: wl hld and plugged on same pce fr over 1f out* **20/1**

3m 29.09s (-0.91) **Going Correction** -0.15s/f (Stan)
**WFA** 4 from 5yo+ 3lb **6** Ran SP% **112.5**
Speed ratings (Par 105): **96,95,94,91,91 91**
CSF £5.49 CT £11.01 TOTE £2.40: £2.90, £1.20; EX 5.30 Trifecta £11.50.
**Owner** A Morse **Bred** Equine Breeding Limited **Trained** Sheriff Hutton, N Yorks

**FOCUS**
A fair staying contest rated around the first two.

## 1224 TOTEPOOL LIVE INFO DOWNLOAD THE APP H'CAP 1m (P)
**8:15** (8:18) (Class 4) (0-80,82) 4-Y-O+ **£6,469** (£1,925; £962; £481) **Stalls** Low

Form RPR

0-01 **1** **Welliesinthewater (IRE)**[14] 984 7-9-7 **79**.....................(v) MartinLane 1 86
(Derek Shaw) *hld up in rr: effrt 2f out: hdwy u.p over 1f out: r.o wl to ld wl ins fnl f: pushed out towards fin* **10/3**[1]

45-4 **2** *¾* **Mr Red Clubs (IRE)**[10] 1065 8-8-7 **72**.........................(p) JaneElliott(7) 3 77
(Michael Appleby) *chsd ldng trio: effrt to chse ldr 2f out: rdn to ld 1f out: hdd and styd on same pce wl ins fnl f* **12/1**

60-2 **3** *1* **Intensical (IRE)**[14] 984 6-8-12 **77**...............................(p) DavidEgan(7) 8 80
(Ivan Furtado) *hld up in tch in midfield: effrt on inner over 1f out: ev ch and edgd rt 1f out: unable qck and kpt on same pce ins fnl f* **9/1**

536- **4** *½* **Frozen Lake (USA)**[157] 7203 5-8-9 **67**.............................. JackMitchell 6 69
(Mary Hambro) *v awkward leaving stalls and s.i.s: t.k.h: hld up in rr: clsd and switching rt over 1f out: kpt on wl ins fnl f: nt rch ldrs* **7/1**

-423 **5** *2¼* **King Of Dreams**[8] 1085 4-8-12 **75**..........................(p) SophieKilloran(5) 9 72
(David Simcock) *hld up in tch in rr: effrt wd wl over 1f out: sn rdn: kpt on same pce and no threat to ldrs ins fnl f* **9/2**[3]

5254 **6** *1¼* **Byres Road**[12] 1032 4-9-10 **82**............................................... JoeFanning 4 76
(Mark Johnston) *sn led and hdd over 1f out: losing pl whn sltly short of room jst ins fnl f: sn wknd* **4/1**[2]

6-60 **7** *nk* **False Id**[14] 984 4-8-2 **67**.............................................. DarraghKeenan(7) 2 60
(Robert Eddery) *chsd ldr on inner tl unable qck ent fnl 2f out: outpcd over 1f out: wknd ins fnl f* **14/1**

00-0 **8** *shd* **Passing Star**[68] 117 6-9-2 **79**.......................................... PaddyPilley(5) 7 72
(Daniel Kubler) *swtchd lft after s: hld up in tch in midfield: effrt u.p over 1f out: no imp and kpt on same pce ins fnl f* **10/1**

6- **9** 14 **Theodorico (IRE)**[48] 3931 4-9-2 **81**..............................(p) GerO'Neill(7) 5 42
(David Loughnane) *t.k.h: chsd ldrs: lost pl u.p and sltly impeded over 1f out: bhd fnl f* **20/1**

60-0 **P** **Cambodia (IRE)**[68] 122 4-8-13 **71**..............................(h) TedDurcan 10
(Chris Wall) *rdr unable to remove hood and v.s.a: sn p.u* **14/1**

1m 37.54s (-2.36) **Going Correction** -0.15s/f (Stan) **10** Ran SP% **118.6**
Speed ratings (Par 105): **105,104,103,102,100 99,98,98,84,**
CSF £45.44 CT £342.27 TOTE £4.60: £1.60, £4.40, £3.20; EX 51.00 Trifecta £675.80.
**Owner** Shawthing Racing Partnership **Bred** Brendan Ryan **Trained** Sproxton, Leics

**FOCUS**
This was run at a sound gallop. The placed horses' best 2016 form sets the level with the winner back to his best.

## 1225 COLLECT TOTEPOOL WINNINGS AT BETFRED SHOPS H'CAP 1m (P)
**8:45** (8:47) (Class 6) (0-60,62) 4-Y-0+ **£3,234** (£962; £481; £240) **Stalls** Low

Form RPR

4-36 **1** **Scribner Creek (IRE)**[26] 812 4-9-7 **60**.............................. DaleSwift 2 66
(Daniel Mark Loughnane) *t.k.h: hld up in tch: hdwy ent fnl f: drvn to chal ins fnl f: r.o to ld last strides: jst hld on* **4/1**[3]

6002 **2** *nse* **Sheer Intensity (IRE)**[6] 1125 4-8-11 **50**.............................. JFEgan 1 56
(David Evans) *hld up in tch in last pair: rdn and hdwy jst over 1f out: r.o strly ins fnl f: wnt 2nd last strides: jst failed* **7/1**

-620 **3** *nk* **Little Choosey**[51] 390 7-9-7 **60**..............................(bt) MartinLane 5 65
(Roy Bowring) *led and sn crossed to rail: t.k.h and set stdy gallop tl hdd 5f out: styd w ldr: rdn to ld again jst over 1f out: drvn ins fnl f: hdd and lost 2 pls last strides* **20/1**

000- **4** *¾* **Cleverconversation (IRE)**[207] 5677 4-9-7 **60**..............(h) DannyBrock 4 63
(Jane Chapple-Hyam) *dwlt and flashed tail leaving stalls: hld up in tch in midfield: effrt on inner over 1f out: kpt on wl ins fnl f* **33/1**

0-40 **5** *¾* **Lord Of The Storm**[35] 641 9-9-9 **62**.............................. LukeMorris 8 64
(Michael Attwater) *hld up in tch: rdn over 2f out: drvn over 1f out: kpt on ins fnl f* **25/1**

4211 **6** *½* **Hold Firm**[5] 1139 5-8-11 **57**.............................. GabrieleMalune(7) 6 58
(Mark H Tompkins) *t.k.h: w ldr tl led 5f out: rdn over 1f out: sn hdd and unable qck: edgd lft and short of room jst ins fnl f: wknd fnl 75yds* **11/4**[2]

1340 **7** *nse* **Samphire Coast**[26] 812 4-9-6 **59**..............................(v) TonyHamilton 9 59
(Derek Shaw) *stdd s: t.k.h: hld up in tch in last pair: hdwy and swtchd lft 1f out: kpt on ins fnl f: nvr trbld ldrs* **7/1**

00-5 **8** *hd* **One For Jodie (IRE)**[29] 747 6-9-7 **60**.............................. SilvestreDeSousa 3 60
(Michael Appleby) *t.k.h: chsd ldrs: rdn to press ldrs 2f out: unable qck over 1f out: wknd ins fnl f* **5/2**[1]

0-26 **9** *3* **Strictly Art (IRE)**[22] 865 4-8-13 **52**..............................(p) FranBerry 7 45
(Alan Bailey) *hld up in tch in last trio: rdn over 3f out: drvn and no hdwy over 2f out: bhd 1f out* **8/1**

1m 40.29s (0.39) **Going Correction** -0.15s/f (Stan) **9** Ran SP% **122.9**
Speed ratings (Par 101): **92,91,91,90,90 89,89,89,86**
CSF £33.43 CT £518.45 TOTE £5.40: £2.00, £2.10, £3.90; EX 36.60 Trifecta £398.90.
**Owner** David Slater **Bred** Holborn Trust Co **Trained** Rock, Worcs

**FOCUS**
A tight finish to this handicap.

## 1226 UB40 HERE ON 12TH AUGUST MAIDEN STKS 1m 2f (P)
**9:15** (9:19) (Class 5) 3-Y-0+ **£5,175** (£1,540; £769; £384) **Stalls** Low

Form RPR

522 **1** **Specialist (IRE)**[10] 1069 3-8-8 0.............................. JoeFanning 5 72
(Mark Johnston) *sn led and mde rest: rdn over 1f out: keeping on u.p whn lft in command 100yds out* **11/4**[2]

65 **2** *6* **Gee Sixty Six**[41] 552 3-8-10 0 ow2.............................. StevieDonohoe 4 63
(Mark H Tompkins) *dwlt and bhd: clsd and in tch 5f out: swtchd rt and hdwy 3f out: 3rd and u.p over 1f out: no imp and wl hld whn lft 2nd 100yds out* **14/1**

65 **3** *3½* **Swilly Bay (IRE)**[22] 863 3-8-8 0.............................. SilvestreDeSousa 1 54
(Charles Hills) *restless in stalls: chsd ldr tl 1/2-way: rdn over 2f out: sn outpcd: 4th and wl hld 1f out: lft modest 3rd 100yds out* **7/1**[3]

**4** *17* **Yemnaak (FR)** 3-8-8 0.............................. LukeMorris 2 22
(George Peckham) *racd in 4th tl dropped to last 3f out: sn rdn and struggling: bhd over 1f out: lft poor 4th 100yds out* **25/1**

3 **R** **Royalistic (IRE)**[33] 681 3-8-8 0.............................. NickyMackay 3 68
(John Gosden) *t.k.h: chsd ldrs tl wnt 2nd 1/2-way: effrt 2f out: rdn and hung bdly rt ent fnl f: stl chsng wnr whn crashed through rail and uns rdr 100yds out* **8/13**[1]

2m 5.08s (-3.52) **Going Correction** -0.15s/f (Stan) **5** Ran SP% **111.6**
Speed ratings (Par 103): **108,103,100,86,**
CSF £33.25 TOTE £3.10: £3.70, £4.40; EX 21.40 Trifecta £93.70.
**Owner** The Goodmove Syndicate **Bred** Lynn Lodge Stud **Trained** Middleham Moor, N Yorks

**FOCUS**
A dramatic finish to this maiden.
T/Plt: £60.50 to a £1 stake. Pool: £84,533.97 - 1019.94 winning units. T/Qpdt: £14.50 to a £1 stake. Pool: £8,655.45 - 439.64 winning units. **Steve Payne**

1227 - 1232a (Foreign Racing) - See Raceform Interactive

# 1128 DUNDALK (A.W) (L-H)
Thursday, March 16

**OFFICIAL GOING: Polytrack: standard**

## 1233a WWW.DUNDALKSTADIUM.COM H'CAP 7f (P)
**8:30** (8:31) 4-Y-0+ **£8,410** (£2,598; £1,230; £547; £205)

RPR

**1** **Shannon Soul (IRE)**[20] 907 5-9-1 **80**..............................(bt) ShaneFoley 2 89
(M Halford, Ire) *dwlt and settled in rr: pushed along into st: sn rdn and u.p stl in rr over 1f out: r.o wl nr side ins fnl f to ld fnl stride* **11/4**[1]

**2** *hd* **Split The Atom (IRE)**[13] 1009 5-8-12 **77**....................(b) WayneLordan 7 85
(David Marnane, Ire) *towards rr: pushed along in 5th fr 1/2-way: rdn 2f out and clsd u.p nr side to ld ins fnl f where edgd sltly lft: all out clsng stages where strly pressed and hdd fnl stride* **13/2**

**3** *¾* **Ishebayorgrey (IRE)**[55] 340 5-9-2 **86**.............................. OisinOrr(5) 3 92
(Patrick Martin, Ire) *hld up bhd ldrs: 4th 1/2-way: prog far side over 1f out: rdn to chal ins fnl f: no ex in 3rd cl home* **3/1**[2]

**4** *1¼* **Pearl Spectre (USA)**[13] 999 6-9-10 **89**................. JosephineGordon 5 92
(Phil McEntee) *led briefly tl sn hdd and settled bhd ldr: 2nd 1/2-way: lost pl over 2f out: sn rdn bhd ldrs and u.p in 6th wl ins fnl f: kpt on clsng stages to snatch 4th fnl strides* **5/1**

**5** *nk* **Ducky Mallon (IRE)**[148] 7475 6-8-1 **76**.............(t) MichelleHamilton(10) 4 78
(Donal Kinsella, Ire) *hooded to load: chsd ldrs: racd keenly early: 3rd 1/2-way: hdwy to ld narrowly 1 1/2f out: hdd ins fnl f where sltly hmpd: no ex and wknd clsng stages: denied 4th fnl strides* **22/1**

**6** *¾* **Geological (IRE)**[13] 1011 5-9-3 **87**.............................. DonaghO'Connor(5) 6 87
(Damian Joseph English, Ire) *cl up and sn led narrowly: rdn and hdd 1 1/2f out: no ex ins fnl f and wknd clsng stages* **9/2**[3]

**7** *shd* **Guanabara Bay (IRE)**[34] 673 4-8-6 **71**.............................. ConorHoban 1 70
(Adrian McGuinness, Ire) *hooded to load: towards rr: 6th 1/2-way: pushed along in 6th under 2f out and no ex u.p far side ins fnl f: one pce clsng stages* **10/1**

1m 24.52s (-0.58) **Going Correction** +0.125s/f (Slow) **7** Ran SP% **113.3**
Speed ratings: **108,107,106,105,105 104,104**
CSF £20.52 TOTE £3.30: £1.90, £2.90; DF 19.50 Trifecta £95.80.
**Owner** M J Enright **Bred** Mr M Enright **Trained** Doneany, Co Kildare

**FOCUS**
They didn't go that slowly here yet they finished in a bit of a heap. The winner would have been an unlucky loser. The race has been rated around the balance of the first four.

1234 - 1236a (Foreign Racing) - See Raceform Interactive

# 1086 LINGFIELD (L-H)
Friday, March 17

**OFFICIAL GOING: Polytrack: standard**
Wind: medium, across Weather: overcast

## 1237 32RED.COM FILLIES' H'CAP 1m 1y(P)
**1:10** (1:11) (Class 5) (0-70,67) 4-Y-0+ **£2,911** (£866; £432; £216) **Stalls** High

Form RPR

0-3 **1** **Ixelles Diamond (IRE)**[30] 739 6-8-5 **51**..............................(h) KieranO'Neill 5 58
(Lee Carter) *dwlt and pushed along leaving stalls: hdwy to chse ldr over 6f out: rdn to ld over 2f out: kpt on wl ins fnl f* **5/1**[3]

30-4 **2** *1½* **Little Kipling**[22] 883 4-9-5 **65**.............................. OisinMurphy 1 68
(Stuart Williams) *chsd ldr tl over 6f out: styd trcking ldrs tl effrt to chse wnr 2f out: drvn ent fnl f: kpt on same pce* **1/1**[1]

4120 **3** *1¼* **Welsh Inlet (IRE)**[23] 860 9-7-13 **52**.............................. JaneElliott(7) 6 52
(John Bridger) *hld up in tch: effrt in 4th 2f out: chsd ldng pair 1f out: styd on same pce ins fnl f* **10/1**

3222 **4** *2¼* **Ms Gillard**[15] 993 4-9-2 **67**.............................. SophieKilloran(5) 4 62
(David Simcock) *stdd s: hld up in rr: effrt but stl plenty to do 2f out: wnt 4th jst ins fnl f: nvr trbld ldrs* **3/1**[2]

5F0- **5** *5* **Nellie Deen (IRE)**[79] 8559 4-8-13 **59**.............................. ShaneKelly 3 42
(David Elsworth) *led tl hdd and rdn over 2f out: 3rd and outpcd 2f out: wknd over 1f out* **7/1**

-000 **6** *25* **Rubheira**[17] 961 5-7-9 **48** oh3..............................(h) RPWalsh(7) 2
(Paul Burgoyne) *taken down early and led to post: stdd after s: t.k.h in last pair: swtchd rt and hdwy into midfield over 6f out: rdn and struggling 3f out: sn bhd* **66/1**

1m 38.48s (0.28) **Going Correction** +0.125s/f (Slow) **6** Ran SP% **114.8**
Speed ratings (Par 100): **103,101,100,98,93 68**
CSF £10.84 TOTE £6.20: £2.40, £1.20; EX 14.40 Trifecta £52.00.
**Owner** Clear Racing **Bred** Lynn Lodge Stud **Trained** Epsom, Surrey

**FOCUS**
A very modest fillies' handicap. The winner was well in on old form.

## 1238 SUNBETS.CO.UK CLAIMING STKS 7f 1y(P)
**1:45** (1:46) (Class 6) 3-Y-0+ **£2,264** (£673; £336; £168) **Stalls** Low

Form RPR

-05 **1** **Willwams (IRE)**[22] 882 3-8-6 0.............................. RossaRyan(7) 7 69
(Richard Hannon) *led for 2f: trckd ldrs 4f out: effrt to chal and edgd rt u.p over 1f out: led jst ins fnl f: hld on wl u.p: rdn out* **33/1**

4-60 **2** *shd* **Sans Souci Bay**[6] 1149 3-8-10 75.............................. HollieDoyle(3) 3 69
(Richard Hannon) *hld up in tch: rdn and hdwy over 1f out: ev ch ins fnl f: kpt on: jst hld* **5/2**[2]

4-00 **3** *shd* **Aqua Libre**[42] 551 4-9-4 79..............................(t[1]) PaddyBradley(5) 9 68
(Philip McBride) *chsd ldrs after 2f: wnt 2nd 4f out: rdn and ev ch over 1f out: kpt on tl unable qck and hld towards fin* **20/1**

1162 **4** *shd* **Gold Flash**[11] 1065 5-10-0 78..............................(v) PhillipMakin 4 73
(Keith Dalgleish) *hld up in tch: effrt over 1f out: swtchd rt ins fnl f: styd on wl fnl 75yds: nt quite rch ldrs* **9/4**[1]

-600 **5** *½* **Luis Vaz De Torres (IRE)**[8] 1103 5-9-11 78.....(h) AdamMcNamara(3) 2 72
(Richard Fahey) *in tch in midfield: effrt over 1f out: chsd ldrs 1f out: kpt on same pce u.p wl ins fnl f* **9/1**

0506 **6** *¾* **Macho Mac**[8] 1109 4-9-4 69.............................. CharlieBennett(5) 8 65
(Hughie Morrison) *chsd ldr tl led after 2f: rdn 2f out: hdd jst ins fnl f: no ex and wknd towards fin* **18/1**

0-20 **7** *nk* **Aqua Ardens (GER)**[10] 1074 9-9-9 72..........................(tp) PatCosgrave 5 64
(George Baker) *dwlt: hld up in tch towards rr: effrt 2f out: kpt on ins fnl f: nt rch ldrs* **9/2**[3]

51-6 **8** *hd* **Chelwood Gate (IRE)**[60] 267 7-9-8 72................(v) HectorCrouch(3) 10 65
(Patrick Chamings) *hld up in tch in rr: hdwy ent fnl f: styng in but nvr gng to rch ldrs whn nt clr run and eased towards fin* **8/1**

645- **9** *nk* **Sexton Blake (IRE)**[100] 8248 4-9-9 60..............................(p) TimmyMurphy 1 63
(Gary Moore) *in tch in midfield: effrt on inner over 1f out: rdn to chse ldrs 1f out: no ex ins fnl f: wknd fnl 75yds* **18/1**

16-6 **10** *6* **Seek The Fair Land**[42] 551 11-8-13 66..............................(b) JaneElliott(7) 6 43
(Lee Carter) *hld up in rr: struggling and rdn over 2f out: wknd over 1f out* **25/1**

1m 24.58s (-0.22) **Going Correction** +0.125s/f (Slow)
**WFA** 3 from 4yo+ 15lb **10** Ran SP% **120.7**
Speed ratings (Par 101): **106,105,105,105,105 104,103,103,103,96**
CSF £116.63 TOTE £33.50: £7.80, £1.30, £6.30; EX 241.00 Trifecta £3852.70.Gold Flash was claimed by Mr Hugo Froud for £10,000. Willwams was the subject of a friendly claim by Mr Richard Hannon for £10,000.
**Owner** Sullivan Bloodstock Limited **Bred** Pat McCarthy **Trained** East Everleigh, Wilts
■ Stewards' Enquiry : Rossa Ryan four-day ban; used whip above the permitted level (31st Mat, 1st-2nd Apr, 4th Apr)

**FOCUS**
An ordinary claimer and the first four finished almost in a line. A 1-2 for trainer Richard Hannon with the only 3yos in the race, but not in the order most would have expected. The form is far from convincing.

## 1239 £10 FREE AT 32RED.COM MAIDEN STKS 1m 4f (P)
**2:25** (2:29) (Class 5) 3-Y-O **£2,911** (£866; £432; £216) **Stalls** Low

Form RPR
2 **1** **Here And Now**$^{23}$ 855 3-9-5 0 FranBerry 4 77
(Ralph Beckett) *mostly chsd ldr tl led and travelling strly 2f out: sn rdn: kpt on and a doing enough fnl f: rdn out* **1/1**$^{1}$
43-3 **2** *1 1/4* **Balashakh (USA)**$^{23}$ 855 3-9-5 74 OisinMurphy 3 75
(David Simcock) *t.k.h: led for 2f: trckd ldr 9f out: swtchd rt and effrt 2f out: chsd wnr wl over 1f out: drvn and hung lft ins fnl f: kpt on but a hld* **6/4**$^{2}$
5 **3** *6* **Temir Kazyk**$^{16}$ 970 3-9-5 0 LiamKeniry 1 65
(David Simcock) *hld up in tch: rdn 4f out: 3rd and outpcd over 1f out: wknd fnl f* **16/1**
0-03 **4** *9* **Born Legend (IRE)**$^{49}$ 437 3-9-5 72 (b) DavidProbert 2 51
(Charles Hills) *hld up in rr: t.k.h and hdwy to ld after 2f: rdn and hdd 2f out: sn lost pl: bhd fnl f* **8/1**$^{3}$

2m 34.06s (1.06) **Going Correction** +0.125s/f (Slow) **4** Ran SP% **107.0**
Speed ratings (Par 98): **101,100,96,90**
CSF £2.66 TOTE £1.80; EX 2.40 Trifecta £5.40.
**Owner** J H Richmond-Watson **Bred** Lawn Stud **Trained** Kimpton, Hants
■ Indian Red was withdrawn. Price at time of withdrawal 14-1. Rule 4 applies to all bets - deduction 5p in the pound.
**FOCUS**
A modest middle-distance 3yo maiden reduced by one when Indian Red was withdrawn after getting upset in the stalls, but the pace was fair enough considering the small field. The first two finished second and third in a Kempton maiden last month and the form was confirmed. Not a race to be confident in.

## 1240 BET ON THE FESTIVAL WITH BETWAY H'CAP 1m 4f (P)
**3:05** (3:05) (Class 3) (0-95,94) 4-Y-O **£7,246** (£2,168; £1,084; £542; £270) **Stalls** Low

Form RPR
1-12 **1** **Petite Jack**$^{28}$ 779 4-9-6 92 JackMitchell 6 100+
(Neil King) *hld up in tch: swtchd rt wl over 1f out: clsng but hanging lft over 1f out: led and stl gng lft ins fnl f: sn in command and r.o wl: comf* **11/8**$^{1}$
-245 **2** *1 1/2* **Masterpaver**$^{20}$ 921 6-9-1 88 AdamMcNamara$^{(3)}$ 1 92
(Richard Fahey) *chsd ldr for 2f: styd chsng ldrs: rdn wl over 1f out: nt clr run 1f out: swtchd rt ins fnl f: kpt on wl fnl 75yds to snatch 2nd on post: no threat to wnr* **6/1**
1/52 **3** *nse* **Every Chance (IRE)**$^{27}$ 809 4-9-4 90 TimmyMurphy 4 94
(Jamie Osborne) *chsd ldr after 2f: rdn and ev ch wl over 1f out: led jst ins fnl f: sn hdd: swtchd rt and kpt on same pce fnl 100yds: lost 2nd on post* **7/2**$^{2}$
-005 **4** *1/2* **Castilo Del Diablo (IRE)**$^{13}$ 1027 8-8-13 83 OisinMurphy 2 86
(David Simcock) *in tch in 4th: effrt 2f out: swtchd rt and kpt on same pce ins fnl f* **9/1**
4315 **5** *hd* **Sennockian Star**$^{17}$ 963 7-9-10 94 JoeFanning 5 96
(Mark Johnston) *led: rdn wl over 1f out: hdd jst ins fnl f: no ex and kpt on same pce after* **9/2**$^{3}$
05-0 **6** *2 1/4* **Zamperini (IRE)**$^{57}$ 306 5-9-0 84 (b) TedDurcan 3 83
(Mike Murphy) *stdd and swtchd lft after s: hld up in tch in rr: effrt over 1f out: no imp* **16/1**

2m 33.49s (0.49) **Going Correction** +0.125s/f (Slow)
**WFA** 4 from 5yo+ 1lb **6** Ran SP% **112.7**
Speed ratings (Par 107): **103,102,101,101,101 100**
CSF £10.30 TOTE £2.10: £1.40, £3.20; EX 11.40 Trifecta £32.20.
**Owner** W Burn **Bred** Mrs Liz Nelson Mbe **Trained** Barbury Castle, Wiltshire
**FOCUS**
A decent middle-distance handicap and another spectacular effort from the winner. The form is straightforward around the second and third.

## 1241 32RED CASINO MAIDEN STKS 1m 1y(P)
**3:45** (3:45) (Class 5) 3-Y-O **£2,911** (£866; £432; £216) **Stalls** High

Form RPR
3 **1** **Island Brave (IRE)**$^{17}$ 962 3-9-5 0 LiamKeniry 4 74
(J S Moore) *mde all and set stdy gallop: rdn and qcknd ent fnl 2f: kpt on and a doing enough ins fnl f* **14/1**
**2** *1* **Bless Him (IRE)** 3-9-5 0 OisinMurphy 5 71+
(David Simcock) *t.k.h: chsd wnr over 6f out: rdn ent fnl 2f: kpt on u.p ins fnl f but nvr getting on terms w wnr* **4/9**$^{1}$
620- **3** *1/2* **Mr Tyrrell (IRE)**$^{170}$ 6881 3-9-5 79 TomMarquand 3 70
(Richard Hannon) *t.k.h: chsd wnr tl over 6f out: rdn ent fnl 2f: kpt on u.p ins fnl f: nvr enough pce to chal wnr* **5/2**$^{2}$
**4** *3 1/4* **Gunmaker (IRE)** 3-9-5 0 PatCosgrave 1 63+
(David Simcock) *s.i.s: hld up in tch: effrt in 4th 2f out: no imp and wl hld whn rn green and hung lft ins fnl f* **12/1**$^{3}$
**5** *5* **Lord E (IRE)** 3-9-2 0 HectorCrouch$^{(3)}$ 2 50+
(Gary Moore) *hld up in tch: rdn 3f out: outpcd ent fnl 2f: n.d after* **50/1**
**6** *31* **Moorea** 3-8-12 0 JaneElliott$^{(7)}$ 6
(John Bridger) *s.i.s: in tch on outer: rdn 3f out: sn outpcd: bhd 2f out* **66/1**

1m 42.14s (3.94) **Going Correction** +0.125s/f (Slow) **6** Ran SP% **115.6**
Speed ratings (Par 98): **85,84,83,80,75 44**
CSF £21.97 TOTE £16.40: £4.70, £1.10; EX 35.90 Trifecta £86.80.
**Owner** Donald M Kerr **Bred** Tally-Ho Stud **Trained** Upper Lambourn, Berks
**FOCUS**
An uncompetitive 3yo maiden run in a slow time. The order barely changed and there was a bit of a turn-up. Very hard to pin down the form.

## 1242 32REDSPORT.COM H'CAP 7f 1y(P)
**4:25** (4:26) (Class 5) (0-70,69) 3-Y-O **£2,911** (£866; £432; £216) **Stalls** Low

Form RPR
213- **1** **Altiko Tommy (IRE)**$^{177}$ 6670 3-9-2 64 LiamKeniry 5 70
(George Baker) *trckd ldrs: wnt 2nd and swtchd rt 2f out: pushed into ld 1f out: sn rdn and asserted: r.o wl* **11/2**
530- **2** *3/4* **Widnes**$^{100}$ 8244 3-9-7 69 (b$^{1}$) DavidProbert 6 72
(Alan Bailey) *dwlt: hld up in tch: effrt on outer bnd wl over 1f out: hdwy 1f out: styd on wl u.p to go 2nd towards fin: nvr getting to wnr* **6/1**
1-55 **3** *3/4* **Wily Rumpus (IRE)**$^{49}$ 434 3-9-2 64 ThomasBrown 2 65
(Ed Walker) *led: rdn 2f out: hdd and no ex u.p 1f out: kpt on same pce ins fnl f* **4/1**$^{2}$
55-0 **4** *1 3/4* **Ivor's Magic (IRE)**$^{29}$ 763 3-8-13 61 ShaneKelly 1 57
(David Elsworth) *hld up in tch in midfield: hdwy on inner over 1f out: chsd ldrs and kpt on same pce u.p fnl f* **20/1**
-042 **5** *1 3/4* **Masquerade Bling (IRE)**$^{21}$ 897 3-8-7 55 RobHornby 7 47
(Simon Hodgson) *in tch in midfield: effrt 2f out: kpt on same pce and no imp ins fnl f* **9/1**
-131 **6** *nse* **Mia Cara**$^{29}$ 763 3-9-5 67 JFEgan 10 58
(David Evans) *in tch in midfield: effrt to chse ldrs and drvn ent fnl f: sn outpcd* **7/2**$^{1}$
00-4 **7** *3 1/4* **Baby Gal**$^{37}$ 625 3-9-4 66 PatCosgrave 4 49
(Jim Boyle) *t.k.h: early: wl in tch in midfield: nt clrest of runs and shuffled bk bnd 2f out: nudged along and hdwy 1f out: eased wl ins fnl f* **8/1**
6-65 **8** *3 1/2* **Dixie's Double**$^{9}$ 1088 3-9-3 65 OisinMurphy 3 38
(Daniel Kubler) *t.k.h: chsd ldr tl unable qck and lost 2nd 2f out: wknd fnl f* **16/1**
406- **9** *1 1/4* **Jasmincita (IRE)**$^{204}$ 5796 3-9-3 65 SteveDrowne 8 35
(George Baker) *nvr travelling wl in rr: wknd over 1f out* **33/1**
2143 **10** *nk* **Auric Goldfinger (IRE)**$^{21}$ 895 3-8-10 65 (b) TinaSmith$^{(7)}$ 9 34+
(Richard Hannon) *v slwly away: clsd onto bk of field 4f out: effrt on inner over 1f out: no hdwy and wknd fnl f* **5/1**$^{3}$

1m 26.32s (1.52) **Going Correction** +0.125s/f (Slow) **10** Ran SP% **123.3**
Speed ratings (Par 98): **96,95,94,92,90 90,86,82,81,80**
CSF £40.92 CT £151.09 TOTE £6.80: £1.80, £2.60, £1.90; EX 56.50 Trifecta £281.10.
**Owner** P Bowden **Bred** Fergus Cousins **Trained** Manton, Wilts
**FOCUS**
A modest 3yo handicap, but the winner did it nicely and showed improvement.
T/Plt: £45.30 to a £1 stake. Pool: £47,986.66 - 771.83 winning units. T/Qpdt: £12.10 to a £1 stake. Pool: £3,098.80 - 188.01 winning units. **Steve Payne**

# 1189 WOLVERHAMPTON (A.W) (L-H)
### Friday, March 17

**OFFICIAL GOING: Tapeta: standard**
Wind: Strong behind Weather: Overcast

## 1243 32RED CASINO FILLIES' H'CAP 7f 36y (Tp)
**5:45** (5:46) (Class 5) (0-70,70) 3-Y-O+ **£3,072** (£914; £456; £228) **Stalls** High

Form RPR
0-12 **1** **Toy Theatre**$^{22}$ 875 3-8-7 64 SilvestreDeSousa 2 76+
(Michael Appleby) *chsd ldr tl led and edgd lft over 2f out: pushed clr fr over 1f out: easily* **5/4**$^{1}$
1-36 **2** *5* **Coquine**$^{20}$ 929 4-9-9 65 (p) DanielTudhope 9 68
(David O'Meara) *s.i.s: hld up: hdwy and hung lft fr over 1f out: wnt 2nd ins fnl f: no ch w wnr* **8/1**$^{3}$
4-4 **3** *nk* **World Of Good**$^{15}$ 986 4-9-12 68 (b) SeanLevey 4 70
(Anabel K Murphy) *chsd ldrs: rdn over 2f out: chsd wnr over 1f out tl no ex ins fnl f* **10/1**
3123 **4** *1 1/2* **Killermont Street (IRE)**$^{25}$ 846 3-8-12 69 FrannyNorton 3 63
(Mark Johnston) *s.i.s and hmpd s: hld up: pushed along over 2f out: hdwy over 1f out: sn hung lft: no ex ins fnl f* **2/1**$^{2}$
-323 **5** *1 3/4* **Bloomin Lovely (IRE)**$^{31}$ 731 3-8-12 69 JasonHart 7 58
(John Quinn) *chsd ldrs: rdn over 2f out: wknd fnl f* **16/1**
030/ **6** *4 1/2* **Cline**$^{457}$ 8253 4-9-2 65 SeamusCronin$^{(7)}$ 8 48
(Kevin Ryan) *chsd ldrs: rdn over 2f out: wknd over 1f out* **50/1**
1-06 **7** *3 1/4* **Right Rebel**$^{48}$ 460 5-9-9 70 DavidParkes$^{(5)}$ 1 45
(Alan Bailey) *led: rdn and hdd over 2f out: n.m.r sn after: hung lft and wknd over 1f out* **10/1**

1m 28.42s (-0.38) **Going Correction** 0.0s/f (Stan)
**WFA** 3 from 4yo+ 15lb **7** Ran SP% **114.9**
Speed ratings (Par 100): **102,96,95,94,92 87,83**
CSF £12.54 CT £70.55 TOTE £2.20: £1.20, £2.90; EX 13.70 Trifecta £54.50.
**Owner** L J Vaessen **Bred** Darley **Trained** Oakham, Rutland
**FOCUS**
An uncompetitive race, but a progressive winner who was value for at least a little extra.

## 1244 32RED.COM MAIDEN STKS 7f 36y (Tp)
**6:15** (6:16) (Class 5) 3-Y-O **£3,234** (£962; £481; £240) **Stalls** High

Form RPR
**1** **Giant's Treasure (IRE)** 3-9-5 0 SeanLevey 6 86+
(Richard Hannon) *chsd ldr tl led over 1f out: qcknd clr ins fnl f: impressive* **7/4**$^{1}$
42 **2** *4 1/2* **Trenchard (USA)**$^{16}$ 970 3-9-5 0 AdamKirby 1 72+
(John Gosden) *hld up: rdn over 2f out: swtchd rt and hdwy over 1f out: r.o to go 2nd wl ins fnl f: no ch w wnr* **9/4**$^{2}$
-443 **3** *3/4* **Atteq**$^{35}$ 657 3-9-5 72 TonyHamilton 2 70
(Richard Fahey) *chsd ldrs: rdn over 2f out: r.o to go 3rd nr fin* **5/1**
5 **4** *1/2* **Channel Packet**$^{31}$ 731 3-9-5 0 SilvestreDeSousa 4 69
(Michael Appleby) *led at stdy pce tl rdn and qcknd over 2f out: hdd over 1f out: styd on same pce ins fnl f* **16/1**
55- **5** *3* **Teodoro (IRE)**$^{130}$ 7849 3-9-5 0 RichardKingscote 7 61
(Tom Dascombe) *hld up: shkn up over 1f out: nvr nr to chal* **4/1**$^{3}$
**6** *4* **Mahna Mahna (IRE)** 3-9-5 0 WilliamCarson 5 51
(David W Drinkwater) *plld hrd and prom: rdn over 2f out: wknd wl over 1f out* **50/1**
06- **7** *1* **Majestic Stone (IRE)**$^{151}$ 7414 3-9-5 0 JoeDoyle 3 49
(Julie Camacho) *hld up in tch: plld hrd: rdn over 2f out: wknd over 1f out* **20/1**
000- **8** *25* **Henrietta's Dream**$^{177}$ 6678 3-9-0 25 (p) TomEaves 8
(John Wainwright) *hld up: wknd over 2f out* **100/1**

1m 30.66s (1.86) **Going Correction** 0.0s/f (Stan) **8** Ran SP% **117.4**
Speed ratings (Par 98): **89,83,83,82,79 74,73,44**
CSF £6.05 TOTE £2.80: £1.40, £1.10, £1.20; EX 6.20 Trifecta £21.80.
**Owner** M J Jooste & China Horse Club **Bred** Yeguada De Milagro Sa **Trained** East Everleigh, Wilts
**FOCUS**
The pace was steady and the form looks nothing special, but the winner is a very decent prospect.

## 1245 £10 FREE AT 32RED.COM FILLIES' H'CAP 1m 1f 104y (Tp)
**6:45** (6:45) (Class 5) (0-75,75) 4-Y-O+ **£3,072** (£914; £456; £228) **Stalls** Low

Form RPR
15-5 **1** **Auntie Barber (IRE)**$^{22}$ 885 4-8-13 70 AaronJones$^{(3)}$ 1 77
(Stuart Williams) *chsd ldrs: shkn up to ld over 1f out: r.o wl* **2/1**$^{1}$
1-62 **2** *2 1/4* **Amber Mystique**$^{13}$ 1032 4-9-7 75 TonyHamilton 3 77
(Richard Fahey) *chsd ldr tl led 2f out: rdn and hdd over 1f out: styd on same pce ins fnl f* **3/1**$^{3}$

60-0 **3** *hd* **Moi Aussie**[11] 1062 4-8-2 **56** ........ FrannyNorton 5 57
(Michael Appleby) *stdd s: sn swtchd lft and hld up: hdwy over 1f out: sn rdn: r.o* **20/1**

06- **4** *5* **Rock On Rosie (IRE)**[15] 8020 8-8-9 **63** ........ (h) LukeMorris 4 55
(Adrian Brendan Joyce, Ire) *hld up: hdwy 5f out: sn pushed along: rdn over 2f out: edgd lft and wknd fnl f* **5/1**

4022 **5** *15* **Heartstone (IRE)**[6] 1151 4-9-3 **71** ........ AdamKirby 2 34
(David Evans) *led at stdy pce: qcknd over 3f out: rdn and hdd 2f out: sn hung rt: wknd and eased fnl f* **9/4**[2]

2m 0.7s (-0.10) **Going Correction** 0.0s/f (Stan) **5** Ran SP% **110.5**
Speed ratings (Par 100): **100,98,97,93,80**
CSF £8.36 TOTE £2.80: £1.60, £1.70; EX 8.40 Trifecta £53.90.
**Owner** J W Parry **Bred** Mrs Martin Armstrong **Trained** Newmarket, Suffolk

**FOCUS**
This race rather fell apart, but the winner is unexposed. She's rated back to her best.

## 1246 BETWAY SPRINT H'CAP (DIV I) 6f 20y (Tp)
**7:15** (7:16) (Class 6) (0-55,56) 3-Y-0+ **£2,587** (£770; £384; £192) **Stalls** Low

Form RPR

0644 **1** **Tasaaboq**[10] 1075 6-9-2 **47** ........ (t) JosephineGordon 9 52
(Phil McEntee) *hld up: hdwy over 1f out: rdn to ld wl ins fnl f: r.o* **13/2**

02/0 **2** *nk* **Pillar**[7] 1129 4-9-4 **49** ........ StevieDonohoe 7 53
(Adrian McGuinness, Ire) *chsd ldrs: wnt 2nd over 2f out: led over 1f out: rdn: edgd lft and hdd wl ins fnl f* **6/1**[3]

0555 **3** *1* **Lizzy's Dream**[21] 899 9-9-1 **46** ........ DanielTudhope 5 47
(Rebecca Bastiman) *prom: rdn and hung lft over 1f out: r.o* **9/1**

-213 **4** *1* **Castlerea Tess**[11] 1062 4-9-7 **52** ........ (p) AdamKirby 3 50
(Sarah Hollinshead) *s.i.s: pushed along early in rr: hdwy u.p over 1f out: nt rch ldrs* **9/4**[1]

2104 **5** *½* **Swendab (IRE)**[1] 1221 9-9-5 **55** ........ MitchGodwin(5) 4 52
(John O'Shea) *chsd ldr over 3f: rdn and ev ch over 1f out: styd on same pce ins fnl f* **12/1**

-351 **6** *2 ½* **Dream Ally (IRE)**[15] 981 7-9-5 **50** ........ (be) LukeMorris 10 39
(John Weymes) *hld up: shkn up over 2f out: nvr trbld ldrs* **9/2**[2]

4 **7** *3 ¼* **Mr Michael (IRE)**[30] 743 4-9-11 **56** ........ (tp) MartinHarley 12 35
(Adrian Brendan Joyce, Ire) *led: rdn and hdd over 1f out: wknd ins fnl f* **7/1**

06-0 **8** *1 ¼* **Let It Go**[59] 274 5-9-1 **46** oh1 ........ (h) GeorgeDowning 1 22
(Tony Carroll) *prom: rdn over 2f out: wknd over 1f out* **150/1**

20-0 **9** *9* **Cooperess**[32] 724 4-9-9 **54** ........ TimmyMurphy 2 3
(John O'Shea) *stdd s: hld up: nvr on terms* **33/1**

06-0 **10** *3* **Love And Be Loved**[49] 435 3-8-11 **55** ........ DanielMuscutt 13
(John Flint) *hld up: rdn over 2f out: sn wknd* **66/1**

1m 13.93s (-0.57) **Going Correction** 0.0s/f (Stan)
**WFA** 3 from 4yo+ 13lb **10** Ran SP% **111.9**
Speed ratings (Par 101): **103,102,101,99,99 95,91,89,77,73**
CSF £43.01 CT £346.48 TOTE £7.80: £2.10, £1.80, £3.30; EX 48.80 Trifecta £287.80.
**Owner** Mrs Rita Baker **Bred** Tim Bostwick **Trained** Newmarket, Suffolk

**FOCUS**
A moderate sprint handicap. The second and third help with the form, which is limited.

## 1247 BETWAY SPRINT H'CAP (DIV II) 6f 20y (Tp)
**7:45** (7:46) (Class 6) (0-55,55) 3-Y-0+ **£2,587** (£770; £384; £192) **Stalls** Low

Form RPR

-004 **1** **Broughtons Fancy**[36] 640 4-8-12 **50** ........ BenRobinson(7) 2 59
(Gary Moore) *sn pushed along and prom: led over 1rf out: rdn out* **5/2**[2]

/-12 **2** *¾* **Oor Jock (IRE)**[42] 562 9-9-10 **55** ........ (b) StevieDonohoe 5 62
(Adrian McGuinness, Ire) *hld up: hdwy over 1f out: sn rdn: r.o* **13/8**[1]

2302 **3** *½* **Mr Chuckles (IRE)**[21] 899 4-8-13 **49** ........ (p) CharlieBennett(5) 3 54
(Daniel Mark Loughnane) *hld up in tch: rdn and ev ch ins fnl f: styd on same pce towards fin* **13/2**

0063 **4** *1 ¼* **Virile (IRE)**[15] 981 6-9-9 **54** ........ (b) LukeMorris 1 56
(Sylvester Kirk) *s.i.s: hld up: swtchd rt and hdwy over 1f out: r.o: nt rch ldrs* **6/1**[3]

2432 **5** *½* **Justice Rock**[15] 981 4-9-2 **47** ........ JosephineGordon 4 47
(Phil McEntee) *mid-div: hdwy over 1f out: sn rdn: no ex wl ins fnl f* **14/1**

-360 **6** *6* **Local Artist (IRE)**[44] 511 3-8-11 **55** ........ (b[1]) JasonHart 9 33
(John Quinn) *w ldr tl led over 1f out: sn rdn and hdd: wknd ins fnl f* **22/1**

30-0 **7** *¾* **Bogsnog (IRE)**[14] 1006 7-9-9 **54** ........ JamesSullivan 8 34
(Ruth Carr) *led 2f: led again over 2f out: rdn and hdd over 1f out: wknd ins fnl f* **16/1**

0-34 **8** *1 ¼* **Sparkling Cossack**[13] 1024 3-8-7 **51** ........ AdamBeschizza 6 23
(Jeremy Gask) *sn pushed along in rr: rdn over 1f out: wknd fnl f* **18/1**

-005 **9** *½* **Louis Vee (IRE)**[15] 981 9-8-10 **46** oh1 ........ (tp) PatrickO'Donnell(5) 12 21
(John O'Shea) *s.i.s: hdwy over 4f out: sn rdn: wknd over 1f out* **33/1**

0-66 **10** *nse* **Ambitious Boy**[21] 899 8-9-2 **47** ........ (p) TimmyMurphy 7 21
(John O'Shea) *hld up: rdn over 2f out: nvr on terms* **14/1**

0030 **11** *8* **Barnsdale**[14] 1006 4-8-8 **46** oh1 ........ (p) MeganEllingworth(7) 11
(John Holt) *racd keenly: prom: led 4f out: hdd over 2f out: wknd over 1f out* **80/1**

1m 14.12s (-0.38) **Going Correction** 0.0s/f (Stan)
**WFA** 3 from 4yo+ 13lb **11** Ran SP% **127.3**
Speed ratings (Par 101): **102,101,100,98,98 90,89,87,86,86 75**
CSF £7.53 CT £25.45 TOTE £3.80: £2.00, £1.10, £2.50; EX 11.30 Trifecta £55.40.
**Owner** The Fancy Partnership **Bred** Michael E Broughton **Trained** Lower Beeding, W Sussex

**FOCUS**
This looked a fair race for the grade although the time was slightly slower than the first division. The winner was well in on old form.

## 1248 BETWAY STAYERS H'CAP 1m 5f 194y
**8:15** (8:15) (Class 4) (0-85,84) 4-Y-0+ **£4,851** (£1,443; £721; £360) **Stalls** Low

Form RPR

12-4 **1** **Charismatic Man (IRE)**[50] 422 4-9-6 **82** ........ FranBerry 5 90
(Ralph Beckett) *chsd ldr over 5f: remained handy: tk clsr order and wnt 2nd over 2f out: rdn to ld and edgd lft ins fnl f: styd on* **4/6**[1]

0-0 **2** *2 ¾* **Takbeer (IRE)**[39] 599 5-9-2 **74** ........ (p) DavidProbert 4 78
(Nikki Evans) *hld up: plld hrd: wnt prom 12f out: wnt 2nd over 8f out: led over 5f out: clr over 2f out tl rdn over 1f out: hdd ins fnl f: styd on same pce* **16/1**

0-30 **3** *½* **Tetradrachm**[14] 1002 4-9-5 **81** ........ TomEaves 1 84
(David Simcock) *hld up: hdwy over 2f out: rdn over 1f out: swtchd rt ins fnl f: styd on* **7/1**[3]

53-2 **4** *8* **Dolphin Village (IRE)**[72] 38 7-9-7 **84** ........ CharlieBennett(5) 2 76
(Shaun Harris) *hld up: racd keenly: rdn over 2f out: nvr on terms* **6/1**[2]

4-15 **5** *3 ¼* **Persian Steel (IRE)**[38] 613 5-8-10 **75** ........ BenRobinson(7) 7 63
(Brian Ellison) *s.i.s: hld up: rdn over 3f out: nvr on terms* **8/1**

000/ **6** *38* **Marmion**[506] 7556 5-9-8 **80** ........ JasonHart 6 15
(Les Eyre) *led and sn clr: hung rt: c bk to the field 9f out: hdd over 5f out: wknd over 2f out* **16/1**

3m 3.7s (-1.10) **Going Correction** 0.0s/f (Stan)
**WFA** 4 from 5yo+ 2lb **6** Ran SP% **109.6**
Speed ratings (Par 105): **103,101,101,96,94 73**
CSF £12.29 TOTE £1.60: £1.10, £5.80; EX 12.10 Trifecta £38.20.
**Owner** S Hanson **Bred** Salinity Service Ab **Trained** Kimpton, Hants

**FOCUS**
A muddling contest, with the runner-up and last-placed horse clear of the others for much of the way, but the favourite proved too good. The second and third fit the form.

## 1249 BETWAY H'CAP 1m 1f 104y (Tp)
**8:45** (8:45) (Class 6) (0-60,60) 4-Y-0+ **£2,587** (£770; £384; £192) **Stalls** Low

Form RPR

**1** **Lucent Dream (IRE)**[21] 911 6-9-5 **58** ........ (t) BenCurtis 9 65
(John C McConnell, Ire) *hld up: hdwy over 2f out: rdn over 1f out: r.o to ld wl ins fnl f* **4/1**[1]

00-0 **2** *¾* **Victor's Bet (SPA)**[11] 1067 8-9-7 **60** ........ DougieCostello 13 66
(Ralph J Smith) *s.i.s: hld up: hdwy over 1f out: edgd lft: r.o* **14/1**

04-5 **3** *¾* **Star Ascending (IRE)**[71] 68 5-9-2 **55** ........ (p) ConnorBeasley 8 59
(Jennie Candlish) *prom: led over 2f out: rdn over 1f out: hdd wl ins fnl f* **6/1**[2]

550- **4** *1 ½* **The Greedy Boy**[21] 7532 4-8-7 **46** oh1 ........ (p[1]) JoeDoyle 4 48
(Steve Flook) *hld up: hdwy and nt clr run over 1f out: styd on* **50/1**

-006 **5** *nk* **Turnbury**[11] 1067 6-9-7 **60** ........ (p) LukeMorris 6 61
(Nikki Evans) *chsd ldrs: rdn over 2f out: styd on same pce ins fnl f* **12/1**

0-00 **6** *2 ¼* **El Tel**[16] 969 5-9-0 **53** ........ JosephineGordon 5 49
(Shaun Harris) *hld up in tch: racd keenly: rdn over 1f out: no ex ins fnl f* **22/1**

4-50 **7** *nk* **Monna Valley**[34] 690 5-9-3 **59** ........ AaronJones(3) 12 55
(Stuart Williams) *disp ld tl over 2f out: sn rdn: wknd ins fnl f* **6/1**[2]

-534 **8** *¾* **Paddy's Rock (IRE)**[31] 726 6-8-11 **50** ........ (p) PaddyAspell 2 44
(Lynn Siddall) *chsd ldrs: rdn over 2f out: wknd ins fnl f* **8/1**

0042 **9** *2 ½* **Arcanista (IRE)**[27] 811 4-9-4 **57** ........ (be) ShaneKelly 3 47
(Richard Hughes) *hld up: rdn over 2f out: n.d* **7/1**[3]

-426 **10** *3 ¼* **Dove Mountain (IRE)**[50] 420 6-9-6 **59** ........ (tp) AdamKirby 10 43
(Anabel K Murphy) *hld up: rdn over 2f out: no rspnse* **10/1**

-030 **11** *11* **Raise The Game (IRE)**[23] 860 4-9-1 **59** ........ RyanWhile(5) 7 22
(Bill Turner) *disp ld tl rdn over 2f out: wknd over 1f out* **9/1**

665 **12** *32* **Dibloam (USA)**[24] 849 4-8-12 **51** ........ FranBerry 1
(David Evans) *plld hrd and prom: rdn over 3f out: sn wknd* **8/1**

1m 59.48s (-1.32) **Going Correction** 0.0s/f (Stan) **12** Ran SP% **123.1**
Speed ratings (Par 101): **105,104,103,102,102 100,99,99,96,94 84,55**
CSF £65.72 CT £343.90 TOTE £4.90: £2.00, £4.10, £2.80; EX 57.00 Trifecta £674.80.
**Owner** Ms Caroline Ahearn **Bred** Roland H Alder **Trained** Stamullen, Co Meath

**FOCUS**
Moderate but competitive. The principals came from the rear and the winner is rated near his best Irish winter form.
T/Plt: £33.20 to a £1 stake. Pool: £62,155.00 - 1,872.03 winning units. T/Qpdt: £15.50 to a £1 stake. Pool: £6,391.00 - 410.32 winning units. **Colin Roberts**

1250 - 1255a (Foreign Racing) - See Raceform Interactive

# 1243 WOLVERHAMPTON (A.W) (L-H)
Saturday, March 18

**OFFICIAL GOING: Tapeta: standard**
Weather: Cloudy

## 1256 BETWAY STAYERS H'CAP 1m 5f 194y
**5:45** (5:45) (Class 6) (0-60,61) 4-Y-0+ **£2,264** (£673; £336; £168) **Stalls** Low

Form RPR

62-0 **1** **Cosmic Tigress**[16] 990 6-9-8 **58** ........ JasonHart 8 62
(John Quinn) *mid div: 3rd 4f out: hdwy to ld over 2f out: sn hrd rdn: briefly hdd wl ins fnl f: regained ld post* **14/1**

-001 **2** *nse* **Par Three (IRE)**[16] 988 6-9-3 **53** ........ (p) AdamKirby 5 57
(Tony Carroll) *2nd early: trckd ldrs into st: rdn and chal ins fnl f: led briefly tl hdd line* **11/4**[1]

065 **3** *½* **Penny Poet (IRE)**[33] 717 4-8-10 **50** ........ LiamKeniry 2 53
(Neil Mulholland) *mid div: hdwy on ins ent st: rdn and n.m.r ins fnl f: unlucky* **9/1**

2606 **4** *1 ¼* **Ali Bin Nayef**[10] 1081 5-9-1 **51** ........ JosephineGordon 7 52
(Michael Wigham) *hld up: hdwy on outer 3f out: c wd into st and sn ever ch: rdn and no ex fnl f* **11/1**

-604 **5** *1 ¾* **Kilim**[21] 924 4-9-0 **54** ........ (t[1]) FrannyNorton 6 53
(John Berry) *hld up: effrt 3f out: c wd: rdn and no ex last 2f* **7/1**

2-51 **6** *½* **Kay Sera**[30] 762 9-9-11 **61** ........ MartinDwyer 3 59
(Tony Newcombe) *slowly away and in rr: keen early: effrt and rdn 3f out: no imp* **10/3**[2]

3433 **7** *2 ¼* **Stonecoldsoba**[21] 924 4-9-6 **60** ........ (v) LukeMorris 4 55
(Denis Quinn) *prom: rdn and lost pl 2f out: wknd* **7/2**[3]

6000 **8** *13* **Zeteah**[10] 1081 7-8-10 **46** oh1 ........ GeorgeDowning 1 22
(Tony Carroll) *led: 3l clr 1/2-way: pushed along 3f out: hdd over 2f out: rdn and wknd qckly* **66/1**

3m 3.08s (-1.72) **Going Correction** -0.075s/f (Stan)
**WFA** 4 from 5yo+ 2lb **8** Ran SP% **111.0**
Speed ratings (Par 101): **101,100,100,99,98 98,97,89**
CSF £49.51 CT £359.21 TOTE £13.80: £2.80, £1.20, £2.80; EX 63.50 Trifecta £655.30.
**Owner** The Cosmic Cases **Bred** The Cosmic Cases **Trained** Settrington, N Yorks

**FOCUS**
Not a bad race of its type; competitive enough at its lowly level.

## 1257 BETWAY H'CAP 1m 4f 51y (Tp)
**6:15** (6:16) (Class 5) (0-70,72) 4-Y-0+ **£2,911** (£866; £432; £216) **Stalls** Low

Form RPR

**1** **Shamash (IRE)**[36] 675 5-9-1 **64** ........ (t) PaulHanagan 4 72
(John C McConnell, Ire) *led 2f: remained prom: pushed along to ld ent st: sn clr: rdn and r.o wl fnl f: comf* **2/1**[1]

3145 **2** *2* **What Usain**[3] 1210 5-9-5 **68** ........ (h) OisinMurphy 10 73
(Michael Appleby) *mid div: effrt 3f out: hdwy to trck ldr into st: rdn and r wl: but no imp on wnr* **5/1**[2]

1250 **3** *¾* **Trending (IRE)**[21] 928 8-9-0 **68** ........ (t) DavidParkes(5) 3 71
(Jeremy Gask) *mid div: pushed along 3f out: hdwy 2f out: hrd rdn and styd on into 3rd fnl f* **16/1**

0/20 **4** *hd* **Magistral**[16] 992 7-9-2 **72**....................(p) CallumRodriguez[(7)] 9 74
(Iain Jardine) *in rr: plld wd and hdwy ent st: rdn and r.o fnl 2f: nrst fin* **13/2**[3]

0-06 **5** *hd* **Grand Meister**[19] 958 6-9-7 **70**....................(b) JasonHart 6 72
(John Quinn) *mid div tl wnt prom to press ldr after 3f: stdy handy and led briefly ent st: sn hdd: rdn and one pce* **16/1**

06-4 **6** *1* **Rock On Rosie (IRE)**[1] 1245 8-9-0 **63**....................(h) StevieDonohoe 5 63
(Adrian Brendan Joyce, Ire) *trckd ldrs: pushed along 3f out: rdn over 2f out: one pce* **12/1**

/666 **7** *1* **Thorntoun Care**[16] 990 6-9-0 **63**.................... TomEaves 1 62
(Iain Jardine) *hld up: hdwy 2f out: sn rdn and no further prog* **18/1**

/324 **8** *1* **Pour L'Amour (IRE)**[19] 954 4-8-12 **63**.................... LukeMorris 8 60
(Daniel Mark Loughnane) *hld up: hrd rdn ent st: no imp* **7/1**

-030 **9** *1 ¾* **Uphold**[28] 822 10-8-1 **57**....................(p) DavidEgan[(7)] 2 51
(Gay Kelleway) *mid div: 6th st: rdn over 2f out: wknd* **20/1**

2-00 **10** *½* **Dovils Date**[7] 1153 8-9-3 **66**.................... DavidProbert 11 60
(Tim Vaughan) *led after 2f: hrd rdn and hdd ent st: wknd qckly* **40/1**

-300 **11** *2* **Handsome Dan (IRE)**[35] 688 11-9-3 **66**.................... AdamKirby 7 56
(Sarah Hollinshead) *a in rr* **20/1**

2m 39.13s (-1.67) **Going Correction** -0.075s/f (Stan)
**WFA** 4 from 5yo+ 1lb **11** Ran SP% **112.5**
Speed ratings (Par 103): **102,100,100,100,99 99,98,97,96,96 95**
CSF £10.26 CT £119.61 TOTE £2.70: £1.30, £1.90, £4.70; EX 12.50 Trifecta £101.50.
**Owner** Derek Kierans **Bred** His Highness The Aga Khan's Studs S C **Trained** Stamullen, Co Meath

**FOCUS**
A modest handicap and straightforward form.

## 1258 BETWAY INSIDER H'CAP — 1m 1f 104y (Tp)

**6:45** (6:45) (Class 3) (0-95,95) 4-Y-O **£7,246** (£2,168; £1,084; £542; £270) **Stalls** Low

Form RPR

0-31 **1** **Winners Follow Me (GER)**[23] 885 4-9-3 **91**.................... LukeMorris 3 100
(James Tate) *settled in 4th: hdwy and 3rd ent st: pushed along and led over 1f out: r.o wl under hand riding. comf* **7/4**[1]

2-20 **2** *1 ½* **Bunbury**[14] 1023 5-9-1 **89**.................... ShaneKelly 9 95
(Richard Hughes) *keen: trckd ldr: ev ch and rdn 2f out: kpt on ins fnl f: but a hld* **8/1**[3]

2-36 **3** *nk* **Perfect Cracker**[33] 720 9-9-1 **89**.................... AdamKirby 4 95
(Clive Cox) *mid div: effrt ent st: rdn 2f out: styd on wl ins fnl f* **9/1**

6-06 **4** *1* **Intrude**[21] 918 5-9-3 **91**....................(t[1]) OisinMurphy 8 95
(Stuart Williams) *hld up on inner: swtchd wd ent st: rdn 2f out: r.o wl ins fnl f* **10/1**

2612 **5** *¾* **Dutch Uncle**[18] 963 5-9-3 **91**.................... JosephineGordon 10 93
(Ed Dunlop) *keen: led: pushed along 3f out: rdn 2f out: hdd and no ex over 1f out: grad wknd* **7/1**[2]

46-0 **6** *1 ½* **High Baroque (USA)**[66] 173 5-8-10 **84**.................... PaulHanagan 2 83
(Richard Fahey) *trckd ldrs: 4th st: sn rdn and wknd* **12/1**

534 **7** *½* **Coillte Cailin (IRE)**[18] 963 7-9-7 **95**.................... DanielTudhope 1 93
(David O'Meara) *hld up: racd wd entering st: rdn and no imp* **12/1**

1/4 **8** *1* **Andastra (GER)**[31] 744 4-9-0 **88**.................... FranBerry 5 85
(Ralph Beckett) *a in rr: rdn and no hdwy st* **8/1**[3]

224- **9** *2* **Cote D'Azur**[161] 7154 4-9-7 **95**.................... JasonHart 7 88
(Les Eyre) *plld hrd: mid div: pushed along 3f out: rdn and wknd st* **12/1**

1m 59.02s (-1.78) **Going Correction** -0.075s/f (Stan) **9** Ran SP% **113.3**
Speed ratings (Par 107): **104,102,102,101,100 99,99,98,96**
CSF £15.73 CT £97.57 TOTE £2.60: £1.20, £2.60, £2.70; EX 18.40 Trifecta £130.10.
**Owner** Sheikh Juma Dalmook Al Maktoum **Bred** Gestut Ammerland **Trained** Newmarket, Suffolk

**FOCUS**
A good handicap, but the early pace didn't look that quick and few got seriously involved. The winner continues to progress.

## 1259 32RED CASINO MAIDEN STKS — 1m 142y (Tp)

**7:15** (7:15) (Class 5) 3-Y-O **£2,911** (£866; £432; £216) **Stalls** Low

Form RPR

0- **1** **Weloof (FR)**[148] 7501 3-9-5 0.................... AdamKirby 1 80+
(Ed Dunlop) *mid div: gd hdwy on outer ent st: rdn and led over 1f out: sn clr: comf* **3/1**[3]

4- **2** *2 ¼* **Everything For You (IRE)**[148] 7496 3-9-5 0.................... TomEaves 6 75
(Kevin Ryan) *led: pushed along 3f out: rdn st: hdd over 1f: kpt on ins fnl f* **11/4**[2]

42- **3** *hd* **Sufi**[149] 7483 3-9-5 0.................... TomMarquand 5 75
(Richard Hannon) *trckd ldr: pushed along ent st: sn rdn: one pce fnl 2f* **11/8**[1]

6 **4** *6* **Magic Pass**[23] 882 3-9-5 0....................(h) DavidProbert 2 62
(Andrew Balding) *hld up: 5th st: rdn and styd on to take 4th ins fnl f* **14/1**

33 **5** *¾* **Dalavida (FR)**[7] 1143 3-9-0 0....................(h) OisinMurphy 3 55
(David Simcock) *4th early: tk 3rd 1/2-way: pushed along over 2f out: sn rdn and wknd* **11/1**

**6** *31* **Nonnie And Norny** 3-8-9 0.................... CharlieBennett[(5)] 4
(Shaun Harris) *in rr: chsd along early: rdn and lost tch fr 1/2-way* **100/1**

1m 48.91s (-1.19) **Going Correction** -0.075s/f (Stan) **6** Ran SP% **109.8**
Speed ratings (Par 98): **102,100,99,94,93 66**
CSF £11.10 TOTE £4.20: £2.10, £1.60; EX 12.20 Trifecta £23.90.
**Owner** Abdullah Saeed Al Naboodah **Bred** Dream With Me Stable Inc **Trained** Newmarket, Suffolk

**FOCUS**
This looked at least a fair maiden, with a trip clear. The third is rated near his 2yo form.

## 1260 SUNBETS.CO.UK H'CAP — 1m 142y (Tp)

**7:45** (7:47) (Class 6) (0-55,60) 4-Y-O+ **£2,264** (£673; £336; £168) **Stalls** Low

Form RPR

-026 **1** **Vivre La Reve**[25] 852 5-9-2 **50**....................(h) RyanPowell 7 58
(James Unett) *broke wl: remained prom: gd hdwy 3f out: 2nd st: rdn and led over 1f out: drvn out* **25/1**

02-2 **2** *1 ½* **Simply Clever**[40] 605 4-9-7 **55**.................... TomEaves 10 60
(David Brown) *led after 2f: pushed along ent st: rdn 2f out: hdd over 1f out: styd on one pce* **9/2**[3]

1-40 **3** *1 ¾* **Pipers Piping (IRE)**[10] 1084 11-9-1 **49**.................... RobHornby 6 50
(Mandy Rowland) *hld up: pushed along 3f out: chal wd into st: rdn and swtchd to ins: tk 3rd ins fnl f* **25/1**

-240 **4** *¾* **Canford Belle**[40] 605 4-8-12 **53**.................... PatrickVaughan[(7)] 3 53
(Grant Tuer) *mid div: 5th st gng wl: rdn 2f out: one pce* **7/1**

0303 **5** *1 ½* **Mount Cheiron (USA)**[39] 608 6-8-9 **50**..........(b) CallumRodriguez[(7)] 11 49
(Richard Ford) *slowly away: hdwy appr st: rdn 2f out: r.o: nrst fin* **9/1**

6-60 **6** *1* **Foylesideview (IRE)**[51] 425 5-8-12 **46** oh1................(h) SteveDrowne 4 40
(Harry Chisman) *in rr: effrt 3f out: rdn over 2f out: one pce* **22/1**

6061 **7** *2* **Hannington**[7] 1145 6-9-12 **60**....................(t) OisinMurphy 9 50
(Michael Appleby) *racd wd: prom tl rdn and lost pl 3f out* **9/4**[1]

0004 **8** *¾* **Way Up High**[18] 964 5-8-12 **46** oh1....................(p[1]) TomMarquand 5 35
(Steve Flook) *mid div: rdn st and no imp* **33/1**

01-0 **9** *¾* **Turaathy (IRE)**[30] 761 4-9-6 **54**.................... MartinDwyer 2 41
(Tony Newcombe) *a in rr* **16/1**

03/- **10** *14* **Coach Bombay (IRE)**[50] 454 9-9-9 **57**....................(bt) StevieDonohoe 1 15
(Adrian Brendan Joyce, Ire) *led 2f: styd prom tl wknd qckly 3f out* **4/1**[2]

000- **11** *23* **Overrider**[263] 1556 7-9-0 **48**....................(bt) LukeMorris 8
(Shaun Lycett) *mid div: rdn 3f out and no rspnse: wknd qckly and eased* **40/1**

1m 48.66s (-1.44) **Going Correction** -0.075s/f (Stan) **11** Ran SP% **114.8**
Speed ratings (Par 101): **103,101,100,99,98 97,95,94,94,81 61**
CSF £125.28 CT £2866.61 TOTE £28.50: £5.80, £1.70, £5.80; EX 167.00 Trifecta £4355.90.
**Owner** James Unett **Bred** P Balding **Trained** Wolverhampton, West Midlands

**FOCUS**
A moderate handicap and the form should prove reliable enough.

## 1261 32RED.COM EBF FILLIES' H'CAP — 7f 36y (Tp)

**8:15** (8:16) (Class 3) (0-90,84) 4-Y-O£ **£10,396** (£3,111; £1,555; £778; £387) **Stalls** High

Form RPR

-036 **1** **Shypen**[22] 896 4-9-2 **79**.................... PaulHanagan 9 85
(Richard Fahey) *trckd ldr: rdn and led over 1f out: hld on wl cl home* **3/1**[2]

0-00 **2** *¾* **Staintondale Lass (IRE)**[10] 1091 4-9-6 **83**.................... OisinMurphy 8 87
(Ed Vaughan) *settled in 4th: chal st: rdn over 1f out: r.o wl: but a hld by wnr* **16/1**

/06- **3** *1* **Hells Babe**[148] 7505 4-9-0 **77**.................... TomMarquand 10 79
(Michael Appleby) *led: kicked on ent st: but sn chal and hdd over 1f out: kpt on* **10/1**

-161 **4** *½* **Bint Arcano (FR)**[16] 994 4-9-7 **84**.................... JoeDoyle 4 86
(Julie Camacho) *hld up in rr tl hdwy over 2f out: r.o u.p ins fnl f: nvr nrr* **5/2**[1]

-434 **5** *nk* **Rebel Surge (IRE)**[28] 810 4-9-6 **83**....................(p) StevieDonohoe 2 83
(Richard Spencer) *mid div: hrd rdn over 2f out: styd on ins fnl f* **7/1**[3]

3222 **6** *1* **First Experience**[15] 996 6-8-13 **76**....................(p) JosephineGordon 1 74
(Lee Carter) *mid div: effrt on inner st: sn rdn and no imp* **10/1**

2-32 **7** *2 ½* **Pacolita (IRE)**[16] 994 5-8-13 **76**.................... LukeMorris 6 68
(Sylvester Kirk) *in rr: racd wd ent st: one pce u.p* **7/1**[3]

50-0 **8** *½* **Nouvelli Dancer (IRE)**[16] 994 4-9-6 **83**.................... FranBerry 5 74
(David C Griffiths) *plld hrd early: trckd ldrs: 3rd ent st: rdn over 1f out: wknd* **40/1**

5651 **9** *½* **Lady Lydia (IRE)**[12] 1066 6-9-1 **78**....................(tp) DanielMuscutt 7 67
(Gay Kelleway) *hld up: rdn fr 2f out: nvr a factor* **9/1**

04/0 **10** *8* **Dr Doro (IRE)**[28] 816 4-8-12 **75**....................(h) GeorgeDowning 3 46
(Ian Williams) *a in rr* **50/1**

1m 28.53s (-0.27) **Going Correction** -0.075s/f (Stan) **10** Ran SP% **117.0**
Speed ratings (Par 104): **98,97,96,95,95 93,91,90,89,80**
CSF £50.50 CT £354.37 TOTE £4.00: £1.40, £4.90, £3.60; EX 50.70 Trifecta £618.10.
**Owner** Nick Bradley Racing 27 **Bred** F Butler **Trained** Musley Bank, N Yorks

**FOCUS**
A decent fillies' handicap. The winner is rated to her best.
T/Plt: £139.60 to a £1 stake. Pool: £99,635.77 - 520.79 winning units T/Qpdt: £36.30 to a £1 stake. Pool: £10,555.07 - 215.03 winning units **Keith McHugh**

1262 - 1269a (Foreign Racing) - See Raceform Interactive

# 1157 SAINT-CLOUD (L-H)

Sunday, March 19

**OFFICIAL GOING: Turf: soft**

## 1270a PRIX LA CAMARGO (LISTED RACE) (3YO FILLIES) (TURF) — 1m

**3:20** 3-Y-O **£23,504** (£9,401; £7,051; £4,700; £2,350)

RPR

**1** **Melesina (IRE)**[24] 889 3-9-0 0.................... AlexisBadel 6 102
(Richard Fahey) *pressed ldr on outer: led appr end of first 2f: mde rest: drvn and 2 l clr 2 1/2f out: rdn ent fnl f: styd on wl* **53/10**[3]

**2** *¾* **Heuristique (IRE)**[128] 7928 3-9-0 0.................... Pierre-CharlesBoudot 1 100+
(F-H Graffard, France) **17/10**[1]

**3** *1 ¾* **Grecian Light (IRE)**[163] 7114 3-9-0 0.................... MickaelBarzalona 3 96
(Charlie Appleby) *t.k.h: chsd ldr on outer: drvn but no real imp 2 1/2f out: sn rdn and nt qckn dropped to 3rd 1f out: one pce fnl f* **56/10**

**4** *nk* **Gokena (FR)**[15] 3-9-0 0.................... JulienAuge 7 96?
(P Sogorb, France) **37/1**

**5** *snk* **Body Sculpt (FR)**[168] 6986 3-9-0 0.................... GregoryBenoist 2 95
(S Kobayashi, France) **175/10**

**6** *1 ¼* **Flower Fashion (FR)**[62] 3-9-0 0.................... StephanePasquier 11 92
(N Clement, France) **43/10**[2]

**7** *1 ¼* **Invincible Queen (FR)**[151] 7480 3-9-0 0.................... OlivierPeslier 4 89
(F Head, France) **43/5**

**8** *hd* **Lilly Kafeine (FR)**[30] 799 3-9-0 0.................... IoritzMendizabal 10 89
(J C Napoli, France) **35/1**

**9** *snk* **La Sardane (FR)**[14] 3-9-0 0....................(p) FranckBlondel 8 89
(B De Montzey, France) **177/10**

**10** *nk* **Westit**[23] 3-9-0 0.................... MaximeGuyon 5 88
(C Laffon-Parias, France) **119/10**

1m 44.11s (-3.39) **Going Correction** -0.425s/f (Firm) **10** Ran SP% **121.3**
Speed ratings: **99,98,96,96,96 94,93,93,93,92**
PARI-MUTUEL (all including 1 euro stake): WIN 6.30 PLACE 1.70, 1.30, 1.80 DF 8.60 SF 23.80.
**Owner** Nick Bradley Racing (Lastroseofsummer) **Bred** Duggan Bloodstock **Trained** Musley Bank, N Yorks

## 1271a PRIX EXBURY (GROUP 3) (4YO+) (TURF) — 1m 2f

**3:50** 4-Y-O+ **£34,188** (£13,675; £10,256; £6,837; £3,418)

RPR

**1** **Cloth Of Stars (IRE)**[248] 4332 4-9-4 0.................... MickaelBarzalona 3 114+
(A Fabre, France) *w.w in fnl trio: angled out and smooth prog 2f out: led under 1 1/2f out: pushed out fnl f: cosily* **11/8**[1]

**2** *1 ¼* **Star Victory (FR)**[98] 8336 6-9-0 0.................... IoritzMendizabal 4 108+
(J-L Dubord, France) *racd in midfield: drvn to cl 1 1/2f out: chsd ldr into fnl f: styd on but no match for wnr* **14/1**

**3** *3 ½* **Cafe Royal (GER)**[120] 8042 6-8-11 0.................... GregoryBenoist 2 98
(A Schutz, France) *chsd ldrs on inner: 2nd and drvn 2f out: rdn but nt qckn 1 1/2f out: one pce fnl f* **14/1**

**4** *3* **Savoken (FR)**[35] 711 6-8-11 0.................... Pierre-CharlesBoudot 10 92
(Cedric Rossi, France) *led after 1f: rdn and hdd under 1 1/2f out: grad lft bhd by ldrs* **11/4**[2]

5 4 **Palace Prince (GER)**[133] 7843 5-9-2 0 ChristopheSoumillon 8 89
(Jean-Pierre Carvalho, Germany) *cl up on outer: 2nd and ev ch 2 1/2f out: outpcd by ldrs 1 1/2f out: kpt on at same pce fnl f* **10/1**
6 3 **Subway Dancer (IRE)**[17] 5-9-2 0 RadekKoplik 5 83
(Z Koplik, Czech Republic) *hld up in fnl trio: plld way to chse ldrs bef 1/2-way: rdn 2 1/2f out: sn lost pl: wl hld last 1 1/2f* **25/1**
7 4 **Banzari**[154] 7404 5-8-13 0 AlexisBadel 7 72
(H-F Devin, France) *cl up: dropped into midfield bef 1/2-way: drvn wl over 2f out but no imp: wknd ins fnl 1 1/2f* **7/1**
8 4 **Primero (FR)**[39] 4-8-11 0 JulienAuge 9 62
(C Ferland, France) *dwlt and fly j. leaving stalls: in rr and sn racing keenly: last and drvn 2 1/2f out: sn lost tch* **13/2**[3]
9 2 **Restorer**[127] 7934 5-8-11 0 TonyPiccone 1 58
(William Muir) *broke wl and led: hdd after 1f: chsd ldng trio on inner: lost pl wl bef 1/2-way: towards rr and labouring 3f out: wknd fnl 1 1/2f* **25/1**

2m 7.05s (-8.95) **Going Correction** -0.55s/f (Hard) **9 Ran SP% 124.7**
Speed ratings: **113,112,109,106,103 101,98,94,93**
PARI-MUTUEL (all including 1 euro stake): WIN 2.60 PLACE 1.40, 2.50, 3.20 DF 12.20 SF 22.80.
**Owner** Godolphin SNC **Bred** Peter Anastasiou **Trained** Chantilly, France

1272 - 1281a (Foreign Racing) - See Raceform Interactive

# 1114 FONTAINEBLEAU
Friday, March 17

**OFFICIAL GOING: Turf: very soft**

## 1282a PRIX DU MONT PIERREUX (CLAIMER) (2YO) (TURF) 4f 110y
1:05 2-Y-O **£9,829** (£3,931; £2,948; £1,965; £982)

RPR

1 **Lamchope (FR)** 2-8-8 0 (p) JulienAuge 11
(A Chopard, France) **17/2**
2 4 1/2 **Thousand Oaks (FR)** 2-9-1 0 Jean-BernardEyquem 3
(B De Montzey, France) **53/10**[3]
3 4 1/2 **Vida Loca (FR)** 2-8-11 0 AntoineHamelin 9
(R Chotard, France) **9/1**
4 2 **Ormixa (FR)** 2-8-8 0 CristianDemuro 4
(J-V Toux, France) **12/1**
5 2 **Evaguei (FR)** 2-8-8 0 AntonioPolli 2
(W Menuet, France) **71/1**
6 1/2 **Double Pouvoir (FR)** 2-8-11 0 (p) ChristopheSoumillon 10
(A De Watrigant, France) **14/5**[1]
7 1 3/4 **Kiunguja (FR)** 2-9-1 0 Pierre-CharlesBoudot 8
(M Boutin, France) **5/1**[2]
8 3/4 **Out Of Money** 2-9-1 0 IrineuGoncalves 6
(Jo Hughes) **22/1**
9 3/4 **Auguri Pyla (FR)** 2-9-1 0 GregoryBenoist 5
(C Baillet, France) **8/1**
10 9 **Fast Pepite (FR)** 2-8-11 0 DavidMichaux 7
(C Plisson, France) **47/1**
11 4 1/2 **Lannister (FR)** 2-9-4 0 IoritzMendizabal 1
(M Boutin, France) **7/1**

PARI-MUTUEL (all including 1 euro stake): WIN 9.50; PLACE 3.50, 2.20, 3.80; DF 30.20; SF 70.10.
**Owner** Alain Chopard **Bred** A Chopard **Trained** France

# 1079 KEMPTON (A.W) (R-H)
Monday, March 20

**OFFICIAL GOING: Polytrack: standard**
Wind: First 3 races, strong, half behind; remainder, across, moderate Weather: Overcast, heavy shower race 3

## 1283 BETTER ODDS WITH MATCHBOOK BETTING EXCHANGE H'CAP (DIV I) 1m 2f 219y(P)
**2:00** (2:00) (Class 6) (0-65,67) 4-Y-O+ **£2,264** (£673; £336; £168) **Stalls** Low

Form RPR

-311 1 **Moayadd (USA)**[33] 733 5-9-2 **62** HollieDoyle(3) 9 72+
(Neil Mulholland) *trckd ldr 3f: styd cl up: effrt to ld 2f out: drawing clr whn hung lft 1f out: comf* **11/8**[1]
-000 2 4 1/2 **Solveig's Song**[23] 922 5-9-10 **67** (p) JackMitchell 3 69
(Steve Woodman) *hld up towards rr: swtchd sharply rt to inner jst over 2f out: prog after and styd on to take 2nd last 100yds: no ch w wnr* **14/1**
40-4 3 3/4 **Estibdaad (IRE)**[23] 922 7-9-3 **60** (t) DannyBrock 1 61
(Paddy Butler) *led: pressed and kicked on 4f out: rdn and hdd 2f out: no ch w wnr after and lost 2nd last 100yds* **15/2**[3]
5P05 4 1 1/2 **Fantasy Gladiator**[18] 992 11-9-7 **64** (p) AndrewMullen 2 62
(Michael Appleby) *trckd ldr after 3f to 4f out: sn urged along: nt qckn over 2f out: one pce after* **7/1**[2]
1-00 5 1 3/4 **Munsarim (IRE)**[20] 965 10-9-0 **57** (b) JosephineGordon 4 53
(Lee Carter) *s.i.s: hld up towards rr: rdn over 2f out: one pce and no ch w ldrs* **20/1**
0453 6 1 1/4 **Jersey Bull (IRE)**[24] 893 5-9-5 **62** (h) LiamKeniry 8 56+
(Michael Madgwick) *hld up and sn in rr: quick move 5f out to chse ldr 4f out: lost 2nd over 2f out: wknd over 1f out* **7/1**[2]
4-06 7 1 **Golden Muscade (USA)**[33] 747 4-8-12 **56** JoeDoyle 7 48
(Brian Barr) *t.k.h: in tch: rdn and no prog over 2f out: sn wknd* **33/1**
00-3 8 1/2 **The Detainee**[30] 820 4-8-8 **57** DavidParkes(5) 10 48
(Jeremy Gask) *mostly in last pair: urged along over 3f out: no prog* **15/2**[3]
4-05 9 4 1/2 **Goodby Inheritence**[24] 893 5-9-6 **63** (tp) AdamKirby 6 47
(Seamus Durack) *in tch: rdn and no prog over 2f out: wl btn over 1f out: eased* **12/1**
0 10 6 **Tsundoku (IRE)**[12] 1086 6-8-13 **59** LouisSteward(3) 5 33
(Alexandra Dunn) *s.i.s: in a last: lost tch 4f out: bhd after* **100/1**

2m 23.02s (1.12) **Going Correction** +0.05s/f (Slow) **10 Ran SP% 113.7**
Speed ratings (Par 101): **97,93,93,92,90 89,89,88,85,81**
CSF £21.99 CT £108.84 TOTE £1.90: £1.10, £6.80, £3.80; EX 23.50 Trifecta £107.20.
**Owner** P & Mrs K E Malcolm **Bred** Darley **Trained** Limpley Stoke, Wilts

**FOCUS**
The first division of an ordinary middle-distance handicap. They went a modest gallop into a strong headwind in the back-straight on standard Polytrack. The balance of the second and third set the level.

## 1284 BETTER ODDS WITH MATCHBOOK BETTING EXCHANGE H'CAP (DIV II) 1m 2f 219y(P)
**2:30** (2:30) (Class 6) (0-65,65) 4-Y-O+ **£2,264** (£673; £336; £168) **Stalls** Low

Form RPR

6-50 1 **Tommys Geal**[23] 922 5-8-11 **55** DanielMuscutt 8 61
(Michael Madgwick) *settled in midfield: prog fr 3f out to trck ldr 2f out: rdn to ld over 1f out: wandered sltly and drvn out* **8/1**
05-3 2 1 1/4 **Halling's Wish**[45] 555 7-9-6 **64** (b) TimmyMurphy 6 68
(Gary Moore) *trckd ldr: upsides 5f out tl led 3f out gng wl: rdn and hdd over 1f out: clr of rest but nt qckn: one pce after* **5/1**[2]
050- 3 3/4 **McDelta**[145] 7613 7-8-11 **60** PaddyPilley(5) 9 63
(Geoffrey Deacon) *hld up in last pair: rdn wl over 2f out: prog on wd outside over 1f out: styd on to take 3rd last 150yds: nrst fin* **40/1**
61-0 4 3 **Mr Frankie**[30] 806 6-8-13 **57** JoeDoyle 7 55
(John Spearing) *t.k.h: trckd ldrs: rdn over 2f out and sn outpcd: n.d after* **20/1**
-416 5 1 1/4 **Shining Romeo**[20] 965 5-9-4 **62** (v) LukeMorris 4 58
(Denis Quinn) *t.k.h: trckd ldrs: rdn over 2f out: hung lft and outpcd by ldng pair after: fdd ins fnl f* **5/1**[2]
-310 6 hd **Henry Grace (IRE)**[26] 865 6-8-9 **56** (b) HollieDoyle(3) 10 52
(Jimmy Fox) *pushed along in last early: rdn over 2f out: plugged on but nvr a threat* **7/1**
0-34 7 1 1/4 **Betsalottie**[20] 966 4-8-3 **55** JaneElliott(7) 5 49
(John Bridger) *led: edgd lft off rail and hdd 5f out: rdn 4f out: fdd fnl 2f* **13/2**[3]
3416 8 3 1/2 **Runaiocht (IRE)**[23] 922 7-9-2 **65** (b) DavidParkes(5) 2 53
(Paul Burgoyne) *taken down early: trckd ldr: led 5f out to 3f out: sn drvn and wknd over 1f out* **13/2**[3]
-045 9 3 1/2 **Zephyros (GER)**[32] 769 6-9-5 **63** OisinMurphy 1 45
(David Bridgwater) *dwlt sltly: in midfield: rdn and effrt over 2f out: sn wknd* **4/1**[1]
40-P 10 28 **Power Up**[46] 517 6-9-1 **59** JackMitchell 3
(Roger Ingram) *a in rr: wknd 3f out: t.o and eased fnl f* **28/1**

2m 20.55s (-1.35) **Going Correction** +0.05s/f (Slow) **10 Ran SP% 114.3**
Speed ratings (Par 101): **106,105,104,102,101 101,100,97,95,74**
CSF £45.71 CT £1503.24 TOTE £11.60: £3.20, £2.30, £9.00; EX 58.80 Trifecta £1518.10.
**Owner** Recycled Products Limited **Bred** Recycled Products Limited **Trained** Denmead, Hants

**FOCUS**
The second division of a modest middle-distance handicap. The winning time was 2.5 seconds quicker off a stronger gallop. The first two have been rated near this winter's levels.

## 1285 MATCHBOOK BETTING PODCAST H'CAP 7f (P)
**3:00** (3:01) (Class 6) (0-65,66) 4-Y-O+ **£2,264** (£673; £336; £168) **Stalls** Low

Form RPR

60-1 1 **Magic Mirror**[61] 282 4-8-8 **52** (v) TomMarquand 7 60
(Mark Rimell) *hld up in last pair: shkn up over 2f out: stl only 9th over 1f out: str run fnl f to ld last strides* **7/1**[3]
-110 2 hd **Bounty Pursuit**[11] 1109 5-9-8 **66** (h) SilvestreDeSousa 5 73
(Michael Appleby) *trckd ldrs: rdn over 2f out: clsd to ld over 1f out: sn hrd pressed: kpt on wl but hdd last strides* **7/4**[1]
0025 3 1/2 **Freddy With A Y (IRE)**[12] 1086 7-9-5 **63** PaddyAspell 1 69
(J R Jenkins) *wl in tch on inner: shkn up and clsd jst over 2f out: rdn to chal and w ldr 1f out: styd on but lost 2nd nr fin* **4/1**[2]
-436 4 1 1/2 **Keene's Pointe**[35] 724 7-9-1 **59** AdamBeschizza 3 61
(Steph Hollinshead) *hld up in midfield: rdn and nt qckn over 2f out: tried to cl over 1f out: kpt on same pce* **16/1**
00-5 5 shd **Caledonian Gold**[7] 1180 4-9-1 **59** JoeyHaynes 6 61
(Paul D'Arcy) *trckd ldrs: rdn over 2f out: cl enough over 1f out: nt qckn* **20/1**
5-02 6 1 **Hipz (IRE)**[26] 860 6-9-2 **60** (p) LiamKeniry 10 59
(Laura Mongan) *n.m.r s: t.k.h: hld up towards rr: rdn over 2f out: kpt on one pce and nvr landed a blow* **14/1**
30-0 7 1 3/4 **Royal Rettie**[33] 735 5-8-13 **57** (h) DannyBrock 11 52
(Paddy Butler) *pressed ldr: drvn to ld wl over 2f out: hdd and fdd over 1f out* **66/1**
-464 8 nse **Quintus Cerialis (IRE)**[33] 734 5-8-4 **53** (tp) PatrickO'Donnell(5) 4 48
(Karen George) *s.v.s and detached in last tl 4f out: shkn up over 2f out: kpt on fr over 1f out: no ch but nrst fin* **7/1**[3]
4460 9 nk **Mime Dance**[18] 986 6-9-5 **66** (p) HectorCrouch(3) 8 60
(John Butler) *hld up in midfield on outer: rdn and nt qckn over 2f out: one pce and n.d after* **25/1**
600- 10 1 1/2 **Secret Look**[167] 7059 7-9-7 **65** (p) TimmyMurphy 13 55
(Richard Phillips) *led to wl over 2f out: shkn up and steadily lost pl fr over 1f out* **66/1**
3-00 11 2 3/4 **Qortaaj**[48] 169 4-9-0 **65** GerO'Neill(7) 9 48
(David Loughnane) *towards rr on outer: rdn and wknd over 2f out* **12/1**
0-00 12 8 **Star Of The Stage**[44] 570 5-9-6 **64** (p) AdamKirby 2 26
(John Butler) *towards rr on inner: shkn up and fnd nil wl over 2f out: sn bhd* **10/1**

1m 27.13s (1.13) **Going Correction** +0.05s/f (Slow) **12 Ran SP% 122.3**
Speed ratings (Par 101): **95,94,94,92,92 91,89,89,88,87 83,74**
CSF £19.65 CT £59.65 TOTE £8.10: £2.80, £1.30, £1.90; EX 26.00 Trifecta £178.00.
**Owner** William Wood **Bred** Hesmonds Stud Ltd **Trained** Leafield, Oxon
■ Captain Joe was withdrawn. Price at time of withdrawal 66-1. Rule 4 does not apply

**FOCUS**
A modest handicap. They went a respectable gallop and the first three home had sound form claims beforehand. Straightforward form.

## 1286 WINNERS WELCOME AT MATCHBOOK EXCHANGE MAIDEN FILLIES' STKS (PLUS 10 RACE) 7f (P)
**3:30** (3:31) (Class 5) 3-Y-O **£2,911** (£866; £432; £216) **Stalls** Low

Form RPR

25-3 1 **Preobrajenska**[74] 76 3-9-0 70 (h) JosephineGordon 5 72
(William Jarvis) *trckd ldr: shkn up over 2f out: rdn to chal over 1f out: styd on to ld last 100yds* **14/1**
2 1/2 **Global Alexander (IRE)** 3-9-0 0 AdamKirby 3 71
(Clive Cox) *led: rdn and pressed over 1f out: edgd lft and hdd last 100yds: styd on* **5/4**[1]
3 2 1/2 **Western Safari (IRE)** 3-9-0 0 SeanLevey 4 64
(Richard Hannon) *in tch: rdn 2f out: prog to chse ldng pair over 1f out: kpt on but no imp* **12/1**

33 **4** 3 1/2 **Secret Salvage (IRE)**[11] 1111 3-9-0 0 FergusSweeney 1 55
(Jamie Osborne) *dwlt: hld up in rr: pushed along over 2f out: prog and one reminder over 1f out: tk 4th fnl f: fdd nr fin* **10/1**[3]

5 **5** 2 1/4 **From A Distance (IRE)**[18] 983 3-9-0 0 LiamKeniry 8 49+
(David Simcock) *t.k.h: hld up in rr: rn green whn shkn up over 2f out: one pce after* **40/1**

4- **6** 3/4 **Double Spin**[264] 3782 3-9-0 0 AndreaAtzeni 7 47
(John Gosden) *trckd ldng pair on outer: rdn and nt qckn over 2f out: steadily wknd* **15/8**[2]

**7** 3 1/4 **Irish Sky (IRE)** 3-9-0 0 KieranO'Neill 2 39
(Henry Spiller) *cl up on inner: wl in tch 2f out: wknd qckly over 1f out* **33/1**

**8** 4 **Garnetta** 3-9-0 0 JackMitchell 9 28
(Amanda Perrett) *slowly away: rn v green and virtually t.o early: kpt on fnl 2f* **33/1**

**9** 6 **Reckless Woman (IRE)** 3-9-0 0 JFEgan 6 13
(Jeremy Noseda) *dwlt: towards rr: hung lft and racd awkwardly bnd 4f out to 3f out: sn wknd* **20/1**

1m 26.5s (0.50) **Going Correction** +0.05s/f (Slow) **9** Ran SP% **115.8**
Speed ratings (Par 95): **99,98,95,91,89 88,84,79,73**
CSF £31.31 TOTE £11.40: £3.10, £1.10, £3.00; EX 40.10 Trifecta £262.40.
**Owner** W J and T C O Gredley **Bred** Stetchworth & Middle Park Studs Ltd **Trained** Newmarket, Suffolk

**FOCUS**
A fair 3yo fillies' maiden. They went a respectable gallop. The level is fluid.

## 1287 MATCHBOOK TRADERS CONFERENCE MAIDEN STKS 6f (P)
**4:00** (4:00) (Class 5) 3-Y-O+ **£2,911** (£866; £432; £216) **Stalls** Low

Form RPR

32- **1** **Ashwaq**[110] 8152 3-8-10 0 TomMarquand 9 69
(Richard Hannon) *mde all: kicked for home over 2f out: decisive ld over 1f out: rdn out and kpt on* **8/11**[1]

0- **2** 1 1/4 **Hisar (IRE)**[256] 4053 3-9-1 0 (h[1]) LukeMorris 6 69
(Ronald Harris) *cl up on inner: rdn over 1f out: kpt on to win battle for 2nd: nvr able to chal* **20/1**

5 **3** shd **Essential**[25] 878 3-9-1 0 OisinMurphy 11 69
(George Scott) *mostly chsd wnr: rdn and no imp over 1f out: kpt on but lost 2nd nr fin* **3/1**[2]

**4** hd **Sparkalot** 3-9-1 0 JFEgan 7 68+
(Simon Dow) *t.k.h early: cl up: rdn to dispute 2nd fr over 1f out: kpt on* **10/1**[3]

**5** 2 1/4 **Napping** 4-9-9 0 GeorgeDowning 5 60
(Anabel K Murphy) *trckd ldrs: shkn up and nt qckn over 2f out: one pce after* **50/1**

06 **6** 1/2 **Pocket Warrior**[16] 1024 6-9-9 0 GeorgeWood(5) 3 63+
(Martin Bosley) *hld up in midfield on inner: pushed along over 2f out: nvr on terms w ldrs but kpt on steadily whn rdn fnl f* **66/1**

**7** 3 3/4 **Mister Chow** 3-9-1 0 TimmyMurphy 4 47
(Gary Moore) *s.s: hld up in detached last: pushed along and kpt on steadily fr 2f out: nt disgracd* **33/1**

00 **8** shd **Tilly's Bridge**[26] 863 4-9-9 0 JackMitchell 1 46
(Steve Woodman) *nvr beyond midfield: lft bhd fr over 2f out* **66/1**

0 **9** nk **Spare Parts (IRE)**[30] 807 3-8-12 0 CallumShepherd(3) 10 46
(Charles Hills) *t.k.h: chsd ldrs on outer: wknd over 2f out* **25/1**

6 **10** 1 1/2 **Tojosimbre**[30] 807 3-9-1 0 (h[1]) ShaneKelly 2 41
(Richard Hughes) *nvr beyond midfield: wknd over 2f out* **14/1**

00 **11** 1 **Zerafino (BEL)**[30] 807 4-10-0 0 KieranO'Neill 12 42
(Jimmy Fox) *dwlt and wnt lft s: a wl in rr* **150/1**

5- **12** 1 3/4 **Double Dutch**[327] 1783 3-9-1 0 AdamKirby 8 32
(John Butler) *hld up: a towards rr: wknd over 2f out* **10/1**[3]

1m 14.02s (0.92) **Going Correction** +0.05s/f (Slow)
**WFA** 3 from 4yo+ 13lb **12** Ran SP% **124.9**
Speed ratings (Par 103): **95,93,93,92,89 89,84,84,83,81 80,78**
CSF £25.32 TOTE £1.80: £1.10, £4.50, £1.40; EX 17.10 Trifecta £49.40.
**Owner** Al Shaqab Racing **Bred** Stowell Hill Ltd **Trained** East Everleigh, Wilts

**FOCUS**
An ordinary maiden. The short-priced favourite proved thoroughly dominant off her own tempo from a modest draw. The winner hs been rated 5lb off her debut form.

## 1288 SMARTER BETS WITH MATCHBOOK BETTING EXCHANGE H'CAP 1m (P)
**4:30** (4:30) (Class 4) (0-85,87) 4-Y-O+ **£4,690** (£1,395; £697; £348) **Stalls** Low

Form RPR

-151 **1** **Gossiping**[51] 460 5-9-1 79 ShaneKelly 7 88
(Gary Moore) *trckd ldng trio: clsd gng strly over 2f out: led over 1f out: drvn out fnl f* **5/2**[1]

45-3 **2** 1 1/4 **The Warrior (IRE)**[24] 896 5-9-6 84 JackMitchell 8 90
(Amanda Perrett) *hld up in 5th: shkn up over 2f out: prog over 1f out: styd on fnl f to take 2nd last strides* **5/2**[1]

5-01 **3** nk **Alejandro (IRE)**[33] 736 8-9-9 87 JosephineGordon 1 92
(David Loughnane) *cl up in 3rd: tried to chal on inner 2f out: chsd wnr over 1f out: kpt on but no real imp: lost 2nd last strides* **15/2**[3]

230- **4** 2 1/2 **Kestrel Dot Com**[172] 6899 5-9-2 80 (h) DavidProbert 2 80
(Chris Dwyer) *sltly awkward and stdd s: hld up in last: pushed along over 3f out: rdn and kpt on fr over 2f out to take 4th nr fin* **25/1**

00-0 **5** 1 **Thaqaffa (IRE)**[32] 760 4-9-0 78 SilvestreDeSousa 3 75
(Amy Murphy) *led at gd pce: rdn over 2f out: hdd over 1f out: wknd* **6/1**[2]

1/4- **6** nk **Jufn**[342] 1398 4-9-4 82 LiamKeniry 6 79
(John Butler) *taken down early: settled in rr: rdn over 2f out: hanging and no great prog* **16/1**

-045 **7** 4 **Presumido (IRE)**[23] 918 7-9-2 85 PaddyBradley(5) 5 72
(Simon Dow) *hld up in rr: hld together fr over 2f out tl rdn and no rspnse over 1f out* **8/1**

230- **8** 7 **Harlequin Striker (IRE)**[168] 7017 5-9-4 82 RobertWinston 4 53
(Dean Ivory) *chsd ldr to over 2f out: wknd qckly* **12/1**

1m 38.22s (-1.58) **Going Correction** +0.05s/f (Slow) **8** Ran SP% **111.7**
Speed ratings (Par 105): **109,107,107,104,103 103,99,92**
CSF £7.80 CT £37.82 TOTE £3.30: £1.10, £1.70, £2.20; EX 9.70 Trifecta £27.80.
**Owner** G L Moore & Partners **Bred** Darley **Trained** Lower Beeding, W Sussex

**FOCUS**
A decent handicap. They went a proper gallop and an improving horse won this contest in taking fashion. It's been rated through the runner-up.

## 1289 MATCHBOOK TRADERS CONFERENCE H'CAP 1m 3f 219y(P)
**5:00** (5:02) (Class 4) (0-80,82) 4-Y-O+ **£4,690** (£1,395; £697; £348) **Stalls** Centre

Form RPR

/50- **1** **Instant Karma (IRE)**[84] 4634 6-9-4 80 LouisSteward(3) 4 86
(Michael Bell) *trckd ldng pair: pushed along 3f out: clsd fr 2f out: rdn to ld 1f out: hung lft ins fnl f: hld on* **10/1**

6-63 **2** 3/4 **Safira Menina**[26] 856 5-8-6 72 MillyNaseb(7) 8 78
(Martin Smith) *hld up in last: shkn up 3f out: stl last over 1f out: gd prog after: tk 2nd nr fin and clsng on wnr whn sltly impeded last strides* **12/1**

0-10 **3** 1/2 **Elysian Prince**[51] 467 6-9-8 81 JackMitchell 7 85
(Neil King) *hld up in 6th: rdn over 2f out: prog over 1f out: styd on fnl f to take 3rd last stride* **9/2**[2]

6-23 **4** shd **Light Of Air (FR)**[20] 965 4-8-9 70 (b) ShaneKelly 5 74
(Gary Moore) *trckd ldr: chal 4f out: led over 2f out and cajoled along: hdd and nt qckn 1f out* **5/1**[3]

6-00 **5** 2 1/4 **Giantstepsahead (IRE)**[47] 507 8-9-6 79 (t[1]) DanielMuscutt 2 79
(Alan Bailey) *led: pressed 4f out: hdd over 1f out: fdd over 1f out* **8/1**

-224 **6** 1 **Alcatraz (IRE)**[30] 809 5-9-6 79 (vt) AdamKirby 3 78
(George Baker) *stdd s: hld up in last pair: rdn and no prog over 2f out: n.d after* **9/4**[1]

322/ **7** 5 **Bostonian**[868] 5286 7-9-6 79 LukeMorris 6 70
(Shaun Lycett) *chsd ldng trio: rdn over 2f out: wknd over 1f out* **50/1**

-453 **8** 6 **Tangramm**[42] 599 5-9-9 82 (p) RobertWinston 1 63
(Dean Ivory) *in tch in 5th: rdn over 2f out: wknd qckly over 1f out* **9/2**[2]

2m 33.72s (-0.78) **Going Correction** +0.05s/f (Slow)
**WFA** 4 from 5yo+ 1lb **8** Ran SP% **113.7**
Speed ratings (Par 105): **104,103,103,103,101 100,97,93**
CSF £118.08 CT £615.25 TOTE £12.90: £2.90, £2.70, £1.80; EX 111.60 Trifecta £792.90.
**Owner** J Barnett & Partner **Bred** Glashare House Stud **Trained** Newmarket, Suffolk

**FOCUS**
A fairly decent middle-distance handicap. They went a respectable gallop and a now decent hurdler won well reverting to the Flat off a break. The level is straightforward.

## 1290 MATCHBOOK BETTING EXCHANGE H'CAP 6f (P)
**5:30** (5:31) (Class 5) (0-70,76) 4-Y-O+ **£2,911** (£866; £432; £216) **Stalls** Low

Form RPR

1-04 **1** **Major Valentine**[28] 844 5-8-10 66 BenRobinson(7) 2 74
(John O'Shea) *trckd ldr: pushed into ld jst over 2f out: rdn over 1f out: hld on wl fnl f* **15/2**

1-06 **2** nk **Nezar (IRE)**[14] 1062 6-9-8 71 (h) RobertWinston 10 78
(Dean Ivory) *hld up towards rr: prog 2f out: squeezed through over 1f out: drvn to chse wnr ins fnl f: clsng at fin but a hld* **16/1**

4111 **3** 3/4 **Athassel**[4] 1219 8-9-6 76 6ex KatherineGlenister(7) 4 81
(David Evans) *hld up in 7th: prog on inner 2f out: rdn to dispute 2nd fr jst over 1f out: styd on but nvr able to chal* **3/1**[1]

530 **4** 1 1/4 **Higher Court (USA)**[9] 1140 9-9-7 70 GeorgeWood 5 71
(Emma Owen) *prom: rdn over 2f out: tried to mount an effrt over 1f out: but kpt on same pce* **10/1**

064- **5** nk **Muatadel**[137] 7782 4-9-7 70 (b[1]) SilvestreDeSousa 1 70
(Ed Dunlop) *trckd ldrs: rdn over 2f out: chsd wnr over 1f out: edgd lft and fnd little: one pce fnl f* **7/2**[2]

400- **6** 1 1/4 **Classic Pursuit**[144] 7644 6-9-4 67 (p) OisinMurphy 11 63+
(Michael Appleby) *blindfold off sltly late and slowly away: swtchd fr wd draw to inner and hld up in last trio: pushed along over 2f out: rdn and styd on fnl f: no ch* **14/1**

151 **7** 3/4 **K'Gari Spirit**[14] 1062 4-9-1 69 (t) DavidParkes(5) 7 62
(Jeremy Gask) *trckd ldrs: rdn over 2f out: nt qckn over 1f out: one pce after* **7/1**[3]

5604 **8** 1 1/4 **Indian Affair**[14] 1063 7-8-11 60 (bt) LukeMorris 6 52
(Milton Bradley) *hld up towards rr: shkn up over 2f out: sme prog but no ch whn nt clr run jst over 1f out: kpt on* **16/1**

0-55 **9** 3 3/4 **Panther Patrol (IRE)**[14] 1062 7-9-4 70 EdwardGreatrex(3) 12 47
(Eve Johnson Houghton) *dropped in fr wd draw and hld up in last: shkn up and bhd over 2f out: nvr in it* **14/1**

0-03 **10** 1/2 **Bush Warrior (IRE)**[12] 1087 6-9-6 69 (v) AdamKirby 3 45
(Anabel K Murphy) *led at str pce: hdd jst over 2f out: wknd qckly over 1f out* **12/1**

0000 **11** 5 **King Of Swing**[37] 682 4-9-4 67 (h) ShaneKelly 8 27
(Richard Hughes) *a wl in rr: no prog over 2f out: wknd* **16/1**

0400 **12** 1/2 **Waneen (IRE)**[13] 1071 4-9-3 66 JFEgan 9 24
(John Butler) *chsd ldrs on wd outside to 1/2-way: sn wknd* **50/1**

1m 11.85s (-1.25) **Going Correction** +0.05s/f (Slow) **12** Ran SP% **121.2**
Speed ratings (Par 103): **110,109,108,106,106 104,103,102,97,96 89,89**
CSF £124.04 CT £450.53 TOTE £9.10: £2.80, £5.20, £1.60; EX 146.20 Trifecta £1112.20.
**Owner** Pete Smith **Bred** J R Salter **Trained** Elton, Gloucs

**FOCUS**
A fair handicap. They went a decent gallop and it is sound form. The third confirmed he hasn't been flattered by his recent progressive form.
T/Plt: £17.80 to a £1 atake. Pool: £76,556.87 - 3134.03 winning units T/Qpdt: £2.90 to a £1 stake. Pool: £6,158.47 - 1558.76 winning units **Jonathan Neesom**

# 1204 SOUTHWELL (L-H)
### Tuesday, March 21

**OFFICIAL GOING: Fibresand: standard**
Wind: Strong across moving to half behind after 3.15 race Weather: Fine and dry,but blustery and wintry showers later

## 1291 BETWAY STAYERS' H'CAP 1m 6f 21y(F)
**2:10** (2:10) (Class 5) (0-75,77) 4-Y-O+ **£3,234** (£962; £481; £240) **Stalls** Low

Form RPR

2223 **1** **Eurato (FR)**[14] 1073 7-9-2 72 (p) FinleyMarsh(7) 5 78
(Steve Gollings) *trckd ldng pair: hdwy on outer 3f out: chsd ldr over 2f out: sn chal: rdn to ld over 1f out: drvn and edgd lft ins fnl f: kpt on wl towards fin* **9/4**[2]

2231 **2** nk **Brigadoon**[6] 1207 10-10-0 77 6ex SilvestreDeSousa 4 83
(Michael Appleby) *trckd ldr: cl up 6f out: led 4f out: pushed along over 2f out: sn jnd and rdn: hdd over 1f out: sn drvn and ev ch ins fnl f: kpt on same pce towards fin* **8/11**[1]

6-54 **3** *28* **Mister Bob (GER)**[18] 1002 8-9-12 **75**................................(p) TedDurcan 2 45
(James Bethell) *trckd ldng pair on inner: pushed along wl over 3f out: rdn wl over 2f out: sn one pce* **6/1**[3]

-000 **4** *9* **With Hindsight (IRE)**[22] 958 9-8-11 **60**................................ TomEaves 3 18
(Steve Gollings) *led: jnd 6f out: pushed along and hdd 4f out: sn rdn: outpcd and bhd fnl 3f* **50/1**

3m 9.46s (1.16) **Going Correction** +0.20s/f (Slow) **4** Ran SP% **104.9**
Speed ratings (Par 103): **104,103,87,82**
CSF £4.06 TOTE £3.50; EX 4.90 Trifecta £6.20.

**Owner** Lloyd Martell **Bred** Wertheimer & Frere **Trained** Scamblesby, Lincs

**FOCUS**
The first two drew well clear in the straight. A small step forward from the winner.

## 1292 BETWAY H'CAP 1m 4f 14y(F)
**2:40** (2:40) (Class 5) (0-75,77) 4-Y-O+ **£3,234** (£962; £481; £240) **Stalls** Low

Form RPR

1-10 **1** **Tatting**[56] 389 8-9-10 **77**................................ PaulMulrennan 2 86
(Lawrence Mullaney) *hld up towards rr: pushed along wl over 3f out: hdwy 2f out: swtchd rt to outer and gd hdwy over 1f out: rdn to chal ins fnl f: edgd lft and styd on wl to ld last 100 yds* **14/1**

00-2 **2** *½* **Busy Street**[7] 1182 5-9-7 **74**................................ JoeFanning 4 81
(Alan Swinbank) *prom: trckd ldr after 4f: cl up 4f out: led 3f out: rdn along wl over 1f out: drvn and edgd rt ins fnl f: hdd and no ex last 100 yds* **1/1**[1]

0-40 **3** *3 ¼* **Major Rowan**[19] 991 6-9-4 **71**................................ PhillipMakin 5 73
(John Davies) *trckd ldrs: hdwy 3f out: swtchd lft and rdn wl over 1f out: sn drvn: kpt on same pce fnl f* **12/1**

-061 **4** *¾* **Muqarred (USA)**[7] 1186 5-9-2 **69** 6ex................................(p) DanielTudhope 8 70
(Roger Fell) *trckd ldrs: hdwy over 3f out: chsd ldr over 2f out: rdn to chal wl over 1f out: son drvn and kpt on one pce* **9/4**[2]

03-5 **5** *3 ½* **Alshan Fajer**[7] 1182 7-8-13 **73**................................ GinaMangan(7) 7 68
(J R Jenkins) *hld up: hdwy over 3f out: chsd ldrs 2f out: sn rdn and wknd over 1f out* **66/1**

3613 **6** *8* **The Lock Master (IRE)**[12] 1113 10-9-3 **70**..........(v) SilvestreDeSousa 1 52
(Michael Appleby) *trckd ldng pair on inner: pushed along over 4f out: rdn along 3f out: sn drvn and wknd wl over 1f out* **8/1**[3]

510- **7** *16* **Torremar (FR)**[134] 7846 4-9-5 **74**................................(p) TomEaves 3 31
(Kevin Ryan) *led: rdn along 4f out: hdd over 3f out and sn wknd* **20/1**

00-5 **8** *24* **Falcon's Fire (IRE)**[12] 1113 4-8-12 **72**................................ ShirleyTeasdale(5) 6 +
(Keith Dalgleish) *rrd bdly s and lost many l: a bhd* **50/1**

2m 43.5s (2.50) **Going Correction** +0.20s/f (Slow)
**WFA** 4 from 5yo+ 1lb **8** Ran SP% **114.5**
Speed ratings (Par 103): **99,98,96,96,93 88,77,61**
CSF £28.53 CT £185.35 TOTE £11.60: £3.30, £1.10, £2.80; EX 31.30 Trifecta £155.20.

**Owner** The Usual Suspects **Bred** Darley **Trained** Great Habton, N Yorks

**FOCUS**
A fair handicap. The winner has been rated to his best of recent years.

## 1293 SUNBETS.CO.UK MEDIAN AUCTION MAIDEN STKS 1m 13y(F)
**3:15** (3:16) (Class 5) 3-5-Y-O **£3,234** (£962; £481; £240) **Stalls** Low

Form RPR

3 **1** **Whosyourhousemate**[66] 236 3-8-11 0................................ JoeFanning 1 77
(Ed Vaughan) *trckd ldrs on inner: pushed along over 3f out: hdwy to chse ldr over 2f out: sn rdn: drvn over 1f out: swtchd rt ins fnl f: styd on wl to ld nr fin* **8/11**[1]

2-50 **2** *½* **Magical Forest (IRE)**[26] 889 3-8-6 73................................(b) LukeMorris 6 71
(Marco Botti) *sn slt ld: pushed clr wl over 2f out: rdn wl over 1f out: drvn and hung lft to far rail appr fnl f: hdd and no ex towards fin* **13/8**[2]

- **3** *6* **Testbourne (IRE)** 3-8-8 0................................ JordanVaughan(3) 5 62
(K R Burke) *prom: cl up 1/2-way: pushed along 3f out: rdn over 2f out: kpt on same pce* **10/1**[3]

**4** *3 ¼* **Lakeski** 3-8-6 0................................ KieranO'Neill 3 49
(Scott Dixon) *chsd ldrs: rdn along wl over 2f out: sn one pce* **40/1**

0-0 **5** *2* **Melo Magic**[12] 1111 3-7-13 0................................ GinaMangan(7) 4 44
(J R Jenkins) *fly j. s and slowly away: bhd: hdwy over 3f out: rdn along and in tch on inner over 2f out: sn one pce* **200/1**

50 **6** *29* **Billys Connoisseur (IRE)**[45] 580 4-10-0 0................ DuranFentiman 2
(Tim Easterby) *prom: pushed along over 4f out: sn lost pl and bhd* **100/1**

1m 48.4s (4.70) **Going Correction** +0.20s/f (Slow)
**WFA** 3 from 4yo 17lb **6** Ran SP% **109.0**
Speed ratings (Par 103): **84,83,77,74,72 43**
CSF £1.97 TOTE £1.80: £1.40, £1.10; EX 2.50 Trifecta £4.00.

**Owner** Ballymore Downunder Syndicate **Bred** Heather Raw **Trained** Newmarket, Suffolk

**FOCUS**
An ordinary maiden. The runner-up has been rated a fraction off last year's domestic level.

## 1294 32RED.COM H'CAP 4f 214y(F)
**3:50** (3:50) (Class 4) (0-85,80) 3-Y-O **£5,175** (£1,540; £769; £384) **Stalls** Centre

Form RPR

1260 **1** **Erissimus Maximus (FR)**[11] 1124 3-9-7 **76**........(b[1]) SilvestreDeSousa 4 85
(Chris Dwyer) *racd towards stands side: chsd ldrs: hdwy wl over 1f out: rdn jst over 1f out: styd on strly to ld last 75 yds* **5/2**[2]

3111 **2** *1* **Fiery Spice (IRE)**[6] 1204 3-9-2 **71** 6ex................................ LukeMorris 2 76
(Robert Cowell) *cl up centre: led after 1f: rdn and hung bdly lft to far rail over 1f out: sn drvn: hdd and no ex last 75 yds* **5/6**[1]

400- **3** *2* **Camargue**[161] 7258 3-9-9 **78**................................ JoeFanning 3 76
(Mark Johnston) *racd centre: prom: cl up 1/2-way: rdn along wl over 1f out: kpt on same pce* **5/1**[3]

120- **4** *3 ¾* **Reckless Serenade (IRE)**[129] 7938 3-9-2 **71**............. ConnorBeasley 1 56
(Keith Dalgleish) *racd towards far side: slt ld 1f: cl up: rdn along 1/2-way: sn wknd* **14/1**

0-04 **5** *2 ¾* **Grecian Divine (IRE)**[13] 1090 3-9-4 **80**................ SophieScardifield(7) 5 55
(Joseph Tuite) *trckd ldrs: pushed along bef 1/2-way: sn outpcd and bhd* **50/1**

59.33s (-0.37) **Going Correction** -0.05s/f (Stan) **5** Ran SP% **108.4**
Speed ratings (Par 100): **100,98,95,89,84**
CSF £4.81 TOTE £3.50: £1.70, £1.10; EX 4.80 Trifecta £8.80.

**Owner** P Venner **Bred** Derek Clee **Trained** Newmarket, Suffolk

**FOCUS**
A fair little sprint in which the favourite threw his chance away by hanging. The runner-up has been rated to form.

## 1295 SUNBETS.CO.UK H'CAP 7f 14y(F)
**4:25** (4:25) (Class 2) (0-105,99) 4-Y-O+
**£12,450** (£3,728; £1,864; £932; £466; £234) **Stalls** Low

Form RPR

5206 **1** **Supersta**[10] 1148 6-9-1 **93**................................(p) SilvestreDeSousa 4 105
(Michael Appleby) *cl up: led 2f out: rdn and qcknd clr over 1f out: readily* **5/1**[3]

0012 **2** *3 ¾* **Outer Space**[6] 1208 6-9-0 **92**................................ TimmyMurphy 7 94
(Jamie Osborne) *trckd ldrs on outer: pushed along wl over 2f out: rdn wl over 1f out: kpt on fnl f: tk 2nd nr fin* **9/2**[2]

23-3 **3** *nk* **Twin Appeal (IRE)**[12] 1105 6-8-10 **88**................................(b) PhillipMakin 5 89
(David Barron) *trckd ldng pair: hdwy 3f out: chsd wnr wl over 1f out and sn rdn: drvn and kpt on same pce fnl f* **2/1**[1]

0-13 **4** *3 ¼* **Sir Billy Wright (IRE)**[12] 1110 6-8-8 **86**................................ AndrewMullen 8 78
(David Evans) *hld up in rr: hdwy 3f out: sn rdn: kpt on fnl f* **10/1**

3541 **5** *hd* **Dusky Dawn**[12] 1104 5-8-2 **80**................................ JoeFanning 6 72
(Alan Swinbank) *trckd ldrs: rdn along wl over 2f out: sn drvn and btn* **11/1**

0412 **6** *4* **War Department (IRE)**[12] 1105 4-8-12 **90**...............(v) ConnorBeasley 1 71
(Keith Dalgleish) *chsd ldrs on inner: rdn along wl over 2f out: sn drvn and grad wknd* **5/1**[3]

/05- **7** *nk* **Ascription (IRE)**[176] 6837 8-9-7 **99**................................ DanielTudhope 2 79
(Keith Dalgleish) *sn slt ld: rdn along over 2f out: sn hdd: drvn and wknd* **11/1**

1m 29.88s (-0.42) **Going Correction** +0.20s/f (Slow) **7** Ran SP% **110.6**
Speed ratings (Par 109): **110,105,105,101,101 96,96**
CSF £25.66 CT £55.46 TOTE £5.10: £2.20, £2.70; EX 29.40 Trifecta £93.20.

**Owner** Rod In Pickle Partnership **Bred** Cheveley Park Stud Ltd **Trained** Oakham, Rutland

**FOCUS**
The early pace wasn't strong but it was hard not to be taken by the way the winner drew right away in the straight, proving himself very much at home on this surface. A clear pb from the winner, with the runner-up rated to form.

## 1296 BETWAY SPRINT H'CAP 6f 16y(F)
**5:00** (5:02) (Class 5) (0-75,77) 4-Y-O+ **£3,234** (£962; £481; £240) **Stalls** Low

Form RPR

1503 **1** **Big Amigo (IRE)**[10] 1147 4-9-4 **67**................................ SilvestreDeSousa 7 77
(Daniel Mark Loughnane) *in tch: hdwy to chse ldrs over 2f out: rdn to ld over 1f out: drvn and kpt on strly fnl f* **10/1**

-055 **2** *2 ½* **Red Touch (USA)**[14] 1074 5-9-13 **76**................................(h) LukeMorris 9 79
(Michael Appleby) *towards rr: pushed along 3f out: rdn along and wd st: hdwy on outer 2f out: chsd wnr enterinmg fnl f: sn drvn: edgd lft and no imp* **8/1**[3]

00-3 **3** *2 ¼* **Meshardal (GER)**[20] 971 7-9-3 **66**................................ JamesSullivan 8 65
(Ruth Carr) *trckd ldrs: effrt and sltly hmpd 3f out: wd st: and rdn to chse ldrs 2f out: drvn over 1f out: kpt on same pce* **6/1**[2]

14/2 **4** *1* **Dark Profit (IRE)**[12] 1109 5-9-1 **69**................................(p) ShirleyTeasdale(5) 10 62
(Keith Dalgleish) *dwlt: sn trcking ldrs on outer: hdwy and cl up over 2f out: rdn wl over 1f out: drvn appr fnl f: kpt on same pce* **9/2**[1]

4231 **5** *¾* **Crosse Fire**[7] 1185 5-9-13 **76** 6ex................................ KieranO'Neill 5 67
(Scott Dixon) *dwlt: sn chsng ldrs: hdwy 3f out: chal over 2f out: sn rdn and ev ch: drvn wl over 1f out: grad wknd* **9/2**[1]

1660 **6** *nk* **Bring On A Spinner**[7] 1185 4-9-11 **77**................................(be) AaronJones(3) 6 73
(Stuart Williams) *trckd ldrs: hdwy 3f out: rdn along 2f out: no imp appr fnl f* **6/1**[2]

435- **7** *½* **African Blessing**[213] 5643 4-9-7 **70**................................ PhillipMakin 3 58
(David Barron) *cl up: rdn along 2f out: sn drvn and grad wknd* **9/2**[1]

0405 **8** *½* **Ebony N Ivory**[5] 1219 4-9-5 **68**................................(p) OisinMurphy 1 55
(Archie Watson) *slt ld: rdn along 3f out: drvn 2f out: sn hdd & wknd* **16/1**

4/00 **9** *15* **Baron Run**[48] 514 7-8-7 **63**................................ RussellHarris(7) 4 5
(K R Burke) *chsd ldrs on inner: rdn along wl over 2f out: sn wknd* **66/1**

500- **10** *¾* **Coiste Bodhar (IRE)**[98] 8349 6-8-12 **68**................................ RPWalsh(7) 2 10+
(Scott Dixon) *cl up: rdn along whn hmpd jst over 3f out: sn wknd* **40/1**

1m 17.3s (0.80) **Going Correction** +0.20s/f (Slow) **10** Ran SP% **113.1**
Speed ratings (Par 103): **102,98,95,94,93 92,92,91,71,70**
CSF £84.76 CT £402.48 TOTE £9.80: £2.60, £5.00, £1.80; EX 49.50 Trifecta £434.50.

**Owner** The Friday Morning Fourball **Bred** Kildaragh Stud **Trained** Rock, Worcs

**FOCUS**
They went a good gallop and the first two came from the back of the field. The runner-up has been rated to his recent form.

## 1297 32RED APPRENTICE H'CAP 1m 13y(F)
**5:35** (5:35) (Class 6) (0-60,61) 3-Y-O **£2,587** (£770; £384; £192) **Stalls** Low

Form RPR

00-6 **1** **Chamasay**[12] 1107 3-8-10 **47**................................ DavidEgan(5) 3 64+
(David Evans) *trckd ldng pair: cl up 3f out: led 2f out: rdn clr over 1f out: hung rt ins fnl f: kpt on strly* **16/1**

302- **2** *5* **Bonnie Arlene (IRE)**[161] 7244 3-9-8 **61**............... SharnaArmstrong(7) 5 66
(Mark Johnston) *towards rr: wd st: hdwy over 2f out: rdn to chse ldrs and hung lft over 1f out: kpt on* **13/2**[3]

63-3 **3** *3 ½* **Topmeup**[12] 1107 3-9-2 **53**................................ KatherineGlenister(5) 11 50
(David Evans) *hld up: hdwy on outer over 3f out: slt ld wl over 2f out and sn rdn: hdd 2f out: sn drvn and grad wknd appr fnl f* **9/4**[1]

0-00 **4** *1 ½* **Greyjoy (IRE)**[25] 895 3-10-1 **61**................................ MitchGodwin 6 54
(Sylvester Kirk) *chsd ldrs: rdn along wl over 2f out: kpt on same pce* **11/1**

000 **5** *2* **River Warrior**[32] 777 3-8-6 **45**................................(b[1]) ConnorMurtagh(3) 4 33
(Richard Fahey) *dwlt and rr: rdn and hdwy 2f out: kpt on fnl f: nrst fin* **14/1**

440- **6** *6* **Flawed Diamond (FR)**[202] 6026 3-9-5 **51**................................ CliffordLee 1 25
(K R Burke) *chsd ldrs: rdn along wl over 2f out: sn no hdwy* **16/1**

4-00 **7** *3 ½* **Our Lois (IRE)**[20] 967 3-9-1 **50**................................(v) RowanScott(3) 8 15
(Keith Dalgleish) *a rr* **20/1**

0640 **8** *nse* **Rockalater**[25] 897 3-8-7 **46**................................ FinleyMarsh(7) 10 11
(Sylvester Kirk) *chsd ldrs: rdn along 3f out: sn drvn and wknd* **16/1**

-036 **9** *2 ½* **Panther In Pink (IRE)**[17] 1034 3-8-13 **45**................................ CallumShepherd 7 4
(Ann Duffield) *slt ld: rdn along 3f out: sn hdd & wknd* **10/1**

0446 **10** *nk* **State Residence (IRE)**[25] 895 3-10-1 **61**................................ JoshDoyle 9 20
(David O'Meara) *dwlt: in tch on outer: hdwy to chse ldrs 1/2-way: rdn along over 3f out: sn wknd* **7/2**[2]

6-60 **11** *2 ¾* **Red Shanghai (IRE)**[12] 1107 3-8-10 **45**................................ BenRobinson(3) 2
(Charles Smith) *cl up on inner: rdn along pover 3f out:. sn wknd* **66/1**

1m 45.31s (1.61) **Going Correction** +0.20s/f (Slow) **11** Ran SP% **114.3**
Speed ratings (Par 96): **99,94,90,89,87 81,77,77,74,74 71**
CSF £113.30 CT £332.43 TOTE £18.90: £4.80, £2.10, £1.90; EX 96.10 Trifecta £506.80.

**Owner** E A R Morgans **Bred** E A R Morgans **Trained** Pandy, Monmouths


The Form Book Flat, Raceform Ltd, Newbury, RG14 5SJ

**FOCUS**
An ordinary race but there was plenty to like about the way the winner did it.
T/Plt: £88.00 to a £1 stake. Pool: £72,466.68 - 600.97 winning units. T/Qpdt: £13.20 to a £1 stake. Pool: £6,145.55 - 342.82 winning units. **Joe Rowntree**

## [1283]KEMPTON (A.W) (R-H)
Wednesday, March 22

**OFFICIAL GOING: Polytrack: standard**
Wind: nil Weather: cloudy, mild

### 1298 RACING UK ANYWHERE H'CAP 1m (P)
**5:45** (5:46) (Class 7) (0-50,56) 4-Y-0+ **£1,940** (£577; £288; £144) **Stalls** Low

Form RPR
003- **1** **Monologue (IRE)**[172] 6967 4-9-6 **50**.................................. RobHornby 11 56+
(Simon Hodgson) *settled in mid-div on outer: rdn over 1f out: kpt on wl and led jst ins fnl f: rdn out* **20/1**
-650 **2** ½ **Altaira**[28] 854 6-9-3 **47**..............................................(p) WilliamCarson 13 52
(Tony Carroll) *hld up in rr: angled wd ent st: shkn up and prog over 2f out: rdn 2f out: kpt on wl fr over 1f out* **25/1**
03-3 **3** 2¼ **Rafaaf (IRE)**[28] 854 9-8-12 **49**..............................(p) KieranSchofield(7) 4 48
(Peter Hiatt) *racd keenly covered up bhd ldrs: swtchd to rail and rdn 2f out: kpt on wl and led ent fnl f: hdd jst ins fnl f: wknd fnl 110yds* **11/1**
0041 **4** *hd* **Broughtons Fancy**[5] 1247 4-9-5 **56** 6ex.................... BenRobinson(7) 10 55
(Gary Moore) *chsd ldrs: gng wl over 2f out: rdn over 1f out: hung lft and nt qckn: kpt on: lame* **5/1**[2]
-005 **5** 1¼ **Rising Sunshine (IRE)**[14] 1084 4-9-5 **49**....................(bt) LukeMorris 14 45
(Milton Bradley) *cl up bhd ldrs: rdn 2f out: no ex fr 1f out* **20/1**
5-05 **6** *nk* **Caius College Girl (IRE)**[44] 605 5-9-1 **50**................. DavidParkes(5) 3 45
(Natalie Lloyd-Beavis) *led: rdn over 2f out: hdd ent fnl f: no ex sn after* **20/1**
4023 **7** ½ **A Boy Named Sue**[12] 1125 4-9-5 **49**...............................(v) AdamKirby 7 43
(Peter Niven) *mid-div and t.k.h: rdn over 1f out: kpt on wl ins fnl f* **4/1**[1]
0-02 **8** ½ **Free To Roam (IRE)**[14] 1084 4-9-0 **49**........................ GeorgeWood(5) 6 42
(Luke McJannet) *briefly led: t.k.h bhd ldr after: rdn over 2f out: no ex over 1f out and wknd* **9/1**
5-53 **9** 1¼ **Gavarnie Encore**[14] 1084 5-9-4 **48**................................. DavidProbert 1 38
(Michael Blanshard) *in rr-div on inner: short of room over 3f out where pushed along to hold pl: rdn over 2f out: kpt on one pce* **11/2**[3]
-634 **10** 1¾ **West Leake (IRE)**[35] 740 11-9-2 **46**.................................. LiamKeniry 9 32
(Paul Burgoyne) *t.k.h in rr-div: rdn over 2f out: kpt on: nt picked up* **16/1**
06-0 **11** 1½ **Zebedee's Son (IRE)**[14] 1084 4-8-9 **46**...................... RhiainIngram(7) 2 29
(Roger Ingram) *in rr-div on inner: n.m.r on bnd 4f out where lost pl* **33/1**
-044 **12** *nk* **Misu Pete**[33] 784 5-9-5 **49**..............................................(p[1]) SteveDrowne 8 30
(Mark Usher) *mid-div on outer: rdn over 2f out: no ex fr over 1f out* **12/1**
6020 **13** 2 **Breakheart (IRE)**[22] 966 10-8-13 **50**.......................(v) JasonWatson(7) 5 26
(Andrew Balding) *s.s: in rr: rdn over 2f out: no imp* **10/1**
0-06 **14** 7 **Never To Be (USA)**[14] 1084 6-8-13 **48**...................(vt) LuluStanford(5) 12 8
(Nikki Evans) *mid-div: rdn over 2f out: wknd qckly after: b.b.v* **20/1**

1m 40.04s (0.24) **Going Correction** +0.05s/f (Slow) **14** Ran SP% **118.9**
Speed ratings (Par 97): **100,99,97,97,95 95,95,94,93,91 90,89,87,80**
CSF £412.58 CT £5823.02 TOTE £20.10: £5.70, £8.00, £3.70; EX 700.60 Trifecta £4987.00.
**Owner** C E Weare **Bred** Darley **Trained** Queen Camel, Somerset

**FOCUS**
They didn't seem to go that quick early but the first two came from well back, finishing a little clear of the rest. The runner-up has been rated near his better recent form.

### 1299 32RED CASINO MAIDEN STKS 1m (P)
**6:15** (6:15) (Class 5) 3-Y-0+ **£2,911** (£866; £432; £216) **Stalls** Low

Form RPR
4- **1** **Sabador (FR)**[155] 7431 3-8-11 0..................................... ThomasBrown 7 79+
(Ed Walker) *t.k.h in mid-div on outer: settled bttr at 1/2-way: tk clsr order on outer over 2f out: shkn up over 1f out and almost upsides ent fnl f: qcknd again and led 100yds out: won gng away: tk 6f to pull up* **9/2**[2]
4 **2** 1¼ **Wonderfillo (IRE)**[14] 1083 3-8-11 0................................ LukeMorris 14 74
(Paul Cole) *broke wl and sn cl up bhd ldrs: shkn up wl over 1f out: rdn ent fnl f where led: kpt on wl tl hdd 100yds out* **9/2**[2]
6 **3** 2¼ **Entangling (IRE)**[14] 1083 3-8-11 0..................................... TedDurcan 5 71+
(Chris Wall) *hld up in mid-div on inner: gng wl whn ct on heels fr over 1f out tl ent fnl f: pushed out after for 3rd* **7/2**[1]
4 **4** ½ **Deep Challenger (IRE)**[7] 1205 5-10-0 0.................. FergusSweeney 1 72
(Jamie Osborne) *mid-div on inner: shkn up and prog over 2f out: rdn 2f out: kpt on wl fr over 1f out* **7/1**
00- **5** *nk* **Power Power (IRE)**[117] 8088 3-8-6 0........................ GeorgeWood(5) 10 67
(Marco Botti) *hld up in rr-div on inner: shkn up and swtchd to outer over 2f out: rdn 2f out: kpt on wl fr over 1f out: nvr nrr* **10/1**
**6** 2¾ **Chance To Dream (IRE)** 3-8-11 0..................................... KierenFox 2 60
(John Best) *in rr on inner: rdn over 2f out: kpt on past btn horse fr over 1f out* **25/1**
5- **7** ¾ **Meteoric Riser (USA)**[168] 7065 3-8-11 0.......................... ShaneKelly 8 58
(Richard Hughes) *t.k.h bhd ldrs: rdn over 2f out: wknd ins fnl f* **5/1**[3]
54 **8** ½ **Bob Hopeful**[35] 747 4-10-0 0.............................(h) RobertWinston 6 62
(Mike Murphy) *chsd ldr: upsides and rdn 2f out: sn led: hdd ent fnl f: one pce in 3rd ent fnl f: wknd qckly last 100yds* **25/1**
52/ **9** 2½ **Impressive Day (IRE)**[510] 7585 4-9-9 0........................... AdamKirby 12 51
(Gary Moore) *mid-div on outer: rdn over 2f out: sn no imp* **12/1**
**10** 1¾ **Duke Of Bronte** 3-8-11 0.................................................. RyanTate 4 47
(Rod Millman) *s.s: a in rr* **66/1**
**11** 1½ **Somes Sound (IRE)** 3-8-6 0...................................... CharlieBennett(5) 3 43
(Jane Chapple-Hyam) *mid-div on outer: rdn over 2f out: sn hld* **40/1**
00-0 **12** 3¾ **Magical Peak**[63] 282 5-9-4 27...................................(b[1]) MitchGodwin(5) 9 34
(John O'Shea) *sn led: clr ldr over 4f out: rdn wl over 2f out: hdd wl over 1f out: wknd after* **200/1**
6 **13** 10 **Taurean Gold**[22] 962 3-8-4 0........................................... JaneElliott(7) 13 10
(John Bridger) *in rr and t.k.h: rdn ent st: btn fr 2f out* **150/1**

1m 40.2s (0.40) **Going Correction** +0.05s/f (Slow)
**WFA** 3 from 4yo+ 17lb **13** Ran SP% **117.3**
Speed ratings (Par 103): **100,98,96,96,95 92,92,91,89,87 85,82,72**
CSF £23.63 TOTE £6.20: £2.00, £2.60, £1.70; EX 29.70 Trifecta £144.70.
**Owner** P K Siu **Bred** Guy Pariente Holding Sprl **Trained** Upper Lambourn, Berks

**FOCUS**
An ordinary maiden but a nice performance from the winner. The level is fluid.

### 1300 100% PROFIT BOOST AT 32REDSPORT.COM MEDIAN AUCTION MAIDEN STKS 1m 3f 219y(P)
**6:45** (6:45) (Class 6) 3-4-Y-0 **£2,264** (£673; £336; £168) **Stalls** Centre

Form RPR
**1** **Villette (IRE)** 3-8-3 0............................................................. LukeMorris 6 76+
(Dean Ivory) *racd in 5th on outer: shkn up to take clsr order on outer over 2f out: rdn 2f out where qcknd up and breezed by ldrs: in n.d ent fnl f: nudged out cl home* **20/1**
054- **2** *shd* **Red Caravel (IRE)**[183] 6655 3-8-8 72................................. ShaneKelly 4 67
(Richard Hughes) *settled bhd ldr on outer: pushed along over 3f out: rdn ent st: lft bhd by wnr 2f out: kpt on one pce after in duel for 2nd: sltly hmpd cl home: jst hld by runner-up: fin 3rd: awrdd 2nd* **4/6**[1]
220- **3** 6 **Akkadian Empire**[152] 7511 3-8-8 76............................. GeorgeDowning 3 67
(Mick Channon) *led: shkn up over 3f out: rdn 2f out: lft bhd by wnr 2f out: kpt on one pce in duel for 2nd: hung lft cl home: fin 2nd: disqualified and plcd 3rd - caused interference* **10/3**[2]
**4** 8 **Pourquoi Moi**[41] 4-9-9 0.............................................(h[1]) AdamKirby 2 51
(George Scott) *settled bhd ldr on inner: rdn and wknd fr over 2f out* **14/1**
**5** ¾ **Lagopus** 4-9-9 0........................................................... FergusSweeney 5 50
(David Simcock) *racd in last: pushed along over 3f out: no ex fr over 2f out* **5/1**[3]

2m 39.37s (4.87) **Going Correction** +0.05s/f (Slow)
**WFA** 3 from 4yo 22lb **5** Ran SP% **111.2**
Speed ratings (Par 101): **85,80,81,75,75**
CSF £35.37 TOTE £15.40: £4.40, £1.10; EX 31.40 Trifecta £108.70.
**Owner** Radlett Racing **Bred** S Roy **Trained** Radlett, Herts

**FOCUS**
A bit of a shock here.

### 1301 32RED H'CAP 7f (P)
**7:15** (7:15) (Class 4) (0-85,85) 4-Y-0+ **£4,690** (£1,395; £697; £348) **Stalls** Low

Form RPR
132 **1** **Saleh (IRE)**[14] 1085 4-8-8 **72**............................................ KieranO'Neill 3 79
(Lee Carter) *settled bhd ldrs on rail: travelling wl on heels over 2f out: swtchd to inner and rdn 2f out: sn led: kpt on wl fnl f* **7/2**[1]
50-3 **2** 1½ **Until Midnight (IRE)**[34] 760 7-8-11 **80**........................ LuluStanford(5) 8 83
(Eugene Stanford) *rrd up leaving stalls: stl in rr over 3f out: trckd wnr over 2f out: rdn 2f out: kpt on wl but no ch w wnr* **6/1**[3]
-300 **3** ¾ **Dutiful Son (IRE)**[49] 506 7-8-13 **77**................................... LukeMorris 6 78
(Simon Dow) *in rr-div on outer: rdn over 2f out: kpt on wl ent fnl f to take 3rd* **15/2**
6-14 **4** *hd* **Varsovian**[14] 1091 7-8-12 **79**............................................. JackDuern(3) 1 79
(Dean Ivory) *mid-div on rail: rdn 2f out: kpt on one pce* **8/1**
040- **5** 1¾ **Highly Sprung (IRE)**[137] 7821 4-9-7 **85**........................ FrannyNorton 5 81
(Mark Johnston) *sn led: qcknd pce ent st: rdn 2f out and sn hdd: kpt on one pce tl wknd ins fnl f* **5/1**[2]
0-00 **6** *hd* **Major Crispies**[28] 857 6-8-10 **74**....................................... RyanTate 4 69
(Jeremy Gask) *settled bhd ldrs on rail: rdn 2f out: kpt on one pce* **10/1**
003- **7** *shd* **Black Bess**[178] 6806 4-9-7 **85**............................................ AdamKirby 7 80
(Jim Boyle) *settled bhd ldr: rdn 2f out: one pce fnl f* **7/1**
150- **8** ½ **Mezmaar**[224] 5301 8-9-1 **79**...............................................(h) LiamKeniry 2 73
(Mark Usher) *tk fierce hold early in rr-div: rdn wdst 2f out: no imp fnl f* **7/1**

1m 25.19s (-0.81) **Going Correction** +0.05s/f (Slow) **8** Ran SP% **110.1**
Speed ratings (Par 105): **106,104,103,103,101 100,100,100**
CSF £22.56 CT £136.87 TOTE £2.90: £3.00, £1.90, £2.10; EX 29.00 Trifecta £168.80.
**Owner** Only One Bid Partnership **Bred** Stowell Park Stud **Trained** Epsom, Surrey

**FOCUS**
The early gallop wasn't strong but there was a comfortable winner. The runner-up has been rated near his best.

### 1302 32RED.COM H'CAP 6f (P)
**7:45** (7:46) (Class 4) (0-85,84) 4-Y-0+ **£4,690** (£1,395; £697; £348) **Stalls** Low

Form RPR
0-03 **1** **Bouclier (IRE)**[20] 989 7-9-2 **79**..................................... FrannyNorton 3 85
(David Loughnane) *in rr-div on inner: shkn up and gd prog past rivals fr over 1f out: rdn ent fnl f: led fnl 110yds: on top cl home* **7/1**[3]
243- **2** ¾ **Cultured Knight**[284] 3144 4-8-13 **76**................................. ShaneKelly 1 80
(Richard Hughes) *chsd ldr: rdn 2f out and led ent fnl f: hdd fnl 110yds: no ex cl home* **7/1**[3]
1-02 **3** *nk* **Under Siege (IRE)**[28] 857 5-9-3 **83**......................(t) AaronJones(3) 7 86
(Stuart Williams) *settled bhd ldrs: rdn over 2f out: kpt on wl on outer ent fnl f: no ex fnl strides* **7/2**[2]
6000 **4** ½ **Swiss Cross**[14] 1091 10-9-1 **78**.......................................(tp) LukeMorris 8 79
(Phil McEntee) *in rr: rdn 2f out: briefly threatened ins fnl f: kpt on again cl home* **20/1**
4-1 **5** 1¾ **Artscape**[32] 807 5-8-12 **75**..........................................(h) RobertWinston 4 71
(Dean Ivory) *chsd ldrs: rdn 2f out: kpt on one pce fnl f* **7/2**[2]
150- **6** *hd* **Red Tycoon (IRE)**[179] 6780 5-8-13 **76**.............................. LiamKeniry 5 72
(Ken Cunningham-Brown) *in rr: rdn 2f out: kpt on one pce fr over 1f out* **50/1**
30-0 **7** 1½ **Gwendolyn (GER)**[32] 816 4-9-5 **82**.................................. AdamKirby 9 73
(Amy Murphy) *sn led: rdn over 2f out: hdd ent fnl f: wknd after* **25/1**
6-51 **8** ½ **Florencio**[28] 857 4-9-2 **84**..........................................(t) GeorgeWood(5) 6 74
(Marco Botti) *in rr-div: rdn out wd over 2f out: kpt on one pce* **5/2**[1]
606- **9** ½ **Major Pusey**[161] 7289 5-9-3 **80**........................................ MartinDwyer 2 68+
(John Gallagher) *rrd up s: a bhd* **14/1**

1m 11.83s (-1.27) **Going Correction** +0.05s/f (Slow) **9** Ran SP% **115.3**
Speed ratings (Par 105): **110,109,108,107,105 105,103,102,102**
CSF £53.45 CT £202.49 TOTE £7.50: £2.00, £2.10, £4.30; EX 56.10 Trifecta £248.30.
**Owner** M Chung **Bred** Dayton Investments Ltd **Trained** Market Drayton, Shropshire

**FOCUS**
The pace collapsed here and that set things up for a closer. The winner has been rated to his Polytrack form this time last year.

### 1303 32RED ON THE APP STORE H'CAP 1m 7f 218y(P)
**8:15** (8:16) (Class 6) (0-65,65) 4-Y-0+ **£2,264** (£673; £336; £168) **Stalls** Low

Form RPR
0-01 **1** **Briac (FR)**[14] 1081 6-8-8 **50**......................................... HectorCrouch(3) 3 55
(Mark Pattinson) *mid-div on inner: swtchd to inner and rdn 2f out: kpt on wl and disp ld over 1f out: jst hld on* **9/2**[2]

3244 **2** *shd* **Tasty Ginger (IRE)**[15] 1072 4-9-3 **61** .................................. AdamKirby 6 66
(J R Jenkins) *hld up in rr: travelling wl on heels w nowhere to go 2f out: no gap tl squeezed through rivals ent fnl f: slowly gaining on ldng pair tl styd on strly cl home: jst hld* **7/2**[1]

0-31 **3** *½* **Iona Island**[26] 900 4-9-0 **63** .......................................... DavidParkes(5) 2 67
(Peter Hiatt) *settled bhd ldrs: rdn 2f out: disp ld fr over 1f out: kpt on wl and only dropped to 3rd fnl strides* **10/1**

5/44 **4** *2½* **Money Talks**[28] 859 7-8-13 **57** .................................. GeorgeWood(5) 10 58
(Michael Madgwick) *chsd ldrs: rdn over 2f out: kpt on one pce fnl f* **8/1**

60-0 **5** *1* **Art History (IRE)**[18] 1028 9-9-4 **57** ..............................(t) JohnFahy 4 57
(Zoe Davison) *chsd clr ldrs: led 6f out: rdn over 2f out: hdd over 1f out: one pce after* **66/1**

2663 **6** *shd* **Treble Strike (USA)**[14] 1092 4-9-4 **65** ..........................(p) JackDuern(3) 9 65
(Dean Ivory) *mid-div on outer: hrd rdn over 3f out: one pce after* **9/1**

/4-3 **7** *nse* **Shalianzi (IRE)**[28] 859 7-9-7 **60** ....................................(b) LukeMorris 5 60
(Chris Gordon) *mid-div on inner: rdn over 2f out: no imp on ldrs* **7/1**[3]

0-35 **8** *2¼* **Newtown Cross (IRE)**[28] 859 7-8-8 **47** ........................ KieranO'Neill 8 44
(Jimmy Fox) *in rr-div: rdn over 2f out: no imp* **8/1**

-040 **9** *¾* **Movie Magic**[14] 1081 6-8-4 **46** oh1 ................................(b) AaronJones(3) 7 42
(Mark Hoad) *sn led: hdd 6f out: rdn and wknd fr over 1f out* **80/1**

34-2 **10** *5* **Forecast**[25] 924 5-9-5 **58** ...............................................(t) TomQueally 11 48
(Martin Keighley) *mid-div on outer: began to hang bdly lft on bnd over 6f out: pushed out after* **9/2**[2]

3m 34.34s (4.24) **Going Correction** +0.05s/f (Slow)
**WFA** 4 from 5yo+ 3lb **10** Ran SP% **115.1**
Speed ratings (Par 101): **91,90,90,89,88 88,88,87,87,84**
CSF £20.34 CT £148.72 TOTE £5.50: £1.90, £1.50, £3.20; EX 28.00 Trifecta £216.60.
**Owner** O S Harris **Bred** P J Loivel & R Dugardin **Trained** Epsom, Surrey

**FOCUS**
This developed into a sprint from the turn in. The runner-up has been rated to his mark.

## 1304 WATCH RACING UK IN HD H'CAP (DIV I) — 6f (P)
**8:45** (8:45) (Class 6) (0-55,57) 4-Y-0+ **£2,264** (£673; £336; £168) **Stalls** Low

Form RPR

0244 **1** **Nasri**[9] 1180 11-9-7 **54** ..........................................(v) TomQueally 2 60
(Emma Owen) *restrained in rr-div on inner: rdn over 1f out: kpt on wl and gaining on ldr w ev stride ins fnl f: led cl home* **3/1**[2]

-010 **2** *¾* **Encapsulated**[34] 768 7-9-3 **57** .............................. RhiainIngram(7) 4 61
(Roger Ingram) *settled bhd ldr: rdn to ld 2f out: kpt on wl tl wknd nr fin: hdd last strides* **8/1**

0-40 **3** *1½* **Blistering Dancer (IRE)**[20] 982 7-8-12 **45** .............. GeorgeDowning 6 44
(Tony Carroll) *sn led: rdn over 2f out: sn hdd: kpt on one pce* **12/1**

6505 **4** *¾* **Multi Quest**[20] 982 5-9-6 **53** ..........................................(b) FrannyNorton 8 50
(John E Long) *chsd ldr: rdn 2f out: sn hld and kpt on one pce: fin 5th: plcd 4th* **6/1**

0000 **5** *½* **Catalyze**[6] 1219 9-8-5 **45** ..................................................(t) JaneElliott(7) 1 41
(Paddy Butler) *in rr-div on inner: tk clsr order over 2f out: sn rdn: wknd fnl f: fin 6th: plcd 5th* **33/1**

2121 **6** *1¾* **Krazy Paving**[20] 982 5-9-10 **57** .......................................(b) AdamKirby 5 47
(Anabel K Murphy) *settled in mid-div: shkn up over 2f out: no imp fr over 1f out on outer: fin 7th: plcd 6th* **6/4**[1]

-300 **7** *13* **Willow Spring**[18] 1022 5-8-10 **46** ...................................... TimClark(3) 9
(Denis Quinn) *in rr on outer: rdn over 2f out: no imp: fin 8th: plcd 7th* **33/1**

0-15 **D** *2* **Little Indian**[35] 739 7-9-5 **52** ............................................ ShaneKelly 7 51
(J R Jenkins) *in rr-div: rdn between horses over 1f out: kpt on wl tl one pce ins fnl f: fin 4th: disqualified and plcd last - rdr failed to weigh in* **5/1**[3]

1m 12.43s (-0.67) **Going Correction** +0.05s/f (Slow) **8** Ran SP% **120.6**
Speed ratings (Par 101): **106,105,103,99,98 96,79,100**
CSF £28.88 CT £255.26 TOTE £3.70: £1.40, £2.00, £2.90; EX 29.00 Trifecta £192.10.
**Owner** Miss Emma L Owen **Bred** Lady Hardy **Trained** Nether Winchendon, Bucks

**FOCUS**
A moderate sprint.

## 1305 WATCH RACING UK IN HD H'CAP (DIV II) — 6f (P)
**9:15** (9:15) (Class 6) (0-55,57) 4-Y-0+ **£2,264** (£673; £336; £168) **Stalls** Low

Form RPR

1045 **1** **Swendab (IRE)**[5] 1246 9-9-2 **55** ....................................(b) MitchGodwin(5) 3 60
(John O'Shea) *settled bhd ldrs on rail: shkn up 2f out: rdn between horses ent fnl f: kpt on wl to ld cl home* **3/1**[1]

4325 **2** *nk* **Justice Rock**[5] 1247 4-8-8 **47** ........................................ LuluStanford(5) 5 51
(Phil McEntee) *blindfold removed late: in rr on inner: hrd rdn over 2f out: led ent fnl f: kpt on wl tl hdd fnl strides* **11/2**[3]

34-0 **3** *1¼* **Wattaboutsteve**[72] 143 6-8-12 **46** oh1 ........................... DavidProbert 6 46
(Ralph J Smith) *settled bhd ldrs and t.k.h: rdn over 1f out: ev ch ent fnl f: no ex cl home: jst hld 3rd* **15/2**

-314 **4** *shd* **Pick Of Any (IRE)**[13] 1112 4-9-5 **53** ..........................(h) DavidParkes(5) 4 58
(David Loughnane) *in rr on inner: rdn over 1f out: kpt on strly wl ins fnl f: jst failed for 3rd* **7/2**[2]

2400 **5** *1¾* **Spirit Of Gondree (IRE)**[11] 1139 9-9-4 **52** ....................(b) LukeMorris 8 47
(Milton Bradley) *tk fierce hold early to settled bhd ldrs: swtchd wd over 2f out: sn rdn and kpt on one pce* **7/1**

3660 **6** *½* **Whaleweigh Station**[15] 1076 6-9-2 **57** .........................(v) GinaMangan(7) 2 50
(J R Jenkins) *pressed ldr: rdn over 1f out: one pce after* **6/1**

0-06 **7** *2¾* **Storming Ambition**[53] 455 4-8-12 **46** oh1 ...................(t) MartinDwyer 1 31
(Conrad Allen) *sn led: pressed for ld after 2f: hdd ent fnl f: wknd sn after* **14/1**

-000 **8** *nk* **Just Over**[37] 722 4-8-12 **46** oh1 ................................(v[1]) AdamBeschizza 7 30
(Robert Cowell) *mid-div on outer: rdn 2f out: kpt on one pce* **25/1**

00-0 **9** *17* **Dramatic Voice**[15] 1075 4-8-12 **46** oh1 ...........................(t) LiamKeniry 9
(Ken Cunningham-Brown) *a in rr: eased fr over 1f out* **100/1**

1m 13.03s (-0.07) **Going Correction** +0.05s/f (Slow) **9** Ran SP% **112.7**
Speed ratings (Par 101): **102,101,99,99,97 96,93,92,70**
CSF £19.18 CT £110.28 TOTE £4.40: £1.10, £5.20, £2.10; EX 21.30 Trifecta £117.00.
**Owner** E&G Racing: Swendab **Bred** P Brady **Trained** Elton, Gloucs
■ Stewards' Enquiry : Lulu Stanford four-day ban: used whip above permitted level (5-8 Apr)

**FOCUS**
The slower of the two divisions by 0.6sec. The runner-up has been rated to his mark.

T/Jkpt: Not won. T/Plt: £160.40 to a £1 stake. Pool: £104,028.74 - 473.23 winning units. T/Qpdt: £9.80 to a £1 stake. Pool: £12,400.23 - 931.32 winning units. **Cathal Gahan**

# [1197] NEWCASTLE (A.W) (L-H)
Wednesday, March 22

**OFFICIAL GOING: Tapeta: standard**
Wind: Breezy, half behind Weather: Overcast

## 1306 32RED.COM CLASSIFIED STKS — 7f 14y (Tp)
**2:00** (2:00) (Class 5) 3-Y-O **£3,881** (£1,155; £577; £288) **Stalls** Centre

Form RPR

006- **1** **Alemaratalyoum (IRE)**[152] 7502 3-9-0 **70** ................ SilvestreDeSousa 2 76+
(Ed Dunlop) *mde virtually all: set modest gallop: shkn up over 1f out: edgd lft ins fnl f: pushed out: comf* **4/5**[1]

1316 **2** *1¾* **Mia Cara**[5] 1242 3-9-0 **67** .................................................(v) AndrewMullen 3 69
(David Evans) *prom: effrt and pushed along over 2f out: hung lft and chsd wnr over 1f out: kpt on fnl f: nt pce to chal* **6/1**[3]

1-02 **3** *5* **Touch Me (IRE)**[19] 1000 3-8-11 **67** ........................(h) JordanVaughan(3) 1 56
(K R Burke) *t.k.h: chsd wnr to over 1f out: sn rdn and edgd lft: wknd fnl f* **10/1**

3134 **4** *8* **Tranquil Daze (IRE)**[19] 1005 3-9-0 **70** ................................ SeanLevey 4 34
(David Brown) *plld hrd in falsely run r: cl up tl wknd 2f out: sn hung lft and eased* **5/2**[2]

1m 27.35s (1.15) **Going Correction** -0.175s/f (Stan) **4** Ran SP% **107.5**
Speed ratings (Par 98): **86,84,78,69**
CSF £5.83 TOTE £1.80; EX 6.50 Trifecta £10.60.
**Owner** Mohammed Jaber **Bred** Ammerland Verwaltung Gmbh & Co Kg **Trained** Newmarket, Suffolk

**FOCUS**
A modest classified event which was run at a farcical pace for the first 5f and the winner was in the ideal position. They started off up the centre of the track, but all four ended up against the far rail. The runner-up has been rated to her mark.

## 1307 BETWAY H'CAP — 1m 4f 98y (Tp)
**2:30** (2:31) (Class 4) (0-85,87) 4-Y-0+ **£5,498** (£1,636; £817; £408) **Stalls** High

Form RPR

-212 **1** **Final**[9] 1178 5-9-11 **87** ......................................................... JoeFanning 5 95
(Mark Johnston) *chsd clr ldr: clsd 1/2-way: rdn to ld ins fnl f: kpt on wl* **9/4**[2]

-221 **2** *1½* **On Fire**[20] 993 4-8-6 **70** ...............................................(p) PaulHanagan 3 76
(James Bethell) *hld up in tch: pushed along over 2f out: hdwy and edgd lft over 1f out: kpt on to take 2nd nr fin: nt rch wnr* **7/2**[3]

-311 **3** *nk* **Codeshare**[20] 991 5-9-7 **83** ........................................ SilvestreDeSousa 1 88
(Alan Swinbank) *plld hrd early: chsd ldrs: effrt over 2f out: rdn and veered rt over 1f out: chsd wnr ins fnl f tl no ex nr fin* **6/4**[1]

55-0 **4** *1¼* **Be Perfect (USA)**[20] 991 8-9-3 **79** ...............................(p) JamesSullivan 7 82
(Ruth Carr) *led: clr to 1/2-way: rdn over 2f out: hdd ins fnl f: sn no ex* **20/1**

1120 **5** *1¾* **L'Inganno Felice (FR)**[20] 991 7-9-11 **87** ....................(h) PJMcDonald 8 88
(Iain Jardine) *hld up: rdn over 2f out: hdwy over 1f out: no imp fnl f* **13/2**

60-0 **6** *shd* **Card High (IRE)**[49] 509 7-8-11 **73** ..........................(t) PaulMulrennan 9 74
(Wilf Storey) *in tch: rdn along over 2f out: shortlived effrt over 1f out: sn outpcd* **50/1**

06-0 **7** *5* **Euchen Glen**[33] 779 4-9-5 **83** ..........................................(h[1]) SamJames 6 76
(Jim Goldie) *t.k.h: stdd s: pushed along and outpcd over 2f out: sn btn* **20/1**

0 **8** *7* **Main Fact (USA)**[33] 782 4-8-6 **70** ..............................(h[1]) BarryMcHugh 4 53
(Dianne Sayer) *hld up midfield: drvn and struggling 3f out: btn fnl 2f* **150/1**

0-00 **9** *5* **Buthelezi (USA)**[19] 1002 9-9-0 **76** ............................................ BenCurtis 2 51
(Brian Ellison) *hld up: rdn and struggling over 3f out: sn wknd* **66/1**

2m 42.96s (1.86) **Going Correction** +0.175s/f (Slow)
**WFA** 4 from 5yo+ 1lb **9** Ran SP% **120.0**
Speed ratings (Par 105): **100,99,98,97,96 96,93,88,85**
CSF £10.61 CT £15.18 TOTE £3.10: £1.10, £1.80, £1.30; EX 12.30 Trifecta £29.10.
**Owner** C H Greensit & W A Greensit **Bred** C H And W A Greensit **Trained** Middleham Moor, N Yorks

**FOCUS**
A fair middle-distance handicap and they were soon well spread out, but even so few got into it. The winner has been rated as improving fractionally on his Chelmsford form.

## 1308 BETWAY MAIDEN STKS — 1m 2f 42y (Tp)
**3:00** (3:00) (Class 5) 3-Y-0+ **£4,528** (£1,347; £673; £336) **Stalls** High

Form RPR

203- **1** **Lopes Dancer (IRE)**[299] 2662 5-10-0 **74** ................................... NeilFarley 1 77
(Alan Swinbank) *t.k.h early: trckd ldrs: hdwy to ld over 2f out: pushed out fnl f: comf* **6/1**[3]

35- **2** *2¼* **Wefait (IRE)**[126] 7975 3-8-8 **0** ........................................ TomMarquand 5 69
(Richard Hannon) *led at stdy pce: hdd 4f out: rallied and ev ch over 2f out: sn rdn: hung lft and hit rail ent fnl f sn one pce* **2/1**[1]

04 **3** *3* **Delphyne**[16] 1069 5-9-2 **0** .......................................... AidenBlakemore(7) 8 63
(Shaun Harris) *t.k.h: pressed ldr to 4f out: ev ch gng wl over 2f out: sn rdn: hung lft over 1f out: kpt on same pce* **40/1**

50-3 **4** *1¼* **Cray (IRE)**[21] 970 3-8-8 **72** .................................................. PJMcDonald 6 61+
(James Bethell) *prom: drvn and outpcd over 2f out: rallied over 1f out: kpt on fnl f: nvr able to chal* **2/1**[1]

**5** *nk* **Hurricane Hollow**[459] 7-10-0 **0** ........................................ PhillipMakin 9 65+
(David Barron) *hld up: stdy hdwy over 3f out: shkn up over 2f out: no imp fr over 1f out* **5/2**[2]

5 **6** *2¼* **Absolute Angel**[20] 993 6-9-9 **0** ............................................ TomEaves 2 56
(Peter Niven) *hld up: rdn and outpcd over 2f out: n.d after* **40/1**

0-4 **7** *½* **Redarna**[33] 777 3-8-8 **0** .................................................. BarryMcHugh 7 56
(Dianne Sayer) *t.k.h: hld up: hdwy on outside to ld 4f out: rdn and hdd over 2f out: sn wknd* **33/1**

0 **8** *1¾* **Heavenly Gait**[20] 993 5-9-9 **0** ..........................................(h) ShaneGray 11 52
(Jason Ward) *prom: rdn over 2f out: wknd over 1f out* **200/1**

4 **9** *¾* **Dan's Hopefoglory**[20] 993 5-9-9 **0** ................................ AndrewMullen 4 50
(Peter Niven) *hld up: pushed along and struggling 3f out: sn btn* **33/1**

0- **10** *3* **Hot Gossip (IRE)**[301] 2570 3-8-3 **0** ................................. JamesSullivan 3 41
(Dianne Sayer) *t.k.h: hld up: rdn and struggling over 3f out: sn btn* **125/1**

2m 20.82s (10.42) **Going Correction** +0.175s/f (Slow)
**WFA** 3 from 4yo+ 20lb **10** Ran SP% **121.6**
Speed ratings (Par 103): **65,63,60,59,59 57,57,55,55,52**
CSF £18.98 TOTE £7.00: £2.20, £1.50, £8.10; EX 24.20 Trifecta £566.40.
**Owner** D G Clayton Racing **Bred** Carol Burke & Lope De Vega Syndicate **Trained** Melsonby, N Yorks

**FOCUS**
A routine maiden run at an ordinary gallop. The runner-up has been rated roughly to his 2yo debut.

## 1309 BETWAY STAYERS' H'CAP 2m 56y (Tp)
**3:30** (3:30) (Class 2) (0-100,98) 4-Y-0+
**£14,628** (£4,380; £2,190; £1,095; £547; £274) **Stalls** Low

| Form | | | | RPR |
|---|---|---|---|---|
| 00-4 | 1 | | **Gavlar**[35] [746] 6-9-1 **90**...(v) CallumShepherd(3) 3 (William Knight) *hld up: stdy hdwy over 3f out: led on outside over appr fnl f: edgd lft: kpt on wl last 100yds* **14/1** | 98 |
| /01- | 2 | 3/4 | **Good Run (FR)**[114] [8133] 4-9-5 **96**... KevinStott 4 (Saeed bin Suroor) *in tch: hdwy to chse ldrs over 3f out: rdn to chal over 1f out: kpt on fnl f: hld towards fin* **5/2**[1] | 103 |
| 113- | 3 | 4 1/2 | **Swashbuckle**[199] [6163] 4-8-8 **85**... OisinMurphy 7 (Andrew Balding) *w ldr: led 4f out to 2f out: drvn and outpcd fnl f* **4/1**[2] | 87 |
| 4-12 | 4 | nk | **Byron Flyer**[35] [746] 6-9-1 **87**... StevieDonohoe 2 (Ian Williams) *in tch: stdy hdwy over 6f out: chal 4f out: led 2f out to appr fnl f: sn rdn and outpcd* **9/2**[3] | 88 |
| 04-1 | 5 | 7 | **Hamelin (IRE)**[33] [779] 7-9-12 **98**... SilvestreDeSousa 8 (George Scott) *stdd and swtchd lft s: hld up: pushed along over 3f out: no imp fnl 2f* **9/2**[3] | 91 |
| 111- | 6 | 3 1/2 | **Silva Eclipse**[204] [6011] 4-8-3 **80**... JamesSullivan 6 (Jedd O'Keeffe) *in tch: rdn and outpcd over 3f out: n.d after* **9/1** | 69 |
| 1-55 | 7 | 1 3/4 | **Calvinist**[20] [985] 4-8-8 **90**...(p[1]) CliffordLee(5) 5 (Archie Watson) *t.k.h: led to 4f out: rdn and wknd over 2f out* **6/1** | 77 |
| 100- | 8 | 41 | **Injam (IRE)**[159] [7320] 4-8-5 **82**... PaulHanagan 1 (Jedd O'Keeffe) *t.k.h: trckd ldrs to 4f out: sn struggling: eased whn no ch fnl 2f* **33/1** | 19 |

3m 30.89s (-4.31) **Going Correction** +0.175s/f (Slow)
**WFA** 4 from 6yo+ 3lb **8** Ran SP% **118.8**
Speed ratings (Par 109): **117,116,114,114,110 108,108,87**
CSF £51.22 CT £174.20 TOTE £17.40: £4.00, £1.10, £2.00; EX 56.40 Trifecta £554.60.
**Owner** Canisbay Bloodstock **Bred** A Black **Trained** Patching, W Sussex

**FOCUS**
A decent staying handicap, but the pace was modest and it only quickened once into the straight. A pb from the winner.

## 1310 BETWAY CLAIMING STKS 6f (Tp)
**4:00** (4:00) (Class 6) 3-Y-0+ **£3,234** (£962; £481; £240) **Stalls** Centre

| Form | | | | RPR |
|---|---|---|---|---|
| 0064 | 1 | | **Ticks The Boxes (IRE)**[19] [1007] 5-9-1 75...(p) CliffordLee(5) 6 (Michael Herrington) *trckd ldrs: hdwy over 1f out: sn rdn: edgd lft and led wl ins fnl f: kpt on* **13/8**[1] | 74 |
| -665 | 2 | nk | **Semana Santa**[18] [1030] 4-9-4 71... PhillipMakin 4 (David Barron) *led: rdn 2f out: hdd wl ins fnl f: kpt on: hld cl home* **11/4**[2] | 71 |
| 000- | 3 | 1 1/4 | **Compton Park**[208] [5859] 10-9-7 73...(t) DavidAllan 3 (Les Eyre) *in tch: hdwy to press ldrs over 1f out: kpt on same pce ins fnl f* **5/1** | 70 |
| -000 | 4 | 3 | **Masarzain (IRE)**[25] [923] 4-9-7 67... AndrewMullen 1 (James Given) *trckd ldrs: rdn over 2f out: edgd lft and outpcd fnl f* **22/1** | 61 |
| 0350 | 5 | 2 | **Disclosure**[7] [1203] 6-9-4 58...(h) JasonHart 5 (Les Eyre) *missed break: bhd: rdn over 2f out: rallied over 1f out: sn no imp* **18/1** | 52 |
| 0-35 | 6 | 2 1/2 | **Endeavour (IRE)**[32] [819] 3-8-10 63... SeanLevey 2 (Richard Hannon) *t.k.h: pressed ldr: rdn over 2f out: wknd over 1f out* **3/1**[3] | 46 |

1m 11.29s (-1.21) **Going Correction** -0.175s/f (Stan)
**WFA** 3 from 4yo+ 13lb **6** Ran SP% **116.0**
Speed ratings (Par 101): **101,100,98,94,92 88**
CSF £6.72 TOTE £3.30: £2.00, £1.30; EX 6.00 Trifecta £22.50.Disclosure was claimed by Mrs Sarah Bryan for £3000
**Owner** Darren & Annaley Yates **Bred** John B Hughes **Trained** Cold Kirby, N Yorks

**FOCUS**
A moderate claimer and they finished very much as adjusted official ratings suggested they should. It's been rated a shade negatively around the runner-up's more recent form.

## 1311 32RED CASINO H'CAP 6f (Tp)
**4:30** (4:31) (Class 2) (0-103,99) 3-Y-0 **£15,202** (£4,523; £2,260; £1,130) **Stalls** Centre

| Form | | | | RPR |
|---|---|---|---|---|
| 035- | 1 | | **Unabated (IRE)**[186] [6572] 3-9-2 **94**...(t) DanielMuscutt 8 (Marco Botti) *taken early to post: hld up: hdwy nr side of gp and led appr fnl f: hrd rdn and drifted lft ins fnl f: styd on wl* **12/1** | 99 |
| 4560 | 2 | nk | **Letmestopyouthere (IRE)**[11] [1149] 3-8-7 **85**... SilvestreDeSousa 3 (David Evans) *in tch: hdwy to ld over 2f out: rdn and hdd appr fnl f: rallied: kpt on same pce towards fin* **20/1** | 89 |
| 2-31 | 3 | 1 1/2 | **Tomily (IRE)**[41] [643] 3-9-7 **99**... SeanLevey 1 (Richard Hannon) *hld up: effrt on far side of gp and cl up over 1f out: rdn and kpt on same pce ins fnl f* **9/1** | 99 |
| 1-31 | 4 | hd | **Wick Powell**[12] [1124] 3-9-3 **95**... AndrewMullen 7 (David Barron) *cl up: rdn over 2f out: edgd lft over 1f out: kpt on same pce ins fnl f* **15/8**[1] | 94 |
| 110- | 5 | 2 1/4 | **Leontes**[195] [6260] 3-8-13 **91**... OisinMurphy 4 (Andrew Balding) *taken early to post: s.i.s: hld up in tch: rdn over 2f out: outpcd fr over 1f out* **11/1** | 83 |
| 62-1 | 6 | 1 1/4 | **Glorious Politics**[78] [27] 3-8-7 **85**... BenCurtis 2 (David Barron) *cl up on outside of gp: rdn over 2f out: wknd over 1f out* **7/1**[3] | 73 |
| 1-53 | 7 | 1 3/4 | **Zamjar**[12] [1124] 3-8-4 **82**...(b) JosephineGordon 5 (Ed Dunlop) *led to over 2f out: rdn and wknd wl over 1f out* **7/1**[3] | 65 |
| 10-2 | 8 | 1/2 | **Hemingway (IRE)**[12] [1124] 3-8-2 **80**... JoeDoyle 6 (Kevin Ryan) *trckd ldrs: drvn and outpcd over 2f out: wknd wl over 1f out* **3/1**[2] | 62 |

1m 9.86s (-2.64) **Going Correction** -0.175s/f (Stan) course record **8** Ran SP% **115.6**
Speed ratings (Par 104): **110,109,107,107,104 102,100,99**
CSF £214.84 CT £2265.70 TOTE £12.00: £2.90, £3.60, £1.80; EX 144.40 Trifecta £793.40.
**Owner** Mubarak Al Naemi **Bred** Mubarak Al Naemi **Trained** Newmarket, Suffolk

**FOCUS**
A decent 3yo sprint handicap and the form should work out. They raced centre to nearside. The runner-up has been rated to his mark.

## 1312 BETWAY APPRENTICE H'CAP 1m 2f 42y (Tp)
**5:00** (5:00) (Class 6) (0-65,67) 4-Y-0+ **£3,234** (£962; £481; £240) **Stalls** High

| Form | | | | RPR |
|---|---|---|---|---|
| 0-00 | 1 | | **Mazaaher**[25] [928] 7-9-7 **63**... CliffordLee 7 (David Evans) *prom: rdn along over 2f out: hdwy to ld ins fnl f: kpt on wl* **20/1** | 70 |
| 6141 | 2 | 2 1/4 | **Spirit Of The Vale (IRE)**[13] [1101] 4-8-7 **56**...(t) ConnorMurtagh(7) 10 (Oliver Greenall) *reluctant to enter stalls: s.i.s: hld up in last pl: shkn up and hdwy on outside over 2f out: hung lft: chsd wnr ins fnl f: kpt on same pce* **9/4**[1] | 59 |
| 5-34 | 3 | 1 | **Lord Rob**[43] [607] 6-8-7 **49** oh4...(p) PaddyPilley 9 (David Thompson) *trckd ldrs: led briefly over 2f out: ev ch to ins fnl f: kpt on same pce last 100yds* **10/1** | 50 |
| 014- | 4 | nse | **Strummer (IRE)**[145] [7656] 4-8-13 **62**...(p) SeamusCronin(7) 1 (Kevin Ryan) *t.k.h: hld up in tch on ins: hdwy to ld 2f out: sn rdn and edgd rt: hdd ins fnl f: one pce* **5/1** | 63 |
| 400- | 5 | 1 1/4 | **Lady Clitico (IRE)**[285] [3118] 6-9-6 **67**... PaulaMuir(5) 2 (Rebecca Menzies) *t.k.h: hld up in tch: pushed along over 2f out: kpt on same pce fnl f* **33/1** | 66 |
| 5255 | 6 | 1/2 | **King Oswald (USA)**[23] [954] 4-9-7 **63**... JoshDoyle 12 (James Unett) *hld up: pushed along over 2f out: hdwy over 1f out: kpt on fnl f: nt pce to chal* **7/2**[2] | 61 |
| -303 | 7 | 1/2 | **Leonard Thomas**[18] [1028] 7-9-0 **63**...(p) AledBeech(7) 6 (Tony Carroll) *hld up midfield: rdn over 2f out: edgd lft: no imp over 1f out* **8/1** | 60 |
| 60-0 | 8 | 5 | **Bilko's Back (IRE)**[20] [990] 5-8-0 **49** oh2...(t) TheodoreLadd(7) 3 (Susan Corbett) *dwlt: t.k.h: hld up: rdn along over 2f out: sn outpcd* **100/1** | 37 |
| 200- | 9 | 2 | **Whitchurch**[96] [8400] 5-8-11 **53**... ShirleyTeasdale 5 (Philip Kirby) *hld up: rdn and outpcd over 2f out: sn btn* **33/1** | 37 |
| 406- | 10 | 1/2 | **My Valentino (IRE)**[78] [3215] 4-8-9 **58**... TristanPrice(7) 11 (Dianne Sayer) *rn wout declared tongue-tie: s.i.s: bhd: rdn over 3f out: sn btn* **40/1** | 42 |
| -523 | 11 | 2 1/4 | **Kicking The Can (IRE)**[30] [841] 6-9-7 **66**... CallumRodriguez(3) 4 (David Thompson) *cl up: rdn and ev ch over 2f out: wknd over 1f out* **9/2**[3] | 46 |
| 060- | 12 | 3 1/2 | **In Focus (IRE)**[190] [6432] 6-9-7 **63**... PhilDennis 8 (Philip Kirby) *t.k.h: led to over 2f out: sn rdn and wknd* **33/1** | 36 |

2m 10.75s (0.35) **Going Correction** +0.175s/f (Slow) **12** Ran SP% **125.1**
Speed ratings (Par 101): **105,103,102,102,101 100,100,96,94,94 92,89**
CSF £66.01 CT £515.91 TOTE £21.70: £5.00, £1.60, £3.90; EX 137.00 Trifecta £1627.80.
**Owner** Diamond Racing Ltd **Bred** Shadwell Estate Company Limited **Trained** Pandy, Monmouths
■ Stewards' Enquiry : Theodore Ladd five-day ban (5-8 & 10 Apr): used whip when out of contention
Connor Murtagh filly stumbled and lay on its side when being reluctant to go to post. Having been checked by the Veterinary Surgeon at the start, the filly was deemed fit to race.

**FOCUS**
A moderate apprentice handicap. The runner-up has been rated as matching her latest C&D form.
T/Plt: £54.70 to a £1 stake. Pool: £77,153.79 - 1028.75 winning units. T/Qpdt: £54.70 to a £1 stake. Pool: £77,153.79 - 1028.75 winning units. **Richard Young**

1313 - 1320a (Foreign Racing) - See Raceform Interactive

# [1219]CHELMSFORD (A.W) (L-H)
Thursday, March 23

**OFFICIAL GOING: Polytrack: standard**
Wind: medium to strong, half against Weather: dry

## 1321 GOING RACING? STAY AT CHANNELS CHANNELSLODGE.CO.UK MAIDEN STKS 5f (P)
**5:50** (5:51) (Class 5) 3-Y-0+ **£5,175** (£1,540; £769; £384) **Stalls** Low

| Form | | | | RPR |
|---|---|---|---|---|
| 2 | 1 | | **Midnightly**[33] [819] 3-8-11 0... AdamBeschizza 1 (Rae Guest) *mde virtually all: rdn over 1f out: r.o wl and a doing enough ins fnl f: eased towards fin* **9/2**[2] | 71 |
| 32- | 2 | 2 | **Kowaiyess (IRE)**[162] [7269] 3-9-2 0... DavidProbert 3 (Owen Burrows) *stdd s: t.k.h: hld up in tch: effrt to chse wnr over 1f out: sn rdn: kpt on same pce and no imp ins fnl f* **2/5**[1] | 69 |
| 0 | 3 | 1 1/4 | **Tooty Fruitti**[9] [1192] 3-8-11 0... IrineuGoncalves 6 (Jo Hughes) *stdd after s: hld up in rr: pushed along and effrt on inner over 1f out: chsd ldng pair and kpt on same pce fnl f* **33/1** | 60 |
| 243- | 4 | 3 1/4 | **Three C's (IRE)**[230] [5099] 3-9-2 77... DougieCostello 5 (David Dennis) *in tch: pushed rt over 4f out: effrt over 1f out: wl hld 4th and kpt on same pce ins fnl f* **7/1**[3] | 53 |
| 00- | 5 | 1 1/4 | **Vicky Park**[142] [7748] 3-8-4 0... JaneElliott(7) 4 (George Margarson) *w ldrs: rn green and wnt rt over 4f out: chsd wnr 2f out tl rdn and outpcd over 1f out: wknd ins fnl f* **50/1** | 43 |
| | 6 | 12 | **Tartufo Classico** 4-10-0 0... MartinLane 2 (Derek Shaw) *t.k.h: w wnr tl 2f out: sn rdn and lost pl: wknd fnl f* **25/1** | 10 |

59.97s (-0.23) **Going Correction** -0.125s/f (Stan)
**WFA** 3 from 4yo 12lb **6** Ran SP% **110.9**
Speed ratings (Par 103): **96,92,90,85,83 64**
CSF £6.63 TOTE £4.50: £2.00, £1.10; EX 7.30 Trifecta £51.40.
**Owner** Bradmill Ltd **Bred** C J Mills **Trained** Newmarket, Suffolk

**FOCUS**
An ordinary maiden but a pleasing performance from the winner. The level is fluid.

## 1322 TOTEPOOL LIVE INFO DOWNLOAD THE APP H'CAP 1m 2f (P)
**6:20** (6:22) (Class 7) (0-50,49) 4-Y-0+ **£2,587** (£770; £384; £192) **Stalls** Low

| Form | | | | RPR |
|---|---|---|---|---|
| -020 | 1 | | **Street Art (IRE)**[15] [1082] 5-9-1 **47**...(bt) HollieDoyle(3) 11 (Mike Murphy) *awkward leaving stalls and slowly away: hdwy to ld after 2f and mde rest: rdn 2f out: clr w chalr 1f out: hld on wl u.p towards fin* **12/1** | 56 |
| 3062 | 2 | shd | **Cahar Fad (IRE)**[12] [1145] 5-9-5 **48**...(bt) AdamBeschizza 10 (Steph Hollinshead) *mostly 2nd: rdn 2f out: clr w wnr 1f out: kpt on wl u.p towards fin: jst failed* **4/1**[2] | 57 |
| /300 | 3 | 6 | **Flying Author (IRE)**[21] [988] 6-9-2 **45**...(tp) JosephineGordon 4 (Phil McEntee) *chsd ldrs: effrt 2f out: outpcd over 1f out: wnt 3rd and kpt on same pce ins fnl f* **9/1** | 43 |
| 5-00 | 4 | 2 | **Understory (USA)**[33] [820] 10-9-3 **46**... MartinLane 5 (Tim McCarthy) *chsd ldr for 2f: chsd ldng pair after: rdn 2f out: outpcd over 1f out: wl hld 4th and plugged on same pce fnl f* **14/1** | 40 |

-206 **5** *nse* **Moving Robe (IRE)**[35] 761 4-9-2 **45**..........................(t) WilliamCarson 2 39
(Conrad Allen) *wl in tch in midfield: rdn over 2f out: drvn and outpcd over 1f out: wl hld and kpt on same pce fnl f* **12/1**

-334 **6** *3/4* **Rezwaan**[15] 1082 10-9-5 **48**..........................(b) TomQueally 9 40+
(Murty McGrath) *hld up in midfield: swtchd rt and hdwy jst over 2f out: outpcd and btn over 1f out and plugged on same pce after* **12/1**

0243 **7** *nk* **Jazri**[12] 1145 6-9-6 **49**..........................(b) FrannyNorton 3 41+
(Milton Bradley) *hld up off the pce in midfield: effrt but stl plenty to do over 1f out: no ch but kpt on ins fnl f* **3/1[1]**

4-06 **8** *hd* **Just Fred (IRE)**[62] 334 4-9-6 **49**..........................(tp) LiamKeniry 8 40+
(Neil Mulholland) *t.k.h: hld up in tch in midfield: effrt 2f out: outpcd u.p over 1f out: wl hld and kpt on same pce fnl f* **8/1[3]**

0/06 **9** *1 1/4* **Gamesters Lad**[16] 1072 5-9-3 **46**..........................(b) KevinStott 7 35+
(Oliver Greenall) *s.i.s: hld up in rr: effrt 2f out: nvr trbld ldrs* **10/1**

2500 **10** *3/4* **Awesome Rock (IRE)**[15] 1081 8-9-2 **45**.......................... KieranO'Neill 14 33+
(Roger Ingram) *t.k.h: hld up off the pce in last trio: effrt wl over 1f out: no prog: n.d* **33/1**

0026 **11** *nk* **Ertidaad (IRE)**[12] 1146 5-8-11 **45**..........................(b) DavidParkes(5) 13 32
(Emma Owen) *wl in tch in midfield: rdn over 2f out: drifted rt u.p and wknd over 1f out* **14/1**

00/0 **12** *14* **Swinford Lass**[64] 283 5-9-6 **49**.......................... GeorgeDowning 12 9+
(Tony Carroll) *s.i.s: hld up in rr: reminders 5f out: lost tch over 2f out* **33/1**

5-64 **13** *2 3/4* **Zebedee's Girl (IRE)**[15] 1084 4-9-3 **46**.......................... AdamKirby 6
(David Evans) *hld up off the pce in midfield: rdn 3f out: wknd over 1f out: bhd ins fnl f* **12/1**

2m 7.83s (-0.77) **Going Correction** -0.125s/f (Stan) **13 Ran SP% 125.2**
Speed ratings (Par 97): **98,97,93,91,91 90,90,90,89,88 88,77,75**
CSF £62.33 CT £470.18 TOTE £14.20: £3.60, £3.00, £2.90; EX 74.00 Trifecta £796.40.
**Owner** Ms Denise Tibbett **Bred** Minch Bloodstock **Trained** Westoning, Beds

**FOCUS**
Few got into this, the pace holding up well. It's been rated around the winner back to his best.

## 1323 TOTEPOOLLIVEINFO.COM VISIT FOR RACING RESULTS H'CAP 1m 2f (P)
**6:50** (6:52) (Class 4) (0-80,80) 4-Y-O+ **£6,469** (£1,925; £962; £481) **Stalls Low**

Form RPR

056- **1** **Celebration Day (IRE)**[286] 3102 4-9-3 **76**.......................... RyanPowell 7 83
(Simon Crisford) *led after 1f: mde rest: rdn wl over 1f out: edgd lft u.p 1f out: in command and kpt on wl ins fnl f: rdn out* **7/1**

40-0 **2** *1 3/4* **Bluff Crag**[15] 1085 4-8-3 **69** ow1..........................(h[1]) FinleyMarsh(7) 2 73
(Richard Hughes) *stdd s: hld up in tch in rr: clsd: nt clr run and swtchd rt over 1f out: rdn and hdwy ent fnl f: hung lft ins fnl f: kpt on to go 2nd towards fin* **8/1**

0045 **3** *1* **Ravenhoe (IRE)**[15] 1085 4-8-11 **70**.......................... FrannyNorton 4 72
(Mark Johnston) *led for 1f: chsd ldrs after: effrt over 1f out: chsd wnr and swtchd rt 1f out: kpt on same pce after and lost 2nd towards fin* **8/1**

0-23 **4** *3/4* **Intensical (IRE)**[7] 1224 6-8-11 **77**..........................(p) DavidEgan(7) 1 77
(Ivan Furtado) *hld up in tch: pushed along and swtchd rt over 3f out: rdn to chse wnr 2f out tl 1f out: keeping on same pce and hld whn sltly squeezed for room ins fnl f* **7/2[2]**

253- **5** *2 1/4* **Taper Tantrum (IRE)**[131] 4208 5-9-4 **80**..........................(v) LouisSteward(3) 3 76
(Michael Bell) *t.k.h: hld up wl in tch in midfield: swtchd rt over 2f out: effrt u.p over 1f out: sn hung bdly rt and no imp: wl hld and one pced fnl f* **15/8[1]**

006- **6** *4* **Inke (IRE)**[132] 7902 5-9-5 **78**..........................(p) AdamKirby 5 66
(Jim Boyle) *hld up wl in tch in midfield: pushed rt and rdn over 2f out: lost pl and btn over 1f out: wknd fnl f* **9/2[3]**

000- **7** *1/2* **Invictus (GER)**[36] 3435 5-9-0 **80**.......................... GerO'Neill(7) 6 68
(David Loughnane) *t.k.h: chsd ldr after 1f tl 2f out: sn rdn and lost pl: wknd fnl f* **25/1**

2m 6.37s (-2.23) **Going Correction** -0.125s/f (Stan) **7 Ran SP% 113.8**
Speed ratings (Par 105): **103,101,100,100,98 95,94**
CSF £59.07 TOTE £7.50: £2.90, £3.60; EX 60.30 Trifecta £392.50.
**Owner** Mohammed Al Nabouda **Bred** Rabbah Bloodstock Limited **Trained** Newmarket, Suffolk
■ Stewards' Enquiry : Finley Marsh cautioned to his future conduct in races

**FOCUS**
The winner had his own way out in front and was able to hold off his pursuers. The second and third help set the level.

## 1324 @TOTEPOOLRACING WIN TICKETS ON TWITTER H'CAP 1m (P)
**7:20** (7:23) (Class 4) (0-80,80) 4-Y-O+ **£6,469** (£1,925; £962; £481) **Stalls Low**

Form RPR

0-11 **1** **Hammer Gun (USA)**[9] 1187 4-8-10 **69** 6ex..........................(v) MartinLane 6 79
(Derek Shaw) *stdd s: hld up in 4th: effrt over 2f out: hdwy u.p to chse wnr jst ins fnl f: styd on wl to ld last strides* **8/1**

-066 **2** *nk* **London (FR)**[16] 1074 4-9-3 **76**..........................(h) JosephineGordon 2 85
(Phil McEntee) *led: clr and shkn up 2f out: rdn over 1f out: drvn and kpt on ins fnl f tl hdd and no ex last strides* **5/1**

-221 **3** *2 3/4* **Kenstone (FR)**[21] 986 4-8-12 **74**..........................(p) HollieDoyle(3) 5 76
(Adrian Wintle) *t.k.h: chsd ldr for 1f: chsd ldrs after: effrt wl over 1f out: chsd ldr jst over 1f out: no imp: 3rd and kpt on same pce ins fnl f* **3/1[2]**

145- **4** *3* **Duke Of North (IRE)**[232] 5017 5-8-3 **67**.......................... CharlieBennett(5) 1 62
(Jim Boyle) *chsd ldr after 1f: rdn and unable qck over 1f out: 4th and btn 1f out: wknd ins fnl f* **12/1**

-322 **5** *4 1/2* **Mariee**[34] 781 4-9-7 **80**.......................... FrannyNorton 4 64
(Mark Johnston) *rousted along leaving stalls: nvr gng wl in last pair: no imp u.p over 1f out: wl hld fnl f* **2/1[1]**

322- **6** *1/2* **Archimento**[281] 3281 4-9-7 **80**.......................... AdamKirby 3 63
(Ed Dunlop) *dwlt: off the pce in rr: rdn over 2f out: no prog and wl hld fnl f* **4/1[3]**

1m 36.87s (-3.03) **Going Correction** -0.125s/f (Stan) **6 Ran SP% 113.8**
Speed ratings (Par 105): **110,109,106,103,99 98**
CSF £47.06 TOTE £8.50: £4.00, £3.10; EX 38.90 Trifecta £176.60.
**Owner** A Flint **Bred** Her Majesty The Queen **Trained** Sproxton, Leics

**FOCUS**
The leader set a good gallop and soon had them well strung out.

## 1325 TOTEPOOL LIKE US ON FACEBOOK H'CAP 7f (P)
**7:50** (7:52) (Class 6) (0-60,61) 4-Y-O+ **£3,234** (£962; £481; £240) **Stalls Low**

Form RPR

0006 **1** **Athletic**[22] 969 8-9-4 **57**..........................(v) AdamKirby 6 65
(David Evans) *in tch in rr: rdn 2f out: hdwy to chse ldrs and swtchd lft 1f out: str run on inner to ld 50yds out: gng away at fin* **7/2[2]**

6-20 **2** *1 1/2* **Hidden Gem**[34] 784 4-9-2 **58**..........................(vt) AaronJones(3) 1 62
(Stuart Williams) *sn bustled up to chse ldrs: drifted rt u.p over 1f out: ev ch ins fnl f: kpt on same pce fnl 75yds: wnt 2nd cl home* **6/1**

4303 **3** *hd* **Jack The Laird (IRE)**[27] 901 4-9-4 **60**..........................(p) JackDuern(3) 9 63
(Dean Ivory) *chsd ldrs: wnt 2nd 5f out tl pushed into ld over 1f out: rdn 1f out: hdd and one pced fnl 50yds: lost 2nd cl home* **12/1**

15- **4** *nk* **Quiet Warrior (IRE)**[92] 8483 6-9-8 **61**..........................(h) JosephineGordon 7 64
(David Loughnane) *dwlt and sltly hmpd leaving stalls: in tch in midfield on outer: effrt wl over 1f out: ev ch ins fnl f: one pced fnl 50yds* **5/2[1]**

40-3 **5** *1* **Rosie Crowe (IRE)**[35] 761 5-8-6 **50**..........................(v) CharlieBennett(5) 4 50
(Shaun Harris) *led: rdn 2f out: hdd over 1f out: kpt on and stl ev ch tl no ex wl ins fnl f: wknd towards fin* **5/1[3]**

0/52 **6** *1 1/4* **Lily Ash (IRE)**[21] 983 4-9-6 **59**.......................... ShaneKelly 8 56
(Mike Murphy) *hld up in tch: rdn over 2f out: kpt on u.p ins fnl f: nvr enough pce to chal* **25/1**

-000 **7** *1* **Just Fab (IRE)**[15] 1084 4-8-8 **47**..........................(v[1]) KieranO'Neill 3 41
(Lee Carter) *in tch towards rr: rdn 3f out: no imp and kpt on same pce fr over 1f out* **33/1**

5454 **8** *3 1/4* **Limerick Lord (IRE)**[9] 1187 5-8-6 **48**..........................(p) ShelleyBirkett(3) 5 33
(Julia Feilden) *chsd ldr for 2f: sn dropped into midfield: 5th and rdn over 2f out: no imp: wknd fnl f* **11/1**

4364 **9** *shd* **Keene's Pointe**[3] 1285 7-9-6 **59**..........................(v[1]) AdamBeschizza 2 44
(Steph Hollinshead) *dwlt: hld up in tch towards rr: effrt u.p over 1f out: no imp over 1f out: wknd ins fnl f* **6/1**

1m 25.48s (-1.72) **Going Correction** -0.125s/f (Stan) **9 Ran SP% 118.8**
Speed ratings (Par 101): **104,102,102,101,100 99,98,94,94**
CSF £25.72 CT £231.97 TOTE £4.40: £1.30, £2.20, £3.70; EX 28.90 Trifecta £300.10.
**Owner** J E Abbey **Bred** A S Reid **Trained** Pandy, Monmouths

**FOCUS**
A moderate handicap. The winner has been rated to his January form, and the runner-up near her recent C&D form.

## 1326 TOTEPOOL BETTING ON ALL UK RACING FILLIES' H'CAP 6f (P)
**8:20** (8:20) (Class 5) (0-75,75) 4-Y-O+ **£3,357** (£3,357; £769; £384) **Stalls Centre**

Form RPR

2322 **1** **Fredricka**[12] 1140 6-9-6 **74**..........................(v) RenatoSouza 5 82
(Jose Santos) *t.k.h: chsd ldrs: effrt to chal over 1f out: sustained effrt u.p and battled on wl ins fnl f: jnd ldr on post* **5/1[2]**

34-1 **1** *dht* **Atalante**[21] 983 4-9-3 **71**..........................(h) AdamKirby 2 79
(Jeremy Noseda) *chsd ldr: swtchd rt over 1f out: rdn to ld jst over 1f out: hrd pressed after and battled on wl u.p: jnd on post* **6/4[1]**

1-21 **3** *2* **Assertive Agent**[36] 735 7-8-12 **66**.......................... DavidProbert 4 68
(Tony Carroll) *in tch in midfield: rdn over 3f out: hdwy u.p and swtchd rt 1f out: kpt on ins fnl f* **6/1[3]**

6-06 **4** *1* **Saved My Bacon (IRE)**[14] 1110 6-9-7 **75**..........................(h) JosephineGordon 7 74
(Chris Dwyer) *in tch in midfield: effrt jst over 1f out: kpt on same pce ins fnl f* **16/1**

3-04 **5** *hd* **Noble Act**[21] 984 4-8-8 **67**.......................... LuluStanford(5) 3 65
(Phil McEntee) *led: rdn and hdd jst over 1f out: wknd ins fnl f* **7/1**

06-4 **6** *9* **Himalayan Queen**[12] 1140 4-8-6 **65**.......................... SophieKilloran(5) 1 36
(William Jarvis) *stdd s: hld up in last pair: pushed along over 1f out: no imp: wknd fnl f* **5/1[2]**

220- **7** *1* **Tigserin (IRE)**[159] 7363 4-9-2 **70**.......................... JackMitchell 6 38
(Giles Bravery) *stdd s: hld up in last pair: rdn 3f out: no imp over 1f out: wknd fnl f* **6/1[3]**

1m 11.97s (-1.73) **Going Correction** -0.125s/f (Stan) **7 Ran SP% 120.3**
Speed ratings (Par 100): **106,106,103,102,101 89,88**
WIN: FR 3.40, AT 1.40; PL: FR 2.80, AT 2.60; EX: FR/AT 9.50, AT/FR 5.10; CSF: FR/AT 6.95, AT/FR 5.11; TF: FR/AT/AA 39.60, AT/FR/AA 26.00.
**Owner** J Melo **Bred** J C Parsons & J J Gilmartin **Trained** Upper Lambourn, Berks
**Owner** M Swinburn & Exors Late Walter Swinburn **Bred** Rockwell Bloodstock **Trained** Newmarket, Suffolk
■ Stewards' Enquiry : Renato Souza four-day ban: used whip above permitted level (6-10 Apr)

**FOCUS**
The judge couldn't split the first two at the line. Not a race with much depth.

## 1327 COLLECT TOTEPOOL WINNINGS AT BETFRED SHOPS H'CAP 5f (P)
**8:50** (8:51) (Class 5) (0-75,77) 4-Y-O+ **£5,175** (£1,540; £769; £384) **Stalls Low**

Form RPR

2241 **1** **Malaysian Boleh**[12] 1147 7-9-3 **69**..........................(v) JosephineGordon 7 75
(Phil McEntee) *off the pce in 4th: rdn 1/2-way: hdwy u.p 1f out: styd on wl fnl 100yds to ld on post* **5/1[3]**

-005 **2** *nse* **Normal Equilibrium**[28] 886 7-9-7 **73**.......................... DavidNolan 4 79
(Ivan Furtado) *led: rdn ent fnl f: drvn ins fnl f: forged ahd wl ins fnl f: hdd on post* **9/4[1]**

2544 **3** *3/4* **Temple Road (IRE)**[24] 955 9-9-1 **67**..........................(bt) FrannyNorton 3 70
(Milton Bradley) *trckd ldrs: swtchd out rt 1f out: rdn hands and heels and kpt on same pce ins fnl f* **9/2[2]**

2-04 **4** *3/4* **Come On Dave (IRE)**[33] 816 8-9-11 **77**..........................(v) LiamKeniry 6 77
(John Butler) *chsd ldr: effrt over 1f out: drvn and upsides jst ins fnl f: no ex and btn wl ins fnl f: wknd towards fin* **9/2[2]**

660- **5** *2 1/4* **Soaring Spirits (IRE)**[110] 8205 7-9-0 **69**.......................... JackDuern(3) 2 61
(Dean Ivory) *bmpd s: outpcd in last pair: rdn over 2f out: kpt on same pce ins fnl f: nvr trbld ldrs* **8/1**

0-00 **6** *3/4* **Secret Asset (IRE)**[21] 995 12-9-7 **73**..........................(v) RobHornby 1 63
(Lisa Williamson) *dwlt and bmpd s: hld up off the pce in rr: effrt u.p over 1f out: no imp: n.d* **12/1**

(-0.20) **Going Correction** -0.125s/f (Stan) **6 Ran SP% 102.6**
Speed ratings (Par 103): **96,95,94,93,89 88**
CSF £13.87 CT £37.51 TOTE £3.80: £6.70, £1.40; EX 16.70 Trifecta £48.10.
**Owner** Mrs Rebecca McEntee **Bred** John & Sue Davis **Trained** Newmarket, Suffolk
■ Welease Brian was withdrawn. Price at time of withdrawal 7-1. Rule 4 applies to all bets - deduction 10p in the pound.

**FOCUS**
A competitive little sprint run at a good gallop. The second and third pin the limited level.

T/Plt: £331.40 to a £1 stake. Pool: £86,192.96 - 189.92 winning units. T/Qpdt: £188.90 to a £1 stake. Pool: £9,266.60 - 36.30 winning units. **Steve Payne**

# 1256 WOLVERHAMPTON (A.W) (L-H)

Thursday, March 23

**OFFICIAL GOING: Tapeta: standard**

Wind: Fresh against Weather: Cloudy with sunny spells

## 1328 BETWAY SPRINT H'CAP 5f 21y (Tp)

**1:50** (1:50) (Class 6) (0-65,67) 3-Y-0+ **£2,587** (£770; £384; £192) **Stalls** Low

Form RPR

0201 **1** **Dashing Poet**[7] 1221 3-8-11 **62** 6ex....(h) MartinLane 5 65
(Jeremy Gask) *s.i.s: hld up: hdwy over 1f out: sn rdn: edgd lft and r.o to ld wl ins fnl f* **5/1**[2]

0-41 **2** *nk* **Powerful Dream (IRE)**[24] 955 4-10-0 **67**....(p) OisinMurphy 4 74
(Ronald Harris) *hld up: shkn up and nt clr run 1f out: rdn: edgd lft and r.o ins fnl f: wnt 2nd nr fin* **5/1**[2]

0033 **3** *½* **Loumarin (IRE)**[17] 1063 5-9-5 **58**....(p) SilvestreDeSousa 6 63
(Michael Appleby) *led 2f: remained w ldr: hung rt 1/2-way: rdn to ld ins fnl f: sn hdd: styd on same pce towards fin* **11/2**[3]

-215 **4** *½* **Annie Salts**[23] 961 4-9-12 **65**....(h) JoeFanning 7 68
(Chris Dwyer) *w ldrs: shkn up over 1f out: ev ch ins fnl f: no ex nr fin* **8/1**

00-5 **5** *nse* **Ryedale Rio (IRE)**[16] 1071 4-9-6 **62**.... RachelRichardson(3) 2 65
(Tim Easterby) *sn chsng ldr: led 3f out: rdn and hdd ins fnl f: styd on same pce* **8/1**

-622 **6** *½* **Goodwood Crusader (IRE)**[15] 1088 3-9-0 **65**.... ShaneKelly 1 65+
(Richard Hughes) *s.i.s: sn pushed along in rr: nt clr run over 1f out: and ins fnl f: r.o towards fin* **11/4**[1]

-543 **7** *nk* **Noble Asset**[45] 604 6-9-9 **62**.... LukeMorris 9 62
(Milton Bradley) *prom: racd keenly: rdn over 1f out: styd on same pce ins fnl f* **16/1**

5406 **8** *nk* **Doctor Parkes**[12] 1147 11-9-5 **65**.... MillyNaseb(7) 3 64
(Stuart Williams) *chsd ldrs: rdn over 1f out: no ex wl ins fnl f* **11/1**

1m 1.66s (-0.24) **Going Correction** +0.025s/f (Slow)
**WFA** 3 from 4yo+ 12lb **8** Ran SP% **111.8**
Speed ratings (Par 101): **102,101,100,99,99 99,98,98**
CSF £28.71 CT £139.04 TOTE £5.60: £1.30, £2.20, £1.20; EX 21.70 Trifecta £126.20.
**Owner** The Dashing Poets **Bred** Qatar Bloodstock Ltd **Trained** Stockbridge, Hants

**FOCUS**
A moderate if competitive sprint handicap and luck in running played its part. Straightforward form.

## 1329 BETWAY (S) STKS 1m 1f 104y (Tp)

**2:20** (2:20) (Class 6) 4-Y-0+ **£2,587** (£770; £384; £192) **Stalls** Low

Form RPR

5-42 **1** **Mr Red Clubs (IRE)**[7] 1224 8-8-11 70....(p) JaneElliott(7) 4 73
(Michael Appleby) *hld up: hdwy over 2f out: led over 1f out: rdn out* **15/8**[1]

100- **2** *3 ½* **Bling King**[183] 6683 8-9-4 55.... SamJames 7 66
(Geoffrey Harker) *hld up: hdwy over 3f out: rdn over 2f out: styd on same pce fr over 1f out: wnt 2nd wl ins fnl f* **50/1**

6002 **3** *½* **Pool House**[9] 1186 6-8-12 60.... ShaneKelly 5 59
(Mike Murphy) *prom: lost pl after 1f: pushed along and hdwy 2f out: styd on to go 3rd nr fin* **14/1**

115- **4** *½* **Drago (IRE)**[118] 8101 5-9-3 73....(h) PatrickVaughan(7) 6 70
(David O'Meara) *plld hrd and prom: wnt 2nd over 6f out: ev ch wl over 1f out: no ex ins fnl f* **7/2**[2]

-240 **5** *2 ¼* **Anton Chigurh**[16] 1074 8-10-2 74.... RichardKingscote 8 72
(Tom Dascombe) *led after 1f: rdn and hdd wl over 1f out: wknd ins fnl f* **15/2**

0-60 **6** *2 ¾* **Ready (IRE)**[66] 266 7-9-4 83.... SteveDrowne 1 57
(Clare Ellam) *led 1f: lost pl over 6f out: rdn over 3f out: outpcd over 2f out: eased whn btn fnl f* **6/1**[3]

000- **7** *6* **Little Lotte (IRE)**[17] 7230 4-8-2 51....(b) GeorgeWood(5) 2 32
(Tom Gretton) *hld up in tch: plld hrd: pushed along 1/2-way: rdn and wknd over 2f out* **66/1**

203- **8** *2* **Port Paradise**[44] 7653 4-9-4 68....(h) JoeFanning 3 45
(William Jarvis) *chsd ldrs: pushed along over 3f out: wknd and eased wl over 1f out* **7/2**[2]

2m 2.22s (1.42) **Going Correction** +0.025s/f (Slow) **8** Ran SP% **115.4**
Speed ratings (Par 101): **94,90,90,90,88 85,80,78**
CSF £98.42 TOTE £2.20: £1.02, £9.50, £3.40; EX 77.10 Trifecta £2406.10.No bids for the winner.
**Owner** Ferrybank Properties Limited **Bred** Tally-Ho Stud **Trained** Oakham, Rutland

**FOCUS**
An ordinary seller with the eight runners officially rated between 51 and 83. The runner-up has been rated to last year's best.

## 1330 BETWAY H'CAP 1m 4f 51y (Tp)

**2:55** (2:55) (Class 6) (0-65,67) 4-Y-0+ **£2,587** (£770; £384; £192) **Stalls** Low

Form RPR

0-01 **1** **Dunquin (IRE)**[31] 841 5-9-7 **65**.... LukeMorris 4 76
(John Mackie) *chsd ldr tl led at stdy pce 10f out: qcknd over 2f out: rdn over 1f out: styd on* **2/1**[1]

2-32 **2** *1 ¼* **Surround Sound**[9] 1191 7-8-9 **56**....(t) RachelRichardson(3) 7 65
(Tim Easterby) *dwlt: hld up: hdwy 2f out: rdn to chse wnr ins fnl f: r.o* **6/1**

6300 **3** *7* **Playtothewhistle**[16] 1074 6-9-7 **65**....(v) SilvestreDeSousa 6 63
(Michael Appleby) *prom: chsd wnr 9f out: rdn over 2f out: wknd ins fnl f* **7/2**[3]

4-31 **4** *6* **Lady Turpin (IRE)**[9] 1188 4-8-0 **53**.... ConnorMurtagh(7) 5 41
(Richard Fahey) *hld up in tch: rdn: edgd lft and wknd over 1f out* **5/2**[2]

0-45 **5** *2 ¼* **Mamnoon (IRE)**[29] 855 4-9-0 **60**.... TomMarquand 1 45
(Roy Brotherton) *prom: rdn over 2f out: sn wknd* **33/1**

0260 **6** *1* **English Summer**[24] 958 10-9-7 **65**....(vt[1]) StevieDonohoe 2 50
(Ian Williams) *led 2f: chsd ldrs: rdn over 2f out: wknd wl over 1f out* **25/1**

12-4 **7** *71* **Consortium (IRE)**[34] 786 5-9-6 **67**....(t[1]) CallumShepherd(3) 3
(Miss Imogen Pickard) *pushed along in rr early: rdn and wknd over 2f out: eased* **11/1**

2m 41.67s (0.87) **Going Correction** +0.025s/f (Slow)
**WFA** 4 from 5yo+ 1lb **7** Ran SP% **113.5**
Speed ratings (Par 101): **98,97,92,88,87 86,39**
CSF £14.43 TOTE £3.00: £2.80, £2.00; EX 13.80 Trifecta £43.30.
**Owner** Mrs Carolyn Seymour **Bred** Darley **Trained** Church Broughton , Derbys

**FOCUS**
A moderate middle-distance handicap. They went steadily and that was a big help to the winner. The winner has been rated close to last year's form over this trip.

## 1331 32REDSPORT.COM H'CAP 1m 4f 51y (Tp)

**3:25** (3:25) (Class 6) (0-65,64) 3-Y-O **£2,587** (£770; £384; £192) **Stalls** Low

Form RPR

-546 **1** **Ladofash**[22] 967 3-9-1 **58**....(v) PJMcDonald 4 65
(K R Burke) *hld up: hdwy over 2f out: led ins fnl f: rdn clr* **9/1**

6452 **2** *4* **Av A Word**[14] 1107 3-8-12 **55**....(p) LukeMorris 1 56
(Daniel Kubler) *chsd ldrs: rdn to ld wl over 1f out: sn hung lft: hdd ins fnl f: styd on same pce* **10/1**

60-3 **3** *1 ½* **Spirit Of Rome (IRE)**[28] 881 3-9-3 **60**.... TedDurcan 9 58
(James Bethell) *hld up: hdwy 2f out: styd on to go 3rd nr fin* **13/2**

-001 **4** *¾* **Bessemer Lady**[28] 881 3-9-6 **63**....(b) RichardKingscote 3 60
(Ralph Beckett) *prom: chsd ldr 4f out: ev ch over 2f out: sn rdn: no ex ins fnl f* **11/4**[1]

-522 **5** *7* **The Last Debutante**[43] 627 3-9-7 **64**.... JoeFanning 7 50
(Mark Johnston) *chsd ldr tl led 5f out: rdn and hdd wl over 1f out: wknd fnl f* **3/1**[2]

3155 **6** *1* **Log Off (IRE)**[30] 848 3-9-2 **59**.... AndrewMullen 6 43+
(David Evans) *hld up: carried rt and lost pl 10f out: nvr on terms after* **14/1**

-662 **7** *2 ¼* **Knightsbridge Liam (IRE)**[38] 718 3-8-12 **58**.... NathanEvans(3) 2 39+
(Michael Easterby) *hld up: hung rt and lost pl 10f out: sn bhd: n.d after* **5/1**[3]

0-65 **8** *8* **Affair**[35] 766 3-8-4 **54**.... TheodoreLadd(7) 5 22
(Hughie Morrison) *led 7f: rdn and wknd over 2f out* **100/1**

040- **9** *42* **Intisha (IRE)**[203] 6060 3-9-2 **64**....(t[1]) MitchGodwin(5) 8
(Jonathan Portman) *hld up: reminder 5f out: hdwy over 3f out: sn pushed along: hung rt and wknd over 2f out* **22/1**

2m 40.83s (0.03) **Going Correction** +0.025s/f (Slow) **9** Ran SP% **112.8**
Speed ratings (Par 96): **100,97,96,95,91 90,89,83,55**
CSF £92.07 CT £622.99 TOTE £10.90: £2.30, £3.70, £4.50; EX 92.40 Trifecta £553.80.
**Owner** John Dance **Bred** Horizon Bloodstock Limited **Trained** Middleham Moor, N Yorks

**FOCUS**
Another moderate middle-distance handicap, this time for 3yos. The winner has been rated within 5lb of his 2yo peak.

## 1332 32RED.COM H'CAP 6f 20y (Tp)

**4:00** (4:01) (Class 5) (0-75,75) 3-Y-0 **£3,234** (£962; £481; £240) **Stalls** Low

Form RPR

-511 **1** **Lord Cooper**[27] 903 3-9-7 **75**....(tp) RenatoSouza 2 80
(Jose Santos) *a.p: rdn to ld wl ins fnl f: r.o* **15/2**

-123 **2** *hd* **Cappananty Con**[28] 877 3-9-6 **74**.... RobertWinston 5 78
(Dean Ivory) *hld up: hdwy over 1f out: rdn and ev ch wl ins fnl f: r.o* **7/4**[1]

0-1 **3** *shd* **Derek Duval (USA)**[17] 1064 3-9-1 **72**....(t) AaronJones(3) 6 76
(Stuart Williams) *trckd ldrs: lost pl over 3f out: hdwy over 1f out: r.o wl* **9/2**[3]

-11 **4** *1* **Intense Romance (IRE)**[20] 1005 3-9-2 **70**.... ConnorBeasley 4 71
(Michael Dods) *chsd ldr 5f out: rdn and ev ch fr over 1f out tl no ex towards fin* **13/2**

3342 **5** *shd* **Arzaak (IRE)**[22] 972 3-9-5 **73**....(p) SilvestreDeSousa 8 73
(Chris Dwyer) *led: rdn over 1f out: hdd and unable qck wl ins fnl f* **4/1**[2]

100- **6** *4 ½* **Compton Lane**[164] 7217 3-9-5 **73**.... RyanTate 1 62
(Rod Millman) *chsd ldr 1f: remained handy: rdn over 1f out: wknd ins fnl f* **18/1**

0-63 **7** *4* **Who Told Jo Jo (IRE)**[27] 898 3-9-0 **68**.... OisinMurphy 3 43
(Joseph Tuite) *sn pushed along in rr: bhd fr 1/2-way* **22/1**

130- **8** *5* **Bobby Vee**[191] 6440 3-8-9 **68**.... LuluStanford(5) 7 37
(Dean Ivory) *hld up: hdwy over 3f out: wknd over 1f out* **28/1**

1m 14.01s (-0.49) **Going Correction** +0.025s/f (Slow) **8** Ran SP% **112.7**
Speed ratings (Par 98): **104,103,103,102,102 96,90,84**
CSF £20.45 CT £66.77 TOTE £8.20: £1.80, £1.20, £1.50; EX 19.70 Trifecta £84.00.
**Owner** R Cooper Racing Ltd **Bred** Miss K Rausing **Trained** Upper Lambourn, Berks

**FOCUS**
An ordinary 3yo sprint handicap and they finished in a bit of a heap. The second has been rated just above his previous C&D form.

## 1333 32RED CASINO MAIDEN FILLIES' STKS 1m 142y (Tp)

**4:30** (4:30) (Class 5) 3-Y-0+ **£3,234** (£962; £481; £240) **Stalls** Low

Form RPR

**1** **Hidden Charms (IRE)** 3-8-7 0.... JoeFanning 9 75+
(David Simcock) *s.i.s: hld up: hdwy over 1f out: shkn up and r.o to ld wl ins fnl f* **9/1**

**2** *¾* **Rinaria (IRE)** 3-8-4 0.... JordanVaughan(3) 6 70
(K R Burke) *hld up in tch: racd keenly: rdn and edgd lft ins fnl f: r.o* **33/1**

5- **3** *¾* **Angel Of Rome (IRE)**[128] 7963 3-8-7 0.... ShaneKelly 3 69
(Richard Hughes) *plld hrd and prom: chsd ldr over 2f out: led and hung lft over 1f out: rdn and hdd wl ins fnl f* **6/1**[2]

6-3 **4** *¾* **Kassandra (IRE)**[10] 1179 3-8-7 0.... TomMarquand 10 67
(Richard Hannon) *mid-div: rdn over 2f out: hdwy over 1f out: r.o* **10/1**

**5** *¾* **Shift Cross** 3-8-7 0.... SilvestreDeSousa 1 66
(Marco Botti) *chsd ldrs: pushed along over 2f out: no ex ins fnl f* **11/4**[1]

63 **6** *3* **Miss M (IRE)**[12] 1151 3-8-7 0.... MartinDwyer 2 59
(William Muir) *led 1f: chsd ldr tl led again 3f out: rdn and hdd over 1f out: wknd ins fnl f* **16/1**

42 **7** *hd* **Dusky Maid (IRE)**[14] 1102 3-8-7 0.... AndrewMullen 5 63+
(James Given) *hld up: nvr on terms* **9/1**

64 **8** *nk* **Melodine**[41] 658 3-8-7 0.... LukeMorris 8 58
(Sir Mark Prescott Bt) *hld up: pushed along over 2f out: nvr on terms* **6/1**[2]

030- **9** *1 ¾* **Patching**[133] 7885 3-8-4 68.... AaronJones(3) 4 55
(Giles Bravery) *mid-div: pushed along over 2f out: n.d* **14/1**

**10** *7* **Almerita Moon (IRE)** 3-8-2 0.... GeorgeWood(5) 7 40
(Marco Botti) *s.i.s: sn pushed along and a in rr* **18/1**

42 **11** *½* **Never Folding (IRE)**[23] 962 3-8-7 0.... OisinMurphy 11 39
(Seamus Durack) *racd keenly: w ldr tl led over 7f out: hdd 3f out: wknd over 1f out* **8/1**[3]

1m 50.67s (0.57) **Going Correction** +0.025s/f (Slow) **11** Ran SP% **116.2**
Speed ratings (Par 100): **98,97,96,96,95 92,92,92,90,84 84**
CSF £261.24 TOTE £7.50: £2.50, £7.30, £2.50; EX 311.40 Trifecta £2559.90.
**Owner** Mrs Doreen Tabor **Bred** Lynchbages Edgeridge Ltd & Glenvale Stud **Trained** Newmarket, Suffolk

**FOCUS**
Quite an interesting maiden and a strange betting market. Two of the four newcomers filled the first two places. The opening level is fluid.

## 1334 SUNBETS.CO.UK H'CAP 1m 142y (Tp)
5:00 (5:01) (Class 6) (0-65,67) 4-Y-0+ £2,587 (£770; £384; £192) Stalls Low

Form RPR
0114 1 **Celtic Artisan (IRE)**[35] 757 6-9-9 **67**......................(bt) OisinMurphy 10 74
(Rebecca Menzies) *a.p: chsd ldr over 5f out: led over 1f out: rdn and edgd lft ins fnl f: r.o* **11/1**
-060 2 *hd* **All You (IRE)**[26] 928 5-9-9 **67**......................(v) PhillipMakin 2 73
(David O'Meara) *hld up: hdwy and nt clr run over 1f out: sn rdn: r.o to go 2nd wl ins fnl f: nt quite rch wnr* **12/1**
0066 3 *1 ¼* **Hard To Handel**[17] 1065 5-9-7 **65**......................(b[1]) PaddyAspell 12 69
(Clare Ellam) *hld up: hdwy and nt clr run over 1f out: r.o to go 3rd nr fin* **33/1**
3255 4 *hd* **Roman De Brut (IRE)**[26] 928 5-9-1 **66**...................... TobyEley(7) 11 69
(Daniel Mark Loughnane) *hld up: hdwy on outer over 2f out: rdn and edgd lft ins fnl f: styd on same pce towards fin* **9/1[3]**
1102 5 *¾* **Bounty Pursuit**[3] 1285 5-9-8 **66**......................(p[1]) SilvestreDeSousa 1 67
(Michael Appleby) *prom: rdn over 1f out: styd on same pce ins fnl f* **15/8[1]**
/50- 6 *1 ¼* **Pretty Jewel**[283] 3236 4-9-4 **62**...................... RobHornby 13 60+
(Sarah Hollinshead) *s.i.s: hld up: rdn over 2f out: r.o towards fin: nvr nrr* **150/1**
1123 7 *shd* **Gabrial The Thug (FR)**[24] 954 7-9-4 **62**...................... RichardKingscote 3 61
(Ian Williams) *chsd ldrs: rdn over 2f out: no ex ins fnl f* **9/2[2]**
-064 8 *nk* **Cabal**[22] 968 10-9-7 **65**......................(v) SamJames 5 65
(Geoffrey Harker) *hld up: nt clr run fr over 1f out: nt trble ldrs* **33/1**
0-62 9 *½* **Foie Gras**[22] 968 7-9-8 **66**......................(p) JoeFanning 8 62
(Chris Dwyer) *hld up: hdwy 3f out: rdn over 1f out: no ex fnl f* **18/1**
0-05 10 *nk* **Rustique**[20] 996 5-9-6 **64**......................(p[1]) ThomasBrown 9 60
(Ed Walker) *chsd ldr tl led over 6f out: rdn over 2f out: hdd over 1f out: wknd wl ins fnl f* **14/1**
2021 11 *1 ¾* **Siouxperhero (IRE)**[17] 1067 8-9-5 **63**......................(p) MartinDwyer 4 55
(William Muir) *sn led: hdd over 6f out: chsd ldrs: rdn over 2f out: wknd ins fnl f* **10/1**
00-0 12 *1 ½* **Shamlan (IRE)**[31] 841 5-9-2 **60**......................(tp) StevieDonohoe 6 49
(Johnny Farrelly) *in rr: bhd and pushed along over 5f out: n.d* **10/1**
1m 49.8s (-0.30) **Going Correction** +0.025s/f (Slow) 12 Ran SP% **115.6**
Speed ratings (Par 101): **102,101,100,100,99 98,98,98,97,97 96,94**
CSF £131.37 CT £4202.89 TOTE £8.50: £2.90, £3.40, £7.20; EX 119.70 Trifecta £2472.20.
**Owner** EPDS Racing Partnership 11 **Bred** Fortbarrington Stud **Trained** Mordon, Durham

**FOCUS**
A moderate if competitive handicap. The winner has been rated in keeping with the best interpretation of his Chelmsford February win.
T/Jkpt: Not won. T/Plt: £312.80 to a £1 stake. Pool: £84,249.29 - 196.61 winning units. T/Qpdt: £55.10 to a £1 stake. Pool: £5,806.99 - 77.90 winning units. **Colin Roberts**

# 1269 SAINT-CLOUD (L-H)
Thursday, March 23

**OFFICIAL GOING: Turf: soft**

## 1335a PRIX DU DEBUT - ETALON KENDARGENT (MAIDEN) (UNRACED 2YO) (TURF) 4f 110y
11:40 2-Y-0 £11,538 (£4,615; £3,461; £2,307; £1,153)

RPR
1 **Evabienchope (FR)** 2-8-13 0...................... Pierre-CharlesBoudot 7 75
(P Sogorb, France) **23/10[1]**
2 *1 ¾* **Get Even** 2-8-13 0...................... MickaelBarzalona 11 68
(Jo Hughes) *qckly into stride: disp ld early: remained cl up: pushed along over 1f out: rdn and styd on one pce fnl f* **246/10**
3 *½* **Jurisprudance (FR)** 2-8-13 0...................... MaximeGuyon 10 66
(George Baker) *slowly away: pushed along early: impr over 2f out: drvn over 1 out and r.o wl ins fnl f to take 3rd cl home* **11/1**
4 *nk* **Dann (FR)** 2-9-2 0...................... AlexandreGavilan 12 68
(D Guillemin, France) **111/10**
5 *nk* **Uchronique (FR)** 2-8-13 0...................... AlexisBadel 17 64
(M Boutin, France) **42/1**
6 *¾* **Rioticism (FR)** 2-8-13 0...................... EddyHardouin 14 61
(Matthieu Palussiere, France) **52/1**
7 *hd* **Kyvon Des Aigles (FR)** 2-9-2 0...................... RonanThomas 16 63
(Mme C Barande-Barbe, France) **98/10**
8 *snk* **Alets (FR)** 2-8-13 0......................(p) FabriceVeron 3 59
(C Baillet, France) **184/10**
9 *hd* **Belgrano (FR)** 2-9-2 0...................... ChristopheSoumillon 4 61
(C Lerner, France) **17/2[3]**
10 *nk* **Acapella Style (FR)** 2-8-13 0...................... AntoineHamelin 2 57
(Matthieu Palussiere, France) **154/10**
11 *2 ½* **Marina Palace (FR)** 2-8-7 0...................... KyllanBarbaud(6) 9 47
(A Junk, France) **51/1**
12 *½* **Popsi** 2-8-7 0...................... GuillaumeTrolleyDePrevaux(6) 8 45
(Jo Hughes) *wl into stride: pushed along over 2f out: rdn over 1f out and grad wknd* **66/1**
13 *½* **Qatar Sunshine** 2-8-13 0...................... OlivierPeslier 15 43
(H-A Pantall, France) **56/10[2]**
14 *1 ½* **Fidji D'Emra (FR)** 2-8-13 0...................... DavidMichaux 5 37
(C Plisson, France) **58/1**
15 *hd* **Zie De Ket (FR)** 2-9-2 0...................... IoritzMendizabal 6 39
(M Boutin, France) **228/10**
16 *3* **Golfindia (FR)** 2-8-13 0...................... CristianDemuro 1 24
(J-V Toux, France) **23/1**
17 *4* **Lastyouni (FR)** 2-8-13 0...................... TonyPiccone 13 8
(Matthieu Palussiere, France) **33/1**

PARI-MUTUEL (all including 1 euro stake): WIN 3.30; PLACE 1.80, 6.00, 3.60; DF 41.90; SF 84.30.
**Owner** Guy Pariente **Bred** A Chopard **Trained** France

## 1337a PRIX KIZIL KOURGAN (CONDITIONS) (3YO) (TURF) 1m
2:20 3-Y-0 £11,111 (£4,444; £3,333; £2,222; £1,111)

RPR
1 **Livrable**[22] 3-8-10 0......................(b[1]) MaximeGuyon 4 92
(C Ferland, France) **7/1**
2 *hd* **Mille Pieds (FR)**[156] 3-8-10 0...................... ChristopheSoumillon 7 91
(J-C Rouget, France) **4/5[1]**
3 *shd* **Charly Nova (FR)**[121] 8062 3-8-11 0...................... ThierryThulliez 1 92
(F Rossi, France) **19/5[2]**
4 *1 ¾* **Prost (GER)**[97] 8420 3-9-1 0...................... GregoryBenoist 2 92
(Ed Vaughan) *in tch: rdn to chal 2f out: ev ch over 1f out: no ex fnl f* **19/1**
5 *3 ½* **Birmano (USA)**[22] 3-8-7 0...................... MathieuPelletan(8) 3 84
(A Fabre, France) *led to 1/2-way then trckd ldr: led again whn rdn 2f out: sn hdd: no ex and wknd on rail fnl f* **6/1[3]**
6 *8* **Quindiana (FR)**[126] 7996 3-8-11 0...................... Pierre-CharlesBoudot 6 62
(H-A Pantall, France) **83/10**
1m 43.82s (-3.68) 6 Ran SP% **118.9**
PARI-MUTUEL (all including 1 euro stake): WIN 8.00; PLACE 2.30, 1.30; SF 19.70.
**Owner** Wertheimer & Frere **Bred** J Wertheimer Et Frere **Trained** France

1336 - 1337a (Foreign Racing) - See Raceform Interactive

# 1237 LINGFIELD (L-H)
Friday, March 24

**OFFICIAL GOING: Polytrack: standard**
Wind: Half against, mostly fresh Weather: Cloudy becoming fine

## 1338 SUN BETS ON THE APP STORE H'CAP 1m 1y(P)
2:20 (2:21) (Class 6) (0-65,63) 4-Y-0+ £2,264 (£673; £336; £168) Stalls High

Form RPR
00-0 1 **Shifting Star (IRE)**[16] 1086 12-9-2 **58**......................(vt) WilliamCarson 10 66
(John Bridger) *t.k.h: cl up: trckd ldr over 1f out: rdn to ld last 120yds: edgd lft but kpt on wl* **16/1**
0022 2 *¾* **Sheer Intensity (IRE)**[8] 1225 4-8-4 **53**...................... DavidEgan(7) 4 59
(David Evans) *hld up in midfield: pushed along over 1f out: prog fnl f: tk 2nd last 75yds: rdn and styd on: nt rch wnr* **7/1[3]**
5-03 3 *nk* **Bloodsweatandtears**[34] 811 9-9-3 **59**...................... JosephineGordon 6 64
(William Knight) *hld up in rr: drvn over 1f out: r.o fnl f and tk 3rd last strides: nrst fin* **11/1**
0253 4 *¾* **Freddy With A Y (IRE)**[4] 1285 7-9-7 **63**......................(v) PaddyAspell 3 66
(J R Jenkins) *dwlt: rcvrd into midfield after 1f: cl up 2f out: rdn and nt qckn over 1f out: hung rt fnl f and ended against nr side rail: kpt on* **4/1[1]**
0342 5 *shd* **Tavener**[27] 929 5-8-8 **57**......................(p) FinleyMarsh(7) 8 60
(David C Griffiths) *t.k.h: mde most: rdn over 1f out: hdd & wknd last 120yds* **6/1[2]**
0503 6 *nse* **With Approval (IRE)**[21] 998 5-9-4 **60**......................(p) LiamKeniry 1 63
(Laura Mongan) *cl up on inner: rdn to dispute 2nd over 1f out: nt qckn ins fnl f: one pce nr fin* **10/1**
3620 7 *½* **Dukes Meadow**[24] 966 6-8-4 **53**...................... RhiainIngram(7) 7 55
(Roger Ingram) *hld up in last pair: stl there over 1f out: pushed along and prog fnl f: nvr nr to chal* **14/1**
0-02 8 *¾* **Mulled Wine**[37] 740 4-8-10 **52**...................... KierenFox 12 54
(John Best) *hld up in last: rdn over 1f out: prog fnl f: keeping on but no ch whn rn out of room nr fin* **11/1**
05-6 9 *½* **Golly Miss Molly**[41] 677 6-9-6 **62**......................(b) MartinLane 9 61
(Jeremy Gask) *hld up in rr: effrt and sme prog on inner over 1f out: nvr rchd ldrs and no hdwy fnl f* **14/1**
0-03 10 *5* **Moi Aussie**[7] 1245 4-8-11 **53**...................... TomMarquand 11 40
(Michael Appleby) *t.k.h: cl up bhd ldrs tl wknd 2f out* **10/1**
33-2 11 *3 ¾* **Muzaahim (IRE)**[13] 1146 6-9-2 **58**......................(p[1]) ShaneKelly 2 36
(Laura Morgan) *mostly pressed ldr to over 1f out: wknd qckly* **6/1[2]**
00-0 12 *5* **Marmalad (IRE)**[41] 689 5-9-1 **57**...................... FergusSweeney 5 23
(Shaun Lycett) *racd wd: nudged by rival after 1f: rdn over 3f out: wknd over 2f out: sn bhd* **25/1**
1m 38.54s (0.34) **Going Correction** +0.05s/f (Slow) 12 Ran SP% **119.0**
Speed ratings (Par 101): **100,99,98,98,98 98,97,96,96,91 87,82**
CSF £124.42 CT £1319.98 TOTE £19.90: £5.20, £1.80, £3.00; EX 148.00 Trifecta £692.60.
**Owner** Night Shadow Syndicate **Bred** Hardys Of Kilkeel Ltd **Trained** Liphook, Hants
■ Stewards' Enquiry : William Carson two-day ban; careless riding (7th-8th Apr)

**FOCUS**
A moderate if competitive handicap and a typically tight finish. The winner didn't need to match his September C&D form.

## 1339 BETWAY SPRINT H'CAP 6f 1y(P)
2:55 (2:57) (Class 5) (0-70,71) 4-Y-0+ £2,911 (£866; £432; £216) Stalls Low

Form RPR
0-10 1 **Top Of The Bank**[20] 1031 4-9-2 **63**......................(p) TonyHamilton 7 75
(Kristin Stubbs) *mde all: shkn up and drew clr wl over 1f out: in n.d after: rdn out* **20/1**
41-2 2 *2 ¼* **El Principe**[16] 1080 4-9-6 **67**......................(h) DavidAllan 1 72
(Les Eyre) *trckd ldrs on inner: shkn up 2f out and racd awkwardly: kpt on fr over 1f out to take 2nd last 120yds: no ch w wnr* **11/8[1]**
0665 3 *1 ½* **Colourbearer (IRE)**[13] 1140 10-8-13 **67**......................(t) JoshuaBryan(7) 8 67
(Charlie Wallis) *chsd wnr: outpcd wl over 1f out: n.d after and lost 2nd last 120yds* **20/1**
5043 4 *hd* **Head Space (IRE)**[9] 1206 9-9-4 **65**......................(b) AdamKirby 3 64
(David Evans) *hld up in rr: bmpd along over 1f out: styd on ins fnl f: rdn and nrly snatched 3rd* **8/1**
4156 5 *1 ¼* **Bridge Builder**[34] 808 7-9-10 **71**......................(p) TomMarquand 6 66+
(Peter Hedger) *hld up in rr: shkn up 2f out: nt qckn over 1f out and nvr posed a threat* **7/2[2]**
0534 6 *½* **Compton Prince**[16] 1080 8-9-3 **64**......................(b) JoeFanning 5 58
(Milton Bradley) *t.k.h: hld up in tch: shkn up and nt qckn over 1f out: fdd ins fnl f* **12/1**
34-3 7 *1 ¾* **Dance Rebel**[34] 807 4-9-1 **67**...................... GeorgeWood(5) 9 55
(Dr Jon Scargill) *racd on outer: hld up in rr: shkn up 2f out: no great prog* **14/1**
-030 8 *9* **Aragon Knight**[18] 1062 4-9-4 **68**......................(p[1]) HectorCrouch(3) 4 27
(Heather Main) *disp 2nd pl to wl over 1f out: wknd rapidly* **6/1[3]**
-000 9 *10* **Something Lucky (IRE)**[34] 808 5-9-3 **64**......................(h) StevieDonohoe 2
(Daniel Steele) *blindfold late off and slowly away: outpcd and sn t.o* **40/1**
1m 11.73s (-0.17) **Going Correction** +0.05s/f (Slow) 9 Ran SP% **116.0**
Speed ratings (Par 103): **103,100,98,97,96 95,93,81,67**
CSF £47.34 CT £601.50 TOTE £18.40: £3.90, £1.10, £4.10; EX 63.10 Trifecta £480.20.

**Owner** R Whichelow, T Baker & Partners **Bred** D Carroll **Trained** Norton, N Yorks
**FOCUS**
An ordinary sprint handicap. A few of these normally like to force it, but the winner had this very much own way and the race was his passing the furlong pole. He's rated to last year's mark.

## 1340 BETWAY DASH H'CAP — 5f 6y(P)
**3:30** (3:31) (Class 6) (0-60,62) 4-Y-0+ **£2,264** (£673; £336; £168) **Stalls** High

Form RPR
0060 **1** **Red Invader (IRE)**[17] 1071 7-9-7 **60**.................................(p) LiamKeniry 6 69
(John Butler) *dwlt: hld up in last: stl there over 1f out: jst shkn up and swept past rivals ins fnl f to ld last 50yds: cleverly* **16/1**
3354 **2** 3/4 **Roy's Legacy**[20] 1022 8-8-8 **52**.................................. CharlieBennett(5) 8 58
(Shaun Harris) *kpt away fr rest at s spd fr wd draw to press ldr: led 2f out: drvn over 1f out: hrd pressed after: kpt on but hdd and outpcd last 50yds* **9/1**
6251 **3** *nk* **Frank The Barber (IRE)**[20] 1022 5-9-7 **60**...................(vt[1]) AdamKirby 7 65
(Steph Hollinshead) *cl up: drvn to chal jst over 1f out: nt qckn ins fnl f: kpt on* **9/4[1]**
-063 **4** *nk* **Hurricane Alert**[8] 1220 5-8-7 **46** oh1............................ AdamBeschizza 4 50
(Mark Hoad) *taken down early: dwlt: hld up in last trio: prog over 1f out: clsd on ldrs and looked a threat ins fnl f: one pce last 75yds* **16/1**
3424 **5** *nse* **Pharoh Jake**[24] 961 9-8-12 **58**...................................... JaneElliott(7) 5 62
(John Bridger) *in tch: drvn and tried to chal fr over 1f out: nt qckn after and kpt on same pce* **8/1**
0-13 **6** *hd* **Hot Stuff**[24] 961 4-9-5 **58**............................................. GeorgeDowning 3 61
(Tony Carroll) *hld up in last trio: shkn up over 1f out: kpt on same pce fnl f: nt btn far but nvr a real threat* **6/1[3]**
5430 **7** 3/4 **Noble Asset**[1] 1328 6-9-9 **62**............................................. JoeFanning 2 64
(Milton Bradley) *taken down early: led to 2f out: stl on terms w ldr fnl f: one pce last 150yds and lost many pls* **7/2[2]**
-005 **8** *shd* **Ask The Guru**[20] 1022 7-8-13 **52**...........................(p) JosephineGordon 1 52
(Michael Attwater) *cl up on inner: drvn and tried to chal over 1f out: one pce and lost pl last 150yds* **7/1**
59.79s (0.99) **Going Correction** +0.05s/f (Slow) 8 Ran SP% **112.7**
Speed ratings (Par 101): **94,92,92,91,91 91,90,90**
CSF £144.60 CT £397.60 TOTE £16.80: £3.80, £1.90, £1.40; EX 117.10 Trifecta £588.00.
**Owner** Sterling Racing **Bred** Tally-Ho Stud **Trained** Newmarket, Suffolk
**FOCUS**
A moderate sprint handicap and a large horse blanket would have covered all eight runners 50yds from the line. Straightforward form.

## 1341 BETWAY H'CAP — 1m 4f (P)
**4:00** (4:00) (Class 2) (0-105,103) 4-Y0+ £11,971 (£3,583; £1,791; £896; £446) **Stalls** Low

Form RPR
0-10 **1** **Abareeq**[13] 1148 4-8-13 **94**................................................ JoeFanning 8 104+
(Mark Johnston) *hld up in last pair: gd prog on outer over 1f out: swept into the ld 150yds out: edgd lft but sn clr* **5/1[3]**
052- **2** 2 1/2 **Gawdawpalin (IRE)**[128] 7980 4-8-6 **87**........................ TomMarquand 6 93
(Sylvester Kirk) *hld up in midfield: prog over 2f out: chsd ldr over 1f out and sn chalng: hanging lft and nt qckn fnl f: styd on* **10/3[2]**
3155 **3** 1 1/4 **Sennockian Star**[7] 1240 7-8-10 **94**............................. RichardOliver(5) 7 98
(Mark Johnston) *pressed ldr: led 3f out: drvn and jnd over 2f out: kpt on but hdd and readily outpcd last 150yds* **8/1**
153- **4** 3/4 **Great Hall**[139] 7814 7-9-10 **103**.................................... WilliamCarson 1 106
(Mick Quinn) *trckd ldrs: looked poised to chal 2f out: shuffled along and outpcd by ldng trio fnl f: styd on nr fin but no ch by then* **20/1**
300- **5** 4 **Ballynanty (IRE)**[216] 5655 5-9-9 **102**............................... LiamKeniry 4 99
(Andrew Balding) *hld up in midfield: clsd on ldrs fr 3f out: appeared to be gng wl whn nt clr run 2f out to over 1f out: wknd tamely* **10/1**
2-55 **6** *nse* **Barye**[18] 1068 6-9-6 **99**........................................................ ShaneKelly 2 95
(Richard Hughes) *hld up in last pair: rdn on inner wl over 1f out: no prog* **5/2[1]**
5414 **7** 1/2 **Retrieve (AUS)**[22] 985 9-9-4 **97**..................................(t) AdamKirby 5 93
(Jamie Osborne) *chsd ldrs: urged along 5f out: rdn to join ldr over 2f out to over 1f out: wknd qckly* **9/1**
50-5 **8** *hd* **Dashing Star**[36] 767 7-9-2 **98**..................................(h) TimClark(3) 3 93
(David Elsworth) *rousted to ld: drvn and hdd 3f out: dropped to last by 2f out and wl btn after* **9/1**
2m 29.87s (-3.13) **Going Correction** +0.05s/f (Slow)
**WFA** 4 from 5yo+ 1lb 8 Ran SP% **113.3**
Speed ratings (Par 109): **112,110,109,109,106 106,105,105**
CSF £21.60 CT £129.50 TOTE £6.80: £1.80, £1.50, £2.30; EX 26.40 Trifecta £112.10.
**Owner** A D Spence & M B Spence **Bred** Shadwell Estate Company Limited **Trained** Middleham Moor, N Yorks
**FOCUS**
A decent middle-distance handicap, but even though the pace looked ordinary the first four still pulled well clear. The third is a reasonable benchmark.

## 1342 32RED.COM MAIDEN STKS — 1m 4f (P)
**4:35** (4:37) (Class 5) 3-Y-O **£2,911** (£866; £432; £216) **Stalls** Low

Form RPR
**1** **Voski (USA)** 3-9-5 0............................................................ JoeFanning 2 76+
(Mark Johnston) *mde all: rn green early: shkn up and drew clr fr 2f out: unchal* **2/1[2]**
2 **2** 6 **Ulysses (GER)**[21] 1001 3-9-5 0............................................... FranBerry 5 64
(Ralph Beckett) *rn in snatches: chsd wnr after 2f: rdn 5f out and dropped to 3rd 3f out: kpt on to take 2nd again last 150yds: no ch* **10/11[1]**
0- **3** 1 1/2 **Sheila's Fancy (IRE)**[129] 7962 3-9-5 0.......................... MichaelJMMurphy 4 62
(J S Moore) *in tch: rdn over 3f out: chsd ldng trio over 2f out: kpt on same pce after* **33/1**
**4** 1 **Asanta Sana (IRE)** 3-9-0 0.................................................. AdamKirby 7 55
(John Gosden) *chsd wnr 2f: styd prom: tk 2nd again 3f out: drvn and readily lft bhd fr 2f out: wknd last 150yds* **9/2[3]**
0-0 **5** 4 1/2 **Lyrica's Lion (IRE)**[69] 237 3-9-5 0........................................ AdamBeschizza 1 53
(Paddy Butler) *hld up in last pair: rdn 3f out: sme late prog bttr than sme but outpcd fr 3f out: shkn up over 1f out: one pce and nvr a threat* **100/1**
5 **6** 1/2 **Cookie's Star**[16] 1089 3-9-0 0............................................... DavidProbert 6 47
(Philip McBride) *hld up in last pair: rdn over 3f out: sn outpcd and n.d after* **33/1**
6 **7** 55 **Dashanti**[30] 862 3-9-0 0........................................................ RyanTate 3
(Jonathan Portman) *in tch: rdn 5f out: wknd 3f out: t.o* **66/1**
2m 33.04s (0.04) **Going Correction** +0.05s/f (Slow) 7 Ran SP% **112.3**
Speed ratings (Par 98): **101,97,96,95,92 92,55**
CSF £4.01 TOTE £2.90: £1.70, £1.10; EX 4.20 Trifecta £34.30.
**Owner** Sheikh Hamdan bin Mohammed Al Maktoum **Bred** Darley **Trained** Middleham Moor, N Yorks
**FOCUS**
A particularly uncompetitive maiden, but a nice debut from the winner who dictated a slow pace. It's hard to set the level of the form with confidence.

## 1343 SUNBETS.CO.UK APPRENTICE H'CAP — 1m 1y(P)
**5:05** (5:05) (Class 5) (0-75,75) 3-Y-O **£2,911** (£866; £432; £216) **Stalls** High

Form RPR
10- **1** **Cheval Blanche (USA)**[280] 3336 3-9-3 **71**....................... LuluStanford 2 78+
(Michael Bell) *t.k.h: hld up in 4th tl chsd ldng pair over 2f out: clsd qckly to ld 1f out: sn clr: readily* **9/2[3]**
4-15 **2** 2 1/4 **Spirit Of Sarwan (IRE)**[28] 902 3-9-4 **75**........................ MillyNaseb(3) 3 76
(Julia Feilden) *slowly away: w.w in detached last: urged along furiously over 1f out: r.o fnl f to take 2nd last strides: no ch to threaten* **4/1[2]**
-221 **3** 1/2 **Delfie Lane**[22] 987 3-8-10 **69**......................................(p) FinleyMarsh(5) 5 69
(Richard Hughes) *trckd ldr: asked to chal over 1f out but hanging bdly and sn dropped to 3rd: kpt on to chse wnr ins fnl f but no ch: lost 2nd last strides* **6/4[1]**
23-1 **4** 3/4 **Millie's Kiss**[21] 997 3-9-6 **74**........................................... PaddyBradley 1 72
(Philip McBride) *chsd ldng pair to over 2f out: sn rdn: kpt on one pce after* **7/1**
2551 **5** 2 1/2 **Things Happen**[39] 718 3-9-1 **72**................................(v) DavidEgan(3) 4 64
(David Evans) *led: tried to stretch on 2f out: hdd & wknd 1f out* **4/1[2]**
1m 39.42s (1.22) **Going Correction** +0.05s/f (Slow) 5 Ran SP% **110.7**
Speed ratings (Par 98): **95,92,92,91,89**
CSF £21.97 TOTE £4.70: £4.60, £2.00; EX 19.70 Trifecta £60.90.
**Owner** The Hon Mrs J M Corbett & C Wright **Bred** Klawervlei Stud **Trained** Newmarket, Suffolk
**FOCUS**
A modest 3yo apprentice handicap, but the impressive winner looks a lot better than this grade.
T/Jkpt: Not won. T/Plt: £111.70 to a £1 stake. Pool: £62,268 - 557.24 winning units. T/Qpdt: £12.40 to a £1 stake. Pool: £5,173.00 - 415.60 winning units. **Jonathan Neesom**

# 1306 NEWCASTLE (A.W) (L-H)
Friday, March 24

**OFFICIAL GOING: Tapeta: standard**
Wind: virtually nil Weather: Fine

## 1344 BETWAY STAYERS' H'CAP — 2m 56y (Tp)
**5:45** (5:45) (Class 5) (0-75,75) 4-Y-O+ **£2,911** (£866; £432; £216) **Stalls** Low

Form RPR
-240 **1** **Medicine Hat**[25] 958 6-9-9 **72**.......................................... PhillipMakin 3 79+
(Marjorie Fife) *trckd ldr: jnd ldr on bit wl over 2f out: led 2f out: rdn and kpt on* **6/4[1]**
35-1 **2** 1 1/2 **Stoneham**[22] 990 6-9-0 **70**.................................(h) CallumRodriguez(7) 6 75
(Iain Jardine) *hld up in rr: hdwy on outer over 2f out: rdn over 1f out: wnt 2nd ins fnl f: styd on but nvr rching wnr* **3/1[2]**
3306 **3** 1/2 **Cavalieri (IRE)**[36] 759 7-9-3 **66**...........................................(tp) KevinStott 2 71
(Philip Kirby) *led: rdn whn jnd wl over 2f out: hdd 2f out: plugged on* **15/2**
00/2 **4** 1 1/4 **Fair Loch**[21] 1002 9-8-10 **66**......................................... KieranSchofield(7) 1 69
(Brian Ellison) *trckd ldrs: rdn over 2f out: chal for 2nd ins fnl f: wknd towards fin* **4/1[3]**
0524 **5** 2 3/4 **Jan Smuts (IRE)**[22] 990 9-8-7 **59**..................................(t) HollieDoyle(3) 4 59
(Wilf Storey) *hld up: rdn 3f out: no imp* **10/1**
12/0 **6** 24 **Masterful Act (USA)**[29] 885 10-9-12 **75**.................................. BenCurtis 5 46
(John Balding) *midfield: pushed along 3f out: wknd and eased* **20/1**
3m 38.76s (3.56) **Going Correction** +0.20s/f (Slow)
**WFA** 4 from 6yo+ 3lb 6 Ran SP% **110.6**
Speed ratings (Par 103): **99,98,98,97,96 84**
CSF £5.97 TOTE £2.20: £1.20, £1.50; EX 6.50 Trifecta £19.30.
**Owner** Mrs Sarah Pearson **Bred** Mrs S M Pearson **Trained** Stillington, N Yorks
**FOCUS**
They raced in single file most of the way but the pace held up reasonably well. The winner remains open to more progress at this trip.

## 1345 32RED.COM FILLIES' H'CAP — 1m 2f 42y (Tp)
**6:15** (6:15) (Class 5) (0-75,75) 4-Y-O+ **£2,911** (£866; £432; £216) **Stalls** High

Form RPR
1 **1** **Signe (IRE)**[42] 658 4-9-7 **75**............................................... PaulHanagan 5 86+
(William Haggas) *s.i.s: hld up: pushed along over 2f out: nt qckn immediately: r.o wl fnl f: led towards fin: cosily* **1/3[1]**
6254 **2** 1 1/4 **Mercy Me**[13] 1144 5-9-0 **71**........................................... LouisSteward(3) 1 76
(John Ryan) *led: hdd 8f out: trckd ldr: led again 2f out: rdn over 1f out: kpt on but hdd towards fin* **7/1[2]**
2/5- **3** 2 1/4 **Star Of Lombardy (IRE)**[111] 8212 4-8-11 **65**................ FrannyNorton 4 66
(Mark Johnston) *prom on outer racing keenly: led 8f out: sn stdd pce: hdd 2f out: rdn and one pce* **10/1[3]**
62-3 **4** 1 3/4 **Henpecked**[20] 30 7-9-2 **70**.............................................(p) PJMcDonald 3 68
(Alistair Whillans) *in tch: rdn over 2f out: outpcd and no threat after* **7/1[2]**
240- **5** 1/2 **Perceived**[154] 7504 5-9-6 **74**.................................................. CamHardie 2 71
(Antony Brittain) *prom for 2f: dropped bk and in tch: rdn over 2f out: sn outpcd* **50/1**
2m 11.37s (0.97) **Going Correction** +0.20s/f (Slow) 5 Ran SP% **111.1**
Speed ratings (Par 100): **104,103,101,99,99**
CSF £3.39 TOTE £1.10: £1.10, £2.20; EX 2.80 Trifecta £9.40.
**Owner** Fiona and Ian Carmichael-Jennings **Bred** Vimal And Gillian Khosla **Trained** Newmarket, Suffolk
**FOCUS**
The short-priced favourite made her backers sweat here. It was a weak race in terms of depth and the second sets the level.

## 1346 BETWAY SPRINT H'CAP — 6f (Tp)
**6:45** (6:45) (Class 4) (0-80,80) 4-Y-O+ **£5,175** (£1,540; £769; £384) **Stalls** Centre

Form RPR
-032 **1** **Aprovado (IRE)**[22] 995 5-9-0 **80**.........................(p) CallumRodriguez(7) 8 86
(Michael Dods) *mde all: rdn over 2f out: strly pressed ent fnl f: kpt on wl* **9/2[3]**
4150 **2** 3/4 **Burtonwood**[23] 971 5-8-0 **66** oh1............................ KieranSchofield(7) 5 70
(Julie Camacho) *chsd ldr: rdn over 2f out: kpt on ins fnl f* **10/1**
20-4 **3** 3/4 **Parkour (IRE)**[30] 857 4-9-6 **79**.........................................(b) LukeMorris 4 81
(Marco Botti) *in tch: rdn and hdwy 2f out: chal strly ent fnl f: sn edgd lft: one pce fnl 110yds* **7/2[2]**
20-4 **4** *hd* **Enjoy Life (IRE)**[15] 1105 4-9-0 **73**.................................(p) KevinStott 2 74
(Kevin Ryan) *chsd ldr: rdn over 2f out: kpt on same pce* **3/1[1]**
020- **5** 3/4 **Explain**[169] 7094 5-9-6 **79**.......................................(p) JamesSullivan 7 78
(Ruth Carr) *in tch: rdn over 2f out: one pce and nvr threatened ldrs* **15/2**

200- 6 shd **Money Team (IRE)**[120] 8083 6-9-6 **79**.... PhillipMakin 6 77
(David Barron) *hld up pushed along over 2f out: kpt on ins fnl f: nvr threatened* **15/2**
0-00 7 1 3/4 **Newstead Abbey**[22] 989 7-9-2 **75**.... TomEaves 1 68
(Michael Herrington) *in tch: rdn over 2f out: wknd ins fnl f* **20/1**
0- 8 1/2 **Strada Di Carsoli**[161] 7340 4-9-3 **79**.... LouisSteward(3) 3 71
(Henry Spiller) *dwlt: hld up: rdn over 2f out: edgd lft over 1f out: nvr threatened* **15/2**
1m 10.92s (-1.58) **Going Correction** +0.20s/f (Slow) **8 Ran SP% 114.6**
Speed ratings (Par 105): **118,117,116,115,114 114,112,111**
CSF £48.05 CT £175.79 TOTE £4.10: £1.60, £3.30, £1.70; EX 56.80 Trifecta £245.80.
**Owner** Hanson, McKiver, Percival **Bred** R N Auld **Trained** Denton, Co Durham
**FOCUS**
An open sprint on paper, but the winner was allowed a free hand in front. The second is the best guide.

## 1347 32RED CASINO MAIDEN STKS 1m 5y (Tp)
**7:15** (7:15) (Class 5) 3-Y-O **£3,234** (£962; £481; £240) **Stalls** Centre

Form RPR
1 **Musikel (IRE)**[152] 7557 3-9-2 0.... JordanVaughan(3) 5 73
(K R Burke) *prom: pushed along to ld over 2f out: rdn over 1f out: edgd rt ent fnl f: kpt on wl* **5/2**[2]
2 1 **Globetrotter (IRE)** 3-9-5 0.... LukeMorris 7 71
(James Tate) *s.i.s: sn trckd ldrs racing keenly: pushed along 2f out: rdn fnl f: kpt on but a hld* **13/8**[1]
3 nk **Ninepin Bowler** 3-9-5 0.... PaulMulrennan 6 70
(Michael Dods) *racd keenly in tch: pushed along to chse ldr over 1f out: rn green and bit tight for room ent fnl f: kpt on fnl 75yds* **5/1**
50- 4 nse **Alfred Richardson**[143] 7741 3-9-5 0.... PhillipMakin 2 70
(John Davies) *trckd ldrs: pushed along over 2f out: kpt on same pce* **9/1**
5 4 1/2 **Circling Vultures** 3-9-5 0.... CamHardie 4 59
(Antony Brittain) *dwlt: hld up: pushed along 3f out: sn struggling* **66/1**
6 nk **Marqoom** 3-9-5 0.... FrannyNorton 1 58
(Mark Johnston) *led at stdy pce: rdn along whn hdd over 2f out: sn btn* **4/1**[3]
1m 41.67s (3.07) **Going Correction** +0.20s/f (Slow) **6 Ran SP% 114.8**
Speed ratings (Par 98): **92,91,90,90,86 85**
CSF £7.24 TOTE £3.40: £1.60, £1.90; EX 8.00 Trifecta £31.60.
**Owner** Mrs Elaine M Burke **Bred** Rathbarry Stud **Trained** Middleham Moor, N Yorks
**FOCUS**
They went a fairly steady pace early on and the first four finished close up. The winner could leave the bare form miles behind in time.

## 1348 SUNBETS.CO.UK H'CAP 7f 14y (Tp)
**7:45** (7:46) (Class 6) (0-65,67) 3-Y-O **£2,587** (£770; £384; £192) **Stalls** Centre

Form RPR
-601 1 **Man About Town (IRE)**[14] 1127 3-9-4 **66**.... CliffordLee(5) 8 71
(K R Burke) *led after 1f: mde rest: rdn over 1f out: edgd lft ent fnl f: kpt on* **11/4**[1]
0-50 2 3/4 **Stretewise (IRE)**[23] 970 3-9-4 **61**.... ShaneGray 7 64
(Jason Ward) *chsd ldrs: rdn over 2f out: kpt on* **40/1**
60-0 3 shd **Rosemay (FR)**[21] 1003 3-9-9 **66**.... JamesSullivan 5 69
(Iain Jardine) *hld up: rdn and outpcd over 2f out: swtchd rt ins fnl f: r.o wl: gaining at fin* **25/1**
6331 4 1 **Scala Regia (FR)**[14] 1123 3-9-7 **64**.... LukeMorris 1 65
(Sir Mark Prescott Bt) *dwlt: sn trckd ldrs: rdn and outpcd over 2f out: kpt on fnl f* **4/1**[2]
05-6 5 1/2 **Canberra Cliffs (IRE)**[16] 1088 3-9-6 **63**.... PaulHanagan 6 62
(Don Cantillon) *hld up in midfield: pushed along and sme hdwy over 2f out: rdn over 1f out: one pce and nvr threatened ldrs* **11/4**[1]
225- 6 3/4 **Tagur (IRE)**[133] 7898 3-9-10 **67**.... (p) TomEaves 4 64
(Kevin Ryan) *led for 1f: trckd ldr: racd quite keenly: rdn 2f out: wknd fnl 110yds* **9/2**[3]
-035 7 1/2 **Magic Journey (IRE)**[14] 1123 3-8-12 **55**.... (b) JasonHart 3 51
(John Quinn) *racd keenly in midfield: rdn 2f out: wknd fnl 110yds* **12/1**
06-2 8 1/2 **Kazanan (IRE)**[20] 1034 3-8-7 **50**.... AndrewMullen 9 45
(Michael Dods) *dwlt: hld up: rdn over 2f out: nvr threatened* **16/1**
0-52 9 1 **Magical Molly Joe**[45] 612 3-9-7 **64**.... PhillipMakin 2 56
(David Barron) *hld up in midfield: rdn over 2f out: wknd fnl f* **16/1**
1m 27.08s (0.88) **Going Correction** +0.20s/f (Slow) **9 Ran SP% 117.3**
Speed ratings (Par 96): **102,101,101,99,99 98,97,97,96**
CSF £117.88 CT £2299.28 TOTE £3.70: £1.40, £8.60, £5.80; EX 107.30 Trifecta £3116.60.
**Owner** Clipper Logistics **Bred** Ballyhane Stud Ltd **Trained** Middleham Moor, N Yorks
■ Stewards' Enquiry : Clifford Lee two-day ban; used whip above the permitted level (7th-8th Apr)
**FOCUS**
A modest handicap. The winner quickened off steady fractions he'd set, and the next two are the key to the level.

## 1349 BETWAY MEDIAN AUCTION MAIDEN STKS 5f (Tp)
**8:15** (8:15) (Class 6) 3-5-Y-O **£2,587** (£770; £384; £192) **Stalls** Centre

Form RPR
1 **Melonade** 3-8-10 0 ow1.... PhillipMakin 3 69+
(David Barron) *trckd ldrs: pushed along to ld appr fnl f: rdn ins fnl f: kpt on wl* **6/4**[2]
405- 2 1 1/4 **Sheepscar Lad (IRE)**[158] 7407 3-9-0 68.... TomEaves 5 66
(Nigel Tinkler) *dwlt: hld up: rdn over 1f out: hdwy to go 2nd ins fnl f: kpt on but no ch w wnr* **5/1**[3]
0-3 3 1 **Darvie**[10] 1183 3-9-0 0.... SamJames 1 62
(David Barron) *led after 1f out: rdn whn hdd over 1f out: one pce* **8/1**
2 4 hd **Royal Request (IRE)**[10] 1192 3-8-9 0.... LukeMorris 2 57
(James Tate) *led for 1f: remained cl up racing keenly: rdn to ld again over 1f out: sn hdd: no ex ins fnl f* **11/8**[1]
00 5 6 **Six Of The Best**[25] 956 5-9-7 0.... AndrewMullen 4 40
(Ollie Pears) *hld up: rdn 1/2-way: sn btn* **66/1**
1m 1.28s (1.78) **Going Correction** +0.20s/f (Slow)
**WFA** 3 from 5yo 12lb **5 Ran SP% 111.4**
Speed ratings (Par 101): **93,91,89,89,79**
CSF £9.37 TOTE £2.50: £1.30, £2.00; EX 8.20 Trifecta £21.10.
**Owner** Theakston Stud Syndicate & Partner **Bred** Theakston Stud **Trained** Maunby, N Yorks
**FOCUS**
The market told the story here. It was run at a typically steady pace but the form has been given a chance.
T/Plt: £80.30 to a £1 stake. Pool: £60,148.00 - 748.36 winning units. T/Qpdt: £38.00 to a £1 stake. Pool: £6,079.00 - 159.89 winning units. **Andrew Sheret**

1350 - 1352a (Foreign Racing) - See Raceform Interactive

# 1227 DUNDALK (A.W) (L-H)
Friday, March 24
**OFFICIAL GOING: Polytrack: standard**

## 1353a DOWNLOAD THE AWARD-WINNING AT THE RACES APP RACE 6f (P)
**7:30** (7:33) 3-Y-0+ **£13,141** (£4,059; £1,923; £854; £320)

RPR
1 **Sign Of The Kodiac (IRE)**[27] 917 4-9-10 94.... PatSmullen 4 97
(James Given) *broke wl and sn trckd ldr in 2nd: rdn to ld appr fnl f: kpt on wl clsng stages* **9/2**[2]
2 1/2 **Gordon Lord Byron (IRE)**[57] 433 9-10-3 104.... WayneLordan 9 102
(T Hogan, Ire) *sn chsd ldrs in 3rd: rdn and no imp 1f out: kpt on strly into 2nd ins fnl 100yds: nt quite rch wnr* **4/1**[1]
3 3/4 **Pearl Spectre (USA)**[8] 1233 6-9-10 89.... ColinKeane 6 93
(Phil McEntee) *racd in mid-div: 5th at 1/2-way: clsr whn short of room 1f out: kpt on wl into 3rd cl home* **11/2**[3]
4 1/2 **Ostatnia (IRE)**[201] 6167 5-9-5 91.... (v) WJLee 3 86
(W McCreery, Ire) *racd in mid-div: 4th at 1/2-way: briefly clsr in 3rd ent fnl f: no ex and dropped to 4th cl home* **4/1**[1]
5 nk **Patrick (IRE)**[35] 795 5-9-3 88.... ETDaly(7) 1 90
(Richard John O'Brien, Ire) *quite keen on inner in 6th: rdn to chse ldrs under 2f out: no imp fnl 100yds: kpt on same pce* **7/1**
6 3/4 **Togoville (IRE)**[21] 1008 7-9-10 96.... (b) DeclanMcDonogh 8 88
(Georgios Pakidis, Ire) *sn led tl hdd appr fnl f: wknd fnl 100yds* **4/1**[1]
7 2 **Turbine (IRE)**[307] 2466 4-9-7 91.... GaryHalpin(3) 7 82
(Denis Gerard Hogan, Ire) *racd towards rr: rdn over 2f out: hung rt on outer fr 1f out: sn wknd: eased clsng stages* **12/1**
8 4 3/4 **Power Of Ten (IRE)**[28] 908 3-8-4 0.... (bt) SeanDavis(7) 2 62
(R P McNamara, Ire) *a in rr: rdn over 2f out: detached appr fnl f* **66/1**
1m 12.37s (-0.03) **Going Correction** +0.25s/f (Slow)
**WFA** 3 from 4yo+ 13lb **8 Ran SP% 115.3**
Speed ratings: **110,109,108,107,107 106,103,97**
CSF £23.05 TOTE £5.20: £1.50, £1.60, £2.00; DF 19.60 Trifecta £139.10.
**Owner** The Cool Silk Partnership **Bred** Mrs Claire Doyle **Trained** Willoughton, Lincs
**FOCUS**
All roads lead to Lingfield for the impressive winner Sign Of The Kodiac.

## 1355a VISIT ATTHERACES.COM RACE 1m 2f 150y(P)
**8:30** (8:32) 4-Y-0+ **£13,141** (£4,059; £1,923; £854; £320)

RPR
1 **Elbereth**[159] 7402 6-9-0 100.... ColinKeane 4 102+
(Andrew Balding) *chsd ldr in 2nd: rdn in 3rd appr fnl f: styd on wl on outer to ld cl home* **11/2**[3]
2 1/2 **Fire Fighting (IRE)**[209] 5894 6-9-2 112.... (b) PatSmullen 5 103+
(Mark Johnston) *attempted to make all: rdn and strly pressed 1f out: kpt on wl: hdd cl home* **5/4**[1]
3 hd **Elleval (IRE)**[20] 1046 7-8-11 101.... (p) OisinOrr(5) 6 103
(David Marnane, Ire) *racd in rr tl tk clsr order to chse ldrs in 4th appr fnl f: kpt on strly into 3rd clsng stages: nvr nrr* **7/1**
4 1 1/2 **Stronger Than Me (IRE)**[126] 8018 9-9-2 97.... WJLee 1 100
(W T Farrell, Ire) *chsd ldrs in 3rd: clsr to press ldr in 2nd 1f out: no ex fnl 50yds and dropped to 4th cl home* **8/1**
5 3 1/2 **Sanus Per Aquam (IRE)**[271] 3692 4-9-2 102.... KevinManning 2 94
(J S Bolger, Ire) *hld up in 5th: pushed along over 2f out: no imp appr fnl f* **9/2**[2]
6 2 1/2 **Pique Sous (FR)**[22] 985 10-9-2 97.... (t) DeclanMcDonogh 7 88
(W P Mullins, Ire) *settled off ldrs in 4th: pushed along over 2f out: no imp appr fnl f: nt hrd rdn once btn* **12/1**
7 1 1/4 **Shalaman (IRE)**[35] 797 8-9-2 91.... (tp) WayneLordan 3 86
(Matthew J Smith, Ire) *racd in 6th tl dropped to rr 3f out: no imp over 1f out* **20/1**
2m 15.29s (-0.21) **Going Correction** +0.25s/f (Slow) **7 Ran SP% 114.1**
Speed ratings: **110,109,109,108,105 104,103**
CSF £12.78 TOTE £6.00: £5.80, £1.10; DF 13.00 Trifecta £68.90.
**Owner** David Taylor **Bred** David Taylor **Trained** Kingsclere, Hants
**FOCUS**
A cracking finish served up by the Brits who were both running after decent layoffs and should progress from this. Another pb from the winner.

1354 - 1357a (Foreign Racing) - See Raceform Interactive

# 1338 LINGFIELD (L-H)
Saturday, March 25
**OFFICIAL GOING: Polytrack: standard**
Wind: mild breeze, half against Weather: sunny

## 1358 SUNBETS.CO.UK MAIDEN STKS 1m 1y(P)
**2:00** (2:00) (Class 5) 3-Y-0+ **£2,911** (£866; £432; £216) **Stalls** High

Form RPR
0- 1 **Glorious Power (IRE)**[247] 4552 3-8-11 0.... DavidProbert 5 77
(Charles Hills) *mde all: shifted briefly lft u.p jst ins fnl f: kpt on strly: rdn out* **10/1**
2 1 1/4 **Detachment**[165] 4-10-0 0.... DavidAllan 3 79
(Les Eyre) *in tch: rdn whn c wdst ent st: r.o ins fnl f: wnt 2nd cl home* **11/2**[3]
3 shd **Tristram** 3-8-11 0.... ShaneKelly 4 74+
(Richard Hughes) *trckd ldrs: rdn over 1f out: kpt on wl ins fnl f: wnt 3rd cl home* **20/1**
32-3 4 1/2 **Arnarson**[56] 464 3-8-11 80.... JosephineGordon 1 75
(Ed Dunlop) *trckd ldrs: rdn to chal over 1f out: short of room and briefly whn snatched up jst ins fnl f: sn hld: no ex and lost 2 pls cl home* **11/8**[1]
5 4 1/2 **Hippocampus (IRE)** 3-8-11 0.... SeanLevey 2 62
(Richard Hannon) *s.i.s: last pair: rdn 2f out: little imp* **4/1**[2]
5 6 1 **The Raven Master (IRE)**[17] 1083 3-8-11 0.... (h) StevieDonohoe 8 59
(Michael Bell) *trckd ldrs: rdn 2f out: wknd over 1f out* **11/2**[3]
0- 7 3 1/2 **Pushjockeypush**[157] 7468 3-8-11 0.... (t[1]) JoeFanning 6 51
(Stuart Williams) *sn pushed along: alway towards rr* **40/1**

8 13 **Mister Flip Flop (IRE)**98 4-10-0 0 MartinDwyer 7 25
(Adam West) *s.i.s: racd keenly: hdwy to press ldr after 2f: rdn over 2f out: wknd wl over 1f out* **25/1**

1m 39.71s (1.51) **Going Correction** +0.175s/f (Slow)
**WFA** 3 from 4yo 17lb 8 Ran SP% **113.0**
Speed ratings (Par 103): **99,97,97,97,92 91,88,75**
CSF £61.05 TOTE £11.80: £3.30, £2.40, £4.60; EX 78.10 Trifecta £2837.30.
**Owner** Kangyu International Racing (HK) Limited **Bred** Barronstown Stud **Trained** Lambourn, Berks

**FOCUS**
An ordinary maiden, rated at the lower ebd of the race average.

## 1359 BETWAY SPRINT H'CAP 6f 1y(P)
**2:35** (2:35) (Class 6) (0-55,57) 3-Y-0+ **£2,264** (£673; £336; £168) **Stalls** Low

Form RPR
660- 1 **Termsnconditions (IRE)**88 8537 3-8-12 **56** KieranO'Neill 3 57
(Tim Vaughan) *prom: rdn whn hung rt turning: disputing 1 l 2nd ent fnl f: r.o wl to chal fnl 120yds: led fnl stride* **4/1**2
660- 2 *nse* **Sir Harry Collins (IRE)**224 5410 3-8-10 **54** ow1 StevieDonohoe 2 55
(Richard Spencer) *led for over 1f: trckd ldrs: rdn over 1f out: r.o to ld fnl 120yds: hdd fnl stride* **7/1**
3500 3 *nk* **Major Muscari (IRE)**18 1076 9-9-10 **55** (p) JosephineGordon 7 59
(Shaun Harris) *s.i.s: sn chsng ldrs: chal over 2f out: rdn over 1f out: r.o wl to have ev ch fnl 120yds: no ex cl home* **11/4**1
400- 4 ½ **Refuse Colette (IRE)**158 7442 8-9-12 **57** WilliamCarson 1 62
(Mick Quinn) *hld up: hdwy 2f out: nt clr run bhd ldrs whn snatched up and swtchd rt ent fnl f: no ch after but r.o wl ins fnl 120yds to go 4th cl home* **5/1**3
-002 5 1 **Culloden**9 1220 5-9-6 **56** CharlieBennett(5) 6 55
(Shaun Harris) *sn prom: led over 1f out: rdn over 1f out: no ex whn hdd fnl 120yds* **4/1**2
-340 6 1 ¼ **Great Expectations**22 1006 9-9-5 **50** (vt) TomQueally 4 46
(J R Jenkins) *slowly away: last: drvn and sme prog over 1f out: fdd fnl 100yds* **6/1**
0500 7 4 ½ **Diamond Vine (IRE)**47 602 9-9-1 **46** oh1 (p) LukeMorris 5 28
(Ronald Harris) *slowly away: sn struggling: a last pair* **16/1**

1m 13.06s (1.16) **Going Correction** +0.175s/f (Slow)
**WFA** 3 from 5yo+ 13lb 7 Ran SP% **116.0**
Speed ratings (Par 101): **99,98,98,97,96 94,88**
CSF £32.35 TOTE £5.30: £2.90, £4.00; EX 39.50 Trifecta £180.70.
**Owner** T Vaughan **Bred** Tally-Ho Stud **Trained** Aberthin, Vale of Glamorgan

**FOCUS**
A moderate sprint handicap and a tight finish between the two 3yos making their handicap debuts on their fourth outings. The third helps the level.

## 1360 BETWAY CONDITIONS STKS (ALL-WEATHER CHAMPIONSHIPS FAST-TRACK QUALIFIER) 1m 7f 169y(P)
**3:10** (3:10) (Class 2) 4-Y-0+ **£11,971** (£3,583; £1,791; £896; £446) **Stalls** Low

Form RPR
02-3 1 **First Mohican**31 858 9-9-0 101 (h) HollieDoyle 3 98
(Alan King) *trckd ldrs: smooth run on inner turning in to ld over 1f out: styd on wl to assert fnl f: rdn out* **9/2**3
-113 2 1 ¾ **Isharah (USA)**38 746 4-8-9 93 JoeFanning 4 96
(Mark Johnston) *trckd ldr: chal wl over 2f out: rdn and ev ch over 1f out: styd on same pce fnl f* **5/2**2
52 3 ½ **Vettori Rules**31 858 4-8-9 101 (h1) LukeMorris 5 95
(Gay Kelleway) *taken to s early: racd keenly early: trckd ldrs: pushed along 3f out: c wd to chal briefly ent st: sn hung lft: kpt on same pce* **8/1**
6000 4 ½ **John Reel (FR)**19 1068 8-9-0 93 JFEgan 1 95
(David Evans) *led: qcknd pce 3f out: rdn and edgd sltly off rails turning in: hdd over 1f out: kpt on same pce fnl f* **10/1**
1212 5 2 ¼ **Winterlude (IRE)**19 1068 7-9-0 105 PaulHanagan 2 93
(Jennie Candlish) *hld up: pushed long 3f out: c wdst ent st: sn hung lft: nt pce to get on terms* **11/8**1

3m 21.2s (-4.50) **Going Correction** +0.175s/f (Slow)
**WFA** 4 from 7yo+ 3lb 5 Ran SP% **109.1**
Speed ratings (Par 109): **118,117,116,116,115**
CSF £15.66 TOTE £5.50: £3.10, £1.80; EX 12.80 Trifecta £45.40.
**Owner** HP Racing First Mohican **Bred** Bottisham Heath Stud **Trained** Barbury Castle, Wilts

**FOCUS**
An interesting conditions event, despite the small field, and a qualifier for the Marathon Championship over C&D next month. They went just an even pace. Three of these met at Kempton last month and the 1-2-3 from there finished 5-3-1 here. The form could have been rated a shade higher.

## 1361 BETWAY STAYERS H'CAP 1m 5f (P)
**3:45** (3:45) (Class 3) (0-95,95) 4-Y-0 **£7,246** (£2,168; £1,084; £542; £270) **Stalls** Low

Form RPR
45R3 1 **Royal Marskell**21 1027 8-8-4 **85** (h) DavidEgan(7) 2 93
(Gay Kelleway) *trckd ldrs: pushed along over 3f out: rdn wl over 1f out: styd on wl fnl f: led nring fin* **8/1**
210- 2 ½ **Manjaam (IRE)**169 7117 4-9-4 **95** LukeMorris 3 102
(Ed Dunlop) *trckd ldr: led over 1f out: sn rdn and edgd lft: kpt on: hdd nring fin* **15/8**1
6131 3 1 ½ **Midtech Star (IRE)**14 1153 5-8-12 **86** (v) StevieDonohoe 1 91
(Ian Williams) *trckd ldrs: pushed along over 3f out: rdn over 1f out: r.o w wnr fnl f tl no ex towards fin* **7/2**3
1112 4 1 ¾ **Start Seven**43 666 5-9-0 **88** AdamKirby 5 90
(Jamie Osborne) *led: qcknd pce over 3f out: rdn and hdd over 1f out: no ex ins fnl f* **3/1**2
10-0 5 6 **Oceane (FR)**38 746 5-9-4 **92** (p) FergusSweeney 4 85
(Alan King) *hld up bhd ldrs: outpcd over 3f out: n.d after* **9/2**

2m 46.63s (0.63) **Going Correction** +0.175s/f (Slow)
**WFA** 4 from 5yo+ 1lb 5 Ran SP% **111.3**
Speed ratings (Par 107): **105,104,103,102,99**
CSF £23.67 TOTE £10.60: £4.30, £1.50; EX 25.00 Trifecta £64.50.
**Owner** Miss Chantal Wootten **Bred** Miss V Woodward **Trained** Exning, Suffolk

**FOCUS**
Again a decent staying handicap despite the small field, but it became a 3f sprint. The winner is rated just below his best.

## 1362 BETWAY DASH H'CAP 5f 6y(P)
**4:20** (4:20) (Class 2) (0-105,102) 3-Y-0+ **£11,971** (£3,583; £1,791; £896; £446) **Stalls** High

Form RPR
336- 1 **Kimberella**124 8050 7-9-12 **102** PaulHanagan 7 112
(Richard Fahey) *hld up: swtchd rt over 1f out: hdwy ent fnl f: r.o strly to ld fnl 75yds* **11/2**
5325 2 1 **Bowson Fred**14 1152 5-9-6 **99** NathanEvans(3) 4 105
(Michael Easterby) *prom early: trckd ldrs after 2f: r.o ent fnl f: ev ch fnl 75yds: nt quite pce of wnr* **3/1**2
500- 3 ½ **Iseemist (IRE)**155 7497 6-9-2 **92** LukeMorris 6 97
(John Gallagher) *hld up: rdn and hdwy ent fnl f: led v briefly fnl 90yds: kpt on but no ex* **33/1**
0450 4 ¾ **Watchable**21 1044 7-9-9 **99** (p) AdamKirby 5 101
(David O'Meara) *prom: rdn for str chal fr 2f out tl no ex fnl 90yds* **7/2**3
3212 5 *nse* **Zac Brown (IRE)**21 1025 6-8-12 **95** (t) JoshuaBryan(7) 2 97
(Charlie Wallis) *led: rdn whn strly pressed fr 2f out: hdd fnl 90yds: no ex* **9/2**
5113 6 1 ¼ **Verne Castle**28 917 4-9-9 **99** (h) DavidProbert 1 96
(Andrew Balding) *chsd ldrs: rdn over 1f out: ev ch fnl 120yds: fdd nring fin* **5/2**1
0 7 5 **Old Fashioned (CHI)**14 1152 4-9-8 **98** (t) JFEgan 3 77
(Rune Haugen) *s.i.s: sn chsng ldrs: rdn over 2f out: sn outpcd* **50/1**

57.6s (-1.20) **Going Correction** +0.175s/f (Slow) 7 Ran SP% **114.3**
Speed ratings (Par 109): **116,114,113,112,112 110,102**
CSF £22.30 TOTE £6.30: £3.20, £2.10; EX 23.00 Trifecta £289.30.
**Owner** C Titcomb **Bred** P And Mrs A G Venner **Trained** Musley Bank, N Yorks

**FOCUS**
A warm sprint handicap, but the leaders may have gone a bit quick and the first two came late and widest. Straightforward form.

## 1363 32RED H'CAP 5f 6y(P)
**4:55** (4:59) (Class 6) (0-60,60) 3-Y-0 **£2,264** (£673; £336; £168) **Stalls** High

Form RPR
40-6 1 **Snoozy Sioux (IRE)**42 679 3-9-3 **59** NoelGarbutt(3) 6 63
(Martin Smith) *mde all: kicked clr turning in: kpt on wl and in command fnl f* **33/1**
-500 2 ½ **Billy's Boots**26 960 3-9-7 **60** TomQueally 4 62
(J R Jenkins) *in tch: c wdst ent st: sn rdn: r.o strly fnl f: wnt 2nd fnl 50yds: clsng on wnr at fin* **10/1**
-231 3 ¾ **Gnaad (IRE)**11 1183 3-9-5 **58** (p) LukeMorris 2 57
(Robert Cowell) *chsd wnr: rdn over 1f out: nt pce to get on terms: no ex whn lost 2nd fnl 50yds* **4/5**1
-526 4 2 **Glam'Selle**26 960 3-8-9 **48** (p) LiamKeniry 5 40
(Ronald Harris) *hld up: travelling wl whn nt clr run turning in or whn swtchd rt jst over 1f out: swtchd lft and r.o fnl f but no ch* **14/1**
0-00 5 ½ **Cherry Leyf**45 624 3-9-4 **57** AdamKirby 1 47
(Stuart Williams) *trckd wnr: rdn wl over 1f out: no ex fnl 120yds* **7/1**2
4226 6 *nk* **Celerity (IRE)**9 1221 3-8-12 **51** (b) JFEgan 7 40
(David Evans) *trckd ldrs: pressed wnr after 2f tl wl over 1f out: one pce after* **8/1**3
-124 7 *nk* **Popsilca**29 898 3-9-2 **55** WilliamCarson 8 43
(Mick Quinn) *sn rousted along to chse ldrs on outer: one pce fr over 1f out* **8/1**3
5000 8 4 **Alfolk (IRE)**11 1193 3-9-0 **53** (h) MartinLane 3 27
(David Simcock) *sn outpcd: a in rr* **12/1**

1m 0.87s (2.07) **Going Correction** +0.175s/f (Slow) 8 Ran SP% **116.7**
Speed ratings (Par 96): **90,89,88,84,84 83,83,76**
CSF £327.81 CT £592.10 TOTE £22.80: £5.80, £2.30, £1.10; EX 96.60 Trifecta £509.60.
**Owner** M & M Bloodstock **Bred** Mrs Michelle Smith **Trained** Newmarket, Suffolk

**FOCUS**
Much lesser fare than the previous contest over the same trip and quite a shock. The front pair were near their respective bests.

## 1364 BETWAY H'CAP 1m 4f (P)
**5:30** (5:30) (Class 5) (0-70,71) 4-Y-0+ **£2,911** (£866; £432; £216) **Stalls** Low

Form RPR
5311 1 **Synodic (USA)**21 1028 5-9-7 **70** (t) JoeFanning 2 76+
(Seamus Durack) *in tch: travelling wl on heels of ldrs turning in: led jst ins fnl f: drifted rt: kpt on wl: pushed out* **10/3**2
3-45 2 ½ **Duck A L'Orange (IRE)**45 619 4-9-3 **71** LouisSteward(3) 1 76
(Michael Bell) *trckd ldr: led over 3f out: rdn and hdd jst ins fnl f: kpt on but a being hld* **3/1**1
1452 3 *shd* **Attain**21 1028 8-9-4 **70** EdwardGreatrex(3) 6 75
(Archie Watson) *mid-div: rdn and hdwy over 1f out: kpt on ins fnl f* **7/1**
-232 4 ½ **Miss Tiger Lily**49 571 7-9-7 **70** LukeMorris 8 74
(Harry Dunlop) *trckd ldr: rdn over 1f out: kpt on same pce fnl f* **7/1**
320- 5 *shd* **Pearly Prince**268 3817 5-9-3 **69** (h) HectorCrouch(3) 3 75+
(Martin Bosley) *s.i.s: towards rr: travelling wl but nt clr run over 1f out tl ins fnl f: r.o strly but no ch fnl 120yds* **25/1**
-000 6 ½ **Dovils Date**7 1257 8-9-0 **63** DavidProbert 5 66
(Tim Vaughan) *mid-div: rdn 2f out: kpt on fnl f but nt pce to get on terms* **22/1**
1424 7 *nk* **Bamako Du Chatelet (FR)**25 965 6-9-8 **71** (v) AdamKirby 11 74
(Ian Williams) *dwlt: towards rr: hdwy on outer fr over 3f out: rdn to chse ldrs turning in: kpt on same pce fnl f* **4/1**3
/10- 8 *nk* **The Way You Dance (IRE)**165 1456 5-9-2 **65** (p) LiamKeniry 9 67
(Neil Mulholland) *in tch: rdn to chse ldng pair over 1f out tl ent fnl f: kpt on same pce* **8/1**
1005 9 ½ **Karam Albaari (IRE)**21 1028 9-9-6 **69** (v) TomQueally 7 72
(J R Jenkins) *hld up: travelling wl but nt clr run over 1f out or whn jst ins fnl f: swtchd rt sn after but no ch* **33/1**
-000 10 30 **Genuine Approval (IRE)**21 1028 4-9-2 **67** RobertWinston 10 21
(John Butler) *led tl over 3f out: sn wknd* **33/1**

2m 34.87s (1.87) **Going Correction** +0.175s/f (Slow)
**WFA** 4 from 5yo+ 1lb 10 Ran SP% **118.3**
Speed ratings (Par 103): **100,99,99,99,99 98,98,98,98,78**
CSF £13.38 CT £64.67 TOTE £5.00: £1.70, £1.60, £2.60; EX 17.30 Trifecta £70.50.
**Owner** A M Gibbons **Bred** Flaxman Holdings Limited **Trained** Upper Lambourn, Berkshire

**FOCUS**
An ordinary middle-distance handicap run at a fair pace. The progressive winner took another step forward.

T/Plt: £1,393.80 to a £1 stake. Pool: £60,718.52 - 31.80 winning units T/Qpdt: £22.50 to a £1 stake. Pool: £4,638.85 - 152.20 winning units **Tim Mitchell**

## [1328]WOLVERHAMPTON (A.W) (L-H)

Saturday, March 25

**OFFICIAL GOING: Tapeta: standard**

Wind: Light against Weather: Fine

### 1365 SUNBETS.CO.UK H'CAP 7f 36y (Tp)

5:45 (5:45) (Class 5) (0-75,77) 4-Y-O+ £3,234 (£962; £481; £240) Stalls High

Form RPR

6311 **1** **Call Out Loud**[11] 1189 5-9-3 74 (vt) AlistairRawlinson(3) 8 82
(Michael Appleby) *mde all: set stdy pce tl qcknd over 2f out: rdn over 1f out: styd on* 11/4[1]

1314 **2** 1 **Custard The Dragon**[32] 850 4-9-7 75 (p) BenCurtis 1 80
(John Mackie) *prom: hmpd over 6f out: nt clr and outpcd over 2f out: hdwy over 1f out: r.o u.p to go 2nd nr fin: no ch w wnr* 7/2[2]

-400 **3** ½ **Gramercy (IRE)**[36] 783 10-9-7 75 (p) BarryMcHugh 5 78
(Patrick Morris) *chsd wnr: rdn over 1f out: hung lft ins fnl f: kpt on* 33/1

101- **4** 1¼ **Faintly (USA)**[128] 7995 6-8-11 65 (b) JamesSullivan 7 66
(Ruth Carr) *hld up: hdwy and nt clr run over 1f out: nt trble ldrs* 12/1

-023 **5** 1¾ **Rockley Point**[23] 984 4-9-4 77 (p) CliffordLee(5) 9 72
(Paul D'Arcy) *hld up: pushed along over 2f out: styd on ins fnl f: nvr on terms* 4/1[3]

1113 **6** ¾ **Athassel**[5] 1290 8-8-12 73 KatherineGlenister(7) 11 66+
(David Evans) *s.i.s: hld up: rdn and edgd lft over 1f out: n.d* 5/1

6-05 **7** nse **Corporal Maddox**[50] 551 10-9-4 72 (p) TomMarquand 3 65
(Ronald Harris) *hld up: rdn over 1f out: nvr nrr* 14/1

400- **8** 1¼ **Mister Musicmaster**[177] 6889 8-8-4 65 FinleyMarsh(7) 2 55
(Ron Hodges) *chsd ldrs: rdn over 2f out: wknd fnl f* 12/1

4/00 **9** nse **Dr Doro (IRE)**[7] 1261 4-9-3 71 (h) GeorgeDowning 4 61
(Ian Williams) *hld up: shkn up over 1f out: n.d* 40/1

245- **10** 7 **Rock'n Gold**[156] 7487 4-9-9 77 ShaneKelly 10 48
(Adrian Wintle) *chsd ldrs: rdn over 2f out: wknd over 1f out* 22/1

1m 30.03s (1.23) **Going Correction** +0.075s/f (Slow) **10 Ran SP% 117.3**
Speed ratings (Par 103): **95,93,93,91,89 89,88,87,87,79**
CSF £12.17 CT £263.15 TOTE £4.20: £1.20, £2.10, £7.90; EX 14.40 Trifecta £453.70.

**Owner** Kings Head Duffield Racing Partnership **Bred** Rabbah Bloodstock Limited **Trained** Oakham, Rutland

**FOCUS**

This looked quite a competitive heat for the grade but the winner took the field apart from the front and never looked like getting caught. The runner-up fits.

### 1366 SUNBETS.CO.UK DOWNLOAD THE APP MAIDEN STKS 7f 36y (Tp)

6:15 (6:15) (Class 5) 3-Y-O+ £3,234 (£962; £481; £240) Stalls High

Form RPR

6- **1** **Jupiter Light**[200] 6211 3-8-11 0 RobertTart 3 84+
(John Gosden) *sn chsng ldr: shkn up over 1f out: r.o to ld post* 11/4[2]

32-2 **2** shd **Tafaakhor (IRE)**[14] 1149 3-8-11 85 KieranO'Neill 4 83+
(Richard Hannon) *led: qcknd over 2f out: rdn and edgd rt ins fnl f: hdd post* 2/7[1]

0- **3** 8 **Barwell (IRE)**[120] 8089 3-8-11 0 PaulMulrennan 2 61
(Michael Dods) *plld hrd and prom: stdd and lost pl after 1f: hdwy over 2f out: outpcd fr over 1f out* 16/1[3]

6 **4** 11 **Stragar**[16] 1111 3-8-11 0 BenCurtis 1 31
(Michael Appleby) *chsd ldrs: pushed along over 2f out: sn wknd* 33/1

1m 30.4s (1.60) **Going Correction** +0.075s/f (Slow) **4 Ran SP% 113.3**
Speed ratings (Par 103): **93,92,83,71**
CSF £4.22 TOTE £3.90; EX 3.90 Trifecta £7.90.

**Owner** George Strawbridge **Bred** George Strawbridge **Trained** Newmarket, Suffolk

**FOCUS**

This looked straightforward for the long odds-on favourite but he wasn't able to put this to bed and was collared late on by what must be a promising colt. The time was poor and the third and fourth are the keys to the form.

### 1367 32RED CASINO H'CAP 7f 36y (Tp)

6:45 (6:46) (Class 6) (0-60,60) 3-Y-O £2,911 (£866; £432; £216) Stalls High

Form RPR

40-4 **1** **Jack Blane**[29] 904 3-9-1 54 GeorgeDowning 5 57
(Daniel Kubler) *chsd ldrs: led over 1f out: sn rdn: styd on* 13/2

0006 **2** nk **Tink**[11] 1193 3-8-5 49 oh1 ow3 (p) CharlieBennett(5) 9 51
(Mark Brisbourne) *sn prom: rdn over 1f out: r.o* 33/1

230- **3** ¾ **Luduamf (IRE)**[155] 7510 3-9-0 60 RossaRyan(7) 8 61
(Richard Hannon) *hld up: nt clr run over 2f out: hdwy over 1f out: sn rdn and hung lft: r.o* 9/2[3]

0414 **4** nk **Viola Park**[16] 1107 3-8-12 51 (p) RyanPowell 1 51
(Ronald Harris) *a.p: rdn over 1f out: styd on* 11/4[1]

6020 **5** ¾ **Lady Volante (IRE)**[15] 1123 3-8-11 57 KatherineGlenister(7) 2 56
(David Evans) *led early: sn stdd and lost pl: hmpd wl over 5f out: hung rt 1/2-way: hdwy over 1f out: rdn ins fnl f: styd on same pce* 15/2

00-4 **6** 1 **Fast Kar (IRE)**[15] 1127 3-8-13 52 BenCurtis 4 47
(Barry John Murphy, Ire) *in rr: pushed along 4f out: hdwy over 1f out: sn rdn and hung lft: styd on same pce ins fnl f: sddle slipped* 7/1

00-0 **7** 4 **Lily Fontana (IRE)**[75] 139 3-8-9 48 BarryMcHugh 10 34
(Richard Fahey) *s.i.s: hld up: rdn over 2f out: nvr on terms* 20/1

4 **8** 2½ **Lady Morel (IRE)**[23] 987 3-9-5 58 (b[1]) JosephineGordon 3 38
(Joseph Tuite) *pushed along to ld over 6f out: hdd over 4f out: led again over 2f out: rdn and hdd over 1f out: wknd ins fnl f* 4/1[2]

403 **9** 5 **Scealtara (IRE)**[23] 983 3-9-3 59 ShelleyBirkett(3) 6 27
(David O'Meara) *hld up: rdn and hung lft over 1f out: sn wknd* 16/1

0-50 **10** 3 **Sallee**[23] 987 3-8-4 46 oh1 HollieDoyle(3) 12 7
(Adrian Wintle) *racd keenly: hdwy to join ldr over 5f out: led over 4f out: hdd over 2f out: wknd fnl f* 40/1

1m 30.39s (1.59) **Going Correction** +0.075s/f (Slow) **10 Ran SP% 118.5**
Speed ratings (Par 96): **93,92,91,91,90 89,84,82,76,72**
CSF £203.45 CT £1068.85 TOTE £8.40: £2.60, £7.30, £2.20; EX 195.80 Trifecta £841.10.

**Owner** Patrick Whitten **Bred** P J H Whitten **Trained** Lambourn, Berks

**FOCUS**

A weak handicap but it was at least won by one of the least exposed runners. THe beaten favourite limits the form.

### 1368 32RED.COM FILLIES' H'CAP 1m 142y (Tp)

7:15 (7:16) (Class 4) (0-85,87) 4-Y-O+ £5,498 (£1,636; £817; £408) Stalls Low

Form RPR

230- **1** **Toboggan's Fire**[150] 7623 4-9-2 79 JoeyHaynes 3 84
(Ann Duffield) *s.i.s: hld up: hdwy over 1f out: rdn and r.o to ld post* 8/1

5-51 **2** hd **Auntie Barber (IRE)**[8] 1245 4-8-9 75 AaronJones(3) 4 80
(Stuart Williams) *chsd ldr: shkn up to ld over 1f out: rdn ins fnl f: hdd post* 9/4[1]

-320 **3** 1½ **Bint Dandy (IRE)**[35] 810 6-9-10 87 (p) ConnorBeasley 7 88
(Chris Dwyer) *chsd ldrs: rdn over 1f out: styd on same pce ins fnl f* 10/1

200- **4** 2 **Hidden Rebel**[140] 7825 5-9-10 87 PaulMulrennan 6 84
(Alistair Whillans) *s.i.s: hld up: rdn over 1f out: nt trble ldrs* 8/1

06-3 **5** 2 **Hells Babe**[7] 1261 4-9-0 77 TomMarquand 2 70
(Michael Appleby) *led: shkn up over 2f out: hdd over 1f out: wknd wl ins fnl f* 10/3[3]

1113 **6** 2¾ **Simply Me**[19] 1066 4-9-3 80 (p) RichardKingscote 1 67
(Tom Dascombe) *trckd ldrs: shkn up over 1f out: wknd ins fnl f* 11/4[2]

1m 49.19s (-0.91) **Going Correction** +0.075s/f (Slow) **6 Ran SP% 111.8**
Speed ratings (Par 102): **107,106,105,103,101 99**
CSF £26.16 TOTE £8.60: £3.70, £1.20; EX 28.10 Trifecta £232.50.

**Owner** Grange Park Racing X, T P & D McMahon **Bred** D McMahon **Trained** Constable Burton, N Yorks

**FOCUS**

A reasonably competitive little class 4 handicap and it served up a good finish as the front two came clear down the middle of the track. The pace looked fairly even and the runner-up came here bang in form so the form looks solid enough. The winner basically ran to her best.

### 1369 BETWAY H'CAP 2m 120y (Tp)

7:45 (7:45) (Class 6) (0-60,62) 4-Y-O+ £2,749 (£818; £408; £204) Stalls Low

Form RPR

00-3 **1** **Mr Globetrotter (USA)**[10] 1197 4-9-6 62 CliffordLee(5) 8 69+
(Iain Jardine) *hld up: hdwy over 2f out: hmpd over 1f out: rdn to ld wl ins fnl f: styd on* 9/2[2]

/00- **2** nk **Author's Dream**[301] 2700 4-9-1 55 CallumShepherd(3) 7 61
(William Knight) *s.i.s: hld up: hdwy u.p over 3f out: led ins fnl f: sn edgd lft and hdd: styd on* 2/1[1]

2132 **3** 3 **Ryan The Giant**[10] 1197 4-9-1 52 (v) ConnorBeasley 1 54
(Keith Dalgleish) *chsd clr ldrs: tk clsr order over 3f out: led over 2f out: rdn and hung lft over 1f out: hdd and no ex ins fnl f* 9/2[2]

6020 **4** 1¼ **Cold Fusion (IRE)**[4] 1082 4-8-13 53 HollieDoyle(3) 9 54
(David Flood) *hld up: hdwy over 1f out: styd on same pce wl ins fnl f* 16/1

5534 **5** nk **Oyster Card**[11] 1191 4-8-9 46 (p) BenCurtis 2 46
(Michael Appleby) *sn led: hdd over 13f out: chsd ldr who sn wnt clr: tk clsr order over 5f out: led over 3f out: hdd over 2f out: no ex ins fnl f* 10/1

2420 **6** nk **Cape Spirit (IRE)**[11] 1191 5-9-9 55 (p) ThomasBrown 3 55
(Andrew Balding) *hld up: pushed along over 7f out: hdwy over 2f out: hmpd over 1f out: styd on same pce ins fnl f* 8/1

-250 **7** 1¾ **Lineman**[29] 900 7-9-10 56 (b) KieranO'Neill 4 54
(Sarah Hollinshead) *chsd clr ldrs: tk clsr order over 3f out: rdn and ev ch over 2f out: wknd ins fnl f* 16/1

50- **8** 1¾ **The Quarterjack**[196] 6335 8-9-2 55 FinleyMarsh(7) 6 51
(Ron Hodges) *hld up: hdwy on outer over 2f out: sn rdn: wknd ins fnl f* 20/1

0034 **9** 2 **Tempuran**[18] 1073 8-9-11 62 (t[1]) GeorgeWood(5) 5 55
(David Bridgwater) *jnd ldr after 1f tl led over 13f out: sn clr: c bk to the field over 5f out: hdd over 3f out: rdn and wknd over 1f out* 7/1[3]

3m 41.77s (-1.93) **Going Correction** +0.075s/f (Slow)
**WFA** 4 from 5yo+ 3lb **9 Ran SP% 118.9**
Speed ratings (Par 101): **107,106,105,104,104 104,103,102,101**
CSF £14.37 CT £43.57 TOTE £6.00: £1.70, £1.70, £1.60; EX 20.30 Trifecta £90.20.

**Owner** New Approach Racing Limited **Bred** Jane Schosberg **Trained** Carrutherstown, D'fries & G'way

■ Stewards' Enquiry : Clifford Lee two day ban (10-11 April) - guilty of careless riding

**FOCUS**

A low grade staying handicap in which the first two pulled well clear. THe third is a solid guide.

### 1370 BETWAY DASH H'CAP 5f 21y (Tp)

8:15 (8:16) (Class 4) (0-80,81) 4-Y-O+ £5,498 (£1,636; £817; £408) Stalls Low

Form RPR

0320 **1** **Foxy Forever (IRE)**[9] 1222 7-9-8 81 (t) ConnorBeasley 11 87
(Michael Wigham) *s.i.s: hld up: shkn up over 1f out: str run ins fnl f to ld post* 9/1

00-6 **2** hd **Excellent George**[31] 857 5-9-3 79 (t) AaronJones(3) 3 84
(Stuart Williams) *chsd ldrs: shkn up 1/2-way: rdn and edgd rt over 1f out: r.o* 5/2[1]

100- **3** shd **Van Gerwen**[135] 7892 4-9-4 77 PJMcDonald 6 82
(Les Eyre) *w ldr tl led over 1f out: sn rdn: hdd post* 20/1

-062 **4** ½ **Rosealee (IRE)**[17] 1091 4-8-13 77 DavidParkes(5) 2 80
(Jeremy Gask) *chsd ldrs: rdn over 1f out: sn edgd rt: unable qck nr fin* 11/2[3]

0-16 **5** ½ **Zipedeedodah (IRE)**[35] 816 5-9-5 78 (t) JosephineGordon 8 79
(Joseph Tuite) *mid-div: hdwy over 1f out: sn rdn: styd on same pce towards fin* 10/1

0630 **6** 1 **Ballesteros**[24] 971 8-9-2 75 PaulHanagan 7 73
(Richard Fahey) *hld up: hdwy over 1f out: styd on* 14/1

600- **7** nk **Foxtrot Knight**[193] 6449 5-9-5 78 JamesSullivan 9 75
(Ruth Carr) *hld up: edgd lft and r.o ins fnl f: nt trble ldrs* 16/1

-622 **8** ½ **Invincible Ridge (IRE)**[28] 923 9-9-2 75 NeilFarley 4 72
(Eric Alston) *s.i.s: sn pushed along in rr: rdn: nt clr run and swtchd rt ins fnl f: nt trble ldrs* 10/1

0052 **9** 1¼ **Normal Equilibrium**[2] 1327 7-8-7 73 DavidEgan(7) 5 63
(Ivan Furtado) *led: rdn and hdd over 1f out: wknd wl ins fnl f* 5/1[2]

-003 **10** ½ **Miracle Garden**[26] 955 5-9-1 74 (p) TomMarquand 10 63
(Roy Brotherton) *mid-div: hdwy over 3f out: pushed along on outer 1/2-way: wknd ins fnl f* 7/1

100- **11** 5 **Sandra's Secret (IRE)**[176] 6926 4-9-4 80 NathanEvans(3) 1 51
(Les Eyre) *mid-div: hdwy over 1f out: sn rdn: wknd fnl f* 20/1

1m 1.04s (-0.86) **Going Correction** +0.075s/f (Slow) **11 Ran SP% 123.4**
Speed ratings (Par 105): **109,108,108,107,106 105,104,104,102,101 93**
CSF £33.34 CT £460.21 TOTE £11.10: £3.20, £1.70, £7.50; EX 42.90 Trifecta £826.10.

**Owner** D Hassan, J Cullinan **Bred** Tally-Ho Stud **Trained** Newmarket, Suffolk

■ Stewards' Enquiry : Connor Beasley trainer could offer no explanation for the apparent improvement in form

**FOCUS**
A wide open sprint handicap run at a strong pace and they were spread right across the track in the closing stages. THe winner is rated to his best winter form.

## 1371 BETWAY SPRINT H'CAP (DIV I) 6f 20y (Tp)
8:45 (8:45) (Class 6) (0-55,57) 3-Y-0+ £2,749 (£818; £408; £204) Stalls Low

Form RPR
0-00 1 Bogsnog (IRE)[8] 1247 7-9-9 52 JamesSullivan 6 59
(Ruth Carr) *broke wl: sn lost pl: hdwy over 2f out: rdn to ld and edgd lft ins fnl f: r.o* 11/1
3023 2 3/4 Mr Chuckles (IRE)[8] 1247 4-9-2 50 (p) CharlieBennett(5) 9 55
(Daniel Mark Loughnane) *chsd ldrs: led over 1f out: rdn and hdd ins fnl f: styd on* 10/3[2]
0654 3 2 Socialites Red[10] 1200 4-9-5 55 RPWalsh(7) 4 54
(Scott Dixon) *awkward s: sn pushed along in rr: rdn over 1f out: hung lft and r.o ins fnl f: nt rch ldrs* 10/1
53-1 4 1 1/2 Strictly Carter[47] 602 4-9-9 57 GeorgeWood(5) 7 51
(Alan Bailey) *hld up: hdwy over 1f out: sn rdn and edgd lft: styd on same pce fnl f* 5/2[1]
600- 5 2 Clon Rocket (IRE)[168] 7145 4-9-0 50 MeganEllingworth(7) 3 41+
(John Holt) *s.i.s: racd wd over 2f out: hung lft and r.o ins fnl f: nvr nrr* 20/1
-402 6 1 1/2 Gettin' Lucky[32] 852 4-9-4 47 (p) BenCurtis 8 31
(John Balding) *led: rdn and hdd over 1f out: wknd ins fnl f* 4/1[3]
54-6 7 1 1/2 George Bailey (IRE)[57] 445 5-9-0 46 oh1 NathanEvans(3) 5 25
(Suzzanne France) *plld hrd and prom: rdn over 1f out: wknd fnl f* 12/1
00-4 8 4 1/2 African Girl[59] 393 3-8-10 55 SimonPearce(3) 2 17
(Lydia Pearce) *s.i.s: hdwy into mid-div over 4f out: rdn over 2f out: wknd over 1f out* 20/1
0463 9 24 Lady Bacchus[9] 1221 4-9-11 54 (b) ShaneKelly 1
(Richard Guest) *sn w ldr tl rdn over 2f out: eased wl over 1f out* 8/1

1m 13.85s (-0.65) **Going Correction** +0.075s/f (Slow)
**WFA** 3 from 4yo+ 13lb 9 Ran SP% **117.4**
Speed ratings (Par 101): **107,106,103,101,98 96,94,88,56**
CSF £48.48 CT £383.48 TOTE £12.20: £3.00, £1.90, £2.80; EX 58.50 Trifecta £446.60.
**Owner** Facts & Figures **Bred** J R Weston **Trained** Huby, N Yorks
■ Stewards' Enquiry : Shane Kelly jockey said the filly stopped quickly as if something were amiss; vet reported that a post-race examination failed to reveal any abnormalities

**FOCUS**
A modest heat and very few got into it. The second and third set the level.

## 1372 BETWAY SPRINT H'CAP (DIV II) 6f 20y (Tp)
9:15 (9:15) (Class 6) (0-55,56) 3-Y-0+ £2,749 (£818; £408; £204) Stalls Low

Form RPR
6441 1 Tasaaboq[8] 1246 6-9-7 50 (t) JosephineGordon 8 56
(Phil McEntee) *hld up: hdwy over 1f out: rdn to ld ins fnl f: styd on u.p* 5/2[2]
3144 2 nk Pick Of Any (IRE)[3] 1305 4-9-3 53 (h) GerO'Neill(7) 4 58
(David Loughnane) *plld hrd: w ldr: rdn over 1f out: ev ch ins fnl f: styd on* 9/4[1]
6-00 3 1 1/2 Little Belter (IRE)[15] 1126 5-9-7 50 (p) ConnorBeasley 6 51
(Keith Dalgleish) *plld hrd and prom: rdn over 1f out: styd on same pce wl ins fnl f* 12/1
6030 4 nk National Service (USA)[23] 982 6-9-5 48 (tp) RyanPowell 10 48
(Clare Ellam) *hld up: r.o ins fnl f: nt rch ldrs* 25/1
3546 5 nk David's Beauty (IRE)[15] 1126 4-9-12 55 (p) PaulMulrennan 1 54
(Brian Baugh) *chsd ldrs: rdn and ev ch ins fnl f: styd on same pce* 10/1
0040 6 nk Jessie Allan (IRE)[15] 1125 6-9-3 46 oh1 SamJames 9 44
(Jim Goldie) *hld up: rdn over 2f out: r.o ins fnl f: nt trble ldrs* 25/1
00-2 7 shd Blastofmagic[11] 1193 3-9-0 56 (p) DougieCostello 5 50
(David Dennis) *hld up: hdwy over 1f out: nt clr run sn after: styd on same pce wl ins fnl f* 7/1[3]
0025 8 1 1/4 Spowarticus[10] 1209 8-9-2 52 (b) RPWalsh(7) 7 46
(Scott Dixon) *hld up: hdwy over 3f out: hung rt over 2f out: no ex fnl f* 16/1
004 9 1/2 Vocalisation (IRE)[11] 1193 3-8-4 46 oh1 JimmyQuinn 3 34
(John Weymes) *led: rdn over 1f out: hdd and no ex ins fnl f* 12/1
00-0 10 1 Frangarry (IRE)[9] 1219 5-9-7 55 (b) DavidParkes(5) 2 44+
(Alan Bailey) *s.s: latched on to the bk of the field 4f out: rdn over 2f out: btn over 1f out* 12/1

1m 15.39s (0.89) **Going Correction** +0.075s/f (Slow)
**WFA** 3 from 4yo+ 13lb 10 Ran SP% **117.6**
Speed ratings (Par 101): **97,96,94,94,93 93,93,91,90,89**
CSF £8.63 CT £52.95 TOTE £3.30: £1.40, £1.10, £3.80; EX 9.90 Trifecta £90.20.
**Owner** Mrs Rita Baker **Bred** Tim Bostwick **Trained** Newmarket, Suffolk
■ Stewards' Enquiry : David Parkes jockey said the gelding missed the break

**FOCUS**
A modest finale but the form horses came to the fore. Those close up confirm the level.
T/Plt: £363.20 to a £1 stake. Pool: £94,513.22 - 189.95 winning units T/Qpdt: £58.20 to a £1 stake. Pool: £12,332.96 - 156.70 winning units **Colin Roberts**

# 1115 MEYDAN (L-H)
Saturday, March 25
**OFFICIAL GOING: Turf: yielding; dirt: muddy**

## 1373a GODOLPHIN MILE SPONSORED BY MEYDAN SOBHA (GROUP 2) (DIRT) 1m (D)
11:45 (11:45) 3-Y-0+
£487,804 (£162,601; £81,300; £40,650; £24,390; £16,260)

RPR
1 Second Summer (USA)[21] 1045 5-9-0 111 (vt) PatDobbs 5 113
(Doug Watson, UAE) *s.i.s: settled in rr: rdn 3f out: r.o wl to ld fnl 110yds* 20/1
2 nk Ross (IRE)[21] 1043 5-9-0 104 AndreaAtzeni 1 112
(P Schiergen, Germany) *mid-div: r.o wl fnl 2f: jst failed* 28/1
3 3/4 Sharp Azteca (USA)[42] 4-9-0 115 (bt) EdgardJZayas 6 114+
(Jorge Navarro, U.S.A) *trckd ldng pair: led 3f out: rdn 2f out: hdd fnl 110yds* 9/4[2]
4 4 1/4 Fitzgerald (USA)[51] 541 5-9-0 106 (t) ColmO'Donoghue 12 101
(A bin Harmash, UAE) *nvr nr to chal but r.o fnl 2f* 50/1
5 1 1/2 Kafuji Take (JPN)[34] 836 5-9-0 114 (h) YuichiFukunaga 13 97
(Sachio Yukubo, Japan) *nvr nr to chal but r.o fnl 2f* 12/1
6 2 1/4 Farrier (USA)[6] 1268 9-9-0 108 (p) PatCosgrave 2 92
(S Seemar, UAE) *slowly away: nvr nr to chal but r.o fnl 2f* 66/1
7 6 Etijaah (USA)[30] 891 7-9-0 107 (h) JimCrowley 10 78
(Doug Watson, UAE) *mid-div: rdn 4f out: sn btn* 25/1
8 8 1/4 Heavy Metal[21] 1043 7-9-0 113 MickaelBarzalona 8 59+
(S bin Ghadayer, UAE) *trckd ldr: ev ch 2f out: wknd fnl f* 5/1[3]
9 1 Gifted Master (IRE)[37] 774 4-9-0 110 (b) RyanMoore 4 57+
(Hugo Palmer) *trckd ldrs tl wknd fnl 2f* 25/1
10 2 North America[42] 695 5-9-0 113 (t) RichardMullen 7 53+
(S Seemar, UAE) *sn led: hdd 3f out: wknd fnl f* 15/8[1]
11 29 Triple Nine (KOR)[21] 1045 5-9-0 105 (e) MichaelRodd 11
(Kim Young Kwan, Korea) *nvr nr to chal* 66/1
12 4 1/2 Le Bernardin (USA)[21] 1043 8-9-0 110 (t) TadhgO'Shea 3
(A R Al Rayhi, UAE) *nvr bttr than mid-div* 16/1
U Stormardal (IRE)[21] 1043 6-9-0 104 (p) AdriedeVries 9
(Ismail Mohammed) *nvr bttr than mid-div: uns rdr 1 1/2f out* 25/1

1m 35.62s (-1.88) **Going Correction** +0.075s/f (Slow) 13 Ran SP% **120.5**
Speed ratings: **112,111,110,106,105 102,96,88,87,85 56,52,**
CSF: 455.29; TRICAST: 1,756.52.
**Owner** Sheikh Rashid bin Humaid Al Nuaimi **Bred** Richard Shultz **Trained** United Arab Emirates

**FOCUS**
TRAKUS: 2nd -1, 3rd +8, 4th +11, 5th +11, 6th +2, 7th +7, 8th +5, 9th 0, 10th -2, 11th +13, 12th +4. There was loads of rain overnight and into the early part of the afternoon and the dirt, which was sealed (packed down), was officially described as muddy, with the turf track given as yielding. Four horses helped to force a furious pace - 23.22 (from standing start), 22.34, 24.04, with the winner home in 25.26 - and a couple of late closers filled the first two places. The final time was 0.41sec off the track record set by One Man Band (also Doug Watson) in this race the previous year. The form can't be rated any higher.

## 1374a DUBAI GOLD CUP SPONSORED BY AL TAYER MOTORS (GROUP 2) (TURF) 2m
12:50 (12:50) 3-Y-0+
£487,804 (£162,601; £81,300; £40,650; £24,390; £16,260)

RPR
1 Vazirabad (FR)[30] 890 5-9-1 117 ChristopheSoumillon 3 117+
(A De Royer-Dupre, France) *settled in rr: smooth prog 4f out: rdn 2 1/2f out: r.o wl to ld cl home* 9/4[1]
2 nk Beautiful Romance[30] 890 5-8-10 110 OisinMurphy 11 112
(Saeed bin Suroor) *trckd ldr: led 3f out: r.o wl but hdd cl home* 5/1[3]
3 1 1/4 Sheikhzayedroad[30] 890 8-9-1 118 (h) MartinHarley 1 116
(David Simcock) *trckd ldrs: ev ch 2f out: n.m.r a f out: r.o wl* 8/1
4 1/2 Big Orange[104] 8329 6-9-1 117 (p) FrankieDettori 7 115
(Michael Bell) *sn led: hdd 3f out but r.o wl* 12/1
5 4 1/2 Zamaam[6] 1268 7-9-1 104 (t) JimCrowley 5 110
(E Charpy, UAE) *nvr nr to chal but r.o fnl 2f* 100/1
6 2 1/2 Wall Of Fire (IRE)[197] 6283 4-8-9 107 (b) WilliamBuick 4 106
(Hugo Palmer) *nvr nr to chal but r.o fnl 2f* 12/1
7 1 1/2 Rembrandt Van Rijn (IRE)[21] 1042 6-9-1 110 (b) MickaelBarzalona 9 106
(S bin Ghadayer, UAE) *s.i.s: nvr nr to chal: r.o same pce fnl 3f* 25/1
8 3 Basateen (IRE)[30] 890 5-9-1 107 (v) DaneO'Neill 13 102
(Doug Watson, UAE) *nvr nr to chal* 66/1
9 1/2 Quest For More (IRE)[161] 7349 7-9-1 117 (b) JamieSpencer 6 102
(Roger Charlton) *trckd ldrs tl wknd fnl 3f* 11/1
10 4 Famous Kid (USA)[21] 1042 6-9-1 108 SilvestreDeSousa 2 97
(Saeed bin Suroor) *trckd ldr tl wknd 3 1/2f out* 40/1
11 2 3/4 Heartbreak City (FR)[62] 7756 7-9-1 118 (t) JoaoMoreira 12 94
(A J Martin, Ire) *nvr able to chal* 4/1[2]
12 5 1/2 Quechua (ARG)[29] 6-9-1 114 BVorster 10 88
(Ricardo Le Grange, Singapore) *nvr bttr than mid-div* 150/1
13 36 Trip To Paris (IRE)[195] 6387 6-9-1 112 AndreaAtzeni 14 49
(Ed Dunlop) *nvr nr to chal* 33/1
14 25 Kingfisher (IRE)[508] 7697 6-9-1 110 RyanMoore 8 21
(A P O'Brien, Ire) *nvr bttr than mid-div: virtually p.u 3 1/2f out* 16/1

3m 22.52s (-1.98) **Going Correction** +0.275s/f (Good)
**WFA** 4 from 5yo+ 3lb 14 Ran SP% **120.5**
Speed ratings: **115,114,114,113,111 110,109,108,107,105 104,101,83,71**
CSF: 12.66 TRICAST: 79.23.
**Owner** H H Aga Khan **Bred** Haras De Son Altesse L'Aga Khan Scea **Trained** Chantilly, France

**FOCUS**
A strong line-up for this stayers' contest, and on the rain-softened ground (time was 2.96sec slower than last year) the pace more or less held up (second, third and fourth raced in the first five throughout). Given he was held up towards the back, it was top-class performance from the winner to get up. They went 51.80 (800m), 51.43 (1600m), 50.82 (2400m), before finishing in 23.75 (2800m) and 24.72. TRAKUS (metres covered compared to winner): 2nd +2, 3rd -4, 4th -4, 5th 0, 6th -3, 7th -6, 8th +6, 9th +3, 10th -10, 11th -6, 12th +2, 13th +2, 14th -7

## 1375a UAE DERBY SPONSORED BY THE SAEED & MOHAMMED AL NABOODAH GROUP (GROUP 2) (DIRT) 1m 1f 110y(D)
1:25 (1:25) 3-Y-0
£975,609 (£325,203; £162,601; £81,300; £48,780; £32,520)

RPR
1 Thunder Snow (IRE)[42] 697 3-8-9 118 ChristopheSoumillon 13 115+
(Saeed bin Suroor) *trckd ldrs: rdn 2f out: r.o wl: led on line* 11/4[1]
2 shd Epicharis (JPN)[34] 3-8-9 112 Christophe-PatriceLemaire 10 114
(Kiyoshi Hagiwara, Japan) *sn led: rdn 3f out: r.o wl: hdd fnl strides* 9/2[2]
3 1 1/4 Master Plan (USA)[60] 3-8-9 105 (b) JohnRVelazquez 2 111+
(Todd Pletcher, U.S.A) *nvr nr to chal but r.o fnl 3f* 7/1
4 3/4 Lancaster Bomber (USA)[141] 7807 3-8-9 117 RyanMoore 3 110+
(A P O'Brien, Ire) *s.i.s: nvr nr to chal but r.o wl fnl 2f* 6/1[3]
5 2 Fly At Dawn (USA)[30] 887 3-8-9 108 (t) WilliamBuick 9 106
(Charlie Appleby) *settled in rr: r.o fnl 2f but nvr able to chal* 16/1
6 2 3/4 Qatar Man (IRE)[21] 1040 3-8-9 106 (b) ColmO'Donoghue 1 100
(Marco Botti) *trckd ldrs: ev ch 2 1/2f out: wknd fnl f* 14/1
7 5 Fawree (USA)[21] 1040 3-8-9 104 BernardFayd'Herbe 6 90
(M F De Kock, South Africa) *trckd ldr: rdn 4f out: wknd and hmpd 2f out: nt rcvr* 9/1
8 1/2 Spirit Of Valor (USA)[153] 7559 3-8-9 102 (bt) SeamieHeffernan 12 89
(A P O'Brien, Ire) *s.i.s: nvr nr to chal* 20/1
9 4 1/4 Goldfield (ARG)[98] 3-9-5 113 (t) SilvestreDeSousa 11 81
(Ricardo Colombo, Uruguay) *nvr nr to chal* 20/1
10 nk Vettori Kin (BRZ)[98] 3-9-5 113 JoelRosario 8 81
(Kenneth McPeek, U.S.A) *nvr bttr than mid-div* 33/1
11 nk Top Score[30] 887 3-8-9 109 AdriedeVries 5 79
(Saeed bin Suroor) *v.s.a: nvr nr to chal* 14/1
12 2 Adirato (JPN)[34] 3-8-9 108 YutakaTake 16 75
(Naosuke Sugai, Japan) *trckd ldrs: ev ch 3f out: wknd fnl 2f* 33/1

13 16 **Cosmo Charlie (USA)**[21] 1040 3-8-9 108........................(v) PatDobbs 15 42
(Doug Watson, UAE) *trckd ldrs tl wknd 4f out* **25/1**

14 23 **Nomorerichblondes (USA)**[30] 889 3-8-5 100.......(tp) AntonioFresu 14
(A bin Harmash, UAE) *a in rr* **100/1**

15 1 1/4 **Bee Jersey (USA)**[42] 697 3-8-9 105............................(t) SamHitchcott 7
(Doug Watson, UAE) *mid-div tl wknd 4f out* **40/1**

16 nse **Midnight Chica (USA)**[30] 889 3-8-5 97.........................(t) ChrisHayes 4
(D Selvaratnam, UAE) *mid-div tl wknd 4f out* **150/1**

1m 57.76s (-1.04) **Going Correction** +0.15s/f (Slow) **16** Ran SP% **124.2**
Speed ratings: **110,109,108,108,106 104,100,100,96,96 96,94,81,63,62 62**
CSF: 13.15 TRICAST: 82.76.
**Owner** Godolphin **Bred** Darley **Trained** Newmarket, Suffolk

**FOCUS**
TRAKUS (metres covered compared to winner): 2nd -15, 3rd -17, 4th -18, 5th -9, 6th -20, 7th -10, 8th +2, 9th 0, 10th +3, 11th -13, 12th -1, 13th +6, 14th +10, 15th -4, 16th -16. This looked a decent enough UAE Derby and the well-ridden runner-up set a sensible pace, getting a breather in down the back straight: 24.8 (400m), 23.4 (800m), 25.66 (1200m), 24.84 (1600m).

## 1376a AL QUOZ SPRINT SPONSORED BY AZIZI DEVELOPMENTS (GROUP 1) (TURF) 6f
**2:00** (2:00) 3-Y-O+

**£487,804** (£162,601; £81,300; £40,650; £24,390; £16,260)

RPR

1 **The Right Man**[21] 1044 5-9-0 113...................... Francois-XavierBertras 3 120
(D Guillemin, France) *trckd ldr: rdn to ld 1f out: r.o wl: jst hld on* **12/1**

2 nse **Long On Value (USA)**[56] 6-9-0 112...............................(t) JoelRosario 7 120
(William Mott, U.S.A) *settled in rr: r.o wl fnl 2f: jst failed* **66/1**

3 1 1/4 **Ertijaal (IRE)**[37] 773 6-9-0 119........................................... JimCrowley 6 116+
(A R Al Rayhi, UAE) *sn led: hdd 1f out: r.o same pce* **2/1**[1]

4 nse **Jungle Cat (IRE)**[21] 1044 5-9-0 113..............................(p) WilliamBuick 5 116
(Charlie Appleby) *trckd ldrs: ev ch 2f out: r.o same pce fnl f* **9/2**[3]

5 1 1/4 **Richard's Boy (USA)**[28] 5-9-0 109........................... NorbertoArroyoJr 9 112
(Peter Miller, U.S.A) *trckd ldrs: ev ch 2f out: wknd fnl 110yds* **80/1**

6 1 1/2 **Amazing Kids (NZ)**[54] 486 5-9-0 119.................................. JoaoMoreira 1 107
(J Size, Hong Kong) *settled in rr: r.o same pce fnl 2f* **6/1**

7 1/2 **Washington DC (IRE)**[140] 7833 4-9-0 113....................(t) RyanMoore 10 105
(A P O'Brien, Ire) *nvr nr to chal but r.o fnl 2f* **14/1**

8 1 1/2 **Final Venture**[21] 1044 5-9-0 111........................................(h) PatDobbs 4 101
(Paul Midgley) *s.i.s: trckd ldrs tl outpcd fnl 2f* **40/1**

9 1 **Medicean Man**[28] 932 11-9-0 110................................(tp) AdriedeVries 2 97
(Jeremy Gask) *nvr bttr than mid-div* **66/1**

10 2 1/4 **Limato (IRE)**[140] 7837 5-9-0 122........................................ HarryBentley 11 90
(Henry Candy) *nvr bttr than mid-div* **11/4**[2]

11 2 1/4 **Baccarat (IRE)**[21] 1044 8-9-0 111........................... ColmO'Donoghue 12 83
(Charlie Appleby) *nvr bttr than mid-div* **20/1**

12 11 **Finsbury Square (IRE)**[23] 5-9-0 111..............(b) ChristopheSoumillon 8 48
(F Chappet, France) *s.i.s: a in rr* **50/1**

1m 9.59s (0.59) **Going Correction** +0.35s/f (Good) **12** Ran SP% **120.2**
Speed ratings: **110,109,108,108,106 104,103,101,100,97 94,79**
CSF: 640.24; TRICAST: 2,239.26.
**Owner** Pegase Bloodstock **Bred** Mrs James Wigan **Trained** France

**FOCUS**
This race reverted to 6f for the first time since 2010, when it only held Group 3 status. The rain-softened ground played against the strengths of the first two in the betting, leaving this an open race. The pace was towards the far rail. They went 24.22 (400m), 21.50 (800m) and finished in 23.87. TRAKUS (metres covered compared to winner): 2nd -1, 3rd -1, 4th -1, 5th -1, 6th -1, 7th -1, 8th 0, 9th -1, 10th 0, 11th 0, 12th 0. The form is rated around the runner-up and the fifth.

## 1377a DUBAI GOLDEN SHAHEEN SPONSORED BY GULF NEWS (GROUP 1) (DIRT) 6f (D)
**2:35** (2:35) 3-Y-O+

**£975,609** (£325,203; £162,601; £81,300; £48,780; £32,520)

RPR

1 **Mind Your Biscuits (USA)**[28] 4-9-6 115...................(bt) JoelRosario 14 123+
(Chad Summers, U.S.A) *settled in rr: rdn 3f out: r.o wl to ld 110yds out* **9/2**[1]

2 3 **Comicas (USA)**[21] 1041 4-9-6 104...............................(b) WilliamBuick 13 113
(Charlie Appleby) *mid-div: smooth prog to chse ldrs 2f out: ev ch 110yds: one pce fnl 55yds* **50/1**

3 shd **Morawij**[21] 1041 7-9-6 112.................................................. ChrisHayes 2 113
(D Selvaratnam, UAE) *trckd ldr: rdn 3 1/2f out: r.o wl fnl f but no ch w wnr* **8/1**

4 1/2 **St. Joe Bay (USA)**[49] 5-9-6 110.........................(bt) NorbertoArroyoJr 11 111
(Peter Miller, U.S.A) *trckd ldr: led 1 1/2f out: hdd 110yds out: wknd* **6/1**[2]

5 1 3/4 **Cool Cowboy (USA)**[21] 1041 6-9-6 112.................................. PatDobbs 5 105
(Doug Watson, UAE) *nvr nr to chal but r.o fnl 2f* **9/2**[1]

6 hd **Stallwalkin' Dude (USA)**[35] 7-9-6 112...............(bt) FlorentGeroux 1 105
(David Jacobson, U.S.A) *mid-div: r.o same pce fnl 2f* **10/1**

7 3/4 **Not Listenin'tome (AUS)**[20] 1053 6-9-6 118............(bt) TommyBerry 10 102
(John Moore, Hong Kong) *s.i.s: nvr nr to chal* **14/1**

8 1 1/4 **Reynaldothewizard (USA)**[72] 206 11-9-6 113.....(bt) RichardMullen 12 98
(S Seemar, UAE) *nvr bttr than mid-div* **9/1**

9 3/4 **Dundonnell (USA)**[21] 1041 7-9-6 110...............(h) ChristopheSoumillon 4 96
(C Fownes, Hong Kong) *settled in rr: r.o same pce fnl 2f* **16/1**

10 shd **My Catch (IRE)**[100] 8395 6-9-6 112.................................. SamHitchcott 8 96
(Doug Watson, UAE) *sn led: hdd 1 1/2f out: wknd fnl f* **16/1**

11 2 1/2 **Dios Corrida (JPN)**[21] 1041 3-8-11 103..............................(t) ShaneFoley 7 88
(Yoshitada Takahashi, Japan) *nvr bttr than mid-div* **66/1**

12 3/4 **High On Life**[8] 1254 6-9-6 104...................................(t) RoystonFfrench 9 85
(S bin Ghadayer, UAE) *trckd ldrs tl wknd fnl 2f* **100/1**

13 6 **Wild Dude (USA)**[21] 1041 7-9-6 103...............................(bt) JoaoMoreira 3 66
(M Halford, Ire) *nvr nr to chal* **25/1**

14 1/2 **Muarrab**[21] 1041 8-9-6 110.................................................. JimCrowley 6 65
(A R Al Rayhi, UAE) *trckd ldr tl wknd fnl 3f* **15/2**[3]

1m 10.91s (-0.69) **Going Correction** +0.225s/f (Slow)
**WFA** 3 from 4yo+ 13lb **14** Ran SP% **119.3**
Speed ratings: **113,109,108,108,105 105,104,102,101,101 98,97,89,88**
CSF: 254.41 TRICAST: 1,804.49.
**Owner** J Stables, Head Of Plains Partners LLC Et Al **Bred** Jumping Jack Racing Llc **Trained** North America

**FOCUS**
TRAKUS (metres covered compared to winner): 2nd -1, 3rd -13, 4th -9, 5th -7, 6th -16, 7th -4, 8th -5, 9th -12, 10th -15, 11th -10, 12th -8, 13th -14, 14th -10. There was further heavy rain before and during this race and the track didn't seem as fast as for the Godolphin Mile, and at this point the outside was no disadvantage, with the first two home coming from the top two stalls. In particular, the runner-up surely needed some help from the track to run so well whilst wide. The splits were 23.9, 23.03, with the winner finishing in 23.23.

## 1378a DUBAI TURF SPONSORED BY DP WORLD (GROUP 1) (TURF) 1m 1f (T)
**3:30** (3:30) 3-Y-O+

**£2,926,829** (£975,609; £487,804; £243,902; £146,341; £97,560)

RPR

1 **Vivlos (JPN)**[27] 4-8-9 112...............................................(h) JoaoMoreira 9 116
(Yasuo Tomomichi, Japan) *settled in rr: prog 3f out: plld wd 2f out: r.o wl: led fnl 55yds* **14/1**

2 1/2 **Heshem (IRE)**[23] 4-9-0 115.......................................... GregoryBenoist 3 120
(C Ferland, France) *mid-div: smooth prog 3f out: rdn to ld 110yds out: hdd fnl 55yds* **20/1**

3 1/2 **Ribchester (IRE)**[161] 7352 4-9-0 122................................ WilliamBuick 1 119+
(Richard Fahey) *sn led: hdd 6f out: led again 2 1/2f out: hdd 110yds out but r.o* **11/4**[2]

4 1 3/4 **Zarak (FR)**[37] 776 4-9-0 116.................................. ChristopheSoumillon 2 115
(A De Royer-Dupre, France) *trckd ldng trio: ev ch 3f out: n.m.r over 1f out: r.o same pce* **2/1**[1]

5 3 **Mutakayyef**[189] 6601 6-9-0 120.........................................(p) JimCrowley 6 109
(William Haggas) *trckd ldng pair: ev ch 2f out: one pce fnl f* **6/1**[3]

6 1 1/4 **Decorated Knight**[21] 1046 5-9-0 114................................ AndreaAtzeni 4 106
(Roger Charlton) *nvr nr to chal but r.o same pce fnl 2f* **15/2**

7 nk **Deauville (IRE)**[224] 5431 4-9-0 113.....................................(t) RyanMoore 12 105
(A P O'Brien, Ire) *nvr bttr than mid-div* **16/1**

8 1 1/4 **Cougar Mountain (IRE)**[29] 914 6-9-0 113........(tp) DonnachaO'Brien 11 103+
(A P O'Brien, Ire) *s.i.s: nvr nr to chal but r.o fnl 2f* **66/1**

9 1 1/4 **Debt Collector (NZ)**[22] 4-9-0 115...................................... MichaelRodd 10 100
(Cliff Brown, Singapore) *nvr nr to chal* **50/1**

10 4 1/2 **Very Special (IRE)**[37] 771 5-8-9 114....................(h) SilvestreDeSousa 8 86
(Saeed bin Suroor) *trckd ldr: led 6f out: rdn 3 1/2f out: hdd 2 1/2f out: sn btn* **25/1**

11 4 1/4 **Mondialiste (IRE)**[140] 7835 7-9-0 115.............................. DanielTudhope 7 82
(David O'Meara) *nvr nr to chal* **25/1**

12 2 **Long Island Sound (USA)**[176] 6932 4-9-0 111..(vt) SeamieHeffernan 13 78
(A P O'Brien, Ire) *nvr nr to chal* **40/1**

13 18 **Opal Tiara (IRE)**[37] 771 4-8-9 111.................................... OisinMurphy 5 35
(Mick Channon) *nvr bttr than mid-div* **66/1**

1m 50.2s (1.10) **Going Correction** +0.425s/f (Yiel) **13** Ran SP% **118.4**
Speed ratings: **112,111,111,109,106 105,105,104,103,99 95,93,77**
CSF: 262.82; TRICAST: 1,032.43.
**Owner** Kazuhiro Sasaki **Bred** Northern Racing **Trained** Japan

**FOCUS**
A competitive Group 1 and a nice performance from the winner, enhancing Japan's recent record in this race. They went 26.38 (400m), 23.95 (800m), 24.62 (1200m), 23.63 (1600m) and finished in 11.62. TRAKUS (metres covered compared to winner): 2nd -1, 3rd 0, 4th -3, 5th +3, 6th +2, 7th +5, 8th +3, 9th +6, 10th +7, 11th +5, 12th +6, 13th +3. A Step up from Vivlos.

## 1379a LONGINES DUBAI SHEEMA CLASSIC (GROUP 1) (TURF) 1m 4f 11y(T)
**4:05** (4:05) 3-Y-O+

**£2,926,829** (£975,609; £487,804; £243,902; £146,341; £97,560)

RPR

1 **Jack Hobbs**[161] 7353 5-9-0 120.......................................(b) WilliamBuick 2 123+
(John Gosden) *trckd ldr: smooth prog to ld 2f out: r.o wl* **4/1**[3]

2 2 1/4 **Seventh Heaven (IRE)**[140] 7831 4-8-8 119.............. SeamieHeffernan 6 114+
(A P O'Brien, Ire) *s.i.s: settled in rr: r.o fnl 2f: nrst fin* **8/1**

3 1 3/4 **Postponed (IRE)**[21] 1042 6-9-0 124.................................. AndreaAtzeni 7 116
(Roger Varian) *trckd ldr: ev ch 1 1/2f out: one pce fnl f* **7/4**[1]

4 1/2 **Prize Money**[21] 1042 4-8-13 115.......................................(h) AdriedeVries 5 116
(Saeed bin Suroor) *mid-div: rdn 4f out: chsd ldrs and ev ch 2f out: one pce fnl f* **9/1**

5 2 1/4 **Earnshaw (USA)**[21] 1046 6-9-0 110.........................(t) MickaelBarzalona 1 111
(S bin Ghadayer, UAE) *nvr nr to chal* **66/1**

6 3 3/4 **Sounds Of Earth (JPN)**[90] 8523 6-9-0 118 Christophe-PatriceLemaire 4 105
(Kenichi Fujioka, Japan) *nvr bttr than mid-div* **20/1**

7 1 1/2 **Highland Reel (IRE)**[104] 8329 5-9-0 123................................ RyanMoore 3 103+
(A P O'Brien, Ire) *sn led: hdd & wknd 2f out* **5/2**[2]

2m 32.39s (0.59) **Going Correction** +0.50s/f (Yiel)
**WFA** 4 from 5yo+ 1lb **7** Ran SP% **112.3**
Speed ratings: **118,116,115,115,113 111,110**
CSF: 33.68.
**Owner** Godolphin & Partners **Bred** Minster Stud **Trained** Newmarket, Suffolk

**FOCUS**
The pace was controlled by Ryan Moore aboard Highland Reel, and they went 28.72 (400m), 25.74 (800m), 23.89 (1200m), 24.82 (1600m), 24.67 (2000m) before finishing in 24.55. They were pretty well bunched turning in but the winner quickened away in impressive style. TRAKUS (metres covered compared to winner): 2nd +4, 3rd +9, 4th -4, 5th -9, 6th +7, 7th +1. The form makes sense around the third, fourth and seventh.

## 1380a DUBAI WORLD CUP SPONSORED BY EMIRATES AIRLINE (GROUP 1) (DIRT) 1m 2f (D)
**4:45** (4:45) 3-Y-O+

**£4,878,048** (£1,626,016; £813,008; £406,504; £243,902; £162,601)

RPR

1 **Arrogate (USA)**[56] 469 4-9-0 134.......................................(t) MikeESmith 9 130+
(Bob Baffert, U.S.A) *hmpd at s: settled in rr: smooth prog 4f out: rdn to ld over 1f out: comf* **1/3**[1]

2 2 1/4 **Gun Runner (USA)**[33] 4-9-0 118.................................(t) FlorentGeroux 5 124
(Steven Asmussen, U.S.A) *trckd ldr: led 4f out: hdd over 1f out but r.o wl* **7/1**[2]

3 5 **Neolithic (USA)**[56] 469 4-9-0 114..........................(b) JohnRVelazquez 11 114
(Todd Pletcher, U.S.A) *trckd ldr: ev ch 2f out: r.o same pce fnl f* **25/1**

4 1 3/4 **Mubtaahij (IRE)**[30] 891 5-9-0 117......................... ChristopheSoumillon 14 111
(M F De Kock, South Africa) *trckd ldng trio: rdn 4f out: ev ch 2f out: one pce fnl f* **16/1**[3]

5 1 1/2 **Awardee (USA)**[86] 7-9-0 118..............................................(b) YutakaTake 7 108+
(Mikio Matsunaga, Japan) *mid-div: r.o same pce fnl 3f* **66/1**

6 *nk* **Hoppertunity (USA)**[49] 587 6-9-0 117.........................(bt) FlavienPrat 12 107+
(Bob Baffert, U.S.A) *nvr nr to chal but r.o fnl 2f* **16/1**[3]
7 *1* **Keen Ice (USA)**[56] 469 5-9-0 115............................ JavierCastellano 10 105+
(Todd Pletcher, U.S.A) *nvr nr to chal* **33/1**
8 *4* **Lani (USA)**[21] 1045 4-9-0 112............................................. RyanMoore 4 97+
(Mikio Matsunaga, Japan) *nvr nr to chal but r.o fnl 2f* **100/1**
9 *5* **Apollo Kentucky (USA)**[86] 5-9-0 117........ Christophe-PatriceLemaire 1 87+
(Kenji Yamauchi, Japan) *nvr bttr than mid-div* **66/1**
10 *2 3/4* **Move Up**[21] 1045 4-9-0 115.............................................. AdriedeVries 6 81+
(Saeed bin Suroor) *a in rr* **16/1**[3]
11 *8* **Long River (USA)**[21] 1045 7-9-0 115......................(b) MickaelBarzalona 2 65
(S bin Ghadayer, UAE) *sn led: hdd 4f out: sn btn* **50/1**
12 *15* **Special Fighter (IRE)**[21] 1045 6-9-0 115...................... FernandoJara 13 35
(Maria Ritchie, UAE) *trckd ldrs tl outpcd 4f out* **40/1**
13 *1/2* **Furia Cruzada (CHI)**[21] 1045 5-8-9 108........................ AntonioFresu 8 29
(E Charpy, UAE) *s.i.s: nvr bttr than mid-div: r.o fnl 2f* **100/1**
14 *13 1/2* **Gold Dream (JPN)**[34] 836 4-9-0 116...........................(h) JoaoMoreira 3 7
(Osamu Hirata, Japan) *slowly away: nvr nr to chal* **50/1**

2m 2.15s (-2.55) **Going Correction** +0.30s/f (Slow) 14 Ran SP% **123.3**
Speed ratings: **122,120,116,114,113 113,112,109,105,103 96,84,84,73**
CSF: 2.91 TRICAST: 30.49. Placepot: £183.20 to a £1 stake. Pool: £10,545.70 - 42.00 winning units. Quadpot: £84.10 to a £1 stake. Pool: £693.50 - 6.10 winning units..
**Owner** Juddmonte Farms Inc **Bred** Clearsky Farms **Trained** USA

**FOCUS**
TRAKUS (metres covered compared to winner): 2nd -13, 3rd -4, 4th -12, 5th -18, 6th -9, 7th -11, 8th -16, 9th -21, 10th -12, 11th -21, 12th 0, 13th -6, 14th -10. The Dubai World Cup is no longer the richest race around but this latest edition saw an astonishing performance from a great horse. After 400 metres the 2nd, 3rd, 4th and 5th-placed finishers filled those very positions, and Arrogate was 13th. He'd blown the start, the pace was not strong - 24.81 (400m), 23.47 (800m), 24.65 (1200m), 24.93 (1600m) - and no runner covered more ground yet, remarkably, he was in front more than a furlong out, quickening to the line in 23.82 for the last 400m. And he missed the track record, set by the brilliant California Chrome in this race the previous year, by only 0.32sec. Arrogate didn't need to run to his best, but the second and third have been awarded pbs.

1381 - 1384a (Foreign Racing) - See Raceform Interactive

# NAAS (L-H)
Sunday, March 26

**OFFICIAL GOING: Soft to heavy (soft in places)**

## 1385a NAAS RACECOURSE LAUCHES THE 2017 FLAT SEASON H'CAP 6f
**3:10** (3:11) 3-Y-0+ **£13,141** (£4,059; £1,923; £854; £320)

RPR

1 **Gymkhana**[161] 4-9-1 **89**......................................................... ColinKeane 3 98+
(G M Lyons, Ire) *hld up in rr of mid-div: hdwy gng wl under 2f out and sn pushed along between horses: rdn to ld ins fnl f and kpt on wl to assert clsng stages* **12/1**
2 *2 1/4* **Athas An Bhean**[144] 7773 4-8-6 **80**..............................(t) WayneLordan 1 82
(Adrian Paul Keatley, Ire) *sn chsd ldrs: rdn over 2f out and clsd u.p to ld narrowly far side over 1f out: hdd ins fnl f and no imp on wnr clsng stages* **25/1**
3 *1/2* **Maarek**[144] 7771 10-10-2 **104**........................................................ WJLee 9 104
(Miss Evanna McCutcheon, Ire) *mid-div tl tk clsr order fr 1/2-way: rdn 2f out and clsd u.p to dispute 3rd ent fnl f: kpt on same pce: nt trble wnr* **16/1**
4 *shd* **Imagine If (IRE)**[158] 7473 3-7-11 **91** oh6.......................... SeanDavis(7) 5 87
(G M Lyons, Ire) *hld up towards rr: rdn and hdwy under 2f out to chse ldr between horses ins fnl f: kpt on clsng stages: nrst fin* **9/1**
5 *shd* **Bubbly Bellini (IRE)**[10] 1234 10-7-11 **78** oh7......(p) AndrewBreslin(7) 12 77
(Adrian McGuinness, Ire) *chsd ldrs: effrt 1 1/2f out: no imp on wnr u.p in 5th wl ins fnl f: kpt on same pce* **10/1**
6 *3/4* **Ducky Mallon (IRE)**[10] 1233 6-8-4 **78** oh2.................(t) NGMcCullagh 15 75
(Donal Kinsella, Ire) *dwlt: sn settled in mid-div: rdn and sme hdwy under 2f out to chse ldrs u.p ent fnl f: disp 2nd briefly tl no ex and wknd clsng stages* **11/1**
7 *nk* **Dinkum Diamond (IRE)**[141] 7821 9-9-7 **98**................ RossCoakley(3) 2 94
(Andrew Slattery, Ire) *w ldrs: rdn under 2f out and no ex u.p far side ent fnl f: sn wknd* **16/1**
8 *3/4* **Mizaah (IRE)**[175] 6984 4-8-13 **90**.................................... GaryHalpin(3) 17 84
(Kevin Prendergast, Ire) *s.i.s and in rr: pushed along after 1f: tk clsr order ent fnl f where short of room between horses briefly: r.o wl clsng stages: nvr nrr* **7/2**[1]
9 *1 1/4* **Dark Defender**[163] 7315 4-8-12 **86**...........................(v) ConnorBeasley 13 76
(Keith Dalgleish) *led and disp: rdn 2f out and sn hdd: no ex and wknd ins fnl f* **12/1**
10 *1* **Barron's Lad**[202] 6199 4-7-8 **78** oh8....................(t) ScottMcCullagh(10) 19 64
(Mark Michael McNiff, Ire) *dwlt and wnt sltly rt s: sn settled in mid-div tl impr to chse ldrs bef 1/2-way: rdn 2f out and sn no ex: one pce fnl f* **50/1**
11 *2 3/4* **Sahreej (IRE)**[114] 8197 4-8-6 **80**.................................... MichaelHussey 6 58
(Adrian Paul Keatley, Ire) *chsd ldrs: almost on terms fr 1/2-way: rdn far side over 2f out and sn no imp on ldrs: wknd fnl f* **20/1**
12 *shd* **St Brelades Bay (IRE)**[275] 3628 5-8-6 **80**..................(p) ConorHoban 11 57
(Mrs John Harrington, Ire) *w ldrs and disp bef 1/2-way: rdn on terms 2f out and sn hdd: wknd and eased fnl f* **9/1**
13 *3 1/2* **Sixties Sue**[23] 1009 4-7-13 **80** oh7 ow2....................... DamienMelia(7) 18 46
(Luke Comer, Ire) *dwlt: sn chsd ldrs nr side: rdn and no ex after 1/2-way: wknd fnl 2f* **40/1**
14 *2* **Bluesbreaker (IRE)**[16] 1133 5-8-4 **78** oh6....................(vt) RoryCleary 16 38
(Damian Joseph English, Ire) *w ldrs: rdn over 2f out and no ex whn hmpd between horses 1 1/2f out: wknd* **20/1**
15 *1/2* **Geological (IRE)**[10] 1233 5-8-13 **87**.................................. ShaneFoley 8 45
(Damian Joseph English, Ire) *chsd ldrs: rdn nr side over 2f out and sn no ex: wknd over 1f out* **16/1**
16 *1 3/4* **An Saighdiur (IRE)**[175] 6984 10-9-6 **94**.............(b) DeclanMcDonogh 14 47
(Andrew Slattery, Ire) *chsd ldrs: tk clsr order almost on terms gng wl over 2f out: sn rdn and wknd 1 1/2f out* **18/1**
17 *21* **Tatlisu (IRE)**[17] 1103 7-9-2 **90**................................................ PaulHanagan 7
(Richard Fahey) *s.i.s and towards rr thrght: pushed along after 1f: rdn and no imp trailing under 2f out: nvr a factor* **8/1**[3]
18 *49* **Sharliyna (IRE)**[169] 7162 4-9-1 **89**........................................ PatSmullen 4
(D K Weld, Ire) *dwlt sltly: settled in rr of mid-div early: wknd and eased fr 1/2-way: t.o: lame* **7/1**[2]

1m 16.24s (3.04)
**WFA** 3 from 4yo+ 13lb 18 Ran SP% **139.3**
CSF £312.60 CT £4957.51 TOTE £15.10: £3.00, £7.40, £1.90, £3.60; DF 507.40 Trifecta £4164.90.
**Owner** Patrick Cassidy **Bred** Juddmonte Farms Ltd **Trained** Dunsany, Co Meath

**FOCUS**
A French import proved too good for the opposition on his Irish debut. The form is rated around the next five.

## 1386a PALMERSTOWN HOUSE MADRID H'CAP 7f
**3:40** (3:40) 3-Y-0

**£25,213** (£8,119; £3,846; £1,709; £854; £427)

RPR

1 **Gino Severini (IRE)**[167] 7235 3-8-4 **73** oh1....................... ChrisHayes 12 84+
(J A Stack, Ire) *chsd ldrs: pushed along in 6th at 1/2-way: rdn bhd ldrs over 2f out and clsd u.p to ld narrowly 1f out: kpt on wl to assert clsng stages* **8/1**
2 *1 1/2* **Hailstone (IRE)**[16] 1128 3-7-13 **75**................................(h) SeanDavis(7) 8 82
(P J Prendergast, Ire) *cl up tl sn disp and led narrowly: jnd into st: rdn to ld 2f out: strly pressed and hdd narrowly 1f out: kpt on wl wout matching wnr clsng stages* **7/1**
3 *1 1/2* **Zelaniya (IRE)**[159] 7448 3-9-2 **85**.......................................... PatSmullen 1 88
(D K Weld, Ire) *chsd ldrs: pushed along in 3rd over 2f out and impr to chal briefly between horses 1 1/2f out: no ex u.p in 3rd ins fnl f: kpt on same pce* **7/1**
4 *1/2* **Mr Adjudicator**[276] 3583 3-8-7 **76**................................... NGMcCullagh 2 78
(Joseph G Murphy, Ire) *dwlt and in rr early tl sn settled in mid-div: tk clsr order bhd ldrs into st: rdn 2f out and no imp on ldrs in 4th ins fnl f: kpt on same pce* **20/1**
5 *nse* **Ultimate Dream (IRE)**[161] 7390 3-8-13 **82**......................... ColinKeane 5 83
(G M Lyons, Ire) *w.w towards rr: rdn and sme hdwy 2f out: no imp on ldrs u.p in 5th ent fnl f: kpt on same pce* **6/1**[3]
6 *3 1/4* **Elusive Beauty (IRE)**[148] 7705 3-9-4 **87**......................... ShaneFoley 10 80
(K J Condon, Ire) *hld up towards rr: rdn and sme hdwy 2f out: no imp on ldrs disputing 6th ent fnl f: kpt on one pce* **14/1**
7 *4 1/2* **Circus Ring (IRE)**[23] 1010 3-8-7 **81**...........................(tp) AnaO'Brien(5) 9 65
(Joseph Patrick O'Brien, Ire) *chsd ldrs: 5th 1/2-way: sn pushed along and dropped towards rr u.p over 2f out: rdn to dispute 6th ent fnl f and sn no ex: one pce in 7th wl ins fnl f* **8/1**
8 *1* **Vociferous Marina (IRE)**[182] 6814 3-9-10 **93**.............. KevinManning 4 71
(J S Bolger, Ire) *in rr of mid-div early: rdn towards rr 2f out and no imp: kpt on one pce ins fnl f* **8/1**
9 *3 3/4* **Red Sabor**[161] 7389 3-8-12 **81**.................................................... WJLee 7 49
(Andrew Slattery, Ire) *led narrowly tl sn jnd and hdd: disp ld into st: rdn and hdd 2f out: wknd over 1f out* **22/1**
10 *hd* **Party Tiger**[37] 788 3-8-5 **74**.....................................(p) PaulHanagan 3 41
(Richard Fahey) *mid-div: pushed along over 2f out and sn no ex u.p: wknd fr over 1f out* **11/2**[2]
11 *3/4* **Massif Central (IRE)**[149] 7674 3-9-0 **83**................ DeclanMcDonogh 11 48
(John Joseph Murphy, Ire) *towards rr thrght: pushed along under 3f out and no imp: one pce fnl 2f* **5/1**[1]
12 *4 3/4* **Oh Grace (IRE)**[161] 7389 3-8-11 **90**...........................(p) WillieByrne(10) 6 42
(J S Bolger, Ire) *chsd ldrs: 4th 1/2-way: wknd over 2f out* **16/1**

1m 31.5s (4.00) 12 Ran SP% **126.3**
CSF £67.43 CT £431.39 TOTE £12.40: £3.50, £2.40, £2.90; DF 92.70 Trifecta £1516.40.
**Owner** Next Pension Fund Syndicate **Bred** Stonethorn Stud Farms Ltd **Trained** Golden, Co. Tipperary

**FOCUS**
A first winner in his own right for Fozzy Stack, former assistant to his father Tommy who often managed to saddle a winner on the opening day of the season. His lightly-weighted runner did well to beart a horse who was fit from action at Dundalk. The fourth and fifth help with the standard.

## 1387a LODGE PARK STUD EUROPEAN BREEDERS FUND PARK EXPRESS STKS (GROUP 3) (F&M) 1m
**4:10** (4:10) 3-Y-0+

**£39,081** (£12,585; £5,961; £2,649; £1,324; £662)

RPR

1 **Czabo**[15] 1159 4-9-11 99..................................................... GrahamLee 10 97
(Mick Channon) *chsd ldrs: 4th 1/2-way: gng wl bhd ldrs 2f out: rdn on outer over 1f out and clsd u.p to ld wl ins fnl f: kpt on wl* **8/1**
2 *1/2* **Somehow (IRE)**[210] 5939 4-10-0 114.................(v) DonnachaO'Brien 3 99
(A P O'Brien, Ire) *chsd ldrs: 6th 1/2-way: gng wl bhd ldrs over 2f out: rdn to ld narrowly over 1f out: strly pressed and hdd wl ins fnl f: no ex* **7/4**[1]
3 *1* **Flying Fairies (IRE)**[154] 7558 4-9-11 99................ DeclanMcDonogh 11 94
(John M Oxx, Ire) *hld up bhd ldrs on outer: disp 5th into st: effrt 1 1/2f out: u.p in 4th ins fnl f and sn no imp on wnr: kpt on same pce in 3rd wl ins fnl f* **5/1**[2]
4 *nk* **Queen Anne's Lace (USA)**[148] 7707 3-8-9 96................. PatSmullen 1 89
(D K Weld, Ire) *settled bhd ldrs: 3rd 1/2-way: clsr in 2nd fr 3f out: rdn to ld briefly 1 1/2f out tl sn hdd: no imp on ldrs wl ins fnl f and one pce in 4th clsng stages* **11/2**[3]
5 *nk* **Wild As The Wind (IRE)**[167] 7236 4-9-11 81.......................... WJLee 7 93+
(W McCreery, Ire) *w.w towards rr: 10th over 2f out: sn rdn and sme late hdwy u.p into nvr threatening 5th cl home: nrst fin* **25/1**
6 *1/2* **Shes Ranger (IRE)**[10] 1230 3-8-9 78................................. ShaneFoley 5 87
(Adrian Murray, Ire) *towards rr: rdn 2f out and tk clsr order whn stmbld sltly 1 1/2f out: no imp on ldrs u.p in 6th over 1f out: kpt on one pce* **16/1**
7 *2 1/2* **Ce La Vie**[162] 7356 3-8-9 0................................................ ConnorBeasley 6 82
(Keith Dalgleish) *towards rr: pushed along in 10th into st and no imp u.p in 8th ent fnl f: kpt on one pce* **16/1**
8 *3/4* **Legitimus (IRE)**[182] 6815 3-8-9 95................................... RonanWhelan 4 80
(J S Bolger, Ire) *sn led: rdn and hdd 1 1/2f out: sn wknd* **8/1**
9 *2* **Chilli Spice (IRE)**[163] 7342 4-9-11 87................................ ConnorKing 2 79
(J P Murtagh, Ire) *hld up bhd ldrs: disp 5th into st: rdn 2f out and sn no ex: wknd fnl f* **33/1**
10 *nk* **Dew Line (IRE)**[158] 7478 5-9-11 90....................................... ChrisHayes 9 79
(Michael Mulvany, Ire) *settled bhd ldr: 2nd 1/2-way rdn and lost pl 3f out: sn no ex and lost tch fnl 2f* **28/1**
11 *5 1/2* **Cirin Toinne (IRE)**[149] 7676 4-9-11 95............................ KevinManning 8 66
(J S Bolger, Ire) *hld up: 8th 1/2-way: rdn and no ex over 2f out* **12/1**
12 *11* **Camellia Japonica (IRE)**[259] 4180 4-9-11 75.................. GaryCarroll 12 41
(Joseph G Murphy, Ire) *hld up: rdn in 9th into st and sn wknd* **66/1**

1m 48.14s (8.14)
**WFA** 3 from 4yo+ 17lb 12 Ran SP% **121.8**
CSF £22.30 TOTE £11.10: £2.40, £1.02, £1.80; DF 34.40 Trifecta £96.30.
**Owner** D Wachman, MV Magnier & Mrs L Shanahan **Bred** Norman Court Stud **Trained** West Ilsley, Berks

**FOCUS**
An up-to-scratch running of this Group 3. The runner-up was the only one with a three-figure rating but she was unable to repel the gutsy winner, who was officially rated 15lb superior to her. Less than 3l seperated the first six home. The fifth and sixth potentially limit the form.

## 1388a TOTE IRISH LINCOLNSHIRE (PREMIER H'CAP) 1m
4:40 (4:41) 4-Y-O+
£50,427 (£16,239; £7,692; £3,418; £1,709; £854)

RPR
1 **Brendan Brackan (IRE)**[162] 7372 8-9-12 **105**.................... GaryCarroll 3 114
(G M Lyons, Ire) *hld up in rr of mid-div: 10th 1/2-way: tk clsr order far side fr 3f out and impr bhd ldrs: rdn to ld 1f out and kpt on wl clsng stages* **16/1**
2 1 ½ **Aussie Valentine (IRE)**[30] 907 6-8-8 **87**........................(t) ChrisHayes 8 93+
(P D Deegan, Ire) *chsd ldrs: disp 3rd at 1/2-way: rdn bhd ldrs 2f out and no imp on wnr ins fnl f where wnt 2nd: kpt on same pce* **7/1**[3]
3 ½ **Sea Wolf (IRE)**[162] 7354 5-9-7 **100**...................................... ColinKeane 1 104+
(G M Lyons, Ire) *in tch: 8th 1/2-way: tk clsr order bhd ldrs over 2f out: sn rdn in 5th and clsd u.p to dispute 2nd briefly ins fnl f where no imp on wnr: kpt on same pce in 3rd clsng stages* **5/1**[2]
4 2 ¼ **Tribal Path (IRE)**[16] 1133 7-8-7 **86** ow2..........................(t) ShaneFoley 2 85
(Damian Joseph English, Ire) *broke wl to sn ld: rdn under 2f out and hdd 1f out: no imp on wnr ins fnl f: kpt on one pce clsng stages to jst hold 4th* **20/1**
5 hd **Spring Offensive (IRE)**[232] 5156 5-9-1 **94**...................... PaulHanagan 5 93
(Richard Fahey) *chsd ldrs: disp 3rd at 1/2-way: tk clsr order bhd ldr gng wl into st: pushed along in 2nd 2f out and no ex in 3rd ent fnl f: sn wknd* **9/1**
6 1 ¼ **Brokopondo (IRE)**[30] 910 5-7-11 **83** oh3....................... SeanDavis(7) 4 79
(J F Levins, Ire) *s.i.s and in rr early: sme hdwy into mid-div 2f out: kpt on u.p into 6th ins fnl f: nvr trbld ldrs* **25/1**
7 hd **Canary Row (IRE)**[154] 7561 7-8-8 **87**........................(v) RonanWhelan 12 82
(P J Prendergast, Ire) *in tch: rdn in mid-div under 2f out and u.p in 9th ent fnl f: kpt on wl clsng stages* **9/1**
8 1 ½ **Onenightidreamed (IRE)**[343] 1509 6-9-7 **107**...(p) KillianHennessy(7) 16 99
(J A Stack, Ire) *chsd ldrs: 5th 1/2-way: wd into st: rdn 2f out and no imp on ldrs over 1f out: one pce after* **12/1**
9 2 ½ **Sikandarabad (IRE)**[197] 6355 4-9-4 **97**..........................(v) PatSmullen 7 83
(D K Weld, Ire) *mid-div: disp 6th at 1/2-way: rdn and no imp on ldrs 2f out: wknd into 9th ins fnl f* **4/1**[1]
10 2 ½ **Marshall Jennings (IRE)**[221] 5564 5-9-4 **97**......... ColmO'Donoghue 15 77
(Mrs John Harrington, Ire) *hld up: rdn towards rr under 2f out and sme hdwy into 11th ent fnl f: kpt on one pce* **16/1**
11 ¾ **Mr Right (IRE)**[210] 5941 5-8-6 **85**...........................(h) MichaelHussey 13 64
(J F Levins, Ire) *mid-div: 9th 1/2-way: c wd into st: sn rdn and no imp over 1f out: kpt on one pce* **22/1**
12 2 ½ **Gentil J (IRE)**[162] 7374 4-8-6 **85**.............................(t) WayneLordan 11 58
(H Rogers, Ire) *towards rr: rdn and no imp 2f out: one pce after* **10/1**
13 1 ¼ **Lean And Keen (IRE)**[196] 4467 7-8-4 **83** oh5............(p[1]) ConorHoban 17 53
(Sean Byrne, Ire) *prom tl sn settled bhd ldr: 2nd 1/2-way: rdn over 2f out and sn wknd* **50/1**
14 3 **Stenographer (USA)**[169] 7162 4-8-12 **91**.................... KevinManning 14 54
(J S Bolger, Ire) *in tch: rn freely early and disp 6th at 1/2-way: c wd into st: rdn and wknd over 2f out* **12/1**
15 4 ¼ **Tithonus (IRE)**[155] 7537 6-8-7 **89**.........................(tp) GaryHalpin(3) 9 42
(Denis Gerard Hogan, Ire) *mid-div early: 12th 1/2-way: rdn under 3f out and sn no ex: wknd* **16/1**
16 1 ¾ **Specific Gravity (FR)**[16] 1134 9-8-7 **86**........................(b) LeighRoche 6 35
(Adrian McGuinness, Ire) *s.i.s: sn settled in mid-div whn n.m.r and checked after 1f: in rr of mid-div bef 1/2-way: sme hdwy under 3f out: rdn over 2f out and sn no ex: wknd 1 1/2f out* **33/1**
17 18 **Red Avenger (USA)**[16] 1133 7-8-13 **92**.......................... RoryCleary 18
(Damian Joseph English, Ire) *rrd s and s.i.s: towards rr thrght: pushed along and no imp 2f out: wknd and eased* **33/1**

1m 47.42s (7.42) **17** Ran SP% **132.1**
CSF £123.98 CT £692.22 TOTE £21.10: £4.90, £2.30, £1.80, £4.20; DF 177.10 Trifecta £2036.70.
**Owner** David Spratt & Sean Jones **Bred** Anamoine Ltd **Trained** Dunsany, Co Meath
■ A change of venue for this race, due to redevelopment at the Curragh.

**FOCUS**
A triumph for Ger Lyons who supplied the winner and third, but spare a thought for the connections of Aussie Valentine, second in the race for the third year in a row. The placed horses help with the standard.

## 1389a IRISH STALLION FARMS EUROPEAN BREEDERS FUND MAIDEN (PLUS 10 RACE) 1m
5:10 (5:13) 3-Y-O £8,423 (£2,611; £1,244; £560; £218)

RPR
1 **Orderofthegarter (IRE)**[148] 7704 3-9-0 0..................(t) AnaO'Brien(5) 5 105+
(A P O'Brien, Ire) *sn led briefly tl hdd narrowly after 1f: regained advantage bef 1/2-way: stl travelling wl over 2f out where extended advantage: styd on strly and drew further clr fr over 1f out: v easily* **11/4**[2]
2 11 **Tommy Hallinan (IRE)**[174] 7020 3-9-5 0................................ WJLee 15 80
(W McCreery, Ire) *cl up and led narrowly after 1f: hdd bef 1/2-way: rdn in 2nd over 2f out and sn no imp on easy wnr: kpt on same pce* **25/1**
3 8 ½ **Port Moody (IRE)**[175] 6982 3-9-5 63.......................... NGMcCullagh 2 60
(Patrick Tallis, Ire) *chsd ldrs: 7th 1/2-way: rdn and no imp over 2f out: mod 5th ent fnl f: kpt on u.p into mod 3rd ins fnl f* **66/1**
4 2 ¾ **Pocketfullofdreams (FR)**[210] 5937 3-9-0 0..............(h[1]) WayneLordan 3 49
(A P O'Brien, Ire) *chsd ldrs: 3rd 1/2-way: pushed along under 3f out and no imp on easy wnr: one pce fnl 2f* **5/1**[3]
5 1 ¼ **Gold Spinner (IRE)** 3-9-5 0........................................... ColinKeane 9 51
(G M Lyons, Ire) *mid-div: pushed along into st and no imp on ldrs: sn rdn and kpt on u.p into mod 5th* **10/1**
6 ½ **Toursoun (IRE)** 3-9-5 0................................................ PatSmullen 7 50
(D K Weld, Ire) *chsd ldrs: disp 4th at 1/2-way: rdn over 2f out and no imp on ldrs: disp mod 3rd briefly 1 1/2f out: one pce fnl f* **17/2**
7 2 ¾ **Inca Gold (IRE)**[273] 3691 3-9-2 0.......................... DonnachaO'Brien(3) 17 44
(A P O'Brien, Ire) *in rr of mid-div: pushed along in mod 13th under 3f out: sn rdn and sme hdwy over 1f out: kpt on one pce* **5/2**[1]
8 ¾ **Great Uncle (IRE)**[161] 7387 3-9-5 0.............................. RoryCleary 1 42
(Brendan W Duke, Ire) *cl up early tl sn settled bhd ldrs: 4th 1/2-way: rdn in 5th under 3f out and sn no ex: one pce fnl 2f* **50/1**
9 1 ½ **Karaganda (IRE)** 3-9-0 0............................................ LeighRoche 4 34
(D K Weld, Ire) *mid-div: pushed along in 9th over 2f out and no imp: one pce after* **25/1**
10 2 **Erquy (FR)** 3-9-2 0.......................................... ShaneBKelly(3) 8 34
(Anthony Mullins, Ire) *s.i.s and towards rr: n.m.r on inner into st: sn pushed along and sme hdwy 2f out: kpt on one pce* **50/1**
11 1 ¼ **Freedom Chimes**[158] 7476 3-9-0 0.................................. OisinOrr(5) 12 31
(Edward Lynam, Ire) *towards rr: pushed along under 3f out and sme hdwy under 2f out: kpt on one pce ins fnl f* **50/1**
12 4 ¾ **Khudha (IRE)**[149] 7674 3-9-5 0......................................... ConnorKing 19 20
(J P Murtagh, Ire) *prom early tl sn settled in mid-div: rdn in rr of mid-div over 2f out and no imp: one pce after* **50/1**
13 1 ¼ **The Eagle's Nest (IRE)**[54] 500 3-9-5 0................ ColmO'Donoghue 10 17
(Richard Fahey) *chsd ldrs: rdn into st wknd 2f out* **12/1**
14 5 ½ **Feathery**[167] 7232 3-9-0 84.....................................(t) KevinManning 11
(J S Bolger, Ire) *in tch: 8th 1/2-way: rdn and no imp under 3f out: wknd and eased fnl 2f* **8/1**
15 2 ½ **Algebra**[137] 7872 3-9-5 0..................................... DeclanMcDonogh 16
(John Joseph Murphy, Ire) *dwlt and wnt sltly lft s: settled towards rr: tk clsr order briefly into st: no imp under 3f out: one pce fnl 2f* **66/1**
16 shd **You Bank (IRE)** 3-9-5 0................................................ RonanWhelan 13
(Kieran P Cotter, Ire) *mid-div: pushed along fr 1/2-way and no imp into st: wknd fnl 2f* **66/1**
17 2 ¼ **Claregate Street (IRE)**[148] 7703 3-9-0 0......................... ConorHoban 6
(M Halford, Ire) *towards rr thrght: rdn and no imp 3f out* **66/1**
18 3 ¼ **Conron (IRE)**[174] 7020 3-9-5 0.......................................... ShaneFoley 14
(M Halford, Ire) *towards rr thrght: rdn and no imp 3f out* **20/1**
19 4 ½ **Compatriot (IRE)**[72] 225 3-8-9 0......................... MikeyO'Sullivan(10) 18
(John Joseph Murphy, Ire) *hld up in tch: rdn in 9th fr 1/2-way and no imp into st: sn wknd* **66/1**
20 ½ **Mister Saxman**[247] 4617 3-9-5 0........................................ GaryCarroll 20
(G M Lyons, Ire) *towards rr thrght: rdn and no imp over 3f out* **50/1**

1m 46.9s (6.90) **20** Ran SP% **136.8**
Tote Aggregate: 2017: 442,642.00 - 2016: 398,806.00. Pick Six: Not won. Pool of 20,270.31 carried forward to Sunday 2nd April. CSF £84.97 TOTE £3.60: £1.60, £4.00, £17.10; DF 60.20 Trifecta £3436.00.
**Owner** Derrick Smith & Mrs John Magnier & Michael Tabor **Bred** Barronstown Stud **Trained** Cashel, Co Tipperary

**FOCUS**
Aidan O'Brien supplied the first three in the market, with the second-favourite bolting up to complete a double for the trainer and rider. It looks as though the Ballydoyle three-year-olds are well forward. The time was quicker than the Irish Lincolnshire.
T/Jkpt: Not won. T/Plt: @489.00. Pool: @48,145.86 **Brian Fleming**

1390 - 1399a (Foreign Racing) - See Raceform Interactive

# MORNINGTON
Saturday, March 25
**OFFICIAL GOING: Turf: good**

## 1400a LADBROKES MORNINGTON CUP (LISTED H'CAP) (3YO+) (TURF) 1m 4f
5:30 3-Y-O+
£105,263 (£31,578; £15,789; £7,894; £4,385; £3,508)

RPR
1 **Tally (AUS)**[14] 1155 4-9-4 **0**...............................(b) AndrewMallyon 8 110+
(J O'Shea, Australia) **7/1**[2]
2 shd **Vengeur Masque (IRE)**[28] 5-8-7 **0**......................... PatrickMoloney 1 99
(Michael Moroney, Australia) **20/1**
3 1 ¼ **Settler's Stone (AUS)**[21] 5-8-7 **0**.......................(bt) CraigNewitt 7 97+
(Troy Blacker, Australia) **40/1**
4 hd **Gold Trail (IRE)**[58] 428 6-9-3 **0**............................. CraigAWilliams 6 107
(Charlie Appleby) **11/10**[1]
5 hd **Boom Time (AUS)**[14] 1155 5-9-1 **0**...........................(b[1]) DwayneDunn 3 104
(David A & B Hayes & Tom Dabernig, Australia) **8/1**[3]
6 1 **Self Sense (AUS)**[749] 6-8-7 **0**.................................(bt) ChrisSymons 11 95
(David Brideoake, Australia) **25/1**
7 1 ½ **Almoonqith (USA)**[21] 7-9-6 **0**..................................(b) MichaelDee 12 105
(David A & B Hayes & Tom Dabernig, Australia) **30/1**
8 ½ **Cadillac Mountain (AUS)**[21] 6-8-7 **0**.........................(b) DeanYendall 9 92
(Darren Weir, Australia) **18/1**
9 1 ¼ **Unfurl (NZ)** 5-8-7 **0**......................................................(b) BenAllen 13 90
(Darren Weir, Australia) **80/1**
10 ¾ **Youl Dash For Cash (AUS)** 5-8-7 **0**............................(b) JyeMcNeil 5 88
(Peter Gelagotis, Australia) **80/1**
11 2 ¼ **Dark Eyes (AUS)**[35] 4-8-10 **0**................................(b) StephenBaster 2 88
(Gai Waterhouse & Adrian Bott, Australia) **11/1**
12 1 **Big Memory (FR)**[21] 7-9-0 **0**....................................(tp) LukeCurrie 10 90
(Tony McEvoy, Australia) **10/1**
13 1 **Annus Mirabilis (IRE)**[12] 6-9-1 **0**..............................(b) JamieMott 4 90
(Stuart Webb, Australia) **14/1**

2m 27.02s
**WFA** 4 from 5yo+ 1lb **13** Ran SP% **117.3**
**Owner** Godolphin **Bred** Darley **Trained** Australia

# 1365 WOLVERHAMPTON (A.W) (L-H)
Monday, March 27
**OFFICIAL GOING: Tapeta: standard**
Wind: light, across Weather: cloud clearing, bright spells

## 1401 32RED.COM MAIDEN FILLIES' STKS 7f 36y (Tp)
1:50 (1:51) (Class 5) 3-Y-O+ £3,881 (£1,155; £577; £288) Stalls High

Form RPR
35- 1 **Wurood**[142] 7819 3-8-11 0............................................ JimCrowley 6 74+
(William Haggas) *sn pressing ldr: led travelling strly wl over 1f out: sn rdn: and r.o wl and in command fnl f: readily* **11/10**[1]
3- 2 2 **Castle Hill Cassie (IRE)**[187] 6682 3-8-11 0.................... GrahamLee 9 69
(Ben Haslam) *wl in tch in midfield: effrt and hdwy wl over 1f out: chsd wnr jst ins fnl f: r.o but a hld* **12/1**
3 1 ½ **Art's Desire (IRE)** 3-8-11 0........................................ ThomasBrown 2 65+
(Ed Walker) *hld up in tch in last trio: shkn up and hdwy over 1f out: r.o wl ins fnl f to go 3rd 50yds out: no threat to wnr* **11/1**

0- **4** *2* **Sherbert**[164] 7314 3-8-11 0 TomMarquand 1 61
(Richard Hannon) *broke wl: sn stdd to chse ldrs: rdn and unable qck over 2f out: kpt on same pce u.p fnl 2f* **14/1**

0- **5** *3/4* **Mythical Spirit (IRE)**[263] 4064 3-8-11 0 MartinHarley 8 59
(James Tate) *chsd ldrs: effrt to press ldng pair 2f out: unable qck over 1f out: wknd ins fnl f* **4/1**[2]

**6** *3/4* **Al Jawza** 3-8-11 0 SeanLevey 5 57
(Richard Hannon) *dwlt: sn rcvrd and in tch in midfield: effrt 2f out: rn green and edgd lft ent fnl f: swtchd rt and kpt on same pce ins fnl f* **5/1**[3]

34-0 **7** *1* **Ok By Me (IRE)**[26] 967 3-8-11 64 JFEgan 4 54
(David Evans) *sn led: rdn 2f out: sn hdd and unable qck over 1f out: wknd ins fnl f* **33/1**

05 **8** *nk* **Seeking Attention (USA)**[12] 1205 3-8-11 0 JosephineGordon 3 54
(George Scott) *dwlt: sn rcvrd and hld up in tch in midfield: rdn 2f out: sn outpcd: wknd ins fnl f* **20/1**

-06 **9** *3 1/2* **Anna Medici**[14] 1179 3-8-11 0 LukeMorris 12 45
(Sir Mark Prescott Bt) *s.i.s: in tch in rr: rdn over 2f out: no imp: nvr trbld ldrs* **66/1**

55 **10** *3/4* **From A Distance (IRE)**[7] 1286 3-8-11 0 (h[1]) LiamKeniry 10 43
(David Simcock) *stdd s: t.k.h in rr: n.d* **66/1**

1m 30.11s (1.31) **Going Correction** +0.025s/f (Slow)
**WFA** 3 from 4yo 15lb **10** Ran SP% **117.7**
Speed ratings (Par 100): **93,90,89,86,85 85,83,83,79,78**
CSF £16.26 TOTE £2.20: £2.00, £2.80, £3.10; EX 18.80 Trifecta £203.60.
**Owner** Hamdan Al Maktoum **Bred** Kilshannig Stud **Trained** Newmarket, Suffolk
**FOCUS**
Just an ordinary maiden. The winner built on last year's 6f form here.

## 1402 BETWAY INSIDER H'CAP 1m 4f 51y (Tp)
**2:20** (2:20) (Class 7) (0-50,48) 4-Y-0+ **£2,264** (£673; £336; £168) **Stalls** Low

Form RPR

**1** **Bottleofsmoke (IRE)**[31] 912 4-9-3 47 (h) AdamKirby 9 62+
(Gavin Cromwell, Ire) *in tch in midfield: rdn and hdwy to chse ldrs over 2f out: led wl over 1f out: sn drew clr andf in command 1f out: readily* **15/8**[1]

5-35 **2** *6* **Ted's Brother (IRE)**[19] 1081 9-9-6 48 (h) ShaneKelly 5 51
(Laura Morgan) *stdd s: hld up in rr: pushed along and hdwy over 1f out: swtchd rt over 1f out: drvn to chse clr ldr 1f out: no ch w wnr but kpt on for clr 2nd* **9/1**[3]

30-0 **3** *5* **King Julien (IRE)**[60] 425 4-9-2 46 JosephineGordon 12 41
(John Ryan) *rousted along early: chsd ldrs after 2f: rdn 5f out: outpcd u.p 2f out: no ch but kpt on ins fnl f to go 3rd fnl 75yds* **20/1**

000- **4** *1 1/4* **Mister Marcasite**[151] 7641 7-9-5 47 CamHardie 8 40
(Antony Brittain) *t.k.h: short of room sn after s: hld up in midfield: effrt jst over 2f out: styd on u.p ins fnl f: swtchd rt wl ins fnl f: snatched 4th last strides* **25/1**

2-55 **5** *hd* **Brooke's Point**[46] 646 4-9-3 47 (p) DougieCostello 2 40
(Neil Mulholland) *w ldr tl after 2: hdd 8f and pressed ldr after: rdn to ld 2f out: sn hdd and unable qck : wknd 1f out: lost 2 pls fnl 75yds* **7/2**[2]

-066 **6** *1 1/4* **Celestial Dancer (FR)**[40] 741 5-9-3 45 AndrewMullen 1 36
(Nigel Twiston-Davies) *chsd ldrs: rdn over 2f out: sn outpcd and btn over 1f out: wknd fnl f* **22/1**

063/ **7** *1 1/4* **Jebulani**[328] 6582 7-8-10 45 ConnorMurtagh(7) 3 34
(Barry Murtagh) *wl in tch in midfield: rdn over 2f out: sn outpcd: wknd fnl f* **66/1**

0622 **8** *3/4* **Cahar Fad (IRE)**[4] 1322 5-9-6 48 (bt) AdamBeschizza 10 36
(Steph Hollinshead) *chsd ldrs tl hdwy to ld 8f out: rdn over 2f out: hdd 2f out: sn outpcd: wknd fnl f* **7/2**[2]

0-05 **9** *nse* **Ledbury (IRE)**[33] 865 5-9-5 47 MartinHarley 11 36
(Lee Carter) *stdd s: hld up in rr: effrt and c wd bnd wl over 1f out: sn wknd* **12/1**

-000 **10** *15* **Silver Lining (IRE)**[47] 621 5-9-3 45 (vt[1]) TimmyMurphy 7 9
(Mark Hoad) *hld up in last trio: rdn over 2f out: sn wknd* **66/1**

00-0 **11** *56* **Overrider**[9] 1260 7-9-1 46 (bt) CallumShepherd(3) 4
(Shaun Lycett) *led for 2f: lost pl 7f out: rdn 5f out: last and lost tch over 2f out: t.o* **66/1**

2m 38.98s (-1.82) **Going Correction** +0.025s/f (Slow)
**WFA** 4 from 5yo+ 1lb **11** Ran SP% **114.4**
Speed ratings (Par 97): **107,103,99,98,98 97,97,96,96,86 49**
CSF £17.90 CT £249.62 TOTE £3.00: £1.10, £2.20, £3.40; EX 22.40 Trifecta £284.30.
**Owner** IFHS Syndicate **Bred** Kevin Blake **Trained** Navan, Co. Meath
■ Stewards' Enquiry : Adam Beschizza caution: guilty of careless riding in that he had allowed his mount to angle left
**FOCUS**
A soundly run low-grade handicap which was all about the winner.

## 1403 BETWAY H'CAP 1m 1f 104y (Tp)
**2:50** (2:50) (Class 6) (0-60,60) 4-Y-0+ **£2,749** (£818; £408; £204) **Stalls** Low

Form RPR

/00- **1** **Voice Of A Leader (IRE)**[403] 621 6-9-7 60 (h) JoeyHaynes 11 65
(Andi Brown) *mounted on crse and taken down early: hld up in tch: rdn and hdwy on outer over 2f out: chal u.p 1f out: led ins fnl f: r.o wl* **5/1**[1]

0524 **2** *1 1/4* **Powered (IRE)**[13] 1188 4-9-2 55 AdamKirby 12 58
(David Evans) *hld up in last trio: clsd and nt clr run 2f out: swtchd lft 1f out and hdwy between rivals to press ldrs ins fnl f: wnt 2nd and kpt on same pce towards fin* **6/1**[3]

6145 **3** *1/2* **Outlaw Torn (IRE)**[16] 1145 8-9-3 56 (e) DougieCostello 8 58
(Richard Guest) *wl in tch in midfield: hdwy to chse ldrs 6f out: wnt 2nd 2f out: sn rdn and led 1f out: hdd and styd on same pce fnl 100yds: lost 2nd towards fin* **16/1**

-500 **4** *1/2* **Monna Valley**[10] 1249 5-9-1 57 AaronJones(3) 3 58
(Stuart Williams) *chsd ldrs: effrt ent fnl 2f: drvn and ev ch 1f out: kpt on same pce ins fnl f* **5/1**[1]

-405 **5** *shd* **John Caesar (IRE)**[17] 1125 6-9-3 56 (tp) DanielTudhope 4 57
(Rebecca Bastiman) *stdd s: hld up in tch: clsd and n.m.r 2f out: swtchd rt and effrt jst over 1f out: kpt on same pce ins fnl f* **8/1**

546/ **6** *1/2* **Mosman**[31] 912 7-8-7 46 oh1 (vt) TomMarquand 1 47
(Paul W Flynn, Ire) *t.k.h: hld up in tch in midfield: nt clr run on inner 2f out: swtchd rt wl over 1f out and then bk lft again: drvn and hdwy to press ldrs 1f out: no ex and outpcd fnl 100yds* **6/1**[3]

-066 **7** *nse* **Cosmic Ray**[19] 1086 5-9-6 59 (h) JasonHart 5 58
(Les Eyre) *t.k.h: chsd ldrs tl led 7f out: rdn wl over 1f out: hdd 1f out: no ex: wknd wl ins fnl f* **16/1**

6- **8** *nk* **Balmont Belle (IRE)**[321] 2127 7-8-10 52 TimClark(3) 13 51
(Barry Leavy) *stdd and dropped in bhd after s: in tch in rr: clsd and swtchd rt 2f out: hung lft 1f out: kpt on ins fnl f: no threat to ldrs* **100/1**

00-3 **9** *2 3/4* **Filament Of Gold (USA)**[21] 1067 6-9-1 54 (p) JosephineGordon 9 48
(Roy Brotherton) *chsd ldrs tl unable qck u.p 2f out: wknd ins fnl f* **11/2**[2]

0-04 **10** *3 1/2* **Frap**[44] 689 4-9-2 55 (h) StevieDonohoe 2 42
(Ian Williams) *in tch in midfield: rdn and lost pl jst over 2f out: bhd 1f out* **12/1**

500- **11** *2 1/2* **Mayfield Boy**[151] 7642 6-9-1 54 CamHardie 10 37
(Antony Brittain) *t.k.h: hld up in tch in rr: struggling over 2f out: bhd 1f out* **50/1**

-500 **12** *2* **Lemon Thyme**[21] 1067 4-9-4 57 (v[1]) ShaneKelly 7 35
(Mike Murphy) *led tl 7f out: chsd ldrs after tl lost pl u.p 2f out: bhd fnl f* **28/1**

2m 1.95s (1.15) **Going Correction** +0.025s/f (Slow) **12** Ran SP% **114.3**
Speed ratings (Par 101): **95,93,93,93,92 92,92,92,89,86 84,82**
CSF £32.91 CT £443.88 TOTE £8.20: £3.20, £1.40, £3.70; EX 47.90 Trifecta £620.40.
**Owner** Miss Linsey Knocker **Bred** Lynch Bages Ltd **Trained** Newmarket, Suffolk
**FOCUS**
A moderate handicap but a competitive one. They finished in a heap behind the winner.

## 1404 BETWAY MIDDLE H'CAP 1m 1f 104y (Tp)
**3:20** (3:20) (Class 4) (0-80,75) 3-Y-0 **£4,690** (£1,395; £697; £348) **Stalls** Low

Form RPR

2-21 **1** **Enfolding (IRE)**[21] 1069 3-9-6 74 SilvestreDeSousa 6 86+
(James Fanshawe) *stdd and dropped in after s: hld up in tch in rr: rdn and hdwy on outer 2f out: led and edgd lft u.p 1f out: sn clr and r.o wl: readily* **7/2**[3]

031- **2** *3 1/4* **Peace And Plenty**[123] 8080 3-9-2 70 MartinDwyer 3 73
(William Muir) *t.k.h: pressed ldr: rdn to ld over 1f out: hdd 1f out: outpcd by wnr but kpt on to hold 2nd ins fnl f* **8/1**

641- **3** *nk* **Hertford Dancer**[105] 8340 3-9-4 72 AdamKirby 4 75
(John Gosden) *in tch: rdn and effrt to chse ldrs 2f out: nt clr run over 1f out: no ch w wnr but rallied to battle for 2nd ins fnl f: kpt on* **5/2**[2]

52-2 **4** *2 1/4* **Muqaatil (USA)**[16] 1141 3-9-7 75 JimCrowley 1 73
(Richard Hannon) *led: rdn 2f out: hdd and unable qck over 1f out: wknd ins fnl f* **9/1**

55-1 **5** *1 1/2* **Earthly (USA)**[52] 552 3-9-5 73 FranBerry 2 68
(Ralph Beckett) *dwlt and rousted along leaving stalls: rdn 2f out: outpcd and btn over 1f out: wknd ins fnl f* **9/4**[1]

001- **6** *6* **Mary Anne Evans**[206] 6077 3-9-3 71 RobertTart 5 53
(John Gosden) *in tch in midfield but wd: rdn and dropped to rr 3f out: hung rt 2f out: sn wknd* **12/1**

2m 0.58s (-0.22) **Going Correction** +0.025s/f (Slow) **6** Ran SP% **110.4**
Speed ratings (Par 100): **101,98,97,95,94 89**
CSF £28.82 TOTE £4.10: £7.80, £3.10; EX 25.10 Trifecta £74.60.
**Owner** Ben CM Wong **Bred** Kenilworth Partnership **Trained** Newmarket, Suffolk
**FOCUS**
Quite an interesting 3yo handicap and a good performance from the winner off a steady pace. He's on the up now.

## 1405 BETWAY STAYERS H'CAP 2m 120y (Tp)
**3:50** (3:50) (Class 4) (0-85,83) 4-Y-0+ **£5,498** (£1,636; £817; £408) **Stalls** Low

Form RPR

004- **1** **Grumeti**[150] 7670 9-9-10 81 FergusSweeney 6 87
(Alan King) *chsd ldrs: wnt 2nd over 4f out: rdn and clsd on ldr 3f out: styd on wl u.p ins fnl f: led towards fin* **5/1**[3]

/55- **2** *1/2* **All For The Best (IRE)**[67] 2392 5-9-1 72 (t[1]) LukeMorris 2 77
(Robert Stephens) *hld up in midfield: clsd 3f out: swtchd rt and effrt 2f out: edging lft ins fnl f: styd on wl fnl 100yds: wnt 2nd cl home* **13/2**

4660 **3** *1/2* **Entihaa**[16] 1153 9-9-10 81 MartinHarley 3 86
(Dai Burchell) *s.i.s and swtchd rt after s: hdwy to ld after 1f: sn clr: c bk to field but stl travelling wl 3f out: rdn and fnd ex wl over 1f out: kpt on tl hdd and no ex towards fin: lost 2nd cl home* **16/1**

143- **4** *1* **Fire Jet (IRE)**[152] 7624 4-9-3 79 TomQueally 8 83
(John Mackie) *hld up in 6th: sme hdwy 1/2-way: clsd but wd over 2f out: unable qck over 1f out: styd on again ins fnl f* **7/2**[2]

/0P1 **5** *nk* **Rowlestone Lass**[14] 1175 7-9-1 77 CliffordLee(5) 4 80
(Richard Price) *midfield: clsd 3f out: chsd ldrs and rdn over 1f out unable qck and kpt on same pce ins fnl f* **8/1**

0332 **6** *1 3/4* **Icebuster**[19] 1092 9-9-4 75 RyanTate 1 76
(Rod Millman) *stdd s: hld up in rr: sme hdwy 7f out: clsd 3f out: no hdwy u.p over 1f out: kpt on same pce fnl f* **9/1**

1231 **7** *2* **Aldreth**[11] 1223 6-9-9 83 (p) NathanEvans(3) 7 82
(Michael Easterby) *led for 1f: chsd ldr tl over 4f out: styd chsng ldrs: clsd and rdn 3f out: unable qck over 1f out: wknd ins fnl f* **3/1**[1]

155- **8** *5* **Lady Makfi (IRE)**[191] 6591 5-9-7 78 StevieDonohoe 5 71
(Johnny Farrelly) *hld up in rr: effrt and no imp over 2f out: n.d* **9/1**

3m 40.84s (-2.86) **Going Correction** +0.025s/f (Slow)
**WFA** 4 from 5yo+ 3lb **8** Ran SP% **114.2**
Speed ratings (Par 105): **107,106,106,106,105 105,104,101**
CSF £37.07 CT £480.85 TOTE £6.30: £2.00, £2.00, £5.10; EX 37.60 Trifecta £504.10.
**Owner** McNeill Family **Bred** Catridge Farm Stud **Trained** Barbury Castle, Wilts
**FOCUS**
A fair staying handicap. The runner-up is the best guide and the third fits.

## 1406 SUNBETS.CO.UK DOWNLOAD THE APP H'CAP 1m 142y (Tp)
**4:20** (4:21) (Class 6) (0-55,55) 4-Y-0+ **£2,749** (£818; £408; £204) **Stalls** Low

Form RPR

00-0 **1** **Lord Murphy (IRE)**[47] 614 4-8-12 46 oh1 LiamKeniry 4 52+
(Daniel Mark Loughnane) *hld up in tch in midfield: travelling strly but nt clr run over 2f out: swtchd rt over 1f out: rdn and hdwy to chse ldr ins fnl f: r.o wel to ld cl home* **8/1**

0-03 **2** *1/2* **Sublimation (IRE)**[16] 1146 7-9-4 55 KieranShoemark(3) 6 60
(Steve Gollings) *chsd ldrs: rdn to ld jst over 1f out: kpt on wl u.p tl hdd and no ex cl home* **13/2**[3]

6046 **3** *3* **Lutine Charlie (IRE)**[16] 1145 10-8-12 46 oh1 (p) TomQueally 8 45
(Emma Owen) *chsd ldr tl led 5f out: rdn and hdd over 1f out: lost 2nd ins fnl f: wknd towards fin* **25/1**

-050 **4** *nse* **Sarakova (IRE)**[60] 425 4-8-12 46 oh1 (b) DougieCostello 5 45
(Kevin Frost) *t.k.h: hld up in tch in rr: swtchd rt and effrt wl over 1f out: hdwy 1f out: styd on wl ins fnl f: nvr trbld ldrs* **12/1**

3035 **5** *nk* **Mount Cheiron (USA)**[9] 1260 6-8-8 49 (p) CallumRodriguez(7) 10 47
(Richard Ford) *s.i.s: hld up in tch in last pair: effrt on inner over 1f out: swtchd rt and styd on wl ins fnl f: nvr trbld ldrs* **7/1**

0222 **6** *2 1/2* **Sheer Intensity (IRE)**[3] 1338 4-9-5 53 AdamKirby 9 46
(David Evans) *hld up in tch towards rr: effrt and switching rt 2f out: kpt on same pce and no imp ins fnl f* **4/1**[1]

-403 **7** *1 1/4* **Pipers Piping (IRE)**[9] 1260 11-9-1 **49**.............................. RobHornby 1 39
(Mandy Rowland) *chsd ldrs: rdn over 2f out: sn outpcd: wl hld and kpt on same pce ins fnl f* **14/1**

0261 **8** *1/2* **Vivre La Reve**[9] 1260 5-9-7 **55**.............................(h) RyanPowell 4 44
(James Unett) *led tl 5f out: styd w ldr: rdn 2f out: unable qck over 1f out: wknd ins fnl f* **6/1**[2]

-640 **9** *1 1/4* **Zebedee's Girl (IRE)**[4] 1322 4-8-12 **46**.................................... JFEgan 3 32
(David Evans) *hld in in tch towards rr: effrt over 1f out: no imp: wknd ins fnl f* **20/1**

-006 **10** *4 1/2* **El Tel**[10] 1249 5-9-2 **50**............................................. JosephineGordon 12 27
(Shaun Harris) *t.k.h: chsd ldrs tl 4th and outpcd u.p 2f out: wknd ins fnl f* **9/1**

5260 **11** *3/4* **Bassino (USA)**[40] 740 4-9-2 **55**........................(h) RachealKneller(5) 13 30
(James Bennett) *hld up in rr: pushed along and hung lft over 1f out: wknd ins fnl f* **9/1**

000- **12** *3* **Rock Of Monaco**[164] 7323 4-9-6 **54**........................................ CamHardie 2 23
(Antony Brittain) *t.k.h: hld up in midfield: rdn over 3f out: lost pl over 1f out: wknd ins fnl f* **50/1**

-000 **P** **Bella's Boy (IRE)**[16] 1139 4-8-12 **46** oh1..................(b[1]) MartinHarley 11
(John Ryan) *v.s.a and immediately p.u* **100/1**

1m 50.3s (0.20) **Going Correction** +0.025s/f (Slow) **13** Ran SP% **117.1**
Speed ratings (Par 101): **100,99,96,96,96 94,93,92,91,87 87,84,**
CSF £56.21 CT £1250.09 TOTE £8.70: £3.00, £4.30, £6.20; EX 62.00 Trifecta £1215.00.
**Owner** Eclipse Horse Racing **Bred** Nanallac Stud **Trained** Rock, Worcs
■ Stewards' Enquiry : Liam Keniry two day ban (10-11 April) - used whip above the permitted level

**FOCUS**
Moderate fare, but the winner is unexposed and should progress. The second and third are the key to the level.

## 1407 SUNBETS.CO.UK H'CAP (DIV I) 7f 36y (Tp)
**4:50** (4:51) (Class 6) (0-55,57) 4-Y-0+ **£2,749** (£818; £408; £204) **Stalls** High

Form RPR

3425 **1** **Tavener**[3] 1338 5-9-9 **57**.....................................................(p) DavidAllan 9 65
(David C Griffiths) *mde all: rdn and fnd ex over 1f out: in command and styd on ins fnl f: rdn out* **9/4**[1]

06-0 **2** *1 1/4* **Magic Moments**[30] 929 4-9-7 **55**.................................... MartinHarley 5 60
(Alan King) *wnt rt s: chsd ldrs: rdn wl over 1f out: kpt on but no imp on wnr ins fnl f: wnt 2nd cl home* **7/1**

6-43 **3** *nk* **Frank Cool**[19] 1080 4-9-6 **54**....................................... GeorgeDowning 10 58
(Tony Carroll) *t.k.h: chsd wnr: rdn wl over 1f out: kpt on same pce ins fnl f: lost 2nd cl home* **4/1**[2]

0-55 **4** *1 1/2* **Caledonian Gold**[7] 1285 4-9-9 **57**.................................... JoeyHaynes 3 58
(Paul D'Arcy) *mounted on crse and taken down early: rousted along leaving stalls: in tch in midfield: effrt over 1f out: kpt on same pce ins fnl f* **13/2**[3]

5301 **5** *1 1/4* **Fossa**[20] 1075 7-8-12 **51**.........................................(h) CharlieBennett(5) 2 50+
(Mark Brisbourne) *hld up in tch towards rr: nt clr run over 1f out: pushed along and hdwy 1f out: r.o ins fnl f: no threat to ldrs* **8/1**

4640 **6** *nk* **Quintus Cerialis (IRE)**[7] 1285 5-9-5 **53**........................(tp) TimmyMurphy 11 50
(Karen George) *rousted along leaving stalls: in tch in midfield: effrt 2f out: unable qck and kpt on same pce ins fnl f* **14/1**

00-0 **7** *1 1/4* **Tom's Anna (IRE)**[51] 579 7-8-5 **46** oh1.......................... PaulaMuir(7) 6 40
(Sean Regan) *dwlt and sltly hmpd leaving stalls: hld up in tch in rr: effrt wd over 1f out: kpt on: nvr trbld ldrs* **33/1**

0000 **8** *nk* **Insolenceofoffice (IRE)**[25] 981 9-8-7 **48**.........(v) CallumRodriguez(7) 8 42
(Richard Ford) *chsd ldrs: rdn 2f out: edgd lft and outpcd 1f out: wknd ins fnl f* **25/1**

0304 **9** *1 1/4* **National Service (USA)**[2] 1372 6-9-0 **48**......................(tp) RyanPowell 1 39
(Clare Ellam) *t.k.h: hld up in tch in rr: effrt over 1f out: no imp* **12/1**

60-0 **10** *6* **Hab Reeh**[12] 1209 9-9-2 **50**...............................................(p) JamesSullivan 4 27
(Ruth Carr) *in tch in midfield: rdn and unable qck over 1f out: wknd fnl f* **25/1**

0-00 **11** *25* **Love In The Dark**[46] 644 4-8-12 **46** oh1..........................(h) LukeMorris 7
(Nikki Evans) *hung rt and plld hrd: in tch in rr: hung bdly rt 3f out: sn lost tch and eased: t.o* **100/1**

1m 28.43s (-0.37) **Going Correction** +0.025s/f (Slow) **11** Ran SP% **113.7**
Speed ratings (Par 101): **103,101,101,99,98 97,96,95,94,87 59**
CSF £16.90 CT £59.58 TOTE £3.40: £1.30, £2.20, £2.40; EX 20.80 Trifecta £86.10.
**Owner** Baker, Hensby, Longden, Baker **Bred** Car Colston Hall Stud **Trained** Bawtry, S Yorks

**FOCUS**
The pace held up and few got involved.

## 1408 SUNBETS.CO.UK H'CAP (DIV II) 7f 36y (Tp)
**5:20** (5:20) (Class 6) (0-55,57) 4-Y-0+ **£2,749** (£818; £408; £204) **Stalls** High

Form RPR

566- **1** **Grey Destiny**[143] 7794 7-9-7 **55**.............................................. CamHardie 8 61
(Antony Brittain) *dwlt: t.k.h: hld up in tch in last trio: hdwy to chse ldrs 1f out: swtchd rt ins fnl f: rdn and r.o to ld cl home* **14/1**

2R33 **2** *hd* **Prince Of Time**[26] 969 5-8-7 **48**............................ CallumRodriguez(7) 9 54
(Richard Ford) *in tch in midfield: effrt over 1f out: hdwy u.p and ev ch wl ins fnl f: kpt on* **4/1**[2]

-560 **3** *nk* **Kingstreet Lady**[14] 1180 4-8-12 **46** oh1............................ MartinHarley 7 51
(Richard Price) *chsd ldrs tl rdn to ld ent fnl f: kpt on wl u.p tl hdd and lost 2 pls cl home* **9/1**

0055 **4** *3/4* **Rising Sunshine (IRE)**[5] 1298 4-9-1 **49**..........................(bt) LukeMorris 1 52
(Milton Bradley) *t.k.h: chsd ldrs: effrt and hrd drvn to chse ldr 1f out: edgd lft and kpt on same pce ins fnl f: lost 2 pls towards fin* **15/2**

4514 **5** *1 1/2* **Mr Potter**[18] 1106 4-9-9 **57**........................................(v) ConnorBeasley 10 57
(Richard Guest) *taken down early: stdd after s: hld up in tch in last trio: effrt u.p over 1f out: hung lft 1f out: styd on ins fnl f: nvr trbld ldrs* **9/2**[3]

00-1 **6** *1* **Symbolic Star (IRE)**[26] 969 5-8-13 **54**...............(p) ConnorMurtagh(7) 6 51
(Barry Murtagh) *s.i.s: hld up in tch in last trio: swtchd rt and effrt 2f out: kpt on same pce ins fnl f* **11/4**[1]

00-6 **7** *1 1/2* **Harbour Patrol (IRE)**[18] 1106 5-9-3 **51**........................... DanielTudhope 4 45
(Rebecca Bastiman) *chsd ldr tl rdn to ld 2f out: hdd and no ex jst over 1f out: wknd ins fnl f* **9/1**

-015 **8** *1 3/4* **Dr Red Eye**[38] 784 9-9-4 **52**...........................................(p) KieranO'Neill 2 42
(Scott Dixon) *chsd ldrs: rdn and struggling over 2f out: lost pl over 1f out: wknd fnl f* **12/1**

0-6 **9** *2 3/4* **Any Joy (IRE)**[32] 883 4-9-0 **48**....................................(p[1]) PJMcDonald 3 31
(Ben Haslam) *led: rdn and hdd 2f out: lost pl over 1f out: wknd fnl f* **40/1**

1m 28.51s (-0.29) **Going Correction** +0.025s/f (Slow) **9** Ran SP% **113.4**
Speed ratings (Par 101): **102,101,101,100,98 97,96,94,90**
CSF £68.07 CT £538.81 TOTE £13.30: £3.80, £1.50, £2.80; EX 72.10 Trifecta £693.80.
**Owner** Antony Brittain **Bred** Northgate Lodge Stud Ltd **Trained** Warthill, N Yorks

**FOCUS**
This was run in a similar time to the first division, but this one set up well for the closers. Very modest form.
T/Jkpt: £11,177.50 to a £1 stake. Pool: £22,355.04 - 2.0 winning units. T/Plt: £404.90 to a £1 stake. Pool: £80,609.41 - 145.32 winning units. T/Qpdt: £234.10 to a £1 stake. Pool: £6,862.44 - 21.69 winning units. **Steve Payne**

# 1401 WOLVERHAMPTON (A.W) (L-H)
Tuesday, March 28

**OFFICIAL GOING: Tapeta: standard**
Wind: light, behind Weather: cloud clearing, bright spells

## 1409 SUNBETS.CO.UK DOWNLOAD THE APP APPRENTICE H'CAP 1m 142y (Tp)
**2:20** (2:20) (Class 6) (0-65,67) 4-Y-0+ **£2,587** (£770; £384; £192) **Stalls** Low

Form RPR

-003 **1** **Spiritual Star (IRE)**[20] 1086 8-9-9 **67**.............................. PaddyBradley 5 73
(Lee Carter) *hld up in midfield: effrt over 1f out: hdwy and edgd lft 1f out: rdn to ld ins fnl f: r.o wl* **13/2**[3]

1 **2** *1 1/4* **Lucent Dream (IRE)**[11] 1249 6-9-4 **62**.......................(t) BenRobinson 8 65+
(John C McConnell, Ire) *t.k.h: hld up in last trio: effrt on outer over 1f out: styd on strly ins fnl f: wnt 2nd last strides: nvr getting to wnr* **6/4**[1]

0602 **3** *nk* **All You (IRE)**[5] 1334 5-9-9 **67**..............................(v) PatrickVaughan 2 70+
(David O'Meara) *stdd and dropped in bhd s: hld up in last pair: clsd and nt clr run over 1f out: swtchd rt 1f out: styd on strly fnl 100yds: snatched 3rd last strides: nvr getting to wnr* **4/1**[2]

0-50 **4** *shd* **One For Jodie (IRE)**[12] 1225 6-9-0 **58**.............................(p) JaneElliott 6 61
(Michael Appleby) *t.k.h: led for 1f: chsd ldrs after: clsd and wnt 2nd over 2f out: rdn and ev ch 2f out: led jst ins fnl f: hdd and one pce ins fnl f: lost 2 pls last strides* **12/1**

2116 **5** *nk* **Hold Firm**[12] 1225 5-8-11 **60**......................................... GabrieleMalune(5) 9 62
(Mark H Tompkins) *t.k.h: w ldrs tl dropped bk into 4th over 6f out: effrt over 1f out: kpt on same pce ins fnl f* **9/1**

-606 **6** *1/2* **Green Howard**[27] 968 9-9-9 **67**...................................... MeganNicholls 1 68
(Rebecca Bastiman) *hld up in last pair: effrt over 1f out: clsd and swtchd lft 1f out: kpt on ins fnl f: no threat to wnr* **16/1**

55-0 **6** *dht* **Stormbound (IRE)**[20] 1086 8-8-12 **63**.................. PaulStJohn-Dennis(7) 3 64
(Paul Cole) *midfield: effrt 2f out: hdwy and swtchd lft ent fnl f: kpt on same pce ins fnl f* **16/1**

000- **8** *2* **Gambino (IRE)**[245] 4729 7-9-2 **65**............................ ConnorMurtagh(5) 7 62
(John David Riches) *awkward leaving stalls: t.k.h: led after 1f and set v slow gallop: strode on and wnt clr 6f out: shkn up over 1f out: rdn and hdd jst ins fnl f: wknd wl ins fnl f* **20/1**

00-0 **9** *hd* **Pc Dixon**[66] 351 4-8-10 **61**............................................. LenkaHelmecka(7) 4 57
(Mick Channon) *t.k.h: chsd ldr after 1f: lost 2nd but stl clsng on ldr over 2f out: rdn and outpcd 2f out: wknd ins fnl f: sddle slipped* **14/1**

1m 55.65s (5.55) **Going Correction** -0.05s/f (Stan) **9** Ran SP% **114.2**
Speed ratings (Par 101): **73,71,71,71,71 70,70,69,68**
CSF £16.43 CT £44.34 TOTE £8.00: £1.90, £1.50, £1.30; EX 20.40 Trifecta £72.30.
**Owner** Wackey Racers Harefield **Bred** John Quigley **Trained** Epsom, Surrey

**FOCUS**
Muddling form. They hacked around at a steady pace early on, so this wasn't a true test, and several of these were keen. The form is unlikely to prove much of a literal guide.

## 1410 SUNBETS.CO.UK MEDIAN AUCTION MAIDEN STKS 1m 142y (Tp)
**2:50** (2:51) (Class 6) 3-5-Y-0 **£2,587** (£770; £384; £192) **Stalls** Low

Form RPR

0 **1** **William Sayle**[55] 503 3-8-9 0......................................... AndreaAtzeni 2 79+
(John Gosden) *bmpd leaving stalls: chsd clr ldr: clsd on ldr 3f out: rdn to ld 1f out: styd on strly and sn in command: readily* **7/4**[1]

3- **2** *2* **Golden Wolf (IRE)**[139] 7865 3-8-9 0................................. ShaneKelly 1 73
(Richard Hughes) *t.k.h: stdd after s: hld up off the pce in 4th: wnt 3rd 4f out: clsd on ldr 3f out: rdn and unable qck over 1f out: edgd lft 1f out: kpt on to go 2nd wl ins fnl f: no threat to wnr* **2/1**[2]

002- **3** *1* **Armagnac (IRE)**[136] 7941 3-8-9 69........................... JamieSpencer 6 71
(Michael Bell) *led and sn clr: pressed and drvn 2f out: hdd 1f out: sn outpcd: wknd and lost 2nd wl ins fnl f* **5/2**[3]

2-30 **4** *3 3/4* **Major Cornwallis (IRE)**[24] 1029 3-8-9 69........................ PaulHanagan 4 63
(Richard Fahey) *racd off the pce in 3rd tl over 3f out: 4th and sme hdwy over 2f out: no imp over 1f out: wknd ins fnl f* **8/1**

6-0 **5** *8* **Diamante (IRE)**[38] 814 3-8-4 0..................................... KieranO'Neill 3 41
(Daniel Kubler) *stdd and wnt lft leaving s: a same pl and nvr on terms: rdn over 2f out: wl btn over 1f out* **150/1**

**6** *20* **Forestry** 3-8-2 0............................................. Pierre-LouisJamin(7) 7 4
(Jonathan Portman) *s.i.s: a off the pce in 6th: lost tch over 2f out* **50/1**

**7** *4 1/2* **Bite My Tongue (IRE)** 4-9-7 0..................................... AledBeech(7) 5
(Tony Carroll) *uns rdr on way to s: stdd and awkward laving stalls: a wl off the pce in rr: lost tch 3f out: t.o* **200/1**

1m 49.43s (-0.67) **Going Correction** -0.05s/f (Stan)
**WFA** 3 from 4yo 19lb **7** Ran SP% **112.5**
Speed ratings (Par 101): **100,98,97,94,86 69,65**
CSF £5.40 TOTE £2.80: £1.10, £1.70; EX 6.70 Trifecta £10.80.
**Owner** HRH Princess Haya Of Jordan **Bred** Lady Hardy **Trained** Newmarket, Suffolk

**FOCUS**
Probably no more than a fair maiden but the winner looks quite nice. The form is rated around the third's last run.

## 1411 32RED.COM H'CAP 7f 36y (Tp)
**3:20** (3:21) (Class 5) (0-75,77) 3-Y-0 **£3,881** (£1,155; £577; £288) **Stalls** High

Form RPR

0-21 **1** **Dark Destroyer (IRE)**[53] 545 3-9-7 **75**................................... JFEgan 10 82
(Joseph Tuite) *hld up in tch in midfield: hdwy to chse ldrs on outer 4f out: rdn and qcknd to ld over 1f out: in command and r.o wl ins fnl f* **3/1**[1]

-253 **2** *3/4* **Sidewinder (IRE)**[17] 1149 3-9-4 **72**............................ RichardKingscote 1 77
(Tom Dascombe) *chsd ldr for 1f: trckd ldrs after: nt clr run jst over 2f out: swtchd rt and effrt over 1f out: rdn and hdwy to chse wnr jst ins fnl f: r.o but no threat wnr* **7/2**[2]

0-41 **3** *1 1/2* **Revel**[69] 284 3-9-9 **77**..................................................(t) JamieSpencer 9 78
(Stuart Williams) *stdd s: t.k.h: hld up in tch in last trio: effrt wd wl over 1f out: styd on u.p ins fnl f: no threat to wnr* **4/1**[3]

3162 **4** *1/2* **Mia Cara**[6] 1306 3-8-13 **67**.........................................(v) AndrewMullen 6 67
(David Evans) *t.k.h: hld up in tch: hmpd and snatched up after 1f: effrt on inner over 1f out: chsd ldrs and kpt on same pce u.p ins fnl f* **8/1**

2331 **5** ¾ **Bazwind (IRE)**$^{36}$ [846] 3-8-12 **66**........(p) SeanLevey 7 64
(David Evans) *chsd ldrs: effrt 2f out: keeping on same pce and hld whn sltly impeded ins fnl f* **8/1**

00-3 **6** 1 ¾ **Hidden Stash**$^{14}$ [1194] 3-9-0 **68**........ DavidProbert 8 61
(Andrew Balding) *rousted along leaving stalls: chsd ldr after 1f: rdn and ev ch 2f out tl unable qck w wnr 1f out: wknd ins fnl f* **14/1**

10-0 **7** 2 **Tor**$^{17}$ [1149] 3-9-7 **75**........ TomEaves 2 63
(Iain Jardine) *stdd s: hld up in tch in last trio: effrt 2f out: edgd lft and no hdwy over 1f out: nvr trbld ldrs* **66/1**

045- **8** nk **Justice Frederick (IRE)**$^{160}$ [7469] 3-9-8 **76**........ JoeyHaynes 3 63
(Paul D'Arcy) *led: rdn 2f out: hdd and unable qck w wnr over 1f out: wknd ins fnl f* **14/1**

523- **9** 3 **Lightoller (IRE)**$^{226}$ [5433] 3-8-13 **67**........ RobHornby 5 47
(Mick Channon) *in tch in midfield: dropped to last trio over 3f out: no hdwy u.p over 1f out: wknd ins fnl f* **20/1**

0356 **10** nse **Naupaka**$^{24}$ [1029] 3-8-4 **65**........ BenRobinson$^{(7)}$ 4 44
(Brian Ellison) *stdd s: hld up in tch in rr: effrt jst over 2f out: no prog: n.d* **25/1**

1m 28.92s (0.12) **Going Correction** -0.05s/f (Stan) **10** Ran SP% **112.9**
Speed ratings (Par 98): **97,96,94,93,93 91,88,88,84,84**
CSF £12.64 CT £41.62 TOTE £4.00: £1.40, £1.30, £1.80; EX 15.20 Trifecta £41.40.
**Owner** P Gleeson & Goldrush Thoroughbreds **Bred** Castle Estates **Trained** Lambourn, Berks

**FOCUS**
A fair race of its type and a winner to follow. Good efforts from the next two aswell.

## 1412 BETWAY H'CAP — 1m 5f 194y
**3:50** (3:51) (Class 5) (0-75,72) 4-Y-O+ **£3,881** (£1,155; £577; £288) **Stalls** Low

Form RPR

55-1 **1** **Monjeni**$^{14}$ [1191] 4-9-2 **66**........(p) StevieDonohoe 1 75+
(Ian Williams) *trckd ldrs: nt clr run 3f out tl gap opened and effrt to chse ldr over 1f out: edgd lft u.p to rail ins fnl f: r.o wl to ld 50yds out: sn in command* **9/4**$^{2}$

1 **2** ½ **Shamash (IRE)**$^{10}$ [1257] 5-9-10 **70**........(t) PaulHanagan 4 77
(John C McConnell, Ire) *t.k.h and styd wd early: chsd ldr tl 9f out: dropped to last but stl wl in tch 8f out: hdwy to ld 2f out: sn rdn: hdd and no ex fnl 50yds* **10/11**$^{1}$

1654 **3** 4 ½ **Oratorio's Joy (IRE)**$^{15}$ [1175] 7-9-12 **72**........(p) TimmyMurphy 3 72
(Jamie Osborne) *s.i.s and bustled along early: hdwy to chse ldr 9f out: rdn over 3f out: outpcd 2f out: wknd ins fnl f* **8/1**

4144 **4** 10 **Free Bounty**$^{20}$ [1092] 4-9-4 **68**........(t) DavidProbert 2 54
(Philip McBride) *led tl drvn and hdd 2f out: sn outpcd and wknd* **11/2**$^{3}$

3m 1.99s (-2.81) **Going Correction** -0.05s/f (Stan)
**WFA** 4 from 5yo+ 2lb **4** Ran SP% **109.6**
Speed ratings (Par 103): **106,105,103,97**
CSF £4.81 TOTE £2.10; EX 5.10 Trifecta £10.80.
**Owner** Ian Williams **Bred** The Kathryn Stud **Trained** Portway, Worcs

**FOCUS**
Only four runners, but the front two are progressive.

## 1413 BETWAY SPRINT H'CAP — 5f 21y (Tp)
**4:20** (4:20) (Class 6) (0-60,60) 4-Y-O+ **£2,587** (£770; £384; £192) **Stalls** Low

Form RPR

620 **1** **Cruise Tothelimit (IRE)**$^{22}$ [1062] 9-9-0 **60**........(vt) CallumRodriguez$^{(7)}$ 6 68
(Patrick Morris) *sn led and mde rest: drifted rt wl over 1f out: kpt on wl u.p ins fnl f: rdn out* **6/1**$^{3}$

0534 **2** 1 ¼ **See Vermont**$^{18}$ [1126] 9-9-3 **56**........(p) DanielTudhope 5 63
(Rebecca Bastiman) *dwlt: hld up in tch in last pair: clsd whn hmpd over 1f out: swtchd rt 1f out: hdwy ins fnl f: wnt 2nd wl ins fnl f: styd on: nvr getting to wnr* **3/1**$^{2}$

0333 **3** hd **Loumarin (IRE)**$^{5}$ [1328] 5-9-5 **58**........(p) SilvestreDeSousa 7 61
(Michael Appleby) *in tch in 4th but sn pushed along: lost pl and hung rt 2f out: rallied u.p ins fnl f: styd on wl fnl 100yds: nvr getting to wnr* **13/8**$^{1}$

4336 **4** 1 ¼ **Penny Dreadful**$^{15}$ [1180] 5-9-4 **57**........(p) KieranO'Neill 3 55
(Scott Dixon) *broke wl: sn restrained and t.k.h in 3rd: effrt 2f out: no ex u.p jst ins fnl f: wknd wl ins fnl f* **13/2**

2642 **5** nse **Pearl Noir**$^{25}$ [1006] 7-8-9 **55**........(b) RPWalsh$^{(7)}$ 1 53
(Scott Dixon) *bustled along leaving stalls: sn chsng ldr: swtchd lft over 1f out: no ex u.p jst ins fnl f: wknd wl ins fnl f* **8/1**

0-00 **6** 1 ¼ **Toni's A Star**$^{41}$ [743] 5-9-4 **57**........ GeorgeDowning 2 51
(Tony Carroll) *hld up in last pair: effrt over 1f out: no imp fnl f* **10/1**

1m 1.58s (-0.32) **Going Correction** -0.05s/f (Stan) **6** Ran SP% **110.9**
Speed ratings (Par 101): **100,98,97,95,95 93**
CSF £23.57 TOTE £6.10: £2.00, £6.30; EX 22.20 Trifecta £61.40.
**Owner** Odysian Ltd T/A Cruise Nightspot **Bred** D And Mrs D Veitch **Trained** Prescot, Merseyside

**FOCUS**
A moderate sprint handicap. The winner is rated to last November's form here.

## 1414 BETWAY MAIDEN STKS — 1m 4f 51y (Tp)
**4:50** (4:50) (Class 5) 3-Y-O **£3,881** (£1,155; £577; £288) **Stalls** Low

Form RPR

3- **1** **Count Octave**$^{170}$ [7187] 3-9-5 0........ DavidProbert 4 92+
(Andrew Balding) *trckd ldr tl clsd and upsides 2f out: pushed along to ld 1f out: rn green but asserted ins fnl f: pushed out* **30/100**$^{1}$

44 **2** 3 **Utopian Dream**$^{34}$ [862] 3-9-0 0........(b$^{1}$) AndreaAtzeni 5 82
(John Gosden) *led: rdn wl over 1f out: hdd 1f out: no ex and outpcd ins fnl f* **3/1**$^{2}$

66 **3** 30 **Elite Icon**$^{39}$ [777] 3-9-5 0........ MartinDwyer 1 39
(Iain Jardine) *hld up off the pce in 3rd: clsd over 4f out: rdn and outpcd over 3f out: no ch after* **66/1**

06 **4** 1 ¾ **Astrostorm**$^{34}$ [855] 3-9-5 0........ StevieDonohoe 3 36
(Mark H Tompkins) *hld up off the pce in 4th: clsd over 4f out: rdn and outpcd over 3f out: no ch after* **66/1**

**5** 7 **Piccoloro** 3-9-5 0........ RenatoSouza 2 25
(Jonathan Portman) *s.i.s: hld up in rr: nvr on terms: lost tch 3f out: t.o* **25/1**$^{3}$

2m 37.98s (-2.82) **Going Correction** -0.05s/f (Stan) **5** Ran SP% **108.8**
Speed ratings (Par 98): **107,105,85,83,79**
CSF £1.40 TOTE £1.40: £1.10, £1.30; EX 1.60 Trifecta £5.80.
**Owner** Qatar Racing Limited **Bred** Qatar Bloodstock Ltd **Trained** Kingsclere, Hants

**FOCUS**
Essentially a race match race. It's worth giving a chance to this form.
T/Plt: £12.30 to a £1 stake. Pool: £69,128.97 - 4,100.47 winning units T/Qpdt: £8.00 to a £1 stake. Pool: £4,379.24 - 403.59 winning units **Steve Payne**

1415 - 1416a (Foreign Racing) - See Raceform Interactive

# $^{1335}$SAINT-CLOUD (L-H)
Tuesday, March 28

**OFFICIAL GOING: Turf: soft**

## 1417a PRIX DE CHATOU (CLAIMER) (3YO) (TURF) — 7f
**2:50** 3-Y-O **£9,829** (£3,931; £2,948; £1,965; £982)

RPR

**1** **Zouk (FR)**$^{14}$ 3-9-1 0........ LouisBeuzelin 9 77
(P Bary, France) **36/5**

**2** ¾ **Weekfair (FR)**$^{21}$ 3-8-8 0........(p) RonanThomas 2 68
(J Phelippon, France) **217/10**

**3** shd **Elusive Blue (GER)**$^{20}$ 3-9-1 0........ Pierre-CharlesBoudot 6 75
(J Phelippon, France) **19/5**$^{2}$

**4** 1 ¼ **Sirma Traou Land (FR)**$^{159}$ [7490] 3-8-5 0........ MlleAdelineMerou$^{(10)}$ 10 67
(B De Montzey, France) **41/5**

**5** nk **Tap Tap Boom**$^{146}$ [7768] 3-9-4 0........ MaximeGuyon 11 74
(George Baker) *wl into stride: settled bhd ldr: rdn to chal over 2f out: drvn over 1f out and styd on one pce fnl f* **39/10**$^{3}$

**6** 3 **La Undecima (FR)**$^{47}$ 3-8-8 0........ VincentCheminaud 7 55
(M Delcher Sanchez, France) **152/10**

**7** ¾ **Danarosa (IRE)**$^{34}$ 3-9-3 0........ JeffersonSmith$^{(5)}$ 8 67
(Simone Brogi, France) **11/5**$^{1}$

**8** 3 **Silver Poker (FR)**$^{167}$ [7293] 3-8-11 0........ ThibaultSpeicher$^{(4)}$ 5 52
(D Chenu, France) **69/1**

**9** 10 **Tawaret (FR)**$^{18}$ [1137] 3-9-1 0........(p) AntoineHamelin 1 25
(Mme M-C Naim, France) **158/10**

**10** shd **La Testerine (FR)**$^{239}$ [4965] 3-8-0 0........ FlorentMalbran$^{(8)}$ 3 18
(F Chappet, France) **70/1**

**11** 3 ½ **Tu Te Calmes (FR)**$^{17}$ 3-8-11 0........(b) TonyPiccone 4 12
(F Chappet, France) **26/1**

1m 28.55s (-3.65) **11** Ran SP% **118.6**
PARI-MUTUEL (all including 1 euro stake): WIN 8.20 PLACE 2.10, 3.00, 2.10 DF 51.00 SF 82.90.
**Owner** Galileo Racing Inc **Bred** Haras De La Huderie **Trained** Chantilly, France

# $^{1298}$KEMPTON (A.W) (R-H)
Wednesday, March 29

**OFFICIAL GOING: Polytrack: standard**
Wind: Moderate, across (away from stands) Weather: Cloudy

## 1418 100% PROFIT BOOST AT 32REDSPORT.COM APPRENTICE H'CAP — 6f (P)
**5:55** (5:55) (Class 6) (0-60,62) 3-Y-O **£2,264** (£673; £336; £168) **Stalls** Low

Form RPR

-650 **1** **Brother In Arms (IRE)**$^{21}$ [1088] 3-8-11 **60**........ AledBeech$^{(10)}$ 4 66
(Tony Carroll) *hld up in last pair: prog on inner fr 2f out: sustained effrt to ld jst ins fnl f: styd on wl* **5/1**$^{2}$

**2** ½ **Dulcina**$^{145}$ [7799] 3-8-1 **47**........ SeanDavis$^{(7)}$ 6 51
(R P McNamara, Ire) *hld up in last pair: prog on outer over 1f out: rdn to chal jst ins fnl f: styd on but jst outpcd by wnr* **3/1**$^{1}$

406- **3** 1 ½ **Tea El Tee (IRE)**$^{106}$ [8344] 3-8-9 **53**........(p) DavidEgan$^{(5)}$ 5 53
(Gay Kelleway) *t.k.h: hld up in 5th: clsd on ldrs 2f out: rdn to chal and edgd lft 1f out: outpcd by ldng pair after* **5/1**$^{2}$

2266 **4** ¾ **Celerity (IRE)**$^{4}$ [1363] 3-8-2 **51**........(v) KeelanBaker$^{(10)}$ 2 48
(David Evans) *n.m.r s: sn rcvrd and chsd ldr after 2f: rdn and tried to chal fr 2f out: nt qckn over 1f out: one pce after* **12/1**

640 **5** hd **Fun Raiser (IRE)**$^{21}$ [1083] 3-9-6 **59**........(v$^{1}$) CharlieBennett 1 56
(Harry Dunlop) *t.k.h: led: pressed fr over 1f out: hdd and fdd jst ins fnl f* **14/1**

05-4 **6** 2 ½ **Coping Stone**$^{21}$ [1088] 3-9-1 **61**........(p$^{1}$) FinleyMarsh$^{(7)}$ 9 50
(David Brown) *hld up in 6th: rdn to cl on ldrs fr 2f out: finding little whn nt clr run fnl f: wknd* **11/2**$^{3}$

60-2 **7** 5 **Sir Harry Collins (IRE)**$^{4}$ [1359] 3-8-11 **53**........ JoshuaBryan$^{(3)}$ 7 27
(Richard Spencer) *t.k.h: trckd ldrs: shkn up over 2f out: hanging lft and no rspnse: sn wknd* **3/1**$^{1}$

-650 **8** 2 ¾ **Dixie's Double**$^{12}$ [1242] 3-9-9 **62**........ GeorgeWood 8 28
(Daniel Kubler) *chsd ldr 2f: rdn whn hung bdly lft bnd 3f out: sn bhd* **16/1**

1m 13.6s (0.50) **Going Correction** 0.0s/f (Stan) **8** Ran SP% **119.0**
Speed ratings (Par 96): **96,95,93,92,92 88,82,78**
CSF £21.34 CT £80.43 TOTE £5.30: £1.60, £2.10, £1.70; EX 34.90 Trifecta £167.20.
**Owner** Cover Point Racing **Bred** Patrick Roche **Trained** Cropthorne, Worcs

**FOCUS**
The finish was contested by a lightly raced pair who both came from the rear. Fair form for the grade, rated around the second.

## 1419 32RED CASINO H'CAP — 7f (P)
**6:25** (6:25) (Class 5) (0-70,72) 4-Y-O+ **£2,911** (£866; £432; £216) **Stalls** Low

Form RPR

360- **1** **Gulland Rock**$^{97}$ [8490] 6-9-6 **68**........ WilliamCarson 4 74
(Anthony Carson) *mde all: rdn and sent for home jst over 2f out: kpt on u.p: jst clung on* **12/1**

0-30 **2** nk **Light From Mars**$^{21}$ [1085] 12-9-5 **67**........ LukeMorris 5 72
(Ronald Harris) *hld up in last trio: u.p and no prog over 2f out: sed to run on over 1f out: str fin to take 2nd last strides but jst too late* **10/1**

0-06 **3** ½ **Picket Line**$^{23}$ [1063] 5-9-9 **71**........ TimmyMurphy 3 75
(Geoffrey Deacon) *t.k.h: hld up disputing 5th: prog jst over 2f out: rdn to chse wnr ins fnl f: kpt on but a hld and lost 2nd last strides* **8/1**

1-01 **4** ¾ **Admirable Art (IRE)**$^{30}$ [954] 7-9-6 **68**........ AdamKirby 2 70
(Tony Carroll) *pressed ldng pair tl chsd wnr jst over 2f out: tried to cl over 1f out: kpt on but lost 2nd ins fnl f* **8/1**

5 **5** nk **The Yellow Bus**$^{23}$ [1066] 4-9-10 **72**........ JosephineGordon 6 73
(Michael Wigham) *hld up in last trio: rdn 2f out: kpt on fr over 1f out but nvr pce to threaten* **9/2**$^{2}$

00-6 **6** 1 **Classic Pursuit**$^{9}$ [1290] 6-9-5 **67**........(p) SilvestreDeSousa 8 65
(Michael Appleby) *t.k.h: sn chsd wnr: rdn and fnd little over 2f out: sn lost 2nd: one pce after* **4/1**$^{1}$

0-00 **7** ½ **Flying Fantasy**$^{41}$ [760] 5-9-7 **69**........ SeanLevey 1 66
(Stuart Williams) *hld up disputing 5th: effrt on inner 2f out: nt qckn jst over 1f out: steadily fdd* **6/1**$^{3}$

6050 **8** *nse* **Dominium (USA)**[21] 1080 10-8-10 **63**........................(b) DavidParkes(5) 9 60+
(Jeremy Gask) *stdd after s fr wd draw and hld up in last: rdn over 2f out: stl last 1f out and nvr any hope: styd on nr fin* **14/1**

2-53 **9** *nk* **Inshaa**[14] 1203 5-9-4 **66**........................ TomEaves 7 64
(Michael Herrington) *t.k.h: trckd ldrs: rdn over 2f out: losing pl whn nudged by rival fnl f: eased* **9/2**[2]

1m 25.51s (-0.49) **Going Correction** 0.0s/f (Stan) **9** Ran SP% **116.3**
Speed ratings (Par 103): **102,101,101,100,99 98,98,98,97**
CSF £125.52 CT £1023.82 TOTE £14.30: £3.50, £2.80, £11.70; EX 101.10 Trifecta £1315.30.
**Owner** W H Carson **Bred** Whitsbury Manor Stud **Trained** Newmarket, Suffolk

**FOCUS**
The winner dictated an ordinary initial pace in this modest handicap. They finished in a heap, covered by around three and a half lengths at the line. A small pb from the winner.

## 1420 32RED ON THE APP STORE MAIDEN STKS 1m 2f 219y(P)
**6:55** (6:57) (Class 5) 3-4-Y-O **£2,911** (£866; £432; £216) **Stalls** Low

Form RPR

**1** **Eskendash (USA)**[53] 4-10-0 0........................ AdamKirby 9 74+
(Pam Sly) *dwlt: hld up towards rr: prog over 3f out: tk 2nd 2f out and sn chalng: edgd rt but led jst over 1f out: styd on wl and a jst holding on* **5/2**[1]

03 **2** *nk* **Chippenham (IRE)**[15] 1190 3-8-8 0........................(b) SilvestreDeSousa 2 71
(John Gosden) *prom: trckd ldr 1/2-way: led 3f out: sn pressed and shkn up: pressed again 2f out: hdd and edgd rt jst over 1f out: kpt on wl fnl f but a jst hld* **11/4**[2]

53 **3** *4 ½* **Temir Kazyk**[12] 1239 3-8-8 0........................ TomEaves 4 64+
(David Simcock) *towards rr: pushed along over 2f out: prog to take 3rd jst over 1f out: no threat to ldng pair but styd on to draw clr of rest* **10/1**

0- **4** *5* **Sehail (USA)**[148] 7753 4-10-0 0........................ StevieDonohoe 3 59
(George Peckham) *chsd ldr to 1/2-way: rdn and lost pl over 3f out: plugged on to take 4th last strides* **66/1**

**5** *½* **Reel Leisure (GR)**[43] 4-9-9 0........................(e[1]) JimCrowley 8 53
(Amanda Perrett) *t.k.h: hld up in midfield: prog 4f out: pressed ldr wl over 2f out to 2f out: sn wknd: lost 4th last strides* **16/1**

0/ **6** *¾* **Hawkerland (IRE)**[606] 4859 4-9-7 0........................ TylerSaunders(7) 1 57
(Marcus Tregoning) *coltish preliminaries: chsd ldng trio to 5f out: steadily lost pl: shkn up in rr over 2f out: plugged on* **7/2**[3]

**7** *2* **I'm Running Late** 3-8-8 0........................ RobHornby 7 51
(Dean Ivory) *rn green and mostly in last: sme prog fr 2f out: no hdwy 1f out and nvr a threat* **25/1**

**8** *1 ¾* **Altyn Alqa** 3-8-3 0........................ LukeMorris 6 43
(Clive Cox) *chsd ldrs but rn green and sn pushed along: steadily wknd fr 3f out* **4/1**

**9** *1 ¾* **C'Est No Mour (GER)**[20] 4-10-0 0........................ MartinLane 5 48
(Peter Hedger) *slowly away: hld up in last pair: shkn up and no prog 3f out* **40/1**

6 **10** *24* **Moorea**[12] 1241 3-8-8 0........................ AdamBeschizza 10 7
(John Bridger) *led to 3f out: wknd rapidly: t.o* **250/1**

2m 23.0s (1.10) **Going Correction** 0.0s/f (Stan)
**WFA** 3 from 4yo 21lb **10** Ran SP% **120.6**
Speed ratings (Par 103): **96,95,92,88,88 87,86,85,83,66**
CSF £9.90 TOTE £3.40: £1.10, £1.50, £2.40; EX 14.10 Trifecta £70.10.
**Owner** Boyle Racing **Bred** B D Gibbs Farm Llc & Chancey Mill Farm **Trained** Thorney, Cambs

**FOCUS**
The pace slowed appreciably mid-race and the first two did well to pull clear. Probably ordinary maiden form overall.

## 1421 RACING UK IN GLORIOUS HD H'CAP 1m (P)
**7:25** (7:25) (Class 6) (0-60,62) 3-Y-O **£2,264** (£673; £336; £168) **Stalls** Low

Form RPR

032- **1** **Sir Plato (IRE)**[200] 6313 3-9-4 **57**........................ OisinMurphy 11 63
(Rod Millman) *led after 1f and dictated mod pce: committed for home jst over 2f out: drvn over 1f out: kpt on wl after* **8/1**

5-35 **2** *1 ¼* **Whatalove**[27] 987 3-8-2 **46**........................ GeorgeWood(5) 5 49
(Martin Keighley) *led 1f: sn in 3rd: chsd wnr wl over 1f out: drvn and styd on but nvr quite able to chal* **7/1**[3]

-362 **3** *¾* **No Not Again (IRE)**[27] 987 3-9-6 **62**........................ HollieDoyle(3) 7 63
(Richard Hannon) *cl up on inner: rdn whn pce lifted jst over 2f out: wnt 3rd over 1f out: styd on but no imp last 150yds* **4/1**[2]

0425 **4** *1* **Masquerade Bling (IRE)**[12] 1242 3-9-2 **55**........................ RobHornby 3 54
(Simon Hodgson) *hld up in 8th in modly run contest: rdn and prog fr 2f out: tk 4th ins fnl f but no ch to threaten* **8/1**

-503 **5** *nse* **De Vegas Kid (IRE)**[19] 1123 3-9-5 **58**........................(p) GeorgeDowning 6 57+
(Tony Carroll) *hld up in 7th: rdn and outpcd whn pce lifted jst over 2f out: no ch after but styd on wl on wd outside ins fnl f* **10/1**

-000 **6** *¾* **Dragon Dream (IRE)**[26] 1000 3-9-4 **57**........................ MartinLane 2 54
(Roger Ingram) *sn hld up in midfield: rdn whn pce lifted jst over 2f out: tk 4th briefly 1f out but no ch to threaten ldrs* **14/1**

500- **7** *¾* **Legendoire (IRE)**[119] 8153 3-9-6 **59**........................ FergusSweeney 8 54
(John Gallagher) *t.k.h: plld way through to press wnr after 2f: rdn over 2f out: lost 2nd and fdd wl over 1f out* **14/1**

00-0 **8** *hd* **Follow Me (IRE)**[39] 814 3-9-3 **56**........................ KieranO'Neill 4 51
(Lee Carter) *hld up in last pair in modly run contest: rdn over 2f out: no great prog* **40/1**

0-61 **9** *1 ¼* **Chamasay**[8] 1297 3-8-1 **47**........................ DavidEgan(7) 9 39
(David Evans) *trapped out wd in midfield: rdn over 2f out: steadily wknd* **15/8**[1]

6410 **10** *hd* **Oakley Pride (IRE)**[33] 895 3-9-4 **62**........................(bt) CliffordLee(5) 1 54
(Gay Kelleway) *hld up in last pair in modly run contest: effrt on inner 2f out but ldrs already gone: no prog* **14/1**

1m 41.3s (1.50) **Going Correction** 0.0s/f (Stan) **10** Ran SP% **121.0**
Speed ratings (Par 96): **92,90,90,89,88 88,87,87,86,85**
CSF £65.44 CT £268.49 TOTE £10.40: £2.80, £2.30, £1.50; EX 67.90 Trifecta £467.30.
**Owner** The Sir Plato Partnership **Bred** Noel Finegan **Trained** Kentisbeare, Devon

**FOCUS**
This was steadily run, the winner setting his own fractions, and it paid to be prominent.

## 1422 32RED H'CAP (LONDON MILE SERIES QUALIFIER) 1m (P)
**7:55** (7:56) (Class 4) (0-85,87) 4-Y-O+ **£4,690** (£1,395; £697; £348) **Stalls** Low

Form RPR

5-32 **1** **The Warrior (IRE)**[9] 1288 5-9-6 **84**........................(e[1]) JimCrowley 4 91
(Amanda Perrett) *hld up in 5th: waiting for a gap 2f out: prog over 1f out: rdn to ld last 150yds: styd on wl* **9/4**[1]

454- **2** *½* **Ballard Down (IRE)**[282] 3465 4-9-6 **84**........................ AdamKirby 9 90
(William Knight) *hld up in rr: shkn up over 2f out: prog over 1f out w hd quite high: r.o wl fnl f to take 2nd last strides* **15/2**[3]

1511 **3** *hd* **Gossiping**[9] 1288 5-9-7 **85** 6ex........................ ShaneKelly 8 90
(Gary Moore) *t.k.h in midfield: prog 2f out: hrd rdn to cl over 1f out: chal ins fnl f: hld by wnr last 100yds and lost 2nd fnl strides* **11/4**[2]

4605 **4** *nk* **Kingston Kurrajong**[14] 1208 4-9-8 **86**........................ AdamBeschizza 10 91
(Michael Attwater) *hld up wl in rr: rdn over 2f out: prog on outer over 1f out: fin wl but too late to rch ldrs* **40/1**

-024 **5** *½* **Special Season**[14] 1208 4-9-9 **87**........................ FergusSweeney 5 91
(Jamie Osborne) *hld up in midfield: prog on inner over 2f out: rdn to ld over 1f out: hdd and no ex last 150yds* **14/1**

5416 **6** *¾* **Berrahri (IRE)**[16] 1178 6-8-9 **73**........................ KierenFox 2 75
(John Best) *led at gd pce: rdn over 2f out: hdd and one pce over 1f out* **20/1**

-013 **7** *nse* **Alejandro (IRE)**[9] 1288 8-9-9 **87**........................ JosephineGordon 1 89
(David Loughnane) *trckd ldng pair: wnt 2nd 2f out to over 1f out: one pce and lost pls after* **8/1**

0345 **8** *4* **Black Dave (IRE)**[26] 998 7-8-0 **71**........................ DavidEgan(7) 6 64
(David Evans) *chsd ldr to 2f out: sn wknd* **25/1**

-061 **9** *5* **Lacan (IRE)**[23] 1065 6-9-7 **85**........................ OisinMurphy 11 66
(Brett Johnson) *trapped out wd: chsd ldrs to over 2f out: sn wknd* **16/1**

-000 **10** *nk* **Arrowzone**[16] 1178 6-9-2 **80**........................ RyanPowell 7 60
(Kevin Frost) *hld up in rr: rdn and struggling over 2f out: no ch* **50/1**

450- **11** *1 ½* **Royal Reserve**[35] 7189 4-9-2 **80**........................ StevieDonohoe 3 57
(Ian Williams) *sn in last: lost tch 3f out: bhd after* **9/1**

1m 38.31s (-1.49) **Going Correction** 0.0s/f (Stan) **11** Ran SP% **115.9**
Speed ratings (Par 105): **107,106,106,106,105 104,104,100,95,95 93**
CSF £18.54 CT £48.78 TOTE £3.30: £1.30, £2.60, £1.30; EX 21.80 Trifecta £76.30.
**Owner** The Warrior Partnership **Bred** Glenvale Stud **Trained** Pulborough, W Sussex

**FOCUS**
A decent handicap in which the field finished compressed. The time was three seconds quicker than the earlier Class 6 handicap and the form is straightforward.

## 1423 32RED.COM H'CAP 6f (P)
**8:25** (8:25) (Class 4) (0-85,85) 4-Y-O+ **£4,690** (£1,395; £697; £348) **Stalls** Low

Form RPR

3003 **1** **Dutiful Son (IRE)**[7] 1301 7-8-13 **77**........................ JimCrowley 2 85
(Simon Dow) *cl up: trckd ldr over 2f out and sn chalng: rdn to ld over 1f out: kpt on wl fnl f* **4/1**[3]

2350 **2** *1* **Steelriver (IRE)**[30] 957 7-9-4 **82**........................ AdamKirby 5 87
(David Barron) *urged into ld: rdn and pressed 2f out: hdd over 1f out: kpt on u.p* **4/1**[3]

5-12 **3** *1* **Escalating**[15] 1185 5-9-5 **83**........................(t) SilvestreDeSousa 8 85
(Michael Appleby) *t.k.h: trapped out wd in midfield: rdn 2f out: kpt on to take 3rd ins fnl f: nvr pce to chal* **9/4**[1]

0004 **4** *¾* **Swiss Cross**[7] 1302 10-9-0 **78**........................(tp) LukeMorris 6 78
(Phil McEntee) *hld up in last: shkn up over 2f out: sme prog over 1f out: drvn and kpt on same pce: nvr able to threaten* **11/1**

1-22 **5** *1 ¼* **Pretty Bubbles**[47] 660 8-9-7 **85**........................(v) TomQueally 3 81
(J R Jenkins) *hld up in midfield: drvn wl over 1f out: nt qckn and no imp ldrs* **12/1**

34/0 **6** *shd* **Mansfield**[25] 1023 4-9-6 **84**........................ JosephineGordon 1 80
(Michael Wigham) *stdd s: t.k.h: hld up in last pair: prog on inner to chse ldng pair 2f out: no imp over 1f out: fdd ins fnl f* **20/1**

-523 **7** *4* **Sophisticated Heir (IRE)**[54] 551 7-8-11 **80**........................(b) CliffordLee(5) 7 64
(Michael Herrington) *chsd ldr to over 2f out: sn wknd* **7/2**[2]

1m 11.82s (-1.28) **Going Correction** 0.0s/f (Stan) **7** Ran SP% **113.8**
Speed ratings (Par 105): **108,106,105,104,102 102,97**
CSF £20.08 CT £43.42 TOTE £4.90: £2.10, £3.00; EX 22.10 Trifecta £71.40.
**Owner** J C G Chua & Partner **Bred** Lodge Park Stud **Trained** Ashtead, Surrey

**FOCUS**
An ordinary sprint handicap. The winner can rate a bit higher than this.
T/Jkpt: Not won. T/Plt: £178.40 to a £1 stake. Pool: £112,926.96. 462.04 winning units. T/Qpdt: £12.20 to a £1 stake. Pool: £14,957.07. 904.93 winning units. **Jonathan Neesom**

# 1358 LINGFIELD (L-H)
Wednesday, March 29

**OFFICIAL GOING: Polytrack: standard**
Wind: light, behind Weather: drizzle until race 3

## 1424 32RED MEDIAN AUCTION MAIDEN FILLIES' STKS 1m 4f (P)
**2:20** (2:20) (Class 6) 3-Y-O **£2,587** (£770; £384; £192) **Stalls** Low

Form RPR

323 **1** **Bishops Cannings (IRE)**[26] 1001 3-9-0 73........................ RyanMoore 1 67+
(David Elsworth) *trckd ldr tl led 2f out: shkn up and shifted lft jst over 1f out: reminder jst ins fnl f: kpt on and a holding chalr ins fnl f* **1/4**[1]

**2** *1* **Stepney** 3-8-11 0........................ HollieDoyle(3) 2 65+
(Robyn Brisland) *t.k.h: trckd ldrs: dropped to rr and stuck bhd rivals over 2f out: gap opened and rdn to chal on inner whn bmpd jst over 1f out: kpt on but a hld ins fnl f: wandered rt towards fin* **6/1**[2]

66- **3** *10* **Mystical Nelly**[209] 6062 3-9-0 0........................ RichardKingscote 5 49
(Jonathan Portman) *trckd ldrs: pushed along to press ldrs over 2f out: outpcd u.p over 1f out: wl btn after: wnt modest 3rd ins fnl f* **8/1**[3]

0-00 **4** *2* **Lady Parker (IRE)**[48] 637 3-9-0 47........................(p[1]) LiamKeniry 4 46
(J S Moore) *led and set stdy gallop: rdn and hdd 2f out: outpcd u.p and btn over 1f out: wknd ins fnl f* **66/1**

0- **5** *nse* **Sheltered Waters**[161] 7458 3-8-11 0........................ EdwardGreatrex(3) 3 46
(Eve Johnson Houghton) *hld up in tch in rr: swtchd rt and hdwy on outer over 3f out: pressed ldrs and rdn over 2f out: wd and lost pl bnd 2f out: hung lft and wl btn over 1f out* **14/1**

2m 36.9s (3.90) **Going Correction** 0.0s/f (Stan) **5** Ran SP% **113.6**
Speed ratings (Par 93): **87,86,79,78,78**
CSF £2.56 TOTE £1.10: £1.02, £2.40; EX 2.70 Trifecta £5.30.
**Owner** Elsworth & Nettlefold **Bred** Joseph Hernon **Trained** Newmarket, Suffolk

**FOCUS**
This weak fillies' maiden was a falsely run affair. The bare form is very modest.

## 1425 SUNBETS.CO.UK H'CAP 1m 1y(P)
**2:50** (2:50) (Class 6) (0-55,55) 4-Y-O+ **£2,587** (£770; £384; £192) **Stalls** High

Form RPR

0-01 **1** **Living Leader**[35] 854 8-8-10 **51**........................ BenRobinson(7) 4 57+
(Grace Harris) *wl in tch in midfield: effrt to chse ldrs 2f out: styd on to ld jst ins fnl f: r.o wl: rdn out* **4/1**[2]

-530 **2** *1 ½* **Sir Jamie**[49] 621 4-8-12 **46** oh1........................ GeorgeDowning 3 50
(Tony Carroll) *in tch in midfield: nt clr run jst over 2f out: effrt over 1f out: styd on wl u.p ins fnl f: wnt 2nd last strides* **7/1**[3]

6340 **3** *shd* **West Leake (IRE)**[7] 1298 11-8-12 **46**.............................. LiamKeniry 12 49
(Paul Burgoyne) *hld up in last quartet: nt clr run over 2f out: swtchd lft over 1f out: hdwy 1f out: styd on strly ins fnl f: snatched 3rd on post* **10/1**

1203 **4** *nse* **Welsh Inlet (IRE)**[12] 1237 9-9-4 **52**.............................. LukeMorris 1 54
(John Bridger) *chsd ldrs: effrt to chse ldng pair jst over 2f out: chsd wnr ins fnl f: kpt on same pce fnl 100yds: lost 2 pls last strides* **7/1**[3]

-300 **5** *½* **Kristoff (IRE)**[18] 1139 4-8-7 **46** oh1.............................. CharlieBennett(5) 6 47
(Jim Boyle) *led for 2f: styd w ldr tl led 3f: rdn 2f out: hdd jst ins fnl f: no ex and one pced fnl 100yds* **8/1**

506- **6** *½* **Fairy Mist (IRE)**[167] 7299 10-9-4 **52**..............................(v) WilliamCarson 5 54
(John Bridger) *hld up in tch in midfield: nt clr run over 2f out: rdn and hdwy jst over 1f out: chsng ldrs and nt clr run again ins fnl f: swtchd rt and kpt on fnl 100yds* **20/1**

360- **7** *2 ¼* **Coup De Vent**[274] 3748 6-9-2 **50**.............................. TimmyMurphy 8 46
(John O'Shea) *hmpd and stdd after s: hld up in rr: nt clr run ent fnl 2f: hmpd wl over 1f out and sn swtchd lft: pushed along and no imp ins fnl f* **33/1**

6-03 **8** *1 ½* **The Special One (IRE)**[18] 1139 4-9-7 **55**..............................(h) AdamKirby 10 46
(Ali Stronge) *wl in tch in midfield: effrt to chse ldr 2f out: unable qck over 1f out: wknd ins fnl f* **3/1**[1]

0-00 **9** *½* **Fishergate**[16] 1181 4-8-9 **50**..............................(b) GabrieleMalune(7) 7 40+
(Richard Rowe) *hmpd leaving stalls and sn detached in last: steadily rcvrd: hdwy into midfield over 3f out: rdn over 2f out: lost pl on outer bnd 2f out: wl hld and kpt on same pce fnl f* **33/1**

0-06 **10** *1 ½* **Palace Moon**[42] 740 12-9-2 **50**..............................(t) KierenFox 11 38
(Michael Attwater) *hld up in tch in last quartet: nt clr run over 2f: effrt wl over 1f out: no prog and wl hld fnl f* **8/1**

0040 **11** *5* **Way Up High**[11] 1260 5-8-5 **46** oh1..............................(b[1]) JoshuaBryan(7) 9 21
(Steve Flook) *bustled along leaving stalls: hdwy to chse ldrs after 1f: lost pl wl over 1f out: sn wknd* **50/1**

000- **12** *26* **Spice Boat**[181] 6891 5-8-9 **46** oh1..............................(p) HollieDoyle(3) 2
(Paddy Butler) *w ldr tl led after 2f: hdd 3f out: losing pl qckly ent fnl 2f: bhd fnl f: t.o: burst blood vessel* **50/1**

1m 38.45s (0.25) **Going Correction** 0.0s/f (Stan) **12** Ran SP% **115.9**
Speed ratings (Par 101): **98,96,96,96,95 95,93,91,91,89 84,58**
CSF £29.61 CT £261.88 TOTE £4.90: £2.00, £1.90, £3.90; EX 36.00 Trifecta £296.60.
**Owner** Ms Michelle Harris **Bred** D J And Mrs Deer **Trained** Shirenewton, Monmouthshire

**FOCUS**
They went a solid early pace in this moderate handicap, which was a pretty rough race. The winner found a bit more on his Kempton win.

## 1426 32RED MAIDEN AUCTION STKS 7f 1y(P)
**3:20** (3:22) (Class 5) 3-Y-O **£2,911** (£866; £432; £216) **Stalls** Low

Form RPR

43- **1** **Hajjam**[153] 7649 3-9-5 0..............................(h[1]) JimCrowley 3 73
(William Knight) *keen to post. chsd ldr: rdn and ev ch 2f out: drvn to ld ent fnl f: forged ahd 100yds out: styd on: rdn out* **8/11**[1]

0- **2** *1* **Wonder Of Dubai (IRE)**[139] 7882 3-9-5 0.............................. AdamKirby 2 70
(Michael Bell) *led: jnd and rdn 2f out: no ex u.p jst ins fnl f: styd on same pce fnl 100yds* **3/1**[2]

043- **3** *shd* **Spiritofedinburgh (IRE)**[189] 6672 3-9-5 70.............................. FranBerry 6 70
(Brendan Powell) *chsd ldng pair: effrt jst over 2f out: kpt on u.p ins fnl f: alomost snatched 2nd but nvr enough pce to chal wnr* **9/2**[3]

**4** *3 ¾* **Happy Escape** 3-9-0 0..............................(t[1]) LiamKeniry 5 55+
(Joseph Tuite) *s.i.s: hld up in rr: shkn up wl over 1f out: pushed along and hdwy 1f out: wnt 4th ins fnl f: kpt on steadily but nvr threatened ldrs* **25/1**

6 **5** *1 ¾* **Mahna Mahna (IRE)**[12] 1244 3-9-5 0.............................. WilliamCarson 7 55
(David W Drinkwater) *stdd and swtchd lft after s: t.k.h: hld up in last pair: hdwy into 4th over 2f out: sn rdn and outpcd: wl hld fnl f* **66/1**

0- **6** *hd* **La Isla Bonita**[104] 8377 3-9-0 0.............................. StevieDonohoe 8 50
(Richard Spencer) *t.k.h: hld up in tch in midfield: rdn ent fnl 2f: outpcd and btn over 1f out: wknd ins fnl f* **25/1**

5 **7** *hd* **Lord E (IRE)**[12] 1241 3-9-5 0.............................. TimmyMurphy 1 54
(Gary Moore) *in tch in midfield: pushed along and lost pl over 1f out: bhd fnl f* **25/1**

1m 26.16s (1.36) **Going Correction** 0.0s/f (Stan) **7** Ran SP% **114.1**
Speed ratings (Par 98): **92,90,90,86,84 84,84**
CSF £3.03 TOTE £1.60: £1.10, £1.50; EX 3.90 Trifecta £6.20.
**Owner** Sheikh Abdullah Almalek Alsabah **Bred** Mrs Janis Macpherson **Trained** Patching, W Sussex

**FOCUS**
An ordinary 3yo maiden, rated around the third. The winner is rated to his mark.

## 1427 SUNBETS ON THE APP STORE H'CAP 7f 1y(P)
**3:50** (3:52) (Class 6) (0-60,63) 4-Y-O+ **£2,587** (£770; £384; £192) **Stalls** Low

Form RPR

00-0 **1** **Locommotion**[29] 966 5-8-7 **46** oh1..............................(bt) FrannyNorton 10 54
(Matthew Salaman) *dwlt: rcvrd and hdwy to ld after 1f: sn clr and mde rest: c towards centre wl over 1f out: sn rdn: kpt on wl fnl f: unchal* **20/1**

0-00 **2** *3 ½* **Evanescent (IRE)**[22] 1071 8-9-8 **61**.............................. RobertWinston 3 60
(Tony Carroll) *taken down early: t.k.h: chsd ldrs tl chsd clr wnr over 3f out: rdn 2f out: kpt on but no imp on wnr ins fnl f* **12/1**

1202 **3** *shd* **Bookmaker**[29] 966 7-8-12 **58**..............................(p) SophieRalston(7) 9 56
(John Bridger) *led for 1f: chsd clr wnr after tl over 3f out: rdn 2f out: battling for 2nd but no imp on wnr fnl f: kpt on* **8/1**

5036 **4** *nk* **Noble Deed**[21] 1080 7-9-9 **62**..............................(p) LukeMorris 8 59
(Michael Attwater) *hld up in tch in midfield: swtchd rt and effrt over 2f out: battling for 2nd 1f out: kpt on but no imp ins fnl f* **14/1**

00-2 **5** *1 ¼* **Muthraab Aldaar (IRE)**[42] 734 4-9-7 **60**.............................. JackMitchell 5 54+
(Jim Boyle) *t.k.h: hld up in rr: effrt and pushed lft over 1f out: barging match w rival ins fnl f: kpt on: nvr threatened ldrs* **4/1**[2]

0-05 **6** *1 ¼* **Indus Valley (IRE)**[29] 966 10-8-8 **47**..............................(b) KieranO'Neill 7 38+
(Lee Carter) *t.k.h: hld up in midfield: effrt over 1f out: no imp u.p ins fnl f* **16/1**

0455 **7** *½* **Blackthorn Stick (IRE)**[18] 1139 8-9-2 **55**..............................(p) JimmyQuinn 1 44
(Paul Burgoyne) *taken down early: wl in tch in midfield: unable qck u.p over 1f out: wknd ins fnl f* **7/1**[3]

314- **8** *nk* **Intimately**[176] 7062 4-8-13 **57**.............................. GeorgeWood(5) 6 48
(Jonathan Portman) *dwlt: in tch: swtchd lft and effrt over 1f out: barging match w rival jst ins fnl f: squeezed out 100yds: nvr trbld ldrs* **12/1**

30-0 **9** *1 ¼* **Hurricane Rock**[39] 807 4-9-7 **60**.............................. JFEgan 4 45+
(Simon Dow) *t.k.h: hld up in rr: hmpd 5f out: effrt and no imp over 1f out: n.d* **10/1**

0061 **P** **Athletic**[6] 1325 8-9-10 **63** 6ex..............................(v) AdamKirby 2
(David Evans) *dwlt: hld up towards rr tl lost action and p.u 5f out: fatally injured* **2/1**[1]

1m 24.47s (-0.33) **Going Correction** 0.0s/f (Stan) **10** Ran SP% **118.7**
Speed ratings (Par 101): **101,97,96,96,95 93,93,92,91,**
CSF £242.71 CT £2138.72 TOTE £24.10: £5.40, £4.40, £2.40; EX 332.90 Trifecta £2760.50.
**Owner** Susannah Green,N J Milner,Deb Hughes **Bred** Gracelands Stud **Trained** Tonyrefail, Rhondda Cynon Taff

**FOCUS**
Suspect form as the winner set a crawl.

## 1428 32RED POKER H'CAP 7f 1y(P)
**4:20** (4:25) (Class 6) (0-60,62) 3-Y-O **£2,587** (£770; £384; £192) **Stalls** Low

Form RPR

053- **1** **Gala Celebration (IRE)**[156] 7570 3-9-8 **61**.............................. MartinDwyer 9 71+
(John Gallagher) *taken down early: nt best away but sn rcvrd to ld and clr: rdn over 1f out: styd on wl: unchal* **7/1**

3-33 **2** *4* **Topmeup**[8] 1297 3-9-0 **53**.............................. JFEgan 5 52
(David Evans) *hld up in midfield: effrt to chse ldrs 2f out: chsd clr wnr 1f out: kpt on but no imp fnl f* **7/2**[2]

-035 **3** *shd* **Hold Me Tight (IRE)**[20] 1107 3-9-2 **55**..............................(b) LiamKeniry 3 54
(J S Moore) *hld up in last trio: nt clrest run ent fnl 2f: effrt u.p over 1f out: styd on ins fnl f: almost snatched 2nd: no ch w wnr* **9/1**

040- **4** *1 ¼* **Luxford**[139] 7884 3-8-9 **48**.............................. KierenFox 1 43
(John Best) *hld up in tch: effrt and hdwy u.p on inner over 1f out: no imp fnl f: nvr nr wnr* **28/1**

02-1 **5** *¾* **Beepeecee**[65] 377 3-9-9 **62**..............................(p) ShaneKelly 4 55
(Richard Hughes) *chsd ldng trio: 3rd and rdn 2f out: sn drvn and unable qck: wl hld and kpt on same pce ins fnl f* **3/1**[1]

4-33 **6** *½* **Sheila's Palace**[15] 1193 3-9-7 **60**.............................. JosephineGordon 7 52
(J S Moore) *chsd clr wnr: rdn jst over 2f out: unable qck u.p over 1f out: wknd ins fnl f* **5/1**[3]

060- **7** *½* **Baker Street**[200] 6319 3-9-9 **62**.............................. RichardKingscote 8 53
(Tom Dascombe) *stdd s and dropped in bhd: hld up in rr: swtchd rt and effrt wd bnd 2f out: sme hdwy 1f out: kpt on same pce and no imp ins fnl f* **6/1**

-044 **8** *2 ¼* **Captain Sedgwick (IRE)**[15] 1192 3-8-8 **47**.............................. LukeMorris 6 32
(John Spearing) *chsd ldrs: lost pl and u.p whn hung lft jst over 1f out: wknd ins fnl f* **25/1**

004- **9** *1* **Ciel Rouge**[181] 6896 3-9-0 **53**.............................. AdamBeschizza 2 35
(Charlie Wallis) *hld up in midfield: pushed along and lost pl wl over 1f out: bhd fnl f* **25/1**

1m 24.34s (-0.46) **Going Correction** 0.0s/f (Stan) **9** Ran SP% **111.8**
Speed ratings (Par 96): **102,97,97,95,95 94,93,91,90**
CSF £29.93 CT £220.97 TOTE £8.10: £2.70, £1.20, £2.40; EX 35.70 Trifecta £262.30.
**Owner** Caveat Emptor Partnership **Bred** Haras Du Logis St Germain **Trained** Chastleton, Oxon

**FOCUS**
This moderate 3yo handicap looks straightforward rated around the placed horses. Improved form from the winner.

## 1429 BETWAY SPRINT H'CAP 5f 6y(P)
**4:55** (4:56) (Class 5) (0-70,70) 4-Y-O+ **£2,911** (£866; £432; £216) **Stalls** High

Form RPR

3121 **1** **Menelik (IRE)**[16] 1180 8-9-5 **68**..............................(bt) DavidProbert 3 84
(Des Donovan, Ire) *chsd ldrs: effrt in 3rd wl over 1f out: r.o to ld 100yds out: r.o strly and drew clr towards fin* **3/1**[1]

-004 **2** *3* **Powerful Wind (IRE)**[22] 1071 8-9-1 **64**..............................(t) WilliamCarson 1 69
(Charlie Wallis) *taken down early and led to s: sn led and clr: rdn over 1f out: hdd 100yds: no ex and kpt on to hold 2nd* **14/1**

2-41 **3** *¾* **Mossgo (IRE)**[29] 961 7-7-9 **70**..............................(t) KierenFox 4 72
(John Best) *chsd ldr: rdn over 1f out: 3rd and kpt on same pce ins fnl f* **7/1**

5443 **4** *1* **Temple Road (IRE)**[6] 1327 9-9-4 **67**..............................(bt) FrannyNorton 7 66
(Milton Bradley) *hld up in midfield: effrt over 1f out: rdn and styd on same pce ins fnl f* **7/1**

1-02 **5** *¾* **Picansort**[29] 961 10-9-2 **65**..............................(b) ShaneKelly 6 61
(Peter Crate) *short of room leaving stalls and sn dropped to rr: swtchd rt and effrt over 1f out: kpt on ins fnl f: nvr trbld ldrs* **7/1**

20-5 **6** *nk* **Taajub (IRE)**[53] 573 10-9-7 **70**.............................. TomQueally 2 65
(Peter Crate) *taken down early: hld up in last pair: effrt over 1f out: kpt on ins fnl f: nvr trbld ldrs* **13/2**[3]

634- **7** *1 ¾* **Equijade**[130] 8040 4-9-1 **64**.............................. LukeMorris 5 53
(Robert Stephens) *midfield: rdn 1/2-way: no imp over 1f out: wknd ins fnl f* **17/2**

053- **8** *1 ½* **Cherry Kool**[102] 8429 4-9-7 **70**.............................. OisinMurphy 8 53
(Stuart Williams) *chsd ldrs: outpcd and btn over 1f out: wknd ins fnl f* **4/1**[2]

57.58s (-1.22) **Going Correction** 0.0s/f (Stan) **8** Ran SP% **113.0**
Speed ratings (Par 103): **109,104,103,101,100 99,96,94**
CSF £44.57 CT £268.84 TOTE £3.80: £1.40, £3.60, £2.00; EX 44.30 Trifecta £194.60.
**Owner** D Donovan **Bred** Irish National Stud **Trained** Dualla, Co Tipperary

**FOCUS**
They went hard up front in this ordinary sprint handicap. The second and third help the level.

## 1430 BETWAY H'CAP 1m 4f (P)
**5:25** (5:27) (Class 5) (0-75,74) 4-Y-O+ **£3,234** (£962; £481; £240) **Stalls** Low

Form RPR

341- **1** **Balancing Time**[102] 8428 4-9-0 **69**..............................(p) JimCrowley 4 77+
(Amanda Perrett) *trckd ldr: effrt 2f out: rdn to ld over 1f out: hrd pressed and drvn jst ins fnl f: hdd 50yds out: battled bk u.p to ld again last strides* **15/8**[2]

3111 **2** *hd* **Moayadd (USA)**[9] 1283 5-8-12 **68** 6ex.............................. HollieDoyle(3) 1 76+
(Neil Mulholland) *trckd ldng pair: swtchd rt and effrt between rivals whn struck by rivals whip 1f out: rdn and str chal ins fnl f: led 50yds out: kpt on tl hdd and no ex last strides* **6/4**[1]

60-3 **3** *4 ½* **Bridge Of Sighs**[82] 92 5-9-7 **74**.............................. RichardKingscote 5 73
(Martin Smith) *stdd and dropped in bhd after s: hld up in rr: swtchd rt and effrt wl over 1f out: sn rdn and outpcd: wnt 3rd but no ch w ldrs ins fnl f* **7/2**[3]

4523 **4** *¾* **Attain**[4] 1364 8-9-0 **70**.............................. EdwardGreatrex(3) 3 68
(Archie Watson) *led tl rdn and hdd over 1f out: 3rd and outpcd 1f out: wknd ins fnl f* **7/1**

2m 31.69s (-1.31) **Going Correction** 0.0s/f (Stan)
**WFA** 4 from 5yo+ 1lb **4** Ran SP% **109.5**
Speed ratings (Par 103): **104,103,100,100**
CSF £5.14 TOTE £3.30; EX 5.90 Trifecta £8.30.
**Owner** John Connolly & Odile Griffith **Bred** W And R Barnett Ltd **Trained** Pulborough, W Sussex

**FOCUS**
Two progressive colts came clear in a bobbing finish off a tactical pace. THe form could prove better than rated.
T/Plt: £103.70 to a £1 stake. Pool: £68,875.30. 484.73 winning units. T/Qpdt: £38.00 to a £1 stake. Pool: £5,024.31. 97.71 winning units. **Steve Payne**

## 1291 SOUTHWELL (L-H)
Wednesday, March 29

**OFFICIAL GOING: Fibresand: standard**
Wind: Moderate, across Weather: Cloudy

### 1431 BETWAY SPRINT H'CAP 6f 16y(F)
**2:00** (2:01) (Class 5) (0-70,72) 4-Y-O+ **£3,234** (£962; £481; £240) **Stalls** Low

Form RPR
2412 1 **Treaty Of Rome (USA)**[22] 1071 5-9-4 **67**.....................(v) TonyHamilton 2 74
(Derek Shaw) *trckd ldng pair: : hdwy 2f out: chal on inner over 1f out: sn rdn: kpt on wl to ld last 75 yds* **9/2**[2]
0-33 2 *nk* **Captain Bob (IRE)**[32] 929 6-9-3 **66**......................... SilvestreDeSousa 7 72+
(Robert Cowell) *dwlt and sn swtchd lft towards inner: in tch: hdwy on inner and cl up 3f out: chal 2f out and sn rdn: drvn to take slt ld briefly ins fnl f: hdd and no ex last 75 yds* **10/3**[1]
50-6 3 *½* **Vallarta (IRE)**[15] 1185 7-9-9 **72**....................................... JamesSullivan 3 77
(Ruth Carr) *led: jnd 1/2-way: pushed along over 2f out: rdn wl over 1f out: drvn and hdd ins fnl f: kpt on* **7/1**[3]
-011 4 *nk* **Viva Verglas (IRE)**[14] 1209 6-9-0 **70**................................... TobyEley(7) 4 74
(Daniel Mark Loughnane) *in tch: hdwy to chse ldrs 2f out: rdn and n.m.r over 1f out: : styd on wl fnl f* **9/1**
0-02 5 *2 ¼* **Monsieur Jimmy**[22] 1076 5-8-6 **60**................................... PhilDennis(5) 11 57
(Declan Carroll) *towards rr: hdwy on inner 3f out: rdn to chse ldrs over 1f out: kpt on same pce* **14/1**
1533 6 *1 ¾* **Fortinbrass (IRE)**[14] 1209 7-8-8 **62**............................. LewisEdmunds(5) 10 54
(John Balding) *prom: rdn along over 2f out: drvn wl over 1f out: sn one pce* **9/1**
000- 7 *3 ¾* **Kestrel Call (IRE)**[145] 7798 4-9-7 **70**...................................(t) BenCurtis 6 50
(Michael Appleby) *chsd ldrs on outer: rdn along and edgd lft wl over 1f out: one pce after* **10/1**
020- 8 *shd* **Silver Bid (USA)**[257] 4360 5-8-11 **65**............................ GemmaTutty(5) 1 45+
(Karen Tutty) *dwlt: a rr* **9/1**
5405 9 *1* **Harwoods Star (IRE)**[20] 1109 7-9-6 **69**.......................(be) DannyBrock 9 46
(John Butler) *dwlt: a rr* **20/1**
00-0 10 *¾* **Coiste Bodhar (IRE)**[8] 1296 6-8-12 **68**............................. RPWalsh(7) 5 43
(Scott Dixon) *cl up: rdn along 3f out: sn wknd* **66/1**
10-0 11 *¾* **Be Bold**[28] 971 5-9-2 **65**................................................. DanielTudhope 8 38
(Rebecca Bastiman) *a towards rr* **20/1**

1m 16.34s (-0.16) **Going Correction** +0.125s/f (Slow) 11 Ran SP% **110.5**
Speed ratings (Par 103): **106,105,104,104,101 99,94,94,92,91 90**
CSF £18.01 CT £97.79 TOTE £4.40: £1.60, £1.50, £2.60; EX 17.70 Trifecta £76.80.
**Owner** John R Saville **Bred** Fred W Hertrich III & John D Fielding **Trained** Sproxton, Leics

**FOCUS**
An ordinary sprint handicap and a tight finish with not much covering the first four at the line. The winner is up slightly on his previous good effort.

### 1432 BETWAY MAIDEN STKS 6f 16y(F)
**2:30** (2:30) (Class 5) 3-Y-O+ **£3,234** (£962; £481; £240) **Stalls** Low

Form RPR
32- 1 **Comprise**[187] 6731 3-9-1 0............................................. JamieSpencer 6 73+
(Michael Bell) *trckd ldrs on outer: hdwy on bit 1/2-way: led 2f out: pushed clr appr fnl f: readily* **30/100**[1]
52 2 *2 ¾* **Hungarian Rhapsody**[15] 1183 3-9-1 0............................ DougieCostello 3 58
(Jamie Osborne) *trckd ldrs on inner: hdwy over 2f out: rdn to chse wnr and edgd lft ent fnl f: no imp* **4/1**[2]
00- 3 *1 ½* **Maggi May (IRE)**[238] 5029 3-8-4 0 ow1.......................... TomDonoghue(7) 4 50
(David Brown) *sn led: pushed along 3f out: rdn over 2f out and sn hdd: edgd lft ent fnl f: kpt on same pce* **50/1**
60-6 4 *1 ¼* **Ejabah (IRE)**[14] 1205 3-8-10 59.......................................... JoeyHaynes 2 45
(Charles Smith) *cl up on inner: rdn along wl over 2f out: drvn wl over 1f out: n.m.r and swtchd rt ent fnl f: kpt on* **20/1**[3]
260- 5 *11* **Waves (IRE)**[189] 6670 3-8-10 61............................................... JohnFahy 5 12
(Eve Johnson Houghton) *cl up: rdn along 3f out: wknd 2f out* **20/1**[3]

1m 17.47s (0.97) **Going Correction** +0.125s/f (Slow) 5 Ran SP% **108.4**
Speed ratings (Par 103): **98,94,92,90,76**
CSF £1.62 TOTE £1.10: £1.10, £1.30; EX 1.90 Trifecta £15.00.
**Owner** The Royal Ascot Racing Club **Bred** Cheveley Park Stud Ltd **Trained** Newmarket, Suffolk

**FOCUS**
A particularly uncompetitive maiden. An easy winner but a feet-on-the-ground view of the form.

### 1433 SUNBETS.CO.UK H'CAP 1m 13y(F)
**3:00** (3:00) (Class 4) (0-80,80) 4-Y-O+ **£5,175** (£1,540; £769; £384) **Stalls** Low

Form RPR
-111 1 **Hammer Gun (USA)**[6] 1324 4-9-2 **75** 6ex.......................(v) MartinLane 7 87+
(Derek Shaw) *trckd ldrs: smooth hdwy on outer over 3f out and sn cl up: led 2f out: rdn clr over 1f out: easily* **9/4**[2]
0614 2 *4 ½* **Muqarred (USA)**[8] 1292 5-9-2 **75**..............................(p) DanielTudhope 3 75
(Roger Fell) *hld up in tch: hdwy over 2f out: rdn to chse ldrs over 1f out: drvn and kpt on same pce ins fnl f* **6/1**[3]
-052 3 *½* **Order Of Service**[14] 1210 7-9-1 **74**..............................(e) MartinHarley 5 73
(Shaun Harris) *s.i.s and bhd: tk clsr order over 3f out: wd st and hdwy over 2f out: rdn to chse ldrs wl over 1f out: drvn and kpt on same pce fnl f* **10/1**
4100 4 *1* **Sands Chorus**[34] 876 5-9-7 **80**...................................... AndrewMullen 4 77
(James Given) *led: pushed along and hdd 3f out: rdn over 2f out: drvn wl over 1f out: sn one pce* **10/1**
-155 5 *1 ¼* **House Of Commons (IRE)**[44] 719 4-9-5 **78**......... SilvestreDeSousa 2 72
(Michael Appleby) *trckd ldrs on inner: pushed along wl over 2f out: rdn to chse wnr wl over 1f out: drvn appr fnl f: sn wknd* **15/8**[1]
4043 6 *1* **Boots And Spurs**[20] 1109 8-8-11 **70**..............................(vt) BenCurtis 6 61
(Scott Dixon) *cl up: led 3f out: rdn and hdd 2f out: sn drvn and wknd* **9/1**
000- 7 *21* **Ellaal**[173] 7108 8-9-3 **76**................................................. JamesSullivan 1 19+
(Ruth Carr) *chsd ldng pair on inner: rdn along over 3f out: sn lost pl and bhd* **100/1**

1m 43.22s (-0.48) **Going Correction** +0.125s/f (Slow) 7 Ran SP% **109.0**
Speed ratings (Par 105): **107,102,102,101,99 98,77**
CSF £14.48 TOTE £2.60: £1.30, £2.70; EX 13.60 Trifecta £59.10.
**Owner** A Flint **Bred** Her Majesty The Queen **Trained** Sproxton, Leics

■ Stewards' Enquiry : Andrew Mullen four-day ban; used whip above the permitted level (12th-15th Apr)

**FOCUS**
Not a bad handicap, but a one-horse race with another extraordinary performance from a gelding on a hot roll. The second and third help with the level.

### 1434 32RED.COM H'CAP 1m 13y(F)
**3:30** (3:31) (Class 5) (0-75,77) 3-Y-O **£3,234** (£962; £481; £240) **Stalls** Low

Form RPR
0-41 1 **Vantage Point (IRE)**[58] 479 3-9-12 **77**..................(p) HectorCrouch(3) 3 82
(Gary Moore) *prom on outer: hdwy and cl up over 2f out: chal wl over 1f out and sn rdn: drvn to take slt ld ins fnl f: kpt on wl towards fin* **2/1**[1]
3-12 2 *shd* **Seaview**[78] 160 3-9-4 **66**.............................................. DanielTudhope 1 70
(David Brown) *led: jnd and pushed along wl over 1f out: rdn whn edgd sharply rt and rdr dropped rein jst over 1f out: drvn and hdd narrowly ins fnl f: rallied and kpt on wl* **2/1**[1]
440- 3 *3* **Midnight Man (FR)**[160] 7482 3-9-1 **63**.............................. JoeyHaynes 4 60
(K R Burke) *hld up: hdwy on outer over 2f out: rdn over 1f out: kpt on same pce fnl f* **9/1**[3]
056- 4 *1 ¼* **Shambra (IRE)**[133] 7977 3-8-5 **60**................................ BenSanderson(7) 2 54
(Roger Fell) *trckd ldr: cl up 3f out: rdn along over 2f out: drvn and wknd over 1f out* **16/1**
1234 5 *12* **Killermont Street (IRE)**[12] 1243 3-9-7 **69**......................... JoeFanning 5 35
(Mark Johnston) *trckd ldrs on outer: swtchd lft to inner after 2f: hdwy 3f out and sn cl up: rdn along over 2f out: sn drvn and wknd* **3/1**[2]

1m 44.49s (0.79) **Going Correction** +0.125s/f (Slow) 5 Ran SP% **107.5**
Speed ratings (Par 98): **101,100,97,96,84**
CSF £5.91 TOTE £2.40: £1.10, £1.40; EX 5.60 Trifecta £24.40.
**Owner** R A Green **Bred** Smithfield Inc **Trained** Lower Beeding, W Sussex

**FOCUS**
An ordinary 3yo handicap lacking depth, but a thrilling finish between the joint-favourites, both previous course winners. Both are rated to their respective marks.

### 1435 BETWAY DASH H'CAP 4f 214y(F)
**4:00** (4:00) (Class 6) (0-58,58) 4-Y-O+ **£2,264** (£673; £336; £168) **Stalls** Centre

Form RPR
3542 1 **Roy's Legacy**[5] 1340 8-9-1 **52**.......................................... AndrewMullen 1 59
(Shaun Harris) *mde most: rdn clr jst over 1f out: drvn ins fnl f: kpt on* **5/2**[1]
-045 2 *nk* **Novabridge**[19] 1126 9-9-2 **58**.....................................(b) GemmaTutty(5) 4 64
(Karen Tutty) *dwlt: sn rdn along and outpcd in rr:. swtchd rt towards stands side over 3f out: hdwy 2f out: styd on strly fnl f* **4/1**[3]
000- 3 *3* **Under Approval**[141] 7859 6-8-9 **46**................................(b) SamJames 2 41
(Karen Tutty) *dwlt: sn chsng ldrs: cl up over 3f out: disp ld 1/2-way: rdn along wl over 1f out: drvn and kpt on same pce fnl f* **11/1**
0006 4 *nk* **Misu Moneypenny**[14] 1209 4-9-6 **57**..................................(p) DaleSwift 3 51
(Scott Dixon) *dwlt and sn rdn along: chsd ldrs: hdwy over 2f out: drvn over 1f out: kpt on same pce* **9/1**
0426 5 *½* **Excellent Aim**[22] 1076 10-8-13 **57**................................... JaneElliott(7) 6 49
(George Margarson) *in tch: hdwy 2f out and sn rdn: drvn over 1f out: one pce* **4/1**[3]
6332 6 *6* **Red Flute**[14] 1206 5-8-7 **47**.............................................(v) TimClark(3) 5 18
(Denis Quinn) *cl up: rdn along bef 1/2-way: drvn and wknd wl over 1f out* **7/2**[2]

1m 0.15s (0.45) **Going Correction** +0.125s/f (Slow) 6 Ran SP% **109.1**
Speed ratings (Par 101): **101,100,95,95,94 84**
CSF £11.93 TOTE £3.60: £1.60, £2.80; EX 11.50 Trifecta £71.20.
**Owner** Notts Racing, S Mohammed & S Rowley **Bred** A Christou **Trained** Carburton, Notts

**FOCUS**
A moderate sprint handicap. The winner is rated only to his recent best.

### 1436 BETWAY AMATEUR RIDERS' H'CAP 1m 6f 21y(F)
**4:35** (4:35) (Class 6) (0-65,65) 4-Y-O+ **£2,183** (£677; £338; £169) **Stalls** Low

Form RPR
05-3 1 **Rainbow Lad (IRE)**[79] 146 4-9-13 **54**........................ MissSBrotherton 5 62
(Michael Appleby) *hld up in tch: hdwy to trck ldrs 1/2-way: chsd clr ldr over 3f out: hdwy to ld 2f out: sn rdn clr* **11/4**[2]
552 2 *4 ½* **Paris Bound**[20] 1108 4-10-0 **60**............................... PoppyBridgwater(5) 10 62+
(Andrew Balding) *prom: pushed along and lost pl over 4f out: rdn along and hdwy 2f out: styd on to chse wnr ins fnl f: no imp* **9/4**[1]
3304 3 *3 ¼* **Thackeray**[14] 1207 10-9-9 **46**......................................... MissBeckySmith 3 43
(Chris Fairhurst) *hld up towards rr: hdwy over 4f out: chsd ldng pair 3f out: sn rdn and chsng wnr wl over 1f out: kpt on same pce* **14/1**
5/6- 4 *3* **Three Colours Red (IRE)**[25] 3064 5-10-7 **65**... MrMorganWinstone(7) 4 58
(Robert Stephens) *trckd ldrs: hdwy 5f out: pushed along 4f out: rdn 3f out: sn drvn and one pce* **22/1**
2026 5 *¾* **Noguchi (IRE)**[22] 1073 12-10-7 **65**..............................(p) MissEBushe(7) 1 57
(Chris Dwyer) *led: hdd after 6f: prom on inner: rdn along over 3f out: sn drvn and grad wknd* **10/1**
0-30 6 *3 ¾* **Monzino (USA)**[14] 1207 9-9-4 **46**......................... MrRomainClavreul(5) 9 33
(Michael Chapman) *hld up towards rr: gd hdwy on wd outside over 6f out: led 5f out and sn clr: rdn along 3f out: hdd 2f out and sn wknd* **33/1**
0-46 7 *1 ¼* **Crakehall Lad (IRE)**[15] 1188 6-9-9 **46** oh1.................(h[1]) MissCWalton 2 32
(Andrew Crook) *trckd ldrs on inner: pushed along and lost pl over 7f out: rdn along over 4f out: nvr a factor* **16/1**
2-01 8 *18* **Cosmic Tigress**[11] 1256 6-10-9 **60**..................................... MrSWalker 6 22
(John Quinn) *trckd ldrs: effrt over 4f out: rdn along over 3f out: sn drvn and wknd* **4/1**[3]
040- 9 *6* **Duc De Seville (IRE)**[57] 7895 5-9-6 **50**........................(b) MrCAJones(7) 8 4
(Michael Chapman) *trckd ldrs: cl up after 4f: led 1m out: hdd and pushed along over 5f out: sn lost pl and bhd* **100/1**
44-0 10 *18* **Toboggan's Gift**[15] 1188 5-9-12 **49**............................. MissJoannaMason 7
(Ann Duffield) *towards rr: pushed along over 5f out: rdn over 4f out and sn bhd* **14/1**

3m 11.98s (3.68) **Going Correction** +0.125s/f (Slow)
**WFA** 4 from 5yo+ 2lb 10 Ran SP% **114.0**
Speed ratings (Par 101): **94,91,89,87,87 85,84,74,70,60**
CSF £8.94 CT £69.49 TOTE £3.70: £1.40, £1.40, £3.20; EX 11.30 Trifecta £90.20.
**Owner** Michael Appleby **Bred** Rathbarry Stud **Trained** Oakham, Rutland

**FOCUS**
A moderate staying handicap for amateur riders and they finished well spread out. The winner is rated back to his best.
T/Plt: £13.40 to a £1 stake. Pool: £69,366.99. 3,761.71 winning units. T/Qpdt: £7.90 to a £1 stake. Pool: £3,395.94. 316.17 winning units. **Joe Rowntree**

1437 - 1444a (Foreign Racing) - See Raceform Interactive

# 1321 CHELMSFORD (A.W) (L-H)

Thursday, March 30

**OFFICIAL GOING: Polytrack: standard**

Wind: light, behind final 2f Weather: dry

## 1445 BET TOTEPLACEPOT AT BETFRED.COM APPRENTICE H'CAP 1m 2f (P)

5:45 (5:48) (Class 6) (0-65,66) 3-Y-0 **£3,234** (£962; £481; £240) **Stalls** Low

Form RPR

3-22 **1** **Moneyoryourlife**[36] 864 3-9-6 **58** HollieDoyle 7 65+
(Richard Hannon) *chsd ldrs: wnt 2nd 4f out: rdn to ld over 1f out: in command and r.o wl ins fnl f: readily* **3/1**[1]

6-34 **2** *3* **Lady Hester (USA)**[27] 1003 3-10-0 **66** KieranShoemark 9 67
(John Gosden) *styd wd early: chsd ldr tl led after 2f: rdn and hdd over 1f out: no ch w wnr but kpt on for clr 2nd fnl f* **12/1**

02-2 **3** *3* **Bonnie Arlene (IRE)**[9] 1297 3-9-2 **61** SharnaArmstrong(7) 6 56
(Mark Johnston) *taken down early: bustled along leaving stalls: wl in tch in midfield on outer: clsd to chse ldrs 4f out: outpcd and rdn over 1f out: wl hld and kpt on same pce fnl f* **5/1**[3]

40-0 **4** *1 3/4* **Conkering Hero (IRE)**[71] 284 3-9-4 **63** DavidEgan(7) 2 55
(Joseph Tuite) *chsd ldrs: effrt 2f out: sn outpcd: wl hld and kpt on same pce fnl f* **12/1**

-334 **5** *3/4* **Beauchamp Opal**[34] 895 3-9-3 **60** PaddyBradley(5) 1 51
(Charlie Fellowes) *taken down early: hld up in midfield: effrt over 1f out: kpt on ins fnl f: nvr trbld ldrs* **7/2**[2]

600- **6** *1* **Jive Factor (USA)**[161] 7483 3-9-8 **63** GeorgeWood(3) 3 52
(Ed Dunlop) *t.k.h: led for 2f: chsd ldr tl 4f out: styd handy tl rdn and btn over 1f out: sn wknd* **7/2**[2]

1556 **7** *1/2* **Log Off (IRE)**[7] 1331 3-9-7 **59** PhilipPrince 4 47
(David Evans) *dwlt hld up in last pair: nt clrest of runs over 2f out: sme hdwy fnl f: nvr trbld ldrs* **14/1**

046 **8** *1 1/4* **Navajo Star (IRE)**[19] 1143 3-8-11 **54** JaneElliott(5) 5 39
(Michael Appleby) *dwlt: nvr bttr than midfield: rdn and no hdwy 3f out: wknd over 1f out* **28/1**

05-6 **9** *2* **Zenovia (IRE)**[40] 814 3-9-9 **64** (h) GeorgeBuckell(3) 8 46
(David Simcock) *hld up in rr: swtchd rt and effrt over 2f out: no prog and wknd over 1f out* **14/1**

2m 5.42s (-3.18) **Going Correction** -0.125s/f (Stan) **9** Ran SP% **118.3**
Speed ratings (Par 96): **107,104,102,100,100 99,99,98,96**
CSF £41.29 CT £177.93 TOTE £3.50: £1.40, £3.00, £2.30; EX 24.10 Trifecta £69.50.

**Owner** R Hannon **Bred** Trinity Park Stud **Trained** East Everleigh, Wilts

**FOCUS**
Not that many got into this. The winner was slightly improved.

## 1446 BET TOTETRIFECTA AT BETFRED.COM H'CAP 1m 2f (P)

6:15 (6:17) (Class 2) (0-100,100) 4-Y-0+ **£12,291** (£3,657; £1,827; £913) **Stalls** Low

Form RPR

-451 **1** **Ickymasho**[17] 1178 5-9-0 **88** RichardKingscote 3 94
(Jonathan Portman) *mde all and set stdy gallop: rdn and qcknd 2f out: hld on gamely u.p ins fnl f* **7/2**[3]

-010 **2** *1/2* **Pactolus (IRE)**[19] 1148 6-9-7 **95** (t) PatCosgrave 2 100
(Stuart Williams) *sn trcking ldr: effrt wl over 1f out: drvn and ev ch fnl f: r.o but a jst hld* **6/1**

-021 **3** *hd* **Qaffaal (USA)**[17] 1177 6-9-0 **91** NathanEvans(3) 6 96
(Michael Easterby) *stdd and dropped in bhd: effrt and swtchd rt over 1f out: drvn and r.o wl fnl 100yds: snatched 3rd last stride* **10/3**[2]

3234 **4** *shd* **Ice Royal (IRE)**[17] 1177 4-9-0 **88** TimmyMurphy 5 92
(Jamie Osborne) *in tch in last pair: hdwy on outer to chse ldrs 5f out: rdn over 1f out: ev ch fnl f: styd on but unable qck fnl 100yds* **6/1**

-101 **5** *1/2* **Abareeq**[6] 1341 4-9-12 **100** 6ex JoeFanning 1 104
(Mark Johnston) *hld up in tch in midfield: trapped on inner over 2f out: swtchd rt jst ins fnl f: stl nt enough room and swtchd bk lft 100yds out: kpt on same pce after* **2/1**[1]

3052 **6** *2* **Forceful Appeal (USA)**[19] 1148 9-9-4 **92** LukeMorris 4 92
(Simon Dow) *trckd ldrs tl 5f out: styd wl in tch: swtchd rt and effrt over 1f out: no imp: outpcd fnl f* **14/1**

2m 6.95s (-1.65) **Going Correction** -0.125s/f (Stan) **6** Ran SP% **113.9**
Speed ratings (Par 109): **101,100,100,100,99 98**
CSF £24.49 TOTE £4.10: £1.80, £4.40; EX 26.20 Trifecta £60.90.

**Owner** C R Lambourne, M Forbes, D Losse **Bred** Allseasons Bloodstock **Trained** Upper Lambourn, Berks

**FOCUS**
A good handicap, but they went steady and the leader held on in a bunched finish. The winner is just rated to her recent level.

## 1447 BET TOTEQUADPOT AT BETFRED.COM FILLIES' H'CAP 1m (P)

6:45 (6:47) (Class 5) (0-75,74) 4-Y-0+ **£5,175** (£1,540; £769; £384) **Stalls** Low

Form RPR

434- **1** **Ejayteekay**[171] 7220 4-9-2 **74** GeorgeWood(5) 5 79
(Hughie Morrison) *pressed ldr: rdn and chal over 1f out: sustained effrt u.p and kpt on wl to ld cl home* **7/4**[1]

1244 **2** *nk* **Skidby Mill (IRE)**[27] 996 7-9-7 **74** PatCosgrave 6 78
(Laura Mongan) *t.k.h: led: rdn over 1f out: sustained duel w wnr: kpt on wl u.p ins fnl f: tl hdd and no ex cl home* **4/1**

2226 **3** *1 3/4* **Sheer Intensity (IRE)**[3] 1406 4-7-9 **55** oh2 DavidEgan(7) 1 55
(David Evans) *hld up in tch in last pair: rdn 3f out: wnt 3rd over 2f out: rdn and effrt on inner over 1f out: kpt on same pce ins fnl f* **7/2**[3]

0-31 **4** *1* **Ixelles Diamond (IRE)**[13] 1237 6-8-4 **57** (h) KieranO'Neill 4 55
(Lee Carter) *t.k.h: trckd ldrs tl over 2f out: swtchd rt and effrt over 1f out: unable qck u.p: kpt on same pce ins fnl f* **3/1**[2]

064- **5** *hd* **Chelabella**[113] 8255 4-8-10 **63** (v[1]) MartinLane 2 60
(Derek Shaw) *hld up in tch: effrt u.p and unable qck over 1f out: kpt on same pce ins fnl f* **12/1**

1m 39.72s (-0.18) **Going Correction** -0.125s/f (Stan) **5** Ran SP% **111.3**
Speed ratings (Par 100): **95,94,92,91,91**
CSF £9.16 TOTE £2.20: £2.50, £2.10; EX 8.60 Trifecta £22.70.

**Owner** Miss Magdalena Gut **Bred** Pinehurst Stud **Trained** East Ilsley, Berks

**FOCUS**
The early pace wasn't strong and the two in front had the race between them from the turn in. Not form to treat too seriously.

## 1448 BET TOTEEXACTA AT BETFRED.COM MEDIAN AUCTION MAIDEN STKS 1m (P)

7:15 (7:16) (Class 5) 3-5-Y-0 **£5,175** (£1,540; £769; £384) **Stalls** Low

Form RPR

3- **1** **Itsakindamagic**[155] 7622 3-8-11 0 (h) OisinMurphy 3 86+
(Andrew Balding) *plld hrd: chsd ldrs tl lft in ld after 1f: mde rest: awkward hd carriage but qcknd clr over 1f out: eased wl ins fnl f: easily* **5/6**[1]

0- **2** *8* **Royal Peace (IRE)**[148] 7763 3-8-6 0 KieranO'Neill 4 62
(Richard Hannon) *plld hrd: led tl wnt lft and hdd after 1f: chsd wnr after: rdn and outpcd over 1f out: wnt lft u.p 1f out: no ch w wnr but kpt to hold 2nd ins fnl f* **8/1**

**3** *1 1/2* **Stararchitecture (IRE)** 3-8-11 0 (t[1]) PatCosgrave 5 63+
(William Haggas) *v.s.a: sn in tch in rr: wnt 3rd and effrt jst over 2f out: outpcd by wnr over 1f out: wl hld and kpt on same pce fnl f* **9/2**[3]

**4** *3/4* **Zillion (IRE)** 3-8-11 0 WilliamBuick 2 61+
(John Gosden) *s.i.s: in tch: wnt 3rd 6f out: rdn and unable qck over 2f out: 4th and outpcd whn hung lft fr over 1f out: no ch w wnr and kpt on same pce after: fin lame* **3/1**[2]

60- **5** *3/4* **Duke's Girl**[148] 7761 3-8-6 0 (h) DannyBrock 1 55
(Michael Bell) *plld hrd: chsd ldr for 1f: in tch after tl dropped to last and outpcd whn rdn over 2f out: wl hld and kpt on same pce fr over 1f out* **25/1**

1m 39.16s (-0.74) **Going Correction** -0.125s/f (Stan) **5** Ran SP% **112.7**
Speed ratings (Par 103): **98,90,88,87,87**
CSF £8.63 TOTE £1.70: £1.10, £3.90; EX 8.60 Trifecta £22.90.

**Owner** Sheikh Juma Dalmook Al Maktoum **Bred** Newsells Park & Mr & Mrs Flannigan **Trained** Kingsclere, Hants

**FOCUS**
The favourite came home a wide-margin winner having been allowed a very soft lead, but didn't look entirely straightforward.

## 1449 TOTEPOOL BETTING AT BETFRED.COM H'CAP 1m (P)

7:45 (7:45) (Class 6) (0-65,73) 4-Y-0+ **£3,234** (£962; £481; £240) **Stalls** Low

Form RPR

-620 **1** **Foie Gras**[7] 1334 7-9-1 **66** (p) JoshuaBryan(7) 2 70
(Chris Dwyer) *hld up in tch in midfield: swtchd rt and hdwy over 1f out: sn chsng ldrs: rdn to ld jst ins fnl f: r.o wl: rdn out* **7/1**[3]

2-04 **2** *1/2* **Almanack**[16] 1186 7-9-3 **64** NathanAlison(3) 10 67
(Mark Pattinson) *in tch in midfield: rdn over 2f out: hdwy u.p 1f out: chal and wnt clr w wnr ins fnl f: r.o but hld towards fin* **8/1**

5-20 **3** *2 1/4* **Cat Royale (IRE)**[31] 954 4-9-1 **66** (p) DarraghKeenan(7) 6 63
(John Butler) *trckd ldrs: effrt over 1f out: sn drvn: unable qck ins fnl f: kpt on same pce fnl 100yds* **14/1**

6203 **4** *3/4* **Little Choosey**[14] 1225 7-9-3 **61** (bt) JFEgan 4 57
(Roy Bowring) *trckd ldrs on inner effrt over 1f out: no ex u.p and outpcd fnl 100yds* **7/1**[3]

1141 **5** *1/2* **Celtic Artisan (IRE)**[7] 1334 6-10-1 **73** 6ex (bt) OisinMurphy 7 67
(Rebecca Menzies) *t.k.h: w ldr tl rdn to ld over 1f out: hdd after 1f out and no ex jst ins fnl f: outpcd fnl 100yds* **7/2**[1]

5036 **6** *1* **With Approval (IRE)**[6] 1338 5-9-2 **60** (p) LiamKeniry 8 52
(Laura Mongan) *chsd ldrs: unable qck u.p over 1f out: wknd ins fnl f* **8/1**

-412 **7** *1/2* **Polar Kite (IRE)**[22] 1086 9-9-8 **66** (h) KierenFox 3 57
(Michael Attwater) *hld up in tch in last pair: effrt over 1f out: rdn 1f out: kpt on same pce and no imp ins fnl f* **5/1**[2]

0443 **8** *2 1/2* **Greyfriarschorista**[16] 1186 10-8-11 **62** (vt) KatherineGlenister(7) 5 47
(David Evans) *t.k.h: hld up in tch: effrt u.p over 1f out: sn switching rt and no hdwy: wknd ins fnl f* **14/1**

14/0 **9** *1 1/4* **Swilly Sunset**[21] 1109 4-9-2 **60** WilliamCarson 11 42
(Anthony Carson) *s.i.s: swtchd lft and hld up in rr: effrt on inner over 1f out: no imp: n.d* **8/1**

0-06 **10** *nk* **Starfield**[16] 1186 8-9-7 **65** (p) JosephineGordon 1 46
(Mandy Rowland) *led: rdn ent fnl 2f: hdd over 1f out: no ex u.p and wknd ins fnl f* **9/1**

1m 37.85s (-2.05) **Going Correction** -0.125s/f (Stan) **10** Ran SP% **120.6**
Speed ratings (Par 101): **105,104,102,101,101 100,99,97,95,95**
CSF £64.07 CT £789.52 TOTE £8.30: £3.10, £3.60, £6.40; EX 69.90 Trifecta £533.70.

**Owner** Mrs Shelley Dwyer **Bred** Sir Eric Parker **Trained** Newmarket, Suffolk

**FOCUS**
A modest handicap, rated around the first two.

## 1450 COLLECT TOTEPOOL WINNINGS AT BETFRED SHOPS H'CAP 7f (P)

8:15 (8:16) (Class 5) (0-75,81) 4-Y-0+ **£5,175** (£1,540; £769; £384) **Stalls** Low

Form RPR

0662 **1** **London (FR)**[7] 1324 4-9-9 **76** (h) JosephineGordon 6 84
(Phil McEntee) *mde all: rdn over 1f out: styd on wl and a doing enough ins fnl f: rdn out* **11/8**[1]

14-5 **2** *3/4* **Capolavoro (FR)**[57] 513 6-9-6 **73** LukeMorris 9 79
(Robert Cowell) *hld up in 5th: clsd and swtchd rt over 1f out: styd on u.p ins fnl f: wnt 2nd last strides: nvr quite getting to wnr* **6/1**[3]

304 **3** *nk* **Higher Court (USA)**[10] 1290 9-8-12 **70** GeorgeWood(5) 4 75
(Emma Owen) *t.k.h: chsd wnr: rdn over 1f out: kpt on u.p but a hld ins fnl f: lost 2nd last strides* **8/1**

0513 **4** *1 1/2* **Space War**[14] 1219 10-8-10 **66** (t) NathanEvans(3) 1 67
(Michael Easterby) *chsd ldng pair: drvn over 1f out: unable qck and styd on same pce ins fnl f* **6/1**[3]

-602 **5** *5* **Out Of The Ashes**[27] 1007 4-9-2 **76** (vt) DavidEgan(7) 2 64
(Mohamed Moubarak) *in tch in midfield: effrt over 1f out: no rspnse and btn 1f out: wknd ins fnl f* **9/2**[2]

402- **6** *27* **Let's Twist**[111] 8287 5-9-7 **74** (b) ShaneGray 5
(Kristin Stubbs) *rring in stalls: s.i.s: a detached in last: rdn and no hdwy 3f out: eased over 1f out* **6/1**[3]

1m 24.51s (-2.69) **Going Correction** -0.125s/f (Stan) **6** Ran SP% **114.3**
Speed ratings (Par 103): **110,109,108,107,101 70**
CSF £10.47 CT £47.85 TOTE £2.00: £1.40, £3.10; EX 9.30 Trifecta £47.90.

**Owner** Eventmaker Racehorses **Bred** Jean-Pierre Dubois **Trained** Newmarket, Suffolk

**FOCUS**
A fair handicap. The winner had an uncontested lead and the form is rated around the runner-up.

## 1451 UB40 HERE ON 12TH AUGUST H'CAP — 7f (P)
8:45 (8:45) (Class 6) (0-52,56) 3-Y-O+ £3,234 (£962; £481; £240) Stalls Low

Form RPR
606- 1 **Isntshesomething**[104] 8401 5-9-4 **46** oh1................(v[1]) DougieCostello 9 56
(Richard Guest) *chsd ldng trio: swtchd rt and effrt to chse ldr ent fnl f: hdwy u.p to ld ins fnl f: r.o strly* **33/1**
0-23 2 2 1/4 **Home Again**[28] 982 4-9-10 **52**..........................(v[1]) KierenFox 8 56
(Lee Carter) *led: rdn over 1f out: drvn and hdd jst ins fnl f: outpcd by wnr but kpt on for 2nd fnl 100yds* **5/1**
0363 3 1 1/4 **Bold Max**[30] 966 6-9-4 **46** oh1..........................(v) LukeMorris 3 47
(Zoe Davison) *t.k.h: chsd ldrs: drvn over 1f out: unable qck and styd on same pce ins fnl f* **10/1**
4411 4 nk **Tasaaboq**[5] 1372 6-10-0 **56** 6ex..................(t) JosephineGordon 1 56
(Phil McEntee) *hld up in tch in midfield: effrt on inner over 1f out: styd on same pce u.p ins fnl f* **9/2[3]**
5311 5 1/2 **Tigerfish (IRE)**[34] 897 3-8-7 **53**..................(p) HollieDoyle(3) 7 46
(William Stone) *dwlt: hld up in last pair: swtchd rt and effrt over 1f out: kpt on u.p ins fnl f: nvr trbld ldrs* **15/8[1]**
000- 6 nk **Wild Flower (IRE)**[154] 7641 5-9-7 **49**.................. KieranO'Neill 2 47
(Jimmy Fox) *trckd ldng pair: rdn over 2f out: unable qck u.p ent fnl f: wknd ins fnl f* **10/1**
0005 7 1 1/4 **Zebelini (IRE)**[14] 1220 5-9-4 **46** oh1.................. JFEgan 6 41
(Roy Bowring) *t.k.h: hld up in tch: rdn ent fnl 2f: unable qck over 1f out: wknd ins fnl f* **20/1**
0-01 8 1/2 **Locommotion**[1] 1427 5-9-9 **51** 6ex..................(bt) JohnFahy 4 45
(Matthew Salaman) *s.i.s: t.k.h: hld up in rr: effrt over 1f out: no prog and nvr threatened ldrs: eased towards fin* **5/2[2]**
1m 25.81s (-1.39) **Going Correction** -0.125s/f (Stan)
**WFA** 3 from 4yo+ 15lb 8 Ran SP% **124.1**
Speed ratings (Par 101): **102,99,98,97,97 96,95,94**
CSF £204.23 CT £1840.04 TOTE £29.30: £10.00, £2.30, £1.70; EX 178.20 Trifecta £890.70.
**Owner** Chris Penney **Bred** P Balding **Trained** Ingmanthorpe, W Yorks
**FOCUS**
The two first-time visored runners finished 1-2 here. Very modest but straightforward form.
T/Plt: £140.20 to a £1 stake. Pool: £96,676.89 - 503.08 winning units. T/Qpdt: £33.20 to a £1 stake. Pool: £10,349.54 - 230.65 winning units. **Steve Payne**

# 1409 WOLVERHAMPTON (A.W) (L-H)
Thursday, March 30
**OFFICIAL GOING: Tapeta: standard**
Wind: Light behind Weather: Overcast

## 1452 BETWAY SPRINT H'CAP — 5f 21y (Tp)
2:10 (2:10) (Class 7) (0-50,50) 3-Y-O+ £2,264 (£673; £336; £168) Stalls Low

Form RPR
04-5 1 **Quality Art (USA)**[76] 215 9-9-7 **50**..................(h) RobHornby 5 58
(Simon Hodgson) *s.i.s: hld up: hdwy over 1f out: r.o to ld wl ins fnl f: comf* **11/2[3]**
0-00 2 1 3/4 **Camino**[49] 640 4-8-11 **45**..................(p[1]) LuluStanford(5) 1 47
(Andi Brown) *sn pushed along and prom: chsd ldr 3f out: rdn to ld 1f out: hdd wl ins fnl f* **9/1**
5553 3 nk **Lizzy's Dream**[13] 1246 9-9-3 **46**.................. DanielTudhope 6 49
(Rebecca Bastiman) *prom: hmpd and lost pl over 4f out: swtchd wd wl over 1f out: rdn and r.o ins fnl f: nt rch ldrs* **5/2[1]**
3252 4 2 1/4 **Justice Rock**[8] 1305 4-9-4 **47**.................. JosephineGordon 7 42
(Phil McEntee) *prom: hmpd over 4f out: lost pl over 3f out: hdwy over 1f out: abt to be rdn whn rdr dropped whip over 1f out: kpt on* **7/2[2]**
-201 5 nk **Teepee Time**[45] 723 4-9-0 **48**.................. PhilDennis(5) 9 39
(Michael Mullineaux) *chsd ldr 2f: sn pushed along: styd on same pce fnl f* **9/1**
3326 6 1/2 **Red Flute**[1] 1435 5-9-1 **47**..................(v) TimClark(3) 2 37
(Denis Quinn) *led: rdn and hdd 1f out: wknd ins fnl f* **13/2**
5500 7 hd **Rojina (IRE)**[14] 1221 4-8-11 **45**..................(b) DavidParkes(5) 8 34
(Lisa Williamson) *s.i.s: hld up: r.o ins fnl f: nvr nrr* **80/1**
-000 8 1 1/4 **Rat Catcher (IRE)**[14] 1221 7-9-2 **45**..................(b) LukeMorris 3 29
(Lisa Williamson) *mid-div: hdwy 1/2-way: rdn over 1f out: wknd fnl f* **22/1**
0006 9 2 **Allen's Folly**[16] 1192 4-8-10 **46**.................. MollyKing(7) 4 23
(Peter Hiatt) *hld up: effrt over 1f out: wknd fnl f* **28/1**
-000 10 1 3/4 **Master Pekan**[19] 1147 4-9-2 **45**..................(b) BenCurtis 10 16
(Roy Brotherton) *sn chsng ldrs: hung rt fr over 3f out: wknd over 1f out* **33/1**
1m 2.08s (0.18) **Going Correction** -0.025s/f (Stan) 10 Ran SP% **111.5**
Speed ratings (Par 97): **97,94,93,90,89 88,88,86,83,80**
CSF £49.04 CT £153.96 TOTE £6.10: £1.70, £2.90, £1.40; EX 56.70 Trifecta £235.70.
**Owner** Mrs Lisa Clarke **Bred** Farfellow Farms & Darley Stud Management **Trained** Queen Camel, Somerset
**FOCUS**
The third meeting of the week here and clerk of the course Fergus Cameron said of the track: "It was worked to a depth of three and a half inches again this morning, but it has been reinstated and gallop-mastered and I don't think it will ride very differently." A basement-level sprint handicap to start. The winner took advantage of the drop in grade.

## 1453 BETWAY SPRINT MAIDEN STKS — 5f 21y (Tp)
2:40 (2:40) (Class 5) 3-Y-O+ £3,234 (£962; £481; £240) Stalls Low

Form RPR
225- 1 **Full Intention**[175] 7090 3-9-1 84.................. PJMcDonald 6 77+
(Tom Dascombe) *sn chsng ldr: rdn to ld over 1f out: r.o wl* **2/5[1]**
2 2 1/2 **Secret Strategy (IRE)** 3-9-1 0.................. AdamBeschizza 5 67
(Julia Feilden) *s.i.s: pushed along 1/2-way: hdwy over 1f out: r.o to go 2nd wl ins fnl f: no ch w wnr* **33/1**
6-4 3 2 **Wishing Time (IRE)**[27] 1004 3-8-10 0.................. OisinMurphy 4 55
(David O'Meara) *led: rdn and hdd over 1f out: no ex ins fnl f* **16/1**
00- 4 2 1/2 **Charlie Victor**[266] 4053 3-9-1 0.................. AdamKirby 1 51
(Clive Cox) *trckd ldrs: shkn up and hung rt over 1f out: sn btn* **5/1[2]**
55 5 1 **Seneca Chief**[24] 1064 3-9-1 0.................. GeorgeDowning 3 47
(Daniel Kubler) *hld up: plld hrd: shkn up 1/2-way: wknd over 1f out* **33/1**
0-2 6 4 **Hisar (IRE)**[10] 1287 3-9-1 0..................(h) LukeMorris 7 33
(Ronald Harris) *s.i.s: hdwy over 3f out: rdn and wknd over 1f out* **8/1[3]**
1m 1.59s (-0.31) **Going Correction** -0.025s/f (Stan) 6 Ran SP% **111.0**
Speed ratings (Par 103): **101,97,93,89,88 81**
CSF £17.21 TOTE £1.30: £1.02, £10.40; EX 14.80 Trifecta £73.60.
**Owner** John Dance **Bred** Springcombe Park Stud **Trained** Malpas, Cheshire
**FOCUS**
An uncompetitive maiden with the long-odds-on favourite winning as he liked. He's rated in line with his solid Thirsk run.

## 1454 BETWAY APP H'CAP — 6f 20y (Tp)
3:10 (3:12) (Class 3) (0-95,92) 3-Y-O+ £7,246 (£2,168; £1,084; £542; £270) Stalls Low

Form RPR
511- 1 **Dubai One (IRE)**[117] 8209 3-8-11 **88**.................. OisinMurphy 4 93
(Saeed bin Suroor) *chsd ldrs: led over 1f out: rdn out* **7/4[1]**
0-01 2 nk **King Robert**[31] 957 4-10-0 **92**..................(v) BenCurtis 8 100
(Bryan Smart) *pushed along in rr early: hdwy over 1f out: nt clr run sn after: rdr dropped whip ins fnl f: r.o wl to go 2nd nr fin: nt quite rch wnr* **8/1[3]**
-143 3 1/2 **Fast Track**[31] 957 6-9-10 **88**.................. PhillipMakin 5 95
(David Barron) *a.p: rdn over 1f out: r.o* **4/1[2]**
4400 4 1/2 **Gentlemen**[19] 1152 6-9-12 **90**.................. JosephineGordon 1 95
(Phil McEntee) *mid-div: pushed along over 3f out: hdwy over 1f out: sn rdn and edgd rt: r.o* **14/1**
6056 5 1 **Aguerooo (IRE)**[21] 1103 4-9-9 **87**..................(p) PaulHanagan 6 89
(Ollie Pears) *hld up: hung lft over 3f out: hdwy over 1f out: r.o: nt rch ldrs* **20/1**
3132 6 2 1/2 **Captain Dion**[21] 1103 4-9-8 **91**..................(v) LewisEdmunds(5) 3 86
(Kevin Ryan) *led: hdd over 4f out: led again over 3f out: rdn and hdd over 1f out: wknd wl ins fnl f* **4/1[2]**
610- 7 1/2 **Cosmic Chatter**[142] 7858 7-9-5 **83**..................(p) JamesSullivan 2 76
(Ruth Carr) *s.i.s: outpcd: r.o ins fnl f: nvr nrr* **80/1**
30-1 8 1/2 **Jaywalker (IRE)**[21] 1103 6-9-10 **88**.................. PJMcDonald 7 80
(Rebecca Bastiman) *sn w ldr: led over 4f out tl over 3f out: ev ch over 2f out: rdn over 1f out: wknd ins fnl f* **14/1**
06-5 9 nk **Ninjago**[31] 957 7-9-11 **89**..................(p) RobertWinston 10 82
(Paul Midgley) *hld up: swtchd rt and effrt over 1f out: eased whn hld ins fnl f* **8/1[3]**
00/- 10 2 1/2 **Steve Prescott**[558] 6515 5-9-9 **87**.................. JackGarritty 9 70
(Patrick Morris) *prom: racd keenly: shkn up over 2f out: wknd over 1f out* **125/1**
2530 11 1 **Oriental Relation (IRE)**[36] 857 6-9-5 **83**..................(v) AndrewMullen 11 63
(James Given) *sn pushed along to chse ldrs: rdn over 2f out: wknd over 1f out* **50/1**
1m 13.38s (-1.12) **Going Correction** -0.025s/f (Stan)
**WFA** 3 from 4yo+ 13lb 11 Ran SP% **120.7**
Speed ratings (Par 107): **106,105,104,104,102 99,98,98,97,94 93**
CSF £17.27 CT £52.44 TOTE £3.10: £1.10, £3.00, £1.80; EX 20.50 Trifecta £87.40.
**Owner** Godolphin **Bred** Darley **Trained** Newmarket, Suffolk
**FOCUS**
A decent sprint handicap in which a few of these had met each other within the past month, while a strong pace was always likely with some confirmed trailblazers in the field. The form should work out and the winner should have more progress to come.

## 1455 32RED CASINO FILLIES' H'CAP — 1m 1f 104y (Tp)
3:45 (3:45) (Class 5) (0-75,73) 4-Y-O+ £3,234 (£962; £481; £240) Stalls Low

Form RPR
/5-3 1 **Star Of Lombardy (IRE)**[6] 1345 4-8-13 **65**.................. FrannyNorton 1 77
(Mark Johnston) *chsd ldr tl led 2f out: rdn over 1f out: styd on* **4/1[2]**
2224 2 2 3/4 **Ms Gillard**[13] 1237 4-9-0 **66**..................(b[1]) JamieSpencer 4 72
(David Simcock) *hld up: hdwy over 2f out: rdn to chse wnr and hung lft ins fnl f: styd on same pce* **5/1[3]**
2542 3 2 1/2 **Mercy Me**[6] 1345 5-9-5 **71**.................. AdamKirby 5 72
(John Ryan) *sn pushed along to ld at stdy pce: rdn and qcknd 3f out: hdd 2f out: no ex ins fnl f* **5/4[1]**
-213 4 1 **Remember Me**[27] 996 4-9-2 **73**.................. CharlieBennett(5) 2 72
(Hughie Morrison) *chsd ldrs: shkn up over 1f out: no ex fnl f* **5/1[3]**
6-06 5 20 **Indigo Princess**[62] 444 4-8-10 **62**.................. BenCurtis 3 19
(Michael Appleby) *s.i.s: hld up: rdn and wknd over 2f out* **15/2**
1m 59.49s (-1.31) **Going Correction** -0.025s/f (Stan) 5 Ran SP% **109.5**
Speed ratings (Par 100): **104,101,99,98,80**
CSF £22.56 TOTE £4.70: £2.00, £2.30; EX 24.80 Trifecta £43.00.
**Owner** Paul Dean **Bred** Tom Darcy And Vincent McCarthy **Trained** Middleham Moor, N Yorks
**FOCUS**
An ordinary fillies' handicap and limited form for the grade.

## 1456 SUNBETS.CO.UK H'CAP — 1m 142y (Tp)
4:20 (4:22) (Class 6) (0-52,56) 4-Y-O+ £2,587 (£770; £384; £192) Stalls Low

Form RPR
1 **Society Ranger (IRE)**[6] 1354 4-9-1 **46** oh1..................(p) RobertWinston 4 57
(S M Duffy, Ire) *hld up: hdwy over 1f out: r.o to ld wl ins fnl f* **4/1[2]**
6040 2 1 3/4 **The Dukkerer (IRE)**[35] 880 6-9-7 **52**.................. TomEaves 6 59
(James Given) *chsd ldrs: led over 1f out: rdn and hdd wl ins fnl f* **14/1**
3/0- 3 2 1/2 **Appease**[41] 793 8-8-11 **47**..................(bt) PatrickO'Donnell(5) 5 49
(E Sheehy, Ire) *chsd ldr tl led over 5f out: rdn and hdd over 1f out: no ex ins fnl f* **7/1[3]**
03-1 4 nk **Monologue (IRE)**[8] 1298 4-9-11 **56** 6ex.................. RobHornby 8 57
(Simon Hodgson) *prom: rdn over 2f out: styd on same pce fnl f* **5/2[1]**
3-33 5 3 **Rafaaf (IRE)**[8] 1298 9-8-11 **49**.................. KieranSchofield(7) 9 44
(Peter Hiatt) *hld up: hdwy over 1f out: nvr rchd ldrs* **15/2**
0-U1 6 nse **Secret Lightning (FR)**[22] 1084 5-9-4 **52**.................. AlistairRawlinson(3) 7 47
(Michael Appleby) *s.i.s: hld up: rdn over 2f out: nvr on terms* **8/1**
2404 7 1 1/4 **Canford Belle**[12] 1260 4-9-0 **52**.................. PatrickVaughan(7) 10 44
(Grant Tuer) *hld up: hdwy u.p over 1f out: wknd fnl f* **11/1**
30-0 8 3 1/4 **Poor Duke (IRE)**[75] 239 7-9-4 **54**.................. PhilDennis(5) 3 40
(Michael Mullineaux) *chsd ldrs: rdn over 2f out: wknd ins fnl f* **50/1**
000- 9 hd **Adiator**[149] 7747 9-9-6 **51**.................. DaleSwift 11 36
(Neville Bycroft) *s.i.s: hld up: a in rr* **50/1**
60-0 10 3 3/4 **Bold Grove**[23] 1075 5-8-12 **46** oh1.................. CallumShepherd(3) 1 24
(Edward Bevan) *hld up in tch: hung rt 1/2-way: rdn over 2f out: wkng whn hmpd over 1f out* **50/1**
50-4 11 2 1/4 **The Greedy Boy**[13] 1249 4-9-1 **46** oh1..................(p) JoeDoyle 2 19
(Steve Flook) *led: hdd over 5f out: chsd ldr tl rdn over 2f out: wknd over 1f out* **11/1**
1m 49.49s (-0.61) **Going Correction** -0.025s/f (Stan) 11 Ran SP% **113.2**
Speed ratings (Par 101): **101,99,97,96,94 94,93,90,90,86 84**
CSF £55.67 CT £375.00 TOTE £4.80: £1.80, £3.10, £2.70; EX 56.30 Trifecta £366.90.
**Owner** The Superb Partnership **Bred** Mrs Natasha Drennan **Trained** Errill, Co. Laois
■ Shay Duffy's first winner in Britain.


The Form Book Flat, Raceform Ltd, Newbury, RG14 5SJ

**FOCUS**
Another particularly moderate handicap and a 1-3 for Ireland. The winner is rated close to his October Dundalk form.

## 1457 BETWAY H'CAP 1m 4f 51y (Tp)
4:55 (4:55) (Class 4) (0-85,83) 4-Y-O+ £4,851 (£1,443; £721; £360) Stalls Low

Form RPR
12 1 **Shamash (IRE)**[2] 1412 5-8-8 70 .....(t) PaulHanagan 3 77
(John C McConnell, Ire) *chsd ldr tl led over 2f out: rdn over 1f out: styd on* 13/8[1]
234- 2 ½ **Lexington Law (IRE)**[36] 4265 4-9-4 82 ..... AdamKirby 8 88+
(Alan King) *hld up: racd keenly: hdwy u.p over 1f out: r.o wl: nt quite rch wnr* 6/1[3]
0014 3 2 **Ravens Quest**[19] 1153 4-8-11 75 ..... StevieDonohoe 6 78
(John Ryan) *chsd ldrs: rdn over 1f out: hung lft ins fnl f: styd on same pce* 9/2[2]
2546 4 2 **Byres Road**[14] 1224 4-9-3 81 ..... JasonHart 5 81
(Mark Johnston) *led: hdd over 2f out: sn rdn: no ex ins fnl f* 15/2
560- 5 ½ **Viewpoint (IRE)**[242] 4919 8-9-2 81 ..... AlistairRawlinson(3) 2 80
(Michael Appleby) *prom: rdn over 2f out: no ex wl ins fnl f* 16/1
0054 6 2¼ **Castilo Del Diablo (IRE)**[13] 1240 8-9-6 82 .....(p) JamieSpencer 4 77
(David Simcock) *hld up: shkn up over 2f out: hdwy over 1f out: sn rdn: edgd lft and no ex ins fnl f* 6/1[3]
56-P 7 ½ **Precision Five**[33] 921 8-9-0 83 ..... JordanUys(7) 7 78
(Nick Lampard) *hld up: hmpd over 2f out: n.d* 150/1
0044 8 ½ **The Gay Cavalier**[27] 998 6-8-4 73 .....(t) JonathanFisher(7) 1 67
(John Ryan) *s.s: hld up: pushed along over 2f out: nvr on terms* 33/1
050- 9 hd **Renfrew Street**[173] 7139 4-9-2 80 ..... FrannyNorton 9 73
(Mark Johnston) *chsd ldrs: rdn over 2f out: wknd over 1f out* 20/1

2m 39.21s (-1.59) **Going Correction** -0.025s/f (Stan)
**WFA** 4 from 5yo+ 1lb 9 Ran SP% **110.9**
Speed ratings (Par 105): **104,103,102,101,100 99,98,98,98**
CSF £10.76 CT £33.93 TOTE £2.80: £1.30, £1.90, £1.70; EX 12.90 Trifecta £39.50.
**Owner** Derek Kierans **Bred** His Highness The Aga Khan's Studs S C **Trained** Stamullen, Co Meath
■ Stewards' Enquiry : Jonathan Fisher two day ban (13-14 April) - used whip with his above shoulder height

**FOCUS**
Not a bad middle-distance handicap, but they didn't go a great pace and it saw another win for the visitors. The winner basically repeated his latest form.

## 1458 BETWAY INSIDER H'CAP 1m 4f 51y (Tp)
5:25 (5:25) (Class 6) (0-60,62) 4-Y-O+ £2,587 (£770; £384; £192) Stalls Low

Form RPR
-322 1 **Surround Sound**[7] 1330 7-9-2 58 .....(tp) RachelRichardson(3) 6 66
(Tim Easterby) *s.i.s: hld up: hdwy on outer over 3f out: led and hung lft fr wl over 1f out: shkn up ins fnl f: comf* 9/4[1]
3240 2 2¼ **Pour L'Amour (IRE)**[12] 1257 4-9-7 62 ..... AdamKirby 3 66
(Daniel Mark Loughnane) *hld up in tch: rdn over 1f out: chsd wnr ins fnl f: styd on* 9/2[2]
300- 3 2 **Percys Princess**[199] 6424 6-9-2 58 ..... AlistairRawlinson(3) 5 59
(Michael Appleby) *led over 4f: chsd ldr tl led again over 2f out: rdn and hdd wl over 1f out: no ex ins fnl f* 10/1
0-03 4 6 **King Julien (IRE)**[3] 1402 4-7-12 46 .....(p) JackOsborn(7) 8 37
(John Ryan) *chsd ldrs: rdn over 2f out: wkng whn hung lft fnl f* 7/1
4206 5 ¾ **Cape Spirit (IRE)**[5] 1369 5-8-9 55 .....(p) JasonWatson(7) 10 45
(Andrew Balding) *s.s: hdwy over 10f out: rdn over 2f out: hung lft and wknd over 1f out* 5/1[3]
000- 6 2¾ **Put The Boot In (IRE)**[9] 8469 5-8-13 57 .....(p) CharlieBennett(5) 2 43
(Barry Brennan) *pushed along to chse ldrs: rdn over 3f out: wknd wl over 1f out* 80/1
6660 7 1 **Thorntoun Care**[12] 1257 6-9-7 60 ..... TomEaves 9 44
(Iain Jardine) *prom: led over 7f out: rdn and hdd over 2f out: wknd over 1f out* 13/2
-340 8 4 **Sir Jack**[22] 1082 4-8-11 52 .....(v[1]) GeorgeDowning 7 30
(Tony Carroll) *hld up: pushed along over 4f out: wknd over 2f out: hung lft over 1f out* 12/1
0-00 9 25 **Haabis (USA)**[19] 1146 4-8-11 52 ow1 .....(t) StevieDonohoe 4
(George Peckham) *hld up: rdn over 3f out: wknd over 2f out* 25/1

2m 39.68s (-1.12) **Going Correction** -0.025s/f (Stan)
**WFA** 4 from 5yo+ 1lb 9 Ran SP% **113.3**
Speed ratings (Par 101): **102,100,99,95,94 92,92,89,72**
CSF £11.94 CT £81.34 TOTE £3.70: £1.50, £1.80, £2.90; EX 12.40 Trifecta £73.70.
**Owner** Craig Wilson **Bred** D & N Leggate, R Kent & I Henderson **Trained** Great Habton, N Yorks

**FOCUS**
A more moderate event than the previous race over the same trip and the front three came well clear. The form is rated slightly positively.
T/Plt: £83.50 to a £1 stake. Pool: £67,679.00 - 591.18 winning units. T/Qpdt: £35.60 to a £1 stake. Pool: £5,854.74 - 121.53 winning units. **Colin Roberts**

# 1282 FONTAINEBLEAU
Thursday, March 30

**OFFICIAL GOING: Turf: soft**

## 1459a PRIX DE MONTEREAU (MAIDEN) (3YO FILLIES) (TURF) 1m
11:40 3-Y-O £10,683 (£4,273; £3,205; £2,136; £1,068)

RPR
1 **Dallas Affair**[16] 3-9-2 0 ..... AurelienLemaitre 3
(F Head, France) 61/10[3]
2 ¾ **Baltic Duchess (IRE)** 3-8-11 0 ..... Pierre-CharlesBoudot 2
(A Fabre, France) 7/10[1]
3 ¾ **Sri Prada (FR)**[155] 3-9-2 0 ..... AlexisBadel 7
(G Doleuze, France) 15/1
4 ¾ **Hug (IRE)** 3-8-11 0 ..... IoritzMendizabal 4
(F Chappet, France) 12/1
5 1½ **Selati (IRE)**[181] 6929 3-9-2 0 ..... StephanePasquier 6
(N Clement, France) 23/1
6 1¼ **Canterbury Quad (FR)**[167] 7346 3-9-2 0 ..... ChristopheSoumillon 8
(Henry Spiller) 43/10[2]
7 ¾ **Manouka (FR)**[35] 3-8-6 0 ..... MlleMargotRomary(10) 1
(Mlle B Renk, France) 55/1
8 6 **Babylove (FR)**[20] 3-9-2 0 ..... OlivierPeslier 5
(H-A Pantall, France) 11/1

PARI-MUTUEL (all including 1 euro stake): WIN 7.10; PLACE 1.40, 1.10, 1.80; DF 5.70; SF 13.90.
**Owner** George Strawbridge **Bred** Gestut Haus Ittlingen **Trained** France

## 1460a PRIX DE LARCHANT (MAIDEN) (3YO COLTS & GELDINGS) (TURF) 1m
12:10 3-Y-O £10,683 (£4,273; £3,205; £2,136; £1,068)

RPR
1 **Mask Of Time (IRE)**[28] 3-9-2 0 ..... Pierre-CharlesBoudot 8
(A Fabre, France) 13/5[2]
2 hd **Called To The Bar (IRE)**[203] 3-9-2 0 ..... MaximeGuyon 3
(Mme Pia Brandt, France) 1/1[1]
3 2 **Take Me Home (FR)** 3-9-2 0 ..... MickaelBarzalona 6
(H-A Pantall, France) 45/1
4 snk **Nahuel**[281] 3-9-2 0 ..... VincentCheminaud 2
(M Delzangles, France) 14/1
5 hd **Real Value (FR)**[144] 7842 3-9-2 0 ..... ChristopheSoumillon 5
(Mario Hofer, Germany) 11/2[3]
6 3 **Savile Row (FR)**[144] 7842 3-9-2 0 .....(p) EddyHardouin 7
(Frau Erika Mader, Germany) 22/1
7 1 **Staff College (FR)**[167] 7345 3-9-2 0 ..... OlivierPeslier 4
(Henry Spiller) 87/10
8 1¼ **Tioman (FR)**[20] 3-8-10 0 ..... AdrienMoreau(6) 1
(Mlle B Renk, France) 68/1
9 7 **Heaven's Door (FR)**[17] 3-9-2 0 ..... StephanePasquier 9
(P Demercastel, France) 48/1

PARI-MUTUEL (all including 1 euro stake): WIN 3.60; PLACE 1.40, 1.10, 4.80; DF 3.00; SF 7.70.
**Owner** Ballymore Thoroughbred Ltd **Bred** Dayton Investments (breeding) Limited **Trained** Chantilly, France

1461 - (Foreign Racing) - See Raceform Interactive

# 1424 LINGFIELD (L-H)
Friday, March 31

**OFFICIAL GOING: Polytrack: standard**
Wind: Fresh, behind in home straight Weather: Cloudy

## 1462 SUNBETS.CO.UK H'CAP 1m 1y(P)
2:00 (2:00) (Class 5) (0-75,78) 4-Y-O+ £2,911 (£866; £432; £216) Stalls High

Form RPR
5-02 1 **Zain Emperor (IRE)**[62] 460 4-9-9 77 ..... JFEgan 6 82
(John Butler) *trckd ldng pair: shkn up 2f out: clsd to ld 1f out: drvn out and hld on* 6/1
5141 2 ½ **Wink Oliver**[23] 1086 5-8-7 68 .....(p) LauraCoughlan(7) 4 72
(Jo Hughes) *hld up in 5th: gng easily 2f out: pushed along over 1f out: r.o fnl f to take 2nd nr fin: too late to chal* 14/1
260- 3 nk **Thundering Blue (USA)**[163] 7461 4-9-7 75 ..... JimmyFortune 3 78
(David Menuisier) *t.k.h early: hld up in last: shake up 2f out: prog on outer jst over 1f out: r.o to take 3rd last strides:: nvr nrr* 11/1
321 4 nk **Saleh (IRE)**[9] 1301 4-9-10 78 6ex ..... AdamKirby 1 80
(Lee Carter) *trckd ldng pair: gng easily and waiting for a gap 2f out: squeezed through to chal fnl f: one pce on inner last 100yds* 2/1[1]
2-21 5 ½ **Captain Courageous (IRE)**[50] 641 4-9-7 75 ..... ThomasBrown 5 76
(Ed Walker) *t.k.h: w ldr: rdn to ld 2f out: hdd 1f out: one pce after* 3/1[2]
0612 6 4 **Russian Reward (IRE)**[20] 1144 5-9-6 74 .....(p) SilvestreDeSousa 2 66
(Amanda Perrett) *mde most to 2f out: wknd u.p 1f out* 7/2[3]

1m 37.39s (-0.81) **Going Correction** -0.075s/f (Stan) 6 Ran SP% **109.8**
Speed ratings (Par 103): **101,100,100,99,99 95**
CSF £72.06 TOTE £6.80: £7.70, £6.10; EX 61.20 Trifecta £389.70.
**Owner** Asaad Al Banwan **Bred** Kevin J Molloy **Trained** Newmarket, Suffolk

**FOCUS**
A fair handicap. The winner has been rated to form.

## 1463 32RED CASINO H'CAP 6f 1y(P)
2:30 (2:30) (Class 5) (0-75,77) 3-Y-O £2,911 (£866; £432; £216) Stalls Low

Form RPR
534- 1 **Sword Exceed (GER)**[198] 6477 3-9-3 71 ..... SilvestreDeSousa 3 82+
(Ivan Furtado) *hld up in 5th: swtchd rt over 1f out: sn clsd on ldrs and nudged into ld last 100yds: nt extended* 5/2[2]
2542 2 1½ **Allegheny Bay (IRE)**[27] 1024 3-8-9 63 ..... LiamKeniry 2 63
(J S Moore) *mde most: drvn over 1f out: kpt on but hdd and easily outpcd last 100yds* 9/2[3]
1331 3 ½ **Peachey Carnehan**[17] 1194 3-9-7 75 .....(v) WilliamCarson 7 74
(Michael Attwater) *chsd ldr: rdn 2f out: tried to chal jst over 1f out: kpt on but outpcd last 100yds* 8/1
5-12 4 ½ **Right Action**[36] 877 3-9-5 73 ..... TonyHamilton 1 71
(Richard Fahey) *t.k.h: trckd ldng pair: rdn wl over 1f out: tried to chal fnl f: one pce last 150yds* 9/4[1]
3-51 5 nk **Porto Ferro (IRE)**[43] 764 3-9-4 72 .....(p) LukeMorris 6 68
(Dr Jon Scargill) *chsd ldng trio: rdn over 2f out: nt qckn over 1f out: kpt on again nr fin* 12/1
140- 6 ¾ **Quench Dolly**[188] 6763 3-9-9 77 ..... MartinDwyer 4 71
(John Gallagher) *n.m.r s and stdd: hld up in last: shkn up on inner over 1f out: one pce and nvr involved* 12/1
000- 7 1¼ **Stringybark Creek**[160] 7549 3-9-2 70 ..... GeorgeDowning 5 60
(Mick Channon) *mostly in 6th: rdn over 2f out: no prog and btn over 1f out* 12/1

1m 11.61s (-0.29) **Going Correction** -0.075s/f (Stan) 7 Ran SP% **111.7**
Speed ratings (Par 98): **98,96,95,94,94 93,91**
CSF £13.48 TOTE £2.90: £1.50, £2.20; EX 14.90 Trifecta £69.80.
**Owner** 21st Century Racing, C Hodgson & Bgc **Bred** Gestut Wittekindshof **Trained** Wiseton, Nottinghamshire

**FOCUS**
The beaten runners did not look obviously progressive or well handicapped, but the winner is a horse woth potential and he won with a significant amount in hand. The second and third have been rated close to their marks and help set the level.

## 1464 BETWAY CLAIMING STKS 1m 5f (P)
3:00 (3:00) (Class 6) 4-Y-O+ £2,264 (£673; £336; £168) Stalls Low

Form RPR
3401 1 **Luv U Whatever**[22] 1108 7-9-6 83 ..... WilliamCarson 1 81
(Michael Attwater) *led at slow pce 1f: trckd ldr: led again 3f out: sn rdn: hdd over 1f out: drifted rt but rallied to ld last 75yds* 9/4[2]

-255 **2** *1* **El Campeon**[20] 1153 5-9-8 78 .......... JFEgan 6 82
(Simon Dow) *hld up: trckd ldng pair 4f out: clsd over 2f out: rdn to ld over 1f out: hdd and nt qckn last 75yds* **10/3**[3]

01-1 **3** *2 ½* **King Olav (UAE)**[63] 436 12-8-13 67 .......... GeorgeDowning 5 69
(Tony Carroll) *chsd ldng pair to 4f out: sn rdn: nt on terms after: kpt on fnl f* **16/1**

**4** *¾* **Soiesauvage (FR)**[30] 6-9-2 0 .......... HectorCrouch(3) 3 74
(Gary Moore) *t.k.h early: hld up: urged along over 4f out: nt on terms after: kpt on fnl f* **8/1**

-405 **5** *6* **Our Channel (USA)**[23] 1079 6-9-10 99 .......... AdamKirby 4 70
(Jamie Osborne) *stdd s and initially hld up: quick move to ld after 1f: rdn and hdd 3f out: wknd over 1f out* **6/4**[1]

2m 45.59s (-0.41) **Going Correction** -0.075s/f (Stan) **5** Ran SP% **110.8**
Speed ratings (Par 101): **98,97,95,95,91**
CSF £10.10 TOTE £2.70: £1.20, £2.00; EX 9.80 Trifecta £37.90.Our Channel was claimed by Miss A. Mooney for £14,000. Soiesauvage was claimed by Mrs S. V. O. Leech for £14,000.
**Owner** Richard and Nicola Hunt **Bred** Richard Hunt **Trained** Epsom, Surrey

**FOCUS**
The early pace was slow and the favourite was nowhere near form, but this was still a fair race of its type. The first three have been rated to their recent form.

## 1465 BETWAY DASH H'CAP — 5f 6y(P)
3:30 (3:30) (Class 4) (0-85,87) 4-Y-O+ £4,690 (£1,395; £697; £348) Stalls High

Form RPR

4264 **1** **Monumental Man**[15] 1222 8-9-6 83 .......... (p) WilliamCarson 3 87
(Michael Attwater) *led: hung rt bnd 2f out: hdd over 1f out: kpt on wl to ld again last 50yds* **9/2**[3]

-050 **2** *nk* **Sandfrankskipsgo**[41] 816 8-9-0 77 .......... TomQueally 1 80
(Peter Crate) *chsd wnr to over 3f out and again 2f out as others wnt wd: rdn to ld over 1f out: edgd rt and hdd last 50yds* **12/1**

-513 **3** *5* **Just Us Two (IRE)**[15] 1222 5-9-0 84 .......... (p) DavidEgan(7) 2 69
(Robert Cowell) *s.i.s: rcvrd to chse wnr over 3f out tl carried wd bnd 2f out: fdd over 1f out* **11/4**[2]

00-2 **4** *hd* **Stepper Point**[15] 1222 8-9-10 87 .......... (p) MartinDwyer 4 71
(William Muir) *in tch: pressed ldng pair on outer 3f out tl carried wd bnd 2f out: fdd over 1f out* **11/10**[1]

-235 **5** *hd* **Burning Thread (IRE)**[23] 1087 10-8-12 75 .......... (b) ShaneKelly 5 58
(David Elsworth) *outpcd in last: nvr on terms: kpt on to press for modest 3rd nr fin* **8/1**

57.54s (-1.26) **Going Correction** -0.075s/f (Stan) **5** Ran SP% **111.3**
Speed ratings (Par 105): **107,106,98,98,97**
CSF £46.61 TOTE £4.50: £2.20, £3.80; EX 29.60 Trifecta £78.80.
**Owner** Richard and Nicola Hunt **Bred** Christopher Chell **Trained** Epsom, Surrey

**FOCUS**
No unexposed runners and the winner got things his own way in front. The first two have been rated close to their recent bests.

## 1466 BETWAY STAYERS H'CAP — 1m 7f 169y(P)
4:00 (4:00) (Class 4) (0-80,81) 4-Y-O+ £4,690 (£1,395; £697; £348) Stalls Low

Form RPR

-113 **1** **Tartan Bute**[20] 1153 4-9-8 81 .......... (p) JoeFanning 4 89
(Mark Johnston) *trckd ldrs: wnt 2nd 1/2-way: shkn up to ld over 2f out: edgd rt fr over 1f out but styd on wl* **6/4**[1]

36-1 **2** *2 ¾* **Amanto (GER)**[31] 965 7-9-4 72 .......... (t) TomMarquand 3 77
(Ali Stronge) *hld up in rr: drvn in 4th pl 3f out and no prog: styd on fr over 1f out to take 2nd last strides* **4/1**[2]

022 **3** *hd* **Marshall Aid (IRE)**[42] 786 4-8-6 65 .......... (p) KieranO'Neill 2 70
(Mark Usher) *trckd ldrs: shkn up over 2f out: nt qckn wl over 1f out: kpt on to chse wnr ins fnl f: no imp and lost 2nd last strides* **7/1**

652- **4** *1 ¼* **Corpus Chorister (FR)**[156] 7625 4-9-7 80 .......... JimmyFortune 5 83
(David Menuisier) *t.k.h: led: rdn and hdd over 2f out: wl hld over 1f out: fdd ins fnl f* **6/1**

20-0 **5** *8* **Chartbreaker (FR)**[43] 759 6-9-7 75 .......... (v) LukeMorris 1 69
(Chris Gordon) *rousted early but unable to ld: chsd ldr to 1/2-way: sn urged along: dropped to rr and btn 4f out: sn bhd* **12/1**

-033 **6** *26* **River Dart (IRE)**[55] 571 5-9-9 77 .......... AdamKirby 6 39
(Tony Carroll) *hld up in last: nt gng wl fr 7f out: drvn and btn 4f out: virtually p.u over 1f out* **5/1**[3]

3m 20.5s (-5.20) **Going Correction** -0.075s/f (Stan)
**WFA** 4 from 5yo+ 3lb **6** Ran SP% **111.1**
Speed ratings (Par 105): **110,108,108,107,103 90**
CSF £7.50 TOTE £2.60: £1.60, £2.40; EX 7.70 Trifecta £30.10.
**Owner** Frank Bird **Bred** Newsells Park Stud **Trained** Middleham Moor, N Yorks

**FOCUS**
This race fell apart a bit. Another step forward from the winner, with the runner-up rated to his latest form.

## 1467 BETWAY SPRINT H'CAP — 6f 1y(P)
4:30 (4:31) (Class 5) (0-75,77) 4-Y-O+ £2,911 (£866; £432; £216) Stalls Low

Form RPR

-101 **1** **Top Of The Bank**[7] 1339 4-9-2 69 6ex .......... (p) TonyHamilton 7 77
(Kristin Stubbs) *mde virtually all: rdn over 1f out: hld on wl* **8/1**

11- **2** *½* **Don't Blame Me**[200] 6418 4-9-7 74 .......... AdamKirby 6 80
(Clive Cox) *pressed wnr: rdn over 2f out: chal 1f out: kpt on but a hld* **9/2**[3]

2112 **3** *¾* **Spirit Of Zebedee (IRE)**[16] 1203 4-9-0 67 .......... (p) SilvestreDeSousa 5 71
(John Quinn) *chsd ldng pair: rdn over 2f out: tried to chal on inner 1f out: kpt on same pce* **3/1**[2]

5-04 **4** *1 ¼* **Anonymous John (IRE)**[41] 808 5-9-7 74 .......... JFEgan 3 74
(Dominic Ffrench Davis) *trckd ldrs in 5th: shkn up 2f out: tk 4th over 1f out but nt qckn: one pce after* **7/1**

-131 **5** *1 ¼* **Dream Farr (IRE)**[41] 808 4-9-9 76 .......... (t) ThomasBrown 2 73
(Ed Walker) *hld up in last: nt clr run over 2f out and no ch after: shkn up and kpt on fr over 1f out: nrst fin* **2/1**[1]

30-6 **6** *1* **Chetan**[20] 1140 5-9-5 72 .......... (tp) AdamBeschizza 1 65
(Charlie Wallis) *a abt same pl: rdn over 3f out and no prog: one pce after* **16/1**

6-00 **7** *½* **Very Honest (IRE)**[56] 547 4-9-10 77 .......... StevieDonohoe 4 68
(Brett Johnson) *trckd ldng trio: shkn up over 2f out: wknd jst over 1f out* **16/1**

-020 **8** *10* **Bertie Blu Boy**[20] 1140 9-9-4 71 .......... (b) LukeMorris 8 30
(Lisa Williamson) *a in last pair: rdn after 2f: bhd over 1f out* **25/1**

1m 10.87s (-1.03) **Going Correction** -0.075s/f (Stan) **8** Ran SP% **115.7**
Speed ratings (Par 103): **103,102,101,99,98 96,96,82**
CSF £44.32 CT £133.63 TOTE £9.40: £2.80, £1.10, £1.20; EX 48.20 Trifecta £313.70.
**Owner** R Whichelow, T Baker & Partners **Bred** D Carroll **Trained** Norton, N Yorks

**FOCUS**
The first two finishers filled the top two spots throughout, with the third never far away. The third helps pin the level.

## 1468 32RED MAIDEN FILLIES' STKS — 1m 2f (P)
5:00 (5:01) (Class 5) 3-Y-O+ £2,911 (£866; £432; £216) Stalls Low

Form RPR

220- **1** **Ajman Princess (IRE)**[258] 4416 4-10-0 107 .......... AndreaAtzeni 5 64+
(Roger Varian) *mde all: set stdy pce to 4f out: in command whn edgd rt fr over 1f out and briefly pushed along: easily* **1/20**[1]

**2** *3 ¾* **Tapdancealltheway** 3-8-8 0 .......... JoeFanning 4 49
(Amanda Perrett) *chsd wnr to 3f out: sn outpcd in 3rd: styd on again fnl f to take 2nd last stride* **10/1**[2]

0 **3** *hd* **Lady Maritime (IRE)**[48] 681 3-8-8 0 .......... DannyBrock 6 48
(Brett Johnson) *trckd ldng pair: rdn to chse wnr 3f out: no imp and a wl hld: lost 2nd last stride* **50/1**

00- **4** *7* **Our Cilla**[153] 7696 3-8-8 0 .......... AdamBeschizza 3 35
(Julia Feilden) *a in last: shkn up and struggling over 3f out* **33/1**[3]

2m 9.21s (2.61) **Going Correction** -0.075s/f (Stan)
**WFA** 3 from 4yo 20lb **4** Ran SP% **109.2**
Speed ratings (Par 100): **86,83,82,77**
CSF £1.41 TOTE £1.10; EX 1.50 Trifecta £3.70.
**Owner** Sheikh Mohammed Obaid Al Maktoum **Bred** Darley **Trained** Newmarket, Suffolk

**FOCUS**
Not much of a contest. The second, third and fourth are the key to the level, and time will tell what that is.
T/Plt: £826.40 to a £1 stake. Pool: £49,915.00 - 60.40 winning units. T/Qpdt: £25.50 to a £1 stake. Pool: £5,005.00 - 196 winning units. **Jonathan Neesom**

# 1344 NEWCASTLE (A.W) (L-H)
Friday, March 31

**OFFICIAL GOING: Tapeta: standard**
Wind: Fresh, half against for 3.5f in home straight in race 1, half against for all other races on the str Weather: Cloudy, mild

## 1469 BETWAY H'CAP — 1m 4f 98y (Tp)
5:45 (5:45) (Class 6) (0-65,67) 4-Y-O+ £2,587 (£770; £384; £192) Stalls High

Form RPR

/4-1 **1** **Up Ten Down Two (IRE)**[16] 1197 8-9-5 61 .......... (t) NathanEvans(3) 9 72+
(Michael Easterby) *trckd ldrs: led gng wl over 2f out: shkn up and clr over 1f out: pushed out fnl f: comf* **9/4**[1]

-001 **2** *3 ¾* **Mazaaher**[9] 1312 7-9-5 63 .......... CliffordLee(5) 10 68
(David Evans) *t.k.h: hld up: hdwy and prom 5f out: rdn: edgd lft and chsd (clr) wnr over 1f out: kpt on fnl f: nt pce to chal* **5/2**[2]

000- **3** *1 ½* **Toola Boola**[26] 7656 7-9-1 54 .......... (v[1]) JackGarritty 8 57
(Jedd O'Keeffe) *hld up: stdy hdwy 3f out: rdn along over 1f out: kpt on ins fnl f: no imp* **33/1**

-104 **4** *1 ½* **Tred Softly (IRE)**[35] 900 4-9-3 58 .......... (b) JasonHart 5 59
(John Quinn) *hld up in tch: pushed along and effrt over 2f out: hmpd wl over 1f out: sn rdn and edgd lft: kpt on same pce fnl f* **9/2**[3]

6004 **5** *3* **Psychology**[16] 1197 4-9-0 55 .......... DougieCostello 1 51
(Kenny Johnson) *hld up in rr: stdy hdwy over 2f out: rdn and edgd lft over 1f out: outpcd fnl f* **20/1**

-343 **6** *½* **Lord Rob**[9] 1312 6-8-6 45 .......... (p) AndrewMullen 12 40
(David Thompson) *in tch: hdwy to chal over 2f out: rdn and edgd rt over 1f out: wknd ins fnl f* **13/2**

030- **7** *13* **Rajapur**[300] 2308 4-8-10 51 .......... PaddyAspell 2 27
(Philip Kirby) *hld up on ins: drvn and outpcd over 2f out: n.d after* **33/1**

6-55 **8** *½* **Highwayman**[21] 1122 4-9-4 59 .......... PaulMulrennan 7 34
(David Thompson) *hdwy to press ldr after 2f: led over 3f out to over 2f out: wknd wl over 1f out* **16/1**

00P- **9** *½* **Akavit (IRE)**[106] 7274 5-10-0 67 .......... MichaelJMMurphy 11 41
(Ed de Giles) *t.k.h early: led: hdd and rdn over 3f out: rallied: wknd fr 2f out* **16/1**

634/ **10** *2 ¼* **Sandgate**[179] 5950 5-9-1 57 .......... SammyJoBell(3) 6 28
(Kenny Johnson) *in tch: rdn along over 2f out: sn wknd* **66/1**

0-00 **11** *5* **Bilko's Back (IRE)**[9] 1312 5-8-1 47 .......... (t) TheodoreLadd(7) 4 10
(Susan Corbett) *hld up on ins: drvn and outpcd 3f out: btn fnl 2f* **125/1**

000- **12** *10* **Spokesperson (USA)**[217] 5842 9-8-13 52 .......... (p) GrahamLee 3
(Fred Watson) *in tch on ins: drvn and outpcd over 3f out: sn wknd* **66/1**

2m 40.68s (-0.42) **Going Correction** 0.0s/f (Stan)
**WFA** 4 from 5yo+ 1lb **12** Ran SP% **117.0**
Speed ratings (Par 101): **101,98,97,96,94 94,85,85,84,83 80,73**
CSF £7.42 CT £140.49 TOTE £3.10: £1.10, £1.20, £10.30; EX 8.80 Trifecta £176.20.
**Owner** A Chandler, L Westwood & Mrs C Daurge **Bred** Ammerland Verwaltung Gmbh **Trained** Sheriff Hutton, N Yorks

**FOCUS**
Two well handicapped horses finished 1-2 here. The winner has been rated back towards his better figures. The third is among those who confirm the level.

## 1470 32RED.COM H'CAP — 1m 5y (Tp)
6:15 (6:15) (Class 5) (0-70,71) 3-Y-O £3,234 (£962; £481; £240) Stalls Centre

Form RPR

03-3 **1** **Nick Vedder**[78] 198 3-8-13 67 .......... CliffordLee(5) 4 75+
(K R Burke) *trckd ldrs: hdwy to ld 2f out: sn rdn and hrd pressed: edgd rt ins fnl f: kpt on wl* **7/2**[2]

10-1 **2** *1 ¾* **Cheval Blanche (USA)**[7] 1343 3-9-8 71 .......... JamieSpencer 5 77
(Michael Bell) *t.k.h: stdd in last pl: smooth hdwy on nr side of gp over 2f out: ev ch over 1f out: sn rdn: one pce whn checked and eased wl ins fnl f* **4/7**[1]

60-0 **3** *3* **Dreamofdiscovery (IRE)**[86] 40 3-8-13 62 .......... JoeDoyle 3 60
(Julie Camacho) *dwlt: sn w ldr: rdn over 2f out: outpcd by first two fr over 1f out* **22/1**

5-1 **4** *7* **Elusive Olivia (USA)**[58] 510 3-9-6 69 .......... (t) OisinMurphy 7 52
(Joseph Tuite) *trckd ldrs: hdwy to press wnr briefly 2f out: sn rdn and wknd* **7/1**[3]

000- **5** *¾* **Servo (IRE)**[217] 5840 3-8-12 61 .......... NeilFarley 1 42
(Alan Swinbank) *taken early to post: plld hrd: in tch: hdwy 3f out: rdn and wknd wl over 1f out* **22/1**

**6** *11* **Dapper Man (IRE)**[229] 5440 3-9-7 70 .......... JackGarritty 2 27
(Roger Fell) *led tl rdn and hdd 2f out: sn rdn and wknd* **33/1**

1m 40.31s (1.71) **Going Correction** +0.10s/f (Slow) **6** Ran SP% **110.0**
Speed ratings (Par 98): **95,93,90,83,82 71**
CSF £5.67 TOTE £3.70: £2.10, £1.10; EX 6.60 Trifecta £33.20.
**Owner** Seamus Burns **Bred** Petches Farm Ltd **Trained** Middleham Moor, N Yorks



The Form Book Flat, Raceform Ltd, Newbury, RG14 5SJ

**FOCUS**
An interesting little handicap for 3yos. It's been rated at face value.

## 1471 32RED CASINO MAIDEN FILLIES' STKS (PLUS 10 RACE) 1m 5y (Tp)
6:45 (6:45) (Class 5) 3-Y-O £3,234 (£962; £481; £240) Stalls Centre

Form RPR
1 **The Sky Is Blazing (IRE)** 3-9-0 0 PatCosgrave 11 83+
(William Haggas) *dwlt: hld up: pushed along and rn green over 2f out: gd hdwy to ld over 1f out: qcknd clr: promising* **6/4**[2]
4- 2 4 **Multicultural (IRE)**[153] 7695 3-9-0 0 MartinHarley 7 73
(James Tate) *trckd ldrs gng wl: smooth hdwy to ld over 2f out: rdn and hdd over 1f out: kpt on: no ch w promising wnr* **11/8**[1]
3- 3 2 ½ **Fortuities (IRE)**[221] 5728 3-9-0 0 JackGarritty 6 68
(Jedd O'Keeffe) *hld up in tch: pushed along over 2f out: rallied over 1f out: kpt on fnl f: no imp* **20/1**
420 4 3 ½ **Dusky Maid (IRE)**[8] 1333 3-9-0 0 AndrewMullen 9 60
(James Given) *cl up on nr side of gp: rdn and ev ch over 2f out to wl over 1f out: sn drvn and outpcd* **25/1**
5 2 **England Expects** 3-8-9 0 CliffordLee(5) 4 55
(K R Burke) *t.k.h: pressed ldr: rdn over 2f out: wknd over 1f out* **5/1**[3]
0- 6 4 **Davinci Dawn**[267] 4037 3-9-0 0 ShaneGray 10 47
(Ann Duffield) *t.k.h: hld up: rdn and outpcd over 2f out: sn wknd* **100/1**
0-23 7 12 **Sulafah (IRE)**[16] 1199 3-9-0 69 (p) JasonHart 5 20
(Simon West) *led to over 2f out: sn rdn and wknd* **16/1**
8 7 **Navajo Grey (IRE)** 3-9-0 0 BenCurtis 3 5
(Michael Appleby) *missed break: rn green and a struggling* **50/1**
5- 9 3 ½ **Royal Flute**[111] 8305 3-9-0 0 DougieCostello 2
(Mark Walford) *hld up: rdn and outpcd 3f out: sn btn* **100/1**
6 10 3 ½ **Nonnie And Norny**[13] 1259 3-9-0 0 TomEaves 8
(Shaun Harris) *chsd ldrs 3f: sn lost pl and struggling: no ch fnl 3f* **100/1**

1m 39.34s (0.74) **Going Correction** +0.10s/f (Slow) **10** Ran SP% **118.2**
Speed ratings (Par 95): **100,96,93,90,88 84,72,65,61,58**
CSF £3.80 TOTE £2.30: £1.10, £1.10, £6.80; EX 3.80 Trifecta £31.40.
**Owner** M J Jooste **Bred** Sunderland Holding Inc & Mabaki Inv **Trained** Newmarket, Suffolk
**FOCUS**
A fair maiden and a rather taking performance from the winner. The level is a bit fluid.

## 1472 SUNBETS.CO.UK H'CAP 7f 14y (Tp)
7:15 (7:16) (Class 4) (0-80,82) 3-Y-O+ £5,175 (£1,540; £769; £384) Stalls Centre

Form RPR
3-41 1 **Foolaad**[30] 971 6-9-5 70 (t) BenCurtis 2 81
(Roy Bowring) *taken early to post: mde all: rdn and edgd rt over 1f out: drvn and styd on strly fnl f* **7/2**[1]
115 2 2 **Espresso Freddo (IRE)**[20] 1149 3-8-13 79 (p) OisinMurphy 10 80
(Robert Stephens) *trckd ldrs: hdwy to press wnr over 2f out: effrt and ch over 1f out: kpt on same pce ins fnl f* **4/1**[2]
-045 3 ½ **Tadaawol**[16] 1202 4-9-4 69 (p) PJMcDonald 11 74
(Roger Fell) *in tch on nr side of gp: hdwy to chse ldng pair 2f out: sn rdn and edgd lft: kpt on same pce ins fnl f* **7/1**[3]
623- 4 1 ½ **Athollblair Boy (IRE)**[154] 7662 4-9-0 70 LewisEdmunds(5) 7 71
(Nigel Tinkler) *hld up on nr side of gp: pushed along and effrt 2f out: kpt on fnl f: no imp* **4/1**[2]
-050 5 1 **Shamaheart (IRE)**[16] 1202 7-9-11 76 (p) DavidAllan 8 74
(Geoffrey Harker) *s.i.s: hld up: stdy hdwy over 2f out: rdn and one pce fr over 1f out* **12/1**
400- 6 nk **Abushamah (IRE)**[181] 6956 6-10-3 82 JamesSullivan 5 79
(Ruth Carr) *t.k.h: trckd ldrs on far side of gp tl rdn and wknd over 1f out* **25/1**
000- 7 nk **Avenue Of Stars**[175] 7111 4-9-9 74 (p) DavidNolan 6 70
(Karen McLintock) *pressed wnr to over 2f out: drvn and wknd over 1f out* **33/1**
501- 8 1 ½ **Amood (IRE)**[154] 7662 6-9-11 76 (p) JasonHart 4 69
(Simon West) *plld hrd: hld up: effrt on far side of gp over 2f out: wknd over 1f out* **17/2**
4503 9 2 ¼ **Testa Rossa (IRE)**[27] 1032 7-10-0 79 (b) SamJames 1 66
(Jim Goldie) *hld up: drvn and outpcd over 2f out: n.d after* **12/1**
0-56 10 6 **Trinity Star (IRE)**[16] 1201 6-9-6 71 PaulMulrennan 9 42
(Michael Dods) *s.i.s: sn in tch: rdn 3f out: edgd lft and sn wknd* **20/1**
430- 11 3 **Slemy (IRE)**[199] 6437 6-9-13 78 TomEaves 3 41
(Ruth Carr) *t.k.h: hld up: struggling over 2f out: sn wknd* **20/1**

1m 27.26s (1.06) **Going Correction** +0.10s/f (Slow)
**WFA** 3 from 4yo+ 15lb **11** Ran SP% **116.9**
Speed ratings (Par 105): **97,94,94,92,91 90,90,88,86,79 76**
CSF £16.24 CT £94.64 TOTE £4.00: £1.30, £1.80, £2.80; EX 22.30 Trifecta £98.30.
**Owner** K Nicholls **Bred** Darley **Trained** Edwinstowe, Notts
**FOCUS**
They went steady early on and there were a few racing keenly in behind the winner. The winner has been rated back to his best, and the third fits.

## 1473 SUN BETS ON THE APP STORE APPRENTICE H'CAP 1m 5y (Tp)
7:45 (7:45) (Class 6) (0-65,67) 4-Y-O+ £2,587 (£770; £384; £192) Stalls Centre

Form RPR
2-43 1 **Newmarket Warrior (IRE)**[49] 655 6-9-0 65 (p) JamieGormley(7) 4 72
(Iain Jardine) *t.k.h: hld up: stdy hdwy over 2f out: effrt and swtchd lft over 1f out: led ins fnl f: hld on towards fin* **9/2**[3]
21-2 2 nk **Swansway**[69] 360 4-8-13 64 HarrisonShaw(7) 6 70
(Michael Easterby) *hld up in tch on far side of gp: pushed along over 2f out: rallied over 1f out: ev ch briefly ins fnl f: kpt on: hld nr fin* **3/1**[1]
0014 3 1 **Kiwi Bay**[21] 1125 12-9-5 66 CallumRodriguez(3) 5 70
(Michael Dods) *trckd ldrs on far side of gp: led wl over 1f out: hdd ins fnl f: kpt on same pce* **10/1**
600- 4 nse **Overhaugh Street**[305] 2741 4-9-5 63 CallumShepherd 13 67
(Ed de Giles) *in tch: effrt and rdn 2f out: kpt on same pce ins fnl f* **20/1**
6-66 5 1 **Mr Sundowner (USA)**[21] 1125 5-8-0 51 oh2 (t) ConnorMurtagh(7) 12 53
(Wilf Storey) *dwlt: t.k.h: hld up on nr side of gp: hdwy 2f out: rdn and kpt on fnl f: no imp* **9/1**
10-0 6 ½ **Adventureman**[30] 969 5-9-2 60 (p) JoshDoyle 11 61
(Ruth Carr) *led: rdn over 2f out: edgd lft and hdd over 1f out: sn outpcd* **25/1**
0-00 7 2 **Pacommand**[30] 968 4-9-2 63 BenRobinson(3) 3 59
(David Barron) *hld up: pushed along over 3f out: hdwy over 1f out: drvn and outpcd ins fnl f* **16/1**
22-1 8 1 ¾ **First Excel**[69] 362 5-9-2 63 (v[1]) KevinLundie(3) 9 55
(Roy Bowring) *t.k.h early: trckd ldrs: rdn over 2f out: rallied over 1f out: wknd ins fnl f* **10/3**[2]
000- 9 1 ¼ **Danot (IRE)**[168] 7333 5-9-4 62 LewisEdmunds 7 52
(Jedd O'Keeffe) *w ldr: rdn over 2f out: wknd fnl f* **14/1**
-066 10 5 **Scannermandango**[49] 655 4-8-9 53 NathanEvans 2 32
(Jim Goldie) *hld up: rdn over 2f out: nvr rchd ldrs* **66/1**
000/ 11 hd **Conjuror's Bluff**[555] 6656 9-8-7 51 oh6 (p) ShelleyBirkett 8 29
(Fred Watson) *in tch: rdn along 3f out: wknd over 1f out* **100/1**
-001 12 5 **Nelson's Bay**[21] 1125 8-8-8 57 PaulaMuir(5) 10 24
(Wilf Storey) *t.k.h: hld up on nr side of gp: rdn over 2f out: sn wknd* **8/1**

1m 40.17s (1.57) **Going Correction** +0.10s/f (Slow) **12** Ran SP% **120.1**
Speed ratings (Par 101): **96,95,94,94,93 93,91,89,88,83 82,77**
CSF £18.09 CT £131.47 TOTE £6.10: £1.90, £1.10, £3.30; EX 22.10 Trifecta £170.30.
**Owner** Ms S A Booth & Partner **Bred** Newtown Stud And T J Pabst **Trained** Carrutherstown, D'fries & G'way
■ Stewards' Enquiry : Callum Shepherd 18-day ban: 21 Apr-3 May with 6 days deferred until 3 Jul; used his whip above the permitted level
**FOCUS**
A couple of the closers came through to fight out the finish here. Straightforward form. The winner has been rated to his 2016 level, and the second and third close to their recent form.

## 1474 32REDSPORT.COM H'CAP 5f (Tp)
8:15 (8:15) (Class 6) (0-65,67) 3-Y-O £2,587 (£770; £384; £192) Stalls Centre

Form RPR
1 **Suwaan (IRE)**[216] 5898 3-9-7 65 JamesSullivan 1 73+
(Ruth Carr) *t.k.h: mde all: pushed along and clr over 1f out: edgd rt: kpt on wl fnl f* **14/1**
6-21 2 1 **Little Miss Daisy**[51] 623 3-9-4 67 LewisEdmunds(5) 5 70
(William Muir) *t.k.h: hld up: rdn and gd hdwy over 1f out: chsd wnr ins fnl f: kpt on* **2/1**[1]
503- 3 nk **Emerald Secret (IRE)**[187] 6807 3-9-1 59 (p[1]) GrahamLee 8 61
(Paul Midgley) *chsd wnr: rdn 2f out: lost 2nd ins fnl f: kpt on same pce* **33/1**
5002 4 2 ¼ **Billy's Boots**[6] 1363 3-9-2 60 FrannyNorton 10 54
(J R Jenkins) *hld up in tch: effrt and rdn 2f out: kpt on same pce ins fnl f* **7/1**
434- 5 ¾ **Ocean Princess (IRE)**[166] 7380 3-9-6 64 PaulMulrennan 6 55
(Michael Dods) *hld up in tch: rdn along 2f out: no imp fnl f* **9/2**[2]
56- 6 3 **Dontforgettocall**[140] 7900 3-9-6 64 OisinMurphy 12 44
(Joseph Tuite) *hld up on nr side of gp: rdn over 2f out: hdwy over 1f out: nvr able to chal* **5/1**[3]
5-33 7 ¾ **Prazeres**[25] 1064 3-9-9 67 JasonHart 2 45
(Les Eyre) *t.k.h: trckd ldrs on far side of gp: rdn over 2f out: wknd over 1f out* **9/1**
06-0 8 2 ¼ **Majestic Stone (IRE)**[14] 1244 3-8-10 54 JoeDoyle 7 24
(Julie Camacho) *taken early to post: hld up: rdn over 2f out: sn no imp: btn over 1f out* **12/1**
00-5 9 5 **Violet Mist (IRE)**[28] 1004 3-8-7 51 oh1 (t) CamHardie 4 3
(Ben Haslam) *t.k.h: in tch: lost pl 3f out: sn rdn: btn over 1f out* **50/1**
0205 10 1 ¼ **Flying Hope (IRE)**[32] 960 3-8-7 51 oh2 (t) AndrewMullen 11
(Nigel Tinkler) *s.i.s: prom on nr side of gp: rdn over 2f out: wknd over 1f out* **16/1**
000- 11 shd **Slave To Freedom**[105] 8406 3-8-9 53 JoeyHaynes 3
(Ann Duffield) *s.i.s: bhd on far side of gp: struggling over 2f out: sn btn* **66/1**

59.77s (0.27) **Going Correction** +0.10s/f (Slow) **11** Ran SP% **117.3**
Speed ratings (Par 96): **101,99,98,95,94 89,88,84,76,74 74**
CSF £41.87 CT £970.08 TOTE £19.20: £4.50, £1.10, £5.30; EX 52.60 Trifecta £3155.70 Part won..
**Owner** J A Swinburne **Bred** Shadwell Estate Company Limited **Trained** Huby, N Yorks
**FOCUS**
A modest sprint in which the pace held up pretty well. The third and fourth support this level and the winner could be a bit better than rated.

## 1475 BETWAY SPRINT H'CAP 5f (Tp)
8:45 (8:46) (Class 5) (0-75,77) 4-Y-O+ £3,234 (£962; £481; £240) Stalls Centre

Form RPR
60- 1 **Art Collection (FR)**[177] 7066 4-9-8 76 JamesSullivan 6 82
(Ruth Carr) *hld up: hdwy over 1f out: rdn and edgd lft ins fnl f: kpt on wl to ld towards fin* **14/1**
0-00 2 hd **Orient Class**[38] 851 6-9-4 77 CliffordLee(5) 3 82
(Paul Midgley) *in tch on far side of gp: effrt and hdwy over 1f out: led ent fnl f: edgd lft u.p: kpt on: hdd towards fin* **16/1**
604- 3 ½ **Lydia's Place**[198] 6476 4-9-7 75 DougieCostello 7 78
(Richard Guest) *led on nr side of gp: rdn and hdd over 1f out: kpt on same pce ins fnl f* **25/1**
4-14 4 hd **Ambitious Icarus**[16] 1203 8-8-10 64 (e) ConnorBeasley 9 67
(Richard Guest) *taken early to post: hld up: rdn along 1/2-way: hdwy fnl f: kpt on: nvr able to chal* **7/1**[3]
065- 5 ½ **Swirral Edge**[149] 7773 4-9-7 75 OisinMurphy 8 76
(David Brown) *trckd ldrs: hdwy to ld over 1f out: rdn and hdd ent fnl f: kpt on same pce* **16/1**
000- 6 nk **Lucky Beggar (IRE)**[157] 7593 7-9-8 76 DavidAllan 1 76
(David C Griffiths) *racd on far side of gp: disp ld to over 1f out: rdn and no ex ins fnl f* **10/1**
31-4 7 ¾ **Royal Brave (IRE)**[29] 995 6-9-5 73 PJMcDonald 14 70
(Rebecca Bastiman) *rrd in stall: hld up on nr side of gp: drvn and outpcd 1/2-way: rallied fnl f: no imp* **7/1**[3]
2123 7 dht **Poppy In The Wind**[27] 1030 5-9-3 76 (v) JoshDoyle(5) 5 73
(Alan Brown) *towards rr: rdn 1/2-way: hdwy and edgd lft over 1f out: kpt on fnl f: no imp* **6/1**[2]
5121 9 ½ **You're Cool**[36] 886 5-8-13 72 LewisEdmunds(5) 11 67
(John Balding) *prom: rdn over 2f out: one pce fr over 1f out* **4/1**[1]
0-00 10 nk **Extrasolar**[22] 1110 7-9-7 75 SamJames 2 69
(Geoffrey Harker) *hld up on far side of gp: rdn and effrt 2f out: sn no imp: btn fnl f* **66/1**
00-6 11 1 **Willbeme**[63] 443 9-8-9 70 BenRobinson(7) 12 61
(Neville Bycroft) *dwlt: sn midfield on nr side of gp: rdn and outpcd 1/2-way: sn btn* **12/1**
-212 12 ½ **Indian Pursuit (IRE)**[16] 1200 4-8-11 65 JasonHart 4 54
(John Quinn) *trckd ldrs: rdn over 2f out: wknd over 1f out* **7/1**[3]
5020 13 4 ½ **It Must Be Faith**[35] 901 7-9-0 68 (v[1]) BenCurtis 13 41
(Michael Appleby) *prom on nr side of gp: lost pl over 2f out: sn btn* **10/1**

59.11s (-0.39) **Going Correction** +0.10s/f (Slow) **13** Ran SP% **121.4**
Speed ratings (Par 103): **107,106,105,105,104 104,103,103,102,101 100,99,92**
CSF £223.89 CT £5457.42 TOTE £14.90: £3.80, £5.50, £5.40; EX 259.60 Trifecta £1714.90.
**Owner** N Chapman **Bred** D Aviez, S Gesbert & C Gesbert **Trained** Huby, N Yorks
■ Stewards' Enquiry : James Sullivan caution; careless riding

**FOCUS**
A fair sprint, and a notable double on the card with new recruits for Ruth Carr. The winner has been rated in line with his best for his previous trainer. The fourth fits on his form of recent months.
T/Jkpt: Not won. T/Plt: £4.80 to a £1 stake. Pool: £104,499.48 - 15,572.49 winning units. T/Qpdt: £3.40 to a £1 stake. Pool: £10,480.58 - 2,274.74 winning units. **Richard Young**

1476- 1478a (Foreign Racing) - See Raceform Interactive

## 1350 DUNDALK (A.W) (L-H)
Friday, March 31

**OFFICIAL GOING: Polytrack: standard**

### 1479a RACE & STAY AT CROWNE PLAZA DUNDALK H'CAP — 7f (P)
7:30 (7:30) 3-Y-0+ — £8,950 (£2,775; £1,322; £595; £232)

RPR

1 — **Split The Atom (IRE)**[15] 1233 5-8-10 **78**.....(b) WayneLordan 7 — 86
(David Marnane, Ire) *hld up: pushed along in rr fr 1/2-way: swtchd rt 1 1/2f out and r.o wl u.p ins fnl f to ld clsng stages: readily* **9/2**[3]

2 ¾ **Tribal Path (IRE)**[5] 1388 7-9-2 **84**.....(t) ShaneFoley 5 — 90
(Damian Joseph English, Ire) *sn led tl hdd narrowly after 2f: regained narrow advantage fr 1/2-way: rdn and pressed clly over 1f out: hdd u.p clsng stages: no ex* **4/1**[2]

3 1½ **Ishebayorgrey (IRE)**[15] 1233 5-8-13 **86**..... OisinOrr(5) 4 — 88
(Patrick Martin, Ire) *w.w towards rr: 7th 1/2-way: tk clsr order 1 1/2f out where n.m.r bhd horses: swtchd rt ins fnl f and kpt on same pce in 3rd clsng stages: nt trble wnr* **7/2**[1]

4 1½ **Northern Surprise (IRE)**[42] 795 6-9-1 **83**..... ColinKeane 3 — 81
(Timothy Doyle, Ire) *w.w towards rr: 6th 1/2-way: hdwy far side under 2f out to chal over 1f out where rdn: no ex wl ins fnl f and one pce clsng stages* **6/1**

5 hd **Peticoatgovernment (IRE)**[173] 7191 4-8-13 **81**..... WJLee 6 — 78
(W McCreery, Ire) *chsd ldrs: 5th 1/2-way: gng wl on outer into st and sme hdwy under 2f out where rdn: no ex bhd ldrs wl ins fnl f: kpt on one pce* **10/1**

6 ½ **Pearl Spectre (USA)**[7] 1353 6-9-10 **92**..... PatSmullen 1 — 88
(Phil McEntee) *prom tl sn settled bhd ldrs: disp 3rd at 1/2-way: effrt under 2f out: edgd sltly rt ent fnl f and sn no imp on ldrs: one pce and eased clsng stages* **4/1**[2]

7 nk **Patrick (IRE)**[7] 1353 5-9-4 **89**..... GaryHalpin(3) 8 — 84
(Richard John O'Brien, Ire) *cl up and led narrowly after 2f: hdd narrowly fr 1/2-way: rdn in cl 2nd 2f out and no ex ent fnl f: wknd* **14/1**

8 1¾ **Strait Of Zanzibar (USA)**[142] 7875 8-7-12 **73**.....(tp) AndrewBreslin(7) 2 — 63
(K J Condon, Ire) *cl up early: disp 3rd at 1/2-way: rdn over 2f out and sn wknd* **20/1**

1m 24.47s (-0.63) **Going Correction** +0.125s/f (Slow) — **8** Ran SP% **115.2**
Speed ratings: **108,107,105,103,103 102,102,100**
CSF £23.04 CT £69.67 TOTE £5.40: £1.80, £1.40, £1.60; DF 21.40 Trifecta £73.20.
**Owner** Bet Alchemist Racing Syndicate **Bred** Thistle Bloodstock Limited **Trained** Bansha, Co Tipperary

**FOCUS**
Plenty of Dundalk regulars going toe-to-toe and the winner's confidence is sky high at present.

1480 - 1483a (Foreign Racing) - See Raceform Interactive

## 1445 CHELMSFORD (A.W) (L-H)
Saturday, April 1

**OFFICIAL GOING: Polytrack: standard**
Wind: light tailwind in home straight, of no consequence Weather: dry until rain race 6

### 1484 TOTEPOOL APRIL FOOLS DAY H'CAP — 1m (P)
5:45 (5:46) (Class 6) (0-60,61) 4-Y-0+ — £3,234 (£721; £721; £240) Stalls Low

Form — RPR

3400 1 — **Samphire Coast**[16] 1225 4-9-5 **58**.....(v) MartinLane 9 — 65
(Derek Shaw) *rrd as stalls opened and slowly away: hld up in rr: effrt and wd 2f out: hdwy u.p over 1f out: led jst ins fnl f: r.o wl* **5/1**[3]

0610 2 1½ **Hannington**[14] 1260 6-9-7 **60**.....(t) DaleSwift 5 — 63
(Michael Appleby) *rousted along leaving stalls: in tch in midfield: effrt on inner over 1f out: hdwy to chse ldrs 1f out: kpt on wl ins fnl f* **9/2**[2]

5202 2 dht **Mowhoob**[21] 1139 7-8-6 **52**..... JoshuaBryan(7) 6 — 55
(Brian Barr) *hld up in midfield: effrt over 1f out: hdwy and rdn to chse wnr jst ins fnl f: styd on same pce fnl 100yds* **10/1**

45-0 4 1¼ **Sexton Blake (IRE)**[15] 1238 4-9-7 **60**.....(p) DaneO'Neill 1 — 60
(Gary Moore) *chsd ldrs: effrt 2f out: swtchd lft and hdwy u.p over 1f out: ev ch 1f out: no ex ins fnl f: wknd towards fin* **5/2**[1]

00-4 5 shd **Cleverconversation (IRE)**[16] 1225 4-9-2 **60**.....(h) PaddyBradley(5) 7 — 60
(Jane Chapple-Hyam) *chsd ldrs: effrt over 1f out: unable qck 1f out: wknd ins fnl f* **14/1**

1165 6 nse **Hold Firm**[4] 1409 5-9-0 **60**..... GabrieleMalune(7) 10 — 60
(Mark H Tompkins) *hld up in tch in last trio: effrt and shifting lft over 1f out: chsd ldrs and swtchd lft again jst ins fnl f: kpt on same pce fnl 100yds* **8/1**

0023 7 1¾ **Pool House**[9] 1329 6-9-6 **59**..... ShaneKelly 3 — 55
(Mike Murphy) *led: rdn over 1f out: hdd jst ins fnl f: sn edgd rt and fnd little: wknd wl ins fnl f* **6/1**

1500 8 1¼ **Sir Lancelott**[35] 928 5-9-2 **60**..... RachealKneller(5) 4 — 55
(Brian Barr) *chsd ldr: rdn over 2f out: unable qck over 1f out: losing pl and btn whn squeezed for room ins fnl f* **16/1**

-405 9 1 **Lord Of The Storm**[16] 1225 9-9-8 **61**..... LukeMorris 8 — 51
(Michael Attwater) *s.i.s and rousted along early: a towards rr: bhd and u.p over 2f out: wknd fnl f* **14/1**

004/ 10 8 **Hustle (IRE)**[296] 6713 12-8-13 **59**..... GinaMangan(7) 2 — 30
(Clare Hobson) *dwlt and bmpd leaving stalls: rousted along and sn rcvrd to r in midfield: n.m.r on inner 3f out: sn rdn and lost pl: bhd fnl f* **25/1**

1m 38.66s (-1.24) **Going Correction** -0.20s/f (Stan) — **10** Ran SP% **121.0**
Speed ratings (Par 101): **98,96,96,95,95 95,93,92,91,83**
WIN: 7.00 SC; PL: 2.10 SC, 2.90 MH, 1.60 HAN; EX: SC/HAN 18.60, SC/MH 29.50; CSF: SC/MH 28.17, SC/HAN 14.49; TC: SC/MH/HAN 123.06, SC/HAN/MH 111.32; TF: SC/HAN/MH 136.70, SC/MH/HAN 155.90;.
**Owner** Paddy Barrett **Bred** P E Barrett **Trained** Sproxton, Leics

**FOCUS**
A moderate affair.

### 1485 @TOTEPOOLRACING TWEET US YOUR APRIL FOOLS MAIDEN STKS — 1m (P)
6:15 (6:17) (Class 5) 3-4-Y-0 — £5,175 (£1,540; £769; £384) Stalls Low

Form — RPR

2 1 — **Bless Him (IRE)**[15] 1241 3-8-13 0..... OisinMurphy 5 — 82+
(David Simcock) *t.k.h: trckd ldng pair: effrt and shkn up to ld jst over 1f out: qcknd 2 l clr and rdn ins fnl f: kpt on and a doing enough after* **9/4**[1]

0- 2 ¾ **Highland Cradle**[199] 6486 3-8-13 0..... TedDurcan 1 — 80+
(Sir Michael Stoute) *chsd ldng trio: effrt over 2f out: hdwy to chse clr wnr jst ins fnl f: styd on wl for clr 2nd and clsng on wnr towards fin* **5/1**[2]

0- 3 3½ **Bahar (USA)**[141] 7907 3-8-13 0..... SeanLevey 3 — 72
(Richard Hannon) *t.k.h: w ldr: rdn and jostling w rival over 1f out: 3rd and btn 150yds out: sn wknd* **9/4**[1]

4 ¾ **Mudaarab (USA)** 3-8-13 0..... JimCrowley 9 — 70
(Sir Michael Stoute) *broke wl: sn dropped to midfield but wl in tch: rdn over 2f out: swtchd rt wl over 1f out: unable qck and kpt on same pce ins fnl f* **6/1**[3]

625- 5 1½ **Redgrave (IRE)**[172] 7243 3-8-10 **77**.....(h[1]) CallumShepherd(3) 8 — 66
(Charles Hills) *in tch in rr of main gp: rdn 3f out: c wd wl over 1f out: no imp over 1f out: wl hld and plugged on same pce ins fnl f* **10/1**

422 6 hd **Trenchard (USA)**[15] 1244 3-8-13 **73**.....(b[1]) RobertTart 4 — 66
(John Gosden) *t.k.h: mde most: rdn: edgd lft and jostling w rival over 1f out: sn hdd: wknd ins fnl f* **8/1**

7 nk **Zoffany Bay (IRE)** 3-8-13 0.....(h[1]) LukeMorris 7 — 65
(George Peckham) *rn in snatches: in tch in rr of main gp: rdn over 3f out: outpcd wl over 1f out: no ch but kpt on ins fnl f* **50/1**

8 1 **Free Forum (IRE)** 3-8-10 0..... AaronJones(3) 6 — 63
(David Simcock) *sn dropped to detached last and rn green: rdn 3f out: no ch but kpt on ins fnl f* **25/1**

1m 37.22s (-2.68) **Going Correction** -0.20s/f (Stan)
**WFA** 3 from 4yo 15lb — **8** Ran SP% **118.5**
Speed ratings (Par 103): **105,104,100,100,98 98,98,97**
CSF £14.71 TOTE £2.90: £1.10, £2.10, £1.50; EX 17.00 Trifecta £53.40.
**Owner** Qatar Racing Limited **Bred** Knocklong House Stud **Trained** Newmarket, Suffolk

**FOCUS**
This looked a fair maiden.

### 1486 TOTEPOOL RACECOURSE DEBIT CARD BETTING AVAILABLE H'CAP — 2m (P)
6:45 (6:47) (Class 6) (0-65,65) 4-Y-0+ — £3,234 (£962; £481; £240) Stalls Low

Form — RPR

234- 1 — **Masterson (IRE)**[77] 7223 4-9-8 **65**..... SilvestreDeSousa 2 — 72
(Mick Channon) *t.k.h: hld up in tch in midfield: clsd to ld and travelling strly 2f out: rdn and asserted over 1f out: clr and r.o wl ins fnl f* **5/2**[1]

-430 2 2½ **Topalova**[18] 1191 4-7-11 **47**..... GabrieleMalune(7) 1 — 51
(Mark H Tompkins) *hld up in tch: clsd to chse ldrs 2f out: hdwy u.p over 1f out: chsd clr wnr over 1f out: styd on to hold 2nd but no imp* **8/1**

2442 3 ½ **Tasty Ginger (IRE)**[10] 1303 4-9-6 **63**..... OisinMurphy 7 — 66
(J R Jenkins) *hld up in tch: rdn and effrt on outer 3f out: hdwy over 1f out: battling for 2nd fnl f: kpt on but no imp on wnr* **3/1**[2]

-220 4 4 **Le Tissier**[38] 859 4-8-13 **56**.....(p) RobHornby 3 — 55
(Michael Attwater) *chsd ldr for 2f: styd chsng ldrs: effrt on inner wl over 1f out: sn outpcd: 4th and plugged on same pce ins fnl f* **7/1**

0204 5 nk **Cold Fusion (IRE)**[7] 1369 4-8-6 **52**..... HollieDoyle(3) 5 — 50
(David Flood) *stdd and dropped in bhd after s: hld up in tch in rr: effrt wl over 1f out: n.d whn nt clr run 1f out: swtchd lft and kpt on ins fnl f* **12/1**

0012 6 1 **Par Three (IRE)**[14] 1256 6-9-1 **54**..... LiamKeniry 6 — 51
(Tony Carroll) *rousted along leaving stalls: chsd ldr after 2f: rdn 3f out: outpcd and btn over 1f out* **6/1**[3]

3415 7 1¼ **Dream Serenade**[36] 900 4-8-8 **51**.....(h) LukeMorris 4 — 47
(Michael Appleby) *t.k.h: led and set stdy gallop: shkn up over 3f out: hdd and rdn 2f out: sn outpcd: bhd ins fnl f* **6/1**[3]

3m 27.31s (-2.69) **Going Correction** -0.20s/f (Stan)
**WFA** 4 from 6yo 2lb — **7** Ran SP% **113.4**
Speed ratings (Par 101): **98,96,96,94,94 93,93**
CSF £22.49 TOTE £2.70: £1.30, £5.70; EX 25.20 Trifecta £90.80.
**Owner** Box 41 Racing **Bred** Star Pointe Ltd **Trained** West Ilsley, Berks

**FOCUS**
An ordinary staying race and the winner landed a bit of a punt.

### 1487 TOTEPOOL LIVE INFO DOWNLOAD THE APP H'CAP — 5f (P)
7:15 (7:17) (Class 4) (0-80,83) 3-Y-0+ — £6,469 (£1,925; £962; £481) Stalls Low

Form — RPR

-645 1 — **Captain Lars (SAF)**[18] 1185 7-10-0 **80**.....(v) MartinLane 8 — 88
(Derek Shaw) *hld up in tch in last trio: c wd and effrt over 1f out: drvn and hdwy 1f out: str run ins fnl f to ld cl home* **10/1**[3]

1 2 nk **Rock Of America (USA)**[29] 1004 3-9-3 **80**..... DanielTudhope 4 — 82
(David O'Meara) *t.k.h: hdwy to ld after 1f: hdd and rdn over 1f out: drvn 1f out: kpt on wl u.p to ld again towards fin: hdd cl home* **8/11**[1]

-165 3 shd **Zipedeedodah (IRE)**[7] 1370 5-9-12 **78**.....(t) OisinMurphy 1 — 85
(Joseph Tuite) *led for 1f: styd w ldr tl rdn to ld again over 1f out: drvn 1f out: hdd and no ex nr fin* **5/1**[2]

-033 4 1¾ **Seamster**[24] 1091 10-9-9 **82**.....(t) GerO'Neill(7) 6 — 82
(David Loughnane) *chsd ldng trio: effrt over 1f out: drvn to chse ldrs 1f out: kpt on same pce ins fnl f* **12/1**

2411 5 1¼ **Malaysian Boleh**[9] 1327 7-9-5 **71**.....(v) JosephineGordon 7 — 67
(Phil McEntee) *chsd ldrs: rdn over 1f out: unable qck u.p 1f out: outpcd ins fnl f* **14/1**

-006 6 nk **Secret Asset (IRE)**[9] 1327 12-9-3 **69**.....(v) LukeMorris 2 — 64
(Lisa Williamson) *trckd ldrs: effrt over 1f out: unable qck u.p 1f out: edgd lft and outpcd ins fnl f* **50/1**

3201 7 ¾ **Foxy Forever (IRE)**[7] 1370 7-10-3 **83**.....(t) ConnorBeasley 9 — 75
(Michael Wigham) *stdd and dropped in bhd: effrt jst over 1f out: rdn and swtchd lft ins fnl f: kpt on: nvr trbld ldrs* **5/1**[2]

-045 8 2¼ **Grecian Divine (IRE)**[11] 1294 3-8-5 **75**..... SophieScardifield(7) 3 — 54
(Joseph Tuite) *hld up in tch in midfield: effrt over 1f out: no imp: wknd ins fnl f* **66/1**

200- 9 8 **Jaarih (IRE)**[157] 7626 5-9-1 **74**.....(t[1]) FletcherYarham(7) 5 — 29
(George Scott) *awkward leaving stalls: a towards rr: edgd lft u.p and no hdwy over 1f out: sn wknd* **22/1**

58.99s (-1.21) **Going Correction** -0.20s/f (Stan)
**WFA** 3 from 5yo+ 11lb — **9** Ran SP% **122.5**
Speed ratings (Par 105): **101,100,100,97,95 95,93,90,77**
CSF £18.73 CT £48.25 TOTE £12.70: £3.10, £1.10, £2.00; EX 27.00 Trifecta £95.20.



The Form Book Flat, Raceform Ltd, Newbury, RG14 5SJ

**Owner** Chris Hamilton **Bred** Klawervlei Stud **Trained** Sproxton, Leics

**FOCUS**

The leaders rather took each other on and this was set up for a closer.

## 1488 TOTEPOOLRACING LIKE US ON FACEBOOK MAIDEN STKS 7f (P)

**7:45** (7:47) (Class 5) 3-Y-0+ **£5,175** (£1,540; £769; £384) **Stalls** Low

Form RPR

1 **Moolazim** 3-9-0 0 DanielMuscutt 2 81+
(Marco Botti) *wl in tch in midfield: effrt on inner to chse clr ldr and swtchd rt 1f out: rdn and qcknd ins fnl f: r.o strly to ld last strides* **12/1**

024- 2 *hd* **Farook (IRE)**[164] 7468 3-9-0 75 JimCrowley 8 80
(Charles Hills) *led: rdn and qcknd over 1f out: drvn and kpt on ins fnl f: hdd and no ex last strides* **11/4**[2]

3- 3 *3 ½* **Carigrad (IRE)**[156] 7648 3-9-0 0 JosephineGordon 7 71
(Hugo Palmer) *keen to post: t.k.h: chsd ldr: hmpd and pushed rt 5f out: rdn and unable qck w ldr over 1f out: 3rd and outpcd fnl f* **5/4**[1]

06- 4 *½* **Mulzim**[159] 7574 3-9-0 0 DaneO'Neill 5 69
(Ed Dunlop) *chsd ldng trio: swtchd rt and effrt over 1f out: unable qck u.p and kpt on same pce ins fnl f* **6/1**[3]

4 5 *2* **Gunmaker (IRE)**[15] 1241 3-9-0 0 LiamKeniry 6 64
(David Simcock) *t.k.h: hld up in tch in midfield: effrt over 1f out: sn outpcd: shifting lft and kpt on same pce ins fnl f* **20/1**

43 6 *hd* **Miss Mirabeau**[28] 1024 3-8-9 0 LukeMorris 3 58
(Sir Mark Prescott Bt) *t.k.h: trckd ldrs: shkn up over 1f out: sn outpcd: wl hld and hung rt ins fnl f* **16/1**

54 7 *4 ½* **Badenscoth**[21] 1141 3-8-11 0 JackDuern(3) 4 51
(Dean Ivory) *t.k.h: hld up in last trio: hdwy into midfield 3f out: shkn up 2f out: sn u.p and lost pl: wknd fnl f* **50/1**

8 *¾* **Time's Arrow (IRE)** 3-9-0 0 TedDurcan 10 49
(Sir Michael Stoute) *stdd and dropped in bhd after s: hld up in rr: effrt and stl plenty to do over 1f out: no hdwy: n.d* **7/1**

6 9 *8* **Bobbio (IRE)**[21] 1141 3-9-0 0 TomMarquand 1 27
(Marco Botti) *dwlt and early reminder: a towards rr: struggling u.p over 2f out: bhd over 1f out* **33/1**

0 10 *½* **Tilsworth Lukey**[21] 1141 4-9-7 0 GinaMangan(7) 9 31
(J R Jenkins) *t.k.h: hld up in rr: rdn and struggling 3f out: bhd whn hung lft over 1f out* **100/1**

1m 25.83s (-1.37) **Going Correction** -0.20s/f (Stan)
**WFA** 3 from 4yo 14lb **10** Ran SP% **122.1**
Speed ratings (Par 103): **99,98,94,94,91 91,86,85,76,75**
CSF £46.44 TOTE £16.10: £3.80, £1.40, £1.10; EX 58.80 Trifecta £158.80.
**Owner** Sheikh Mohammed Bin Khalifa Al Maktoum **Bred** Essafinaat **Trained** Newmarket, Suffolk

**FOCUS**

A fair maiden and a good performance from the winner.

## 1489 COLLECT TOTEPOOL WINNINGS AT BETFRED SHOPS FILLIES' H'CAP 7f (P)

**8:15** (8:15) (Class 5) (0-75,76) 3-Y-0+ **£5,175** (£1,540; £769; £384) **Stalls** Low

Form RPR

000- 1 **La Casa Tarifa (IRE)**[147] 7820 3-9-4 **76** JoeFanning 5 80+
(Mark Johnston) *s.i.s: hld up in rr: wnt 3rd jst over 2f out: shkn up over 1f out: rdn and hdwy to chse ldr ins fnl f: r.o wl to ld cl home* **15/8**[1]

6632 2 *½* **East Coast Lady (IRE)**[26] 1066 5-9-7 **68** HollieDoyle(3) 1 75
(William Stone) *broke fast: led: rdn ent fnl 2f: drvn over 1f out: kpt on tl hdd and no ex cl home* **5/2**[2]

20-5 3 *3 ¾* **Be Royale**[72] 308 7-9-10 **68** (t) RobertWinston 2 65
(Michael Appleby) *chsd ldng pair tl wnt 2nd over 2f out: drvn and unable qck over 1f out: lost 2nd and wknd ins fnl f* **7/1**

0-42 4 *1* **Zilza (IRE)**[58] 520 3-8-8 **66** (t[1]) MartinDwyer 6 55
(Conrad Allen) *hld up in tch in last pair: effrt in 4th 2f out: no imp over 1f out: wknd ins fnl f* **3/1**[3]

160- 5 *14* **Iceaxe**[176] 7111 4-9-7 **68** AaronJones(3) 4 24
(John Holt) *chsd ldr tl over 2f out: sn u.p and dropped to rr: wl bhd fnl f* **9/1**

1m 24.82s (-2.38) **Going Correction** -0.20s/f (Stan)
**WFA** 3 from 4yo+ 14lb **5** Ran SP% **110.9**
Speed ratings (Par 100): **105,104,100,99,83**
CSF £6.90 TOTE £2.60: £1.50, £1.90; EX 7.20 Trifecta £17.70.
**Owner** Kingsley Park 5 **Bred** Tony Kilduff **Trained** Middleham Moor, N Yorks

**FOCUS**

An ordinary fillies' handicap.

## 1490 BLUE AT LADIES DAY 22ND JUNE H'CAP 6f (P)

**8:45** (8:45) (Class 6) (0-60,62) 4-Y-0+ **£3,234** (£962; £481; £120; £120) **Stalls** Centre

Form RPR

1231 1 **Mighty Zip (USA)**[16] 1220 5-8-8 **54** (p) JordanUys(7) 8 61
(Lisa Williamson) *mde all: rdn over 1f out: drvn and kpt on wl ins fnl f* **6/1**[3]

4114 2 *¾* **Tasaaboq**[2] 1451 6-9-0 **53** (t) JosephineGordon 5 58
(Phil McEntee) *in tch in midfield: edgd lft and effrt on inner over 1f out: hdwy to chse wnr and swtchd rt ins fnl f: kpt on u.p but nvr getting to wnr* **7/2**[2]

2441 3 *1 ¼* **Nasri**[10] 1304 11-9-3 **56** (v) RobertWinston 4 57
(Emma Owen) *chsd ldr: rdn ent fnl 2f: lost 2nd and unable qck over 1f out: styd on same pce ins fnl f* **7/2**[2]

0634 4 *½* **Hurricane Alert**[8] 1340 5-8-7 **46** AdamBeschizza 2 46
(Mark Hoad) *t.k.h: chsd ldng pair: wnt 2nd and swtchd rt over 1f out: drvn and unable qck 1f out: wknd wl ins fnl f* **16/1**

6042 4 *dht* **Borough Boy (IRE)**[18] 1184 7-9-9 **62** (v) MartinLane 10 62
(Derek Shaw) *hld up in last pair: effrt over 1f out: rdn 1f out: styd on ins fnl f: nvr trbld ldrs* **9/4**[1]

4-00 6 *¾* **Jeanie's Place**[19] 1180 4-9-4 **57** (t) WilliamCarson 9 54
(Charlie Wallis) *hld up in tch in last pair: effrt and hdwy over 1f out: nt clrest of runs 1f out: rdn and kpt on same pce ins fnl f* **50/1**

0-56 7 *7* **Last Star Falling (IRE)**[72] 308 4-9-6 **62** (b) LouisSteward(3) 6 38
(Henry Spiller) *chsd ldng trio: rdn over 2f out: lost pl u.p over 1f out: wknd fnl f* **14/1**

01P0 P **Tilsworth Micky**[19] 1180 5-9-7 **60** OisinMurphy 3
(J R Jenkins) *hld up in tch in midfield: lost pl and dropped to rr over 1f out: sn eased and p.u* **6/1**[3]

00-R R **Ghost Train (IRE)**[44] 768 8-9-6 **59** (p) LukeMorris 1
(Tim McCarthy) *ref to r: tk no part* **25/1**

1m 11.61s (-2.09) **Going Correction** -0.20s/f (Stan) **9** Ran SP% **122.1**
Speed ratings (Par 101): **105,104,102,101,101 100,91, ,**
CSF £29.03 CT £87.73 TOTE £7.60: £2.60, £1.40, £1.70; EX 33.80 Trifecta £75.80.
**Owner** Heath House Racing **Bred** Dr Catherine Wills **Trained** Saighton, Cheshire

**FOCUS**

A moderate sprint dominated from the front by the winner.

T/Plt: £24.70 to a £1 stake. Pool: £88,445.01 - 2,606.25 winning units. T/Qpdt: £5.10 to a £1 stake. Pool: £9,887.41 - 1,409.41 winning units. **Steve Payne**

# DONCASTER (L-H)

Saturday, April 1

**OFFICIAL GOING: Good to soft (good in places; 7.4)**

Wind: Light against Weather: Cloudy

## 1491 BETWAY CAMMIDGE TROPHY STKS (LISTED RACE) 6f 2y

**1:50** (1:51) (Class 1) 3-Y-0+

**£20,982** (£7,955; £3,981; £1,983; £995; £499) **Stalls** Centre

Form RPR

-004 1 **Tupi (IRE)**[28] 1044 5-9-5 101 RyanMoore 4 114
(Richard Hannon) *hld up towards rr: hdwy 1/2-way: trckd ldrs 2f out: rdn to ld ent fnl f: sn clr* **7/1**[3]

100- 2 *4* **Captain Colby (USA)**[140] 7932 5-9-5 100 (b) ThomasBrown 12 102
(Ed Walker) *chsd ldrs: hdwy 2f out: rdn over 1f out: drvn and kpt on fnl f* **11/1**

040- 3 *nk* **Pipers Note**[168] 7358 7-9-5 99 JamesSullivan 1 101
(Ruth Carr) *t.k.h early: hld up: hdwy on wd outside 2f out: rdn over 1f out: edgd rt ins fnl f: kpt on wl towards fin* **33/1**

/00- 4 *hd* **Blue Bayou**[290] 3274 4-9-0 102 FrankieDettori 13 96
(Brian Meehan) *racd towards stands rail: in tch: hdwy 2f out: rdn to chse ldrs over 1f out: drvn and kpt on same pce fnl f* **8/1**

106- 5 *hd* **Nameitwhatyoulike**[174] 7191 8-9-8 105 BenCurtis 10 103
(Bryan Smart) *led: rdn along 2f out: drvn and hdd ent fnl f: grad wknd* **11/1**

2-60 6 *¾* **Buying Trouble (USA)**[35] 917 4-9-1 100 ow1 AdamKirby 2 94
(David Evans) *towards rr: hdwy 2f out: rdn over 1f out: kpt on u.p fnl f* **20/1**

31-0 7 *1* **Scrutineer (IRE)**[51] 651 4-9-5 100 GrahamLee 6 95
(Mick Channon) *prom: rdn along over 2f out: drvn over 1f out: sn wknd and hld whn n.m.r ins fnl f* **14/1**

056- 8 *nk* **Birchwood (IRE)**[181] 6991 4-9-5 110 WilliamBuick 8 94
(Richard Fahey) *prom: hdwy and cl up over 2f out: rdn and ev ch over 1f out: wknd fnl f* **9/2**[1]

30-0 9 *nse* **Ride Like The Wind (IRE)**[35] 917 5-9-5 105 (h[1]) JamieSpencer 11 95+
(Kevin Ryan) *hld up in rr: hdwy over 2f out: nt clr run and swtchd rt over 1f out: sn rdn and no imp* **11/1**

-205 10 *1 ¾* **Rene Mathis (GER)**[21] 1150 7-9-5 102 PaulHanagan 5 88
(Richard Fahey) *nvr bttr than midfield* **16/1**

166- 11 *¾* **Mobsta (IRE)**[150] 7771 5-9-5 108 AndreaAtzeni 3 86
(Mick Channon) *a towards rr* **6/1**[2]

635- 12 *nk* **Absolutely So (IRE)**[147] 7822 7-9-5 107 OisinMurphy 9 85
(Andrew Balding) *t.k.h: chsd ldrs: rdn along over 2f out: sn wknd* **7/1**[3]

11-0 13 *5* **Swift Approval (IRE)**[21] 1150 5-9-8 98 (t[1]) DanielTudhope 7 73
(Stuart Williams) *chsd ldrs: rdn along over 2f out: sn wknd* **25/1**

1m 11.28s (-2.32) **Going Correction** 0.0s/f (Good) **13** Ran SP% **117.7**
Speed ratings (Par 111): **115,109,109,109,108 107,106,106,105,103 102,102,95**
CSF £78.49 TOTE £8.00: £2.70, £3.80, £11.80; EX 88.70 Trifecta £4279.30.
**Owner** Michael Kerr-Dineen & Martin Hughes **Bred** Kabansk Ltd & Rathbarry Stud **Trained** East Everleigh, Wilts

**FOCUS**

A fair day weather wise for the opening of the turf season and the going looked in decent nick through the opener.\n\x\x This was a competitive looking Cammidge. They kept mid-track and form ought to work out. The winner has been rated back to his best.

## 1492 BETWAY SPRING MILE H'CAP 1m (S)

**2:25** (2:30) (Class 2) 4-Y-0+

**£28,012** (£8,388; £4,194; £2,097; £1,048; £526) **Stalls** Centre

Form RPR

112- 1 **Ballet Concerto**[210] 6132 4-9-9 **97** RyanMoore 6 106+
(Sir Michael Stoute) *hld up in midfield towards far side: hdwy 2f out: chsd ldrs over 1f out: rdn to chal ent fnl f: styd on wl to ld last 100yds* **8/1**[3]

426- 2 *¾* **Sinfonietta (FR)**[215] 5956 5-9-2 **90** JimmyFortune 3 97
(David Menuisier) *trckd ldrs towards far side: hdwy and cl up over 3f out: led over 1f out and sn rdn: drvn and edgd rt ins fnl f: hdd last 100yds: kpt on* **12/1**

330- 3 *1* **Candelisa (IRE)**[206] 6225 4-9-6 **94** (p) GrahamLee 1 99
(Jedd O'Keeffe) *in tch towards far side: pushed along 3f out: rdn to chse ldrs 1 1/2f out: sn drvn and kpt on wl fnl f* **25/1**

6-41 4 *nk* **Swift Emperor (IRE)**[28] 1032 5-9-4 92 5ex PhillipMakin 9 96
(David Barron) *racd towards far side: prom: cl up 1/2-way: rdn to ld 2f out: drvn and hdd jst over 1f out: kpt on wl u.p fnl f* **20/1**

254- 5 *2 ¼* **Mount Tahan (IRE)**[147] 7821 5-9-3 **91** KevinStott 7 90
(Kevin Ryan) *dwlt: hld up in tch towards far side: hdwy 3f out: chsd ldrs wl over 1f out: sn rdn and ev ch: drvn ent fnl f: kpt on same pce* **25/1**

516- 6 *¾* **Strong Steps**[242] 4976 5-8-11 **92** BenSanderson(7) 19 90+
(Roger Fell) *hld up in tch: hdwy over 2f out: rdn to chse ldrs over 1f out: sn drvn and kpt on same pce* **50/1**

423- 7 *½* **Fuwairt (IRE)**[101] 8478 5-8-10 **91** CameronNoble(7) 2 88
(Roger Fell) *dwlt and in bhd far side: hdwy 3f out: rdn to chse ldrs over 1f out: kpt on same pce ins fnl f* **33/1**

530- 8 *shd* **London Protocol (FR)**[147] 7821 4-9-3 **94** (p) JordanVaughan(3) 10 90
(K R Burke) *chsd ldrs towards far side: hdwy over 2f out: rdn along wl over 1f out: sn no imp* **33/1**

2/1- 9 *nk* **Sacred Act**[204] 6298 6-9-8 **96** AndreaAtzeni 13 92
(John Gosden) *racd towards stands' side: chsd ldrs: rdn along 2f out: sn no imp* **9/2**[1]

000- 10 *1 ¼* **Lat Hawill (IRE)**[189] 6786 6-9-2 **95** (v) ShirleyTeasdale(5) 14 88+
(Keith Dalgleish) *racd in centre: chsd ldrs: rdn along over 2f out: sn one pce* **66/1**

00-5 11 *¾* **Mutarakez (IRE)**[28] 1023 5-9-5 **93** DougieCostello 12 84
(Brian Meehan) *chsd ldrs towards centre: rdn along 2f out: sn one pce* **20/1**

200- 12 *hd* **Sir Roderic (IRE)**[196] 6573 4-9-8 **96** RyanTate 18 87
(Rod Millman) *racd towards stands' side: towards rr: hdwy over 2f out: rdn along wl over 1f out: n.d* **25/1**

06-5 13 *2* **God Willing**[23] 1103 6-9-4 **92** DanielTudhope 16 79
(Declan Carroll) *racd towards stands' side: a towards rr* **20/1**

1423 14 *shd* **Holiday Magic (IRE)**[21] 1148 6-9-3 **94** NathanEvans(3) 22 80
(Michael Easterby) *racd stands' side: cl up: rdn along over 2f out: sn wknd* **25/1**

006- **15** *nk* **Gabrial's Kaka (IRE)**[224] 5640 7-9-3 **94**................ AdamMcNamara(3) 5 80
(Richard Fahey) *dwlt and towards rr whn swtchd rt after 1f: n.d* **25/1**

330- **16** *nk* **Father Bertie**[131] 8049 5-9-4 **92**......................................(tp) DavidAllan 8 77
(Tim Easterby) *prom far side: cl up 1/2-way: rdn along 2f out: sn drvn and wknd* **25/1**

2- **17** *½* **Another Touch**[175] 7153 4-9-8 **96**................................. PaulHanagan 11 80
(Richard Fahey) *a towards rr* **11/1**

35-4 **18** *½* **Examiner (IRE)**[21] 1148 6-9-5 **93**.........................(t[1]) OisinMurphy 20 76
(Stuart Williams) *racd towards stands' side: towards rr: sme hdwy 3f out: rdn along and n.m.r 2f out: n.d* **14/1**

100- **19** *5* **Lord Of The Rock (IRE)**[282] 3566 5-9-5 **93**.............. PaulMulrennan 15 65
(Michael Dods) *racd towards stands' side: led: pushed along 3f out: hdd over 2f out and sn wknd* **33/1**

-611 **20** *30* **Nimr**[21] 1148 4-9-7 **95** 5ex............................................... FrankieDettori 17 1
(Richard Fahey) *racd towards stands' side: hld up towards rr: pushed along 3f out: sn rdn and wknd: bhd and eased wl over 1f out* **5/1**[2]

110- **P** **Raising Sand**[157] 7608 5-9-6 **94**...................................... AdamKirby 4
(Jamie Osborne) *racd towards far side: a in rr: lost tch and bhd whn p.u over 3f out* **8/1**[3]

1m 38.3s (-1.00) **Going Correction** +0.175s/f (Good) **21** Ran SP% **129.4**
Speed ratings (Par 109): **112,111,110,109,107 106,106,106,106,104 104,103,101,101,101 101,100,100,95,65**
CSF £83.25 CT £1417.76 TOTE £8.00: £2.40, £4.30, £8.60, £5.30; EX 132.90 Trifecta £1738.60.

**Owner** Saeed Suhail **Bred** Meon Valley Stud **Trained** Newmarket, Suffolk

**FOCUS**
This looked a strong consolation race. It's been rated around those close up.

## 1493 BETWAY DONCASTER MILE STKS (LISTED RACE) 7f 213y(R)

**3:00** (3:01) (Class 1) 4-Y-O+

**£20,982** (£7,955; £3,981; £1,983; £995; £499) **Stalls** Low

Form RPR

/42- **1** **Kool Kompany (IRE)**[154] 7701 5-9-0 108.......................... RyanMoore 4 112
(Richard Hannon) *racd keenly in midfield: in tch on bit over 2f out: swtchd rt ent fnl f: rdn and r.o strly: led post* **7/1**[3]

206- **2** *shd* **Stormy Antarctic**[168] 7352 4-9-0 114............................. JamieSpencer 9 112
(Ed Walker) *hld up: hdwy over 2f out: pushed along to chal over 1f out: led ins fnl f: rdn and edgd rt: kpt on but hdd post* **10/3**[2]

541- **3** *½* **Dawn Of Hope (IRE)**[123] 8148 4-8-12 99.......................... AndreaAtzeni 5 109
(Roger Varian) *in tch: hdwy to trck ldr gng wl over 2f out: rdn to ld narrowly ent fnl f: hdd ins fnl f: kpt on same pce* **10/1**

310- **4** *1 ¾* **Toscanini (IRE)**[202] 6384 5-9-0 112.................................. PaulHanagan 3 107
(Richard Fahey) *led: rdn over 1f out: hdd ent fnl f: no ex fnl 110yds* **12/1**

020- **5** *½* **Tullius (IRE)**[168] 7354 9-9-0 110................................(v) OisinMurphy 1 106
(Andrew Balding) *midfield: rdn over 2f out: kpt on ins fnl f: nvr threatened ldrs* **12/1**

250- **6** *nk* **Custom Cut (IRE)**[175] 7152 8-9-0 112.......................... DanielTudhope 2 105
(David O'Meara) *in tch: rdn to chse ldr over 1f out: no ex ins fnl f* **14/1**

0-13 **7** *2 ¾* **Cymric (USA)**[44] 774 4-9-0 109.................................(p) WilliamBuick 6 99
(Charlie Appleby) *trckd ldrs: rdn over 2f out: bit short of room ent fnl f: wknd* **7/1**[3]

122- **8** *3* **Crazy Horse**[127] 8117 4-9-0 112.......................................... FrankieDettori 7 92
(John Gosden) *hld up: rdn over 2f out: nvr threatened* **3/1**[1]

630- **9** *1* **Castle Harbour**[140] 7933 4-9-0 105................................ JimmyFortune 8 90
(John Gosden) *dwlt: hld up: rdn over 2f out: nvr threatened* **12/1**

640- **10** *16* **Big Baz (IRE)**[175] 7152 7-9-0 108................................... MartinDwyer 11 55
(William Muir) *a rr* **33/1**

-500 **11** *31* **Dark Emerald (IRE)**[37] 892 7-9-1 106 ow1..................(t) AdamKirby 10
(Brendan Powell) *prom: rdn and lost pl over 3f out: wknd and eased* **50/1**

1m 36.99s (-2.71) **Going Correction** +0.025s/f (Good) **11** Ran SP% **116.8**
Speed ratings (Par 111): **114,113,113,111,111 110,108,105,104,88 57**
CSF £30.30 TOTE £7.40: £2.40, £1.50, £3.40; EX 28.30 Trifecta £392.30.

**Owner** Kool Kompany Partnership **Bred** Miss Imelda O'Shaughnessy **Trained** East Everleigh, Wilts

**FOCUS**
This Listed event was given a real boost by the subsequent efforts of last year's winner Belardo. It was run at a strong pace this time around and served up a cracking finish. It's been rated around the winner for now.

## 1494 BETWAY LINCOLN (HERITAGE H'CAP) 1m (S)

**3:35** (3:36) (Class 2) 4-Y-O+

**£62,250** (£18,640; £9,320; £4,660; £2,330; £1,170) **Stalls** Centre

Form RPR

004- **1** **Bravery (IRE)**[167] 7394 4-9-1 **100**................................. DanielTudhope 20 108
(David O'Meara) *rr and swtchd markedly rt towards far side s: hld up and bhd: smooth hdwy on wd outside wl over 1f out: rdn to chal ins fnl f: drvn and styd on wl to ld towards fin* **20/1**

1-35 **2** *nk* **Oh This Is Us (IRE)**[37] 892 4-9-6 **105**............................. RyanMoore 2 112
(Richard Hannon) *racd towards far side: in tch: hdwy over 2f out: rdn to ld jst over 1f out: drvn ins fnl f: hdd and no ex towards fin* **7/2**[1]

004- **3** *nk* **Donncha (IRE)**[154] 7701 6-9-1 **100**............................... JamieSpencer 21 106
(Robert Eddery) *swtchd lft after s: hld up and bhd centre: hdwy wl over 1f out: swtchd rt and rdn jst over 1f out: styd on strly* **7/1**[3]

-050 **4** *½* **Gabrial (IRE)**[35] 934 8-9-6 **108**................................ AdamMcNamara(3) 4 113
(Richard Fahey) *dwlt and towards rr far side: hdwy on outer 2f out: rdn to chal over 1f out: ev ch and drvn ins fnl f: kpt on* **16/1**

615- **5** *1 ¼* **Dolphin Vista (IRE)**[175] 7154 4-9-0 **99**......................... PaulHanagan 10 101
(Richard Fahey) *in tch centre: hdwy over 2f out: rdn over 1f out: drvn and kpt on fnl f* **12/1**

/340 **6** *nk* **Eddystone Rock (IRE)**[41] 835 5-9-1 **100**...................(h[1]) KierenFox 5 102
(John Best) *in tch towards far side: hdwy over 2f out: rdn to chse ldrs over 1f out: drvn and kpt on same pce fnl f* **33/1**

-000 **7** *shd* **Steel Train (FR)**[21] 1148 6-8-12 **100**.......................... ShelleyBirkett(3) 16 102
(David O'Meara) *towards rr stands side. hdwy 2f out: rdn over 1f out: styd on fnl f: nrst fin* **28/1**

50-4 **8** *nk* **Zhui Feng (IRE)**[35] 919 4-9-3 **102**................................. MartinDwyer 13 103
(Amanda Perrett) *racd towards stands side: led: rdn along 2f out: drvn and hdd jst over 1f out: grad wknd* **14/1**

020- **9** *shd* **Withernsea (IRE)**[147] 7821 6-8-12 **97**.......................... TonyHamilton 7 98
(Richard Fahey) *racd towards far side: in tch: pushed along and outpcd over 2f out: rdn wl over 1f out: kpt on fnl f* **25/1**

2-60 **10** *shd* **You're Fired (IRE)**[35] 919 6-9-5 **107**..................... JordanVaughan(3) 11 109
(K R Burke) *hld up in rr towards stands side: hdwy 2f out: sn rdn: styd on wl fnl f: nrst fin* **33/1**

200- **11** *nk* **Instant Attraction (IRE)**[216] 5941 6-9-0 **99**..................... JackGarritty 15 99
(Jedd O'Keeffe) *chsd ldrs towards stands side: rdn along 2f out: drvn over 1f out: kpt on same pce* **25/1**

546- **12** *½* **Master Carpenter (IRE)**[185] 6884 6-8-9 **99**............... LuluStanford(5) 19 98
(Rod Millman) *hld up in rr stands side: hdwy 2f out: rdn over 1f out: kpt on fnl f* **20/1**

41-3 **13** *1* **Yufteen**[21] 1150 6-9-6 **105**................................................... AndreaAtzeni 14 102
(Roger Charlton) *trckd ldrs towards stands side: hdwy over 2f out: rdn wl over 1f out: sn drvn and wknd* **4/1**[2]

02-0 **14** *nk* **Top Notch Tonto (IRE)**[21] 1148 7-8-13 **105**.............. BenRobinson(7) 8 101
(Brian Ellison) *trckd ldrs towards far side: rdn along wl over 2f out: sn btn* **14/1**

00-0 **15** *3 ¼* **Emell**[21] 1148 7-9-1 **100**...............................................(b) TimmyMurphy 22 89
(Richard Hannon) *racd towards stands side: a towards rr* **33/1**

350- **16** *shd* **Lucy The Painter (IRE)**[190] 6746 5-9-1 **100**.............. DougieCostello 12 89
(Ed de Giles) *a towards rr* **50/1**

-413 **17** *½* **Third Time Lucky (IRE)**[28] 1023 5-9-0 **106** 5ex...... ConnorMurtagh(7) 1 93
(Richard Fahey) *racd towards far side: prom: rdn along 2f out: sn drvn and wknd* **12/1**

165- **18** *1 ¼* **Highland Colori (IRE)**[159] 7573 9-9-0 **99**...................(v) DavidProbert 17 84
(Andrew Balding) *racd towards stands side: chsd ldr: rdn along over 2f out: wknd over 1f out* **33/1**

30-0 **19** *1 ½* **Dream Walker (FR)**[21] 1148 8-9-2 **101**..............................(t) BenCurtis 9 82
(Brian Ellison) *racd towards far side: prom: rdn along 3f out: sn wknd* **66/1**

000- **20** *hd* **Heaven's Guest (IRE)**[182] 6942 7-8-12 **100**............. SammyJoBell(3) 18 81
(Richard Fahey) *racd towards stands side: rr: sme hdwy 2f out: sn rdn and nvr a factor* **33/1**

0-61 **21** *12* **George Cinq**[17] 1208 7-9-1 **100** 5ex.................................. OisinMurphy 6 55
(George Scott) *racd towards far side: trckd ldrs: pushed along over 2f out: sn rdn and btn* **33/1**

250- **22** *¾* **Battle Of Marathon (USA)**[266] 4127 5-9-10 **109**............(v) AdamKirby 3 62
(John Ryan) *racd towards far side: prom: rdn along over 3f out: sn lost pl and bhd* **25/1**

1m 38.38s (-0.92) **Going Correction** +0.175s/f (Good) **22** Ran SP% **134.9**
Speed ratings (Par 109): **111,110,110,109,108 108,108,107,107,107 107,106,105,105,102 102,101,100,99,98 86,86**
CSF £82.72 CT £589.73 TOTE £27.70: £5.60, £2.00, £2.20, £4.10; EX 214.60 Trifecta £1562.90.

**Owner** Sprint Thoroughbred Racing **Bred** Whisperview Trading Ltd **Trained** Upper Helmsley, N Yorks

**FOCUS**
A highly competitive Lincoln, even though a few ante-post gambles failed to to make the cut. They went mid-track and the runner-up is solid guide, as is the fourth. The winner has been rated up 6lb on his previous best in Ireland. The third has ben rated to his Spring Mile form at this meeting last year.

## 1495 BETWAY BROCKLESBY CONDITIONS STKS (PLUS 10 RACE) (DIV I) 5f 3y

**4:10** (4:12) (Class 4) 2-Y-O **£6,469** (£1,925; £962; £481) **Stalls** Centre

Form RPR

**1** **Santry (IRE)** 2-9-3 0............................................................ NeilFarley 2 77
(Declan Carroll) *chsd ldrs: rdn 2f out: led 1f out: idled fnl 75yds and jst hld on* **4/1**[3]

**2** *hd* **Last Page** 2-9-3 0...................................................................... JFEgan 8 76
(David Evans) *dwlt: hld up: sn pushed along: hdwy 2f out: kpt on wl fnl f* **13/2**

**3** *1 ¼* **Benadalid** 2-9-3 0.............................................................. PaulMulrennan 5 72
(Chris Fairhurst) *hld up: sn pushed along: kpt on fnl f: wnt 3rd towards fin* **50/1**

**4** *nk* **Almane (IRE)** 2-9-3 0........................................................ PaulHanagan 9 71+
(Richard Fahey) *chsd ldrs: rdn 2f out: one pce ins fnl f* **2/1**[1]

**5** *1* **Autumn Lodge** 2-9-3 0................................................ MichaelJMMurphy 1 67+
(J S Moore) *dwlt and wnt sltly lft s: outpcd in rr tl kpt on ins fnl f* **50/1**

**6** *1 ¾* **Billiebrookedit (IRE)** 2-9-3 0.......................................... RobertWinston 3 61
(Steph Hollinshead) *hld up: sn pushed along: nvr threatened* **20/1**

**7** *1 ¾* **Rocket Man Dan (IRE)** 2-9-3 0.................................... ConnorBeasley 6 55
(Keith Dalgleish) *pressed ldr: rdn 2f out: carried lft over 1f out: wknd ins fnl f* **5/2**[2]

**8** *½* **Furni Factors** 2-9-0 0........................................................ NathanEvans(3) 11 53
(Ronald Thompson) *chsd ldrs: rdn and lost pl 3f out: no threat after* **25/1**

**9** *¾* **Dragon's Teeth (IRE)** 2-9-3 0......................................... RenatoSouza 7 50
(Jo Hughes) *led narrowly: pushed along 3f out: edgd lft over 1f out: hdd 1f out: wknd* **22/1**

**10** *10* **Afterthisone** 2-9-3 0.......................................................... DougieCostello 10 14
(Robin Dickin) *slowly away: a bhd* **50/1**

**11** *31* **Primo's Comet** 2-9-3 0............................................................ SamJames 4
(Jim Goldie) *slowly away: bucked: swished tail and veered bdly rt sn after leaving stalls: t.o thrght* **20/1**

1m 1.09s (0.59) **Going Correction** +0.175s/f (Good) **11** Ran SP% **118.8**
Speed ratings (Par 94): **102,101,99,99,97 94,92,91,90,74 24**
CSF £27.57 TOTE £5.40: £1.90, £2.20, £12.40; EX 33.30 Trifecta £869.80.

**Owner** Ray Flegg, John Bousfield & Steve Ryan **Bred** Peter Molony **Trained** Malton, N Yorks

**FOCUS**
The opening 2yo race of 2017 and divided this year. The first pair fought it out down the middle. It's been rated at the lower end of the race averages.

## 1496 BETWAY BROCKLESBY CONDITIONS STKS (PLUS 10 RACE) (DIV II) 5f 3y

**4:45** (4:47) (Class 4) 2-Y-O **£6,469** (£1,925; £962; £481) **Stalls** Centre

Form RPR

**1** **Requinto Dawn (IRE)** 2-9-3 0...................................... TonyHamilton 10 80+
(Richard Fahey) *trckd ldrs: hdwy over 2f out: sn cl up: rdn to ld ent fnl f: kpt on strly* **6/1**

**2** *2 ¼* **The Love Doctor (IRE)** 2-9-3 0.............................................. JFEgan 8 69+
(David Evans) *cl up: green and rdn along over 2f out: edgd rt and drvn over 1f out: kpt on fnl f* **9/2**[3]

**3** *nk* **Black Orange** 2-8-10 0......................................(p[1]) DavidEgan(7) 6 68
(Gay Kelleway) *cl up: rdn to take slt ld wl over 1f out: hdd ent fnl f: sn edgd rt and kpt on* **14/1**

**4** *2 ½* **Hellovaqueen** 2-8-7 0........................................................ RyanWhile(5) 7 54
(Bill Turner) *slt ld: pushed along over 2f out: rdn and hdd wl over 1f out: grad wknd* **10/1**

**5** *1* **Cruel Clever Cat** 2-8-12 0................................................ MartinDwyer 5 50
(John Gallagher) *chsd ldrs: rdn along and green 2f out: kpt on fnl f* **25/1**

3 **6** *½* **Jurisprudance (FR)**[9] 1335 2-8-12 0.............................. SteveDrowne 2 48
(George Baker) *cl up: rdn along over 2f out: sn drvn and wknd wl over 1f out* **11/4**[1]
**7** *1* **Quick Skips Lad (IRE)** 2-9-3 0........................................ LiamJones 1 50
(J S Moore) *chsd ldrs: rdn along over 2f out: sn one pce* **66/1**
**8** *4* **Captain Kissinger** 2-9-3 0........................................ IrineuGoncalves 3 35
(Jo Hughes) *dwlt: sn chsng ldrs on outer: rdn along over 2f out: sn wknd* **33/1**
**9** *shd* **Bee Machine (IRE)** 2-9-3 0................................................ NeilFarley 9 35
(Declan Carroll) *chsd ldrs on outer: rdn along over 2f out: grad wknd* **8/1**
**10** *1* **One Last Hug** 2-9-3 0.................................................. SamJames 4 31
(Jim Goldie) *dwlt: green and a towards rr* **33/1**
**11** *3¾* **Move To The Front (IRE)** 2-9-3 0................................ AdamKirby 11 18
(Clive Cox) *in tch: green and hung lft after 1f: sn outpcd and bhd* **7/2**[2]

1m 1.31s (0.81) **Going Correction** +0.175s/f (Good) **11** Ran SP% **119.4**
Speed ratings (Par 94): **100,96,95,91,90 89,87,81,81,79 73**
CSF £32.77 TOTE £7.40: £2.30, £1.80, £4.90; EX 31.20 Trifecta £458.70.
**Owner** The Phoenix Racing C O & Partner **Bred** Thomas J Murphy **Trained** Musley Bank, N Yorks

**FOCUS**
This second division of the Brocklesby was 0.22secs slower but the winner impressed. This leg has also been rated towards the lower end of the race averages.

## 1497 BETWAY MAIDEN STKS 1m 2f 43y
**5:20** (5:23) (Class 5) 3-Y-O **£3,234** (£962; £481; £240) **Stalls** Low

Form RPR
02- **1** **Dubawi Prince**[169] 7318 3-9-5 0.................................... AndreaAtzeni 13 85+
(Roger Varian) *trckd ldr: hdwy to ld wl over 2f out: rdn wl over 1f out: kpt on wl towards fin* **3/1**[1]
442- **2** *½* **Never Surrender (IRE)**[182] 6945 3-9-5 82.................... JamieSpencer 9 84
(Charles Hills) *in tch: hdwy over 2f out: chsd ldrs whn n.m.r and swtchd lft over 1f out: sn rdn and ev ch ins fnl f: drvn and kpt on towards fin* **8/1**
2 **3** *shd* **Hold Sway (IRE)**[24] 1083 3-9-5 0................................. WilliamBuick 15 84
(Charlie Appleby) *trckd ldrs: hdwy on outer over 3f out: chsd wnr 2f out: rdn over 1f out: ev ch tl drvn ins fnl f and kpt on same pce* **4/1**[2]
3- **4** *4* **Wasatch Range**[150] 7770 3-9-5 0................................... FrankieDettori 4 77
(John Gosden) *trckd ldrs on inner: hdwy over 3f out: cl up over 2f out: rdn and hung lft wl over 1f out: sn drvn and kpt on one pce* **3/1**[1]
5- **5** *2* **Joshua Reynolds**[173] 7226 3-9-5 0................................ GrahamLee 8 73
(John Gosden) *trckd ldrs: hdwy over 3f out: rdn along and cl up whn hmpd wl over 1f out: sn one pce* **7/1**[3]
**6** *1¼* **Albert's Back** 3-9-2 0................................................ NathanEvans(3) 10 71
(Michael Easterby) *towards rr: hdwy on outer 3f out: rdn along wl over 1f out: styd on fnl f* **66/1**
64- **7** *1¾* **Mr Davies**[135] 7982 3-9-5 0........................................... AdamKirby 17 68
(David Brown) *led: pushed along 4f out: rdn over 3f out: hdd wl over 2f out: grad wknd* **40/1**
**8** *1¾* **Kilowatt** 3-9-5 0........................................................ DavidAllan 12 64
(Tim Easterby) *towards rr: hdwy 3f out: rdn along over 2f out: n.d* **100/1**
**9** *½* **Immortalised** 3-9-5 0.................................................. PJMcDonald 3 64+
(K R Burke) *a towards rr* **10/1**
**10** *¾* **Theglasgowwarrior** 3-9-2 0...................................... LouisSteward(3) 11 62
(Michael Bell) *midfield: hdwy to chse ldrs over 3f out: rdn along wl over 2f out: sn wknd* **50/1**
04- **11** *nk* **Lunar Jet**[129] 8073 3-9-5 0............................................ BenCurtis 16 63
(John Mackie) *towards rr: hdwy 4f out: chsd ldrs on inner wl over 2f out: rdn along whn hmpd wl over 1f out: sn wknd* **80/1**
**12** *1¼* **Air Ministry (IRE)** 3-9-5 0........................................(b[1]) DannyBrock 7 59
(Michael Bell) *towards rr: hdwy 4f out: effrt on inner to chse ldrs 3f out: sn rdn and wknd* **50/1**
4 **13** *9* **Yemnaak (FR)**[16] 1226 3-9-5 0....................................(t[1]) PaulMulrennan 5 43
(George Peckham) *midfield: rdn along over 3f out: sn wknd* **100/1**
**14** *1½* **Jump Around** 3-8-9 0................................................ CliffordLee(5) 14 36
(K R Burke) *a towards rr* **33/1**
0- **15** *hd* **Seventii**[165] 7441 3-9-0 0.............................................. JFEgan 6 35
(Robert Eddery) *a towards rr* **100/1**
**P** **Avago Josh** 3-9-5 0................................................... DavidNolan 1
(Ivan Furtado) *v.s.a and t.o: p.u after 2f* **80/1**

2m 12.46s (3.06) **Going Correction** +0.25s/f (Good) **16** Ran SP% **118.9**
Speed ratings (Par 98): **97,96,96,93,91 90,89,87,87,86 86,85,78,77,77**
CSF £24.30 TOTE £4.10: £1.60, £2.40, £1.80; EX 27.70 Trifecta £113.90.
**Owner** Sheikh Mohammed Obaid Al Maktoum **Bred** Newsells Park Stud **Trained** Newmarket, Suffolk
■ Sable Island was withdrawn. Price at time of withdrawal 6-1. Rule 4 applies to all bets - deduction 10p in the pound.

**FOCUS**
Traditionally a fair maiden. The runner-up sets a solid standard.

## 1498 BETWAY APPRENTICE H'CAP (ROUND 1 OF THE GO RACING IN YORKSHIRE FUTURE STARS SERIES) 1m 2f 43y
**5:50** (5:54) (Class 5) (0-70,70) 4-Y-O+ **£3,234** (£962; £481; £240) **Stalls** Low

Form RPR
03-6 **1** **Boycie**[58] 517 4-9-3 69............................................... TinaSmith(5) 7 77
(Richard Hannon) *trckd ldrs: rdn to ld 2f out: wandered ins fnl f: styd on* **10/1**
-304 **2** *¾* **Deeley's Double (FR)**[24] 1085 4-9-2 63........................ CliffordLee 16 70
(Tony Carroll) *midfield: rdn and hdwy over 2f out: wnt 3rd appr fnl f: kpt on* **10/1**
0/ **3** *nk* **Volpone Jelois (FR)**[30] 4-9-6 70..........................(p) MeganNicholls(3) 2 76
(Paul Nicholls) *midfield: pushed along and hdwy fr over 3f out: chsd ldr 2f out: sn rdn: kpt on but a hld* **11/2**[2]
3644 **4** *2* **Take Two**[30] 992 8-9-5 69........................................ CameronNoble(3) 9 72
(Alex Hales) *hld up: pushed along and stl plenty to do 2f out: styd on wl fr over 1f out* **9/1**
1112 **5** *nk* **Boychick (IRE)**[42] 806 4-9-7 68.................................. MitchGodwin 6 70
(Ed Walker) *trckd ldrs: rdn over 2f out: one pce* **13/2**[3]
5-06 **6** *1½* **Al Khafji**[24] 1085 4-9-8 69.........................................(b) DavidParkes 10 68
(Jeremy Gask) *hld up in midfield: rdn 3f out: edgd rt to wd outside over 2f out: styd on fnl f* **14/1**
0321 **7** *hd* **Glorious Asset**[17] 1210 5-9-3 64................................ LewisEdmunds 5 63
(Ivan Furtado) *in tch on inner: rdn over 1f out: styd on same pce* **10/1**
450- **7** *dht* **Ice Galley (IRE)**[179] 7043 4-9-8 69.............................. RichardOliver 20 68
(Philip Kirby) *midfield on outer: rdn over 2f out: styd on fnl f* **40/1**
2-60 **9** *5* **Gatillo**[30] 986 4-9-2 68........................................ FinleyMarsh(5) 13 58
(Julia Feilden) *trckd ldrs: rdn 3f out: wknd fnl f* **50/1**
030- **10** *1¼* **Clayton Hall (IRE)**[126] 8124 4-9-3 67......................... BenRobinson(3) 1 55
(John Wainwright) *hld up in midfield: rdn 3f out: nvr threatened* **66/1**

035- **11** *hd* **Match My Fire (IRE)**[162] 7500 4-9-2 66................ CallumRodriguez(3) 4 53
(Michael Dods) *midfield: rdn over 2f out: wknd ins fnl f* **5/1**[1]
230- **12** *2¾* **Miningrocks (FR)**[136] 7973 5-9-6 67................................ PhilDennis 11 49
(Declan Carroll) *led: rdn whn hdd 2f out: wknd appr fnl f* **25/1**
0663 **13** *shd* **Hard To Handel**[9] 1334 5-9-4 65...................................(b) PaddyPilley 15 47
(Clare Ellam) *hld up: rdn and sme hdwy on inner 3f out: wknd over 1f out* **16/1**
-104 **14** *2* **Hernando Torres**[18] 1189 9-9-1 69.............................(t) RyanTimby(7) 19 48
(Michael Easterby) *dwlt: hld up: rdn and sme hdwy 2f out: wknd fnl f* **33/1**
**15** *3¼* **Fisherman's Blues (IRE)**[57] 556 4-9-7 68....................... JoshDoyle 17 41
(Peter Niven) *hld up: nvr threatened* **40/1**
3-00 **16** *nse* **Rivers Of Asia**[35] 928 4-9-9 70..................................... GeorgeWood 12 43
(Martin Smith) *midfield: rdn over 2f out: wknd over 1f out* **33/1**
102- **17** *1* **We'll Shake Hands (FR)**[216] 5929 6-9-0 66............... RussellHarris(5) 3 37
(K R Burke) *in tch: rdn 3f out: wknd 2f out* **25/1**
1-00 **18** *hd* **Moojaned (IRE)**[65] 414 6-9-4 70..................... KatherineGlenister(5) 18 40
(David Evans) *prom: rdn 3f out: wknd 2f out* **25/1**
323- **19** *2* **Bahamian C**[150] 7775 6-8-9 63...........................(t) SebastianWoods(7) 8 30
(Richard Fahey) *a towards rr* **10/1**
360- **20** *13* **First Wheat**[116] 8240 4-9-2 70................................... HarrisonShaw(7) 14 13
(Michael Easterby) *a rr* **33/1**

2m 11.07s (1.67) **Going Correction** +0.25s/f (Good) **20** Ran SP% **133.0**
Speed ratings (Par 103): **103,102,102,100,100 99,98,98,94,93 93,91,91,89,87 87,86,86,84,74**
CSF £103.75 CT £630.58 TOTE £11.90: £3.00, £3.10, £2.00, £2.90; EX 202.60 Trifecta £866.70.
**Owner** Mrs V Hubbard & K T Ivory **Bred** Highclere Stud **Trained** East Everleigh, Wilts

**FOCUS**
This apprentice handicap was not as competitive as the numbers suggested. A small step forward from the runner-up.
T/Jkpt: Not Won. T/Plt: £2,231.20 to a £1 stake. Pool: £232,019.94 - 75.91 winning units. T/Qpdt: £65.70 to a £1 stake. Pool: £15,966.86 - 179.64 winning units. **Joe Rowntree & Andrew Sheret**

# 1418 KEMPTON (A.W) (R-H)
Saturday, April 1

**OFFICIAL GOING: Polytrack: standard**
Wind: Moderate, across (away from stands) Weather: Fine but cloudy, shower race 3

## 1499 BETFRED TV EBF MAIDEN STKS 1m 1f 219y(P)
**1:30** (1:31) (Class 5) 3-Y-O **£4,204** (£1,251; £625; £312) **Stalls** Low

Form RPR
35-2 **1** **Wefait (IRE)**[10] 1308 3-9-5 74........................................ SeanLevey 8 79
(Richard Hannon) *trckd ldr 2f: styd cl up: rdn 3f out: styd on fr over 1f out to ld last 100yds: drvn out* **16/1**
4 **2** *nk* **Many Waters (USA)**[35] 916 3-9-0 0................................. LiamKeniry 1 73
(Andrew Balding) *trckd ldng pair: effrt whn short of room and briefly unbalanced bnd 2f out: rcvrd and rdn to ld jst ins fnl f: hdd last 100yds: kpt on* **5/1**[3]
004- **3** *1½* **Amlad (IRE)**[218] 5848 3-9-5 79............................... SilvestreDeSousa 3 75
(Ed Dunlop) *dwlt and shoved along early: rapid prog to join ldr after 2f: rdn to ld 2f out: hdd and one pce jst ins fnl f* **11/10**[1]
54- **4** *3* **Secret Soul**[179] 7050 3-9-0 0.......................................... FranBerry 7 64
(Ralph Beckett) *led: jnd after 2f out: shkn up and hdd 2f out: wknd fnl f* **9/2**[2]
0- **5** *2¼* **Inscribe (USA)**[202] 6368 3-9-5 0..................................... TedDurcan 2 65
(Sir Michael Stoute) *awkward s: in tch in midfield but rn green: bdly outpcd fr 3f out: kpt on steadily over 1f out* **8/1**
**6** *½* **Ragtag Rascal (IRE)** 3-9-5 0...................................... JackMitchell 6 64
(Amanda Perrett) *s.s: hld up in last: bdly outpcd 3f out: kpt on steadily fr over 1f out* **40/1**
00- **7** *6* **Light Gunner (IRE)**[127] 8088 3-9-5 0..................... RichardKingscote 4 52
(Henry Tett) *in tch: bdly outpcd 3f out: wknd over 1f out* **200/1**
4-5 **8** *2* **Mesophere**[80] 175 3-9-5 0.............................................(b[1]) JimCrowley 5 48
(John Gosden) *rn green in last pair: bdly outpcd 3f out: wknd over 1f out* **8/1**

2m 5.86s (-2.14) **Going Correction** 0.0s/f (Stan) **8** Ran SP% **113.5**
Speed ratings (Par 98): **108,107,106,104,102 101,97,95**
CSF £92.13 TOTE £9.50: £2.80, £2.00, £1.10; EX 44.00 Trifecta £121.00.
**Owner** Mohamed Saeed Al Shahi **Bred** Conor Murphy & Rathmore Stud **Trained** East Everleigh, Wilts

**FOCUS**
A fair 3yo maiden. They went a respectable gallop on standard Polytrack. The opening level is a bit fluid.

## 1500 BETFRED MOBILE MAGNOLIA STKS (LISTED RACE) 1m 1f 219y(P)
**2:05** (2:05) (Class 1) 4-Y-O+
**£22,684** (£8,600; £4,304; £2,144; £1,076; £540) **Stalls** Low

Form RPR
1123 **1** **Absolute Blast (IRE)**[35] 919 5-8-9 105.......................... LukeMorris 2 102
(Archie Watson) *trckd ldrs: shkn up 2f out: gap appeared on inner and chal jst over 1f out: led last 150yds: r.o wl* **4/1**[3]
220- **2** *nk* **Linguistic (IRE)**[288] 3337 4-9-0 103............................ JimCrowley 7 106
(John Gosden) *trckd ldr: rdn over 2f out: clsd to chal jst over 1f out: w wnr 150yds out: styd on but jst outpcd* **9/4**[1]
32-1 **3** *nk* **Sovereign Debt (IRE)**[36] 914 8-9-3 110.................... AndrewMullen 3 109
(Ruth Carr) *hld up in 5th: gng wl 2f out: nt clr run over 1f out to last 150yds: r.o wl whn in the clr but too late to chal* **6/1**
460- **4** *nk* **Very Dashing**[144] 7862 4-8-9 94............................ RichardKingscote 1 100
(Ralph Beckett) *led at average pce: kicked for home over 2f out: kpt on but worn down last 150yds* **8/1**
05-2 **5** *2* **Fire Fighting (IRE)**[8] 1355 6-9-0 112............................(b) FranBerry 8 103
(Mark Johnston) *pushed along early: chsd ldrs but trapped wd and then t.k.h: rdn over 2f out: nt qckn over 1f out: hld fnl f and sharply eased last strides* **7/2**[2]
010- **6** *½* **Quarterback (GER)**[161] 7545 5-9-5 110................(t[1]) SilvestreDeSousa 6 105
(Rune Haugen) *t.k.h early: hld up in last pair: poorly plcd and struggling whn pce lifted over 2f out: nvr able to threaten* **16/1**
106- **7** *1½* **Poeta Diletto**[160] 4-9-0 108....................................... TomMarquand 4 97
(Marco Botti) *t.k.h early: hld up in last pair: poorly plcd and struggling whn pce lifted over 2f out: no imp after* **16/1**

2m 5.72s (-2.28) **Going Correction** 0.0s/f (Stan) **7** Ran SP% **110.2**
Speed ratings (Par 111): **109,108,108,108,106 106,105**
CSF £12.40 TOTE £4.00: £1.80, £1.80; EX 15.40 Trifecta £34.20.

**Owner** K Sohi **Bred** Mrs O M E McKeever **Trained** Upper Lambourn, W Berks

**FOCUS**

A good quality renewal of this Listed prize. They went a muddling gallop, though, and the winning time was barely better than the previous maiden. A minor pb from the second.

## 1501 BETFRED "LIKE US ON FACEBOOK" H'CAP 6f (P)

**2:40** (2:42) (Class 2) (0-105,101) 4-Y-O+

**£11,827** (£3,541; £1,770; £885; £442; £222) **Stalls** Low

Form RPR

06-1 **1** **Hakam (USA)**[86] [66] 5-8-10 **90**.............................. SilvestreDeSousa 10 98
(Michael Appleby) *trckd ldrs on outer: rdn over 2f out: clsd into 2nd over 1f out: drvn ahd last 75yds: jst hld on* **6/1**[3]

3-00 **2** *nse* **Solar Flair**[28] [1044] 5-9-4 **98**................................................ JimCrowley 8 106
(William Knight) *led: rdn 2f out: hdd last 75yds: rallied wl: jst pipped* **7/1**

240- **3** *1* **Stellarta**[175] [7146] 6-8-12 **92**.................................... TomMarquand 3 97
(Michael Blanshard) *hld up towards rr: prog on inner fr 2f out: styd on to take 3rd ins fnl f: nvr able to chal: only one fr off the pce to figure* **25/1**

2124 **4** *¾* **Kasbah (IRE)**[28] [1025] 5-9-5 **99**........................................ JackMitchell 11 102
(Amanda Perrett) *trckd ldr: rdn over 2f out: lost 2nd over 1f out: one pce after* **16/1**

3-06 **5** *¾* **Judicial (IRE)**[21] [1152] 5-9-4 **98**..........................................(e) JoeDoyle 2 99
(Julie Camacho) *t.k.h: hld up in 6th: shkn up 2f out: nt qckn over 1f out: kpt on same pce* **11/2**[2]

-101 **6** *shd* **Dutch Golden Age (IRE)**[57] [547] 5-8-10 **90**.................... TomQueally 4 90
(Gary Moore) *chsd ldng pair on inner: rdn and nt qckn over 1f out: one pce after* **6/1**[3]

0/50 **7** *¾* **Professor**[23] [1103] 7-8-9 **89**........................................... AdamBeschizza 6 87
(Michael Attwater) *chsd ldrs: shkn up over 2f out: one pce and no imp fnl f* **33/1**

000- **8** *1 ½* **Mont Kiara (FR)**[161] [7537] 4-8-11 **91**.................................... TomEaves 1 84
(Kevin Ryan) *dwlt: t.k.h: hld up in last trio: pushed along on inner over 2f out: reminder and kpt on fnl f: nvr involved* **9/1**

1-26 **9** *2 ¼* **Justice Good (IRE)**[56] [572] 5-9-7 **101**.............................. ShaneKelly 5 88
(David Elsworth) *nvr beyond midfield: rdn and no prog 2f out* **5/1**[1]

35-3 **10** *¾* **Dougan**[79] [200] 5-9-6 **100**................................................ AndrewMullen 9 84
(David Evans) *dwlt: hld up in last trio: shkn up and no prog over 2f out: no ch* **14/1**

13-5 **11** *10* **Memories Galore (IRE)**[77] [234] 5-8-9 **89**.......................... LukeMorris 7 43
(Harry Dunlop) *s.i.s: rcvrd into midfield on outer: no prog 2f out: wknd qckly jst over 1f out: eased* **8/1**

0-41 **12** *9* **Go Far**[21] [1152] 7-9-4 **98**...........................................................(v) FranBerry 12 25
(Alan Bailey) *trapped out wd and had to be hld up in last trio: racd awkwardly and wknd over 2f out: t.o* **25/1**

1m 11.54s (-1.56) **Going Correction** 0.0s/f (Stan) **12** Ran SP% **117.4**
Speed ratings (Par 109): **110,109,108,107,106 106,105,103,100,99 86,74**
CSF £46.14 CT £997.06 TOTE £6.40: £2.50, £2.60, £5.80; EX 48.60 Trifecta £663.40.

**Owner** The Horse Watchers **Bred** Jay W Bligh **Trained** Oakham, Rutland

**FOCUS**

A good 6f handicap. They went a proper gallop. It produced a thrilling duel in the final furlong and a tight photo-finish. The third and fourth help set the opening level.

## 1502 BETFRED "HOME OF GOALS GALORE" ROSEBERY H'CAP (LONDON MIDDLE DISTANCE SERIES QUALIFIER) 1m 2f 219y(P)

**3:15** (3:17) (Class 2) (0-105,112) 4-Y-O+ £28,012 (£8,388; £4,194; £2,097; £1,048; £526) **Stalls** Low

1 **1** **Big Country (IRE)**[49] [687] 4-8-6 **84**......................... SilvestreDeSousa 9 98+
(Michael Appleby) *led 2f: trckd ldr: led again jst over 2f out and sent for home: rdn out fnl f: nvr threatened and readily* **4/1**[1]

141- **2** *1 ½* **Wild Hacked (USA)**[180] [7015] 4-9-5 **97**......................... DanielMuscutt 5 107
(Marco Botti) *wl plcd on inner: rdn to chse wnr over 1f out: styd on wl but no imp* **13/2**[2]

014- **3** *2 ¼* **Prince Of Arran**[129] [8068] 4-9-10 **102**.......................... TomQueally 2 108
(Charlie Fellowes) *trckd ldrs in 6th: nt clr run briefly over 2f out: prog wl over 1f out: styd on wl to take 3rd ins fnl f: no threat to ldng pair* **13/2**[2]

52-2 **4** *1 ¼* **Gawdawpalin (IRE)**[8] [1341] 4-8-11 **89**......................... TomMarquand 10 93
(Sylvester Kirk) *chsd ldrs: urged along wl over 3f out: nvr pce to chal but kpt on fnl 2f* **12/1**

2 **5** *1 ½* **Getback In Paris (IRE)**[24] [1079] 4-8-9 **87**......................... ShaneKelly 6 89
(Richard Hughes) *led after 2f: rdn and hdd jst over 2f out: steadily fdd* **16/1**

563- **6** *½* **Noble Gift**[150] [7765] 7-8-13 **94**................................. CallumShepherd(3) 3 95+
(William Knight) *plld hrd: hld up in midfield: snatched up 4f out: kpt on fnl 2f on inner: no ch to threaten* **16/1**

-211 **7** *½* **General Hazard (IRE)**[21] [1144] 4-8-6 **84**......................... LukeMorris 15 84+
(Archie Watson) *hld up wl in rr fr wdst draw: rdn and kpt on fr over 2f out: nrst fin but no ch* **16/1**

164- **8** *nk* **William Hunter**[147] [7824] 5-8-6 **87**................................. HollieDoyle(3) 1 87+
(Alan King) *hld up in midfield on inner: rdn and nt qckn over 2f out: wknd fnal f* **12/1**

2121 **9** *hd* **Final**[10] [1307] 5-8-13 **91**.......................................................... JoeFanning 8 90+
(Mark Johnston) *racd on outer: hld up wl in rr: rdn and no prog over 2f out: plugged on fr over 1f out: no ch* **8/1**

315- **10** *1 ¼* **Southdown Lad (IRE)**[174] [7188] 4-9-2 **94**......................... JimCrowley 7 91
(William Knight) *trapped out wd: trckd ldrs: rdn over 2f out: wknd over 1f out* **7/1**[3]

0/3- **11** *1 ½* **Fergall (IRE)**[105] [6089] 10-8-6 **84**.............................. JosephineGordon 4 79
(Seamus Mullins) *dwlt: nvr gng wl and urged along most of way in rr: nvr a factor* **14/1**

1553 **12** *5* **Sennockian Star**[8] [1341] 7-9-2 **94**.................................. FrannyNorton 11 80
(Mark Johnston) *trckd ldng pair: rdn wl over 2f out: sn wknd* **20/1**

150- **13** *3 ¾* **Storm Rock**[143] [7869] 5-8-13 **91**...................................... FranBerry 12 71+
(Harry Dunlop) *hld up in last fr wd draw: rdn and no prog over 2f out* **33/1**

**14** *4 ½* **Diana Lady (CHI)**[240] 4-9-3 **95**...................................... JackMitchell 13 68+
(Rune Haugen) *s.i.s: a in rr: bhd fnl 2f* **100/1**

2m 18.27s (-3.63) **Going Correction** 0.0s/f (Stan) **14** Ran SP% **118.7**
Speed ratings (Par 109): **113,111,110,109,108 107,107,107,107,106 105,101,98,95**
CSF £27.39 CT £168.06 TOTE £3.30: £1.50, £2.80, £2.50; EX 30.40 Trifecta £201.90.

**Owner** The Horse Watchers **Bred** Mrs Jacqueline O'Brien **Trained** Oakham, Rutland

**FOCUS**

A good renewal of this middle-distance handicap. They went a modest gallop and it paid to race prominently. Although, the outcome is unlikely to have changed whichever way this race was run. The second and third help set the level.

## 1503 BETFRED LOTTO MAIDEN FILLIES' STKS 7f (P)

**3:50** (3:50) (Class 4) 3-Y-O+ **£5,175** (£1,540; £769; £384) **Stalls** Low

Form RPR

4- **1** **Arabian Hope (USA)**[323] [2211] 3-9-0 0.................(h[1]) JosephineGordon 3 83+
(Saeed bin Suroor) *trckd ldr: shkn up over 2f out: led over 1f out: pushed clr fnl f* **1/1**[1]

**2** *2 ¾* **Manaahil** 3-9-0 0.................................................................. JimCrowley 4 76+
(Charles Hills) *hld up in 6th: pushed along and prog 2f out: rdn and styd on fnl f to take 2nd last strides* **6/1**

24- **3** *hd* **Getna (USA)**[119] [8208] 3-9-0 0...................................... TomMarquand 9 75
(Richard Hannon) *led: shkn up and hdd over 1f out: one pce and no ch w wnr after: lost 2nd last strides* **9/2**[3]

2 **4** *½* **Global Alexander (IRE)**[12] [1286] 3-8-11 0................ HectorCrouch(3) 2 74
(Clive Cox) *t.k.h and hld up in 3rd: tried to chal on inner over 1f out: one pce fnl f* **3/1**[2]

40- **5** *2 ¾* **Star Of Bristol (USA)**[184] [6897] 3-9-0 0.............................. ShaneKelly 7 66
(Richard Hughes) *chsd ldng trio: shkn up over 2f out: sn outpcd: n.d after* **50/1**

**6** *2 ¼* **Foxy Lass** 3-9-0 0.............................................................. PatCosgrave 5 60
(William Haggas) *dwlt: hld up in last trio: outpcd over 2f out: pushed along and one pce after* **9/1**

4 **7** *½* **Happy Escape**[3] [1426] 3-8-7 0.............................(t) SophieScardifield(7) 1 59
(Joseph Tuite) *dwlt: chsd ldrs in 5th: shkn up over 2f out: fdd over 1f out* **50/1**

**8** *3 ½* **Coya** 3-8-11 0.............................................................(h[1]) CallumShepherd(3) 6 49
(Charles Hills) *a in rr: pushed along 1/2-way: no prog and nvr a factor* **50/1**

0 **9** *1 ½* **Garnetta**[12] [1286] 3-9-0 0............................................... JackMitchell 8 45
(Amanda Perrett) *a in last trio: shkn up and no prog 1/2-way* **100/1**

1m 26.08s (0.08) **Going Correction** 0.0s/f (Stan) **9** Ran SP% **124.3**
Speed ratings (Par 102): **99,95,95,95,91 89,88,84,83**
CSF £8.86 TOTE £1.80: £1.10, £2.30, £2.00; EX 9.80 Trifecta £33.40.

**Owner** Godolphin **Bred** Hill 'N' Dale Equine Holdings Inc Et Al **Trained** Newmarket, Suffolk

**FOCUS**

A fair fillies' maiden. The favourite outclassed this opposition. The third, fourth and fifth have been rated near their pre-race marks.

## 1504 BETFRED SUPPORTS JACK BERRY HOUSE H'CAP (LONDON MIDDLE DISTANCE SERIES QUALIFIER) 1m 2f 219y(P)

**4:25** (4:25) (Class 4) (0-85,85) 4-Y-O+ **£5,175** (£1,540; £769; £384) **Stalls** Low

Form RPR

430- **1** **Jacob Cats**[174] [7188] 8-9-7 **85**...................................(v) SilvestreDeSousa 5 95
(William Knight) *dwlt sltly: hld up in last trio: prog on inner jst over 2f out: rdn to ld over 1f out: styd on wl fnl f* **3/1**[2]

150- **2** *2 ¾* **Aldeburgh**[55] [8539] 8-9-3 **81**............................................ TomMarquand 7 85
(Nigel Twiston-Davies) *t.k.h: hld up in last: swift move on outer to ld 2f out: hdd over 1f out: styd on but wl hld fnl f* **10/1**

0-56 **3** *4* **Archangel Raphael (IRE)**[42] [809] 5-8-12 **79**....(p) KieranShoemark(3) 6 76
(Amanda Perrett) *hld up in last trio: effrt over 2f out: sn outpcd: kpt on to take 3rd nr fin: no ch* **14/1**

521- **4** *½* **Brief Visit**[248] [4761] 4-9-5 **83**............................................ LiamKeniry 4 79
(Andrew Balding) *led: rdn over 2f out: sn hdd and outpcd: lost 3rd nr fin* **5/2**[1]

3-24 **5** *3 ¾* **Dolphin Village (IRE)**[15] [1248] 7-9-1 **84**.................(t[1]) CharlieBennett(5) 1 73
(Shaun Harris) *trckd ldrs: rdn and cl up jst over 2f out: sn wknd* **6/1**[3]

0/0 **6** *1* **Red Turtle (FR)**[75] [269] 6-9-2 **80**................................ AdamBeschizza 2 67
(Rune Haugen) *trckd ldr 2f and rdn to go 2nd again briefly wl over 2f out: sn wknd* **40/1**

0143 **7** *2 ¼* **Ravens Quest**[2] [1457] 4-8-11 **75**.................................... TomQueally 3 58
(John Ryan) *trckd ldr after 2f to wl over 2f out: lost pl qckly and sn wknd* **5/2**[1]

2m 19.66s (-2.24) **Going Correction** 0.0s/f (Stan) **7** Ran SP% **114.6**
Speed ratings (Par 105): **108,106,103,102,100 99,97**
CSF £32.15 TOTE £4.30: £2.20, £4.60; EX 34.30 Trifecta £197.40.

**Owner** Canisbay Bloodstock **Bred** Highclere Stud **Trained** Patching, W Sussex

**FOCUS**

A decent middle-distance handicap. They went a modest gallop but sound form in all probability. The runner-up has been rated a bit below his best of recent years.

## 1505 BETFRED "WATCH SKY SPORTS IN OUR SHOPS" H'CAP 1m 7f 218y(P)

**5:00** (5:00) (Class 4) (0-85,81) 4-Y-O+ **£5,175** (£1,540; £769; £384) **Stalls** Low

Form RPR

423- **1** **Endless Acres (IRE)**[173] [7215] 4-9-7 **81**........................(v) StevieDonohoe 3 88+
(Charlie Fellowes) *led 3f: trckd ldr: led wl over 2f out: rdn over 1f out: sn drew clr* **4/7**[1]

0-03 **2** *4 ½* **Glan Y Gors (IRE)**[16] [1223] 5-9-9 **79**..............................(p[1]) MartinHarley 4 81
(David Simcock) *slowly away: hld up in last: prog over 2f out: shkn up to chse wnr over 1f out: no imp and sn outpcd: jst hld on for 2nd* **8/1**[3]

5-24 **3** *hd* **Lord Napier (IRE)**[35] [921] 4-9-5 **79**.................................... TomQueally 1 80
(John Ryan) *trckd ldng pair: rdn to chse wnr over 2f out: outpcd over 1f out and lost 2nd: kpt on nr fin* **10/1**

-511 **4** *nk* **Ayr Of Elegance**[24] [1092] 5-9-3 **73**............................ RichardKingscote 2 74
(Philip Hide) *trckd ldng trio: rdn to dispute 2nd over 2f out: kpt on same pce fr over 1f out and no ch w wnr* **7/1**[2]

40-5 **5** *8* **Golden Jubilee (USA)**[80] [173] 8-9-2 **75**............(p) KieranShoemark(3) 5 66
(Nigel Twiston-Davies) *hld up in 5th: rdn and outpcd over 2f out: no ch after* **20/1**

1-11 **6** *63* **Canadian Diamond (IRE)**[38] [508] 10-9-0 **70**............ AdamBeschizza 6
(Richard Rowe) *t.k.h: led after 3f to wl over 2f out: wknd rapidly: t.o and virtually p.u fnl f* **17/2**

3m 30.77s (0.67) **Going Correction** 0.0s/f (Stan)
**WFA** 4 from 5yo+ 2lb **6** Ran SP% **111.6**
Speed ratings (Par 105): **98,95,95,95,91 60**
CSF £5.81 TOTE £1.60: £1.10, £2.80; EX 5.80 Trifecta £30.20.

**Owner** Saffron House Stables And K Sohi **Bred** Anthony Morris **Trained** Newmarket, Suffolk

**FOCUS**

A fairly decent staying handicap. Once again it wasn't a true test at the trip, but no denying the winner's potential over this sort of distance. The opening level is straightforward.

T/Plt: £165.60 to a £1 stake. Pool: £65,338.00 - 394.41 winning units. T/Qpdt: £48.50 to a £1 stake. Pool: £4,312.00 - 88.78 winning units. **Jonathan Neesom**

1506 - 1511a (Foreign Racing) - See Raceform Interactive

# [1491]DONCASTER (L-H)

Sunday, April 2

**OFFICIAL GOING: Good (good to soft in places; 7.6)**
Wind: virtually nil Weather: cloudy

## 1512 GET DONCASTER MOVING H'CAP 7f 6y
**1:45** (1:49) (Class 4) (0-85,85) 4-Y-0+ **£4,851** (£1,443; £721; £360) **Stalls** Centre

Form RPR
-102 1 **Zoravan (USA)**[26] [1074] 4-8-11 **80**............................(v) RowanScott(5) 13 86
(Keith Dalgleish) *mde all: rdn over 1f out: kpt on* **28/1**
514- 2 1 1/4 **Invermere**[156] [7671] 4-9-1 **79**.............................................. PaulHanagan 6 82
(Richard Fahey) *trckd ldrs: rdn over 2f out: chsd ldr over 1f out: kpt on* **10/1**
151- 3 nk **Timeless Art (IRE)**[156] [7671] 4-9-2 **85**.............................. CliffordLee(5) 7 87
(K R Burke) *trckd ldrs: rdn to chse ldr wl over 1f out: kpt on* **7/2**[1]
544- 4 nk **Ballymore Castle (IRE)**[148] [7825] 5-9-4 **82**................... TonyHamilton 2 83
(Richard Fahey) *midfield: rdn and hdwy over 1f out: kpt on* **8/1**[2]
0436 5 1/2 **Boots And Spurs**[4] [1433] 8-9-1 **79**......................................(v) DaleSwift 1 79
(Scott Dixon) *hld up in midfield: rdn over 2f out: kpt on wl fnl f* **20/1**
435- 6 1/2 **Florenza**[212] [6096] 4-9-3 **81**.................................................. PJMcDonald 3 80
(Chris Fairhurst) *prom: rdn over 2f out: no ex fnl f* **25/1**
110- 7 1/2 **Royal Connoisseur (IRE)**[149] [7798] 6-8-13 **80**........ SammyJoBell(3) 15 77
(Richard Fahey) *chsd ldrs towards stands' side and wd of main gp tl 1/2-way: rdn over 2f out: one pce* **50/1**
000- 8 shd **Zealous (IRE)**[158] [7623] 4-9-1 **79**............................. SilvestreDeSousa 20 77+
(Alan Swinbank) *in tch: rdn over 2f out: briefly short of room appr fnl f: kpt on* **16/1**
300- 9 shd **Khelman (IRE)**[159] [7593] 7-9-1 **82**........................... AdamMcNamara(3) 5 79
(Richard Fahey) *in tch: rdn over 2f out: sltly short of room appr fnl f: one pce* **16/1**
422- 10 nk **Brilliant Vanguard (IRE)**[139] [7958] 4-9-1 **79**...................... ShaneGray 4 75
(Kevin Ryan) *in tch: rdn over 2f out: no ex ins fnl f* **14/1**
001- 11 nk **King Of Naples**[162] [7540] 4-9-1 **84**............................... GeorgeWood(5) 19 79
(James Fanshawe) *midfield: rdn 2f out: kpt on ins fnl f: nvr threatened* **9/1**[3]
206- 12 1 **Gambit**[174] [7221] 4-9-1 **79**.......................................... RichardKingscote 10 72
(Tom Dascombe) *chsd ldrs: rdn over 2f out: edgd lft appr fnl f: wknd ins fnl f* **10/1**
040- 13 nk **Dubai Dynamo**[176] [7159] 12-9-2 **80**.............................. JamesSullivan 16 72
(Ruth Carr) *midfield: pushed along over 2f out: nvr threatened* **50/1**
000- 14 nk **Johnny Cavagin**[155] [7702] 8-9-5 **83**...................................(t) TomEaves 17 74
(Ronald Thompson) *hld up: pushed along over 2f out: rdn over 1f out: kpt on: nvr threatened* **25/1**
030- 15 1/2 **Finn Class (IRE)**[160] [7573] 6-9-7 **85**........................... PaulMulrennan 21 75
(Michael Dods) *hld up: nvr threatened* **25/1**
350- 16 hd **Eastern Racer (IRE)**[198] [6539] 5-9-4 **82**.............................. BenCurtis 12 71
(Brian Ellison) *midfield: rdn over 2f out: wknd fnl f* **16/1**
-104 17 shd **Dutch Art Dealer**[31] [989] 6-9-7 **85**............................(be[1]) DavidNolan 11 74
(Ivan Furtado) *slowly away and bit rel to r: hld up in rr: minor late hdwy: nvr threatened* **25/1**
200- 18 1 1/2 **Tiger Jim**[113] [8311] 7-9-7 **85**................................................ SamJames 14 70
(Jim Goldie) *hld up: nvr threatened* **33/1**
1663 19 1 **Free Code (IRE)**[18] [1202] 6-9-5 **83**......................................... FranBerry 8 66
(David Barron) *a towards rr* **16/1**
3-43 20 2 3/4 **Mister Music**[46] [736] 8-9-1 **79**..................................... GeorgeDowning 22 54
(Tony Carroll) *a towards rr* **25/1**
010- 21 8 **Kalk Bay (IRE)**[132] [8052] 10-8-13 **84** ow3......................(t) RyanTimby(7) 9 39+
(Michael Easterby) *awkward and half rrd s: v.s.a: hld up in rr: rdn over 3f out: wknd 2f out* **50/1**

1m 25.53s (-0.77) **Going Correction** -0.20s/f (Firm) **21 Ran SP% 128.0**
Speed ratings (Par 105): **96,94,94,93,93 92,92,92,91,91 91,90,89,89,88 88,88,86,85,82 73**
CSF £263.45 CT £1268.18 TOTE £36.60: £6.50, £2.30, £1.60, £2.70; EX 386.30 Trifecta £4003.70.
**Owner** Ontoawinner 8 & Partner **Bred** His Highness The Aga Khan Studs S C **Trained** Carluke, S Lanarks

■ Stewards' Enquiry : Sammy Jo Bell caution; entered the wrong stall

**FOCUS**
The going was given as good, good to soft in places (GoingStick: 7.6). After riding in the opener Ben Curtis and Fran Berry called the ground 'dead' while Sammy Jo Bell and Adam McNamara said it was 'good'. The field initially split into two groups, the larger one racing more centre to far side, but the gap between them wasn't great. The pace held up well, those in behind struggling to get involved, perhaps on account of the dead ground. The winner, who made all, led home a bunch of low-drawn horses. A small step forward from the winner.

## 1513 PURPLE VOUCHERS MAIDEN STKS (DIV I) 7f 6y
**2:15** (2:20) (Class 5) 3-Y-0 **£3,234** (£962; £481; £240) **Stalls** Centre

Form RPR
1 **Benbatl** 3-9-5 0............................................................ JosephineGordon 8 96+
(Saeed bin Suroor) *trckd ldng pair: hdwy and cl up over 3f out: led wl over 2f out: pushed clr wl over 1f out: readily* **15/8**[1]
2 7 **Made Of Honour (IRE)** 3-9-0 0.................................... DougieCostello 1 68+
(K R Burke) *trckd ldrs: hdwy over 2f out: rdn wl over 1f out: kpt on fnl f: no ch w wnr* **25/1**
052- 3 1 1/2 **Jewel House**[181] [7012] 3-9-5 80........................................ FrankieDettori 10 69
(John Gosden) *led: jinked rt 1/2-way: sn jnd: hdd wl over 2f out and sn rdn: drvn over 1f out: kpt on same pce* **11/4**[3]
4 1 3/4 **Oregon Point (USA)** 3-9-5 0.................................................. DavidAllan 4 64
(Tim Easterby) *midfield: hdwy over 2f out: sn rdn along: styd on appr fnl f* **66/1**
5 nk **Bob Maxwell (IRE)** 3-9-5 0................................................. PhillipMakin 3 64+
(David Barron) *dwlt: green and bhd: hdwy over 2f out: n.m.r and swtchd rt wl over 1f out: sn rdn and styd on wl fnl f* **20/1**
6 1/2 **Rock Island Line** 3-9-5 0...................................................... JasonHart 11 62
(Mark Walford) *chsd ldr: pushed along 1/2-way: rdn over 2f out: sn drvn and kpt on one pce* **150/1**
50- 7 1 3/4 **Aelius**[176] [7157] 3-9-2 0.................................................. NathanEvans(3) 2 58
(Michael Easterby) *rr: hdwy over 2f out: sn rdn and n.d* **20/1**
4- 8 1 **Eburaci (IRE)**[174] [7208] 3-9-5 0......................................... TomQueally 12 55
(Charlie Fellowes) *chsd ldrs: rdn along wl over 2f out: grad wknd* **16/1**
2- 9 1/2 **Natajack**[198] [6542] 3-9-5 0.................................................. PaulHanagan 5 54
(Richard Fahey) *trckd ldrs: pushed along wl over 2f out: sn rdn and btn* **5/2**[2]
6- 10 1 1/4 **Mr Skinnylegs**[296] [3114] 3-9-5 0........................................... BenCurtis 9 51
(Brian Ellison) *midfield: rdn along 3f out: sn outpcd* **50/1**
00- 11 3/4 **Kaeso**[148] [7818] 3-9-5 0........................................................ TomEaves 6 49
(Nigel Tinkler) *towards rr: hdwy over 3f out: in tch and rdn along over 2f out: sn wknd* **150/1**
12 2 **New Tale** 3-9-5 0............................................................. DuranFentiman 7 44
(Olly Williams) *dfwelt: a rr* **100/1**

1m 25.65s (-0.65) **Going Correction** -0.20s/f (Firm) **12 Ran SP% 115.0**
Speed ratings (Par 98): **95,87,85,83,82 82,80,79,78,77 76,74**
CSF £56.34 TOTE £3.00: £1.40, £4.00, £1.50; EX 61.10 Trifecta £228.40.
**Owner** Godolphin **Bred** Darley **Trained** Newmarket, Suffolk

**FOCUS**
With the second-favourite disappointing and the third-favourite looking a difficult ride, this probably didn't take much winning, but there was still plenty to like about the way the winner settled matters. The opening level is tricky but the winner looks a smart prospect.

## 1514 PURPLE VOUCHERS MAIDEN STKS (DIV II) 7f 6y
**2:45** (2:51) (Class 5) 3-Y-0 **£3,234** (£962; £481; £240) **Stalls** Centre

Form RPR
1 **Dream Castle** 3-9-5 0........................................................ OisinMurphy 9 89+
(Saeed bin Suroor) *t.k.h early: trckd ldr: cl up over 2f out: led 11/2f out: sn pushed clr: readily* **4/7**[1]
5- 2 3 1/2 **To Dibba**[163] [7495] 3-9-5 0................................................ AndreaAtzeni 6 77
(Roger Varian) *trckd ldng pair: hdwy to chse wnr 1f out: sn rdn and kpt on* **9/2**[3]
65- 3 1 1/2 **Lamloom (IRE)**[173] [7247] 3-9-5 0.................................. DanielTudhope 3 73+
(David O'Meara) *led: pushed along over 2f out: rdn and hdd 11/2f out:. sn drvn and kpt on same pce* **25/1**
3- 4 3 1/4 **Loujain (IRE)**[156] [7665] 3-9-5 0........................................... JimCrowley 7 65
(John Gosden) *in tch: hdwy to chse ldrs over 2f out: rdn along wl over 1f out: sn one pce* **3/1**[2]
5 1/2 **Give It Some Teddy** 3-9-5 0............................................... NeilFarley 11 63
(Alan Swinbank) *in tch: hdwy wl over 2f out: rdn along wl over 1f out: kpt on same pce* **40/1**
6 3 **Chunkyfunkymonkey** 3-9-2 0...............................(b[1]) LouisSteward(3) 8 56
(John Ryan) *towards rr: hdwy over 2f out: sn rdn along and n.d* **80/1**
7 2 1/4 **Never You Mind (IRE)** 3-9-5 0................................ RichardKingscote 4 50+
(Charles Hills) *green and sn rdn along: a rr* **20/1**
8 1 3/4 **Our Kim (IRE)** 3-9-5 0............................................................ JFEgan 5 45
(Mohamed Moubarak) *a towards rr* **40/1**
60- 9 5 **Flying Onsite (FR)**[148] [7819] 3-9-5 0.................................... TomEaves 1 32
(Nigel Tinkler) *swtchd rt s: green and a rr* **100/1**
05- 10 nse **Paco Lady**[146] [7845] 3-9-0 0...................................... SilvestreDeSousa 2 27
(Ivan Furtado) *chsd ldrs: rdn along 3f out: sn wknd* **50/1**
0-0 11 nk **Hot Gossip (IRE)**[11] [1308] 3-9-0 0.................................. JamesSullivan 12 26
(Dianne Sayer) *a rr* **150/1**

1m 25.58s (-0.72) **Going Correction** -0.20s/f (Firm) **11 Ran SP% 125.2**
Speed ratings (Par 98): **96,92,90,86,86 82,80,78,72,72 71**
CSF £3.87 TOTE £1.60: £1.10, £1.40, £4.90; EX 4.50 Trifecta £33.40.
**Owner** Godolphin **Bred** Darley **Trained** Newmarket, Suffolk

**FOCUS**
The winner completed a double in the two divisions of the maiden for Saeed bin Suroor, this Frankel newcomer recording a time marginally quicker (0.07sec) than the Dubawi colt in the first leg. The opening level is fluid but there was more depth to this division.

## 1515 ROSINA MAY GODFREY MEMORIAL H'CAP 6f 2y
**3:20** (3:23) (Class 3) (0-95,94) 4-Y-0+ **£7,762** (£2,310; £1,154; £577) **Stalls** Centre

Form RPR
01-0 1 **Wentworth Falls**[40] [851] 5-9-1 **88**...................................... FrannyNorton 8 96
(Geoffrey Harker) *dwlt: hld up centre: stl plenty to do whn angled lft into clr appr fnl f: rdn and r.o strly: led towards fin* **33/1**
001- 2 1/2 **Muntadab (IRE)**[163] [7497] 5-9-6 **93**.......................... SilvestreDeSousa 15 100
(Roger Fell) *chsd ldrs centre: rdn 2f out: led 1f out: kpt on but hdd towards fin* **13/2**[1]
6-50 3 nse **Ninjago**[3] [1454] 7-9-2 **89**.................................................... CamHardie 13 95
(Paul Midgley) *hld up: hdwy into midfield 1/2-way: rdn to chse ldrs appr fnl f: kpt on* **16/1**
101- 4 1/2 **Naggers (IRE)**[178] [7094] 6-8-11 **84**................................. PaulMulrennan 14 89+
(Paul Midgley) *s.i.s: hld up in rr centre: angled rt and bit short of room over 1f out: stl lot to do whn swtchd lft appr fnl f: rdn and r.o wl: nrst fin* **20/1**
-440 5 1/2 **Golden Amber (IRE)**[43] [810] 6-9-4 **91**........................... RobertWinston 1 94
(Dean Ivory) *hld up towards far side: rdn along over 3f out: kpt on wl fnl f* **16/1**
200- 6 nk **Northgate Lad (IRE)**[197] [6560] 5-8-9 **89**................... BenRobinson(7) 10 91
(Brian Ellison) *chsd ldrs towards centre: rdn over 2f out: kpt on same pce* **50/1**
041- 7 nk **Ower Fly**[165] [7461] 4-8-13 **89**.......................................... HollieDoyle(3) 2 91
(Richard Hannon) *chsd ldrs towards centre: rdn over 2f out: one pce* **16/1**
440- 8 3/4 **Eccleston**[170] [7315] 6-9-3 **90**..........................................(p) DanielTudhope 3 89
(David O'Meara) *midfield towards far side: rdn over 2f out: kpt on same pce and nvr threatened* **10/1**[3]
000- 9 1/2 **Another Wise Kid (IRE)**[113] [8308] 9-9-1 **88**.................... LukeMorris 22 86+
(Paul Midgley) *hld up towards stands' side: rdn 1/2-way: kpt on fnl f* **40/1**
60-1 10 hd **Handsome Dude**[44] [783] 5-9-1 **88**..................................(b) PhillipMakin 4 85
(David Barron) *prom centre: rdn over 2f out: no ex ins fnl f* **14/1**
043- 11 nk **Bogart**[162] [7537] 8-8-11 **84**.................................................(p) TomEaves 6 80
(Kevin Ryan) *led centre: rdn 2f out: hdd 1f out: wknd fnl 110yds* **25/1**
600- 12 nk **Lincoln (IRE)**[163] [7497] 6-9-7 **94**.......................................... GrahamLee 5 89
(Mick Channon) *in tch towards centre: rdn 2f out: outpcd whn sltly short of room ins fnl f* **20/1**
655- 13 nk **George Bowen (IRE)**[148] [7821] 5-9-4 **91**........................ PaulHanagan 9 86
(Richard Fahey) *s.i.s: hld up centre: rdn over 2f out: kpt on ins fnl f: nvr threatened* **13/2**[1]
-134 14 1 **Sir Billy Wright (IRE)**[12] [1295] 6-8-7 **85**....................... CliffordLee(5) 12 77
(David Evans) *in tch towards centre: rdn over 2f out: wknd ins fnl f* **20/1**
000- 15 hd **Toofi (FR)**[163] [7497] 6-9-7 **94**............................................... AdamKirby 21 85+
(John Butler) *hld up towards stands' side: pushed along over 2f out: rdn appr fnl f: minor late hdwy: nvr threatened* **33/1**
00-4 16 3/4 **Intense Style (IRE)**[24] [1103] 5-9-1 **88**..................................(b) JasonHart 7 77
(Les Eyre) *midfield centre: rdn over 2f out: nvr threatened* **14/1**
536- 17 1/2 **Lagenda**[156] [7668] 4-8-12 **85**..........................................(p) KevinStott 17 72+
(Kevin Ryan) *prom towards stands' side: rdn over 2f out: wknd over 1f out* **33/1**

054- **18** *nk* **Gunmetal (IRE)**[218] 5881 4-8-11 **87**...................... CallumShepherd(3) 20 73
(Charles Hills) *prom towards stands' side: rdn over 2f out: wknd over 1f out* **14/1**
056- **19** *hd* **Flying Pursuit**[170] 7315 4-9-3 **90**........................................ DavidAllan 11 76+
(Tim Easterby) *chsd ldrs: rdn 1/2-way: wknd over 1f out* **14/1**
460- **20** *1* **My Name Is Rio (IRE)**[162] 7537 7-9-1 **88**.................. ConnorBeasley 19 71+
(Michael Dods) *chsd ldrs towards stands' side: rdn 1/2-way: wknd over 1f out* **33/1**
313- **21** *½* **My Amigo**[291] 3292 4-8-13 **86**.......................................... PJMcDonald 18 67
(K R Burke) *racd centre: midfield: rdn 1/2-way: wknd over 1f out* **7/1**[2]
321- **22** *2¾* **Kenny The Captain (IRE)**[145] 7858 6-8-12 **88**. RachelRichardson(3) 16 61+
(Tim Easterby) *chsd ldrs towards stands' side: rdn 1/2-way: sn wknd* **25/1**

1m 11.19s (-2.41) **Going Correction** -0.20s/f (Firm) **22** Ran SP% **130.7**
Speed ratings (Par 107): **108,107,107,106,105 105,105,104,103,103 102,102,102,100,100 99,98,98,98,96 96,92**
CSF £217.45 CT £3688.88 TOTE £55.70: £8.70, £2.00, £4.60, £6.00; EX 671.00 Trifecta £5831.40 Part won..
**Owner** Stockhill Racing Partnership **Bred** Newsells Park Stud **Trained** Thirkleby, N Yorks

**FOCUS**
A competitive handicap. The race developed centre-to-far side. The winner has been rated back towards his best form.

## 1516 ADWICK KINGPIN CONDITIONS STKS 1m 3f 197y
3:55 (3:56) (Class 2) 4-Y-O+ **£12,938** (£3,850; £1,924; £962) **Stalls** Low

Form RPR
222- **1** **Chemical Charge (IRE)**[112] 8336 5-9-0 107.................... OisinMurphy 1 105
(Ralph Beckett) *hld up in tch: hdwy on inner 3f out: sn chsng ldng pair: swtchd rt and effrt 2f out: rdn to ld appr fnl f: kpt on strly* **15/8**[1]
153- **2** *2* **Saigon City**[239] 5144 7-9-0 93............................................ TomEaves 2 102
(Declan Carroll) *trckd ldng pair: pushed along 3f out: rdn and sltly outpcd 2f out: styd on wl to chse wnr ins fnl f: no imp towards fin* **50/1**
314- **3** *1¾* **Muntahaa (IRE)**[204] 6329 4-9-6 113.................................(h) JimCrowley 3 106+
(John Gosden) *sn trcking ldr: cl up 4f out: chal 3f out: rdn to take slt ld wl over 1f out: drvn and hdd appr fnl f: kpt on same pce* **2/1**[2]
416- **4** *1½* **Frontiersman**[162] 7545 4-9-3 101...................................... WilliamBuick 4 102+
(Charlie Appleby) *sn led: jnd 4f out: pushed along 3f out: rdn and hdd narrowly wl over 1f out: sn drvn and wknd appr fnl f* **3/1**[3]
400- **5** *7* **Maleficent Queen**[148] 7823 5-9-2 103.............................. ConnorBeasley 8 89
(Keith Dalgleish) *t.k.h: hld up in rr: sme hdwy over 3f out: sn rdn along and nvr a factor* **14/1**
315- **6** *½* **Tawdeea**[148] 7824 5-9-4 106.........................................(p) DanielTudhope 6 90
(David O'Meara) *.trckd ldrs: hdwy over 3f out: rdn along over 2f out: drvn wl over 1f out and sn wknd* **10/1**

2m 32.99s (-1.91) **Going Correction** +0.05s/f (Good) **6** Ran SP% **110.8**
Speed ratings (Par 109): **108,106,105,104,99 99**
CSF £63.74 TOTE £2.70: £2.10, £9.60; EX 49.30 Trifecta £166.10.
**Owner** Qatar Racing Limited **Bred** Viktor Timoshenko **Trained** Kimpton, Hants

**FOCUS**
This set up nicely for the winner as his main market rivals took each other on from a long way out. The winner has been rated a bit below his best.

## 1517 CHOOSE FITNESS H'CAP 1m 2f 43y
4:30 (4:31) (Class 4) (0-85,85) 4-Y-O+ **£4,851** (£1,443; £721; £360) **Stalls** Low

Form RPR
100- **1** **Archippos**[152] 7744 4-8-13 **77**............................................ PaddyAspell 2 85
(Philip Kirby) *midfield on inner: hdwy over 2f out: rdn to chse ldr over 1f out: led 110yds out: styd on* **20/1**
-405 **2** *¾* **Hail Clodius (IRE)**[24] 1105 5-9-5 **83**......................... SilvestreDeSousa 9 90
(Roger Fell) *prom: rdn to ld over 2f out: hdd 110yds out: kpt on* **14/1**
000- **3** *1* **Chancery (USA)**[168] 7383 9-9-7 **85**............................ DanielTudhope 19 91
(David O'Meara) *hld up: hdwy 3f out: rdn over 2f out: styd on wl fnl f: wnt 3rd post* **8/1**[3]
000- **4** *shd* **Navajo War Dance**[163] 7505 4-9-4 **82**............................. JoeyHaynes 8 86
(K R Burke) *trckd ldrs: rdn over 2f out: kpt on same pce: lost 3rd post* **9/1**
123- **5** *hd* **Lime And Lemon (IRE)**[167] 7419 4-8-9 **76**.............. HectorCrouch(3) 10 80
(Clive Cox) *in tch: rdn over 2f out: kpt on* **15/2**[2]
26-5 **6** *¾* **Briardale (IRE)**[82] 156 5-9-6 **84**................................... PJMcDonald 11 86
(James Bethell) *midfield: rdn over 2f out: hdwy and chsd ldrs over 1f out: one pce ins fnl f* **14/1**
366- **7** *1* **Hanseatic**[167] 7408 8-8-5 **76**......................................(t) HarrisonShaw(7) 16 76
(Michael Easterby) *hld up in rr: gd hdwy on inner over 3f out: rdn 2f out: wknd ins fnl f* **20/1**
101- **8** *¾* **Carnageo (FR)**[158] 7623 4-9-4 **82**.................................... PaulHanagan 5 81
(Richard Fahey) *in tch: rdn over 2f out: chsd ldr over 1f out: wknd ins fnl f* **9/2**[1]
422- **9** *shd* **Tamayuz Magic (IRE)**[159] 7594 6-9-1 **82**..............(b) NathanEvans(3) 13 81
(Michael Easterby) *hld up in midfield: rdn over 2f out: one pce and nvr threatened* **11/1**
610- **10** *1* **Save The Bees**[176] 7159 9-9-4 **82**.................................... TonyHamilton 1 79
(Declan Carroll) *led: rdn whn hdd over 2f out: grad wknd over 1f out* **25/1**
000- **11** *1¼* **Another Go (IRE)**[117] 8239 4-8-13 **77**............................. JoeFanning 20 71
(Alan Swinbank) *dwlt: hld up: rdn over 2f out: nvr threatened* **25/1**
000- **12** *1¾* **Mysterial**[137] 7980 7-8-7 **76**........................................ PhilDennis(5) 12 67
(Declan Carroll) *chsd ldrs: rdn 3f out: wknd over 1f out* **66/1**
10-0 **13** *4½* **Top Of The Glas (IRE)**[42] 197 6-8-12 **81**............ MeganNicholls(5) 15 63
(Brian Ellison) *hld up in midfield: rdn over 2f out: sn btn* **10/1**
000- **14** *1¼* **Palmerston**[149] 7796 4-9-0 **78**........................................ BenCurtis 17 57
(Michael Appleby) *midfield: rdn and sme hdwy 3f out: wknd over 1f out* **20/1**
0- **15** *2¼* **Foresee (GER)**[54] 8249 4-9-3 **81**............................. GeorgeDowning 18 56
(Tony Carroll) *chsd ldrs: rdn over 2f out: sn wknd* **50/1**
016- **16** *shd* **Suitor**[260] 4417 5-9-0 **78**.................................................. DaleSwift 6 53
(Brian Ellison) *slowly away: a towards rr* **16/1**
00/6 **17** *½* **Marmion**[16] 1248 5-8-13 **77**............................................ DavidAllan 4 51
(Les Eyre) *midfield: rdn over 3f out: sn wknd* **25/1**
400- **18** *3* **Buonarroti (IRE)**[137] 7979 6-9-7 **85**.............................. NeilFarley 14 53
(Declan Carroll) *dwlt: a towards rr* **25/1**
/50- **19** *1¼* **Sikandar (IRE)**[295] 3162 5-8-7 **78**............................. BenRobinson(7) 3 43
(Brian Ellison) *slowly away: a towards: rr* **16/1**

2m 8.34s (-1.06) **Going Correction** +0.05s/f (Good) **19** Ran SP% **127.6**
Speed ratings (Par 105): **106,105,104,104,104 103,102,102,102,101 100,99,95,94,92 92,92,89,88**
CSF £255.74 CT £2452.79 TOTE £26.80: £4.90, £3.80, £3.00, £2.90; EX 554.00 Trifecta £7529.60 Part won..
**Owner** Well Oiled Partnership & Friend **Bred** Mrs K E Collie **Trained** East Appleton, N Yorks

**FOCUS**
A wide-open handicap. The runner-up has been rated back to his turf level.

## 1518 YORKSHIRE WILDLIFE PARK H'CAP 1m 2f 43y
5:05 (5:06) (Class 3) (0-95,93) 3-Y-O **£7,762** (£2,310; £1,154; £577) **Stalls** Low

Form RPR
10- **1** **Bin Battuta**[267] 4150 3-8-13 **85**........................................ JimCrowley 4 98+
(Saeed bin Suroor) *hld up towards rr: stdy hdwy on outer 3f out: chsd ldrs over 1f out: sn rdn: styd on to chal jst ins fnl f: drvn and led last 75 yds* **4/1**[2]
61- **2** *nk* **First Nation**[142] 7907 3-8-11 **83**...................................... WilliamBuick 1 95+
(Charlie Appleby) *trckd ldrs: hdwy 3f out: cl up 2f out: rdn to ld over 1f out: jnd and drvn ins fnl f: edgd lft and hdd last 75 yds* **11/2**[3]
411- **3** *2½* **Khalidi**[204] 6330 3-9-7 **93**............................................ FrankieDettori 10 101
(John Gosden) *hld up: hdwy over 3f out: chsd ldrs over 2f out: rdn over 1f out: kpt on fnl f* **7/2**[1]
21 **4** *2¼* **Bush House (IRE)**[41] 840 3-8-9 **81**.......................(b) JosephineGordon 8 84
(Hugo Palmer) *trckd ldng pair: hdwy on outer and cl up wl over 2f out: rdn to dispute ld and ev ch 11/2f out: sn drvn and kpt on same pce* **20/1**
221- **5** *2½* **Celestial Spheres (IRE)**[193] 6663 3-8-13 **85**.................(p) MartinLane 3 84+
(Charlie Appleby) *led 2f: cl up: led again over 3f out: rdn over 2f out: drvn and hdd over 1f out: wknd fnl f* **11/1**
5-11 **6** *1½* **Flood Warning**[19] 1195 3-8-11 **83**.................................... LukeMorris 7 79
(Clive Cox) *hld up in rr: hdwy 3f out: rdn along 2f out: kpt on fnl f* **22/1**
512- **7** *1* **Western Duke (IRE)**[229] 5519 3-9-3 **89**............................... FranBerry 5 83
(Ralph Beckett) *dwlt: a towards rr* **9/1**
22-1 **8** *3½* **Native Prospect**[40] 849 3-8-8 **80**.................................. OisinMurphy 6 68+
(Andrew Balding) *t.k.h: chsd ldr tl led after 2f: pushed along and hdd over 3f out: sn rdn and wknd 2f out* **7/1**
325- **9** *hd* **Devil's Bridge (IRE)**[147] 7839 3-9-2 **88**............................ SeanLevey 9 76
(Richard Hannon) *chsd ldrs: rdn along 3f out: sn btn* **14/1**
2- **10** *11* **Mushaireb**[216] 5966 3-8-9 **81**......................................... PaulHanagan 2 49
(Richard Fahey) *rr: pushed along over 4f out: rdn over 3f out: sn outpcd and bhd* **7/1**

2m 6.65s (-2.75) **Going Correction** +0.05s/f (Good) **10** Ran SP% **116.7**
Speed ratings (Par 102): **113,112,110,108,106 105,104,102,102,93**
CSF £26.40 CT £84.43 TOTE £4.80: £1.90, £2.40, £1.70; EX 28.80 Trifecta £143.90.
**Owner** Godolphin **Bred** Darley **Trained** Newmarket, Suffolk
■ Stewards' Enquiry : Sean Levey caution; had allowed his mount to edge left causing slight interference

**FOCUS**
An interesting handicap featuring a host of potential improvers. It was run at a good gallop. It's been rated positively.

## 1519 COUNTING HOUSE BESSACARR AMATEUR RIDERS' H'CAP 1m 3f 197y
5:35 (5:35) (Class 5) (0-70,70) 4-Y-O+ **£3,119** (£967; £483; £242) **Stalls** Low

Form RPR
-412 **1** **Royal Flag**[31] 990 7-10-7 **66**......................................... JonjoO'Neill(3) 18 76+
(Brian Ellison) *hld up in midfield: stdy hdwy fr over 3f out: rdn to chse ldr over 1f out: led 110yds out: styd on* **4/1**[1]
30-5 **2** *1¾* **Nafaath (IRE)**[33] 19 11-9-9 **58**...............................(p) MissAMcCain(7) 6 65
(Donald McCain) *in tch: hdwy over 3f out: rdn to ld over 2f out: hdd 110yds out: no ex* **18/1**
54-1 **3** *5* **Deep Resolve (IRE)**[26] 1072 6-11-0 **70**...........................(b) MrSWalker 1 70
(Alan Swinbank) *midfield: hdwy 3f out: rdn to chse ldr 2f out: no ex fnl f* **9/2**[2]
4460 **4** *1½* **Spiritoftomintoul**[26] 1073 8-10-4 **67**........................ MrGGilbertson(7) 16 64+
(Tony Carroll) *slowly away: hld up: hdwy 3f out: styd on fnl 2f* **10/1**
30-4 **5** *3½* **Rahmah (IRE)**[81] 169 5-10-12 **68**................................ MissSBrotherton 4 60
(Geoffrey Deacon) *midfield: rdn over 3f out: one pce and nvr threatened* **6/1**[3]
340- **6** *4½* **Whitecliff Park (IRE)**[344] 1619 4-9-9 **59**...................... MrMWBrown(7) 12 44
(Brian Ellison) *slowly away: hld up in rr: styd on fnl 2f: nvr threatened* **25/1**
006- **7** *nk* **Maskoon**[108] 8387 6-9-11 **60**................................... MissCarlyScott(7) 13 45
(Philip Kirby) *dwlt: hld up: hdwy over 3f out: rdn and no further imp fr over 2f out* **14/1**
030- **8** *1* **Longside**[166] 7429 5-10-10 **66**..................................... MrAlexFerguson 9 49
(James Eustace) *trckd ldrs: prom over 5f out: rdn over 3f out: grad wknd over 2f out* **12/1**
5-00 **9** *shd* **Archipeligo**[18] 1201 6-10-7 **68**........................................ MrBLynn(5) 3 51
(Iain Jardine) *trckd ldrs: rdn over 3f out: grad wknd* **12/1**
023- **10** *1* **Silver Shuffle (IRE)**[12] 5758 10-10-5 **61**..................... MissEmmaSayer 5 43
(Dianne Sayer) *hld up: nvr threatened* **25/1**
3/0- **11** *2½* **The Yank**[136] 2616 8-10-2 **65**.................................. PoppyBridgwater(7) 17 43
(David Bridgwater) *led: rdn whn hdd over 2f out: wknd* **33/1**
640- **12** *3* **Tayaar (IRE)**[109] 8366 4-9-12 **62**............................ MissHVKnowles(7) 14 35
(John Ryan) *prom: lost pl over 5f out: wknd over 3f out* **40/1**
-646 **13** *5* **Sandy Cove**[39] 856 6-10-5 **68**................................. MrJamesSmith(7) 15 34
(James Eustace) *dwlt: hld up: hdwy and in tch on outer over 5f out: rdn over 3f out: sn wknd* **11/1**
010/ **14** *7* **Sergeant Pink (IRE)**[12] 5765 11-9-7 **56**........................ MissAMSlack(7) 8 11
(Dianne Sayer) *a towards rr* **66/1**
210- **15** *9* **Duke Of Yorkshire**[163] 7500 7-10-11 **70**..............(p) MissEEasterby(3) 11 12
(Tim Easterby) *prom: lost pl over 4f out: sn wknd and bhd* **12/1**

2m 33.58s (-1.32) **Going Correction** +0.05s/f (Good) **15** Ran SP% **119.5**
Speed ratings (Par 103): **106,104,101,100,98 95,94,94,94,93 91,89,86,81,75**
CSF £72.18 CT £342.58 TOTE £4.80: £2.40, £5.40, £2.20; EX 80.70 Trifecta £611.30.
**Owner** Dean Woodhouse & Brian Ellison **Bred** Darley **Trained** Norton, N Yorks

**FOCUS**
An ordinary handicap for amateur riders. The runner-up has been rated close to last year's level.
T/Jkpt: Not won. T/Plt: £160.00 to a £1 stake. Pool: £156,004.12 - 711.61 winning units. T/Qpdt: £51.20 to a £1 stake. Pool: £10,699.08 - 154.34 winning units. **Andrew Sheret & Joe Rowntree**

# CORK (R-H)

Sunday, April 2

**OFFICIAL GOING: Heavy**

## 1520a CORK STKS (LISTED RACE) 6f
2:05 (2:06) 3-Y-0+

£22,692 (£7,307; £3,461; £1,538; £769; £384)

RPR

1 **Downforce (IRE)**155 7706 5-9-7 102 ... WJLee 5 111+
(W McCreery, Ire) *quite keen and sn trckd ldr in 2nd: travelled easily to press ldr under 2f out: led over 1f out and sn clr: impressive* **3/1**2

2 12 **Penny Pepper (IRE)**155 7706 5-9-2 89 ... GaryHalpin 1 68
(Kevin Prendergast, Ire) *racd in mid-div on outer: pushed along 1/2-way: 6th appr fnl f: kpt on wl far side into 2nd clsng stages: nt trble wnr* **16/1**

3 hd **Only Mine (IRE)**203 6384 4-9-7 106 ... GaryCarroll 10 72
(Joseph G Murphy, Ire) *hld up: rdn after 1/2-way: short of room and swtchd rt under 2f out: wnt 4th 1f out: kpt on wl in 3rd ins fnl f* **8/1**

4 1/2 **Dandyman Port (IRE)**152 3-8-4 93 ... NGMcCullagh 8 63
(Des Donovan, Ire) *hld up: clsr in mid-div at 1/2-way: rdn in 4th appr fnl f: sn no imp: kpt on same pce* **20/1**

5 hd **Great Minds (IRE)**370 1127 7-9-7 102 ... (p1) ChrisHayes 2 70
(J A Stack, Ire) *chsd ldrs in 4th: 3rd at 1/2-way: rdn and nt qckn appr fnl f: kpt on same pce: lame* **14/1**

6 hd **Sors (IRE)**189 6819 5-9-7 94 ... DeclanMcDonogh 9 69
(Andrew Slattery, Ire) *trckd ldr early in 2nd: sn 3rd: 4th at 1/2-way: nt qckn over 1f out: swtchd lft to stands' side and kpt on again clsng stages* **16/1**

7 2 **Spirit Quartz (IRE)**73 321 9-9-10 104 ... JulianResimont 3 66
(Daniel Rabhi, France) *sn led: strly pressed under 2f out: hdd over 1f out and sn no match for wnr: wknd ins fnl f* **12/1**

8 20 **Giant Spark**24 1103 5-9-7 95 ... PatSmullen 11
(Paul Midgley) *chsd ldrs on stands' side: 5th at 1/2-way: rdn and nt qckn over 1f out: sn no ex: slt abrasion on the rt hind fetlock* **13/2**3

9 4 1/4 **Heroic Heart (FR)**234 4-9-2 81 ... WayneLordan 7
(W McCreery, Ire) *a towards rr: rdn 1/2-way: sn no ex* **66/1**

10 27 **Gymkhana**7 1385 4-9-7 97 ... ColinKeane 6
(G M Lyons, Ire) *racd in mid-div to 1/2-way: sn rdn and no imp under 2f out: wknd qckly and eased: slt abrasion on the rt hind fetlock* **11/4**1

S **Master Speaker (IRE)**155 7706 7-9-7 101 ... (bt) ColmO'Donoghue 4 69
(Martin Hassett, Ire) *little slowly away and sn racd in rr: swtchd rt under 2f out and prog: no imp appr fnl f: kpt on same pce in 7th whn clipped heels and fell clsng stages* **11/1**

1m 20.82s (8.22)
**WFA** 3 from 4yo+ 12lb **11 Ran SP% 116.8**
CSF £50.29 TOTE £3.60: £1.40, £4.60, £2.60; DF 57.70 Trifecta £372.20.
**Owner** Donal Finnan **Bred** P Burns **Trained** Rathbride, Co Kildare

**FOCUS**
The ground was described by trainers and jockeys alike as borderline unraceable but it didn't inconvenience Downforce. A son of Fast Company, whose progeny love testing conditions, namely Jet Setting who actually shed her maiden tag on this card last season, this winner powered through the heavy going and annihilated his rivals. He has a lovely future on this evidence. The rating given to the winner is a bit guessy.

1521 - 1530a (Foreign Racing) - See Raceform Interactive

# 1415 SAINT-CLOUD (L-H)

Sunday, April 2

**OFFICIAL GOING: Turf: good**

## 1531a PRIX EDMOND BLANC (GROUP 3) (4YO+) (TURF) 1m
3:30 4-Y-0+ £34,188 (£13,675; £10,256; £6,837; £3,418)

RPR

1 **Jimmy Two Times (FR)**182 6991 4-9-2 0 ... VincentCheminaud 5 114+
(A Fabre, France) *w.w towards rr: hdwy on outer over 2f out: drvn to chse ldr more than 1f out: styd on strly to ld ins fnl f: sn clr: comf* **18/5**2

2 3 1/2 **Dicton**183 6975 4-9-0 0 ... OlivierPeslier 11 104+
(Gianluca Bietolini, Italy) *w.w towards rr: drvn and hdwy over 1 1/2f out: styd on fnl f: no ch w wnr* **7/1**

3 nk **Attendu (FR)**182 6991 4-9-2 0 ... MaximeGuyon 4 105
(C Laffon-Parias, France) *settled in midfield on outer: 6th and rdn wl over 2f out: styd on fnl f: nt pce to chal* **13/2**

4 nk **Kourkan (FR)**22 1159 4-9-0 0 ... ChristopheSoumillon 12 103+
(J-M Beguigne, France) *dwlt: w.w in rr: last and at least 12l off pce 3f out: drvn and began to cl 2f out: styd on fnl 1 1/2f: nrest at fin* **3/1**1

5 nk **Dhevanafushi**22 1159 4-9-0 0 ... MickaelBarzalona 2 102
(H-A Pantall, France) *chsd ldrs: drvn to ld 2f out: sn rdn and hdd ins fnl f: no ex and lost three pl fnl 50yds* **143/10**

6 snk **Djiguite (FR)**22 1159 5-9-0 0 ... GregoryBenoist 8 102
(D Smaga, France) *prom on outer: drvn to chse ldrs 1 1/2f out: kpt on at same pce fnl f* **5/1**3

7 2 **Maimara (FR)**291 3271 5-8-10 0 ... AurelienLemaitre 7 93
(M Delzangles, France) *half rrd as stalls opened: sn rcvrd and settled in midfield: rdn and nt qckn 2f out: plugged on at one pce* **47/1**

8 snk **Aim To Please (FR)**168 7404 4-8-13 0 ... GeraldMosse 10 96
(F Doumen, France) *hld up in fnl pair: kpt on ins fnl f: nt pce to be involved* **138/10**

9 1/2 **Narnia Dawn (IRE)**136 7998 4-8-10 0 ... Pierre-CharlesBoudot 3 91
(F-H Graffard, France) *missed break: rcvrd into midfield on inner: rdn in pursuit of ldng gp 1 1/2f out: wknd ins fnl f* **93/10**

10 15 **Rakhsh (FR)**283 5-9-0 0 ... EddyHardouin 1 61
(Carina Fey, France) *led racing keenly under restraint: 3l clr 1/2-way: scrubbed along and hdd 2f out: sn wknd* **39/1**

11 dist **Via Cassia**52 4-9-0 0 ... PierreBazire 6
(Gianluca Bietolini, Italy) *dwlt: scrubbed along to chse ldr: drvn 1/2-way: lost pl over 2f out: wknd qckly: ins ins fnl 1 1/2f* **107/1**

1m 37.78s (-9.72) **11 Ran SP% 117.7**
PARI-MUTUEL (all including 1 euro stake): WIN: 4.60; PLACE: 1.90, 2.50, 2.50; DF: 17.80; SF: 24.60.
**Owner** Scea Haras De Saint Pair **Bred** F Teboul & J Boniche **Trained** Chantilly, France

**FOCUS**
The standard is set by the winner and fifth.

1532 - 1541a (Foreign Racing) - See Raceform Interactive

# 1431 SOUTHWELL (L-H)

Tuesday, April 4

**OFFICIAL GOING: Fibresand: standard**
Wind: Moderate across veering to half behind Weather: Grey cloud

## 1542 BETWAY H'CAP 6f 16y(F)
2:10 (2:15) (Class 5) (0-75,77) 3-Y-0+ £2,911 (£866; £432; £216) Stalls Low

Form RPR

2315 1 **Crosse Fire**14 1296 5-9-12 75 ... KieranO'Neill 5 83
(Scott Dixon) *qckly away and mde all: rdn along 2f out: drvn over 1f out: kpt on strly* **4/1**3

0-33 2 1 1/4 **Meshardal (GER)**14 1296 7-9-2 65 ... JamesSullivan 3 69+
(Ruth Carr) *towards rr: wd st: hdwy on outer over 2f out: rdn over 1f out: chsd wnr ent fnl f: sn drvn: edgd lft and kpt on same pce* **5/2**2

010- 3 1 **Appleberry (IRE)**153 7772 5-9-9 75 ... (h) AlistairRawlinson(3) 7 76
(Michael Appleby) *chsd ldrs: hdwy over 2f out: rdn wl over 1f out: kpt on u.p fnl f* **20/1**

5031 4 nk **Big Amigo (IRE)**14 1296 4-9-9 72 ... SilvestreDeSousa 2 72+
(Daniel Mark Loughnane) *trckd ldrs on inner: rdn along and outpcd over 3f out: hdwy 2f out: drvn and kpt on same pce fnl f* **7/4**1

650- 5 2 1/4 **L C Saloon**209 6234 4-10-0 77 ... DavidAllan 4 70
(David C Griffiths) *prom: rdn along over 2f out: drvn over 1f out: grad wknd* **10/1**

2220 6 2 1/4 **Spiraea**29 1063 7-9-5 68 ... TomEaves 8 53
(Ivan Furtado) *prom: cl up 4f out: rdn along over 2f out: drvn wl over 1f out: sn wknd* **20/1**

030- 7 2 1/2 **Specialv (IRE)**136 8036 4-9-9 72 ... (p) BenCurtis 1 49
(Brian Ellison) *dwlt: a rr* **14/1**

1m 16.61s (0.11) **Going Correction** +0.15s/f (Slow) **7 Ran SP% 110.2**
Speed ratings (Par 103): **105,103,102,101,98 95,92**
CSF £13.34 CT £160.26 TOTE £4.40: £1.90, £1.80; EX 13.10 Trifecta £117.40.
**Owner** Paul J Dixon & Darren Lucas **Bred** Dr A Gillespie **Trained** Babworth, Notts

**FOCUS**
A fair, competitive-looking sprint, in which the winner made all at a good pace.

## 1543 BETWAY MEDIAN AUCTION MAIDEN STKS 4f 214y(F)
2:40 (2:46) (Class 6) 3-5-Y-0 £2,264 (£673; £336; £168) Stalls Centre

Form RPR

3425 1 **Arzaak (IRE)**12 1332 3-9-0 73 ... (b1) SilvestreDeSousa 1 77
(Chris Dwyer) *mde all: rdn along and edgd rt over 1f out: sn clr: kpt on strly* **4/7**1

03 2 4 1/2 **Tooty Fruitti**12 1321 3-8-9 0 ... JFEgan 5 56
(Jo Hughes) *chsd ldrs: hdwy over 2f out: rdn wl over 1f out: styd on fnl f* **10/1**

05-2 3 shd **Sheepscar Lad (IRE)**11 1349 3-9-0 68 ... TomEaves 6 60
(Nigel Tinkler) *chsd ldrs: rdn along 2f out: drvn over 1f out: kpt on same pce* **7/1**3

3-3 4 3/4 **Hart Stopper**81 221 3-9-0 0 ... JamieSpencer 8 58
(Michael Bell) *prom: chsd wnr after 2f: rdn along over 2f out: drvn over 1f out: one pce* **11/4**2

05-6 5 3 **Joysunny**21 1183 3-8-2 40 ... HarrisonShaw(7) 3 44+
(Michael Easterby) *prom: pushed along 1/2-way: rdn 2f out: sn one pce* **100/1**

5-4 6 6 **Stopdworldnletmeof**21 1183 3-8-11 0 ... HollieDoyle(3) 4 25
(David Flood) *in tch: rdn along over 2f out: sn outpcd and bhd* **16/1**

00 7 1 3/4 **Slipalongtrevaskis**22 1179 4-9-4 0 ... GinaMangan(7) 2 24
(J R Jenkins) *in tch: rdn along over 2f out: sn outpcd and bhd* **125/1**

6 8 19 **Tartufo Classico**12 1321 4-9-11 0 ... MartinLane 7
(Derek Shaw) *sn rdn along and outpcd: bhd fnl 3f* **40/1**

58.51s (-1.19) **Going Correction** -0.175s/f (Stan)
**WFA** 3 from 4yo 11lb **8 Ran SP% 122.0**
Speed ratings (Par 101): **102,94,94,93,88 79,76,45**
CSF £9.16 TOTE £1.50: £1.10, £2.70, £1.90; EX 10.20 Trifecta £30.80.
**Owner** M M Foulger **Bred** Gerard Kerin **Trained** Newmarket, Suffolk

**FOCUS**
An ordinary maiden which was dominated by the favourite who has been rated to form.

## 1544 SUNBETS.CO.UK DOWNLOAD THE APP H'CAP (DIV I) 1m 13y(F)
3:15 (3:20) (Class 6) (0-55,57) 3-Y-0+ £2,264 (£673; £336; £168) Stalls Low

Form RPR

6-06 1 **Gunner Moyne**59 570 5-9-11 57 ... (v1) HectorCrouch(3) 10 63
(Gary Moore) *dwlt: hdwy on outer and cl up after 2f: led over 3f out: rdn over 1f out: edgd lft ins fnl f: kpt on* **3/1**1

606- 2 1/2 **I'm Super Too (IRE)**151 7795 10-9-7 55 ... GemmaTutty(5) 9 60
(Karen Tutty) *in tch: hdwy 3f out: chsd wnr over 2f out: rdn wl over 1f out: sn drvn and kpt on fnl f* **8/1**

0260 3 1 **Ertidaad (IRE)**12 1322 5-9-3 46 oh1 ... (v) JFEgan 5 49
(Emma Owen) *reminders after 1f: in tch: hdwy on inner 3f out: rdn to chse ldrs 2f out: drvn and kpt on fnl f* **15/2**3

-004 4 1 1/2 **Quadriga (IRE)**53 661 7-9-5 48 ... (b) TonyHamilton 1 47
(Chris Grant) *chsd ldrs: rdn over 2f out: drvn over 1f out: kpt on one pce* **14/1**

655- 5 4 **Joaldo**350 1556 5-9-3 46 oh1 ... CamHardie 3 36
(Antony Brittain) *towards rr: pushed along over 3f out: rdn wl over 2f out: kpt on appr fnl f: n.d* **33/1**

000- 6 5 **Border Bandit (USA)**138 7995 9-9-4 47 ... (p) BenCurtis 6 26
(Tracy Waggott) *rr and swtchd rt to outer after 1f: a rr* **5/1**2

000 7 2 1/4 **Clean Cut**45 819 3-8-4 48 ... SilvestreDeSousa 8 17
(Ivan Furtado) *chsd ldrs: rdn along 3f out: drvn 2f out: grad wknd* **8/1**

60-6 8 4 1/2 **Ada Misobel (IRE)**74 332 4-9-1 51 ... (p) KevinLundie(7) 7 14
(Roy Bowring) *sltly hmpd after s and sn t.k.h: hdwy to chse ldng trio after 2f: rdn along wl over 2f out: sn wknd* **17/2**

040- 9 8 **Funny Oyster (IRE)**22 7628 4-9-9 52 ... LukeMorris 4
(Chris Gordon) *cl up: rdn along and lost pl 1/2-way: sn bhd* **12/1**

-030 10 3/4 **Moi Aussie**11 1338 4-9-9 55 ... AlistairRawlinson(3) 2
(Michael Appleby) *ledf: rdn along and hdd over 3f out: sn wknd* **8/1**

1m 46.01s (2.31) **Going Correction** +0.15s/f (Slow)
**WFA** 3 from 4yo+ 15lb **10 Ran SP% 114.6**
Speed ratings (Par 101): **94,93,92,91,87 82,79,75,67,66**
CSF £26.78 CT £167.84 TOTE £3.70: £1.50, £2.80, £2.80; EX 28.70 Trifecta £176.80.
**Owner** G L Moore **Bred** Five Horses Ltd **Trained** Lower Beeding, W Sussex

**FOCUS**
A moderate handicap. The winner looks up to matching his best form around here.

## 1545 SUNBETS.CO.UK DOWNLOAD THE APP H'CAP (DIV II) 1m 13y(F)
**3:50** (3:57) (Class 6) (0-55,57) 3-Y-0+ **£2,264** (£673; £336; £168) **Stalls** Low

Form RPR

-610 **1** **Chamasay**[6] 1421 3-8-11 **55** ........................ JFEgan 3 68+
(David Evans) *trckd ldrs: hdwy over 3f out: led wl over 2f out: rdn clr wl over 1f out: readily* **6/4**[1]

2-22 **2** *6* **Simply Clever**[17] 1260 4-10-0 **57** ........................ TomEaves 9 60
(David Brown) *dwlt: sn in tch on outer: wd st and rdn along wl over 2f out: hdwy wl over 1f out: drvn and kpt on fnl f: no ch w wnr* **8/1**

2022 **3** *2* **General Tufto**[21] 1187 12-9-8 **51** ........................(b) JoeyHaynes 2 49
(Charles Smith) *chsd ldrs on inner: effrt over 2f out: sn rdn: drvn over 1f out: kpt on same pce* **7/2**[2]

55-0 **4** *hd* **Albert Boy (IRE)**[70] 390 4-9-5 **48** ........................ DaleSwift 10 46
(Scott Dixon) *midfield: hdwy over 3f out: rdn along to chse ldrs over 2f out: sn drvn and kpt on fnl f* **14/1**

66-0 **5** *4* **Demand Respect**[66] 462 4-9-3 **46** oh1........................(b) KieranO'Neill 4 35
(Henry Spiller) *cl up: rdn along 3f out: drvn over 2f out: sn wknd* **33/1**

-000 **6** *1* **Port Lairge**[8] 853 7-9-5 **53** ........................(b) PhilDennis(5) 8 39
(Michael Chapman) *dwlt and bhd: rdn along and hdwy on inner over 3f out: kpt on u.p fnl 2f* **33/1**

4-53 **7** *nse* **Star Ascending (IRE)**[18] 1249 5-9-12 **55** ........................(v) JoeFanning 1 41
(Jennie Candlish) *sn led: rdn along over 3f out: hdd wl over 2f out: sn drvn and wknd over 1f out* **5/1**[3]

0-00 **8** *5* **Chillilililli**[70] 385 3-7-9 **46** oh1........................ RPWalsh(7) 6 17
(Michael Appleby) *prom: rdn along 3f out: wd st and sn wknd* **50/1**

665- **9** *34* **Natalia**[176] 7211 8-9-3 **46** oh1........................(t) RobHornby 7
(Sarah Hollinshead) *sn rdn along: a outpcd and bhd* **22/1**

030- **10** *1 ½* **Ginger Charlie**[180] 7096 4-9-7 **50** ........................ JamesSullivan 5
(Ruth Carr) *dwlt: a outpcd and bhd* **16/1**

1m 45.13s (1.43) **Going Correction** +0.15s/f (Slow)
**WFA** 3 from 4yo+ 15lb 10 Ran SP% **114.7**
Speed ratings (Par 101): **98,92,90,89,85 84,84,79,45,44**
CSF £13.58 CT £37.33 TOTE £2.60: £1.30, £2.00, £1.50; EX 15.10 Trifecta £42.10.
**Owner** E A R Morgans **Bred** E A R Morgans **Trained** Pandy, Monmouths

**FOCUS**
The second leg of a moderate handicap, but hard not to be impressed by the winner. The race has been rated around the second.

## 1546 SUNBETS.CO.UK H'CAP 7f 14y(F)
**4:20** (4:25) (Class 3) (0-90,90) 3-Y-0 **£7,158** (£2,143; £1,071; £535; £267) **Stalls** Low

Form RPR

3142 **1** **Custard The Dragon**[10] 1365 4-9-1 **77** ........................(p) BenCurtis 5 89
(John Mackie) *trckd ldrs: hdwy 3f out: chsd ldr 2f out: rdn to chal over 1f out: drvn ins fnl f: led last 100 yds* **5/2**[2]

3111 **2** *nk* **Call Out Loud**[10] 1365 5-9-0 **79** ........................(vt) AlistairRawlinson(3) 1 90
(Michael Appleby) *led: rdn along 2f out and sn jnd: drvn appr fnl f: hdd and no ex last 100 yds* **10/1**

41F- **3** *5* **Thomas Cranmer (USA)**[207] 6275 3-8-8 **84** ........................ JoeFanning 4 77
(Mark Johnston) *t.k.h: trckd ldng pair: pushed along on inner wl over 2f out: rdn wl over 1f out: kpt on same pce* **9/4**[1]

-343 **4** *1* **Bold Prediction (IRE)**[22] 1177 7-9-12 **88** ........................(p[1]) ThomasBrown 2 83
(Ed Walker) *blind removed late and stmbld s: trckd ldr: rdn along wl over 2f out: sn drvn and kpt on same pce appr fnl f* **7/1**[3]

00-4 **5** *24* **Quixote (GER)**[77] 275 7-10-0 **90** ........................ PaulMulrennan 3 20
(David Loughnane) *s.i.s and lost several l s: a bhd* **5/2**[2]

1m 30.24s (-0.06) **Going Correction** +0.15s/f (Slow)
**WFA** 3 from 4yo+ 14lb 5 Ran SP% **109.5**
Speed ratings (Par 107): **106,105,99,98,71**
CSF £23.80 TOTE £3.50: £1.70, £3.80; EX 9.50 Trifecta £28.30.
**Owner** Derbyshire Racing **Bred** Mr & Mrs Kevan Watts **Trained** Church Broughton , Derbys

**FOCUS**
Not the strongest handicap for the grade and the two principals fought out a thrilling finish, but they have both been rated as improving.

## 1547 BETWAY SPRINT H'CAP 4f 214y(F)
**4:55** (5:00) (Class 6) (0-65,67) 3-Y-0+ **£2,264** (£673; £336; £168) **Stalls** Centre

Form RPR

0- **1** **Zylan (IRE)**[160] 7631 5-8-12 **59** ........................ BenSanderson(7) 3 69+
(Roger Fell) *racd centre: trckd ldrs: hdwy over 2f out: rdn to ld over 1f out: kpt on wl towards fin* **7/1**

603- **2** *nk* **Henley**[170] 7386 5-9-12 **66** ........................ DaleSwift 6 75
(Tracy Waggott) *t.k.h: racd towards stands side: trckd ldrs: hdwy to chse ldr 1/2-way: cl up and rdn along over 1f out: sn edgd lft and ev ch: drvn ins fnl f: kpt on* **10/1**

0-01 **3** *1 ¾* **Dusty Blue**[28] 1071 5-9-9 **63** ........................ DavidProbert 8 66
(David Loughnane) *racd towards stands side: chsd ldrs: hdwy 2f out: rdn over 1f out: kpt on same pce fnl f* **3/1**[1]

0424 **4** *nk* **Borough Boy (IRE)**[3] 1490 7-9-8 **62** ........................(v) TonyHamilton 2 64
(Derek Shaw) *sn led in centre: rdn along 2f out: drvn and hdd over 1f out: kpt on same pce* **4/1**[2]

0452 **5** *1 ¾* **Novabridge**[6] 1435 9-8-13 **58** ........................(b) GemmaTutty(5) 1 53
(Karen Tutty) *racd towards far side: chsd ldrs: rdn along 2f out: drvn over 1f out: no imp fnl f* **9/2**[3]

0401 **6** *2* **Jacob's Pillow**[21] 1184 6-9-11 **65** ........................ DanielTudhope 4 53
(Rebecca Bastiman) *cl up centre: pushed along 1/2-way: rdn wl over 1f out: sn drvn and wknd* **9/2**[3]

4515 **7** *4 ½* **Pulsating (IRE)**[27] 1090 3-9-2 **67** ........................ StevieDonohoe 5 34
(Daniel Steele) *dwlt and a rr towards stands side* **20/1**

2154 **8** *¾* **Annie Salts**[12] 1328 4-9-10 **64** ........................(h) SilvestreDeSousa 7 33
(Chris Dwyer) *racd nr stands rail: in tch: rdn along over 2f out: sn wknd* **10/1**

58.81s (-0.89) **Going Correction** -0.175s/f (Stan)
**WFA** 3 from 4yo+ 11lb 8 Ran SP% **116.8**
Speed ratings (Par 101): **100,99,96,96,93 90,83,81**
CSF £74.75 CT £257.44 TOTE £8.50: £2.50, £3.00, £1.50; EX 65.00 Trifecta £412.90.
**Owner** R G Fell **Bred** Philip And Mrs Jane Myerscough **Trained** Nawton, N Yorks

**FOCUS**
A modest but competitive sprint handicap and they went a good pace. The race has been rated around the runner-up.

## 1548 BETWAY STAYERS H'CAP 1m 6f 21y(F)
**5:25** (5:30) (Class 5) (0-75,75) 4-Y-0+ **£2,911** (£866; £432; £216) **Stalls** Low

Form RPR

040- **1** **Sisyphus**[203] 6457 5-9-10 **75** ........................ AndrewMullen 4 85+
(Ollie Pears) *trckd ldr: cl up 6f out: led wl over 2f out: rdn clr wl over 1f out: styd on strly* **16/1**

2-14 **2** *4 ½* **Ominotago**[84] 162 5-9-3 **68** ........................ SilvestreDeSousa 3 70
(Michael Appleby) *led: pushed along 3f out: sn rdn and hdd: drvn wl over 1f out: kpt on same pce* **6/5**[1]

2231 **3** *nse* **Eurato (FR)**[14] 1291 7-9-2 **74** ........................(p) FinleyMarsh(7) 1 76
(Steve Gollings) *trckd ldng pair on inner: pushed along: outpcd and swtchd rt to outer 5f out: rdn along 3f out: drvn and styd on fnl 2f* **11/4**[2]

13-2 **4** *14* **Denmead**[20] 1207 4-9-1 **69** ........................ RobertWinston 2 51
(John Butler) *sltly hmpd after 200 yds and t.k.h: trckd ldrs: pushed along over 3f out: rdn wl over 2f out: sn wknd* **9/2**[3]

6232 **5** *10* **Go On Gal (IRE)**[21] 1188 4-8-1 **58** ........................(p[1]) ShelleyBirkett(3) 5 26
(Julia Feilden) *trckd ldng pair: pushed along over 4f out: rdn along over 3f out: sn drvn and outpcd* **7/1**

3m 9.21s (0.91) **Going Correction** +0.15s/f (Slow)
**WFA** 4 from 5yo+ 1lb 5 Ran SP% **108.7**
Speed ratings (Par 103): **103,100,100,92,86**
CSF £35.38 TOTE £9.30: £4.30, £1.40; EX 28.20 Trifecta £164.80.
**Owner** Charles Wentworth **Bred** Charles Wentworth **Trained** Norton, N Yorks

**FOCUS**
A fair staying handicap with the winner rated in line with his turf form.

## 1549 BETWAY MIDDLE DISTANCE H'CAP 1m 3f 23y(F)
**5:55** (6:00) (Class 5) (0-75,76) 4-Y-0+ **£2,911** (£866; £432; £216) **Stalls** Low

Form RPR

5-31 **1** **Star Of Lombardy (IRE)**[5] 1455 4-9-4 **70** 6ex........................ FrannyNorton 4 82
(Mark Johnston) *trckd ldr: cl up 1/2-way: chal 3f out: rdn wl over 1f out: drvn to take slt advantage ins fnl f: kpt on wl towards fin* **5/2**[2]

4613 **2** *nk* **Storm King**[21] 1182 8-9-10 **76** ........................ DavidAllan 5 87
(David C Griffiths) *led: jnd 3f out and sn rdn: drvn 2f out: hdd ins fnl f: kpt on gamely towards fin* **2/1**[1]

6136 **3** *9* **The Lock Master (IRE)**[14] 1292 10-9-1 **70** ........(p) AlistairRawlinson(3) 3 66
(Michael Appleby) *dwlt: sn trcking ldrs: hdwy to chse ldng pair 1/2-way: rdn along over 3f out: drvn 2f out: kpt on one pce* **11/2**[3]

-423 **4** *5* **Glenalmond (IRE)**[38] 928 5-9-4 **70** ........................ StevieDonohoe 1 57
(Daniel Steele) *trckd ldrs on inner: pushed along over 5f out: lost pl over 4f out and bhd: plugged on u.p fnl 2f* **8/1**

00-0 **5** *1 ¾* **Balducci**[21] 1187 10-8-7 **59** ........................ BenCurtis 2 43
(Roger Fell) *hld up: a towards rr* **14/1**

40-5 **6** *1 ¾* **Perceived**[11] 1345 5-9-7 **73** ........................ CamHardie 6 54
(Antony Brittain) *trckd ldrs: pushed along over 4f out: rdn over 3f out: drvn wl over 2f out and sn wknd* **28/1**

000- **7** *8* **Indian Chief (IRE)**[153] 7775 7-9-7 **73** ........................ DanielTudhope 7 41
(Rebecca Bastiman) *dwlt and hld up in rr: hdwy on outer 5f out: chsd ;ldrs over 3f out: sn rdn and wknd over 2f out* **8/1**

2m 27.77s (-0.23) **Going Correction** +0.15s/f (Slow) 7 Ran SP% **109.6**
Speed ratings (Par 103): **106,105,99,95,94 93,87**
CSF £7.20 TOTE £3.10: £2.30, £1.30; EX 7.60 Trifecta £18.40.
**Owner** Paul Dean **Bred** Tom Darcy And Vincent McCarthy **Trained** Middleham Moor, N Yorks

**FOCUS**
A fair handicap, but little depth and not many got into it, with the two market leaders up there throughout.
T/Plt: £54.80 to a £1 stake. Pool: £101,933.45 - 1,356.72 winning units. T/Qpdt: £13.90 to a £1 stake. Pool: £8,535.90 - 451.50 winning units. **Joe Rowntree**

# 1499 KEMPTON (A.W) (R-H)
### Wednesday, April 5

**OFFICIAL GOING: Polytrack: standard**
Wind: Light, half against Weather: Bright, white cloud

## 1550 100% PROFIT BOOST AT 32REDSPORT.COM H'CAP 1m (P)
**5:45** (5:45) (Class 5) (0-70,72) 3-Y-0 **£2,911** (£866; £432; £216) **Stalls** Low

Form RPR

4-53 **1** **Arctic Sea**[42] 863 3-9-7 **69** ........................ LukeMorris 5 74
(Paul Cole) *pushed along leaving stalls to sit handy bhd ldrs: shkn up 2f out: 2 l down on ldng trio ent fnl f: kpt on strly on outer fnl 110yds to ld cl home* **16/1**

00-5 **2** *¾* **Power Power (IRE)**[14] 1299 3-8-13 **66** ........................ GeorgeWood(5) 2 69
(Marco Botti) *t.k.h bhd ldrs: rdn over 1f out: kpt on wl ins fnl f: led 110yds out: hdd post* **9/1**[3]

444- **3** *½* **Al Mansor (IRE)**[165] 7527 3-9-6 **68** ........................ FrankieDettori 4 70
(Richard Hannon) *led for 1f out: settled bhd ldr after: shkn up 2f out and sn rdn: led ent fnl f: hdd 110yds out: no ex* **3/1**[2]

400- **4** *1* **Paddy A (IRE)**[145] 7898 3-9-0 **67** ........................ PaddyBradley(5) 7 67
(Philip McBride) *hld up in rr-div: shkn up over 2f out: rdn 2f out: stuck on wl ins fnl f* **33/1**

420 **5** *½* **Never Folding (IRE)**[13] 1333 3-9-0 **62** ........................(t[1]) OisinMurphy 8 61
(Seamus Durack) *mid-div: rdn 2f out: kpt on one pce tl styd on wl cl home* **40/1**

06-1 **6** *shd* **Alemaratalyoum (IRE)**[14] 1306 3-9-10 **72** ........................ SilvestreDeSousa 3 70
(Ed Dunlop) *led after 1f: rdn 2f out: hdd ent fnl f: stuck on tl wknd ins fnl f* **5/4**[1]

056- **7** *shd* **Famous Dynasty (IRE)**[184] 7016 3-9-2 **64** ........................ DavidProbert 6 62
(Michael Blanshard) *in rr-div: rdn 2f out: kpt on one pce* **12/1**

0-45 **8** *2 ½* **Malt Teaser (FR)**[48] 763 3-9-3 **65** ........................ KierenFox 11 57
(John Best) *settled in rr: rdn over 1f out: no imp* **14/1**

531- **9** *hd* **Arthurthedelegator**[110] 8398 3-9-3 **65** ........................ KevinStott 10 57
(Oliver Greenall) *cl up bhd ldrs: shkn up 2f out: kpt on one pce fr over 1f out* **16/1**

006- **10** *2* **Ashazuri**[183] 7049 3-9-7 **69** ........................ JimCrowley 9 56
(Jonathan Portman) *mid-div on outer: rdn over 2f out: wknd fr over 1f out* **40/1**

045- **11** *6* **The Secrets Out**168 7460 3-8-12 **60** KieranO'Neill 1 33
(Luke Dace) *settled bhd ldrs on rail rdn 2f out: no ex and wknd fr over 1f out* **20/1**
1m 39.97s (0.17) **Going Correction** -0.05s/f (Stan) 11 Ran SP% **118.1**
Speed ratings (Par 98): **97,96,95,94,94 94,94,91,91,89 83**
CSF £147.12 CT £555.68 TOTE £14.10: £3.50, £3.10, £1.80; EX 80.30 Trifecta £327.70.
**Owner** P F I Cole Ltd **Bred** Waratah Thoroughbreds Pty Ltd **Trained** Whatcombe, Oxon
**FOCUS**
This was fairly steadily run. The race has been rated around the third, with the first two improvers on their handicap debuts.

## 1551 32RED.COM MAIDEN STKS (DIV I) 1m (P)
**6:15** (6:15) (Class 5) 3-Y-0+ **£2,911** (£866; £432; £216) **Stalls** Low

Form RPR
2- **1** **Bowerman**149 7849 3-8-13 0 AndreaAtzeni 7 86+
(Roger Varian) *sluggish s: pushed up to sit on outer of ldr after 2f: shkn up 2f out and sprinted clr ent fnl f: in n.d and pushed out: easily* **1/3**1
**2** *3 ¾* **Ply** 3-8-10 0 KieranShoemark(3) 9 75+
(Roger Charlton) *s.s and settled in rr: shkn up over 2f out: kpt on wl fr over 1f out to take comfortable 2nd: no ch w wnr* **20/1**
45- **3** *¾* **Blue On Blue (USA)**159 7664 3-8-13 0 (h) FrankieDettori 1 73
(John Gosden) *led: rdn over 2f out: hdd 2f out: kpt on one pce* **4/1**2
3 **4** *1* **Bosphorus Prince (IRE)**30 1069 5-10-0 0 JohnFahy 5 75
(Matthew Salaman) *settled bhd ldrs: rdn 2f out: kpt on one pce fr over 1f out* **33/1**
6 **5** *3 ½* **Chance To Dream (IRE)**14 1299 3-8-13 0 KierenFox 6 62
(John Best) *mid-div on rail: rdn 2f out: no imp on ldrs fr over 1f out* **40/1**
60- **6** *1 ¼* **Delannoy**189 6881 3-8-13 0 RobertWinston 8 59+
(Eve Johnson Houghton) *in rr-div: shuffled along in centre over 1f out: likely improver* **14/1**
5 **7** *1 ½* **Hippocampus (IRE)**11 1358 3-8-13 0 SeanLevey 2 56
(Richard Hannon) *cl up bhd ldrs: rdn 2f out: no ex ent fnl f* **10/1**3
**8** *nk* **Higgy's Heartbeat** 3-8-13 0 LukeMorris 4 55
(Dean Ivory) *in rr: rdn over 2f out: no ex fr over 1f out* **66/1**
56 **9** *1 ¾* **The Raven Master (IRE)**11 1358 3-8-6 0 (h) TristanPrice(7) 3 51
(Michael Bell) *settled bhd ldrs: rdn over 2f out: kpt on tl wknd qckly ent fnl f* **40/1**
1m 38.89s (-0.91) **Going Correction** -0.05s/f (Stan)
**WFA** 3 from 5yo 15lb 9 Ran SP% **124.8**
Speed ratings (Par 103): **102,98,97,96,93 91,90,89,88**
CSF £16.25 TOTE £1.30: £1.10, £3.70, £1.50; EX 14.30 Trifecta £35.50.
**Owner** Paul Smith **Bred** Cheveley Park Stud Ltd **Trained** Newmarket, Suffolk
■ Stewards' Enquiry : John Fahy cautioned - guilty of careless riding
**FOCUS**
This proved pretty straightforward for the well-backed favourite.

## 1552 32RED.COM MAIDEN STKS (DIV II) 1m (P)
**6:45** (6:48) (Class 5) 3-Y-0+ **£2,911** (£866; £432; £216) **Stalls** Low

Form RPR
222- **1** **Archer's Arrow (USA)**145 7906 3-8-13 82 OisinMurphy 5 76+
(Saeed bin Suroor) *broke wl and sent st into ld: shkn up 2f out: sn rdn and 2 l up ent fnl f: kpt on wl to hold runner-up nring fin: jst hld on* **5/4**1
**2** *nk* **Dhalam (USA)** 3-8-13 0 FrankieDettori 2 75+
(John Gosden) *settled bhd ldr: rdn 2f out: no immediate imp on wnr: gaining ent fnl f: clsng nr line: jst hld* **9/4**2
- **3** *2 ½* **Desert Explorer (IRE)** 3-8-10 0 EdwardGreatrex(3) 3 69+
(Eve Johnson Houghton) *s.s: in rr: clsr over 2f out: sn rdn on inner and kpt on to take 3rd 1f out: nvr nrr* **33/1**
400- **4** *¾* **Koeman**166 7502 3-8-13 76 SilvestreDeSousa 1 67
(Mick Channon) *pushed along early in rr-div to hold pl: rdn 2f out: kpt on one pce fr over 1f out* **9/1**
6- **5** *1 ¼* **Zamalight**182 7064 3-8-13 0 JimCrowley 8 64
(Amanda Perrett) *racd in 3rd on outer: rdn 2f out: kpt on one pce* **4/1**3
**6** *1* **Doodle Dandy (IRE)**39 4-9-9 0 JimmyQuinn 6 61
(David Bridgwater) *settled in rr-div: effrt 2f out: kpt on one pce* **250/1**
00- **7** *9* **Darcey Lou**189 6866 3-8-8 0 KierenFox 7 35
(John Best) *mid-div: pushed along over 2f out: lft bhd fr over 1f out* **100/1**
- **8** *3 ¾* **Vaudieu** 3-8-5 0 (b1) JackDuern(3) 4 26
(Dean Ivory) *reluctant to load: in mid-div: rdn over 2f out: urged along over 2f out: sn no ex and shuffled along fr over 1f out* **100/1**
50- **9** *3* **Leopard (IRE)**133 8073 3-8-13 0 LukeMorris 9 24
(Paul Cole) *tk fierce hold in rr: rdn over 2f out: sn no imp and allowed to coast home* **16/1**
1m 38.99s (-0.81) **Going Correction** -0.05s/f (Stan)
**WFA** 3 from 4yo 15lb 9 Ran SP% **116.4**
Speed ratings (Par 103): **102,101,99,98,97 96,87,83,80**
CSF £4.27 TOTE £2.10: £1.10, £1.20, £9.00; EX 4.60 Trifecta £67.40.
**Owner** Godolphin **Bred** Gary Chervenell **Trained** Newmarket, Suffolk
**FOCUS**
Very marginally the slower of the divisions. The first two, both sired by Lonhro, had this between them from some way out. The winner has been rated close to form.

## 1553 32RED ON THE APP STORE H'CAP 1m (P)
**7:15** (7:15) (Class 5) (0-70,72) 4-Y-0+ **£2,911** (£866; £432; £216) **Stalls** Low

Form RPR
430- **1** **Selection (FR)**171 7384 4-9-4 72 GeorgiaCox(5) 3 83+
(William Haggas) *marginal ld on rail: shkn up over 1f out w a line of chalrs in bhd: shuffled along in ld ent fnl f: chal on inner fr over 110yds out: nudged out cl home to fend off runner-up: snug* **2/1**1
0031 **2** *nk* **Spiritual Star (IRE)**8 1409 8-8-13 67 PaddyBradley(5) 6 77
(Lee Carter) *hld up in rr: shkn up and gd prog between horses over 1f out: swtchd to inner ent fnl f: pressed wnr fr over 110yds out: no ex fnl strides* **7/1**
-412 **3** *3* **Tee It Up Tommo (IRE)**34 986 8-9-8 71 (t) StevieDonohoe 9 74
(Daniel Steele) *dropped out leaving stalls and settled in rr: rdn 2f out: kpt on wl on outer past btn horse: tk 3rd ins fnl f: no imp on ldrs* **8/1**
1412 **4** *½* **Wink Oliver**5 1462 5-9-5 68 (p) JFEgan 8 70
(Jo Hughes) *in rr-div: rdn over 2f out: 3rd ins fnl f: wknd and lost 3rd cl home* **11/2**2
00-0 **5** *½* **Mister Musicmaster**11 1365 8-9-1 64 LukeMorris 1 64
(Ron Hodges) *cl up bhd ldrs on rail: rdn over 1f out: ev ch ent fnl f: wknd qckly last 110yds* **33/1**
6-15 **6** *4* **Music Major**25 1144 4-9-7 70 AdamBeschizza 7 61
(Michael Attwater) *t.k.h on outer bhd ldrs: rdn wl over 1f out: no ex fnl f* **13/2**3
00-4 **7** *3 ½* **Thecornishbarron (IRE)**21 1201 5-9-9 72 RobertWinston 5 54
(John Ryan) *disp ld: rdn 2f out: wknd fr over 1f out* **9/1**
0-36 **8** *3 ¼* **Rightway (IRE)**62 524 6-9-5 68 JimCrowley 2 43
(Tony Carroll) *chsd ldrs: pushed along over 1f out: wknd qckly after* **9/1**
-000 **9** *¾* **Freight Train (IRE)**28 1085 5-8-11 60 SamHitchcott 4 33
(Adrian Wintle) *in rr: shkn up ent st: sn rdn and no imp fr 2f out* **150/1**
1m 38.86s (-0.94) **Going Correction** -0.05s/f (Stan) 9 Ran SP% **109.3**
Speed ratings (Par 103): **102,101,98,98,97 93,90,86,86**
CSF £14.73 CT £81.27 TOTE £2.60: £1.20, £2.70, £1.30; EX 16.00 Trifecta £100.70.
**Owner** Highclere Thoroughbred Racing - Siyouni **Bred** F Bozo, M Bozo, M Bozo & J Bozo **Trained** Newmarket, Suffolk
**FOCUS**
The unexposed favourite proved too good for these on his handicap debut.

## 1554 32RED CASINO H'CAP 7f (P)
**7:45** (7:45) (Class 5) (0-75,77) 3-Y-0 **£2,911** (£866; £432; £216) **Stalls** Low

Form RPR
340- **1** **Glory Of Paris (IRE)**208 6289 3-9-2 69 OisinMurphy 1 81
(Rod Millman) *chsd ldrs on inner: shkn up and smooth prog bhd ldr 2f out: sn swtchd off inner to centre and rdn over 1f out: led ent fnl f: rdn out* **10/1**
210- **2** *4* **Sea Shack**186 6950 3-9-10 77 JimCrowley 4 78
(William Knight) *t.k.h and chsd ldr: rdn over 2f out: no immediate imp: kpt on wl fr over 1f out to take 2nd fnl 110yds* **2/1**1
53-1 **3** *1 ½* **Gala Celebration (IRE)**7 1428 3-9-0 67 6ex MartinDwyer 3 64
(John Gallagher) *tk fierce hold in ld: rdn over 2f out and edgd to rail: hdd ent fnl f: kpt on wl tl wknd and lost 2nd fnl 110yds* **2/1**1
-602 **4** *2* **Sans Souci Bay**19 1238 3-9-7 74 TomMarquand 6 66
(Richard Hannon) *in rr-div: rdn over 2f out: no imp ldrs wl over 1f out: kpt on ent fnl f* **8/1**3
642- **5** *1 ½* **Challow (IRE)**158 7697 3-9-5 72 LiamKeniry 7 60
(Sylvester Kirk) *in rr: rdn over 2f out: no ex fr over 1f out and kpt on one pce* **11/1**
5-31 **6** *3 ½* **Preobrajenska**16 1286 3-9-3 70 (h) JosephineGordon 9 48
(William Jarvis) *in rr-div on outer: rdn over 2f out: kpt on one pce* **7/1**2
00-0 **7** *4 ½* **Seeing Things (IRE)**74 354 3-8-8 61 SilvestreDeSousa 5 27
(Philip McBride) *in rr on inner: rdn over 2f out: no imp and eased wl ins fnl f* **25/1**
30-0 **8** *35* **Bobby Vee**13 1332 3-8-13 66 RobertWinston 8
(Dean Ivory) *cl up bhd ldrs: niggled along and wl over 3f out w jockey looking bhd: wknd qckly ent st: t.o* **66/1**
1m 24.6s (-1.40) **Going Correction** -0.05s/f (Stan) 8 Ran SP% **113.0**
Speed ratings (Par 98): **106,101,99,97,95 91,86,46**
CSF £29.73 CT £56.87 TOTE £11.60: £2.90, £1.20, £1.30; EX 37.60 Trifecta £86.60.
**Owner** David Little The Links Partnership **Bred** Peter Grimes & The Late Jackie Grimes **Trained** Kentisbeare, Devon
**FOCUS**
A fair handicap and a good performance from the winner.

## 1555 32RED H'CAP 1m 3f 219y(P)
**8:15** (8:19) (Class 4) (0-85,91) 4-Y-0+ **£4,690** (£1,395; £697; £348) **Stalls** Centre

Form RPR
30-1 **1** **Jacob Cats**4 1504 8-9-13 91 6ex (v) SilvestreDeSousa 4 97
(William Knight) *hld up patiently in last: clsr in rr at 1/2-way: rdn wdst over 2f out: clsng but stl in last pl ent fnl f: str run ins fnl f and led cl home* **2/1**1
301- **2** *½* **Marmajuke Bay**161 7618 4-9-5 84 (p) SteveDrowne 1 89
(Mark Usher) *led for 1f: settled bhd clr ldr after: rdn to cl over 2f out: kpt on wl and led jst ins fnl f: trying hrd but hdd cl home* **7/2**3
15/ **3** *nk* **Sgt Reckless**205 10-9-4 82 RobHornby 5 86
(Simon Hodgson) *in rr: rdn over 2f out in centre: kpt on wl fnl f: no ex* **20/1**
1-3 **4** *1 ½* **Dream Love**82 213 4-8-11 76 ow1 JimCrowley 6 78
(Simon Dow) *in rr-div: effrt over 2f out: kpt on one pce fr over 1f out: no imp on ldrs* **8/1**
0/50 **5** *nk* **Lanceur (FR)**23 1178 8-9-2 83 HollieDoyle(3) 3 84
(William Stone) *in rr-div: rdn over 2f out: one pce ent fnl f* **16/1**
1325 **6** *1 ¼* **Pinwood (IRE)**29 1073 4-8-0 72 (t) JordanUys(7) 7 71
(Adam West) *led after 1f: t.k.h and build up 6 l ld at 1/2-way: pack clsng whn rdn 2f out: kpt on wl tl hdd jst ins fnl f: wknd after* **14/1**
1-42 **7** *hd* **Priors Brook**27 1113 6-8-13 77 OisinMurphy 2 76
(Andrew Balding) *racd in 3rd: rdn over 2f out: kpt on tl one pce fnl f* **3/1**2
2m 32.89s (-1.61) **Going Correction** -0.05s/f (Stan) 7 Ran SP% **109.0**
Speed ratings (Par 105): **103,102,102,101,101 100,100**
CSF £8.24 TOTE £2.90: £1.70, £1.90; EX 8.40 Trifecta £95.40.
**Owner** Canisbay Bloodstock **Bred** Highclere Stud **Trained** Patching, W Sussex
**FOCUS**
This was run at a good gallop. The winner put up his best performance since he was a 3yo and a small personal best from thr runner-up.

## 1556 RACINGUK.COM/HD H'CAP 1m 3f 219y(P)
**8:45** (8:46) (Class 6) (0-60,60) 4-Y-0+ **£2,264** (£673; £336; £168) **Stalls** Centre

Form RPR
1303 **1** **Rail Dancer**28 1081 5-9-1 54 (v) AdamBeschizza 4 67
(Richard Rowe) *hld up in in mid-div: shkn up over 2f out: qcknd up in centre and swept into ld 2f out: kpt up to work ent fnl f: rdn out* **15/2**3
236- **2** *1 ¼* **Desert Cross**170 7421 4-9-3 57 FranBerry 2 68
(Jonjo O'Neill) *in rr: shkn up over 3f out and smooth prog on rail: rdn 2f out and almost upsides on rail: kpt on wl but nt getting to wnr* **6/1**2
5-04 **3** *4 ½* **Party Royal**32 1028 7-9-7 60 (p1) MartinLane 13 64
(Nick Gifford) *in rr-div: shkn up over 2f out bhd horses and sn angled out to centre: kpt on wl past btn horse to take 3rd 2f out: no ch w ldrs* **20/1**
-632 **4** *1* **Graceful Lady**28 1082 4-9-3 57 LukeMorris 7 59
(Robert Eddery) *mid-div: rdn bhd ldrs over 2f out: kpt on wl tl wknd ent fnl f* **8/1**
50-3 **5** *1* **McDelta**16 1284 7-9-2 60 PaddyPilley(5) 1 61
(Geoffrey Deacon) *in rr-div on outer: c v wd st and lost momentum: kpt on wl fr over 1f out: nrst fin* **8/1**
-340 **6** *hd* **Betsalottie**16 1284 4-9-0 54 WilliamCarson 11 54
(John Bridger) *led tl 7f: pressed ldr after: rdn over 2f out: wknd fr 2f out* **12/1**
0323 **7** *1* **Tingo In The Tale (IRE)**15 1191 8-9-2 55 (tp) JosephineGordon 6 54
(Sophie Leech) *settled in mid-div: rdn on inner over 2f out: plugged on fr over 1f out* **14/1**
00 **8** *1 ¾* **Tsundoku (IRE)**16 1283 6-9-0 53 CamHardie 12 49
(Alexandra Dunn) *in rr: rdn over 2f out: no imp* **100/1**

6 **9** *2 ½* **Mr Magill (FR)**[22] 1190 5-9-2 **55** TimmyMurphy 5 47
(Karen George) *tk v t.k.h bhd ldrs on rail: rdn over 2f out: no ex over 1f out and wknd* **50/1**

-011 **10** *2 ½* **Briac (FR)**[14] 1303 6-9-0 **53** DanielMuscutt 10 41
(Mark Pattinson) *settled bhd ldrs between horses: rdn over 2f out: fnd nil and wknd* **9/4**[1]

-455 **11** *nk* **Mamnoon (IRE)**[13] 1330 4-9-3 **57** TomMarquand 8 44
(Roy Brotherton) *pressed ldr tl led after 7f: rdn over 2f out: wknd over 1f out* **25/1**

000- **12** *16* **Cockney Boy**[244] 5053 4-9-1 **55** (h[1]) MartinDwyer 3 17
(John Gallagher) *in rr: ridde along over 4f out: sn hld: t.o* **14/1**

60-5 **13** *8* **Brahma**[29] 1072 4-9-4 **58** (b[1]) RobertWinston 14 7
(Hughie Morrison) *chsd ldrs: rdn along over 4f out: losing grnd and eased st: eased: t.o* **16/1**

2m 32.65s (-1.85) **Going Correction** -0.05s/f (Stan) **13** Ran SP% **117.5**
Speed ratings (Par 101): **104,103,100,99,98 98,98,96,95,93 93,82,77**
CSF £49.53 CT £871.83 TOTE £10.00: £2.60, £2.00, £5.70; EX 62.10 Trifecta £1826.50.
**Owner** Mark Cashmore **Bred** Scuderia Blueberry SRL **Trained** Sullington, W Sussex

**FOCUS**
The first two, who came well clear, look nicely ahead of their marks.

## 1557 RACING UK ANYWHERE H'CAP 6f (P)
**9:15** (9:15) (Class 6) (0-55,55) 4-Y-0+ **£2,264** (£673; £336; £168) **Stalls** Low

Form RPR

0-60 **1** **Fleeting Glimpse**[77] 293 4-9-7 **55** (h) DavidProbert 5 63
(Andrew Balding) *hld up in rr: stl plenty to do over 1f out: shkn up and prog between horses ent fnl f: kpt on wl and led cl home* **6/1**[3]

0634 **2** *½* **Virile (IRE)**[19] 1247 6-9-6 **54** (bt) OisinMurphy 1 59
(Sylvester Kirk) *pushed along leaving stalls: settled in rr-div on rail: rdn 2f out and led ent fnl f: kpt on wl tl hdd cl home* **7/2**[1]

2224 **3** *1* **Fabulous Flyer**[20] 1220 4-8-11 **50** DavidParkes(5) 4 52
(Jeremy Gask) *t.k.h in mid-div on outer: rdn 2f out: kpt on wl and ev ch ent fnl f: tk 3rd post* **15/2**

-154 **4** *nse* **Little Indian**[14] 1304 7-9-4 **52** SilvestreDeSousa 3 54
(J R Jenkins) *chsd ldrs on inner: rdn 2f out: ev ch ent fnl f: kpt on but lost 3rd post* **5/1**[2]

060- **5** *½* **Staffa (IRE)**[270] 4156 4-9-5 **53** TomQueally 9 53
(Denis Coakley) *t.k.h in mid-div on outer: rdn wdst 2f out and ev ch ent fnl f: no ex cl home* **25/1**

-30P **6** *½* **Wedgewood Estates**[34] 981 6-9-4 **52** GeorgeDowning 12 51
(Tony Carroll) *in rr: shkn up in centre over 1f out: nt clr run and swtchd to rail ent fnl f: pushed along bhd runner-up w n.m.r ent fnl f: nvr nrr* **25/1**

2524 **7** *nk* **Justice Rock**[6] 1452 4-9-0 **48** JosephineGordon 8 46
(Phil McEntee) *chsd ldrs: rdn 2f out: kpt on tl wknd ent fnl f* **11/1**

0-00 **8** *½* **Royal Rettie**[16] 1285 5-9-7 **55** (h) DannyBrock 2 51
(Paddy Butler) *mid-div and covered up: shkn up over 1f out w n.m.r: ev ch ent fnl f: no ex 110yds* **16/1**

-056 **9** *1 ½* **Indus Valley (IRE)**[7] 1427 10-8-13 **47** (p) KierenFox 11 38
(Lee Carter) *in rr: rdn on outer 2f out: no imp on ldrs* **16/1**

-300 **10** *1* **Deer Song**[28] 1080 4-9-3 **51** FrannyNorton 6 39+
(John Bridger) *led: rdn 2f out: kpt on swamped and wknd ent fnl f* **10/1**

452- **11** *1* **Foxford**[232] 5509 6-9-2 **55** MitchGodwin(5) 7 40+
(Patrick Chamings) *pressed ldr: rdn 2f out: briefly led ent fnl f: sn wknd* **9/1**

1m 12.85s (-0.25) **Going Correction** -0.05s/f (Stan) **11** Ran SP% **111.8**
Speed ratings (Par 101): **99,98,97,96,96 95,95,94,92,91 89**
CSF £25.77 CT £156.46 TOTE £7.00: £2.20, £2.10, £1.90; EX 26.90 Trifecta £164.30.
**Owner** Mildmay Racing & D H Caslon **Bred** Mildmay Bloodstock Ltd **Trained** Kingsclere, Hants

**FOCUS**
A good gallop set this up for the closers. The winner has been rated back to her debut effort.
T/Plt: £11.60 to a £1 stake. Pool: £84,716.40. 5,327.78 winning units. T/Qpdt: £3.20 to a £1 stake. Pool: £8,155.63. 1,848.79 winning units. **Cathal Gahan**

# 1452 WOLVERHAMPTON (A.W) (L-H)
Wednesday, April 5

**OFFICIAL GOING: Tapeta: standard**
Wind: Fresh, across into the stands Weather: Cloudy

## 1558 BETWAY SPRINT H'CAP 5f 21y (Tp)
**2:10** (2:10) (Class 5) (0-70,70) 4-Y-0+ **£2,911** (£866; £432; £216) **Stalls** Low

Form RPR

-142 **1** **Bahango (IRE)**[37] 955 5-9-2 **70** (p) LewisEdmunds(5) 1 78
(Patrick Morris) *trckd ldrs: plld hrd: shkn up over 1f out: led and edgd rt ins fnl f: r.o wl* **9/4**[1]

0-50 **2** *2* **Vale Of Flight (IRE)**[28] 1080 4-9-0 **63** LukeMorris 2 64
(Luke McJannet) *led: pushed along 2f out: rdn and hdd ins fnl f: edgd rt: styd on same pce* **7/1**

-412 **3** *nse* **Powerful Dream (IRE)**[13] 1328 4-9-6 **69** (p) LiamKeniry 5 70+
(Ronald Harris) *edgd rt s: hmpd sn after: hld up: hdwy over 1f out: r.o* **9/2**[2]

10-6 **4** *1* **Groundworker (IRE)**[21] 1200 6-8-13 **62** (t) PaulMulrennan 7 59
(Paul Midgley) *plld hrd and prom: rdn over 1f out: styd on same pce ins fnl f* **15/2**

100- **5** *¾* **China Excels**[144] 7945 10-9-4 **67** RobHornby 3 61
(Mandy Rowland) *plld hrd in 2nd pl: hung rt 1/2-way: rdn over 1f out: styd on same pce ins fnl f* **20/1**

2-66 **6** *nk* **Compton River**[32] 1031 5-9-7 **70** BenCurtis 8 63
(Bryan Smart) *chsd ldrs: pushed along 1/2-way: styd on same pce fr over 1f out* **5/1**[3]

4434 **7** *1 ½* **Temple Road (IRE)**[7] 1429 9-8-11 **67** (bt) BenRobinson(7) 6 55
(Milton Bradley) *s.i.s and hmpd sn after s: hld up: pushed along 1/2-way: rdn over 1f out: nvr on terms* **15/2**

1-50 **8** *¾* **Monsieur Paddy**[50] 732 4-8-12 **61** GeorgeDowning 4 46
(Tony Carroll) *hld up: racd keenly: hmpd 4f out: rdn over 1f out: nvr on terms* **8/1**

1m 1.68s (-0.22) **Going Correction** -0.05s/f (Stan) **8** Ran SP% **117.5**
Speed ratings (Par 103): **99,95,95,94,92 92,90,88**
CSF £19.32 CT £67.14 TOTE £2.70: £1.50, £2.30, £1.40; EX 19.40 Trifecta £67.80.
**Owner** L P Richards **Bred** Corduff Stud Ltd **Trained** Prescot, Merseyside
■ Stewards' Enquiry : Ben Curtis caution - guilty of careless riding in that he made insufficient effort to prevent his mount from drifting left

**FOCUS**
A fairly competitive, if modest, sprint with the first two close to form.

## 1559 BETWAY MEDIAN AUCTION MAIDEN STKS 1m 4f 51y (Tp)
**2:40** (2:41) (Class 5) 3-5-Y-0 **£2,911** (£866; £432; £216) **Stalls** Low

Form RPR

036- **1** **Jukebox Jive (FR)**[163] 7580 3-8-7 **74** FrannyNorton 2 84
(Anthony Honeyball) *chsd ldr over 2f: wnt 2nd again over 7f out: shkn up over 2f out: rdn over 1f out: r.o to ld wl ins fnl f: comf* **14/1**

2- **2** *1 ½* **Pealer (GER)**[178] 7187 3-8-7 **0** AndreaAtzeni 4 81
(John Gosden) *prom: racd keenly: led over 9f out: shkn up over 1f out: edgd lft and hdd wl ins fnl f* **1/6**[1]

**3** *10* **Investigation** 3-8-7 **0** RobHornby 5 65
(Andrew Balding) *s.s: plld hrd and ct up w the field after 1f: hdwy 7f out: rdn over 2f out: wknd over 1f out* **7/1**[2]

04 **4** *2 ½* **Indian Red**[33] 1001 3-8-0 **0** GabrieleMalune(7) 1 61
(Mark H Tompkins) *led over 2f: chsd ldr tl over 7f out: remained handy: rdn over 3f out: wknd over 2f out* **40/1**

630- **5** *¾* **Spirit Of Belle**[106] 8466 3-8-7 **71** AndrewMullen 3 60
(David Evans) *prom tl rdn and wknd over 2f out* **12/1**[3]

2m 38.44s (-2.36) **Going Correction** -0.05s/f (Stan) **5** Ran SP% **115.0**
Speed ratings (Par 103): **105,104,97,95,95**
CSF £18.35 TOTE £14.50: £3.40, £1.10; EX 30.90 Trifecta £63.50.
**Owner** R W Huggins **Bred** Ronald Wallace Huggins **Trained** Mosterton, Dorset

**FOCUS**
The betting suggested that the favourite was unassailable, but a fair performance from the winner who lowered his colours. He has been rated to his 2yo form.

## 1560 BETWAY H'CAP 1m 4f 51y (Tp)
**3:10** (3:10) (Class 6) (0-65,65) 4-Y-0+ **£2,328** (£693; £346; £173) **Stalls** Low

Form RPR

6111 **1** **Smiley Bagel (IRE)**[28] 1082 4-9-4 **63** RichardKingscote 7 73+
(Ed Walker) *a.p: chsd ldr 8f out: shkn up over 2f out: led ins fnl f: edgd rt: pushed out* **15/8**[1]

044- **2** *2 ½* **Inflexiball**[166] 7516 5-8-13 **57** FrannyNorton 5 61
(John Mackie) *chsd ldrs: rdn over 1f out: styd on same pce ins fnl f* **6/1**[3]

2402 **3** *hd* **Pour L'Amour (IRE)**[6] 1458 4-8-12 **62** CharlieBennett(5) 4 66
(Daniel Mark Loughnane) *led: rdn over 2f out: edgd rt: hdd and no ex ins fnl f* **5/2**[2]

4-60 **4** *3 ½* **Innoko (FR)**[27] 1101 7-8-13 **57** (h) GeorgeDowning 3 55
(Tony Carroll) *hld up: hdwy over 7f out: rdn over 2f out: styd on same pce fr over 1f out* **12/1**

-040 **5** *3 ½* **Frap**[9] 1403 4-8-10 **55** (h) StevieDonohoe 8 47
(Ian Williams) *hld up: rdn over 2f out: nvr nrr* **22/1**

2556 **6** *1 ¾* **King Oswald (USA)**[14] 1312 4-9-3 **62** RyanPowell 2 52
(James Unett) *prom: lost pl over 7f out: hdwy over 1f out: sn rdn: wknd ins fnl f* **8/1**

606/ **7** *hd* **Dembaba (IRE)**[713] 1614 5-8-13 **57** (p[1]) LiamKeniry 1 46
(Gordon Elliott, Ire) *hld up: rdn over 2f out: nvr on terms* **22/1**

00-5 **8** *hd* **Lady Clitico (IRE)**[14] 1312 6-9-0 **65** PaulaMuir(7) 6 54
(Rebecca Menzies) *s.i.s: hld up: hdwy over 7f out: rdn over 2f out: wknd over 1f out* **14/1**

2m 42.01s (1.21) **Going Correction** -0.05s/f (Stan) **8** Ran SP% **111.8**
Speed ratings (Par 101): **93,91,91,88,86 85,85,85**
CSF £13.00 CT £27.09 TOTE £2.10: £1.10, £2.80, £1.20; EX 12.10 Trifecta £35.40.
**Owner** Laurence Bellman **Bred** Max Morris **Trained** Upper Lambourn, Berks

**FOCUS**
Moderate fare, but the winner continues on the upgrade.

## 1561 BETWAY STAYERS H'CAP 2m 120y (Tp)
**3:45** (3:45) (Class 5) (0-75,77) 4-Y-0+ **£2,911** (£866; £432; £216) **Stalls** Low

Form RPR

2162 **1** **Bracken Brae**[20] 1223 5-9-4 **72** StevieDonohoe 3 80
(Mark H Tompkins) *chsd ldrs: wnt 2nd over 13f out tl led over 2f out: rdn over 1f out: styd on u.p* **4/5**[1]

45-4 **2** *½* **Ruler Of The Nile**[20] 1223 5-9-3 **71** LiamKeniry 5 77
(Robert Stephens) *prom: lost pl 14f out: hdwy to chse wnr over 2f out: rdn over 1f out: styd on* **5/1**[3]

460- **3** *10* **See And Be Seen**[206] 6362 7-8-11 **70** (p) MitchGodwin(5) 1 64
(Sylvester Kirk) *hld up: hdwy over 6f out: rdn over 3f out: wknd over 1f out* **9/2**[2]

400- **4** *3 ¾* **Arabian Oasis**[22] 3118 5-9-4 **72** PaddyAspell 4 62
(Philip Kirby) *chsd ldr 3f: remained handy: rdn over 3f out: wknd 2f out* **8/1**

060/ **5** *14* **Deinonychus**[504] 7893 6-9-6 **77** (h) AlistairRawlinson(3) 2 50
(Michael Appleby) *led: rdn and hdd over 2f out: sn wknd* **10/1**

3m 40.48s (-3.22) **Going Correction** -0.05s/f (Stan) **5** Ran SP% **110.6**
Speed ratings (Par 103): **105,104,100,98,91**
CSF £5.24 TOTE £1.60: £1.10, £2.50; EX 4.80 Trifecta £8.60.
**Owner** David P Noblett **Bred** Dullingham Park Stud & Mr D Noblett **Trained** Newmarket, Suffolk
■ Stewards' Enquiry : Liam Keniry 2 day ban - used whip above the permitted level

**FOCUS**
A lot of imponderables and not many solid propositions in this modest staying handicap, but a solid winner.

## 1562 SUNBETS.CO.UK H'CAP 1m 142y (Tp)
**4:15** (4:15) (Class 4) (0-85,82) 4-Y-0+ **£4,851** (£1,443; £721; £360) **Stalls** Low

Form RPR

100- **1** **Calvados Spirit**[158] 7702 4-9-6 **81** PhillipMakin 5 90+
(William Muir) *hld up in tch: shkn up to ld ins fnl f: edgd lft: r.o: comf* **5/2**[1]

-421 **2** *1 ¾* **Mr Red Clubs (IRE)**[13] 1329 8-8-6 **74** (p) JaneElliott(7) 8 78
(Michael Appleby) *hld up: swtchd rt and hdwy over 1f out: rdn and edgd lft ins fnl f: styd on to go 2nd nr fin* **13/2**

-130 **3** *nk* **Shah Of Armaan (IRE)**[29] 1074 4-8-12 **73** TomEaves 4 76
(Kevin Ryan) *chsd ldr tl led 2f out: rdn over 1f out: hdd ins fnl f: styd on same pce* **9/2**[2]

-000 **4** *nse* **Jack Of Diamonds (IRE)**[28] 1085 8-8-12 **73** (b[1]) JackMitchell 1 76
(Roger Teal) *a.p: rdn over 1f out: styd on same pce ins fnl f* **6/1**[3]

033- **5** *2 ½* **Red Tea**[145] 7903 4-9-7 **82** LiamKeniry 7 79
(Peter Hiatt) *hld up: shkn up over 2f out: nt trble ldrs* **13/2**

100- **6** *nk* **Rock Song**[316] 2556 8-8-12 **73** FrannyNorton 6 70
(John Mackie) *chsd ldrs: rdn over 1f out: edgd lft and wknd ins fnl f* **9/1**

-563 **7** *1* **Captain Revelation**[29] 1074 5-9-7 **82** RichardKingscote 3 76
(Tom Dascombe) *led: pushed along and hdd 2f out: wknd ins fnl f* **7/1**

0-00 **8** *8* **Freud (FR)**[37] 958 7-8-11 **72**......(t) StevieDonohoe 2 48
(Ian Williams) *s.s: a in rr* **25/1**

1m 49.63s (-0.47) **Going Correction** -0.05s/f (Stan) 8 Ran SP% **114.1**
Speed ratings (Par 105): **100,98,98,98,95 95,94,87**
CSF £19.06 CT £69.21 TOTE £4.20: £1.70, £2.40, £1.80; EX 20.50 Trifecta £109.10.
**Owner** Muir Racing Partnership - Deauville **Bred** Newsells Park Stud **Trained** Lambourn, Berks

**FOCUS**
Only three horses with ratings north of 80 and the form is below-par for Class 4 AW events. That said, the winner could be one to follow. The race has been rated around the placed horses.

## 1563 SUNBETS.CO.UK DOWNLOAD THE APP H'CAP 1m 142y (Tp)
**4:45** (4:47) (Class 7) (0-50,51) 4-Y-0+ **£2,264** (£673; £336; £168) **Stalls** Low

Form RPR

5302 **1** **Sir Jamie**[7] 1425 4-9-2 **45**...... GeorgeDowning 12 53
(Tony Carroll) *hld up: carried rt over 2f out: hdwy over 1f out: r.o u.p to ld post* **7/1**

0-01 **2** *nse* **Lord Murphy (IRE)**[9] 1406 4-9-8 **51** 6ex...... LiamKeniry 4 58
(Daniel Mark Loughnane) *a.p: chsd ldr over 1f out: rdn to ld ins fnl f: hdd post* **6/4**[1]

5245 **3** *1 1/4* **Captain K (IRE)**[12] 1356 5-8-11 **47**......(h) FinleyMarsh(7) 2 51
(Gordon Elliott, Ire) *chsd ldrs tl led over 2f out: rdn and hdd ins fnl f: styd on same pce* **13/2**[3]

3403 **4** *4 1/2* **West Leake (IRE)**[7] 1425 11-8-11 **45**...... DavidParkes(5) 13 39+
(Paul Burgoyne) *hld up: hmpd over 2f out: r.o ins fnl f: nt rch ldrs* **16/1**

4030 **5** *1/2* **Pipers Piping (IRE)**[9] 1406 11-9-6 **49**...... RobHornby 6 42
(Mandy Rowland) *mid-div: hmpd over 2f out: hdwy over 1f out: styd on same pce fnl f* **22/1**

/060 **6** *nk* **Gamesters Lad**[13] 1322 5-9-2 **45**......(p) JamesSullivan 7 37
(Oliver Greenall) *prom: jnd ldr over 2f out: sn rdn: wknd ins fnl f* **28/1**

6650 **7** *1/2* **Dibloam (USA)**[19] 1249 4-9-7 **50**...... AndrewMullen 9 41
(David Evans) *mid-div: hdwy and hung lft over 2f out: rdn over 1f out: styd on same pce fnl f* **28/1**

0355 **8** *1 1/4* **Mount Cheiron (USA)**[9] 1406 6-8-13 **49**......(v) CallumRodriguez(7) 3 37+
(Richard Ford) *s.s: hld up: hmpd over 2f out: nvr nrr* **8/1**

0-00 **9** *13* **Overrider**[9] 1402 7-9-0 **46**......(bt) CallumShepherd(3) 8 4
(Shaun Lycett) *chsd ldrs: led over 3f out: rdn and hdd over 2f out: wknd over 1f out* **50/1**

/00- **10** *32* **Zubaidah**[434] 347 5-9-5 **48**......(p) DanielTudhope 5
(Jane Chapple-Hyam) *chsd ldr tl led over 6f out: hdd over 3f out: sn rdn: wknd wl over 1f out: eased* **9/2**[2]

06-0 **11** *7* **Ormering**[27] 1112 4-9-2 **45**......(p) JackMitchell 1
(Roger Teal) *led: hdd over 6f out: chsd ldr tl over 4f out: rdn whn nt clr run and hmpd over 2f out: sn eased* **50/1**

0504 **12** *4* **Sarakova (IRE)**[9] 1406 4-9-2 **45**......(b) DougieCostello 10
(Kevin Frost) *s.i.s: hld up: hmpd over 2f out: eased* **16/1**

1m 49.7s (-0.40) **Going Correction** -0.05s/f (Stan) 12 Ran SP% **122.1**
Speed ratings (Par 97): **99,98,97,93,93 93,92,91,80,51 45,41**
CSF £17.57 CT £76.48 TOTE £8.70: £2.40, £1.20, £2.40; EX 26.60 Trifecta £138.20.
**Owner** Mayden Stud **Bred** Mayden Stud, J A And D S Dewhurst **Trained** Cropthorne, Worcs

**FOCUS**
No better than plating-class form and the race has been rated around the third, but another small step up from the winner. There was trouble as they turned for home and a fair few, including the winner, got hampered.

## 1564 32RED.COM H'CAP 7f 36y (Tp)
**5:15** (5:17) (Class 6) (0-60,60) 3-Y-O **£2,587** (£770; £384; £192) **Stalls** High

Form RPR

011- **1** **A Sure Welcome**[155] 7750 3-9-2 **55**......(p) FrannyNorton 1 62
(John Spearing) *led early: chsd ldrs: wnt 2nd over 1f out: rdn to ld wl ins fnl f: styd on* **9/2**[2]

4144 **2** *hd* **Viola Park**[11] 1367 3-8-12 **51**......(p) RyanPowell 9 57
(Ronald Harris) *pushed along and hdwy to chse ldr over 5f out: led over 4f out: hung lft fr 1/2-way: rdn and hdd ins fnl f: styd on* **8/1**

6-00 **3** *1 1/2* **Love And Be Loved**[19] 1246 3-8-11 **50**...... DanielMuscutt 4 52+
(John Flint) *hld up: hdwy and nt clr run over 1f out: r.o to go 3rd nr fin: nt rch ldrs* **66/1**

30-3 **4** *nk* **Luduamf (IRE)**[11] 1367 3-9-3 **59**...... HollieDoyle(3) 2 60
(Richard Hannon) *chsd ldrs: rdn and hung lft fr over 1f out: styd on same pce ins fnl f* **3/1**[1]

0-41 **5** *1/2* **Jack Blane**[11] 1367 3-9-3 **56**...... GeorgeDowning 8 56
(Daniel Kubler) *mid-div: hdwy over 2f out: rdn and hung lft fr over 1f out: styd on* **9/2**[2]

4-52 **6** *1 1/2* **Hollywood Harry (IRE)**[26] 1123 3-9-4 **57**......(v[1]) PhillipMakin 6 54
(Keith Dalgleish) *hld up: hdwy and nt clr run over 1f out: swtchd lft: nt trble ldrs* **7/1**[3]

000 **7** *3 1/2* **Newton Heath (IRE)**[54] 662 3-9-0 **53**......(p[1]) TomEaves 11 40
(Daniel Mark Loughnane) *s.i.s: hld up: rdn over 2f out: nvr nrr* **33/1**

0205 **8** *nse* **Lady Volante (IRE)**[11] 1367 3-8-10 **56**...... KatherineGlenister(7) 7 43
(David Evans) *chsd ldrs: hmpd wl over 1f out: nt clr run ent fnl f: no ex* **14/1**

-004 **9** *nk* **Greyjoy (IRE)**[15] 1297 3-9-2 **60**...... MitchGodwin(5) 10 46
(Sylvester Kirk) *dwlt: hld up: nt clr run 1f out: nvr on terms* **10/1**

0-46 **10** *1/2* **Fast Kar (IRE)**[11] 1367 3-8-13 **52**...... BenCurtis 12 37
(Barry John Murphy, Ire) *hld up: rdn over 2f out: n.d* **20/1**

4030 **11** *3 1/4* **Scealtara (IRE)**[11] 1367 3-9-3 **56**...... DanielTudhope 3 32
(David O'Meara) *mid-div: hdwy and nt clr run over 1f out: wknd fnl f* **25/1**

0062 **12** *1 1/2* **Tink**[11] 1367 3-8-6 **50**......(p) CharlieBennett(5) 5 22
(Mark Brisbourne) *sn led: hdd over 4f out: chsd ldr tl rdn over 2f out: wknd fnl f* **20/1**

1m 28.76s (-0.04) **Going Correction** -0.05s/f (Stan) 12 Ran SP% **118.5**
Speed ratings (Par 96): **98,97,96,95,95 93,89,89,89,88 84,83**
CSF £37.42 CT £2123.88 TOTE £5.50: £2.00, £3.00, £13.10; EX 45.10 Trifecta £2199.40.
**Owner** Kinnersley Partnership 3 **Bred** Richard Evans Bloodstock **Trained** Kinnersley, Worcs

**FOCUS**
Modest fare, but a sound pace.

T/Plt: £4.40 to a £1 stake. Pool: £66,053.50. 10,798.89 winning units. T/Qpdt: £3.10 to a £1 stake. Pool: £4,223.94. 1,001.75 winning units. **Colin Roberts**

1565 - 1567a (Foreign Racing) - See Raceform Interactive

# LEOPARDSTOWN (L-H)
Wednesday, April 5

**OFFICIAL GOING: Soft (yielding in places)**

## 1568a HERITAGE STKS (LISTED RACE) 1m
**5:00** (5:02) 4-Y-0+

**£22,692** (£7,307; £3,461; £1,538; £769; £384)

RPR

**1** **Rose De Pierre (IRE)**[158] 7706 4-9-3 102...... PatSmullen 4 103+
(D K Weld, Ire) *chsd ldrs: 5th 1/2-way: prog on outer to ld ent fnl f and kpt on wl u.p clsng stages where strly pressed to jst hold on: all out* **11/4**[2]

**2** *hd* **Marshall Jennings (IRE)**[10] 1388 5-9-5 96...... ColmO'Donoghue 5 105+
(Mrs John Harrington, Ire) *w.w: last 3f out: tk clsr order into st: hdwy on outer in 6th fr 1 1/2f out: rdn into 2nd wl ins fnl f and strly pressed wnr clsng stages: jst failed* **16/1**

**3** *1 1/4* **Onenightidreamed (IRE)**[10] 1388 6-9-5 106......(b[1]) ChrisHayes 1 102
(J A Stack, Ire) *hld up bhd ldrs: 4th 1/2-way: pushed along bhd ldrs under 3f out: sn rdn and u.p in 4th over 1f out: wnt 3rd wl ins fnl f and kpt on same pce: nt trble wnr* **9/4**[1]

**4** *2 1/4* **Flying Fairies (IRE)**[10] 1387 4-9-3 99...... DeclanMcDonogh 7 94
(John M Oxx, Ire) *led: rdn and jnd briefly 1 1/2f out: sn hdd and no imp on wnr: wknd into 4th ins fnl f* **9/2**[3]

**5** *3* **Round Two (IRE)**[164] 7558 4-9-5 98...... KevinManning 2 90
(J S Bolger, Ire) *settled bhd ldr in 2nd: pushed along into st: rdn to dispute ld briefly 1 1/2f out where wandered sltly: sn no ex in 3rd and wknd fnl f* **12/1**

**6** *1/2* **Sruthan (IRE)**[172] 7372 7-9-8 107......(p) ShaneFoley 6 91
(P D Deegan, Ire) *chsd ldrs: 3rd 1/2-way: rdn bhd ldrs 2f out and wknd over 1f out* **6/1**

**7** *1/2* **Wild As The Wind (IRE)**[10] 1387 4-9-0 89...... WJLee 3 82
(W McCreery, Ire) *towards rr: 7th 3f out: rdn and no imp 2f out: one pce after* **11/1**

**8** *4 1/2* **Stronger Than Me (IRE)**[12] 1355 9-9-5 98...... WayneLordan 8 77
(W T Farrell, Ire) *hld up in tch: 6th 3f out: lost pl into st and rdn in rr under 2f out: no ex* **25/1**

1m 45.01s (3.81) **Going Correction** +0.75s/f (Yiel) 8 Ran SP% **115.7**
Speed ratings: **110,109,108,106,103 102,102,97**
CSF £45.40 TOTE £3.30: £1.30, £4.60, £1.30; DF 45.00 Trifecta £186.80.
**Owner** Moyglare Stud Farm **Bred** Moyglare Stud Farm **Trained** Curragh, Co Kildare

**FOCUS**
Not the strongest Listed race, with only three of the eight runners boasting an official rating in three figures. The winner has a fine strike-rate and could progress to Group 3 level now.

1569 - 1579a (Foreign Racing) - See Raceform Interactive

# 1484 CHELMSFORD (A.W) (L-H)
Thursday, April 6

**OFFICIAL GOING: Polytrack: standard**
Wind: very light half against in home straight, of no consequence Weather: dry, sunny until race 6

## 1580 SHIRES PERFORMING HERE 7TH JULY H'CAP 6f (P)
**5:45** (5:45) (Class 6) (0-60,62) 3-Y-O **£3,234** (£962; £481; £240) **Stalls** Centre

Form RPR

000- **1** **See You Mush**[189] 6895 3-9-2 **55**......(b) AdamBeschizza 2 60
(Mrs Ilka Gansera-Leveque) *t.k.h: w ldr tl led over 2f out: rdn wl over 1f out: sustained battle w runner up after: kpt on wl u.p ins fnl f and a jst holding runner up* **16/1**

3623 **2** *hd* **No Not Again (IRE)**[8] 1421 3-9-6 **62**...... HollieDoyle(3) 6 66
(Richard Hannon) *led tl over 2f out: rdn and ev ch whn edgd rt bnd 2f out: sustained effrt u.p fr over 1f out: kpt on u.p but a jst hld ins fnl f* **5/2**[1]

453- **3** *nk* **Coverham (IRE)**[197] 6678 3-9-3 **56**...... RyanTate 7 59
(James Eustace) *in tch in midfield: : effrt over 1f out: drvn to chse ldng pair ent fnl f: edging lft ins fnl f: swtchd rt and styd on wl fnl 75yds: nvr quite getting to ldrs* **5/2**[1]

6501 **4** *1 3/4* **Brother In Arms (IRE)**[8] 1418 3-9-0 **60**...... AledBeech(7) 5 58
(Tony Carroll) *hld up in pair: effrt but stl plenty to do over 1f out: hdwy 1f out: chsd ldng trio 100yds out: styd on but nvr getting to ldrs* **10/3**[2]

2664 **5** *4 1/2* **Celerity (IRE)**[8] 1418 3-8-8 **50**......(v) PhilipPrince(3) 1 34
(David Evans) *chsd ldr : rdn and little rspnse over 1f out: wknd ins fnl f* **10/1**

000- **6** *2 3/4* **Silver Mist**[167] 7502 3-8-7 **46**...... LukeMorris 3 22
(Sylvester Kirk) *wl in tch in midfield: rdn over 2f out: wknd over 1f out* **9/2**[3]

040 **7** *5* **Raspberry Princess**[42] 878 3-8-7 **46** oh1...... RyanPowell 4 7
(Phil McEntee) *dwlt and jostled leaving stalls: a towards rr: wknd u.p over 1f out: bhd fnl f* **100/1**

1m 12.54s (-1.16) **Going Correction** -0.30s/f (Stan) 7 Ran SP% **114.4**
Speed ratings (Par 96): **95,94,94,92,86 82,75**
CSF £56.06 TOTE £15.10: £6.10, £1.80; EX 58.60 Trifecta £215.20.
**Owner** Strawberry Fields Stud **Bred** G & J Equestrian Of Newmarket **Trained** Newmarket, Suffolk

**FOCUS**
Few got into this, the first two battling it out from some way out.

## 1581 UB40 AFTER RACING 12TH AUGUST MAIDEN FILLIES' STKS 1m (P)
**6:15** (6:16) (Class 5) 3-Y-O+ **£5,175** (£1,540; £769; £384) **Stalls** Low

Form RPR

222- **1** **Interweave**[167] 7494 3-8-13 78...... RyanMoore 3 77
(Sir Michael Stoute) *hld up wl in tch: rdn over 2f out: 3rd and outpcd whn swtchd rt over 1f out: clsd jst ins fnl f: styd on to ld last strides* **1/1**[1]

-3 **2** *hd* **Fiendish (USA)**[34] 1003 3-8-13 0...... JoeFanning 2 76
(Mark Johnston) *t.k.h: led: shkn up over 1f out: wanting to hang but forged ahd ent fnl f: rdn hands and heels and racing awkwardly ins fnl f: hdd last strides* **8/1**

25 **3** *1* **Dubai Waves**[26] 1143 3-8-13 0...... JosephineGordon 4 73
(Hugo Palmer) *w ldr: rdn over 2f out: unable qck over 1f out: kpt on same pce u.p ins fnl f* **14/1**

**4** *4 1/2* **Extra Mile** 3-8-13 0...... JimCrowley 5 63
(Saeed bin Suroor) *wl in tch: rdn and m green over 3f out: outpcd over 2f out: wl hld after* **9/4**[2]

5 *20* **La Goulue** 3-8-13 0 LukeMorris 1 17
(John Gallagher) *v.s.a: rn green in detached last: nvr on terms* **100/1**

2- **6** *10* **Fairy Lights**[176] [7277] 3-8-13 0 AndreaAtzeni 6
(Roger Varian) *t.k.h: in tch on outer: rdn over 2f out: hung rt and btn bnd 2f out: sn eased and rdr looking down: t.o* **6/1**[3]

1m 38.2s (-1.70) **Going Correction** -0.30s/f (Stan) **6** Ran SP% **113.8**
Speed ratings (Par 100): **96,95,94,90,70 60**
CSF £10.40 TOTE £2.10: £1.30, £3.40; EX 10.50 Trifecta £51.10.
**Owner** Cheveley Park Stud **Bred** Cheveley Park Stud Ltd **Trained** Newmarket, Suffolk

**FOCUS**
A fair maiden in which the winner set the form standard.

## 1582 BOOKEE SWIPE BET DONE APP H'CAP 1m (P)
**6:45** (6:46) (Class 4) (0-85,85) 3-Y-O **£6,469** (£1,925; £962; £481) **Stalls** Low

Form RPR

31- **1** **Mustarrid (IRE)**[125] [8189] 3-9-6 **84** JimCrowley 1 93
(Richard Hannon) *w ldr tl led 1/2-way: rdn and edgd lft over 1f out: styd on wl: rdn out* **13/8**[1]

216- **2** *1 1/4* **Drochaid**[208] [6330] 3-9-0 **78** OisinMurphy 3 84
(Andrew Balding) *t.k.h: hld up in tch: hdwy to chse ldrs 1/2-way: wnt 2nd and swtchd rt over 1f out: kpt on same pce ins fnl f* **7/1**

1 **3** *1* **Harlow**[36] [970] 3-9-6 **84** (h) JosephineGordon 8 88
(Hugo Palmer) *taken down early: s.i.s: hld up in tch in rr: effrt on inner to chse ldrs and swtchd rt jst over 1f out: hung rt and kpt on same pce ins fnl f* **4/1**[3]

41- **4** *2 1/4* **Me Too Nagasaki (IRE)**[113] [8353] 3-9-2 **80** JFEgan 2 80
(Jeremy Noseda) *wl in tch in midfield: effrt over 1f out: keeping on same pce and btn whn impeded and wnt lft ins fnl f* **7/2**[2]

-121 **5** *1 1/2* **Toy Theatre**[20] [1243] 3-8-10 **74** LukeMorris 7 69
(Michael Appleby) *hld up in tch in last pair: effrt and nt clrest of runs wl over 1f out: no imp and wl hld fnl f* **20/1**

41-0 **6** *hd* **Annie Fior (IRE)**[33] [1026] 3-9-2 **80** (h) TomQueally 6 75
(Denis Coakley) *led tl 1/2-way: unable qck u.p over 1f out: btn whn impeded ins fnl f: no ch whn hmpd sn after* **25/1**

31- **7** *13* **Daschas**[113] [8354] 3-9-4 **82** (t) RyanMoore 5 47
(Amanda Perrett) *pressed ldrs early: dropped into midfield on outer after 2f: last whn hung rt bnd over 2f out: bhd and eased ins fnl f* **7/1**

1m 36.72s (-3.18) **Going Correction** -0.30s/f (Stan) **7** Ran SP% **113.9**
Speed ratings (Par 100): **103,101,100,98,97 96,83**
CSF £13.78 CT £38.85 TOTE £2.40: £1.60, £3.30; EX 15.00 Trifecta £60.60.
**Owner** Hamdan Al Maktoum **Bred** John Malone **Trained** East Everleigh, Wilts

**FOCUS**
A fair little handicap and a nice performance from the winner, who has more to offer. The form has been rated slightly positively.

## 1583 DOWNLOAD BOOKEE IN THE APP STORE H'CAP 1m 2f (P)
**7:15** (7:17) (Class 4) (0-85,80) 4-Y-O+ **£6,469** (£1,925; £962; £481) **Stalls** Low

Form RPR

201- **1** **Alf Guineas (IRE)**[156] [7753] 4-9-7 **80** TomQueally 1 90+
(John Gosden) *t.k.h: trckd ldr tl 7f out: styd handy: shkn up and qcknd between horses to ld 1f out: r.o wl and a in command after: readily* **15/8**[1]

-233 **2** *3/4* **Hairdryer**[26] [1144] 4-9-4 **77** OisinMurphy 3 83
(Andrew Balding) *t.k.h: trckd ldrs tl wnt 2nd 7f out: rdn to ld over 1f out: hdd 1f out: styd on same pce u.p after* **5/2**[2]

322- **3** *shd* **Cape Peninsular**[198] [6661] 4-9-6 **79** LukeMorris 2 84
(James Tate) *t.k.h: hld up wl in tch in 4th: effrt over 1f out: hung lft 1f out: kpt on wl fnl 100yds* **4/1**[3]

0440 **4** *1 3/4* **The Gay Cavalier**[7] [1457] 6-8-7 **73** (t) JackOsborn(7) 7 74
(John Ryan) *s.i.s and niggled along early: in tch in rr: effrt over 1f out: kpt on same pce ins fnl f* **25/1**

3201 **5** *3/4* **Magic City (IRE)**[22] [1201] 8-9-2 **78** NathanEvans(3) 4 78
(Michael Easterby) *stdd and awkward leaving stalls: t.k.h: hld up in tch in 5th: effrt u.p over 1f out: styd on same pce and no imp ins fnl f* **6/1**

10-0 **6** *3* **Inniscastle Lad**[24] [1178] 5-9-7 **80** (v) RyanMoore 5 74
(Stuart Williams) *led and set stdy gallop: rdn 2f out: hdd and no ex over 1f out: wknd ins fnl f* **8/1**

2m 5.39s (-3.21) **Going Correction** -0.30s/f (Stan) **6** Ran SP% **112.6**
Speed ratings (Par 105): **100,99,99,97,97 94**
CSF £6.86 TOTE £2.40: £1.50, £1.70; EX 7.20 Trifecta £20.10.
**Owner** Mohamed Obaida **Bred** Rabbah Bloodstock Limited **Trained** Newmarket, Suffolk

**FOCUS**
This was steadily run and the winner quickened up well. She's capable of better, with the form set around the second and third at face value.

## 1584 BOOKEE SWIPE BET DONE APP MAIDEN STKS 1m 2f (P)
**7:45** (7:46) (Class 5) 3-Y-O **£5,175** (£1,540; £769; £384) **Stalls** Low

Form RPR

4- **1** **Weekender**[174] [7317] 3-9-5 0 FrankieDettori 4 78+
(John Gosden) *trckd ldr after 2f: rdn to ld wl over 1f out: hdd jst ins fnl f: battled bk gamely to ld again wl ins fnl f: styd on* **5/1**[3]

2- **2** *1/2* **Maghfoor**[174] [7329] 3-9-5 0 JimCrowley 5 77+
(Saeed bin Suroor) *trckd ldr tl 8f out: styd trcking ldrs: rdn to chal over 1f out: led jst ins fnl f: hdd and one pced wl ins fnl f* **4/5**[1]

5- **3** *1 3/4* **Fibonacci**[169] [7470] 3-9-5 0 RyanMoore 1 73+
(Hugo Palmer) *led: rdn 2f out: hdd over 1f out: kpt on u.p and stl ev ch tl no ex 100yds out: wknd towards fin* **2/1**[2]

064- **4** *7* **Bizet (IRE)**[136] [8047] 3-9-5 65 JosephineGordon 2 59
(John Ryan) *t.k.h: hld up in tch in last pair: effrt over 2f out: outpcd over 1f out: wknd fnl f* **66/1**

54 **5** *4* **Channel Packet**[20] [1244] 3-9-5 0 SilvestreDeSousa 3 54
(Michael Appleby) *t.k.h: stdd bk to last pair after 1f: effrt over 2f out: outpcd and btn over 1f out: sn wknd* **33/1**

2m 5.02s (-3.58) **Going Correction** -0.30s/f (Stan) **5** Ran SP% **110.0**
Speed ratings (Par 98): **102,101,100,94,91**
CSF £9.57 TOTE £4.70: £2.50, £1.02; EX 8.40 Trifecta £13.50.
**Owner** K Abdullah **Bred** Juddmonte Farms Ltd **Trained** Newmarket, Suffolk

**FOCUS**
An interesting maiden featuring some useful types. The fourth lends a note of caution to the form.

## 1585 DOWNLOAD BOOKEE IN THE APP STORE H'CAP 1m 6f (P)
**8:15** (8:15) (Class 6) (0-65,71) 4-Y-O+ **£3,234** (£962; £481; £240) **Stalls** Low

Form RPR

34-1 **1** **Masterson (IRE)**[5] [1486] 4-9-13 **71** 6ex SilvestreDeSousa 1 76
(Mick Channon) *t.k.h: mde all: rdn and kicked 2 l clr over 1f out: in command after: eased towards fin: comf* **2/5**[1]

54-0 **2** *1 1/2* **The Lampo Genie**[23] [1191] 5-9-3 **58** (b) StevieDonohoe 2 59
(Johnny Farrelly) *hld up in tch: wnt 3rd 10f out: effrt to chse wnr and swtchd rt over 1f out: styd on same pce fnl f* **11/1**

5345 **3** *1 3/4* **Oyster Card**[12] [1369] 4-8-2 **46** oh1 (p) LukeMorris 3 45
(Michael Appleby) *chsd wnr: rdn 3f out: 3rd and styd on same pce fr over 1f out* **6/1**[2]

-034 **4** *1 1/4* **King Julien (IRE)**[7] [1458] 4-7-9 **46** (p) DarraghKeenan(7) 5 43
(John Ryan) *chsd ldng pair tl 10f out: effrt wl over 2f out: swtchd rt over 1f out: hung lft and no imp ins fnl f* **12/1**

0-04 **5** *4 1/2* **Soundbyte**[35] [988] 12-8-6 **47** (v) MartinDwyer 4 38
(John Gallagher) *veru slowly away: hld up in tch in rr: rdn over 3f out: wknd over 1f out* **10/1**[3]

3m 0.2s (-3.00) **Going Correction** -0.30s/f (Stan)
**WFA** 4 from 5yo+ 1lb **5** Ran SP% **110.8**
Speed ratings (Par 101): **96,95,94,93,90**
CSF £5.90 TOTE £1.30: £1.10, £3.40; EX 5.90 Trifecta £14.90.
**Owner** Box 41 Racing **Bred** Star Pointe Ltd **Trained** West Ilsley, Berks

**FOCUS**
A weak staying race and a perfect opportunity for the winner to follow up his recent win here.

## 1586 LADIES DAY 22ND JUNE BUY TICKETS H'CAP 6f (P)
**8:45** (8:46) (Class 4) (0-85,87) 4-Y-O+ **£6,469** (£1,925; £962; £481) **Stalls** Centre

Form RPR

2651 **1** **Fujin**[26] [1140] 6-8-13 **80** (v) CharlieBennett(5) 2 90
(Shaun Harris) *chsd ldr tl led 2f out: sn rdn and wnt clr: in command and styd on strly ins fnl f* **8/1**

222- **2** *1 3/4* **Lightning Charlie**[179] [7186] 5-9-11 **87** JimCrowley 6 91
(Amanda Perrett) *chsd ldrs: effrt and jostled over 1f out: drvn to chse clr wnr jst over 1f out: no imp on wnr but kpt on to hold 2nd* **7/2**[2]

0-63 **3** *nk* **Vallarta (IRE)**[8] [1431] 7-8-10 **72** JamesSullivan 1 75
(Ruth Carr) *chsd ldrs: c to centre and effrt over 1f out: battling for 2nd and kpt on u.p ins fnl f: no imp on wnr* **6/1**

-253 **4** *2* **Vimy Ridge**[35] [995] 5-8-12 **74** LukeMorris 9 71
(Alan Bailey) *midfield: swtchd rt and effrt over 1f out: kpt on ins fnl f: no threat to wnr* **12/1**

6451 **5** *nse* **Captain Lars (SAF)**[5] [1487] 7-9-10 **86** 6ex (v) MartinLane 4 82+
(Derek Shaw) *s.i.s: bhd: c wd and effrt wl over 1f out: hdwy ins fnl f: styd on fnl 100yds: nvr trbld ldrs* **5/1**[3]

1136 **6** *3/4* **Athassel**[12] [1365] 8-8-8 **77** KatherineGlenister(7) 7 71
(David Evans) *restless in stalls: hld up in last trio: effrt towards inner over 1f out: edgd lft 1f out: kpt on ins fnl f: no threat to wnr* **14/1**

00-0 **7** *1/2* **Brother Tiger**[21] [1222] 8-9-7 **83** DavidAllan 8 75
(David C Griffiths) *taken down early: led tl 2f out: edgd rt and unable qck wl over 1f out: lost 2nd jst over 1f out: wknd ins fnl f* **16/1**

304- **8** *2 1/4* **Quick Look**[170] [7443] 4-9-1 **80** NathanEvans(3) 3 70
(Michael Easterby) *restless in stalls: fly j. as stalls opened and slowly away: hld up in last pair: effrt towards inner over 1f out: stl plenty to do whn squeezed for room jst ins fnl f: no ch after* **5/2**[1]

0-00 **9** *nk* **Nouvelli Dancer (IRE)**[19] [1261] 4-9-5 **81** OisinMurphy 5 65
(David C Griffiths) *in tch in midfield: effrt on inner over 1f out: no imp and edgd rt 1f out: wknd ins fnl f* **25/1**

1m 10.66s (-3.04) **Going Correction** -0.30s/f (Stan) **9** Ran SP% **116.9**
Speed ratings (Par 105): **108,105,105,102,102 101,100,97,97**
CSF £36.65 CT £184.45 TOTE £8.40: £2.50, £1.60, £2.10; EX 40.10 Trifecta £131.70.
**Owner** Mrs S L Robinson **Bred** Juddmonte Farms Ltd **Trained** Carburton, Notts

**FOCUS**
A competitive sprint handicap and another clear pb from the winner.
T/Plt: £15.60 to a £1 stake. Pool: £72,370.70 - 3384.63 winning units. T/Qpdt: £4.10 to a £1 stake. Pool: £8,768.83 - 1551.08 winning units. **Steve Payne**

# 1542 SOUTHWELL (L-H)
### Thursday, April 6

**OFFICIAL GOING: Fibresand: standard**
Wind: Light behind straight course and final 3f on the round course Weather: Sunny spells

## 1587 SUNBETS.CO.UK H'CAP 7f 14y(F)
**1:55** (1:55) (Class 6) (0-55,57) 4-Y-O+ **£2,264** (£673; £336; £168) **Stalls** Low

Form RPR

R332 **1** **Prince Of Time**[10] [1408] 5-8-7 **48** CallumRodriguez(7) 9 60+
(Richard Ford) *hld up: hdwy over 2f out: led over 1f out: pushed clr fnl f: eased nr fin* **6/4**[1]

0-04 **2** *3* **Trust Me Boy**[66] [481] 9-9-7 **55** FrannyNorton 5 57
(John E Long) *prom: pushed along over 4f out: rdn to chse wnr over 1f out: styd on ins fnl f* **7/1**[3]

-554 **3** *3/4* **Caledonian Gold**[10] [1407] 4-9-9 **57** JoeyHaynes 8 57
(Paul D'Arcy) *chsd ldrs: rdn 1/2-way: ev ch over 2f out: styd on same pce fnl f* **15/2**

3006 **4** *1 3/4* **Cuban Queen (USA)**[43] [854] 4-8-6 **47** FinleyMarsh(7) 2 42
(Julia Feilden) *hdwy over 4f out: rdn over 1f out: styd on same pce* **12/1**

0-35 **5** *1/2* **Rupert Boy (IRE)**[23] [1187] 4-9-1 **49** (b) DavidAllan 1 43
(Scott Dixon) *sn drvn along to chse ldrs: led 1/2-way: rdn and hdd over 1f out: styd on same pce* **10/1**

0-60 **6** *9* **Harbour Patrol (IRE)**[10] [1408] 5-9-3 **51** DanielTudhope 7 21
(Rebecca Bastiman) *led 1f: chsd ldrs: rdn 1/2-way: wknd over 1f out* **10/1**

0-06 **7** *1 1/4* **Wotabond**[23] [1187] 4-8-12 **46** oh1 (b[1]) PaulQuinn 6 12
(Richard Whitaker) *sn pushed along in rr: nvr on terms* **33/1**

0463 **8** *3/4* **Lutine Charlie (IRE)**[10] [1406] 10-8-12 **46** oh1 (p) TonyHamilton 10 10
(Emma Owen) *chsd ldrs: rdn 1/2-way: wknd over 2f out* **14/1**

0-04 **9** *1/2* **Spryt (IRE)**[26] [1146] 5-8-10 **51** (h) DarraghKeenan(7) 3 14
(John Butler) *led 6f out: hdd 1/2-way: rdn and wknd over 2f out* **11/2**[2]

1m 31.81s (1.51) **Going Correction** +0.225s/f (Slow) **9** Ran SP% **115.1**
Speed ratings (Par 101): **100,96,95,93,93 82,81,80,80**
CSF £12.32 CT £60.58 TOTE £2.00: £1.10, £2.30, £2.10; EX 11.40 Trifecta £61.30.
**Owner** B Hartley **Bred** D Curran **Trained** Garstang, Lancs

**FOCUS**
A moderate handicap and the favourite took it easily.

## 1588 32RED.COM EBF NOVICE STKS 4f 214y(F)
**2:30** (2:33) (Class 5) 2-Y-O **£2,911** (£866; £432; £216) **Stalls** Centre

Form RPR

**1** **Jasi (IRE)** 2-9-2 0 PaulHanagan 2 68
(Richard Fahey) *mde virtually all: edgd lft 3f out: rdn over 1f out: styd on* **5/4**[2]

2 hd **Kheleyf's Girl** 2-8-11 0 JFEgan 4 62
(David Evans) *w wnr: rdn 1/2-way: styd on* **12/1**
3 3 1/4 **Ventura Knight (IRE)** 2-9-2 0 FrannyNorton 1 56+
(Mark Johnston) *s.i.s: sn chsng ldrs: pushed along 1/2-way: rdn: swvd lft and no ex ins fnl f* **1/1**[1]
4 12 **Glen Valley (IRE)** 2-8-11 0 PhillipMakin 6 7
(Keith Dalgleish) *s.i.s: sn pushed along in rr: bhd fr 1/2-way* **10/1**[3]
1m 0.64s (0.94) **Going Correction** 0.0s/f (Stan) 4 Ran SP% **111.2**
Speed ratings (Par 92): **92,91,86,67**
CSF £13.26 TOTE £2.20; EX 11.60 Trifecta £18.40.
**Owner** Sheikh Abdullah Almalek Alsabah **Bred** Sherborough Developments Co Ltd **Trained** Musley Bank, N Yorks

**FOCUS**
Four newcomers finally lined up for this novice event, which was won by the subsequent Redcar Two-Year-Old Trophy winner Wick Powell last year. The first three disputed the lead to past halfway.

## 1589 32RED CASINO MAIDEN AUCTION STKS 7f 14y(F)
**3:00** (3:01) (Class 5) 3-Y-O **£2,911** (£866; £432; £216) **Stalls** Low

Form RPR
636- 1 **Copper Baked (FR)**[220] [5986] 3-8-6 0 JoeyHaynes 3 63
(K R Burke) *led: rdn and hdd over 2f out: rallied to ld wl ins fnl f: r.o* **11/8**[1]
65 2 1/2 **Eddiebet**[24] [1179] 3-8-13 0 ShelleyBirkett(3) 4 71
(David O'Meara) *chsd ldrs: rdn over 1f out: edgd rt wl ins fnl f: styd on to go 2nd towards fin* **8/1**
00- 3 1/2 **Stevie Brown**[160] [7659] 3-8-2 63 KevinLundie(7) 6 63
(David Brown) *w wnr tl led and hung lft fr over 2f out: sn rdn: hdd and unable qck wl ins fnl f* **9/2**[3]
-502 4 hd **Stretewise (IRE)**[13] [1348] 3-8-4 63 ShaneGray 5 57
(Jason Ward) *dwlt: outpcd: r.o wl ins fnl f: nt quite rch ldrs* **11/4**[2]
000- 5 7 **Pitch High (IRE)**[176] [7286] 3-8-4 62 FinleyMarsh(7) 1 46
(Julia Feilden) *sn pushed along in rr: outpcd fnl 3f* **12/1**
4 6 9 **Lakeski**[16] [1293] 3-8-4 0 KieranO'Neill 2 16
(Scott Dixon) *w ldrs tl pushed along over 4f out: rdn and wknd over 2f out* **28/1**
1m 32.71s (2.41) **Going Correction** +0.225s/f (Slow) 6 Ran SP% **109.2**
Speed ratings (Par 98): **95,94,93,93,85 75**
CSF £12.34 TOTE £2.10: £1.50, £2.50; EX 10.40 Trifecta £51.40.
**Owner** Nick Bradley Racing 5 & E Burke **Bred** M Daguzan-Garros, F Bragato Et Al **Trained** Middleham Moor, N Yorks

**FOCUS**
A moderate maiden, but a tight finish. The form is rated around the third.

## 1590 BETWAY H'CAP 2m 102y(F)
**3:35** (3:35) (Class 4) (0-85,85) 4-Y-O+ **£4,690** (£1,395; £697; £348) **Stalls** Low

Form RPR
4-43 1 **Virnon**[22] [1207] 6-8-10 **69** SilvestreDeSousa 4 76
(Alan Swinbank) *chsd ldr: wnt upsides 1/2-way: led over 6f out: clr over 3f out: pushed along and hung rt over 2f out: drvn out* **10/3**[2]
4250 2 1/2 **Silver Quay (IRE)**[26] [1153] 5-9-12 **85** TimmyMurphy 5 91
(Jamie Osborne) *s.i.s: hld up: racd keenly: hdwy over 5f out: chsd wnr over 3f out: rdn and ev ch ins fnl f: no ex towards fin* **7/2**[3]
51-1 3 23 **Fern Owl**[55] [666] 5-9-11 **84** (b) LiamKeniry 1 62
(Hughie Morrison) *trckd ldrs: racd keenly: wnt 2nd over 5f out: pushed along over 4f out: lost 2nd over 3f out: sn rdn and wknd* **4/5**[1]
60-4 4 99 **Brassbound (USA)**[28] [1108] 9-9-6 **79** (p) AndrewMullen 3
(Michael Appleby) *led: rdn and hdd over 6f out: sn swtchd rt: wknd over 5f out: virtually p.u fnl 3f* **16/1**
3m 48.72s (3.22) **Going Correction** +0.225s/f (Slow) 4 Ran SP% **106.7**
Speed ratings (Par 105): **100,99,88,38**
CSF £13.84 TOTE £3.50; EX 13.80 Trifecta £17.20.
**Owner** Mrs J Porter **Bred** World Racing Network **Trained** Melsonby, N Yorks

**FOCUS**
A fair staying handicap, but a disappointingly small field and the pace was modest. The form is best rated around the second.

## 1591 32RED.COM H'CAP 1m 4f 14y(F)
**4:15** (4:17) (Class 5) (0-70,66) 3-Y-O **£2,911** (£866; £432; £216) **Stalls** Low

Form RPR
205- 1 **Taxmeifyoucan (IRE)**[164] [7580] 3-8-11 **65** (p[1]) RowanScott(5) 4 76
(Keith Dalgleish) *s.i.s: hld up: outpcd over 8f out: sn drvn along: tk clsr order over 4f out: chsd ldr over 3f out: led over 2f out: rdn clr fr over 1f out* **9/2**
0-44 2 15 **Alexander M (IRE)**[50] [737] 3-9-3 **66** FrannyNorton 1 57
(Mark Johnston) *led: hung rt over 9f out: hdd over 8f out: chsd ldr tl led again 4f out: rdn: hung lft and hdd over 2f out: sn wknd* **7/2**[3]
450- 3 9 **Percy Thrower (IRE)**[190] [6875] 3-9-3 **66** SilvestreDeSousa 2 39
(Charles Hills) *s.i.s: sn chsng ldrs: outpcd over 8f out: hdwy over 5f out: rdn and ev ch over 3f out: sn hung rt and wknd* **7/4**[1]
5461 4 3/4 **Ladofash**[14] [1331] 3-9-3 **66** (v) PJMcDonald 3 37
(K R Burke) *chsd ldr: carried rt over 9f out: led over 8f out: clr over 7f out: rdn and hdd 4f out: sn wknd* **9/4**[2]
2m 43.6s (2.60) **Going Correction** +0.225s/f (Slow) 4 Ran SP% **107.5**
Speed ratings (Par 98): **100,90,84,83**
CSF £18.52 TOTE £8.20; EX 17.70 Trifecta £49.20.
**Owner** Straightline Bloodstock **Bred** E Lonergan **Trained** Carluke, S Lanarks

**FOCUS**
An ordinary 3yo middle-distance handicap. All four were making their Fibresand debuts and they finished spread out the length of the straight. The leaders might have done too much early so it may be best not to take the form at face value, with only the winner running his race.

## 1592 BETWAY CLAIMING STKS 6f 16y(F)
**4:50** (4:50) (Class 6) 3-Y-O+ **£2,264** (£673; £336; £168) **Stalls** Low

Form RPR
3124 1 **Vroom (IRE)**[23] [1185] 4-9-6 75 (p) RhiainIngram(7) 2 81
(Gay Kelleway) *racd keenly: led 5f out: rdn over 1f out: edgd lft and hdd ins fnl f: rallied to ld post* **10/3**[2]
0641 2 hd **Ticks The Boxes (IRE)**[15] [1310] 5-9-2 75 (p) JordanVaughan(3) 1 72
(Michael Herrington) *chsd ldrs: rdn over 1f out: led and edgd lft ins fnl f: hdd post* **6/1**
5415 3 3 **Dusky Dawn**[16] [1295] 5-9-7 80 SilvestreDeSousa 6 65
(Alan Swinbank) *hld up: pushed along 1/2-way: hdwy u.p over 1f out: styd on same pce ins fnl f* **10/11**[1]
55-4 4 8 **Yeeoow (IRE)**[83] [211] 8-9-10 75 JoeyHaynes 3 44
(K R Burke) *led 1f: remained handy: rdn over 2f out: wknd and eased fnl f* **5/1**[3]
1m 17.43s (0.93) **Going Correction** +0.225s/f (Slow) 4 Ran SP% **106.4**
Speed ratings (Par 101): **102,101,97,87**
CSF £19.02 TOTE £4.00; EX 14.30 Trifecta £18.90.Ticks The Boxes was claimed by Mr J. S. Wainwright for £5000
**Owner** Buy,Clarke,Whatley & Panther Racing **Bred** Paul & T J Monaghan **Trained** Exning, Suffolk

**FOCUS**
A moderate claimer with a tight finish fought out between the two previous C&D winners. The winner dictates the level.

## 1593 BETWAY SPRINT H'CAP 6f 16y(F)
**5:25** (5:25) (Class 6) (0-60,62) 4-Y-O+ **£2,264** (£673; £336; £168) **Stalls** Low

Form RPR
1303 1 **Dark Forest**[23] [1187] 4-9-7 **60** (p) BarryMcHugh 4 71
(Marjorie Fife) *sn pushed along in rr: hdwy over 2f out: rdn to ld ins fnl f: r.o wl* **6/4**[1]
2106 2 3 **All Or Nothin (IRE)**[30] [1075] 8-8-13 **52** DannyBrock 1 54
(Paddy Butler) *chsd ldrs: led 5f out: rdn over 1f out: hdd ins fnl f: styd on same pce* **33/1**
-504 3 1 1/4 **One For Jodie (IRE)**[9] [1409] 6-9-2 **58** (p) AlistairRawlinson(3) 8 56
(Michael Appleby) *chsd ldrs: chsd ldr over 4f out: rdn over 2f out: hung lft over 1f out: styd on same pce fnl f* **17/2**
140- 4 1 **Gaelic Wizard (IRE)**[153] [7797] 9-9-0 **58** (v) GemmaTutty(5) 6 53
(Karen Tutty) *s.i.s: sn pushed along in rr: hdwy over 1f out: styd on same pce fnl f* **25/1**
0006 5 1 1/4 **Silhuette (IRE)**[22] [1210] 4-9-2 **55** (v) JamesSullivan 9 47
(Colin Teague) *s.i.s: sn prom: rdn over 2f out: no ex fnl f* **33/1**
5336 6 2 **Fortinbrass (IRE)**[8] [1431] 7-9-4 **62** LewisEdmunds(5) 7 48
(John Balding) *prom: lost pl after 1f: sn pushed along: n.d after* **6/1**[3]
-025 7 1 3/4 **Monsieur Jimmy**[8] [1431] 5-9-7 **60** DanielTudhope 11 40
(Declan Carroll) *s.i.s: hld up: rdn over 2f out: sn hung lft: nvr on terms* **3/1**[2]
5055 8 3/4 **Multi Quest**[15] [1304] 5-8-13 **52** (b) FrannyNorton 10 30
(John E Long) *chsd ldrs: rdn over 2f out: wknd over 1f out* **16/1**
5402 9 3 3/4 **Cadeaux Pearl**[22] [1209] 9-8-1 **47** RPWalsh(7) 3 14
(Scott Dixon) *chsd ldrs: rdn over 3f out: wknd over 2f out* **16/1**
-060 10 nk **Storming Ambition**[15] [1305] 4-8-7 **46** oh1 (t) JimmyQuinn 2 12
(Conrad Allen) *s.i.s: sn pushed along and prom: rdn over 3f out: wknd over 1f out* **33/1**
004- 11 8 **Goadby**[146] [7913] 6-8-13 **52** (p) RoystonFfrench 5
(John Holt) *prom: lost pl over 4f out: wknd 1/2-way* **40/1**
1m 17.13s (0.63) **Going Correction** +0.225s/f (Slow) 11 Ran SP% **116.7**
Speed ratings (Par 101): **104,100,98,97,95 92,90,89,84,83 73**
CSF £69.52 CT £340.00 TOTE £2.40: £1.10, £5.80, £3.00; EX 53.90 Trifecta £428.30.
**Owner** David Haddrell **Bred** Genesis Green Stud Ltd **Trained** Stillington, N Yorks

**FOCUS**
A moderate sprint handicap, but the favourite did it nicely.
T/Plt: £1,837.00 to a £1 stake.. Pool: £46,731.29 - 18.57 winning units. T/Qpdt: £187.40 to a £1 stake. Pool: £2,880.45 - 11.37 winning units. **Colin Roberts**

# 1528 SAINT-CLOUD (L-H)
Thursday, April 6

**OFFICIAL GOING: Turf: good**

## 1594a PRIX DE LA MARCHE (CLAIMER) (2YO) (TURF) 4f 110y
**11:40** 2-Y-O **£9,829** (£3,931; £2,948; £1,965; £982)

RPR
1 **So Sora (FR)** 2-9-1 0 AlexandreGavilan 4 72
(D Guillemin, France) **37/10**[1]
2 3 **The Full Swipe (IRE)** 2-9-1 0 MaximeGuyon 7 60
(Tom Dascombe) *slowly away: impr over 2f out: rdn over 1f out: styd on wl fnl f to take 2nd cl home* **112/10**
3 hd **Canouville (FR)** 2-9-1 0 (p) CristianDemuro 6 59
(P Sogorb, France) **4/1**[2]
4 nk **Quick Skips Lad (IRE)**[5] [1496] 2-9-1 0 LiamJones 9 58
(J S Moore) *dwlt: in rr early: pushed along over 2f out: drvn and r.o wl fnl f* **132/10**
5 3 **Popsi**[14] [1335] 2-8-6 0 GuillaumeTrolleyDePrevaux(5) 10 42
(Jo Hughes) *pushed along early: settled midfield: drvn over 1f out: styd on same pce fnl f* **62/1**
6 shd **Vida Loca (FR)**[20] [1282] 2-8-11 0 AntoineHamelin 11 42
(R Chotard, France) **5/1**[3]
7 3 **Fas Le Fios (IRE)** 2-8-11 0 IoritzMendizabal 12 30
(J S Moore) *settled midfield: rdn over 2f out: drvn and styd on same pce fnl f* **157/10**
8 1 3/4 **Ormixa (FR)**[20] [1282] 2-8-11 0 Pierre-CharlesBoudot 14 23
(F Vermeulen, France) **15/2**
9 shd **Manas Ata (FR)** 2-9-4 0 GuillaumeMandel 5 29
(M Pimbonnet, France) **59/1**
10 1 1/2 **Acapella Style (FR)**[14] [1335] 2-9-1 0 FabriceVeron 8 20
(Matthieu Palussiere, France) **77/10**
11 2 **Espaldinha (FR)** 2-8-8 0 TheoBachelot 1
(Y Barberot, France) **183/10**
12 hd **Lastyouni (FR)**[14] [1335] 2-8-9 0 ErwannLebreton(6) 3 11
(Matthieu Palussiere, France) **69/1**
13 2 1/2 **Becquasiki (FR)** 2-8-11 0 AntoineWerle 13
(T Lemer, France) **30/1**
14 nk **Evaguei (FR)**[20] [1282] 2-8-8 0 AntonioPolli 2
(W Menuet, France) **39/1**

PARI-MUTUEL (all including 1 euro stake): WIN 4.70 PLACE 1.60, 3.00, 1.70 DF 26.80 SF 36.90.
**Owner** Ecurie Jarlan **Bred** Ecurie Jarlan **Trained** France

1595 - (Foreign Racing) - See Raceform Interactive

# 1550 KEMPTON (A.W) (R-H)

Friday, April 7

**OFFICIAL GOING: Polytrack: standard**

Wind: very light, of no consequence Weather: dry, sunny until race 5

## 1596 32RED ON THE APP STORE H'CAP (DIV I) 1m (P)

5:45 (5:45) (Class 6) (0-55,57) 3-Y-O **£2,264** (£673; £336; £168) **Stalls** Low

Form RPR

050- **1** **Fleeting Francesca**[165] 7570 3-9-4 **52**........ DaneO'Neill 3 59+
(Chris Gordon) *hld up in rr of main gp: swtchd lft and effrt over 2f out: hdwy u.p over 1f out: led ins fnl f: r.o wl and gng away at fin* **16/1**

600- **2** 1 ½ **A Bit Of Ginger**[185] 7041 3-9-7 **55**........ ShaneGray 4 59
(Ann Duffield) *led early: sn hdd and chsd ldrs after: effrt on inner ent fnl 2f: hdwy u.p to chal 1f out: led ins fnl f: hdd and outpcd fnl 100yds* **33/1**

365- **3** nk **Epsom Secret**[228] 5719 3-8-12 **51**........(h) PaddyBradley(5) 7 54
(Pat Phelan) *chsd ldrs: effrt 2f out: hdwy u.p to chal jst over 1f out: styd on same pce ins fnl f* **16/1**

00-4 **4** ¾ **Rey Loopy (IRE)**[34] 1034 3-9-4 **52**........ TedDurcan 10 53
(Ben Haslam) *hld up in rr of main gp: effrt u.p over 2f out: hdwy 1f out: styd on wl ins fnl f: nt rch ldrs* **9/1**

**5** nse **Les Arceaux (IRE)**[277] 3960 3-9-1 **49**........ DavidProbert 12 50
(J P Murtagh, Ire) *chsd ldrs: effrt ent fnl 2f: sn drvn: styd on same pce ins fnl f* **6/4**[1]

-352 **6** 1 **Whatalove**[9] 1421 3-8-12 **46**........ TomQueally 11 45
(Martin Keighley) *led over 6f out: rdn over 1f out: hdd ins fnl f: no ex and wknd fnl 75yds* **4/1**[2]

0-05 **7** 2 ¾ **Noreena**[27] 1141 3-9-6 **54**........ JoeyHaynes 2 46
(Paul D'Arcy) *wl in tch in midfield: effrt ent fnl 2f out: drvn and unable qck over 1f out: wknd ins fnl f* **16/1**

020- **8** 1 ¼ **How's Lucy**[120] 8276 3-9-5 **53**........ DannyBrock 8 43+
(Jane Chapple-Hyam) *prom: chsd ldr over 6f out: rdn jst over 2f out: unable qck u.p over 1f out: wknd ins fnl f* **11/2**[3]

643 **9** nk **Toolatetodelegate**[27] 1141 3-9-2 **57**........ JoshuaBryan(7) 9 46
(Brian Barr) *hld up in midfield: effrt and swtchd rt over 1f out: no imp fnl f: nvr trbld ldrs* **20/1**

200- **10** 1 ¼ **Swan Serenade**[207] 6412 3-9-2 **55**........ GeorgeWood(5) 5 41
(Jonathan Portman) *in tch in midfield: rdn over 2f out: outpcd and btn over 1f out: wknd fnl f* **25/1**

000- **11** nk **Zipedee**[111] 8425 3-8-12 **46** oh1........ JosephineGordon 1 31
(John Ryan) *a towards rr of main gp: n.d* **25/1**

0-05 **12** 31 **Melo Magic**[17] 1293 3-8-11 **52**........ GinaMangan(7) 6
(J R Jenkins) *awkward leaving stalls: flying leaping early and sn lost tch: nvr on terms: eased over 1f out: t.o* **66/1**

1m 39.21s (-0.59) **Going Correction** -0.125s/f (Stan) **12** Ran SP% **119.9**
Speed ratings (Par 96): **97,95,95,94,94 93,90,89,89,87 87,56**
CSF £468.73 CT £8279.45 TOTE £25.60: £5.30, £7.60, £5.60; EX 822.00 TRIFECTA Not Won..
**Owner** P J & Mrs J P Haycock **Bred** P J Haycock **Trained** Morestead, Hampshire

**FOCUS**
A beautiful dry sunny evening in Sunbury for an eight-race card. The line-up for this opening leg of a low-grade mile handicap boasted a collective record of 0-54, but they went a decent gallop and the winner could yet prove mildly progressive.

## 1597 32RED ON THE APP STORE H'CAP (DIV II) 1m (P)

6:15 (6:17) (Class 6) (0-55,56) 3-Y-O **£2,264** (£673; £336; £168) **Stalls** Low

Form RPR

0-00 **1** **London Grammar (IRE)**[42] 895 3-9-4 **52**........ RyanTate 1 56
(Ralph J Smith) *midfield: clsd jst over 2f out: rdn to chse ldrs over 1f out: ev ch ins fnl f: r.o wl to ld last strides* **10/1**

4254 **2** nk **Masquerade Bling (IRE)**[9] 1421 3-9-7 **55**........ RobHornby 5 58
(Simon Hodgson) *sn dropped to rr: swtchd lft and clsd over 2f out: rdn to ld over 1f out: kpt on wl u.p tl hdd and no ex last strides* **9/2**[2]

-335 **3** nk **Metronomic (IRE)**[69] 463 3-9-7 **55**........(p) SeanLevey 9 58
(Richard Hannon) *led and clr w rival: rdn 2f out: hdd over 1f out: kpt on wl u.p and ev ch after: unable qck nr fin* **9/4**[1]

40-4 **4** 1 ¾ **Luxford**[9] 1428 3-9-0 **48**........ KierenFox 4 47
(John Best) *midfield: effrt u.p over 2f out: clsd and swtchd rt over 1f out: styd on same pce ins fnl f* **12/1**

000- **5** ¾ **Crucial Moment**[156] 7768 3-9-1 **54**........ RyanWhile(5) 6 51
(Bill Turner) *chsd ldr and clr of field: rdn ent fnl 2f: 4th and no ex u.p ins fnl f: wknd ins fnl f* **8/1**

063- **6** hd **Pentito Rap (USA)**[211] 6253 3-9-3 **51**........ DanielMuscutt 10 47+
(Rod Millman) *rrd as stalls opened and v.s.a: clsd onto rr of main gp after 2f: effrt 2f out: hdwy whn nt clr run and swtchd lft ins fnl f: styd on but nvr threatened ldrs* **5/1**[3]

005- **7** 3 **Skilful Lord (IRE)**[165] 7570 3-9-1 **49**........(h[1]) TedDurcan 11 39
(Stuart Kittow) *stdd and dropped in bhd after s: hld up in rr: effrt on inner 2f out: sme hdwy over 1f out: no imp 1f out: eased ins fnl f* **8/1**

00-0 **8** 2 ½ **Secret Willow**[63] 545 3-9-4 **52**........ SamHitchcott 2 36
(John E Long) *pressed ldng pair and clr of field tl squeezed for room and dropped to 3rd 5f out: rdn and effrt jst over 2f out: no imp and btn jst over 1f out: wknd ins fnl f* **33/1**

000- **9** 18 **Myredbush (IRE)**[244] 5165 3-8-12 **46**........ JFEgan 3
(Simon Dow) *chsd clr ldng trio: rdn 1/2-way: lost pl and bhd 2f out: sn lost tch* **25/1**

1m 39.86s (0.06) **Going Correction** -0.125s/f (Stan) **9** Ran SP% **111.4**
Speed ratings (Par 96): **94,93,93,91,90 90,87,85,67**
CSF £51.86 CT £135.01 TOTE £10.20: £2.50, £1.80, £1.10; EX 44.30 Trifecta £136.20.
**Owner** Kevin Old **Bred** Pier House Stud **Trained** Epsom, Surrey
■ Stewards' Enquiry : Ryan Tate two-day ban: used whip above permitted level (21-22 Apr)

**FOCUS**
Another generous pace from the onset here which, combined with a couple of very slow starters, gave rise to a pretty strung out field from a very early stage.

## 1598 32RED H'CAP 1m (P)

6:45 (6:47) (Class 4) (0-85,85) 4-Y-O+ **£4,690** (£1,395; £697; £348) **Stalls** Low

Form RPR

-401 **1** **Believe It (IRE)**[30] 1085 5-8-3 **74**........(b) StephenCummins(7) 7 82
(Richard Hughes) *mde all: rdn 2f out: hrd pressed over 1f out: hld on gamely ins fnl f: all out* **5/1**[2]

241- **2** shd **Cape Banjo (USA)**[155] 7780 4-8-10 **79**........ PatrickO'Donnell(5) 2 86
(Ralph Beckett) *chsd wnr: effrt 2f out: chal u.p over 1f out: kpt on wl towards fin: jst hld* **7/2**[1]

315- **3** 1 ¼ **New Agenda**[106] 8498 5-9-4 **82**........(h) DaneO'Neill 6 86
(Paul Webber) *chsd ldrs: rdn 2f out: drvn and kpt on ins fnl f: nvr enough pce to chal ldrs* **15/2**[3]

1111 **4** ¾ **Hammer Gun (USA)**[9] 1433 4-9-3 **81** 6ex........(v) MartinLane 9 83
(Derek Shaw) *midfield: wnt 4th after 2f out: rdn over 2f out: drvn over 1f out: kpt on u.p ins fnl f: nvr enough pce to chal ldrs* **7/2**[1]

0-25 **5** 1 ¾ **Lunar Deity**[55] 680 8-9-0 **85**........ MillyNaseb(7) 4 83
(Stuart Williams) *hld up off the pce towards rr: effrt 2f out: kpt on ins fnl f: nvr trbld ldrs* **10/1**

30-4 **6** ½ **Kestrel Dot Com**[18] 1288 5-9-1 **79**........(h) DavidProbert 5 76
(Chris Dwyer) *stdd s: t.k.h: hld up off the pce in last pair: effrt over 1f out: nt clrest run and swtchd lft ins fnl f: styd on fnl 100yds: nt rch ldrs* **15/2**[3]

2430 **7** ½ **Zabeel Star (IRE)**[10] 992 5-8-9 **73**........ LiamKeniry 1 69
(Graeme McPherson) *s.i.s: midfield: effrt ent fnl 2f: styd on same pce fr over 1f out* **14/1**

**8** nk **Golden Raven (IRE)**[313] 2721 5-9-7 **85**........ DougieCostello 8 80
(Jamie Osborne) *stdd s: hld up mainly in midfield: effrt ent fnl 2f: no imp 1f out: kpt on same pce ins fnl f* **9/1**

0610 **9** nse **Lacan (IRE)**[9] 1422 6-9-7 **85**........ LukeMorris 10 80
(Brett Johnson) *stdd s: t.k.h: hld up in last pair: swtchd rt and effrt 2f out: nvr trbld ldrs* **25/1**

45-0 **10** 54 **Rock'n Gold**[13] 1365 4-8-10 **74**........ JoeDoyle 3
(Adrian Wintle) *chsd ldng trio for 2f: dropped to rr 3f out: sn lost tch: eased over 1f out: t.o* **100/1**

1m 38.7s (-1.10) **Going Correction** -0.125s/f (Stan) **10** Ran SP% **115.2**
Speed ratings (Par 105): **100,99,98,97,96 95,95,94,94,40**
CSF £22.56 CT £133.00 TOTE £6.20: £1.50, £1.60, £3.00; EX 31.00 Trifecta £183.70.
**Owner** Richard Hughes **Bred** The Kathryn Stud **Trained** Upper Lambourn, Berks

**FOCUS**
This essentially just concerned the front two throughout, and the winning time was half a second faster than the quicker of the two preceding 0-55 events. The winner's C&D latest has been franked by the second since.

## 1599 32RED.COM FILLIES' H'CAP 6f (P)

7:15 (7:15) (Class 5) (0-75,73) 4-Y-O+ **£2,911** (£866; £432; £216) **Stalls** Low

Form RPR

100- **1** **Nightingale Valley**[191] 6883 4-9-7 **73**........ TomQueally 5 81
(Stuart Kittow) *hld up in rr: pushed along 1/2-way: hdwy u.p 1f out: swtchd rt ins fnl f: r.o strly to ld last strides* **14/1**

-000 **2** nk **Nag's Wag (IRE)**[48] 808 4-9-5 **71**........ LiamKeniry 8 78
(George Baker) *t.k.h: hld up in last trio: clsd on inner over 2f out: swtchd rt jst over 2f out: rdn and hdwy over 1f out: led jst ins fnl f: r.o wl tl hdd and no ex last strides* **14/1**

-364 **3** nse **Childesplay**[32] 1066 6-9-2 **73**........ GeorgeWood(5) 4 80
(Heather Main) *midfield on outer: effrt over 1f out: hdwy u.p 1f out: ev ch ins fnl f: r.o* **15/8**[1]

-213 **4** 1 ¼ **Assertive Agent**[15] 1326 7-9-0 **66**........ DavidProbert 9 69
(Tony Carroll) *t.k.h: hld up in last trio: hdwy u.p 1f out: kpt on wl ins fnl f* **7/1**

300- **5** ½ **Monarch Maid**[177] 7267 6-8-10 **69**........ MollyKing(7) 7 70
(Peter Hiatt) *led and crossed to inner: clr 1/2-way: rdn over 1f out: hdd jst ins fnl f: no ex and wknd towards fin* **25/1**

0-53 **6** ½ **Be Royale**[6] 1489 7-9-2 **68**........(t) RobertWinston 1 68
(Michael Appleby) *chsd ldrs: effrt 2f out: unable qck u.p 1f out: wknd ins fnl f* **5/1**[2]

00-6 **7** shd **Andalusite**[22] 1220 4-8-2 **54**........(v[1]) LukeMorris 3 53
(John Gallagher) *chsd ldrs: edgd lft 2f out: no ex 1f out: wknd ins fnl f* **16/1**

510 **8** 1 ½ **K'Gari Spirit**[18] 1290 4-8-12 **69**........(t) DavidParkes(5) 6 64
(Jeremy Gask) *t.k.h: hld up in midfield: nt clr run and hmpd 2f out: no threat to ldrs and kpt on same pce fnl f* **6/1**[3]

1-24 **9** 4 **Arize (IRE)**[72] 394 4-9-2 **68**........ DaneO'Neill 2 50
(Jim Boyle) *chsd ldr tl over 1f out: wknd fnl f* **8/1**

1m 12.27s (-0.83) **Going Correction** -0.125s/f (Stan) **9** Ran SP% **112.4**
Speed ratings (Par 100): **100,99,99,97,97 96,96,94,89**
CSF £184.96 CT £540.00 TOTE £14.20: £3.50, £3.40, £1.40; EX 153.60 Trifecta £784.30.
**Owner** M E Harris **Bred** M Harris **Trained** Blackborough, Devon
■ Stewards' Enquiry : George Wood caution: careless riding

**FOCUS**
More competitive a fillies' handicap in practice than the market predicted it might be, with the first three home pretty hard to split. The pace was good and the form is rated around the runner-up.

## 1600 32RED MAIDEN STKS 6f (P)

7:45 (7:48) (Class 4) 3-Y-O+ **£4,690** (£1,395; £697; £348) **Stalls** Low

Form RPR

4 **1** **Sparkalot**[18] 1287 3-9-2 0........ JFEgan 4 77+
(Simon Dow) *led tl over 4f out: chsd ldr tl led again over 1f out: sn rdn: styd on wl and a holding runner up ins fnl f* **5/2**[2]

**2** 1 ¼ **Desert Rain (IRE)** 3-8-11 0........ JosephineGordon 1 68+
(Saeed bin Suroor) *chsd ldrs: wnt 3rd and rdn jst over 2f out: chsd clr wnr 1f out: styd on wl for clr 2nd but nvr threatening wnr* **10/11**[1]

36- **3** 5 **Raffle King (IRE)**[335] 2023 3-9-2 0........ RobertWinston 12 57+
(Mick Channon) *stdd and dropped in bhd after s: off the pce in rr: clsd and nt clrest of runs 2f out: swtchd rt and hdwy over 1f out: r.o wl to go 3rd ins fnl f: nvr trbld ldrs* **12/1**

**4** 1 ¾ **Chatoyer (FR)** 3-9-2 0........ SeanLevey 10 51
(Richard Hannon) *t.k.h: w ldrs tl led over 4f out: rdn and hdd over 1f out: 3rd and btn 1f out: wknd ins fnl f* **7/1**[3]

60- **5** nk **Verdi (IRE)**[167] 7527 3-8-13 0........ LouisSteward(3) 8 50
(John Ryan) *hld up off the pce towards rr: swtchd lft and effrt 3f out: chsd clr ldng trio 2f out: no imp and kpt on same pce after* **100/1**

**6** 8 **Joy** 3-8-11 0........ TedDurcan 7 20
(Laura Mongan) *a midfield but nvr on terms w ldrs: rdn over 2f out: no prog: wknd over 1f out* **25/1**

60 **7** nk **Taurean Gold**[16] 1299 3-9-2 0........ LukeMorris 9 24
(John Bridger) *off the pce in midfield: rdn over 2f out: swtchd rt and no imp 2f out: wknd over 1f out* **200/1**

00 **8** 1 ¼ **Spare Parts (IRE)**[18] 1287 3-8-13 0........ CallumShepherd(3) 2 20
(Charles Hills) *broke wl: sn off the pce in midfield: rdn and no prog over 2f out: sn wknd* **50/1**

0-5 **9** hd **Shouldertoshoulder**[34] 1024 3-8-13 0........ AaronJones(3) 3 19
(Stuart Williams) *sn outpcd in last pair: n.d* **25/1**

**10** 1 ½ **Imbucato**[12] 1384 3-9-2 0........ DavidProbert 11 14
(J P Murtagh, Ire) *midfield but nvr on terms w ldrs: rdn 2f out: no imp and wknd over 1f out* **16/1**

0- 11 ½ **Artsteelwork**[302] 3073 3-8-4 0 ........................ DarraghKeenan[(7)] 6 8
(John Butler) *chsd ldrs: 4th and struggling 2f out: wknd over 1f out:* **100/1**

\- 12 7 **Charlie Alpha (IRE)** 3-9-2 0 ........................ KierenFox 5
(Roger Ingram) *sn outpcd in rr* **66/1**

1m 11.6s (-1.50) **Going Correction** -0.125s/f (Stan) **12** Ran SP% **120.7**
Speed ratings (Par 105): **105,103,96,94,93 83,82,81,80,78 78,68**
CSF £5.03 TOTE £3.30: £1.10, £1.40, £2.70; EX 6.50 Trifecta £26.80.
**Owner** R Moss, C Brennan, H Redknapp **Bred** Mrs James Wigan **Trained** Ashtead, Surrey

**FOCUS**
Ostensibly an all-age maiden, but in practice every runner was a 3yo. The winning time was the quickest of the three 6f contests on the evening, 0.72sec quicker than that of the 80-rated scorer in the following handicap. The first pair were clear and the winner built on his debut promise.

## 1601 32RED CASINO H'CAP 6f (P)
8:15 (8:16) (Class 4) (0-85,86) 3-Y-O **£4,690** (£1,395; £697; £348) **Stalls** Low

Form RPR

1 1 **Family Fortunes**[41] 920 3-9-7 **80** ........................ JimCrowley 7 86+
(Sylvester Kirk) *pushed lft s: sn rcvrd and racd in 4th: effrt 2f out: clsng whn impeded and pushed lft ent fnl f: rdn to ld ins fnl f: r.o and jst hld runner up* **5/2[2]**

020- 2 hd **Berkshire Boy (IRE)**[211] 6260 3-9-7 **80** ........................ (b[1]) RobHornby 4 83
(Andrew Balding) *dwlt and hmpd leaving stalls: racd in 6th: effrt jst over 2f out: clsng whn impeded ent fnl f: hdwy u.p and swtchd rt ins fnl f: r.o wl fnl 75yds: nt quite get to wnr* **8/1**

4231 3 1 **Juan Horsepower**[30] 1090 3-9-7 **80** ........................ (p) KieranO'Neill 1 80
(Richard Hannon) *led: rdn over 2f out: veered sharply lft u.p ent fnl f: hdd ins fnl f: no ex and outpcd towards fin* **9/2[3]**

000- 4 ½ **Sayesse**[167] 7549 3-9-13 **86** ........................ JFEgan 6 84
(Mick Channon) *wnt lft s: hld up in midfield: rdn and clsd over 1f out: ev ch u.p ins fnl f: no ex and outpcd towards fin* **25/1**

411- 5 2¾ **Ventura Blues (IRE)**[300] 3134 3-9-5 **78** ........................ SeanLevey 3 68
(Richard Hannon) *chsd ldrs: swtchd rt and effrt 2f out: sn chalng tl no ex ins fnl f: wknd fnl 100yds* **5/1**

410- 6 8 **Hyperfocus (IRE)**[272] 4150 3-9-13 **86** ........................ JosephineGordon 2 50+
(Hugo Palmer) *t.k.h: chsd ldr: jnd ldr 4f out tl rdn and unable qck over 1f out: sn wknd* **7/4[1]**

233- 7 6 **Captain Sue (IRE)**[163] 7605 3-8-9 **68** ........................ StevieDonohoe 5 13
(Ian Williams) *hld up in rr: lost tch 3f out* **25/1**

1m 11.78s (-1.32) **Going Correction** -0.125s/f (Stan) **7** Ran SP% **118.6**
Speed ratings (Par 100): **103,102,101,100,97 86,78**
CSF £23.83 TOTE £4.70: £2.70, £5.00; EX 29.90 Trifecta £147.40.
**Owner** Highclere T'Bred Racing-Family Fortunes **Bred** A Parrish & Mrs L Sadler **Trained** Upper Lambourn, Berks

**FOCUS**
A good sprint handicap for the class in which the whole field was covered by 5lb on adjusted RPRs, and an eventful conclusion. The winner was value for a bit extra.

## 1602 100% PROFIT BOOST AT 32REDSPORT.COM H'CAP 1m 3f 219y(P)
8:45 (8:47) (Class 5) (0-75,75) 4-Y-O+ **£2,911** (£866; £432; £216) **Stalls** Centre

Form RPR

1452 1 **What Usain**[20] 1257 5-8-12 **69** ........................ (p) AlistairRawlinson[(3)] 3 74
(Michael Appleby) *chsd ldrs: rdn ent fnl 2f out: hdwy to ld jst over 1f out: hld on wl u.p ins fnl f: all out* **6/1**

-026 2 hd **Clovelly Bay (IRE)**[58] 619 6-9-0 **75** ........................ TylerSaunders[(7)] 7 79
(Marcus Tregoning) *dropped in bhd after s: hld up in rr: rdn and effrt over 1f out: hdwy to chse ldrs ins fnl f: str chal to wl ins fnl f: r.o but hld towards fin* **7/1**

3111 3 nk **Synodic (USA)**[13] 1364 5-9-6 **74** ........................ (t) JoeFanning 6 78
(Seamus Durack) *stdd s: hld up in last pair: effrt and edging rt over 1f out: swtchd out lft jst ins fnl f: hdwy to press ldrs wl ins fnl f: styd on* **11/4[1]**

22/0 4 ½ **Bostonian**[18] 1289 7-9-7 **75** ........................ LukeMorris 1 78
(Shaun Lycett) *chsd ldrs: rdn jst over 2f out: styd on and ev ch u.p ins fnl f: styd on same pce fnl 100yds* **25/1**

054- 5 ½ **Mazalto (IRE)**[191] 6886 4-8-11 **71** ........................ PaddyBradley[(5)] 4 73
(Pat Phelan) *hld up in midfield: rdn over 2f out: drvn over 1f out: styd on ins fnl f: nvr quite getting to ldrs* **16/1**

3-21 6 4 **Choral Clan (IRE)**[79] 286 6-9-6 **74** ........................ JackMitchell 5 70
(Brendan Powell) *hld up in tch in midfield: swtchd rt and effrt 2f out: unable qck u.p 1f out: wknd ins fnl f* **7/2[3]**

206- 7 1 **Maestro Mac (IRE)**[163] 7618 4-9-6 **75** ........................ FranBerry 8 69
(Hughie Morrison) *rousted along leaving stalls: chsd ldr tl led jst over 2f out: rdn over 1f out: hdd jst over 1f out: sn btn and wknd ins fnl f* **10/3[2]**

140- 8 17 **Hard Toffee (IRE)**[141] 7993 6-9-4 **72** ........................ JimCrowley 2 39
(Conrad Allen) *led: rdn over 2f out: sn hdd and lost pl qckly over 1f out: bhd and eased ins fnl f* **6/1**

2m 31.64s (-2.86) **Going Correction** -0.125s/f (Stan) **8** Ran SP% **122.8**
Speed ratings (Par 103): **104,103,103,103,103 100,99,88**
CSF £50.73 CT £145.00 TOTE £6.20: £2.00, £2.10, £1.60; EX 41.20 Trifecta £198.60.
**Owner** Michael Appleby **Bred** Bond Thoroughbred Corporation **Trained** Oakham, Rutland

**FOCUS**
A bunch finish here at the end of a race run more sedately than many on the evening. The form is rated cautiously around the runner-up.

## 1603 RACINGUK.COM/HD H'CAP 7f (P)
9:15 (9:16) (Class 6) (0-65,64) 4-Y-O+ **£2,264** (£673; £336; £168) **Stalls** Low

Form RPR

505- 1 **Olympic Duel (IRE)**[240] 5309 4-8-11 **54** ........................ LukeMorris 9 63
(Peter Hiatt) *racd in midfield: rdn and hdwy 2f out: led jst ins fnl f: r.o wl and drew clr fnl 100yds: rdn out* **20/1**

4-22 2 2½ **Tidal's Baby**[50] 768 8-9-0 **57** ........................ GeorgeDowning 1 59
(Tony Carroll) *chsd ldrs: effrt 2f out: drvn and ev ch jst over 1f out: led 1f out: sn hdd: 2nd and outpcd by wnr fnl 100yds* **8/1[2]**

150- 3 ½ **Fantasy Queen**[200] 6635 4-9-6 **63** ........................ JohnFahy 8 64
(Eve Johnson Houghton) *off the pce in midfield: hdwy u.p over 1f out: styd on wl ins fnl f: snatched 3rd last strides: no threat to wnr* **14/1**

3033 4 nk **Jack The Laird (IRE)**[15] 1325 4-9-0 **60** ........................ (p) JackDuern[(3)] 11 60
(Dean Ivory) *trckd ldng pair: rdn to ld wl over 1f out: hdd 1f out: no ex and wknd wl ins fnl f: lost 2 pls last strides* **12/1**

-042 5 shd **Almanack**[8] 1449 7-9-4 **64** ........................ NathanAlison[(3)] 6 64
(Mark Pattinson) *wl off the pce in last quintet: rdn and hdwy over 1f out: styd on ins fnl f: no threat to wnr* **6/4[1]**

06/3 6 2¼ **Talksalot (IRE)**[51] 734 6-9-6 **63** ........................ (t[1]) DougieCostello 13 57
(Mark Bradstock) *t.k.h: hld up in midfield: rdn and sme hdwy over 1f out: kpt on same pce ins fnl f* **12/1**

4550 7 1½ **Blackthorn Stick (IRE)**[9] 1427 8-8-12 **55** ........................ (p) JimmyQuinn 4 45
(Paul Burgoyne) *chsd ldrs: swtchd rt and effrt to press ldrs wl over 1f out: no ex 1f out: wknd ins fnl f* **9/1[3]**

0400 8 1 **I Can't Stop**[51] 740 4-8-7 **50** oh5 ........................ (b) DavidProbert 12 37
(Milton Bradley) *dwlt and rdn along leaving stalls: wl off the pce in last quintet: drvn over 2f out: n.d* **33/1**

544- 9 ¾ **Sir Compton**[212] 6238 4-9-5 **62** ........................ TedDurcan 5 47
(Stuart Kittow) *dwlt and short of room leaving stalls: wl off the pce in last quintet: swtchd rt and effrt 2f out: sme hdwy over 1f out: nvr trbld ldrs* **11/1**

0420 10 nk **Arcanista (IRE)**[21] 1249 4-8-7 **57** ........................ (b) NicolaCurrie[(7)] 14 41
(Richard Hughes) *dropped in after s: hld up off the pce in last quintet: rdn and sme hdwy over 1f out: n.d* **16/1**

4600 11 1¾ **Mime Dance**[18] 1285 6-9-4 **64** ........................ (p) HectorCrouch[(3)] 7 43+
(John Butler) *led tl rdn and hdd wl over 1f out: lost pl over 1f out: sn wknd* **16/1**

6-00 12 3 **St Andrews (IRE)**[13] 685 4-9-0 **57** ........................ (t) StevieDonohoe 10 28
(Ian Williams) *a off the pce in rr: n.d* **25/1**

-560 13 3¼ **George Baker (IRE)**[30] 1086 10-8-9 **59** ........................ AmeliaGlass[(7)] 3 22
(George Baker) *midfield: c wd and pushed along over 2f out: no hdwy and wknd over 1f out: bhd ins fnl f* **12/1**

626/ 14 6 **Captain Joe**[704] 7592 6-8-10 **60** ........................ (t[1]) JoshuaBryan[(7)] 2 6+
(Brian Barr) *chsd ldr tl ent fnl 2f: lost pce qckly over 1f out: bhd and eased ins fnl f* **66/1**

1m 24.89s (-1.11) **Going Correction** -0.125s/f (Stan) **14** Ran SP% **124.0**
Speed ratings (Par 101): **101,98,97,97,97 94,92,91,90,90 88,85,81,74**
CSF £172.53 CT £2418.56 TOTE £19.00: £4.40, £1.80, £5.90; EX 117.10 Trifecta £3147.50 Part Won..
**Owner** R G Robinson & R D Robinson **Bred** Mrs T Mahon **Trained** Hook Norton, Oxon

**FOCUS**
A moderate finale, but another strong pace and a winner with potentially a bit more to offer.
T/Plt: £561.40 to a £1 stake. Pool: £69,531.21 - 90.41 winning units T/Qpdt: £13.30 to a £1 stake. Pool: £9,763.31 - 539.38 winning units **Steve Payne**

# LEICESTER (R-H)
Friday, April 7

**OFFICIAL GOING: Round course - good to soft (good in places; 6.9); straight course - good (good to soft in places; 7.3)**
Wind: Straight course light against, while on the round course it was light against final 4 1/2 furlongs Weather: Sunny spells

## 1604 GRANBY NOVICE STKS 5f
2:00 (2:02) (Class 5) 2-Y-O **£3,881** (£1,155; £577; £288) **Stalls** High

Form RPR

1 **Kick On Kick On** 2-9-2 0 ........................ AdamKirby 4 80+
(Clive Cox) *pushed along leaving stalls: led 4f out: shkn up over 1f out: rdn clr ins fnl f* **8/1**

2 4 **Zain Flash** 2-9-2 0 ........................ JFEgan 7 66
(David Evans) *led 1f: remained w wnr tl rdn over 1f out: styd on same pce fnl f* **10/3[1]**

3 ½ **Airshow** 2-9-2 0 ........................ (h[1]) RyanTate 5 64
(Rod Millman) *s.i.s: pushed along early in rr: hdwy 2f out: rdn over 1f out: edgd lft and styd on same pce fnl f* **5/1**

4 ½ **Shovel It On (IRE)** 2-9-2 0 ........................ DannyBrock 8 62+
(David Evans) *sn outpcd: r.o ins fnl f: nrst fin* **28/1**

5 1½ **Straight Ash (IRE)** 2-9-2 0 ........................ TomMarquand 6 57+
(Richard Hannon) *prom: rdn 1/2-way: outpcd fr over 1f out* **7/2[2]**

6 ½ **Jedi Master (IRE)** 2-9-2 0 ........................ PaulHanagan 9 55
(Richard Fahey) *pushed along early in rr: styng on whn nt clr run and swtchd lft ins fnl f: nt trble ldrs* **4/1[3]**

7 ¾ **Poignant** 2-9-2 0 ........................ JackMitchell 1 52
(Archie Watson) *in tch and pushed along early: hdwy 2f out: rdn over 1f out: wknd ins fnl f* **16/1**

8 1 **Rockesbury** 2-9-2 0 ........................ DougieCostello 3 49
(Kevin Frost) *w ldrs tl pushed along over 3f out: wknd over 1f out* **100/1**

9 1¼ **Manco Inca (IRE)** 2-9-2 0 ........................ OisinMurphy 2 44
(Joseph Tuite) *chsd ldrs: rdn 1/2-way: wknd fnl f* **20/1**

10 17 **Bunch Of Thyme (IRE)** 2-8-11 0 ........................ RyanWhile[(5)] 10
(Bill Turner) *s.i.s: outpcd* **25/1**

1m 0.55s (0.55) **Going Correction** -0.175s/f (Firm) **10** Ran SP% **112.0**
Speed ratings (Par 92): **88,81,80,80,77 76,75,74,72,44**
CSF £32.14 TOTE £6.90: £2.60, £1.60, £2.00; EX 33.60 Trifecta £235.30.
**Owner** Paul & Clare Rooney **Bred** Fifehead Farms M C Denning **Trained** Lambourn, Berks

**FOCUS**
The ground had dried out slightly and was now good to soft, good in places on the round course and good, good to soft in places on the straight track (GoingStick: round 6.9, straight 7.3). False rail from top of the hill on the back straight to the winning line, increasing race distances on the round course by 8yds. The jockeys felt that the ground was on the fast side of good. Ten newcomers contested this opening novice event and the first two home dominated from the start. The form is rated towards the top end of the race average.

## 1605 BURTON OVERY (S) STKS 6f
2:30 (2:31) (Class 6) 3-Y-O **£3,234** (£962; £481; £240) **Stalls** High

Form RPR

-356 1 **Endeavour (IRE)**[16] 1310 3-9-0 62 ........................ TomMarquand 3 60
(Richard Hannon) *mde all: rdn over 1f out: all out* **4/1[1]**

-635 2 shd **Champagne Queen**[24] 1193 3-8-6 45 ........................ (t) HollieDoyle[(3)] 6 55
(Rae Guest) *prom: lost pl and pushed along over 4f out: hdwy u.p over 1f out: r.o* **10/1**

0 3 ½ **Irish Sky (IRE)**[18] 1286 3-8-9 0 ........................ KieranO'Neill 7 53
(Henry Spiller) *hld up: racd keenly: hdwy over 1f out: sn rdn: r.o* **12/1**

3420 4 1 **Jet Setter (IRE)**[28] 1127 3-9-0 68 ........................ GeorgeDowning 4 55
(Tony Carroll) *hld up in tch: rdn and edgd rt over 1f out: styd on* **4/1[1]**

2050 5 ¾ **Lady Volante (IRE)**[2] 1564 3-8-9 56 ........................ JFEgan 2 48
(David Evans) *w wnr tl rdn over 2f out: no ex wl ins fnl f* **6/1[3]**

4 6 ¾ **Ivor's Fantasy (IRE)**[41] 920 3-8-6 0 ........................ TimClark[(3)] 9 46
(David Elsworth) *s.i.s: in rr: rdn over 2f out: r.o ins fnl f: nvr nrr* **7/1**

56-6 7 ½ **Dontforgettocall**[7] 1474 3-9-0 64 ........................ OisinMurphy 1 49
(Joseph Tuite) *prom: racd keenly: rdn over 1f out: no ex wl ins fnl f* **5/1[2]**

6445 8 hd **Joyful Dream (IRE)**[42] 897 3-8-2 53 ........................ (p) GeorgiaDobie[(7)] 11 44
(J S Moore) *in rr: hdwy over 3f out: hung lft and racd alone fnl 2f: styd on same pce fnl f* **10/1**

000- **9** *13* **Newz Watch**[155] 7777 3-8-9 54 ........ LukeMorris 8 5
(Mick Quinn) *prom: rdn 1/2-way: wknd wl over 1f out* **40/1**

-600 **10** *1 1/2* **Red Shanghai (IRE)**[17] 1297 3-8-4 35 ow2 ........ (p[1]) BenRobinson(7) 5 2
(Charles Smith) *prom: rdn and lost pl over 3f out: wknd over 2f out* **200/1**

1m 12.93s (-0.07) **Going Correction** -0.175s/f (Firm) **10** Ran SP% **112.3**
Speed ratings (Par 96): **93,92,92,90,89 88,88,87,70,68**
CSF £43.10 TOTE £5.20: £1.70, £3.50, £3.90; EX 41.00 Trifecta £645.60.No claims for this race
**Owner** P D Player **Bred** D G Hardisty Bloodstock **Trained** East Everleigh, Wilts

**FOCUS**
A moderate 3yo seller contested by ten maidens and, unlike in the opener, the runners made straight for the centre of the track. The form looks held down by the proximity of the 45-rated runner-up.

## 1606 H.A.C. PIPELINE SUPPLIES H'CAP 7f
**3:05** (3:06) (Class 4) (0-85,86) 4-Y-0+ **£6,469** (£1,925; £962; £481) **Stalls** High

Form RPR

206- **1** **Gallipoli (IRE)**[121] 8256 4-9-9 86 ........ PaulHanagan 8 94
(Richard Fahey) *racd far side: hld up: hdwy over 1f out: r.o to ld post: 1st of 9 in gp* **6/1**[1]

1-45 **2** *shd* **Evening Attire**[50] 760 6-9-0 80 ........ HollieDoyle(3) 7 87
(William Stone) *overall ldr far side: shkn up over 2f out: rdn over 1f out: hdd post: 2nd of 9 in gp* **10/1**

-430 **3** *nk* **Mister Music**[5] 1512 8-9-2 79 ........ GeorgeDowning 6 85
(Tony Carroll) *racd far side: hld up: hdwy over 1f out: r.o: 3rd of 9 in gp* **16/1**

100- **4** *2 1/4* **Mamillius**[204] 6529 4-9-6 83 ........ PatCosgrave 14 83
(George Baker) *racd towards stands' side: a.p: chsd ldr that gp over 4f out: rdn over 1f out: led that gp ins fnl f: styd on same pce: 1st of 9 in gp* **14/1**

540- **5** *1 1/4* **Prying Pandora (FR)**[167] 7540 4-9-1 78 ........ TonyHamilton 18 75
(Richard Fahey) *racd towards stands' side: hld up: hdwy u.p over 1f out: nt trble ldrs: 2nd of 9 in gp* **12/1**

343- **6** *hd* **Handytalk (IRE)**[256] 4709 4-8-13 76 ........ OisinMurphy 10 72
(Rod Millman) *led stands' side gp: hung rt and chse overall ldr over 2f out: rdn over 1f out: no ex ins fnl f: 3rd of 9 in gp* **7/1**[2]

01-0 **7** *1 1/2* **Glorious Poet**[29] 1105 4-9-0 77 ........ AndrewMullen 12 69
(Tony Carroll) *racd towards stands' side: hld up: rdn over 2f out: swtchd lft over 1f out: styd on ins fnl f: nt trble ldrs: 4th of 9 in gp* **66/1**

005- **8** *1 1/2* **Rio Ronaldo (IRE)**[157] 7737 5-9-5 82 ........ JamieSpencer 11 70
(Mike Murphy) *stdd s: hld up: racd towards stands' side: swtchd lft over 1f out: rdn and hung rt ins fnl f: nvr on terms: 5th of 9 in gp* **12/1**

0-32 **9** *nk* **Flexible Flyer**[63] 551 8-9-3 80 ........ (h) SilvestreDeSousa 15 67
(Chris Dwyer) *racd towards stands' side: chsd ldr tl over 4f out: remained handy: rdn over 2f out: styd on same pce fr over 1f out: 6th of 9 in gp* **14/1**

260- **10** *1* **My Lucille (IRE)**[204] 6504 4-8-13 76 ........ AdamBeschizza 2 61
(Chris Wall) *racd far side: mid-div: hdwy over 2f out: sn rdn: wknd over 1f out: 4th of 9 in gp* **20/1**

606- **11** *2 1/4* **Gabrial The Tiger (IRE)**[195] 6764 5-9-6 86 ........ AdamMcNamara(3) 5 65
(Richard Fahey) *racd far side: chsd ldr tl rdn over 2f out: wknd over 1f out: 5th of 9 in gp* **12/1**

000- **12** *hd* **Our Boy Jack (IRE)**[122] 8240 8-9-3 80 ........ (p) PaulMulrennan 13 58
(Conor Dore) *racd towards stands' side: hld up: nvr on terms: 7th of 9 in gp* **100/1**

0-15 **13** *1 1/2* **Tripartite (IRE)**[36] 984 4-8-10 73 ........ LukeMorris 1 47
(Jeremy Gask) *racd far side: chsd ldrs: rdn over 2f out: wknd over 1f out: 6th of 9 in gp* **8/1**[3]

430- **14** *1 3/4* **Steal The Scene (IRE)**[204] 6501 5-8-10 73 ........ RyanPowell 3 42
(Kevin Frost) *racd far side: hld up: rdn over 2f out: wknd over 1f out: 7th of 9 in gp* **18/1**

03-0 **15** *2 3/4* **He's My Cracker**[44] 857 4-9-2 79 ........ AdamKirby 4 41
(Clive Cox) *racd far side: chsd ldrs: rdn over 2f out: wkng whn hung lft over 1f out: 8th of 9 in gp* **9/1**

056- **16** *1 1/2* **Eqleem**[279] 3884 4-9-7 84 ........ JimCrowley 17 42
(David Evans) *racd towards stands' side: chsd ldrs over 4f: 8th of 9 in gp* **22/1**

-006 **17** *1/2* **Major Crispies**[16] 1301 6-8-10 73 ........ RyanTate 16 29
(Jeremy Gask) *racd towards stands' side: s.i.s: nvr on terms: last of 9 in gp* **20/1**

200- **18** *1* **Le Roi Du Temps (USA)**[169] 7486 4-9-0 77 ........ JamesSullivan 9 31
(Tom Tate) *racd far side: hld up: rdn over 2f out: btn whn hmpd over 1f out: last of 9 in gp* **20/1**

1m 23.78s (-2.42) **Going Correction** -0.175s/f (Firm) **18** Ran SP% **125.7**
Speed ratings (Par 105): **106,105,105,102,101 101,99,97,97,96 93,93,91,89,86 85,84,83**
CSF £59.63 CT £940.08 TOTE £6.80: £2.40, £3.00, £4.30, £3.50; EX 62.80 Trifecta £932.20.
**Owner** Peter Timmins **Bred** Lester Cullen & Whitsbury Manor Stud **Trained** Musley Bank, N Yorks

**FOCUS**
A decent and open handicap. The field soon split into two equal groups of nine and the far-side group held sway, providing the first three home. The runner-up is the key to the form.

## 1607 KIBWORTH MAIDEN STKS (PLUS 10 RACE) 1m 3f 179y
**3:40** (3:40) (Class 3) 3-Y-O **£9,703** (£2,887; £1,443; £721) **Stalls** Low

Form RPR

2-23 **1** **Flight Of Fantasy**[48] 814 3-9-0 75 ........ RichardKingscote 3 77
(Harry Dunlop) *led: qcknd 4f out: hdd over 2f out: sn rdn: carried hd high and flashed tail: rallied to ld wl ins fnl f: r.o* **12/1**

2- **2** *1* **Face The Facts (IRE)**[163] 7622 3-9-5 0 ........ (h[1]) FrankieDettori 1 80
(John Gosden) *s.i.s: hld up: outpcd over 3f out: hdwy over 1f out: r.o to go 2nd post* **13/8**[1]

- **3** *nse* **Glassy Waters (USA)** 3-9-5 0 ........ SilvestreDeSousa 4 80+
(Saeed bin Suroor) *s.i.s: hdwy to chse wnr over 9f out: shkn up to ld over 2f out: rdn over 1f out: hdd wl ins fnl f* **7/4**[2]

42-3 **4** *2* **Sufi**[20] 1259 3-9-5 79 ........ RyanMoore 5 78
(Richard Hannon) *chsd ldrs: pushed along over 3f out: styd on same pce wl ins fnl f* **4/1**[3]

32 **5** *6* **Waterville Dancer (IRE)**[30] 1089 3-9-5 0 ........ JamieSpencer 2 67
(Richard Hughes) *chsd ldrs: lost pl 10f out: pushed along over 3f out: n.d after* **16/1**

2m 33.81s (-0.09) **Going Correction** +0.025s/f (Good) **5** Ran SP% **108.0**
Speed ratings (Par 102): **101,100,100,98,94**
CSF £30.92 TOTE £11.50: £3.60, £1.10; EX 31.70 Trifecta £126.00.
**Owner** P A Deal & G Lowe **Bred** Hermes Services Ltd **Trained** Lambourn, Berks

**FOCUS**
Race distance increased by 8yds. An interesting maiden with a well-bred newcomer up against four with proven form. It provided quite a dramatic conclusion.The winner is rated in line with his better AW form.

## 1608 LODDINGTON H'CAP 1m 3f 179y
**4:15** (4:15) (Class 3) (0-90,90) 4-Y-O **£8,821** (£2,640; £1,320; £660; £329) **Stalls** Low

Form RPR

- **1** **Galapiat**[239] 5347 4-9-1 85 ........ JoeFanning 7 97+
(Mark Johnston) *a.p: chsd ldr over 2f out: led over 1f out: shkn up and c clr ins fnl f: easily* **9/1**

4513 **2** *5* **Faithful Creek (IRE)**[36] 991 5-9-0 83 ........ (p) SilvestreDeSousa 10 87
(Michael Appleby) *chsd ldr tl led over 2f out: rdn and hdd over 1f out: no ex ins fnl f* **4/1**[2]

422- **3** *2* **Rainbow Dreamer**[23] 5331 4-9-4 88 ........ (v) FergusSweeney 2 89+
(Alan King) *s.i.s: hld up: shkn up and nt clr run over 2f out: swtchd lft over 1f out: r.o to go 3rd nr fin* **6/1**

240- **4** *1/2* **Duke Of Diamonds**[163] 7624 5-8-4 76 oh3 ........ ShelleyBirkett(3) 6 76
(Julia Feilden) *chsd ldrs: rdn over 2f out: styd on same pce fr over 1f out* **25/1**

040- **5** *3/4* **Carrington (FR)**[253] 4797 4-9-6 90 ........ WilliamBuick 3 89
(Charlie Appleby) *hld up: plld hrd: hdwy u.p over 1f out: no imp fnl f* **5/1**[3]

5-06 **6** *shd* **Zamperini (IRE)**[21] 1240 5-8-13 82 ........ (b) JimCrowley 1 81
(Mike Murphy) *hld up: hdwy over 5f out: rdn and carried hd high over 1f out: hung rt and no ex fnl f* **14/1**

022/ **7** *2 1/4* **Tobacco Road (IRE)**[42] 6987 7-9-1 84 ........ (h) PatCosgrave 9 79
(David Pipe) *led: rdn and hdd over 2f out: wknd over 1f out* **33/1**

341/ **8** *hd* **Mr Cripps**[609] 5101 5-9-4 87 ........ FranBerry 4 82
(Ralph Beckett) *hld up: hdwy over 5f out: rdn over 2f out: wknd fnl f* **13/8**[1]

-000 **9** *8* **Buthelezi (USA)**[16] 1307 9-8-7 76 oh1 ........ BenCurtis 5 58
(Brian Ellison) *s.i.s: rdn over 4f out: nvr on terms* **50/1**

003- **10** *15* **Primogeniture (IRE)**[197] 6711 6-9-4 87 ........ OisinMurphy 8 45
(Mary Hambro) *prom: lost pl 1/2-way: shkn up over 2f out: wknd and eased over 1f out* **25/1**

2m 31.05s (-2.85) **Going Correction** +0.025s/f (Good) **10** Ran SP% **118.3**
Speed ratings (Par 107): **110,106,105,105,104 104,102,102,97,87**
CSF £44.10 CT £238.96 TOTE £8.90: £2.30, £1.30, £2.10; EX 31.70 Trifecta £163.40.
**Owner** Miss K Rausing **Bred** Miss K Rausing **Trained** Middleham Moor, N Yorks

**FOCUS**
Race distance increased by 8yds. A decent middle-distance handicap, but the winner was in a different league. The form can be rated around the second.

## 1609 BARKBY MAIDEN STKS 1m 53y
**4:50** (4:51) (Class 5) 3-Y-O **£3,881** (£1,155; £577; £288) **Stalls** Low

Form RPR

**1** **Zamfir** 3-9-5 0 ........ WilliamBuick 5 84+
(Charlie Appleby) *a.p: pushed along over 3f out: rdn over 1f out: edgd rt and r.o to ld wl ins fnl f* **7/1**[2]

0- **2** *1 1/2* **Mostahel**[168] 7502 3-9-5 0 ........ TomMarquand 2 81
(Richard Hannon) *chsd ldrs: wnt 2nd over 2f out: rdn over 1f out: styng on same pce whn nt clr run wl ins fnl f* **12/1**

5- **3** *nk* **Ifubelieveindreams (IRE)**[114] 8362 3-9-0 0 ........ SilvestreDeSousa 1 75
(Ismail Mohammed) *led: rdn over 1f out: hdd and unable qck wl ins fnl f* **14/1**

**4** *3 1/4* **Albizzia** 3-9-0 0 ........ FranBerry 10 68+
(Ralph Beckett) *prom: rdn over 1f out: styd on same pce* **6/1**

0- **5** *1/2* **Desert Dream**[175] 7317 3-9-5 0 ........ RyanMoore 6 71
(Sir Michael Stoute) *hld up: hdwy over 2f out: rdn over 1f out: styd on same pce* **5/1**[3]

35- **6** *4* **Teqany (IRE)**[170] 7468 3-9-5 0 ........ JimCrowley 7 62
(Owen Burrows) *chsd ldr tl rdn over 2f out: wknd over 1f out* **5/1**[3]

**7** *4 1/2* **Present Tense** 3-9-0 0 ........ FrankieDettori 8 47+
(John Gosden) *hld up: pushed along and hdwy over 3f out: nt clr run over 2f out: wknd wl over 1f out* **3/1**[1]

6 **8** *6* **California Cliffs (IRE)**[27] 1151 3-9-0 0 ........ AdamBeschizza 4 33
(Rae Guest) *hld up: rdn and wknd over 2f out* **100/1**

**9** *1 1/2* **Mushareefa (IRE)** 3-9-0 0 ........ OisinMurphy 9 30
(Ed Dunlop) *s.s: hld up: a bhd* **25/1**

**10** *14* **Book Of Dust** 3-9-0 0 ........ JackMitchell 3
(Giles Bravery) *s.s: a bhd* **100/1**

1m 44.88s (-0.22) **Going Correction** +0.025s/f (Good) **10** Ran SP% **115.0**
Speed ratings (Par 98): **102,100,100,96,96 92,87,81,80,66**
CSF £43.74 TOTE £4.20: £1.70, £4.10, £2.80; EX 45.70 Trifecta £440.80.
**Owner** Godolphin **Bred** Darley **Trained** Newmarket, Suffolk

**FOCUS**
Race distance increased by 8yds. An interesting maiden with several top stables represented and some newcomers boasting tasty pedigrees, including the winner. The third is perhaps the key.

## 1610 SIMON DE MONTFORT H'CAP 1m 53y
**5:25** (5:26) (Class 5) (0-70,69) 4-Y-O+ **£3,881** (£1,155; £577; £288) **Stalls** Low

Form RPR

1400 **1** **Pivotman**[36] 992 9-9-2 67 ........ (bt) NathanEvans(3) 2 74
(Michael Easterby) *mde all: rdn over 1f out: edgd lft ins fnl f: hld on* **6/1**[3]

0660 **2** *1/2* **Cosmic Ray**[11] 1403 5-8-11 59 ........ (h) DavidAllan 10 65
(Les Eyre) *chsd wnr: rdn over 2f out: styd on u.p* **9/1**

3-10 **3** *nse* **Ross Raith Rover**[62] 570 4-9-1 63 ........ (b[1]) AndreaAtzeni 1 69+
(Robert Eddery) *hld up: hdwy over 2f out: rdn over 1f out: running on whn hmpd nr fin* **6/1**[3]

420- **4** *2 3/4* **Harlequin Rock**[211] 6265 4-8-12 60 ........ PatCosgrave 5 60
(Mick Quinn) *plld hrd and prom: rdn over 2f out: styd on same pce ins fnl f* **10/1**

6066 **5** *1/2* **Green Howard**[10] 1409 9-9-5 67 ........ DanielTudhope 9 66+
(Rebecca Bastiman) *hld up: hdwy over 1f out: rdn and edgd rt ins fnl f: styd on: nt rch ldrs* **5/1**[1]

305- **6** *1 3/4* **Billy Bond**[98] 8587 5-9-3 65 ........ (v) PaulHanagan 6 60+
(Richard Fahey) *hld up: hdwy u.p over 1f out: no imp ins fnl f* **11/2**[2]

0/ **7** *1/2* **Dragon Khan (IRE)**[6] 6727 8-8-10 58 ........ FergusSweeney 4 52+
(John O'Shea) *s.i.s: hld up: rdn over 2f out: nt trble ldrs* **16/1**

462/ **8** *1 3/4* **Jeremy's Jet (IRE)**[203] 6552 6-8-11 59 ........ GeorgeDowning 3 49+
(Tony Carroll) *hld up: rdn over 2f out: nvr on terms* **15/2**

13-0 **9** *1/2* **London Glory**[35] 1007 4-9-7 69 ........ AdamKirby 7 58
(David Thompson) *chsd ldrs: rdn over 2f out: wknd over 1f out* **12/1**

261- **10** *3/4* **Infiniti (IRE)**[165] 7572 4-8-9 60 ........ (p) HollieDoyle(3) 8 47+
(Barry Leavy) *hld up: rdn over 2f out: n.d* **10/1**

1m 46.28s (1.18) **Going Correction** +0.025s/f (Good) **10** Ran SP% **114.1**
Speed ratings (Par 103): **95,94,94,91,91 89,88,87,86,85**
CSF £57.58 CT £345.04 TOTE £6.70: £2.20, £2.90, £2.10; EX 73.10 Trifecta £699.00.

**Owner** K Wreglesworth **Bred** Cheveley Park Stud Ltd **Trained** Sheriff Hutton, N Yorks
**FOCUS**
Race distance increased by 8yds. An ordinary handicap and few got into it with the first two holding those positions throughout. The winner is entitled to rate a bit higher on turf.
T/Plt: £248.60 to a £1 stake. Pool: £66,458.12 - 195.09 winning units T/Qpdt: £28.00 to a £1 stake. Pool: £4,743.28 - 125.06 winning units **Colin Roberts**

1611- 1617a (Foreign Racing) - See Raceform Interactive

# 1462 LINGFIELD (L-H)
## Saturday, April 8

**OFFICIAL GOING: Polytrack: standard**
Wind: Light breeze Weather: Warm and sunny

### 1618 32REDPOKER FILLIES' H'CAP 7f 1y(P)
**2:00** (2:00) (Class 5) (0-70,71) 4-Y-O+ **£2,911** (£866; £432; £216) **Stalls** Low

Form RPR
1/1- **1** **Burren View Lady (IRE)**[23] 1234 7-8-9 **56**..................(bt) OisinMurphy 5 62
(Denis Gerard Hogan, Ire) *mid div: hdwy 2f out: qcknd to ld 1f out: rdn and hld on wl: comf* **11/4**[1]
065- **2** *1* **Anastazia**[149] 7887 5-9-6 **67**................................ JoeyHaynes 4 70
(Paul D'Arcy) *hld up: hdwy on outer 2f out: rdn over 1f out: r.o to take 2nd ins fnl f* **3/1**[2]
0-42 **3** *shd* **Little Kipling**[22] 1237 4-9-3 **67**........................ AaronJones(3) 2 70
(Stuart Williams) *hld up: trckd wnr: rdn over 1f out: r.o ins fnl f* **9/2**[3]
-314 **4** *3/4* **Ixelles Diamond (IRE)**[9] 1447 6-8-10 **57**.............(h) JosephineGordon 6 58
(Lee Carter) *prom: disp ld after 2f: led briefly over 1f out: sn hdd and no ex* **8/1**
2034 **5** *hd* **Welsh Inlet (IRE)**[10] 1425 9-8-7 **54** oh3......................... WilliamCarson 8 54
(John Bridger) *led briefly: hdd and remained prom: rdn 2f out: one pce* **20/1**
2200 **6** *2 1/4* **Prisom (IRE)**[61] 606 4-8-6 **60**..........................(p) DavidEgan(7) 1 54
(Gay Kelleway) *hld up: nvr a factor* **17/2**
4-43 **7** *4 1/2* **World Of Good**[22] 1243 4-9-7 **68**..........................(b) AdamKirby 7 50
(Anabel K Murphy) *prom and sn led: disp ld after 2f: hdd over 1f out: wknd and eased* **5/1**
1m 24.55s (-0.25) **Going Correction** -0.075s/f (Stan) 7 Ran SP% **112.9**
Speed ratings (Par 100): **98,96,96,95,95 93,87**
CSF £10.96 CT £34.18 TOTE £3.30: £2.00, £2.50; EX 12.20 Trifecta £51.00.
**Owner** Is That All Syndicate **Bred** L Mulryan **Trained** Cloughjordan, Co Tipperary
**FOCUS**
An ordinary fillies' handicap, but another successful raid on the AW by an Irish-trained horse and the market knew.

### 1619 32REDCASINO MAIDEN STKS 7f 1y(P)
**2:35** (2:35) (Class 5) 3-Y-O **£2,911** (£866; £432; £216) **Stalls** Low

Form RPR
3- **1** **Horroob**[273] 4161 3-9-5 0................................ AndreaAtzeni 3 85+
(Roger Varian) *trckd ldrs in 3rd: swtchd to chal on outer over 1f out: qcknd to ld 1f out: r.o strly under hand riding: easily* **4/11**[1]
20-3 **2** *1 3/4* **Mr Tyrrell (IRE)**[22] 1241 3-9-5 79................................ PatDobbs 8 80
(Richard Hannon) *trckd ldr: pushed along and led over 1f out: hdd 1f out: kpt on but nt pce of wnr* **7/1**[2]
24- **3** *4* **Fastar (IRE)**[302] 3100 3-9-5 0................................ JimmyFortune 4 69
(Brian Meehan) *hld up: pushed along over 2f out: wnt 3rd appr fnl f: r.o steadily towards fin* **10/1**
0- **4** *1* **Milburn Jack**[122] 8243 3-9-5 0................................ AdamKirby 1 67
(Clive Cox) *led: rdn 2f out: hdd over 1f out: grad wknd* **15/2**[3]
5-0 **5** *3 1/2* **Meteoric Riser (USA)**[17] 1299 3-9-5 0........................ ShaneKelly 7 57
(Richard Hughes) *mid div: rdn and racd wd over 2f out: no ex* **33/1**
**6** *4 1/2* **Agnethe (IRE)** 3-9-0 0................................ TomMarquand 5 40
(Paul D'Arcy) *dwlt: a in rr: rdn over 2f out: no imp* **66/1**
00- **7** *2* **Peking Flyer (IRE)**[143] 7976 3-9-5 0........................ ThomasBrown 2 40
(Ed Walker) *slowly away: a in rr* **50/1**
1m 23.71s (-1.09) **Going Correction** -0.075s/f (Stan) 7 Ran SP% **113.1**
Speed ratings (Par 98): **103,101,96,95,91 86,83**
CSF £3.44 TOTE £1.20: £1.10, £2.70; EX 3.30 Trifecta £9.10.
**Owner** Sheikh Ahmed Al Maktoum **Bred** Whitsbury Manor Stud And Mrs M E Slade **Trained** Newmarket, Suffolk
**FOCUS**
An uncompetitive maiden and all very straightforward for the long-odds-on favourite. The 79-rated runner-up sets the level.

### 1620 BETWAY INSIDER H'CAP 1m 2f (P)
**3:10** (3:10) (Class 6) (0-65,67) 4-Y-O+ **£2,264** (£673; £336; £168) **Stalls** Low

Form RPR
0-43 **1** **Embankment**[30] 1101 8-8-13 **57**................................ AdamBeschizza 1 63
(Michael Attwater) *trckd ldrs: rdn 2f out: hdwy over 1f out: led wl ins fnl f: rdn out* **11/1**
1-00 **2** *1* **Fast And Hot (IRE)**[42] 922 4-9-9 **67**........................(b) KieranO'Neill 6 71
(Richard Hannon) *trckd ldr: led gng wl 2f out: kicked 3l clr over 1f out: rdn and hdd wl ins fnl f: no ex* **9/2**[3]
2554 **3** *nk* **Roman De Brut (IRE)**[16] 1334 5-9-3 **66**.................... CharlieBennett(5) 3 70
(Daniel Mark Loughnane) *mid div: wnt 2nd over 1f out: rdn and r.o one pce* **11/4**[1]
0-43 **4** *2 1/2* **Estibdaad (IRE)**[19] 1283 7-9-2 **60**..........................(t[1]) DannyBrock 2 59
(Paddy Butler) *led: rdn and hdd 2f out: grad wknd* **7/2**[2]
4160 **5** *shd* **Runaiocht (IRE)**[19] 1284 7-9-1 **64**......................(b) DavidParkes(5) 4 63
(Paul Burgoyne) *hld up: effrt u.p over 2f out: sme late hdwy* **15/2**
2-51 **6** *1 1/4* **Ruby Wednesday**[64] 549 4-9-7 **65**................................ KierenFox 8 61
(John Best) *mid div: rdn over 2f out: one pce* **13/2**
-606 **7** *1 1/2* **Foylesideview (IRE)**[21] 1260 5-8-7 **51** oh6...........(h) SilvestreDeSousa 5 44
(Harry Chisman) *mid div: rdn 2f out: no imp* **25/1**
5-60 **8** *2* **Golly Miss Molly**[15] 1338 6-9-3 **61**..........................(b) MartinLane 9 51
(Jeremy Gask) *in rr: rdn 4f out: rn wd over 1f out: wknd* **16/1**
-005 **9** *28* **Munsarim (IRE)**[19] 1283 10-8-12 **56**..........................(v) DavidProbert 7
(Lee Carter) *hld up: veered rt towards stands' rail wl ent st: no ch after* **20/1**
2m 6.85s (0.25) **Going Correction** -0.075s/f (Stan) 9 Ran SP% **115.0**
Speed ratings (Par 101): **96,95,94,92,92 91,90,89,66**
CSF £59.66 CT £176.53 TOTE £9.90: £3.10, £1.40, £1.60; EX 67.90 Trifecta £555.50.
**Owner** Canisbay Bloodstock **Bred** Juddmonte Farms Ltd **Trained** Epsom, Surrey

**FOCUS**
A moderate handicap and not many got into it.

### 1621 32RED INTERNATIONAL TRIAL STKS (LISTED RACE) 1m 1y(P)
**3:45** (3:49) (Class 1) 3-Y-O
**£22,684** (£8,600; £4,304; £2,144; £1,076; £540) **Stalls** High

Form RPR
503- **1** **Law And Order (IRE)**[168] 7544 3-9-0 104........................ MartinHarley 7 100
(James Tate) *mid div: racd wd and hdwy u.p over 1f out: led ins fnl f: r.o wl and on top fin* **11/4**[2]
1-41 **2** *nk* **Mr Scaramanga**[42] 933 3-9-3 97................................ HarryBentley 3 102
(Simon Dow) *trckd ldrs: hdwy on ins wl over 1f out: rdn to ld appr fnl f: hdd ins last 150 yds: kpt on wl* **16/1**
132- **3** *1* **Eqtiraan (IRE)**[192] 6882 3-9-0 100........................ JimCrowley 5 97
(Richard Hannon) *led: rdn and hdd over 1f out: kpt on one pce* **15/8**[1]
214- **4** *3 1/2* **Paco's Angel**[183] 7114 3-8-9 97................................ ShaneKelly 6 84
(Richard Hughes) *trckd ldr: rdn and wknd wl over 1f out* **8/1**
154- **5** *1* **Majoris (IRE)**[211] 6285 3-9-0 97................................(t) AndreaAtzeni 2 86
(Hugo Palmer) *s.i.s: pushed along 1/2-way: rdn and sme hdwy fnl 2 fs* **5/1**[3]
1-24 **6** *1* **Ay Ay (IRE)**[59] 626 3-9-0 89................................ FranBerry 1 84
(David Elsworth) *hld up: pushed along over 2f out: sn rdn and no imp* **16/1**
330- **7** *4 1/2* **Baileys Showgirl (FR)**[188] 6986 3-8-9 101.............. SilvestreDeSousa 4 69
(Mark Johnston) *mid div: rdn 2f out: wknd qckly* **8/1**
1m 35.37s (-2.83) **Going Correction** -0.075s/f (Stan) 7 Ran SP% **112.1**
Speed ratings (Par 106): **111,110,109,106,105 104,99**
CSF £41.42 TOTE £3.30: £1.80, £5.80; EX 37.30 Trifecta £144.00.
**Owner** Saeed Manana **Bred** Mr & Mrs Clive Martin **Trained** Newmarket, Suffolk
**FOCUS**
An interesting 3yo Listed event with Dubawi Gold and Bow Creek amongst the better recent winners. The first three came clear in this year's renewal.

### 1622 SUNBETS H'CAP 7f 1y(P)
**4:15** (4:17) (Class 3) (0-95,92) 4-Y-O+ **£7,246** (£2,168; £1,084; £542; £270) **Stalls** Low

Form RPR
0212 **1** **Take The Helm**[26] 1177 4-9-2 **87**................................ KierenFox 3 96
(Brian Meehan) *disp ld tl gained advantage over 1f out: rdn fnl f: briefly hdd fnl 150 yds: rallied gamely u.str.p to ld again cl home: all out* **9/2**[2]
230- **2** *hd* **War Glory (IRE)**[198] 6710 4-9-5 **90**........................ TomMarquand 1 98
(Richard Hannon) *trckd ldrs: chal on inner over 1f out: rdn and led briefly ins fnl f: hdd nr fin: r.o wl* **9/2**[2]
-034 **3** *1 3/4* **Suqoor**[36] 999 4-9-3 **88**................................(p) SilvestreDeSousa 6 92
(Chris Dwyer) *hld up: pushed along over 2f out: hdwy u.p appr fnl f: fin wl* **10/1**
165- **4** *1/2* **Takatul (USA)**[196] 6778 4-9-2 **87**................................ JimCrowley 7 89+
(Charles Hills) *hld up: hdwy on ins 2f out: pushed along and r.o: should improve* **10/3**[1]
0-32 **5** *nk* **Until Midnight (IRE)**[17] 1301 7-8-9 **80**........................ WilliamCarson 9 82
(Eugene Stanford) *trckd ldrs: rdn over 1f out: wknd* **25/1**
162- **6** *1/2* **Viscount Barfield**[211] 6276 4-9-7 **92**........................(h) DavidProbert 4 92
(Andrew Balding) *disp ld tl rdn and fdd over 1f out* **7/1**
651- **7** *nse* **Gothic Empire (IRE)**[190] 6914 5-9-4 **89**.................... DanielMuscutt 8 89+
(James Fanshawe) *in rr: rdn over 2f out: no imp* **5/1**[3]
4004 **8** *1* **Gentlemen**[9] 1454 6-9-5 **90**................................ JosephineGordon 5 87
(Phil McEntee) *mid div: rdn and racd wd wl over 1f out: fdd* **12/1**
000- **9** *3 1/4* **Grand Inquisitor**[218] 6075 5-9-7 **92**........................ StevieDonohoe 2 81
(Ian Williams) *hld up in last: rdn 2f out: no rspnse* **18/1**
1m 24.11s (-0.69) **Going Correction** -0.075s/f (Stan) 9 Ran SP% **114.5**
Speed ratings (Par 107): **100,99,97,97,96 96,96,95,91**
CSF £24.84 CT £191.79 TOTE £5.60: £2.10, £1.40, £3.00; EX 28.20 Trifecta £195.70.
**Owner** J S Threadwell **Bred** Wilsdon & Habton **Trained** Manton, Wilts
**FOCUS**
A decent handicap with a cracking finish.

### 1623 32REDSPORT.COM H'CAP 1m 4f (P)
**4:50** (4:50) (Class 6) (0-60,65) 3-Y-O **£2,264** (£673; £336; £168) **Stalls** Low

Form RPR
3606 **1** **Bartholomew J (IRE)**[37] 987 3-8-4 **46** oh1................ SimonPearce(3) 5 56
(Lydia Pearce) *hld up: hdwy and circled field to ld over 3f out: pushed along 2f out: sn clr: rdn briefly appr fnl f: easily* **28/1**
-440 **2** *5* **Too Many Shots**[46] 848 3-9-4 **57**................................ KierenFox 2 59
(John Best) *2nd early: 3rd after 2f: remained prom: urged along over 1f out: sn rdn and no imp on wnr* **13/2**
060- **3** *1/2* **Look My Way**[122] 8245 3-9-9 **62**................................ DavidProbert 3 63
(Andrew Balding) *mid div: hdwy 3f out: rdn wl over 1f out: styd on one pce* **6/1**[3]
-221 **4** *1/2* **Moneyoryourlife**[9] 1445 3-9-9 **65**........................ HollieDoyle(3) 4 65
(Richard Hannon) *hld up in rr: drvn 2f out: r.o one pce fr over 1f out* **5/6**[1]
4522 **5** *3 3/4* **Av A Word**[16] 1331 3-9-3 **56**................................(p) AdamKirby 6 50
(Daniel Kubler) *2nd after 2f: styd prom tl rdn and wknd 2f out* **7/2**[2]
0-46 **6** *15* **Nothing Compares**[44] 881 3-9-5 **58**........................(b[1]) JoeFanning 1 28
(Mark Johnston) *led: rdn and hdd over 3f out: wknd rapidly* **14/1**
2m 33.08s (0.08) **Going Correction** -0.075s/f (Stan) 6 Ran SP% **114.5**
Speed ratings (Par 96): **96,92,92,92,89 79**
CSF £192.21 TOTE £25.70: £9.00, £3.00; EX 185.70 Trifecta £577.10.
**Owner** P J Stephenson **Bred** Bernard Colclough **Trained** Newmarket, Suffolk
**FOCUS**
A moderate 3yo handicap, with only one of these having scored before, and quite a shock result.

### 1624 32RED.COM MAIDEN STKS 1m 2f (P)
**5:40** (5:42) (Class 5) 3-Y-O **£2,911** (£866; £432; £216) **Stalls** Low

Form RPR
22- **1** **Dubai Horizon (IRE)**[163] 7649 3-9-5 0..........................(p[1]) AdamKirby 1 90
(Saeed bin Suroor) *broke wl and led early: sn hdd: trckd ldr gng wl: rdn to chal wl over 1f out: led appr fnl f: sn clr: comf* **4/6**[1]
**2** *3* **Impact Point (JPN)** 3-9-5 0................................ OisinMurphy 5 83
(Andrew Balding) *dwlt: rcvrd to go 5th after 2f: sn mid-div: rdn and outpcd 3f out: r.o wl fnl 2f: promising* **10/1**
**3** *nk* **Roc Astrale (IRE)** 3-9-5 0................................ JimCrowley 6 82
(Amanda Perrett) *racd in 3rd: pushed along 2f out: r.o under hand and heels fnl 2f: should improve* **7/1**[2]
34- **4** *4 1/2* **Nathania**[221] 5995 3-9-0 0................................ ShaneKelly 2 68
(Richard Hughes) *sn led: drvn 2f out: rdn and hdd over 1f out: wknd fnl f* **9/1**

5 6 **Akamanto (IRE)** 3-9-5 0 TomMarquand 7 61
(Richard Hannon) *hld up: pushed along 3f out: sn rdn and wknd* **8/1**3

6 7 **Intellect (IRE)** 3-9-5 0 TedDurcan 3 47
(Sir Michael Stoute) *trckd ldrs: rdn 3f out: fdd* **10/1**

60 7 31 **Moorea**[10] 1420 3-9-5 0 AdamBeschizza 4
(John Bridger) *s.i.s: a in rr: wl bhd fnl 3f* **100/1**

2m 4.49s (-2.11) **Going Correction** -0.075s/f (Stan) 7 Ran SP% **112.8**
Speed ratings (Par 98): **105,102,102,98,93 88,63**
CSF £8.25 TOTE £1.50: £1.10, £4.40; EX 8.00 Trifecta £38.40.
**Owner** Godolphin **Bred** Mrs James Wigan **Trained** Newmarket, Suffolk

**FOCUS**
An interesting 3yo maiden with some big yards represented.
T/Plt: £329.80 to a £1 stake. Pool: £55,347.43 - 122.50 winning units T/Qpdt: £239.70 to a £1 stake. Pool: £3,532.00 - 10.90 winning units **Keith McHugh**

## 1558 WOLVERHAMPTON (A.W) (L-H)

Saturday, April 8

**OFFICIAL GOING: Tapeta: standard**
Wind: Light behind final 2f Weather: Fine

### 1625 32RED.COM H'CAP 7f 36y (Tp)

**6:20** (6:22) (Class 5) (0-75,77) 3-Y-O £2,911 (£866; £432; £216) **Stalls** High

Form RPR

24-3 1 **Glorious Artist (IRE)**[35] 1033 3-9-7 **75** LukeMorris 2 85
(Charles Hills) *hld up: hdwy over 2f out: shkn up to ld over 1f out: hung lft and rdn clr ins fnl f* **6/1**3

1215 2 3¼ **Toy Theatre**[2] 1582 3-9-3 **74** AlistairRawlinson(3) 4 75
(Michael Appleby) *prom: rdn over 1f out: styd on to go 2nd wl ins fnl f* **6/4**1

51-4 3 1¼ **El Hombre**[38] 972 3-9-4 **77** ShirleyTeasdale(5) 6 75
(Keith Dalgleish) *plld hrd: led 6f out: rdn and hdd over 1f out: no ex ins fnl f* **14/1**

30-2 4 1¾ **Widnes**[22] 1242 3-9-3 **71** (b) FrannyNorton 3 64
(Alan Bailey) *s.s: hld up: rdn over 2f out: hdwy over 1f out: hung lft and no ex ins fnl f* **11/4**2

2410 5 2½ **Blue Bahia (IRE)**[29] 1124 3-9-3 **71** PJMcDonald 7 57
(Mark Johnston) *prom: chsd ldr over 5f out tl rdn over 1f out: wknd ins fnl f* **10/1**

1430 6 3 **Auric Goldfinger (IRE)**[22] 1242 3-8-5 **66** ow1 (b) RossaRyan(7) 5 44
(Richard Hannon) *hld up: plld hrd: hdwy on outer 1/2-way: rdn and wknd over 1f out* **8/1**

23-0 7 28 **Lightoller (IRE)**[11] 1411 3-8-4 **65** KeithQuinn(7) 1
(Mick Channon) *led 1f: chsd ldrs tl rdn and wknd over 2f out* **28/1**

1m 28.23s (-0.57) **Going Correction** -0.05s/f (Stan) 7 Ran SP% **111.3**
Speed ratings (Par 98): **101,97,95,93,91 87,55**
CSF £14.62 TOTE £5.50: £2.70, £1.90; EX 19.20 Trifecta £65.10.
**Owner** Kangyu International Racing (HK) Limited **Bred** N Hartery **Trained** Lambourn, Berks

**FOCUS**
A modest 3yo handicap and the pace was solid. The winner did it nicely enough.

### 1626 32RED CASINO MAIDEN FILLIES' STKS 6f 20y (Tp)

**6:50** (6:51) (Class 5) 3-Y-O+ £2,911 (£866; £432; £216) **Stalls** Low

Form RPR

3- 1 **Qatari Riyals (IRE)**[178] 7279 3-9-0 0 SeanLevey 6 76
(Richard Hannon) *led: hdd over 3f out: chsd ldr tl shkn up to ld over 1f out: rdn out* **9/4**1

2 nk **Historic Event (IRE)** 3-9-0 0 PatCosgrave 3 75
(Saeed bin Suroor) *prom: racd keenly: wnt 2nd over 4f out: led over 3f out: rdn and hdd over 1f out: rallied ins fnl f: r.o* **9/4**1

-5 3 4 **Exquisite Ruby**[93] 75 3-9-0 0 RichardKingscote 5 62
(Charles Hills) *hld up: swtchd lft and hdwy over 1f out: styd on to go 3rd wl ins fnl f: nt trble ldrs* **5/1**3

0- 4 2 **Miss Patience**[161] 7696 3-9-0 0 LukeMorris 2 56
(Peter Chapple-Hyam) *prom: racd keenly: rdn over 1f out: wknd ins fnl f* **11/4**2

54 5 1¾ **Play With Me**[24] 1198 3-9-0 0 ConnorBeasley 8 50
(Keith Dalgleish) *broke wl sn lost pl: n.d after* **50/1**

043- 6 2¾ **Paquita Bailarina**[156] 7776 3-9-0 56 AndrewMullen 7 41
(James Given) *racd keenly in 2nd pl tl over 4f out: hmpd wl over 3f out: sn hung rt: rdn over 2f out: wknd over 1f out* **16/1**

7 3¼ **Tisa River (IRE)** 3-9-0 0 FrannyNorton 4 31
(Milton Bradley) *dwlt: hld up: pushed along 2f out: wkng whn n.m.r over 1f out* **80/1**

6- 8 2¾ **Sweet Amazement**[301] 3143 3-9-0 0 SteveDrowne 1 22
(Mark Usher) *hmpd sn after s: plld hrd and prom: rdn and wknd over 1f out* **66/1**

1m 14.46s (-0.04) **Going Correction** -0.05s/f (Stan) 8 Ran SP% **115.4**
Speed ratings (Par 100): **98,97,92,89,87 83,79,75**
CSF £7.65 TOTE £3.20: £1.30, £1.10, £1.50; EX 8.40 Trifecta £25.20.
**Owner** Mubarak Al Naemi **Bred** Mubarak Al Naemi **Trained** East Everleigh, Wilts
■ Stewards' Enquiry : Sean Levey three-day ban: careless riding (22-25 Apr)

**FOCUS**
An interesting fillies' maiden. The pace was solid and winners will no doubt come from this. The first two home look useful.

### 1627 32REDSPORT.COM EBF FILLIES' NOVICE STKS (PLUS 10 RACE) 5f 21y (Tp)

**7:20** (7:20) (Class 5) 2-Y-O £2,911 (£866; £432; £216) **Stalls** Low

Form RPR

2 1 **Get Even**[16] 1335 2-9-0 0 PatCosgrave 5 69
(Jo Hughes) *led 1f: chsd ldrs: rdn to ld wl ins fnl f: r.o* **3/1**2

2 ½ **Auntie Pam (IRE)** 2-9-0 0 RichardKingscote 10 67
(Tom Dascombe) *chsd ldrs: led 4f out: rdn and hdd wl ins fnl f* **16/1**

3 ½ **Aquadabra (IRE)** 2-9-0 0 GrahamLee 6 65+
(Mick Channon) *hld up: hdwy 1/2-way: nt clr run over 1f out: r.o* **16/1**

4 nk **Felisa** 2-9-0 0 ConnorBeasley 4 64+
(David Evans) *s.i.s and hmpd s: outpcd: swtchd rt over 1f out: r.o wl ins fnl f* **25/1**

5 ½ **Diamond Pursuit** 2-9-0 0 AndrewMullen 7 63
(Jo Hughes) *sn pushed along in rr: hdwy over 1f out: rdn and edgd lft ins fnl f: r.o* **50/1**

6 2¼ **Faithful Promise** 2-9-0 0 FrannyNorton 2 54
(Mark Johnston) *prom: chsd ldr 3f out: shkn up and edgd lft fr over 1f out: no ex ins fnl f* **3/1**2

4 7 ¾ **Hellovaqueen**[7] 1496 2-8-9 0 RyanWhile(5) 1 52
(Bill Turner) *chsd ldrs: lost pl over 3f out: rdn over 1f out: no ex ins fnl f* **12/1**

8 nk **Campion** 2-9-0 0 SeanLevey 3 51
(Richard Hannon) *edgd rt s: prom: jnd ldrs 1/2-way: rdn over 1f out: wknd wl ins fnl f* **5/2**1

9 1½ **Yogi's Girl (IRE)** 2-9-0 0 JFEgan 8 45+
(David Evans) *chsd ldrs: ct wd: rdn and hung rt on outer 3f out: wknd fnl f* **10/1**3

10 2½ **Hypnotic Dancer (IRE)** 2-9-0 0 PhillipMakin 9 36
(Keith Dalgleish) *s.i.s: hld up: rdn and wknd over 1f out* **16/1**

1m 2.18s (0.28) **Going Correction** -0.05s/f (Stan) 10 Ran SP% **118.8**
Speed ratings (Par 89): **95,94,93,92,92 88,87,86,84,80**
CSF £51.40 TOTE £4.50: £1.90, £3.80, £3.90; EX 58.00 Trifecta £383.90.
**Owner** Richard Kent & Jo Hughes **Bred** Mickley Stud & Mr C J Whiston **Trained** Lambourn, Berks

**FOCUS**
A decent fillies' novices' sprint and it would be no surprise to see plenty of winners coming out of it. The front two were up there all the way.

### 1628 BETWAY STAYERS H'CAP 1m 5f 194y

**7:50** (7:52) (Class 3) (0-95,95) 4-Y-O- **£7,246** (£2,168; £1,084; £542; £270) **Stalls** Low

Form RPR

/523 1 **Every Chance (IRE)**[22] 1240 4-9-2 **90** TimmyMurphy 2 97
(Jamie Osborne) *chsd ldrs: rdn to ld over 1f out: sn hung lft: all out* **7/2**3

1313 2 hd **Midtech Star (IRE)**[14] 1361 5-9-1 **86** (v) RichardKingscote 5 92
(Ian Williams) *broke wl: sn lost pl: hdwy over 1f out: rdn and r.o: nt quite get there* **9/4**2

-632 3 nse **Ardamir (FR)**[28] 1153 5-8-10 **81** (h[1]) FergusSweeney 1 87+
(Alan King) *prom: racd keenly: pushed along 3f out: nt clr run fr over 2f out tl 1f out: sn rdn: edgd lft and r.o wl towards fin* **2/1**1

4011 4 1¾ **Luv U Whatever**[8] 1464 7-8-12 **83** AndrewMullen 4 86
(Michael Attwater) *chsd ldr: pushed along over 3f out: led over 2f out: rdn and hdd over 1f out: styd on same pce ins fnl f* **8/1**

0004 5 nse **John Reel (FR)**[14] 1360 8-9-1 **93** KatherineGlenister(7) 7 96
(David Evans) *led at stdy pce: qcknd 4f out: rdn and hdd over 2f out: ev ch over 1f out: styd on same pce ins fnl f* **7/1**

3m 1.05s (-3.75) **Going Correction** -0.05s/f (Stan)
**WFA** 4 from 5yo+ 1lb 5 Ran SP% **109.9**
Speed ratings (Par 107): **108,107,107,106,106**
CSF £11.70 TOTE £3.70: £1.80, £1.50; EX 11.90 Trifecta £23.20.
**Owner** Melbourne 10 Racing **Bred** John O'Connor **Trained** Upper Lambourn, Berks

**FOCUS**
A decent stayers' handicap despite the paucity of runners and they finished in a heap. Solid form.

### 1629 BETWAY (S) H'CAP 1m 4f 51y (Tp)

**8:20** (8:20) (Class 6) (0-60,59) 4-Y-O+ £2,587 (£770; £384; £192) **Stalls** Low

Form RPR

6600 1 **Thorntoun Care**[9] 1458 6-9-6 **58** (b[1]) TomEaves 2 63
(Iain Jardine) *hld up in tch: shkn up over 1f out: rdn to ld and hung lft wl ins fnl f: all out* **6/1**2

4000 2 hd **Senor George (IRE)**[31] 1084 10-8-8 **46** LukeMorris 9 51
(Simon Hodgson) *hld up: hdwy over 1f out: rdn and edgd lft ins fnl f: r.o* **8/1**

062/ 3 ½ **Rembrandt**[58] 5-9-7 **59** GrahamLee 4 64
(Rebecca Menzies) *hld up: hdwy over 1f out: nt clr run ins fnl f: r.o* **7/2**1

2045 4 ½ **Cold Fusion (IRE)**[7] 1486 4-8-9 **51** (v[1]) HollieDoyle(3) 1 54
(David Flood) *chsd ldrs: rdn over 1f out: styd on* **13/2**3

-060 5 1 **Just Fred (IRE)**[16] 1322 4-8-8 **47** (tp) JFEgan 8 49
(Neil Mulholland) *led: rdn over 2f out: hdd and hmpd wl ins fnl f: no ex* **7/1**

0613 6 1½ **Thou Swell (IRE)**[25] 1188 5-9-6 **58** GeorgeDowning 3 57
(Shaun Harris) *chsd ldr: rdn over 3f out: no ex ins fnl f* **10/1**

0000 7 ¾ **Steady Major (IRE)**[45] 865 5-8-10 **53** CharlieBennett(5) 5 51
(Mark Brisbourne) *prom: rdn over 1f out: no ex ins fnl f* **17/2**

330- 8 ¾ **Cool Music (IRE)**[169] 7516 7-9-4 **56** CamHardie 7 53
(Antony Brittain) *hld up: hdwy over 2f out: sn rdn: styd on same pce fr over 1f out* **12/1**

2500 9 shd **Lineman**[14] 1369 7-9-3 **55** (b) KieranO'Neill 12 52
(Sarah Hollinshead) *hld up: rdn over 2f out: nvr on terms* **15/2**

40-0 10 26 **Haaffa Sovereign**[22] 281 6-8-8 **46** (p[1]) AndrewMullen 6
(Laura Morgan) *s.i.s: pushed along early in rr: rdn and wknd over 2f out* **14/1**

150- P **Lady Rocka**[26] 4021 4-8-7 **53** (b) JoshuaBryan(7) 10 +
(Anabel K Murphy) *prom: racd keenly: sddle slipped over 8f out: lost pl over 4f out: p.u wl over 2f out* **28/1**

2m 40.35s (-0.45) **Going Correction** -0.05s/f (Stan) 11 Ran SP% **122.6**
Speed ratings (Par 101): **99,98,98,98,97 96,96,95,95,78**
CSF £55.90 CT £198.46 TOTE £7.10: £2.40, £2.90, £1.80; EX 65.00 Trifecta £375.80.There was no bid for the winner.
**Owner** W M Johnstone **Bred** W M Johnstone **Trained** Carrutherstown, D'fries & G'way

**FOCUS**
A very modest event, even for this standard. As so often the case, the place to be was near the front.

### 1630 BETWAY MIDDLE H'CAP 1m 4f 51y (Tp)

**8:50** (8:50) (Class 5) (0-70,72) 4-Y-O+ £2,911 (£866; £432; £216) **Stalls** Low

Form RPR

00-3 1 **Percys Princess**[9] 1458 6-8-2 **57** JaneElliott(7) 2 64
(Michael Appleby) *chsd ldr tl led 4f out: rdn over 2f out: styd on* **7/2**2

-134 2 1 **Go George Go (IRE)**[30] 1113 4-9-8 **71** JoeFanning 1 76+
(Alan Swinbank) *chsd ldrs: nt clr run over 3f out: sn lost pl: shkn up over 1f out: r.o to go 2nd wl ins fnl f* **11/10**1

220- 3 nk **Rum Swizzle**[210] 6315 5-9-7 **69** LukeMorris 5 73
(Harry Dunlop) *hld up: hdwy 3f out: nt clr run over 2f out: rdn to chse wnr over 1f out: styd on* **10/1**

200- 4 ½ **Hussar Ballad (USA)**[172] 7435 8-9-3 **65** CamHardie 6 68
(Antony Brittain) *hld up: racd keenly: hdwy 3f out: rdn over 1f out: styd on* **9/1**

436- 5 1¼ **Saint Thomas (IRE)**[175] 7361 10-8-10 **58** FrannyNorton 3 59
(John Mackie) *chsd ldrs: wnt 2nd over 2f out tl rdn over 1f out: no ex ins fnl f* **8/1**

006- 6 7 **Teak (IRE)**[138] 8051 10-9-3 **72** (p) LukeCatton(7) 4 62
(Ian Williams) *led at stdy pce 8f: sn rdn: wknd over 1f out* **6/1**3

2m 45.53s (4.73) **Going Correction** -0.05s/f (Stan) 6 Ran SP% **114.3**
Speed ratings (Par 103): **82,81,81,80,79 75**
CSF £8.01 TOTE £4.40: £2.00, £1.10; EX 8.40 Trifecta £50.00.
**Owner** C A Blyth **Bred** Norman A Blyth **Trained** Oakham, Rutland

**FOCUS**
No pace on early in this modest handicap. The winner got first run, but the form should work out.

## 1631 BETWAY SPRINT H'CAP — 6f 20y (Tp)
**9:20** (9:21) (Class 5) (0-75,75) 4-Y-0+ — **£2,911** (£866; £432; £216) **Stalls** Low

Form — RPR

-062 **1** **Nezar (IRE)**[19] 1290 6-9-6 **74**........................................ RobertWinston 3 — 83
(Dean Ivory) *chsd ldrs: shkn up to ld and hung lft wl ins fnl f: r.o* **11/4**[2]

5-03 **2** 1 1/4 **Gold Club**[28] 1140 6-9-7 **75**........................................(p) PatCosgrave 4 — 80
(Tom Clover) *chsd ldr: rdn to ld over 1f out: edgd lft and hdd wl ins fnl f* **4/1**[3]

400- **3** 2 3/4 **Lucky Lodge**[155] 7798 7-8-10 **64**........................................(p) CamHardie 7 — 60
(Antony Brittain) *hld up: rdn over 1f out: r.o ins fnl f: nt rch ldrs* **22/1**

/00- **4** nk **Tafteesh (IRE)**[151] 7857 4-9-0 **71**........................................ NathanEvans(3) 2 — 66
(Michael Easterby) *hld up: hdwy over 1f out: styd on same pce ins fnl f* **8/1**

1011 **5** nk **Top Of The Bank**[8] 1467 4-9-5 **73**........................................(p) TonyHamilton 1 — 67
(Kristin Stubbs) *led: rdn and hdd over 1f out: wknd wl ins fnl f* **5/2**[1]

4216 **6** 1 1/2 **Commanche**[23] 1219 8-8-6 **67**........................................(p) JoshuaBryan(7) 6 — 56
(Chris Dwyer) *prom: pushed along 4f out: rdn over 2f out: wknd fnl f* **12/1**

00-3 **7** 3/4 **Compton Park**[17] 1310 10-9-4 **72**........................................(t) DavidAllan 5 — 59
(Les Eyre) *s.i.s: hld up: rdn over 2f out: nvr on terms* **8/1**

1145 **8** 1 3/4 **Hamish McGonagain**[56] 685 4-8-13 **72**........................................(p) DavidParkes(5) 8 — 53
(Jeremy Gask) *hld up: rdn over 1f out : no rspnse* **5/1**

1m 13.16s (-1.34) **Going Correction** -0.05s/f (Stan) — **8** Ran SP% **126.2**
Speed ratings (Par 103): **106,104,100,100,99 97,96,94**
CSF £16.09 CT £215.57 TOTE £4.00: £1.50, £1.70, £5.20; EX 15.70.
**Owner** Luxham Racing **Bred** Edgeridge Ltd And Glenvale Stud **Trained** Radlett, Herts

**FOCUS**
The pace was sound for this low-grade handicap and those near the pace again saw the benefit.
T/Plt: £86.20 to a £1 stake. Pool: £72,235.13 - 611.35 winning units T/Qpdt: £36.20 to a £1 stake. Pool: £7,842.26 - 159.97 winning units **Colin Roberts**

1632 - (Foreign Racing) - See Raceform Interactive

# 1565 LEOPARDSTOWN (L-H)
Saturday, April 8
**OFFICIAL GOING: Good to yielding**

## 1633a LEOPARDSTOWN 2,000 GUINEAS TRIAL STKS (LISTED RACE) (C&G) — 1m
**2:20** (2:20) 3-Y-O
**£23,952** (£7,713; £3,653; £1,623; £811; £405)

RPR

**1** **Orderofthegarter (IRE)**[13] 1389 3-9-3 103........................................(t) SeamieHeffernan 7 — 112
(A P O'Brien, Ire) *sn led and mde rest: 2 l clr at 1/2-way: rdn further clr over 1f out and kpt on wl ins fnl f: easily* **5/4**[1]

**2** 3 3/4 **The Taj Mahal (IRE)**[160] 7722 3-9-3 108........................................(t) RyanMoore 1 — 103+
(A P O'Brien, Ire) *dwlt and pushed along briefly towards rr early: last at 1/2-way: prog into mod 4th under 2f out: rdn into mod 2nd ins fnl f and kpt on wl clsng stages wout ever troubling easy wnr* **5/1**[3]

**3** 5 **Zorion**[236] 5490 3-9-3 0........................................ KevinManning 5 — 92
(J S Bolger, Ire) *cl up: 2nd 1/2-way: jnd for 2nd appr st where short of room briefly: sn rdn in 3rd and no imp on easy wnr in mod 2nd briefly over 1f out: kpt on one pce in 3rd wl ins fnl f* **7/1**

**4** nk **Firey Speech (USA)**[210] 6349 3-9-3 105........................................ PatSmullen 6 — 91
(D K Weld, Ire) *settled bhd ldrs: 4th 1/2-way: impr to dispute 2nd on outer appr st: rdn in 2nd under 2f out and no imp on easy wnr u.p in 3rd over 1f out: kpt on one pce in 4th wl ins fnl f* **7/1**

**5** 2 1/4 **Glastonbury Song (IRE)**[190] 6930 3-9-3 0........................................ ColinKeane 2 — 86
(G M Lyons, Ire) *s.i.s and in rr early: 6th 1/2-way: rdn into st and no imp on ldrs u.p in 5th over 1f out: kpt on one pce ins fnl f* **9/2**[2]

**6** 6 **Spanish Tenor (IRE)**[167] 7559 3-9-3 100........................................ WJLee 4 — 72
(Timothy Doyle, Ire) *hld up bhd ldrs: 5th 1/2-way: tk clsr order between horses in 4th briefly appr st: sn rdn and no ex fr 2f out: one pce in mod 6th fr over 1f out* **14/1**

**7** 11 **Maximus Daia (IRE)**[6] 1522 3-9-3 0........................................ ConnorKing 3 — 47
(J P Murtagh, Ire) *prom tl sn settled bhd ldr: 3rd 1/2-way: sn rdn and wknd to rr into st* **33/1**

1m 41.06s (-0.14) **Going Correction** +0.25s/f (Good) — **7** Ran SP% **113.9**
Speed ratings: **110,106,101,100,98 92,81**
CSF £7.80 TOTE £1.80: £1.20, £1.70; DF 7.10 Trifecta £36.00.
**Owner** Derrick Smith & Mrs John Magnier & Michael Tabor **Bred** Barronstown Stud **Trained** Cashel, Co Tipperary

**FOCUS**
A straightforward success here for the well-backed winner, who seemed the stable second string on jockey bookings, but usurped his stablemate as favourite early in the day and won comfortably.

## 1634a BALLYLINCH STUD 1,000 GUINEAS TRIAL STKS (GROUP 3) (FILLIES) — 7f
**2:55** (2:57) 3-Y-O
**£32,777** (£10,555; £5,000; £2,222; £1,111; £555)

RPR

**1** **Hydrangea (IRE)**[155] 7809 3-9-0 111........................................ PBBeggy 7 — 110
(A P O'Brien, Ire) *sn led briefly tl hdd after 1f: 2nd 1/2-way: led again over 2f out: sn rdn and strly pressed fr over 1f out: kpt on wl u.p ins fnl f: all out* **5/1**[2]

**2** hd **Winter (IRE)**[237] 5443 3-9-0 89........................................ WayneLordan 12 — 109+
(A P O'Brien, Ire) *chsd ldrs: 4th 1/2-way: effrt on outer in cl 3rd over 1f out: rdn into cl 2nd ins fnl f and kpt on wl clsng stages wout matching wnr* **6/1**[3]

**3** 3/4 **Rehana (IRE)**[209] 6385 3-9-0 107........................................ PatSmullen 10 — 107
(M Halford, Ire) *chsd ldrs: 3rd 1/2-way: impr into 2nd under 2f out: rdn between horses ent fnl f and no imp on wnr u.p in 3rd wl ins fnl f: kpt on same pce* **13/2**

**4** 3/4 **Intricately (IRE)**[155] 7809 3-9-3 112........................................ DonnachaO'Brien 1 — 108
(Joseph Patrick O'Brien, Ire) *prom tl sn settled bhd ldrs: disp 6th at 1/2-way: prog on inner into 4th 1 1/2f out: rdn and no imp on ldrs ins fnl f: kpt on same pce* **7/1**

**5** 1 3/4 **Bean Feasa**[231] 5658 3-9-0 83........................................ KevinManning 9 — 100
(J S Bolger, Ire) *chsd ldrs: 5th 1/2-way: lost pl briefly 2f out and sn rdn in 6th: no imp on ldrs ins fnl f: kpt on same pce in 5th clsng stages* **20/1**

**6** 1/2 **Promise To Be True (IRE)**[160] 7721 3-9-0 112........................................ RyanMoore 11 — 99
(A P O'Brien, Ire) *hld up in tch: disp 6th at 1/2-way: sme hdwy on outer into 5th briefly ent fnl f: no ex and one pce in 6th clsng stages: nvr trbld ldrs* **9/4**[1]

**7** nk **Rain Goddess (IRE)**[210] 6348 3-9-0 96........................................ SeamieHeffernan 4 — 98
(A P O'Brien, Ire) *hld up: 10th 1/2-way: pushed along 2f out and sme hdwy into 7th ent fnl f: kpt on one pce clsng stages: nvr trbld ldrs* **6/1**[3]

**8** 1 1/2 **Drumfad Bay (IRE)**[203] 6555 3-9-0 97........................................ ColmO'Donoghue 2 — 94
(Mrs John Harrington, Ire) *hld up: 9th 1/2-way: tk clsr order between horses under 2f out and n.m.r 1 1/2f out where checked sltly and dropped to 9th: kpt on one pce in 8th ins fnl f* **16/1**

**9** 3/4 **Tinder (IRE)**[174] 7389 3-9-0 96........................................ ShaneFoley 3 — 92
(Mrs John Harrington, Ire) *settled in rr: racd keenly early: last at 1/2-way: kpt on one pce fnl 2f: nvr a factor* **16/1**

**10** 4 1/2 **Stormy Belle (IRE)**[182] 7160 3-9-0 88........................................ LeighRoche 5 — 80
(P A Fahy, Ire) *hld up: 8th 1/2-way: rdn and no ex under 2f out: one pce fnl f* **50/1**

**11** hd **Connacht Girl (IRE)**[163] 7655 3-9-0 88........................................ DeclanMcDonogh 8 — 79
(Adrian Paul Keatley, Ire) *cl up and led after 1f: 1 l clr at 1/2-way: rdn and hdd over 2f out: sn wknd* **50/1**

1m 28.43s (-0.27) **Going Correction** +0.25s/f (Good) — **11** Ran SP% **122.3**
Speed ratings: **111,110,109,109,107 106,106,104,103,98 98**
CSF £36.13 TOTE £6.50: £1.80, £2.20, £2.30; DF 46.30 Trifecta £341.70.
**Owner** Derrick Smith & Mrs John Magnier & Michael Tabor **Bred** Beauty Is Truth Syndicate **Trained** Cashel, Co Tipperary

**FOCUS**
As strong a renewal of this usually classy event as there has ever been in all likelihood, with four of the first five from the Moyglare Stud Stakes in opposition and that form held up, though there was a turnaround with the winner only finishing fourth here. Previously, Virginia Waters and Homecoming Queen won this before winning the 1,000 Guineas while Legatissimo was fourth here two years ago before winning that Classic. It wouldn't surprise if there was another winner among this classy bunch.

1635a (Foreign Racing) - See Raceform Interactive

## 1636a P.W. MCGRATH MEMORIAL BALLYSAX STKS (GROUP 3) — 1m 2f
**4:00** (4:00) 3-Y-O
**£30,256** (£9,743; £4,615; £2,051; £1,025; £512)

RPR

**1** **Rekindling**[160] 7722 3-9-3 96........................................ WayneLordan 1 — 114
(Joseph Patrick O'Brien, Ire) *hld up in tch: 5th 1/2-way: gng wl bhd ldrs into st and impr into 2nd over 1f out: rdn to ld ins fnl f and kpt on wl clsng stages* **16/1**

**2** 1/2 **Douglas Macarthur (IRE)**[160] 7722 3-9-3 110........................................ DonnachaO'Brien 2 — 113
(A P O'Brien, Ire) *chsd ldrs: 3rd 1/2-way: gng wl into st and led fr under 2f out: rdn and strly pressed over 1f out: hdd ins fnl f and kpt on wl wout matching wnr clsng stages* **8/1**[3]

**3** 1/2 **Yucatan (IRE)**[168] 7539 3-9-3 111........................................ RyanMoore 3 — 112
(A P O'Brien, Ire) *hld up: 6th 1/2-way: hdwy 2f out: rdn in 3rd over 1f out and no imp on wnr wl ins fnl f: kpt on same pce* **2/1**[1]

**4** 3 1/4 **Capri (IRE)**[160] 7722 3-9-8 113........................................ SeamieHeffernan 7 — 111
(A P O'Brien, Ire) *w.w towards rr: last at 1/2-way: gng wl into st where n.m.r between horses under 2f out: impr into 5th over 1f out: rdn into 4th ins fnl f and kpt on same pce under hands and heels clsng stages* **5/2**[2]

**5** 1 1/2 **Dubai Sand (IRE)**[161] 7707 3-9-3 104........................................ KevinManning 9 — 103
(J S Bolger, Ire) *trckd ldr: 2nd 1/2-way: rdn to ld briefly over 2f out: sn hdd and no ex whn short of room and hmpd on inner 1 1/2f out: one pce in 5th ins fnl f* **8/1**[3]

**6** 3 1/2 **Grandee (IRE)**[180] 7235 3-9-3 97........................................ ColmO'Donoghue 4 — 96
(Mrs John Harrington, Ire) *settled bhd ldrs: 4th 1/2-way: rdn over 2f out and sn no imp on ldrs: one pce in 6th ins fnl f* **10/1**

**7** hd **Brutal (IRE)**[168] 7539 3-9-3 107........................................(t) ColinKeane 8 — 95
(G M Lyons, Ire) *dwlt and settled in rr: pushed along in 8th fr 1/2-way and no imp u.p 2f out: kpt on one pce* **14/1**

**8** 6 **Legitimus (IRE)**[13] 1387 3-9-0 95........................................ RonanWhelan 5 — 80
(J S Bolger, Ire) *sn led: 1 l clr at 1/2-way: hdd over 2f out and sn wknd* **33/1**

**9** 5 **Saltonstall**[161] 7707 3-9-3 99........................................ WilliamBuick 6 — 73
(M Halford, Ire) *hld up towards rr: 7th 1/2-way: rdn under 3f out and no ex into st: sn wknd* **8/1**[3]

2m 8.88s (0.68) **Going Correction** +0.25s/f (Good) — **9** Ran SP% **119.8**
Speed ratings: **107,106,106,103,102 99,99,94,90**
CSF £141.90 TOTE £22.50: £4.60, £1.90, £1.10; DF 316.20 Trifecta £2190.90.
**Owner** Lloyd J Williams **Bred** The Pocock Family **Trained** Owning Hill, Co Kilkenny
■ Stewards' Enquiry : Donnacha O'Brien one-day ban: careless riding

**FOCUS**
A Group 3 which traditionally has a major bearing on the season with the mighty Galileo, High Chaparral, Yeats and last year's winners Harzand amongst an impressive list of past winners.

1637 - 1652a (Foreign Racing) - See Raceform Interactive

# 1383 NAAS (L-H)
Sunday, April 9
**OFFICIAL GOING: Yielding (soft in places on round course)**

## 1653a GLADNESS STKS (GROUP 3) — 7f
**3:30** (3:30) 3-Y-O+ — **£30,256** (£9,743; £4,615; £2,051; £1,025)

RPR

**1** **Diamond Fields (IRE)**[204] 6595 4-9-4 106........................................ ChrisHayes 4 — 105+
(J A Stack, Ire) *w.w in rr: last at 1/2-way: pushed along fr 2f out: rdn in 4th 1 1/2f out and r.o wl ins fnl f to ld cl home: readily* **9/2**[3]

**2** 1/2 **Alice Springs (IRE)**[155] 7837 4-9-9 118........................................ RyanMoore 5 — 109+
(A P O'Brien, Ire) *settled bhd ldr in 2nd: gng wl over 2f out: sn pushed along and impr to ld briefly wl ins fnl f: hdd cl home* **6/4**[1]

**3** 1/2 **Blue De Vega (GER)**[162] 7706 4-9-7 105........................................ PatSmullen 3 — 106
(M D O'Callaghan, Ire) *led: stl gng wl over 2f out: rdn ins fnl f and sn strly pressed: hdd wl ins fnl f and sn no ex in 3rd* **2/1**[2]

**4** 1 3/4 **Smash Williams (IRE)**[315] 2719 4-9-7 105........................................ KevinManning 1 — 101
(J S Bolger, Ire) *hld up bhd ldrs in 4th: 3rd 1/2-way: pushed along 2f out and no imp on ldrs u.p in rr ent fnl f: kpt on same pce in 4th ins fnl f* **13/2**

**5** 1 **Gordon Lord Byron (IRE)**[16] 1353 9-9-12 103........................................ WayneLordan 2 — 103
(T Hogan, Ire) *trckd ldrs in 3rd early: racd keenly: 4th 1/2-way: wnt 3rd again over 2f out: rdn and no ex 1 1/2f out: wknd to rr ins fnl f* **16/1**

1m 30.05s (2.55) — **5** Ran SP% **110.7**
CSF £11.84 TOTE £5.80: £2.70, £1.10; DF 13.20 Trifecta £24.50.
**Owner** Ms Mary Slack **Bred** Sweetmans Bloodstock **Trained** Golden, Co. Tipperary

**FOCUS**
A fairly steady pace, with the winner quickening well to give Fozzy Stack his first Group-race success in his own right. The winner and third are rated in line with last year's pick.

## 1654a DR VINCENT O'BRIEN CENTENARY ALLEGED STKS (GROUP 3) 1m 2f
4:05 (4:05) 4-Y-0+ £31,769 (£10,230; £4,846; £2,153; £1,076)

RPR

1 **Air Pilot**232 5652 8-9-6 113 FranBerry 5 115+
(Ralph Beckett) *hld up: 4th 1/2-way: tk clsr order fr 3f out and impr into 2nd fr 2f out: rdn and clsd u.p ins fnl f to dispute cl home and led fnl strides* **6/1**3

2 *hd* **Success Days (IRE)**211 6354 5-9-6 114 ShaneFoley 4 115
(K J Condon, Ire) *attempted to make all: over 1 l clr at 1/2-way: stl gng wl over 2f out: sn pushed along: rdn ins fnl f and reduced advantage: all out cl home where jnd and hdd fnl strides* **11/4**2

3 3 1/4 **US Army Ranger (IRE)**176 7353 4-9-6 119 RyanMoore 1 109+
(A P O'Brien, Ire) *chsd ldrs in 3rd: racd keenly early: lost pl over 2f out: sn pushed along and regained 3rd under 2f out: rdn and no imp on ldrs ent fnl f: kpt on same pce* **1/1**1

4 3 3/4 **Stellar Mass (IRE)**182 7196 4-9-6 113 KevinManning 2 101
(J S Bolger, Ire) *settled bhd ldr in 2nd: pushed along fr 3f out and sn no imp on ldr u.p in 3rd: one pce in 4th ins fnl f: jst hld 4th* **9/1**

5 *shd* **Lustrous Light (IRE)**248 5095 4-9-3 100 ColinKeane 3 98
(G M Lyons, Ire) *w.w in rr: last at 1/2-way: short of room on inner 2f out and sn swtchd rt: kpt on one pce ins fnl f: jst failed for 4th: nvr trbld ldrs* **8/1**

2m 18.75s (3.15) 5 Ran SP% 112.1
CSF £22.83 TOTE £5.30: £1.80, £2.00; DF 20.00 Trifecta £37.20.
**Owner** Lady Cobham **Bred** Lady Cobham **Trained** Kimpton, Hants

**FOCUS**
The home defence, including last season's Derby second as well as the Irish Derby third, proved inadequate against a 113-rated British raider. The runner-up is the best guide to the form.

1655 - 1656a (Foreign Racing) - See Raceform Interactive

# 1235 CHANTILLY (R-H)
Sunday, April 9

**OFFICIAL GOING: Turf: good; polytrack: standard**

## 1657a PRIX VANTEAUX (GROUP 3) (3YO FILLIES) (TURF) 1m 1f
2:45 (2:45) 3-Y-0 £34,188 (£13,675; £10,256; £6,837; £3,418)

RPR

1 **Gold Luck (FR)**171 7491 3-9-0 MaximeGuyon 7 104
(F Head, France) *a cl up on outer: drvn to chal 2f out: jnd ldr 1 1/2f out: hdd 150yds out: r.o gamely to ld cl home* **7/2**2

2 *shd* **Monroe Bay (IRE)**213 3-9-0 Pierre-CharlesBoudot 9 104
(P Bary, France) *racd keenly: sn pressing ldr under restraint: led after 3f: drvn whn chal 2f out: jnd 1 1/2f out: rallied u.p and led again 150yds out: r.o gamely: hdd cl home* **11/8**1

3 *hd* **Hebah (IRE)**171 7491 3-9-0 ChristopheSoumillon 1 103+
(J-C Rouget, France) *dwlt: w.w in tch on inner: dropped into fnl pair 3f out gng wl: clsd but nt clr run over 1 1/2f out: sn rdn and r.o fnl f: nt quite get there* **6/1**3

4 3/4 **Vue Fantastique (FR)**21 3-9-0 OlivierPeslier 2 102+
(F Chappet, France) *cl up tl led on inner after 2f: hdd after 3f but remained handy: 3rd and nt clr run 1 1/2f out: styd on u.p fnl f: nt pce to chal* **18/1**

5 1 **Penny Lane (GER)**162 7717 3-9-0 GeraldMosse 6 100
(F-H Graffard, France) *hld up in rr: clsd on outer 3f out: rdn 1 1/2f fr home: kpt on u.p ins fnl f: nvr on terms* **10/1**

6 1 3/4 **Uni**56 712 3-9-0 TonyPiccone 4 96
(F Chappet, France) *racd keenly and led: hdd after 2f and settled in midfield: drvn in 5th and nt qckn 2f out: kpt on same pce fnl f* **7/1**

7 3 **Szolnok (USA)**113 3-9-0 (b1) CristianDemuro 3 90
(S Cerulis, France) *w.w towards rr: last and pushed along 3f out but no imp: kpt on past btn horse ins fnl f: nvr in contention* **22/1**

8 1 1/2 **Ghurfah**48 3-9-0 IoritzMendizabal 5 87
(J-C Rouget, France) *towards rr early: moved into midfield bef 1/2-way: 4th whn outpcd under 2f out and rdn: wknd fnl f* **10/1**

1m 50.21s (-0.89) **Going Correction** -0.225s/f (Firm) 8 Ran SP% 118.9
Speed ratings: **94,93,93,93,92 90,87,86**
PARI-MUTUEL (all including 1 euro stake): WIN 4.20 PLACE 1.30, 1.20, 1.60 DF 4.20 SF 11.10.
**Owner** Wertheimer & Frere **Bred** Wertheimer & Frere **Trained** France

## 1658a PRIX LA FORCE (GROUP 3) (3YO COLTS & GELDINGS) (TURF) 1m 1f
3:30 (3:30) 3-Y-0 £34,188 (£13,675; £10,256; £6,837; £3,418)

RPR

1 **Graphite (FR)**164 3-9-2 Pierre-CharlesBoudot 1 104
(A Fabre, France) *w.w in midfield on inner: clsd to be 4th travelling wl 2f out: angled out and drvn over 1 1/2f out: qcknd to ld ent fnl f: r.o u.p* **6/1**3

2 *nk* **Phelps Win (FR)**21 3-9-2 MaximeGuyon 9 104
(H-A Pantall, France) *chsd ldng trio: rdn to chal ins fnl f: r.o u.p: a jst hld* **11/1**

3 *hd* **Franz Schubert**183 3-9-2 MickaelBarzalona 6 104+
(A Fabre, France) *w.w towards rr on outer: in fnl trio and plenty to do 2 1/2f out: hdwy 1 1/2f out: r.o fnl f: nt quite get there* **11/10**1

4 3/4 **Kensai (FR)**22 3-9-2 CristianDemuro 10 102
(Simone Brogi, France) *settled in rr: in fnl trio and plenty to do 2 1/2f out: drvn and hdwy 2f out: styd on to chal ent fnl f: run flattened out last 75yds* **20/1**

5 *nk* **Saglawy (FR)**31 1114 3-9-2 StephanePasquier 4 101
(N Clement, France) *cl up on inner: angled out and led w over 1 1/2f to run: sn rdn: hdd ent fnl f: no ex* **12/1**

6 1 1/4 **Be My Sheriff (GER)**41 3-9-2 TheoBachelot 7 98
(M Rulec, Germany) *settled in midfield: 6th and drvn 2f out: sn rdn and no imp: styd on fnl 150yds: nt pce to get on terms* **33/1**

7 1/2 **Phoceen (FR)**31 1114 3-9-2 IoritzMendizabal 3 97
(F Chappet, France) *hld up towards rr: tk clsr or 3f out: nt clr run 2f out: hrd rdn and kpt on fnl f: nvr able to get involved* **12/1**

8 2 1/2 **Prinz Hlodowig (FR)**161 7722 3-9-2 VincentCheminaud 12 92
(M Delzangles, France) *w.w in fnl pair: sme prog 1 1/2f out but effrt sn petered out: nvr in contention* **10/1**

9 4 **King Of Spades (FR)**13 3-9-2 AntoineHamelin 5 84
(F Vermeulen, France) *hld up in midfield: drvn and lost pl over 2 1/2f out: nvr a factor* **25/1**

10 2 **Chapa (FR)**21 3-9-2 OlivierPeslier 8 79
(N Bellanger, France) *chsd ldr: drvn and nt qckn 2f out: wknd 1 1/2f out* **40/1**

11 6 **High Alpha (FR)**183 7169 3-9-2 ChristopheSoumillon 11 67
(Mario Hofer, Germany) *broke wl fr wd draw and led: sn swtchd ins to rail: hdd over 1 1/2f out: sn wknd* **5/1**2

1m 48.27s (-2.83) **Going Correction** -0.225s/f (Firm) 11 Ran SP% 125.4
Speed ratings: **103,102,102,101,101 100,100,97,94,92 87**
PARI-MUTUEL (all including 1 euro stake): WIN 1.80 PLACE 2.10, 1.90, 1.30 DF 18.60 SF 31.20.
**Owner** Godolphin SNC **Bred** Scea Haras De Saint Pair **Trained** Chantilly, France

## 1659a PRIX D'HARCOURT (GROUP 2) (4YO+) (TURF) 1m 2f
4:10 (4:10) 4-Y-0+ £63,333 (£24,444; £11,666; £7,777; £3,888)

RPR

1 **Cloth Of Stars (IRE)**21 1271 4-9-0 MickaelBarzalona 10 116+
(A Fabre, France) *racd keenly: hld up in fnl quartet: drvn and hdwy on outer w 1 1/2f to run: wnt 3l 3rd ent fnl f: r.o to ld cl home* **4/5**1

2 *nk* **Mekhtaal**204 6597 4-9-0 GregoryBenoist 8 115
(J-C Rouget, France) *cl up: led after 2f: hdd 3 1/2f out but remained cl up: rdn to ld 1f out: styd on gamely u.p: hdd cl home* **15/2**3

3 1 1/2 **Maniaco**173 7456 4-9-0 MaximeGuyon 3 112
(A Fabre, France) *chsd ldng trio: 3rd and pushed along over 2f out: unable qck appr 1f out: styd on fnl 150yds: tk 3rd cl home* **20/1**

4 *nk* **Robin Of Navan (FR)**154 7841 4-9-0 CristianDemuro 6 111
(Harry Dunlop) *sn led: hdd after 2f but styd cl up: led again 3 1/2f out: drvn and rallied 2 1/2f out: rdn and hdd 1f out: same pce fnl f: lost 3rd cl home* **16/1**

5 2 **Palace Prince (GER)**21 1271 5-9-0 (p) EddyHardouin 9 107
(Jean-Pierre Carvalho, Germany) *settled midfield on outer: drvn 2f out: kpt on ins fnl f: nvr able to chal* **40/1**

6 *hd* **Best Fouad (FR)**38 6-9-0 StephanePasquier 4 107
(F Rohaut, France) *w.w in fnl pair: last and drvn 2f out: styd on fnl f: nvr in contention* **10/1**

7 *nse* **One Foot In Heaven (IRE)**119 8329 5-9-3 ChristopheSoumillon 7 110
(A De Royer-Dupre, France) *w.w in fnl pair: drvn over 1 1/2f out: styd on ins fnl f: nt pce to get involved* **4/1**2

8 *nse* **Cafe Royal (GER)**21 1271 6-9-0 OlivierPeslier 1 107
(A Schutz, France) *settled towards rr: clsd into midfield 3 1/2f out: one pce u.p fnl 1 1/2f* **25/1**

9 5 **Raseed**266 4439 4-9-0 AurelienLemaitre 5 97
(F Head, France) *w.w towards rr: drvn into midfield over 2f out: sn rdn and btn* **33/1**

10 7 **Star Victory (FR)**21 1271 6-9-0 IoritzMendizabal 2 83
(J-L Dubord, France) *chsd ldrs: rdn and nt qckn 2f out: dropped away wl over 1f out* **16/1**

11 9 **Gambissara (FR)**149 7929 4-8-10 AntoineHamelin 11 61
(Lennart Hammer-Hansen, Germany) *cl up on outer: drvn but no imp 2 1/2f out: sn rdn and wknd* **50/1**

1m 58.77s (-6.03) **Going Correction** -0.225s/f (Firm) 11 Ran SP% 124.1
Speed ratings: **115,114,113,113,111 111,111,111,107,101 94**
PARI-MUTUEL (all including 1 euro stake): WIN 1.90 PLACE 1.10, 1.90, 2.60 DF 6.50 SF 8.20.
**Owner** Godolphin SNC **Bred** Peter Anastasiou **Trained** Chantilly, France

## 1660a PRIX SIGY (GROUP 3) (3YO) (TURF) 6f
4:50 (4:50) 3-Y-0 £34,188 (£13,675; £10,256; £6,837; £3,418)

RPR

1 **Fas (IRE)**24 1235 3-9-0 MaximeGuyon 9 113+
(Mme Pia Brandt, France) *a in ldng pair: led appr 1/2-way: kicked for home wl over 1 1/2f out: clr fnl f: pushed out* **5/1**2

2 3 1/2 **Precieuse (IRE)**23 3-8-10 Pierre-CharlesBoudot 4 98
(F Chappet, France) *dwlt: settled in fnl trio: hdwy 1 1/2f out: rdn to go 2nd ins fnl f: no ch w wnr* **6/1**3

3 2 1/2 **Spanish Fly (IRE)**24 1235 3-8-10 VincentCheminaud 2 90+
(M Delcher Sanchez, France) *w.w in rr: last 1/2-way: hdwy wl over 1f out: r.o to go 3rd cl home: nvr trbld ldrs* **20/1**

4 *nk* **Capchop (FR)**27 3-9-0 (b) Jean-BernardEyquem 8 93
(P Sogorb, France) *chsd ldrs: 6th and drvn 1 1/2f out: styd on u.p fnl f* **16/1**

5 *nse* **Tresorier**24 1235 3-9-0 ThierryThulliez 6 93
(Mme C Head-Maarek, France) *chsd ldrs: 3rd and hrd rdn under 1 1/2f out: kpt on ent fnl f: run flattened out last 50yds and dropped two pls* **17/2**

6 3 **Mrs Danvers**184 7113 3-9-0 RichardKingscote 10 83
(Jonathan Portman) *prom on outer under a firm hold: 3rd and drvn 1 1/2f out but no imp: dropped away fnl f* **8/11**1

7 3/4 **Farshad (GER)**159 3-9-0 (b) AntoineHamelin 7 81
(Henk Grewe, Germany) *led on stands' rail: hdd bef 1/2-way: remained prom tl wknd over 1f out* **33/1**

8 1 **Tahoo (IRE)**145 7972 3-8-10 AlexisBadel 3 74
(K R Burke) *chsd ldrs: rdn and no imp 1 1/2f out: sn btn* **33/1**

9 4 **Upendi (FR)**24 1235 3-8-10 IoritzMendizabal 5 61
(Robert Collet, France) *settled in midfield on outer: rdn and wknd ins fnl 1 1/2f* **22/1**

10 3 **Hyper Hyper**102 8564 3-9-0 ChristopheSoumillon 1 55
(Mario Hofer, Germany) *hld up towards rr: bhd whn eased ins fnl f* **22/1**

1m 8.43s (-2.97) **Going Correction** -0.225s/f (Firm) 10 Ran SP% 124.6
Speed ratings: **110,105,102,101,101 97,96,95,89,85**
PARI-MUTUEL (all including 1 euro stake): WIN 6.60 PLACE 1.90, 1.80, 2.80 DF 8.10 SF 20.30.
**Owner** A Jathiere & Z Bifov **Bred** Zalim Bifov **Trained** France

# DUSSELDORF (R-H)
Sunday, April 9

**OFFICIAL GOING: Turf: good**

## 1661a XTIP FRUHJAHRSMEILE (GROUP 3) (4YO+) (TURF) 1m
4:30 4-Y-0+ £27,350 (£10,256; £5,128; £2,564; £1,709)

RPR

1 **Wonnemond (GER)**161 4-9-0 BayarsaikhanGanbat 7 108
(S Smrczek, Germany) *w.w in midfield: drvn to cl on outer fr 2f out: sustained run to ld ent fnl f: rdn out* **42/10**2

2 1 **Degas (GER)**[161] 4-9-0 0 AdriedeVries 5 106
(Markus Klug, Germany) *w.w in fnl trio: clsd u.p 1 1/2f out: styd on fnl f: a hld by wnr* **23/10**[1]
3 3/4 **Diplomat (GER)**[44] 914 6-9-4 0 StephenHellyn 1 108
(Mario Hofer, Germany) *racd keenly: hld up in midfield: 5th and drvn 2f out: styd on u.p fnl f: nvr able to chal* **112/10**
4 hd **Millowitsch (GER)**[328] 2315 4-8-11 0 AndreasHelfenbein 6 101
(Markus Klug, Germany) *pressed ldr on outer: drvn to ld under 1 1/2f out: hdd ent fnl f: kpt on u.p* **23/10**[1]
5 1/2 **De Treville**[365] 5-8-11 0 EduardoPedroza 3 100
(A Wohler, Germany) *chsd ldrs: rdn and ev ch 1 1/2f out: same pce fnl f* **47/10**
6 1/2 **Nordico (GER)**[135] 8117 6-8-11 0 (p) AlexanderPietsch 8 99
(Mario Hofer, Germany) *settled in last: hdwy on outer 1 1/2f out: styd on ins fnl f: nvr plcd to chal* **31/1**
7 2 1/4 **Palang (USA)**[144] 5-9-0 0 FilipMinarik 4 96
(Andreas Suborics, Germany) *racd in fnl pair: rdn and effrt 1 1/2f out: wl hld fnl f* **187/10**
8 1 3/4 **Baroncello (GER)**[26] 4-8-11 0 IanFerguson 2 89
(Andreas Suborics, Germany) *led: pushed along 2 1/2f out: hdd under 1 1/2f out: wknd fnl f* **22/5**[3]

1m 34.99s (-6.17) **8** Ran SP% **132.3**
PARI-MUTUEL (all including 10 euro stake): WIN 52 PLACE: 12, 12, 18; SF: 158.
**Owner** Stall Frohnbach **Bred** K H Schmoock **Trained** Germany

1662 - 1672a (Foreign Racing) - See Raceform Interactive

# REDCAR (L-H)

## Monday, April 10

**OFFICIAL GOING: Good to firm (good in places; 8.5)**
Wind: Light half against Weather: Cloudy

## 1673 RACING UK DAY PASS JUST £10 NOVICE STKS 5f
**2:20** (2:20) (Class 5) 2-Y-O **£3,234** (£962; £481; £240) **Stalls** Centre

Form RPR
1 **Inviolable Spirit (IRE)** 2-9-2 0 TonyHamilton 5 70+
(Richard Fahey) *towards rr early and sn niggled along: hdwy to trck ldrs 1/2-way: effrt and nt clr run over 1f out: sn swtchd lft and rdn to ld ent fnl f: kpt on wl* **17/2**
2 3/4 **Tember** 2-9-2 0 AndrewMullen 12 67
(David Barron) *wnt rt s: in tch on outer: hdwy over 2f out: chsd ldrs over 1f out: sn rdn and edgd lft ins fnl f: kpt on* **4/1**[1]
3 3/4 **Rockin Fella (IRE)** 2-9-2 0 PJMcDonald 11 65
(K R Burke) *trckd ldrs: hdwy 1/2-way: cl up 2f out: rdn to chal and ev ch over 1f out: carried sltly rt ins fnl f: kpt on* **5/1**[2]
4 1/2 **Nobrassnolass (IRE)** 2-8-11 0 RichardKingscote 2 58
(Tom Dascombe) *cl up: effrt 2f out: sn rdn along and ev ch: drvn and kpt on same pce fnl f* **6/1**[3]
5 1/2 **Marnie James** 2-9-2 0 TomEaves 4 61
(Iain Jardine) *t.k.h: sn slt ld: pushed along 2f out: rdn over 1f out: drvn and hdd ent fnl f: sn edgd rt and kpt on same pce* **7/1**
6 1 **Ventura Gold (IRE)** 2-9-2 0 PaulHanagan 3 60
(Richard Fahey) *green and sn pushed along towards rr: hdwy 2f out: chsd ldrs whn n.m.r over 1f out: sn swtchd rt and rdn whn hmpd ins fnl f: no ch after* **5/1**[2]
7 1 **Just For The Craic (IRE)** 2-9-2 0 JamesSullivan 1 54
(Ruth Carr) *t.k.h early: in tch: hdwy to chse ldrs 1/2-way: rdn along wl over 1f out: sn one pce* **25/1**
8 3/4 **Lady Lintera (IRE)** 2-8-11 0 BenCurtis 7 46
(Ann Duffield) *cl up: rdn along over 2f out: sn wknd* **20/1**
9 1 1/2 **Sandytown (IRE)** 2-9-2 0 ShaneGray 10 46+
(Kevin Ryan) *rrd and lost several l s: detached tl styd on appr fnl f* **12/1**
10 3 **Brandy Station (IRE)** 2-9-2 0 BarryMcHugh 6 35
(Tony Coyle) *t.k.h early: chsd ldrs: rdn along over 2f out: sn wknd* **40/1**
11 1 1/2 **Savannah's Show** 2-8-11 0 CamHardie 9 25
(Richard Guest) *a towards rr* **20/1**

58.72s (0.12) **Going Correction** -0.075s/f (Good) **11** Ran SP% **114.1**
Speed ratings (Par 92): **96,94,93,92,92 90,88,87,85,80 78**
CSF £39.05 TOTE £10.60: £3.30, £1.70, £1.70; EX 44.50 Trifecta £364.00.
**Owner** D Bardsley **Bred** Tally-Ho Stud **Trained** Musley Bank, N Yorks

**FOCUS**
The going was going to firm. All 12 were making their debut for this interesting contest which was run at a sound pace.

## 1674 RACINGUK.COM/HD (S) STKS 5f 217y
**2:50** (2:52) (Class 6) 3-Y-O+ **£2,897** (£855; £427) **Stalls** Centre

Form RPR
0-03 1 **Noah Amor (IRE)**[55] 732 4-9-10 65 BarryMcHugh 8 60+
(Richard Fahey) *trckd ldr: hdwy to chal over 1f out: rdn to ld ins fnl f: drvn out* **2/1**[2]
-055 2 hd **The Magic Pencil (IRE)**[38] 1007 4-9-3 63 (v[1]) SeamusCronin(7) 6 59
(Kevin Ryan) *led: rdn along over 1f out: drvn and hdd ins fnl f: kpt on wl u.p* **9/2**[3]
40-0 3 1 1/2 **A J Cook (IRE)**[38] 1006 7-9-10 46 DavidAllan 3 55
(Ron Barr) *trckd ldng pair: hdwy over 2f out: rdn along wl over 1f out: drvn and kpt on same pce fnl f* **25/1**
4003 4 1 3/4 **Gramercy (IRE)**[16] 1365 10-9-7 76 (p) PaulHanagan 4 46
(Patrick Morris) *hld up in tch: hdwy over 2f out: rdn to chse ldng pair on outer over 1f out: sn drvn and btn* **11/10**[1]
300- 5 1 1/2 **Secret City (IRE)**[226] 5889 11-9-7 52 (b) DanielTudhope 1 41
(Rebecca Bastiman) *in tch: hdwy over 2f out: rdn along wl over 1f out: sn drvn and btn* **16/1**

1m 11.04s (-0.76) **Going Correction** -0.075s/f (Good) **5** Ran SP% **108.9**
Speed ratings (Par 101): **102,101,99,97,95**
CSF £10.81 TOTE £3.10: £1.90, £2.70; EX 10.50 Trifecta £52.40.There was no bid for the winner.
**Owner** Middleham Park Racing XIV **Bred** Mrs Claire Doyle **Trained** Musley Bank, N Yorks

**FOCUS**
A typically weak contest for the grade. It's been rated negatively around the third.

## 1675 BECOME A REDCAR ANNUAL BADGEHOLDER TODAY MAIDEN STKS (DIV I) 1m 2f 1y
**3:20** (3:21) (Class 5) 3-4-Y-O **£3,234** (£962; £481; £240) **Stalls** Low

Form RPR
430- 1 **Redicean**[184] 7151 3-8-9 85 PaulMulrennan 2 77
(Peter Chapple-Hyam) *prom on inner: hdwy and cl up over 3f out: rdn along over 2f out: drvn over 1f out: styd on along inner to ld ins fnl f: kpt on strly* **5/4**[1]
-3 2 2 3/4 **Testbourne (IRE)**[20] 1293 3-8-6 0 JordanVaughan(3) 8 72
(K R Burke) *led: pushed clr jst over 2f out: rdn wl over 1f out: hdd and drvn ins fnl f: kpt on same pce* **20/1**
2- 3 1 1/2 **Migyaas (USA)**[268] 4387 3-8-4 0 GeorgeWood(5) 6 69
(Saeed bin Suroor) *trckd ldng pair: pushed along over 3f out: rdn and sltly outpcd over 2f out: styd on wl appr fnl f* **7/2**[3]
3- 4 8 **Lord Commander**[185] 7125 3-8-9 0 PaulHanagan 5 53
(Richard Fahey) *trckd ldrs: hdwy on outer over 3f out: rdn along over 2f out: drvn wl over 1f out: sn wknd* **2/1**[2]
0- 5 1 **Bing Bang Bank (IRE)**[160] 7740 3-8-9 0 SamJames 1 51+
(David Barron) *towards rr: pushed along 4f out: hdwy 3f out: plugged on u.p appr fnl f* **14/1**
06 6 2 1/2 **Ibreeq (IRE)**[31] 1122 4-10-0 0 JackGarritty 4 50?
(Roger Fell) *chsd ldrs: rdn along 4f out: sn outpcd* **150/1**
7 15 **Silk Trader (IRE)** 3-8-4 0 JamesSullivan 9 11
(Sharon Watt) *a rr: bhd fnl 3f* **66/1**
8 37 **Jacques** 4-10-0 0 BenCurtis 7
(John Balding) *a rr: bhd fnl 3f* **100/1**

2m 5.79s (-1.31) **Going Correction** -0.075s/f (Good)
**WFA** 3 from 4yo 19lb **8** Ran SP% **114.6**
Speed ratings (Par 103): **102,99,98,92,91 89,77,47**
CSF £28.21 TOTE £1.90: £1.10, £4.70, £1.80; EX 26.20 Trifecta £93.90.
**Owner** Dreaming Victory **Bred** Cheveley Park Stud Ltd **Trained** Newmarket, Suffolk

**FOCUS**
Not the strongest maiden. The winner has been rated close to his best.

## 1676 BECOME A REDCAR ANNUAL BADGEHOLDER TODAY MAIDEN STKS (DIV II) 1m 2f 1y
**3:50** (3:52) (Class 5) 3-4-Y-O **£3,234** (£962; £481; £240) **Stalls** Low

Form RPR
3- 1 **Kensington Star**[310] 2914 4-9-9 0 (p[1]) ShirleyTeasdale(5) 6 77+
(Keith Dalgleish) *hld uptowards rr: gd hdwy on outer over 3f out: chal over 2f out: rdn to ld wl over 1f out: sn edgd lft: drvn and edgd lft ins fnl f: kpt on* **11/4**[2]
2 1 1/4 **Sketch Book Venue (IRE)** 3-8-9 0 NeilFarley 5 68
(Alan Swinbank) *trckd ldng pair: cl up over 3f out: pushed along wl over 2f out: ev ch whn n.m.r 1 1/2f out: sn swtchd rt and rdn: styd on fnl f* **5/2**[1]
4-3 3 1/2 **The Grey Warrior (IRE)**[26] 1198 3-8-9 0 TomEaves 7 67
(Kevin Ryan) *led: rdn along wl over 2f out: hdd wl over 1f out: drvn to chse wnr and styng on along inner whn n.m.r ins fnl f: kpt on same pce* **5/2**[1]
4 3 **Royal Headley (IRE)** 3-8-9 0 SamJames 9 61
(David O'Meara) *chsd ldrs: rdn along wl over 2f out: sn one pce* **7/2**[3]
0- 5 3 1/2 **Kelpie Spirit (IRE)**[261] 4642 3-8-4 0 PhilDennis(5) 2 54
(John Weymes) *trckd ldrs on inner: pushed along 4f out: rdn 3f out: sn wknd* **66/1**
6 3 **Nightdress (IRE)** 3-8-4 0 DuranFentiman 1 43
(Tony Coyle) *a rr* **25/1**
5/6- 7 1 1/4 **Druid's Diamond**[372] 1217 4-10-0 0 DougieCostello 8 50
(Mark Walford) *trckd ldr: cl up after 3f: pushed along over 4f out: rdn over 3f out: sn drvn and wknd* **66/1**
00- 8 24 **Bobbys Helmet (IRE)**[221] 6054 3-8-9 0 DavidAllan 4
(David C Griffiths) *a towards rr* **100/1**

2m 7.64s (0.54) **Going Correction** -0.075s/f (Good)
**WFA** 3 from 4yo 19lb **8** Ran SP% **113.9**
Speed ratings (Par 103): **94,93,92,90,87 85,84,64**
CSF £9.90 TOTE £3.30: £1.30, £1.10, £1.30; EX 12.80 Trifecta £28.10.
**Owner** J S Morrison **Bred** Cheveley Park Stud Ltd **Trained** Carluke, S Lanarks

**FOCUS**
Not the strongest of maidens. The time was modest and there's some doubt about the level of the form.

## 1677 RACING UK PROFITS RETURNED TO RACING H'CAP 7f 219y
**4:20** (4:25) (Class 4) (0-85,86) 4-Y-O+ **£6,469** (£1,925; £962; £481) **Stalls** Centre

Form RPR
502- 1 **Torrid**[166] 7623 6-8-11 77 NathanEvans(3) 3 85
(Michael Easterby) *trckd ldrs: hdwy and cl up 3f out: led over 1f out: sn rdn and kpt on strly* **8/1**[2]
301- 2 1 3/4 **Heir To A Throne (FR)**[216] 6217 4-9-4 86 LewisEdmunds(5) 9 90
(Kevin Ryan) *trckd ldng pair: cl up 1/2-way: led wl over 2f out: rdn and hdd over 1f out: sn drvn and kpt on* **4/1**[1]
-431 3 1/2 **Newmarket Warrior (IRE)**[10] 1473 6-8-0 70 oh2(p) JamieGormley(7) 18 73
(Iain Jardine) *dwlt and rr: grad swtchd lft to far side 1/2-way: hdwy to chse ldrs wl over 1f out: rdn and kpt on wl fnl f: nrst fin* **18/1**
000- 4 hd **Character Onesie (IRE)**[136] 8092 5-8-12 75 PaulHanagan 16 78
(Richard Fahey) *hld up towards rr: hdwy on outer 2f out: rdn to chse ldrs ins fnl f: sn drvn: edgd lft and kpt on* **16/1**
/5-6 5 shd **Pullman Brown (USA)**[48] 850 5-8-12 75 PaddyAspell 1 77
(Philip Kirby) *cl up: over 5f out: pushed along and hdd 3f out: rdn wl over 1f out: drvn and kpt on same pce fnl f* **10/1**[3]
00-6 6 shd **Abushamah (IRE)**[10] 1472 6-9-4 81 JamesSullivan 17 83
(Ruth Carr) *rr: hdwy 2f out: rdn over 1f out: kpt on fnl f: nrst fin* **16/1**
0505 7 3/4 **Shamaheart (IRE)**[10] 1472 7-9-5 82 (p) DavidAllan 13 82
(Geoffrey Harker) *hld up towards rr: hdwy over 2f out: rdn to chse ldrs over 1f out: kpt on fnl f* **20/1**
50-0 8 3/4 **Nicholas T**[52] 782 5-8-10 73 SamJames 12 71
(Jim Goldie) *hld up in midfield: effrt over 2f out: sn rdn along and n.d* **20/1**
411- 9 hd **Maifalki (FR)**[109] 8498 4-9-5 82 DougieCostello 4 80
(Mark Walford) *stmbld s: trckd ldrs: hdwy over 2f out: rdn along wl over 1f out: grad wknd* **12/1**
330- 10 nk **Bernie's Boy**[205] 6576 4-9-0 77 TonyHamilton 10 74
(Roger Fell) *stmbld s: led: hdd over 5f out: cl up: rdn along wl over 2f out: grad wknd* **25/1**
550- 11 1 3/4 **Flyboy (IRE)**[164] 7671 4-9-2 79 DanielTudhope 15 72
(David O'Meara) *nvr bttr than midfield* **8/1**[2]

00-0 **12** *nk* **Zealous (IRE)**[8] 1512 4-9-2 **79** JoeFanning 7 71
(Alan Swinbank) *in tch: rdn along wl over 12f out: sn wknd* **10/1**[3]

033- **13** *shd* **Mustaqbal (IRE)**[245] 5223 5-8-10 **73** PaulMulrennan 11 65
(Michael Dods) *t.k.h: trckd ldrs: pushed along over 2f out: sn rdn and wknd over 1f out* **16/1**

301- **14** *shd* **Be Kool (IRE)**[214] 6265 4-8-9 **72** CamHardie 14 64
(Brian Ellison) *hld up: a towards rr* **50/1**

613- **15** *1 ½* **Alexandrakollontai (IRE)**[147] 7957 7-9-2 **84** (b) RowanScott(5) 8 72
(Alistair Whillans) *stmbld and dwlt s: a rr* **40/1**

1m 36.24s (-0.36) **Going Correction** -0.075s/f (Good) **15** Ran SP% **108.8**
Speed ratings (Par 105): **98,96,95,95,95 95,94,93,93,93 91,91,91,91,89**
CSF £30.11 CT £425.49 TOTE £8.90: £3.80, £1.90, £4.40; EX 35.60 Trifecta £691.30.
**Owner** J Blackburn, Mrs A Bartram & S Winter **Bred** Juddmonte Farms Ltd **Trained** Sheriff Hutton, N Yorks

■ Midnight Macchiato was withdrawn. Price at time of withdrawal 13/2. Rule 4 applies to all bets - deduction 10 pence in the pound.

**FOCUS**
The pace was steady for this competitive handicap. Its been rated as ordinary form.

## 1678 RACING UK STRAIGHT MILE H'CAP (REDCAR STRAIGHT MILE SERIES QUALIFIER) 7f 219y
**4:55** (4:56) (Class 5) (0-75,72) 3-Y-O **£3,234** (£962; £481; £240) **Stalls** Centre

Form RPR

446- **1** **Miss Sheridan (IRE)**[115] 8405 3-8-9 **63** NathanEvans(3) 10 70
(Michael Easterby) *mde all: rdn over 1f out: kpt on strly* **15/2**[3]

50-6 **2** *2 ¼* **Heir Of Excitement (IRE)**[30] 1149 3-9-7 **72** ShaneGray 8 74
(Kevin Ryan) *trckd ldrs: hdwy to chse wnr over 1f out: rdn and edgd lft ins fnl f: kpt on* **11/2**[2]

334- **3** *1 ½* **Golconda Prince (IRE)**[198] 6771 3-8-13 **64** PaulHanagan 3 62
(Richard Fahey) *cl up: rdn along 2f out: drvn over 1f out: kpt on same pce ins fnl f* **11/4**[1]

160- **4** *nk* **Geophony (IRE)**[205] 6563 3-9-7 **72** JoeFanning 5 70
(Mark Johnston) *hld up in tch: hdwy over 2f out: rdn over 1f out: drvn and kpt on same pce fnl f* **8/1**

600- **5** *nse* **Breakwater Bay (IRE)**[226] 5884 3-8-12 **63** DavidAllan 6 61
(Tim Easterby) *chsd ldrs: rdn along 2f out: drvn over 1f out: kpt on same pce* **20/1**

551- **6** *4* **Lucy's Law (IRE)**[192] 6923 3-9-3 **68** JamesSullivan 4 56
(Tom Tate) *hld up towards rr: swtchd rt over 4f out: effrt on outer to chse ldrs 2f out: sn rdn and wknd* **10/1**

020- **7** *4 ½* **Conistone**[200] 6713 3-8-13 **64** PJMcDonald 7 42
(James Bethell) *towards rr: hdwy 3f out: in tch and rdn along 2f out: sn no imp* **12/1**

446- **8** *2 ¼* **Iron Islands**[160] 7741 3-9-6 **71** DougieCostello 1 44
(K R Burke) *chsd ldrs: rdn along 3f out: sn wknd* **15/2**[3]

046- **9** *11* **Rebounded**[231] 5727 3-8-8 **59** JasonHart 2 7
(Mark Walford) *chsd ldrs: rdn along 3f out: sn wknd* **12/1**

644- **10** *7* **Vintage Dream (IRE)**[260] 4678 3-9-1 **66** (h[1]) PaulMulrennan 9
(Noel Wilson) *dwlt and t.k.h: a rr* **16/1**

1m 36.84s (0.24) **Going Correction** -0.075s/f (Good) **10** Ran SP% **111.8**
Speed ratings (Par 98): **95,92,91,90,90 86,82,80,69,62**
CSF £46.34 CT £142.63 TOTE £7.30: £2.00, £2.00, £1.80; EX 46.80 Trifecta £170.10.
**Owner** J Blackburn & A Turton & Partner **Bred** Drumlin Bloodstock **Trained** Sheriff Hutton, N Yorks

**FOCUS**
A truly run contest. A small pb from the winner, and she could be rated 2-3lb higher through the second and third.

## 1679 RACINGUK.COM/DAYPASS FILLIES' H'CAP 1m 2f 1y
**5:25** (5:26) (Class 5) (0-70,72) 4-Y-0+ **£3,234** (£962; £481; £240) **Stalls** Low

Form RPR

-522 **1** **Kerry Icon**[32] 1101 4-7-11 **49** oh3 (h) RichardOliver(5) 6 52
(Iain Jardine) *prom: trckd ldr 7f out: cl up over 3f out: slt ld 2f out and sn rdn: drvn ins fnl f: hld on wl towards fin* **11/1**

651- **2** *nse* **Ronya (IRE)**[168] 7581 6-9-2 **63** RoystonFfrench 8 66
(Tracy Waggott) *trckd ldr: led after 2f: jnd over 2f out: sn hdd and rdn: drvn and rallied ins fnl f: jst hld* **16/1**

111- **3** *1 ¼* **Canny Style**[181] 7249 4-9-7 **68** KevinStott 3 69
(Kevin Ryan) *hld up in rr: stdy hdwy 3f out: chsd ldrs wl over 1f out and sn rdn: kpt on u.p fnl f* **5/1**[3]

235- **4** *nk* **Monaco Rose**[198] 6767 4-9-4 **65** PaulHanagan 4 65
(Richard Fahey) *hld up towards rr: hdwy over 3f out: rdn along to chse ldrs 2f out: drvn and kpt on same pce fnl f* **2/1**[1]

1412 **5** *1 ½* **Spirit Of The Vale (IRE)**[19] 1312 4-8-10 **57** (t) ShaneGray 2 54
(Oliver Greenall) *s.i.s and bhd: hdwy over 3f out: rdn along on outer to chse ldrs 2f out: drvn and no imp fnl f* **8/1**

55-4 **6** *hd* **Livella Fella (IRE)**[32] 1104 4-9-11 **72** PhillipMakin 7 69
(Keith Dalgleish) *led 2f: trckd ldng pair: effrt 3f out and sn pushed along: rdn 2f out: sn drvn and wknd ent fnl f* **7/1**

610- **7** *2 ¼* **Graceful Act**[177] 7361 9-8-2 **49** oh2 AndrewMullen 9 41
(Ron Barr) *chsd ldrs: hdwy 3f out: rdn along over 2f out: sn wknd* **66/1**

043 **8** *7* **Delphyne**[19] 1308 5-9-2 **63** BenCurtis 1 41
(Shaun Harris) *trckd ldrs on inner: pushed along 4f out: rdn over 3f out: sn wknd* **16/1**

013- **9** *8* **Calliope**[223] 6006 4-9-1 **62** JamesSullivan 5 24
(Kenneth Slack) *trckd ldrs: hdwy over 4f out: rdn along 3f out: sn wknd* **4/1**[2]

2m 6.5s (-0.60) **Going Correction** -0.075s/f (Good) **9** Ran SP% **115.2**
Speed ratings (Par 100): **99,98,97,97,96 96,94,88,82**
CSF £168.73 CT £991.19 TOTE £12.00: £2.60, £4.00, £1.40; EX 229.00 Trifecta £1029.50.
**Owner** Michael Wares **Bred** Patrick & Simon Trant **Trained** Carrutherstown, D'fries & G'way

**FOCUS**
A modest handicap run at an even pace. It suited those who raced prominently, and it's been rated negatively around the first two.

## 1680 FOLLOW REDCARRACING ON FACEBOOK & TWITTER APPRENTICE MEDIAN AUCTION MAIDEN STKS 7f
**5:55** (5:55) (Class 6) 3-4-Y-O **£2,749** (£818; £408; £204) **Stalls** Centre

Form RPR

**1** **Sir Reginald Brown** 3-8-7 0 ConnorMurtagh(7) 16 76+
(Richard Fahey) *trckd ldrs: hdwy on outer to ld jst over 1f out: rdn ins fnl f: hld on wl towards fin* **11/1**

22- **2** *shd* **Benjamin Thomas (IRE)**[175] 7407 3-9-0 0 GeorgeWood 1 76
(John Quinn) *in tch: hdwy 2f out: rdn to chal ent fnl f: sn drvn and ev ch whn edgd rt and no ex towards fin* **5/4**[1]

524- **3** *2 ¼* **Royal Icon**[151] 7891 3-8-9 65 LewisEdmunds 3 65
(Kevin Ryan) *in tch: hdwy 2f out: chsd ldrs over 1f out: sn rdn and kpt on fnl f* **9/1**

**4** *hd* **Komodo (IRE)** 3-9-0 0 JoshDoyle 12 69+
(Jedd O'Keeffe) *hld up: hdwy 2f out: rdn over 1f out: styd on wl fnl f: nrst fin* **28/1**

52- **5** *nk* **Nature Boy (IRE)**[178] 7328 3-8-11 0 JoshuaBryan(3) 6 69
(Peter Chapple-Hyam) *led: rdn along over 2f out: drvn and hdd jst over 1f out: one pce fnl f* **11/2**[2]

33- **6** *2 ½* **Mr Coco Bean (USA)**[181] 7247 3-9-0 0 RowanScott 13 62
(Ann Duffield) *cl up: disp ld 1/2-way: rdn along wl over 1f out: grad wknd appr fnl f* **14/1**

506- **7** *¾* **The Name's Paver**[181] 7254 4-9-9 57 GerO'Neill(5) 7 66
(Noel Wilson) *prom: rdn along 2f out: grad wknd appr fnl f* **40/1**

0-03 **8** *1* **Rosemay (FR)**[17] 1348 3-8-2 67 JamieGormley(7) 10 52
(Iain Jardine) *chsd ldrs: rdn along 2f out: kpt on one pce* **15/2**[3]

000- **9** *1* **Ching Ching Lor (IRE)**[160] 7741 3-9-0 38 PhilDennis 9 54
(Declan Carroll) *chsd ldrs: rdn along 2f out: sn one pce* **100/1**

**10** *hd* **Tilly Tinker** 3-8-2 0 HarrisonShaw(7) 14 49
(Michael Easterby) *a towards rr* **25/1**

5-2 **11** *½* **Prancing Oscar (IRE)**[26] 1198 3-8-11 0 CameronNoble(3) 15 53
(Ben Haslam) *a towards rr* **16/1**

00- **12** *7* **Regal Mirage (IRE)**[171] 7496 3-8-7 0 SeamusCronin(7) 11 34
(Tim Easterby) *a towards rr* **66/1**

6- **13** *5* **Ginger Love**[201] 6682 3-9-0 0 RichardOliver 8 20
(Bryan Smart) *dwlt: a rr* **33/1**

0- **14** *4* **Chionodoxa**[160] 7740 3-8-6 0 CallumRodriguez(3) 5 4
(Tim Easterby) *a towards rr* **100/1**

36 **15** *1 ¾* **Slaying The Dragon (IRE)**[39] 993 4-9-7 0 FayeMcManoman(7) 2 10
(Nigel Tinkler) *a rr* **100/1**

**16** *8* **Ay Up Mrs**[86] 4-9-6 0 MeganNicholls(3) 4
(Rebecca Bastiman) *dwlt: a rr* **100/1**

1m 23.43s (-1.07) **Going Correction** -0.075s/f (Good)
**WFA** 3 from 4yo 14lb **16** Ran SP% **120.6**
Speed ratings (Par 101): **103,102,100,100,99 96,96,94,93,93 92,84,79,74,72 63**
CSF £23.68 TOTE £15.30: £4.70, £1.20, £2.40; EX 43.70 Trifecta £274.30.
**Owner** P D Smith Holdings Ltd **Bred** P D Smith Holdings Ltd **Trained** Musley Bank, N Yorks

**FOCUS**
A modest maiden. The runner-up has been rated near last year's form.
T/Plt: £31.90 to a £1 stake. Pool: £64,310.88 - 1,467.89 winning units T/Qpdt: £6.50 to a £1 stake. Pool: £5,257.73 - 595.80 winning units **Joe Rowntree**

# WINDSOR (R-H)
Monday, April 10

**OFFICIAL GOING: Good (good to firm in places; 8.5) (watered)**
Wind: Fresh, half behind in home straight Weather: Cloudy

## 1681 EBF RACING WELFARE NOVICE STKS 5f 21y
**2:00** (2:02) (Class 5) 2-Y-O **£2,911** (£866; £432; £216) **Stalls** Low

Form RPR

**1** **Rock Of Estonia (IRE)** 2-9-2 0 JamieSpencer 10 82+
(Charles Hills) *mde virtually all: hrd pressed fr 2f out: pushed along and a holding narrow but decisive ld* **5/1**[2]

**2** *nk* **Angel Of The South (IRE)** 2-8-11 0 RobertWinston 2 75
(Dean Ivory) *cl up on inner: pressed wnr jst over 2f out: styd on fnl f but a hld* **5/1**[2]

**3** *½* **Daddies Girl (IRE)** 2-8-11 0 OisinMurphy 9 73
(Rod Millman) *s.i.s: rcvrd and w ldrs: chal 2f out: nt qckn over 1f out: styd on ins fnl f* **9/1**

**4** *1* **Declarationoflove (IRE)** 2-9-2 0 PatCosgrave 11 75
(Tom Clover) *pressed ldrs: shkn up over 1f out: kpt on same pce* **10/1**

**5** *¾* **May Remain** 2-9-2 0 LukeMorris 4 72+
(Paul Cole) *s.i.s: in rr: shkn up 1/2-way and chsd ldrs 2f out: kpt on same pce and no prog fnl f* **8/1**

**6** *2* **Milton Road** 2-9-2 0 GrahamLee 3 65
(Mick Channon) *trckd ldrs: waiting for a gap 2f out to over 1f out: fdd fnl f* **20/1**

**7** *¾* **Lethal Lunch** 2-9-2 0 RyanMoore 5 62
(Richard Hannon) *towards rr: taken to outer 2f out: pushed along and no prog over 1f out* **85/40**[1]

**8** *1 ¾* **Controversial Lady (IRE)** 2-8-11 0 JFEgan 1 51
(J S Moore) *pressed wnr to jst over 2f out: fdd and eased* **50/1**

**9** *7* **Give Em A Clump (IRE)** 2-9-2 0 AdamKirby 7 30
(David Evans) *s.i.s: a in rr: bhd fnl 2f* **13/2**[3]

**10** *4 ½* **Glimpse Of Dirhams** 2-8-11 0 SamHitchcott 6 9
(Chris Gordon) *slowly to stride: a in rr: bhd fnl 2f* **100/1**

**11** *1 ¼* **Mullion Star** 2-9-2 0 DanielMuscutt 8 10
(Michael Madgwick) *rdn in rr bef 1/2-way: bhd fnl 2f* **100/1**

1m 0.79s (0.49) **Going Correction** -0.175s/f (Firm) **11** Ran SP% **117.6**
Speed ratings (Par 92): **89,88,87,86,84 81,80,77,66,59 57**
CSF £29.67 TOTE £6.10: £2.00, £1.80, £2.90; EX 34.40 Trifecta £174.80.
**Owner** Kangyu Int Racing (HK) Ltd & F Ma **Bred** Colin Kennedy **Trained** Lambourn, Berks

**FOCUS**
Races of one mile and over increased by 23yds. Probably a fair little novice, it's a race that should produce winners. It's been rated towards the top end of the average for the race.

## 1682 WINDSOR VEHICLE LEASING MAIDEN STKS 1m 1f 194y
**2:30** (2:31) (Class 5) 3-Y-O **£2,911** (£866; £432; £108; £108) **Stalls** Centre

Form RPR

**1** **Comrade Conrad (IRE)** 3-9-5 0 HarryBentley 6 79+
(Roger Charlton) *in tch in 6th: prog over 2f out: rdn to chal jst over 1f out: narrow ld last 100yds: jst hld on* **12/1**

4- **2** *hd* **Mistress Quickly (IRE)**[194] 6874 3-9-0 0 FranBerry 2 73
(Ralph Beckett) *trckd ldng pair: wnt 2nd over 3f out: rdn to ld 1f out: hdd last 100yds: kpt on wl: jst pipped* **5/2**[2]

**3** *shd* **Bristol Missile (USA)** 3-9-5 0 SeanLevey 8 78+
(Richard Hannon) *in tch in 7th: prog over 2f out: rdn to cl on ldrs over 1f out: styd on ins fnl f: jst failed* **11/2**[3]

04- **4** *1 ½* **Master Archer (IRE)**[124] 8245 3-9-5 0 TomQueally 1 75+
(James Fanshawe) *trckd ldrs in 5th: cl up bhd them whn nt clr run over 1f out: swtchd lft and nudged along: nvr chal but shaped w promise* **10/1**

23- **4** *dht* **Radjash**[171] 7495 3-9-5 0 (p[1]) AdamKirby 11 75
(Charlie Appleby) *led: drvn over 2f out: hdd and one pce u.p 1f out* **2/1**[1]



The Form Book Flat, Raceform Ltd, Newbury, RG14 5SJ

6 4 **Breaking Bread** 3-9-5 0 RobertTart 10 67
(John Gosden) *slowly away: mostly in last: effrt on outer 3f out: plugged on but no ch w ldrs* **16/1**

50- 7 *nk* **Penny Red**[159] 7761 3-8-11 0 CallumShepherd(3) 4 61+
(William Knight) *hld up in 8th: nudged along fr over 2f out: nvr a threat but kpt on steadily and shaped w promise* **25/1**

8 *shd* **Key Bid** 3-9-5 0 MartinLane 3 66
(Charlie Appleby) *chsd ldrs: urged along bef 1/2-way: lost pl over 2f out: fdd* **12/1**

5 9 *37* **Piccoloro**[13] 1414 3-8-12 0 Pierre-LouisJamin(7) 9
(Jonathan Portman) *pressed ldr to over 3f out: wknd rapidly: t.o* **100/1**

2m 9.37s (0.67) **Going Correction** -0.175s/f (Firm) 9 Ran SP% **112.5**
Speed ratings (Par 98): **90,89,89,88,88 85,85,85,55**
CSF £40.94 TOTE £15.10: £3.00, £1.30, £1.90; EX 48.60 Trifecta £365.70.
**Owner** Michael Pescod **Bred** Desert Star Phoenix Jvc **Trained** Beckhampton, Wilts
■ Stewards' Enquiry : Fran Berry two-day ban: used whip above permitted level (Apr 24-25)

**FOCUS**
Distance increased by 23yds. Probably a decent maiden, although there was hardly anything between the front four at the line. It's been rated around the runner-up and Radjash to their marks.

## 1683 MPM FLOORING LTD H'CAP 1m 1f 194y
**3:00** (3:03) (Class 5) (0-75,74) 4-Y-0+ **£2,911** (£866; £432; £216) **Stalls** Centre

Form RPR

513- 1 **Perfect Quest**[208] 6485 4-9-3 **70** (t) AdamKirby 13 79+
(Clive Cox) *dwlt: towards rr and off the pce: pushed along and prog on outer fr 3f out: drvn to chse ldr fnl f: sustained effrt to ld last stride* **8/1**[3]

253- 2 *shd* **Capton**[188] 7052 4-9-4 **71** DaneO'Neill 1 79
(Henry Candy) *mde most: set gd pce and stretched field: rdn and jnd over 2f out to over 1f out: kpt on wl but hdd last stride* **8/1**[3]

002- 3 *1 ½* **Cordite (IRE)**[175] 7418 6-9-5 **72** (h) SamHitchcott 4 77
(Jim Boyle) *taken down early: mostly chsd ldng pair: rdn over 2f out: hanging and nt qckn against rail over 1f out: kpt on* **16/1**

-234 4 *½* **Light Of Air (FR)**[21] 1289 4-9-3 **70** (b) RyanMoore 10 74
(Gary Moore) *chsd ldrs disputing 5th: rdn and prog over 2f out: tried to chal over 1f out: one pce ins fnl f* **7/1**[2]

001- 5 *shd* **Isis Blue**[196] 6827 7-8-12 **65** OisinMurphy 2 69
(Rod Millman) *pressed ldr: rdn and upsides over 2f out to over 1f out: one pce* **12/1**

-600 6 *1 ¼* **False Id**[25] 1224 4-8-12 **65** JackMitchell 15 66
(Robert Eddery) *hld up in midfield: pushed along and prog over 2f out: rchd 6th fnl f and clr of rest: kpt on but nvr able to chal* **25/1**

040- 7 *5* **Live Dangerously**[166] 7613 7-8-7 **60** oh3 WilliamCarson 8 51
(John Bridger) *settled in rr and wl off the pce: pushed along fr 3f out: nvr involved but passed several rivals fr 2f out* **40/1**

513- 8 *1 ¼* **Tom's Rock (IRE)**[182] 7227 4-9-6 **73** TomQueally 7 62
(John Butler) *t.k.h: trckd ldrs disputing 5th: rdn over 2f out: wknd wl over 1f out* **17/2**

216- 9 *2 ¼* **Eez Eh (IRE)**[167] 7594 4-9-7 **74** (p) ConnorBeasley 6 58
(Keith Dalgleish) *chsd ldng trio: drvn over 3f out: wknd over 2f out* **16/1**

4404 10 *nk* **The Gay Cavalier**[4] 1583 6-8-12 **72** (t) JackOsborn(7) 16 56
(John Ryan) *s.v.s: wl in rr and off the pce: rdn 3f out: modest late prog* **20/1**

25 11 *1 ¼* **Zorba The Greek**[60] 641 5-9-3 **70** JamieSpencer 12 51
(Ed Vaughan) *stdd s: hld up and sn in last and also wl off the pce: shkn up 3f out but nvr any ch* **9/2**[1]

-012 12 *1* **Etaad (USA)**[44] 922 6-8-8 **64** (b) HectorCrouch(3) 11 43
(Gary Moore) *in tch in abt 8th: rdn and no prog over 2f out: fdd* **25/1**

063- 13 *½* **Spinart**[160] 7753 4-9-2 **69** RobHornby 9 47
(Pam Sly) *hld up: a off the pce towards rr: shkn up and no prog 3f out* **8/1**[3]

4-00 14 *9* **Red Cossack (CAN)**[33] 1085 6-9-0 **67** (t) RobertWinston 14 27
(Paul Webber) *hld up wl in rr: nudged by rival 4f out: no prog 3f out: eased over 1f out* **33/1**

000- 15 *2 ¾* **Outback Blue**[138] 8077 4-9-6 **73** (t) JFEgan 5 28
(David Evans) *s.s: a in rr: shkn up and no prog 3f out: eased over 1f out* **12/1**

500- 16 *35* **Della Valle (GER)**[171] 7504 4-9-5 **72** TedDurcan 3
(Mike Murphy) *in tch tl wknd 3f out: eased and t.o* **50/1**

2m 6.77s (-1.93) **Going Correction** -0.175s/f (Firm) 16 Ran SP% **121.5**
Speed ratings (Par 103): **100,99,98,98,98 97,93,92,90,90 89,88,88,80,78 50**
CSF £64.78 CT £1017.36 TOTE £8.40: £2.30, £2.00, £4.30, £2.00; EX 82.00 Trifecta £885.70.
**Owner** Hants and Herts **Bred** Mrs S J Walker **Trained** Lambourn, Berks

**FOCUS**
Distance increased by 23yds. Not many got into this and so the winner can have her effort upgraded, coming from off the pace and challenging wide in the straight. It's been rated around the third to his C&D form on his final start last year.

## 1684 BGC RACING MEMBERSHIP £125 H'CAP 1m 3f 99y
**3:30** (3:32) (Class 5) (0-75,75) 4-Y-0+ **£2,911** (£866; £432; £216) **Stalls** Centre

Form RPR

335- 1 **Captain Peacock**[166] 7624 4-9-6 **75** (v) RyanMoore 6 83+
(William Knight) *trckd ldng pair gng wl: clsd to ld over 1f out: racd sltly awkwardly but cajoled along to assert ins fnl f* **1/1**[1]

-632 2 *¾* **Safira Menina**[21] 1289 5-8-12 **73** MillyNaseb(7) 9 79
(Martin Smith) *hld up bhd ldrs: prog on outer over 2f out: chal and w wnr over 1f out: kpt on but readily hld last 150yds* **7/1**

62-5 3 *5* **Maroc**[15] 220 4-9-3 **72** (p) LukeMorris 5 70
(Nikki Evans) *led 5f: trckd ldr: rdn 3f out: stl upsides over 1f out: wknd* **50/1**

0-02 4 *1 ¼* **Bluff Crag**[18] 1323 4-9-0 **69** (h) ShaneKelly 7 65
(Richard Hughes) *t.k.h: hld up in tch: shkn up over 2f out: tried to cl over 1f out but nt qckn and sn outpcd* **5/1**[2]

-066 5 *1 ¾* **Al Khafji**[9] 1498 4-8-8 **68** (b) DavidParkes(5) 8 61
(Jeremy Gask) *mostly in last pair: shkn up 3f out: no imp on ldrs fnl 2f* **11/2**[3]

-000 6 *6* **Moojaned (IRE)**[9] 1498 6-9-0 **68** JFEgan 4 51
(David Evans) *trckd ldr: led after 5f: drvn 3f out: hdd & wknd rapidly over 1f out* **8/1**

040- 7 *10* **Bohemian Rhapsody (IRE)**[124] 5963 8-9-2 **70** FranBerry 2 36
(Brendan Powell) *mostly in last pair: lost tch 3f out: sn wl bhd* **20/1**

2m 26.13s (-3.37) **Going Correction** -0.175s/f (Firm) 7 Ran SP% **112.4**
Speed ratings (Par 103): **104,103,100,99,98 94,87**
CSF £8.40 CT £200.96 TOTE £1.90: £1.10, £2.70; EX 6.80 Trifecta £50.10.
**Owner** Chasemore Farm **Bred** Chasemore Farm **Trained** Patching, W Sussex

**FOCUS**
Distance increased by 23yds. A pretty modest handicap, all the money was for the favourite and he duly obliged. It's been rated around the runner-up to the better view of her AW form.

## 1685 BGC RACING OWNERSHIP FROM £125 H'CAP (DIV I) 1m 31y
**4:00** (4:01) (Class 5) (0-70,72) 3-Y-O **£2,911** (£866; £432; £216) **Stalls** Low

Form RPR

016- 1 **Masterofdiscovery**[194] 6875 3-9-7 **70** (b) JohnFahy 1 77
(Clive Cox) *mde all: kicked for home over 2f out: styd on wl fr over 1f out: readily* **17/2**

2213 2 *1 ½* **Delfie Lane**[17] 1343 3-9-6 **69** (p) JamieSpencer 4 72
(Richard Hughes) *hld up in 5th gng wl: shkn up and prog to chse wnr wl over 1f out: kpt on but no imp fnl f* **8/1**[3]

543- 3 *½* **Know Your Limit (IRE)**[117] 8354 3-9-8 **71** ThomasBrown 10 73+
(Ed Walker) *t.k.h: hld up towards rr: shkn up over 2f out: prog after and styd on to take 3rd nr fin: nvr able to chal* **4/1**[2]

131- 4 *nk* **Glenys The Menace (FR)**[201] 6670 3-9-3 **66** (h[1]) KierenFox 5 67
(John Best) *wl in tch: rdn over 2f out: styd on fr over 1f out to press for a pl nr fin* **8/1**[3]

246- 5 *2 ½* **Fields Of Fortune**[187] 7074 3-9-4 **70** HollieDoyle(3) 2 65+
(Richard Hannon) *towards rr: trying to make prog fr 2f out but had to twice switch lft: tk 5th fnl f but no prog after* **15/8**[1]

530- 6 *3* **Moonstone Rock**[145] 7974 3-9-0 **63** PatCosgrave 8 52
(Jim Boyle) *chsd ldng pair: drvn over 2f out: tried to cl over 1f out: sn wknd* **16/1**

056- 7 *nse* **Latest Quest (IRE)**[123] 8276 3-8-3 **57** MitchGodwin(5) 6 45
(Sylvester Kirk) *s.i.s: wl in rr: sme prog on inner 2f out: nt clr run after and swtchd to outer: no hdwy fnl f* **28/1**

45-0 8 *1* **Justice Frederick (IRE)**[13] 1411 3-9-9 **72** (t[1]) JoeyHaynes 3 58
(Paul D'Arcy) *chsd wnr to wl over 1f out: wknd* **18/1**

400- 9 *5* **Unzipped**[150] 7898 3-9-2 **65** StevieDonohoe 9 40
(Stuart Edmunds) *slowly away: mostly in last pair: no prog over 2f out: wl btn after* **33/1**

40-0 10 *¾* **Intisha (IRE)**[18] 1331 3-9-1 **64** LukeMorris 11 37
(Jonathan Portman) *hung lft bnd 6f out and dropped to rr: effrt over 3f out: wknd over 2f out* **66/1**

560- 11 *2* **Every Nice Girl (USA)**[193] 6897 3-9-1 **64** JosephineGordon 7 32
(Marco Botti) *chsd ldng pair: rdn over 2f out: wknd rapidly over 1f out* **25/1**

021- 12 *¾* **Claire's Secret**[179] 7304 3-9-6 **69** DavidProbert 12 36
(Philip McBride) *a in rr: shkn up and no prog over 2f out: wknd* **12/1**

06-0 13 *10* **Jasmincita (IRE)**[24] 1242 3-8-13 **62** SteveDrowne 13 6
(George Baker) *a wl in rr: wknd over 2f out: eased over 1f out* **50/1**

1m 42.88s (-1.82) **Going Correction** -0.175s/f (Firm) 13 Ran SP% **120.1**
Speed ratings (Par 98): **102,100,100,99,97 94,94,93,88,87 85,84,74**
CSF £72.02 CT £328.07 TOTE £10.40: £2.60, £2.50, £1.60; EX 72.90 Trifecta £437.50.
**Owner** The Voyagers **Bred** Meon Valley Stud **Trained** Lambourn, Berks

**FOCUS**
Distance increased by 23yds. Division one of a modest handicap. The runner-up has been rated as building on his recent AW form, with the fourth to her nursery form.

## 1686 BGC RACING OWNERSHIP FROM £125 H'CAP (DIV II) 1m 31y
**4:30** (4:31) (Class 5) (0-70,72) 3-Y-O **£2,911** (£866; £432; £216) **Stalls** Low

Form RPR

32-1 1 **Sir Plato (IRE)**[12] 1421 3-8-12 **61** OisinMurphy 8 74+
(Rod Millman) *pressed ldr: led 4f out: drew rt away over 1f out: heavily eased last 100yds* **7/2**[1]

245- 2 *4 ½* **Golden Guest**[217] 6191 3-9-2 **65** TomQueally 5 64
(George Margarson) *hld up towards rr: prog on outer fr 3f out: rdn and styd on fr 2f out to take 2nd ins fnl f: no ch w wnr* **10/1**

500- 3 *¾* **Sakurajima (IRE)**[180] 7286 3-9-1 **67** (t[1]) CallumShepherd(3) 13 64+
(Charles Hills) *hld up in rr fr wd draw: sme prog 2f out: hmpd sn after and swtchd: str run fnl f to take 3rd last strides* **16/1**

330- 4 *½* **Singing Sands (IRE)**[198] 6762 3-9-9 **72** (t[1]) JamieSpencer 12 68+
(Seamus Durack) *dropped in fr wd draw and hld up towards rr: effrt in midfield over 2f out gng wl enough: nt clr run 2f out and sn swtchd rt: styd on but nvr able to threaten* **12/1**

060- 5 *½* **Whiteley (IRE)**[183] 7185 3-9-0 **63** GrahamLee 11 58
(Mick Channon) *in tch in midfield: effrt over 2f out: kpt on but nvr a real threat* **16/1**

010- 6 *½* **Bayston Hill**[191] 6950 3-9-7 **70** DanielMuscutt 3 64
(Mark Usher) *chsd ldrs: drvn wl over 2f out: no ch w wnr and fdd ins fnl f* **11/1**

1 7 *1 ¼* **Broad Appeal**[68] 503 3-9-1 **69** MitchGodwin(5) 2 60
(Jonathan Portman) *led: hung lft bnd over 4f out: sn hdd: chsd wnr but lft bhd over 1f out: wknd fnl f* **6/1**[2]

060- 8 *2 ½* **Mr Scaff (IRE)**[171] 7502 3-9-1 **64** MartinLane 4 49
(Paul Henderson) *hld up in rr: pushed along wl over 2f out: nvr a factor* **9/1**

540- 9 *1* **Lemon Drop**[210] 6412 3-8-8 **57** SamHitchcott 10 40
(Jim Boyle) *trapped out wd and in rr after 3f: nvr a threat* **50/1**

6-34 10 *1* **Kassandra (IRE)**[18] 1333 3-9-7 **70** SeanLevey 7 50
(Richard Hannon) *hld up wl in rr: shkn up over 2f out: no real prog and nvr involved* **8/1**[3]

063- 11 *3 ½* **Expectation (IRE)**[182] 7208 3-9-1 **64** TomMarquand 9 36
(Michael Blanshard) *chsd ldrs: wknd u.p fr wl over 2f out* **16/1**

5515 12 *1 ¼* **Things Happen**[17] 1343 3-9-8 **71** (v) AdamKirby 1 41
(David Evans) *chsd ldrs: rdn 3f out: wknd 2f out* **9/1**

035- 13 *6* **Golden Eye**[149] 7941 3-9-2 **65** DaneO'Neill 6 21
(Sylvester Kirk) *a in last: rdn and no prog 3f out: bhd over 1f out* **12/1**

1m 42.7s (-2.00) **Going Correction** -0.175s/f (Firm) 13 Ran SP% **120.0**
Speed ratings (Par 98): **103,98,97,97,96 96,95,92,91,90 87,85,79**
CSF £38.85 CT £523.76 TOTE £3.40: £1.60, £3.90, £5.50; EX 51.60 Trifecta £1023.90.
**Owner** The Sir Plato Partnership **Bred** Noel Finegan **Trained** Kentisbeare, Devon

**FOCUS**
Distance increased by 23yds. Probably less competitive than the first division and Sir Plato, who had finished runner-up to the winner of the first division in a race last season, bolted up. The runner-up has been rated close to form.

## 1687 ROYAL WINDSOR HORSE SHOW H'CAP 1m 31y
**5:00** (5:01) (Class 5) (0-75,76) 4-Y-O+ **£2,911** (£866; £432; £216) **Stalls** Low

Form RPR

636- 1 **Commodity (IRE)**[166] 7616 4-9-7 **75** RyanMoore 10 82+
(Sir Michael Stoute) *trckd ldrs: pushed along 3f out: clsd fr 2f out: drvn to ld ins fnl f: styd on wl* **6/4**[1]

245- **2** *nk* **Marcano (IRE)**[241] 5357 5-9-7 **75**........................................(t) RyanTate 11 81
(Rod Millman) *hld up in rr: prog on outer fr over 2f out: drvn to chal ins fnl f: styd on but a jst hld* **10/1**

0-01 **3** *1/2* **Shifting Star (IRE)**[17] 1338 12-8-7 **61** oh1................(vt) WilliamCarson 1 66
(John Bridger) *led: rdn 2f out: hdd ins fnl f: kpt on wl nr fin* **8/1**[3]

45-4 **4** *1 1/4* **Duke Of North (IRE)**[18] 1324 5-8-8 **67**.................... CharlieBennett(5) 14 69
(Jim Boyle) *in tch: effrt over 2f out: clsd on ldrs over 1f out: one pce fnl f* **14/1**

120- **5** *3/4* **Here's Two**[264] 4534 4-9-5 **73**................................................ LukeMorris 6 73
(Ron Hodges) *t.k.h: hld up towards rr: sme prog over 2f out: kpt on fr over 1f out but nvr pce to rch ldrs* **16/1**

550- **6** *1/2* **Ghinia (IRE)**[164] 7671 6-9-8 **76**.......................................... RobHornby 13 75
(Pam Sly) *spd fr wd draw to press ldr: stl upsides jst over 1f out: wknd u.p ins fnl f* **6/1**[2]

1606 **7** *1* **Essenaitch (IRE)**[38] 1007 4-9-2 **70**.......................................... JFEgan 5 67
(David Evans) *in tch in midfield: tried to cl on ldrs fr 2f out: fdd u.p fnl f* **16/1**

435- **8** *1 1/4* **Tarseekh**[119] 8342 4-9-3 **71**................................................. DaneO'Neill 2 65
(Chris Gordon) *nvr beyond midfield: rdn and no imp ldrs on inner fr 2f out* **66/1**

4166 **9** *nk* **Berrahri (IRE)**[12] 1422 6-9-4 **72**........................................... KierenFox 7 65
(John Best) *a towards rr: rdn and no prog over 2f out* **8/1**[3]

600- **10** *1 1/4* **Good Luck Charm**[160] 7738 8-9-3 **74**........................ HectorCrouch(3) 8 64
(Gary Moore) *hld up in last trio: pushed along over 2f out: nvr involved but plugged on fr over 1f out* **28/1**

52/0 **11** *1 1/2* **Impressive Day (IRE)**[19] 1299 4-9-5 **73**........................... AdamKirby 3 60
(Gary Moore) *sn in last and nt gng that wl: looked like fining wl btn 2f out: styd on ins fnl f* **20/1**

60-5 **12** *8* **Soaring Spirits (IRE)**[18] 1327 7-9-6 **74**........................ RobertWinston 9 43
(Dean Ivory) *chsd ldrs: wknd qckly over 2f out: t.o* **33/1**

0-40 **13** *3/4* **Thecornishbarron (IRE)**[5] 1553 5-9-1 **72**................. LouisSteward(3) 4 39
(John Ryan) *nvr beyond midfield: wknd qckly over 2f out: t.o* **14/1**

1m 42.91s (-1.79) **Going Correction** -0.175s/f (Firm) **13** Ran SP% **123.3**
Speed ratings (Par 103): **101,100,100,98,98 97,96,95,95,93 92,84,83**
CSF £17.40 CT £103.53 TOTE £2.30: £1.10, £3.30, £2.70; EX 19.10 Trifecta £82.10.
**Owner** Highclere T'bred Racing (Wellington) **Bred** Stowell Park Stud **Trained** Newmarket, Suffolk

**FOCUS**
Distance increased by 23yds. A fair handicap and a winner capable of rating a fair bit higher. It's been rated around the third to his recent form, with the fourth close to form.

## 1688 HAPPY RETIREMENT JOE WALSH H'CAP — 5f 21y
**5:30** (5:31) (Class 6) (0-65,67) 3-Y-O **£2,264** (£673; £336; £168) **Stalls** Low

Form RPR

-630 **1** **Who Told Jo Jo (IRE)**[18] 1332 3-9-7 **65**........................ OisinMurphy 10 72
(Joseph Tuite) *pressed ldrs: rdn to ld jst over 1f out and edgd rt: hung lft u.p ins fnl f: hld on* **7/1**[3]

0-20 **2** *nk* **Met By Moonlight**[33] 1088 3-9-4 **62**................................ DavidProbert 8 68
(Ron Hodges) *wl in tch: prog 2f out: rdn to take 2nd ins fnl f: carried lft whn chalng last 100yds: a hld* **14/1**

0-60 **3** *1 1/2* **Beach Dancer (IRE)**[37] 1024 3-8-4 **51** oh1........... EdwardGreatrex(3) 13 51
(William Knight) *racd on wd outside: prom: shkn up and racd awkwardly 1/2-way: clsd over 1f out: nt qckn ins fnl f* **8/1**

300- **4** *2* **Hamidans Girl (IRE)**[135] 8118 3-9-9 **67**...................... ConnorBeasley 12 60
(Keith Dalgleish) *hld up and in last pair early: prog on outer fr 1/2-way: cl up jst over 1f out: outpcd fnl f* **4/1**[1]

2011 **5** *3/4* **Dashing Poet**[18] 1328 3-9-8 **66**............................................(h) MartinLane 2 56
(Jeremy Gask) *chsd ldrs: rdn wl over 1f out: one pce fnl f* **9/2**[2]

10-0 **6** *1 3/4* **Prancelina (IRE)**[33] 1088 3-9-4 **62**............................ JosephineGordon 6 46
(Phil McEntee) *chsd ldr to over 1f out: impeded sn after and fdd* **20/1**

06-3 **7** *nk* **Tea El Tee (IRE)**[12] 1418 3-8-2 **53**........................(p) DavidEgan(7) 5 36
(Gay Kelleway) *towards rr: shkn up 1/2-way: nvr a factor but kpt on ins fnl f* **10/1**

060- **8** *1/2* **Miss Rosina (IRE)**[130] 8174 3-8-12 **63**........................ JaneElliott(7) 14 44
(George Margarson) *chsd ldrs tl fdd jst over 1f out* **8/1**

6645 **9** *hd* **Celerity (IRE)**[4] 1580 3-8-7 **51** oh1..........................................(b) JFEgan 3 31
(David Evans) *gd spd and led against nr side rail: hdd & wknd jst over 1f out* **14/1**

00-0 **10** *1/2* **Stringybark Creek**[10] 1463 3-9-9 **67**.................................... GrahamLee 11 46
(Mick Channon) *nvr on terms w ldrs: shkn up and no prog 2f out* **11/1**

0-61 **11** *5* **Snoozy Sioux (IRE)**[16] 1363 3-9-1 **62**........................ NoelGarbutt(3) 7 23
(Martin Smith) *a struggling to go the pce: rdn in last 1/2-way and no prog* **16/1**

5264 **12** *1 3/4* **Glam'Selle**[16] 1363 3-8-7 **51** oh4.........................................(p) LukeMorris 9 5
(Ronald Harris) *s.i.s: rchd midfield after 2f out: wknd wl over 1f out* **16/1**

000- **13** *4 1/2* **Percy Toplis**[163] 7688 3-9-0 **65**.................................... JacobMitchell(7) 1 3
(Christine Dunnett) *s.i.s: nvr bttr than midfield: wknd over 1f out: eased* **66/1**

59.66s (-0.64) **Going Correction** -0.175s/f (Firm) **13** Ran SP% **121.7**
Speed ratings (Par 96): **98,97,95,91,90 87,87,86,86,85 77,74,67**
CSF £103.23 CT £813.38 TOTE £9.40: £2.70, £5.30, £2.40; EX 176.90 Trifecta £854.60.
**Owner** The Harefield Racing Club **Bred** James And Joe Brannigan **Trained** Lambourn, Berks
■ Stewards' Enquiry : J F Egan one-day ban: in breach of Rule (B) 67.4.3 (24th Apr)
Oisin Murphy cautioned to future conduct in races.

**FOCUS**
A competitive sprint, the front pair came close late on. The winner has been rated back towards the best of his 2yo form.
T/Jkpt: Not Won. T/Plt: £88.00 to a £1 stake. Pool: £86,450.22 - 716.37 winning units T/Qpdt: £13.00 to a £1 stake. Pool: £7,855.44 - 447.10 winning units **Jonathan Neesom**

# 1483 MAISONS-LAFFITTE (R-H)
Monday, April 10

**OFFICIAL GOING: Turf: good**

## 1689a PRIX DJEBEL (GROUP 3) (3YO COLTS & GELDINGS) (STRAIGHT) (TURF) — 7f
**2:20** (2:20) 3-Y-O **£34,188** (£13,675; £10,256; £6,837; £3,418)

RPR

**1** **Al Wukair (IRE)**[172] 7491 3-9-2 0.................................. GregoryBenoist 1 117+
(A Fabre, France) *in rr: last and nrly 10l off ldr appr 1/2-way: gd hdwy on outer 1 1/2f out: drvn to ld fnl 125yds out: sn in command* **9/10**[1]

**2** *1* **National Defense**[190] 6987 3-9-2 0..................... Pierre-CharlesBoudot 7 115
(Mme C Head-Maarek, France) *racd keenly: trckd ldr: led bef 1/2-way and swtchd to stands' rail: jnd (and possibly hdd briefly under 1 1/2f out): drvn to go on appr fnl f: hdd last 125yds: kpt on but wl hld by wnr* **2/1**[2]

**3** *2 1/2* **African Ride**[25] 1236 3-9-2 0........................................(h) MaximeGuyon 3 108
(C Laffon-Parias, France) *racd keenly: hld up bhd ldr: outpcd and rdn over 1 1/2f out: styd on u.p fnl f: nvr on terms* **15/2**[3]

**4** *snk* **Straight Right (FR)**[57] 712 3-9-2 0.................................. OlivierPeslier 6 108
(C Ferland, France) *chsd ldrs: drvn to join ldr (and possibly ld briefly) under 1 1/2f out: sn rdn and nt qckn: one pce fnl f: lost 3rd cl home* **79/10**

**5** *1 3/4* **Ajmal (IRE)**[187] 7086 3-9-2 0.......................................... VincentCheminaud 5 103
(A Fabre, France) *w.w towards rr on inner: drvn and nt qckn 1 1/2f out: one pce fnl f* **29/1**

**6** *7* **Red Onion**[139] 8062 3-9-2 0..................................(p) ChristopheSoumillon 8 84
(C Lerner, France) *wnt rt s. racd towards rr: drvn bef 1/2-way but no imp: wl hld whn eased ins fnl f* **228/10**

**7** *4* **Oriental (JPN)**[7] 3-9-2 0.................................................. FrankPanicucci 4 73
(C Laffon-Parias, France) *led: hdd appr 1/2-way: wknd 1 1/2f out: sn bhd* **56/1**

1m 23.03s (-4.97) **7** Ran SP% **118.3**
PARI-MUTUEL (all including 1 euro stake): WIN 1.90 PLACE 1.10, 1.10, 1.10 DF 2.50 SF 3.70.
**Owner** Al Shaqab Racing **Bred** Ballylinch Stud **Trained** Chantilly, France

**FOCUS**
This was run at a good gallop and the winning time was much faster (2.77sec) than the following fillies' trial.

## 1690a PRIX IMPRUDENCE (GROUP 3) (3YO FILLIES) (STRAIGHT) (TURF) — 7f
**2:55** (2:55) 3-Y-O **£34,188** (£13,675; £10,256; £6,837; £3,418)

RPR

**1** **Via Ravenna (IRE)**[39] 3-9-0 0.................................. VincentCheminaud 5 108
(A Fabre, France) *w.w in rr: gd prog on outer w 1 1/2f to run: led ins fnl f: edgd lft but r.o under driving* **76/10**

**2** *1* **Thais (FR)**[160] 7757 3-9-0 0.................................. ChristopheSoumillon 6 105
(P Bary, France) *led: kicked for home 1 1/2f out: sn drvn: hdd ins fnl f: r.o but no match for wnr* **59/10**[2]

**3** *1 1/2* **Silver Storm (FR)**[36] 3-9-0 0.......................................... OlivierPeslier 3 101
(C Ferland, France) *racd keenly: pressed ldr: drvn 1 1/2f out but nt pce of ldr: kpt on wout qckning fnl f* **199/10**

**4** *3/4* **Speed As (FR)**[31] 3-9-0 0............................................ IoritzMendizabal 1 99
(F Chappet, France) *plld hrd: hld up in fnl pair: scrubbed along and clsd fr 1 1/2f out: styd on ins fnl f: nvr on terms* **89/10**

**5** *hd* **Gokena (FR)**[22] 1270 3-9-0 0................................ Jean-BernardEyquem 2 98
(P Sogorb, France) *hld up among bkmarkers: last and drvn appr fnl f: styd on u.p: nvr trbld ldrs* **219/10**

**6** *1 3/4* **Normandel (FR)**[190] 6986 3-9-0 0................................... CristianDemuro 7 94
(Mme Pia Brandt, France) *racd v keenly: hld up wl in tch on outer: drvn to chse ldrs wl over 1f out: grad dropped away ins fnl f* **69/10**[3]

**7** *hd* **Double Lady (FR)**[185] 7114 3-9-0 0....................... Pierre-CharlesBoudot 4 93
(A Fabre, France) *racd keenly: hld up in tch between horses: drvn and short-lived effrt wl over 1f out: lft bhd ins fnl f* **9/10**[1]

**8** *nse* **Deep Inside (FR)**[289] 3-9-0 0.......................................... MaximeGuyon 8 93
(Mme Pia Brandt, France) *racd keenly: hld up towards rr: midfield 1/2-way: outpcd and drvn 1 1/2f out: dropped away ins fnl f* **10/1**

1m 25.8s (-2.20) **8** Ran SP% **119.8**
PARI-MUTUEL (all including 1 euro stake): WIN 8.60 PLACE 2.40, 2.00, 4.10 DF 17.00 SF 47.90.
**Owner** Scea Haras De Saint Pair **Bred** Scea Haras De Saint Pair **Trained** Chantilly, France

**FOCUS**
Far more steadily run than the Djebel, the time was 2.77sec slower. The fifth and seventh help set the standard.

## 1691a PRIX JACQUES LAFFITTE (LISTED RACE) (4YO+) (STRAIGHT) (TURF) — 1m 1f
**3:25** (3:25) 4-Y-O+ **£22,222** (£8,888; £6,666; £4,444; £2,222)

RPR

**1** **Ultra (IRE)**[238] 5499 4-9-0 0.......................................... MickaelBarzalona 1 111+
(A Fabre, France) *a cl up on stands' rail: angled out to chse ldr under 1 1/2f out: drvn and r.o to ld 125yds out: wl on top at fin* **17/10**[1]

**2** *1 1/4* **Wireless (FR)**[155] 7841 6-9-0 0.......................................... TheoBachelot 4 108
(V Luka Jr, Czech Republic) **10/1**

**3** *3 1/2* **Le Juge (IRE)**[20] 4-9-0 0.......................................... Pierre-CharlesBoudot 9 101
(A Fabre, France) **142/10**

**4** *2* **Bravo Zolo (IRE)**[46] 892 5-9-4 0.......................................... WilliamBuick 3 101
(Charlie Appleby) *led gp of six on stands' rail: drvn whn pressed appr 2f out: hdd over 1 1/2f out: edgd rt then veered lft: one pce fnl f* **29/10**[2]

**5** *2 1/2* **Instant De Reve (FR)**[57] 711 4-9-0 0.......................................... ThierryThulliez 6 92
(Mme C Barande-Barbe, France) **92/10**

**6** *3 1/2* **Saunter (FR)**[151] 7897 4-9-0 0.......................................... GeraldMosse 8 84
(David Menuisier) *sn chsng ldr in gp of four towards centre of trck: drvn to ld gp 1/2-way but a little bhd stands' side ldrs: rdn and btn appr fnl f* **269/10**

**7** *12* **Landym (FR)**[163] 7718 6-9-4 0.......................................... OlivierPeslier 10 63
(H-A Pantall, France) **45/1**

**8** *1/2* **Line Drummer (FR)**[162] 7-9-0 0.......................................... GuillaumeMillet 5 58
(J Reynier, France) **163/10**

**9** *15* **Prestige Vendome (FR)**[13] 1416 6-9-0 0........(p) ChristopheSoumillon 2 26
(Yannick Fouin, France) **69/10**[3]

**10** *1 1/4* **Bonusdargent (FR)**[179] 7312 5-9-0 0.......................................... MaximeGuyon 7 24
(Mme Pia Brandt, France) **194/10**

1m 47.5s (-7.20) **10** Ran SP% **117.3**
PARI-MUTUEL (all including 1 euro stake): WIN 1.50 PLACE 1.50, 2.60, 3.00 DF 12.00 SF 15.90.
**Owner** Godolphin SNC **Bred** Darley **Trained** Chantilly, France

**FOCUS**
The second and third help set the standard.

# [1618]LINGFIELD (L-H)
Tuesday, April 11

**OFFICIAL GOING: Polytrack: standard**
Wind: Moderate, across (towards stands) Weather: Fine

## 1692 32RED MAIDEN STKS 1m 1y(P)
**2:00** (2:01) (Class 5) 3-Y-O **£2,911** (£866; £432; £216) **Stalls** High

Form RPR
5- **1** **Eagle Creek (IRE)**[172] 7503 3-9-5 0 AndreaAtzeni 10 97+
(Simon Crisford) *mde all: pushed along and drew clr wl over 1f out: v comf* **9/4**[1]
02- **2** *6* **Mathix (FR)**[172] 7503 3-9-5 0 PatCosgrave 8 79
(William Haggas) *chsd wnr: rdn and easily lft bhd fr 2f out: kpt on to hold 2nd pl nr fin* **4/1**[2]
2-34 **3** *3/4* **Arnarson**[17] 1358 3-9-5 80 FrankieDettori 12 77
(Ed Dunlop) *chsd ldng pair: clr of rest over 2f out: kpt on to press for 2nd fnl f: no ch w wnr* **8/1**
0- **4** *3 1/4* **Azaly (IRE)**[188] 7064 3-9-5 0 JimCrowley 9 69
(Owen Burrows) *rring in stalls bef s: chsd ldrs in 5th: outpcd wl over 2f out: shkn up and kpt on fr over 1f out to win battle for modest 4th* **12/1**
422- **5** *hd* **Prerogative (IRE)**[187] 7100 3-9-5 79 (p) TomMarquand 6 69
(Richard Hannon) *mostly in 7th: outpcd wl over 2f out: shkn up over 1f out: kpt on steadily to press for modest 4th nr fin* **9/2**[3]
0 **6** *hd* **Coya**[10] 1503 3-8-11 0 (h) CallumShepherd[(3)] 1 63
(Charles Hills) *chsd ldrs in 5th: outpcd wl over 2f out: tk modest 4th fnl f tl nr fin* **100/1**
03- **7** *2* **Daimochi (IRE)**[147] 7962 3-9-5 0 AdamKirby 2 63
(Clive Cox) *plld hrd: chsd ldng trio: outpcd wl over 2f out: lost modest 4th fnl f* **8/1**
66- **8** *2 1/4* **Spun Gold**[285] 3819 3-9-5 0 JamieSpencer 3 58+
(Luca Cumani) *hld up towards rr and off the pce: shkn up and no prog over 2f out* **10/1**
63 **9** *2 1/2* **Entangling (IRE)**[20] 1299 3-9-5 0 TedDurcan 5 52+
(Chris Wall) *hld up and racd v wd thrght: nvr on terms and no prog whn shkn up over 2f out* **16/1**
0 **10** *nk* **Duke Of Bronte**[20] 1299 3-9-5 0 RyanTate 7 51
(Rod Millman) *a wl off the pce in last pair: bhd 3f out: kpt on ins fnl f* **100/1**
0 **11** *3 1/2* **Free Forum (IRE)**[10] 1485 3-9-2 0 AaronJones[(3)] 11 43
(David Simcock) *s.i.s fr wd draw: a wl in rr: pushed along 1/2-way: sn bhd* **66/1**
40 **12** *2* **Yemnaak (FR)**[10] 1497 3-9-5 0 (t) LukeMorris 4 38
(George Peckham) *t.k.h early: a wl in rr: bhd fnl 3f* **100/1**

1m 36.71s (-1.49) **Going Correction** -0.10s/f (Stan) 12 Ran SP% **118.3**
Speed ratings (Par 98): **103,97,96,93,92 92,90,88,85,85 82,80**
CSF £10.88 TOTE £3.10: £1.50, £1.80, £2.30; EX 12.80 Trifecta £69.20.
**Owner** Sheikh Mohammed Obaid Al Maktoum **Bred** Ruskerne Ltd **Trained** Newmarket, Suffolk

**FOCUS**
What looked a fair maiden beforehand was turned into a procession by the easy winner, who looks potentially very useful. The gallop was an ordinary one and the winner raced towards the far rail in the straight. It's been rated around the third.

## 1693 32RED.COM H'CAP 6f 1y(P)
**2:30** (2:30) (Class 5) (0-70,71) 3-Y-O **£2,911** (£866; £432; £216) **Stalls** Low

Form RPR
36-2 **1** **Angel Of Darkness**[90] 168 3-9-5 71 CallumShepherd[(3)] 3 76
(Charles Hills) *trckd ldrs: effrt on outer over 1f out: rdn and r.o to ld last 75yds* **12/1**[3]
4136 **2** *1/2* **Lady Cristal (IRE)**[27] 1203 3-9-2 65 (p) JosephineGordon 2 68
(K R Burke) *led: rdn 2f out: kpt on wl but hdd and outpcd last 75yds* **20/1**
1- **3** *1/2* **Team Meeting (USA)**[151] 7900 3-9-7 70 OisinMurphy 4 71
(Saeed bin Suroor) *free to post: t.k.h: trckd ldr: asked to chal over 1f out: fnd little and lost 2nd ins fnl f* **4/7**[1]
640- **4** *nk* **Tawaafoq**[185] 7157 3-9-8 71 (h[1]) JimCrowley 1 71
(Richard Hannon) *trckd ldng pair: waiting for a gap 2f out: nt clr run over 1f out and swtchd ins: shkn up to cl but limited rspnse and readily hld* **11/4**[2]
6-43 **5** *3* **Atlanta Belle (IRE)**[28] 1192 3-9-3 66 TedDurcan 6 57
(Chris Wall) *hld up in last: sltly detached over 2f out: pushed along over 1f out: nvr a threat but kpt on steadily* **33/1**
0-36 **6** *7* **Hidden Stash**[14] 1411 3-9-2 65 DavidProbert 5 33
(Andrew Balding) *rousted early: chsd ldrs on outer: rdn 1/2-way: wknd 2f out* **16/1**

1m 11.88s (-0.02) **Going Correction** -0.10s/f (Stan) 6 Ran SP% **111.6**
Speed ratings (Par 98): **96,95,94,94,90 80**
CSF £180.75 TOTE £10.00: £2.60, £6.40; EX 94.60 Trifecta £97.70.
**Owner** D James, J Gompertz, S Jenkins **Bred** Stratford Place Stud **Trained** Lambourn, Berks

**FOCUS**
A fair handicap but not too much early pasce on and the first four finished in a heap. The winner made her ground on the outside of the field. The second has been rated to her AW handicap latest.

## 1694 32REDSPORT NOVICE MEDIAN AUCTION STKS 5f 6y(P)
**3:00** (3:01) (Class 5) 2-Y-O **£2,911** (£866; £432; £216) **Stalls** High

Form RPR
**1** **Corinthia Knight (IRE)** 2-9-2 0 OisinMurphy 4 80+
(Archie Watson) *pressed ldr after 1f: rdn over 1f out: led last 150yds: sn clr* **13/2**
3 **2** *3 1/2* **Black Orange**[10] 1496 2-8-9 0 (b[1]) DavidEgan[(7)] 1 66
(Gay Kelleway) *led: tried to kick away 2f out: hdd and readily outpcd 150yds out* **11/10**[1]
**3** *1 1/4* **Crownthorpe** 2-9-2 0 TonyHamilton 6 62
(Richard Fahey) *dwlt: hld up: outpcd 1/2-way: shkn up and kpt on to take 3rd ins fnl f* **13/2**
**4** *1* **Our Man In Havana** 2-9-2 0 LukeMorris 7 58
(Tom Dascombe) *t.k.h: trckd ldrs: outpcd over 2f out: no imp after: lost 3rd ins fnl f* **11/2**[3]
**5** *2 1/4* **Brian Ryan** 2-9-2 0 TomMarquand 5 50
(Robyn Brisland) *chsd ldrs: outpcd 1/2-way: nvr on terms after* **5/1**[2]
**6** *14* **Swiss Psalm** 2-8-11 0 RobHornby 3
(Simon Hodgson) *dwlt: outpcd and sn t.o* **25/1**
**7** *1 1/4* **Tie Em Up Tel (IRE)** 2-9-2 0 AdamKirby 2
(David Evans) *dwlt: rousted to press ldr but hung rt bnd after 1f and lost pce: hung bdly rt bnd 2f out and virtually unsteerable: t.o after* **16/1**

58.87s (0.07) **Going Correction** -0.10s/f (Stan) 7 Ran SP% **116.1**
Speed ratings (Par 92): **95,89,87,85,82 59,57**
CSF £14.57 TOTE £6.60: £2.70, £1.30; EX 16.50 Trifecta £78.20.
**Owner** Ontoawinner & Partner **Bred** Tally-Ho Stud **Trained** Upper Lambourn, W Berks

**FOCUS**
Not much form to go on but a fair effort at least from Corinthia Knight, who was well on top at the finish. The gallop was sound and the winner raced just off the inside rail in the straight. The runner-up probably limits the level.

## 1695 BETWAY (S) STKS 1m 2f (P)
**3:30** (3:30) (Class 6) 3-Y-O+ **£2,264** (£673; £336; £168) **Stalls** Low

Form RPR
60-5 **1** **Viewpoint (IRE)**[12] 1457 8-9-11 80 AlistairRawlinson[(3)] 3 71+
(Michael Appleby) *trckd ldr: shkn up to ld 2f out: clr fnl f: pushed out* **4/6**[1]
2405 **2** *6* **Anton Chigurh**[19] 1329 8-10-4 73 JimCrowley 1 61+
(Tom Dascombe) *hld up in tch: chsd ldng pair over 2f out: sn no imp: rdn and kpt on to take 2nd last 75yds* **9/2**[3]
-000 **3** *1/2* **Haabis (USA)**[12] 1458 4-9-3 48 (h[1]) DavidEgan[(7)] 7 52
(George Peckham) *led at decent pce: rdn and hdd 2f out: no ch w wnr after: lost 2nd last 75yds* **100/1**
3060 **4** *2 1/2* **Firestorm (GER)**[28] 1191 6-9-10 58 (e) AdamKirby 6 47
(Michael Attwater) *hld up in last pair: drvn up on outer over 2f out: sn outpcd and wl btn* **8/1**
2-52 **5** *20* **Gaelic Silver (FR)**[39] 998 11-9-11 71 (p) HectorCrouch[(3)] 4 13
(Gary Moore) *trckd ldng pair: lost pl over 2f out and wknd tamely: t.o* **7/2**[2]
0 **6** *4 1/2* **Mister Flip Flop (IRE)**[17] 1358 4-9-10 0 (h[1]) JimmyQuinn 2 1
(Adam West) *dwlt: in tch in last pair to 3f out: wknd and sn t.o* **100/1**

2m 5.47s (-1.13) **Going Correction** -0.10s/f (Stan) 6 Ran SP% **113.5**
Speed ratings (Par 101): **100,95,94,92,76 73**
CSF £4.33 TOTE £1.50: £1.10, £2.30; EX 4.60 Trifecta £51.30.The winner was bought in for 6,000gns
**Owner** Mick Appleby Racing **Bred** F Dunne **Trained** Oakham, Rutland

**FOCUS**
Not a competitive seller, especially with Gaelic Silver underperforming. The gallop was an ordinary one and the proximity of the third holds the form down. The time, and the proximity of the third hold the level of the form down.

## 1696 BETWAY H'CAP 6f 1y(P)
**4:00** (4:01) (Class 4) (0-80,82) 4-Y-O+ **£4,690** (£1,395; £697; £348) **Stalls** Low

Form RPR
010- **1** **Alkhor**[117] 8380 4-9-9 82 FrankieDettori 7 93
(Richard Hannon) *trckd ldng pair: shkn up 2f out: clsd over 1f out: rdn to ld last 150yds: styd on wl* **7/2**[1]
4606 **2** *1* **Salvatore Fury (IRE)**[34] 1091 7-9-3 76 (p) JamieSpencer 2 83
(Keith Dalgleish) *dwlt: sn in 6th: racd awkwardly whn asked to make prog over 1f out: hanging but r.o to take 2nd nr fin* **5/1**[2]
5300 **3** *1 1/4* **Oriental Relation (IRE)**[12] 1454 6-9-8 81 (b) JimCrowley 6 84
(James Given) *pressed ldr w field strung out: led over 2f out: drvn and hdd last 150yds: lost 2nd nr fin* **11/2**[3]
-144 **4** *1/2* **Varsovian**[20] 1301 7-9-2 78 JackDuern[(3)] 9 79
(Dean Ivory) *chsd ldrs: rdn 2f out: one pce and nvr able to chal* **8/1**
50-6 **5** *1/2* **Red Tycoon (IRE)**[20] 1302 5-9-1 74 PatDobbs 10 74
(Ken Cunningham-Brown) *hld up in 9th and wl off the pce: pushed along 2f out: no prog tl rdn and styd on quite wl fnl f: nvr involved* **25/1**
1131 **6** *nk* **Born To Finish (IRE)**[59] 682 4-9-2 80 (p) DavidParkes[(5)] 8 79
(Jeremy Gask) *off the pce disputing 7th: rdn and prog on inner jst over 1f out: styd on but no ch to threaten* **5/1**[2]
0044 **7** *2 1/4* **Swiss Cross**[13] 1423 10-9-1 77 (tp) CallumShepherd[(3)] 11 69
(Phil McEntee) *off the pce disputing 7th: shkn up over 2f out: kpt on fnl f: no ch* **16/1**
1624 **8** *1/2* **Gold Flash**[25] 1238 5-9-7 80 KieranO'Neill 1 70
(Hugo Froud) *moslty in last pair: rdn 2f out: nvr in it but styd on ins fnl f* **12/1**
50-0 **9** *3/4* **Mezmaar**[20] 1301 8-9-4 77 (h) LiamKeniry 5 65
(Mark Usher) *slowly away: hld up in last pair and wl off the pce: pushed along 2f out: nvr involved but kpt on fnl f* **12/1**
0200 **10** *1/2* **Bertie Blu Boy**[11] 1467 9-8-10 69 (b) JFEgan 3 55
(Lisa Williamson) *led but pressed: hdd over 2f out: wknd qckly over 1f out* **25/1**
6306 **11** *1/2* **Ballesteros**[17] 1370 8-9-1 74 TonyHamilton 4 58
(Richard Fahey) *chsd ldng trio to over 2f out: wknd qckly over 1f out* **16/1**

1m 10.43s (-1.47) **Going Correction** -0.10s/f (Stan) 11 Ran SP% **116.9**
Speed ratings (Par 105): **105,103,102,101,100 100,97,96,95,94 94**
CSF £20.25 CT £94.37 TOTE £3.80: £1.70, £1.70, £2.60; EX 27.90 Trifecta £127.30.
**Owner** Al Shaqab Racing **Bred** Whatton Manor Stud **Trained** East Everleigh, Wilts

**FOCUS**
A strongly run race but one in which very frew figured. The winner, who came down the centre in the straight, is the type to win more races. The runner-up has been rated to this year's best.

## 1697 BETWAY STAYERS H'CAP 1m 7f 169y(P)
**4:30** (4:30) (Class 5) (0-70,72) 4-Y-O+ **£2,911** (£866; £432; £216) **Stalls** Low

Form RPR
6-12 **1** **Amanto (GER)**[11] 1466 7-10-0 72 (t) TomMarquand 10 80
(Ali Stronge) *trckd ldrs: clsd over 2f out: rdn to ld 1f out: pressed again 100yds out: kpt on* **7/2**[1]
2324 **2** *hd* **Miss Tiger Lily**[17] 1364 7-9-12 70 JimCrowley 9 77
(Harry Dunlop) *trckd ldrs: clsd 6f out: led over 2f out: drvn and hdd 1f out: rallied to press wnr 100yds out: no ex nr fin* **9/2**[2]
223 **3** *2 1/2* **Marshall Aid (IRE)**[11] 1466 4-9-3 65 (p) KieranO'Neill 1 69
(Mark Usher) *trckd ldrs: rdn to go 3rd over 1f out and tried to chal: one pce fnl f* **9/2**[2]
05-6 **4** *hd* **Aumerle**[38] 1027 5-9-9 67 LukeMorris 3 71
(Shaun Lycett) *in tch: rdn to chse ldrs wl over 2f out: kpt on u.p fnl f to press for 3rd nr fin* **12/1**
023- **5** *hd* **Southern States**[114] 8445 4-9-1 63 SteveDrowne 6 67
(Lydia Richards) *hld up in rr: prog over 4f out to chse ldrs over 2f out: sn drvn: kpt on fnl f but nvr able to threaten* **6/1**[3]
50-0 **6** *1 1/4* **The Quarterjack**[17] 1369 8-8-2 53 FinleyMarsh[(7)] 8 55
(Ron Hodges) *hld up in rr: effrt over 3f out: rdn over 2f out: kpt on same pce fr over 1f out and n.d* **16/1**
154- **7** *6* **Onorina (IRE)**[195] 6885 5-9-11 69 SamHitchcott 2 64
(Jim Boyle) *racd freely: led and clr after 3f to 6f out: rdn and hdd over 2f out: wknd qckly over 1f out* **10/1**

0440 **8** *3 3/4* **Dalavand (IRE)**[40] 988 4-7-10 **51** oh1 OllieJago(7) 5 41
(Laura Mongan) *a in rr: urged along and no prog over 4f out: lost tch 3f out* **20/1**

3-55 **9** *3 1/2* **Alshan Fajer**[21] 1292 7-9-5 **70** GinaMangan(7) 7 56
(J R Jenkins) *hld up in last: urged along 4f out: no prog and lost tch 3f out* **28/1**

032- **10** *119* **Shrubland**[31] 7309 4-8-6 **54** (b) JosephineGordon 4
(Alexandra Dunn) *chsd ldng trio: urged along bef 1/2-way: wknd rapidly over 5f out: t.o and virtually p.u fnl 2f* **7/1**

3m 22.31s (-3.39) **Going Correction** -0.10s/f (Stan)
**WFA** 4 from 5yo+ 2lb **10** Ran SP% **116.2**
Speed ratings (Par 103): **104,103,102,102,102 101,98,96,95,**
CSF £18.92 CT £71.82 TOTE £3.90: £1.50, £1.80, £1.60; EX 14.10 Trifecta £42.30.
**Owner** Shaw Racing Partnership 2 **Bred** Gestut Hof Ittlingen **Trained** Eastbury, Berks
■ Stewards' Enquiry : Gina Mangan five-day ban: used whip when out of contention (Apr 25-29)

**FOCUS**
Not many progressive sorts in an ordinary handicap. The gallop was only fair and the winner came down the centre. The runner-up has been rated pretty much to her old best.

## 1698 BETWAY APPRENTICE H'CAP (DIV I) 1m 4f (P)
**5:00** (5:00) (Class 6) (0-60,61) 4-Y-0+ **£2,264** (£673; £336; £168) **Stalls** Low

Form RPR

0-02 **1** **Victor's Bet (SPA)**[25] 1249 8-9-7 **61** PaddyBradley(5) 10 66
(Ralph J Smith) *hld up in last: stl there 3f out: gd prog and circled field fr 2f out: clsd over 1f out: rdn to ld last 80yds* **6/1**

0-30 **2** *3/4* **The Detainee**[22] 1283 4-9-4 **57** DavidParkes(3) 5 61
(Jeremy Gask) *awkward s: sn prom: pushed along over 4f out: prog u.p to chse ldr over 2f out: led ins fnl f: kpt on but hdd and hld last 80yds* **4/1**[2]

0065 **3** *3* **Turnbury**[25] 1249 6-9-9 **58** (p) EdwardGreatrex 8 57
(Nikki Evans) *chsd ldr: led 3f out: drvn 2f out: hdd and one pce ins fnl f* **8/1**

5242 **4** *1 1/2* **Powered (IRE)**[15] 1403 4-9-5 **55** HollieDoyle 6 52
(David Evans) *in tch: pushed along over 4f out: no prog tl kpt on fr over 1f out to take 4th ins fnl f: no threat* **7/2**[1]

0-54 **5** *3/4* **Smoky Hill (IRE)**[69] 279 8-8-11 **53** AledBeech(7) 2 48
(Tony Carroll) *hld up in tch: hanging on inner fr over 3f out: no prog 2f out: kpt on fnl f* **8/1**

-050 **6** *nse* **Ledbury (IRE)**[15] 1402 5-8-6 **46** JoshuaBryan(5) 9 41
(Lee Carter) *racd on outer: in tch: pushed along over 4f out: prog to press ldrs over 2f out: wknd over 1f out* **12/1**

05/4 **7** *1* **Hong Kong Joe**[34] 1081 7-9-0 **49** (e) HectorCrouch 1 43
(Lydia Richards) *prom: rdn 3f out: cl up bhd ldrs over 2f out: wknd over 1f out* **9/2**[3]

0-00 **8** *1/2* **Abertillery**[34] 1082 5-8-3 **45** LauraCoughlan(7) 3 38
(Michael Blanshard) *hld up in rr: pushed along and no great prog over 2f out* **16/1**

00-6 **9** *9* **Put The Boot In (IRE)**[12] 1458 5-9-1 **53** (p) CharlieBennett(3) 7 32
(Barry Brennan) *awkward s: sn wl in tch: urged along 4f out: wknd wl over 2f out* **50/1**

3003 **10** *2 1/2* **Flying Author (IRE)**[19] 1322 6-8-10 **45** (p) CallumShepherd 4 28
(Phil McEntee) *led: stdd pce after 3f and stretched on 5f out: hdd 3f out: wknd 2f out: heavily eased sn after* **11/1**

2m 32.68s (-0.32) **Going Correction** -0.10s/f (Stan) **10** Ran SP% **120.8**
Speed ratings (Par 101): **97,96,94,93,93 92,92,91,85,84**
CSF £31.44 CT £198.75 TOTE £5.80: £2.00, £1.90, £3.00; EX 39.10 Trifecta £163.80.
**Owner** Homecroft Wealth Racing & Kevin Old **Bred** Jose Simo Vazquez **Trained** Epsom, Surrey

**FOCUS**
Not a strong race and just an ordinary gallop but the winner, who came down the centre in the straight, won decisively. Straightforward form, with the runner-up rated to his best AW form to date.

## 1699 BETWAY APPRENTICE H'CAP (DIV II) 1m 4f (P)
**5:30** (5:30) (Class 6) (0-60,60) 4-Y-0+ **£2,264** (£673; £336; £168) **Stalls** Low

Form RPR

0-12 **1** **Willyegolassiego**[36] 762 4-9-3 **54** HollieDoyle 1 62+
(Neil Mulholland) *nudged along in rr: urged along more firmly and no prog over 4f out: laboured prog into 3rd wl over 1f out but sme way adrift: picked up fnl f and clsd qckly to ld last 50yds* **10/11**[1]

600- **2** *1 1/4* **Hallingham**[279] 3999 7-9-5 **55** HectorCrouch 2 61
(Ken Cunningham-Brown) *led 2f: chsd ldr: pushed along 5f out: rdn to ld 3f out and sent for home: looked like holding on tl mown down last 50yds* **13/2**[3]

0400 **3** *4* **Movie Magic**[20] 1303 6-8-3 **46** oh1 (b) DavidEgan(7) 4 46
(Mark Hoad) *led after 2f: clr w one rival 4f out: hdd 3f out: one pce after and lost 2nd ins fnl f* **20/1**

2010 **4** *1 3/4* **Nouvelle Ere**[36] 1067 6-9-3 **60** (t) AledBeech(7) 8 57
(Tony Carroll) *trckd ldng pair: outpcd 4f out: lost pl 3f out: no ch over 1f out but then styd on fnl f* **5/1**[2]

0-00 **5** *5* **Fleetwood Poppy**[61] 646 5-8-11 **47** CallumShepherd 7 36
(Michael Attwater) *in tch: outpcd fr 4f out: no hdwy and wl btn 2f out* **16/1**

-006 **6** *1 1/2* **Athenian Garden (USA)**[34] 1082 10-8-5 **46** oh1 JaneElliott(5) 9 33
(Paddy Butler) *hld up in last pair: no ch whn urged along on inner 2f out: sn no prog* **25/1**

300- **7** *2 3/4* **Bennelong**[175] 7427 11-8-11 **52** (v) PaddyBradley(5) 5 34
(Lee Carter) *in tch: chsd clr ldng pair over 3f out to wl over 1f out: wknd* **25/1**

5550 **8** *nse* **Galuppi**[52] 820 6-8-7 **50** (v) GinaMangan(7) 6 32
(J R Jenkins) *in tch: outpcd fr 4f out: no hdwy 2f out: no ch after* **12/1**

003- **P** **Fair Comment**[114] 8448 7-9-0 **57** StephenCummins(7) 3
(Michael Blanshard) *hld up in last pair: p.u and dismntd 4f out* **7/1**

2m 32.15s (-0.85) **Going Correction** -0.10s/f (Stan) **9** Ran SP% **120.9**
Speed ratings (Par 101): **98,97,94,93,90 89,87,87,**
CSF £7.64 CT £72.86 TOTE £1.80: £1.10, £1.90, £5.70; EX 6.90 Trifecta £146.40.
**Owner** John Hobbs **Bred** Southcourt Stud **Trained** Limpley Stoke, Wilts

**FOCUS**
Division two of a very ordinary event and a race in which the gallop picked up appreciably in the last 3f. The winner came down the centre. The third has been rated to her C&D form last February.
T/Plt: £90.30 to a £1 stake. Pool: £68,070.81 - 549.75 winning units. T/Qpdt: £3.80 to a £1 stake. Pool: £6,667.59 - 1268.36 winning units. **Jonathan Neesom**

# PONTEFRACT (L-H)
Tuesday, April 11

**OFFICIAL GOING: Good (good to firm in places; 9.0)**
Wind: Strong behind Weather: Cloudy with sunny periods

## 1700 ROA/RACING POST OWNERS JACKPOT H'CAP (DIV I) 1m 6y
**2:10** (2:10) (Class 5) (0-75,77) 4-Y-0+ **£3,881** (£1,155; £577; £288) **Stalls** Low

Form RPR

00-0 **1** **Billy Roberts (IRE)**[38] 1032 4-9-6 **74** ConnorBeasley 14 80
(Richard Guest) *sn trcking ldrs: hdwy over 2f out: rdn to ld jst over 1f out: styd on* **25/1**

606- **2** *1/2* **Desert Ruler**[161] 7743 4-9-2 **70** JackGarritty 13 75+
(Jedd O'Keeffe) *hld up and bhd: hdwy on inner 2f out: n.m.r and squeezed through jst ins fnl f: sn swtchd rt and rdn: fin strly* **12/1**

1555 **3** *3/4* **House Of Commons (IRE)**[13] 1433 4-9-9 **77** SilvestreDeSousa 10 80
(Michael Appleby) *cl up: led wl over 2f out: rdn and hdd jst over 1f out: drvn and kpt on fnl f* **6/1**[1]

-110 **4** *2* **Shearian**[35] 1074 7-9-0 **73** PhilDennis(5) 2 71
(Declan Carroll) *trckd ldrs: hdwy 3f out: rdn along over 2f out: drvn over 1f out: kpt on same pce* **16/1**

600- **5** *hd* **Sunnua (IRE)**[143] 8028 4-9-0 **75** SebastianWoods(7) 1 73
(Richard Fahey) *trckd ldrs on inner: n.m.r and swtchd rt over 1f out: sn rdn and kpt on same pce* **13/2**[2]

426- **6** *3/4* **Rockliffe**[159] 7582 4-8-7 **61** oh1 PJMcDonald 4 57
(Micky Hammond) *midfield: hdwy 3f out: rdn to chse ldrs over 1f out: drvn and kpt on same pce fnl f* **66/1**

114- **7** *1* **Fine Example**[183] 7203 4-8-12 **66** (p) KevinStott 9 60
(Kevin Ryan) *midfield: hdwy 3f out: rdn along 2f out: no imp* **12/1**

-560 **8** *nk* **Trinity Star (IRE)**[11] 1472 6-9-1 **69** (p) PaulMulrennan 12 62
(Michael Dods) *hld up towards rr: hdwy 2f out: sn rdn and n.d* **12/1**

515- **9** *shd* **Stanley (GER)**[167] 7623 6-9-8 **76** GrahamLee 6 69
(Jonjo O'Neill) *towards rr: hdwy on outer over 2f out: sn rdn along and n.d* **13/2**[2]

430- **10** *3/4* **Red Charmer (IRE)**[194] 6907 7-9-0 **68** ShaneGray 7 59
(Ann Duffield) *hld up: a towards rr* **33/1**

6023 **11** *4* **All You (IRE)**[14] 1409 5-9-3 **71** (v) DanielTudhope 5 53
(David O'Meara) *a towards rr* **7/1**[3]

540- **12** *5* **High Draw (FR)**[176] 7408 4-9-6 **77** JordanVaughan(3) 11 48
(K R Burke) *chsd ldrs on outer: hdwy over 3f out: rdn along over 2f out: sn wknd* **8/1**

00-0 **13** *1* **Ellaal**[13] 1433 8-9-6 **74** JamesSullivan 15 42
(Ruth Carr) *trckd ldrs: effrt over 3f out: rdn along wl over 2f out: sn wknd* **66/1**

6142 **14** *17* **Muqarred (USA)**[13] 1433 5-9-7 **75** (p) BenCurtis 3 4
(Roger Fell) *led: pushed along over 3f out: rdn and hdd wl over 2f out: sn wknd* **15/2**

1m 43.88s (-2.02) **Going Correction** -0.125s/f (Firm) **14** Ran SP% **115.1**
Speed ratings (Par 103): **105,104,103,101,101 100,99,99,99,98 94,89,88,71**
CSF £283.36 CT £2035.29 TOTE £24.90: £6.90, £4.30, £2.40; EX 285.10 Trifecta £2290.80.
**Owner** www.primelawns.co.uk **Bred** Burgage Stud **Trained** Ingmanthorpe, W Yorks

**FOCUS**
No watering, and the going was given as good, good to firm in places (GoingStick: 8.9). After riding in the opener Graham Lee called the ground good and Danny Tudhope said: "It is good, fast ground," but Ben Curtis said: "It is quick." It paid to be fairly handy. The winner has been rated close to his 3yo form, and the third to his best.

## 1701 BREEDERS BACKING RACING "HIGH-RISE" EBF MAIDEN STKS (PLUS 10 RACE) 1m 4f 5y
**2:40** (2:41) (Class 3) 3-Y-O
**£9,337** (£2,796; £1,398; £699; £349; £175) **Stalls** Low

Form RPR

**1** **Above Normal** 3-9-5 0 KevinStott 3 80+
(Saeed bin Suroor) *dwlt: sn trcking ldrs: hdwy over 2f out and sn cl up: rdn and qcknd wl to ld appr fnl f: sn clr: readily* **15/8**[1]

6 **2** *4 1/2* **Marqoom**[18] 1347 3-9-5 0 DaneO'Neill 2 73
(Mark Johnston) *led: pushed along 3f out: jnd and rdn over 2f out: drvn and hdd appr fnl f: kpt on same pce* **5/1**[2]

0-34 **3** *2 1/4* **Cray (IRE)**[20] 1308 3-9-5 72 PJMcDonald 5 69
(James Bethell) *trckd ldng pair on inner: effrt 2f out and sn rdn: kpt on same pce fnl f* **6/1**[3]

4 **4** *3 1/4* **Asanta Sana (IRE)**[18] 1342 3-9-0 0 WilliamBuick 6 59
(John Gosden) *trckd ldr: cl up 1/2-way: chal over 2f out: sn rdn and ev ch: drvn over 1f out: sn btn* **15/8**[1]

- **5** *15* **Full Tilt Lad (IRE)** 3-9-5 0 BenCurtis 1 40
(Tim Easterby) *in tch: pushed along over 3f out: rdn wl over 2f out: sn outpcd* **33/1**

**6** *2 3/4* **Company Trader (IRE)** 3-9-5 0 PaddyAspell 7 35
(Sharon Watt) *dwlt and wnt rt s: in tch: rdn along 3f out: sn outpcd* **50/1**

- **7** *69* **Sambuca Nera** 3-9-0 0 TomEaves 4
(James Given) *a rr: rdn along 1/2-way: sn outpcd and wl bhd* **20/1**

2m 44.92s (4.12) **Going Correction** -0.125s/f (Firm) **7** Ran SP% **110.2**
Speed ratings (Par 102): **81,78,76,74,64 62,16**
CSF £10.93 TOTE £2.40: £1.50, £2.50; EX 10.40 Trifecta £33.90.
**Owner** Godolphin **Bred** Darley **Trained** Newmarket, Suffolk

**FOCUS**
This didn't look the strongest of maidens beforehand, but there was quite a bit to like about the way the winner settled matters. It's been rated around the third to the better view of his form.

## 1702 RACING UK ANYWHERE AVAILABLE NOW H'CAP 6f
**3:10** (3:10) (Class 3) (0-95,95) 3-Y-O **£7,762** (£2,310; £1,154; £577) **Stalls** Low

Form RPR

11- **1** **Brian The Snail (IRE)**[168] 7589 3-9-7 **95** WilliamBuick 1 102+
(Richard Fahey) *trckd ldrs: hdwy over 2f out: cl up over 1f out: rdn and qcknd to ld ent fnl f: readily* **6/5**[1]

140- **2** *1 3/4* **Jule In The Crown**[300] 3270 3-8-11 **85** GrahamLee 5 86+
(Mick Channon) *trckd ldrs: effrt over 2f out and sn pushed along: rdn over 1f out: styd on wl u.p fnl f* **25/1**

0-20 **3** *shd* **Hemingway (IRE)**[20] 1311 3-8-6 **80** (p1) ShaneGray 10 81
(Kevin Ryan) *cl up: rdn 2f out: slt ld briefly jst over 1f out: hdd and drvn ent fnl f: kpt on same pce* **25/1**

046- **4** 1 **Seduce Me**[185] 7147 3-8-4 **78**.....(p) JoeyHaynes 4 76
(K R Burke) *hld up and bhd: hdwy over 2f out: rdn wl over 1f out: styd on strly fnl f* **16/1**

312- **5** nk **Battered**[186] 7120 3-8-8 **82**.....BenCurtis 6 79
(William Haggas) *trckd ldng pair: pushed along 3f out: rdn 2f out: drvn and no imp appr fnl f* **3/1**[2]

216- **5** dht **Arc Royal**[186] 7120 3-8-11 **85**.....RichardKingscote 3 82
(Tom Dascombe) *led: pushed along wl over 2f out: sn rdn: drvn and hdd over 1f out: grad wknd* **10/1**

341- **7** 2 ¾ **Mjjack (IRE)**[200] 6731 3-8-6 **80**.....PJMcDonald 9 68
(K R Burke) *dwlt and towards rr: hdwy over 2f out: rdn along wl over 1f out: n.d* **16/1**

31- **8** 1 ¼ **Chipping (IRE)**[169] 7578 3-8-3 **77**.....AndrewMullen 2 61
(Michael Dods) *chsd ldrs on inner: rdn along wl over 1f out: sn wknd* **8/1**[3]

602- **9** ¾ **Monks Stand (USA)**[244] 5299 3-8-12 **86**.....DavidAllan 7 68
(Tim Easterby) *chsd ldrs: rdn along over 2f out: sn wknd* **40/1**

1m 14.73s (-2.17) **Going Correction** -0.125s/f (Firm) **9** Ran SP% **112.6**
Speed ratings (Par 102): **109,106,106,105,104 104,101,99,98**
CSF £39.22 CT £500.73 TOTE £2.10: £1.10, £4.10, £5.20; EX 30.20 Trifecta £353.60.
**Owner** Godolphin **Bred** A Kirwan **Trained** Musley Bank, N Yorks
■ Stewards' Enquiry : Joey Haynes cautioned to future conduct in races

**FOCUS**
A good performance from the winner, who is well regarded and is likely to be upped in grade very soon. The third has been rated as improving, with the fourth fitting based on her form since her maiden win.

## 1703 JAMAICAN FLIGHT H'CAP (ROUND 1 OF THE PONTEFRACT STAYERS CHAMPIONSHIP 2017) 2m 2f 2y
**3:40** (3:40) (Class 5) (0-75,75) 4-Y-0+ **£3,234** (£962; £481; £240) **Stalls** Low

Form RPR

246 **1** **Uncle Bernie (IRE)**[31] 1153 7-9-8 **71**.....(p) JamesSullivan 1 77
(Sarah Hollinshead) *hld up in rr: smooth hdwy 4f out: trckd ldrs over 2f out: sn n.m.r and swtchd rt: rdn over 1f out: styd on strly to ld ins fnl f* **7/1**[3]

006- **2** 2 **Tuscan Gold**[58] 7006 10-8-11 **60**.....(p) PJMcDonald 8 63
(Micky Hammond) *hld up towards rr: hdwy over 4f out: trckd ldrs 3f out: effrt to chse ldr over 1f out: sn rdn and ev ch: drvn and kpt on same pce last 100yds* **12/1**

2401 **3** 1 ¼ **Medicine Hat**[18] 1344 6-9-12 **75**.....PhillipMakin 10 76+
(Marjorie Fife) *led 2f: trckd ldng pair: smooth hdwy and cl up 4f out: led 3f out: rdn wl over 1f out: drvn and hdd ins fnl f: kpt on same pce* **7/4**[1]

4150 **4** nse **Dream Serenade**[10] 1486 4-8-2 **56** oh5.....(h) RoystonFfrench 3 57
(Michael Appleby) *prom: chsd ldr over 2f out: rdn wl over 1f out: drvn and kpt on same pce fnl f* **10/1**

500- **5** 3 **Madam Lilibet (IRE)**[190] 7006 8-8-7 **56** oh2.....JoeyHaynes 4 54
(Sharon Watt) *trckd ldrs: hdwy 4f out: rdn over 2f out: drvn wl over 1f out: no imp fnl f* **12/1**

00- **6** 6 **Gran Paradiso (IRE)**[171] 3437 5-9-4 **67**.....(tp) PaulMulrennan 5 57
(Micky Hammond) *hld up towards rr: hdwy on inner over 4f out: chsd ldrs wl over 2f out: sn rdn and no imp* **33/1**

030- **7** 6 **Riptide**[176] 7411 11-9-4 **67**.....DougieCostello 11 50
(Michael Scudamore) *chsd ldrs: rdn along 4f out: wknd and hld whn hmpd 2f out* **25/1**

435- **8** 5 **Our Folly**[175] 3746 9-9-1 **64**.....(t) TomQueally 6 41
(Stuart Kittow) *a towards rr* **8/1**

20-6 **9** 29 **Hier Encore (FR)**[28] 1191 5-8-7 **56**.....PaulHanagan 12
(David Menuisier) *cl up: led after 2f: rdn along 4f out: hdd 3f out: sn drvn and wknd* **6/1**[2]

066- **10** 26 **Hartside (GER)**[21] 3437 8-8-13 **62**.....GrahamLee 7
(Peter Winks) *trckd ldrs: hdwy on outer and cl up over 5f out: rdn along over 4f out: sn drvn and wknd* **10/1**

4m 3.62s (7.42) **Going Correction** -0.125s/f (Firm)
**WFA** 4 from 5yo+ 2lb **10** Ran SP% **114.6**
Speed ratings (Par 103): **78,77,76,76,75 72,69,67,54,43**
CSF £85.86 CT £209.79 TOTE £7.50: £2.50, £3.30, £1.30; EX 126.70 Trifecta £438.90.
**Owner** Graham Brothers Racing Partnership **Bred** Roundhill Stud & Gleadhill House Stud Ltd **Trained** Upper Longdon, Staffs
■ Stewards' Enquiry : James Sullivan three-day ban: careless riding (Apr 25-27)

**FOCUS**
This was run at a good gallop.

## 1704 WATCH RACING UK ON 3 DEVICES H'CAP 1m 2f 5y
**4:10** (4:10) (Class 2) (0-105,103) 4-Y-0+
**£15,562** (£4,660; £2,330; £1,165; £582; £292) **Stalls** Low

Form RPR

510- **1** **Snoano**[185] 7154 5-8-13 **95**.....DavidAllan 8 106+
(Tim Easterby) *trckd ldrs on inner: hdwy 3f out: swtchd rt and rdn to chse ldr over 1f out: sn led: kpt on strly* **6/1**[2]

1210 **2** 2 ¼ **Final**[10] 1502 5-8-9 **91**.....FrannyNorton 9 96+
(Mark Johnston) *dwlt and rr: hdwy 3f out: effrt on inner over 1f out: sn rdn and squeezed through entering fnl f: styd on wl towards fin* **11/2**[1]

510- **3** 1 ¼ **Innocent Touch (IRE)**[206] 6559 6-8-12 **94**.....JackGarritty 7 96
(Richard Fahey) *hld up in tch: hdwy over 2f out: rdn to chse ldrs over 1f out: kpt on fnl f* **7/1**

10-6 **4** ¾ **Bahama Moon (IRE)**[27] 1208 5-8-6 **88**.....PJMcDonald 4 89
(David Barron) *trckd ldng pair: pushed along wl over 2f out: rdn wl over 1f out: drvn and kpt on same pce fnl f* **6/1**[2]

24-0 **5** shd **Cote D'Azur**[24] 1258 4-8-12 **94**.....WilliamBuick 13 94
(Les Eyre) *led: rdn along over 2f out: drvn and hdd over 1f out: wknd* **6/1**[2]

014- **6** 2 ½ **Cymro (IRE)**[207] 6545 5-9-5 **101**.....RichardKingscote 11 96
(Tom Dascombe) *hld up and bhd: hdwy over 2f out: rdn and kpt on fnl f: nrst fin* **6/1**[2]

53-4 **7** hd **Great Hall**[18] 1341 7-9-7 **103**.....WilliamCarson 10 98
(Mick Quinn) *in tch on outer: rdn along over 2f out: sn wknd* **14/1**

3/ **8** 4 ½ **Ashkoul (FR)**[201] 4-8-12 **94**.....BenCurtis 5 80
(Michael Appleby) *chsd ldr: hdwy 3f out: cl up over 2f out: rdn and ev ch wl over 1f out: sn drvn and wknd* **13/2**[3]

340- **9** 3 ¾ **Imshivalla (IRE)**[157] 7823 6-8-7 **89**.....(h) PaulHanagan 14 67
(Richard Fahey) *chsd ldrs: rdn along 3f out: sn wknd* **10/1**

2m 10.97s (-2.73) **Going Correction** -0.125s/f (Firm) **9** Ran SP% **114.1**
Speed ratings (Par 109): **105,103,102,101,101 99,99,95,92**
CSF £38.42 CT £235.44 TOTE £7.40: £2.30, £2.10, £2.40; EX 47.40 Trifecta £321.10.
**Owner** M J Macleod **Bred** Minster Stud **Trained** Great Habton, N Yorks

**FOCUS**
The free-going Cote D'Azur took them along at a pretty good gallop. The third has been rated close to form.

## 1705 INTO THE SKY MAIDEN FILLIES' STKS (PLUS 10 RACE) 6f
**4:40** (4:42) (Class 5) 3-Y-O **£3,881** (£1,155; £577; £288) **Stalls** Low

Form RPR

2 **1** **Acadian Angel (IRE)**[27] 1199 3-9-0 0.....JasonHart 7 70
(John Quinn) *trckd ldrs: hdwy on outer over 2f out: rdn jst over 1f out: styd on wl fnl f to ld nr fin* **10/1**

45- **2** ½ **Always Thankful**[187] 7099 3-9-0 0.....SilvestreDeSousa 3 68
(Ismail Mohammed) *slt ld: hdd 3f out: cl up and rdn to ld again jst over 1f out: drvn ins fnl f: hdd and no ex nr fin* **11/10**[1]

040- **3** 1 ¾ **Doria Road (USA)**[145] 7988 3-9-0 63.....KevinStott 10 63
(Kevin Ryan) *hld up in rr: hdwy on outer wl over 1f out: rdn and styd on strly fnl f: nrst fin* **25/1**

255- **4** hd **Sugar Beach (FR)**[201] 6712 3-9-0 72.....JoeyHaynes 2 62
(Ann Duffield) *t.k.h: trckd ldrs: hdwy over 2f out effrt and nt clr run over 1f out: swtchd rt and rdn ins fnl f: kpt on* **8/1**[3]

450- **5** nk **Incentive**[169] 7571 3-9-0 62.....TomQueally 1 61
(Stuart Kittow) *cl up on inner: led 3f out: rdn along 2f out: hdd over 1f out: sn drvn and grad wknd* **16/1**

5 **6** 1 **England Expects**[11] 1471 3-9-0 0.....DougieCostello 6 59
(K R Burke) *t.k.h: trckd ldrs on inner: hdwy over 2f out: nt clr run over 1f out: rdn and kpt on fnl f* **9/1**

04- **7** 1 ¾ **Chicago Star**[164] 7696 3-9-0 0.....GrahamLee 4 52+
(Mick Channon) *t.k.h: trckd ldrs: pushed along over 2f out: rdn wl over 1f out: sn drvn and wknd* **5/1**[2]

**8** 1 **Mabs Cross** 3-9-0 0.....PaulMulrennan 8 49+
(Michael Dods) *dwlt: a towards rr* **8/1**[3]

**9** 4 ½ **Decima (IRE)** 3-8-7 0.....HarrisonShaw(7) 9 35
(Michael Easterby) *s.i.s: a rr* **50/1**

4- **10** 7 **Suited**[145] 7988 3-9-0 0.....DuranFentiman 11 12
(Tim Easterby) *in tch on outer: pushed along 3f out: rdn over 2f out: sn wknd* **25/1**

1m 17.04s (0.14) **Going Correction** -0.125s/f (Firm) **10** Ran SP% **121.1**
Speed ratings (Par 95): **94,93,91,90,90 89,86,85,79,70**
CSF £21.95 TOTE £8.50: £2.60, £1.10, £6.60; EX 21.60 Trifecta £370.90.
**Owner** The Desperados **Bred** R Hannon & J Cullinan **Trained** Settrington, N Yorks

**FOCUS**
They went steady early, with plenty racing keenly, and they finished in a bit of a heap. It's been rated around the fifth, with the first two close to form.

## 1706 ROA/RACING POST OWNERS JACKPOT H'CAP (DIV II) 1m 6y
**5:10** (5:10) (Class 5) (0-75,77) 4-Y-0+ **£3,881** (£1,155; £577; £288) **Stalls** Low

Form RPR

303- **1** **Rockwood**[144] 8007 6-9-5 **73**.....(v) TomEaves 13 79
(Karen McLintock) *swtchd lft s and rr: hdwy over 2f out: sn swtchd rt to outer and rdn over 1f out: styd on strly fnl f to ld nr fin* **40/1**

-310 **2** ¾ **Chiswick Bey (IRE)**[41] 968 9-9-0 **71**.....AdamMcNamara(3) 12 75
(Richard Fahey) *trckd ldr: cl up over 2f out: rdn to chal over 1f out: drvn ins fnl f: slt advantage last 75 yds: hdd and no ex nr fin* **25/1**

050- **3** hd **Buckland Beau**[222] 6048 6-9-6 **74**.....StevieDonohoe 1 78+
(Charlie Fellowes) *in tch: hdwy over 2f out: rdn and n.m.r over 1f out: swtchd rt and drvn ins fnl f: kpt on wl towards fin* **6/1**[3]

0143 **4** hd **Kiwi Bay**[11] 1473 12-8-5 **66**.....CallumRodriguez(7) 8 69
(Michael Dods) *trckd ldrs: hdwy 2f out: rdn over 1f out: drvn and ev ch ins fnl f: kpt on* **16/1**

000- **5** ¾ **Off Art**[185] 7159 7-9-7 **75**.....(p) DavidAllan 2 76
(Tim Easterby) *led: jnd and rdn 2f out: drvn over 1f out: hdd wl ins fnl f: kpt on same pce* **5/2**[1]

0-05 **6** 1 ¼ **Thaqaffa (IRE)**[22] 1288 4-9-8 **76**.....SilvestreDeSousa 3 77+
(Amy Murphy) *trckd ldrs on inner: hdwy 2f out: nt clr run jst ins fnl f: nt rcvr* **4/1**[2]

411- **7** nk **Zeshov (IRE)**[203] 6643 6-9-5 **73**.....DanielTudhope 5 72
(Rebecca Bastiman) *trckd ldrs: hdwy over 2f out: rdn to chal over 1f out: ev ch tl drvn and wknd fnl f* **9/1**

620- **8** nk **Jabbaar**[189] 7051 4-9-7 **75**.....PhillipMakin 9 72
(David Barron) *midfield: pushed along and outpcd over 2f out: rdn wl over 1f out: kpt on fnl f* **16/1**

660- **9** 1 **Ataman (IRE)**[183] 7222 5-9-3 **74**.....LouisSteward(3) 10 69
(Chris Wall) *towards rr: hdwy on outer 3f out: rdn to chse ldrs 2f out: sn drvn and wknd* **16/1**

-100 **10** shd **Pickett's Charge**[41] 968 4-9-2 **70**.....(h[1]) DougieCostello 6 65
(Richard Guest) *a towards rr* **20/1**

/62- **11** 1 ½ **Cornborough**[122] 1631 6-9-3 **71**.....(p) JasonHart 7 62
(Mark Walford) *a towards rr* **12/1**

60-0 **12** 2 ¼ **First Wheat**[10] 1498 4-8-12 **69**.....(b[1]) NathanEvans(3) 4 55
(Michael Easterby) *t.k.h: midfield: pushed along on inner: rdn along 3f out: sn wknd* **20/1**

330- **13** 1 ½ **Arithmetic (IRE)**[192] 6956 4-8-13 **67**.....JamesSullivan 11 49
(Ruth Carr) *a rr* **16/1**

0000 **14** nk **Arrowzone**[13] 1422 6-9-9 **77**.....RyanPowell 14 59
(Kevin Frost) *a rr* **33/1**

1m 44.86s (-1.04) **Going Correction** -0.125s/f (Firm) **14** Ran SP% **122.8**
Speed ratings (Par 103): **100,99,99,98,98 96,96,96,95,95 93,91,89,89**
CSF £806.34 CT £6853.84 TOTE £39.90: £7.80, £7.60, £2.50; EX 531.20 Trifecta £6358.70 Part won..
**Owner** I R Clements & Dr L G Parry **Bred** Norcroft Park Stud **Trained** Ingoe, Northumberland

**FOCUS**
A fair handicap. It's been rated around the runner-up, with the fourth to his recent AW form.

## 1707 SEE BANANARAMA AT PONTEFRACT 80S NIGHT APPRENTICE H'CAP 1m 2f 5y
**5:40** (5:44) (Class 5) (0-75,77) 4-Y-0+ **£3,234** (£962; £481; £240) **Stalls** Low

Form RPR

000- **1** **Gulf Of Poets**[176] 7412 5-9-2 **70**.....NathanEvans 6 85+
(Michael Easterby) *in tch: hdwy 3f out: chsd ldr over 1f out: rdn to ld appr fnl f: sn clr: kpt on strly* **7/2**[3]

226- **2** 3 ¾ **Bit Of A Quirke**[210] 6432 4-8-7 **61** oh1.....JordanVaughan 7 67
(Mark Walford) *cl up: led over 7f out: rdn clr 2f out: hdd appr fnl f: kpt on same pce* **14/1**

-131 **3** 1 ¾ **Kingthistle**[52] 809 4-9-2 **73**.....LewisEdmunds(3) 3 76
(Rebecca Menzies) *t.k.h: hld up: hdwy 3f out: rdn along to chse ldrs 2f out: no imp fnl f* **11/4**[1]

0-54 **4** *5* **Melabi (IRE)**[56] 727 4-8-8 **67**.............................. CallumRodriguez(5) 11 60
(Richard Ford) *hld up towards rr: hdwy 3f out: rdn along 2f out: kpt on one pce* **10/1**

600- **5** *1 1/4* **Theos Lolly (IRE)**[144] 8007 4-9-0 **75**........................ ConnorMurtagh(7) 5 65
(Richard Fahey) *prom: cl up 4f out: rdn to chal over 2f out: drvn over 1f out: wknd* **3/1**[2]

00-0 **6** *hd* **Framley Garth (IRE)**[20] 992 5-8-12 **71**........................... PaulaMuir(5) 2 61
(Patrick Holmes) *rr tl sme late hdwy* **14/1**

02-0 **7** *7* **We'll Shake Hands (FR)**[10] 1498 6-8-4 **65**.............. RussellHarris(7) 14 41
(K R Burke) *a rr* **25/1**

0453 **8** *nk* **Ravenhoe (IRE)**[19] 1323 4-9-2 **73**............................. RichardOliver(3) 8 48
(Mark Johnston) *trckd ldrs on outer: hdwy and cl up over 2f out: sn rdn along and wknd* **10/1**

30-0 **9** *9* **Clayton Hall (IRE)**[10] 1498 4-8-6 **65**....................(p[1]) BenRobinson(5) 12 22
(John Wainwright) *in tch on outer: rdn along over 3f out: sn wknd* **33/1**

0-00 **10** *9* **Silver Alliance**[52] 806 9-8-11 **65**................................(b) ShelleyBirkett 10
(Julia Feilden) *led: hdd over 7f out: cl up on inner: rdn along 3f out: sn wknd* **20/1**

2m 12.61s (-1.09) **Going Correction** -0.125s/f (Firm) **10** Ran SP% **117.0**
Speed ratings (Par 103): **99,96,94,90,89 89,83,83,76,69**
CSF £49.94 CT £154.31 TOTE £4.50: £1.30, £4.00, £1.50; EX 59.10 Trifecta £231.30.
**Owner** L Westwood, A Chandler & L Hall **Bred** Juddmonte Farms Ltd **Trained** Sheriff Hutton, N Yorks

**FOCUS**

The winner proved to be in a different league to the rest. It's been rated around the runner-up to the better view of his form.

T/Jkpt: Not won. T/Plt: £37.80 to a £1 stake. Pool: £81,409.30 - 1571.70 winning units. T/Qpdt: £5.30 to a £1 stake. Pool: £5,709.14 - 789.50 winning units. **Joe Rowntree**

1708 - 1714a (Foreign Racing) - See Raceform Interactive

# CATTERICK (L-H)

Wednesday, April 12

**OFFICIAL GOING: Good to firm (good in places; 8.7) (watered)**

Wind: fairly strong, predominantly against runners in home straight Weather: Fine

## 1715 FLAT SEASON STARTS TODAY H'CAP 5f

**2:00** (2:01) (Class 6) (0-60,60) 3-Y-O **£2,264** (£673; £336; £168) **Stalls** Low

Form RPR

6-43 **1** **Wishing Time (IRE)**[13] 1453 3-9-5 **58**........................ DanielTudhope 14 66+
(David O'Meara) *chsd ldr towards outer: rdn to ld narrowly 1f out: drvn and hld on all out* **4/1**[1]

5-65 **2** *hd* **Joysunny**[8] 1543 3-8-4 **46** oh1.................................... NathanEvans(3) 12 53+
(Michael Easterby) *chsd ldrs: rdn 1/2-way: chal strly ent fnl f: kpt on: jst failed* **9/1**

200- **3** *2* **Flashing Light**[124] 8285 3-9-5 **58**........................................ DavidAllan 1 58
(Tim Easterby) *chsd ldrs: rdn 1/2-way: kpt on same pce* **8/1**[3]

316- **4** *nk* **Jorvik Prince**[138] 8097 3-9-7 **60**........................................... SamJames 6 59
(Karen Tutty) *midfield: rdn 1/2-way: kpt on fnl f* **4/1**[1]

000- **5** *3 1/4* **Nifty Niece (IRE)**[203] 6678 3-8-13 **52**............................. GrahamLee 11 39
(Ann Duffield) *outpcd in rr tl kpt on fnl f: nrst fin* **22/1**

0-50 **6** *2* **Violet Mist (IRE)**[12] 1474 3-8-9 **48**.............................. PaulMulrennan 8 28
(Ben Haslam) *midfield: rdn 1/2-way: no imp* **33/1**

2050 **6** *dht* **Flying Hope (IRE)**[12] 1474 3-8-5 **47**..................(v) RachelRichardson(3) 7 27
(Nigel Tinkler) *led: rdn 2f out: hdd 1f out: wknd* **14/1**

0040 **8** *nk* **Vocalisation (IRE)**[18] 1372 3-8-7 **46** oh1........................ JimmyQuinn 15 25
(John Weymes) *slowly away: sn midfield: rdn 1/2-way and no imp* **14/1**

000- **9** *1 1/4* **Miss Pepper (IRE)**[204] 6641 3-8-7 **46** oh1....................(p[1]) CamHardie 9 20
(Paul Midgley) *hld up: nvr threatened* **25/1**

500- **10** *hd* **Nyx**[199] 6807 3-8-7 **46** oh1...........................................(h[1]) BenCurtis 5 20
(Richard Guest) *chsd ldrs: wknd fnl 2f* **25/1**

600- **11** *4* **Lights**[199] 6807 3-8-2 **46** oh1............................................ PhilDennis(5) 2 5
(Declan Carroll) *dwlt: sn in tch: rdn 1/2-way: sn wknd* **66/1**

300- **12** *14* **Redrosezorro**[180] 7313 3-9-6 **59**.......................................... JasonHart 4
(Eric Alston) *s.i.s: sn midfield: pushed along and outpcd 1/2-way: wknd over 1f out and eased* **11/2**[2]

6500 **13** *20* **Dixie's Double**[14] 1418 3-9-7 **60**...................................(b[1]) JoeFanning 13
(Daniel Kubler) *sn bdly outpcd in rr: eased fr over 1f out* **14/1**

1m 1.09s (1.29) **Going Correction** +0.05s/f (Good) **13** Ran SP% **113.0**
Speed ratings (Par 96): **91,90,87,87,81 78,78,78,76,75 69,47,15**
CSF £35.24 CT £279.75 TOTE £4.20: £1.80, £3.00, £2.80; EX 46.00 Trifecta £273.90.
**Owner** Qatar Racing & Clipper Logistics **Bred** Southacre Bloodstock **Trained** Upper Helmsley, N Yorks

■ Stewards' Enquiry : Joe Fanning jockey said filly lost its action

**FOCUS**

All distances as advertised. Drying ground on a sunny day for Catterick's opening Flat fixture, and the wind was against them in the straight. After riding in the opener Paul Mulrennan said: "It is quick ground" while Joe Fanning and Danny Tudhope called it "good, fast ground". Not many got into this lowly sprint handicap. The balance of the third and fourth suggest this is a sensible starting point.

## 1716 NAGS HEAD SUPPORTS CATTERICK CHAMPIONS' AWARDS H'CAP 1m 5f 192y

**2:30** (2:31) (Class 5) (0-75,77) 4-Y-O+ **£2,911** (£866; £432; £216) **Stalls** Low

Form RPR

313- **1** **Kajaki (IRE)**[225] 6011 4-9-6 **71**..........................................(p) KevinStott 6 78
(Kevin Ryan) *trckd ldrs: pushed along to chse ldr over 2f out: rdn to ld ins fnl f: styd on* **4/1**[1]

0-50 **2** *1 1/2* **Falcon's Fire (IRE)**[22] 1292 4-9-2 **72**......................... RowanScott(5) 11 77
(Keith Dalgleish) *prom: led over 3f out: sn rdn: hdd ins fnl f: one pce* **33/1**

1342 **3** *2* **Go George Go (IRE)**[4] 1630 4-9-6 **71**................................. JoeFanning 3 73
(Alan Swinbank) *trckd ldrs: rdn over 2f out: styd on same pce* **5/1**[2]

3221 **4** *hd* **Surround Sound**[13] 1458 7-8-12 **63**..............(tp) RachelRichardson(3) 12 65
(Tim Easterby) *hld up: pushed along and hdwy towards outer fr over 2f out: disp 3rd ent fnl f: rdn and one pce* **8/1**

/51- **5** *2 1/2* **Gold Chain (IRE)**[39] 4935 7-8-8 **61**................................. PhilDennis(5) 9 60
(Dianne Sayer) *slowly away: hld up in rr: rdn and sme hdwy on outer 2f out: styd on fnl f: nrst fin* **50/1**

5245 **6** *hd* **Jan Smuts (IRE)**[19] 1344 9-8-11 **66**......................(tp) ConnorMurtagh(7) 1 64
(Wilf Storey) *midfield: rdn over 2f out: styd on same pce and nvr threatened* **33/1**

/204 **7** *3/4* **Magistral**[25] 1257 7-9-7 **72**.........................................(p) NathanEvans(3) 4 69
(Iain Jardine) *in tch: rdn over 2f out: one pce* **11/2**[3]

440- **8** *3/4* **Brandon Castle**[201] 6730 5-9-7 **69**.........................(h) DougieCostello 15 65
(Simon West) *dwlt: sn midfield towards outer: rdn over 2f out: one pce* **18/1**

224- **9** *6* **Satish**[174] 7487 4-9-11 **76**.............................................. DanielTudhope 10 64
(David O'Meara) *hld up in midfield: pushed along and sme hdwy over 2f out: wknd over 1f out* **8/1**

00 **10** *nk* **Main Fact (USA)**[21] 1307 4-9-0 **65**...........................(h) JamesSullivan 14 52
(Dianne Sayer) *hld up: nvr threatened* **100/1**

400- **11** *1 1/4* **Russian Royale**[167] 6083 7-9-7 **69**........................................ GrahamLee 5 55
(Micky Hammond) *in tch: rdn over 2f out: wknd over 1f out* **28/1**

-065 **12** *3* **Grand Meister**[25] 1257 6-9-7 **69**.......................................(b) JasonHart 13 50
(John Quinn) *in tch towards outer: rdn over 3f out: wknd over 2f out* **16/1**

065- **13** *3 1/2* **Cloud Monkey (IRE)**[19] 7043 7-9-7 **69**............................. DavidNolan 8 45
(Martin Todhunter) *hld up: rdn over 2f out: nvr threatened* **16/1**

134- **14** *1* **Bell Weir**[48] 6227 9-9-6 **68**........................................(bt) PaulMulrennan 7 43
(Kenneth Slack) *midfield towards inner: pushed along and lost pl over 3f out: sn btn* **8/1**

60/5 **15** *6* **Deinonychus**[7] 1561 6-9-12 **77**..........................(h) AlistairRawlinson(3) 2 44
(Michael Appleby) *led: hdd over 3f out: wknd* **40/1**

3m 2.68s (-0.92) **Going Correction** -0.175s/f (Firm)
**WFA** 4 from 5yo+ 1lb **15** Ran SP% **117.1**
Speed ratings (Par 103): **95,94,93,92,91 91,90,90,87,86 86,84,82,81,78**
CSF £149.89 CT £678.39 TOTE £5.00: £1.70, £6.80, £2.40; EX 121.50 Trifecta £1811.00.
**Owner** F Gillespie **Bred** Epona Bloodstock Ltd **Trained** Hambleton, N Yorks

**FOCUS**

They didn't go a particularly strong gallop in this modest staying event. The second has been rated back to form, with the fourth to his recent AW form.

## 1717 TEXT TO WIN A SPONSORSHIP EXPERIENCE H'CAP 7f 6y

**3:00** (3:03) (Class 5) (0-75,77) 4-Y-O+ **£2,911** (£866; £432; £216) **Stalls** Low

Form RPR

250- **1** **Bahamian Bird**[166] 7662 4-8-10 **67**...................... AdamMcNamara(3) 10 77
(Richard Fahey) *chsd ldrs: rdn 2f out: led ent fnl f: kpt on* **9/1**

0453 **2** *1 1/4* **Tadaawol**[12] 1472 4-9-1 **69**...............................................(p) GrahamLee 2 76
(Roger Fell) *chsd ldrs: rdn over 2f out: edgd rt ins fnl f: kpt on* **13/2**[3]

300- **3** *1* **Dutch Artist (IRE)**[187] 7126 5-9-9 **77**............................. DanielTudhope 5 81
(David O'Meara) *in tch towards inner: rdn over 2f out: bit tight for room and angled rt ent fnl f: kpt on* **4/1**[1]

322- **4** *1/2* **Someone Exciting**[162] 7747 4-8-9 **63**.................................. JasonHart 11 66
(David Thompson) *in tch: pushed along over 3f out: rdn over 2f out: sltly hmpd and swtchd lft ins fnl f: kpt on* **16/1**

-320 **5** *1/2* **Curzon Line**[55] 760 8-9-3 **74**....................................... NathanEvans(3) 9 77
(Michael Easterby) *midfield: pushed along and hdwy over 1f out: short of room 110yds out: rdn and kpt on* **6/1**[2]

000- **6** *3/4* **Crazy Tornado (IRE)**[145] 8011 4-8-8 **67**.................(h) RowanScott(5) 13 67
(Keith Dalgleish) *midfield: rdn over 2f out: kpt on ins fnl f* **12/1**

4251 **7** *1 1/4* **Tavener**[16] 1407 5-8-7 **61**...........................................................(p) BenCurtis 4 57
(David C Griffiths) *led: hdd over 5f out: led again over 2f out: hdd ent fnl f: wknd fnl 110yds* **11/1**

130- **8** *3/4* **Beatbybeatbybeat**[155] 7857 4-9-7 **75**................................ CamHardie 12 69
(Antony Brittain) *in tch: rdn over 2f out: wknd ins fnl f* **50/1**

226- **9** *nk* **Mr Orange (IRE)**[166] 7663 4-9-1 **69**........................(p) DougieCostello 14 62
(Paul Midgley) *prom on outer: led over 5f out: rdn whn hdd over 2f out: wknd and eased fnl f* **14/1**

01-4 **10** *2 1/2* **Faintly (USA)**[18] 1365 6-8-11 **65**..............................(b) JamesSullivan 3 52
(Ruth Carr) *s.i.s: hld up: nvr threatened* **8/1**

350- **11** *3/4* **Willsy**[138] 8101 4-8-9 **68**............................................. GemmaTutty(5) 15 53
(Karen Tutty) *hld up in rr: nvr threatened* **20/1**

30-0 **12** *8* **Slemy (IRE)**[12] 1472 6-9-9 **77**........................................... PaulMulrennan 7 40
(Ruth Carr) *dwlt: hld up: rdn over 2f out: sn wknd* **11/1**

056- **13** *8* **Steccando (IRE)**[227] 5919 4-9-0 **68**.................................... JoeFanning 6 9
(Alan Swinbank) *hld up: pushed along over 2f out: wknd and eased over 1f out* **20/1**

1m 25.16s (-1.84) **Going Correction** -0.175s/f (Firm) **13** Ran SP% **117.1**
Speed ratings (Par 103): **103,101,100,99,99 98,97,96,95,92 92,82,73**
CSF £63.53 CT £283.69 TOTE £10.90: £3.80, £2.40, £1.80; EX 74.40 Trifecta £409.50.
**Owner** Lady Juliet Tadgell **Bred** Lady Juliet Tadgell **Trained** Musley Bank, N Yorks

**FOCUS**

Modest form. Three of the first four raced up with the pace. The runner-up has been rated to the better view of his AW form.

## 1718 RACING UK IN GLORIOUS HD CLAIMING STKS 7f 6y

**3:30** (3:30) (Class 6) 3-Y-O+ **£2,264** (£673; £336; £168) **Stalls** Low

Form RPR

0-01 **1** **Fingal's Cave (IRE)**[40] 1007 5-9-7 83......................... JamieGormley(7) 6 86
(Iain Jardine) *prom: pushed along to ld 1f out: rdn and kpt on* **3/1**[2]

100- **2** *1 3/4* **Victoire De Lyphar (IRE)**[209] 6500 10-9-8 80...........(e) JamesSullivan 5 75
(Ruth Carr) *chsd ldrs: pushed along over 2f out: kpt on ins fnl f* **12/1**

-240 **3** *3/4* **Joey's Destiny (IRE)**[47] 896 7-9-11 86............................ DanielTudhope 4 76
(George Baker) *hld up: rdn and hdwy 2f out: chsd ldr ent fnl f: one pce fnl 110yds* **10/11**[1]

5-00 **4** *4* **Llewellyn**[50] 852 9-9-0 55.................................................(v) PhilDennis(5) 3 59
(Declan Carroll) *led: rdn 2f out: hdd 1f out: wknd* **25/1**

6334 **5** *1* **Jubilee Brig**[28] 1210 7-9-8 69.............................................. JoeFanning 2 60
(Alan Swinbank) *chsd ldrs: rdn over 2f out: sn outpcd and btn* **16/1**

6-32 **6** *2 1/4* **Secret Glance**[72] 481 5-10-0 78........................................ DougieCostello 7 60
(Philip Kirby) *midfield: rdn over 2f out: wknd ins fnl f* **14/1**

-003 **7** *1* **Aqua Libre**[26] 1238 4-9-2 75.........................................(t) LouisSteward(3) 1 48
(Philip McBride) *slowly away: hld up: nvr threatened* **8/1**[3]

00-0 **8** *16* **Slave To Freedom**[12] 1474 3-8-1 48....................................... JimmyQuinn 8
(Ann Duffield) *dwlt: hld up: bhd fr 1/2-way* **150/1**

1m 24.97s (-2.03) **Going Correction** -0.175s/f (Firm)
**WFA** 3 from 4yo+ 14lb **8** Ran SP% **113.2**
Speed ratings (Par 101): **104,102,101,96,95 92,91,73**
.Joey's Destiny was claimed by Mr Antony Brittain for £9000. Secret Glance was claimed by Mr Adrian Wintle for £12000. \n\x\x
**Owner** S Middleton **Bred** Rathasker Stud **Trained** Carrutherstown, D'fries & G'way

**FOCUS**

This claimer was run at what looked like a decent pace, and the time was slightly quicker than the preceding handicap. The winner has been rated near his recent form.

## 1719 2017 CATTERICK TWELVE FURLONG SERIES H'CAP (QUALIFIER) 1m 4f 13y

**4:00** (4:01) (Class 4) (0-85,87) 4-Y-O+ **£6,469** (£1,925; £962; £481) **Stalls** Low

Form RPR

5-04 **1** **Be Perfect (USA)**[21] 1307 8-9-2 **78**..........................(p) JamesSullivan 13 86
(Ruth Carr) *mde all: pushed along over 2f out: 2 1/2 l up over 1f out: rdn and reduced advantage ins fnl f: hld on all out* **10/1**

050- **2** *nk* **Sellingallthetime (IRE)**[200] 6794 6-8-8 **70**.....................(p) BenCurtis 4 77
(Michael Appleby) *trckd ldrs: rdn over 2f out: styd on ins fnl f* **8/1**

0-22 **3** *nse* **Busy Street**[22] 1292 5-9-0 **76** JoeFanning 6 83
(Alan Swinbank) *trckd ldrs: rdn over 2f out: styd on ins fnl f* **9/2**[1]
0-06 **4** *3* **Card High (IRE)**[21] 1307 7-8-11 **73** (t) PaulMulrennan 1 76
(Wilf Storey) *in tch: rdn 3f out: styd on same pce* **18/1**
010- **5** *3 1/2* **Syncopate**[147] 7980 8-9-4 **80** RobHornby 9 77
(Pam Sly) *trckd ldrs: rdn and outpcd 3f out: plugged on fnl f* **14/1**
100- **6** *1 1/2* **Mukhayyam**[158] 7824 5-9-7 **86** (p) RachelRichardson(3) 2 81
(Tim Easterby) *prom: rdn 3f out: grad wknd over 2f out* **13/2**[3]
045- **7** *3/4* **Master Of Irony (IRE)**[84] 7015 5-9-11 **87** (v) JasonHart 11 80
(John Quinn) *s.i.s: sn midfield: rdn over 3f out: no imp* **11/2**[2]
231- **8** *1 3/4* **Wishing Well**[165] 7332 5-8-9 **71** GrahamLee 8 62
(Micky Hammond) *hld up: pushed along over 2f out: minor late hdwy: nvr threatened* **25/1**
0/0- **9** *3 1/2* **Buyer Beware (IRE)**[200] 6794 5-9-1 **77** DougieCostello 10 62
(Patrick Holmes) *hld up: nvr threatened* **100/1**
445- **10** *2 3/4* **Itlaaq**[186] 7158 11-8-10 **79** (t) HarrisonShaw(7) 7 60
(Michael Easterby) *hld up: nvr threatened* **40/1**
50-1 **11** *10* **Instant Karma (IRE)**[23] 1289 6-9-4 **83** LouisSteward(3) 12 48
(Michael Bell) *midfield: rdn over 3f out: wknd over 1f out* **11/2**[2]
421- **12** *13* **Airton**[118] 8387 4-8-4 **74** BenRobinson(7) 3 18+
(James Bethell) *midfield: stmbld and rdr lost irons over 8f out: wknd over 2f out* **17/2**
250- **13** *3 3/4* **Wotabreeze (IRE)**[200] 6794 4-9-1 **78** CamHardie 5 16
(John Quinn) *a towards rr* **25/1**

2m 34.69s (-4.21) **Going Correction** -0.175s/f (Firm) **13** Ran SP% **116.1**
Speed ratings (Par 105): **107,106,106,104,102 101,100,99,97,95 88,80,77**
CSF £82.65 CT £413.83 TOTE £11.00: £3.80, £3.20, £2.20; EX 151.60 Trifecta £908.30.
**Owner** The Beer Stalkers & Ruth Carr **Bred** Joseph Allen **Trained** Huby, N Yorks

**FOCUS**
Fair handicap form, but another race in which the principals raced up with the pace. The third has been rated close to form.

## 1720 RACINGUK.COM H'CAP (DIV I) 5f 212y
4:30 (4:31) (Class 6) (0-65,65) 4-Y-0+ £2,264 (£673; £336; £168) Stalls Low

Form RPR
041 **1** **Major Valentine**[23] 1290 5-8-9 **60** BenRobinson(7) 8 67
(John O'Shea) *mde all: rdn over 1f out: kpt on* **3/1**[1]
05-4 **2** *3/4* **Clergyman**[28] 1209 5-8-9 **53** DuranFentiman 9 57
(Rebecca Bastiman) *hld up: rdn and hdwy over 1f out: kpt on* **11/1**
2120 **3** *shd* **Indian Pursuit (IRE)**[12] 1475 4-9-7 **65** JasonHart 12 69
(John Quinn) *chsd ldrs: rdn over 2f out: kpt on* **9/1**[3]
6543 **4** *1/2* **Socialites Red**[18] 1371 4-8-13 **60** (p) AlistairRawlinson(3) 10 63
(Scott Dixon) *prom: rdn over 2f out: no ex fnl 110yds* **10/1**
-362 **5** *1 1/2* **Coquine**[26] 1243 4-9-7 **65** (v1) DanielTudhope 7 63
(David O'Meara) *chsd leders: rdn over 2f out: no ex ins fnl f* **7/1**[2]
0004 **6** *hd* **Masarzain (IRE)**[21] 1310 4-9-7 **65** (b1) PaulMulrennan 11 62
(James Given) *s.i.s: hld up in rr: rdn over 2f out: kpt on ins fnl f: nvr threatened* **9/1**[3]
033- **7** *shd* **Bold Spirit**[170] 7584 6-8-12 **61** (t) PhilDennis(5) 1 58
(Declan Carroll) *chsd ldrs: rdn over 2f out: no ex fnl f* **11/1**
600- **8** *shd* **Dalalah**[253] 4972 4-8-7 **51** oh5 (v) JoeFanning 2 48
(Richard Guest) *dwlt: hld up: pushed along and sme hdwy over 1f out: one pce fnl f* **20/1**
0-55 **9** *2 1/4* **Ryedale Rio (IRE)**[20] 1328 4-8-13 **57** DavidAllan 5 47
(Tim Easterby) *midfield: rdn over 2f out: wknd fnl f* **10/1**
0320 **10** *1* **Kyllach Me (IRE)**[50] 852 5-8-8 **57** (b) RichardOliver(5) 4 44
(Bryan Smart) *hld up: rdn 1/2-way: nvr threatened* **9/1**[3]
2000 **11** *3 1/4* **Doeadeer (IRE)**[36] 1076 4-8-6 **55** (p) RowanScott(5) 3 32
(Keith Dalgleish) *s.i.s: a towards rr* **12/1**

1m 11.78s (-1.82) **Going Correction** -0.175s/f (Firm) **11** Ran SP% **114.8**
Speed ratings (Par 101): **105,104,103,103,101 100,100,100,97,96 92**
CSF £36.07 CT £266.20 TOTE £3.50: £1.40, £4.30, £2.10; EX 46.10 Trifecta £392.20.
**Owner** Pete Smith **Bred** J R Salter **Trained** Elton, Gloucs

**FOCUS**
Another race won from the front. Probably not bad form for the grade. The third has not rated higher than this since 2015 so that points to this being a sensible level.

## 1721 RACINGUK.COM H'CAP (DIV II) 5f 212y
5:00 (5:03) (Class 6) (0-65,65) 4-Y-0+ £2,264 (£673; £336; £168) Stalls Low

Form RPR
20-0 **1** **Blue Jacket (USA)**[60] 684 6-9-2 **60** PaulMulrennan 8 66
(Dianne Sayer) *prom: pushed along to ld narrowly over 1f out: rdn and edgd persistently lft: a maintained slt advantage* **11/2**[3]
6421 **2** *nk* **Windforpower (IRE)**[28] 1200 7-9-4 **62** (p) BenCurtis 9 67
(Tracy Waggott) *chsd ldrs: rdn over 2f out: ev ch ins fnl f: kpt on* **10/1**
3364 **3** *shd* **Penny Dreadful**[15] 1413 5-8-11 **55** (p) DavidAllan 10 60
(Scott Dixon) *led: rdn whn hdd over 1f out: remained w ev ch tl sltly impeded by wnr on rail nr fin* **5/1**[2]
-001 **4** *1 1/4* **Bogsnog (IRE)**[18] 1371 7-8-13 **57** JamesSullivan 6 62
(Ruth Carr) *in tch: pushed along to chse ldrs over 1f out: persistently short of room towards inner ins fnl f* **9/2**[1]
-144 **5** *1 1/4* **Ambitious Icarus**[12] 1475 8-9-6 **64** (e) DougieCostello 7 61
(Richard Guest) *midfield: rdn along 3f out: kpt on fnl f* **7/1**
000- **6** *2* **French**[159] 7797 4-9-2 **60** CamHardie 5 51+
(Antony Brittain) *s.i.s: hld up: collided w rail 3f out: dropped to rr and sn rdn along: minor late hdwy: nvr threatened* **14/1**
3505 **7** *nse* **Disclosure**[21] 1310 6-8-6 **55** PhilDennis(5) 12 46
(Declan Carroll) *stdd s and hld up in rr: rdn and hdwy 2f out: no ex fnl 110yds* **9/1**
050 **8** *3 1/2* **Louis Vee (IRE)**[26] 1247 9-8-3 **54** oh6 ow3 BenRobinson(7) 11 35
(John O'Shea) *hld up in rr: rdn over 2 out: nvr threatened* **40/1**
-040 **9** *3 1/4* **Life Of Fame**[78] 386 4-8-6 **53** (t1) NathanEvans(3) 4 24
(Rebecca Menzies) *midfield: rdn over 2f out: sn wknd* **8/1**
400- **10** *1 1/2* **Native Falls (IRE)**[169] 7596 6-9-0 **58** JoeFanning 1 24
(Alan Swinbank) *dwlt: sn prom: rdn over 2f out: sn wknd* **9/1**

1m 12.19s (-1.41) **Going Correction** -0.175s/f (Firm) **10** Ran SP% **112.0**
Speed ratings (Par 101): **102,101,101,99,98 95,95,90,86,84**
CSF £56.79 CT £288.95 TOTE £5.50: £2.00, £2.20, £1.60; EX 52.90 Trifecta £241.80.
**Owner** Andrew Sayer **Bred** Juddmonte Farms Inc **Trained** Hackthorpe, Cumbria

**FOCUS**
Once again the pace held up. It was the slower division by 0.41sec. The second, third and fourth set the level.

## 1722 RACING AGAIN 26TH APRIL APPRENTICE H'CAP 5f
5:30 (5:31) (Class 6) (0-65,65) 4-Y-0+ £2,264 (£673; £336; £168) Stalls Low

Form RPR
23-1 **1** **Kinloch Pride**[40] 1006 5-8-11 **52** (p) PhilDennis 12 61+
(Noel Wilson) *chsd ldrs: pushed along to ld appr fnl f: rdn and kpt on* **15/2**
0025 **2** *nk* **Culloden**[18] 1359 5-9-1 **56** PaddyPilley 9 63
(Shaun Harris) *prom: rdn to ld 2f out: hdd appr fnl f: kpt on but a hld* **16/1**
0-1 **3** *1/2* **Zylan (IRE)**[8] 1547 5-9-2 **65** 6ex BenSanderson(8) 15 70
(Roger Fell) *hld up on outer: rdn and gd hdwy over 1f out: kpt on* **7/2**[1]
603- **4** *nk* **The Armed Man**[170] 7585 4-8-10 **56** PaulaMuir(5) 13 60
(Chris Fairhurst) *hld up: pushed along and hdwy over 1f out: kpt on* **11/1**
5342 **5** *1/2* **See Vermont**[15] 1413 9-9-7 **62** (p) LouisSteward 1 64
(Rebecca Bastiman) *chsd ldrs: rdn 1/2-way: kpt on same pce* **18/1**
553- **6** *1* **Searanger (USA)**[118] 8390 4-9-6 **61** RowanScott 8 60
(Rebecca Menzies) *in tch: rdn 2f out: kpt on* **14/1**
416 **7** *2 1/4* **Roaring Rory**[47] 901 4-9-10 **65** (p) NathanEvans 6 55
(Ollie Pears) *midfield: pushed along 1/2-way: rdn over 1f out: nvr threatened* **16/1**
606- **8** *3* **Noodles Blue Boy**[200] 6774 11-9-5 **60** AdamMcNamara 4 40
(Ollie Pears) *dwlt: hld up: hdwy and in tch 1/2-way: briefly short of room over 1f out: sn wknd* **22/1**
2310 **9** *3 1/4* **Dandilion (IRE)**[33] 1126 4-8-13 **57** (t) BenRobinson(3) 11 25
(Alex Hales) *s.i.s: hld up: nvr threatened* **6/1**[2]
6201 **10** *3/4* **Cruise Tothelimit (IRE)**[15] 1413 9-9-5 **63** (vt) CallumRodriguez(3) 3 28
(Patrick Morris) *pressed ldr: rdn 1/2-way: wknd over 1f out* **7/1**[3]
040- **11** *1 1/2* **Lady Joanna Vassa (IRE)**[112] 8485 4-8-12 **56** PatrickVaughan(3) 2 16
(Richard Guest) *sn pressed ldr: rdn 1/2-way: wknd over 1f out* **22/1**
2365 **12** *hd* **Archie Stevens**[32] 1147 7-9-9 **64** (t1) CliffordLee 7 23
(Clare Ellam) *a towards rr* **16/1**
00-3 **13** *1 3/4* **Under Approval**[14] 1435 6-8-7 **51** oh1 (b) GemmaTutty(3) 14 4
(Karen Tutty) *slowly away: a rr* **28/1**
6425 **14** *3/4* **Pearl Noir**[15] 1413 7-9-9 **64** (b) DavidParkes 5 14
(Scott Dixon) *led narrowly: rdn whn hdd 2f out: wknd* **16/1**

59.68s (-0.12) **Going Correction** +0.05s/f (Good) **14** Ran SP% **116.7**
Speed ratings (Par 101): **102,101,100,100,99 97,94,89,84,83 80,80,77,76**
CSF £114.78 CT £495.35 TOTE £6.70: £2.10, £6.00, £1.70; EX 133.20 Trifecta £1683.10.
**Owner** G J Paver **Bred** Mrs C K Paver **Trained** Marwood, Co Durham

**FOCUS**
A moderate apprentice handicap in which high numbers emerged on top. So did offspring of Kyllachy, who's sire of the first three home as well as the fifth. The second and third pin the modest level.
T/Jkpt: Not Won. T/Plt: £39.00 to a £1 stake. Pool: £66,764.35 - 1,248.88 winning units. T/Qpdt: £8.70 to a £1 stake. Pool: £5,357.86 - 452.77 winning units. **Andrew Sheret**

# 1596 KEMPTON (A.W) (R-H)
Wednesday, April 12

**OFFICIAL GOING: Polytrack: standard**
Wind: Fresh, mostly across (away from stands) Weather: Becoming cloudy

## 1723 32RED.COM H'CAP 6f (P)
5:45 (5:50) (Class 6) (0-65,64) 4-Y-0+ £2,264 (£673; £336; £168) Stalls Low

Form RPR
340- **1** **Go Amber Go**[191] 7018 5-8-8 **56** LuluStanford(5) 5 66
(Rod Millman) *reluctant to s and to enter stall: mde all: decisive ld fr 1/2-way: urged along and kpt on wl: unchal* **13/2**
5346 **2** *2 3/4* **Compton Prince**[19] 1339 8-9-5 **62** (b) DavidProbert 10 64
(Milton Bradley) *sn chsd wnr: shkn up over 2f out: one pce and no imp wnr fr over 1f out* **9/1**
04-0 **3** *3/4* **Spellmaker**[96] 95 8-9-7 **64** MartinLane 11 64+
(Tony Newcombe) *towards rr: rdn and prog jst over 2f out: styd on to take 3rd nr fin* **16/1**
4000 **4** *3/4* **Rigolleto (IRE)**[35] 1080 9-9-6 **63** (p) JosephineGordon 9 61
(Anabel K Murphy) *chsd ldrs: rdn over 2f out: kpt on same pce and nvr threatened* **20/1**
0451 **5** *1/2* **Swendab (IRE)**[21] 1305 9-8-9 **57** (b) MitchGodwin(5) 4 53
(John O'Shea) *restless stalls: chsd ldng pair: rdn and no imp 2f out: fdd ins fnl f* **11/2**[3]
-062 **6** *1* **Mambo Spirit (IRE)**[30] 1180 13-9-5 **62** SteveDrowne 12 55
(Tony Newcombe) *wl in rr: shkn up over 2f out: kpt on fr over 1f out: nrst fin but no ch* **20/1**
00-0 **7** *1/2* **Hellarious**[65] 602 4-8-7 **50** oh5 (t) KieranO'Neill 1 42
(Geoffrey Deacon) *mostly in last pair tl plugged on fr over 1f out on inner: no ch* **50/1**
066 **8** *nk* **Pocket Warrior**[23] 1287 6-9-1 **63** GeorgeWood(5) 2 54
(Martin Bosley) *w.w in midfield: shkn up and no prog over 2f out: sn btn* **8/1**
2040 **9** *3/4* **New Rich**[35] 1080 7-9-3 **60** (v) JohnFahy 8 48
(Eve Johnson Houghton) *trapped out wd towards rr early: nvr a factor* **5/1**[2]
0006 **10** *nk* **Catalyze**[21] 1304 9-8-7 **50** oh5 (t1) DannyBrock 3 37
(Paddy Butler) *chsd ldng trio to over 1f out: wknd* **50/1**
4413 **11** *shd* **Nasri**[11] 1490 11-8-13 **56** (v) PatCosgrave 7 43+
(Emma Owen) *nrly sat down as stalls opened: lost abt 10 l and a bhd* **9/2**[1]
0102 **12** *1 3/4* **Encapsulated**[21] 1304 7-8-7 **57** RhiainIngram(7) 6 39
(Roger Ingram) *reluctant to post: nvr bttr than midfield: wknd over 1f out* **15/2**

1m 13.37s (0.27) **Going Correction** -0.075s/f (Stan) **12** Ran SP% **115.8**
Speed ratings (Par 101): **95,91,90,89,88 87,86,86,85,84 84,82**
CSF £59.49 CT £907.06 TOTE £6.90: £2.60, £2.60, £4.30; EX 68.50 Trifecta £1460.60.
**Owner** AJ & CS Bricknell-Webb **Bred** Percys (north Harrow) Ltd **Trained** Kentisbeare, Devon

**FOCUS**
Few got competitive here, the winner dominating throughout. A pb from the winner, but the form has been rated conservatively around the second and third.

## 1724 32RED CASINO CLASSIFIED STKS — 7f (P)
6:15 (6:16) (Class 5) 3-Y-O — £2,911 (£866; £432; £216) Stalls Low

Form — RPR

4226 **1** **Trenchard (USA)**$^{11}$ 1485 3-9-0 72.....(p$^1$) AdamKirby 2 — 78
(John Gosden) *trckd ldng pair: clsd to ld wl over 1f out: hrd rdn and kpt on wl fnl f* — **6/1$^3$**

330- **2** 1 ½ **On To Victory**$^{187}$ 7125 3-9-0 75.....(h) TomMarquand 1 — 74
(Eve Johnson Houghton) *urged along early and sn in 5th: rdn over 2f out: styd on fr over 1f out to take 2nd last 120yds: unable to chal* — **6/1$^3$**

4-31 **3** ½ **Glorious Artist (IRE)**$^4$ 1625 3-9-3 75..... CallumShepherd$^{(3)}$ 6 — 79
(Charles Hills) *dropped in fr wd draw and hld up in 6th: rdn and nt qckn over 2f out: kpt on fr over 1f out to take 3rd nr fin* — **11/8$^1$**

0-26 **4** ¾ **Hisar (IRE)**$^{13}$ 1453 3-9-0 73.....(h) LukeMorris 4 — 71
(Ronald Harris) *chsd ldng trio: rdn and nt qckn over 2f out: kpt on u.p fnl f: n.d* — **66/1**

00-3 **5** ¾ **Camargue**$^{22}$ 1294 3-9-0 75..... DaneO'Neill 3 — 69
(Mark Johnston) *led at decent pce: tried to kick on over 2f out: hdd wl over 1f out: fdd ins fnl f* — **9/1**

4-44 **6** nk **El Torito (IRE)**$^{30}$ 1176 3-9-0 74..... PatCosgrave 5 — 68
(Jim Boyle) *t.k.h early: trckd ldr: rdn over 2f out: one pce over 1f out: fdd ins fnl f* — **9/2$^2$**

31 **7** 4 ½ **Island Brave (IRE)**$^{26}$ 1241 3-9-0 74..... LiamKeniry 7 — 56
(J S Moore) *a in last: racd awkwardly after 2f: no prog and struggling over 2f out* — **8/1**

1m 25.35s (-0.65) **Going Correction** -0.075s/f (Stan) — 7 Ran SP% **111.5**
Speed ratings (Par 98): **100,98,97,96,96 95,90**
CSF £38.92 TOTE £3.70: £2.10, £4.30; EX 45.80 Trifecta £137.90.
**Owner** Godolphin **Bred** Ron Magers & Robert Marcocchio **Trained** Newmarket, Suffolk

**FOCUS**
A tight affair on paper but the winner was comfortably on top at the finish. The second has been rated a bit below his 2yo best, with the thrd also below his latest Wolverhampton win.

## 1725 32RED H'CAP (LONDON MIDDLE DISTANCE SERIES QUALIFIER) — 1m 2f 219y(P)
6:45 (6:46) (Class 3) (0-90,90) 3-Y-O
£7,158 (£2,143; £1,071; £535; £267; £134) Stalls Low

Form — RPR

21- **1** **Monarchs Glen**$^{185}$ 7187 3-9-4 **87**..... FrankieDettori 3 — 100+
(John Gosden) *taken down early: racd quite freely: mde all: qcknd clr smartly over 2f out: jst pushed along and 6 l ahd fnl f: heavily eased last 100yds* — **7/4$^2$**

1- **2** 1 **Big Challenge (IRE)**$^{161}$ 7770 3-9-6 **89**..... JosephineGordon 6 — 91
(Saeed bin Suroor) *t.k.h: trckd wnr: completely outpcd over 2f out: kpt on fr over 1f out but flattered by proximity* — **6/4$^1$**

21 **3** 2 **Here And Now**$^{26}$ 1239 3-8-8 **77**..... OisinMurphy 1 — 76
(Ralph Beckett) *restless stalls: chsd ldng pair: bdly outpcd over 2f out: kpt on fr over 1f out but nvr any ch* — **7/1**

043- **4** 1 ½ **Jackhammer (IRE)**$^{196}$ 6868 3-9-7 **90**.....(h$^1$) AdamKirby 2 — 86
(William Knight) *a abt same pl: shkn up and bdly outpcd by wnr over 2f out: no ch after: briefly pressed for 3rd ins fnl f* — **25/1**

41- **5** nk **Andrassy Avenue (USA)**$^{151}$ 7940 3-8-12 **81**.....(b$^1$) MartinLane 5 — 76
(Charlie Appleby) *awkward s: hld up in last: rdn 3f out: tried to raise an effrt 2f out but no real impact* — **13/2$^3$**

1 **6** 6 **Villette (IRE)**$^{21}$ 1300 3-8-11 **80**..... LukeMorris 4 — 65
(Dean Ivory) *a in last trio: rdn over 2f out: wknd over 1f out* — **25/1**

2m 18.44s (-3.46) **Going Correction** -0.075s/f (Stan) — 6 Ran SP% **109.9**
Speed ratings (Par 102): **109,108,106,105,105 101**
CSF £4.51 TOTE £2.60: £1.50, £1.40; EX 5.30 Trifecta £13.30.
**Owner** K Abdullah **Bred** Juddmonte Farms Ltd **Trained** Newmarket, Suffolk

**FOCUS**
This looked an interesting handicap, with all but one in the line-up coming off maiden wins. The positions barely changed throughout but the winner stretched right away and was impressive. The third has been rated in line with the better view of his maiden form.

## 1726 RACING UK IN GLORIOUS HD H'CAP — 1m 2f 219y(P)
7:15 (7:15) (Class 6) (0-60,61) 3-Y-O — £2,264 (£673; £336; £168) Stalls Low

Form — RPR

550- **1** **Arab Moon**$^{148}$ 7962 3-9-8 **61**..... AdamKirby 4 — 68+
(William Knight) *hld up in last trio: bmpd along in last pl 3f out: prog over 2f out: chsd ldr fnl f: urged along and styd on to ld last 50yds* — **7/2$^2$**

2-23 **2** hd **Bonnie Arlene (IRE)**$^{13}$ 1445 3-9-7 **60**..... RichardKingscote 9 — 66
(Mark Johnston) *trckd ldrs: shkn up to ld wl over 1f out: drvn and kpt on wl fnl f but hdd last 50yds* — **2/1$^1$**

000- **3** 2 ¾ **Black Prince (FR)**$^{147}$ 7977 3-9-0 **53**..... JFEgan 5 — 55
(Anthony Honeyball) *hld up in last trio: quick move to press ldr 1/2-way: rdn to ld over 2f out: hdd wl over 1f out: one pce* — **6/1**

065- **4** 1 ¼ **Perla Blanca (USA)**$^{163}$ 7726 3-9-2 **55**..... SteveDrowne 6 — 55
(Marcus Tregoning) *hld up in tch: rdn over 2f out: kpt on same pce and nvr able to chal* — **5/1$^3$**

006- **5** 8 **Netley Abbey**$^{205}$ 6623 3-9-6 **59**.....(v$^1$) JosephineGordon 8 — 46
(Harry Dunlop) *urged along early then t.k.h on outer: chsd ldrs: rdn over 2f out: sn wknd* — **7/1**

0-04 **6** 1 ½ **Hi There Silver (IRE)**$^{63}$ 627 3-8-7 **46** oh1..... KieranO'Neill 1 — 31
(Michael Madgwick) *trckd ldrs: lost pl 1/2-way: rdn 4f out: lost tch 2f out* — **12/1**

40-6 **7** nse **Flawed Diamond (FR)**$^{22}$ 1297 3-8-7 **49**..... JordanVaughan$^{(3)}$ 3 — 34
(K R Burke) *hld up in last trio: urged along over 3f out: struggling in last over 2f out: sn no ch* — **16/1**

04-0 **8** nk **Ciel Rouge**$^{14}$ 1428 3-8-11 **50**.....(t$^1$) AdamBeschizza 2 — 34
(Charlie Wallis) *led: set modest pce tl pressed 1/2-way: hdd over 2f out: wknd rapidly over 1f out* — **33/1**

2m 21.08s (-0.82) **Going Correction** -0.075s/f (Stan) — 8 Ran SP% **115.5**
Speed ratings (Par 96): **99,98,96,95,90 89,89,88**
CSF £11.06 CT £39.62 TOTE £5.60: £1.70, £1.40, £2.80; EX 12.10 Trifecta £64.80.
**Owner** Angmering Park Thoroughbreds Iv **Bred** Genesis Green Stud Ltd **Trained** Patching, W Sussex

**FOCUS**
A modest affair, but one or two noteworthy performances. The runner-up has been rated to his best.

## 1727 WATCH RACING UK IN HD MEDIAN AUCTION MAIDEN STKS — 7f (P)
7:45 (7:47) (Class 6) 3-5-Y-O — £2,264 (£673; £336; £168) Stalls Low

Form — RPR

**1** **Yamarhaba Malayeen (IRE)** 3-9-0 0..... OisinMurphy 14 — 83+
(Simon Crisford) *t.k.h: sn trckd ldr: led after 3f: shkn up 2f out: clr whn hung lft fnl f: styd on* — **5/1**

**2** 3 ¾ **Del Parco** 3-9-0 0..... AdamKirby 12 — 73+
(Clive Cox) *dwlt: rcvrd into 5th after 1f: drvn 2f out: styd on to dispute 2nd fnl f: no imp on wnr* — **7/2$^2$**

**3** nk **Yabrave** 3-9-0 0..... AndreaAtzeni 11 — 72+
(Roger Varian) *cl up: shkn up and rn green over 2f out: chsd wnr over 1f out: no imp but kpt on and jst lost out for 2nd nr fin* — **3/1$^1$**

0-5 **4** 3 **Mythical Spirit (IRE)**$^{16}$ 1401 3-8-9 0..... LukeMorris 10 — 59+
(James Tate) *mounted on crse: chsd ldng trio: shkn up 2f out: outpcd over 1f out* — **8/1**

**5** 3 ¼ **Patchwork** 3-9-0 0..... ShaneKelly 13 — 55
(Richard Hughes) *t.k.h: sn led: hdd after 3f: chsd wnr to over 1f out: wknd qckly* — **16/1**

**6** ½ **Tadween (IRE)** 3-9-0 0..... DaneO'Neill 1 — 54+
(Richard Hannon) *s.s: rcvrd into midfield disputing 8th but off the pce: sltly impeded over 2f out: kpt on but nvr a real threat* — **4/1$^3$**

**7** 1 **Lady Prima** 3-8-9 0..... KieranO'Neill 8 — 46
(Mike Murphy) *off the pce in midfield disputing 8th: outpcd over 2f out: nvr a factor but keeping on at fin* — **66/1**

00- **8** ¾ **Pursuing Steed**$^{258}$ 4805 3-9-0 0..... LiamKeniry 3 — 49
(Hughie Morrison) *chsd ldrs disputing 6th: pushed along and outpcd fr 2f out* — **14/1**

**9** ¾ **Luna Bear** 3-8-6 0..... NoelGarbutt$^{(3)}$ 5 — 42
(Gary Moore) *sn wl bhd in last quartet: urged along over 2f out and plugged on one pce* — **50/1**

**10** 1 ½ **Three's A Crowd (IRE)** 3-8-11 0..... CallumShepherd$^{(3)}$ 4 — 43
(Ed de Giles) *sn wl bhd in last quartet: nvr a factor* — **33/1**

0-0 **11** ¾ **Pushjockeypush**$^{18}$ 1358 3-8-11 0.....(t) AaronJones$^{(3)}$ 7 — 41
(Stuart Williams) *sn pushed along and wl bhd in last quartet: nvr a factor* — **100/1**

0-6 **12** 1 ¾ **La Isla Bonita**$^{14}$ 1426 3-8-9 0..... JosephineGordon 9 — 31
(Richard Spencer) *chsd ldrs disputing 6th: shifted lft over 2f out: sn wknd* — **50/1**

**13** 9 **Hell Of A Lady** 3-8-9 0..... AdamBeschizza 6 — 7
(Michael Attwater) *s.v.s: a wl bhd in last quartet* — **100/1**

1m 25.68s (-0.32) **Going Correction** -0.075s/f (Stan)
**WFA** 3 from 4yo 14lb — 13 Ran SP% **117.9**
Speed ratings (Par 101): **98,93,93,89,86 85,84,83,82,81 80,78,67**
CSF £22.07 TOTE £6.70: £2.20, £2.20, £1.40; EX 31.30 Trifecta £113.50.
**Owner** Ahmad Abdulla Al Shaikh **Bred** Mountarmstrong Stud **Trained** Newmarket, Suffolk

**FOCUS**
The pace wasn't that strong and it probably paid to be prominent. The fourth has been rated to her pre-race mark.

## 1728 100% PROFIT BOOST AT 32REDSPORT.COM H'CAP — 7f (P)
8:15 (8:17) (Class 5) (0-70,72) 4-Y-O+ — £2,911 (£866; £432; £216) Stalls Low

Form — RPR

-401 **1** **Papou Tony**$^{53}$ 812 4-9-5 **68**..... LiamKeniry 8 — 79+
(George Baker) *stdd s: hld up in last pair: prog 2f out: pushed along and swept past four rivals to ld 150yds out: sn clr: readily* — **5/1$^2$**

3043 **2** 2 ¼ **Higher Court (USA)**$^{13}$ 1450 9-9-8 **71**..... AdamKirby 7 — 75
(Emma Owen) *pressed ldr: rdn to chal 2f out: upsides whn wnr swept past 150yds out: kpt on* — **5/1$^2$**

60-1 **3** 1 ¼ **Gulland Rock**$^{14}$ 1419 6-9-7 **70**..... WilliamCarson 1 — 71
(Anthony Carson) *led: rdn and hrd pressed fr 2f out: hdd and one pce last 150yds* — **8/1$^3$**

540 **4** hd **Bob Hopeful**$^{21}$ 1299 4-9-2 **65**..... ShaneKelly 4 — 65
(Mike Murphy) *t.k.h: trckd ldrs: rdn to chal over 1f out: outpcd ins fnl f* — **25/1**

1440 **5** nk **Fire Diamond**$^{47}$ 896 4-9-7 **70**.....(p) RichardKingscote 3 — 69
(Tom Dascombe) *n.m.r s: hld up in last: pushed along and stl there over 1f out: styd on ins fnl f: too late to be involved* — **9/4$^1$**

0-66 **6** nk **Chetan**$^{12}$ 1467 5-9-7 **70**.....(tp) AdamBeschizza 2 — 68
(Charlie Wallis) *wnt lft s: in tch: rdn over 2f out: nvr pce to threaten but kpt on ins fnl f* — **10/1**

-063 **7** 1 **Picket Line**$^{14}$ 1419 5-9-8 **71**..... TimmyMurphy 5 — 67
(Geoffrey Deacon) *t.k.h: trckd ldrs: chal on inner 2f out: wknd jst ins fnl f* — **9/1**

-302 **8** ¾ **Light From Mars**$^{14}$ 1419 12-9-4 **67**..... LukeMorris 9 — 61
(Ronald Harris) *t.k.h: cl up on outer: rdn over 2f out: sn lost pl and btn* — **11/1**

1-60 **9** nk **Chelwood Gate (IRE)**$^{26}$ 1238 7-9-6 **72**.....(v) HectorCrouch$^{(3)}$ 6 — 65
(Patrick Chamings) *t.k.h: hld up and racd on outer: pushed along and no prog 2f out: fdd* — **16/1**

1m 26.62s (0.62) **Going Correction** -0.075s/f (Stan) — 9 Ran SP% **112.4**
Speed ratings (Par 103): **93,90,89,88,88 88,86,86,85**
CSF £29.14 CT £194.68 TOTE £6.00: £1.90, £1.60, £1.90; EX 28.80 Trifecta £206.90.
**Owner** PJL, Clark & Moore **Bred** Litex Commerce **Trained** Manton, Wilts

**FOCUS**
They didn't go that quick early but the winner had the pace to come from behind. The runner-up has been rated to form, with the third confirming his C&D latest.

## 1729 32RED ON THE APP STORE H'CAP — 1m (P)
8:45 (8:46) (Class 6) (0-65,66) 4-Y-O+ — £2,264 (£673; £336; £168) Stalls Low

Form — RPR

45-0 **1** **Ebbisham (IRE)**$^{62}$ 641 4-9-6 **64**.....(p) PatCosgrave 10 — 72
(Jim Boyle) *trckd ldrs: prog to ld over 1f out and sn dashed clr: rdn out* — **11/2$^3$**

0201 **2** 1 ¼ **Lucky Louie**$^{49}$ 860 4-9-4 **62**.....(p) JackMitchell 12 — 67
(Roger Teal) *hld up off the pce disputing 9th: nt clr run over 2f out: gd prog over 1f out: r.o to take 2nd last 100yds: nt rch wnr* — **8/1**

025- **3** 1 ¾ **Rattle On**$^{139}$ 8085 4-9-3 **61**..... AdamKirby 3 — 62
(Jim Boyle) *hld up in midfield disputing 7th: prog over 2f out: rdn to chse wnr jst ins fnl f: one pce and lost 2nd last 100yds* — **7/2$^1$**

00-4 **4** nk **Makhfar (IRE)**$^{32}$ 1139 6-8-11 **55**.....(p) LiamKeniry 6 — 55
(Mark Usher) *dwlt: hld up in off the pce disputing 9th: rdn over 2f out: kpt on wl fr over 1f out: nrst fin but n.d* — **20/1**

6200 **5** *2* **Dukes Meadow**[19] 1338 6-8-1 **52** RhiainIngram(7) 4 48
(Roger Ingram) *trckd ldrs: rdn and fnd nil over 2f out: one pce after* **14/1**

000- **6** *nk* **Sunlit Waters**[252] 5011 4-8-12 **56** TomQueally 5 51
(Eve Johnson Houghton) *wl in rr: shkn up over 2f out: kpt on one pce fr over 1f out: no ch* **20/1**

0-11 **7** *nk* **Magic Mirror**[23] 1285 4-8-12 **56** (v) TomMarquand 8 50
(Mark Rimell) *hld up in midfield disputing 7th: drvn on outer over 2f out: no prog* **9/2**[2]

-203 **8** *1/2* **Cat Royale (IRE)**[13] 1449 4-9-1 **66** (p) DarraghKeenan(7) 9 59+
(John Butler) *chsd ldr to wl over 1f out: wknd* **14/1**

-330 **9** *1* **Suitsus**[37] 1067 6-9-0 **58** (t) TimmyMurphy 14 49
(Geoffrey Deacon) *stdd s fr wdst draw: hld up in last of main gp and wl off the pce: smooth prog 2f out: nudged along and no hdwy fnl f* **16/1**

2351 **10** *1 1/4* **Zabdi**[56] 739 4-9-6 **64** JosephineGordon 13 52+
(Lee Carter) *led at gd pce and stretched field: hdd & wknd qckly over 1f out* **9/1**

631- **11** *10* **Carcharias (IRE)**[181] 7299 4-9-3 **64** CallumShepherd(3) 2 29+
(Ed de Giles) *v awkward s and lost many l: a t.o* **16/1**

20-0 **12** *10* **Mossy's Lodge**[53] 812 4-9-7 **65** WilliamCarson 1 7
(Anthony Carson) *dwlt: rushed up to press ldrs: wknd rapidly over 2f out: t.o* **16/1**

000/ **13** *2* **A Definite Diamond**[542] 7310 4-8-4 **51** oh6 AaronJones(3) 7
(Grace Harris) *t.k.h: prom to 1/2-way: wknd qckly: t.o* **100/1**

1m 38.12s (-1.68) **Going Correction** -0.075s/f (Stan) **13** Ran SP% **118.4**
Speed ratings (Par 101): **105,103,102,101,99 99,99,98,97,96 86,76,74**
CSF £47.59 CT £183.18 TOTE £5.70: £2.20, £2.30, £1.80; EX 48.30 Trifecta £286.90.
**Owner** The 'In Recovery' Partnership **Bred** John Quigley **Trained** Epsom, Surrey

**FOCUS**
There was a fair gallop on here. The winner has been rated back to his C&D win in November, with the runner-up and third fitting.
T/Plt: £145.40 to a £1 stake. Pool: £85,099.96 - 426.97 winning units. T/Qpdt: £4.50 to a £1 stake. Pool: £8,582.94 - 1,388.68 winning units. **Jonathan Neesom**

# NOTTINGHAM (L-H)
Wednesday, April 12
**OFFICIAL GOING: Good to firm (good in places; 8.4) (watered)**
Wind: Strong against in straight Weather: Cloudy

## 1730 TOTEPLACEPOT SIX PLACES IN SIX RACES MAIDEN STKS 1m 72y
**1:50** (1:53) (Class 5) 3-Y-O **£3,234** (£962; £481; £240) **Stalls** Centre

Form RPR

0- **1** **Valcartier (IRE)**[173] 7496 3-9-5 0 WilliamBuick 7 89+
(John Gosden) *mde all: qcknd clr over 2f out: readily* **11/4**[1]

30- **2** *3 3/4* **Endless Gold**[231] 5764 3-9-5 0 AdamKirby 17 75+
(Charlie Appleby) *hld up in midfield: hdwy on outer over 3f out: rdn over 2f out: styd on to chse wnr appr fnl f: no imp* **8/1**[3]

**3** *1 1/2* **Born To Boom (IRE)** 3-9-0 0 CliffordLee(5) 1 71+
(K R Burke) *in tch: hdwy over 2f out: rdn along wl over 1f out: kpt on fnl f* **25/1**

0 **4** *1/2* **Zoffany Bay (IRE)**[11] 1485 3-9-5 0 LukeMorris 2 70
(George Peckham) *trckd ldng pair on inner: swtchd rt and hdwy over 2f out: rdn wl over 1f out: kpt on same pce* **50/1**

0- **5** *1/2* **Cribbs Causeway (IRE)**[182] 7284 3-8-11 0 KieranShoemark(3) 12 64
(Roger Charlton) *towards rr: hdwy on outer 3f out: pushed along 2f out: rdn and kpt on fnl f* **50/1**

0- **6** *1 3/4* **Legato (IRE)**[180] 7317 3-9-5 0 MartinHarley 14 66
(Tom Dascombe) *midfield: hdwy and in tch over 3f out: rdn along over 2f out: sn no imp* **100/1**

0- **7** *1* **Nigh Or Never (IRE)**[218] 6211 3-9-5 0 RichardKingscote 11 63
(Tom Dascombe) *midfield: hdwy on inner 3f out: rdn along 2f out: kpt on same pce* **12/1**

**8** *hd* **Al Galayel (IRE)** 3-9-5 0 FrankieDettori 3 62+
(Luca Cumani) *towards rr: hdwy on outer wl over 2f out: rdn over 1f out: kpt on fnl f* **8/1**[3]

**9** *2 1/4* **Wasm** 3-9-5 0 (t[1]) JimCrowley 6 57+
(Simon Crisford) *t.k.h in rr: hdwy wl over 2f out: n.m.r and swtchd lft wl over 1f out: n.d* **10/1**

00- **10** *nk* **Belisa (IRE)**[138] 8088 3-9-0 0 TomEaves 4 51
(Ivan Furtado) *trckd ldrs: hdwy over 3f out: rdn along over 2f out: wknd over 1f out* **100/1**

**11** *shd* **Tango Fire (USA)** 3-9-5 0 PatDobbs 13 56+
(Richard Hannon) *stmbld s and bhd: hdwy on inner 2f out: kpt on fnl f* **9/2**[2]

65- **12** *3 1/2* **Cryptonite (IRE)**[180] 7331 3-9-5 0 SilvestreDeSousa 9 48
(Michael Appleby) *a towards rr* **12/1**

04- **13** *1 1/4* **Go On Mayson**[248] 5203 3-9-5 0 JFEgan 15 45
(David Evans) *chsd ldrs on outer: rdn along 3f out: wknd over 2f out* **16/1**

0 **14** *2 1/2* **Somes Sound (IRE)**[21] 1299 3-9-5 0 DannyBrock 16 39
(Jane Chapple-Hyam) *chsd wnr: rdn along 3f out: sn wknd* **100/1**

0 **15** *3 1/4* **Never You Mind (IRE)**[10] 1514 3-9-5 0 DavidProbert 10 32
(Charles Hills) *a towards rr* **50/1**

24- **16** *38* **Sue's Angel (IRE)**[229] 5854 3-9-0 0 JackGarritty 8
(Richard Fahey) *v.s.a and lost many l s: a t.o* **14/1**

1m 46.17s (-2.83) **Going Correction** -0.425s/f (Firm) **16** Ran SP% **116.8**
Speed ratings (Par 98): **97,93,91,91,90 89,88,87,85,85 85,81,80,77,74 36**
CSF £22.60 TOTE £3.80: £1.70, £2.80, £7.20; EX 33.30 Trifecta £422.40.
**Owner** Godolphin **Bred** Barronstown Stud **Trained** Newmarket, Suffolk

**FOCUS**
Inner Track: standard distances. Runners faced a stiff headwind off the home bend. It paid to be handy in this interesting maiden. Winning rider William Buick afterwards reported it was 'good to firm ground, good on the bends.' The level is a bit fluid. The fourth has been rated similar to his debut effort.

## 1731 TOTEPOOLLIVEINFO.COM VISIT FOR RACING RESULTS H'CAP 5f 8y
**2:20** (2:22) (Class 4) (0-80,82) 3-Y-O **£5,175** (£1,540; £769; £384) **Stalls** Centre

Form RPR

213- **1** **Justanotherbottle (IRE)**[207] 6564 3-9-0 **73** NeilFarley 1 86
(Declan Carroll) *racd centre: mde most: rdn and qcknd clr ent fnl f: edgd lft: styd on* **25/1**

50-1 **2** *4 1/2* **Scuzeme**[81] 357 3-9-7 **80** PhillipMakin 2 77+
(David Barron) *hld up in rr centre: hdwy on outer 2f out: rdn over 1f out: styd on fnl f* **9/1**

2601 **3** *hd* **Erissimus Maximus (FR)**[22] 1294 3-9-6 **79** (b) SilvestreDeSousa 7 75
(Chris Dwyer) *trckd ldrs centre: hdwy wl over 1f out: rdn to chse wnr ins fnl f: sn drvn and kpt on same pce* **8/1**[3]

2 **4** *3/4* **Blitz**[46] 926 3-9-9 **82** AdamKirby 8 75
(Clive Cox) *in tch centre: hdwy 2f out: rdn over 1f out: drvn and kpt on fnl f* **6/1**[1]

102- **5** *1 1/4* **Father McKenzie**[180] 7313 3-9-5 **78** RyanTate 13 67
(James Eustace) *racd towards stands side: hld up: hdwy over 2f out: rdn wl over 1f out: kpt on fnl f* **12/1**

320- **6** *1/2* **Coolfitch (IRE)**[169] 7600 3-9-4 **82** JoshDoyle(5) 9 69
(David O'Meara) *hld up towards rr centre: hdwy 2f out: rdn over 1f out: kpt on fnl f* **14/1**

042- **7** *3/4* **Blue Suede (IRE)**[135] 8136 3-9-5 **78** PaulHanagan 3 62
(Richard Fahey) *cl up centre: chal wl over 1f out and sn rdn: drvn and wknd ent fnl f* **6/1**[1]

40-6 **8** *nk* **Quench Dolly**[12] 1463 3-9-2 **75** FergusSweeney 14 58
(John Gallagher) *racd nr stands rail: chsd ldrs: rdn along 2f out: sn one pce* **25/1**

460- **9** *1/2* **Twizzell**[201] 6734 3-9-4 **77** PJMcDonald 11 58
(K R Burke) *in tch towards stands side: hdwy 1/2-way: rdn to chse ldrs wl over 1f out: sn drvn and wknd* **10/1**

014- **10** *1/2* **Savannah Slew**[158] 7820 3-9-6 **79** (h) LukeMorris 10 59
(James Given) *dwlt: a rr* **14/1**

601- **11** *nk* **Awesome Allan (IRE)**[189] 7073 3-9-8 **81** (t) JFEgan 5 60
(David Evans) *chsd ldrs centre: rdn along over 2f out: sn drvn and wknd* **14/1**

100- **12** *1 1/2* **Diable D'Or (IRE)**[189] 7073 3-9-3 **79** EdwardGreatrex(3) 6 52+
(Eve Johnson Houghton) *a towards rr* **10/1**

121 **13** *1 3/4* **Jack Flash (FR)**[55] 765 3-9-6 **79** RyanMoore 12 46
(Les Eyre) *racd towards stands side: chsd ldrs: rdn along over 2f out: sn wknd* **7/1**[2]

0450 **14** *1 1/4* **Grecian Divine (IRE)**[11] 1487 3-8-9 **75** SophieScardifield(7) 4 37
(Joseph Tuite) *chsd ldrs centre: rdn along bef 1/2-way: sn lost pl and bhd* **100/1**

59.57s (-1.93) **Going Correction** -0.175s/f (Firm) **14** Ran SP% **116.7**
Speed ratings (Par 100): **108,100,100,99,97 96,95,94,94,93 92,90,87,85**
CSF £226.89 CT £2031.18 TOTE £30.60: £7.00, £3.80, £2.70; EX 286.60 Trifecta £856.60.
**Owner** Steve Ryan & M J Tedham **Bred** John O'Connor **Trained** Malton, N Yorks

**FOCUS**
This 3yo sprint handicap looked highly competitive but the winner took it apart. The middle was the place to be and, despite the headwind, again it paid to be up there. The third has been rated a bit below his AW form.

## 1732 TOTEQUADPOT INSURE YOUR PLACEPOT LAST FOUR CONDITIONS STKS (PLUS 10 RACE) 5f 8y
**2:50** (2:50) (Class 3) 3-Y-O
**£9,337** (£2,796; £1,398; £699; £349; £175) **Stalls** Centre

Form RPR

012- **1** **Kyllang Rock (IRE)**[201] 6734 3-8-12 91 MartinHarley 3 92+
(James Tate) *rrd s and rr: smooth hdwy over 2f out: chsd ldrs over 1f out: rdn to chal ent fnl f: led and edgd lft last 100 yds: kpt on* **2/1**[1]

2121 **2** *nk* **Major Jumbo**[46] 926 3-8-7 89 LewisEdmunds(5) 2 91+
(Kevin Ryan) *chsd ldrs: hdwy over 2f out: rdn along wl over 1f out: drvn and styd on wl fnl f* **9/4**[2]

103- **3** *1 1/4* **Plata O Plomo**[278] 4091 3-8-12 85 BarryMcHugh 4 86
(Tony Coyle) *chsd clr ldr: hdwy wl over 1f out: rdn to ld ent fnl f: sn drvn and edgd lft: hdd and no ex last 100 yds* **20/1**

1-32 **4** *3 1/4* **Merry Banter**[35] 1090 3-8-4 85 EdwardGreatrex(3) 6 70
(Paul Midgley) *set str pce and sn clr: rdn 11/2f out: hdd ent fnl f: sn wknd* **7/1**

310- **5** *1/2* **Smokey Lane (IRE)**[186] 7155 3-9-4 95 RyanMoore 5 79
(David Evans) *chsd ldrs: rdn along wl over 1f out: sn drvn and wknd* **9/2**[3]

3234 **6** *1 1/2* **Dazacam**[33] 1124 3-8-7 84 PaulHanagan 7 63
(Michael Herrington) *a rr* **12/1**

10- **7** *hd* **Reedanjas (IRE)**[148] 7972 3-8-0 79 (p) DavidEgan(7) 1 62
(Gay Kelleway) *t.k.h: chsd ldng pair: rdn along 2f out: sn wknd* **25/1**

59.8s (-1.70) **Going Correction** -0.175s/f (Firm) **7** Ran SP% **111.1**
Speed ratings (Par 102): **106,105,103,98,97 95,94**
CSF £6.32 TOTE £3.80: £1.60, £1.60; EX 7.00 Trifecta £51.40.
**Owner** Sheikh Juma Dalmook Al Maktoum **Bred** Old Carhue & Graeng Bloodstock **Trained** Newmarket, Suffolk

**FOCUS**
A fair 3yo conditions sprint, run at a blistering early pace. It was 0.23secs slower than the preceding 0-80 handicap.

## 1733 TOTEPOOL BARRY HILLS FURTHER FLIGHT STKS (LISTED RACE) 1m 6f
**3:20** (3:20) (Class 1) 4-Y-O+ **£22,684** (£8,600; £4,304; £2,144; £1,076) **Stalls** Low

Form RPR

100- **1** **Elidor**[215] 6283 7-9-1 108 SilvestreDeSousa 3 111
(Mick Channon) *hld up in rr: tk clsr order over 6f out: trckd ldrs over 4f out: hdwy 3f out: chal 2f out: sn rdn and ev ch: drvn to slt ld wl ins fnl f: jst hld on* **6/1**[3]

11-6 **2** *nse* **Wall Of Fire (IRE)**[18] 1374 4-8-12 107 (b) WilliamBuick 5 110
(Hugo Palmer) *trckd ldr: hdwy and cl up 3f out: rdn to take narrow ld wl over 1f out: drvn and hdd wl ins fnl f: kpt on wl towards fin: jst hld* **11/8**[1]

/11- **3** *3* **Moonrise Landing (IRE)**[326] 2486 6-8-10 105 FranBerry 1 101
(Ralph Beckett) *trckd ldng pair: hdwy over 4f out: cl up over 2f out :sn rdn: kpt on same pce appr fnl f* **2/1**[2]

43-0 **4** *1* **Trip To Paris (IRE)**[18] 1374 6-9-1 110 (b) RyanMoore 2 104
(Ed Dunlop) *set stdy pce: qcknd clr 10f out: pushed along 3f out: jnd and rdn over 2f out: hdd wl over 1f out: sn one pce* **6/1**[3]

**5** *4* **Culmination**[33] 5-9-1 0 PaulHanagan 4 99?
(Donald McCain) *hld up: a towards rr* **50/1**

3m 7.24s (0.24) **Going Correction** -0.425s/f (Firm)
**WFA** 4 from 5yo+ 1lb **5** Ran SP% **106.0**
Speed ratings (Par 111): **82,81,80,79,77**
CSF £13.72 TOTE £5.10: £2.60, £1.60; EX 16.60 Trifecta £29.80.
**Owner** Jon and Julia Aisbitt **Bred** Ashley House Stud **Trained** West Ilsley, Berks

**FOCUS**
A small, yet select edition of the feature Listed event for stayers. Thankfully there was a fair early pace on. The runner-up has been rated to form, with the winner close to his best.

## 1734 TOTEPOOL RACECOURSE DEBIT CARD BETTING AVAILABLE H'CAP 1m 72y

**3:50** (3:53) (Class 3) (0-95,94) 4-Y-0+ **£9,703** (£2,887; £1,443; £721) **Stalls** Centre

Form RPR

551- **1** **George William**[172] 7530 4-9-3 **90** RyanMoore 2 98+
(Richard Hannon) *trckd ldrs on inner: effrt and nt clr run over 1f out: sn swtchd rt and rdn to chal ins fnl f: drvn and kpt on wl to ld towards fin* **9/2**[1]

/50- **2** *nk* **G K Chesterton (IRE)**[173] 7499 4-8-13 **86** WilliamBuick 1 93
(Charlie Appleby) *slt ld: hdd over 4f out: cl up: rdn to ld wl over 1f out and sn edgd lft: jnd and drvn ent fnl f: sn edgd rt: hdd and no ex towards fin* **5/1**[2]

431- **3** *1 ¼* **Weekend Offender (FR)**[186] 7153 4-9-2 **89** TomEaves 11 94+
(Kevin Ryan) *dwlt and rr: hdwy over 3f out: swtchd rt to outer 2f out and sn rdn: styd on wl appr fnl f* **6/1**[3]

200- **4** *nk* **Midhmaar**[278] 4108 4-9-2 **89** JimCrowley 8 93
(Owen Burrows) *trckd ldrs: hdwy on outer and cl up over 3f out: chal 2f out: sn rdn and ev ch: kpt on same pce fnl f* **8/1**

060- **5** *shd* **King's Pavilion (IRE)**[186] 7153 4-8-13 **86** PhillipMakin 6 90
(David Barron) *trckd ldrs: pushed along and sltly outpcd wl over 2f out: rdn wl over 1f out: kpt on fnl f* **16/1**

000- **6** *nk* **Two For Two (IRE)**[112] 8478 9-9-1 **88** (p) TonyHamilton 12 91
(Roger Fell) *dwlt and rr: hdwy 3f out: rdn along on inner over 2f out: kpt on u.p fnl f* **33/1**

320- **7** *1 ½* **Marsh Pride**[158] 7823 5-9-1 **88** PJMcDonald 4 88
(K R Burke) *chsd ldrs: rdn along wl over 2f out: sn drvn and wknd* **14/1**

/40- **8** *nk* **Heatstroke (IRE)**[280] 4026 5-8-13 **86** JamieSpencer 10 85
(Charles Hills) *hld up towards rr: effrt and sme hdwy on outer over 3f out: rdn along wl over 2f out: n.d* **8/1**

130- **9** *nse* **Interconnection**[200] 6786 6-9-3 **90** (p) AdamBeschizza 14 89
(Ed Vaughan) *chsd ldng pair: rdn along 3f out: wknd over 2f out* **10/1**

404- **10** *nk* **Ice Slice (IRE)**[187] 7121 6-9-7 **94** RyanTate 7 92
(James Eustace) *cl up: slt ld over 4f out: rdn along 3f out: drvn 2f out: sn hdd & wknd* **10/1**

040- **11** *7* **Shady McCoy (USA)**[158] 7821 7-9-3 **90** RobertWinston 3 72
(Ian Williams) *rr: rdn along and outpcd fr 3f out* **10/1**

1m 43.78s (-5.22) **Going Correction** -0.425s/f (Firm) **11** Ran SP% **114.1**
Speed ratings (Par 107): **109,108,107,107,107 106,105,104,104,104 97**
CSF £25.63 CT £137.09 TOTE £4.50: £1.80, £2.00, £2.10; EX 23.00 Trifecta £83.90.
**Owner** Lady Coventry & Partners **Bred** Rachel Countess Of Coventry **Trained** East Everleigh, Wilts

**FOCUS**
Competitive stuff. They went a sound pace and it's handicap form to follow, despite a bunched finish.

## 1735 @TOTEPOOL FOLLOW US ON TWITTER H'CAP 1m 72y

**4:20** (4:25) (Class 5) (0-70,70) 4-Y-0+ **£3,234** (£962; £481; £240) **Stalls** Centre

Form RPR

6602 **1** **Cosmic Ray**[5] 1610 5-8-8 **57** (h) PaulHanagan 3 63
(Les Eyre) *trckd ldng pair: hdwy 3f out: cl up 2f out: rdn over 1f out: drvn to chal ins fnl f: led last 75 yds: hld on gamely* **11/2**[3]

-361 **2** *nse* **Scribner Creek (IRE)**[27] 1225 4-8-13 **62** RobertWinston 5 68
(Daniel Mark Loughnane) *hld up: hdwy over 3f out: chsd ldrs 2f out: swtchd rt and rdn ent fnl f: sn drvn and ev ch: jst hld* **8/1**

P054 **3** *nk* **Fantasy Gladiator**[23] 1283 11-9-0 **63** (p) SilvestreDeSousa 2 68+
(Michael Appleby) *rr: hdwy on inner 3f out: chsd ldrs wl over 1f out and sn n.m.r: rdn ent fnl f and sn ev ch: kpt on wl* **4/1**[2]

0-06 **4** *hd* **Adventureman**[12] 1473 5-8-10 **59** (p) JackGarritty 12 64
(Ruth Carr) *led: pushed along 3f out: rdn 2f out: drvn over 1f out: hdd and no ex last 75 yds* **20/1**

3 **5** *nk* **Fire Tree (IRE)**[46] 922 4-9-7 **70** (t) StevieDonohoe 1 74
(Charlie Fellowes) *trckd ldrs: hdwy 3f out: chal 2f out: sn rdn and ev ch: drvn and kpt on same pce fnl f* **5/2**[1]

00-2 **6** *1 ½* **Bling King**[20] 1329 8-8-12 **61** (p) PhillipMakin 8 62
(Geoffrey Harker) *in tch: hdwy over 2f out: rdn wl over 1f out: no imp fnl f* **12/1**

220- **7** *½* **Stoneboat Bill**[166] 7656 5-9-0 **63** NeilFarley 6 63
(Declan Carroll) *rr: hdwy on inner over 2f out: rdn along wl over 1f out: kpt on fnl f* **8/1**

1-06 **8** *2* **Candesta (USA)**[69] 516 7-8-12 **64** ShelleyBirkett(3) 14 59
(Julia Feilden) *cl up: disp ld over 2f out: rdn wl over 1f out: sn drvn and wknd fnl f* **33/1**

561- **9** *2 ¾* **Walking In Rhythm (IRE)**[205] 6631 4-8-8 **60** HollieDoyle(3) 10 49
(Barry Leavy) *a towards rr* **25/1**

600- **10** *2 ¼* **Poppy Time**[168] 7627 4-9-0 **63** RyanTate 7 46
(James Eustace) *chsd ldrs: rdn along 3f out: wknd 2f out* **20/1**

-200 **11** *4 ½* **Swiftee (IRE)**[64] 607 4-8-11 **60** (p) TonyHamilton 11 33
(Ivan Furtado) *chsd ldrs on outer: rdn along over 3f out: wknd over 2f out* **50/1**

23-4 **12** *1 ¾* **Athollblair Boy (IRE)**[12] 1472 4-9-7 **70** TomEaves 13 39
(Nigel Tinkler) *a rr* **20/1**

1m 44.9s (-4.10) **Going Correction** -0.425s/f (Firm) **12** Ran SP% **116.9**
Speed ratings (Par 103): **103,102,102,102,102 100,100,98,95,93 88,86**
CSF £42.80 CT £171.38 TOTE £6.40: £2.60, £2.70, £1.20; EX 55.80 Trifecta £375.00.
**Owner** Over The Moon Racing III **Bred** Winterbeck Manor Stud **Trained** Catwick, N Yorks

**FOCUS**
This moderate handicap saw another tight finish. The runner-up has been rated as improving a bit on his AW win, with the fourth rated to form.

## 1736 COLLECT TOTEPOOL WINNINGS AT BETFRED SHOPS H'CAP (DIV I) 1m 2f 52y

**4:50** (4:53) (Class 5) (0-75,77) 3-Y-0 **£3,234** (£962; £481; £240) **Stalls** Low

Form RPR

3-23 **1** **Mullarkey**[40] 1000 3-9-0 **68** JimCrowley 13 76
(John Best) *hld up in rr: gd hdwy over 3f out and sn swtchd lft to inner: chsd ldrs over 1f out: rdn to ld ins fnl f: drvn out* **12/1**

41-3 **2** *1 ¼* **Hertford Dancer**[16] 1404 3-9-4 **72** WilliamBuick 9 77+
(John Gosden) *midfield: hdwy wl over 2f out: swtchd rt to outer and rdn over 1f out: styd on wl fnl f* **9/1**

31-4 **3** *nk* **Plead**[29] 1195 3-9-7 **75** JackMitchell 12 79
(Archie Watson) *hld up towards rr: swtchd rt to outer and hdwy over 2f out: rdn to chal and hung lft ent fnl f: sn drvn and kpt on* **15/2**[2]

-211 **4** *shd* **Serenade The Stars (IRE)**[63] 627 3-9-7 **75** (v) MartinHarley 1 79
(James Tate) *rdn along s and led after 1f: pushed along 3f out: rdn 2f out: drvn over 1f out: hdd ins fnl f: kpt on* **8/1**[3]

05-4 **5** *1 ¼* **Road To Dubai (IRE)**[49] 863 3-9-2 **70** SilvestreDeSousa 5 71+
(George Scott) *in tch: hdwy 3f out: rdn to chse ldrs over 1f out: no imp ins fnl f* **10/1**

2-11 **6** *3* **Daily Trader**[42] 967 3-9-0 **68** ConnorBeasley 10 63
(David Evans) *hld up: hdwy on wd outside 3f out: chsd ldrs 2f out: sn rdn: drvn over 1f out: sn one pce* **16/1**

045- **7** *1 ¼* **Chaparrachik (IRE)**[205] 6623 3-9-5 **73** PatDobbs 7 66
(Amanda Perrett) *chsd ldrs: hdwy over 3f out: rdn along over 2f out: sn drvn and grad wknd* **25/1**

221- **8** *2 ¾* **Snookered (IRE)**[183] 7244 3-8-7 **61** oh1 PaulHanagan 2 48
(Richard Fahey) *in tch: hdwy over 3f out: rdn along over 2f out: sn drvn and wknd* **14/1**

012- **9** *shd* **Phoenix Dawn**[161] 7768 3-9-1 **69** (p) FranBerry 6 56
(Brendan Powell) *led 1f: chsd ldr: rdn over 2f out: sn drvn and wknd* **33/1**

31-2 **10** *5* **Peace And Plenty**[16] 1404 3-9-2 **70** MartinDwyer 3 47
(William Muir) *trckd ldrs: hdwy over 3f out: rdn over 2f out: sn drvn and wknd* **8/1**[3]

006- **11** *5* **Casado (IRE)**[140] 8063 3-8-8 **62** KierenFox 8 29
(John Best) *.trckd ldrs: hdwy on outer 4f out: rdn along 3f out: sn wknd* **25/1**

0-05 **12** *4* **Costa Percy**[67] 580 3-8-11 **65** JoeyHaynes 4 24
(K R Burke) *a rr* **20/1**

1 **13** *2 ¼* **Mori Yoshinari (IRE)**[46] 916 3-9-9 **77** RyanMoore 11 31
(Richard Hannon) *dwlt and bhd: hdwy 1/2-way: in tch 4f out: rdn along over 3f out: sn wknd* **11/4**[1]

2m 11.77s (-2.53) **Going Correction** -0.425s/f (Firm) **13** Ran SP% **115.4**
Speed ratings (Par 98): **93,92,91,91,90 88,87,85,85,81 77,73,72**
CSF £106.29 CT £869.93 TOTE £11.50: £3.20, £2.90, £2.80; EX 124.80 Trifecta £1192.20.
**Owner** Thomson, Tobin & Sheridan **Bred** Best Breeding **Trained** Oad Street, Kent

**FOCUS**
There was a sound pace on in this modest 3yo handicap, which can be rated around the third. The third and fourth help set the standard on their AW form.

## 1737 COLLECT TOTEPOOL WINNINGS AT BETFRED SHOPS H'CAP (DIV II) 1m 2f 52y

**5:20** (5:21) (Class 5) (0-75,76) 3-Y-0 **£3,234** (£962; £481; £240) **Stalls** Low

Form RPR

003- **1** **Outcrop (IRE)**[126] 8245 3-9-0 **68** RobertWinston 2 74
(Hughie Morrison) *mde all: rdn clr wl over 1f out: styd on strly* **8/1**

565- **2** *1 ½* **Bedouin (IRE)**[158] 7812 3-9-4 **72** JamieSpencer 12 75+
(Luca Cumani) *hld up towards rr: hdwy on outer 3f out: rdn along 2f out: drvn over 1f out: chsd wnr and edgd lft ins fnl f: kpt on* **3/1**[1]

002- **3** *1 ¼* **Shadow Warrior**[165] 7688 3-9-1 **69** JoeyHaynes 11 70+
(Paul D'Arcy) *hld up in rr: hdwy 3f out: chsd ldrs over 1f out: drvn and kpt on fnl f* **9/1**

003- **4** *1 ¼* **I'vegotthepower (IRE)**[214] 6314 3-8-7 **68** JordanUys(7) 1 66
(Brian Meehan) *trckd wnr: lost pl and pushed along 3f out: hdwy 2f out: sn rdn and kpt on same pce fnl f* **9/1**

01-6 **5** *hd* **Mary Anne Evans**[16] 1404 3-9-1 **69** RobertTart 3 67
(John Gosden) *prom: chsd wnr over 3f out: rdn 2f out: drvn over 1f out: grad wknd fnl f* **14/1**

340- **6** *nk* **Mistress Viz (IRE)**[202] 6713 3-8-8 **62** RoystonFfrench 9 59
(John Mackie) *midfield: hdwy on outer to chse ldrs 3f out: rdn along 2f out: sn drvn and grad wknd* **16/1**

316- **7** *1 ½* **Gravity Wave (IRE)**[217] 6240 3-9-8 **76** JimCrowley 7 70+
(Sylvester Kirk) *dwlt and rr: hdwy on outer over 3f out: rdn along 2f out: no imp fnl f* **9/2**[2]

00-4 **8** *½* **Padrinho (IRE)**[35] 1089 3-8-11 **65** KierenFox 6 58
(John Best) *nvr bttr than midfield* **10/1**

614- **9** *2 ¼* **See The City (IRE)**[244] 5318 3-9-7 **75** RyanTate 8 64
(James Eustace) *chsd ldrs: rdn along over 3f out: sn wknd* **7/1**[3]

105- **10** *½* **Kiruna Peak (IRE)**[189] 7075 3-9-2 **70** GeorgeDowning 5 58
(Mick Channon) *hld up towards rr: hdwy into midfield 1/2-way: chsd ldrs over 3f out: sn rdn and wknd over 2f out* **14/1**

2m 15.64s (1.34) **Going Correction** -0.425s/f (Firm) **10** Ran SP% **115.1**
Speed ratings (Par 98): **77,75,74,73,73 73,72,71,70,69**
CSF £31.79 CT £223.03 TOTE £9.60: £2.20, £1.20, £3.60; EX 42.80 Trifecta £293.80.
**Owner** J H Richmond-Watson **Bred** J H Richmond-Watson **Trained** East Ilsley, Berks

**FOCUS**
This second division of the modest 3yo handicap was run at an uneven pace, resulting in a 5.67secs slower winning time. The fourth, fifth and sixth have been rated a bit below form.
T/Plt: £62.10 to a £1 stake. Pool: £67,162.99 - 789.34 winning units. T/Qpdt: £9.80 to a £1 stake. Pool: £4,470.43 - 334.18 winning units. **Joe Rowntree**

1738 - 1741a (Foreign Racing) - See Raceform Interactive

# 1611 DUNDALK (A.W) (L-H)

Wednesday, April 12

**OFFICIAL GOING: Polytrack: standard**

## 1742a AVENUE INN, DUNDALK PATTON STKS (LISTED) 7f (P)

**7:30** (7:31) 3-Y-0

**£22,692** (£7,307; £3,461; £1,538; £769; £384)

RPR

**1** **War Secretary (USA)**[168] 7630 3-9-3 94 (t) SeamieHeffernan 4 106
(A P O'Brien, Ire) *cl up tl sn disp and led: rdn over 1f out and sn strly pressed: jnd briefly ins fnl f tl kpt on wl u.p w narrow advantage clsng stages* **5/2**[2]

**2** *nk* **Noivado (IRE)**[178] 7390 3-9-3 93 ColinKeane 3 105+
(G M Lyons, Ire) *settled bhd ldrs: 4th 1/2-way: rdn nr side 1 1/2f out and impr to chal on terms briefly ins fnl f: sn hdd and kpt on wl wout matching wnr clsng stages where hung sltly rt* **8/1**

**3** *2* **Ambassadorial (USA)**[187] 7130 3-9-3 106 ShaneFoley 6 100+
(M Halford, Ire) *w.w towards rr: 5th 1/2-way: pushed along 2f out and sme hdwy u.p into 3rd wl ins fnl f: kpt on same pce clsng stages: nvr trbld ldrs* **6/4**[1]

**4** *1* **Intelligence Cross (USA)**[159] 7807 3-9-6 110 (t) DonnachaO'Brien 2 100
(A P O'Brien, Ire) *cl up and sn disp 2nd: edgd sltly rt over 2f out: sn rdn in 3rd and no imp on ldrs u.p in 4th wl ins fnl f: kpt on same pce* **3/1**[3]

5 3 **Holistic Approach (IRE)**[171] 7559 3-9-3 93................. KevinManning 5 89
(J S Bolger, Ire) *dwlt sltly and settled in rr: last at 1/2-way: tk clsr order into st: rdn briefly under 2f out and no imp on ldrs in 5th ins fnl f: kpt on one pce* **12/1**

6 12 **Hit The Bid**[215] 6282 3-9-6 100.......................................... LeighRoche 1 59
(D J Bunyan, Ire) *led narrowly tl sn jnd and hdd: t.k.h early: disp 2nd for most tl rdn to chal far side briefly 1 1/2f out: sn no ex and wknd* **14/1**

1m 24.76s (-0.34) **Going Correction** +0.125s/f (Slow) 6 Ran SP% **119.0**
Speed ratings: **106,105,103,102,98 85**
CSF £23.53 TOTE £3.90: £3.10, £2.90; DF 21.80 Trifecta £65.40.
**Owner** Derrick Smith & Mrs John Magnier & Michael Tabor **Bred** Town & Country Farms Corp **Trained** Cashel, Co Tipperary

**FOCUS**
The winner had the run of a messy race and, despite not looking the most straightforward at the end of the contest, he got the job done. The third and fourth support the level.

1743 - 1753a (Foreign Racing) - See Raceform Interactive

# 1580 CHELMSFORD (A.W) (L-H)

Thursday, April 13

**OFFICIAL GOING: Polytrack: standard**
Wind: light, half against in home straight, of no consequence Weather: light cloud

## 1754 BET TOTEPLACEPOT AT TOTESPORT.COM H'CAP 1m 6f (P)

**2:10** (2:11) (Class 6) (0-65,64) 4-Y-0+ **£3,234** (£962; £481; £240) **Stalls** Low

Form RPR

651- 1 **Regal Gait (IRE)**[31] 7692 4-9-7 63.................................... HarryBentley 3 71+
(Harry Whittington) *hld up wl in tch: effrt ent fnl 2f: rdn and hdwy to ld jst over 1f out: r.o strly and drew clr fnl f: comf* **11/10**[1]

0265 2 2 3/4 **Noguchi (IRE)**[15] 1436 12-9-11 64.......................(b) SilvestreDeSousa 6 67
(Chris Dwyer) *pressed ldr: drvn to ld over 1f out: sn hdd: outpcd by wnr but kpt on u.p to hold 2nd ins fnl f* **10/3**[2]

-352 3 hd **Ted's Brother (IRE)**[17] 1402 9-8-9 48...............................(h) ShaneKelly 7 51
(Laura Morgan) *hld up in tch in last pair: effrt and swtchd lft over 1f out: no ch w wnr but battling for 2nd ins fnl f: kpt on* **16/1**

632- 4 1 3/4 **The Juggler**[162] 7767 4-8-11 53......................................... JimmyQuinn 5 54
(William Knight) *taken down early: led: drvn and hdd over 1f out: unable qck 1f out: 4th and wl hld whn eased wl ins fnl f* **4/1**[3]

2065 5 1 **Cape Spirit (IRE)**[14] 1458 5-8-7 53..............................(v) WilliamCox(7) 4 53
(Andrew Balding) *hld up wl in tch in midfield: effrt and c centre st: no imp u.p over 1f out: kpt on same pce after* **7/1**

402/ 6 13 **Blue Valentino**[864] 7990 8-8-3 49 ow1.............................. JordanUys(7) 2 32
(Lisa Williamson) *s.i.s: t.k.h: hld up in tch in last pair: effrt ent fnl 2f: sn drifted rt and wknd over 1f out* **80/1**

00- 7 13 **Lady Emma**[305] 3194 4-8-13 55..........................................(p1) RoystonFfrench 1 21
(Steph Hollinshead) *chsd ldrs: rdn wl over 2f out: sn lost pl: bhd fnl f* **40/1**

3m 1.09s (-2.11) **Going Correction** -0.30s/f (Stan)
**WFA** 4 from 5yo+ 1lb 7 Ran SP% **112.8**
Speed ratings (Par 101): **94,92,92,91,90 83,75**
CSF £4.82 CT £33.33 TOTE £2.00: £1.30, £2.90; EX 5.60 Trifecta £33.70.
**Owner** Paul G Jacobs **Bred** Peter Molony **Trained** Sparsholt, Oxfordshire

**FOCUS**
A weak race that went the way of the unexposed favourite. Straightforward form.

## 1755 BET TOTETRIFECTA AT TOTESPORT.COM H'CAP 7f (P)

**2:40** (2:41) (Class 6) (0-65,66) 4-Y-0+ **£3,234** (£962; £481; £240) **Stalls** Low

Form RPR

-026 1 **Hipz (IRE)**[24] 1285 6-9-3 60.......................................(p) IrineuGoncalves 8 67
(Ivan Furtado) *chsd ldr tl led wl over 1f out: pushed along and wnt clr ent fnl f: rdn and a doing enough ins fnl f: kpt on* **10/1**

06-1 2 1 1/2 **Isntshesomething**[14] 1451 5-8-9 52...............................(v) JoeFanning 6 55
(Richard Guest) *hld up in tch in midfield: effrt over 1f out: hdwy u.p 1f out: styd on ins fnl f to snatch 2nd last strides: no threat to wnr* **5/1**[2]

0334 3 hd **Jack The Laird (IRE)**[6] 1603 4-9-0 60.......................(p) JackDuern(3) 3 62
(Dean Ivory) *t.k.h: trckd ldrs: effrt over 1f out: chsd wnr and kpt on same pce ins fnl f* **5/1**[2]

5134 4 2 **Space War**[14] 1450 10-9-6 66.....................................(t) NathanEvans(3) 5 63
(Michael Easterby) *hld up in tch in last quartet: effrt over 1f out: sn drvn: swtchd lft 1f out: styd on ins fnl f: nvr trbld ldrs* **7/2**[1]

440- 5 1/2 **Helfire**[198] 6851 4-9-4 66.............................................. CharlieBennett(5) 10 62
(Hughie Morrison) *taken down early: chsd ldrs: swtchd rt and effrt wl over 1f out: sn drvn: chsd clr wnr briefly ent fnl f: wknd ins fnl f* **5/1**[2]

4-30 6 3/4 **Dance Rebel**[20] 1339 4-9-6 63......................................... RichardKingscote 1 57
(Dr Jon Scargill) *chsd ldrs: effrt u.p on inner over 1f out: no imp: wknd ins fnl f* **5/1**[2]

-U16 7 3/4 **Secret Lightning (FR)**[14] 1456 5-8-9 52..............(p) SilvestreDeSousa 2 44
(Michael Appleby) *sn dropped to last pair: nvr gng wl and sn rdn along: kpt on u.p ins fnl f: nvr trbld ldrs* **8/1**[3]

045 8 2 3/4 **Noble Act**[21] 1326 4-9-9 66......................................... JosephineGordon 7 50
(Phil McEntee) *sn bustled up to ld: rdn and hdd wl over 1f out: unable qck and lost 2nd ent fnl f: sn edgd rt and wknd fnl 150yds* **12/1**

603- 9 nk **The Firm (IRE)**[272] 4348 8-9-0 64................................ GinaMangan(7) 4 47
(J R Jenkins) *sn stdd and hld up in last pair: c centre and shkn up over 1f out: no imp: n.d* **40/1**

1m 24.51s (-2.69) **Going Correction** -0.30s/f (Stan) 9 Ran SP% **119.2**
Speed ratings (Par 101): **103,101,101,98,98 97,96,93,93**
CSF £61.27 CT £288.09 TOTE £12.20: £3.00, £1.70, £1.70; EX 102.80 Trifecta £439.60.
**Owner** J Melo **Bred** Mrs Noelle Walsh **Trained** Wiseton, Nottinghamshire

**FOCUS**
A modest but competitive handicap. The winner has been rated as repeating his best figure from 2016 on his first start for his new stable.

## 1756 BET TOTEQUADPOT AT TOTESPORT.COM MAIDEN FILLIES' STKS (PLUS 10 RACE) 1m 2f (P)

**3:10** (3:13) (Class 4) 3-Y-O **£8,086** (£2,406; £1,202; £601) **Stalls** Low

Form RPR

20- 1 **Curlew River**[166] 7696 3-9-0 0.......................................... SilvestreDeSousa 5 81
(Mark Johnston) *mde all: rdn: rn green and edgd lft over 1f out: edging bk rt but asserting u.p ins fnl f: r.o strly and drew clr fnl 100yds* **3/1**[3]

4- 2 2 1/4 **Pure Shores**[140] 8081 3-9-0 0............................................ WilliamBuick 4 76
(Charlie Appleby) *t.k.h: trckd ldr: rdn over 1f out: drvn and stl pressing wnr 1f out: no ex and outpcd fnl 100yds* **1/1**[1]

-32 3 nk **Fiendish (USA)**[7] 1581 3-9-0 0............................................ JoeFanning 2 75
(Mark Johnston) *trckd ldng pair: effrt and hung lft over 1f out: r.o same pce ins fnl f* **2/1**[2]

4 11 **Luna Magic** 3-8-11 0.......................................................... SimonPearce(3) 3 53
(Lydia Pearce) *t.k.h: hld up in tch: pushed along ent fianl 2f: sn outpcd and wknd over 1f out* **50/1**

0- 5 1/2 **Piaffe (USA)**[114] 8464 3-8-9 0...................................... CharlieBennett(5) 1 52
(Jane Chapple-Hyam) *s.i.s: rn green in rr: rdn ent fnl 2f: sn outpcd and wknd over 1f out* **40/1**

2m 7.82s (-0.78) **Going Correction** -0.30s/f (Stan) 5 Ran SP% **112.7**
Speed ratings (Par 97): **91,89,88,80,79**
CSF £6.64 TOTE £3.90: £2.20, £1.50; EX 7.10 Trifecta £8.60.
**Owner** Sheikh Hamdan bin Mohammed Al Maktoum **Bred** Darley **Trained** Middleham Moor, N Yorks

**FOCUS**
This was fairly steadily run, and the winner dominated from the front. Nevertheless, she looked the best long-term prospect of the bunch. The third has been rated close to her latest form.

## 1757 BET TOTEEXACTA AT TOTESPORT.COM H'CAP 1m 2f (P)

**3:40** (3:46) (Class 2) 3-Y-O+ **£29,110** (£8,662; £4,329; £2,164) **Stalls** Low

Form RPR

412- 1 **Poet's Word (IRE)**[217] 6261 4-9-4 104................................ RyanMoore 1 113
(Sir Michael Stoute) *trckd ldng pair: swtchd rt and effrt to chal over 1f out: led jst ins fnl f: r.o strly and gng away towards fin: readily* **8/11**[1]

-064 2 1 1/2 **Intrude**[26] 1258 5-8-5 91 ow1............................................ SilvestreDeSousa 7 97
(Stuart Williams) *t.k.h: pressed ldr: rdn and ev ch over 1f out: chsd wnr and kpt on same pce ins fnl f* **20/1**

0102 3 3/4 **Pactolus (IRE)**[14] 1446 6-8-6 95.................................(t) AaronJones(3) 2 99
(Stuart Williams) *led: rdn wl over 1f out: hdd jst ins fnl f: no ex and styd on same pce after* **16/1**

211- 4 hd **Lionrockspirit (IRE)**[189] 7101 4-9-4 104......................... AndreaAtzeni 3 108
(Marco Botti) *t.k.h: hld up in tch in midfield: nt clrest of runs over 2f out: effrt u.p over 1f out: wnt 4th 1f out: styd on wl but no threat to wnr* **3/1**[2]

433- 5 1 **Brorocco**[208] 6581 4-8-0 86 oh1....................................(h) JimmyQuinn 4 88
(Andrew Balding) *stdd s: t.k.h: hld up in tch in last trio: nt clrest of runs over 2f out: pushed along and effrt on inner over 1f out: kpt on under hands and heels ins fnl f: nvr trbld ldrs* **20/1**

0213 6 hd **Qaffaal (USA)**[14] 1446 6-8-2 91..................................... NathanEvans(3) 5 92
(Michael Easterby) *hld up wl in tch in midfield: effrt over 1f out: sn drvn: kpt on ins fnl f but no threat to wnr* **8/1**[3]

5-25 7 nk **Fire Fighting (IRE)**[12] 1500 6-9-10 110.......................(b) AdamKirby 6 111
(Mark Johnston) *hld up in last pair: rdn and effrt on outer over 2f out: styd on ins fnl f: nvr threatened ldrs* **10/1**

2344 8 5 **Ice Royal (IRE)**[14] 1446 4-8-2 88..................................(p) LiamJones 9 79
(Jamie Osborne) *chsd ldng trio: effrt over 2f out: unable qck over 1f out: wknd ins fnl f* **40/1**

0 9 12 **Diana Lady (CHI)**[12] 1502 4-8-5 91.................................(t1) LukeMorris 8 58
(Rune Haugen) *dwlt: in tch in lst trio: rdn and dropped to last 3f out: lost tch over 1f out* **100/1**

2m 4.06s (-4.54) **Going Correction** -0.30s/f (Stan) 9 Ran SP% **121.9**
Speed ratings (Par 109): **106,104,104,104,103 103,102,98,89**
CSF £24.72 CT £157.37 TOTE £1.80: £1.10, £3.90, £4.00; EX 19.20 Trifecta £168.90.
**Owner** Saeed Suhail **Bred** Woodcote Stud Ltd **Trained** Newmarket, Suffolk

**FOCUS**
The early pace wasn't that strong, but the well-backed winner proved he's destined for a higher grade. It's been rated around the well placed second and third.

## 1758 TOTEPOOL BETTING AT TOTESPORT.COM H'CAP 1m 2f (P)

**4:10** (4:13) (Class 6) (0-65,67) 4-Y-O+ **£3,234** (£962; £481; £240) **Stalls** Low

Form RPR

111- 1 **Estrella Eria (FR)**[169] 7609 4-9-7 65...............................(h) LukeMorris 4 73
(George Peckham) *chsd ldrs: wnt 2nd 4f out: rdn to chal 2f out: drvn ahd 1f out: wandered lft u.p but styd on wl ins fnl f: rdn out* **7/2**[1]

6102 2 2 3/4 **Hannington**[12] 1484 6-9-2 60.......................................(t) SilvestreDeSousa 9 63
(Michael Appleby) *hld up in tch in midfield: 4th and rdn over 3f out: unable qck u.p over 1f out: no threat to wnr but kpt on u.p ins fnl f to snatch 2nd last stride* **9/2**[2]

4050 3 shd **Einstein**[47] 924 4-8-12 56..........................................(t) AdamBeschizza 10 59
(Mrs Ilka Gansera-Leveque) *led: rdn wl over 1f out: hdd 1f out: outpcd by wnr and wknd wl ins fnl f: lost 2nd last stride* **16/1**

6006 4 hd **False Id**[3] 1683 4-9-7 65.................................................. AndreaAtzeni 1 67
(Robert Eddery) *t.k.h: hld up in tch in midfield: effrt but unable qck over 1f out: kpt on but no threat to wnr ins fnl f* **7/2**[1]

-002 5 2 1/4 **Fast And Hot (IRE)**[5] 1620 4-9-9 67..............................(b) KieranO'Neill 8 65+
(Richard Hannon) *hld up in last pair: effrt but stl plenty to do whn swtchd rt over 1f out: kpt on ins fnl f: nvr threatened ldrs* **9/2**[2]

64-5 6 1 1/2 **Chelabella**[14] 1447 4-9-3 61...........................................(v) MartinLane 2 56
(Derek Shaw) *hld up in tch: rdn and unable qck over 2f out: styd on same pce after* **28/1**

1453 7 3 1/2 **Outlaw Torn (IRE)**[17] 1403 8-8-12 56........................(e) DougieCostello 3 45
(Richard Guest) *taken down early: t.k.h: chsd ldr tl 4f out: lost pl over 1f out: sn wknd* **20/1**

2-62 8 nk **The Ginger Berry**[48] 893 7-9-7 65..............................(h) RobertWinston 6 53
(Dr Jon Scargill) *stdd and short of room sn after s: hld up in last pair: swtchd and stl plenty to do whn pushed along over 1f out: no imp: n.d* **9/1**

0/6- 9 2 1/2 **Lawman's Justice (IRE)**[273] 4313 4-9-4 62.................... JasonHart 11 45
(John Quinn) *hld up in tch: rdn and struggling over 2f out: bhd over 1f out* **50/1**

000- 10 nse **My Mo (FR)**[165] 5392 5-9-7 65......................................(p) OisinMurphy 5 48
(David Dennis) *bmpd leaving stalls and rousted along: midfield on outer but a niggled along: rdn 4f out: steadily lost pl and bhd over 1f out* **6/1**[3]

2m 5.11s (-3.49) **Going Correction** -0.30s/f (Stan) 10 Ran SP% **121.1**
Speed ratings (Par 101): **101,98,98,98,96 95,92,92,90,90**
CSF £19.79 CT £228.79 TOTE £3.90: £1.70, £1.90, £4.70; EX 14.20 Trifecta £226.70.
**Owner** Fawzi Abdulla Nass **Bred** D Chassagneux & E A R L Ecurie Loire **Trained** Newmarket, Suffolk

**FOCUS**
A modest handicap run at a fairly ordinary gallop. Straightforward form rated around the second, third and fourth.

## 1759 TOTEPOOL BETTING ON ALL UK RACING H'CAP 5f (P)

**4:40** (4:41) (Class 6) (0-60,60) 4-Y-O+ **£3,234** (£962; £481; £240) **Stalls** Low

Form RPR

5421 1 **Roy's Legacy**[15] 1435 8-8-10 54................................ CharlieBennett(5) 10 64
(Shaun Harris) *pressed ldr tl led 2f out: sn rdn: kpt on wl ins fnl f: rdn out* **12/1**

6344 **2** 1 **Hurricane Alert**[12] 1490 5-8-7 **46** ........ AdamBeschizza 8 52
(Mark Hoad) *taken down early: t.k.h: chsd ldrs: rdn to chse wnr over 1f out: drvn and kpt on ins fnl f but nvr quite getting to wnr* **20/1**

2513 **3** 1 ¼ **Frank The Barber (IRE)**[20] 1340 5-9-7 **60** ........(t) AdamKirby 2 62
(Steph Hollinshead) *chsd ldrs: effrt over 1f out: 3rd and kpt on same pce u.p ins fnl f* **11/4**[1]

2311 **4** nk **Mighty Zip (USA)**[12] 1490 5-8-12 **58** ........(p) JordanUys(7) 12 59
(Lisa Williamson) *hld up in tch in midfield: effrt over 1f out: edging lft and kpt on wl u.p ins fnl f: nvr enough pce to threaten ldrs* **7/1**[3]

1142 **5** 1 ¾ **Tasaaboq**[12] 1490 6-9-2 **55** ........(t) JosephineGordon 9 50
(Phil McEntee) *dwlt: in rr: rdn over 2f out: swtchd rt and hdwy 1f out: styd on wl ins fnl f: nvr trbld ldrs* **8/1**

6-46 **6** hd **Fuel Injection**[76] 446 6-8-13 **52** ........(p) JackGarritty 1 46
(Paul Midgley) *bustled along leaving stalls: in tch in midfield: rdn over 1f out: no threat to wnr but kpt on ins fnl f* **8/1**

0300 **7** nk **Barnsdale**[27] 1247 4-8-0 **46** oh1 ........ MeganEllingworth(7) 4 39
(John Holt) *racd in last quartet: pushed along over 1f out: styd on ins fnl f: nvr trbld ldrs* **50/1**

3333 **8** 1 ½ **Loumarin (IRE)**[16] 1413 5-9-5 **58** ........(p) SilvestreDeSousa 11 45
(Michael Appleby) *in rr: hung rt 3f out: rdn and c wd wl over 1f out: sme late hdwy: n.d* **6/1**[2]

-002 **9** 1 ¾ **Camino**[14] 1452 4-8-2 **46** oh1 ........(p) LuluStanford(5) 7 27
(Andi Brown) *led tl 2f out: 4th and btn over 1f out: wknd ins fnl f* **12/1**

00-0 **10** 1 ¼ **Secret Clause**[93] 158 4-9-3 **56** ........ MartinLane 3 33
(Derek Shaw) *s.i.s: a towards rr: rdn over 2f out: no prog* **14/1**

2051 **11** 1 ¾ **Autumn Tonic (IRE)**[35] 1112 5-9-3 **56** ........(b) WilliamCarson 5 26
(Charlie Wallis) *hld up in midfield: rdn and lost pl over 1f out: wknd fnl f* **12/1**

4-51 **P** **Quality Art (USA)**[14] 1452 9-9-2 **55** ........ RobHornby 6
(Simon Hodgson) *midfield: rdn 2f out: dropped to rr and lost action over 1f out: p.u and collapsed ins fnl f (fatally injured)* **7/1**[3]

58.4s (-1.80) **Going Correction** -0.30s/f (Stan) **12** Ran SP% **124.6**
Speed ratings (Par 101): **102,100,98,97,95 94,94,91,89,87 84,**
CSF £240.59 CT £871.24 TOTE £14.60: £3.70, £4.90, £1.60; EX 319.40 Trifecta £4162.20.
**Owner** Notts Racing, S Mohammed & S Rowley **Bred** A Christou **Trained** Carburton, Notts

**FOCUS**
An ordinary race in which the pace held up pretty well. The runner-up has been rated to his mark and limits the form.

## 1760 PAUL GOODWIN 50TH AT CHARLIE LOCKRAMS'S BAR H'CAP 1m (P)
**5:10** (5:13) (Class 4) (0-80,81) 3-Y-O **£6,469** (£1,925; £962; £481) **Stalls** Low

Form RPR

1- **1** **Son Of The Stars**[127] 8245 3-9-8 **81** ........ RyanMoore 3 90+
(Richard Hannon) *t.k.h: trckd ldrs tl wnt 2nd after 2f: carried rt wl over 1f out: rdn to ld over 1f out: in command whn rn green and wandered ins fnl f: pushed out: readily* **8/13**[1]

1- **2** 2 **Prosper**[162] 7761 3-9-5 **78** ........ AndreaAtzeni 6 81+
(Roger Varian) *hld up in tch: shkn up ent fnl 2f: chsd clr wnr and battling for 2nd fnl f: kpt on but no imp on wnr* **5/1**[2]

010- **3** shd **Illaunmore (USA)**[166] 7698 3-9-7 **80** ........ RichardKingscote 2 83+
(John Gosden) *t.k.h: hld up in midfield: clsd whn impeded and swtchd rt over 1f out: hdwy and battling for 2nd fnl f: kpt on but no imp on wnr* **12/1**

52-1 **4** 1 ¼ **Ray's The Money (IRE)**[40] 1033 3-9-6 **79** ........(v) JamieSpencer 5 79
(Michael Bell) *stdd s: hld up in rr: clsd and swtchd rt over 1f out: effrt ent fnl f: edgd lft and kpt on same pce fnl 100yds* **7/1**[3]

02-6 **5** 1 ½ **Masonic (IRE)**[63] 642 3-8-13 **72** ........ TomMarquand 7 68
(Robyn Brisland) *led: edgd rt wl over 1f out: rdn and hdd over 1f out: unable qck and wknd ins fnl f* **33/1**

3-24 **6** shd **Jumping Jack (IRE)**[52] 846 3-8-10 **76** ........ StephenCummins(7) 4 72
(Richard Hughes) *dwlt: hld up in tch towards rr: nt clrest of runs on inner over 2f out: effrt over 1f out: no imp and wknd ins fnl f* **14/1**

-122 **7** 4 ½ **Seaview**[15] 1434 3-8-6 **68** ........ AaronJones(3) 1 53
(David Brown) *taken down early: chsd ldr for 2f: styd chsng ldrs: rdn over 1f out: unable qck and sn wknd: bhd ins fnl f* **14/1**

1m 36.86s (-3.04) **Going Correction** -0.30s/f (Stan) **7** Ran SP% **115.1**
Speed ratings (Par 100): **103,101,100,99,98 98,93**
CSF £4.18 CT £18.45 TOTE £1.70: £1.40, £2.30; EX 4.40 Trifecta £20.90.
**Owner** Ahmad Abdulla Al Shaikh **Bred** Southill Stud **Trained** East Everleigh, Wilts

**FOCUS**
An easy-enough win for the well-backed favourite. The first three can all potentially rate higher, while the fifth is perhaps the key to the form.
T/Jkpt: Part Won. £10,000.00 to a £1 stake. Pool: £8,874.66 - 0.5 winning unit. T/Plt: £27.40 to a £1 stake. Pool: £97,646.46 - 2,600.44 winning units T/Qpdt: £7.00 to a £1 stake. Pool: £7,195.44 - 752.83 winning units **Steve Payne**

# BATH (L-H)
Friday, April 14

**OFFICIAL GOING: Firm (good to firm in places; 10.00)**
Wind: quite strong half against Weather: cloudy

## 1761 BETWAY MAIDEN STKS (DIV I) 5f 160y
**2:00** (2:00) (Class 4) 3-Y-O+ **£4,883** (£1,461; £730; £365; £182) **Stalls** Centre

Form RPR

62- **1** **Esprit De Corps**[149] 7976 3-8-13 0 ........ KieranShoemark(3) 3 81
(Roger Charlton) *in last pair but wl in tch: hdwy 3f out: swtchd rt 2f out: led ent fnl f: r.o wl: readily* **7/4**[1]

24 **2** 3 ¼ **Global Alexander (IRE)**[13] 1503 3-8-11 0 ........ SamHitchcott 9 65
(Clive Cox) *trckd ldrs: led over 2f out: rdn and hdd ent fnl f: kpt on but sn hld by wnr* **11/4**[2]

42- **3** 3 **Sumou (IRE)**[273] 4347 4-10-0 0 ........ RichardKingscote 10 63
(Milton Bradley) *prom: led over 3f out: rdn and hdd over 2f out: kpt on tl no ex ins fnl f* **8/1**

-622 **4** 14 **Trotter**[39] 1064 3-9-2 71 ........ MartinDwyer 2 14
(Stuart Kittow) *trckd ldrs: rdn over 2f out: wknd over 1f out* **4/1**[3]

5- **5** ¾ **Delahay**[230] 5890 3-8-11 0 ........ TomMarquand 8 6
(Michael Blanshard) *in tch: effrt over 2f out: wknd over 1f out* **20/1**

06- **6** 1 **Amberine**[260] 4790 3-8-11 0 ........ RoystonFfrench 6 3
(Malcolm Saunders) *slowly away: a outpcd in rr* **33/1**

43-4 **P** **Three C's (IRE)**[22] 1321 3-9-2 75 ........ FranBerry 7
(David Dennis) *rousted along to ld: hdd over 3f out: wknd over 1f out: lost action and p.u fnl f (dismntd)* **13/2**

1m 10.59s (-0.61) **Going Correction** -0.075s/f (Good)
**WFA** 3 from 4yo 12lb **7** Ran SP% **115.2**
Speed ratings (Par 105): **101,96,92,74,73 71,**
CSF £6.87 TOTE £2.70: £1.60, £1.80; EX 6.60 Trifecta £30.70.
**Owner** P Hearson & P Inglett **Bred** David Jamison & Gordon Roddick **Trained** Beckhampton, Wilts

**FOCUS**
This was a modest maiden and it's straightforward enough form. The runner-up has been rated a bit off her AW form.

## 1762 BETWAY MAIDEN STKS (DIV II) 5f 160y
**2:30** (2:38) (Class 4) 3-Y-O+ **£4,883** (£1,461; £730; £365; £182) **Stalls** Centre

Form RPR

6226 **1** **Goodwood Crusader (IRE)**[22] 1328 3-8-9 65 ........ FinleyMarsh(7) 4 75
(Richard Hughes) *hld up last pair but wl in tch: swtchd rt and hdwy over 1f out: shkn up to ld ent fnl f: r.o wl* **6/1**

03- **2** 3 ¼ **Bahamian Paradise**[164] 7733 3-8-6 0 ........ CharlieBennett(5) 9 59
(Hughie Morrison) *hld up in tch: hdwy over 2f out: led over 1f out: drifted lft: hdd ent fnl f: nt pce of wnr* **16/1**

034- **3** 3 **Glacier Point**[182] 7314 3-8-11 73 ........ JohnFahy 6 49
(Clive Cox) *trckd ldrs: rdn 2f out: kpt on same pce fnl f* **7/4**[1]

4 **4** 5 **Chatoyer (FR)**[7] 1600 3-9-2 0 ........ TomMarquand 3 38
(Richard Hannon) *s.i.s: last pair but in tch: rdn over 2f out: kpt on into hld 4th ent fnl f: nvr gng pce to get involved* **11/4**[2]

32-2 **5** 1 **Kowaiyess (IRE)**[22] 1321 3-9-2 70 ........ FranBerry 7 35
(Owen Burrows) *racd keenly: trckd ldrs: chal 3f out: rdn over 1f out: hung lft and wknd fnl f* **10/3**[3]

**6** ½ **Clever Lady (IRE)** 3-8-11 0 ........ SteveDrowne 1 28
(David Evans) *s.i.s: sn rcvrd to ld: hdd over 2f out: wknd jst over 1f out* **20/1**

0 **7** shd **Tisa River (IRE)**[6] 1626 3-8-11 0 ........ RichardKingscote 8 28
(Milton Bradley) *prom: led over 2f out: rdn and hdd over 1f out: fdd fnl f* **100/1**

1m 10.55s (-0.65) **Going Correction** -0.075s/f (Good)
**WFA** 3 from 4yo 12lb **7** Ran SP% **112.0**
Speed ratings (Par 105): **101,96,92,86,84 84,83**
CSF £85.44 TOTE £7.20: £2.60, £4.30; EX 97.30 Trifecta £296.10.
**Owner** Goodwood Racehorse Owners Group (23) Ltd **Bred** Tally-Ho Stud **Trained** Upper Lambourn, Berks

■ Under The Covers and Ballysampson were withdrawn. Prices at time of withdrawal 50-1. Rule 4 does not apply.

**FOCUS**
Modest form. At face value the winner could rate higher, while the runner-up would back at least 6lb higher on her AW latest.

## 1763 BETWAY H'CAP 1m 5f 11y
**3:00** (3:00) (Class 4) (0-85,81) 4-Y-O+
**£4,513** (£1,351; £675; £337; £168; £84) **Stalls** High

Form RPR

3132 **1** **Midtech Star (IRE)**[6] 1628 5-8-7 **64** ........(v) FrannyNorton 3 69
(Ian Williams) *trckd ldr: rdn to ld over 2f out: sn strly chal: hld on wl ins fnl f* **6/4**[1]

514/ **2** nk **Eddiemaurice (IRE)**[8] 7161 6-9-3 **74** ........ DanielMuscutt 2 78
(John Flint) *trckd ldrs: sltly outpcd over 3f out: hdwy over 2f out: str chal ins fnl f: kpt on* **6/1**

0044 **3** 1 **Wordiness**[69] 571 9-8-0 **64** ........ DavidEgan(7) 1 67
(David Evans) *in tch: hdwy over 3f out: str chal over 2f out: sn rdn: kpt on w ev ch tl no ex ins fnl f* **10/1**

3326 **4** 1 ¾ **Icebuster**[18] 1405 9-9-4 **75** ........ RyanTate 4 75
(Rod Millman) *racd keenly: hld up: hdwy to ld over 7f out where qcknd pce: sn 4 l clr: rdn and hdd over 2f out: kpt on same pce* **5/2**[2]

000- **5** 6 **Urban Space**[184] 7270 11-8-8 **65** ........(t) KieranO'Neill 6 56
(John Flint) *trckd ldrs tl outpcd 3f out: nvr bk on terms* **33/1**

540- **6** nk **Togetherness (IRE)**[192] 7060 4-9-5 **78** ........ RichardKingscote 5 68
(Harry Dunlop) *led tl over 7f out: chsd ldrs: rdn wl over 2f out: wknd fnl f* **9/2**[3]

2m 56.27s (4.27) **Going Correction** -0.075s/f (Good) **6** Ran SP% **113.1**
Speed ratings (Par 105): **83,82,82,81,77 77**
CSF £11.32 CT £64.67 TOTE £1.90: £1.30, £3.40; EX 12.80 Trifecta £53.10.
**Owner** Midtech **Bred** Denis McDonnell **Trained** Portway, Worcs

■ Stewards' Enquiry : Daniel Muscutt 2 day ban (28-29 April) - used whip above the permitted level

**FOCUS**
Not a bad staying handicap. Muddling form. The runner-up has been rated to his old form.

## 1764 BATHWICK TYRES H'CAP 1m 3f 137y
**3:30** (3:33) (Class 2) (0-100,100) 3-Y-O
**£37,350** (£11,184; £5,592; £2,796; £1,398; £702) **Stalls** Low

Form RPR

614- **1** **Hushood (IRE)**[211] 6499 3-8-7 **86** ........ TomMarquand 5 92
(Richard Hannon) *slowly away: in last trio but in tch: hdwy over 2f out: rdn over 1f out: kpt on strly ins fnl f: led fnl strides* **11/2**[3]

321- **2** hd **Mister Manduro (FR)**[170] 7605 3-8-6 **85** ........ RoystonFfrench 3 90
(Mark Johnston) *trckd ldr: rdn to chal 2f out: led ent fnl f: kpt on: hdd fnl strides* **11/2**[3]

153- **3** shd **Permian (IRE)**[188] 7151 3-9-7 **100** ........ RichardKingscote 6 105+
(Mark Johnston) *trckd ldrs: rdn and hanging lft fr 2f out: keeping o whn hung bhd ldr ent fnl f: kpt on wl w wnr fnl 120yds* **3/1**[2]

231- **4** ¾ **Sofia's Rock (FR)**[172] 7580 3-8-6 **85** ........ FrannyNorton 8 89
(Mark Johnston) *led: rdn whn strly chal fr 2f out: hdd ent fnl f: kpt on tl no ex cl home* **11/4**[1]

01-1 **5** 4 ½ **Emenem**[77] 439 3-7-9 **81** oh4 ........ DavidEgan(7) 7 77
(Simon Dow) *stdd s: cl up whn rdn 2f out: nt quite pce to mount chal: wknd ins fnl f* **16/1**

23-1 **6** hd **Doctor Bartolo (IRE)**[93] 175 3-8-2 **81** oh1 ........ KieranO'Neill 1 77
(Charles Hills) *trckd ldrs: rdn over 2f out: nt quite pce to chal: wknd ins fnl f* **6/1**

1113 **7** 5 **Poetic Force (IRE)**[34] 1142 3-8-5 **84** ........(t) JoeyHaynes 2 72
(Tony Carroll) *hld up in tch: rdn over 2f out: nt pce to chal: wknd fnl f* **20/1**

2m 26.43s (-4.17) **Going Correction** -0.075s/f (Good) **7** Ran SP% **107.4**
Speed ratings (Par 104): **110,109,109,109,106 106,102**
CSF £30.79 CT £90.77 TOTE £5.70: £2.60, £3.30; EX 34.60 Trifecta £102.50.
**Owner** Hamdan Al Maktoum **Bred** Ringfort Stud **Trained** East Everleigh, Wilts

■ Atkinson Grimshaw was withdrawn. Price at time of withdrawal 10-1. Rule 4 applies to all bets - deduction 5p in the pound.

**FOCUS**
A valuable 3yo handicap, run at a sound pace. The level is fluid, but the race has been rated around the third to the better view of his form for now.

## 1765 BATHWICK TYRES CONDITIONS STKS 5f 160y
**4:00** (4:03) (Class 2) 3-Y-O+ **£12,450** (£3,728; £1,864; £932; £466) **Stalls** Centre

Form RPR
63- **1** **Muthmir (IRE)**[230] 5863 7-9-4 110 FranBerry 5 112
(William Haggas) *trckd ldrs: led jst over 1f out: r.o wl: pushed out* **10/11**[1]
550- **2** 1 1/4 **Mr Lupton (IRE)**[181] 7350 4-9-8 107 JamieSpencer 3 111
(Richard Fahey) *last but in tch: swtchd rt for effrt over 1f out: r.o: wnt 2nd fnl 120yds but nvr threatening wnr* **7/2**[2]
424- **3** 3/4 **Willytheconqueror (IRE)**[195] 6943 4-9-4 104 MartinDwyer 2 105
(William Muir) *trckd ldr: rdn over 1f out: kpt on same pce fnl f* **11/2**[3]
236- **4** 1 1/4 **Equimou**[217] 6282 3-8-1 103 JimmyQuinn 7 93
(Robert Eddery) *led: rdn and hdd jst over 1f out: kpt on but sn no ex* **11/2**[3]
320- **5** 2 1/2 **Pixeleen**[188] 7146 5-8-13 86 PatDobbs 6 88
(Malcolm Saunders) *trckd ldr: rdn over 1f out: wknd ins fnl f* **12/1**

1m 10.28s (-0.92) **Going Correction** -0.075s/f (Good)
**WFA** 3 from 4yo+ 12lb **5 Ran SP% 113.1**
Speed ratings (Par 109): **103,101,100,98,95**
CSF £4.58 TOTE £1.60: £1.10, £2.10; EX 4.70 Trifecta £7.50.
**Owner** Hamdan Al Maktoum **Bred** Sunderland Holdings Ltd **Trained** Newmarket, Suffolk

**FOCUS**
A good-quality conditions sprint. The runner-up has been rated to his best, with the third close to form.

## 1766 DRIBUILD H'CAP 1m 5y
**4:30** (4:31) (Class 2) 4-Y-O+
**£31,125** (£9,320; £4,660; £2,330; £1,165; £585) **Stalls** Low

Form RPR
-352 **1** **Oh This Is Us (IRE)**[13] 1494 4-9-10 107 PatDobbs 9 115
(Richard Hannon) *in tch: hdwy over 2f out: led narrowly over 1f out: kpt on wl: rdn out* **3/1**[2]
5-23 **2** nk **Hors De Combat**[64] 654 6-9-5 102 JimmyFortune 12 109
(Denis Coakley) *hld up last pair: hdwy fr 2f out: swtchd rt over 1f out: r.o strly fnl f: wnt 2nd fnl 100yds: clsng on wnr at fin* **9/1**
431- **3** 3/4 **El Vip (IRE)**[172] 7573 4-8-11 94 JamieSpencer 3 99
(Luca Cumani) *slowly away: sn trcking ldrs: chal gng wl 2f out: led briefly over 1f out: sn drvn: kpt on: no ex fnl 75yds* **9/4**[1]
-321 **4** 1 1/2 **The Warrior (IRE)**[16] 1422 5-8-3 86 (e) FrannyNorton 1 88
(Amanda Perrett) *in tch: hdwy on inner over 1f out: cl up whn rdn ent fnl f: nt qckn* **6/1**[3]
0-16 **5** 1 1/4 **Worlds His Oyster**[56] 782 4-7-13 89 DavidEgan(7) 10 88
(John Quinn) *trckd ldrs tl lost pl over 4f out: hdwy 2f out: sn rdn: kpt on same pce fnl f* **14/1**
3434 **6** 1 1/4 **Bold Prediction (IRE)**[10] 1546 7-7-12 88 JaneElliott(7) 6 84
(Ed Walker) *led tl over 3f out: regained ld over 2f out: rdn and hdd wl over 1f out: no ex fnl f* **16/1**
00-0 **7** 1 **Heaven's Guest (IRE)**[13] 1494 7-8-8 98 ConnorMurtagh(7) 4 92
(Richard Fahey) *hld up towards rr: sme prog 2f out: no further imp fnl f* **16/1**
14-2 **8** shd **Invermere**[12] 1512 4-8-0 83 oh4 JoeyHaynes 8 77
(Richard Fahey) *hld up towards rr: hdwy u.p on outer 2f out: drifted lft and fdd fnl f* **14/1**
-202 **9** 2 1/4 **Bunbury**[27] 1258 5-8-7 90 ShaneKelly 11 79
(Richard Hughes) *a towards rr* **12/1**
000- **10** 1 3/4 **Winklemann (IRE)**[160] 7825 5-8-2 85 (p[1]) KieranO'Neill 5 70
(John Flint) *mid-div: struggling over 3f out: wknd jst over 1f out* **50/1**
6054 **11** 2 1/4 **Kingston Kurrajong**[16] 1422 4-8-3 86 JimmyQuinn 7 65
(Michael Attwater) *pressed ldr: led over 3f out tl over 2f out: wknd over 1f out* **16/1**

1m 38.08s (-2.72) **Going Correction** -0.075s/f (Good) **11 Ran SP% 120.7**
Speed ratings (Par 109): **110,109,108,107,106 104,103,103,101,99 97**
CSF £31.47 CT £74.15 TOTE £3.70: £1.80, £2.70, £1.30; EX 24.60 Trifecta £60.40.
**Owner** Team Wallop **Bred** Herbertstown House Stud **Trained** East Everleigh, Wilts

**FOCUS**
A classy handicap and solid form. The runner-up has been rated to his best since late 2015, with the fourth close to his recent AW form.

## 1767 BATHWICK TYRES SOUTH WEST CONDITIONS STKS (PLUS 10 RACE) 5f 10y
**5:00** (5:04) (Class 2) 2-Y-O
**£12,450** (£3,728; £1,864; £932; £466; £234) **Stalls** Centre

Form RPR
**1** **Chagatai (IRE)** 2-9-2 0 SamHitchcott 5 77+
(Clive Cox) *hmpd s: in tch: trcking ldrs travelling strly whn nt clr run and snatched up over 1f out: swtchd rt: shkn up and r.o wl fnl 130yds: led fnl stride* **7/4**[1]
2 **2** hd **Last Page**[13] 1495 2-9-2 0 SteveDrowne 9 74
(David Evans) *s.i.s: sn mid-div: swtchd to outer and hdwy over 2f out: rdn to ld but edging bdly lft ent fnl f: kpt on: hdd fnl stride* **7/1**
5 **3** 1 3/4 **Autumn Lodge**[13] 1495 2-9-2 0 ShaneKelly 10 67
(J S Moore) *trckd ldrs: led wl over 1f out: rdn and hdd ent fnl f: kpt on but no ex* **33/1**
**4** 2 **Jonnysimpson (IRE)** 2-8-11 0 FranBerry 11 54
(Brendan Powell) *in tch on outer: trckd ldrs over 2f out: sn rdn: kpt on same pce fnl f* **10/1**
4 **5** 1 1/2 **Shovel It On (IRE)**[7] 1604 2-9-2 0 DannyBrock 6 53
(David Evans) *in tch: rdn over 2f out: kpt on but nt pce to get on terms* **14/1**
**6** nk **Uther Pendragon (IRE)** 2-9-2 0 KieranO'Neill 2 52+
(J S Moore) *outpcd towards rr: hung rt over 2f out: hdwy over 1f out: kpt on nicely fnl f but nvr any dager* **66/1**
**7** shd **Zalshah** 2-9-2 0 TomMarquand 8 51
(Richard Hannon) *disp ld: edgd ahd over 2f out: rdn and hdd wl over 1f out: fdd fnl f* **3/1**[2]
**8** 2 1/2 **My Guy (IRE)** 2-9-2 0 LiamKeniry 1 41
(J S Moore) *uns rdr on way to s: wnt bdly lft and slowly away: bhd: sme late prog: nvr any danger* **40/1**
3 **9** 1 1/4 **Airshow**[7] 1604 2-9-2 0 (h) RyanTate 4 36
(Rod Millman) *wnt rt s: in tch: rdn wl over 2f out: wknd over 1f out* **6/1**
**10** 1 **Demons Rock (IRE)** 2-9-2 0 RichardKingscote 3 32
(Tom Dascombe) *disp ld tl rdn over 2f out: wknd over 1f out* **9/2**[3]
0 **11** 2 **Manco Inca (IRE)**[7] 1604 2-9-2 0 GeorgeDowning 7 24
(Joseph Tuite) *a towards rr* **66/1**

1m 2.97s (0.47) **Going Correction** -0.075s/f (Good) **11 Ran SP% 130.5**
Speed ratings (Par 98): **93,92,89,86,84 83,83,79,77,76 72**
CSF £17.10 TOTE £3.00: £1.60, £2.20, £4.40; EX 17.40 Trifecta £178.90.
**Owner** AlMohamediya Racing **Bred** Thomas Hassett **Trained** Lambourn, Berks

**FOCUS**
Probably a decent little event. The runner-up and third have been rated close to their Doncaster debut form.

## 1768 BETWAY SPRINT H'CAP 5f 10y
**5:30** (5:30) (Class 4) (0-85,84) 4-Y-O+
**£6,225** (£1,864; £932; £466; £233; £117) **Stalls** Centre

Form RPR
520- **1** **Love On The Rocks (IRE)**[189] 7124 4-9-7 84 (h) JamieSpencer 9 91
(Charles Hills) *hld up: hdwy 2f out: sn pushed along: chal ins fnl f: edgd ahd towards fin* **11/4**[1]
0334 **2** hd **Seamster**[13] 1487 10-8-11 81 (t) GerO'Neill(7) 4 87
(David Loughnane) *led: rdn over 1f out: str chal ins fnl f: hdd towards fin* **12/1**
0624 **3** 2 3/4 **Rosealee (IRE)**[20] 1370 4-8-9 77 DavidParkes(5) 11 73
(Jeremy Gask) *mid-div: hdwy in center 2f out: sn rdn: kpt on ins fnl f* **17/2**
1653 **4** nk **Zipedeedodah (IRE)**[13] 1487 5-8-0 70 (t) DavidEgan(7) 8 65
(Joseph Tuite) *trckd ldrs: rdn w ch over 1f out: kpt on same pce fnl f* **7/1**
43-2 **5** 1 1/2 **Cultured Knight**[23] 1302 4-9-0 77 ShaneKelly 5 67
(Richard Hughes) *trckd ldrs: rdn over 1f out: sn one pce* **4/1**[3]
4060 **6** 1 **Silvanus (IRE)**[29] 1222 12-9-2 79 MartinLane 10 65
(Paul Midgley) *trckd ldrs: rdn 2f out: fdd fnl f* **12/1**
100- **7** 3 3/4 **Babyfact**[184] 7267 6-8-8 71 JimmyQuinn 2 44
(Malcolm Saunders) *mid-div: rdn over 2f out: nvr threatened* **20/1**
040- **8** 1/2 **Englishman**[187] 7186 7-9-7 84 FrannyNorton 7 55
(Milton Bradley) *w ldr tl rdn over 2f out: wkng whn short of room over 1f out* **17/2**
2125 **9** 1 1/4 **Zac Brown (IRE)**[20] 1362 6-8-12 75 (t) WilliamCarson 3 41+
(Charlie Wallis) *wl bhd after rring bdly leaving stalls: nvr any ch* **7/2**[2]

1m 1.36s (-1.14) **Going Correction** -0.075s/f (Good) **9 Ran SP% 122.6**
Speed ratings (Par 105): **106,105,101,100,98 96,90,90,88**
CSF £40.00 CT £261.98 TOTE £3.50: £1.30, £3.70, £2.80; EX 38.50 Trifecta £279.40.
**Owner** The Chriselliam Partnership **Bred** Mount Coote New England Barton & Myriad **Trained** Lambourn, Berks

**FOCUS**
A modest sprint handicap. A pb from the winner, with the third rated similar to last year's C&D win.
T/Plt: £193.80 to a £1 stake. Pool: £65,487.00 - 337.85 winning units. T/Qpdt: £8.90 to a £1 stake. Pool: £4,530.00 - 505.98 winning units. **Tim Mitchell**

# 1692 LINGFIELD (L-H)
## Friday, April 14

**OFFICIAL GOING: Polytrack: standard**
Wind: light half behind in home straight, of little consequence Weather: light cloud

## 1769 SUNBETS ALL-WEATHER CHAMPIONSHIPS APPRENTICE H'CAP 7f 1y(P)
**1:40** (1:41) (Class 2) (0-100,100) 4-Y-O+
**£31,125** (£9,320; £4,660; £2,330; £1,165; £585) **Stalls** Low

Form RPR
0526 **1** **Forceful Appeal (USA)**[15] 1446 9-8-13 92 PaddyBradley(5) 1 99
(Simon Dow) *trckd ldrs: rdn to chal over 1f out: drvn to ld ins fnl f: sn hrd pressed: kpt on gamely to win on the nod: all out* **33/1**
30-2 **2** nse **War Glory (IRE)**[6] 1622 4-9-2 90 HollieDoyle 9 97
(Richard Hannon) *t.k.h: hld up in tch in midfield: swtchd rt and effrt over 1f out: hdwy and squeezed between rivals 1f out: str chal wl ins fnl f: r.o but jst hld on the nod* **10/3**[1]
601- **3** nk **Charles Molson**[148] 7984 6-9-9 97 HectorCrouch 11 103
(Patrick Chamings) *hld up in tch in midfield on outer: effrt over 1f out: hdwy: edgd lft u.p and bmpd 1f out: styd on strly ins fnl f: nt quite rch ldng pair* **12/1**
2121 **4** 3/4 **Take The Helm**[6] 1622 4-8-12 93 6ex JordanUys(7) 12 97
(Brian Meehan) *nt that wl away and bustled along early: hdwy to chse ldrs after 1f: effrt over 1f out: ev ch 1f out: kpt on but no ex towards fin* **8/1**
5-60 **5** 1 **Kadrizzi (FR)**[42] 999 4-9-12 100 JackDuern 14 101
(Dean Ivory) *pressed ldr: rdn and ev ch over 1f out: edgd rt u.p 1f out: no ex ins fnl f and wknd towards fin* **33/1**
0-51 **6** nk **Suzi's Connoisseur**[59] 730 6-9-11 99 (vt) AaronJones 6 100
(Stuart Williams) *hld up in tch in midfield: effrt and c wd wl over 1f out: styd on u.p ins fnl f: nvr getting on terms w ldrs* **12/1**
4230 **7** nk **Holiday Magic (IRE)**[13] 1492 6-9-9 97 NathanEvans 3 97
(Michael Easterby) *t.k.h: led: rdn over 1f out: drvn and hdd ins fnl f: no ex 100yds out and wknd towards fin* **11/2**[3]
0-05 **8** 1 1/4 **Baraweez (IRE)**[34] 1148 7-9-5 98 BenRobinson(5) 13 94
(Brian Ellison) *t.k.h: chsd ldrs: effrt over 1f out: drvn and unable qck 1f out: wknd ins fnl f* **18/1**
6-11 **9** 3/4 **Hakam (USA)**[13] 1501 5-9-5 93 AlistairRawlinson 5 87+
(Michael Appleby) *awkward leaving stalls and s.i.s: hld up in tch towards rr: effrt over 1f out: hdwy u.p ins fnl f: styd on: nvr trbld ldrs* **5/1**[2]
1225 **10** 1/2 **Intransigent**[42] 999 8-8-12 93 WilliamCox(7) 4 86
(Andrew Balding) *t.k.h: hld up in tch in midfield: nt clrest of runs ent fnl 2f: effrt on inner over 1f out: no imp and styd on same pce ins fnl f* **16/1**
1-04 **11** nk **Amazour (IRE)**[34] 1150 5-9-7 100 JoshuaBryan(5) 8 92+
(Ismail Mohammed) *s.i.s: hld up in tch in rr: effrt over 1f out: sme hdwy ins fnl f: styd on but nvr threatened ldrs* **6/1**
5-30 **12** nk **Dougan**[13] 1501 5-9-11 99 CallumShepherd 7 90
(David Evans) *hld up in tch in last trio: effrt over 1f out: rdn 1f out: kpt on but nvr threatened ldrs* **16/1**
0365 **13** nk **Al Khan (IRE)**[59] 730 8-9-0 91 LewisEdmunds(3) 10 82
(Kevin Ryan) *s.i.s: hld up in tch towards rr: rdn over 1f out: no imp: n.d* **25/1**
03/0 **14** 1 1/4 **Grey Danube (IRE)**[56] 795 8-8-13 94 (t) DamienMelia(7) 2 81
(D J Bunyan, Ire) *hld up in tch in midfield: rdn and effrt on inner over 1f out: no prog: bhd ins fnl f* **40/1**

1m 23.06s (-1.74) **Going Correction** -0.125s/f (Stan) **14 Ran SP% 125.1**
Speed ratings (Par 109): **104,103,103,102,101 101,100,99,98,98 97,97,97,95**
CSF £142.74 CT £1512.61 TOTE £36.20: £9.20, £1.70, £4.60; EX 193.60 Trifecta £4230.00.
**Owner** Mark McAlister **Bred** Juddmonte Farms Inc **Trained** Ashtead, Surrey

**FOCUS**

The fourth running of the All-Weather Championships and a total prize fund of £1 million up for grabs. The meeting kicked off with a good quality apprentice handicap. It paid to race in the first half of the field, the deep closers never getting involved. The winner has been rated to form, while the second and fourth help set the level.

## 1770 BETWAY ALL-WEATHER MARATHON CHAMPIONSHIPS CONDITIONS STKS — 1m 7f 169y(P)

**2:10** (2:11) (Class 2) 4-Y-O+

**£93,375** (£27,960; £13,980; £6,990; £3,495; £1,755) **Stalls** Low

Form — RPR

61-2 **1** **Winning Story**[43] 985 4-9-1 104..........................(p) SilvestreDeSousa 12 111
(Saeed bin Suroor) *hld up in midfield: swtchd rt and effrt over 2f out: hdwy to chse ldr 2f out: styd on u.p to ld ins fnl f: gng away at fin: rdn out* **7/1**[3]

-311 **2** *1 ¾* **Watersmeet**[43] 985 6-9-5 105.......................................... JoeFanning 14 109
(Mark Johnston) *chsd ldrs: hdwy to ld and wnt clr over 2f out: rdn over 1f out: hdd ins fnl f: no ex and outpcd towards fin* **7/1**[3]

23-3 **3** *¾* **Steve Rogers (IRE)**[88] 268 6-9-5 100............................ AndreaAtzeni 5 108
(Roger Varian) *hld up in tch in midfield: effrt to chse ldr over 2f out: 3rd and kpt on same pce u.p fnl 2f* **16/1**

-431 **4** *3 ¼* **Cohesion**[39] 1068 4-9-1 105................................................. RyanMoore 8 104
(David Bridgwater) *hld up in tch in midfield: nt clr run over 2f out: hdwy 2f out: chsd clr ldng trio over 1f out: styd on but nvr threatened ldrs* **5/1**[2]

14-3 **5** *¾* **Prince Of Arran**[13] 1502 4-9-1 103.................................. TomQueally 13 103
(Charlie Fellowes) *s.i.s: hld up in last pair: pushed along over 2f out: hdwy on outer bnd 2f out: styd on ins fnl f: nvr trbld ldrs* **15/2**

3-11 **6** *nse* **Natural Scenery**[59] 728 4-8-10 103.............................. DavidProbert 11 98
(Saeed bin Suroor) *hld up towards rr: nt clr run and bmpd over 2f out: hdwy into 6th 2f out but nt on terms w ldrs: kpt on but nvr getting on terms* **4/1**[1]

2-31 **7** *1* **First Mohican**[20] 1360 9-9-5 101..................................(h) HollieDoyle 3 102
(Alan King) *short of room leaving stalls: hld up in last pair: rdn briefly over 6f out: sme hdwy u.p on outer bnd 2f out: kpt on ins fnl f: nvr threatened ldrs* **16/1**

0-41 **8** *3 ¾* **Gavlar**[23] 1309 6-9-5 94...............................................(v) CallumShepherd 4 97
(William Knight) *wnt lft and rousted along leaving stalls: in tch in midfield: effrt whn n.m.r on inner over 2f out: no imp and wl hld over 1f out* **25/1**

4-16 **9** *nk* **Haines**[39] 1068 6-9-5 94........................................................ RobHornby 9 97+
(Andrew Balding) *hld up towards rr: clsd whn nt clr run and swtchd lft over 2f out: stl nt clr run and swtchd rt 2f out: stl plenty to do and rdn over 1f out: no ch of getting on terms: nvr trbld ldrs* **33/1**

-121 **10** *¾* **Petite Jack**[28] 1240 4-9-1 98.............................................. JackMitchell 6 96
(Neil King) *hld up towards rr: nt clr run over 2f out: stl plenty to whn effrt and hung lft over 1f out: no ch of getting on terms: kpt on* **8/1**

1-12 **11** *11* **Pinzolo**[48] 919 6-9-5 108...................................................... SeanLevey 7 83
(Ismail Mohammed) *hld up in tch in midfield: hdwy to chse ldrs 1/2-way: 4th and outpcd u.p 2f out: lost pl and btn 1f out: eased ins fnl f* **8/1**

0045 **12** *2 ¼* **John Reel (FR)**[6] 1628 8-9-5 93.........................................(t[1]) JFEgan 1 80
(David Evans) *led tl rdn and hdd 3f out: losing pl whn squeezed for room and snatched up over 2f out: dropped to rr and hmpd again wl over 1f out: bhd and eased wl ins fnl f* **40/1**

523 **13** *15* **Vettori Rules**[20] 1360 4-9-1 101....................................(p[1]) LukeMorris 10 62
(Gay Kelleway) *taken down early: t.k.h: chsd ldr tl rdn to ld 3f out: sn hdd and lost pl 2f out: bhd and eased ins fnl f: t.o* **50/1**

2125 **14** *37* **Winterlude (IRE)**[20] 1360 7-9-5 105................................... DavidNolan 2 18
(Jennie Candlish) *chsd ldrs: rdn 4f out: lost pl over 3f out: bhd fnl 2f: t.o: burst blood vessel* **16/1**

3m 15.18s (-10.52) **Going Correction** -0.125s/f (Stan) course record
**WFA** 4 from 6yo+ 2lb — **14** Ran SP% **124.5**
Speed ratings (Par 109): **121,120,119,118,117 117,117,115,115,114 109,108,100,82**
CSF £55.83 CT £779.34 TOTE £7.80: £2.60, £2.50, £5.20; EX 64.40 Trifecta £1063.10.
**Owner** Godolphin **Bred** Darley **Trained** Newmarket, Suffolk

■ Stewards' Enquiry : Andrea Atzeni 2 day ban (28-29 April) - guilty of careless riding in that he allowed his mount to drift left-handed

**FOCUS**

This looked really open beforehand, but it was run at a good gallop and the first three drew clear of the rest to lower the course record by 1.55sec. A pb from the winner, with the runner-up rated close to his old best.

## 1771 32RED ALL-WEATHER FILLIES' AND MARES' CHAMPIONSHIPS CONDITIONS STKS — 7f 1y(P)

**2:40** (2:41) (Class 2) 4-Y-O+

**£93,375** (£27,960; £13,980; £6,990; £3,495; £1,755) **Stalls** Low

Form — RPR

1-06 **1** **Realtra (IRE)**[57] 771 5-9-0 107...................................(b[1]) AndreaAtzeni 12 95+
(Roger Varian) *trckd ldrs on outer: effrt 2f out: hdwy u.p to chse ldr 1f out: styd on to ld wl ins fnl f: hld on towards fin: drvn out* **6/1**[3]

-333 **2** *nk* **Muffri'Ha (IRE)**[41] 1046 5-9-0 109..................................(p[1]) PatCosgrave 1 94+
(William Haggas) *nt that wl away and rousted along early: hld up in tch in midfield: n.m.r on inner over 2f out: swtchd rt and effrt over 1f out: hdwy u.p 1f out: styd on to go 2nd and pressing wnr wl ins fnl f: kpt on* **1/1**[1]

50-1 **3** *hd* **Ashadihan**[65] 617 4-9-0 105..................................................(p) KevinStott 7 93+
(Kevin Ryan) *t.k.h: hld up in tch in midfield: effrt ent fnl 2f: hdwy u.p 1f out: styd on: wnt 3rd and pressing ldr wl ins fnl f: kpt on* **5/2**[2]

1051 **4** *1 ½* **Make Music**[37] 1091 4-9-0 85.......................................... DavidProbert 10 89
(Andrew Balding) *w ldr: rdn and ev ch 2f out tl no ex wl ins fnl f: outpcd wl ins fnl f* **25/1**

0361 **5** *hd* **Shypen**[27] 1261 4-9-0 83...................................................... PaulHanagan 2 89
(Richard Fahey) *t.k.h: led and set stdy gallop: rdn over 1f out: drvn ins fnl f: hdd and no ex wl ins fnl f: outpcd towards fin* **33/1**

3203 **6** *nk* **Bint Dandy (IRE)**[20] 1368 6-9-0 87..........................(b) SilvestreDeSousa 6 88
(Chris Dwyer) *trckd ldrs: effrt u.p but unable qck over 1f out: styd on same pce ins fnl f* **25/1**

2-11 **7** *1* **Carolinae**[45] 964 5-9-0 88................................................ StevieDonohoe 3 85
(Charlie Fellowes) *t.k.h: hld up in tch in last trio: rdn and hdwy over 1f out: styd on same pce u.p ins fnl f* **10/1**

-002 **8** *2 ¼* **Staintondale Lass (IRE)**[27] 1261 4-9-0 85...................... LukeMorris 8 79
(Ed Vaughan) *broke wl restrained and t.k.h: in midfield: effrt 2f out: no imp u.p over 1f out: styd on same pce ins fnl f* **66/1**

-026 **9** *1* **Volunteer Point (IRE)**[43] 994 5-9-0 95............................ GrahamLee 9 77
(Mick Channon) *wnt lft after s: hld up in tch in midfield: rdn 2f out: no imp u.p over 1f out: wl hld and kpt on same pce ins fnl f* **18/1**

4345 **10** *hd* **Rebel Surge (IRE)**[27] 1261 4-9-0 82................................(p) TomQueally 5 76
(Richard Spencer) *short of room and stdd sn after s: t.k.h: hld up in tch in last trio: effrt on outer bnd 2f out: no imp and one pced after: nvr trbld ldrs* **50/1**

6510 **11** *3* **Lady Lydia (IRE)**[27] 1261 6-9-0 78...........................(tp) ConnorBeasley 11 68
(Gay Kelleway) *a rr: rdn over 1f out: no hdwy and bhd ins fnl f* **80/1**

1m 23.47s (-1.33) **Going Correction** -0.125s/f (Stan) — **11** Ran SP% **122.5**
Speed ratings (Par 96): **102,101,101,99,99 99,98,95,94,94 90**
CSF £12.49 CT £20.92 TOTE £7.20: £2.30, £1.10, £1.30; EX 16.10 Trifecta £39.20.
**Owner** Yasushi Kubota **Bred** Tom & Geraldine Molan **Trained** Newmarket, Suffolk

■ Stewards' Enquiry : Graham Lee caution - guilty of careless riding in that he allowed his mount to drift left-handed when not sufficiently clear

**FOCUS**

This looked a three-horse race on the ratings, but while they filled the frame as expected, it was the outsider of the three who came out on top. They didn't go a great early gallop. The level is set by the fourth, fifth and sixth.

## 1772 BETWAY ALL-WEATHER SPRINT CHAMPIONSHIPS CONDITIONS STKS — 6f 1y(P)

**3:10** (3:13) (Class 2) 4-Y-O+

**£93,375** (£27,960; £13,980; £6,990; £3,495; £1,755) **Stalls** Low

Form — RPR

36-1 **1** **Kimberella**[20] 1362 7-9-5 107............................................. PaulHanagan 5 114
(Richard Fahey) *hld up in tch in midfield: nt clr run and switching rt bnd 2f out: rdn and hdwy over 1f out: chsd ldr ins fnl f: r.o wl to ld 50yds out: rdn out* **4/1**[1]

-444 **2** *½* **Gracious John (IRE)**[48] 932 4-9-5 108.................................... JFEgan 4 112
(David Evans) *t.k.h: pressed ldr tl led over 3f out: rdn over 1f out: hdd 50yds out: kpt on but a hld after* **8/1**

-051 **3** *1 ¾* **Encore D'Or**[41] 1025 5-9-5 101.......................................... LukeMorris 11 106
(Robert Cowell) *hld up in tch in midfield: effrt over 1f out: kpt on u.p ins fnl f to go 3rd fnl 50yds: nvr enough pce to threaten ldng pair* **14/1**

-112 **4** *1 ½* **Lancelot Du Lac (ITY)**[48] 917 7-9-5 107.................... RobertWinston 6 102
(Dean Ivory) *chsd ldrs: effrt over 1f out: chsd ldr 1f out: no imp and lost 2nd ins fnl f: wknd fnl 50yds* **4/1**[1]

2-62 **5** *½* **Mythmaker**[69] 572 5-9-5 107.......................................... ConnorBeasley 1 100
(Bryan Smart) *led: rdn and hdd over 1f out: no ex u.p and wknd ins fnl f* **6/1**[3]

-200 **6** *¾* **Realize**[34] 1150 7-9-5 104....................................................(t) SeanLevey 9 98
(Stuart Williams) *hld up in tch in midfield: effrt over 1f out: kpt on same pce u.p and no imp ins fnl f* **22/1**

0061 **7** *nk* **Sign Of The Kodiac (IRE)**[21] 1353 4-9-5 94...................... JoeFanning 2 97
(James Given) *chsd ldrs: rdn over 1f out: no imp u.p 1f out: wknd ins fnl f* **25/1**

-364 **8** *½* **Boom The Groom (IRE)**[48] 917 6-9-5 105..................... AndreaAtzeni 8 95+
(Tony Carroll) *hld up towards rr of main gp: snatched up after 1f out: effrt on outer bnd 2f out: sme hdwy ins fnl f: nvr trbld ldrs* **12/1**

-031 **9** *shd* **Royal Birth**[48] 917 6-9-5 102...........................................(t) AaronJones 3 95+
(Stuart Williams) *stmbld leaving stalls and slowly away: sn rcvrd and in tch in midfield: nt clr run jst over 2f out: rdn and styd on same pce fr over 1f out* **7/1**

-155 **10** *1 ½* **Pretend (IRE)**[48] 917 6-9-5 107......................................... AdamKirby 12 90
(Charlie Appleby) *s.i.s and swtchd lft after s: a towards rr of main gp: effrt on inner over 1f out: no imp: wknd ins fnl f* **5/1**[2]

1136 **11** *1 ¼* **Verne Castle**[20] 1362 4-9-5 99.....................................(h) DavidProbert 10 86
(Andrew Balding) *hld up towards rr of main gp: effrt u.p over 1f out: no imp and wl hld fnl f* **40/1**

-210 **12** *3 ½* **Doc Sportello (IRE)**[53] 842 5-9-5 102............................(p) GrahamLee 14 75
(Michael Herrington) *sn outpcd in rr: n.d* **28/1**

1m 9.36s (-2.54) **Going Correction** -0.125s/f (Stan) — **12** Ran SP% **123.0**
Speed ratings (Par 109): **111,110,108,106,105 104,103,103,103,101 99,94**
CSF £36.39 CT £427.82 TOTE £5.60: £2.20, £2.80, £4.50; EX 44.40 Trifecta £619.90.
**Owner** C Titcomb **Bred** P And Mrs A G Venner **Trained** Musley Bank, N Yorks

**FOCUS**

This was run at a good pace and the winner once again showed off a strong finishing burst. A small pb from the winner, with the second rated close to his best.

## 1773 SUNBETS ALL-WEATHER MILE CHAMPIONSHIPS CONDITIONS STKS — 1m 1y(P)

**3:40** (3:42) (Class 2) 4-Y-O+

**£93,375** (£27,960; £13,980; £6,990; £3,495; £1,755) **Stalls** High

Form — RPR

2-13 **1** **Sovereign Debt (IRE)**[13] 1500 8-9-5 110...................... JamesSullivan 6 112
(Ruth Carr) *chsd ldrs: effrt 2f out: drvn to chse clr ldr over 1f out: styd on strly u.p to ld wl ins fnl f: hld on towards fin* **8/1**

6110 **2** *nk* **Nimr**[13] 1492 4-9-5 100.................................................... PaulHanagan 3 111+
(Richard Fahey) *hld up in tch in midfield: swtchd rt and effrt over 1f out: str run u.p ins fnl f: wnt 2nd and pressing wnr wl ins fnl f: r.o but nvr quite getting to wnr* **14/1**

0101 **3** *1* **Salateen**[34] 1150 5-9-5 105.............................................. RyanMoore 11 109
(David O'Meara) *led: rdn 2f out: qcknd and wnt clr over 1f out: drvn ins fnl f: hdd and no ex wl ins fnl f* **12/1**

111- **4** *¾* **Ennaadd**[149] 7978 4-9-5 113.......................................... AndreaAtzeni 2 108
(Roger Varian) *t.k.h: trckd ldrs: effrt in 4th 2f out: disputing 2nd 1f out: kpt on to press ldr whn short of room and swtchd rt wl ins fnl f: stl nt enough room and no imp towards fin* **6/5**[1]

521- **5** *¾* **Qurbaan (USA)**[55] 821 4-9-5 106.................................. DaneO'Neill 10 106
(F Rohaut, France) *in tch in midfield: hdwy and rdn in cl 5th 2f out: kpt on same pce u.p ins fnl f* **11/2**[2]

4-12 **6** *¾* **Keystroke**[34] 1150 5-9-5 103.......................................... AdamKirby 12 104
(Jeremy Noseda) *stdd and swtchd lft after s: hld up in tch in midfield: effrt u.p over 1f out: styd on same pce ins fnl f* **7/1**[3]

1116 **7** *1 ½* **My Target (IRE)**[34] 1150 6-9-5 107............................ ConnorBeasley 9 100
(Michael Wigham) *t.k.h: hld up in tch towards rr: effrt over 1f out: kpt on ins fnl f: nvr threatened ldrs* **9/1**

2061 **8** *nk* **Supersta**[24] 1295 6-9-5 102.................................(p) SilvestreDeSousa 14 100
(Michael Appleby) *dwlt: t.k.h: hdwy to chse ldr after 1f: rdn and lost 2nd over 1f out: wknd ins fnl f* **40/1**

-136 **9** *1 ¾* **Alfred Hutchinson**[41] 1023 9-9-5 98................................(p) DavidNolan 1 96
(David O'Meara) *hld up in tch in midfield: rdn and unable qck over 1f out: wknd ins fnl f* **66/1**

0000 **10** *nk* **Steel Train (FR)**[13] 1494 6-9-5 99.................................. ShelleyBirkett 4 95
(David O'Meara) *hld up in tch in last pair: effrt over 1f out: no imp: nvr trbld ldrs* **50/1**

332- **11** 2 1/2 **Donjuan Triumphant (IRE)**[113] 8489 4-9-5 104.........(t[1]) DavidProbert 8 89
(Andrew Balding) *t.k.h: hld up in tch towards rr: no hdwy u.p over 1f out: wknd ins fnl f* **20/1**

1520 **12** 1 1/4 **Mythical Madness**[48] 919 6-9-5 101.............................(p) LukeMorris 13 86
(David O'Meara) *dropped in bhd after s: a in rr* **50/1**

1m 35.9s (-2.30) **Going Correction** -0.125s/f (Stan) **12** Ran SP% **121.4**
Speed ratings (Par 109): **106,105,104,103,103 102,100,100,98,98 96,94**
CSF £111.05 CT £1370.26 TOTE £8.80: £2.30, £4.50, £2.20; EX 132.80 Trifecta £1365.20.
**Owner** Lady O'Reilly & Partners **Bred** Yeomanstown Stud **Trained** Huby, N Yorks

**FOCUS**
Ryan Moore dictated a pace to suit himself and the race developed into a test of speed in the straight. It's been rated around the third, with the winner to his best since last summer.

## 1774 32RED 3 YEAR OLD ALL-WEATHER CHAMPIONSHIPS CONDITIONS STKS 6f 1y(P)
**4:10** (4:13) (Class 2) 3-Y-O
**£93,375** (£27,960; £13,980; £6,990; £3,495; £1,755) **Stalls** Low

Form RPR

1-11 **1** **Second Thought (IRE)**[41] 1026 3-9-5 105.................. RobertWinston 5 102+
(William Haggas) *hld up in tch in midfield: bdly hmpd over 4f out: effrt over 1f out: hdwy and swtchd rt 1f out: r.o wl to ld wl ins fnl f: holding runner up towards fin* **11/8[1]**

-131 **2** 1/2 **Visionary (IRE)**[42] 1012 3-9-5 94........................................ LukeMorris 4 100
(Robert Cowell) *hld up in tch in midfield: effrt in 4th 2f out: swtchd rt over 1f out: str run u.p to press wnr wl ins fnl f: r.o but hld towards fin* **16/1**

-313 **3** 1 **Tomily (IRE)**[23] 1311 3-9-5 99.............................................. SeanLevey 8 97
(Richard Hannon) *chsd ldr: rdn and chal ent fnl f: drvn to ld jst ins fnl f: hdd and no ex wl ins fnl f* **15/2**

-314 **4** 2 **Wick Powell**[23] 1311 3-9-5 95............................................... AdamKirby 9 91
(David Barron) *led: rdn ent 2f out: drvn 1f out: sn hdd and no ex: wknd wl ins fnl f* **9/1**

2212 **5** nk **Sutter County**[41] 1026 3-9-5 103......................................... JoeFanning 1 90
(Mark Johnston) *hld up in tch in midfield: bdly hmpd over 4f out: effrt over 1f out: drvn and kpt on same pce ins fnl f* **4/1[2]**

4251 **6** 1 3/4 **Arzaak (IRE)**[10] 1543 3-9-5 73...........................(b) SilvestreDeSousa 6 84
(Chris Dwyer) *taken down early: t.k.h: chsd ldrs: effrt ent fnl 2f: unable qck over 1f out: wknd ins fnl f* **66/1**

5602 **7** 1 **Letmestopyouthere (IRE)**[23] 1311 3-9-5 89............................ JFEgan 3 81
(David Evans) *sn outpcd and pushed along in last pair: clsd and swtchd rt over 4f out: no imp u.p over 1f out: wknd ins fnl f* **33/1**

11-1 **8** 2 **Dubai One (IRE)**[15] 1454 3-9-0 92...................................... RyanMoore 7 69+
(Saeed bin Suroor) *rrd as stalls opened: hld up in tch in midfield: hmpd over 4f out: dropped to last trio and no rspnse whn rdn 2f out: wknd fnl f* **9/2[3]**

1246 **9** 2 **Marquee Club**[41] 1026 3-9-5 88..............................(b[1]) TimmyMurphy 10 68
(Jamie Osborne) *s.i.s: t.k.h: hdwy to chse ldrs on outer after 2f: rdn and lost pl bnd 2f out: bhd ins fnl f* **66/1**

0- **10** 3/4 **Carlton Choice (IRE)**[14] 3-9-5 88...............................(b) TedDurcan 2 66
(Louis Baudron, France) *nvr travelling and sn outpcd in rr: a bhd* **20/1**

1m 10.08s (-1.82) **Going Correction** -0.125s/f (Stan) **10** Ran SP% **118.6**
Speed ratings (Par 104): **107,106,105,102,101 99,98,95,92,91**
CSF £27.46 CT £129.71 TOTE £2.20: £1.10, £5.50, £2.40; EX 29.10 Trifecta £155.20.
**Owner** Liam Sheridan **Bred** Tally-Ho Stud **Trained** Newmarket, Suffolk

■ Stewards' Enquiry : Sean Levey caution - guilty of careless riding in that he allowed his mount to drift left-handed when not sufficiently clear

**FOCUS**
Although the margin of victory wasn't huge the winner was comfortably the best here. A messy race, the winner doing well to overcome being hampered. The third and fourth have been rated a bit off.

## 1775 BETWAY EASTER CLASSIC ALL-WEATHER MIDDLE DISTANCE CHAMPIONSHIPS CONDITIONS STKS 1m 2f (P)
**4:40** (4:41) (Class 2) 4-Y-O+
**£124,500** (£37,280; £18,640; £9,320; £4,660; £2,340) **Stalls** Low

Form RPR

35-1 **1** **Convey**[48] 919 5-9-5 111.................................................... RyanMoore 4 110+
(Sir Michael Stoute) *t.k.h: stdd bk into midfield after 1f: hdwy to chse ldrs 2f out: rdn to ld jst ins fnl f: sn asserted u.p and in command: r.o wl: readily* **11/10[1]**

1231 **2** 1 3/4 **Absolute Blast (IRE)**[13] 1500 5-9-0 105............................ LukeMorris 9 101
(Archie Watson) *hld up in tch in midfield: effrt wl over 1f out: styd on u.p to go 2nd wl ins fnl f: no threat to wnr* **7/1[3]**

0/0- **3** 1/2 **Allez Henri (IRE)**[43] 6-9-5 97...................................(p) AurelienLemaitre 6 105
(D Prod'Homme, France) *hld up in tch in last trio: effrt over 1f out: styd on wl ins fnl f to go 3rd towards fin: no threat to wnr* **25/1**

33-1 **4** 1/2 **Elbereth**[21] 1355 6-9-0 100................................................. DavidProbert 7 99
(Andrew Balding) *sn chsng ldr: rdn and ev ch over 1f out tl unable qck w wnr ins fnl f: styd on same pce and lost 2 pls wl ins fnl f* **12/1**

4130 **5** nse **Third Time Lucky (IRE)**[13] 1494 5-9-5 101................(h[1]) PaulHanagan 2 104
(Richard Fahey) *led: rdn over 1f out: hdd and unable qck jst ins fnl f: no ex and outpcd fnl 100yds* **14/1**

305- **6** 2 1/2 **Metropol (IRE)**[11] 6-9-5 99............................................. MaximeGuyon 8 99
(Mme Pia Brandt, France) *hld up in rr: effrt but stl plenty to do over 1f out: kpt on ins fnl f: nvr trbld ldrs* **16/1**

2433 **7** 2 **Van Huysen (IRE)**[45] 963 5-9-5 85......................................... JFEgan 3 95?
(Dominic Ffrench Davis) *hld up in tch towards rr: effrt on inner over 1f out: no imp whn n.m.r 1f out: wknd ins fnl f* **66/1**

3-45 **8** hd **Grendisar (IRE)**[48] 919 7-9-5 107.........................(p) SilvestreDeSousa 5 95
(Marco Botti) *dwlt and pushed along early: hdwy into midfield 8f out: rdn and unable qck over 1f out: wknd ins fnl f* **5/1[2]**

1-36 **9** 11 **Battalion (IRE)**[48] 919 7-9-5 108...................................... AdamKirby 1 73
(Jamie Osborne) *dwlt: hdwy on inner to chse ldrs after 2f out: rdn and no rspnse 2f out: sn btn: bhd and eased ins fnl f* **5/1[2]**

2m 2.16s (-4.44) **Going Correction** -0.125s/f (Stan) **9** Ran SP% **119.0**
Speed ratings (Par 109): **112,110,110,109,109 107,106,106,97**
CSF £9.98 CT £129.66 TOTE £2.00: £1.10, £2.00, £4.30; EX 9.10 Trifecta £162.10.
**Owner** Robert Ng **Bred** Juddmonte Farms Ltd **Trained** Newmarket, Suffolk

**FOCUS**
This proved fairly straightforward for the Winter Derby winner, who stamped his class on the race in the straight. The winner has been rated similar to his Winter Derby win, with the fourth and fifth close to their best.

T/Jkpt: Not won. T/Plt: £250.40 to a £1 stake. Pool: £149,405.00 - 596.57 winning units. T/Qpdt: £27.60 to a £1 stake. Pool: £10,100.00 - 365.70 winning units. **Steve Payne**

# 1469 NEWCASTLE (A.W) (L-H)
Friday, April 14

**OFFICIAL GOING: Tapeta: standard**
Wind: Breezy, half against throughout in races on the straight course, half against during last 3.5f on ro Weather: Overcast

## 1776 32RED.COM FILLIES' CONDITIONS STKS (PLUS 10 RACE) 5f (Tp)
**1:50** (1:50) (Class 2) 2-Y-O **£12,602** (£3,772; £1,886; £944; £470) **Stalls** Centre

Form RPR

**1** **Cheeseandpickle** 2-9-0 0............................................... PhillipMakin 3 67+
(Keith Dalgleish) *prom gng wl: shkn up to ld over 1f out: rdn and r.o strly fnl f* **7/2[1]**

**2** 1 1/4 **Thrifty** 2-9-0 0.......................................................... DavidAllan 7 63+
(Tim Easterby) *hld up: smooth hdwy over 1f out: rdn to chse wnr ins fnl f: edgd lft: kpt on: nt pce to chal* **10/1**

**3** shd **Marsh Storm (IRE)** 2-9-0 0.......................................... PJMcDonald 8 62
(K R Burke) *hld up on nr side of gp: hdwy over 1f out: rdn and disp 2nd pl last 75yds: kpt on* **4/1[2]**

0 **4** 1 1/2 **Fas Le Fios (IRE)**[8] 1594 2-9-0 0..................................... LiamJones 4 57
(J S Moore) *cl up: rdn and ev ch briefly over 1f out: kpt on same pce ins fnl f* **40/1**

0 **5** 1/2 **Controversial Lady (IRE)**[4] 1681 2-9-0 0.............. JosephineGordon 6 55
(J S Moore) *sn pushed along in rr: drvn along 1/2-way: kpt on fnl f: nvr able to chal* **16/1**

**6** 2 1/4 **Peace Prevails** 2-9-0 0.............................................. TonyHamilton 1 47
(Richard Fahey) *noisy in paddock: cl up on far side of gp: rdn and rn green over 1f out: hung lft and sn outpcd: btn fnl f* **4/1[2]**

2 **7** 1/2 **Kheleyf's Girl**[8] 1588 2-9-0 0...................................... DanielTudhope 2 45
(David Evans) *cl up: rdn and ev ch over 2f out to over 1f out: sn wknd* **7/2[1]**

**8** nse **Nsnas Alward** 2-9-0 0................................................. TomEaves 9 45
(Kevin Ryan) *led on nr side of gp: rdn and hdd over 1f out: wknd ins fnl f* **17/2[3]**

**9** 9 **Time For Treacle** 2-9-0 0............................................ CamHardie 5 13
(Ben Haslam) *dwlt: bhd and green: hung lft thrght: struggling after 2f: sn btn* **80/1**

1m 2.36s (2.86) **Going Correction** +0.325s/f (Slow) **9** Ran SP% **113.6**
Speed ratings (Par 95): **90,88,87,85,84 81,80,80,65**
CSF £38.63 TOTE £4.80: £1.50, £2.70, £1.70; EX 43.70 Trifecta £223.90.
**Owner** Equus I **Bred** Bumble Bloodstock Ltd **Trained** Carluke, S Lanarks

**FOCUS**
The first Good Friday fixture at Newcastle. A valuable prize for what was essentially a maiden. The form has been rated as relatively modest.

## 1777 BETWAY SPRINT H'CAP 5f (Tp)
**2:20** (2:21) (Class 4) (0-85,85) 4-Y-O+ **£6,469** (£1,925; £962; £481) **Stalls** Centre

Form RPR

0-1 **1** **Art Collection (FR)**[14] 1475 4-9-1 79............................... JackGarritty 1 94
(Ruth Carr) *hld up: shkn up and gd hdwy to ld appr fnl f: edgd lft: sn rdn clr: readily* **11/2[2]**

504- **2** 3 1/4 **Paddy Power (IRE)**[184] 7289 4-8-8 75.................... SammyJoBell[(3)] 4 78
(Richard Fahey) *hld up: pushed along and hdwy 2f out: chsd wnr appr fnl f: kpt on: nt pce to chal* **9/2[1]**

000- **3** 1/2 **Excessable**[202] 6793 4-8-11 78........................... RachelRichardson[(3)] 2 80
(Tim Easterby) *hld up on far side of gp: hdwy over 2f out: effrt and disp 2nd pl 1f out: kpt on same pce ins fnl f* **16/1**

00-6 **4** 1/2 **Money Team (IRE)**[21] 1346 6-9-1 79................................ PhillipMakin 5 79
(David Barron) *in tch: drvn and outpcd 1/2-way: rallied over 1f out: kpt on fnl f: nvr able to chal* **14/1**

410- **5** 1 3/4 **First Bombardment**[181] 7358 4-9-5 83........................ DanielTudhope 11 76
(David O'Meara) *pressed ldr: led briefly over 1f out: rdn and wknd ins fnl f* **7/1**

-002 **6** 1/2 **Orient Class**[14] 1475 6-9-1 79...................................... PaulMulrennan 3 71
(Paul Midgley) *prom on far side of gp: effrt and rdn 2f out: wknd ins fnl f* **12/1**

000- **7** 1/2 **Tylery Wonder (IRE)**[179] 7413 7-9-3 81.......................(b) OisinMurphy 9 71
(Paul Midgley) *led at str gallop to over 1f out: rdn and wknd ins fnl f* **20/1**

303- **8** 3/4 **Bapak Asmara (IRE)**[224] 6079 5-9-4 82............................. ShaneGray 6 69
(Kevin Ryan) *hld up midfield: rdn along over 2f out: wknd over 1f out* **11/1**

302- **9** 2 1/2 **Stanghow**[169] 7643 5-9-7 85............................................ CamHardie 7 63
(Antony Brittain) *hld up midfield: drvn along over 2f out: wknd over 1f out* **28/1**

000- **10** hd **Secret Missile**[195] 6962 7-9-7 85..........................(b) JosephineGordon 13 62
(David C Griffiths) *hld up on nr side of gp: drvn along 1/2-way: wknd wl over 1f out* **25/1**

00-3 **11** 1 1/2 **Van Gerwen**[20] 1370 4-9-0 78........................................... DavidAllan 8 50
(Les Eyre) *chsd ldrs: drvn along over 2f out: wknd wl over 1f out* **6/1[3]**

0321 **12** 1 1/4 **Aprovado (IRE)**[21] 1346 5-8-12 83..................(p) CallumRodriguez[(7)] 12 50
(Michael Dods) *in tch: rdn along 1/2-way: wknd wl over 1f out* **8/1**

6-02 **13** 1 3/4 **New Road Side**[36] 1110 4-9-0 78.................................. DougieCostello 10 39
(Richard Guest) *prom: drvn along 1/2-way: sn wknd* **16/1**

59.84s (0.34) **Going Correction** +0.325s/f (Slow) **13** Ran SP% **118.0**
Speed ratings (Par 105): **110,104,104,103,100 99,98,97,93,93 90,88,86**
CSF £29.17 CT £303.08 TOTE £6.50: £2.10, £2.20, £5.00; EX 41.10 Trifecta £606.60.
**Owner** N Chapman **Bred** D Aviez, S Gesbert & C Gesbert **Trained** Huby, N Yorks

**FOCUS**
Low numbers came out on top in this fair sprint handicap, which was run at a strong pace. The level is a bit fluid, but a pb from the winner.

## 1778 SUNBETS.CO.UK H'CAP 7f 14y (Tp)
**2:55** (2:56) (Class 4) (0-85,85) 4-Y-O+ **£6,469** (£1,925; £962; £481) **Stalls** Centre

Form RPR

345- **1** **Chaplin Bay (IRE)**[181] 7360 5-8-10 74............................ JackGarritty 12 81
(Ruth Carr) *hld up: smooth hdwy and swtchd lft over 1f out: rdn to ld ins fnl f: hld on wl cl home* **11/2[3]**

-511 **2** nk **Inaam (IRE)**[30] 1202 4-9-3 81......................................... TonyHamilton 4 87
(Richard Fahey) *hld up in tch: stdy hdwy gng wl whn n.m.r briefly over 1f out: rdn and kpt on ins fnl f: hld c* **6/1**

10-0 **3** nk **Kalk Bay (IRE)**[12] 1512 10-8-10 81.......................(t) HarrisonShaw[(7)] 8 86
(Michael Easterby) *hld up in tch: hdwy on nr side of gp to ld appr fnl f: hdd ins fnl f: kpt on: hld cl home* **20/1**

523- **4** ¾ **Deansgate (IRE)**[189] 7111 4-8-10 **74**....(e) JoeDoyle 14 77+
(Julie Camacho) *taken early to post: hld up: stdy hdwy 2f out: rdn and kpt on fnl f: hld towards fin* **15/2**

000- **5** *nse* **Mon Beau Visage (IRE)**[144] 8052 4-8-13 **77**....(p) DanielTudhope 11 80+
(David O'Meara) *t.k.h: hld up: smooth hdwy whn nt clr run briefly over 1f out: sn rdn: kpt on ins fnl f: no ex nr fin* **5/1[2]**

0-00 **6** ¾ **Kingsley Klarion (IRE)**[90] 234 4-9-2 **80**.... PJMcDonald 6 81
(Mark Johnston) *led: rdn over 2f out: hdd appr fnl f: sn one pce* **20/1**

01-0 **7** ½ **Amood (IRE)**[14] 1472 6-8-12 **76**.... JasonHart 1 78+
(Simon West) *missed break: hld up: smooth hdwy whn nt clr run over 1f out to wl ins fnl f: nt rcvr* **18/1**

24-2 **8** 3½ **Mutamid**[30] 1202 5-9-5 **83**.... WilliamBuick 3 73
(Ismail Mohammed) *in tch on far side of gp: rdn over 2f out: wknd fnl f* **4/1[1]**

2-00 **9** *hd* **Like No Other**[69] 581 4-8-13 **77**.... DavidAllan 7 66
(Les Eyre) *trckd ldrs: rdn and ev ch briefly over 1f out: n.m.r and wknd ins fnl f* **14/1**

200- **10** 2¼ **Ralphy Boy (IRE)**[178] 7436 8-8-9 **73**.... PaulMulrennan 13 56
(Alistair Whillans) *hld up: rdn and outpcd over 2f out: n.d after* **66/1**

-510 **11** *nk* **Florencio**[23] 1302 4-9-1 **84**....(t) GeorgeWood[(5)] 9 67
(Marco Botti) *trckd ldrs: rdn over 2f out: wknd over 1f out* **12/1**

520- **12** *hd* **Short Work**[175] 7506 4-8-10 **79**.... JoshDoyle[(5)] 10 61
(David O'Meara) *hld up in tch: drvn and outpcd over 2f out: sn btn* **16/1**

020- **13** *1* **Courier**[189] 7126 5-9-7 **85**.... CamHardie 5 64
(Marjorie Fife) *cl up: rdn over 2f out: wknd over 1f out* **40/1**

1m 27.65s (1.45) **Going Correction** +0.325s/f (Slow) **13** Ran SP% **117.1**
Speed ratings (Par 105): **104,103,103,102,102 101,100,96,96,94 93,93,92**
CSF £36.04 CT £636.53 TOTE £6.50: £2.40, £1.80, £8.00; EX 48.70 Trifecta £784.30.
**Owner** Miss B Houlston,Mrs M Chapman,Mrs R Carr **Bred** Stonethorn Stud Farms Ltd **Trained** Huby, N Yorks

**FOCUS**
They went an ordinary gallop in this fair handicap. The winner matched his turf form.

## 1779 BETWAY H'CAP — 1m 4f 98y (Tp)
**3:25** (3:27) (Class 2) 4-Y-0+
**£52,912** (£15,844; £7,922; £3,961; £1,980; £994) **Stalls** High

Form RPR

41-2 **1** **Wild Hacked (USA)**[13] 1502 4-9-4 **101**.... FrankieDettori 14 110
(Marco Botti) *cl up: led gng wl over 2f out: hrd pressed and drvn along over 1f out: asserted ins fnl f: kpt on gamely* **5/1[2]**

6-64 **2** ½ **Mistiroc**[39] 1068 6-8-13 **95**....(v) JasonHart 12 103
(John Quinn) *t.k.h early: cl up: hdwy to chal over 1f out to ins fnl f: kpt on u.p: hld cl home* **20/1**

410- **3** ¾ **Lord George (IRE)**[178] 7456 4-8-5 **93**.... GeorgeWood[(5)] 9 100+
(James Fanshawe) *hld up midfield: effrt and hdwy over 1f out: kpt on ins fnl f: nrst fin* **8/1**

01-3 **4** 2¼ **Fabricate**[39] 1068 5-9-3 **102**....(p) LouisSteward[(3)] 5 105
(Michael Bell) *led 1f: cl up: drvn along over 2f out: rallied over 1f out: kpt on same pce ins fnl f* **10/1**

4-15 **5** *nk* **Hamelin (IRE)**[23] 1309 7-9-2 **98**.... MartinHarley 2 101
(George Scott) *hld up in tch: stdy hdwy and prom over 1f out: sn rdn: no ex ins fnl f* **33/1**

302- **6** 1¼ **Erik The Red (FR)**[160] 7824 5-9-3 **99**.... TomEaves 4 100
(Kevin Ryan) *stdd s: t.k.h: hld up: effrt and hdwy over 2f out: rdn and no imp over 1f out* **11/1**

15-6 **7** ½ **Tawdeea**[12] 1516 5-9-10 **106**....(p) DanielTudhope 7 106+
(David O'Meara) *hld up: rdn and outpcd over 2f out: rallied fnl f: kpt on: nvr able to chal* **25/1**

/11- **8** ½ **To Be Wild (IRE)**[174] 7538 4-9-7 **104**.... JosephineGordon 10 103
(Hugo Palmer) *hld up: stdy hdwy on outside over 2f out: rdn and no imp fr over 1f out* **9/2[1]**

/23- **9** 2¼ **Mustajeer**[190] 7101 4-9-1 **98**.... JimCrowley 1 94
(Owen Burrows) *hld up: rdn and outpcd over 2f out: n.d after* **10/1**

1015 **10** 1¼ **Abareeq**[15] 1446 4-9-5 **102**.... HarryBentley 11 96
(Mark Johnston) *hld up in tch on outside: pushed along over 2f out: edgd lft: wknd over 1f out* **12/1**

01-2 **11** 3½ **Good Run (FR)**[23] 1309 4-8-13 **99**....(b[1]) AdamMcNamara[(3)] 3 87
(Saeed bin Suroor) *t.k.h: cl up: led after 1f to over 2f out: rdn and wknd wl over 1f out* **7/1[3]**

0-64 **12** ¾ **Intense Tango**[51] 858 6-8-9 **96**....(t) CliffordLee[(5)] 6 83
(K R Burke) *t.k.h: hld up: drvn and outpcd 3f out: sn btn* **50/1**

00-5 **13** *1* **Ballynanty (IRE)**[21] 1341 5-9-5 **101**.... OisinMurphy 13 86
(Andrew Balding) *hld up on outside: drvn over 2f out: sn wknd* **28/1**

2102 **U** **Final**[3] 1704 5-8-9 **91**.... PJMcDonald 8
(Mark Johnston) *sn pushed along in rr: clipped heels and uns rdr after 1f* **10/1**

2m 40.16s (-0.94) **Going Correction** +0.075s/f (Slow) **14** Ran SP% **118.7**
Speed ratings (Par 109): **106,105,105,103,103 102,102,101,100,99 97,96,96,**
CSF £108.14 CT £796.10 TOTE £6.20: £2.10, £5.90, £2.50; EX 101.90 Trifecta £1005.50.
**Owner** Khalid Bin Ali Al Khalifa **Bred** Moyglare Stud **Trained** Newmarket, Suffolk
■ Stewards' Enquiry : Oisin Murphy 10 day ban (28 April-7 May) - guilty of careless riding in that he had made a misjudgment in manoeuvering left

**FOCUS**
A big prize for this handicap and a good field, but it wasn't run at a great gallop and nothing could get involved from off the pace. The winner continued his progress, with the 2nd probably the key, earning a small pb.

## 1780 32RED BURRADON CONDITIONS STKS — 1m 5y (Tp)
**3:55** (4:00) (Class 2) 3-Y-0
**£62,250** (£18,640; £9,320; £4,660; £2,330; £1,170) **Stalls** Centre

Form RPR

13- **1** **Forest Ranger (IRE)**[179] 7409 3-9-5 94.... TonyHamilton 1 107
(Richard Fahey) *hld up in last pl: shkn up and gd hdwy to ld appr fnl f: clr ins fnl f: pushed out: readily* **25/1**

11- **2** 2¾ **Syphax (USA)**[240] 5556 3-9-5 110.... WilliamBuick 6 101
(Kevin Ryan) *dwlt: sn pushed along bhd ldng gp: pushed along and hung lft over 2f out: rallied over 1f out: chsd wnr ins fnl f: kpt on: no imp* **4/1[2]**

1- **3** *nse* **Utmost (USA)**[185] 7243 3-9-5 91.... FrankieDettori 7 101+
(John Gosden) *t.k.h: prom on nr side: rdn and outpcd over 2f out: rallied and disp 2nd pl ins fnl f: kpt on fin* **10/3[1]**

15- **4** 2¼ **Taamol (IRE)**[217] 6285 3-9-5 95.... JimCrowley 3 96+
(Sir Michael Stoute) *hld up in tch: smooth hdwy to chal over 1f out: rdn and sn pressing wnr: lost 2nd ins fnl f: sn btn* **4/1[2]**

162- **5** 2 **South Seas (IRE)**[166] 7721 3-9-5 110.... OisinMurphy 2 91
(Andrew Balding) *cl up: led over 2f out: rdn and hdd appr fnl f: sn outpcd* **4/1[2]**

61-3 **6** 4½ **Volatile**[41] 1026 3-9-5 98.... MartinHarley 5 81
(James Tate) *cl up on nr side: drvn and ev ch over 2f out: wknd over 1f out* **14/1**

-064 **7** 1¾ **Masham Star (IRE)**[50] 887 3-9-5 101.... PJMcDonald 4 77
(Mark Johnston) *led to over 2f out: rdn and wknd over 1f out* **33/1**

21- **8** 3¾ **Leshlaa (USA)**[149] 7975 3-9-5 90.... DanielTudhope 8 68
(Saeed bin Suroor) *in tch on nr side of gp: drvn and outpcd over 2f out: sn wknd* **11/2[3]**

1m 39.42s (0.82) **Going Correction** +0.325s/f (Slow) **8** Ran SP% **111.9**
Speed ratings (Par 104): **108,105,105,102,100 96,94,90**
CSF £117.12 TOTE £18.10: £4.30, £1.60, £1.30; EX 95.90 Trifecta £370.80.
**Owner** Mrs H Steel **Bred** Yeguada De Milagro Sa **Trained** Musley Bank, N Yorks

**FOCUS**
A fascinating race for this big prize, several holding Classic entries. They went a good gallop down the straight mile. The level is a bit fluid but this was a big improvement from the winner.

## 1781 BETWAY INSIDER H'CAP — 1m 2f 42y (Tp)
**4:25** (4:28) (Class 4) (0-85,85) 4-Y-0+
**£6,469** (£1,925; £962; £481) **Stalls** High

Form RPR

6-56 **1** **Briardale (IRE)**[12] 1517 5-9-6 **84**.... JimCrowley 2 95
(James Bethell) *mde all: qcknd clr 3f out: kpt on strly fnl f: unchal* **4/1[2]**

1- **2** 3 **Gaelic Tiger**[235] 5716 4-9-7 **85**.... DanielTudhope 5 90+
(David O'Meara) *prom: pushed along over 3f out: rallied and chsd (clr) wnr over 1f out: kpt on fnl f: no imp* **2/1[1]**

-212 **3** 3 **Lac Leman (GER)**[43] 991 6-9-2 **80**....(h) PaulMulrennan 6 79
(Pauline Robson) *stdd and swtchd lft s: hld up: effrt and pushed along 2f out: kpt on fnl f: nvr able to chal* **11/2**

3113 **4** ½ **Codeshare**[23] 1307 5-9-5 **83**.... WilliamBuick 1 81
(Alan Swinbank) *trckd ldrs: effrt and chsd wnr briefly over 1f out: outpcd fnl f* **9/2[3]**

2 **5** 2 **Detachment**[20] 1358 4-9-1 **79**.... DavidAllan 8 73
(Les Eyre) *hld up: effrt and hdwy on outside over 2f out: drvn and no imp over 1f out* **9/1**

03-1 **6** 2¾ **Lopes Dancer (IRE)**[23] 1308 5-9-0 **78**.... NeilFarley 3 67
(Alan Swinbank) *hld up in tch on ins: struggling over 2f out: sn wknd* **15/2**

150/ **7** ½ **Belle De Lawers**[885] 6-9-7 **85**.... JosephineGordon 7 73
(James Bethell) *pressed wnr tl rdn and wknd over 1f out* **25/1**

2/06 **8** 11 **Masterful Act (USA)**[21] 1344 10-8-7 **71** oh2.... BenCurtis 4 37
(John Balding) *hld up: drvn and struggling 3f out: sn btn* **66/1**

2m 9.36s (-1.04) **Going Correction** +0.075s/f (Slow) **8** Ran SP% **114.0**
Speed ratings (Par 105): **107,104,102,101,100 98,97,88**
CSF £12.34 CT £42.78 TOTE £5.20: £1.80, £1.40, £1.80; EX 15.80 Trifecta £75.70.
**Owner** J Carrick&Clarendon Thoroughbred Racing **Bred** Rabbah Bloodstock Limited **Trained** Middleham Moor, N Yorks

**FOCUS**
Ordinary handicap form, and the pace the winner set wasn't a strong one. A clear pb from the winner.

## 1782 BETWAY MAIDEN STKS (PLUS 10 RACE) — 5f (Tp)
**4:55** (4:55) (Class 3) 3-Y-0
**£9,451** (£2,829; £1,414; £708; £352) **Stalls** Centre

Form RPR

02- **1** **Marseille (IRE)**[158] 7845 3-9-0 0.... JoeDoyle 5 71+
(Julie Camacho) *hld up: pushed along and hdwy over 1f out: led wl ins fnl f: kpt on strly* **7/1[3]**

-2 **2** *nk* **Poet's Reward**[42] 1004 3-9-5 0.... PhillipMakin 1 75+
(David Barron) *led: rdn and hrd pressed over 1f out: hdd wl ins fnl f: kpt on: hld nr fin* **1/1[1]**

30- **3** 1½ **Eltanin (IRE)**[265] 4663 3-9-5 0.... JasonHart 7 70
(John Quinn) *t.k.h: trckd ldrs: rdn along 2f out: kpt on same pce wl ins fnl f* **6/1[2]**

0- **4** ½ **Angel's Acclaim (IRE)**[326] 2535 3-9-0 0.... ShaneGray 4 63
(Kevin Ryan) *dwlt: hld up: rdn and hdwy over 1f out: kpt on fnl f: nvr able to chal* **14/1**

2233 **5** *hd* **Alfonso Manana (IRE)**[48] 920 3-9-5 69....(p) JosephineGordon 8 67
(James Given) *pressed ldr: rdn and ev ch over 1f out: no ex ins fnl f* **10/1**

0-3 **6** 1¾ **Barwell (IRE)**[20] 1366 3-9-5 0.... PaulMulrennan 10 61
(Michael Dods) *trckd ldrs: rdn over 2f out: outpcd over 1f out: kpt on ins fnl f: no imp* **20/1**

00- **7** *hd* **Archi's Affaire**[230] 5884 3-9-5 0.... TomEaves 9 63+
(Michael Dods) *hld up: pushed along over 2f out: sme hdwy whn n.m.r ins fnl f: no imp* **25/1**

24- **8** ¾ **Flawlessly (FR)**[317] 2800 3-9-0 0.... PJMcDonald 6 52
(James Bethell) *t.k.h: hld up: hdwy over 2f out: no imp over 1f out* **7/1[3]**

00- **9** *hd* **Pavers Pride**[189] 7122 3-9-5 0.... BarryMcHugh 2 57
(Noel Wilson) *trckd ldrs: rdn over 2f out: wknd ins fnl f* **80/1**

**10** 12 **Definitely Maybe (IRE)** 3-9-0 0.... ShirleyTeasdale[(5)] 3 13
(Keith Dalgleish) *plld hrd: in tch on outside: rdn over 2f out: wknd wl over 1f out* **25/1**

1m 1.16s (1.66) **Going Correction** +0.325s/f (Slow) **10** Ran SP% **118.7**
Speed ratings (Par 102): **99,98,96,95,95 92,91,90,90,71**
CSF £14.15 TOTE £7.10: £2.20, £1.10, £2.10; EX 15.40 Trifecta £82.60.
**Owner** Elite Racing Club **Bred** Elite Racing Club **Trained** Norton, N Yorks

**FOCUS**
A fair race of its type. The form is set around the runner-up and 5th.
T/Plt: £357.30 to a £1 stake. Pool: £81,239.00 - 227.35 winning units. T/Qpdt: £31.90 to a £1 stake. Pool: £6,659.00 - 208.54 winning units. **Richard Young**

1783 - 1784a (Foreign Racing) - See Raceform Interactive

# BRIGHTON (L-H)
Saturday, April 15

**OFFICIAL GOING: Good to firm (good in places) changing to good to firm after race 1 (4.35)**
Wind: light, across, of no consequence Weather: bright spells

## 1785 HERTZ RENTAL CAR MAIDEN STKS — 5f 60y
**4:35** (4:35) (Class 5) 3-Y-0+
**£3,234** (£962; £481; £240) **Stalls** Low

Form RPR

226- **1** **Jumira Bridge**[219] 6260 3-9-2 88.... AndreaAtzeni 1 86+
(Roger Varian) *trckd ldng pair: cruised upsides ldr wl over 1f out: led 1f out: c clr on bit ins fnl f: v easily* **1/12[1]**

2 **2** 2 ½ **Secret Strategy (IRE)**[16] [1453] 3-9-2 0........................ AdamBeschizza 6 72
(Julia Feilden) *t.k.h: pressed ldr tl led jst over 2f out: drvn and jnd by cantering wnr over 1f out: sn hdd: no ch w wnr but kpt on for clr 2nd ins fnl f* **5/1**[2]

0-60 **3** 6 **Andalusite**[8] [1599] 4-9-8 52.........................................(v) FergusSweeney 3 51
(John Gallagher) *racd in 4th: effrt over 2f out: outpcd and wl btn over 1f out: plugged on into modest 3rd ins fnl f* **16/1**[3]

**4** 3 ½ **Lambrini Legacy** 3-8-11 0............................................ JFEgan 4 34
(Lisa Williamson) *v keen to post: sn led: rdn and hdd jst over 2f out: 3rd and wl btn over 1f out: wknd* **33/1**

5000 **5** 1 ½ **Rojina (IRE)**[16] [1452] 4-9-3 42.......................................(b) DavidParkes(5) 2 34
(Lisa Williamson) *a 5th and nvr on terms* **100/1**

000- **6** 66 **Little Lizzie**[154] [7935] 4-9-8 29.......................................... DannyBrock 5
(Paddy Butler) *sn outpcd in rr: t.o 1/2-way* **100/1**

1m 1.3s (-1.00) **Going Correction** -0.10s/f (Good)
**WFA** 3 from 4yo 11lb **6** Ran SP% **119.8**
Speed ratings (Par 103): **104,100,90,84,82**
CSF £1.43 TOTE £1.10: £1.02, £1.40; EX 1.50 Trifecta £2.80.
**Owner** Sheikh Mohammed Obaid Al Maktoum **Bred** Cheveley Park Stud Ltd **Trained** Newmarket, Suffolk

**FOCUS**
All races were run over 2yds further than advertised. The going was changed to Good to firm, (from Good to firm, good in places) after race 1. An uncompetitive-looking maiden with a promising sort from a powerful stable prohibitively priced and winning as he liked.

## 1786 STREAMLINE TAXIS 202020 H'CAP 5f 60y
**5:05** (5:07) (Class 5) (0-70,71) 3-Y-O **£2,911** (£866; £432; £216) **Stalls** Low

Form RPR

3561 **1** **Endeavour (IRE)**[8] [1605] 3-9-0 62.................................. TomMarquand 3 67
(Richard Hannon) *taken down early: chsd ldr: rdn over 1f out: drvn to ld ins fnl f: styd on wl: rdn out* **5/1**

130- **2** 1 ¼ **Yorkshiredebut (IRE)**[210] [6564] 3-9-7 69............................ AdamKirby 5 70
(Paul Midgley) *taken down early: sn led: rdn over 1f out: hdd and edgd rt ins fnl f: no ex and one pced fnl 100yds* **9/2**[3]

0-06 **3** nk **Prancelina (IRE)**[5] [1688] 3-8-7 62.................................. DavidEgan(7) 1 62
(Phil McEntee) *chsd ldng pair: rdn 2f out: styd on same pce ins fnl f* **14/1**

3411 **4** shd **Roundabout Magic (IRE)**[38] [1088] 3-9-5 67............................ JFEgan 6 67+
(Simon Dow) *stdd after s: hld up in last pair: clsd to chse ldrs and hung lft over 1f out: swtchd rt 1f out: kpt on same pce u.p ins fnl f* **5/1**

5150 **5** 5 **Pulsating (IRE)**[11] [1547] 3-9-2 64...................................... DannyBrock 7 46
(Daniel Steele) *dwlt: sn outpcd and in detached in last: n.d* **12/1**

334- **6** 1 ¾ **Katrine (IRE)**[201] [6829] 3-9-9 71........................................... JimCrowley 2 47
(William Knight) *in tch in midfield: pushed along ent fnl 2f: fnd nil and sn btn: wknd over 1f out* **5/2**[1]

-212 **7** 4 ½ **Little Miss Daisy**[15] [1474] 3-9-7 69.................................... MartinDwyer 4 29
(William Muir) *in tch in midfield: trying to switch rt and bmpd 2f out: sn rdn and fnd nil: wknd over 1f out* **4/1**[2]

1m 1.87s (-0.43) **Going Correction** -0.10s/f (Good) **7** Ran SP% **114.4**
Speed ratings (Par 98): **99,97,96,96,88 85,78**
CSF £27.56 TOTE £5.40: £2.60, £3.10; EX 35.00 Trifecta £397.30.
**Owner** P D Player **Bred** D G Hardisty Bloodstock **Trained** East Everleigh, Wilts

**FOCUS**
Run over 2yds further than advertised. An intriguing sprint handicap where it paid to be up with the pace.

## 1787 WINNER RENTAL SERVICES MAIDEN STKS 6f 210y
**5:35** (5:39) (Class 5) 3-Y-O+ **£3,234** (£962; £481; £240) **Stalls** Low

Form RPR

2-22 **1** **Tafaakhor (IRE)**[21] [1366] 3-9-0 85...................................... JimCrowley 2 78+
(Richard Hannon) *chsd ldrs tl wnt 2nd 5f out: pushed into ld over 1f out: styd on and a doing enough ins fnl f* **11/10**[1]

63- **2** ¾ **King Of Paris**[232] [5820] 3-9-0 0.......................................... AndreaAtzeni 1 76+
(Roger Varian) *hld up in tch in midfield: wnt 3rd 2f out: sn rdn and drifting lft: chsd wnr 1f out: kpt on but a hld ins fnl f* **11/8**[2]

00-0 **3** 6 **Legendoire (IRE)**[17] [1421] 3-9-0 56.................................... FergusSweeney 5 60
(John Gallagher) *led: rdn and hdd over 1f out: 3rd and wknd ins fnl f* **20/1**

034- **4** hd **Second Page**[121] [8377] 3-9-0 77.......................................... TomMarquand 8 59
(Richard Hannon) *hld up in tch in midfield: effrt in 4th 2f out: hung lft and no imp over 1f out: wl hld and kpt on same pce ins fnl f* **4/1**[3]

05 **5** 11 **Rocksette**[46] [962] 3-8-9 0.................................................. MartinDwyer 6 25
(Philip Hide) *hld up in tch in rr of main gp: effrt over 2f out: sn struggling: wknd over 1f out* **50/1**

0- **6** 2 **So Much Water (FR)**[348] [1931] 5-9-9 0...................................... JFEgan 7 24
(John Berry) *chsd ldr for 2f: rdn and lost pl over 2f out: wknd over 1f out* **20/1**

60 **7** nk **Tojosimbre**[26] [1287] 3-9-0 0................................................(h) ShaneKelly 4 23
(Richard Hughes) *s.i.s: nvr gng wl and a bhd* **33/1**

**8** 2 ¾ **Golden Cannon**[15] 6-9-9 0.................................................. DannyBrock 3 16
(Sheena West) *s.i.s: hld up in rr of main gp: rdn over 2f out: sn struggling: wknd over 1f out* **66/1**

1m 21.27s (-1.83) **Going Correction** -0.10s/f (Good)
**WFA** 3 from 5yo+ 14lb **8** Ran SP% **125.6**
Speed ratings (Par 103): **106,105,98,98,85 83,82,79**
CSF £3.15 TOTE £2.10: £1.10, £1.10, £4.60; EX 3.40 Trifecta £19.90.
**Owner** Hamdan Al Maktoum **Bred** Ms Ashley O'Leary **Trained** East Everleigh, Wilts

**FOCUS**
Run over 2yds further than advertised. Two promising sorts clashed in this maiden and experience told as they came home alone.

## 1788 WEATHERBYS BANK H'CAP 1m 1f 207y
**6:05** (6:06) (Class 4) (0-85,81) 4-Y-O+ **£4,787** (£1,424; £711; £355) **Stalls** High

Form RPR

/23- **1** **Mornington**[129] [8255] 4-8-5 72.......................................... TylerSaunders(7) 3 84+
(Marcus Tregoning) *t.k.h: chsd ldrs: pushed along to chal and high hd carriage jst over 1f out: led ins fnl f: sn pushed clr: readily* **9/1**

0-06 **2** 2 ¾ **Inniscastle Lad**[9] [1583] 5-9-2 79......................................(v) AaronJones(3) 9 85
(Stuart Williams) *led: rdn 2f out: hdd ins fnl f: no ex and styd on same pce after* **11/1**

3-61 **3** hd **Boycie**[14] [1498] 4-8-7 74.................................................. TinaSmith(7) 2 80
(Richard Hannon) *dwlt: sn rcvrd to chse ldrs and t.k.h: outpcd and rdn 2f out: rallied ins fnl f: styd on wl fnl 110yds to press for 2nd cl home* **7/2**[1]

50-2 **4** 1 ¾ **Aldeburgh**[14] [1504] 8-9-7 81.............................................. TomMarquand 5 83
(Nigel Twiston-Davies) *taken down early: t.k.h: hld up in last pair: clsd on inner to trck ldrs but nt clr run jst over 2f out: fnlly enough room and rdn to go 3rd ins fnl f: no imp and lost 3rd wl ins fnl f* **8/1**[3]

2-05 **5** 1 ¼ **Craftsmanship (FR)**[33] [1178] 6-9-4 78..............................(p) AndreaAtzeni 8 78
(Robert Eddery) *hld up in tch in last pair: clsd and n.m.r 2f out: swtchd rt over 1f out: kpt on ins fnl f: no threat to wnr* **5/1**[2]

5464 **6** hd **Byres Road**[16] [1457] 4-9-7 81............................................ AdamKirby 6 80
(Mark Johnston) *chsd ldrs: rdn ent fnl 2f: unable qck over 1f out: wknd ins fnl f* **5/1**[2]

4234 **7** nk **Glenalmond (IRE)**[11] [1549] 5-8-9 69.................................. DannyBrock 4 68
(Daniel Steele) *in tch in midfield: shkn up over 1f out: no threat to ldrs but kpt on ins fnl f* **10/1**

4235 **8** ¾ **King Of Dreams**[30] [1224] 4-8-9 74.................................... GeorgeBuckell(5) 7 71
(David Simcock) *t.k.h: wl in tch in midfield: effrt 2f out: sn rdn and unable qck: wl hld and one pce ins fnl f* **5/1**[2]

-563 **9** 6 **Archangel Raphael (IRE)**[14] [1504] 5-9-3 77.......................(p) JimCrowley 1 62
(Amanda Perrett) *hld up in tch in last trio: n.m.r jst over 2f out: pushed along and no rspnse 2f out: sn btn and bhd fnl f* **10/1**

2m 4.15s (0.55) **Going Correction** -0.10s/f (Good) **9** Ran SP% **119.8**
Speed ratings (Par 105): **93,90,90,89,88 88,87,87,82**
CSF £106.12 CT £418.54 TOTE £12.00: £2.80, £3.10, £2.30; EX 121.30 Trifecta £889.60.
**Owner** M P N Tregoning **Bred** Dachel Stud **Trained** Whitsbury, Hants

**FOCUS**
Run over 2yds further than advertised. A competitive heat won decisively by a lightly raced sort.

## 1789 WINNER RENTAL FILLIES' H'CAP 1m 1f 207y
**6:35** (6:35) (Class 5) (0-70,67) 4-Y-O+ **£2,911** (£866; £432; £216) **Stalls** High

Form RPR

660- **1** **Pernickety**[198] [6901] 4-9-6 66.............................................(h) JimCrowley 1 73
(Lucy Wadham) *t.k.h: hld up in tch in midfield: swtchd rt and effrt to chse ldr 2f out: sn chalng: drvn to ld ins fnl f: styd on* **6/1**[3]

2242 **2** ¾ **Ms Gillard**[16] [1455] 4-9-6 66..............................................(b) AdamKirby 3 72
(David Simcock) *led: rdn 2f out: hrd pressed and drvn over 1f out: hdd and styd on same pce ins fnl f* **5/1**[2]

-501 **3** 4 ½ **Tommys Geal**[26] [1284] 5-8-13 59........................................ DanielMuscutt 6 56
(Michael Madgwick) *hld up in tch in midfield: clsd and swtchd rt 2f out: rdn and chalng over 1f out tl no ex ins fnl f: wknd fnl 150yds* **13/2**

-423 **4** 3 **Little Kipling**[7] [1618] 4-9-4 67.............................................. AaronJones(3) 7 58
(Stuart Williams) *chsd ldr tl jst over 2f out: 4th and outpcd u.p over 1f out: wl hld fnl f* **8/1**

016- **5** 2 **Becca Campbell (IRE)**[186] [7245] 4-9-4 67.....................(p) HollieDoyle(3) 4 55
(Eve Johnson Houghton) *hld up in last pair: clsd and in tch 5f out: effrt 2f out: sn drifting lft and no imp: wknd fnl f* **7/2**[1]

0002 **6** nk **Solveig's Song**[26] [1283] 5-9-7 67.......................................(p) JackMitchell 5 54
(Steve Woodman) *stdd after s: hld up in rr: clsd and in tch 5f out: effrt jst over 2f out: outpcd over 1f out: sn wknd* **6/1**[3]

60-4 **7** hd **Weardiditallgorong**[98] [121] 5-9-0 60.................................(b) DavidProbert 8 47
(Des Donovan, Ire) *in tch in midfield: rdn jst over 2f out: lost pl and bhd over 1f out: wknd fnl f* **8/1**

512- **8** 84 **Onehelluvatouch**[191] [7103] 4-8-13 59.................................(b) ShaneKelly 2 +
(Philip Hide) *in tch: clipped heels: stmbld and blinkers bec displcd sn after s: stmbld bdly after 1f: styd away fr rivals 7f out: hdwy to ld 4f out tl over 2f out: sn rdn and dropped out and virtually p.u 1f out: t.o* **7/1**

2m 3.96s (0.36) **Going Correction** -0.10s/f (Good) **8** Ran SP% **115.5**
Speed ratings (Par 100): **94,93,89,87,85 85,85,18**
CSF £36.32 CT £201.93 TOTE £7.90: £2.60, £1.90, £2.40; EX 46.30 Trifecta £395.80.
**Owner** Mr And Mrs A E Pakenham **Bred** Mr & Mrs A E Pakenham **Trained** Newmarket, Suffolk

**FOCUS**
Run over 2yds further than advertised. A tight fillies' handicap with a right old tussle up the straight between two jockeys at the top of their game.

## 1790 RETRAINING OF RACEHORSES ROR H'CAP 7f 211y
**7:05** (7:05) (Class 6) (0-65,67) 3-Y-O **£2,587** (£770; £384; £192) **Stalls** Low

Form RPR

040- **1** **Darkroom Angel**[136] [8153] 3-9-5 66.................................. HectorCrouch(3) 6 73+
(Philip Hide) *w ldr tl led 4f out: rdn ent fnl 2f: drvn over 1f out: forged ahd ins fnl f: styd on wl: rdn out* **13/2**[3]

4306 **2** 1 ¾ **Auric Goldfinger (IRE)**[7] [1625] 3-8-13 64.....................(b) RossaRyan(7) 4 67
(Richard Hannon) *t.k.h: chsd ldrs: n.m.r and swtchd rt 2f out: edgd rt u.p in 3rd over 1f out: styd on ins fnl f to 2nd towards fin: no threat to wnr* **9/1**

604- **3** ½ **Il Sicario (IRE)**[305] [3248] 3-9-9 67...................................... AdamKirby 9 69
(Mark Johnston) *pressed ldrs: rdn to chal over 1f out: no ex u.p ins fnl f: styd on same pce and lost 2nd towards fin* **3/1**[2]

000- **4** 1 ¾ **Equal Rights**[219] [6264] 3-9-1 59.......................................... JimCrowley 2 57
(Eve Johnson Houghton) *hld up in tch in midfield: rdn over 2f out: kpt on same pce ins fnl f* **10/1**

023- **5** 2 ¼ **Orithia (USA)**[143] [8072] 3-9-3 61.......................................(t) FergusSweeney 1 54
(Seamus Durack) *stdd after s: hld up in last pair: swtchd rt over 2f out: edging lft u.p over 1f out: wknd ins fnl f* **7/1**

0040 **6** 1 ¾ **Greyjoy (IRE)**[10] [1564] 3-8-9 58...................................... MitchGodwin(5) 5 47
(Sylvester Kirk) *stdd after s: hld up in last pair: effrt 2f out: drifting lft and no imp over 1f out: wknd fnl f* **20/1**

-553 **7** hd **Wily Rumpus (IRE)**[29] [1242] 3-9-7 65.............................. ThomasBrown 7 53
(Ed Walker) *t.k.h: led tl 4f out: rdn 2f out: lost pl over 1f out: wknd fnl f* **11/4**[1]

636 **8** 1 **Miss M (IRE)**[23] [1333] 3-9-7 65.......................................... MartinDwyer 3 51
(William Muir) *hld up in midfield: effrt 2f out: edging lft and no imp whn sltly hmpd over 1f out: sn wknd* **14/1**

500- **9** 1 ¾ **Caspian Gold (IRE)**[186] [7259] 3-9-6 64.............................. ShaneKelly 8 46
(Richard Hughes) *hld up in tch in midfield: impeded 2f out: dropped to rr and nt clr run over 1f out: wknd fnl f* **9/1**

1m 35.74s (-0.26) **Going Correction** -0.10s/f (Good) **9** Ran SP% **118.0**
Speed ratings (Par 96): **97,95,94,93,90 89,88,87,86**
CSF £64.66 CT £214.25 TOTE £7.60: £2.10, £2.40, £2.60; EX 53.10 Trifecta £324.30.
**Owner** The Perfect Smiths **Bred** David Jamison Bloodstock **Trained** Findon, W Sussex

**FOCUS**
Run over 2yds further than advertised. An interesting if modest 3yo handicap where it paid to be prominent. The winner found some improvement.

## 1791 DONATELLO RESTAURANT BRIGHTON H'CAP 5f 215y
**7:35** (7:35) (Class 5) (0-70,69) 4-Y-O+ **£3,169** (£943; £471; £235) **Stalls** Low

Form RPR

0262 **1** **Beau Mistral (IRE)**[30] [1219] 8-9-2 64.............................. WilliamCarson 1 72
(Tony Carroll) *mde all: rdn over 1f out: styd on strly to draw clr ins fnl f* **11/4**[3]

4060 **2** 3 **Doctor Parkes**[23] [1328] 11-8-8 63.................................... MillyNaseb(7) 5 61
(Stuart Williams) *chsd wnr: effrt over 1f out: sn rdn and unable qck: outpcd by wnr ins fnl f: kpt on* **6/1**

-550 **3** *2 ¼* **Panther Patrol (IRE)**[26] 1290 7-9-4 **69**..................(v) EdwardGreatrex(3) 2 60
(Eve Johnson Houghton) *trckd ldng pair: effrt over 1f out: sn u.p and unable qck: wknd ins fnl f* **15/8**[1]

510- **4** *2* **Essaka (IRE)**[155] 7912 5-8-12 **60**........................................ JimCrowley 4 45
(Tony Carroll) *stdd s: hld up in rr: wnt 4th 2f out: sn shkn up and no hdwy: wl hld fnl f* **9/4**[2]

0-00 **5** *3 ¾* **Magical Peak**[24] 1299 5-7-9 **50** oh5.........................(b) SophieRalston(7) 3 23
(John O'Shea) *racd in 4th tl dropped to last and pushed along 2f out: sn wknd* **33/1**

1m 9.86s (-0.34) **Going Correction** -0.10s/f (Good) **5** Ran SP% **109.4**
Speed ratings (Par 103): **98,94,91,88,83**
CSF £18.05 TOTE £3.50: £1.60, £3.00; EX 18.50 Trifecta £41.50.
**Owner** A Mills **Bred** John McEnery **Trained** Cropthorne, Worcs

**FOCUS**
Run over 2yds further than advertised. A modest sprint handicap won from the front.
T/Plt: £54.30 to a £1 stake. Pool: £35,391.00 - 650.81 winning units. T/Qpdt: £14.70 to a £1 stake. Pool: £4,123.00 - 280.40 winning units. **Steve Payne**

# 1723 KEMPTON (A.W) (R-H)

## Saturday, April 15

**OFFICIAL GOING: Polytrack: standard**
Wind: Fresh, across (away from stands) Weather: Fine

## 1792 BRITISH STALLION STUDS EBF NOVICE STKS (PLUS 10 RACE) 5f (P)
**2:00** (2:05) (Class 4) 2-Y-O **£4,592** (£1,366; £683; £341) **Stalls** Low

Form RPR

**1** **Plunger** 2-9-2 0........................................................... JimCrowley 7 70+
(Paul Cole) *pressed ldr: shkn up to ld over 1f out: urged along and kpt on wl* **6/4**[1]

0 **2** *1 ½* **Dragon's Teeth (IRE)**[14] 1495 2-9-2 0.................................. JFEgan 6 65
(Jo Hughes) *led: rdn and hdd over 1f out: one pce* **2/1**[2]

04 **3** *nk* **Quick Skips Lad (IRE)**[9] 1594 2-9-2 0........................... LiamKeniry 5 64
(J S Moore) *chsd ldng pair: pushed along 1/2-way: rdn and kpt on fr over 1f out to press for 2nd nr fin* **12/1**

**4** *2 ¾* **Kodiac Express (IRE)** 2-8-11 0....................................... FranBerry 3 49
(Mike Murphy) *chsd ldng trio: pushed along 1/2-way: shkn up and one pce over 1f out* **7/1**

0 **5** *9* **Afterthisone**[14] 1495 2-9-2 0............................................ KevinStott 4 22
(Robin Dickin) *unruly bef ent stall: sn outpcd: bhd fr 1/2-way* **50/1**

**6** *nk* **Heavenly Pulse (IRE)** 2-9-2 0........................................ JoeyHaynes 1 21
(Ann Duffield) *fractious preliminaries and difficult to load into stall: dwlt: outpcd and a bhd* **9/2**[3]

1m 1.74s (1.24) **Going Correction** -0.025s/f (Stan) **6** Ran SP% **113.7**
Speed ratings (Par 94): **89,86,86,81,67 66**
CSF £4.88 TOTE £2.20: £1.30, £1.60; EX 5.30 Trifecta £16.80.
**Owner** A H Robinson **Bred** A H And C E Robinson Partnership **Trained** Whatcombe, Oxon

**FOCUS**
An ordinary-looking novice race.

## 1793 RACING UK IN STUNNING HD H'CAP 5f (P)
**2:35** (2:35) (Class 2) (0-105,101) 4-Y-O+
**£11,827** (£3,541; £1,770; £885; £442; £222) **Stalls** Low

Form RPR

060- **1** **A Momentofmadness**[175] 7537 4-8-6 **86**..............(h) SilvestreDeSousa 1 94
(Charles Hills) *mde all: rdn over 1f out: kpt on wl fnl f* **7/4**[1]

-013 **2** *¾* **Robot Boy (IRE)**[42] 1025 7-9-7 **101**................................. RyanMoore 4 106
(David Barron) *tried to chse ldrs but nt pce to keep up: urged along in 5th 1/2-way: rdn and styd on fnl f to take 2nd last strides* **2/1**[2]

635- **3** *½* **Just That Lord**[147] 8032 4-8-5 **85**.................................... JimmyQuinn 3 88
(Bill Turner) *trckd ldng pair: rdn to chse wnr over 1f out: kpt on but a hld and lost 2nd last strides* **16/1**

140- **4** *¾* **Southern Belle (IRE)**[212] 6518 4-8-9 **89**.......................... LukeMorris 2 90
(Robert Cowell) *jst in tch: rdn over 1f out: kpt on fnl f but nvr able to chal: impeded last strides* **12/1**

4504 **5** *2 ¼* **Watchable**[21] 1362 7-9-4 **98**.......................................(p) AdamKirby 5 90
(David O'Meara) *pressed wnr to over 1f out: wknd ins fnl f* **4/1**[3]

5133 **6** *6* **Just Us Two (IRE)**[15] 1465 5-8-0 **83**.......................(p) AaronJones(3) 6 54
(Robert Cowell) *hung bdly lft bnd over 3f out: a last and bhd over 1f out* **12/1**

58.93s (-1.57) **Going Correction** -0.025s/f (Stan) **6** Ran SP% **111.0**
Speed ratings (Par 109): **111,109,109,107,104 94**
CSF £5.38 TOTE £2.10: £1.60, £1.70; EX 6.40 Trifecta £43.90.
**Owner** Tony Wechsler & Ann Plummer **Bred** D R Tucker **Trained** Lambourn, Berks

**FOCUS**
A good front-running performance from the winner, who posted a small pb.

## 1794 FOLLOW @RACING_UK ON TWITTER H'CAP 6f (P)
**3:10** (3:11) (Class 2) (0-105,100) 4-Y-O+
**£11,827** (£3,541; £1,770; £885; £442; £222) **Stalls** Low

Form RPR

-002 **1** **Solar Flair**[14] 1501 5-9-7 **100**........................................ JimCrowley 10 108
(William Knight) *spd fr wdst draw to press ldr: rdn to ld over 1f out: kpt on fnl f: jst lasted* **4/1**[2]

40-3 **2** *nse* **Stellarta**[14] 1501 6-8-13 **92**........................................ TomMarquand 3 100
(Michael Blanshard) *in tch: prog on inner over 2f out: drvn to chal fnl f: kpt on wl: jst denied* **10/1**

1433 **3** *1 ¾* **Fast Track**[16] 1454 6-8-10 **89**........................................ GrahamLee 2 91
(David Barron) *chsd ldng pair: rdn and cl enough over 1f out but dropped to 4th: kpt on fnl f to snatch 3rd again post* **13/2**

1326 **4** *shd* **Captain Dion**[16] 1454 4-8-11 **90**.................................(v) KevinStott 1 92
(Kevin Ryan) *led: drvn and hdd over 1f out: kpt on same pce: lost 3rd post* **6/1**

34/0 **5** *2 ¼* **Eltezam (IRE)**[35] 1150 4-9-4 **97**................................(h[1]) FrankieDettori 5 92
(Richard Hannon) *rrd s: in rr: effrt into 5th 2f out but nt on terms: no imp after* **7/2**[1]

440- **6** *3 ½* **Basil Berry**[126] 8311 6-9-1 **94**..........................(b) SilvestreDeSousa 8 78
(Chris Dwyer) *restless stalls: towards rr: rdn and struggling over 2f out: sn lft bhd* **14/1**

1436 **7** *2* **Pearl Spectre (USA)**[15] 1479 6-8-11 **90**.................... JosephineGordon 4 67
(Phil McEntee) *t.k.h early: cl up to over 2f out: sn wknd* **20/1**

1016 **8** *1* **Dutch Golden Age (IRE)**[14] 1501 5-8-7 **89**.............. HectorCrouch(3) 6 63
(Gary Moore) *in tch but forced to r quite wd: rdn and lft bhd over 2f out* **9/1**

-410 **9** *7* **Go Far**[14] 1501 7-8-12 **98**.........................................(v) JoshuaBryan(7) 9 50
(Alan Bailey) *chsd ldrs but trapped out wd and rdn bef 1/2-way: wknd u.p over 2f out: sn bhd* **33/1**

-130 **10** *130* **Eljaddaaf (IRE)**[47] 957 6-8-11 **90**..............................(h) RobertWinston 7
(Dean Ivory) *rel to r and lost all ch: allowed to amble rnd and hanging lft* **11/2**[3]

1m 11.2s (-1.90) **Going Correction** -0.025s/f (Stan) **10** Ran SP% **118.7**
Speed ratings (Par 109): **111,110,108,108,105 100,98,96,87,**
CSF £44.63 CT £265.08 TOTE £5.50: £2.30, £2.90, £2.20; EX 42.00 Trifecta £239.00.
**Owner** Art Of Racing & The Kimber Family **Bred** Farmers Hill Stud **Trained** Patching, W Sussex

**FOCUS**
A decent sprint handicap. The one-two were closely matched on their C&D latest and this rates a small step up on that, which fits a better view of their form.

## 1795 WATCH RACING UK ON SKY 432 SNOWDROP FILLIES' STKS (LISTED RACE) 1m (P)
**3:45** (3:47) (Class 1) 4-Y-O+
**£22,684** (£8,600; £4,304; £2,144; £1,076; £540) **Stalls** Low

Form RPR

140- **1** **Aljazzi**[161] 7823 4-9-0 100.........................................(h) RyanMoore 4 105
(Marco Botti) *wl plcd bhd ldrs: shkn up over 2f out: clsd to ld 1f out: styd on wl and in command after* **4/1**[2]

405- **2** *1 ½* **Materialistic**[161] 7823 4-9-0 96.................................. JamieSpencer 5 101
(Luca Cumani) *wl in tch in midfield: prog 2f out: drvn and styd on to chse wnr last 120yds: no imp* **8/1**

603- **3** *hd* **Zest (IRE)**[197] 6915 4-9-0 87.......................................... TomQueally 6 100
(James Fanshawe) *t.k.h: hld up in rr: prog 2f out: rdn and styd on fnl f to press for 2nd last 100yds* **14/1**

424- **4** *1 ¼* **Robanne**[183] 7348 4-9-0 97.................................. SilvestreDeSousa 3 97
(William Knight) *in tch: prog on inner over 2f out: nt qckn over 1f out: one pce fnl f* **6/1**[3]

121- **5** *nk* **Laugh Aloud**[204] 6746 4-9-3 108........................................(t) WilliamBuick 2 100
(John Gosden) *led and kpt away fr ins rail: asked to kick on over 2f out: drvn and hdd 1f out: fdd* **7/4**[1]

60-5 **6** *1 ¼* **Bahaarah (IRE)**[66] 617 4-9-0 95.................................... SeanLevey 1 94
(Richard Hannon) *hld up in last pair: rdn over 2f out: kpt on fnl f: nrst fin but no ch* **16/1**

1330 **7** *½* **Summer Icon**[35] 1150 4-9-0 95........................................ GrahamLee 8 93
(Mick Channon) *dwlt: hld up in last: shkn up over 2f out: swtchd rt over 1f out: kpt on fnl f: nvr a threat* **25/1**

126- **8** *hd* **Crowning Glory (FR)**[170] 7650 4-9-0 93.............................. PatDobbs 7 92
(Ralph Beckett) *mostly pressed ldr: tried to chal 2f out: lost 2nd over 1f out: wknd qckly last 150yds* **16/1**

50-0 **9** *1 ¾* **Lucy The Painter (IRE)**[14] 1494 5-9-0 97....................... HarryBentley 9 88
(Ed de Giles) *trapped out wd in midfield: rdn and struggling wl over 2f out: wknd* **20/1**

452- **10** *nk* **Desert Haze**[169] 7676 4-9-0 98.......................................... FranBerry 10 87
(Ralph Beckett) *chsd ldrs but forced out wd: rdn over 2f out: nt qckn wl over 1f out: wknd qckly fnl f* **10/1**

1m 37.91s (-1.89) **Going Correction** -0.025s/f (Stan) **10** Ran SP% **117.9**
Speed ratings (Par 108): **108,106,106,105,104 103,103,102,101,100**
CSF £36.56 TOTE £5.00: £1.30, £2.80, £4.00; EX 41.70 Trifecta £446.30.
**Owner** Saleh Al Homaizi & Imad Al Sagar **Bred** Saleh Al Homaizi & Imad Al Sagar **Trained** Newmarket, Suffolk

**FOCUS**
There was a comfortable winner of this Listed contest, but not the one the early market had predicted. The winner has been rated close to her Haydock success from last year.

## 1796 WATCH RACING UK ON VIRGIN 536 FILLIES' CONDITIONS STKS (PLUS 10 RACE) 1m (P)
**4:15** (4:17) (Class 2) 3-Y-O
**£11,827** (£3,541; £1,770; £885; £442; £222) **Stalls** Low

Form RPR

1- **1** **Sibilance**[317] 2817 3-9-4 81............................................ FranBerry 5 94+
(Ralph Beckett) *led 2f: trckd ldr: shkn up over 2f out: clsd qckly to ld jst over 1f out: r.o wl: readily* **6/1**

210- **2** *2 ¼* **Raven's Lady**[190] 7114 3-9-4 85........................................ RyanMoore 7 88
(Marco Botti) *led after 2f: 2 l clr 2f out: rdn: hdd and nt qckn jst over 1f out: one pce* **3/1**[2]

21- **3** *nk* **Indian Blessing**[158] 7855 3-9-4 77................................ JamieSpencer 4 87
(Ed Walker) *hld up in 5th: rdn and prog fr 2f out: tk 3rd fnl f: kpt on but nvr able to threaten* **5/1**[3]

316- **4** *1 ¾* **Blending**[219] 6258 3-9-4 90.......................................... FrankieDettori 6 83
(John Gosden) *trckd ldng pair: shkn up over 2f out: no imp over 1f out: fdd ins fnl f* **5/2**[1]

166- **5** *¾* **Perfect Madge (IRE)**[204] 6748 3-9-4 92.............................. KevinStott 2 81
(Kevin Ryan) *trckd ldng trio: rdn 2f out: no prog over 1f out: fdd ins fnl f* **14/1**

10- **6** *nk* **Hidden Steps**[219] 6258 3-9-4 91....................................(h[1]) ThomasBrown 3 81
(Andrew Balding) *hld up in 6th: shkn up over 2f out and no prog: no ch over 1f out: kpt on nr fin* **10/1**

15- **7** *3 ¾* **Assanilka (FR)**[178] 7480 3-9-4 92............................. RichardKingscote 1 72
(Harry Dunlop) *hld up: a in last: rdn and no prog over 2f out* **11/2**

1m 38.0s (-1.80) **Going Correction** -0.025s/f (Stan) **7** Ran SP% **115.7**
Speed ratings (Par 101): **108,105,105,103,102 102,98**
CSF £24.90 TOTE £6.70: £3.00, £1.60; EX 28.90 Trifecta £111.80.
**Owner** Nigel & Carolyn Elwes **Bred** Aylesfield Farms Stud **Trained** Kimpton, Hants

**FOCUS**
An interesting race and a fair performance from the winner, who looks set to compete in better company. An unexposed field so the level is fluid.

## 1797 OVER 2,800 FLAT RACES ON RACING UK CONDITIONS STKS (PLUS 10 RACE) (C&G) 1m (P)
**4:50** (4:51) (Class 2) 3-Y-O **£11,827** (£3,541; £1,770; £885) **Stalls** Low

Form RPR

134- **1** **Khafoo Shememi (IRE)**[175] 7536 3-9-4 95............................ RyanMoore 5 104
(Richard Hannon) *mde all: shkn up over 2f out: drew clr over 1f out: pushed out firmly* **3/1**[3]

120- **2** *3 ½* **Executive Force**[175] 7544 3-9-4 102.................................. PatCosgrave 1 96
(William Haggas) *hld up in last: rdn over 2f out: kpt on to take 2nd fnl f: no ch w wnr* **5/2**[2]

316- **3** *2 ¾* **Ultimate Avenue (IRE)**[205] 6707 3-9-4 99........................ JamieSpencer 4 89
(Ed Walker) *chsd wnr after 2f to jst over 2f out: steadily fdd u.p* **2/1**[1]

165- **4** 1/2 **Red Ensign (IRE)**[205] 6705 3-9-4 88 .................................. HarryBentley 2 88
(Simon Crisford) *chsd wnr 2f: rdn to go 2nd again jst over 2f out to 1f out: no imp then wknd* **7/2**

1m 36.49s (-3.31) **Going Correction** -0.025s/f (Stan) **4** Ran SP% **109.1**
Speed ratings (Par 104): **115,111,108,108**
CSF £10.55 TOTE £3.10; EX 7.40 Trifecta £15.40.
**Owner** Saeed Suhail **Bred** Mrs M McWey **Trained** East Everleigh, Wilts

**FOCUS**
The winning time compared favourably with that recorded by the fillies in the earlier equivalent race, being 1.51sec faster, and the winner looks much improved at three.

## 1798 FLAT IS BACK ON RACING UK QUEEN'S PRIZE H'CAP 1m 7f 218y(P)
**5:25** (5:26) (Class 2) (0-105,100) 4-Y-O+
**£11,827** (£3,541; £1,770; £885; £442; £222) **Stalls** Low

Form RPR
116- **1** **Blakeney Point**[190] 7123 4-8-8 **89** .......................(p) KieranShoemark(3) 9 99
(Roger Charlton) *mde all: set mod pce tl stepped on it over 3f out: hung lft fr 2f out but already in decisive ld: pushed out fnl f: unchal* **12/1**

221- **2** 1 1/4 **Higher Power**[150] 7979 5-9-12 **100** .................................. TomQueally 5 108
(James Fanshawe) *trckd ldng trio: rdn over 2f out and sn chsd wnr: kpt on but nvr able to chal* **15/8**[1]

23-1 **3** 1 1/2 **Endless Acres (IRE)**[14] 1505 4-8-11 **89** ....................(v) StevieDonohoe 2 96
(Charlie Fellowes) *trckd ldrs in 5th: rdn and lost pl over 2f out: rallied over 1f out to chse ldng pair: kpt on but no imp* **3/1**[2]

141- **4** 1 1/4 **Velvet Revolution**[145] 8051 4-8-7 **85** ......................... JosephineGordon 8 90+
(Marco Botti) *hld up in last pair in modly run event: shkn up over 3f out: swtchd to inner and prog 2f out: pressed for a pl over 1f out: one pce after* **10/1**

143- **5** 2 **Magic Circle (IRE)**[168] 7708 5-9-11 **99** .................................. FranBerry 7 102+
(Ralph Beckett) *hld up in last in modly run event: prog on inner over 2f out: pressed for a pl over 1f out: no ex* **15/2**

3/1- **6** 1 **Beltor**[26] 8250 6-8-7 **81** .......................................................... LiamKeniry 4 82
(Robert Stephens) *hld up in 6th: urged along whn pce lifted over 3f out: no prog fnl 2f* **6/1**[3]

-556 **7** 3/4 **Barye**[22] 1341 6-9-10 **98** ......................................................... RyanMoore 6 99
(Richard Hughes) *hld up in 7th in modly run event: effrt over 2f out: pressed for a pl over 1f out: wknd fnl f* **20/1**

320- **8** 1 1/4 **Against The Odds**[190] 7123 4-8-5 **83** ................................ LukeMorris 1 82
(Paul Cole) *trckd ldng pair: rdn to chse wnr briefly over 2f out: wknd over 1f out* **12/1**

6603 **9** 3 **Entihaa**[19] 1405 9-8-8 **82** ............................................... RoystonFfrench 10 77
(Dai Burchell) *s.i.s: sn chsd wnr: lost 2nd and wknd over 2f out* **66/1**

3m 34.64s (4.54) **Going Correction** -0.025s/f (Stan)
**WFA** 4 from 5yo+ 2lb **9** Ran SP% **116.6**
Speed ratings (Par 109): **87,86,85,85,84 83,83,82,81**
CSF £35.23 CT £88.73 TOTE £15.30: £3.50, £1.50, £1.20; EX 56.10 Trifecta £205.80.
**Owner** Axom LX **Bred** Mr & Mrs A E Pakenham **Trained** Beckhampton, Wilts

**FOCUS**
This was run at a steady gallop and the winner had things easy in front.
T/Plt: £190.20 to a £1 stake. Pool: £42,356.00 - 222.62 winning units. T/Qpdt: £77.90 to a £1 stake. Pool: £2,782.00 - 35.70 winning units. **Jonathan Neesom**

# MUSSELBURGH (R-H)
Saturday, April 15

**OFFICIAL GOING: Good to firm (good in places; 7.7)**
Wind: Fairly strong, against in nearly 4f of home straight Weather: Cloudy, bright

## 1799 TOTEPLACEPOT EASTER SATURDAY H'CAP 7f 33y
**1:50** (1:52) (Class 3) (0-95,93) 4-Y-O+ **£8,409** (£2,502; £1,250; £625) **Stalls** Low

Form RPR
3-33 **1** **Twin Appeal (IRE)**[25] 1295 6-9-3 **89** ..............................(b) PhillipMakin 4 97
(David Barron) *trckd ldrs: led and rdn over 1f out: drvn out fnl f* **11/2**[3]

00-0 **2** 1 3/4 **Lat Hawill (IRE)**[14] 1492 6-9-2 **93** .........................(v) ShirleyTeasdale(5) 1 96
(Keith Dalgleish) *trckd ldrs: n.m.r over 2f out: effrt and swtchd lft over 1f out: chsd wnr ins fnl f: kpt on* **11/2**[3]

200- **3** 1 3/4 **Gurkha Friend**[185] 7287 5-9-1 **87** ......................................... TomEaves 6 86
(Karen McLintock) *trckd ldr: led over 2f out to over 1f out: lost 2nd and no ex ins fnl f* **11/1**

0- **4** 1 3/4 **Eternal**[320] 2744 5-8-11 **88** ................................................ PhilDennis(5) 2 82
(Declan Carroll) *in tch on ins: effrt whn n.m.r over 2f out to over 1f out: sn angled lft: kpt on fnl f: no imp* **25/1**

6-50 **5** 1 3/4 **God Willing**[14] 1492 6-9-5 **91** ........................................ DanielTudhope 8 80
(Declan Carroll) *hld up: stdy hdwy whn nt clr run over 2f out to over 1f out: rdn and kpt on fnl f: nvr able to chal* **13/2**

12-0 **6** 2 **Bertiewhittle**[31] 1208 9-9-2 **93** ........................................ RowanScott(5) 10 77
(David Barron) *missed break: bhd: hdwy 2f out: kpt on fnl f: nvr able to chal* **12/1**

23-0 **7** nse **Mishaal (IRE)**[47] 957 7-9-1 **87** ........................................ BarryMcHugh 5 71
(Michael Herrington) *led to over 2f out: rdn and wknd appr fnl f* **16/1**

612- **8** nk **Roll On Rory**[169] 7668 4-9-7 **93** .......................................(v) OisinMurphy 3 76
(Jason Ward) *t.k.h: in tch: drvn along over 2f out: outpcd over 1f out* **9/2**[1]

141- **9** 1 1/2 **Ionization (IRE)**[266] 4630 4-9-1 **87** ....................................... TadhgO'Shea 7 66
(John Patrick Shanahan, Ire) *t.k.h: hld up: rdn over 2f out: hung rt over 1f out: sn no imp* **20/1**

300- **10** 1 3/4 **Russian Realm**[191] 7095 7-9-3 **89** ................................... PaulMulrennan 9 63
(Paul Midgley) *hld up: drvn and outpcd over 2f out: btn over 1f out* **22/1**

400- **11** 1/2 **B Fifty Two (IRE)**[231] 5880 8-9-7 **93** ...................................... CamHardie 12 66
(Marjorie Fife) *hld up on outside: drvn along over 2f out: sn wknd* **40/1**

001- **12** 1/2 **Penwortham (IRE)**[218] 6276 4-9-2 **88** ................................ PaulHanagan 11 59
(Richard Fahey) *t.k.h: hld up midfield on outside: drvn and outpaced over 2f out: sn wknd* **5/1**[2]

1m 27.81s (-1.19) **Going Correction** +0.05s/f (Good) **12** Ran SP% **116.3**
Speed ratings (Par 107): **108,106,104,102,100 97,97,97,95,93 93,92**
CSF £33.23 CT £327.20 TOTE £6.70: £1.90, £2.30, £3.70; EX 40.80 Trifecta £266.70.
**Owner** Twinacre Nurseries Ltd **Bred** Glashare House Stud **Trained** Maunby, N Yorks

**FOCUS**
Less than 1mm of rain fell the day before racing. 20mm had been placed on the track on Tuesday and Wednesday, with a further 7mm on the bends on Thursday, leaving the going as good, good to firm in places (GoingStick: 7.7). Race distances were as advertised, while the stalls for the 5f and 2m races were placed on the stands' side, and on the inner for the rest. Jockeys riding in the first race were unanimous in reporting the ground as being quick. A competitive handicap on paper, but not that many were able to strike a blow in a steadily run contest dominated by those with low draws. A pb from the winner.

## 1800 TOTESCOOP6 BORDERLESCOTT SPRINT TROPHY CONDITIONS STKS 5f 1y
**2:25** (2:25) (Class 2) 3-Y-O+ **£12,938** (£3,850; £1,924; £962) **Stalls** High

Form RPR
000- **1** **Desert Law (IRE)**[175] 7537 9-9-2 86 .................................. OisinMurphy 6 99
(Paul Midgley) *hld up in last pl: effrt and p.u over 1f out: led ent fnl f: pushed along and qcknd clr: readily* **14/1**

002- **2** 3 1/4 **Lexington Abbey**[189] 7156 6-9-2 96 ................................(p) ShaneGray 7 87
(Kevin Ryan) *trckd ldrs: effrt whn nt clr run over 1f out to ent fnl f: kpt on to take 2nd cl home: no ch w wnr* **4/1**[2]

4650 **3** nk **Line Of Reason (IRE)**[58] 773 7-9-2 100 ...................... PaulMulrennan 4 86
(Paul Midgley) *trckd ldrs: smooth hdwy on outside to ld over 1f out: rdn and hdd ent fnl f: kpt on same pce* **5/2**[1]

5-00 **4** 1 3/4 **Taexali (IRE)**[49] 941 4-9-2 93 ....................................(b[1]) SamHitchcott 2 80
(John Patrick Shanahan, Ire) *w ldr: rdn over 1f out: kpt on same pce ins fnl f* **10/1**

412- **5** 3 1/4 **Monsieur Joe (IRE)**[259] 4905 10-9-2 109 ........................... MartinLane 5 68
(Paul Midgley) *trckd ldrs: drvn along over 2f out: sn outpcd: edgd rt and no imp over 1f out* **5/2**[1]

0-00 **6** 6 **Red Baron (IRE)**[37] 1110 8-9-2 82 ......................................... NeilFarley 3 47
(Eric Alston) *led to over 1f out: sn rdn and btn* **28/1**

112- **7** 85 **Glenrowan Rose (IRE)**[186] 7250 4-9-1 95 ......................... PhillipMakin 1
(Keith Dalgleish) *s.v.s: sn t.o and eased* **9/2**[3]

1m 0.2s (-0.20) **Going Correction** +0.275s/f (Good) **7** Ran SP% **114.5**
Speed ratings (Par 109): **112,106,106,103,98 88,**
CSF £68.81 TOTE £18.50: £6.90, £2.20; EX 84.60 Trifecta £292.90.
**Owner** Taylor's Bloodstock Ltd **Bred** Littleton Stud **Trained** Westow, N Yorks

**FOCUS**
Official ratings counted for nothing as the winner routed his rivals in what had looked to be a competitive sprint. The winner has been rated back to last year's best (109 peak in past); worth more at face value, but not one to be confident in.

## 1801 TOTEPOOLLIVEINFO.COM ROYAL MILE H'CAP 1m 2y
**3:00** (3:01) (Class 2) (0-100,99) 3-Y-O **£32,345** (£9,625; £4,810; £2,405) **Stalls** Low

Form RPR
334- **1** **Cullingworth (IRE)**[218] 6275 3-8-0 **81** ......................... SammyJoBell(3) 3 87
(Richard Fahey) *hld up: stdy hdwy over 2f out: rdn to ld ins fnl f: hld on wl towards fin* **16/1**

-564 **2** hd **Grey Britain**[42] 1026 3-9-5 **97** .......................................(p) PaulMulrennan 9 102
(John Ryan) *t.k.h: pressed ldr: rdn to ld over 2f out: hdd ins fnl f: rallied u.p: hld nr fin* **22/1**

1-20 **3** 3/4 **Dr Julius No**[42] 1026 3-8-12 **90** ......................................... OisinMurphy 12 93+
(Ralph Beckett) *s.i.s: hld up: rdn along over 2f out: gd hdwy over 1f out: kpt on ins fnl f* **9/1**

231- **4** 2 3/4 **Mazyoun**[172] 7599 3-8-12 **90** ...............................................(b) PJMcDonald 8 87
(Hugo Palmer) *hld up midfield: effrt and drvn over 2f out: kpt on same pce fnl f* **13/2**[3]

405- **5** 1 3/4 **Navarone (IRE)**[211] 6535 3-7-11 **78** oh3 ..................... NathanEvans(3) 11 71
(Richard Fahey) *hld up: rdn along over 2f out: hdwy over 1f out: kpt on fnl f: nt pce to chal* **20/1**

262- **6** nk **Society Red**[176] 7493 3-8-2 **80** ......................................... JamesSullivan 4 72
(Richard Fahey) *t.k.h: in tch: hdwy over 2f out: rdn and edgd lft over 1f out: edgd rt and sn one pce* **7/1**

220- **7** 3 1/4 **Rusumaat (IRE)**[219] 6260 3-9-1 **93** .......................................... DaneO'Neill 5 78
(Mark Johnston) *restless in stalls: prom: rdn along over 2f out: edgd rt and wknd over 1f out* **8/1**

032- **8** 1 1/4 **Somnambulist**[169] 7658 3-7-9 **78** oh1 ..................(h) ShirleyTeasdale(5) 2 60
(Keith Dalgleish) *s.i.s: hld up: rdn and hdwy over 2f out: kpt on fnl f: no imp* **14/1**

111- **9** 1 **Rashford's Double (IRE)**[164] 7768 3-8-5 **83** .................. PaulHanagan 7 63
(Richard Fahey) *hld up: drvn along 3f out: no imp fr 2f out* **6/1**[2]

523- **10** 3 1/2 **Novoman (IRE)**[175] 7541 3-8-12 **90** .................................... LiamJones 10 62+
(William Haggas) *t.k.h: hld up on outside: drvn and outpcd over 2f out: sn btn* **9/2**[1]

3121 **11** 1/2 **Mailshot (USA)**[35] 1142 3-9-7 **99** ........................................... JoeFanning 6 69
(Mark Johnston) *in tch: drvn and outpcd over 2f out: sn wknd* **8/1**

-455 **12** 3 1/4 **Chupalla**[63] 678 3-8-6 **84** .................................................. FrannyNorton 1 47
(Mark Johnston) *led: clr 1/2-way to over 2f out: sn hdd & wknd* **25/1**

1m 40.35s (-0.85) **Going Correction** +0.05s/f (Good) **12** Ran SP% **116.0**
Speed ratings (Par 104): **106,105,105,102,100 100,97,95,94,91 90,87**
CSF £324.77 CT £3382.96 TOTE £23.50: £5.80, £4.90, £3.30; EX 411.60 Trifecta £5090.40 Part won..
**Owner** Tiffin Sandwiches Limited & Partner **Bred** John Foley **Trained** Musley Bank, N Yorks

**FOCUS**
A competitive 3yo handicap which produced an exciting finish and the winner has been rated back to his early 2yo level.

## 1802 TOTEPOOL QUEEN'S CUP H'CAP 1m 5f 216y
**3:35** (3:35) (Class 2) 4-Y-O+ **£64,690** (£19,250; £9,620; £4,810) **Stalls** Low

Form RPR
2450 **1** **Carbon Dating (IRE)**[27] 1268 5-9-7 **101** ......................... TadhgO'Shea 7 110
(John Patrick Shanahan, Ire) *hld up in tch: smooth hdwy to ld over 1f out: sn rdn and edgd rt: kpt on strly fnl f* **12/1**

00-5 **2** 1 1/2 **Maleficent Queen**[13] 1516 5-9-8 **102** ................................. PhillipMakin 5 108
(Keith Dalgleish) *hld up: effrt whn nt clr run over 2f out to over 1f out: rdn and chsd wnr ins fnl f: kpt on* **11/1**

006- **3** 1/2 **The Tartan Spartan (IRE)**[197] 6917 4-8-11 **94** ............. SamHitchcott 3 99+
(John Patrick Shanahan, Ire) *hld up on ins: nt clr run over 2f out to ins fnl f: kpt on: nt rch first two* **12/1**

030- **4** 1 1/4 **Angel Gabrial (IRE)**[189] 7150 8-9-2 **96** ............................ PaulHanagan 8 99
(Richard Fahey) *prom: effrt and rdn over 2f out: chsd wnr over 1f out to ins fnl f* **9/1**

036- **5** nse **Sindarban (IRE)**[181] 7383 6-8-11 **91** ......................... ConnorBeasley 12 94
(Keith Dalgleish) *hld up: rdn and hdwy on outside over 2f out: drvn and edgd rt over 1f out: kpt on fnl f: no imp* **9/1**

600- **6** ½ **Sir Chauvelin**[161] 7824 5-8-13 **93**........ SamJames 13 96
(Jim Goldie) *stdd s: hld up: effrt whn nt clr run over 2f out to ins fnl f: nvr able to chal* **25/1**

1132 **7** ¾ **Isharah (USA)**[21] 1360 4-8-12 **95**........ JoeFanning 1 97
(Mark Johnston) *midfield: effrt and drvn along over 2f out: no imp fr over 1f out* **8/1**[3]

030- **8** *nk* **Shrewd**[189] 7150 7-9-2 **101**........ LewisEdmunds(5) 6 102
(Iain Jardine) *hld up on outside: drvn along over 2f out: no imp fr over 1f out* **9/2**[1]

660- **9** ½ **Suegioo (FR)**[182] 7349 8-9-7 **104**........(p) AdamMcNamara(3) 10 105
(Richard Fahey) *hld up: pushed along over 4f out: effrt on outside over 2f out: sn no imp* **14/1**

000- **10** 1½ **Gabrial The Hero (USA)**[176] 7498 8-8-13 **93**........ TonyHamilton 4 91
(Richard Fahey) *prom: n.m.r over 2f out: rdn and wknd over 1f out* **14/1**

000- **11** ½ **My Reward**[175] 7538 5-8-12 **92**........ DavidAllan 2 90
(Tim Easterby) *led 1f: chsd ldrs: rdn and regained ld over 2f out: hdd over 1f out: sn wknd* **9/1**

010- **12** *1* **Soldier In Action (FR)**[29] 7824 4-9-8 **105**........ FrannyNorton 9 101
(Mark Johnston) *chsd ldrs: drvn along over 2f out: wkng whn hmpd over 1f out* **6/1**[2]

660- **13** *7* **Stipulate**[69] 6786 8-9-2 **96**........ BenCurtis 14 83
(Brian Ellison) *led after 1f: rdn and hdd over 2f out: sn wknd* **16/1**

3m 3.06s (-2.24) **Going Correction** +0.05s/f (Good)
**WFA** 4 from 5yo+ 1lb **13** Ran SP% **120.4**
Speed ratings (Par 109): **108,107,106,106,106 105,105,105,104,104 103,103,99**
CSF £138.73 CT £1632.64 TOTE £12.80: £3.70, £3.80, £4.10; EX 170.10 Trifecta £2509.90.
**Owner** Thistle Bloodstock Limited **Bred** Thistle Bloodstock Ltd **Trained** Kells, Co Kilkenny
**FOCUS**
A valuable staying handicap which provided a 1-3 for the trainer. A pb from the winner.

## 1803 TOTEEXACTA EBF STALLIONS CONDITIONS STKS (PLUS 10 RACE) 5f 1y
**4:05** (4:08) (Class 3) 2-Y-O **£9,703** (£2,887; £1,443; £721) **Stalls** High

Form RPR
**1** **Excellently Poised** 2-9-2 0........ ConnorBeasley 9 81+
(Bryan Smart) *hld up in tch: hdwy to ld over 1f out: rdn and r.o wl fnl f* **8/1**[3]

1 **2** ¾ **Requinto Dawn (IRE)**[14] 1496 2-9-6 0........ TonyHamilton 7 82
(Richard Fahey) *pressed ldr: rdn and led briefly over 1f out: kpt on ins fnl f: hld towards fin* **11/8**[1]

3 **3** 3¾ **Rockin Fella (IRE)**[5] 1673 2-9-2 0........ PJMcDonald 5 65
(K R Burke) *led against stands' rail: rdn and hdd over 1f out: kpt on same pce fnl f* **7/2**[2]

**4** 2½ **Washeek (IRE)** 2-9-2 0........ DaneO'Neill 10 56
(Mark Johnston) *t.k.h early: trckd ldrs: rdn and edgd rt over 1f out: sn outpcd: btn ins fnl f* **7/2**[2]

**5** *2* **I Am Dandy (IRE)** 2-9-2 0........ PaulMulrennan 6 48
(James Ewart) *dwlt: sn pushed along bhd ldng gp: drvn and outpcd 1/2-way: n.d after* **22/1**

**6** ¾ **Revenge** 2-9-2 0........ DavidAllan 8 46
(Tim Easterby) *missed break: bhd and outpcd: nvr on terms* **25/1**

**7** *6* **Albarino** 2-9-2 0........ TomEaves 4 24+
(Kevin Ryan) *prom on outside tl rdn: edgd rt and wknd over 1f out* **14/1**

1m 1.4s (1.00) **Going Correction** +0.275s/f (Good) 7 Ran SP% **112.5**
Speed ratings (Par 96): **103,101,95,91,88 87,77**
CSF £18.89 TOTE £9.50: £3.40, £1.90; EX 18.20 Trifecta £66.00.
**Owner** Sir A Ferguson G Lowe H Agustsson **Bred** Crossfields Bloodstock Ltd **Trained** Hambleton, N Yorks
**FOCUS**
A decent-looking juvenile event won by a promising horse. The runner-up gives the form a solid look.

## 1804 TOTETRIFECTA EBF MAIDEN STKS 7f 33y
**4:40** (4:41) (Class 4) 3-Y-O+ **£5,175** (£1,540; £769; £384) **Stalls** Low

Form RPR
222- **1** **What's The Story**[274] 4336 3-9-0 82........ JoeFanning 1 82
(Keith Dalgleish) *chsd ldr: clsd after 3f: rdn 2f out: kpt on wl fnl f to ld last stride* **15/8**[2]

0- **2** *nse* **Sharp Defence (USA)**[107] 8574 3-9-0 0........ TadhgO'Shea 7 81
(John Patrick Shanahan, Ire) *t.k.h: led: stdd over 4f out: rdn wl over 1f out: kpt on wl fnl f: hdd last stride* **7/2**[3]

022- **3** 4½ **War Of Succession**[224] 6122 3-9-0 89........ OisinMurphy 3 69
(Andrew Balding) *dwlt: hld up bhd ldng gp: hdwy over 3f out: rdn over 2f out: kpt on same pce over 1f out* **7/4**[1]

322- **4** *nk* **Manshood (IRE)**[221] 6218 4-10-0 72........ MartinLane 4 73
(Paul Midgley) *in tch: hdwy 1/2-way: drvn over 2f out: kpt on same pce fr over 1f out* **20/1**

00- **5** 2¼ **Helovaplan (IRE)**[183] 7329 3-9-0 0........ ConnorBeasley 2 62
(Bryan Smart) *hld up: pushed along and outpcd over 2f out: n.d after* **14/1**

60 **6** 3¼ **Tambour**[44] 993 4-9-9 0........ RowanScott(5) 6 58
(Keith Dalgleish) *s.i.s: hld up: struggling over 2f out: sn wknd* **40/1**

6 **7** *8* **Chunkyfunkymonkey**[13] 1514 3-9-0 0........(b) PaulHanagan 5 32
(John Ryan) *chsd ldrs: drvn along 3f out: wknd fnl 2* **28/1**

1m 29.72s (0.72) **Going Correction** +0.05s/f (Good)
**WFA** 3 from 4yo 14lb 7 Ran SP% **110.7**
Speed ratings (Par 105): **97,96,91,91,88 85,76**
CSF £8.17 TOTE £2.90: £1.40, £1.70; EX 8.80 Trifecta £16.30.
**Owner** Weldspec Glasgow Limited **Bred** Mrs Liz Nelson Mbe **Trained** Carluke, S Lanarks
**FOCUS**
An ordinary maiden which provided a thrilling finish and a game winner who can go on to better things. The winner, 2nd and 4th set the standard.

## 1805 @TOTEPOOLRACING FOLLOW US ON TWITTER H'CAP 5f 1y
**5:10** (5:10) (Class 5) (0-75,75) 3-Y-O+ **£3,234** (£962; £481; £240) **Stalls** High

Form RPR
1-40 **1** **Royal Brave (IRE)**[15] 1475 6-9-11 **72**........ PJMcDonald 7 80
(Rebecca Bastiman) *trckd ldrs: effrt and rdn over 1f out: led ins fnl f: kpt on strly* **4/1**[1]

0035 **2** ½ **Entertaining Ben**[31] 1200 4-8-10 **64**........ JamieGormley(7) 2 70
(Iain Jardine) *pressed ldr: rdn to ld over 1f out: hdd ins fnl f: kpt on: hld nr fin* **6/1**

1-50 **3** 1¼ **One Boy (IRE)**[44] 995 6-10-0 **75**........ PaulMulrennan 1 77+
(Paul Midgley) *hld up bhd ldng gp: rdn and hdwy over 1f out: kpt on ins fnl f: nt rch first two* **11/2**[3]

010- **4** *hd* **Goninodaethat**[173] 7585 9-8-11 **58**........ SamJames 12 59
(Jim Goldie) *hld up bhd ldng gp: rdn and hdwy over 1f out: kpt on fnl f: nvr able to chal* **40/1**

04-3 **5** 3½ **Lydia's Place**[15] 1475 4-10-0 **75**........ DougieCostello 5 63
(Richard Guest) *led against stands' rail: rdn and hdd over 1f out: wknd ins fnl f* **5/1**[2]

20-4 **6** 2¾ **Reckless Serenade (IRE)**[25] 1294 3-8-7 **70**........ ShirleyTeasdale(5) 11 43
(Keith Dalgleish) *trckd ldrs: drvn along over 2f out: wknd over 1f out* **11/1**

060- **7** 2¾ **Star Cracker (IRE)**[186] 7252 5-8-11 **65**........(p) SeanMooney(7) 3 34
(Jim Goldie) *prom on outside: rdn over 2f out: wknd over 1f out* **33/1**

3220 **8** *17* **Havelock (IRE)**[33] 1179 3-9-0 **72**........ JoeFanning 6
(Mark Johnston) *in tch on outside tl rdn and wknd fr 1/2-way: eased whn no ch fnl f* **11/2**[3]

220- **9** *28* **Twentysvnthlancers**[169] 7660 4-9-8 **69**........ CamHardie 9
(Paul Midgley) *missed break: sn wl bhd: no ch and eased fr 1/2-way* **14/1**

056- **U** **Casterbridge**[180] 7413 5-9-11 **72**........(h) JasonHart 4
(Eric Alston) *rrd and uns rdr s* **13/2**

1m 1.2s (0.80) **Going Correction** +0.275s/f (Good)
**WFA** 3 from 4yo+ 11lb **10** Ran SP% **115.4**
Speed ratings (Par 103): **104,103,101,100,95 90,86,59,14,**
CSF £27.66 CT £135.58 TOTE £4.40: £1.90, £2.30, £2.20; EX 30.60 Trifecta £164.50.
**Owner** James Edgar & William Donaldson **Bred** M Fahy **Trained** Cowthorpe, N Yorks
**FOCUS**
A competitive if ordinary sprint handicap which saw the winner come from just off the pace.
T/Plt: £4,916.10 to a £1 stake. Pool: £85,295.00 - 17.35 winning units. T/Qpdt: £268.90 to a £1 stake. Pool: £5,612.00 - 20.87 winning units. **Richard Young**

1806 - 1807a (Foreign Racing) - See Raceform Interactive

# 1520 CORK (R-H)
Saturday, April 15

**OFFICIAL GOING: Good to yielding**

## 1808a IRISH STALLION FARMS EUROPEAN BREEDERS FUND NOBLESSE STKS (FILLIES) (LISTED RACE) 1m 4f
**2:45** (2:48) 4-Y-O+
**£27,735** (£8,931; £4,230; £1,880; £940; £470)

RPR
**1** **Zhukova (IRE)**[182] 7351 5-9-5 115........ PatSmullen 5 105+
(D K Weld, Ire) *settled bhd ldrs in 3rd: impr into 2nd fr 3f out: sn pushed along and prog on outer to ld gng best over 1f out: rdn briefly ins fnl f and kpt on wl clsng stages* **1/3**[1]

**2** *2* **Island Remede**[70] 7393 6-9-0 90........(b[1]) ColinKeane 7 97
(Henry De Bromhead, Ire) *sn led: 2 l clr at 1/2-way: rdn and reduced advantage fr 2f out: hdd u.p over 1f out and no imp on wnr wl ins fnl f: jst hld 2nd* **20/1**

**3** *hd* **Glamorous Approach (IRE)**[181] 7392 4-9-0 97........ KevinManning 3 98+
(J S Bolger, Ire) *chsd ldrs: 4th 1/2-way: rdn disputing 4th under 3f out and no imp on wnr in 3rd 1f out: kpt on u.p clsng stages and jst hld for 3rd: nrst fin* **12/1**

**4** *2* **Red Stars (IRE)**[273] 4416 4-9-3 101........(h) DeclanMcDonogh 6 97+
(John M Oxx, Ire) *towards rr: disp 5th at 1/2-way: rdn 2f out and sme late hdwy u.p ins fnl f where swtchd lft into 4th clsng stages: nvr trbld ldrs* **10/1**[3]

**5** *1* **Nanabad (IRE)**[13] 1525 4-9-0 84........(h) GaryHalpin 1 93
(Jarlath P Fahey, Ire) *w.w in rr: pushed along over 5f out and no imp appr st: stl in rr u.p over 1f out: r.o between horses ins fnl f: nvr nrr* **16/1**

**6** *hd* **Love Potion (IRE)**[498] 8112 4-9-0 0........ SeamieHeffernan 4 93
(A P O'Brien, Ire) *hld up in tch: disp 5th at 1/2-way: sme hdwy on outer into 2nd briefly fr 2f out: no imp on ldrs in 4th ent fnl f: one pce after and wknd between horses clsng stages* **8/1**[2]

**7** *2* **Dew Line (IRE)**[20] 1387 5-9-0 90........ GaryCarroll 2 88?
(Michael Mulvany, Ire) *broke wl to ld early sn sn hdd and settled bhd ldr: pushed along in 2nd bef st and sn lost pl: sn rdn in 3rd lost tch fr over 2f out: one pce in rr ins fnl f* **50/1**

2m 41.44s (-6.46) 7 Ran SP% **115.5**
CSF £10.27 TOTE £1.20: £1.02, £7.20; DF 11.00 Trifecta £43.90.
**Owner** Mrs C C Regalado-Gonzalez **Bred** Mrs C L Weld **Trained** Curragh, Co Kildare
**FOCUS**
A fairly workmanlike performance from the winner, but she looked like she would need the run and there should be a lot more to come.

1809 - 1812a (Foreign Racing) - See Raceform Interactive

# 1783 KEENELAND (L-H)
Saturday, April 15

**OFFICIAL GOING: Dirt: fast; turf: firm**

## 1813a GIANT'S CAUSEWAY STKS (LISTED RACE) (3YO+ FILLIES & MARES) (TURF) 5f 110y
**9:57** 3-Y-O+
**£48,780** (£16,260; £8,130; £4,065; £2,439; £271)

RPR
**1** **Lady Aurelia (USA)**[203] 6784 3-8-5 0........ JohnRVelazquez 6 111+
(Wesley A Ward, U.S.A) **1/1**[1]

**2** 2½ **Nobody's Fault (USA)**[176] 4-8-8 0........ JoseValdiviaJr 3 94+
(Neil Pessin, U.S.A) **51/1**

**3** *nk* **Ruby Notion (USA)**[533] 7626 4-8-8 0........ JoelRosario 1 93
(Wesley A Ward, U.S.A) **113/10**

**4** 1¼ **Triple Chelsea (USA)**[419] 4-8-8 0........ RobbyAlbarado 2 89
(Anthony Granitz, U.S.A) **69/10**

**5** ½ **Miss Katie Mae (IRE)**[161] 7829 4-8-8 0........ JoseLOrtiz 11 87
(H Graham Motion, U.S.A) **116/10**

**6** ½ **Rapid Rhythm (USA)**[216] 5-8-8 0........ JamesGraham 5 86
(Michael Stidham, U.S.A) **187/10**

**7** *3* **Exaggerated (USA)** 5-8-8 0........ FlavienPrat 4 76
(Arnaud Delacour, U.S.A) **66/10**[3]

**8** *nse* **Pretty Perfection (USA)** 5-8-13 0........(b) NikJuarez 9 81
(Kelly Breen, U.S.A) **31/5**[2]

**9** 2½ **Lots O' Lex (USA)**[35] 6-8-8 0........ JesusLopezCastanon 7 67
(Gerald Russel Aschinger, U.S.A) **94/1**

**10** *nk* **Bibby (USA)**[668] 5-8-8 0........ JoseLezcano 8 66
(Victoria H Oliver, U.S.A) **68/1**



The Form Book Flat, Raceform Ltd, Newbury, RG14 5SJ

11 3¾ **Lajatico**[98] 4-8-8 0 ........ FlorentGeroux 10 54
(Doug O'Neill, U.S.A) 22/1

1m 2.4s
**WFA** 3 from 4yo+ 11lb 11 Ran SP% **119.6**

**Owner** Stonestreet Stables/G Bolton/P Leidel **Bred** Stonestreet Thoroughbred Holdings LLC **Trained** North America

**FOCUS**
The return of last year's European Champion 2yo filly, and she didn't disappoint.

1814 - 1816a (Foreign Racing) - See Raceform Interactive

## [1587]SOUTHWELL (L-H)
### Sunday, April 16

**OFFICIAL GOING: Fibresand: standard**
Wind: light and behind runners in home straight Weather: Overcast

## 1817 ROBINS MILESTONE CELEBRATION H'CAP 1m 13y(F)
**2:15** (2:15) (Class 6) (0-60,65) 3-Y-O **£2,264** (£673; £336; £168) **Stalls** Low

Form RPR
00-5 **1** **Crucial Moment**[9] [1597] 3-8-8 **52** ........ RyanWhile(5) 3 61
(Bill Turner) *trckd ldrs: rdn to chal 2f out: led ent fnl f: kpt on* **20/1**

005- **2** *nk* **Cliff Bay (IRE)**[198] [6923] 3-8-11 **55** ........(p[1]) RowanScott(5) 7 64
(Keith Dalgleish) *trckd ldrs on outside: rdn over 2f out: chal over 1f out: edgd lft ins fnl f: kpt on* **7/1**

6101 **3** 3¾ **Chamasay**[12] [1545] 3-9-5 **65** ........ DavidEgan(7) 5 65
(David Evans) *trckd ldrs: rdn to ld narrowly 2f out: hdd ent fnl f: wknd fnl 110yds* **11/4**[1]

00-6 **4** *1* **Jive Factor (USA)**[17] [1445] 3-9-8 **61** ........ SilvestreDeSousa 4 59
(Ed Dunlop) *w ldr: led narrowly over 2f out: sn rdn: hdd 2f out: one pce in 4th fr appr fnl f* **11/4**[1]

56-4 **5** *3* **Shambra (IRE)**[18] [1434] 3-9-5 **58** ........ TonyHamilton 1 49
(Roger Fell) *dwlt but sn led narrowly: rdn whn hdd over 2f out: wknd over 1f out* **20/1**

6-40 **6** 2½ **Forest Angel (IRE)**[37] [1123] 3-9-7 **60** ........(p[1]) LukeMorris 6 45
(James Tate) *hld up: pushed along over 4f out: rdn 3f out: sn btn* **6/1**[3]

050 **7** *19* **Seeking Attention (USA)**[20] [1401] 3-9-3 **56** ........(h[1]) OisinMurphy 2 +
(George Scott) *sn pushed along in rr: a bhd: eased over 1f out* **3/1**[2]

1m 45.18s (1.48) **Going Correction** +0.15s/f (Slow) 7 Ran SP% **114.6**
Speed ratings (Par 96): **98,97,93,92,89 87,68**
CSF £148.89 TOTE £20.40: £6.00, £4.00; EX 154.00 Trifecta £266.10.
**Owner** E A Brook **Bred** Cheveley Park Stud Ltd **Trained** Sigwells, Somerset

**FOCUS**
Morning market moves suggested we would see improved performances from one or two of these but that failed to materialise and this potentially interesting 3yo handicap was won by the outsider of the field, who has been rated just off his best 2yo figure.

## 1818 LUCKY HOLLINBRIDGE PARTNERSHIP MAIDEN STKS 1m 13y(F)
**2:45** (2:46) (Class 5) 3-Y-O+ **£2,911** (£866; £432; £216) **Stalls** Low

Form RPR
0- **1** **Flashy Snapper**[162] [7812] 3-9-0 0 ........ SilvestreDeSousa 1 91+
(Simon Crisford) *mde all: pushed clr fr 3f out: styd on strly: v easily* **7/4**[1]

40- **2** *11* **Vernatti**[182] [7384] 4-9-9 0 ........ RobHornby 10 62
(Pam Sly) *midfield on outside: rdn and hdwy into modest 2nd 2f out: plugged on but no ch w wnr* **20/1**

64 **3** *6* **Magic Pass**[29] [1259] 3-9-0 0 ........ OisinMurphy 12 49
(Andrew Balding) *chsd ldrs towards outer: rdn 3f out: one pce in poor 3rd fr wl over 1f out* **9/2**[2]

**4** ¾ **Kensington Palace (IRE)** 4-10-0 0 ........ BarryMcHugh 8 51+
(Marjorie Fife) *s.i.s: spoon pushed along towards rr: rdn and hdwy on inner over 2f out* **25/1**

-232 **5** *5* **Ceyhan**[64] [687] 5-10-0 76 ........ TimmyMurphy 11 40
(Jamie Osborne) *prom towards outer: rdn over 2f out: wknd over 1f out* **9/2**[2]

6 **6** 1½ **Albert's Back**[15] [1497] 3-8-7 0 ........ HarrisonShaw(7) 5 33
(Michael Easterby) *dwlt: sn pushed along towards rr: minor late hdwy: nvr threatened* **8/1**[3]

0- **7** 3¼ **Time To Sea (IRE)**[222] [6211] 3-9-0 0 ........ LiamKeniry 7 25
(John Butler) *hld up: pushed along over 3f out: nvr threatened* **14/1**

25 **8** 2¾ **Hot Natured (IRE)**[44] [1003] 3-8-9 0 ........ PJMcDonald 4 14
(K R Burke) *prom: rdn over 3f out: wknd over 2f out* **17/2**

2603 **9** 2¾ **Ertidaad (IRE)**[12] [1544] 5-10-0 45 ........(v) TonyHamilton 3 16
(Emma Owen) *a towards rr* **33/1**

6 **10** *nk* **Doodle Dandy (IRE)**[11] [1552] 4-9-9 0 ........ JimmyQuinn 2
(David Bridgwater) *prom: lost pl qckly 6f and sn towards rr: wknd over 2f out* **28/1**

0-6 **11** *7* **Davinci Dawn**[16] [1471] 3-8-9 0 ........ ShaneGray 6
(Ann Duffield) *chsd ldrs: rdn over 3f out: sn wknd* **66/1**

5-0 **12** *55* **Double Dutch**[27] [1287] 3-9-0 0 ........ RobertWinston 9
(John Butler) *hld up in rr on outside: wknd and eased fr over 1f out* **66/1**

1m 44.04s (0.34) **Going Correction** +0.15s/f (Slow)
**WFA** 3 from 4yo+ 14lb 12 Ran SP% **119.0**
Speed ratings (Par 103): **104,93,87,86,81 79,76,73,71,70 63,8**
CSF £46.61 TOTE £3.00: £1.60, £5.30, £1.80; EX 53.80 Trifecta £197.10.
**Owner** Hamad Rashed Bin Ghedayer **Bred** Cliveden Stud Ltd **Trained** Newmarket, Suffolk

**FOCUS**
No depth to this and the winner proved in a different league.

## 1819 DAVIDS DASH H'CAP 4f 214y(F)
**3:20** (3:20) (Class 5) (0-70,72) 4-Y-O+ **£2,911** (£866; £432; £216) **Stalls** Centre

Form RPR
0-13 **1** **Zylan (IRE)**[4] [1722] 5-8-7 **63** ........ BenSanderson(7) 4 81+
(Roger Fell) *prom: pushed along to ld 2f out: kpt on wl and sn clr: easily* **10/11**[1]

340- **2** *6* **Indian Tinker**[200] [6879] 8-9-3 **66** ........ AdamBeschizza 3 62
(Robert Cowell) *led: rdn whn hdd 2f out: one pce and sn no ch w wnr* **12/1**

0314 **3** ½ **Big Amigo (IRE)**[12] [1542] 4-9-4 **72** ........ LewisEdmunds(5) 6 67
(Daniel Mark Loughnane) *hld up: rdn along 1/2-way: kpt on fnl f: wnt 3rd 110yds out* **3/1**[2]

530- **4** 1¼ **Flash City (ITY)**[187] [7252] 9-9-7 **70** ........ JamesSullivan 2 60
(Ruth Carr) *trckd ldrs: rdn and outpcd 1/2-way: plugged on* **9/1**[3]

20-0 **5** *shd* **Silver Bid (USA)**[18] [1431] 5-8-8 **62** ........ GemmaTutty(5) 5 52
(Karen Tutty) *slowly away: sn pushed along in rr: kpt on fnl f: nvr threatened* **9/1**[3]

500- **6** 1¼ **Corridor Kid (IRE)**[200] [6879] 4-9-7 **70** ........(v) TonyHamilton 8 55
(Derek Shaw) *prom: rdn 1/2-way: wknd fnl f* **25/1**

-000 **7** *9* **King Crimson**[40] [1071] 5-9-4 **67** ........ TimmyMurphy 7 20
(John Butler) *racd keenly: trckd ldrs: pushed along 2f out: edgd lft and wknd over 1f out: eased* **33/1**

4000 **8** 3¼ **Waneen (IRE)**[27] [1290] 4-9-2 **65** ........ RobertWinston 1 6
(John Butler) *chsd ldrs: rdn along and lost pl 3f out: sn in rr and btn* **20/1**

58.99s (-0.71) **Going Correction** 0.0s/f (Stan) 8 Ran SP% **116.6**
Speed ratings (Par 103): **105,95,94,92,92 90,76,70**
CSF £13.81 CT £26.51 TOTE £1.80: £1.10, £2.80, £1.20; EX 13.70 Trifecta £30.60.
**Owner** R G Fell **Bred** Philip And Mrs Jane Myerscough **Trained** Nawton, N Yorks

**FOCUS**
No great depth to this but the winner is 2-2 here now.

## 1820 MASON JAMES YOUNG RACE GOER H'CAP 6f 16y(F)
**3:55** (3:55) (Class 4) (0-80,85) 3-Y-O+ **£4,690** (£1,395; £697; £348) **Stalls** Low

Form RPR
4121 **1** **Treaty Of Rome (USA)**[18] [1431] 5-9-2 **69** ........(v) TonyHamilton 2 80+
(Derek Shaw) *trckd ldr: stalked ldr gng wl 2f out: pushed along to ld 1f out: drvn and kpt on* **7/2**[1]

1241 **2** 1½ **Vroom (IRE)**[10] [1592] 4-9-4 **78** ........(p) RhiainIngram(7) 1 83
(Gay Kelleway) *led narrowly: rdn 2f out: hdd 1f out: kpt on same pce* **8/1**

3031 **3** *nk* **Dark Forest**[10] [1593] 4-9-1 **68** ........(p) BarryMcHugh 9 72
(Marjorie Fife) *hld up on outer: rdn along 3f out: hdwy to chse ldr appr fnl f: kpt on* **7/2**[1]

050- **4** 1¼ **English Hero**[153] [7959] 4-9-1 **68** ........ LukeMorris 7 68
(John Mackie) *midfield: rdn over 2f out: hdwy over 1f out: kpt on same pce* **9/1**

531- **5** *5* **Big Lachie**[148] [8033] 3-9-2 **80** ........ TimmyMurphy 6 61
(Jamie Osborne) *trckd ldrs: pushed along 2f out: wknd over 1f out* **7/1**

3151 **6** 1¾ **Crosse Fire**[12] [1542] 5-9-12 **79** ........ KieranO'Neill 5 57
(Scott Dixon) *pressed ldr: rdn over 2f out: wknd over 1f out* **11/2**[2]

6511 **7** 3¼ **Fujin**[10] [1586] 6-9-13 **85** ........(v) CharlieBennett(5) 4 53
(Shaun Harris) *dwlt: hld up: rdn 3f out: nvr threatened* **6/1**[3]

240- **8** *5* **Pea Shooter**[221] [6234] 8-10-1 **82** ........ BenCurtis 8 34
(Brian Ellison) *hld up: rdn wl over 2f out: sn wknd* **16/1**

1m 17.24s (0.74) **Going Correction** +0.15s/f (Slow)
**WFA** 3 from 4yo+ 11lb 8 Ran SP% **113.6**
Speed ratings (Par 105): **101,99,98,96,90 87,83,76**
CSF £31.68 CT £104.32 TOTE £3.90: £1.40, £2.50, £1.60; EX 28.00 Trifecta £115.50.
**Owner** John R Saville **Bred** Fred W Hertrich III & John D Fielding **Trained** Sproxton, Leics

**FOCUS**
A competitive contest featuring several Fibresand specialists; the front four pulled clear but the result never really looked in doubt all the way up the straight. An improving winner.

## 1821 HAPPY BIRTHDAY LAURA H'CAP 4f 214y(F)
**4:30** (4:30) (Class 6) (0-60,60) 3-Y-O **£2,264** (£673; £336; £168) **Stalls** Centre

Form RPR
2313 **1** **Gnaad (IRE)**[22] [1363] 3-9-5 **58** ........(p) LukeMorris 6 72
(Robert Cowell) *mde all: pushed along 2f: kpt on wl to draw clr fr over 1f out: easily* **11/8**[1]

00-3 **2** *4* **Maggi May (IRE)**[18] [1432] 3-8-11 **50** ........ OisinMurphy 1 51
(David Brown) *pressed ldr: rdn 1/2-way: one pce and hld in 2nd fr over 1f out* **11/4**[2]

0024 **3** 2½ **Billy's Boots**[16] [1474] 3-9-7 **60** ........ SilvestreDeSousa 2 51
(J R Jenkins) *chsd ldrs: rdn 1/2-way: one pce in 3rd fr over 1f out* **11/4**[2]

00-5 **4** 4½ **Vicky Park**[24] [1321] 3-8-0 **46** ........ JaneElliott(7) 4 21
(George Margarson) *prom: rdn 1/2-way: wknd over 1f out* **10/1**[3]

-400 **5** *3* **Mesmeric Moment**[32] [1204] 3-8-7 **46** ........(v) JimmyQuinn 5 10
(Shaun Harris) *dwlt: a outpcd in rr* **16/1**

1m 0.36s (0.66) **Going Correction** 0.0s/f (Stan) 5 Ran SP% **110.4**
Speed ratings (Par 96): **94,87,83,76,71**
CSF £5.46 TOTE £1.60: £1.10, £2.30; EX 4.60 Trifecta £7.90.
**Owner** Ahmed Jaber **Bred** Rabbah Bloodstock Limited **Trained** Six Mile Bottom, Cambs

**FOCUS**
A weak handicap won in good style by the short-priced favourite, who progressed to take his record to 2-2 here.

## 1822 GRAHAMS 57TH BIRTHDAY PARTY H'CAP 1m 4f 14y(F)
**5:05** (5:05) (Class 6) (0-60,62) 3-Y-O **£2,264** (£673; £336; £168) **Stalls** Low

Form RPR
60-3 **1** **Look My Way**[8] [1623] 3-9-9 **62** ........ OisinMurphy 4 73+
(Andrew Balding) *trckd ldrs: pushed along to ld narrowly wl over 2f out: rdn over 1f out: edgd lft but styd on wl to draw clr fnl f: eased towards fin* **5/2**[2]

060- **2** *4* **Dirty Randy (IRE)**[170] [7659] 3-9-2 **60** ........(p[1]) RowanScott(5) 3 63
(Keith Dalgleish) *trckd ldrs: rdn and outpcd over 3f out: styd on fr over 1f: wnt 2nd 110yds out: no ch w wnr* **9/1**

000- **3** 2¾ **Twiston Shout (IRE)**[144] [8063] 3-8-7 **49** ........ HectorCrouch(3) 1 47
(Richard Spencer) *led: rdn whn hdd narrowly wl over 2f out: wknd fnl f: lost 2nd 110yds out* **16/1**

54-1 **4** *7* **Padleyourowncanoe**[38] [1107] 3-9-5 **58** ........ LukeMorris 6 45
(Daniel Mark Loughnane) *sn midfield: wnt in snatches: rdn 4f out: sn btn* **11/10**[1]

00-4 **5** *7* **Our Cilla**[16] [1468] 3-8-4 **46** oh1 ........(b[1]) ShelleyBirkett(3) 2 22
(Julia Feilden) *prom: rdn over 3f out: sn wknd* **50/1**

5560 **6** 1¾ **Log Off (IRE)**[17] [1445] 3-8-10 **56** ........ DavidEgan(7) 7 29
(David Evans) *s.i.s: hld up: rdn over 3f out: sn wknd* **11/2**[3]

053- **7** *30* **Generous Times**[270] [4509] 3-8-8 **47** ........ ConnorBeasley 5
(Chris Grant) *hld up: rdn 4f out: sn wknd and bhd* **40/1**

2m 43.3s (2.30) **Going Correction** +0.15s/f (Slow) 7 Ran SP% **111.9**
Speed ratings (Par 96): **98,95,93,88,84 83,63**
CSF £23.60 TOTE £2.40: £1.70, £4.20; EX 26.40 Trifecta £152.70.
**Owner** Kingsclere Racing Club **Bred** Kingsclere Stud **Trained** Kingsclere, Hants

**FOCUS**
Some of these might do better in the future but this was one-way traffic up the straight, with the winner putting up an improved performance.

## 1823 IMPERIAL D JAY H'CAP 7f 14y(F)
**5:40** (5:40) (Class 6) (0-60,61) 4-Y-O+ **£2,264** (£673; £336; £168) **Stalls** Low

Form RPR
3366 **1** **Fortinbrass (IRE)**[10] [1593] 7-9-4 **61** ........ LewisEdmunds(5) 4 67
(John Balding) *chsd ldr: rdn over 2f out: led 110yds out: kpt on* **11/2**[3]

4040 **2** *hd* **Canford Belle**[17] [1456] 4-8-12 **50** ........ PaddyAspell 8 55
(Grant Tuer) *trckd ldrs towards outer: rdn to ld wl over 1f out: edgd lft ent fnl f: hdd 110yds out: kpt on* **6/1**

0044 **3** ¾ **Quadriga (IRE)**[12] 1544 7-8-7 **45**..............................(b) JimmyQuinn 1 48
(Chris Grant) *trckd ldrs: rdn and ev ch 2f out: one pce in 3rd fnl f* **7/1**
0223 **4** *hd* **General Tufto**[12] 1545 12-8-13 **51**..............................(b) JoeyHaynes 2 54
(Charles Smith) *hld up: rdn over 3f out: kpt on wl fnl f: nrst fin* **5/1**[2]
00-0 **5** *1* **Danot (IRE)**[16] 1473 5-9-7 **59**.............................. JackGarritty 10 59
(Jedd O'Keeffe) *w ldr: rdn over 2f out: already losing position whn sltly hmpd ins fnl f: no ex* **7/1**
66-1 **6** 1 ¾ **Grey Destiny**[20] 1408 7-9-6 **58**.............................. CamHardie 7 53
(Antony Brittain) *s.i.s: hld up on outer: sltly hmpd and carried even wdr on bnd over 4f out: pushed along over 2f out: nvr threatened* **9/2**[1]
0300 **7** *8* **Raise The Game (IRE)**[30] 1249 4-9-1 **58**.............................. RyanWhile(5) 6 32
(Bill Turner) *w ldr: rdn to ld narrowly over 2f out: hdd wl over 1f out: sn wknd and eased* **12/1**
0600 **8** *4* **Storming Ambition**[10] 1593 4-8-7 **45**..............................(t) LukeMorris 3 8
(Conrad Allen) *led narrowly: rdn whn hdd over 2f out: sn wknd* **50/1**
-560 **9** 1 ½ **Last Star Falling (IRE)**[15] 1490 4-9-7 **59**.............................. KieranO'Neill 9 18
(Henry Spiller) *a rr* **20/1**
116- **10** *26* **Amy Blair**[187] 7249 4-8-13 **56**..............................(h) ShirleyTeasdale(5) 5 +
(Keith Dalgleish) *awkward s and rdr lost iron: rdr wout both irons and plld way to be prom on wd outside 5f out: wknd 3f out and sn bhd* **7/1**

1m 33.0s (2.70) **Going Correction** +0.15s/f (Slow) **10** Ran SP% **116.4**
Speed ratings (Par 101): **90,89,88,88,87 85,76,71,70,40**
CSF £38.45 CT £240.26 TOTE £6.00: £2.00, £2.30, £1.70; EX 48.70 Trifecta £360.90.
**Owner** Billy Herring **Bred** Tom Wallace **Trained** Scrooby, S Yorks

**FOCUS**
A modest but open handicap featuring a handful of course winners.
T/Plt: £197.40 to a £1 stake. Pool: £54,897.00 - 277.97 winning units. T/Qpdt: £5.30 to a £1 stake. Pool: £4,367.00 - 809.85 winning units. **Andrew Sheret**

# 1657 CHANTILLY (R-H)

## Sunday, April 16

**OFFICIAL GOING: Polytrack: standard; turf: good**

## 1824a PRIX DE FONTAINEBLEAU (GROUP 3) (3YO COLTS) (TURF) 1m

**2:45** 3-Y-0 **£34,188** (£13,675; £10,256; £6,837; £3,418)

RPR

**1** **Brametot (IRE)**[187] 7263 3-9-2 0.............................. CristianDemuro 5 115+
(J-C Rouget, France) *missed break: detached in rr: grad clsd to be last but in tch 3f out: hdwy on outer 2f out: cl 4th and styng on 1 1/2f out: drvn to ld ent fnl f: sn clr: comf* **41/10**
**2** 2 ½ **Stunning Spirit**[19] 1415 3-9-2 0.............................. AurelienLemaitre 4 109
(F Head, France) *racd v keenly: hld up and bhd ldrs: shkn up to chal between horses over 1f out: rdn and kpt on at same pce fnl f* **22/5**
**3** *hd* **Spotify (FR)**[45] 3-9-2 0..............................(b) MaximeGuyon 7 109
(C Ferland, France) *chsd ldr on outer: scrubbed along to ld 1 1/2f out: hdd ent fnl f: kpt on at same pce u.p* **4/1**[3]
**4** *3* **Markazi (FR)**[28] 1269 3-9-2 0.............................. ChristopheSoumillon 6 102
(J-C Rouget, France) *w.w wl in tch: 6th and rdn over 1 1/2f out but nt qckn: kpt on at one pce fnl f: nvr a threat* **18/5**[2]
**5** 2 ½ **Xaarino (FR)**[245] 5450 3-9-2 0.............................. Pierre-CharlesBoudot 3 96
(A Fabre, France) *hld up in cl 6th: drvn 2 1/2f out and dropped to last: rdn over 1 1/2f out: kpt on past btn horses late on: nvr in contention* **23/10**[1]
**6** ¾ **Greyway (FR)**[31] 1236 3-9-2 0.............................. IoritzMendizabal 2 95
(J-M Lefebvre, France) *racd keenly and led under a tight hold: hdd 1 1/2f out: dropped away fnl f* **31/1**
**7** 3 ½ **Incampo (FR)**[20] 3-9-2 0.............................. MickaelBarzalona 1 87
(H-A Pantall, France) *w.w in tch: outpcd and drvn wl over 1 1/2f out: bhd fnl f* **169/10**

1m 35.18s (-2.82) **7** Ran SP% **118.9**
PARI-MUTUEL (all including 1 euro stake): WIN 5.10 PLACE 2.80, 2.30 SF 20.50.
**Owner** G Augustin-Normand & Mme E Vidal **Bred** H Cardemil **Trained** Pau, France

## 1825a PRIX DE LA GROTTE - ETALON KENDARGENT (GROUP 3) (3YO FILLIES) (TURF) 1m

**3:30** 3-Y-0 **£34,188** (£13,675; £10,256; £6,837; £3,418)

RPR

**1** **Senga (USA)**[196] 6986 3-9-0 0.............................. StephanePasquier 5 108+
(P Bary, France) *racd keenly: hld up in 4th: j. path after 2 1/2f: drvn to cl under 2f out: led ins fnl 1 1/2f: r.o fnl f: won a shade cosily* **1/1**[1]
**2** *1* **La Sardane (FR)**[28] 1270 3-9-0 0..............................(p) FranckBlondel 2 106
(B De Montzey, France) *wnt lft s and led: drvn wl under 2f out: hdd 1 1/2f out: styd on gamely fnl f* **31/1**
**3** ½ **Lady Frankel**[28] 3-9-0 0.............................. Pierre-CharlesBoudot 4 105+
(A Fabre, France) *hld up in fnl pair: angled out and drvn w under 2f to run: styd on fnl f: nt pce to get on terms* **29/10**[2]
**4** *snk* **Toulifaut (IRE)**[196] 6986 3-9-0 0.............................. ChristopheSoumillon 6 104
(J-C Rouget, France) *t.k.h: hld up in fnl pair: clsd between horses 1 1/2f out: chsd ldng pair ins fnl f: one pce u.p: lost 3rd late on* **3/1**[3]
**5** *7* **Body Sculpt (FR)**[28] 1270 3-9-0 0..............................(h) MaximeGuyon 3 88
(S Kobayashi, France) *racd keenly: chsd ldr on outer: cl 2nd and drvn 2f out: sn btn: wknd fnl f* **18/1**
**6** 2 ½ **Beauty Of Love**[198] 6937 3-9-0 0.............................. MickaelBarzalona 1 82
(Mme Pia Brandt, France) *plld hrd: hld up bhd ldr on inner: drvn and no imp 1 1/2f out: wknd fnl f* **81/10**

1m 40.3s (2.30) **6** Ran SP% **120.0**
PARI-MUTUEL (all including 1 euro stake): WIN 2.00 PLACE 1.30, 5.70 SF 42.60.
**Owner** Flaxman Stables Ireland Ltd **Bred** Flaxman Holdings Limited **Trained** Chantilly, France

## 1826a PRIX NOAILLES (GROUP 3) (3YO) (TURF) 1m 2f 110y

**4:10** 3-Y-0 **£34,188** (£13,675; £10,256; £6,837; £3,418)

RPR

**1** **Soleil Marin (IRE)**[24] 1336 3-9-2 0.............................. MickaelBarzalona 3 108+
(A Fabre, France) *settled cl up 4th on outer: drvn to chal outside three rivals 1 1/2f out: led briefly 1f out but sn hdd: rallied to join ldr sn after: r.o u.p: led again fnl 50yds* **29/10**[2]
**2** *hd* **Akihiro (JPN)**[220] 6270 3-9-2 0.............................. MaximeGuyon 5 108+
(A Fabre, France) *w.w in fnl trio: 5th and drvn 2f out: hdwy on outer 1 1/2f fr home: styd on u.p and led ins fnl f: jnd sn after and r.o: hdd narrowly 50yds out: no ex* **2/5**[1]
**3** 1 ½ **Normandy Eagle (IRE)**[36] 1157 3-9-2 0.............................. AurelienLemaitre 1 105
(F Head, France) *racd keenly: hld up bhd front two: drvn to chal between horses 1 1/2f out: kpt on at same pce fnl f* **71/10**[3]
**4** ¾ **Galipad**[11] 3-9-2 0.............................. VincentCheminaud 2 104
(A Fabre, France) *led: hdd 2 1/2f out: rallied gamely u.p and led again 2f out: kpt on wout qckning fnl f* **38/1**
**5** *shd* **Amazing (FR)**[24] 1336 3-9-2 0.............................. AntoineHamelin 6 103+
(F Vermeulen, France) *w.w in fnl trio on inner: drvn and styd on over 1f out: nt pce to get on terms* **20/1**
**6** *snk* **Saldier (FR)**[27] 3-9-2 0.............................. JeromeMoutard 7 103
(T Castanheira, France) *dwlt: w.w in rr: styd on u.p over 1f out: nvr on terms* **68/1**
**7** ½ **Go Fast (IRE)**[24] 1336 3-9-2 0..............................(h) GregoryBenoist 4 102
(N Caullery, France) *pressed ldr on outer: led 2 1/2f out: drvn and no ex whn hdd 2f out: grad dropped away* **33/1**

2m 8.34s (-0.46) **7** Ran SP% **121.1**
PARI-MUTUEL (all including 1 euro stake): WIN 3.90 PLACE 1.20, 1.10 SF 6.70.
**Owner** Godolphin SNC **Bred** Ecurie Peregrine SAS **Trained** Chantilly, France

1827 - (Foreign Racing) - See Raceform Interactive

# 1673 REDCAR (L-H)

## Monday, April 17

**OFFICIAL GOING: Good (good to firm in places; 8.6)**
Wind: light half against, making no material difference Weather: Cloudy

## 1828 TOTEPLACEPOT SIX PLACES IN SIX RACES FILLIES' H'CAP 5f

**2:05** (2:07) (Class 5) (0-75,76) 3-Y-0+ **£3,881** (£1,155; £577; £288) **Stalls** Centre

Form RPR

01- **1** **Carlton Frankie**[192] 7122 3-9-0 **74**.............................. NathanEvans(3) 12 83+
(Michael Easterby) *mde all: pushed along over 1f out: rdn out ins fnl f: shade cosily* **2/1**[1]
3-11 **2** *1* **Kinloch Pride**[5] 1722 5-8-4 **56** oh4..............................(p) PhilDennis(5) 11 65
(Noel Wilson) *chsd ldrs: rdn to chse wnr over 1f out: kpt on but a hld* **6/1**[3]
050- **3** 2 ¼ **Kachess**[206] 6734 3-9-5 **76**.............................. RichardKingscote 4 73+
(Tom Dascombe) *dwlt and squeezed out s: hld up: rdn and outpcd in rr 1/2-way: kpt on wl fnl f: nrst fin* **7/2**[2]
530- **4** ½ **Rose Eclair**[174] 7591 4-9-10 **71**..............................(b) DavidAllan 7 70
(Tim Easterby) *midfield: rdn over 2f out: kpt on fnl f* **16/1**
325- **5** ¾ **Eternalist**[129] 8290 4-8-11 **58**..............................(h) SamJames 3 54
(Jim Goldie) *chsd ldrs: rdn over 2f out: carried lft over 1f out: kpt on same pce fnl f* **28/1**
30-6 **6** *nk* **Lady Molly (IRE)**[33] 1204 3-8-0 **62**..............................(p[1]) RowanScott(5) 10 53
(Keith Dalgleish) *chsd ldrs: rdn and outpcd over 2f out: plugged on ins fnl f* **25/1**
65-5 **7** *1* **Swirral Edge**[17] 1475 4-10-0 **75**.............................. PatCosgrave 5 67
(David Brown) *half stmbld and squeezed out s: hld up: pushed along 2f out: nvr threatened* **8/1**
03-3 **8** ¾ **Emerald Secret (IRE)**[17] 1474 3-8-3 **60**..............................(p) CamHardie 2 45
(Paul Midgley) *hld up towards far side: rdn over 2f out: nvr threatened* **12/1**
510- **9** *1* **Bond Bombshell**[188] 7252 4-9-5 **73**.............................. PatrickVaughan(7) 9 58
(David O'Meara) *prom: rdn over 2f out: hung lft over 1f out and wknd* **20/1**
616- **10** ½ **Mininggold**[188] 7252 4-9-2 **70**.............................. CallumRodriguez(7) 6 54
(Michael Dods) *hld up: pushed along over 2f out: wknd over 1f out* **12/1**
630- **11** 2 ¼ **Caymus**[160] 7860 4-8-9 **56** oh10..............................(t) BenCurtis 1 32
(Tracy Waggott) *dwlt: hld up towards far side: rdn 1/2-way: wknd over 1f out* **66/1**

58.94s (0.34) **Going Correction** -0.025s/f (Good)
**WFA** 3 from 4yo+ 10lb **11** Ran SP% **115.8**
Speed ratings (Par 100): **96,94,90,90,88 88,86,85,83,83 79**
CSF £13.20 CT £40.24 TOTE £3.20: £1.40, £1.90, £1.60; EX 12.70 Trifecta £40.90.
**Owner** Padgett Hollings Hull Fielding Hoskins **Bred** D Curran **Trained** Sheriff Hutton, N Yorks

**FOCUS**
The watered ground (4mm overnight Thursday and Friday, 2mm overnight Saturday) was given as good, good to firm in places (GoingStick 8.6). An ordinary sprint but, with the runner-up very much in form and the winner considered good enough to have been tried in Listed company on her debut, the form looks sound for the grade.

## 1829 TOTEPOOL HAPPY EASTER MAIDEN STKS (DIV I) 7f 219y

**2:35** (2:37) (Class 5) 3-Y-0+ **£3,881** (£1,155; £577; £288) **Stalls** Centre

Form RPR

3-3 **1** **Carigrad (IRE)**[16] 1488 3-9-0 0..............................(h[1]) JosephineGordon 6 76
(Hugo Palmer) *chsd ldrs: rdn over 2f out: drvn and kpt on fnl f: led towards fin* **11/4**[2]
33-6 **2** *nk* **Armandihan (IRE)**[47] 970 3-9-0 80.............................. KevinStott 12 75
(Kevin Ryan) *led: hung lft appr fnl f: rdn and one pce ins fnl f: hdd towards fin* **9/4**[1]
**3** 1 ¼ **Mellor Brook (IRE)** 3-9-0 0.............................. ConnorBeasley 5 73+
(Bryan Smart) *dwlt: sn midfield: pushed along over 2f out: rdn and gd hdwy over 1f out: kpt on fnl f: short of room towards fin* **6/1**
3 **4** *nk* **Ninepin Bowler**[24] 1347 3-9-0 0.............................. PaulMulrennan 10 71
(Michael Dods) *chsd ldrs: pushed along to chse ldr over 2f out: rdn and edgd lft over 1f out: kpt on ins fnl f* **11/2**[3]
54- **5** *1* **Glorvina (IRE)**[206] 6741 3-8-6 0.............................. ShelleyBirkett(3) 4 64
(David O'Meara) *in tch: pushed along over 2f out: kpt on ins fnl f* **11/1**
**6** 2 ¼ **Senatus (FR)**[23] 5-10-0 0..............................(h) GrahamLee 9 67
(Karen McLintock) *v.s.a: hld up in rr: pushed along 3f out: kpt on fr over 1f out: nrst fin* **14/1**
-030 **7** 3 ¾ **Sandstream**[47] 969 4-10-0 46..............................(t) RoystonFfrench 2 58?
(Tracy Waggott) *prom: rdn over 2f out: wknd over 1f out* **100/1**
6 **8** *7* **Rock Island Line**[15] 1513 3-9-0 0.............................. DougieCostello 7 38
(Mark Walford) *midfield: pushed along 3f out: wknd fnl 2f* **20/1**
40 **9** 2 ¼ **Dan's Hopeforglory**[26] 1308 5-9-9 0.............................. AndrewMullen 8 31
(Peter Niven) *s.i.s: hld up: nvr threatened* **80/1**
**10** *nk* **Acid Test** 3-9-0 0.............................. JackGarritty 11 32
(Jedd O'Keeffe) *in tch: pushed along and lost pl over 3f out: sn wknd* **25/1**
0- **11** *7* **Zaytoon (IRE)**[233] 5907 4-10-0 0.............................. TomEaves 1 19
(Micky Hammond) *hld up: nudged along over 2f out: nvr threatened* **125/1**
500/ **12** 2 ¾ **In Due Time (IRE)**[672] 3227 5-10-0 60.............................. NeilFarley 3 12
(Alan Swinbank) *a rr* **66/1**

1m 38.03s (1.43) **Going Correction** -0.025s/f (Good)
**WFA** 3 from 4yo+ 14lb **12** Ran SP% **115.2**
Speed ratings (Par 103): **91,90,89,89,88 85,82,75,72,72 65,62**
CSF £8.62 TOTE £3.70: £1.30, £1.40, £2.30; EX 11.00 Trifecta £44.10.



The Form Book Flat, Raceform Ltd, Newbury, RG14 5SJ

**Owner** V I Araci **Bred** Earl Ecurie Du Grand Chene & N Drion **Trained** Newmarket, Suffolk
**FOCUS**
This was 7lb faster than division two, but the proximity of the 7th clouds bare form.

## 1830 TOTEPOOL HAPPY EASTER MAIDEN STKS (DIV II) 7f 219y
**3:10** (3:13) (Class 5) 3-Y-0+ **£3,881** (£1,155; £577; £288) **Stalls** Centre

Form RPR
4-2 1 **Everything For You (IRE)**[30] 1259 3-9-0 0........................ TomEaves 1 81
(Kevin Ryan) *cl up: led 1/2-way: hrd pressed over 1f out: kpt on gamely to assert towards fin* **11/4**[1]
02- 2 ¾ **Merlin**[214] 6523 3-9-0 0........................ PatCosgrave 10 79
(Michael Bell) *trckd ldrs gng wl: smooth hdwy to chal over 1f out: sn drvn along: kpt on fnl f: hld nr fin* **5/1**[2]
3 4½ **Playwriter (IRE)** 3-9-0 0........................ MartinLane 9 68+
(Charlie Appleby) *dwlt: t.k.h in rr: stdy hdwy on nr side of gp over 2f out: sn pushed along: kpt on fnl f: nt pce to chal* **7/1**[3]
4 1½ **Triangulate**[72] 5-10-0 0........................ JackGarritty 11 69
(Micky Hammond) *in tch: pushed along over 2f out: outpcd fr over 1f out* **250/1**
5 2 **Belgravian (FR)** 3-9-0 0........................ BenCurtis 2 60+
(Archie Watson) *prom: rdn and outpcd 2f out: no imp fnl f* **15/2**
53/ 6 hd **Bumptious**[534] 7628 4-9-9 0........................ SeanLevey 8 59+
(Ismail Mohammed) *dwlt: t.k.h: hld up: stdy hdwy on nr side of gp over 2f out: rdn and no imp fr over 1f out* **15/2**
0- 7 5 **Scoones**[187] 7283 3-9-0 0........................ DanielMuscutt 3 48
(James Fanshawe) *trckd ldrs: rdn over 2f out: wknd over 1f out* **11/4**[1]
8 4½ **Foxy Rebel** 3-9-0 0........................ JamesSullivan 6 37
(Ruth Carr) *t.k.h: hld up: rdn and outpcd over 2f out: sn btn* **50/1**
56 9 ¾ **Absolute Angel**[26] 1308 6-9-9 0........................ AndrewMullen 5 34
(Peter Niven) *dwlt: hld up: drvn and struggling over 2f out: sn btn* **40/1**
5-0 10 9 **Royal Flute**[17] 1471 3-8-9 0........................ JasonHart 7 8
(Mark Walford) *led to 1/2-way: sn rdn: hung lft and wknd fr 2f out* **100/1**
11 ½ **Subotal (IRE)**[50] 4-10-0 0........................ DougieCostello 4 16
(Richard Guest) *hld up on far side of gp: drvn and struggling over 2f out: sn btn* **250/1**

1m 38.5s (1.90) **Going Correction** -0.025s/f (Good)
**WFA** 3 from 4yo+ 14lb **11** Ran SP% **112.2**
Speed ratings (Par 103): **89,88,83,82,80 80,75,70,69,60 60**
CSF £15.89 TOTE £3.70: £1.40, £1.70, £2.60; EX 15.10 Trifecta £59.20.
**Owner** T A Rahman **Bred** Highbank Stud Llp **Trained** Hambleton, N Yorks
■ Stewards' Enquiry : Jack Garritty cautioned - guilty of careless riding in that he moved left when insufficiently clear of those on his inside
**FOCUS**
The slower of the two divisions by 0.47sec. This has been rated through the 2nd for now.

## 1831 MARKET CROSS JEWELLERS H'CAP 5f 217y
**3:45** (3:47) (Class 3) (0-95,92) 4-Y-0+ **£9,703** (£2,887; £1,443; £721) **Stalls** Centre

Form RPR
1-01 1 **Wentworth Falls**[15] 1515 5-9-7 **92**........................ PhillipMakin 12 100+
(Geoffrey Harker) *dwlt sltly: hld up: smooth hdwy 2f out: pushed along to chse ldr appr fnl f: rdn to ld 110yds out: edgd lft: kpt on* **9/2**[1]
00-0 2 ½ **Tiger Jim**[15] 1512 7-8-12 **83**........................ SamJames 4 89
(Jim Goldie) *hld up in rr: pushed along and hdwy over 1f out: r.o strly ins fnl f* **25/1**
000- 3 nk **Grandad's World (IRE)**[166] 7772 5-8-9 **80**........................ PaulHanagan 8 85
(Richard Fahey) *trckd ldrs: pushed along to chal appr fnl f: rdn and kpt on ins fnl f* **15/2**[3]
0-10 4 shd **Jaywalker (IRE)**[18] 1454 6-9-2 **87**........................ DuranFentiman 9 92
(Rebecca Bastiman) *prom: rdn over 2f out: led over 1f out: hdd 110yds out: one pce* **33/1**
0-10 5 1½ **Handsome Dude**[15] 1515 5-9-2 **87**........................(b) BenCurtis 7 87
(David Barron) *midfield: rdn over 2f out: kpt on* **7/1**[2]
-503 6 ½ **Ninjago**[15] 1515 7-9-6 **91**........................ CamHardie 5 90
(Paul Midgley) *midfield: rdn and hdwy to chse ldrs over 1f out: no ex fnl 110yds* **7/1**[2]
156- 7 1¾ **Laughton**[225] 6164 4-8-11 **82**........................ ShaneGray 3 75+
(Kevin Ryan) *s.i.s: hld up: hdwy on bit 2f out: pushed along and one pce ins fnl f* **8/1**
10-0 8 ½ **Cosmic Chatter**[18] 1454 7-9-1 **86**........................(p) JamesSullivan 10 77
(Ruth Carr) *midfield: rdn 1/2-way: no imp* **20/1**
316- 9 1 **Musharrif**[205] 6766 5-8-10 **81**........................ NeilFarley 2 69
(Declan Carroll) *led narrowly: rdn over 2f out: hdd over 1f out: grad wknd* **12/1**
011- 10 3 **Munfallet (IRE)**[185] 7315 6-9-5 **90**........................ PatCosgrave 11 69
(David Brown) *w ldr: rdn 3f out: wknd over 1f out* **9/1**
010- 11 3 **Bossipop**[160] 7858 4-9-1 **86**........................(b) JasonHart 13 55
(Tim Easterby) *racd keenly in tch: rdn 2f out: wknd ins fnl f* **33/1**
21-0 12 1½ **Kenny The Captain (IRE)**[15] 1515 6-8-11 **85**... RachelRichardson(3) 14 49
(Tim Easterby) *hld up: rdn along 1/2-way: nvr threatened* **16/1**
40-5 13 2¾ **Highly Sprung (IRE)**[26] 1301 4-9-0 **85**........................ FrannyNorton 15 40
(Mark Johnston) *chsd ldrs: rdn 1/2-way: wknd over 1f out* **16/1**
000- 14 11 **See The Sun**[216] 6449 6-9-2 **87**........................ DavidAllan 6 7
(Tim Easterby) *chsd ldrs: rdn over 2f out: wknd over 1f out: eased* **14/1**

1m 10.37s (-1.43) **Going Correction** -0.025s/f (Good) **14** Ran SP% **116.7**
Speed ratings (Par 107): **108,107,106,106,104 104,101,101,99,95 91,89,86,71**
CSF £126.98 CT £841.77 TOTE £4.90: £2.30, £8.40, £3.30; EX 139.20 Trifecta £3358.30 Part won..
**Owner** Stockhill Racing Partnership **Bred** Newsells Park Stud **Trained** Thirkleby, N Yorks
**FOCUS**
A pretty competitive sprint on paper, but the winner stamped his class once again.

## 1832 RACING UK STRAIGHT MILE H'CAP (REDCAR STRAIGHT MILE SERIES QUALIFIER) 7f 219y
**4:20** (4:24) (Class 4) (0-85,86) 4-Y-0+ **£5,175** (£1,540; £769; £384) **Stalls** Centre

Form RPR
1-26 1 **Roller**[86] 359 4-9-1 **78**........................ NathanEvans(3) 5 89+
(Michael Easterby) *hld up in tch: smooth hdwy to ld over 1f out: shkn up and sn qcknd clr: eased wl ins fnl f: readily* **3/1**[1]
00-0 2 2 **Palmerston**[15] 1517 4-9-2 **76**........................ BenCurtis 10 81
(Michael Appleby) *prom: hdwy to ld over 2f out: rdn: edgd lft and hdd over 1f out: kpt on ins fnl f: nt pce to chal* **11/1**
00-4 3 2 **Hidden Rebel**[23] 1368 5-9-12 **86**........................ PaulMulrennan 9 86
(Alistair Whillans) *hld up: rdn along over 2f out: hdwy to chse ldrs over 1f out: kpt on fnl f: nvr able to chal* **17/2**
40-0 4 ½ **Dubai Dynamo**[15] 1512 12-9-4 **78**........................ JamesSullivan 7 77
(Ruth Carr) *hld up in last pl: shkn up and hdwy over 1f out: edgd lft: kpt on ins fnl f: nvr nr ldrs* **9/1**
041- 5 ½ **Tellovoi (IRE)**[116] 8487 9-9-0 **74**........................(h[1]) DougieCostello 8 72
(Richard Guest) *hld up in tch: rdn along over 2f out: edgd lft and outpcd over 1f out* **33/1**
000- 6 2 **Mohab**[151] 7984 4-9-12 **86**........................ KevinStott 4 79
(Kevin Ryan) *trckd ldrs: rdn over 2f out: wknd over 1f out* **9/2**[2]
10-0 7 ¾ **Save The Bees**[15] 1517 9-9-7 **81**........................ NeilFarley 3 72
(Declan Carroll) *led: rdn and hdd over 2f out: outpcd over 1f out* **16/1**
1556 8 1¼ **Eastern Dragon (IRE)**[44] 1032 7-8-11 **78**..............(p) JamieGormley(7) 6 66
(Iain Jardine) *dwlt: hld up: rdn over 2f out: edgd lft and sn no imp* **14/1**
140- 9 nk **Pumaflor (IRE)**[164] 7796 5-9-7 **81**........................ ConnorBeasley 1 68
(Richard Whitaker) *trckd ldrs: rdn over 2f out: wknd over 1f out* **11/2**[3]
202- 10 2¾ **Imperial Focus (IRE)**[230] 6014 4-9-4 **78**........................ PaulHanagan 11 59
(Simon Waugh) *pressed ldr: rdn over 2f out: wknd wl over 1f out* **8/1**

1m 37.2s (0.60) **Going Correction** -0.025s/f (Good) **10** Ran SP% **114.0**
Speed ratings (Par 105): **96,94,92,91,91 89,88,87,86,83**
CSF £36.42 CT £257.05 TOTE £3.30: £1.80, £3.30, £3.40; EX 45.20 Trifecta £192.10.
**Owner** Irkroy Racing & Andrew Pollock **Bred** Juddmonte Farms Ltd **Trained** Sheriff Hutton, N Yorks
**FOCUS**
A fairly decent handicap, and the winner took it in good style, building on his AW form.

## 1833 RACINGUK.COM/DAYPASS H'CAP 5f 217y
**4:55** (4:57) (Class 5) (0-75,77) 4-Y-0+ **£3,881** (£1,155; £577; £288) **Stalls** Centre

Form RPR
506- 1 **Gin In The Inn (IRE)**[174] 7590 4-9-6 **74**........................ PaulHanagan 14 85
(Richard Fahey) *hld up: pushed along and hdwy over 1f out: rdn to ld ins fnl f: kpt on wl to draw clr* **6/1**[2]
00-6 2 2¼ **Lucky Beggar (IRE)**[17] 1475 7-9-7 **75**........................ DavidAllan 12 79
(David C Griffiths) *prom: rdn to ld over 1f out: hdd ins fnl f: one pce and sn no ch wnr* **11/1**
1-22 3 nk **El Principe**[24] 1339 4-8-13 **67**........................ JasonHart 7 70
(Les Eyre) *w ldr: rdn to ld over 2f out: hdd over 1f out: kpt on same pce* **13/2**[3]
306- 4 ¾ **Tommy G**[223] 6218 4-9-6 **74**........................ SamJames 1 74+
(Jim Goldie) *stdd s: hld up: pushed along and hdwy over 1f out: rdn and kpt on fnl f* **33/1**
0-44 5 hd **Enjoy Life (IRE)**[24] 1346 4-9-1 **76**........................(p) SeamusCronin(7) 13 76+
(Kevin Ryan) *midfield: pushed along over 1f out: kpt on ins fnl f* **14/1**
-565 6 nk **Buccaneers Vault (IRE)**[40] 1091 5-9-9 **77**........................ PaulMulrennan 10 76
(Paul Midgley) *midfield: pushed along over 2f out: rdn over 1f out: kpt on fnl f* **14/1**
3502 7 ¾ **Steelriver (IRE)**[19] 1423 7-9-5 **73**........................ DougieCostello 11 69
(David Barron) *chsd ldrs: rdn and ev ch over 1f out: wknd ins fnl f* **16/1**
-000 8 hd **Extrasolar**[17] 1475 7-9-4 **72**........................ PhillipMakin 8 68
(Geoffrey Harker) *hld up in midfield: pushed along 2f out: bit short of room appr fnl f and angled lft towards far side: rdn and one pce fnl 110yds* **33/1**
350- 9 ½ **Portland Street (IRE)**[161] 7852 4-9-0 **68**........................(p) ConnorBeasley 9 62
(Bryan Smart) *midfield: rdn over 2f out: no imp* **9/1**
-332 10 hd **Meshardal (GER)**[13] 1542 7-8-12 **66**........................ JamesSullivan 2 60
(Ruth Carr) *hld up: pushed along and hdwy over 1f out: swtchd rt ent fnl f: rdn and no further imp* **5/1**[1]
61-2 11 1¾ **Ad Vitam (IRE)**[39] 1106 9-8-10 **64**........................(bt) TomEaves 15 52
(Suzzanne France) *hld up: minor late hdwy: nvr threatened* **33/1**
241- 12 nk **Tricky Dicky**[175] 7585 4-8-13 **67**........................ DuranFentiman 3 54
(Olly Williams) *midfield: rdn to chse ldrs over 1f out: wknd ins fnl f* **9/1**
520- 13 7 **Bop It**[256] 5060 8-8-13 **70**........................ NathanEvans(3) 5 35
(Michael Easterby) *prom: rdn over 2f out: wknd over 1f out* **11/1**
0-00 14 4½ **Brother Tiger**[11] 1586 8-9-7 **75**........................ JosephineGordon 6 25
(David C Griffiths) *led narrowly: rdn over 2f out: hdd over 1f out: wknd* **12/1**
056- 15 1 **Off The Scale (IRE)**[280] 4191 5-9-2 **70**........................(h[1]) GrahamLee 16 17
(Rebecca Menzies) *slowly away: a rr* **33/1**
00-0 16 1 **Kestrel Call (IRE)**[19] 1431 4-9-0 **68**........................(t) BenCurtis 4 12
(Michael Appleby) *prom: rdn over 2f out: wknd over 1f out* **25/1**

1m 10.77s (-1.03) **Going Correction** -0.025s/f (Good) **16** Ran SP% **123.5**
Speed ratings (Par 103): **105,102,101,100,100 99,98,98,97 95,95,85,79,78 77**
CSF £67.61 CT £459.20 TOTE £8.20: £2.20, £2.80, £2.10, £10.00; EX 82.90 Trifecta £1134.30.
**Owner** Dean Hardman and Stella Hardman **Bred** Colman O'Flynn **Trained** Musley Bank, N Yorks
**FOCUS**
They finished in a bit of a heap behind the impressive winner, who has been rated back to his best.

## 1834 OLIVIA RENSHAW DESIGNED TODAYS RACECARD COVER H'CAP 1m 7f 217y
**5:30** (5:31) (Class 6) (0-65,66) 4-Y-0+ **£3,234** (£962; £481; £240) **Stalls** Low

Form RPR
3063 1 **Cavalieri (IRE)**[24] 1344 7-9-4 **56**........................(tp) KevinStott 2 64
(Philip Kirby) *in tch: smooth hdwy to ld over 2f out: rdn over 1f out: kpt on wl fnl f* **17/2**[3]
62/3 2 1¾ **Rembrandt**[9] 1629 5-9-9 **61**........................ GrahamLee 8 67
(Rebecca Menzies) *hld up: stdy hdwy over 3f out: effrt and chsd wnr over 1f out: kpt on ins fnl f* **8/1**[2]
0-31 3 ¾ **Mr Globetrotter (USA)**[23] 1369 4-9-5 **66**........................ CliffordLee(5) 3 71
(Iain Jardine) *hld up in midfield: rdn and outpcd 3f out: rallied over 1f out: kpt on same pce ins fnl f* **9/5**[1]
-403 4 3 **Major Rowan**[27] 1292 6-9-7 **59**........................ PhillipMakin 5 61+
(John Davies) *hld up: stdy hdwy on outside over 2f out: sn rdn: kpt on same pce fr over 1f out* **10/1**
314- 5 3¼ **Question Of Faith**[227] 6102 6-8-7 **52**........................ ConnorMurtagh(7) 6 50
(Martin Todhunter) *dwlt: hld up: stdy hdwy on outside over 3f out: rdn and edgd lft over 1f out: sn wknd* **9/1**
0-50 6 1 **Adrakhan (FR)**[33] 1197 6-8-7 **45**........................ CamHardie 9 41
(Wilf Storey) *trckd ldrs: chal over 3f out to over 2f out: rdn and wknd over 1f out* **25/1**
306- 7 shd **Stanarley Pic**[266] 4703 6-9-12 **64**........................ NeilFarley 12 60
(Alan Swinbank) *led: clr after 4f: rdn and hdd over 2f out: wknd over 1f out* **25/1**
050- 8 1¼ **Rob's Legacy**[177] 7532 4-8-3 **45**........................ RoystonFfrench 4 40
(Shaun Harris) *dwlt: hld up: drvn and outpcd over 3f out: n.d after* **50/1**
60-0 9 2¾ **Next Edition (IRE)**[33] 1197 9-9-2 **59**........................(p) PhilDennis(5) 13 50
(Philip Kirby) *hld up in tch: rdn and struggling wl over 2f out: sn btn* **10/1**
305/ 10 shd **Dizoard**[599] 5169 7-8-3 **48**........................(h) JamieGormley(7) 11 39
(Iain Jardine) *in tch: drvn and outpcd 4f out: btn over 2f out* **16/1**

0344 **11** *6* **King Julien (IRE)**$^{11}$ [1585] 4-8-3 **45**........................(b) JosephineGordon 1 29
(John Ryan) *chsd clr ldr to over 4f out: rdn and wknd over 2f out* **9/1**
0045 **12** *28* **Psychology**$^{17}$ [1469] 4-8-12 **54**........................................ DougieCostello 7 5
(Kenny Johnson) *dwlt: hld up: rdn along over 3f out: edgd lft and wknd over 2f out: t.o* **28/1**
3m 30.49s (-0.91) **Going Correction** -0.025s/f (Good)
**WFA** 4 from 5yo+ 2lb **12** Ran SP% **114.5**
Speed ratings (Par 101): **101,100,99,98,96 96,96,95,94,94 91,77**
CSF £69.24 CT £176.23 TOTE £8.40: £2.40, £2.50, £1.30; EX 50.90 Trifecta £151.40.
**Owner** The Cavalieri Partnership **Bred** Grange & Manister House Studs **Trained** East Appleton, N Yorks
**FOCUS**
This was run at a good gallop thanks to Stanarley Pic, who soon built up a clear advantage.

## 1835 RACINGUK.COM/HD H'CAP 5f 217y
**6:00** (6:01) (Class 6) (0-60,60) 3-Y-O **£3,234** (£962; £481; £240) **Stalls** Centre

Form RPR
560- **1** **Stubytuesday**$^{167}$ [7741] 3-9-2 **58**........................ NathanEvans(3) 1 64+
(Michael Easterby) *chsd ldrs: rdn over 2f out: led narrowly ins fnl f: kpt on wl* **15/2**$^{3}$
505- **2** *½* **Judy Woods (IRE)**$^{145}$ [8071] 3-9-7 **60**........................ ConnorBeasley 2 65
(Bryan Smart) *hld up: rdn and hdwy 2f out: chal strly ent fnl f: kpt on* **10/1**
550- **3** *1 ¼* **Regal Decree**$^{222}$ [6222] 3-9-0 **53**........................................ JackGarritty 13 54+
(Jedd O'Keeffe) *hld up: rdn and hdwy over 1f out: kpt on* **11/1**
00-0 **4** *1 ¼* **La Haule Lady**$^{38}$ [1123] 3-9-2 **55**........................(p$^{1}$) PaulMulrennan 4 52
(Paul Midgley) *led: rdn over 2f out: edgd lft over 1f out: hdd ins fnl f: no ex* **20/1**
-430 **5** *nse* **Mimic's Memory**$^{34}$ [1193] 3-9-5 **58**........................................ ShaneGray 7 55
(Ann Duffield) *dwlt: midfield: trckd ldrs 1/2-way: rdn 2f out: one pce* **25/1**
006- **6** *1 ¼* **Cosmic Sky**$^{229}$ [6026] 3-9-2 **55**........................................(h$^{1}$) DavidAllan 8 48
(Tim Easterby) *hld up: rdn over 2f out: kpt on fr over 1f out* **28/1**
400- **7** *2 ¼* **Zebedee Star**$^{210}$ [6614] 3-8-12 **56**........................ GemmaTutty(5) 5 46
(Karen Tutty) *chsd ldrs: rdn over 2f out: hmpd appr fnl f: wknd ins fnl f* **33/1**
-526 **8** *1* **Hollywood Harry (IRE)**$^{12}$ [1564] 3-9-4 **57**........................(p) PhillipMakin 15 41
(Keith Dalgleish) *chsd ldrs towards nr side: rdn and outpcd over 2f out: no threat after* **14/1**
0-30 **9** *nse* **Vaux (IRE)**$^{34}$ [1193] 3-9-6 **59**........................................(p) GrahamLee 10 42
(Ben Haslam) *hld up: racd keenly: hmpd by faller 4f out and in rr: pushed along and sme hdwy over 1f out: nvr threatened* **18/1**
1542 **10** *2 ½* **Scotch Myst**$^{33}$ [1204] 3-8-11 **57**........................ ConnorMurtagh(7) 14 33
(Richard Fahey) *chsd ldrs: rdn over 2f out: wknd fnl f* **6/1**$^{2}$
-633 **11** *2 ¼* **Backinanger**$^{38}$ [1127] 3-9-4 **57**........................................(p$^{1}$) TomEaves 16 26
(Kevin Ryan) *hld up: rdn and edgd lft over 1f out: nvr threatened* **16/1**
000- **12** *¾* **Clear As A Bell (IRE)**$^{212}$ [6564] 3-9-5 **58**........................ DuranFentiman 17 25
(Tim Easterby) *hld up towards nr side: nvr threatened* **28/1**
0-41 **13** *¾* **Little Kingdom (IRE)**$^{75}$ [511] 3-9-5 **58**........................ BenCurtis 11 23
(Tracy Waggott) *chsd ldrs: rdn and outpcd lost pl 1/2-way: wknd over 1f out* **10/1**
632- **14** *2 ¼* **Chickenfortea (IRE)**$^{208}$ [6678] 3-9-7 **60**........................ JasonHart 6 18
(Eric Alston) *prom: rdn over 2f out: wknd over 1f out* **4/1**$^{1}$
0-03 **15** *17* **Albizu Campos**$^{44}$ [1034] 3-8-10 **49**........................(p$^{1}$) PaulHanagan 9
(Lawrence Mullaney) *chsd ldrs: rdn 1/2-way: wknd 2f out and eased* **16/1**
6352 **F** **Champagne Queen**$^{10}$ [1605] 3-8-8 **50**........................(t) HollieDoyle(3) 12
(Rae Guest) *dwlt: hld up: clipped heels and fell 4f out* **9/1**
1m 12.82s (1.02) **Going Correction** -0.025s/f (Good) **16** Ran SP% **124.7**
Speed ratings (Par 96): **92,91,89,88,87 86,83,81,81,78 75,74,73,70,47**
CSF £76.85 CT £873.44 TOTE £8.90: £2.20, £2.60, £2.90, £5.30; EX 88.80 Trifecta £1122.00.
**Owner** Stuart Daynes **Bred** The National Stud **Trained** Sheriff Hutton, N Yorks
**FOCUS**
The two drawn in the lowest stalls came through to fight this out. This could be rated a bit higher.
T/Jkpt: Not won. T/Plt: £17.10 to a £1 stake. Pool: £76,407.54 - 3254.20 winning units. T/Qpdt: £10.70 to a £1 stake. Pool: £4,384.65 - 301 winning units. **Andrew Sheret & Richard Young**

# 1625 WOLVERHAMPTON (A.W) (L-H)
Monday, April 17
**OFFICIAL GOING: Tapeta: standard**
Wind: light breeze Weather: sunny spells

## 1836 INVEST CITY OF WOLVERHAMPTON H'CAP 5f 21y (Tp)
**12:30** (12:30) (Class 5) (0-75,77) 4-Y-O+ **£4,140** (£1,232; £615; £307) **Stalls** Low

Form RPR
6220 **1** **Invincible Ridge (IRE)**$^{23}$ [1370] 9-9-5 **73**........................ RobertWinston 3 80
(Eric Alston) *trckd ldrs: effrt and rdn over 1f out: led wl ins fnl f: r.o wl* **5/1**$^{3}$
-164 **2** *nk* **The Big Lad**$^{39}$ [1110] 5-8-13 **74**........................(be$^{1}$) NicolaCurrie(7) 2 80
(Richard Hughes) *mid-div: hdwy on inner over 1f out: rdn and r.o: nrst fin* **9/2**$^{2}$
-044 **3** *2* **Come On Dave (IRE)**$^{25}$ [1327] 8-9-8 **76**........................(v) LiamKeniry 6 75
(John Butler) *disp ld tl tk command 2f out: rdn and hdd ins fnl f: no ex* **9/1**
000- **4** *½* **Dinneratmidnight**$^{193}$ [7094] 6-9-9 **77**........................(e) JoeFanning 4 74
(Richard Guest) *mid-div: pushed along 2f out: rdn 1f out: one pce* **5/1**$^{3}$
0066 **5** *hd* **Secret Asset (IRE)**$^{16}$ [1487] 12-8-6 **67**........................(v) JordanUys(7) 7 63
(Lisa Williamson) *hld up in last: hdwy over 1f out: rdn and styd on ins fnl f* **40/1**
222- **6** *3 ¾* **Showmethewayavrilo**$^{187}$ [7268] 4-8-13 **72**........................ GeorgiaCox(5) 8 55
(Malcolm Saunders) *trckd ldrs: effrt 2f out: sn rdn and one pce* **8/1**
1421 **7** *¾* **Bahango (IRE)**$^{12}$ [1558] 5-9-2 **75**........................(p) LewisEdmunds(5) 5 55
(Patrick Morris) *hld up: pushed along and racd wd over 1f out: rdn and no imp* **11/4**$^{1}$
0-66 **8** *1 ¾* **Tarboosh**$^{46}$ [995] 4-9-4 **75**........................................ AdamMcNamara(3) 1 49
(Paul Midgley) *disp ld tl lost pl and wknd 2f out* **6/1**
1m 1.26s (-0.64) **Going Correction** -0.05s/f (Stan) **8** Ran SP% **116.0**
Speed ratings (Par 103): **103,102,99,98,98 92,91,88**
CSF £28.17 CT £199.58 TOTE £6.30: £2.20, £1.60, £2.20; EX 32.00 Trifecta £330.10.
**Owner** Paul Buist & John Thompson **Bred** Con Harrington **Trained** Longton, Lancs

**FOCUS**
A good pace for the opening sprint handicap with the winner always well positioned. The winner has been rated similarly to his February C&D form.

## 1837 ALL NEW MICRA AT WEST WAY NISSAN MAIDEN STKS 6f 20y (Tp)
**1:00** (1:01) (Class 5) 3-Y-O+ **£4,140** (£1,232; £615; £307) **Stalls** Low

Form RPR
0-2 **1** **Mostahel**$^{10}$ [1609] 3-9-2 0........................................ FrankieDettori 2 94+
(Richard Hannon) *trckd ldrs gng wl: chal over 1f out: led appr fnl f: sn clr under hands and heels riding: easily* **2/1**$^{2}$
24-2 **2** *4* **Farook (IRE)**$^{16}$ [1488] 3-9-2 76........................................ JimCrowley 5 78
(Charles Hills) *trckd ldr: led wl over 1f out: sn jnd: hdd appr fnl f: rdn and kpt on but no ch w wnr* **5/2**$^{3}$
223- **3** *3 ¾* **Hydroxide**$^{194}$ [7074] 3-9-2 82........................................(bt$^{1}$) WilliamBuick 4 66
(Hugo Palmer) *5th early and sn niggled along: effrt over 2f out and racd wd: rdn over 1f out: r.o steadily fnl f* **7/4**$^{1}$
2 **4** *4* **Calypso Jo**$^{53}$ [878] 3-9-2 0........................................ JoeDoyle 6 53
(Kevin Ryan) *racd wd first 2f: rdn over 2f out: one pce* **9/1**
450- **5** *3 ¾* **Coronation Cottage**$^{229}$ [6016] 3-8-6 63........................ GeorgiaCox(5) 3 36
(Malcolm Saunders) *led: rdn and hdd over 1f out: wknd* **100/1**
6-0 **6** *¾* **Sweet Amazement**$^{9}$ [1626] 3-8-11 0........................(h$^{1}$) SteveDrowne 7 34
(Mark Usher) *hld up early: 4th 2f out: sn rdn and no imp* **200/1**
3/ **7** *1* **Flower Cup**$^{602}$ [5697] 4-9-8 0........................................(h$^{1}$) IrineuGoncalves 1 34
(Chris Dwyer) *dwlt: a in rr* **66/1**
1m 12.82s (-1.68) **Going Correction** -0.05s/f (Stan)
**WFA** 3 from 4yo 11lb **7** Ran SP% **111.2**
Speed ratings (Par 103): **109,103,98,93,88 87,86**
CSF £7.00 TOTE £2.70: £1.40, £1.80; EX 6.60 Trifecta £12.40.
**Owner** Al Shaqab Racing **Bred** Newsells Park Stud **Trained** East Everleigh, Wilts
**FOCUS**
Not a bad maiden and the winner looks a decent prospect.

## 1838 BANKS'S AMBER BITTER H'CAP 5f 21y (Tp)
**1:30** (1:31) (Class 4) (0-85,86) 3-Y-O **£6,469** (£1,925; £962; £481) **Stalls** Low

Form RPR
21- **1** **Queen In Waiting (IRE)**$^{240}$ [5631] 3-9-3 **80**........................ JoeFanning 4 91
(Mark Johnston) *broke wl and led: pushed along and wnt clr over 1f out: briefly rdn but wl in command ins fnl f: comf* **4/1**$^{2}$
200- **2** *2 ½* **Evergate**$^{177}$ [7541] 3-9-7 **84**........................................ JimCrowley 3 86
(Robert Cowell) *trckd ldrs: drvn along over 1f out: rdn 1f out: r.o wl ins fnl f* **8/1**
010- **3** *nk* **Nayyar**$^{219}$ [6322] 3-9-9 **86**........................................ WilliamBuick 6 87
(Charles Hills) *trckd ldr: rn wd and lost pl over 1f out: rdn and r.o ins fnl f* **4/1**$^{2}$
12 **4** *nk* **Rock Of America (USA)**$^{16}$ [1487] 3-9-5 **82**........................ DanielTudhope 2 82
(David O'Meara) *trckd ldrs gng wl: pushed along and chsd ldr over 1f out: wknd* **5/2**$^{1}$
25-1 **5** *2* **Full Intention**$^{18}$ [1453] 3-9-7 **84**........................................ PJMcDonald 7 77
(Tom Dascombe) *racd wd in mid-div: effrt over 1f out: rdn and no ex* **11/2**$^{3}$
210- **6** *2* **Rose Berry**$^{192}$ [7113] 3-9-0 **77**........................................(h) SilvestreDeSousa 5 62
(Chris Dwyer) *slowly away: racd keenly: effrt and rdn over 1f out: no imp* **8/1**
-111 **7** *2* **Dandy Flame (IRE)**$^{76}$ [496] 3-8-8 **78**........................ FinleyMarsh(7) 1 56
(Richard Hughes) *hld up: effrt 2f out: sn wknd* **10/1**
022- **8** *4 ½* **Jumping Around (IRE)**$^{220}$ [6292] 3-9-4 **81**........................ GeorgeDowning 8 43
(Ian Williams) *slowly away: a in rr* **33/1**
1m 0.71s (-1.19) **Going Correction** -0.05s/f (Stan) **8** Ran SP% **118.2**
Speed ratings (Par 100): **107,103,102,102,98 95,92,85**
CSF £36.96 CT £137.67 TOTE £6.40: £1.90, £2.60, £1.60; EX 52.80 Trifecta £215.20.
**Owner** Sheikh Hamdan bin Mohammed Al Maktoum **Bred** Darley **Trained** Middleham Moor, N Yorks
**FOCUS**
Some useful 3yos on show but the winner was far too strong, albeit benefiting from a super ride.

## 1839 BANKS'S SUNBEAM H'CAP 1m 1f 104y (Tp)
**2:05** (2:05) (Class 5) (0-70,71) 4-Y-O+ **£4,140** (£1,232; £615; £307) **Stalls** Low

Form RPR
44 **1** **Deep Challenger (IRE)**$^{26}$ [1299] 5-9-5 **68**........................ FergusSweeney 1 75
(Jamie Osborne) *mid-div: effrt and pushed along over 1f out: rdn to chal ent fnl f: responded wl and led last 50 yds* **9/2**$^{2}$
116- **2** *½* **Therthaar**$^{276}$ [4341] 4-9-5 **68**........................................ SilvestreDeSousa 5 74+
(Ismail Mohammed) *trckd ldr gng wl: led 2f out: rdn over 1f out: r.o but hdd last 50 yds* **1/1**$^{1}$
4530 **3** *1 ¾* **Ravenhoe (IRE)**$^{6}$ [1707] 4-9-7 **70**........................................ JoeFanning 4 72
(Mark Johnston) *trckd ldrs: rdn over 1f out: styd on but nt pce of first two* **9/2**$^{2}$
40-6 **4** *1 ¼* **Whitecliff Park (IRE)**$^{15}$ [1519] 4-8-11 **60**........................ BarryMcHugh 3 60
(Brian Ellison) *settled in 5th: rdn 2f out: r.o ins fnl f: nvr nrr* **11/1**
0210 **5** *1 ½* **Siouxperhero (IRE)**$^{25}$ [1334] 8-9-0 **63**........................(p) MartinDwyer 6 60
(William Muir) *led at modest pce: pushed along and hdd 2f out: rdn and wknd* **14/1**
0-0 **6** *18* **Spin Point (IRE)**$^{36}$ [92] 5-9-8 **71**........................................(t$^{1}$) StevieDonohoe 2 30
(Ian Williams) *hld up in last: rdn over 5f out: no rspnse and sn wl bhd* **8/1**$^{3}$
2m 1.81s (1.01) **Going Correction** -0.05s/f (Stan) **6** Ran SP% **112.5**
Speed ratings (Par 103): **93,92,91,89,88 72**
CSF £9.52 TOTE £6.60: £2.50, £1.10; EX 8.80 Trifecta £40.30.
**Owner** D Margolis **Bred** Healing Music Partnership **Trained** Upper Lambourn, Berks
**FOCUS**
A modest handicap run at a steady pace but the two unexposed runners fought out the finish. This has been rated around the 3rd.

## 1840 BANKS'S AMBER BITTER MAIDEN AUCTION STKS 1m 1f 104y (Tp)
**2:40** (2:41) (Class 5) 3-Y-O **£4,204** (£1,251; £625; £312) **Stalls** Low

Form RPR
00- **1** **Lightly Squeeze**$^{215}$ [6480] 3-9-5 0........................(p$^{1}$) SilvestreDeSousa 1 75
(Philip Hide) *settled in 3rd: pushed along 2f out: swtchd and rdn to chal over 1f out: led ent fnl f: readily* **13/2**
25 **2** *1 ¼* **Wedding Breakfast (IRE)**$^{54}$ [862] 3-9-0 0........................(h$^{1}$) WilliamBuick 5 67
(Hugo Palmer) *trckd ldr: chal and led 2f out: rdn over 1f out: hdd jst ins fnl f: r.o* **11/4**$^{2}$
02 **3** *1 ½* **Oxford Don**$^{34}$ [1190] 3-9-2 0........................................ AaronJones(3) 4 69
(David Simcock) *slowly away and last but sn wl in tch: effrt and racd wd 2f out: sn rdn and one pce* **5/4**$^{1}$

-304 **4** 4 ½ **Major Cornwallis (IRE)**[20] 1410 3-9-5 67 TonyHamilton 3 59
(Richard Fahey) *led: hdd and rdn 2f out: wknd: eased fnl f* **3/1**[3]
2m 2.03s (1.23) **Going Correction** -0.05s/f (Stan) **4** Ran SP% **109.4**
Speed ratings (Par 98): **92,90,89,85**
CSF £23.19 TOTE £6.60; EX 28.30 Trifecta £36.60.
**Owner** Wong Yu On **Bred** Highbury Stud Ltd **Trained** Findon, W Sussex
**FOCUS**
A modest maiden run at a steady pace and the outsider of the field landed the money.

## 1841 FCL GLOBAL FORWARDING MAKING LOGISTICS PERSONAL H'CAP 7f 36y (Tp)
**3:10** (3:12) (Class 3) (0-95,88) 3-Y-O **£9,451** (£2,829; £1,414; £708; £352) **Stalls** High

Form RPR
041- **1** **Original Choice (IRE)**[167] 7740 3-8-13 **80** SilvestreDeSousa 1 90
(William Haggas) *led: kicked on 2f out: rdn appr fnl f: r.o strly* **3/1**[2]
1- **2** ¾ **Medahim (IRE)**[131] 8243 3-9-6 **87** FrankieDettori 4 95
(Richard Hannon) *trckd ldrs: pushed along 2f out: swtchd to chal over 1f out: rdn and no imp ins fnl f* **6/4**[1]
401- **3** 2 ½ **Parfait (IRE)**[178] 7502 3-9-6 **87** WilliamBuick 6 88
(John Gosden) *mid div: pushed along and racd wd 2f out: sn rdn: r.o fnl f* **7/2**[3]
20-2 **4** ¾ **Berkshire Boy (IRE)**[10] 1601 3-9-2 **83** (b) RobHornby 7 82
(Andrew Balding) *slowly away: cajoled along 3f out and racd wd 2f out: rdn and darted lft to stands rail ent fnl f: r.o: nrst fin* **12/1**
31-5 **5** *hd* **High Acclaim (USA)**[44] 1026 3-9-7 **88** DanielTudhope 8 86
(Roger Teal) *prom and racd wd early: wnt 2nd 4f out: styd 2nd tl rdn wl over 1f out: fdd* **8/1**
000- **6** 4 **Burrishoole Abbey (IRE)**[213] 6536 3-8-12 **79** PJMcDonald 2 67
(K R Burke) *2nd early: sn eased into mid div and trckd ldrs: effrt and rdn 2f out: wknd* **25/1**
010- **7** ¾ **Abiento (IRE)**[198] 6954 3-8-11 **78** TonyHamilton 3 64
(Richard Fahey) *hld up: outpcd and rdn 2f out: fdd* **20/1**
-150 **8** 1 ½ **Vatican Hill (IRE)**[37] 1149 3-9-1 **82** TimmyMurphy 5 64
(Jamie Osborne) *hld up in rr: pushed along 2f out: rdn over 1f out: no imp* **25/1**
1m 27.98s (-0.82) **Going Correction** -0.05s/f (Stan) **8** Ran SP% **118.5**
Speed ratings (Par 102): **102,101,98,97,97 92,91,90**
CSF £8.03 CT £15.38 TOTE £4.90: £1.40, £1.10, £1.50; EX 9.80 Trifecta £21.30.
**Owner** A A Goodman **Bred** Ballybrennan Stud **Trained** Newmarket, Suffolk
**FOCUS**
The feature race on the card and the finish was dominated by unexposed runners from powerful stables. This has been rated positively.

## 1842 INVEST WOLVERHAMPTON - THE CITY OF OPPORTUNITY H'CAP 7f 36y (Tp)
**3:45** (3:47) (Class 6) (0-65,66) 4-Y-O+ **£2,781** (£827; £413; £206) **Stalls** High

Form RPR
43-4 **1** **Caledonia Laird**[98] 147 6-9-5 **59** IrineuGoncalves 10 66
(Jo Hughes) *mid-div: travelling wl 2f out: effrt and chal wd over 1f out: pushed along to ld wl ins fnl f: readily* **6/1**
5040 **2** ¾ **Miss Goldsmith (IRE)**[42] 1066 4-9-6 **60** (h) TonyHamilton 9 65
(Richard Fahey) *hld up: hdwy 2f out: rdn appr fnl f: fin wl: but hld by wnr* **10/1**
2510 **3** *nk* **Tavener**[5] 1717 5-9-0 **61** (p) FinleyMarsh(7) 5 65
(David C Griffiths) *trckd ldr: led 4f out: kicked a l clr over 1f out: rdn fnl f: ct last 100 yds: no ex* **7/2**[1]
005- **4** 1 ¼ **Bush Beauty (IRE)**[167] 7751 6-8-12 **57** SophieKilloran(5) 6 58+
(Eric Alston) *plld hrd in rr: plenty to do 2f out: effrt over 1f out: briefly rdn and r.o wl ins fnl f: nvr nrr* **12/1**
600B **5** 1 ¼ **Binky Blue (IRE)**[59] 784 5-9-6 **60** SilvestreDeSousa 7 58
(Daniel Mark Loughnane) *hld up: effrt and n.m.r over 1f out: rdn ins fnl f: r.o* **9/2**[2]
-305 **6** *nk* **Top Offer**[51] 929 8-9-2 **61** (p) LewisEdmunds(5) 2 58
(Patrick Morris) *mid div: effrt over 1f out: r.o ins fnl f under hand riding* **9/2**[2]
150- **7** 1 **Mr Cool Cash**[171] 7671 5-9-12 **66** JoeFanning 4 61
(Richard Guest) *trckd ldrs: effrt over 1f out: pushed along and fdd* **5/1**[3]
2134 **8** 2 ¼ **Castlerea Tess**[31] 1246 4-9-1 **55** (p) KieranO'Neill 3 44
(Sarah Hollinshead) *led tl hdd 4f out: hrd rdn 2f out: wknd* **8/1**
060- **9** 3 ¼ **Foxinthehenhouse**[299] 3527 4-9-6 **60** LiamKeniry 1 41
(John Holt) *trckd ldrs: pushed along 2f out: rdn and wknd appr fnl f* **40/1**
1m 28.37s (-0.43) **Going Correction** -0.05s/f (Stan) **9** Ran SP% **119.9**
Speed ratings (Par 101): **100,99,98,97,95 95,94,91,88**
CSF £66.51 CT £247.01 TOTE £7.60: £2.00, £2.60, £1.60; EX 85.50 Trifecta £514.50.
**Owner** Isla & Colin Cage **Bred** Mrs I M Cage And Mr C J Cage **Trained** Lambourn, Berks
**FOCUS**
A low-grade finale and another steadily run event, the winner doing well given he was caught out wide for much of the race. This has been rated around the principals.
T/Plt: £181.30 to a £1 stake. Pool: £44,901.48 - 180.71 winning units. T/Qpdt: £33.30 to a £1 stake. Pool: £3,362.46 - 74.60 winning units. **Keith McHugh**

1843 - 1845a (Foreign Racing) - See Raceform Interactive

# COLOGNE (R-H)
Monday, April 17
**OFFICIAL GOING: Turf: good**

## 1846a KARIN BARONIN VON ULLMANN - SCHWARZGOLD-RENNEN (GROUP 3) (3YO FILLIES) (TURF) 1m
**3:45** 3-Y-O **£27,350** (£10,256; £3,846; £3,846; £1,709)

RPR
**1** **Delectation**[212] 6555 3-9-2 0 EduardoPedroza 9 100
(A Wohler, Germany) *awkward s: settled towards rr: rdn and hdwy ins fnl 2f: led 1f out: wnt clr fnl f: pushed out* **12/5**[2]
**2** 2 **Alicante (GER)** 3-9-2 0 AdriedeVries 7 95
(Markus Klug, Germany) *s.i.s and racd towards rr: pushed along in last over 2f out: styd on wl fnl 2f: no ch w wnr* **56/10**[3]
**3** *nk* **Hargeisa (USA)**[228] 6068 3-9-2 0 StephenHellyn 3 95
(Mario Hofer, Germany) *racd in midfield: hdwy to join ldrs 2f out: kpt on but nt pce of wnr* **41/5**
**3** *dht* **Peace In Motion (USA)**[173] 3-9-2 0 MarcLerner 1 95
(Waldemar Hickst, Germany) *s.i.s but sn racing 2nd bhd clr ldr: led nr side gp at top of st: veered towards rail bef stening to cl on ldr 2f out: led briefly over 1f out: sn hdd: kpt on wl but nt pce of wnr* **2/1**[1]
**5** 1 ¼ **Arazza (GER)**[176] 7563 3-9-2 0 AlexanderPietsch 8 92
(J Hirschberger, Germany) *racd in rr: sme hdwy turning in: rdn over 2f out: kpt on one pce: nvr a danger* **8/1**
**6** ½ **Viva La Flora (GER)**[169] 3-9-2 0 AndraschStarke 6 91
(P Schiergen, Germany) *settled in 3rd: rdn along and ev ch 2f out: lost position fnl 100yds* **17/2**
**7** 1 ¼ **Qool**[239] 3-9-2 0 MartinSeidl 5 88
(Markus Klug, Germany) *midfield: ev ch 2f out: outpcd ent fnl f: no ex* **182/10**
**8** 5 **Alwina (GER)**[176] 7563 3-9-2 0 AntoineHamelin 10 76+
(Henk Grewe, Germany) *away wl to ld: 6 l clr turning in: racd alone far side down st: hdd over 1f out: wknd fnl f* **111/10**
**9** 3 ½ **Djumay (GER)** 3-9-2 0 IanFerguson 4 68
(Andreas Suborics, Germany) *t.k.h early: racd in midfield: rdn and lost position ins fnl 2f: eased fnl f* **148/10**
1m 38.88s (0.49) **9** Ran SP% **130.2**
PARI-MUTUEL (all including 10 euro stake): WIN 34 PLACE: 16, 15, 11 (Hargeisa), 7 (Peace In Motion); SF: 228.
**Owner** Australian Bloodstock **Bred** Crossfields Bloodstock Ltd **Trained** Germany

1847 - 1856a (Foreign Racing) - See Raceform Interactive

# NEWMARKET (R-H)
Tuesday, April 18
**OFFICIAL GOING: Good to firm (good in places; 7.8)**
Wind: light to medium, across Weather: light cloud, bright spells

## 1857 BET365 WOOD DITTON MAIDEN STKS (PLUS 10 RACE) 1m
**1:50** (1:52) (Class 4) 3-Y-O **£6,469** (£1,925; £962; £481) **Stalls** High

Form RPR
**1** **Night Circus (IRE)** 3-9-5 0 WilliamBuick 12 89+
(Charlie Appleby) *str: racd stands side: t.k.h: chsd gp ldr and prom overall: effrt to chse overall ldr over 2f out: sn rdn to chal: drvn over 1f out: led and edgd lft wl ins fnl f: styd on: 1st of 9 in gp* **13/2**[3]
**2** ¾ **Jalela** 3-9-0 0 FrankieDettori 13 83
(Richard Hannon) *unf: racd stands side: led gp and chsd overall ldr tl led 3f out: rdn and hrd pressed wl over 1f out: hdd wl ins fnl f: one pce and hld whn bmpd sn after: 2nd of 9 in gp* **9/1**
**3** *nk* **Mark Of Approval (USA)** 3-9-5 0 JamesDoyle 9 86+
(John Gosden) *tall: racd stands side: awkward leaving stalls and s.i.s: hld up in last trio: hdwy over 2f out: rdn to chse clr ldng pair over 1f out: styd on strly ins fnl f: nvr quite getting to ldrs: 3rd of 9 in gp* **11/2**[2]
**4** 6 **Damocles (GER)** 3-9-5 0 (t[1]) AndreaAtzeni 7 73
(John Gosden) *lengthy: racd stands side: hld up in midfield: rdn and hdwy 3f out: chsd ldrs wl over 1f out: no imp and btn 4th 1f out: kpt on same pce: 4th of 9 in gp* **13/2**[3]
**5** 1 ¼ **Dawaaleeb (USA)** 3-9-5 0 DaneO'Neill 11 70+
(Charles Hills) *tall: racd stands side: racd stands side: dwlt and bustled along early: sn rcvrd to chse ldrs: rdn 3f out: unable qck 2f out: wknd ent fnl f: 5th of 9 in gp* **10/1**
- **6** ¾ **Elyaasaat (USA)** 3-9-5 0 (t[1]) JimCrowley 3 68+
(William Haggas) *str: racd far side: overall ldr tl rdn and hdd 3f out: struggling and lost pl wl over 1f out: wknd fnl f: 1st of 5 in gp* **7/4**[1]
**7** 4 ½ **Buldan** 3-9-5 0 TedDurcan 6 58
(Sir Michael Stoute) *str: racd stands side: stdd and hmpd s: sn swtchd lft and in rr: rdn 3f out: no threat to ldrs but kpt on ins fnl f: 6th of 9 in gp* **16/1**
**8** ½ **Titan** 3-9-5 0 AdamKirby 8 56
(Ed Dunlop) *w'like: racd stands side: in tch in midfield: rdn and swtchd rt wl over 2f out: unable qck over 2f out: wknd over 1f out: 7th of 9 in gp* **33/1**
**9** ¾ **Zack Mayo** 3-9-5 0 DavidProbert 1 55
(Philip McBride) *athletic: racd far side: hld up in rr: rdn 3f out: sn struggling: wknd over 1f out: 2nd of 5 in gp* **66/1**
**10** ¾ **Unit Of Assessment (IRE)** 3-9-5 0 LukeMorris 4 53
(William Knight) *w'like: racd far side: chsd gp ldrs and midfield overall: rdn 3f out: sn struggling: wknd over 1f out: 3rd of 5 in gp* **66/1**
**11** 3 **Tallulah's Quest (IRE)** 3-9-0 0 AdamBeschizza 5 41
(Julia Feilden) *lengthy: racd far side: chsd gp ldrs tl chsd gp ldr over 3f out: sn rdn: lost pl and wknd over 1f out: 4th of 5 in gp* **125/1**
**12** 4 **Shyarch** 3-9-5 0 JFEgan 10 37
(George Margarson) *w'likeL racd stands side: midfield: pushed along 5f out: rdn 1/2-way: wknd 2f out: 8th of 9 in gp* **100/1**
**13** 1 **Dream Start** 3-9-0 0 JosephineGordon 2 30
(John Ryan) *athletic: racd far side: wnt sharply lft s: chsd gp ldr tl over 3f out: sn lost pl: wknd 2f out: 5th of 5 in gp* **66/1**
**14** 5 **Borthwen (IRE)** 3-9-0 0 JamieSpencer 14 18
(Charles Hills) *w'like: racd stands side: stdd s: hld up in rr: rdn 3f out: no imp and hung rt over 2f out: wknd and wl bhd fnl f* **25/1**
1m 38.77s (0.17) **Going Correction** +0.025s/f (Good) **14** Ran SP% **116.4**
Speed ratings (Par 100): **100,99,98,92,91 90,86,85,85,84 81,77,76,71**
CSF £59.81 TOTE £7.50: £2.10, £2.60, £2.10; EX 67.60 Trifecta £309.80.
**Owner** Godolphin **Bred** Darley **Trained** Newmarket, Suffolk
■ Stewards' Enquiry : William Buick cautioned to future conduct in races
**FOCUS**
Far side course used with stalls on stands' side for all races. It was dry on Monday and overnight, and this was another largely dry day. Clerk of the course Michael Prosser said: "I've never seen the grass looking so well. It was supposed to rain last night but didn't so we've changed the ground to good to firm, good in places. There is a stiff cross breeze which may carry them out into the middle of the track." Five of these raced up the middle and were all unplaced, including the favourite, although the others in that bunch were big outsiders. The remainder raced stands' side. This has been rated at the top end of the race averages.

## 1858 MONTAZ RESTAURANT EBF STALLIONS NOVICE STKS (PLUS 10 RACE) 5f
**2:20** (2:23) (Class 4) 2-Y-O **£4,528** (£1,347; £673; £336) **Stalls** High

Form RPR
**1** **Sound And Silence** 2-9-2 0 WilliamBuick 3 83+
(Charlie Appleby) *str: w ldrs tl pushed ahd over 1f out: edgd lft and rdn ins fnl f: r.o wl and a holding chalr* **7/2**[1]
**2** ½ **Never Back Down (IRE)** 2-9-2 0 JamesDoyle 4 80
(Hugo Palmer) *cmpt: in tch: rdn and hdwy to press ldrs 2f out: drvn and str chal over 1f out: sustained effrt u.p: kpt on but a jst hld ins fnl f* **9/2**[2]

3 2 **Areen Faisal (IRE)** 2-9-2 0 .......... PaulHanagan 2 73+
(Richard Fahey) *leggy: rn green in last pair: sme prog 1f out: swtchd rt ins fnl f: styd on strly fnl 100yds to go 3rd last strides: no threat to ldng pair* **5/1**[3]

2 4 *nk* **The Love Doctor (IRE)**[17] [1496] 2-9-2 0 .......... JFEgan 1 72
(David Evans) *str: pressed ldrs: rdn and ev ch 2f out tl no ex ins fnl f: outpcd fnl 150yds: lost 3rd last strides* **7/1**

5 *3/4* **Unfortunately (IRE)** 2-8-11 0 .......... CliffordLee(5) 5 69
(K R Burke) *w'like: wl in tch in midfield: rdn 2f out: chsd ldrs but unable qck ent fnl f: edgd lft and kpt on same pce u.p ins fnl f* **9/1**

6 *1/2* **Shobrom (IRE)** 2-9-2 0 .......... PhillipMakin 8 68
(Richard Fahey) *unf: led: hdd and rdn over 1f out: unable qck ent fnl f: styd on same pce ins fnl f* **8/1**

7 *4 1/2* **Devil's Cowboy (IRE)** 2-9-2 0 .......... JamieSpencer 10 51
(Charles Hills) *athletic: w ldr: rdn ent fnl 2f: outpcd and edgd lft over 1f out: wknd ins fnl f* **10/1**

8 *2 1/2* **Contribute** 2-9-2 0 .......... DavidProbert 9 42
(Martyn Meade) *lengthy: dwlt and short of room leaving stalls: sn in tch in midfield: rdn over 2f out: sn struggling and outpcd: wknd over 1f out* **8/1**

9 *1* **Frozen Angel (IRE)** 2-9-2 0 .......... RichardKingscote 6 39
(Tom Dascombe) *str: bit bkwd: dwlt and short of room leaving stalls: rn green in rr: n.d* **18/1**

59.89s (0.79) **Going Correction** +0.025s/f (Good) **9 Ran SP% 116.1**
Speed ratings (Par 94): **94,93,90,89,88 87,80,76,74**
CSF £19.21 TOTE £4.90: £1.90, £2.10, £1.90; EX 20.40 Trifecta £89.20.
**Owner** Godolphin **Bred** Godolphin **Trained** Newmarket, Suffolk

**FOCUS**
The fourth-placed finisher, who was the only one with experience, had already shown a fair level of ability and this was probably a decent enough novice race.

## 1859 EBF STALLIONS BET365 CONDITIONS STKS (PLUS 10 RACE) 7f
2:55 (2:56) (Class 3) 3-Y-O **£9,056** (£2,695; £1,346; £673) **Stalls High**

Form RPR

1 **Beat The Bank**[53] [908] 3-9-6 0 .......... OisinMurphy 2 104+
(Andrew Balding) *str: stdd s: wl in tch in midfield: effrt to chal over 1f out: led ent fnl f: edgd lft and styd on wl ins fnl f* **7/1**[3]

12- 2 *nk* **Salsabeel (IRE)**[221] [6285] 3-9-6 106 .......... WilliamBuick 4 103+
(Charlie Appleby) *lengthy: t.k.h: trckd ldng pair: effrt to chal and hung rt over 1f out: stl chalng and drvn ins fnl f: kpt on but a hld* **5/4**[1]

351- 3 *5* **Via Egnatia (USA)**[199] [6945] 3-9-6 99 .......... (h[1]) FrankieDettori 6 90
(John Gosden) *taken steadily to s: t.k.h: led after 1f out: rdn 2f out: hdd ent fnl f: no ex and wknd ins fnl f* **15/8**[2]

053- 4 *1 1/4* **Vona (IRE)**[173] [7655] 3-9-1 88 .......... PaulHanagan 3 81
(Richard Fahey) *t.k.h: led for 1f out: chsd ldr tl 4th and outpcd ent fnl f: wknd ins fnl f* **25/1**

1- 5 *1 1/4* **Time Zone**[207] [6750] 3-9-6 82 .......... JamesDoyle 5 83+
(Peter Chapple-Hyam) *w'like: stdd s: t.k.h: hld up in wl in tch in last pair: rdn ent fnl 2f: outpcd and btn over 1f out: wknd ins fnl f* **9/1**

3-31 6 *7* **Mitigate**[55] [863] 3-9-1 77 .......... RyanMoore 1 59
(David Elsworth) *hld up in tch in rr: effrt ent fnl 2f: sn struggling and outpcd: wknd over 1f out* **25/1**

1m 24.4s (-1.00) **Going Correction** +0.025s/f (Good) **6 Ran SP% 109.4**
Speed ratings (Par 102): **106,105,99,98,97 89**
CSF £15.50 TOTE £7.20: £2.50, £1.30; EX 15.70 Trifecta £37.30.
**Owner** Abudiencia Co Ltd **Bred** A S Denniff **Trained** Kingsclere, Hants

**FOCUS**
The big two in the market, both entered in the 2,000 Guineas, were beaten by a gelding who can't go for the Classics, but the winner is not to be underestimated. The level as rated is a bit fluid.

## 1860 PLUSVITAL RACING GENEPAK H'CAP 1m
3:30 (3:31) (Class 2) (0-100,100) 4-Y-O+ **£12,938** (£3,850; £1,924; £962) **Stalls High**

Form RPR

/20- 1 **Next Stage**[300] [3534] 4-8-11 **90** .......... OisinMurphy 7 101
(Saeed bin Suroor) *racd centre: stdd and short of room leaving stalls: t.k.h and sn chsng ldrs: chsd ldr 1/2-way: rdn to ld over 1f out: wandered but styd on wl ins fnl f: rdn out: 1st of 10 in gp* **4/1**[2]

210- 2 *1 1/2* **Shaiyem (IRE)**[332] [2473] 4-8-7 **86** .......... TomMarquand 1 93
(Richard Hannon) *lw: racd centre: t.k.h: hld up towards rr: stdy hdwy 1/2-way: rdn to chse ldrs 2f out: styd on same pce ins fnl f: wnt 2nd towards fin: 2nd of 10 in gp* **12/1**

/1-0 3 *3/4* **Sacred Act**[17] [1492] 6-9-3 **96** .......... FrankieDettori 13 102
(John Gosden) *racd stands' side: t.k.h: hld up in midfield: hdwy chse ldrs 2f out: rdn to press wnr and edgd rt over 1f out: no ex ins fnl f: wknd wl ins fnl f and lost 2nd towards fin: 1st of 3 in gp* **10/3**[1]

65-0 4 *2* **Highland Colori (IRE)**[17] [1494] 9-9-5 **98** .......... (v) DavidProbert 11 99
(Andrew Balding) *racd centre: overall ldr: rdn and hdd over 1f out: no ex and u.p 1f out: styd on same pce ins fnl f: 3rd of 10 in gp* **28/1**

224- 5 *nse* **Brigliadoro (IRE)**[166] [7779] 6-8-11 **90** .......... SilvestreDeSousa 3 91
(Philip McBride) *racd centre: stdd s: hld up in tch in rr: hdwy u.p over 1f out: kpt on ins fnl f: nvr threatened ldrs: 4th of 10 in gp* **10/1**

6 *nk* **Repercussion**[260] 4-9-2 **95** .......... (h[1]) StevieDonohoe 9 95
(Charlie Fellowes) *racd centre: hld up in midfield: effrt 2f out: no imp tl styd on u.p ins fnl f: no threat to ldrs: 5th of 10 in gp* **20/1**

51-3 7 *1/2* **Timeless Art (IRE)**[16] [1512] 4-8-7 **86** oh1 .......... JoeyHaynes 5 85
(K R Burke) *lw: racd centre: hld up in midfield: effrt ent fnl 2f: no imp u.p over 1f out: kpt on same pce ins fnl f: 6th of 10 in gp* **13/2**[3]

0-50 8 *nse* **Mutarakez (IRE)**[17] [1492] 5-8-3 **89** .......... JordanUys(7) 14 88+
(Brian Meehan) *racd centre: t.k.h: hld up in tch in rr: pushed along over 1f out: nt clrest of runs and swtchd lft 1f out: kpt on ins fnl f: nvr trbld ldrs: 7th of 10 in gp* **9/1**

031- 9 *1/2* **Lavetta**[181] [7472] 5-8-9 **88** .......... JoeFanning 8 86
(Alan Swinbank) *racd centre: taken down early: chsd ldrs: rdn ent fnl 2f: unable qck over 1f out: lost pl and btn 1f out: kpt on same pce ins fnl f: 8th 0f 10 in gp* **20/1**

3630 10 *nk* **Brex Drago (ITY)**[45] [1043] 5-9-2 **100** .......... GeorgeWood(5) 6 97
(Marco Botti) *racd centre: t.k.h: hld up in midfield: effrt over 2f out: no imp u.p over 1f out: kpt on same pce ins fnl f: 9th of 10 in gp* **33/1**

16-6 11 *4 1/2* **Strong Steps**[17] [1492] 5-8-13 **92** .......... (p) TonyHamilton 12 79
(Roger Fell) *racd stands' side: led gp and chsd ldrs overall tl midfield and rdn 1/2-way: wknd over 1f out: 2nd of 3 in gp* **8/1**

022- 12 *8* **Briyouni (FR)**[164] [7825] 4-8-8 **87** .......... ShaneGray 15 55
(Kevin Ryan) *racd stands' side: hld up in rr: effrt ent fnl 2f: no imp: bhd and eased wl ins fnl f: 3rd of 3 in gp* **16/1**

500- 13 *14* **Secret Art (IRE)**[193] [7121] 7-9-0 **93** .......... MartinDwyer 4 29
(William Knight) *racd centre: in tch in midfield: rdn over 3f out: sn struggling and dropped to rr 2f out: bhd and eased fnl f* **50/1**

1m 38.02s (-0.58) **Going Correction** +0.025s/f (Good) **13 Ran SP% 118.1**
Speed ratings (Par 109): **103,101,100,98,98 98,97,97,97,97 92,84,70**
CSF £46.86 CT £184.83 TOTE £5.40: £2.30, £3.40, £1.90; EX 57.90 Trifecta £200.20.
**Owner** Godolphin **Bred** Meon Valley Stud **Trained** Newmarket, Suffolk

**FOCUS**
Three of these raced stands' side early on, with the best of those finishing third, but the majority raced up the middle. The groups merged in the closing stages. This has been rated on the positive side.

## 1861 BET365 FEILDEN STKS (LISTED RACE) 1m 1f
4:05 (4:06) (Class 1) 3-Y-O
**£20,982** (£7,955; £3,981; £1,983; £995; £499) **Stalls High**

Form RPR

11-3 1 **Khalidi**[16] [1518] 3-9-0 95 .......... FrankieDettori 2 109
(John Gosden) *lw: hld up in tch: clsd to trck ldrs 2f out: rdn to chal over 1f out: led ins fnl f: r.o wl and a holding rival after* **7/2**[2]

123- 2 *nk* **Salouen (IRE)**[178] [7539] 3-9-0 110 .......... RyanMoore 1 108
(Sylvester Kirk) *t.k.h early: pressed ldr tl rdn to ld 2f out: drvn and hdd ins fnl f: kpt on but a hld by wnr after* **5/2**[1]

03-1 3 *3 1/4* **Law And Order (IRE)**[10] [1621] 3-9-3 104 .......... MartinHarley 3 104
(James Tate) *broke wl: t.k.h and restrained into midfield after 2f: clsd to press ldrs and travelling wl ent fnl 2f: rdn wl over 1f out: unable qck: wknd ins fnl f* **6/1**[3]

013- 4 *3* **Max Zorin (IRE)**[205] [6801] 3-9-0 90 .......... DavidProbert 5 94
(Andrew Balding) *t.k.h: chsd ldrs 7f out: rdn over 2f out: outpcd and sltly impeded over 1f out: wl hld 4th and plugged on same pce fnl f* **25/1**

114- 5 *hd* **Apex King (IRE)**[241] [5646] 3-9-0 99 .......... AndreaAtzeni 4 94
(Ed Dunlop) *t.k.h: hld up in tch: rdn 3f out: unable qck and outpcd over 1f out: wl hld and plugged on same pce fnl f* **15/2**

212- 6 *3 3/4* **Al Hamdany (IRE)**[183] [7409] 3-9-0 97 .......... HarryBentley 6 86
(Marco Botti) *in tch in rr: rdn 3f out: struggling u.p 2f out: wknd and drifted rt ent fnl f* **17/2**

164- 7 *3/4* **Montataire (IRE)**[192] [7148] 3-9-0 103 .......... JoeFanning 7 84
(Mark Johnston) *t.k.h: sn led: hdd 2f out: sn rdn and lost pl qckly over 1f out: wknd fnl f* **7/2**[2]

1m 50.43s (-1.27) **Going Correction** +0.025s/f (Good) **7 Ran SP% 113.4**
Speed ratings (Par 106): **106,105,102,100,100 96,96**
CSF £12.48 TOTE £4.80: £2.30, £1.80; EX 12.60 Trifecta £79.00.
**Owner** Nizar Anwar **Bred** Aston House Stud **Trained** Newmarket, Suffolk

**FOCUS**
This didn't look a strong running of the Feilden Stakes, but the winner is progressive and the runner-up, who has been rated close to form, should come on for the outing.

## 1862 ALEX SCOTT MAIDEN STKS (PLUS 10 RACE) (C&G) 7f
4:35 (4:36) (Class 4) 3-Y-O **£5,175** (£1,540; £769; £384) **Stalls High**

Form RPR

52-3 1 **Jewel House**[16] [1513] 3-9-0 79 .......... FrankieDettori 7 88+
(John Gosden) *mde all: rdn and hrd pressed over 1f out: forged ahd and lft in command ins fnl f: styd on wl and eased cl home* **15/2**[3]

2- 2 *1 3/4* **Top Mission**[172] [7665] 3-9-0 0 .......... SilvestreDeSousa 4 83+
(Saeed bin Suroor) *str: bit bkwd: hld up in tch in midfield: hdwy over 2f out: rdn and str chal over 1f out tl no ex and hung lft ins fnl f: wknd towards fin but hld on for 2nd* **7/4**[1]

232- 3 *nk* **Firefright (IRE)**[179] [7502] 3-9-0 90 .......... RyanMoore 5 82
(Jeremy Noseda) *t.k.h: hld up in tch in midfield: effrt jst over 2f out: chsd ldrs but unable qck over 1f out: kpt on same pce ins fnl f: pressing for 2nd towards fin* **7/4**[1]

4 *hd* **Afaak** 3-9-0 0 .......... DaneO'Neill 6 82+
(Charles Hills) *unf: v.s.a: rn green in tch in rr: rdn 3f out: hdwy jst over 1f out: stl green but styd on wl ins fnl f: pressing for 2nd cl home* **16/1**

2- 5 *4* **Mukalal**[144] [8088] 3-9-0 0 .......... (h[1]) JimCrowley 2 71
(Marcus Tregoning) *tall: chsd ldrs: ev ch 2f out: sn rdn and unable qck: btn 1f out: wknd ins fnl f* **7/1**[2]

0- 6 *1* **Jumira Prince (IRE)**[322] [2756] 3-9-0 0 .......... AndreaAtzeni 3 68
(Roger Varian) *tall: chsd wnr tl over jst over 2f out: sn rdn: lost pl and btn 1f out: wknd ins fnl f* **8/1**

00 7 *6* **Never You Mind (IRE)**[6] [1730] 3-8-11 0 .......... CallumShepherd(3) 9 52
(Charles Hills) *hld up in tch: shkn up jst over 2f out: pushed along and outpcd over 1f out: wknd fnl f* **100/1**

0 8 *17* **Mister Chow**[29] [1287] 3-9-0 0 .......... TimmyMurphy 1 6
(Gary Moore) *a towards rr: lost tch 1/2-way* **100/1**

50 9 *nk* **Lord E (IRE)**[20] [1426] 3-8-11 0 .......... HectorCrouch(3) 8 5
(Gary Moore) *a last trio: struggling 3f out: bhd fnl 2f* **250/1**

1m 24.84s (-0.56) **Going Correction** +0.025s/f (Good) **9 Ran SP% 116.4**
Speed ratings (Par 100): **104,102,101,101,96 95,88,69,69**
CSF £21.39 TOTE £8.50: £1.90, £1.30, £1.10; EX 27.60 Trifecta £42.30.
**Owner** K Abdullah **Bred** Juddmonte Farms Ltd **Trained** Newmarket, Suffolk

**FOCUS**
It's hard to get that excited by this maiden, given the 1st and 3rd had already had a few chances and the winner got things his own way in front, while the 2nd seemed to have an issue late on, but still fair form and the 4th shaped well.

## 1863 QUY MILL HOTEL & SPA H'CAP 5f
5:05 (5:07) (Class 3) (0-95,95) 4-Y-O+ **£9,056** (£2,695; £1,346; £673) **Stalls High**

Form RPR

410- 1 **El Astronaute (IRE)**[227] [6119] 4-9-0 **88** .......... JasonHart 1 93
(John Quinn) *chsd ldr tl rdn to ld over 1f out: hdd 1f out: styd chalng: edgd lft u.p ins fnl f: battled bk gamely to ld on post* **5/1**[2]

000- 2 *shd* **Majestic Hero (IRE)**[193] [7124] 5-9-0 **88** .......... JamieSpencer 5 93
(Ronald Harris) *chsd ldrs: rdn and ev ch over 1f out: led 1f out: drvn and hrd pressed ins fnl f: kpt on gamely u.p: hdd on post* **9/1**

142- 3 *nk* **Oh So Sassy**[274] [4461] 7-9-2 **90** .......... TedDurcan 2 94
(Chris Wall) *hld up in tch towards rr: effrt and hdwy jst over 1f out: rdn and styd on to chal fnl 100yds: kpt on wl* **33/1**

260- 4 *nse* **Olivia Fallow (IRE)**[220] [6327] 5-8-11 **85** .......... GrahamLee 11 89
(Paul Midgley) *hld up in tch in midfield: hdwy u.p to chse ldrs 1f out: ev ch fnl 100yds: kpt on wl* **9/1**

032- 5 *3/4* **Seeking Magic**[168] [7752] 9-9-7 **95** .......... (t) RyanTate 8 96
(Clive Cox) *taken down early: bmpd s: hld up in tch in midfield: effrt u.p over 1f out: styd on wl u.p fnl 100yds* **13/2**[3]

320- **6** ¾ **Vibrant Chords**$^{200}$ [6916] 4-9-2 **90** .................................. HarryBentley 9 92+
(Henry Candy) *hld up in tch in last pair: effrt over 1f out: nt clr run and snatched up 1f out: rdn and hdwy ins fnl f: styd on strly fnl 100yds: nt rcvr* **2/1**$^{1}$

/00- **7** ¾ **Independence Day (IRE)**$^{338}$ [2272] 4-9-5 **93** .................. RyanMoore 3 89
(Robert Cowell) *in tch in midfield: rdn 2f out: chsd ldrs ins fnl f: no ex and one pced fnl 100yds* **5/1**$^{2}$

1461 **8** 1¼ **Dungannon**$^{40}$ [1110] 10-8-6 **87** ..................................(b) JoshuaBryan(7) 10 78
(Andrew Balding) *chsd ldrs: rdn over 1f out: unable qck and edgd rt ins fnl f: wknd towards fin* **12/1**

3/-4 **9** 2¾ **Sir Ottoman (FR)**$^{42}$ [1078] 4-9-7 **95** ........................................ JFEgan 4 76
(Mohamed Moubarak) *hld up in tch in rr: pushed along and trying to cl whn stmbld over 1f out: hld together tl reminders and kpt on same pce ins fnl f* **40/1**

00 **10** 1½ **Old Fashioned (CHI)**$^{24}$ [1362] 4-9-6 **94** ...............................(b) PatDobbs 6 70
(Rune Haugen) *in tch in midfield: lost pl u.p over 1f out: wknd ins fnl f* **80/1**

2010 **11** 1¾ **Foxy Forever (IRE)**$^{17}$ [1487] 7-8-9 **83** ......................(bt) ConnorBeasley 7 53
(Michael Wigham) *bmpd s: sn led: rdn and hdd over 1f out: sn lost pl and wknd ins fnl f* **14/1**

59.04s (-0.06) **Going Correction** +0.025s/f (Good) **11** Ran SP% **121.0**
Speed ratings (Par 107): **101,100,100,100,99 97,96,94,90,87 85**
CSF £50.56 CT £1362.68 TOTE £8.70: £2.40, £2.70, £4.90; EX 77.30 Trifecta £1089.20.
**Owner** Ross Harmon **Bred** T Jones **Trained** Settrington, N Yorks

**FOCUS**
A decent sprint handicap, although the first seven were making their seasonal reappearance.
T/Jkpt: Not won. T/Plt: £17.80 to a £1 stake. Pool: £85,828.48 - winning units. T/Qpdt: £4.00 to a £1 stake. Pool: £6,661.84 - 1227.78 winning units. **Steve Payne**

## 1817 SOUTHWELL (L-H)
### Tuesday, April 18

**OFFICIAL GOING: Fibresand: standard**
Wind: Moderate across Weather: Fine and dry

## 1864 TOTEPLACEPOT AT BETFRED.COM H'CAP 1m 3f 23y(F)
**2:10** (2:10) (Class 6) (0-65,67) 4-Y-0+ **£2,264** (£673; £336; £168) **Stalls** Low

Form RPR

0-05 **1** **Bushel (USA)**$^{34}$ [1207] 7-8-13 **57** ........................................(p) TomEaves 4 62
(Tony Newcombe) *trckd ldrs on inner: pushed along over 3f out: rdn wl over 2f out: drvn over 1f out: swtchd lft and hrd drvn ent fnl f: styd on to ld nr fin* **11/2**$^{3}$

550- **2** hd **Young Tom**$^{176}$ [7582] 4-8-13 **60** .............................. AlistairRawlinson(3) 5 65
(Michael Appleby) *trckd ldr: hdwy and cl up 4f out: chal wl over 2f out and sn rdn: drvn and ev ch ins fnl f: kpt on* **5/2**$^{2}$

010- **3** ½ **Lean On Pete (IRE)**$^{186}$ [7336] 8-9-5 **63** ........................... AndrewMullen 1 67
(Ollie Pears) *led: jnd over 4f out: pushed along 3f out: rdn over 2f out: narrow advantage and drvn over 1f out: hdd and no ex last 50 yds* **10/1**

44-2 **4** nk **Inflexiball**$^{13}$ [1560] 5-9-0 **58** ............................................ FrannyNorton 9 62
(John Mackie) *trckd ldrs: pushed along over 3f out: wd st and sn rdn: chsd ldrs and drvn over 1f out: kpt on u.p fnl f* **9/4**$^{1}$

4550 **5** ¾ **Commissar**$^{41}$ [1081] 8-8-9 **53** ........................................(tp) RobHornby 2 56
(Mandy Rowland) *trckd ldrs: cl up over 4f out: smooth effrt to chal 3f out: rdn to dispute ld 2f out: drvn and ev ch ent fnl f: kpt on same pce* **20/1**

005 **6** 14 **Fire In Babylon (IRE)**$^{35}$ [1188] 9-8-4 **51** oh6............(b) AaronJones(3) 10 31
(Giles Bravery) *rr: hdwy over 4f out: sn pushed along and wd st: rdn over 2f out: n.d* **40/1**

6136 **7** 7 **Thou Swell (IRE)**$^{10}$ [1629] 5-8-8 **57** ........................... CharlieBennett(5) 3 26
(Shaun Harris) *towards rr on inner and sn pushed along: rdn along and sme hdwy over 5f out: drvn over 3f out: nvr a factor* **6/1**

060- **8** 7 **Carragold**$^{327}$ [2618] 11-9-2 **60** .............................................. CamHardie 7 18
(Antony Brittain) *a towards rr: rdn along 5f out: sn outpcd and bhd* **28/1**

230- **9** 25 **Competent**$^{344}$ [2093] 5-9-7 **65** ........................................... BarryMcHugh 6
(Tim Fitzgerald) *stmbld s and rr: hdwy to chse ldrs over 7f out: rdn along 5f out: sn lost pl and bhd* **11/1**

2m 29.86s (1.86) **Going Correction** +0.225s/f (Slow) **9** Ran SP% **117.1**
Speed ratings (Par 101): **102,101,101,101,100 90,85,80,62**
CSF £19.56 CT £135.70 TOTE £6.80: £2.10, £1.20, £2.70; EX 29.00 Trifecta £186.20.
**Owner** Nigel Hardy **Bred** Darley **Trained** Yarnscombe, Devon
■ Stewards' Enquiry : Tom Eaves two-day ban: used whip above permitted level (2-3 May)
Alistair Rawlinson two-day ban: used whip above permitted level (2-3 May)

**FOCUS**
A modest handicap in which an ordinary gallop picked up turning for home. The first five, who finished in a heap, pulled clear of the remainder.

## 1865 TOTETRIFECTA AT BETFRED.COM CLAIMING STKS 1m 3f 23y(F)
**2:45** (2:45) (Class 6) 4-Y-0+ **£2,264** (£673; £336; £168) **Stalls** Low

Form RPR

-101 **1** **Tatting**$^{28}$ [1292] 8-10-0 80 ................................................ PaulMulrennan 4 86
(Lawrence Mullaney) *hld up in rr: hdwy and wd st: pushed along to chse ldng pair 2f out and sn swtchd lft: swtchd rt to outer and effrt ent fnl f: sn rdn and styd on wl to ld nr line* **11/4**$^{2}$

0114 **2** hd **Luv U Whatever**$^{10}$ [1628] 7-10-0 82 ................................ AndrewMullen 5 86
(Michael Attwater) *trckd ldng pair: hdwy 4f out: sn cl up: chal over 2f out: rdn and edgd lft jst over 1f out: drvn to take slt ld ins fnl f: hdd and no ex nr line* **5/2**$^{1}$

2312 **3** ¾ **Brigadoon**$^{28}$ [1291] 10-9-1 79 ................................ AlistairRawlinson(3) 1 74
(Michael Appleby) *led 1f: trckd ldr: cl up 5f out: led over 4f out: rdn along and jnd over 2f out: drvn and carried lft jst over 1f out: hdd narrowly ins fnl f: ev ch tl no ex towards fin* **4/1**$^{3}$

-530 **4** 8 **Esteaming**$^{63}$ [728] 7-8-13 78 ......................................(p) RowanScott(5) 2 62
(Keith Dalgleish) *trckd ldrs on inner: effrt over 3f out and sn rdn along: drvn and outpcd fr wl over 1f out* **7/1**

0-56 **5** 2 **Fattsota**$^{21}$ [921] 9-10-0 89 ............................................(p$^{1}$) DanielTudhope 3 68
(David O'Meara) *pushed along s and led after 1f: rdn along and hdd over 4f out. drvn over 3f out: sn wknd* **4/1**$^{3}$

2m 28.26s (0.26) **Going Correction** +0.225s/f (Slow) **5** Ran SP% **107.7**
Speed ratings (Par 101): **108,107,107,101,100**
CSF £9.51 TOTE £3.00: £1.50, £1.90; EX 9.30 Trifecta £22.30.
**Owner** The Usual Suspects **Bred** Darley **Trained** Great Habton, N Yorks

**FOCUS**
A useful event in which the gallop was no more than fair to the home straight. The winner came down the centre.

## 1866 TOTEQUADPOT AT BETFRED.COM MEDIAN AUCTION MAIDEN STKS 1m 13y(F)
**3:20** (3:22) (Class 5) 3-5-Y-0 **£2,911** (£866; £432; £216) **Stalls** Low

Form RPR

3- **1** **Passcode**$^{181}$ [7466] 3-8-8 0 ................................................ LiamKeniry 6 68
(Andrew Balding) *cl up: rdn along over 2f out: led 1 1/2f out: jnd ent fnl f: drvn and hdd narrowly fnl 100 yds: rallied gamely to ld again nr line* **11/8**$^{1}$

5 **2** shd **Amitie Waltz (FR)**$^{43}$ [1069] 5-9-13 0 .................................... ShaneKelly 4 77
(Richard Hughes) *trckd ldrs: smooth hdwy over 2f out: cl up over 1f out: sn chal and led on bit last 100 yds: sn shkn up: hdd and no ex nr line* **5/1**

652 **3** 5 **Eddiebet**$^{12}$ [1589] 3-8-13 74 ............................................. DanielTudhope 1 61
(David O'Meara) *led: pushed along 3f out: rdn over 2f out: hdd 1 1/2f out: sn drvn and grad wknd fnl f* **5/2**$^{2}$

4-0 **4** 1½ **Eburaci (IRE)**$^{16}$ [1513] 3-8-13 0 .......................................(v$^{1}$) TomQueally 7 58
(Charlie Fellowes) *cl up on outer: rdn along over 2f out: sn drvn and wknd over 1f out* **7/2**$^{3}$

**5** 17 **Toast Of London** 4-9-8 0 .................................................. CamHardie 5 17
(Antony Brittain) *green and sn rdn along in rr: detached 1/2-way: kpt on fnl 3f* **66/1**

P **6** 6 **Avago Josh**$^{17}$ [1497] 3-8-13 0 .............................................. TomEaves 2 5
(Ivan Furtado) *chsd ldrs: rdn along over 3f out: drvn and outpcd over 2f out* **100/1**

1m 46.18s (2.48) **Going Correction** +0.225s/f (Slow)
**WFA** 3 from 4yo+ 14lb **6** Ran SP% **112.0**
Speed ratings (Par 103): **96,95,90,89,72 66**
CSF £8.90 TOTE £2.40: £1.50, £2.40; EX 9.80 Trifecta £15.80.
**Owner** Sheikh Juma Dalmook Al Maktoum **Bred** David & Nicola Leggate **Trained** Kingsclere, Hants

**FOCUS**
No more than a fair maiden and just an ordinary gallop but the first two pulled clear in the closing stages.

## 1867 TOTEEXACTA AT BETFRED.COM H'CAP 7f 14y(F)
**3:55** (3:56) (Class 4) (0-80,80) 4-Y-0+ **£4,690** (£1,395; £697; £348) **Stalls** Low

Form RPR

1421 **1** **Custard The Dragon**$^{14}$ [1546] 4-9-7 **80** ...............................(p) BenCurtis 1 92
(John Mackie) *trckd ldrs on inner: hdwy to trck ldr 3f out: chal 2f out: rdn wl over 1f out: drvn ins fnl f: led and edgd rt towards fin* **7/2**$^{2}$

102- **2** hd **Robero**$^{235}$ [5858] 5-9-0 **76** ........................................ NathanEvans(3) 3 87
(Michael Easterby) *led: jnd over 2f out and sn rdn along: hrd pressed and drvn ent fnl f: hdd narrowly whn sltly hmpd nr fin* **9/4**$^{1}$

5100 **3** 8 **Among Angels**$^{35}$ [1185] 5-9-4 **77** ...............................(b) RobertWinston 2 67
(Daniel Mark Loughnane) *trckd ldrs: hdwy to chse ldng pair over 2f out: sn rdn along and kpt on one pce* **17/2**

0552 **4** nk **Red Touch (USA)**$^{28}$ [1296] 5-9-0 **76** ..................(p$^{1}$) AlistairRawlinson(3) 4 65
(Michael Appleby) *towards rr and sn pushed along: rdn along and outpcd 1/2-way: sme hdwy on inner over 2f out: plugged on: n.d* **7/2**$^{2}$

23 **5** 3½ **Order Of Service**$^{20}$ [1433] 7-8-10 **74** .......................(e) CharlieBennett(5) 5 54
(Shaun Harris) *s.i.s and lost several l s: a rr* **7/1**$^{3}$

-234 **6** 6 **Intensical (IRE)**$^{26}$ [1323] 6-9-4 **77** ......................................(p) DavidNolan 7 42
(Ivan Furtado) *chsd ldrs: rdn along 3f out: sn outpcd* **15/2**

200- **7** 5 **Jay Kay**$^{185}$ [7360] 8-8-8 **74** ........................................(h) PatrickO'Hanlon(7) 6 26
(K R Burke) *prom: rdn along over 3f out: drvn and wknd over 2f out* **25/1**

1m 29.99s (-0.31) **Going Correction** +0.225s/f (Slow) **7** Ran SP% **113.9**
Speed ratings (Par 105): **110,109,100,100,96 89,83**
CSF £11.72 TOTE £4.00: £2.00, £1.70; EX 12.20 Trifecta £46.30.
**Owner** Derbyshire Racing **Bred** Mr & Mrs Kevan Watts **Trained** Church Broughton , Derbys
■ Stewards' Enquiry : Ben Curtis cautioned to his future conduct in races

**FOCUS**
A fair handicap in which the first two pulled clear in the straight.

## 1868 @TOTEPOOLRACING FOLLOW FOR RACING NEWS H'CAP 7f 14y(F)
**4:25** (4:28) (Class 6) (0-60,66) 4-Y-0+ **£2,264** (£673; £336; £168) **Stalls** Low

Form RPR

60-0 **1** **Luath**$^{39}$ [1125] 4-9-4 **57** ............................................................ TomEaves 13 64
(Suzzanne France) *dwlt: sn chsng ldrs on outer: wd st: hdwy to chal 2f out: rdn over 1f out and ev ch: drvn ins fnl f: kpt on wl to ld towards fin* **33/1**

3321 **2** ½ **Prince Of Time**$^{12}$ [1587] 5-8-8 **54** .............................. CallumRodriguez(7) 2 60
(Richard Ford) *in tch: hdwy on inner to trck ldrs 3f out: effrt to ld over 1f out: rdn and edgd rt ins fnl f: hdd and no ex towards fin* **9/2**$^{2}$

000/ **3** 1¼ **Geordie George (IRE)**$^{151}$ 5-9-7 **60** ............................ DougieCostello 11 62
(Rebecca Menzies) *hmpd sn after s: trckd ldrs: hdwy wl over 2f out and sn cl up: rdn to chal wl over 1f out and ev ch: drvn ins fnl f: kpt on same pce fnl 75 yds* **18/1**

0250 **4** 1¾ **Monsieur Jimmy**$^{12}$ [1593] 5-9-6 **59** ................................. DanielTudhope 5 57
(Declan Carroll) *hld up: hdwy over 2f out: chsd ldrs wl over 1f out: swtchd rt and rdn ent fnl f: kpt on towards fin* **8/1**

-042 **5** ¾ **Trust Me Boy**$^{12}$ [1587] 9-9-1 **54** ........................................... FrannyNorton 6 50
(John E Long) *chsd ldrs: rdn along wl over 2f out: drvn over 1f out: kpt on same pce* **10/1**

2234 **6** 1¾ **General Tufto**$^{2}$ [1823] 12-8-12 **51** ......................................(b) MartinLane 9 42
(Charles Smith) *dwlt and sn rdn along in rr: hdwy over 2f out: styd on appr fnl f: nrst fin* **5/1**$^{3}$

312- **7** 1¾ **Eium Mac**$^{398}$ [956] 8-9-0 **53** ..................................................(b) JoeDoyle 4 39
(Neville Bycroft) *cl up on inner: led after 2f: rdn along wl over 2f out: hdd wl over 1f out: grad wknd* **14/1**

0261 **8** 1¼ **Hipz (IRE)**$^{5}$ [1755] 6-9-13 **66** 6ex.............................(p) IrineuGoncalves 10 49
(Ivan Furtado) *midfield on outer: wd st: rdn and sme hdwy 2f out: sn drvn and n.d* **8/1**

0150 **9** nk **Dr Red Eye**$^{22}$ [1408] 9-8-13 **52** ..............................................(p) BenCurtis 12 34
(Scott Dixon) *hmpd sn after s: prom: rdn along wl over 2f out: sn drvn and grad wknd* **28/1**

6-05 **10** 1 **Demand Respect**$^{14}$ [1545] 4-8-7 **46** oh1 .......................... KieranO'Neill 8 25
(Henry Spiller) *dwlt: a towards rr* **66/1**

2006 **11** 2 **Prisom (IRE)**$^{10}$ [1618] 4-8-12 **58** .................................(p) DavidEgan(7) 1 32
(Gay Kelleway) *nvr bttr than midfield* **16/1**

046- **12** ¾ **Sooqaan**$^{185}$ [7368] 6-9-8 61 ........................................................ CamHardie 14 33
(Antony Brittain) *led and swtchd lft sn after s: hdd after 2f and cl up: rdn along wl over 2f out: sn wknd* **20/1**

-000 **13** 17 **Star Of The Stage**$^{29}$ [1285] 5-9-9 **62** ................................(p) LiamKeniry 3
(John Butler) *a rr* **33/1**

233- **14** *10* **Midlight**[245] 5521 5-9-2 **55**................................ JamesSullivan 7
(Ruth Carr) *hmpd sn after s: chsd ldrs: rdn along 1/2-way: sn lost pl and bhd* **3/1**[1]

1m 31.46s (1.16) **Going Correction** +0.225s/f (Slow) **14** Ran SP% **124.6**
Speed ratings (Par 101): **102,101,100,98,97 95,93,91,91,90 87,87,67,56**
CSF £176.03 CT £2921.42 TOTE £37.30: £7.50, £2.00, £6.10; EX 290.40 Trifecta £6646.20 Part won..
**Owner** Miss Kate Dobb & Stuart Dobb **Bred** Stuart Dobb & Miss Kate Dobb **Trained** Norton, N Yorks
■ Stewards' Enquiry : Cam Hardie four-day ban: careless riding (May 2-5)

**FOCUS**
A modest handicap in which the gallop was reasonable throughout. The winner raced towards the stands' side in the straight and bounced back to near his best.

## 1869 TOTEPOOL RACECOURSE DEBIT CARD BETTING AVAILABLE H'CAP 4f 214y(F)

**4:55** (4:56) (Class 6) (0-65,65) 4-Y-0+ **£2,264** (£673; £336; £168) **Stalls** Low

Form RPR

4244 **1** **Borough Boy (IRE)**[14] 1547 7-9-3 **61**................................(v) MartinLane 1 71
(Derek Shaw) *racd towards far side: prom: sltly outpcd and rdn along 2f out: hdwy over 1f out: chal ins fnl f: kpt on u.p to ld last 75 yds* **11/4**[1]

4016 **2** *1 1/4* **Jacob's Pillow**[14] 1547 6-9-7 **65**................................(p) DanielTudhope 7 70
(Rebecca Bastiman) *racd towards stands side: prom: hdwy to chal 2f out: rdn over 1f out: drvn and ev ch ins fnl f: kpt on same pce towards fin* **8/1**

0042 **3** *3/4* **Powerful Wind (IRE)**[20] 1429 8-9-6 **64**................................(t) WilliamCarson 2 66
(Charlie Wallis) *cl up towards far side: led over 3f out: rdn wl over 1f out: drvn ent fnl f: hdd and no ex last 75 yds* **5/1**[2]

0252 **4** *1* **Culloden**[6] 1722 5-8-7 **56**................................ CharlieBennett(5) 3 55
(Shaun Harris) *cl up centre: pushed along over 2f out: rdn over 1f out: sn drvn and kpt on same pce* **15/2**

0-05 **5** *2 3/4* **Silver Bid (USA)**[2] 1819 5-9-4 **62**................................ JamesSullivan 9 51
(Karen Tutty) *racd towards stands side: dwlt and towards rr: hdwy 1/2-way: rdn wl over 1f out: kpt on fnl f: nrst fin* **13/2**[3]

-550 **6** *shd* **Ryedale Rio (IRE)**[6] 1720 4-9-3 **61**................................ DavidAllan 6 49
(Tim Easterby) *racd centre: cl up: pushed along 1/2-way: rdn 2f out: sn drvn and wknd* **5/1**[2]

0-00 **7** *2 1/2* **Coiste Bodhar (IRE)**[20] 1431 6-9-6 **64**................................(p) KieranO'Neill 5 43
(Scott Dixon) *racd centre: led: hdd over 3f out: sn rdn along: wknd wl over 2f out* **25/1**

4525 **8** *3/4* **Novabridge**[14] 1547 9-8-9 **58**................................(b) GemmaTutty(5) 4 35
(Karen Tutty) *dwlt: a rr* **8/1**

403- **9** *9* **Jazz Legend (USA)**[228] 6098 4-9-2 **60**................................(p) RobHornby 8 4
(Mandy Rowland) *racd towards stands side: chsd ldrs: rdn along bef halwfay: sn outpcd* **33/1**

1m 0.46s (0.76) **Going Correction** +0.20s/f (Slow) **9** Ran SP% **114.1**
Speed ratings (Par 101): **101,99,97,96,91 91,87,86,72**
CSF £25.18 CT £104.30 TOTE £4.00: £2.00, £2.40, £1.50; EX 28.40 Trifecta £81.50.
**Owner** Brian Johnson (Northamptonshire) **Bred** E Kopica And M Rosenfeld **Trained** Sproxton, Leics

**FOCUS**
A modest sprint in which the gallop was sound throughout. The first four finished clear and the 2nd helps to set the level.

## 1870 COLLECT TOTEPOOL WINNINGS AT BETFRED SHOPS APPRENTICE H'CAP 1m 6f 21y(F)

**5:25** (5:25) (Class 5) (0-70,72) 4-Y-0+ **£2,911** (£866; £432; £216) **Stalls** Low

Form RPR

3160 **1** **Scrafton**[45] 1027 6-9-3 **62**................................ AledBeech(3) 2 70
(Tony Carroll) *.trckd ldrs: smooth hdwy over 3f out: led 2f out: sn pushed clr: readily* **7/1**

342 **2** *3* **Sugarloaf Mountain (IRE)**[39] 1122 4-10-0 **72**.........(t) KieranSchofield 3 75
(Brian Ellison) *cl up: led after 2f: rdn along over 3f out: hdd 2f out: sn drvn and kpt on same pce* **10/3**[3]

-431 **3** *2* **Virnon**[12] 1590 6-10-0 **70**................................ FinleyMarsh 4 70
(Alan Swinbank) *prom: pushed along 4f out: rdn and lost pl over 3f out: hdwy on wd outside over 2f out: rdn to chse ldng pair wl over 1f out: sn drvn and no imp* **9/4**[1]

006/ **4** *8* **Chivers (IRE)**[36] 8256 6-9-9 **70**................................(t[1]) RossaRyan(5) 7 59
(Daniel Steele) *in tch on outer: trckd ldrs 1/2-way: rdn along 4f out: wd st: sn drvn and plugged on one pce* **25/1**

/00- **5** *1 1/2* **Duke Of Sonning**[16] 4483 5-9-9 **68**................................ AldenBlakemore(3) 1 55
(Shaun Harris) *led 2f: trckd ldrs on inner: pushed along over 4f out: rdn over 3f out: sn drvn and outpcd* **50/1**

3453 **6** *nk* **Oyster Card**[12] 1585 4-8-4 **51** oh6................................(p) GabrieleMalune(3) 5 37
(Michael Appleby) *cl up: disp ld over 4f out: rdn along 3f out: sn drvn and wknd fnl 2f* **7/1**

0/31 **7** *1 3/4* **Ascendant**[55] 859 11-8-12 **59**................................ ConnorMurtagh(5) 6 43
(Johnny Farrelly) *hld up: hdwy on outer to trck ldrs over 7f out: rdn along over 4f out: drvn and wknd 3f out* **11/4**[2]

3m 14.25s (5.95) **Going Correction** +0.225s/f (Slow)
**WFA** 4 from 5yo+ 1lb **7** Ran SP% **111.3**
Speed ratings (Par 103): **92,90,89,84,83 83,82**
CSF £28.83 TOTE £7.40: £3.50, £2.10; EX 34.30 Trifecta £120.90.
**Owner** Mrs P Clark **Bred** Bearstone Stud Ltd **Trained** Cropthorne, Worcs

**FOCUS**
Exposed performers in an ordinary handicap and a steady gallop but a convincing win from Scrafton, who came down the centre in the straight.
T/Plt: £84.70 to a £1 stake. Pool: £64,124.95 - 552.03 winning units. T/Qpdt: £9.20 to a £1 stake. Pool: £5,232.92 - 417.20 winning units. **Joe Rowntree**

# 1689 MAISONS-LAFFITTE (R-H)

Tuesday, April 18

**OFFICIAL GOING: Turf: good**

## 1871a PRIX LORD SEYMOUR (LISTED RACE) (4YO+) (TURF) 1m 4f

**1:50** 4-Y-0+ **£22,222** (£8,888; £6,666; £4,444; £2,222)

RPR

**1** **Talismanic**[21] 1416 4-9-6 0................................ MickaelBarzalona 3 110+
(A Fabre, France) *disp ld early: led after 1f: set stdy pce: qcknd over 2f out under hand riding and styd on strly fnl f* **9/10**[1]

**2** *1 1/2* **Zemindari (FR)**[12] 5-9-0 0................................ AlexisBadel 1 101
(H-F Devin, France) **15/2**

**3** *hd* **Apilobar (FR)**[65] 711 4-9-0 0................................ CristianDemuro 6 101
(F Vermeulen, France) **7/2**[2]

**4** *3* **Launched (IRE)**[240] 5692 5-9-6 0................................ StephanePasquier 4 101
(P Bary, France) **36/5**

**5** *1/2* **Tres Rock Glory (IRE)**[18] 1483 4-9-0 0................................ AurelienLemaitre 5 96
(F Head, France) **198/10**

**6** *snk* **Brave Impact**[26] 6-9-0 0................................ MaximeGuyon 2 94
(Mme Pia Brandt, France) **59/10**[3]

2m 42.96s (162.96) **6** Ran SP% **118.1**
PARI-MUTUEL (all including 1 euro stake): WIN 1.90 PLACE 1.20, 2.50 SF 15.60.
**Owner** Godolphin SNC **Bred** Darley **Trained** Chantilly, France

# BEVERLEY (R-H)

Wednesday, April 19

**OFFICIAL GOING: Good to firm (7.8)**
Wind: Light across (of little effect) Weather: Cloudy

## 1872 GET PROMO CODE OFFERS AT ACEODDS.COM NOVICE AUCTION STKS (DIV I) 5f

**2:15** (2:17) (Class 5) 2-Y-0 **£3,780** (£1,131; £565; £283; £141) **Stalls** Low

Form RPR

4 **1** **Almane (IRE)**[18] 1495 2-9-0 0................................ PaulHanagan 10 78
(Richard Fahey) *unruly bef s: cl up: rdn over 1f out: drvn ins fnl f: kpt on to ld last 50 yds* **6/4**[1]

**2** *1* **Emilia James** 2-8-9 0................................ JoeFanning 5 69
(Mark Johnston) *qckly away and led: pushed along wl over 1f out: rdn ent fnl f: hdd and no ex last 50* **7/2**[2]

0 **3** *2 3/4* **Just For The Craic (IRE)**[9] 1673 2-8-12 0................................ JamesSullivan 4 63
(Ruth Carr) *chsd ldrs: rdn along over 1f out: kpt on fnl f* **14/1**

**4** *1/2* **Floss The Hoss (IRE)** 2-8-11 0................................ AndrewMullen 13 60
(David Evans) *towards rr: pushed along and hdwy 1/2-way: rdn wl over 1f out: swtchd rt and kpt on fnl f* **33/1**

**5** *1/2* **Mistress Of Venice** 2-8-11 0................................ JackGarritty 7 58+
(James Given) *hmpd s and towards rr: n.m.r on inner 1/2-way: swtchd lft and rdn wl over 1f out: kpt on wl fnl f: nrst fin* **16/1**

**6** *1* **Mount Hellvelyn** 2-8-12 0................................ CamHardie 14 55
(Clive Mulhall) *chsd ldrs: rdn along over 1f: grad wknd* **200/1**

**7** *3/4* **Magic Jazz (IRE)** 2-9-0 0................................ KevinStott 3 55+
(Kevin Ryan) *green and outpcd in rr: rdn along 1/2-way: styd on appr fnl f: nrst fin* **11/1**

**8** *1 1/4* **Rock On Bertie (IRE)** 2-9-1 0................................ TomEaves 6 51
(Nigel Tinkler) *wnt lft s: chsd ldrs: rdn along wl over 1f out: grad wknd* **20/1**

0 **9** *2 1/4* **Furni Factors**[18] 1495 2-8-9 0................................ NathanEvans(3) 9 40
(Ronald Thompson) *in tch on outer: rdn along over 2f out: sn wknd* **50/1**

**10** *3 3/4* **Dyson's Girl** 2-8-11 0................................ ConnorBeasley 8 26
(Bryan Smart) *green and a rr* **12/1**

**11** *1 1/4* **Kikini Bamalaam (IRE)** 2-8-11 0................................ PhillipMakin 2 21+
(Keith Dalgleish) *in tch on inner: pushed along 1/2-way: wknd wl over 1f out: eased* **11/2**[3]

**12** *7* **Progressive Jazz (IRE)** 2-9-1 0................................ DougieCostello 1
(K R Burke) *dwlt: green and a rr* **12/1**

1m 3.24s (-0.26) **Going Correction** -0.225s/f (Firm) **12** Ran SP% **124.0**
Speed ratings (Par 92): **93,91,87,86,85 83,82,80,77,71 69,57**
CSF £6.60 TOTE £2.60: £1.10, £1.60, £3.90; EX 10.80 Trifecta £38.40.
**Owner** R A Fahey **Bred** Tally-Ho Stud **Trained** Musley Bank, N Yorks

**FOCUS**
The track's opening meeting of 2017 and the going was upgraded prior to racing and looked in really good nick. Stalls: Inside (all races). The market leaders dominated this modest 2yo novice event. Limited form.

## 1873 GET PROMO CODE OFFERS AT ACEODDS.COM NOVICE AUCTION STKS (DIV II) 5f

**2:50** (2:52) (Class 5) 2-Y-0 **£3,780** (£1,131; £565; £283; £141) **Stalls** Low

Form RPR

**1** **Bengali Boys (IRE)** 2-8-13 0................................ PaulHanagan 12 79+
(Richard Fahey) *t.k.h early: trckd ldrs on outer: hdwy over 1f out: rdn to chal jst ins fnl f: styd on wl to ld last 100 yds* **4/1**[2]

**2** *1* **Wahoo** 2-9-1 0................................ PaulMulrennan 10 77
(Michael Dods) *trckd ldrs: hdwy wl over 1f out: rdn to chal ent fnl f and ev ch: kpt on same pce towards fin* **7/2**[1]

**3** *1* **Starlight Mystery (IRE)** 2-8-9 0................................ JoeFanning 8 68
(Mark Johnston) *prom: hdwy and cl up 2f out: rdn to ld over 1f out: jnd ent fnl f: hdd and no ex last 100 yds* **6/1**[3]

**4** *2 3/4* **Hot Rock (IRE)** 2-9-1 0................................ ConnorBeasley 9 64
(Bryan Smart) *t.k.h early: hld up towards rr on inner: hdwy 2f out: swtchd lft and rdn over 1f out: styd on wl fnl f* **9/1**

**5** *hd* **Poet's Dawn** 2-8-12 0................................ DavidAllan 1 60+
(Tim Easterby) *trckd ldrs: effrt 2f out: nt clr run over 1f out: sn rdn and kpt on* **10/1**

**6** *3 3/4* **Asheena** 2-8-7 0................................ JoeyHaynes 7 42
(Paul D'Arcy) *wnt rt s: sn led: hdd 1/2-way: cl up: rdn wl over 1f out: wknd* **14/1**

**7** *3/4* **Abu Dhabi Doo** 2-8-5 0................................ JordanVaughan(3) 4 40
(K R Burke) *cl up on inner slt ld 1/2-way: rdn along wl over 1f out: sn hdd & wknd* **8/1**

**8** *shd* **Placebo Effect (IRE)** 2-8-12 0................................ AndrewMullen 13 44
(Ollie Pears) *wnt lft s: chsd ldrs on outer: pushed along and outpcd 1/2-way: kpt on fnl f* **66/1**

**9** *1 1/2* **Watching Spirits** 2-9-0 0................................ BenCurtis 5 40
(Ann Duffield) *.trckd ldrs on inner: effrt 2f out: rdn along wl over 1f out: sn wknd* **10/1**

**10** *1* **Dark Hedges** 2-8-8 0................................ DuranFentiman 14 31
(Olly Williams) *dwlt: a towards rr* **66/1**

**11** *3/4* **Bahuta Acha** 2-8-12 0................................ DougieCostello 6 32
(David Loughnane) *s.i.s: a rr* **25/1**

4 **12** *16* **Glen Valley (IRE)**[13] 1588 2-8-9 0................................ JasonHart 11
(Keith Dalgleish) *chsd ldrs: rdn along 1/2-way: sn wknd and bhd* **20/1**

1m 4.21s (0.71) **Going Correction** -0.225s/f (Firm) **12** Ran SP% **114.1**
Speed ratings (Par 92): **85,83,81,77,77 71,69,69,67,65 64,38**
CSF £16.33 TOTE £4.70: £1.90, £1.70, £2.00; EX 17.50 Trifecta £60.10.
**Owner** A Tattersall **Bred** N Hartery **Trained** Musley Bank, N Yorks
■ Reel Mr Bond was withdrawn. Price at time of withdrawal 10-1. Rule 4 applies to all bets - deduction 5p in the pound.

**FOCUS**
The second division of the novice event was 0.97secs slower than the first. Again prominent racers dominated. The form is rated at the bottom end of the race averages.

## 1874 WHITE RABBIT CHOCOLATIERS MAIDEN STKS 1m 1f 207y
**3:25** (3:26) (Class 5) 3-Y-O **£2,911** (£866; £432; £216) **Stalls** Low

Form RPR
04-3 **1** **Amlad (IRE)**[18] 1499 3-9-5 78 PaulMulrennan 2 84
(Ed Dunlop) *sn led at stdy pce: qcknd over 3f out: pushed along 2f out: rdn over 1f out: kpt on wl u.p fnl f* **6/5**[1]

66- **2** ½ **Sable Island (IRE)**[159] 7908 3-9-5 0 TedDurcan 3 83
(Sir Michael Stoute) *trckd wnr: hdwy and cl up over 3f out: rdn to chal wl over 1f out: ev ch ent fnl f: sn drvn and kpt on* **9/4**[2]

**3** ½ **Pleasant Surprise (IRE)** 3-9-0 0 JamieSpencer 4 77
(Luca Cumani) *hld up in rr: hdwy on outer over 2f out: rdn to chse ldng pair over 1f out: kpt on u.p fnl f* **7/1**

032 **4** 6 **Chippenham (IRE)**[21] 1420 3-9-5 75 (b) RobertTart 1 70
(John Gosden) *dwlt: sn trcking ldng pair on inner: effrt 3f out: rdn along 2f out: sn drvn and btn* **11/2**[3]

**5** 4 ½ **Sunrize (IRE)** 3-9-5 0 PhillipMakin 5 61
(David O'Meara) *trckd ldng pair on outer: pushed along wl over 2f out: rdn wl over 1f out: sn wknd* **12/1**

2m 6.62s (-0.38) **Going Correction** -0.275s/f (Firm) **5** Ran SP% **111.8**
Speed ratings (Par 98): **90,89,89,84,80**
CSF £4.23 TOTE £2.10: £1.10, £2.50; EX 4.80 Trifecta £14.50.
**Owner** Abdullah Saeed Al Naboodah **Bred** Barouche Stud Ireland Ltd **Trained** Newmarket, Suffolk

**FOCUS**
This modest 3yo maiden was run at a stop-start pace and threw up a tight three-way finish. The winner had the run of the race but is rated to form.

## 1875 FOLLOW US ON TWITTER @BEVERLEY_RACES H'CAP 1m 1f 207y
**4:00** (4:00) (Class 4) (0-80,80) 3-Y-O **£5,040** (£1,508; £754; £377; £188) **Stalls** Low

Form RPR
541- **1** **Stradivarius (IRE)**[163] 7849 3-9-5 78 RobertTart 1 93
(John Gosden) *hld up in tch: hdwy on outer over 2f out: rdn over 1f out: qcknd to ld ent fnl f: sn clr: readily* **9/4**[1]

511- **2** 6 **Election Day**[187] 7322 3-9-7 80 PJMcDonald 3 83
(Mark Johnston) *led: pushed along over 2f out: rdn over 1f out: drvn and hdd ent fnl f: kpt on: no ch w wnr* **5/1**

1- **3** 1 ¼ **Manangatang (IRE)**[155] 7962 3-9-3 76 JamieSpencer 6 77
(Luca Cumani) *trckd ldrs: hdwy to trck ldng pair 3f out: effrt 2f out: rdn wl over 1f out: drvn appr fnl f: sn one pce* **5/2**[2]

146- **4** 12 **Our Boy (IRE)**[196] 7075 3-9-3 76 AndrewMullen 2 53
(David Evans) *trckd ldng pair: hdwy 3f out: rdn along 2f out: sn drvn and outpcd* **16/1**

500- **5** 1 **Steel Helmet (IRE)**[215] 6535 3-8-5 64 PaulHanagan 5 39
(Brian Ellison) *hld up in rr: tk clsr order over 3f out: rdn along over 2f out: sn outpcd* **28/1**

2-11 **6** 7 **Sir Plato (IRE)**[9] 1686 3-8-8 67 6ex RyanTate 4 28
(Rod Millman) *trckd wnr: hdwy 3f out: cl up 2f out: sn rdn: wknd qckly appr fnl f: sn eased* **3/1**[3]

2m 2.04s (-4.96) **Going Correction** -0.275s/f (Firm) **6** Ran SP% **110.3**
Speed ratings (Par 100): **108,103,102,92,91 86**
CSF £13.32 TOTE £3.70: £1.70, £2.60; EX 15.50 Trifecta £54.70.
**Owner** B E Nielsen **Bred** Bjorn Nielsen **Trained** Newmarket, Suffolk

**FOCUS**
An interesting 3yo handicap. It was run at a solid early pace and the form looks decent. The runner-up may give thuis form a stronger look in time.

## 1876 OPENING DAY SPRINT TROPHY H'CAP 5f
**4:35** (4:35) (Class 3) (0-95,93) 4-Y-O+
**£7,158** (£2,143; £1,071; £535; £267; £134) **Stalls** Low

Form RPR
220- **1** **Edward Lewis**[187] 7315 4-8-12 89 JoshDoyle(5) 8 100+
(David O'Meara) *prom: smooth hdwy and cl up over 1f out: led jst ins fnl f and sn rdn and kpt on wl* **8/1**

120- **2** hd **East Street Revue**[194] 7124 4-9-3 89 (b) DuranFentiman 1 99+
(Tim Easterby) *wnt sharply lft s: in tch on inner and pushed along 1/2-way: hdwy over 1f out: nt clr run and swtchd lft ent fnl f: sn drvn and styd on strly: jst hld* **5/1**[2]

430- **3** 1 ½ **Gamesome (FR)**[179] 7537 6-9-7 93 PaulMulrennan 3 98
(Paul Midgley) *trckd ldng pair on inner: hdwy 2f out: rdn to take narrow ld briefly appr fnl f: sn hdd and drvn: kpt on same pce towards fin* **7/2**[1]

43-0 **4** 2 **Bogart**[17] 1515 8-8-11 83 (p) TomEaves 11 81
(Kevin Ryan) *wnt rt s: chsd ldrs: nt clr run and swtchd lft over 1f out: sn rdn and kpt on wl fnl f* **8/1**

3P0- **5** shd **Bashiba (IRE)**[194] 7124 6-8-8 85 (t) LewisEdmunds(5) 7 82
(Nigel Tinkler) *towards rr: hdwy 2f out: rdn over 1f out: kpt on fnl f* **14/1**

500- **6** ½ **Lexington Place**[232] 6012 7-8-12 84 JamesSullivan 2 80
(Ruth Carr) *dwlt and rr: hdwy on inner wl over 1f out: rdn along and n.m.r ent fnl f: kpt on* **15/2**

00-0 **7** 1 **Sandra's Secret (IRE)**[25] 1370 4-8-8 80 PJMcDonald 6 72
(Les Eyre) *cl up: led over 2f out: rdn wl over 1f out: drvn and hdd appr fnl f: wknd* **20/1**

304/ **8** ¾ **Rasheeq (IRE)**[558] 7087 4-9-7 93 DavidAllan 4 82
(Tim Easterby) *rr: hdwy over 1f out: rdn and kpt on fnl f* **50/1**

016- **9** ¾ **Singeur (IRE)**[194] 7124 10-8-10 87 MeganNicholls(5) 12 74
(Rebecca Bastiman) *a towards rr* **33/1**

200- **10** ½ **Powerallied (IRE)**[207] 6779 4-9-1 87 PaulHanagan 9 72
(Richard Fahey) *a rr* **10/1**

-205 **11** 1 ¾ **Meadway**[68] 664 6-9-3 89 (p) ConnorBeasley 14 68
(Bryan Smart) *sn slt ld: rdn along and hdd jst over 2f out: sn drvn and wknd over 1f out* **22/1**

060- **12** nk **Burnt Sugar (IRE)**[147] 8069 5-9-5 91 JoeFanning 10 68
(Roger Fell) *a towards rr* **7/1**[3]

020- **13** 1 ¾ **Kibaar**[179] 7537 5-9-1 87 KevinStott 13 58
(Kevin Ryan) *chsd ldng pair: rdn along jst over 2f out: sn wknd* **14/1**

1m 1.77s (-1.73) **Going Correction** -0.225s/f (Firm) **13** Ran SP% **121.8**
Speed ratings (Par 107): **104,103,101,98,97 97,95,94,93,92 89,89,86**
CSF £46.76 CT £175.63 TOTE £9.30: £2.80, £2.10, £1.90; EX 46.50 Trifecta £162.50.
**Owner** Akela Construction Ltd **Bred** Pantile Stud **Trained** Upper Helmsley, N Yorks

**FOCUS**
The feature sprint handicap was a frantically run race. Sound form, with progress from the first two.

## 1877 WESTWOOD H'CAP 1m 4f 23y
**5:10** (5:11) (Class 5) (0-75,76) 3-Y-O **£3,780** (£1,131; £565; £283; £141) **Stalls** Low

Form RPR
-321 **1** **Global Revival (IRE)**[69] 647 3-9-7 75 AntonioFresu 4 78
(Ed Dunlop) *trckd ldng pair on outer. hdwy whn carried lft over 2f out: rdn and cl up over 1f out: drvn to ld ins fnl f: edgd rt and kpt on wl towards fin* **4/1**[2]

42-1 **2** ¾ **The Blues Master (IRE)**[103] 91 3-9-8 76 PJMcDonald 5 78
(Mark Johnston) *dwlt and reminders s: led after 1f: pushed along over 2f out: rdn wl over 1f out: drvn and hdd ins fnl f: kpt on* **15/8**[1]

2 **3** ¾ **Baltic Eagle (GER)**[55] 881 3-9-0 68 JackMitchell 1 69
(Rune Haugen) *t.k.h: trckd ldng pair on inner: hdwy over 2f out: rdn over 1f out: drvn and ch ins fnl f: kpt on same pce towards fin* **9/2**[3]

453- **4** 1 ¾ **Lester Kris (IRE)**[250] 5363 3-9-0 75 RossaRyan(7) 6 73
(Richard Hannon) *hld up in rr: hdwy 3f out: carried lft over 2f out: rdn wl over 1f out: kpt on same pce* **5/1**

0-33 **5** 2 ¾ **Spirit Of Rome (IRE)**[27] 1331 3-8-7 61 oh1 JoeFanning 3 55
(James Bethell) *led 1f: trckd ldr: rdn along and hung lft over 2f out: drvn wl over 1f out: sn wknd* **4/1**[2]

2m 38.81s (-0.99) **Going Correction** -0.275s/f (Firm) **5** Ran SP% **109.6**
Speed ratings (Par 98): **92,91,91,89,88**
CSF £11.83 TOTE £5.10: £2.20, £1.40; EX 9.60 Trifecta £25.70.
**Owner** Dr Johnny Hon **Bred** John Cullinan **Trained** Newmarket, Suffolk

**FOCUS**
A modest 3yo handicap, run at a routine sort of pace. The winner continues to progress from the AW.

## 1878 BEVERLEY ANNUAL BADGEHOLDERS H'CAP 7f 96y
**5:45** (5:46) (Class 4) (0-80,81) 3-Y-O **£5,040** (£1,508; £754; £377; £188) **Stalls** Low

Form RPR
203- **1** **Proud Archi (IRE)**[207] 6791 3-9-5 77 PaulMulrennan 6 83
(Michael Dods) *trckd ldrs: hdwy over 2f out: rdn to ld ent fnl f: sn drvn and hld on gamely towards fin* **7/1**

21- **2** shd **Areen Heart (FR)**[211] 6640 3-9-9 81 PaulHanagan 8 86
(Richard Fahey) *t.k.h: hld up towards rr: hdwy over 2f out: swtchd lft to outer and effrt over 1f out: rdn to chal ins fnl f: sn drvn and ev ch: jst hld* **5/2**[1]

34-1 **3** 2 **Lualiwa**[39] 1141 3-9-7 79 KevinStott 4 79+
(Kevin Ryan) *sn led: pushed along over 2f out: rdn wl over 1f out: hdd and drvn ent fnl f: kpt on same pce* **3/1**[2]

130- **4** shd **George Reme (IRE)**[214] 6554 3-9-6 78 JasonHart 5 78
(John Quinn) *hld up in tch on inner: hdwy wl over 2f out: cl up and rdn over 1f out: ev ch tl drvn ent fnl f and kpt on same pce* **10/1**

104- **5** hd **Our Charlie Brown**[202] 6903 3-8-11 69 DavidAllan 1 69
(Tim Easterby) *hld up in rr: tk clsr order 2f out: rdn over 1f out: drvn and kpt on fnl f* **9/1**

321- **6** 1 ¾ **Brogan**[187] 7319 3-9-7 79 PJMcDonald 7 74
(Tom Dascombe) *trckd ldr: hdwy and cl up over 2f out: rdn to dispute ld over 1f out and ev ch tl drvn and wknd fnl f* **7/1**

443- **P** **Actualisation**[184] 7406 3-8-13 71 JackGarritty 3
(John Quinn) *prom on inner: pushed along 3f out: rdn over 2f out: wknd over 1f out: bhd whn lost action and p.u ins fnl f* **5/1**[3]

1m 31.71s (-2.09) **Going Correction** -0.275s/f (Firm) **7** Ran SP% **114.3**
Speed ratings (Par 100): **100,99,97,97,97 95,**
CSF £24.87 CT £63.91 TOTE £8.10: £3.80, £2.30; EX 26.60 Trifecta £98.80.
**Owner** Eagle Racing **Bred** Robert Allcock **Trained** Denton, Co Durham

**FOCUS**
Not a bad 3yo handicap for the class and it was run at a blistering pace. The winner found a bit on his 2yo form.

## 1879 RACING AGAIN NEXT THURSDAY FILLIES' H'CAP 1m 100y
**6:20** (6:20) (Class 5) (0-70,72) 4-Y-O+ **£3,780** (£1,131; £565; £283; £141) **Stalls** Low

Form RPR
04-3 **1** **Make On Madam (IRE)**[41] 1106 5-8-12 61 DavidAllan 4 71
(Les Eyre) *in tch: hdwy 3f out: chsd ldrs over 2f out: rdn to ld ent fnl f: sn clr* **6/1**

0640 **2** 4 ½ **Cabal**[27] 1334 10-9-1 64 (b) SamJames 5 64
(Geoffrey Harker) *hld up in rr: hdwy on outer over 2f out: rdn over 1f out: chse wnr jst ins fnl f: sn drvn and no imp* **8/1**

1235 **3** nk **Dose**[36] 1186 4-9-0 63 PaulHanagan 3 62
(Richard Fahey) *hld up towards rr: hdwy over 2f out: effrt on inner and chsd ldrs over 1f out: n.m.r ins fnl f: kpt on towards fin* **4/1**[1]

00-3 **4** 1 ½ **Forever A Lady (IRE)**[41] 1104 4-9-8 71 JoeFanning 7 67
(Keith Dalgleish) *chsd ldr: hdwy over 3f out: rdn to ld wl over 1f out: drvn and hdd ent fnl f: one pce* **10/1**

210- **5** shd **Beadlam (IRE)**[202] 6908 4-9-2 65 JackGarritty 8 61
(Roger Fell) *dwlt: sn chsng ldrs: hdwy over 2f out: rdn to chal over 1f out: ev ch tl drvn and one pce fnl f* **16/1**

5-46 **6** 2 ¾ **Livella Fella (IRE)**[9] 1679 4-9-9 72 PhillipMakin 2 62
(Keith Dalgleish) *trckd ldrs: hdwy on inner 3f out: rdn along 2f out: sn drvn and btn* **9/2**[2]

206- **7** 8 **Miss Ranger (IRE)**[249] 5392 5-9-5 68 TomEaves 6 40
(Brian Ellison) *a towards rr* **14/1**

250- **8** 4 ½ **Rosamaria (IRE)**[215] 6541 4-9-5 68 JoeDoyle 1 30
(Julie Camacho) *led and sn clr: pushed along 3f out: rdn over 2f out: hdd wl over 1f out and sn wknd* **5/1**[3]

360- **9** 21 **Fidelma Moon (IRE)**[198] 7010 5-9-4 70 JordanVaughan(3) 10
(K R Burke) *chsd clr ldr: hdwy over 3f out: rdn along over 2f out: sn wknd* **6/1**

1m 44.33s (-3.27) **Going Correction** -0.275s/f (Firm) **9** Ran SP% **116.2**
Speed ratings (Par 100): **105,100,100,98,98 95,87,83,62**
CSF £53.34 CT £215.70 TOTE £7.70: £2.60, £2.60, £1.70; EX 35.40 Trifecta £87.40.
**Owner** G Parkinson **Bred** Mrs T Brudenell **Trained** Catwick, N Yorks

**FOCUS**
This competitive fillies' handicap was another one set up for the closers. The form could be worth more at face value.
T/Plt: £14.20 to a £1 stake. Pool: £5,3521.99. 2,732.33 winning units. T/Qpdt: £5.90 to a £1 stake. Pool: £2,502.10. 310.98 winning units. **Joe Rowntree**

# 1857 NEWMARKET (R-H)

Wednesday, April 19

**OFFICIAL GOING: Good to firm (good in places; 7.9)**

Wind: virtually nil Weather: sunny

## 1880 WEATHERBYS GENERAL STUD BOOK ONLINE H'CAP 6f

**1:50** (1:50) (Class 2) (0-100,98) 4-Y-0+ **£12,938** (£3,850; £1,924; £962) **Stalls** Low

Form RPR

54-0 **1** **Gunmetal (IRE)**[17] [1515] 4-8-9 **86**.................................... AndreaAtzeni 8 101
(Charles Hills) *chsd ldr tl led wl over 1f out: rdn and qcknd clr ent fnl f: r.o strly: readily* **9/2**[2]

410- **2** 2 ¾ **Normandy Barriere (IRE)**[193] [7156] 5-9-5 **96**................ WilliamBuick 3 102
(Nigel Tinkler) *in tch in midfield: rdn over 2f out: swtchd lft and effrt to chse wnr over 1f out: styd on same pce ins fnl f* **7/2**[1]

-000 **3** 1 ¼ **Moonraker**[76] [543] 5-9-0 **91**............................................ GrahamLee 2 93
(Mick Channon) *lw: stdd after s: hld up in tch in last trio: effrt over 1f out: rdn and kpt on wl ins fnl f: wnt 2nd towards fin: no threat to wnr* **8/1**

00-0 **4** ½ **Mont Kiara (FR)**[18] [1501] 4-8-13 **90**................................ HarryBentley 10 91
(Kevin Ryan) *lw: taken down early: stdd s: t.k.h: chsd ldrs: rdn wl over 1f out: unable qck ent fnl f: styd on same pce after* **6/1**

120- **5** 1 ½ **Reputation (IRE)**[214] [6556] 4-9-1 **92**............................(b[1]) RyanMoore 5 88
(John Quinn) *hld up in last trio: effrt jst over 2f out: no imp over 1f out: wl hld but kpt on ins fnl f* **6/1**

0343 **6** hd **Suqoor**[11] [1622] 4-8-7 **84** oh1...............................(p) SilvestreDeSousa 1 79
(Chris Dwyer) *lw: stdd s: hld up in rr: effrt jst over 2f out: sme hdwy into midfield over 1f out: wl hld and kpt on same pce ins fnl f* **9/1**

00-0 **7** 4 ½ **Dark Defender**[24] [1385] 4-8-8 **85**.....................................(v) LukeMorris 7 66
(Keith Dalgleish) *chsd ldrs: rdn 2f out: unable qck and btn 1f out: wknd ins fnl f* **16/1**

-012 **8** 5 **King Robert**[20] [1454] 4-9-4 **95**.......................................(v) JimCrowley 4 60
(Bryan Smart) *led tl wl over 1f out: sn rdn and lost pl: bhd ins fnl f* **5/1**[3]

1m 11.02s (-1.18) **Going Correction** +0.05s/f (Good) **8** Ran SP% **113.7**
Speed ratings (Par 109): **109,105,103,103,101 100,94,88**
CSF £20.40 CT £121.58 TOTE £4.90: £1.70, £1.70, £2.90; EX 22.40 Trifecta £239.30.
**Owner** Mrs J K Powell **Bred** Maurice Byrne **Trained** Lambourn, Berks

**FOCUS**
Far side course used. Stalls: all races far side. It was dry overnight and the going was given as good to firm, good in places (GoingStick: 7.9). A wide open sprint handicap on paper, but a cosy winner who could rate a bit higher still.

## 1881 BET365 EUROPEAN FREE H'CAP (LISTED RACE) 7f

**2:25** (2:25) (Class 1) 3-Y-O

**£20,982** (£7,955; £3,981; £1,983; £995; £499) **Stalls** Low

Form RPR

23- **1** **Whitecliffsofdover (USA)**[199] [6987] 3-9-7 **108**...............(t[1]) RyanMoore 8 113
(A P O'Brien, Ire) *tall: lw: mde all: grad increased gallop fr 3f out: rdn and qcknd over 1f out: in command and r.o strly fnl f: readily* **10/3**[2]

100- **2** 2 ¾ **Rodaini (USA)**[166] [7807] 3-9-5 **106**................................(v[1]) JimCrowley 7 104
(Simon Crisford) *t.k.h: chsd ldrs: rdn 2f out: drvn and unable qck w wnr over 1f out: kpt on same pce ins fnl f* **8/1**

110- **3** ½ **Seven Heavens**[193] [7149] 3-9-7 **108**.............................(h[1]) FrankieDettori 2 105
(John Gosden) *taken down early: t.k.h: hld up in tch in midfield: effrt 2f out: unable qck w wnr over 1f out: 3rd and kpt on same pce ins fnl f* **5/2**[1]

201- **4** 2 ½ **Private Matter**[174] [7655] 3-9-5 **106**.................................. TonyHamilton 3 96
(Richard Fahey) *chsd wnr: rdn ent fnl 2f: unable qck and lost pl over 1f out: wl hld 4th and plugged on ins fnl f* **11/2**

316- **5** nk **Sir Dancealot (IRE)**[179] [7539] 3-9-7 **108**............................ ShaneKelly 1 97
(David Elsworth) *lw: stdd s: hld up in tch in last pair: effrt 2f out: swtchd lft and no imp u.p over 1f out: wl hld and plugged on same pce fnl f* **25/1**

214- **6** 3 ¼ **Majeste**[221] [6326] 3-9-2 **103**............................................. SeanLevey 5 83
(Richard Hannon) *str: lw: in tch in midfield: rdn over 2f out: sn struggling: wknd over 1f out* **9/2**[3]

230- **7** 2 **Miss Infinity (IRE)**[194] [7114] 3-9-2 **103**.................... SilvestreDeSousa 6 78
(Mark Johnston) *t.k.h: stdd s: hld up in tch in last pair: rdn wl over 2f out: no imp: wknd over 1f out* **5/1**

1m 24.68s (-0.72) **Going Correction** +0.05s/f (Good) **7** Ran SP% **110.5**
Speed ratings (Par 106): **106,102,102,99,99 95,93**
CSF £27.39 CT £71.72 TOTE £3.40: £1.90, £4.30; EX 24.40 Trifecta £95.80.
**Owner** Michael Tabor & Derrick Smith & Mrs John Magnier **Bred** Claiborne Farm **Trained** Cashel, Co Tipperary

**FOCUS**
This looked competitive, with only 5lb between the top weights and the bottom weight, but the early gallop wasn't that strong and the winner was able to control the race from the front. Whitecliffsofdover has improved with each start. This form is rated around the second and third.

## 1882 BET365 EARL OF SEFTON STKS (GROUP 3) 1m 1f

**3:00** (3:00) (Class 1) 4-Y-0+

**£34,026** (£12,900; £6,456; £3,216; £1,614; £810) **Stalls** Low

Form RPR

550- **1** **Calderon (IRE)**[194] [7117] 4-8-13 106.................................... PatDobbs 4 115
(Richard Hannon) *t.k.h: trckd ldrs tl wnt 2nd 3f out: rdn and clsd to chal over 1f out: sn carried lft: sustained chal u.p to ld wl ins fnl f: styd on* **10/1**

-212 **2** ½ **Folkswood**[46] [1046] 4-8-13 112..................................(p) WilliamBuick 3 114
(Charlie Appleby) *led: rdn 2f out: hrd pressed and edgd lft u.p over 1f out: wnt bk rt u.p 1f out: drvn ins fnl f: hdd and one pced wl ins fnl f* **5/2**[1]

541- **3** 4 **Spark Plug (IRE)**[207] [6786] 6-8-13 112..........................(p) JimmyFortune 8 105
(Brian Meehan) *stdd s: t.k.h: hld up in tch in midfield: rdn over 2f out: chsd ldrs over 1f out: no ex 1f out: battling for 3rd and kpt on same pce ins fnl f* **11/2**[3]

134- **4** ¾ **Abdon**[193] [7152] 4-8-13 109.............................................. FrankieDettori 7 104
(Sir Michael Stoute) *stdd s and sn swtchd rt: t.k.h: hld up in tch in rr: effrt towards far side over 2f out: no imp over 1f out: battling for 3rd and kpt on same pce ins fnl f* **7/1**

1-01 **5** 5 **Viren's Army (IRE)**[55] [888] 4-8-13 111......................(p) JamesDoyle 2 93
(Charlie Appleby) *chsd ldr tl 3f out: sn drvn: lost pl and wknd over 1f out* **7/2**[2]

201- **6** nse **Autocratic**[193] [7154] 4-8-13 102.......................................... RyanMoore 5 92
(Sir Michael Stoute) *bit bkwd: hld up in tch in midfield: rdn 3f out: outpcd and btn over 1f out: sn wknd* **11/2**[3]

04-1 **7** hd **Bravery (IRE)**[18] [1494] 4-8-13 104................................ DanielTudhope 6 92
(David O'Meara) *stdd s: t.k.h: hld up in tch in midfield: rdn over 2f out: sn outpcd: wknd over 1f out* **12/1**

1m 51.27s (-0.43) **Going Correction** +0.05s/f (Good) **7** Ran SP% **110.8**
Speed ratings (Par 113): **103,102,99,98,93 93,93**
CSF £33.12 TOTE £12.80: £5.30, £1.90; EX 38.40 Trifecta £210.60.
**Owner** Michael Pescod **Bred** Jeddah Bloodstock **Trained** East Everleigh, Wilts

**FOCUS**
The pace held up well, the first two home always in the first three. The form is rated around the second.

## 1883 LANWADES STUD NELL GWYN STKS (GROUP 3) (FILLIES) 7f

**3:35** (3:36) (Class 1) 3-Y-O

**£34,026** (£12,900; £6,456; £3,216; £1,614; £810) **Stalls** Low

Form RPR

1- **1** **Daban (IRE)**[168] [7763] 3-9-0 81....................................... FrankieDettori 11 109+
(John Gosden) *t.k.h early: hld up in tch in midfield: effrt over 1f out: hdwy u.p 1f out to ld 75yds out: r.o wl and eased cl home* **12/1**

123- **2** ¾ **Unforgetable Filly**[194] [7114] 3-9-0 99................................ JamesDoyle 8 106
(Hugo Palmer) *unf: pressed ldrs: rdn and ev ch 2f out: drvn and sustained chal over 1f out: led 100yds out: sn hdd and styd on same pce towards fin* **14/1**

411- **3** 1 ¼ **Poet's Vanity**[194] [7114] 3-9-0 104.................................... OisinMurphy 4 103
(Andrew Balding) *lw: t.k.h: led rdn over 1f out: drvn 1f out: hdd 100yds: no ex and outpcd towards fin* **6/1**

**4** 1 ¾ **Pamplemousse (IRE)**[15] 3-9-0 0.......................... Pierre-CharlesBoudot 5 98+
(A Fabre, France) *athletic: stdd s: hld up in tch towards rr: rdn and hdwy over 1f out: styd on steadily ins fnl f: nvr enough pce to threaten ldrs* **4/1**[2]

1- **5** ½ **Sea Of Grace (IRE)**[234] [5937] 3-9-0 107............................. PatCosgrave 6 97+
(William Haggas) *tall: lengthy: restless in stalls: t.k.h: hld up in tch in midfield: effrt 2f out: drvn and ev ch over 1f out: no ex ins fnl f: wknd fnl 100yds* **5/1**[3]

010- **6** ½ **Kilmah**[223] [6258] 3-9-0 101.......................................... SilvestreDeSousa 9 96
(Mark Johnston) *chsd ldr after 2f tl 3f out: sn rdn and unable qck over 1f out: wknd ins fnl f* **25/1**

220- **7** ¾ **Roly Poly (USA)**[166] [7809] 3-9-0 115.................................. RyanMoore 2 94
(A P O'Brien, Ire) *pressed ldr for 2f: rdn and lost pl 3f out: trying to rally over 1f out: no threat to ldrs but kpt on ins fnl f* **7/2**[1]

142- **8** 1 **Kazimiera**[172] [7698] 3-9-0 90........................................... WilliamBuick 10 91
(Charlie Appleby) *t.k.h: hld up in tch in rr: shkn up 2f out: no imp and edgd rt 1f out: wl hld and kpt on same pce fnl f* **16/1**

140- **9** 4 **Tallulah Rose**[250] [5359] 3-9-0 92...................................... AdriedeVries 1 80
(K R Burke) *t.k.h: hld up in tch in midfield: stdd bk towards rr after 2f out: effrt over 1f out: sn edging lft and no hdwy: wknd ins fnl f* **100/1**

661- **10** 2 **Brave Anna (USA)**[207] [6784] 3-9-3 116........................ SeamieHeffernan 7 78
(A P O'Brien, Ire) *stdd s: t.k.h: hld up in tch in last pair: effrt over 2f out: no imp u.p over 1f out: wknd fnl f* **13/2**

416- **11** 4 ½ **Choumicha**[172] [7698] 3-9-0 83.......................................... AndreaAtzeni 3 63
(Hugo Palmer) *chsd ldrs tl rdn and lost pl 3f out: bhd fnl f* **40/1**

1m 24.42s (-0.98) **Going Correction** +0.05s/f (Good) **11** Ran SP% **114.0**
Speed ratings (Par 105): **107,106,104,102,102 101,100,99,95,92 87**
CSF £160.45 TOTE £13.20: £3.70, £3.60, £2.20; EX 176.30 Trifecta £1257.70.
**Owner** Abdullah Saeed Al Naboodah **Bred** Kildaragh Stud **Trained** Newmarket, Suffolk

**FOCUS**
This looked competitive and promised to be an informative Guineas trial. Although the inexperienced winner impressed, several of the other principals will be worth their place in the first fillies' Classic. The time was 0.26sec faster than the Free Handicap. The form is rated to the race average, with the third helping.

## 1884 BET365 EBF MAIDEN FILLIES' STKS (PLUS 10 RACE) 5f

**4:10** (4:10) (Class 4) 2-Y-O **£4,528** (£1,347; £673; £336) **Stalls** Low

Form RPR

**1** **Formidable Kitt** 2-9-0 0........................................... RichardKingscote 3 78+
(Tom Dascombe) *cmpt: mde all: jnd 3f out: pushed along over 1f out: rdn ins fnl f: fnd ex and forged ahd towards fin: gamely* **11/8**[1]

**2** ½ **Take Shelter** 2-9-0 0......................................................... LukeMorris 7 76
(James Tate) *str: chsd ldrs: clsd to join ldr 3f out: rdn wl over 1f out: drvn and ev ch ins fnl f: kpt on but jst outpcd fnl 50yds* **8/1**

**3** ½ **Ziarah (IRE)** 2-9-0 0.............................................(h[1]) MartinHarley 9 74+
(James Tate) *tall: s.i.s and swtchd rt s: hld up in tch: rdn and hdwy over 1f out: styd on wl to go 3rd wl ins fnl f: gng on at fin* **10/1**

**4** 1 ¾ **Noble Manners (IRE)** 2-9-0 0.............................. SilvestreDeSousa 5 68+
(Mark Johnston) *tall: lenghty: wnt rt s: rn green in rr: clsd 3f out: rdn and outpcd again wl over 1f out: hdwy 1f out: no threat to ldrs but kpt on steadily ins fnl f* **13/2**[2]

**5** nk **Queen Of Kalahari** 2-9-0 0.............................................. JamesDoyle 6 67
(Charles Hills) *lengthy: chsd wnr: clsd to join wnr 3f out: 3rd and jst getting outpcd whn edgd rt 1f out: wknd fnl 100yds* **8/1**

**6** 2 ¼ **On A Roll** 2-9-0 0.......................................................... TomMarquand 2 59
(Richard Hannon) *cmpt: bit bkwd: hld up in tch: nt clrest of runs 2f out: sn rdn and no imp over 1f out: wknd ins fnl f* **7/1**[3]

**7** 2 **Cherubic** 2-9-0 0........................................................... DavidProbert 1 52
(Charles Hills) *w'like: rn green: in tch towards rr: effrt and hdwy on far rail 2f out: no imp over 1f out: wknd ins fnl f* **16/1**

**8** ½ **Mraseel (IRE)** 2-9-0 0....................................................... JimCrowley 4 50
(James Tate) *str: bmpd s: sn rcvrd to chse ldrs: rdn jst over 2f out: lost pl over 1f out: bhd ins fnl f* **11/1**

1m 0.88s (1.78) **Going Correction** +0.05s/f (Good) **8** Ran SP% **113.5**
Speed ratings (Par 91): **87,86,85,82,82 78,75,74**
CSF £12.81 TOTE £2.30: £1.10, £2.50, £2.70; EX 13.10 Trifecta £95.40.
**Owner** Chasemore Farm **Bred** Chasemore Farm **Trained** Malpas, Cheshire

**FOCUS**
It's hard to know how strong a race this was, but the winner is bred to make a good early 2yo and won a shade comfortably. She has clear scope to do better.

## 1885 BET365 EBF STALLIONS MAIDEN FILLIES' STKS (PLUS 10 RACE) 1m

**4:45** (4:46) (Class 4) 3-Y-O **£5,175** (£1,540; £769; £384) **Stalls** Low

Form RPR

- **1** **Dancing Breeze (IRE)** 3-9-0 0..................................... FrankieDettori 10 86+
(John Gosden) *athletic: str: acd centre: t.k.h: led gp: chsd overall ldr tl led over 2f out: rdn jst over 1f out: clr w rival ins fnl f: edging rt but styd on wl to assert wl ins fnl f: eased cl home: 1st of 6 in gp* **15/2**

**2** ½ **Natavia** 3-9-0 0.................................................................. JamesDoyle 2 85+
(Roger Charlton) *tall: racd far side: chsd ldrs overall: ev ch 2f out: rdn over 1f out: kpt on u.p tl no ex and btn wl ins fnl f: 1st of 6 in gp* **4/1**[1]

50- **3** 2 3/4 **Crimson Rosette (IRE)**[181] 7484 3-9-0 0................. StevieDonohoe 12 78
(Charlie Fellowes) *leggy: racd centre: in tch in midfield overall: rdn and hdwy over 1f out: chsd clr ldng pair 1f out: kpt on for clr 3rd but nvr threatening ldng pair: 2nd of 6 in gp* **16/1**

**4** 2 **Glittering Jewel (USA)** 3-9-0 0........................................ WilliamBuick 4 74
(Charlie Appleby) *str: bit bkwd: racd far side: in tch in midfield overall: hdwy to chse ldrs 2f out: rdn and unable qck over 1f out: 4th and kpt on same pce fnl f: 2nd of 6 in gp* **5/1**[3]

6- **5** nse **Polly Glide (IRE)**[172] 7696 3-8-7 0............................ GabrieleMalune(7) 1 73
(Luca Cumani) *leggy: racd far side: in tch in midfield overall: effrt jst over 2f out: unable qck over 1f out: kpt on same pce ins fnl f: 3rd of 6 in gp* **33/1**

32- **6** hd **Mouille Point**[191] 7210 3-9-0 0............................................ PatDobbs 13 73+
(Richard Hannon) *str: lengthy: racd centre: stdd and dropped in bhd after s: pushed along and stl plenty to do over 1f out: kpt on ins fnl f: nvr trbld ldrs: 3rd of 6 in gp* **12/1**

**7** 1/2 **Tranquil Star (IRE)** 3-9-0 0.......................................... GeraldMosse 11 72+
(Jeremy Noseda) *athletic: racd centre: t.k.h: hld up in tch towards rr: effrt 3f out: sme hdwy over 1f out: kpt on same pce and no imp ins fnl f: 4th of 6 gp* **8/1**

4- **8** 1 1/2 **Hadeeqa (IRE)**[154] 7976 3-9-0 0........................................ JimCrowley 9 68+
(Simon Crisford) *cmpt: racd centre: dwlt and short of room leaving stalls: in tch in rr: clsd and nt clrest of runs whn swtchd lft 2f out: effrt and sme hdwy over 1f out: no imp 1f out: wknd ins fnl f: 5th of 6 in gp* **8/1**

**9** 2 1/4 **Saniyaat** 3-9-0 0................................................................ HarryBentley 7 63
(George Peckham) *w'like: racd far side: in tch in midfield: rdn over 2f out: unable qck and wknd over 1f out: wl hld whn swtchd rt ins fnl f: 4th of 6 in gp* **33/1**

0- **10** 1/2 **Vice Versa**[172] 7696 3-9-0 0................................................ RyanMoore 5 62
(Sir Michael Stoute) *racd far side: overall ldr tl rdn and hdd over 2f out: lost pl over 1f out: wknd ins fnl f: 5th of 6 in gp* **10/1**

42- **11** 3 1/4 **First Dance (IRE)**[194] 7118 3-9-0 0.................................. MartinHarley 8 54
(James Tate) *w'like: racd centre: t.k.h: in midfield: rdn to chse ldrs 2f out: sn outpcd and lost pl over 1f out: wknd fnl f: 6th of 6 in gp* **9/2**[2]

**12** 3/4 **Charming Loza** 3-9-0 0...................................................... AndreaAtzeni 3 52
(Charlie Fellowes) *str: bit bkwd: racd far side: a towards rr: rdn over 3f out: bhd fnl f: 6th of 6 in gp* **66/1**

1m 38.1s (-0.50) **Going Correction** +0.05s/f (Good) 12 Ran SP% **118.9**
Speed ratings (Par 97): **104,103,100,98,98 98,98,96,94,93 90,89**
CSF £37.24 TOTE £8.90: £3.10, £1.70, £5.70; EX 49.40 Trifecta £626.00.

**Owner** Merry Fox Stud Limited **Bred** Merry Fox Stud II Limited **Trained** Newmarket, Suffolk

**FOCUS**
Probably a decent maiden. The field split into two groups, and one from each came clear to fight it out. The first two are both bred to be smart.

## 1886 BET365 H'CAP 1m 2f
**5:20** (5:22) (Class 3) (0-95,95) 3-Y-O **£9,056** (£2,695; £1,346; £673) **Stalls** Low

Form RPR

1- **1** **Middle Kingdom (USA)**[145] 8088 3-8-12 **86**................ JimmyFortune 3 96+
(John Gosden) *athletic: str: hld up in tch in last trio: hdwy towards far rail over 2f out: rdn to chal and hung lft 1f out: led wl ins fnl f: r.o wl* **7/2**[1]

420- **2** nk **Euginio (IRE)**[193] 7151 3-9-7 **95**........................................ AndreaAtzeni 10 104
(Richard Hannon) *str: chsd ldrs: effrt and hdwy to ld over 1f out: hung rt ins fnl f: hdd and kpt on same pce wl ins fnl f* **20/1**

10-1 **3** 3 1/4 **Bin Battuta**[17] 1518 3-9-0 **93**........................................ GeorgeWood(5) 1 95+
(Saeed bin Suroor) *str: chsd ldng trio: rdn 2f out: jst getting outpcd whn hung lft jst over 1f out: gng bk rt ins fnl f: no ch w ldrs but kpt on to snatch 3rd on post* **4/1**[2]

421- **4** nse **Wahash (IRE)**[211] 6655 3-9-2 **90**....................................... FrankieDettori 5 93
(Richard Hannon) *chsd ldr: rdn and ev ch over 1f out: struggling to qckn and looked hld whn squeezed for room and snatched up ins fnl f: nt rcvr and lost 3rd on post* **12/1**

111- **5** 1/2 **Count Calabash (IRE)**[172] 7697 3-9-1 **89**............................ JimCrowley 11 92
(Paul Cole) *led: rdn and hdd over 1f out: stl ev ch but jst beginning to struggle whn squeezed for room and snatched up ins fnl f: nt rcvr* **25/1**

441- **6** 1 1/2 **Azam**[147] 8063 3-8-13 **87**...................................................... JamesDoyle 6 85
(John Gosden) *bit bkwd: hld up in tch in last trio: hdwy 1/2-way: unable qck u.p and sltly hmpd over 1f out: wknd ins fnl f* **8/1**

31- **7** shd **Elucidation (IRE)**[225] 6211 3-9-0 **88**.................................... RyanMoore 4 86
(Sir Michael Stoute) *cmpt: bit bkwd: hld up in tch in midfield: shuffled bk towards rr 3f out: rdn 2f out: no imp over 1f out: wl hld but kpt on ins fnl f* **9/2**[3]

12-0 **8** 1/2 **Western Duke (IRE)**[17] 1518 3-9-1 **89**................................. FranBerry 7 86
(Ralph Beckett) *lw: s.i.s: hld up in tch in last pair: swtchd rt and effrt over 2f out: no imp and btn over 1f out: sn wknd* **25/1**

613- **9** 7 **Je Suis Charlie**[182] 7471 3-8-2 **76** oh1............................... LukeMorris 8 59
(Michael Bell) *t.k.h: hld up in tch in midfield: rdn and dropped to rr jst over 2f out: wknd over 1f out* **33/1**

61-2 **10** 2 1/4 **First Nation**[17] 1518 3-9-3 **91**........................................... WilliamBuick 2 69
(Charlie Appleby) *cmpt: lw: in tch in midfield: rdn jst over 2f out: struggling whn n.m.r over 1f out: wknd fnl f* **7/2**[1]

2m 4.07s (-1.73) **Going Correction** +0.05s/f (Good) 10 Ran SP% **116.8**
Speed ratings (Par 102): **108,107,105,105,104 103,103,103,97,95**
CSF £77.27 CT £293.94 TOTE £4.80: £1.50, £5.10, £1.80; EX 86.50 Trifecta £439.20.

**Owner** China Horse Club International Limited **Bred** Lofts Hall Stud **Trained** Newmarket, Suffolk

■ Stewards' Enquiry : Andrea Atzeni three-day ban: careless riding (May 3-5)

James Doyle caution: careless riding

**FOCUS**
This is a handicap that has thrown up a number of smart performers in the past, not least the John Gosden-trained Cloudscape and Bronze Cannon, who went on to compete at Group level. His winner this year has the potential to do the same. The fifth is the best guide to the form.

T/Jkpt: Not won. T/Plt: £328.30 to a £1 stake. Pool: £128,289.43. 285.26 winning units. T/Qpdt: £124.10 to a £1 stake. Pool: £7,765.48. 46.30 winning units. **Steve Payne**

# 1836 WOLVERHAMPTON (A.W) (L-H)
Wednesday, April 19

**OFFICIAL GOING: Tapeta: standard**
Wind: Light behind final 2f Weather: Cloudy

## 1887 FCL GLOBAL FORWARDING MAKING LOGISTICS PERSONAL "HANDS AND HEELS" APPRENTICE H'CAP 6f 20y (Tp)
**5:40** (5:40) (Class 6) (0-65,67) 4-Y-0+ **£2,264** (£673; £336; £168) **Stalls** Low

Form RPR

1344 **1** **Space War**[6] 1755 10-9-4 **66**..........................................(t) RyanTimby(5) 3 73
(Michael Easterby) *s.i.s: hld up: swtchd rt and hdwy wl over 1f out: shkn up and edgd lft ins fnl f: r.o to ld nr fin* **6/1**[3]

1135 **2** nk **Pushkin Museum (IRE)**[44] 1063 6-9-6 **66**............... ConnorMurtagh(3) 4 72
(Patrick Morris) *chsd ldr tl led over 1f out: shkn up ins fnl f: hdd nr fin* **9/2**[2]

-530 **3** 1 3/4 **Inshaa**[21] 1419 5-9-4 **64**.........................................(p) SeamusCronin(3) 11 65+
(Michael Herrington) *hld up: hdwy and nt clr run over 1f out: swtchd rt ins fnl f: r.o wl towards fin* **6/1**[3]

0232 **4** 1 **Mr Chuckles (IRE)**[25] 1371 4-8-9 **52**.................................(p) DavidEgan 5 50
(Daniel Mark Loughnane) *chsd ldrs: shkn up over 1f out: styd on same pce ins fnl f* **9/2**[2]

1502 **5** nse **Burtonwood**[26] 1346 5-9-10 **67**...................................... KieranSchofield 6 65
(Julie Camacho) *pushed along early in rr: hdwy to go prom 5f out: shkn up over 1f out: styd on same pce ins fnl f* **4/1**[1]

0064 **6** 1 1/4 **Cuban Queen (USA)**[13] 1587 4-8-7 **50** oh5.................... FinleyMarsh 10 44
(Julia Feilden) *pushed along and prom on outer: lost pl over 4f out: swtchd rt over 1f out: r.o towards fin* **18/1**

1425 **7** 1 **Tasaaboq**[6] 1759 6-8-7 **55**.............................................(t) TristanPrice(5) 1 46
(Phil McEntee) *prom: pushed along over 2f out: wknd ins fnl f* **10/1**

-650 **8** 3/4 **City Of Angkor Wat (IRE)**[79] 482 7-8-11 **54**.....(p) KatherineGlenister 2 43
(Conor Dore) *sn pushed along in rr: hdwy wl over 1f out: wknd ins fnl f* **16/1**

0060 **9** 4 **Allen's Folly**[20] 1452 4-8-4 **50** oh5.................................(b[1]) MollyKing(3) 8 27
(Peter Hiatt) *sn led: pushed along and hdd over 1f out: wknd fnl f* **100/1**

00-5 **10** 8 **Clon Rocket (IRE)**[25] 1371 4-8-2 **50** oh2............. MeganEllingworth(5) 7 3
(John Holt) *chsd ldrs : pushed along 1/2-way: wknd 2f out* **25/1**

0434 **11** 2 1/2 **Head Space (IRE)**[26] 1339 9-9-1 **63**.............................. KeelanBaker(5) 9 8
(David Evans) *prom towards outer: pushed along and lost pl over 3f out: wknd over 2f out* **22/1**

1m 13.69s (-0.81) **Going Correction** -0.125s/f (Stan) 11 Ran SP% **114.4**
Speed ratings (Par 101): **100,99,97,95,95 94,92,91,86,75 72**
CSF £31.58 CT £172.21 TOTE £8.00: £2.60, £1.80, £2.30; EX 35.20 Trifecta £222.50.

**Owner** M W Easterby **Bred** Shutford Stud And O F Waller **Trained** Sheriff Hutton, N Yorks

**FOCUS**
Only apprentices with less than 10 winners to their name were eligible to ride in this moderate sprint handicap. They went a good pace courtesy of \bAllen's Folly\p in the first-time blinkers. The form could have been rated a fraction better.

## 1888 FCL GLOBAL FORWARDING MAKING LOGISTICS PERSONAL H'CAP 7f 36y (Tp)
**6:15** (6:16) (Class 5) (0-70,72) 3-Y-O **£2,911** (£866; £432; £216) **Stalls** High

Form RPR

06-4 **1** **Mulzim**[18] 1488 3-9-6 **69**....................................................... DaneO'Neill 9 76
(Ed Dunlop) *hld up in tch: plld hrd: shkn up over 1f out: rdn to ld wl ins fnl f: r.o* **5/1**[2]

536- **2** nk **Favourite Royal (IRE)**[211] 6648 3-9-9 **72**..................... RobertWinston 3 78
(Eve Johnson Houghton) *hld up: flashed tail at times: nt clr run: hdwy and swtchd lft over 1f out: sn hung lft: r.o wl* **33/1**

3-34 **3** nk **Hart Stopper**[15] 1543 3-9-3 **69**........................................ LouisSteward(3) 8 74
(Michael Bell) *plld hrd and prom: wnt 2nd 1/2-way: shkn up to ld over 1f out: rdn and hdd wl ins fnl f* **15/2**[3]

50-5 **4** 1 1/4 **Rita's Man (IRE)**[96] 212 3-9-1 **64**..................................... KieranO'Neill 1 66
(Richard Hannon) *led: plld hrd: hdd over 6f out: remained handy: pushed along over 2f out: rallied over 1f out: r.o* **16/1**

3315 **5** 3/4 **Bazwind (IRE)**[22] 1411 3-8-12 **66**...............................(p) CliffordLee(5) 10 66
(David Evans) *sn pushed along and prom fr wd draw: led over 5f out: rdn and qcknd over 2f out: hdd over 1f out: no ex ins fnl f* **8/1**

13-1 **6** nk **Altiko Tommy (IRE)**[33] 1242 3-9-6 **69**................................ LiamKeniry 6 68
(George Baker) *hld up in tch: racd keenly: nt clr run and lost pl over 4f out: hdwy over 1f out: sn rdn: styd on* **5/1**[2]

44-3 **7** 1 1/4 **Al Mansor (IRE)**[14] 1550 3-9-5 **68**...................................... SeanLevey 7 63
(Richard Hannon) *plld hrd: led over 6f out: hdd over 5f out: lost 2nd 1/2-way: rdn and edgd lft over 1f out: no ex ins fnl f* **5/2**[1]

0-00 **8** 4 1/2 **Tor**[22] 1411 3-9-7 **70**.............................................................. DavidNolan 4 53
(Iain Jardine) *hld up: rdn over 1f out: a in rr* **14/1**

42-5 **9** 1 1/2 **Challow (IRE)**[14] 1554 3-9-5 **71**................................. EdwardGreatrex(3) 2 50
(Sylvester Kirk) *awkward s: hld up racd keenly: a in rr* **8/1**

1m 28.75s (-0.05) **Going Correction** -0.125s/f (Stan) 9 Ran SP% **111.4**
Speed ratings (Par 98): **95,94,94,92,92 91,90,85,83**
CSF £138.86 CT £1198.98 TOTE £5.80: £1.80, £4.70, £2.20; EX 92.00 Trifecta £607.80.

**Owner** Hamdan Al Maktoum **Bred** Shadwell Estate Company Limited **Trained** Newmarket, Suffolk

**FOCUS**
As usual for 3yo handicaps at this time of year, there were plenty of imponderables and the waters were further muddied by a slow early gallop. It was probably still an okay race of its type, though.

## 1889 FCL GLOBAL FORWARDING MAKING LOGISTICS PERSONAL MAIDEN STKS 7f 36y (Tp)
**6:45** (6:46) (Class 5) 3-4-Y-0 **£2,911** (£866; £432; £216) **Stalls** High

Form RPR

42- **1** **Ejaaby**[160] 7883 3-8-11 0....................................................... DaneO'Neill 8 79+
(Roger Varian) *racd keenly in 2nd pl tl over 4f out: remained handy: rdn to ld and hung lft over 1f out: r.o* **11/10**[1]

0- **2** 1 3/4 **Excellent Sunset (IRE)**[284] 4147 3-8-6 0................. JosephineGordon 1 69
(David Lanigan) *edgd lft s: wnt prom over 5f out: rdn over 1f out: styd on* **12/1**

22- **3** shd **El Cap (USA)**[165] 7812 3-8-11 0........................................... TedDurcan 3 77+
(Sir Michael Stoute) *chsd ldr: effrt and n.m.r over 1f out: styd on* **13/8**[2]

45 **4** 3 **Gunmaker (IRE)**[18] 1488 3-8-11 0........................................ LiamKeniry 2 66+
(David Simcock) *hld up: hdwy and nt clr run over 1f out: swtchd rt and styd on ins fnl f: nt trble ldrs* **50/1**

0/ **5** shd **Under The Covers**[646] 4204 4-9-5 0.................................. RyanPowell 6 66
(Ronald Harris) *plld hrd and sn prom: led over 4f out: hung rt over 2f out: rdn and hdd over 1f out: hmpd ins fnl f: no ex* **200/1**

0-2 **6** *2* **Royal Peace (IRE)**[20] 1448 3-8-6 0 KieranO'Neill 4 55
(Richard Hannon) *led: hdd over 4f out: chsd ldr: rdn and ev ch over 1f out: sn edgd lft: wkng whn edgd rt ins fnl f* **16/1**

4 **7** *hd* **Zillion (IRE)**[20] 1448 3-8-11 0 (p[1]) DanielMuscutt 11 60
(John Gosden) *hld up: rdn over 1f out: nvr on terms* **8/1**[3]

**8** *nk* **Katheefa (USA)** 3-8-8 0 CallumShepherd(3) 10 59
(Charles Hills) *hld up: hdwy over 1f out: edgd lft and wknd fnl f* **25/1**

**9** *4½* **Careyanne** 3-8-6 0 FrannyNorton 9 42
(David Loughnane) *sn prom: shkn up over 1f out: wknd fnl f* **200/1**

**10** *3½* **Tawfeer** 3-8-11 0 RobHornby 5 37
(James Unett) *hld up: a in rr* **200/1**

**11** *32* **Socks And Shares (IRE)** 4-9-10 0 AdamBeschizza 7
(Derek Shaw) *s.v.s: a bhd* **200/1**

1m 27.77s (-1.03) **Going Correction** -0.125s/f (Stan) **11** Ran SP% **118.2**
**WFA** 3 from 4yo 13lb
Speed ratings (Par 103): **100,98,97,94,94 92,91,91,86,82 45**
CSF £16.62 TOTE £2.20: £1.10, £2.60, £1.10; EX 16.80 Trifecta £29.30.
**Owner** Hamdan Al Maktoum **Bred** Tony Webb **Trained** Newmarket, Suffolk

**FOCUS**
An uncompetitive maiden where they went steady early.

## 1890 FCL GLOBAL FORWARDING H'CAP 7f 36y (Tp)

**7:15** (7:17) (Class 5) (0-75,77) 4-Y-O+ **£2,911** (£866; £432; £216) **Stalls** High

Form RPR

-044 **1** **Anonymous John (IRE)**[19] 1467 5-9-5 **73** JosephineGordon 12 80
(Dominic Ffrench Davis) *hld up: hdwy over 2f out: rdn: edgd lft and r.o to ld nr fin* **10/1**

00-3 **2** *nk* **Lucky Lodge**[11] 1631 7-8-9 **63** (p) CamHardie 11 69
(Antony Brittain) *a.p: racd keenly: rdn to ld ins fnl f: hdd nr fin* **20/1**

3-00 **3** *nk* **Air Of York (IRE)**[53] 929 5-8-8 **62** DanielMuscutt 7 67
(John Flint) *hld up: rdn: edgd lft and r.o wl ins fnl f: nt quite rch ldrs* **16/1**

1366 **4** *½* **Athassel**[13] 1586 8-9-1 **76** KatherineGlenister(7) 8 80
(David Evans) *hld up: shkn up over 1f out: r.o wl ins fnl f* **16/1**

00-4 **5** *¾* **Tafteesh (IRE)**[11] 1631 4-8-12 **69** NathanEvans(3) 10 71
(Michael Easterby) *mid-div: pushed along and lost pl 1/2-way: rallied over 1f out: r.o* **11/2**

-000 **6** *1¼* **Newstead Abbey**[26] 1346 7-8-13 **72** (b[1]) CliffordLee(5) 5 71
(Michael Herrington) *racd keenly: wnt 2nd 6f out: led 2f out: rdn and hung lft over 1f out: hdd and no ex ins fnl f* **4/1**[2]

0-00 **7** *½* **Passing Star**[34] 1224 6-8-9 **76** (p[1]) GeorgeDowning 2 73
(Daniel Kubler) *s.i.s: hld up: nt clr run over 2f out: hdwy and nt clr run over 1f out: swtchd rt ins fnl f: r.o: nt trble ldrs* **10/1**

144- **8** *1½* **Little Miss Kodi (IRE)**[189] 7281 4-9-7 **75** FrannyNorton 4 68
(Daniel Mark Loughnane) *chsd ldrs: rdn over 1f out: wknd ins fnl f* **9/2**[3]

-536 **9** *3½* **Be Royale**[12] 1599 7-8-12 **66** (t) RobertWinston 9 50
(Michael Appleby) *hld up in tch: effrt and nt clr run over 1f out: hmpd ins fnl f: eased sn after* **20/1**

43-0 **10** *4* **Mr Christopher (IRE)**[91] 287 5-9-9 **77** (p) RichardKingscote 3 50
(Tom Dascombe) *led: rdn and hdd 2f out: wknd fnl f* **7/2**[1]

104/ **11** *¾* **Rain Wind And Fire (USA)**[623] 5017 5-9-7 **75** RyanPowell 6 46
(Ronald Harris) *dwlt: a in rr* **50/1**

1m 27.8s (-1.00) **Going Correction** -0.125s/f (Stan) **11** Ran SP% **117.2**
Speed ratings (Par 103): **100,99,99,98,97 96,95,94,90,85 84**
CSF £193.31 CT £3186.70 TOTE £9.40: £2.40, £4.60, £4.50; EX 78.70 Trifecta £1537.30.
**Owner** R F Haynes **Bred** Tally-Ho Stud **Trained** Lambourn, Berks

**FOCUS**
They got racing a long way out in this wide open handicap. Those who were ridden more conservatively were favoured.

## 1891 FCLGF.COM H'CAP 1m 4f 51y (Tp)

**7:45** (7:46) (Class 5) (0-70,72) 4-Y-O+ **£2,911** (£866; £432; £216) **Stalls** Low

Form RPR

4300 **1** **Zabeel Star (IRE)**[12] 1598 5-9-8 **71** LiamKeniry 2 77
(Graeme McPherson) *s.i.s: hld up: hdwy over 2f out: rdn to ld ins fnl f: r.o* **10/1**

0012 **2** *nk* **Mazaaher**[19] 1469 7-9-0 **68** CliffordLee(5) 5 73
(David Evans) *a.p: rdn: carried hd high and hung lft fr over 1f out: sn ev ch: nt run on* **7/1**[3]

00-4 **3** *1¼* **Hussar Ballad (USA)**[11] 1630 8-9-2 **65** CamHardie 6 68
(Antony Brittain) *hld up: hdwy over 1f out: sn rdn: r.o* **28/1**

4240 **4** *nse* **Bamako Du Chatelet (FR)**[25] 1364 6-9-7 **70** (p) StevieDonohoe 8 74+
(Ian Williams) *hld up: hdwy and nt clr run over 1f out: nt clr run and swtchd lft wl ins fnl f: r.o* **9/1**

-502 **5** *1¾* **Falcon's Fire (IRE)**[7] 1716 4-9-3 **72** RowanScott(5) 7 72
(Keith Dalgleish) *chsd ldr over 3f: remained handy: rdn and ev ch over 1f out: no ex ins fnl f* **16/1**

1111 **6** *½* **Smiley Bagel (IRE)**[14] 1560 4-9-7 **71** RichardKingscote 3 70
(Ed Walker) *prom: wnt 2nd over 8f out tl over 6f out: remained handy: chsd ldr again over 3f out: rdn to ld over 1f out: hdd and no ex ins fnl f* **2/1**[1]

-000 **7** *3¼* **Archipeligo**[17] 1519 6-9-2 **65** DavidNolan 9 59
(Iain Jardine) *prom: lost pl over 3f out: styd on same pce fr over 1f out* **8/1**

-011 **8** *½* **Dunquin (IRE)**[27] 1330 5-9-7 **70** TomQueally 1 63
(John Mackie) *hld up in tch: racd keenly: wnt 2nd over 6f out: led 5f out: rdn and hdd over 1f out: wknd ins fnl f* **11/4**[2]

06-6 **9** *12* **Teak (IRE)**[11] 1630 10-9-0 **70** (v) LukeCatton(7) 4 44
(Ian Williams) *led 7f: rdn over 3f out: wknd over 2f out* **80/1**

2m 37.17s (-3.63) **Going Correction** -0.125s/f (Stan) **9** Ran SP% **113.3**
Speed ratings (Par 103): **107,106,105,105,104 104,102,101,93**
CSF £76.32 CT £1883.97 TOTE £9.50: £2.60, £2.30, £5.90; EX 92.30 Trifecta £932.20.
**Owner** The Self Preservation Society & Partner **Bred** G Morrin **Trained** Upper Oddington, Gloucs

**FOCUS**
Modest fare with the winning runs of the front two in the market coming to an end.

## 1892 PERSONAL LOGISTICS FROM FCL GLOBAL FORWARDING H'CAP 1m 1f 104y (Tp)

**8:15** (8:17) (Class 5) (0-70,74) 4-Y-O+ **£2,911** (£866; £432; £216) **Stalls** Low

Form RPR

00-1 **1** **Gulf Of Poets**[8] 1707 5-9-4 **70** NathanEvans(3) 4 83+
(Michael Easterby) *hld up: hdwy over 3f out: shkn up to ld over 1f out: sn edgd lft and wnt clr: easily* **4/9**[1]

34 **2** *1¼* **Bosphorus Prince (IRE)**[14] 1551 5-9-8 **71** JohnFahy 3 75
(Matthew Salaman) *hld up: rdn over 2f out: hdwy over 1f out: sn rdn and edgd lft: styd on to go 2nd nr fin: no ch w wnr* **10/1**[3]

4521 **3** *nk* **What Usain**[12] 1602 5-9-5 **71** (p) AlistairRawlinson(3) 5 74
(Michael Appleby) *chsd ldr tl led over 2f out: rdn and hdd over 1f out: styd on same pce* **4/1**[2]

0-56 **4** *7* **Perceived**[15] 1549 5-9-8 **71** CamHardie 1 59
(Antony Brittain) *prom: pushed along over 3f out: outpcd fr over 2f out* **50/1**

3/05 **5** *6* **Instill**[67] 688 5-9-3 **66** RobHornby 6 42
(Mandy Rowland) *sn led: pushed along over 3f out: hdd over 2f out: rdn and wknd over 1f out* **18/1**

1m 59.28s (-1.52) **Going Correction** -0.125s/f (Stan) **5** Ran SP% **105.6**
Speed ratings (Par 103): **101,99,99,93,88**
CSF £5.05 TOTE £1.30: £1.10, £1.70; EX 4.30 Trifecta £8.90.
**Owner** L Westwood, A Chandler & L Hall **Bred** Juddmonte Farms Ltd **Trained** Sheriff Hutton, N Yorks
■ Lord Of The Storm was withdrawn. Price at time of withdrawal 20-1. Rule 4 does not apply.

**FOCUS**
A good opportunity for the favourite to follow up his turf win of the previous week.

## 1893 FCL PERSONALISED GLOBAL FREIGHT SOLUTIONS H'CAP 1m 142y (Tp)

**8:45** (8:45) (Class 5) (0-70,72) 4-Y-O+ **£2,911** (£866; £432; £216) **Stalls** Low

Form RPR

5543 **1** **Roman De Brut (IRE)**[11] 1620 5-8-12 **66** CharlieBennett(5) 6 73+
(Daniel Mark Loughnane) *chsd ldrs: wnt 2nd over 3f out tl led over 2f out: sn rdn clr: eased nr fin* **4/1**[2]

0312 **2** *1* **Spiritual Star (IRE)**[14] 1553 8-9-9 **72** RobertWinston 5 75+
(Lee Carter) *dwlt: hld up: shkn up and hung lft over 1f out: r.o to go 2nd wl ins fnl f: no ch w wnr* **4/1**[2]

5603 **3** *½* **So It's War (FR)**[35] 1201 6-9-2 **65** (p) TomQueally 4 67
(Keith Dalgleish) *hld up: hdwy over 2f out: rdn to chse wnr and hung lft over 1f out: styd on* **6/1**[3]

1-22 **4** *1¼* **Swansway**[19] 1473 4-9-0 **66** NathanEvans(3) 7 65
(Michael Easterby) *hld up: rdn over 2f out: hdwy and nt clr run ins fnl f: nt rch ldrs* **11/4**[1]

6201 **5** *shd* **Foie Gras**[20] 1449 7-9-0 **70** (p) JoshuaBryan(7) 1 68
(Chris Dwyer) *hld up: r.o ins fnl f: nvr nrr* **16/1**

3450 **6** *½* **Black Dave (IRE)**[21] 1422 7-9-6 **69** SeanLevey 8 66
(David Evans) *sn led: rdn and hdd over 2f out: no ex ins fnl f* **13/2**

-222 **7** *½* **Simply Clever**[15] 1545 4-8-6 **58** AaronJones(3) 2 54
(David Brown) *chsd ldr 5f: rdn over 2f out: hung lft over 1f out: styd on same pce* **9/1**

00-0 **8** *14* **Gambino (IRE)**[22] 1409 7-8-7 **63** ConnorMurtagh(7) 3 27
(John David Riches) *rrd s: sn prom: rdn and wknd over 2f out* **25/1**

1m 47.56s (-2.54) **Going Correction** -0.125s/f (Stan) **8** Ran SP% **114.0**
Speed ratings (Par 103): **106,105,104,103,103 103,102,90**
CSF £20.26 CT £93.65 TOTE £4.40: £1.80, £1.40, £2.30; EX 18.10 Trifecta £104.60.
**Owner** Phil Slater **Bred** Tinnakill Bloodstock **Trained** Rock, Worcs

**FOCUS**
Modest stuff, but a case could be made for all of these. Charlie Bennett rather stole the race on the winner.
T/Plt: £285.50 to a £1 stake. Pool: £75,800.63. 193.75 winning units. T/Qpdt: £51.70 to a £1 stake. Pool: £8,181.44. 117.04 winning units. **Colin Roberts**

# 1769 LINGFIELD (L-H)

Thursday, April 20

**OFFICIAL GOING: Polytrack: standard**
Wind: Light behind Weather: Cloudy, cold

## 1894 BARRY BAZ WELLER 80TH BIRTHDAY H'CAP 1m 1y(P)

**4:40** (4:40) (Class 6) (0-55,55) 4-Y-O+ **£2,264** (£673; £336; £168) **Stalls** High

Form RPR

604- **1** **Whispered Kiss**[154] 7986 4-9-3 **51** ShaneKelly 9 59
(Mike Murphy) *led tl hdd after 2f: t.k.h bhd ldrs on inner: swtchd to outer and rdn over 2f out: kpt on wl and led 150yds out: rdn out* **8/1**

-012 **2** *1* **Lord Murphy (IRE)**[15] 1563 4-9-7 **55** AdamKirby 7 61
(Daniel Mark Loughnane) *hld up in rr-div on outer: shkn up wl over 2f out w little rspnse: no imp tl kpt on wl ent fnl f: tk 2nd cl home: nt rch wnr* **5/4**[1]

-232 **3** *nk* **Home Again**[21] 1451 4-8-11 **52** JoshuaBryan(7) 2 57
(Lee Carter) *mid-div on inner: rdn over 2f out on inner: angled between horses coming off bnd: led 1f out: hdd 150yds out: kpt on and lost 2nd cl home* **8/1**

340- **4** *1½* **Caribbean Spring (IRE)**[141] 8156 4-9-0 **55** JaneElliott(7) 12 57
(George Margarson) *mid-div on outer: rdn over 2f out: kpt on ent fnl f: no ex fnl 110yds* **14/1**

-020 **5** *1¼* **Mulled Wine**[27] 1338 4-9-4 **52** KierenFox 4 51
(John Best) *in rr: rdn along wl over 2f out: on inner over 1f out: kpt on one pce* **6/1**[2]

-530 **6** *2* **Gavarnie Encore**[29] 1298 5-9-0 **48** KieranO'Neill 5 42
(Michael Blanshard) *niggled along early in rr: rdn over 2f out: no imp fr over 1f out* **10/1**

60-0 **7** *hd* **Coup De Vent**[22] 1425 6-9-0 **48** TimmyMurphy 6 41
(John O'Shea) *sluggish s: kpt wd and mde up grnd after 2f to sit bhd ldr on outer: led 2f out: drifted lft to rail and bdly hmpd rival jst over 1f out: hdd sn after and wknd* **25/1**

5543 **8** *5* **Caledonian Gold**[14] 1587 4-9-7 **55** RobertWinston 8 56
(Paul D'Arcy) *chsd ldrs tl led after 2f: rdn wl over 2f out: hdd 2f out but remained pressing for ld: wkng whn snatched up on rail over 1f out and jockey had to ease heavily: no imp after* **7/1**[3]

06-6 **9** *1* **Fairy Mist (IRE)**[22] 1425 10-9-3 **51** (v) WilliamCarson 1 30
(John Bridger) *missed break: in rr: rdn over 2f out: no imp fr over 1f out* **16/1**

000 **10** *9* **Tilly's Bridge**[31] 1287 4-9-2 **50** JackMitchell 3 7
(Steve Woodman) *covered up in mid-div: niggled along 1/2-way: rdn over 2f out: no imp fr over 1f out and eased* **33/1**

1m 38.65s (0.45) **Going Correction** -0.15s/f (Stan) **10** Ran SP% **121.9**
Speed ratings (Par 101): **91,90,89,88,86 84,84,79,78,69**
CSF £19.22 CT £91.81 TOTE £8.70: £3.30, £1.10, £2.60; EX 24.80 Trifecta £147.00.
**Owner** D Ellison, B Olkowicz, C Speller **Bred** T Ellison, B Olkowicz And C Speller **Trained** Westoning, Beds


The Form Book Flat, Raceform Ltd, Newbury, RG14 5SJ

**FOCUS**
A moderate handicap. The winner found improvement to get off the mark from a wide draw off a modest gallop. The third helps guide the form.

## 1895 RUDRIDGE LTD H'CAP 7f 1y(P)
**5:15** (5:15) (Class 4) (0-85,84) 3-Y-O **£4,690** (£1,395; £697; £348) **Stalls** Low

Form RPR
264- **1** **Aventinus (IRE)**[143] 8132 3-9-3 **80**.................................... JackMitchell 9 89
(Hugo Palmer) *pressed ldr: rdn along over 2f out and stole a ld w runner-up fr over 1f out: led 150yds out: kpt on wl* **8/1**
22-1 **2** *2 ½* **Archer's Arrow (USA)**[15] 1552 3-9-0 **82**.................... GeorgeWood(5) 7 84
(Saeed bin Suroor) *led: rdn over 2f out w wnr pressing: kpt on wl tl hdd fnl 150yds out: wkng fnl 100yds and jst hld 2nd* **6/1**[3]
34-1 **3** *shd* **Sword Exceed (GER)**[20] 1463 3-9-3 **80**............................ DavidNolan 8 82+
(Ivan Furtado) *racd in 5th on outer: nt clr run 2f out and swtchd to inner: plenty to do and rdn over 1f out: keeping on strly cl home and almost snatched 2nd: nvr nrr* **7/1**
1 **4** *nse* **Moolazim**[19] 1488 3-9-0 **77**.............................................. DanielMuscutt 4 79+
(Marco Botti) *in last on outer: plenty to do over 2f out: c wd st: sn rdn w plenty to do: styd on strly ins fnl f: nvr nrr* **11/4**[1]
20-1 **5** *2* **Cinque Port**[38] 1179 3-9-3 **80**............................................... ShaneKelly 5 76
(Richard Hughes) *racd in 3rd on inner: rdn over 2f out: no imp fr over 1f: kpt on one pce fnl f* **8/1**
531- **6** *½* **Thaaqib**[189] 7306 3-9-3 **80**.................................................... DaneO'Neill 6 75
(Charles Hills) *racd in 4th on outer: rdn over 2f out: outpcd fr over 1f out: kpt on one pce fnl f* **8/1**
413- **7** *3 ¼* **Glorious Rocket**[189] 7305 3-9-3 **80**.................................... AdamKirby 1 66
(Luca Cumani) *racd keenly in 6th on inner: niggled along wl over 2f out: no ex fr over 1f out* **5/1**[2]
301- **P** **Muthmira**[219] 6454 3-9-7 **84**............................................... OisinMurphy 3
(Simon Crisford) *s.s: immediately p.u: lame* **5/1**[2]
1m 23.02s (-1.78) **Going Correction** -0.15s/f (Stan) **8** Ran SP% **120.1**
Speed ratings (Par 100): **104,101,101,100,98 98,94,**
CSF £57.76 CT £291.68 TOTE £8.50: £2.70, £2.10, £2.80; EX 67.90 Trifecta £374.10.
**Owner** Seventh Lap Racing **Bred** Dr Philip J Brown **Trained** Newmarket, Suffolk

**FOCUS**
The feature contest was a decent 3yo handicap. It was marred by an early injury to the 84-rated filly at the head of the weights.

## 1896 RSM CLASSIFIED CLAIMING STKS 6f 1y(P)
**5:50** (5:51) (Class 6) 3-Y-O+ **£2,264** (£673; £336; £168) **Stalls** Low

Form RPR
0060 **1** **Major Crispies**[13] 1606 6-9-9 69.......................................(bt) AdamKirby 2 67
(Jeremy Gask) *hld up in rr off the pce: gng best and swtchd four horses wd ent st: shkn up over 1f out: sn rdn and gaining on ldr w ev stride wl ins fnl f: kpt on wl and led fnl strides* **1/1**[1]
030 **2** *hd* **Bush Warrior (IRE)**[31] 1290 6-9-5 69....................(p) JosephineGordon 1 62
(Anabel K Murphy) *sn led: rdn 2f out: stuck on wl ent fnl f tl hdd fnl strides* **9/4**[2]
500 **3** *2 ¾* **Louis Vee (IRE)**[8] 1721 9-9-6 41..................................(p) TimmyMurphy 3 55
(John O'Shea) *racd in 2nd on outer: rdn 2f out: kpt on tl lft bhd fr 1f out* **33/1**
3650 **4** *3 ¼* **Archie Stevens**[8] 1722 7-8-13 64.............................. RachealKneller(5) 4 43
(Clare Ellam) *racd in 4th on inner: rdn 2f out: no imp st* **7/1**
-000 **5** *½* **Majestic Myles (IRE)**[43] 1086 9-8-11 57...................... JoshuaBryan(7) 5 42
(Lee Carter) *racd in 3rd on outer: rdn along over 2f out: no ex fr 1f out* **4/1**[3]
1m 11.45s (-0.45) **Going Correction** -0.15s/f (Stan) **5** Ran SP% **116.2**
Speed ratings (Par 101): **97,96,93,88,88**
CSF £3.84 TOTE £1.90: £1.10, £1.70; EX 3.80 Trifecta £32.70.
**Owner** Crowd Racing Partnership, Guy Carstairs **Bred** Lowther Racing **Trained** Stockbridge, Hants

**FOCUS**
A modest claimer. They went a respectable gallop and the horse with the best overall form got his head in the front in the closing stages after a wide trip. The third is the key to the level.

## 1897 OYSTER PARTNERSHIP FILLIES' H'CAP 1m 1y(P)
**6:20** (6:20) (Class 5) (0-75,77) 4-Y-O+ **£2,911** (£866; £432; £216) **Stalls** High

Form RPR
132- **1** **Tegara**[119] 8493 4-9-2 **71**............................................. JosephineGordon 3 79+
(David Simcock) *settled bhd ldrs: shkn up wl over 1f out: pushed up between horses ent fnl f and sn upsides: wnt hd to hd w runner-up tl on top cl home* **4/1**[2]
/51- **2** *nk* **Karisma (IRE)**[123] 8449 4-9-7 **76**..................................... JackMitchell 4 83+
(Roger Varian) *hld up in rr on inner: gng wl 2f out: stuck to inner and rdn over 1f out: slt ld jst under 1f out: kpt on wl gng hd to hd w wnr ins fnl f: no ex cl home* **11/8**[1]
40- **3** *1 ¼* **Rayaa**[181] 7500 4-9-2 **71**...................................................(t) TomQueally 5 75
(John Butler) *hld up in rr: rdn over 2f out and c wd st: kpt on strly fr over 1f out: no ex cl home* **12/1**
2442 **4** *1* **Skidby Mill (IRE)**[21] 1447 7-9-7 **76**..................................... AdamKirby 1 78
(Laura Mongan) *sn led: hrd rdn wl over 1f out: kpt on tl hdd & wknd fr 1f out* **12/1**
20-5 **5** *1 ¼* **Here's Two**[10] 1687 4-9-4 **73**................................................ DaneO'Neill 2 72
(Ron Hodges) *settled bhd ldr on inner: rdn 2f out: kpt on wl and ev ch over 1f out: no ex 1f out and wknd* **8/1**
2134 **6** *4* **Remember Me**[21] 1455 4-8-13 **73**............................ CharlieBennett(5) 6 62
(Hughie Morrison) *cl up w ldr and rn free: rdn wl over 2f out: no imp fr over 1f out* **7/1**
34-1 **7** *3* **Ejayteekay**[21] 1447 4-9-3 **77**........................................ GeorgeWood(5) 7 59
(Hughie Morrison) *cl up on outer and t.k.h: rdn over 2f out: sn wknd and one pce* **11/2**[3]
1m 36.62s (-1.58) **Going Correction** -0.15s/f (Stan) **7** Ran SP% **116.5**
Speed ratings (Par 100): **101,100,99,98,97 93,90**
CSF £10.28 TOTE £4.50: £1.70, £1.80; EX 12.30 Trifecta £146.90.
**Owner** Tick Tock Partnership **Bred** Rabbah Bloodstock Limited **Trained** Newmarket, Suffolk

**FOCUS**
A fair fillies' handicap. They went a respectable gallop and it is sound form.

## 1898 HASLEMERE BUILDING COMPANY H'CAP 7f 1y(P)
**6:50** (6:50) (Class 5) (0-70,70) 4-Y-O+ **£2,911** (£866; £432; £216) **Stalls** Low

Form RPR
5103 **1** **Tavener**[3] 1842 5-8-12 **61**................................................(p) OisinMurphy 1 73
(David C Griffiths) *mde all: kicked for home wl over 2f out: big ld ent fnl f: in n.d wl ins fnl f and eased cl home* **9/4**[1]
6342 **2** *4* **Virile (IRE)**[15] 1557 6-8-1 **56** ow1..............................(bt) FinleyMarsh(7) 2 56
(Sylvester Kirk) *chsd ldr on inner: rdn 2f out: kpt on one pce fr over 1f out: no ch w wnr* **8/1**
-000 **3** *2* **Flying Fantasy**[22] 1419 5-9-2 **68**..................................(t[1]) AaronJones(3) 3 62
(Stuart Williams) *hld up in rr on outer: shkn up and c v wd st: plenty to do whn rdn over 1f out: styd on wl: nrst fin* **4/1**[3]
2023 **4** *hd* **Bookmaker**[22] 1427 7-8-2 **58**.........................................(p) JaneElliott(7) 6 51
(John Bridger) *mid-div on outer: rdn over 1f out: kpt on fnl f* **6/1**
54-0 **5** *1* **Torment**[93] 277 4-9-7 **70**.................................................. WilliamCarson 7 60
(Charlie Wallis) *chsd ldr on outer: shkn up over 2f out to hold pl: kpt on one pce fnl f* **15/2**
-430 **6** *nse* **World Of Good**[12] 1618 4-9-4 **67**.............................. JosephineGordon 4 57
(Anabel K Murphy) *settled in mid-divsion on inner: rdn over 2f out to take clsr order: 3rd ent fnl f: wknd qckly after* **16/1**
4120 **7** *shd* **Polar Kite (IRE)**[21] 1449 9-9-3 **66**..................................(h) RobHornby 5 56
(Michael Attwater) *in rr: rdn over 2f out: no imp fr over 1f out* **7/2**[2]
140- **8** *1 ½* **Perfect Pastime**[224] 6269 9-8-12 **61**.............................(h) PatCosgrave 8 47
(Jim Boyle) *hld up in rr on inner: rdn over 2f out: no imp fr over 1f out* **25/1**
1m 23.2s (-1.60) **Going Correction** -0.15s/f (Stan) **8** Ran SP% **119.9**
Speed ratings (Par 103): **103,98,96,95,94 94,94,92**
CSF £22.59 CT £70.72 TOTE £3.00: £1.10, £2.60, £1.60; EX 15.80 Trifecta £121.70.
**Owner** Baker, Hensby, Longden, Baker **Bred** Car Colston Hall Stud **Trained** Bawtry, S Yorks

**FOCUS**
A modest handicap. The winner proved thoroughly dominant from a low draw at a decent tempo throughout. Not strong form for the grade.

## 1899 LYONS O'NEILL FILLIES' H'CAP 6f 1y(P)
**7:20** (7:21) (Class 5) (0-75,77) 4-Y-O+ **£2,911** (£866; £432; £216) **Stalls** Low

Form RPR
560- **1** **Diamond Lady**[136] 8233 6-9-7 **75**................................ AdamBeschizza 8 86
(William Stone) *settled bhd ldr: rdn over 2f out: kpt on wl and led fnl 110yds* **5/1**
11- **2** *1 ¾* **Hackney Road**[127] 8358 4-9-6 **74**........................................ TomQueally 4 78+
(Henry Spiller) *hld up in 5th: rdn over 2f out: kpt on wl fr over 1f out: fin wl and tk 2nd post: nvr nrr* **9/4**[1]
-000 **3** *nk* **Very Honest (IRE)**[20] 1467 4-9-6 **74**...........................(v[1]) DannyBrock 3 77
(Brett Johnson) *led a str clip: rdn over 2f out: stuck on wl tl hdd & wknd fnl 110yds: no ex and lost 2nd post* **11/4**[2]
402- **4** *2 ¼* **Dynamic Girl (IRE)**[185] 7415 4-9-3 **71**............................(h) ShaneKelly 1 67
(Brendan Powell) *racd in 3rd chsng ldng pair: rdn over 2f out: kpt on one pce fr over 1f out* **9/2**[3]
020- **5** *1 ¼* **Bella's Venture**[177] 7591 4-8-4 **63**.............................. GeorgeWood(5) 7 55
(John Gallagher) *dropped out leaving stalls and racd in last pair: rdn over 2f out: kpt on one pce fr over 1f out* **11/1**
203- **6** *1 ¼* **Racing Angel (IRE)**[166] 7811 5-9-2 **70**......................... WilliamCarson 5 58
(Mick Quinn) *racd in 4th chsng ldng pair: rdn over 2f out: one pce st* **8/1**
-240 **7** *3* **Arize (IRE)**[13] 1599 4-8-13 **67**............................................. PatCosgrave 6 46
(Jim Boyle) *in rr: rdn over 2f out: no imp* **14/1**
1m 10.72s (-1.18) **Going Correction** -0.15s/f (Stan) **7** Ran SP% **118.4**
Speed ratings (Par 100): **101,98,98,95,93 91,87**
CSF £17.59 CT £37.65 TOTE £6.60: £2.30, £1.40; EX 22.20 Trifecta £80.00.
**Owner** The Going Great Guns Partnership **Bred** Mickley Stud **Trained** West Wickham, Cambs

**FOCUS**
A fair fillies' handicap. The third horse home nearly skipped her field, setting a strong gallop after sustained market interest, but crucially the winner was able to stay within striking distance. The winner is rated back to last season's C&D form.

## 1900 ASSET FUNDER & FULLER GRAB HIRE MAIDEN STKS 1m 4f (P)
**7:50** (7:50) (Class 5) 3-Y-O **£2,911** (£866; £432; £216) **Stalls** Low

Form RPR
422- **1** **Agathonia (USA)**[198] 7050 3-9-0 77.................................(p[1]) AdamKirby 4 82+
(Charlie Appleby) *settled in mid-div on outer: swtchd out and rdn 3f out: shkn up and led over 2f out: sn rdn and wnt clr of rivals: in n.d and styd on strly ins fnl f: pushed out* **6/4**[1]
3- **2** *7* **Physicist (IRE)**[199] 7003 3-9-5 0........................................ PatCosgrave 1 75
(Paul Cole) *led tl hdd after 2f: chsd ldr on inner: rdn 3f out where swtchd off rail: kpt on fr over 1f out: n.d to wnr and jst hld 2nd post* **11/4**[2]
3 **3** *shd* **Tristram**[26] 1358 3-9-5 0.......................................................... ShaneKelly 2 74
(Richard Hughes) *mid-div on inner: rdn and chsd wnr over 3f out: stuck on wl fr over 1f out: almost tk 2nd post* **5/1**
2 **4** *2* **Tapdancealltheway**[20] 1468 3-8-11 0.................. KieranShoemark(3) 3 66
(Amanda Perrett) *wnt lft s: hld up in rr-div: rdn over 3f out and chsd ldng quartet: kpt on one pce fr over 1f out* **20/1**
**5** *¾* **Touwari (IRE)** 3-9-5 0.......................................................(b[1]) RobertTart 6 70
(John Gosden) *led after 2f: rdn over 3f out: hdd over 2f out: kpt on tl wknd fr over 1f out* **4/1**[3]
**6** *8* **Forward Contract (USA)** 3-9-5 0.............................. RobertWinston 5 57
(Hughie Morrison) *rn green early and wl in rr: pushed along and latched on to rr of gp after 3f: rdn over 3f out: no imp* **25/1**
03 **7** *14* **Lady Maritime (IRE)**[20] 1468 3-9-0 0................................... DannyBrock 7 30
(Brett Johnson) *early pce to press ldr on outer: rdn over 3f out: wknd fr over 2f out: t.o st* **66/1**
**8** *10* **Eyesight** 3-9-5 0.........................................................(v[1]) StevieDonohoe 8 19
(Charlie Fellowes) *s.s: rdn along the whole r and wl adrift: t.o fr 4f out* **20/1**
2m 30.56s (-2.44) **Going Correction** -0.15s/f (Stan) **8** Ran SP% **118.2**
Speed ratings (Par 98): **102,97,97,95,95 90,80,74**
CSF £5.77 TOTE £2.00: £1.02, £1.60, £2.40; EX 6.90 Trifecta £18.40.
**Owner** Godolphin **Bred** Darley **Trained** Newmarket, Suffolk

**FOCUS**
A fair 3yo middle-distance maiden but lacking depth. They only went a respectable gallop but the right three horses came to the fore. The form is rated a bit cautiously.

T/Plt: £14.90 to a £1 stake. Pool: £50,263.72 -2,452.77 winning units. T/Qpdt: £3.20 to a £1 stake. Pool: £4,807.79 - 1,091.77 winning units. **Cathal Gahan**

## [1880]NEWMARKET (R-H)

Thursday, April 20

**OFFICIAL GOING: Good to firm (8.5)**

Wind: light, half behind, of no consequence Weather: overcast

### 1901 BET365.COM H'CAP 6f

**1:50** (1:52) (Class 2) (0-100,99) 3-Y-O **£12,938** (£3,850; £1,924; £962) **Stalls** Low

Form RPR

031- **1** **Victory Angel (IRE)**[166] 7819 3-8-3 **81** SilvestreDeSousa 7 95+
(Roger Varian) *athletic: hld up in tch: hdwy over 1f out to ld 1f out: r.o strly: readily* **11/4**[1]

210- **2** *2 ¼* **Rich And Famous (USA)**[194] 7155 3-8-8 **86** WilliamBuick 8 91
(Mark Johnston) *lw: chsd ldr tl rdn to ld over 1f out: hdd and edgd rt 1f out: no ch w wnr but kpt on for clr 2nd ins fnl f* **13/2**[3]

246- **3** *2 ¼* **Tommy Taylor (USA)**[222] 6326 3-9-5 **97** TomEaves 6 95+
(Kevin Ryan) *taken down early: stdd s: hld up in tch in rr: hdwy and hung rt over 1f out: kpt on same pce ins fnl f* **8/1**

14- **4** *nse* **Akhlaaq**[225] 6228 3-8-12 **90** JimCrowley 5 88
(Owen Burrows) *athletic: hld up in tch: effrt and hdwy over 1f out: kpt on same pce and no imp ins fnl f* **13/2**[3]

324- **5** *2 ¾* **Storm Cry**[210] 6706 3-8-6 **84** JoeFanning 4 73
(Mark Johnston) *lw: wnt rt s: chsd ldrs: rdn over 1f out: sn btn and wknd fnl f* **10/1**

14- **6** *nse* **Castleacre**[180] 7547 3-9-1 **93** JamesDoyle 1 82
(Hugo Palmer) *athletic: t.k.h: led: rdn and hdd over 1f out: sn wknd* **6/1**[2]

560- **7** *1 ¼* **Medici Banchiere**[201] 6954 3-9-2 **99** CliffordLee(5) 2 84
(K R Burke) *in tch in midfield: rdn 2f out: sn outpcd and wknd fnl f* **8/1**

015- **8** *13* **Hilario**[180] 7536 3-9-2 **94** RyanMoore 3 37
(Charles Hills) *w'like: dwlt and hmpd s: rousted along early: a towards rr: rdn over 2f out: no rspnse: bhd and eased fnl f* **7/1**

1m 10.43s (-1.77) **Going Correction** -0.125s/f (Firm) **8** Ran SP% **111.4**
Speed ratings (Par 104): **106,103,100,99,96 96,94,77**
CSF £19.57 CT £112.23 TOTE £2.90: £1.40, £1.80, £2.80; EX 14.60 Trifecta £106.80.

**Owner** Ziad A Galadari **Bred** Max Morris **Trained** Newmarket, Suffolk

**FOCUS**

Far side course used. Stalls: far side. No watering, and the going was given as good to firm all round (GoingStick: 8.5). An interesting sprint handicap, and it produced a very easy winner. He has more to offer.

### 1902 BET365 H'CAP 7f

**2:25** (2:25) (Class 2) (0-105,105) 4-Y-O+ **£12,938** (£3,850; £1,924; £962) **Stalls** Low

Form RPR

240- **1** **Mix And Mingle (IRE)**[201] 6939 4-9-1 **99** TedDurcan 5 110
(Chris Wall) *hld up in tch: smooth hdwy to join ldrs over 2f out: rdn to ld over 1f out: styd on wl: rdn out* **5/1**[3]

/21- **2** *1* **Tabarrak (IRE)**[349] 1991 4-9-7 **105** JimCrowley 2 113
(Richard Hannon) *lw: led for 2f: styd w ldr tl led again wl over 1f out: sn hdd and rdn: styd on same pce ins fnl f* **11/4**[1]

30-0 **3** *3* **Castle Harbour**[19] 1493 4-9-7 **105** FrankieDettori 1 105
(John Gosden) *hld up in tch in last pair: clsd to chse ldrs and rdn over 2f out: 3rd and no ex 1f out: kpt on same pce ins fnl f* **9/2**[2]

1013 **4** *¾* **Salateen**[6] 1773 5-9-7 **105** RyanMoore 4 103
(David O'Meara) *w ldr tl led after 2f: hdd 2f out: sn rdn and unable qck: wl hld 4th and kpt on same pce ins fnl f* **11/4**[1]

233- **5** *1 ¾* **Accession (IRE)**[191] 7241 8-9-2 **100** MartinLane 6 93
(Charlie Fellowes) *chsd ldrs: rdn over 2f out: unable qck and outpcd over 1f out: sn wl btn* **9/1**

/36- **6** *3* **Qeyaadah (IRE)**[226] 6210 4-8-7 **91** oh1 SilvestreDeSousa 7 76
(Michael Appleby) *dropped in bhd after s: hld up in rr: effrt 2f out: no hdwy and edgd rt over 1f out: bhd fnl f* **7/1**

1m 23.34s (-2.06) **Going Correction** -0.125s/f (Firm) **6** Ran SP% **110.7**
Speed ratings (Par 109): **106,104,101,100,98 95**
CSF £18.51 TOTE £5.90: £2.60, £1.80; EX 21.60 Trifecta £116.10.

**Owner** Ms Aida Fustoq **Bred** Deerfield Farm **Trained** Newmarket, Suffolk

**FOCUS**

A pleasing return to form by the winner, who seems to reserve her best for this track. The winner is rated back to his form here early last year.

### 1903 CONNAUGHT ACCESS FLOORING ABERNANT STKS (GROUP 3) 6f

**3:00** (3:00) (Class 1) 3-Y-O+

**£34,026** (£12,900; £6,456; £3,216; £1,614; £810) **Stalls** Low

Form RPR

013- **1** **Brando**[187] 7350 5-9-6 116 TomEaves 4 115
(Kevin Ryan) *hld up in 4th: hdwy to chse clr wnr 2f out: effrt and 3 l down over 1f out: rdn and styd on to ld 75yds out: gng away at fin* **1/1**[1]

222- **2** *1* **Ornate**[202] 6916 4-9-6 104 RyanMoore 5 112
(Robert Cowell) *swtg: sn led: clr 1/2-way: rdn over 1f out: hdd and styd on same pce fnl 75yds* **9/1**

331- **3** *2* **Windfast (IRE)**[236] 5880 6-9-6 109 RichardKingscote 1 106
(Brian Meehan) *hld up in 5th: clsd ent fnl 2f: hdwy u.p to go 3rd 1f out: no imp ins fnl f* **5/1**[2]

211- **4** *2 ¼* **Kassia (IRE)**[194] 7146 4-9-3 100 GrahamLee 2 95
(Mick Channon) *lw: hld up in rr: effrt jst over 2f out: 4th and no imp fnl f: nvr trbld ldrs* **6/1**[3]

040- **5** *1 ¾* **Mayfair Lady**[194] 7156 4-9-3 100 JackGarritty 7 90
(Richard Fahey) *taken down early: chsd ldr tl 2f out: sn rdn and lost pl over 1f out: wl btn fnl f* **16/1**

026- **6** *¾* **Aeolus**[159] 7932 6-9-6 107 JamieSpencer 6 90
(Ed Walker) *racd in 4th: rdn 2f out: sn struggling: bhd ins fnl f* **6/1**[3]

1m 10.19s (-2.01) **Going Correction** -0.125s/f (Firm) **6** Ran SP% **111.1**
Speed ratings (Par 113): **108,106,104,101,98 97**
CSF £10.65 TOTE £1.80: £1.20, £3.30; EX 7.90 Trifecta £22.80.

**Owner** Mrs Angie Bailey **Bred** Car Colston Hall Stud **Trained** Hambleton, N Yorks

**FOCUS**

Not the strongest of Group 3s, and the Group 1-placed winner stood out on ratings beforehand. He was made to work for it, though, with the runner-up being given a good tactical ride. Kevin Ryan was winning the race for the third time in four years. The runner-up is the key.

### 1904 BET365 CRAVEN STKS (GROUP 3) (C&G) 1m

**3:35** (3:36) (Class 1) 3-Y-O

**£34,026** (£12,900; £6,456; £3,216; £1,614; £810) **Stalls** Low

Form RPR

1- **1** **Eminent (IRE)**[210] 6704 3-9-0 87 JimCrowley 4 111+
(Martyn Meade) *tall: scope: racd centre to stands side: chsd gp ldr: rdn over 2f out: ev ch over 1f out: drvn to ld ins fnl f: styd on strly and gng away at fin: 1st of 4 in gp* **8/1**

151- **2** *1 ¾* **Rivet (IRE)**[180] 7539 3-9-0 115 FrankieDettori 5 106
(William Haggas) *racd centre to stands side: overall ldr: rdn ent fnl 2f: drvn and hrd pressed over 1f out: hdd ins fnl f: no ex and styd on same pce: 2nd of 4 in gp* **11/4**[2]

1 **3** *nk* **Benbatl**[18] 1513 3-9-0 95 SilvestreDeSousa 7 105+
(Saeed bin Suroor) *str: lw: racd centre to stands side: t.k.h: hld up in tch in midfield overall: effrt and edging rt jst over 2f out: drvn and ev ch over 1f out: no ex and styd on same pce ins fnl f: 3rd of 4 in gp* **4/1**[3]

210- **4** *2* **Contrapposto (IRE)**[180] 7539 3-9-0 92 JimmyFortune 6 101
(David Menuisier) *racd centre to stands side: stdd s: hld up in rr: rdn over 2f out: styd on to pass btn horses ins fnl f: no threat to ldrs: 4th of 4 in gp* **50/1**

131- **5** *nk* **Larchmont Lad (IRE)**[210] 6707 3-9-0 110 SeanLevey 1 100
(Richard Hannon) *racd centre to far side: wl in tch: effrt jst over 2f out: hdwy u.p and ev ch over 1f out: no ex ins fnl f: wknd fnl 100yds: 1st of 3 in gp* **9/2**

21- **6** *2 ½* **War Decree (USA)**[268] 4732 3-9-0 113 RyanMoore 2 94
(A P O'Brien, Ire) *racd centre to far side: pressed gp ldr and prom overall: rdn ent fnl 2f: unable qck and lost pl ent fnl f: wknd ins fnl f: 2nd of 3 in gp* **9/4**[1]

431- **7** *shd* **Gulliver**[194] 7157 3-9-0 85 (bt) JamesDoyle 3 93
(Hugo Palmer) *str: lw: racd centre to far side: led gp and w overall ldr: rdn over 2f out: lost pl over 1f out: wknd ins fnl f: 3rd of 3 in gp* **25/1**

1m 35.15s (-3.45) **Going Correction** -0.125s/f (Firm) **7** Ran SP% **112.5**
Speed ratings (Par 108): **112,110,109,107,107 105,105**
CSF £29.30 TOTE £9.40: £3.10, £2.10; EX 28.70 Trifecta £126.40.

**Owner** Sir Peter Vela **Bred** Premier Bloodstock **Trained** Newmarket, Suffolk

**FOCUS**

A slightly unsatisfactory Craven, with the field splitting into two groups and the first four all coming from the stands' side bunch. Nevertheless, it was a good performance from the winner, who was one of the two least experienced runners in the line-up. The form has a slightly fluid feel but was a stone faster than the later handicap.

### 1905 ROSSDALES MAIDEN FILLIES' STKS (PLUS 10 RACE) 7f

**4:10** (4:10) (Class 4) 3-Y-O **£5,175** (£1,540; £769; £384) **Stalls** Low

Form RPR

4- **1** **Tomyris**[169] 7763 3-9-0 0 SilvestreDeSousa 7 85+
(Roger Varian) *str: t.k.h early: hld up towards rr and flashed tail early: swtchd to centre over 2f out: rdn and hdwy to ld ent fnl f: r.o strly: pushed out: readily* **11/4**[1]

2- **2** *1 ½* **Spinnaka (IRE)**[241] 5705 3-9-0 0 JamieSpencer 3 81+
(Luca Cumani) *athletic: lw: chsd ldrs: rdn over 2f out: ev ch over 1f out: drvn 1f out: chsd wnr and styd on same pce ins fnl f* **9/2**[3]

52- **3** *1 ¼* **Isabel's On It**[163] 7855 3-9-0 0 PatCosgrave 5 78+
(William Haggas) *str: fly j. leaving stalls: t.k.h: hld up in tch in midfield: effrt to chse ldrs over 1f out: n.m.r jst over 1f out: kpt on same pce ins fnl f* **11/4**[1]

4- **4** *3 ¾* **South Sea Belle (IRE)**[231] 6061 3-9-0 0 JimmyFortune 1 68
(David Menuisier) *led and racd alone in centre: rdn 2f out: edgd lft and hdd over 1f out: wknd ins fnl f* **25/1**

2 **5** *1 ¼* **Manaahil**[19] 1503 3-9-0 0 JimCrowley 2 64
(Charles Hills) *athletic: lw: chsd ldr: rdn and ev ch 2f out: struggling to qckn whn squeezed for room and lost pl over 1f out: sn wknd* **3/1**[2]

0- **6** *nk* **Trilliant (IRE)**[180] 7548 3-9-0 0 WilliamBuick 6 63
(Ed Walker) *tall: in tch in midfield: rdn 3f out: outpcd 2f out and swtchd rt over 1f out: wl hld but kpt on ins fnl f* **11/1**

**7** *nk* **Lyric Harmony (IRE)** 3-9-0 0 PatDobbs 9 63
(Giles Bravery) *dwlt: hld up in rr: pushed along and outpcd 2f out: wl hld but kpt on ins fnl f* **50/1**

06 **8** *16* **Coya**[9] 1692 3-8-11 0 (h) CallumShepherd(3) 4 19
(Charles Hills) *lw: a towards rr: rdn 2f out: sn struggling: bhd ins fnl f* **66/1**

1m 24.75s (-0.65) **Going Correction** -0.125s/f (Firm) **8** Ran SP% **112.1**
Speed ratings (Par 97): **98,96,94,90,89 88,88,70**
CSF £14.83 TOTE £3.70: £1.20, £1.70, £1.40; EX 18.30 Trifecta £46.40.

**Owner** Nurlan Bizakov **Bred** Hesmonds Stud Ltd **Trained** Newmarket, Suffolk

**FOCUS**

Following the Craven and the eclipse of the three who raced up the centre of the track, all but one of the runners in this maiden edged over to race towards the stands' rail. The form is rated around the race averages.

### 1906 BET365 EBF STALLIONS MAIDEN STKS (PLUS 10 RACE) 1m 2f

**4:45** (4:47) (Class 4) 3-Y-O **£5,175** (£1,154; £1,154; £384) **Stalls** Low

Form RPR

3- **1** **Tamleek (USA)**[192] 7226 3-9-5 0 JimCrowley 4 95
(Saeed bin Suroor) *tall: scope: bit bkwd: chsd ldrs: clsd to ld and travelling strly 2f: pushed along and asserting whn hung lft over 1f out: clr and r.o wl ins fnl f: comf* **11/4**[1]

**2** *4* **Oasis Charm** 3-9-5 0 MartinLane 12 87
(Charlie Appleby) *athletic: lw: chsd ldrs: effrt 2f out: chsd wnr and kpt on same pce ins fnl f: jnd 2nd on post* **25/1**

04- **2** *dht* **Mafaaheem (IRE)**[171] 7726 3-9-5 0 SilvestreDeSousa 8 87
(Owen Burrows) *leggy: bit bkwd: t.k.h: hld up in tch in midfield: nt clr run and swtchd rt over 2f out: rdn and hdwy over 1f out: kpt on ins fnl f to join 2nd on line: no ch w wnr* **12/1**

2-2 **4** *1 ¾* **Pealer (GER)**[15] 1559 3-9-5 0 (t[1]) RobertTart 1 83
(John Gosden) *w'like: stdd s: hld up in rr: clsd 3f out: pushed along over 1f out: no ch w wnr but kpt on steadily ins fnl f: wnt 4th on post* **7/2**[2]

**5** *nse* **Grieg Hall** 3-9-5 0 JamesDoyle 2 83
(John Gosden) *w'like: bit bkwd: hld up in tch: hdwy to chse ldrs over 1f out: no ex 1f out: wknd ins fnl f* **13/2**

**6** *nk* **Daawy (IRE)** 3-9-5 0 FrankieDettori 11 82
(William Haggas) *athletic: led: rdn and hdd 2f out: unable qck and swtchd rt jst over 1f out: wknd ins fnl f* **9/2**[3]

5- **7** 2¼ **Rising (IRE)**[181] 7502 3-9-5 0 ........ JimmyFortune 3 79
(Brian Meehan) *tall: w ldr tl unable qck u.p over 1f out: wknd ins fnl f: wl btn: hung lft and eased towards fin* **8/1**

2 **8** 1¾ **Globetrotter (IRE)**[27] 1347 3-9-5 0 ........ MartinHarley 5 74
(James Tate) *tall: lengthy: in tch in midfield: rdn 3f out: outpcd and btn over 1f out: wknd ins fnl f* **14/1**

0-0 **9** 19 **Seventii**[19] 1497 3-9-0 0 ........ JFEgan 10 31
(Robert Eddery) *w'like: hld up in tch in last trio: struggling over 2f out: lost tch over 1f out* **200/1**

0- **10** 4 **About Glory**[181] 7503 3-9-5 0 ........ RyanMoore 6 46
(Richard Hannon) *athletic: hld up in tch in rr: hdwy to join ldrs 5f out: rdn over 3f out: lost pl u.p 2f out: bhd and eased ins fnl f* **12/1**

2m 5.21s (-0.59) **Going Correction** -0.125s/f (Firm) **10** Ran SP% **117.9**
Speed ratings (Par 100): **97,93,93,92,92 92,90,88,73,70**
WIN: £3.80; PL: M £3.40, T £1.60, OC £7.20; EX: T/M£20.90, T/OC £39.50; CSF: T/M £19.06, T/OC £38.30; TF: T/M/OC £485.50,T/OC/M £561.10;.
**Owner** Godolphin **Bred** Shadwell Farm LLC **Trained** Newmarket, Suffolk

**FOCUS**
A maiden that Godolphin like to win, this being the fifth time in the last seven years they have captured it, and the third year in a row the winner has been trained by Saeed bin Suroor. This form fits with the race averages.

## 1907 CLOSE BROTHERS PREMIUM FINANCE 40TH ANNIVERSARY H'CAP 1m
**5:20** (5:21) (Class 4) (0-85,87) 3-Y-O **£6,469** (£1,925; £962; £481) **Stalls** Low

Form RPR

211 **1** **Tricorn (IRE)**[47] 1029 3-9-7 **85** ........ JamesDoyle 3 100+
(John Gosden) *str: swtg: hld up in tch in midfield: shkn up and clsd ent fnl 2f: rdn to chal ent fnl f: c clr w runner up and led ins fnl f: r.o wl* **5/2**[1]

1-32 **2** ½ **Marzouq (USA)**[47] 1029 3-8-12 **76** ........ JFEgan 9 89
(Jeremy Noseda) *leggy: chsd ldr tl led over 2f out: sn rdn: hrd pressed ent fnl f: c clr w wnr but hdd ins fnl f: kpt on wl but a hld* **16/1**

221- **3** 5 **Dubara**[218] 6472 3-9-4 **82** ........ JamieSpencer 6 83
(Luca Cumani) *stdd s: hld up in rr: clsd over 2f out: rdn to chse ldrs 1f out: 3rd and no imp on ldng pair ins fnl f: kpt on* **12/1**

21- **4** 1¾ **Munawer**[187] 7366 3-9-0 **78** ........ JimCrowley 12 75
(Hugo Palmer) *unf: chsd ldrs: rdn ent fnl 2f: 4th and outpcd whn wandered ent fnl f: kpt on same pce* **7/1**[3]

10- **5** 1¾ **Ernststavroblofeld (USA)**[194] 7155 3-9-7 **85** ........ RyanMoore 8 78
(Martyn Meade) *str: hld up off the pce in last pair: rdn 3f out: sme hdwy over 1f out: styd on to pass btn horses ins fnl f* **11/2**[2]

622- **6** hd **Pillar Of Society (IRE)**[197] 7072 3-9-2 **80** ........ PatDobbs 2 72
(Richard Hannon) *t.k.h: hld up in tch in midfield: effrt 2f out: pushed along and no imp over 1f out: wl hld and kpt on same pce fnl f* **20/1**

41- **7** ½ **Marilyn**[268] 4738 3-8-9 **73** ........ TedDurcan 5 64
(Chris Wall) *wl in tch in midfield: rdn 2f out unable qck and btn 1f out: wknd ins fnl f* **25/1**

545- **8** 1¼ **Amelia Dream**[229] 6111 3-8-9 **73** ........ GrahamLee 7 61
(Mick Channon) *hld up in tch in midfield: effrt 2f out: no imp and wknd ins fnl f* **66/1**

5-43 **9** nk **Rock N Roll Global (IRE)**[76] 545 3-8-7 **71** ........ SilvestreDeSousa 10 59
(Richard Hughes) *tall: s.i.s: a towards rr: rdn 3f out: nvr trbld ldrs* **8/1**

-124 **10** ¾ **Shamrokh (IRE)**[40] 1142 3-9-9 **87** ........(tp) FrankieDettori 11 73
(John Gosden) *tall: t.k.h: hld up in tch in midfield: effrt nr stands rail 2f out: no imp and btn over 1f out: wknd fnl f* **8/1**

344- **11** 2½ **Fire Palace**[174] 7668 3-9-0 **78** ........ MartinHarley 15 58
(Robert Eddery) *lw: led tl over 2f out: sn rdn and lost pl over 1f out: wknd fnl f* **16/1**

1 **12** 2½ **Musikel (IRE)**[27] 1347 3-8-6 **73** ........ JordanVaughan(3) 14 48
(K R Burke) *chsd ldrs: rdn 3f out: dropped towards rr and btn whn nt clr run over 1f out: bhd fnl f* **14/1**

1m 36.64s (-1.96) **Going Correction** -0.125s/f (Firm) **12** Ran SP% **114.9**
Speed ratings (Par 100): **104,103,98,96,95 94,94,93,92,92 89,87**
CSF £44.19 CT £411.68 TOTE £3.20: £1.70, £4.40, £3.50; EX 41.30 Trifecta £328.70.
**Owner** HRH Princess Haya Of Jordan **Bred** N Hartery **Trained** Newmarket, Suffolk

**FOCUS**
The first two, who filled the same positions when they met at Newcastle last month, came right away from their rivals in the closing stages. They're clearly ahead of their marks.
T/Plt: £33.80 to a £1 stake. Pool: £127,384.88 - 2,749.10 winning units. T/Qpdt: £9.30 to a £1 stake. Pool: £7,171.51 - 566.43 winning units. **Steve Payne**

# RIPON (R-H)
Thursday, April 20

**OFFICIAL GOING: Good to firm (good in places; 8.4)**
Wind: Light, across Weather: Fine

## 1908 NAGS HEAD PICKHILL EBF FILLIES' NOVICE STKS (PLUS 10 RACE) (DIV I) 5f
**2:15** (2:16) (Class 5) 2-Y-O **£3,234** (£962; £481; £240) **Stalls** High

Form RPR

**1** **Maggies Angel (IRE)** 2-9-0 0 ........ PaulHanagan 4 78+
(Richard Fahey) *racd keenly: sn chsd ldrs: wnt 2nd jst over 2f out: rdn to ld 1f out: r.o wl fnl 110yds: comf* **2/1**[1]

**2** 2¼ **Mount Victoria (IRE)** 2-9-0 0 ........ PaulMulrennan 2 69
(James Given) *led: green and hung rt thrght: rdn and hdd 1f out: nt pce of wnr fnl 110yds* **16/1**

**3** nk **Under Offer (IRE)** 2-9-0 0 ........ LukeMorris 6 68
(James Tate) *in tch: pushed along 3f out: rdn whn chsng ldrs 2f out: kpt on towards fin* **7/2**[3]

**4** 3½ **Che Bella (IRE)** 2-9-0 0 ........ PhillipMakin 7 55
(Keith Dalgleish) *chsd ldrs: rdn and green over 2f out: outpcd over 1f out: kpt on same pce ins fnl f whn no imp* **11/4**[2]

**5** 3¼ **Autumn Belle** 2-9-0 0 ........ JamesSullivan 3 44
(Ollie Pears) *racd keenly: hld up: effrt whn edgd lft ent fnl 2f: one pce fnl f: nvr trbld ldrs* **25/1**

**6** 2¼ **Society's Dream (IRE)** 2-9-0 0 ........ JoeyHaynes 9 35
(K R Burke) *hld up: pushed along over 2f out: nvr a threat* **16/1**

**7** 4 **Runthatbymeagain (IRE)** 2-9-0 0 ........ AndrewMullen 8 21
(David Evans) *towards rr early: pushed along 3f out: hmpd ent fnl 2f: n.d after* **20/1**

**8** 1¾ **St Helens Gate (IRE)** 2-9-0 0 ........ PJMcDonald 1 15
(Rebecca Menzies) *chsd ldr tl rdn jst over 2f out: wknd over 1f out* **50/1**

**9** 1½ **Beau Times (IRE)** 2-9-0 0 ........ DavidAllan 5 9
(Tim Easterby) *s.i.s: in rr: pushed along over 2f out: outpcd sn after* **15/2**

1m 0.05s (0.05) **Going Correction** -0.125s/f (Firm) **9** Ran SP% **116.3**
Speed ratings (Par 89): **94,90,89,84,79 75,69,66,63**
CSF £35.73 TOTE £3.00: £1.20, £3.90, £1.50; EX 28.60 Trifecta £85.50.
**Owner** P D Smith Holdings Ltd **Bred** Grangemore Stud **Trained** Musley Bank, N Yorks

**FOCUS**
The rail on the bend from back straight to home straight was dolled out by 6 yards adding approximately 12 yards to races on the round course. The first division of the novice stakes was taken by a really sharp-looking type who can do better next time.

## 1909 NAGS HEAD PICKHILL EBF FILLIES' NOVICE STKS (PLUS 10 RACE) (DIV II) 5f
**2:50** (2:53) (Class 5) 2-Y-O **£3,234** (£962; £481; £240) **Stalls** High

Form RPR

**1** **Capla Dancer (IRE)** 2-9-0 0 ........ JoeyHaynes 6 73
(K R Burke) *broke wl: led early: continued to chse ldr: rdn over 2f out: upsides over 1f out: intimidated by rival and edgd rt ins fnl f: led narrowly towards fin* **66/1**

6 **2** nk **Faithful Promise**[12] 1627 2-9-0 0 ........ FrannyNorton 8 72
(Mark Johnston) *sn led: rdn whn pressed and edgd ins fnl f: hdd narrowly towards fin* **4/1**[3]

**3** 3½ **Flo's Melody** 2-9-0 0 ........ PaulHanagan 3 60
(Richard Fahey) *a.p: effrt over 1f out: unable qck ins fnl f* **7/2**[2]

**4** 2 **Listen Alexander (IRE)** 2-9-0 0 ........ AndrewMullen 4 52
(David Evans) *prom: rdn over 2f out: kpt on same pce ins fnl f* **12/1**

**5** ¾ **Bow Belles** 2-9-0 0 ........ DavidAllan 1 49
(Tim Easterby) *wnt rt s: hld up: green and edgd lft over 2f out: kpt on fnl f: nvr trbld ldrs* **28/1**

**6** 1 **Showdancing** 2-9-0 0 ........ LukeMorris 9 46
(James Tate) *in tch: pushed along over 2f out: nt clr run and hmpd wl over 1f out: lost pl: sn swtchd rt: no imp after* **7/1**

**7** nk **Kirbec (IRE)** 2-9-0 0 ........ PhillipMakin 7 45
(Keith Dalgleish) *rn green: in rr: drifted rt fr over 2f out: nvr a threat* **11/1**

4 **8** 9 **Nobrassnolass (IRE)**[10] 1673 2-9-0 0 ........ AndreaAtzeni 2 12
(Tom Dascombe) *wnt rt s: in tch: pushed along and outpcd 3f out: lft bhd over 1f out* **7/4**[1]

59.9s (-0.10) **Going Correction** -0.125s/f (Firm) **8** Ran SP% **112.1**
Speed ratings (Par 89): **95,94,88,85,84 82,82,68**
CSF £302.16 TOTE £29.00: £11.40, £1.60, £1.50; EX 278.80 Trifecta £5130.20.
**Owner** Classic Racing (greatest Dancer)&e Burke **Bred** Ballyhane Stud **Trained** Middleham Moor, N Yorks

**FOCUS**
The second division of the novice stakes had two previously raced fillies unlike the first, which had none, but it was a newcomer that collected the prize. It produced the quicker time.

## 1910 PPR FOUNDATION H'CAP 6f
**3:25** (3:25) (Class 4) (0-85,88) 4-Y-O+ **£4,851** (£1,443; £721; £360) **Stalls** High

Form RPR

132- **1** **Magical Effect (IRE)**[229] 6131 5-8-13 **77** ........ JamesSullivan 7 85
(Ruth Carr) *racd stands' side: a.p: rdn ins fnl f: r.o to ld towards fin: 1st of 9 in gp* **9/2**[1]

342- **2** hd **Straightothepoint**[169] 7772 5-9-4 **82** ........ ConnorBeasley 1 89
(Bryan Smart) *racd far side: overall ldr: rdn over 2f out: r.o: hdd towards fin: 1st of 5 in gp* **5/1**[2]

10-1 **3** 1¾ **Alkhor**[9] 1696 4-9-10 **88** 6ex ........ TomMarquand 12 89
(Richard Hannon) *sed awkwardly: racd stands' side: in tch: drifted rt fr over 2f out: sn rdn and in contention: kpt on ins fnl f: nt quite pce of front two: 2nd of 9 fr gp* **11/2**[3]

100- **4** ¾ **Honeysuckle Lil (IRE)**[184] 7434 5-8-11 **78**....(p) RachelRichardson(3) 13 77
(Tim Easterby) *racd stands' side: chsd ldrs: rdn over 1f out: edgd rt ins fnl f: kpt on: nt quite pce to mount serious chal: 3rd of 9 in gp* **40/1**

000- **5** ¾ **Still On Top**[230] 6079 4-8-11 **75** ........(h) DavidAllan 2 72
(Tim Easterby) *racd far side: handy: rdn over 1f out: nt qckn over 1f out: styd on same pce ins fnl f: 2nd of 5 in gp* **33/1**

50-0 **6** nk **Eastern Racer (IRE)**[18] 1512 5-8-9 **80** ........(p) BenRobinson(7) 6 76
(Brian Ellison) *racd stands' side: pushed along to ld gp tl rdn and hung rt fr over 2f out: kpt on same pce fnl 100yds: 4th of 9 in gp* **12/1**

0/0- **7** hd **Taskeen (IRE)**[226] 6209 4-8-7 **78** ........ BenSanderson(7) 9 73
(Roger Fell) *racd stands' side: cl up: rdn and drifted rt fr over 2f out: no ex fnl 100yds: 5th of 9 fr gp* **66/1**

10-0 **8** hd **Royal Connoisseur (IRE)**[18] 1512 6-8-13 **80** ........ SammyJoBell(3) 4 74
(Richard Fahey) *racd far side: in tch: rdn 2f out: one pce ins fnl f: 3rd of 5 in gp* **9/1**

222- **9** 1 **Rantan (IRE)**[279] 4344 4-9-5 **83** ........ PhillipMakin 11 74
(David Barron) *racd stands' side: hld up: rdn wl over 1f out: kpt on ins fnl f: nvr trbld ldrs: 6th of 9 in gp* **15/2**

6062 **10** ¾ **Salvatore Fury (IRE)**[9] 1696 7-8-8 **72** ........(p) AndrewMullen 15 61
(Keith Dalgleish) *racd stands' side: hld up: rdn over 1f out: nvr a threat: 7th of 9 in gp* **14/1**

000- **11** 5 **Best Trip (IRE)**[120] 8482 10-8-9 **80** ........(t) HarrisonShaw(7) 14 53
(Marjorie Fife) *racd stands' side: prom tl rdn and wknd over 1f out: 8th: of 9 in gp* **33/1**

06-0 **12** 2¼ **Gabrial The Tiger (IRE)**[13] 1606 5-9-3 **84** ........ AdamMcNamara(3) 5 50
(Richard Fahey) *racd far side: prom: rdn over 2f out: wknd over 1f out: 4th of 5 in gp* **16/1**

100- **13** hd **Mywayistheonlyway (IRE)**[228] 6164 4-9-3 **81** ........ PaddyAspell 10 46
(Grant Tuer) *racd stands' side: in tch: rdn and wknd over 1f out: wl btn ins fnl f: 9th of 9 in gp* **66/1**

020- **14** 6 **Dragon King (IRE)**[154] 7990 5-9-7 **85** ........ PaulHanagan 3 31
(Iain Jardine) *racd far side: racd keenly: in tch: rdn and wknd over 1f out: 5th of 5 in gp* **13/2**

1m 11.81s (-1.19) **Going Correction** -0.125s/f (Firm) **14** Ran SP% **116.9**
Speed ratings (Par 105): **102,101,99,98,97 97,96,96,95,94 87,84,84,76**
CSF £24.69 CT £129.22 TOTE £5.30: £1.80, £2.40, £2.40; EX 26.70 Trifecta £169.70.
**Owner** Miss Vanessa Church **Bred** W Maxwell Ervine **Trained** Huby, N Yorks

**FOCUS**
A big field of sprinters and the pace was unsurprisingly strong from the outset. Only five went towards the far side of the track, but they ended up all over the place late on. The second helps set the standard.

## 1911 RIPONBET SILVER BOWL H'CAP 1m 1f 170y
**4:00** (4:00) (Class 3) (0-95,96) 4-Y-O- **£7,246** (£2,168; £1,084; £542; £270) **Stalls** Low

Form RPR
316- **1** **UAE Prince (IRE)**[180] 7538 4-9-7 **93**............................. AndreaAtzeni 11 102+
(Roger Varian) *racd wd fr draw for 1f: prom racing in 2nd pl: effrt over 2f out: led ins fnl f: pushed out and kpt on towards fin* **2/1**[1]
102U **2** ¾ **Final**[6] 1779 5-9-5 **91**............................. FrannyNorton 1 98
(Mark Johnston) *s.i.s: towards rr: pushed along over 2f out: hdwy and swtchd lft wl over 1f out: edgd rt fnl 150yds: styd on wl to take 2nd nr fin* **6/1**[2]
0-12 **3** ½ **Count Montecristo (FR)**[56] 885 5-8-11 **83**....................... KevinStott 5 89
(Kevin Ryan) *led: rdn and edgd lft over 1f out: hdd ins fnl f: lost 2nd and kpt on same pce nr fin* **6/1**[2]
2133 **4** 3 **Footlight**[38] 1178 4-8-6 **78**............................. PaulHanagan 4 78
(Richard Fahey) *prom: rdn 2f out: nt qckn over 1f out: edgd rt ins fnl f: kpt on same pce fnl 100yds* **16/1**
614- **5** 1 ¼ **Silvery Moon (IRE)**[208] 6778 10-9-2 **88**....................... DuranFentiman 6 85
(Tim Easterby) *hld up: rdn and hdwy 2f out: hung rt ins fnl f: one pce fnl 100yds* **50/1**
**6** 1 ½ **Mulligatawny (IRE)**[209] 6760 4-9-1 **87**........................ TonyHamilton 2 81
(Roger Fell) *racd keenly: prom: rdn over 1f out and hung rt: wknd ins fnl f* **28/1**
-311 **7** 1 ¼ **Winners Follow Me (GER)**[33] 1258 4-9-10 **96**................. LukeMorris 9 88
(James Tate) *trckd ldrs for 4f: rdn in tch over 2f out: outpcd over 1f out* **15/2**[3]
630- **8** hd **Maraakib (IRE)**[305] 3435 5-8-12 **89**............................. JoshDoyle(5) 7 80
(David O'Meara) *midfield: rdn 2f out: no imp* **40/1**
060- **9** 1 ½ **Dance King**[180] 7535 7-8-6 **81**.........................(p) RachelRichardson(3) 8 69+
(Tim Easterby) *dwlt: in rr: nt clr run 2f out: sn u.p: nvr a threat* **14/1**
00-3 **10** 2 **Chancery (USA)**[18] 1517 9-8-13 **85**.........................(p) DanielTudhope 10 69
(David O'Meara) *hld: struggling over 2f out: nvr a threat* **17/2**
11-0 **11** 1 **Maifalki (FR)**[10] 1677 4-8-7 **82**............................. NathanEvans(3) 3 64
(Mark Walford) *midfield: rdn over 2f out: wknd over 1f out* **8/1**

2m 2.36s (-3.04) **Going Correction** -0.125s/f (Firm) **11 Ran SP% 115.7**
Speed ratings (Par 107): **107,106,106,103,102 101,100,100,99,97 96**
CSF £13.21 CT £61.57 TOTE £2.90: £1.20, £3.40, £2.10; EX 11.60 Trifecta £58.70.
**Owner** Sheikh Mohammed Obaid Al Maktoum **Bred** John Connaughton **Trained** Newmarket, Suffolk

**FOCUS**
Distance increased by 12yds. This contained a favourite who was potentially thought to be better than a handicapper, and he just about hung on after emerging from a tricky stall. It's rated around the third and the winner has clear potential to do better.

## 1912 RIPON "COCK O' THE NORTH" H'CAP 1m
**4:30** (4:31) (Class 3) (0-95,86) 3-Y-O **£7,246** (£2,168; £1,084; £542; £270) **Stalls** Low

Form RPR
00-1 **1** **La Casa Tarifa (IRE)**[19] 1489 3-9-1 **80**........................... FrannyNorton 4 85
(Mark Johnston) *s.i.s: in rr: nt clr run and hdwy over 2f out: led jst over 1f out: kpt on wl towards fin* **8/1**[3]
25-0 **2** 1 **Devil's Bridge (IRE)**[18] 1518 3-9-7 **86**........................... TomMarquand 1 89
(Richard Hannon) *led: rdn 2f out: hdd jst over 1f out: no ex towards fin* **7/2**[2]
251- **3** 2 ¼ **In First Place**[198] 7042 3-9-1 **80**............................. PaulHanagan 2 78
(Richard Fahey) *chsd ldrs: bmpd over 2f out: kpt on same pce fnl 100yds* **7/2**[2]
365- **4** 5 **White Tower (IRE)**[218] 6481 3-9-7 **86**............................. PJMcDonald 5 72
(Mark Johnston) *hld up: effrt and hdwy wl over 2f out: cl up sn after: wknd ent fnl f* **8/1**[3]
1- **5** 14 **Kitten's Johnstown (USA)**[216] 6535 3-9-5 **84**.................... KevinStott 3 36
(Kevin Ryan) *chsd ldr tl rdn over 2f out: wknd over 1f out* **11/8**[1]

1m 39.94s (-1.46) **Going Correction** -0.125s/f (Firm) **5 Ran SP% 108.8**
Speed ratings (Par 102): **102,101,98,93,79**
CSF £33.91 TOTE £8.10: £3.40, £1.60; EX 33.60 Trifecta £98.50.
**Owner** Kingsley Park 5 **Bred** Tony Kilduff **Trained** Middleham Moor, N Yorks

**FOCUS**
Distance increased by 12yds. A small field lined up for this mile event, and it was taken by the only filly. The first two were the only ones with a recent start. Not a strong renewal, the second the key to the form.

## 1913 PETER ROBERTS MEMORIAL H'CAP 6f
**5:05** (5:05) (Class 5) (0-75,76) 3-Y-O **£3,234** (£962; £481; £240) **Stalls** High

Form RPR
340- **1** **Dandy Highwayman (IRE)**[195] 7120 3-9-8 **76**........... DanielTudhope 15 82
(Ollie Pears) *racd stands' side: a.p: led overall over 1f out: r.o towards fin: 1st of 10 in gp* **13/2**[3]
336- **2** 1 ¼ **Suitcase 'N' Taxi**[272] 4602 3-8-11 **65**............................. DavidAllan 3 67
(Tim Easterby) *racd far side: led gp: rdn and hung lft over 1f out whn hdd and ended in stands' side gp: styd on: nt pce of wnr nr fin: 1st of 7 fr original gp* **20/1**
-114 **3** hd **Intense Romance (IRE)**[28] 1332 3-9-2 **70**................... ConnorBeasley 2 71+
(Michael Dods) *racd far side: hld up: rdn and hdwy 2f out: r.o ins fnl f: nt pce of wnr: 2nd of 7 in gp* **9/1**
000- **4** nse **Scofflaw**[195] 7120 3-9-8 **76**............................. PaulHanagan 4 77+
(Richard Fahey) *racd far side: hld up: rdn 2f out: hdwy over 1f out: r.o ins fnl f: 3rd of 7 in gp* **4/1**[1]
-330 **5** nk **Prazeres**[20] 1474 3-8-11 **65**.........................(t[1]) PJMcDonald 18 65
(Les Eyre) *racd stands' side: led gp: rdn and hdd over 1f out: kpt on ins fnl f: 2nd of 10 in gp* **33/1**
-124 **6** hd **Right Action**[20] 1463 3-9-4 **72**............................. TonyHamilton 14 71
(Richard Fahey) *wnt rt s: racd stands' side: chsd ldrs: rdn over 1f out: styd on same pce towards fin: 3rd of 10 in gp* **12/1**
00-1 **7** 1 ¾ **Logi (IRE)**[55] 904 3-9-7 **75**.........................(b) PhillipMakin 13 69
(David Barron) *racd stands' side: chsd ldrs: rdn 2f out: one pce fnl 75yds: 4th of 10 in gp* **11/2**[2]
200- **8** ¾ **Decadent Times (IRE)**[215] 6564 3-8-9 **63**................... BarryMcHugh 7 54
(Marjorie Fife) *racd far side: hld up in tch: rdn over 2f out: edgd lft over 1f out: kpt on ins fnl f: nt quite able to chal: 4th of 7 in gp* **20/1**
0U0- **9** shd **Lexington Sky (IRE)**[193] 7185 3-9-5 **73**................... DougieCostello 1 64
(Roger Fell) *racd far side: chsd ldrs: rdn and edgd lft over 1f out: wl there 1f out: wknd fnl 75yds: 5th of 7 in gp* **50/1**
602- **10** 1 **Cupid's Arrow (IRE)**[198] 7041 3-8-11 **65**................... JamesSullivan 11 53
(Ruth Carr) *racd stands' side: midfield: rdn over 1f out: no imp fnl f: 5th of 10 in gp* **14/1**
6-06 **11** ¾ **Trick Of The Lyte (IRE)**[48] 1005 3-8-12 **66**................... JasonHart 12 51
(John Quinn) *racd stands' side: midfield: pushed along over 3f out: outpcd over 1f out: 6th of 10 in gp* **25/1**
060- **12** 1 ¾ **Greenview Paradise (IRE)**[228] 6162 3-8-5 **62**........... SammyJoBell(3) 9 42
(Richard Fahey) *racd stands' side: towards rr: nt clr run over 1f out: nvr on terms: 7th of 10 in gp* **40/1**
2-22 **13** shd **Rag Tatter**[38] 1179 3-9-7 **75**............................. KevinStott 6 55
(Kevin Ryan) *racd far side: prom: rdn over 2f out: wknd ins fnl f: 6th of 7 in gp* **8/1**
045- **14** 3 **Hamba Kashe (IRE)**[219] 6448 3-8-8 **62**................... DuranFentiman 10 32
(Tim Easterby) *racd stands' side: midfield: rdn over 2f out: wknd over 1f out: 8th of 10 in gp* **28/1**
550- **15** 1 ¼ **Outfox**[201] 6954 3-8-11 **65**............................. PaulMulrennan 8 31
(Bryan Smart) *dwlt: swtchd lft s: racd stands' side: a bhd: nvr on terms: 9th of 10 in gp* **16/1**
643- **16** 1 **Heavenly Angel**[195] 7118 3-9-8 **76**............................. TomMarquand 16 39
(Richard Hannon) *racd stands' side: in tch: pushed along 4f out: wknd over 1f out: 10th of 10 in gp* **10/1**
000- **17** 4 **Melaniemillie**[198] 7041 3-8-7 **61**............................. AndrewMullen 5 11
(Ollie Pears) *racd far side: prom: rdn over 2f out: wknd over 1f out: 7th of 7 in gp* **50/1**

1m 12.31s (-0.69) **Going Correction** -0.125s/f (Firm) **17 Ran SP% 125.3**
Speed ratings (Par 98): **99,97,97,97,96 96,94,93,92,91 90,88,88,84,82 81,75**
CSF £138.61 CT £1226.33 TOTE £6.40: £2.40, £5.10, £2.00, £1.80; EX 191.40 Trifecta £3050.50.
**Owner** Ontoawinner & Ollie Pears **Bred** Michael M Byrne **Trained** Norton, N Yorks

**FOCUS**
Another big field sprint in which the field split but, like the earlier one, there didn't seem a strong bias to either side despite the first two finishing on the stands' side. This fits with the winner's Thirsk form last year.

## 1914 SIS MAIDEN STKS 1m
**5:35** (5:39) (Class 5) 3-Y-O **£3,234** (£962; £481; £240) **Stalls** Low

Form RPR
023- **1** **Fujaira Bridge (IRE)**[191] 7239 3-9-5 78........................... AndreaAtzeni 5 82+
(Roger Varian) *racd keenly: chsd ldr: rdn to ld narrowly over 1f out: kpt on wl and in command nr fin* **4/6**[1]
65-3 **2** ¾ **Lamloom (IRE)**[18] 1514 3-9-5 78........................... DanielTudhope 8 80+
(David O'Meara) *racd keenly: led: rdn and hdd narrowly over 1f out: kpt on: hld nr fin* **5/1**[2]
00- **3** 9 **American Craftsman (IRE)**[184] 7432 3-9-5 0.........(p[1]) TonyHamilton 3 58
(Roger Fell) *in tch: rdn over 3f out: unable to go w front two over 1f out: kpt on but no ch* **100/1**
**4** 2 ½ **El Nino Sea (IRE)** 3-9-5 0............................. PaulHanagan 9 52+
(Richard Fahey) *racd keenly: midfield: pushed along over 2f out: kpt on ins fnl f but no ch* **9/1**[3]
**5** nse **Pilgrim's Treasure (USA)** 3-9-5 0............................. PhillipMakin 4 52+
(Charlie Appleby) *s.i.s: hld up: swtchd lft and sme hdwy wl over 2f out: kpt on ins fnl f but no ch* **5/1**[2]
00- **6** ½ **Indian Vision (IRE)**[166] 7819 3-9-5 0............................. PJMcDonald 1 51
(Micky Hammond) *hld up: sme hdwy over 2f out: kpt on one pce ins fnl f: nvr able to trble ldrs* **33/1**
5- **7** ½ **Tread Lightly**[300] 3598 3-9-5 0............................. DavidAllan 10 50
(Tim Easterby) *hld up: rdn and hdwy over 3f put: chsd ldrs over 1f out but no imp: no ch fnl f* **33/1**
0-0 **8** 8 **Chionodoxa**[10] 1680 3-8-11 0............................. RachelRichardson(3) 6 26
(Tim Easterby) *chsd ldrs tl rdn and wknd over 2f out* **100/1**
00- **9** 5 **Bollin Ted**[243] 5637 3-9-5 0............................. DuranFentiman 11 19
(Tim Easterby) *chsd ldrs tl rdn and lost pl 3f out: wl btn* **100/1**
00- **10** 39 **Sai Kung Star**[280] 4298 3-9-0 0............................. AndrewMullen 7
(Nigel Tinkler) *racd keenly: hld up in rr: pushed along 4f out: lft wl bhd over 2f out: t.o* **100/1**

1m 40.5s (-0.90) **Going Correction** -0.125s/f (Firm) **10 Ran SP% 113.2**
Speed ratings (Par 98): **99,98,89,86,86 86,85,77,72,33**
CSF £3.94 TOTE £1.60: £1.20, £1.30, £3.60; EX 4.60 Trifecta £98.50.
**Owner** Sheikh Mohammed Obaid Al Maktoum **Bred** Aston Mullins Stud **Trained** Newmarket, Suffolk
■ Swanenburg was withdrawn. Price at time of withdrawal 14-1. Rule 4 applies to all bets - deduction 5p in the pound.

**FOCUS**
Distance increased by 12yds. An interesting maiden, in which the market leader was really well backed. The form pair pulled well clear and look nice types.

## 1915 GO RACING IN YORKSHIRE APPRENTICE H'CAP (YORKSHIRE FUTURE STARS APPRENTICE SERIES) 5f
**6:05** (6:07) (Class 4) (0-80,81) 4-Y-O+ **£3,147** (£3,147; £721; £360) **Stalls** High

Form RPR
120- **1** **Black Grass**[272] 4612 4-8-7 **78**............................. HarrisonShaw(10) 3 85
(Michael Easterby) *a.p: led 2f out: rdn and hung rt over 1f out: jnd post* **9/2**[3]
00-0 **1** dht **Foxtrot Knight**[26] 1370 5-8-13 **77**............................. DavidEgan(3) 7 84
(Ruth Carr) *chsd ldrs: rdn over 1f out: effrt between horses whn nt clr run ent fnl f: plld to nr side rail after: r.o to join ldr post* **7/2**[2]
034- **3** 2 **General Alexander (IRE)**[216] 6537 4-9-2 **77**...........(p) MeganNicholls 6 77
(Brian Ellison) *hld up: rdn over 2f out: prog ins fnl f: styd on: nt pce to rch front pair* **11/2**
146- **4** hd **Desert Ace (IRE)**[195] 7112 6-8-10 **79**.....................(p) JamieGormley(8) 1 78
(Iain Jardine) *led: hdd 2f out: rdn and stl ev ch ent fnl f: no ex towards fin* **7/2**[2]
0-00 **5** 3 **Quatrieme Ami**[70] 639 4-9-4 **79**.........................(t) BenRobinson 5 67
(Philip McBride) *in tch: rdn over 1f out: one pce ins fnl f* **3/1**[1]
0-00 **6** 1 ¾ **Gwendolyn (GER)**[29] 1302 4-9-1 **79**.........................(p[1]) JordanUys(3) 2 61
(Amy Murphy) *hld up in tch: rdn over 1f out: wknd ins fnl f* **12/1**

59.35s (-0.65) **Going Correction** -0.125s/f (Firm) **6 Ran SP% 110.7**
Speed ratings (Par 105): **100,100,96,96,91 88**
WIN: 3.50 BG, 1.40 FK; PL: 2.60 BG, 2.20 FK; EX: BG/FK 6.30, FK/BG 5.70; CSF: BG/FK 9.90, FK/BG 9.35; TF: BG/FK/GA 22.30, FK/BG/GA 21.40.
**Owner** Grange Park Racing Xiii **Bred** Whatton Manor Stud & Robert Cornelius **Trained** Huby, N Yorks
**Owner** T Dewhirst, Mrs L Folwell & S Hull **Bred** M W Easterby **Trained** Sheriff Hutton, N Yorks
■ Stewards' Enquiry : Jamie Gormley 10 day ban: dropped hands just before the winning post (May 4-13)

**FOCUS**
Seamster coming out in the morning didn't make this any easier to work out, with the betting really open. Black Grass is rated to form.
T/Plt: £75.10 to a £1 stake. Pool: £63,132.82 - 613.44 winning units. T/Qpdt: £24.80 to a £1 stake. Pool: £4,717.14 - 140.50 winning units. **Darren Owen**

1916 - 1918a (Foreign Racing) - See Raceform Interactive

# [1824] CHANTILLY (R-H)

Thursday, April 20

**OFFICIAL GOING: Polytrack: standard, turf: good**

## 1919a PRIX DU PREMIER PAS (MAIDEN) (UNRACED 2YO) (TURF) 5f

**11:40** (11:40) 2-Y-O **£11,538** (£4,615; £3,461; £2,307; £1,153)

RPR

1 **Kentish Waltz (IRE)** 2-8-13 0 FabriceVeron 9 77
(E J O'Neill, France) **36/1**
2 2 **La Canche (FR)** 2-8-13 0 EddyHardouin 13 69
(T Clout, France) **237/10**
3 shd **White Feather** 2-9-2 0 MickaelBarzalona 7 72
(Jo Hughes) *a cl up: pressed ldr fr 1/2-way: sn rdn: styd on same pce fnl f* **227/10**
4 1 **Hautot (FR)** 2-9-2 0 CristianDemuro 2 68
(P Sogorb, France) **7/5**[1]
5 2 ½ **Joe The Tinker (FR)** 2-9-2 0 AlexisBadel 11 59
(C Boutin, France) **38/1**
6 ½ **Zone Regard (IRE)** 2-8-13 0 StephanePasquier 14 55
(M Delcher Sanchez, France) **116/10**
7 1 ¾ **Fastidious (FR)** 2-9-2 0 ThibaultSpeicher 8 51
(Louis Baudron, France) **37/1**
8 hd **Indian Mistress (IRE)** 2-8-13 0 TheoBachelot 3 48
(S Wattel, France) **206/10**
9 nk **Saint Nicolas (FR)** 2-9-2 0 (p) ChristopheSoumillon 10 50
(C Lerner, France) **115/10**
10 3 ½ **Chante Blu (FR)** 2-9-2 0 Pierre-CharlesBoudot 5 37
(A Giorgi, Italy) **56/10**[2]
11 3 ½ **Salt Lake City (FR)** 2-9-2 0 RonanThomas 1 24
(Robert Collet, France) **37/1**
12 2 ½ **Vanturi (IRE)** 2-9-2 0 AurelienLemaitre 6 15
(J-V Toux, France) **55/1**
13 1 ¼ **Conset Bay** 2-8-13 0 LouisBeuzelin 12 8
(P Bary, France) **19/2**
14 7 **Some Nights (FR)** 2-9-2 0 AntoineHamelin 4
(Matthieu Palussiere, France) **77/10**[3]

59.75s (1.45) **14** Ran SP% **119.0**
PARI-MUTUEL (all including 1 euro stake): WIN 36.50 PLACE 13.00, 7.80, 5.80 DF 361.20 SF 855.00.
**Owner** Mrs Susan Davis & Mrs Melissa O'Neill **Bred** Ballyhane Stud **Trained** France

## 1920a PRIX DU BU (CONDITIONS) (4YO+) (POLYTRACK) 1m

**2:25** (2:25) 4-Y-O+ **£11,965** (£4,786; £3,589; £2,393; £1,196)

RPR

1 **Lord Glitters (FR)**[143] 4-8-11 0 ChristopheSoumillon 16 93
(C Lotoux, France) **97/10**
2 2 **Alberobello (FR)**[12] 4-8-6 0 NicolasLarenaudie(5) 13 88
(M Delcher Sanchez, France) **15/1**
3 hd **Lefortovo (FR)**[131] 8311 4-8-11 0 MickaelBarzalona 11 88
(Jo Hughes) *in tch: rdn 2f out: kpt on fnl f and jst missed 2nd: nt pce of wnr* **23/1**
4 hd **Snaad**[23] 5-8-11 0 GregoryBenoist 6 88
(F-H Graffard, France) **5/2**[1]
5 shd **Motabaary (IRE)**[181] 7524 7-9-0 0 MaximeGuyon 12 90
(Mme Pia Brandt, France) **15/2**[3]
6 1 **Syrita (FR)**[154] 7998 4-8-8 0 CristianDemuro 14 82
(M Nigge, France) **11/1**
7 nk **Phu Hai (FR)**[181] 7525 8-8-11 0 TheoBachelot 9 84
(V Luka Jr, Czech Republic) **10/1**
8 ½ **Maningrey (GER)**[361] 8-8-11 0 MarcLerner 3 83
(Waldemar Hickst, Germany) **26/1**
9 ½ **Moon Trouble (IRE)**[200] 6991 4-8-11 0 FranckBlondel 4 82
(E J O'Neill, France) **9/1**
10 hd **Atlantik Cup (GER)**[158] 7952 4-8-11 0 AntoineHamelin 2 82
(A Kleinkorres, Germany) **17/1**
11 hd **Iron Spirit (FR)**[14] 7-9-0 0 AlexisBadel 10 84
(Mme M Bollack-Badel, France) **63/10**[2]
12 2 ½ **See You Soon (FR)**[103] 6-8-13 0 ClementLecoeuvre(3) 5 80
(C Boutin, France) **28/1**
13 9 **Pont Neuilly (FR)**[56] 7-9-0 0 Pierre-CharlesBoudot 8 58
(Yves de Nicolay, France) **18/1**
14 1 ½ **Moonlight Gambler (FR)**[690] 8-8-6 0 KyllanBarbaud(5) 1 51
(N Caullery, France) **34/1**
15 dist **Debt Of Honour (FR)** 4-8-11 0 SebastienMaillot 15
(C Boutin, France) **60/1**

1m 37.69s **15** Ran SP% **123.7**
PARI-MUTUEL (all including 1 euro stake): WIN 10.70; PLACE 3.70, 4.40, 6.80; DF 57.00; SF 140.60.
**Owner** Ecurie Du Trieux **Bred** S C A Elevage De Tourgeville Et Al **Trained** France

1921 - 1928a (Foreign Racing) - See Raceform Interactive

# NANTES (R-H)

Thursday, April 20

**OFFICIAL GOING: Turf: good**

## 1929a PRIX DU TERTRE (MAIDEN) (2YO) (TURF) 5f 110y

**11:25** (11:25) 2-Y-O **£7,692** (£3,076; £2,307; £1,538; £769)

RPR

1 **Dann (FR)**[28] 1335 2-9-2 0 AlexandreGavilan 2 70
(D Guillemin, France) **4/5**[1]
2 3 **Siyougirl** 2-8-8 0 ChristopherGrosbois 10 52
(A Vetault, France) **242/10**
3 shd **Fancy Dresser (FR)**[16] 2-9-2 0 ValentinSeguy 7 60
(Matthieu Palussiere, France) **124/10**
4 hd **Hurricane Breizh (FR)** 2-8-13 0 (b[1]) MickaelForest 5 56
(W Walton, France) **54/10**[3]
5 snk **Popsi**[14] 1594 2-8-7 0 GuillaumeTrolleyDePrevaux(6) 6 56
(Jo Hughes) *broke wl: racd keenly w ldrs under restraint: 4th and outpcd whn rdn 1 1/2f out: styd on u.p fnl f* **94/10**
6 6 ½ **Playcity (FR)** 2-9-2 0 (b[1]) RichardJuteau 3 37
(J-P Lopez, France) **66/1**
7 5 **Venussio (FR)** 2-8-11 0 SebastienMartino 12 16
(J-L Delaplace, France) **49/1**
8 nk **Numancia (FR)** 2-8-13 0 AlexandreRoussel 1 17
(P Monfort, France) **23/5**[2]
9 nk **Coral Slipper (FR)** 2-8-13 0 JulienGuillochon 9 16
(Matthieu Palussiere, France) **33/1**
10 hd **Evaguei (FR)**[14] 1594 2-8-13 0 MathieuAndrouin 4 15
(W Menuet, France) **50/1**
11 20 **Fast Pepite (FR)**[34] 1282 2-8-8 0 ow1 TristanBaron(6) 8
(C Plisson, France) **81/1**

1m 3.02s **11** Ran SP% **119.7**
PARI-MUTUEL (all including 1 euro stake): WIN 1.80 PLACE 1.10, 4.30, 2.50 DF 24.60 SF 35.10.
**Owner** Ecurie Jarlan **Bred** Ecurie Jarlan **Trained** France

# LES LANDES

Monday, April 17

**OFFICIAL GOING: Turf: firm**

Wind: Moderate, half against towards viewing area Weather: Fine

## 1930a JERSEY BOOKMAKERS H'CAP 1m 4f

**3:05** (3:05) (0-65,0) 3-Y-O+ **£1,780** (£640; £380)

RPR

1 **Rainbow Lad (IRE)**[19] 1436 4-10-11 0 MissSBrotherton 6 62
(Michael Appleby) *hld up: smooth hdwy fr 5f out: shkn up to ld wl over 1f out: pushed out* **4/7**[1]
2 10 **Spring Dixie (IRE)**[218] 5-9-1 0 (h) MrFTett 4 21
(Mrs A Malzard, Jersey) *led: hdd wl over 1f out: no ch w wnr* **9/1**
3 14 **Hawaiian Freeze**[58] 820 8-9-11 0 RyanWhile 3 9
(J Moon, Jersey) *t.k.h: trckd ldrs: rn wd on bnd 6f out: sn outpcd* **4/1**
4 2 **Frivolous Prince (IRE)**[56] 839 4-10-5 0 (bt) PhilipPrince 2 14
(K Kukk, Jersey) *trckd ldr: rdn and wknd over 3f out* **11/4**[2]
5 8 **Mr Opulence**[246] 5459 8-10-3 0 MarkQuinlan 5
(T Le Brocq, Jersey) *hld up: bhd fr 1/2-way* **7/2**[3]

2m 44.0s **5** Ran SP% **142.5**

**Owner** Michael Appleby **Bred** Rathbarry Stud **Trained** Oakham, Rutland

## 1931a MILLBROOK EASTER FEATURE H'CAP 7f

**3:40** (3:40) 3-Y-O+ **£2,380** (£860; £510)

RPR

1 **First Cat**[218] 6401 10-8-7 0 PhilipPrince 6 37
(K Kukk, Jersey) *chsd ldrs: sltly outpcd 4f out: styd on wl fr 2f out: led wl ins fnl f: hung lft: drvn out* **15/2**
2 1 **National Service (USA)**[21] 1407 6-9-1 0 (tp) PaddyAspell 10 42
(Clare Ellam) *chsd ldrs in 3rd: ev ch fnl f: kpt on one pce: tk 2nd on line* **5/2**[2]
3 shd **Country Blue (FR)**[218] 6401 8-10-5 0 (p) MattieBatchelor 4 60
(Mrs A Malzard, Jersey) *pressed ldr: led 5f out: hdd and no ex wl ins fnl f: lost 2nd on line* **9/4**[1]
4 2 ½ **Benoordenhout (IRE)**[218] 6402 6-9-13 0 ow6 MarkQuinlan 11 47
(T Le Brocq, Jersey) *led tl 5f out: ev ch over 1f out: wknd nr fin* **5/1**
5 2 **Brown Velvet**[218] 6401 5-8-8 0 oh2 ow3 (p) RyanWhile 7 23
(K Kukk, Jersey) *chsd ldrs: sn pushed along and outpcd: btn fr 2f out* **12/1**
6 4 **Princess Kodia (IRE)**[189] 7221 4-10-12 0 JemmaMarshall 8 44
(Mrs A Malzard, Jersey) *sn bhd: last at 1/2-way: nvr on terms* **9/1**
7 hd **My Meteor**[551] 7210 10-9-7 0 MissSBrotherton 2 25
(Natalie Lloyd-Beavis) *sn bhd* **5/1**
8 4 **Mendacious Harpy (IRE)**[181] 7426 6-10-6 0 VictoriaMalzard 3 27
(Mrs A Malzard, Jersey) *s.s: a bhd* **10/3**[3]

**Owner** Mrs E C Roberts **Bred** W And R Barnett Ltd **Trained** Jersey

## 1932a TRUMP (NOT HIM) HOLDINGS LIMITED H'CAP 1m 2f

**4:15** (4:15) 3-Y-O+ **£1,780** (£640; £380)

RPR

1 **City Ground (USA)**[194] 7078 10-10-2 0 MissSBrotherton 7 67
(Michael Appleby) *hld up: hdwy fr 4f out: drvn to take narrow ld 1f out: all out: gamely* **5/2**[2]
2 shd **Alcatraz (IRE)**[28] 1289 5-10-12 0 MattieBatchelor 5 77
(George Baker) *t.k.h: hdwy fr wl over 3f out: virtually jnd wnr 1f out: ev ch nr fin: no ex* **4/7**[1]
3 2 ½ **Hard To Handel**[16] 1498 5-9-12 0 PaddyAspell 6 58
(Clare Ellam) *hld up: last 5f out: styd on same pce fr 2f out* **8/1**
4 6 **Flutterbee**[173] 7614 5-10-7 0 JemmaMarshall 3 55
(Mrs A Malzard, Jersey) *led at sedate pce: drvn and hdd 1f out: wknd* **4/1**
5 1 **Gabster (IRE)**[232] 5923 4-9-10 0 PhilipPrince 2 42
(K Kukk, Jersey) *hld up: hdwy fr 3f out: nvr able to chal* **9/1**
6 4 **Grey Panel (FR)**[218] 9-8-5 0 AliceMills 1 15
(T Le Brocq, Jersey) *trckd ldrs in 3rd: rdn and lost pl fr 4f out* **7/2**[3]
7 6 **Honcho (IRE)**[138] 8156 5-9-9 0 MrFTett 8 21
(Mrs A Malzard, Jersey) *t.k.h in mid-div: bhd fr 3f out* **10/1**
8 6 **Frankki M**[218] 7-8-5 0 (p) MissMHooper 4
(Mrs A Corson, Jersey) *trckd ldr in cl 2nd: rdn and wknd rapidly fr over 2f out* **20/1**

2m 13.0s **8** Ran SP% **169.4**

**Owner** Mrs D R Brotherton **Bred** Mrs E Scott Jr & Mrs L Macelree **Trained** Oakham, Rutland

## 1933a BLOODSTOCK ADVISORY SERVICES H'CAP — 1m 100y
4:50 (4:50) (0-50,0) 3-Y-O+ — £1,780 (£640; £380)

RPR

1 **Lucifers Shadow (IRE)**[304] 8-10-3 0 ....(v) AliceMills 6 — 50
(Mrs C Gilbert, Jersey) *trckd ldrs: smooth hdwy to ld 2f out: unchal* **11/4**[2]

2 7 **Granny Anne (IRE)**[1872] 773 9-10-9 0 .... MattieBatchelor 3 — 41
(Natalie Lloyd-Beavis) *trckd ldrs: outpcd 4f out: kpt on again fr wl over 1f out: tk 2nd nr fin* **2/1**[1]

3 ¾ **Engaging Smile**[71] 7738 5-10-9 0 .... RyanWhile 1 — 39
(J Moon, Jersey) *led tl 2f out: no ex: lost 2nd nr fin* **13/2**[3]

4 2 **Carrera**[267] 7-10-1 0 .... VictoriaMalzard 9 — 27
(Mrs A Malzard, Jersey) *s.s: sn detached: passed btn rivals fr 2f out: nvr nrr* **15/2**

5 1½ **Ocean Crystal**[218] 6401 5-10-0 0 .... MrFTett 4 — 23
(Mrs A Malzard, Jersey) *sn detached: passed btn rivals fr 2f out: nvr nrr* **2/1**[1]

6 3 **Ron's Ballad**[167] 7735 4-10-8 0 .... PhilipPrince 7 — 24
(K Kukk, Jersey) *s.s: hdwy into 4th over 5f out: wknd fr 2f out* **10/1**

7 2 **Grey Gem (IRE)**[538] 7543 6-10-12 0 .... MarkQuinlan 2 — 24
(K Kukk, Jersey) *trckd ldr: rdn and wknd fr 2f out* **15/2**

8 9 **Chester'slittlegem (IRE)**[290] 8-9-1 0 ....(p) MissSBrotherton 5
(Mrs A Corson, Jersey) *a bhd: sn t.o* **12/1**

**Owner** Capricorn Racing **Bred** J & M & E Doyle **Trained** Jersey

# 1761 BATH (L-H)
### Friday, April 21

**OFFICIAL GOING: Firm (good to firm in places; 10.5)**
Wind: Almost nil Weather: Overcast

## 1934 BRITISH STALLION STUDS EBF NOVICE MEDIAN AUCTION STKS — 5f 10y
4:55 (4:59) (Class 5) 2-Y-O — £3,557 (£1,058; £529; £264) Stalls Centre

Form — RPR

1 **Mutanaaseq (IRE)** 2-9-2 0 .... DaneO'Neill 4 — 77+
(Richard Hannon) *s.i.s and n.m.r after s: hld up: hdwy over 1f out: chsd ldr fnl f: r.o to ld post* **7/4**[2]

2 shd **Big Time Maybe (IRE)** 2-9-2 0 .... RichardKingscote 6 — 77
(Tom Dascombe) *sn led: clr over 1f out: rdn ins fnl f: hdd post* **1/1**[1]

3 2¾ **Diamond Dougal (IRE)** 2-9-2 0 .... ShaneKelly 2 — 66
(Mick Channon) *plld hrd: led early: sn settled to trck ldrs: shkn up over 1f out: styd on same pce ins fnl f* **8/1**[3]

6 4 1 **Uther Pendragon (IRE)**[7] 1767 2-9-2 0 .... LiamJones 1 — 62
(J S Moore) *chsd ldrs: pushed along 1/2-way: sn outpcd: nt clr run wl over 1f out: styd on u.p ins fnl f* **14/1**

0 5 2½ **Give Em A Clump (IRE)**[11] 1681 2-9-2 0 .... DannyBrock 7 — 52
(David Evans) *chsd ldr tl rdn 1/2-way: wknd over 1f out* **20/1**

6 4 **Storm Doris (IRE)** 2-8-11 0 .... RyanPowell 3 — 31
(James Unett) *prom tl wknd 1/2-way* **66/1**

7 4½ **Mirek (IRE)** 2-9-2 0 .... RenatoSouza 5 — 18+
(Jonathan Portman) *free to post: hdwy over 3f out: chsd ldr 1/2-way tl rdn over 1f out: sn wknd: stmbld ins fnl f* **25/1**

1m 2.57s (0.07) **Going Correction** -0.35s/f (Firm) — 7 Ran SP% **114.2**
Speed ratings (Par 92): **85,84,80,78,74 68,61**
CSF £3.79 TOTE £2.50: £1.20, £1.50; EX 4.90 Trifecta £13.60.
**Owner** Hamdan Al Maktoum **Bred** Patrick F Kelly **Trained** East Everleigh, Wilts

**FOCUS**
The going here was Firm (Good to firm in places) and the first two home in this novice handled it well and are probably above average juveniles.

## 1935 GREGOR HEATING H'CAP — 2m 1f 24y
5:30 (5:33) (Class 6) (0-65,64) 4-Y-O+ — £2,264 (£673; £336; £168) Stalls Centre

Form — RPR

010- 1 **Danglydontask**[191] 7270 6-9-9 **61** .... LukeMorris 5 — 66
(David Arbuthnot) *hld up: hdwy over 9f out: chsd ldr over 6f out: pushed along over 4f out: rdn over 2f out: hung lft over 1f out: styd on u.p to ld last strides* **11/4**[3]

0P-0 2 nk **Akavit (IRE)**[21] 1469 5-9-11 **63** .... RichardKingscote 1 — 68
(Ed de Giles) *led: clr 12f out tl over 6f out: rdn over 2f out: hdd last strides* **2/1**[2]

0443 3 5 **Wordiness**[7] 1763 9-9-5 **64** .... KatherineGlenister(7) 2 — 63
(David Evans) *s.i.s: racd keenly and sn prom: wnt 2nd over 11f out tl over 6f out: disp 2nd over 2f out: sn rdn: no ex fnl f* **7/4**[1]

046- 4 33 **Moon Over Mobay**[124] 8445 4-8-13 **55** .... DavidProbert 4 — 20
(Michael Blanshard) *chsd ldr tl over 11f out: dropped rr over 9f out: rdn over 4f out: wknd over 2f out: eased* **15/2**

3m 48.46s (-3.44) **Going Correction** -0.075s/f (Good)
**WFA** 4 from 5yo+ 2lb — 4 Ran SP% **108.1**
Speed ratings (Par 101): **105,104,102,86**
CSF £8.47 TOTE £2.70; EX 10.60 Trifecta £21.40.
**Owner** Philip Banfield **Bred** P Banfield **Trained** Beare Green, Surrey

**FOCUS**
A modest long distance handicap but it was won in thrilling style. The winner is rated a fraction above last year's level.

## 1936 WHITSBURY MANOR STUD & EBF STALLIONS LANSDOWN STKS (LISTED RACE) (F&M) — 5f 10y
6:00 (6:01) (Class 1) 3-Y-O+
£22,684 (£8,600; £4,304; £2,144; £1,076; £540) Stalls Centre

Form — RPR

241- 1 **Priceless**[226] 6230 4-9-5 105 .... AdamKirby 11 — 111
(Clive Cox) *chsd ldrs: led over 3f out: rdn clr fr over 1f out: edgd lft ins fnl f* **13/8**[1]

200- 2 5 **Futoon (IRE)**[195] 7146 4-9-2 84 .... KevinStott 2 — 90
(Kevin Ryan) *prom: rdn to chse wnr over 1f out: styd on same pce* **20/1**

306- 3 1½ **Imtiyaaz (IRE)**[195] 7146 5-9-2 89 .... AndreaAtzeni 5 — 85+
(Roger Varian) *prom: nt clr run and lost pl over 4f out: pushed along and hdwy over 1f out: r.o to go 3rd ins fnl f: nt trble ldrs* **6/1**[2]

400- 4 ½ **Belledesert**[195] 7146 4-9-2 85 .... RoystonFfrench 8 — 83+
(Steph Hollinshead) *n.m.r sn after s: in rr: hdwy over 1f out: edgd lft and styd on: nt trble ldrs* **25/1**

/03- 5 ¾ **Evil Spell**[166] 7840 5-9-2 101 .... DavidProbert 4 — 80
(Robert Cowell) *sn prom: pushed along 1/2-way: styd on same pce fr over 1f out* **10/1**

00-3 6 ½ **Iseemist (IRE)**[27] 1362 6-9-2 92 .... JoeyHaynes 6 — 78+
(John Gallagher) *sn pushed along in rr: styd on fr over 1f out: nvr on terms* **14/1**

040- 7 1 **Swish (IRE)**[21] 1478 3-8-6 89 .... BenCurtis 9 — 71+
(John James Feane, Ire) *hmpd sn after s: in rr: nt clr run ins fnl f: nvr on terms* **33/1**

-606 8 nk **Buying Trouble (USA)**[20] 1491 4-9-2 98 .... JFEgan 13 — 74
(David Evans) *sn pushed along in rr: effrt on outer over 1f out: n.d* **8/1**[3]

12-0 9 nk **Glenrowan Rose (IRE)**[6] 1800 4-9-2 95 .... PhillipMakin 3 — 73
(Keith Dalgleish) *mid-div: pushed along 1/2-way: wknd ins fnl f* **14/1**

550- 10 1¼ **Shrill**[229] 6167 4-9-2 88 .... LukeMorris 7 — 68
(Robert Cowell) *prom: chsd wnr 1/2-way tl rdn and edgd rt over 1f out: wknd ins fnl f* **25/1**

63-4 11 3 **Ostatnia (IRE)**[28] 1353 5-9-2 91 ....(v) WJLee 10 — 57
(W McCreery, Ire) *mid-div: hdwy 1/2-way: rdn over 1f out: wknd fnl f* **8/1**[3]

600- 12 3¾ **Blithe Spirit**[196] 7124 6-9-2 91 .... JasonHart 1 — 44
(Eric Alston) *led: hdd over 3f out: rdn and wknd over 1f out* **25/1**

3221 13 1 **Fredricka**[29] 1326 6-9-2 77 ....(v) RenatoSouza 12 — 40
(Jose Santos) *sn pushed along in rr: rdn 1/2-way: wknd over 1f out* **66/1**

59.67s (-2.83) **Going Correction** -0.35s/f (Firm)
**WFA** 3 from 4yo+ 10lb — 13 Ran SP% **117.8**
Speed ratings (Par 111): **108,100,97,96,95 94,93,92,92,90 85,79,77**
CSF £43.95 TOTE £2.30: £1.40, £5.70, £1.90; EX 34.90 Trifecta £219.70.
**Owner** A D Spence **Bred** Biddestone Stud Ltd **Trained** Lambourn, Berks

**FOCUS**
A fairly competitive looking Listed contest for fillies and mares, which proved a procession for the penalty-shouldering favourite.

## 1937 CLIFFORD HILLIER H'CAP — 1m 3f 137y
6:30 (6:31) (Class 6) (0-65,63) 4-Y-O+ — £2,264 (£673; £336; £168) Stalls Low

Form — RPR

050- 1 **Avocadeau (IRE)**[207] 6825 6-8-10 **52** ....(p) MartinDwyer 5 — 57
(Stuart Kittow) *racd keenly: w ldr tl led 7f out: qcknd over 2f out: rdn over 1f out: all out* **7/1**

00-0 2 hd **Cockney Boy**[16] 1556 4-8-9 **52** .... JoeyHaynes 6 — 57
(John Gallagher) *led over 4f: remained w wnr: rdn and ev ch fr over 1f out: styd on* **16/1**

5234 3 1¼ **Attain**[23] 1430 8-9-4 **63** .... EdwardGreatrex(3) 4 — 66
(Archie Watson) *hld up: rdn over 2f out: hdwy over 1f out: r.o to go 3rd nr fin: nt rch ldrs* **5/2**[1]

4125 4 ¾ **Spirit Of The Vale (IRE)**[11] 1679 4-9-0 **57** ....(t) KevinStott 3 — 58
(Oliver Greenall) *s.i.s: hld up: rdn over 2f out: hdwy over 1f out: styd on same pce ins fnl f* **11/4**[2]

120- 5 3 **Captain George (IRE)**[43] 7274 6-9-7 **63** .... SteveDrowne 1 — 59
(Michael Blake) *chsd ldrs: rdn over 2f out: eased whn btn ins fnl f* **9/2**[3]

0454 6 3 **Cold Fusion (IRE)**[13] 1629 4-8-8 **51** ....(v) KierenFox 7 — 42
(David Flood) *chsd ldrs: rdn over 2f out: wknd over 1f out* **5/1**

50-P 7 4½ **Lady Rocka**[13] 1629 4-9-1 **58** ....(p[1]) JosephineGordon 2 — 42
(Anabel K Murphy) *prom: racd keenly: rdn over 3f out: wknd over 2f out* **16/1**

2m 32.1s (1.50) **Going Correction** -0.075s/f (Good) — 7 Ran SP% **114.4**
Speed ratings (Par 101): **92,91,91,90,88 86,83**
CSF £102.70 TOTE £8.70: £3.80, £8.50; EX 147.20 Trifecta £610.90.
**Owner** Mrs S Clapp & Mrs L Sharpe **Bred** Wiji Bloodstock & Ceka Ltd **Trained** Blackborough, Devon

**FOCUS**
A modest middle-distance handicap fought out by the two pacesetters. The third helps set the level.

## 1938 CONCEPT4 CREATIVE WORKSPACE FILLIES' H'CAP — 1m 2f 37y
7:00 (7:00) (Class 4) (0-85,81) 4-Y-O+ — £4,690 (£1,395; £697; £348) Stalls Low

Form — RPR

621- 1 **Princess Nia (IRE)**[149] 8075 4-9-4 **78** .... MartinDwyer 4 — 81+
(Brian Meehan) *hld up: hdwy over 2f out: shkn up to ld ins fnl f: edgd lft: r.o: comf* **7/2**[3]

-311 2 ¾ **Star Of Lombardy (IRE)**[17] 1549 4-9-1 **75** .... FrannyNorton 1 — 76
(Mark Johnston) *led at stdy pce: qcknd over 2f out: rdn and hdd wl over 1f out: stl ev ch ins fnl f: styd on* **2/1**[2]

221- 3 ¾ **Apres Midi (IRE)**[246] 5581 4-9-7 **81** .... DougieCostello 3 — 81
(K R Burke) *trckd ldr tl shkn up to ld wl over 1f out: rdn and hdd ins fnl f: n.m.r sn after: unable qck towards fin* **15/8**[1]

225- 4 2 **Tuolumne Meadows**[242] 5723 4-9-4 **78** .... LukeMorris 2 — 74
(Paul Cole) *trckd ldrs: shkn up over 2f out: outpcd wl over 1f out: kpt on ins fnl f* **9/2**

2m 14.66s (3.66) **Going Correction** -0.075s/f (Good) — 4 Ran SP% **108.5**
Speed ratings (Par 102): **82,81,80,79**
CSF £10.68 TOTE £5.10; EX 10.80 Trifecta £14.90.
**Owner** The Pony Club **Bred** Andrew Rosen **Trained** Manton, Wilts

**FOCUS**
A tight little fillies handicap with a progressive winner.

## 1939 MITSUBISHI ECODAN RENEWABLE MAIDEN STKS — 1m 5y
7:30 (7:30) (Class 5) 3-Y-O+ — £2,835 (£848; £424; £212; £105) Stalls Low

Form — RPR

52- 1 **International Law**[182] 7501 3-9-0 0 ....(p[1]) JimmyFortune 1 — 75+
(Brian Meehan) *s.i.s: sn rcvrd to ld shkn up over 1f out: rdn out* **8/11**[1]

/20- 2 ¾ **Manton Grange**[220] 6442 4-10-0 75 .... SteveDrowne 5 — 77
(George Baker) *led early: remained handy: rdn to chse wnr over 1f out: sn ev ch: styd on* **10/1**

-3 3 ¾ **Desert Explorer (IRE)**[16] 1552 3-8-11 0 .... EdwardGreatrex(3) 4 — 71
(Eve Johnson Houghton) *plld hrd and prom: stdd and lost pl over 6f out: hdwy over 1f out: r.o to go 3rd ins fnl f: nt rch ldrs* **11/2**[3]

0- 4 1¼ **Aware (IRE)**[157] 7963 3-9-0 0 .... DavidProbert 6 — 68
(Charles Hills) *sn w wnr tl settled into 2nd over 6f out: rdn and ev ch wl over 1f out: styd on same pce ins fnl f* **12/1**

-323 5 2½ **Fiendish (USA)**[8] 1756 3-8-9 0 .... FrannyNorton 2 — 57
(Mark Johnston) *plld hrd and sn prom: rdn over 2f out: no ex fnl f* **9/2**[2]

005/ **6** 3 ½ **Eben Dubai (IRE)**708 2207 5-10-0 58 RoystonFfrench 8 58
(Tracey Barfoot-Saunt) *stdd s: hld up: shkn up over 2f out: wknd over 1f out* **100/1**

1m 42.09s (1.29) **Going Correction** -0.075s/f (Good)
**WFA** 3 from 4yo+ 14lb **6** Ran SP% **109.2**
Speed ratings (Par 103): **90,89,88,87,84 81**
CSF £8.53 TOTE £1.60: £1.20, £3.70; EX 8.00 Trifecta £26.10.
**Owner** Mrs E O'Leary **Bred** Ed's Stud Ltd **Trained** Manton, Wilts

**FOCUS**
An ordinary maiden won in workmanlike fashion by the favourite.

## 1940 DRIBUILD GROUP H'CAP 5f 160y

**8:00** (8:00) (Class 4) (0-85,86) 3-Y-O **£3,042** (£3,042; £697; £348) **Stalls** Centre

Form RPR
561- **1** **Mr Pocket (IRE)**160 7938 3-9-2 76 (b) LukeMorris 1 83
(Paul Cole) *trckd ldrs: racd keenly: pushed along over 2f out: rdn to ld ins fnl f: edgd rt: jnd post* **7/1**

2261 **1** *dht* **Goodwood Crusader (IRE)**7 1762 3-8-4 71 6ex FinleyMarsh(7) 3 78
(Richard Hughes) *hld up: hdwy u.p over 1f out: edgd lft: r.o to join wnr post* **15/8**1

00-4 **3** 1 ¾ **Sayesse**14 1601 3-9-12 86 JFEgan 8 87
(Mick Channon) *s.i.s: sn pushed along in rr: hdwy 1/2-way: nt clr run wl over 1f out: styd on* **10/1**

1362 **4** *nk* **Lady Cristal (IRE)**10 1693 3-8-5 65 (p) JosephineGordon 2 65
(K R Burke) *led: rdn over 1f out: hdd ins fnl f: styd on same pce* **8/1**

306- **5** 2 ½ **Super Julius**209 6763 3-9-7 81 JohnFahy 5 73
(Eve Johnson Houghton) *chsd ldr: rdn and ev ch over 1f out: no ex ins fnl f* **13/2**3

32-1 **6** 2 ½ **Ashwaq**32 1287 3-9-3 77 TomMarquand 7 61
(Richard Hannon) *sn pushed along in rr: hdwy 1/2-way: rdn over 1f out: wknd ins fnl f* **4/1**2

3313 **7** 7 **Peachey Carnehan**21 1463 3-9-1 75 (v) WilliamCarson 4 36
(Michael Attwater) *chsd ldrs: rdn 1/2-way: wknd over 1f out* **20/1**

062- **8** 2 ¾ **Kings Heart (IRE)**149 8071 3-8-4 64 (h) KieranO'Neill 9 16
(Mark Usher) *s.i.s: a in rr* **11/1**

1m 9.66s (-1.54) **Going Correction** -0.35s/f (Firm) **8** Ran SP% **113.9**
Speed ratings (Par 100): **96,96,93,93,89 86,77,73**
WIN: 1.30 Goodwood Crusader, 3.70 Mr Pocket; PL: 3.10 Sayesse, 1.40 Goodwood Crusader, Mr Pocket; EX: MP&GC11.80,GC&MP 8.30; CSF: MP&GC 10.20, GC&MP 7.73; TC: MP&GC&S £66.19, GC&MP&S £51.65.
**Owner** Gatley & Baines **Bred** Kabansk Ltd & Rathbarry Stud **Trained** Whatcombe, Oxon
**Owner** Goodwood Racehorse Owners Group (23) Ltd **Bred** Tally-Ho Stud **Trained** Upper Lambourn, Berks

**FOCUS**
A tight little handicap and so it proved.
T/Plt: £1,030.10 to a £1 stake. Pool: £36,199.00 - 35.14 winning units. T/Qpdt: £182.30 to a £1 stake. Pool: £2,827.00 - 15.50 winning units. **Colin Roberts**

# NEWBURY (L-H)

Friday, April 21

**OFFICIAL GOING: Good to firm (good in places; 7.1)**
Wind: light breeze against Weather: overcast

## 1941 DREWEATTS NEWCOMERS' EBF STALLIONS MAIDEN STKS (PLUS 10 RACE) 5f 34y

**2:00** (2:02) (Class 4) 2-Y-O **£6,469** (£1,925; £962; £481) **Stalls** Centre

Form RPR
**1** **Gold Town** 2-9-5 0 WilliamBuick 7 84+
(Charlie Appleby) *s.i.s: sn trcking ldrs: shkn up over 1f out: r.o wl ent fnl f: led fnl 120yds: pushed out* **10/3**1

**2** *nk* **Headway** 2-9-5 0 PatCosgrave 10 82+
(William Haggas) *hld up: hdwy over 1f out: rdn for str chal ent fnl f: kpt on wl* **7/1**

**3** *shd* **Embour (IRE)** 2-9-5 0 RyanMoore 5 82+
(Richard Hannon) *led for 1f: prom: rdn into narrow advantage over 1f out: hdd fnl 120yds: kpt on wl* **5/1**3

**4** 2 **Qaaraat** 2-9-5 0 JimCrowley 4 74+
(Ed Dunlop) *prom: rdn over 1f out: ev ch ent fnl f: no ex fnl 120yds* **4/1**2

**5** *shd* **Spoof** 2-9-5 0 JamieSpencer 1 74+
(Charles Hills) *hld up: swtchd lft and hdwy fr 2 f out: rdn over 1f out: ch ent fnl f: no ex fnl 120yds* **8/1**

**6** 1 ¼ **Jim Rockford** 2-9-5 0 FranBerry 8 71
(Ralph Beckett) *racd keenly: trckd ldrs: nt clr run over 1f out: outpcd briefly ent fnl f: kpt on fnl 120yds* **14/1**

**7** 1 ¼ **Mysaan (IRE)** 2-9-5 0 JimmyFortune 9 65
(Brian Meehan) *chsd ldrs: rdn 2f out: nt pce to threaten: fdd fnl f* **20/1**

**8** ½ **Motown Mick (IRE)** 2-9-5 0 TomMarquand 2 63
(Richard Hannon) *a towards rr* **16/1**

**9** 1 ¼ **Tony Soprano (IRE)** 2-9-5 0 DavidProbert 3 59
(Martyn Meade) *led after 1f: rdn and hdd over 1f out: wknd fnl f* **12/1**

**10** 8 **Owen The Law** 2-9-5 0 JFEgan 11 30
(David Evans) *sn pushed along in last trio: nvr threatened ldrs: wknd over 1f out* **25/1**

1m 3.38s (1.98) **Going Correction** +0.05s/f (Good) **10** Ran SP% **112.2**
Speed ratings (Par 94): **86,85,85,82,82 80,78,77,75,62**
CSF £25.70 TOTE £4.10: £1.70, £2.70, £1.30; EX 27.40 Trifecta £70.20.
**Owner** Godolphin **Bred** Godolphin **Trained** Newmarket, Suffolk

**FOCUS**
The going was good to firm, good in places. Some choicely bred newcomers contested this maiden which has been won by some nice types in the past. They went an honest pace and the winner did it well, but the field finished compressed and the form is rated at the lower end of the race averages.

## 1942 COMPTON BEAUCHAMP ESTATES LTD SILVER BAR H'CAP 2m 2f

**2:30** (2:32) (Class 2) (0-100,97) 4-Y-O+ **£16,172** (£4,812; £2,405; £1,202) **Stalls** Low

Form RPR
22-3 **1** **Rainbow Dreamer**14 1608 4-8-12 88 (v) RyanMoore 5 94+
(Alan King) *mid-div: stdy prog fr 3f out: cl 3rd 2f out: swtchd rt over 1f out: shkn up to ld fnl 130yds: readily* **11/4**1

516- **2** 1 ¼ **Champagne Champ**182 7498 5-9-5 90 JimCrowley 9 94
(Rod Millman) *led: rdn whn jnd over 2f out: hdd fnl 130yds: styd on gamely but sn hld by wnr* **5/1**2

13-3 **3** *nk* **Swashbuckle**30 1309 4-8-9 85 OisinMurphy 6 88
(Andrew Balding) *trckd ldr: rdn to dispute fr over 2f out: hdd fnl 130yds: styd on gamely but sn hld by wnr: no ex cl home* **11/4**1

46-5 **4** 2 ¼ **Guard of Honour (IRE)**98 227 6-9-4 89 (b) PatCosgrave 8 90
(George Baker) *mid-div: hdwy into 4th over 2f out: sn rdn: styd on but nt pce to get on terms* **12/1**

0-05 **5** 6 **Oceane (FR)**27 1361 5-9-7 92 (p) FergusSweeney 7 86
(Alan King) *trckd ldrs: rdn 3f out: wknd jst over 1f out* **8/1**3

001- **6** 4 **Star Rider**86 7670 5-9-10 95 (p) JimmyFortune 1 85
(Hughie Morrison) *trckd ldrs: rdn over 2f out: sn hld: wknd over 1f out* **5/1**2

00-0 **7** 2 ¼ **Havana Beat (IRE)**66 728 7-9-7 92 GeorgeDowning 2 80
(Tony Carroll) *hld up in last pair: rdn over 3f out: little imp: wknd 2f out* **33/1**

4/46 **8** 9 **Warrior Of Light (IRE)**78 540 6-9-12 97 FranBerry 3 75
(Brendan Powell) *stdd s: last: rdn 3f out: nvr any imp: wknd 2f out* **33/1**

4m 0.63s (28.63)
**WFA** 4 from 5yo+ 2lb **8** Ran SP% **111.4**
CSF £15.84 CT £38.52 TOTE £3.40: £1.40, £2.00, £1.10; EX 17.30 Trifecta £50.80.
**Owner** The Maple Street Partnership **Bred** Rabbah Bloodstock Limited **Trained** Barbury Castle, Wilts

**FOCUS**
Race run over an additional 12yds. The runner-up gradually wound up the pace in this decent staying handicap, which was run just over ten seconds outside the standard. The winner has the potential to do a bit better.

## 1943 DUBAI DUTY FREE GOLF WORLD CUP EBF STALLIONS CONDITIONS STKS (PLUS 10 RACE) 1m 2f

**3:05** (3:06) (Class 3) 3-Y-O
**£9,960** (£2,982; £1,491; £745; £372; £187) **Stalls** Low

Form RPR
1- **1** **Shutter Speed**185 7441 3-9-1 84 FrankieDettori 2 109+
(John Gosden) *trckd ldng trio: stdy prog to ld 2f out: sn pushed clr: styd on wl: comf* **5/4**1

214- **2** 2 ½ **Raheen House (IRE)**181 7539 3-9-6 110 JimmyFortune 6 108
(Brian Meehan) *sn trcking ldr: led 3f out: rdn and hdd 2f out: styd on but nt pce of comfortable wnr: jst hld on for 2nd* **7/2**2

1- **3** *hd* **Enable**144 8130 3-9-1 84 WilliamBuick 1 103+
(John Gosden) *racd keenly early: trckd ldrs: rdn 2f out to chse ldng pair: styd on ins fnl f to nrly snatch 2nd cl home* **5/1**3

31- **4** 6 **Temple Church (IRE)**217 6546 3-9-6 96 SilvestreDeSousa 3 96
(Hughie Morrison) *stdd s: last but in tch: pushed along over 4f out: chal for hld 4th 2f out: styd on same pce* **8/1**

113- **5** *shd* **Maths Prize**223 6330 3-9-9 90 RyanMoore 4 99
(Roger Charlton) *hld up 5th: rdn over 2f out: chal for hld 4th sn after: styd on same pce* **14/1**

02-1 **6** 14 **Dubawi Prince**20 1497 3-9-6 86 AndreaAtzeni 5 68
(Roger Varian) *led tl 3f out: sn rdn: wknd 2f out* **9/1**

2m 7.34s (-1.46) **Going Correction** +0.05s/f (Good) **6** Ran SP% **111.1**
Speed ratings (Par 102): **107,105,104,100,99 88**
CSF £5.64 TOTE £2.10: £1.40, £1.80; EX 6.30 Trifecta £24.00.
**Owner** K Abdullah **Bred** Juddmonte Farms Ltd **Trained** Newmarket, Suffolk

**FOCUS**
Add 8yds to race distance. A very interesting contest, with the winner looking a bit special. The runner-up set a high standard.

## 1944 BATHWICK TYRES MAIDEN FILLIES' STKS (PLUS 10 RACE) 1m 2f

**3:40** (3:40) (Class 4) 3-Y-O **£5,498** (£1,636; £817; £408) **Stalls** Low

Form RPR
0- **1** **Gracious Diana**170 7769 3-9-0 0 FrankieDettori 2 90+
(John Gosden) *mid-div: pushed along and hdwy fr 3f out: led over 1f out: sn clr: comf* **4/1**3

45- **2** 3 ½ **Star Rock**170 7762 3-9-0 0 RobertWinston 3 81
(Hughie Morrison) *trckd ldrs: rdn over 2f out: styd on to chse wnr ent fnl f but nvr threatening to get on terms* **28/1**

4- **3** 2 **Inconceivable (IRE)**162 7885 3-9-0 0 PatDobbs 6 77
(Ralph Beckett) *hld up towards rr: pushed along and stdy prog fr over 3f out: wnt 3rd ins fnl f: styd on* **10/1**

6- **4** 2 **Cubswin (IRE)**232 6061 3-8-11 0 KieranShoemark(3) 15 73
(Roger Charlton) *mid-div: hdwy to trck ldr 6f out: rdn and ev ch over 2f out: sn hld by wnr: styd on same pce fnl f* **33/1**

**5** *nk* **Mori** 3-9-0 0 RyanMoore 5 72
(Sir Michael Stoute) *s.i.s: sn mid-div: stdy prog fr 2f out: styd on fnl f but nt pce to get on terms* **9/4**1

42 **6** 1 **Many Waters (USA)**20 1499 3-9-0 0 JamieSpencer 8 70
(Andrew Balding) *trckd ldrs: lost pl 6f out: rdn 3f out: styd on same pce fnl 2f* **11/1**

62 **7** *nse* **Zehrah (IRE)**41 1143 3-9-0 0 SilvestreDeSousa 14 70
(Simon Crisford) *sn led: rdn and hdd over 1f out: fdd ins fnl f* **20/1**

6- **8** 2 **Mirzam (IRE)**196 7125 3-9-0 0 GrahamLee 10 66
(Mick Channon) *nvr bttr than mid-div* **80/1**

2- **9** ¾ **The Jean Genie**209 6776 3-9-0 0 AdamKirby 4 64
(Clive Cox) *mid-div: rdn over 2f out: nvr any imp (lame bhd)* **7/2**2

**10** ¾ **Nafaayes (IRE)** 3-9-0 0 JimCrowley 13 63
(Charles Hills) *hmpd s: a towards rr* **20/1**

**11** 2 ¼ **Miss Liguria** 3-9-0 0 ThomasBrown 7 58
(Ed Walker) *a towards rr* **50/1**

0- **12** ½ **Fresh Fox**232 6061 3-8-7 0 Pierre-LouisJamin(7) 9 57
(Jonathan Portman) *got loose in paddock: slowly away: a towards rr* **150/1**

44- **13** 1 ¼ **Harebell (IRE)**153 8034 3-9-0 0 FranBerry 12 55
(Ralph Beckett) *rrd leaving stalls: racd keenly: trckd ldrs: rdn 3f out: wknd 2f out* **12/1**

**14** 10 **Cecilator** 3-9-0 0 OisinMurphy 11 35
(Noel Williams) *s.i.s: a bhd* **250/1**

2m 8.0s (-0.80) **Going Correction** +0.05s/f (Good) **14** Ran SP% **118.3**
Speed ratings (Par 97): **105,102,100,99,98 97,97,96,95,95 93,92,91,83**
CSF £118.19 TOTE £6.20: £2.20, £6.30, £2.90; EX 118.70 Trifecta £1252.00.
**Owner** Al Mirqab Racing **Bred** Mrs P M Ignarski **Trained** Newmarket, Suffolk

**FOCUS**
Race run over an additional 8yds. A miaden which has produced some star fillies over the years, among them Oaks winners Eswarah (2005) and Dancing Rain (2011) and Group 1 winners Islington and Folk Opera. The time was only 0.66sec slower than the preceding Class 3 conditions event, which was also won by a John Gosden filly, and it's a race that should produce winners. The winner is rated above the race's solid average.

## 1945 DUBAI DUTY FREE FULL OF SURPRISES H'CAP 7f (S)
**4:10** (4:12) (Class 2) (0-100,92) 3-Y-O

**£12,450** (£3,728; £1,864; £932; £466; £234) **Stalls** Centre

Form RPR
260- 1 **Bacchus**[211] 6705 3-9-7 **92**........................................(p[1]) WilliamBuick 11 101
(Brian Meehan) *prom: led over 2f out: sn rdn: kpt on wl: drvn out* **25/1**
1- 2 nk **Chessman (IRE)**[156] 7976 3-9-2 **87**.............................. FrankieDettori 15 96+
(John Gosden) *hld up towards rr: hdwy wl over 1f out: str run ins fnl f: wnt 2nd towards fin* **7/4**[1]
4-14 3 nk **Winning Ways (IRE)**[71] 643 3-8-9 **80**........................(t) GeraldMosse 16 88+
(Jeremy Noseda) *hld up bhd: hdwy over 1f out: str run ins fnl f: swtchd lft fnl 75yds: short of room but fin wl to snatch 3rd* **14/1**
21- 4 nk **Omran**[127] 8377 3-9-3 **88**.............................................. DanielMuscutt 13 95
(Marco Botti) *mid-div: hdwy 3f out: rdn to chse wnr over 1f out: hung rt: kpt on but no ex cl home* **7/1**[3]
-530 5 1 ½ **Zamjar**[30] 1311 3-8-10 **81**.......................................................... JimCrowley 9 84
(Ed Dunlop) *mid-div: hdwy 3f out: rdn 2f out: pressed for 2nd ent fnl f: no ex fnl 120yds* **50/1**
011- 6 nk **Graphite Storm**[216] 6575 3-8-12 **86**........................ HectorCrouch(3) 10 88
(Clive Cox) *mid-divsion: rdn and hdwy over 1f out: pressed for 2nd ent fnl f: no ex fnl 120yds* **14/1**
41- 7 1 ½ **Warrior's Spirit (IRE)**[216] 6577 3-8-10 **81**........................ PatDobbs 14 79
(Richard Hannon) *hld up towards rr: hdwy over 1f out: rdn and kpt on ins fnl f but no threat to ldrs* **16/1**
-211 8 1 ½ **Dark Destroyer (IRE)**[24] 1411 3-8-9 **80**.................................. JFEgan 17 74
(Joseph Tuite) *a mid-div* **25/1**
31- 9 nk **Pivoine (IRE)**[184] 7458 3-8-11 **82**........................................ RyanMoore 2 75+
(Sir Michael Stoute) *towards rr: pushed along 1/2-way: kpt on ins fnl f but nvr any threat* **10/1**
251- 10 1 **Intimate Art (IRE)**[198] 7065 3-8-8 **79**.................................... OisinMurphy 6 70
(Andrew Balding) *led tl over 2f out: sn rdn: wknd fnl f* **16/1**
610- 11 ¾ **Solomon's Bay (IRE)**[195] 7148 3-9-3 **88**.................. SilvestreDeSousa 3 77
(Roger Varian) *trckd ldrs: rdn 2f out: wknd fnl f* **11/2**[2]
40-1 12 hd **Glory Of Paris (IRE)**[16] 1554 3-8-9 **80**...................... RobertWinston 12 68
(Rod Millman) *stdd s: racd keenly: a towards rr* **33/1**
60-1 13 ½ **Abatement**[83] 464 3-8-9 **83**............................... KieranShoemark(3) 4 70
(Roger Charlton) *in tch: effrt over 2f out: wknd fnl f* **20/1**
40-2 14 2 ½ **Jule In The Crown**[10] 1702 3-9-0 **85**................................ GrahamLee 5 65
(Mick Channon) *trckd ldrs: rdn over 2f out: wknd ent fnl f* **12/1**
152 15 ¾ **Espresso Freddo (IRE)**[21] 1472 3-8-9 **80**........................(p) LiamKeniry 7 58
(Robert Stephens) *racd freely: mid-div tl wknd over 1f out* **66/1**
1m 26.05s (0.35) **Going Correction** +0.05s/f (Good) **15** Ran SP% **125.0**
Speed ratings (Par 104): **100,99,99,98,97 96,95,93,93,92 91,90,90,87,86**
CSF £67.44 CT £703.12 TOTE £34.90: £6.50, £1.70, £4.80; EX 157.40 Trifecta £1029.00.
**Owner** G P M Morland,D J Erwin,John G S Woodman **Bred** D J Erwin Bloodstock **Trained** Manton, Wilts

**FOCUS**
Traditionally a very useful handicap with plenty of unexposed types. This looked a typically sound renewal and the form looks strong. The pace lasted better towards the stands' side. A clear pb from the winner.

## 1946 DUBAI DUTY FREE H'CAP 5f 34y
**4:40** (4:41) (Class 2) (0-110,107) 4-Y-O+

**£15,562** (£4,660; £2,330; £1,165; £582; £292) **Stalls** Centre

Form RPR
300- 1 **Sir Robert Cheval**[195] 7156 6-8-11 **97**.......................... AdamBeschizza 1 106
(Robert Cowell) *sn rousted along to hold position: travelling wl on heels of ldrs 2f out: r.o strly to ld fnl 120yds: won gng away* **11/2**[3]
3252 2 1 ¼ **Bowson Fred**[27] 1362 5-8-11 **100**.................................. NathanEvans(3) 2 104
(Michael Easterby) *prom: led over 2f out: rdn over 1f out: hdd fnl 120yds: no ex: jst hld on for 2nd* **4/1**[2]
510- 3 hd **Lady Macapa**[167] 7822 4-8-11 **97**.................................. SamHitchcott 4 100
(Clive Cox) *prom: rdn 2f out: kpt on ins fnl f to nrly snatch 2nd fnl strides* **6/1**
501- 4 3 ¼ **Soie D'Leau**[181] 7537 5-8-13 **99**.......................................... TonyHamilton 3 91
(Kristin Stubbs) *led tl over 2f out: rdn over 1f out: sn hld: fdd ins fnl f* **6/1**
304- 5 ½ **Double Up**[170] 7771 6-9-3 **103**..................................(t) SilvestreDeSousa 5 93
(Roger Varian) *slowly away: in last trio but in tch: effrt 2f out: nt pce to threaten* **15/8**[1]
266- 6 1 ¼ **Duke Of Firenze**[192] 7250 8-9-5 **105**.......................................... DavidAllan 6 90
(David C Griffiths) *slowly away: last but in tch: rdn 2f out: no imp* **14/1**
-315 7 6 **Poyle Vinnie**[62] 818 7-9-0 **103**................................(p) AlistairRawlinson(3) 8 67
(Michael Appleby) *slowly away: last pair but in tch: rdn over 2f out: wknd over 1f out* **14/1**
1m 0.17s (-1.23) **Going Correction** +0.05s/f (Good) **7** Ran SP% **112.1**
Speed ratings (Par 109): **111,109,108,103,102 100,91**
CSF £26.45 CT £134.25 TOTE £6.30: £2.80, £2.10; EX 23.30 Trifecta £155.70.
**Owner** Heart Of The South Racing **Bred** John And Caroline Penny **Trained** Six Mile Bottom, Cambs

**FOCUS**
A classy sprint handicap in which those drawn low came out on top. A length pb from the winner.

## 1947 COLN VALLEY STUD BRIDGET MAIDEN FILLIES' STKS (PLUS 10 RACE) (DIV I) 7f (S)
**5:10** (5:13) (Class 4) 3-Y-O **£4,851** (£1,443; £721; £360) **Stalls** Centre

Form RPR
1 **Mulhimatty** 3-9-0 0.................................................................. JimCrowley 3 73+
(Charles Hills) *led: narrowly hdd ent fnl f: sn rdn: kpt on gamely: led fnl stride* **12/1**
2 shd **May Sky** 3-9-0 0.................................................................. WilliamBuick 4 72+
(John Gosden) *prom: narrow advantage ent fnl f: sn rdn: kpt on: hdd fnl stride* **3/1**[1]
3 hd **Omneeya** 3-9-0 0.................................................................. TomMarquand 2 71+
(Marco Botti) *s.i.s: last pair: hdwy 2f out: sn hung lft: rdn and ev ch ent fnl f: kpt on* **5/1**[3]
4 1 ¼ **Highway One (USA)** 3-9-0 0.................................................. PatCosgrave 1 68
(George Baker) *in tch: rdn to chse ldrs over 1f out: kpt on same pce fnl f* **25/1**
5 nk **Jinkie Pink (IRE)** 3-9-0 0.................................................. ThomasBrown 5 67
(Ed Walker) *trckd ldrs: rdn 2f out: kpt on but nt pce to chal* **16/1**
6 ½ **Butterfly Lily** 3-9-0 0.................................................................. FranBerry 8 66+
(Ralph Beckett) *slowly away: last: hdwy 2f out: sn rdn: kpt on same pce fnl f* **10/3**[2]
7 1 **World Power (IRE)** 3-9-0 0.................................................. PatDobbs 9 63
(Paul Cole) *in tch: rdn over 1f out: kpt on but nt pce to get involved* **25/1**
8 shd **Ruxleys Star (USA)** 3-9-0 0.................................................. SeanLevey 6 63
(Richard Hannon) *in tch: rdn 2f out: sn one pce* **16/1**
9 4 ½ **Superioritycomplex (IRE)** 3-9-0 0.......................................... RyanMoore 7 55
(Sir Michael Stoute) *racd green: in last trio but in tch: pushed along 1/2-way: wknd fnl f* **3/1**[1]
1m 28.32s (2.62) **Going Correction** +0.05s/f (Good) **9** Ran SP% **116.9**
Speed ratings (Par 97): **87,86,86,85,84 84,83,83,77**
CSF £48.68 TOTE £10.90: £2.50, £1.40, £1.80; EX 55.30 Trifecta £321.90.
**Owner** Hamdan Al Maktoum **Bred** Shadwell Estate Company Limited **Trained** Lambourn, Berks

**FOCUS**
No form to go on but some nice-looking types in the field. The went a steady pace and finished in a bit of a bunch. The slower division by 2.88sec and the form is rated cautiously.

## 1948 COLN VALLEY STUD BRIDGET MAIDEN FILLIES' STKS (PLUS 10 RACE) (DIV II) 7f (S)
**5:40** (5:44) (Class 4) 3-Y-O **£4,851** (£1,443; £721; £360) **Stalls** Centre

Form RPR
1 **Princess De Lune (IRE)** 3-8-11 0.............................. KieranShoemark(3) 6 90+
(Roger Charlton) *in tch: smooth hdwy 2f out: led over 1f out: hung lft but sn drew clr: easily* **7/2**[3]
2 4 **Alnaas** 3-9-0 0....................................................................(t[1]) JimCrowley 4 79
(John Gosden) *led: rdn and hdd over 1f out: sn no ch w wnr: kpt on same pce* **10/3**[2]
3 2 ½ **Tirania** 3-9-0 0.................................................................. PatCosgrave 1 72
(William Haggas) *in tch: rdn 2f out: kpt on ins fnl f: snatched 3rd cl home: nt pce to get on terms* **4/1**
4 hd **Domitilla** 3-9-0 0.................................................................. TomMarquand 5 71
(Marco Botti) *trckd ldrs: rdn and ev ch 2f out: no ex fnl f* **14/1**
5 3 ½ **Tenby Two** 3-9-0 0....................................................(e[1]) GrahamLee 9 62
(Mick Channon) *hld up: struggling 1/2-way: kpt on past btn horses fnl f: nvr any threat* **33/1**
6 ½ **Majorette** 3-9-0 0.................................................................. RobertWinston 7 61
(Martin Smith) *trckd ldr: rdn 2f out: wknd over 1f out* **28/1**
7 ¾ **Flourishing** 3-9-0 0....................................................(h[1]) OisinMurphy 2 59
(Sir Michael Stoute) *racd keenly: in tch :rdn over 2f out: wknd over 1f out* **9/1**
8 1 ¼ **Dr Goodhead (FR)** 3-9-0 0.................................................. SilvestreDeSousa 8 55
(Charles Hills) *s.i.s: a towards rr* **16/1**
9 2 ¾ **Poana (FR)** 3-9-0 0.................................................................. FrankieDettori 3 48
(John Gosden) *prom tl 2f out: sn wknd* **3/1**[1]
1m 25.44s (-0.26) **Going Correction** +0.05s/f (Good) **9** Ran SP% **119.2**
Speed ratings (Par 97): **103,98,95,95,91 90,89,88,85**
CSF £16.23 TOTE £5.20: £1.70, £1.40, £2.50; EX 20.10 Trifecta £63.80.
**Owner** Kaniz Bloodstock Investments Ltd **Bred** Roundhill Stud **Trained** Beckhampton, Wilts

**FOCUS**
The quicker division by a considerable margin, 2.88sec to be precise, with a very promising performance from Princess De Lune. Previous winners of this maiden for unraced fillies include Group 1 scorer Promising Lead. A positive view has been taken of the form.
T/Jkpt: Now won. T/Plt: £79.90 to a £1 stake. Pool: £71,259.00 - 891.71 winning units. T/Qpdt: £63.50 to a £1 stake. Pool: £4,304.00 - 67.70 winning units. **Tim Mitchell**

1949 - 1956a (Foreign Racing) - See Raceform Interactive

# [1941] NEWBURY (L-H)
Saturday, April 22

**OFFICIAL GOING: Good to firm (6.9)**
Wind: light breeze across Weather: sunny

## 1957 DUBAI DUTY FREE FINEST SURPRISE STKS (REGISTERED AS THE JOHN PORTER STAKES ) (GROUP 3) 1m 4f 5y
**1:55** (1:55) (Class 1) 4-Y-O+

**£34,026** (£12,900; £6,456; £3,216; £1,614; £810) **Stalls** Low

Form RPR
14-3 1 **Muntahaa (IRE)**[20] 1516 4-8-13 113.......................................... JimCrowley 6 114
(John Gosden) *trckd ldrs: rdn to chse ldr 2f out: styd on wl ins fnl f: led fnl 40yds* **9/2**[2]
22-1 2 nk **Chemical Charge (IRE)**[20] 1516 5-9-0 107................(p[1]) OisinMurphy 5 113
(Ralph Beckett) *mid-div: hdwy 3f out: led 2f out: sn rdn: drifted lft and rt u.p: no ex whn hdd fnl 40yds* **9/2**[2]
034- 3 1 ¼ **Second Step (IRE)**[211] 6752 6-9-0 106.............................. JamieSpencer 1 112+
(Roger Charlton) *s.i.s: bhd: rdn and hdwy fr over 2f out: chsd ldng pair over 1f out: styng on but hld whn nt best of runs cl home* **12/1**
11- 4 ½ **Crimean Tatar (TUR)**[150] 8068 4-8-13 109.............................. JamesDoyle 3 110
(Hugo Palmer) *in last trio: rdn along fr over 3f out: stdy prog fr 2f out: styd on ins fnl f: wnt 4th fnl 120yds: nt pce to get involved* **5/1**[3]
520- 5 hd **Midterm**[189] 7353 4-8-13 115.................................................. RyanMoore 8 110
(Sir Michael Stoute) *hld up: rdn over 3f out: stdy prog fr 2f out: styd on ins fnl f: wnt 5th fnl 120yds: nt pce to get on terms* **3/1**[1]
131- 6 1 ¾ **Dal Harraild**[211] 6752 4-8-13 109.............................................. PatCosgrave 2 108
(William Haggas) *trckd ldr tl rdn 2f out: kpt chsng ldrs in 4th tl no ex fnl 120yds* **9/2**[2]
-235 7 5 **Dylan Mouth (IRE)**[49] 1042 6-9-0 110.............................. FrankieDettori 9 99
(Marco Botti) *racd wd in bk st: led: rdn and hdd 2f out: wknd jst over 1f out* **12/1**
10-6 8 nse **Quarterback (GER)**[21] 1500 5-9-3 108..........................(tp) PatDobbs 7 102
(Rune Haugen) *trckd ldrs: rdn over 2f out: wknd over 1f out* **66/1**
2m 31.58s (-3.92) **Going Correction** +0.05s/f (Good) **8** Ran SP% **113.1**
Speed ratings (Par 113): **115,114,113,113,113 112,109,108**
CSF £24.44 TOTE £5.20: £1.70, £1.70, £3.80; EX 21.20 Trifecta £244.00.
**Owner** Hamdan Al Maktoum **Bred** Shadwell Estate Company Limited **Trained** Newmarket, Suffolk

**FOCUS**
This was run over 16yds further than advertised. A competitive renewal of this Group 3 prize won most notably in recent years by the subsequent wide-margin King George victor Harbinger in 2010. They went a decent gallop and it produced a busy finish. The winner was close to form with the third helping the standard.

## 1958 DUBAI DUTY FREE STKS (REGISTERED AS THE FRED DARLING STAKES) (GROUP 3) (FILLIES) 7f (S)
**2:30** (2:33) (Class 1) 3-Y-O

**£34,026** (£12,900; £6,456; £3,216; £1,614; £810) **Stalls** Centre

Form RPR
113- **1** **Dabyah (IRE)**[202] [6986] 3-9-0 112 FrankieDettori 8 104+
(John Gosden) *mde all: kpt on strly: rdn out* **6/4**[1]
313- **2** 1 1/4 **Urban Fox**[197] [7116] 3-9-0 100 MartinHarley 7 101
(James Tate) *trckd ldrs: rdn 2f out: chsd wnr ent fnl f: kpt on but a being hld* **25/1**
232- **3** 3/4 **Promising (IRE)**[238] [5870] 3-9-0 100 PatDobbs 5 99
(Richard Hannon) *in tch: hdwy 2f out: rdn to chal for 3rd ent fnl f: kpt on* **8/1**[3]
0 **4** nk **Rain Goddess (IRE)**[14] [1634] 3-9-0 0 RyanMoore 10 98+
(A P O'Brien, Ire) *mid-div: rdn 2f out: little imp tl r.o ins fnl f: wnt 4th cl home* **8/1**[3]
114- **5** nse **Queen Kindly**[210] [6784] 3-9-0 114 JamieSpencer 4 98+
(Richard Fahey) *stdd s and wnt rt: last pair: swtchd rt and hdwy fr 2f out: rdn ent fnl f: kpt on but nt pce to get on terms* **7/2**[2]
263- **6** nk **Mystic Dawn (IRE)**[176] [7667] 3-9-0 98 JamesDoyle 3 97
(David Simcock) *hmpd s: mid-div: hdwy over 2f out: rdn to chal for 2nd over 1f out tl ins fnl f: no ex fnl 100yds* **14/1**
422- **7** 3/4 **Glitter Girl**[182] [7547] 3-9-0 101 PatCosgrave 11 95
(William Haggas) *in tch: hdwy over 1f out: sn rdn: kpt on same pce fnl f* **8/1**[3]
060- **8** 2 **Arwa (IRE)**[196] [7151] 3-9-0 80 JimCrowley 6 90
(Charles Hills) *trckd ldr: rdn 2f out: wknd fnl f* **100/1**
02- **9** 1/2 **Think Fashion (IRE)**[232] [6078] 3-9-0 0 JimmyFortune 2 88
(Brian Meehan) *bmpd leaving stalls: towards rr: rdn 2f out: hung lft: little imp* **66/1**
103- **10** 4 1/2 **Pichola Dance (IRE)**[182] [7547] 3-9-0 94 AndreaAtzeni 9 76
(Roger Varian) *trckd ldr: rdn over 2f out: wknd over 1f out* **25/1**
020- **11** 9 **Poet's Princess**[182] [7547] 3-9-0 84 RobertWinston 1 52
(Hughie Morrison) *unsettled stalls and jockey slow to remove blindfold: slowly away: a towards rr* **66/1**

1m 24.54s (-1.16) **Going Correction** +0.05s/f (Good) **11** Ran SP% **113.9**
Speed ratings (Par 105): **108,106,105,105,105 104,104,101,101,96 85**
CSF £49.51 TOTE £2.10: £1.30, £5.00, £2.30; EX 33.70 Trifecta £206.50.
**Owner** Abdullah Saeed Al Naboodah **Bred** Rabbah Bloodstock Limited **Trained** Newmarket, Suffolk

**FOCUS**
The last filly to win this and follow up in the 1,000 Guineas was Wince in 1999 and it's hard to get excited by the latest running, with the winner getting things her own way up front and the next six runners finishing in a bit of a bunch. The time was 1.46sec slower than the Greenham. Dabyah didn't need to improve and the form is rated a shade better than the race averages.

## 1959 JLT GREENHAM STKS (GROUP 3) (C&G) 7f (S)
**3:05** (3:06) (Class 1) 3-Y-O

**£34,026** (£12,900; £6,456; £3,216; £1,614; £810) **Stalls** Centre

Form RPR
1- **1** **Barney Roy**[210] [6777] 3-9-0 91 JamesDoyle 1 114
(Richard Hannon) *in tch: rdn and hdwy over 2f out: chsd ldr over 1f out: str run ent fnl f: led fnl 120yds: kpt on strly* **5/2**[2]
1 **2** 2 **Dream Castle**[20] [1514] 3-9-0 90 OisinMurphy 8 108+
(Saeed bin Suroor) *racd freely: prom: led 2f out: sn rdn: kpt on but no ex whn hdd fnl 120yds* **9/4**[1]
312- **3** 4 **Zainhom (USA)**[196] [7148] 3-9-0 109 JimCrowley 9 98+
(Sir Michael Stoute) *hmpd s: sn mid-div: rdn and hdwy over 2f out: kpt on fnl f but nt pce of front pair* **8/1**
102- **4** hd **Kings Gift (IRE)**[182] [7544] 3-9-0 101 PaulMulrennan 4 97
(Michael Dods) *hld up: hdwy 3f out: sn rdn: kpt on fnl f but nt pce to get on terms* **25/1**
331- **5** 2 1/2 **Via Serendipity**[211] [6751] 3-9-0 84 (t[1]) JosephineGordon 3 90
(Hugo Palmer) *led: rdn and hdd 2f out: sn hld: no ex ins fnl f* **20/1**
64-4 **6** 1/2 **Sea Fox (IRE)**[56] [933] 3-9-0 104 JFEgan 6 89
(David Evans) *trckd ldr: rdn 2f out: sn outpcd* **33/1**
21- **7** hd **Make Time (IRE)**[206] [6880] 3-9-0 91 JimmyFortune 5 88
(David Menuisier) *hld up: hdwy over 2f out: sn rdn: nvr threatened: fdd fnl f* **17/2**
-412 **8** 4 1/2 **Mr Scaramanga**[14] [1621] 3-9-0 105 HarryBentley 7 76
(Simon Dow) *trckd ldr: rdn over 2f out: sn wknd* **25/1**
5111 **9** 3/4 **Lord Cooper**[30] [1332] 3-9-0 78 (tp) RenatoSouza 10 74
(Jose Santos) *carried sltly rt s: a towards rr* **100/1**
1 **10** 14 **War Secretary (USA)**[10] [1742] 3-9-0 104 (t) RyanMoore 2 36
(A P O'Brien, Ire) *rrd leaving stalls: racd alone on far side: sn prom: rdn 3f out: wknd qckly* **9/2**[3]

1m 23.08s (-2.62) **Going Correction** +0.05s/f (Good) **10** Ran SP% **115.5**
Speed ratings (Par 108): **116,113,109,108,106 105,105,100,99,83**
CSF £7.88 TOTE £3.30: £1.40, £1.30, £2.10; EX 9.70 Trifecta £39.90.
**Owner** Godolphin **Bred** Eliza Park International Pty Ltd **Trained** East Everleigh, Wilts

**FOCUS**
Traditionally one of the stronger 2,000 Guineas trials. Flat stars such as Frankel in 2011, Kingman in 2014 and the champion sprinter Muhaarar in 2015 are on this race's recent role of honour, but today's favourite was available at 20-1 for the first Classic beforehand. Two promising, once-raced and unbeaten Godolphin colts came nicely clear of the third off a decent gallop but there's a bit of doubt over the depth of this.

## 1960 BE WISER INSURANCE SPRING CUP H'CAP 1m
**3:40** (3:43) (Class 2) 4-Y-O+

**£31,125** (£9,320; £4,660; £2,330; £1,165; £585) **Stalls** Centre

Form RPR
220- **1** **Banksea**[210] [6786] 4-9-4 **100** JamieSpencer 12 109
(Luca Cumani) *mid-div: rdn and hdwy fr 2f out: r.o wl fnl f: led fnl 40yds: drvn out* **9/1**[3]
0 **2** 1/2 **Another Touch**[21] [1492] 4-9-0 **96** PaulMulrennan 8 104
(Richard Fahey) *mid-div: hdwy over 2f out: sn rdn: chsd ldr ent fnl f: r.o w wnr clsng stages but a being jst hld* **16/1**
214- **3** nse **Fastnet Tempest (IRE)**[204] [6915] 4-8-6 **88** (p) FrannyNorton 4 96+
(William Haggas) *trckd ldrs: led 2f out: sn rdn: drifted lft ins fnl f: hdd fnl 40yds: no ex* **10/1**
51-1 **4** hd **George William**[10] [1734] 4-8-12 **94** PatDobbs 7 101+
(Richard Hannon) *s.i.s: towards rr: hdwy over 1f out: sn rdn: r.o strly fnl f: wnt 4th cl home* **10/1**
600- **5** 1/2 **Bossy Guest (IRE)**[273] [4625] 5-9-7 **103** CharlesBishop 5 109
(Mick Channon) *s.i.s: towards rr: making hdwy whn short of room 2f out: sn rdn: r.o wl ins fnl f: wnt 5th cl home* **33/1**
120- **6** 1/2 **El Hayem (IRE)**[273] [4624] 4-8-8 **90** JoeFanning 6 95
(Sir Michael Stoute) *s.i.s: sn mid-div: hdwy over 2f out: chal for 2nd over 1f out: kpt on same pce fnl 120yds* **12/1**
04-3 **7** hd **Donncha (IRE)**[21] [1494] 6-9-5 **101** AndreaAtzeni 11 106+
(Robert Eddery) *hld up towards rr: hdwy over 2f out: sn rdn: kpt on wl ins fnl f* **8/1**[2]
124- **8** 1/2 **Storm Ahead (IRE)**[196] [7153] 4-8-10 **92** JosephineGordon 14 95
(Marcus Tregoning) *trckd ldrs: rdn 2f out: kpt on same pce fnl f* **16/1**
40-0 **9** 1 1/4 **Big Baz (IRE)**[21] [1493] 7-9-9 **105** MartinDwyer 13 105
(William Muir) *led: rdn and hdd over 1f out: no ex ins fnl f* **50/1**
612- **10** hd **Mountain Rescue (IRE)**[186] [7428] 5-8-7 **89** HarryBentley 3 89
(Chris Wall) *trckd ldrs: rdn over 2f out: fdd ins fnl f* **25/1**
-166 **11** 1 **Fanciful Angel (IRE)**[65] [774] 5-9-10 **106** DanielMuscutt 20 104
(Marco Botti) *mid-div: rdn over 1f out: kpt on ins fnl f but nt pce to get involved* **20/1**
220- **12** 3/4 **Pacify**[308] [3383] 5-9-6 **102** FranBerry 2 98
(Ralph Beckett) *hld up towards rr: rdn 2f out: little imp tl kpt on ins fnl f: nvr trbld ldrs* **20/1**
0-40 **13** 2 **Zhui Feng (IRE)**[21] [1494] 4-9-4 **100** JimCrowley 21 91
(Amanda Perrett) *rdn over 2f out: a mid-div* **10/1**
30-0 **14** 1 **London Protocol (FR)**[21] [1492] 4-8-8 **93** (p) JordanVaughan[(3)] 10 82
(K R Burke) *pressed ldr tl rdn over 2f out: wknd over 1f out* **33/1**
46-0 **15** 3/4 **Master Carpenter (IRE)**[21] [1494] 6-8-10 **97** LuluStanford[(5)] 1 84
(Rod Millman) *mid-div: hdwy over 2f out: effrt chsng ldrs over 1f out: wknd ent fnl f* **14/1**
523- **16** 1/2 **Home Cummins (IRE)**[177] [7650] 5-8-9 **94** (p) SammyJoBell[(3)] 9 80
(Richard Fahey) *mid-div: rdn 2f out: no imp: wknd ent fnl f* **20/1**
150- **17** 10 **Boomshackerlacker (IRE)**[237] [5941] 7-9-4 **100** FergusSweeney 16 63
(George Baker) *mid-div tl wknd over 1f out* **33/1**
00-1 **18** nk **In The Red (IRE)**[95] [277] 4-8-2 **87** (b) NoelGarbutt[(3)] 19 49
(Martin Smith) *trckd ldrs: rdn over 2f out: squeezed up whn wkng sn after* **50/1**
00-0 **19** 9 **Sir Roderic (IRE)**[21] [1492] 4-8-13 **95** OisinMurphy 17 37
(Rod Millman) *mid-div: wkng whn squeezed up 2f out* **20/1**
450- **20** 3 **Havre De Paix (FR)**[115] [8563] 5-8-12 **94** JimmyFortune 18 29
(David Menuisier) *a towards rr* **50/1**
/21- **P** **Chelsea Lad (IRE)**[336] [2479] 4-9-0 **96** RyanMoore 15
(Martyn Meade) *mid-div whn eased over 2f out: sn p.u (lame)* **7/2**[1]

1m 36.93s (-2.77) **Going Correction** +0.05s/f (Good) **21** Ran SP% **134.3**
Speed ratings (Par 109): **115,114,114,114,113 113,113,112,111,111 110,109,107,106,105 105,95,94,85,82**
CSF £134.96 CT £1530.68 TOTE £10.30: £2.80, £4.00, £2.60, £2.80; EX 172.10 Trifecta £2682.70.
**Owner** Leonidas Marinopoulos **Bred** Hascombe And Valiant Studs **Trained** Newmarket, Suffolk

**FOCUS**
A typically competitive big-field handicap run at a strong pace and there was no obvious draw/track bias. The winner continues to progress.

## 1961 DUBAI DUTY FREE TENNIS CHAMPIONSHIPS MAIDEN STKS (PLUS 10 RACE) (DIV I) 1m
**4:15** (4:16) (Class 4) 3-Y-O **£5,175** (£1,540; £769; £384) **Stalls** Centre

Form RPR
**1** **Call To Mind** 3-9-5 0 RyanMoore 5 82+
(William Haggas) *chsd ldrs: shkn up 2f out: str run to chal ins fnl f: edgd ahd fnl 70yds: kpt on wl* **6/4**[1]
0- **2** nk **Commander**[183] [7503] 3-9-5 0 AndreaAtzeni 2 81
(Roger Varian) *trckd ldrs: rdn wl over 1f out: chal ent fnl f: ev ch fnl 100yds: kpt on* **5/2**[2]
23- **3** 1/2 **Red Royalist**[203] [6950] 3-9-5 0 MartinDwyer 1 80
(Marcus Tregoning) *led: rdn over 1f out: jnd jst ins fnl f: kpt on but no ex whn hdd fnl 70yds* **4/1**[3]
**4** 1 1/2 **Rumpole** 3-9-5 0 DanielMuscutt 10 76
(Hughie Morrison) *hld up: rdn and hdwy over 1f out: cl 4th ent fnl f: kpt on same pce* **33/1**
**5** 1 3/4 **Alqalsar (IRE)** 3-9-5 0 JimmyFortune 9 72
(Brian Meehan) *prom: rdn 2f out: sn one pce* **25/1**
**6** 1 3/4 **Tinos (GER)** 3-9-5 0 OisinMurphy 8 68
(Ed Walker) *hld up: effrt 2f out: nt pce to chal: wknd fnl f* **50/1**
0- **7** shd **Discovered (IRE)**[168] [7812] 3-9-2 0 KieranShoemark[(3)] 3 68
(Roger Charlton) *racd keenly: hld up: hdwy over 1f out: wknd ins fnl f* **20/1**
**8** 1 1/2 **Najashee (IRE)** 3-9-5 0 JimCrowley 4 64
(Owen Burrows) *slowly away: sn chsng ldrs: hung lft whn trying to mount chal 2f out: wknd ent fnl f* **7/1**
50 **9** 7 **Hippocampus (IRE)**[17] [1551] 3-9-5 0 PatDobbs 7 47
(Richard Hannon) *hld up: rdn over 2f out: wknd over 1f out* **50/1**

1m 41.8s (2.10) **Going Correction** +0.05s/f (Good) **9** Ran SP% **116.5**
Speed ratings (Par 100): **91,90,90,88,86 85,85,83,76**
CSF £5.12 TOTE £2.40: £1.10, £1.20, £1.60; EX 6.00 Trifecta £14.30.
**Owner** The Queen **Bred** The Queen **Trained** Newmarket, Suffolk

**FOCUS**
The first division of a good 3yo maiden won impressively by the subsequent Group 3 winner Intilaaq in 2015. They went a muddling gallop, and the comparative winning time was significantly slower than the previous four races, but the right three horses still came to the fore. It was the slower division and it's hard to rate the form too highly.

## 1962 DUBAI DUTY FREE TENNIS CHAMPIONSHIPS MAIDEN STKS (PLUS 10 RACE) (DIV II) 1m
**4:45** (4:48) (Class 4) 3-Y-O **£5,175** (£1,540; £769; £384) **Stalls** Centre

Form RPR
00 **1** **Duke Of Bronte**[11] [1692] 3-9-5 0 RyanTate 10 83
(Rod Millman) *s.i.s: last: swtchd to centre and hdwy fr 3f out: drifted lft over 1f out: r.o ent fnl f: led fnl 100yds: readily* **100/1**
**2** 2 **Musical Terms** 3-9-5 0 RyanMoore 2 78+
(William Haggas) *in tch: lost pl and pushed along over 3f out: hdwy over 1f out: kpt on ins fnl f: snatched 2nd cl home* **5/2**[2]
2 **3** hd **Dhalam (USA)**[17] [1552] 3-9-5 0 FrankieDettori 7 77+
(John Gosden) *led: rdn and 2 l clr ent fnl f: no ex whn hdd fnl 100yds* **6/5**[1]
**4** 1 1/2 **Archetype (FR)** 3-9-5 0 JamesDoyle 3 74
(Simon Crisford) *prom: rdn to chse ldr over 2f out: one pce fnl f* **12/1**

5 3 3/4 **Anif (IRE)** 3-9-5 0 .......... JimCrowley 4 65
(Charles Hills) *s.i.s: in last trio: pushed along in 5th over 3f out: nvr gng pce to get involved* **25/1**

6 3/4 **Magellan** 3-9-5 0 .......... HarryBentley 9 64
(Roger Charlton) *trckd ldrs: rdn 2f out: sn one pce* **15/2[3]**

00- 7 4 **Noble Behest**[136] 8246 3-8-12 0 .......... TylerSaunders(7) 5 54
(Marcus Tregoning) *in tch: rdn 2f out: sn wknd* **100/1**

0 8 hd **Tango Fire (USA)**[10] 1730 3-9-5 0 .......... PatDobbs 8 54
(Richard Hannon) *a towards rr (fin lame)* **14/1**

9 1 1/4 **Espresso Martini** 3-9-5 0 .......... FranBerry 6 51
(Brian Meehan) *struggling towards rr 1/2-way: wknd 2f out* **40/1**

10 4 1/2 **Saaheq** 3-9-5 0 .......... JimmyFortune 1 41
(Brian Meehan) *trckd ldrs: rdn in cl 3rd 2f out: wknd ent fnl f* **12/1**

1m 39.78s (0.08) **Going Correction** +0.05s/f (Good) **10** Ran SP% **116.1**
Speed ratings (Par 100): **101,99,98,97,93 92,88,88,87,82**
CSF £338.24 TOTE £75.60: £18.40, £1.70, £1.02; EX 197.40 Trifecta £2575.70.

**Owner** Perfect Match **Bred** Harts Farm Stud **Trained** Kentisbeare, Devon

**FOCUS**
Not an easy race to make sense of, but a good time compared with division one. The form is rated a bit cautiously.

## 1963 CARTER JONAS MAIDEN STKS (PLUS 10 RACE) 1m 3f 5y
**5:20** (5:21) (Class 4) 3-Y-O **£6,469** (£1,925; £962; £481) **Stalls** Low

Form RPR

2-2 1 **Face The Facts (IRE)**[15] 1607 3-9-5 0 .......... FrankieDettori 1 85
(John Gosden) *trckd ldr: led 3f out: rdn whn strly pressed 2f out: styd on wl to assert ins fnl f* **7/2[2]**

5- 2 3/4 **Karawaan (IRE)**[220] 6486 3-9-5 0 .......... JimCrowley 3 83
(Sir Michael Stoute) *trckd ldrs: rdn to chal 2f out: kpt on but no ex fnl 120yds* **6/1**

4- 3 1 1/2 **Master Singer (USA)**[171] 7769 3-9-5 0 .......... RyanMoore 5 80
(John Gosden) *trckd ldrs: rdn 2f out: kpt on same pce to go 3rd ins fnl f* **3/1[1]**

4- 4 nk **Really Super**[195] 7187 3-9-0 0 .......... FranBerry 4 74
(Ralph Beckett) *s.i.s: last pair: rdn over 3f out: hdwy 2f out: styd on same pce fnl f* **9/1**

0- 5 nse **UAE King**[183] 7501 3-9-5 0 .......... AndreaAtzeni 6 79
(Roger Varian) *in tch: rdn over 3f out: hdwy over 2f out: cl 3rd w ch over 1f out: no ex ins fnl f* **4/1[3]**

4- 6 1 3/4 **Lethal Impact (JPN)**[166] 7849 3-9-5 0 .......... OisinMurphy 7 76
(David Simcock) *hld up: rdn oer 2f out: styd on fnl f: nt pce to get involved* **8/1**

5 7 nk **Akamanto (IRE)**[14] 1624 3-9-5 0 .......... PatDobbs 2 76
(Richard Hannon) *trckd ldr: rdn 3f out: one pce fnl 2f* **33/1**

8 1/2 **Kazawi** 3-9-2 0 .......... KieranShoemark(3) 9 75
(Roger Charlton) *s.i.s: last pair: rdn over 3 out: nvr gng pce to get involved* **16/1**

9 5 **Rhodes House** 3-9-5 0 .......... (t[1]) JimmyFortune 8 69
(Paul Cole) *led tl 3f out: sn rdn: wknd over 1f out: eased fnl f* **22/1**

2m 22.15s (0.95) **Going Correction** +0.05s/f (Good) **9** Ran SP% **115.8**
Speed ratings (Par 100): **98,97,96,96,96 94,94,94,90**
CSF £24.95 TOTE £3.60: £1.50, £2.40, £1.40; EX 21.80 Trifecta £70.60.

**Owner** George Strawbridge **Bred** George Strawbridge **Trained** Newmarket, Suffolk

**FOCUS**
This was run over 16yds further than advertised. An interesting 3yo middle-distance maiden won in 2014 by the subsequent Group 2 Royal Ascot winner Eagle Top. The winner shaped like an out-and-out stayer, though, and the winning time was modest. The field finished a bit too compressed to be all that positive over the form.

## 1964 DUBAI DUTY FREE MILLENNIUM MILLIONAIRE H'CAP 1m 2f
**5:55** (5:55) (Class 3) (0-90,90) 4-Y-O+ **£7,762** (£2,310; £1,154; £577) **Stalls** Low

Form RPR

11 1 **Signe (IRE)**[29] 1345 4-8-12 **81** .......... PatCosgrave 8 87+
(William Haggas) *trckd ldrs: rdn over 2f out: str run ins fnl f: led fnl stride* **9/4[1]**

402- 2 nse **Grapevine (IRE)**[183] 7505 4-9-4 **87** .......... AndreaAtzeni 1 92
(Charles Hills) *awkward leaving stalls: hld up: racd keenly: smooth hdwy 3f out: shkn up to ld ent fnl f: kpt on: hdd fnl stride* **7/2[2]**

224- 3 1 1/2 **Top Beak (IRE)**[192] 7287 4-9-7 **90** .......... (t) JimmyFortune 4 92
(Hughie Morrison) *in tch: rdn 2f out: kpt on strly ins fnl f: snatched 3rd fnl stride* **8/1**

326- 4 nse **Ripoll (IRE)**[124] 8456 4-8-9 **78** .......... (t) MartinDwyer 12 80
(Sylvester Kirk) *hld up: hdwy 2f out: rdn to chse ldng pair ent fnl f: kpt on same pce: lost 3rd fnl stride* **25/1**

340- 5 hd **Fleeting Visit**[197] 7117 4-9-0 **83** .......... JohnFahy 11 85
(Eve Johnson Houghton) *led: rdn and hdd ent fnl f: no ex* **11/1**

/22- 6 1/2 **Under Attack (IRE)**[364] 1646 4-8-8 **80** .......... (h[1]) KieranShoemark(3) 9 81
(Roger Charlton) *hld up in tch: rdn over 2f out: kpt on ins fnl f but nt pce to get on terms* **5/1**

000- 7 4 **Balmoral Castle**[182] 7546 8-8-13 **89** .......... Pierre-LouisJamin(7) 5 82
(Jonathan Portman) *trckd ldr: rdn over 2f out: wknd over 1f out* **25/1**

00-4 8 nk **Navajo War Dance**[20] 1517 4-8-13 **82** .......... HarryBentley 6 74
(K R Burke) *trckd ldr: rdn wl over 2f out: wknd over 1f out* **4/1[3]**

2m 11.58s (2.78) **Going Correction** +0.05s/f (Good) **8** Ran SP% **116.8**
Speed ratings (Par 107): **90,89,88,88,88 88,84,84**
CSF £10.50 CT £50.83 TOTE £2.50: £1.40, £1.40, £2.60; EX 9.20 Trifecta £33.60.

**Owner** Fiona and Ian Carmichael-Jennings **Bred** Vimal And Gillian Khosla **Trained** Newmarket, Suffolk

**FOCUS**
This was run over 16yds further than advertised. The early pace was steady and it rates as ordinary form for the grade.

T/Plt: £24.50 to a £1 stake. Pool: £153,228.74 - 4,550.19 winning units. T/Qpdt: £4.30 to a £1 stake. Pool: £12,246.03 - 2,100.64 winning units. **Tim Mitchell**

# 1730 NOTTINGHAM (L-H)
### Saturday, April 22

**OFFICIAL GOING: Good to firm (good in places; 8.5)**
Wind: Light across away from the stands Weather: Overcast

## 1965 PARTYPOKER CARL FROCH APPRENTICE H'CAP 5f 8y
**5:30** (5:33) (Class 6) (0-65,65) 4-Y-O+ **£2,587** (£770; £384; £192) **Stalls** High

Form RPR

411 1 **Major Valentine**[10] 1720 5-9-3 **63** .......... BenRobinson(5) 1 73
(John O'Shea) *uns rdr on the way to post: sn chsng ldrs: wnt 2nd 3f out: rdn to ld ins fnl f: r.o* **5/2[1]**

4211 2 1/2 **Roy's Legacy**[9] 1759 8-9-2 **60** .......... CharlieBennett(3) 9 68
(Shaun Harris) *chsd ldr 2f: remained handy: led over 1f out: rdn and hdd ins fnl f: r.o* **14/1**

5133 3 1 3/4 **Frank The Barber (IRE)**[9] 1759 5-8-7 **55** .......... (t) DavidEgan(7) 10 57
(Steph Hollinshead) *chsd ldrs: pushed along 1/2-way: outpcd 2f out: styd on ins fnl f* **14/1**

00-5 4 1/2 **China Excels**[17] 1558 10-9-10 **65** .......... AaronJones 3 65
(Mandy Rowland) *led over 3f: sn rdn: styd on same pce ins fnl f* **33/1**

005- 5 shd **Flicka's Boy**[188] 7386 5-9-10 **65** .......... NathanEvans 6 65
(Tony Coyle) *sn pushed along and prom: rdn over 1f out: no ex ins fnl f* **11/2[3]**

541- 6 1/2 **Chip Or Pellet**[205] 6909 4-8-7 **51** oh2 .......... PhilDennis(3) 8 49
(Nigel Tinkler) *hld up: hdwy over 1f out: r.o: nt rch ldrs* **14/1**

0602 7 1/2 **Doctor Parkes**[7] 1791 11-9-0 **62** .......... MillyNaseb(7) 12 58
(Stuart Williams) *prom: rdn 2f out: styd on same pce fr over 1f out* **11/1**

1445 8 2 **Ambitious Icarus**[10] 1721 8-9-9 **64** .......... (e) EdwardGreatrex 5 59
(Richard Guest) *sn pushed along in rr: sme hdwy whn hung lft and eased fnl f: sddle slipped* **7/1**

500- 9 1/2 **Whitecrest**[191] 7303 9-9-4 **62** .......... GeorgeWood(3) 4 49
(John Spearing) *mid-div: pushed along 1/2-way: wknd over 1f out* **33/1**

0-50 10 1 **Clon Rocket (IRE)**[3] 1887 4-8-3 **51** oh3 .......... MeganEllingworth(7) 7 35
(John Holt) *s.i.s: nvr on terms* **50/1**

000- 11 3 1/2 **Show Palace**[178] 7626 4-9-10 **65** .......... AdamMcNamara 2 36
(Jennie Candlish) *s.i.s and hung lft s: towards rr: rdn and wknd over 1f out* **4/1[2]**

0-00 12 2 **Bilash**[57] 901 10-8-10 **51** oh3 .......... JackDuern 11 15
(Sarah Hollinshead) *chsd ldrs: rdn 1/2-way: wknd over 1f out* **33/1**

58.64s (-2.86) **Going Correction** -0.50s/f (Hard) **12** Ran SP% **115.6**
Speed ratings (Par 101): **102,101,98,97,97 96,95,92,91,90 84,81**
CSF £37.92 CT £417.04 TOTE £3.20: £1.40, £3.00, £3.50; EX 28.60 Trifecta £102.60.

**Owner** Pete Smith **Bred** J R Salter **Trained** Elton, Gloucs

**FOCUS**
A low-grade but competitive sprint handicap, although the first two came clear. The winner could do a bit better still.

## 1966 PARTYPOKER LIVE MILLIONS NOVICE STKS 5f 8y
**6:00** (6:02) (Class 5) 2-Y-O **£3,234** (£962; £481; £240) **Stalls** High

Form RPR

1 **Simmy's Copshop** 2-9-2 0 .......... PaulHanagan 3 84+
(Richard Fahey) *chsd ldrs: shkn up to ld wl ins fnl f: r.o* **11/4[2]**

2 1/2 **Havana Grey** 2-9-2 0 .......... PJMcDonald 8 82+
(K R Burke) *w ldr tl led over 3f out: rdn: edgd lft and hdd wl ins fnl f: styd on* **5/4[1]**

0 3 2 3/4 **Poignant**[15] 1604 2-9-2 0 .......... JackMitchell 6 72
(Archie Watson) *led: hdd over 3f out: chsd ldr: rdn over 1f out: styd on same pce ins fnl f* **11/2[3]**

4 1 1/4 **Choice Encounter** 2-8-13 0 .......... LouisSteward(3) 4 68+
(Michael Bell) *s.i.s: hld up: shkn up over 1f out: styd on: nt trble ldrs* **14/1**

5 nk **Neola** 2-8-11 0 .......... GrahamLee 1 62
(Mick Channon) *in tch on outer: shkn up over 1f out: no ex ins fnl f* **16/1**

6 4 **Mocead Cappall** 2-8-11 0 .......... RoystonFfrench 7 47
(John Holt) *prom: racd keenly: pushed along 1/2-way: wknd over 1f out* **66/1**

7 1 1/2 **Green Power** 2-8-11 0 .......... GeorgeBuckell(5) 5 47
(John Gallagher) *s.i.s: outpcd* **16/1**

8 15 **Snaffled (IRE)** 2-9-2 0 .......... TedDurcan 2
(David Brown) *sn outpcd* **14/1**

1m 0.29s (-1.21) **Going Correction** -0.50s/f (Hard) **8** Ran SP% **113.1**
Speed ratings (Par 92): **89,88,83,81,81 74,72,48**
CSF £6.37 TOTE £3.10: £1.20, £1.20, £1.60; EX 8.00 Trifecta £28.50.

**Owner** Middleham Park Racing CXX & Partner **Bred** Biddestone Stud Ltd **Trained** Musley Bank, N Yorks

**FOCUS**
Mostly speedily bred types in this juvenile novice stakes. The time was 1.65secs slower than the opening handicap and the market leaders came clear. They both created quite a good impression.

## 1967 HUCKNALL SHEET METAL 40TH ANNIVERSARY MAIDEN STKS 1m 2f 52y
**6:30** (6:30) (Class 5) 3-Y-O **£3,234** (£962; £481; £240) **Stalls** Low

Form RPR

2- 1 **Crystal Ocean**[217] 6577 3-9-5 0 .......... TedDurcan 2 87+
(Sir Michael Stoute) *a.p: chsd ldr over 3f out: led over 2f out: pushed clr fr over 1f out: eased nr fin* **7/4[1]**

56- 2 2 **Okool (FR)**[212] 6704 3-9-5 0 .......... DaneO'Neill 4 79
(Owen Burrows) *hld up in tch: rdn to chse wnr over 1f out: styd on same pce ins fnl f* **7/2[2]**

- 3 1 3/4 **Nathan** 3-9-5 0 .......... (h[1]) RyanPowell 7 76+
(Simon Crisford) *dwlt: hld up: hdwy over 1f out: r.o to go 3rd nr fin: nvr nrr* **33/1**

0 4 1/2 **Immortalised**[21] 1497 3-9-5 0 .......... PJMcDonald 5 75
(K R Burke) *led: hung rt thrght: rdn and hdd over 2f out: styd on same pce fnl f* **16/1[3]**

6- 5 6 **Katmandoo (USA)**[233] 6054 3-9-5 0 .......... RichardKingscote 1 63
(Tom Dascombe) *chsd ldrs: shkn up over 2f out: wknd over 1f out* **20/1**

- 6 1 1/4 **Chief Craftsman** 3-9-5 0 .......... JamieSpencer 9 61
(Luca Cumani) *hld up: shkn up over 3f out: nvr nrr* **16/1[3]**

0 7 1/2 **Theglasgowwarrior**[21] 1497 3-9-2 0 .......... LouisSteward(3) 3 60
(Michael Bell) *hld up: rdn over 3f out: wknd over 2f out* **80/1**

0 8 3/4 **Navajo Grey (IRE)**[22] 1471 3-9-0 0 .......... LiamJones 6 54
(Michael Appleby) *hld up: racd keenly: rdn over 3f out: wknd over 2f out* **100/1**

9 4 1/2 **Forever Song** 3-9-5 0 ........ WilliamBuick 8 50
(Charlie Appleby) *chsd ldr tl shkn up over 3f out: wknd over 1f out: eased* **7/4**[1]

10 3/4 **King Kevin** 3-9-5 0 ........ AntonioFresu 10 49
(Ed Dunlop) *s.i.s: hld up: a in rr: wknd over 2f out* **50/1**

2m 13.19s (-1.11) **Going Correction** -0.50s/f (Hard) **10** Ran SP% **118.6**
Speed ratings (Par 98): **84,82,81,80,75 74,74,73,70,69**
CSF £8.19 TOTE £2.50: £1.10, £1.90, £7.80; EX 9.20 Trifecta £142.60.
**Owner** Sir Evelyn De Rothschild **Bred** Southcourt Stud **Trained** Newmarket, Suffolk

**FOCUS**
Rail movements added 6yds to the race distance. The most interesting race of the night, with some expensive types from major yards contesting this 3yo maiden. The time was 20lb slower than the following handicapo, but the winner was value for extra.

## 1968 LEXUS NOTTINGHAM H'CAP 1m 2f 52y
**7:00** (7:03) (Class 6) (0-65,65) 3-Y-O **£2,587** (£770; £384; £192) **Stalls** Low

Form RPR

5-65 1 **Canberra Cliffs (IRE)**[29] [1348] 3-8-13 **62** ........ GeorgeWood(5) 4 72+
(Don Cantillon) *chsd ldrs: wnt 2nd over 3f out: led over 2f out: rdn over 1f out: styd on wl* **7/2**[1]

501- 2 3 **King's Coinage (IRE)**[177] [7640] 3-9-7 **65** ........(h) LiamKeniry 2 67
(Ed Walker) *hld up in tch: rdn over 2f out: styd on to go 2nd post* **10/1**

60-0 3 shd **Baker Street**[24] [1428] 3-9-1 **59** ........ RichardKingscote 1 61
(Tom Dascombe) *sn led: pushed along over 4f out: rdn and hdd over 2f out: styd on same pce fnl f* **25/1**

30-0 4 2 1/2 **Patching**[30] [1333] 3-9-7 **65** ........ JackMitchell 11 62+
(Giles Bravery) *hld up: hdwy over 2f out: nt rch ldrs* **25/1**

006- 5 1 1/4 **Magic Beans**[158] [7963] 3-8-13 **62** ........ CharlieBennett(5) 13 57
(Hughie Morrison) *hdwy over 8f out: rdn over 2f out: styd on same pce fr over 1f out* **7/1**[3]

440- 6 nk **Zamadance**[184] [7482] 3-9-5 **63** ........ AntonioFresu 3 57
(Ed Dunlop) *hld up in tch: racd keenly: rdn over 2f out: styd on* **12/1**

4-44 7 2 3/4 **Tewafeedj**[43] [1122] 3-9-7 **65** ........ KevinStott 6 54
(Kevin Ryan) *chsd ldrs: wnt 2nd over 8f out tl over 6f out: remained handy: rdn over 2f out: wknd fnl f* **5/1**[2]

3560 8 1/2 **Naupaka**[25] [1411] 3-8-9 **60** ........ BenRobinson(7) 5 48+
(Brian Ellison) *s.i.s: in rr: rdn over 3f out: nvr on terms* **25/1**

4446 9 1/2 **Born To Reason (IRE)**[39] [1195] 3-9-3 **61** ........(t[1]) RyanPowell 15 48
(Kevin Frost) *broke wl: plld hrd: sn stdd and lost pl: nvr on terms after* **25/1**

0460 10 2 **Navajo Star (IRE)**[23] [1445] 3-8-8 **52** ........ LiamJones 9 35
(Michael Appleby) *mid-div: hdwy over 7f out: chsd ldr over 6f out: pushed along over 4f out: lost 2nd over 3f out: wknd wl over 1f out* **50/1**

505- 11 2 **Holyroman Princess**[214] [6648] 3-9-0 **58** ........ SteveDrowne 7 38
(Rod Millman) *mid-div: rdn over 2f out: sn wknd* **14/1**

655- 12 1/2 **Kitsey (IRE)**[210] [6762] 3-9-6 **64** ........ TomMarquand 12 43
(Richard Hannon) *prom: lost pl 6f out: rdn and wknd over 2f out* **8/1**

0-14 13 1 1/4 **African Grey**[43] [1123] 3-9-4 **62** ........(b) PhillipMakin 10 38
(David Barron) *hld up: rdn over 2f out: nvr on terms* **12/1**

64-4 14 13 **Bizet (IRE)**[16] [1584] 3-9-7 **65** ........(p) DaneO'Neill 8 17
(John Ryan) *s.i.s: a in rr* **25/1**

00-0 15 8 **Unzipped**[12] [1685] 3-9-2 **60** ........ CamHardie 16
(Stuart Edmunds) *prom: lost pl over 7f out: rdn over 3f out: sn wknd* **33/1**

2m 11.3s (-3.00) **Going Correction** -0.50s/f (Hard) **15** Ran SP% **117.8**
Speed ratings (Par 96): **92,89,89,87,86 86,84,83,83,81 80,79,78,68,61**
CSF £32.44 CT £669.19 TOTE £4.50: £2.20, £3.30, £4.70; EX 46.40 Trifecta £641.80.
**Owner** Mrs Catherine Reed **Bred** Barry Davis **Trained** Newmarket, Suffolk

**FOCUS**
Rail movements added 6yds to the race distance. A big field for this moderate 3yo handicap, which was run 1.89secs faster than the preceding maiden. The winner built on previous promise.

## 1969 1ST SECURITY H'CAP 1m 72y
**7:30** (7:31) (Class 4) (0-80,84) 4-Y-O+ **£5,175** (£1,540; £769; £384) **Stalls** Centre

Form RPR

250- 1 **Reaver (IRE)**[195] [7189] 4-9-7 **80** ........ CharlesBishop 13 89
(Eve Johnson Houghton) *hld up: hdwy over 1f out: rdn to ld ins fnl f: r.o* **25/1**

/05- 2 1/2 **Wannabe Friends**[323] [2861] 4-9-3 **76** ........ JamieSpencer 3 83+
(Luca Cumani) *hld up: hdwy over 1f out: r.o u.p to go 2nd nr fin* **3/1**[2]

-261 3 1/2 **Roller**[5] [1832] 4-9-8 **84** 6ex ........ NathanEvans(3) 8 90
(Michael Easterby) *a.p: led over 1f out: rdn and hdd ins fnl f: styd on same pce* **2/1**[1]

22-0 4 2 **Brilliant Vanguard (IRE)**[20] [1512] 4-9-6 **79** ........ KevinStott 2 81
(Kevin Ryan) *s.i.s: hld up: hdwy u.p over 1f out: styd on* **12/1**

06-0 5 nk **Gambit**[20] [1512] 4-9-3 **76** ........ RichardKingscote 7 77
(Tom Dascombe) *hld up: hdwy over 2f out: rdn and ev ch 1f out: styd on same pce wl ins fnl f* **16/1**

210- 6 5 **British Embassy (IRE)**[168] [7813] 5-9-1 **79** ........(h) RyanWhile(5) 9 69
(Bill Turner) *sn led: clr over 5f out tl rdn over 2f out: hdd over 1f out: wknd fnl f* **66/1**

212- 7 1/2 **Zlatan (IRE)**[178] [7619] 4-9-4 **77** ........(p) ThomasBrown 1 65
(Ed de Giles) *sn prom: chsd ldr over 2f out: ev ch over 1f out: wknd ins fnl f* **20/1**

5553 8 3/4 **House Of Commons (IRE)**[11] [1700] 4-9-1 **77** ........ AlistairRawlinson(3) 6 64
(Michael Appleby) *chsd ldr: rdn over 2f out: wknd fnl f* **8/1**[3]

00-4 9 1 1/4 **Character Onesie (IRE)**[12] [1677] 5-9-2 **75** ........ PaulHanagan 12 59
(Richard Fahey) *s.i.s: hld up: nvr nrr* **10/1**

50-0 10 1 3/4 **Royal Reserve**[24] [1422] 4-9-1 **74** ........ StevieDonohoe 11 54
(Ian Williams) *hld up: a in rr* **50/1**

1040 11 3 1/4 **Hernando Torres**[21] [1498] 9-8-8 **67** ........ CamHardie 10 39
(Michael Easterby) *s.s: a in rr* **50/1**

0-00 12 2 3/4 **Ellaal**[11] [1700] 8-8-13 **72** ........ JamesSullivan 14 38
(Ruth Carr) *prom tl wknd over 2f out* **66/1**

60-3 13 7 **Thundering Blue (USA)**[22] [1462] 4-9-2 **75** ........ DavidNolan 5 25
(David Menuisier) *plld hrd and prom: n.m.r and lost pl after 1f: rdn and wknd over 2f out* **8/1**[3]

010- 14 16 **Acrux**[220] [6484] 4-9-7 **80** ........ TedDurcan 4
(David Lanigan) *plld hrd and prom: wknd wl over 1f out: eased fnl f* **16/1**

1m 43.22s (-5.78) **Going Correction** -0.50s/f (Hard) course record **14** Ran SP% **124.6**
Speed ratings (Par 105): **108,107,107,105,104 99,99,98,97,95 92,89,82,66**
CSF £99.24 CT £237.83 TOTE £22.60: £4.70, £1.70, £1.70; EX 148.80 Trifecta £704.30.
**Owner** Anthony Pye-Jeary **Bred** Kildaragh Stud **Trained** Blewbury, Oxon

**FOCUS**
Rail movements added 6yds to the race distance. The feature race and a fair mile handicap, they went a strong early gallop and the first two came from well off the pace, breaking the track record in the process.

## 1970 PARTYPOKER POWERFEST H'CAP 5f 8y
**8:00** (8:00) (Class 5) (0-75,77) 3-Y-O **£3,234** (£962; £481; £240) **Stalls** High

Form RPR

022- 1 **Tallinski (IRE)**[331] [2617] 3-9-2 **77** ........ BenRobinson(7) 9 80
(Brian Ellison) *s.i.s: hld up: hdwy 1/2-way: shkn up whn rdr dropped whip over 1f out: r.o to ld nr fin* **12/1**

0-00 2 shd **Stringybark Creek**[12] [1688] 3-8-9 **63** ........ GrahamLee 8 65
(Mick Channon) *hld up: rdn and r.o ins fnl f: wnt 2nd post: nt quite rch wnr* **20/1**

1 3 shd **Suwaan (IRE)**[22] [1474] 3-9-2 **70** ........ JamesSullivan 1 72+
(Ruth Carr) *stmbld sn after s: plld hrd and prom: led over 3f out: rdn ins fnl f: hdd nr fin* **7/2**[2]

521- 4 2 **Desert Sport (USA)**[166] [7845] 3-9-7 **75** ........ JamieSpencer 2 70
(Robert Cowell) *chsd ldrs: rdn and ev ch over 1f out: styd on same pce ins fnl f* **11/4**[1]

353- 5 hd **The Big Short**[178] [7615] 3-8-6 **60** ........ FrannyNorton 11 54
(Charles Hills) *chsd ldrs: rdn and ev ch over 1f out: styd on same pce ins fnl f* **13/2**

152- 6 hd **Fabric**[194] [7217] 3-9-6 **74** ........ TomMarquand 4 68
(Richard Hannon) *led: hdd over 3f out: chsd ldr: rdn over 1f out: styd on same pce* **7/2**[2]

3-00 7 2 3/4 **Lightoller (IRE)**[14] [1625] 3-8-11 **65** ........ GeorgeDowning 3 49
(Mick Channon) *chsd ldrs: lost pl over 3f out: wknd over 1f out* **28/1**

250- 8 3 **Champion Harbour (IRE)**[211] [6743] 3-8-8 **62** ........ PaulHanagan 6 35
(Richard Fahey) *hld up: bhd fnl 3f* **6/1**[3]

59.32s (-2.18) **Going Correction** -0.50s/f (Hard) **8** Ran SP% **114.6**
Speed ratings (Par 98): **97,96,96,93,93 92,88,83**
CSF £213.35 CT £1026.55 TOTE £8.00: £1.20, £5.50, £1.70; EX 179.90 Trifecta £1057.60.
**Owner** Mrs J A Martin **Bred** Colin Kennedy **Trained** Norton, N Yorks

**FOCUS**
An ordinary 3yo sprint. The time was 0.68secs slower than the earlier handicap over the trip and it produced a blanket finish.
T/Plt: £23.80 to a £1 stake. Pool: £55,160.56 - 1,688.45 winning units. T/Qpdt: £13.40 to a £1 stake. Pool: £5,381.86 - 295.08 winning units. **Colin Roberts**

# THIRSK (L-H)
Saturday, April 22

**OFFICIAL GOING: Good to firm (good in places; watered; 8.6)**
Wind: Moderate across Weather: Sunny periods

## 1971 BOOK AT THIRSKRACECOURSE.NET FOR DISCOUNTED ENTRY H'CAP (DIV I) 6f
**1:50** (1:50) (Class 5) (0-75,76) 4-Y-O+ **£3,234** (£962; £481; £240) **Stalls** High

Form RPR

-411 1 **Foolaad**[22] [1472] 6-9-9 **76** ........(t) BenCurtis 6 89
(Roy Bowring) *trckd ldrs: hdwy over 2f out: rdn to ld ent fnl f: sn edgd rt: drvn out* **3/1**[1]

-131 2 nk **Zylan (IRE)**[6] [1819] 5-8-11 **71** 6ex ........ BenSanderson(7) 11 83
(Roger Fell) *in tch on inner: swtchd lft and hdwy over 2f out: rdn to chse ldrs over 1f out: chsd wnr and edgd lft ins fnl f: kpt on* **7/2**[2]

0-30 3 2 1/2 **Compton Park**[14] [1631] 10-8-11 **69** ........ LewisEdmunds(5) 12 73
(Les Eyre) *dwlt and rr: hdwy 2f out: rdn over 1f out: styd on wl fnl f* **9/1**

35-0 4 hd **African Blessing**[32] [1296] 4-9-1 **68** ........ PhillipMakin 9 71
(David Barron) *trckd ldrs: hdwy over 2f out: rdn along wl over 1f out: kpt on same pce* **5/1**[3]

140- 5 shd **Meandmyshadow**[159] [7959] 9-9-0 **72** ........(b) JoshDoyle(5) 2 75
(Alan Brown) *cl up: led wl over 2f out: rdn over 1f out: hdd and drvn ent fnl f: grad wknd* **33/1**

120- 6 1 1/4 **Alpine Dream (IRE)**[182] [7540] 4-9-6 **73** ........(b) CamHardie 5 72
(Tim Easterby) *towards rr: hdwy on outer wl over 1f out: sn rdn and kpt on fnl f* **20/1**

0-66 7 1/2 **Classic Pursuit**[24] [1419] 6-9-0 **67** ........(p) RoystonFfrench 13 64
(Michael Appleby) *a towards rr* **12/1**

600- 8 2 1/4 **Fyrecracker (IRE)**[176] [7663] 6-8-9 **62** ........ PaulHanagan 7 52
(Grant Tuer) *chsd ldrs: rdn along 2f out: sn wknd* **9/1**

003- 9 1 3/4 **Racquet**[187] [7415] 4-9-7 **74** ........ JamesSullivan 1 59
(Ruth Carr) *a towards rr* **16/1**

6-53 10 2 3/4 **Storm Trooper (IRE)**[66] [743] 6-8-12 **65** ........ BarryMcHugh 3 41
(Marjorie Fife) *qckly away and slt ld: rdn along and hdd wl over 2f out: wknd over 1f out* **12/1**

0-00 11 9 **Be Bold**[24] [1431] 5-9-2 **69** ........ DanielTudhope 10 16
(Rebecca Bastiman) *chsd ldrs: rdn along over 2f out: sn wknd* **33/1**

1m 11.69s (-1.01) **Going Correction** +0.025s/f (Good) **11** Ran SP% **115.8**
Speed ratings (Par 103): **107,106,103,103,102 101,100,97,95,91 79**
CSF £12.73 CT £83.29 TOTE £4.80: £1.50, £1.40, £3.10; EX 13.20 Trifecta £88.00.
**Owner** K Nicholls **Bred** Darley **Trained** Edwinstowe, Notts

**FOCUS**
Rail movements increased distances in races 4, 6 and 7 by 20yds. The going was good to firm (good in places) for the opener, an average sprint handicap in which the winner came up the stands' rail.

## 1972 BOOK AT THIRSKRACECOURSE.NET FOR DISCOUNTED ENTRY H'CAP (DIV II) 6f
**2:20** (2:23) (Class 5) (0-75,75) 4-Y-O+ **£3,234** (£962; £481; £240) **Stalls** High

Form RPR

053- 1 **Ancient Astronaut**[179] [7590] 4-9-4 **72** ........(h) JasonHart 12 81
(John Quinn) *towards rr and n.m.r on inner: sn swtchd lft and hdwy 2f out: rdn to chse ldrs over 1f out: swtchd rt and chal ent fnl f: styd on wl to ld last 100 yds* **9/4**[1]

0-60 2 3/4 **Willbeme**[22] [1475] 9-8-12 **66** ........ AndrewMullen 5 73
(Neville Bycroft) *cl up: rdn to ld wl over 1f out: jnd and drvn ent fnl f: hdd and no ex last 100 yds* **12/1**

321- 3 1 3/4 **Questo**[172] [7747] 5-8-7 **61** ........ RoystonFfrench 2 62
(Tracy Waggott) *trckd ldrs: hdwy on outer and cl up over 2f out: rdn and ev ch over 1f out: drvn and kpt on same pce fnl f* **8/1**[3]

30-0 4 nk **Specialv (IRE)**[18] [1542] 4-9-2 **70** ........ BenCurtis 11 70
(Brian Ellison) *dwlt and rr: rdn along and hdwy wl over 1f out: kpt on fnl f* **11/1**

23-1 **5** *1* **Epeius (IRE)**[38] 1203 4-8-11 **65** GrahamLee 7 62
(Ben Haslam) *hld up: hdwy on outer over 2f out: rdn to chse ldrs over 1f out: drvn and kpt on same pce fnl f* **6/1**[2]

104- **6** *nk* **Wilde Extravagance (IRE)**[212] 6717 4-9-1 **69** JoeDoyle 9 65
(Julie Camacho) *towards rr: pushed along and hdwy 2f out: rdn to chse ldrs jst over 1f out: kpt on same pce* **9/1**

20-0 **7** *2 ¾* **Bop It**[5] 1833 8-8-13 **70** (t) NathanEvans(3) 6 57
(Michael Easterby) *chsd ldng pair: rdn along over 2f out: drvn wl over 1f out: wknd* **17/2**

6-00 **8** *2 ¾* **Foresight (FR)**[38] 1202 4-9-7 **75** TomEaves 3 53
(Kevin Ryan) *a towards rr* **12/1**

000- **9** *¾* **Etienne Gerard**[190] 7324 5-8-12 **73** (p) FayeMcManoman(7) 8 49
(Nigel Tinkler) *t.k.h: chsd ldrs on inner: n.m.r 1/2-way: nt clr run 2f out: n.d after* **33/1**

0115 **10** *½* **Top Of The Bank**[14] 1631 4-9-5 **73** (p) TonyHamilton 10 47
(Kristin Stubbs) *slt ld: rdn along over 2f out: drvn and hdd wl over 1f out: sn wknd* **6/1**[2]

1m 12.48s (-0.22) **Going Correction** +0.025s/f (Good) **10** Ran SP% **117.6**
Speed ratings (Par 103): **102,101,98,98,96 96,92,89,88,87**
CSF £32.01 CT £192.66 TOTE £2.90: £1.10, £4.30, £2.80; EX 43.60 Trifecta £197.10.
**Owner** Harlen Ltd **Bred** D R Botterill **Trained** Settrington, N Yorks
■ Stewards' Enquiry : Faye McManoman caution; careless riding

**FOCUS**
The second division of this sprint handicap and the winner came more towards the stands' rail than the rest. There was an overly strong pace, resulting in a slower time than the opener.

## 1973 HAMBLETON SUITE - YOUR PERFECT RECEPTION VENUE (S) STKS 5f
**2:55** (2:56) (Class 6) 3-5-Y-0 **£2,726** (£805; £402) **Stalls** High

Form RPR

-031 **1** **Noah Amor (IRE)**[12] 1674 4-9-7 65 ConnorMurtagh(7) 1 70+
(Richard Fahey) *wnt lft s: prom on outer: hdwy 2f out: rdn to ld over 1f out: edgd rt ins fnl f: kpt on* **11/8**[1]

6-0 **2** *1* **Mr Skinnylegs**[20] 1513 3-8-10 0 BenCurtis 6 54
(Brian Ellison) *trckd ldrs on inner: hdwy wl over 1f out: rdn to chse wnr ins fnl f: kpt on* **8/1**

4160 **3** *1 ½* **Roaring Rory**[10] 1722 4-9-9 64 (p) LewisEdmunds(5) 4 61
(Ollie Pears) *towards rr: hdwy 2f out: rdn to chse ldrs over 1f out: n.m.r ent fnl f: kpt on same pce* **9/4**[2]

0065 **4** *1 ½* **Silhuette (IRE)**[16] 1593 4-9-1 65 (p) RoystonFfrench 7 42
(Colin Teague) *dwlt and rr: hdwy wl over 1f out: sn rdn and no imp* **11/2**[3]

-506 **5** *3 ¾* **Violet Mist (IRE)**[10] 1715 3-8-5 46 (p[1]) CamHardie 8 25
(Ben Haslam) *cl up: rdn along 2f out: sltly hmpd over 1f out: sn one pce* **50/1**

6060 **6** *1 ½* **Whispering Wolf**[43] 1126 4-9-1 44 TomEaves 5 23
(Suzzanne France) *chsd ldrs: rdn along 2f out: sn drvn and wknd* **25/1**

4-60 **7** *1 ½* **George Bailey (IRE)**[28] 1371 5-9-6 44 BarryMcHugh 2 23
(Suzzanne France) *a towards rr* **16/1**

0506 **8** *nk* **Flying Hope (IRE)**[10] 1715 3-8-0 46 ow2 (p[1]) BenSanderson(7) 9 15
(Nigel Tinkler) *led: rdn along: hung lft and hdd over 1f out: edgd rt and wknd ent fnl f* **20/1**

630- **9** *6* **Precious Skye (IRE)**[280] 4404 3-8-5 52 JimmyQuinn 3
(Ronald Thompson) *rrd s: sn in tch: rdn along 1/2-way: sn outpcd and bhd* **50/1**

59.33s (-0.27) **Going Correction** +0.025s/f (Good)
**WFA** 3 from 4yo+ 10lb **9** Ran SP% **117.8**
Speed ratings (Par 101): **103,101,99,96,90 88,85,85,75**
CSF £13.31 TOTE £2.30: £1.10, £2.20, £1.20; EX 12.00 Trifecta £39.10.There was no bid for the winner.
**Owner** Middleham Park Racing XVI & Partner **Bred** Mrs Claire Doyle **Trained** Musley Bank, N Yorks

**FOCUS**
A weak seller lacking many in-form contenders bar the favourite, who did what was expected. The winner can match his previous level of form.

## 1974 EBFSTALLIONS.COM MICHAEL FOSTER CONDITIONS STKS 7f
**3:30** (3:32) (Class 3) 4-Y-0+
**£9,337** (£2,796; £1,398; £699; £349; £175) **Stalls** Low

Form RPR

2050 **1** **Rene Mathis (GER)**[21] 1491 7-9-2 100 PaulHanagan 4 101
(Richard Fahey) *in tch: hdwy on outer 3f out: rdn to ld over 1f out: drvn out* **4/1**[3]

50-6 **2** *1 ½* **Custom Cut (IRE)**[21] 1493 8-9-2 110 DanielTudhope 5 97
(David O'Meara) *trckd ldng pair: cl up 1/2-way: rdn to ld 2f out: hdd over 1f out: sn drvn and kpt on* **1/1**[1]

54-5 **3** *½* **Mount Tahan (IRE)**[21] 1492 5-9-2 91 KevinStott 6 96
(Kevin Ryan) *hld up in tch: hdwy on inner over 2f out: rdn to chal and ev ch over 1f out: drvn and kpt on same pce fnl f* **10/3**[2]

520- **4** *1* **Miracle Of Medinah**[210] 6764 6-9-2 94 StevieDonohoe 3 93
(Mark Usher) *led 1f: prom: rdn along over 2f out: drvn wl over 1f out: kpt on same pce* **12/1**

450- **5** *¾* **Kentuckyconnection (USA)**[224] 6328 4-9-2 102 (b) ConnorBeasley 1 91
(Bryan Smart) *cl up: led after 1f: rdn along over 3f out: hdd 2f out: sn drvn and wknd fnl f* **17/2**

**6** *10* **Konig Dax (GER)**[404] 7-9-2 0 TomEaves 2 64
(Alistair Whillans) *a rr: outpcd and bhd fnl 3f* **100/1**

1m 26.33s (-0.87) **Going Correction** +0.025s/f (Good) **6** Ran SP% **112.3**
Speed ratings (Par 107): **105,103,102,101,100 89**
CSF £8.46 TOTE £4.70: £1.50, £1.70; EX 11.80 Trifecta £20.00.
**Owner** Dr Marwan Koukash **Bred** Stall 5-Stars **Trained** Musley Bank, N Yorks

**FOCUS**
The race distance was increased by 20yds for the feature race in which they went a good gallop, though five of the six runners finished close-up, throwing some doubts over the form. The favourite was below par too.

## 1975 WATCH RACING UK IN HD H'CAP 5f
**4:05** (4:06) (Class 3) (0-95,88) 3-Y-0 **£7,762** (£2,310; £1,154; £577) **Stalls** High

Form RPR

105- **1** **Dakota Gold**[203] 6950 3-8-12 **79** ConnorBeasley 2 91
(Michael Dods) *hld up: smooth hdwy on outer over 2f out: rdn to ld ent fnl f: sn drvn and kpt on strly* **9/1**

601- **2** *2* **Computable**[193] 7248 3-8-12 **79** DavidAllan 6 84+
(Tim Easterby) *hld up: hdwy 2f out: rdn to chse ldrs over 1f out: kpt on u.p fnl f* **5/1**[2]

1210 **3** *1 ¼* **Jack Flash (FR)**[10] 1731 3-8-12 **79** JasonHart 1 79
(Les Eyre) *cl up: led 2f out: rdn over 1f out: drvn: edgd lft and hdd ent fnl f: kpt on same pce* **16/1**

00-0 **4** *1 ½* **Tahoo (IRE)**[13] 1660 3-8-13 **85** CliffordLee(5) 11 80+
(K R Burke) *towards rr: nt clr run over 2f out and sn swtchd lft: hdwy over 1f out: n.m.r and swtchd lft to outer ins fnl f: styd on: nrst fin* **14/1**

345- **5** *nse* **Megan Lily (IRE)**[158] 7972 3-9-0 **88** ConnorMurtagh(7) 9 82
(Richard Fahey) *chsd ldrs: rdn along 2f out: kpt on same pce fnl f* **12/1**

0-12 **6** *nk* **Scuzeme**[10] 1731 3-8-13 **80** PhillipMakin 4 73
(David Barron) *t.k.h early: chsd ldrs on outer: rdn along and hld whn n.m.r 1f out* **11/2**[3]

42-0 **7** *nk* **Blue Suede (IRE)**[10] 1731 3-8-10 **77** TonyHamilton 5 69
(Richard Fahey) *t.k.h: chsd ldrs: rdn over 1f out: kpt on same pce* **8/1**

103- **8** *1* **Franca Florio (IRE)**[224] 6322 3-8-6 **73** JoeDoyle 3 62
(Kevin Ryan) *dwlt and swtchd rt to stands rail s: bhd tl hdwy on inner over 1f out: n.d* **12/1**

03-3 **9** *2 ¼* **Plata O Plomo**[10] 1732 3-9-4 **85** BarryMcHugh 7 66
(Tony Coyle) *slt ld: rdn along 1/2-way: sn hdd: drvn and wknd over 1f out* **15/2**

223- **10** *2 ¼* **Valentino Boy (IRE)**[348] 2090 3-9-2 **83** TomEaves 10 55
(Brian Ellison) *chsd ldrs on inner: rdn along 1/2-way: sn wknd* **25/1**

-203 **11** *2 ½* **Hemingway (IRE)**[11] 1702 3-9-0 **81** (p) ShaneGray 8 44
(Kevin Ryan) *rr and rdn along over 3f out: a bhd* **7/2**[1]

58.45s (-1.15) **Going Correction** +0.025s/f (Good) **11** Ran SP% **118.9**
Speed ratings (Par 102): **110,106,104,102,102 101,101,99,96,92 88**
CSF £54.23 CT £736.00 TOTE £10.30: £3.00, £2.40, £4.40; EX 67.50 Trifecta £1789.10 Part won..
**Owner** Doug Graham & Ron Davison **Bred** Redgate Bstock & Peter Bottowley Bstock **Trained** Denton, Co Durham

**FOCUS**
A competitive 3yo sprint handicap with a good history and they went a good pace. There should be plenty of winners to emerge during the coming weeks.

## 1976 NEW "CHERRY TREE" PREMIER RACEGOERS' PACKAGE H'CAP 1m 4f 8y
**4:40** (4:40) (Class 3) (0-90,89) 4-Y-0+ **£7,762** (£2,310; £1,154; £577) **Stalls** High

Form RPR

630- **1** **Gabrial's King (IRE)**[210] 6781 8-9-4 **86** TonyHamilton 5 90
(Richard Fahey) *hld up towards rr: hdwy over 2f out: chsd ldrs whn nt clr run and swtchd rt to outer over 1f out: rdn ent fnl f: styd on strly to ld towards fin* **7/1**

21-0 **2** *¾* **Airton**[10] 1719 4-8-6 **75** oh1 JamesSullivan 6 76
(James Bethell) *hld up towards rr: hdwy over 2f out: chsd ldrs over 1f out: sn rdn: led ins fnl f: drvn and hdd towards fin* **8/1**

-245 **3** *½* **Dolphin Village (IRE)**[21] 1504 7-9-1 **83** (h) AndrewMullen 7 83
(Shaun Harris) *hld up in rr: hdwy over 3f out: chal on outer 2f out: sn rdn: drvn and ev ch ins fnl f: kpt on* **16/1**

000- **4** *¾* **Green Light**[109] 7546 6-9-6 **88** TomEaves 3 87
(Brian Ellison) *trckd ldrs: hdwy over 4f out: cl up on outer over 3f out: rdn to ld wl over 1f out: drvn and hdd jst ins fnl f: kpt on* **14/1**

0-00 **5** *1* **Top Of The Glas (IRE)**[20] 1517 6-8-7 **80** MeganNicholls(5) 10 77
(Brian Ellison) *hld up and bhd: detached 1/2-way: hdwy over 2f out: rdn and kpt on fnl f* **8/1**

300- **6** *hd* **Swaheen**[178] 7624 5-9-0 **82** JoeDoyle 4 79
(Julie Camacho) *in tch: hdwy 2f out: rdn over 1f out: kpt on fnl f* **9/2**[2]

00-6 **7** *nse* **Mukhayyam**[10] 1719 5-9-0 **85** (p) RachelRichardson(3) 9 82
(Tim Easterby) *trckd ldrs: hdwy on outer to ld over 3f out: rdn along and hdd wl over 1f out: cl up tl drvn and wknd ent fnl f* **10/3**[1]

306- **8** *4 ½* **Saved By The Bell (IRE)**[218] 6540 7-9-7 **89** DanielTudhope 8 79
(David O'Meara) *cl up: rdn along 3f out: drvn and wknd fnl 2f* **11/2**[3]

50-0 **9** *21* **Sikandar (IRE)**[20] 1517 5-8-8 **76** (t) BenCurtis 1 32
(Brian Ellison) *led after 1f: pushed along over 4f out: rdn and hdd over 2f out: sn wknd* **18/1**

113- **10** *5* **The Resdev Way**[166] 7847 4-8-9 **78** BarryMcHugh 2 26
(Richard Whitaker) *led 1f: cl up: rdn along over 4f out: wknd over 3f out* **16/1**

2m 37.84s (1.64) **Going Correction** +0.025s/f (Good) **10** Ran SP% **115.1**
Speed ratings (Par 107): **95,94,94,93,93 92,92,89,75,72**
CSF £60.99 CT £863.93 TOTE £7.70: £2.20, £2.90, £4.40; EX 79.30 Trifecta £338.00.
**Owner** Dr Marwan Koukash **Bred** Danella Partnership **Trained** Musley Bank, N Yorks

**FOCUS**
This was run over 20yds further than advertised. A fair handicap if lacking many in-form contenders, and the decent gallop helped set things up for those coming from behind.

## 1977 RACING UK DAY PASS JUST £10 MEDIAN AUCTION MAIDEN STKS 7f
**5:15** (5:16) (Class 5) 3-4-Y-0 **£3,234** (£962; £481; £240) **Stalls** Low

Form RPR

450- **1** **Keyser Soze (IRE)**[203] 6950 3-9-1 83 StevieDonohoe 8 83
(Richard Spencer) *trckd ldrs: smooth hdwy to ld wl over 1f out: clr fnl f* **5/6**[1]

4 **2** *2 ¾* **Komodo (IRE)**[12] 1680 3-9-1 0 JackGarritty 9 75
(Jedd O'Keeffe) *prom: effrt over 2f out: sn rdn: drvn to chse wnr ent fnl f: no imp* **10/3**[2]

400- **3** *1 ¼* **Jamacho**[203] 6954 3-9-1 68 BenCurtis 2 72
(Brian Ellison) *trckd ldr: led after 2f: rdn along 3f out: hdd wl over 1f out: sn drvn and kpt on same pce* **8/1**

**4** *6* **Yorkshire Pudding** 3-8-7 0 RachelRichardson(3) 6 51
(Tim Easterby) *towards rr: hdwy over 2f out: sn rdn and kpt on appr fnl f: n.d* **16/1**

0 **5** *2* **New Tale**[20] 1513 3-9-1 0 DuranFentiman 5 50
(Olly Williams) *led 2f: cl up: rdn along over 2f out: sn drvn and outpcd* **50/1**

000- **6** *2 ¾* **Excellent World (IRE)**[221] 6436 4-9-9 57 BarryMcHugh 3 43
(Tony Coyle) *chsd ldrs: rdn along over 2f out: sn outpcd* **25/1**

60- **7** *1 ½* **Four Kingdoms (IRE)**[172] 7740 3-8-8 0 PatrickO'Hanlon(7) 4 39
(K R Burke) *a rr* **33/1**

4 **8** *1 ½* **Oregon Point (USA)**[20] 1513 3-9-1 0 DavidAllan 1 35
(Tim Easterby) *s.i.s and lost several l s: a bhd* **6/1**[3]

1m 27.03s (-0.17) **Going Correction** +0.025s/f (Good)
**WFA** 3 from 4yo 13lb **8** Ran SP% **117.7**
Speed ratings (Par 103): **101,97,96,89,87 84,82,80**
CSF £3.88 TOTE £1.70: £1.10, £1.40, £2.70; EX 4.80 Trifecta £12.50.
**Owner** Rebel Racing (2) **Bred** J Hanly **Trained** Newmarket, Suffolk

**FOCUS**
The race distance was increased by 20yds for this weak maiden in which the favourite ran out an easy winner. The first three came clear.

## 1978 THIRSK "DISCOVER RACING SUNDAY" 30TH APRIL H'CAP 6f
**5:50** (5:53) (Class 6) (0-60,58) 4-Y-O+ **£3,234** (£962; £481; £240) **Stalls** High

Form RPR
3200 **1** **Kyllach Me (IRE)**[10] 1720 5-9-2 **53**............(v[1]) ConnorBeasley 6 61
(Bryan Smart) *t.k.h: prom far side: hdwy 2f out: rdn over 1f out: led ins fnl f: drvn out: 1st of 8 in gp* **12/1**
040- **2** 1 3/4 **Our Place In Loule**[232] 6100 4-8-13 **50**............ TomEaves 7 53
(Noel Wilson) *cl up far side: slt ld on that side 2f out: rdn and ev ch ent fnl f: sn drvn and kpt on: 2nd of 8 in gp* **33/1**
3643 **3** nse **Penny Dreadful**[10] 1721 5-9-6 **57**............(p) DavidAllan 12 60
(Scott Dixon) *overall ldr stands' side: rdn over 1f out: drvn and hdd ins fnl f: edgd lft and kpt on: 1st of 10 in gp* **7/1[2]**
0333 **4** 1/2 **Hadley**[50] 1006 4-8-13 **50**............(p) TonyHamilton 20 51
(Tracy Waggott) *hld up stands' side: hdwy 2f out: rdn over 1f out: swtchd rt and drvn ins fnl f: kpt on 2nd of 10 in gp* **10/1**
00-0 **5** hd **Dalalah**[10] 1720 4-8-7 **46** ow3............(v) CliffordLee(5) 4 50
(Richard Guest) *trckd ldrs far side: hdwy 2f out: rdn and ev ch ent fnl f: sn drvn and kpt on: 3rd of 8 in gp* **11/1**
034- **6** hd **Young Tiger**[145] 8137 4-9-6 **57**............ AndrewMullen 17 57
(Tom Tate) *towards rr stands' side: hdwy 2f out: rdn to chse ldrs over 1f out: drvn and kpt on fnl f: 3rd of 10 in gp* **11/2[1]**
00-3 **7** 1 **Lackaday**[43] 1126 5-9-7 **58**............(p) BarryMcHugh 1 55
(Noel Wilson) *slt ld far side gp: hdd and rdn along 2f out: drvn over 1f out: kpt on same pce: 4th of 8 in gp* **10/1**
00-5 **8** nk **Secret City (IRE)**[12] 1674 11-8-12 **49**............(b) DuranFentiman 2 45
(Rebecca Bastiman) *in tch far side: rdn along wl over 1f out: kpt on same pce: 5th of 8 in gp* **20/1**
0-03 **9** 1 **A J Cook (IRE)**[12] 1674 7-8-13 **50**............ ShaneGray 8 43
(Ron Barr) *in tch far side: rdn along 2f out: kpt on fnl f: 6th of 8 in gp* **20/1**
600/ **10** nk **New Decade**[656] 1821 8-8-8 **45**............ SamJames 16 37
(Jim Goldie) *in rr stands' side: hdwy over 2f out: sn rdn and edgd lft: no imp 4th of 10 in gp* **50/1**
00-0 **11** 2 1/2 **Pyroclastic (IRE)**[88] 386 5-8-8 **48**............(t[1]) ShelleyBirkett(3) 5 33
(Nick Kent) *chsd ldrs far side: rdn along wl over 1f out: grad wknd: 7th of 8 in gp* **50/1**
400- **12** 3/4 **Carlovian**[155] 8013 4-8-9 **46**............(p[1]) NeilFarley 9 28
(Christopher Kellett) *cl up far side: rdn along 2f out: sn hdd and grad wknd: 8th of 8 in gp* **20/1**
0050 **13** 1 1/2 **Zebelini (IRE)**[23] 1451 5-8-8 **45**............ JimmyQuinn 11 23
(Roy Bowring) *prom stands' side: rdn along 2f out: grad wknd: 5th of 10 in gp* **16/1**
3551 **14** nk **Sea Of Green**[43] 1126 5-8-5 **49**............(p) SeanMooney(7) 13 26
(Jim Goldie) *chsd ldrs stands' side: rdn and edgd lft wl over 1f out: sn drvn and wknd: 5th of 10 in gp* **11/1**
4020 **15** 3/4 **Cadeaux Pearl**[16] 1593 9-8-3 **47**............(b) RPWalsh(7) 18 22
(Scott Dixon) *chsd ldr stands' side: rdn along 2f out: sn drvn and wknd: 6th of 10 in gp* **20/1**
4-40 **16** 2 1/2 **Nuala Tagula (IRE)**[85] 446 4-9-7 **58**............ JasonHart 19 25
(John Quinn) *in tch stands' side: rdn along 2f out: sn wknd: 7th of 10 in gp* **7/1[2]**
020- **17** nk **Tinsill**[165] 7860 6-8-7 **51**............ FayeMcManoman(7) 15 17
(Nigel Tinkler) *hld up stands' side: hdwy over 2f out: rdn wl over 1f out: sn wknd: 8th of 10 in gp* **40/1**
0-00 **18** 2 3/4 **Hab Reeh**[26] 1407 9-8-11 **48**............(p) JackGarritty 10 6
(Ruth Carr) *a towards rr stands' side: 9th of 10 in gp* **25/1**
5043 **19** 6 **One For Jodie (IRE)**[16] 1593 6-9-0 **58**............(p) RayDawson(7) 14
(Michael Appleby) *chsd ldrs stands' side: rdn along over 2f out: sn wknd 10th of 10 in gp* **17/2[3]**

1m 12.74s (0.04) **Going Correction** +0.025s/f (Good) **19** Ran SP% **131.5**
Speed ratings (Par 101): **100,97,97,96,96 95,95,94,93,92 89,88,86,86,85 81,81,77,69**
CSF £382.12 CT £3004.29 TOTE £14.80: £3.80, £8.90, £2.00, £2.20; EX 432.70 Trifecta £1552.80 Part won..
**Owner** The Smart Stoneacre Sarah Partnership **Bred** Tally-Ho Stud **Trained** Hambleton, N Yorks

**FOCUS**
A low-grade, but competitive sprint handicap, in which they split into two groups. The far side (low stalls) held an advantage.
T/Plt: £60.00 to a £1 stake. Pool: £60,887.18 - 740.63 winning units. T/Qpdt: £15.50 to a £1 stake. Pool: £2,838.15 - 135.20 winning units. **Joe Rowntree**

# 1887 WOLVERHAMPTON (A.W) (L-H)
Saturday, April 22

**OFFICIAL GOING: Tapeta: standard**
Wind: Virtually nil Weather: Fine

## 1979 FCL GLOBAL FORWARDING MAKING LOGISTICS PERSONAL AMATEUR RIDERS' H'CAP 6f 20y (Tp)
**5:45** (5:48) (Class 5) (0-70,69) 4-Y-O+ **£2,807** (£870; £435; £217) **Stalls** Low

Form RPR
1340 **1** **Castlerea Tess**[5] 1842 4-10-0 **55**............(p) MissSBrotherton 7 61
(Sarah Hollinshead) *chsd ldr: rdn 2f out: led 1f out: kpt on* **8/1[3]**
1352 **2** 1/2 **Pushkin Museum (IRE)**[3] 1887 6-10-11 **66**............ MrSWalker 3 71
(Patrick Morris) *hld up in tch: pushed along and hdwy to chse ldrs appr fnl f: rdn and one pce ins fnl f: wnt 2nd post* **1/1[1]**
0552 **3** shd **The Magic Pencil (IRE)**[12] 1674 4-10-1 **63**............(v) MissHTLees(7) 4 67
(Kevin Ryan) *sn led: rdn 2f out: hdd 1f out: one pce: lost 2nd post* **11/2[2]**
550- **4** 3 3/4 **Langley Vale**[171] 7774 8-10-7 **65**............(v) MrHHunt(3) 6 63
(Roger Teal) *s.i.s: hld up: bit clsr 1/2-way: hmpd appr fnl f: kpt on but no ch after* **14/1**
1062 **5** 3/4 **All Or Nothin (IRE)**[16] 1593 8-9-12 **55** oh2 ow3............ MissMBryant(5) 9 49
(Paddy Butler) *hld up: pushed along 2f out: kpt on ins fnl f: nvr threatened* **33/1**
606- **6** 3/4 **Spike (IRE)**[212] 6717 4-10-5 **65**............ MissAMcCain(5) 2 53
(Donald McCain) *s.i.s: sn chse ldr: rdn over 2f out: hung lft appr fnl f: wknd ins fnl f* **33/1**
1203 **7** 1 3/4 **Indian Pursuit (IRE)**[10] 1720 4-10-10 **65**............ MrAlexFerguson 1 48
(John Quinn) *chsd ldr: rdn and outpcd 2f out: wknd fnl f* **11/2[2]**
2621 **8** 4 **Beau Mistral (IRE)**[7] 1791 8-10-7 **69**............ MrGGilbertson(7) 8 40
(Tony Carroll) *chsd ldr on outside: rdn over 2f out: wknd over 1f out* **9/1**

1m 14.65s (0.15) **Going Correction** +0.025s/f (Slow) **8** Ran SP% **114.4**
Speed ratings (Par 103): **100,99,99,94,93 92,89,84**
CSF £16.47 CT £47.88 TOTE £9.60: £2.70, £1.10, £1.80; EX 22.60 Trifecta £127.00.
**Owner** Graham Brothers Racing Partnership **Bred** Graham Brothers Racing Partnership **Trained** Upper Longdon, Staffs
■ Stewards' Enquiry : Miss A McCain caution; careless riding

**FOCUS**
Just ordinary sprint handicap form but the pace looked even enough and the favourite had every chance but ultimately proved a touch disappointing. A minor pb from the winner, and the next two fit.

## 1980 FCL GLOBAL FORWARDING H'CAP 6f 20y (Tp)
**6:15** (6:16) (Class 5) (0-70,71) 4-Y-O+ **£3,072** (£914; £456; £228) **Stalls** Low

Form RPR
3235 **1** **Dark Side Dream**[51] 995 5-9-7 **70**............ SilvestreDeSousa 10 78
(Chris Dwyer) *prom on outer: rdn to ld over 1f out: sn drvn: hld on all out* **15/8[1]**
6040 **2** hd **Indian Affair**[33] 1290 7-8-10 **59**............(bt) DavidProbert 2 65
(Milton Bradley) *in tch: rdn to chse wnr over 1f out: kpt on* **9/1**
1450 **3** 1 1/4 **Hamish McGonagain**[14] 1631 4-9-3 **71**............(p) DavidParkes(5) 7 73
(Jeremy Gask) *stdd s: hld up: pushed along and hdwy 2f out: rdn and kpt on fnl f* **10/1**
0114 **4** 1 1/4 **Viva Verglas (IRE)**[24] 1431 6-9-7 **70**............ LukeMorris 5 68
(Daniel Mark Loughnane) *dwlt: hld up in tch: pushed along and sme hdwy whn briefly bit short of room over 1f out: kpt on ins fnl f* **13/2**
3100 **5** 2 1/4 **Dandilion (IRE)**[10] 1722 4-8-8 **57**............(t) KieranO'Neill 6 48
(Alex Hales) *hld up: rdn over 2f out: nvr threatened* **10/1**
6652 **6** 1/2 **Semana Santa**[31] 1310 4-9-7 **70**............ RobHornby 3 60
(David Barron) *prom: rdn and outpcd 1/2-way: grad wknd over 1f out* **9/2[3]**
1123 **7** 2 1/4 **Spirit Of Zebedee (IRE)**[22] 1467 4-9-4 **67**............(v) DougieCostello 1 49
(John Quinn) *led: rdn whn hdd over 1f out: wknd* **4/1[2]**
0-00 **8** 2 1/4 **Secret Clause**[9] 1759 4-8-0 **56** oh3............ JaneElliott(7) 4 31
(Derek Shaw) *midfield: rdn over 2f out: wknd over 1f out* **50/1**

1m 13.53s (-0.97) **Going Correction** +0.025s/f (Slow) **8** Ran SP% **116.4**
Speed ratings (Par 103): **107,106,105,103,100 99,96,93**
CSF £20.64 CT £136.98 TOTE £2.90: £1.30, £2.90, £2.50; EX 21.60 Trifecta £125.50.
**Owner** M M Foulger **Bred** Newsells Park Stud **Trained** Newmarket, Suffolk

**FOCUS**
An opening-looking heat, run at what appeared an even gallop, and the well-backed market leader got the job done, just.

## 1981 CONTACT US ON FCLGF.COM H'CAP 5f 21y (Tp)
**6:45** (6:45) (Class 5) (0-70,71) 4-Y-O+ **£3,072** (£914; £456; £228) **Stalls** Low

Form RPR
1540 **1** **Annie Salts**[18] 1547 4-9-2 **64**............(h) SilvestreDeSousa 1 73
(Chris Dwyer) *mde all: sn pressed: pushed along 2f out: rdn and kpt on wl fnl f: in command fnl 110yds* **6/1[3]**
0352 **2** 2 **Entertaining Ben**[7] 1805 4-8-12 **67**............ JamieGormley(7) 8 69
(Iain Jardine) *pressed ldr: pushed along 2f out: rdn and no ex ins fnl f* **5/1[2]**
1210 **3** nk **You're Cool**[22] 1475 5-9-4 **71**............ LewisEdmunds(5) 2 72
(John Balding) *chsd ldrs: rdn 2f out: kpt on* **9/4[1]**
100 **4** 1 1/4 **K'Gari Spirit**[15] 1599 4-9-6 **68**............(t[1]) MartinLane 3 64
(Jeremy Gask) *hld up: drvn 1/2-way: kpt on fnl f: nvr threatened ldrs* **5/1[2]**
142- **5** shd **Kiringa**[182] 7533 4-9-0 **62**............ AdamBeschizza 6 58
(Robert Cowell) *s.i.s: sn midfield: rdn 2f out: one pce* **9/1**
-502 **6** nk **Vale Of Flight (IRE)**[17] 1558 4-9-1 **63**............ LukeMorris 4 58
(Luke McJannet) *half-rrd s: sn in tch: rdn 1/2-way: wknd ins fnl f* **17/2**
4123 **7** 1 **Powerful Dream (IRE)**[17] 1558 4-9-7 **69**............(p) TomQueally 5 60
(Ronald Harris) *squeezed out s: hld up: pushed along 1/2-way: nvr threatened* **15/2**
4340 **8** 1 3/4 **Temple Road (IRE)**[17] 1558 9-9-3 **65**............(bt) DavidProbert 7 50
(Milton Bradley) *hld up: nvr threatened* **20/1**

1m 0.99s (-0.91) **Going Correction** +0.025s/f (Slow) **8** Ran SP% **115.4**
Speed ratings (Par 103): **108,104,104,102,102 101,100,97**
CSF £36.29 CT £88.06 TOTE £6.20: £2.20, £1.50, £1.30; EX 41.40 Trifecta £90.50.
**Owner** Mrs Shelley Dwyer **Bred** D R Botterill **Trained** Newmarket, Suffolk

**FOCUS**
They seemed to go pretty strong here but the pace held up, with the first three filling those places throughout.

## 1982 FCL GLOBAL FORWARDING MAKING LOGISTICS PERSONAL CLASSIFIED (S) STKS 1m 142y (Tp)
**7:15** (7:15) (Class 6) 3-Y-O+ **£2,425** (£721; £360; £180) **Stalls** Low

Form RPR
4212 **1** **Mr Red Clubs (IRE)**[17] 1562 8-9-4 75............(p) JaneElliott(7) 6 78
(Michael Appleby) *prom: racd keenly: led 3f out: rdn 2f out: kpt on: all out* **6/4[2]**
3122 **2** hd **Spiritual Star (IRE)**[3] 1893 8-9-6 72............ SilvestreDeSousa 1 73
(Lee Carter) *v.s.a: sn hld up in tch racing keenly: trckd ldr over 3f out: rdn over 1f out: carried hd bit awkwardly: one pce: jst hld* **8/11[1]**
-555 **3** 3 1/2 **Dana's Present**[47] 1065 8-9-11 70............ LukeMorris 2 70
(Tom Dascombe) *racd keenly: trckd ldrs: rdn 2f out: wknd ins fnl f* **8/1[3]**
640/ **4** 18 **No Win No Fee**[36] 2961 7-9-6 73............(p) TimmyMurphy 3 25
(Barry Leavy) *led at stdy pce: hdd over 3f out: sn wknd* **50/1**

1m 51.85s (1.75) **Going Correction** +0.025s/f (Slow) **4** Ran SP% **111.0**
Speed ratings (Par 101): **93,92,89,73**
CSF £3.05 TOTE £2.80; EX 4.10 Trifecta £4.20.There was no bid for the winner.
**Owner** Ferrybank Properties Limited **Bred** Tally-Ho Stud **Trained** Oakham, Rutland
■ Stewards' Enquiry : Jane Elliott two-day ban; used whip above the permitted level (8th-9th May)

**FOCUS**
Just four runners and the early pace looked very steady, allowing the slowly away market leader to catch up. All four raced keenly to varying extents in the early stages. There's limited upside in being with this form.

## 1983 WEATHERBYS BANK FOREIGN EXCHANGE H'CAP 1m 142y (Tp)
**7:45** (7:45) (Class 6) (0-65,65) 4-Y-O+ **£2,425** (£721; £360; £180) **Stalls** Low

Form RPR
3612 **1** **Scribner Creek (IRE)**[10] 1735 4-9-6 **64**............ RobertWinston 9 73+
(Daniel Mark Loughnane) *dwlt: hld up: pushed along and hdwy over 1f out: rdn and kpt on fnl f: led towards fin* **9/4[1]**
-032 **2** 1/2 **Sublimation (IRE)**[26] 1406 7-8-6 **57**............ FinleyMarsh(7) 3 64
(Steve Gollings) *in tch: rdn to chse ldrs over 1f out: led narrowly ins fnl f: kpt on but hdd towards fin* **15/2[3]**
031- **3** 1 1/2 **Melgate Melody**[169] 7795 4-8-13 **57**............ PaulMulrennan 8 61
(Michael Easterby) *led: jnd 2f out: sn pushed along: rdn whn hdd ins fnl f: sn no ex* **9/4[1]**
000- **4** nk **Know Your Name**[29] 6737 6-9-4 **62**............ LukeMorris 5 65
(Donald McCain) *trckd ldrs: rdn to join ldr 2f out: no ex fnl 110yds* **14/1**

3003 **5** *1 3/4* **Playtothewhistle**[30] 1330 6-9-0 **65**..............................(v) JaneElliott[(7)] 2 64
(Michael Appleby) *trckd ldr: rdn and outpcd over 2f out: plugged on fnl f* **11/2**[2]

500- **6** *hd* **Berkeley Vale**[157] 7973 6-9-7 **65**..............................(b[1]) JosephineGordon 7 64
(Roger Teal) *hld up: rdn over 2f out: kpt on ins fnl f: nvr threatened* **15/2**[3]

4-56 **7** *1 1/4* **Chelabella**[9] 1758 4-9-1 **59**..............................(v) MartinLane 6 55
(Derek Shaw) *hld up: rdn over 2f out: nvr threatened* **20/1**

61-0 **8** *1 1/2* **Walking In Rhythm (IRE)**[10] 1735 4-8-12 **59**........... SammyJoBell[(3)] 1 52
(Barry Leavy) *fly leapt s: hld up: rdn along 2f out: nvr threatened* **33/1**

011- **9** *2* **Scruffy McGuffy**[243] 5729 4-9-4 **62**.............................. JoeyHaynes 4 51
(Ann Duffield) *midfield on outer: racd quite keenly: pushed along 2f out: sn wknd* **25/1**

1m 50.69s (0.59) **Going Correction** +0.025s/f (Slow) **9** Ran SP% **118.7**
Speed ratings (Par 101): **98,97,96,95,94 94,93,91,90**
CSF £20.78 CT £42.83 TOTE £3.10: £1.10, £2.80, £1.50; EX 24.50 Trifecta £78.00.

**Owner** David Slater **Bred** Holborn Trust Co **Trained** Rock, Worcs

**FOCUS**
A competitive enough heat for the grade but the early gallop looked steady enough, resulting in a few of these racing quite keenly. The winner continues to progress.

## 1984 FCL GLOBAL FORWARDING MAKING LOGISTICS PERSONAL MAIDEN STKS 1m 4f 51y (Tp)
**8:15** (8:15) (Class 5) 3-Y-0+ **£2,911** (£866; £432; £216) **Stalls** Low

Form RPR

2- **1** **Al Zaman (IRE)**[199] 7074 3-8-7 0..............................(t[1]) SilvestreDeSousa 4 81+
(Simon Crisford) *mde all: jnd 11f out: pushed along over 2f out: rdn and styd on and in command fnl f* **1/2**[1]

**2** *2 3/4* **Orsino (IRE)** 3-8-7 0.............................. DavidProbert 10 76
(Andrew Balding) *dwlt: sn jnd ldr: rdn over 2f out: one pce and hld in 2nd fnl f* **9/1**[3]

**3** *8* **Petitioner (IRE)** 3-8-7 0.............................. JosephineGordon 5 63+
(Roger Charlton) *wnt rt s: sn midfield: rn green: pushed along and lost pl over 4f out: only 8th 2f out: styd on: wnt 3rd fnl 110yds: bttr for r* **9/4**[2]

**4** *1 1/2* **Benissimo (IRE)**[21] 7-9-6 0.............................. TobyEley[(7)] 3 62
(Tony Forbes) *hld up: pushed along and sme hdwy over 3f out: kpt on: nvr threatened* **125/1**

0/ **5** *1* **Nachi Falls**[59] 7980 4-9-12 0..............................(t) TomQueally 11 61
(Nigel Hawke) *hld up: pushed along and sme hdwy over 3f out: nvr threatened* **33/1**

**6** *5* **Competition**[32] 5-9-10 0..............................(t) SammyJoBell[(3)] 6 53
(Brian Rothwell) *dwlt: hld up: racd keenly and wnt prom on outside 8f out: rdn 3f out: wknd fnl 2f* **100/1**

0-4 **7** *4* **Sehail (USA)**[24] 1420 4-9-12 0.............................. LukeMorris 8 46
(George Peckham) *trckd ldrs: rdn over 3f out: sn wknd* **33/1**

5 **8** *1 1/2* **Hurricane Hollow**[31] 1308 7-9-13 0.............................. BenCurtis 1 44
(David Barron) *hld up: pushed along over 2f out: nvr threatened* **12/1**

**9** *nse* **Wemyss Point**[13] 5-9-13 0.............................. PaddyAspell 7 44
(Philip Kirby) *midfield: rdn over 4f out: sn wknd* **22/1**

0 **10** *62* **Bite My Tongue (IRE)**[25] 1410 4-9-12 0.............................. JoeyHaynes 2
(Tony Carroll) *midfield: lost pl qckly 8f out: sn in rr: t.o fnl 6f* **125/1**

2m 37.7s (-3.10) **Going Correction** +0.025s/f (Slow)
**WFA** 3 from 4yo+ 20lb **10** Ran SP% **127.9**
Speed ratings (Par 103): **111,109,103,102,102 98,96,95,95,53**
CSF £7.68 TOTE £1.40: £1.02, £2.90, £1.60; EX 10.90 Trifecta £16.40.

**Owner** Abdulla Al Mansoori **Bred** Peter Jones **Trained** Newmarket, Suffolk

**FOCUS**
Not much depth to this maiden and most of these were too inexperienced to make any meaningful impact. The front two came a long way clear and both appear to have bright futures.

## 1985 FCLGF.COM H'CAP 1m 4f 51y (Tp)
**8:45** (8:45) (Class 6) (0-60,61) 4-Y-0+ **£2,587** (£770; £384; £192) **Stalls** Low

Form RPR

-530 **1** **Star Ascending (IRE)**[18] 1545 5-9-3 **55**..............................(p) TomQueally 7 64
(Jennie Candlish) *trckd ldrs: racd quite keenly: led 2f out: rdn over 1f out: edgd rt ent fnl f: drvn and hld on wl* **13/2**[3]

1 **2** *nk* **Bottleofsmoke (IRE)**[26] 1402 4-9-3 **56**..............................(h) RobertWinston 1 65
(Gavin Cromwell, Ire) *in tch: pushed to chse ldrs 2f out: rdn to chal ins fnl f: kpt on but a jst hld* **5/6**[1]

0002 **3** *1 1/4* **Senor George (IRE)**[14] 1629 10-8-10 **48**.............................. LukeMorris 2 55
(Simon Hodgson) *midfield: rdn and sme hdwy over 1f out: styd on fnl f* **9/1**

6001 **4** *1 1/2* **Thorntoun Care**[14] 1629 6-9-2 **61**..............................(b) JamieGormley[(7)] 10 65
(Iain Jardine) *midfield on outside: pushed along and hdwy to chse ldrs 2f out: rdn and no ex ins fnl f* **11/2**[2]

6500 **5** *1 3/4* **Dibloam (USA)**[17] 1563 4-8-8 **47**.............................. KieranO'Neill 3 48
(David Evans) *trckd ldr: led 9f out: rdn over 2f out: hdd 2f out: grad wknd over 1f out* **20/1**

6-0 **6** *shd* **Balmont Belle (IRE)**[26] 1403 7-8-9 **50**.............................. TimClark[(3)] 8 51
(Barry Leavy) *s.i.s: hld up: rdn 2f out: nvr threatened* **25/1**

5000 **7** *3/4* **Barnacle**[38] 1207 8-8-8 **46** oh1..............................(bt) SilvestreDeSousa 4 46
(Emma Owen) *hld up: rdn along over 2f out: nvr threatened* **20/1**

300- **8** *hd* **Ballyfarsoon (IRE)**[172] 7739 6-8-13 **58**.............................. LukeCatton[(7)] 6 58
(Ian Williams) *hld up: rdn 2f out: nvr threatened* **25/1**

4330 **9** *6* **Stonecoldsoba**[35] 1256 4-9-7 **60**.............................. DannyBrock 9 50
(Denis Quinn) *led: hdd 9f out: trckd ldr: pushed along and lost pl over 3f out: wknd over 1f out* **10/1**

2m 42.45s (1.65) **Going Correction** +0.025s/f (Slow) **9** Ran SP% **119.6**
Speed ratings (Par 101): **95,94,93,92,91 91,91,91,87**
CSF £12.19 CT £50.29 TOTE £8.50: £2.70, £1.10, £1.30; EX 20.80 Trifecta £98.60.

**Owner** Paul Wright-Bevans **Bred** Philip Gilligan & Anne Gilligan **Trained** Basford Green, Staffs

■ Stewards' Enquiry : Tom Queally caution; failed to take sufficient steps to correct his mount from hanging right-handed.

**FOCUS**
Only a few in-form contenders for this low-grade staying handicap and the early gallop was very steady, resulting in several pulling for their heads.

T/Plt: £13.60 to a £1 stake. Pool: £69,838.54 - 3,735.90 winning units. T/Qpdt: £6.10 to a £1 stake. Pool: £5,946.49 - 721.10 winning units. **Andrew Sheret**

1986 - 1993a (Foreign Racing) - See Raceform Interactive

# 1815 RANDWICK (L-H)
Saturday, April 22

**OFFICIAL GOING: Turf: soft**

## 1994a SCHWEPPES SYDNEY CUP (GROUP 1 H'CAP) (3YO+) (TURF) 2m
**6:35** 3-Y-0+
**£777,485** (£222,222; £116,959; £52,631; £29,239; £11,695)

RPR

**1** **Polarisation**[14] 1646 5-8-2 **0**..............................(p) CoreyBrown 6 103
(Charlie Appleby) *settled front of midfield: hdwy to move upsides ldr 2 1/2f out: pushed along to ld 2f out: wnt 1 l clr: began to tire 100yds out: kpt on gamely to hold on* **11/2**[3]

**2** *hd* **Who Shot Thebarman (NZ)**[14] 1646 8-9-0 **0**..............................(t) BlakeShinn 13 115
(Chris Waller, Australia) **11/1**

**3** *1/2* **Big Duke (IRE)**[14] 1646 5-8-3 **0**.............................. GlenBoss 2 103+
(Darren Weir, Australia) **27/10**[1]

**4** *5 1/2* **Annus Mirabilis (IRE)**[14] 1646 6-8-3 **0**..............................(b) DeanHolland 4 97
(Stuart Webb, Australia) **30/1**

**5** *shd* **Chance To Dance (IRE)**[14] 1646 7-8-5 **0**..............................(t) ChristianReith 3 99
(Stephen Autridge & Jamie Richards, New Zealand) **18/1**

**6** *hd* **Harlem**[14] 1645 5-8-3 **0**.............................. ChadSchofield 7 97
(David A & B Hayes & Tom Dabernig, Australia) **16/1**

**7** *1 1/2* **Penglai Pavilion (USA)**[14] 1646 7-8-3 **0**..............................(p) KerrinMcEvoy 14 95
(Charlie Appleby) *away wl and prom early: settled 3rd: clsd on clr ldr to ld 3f out: sn u.p and hdd 2f out: lost position but kpt on* **9/2**[2]

**8** *2 3/4* **Mister Impatience**[14] 1646 7-8-3 **0**..............................(t) JayFord 5 92
(Michael Moroney, Australia) **60/1**

**9** *1* **Kinema (IRE)**[14] 1646 6-8-4 **0** ow1..............................(t) TimothyClark 12 92
(Chris Waller, Australia) **20/1**

**10** *shd* **Tally (AUS)**[14] 1646 4-8-9 **0**..............................(b) TommyBerry 1 97
(J O'Shea, Australia) *settled rr of midfield: hdwy 4f out: pushed along turning in: wknd fnl 2f* **11/1**

**11** *19 1/2* **Boom Time (AUS)**[7] 5-8-6 **0**..............................(b) CoryParish 9 73
(David A & B Hayes & Tom Dabernig, Australia) **10/1**

**12** *9* **Lasqueti Spirit (AUS)**[14] 1644 3-8-2 **0**..............................(b) BobbyEl-Issa 8 63
(Lee Curtis, Australia) **18/1**

**13** *30* **Pentathlon (NZ)**[14] 1646 5-8-2 **0**.............................. JeffPenza 11 26
(John Wheeler, New Zealand) **40/1**

**P** **Libran (IRE)**[14] 1646 6-8-13 **0**..............................(t) BrentonAvdulla 10
(Chris Waller, Australia) **18/1**

3m 29.16s
**WFA** 3 from 4yo 24lb 4 from 5yo+ 2lb **14** Ran SP% **120.1**

**Owner** Godolphin **Bred** Darley **Trained** Newmarket, Suffolk

**FOCUS**
A first Group 1 winner in Australia for Charlie Appleby.

1995 - 1998a (Foreign Racing) - See Raceform Interactive

# NAVAN (L-H)
Sunday, April 23

**OFFICIAL GOING: Good**

## 1999a COOLMORE VINTAGE CROP STKS (GROUP 3) 1m 6f
**4:25** (4:25) 4-Y-0+
**£32,777** (£10,555; £5,000; £2,222; £1,111; £555)

RPR

**1** **Torcedor (IRE)**[18] 1571 5-9-4 101..............................(p) ColmO'Donoghue 2 110
(Mrs John Harrington, Ire) *mde all: stl travelled wl to extend advantage 3f out: rdn and styd on wl for press fnl f* **4/1**[2]

**2** *1 1/2* **Order Of St George (IRE)**[190] 7349 5-9-9 120........ SeamieHeffernan 8 113+
(A P O'Brien, Ire) *settled off ldrs in 4th: pushed along over 3f out: rdn in 3rd 2f out: edgd rt u.p ins fnl f: kpt on wl into 2nd cl home: nt trble wnr* **4/5**[1]

**3** *1/2* **Twilight Payment (IRE)**[18] 1571 4-9-3 108..............................(t[1]) KevinManning 6 108
(J S Bolger, Ire) *chsd ldrs in 3rd: clsr in 2nd after 5f: pushed along under 4f out: no imp on wnr ent fnl f: kpt on same pce and dropped to 3rd clsng stages* **4/1**[2]

**4** *6 1/2* **Lustrous Light (IRE)**[14] 1654 4-9-3 100.............................. ColinKeane 7 99
(G M Lyons, Ire) *hld up in 5th: pushed along under 3f out: no imp appr fnl f in 4th: sn one pce* **12/1**[3]

**5** *shd* **Morga (IRE)**[117] 6820 7-9-1 97..............................(h) RonanWhelan 3 95
(Desmond McDonogh, Ire) *racd in rr: pushed along in 6th 3f out: kpt on same pce into 5th ins fnl f: nvr nrr* **25/1**

**6** *1 3/4* **Red Stars (IRE)**[8] 1808 4-9-0 101..............................(h) DeclanMcDonogh 4 94
(John M Oxx, Ire) *chsd ldr in 2nd: 3rd after 5f: rdn in 4th 2f out: no imp appr fnl f: wknd* **16/1**

**7** *15* **Dew Line (IRE)**[8] 1808 5-9-1 89.............................. GaryCarroll 1 72
(Michael Mulvany, Ire) *racd in 6th tl dropped to rr over 3f out: sn detached* **66/1**

3m 2.5s (-12.50)
**WFA** 4 from 5yo+ 1lb **7** Ran SP% **114.5**
CSF £7.59 TOTE £4.60: £2.10, £1.02; DF 8.90 Trifecta £21.80.

**Owner** Te Akau Torcedor (Mngr David Ellis) **Bred** Barronstown Stud **Trained** Moone, Co Kildare

**FOCUS**
No fluke about this as the winner made all at a proper gallop and showed that he definitely belongs in the Gold Cup conversation. He picked up from his 2015 improvement.



The Form Book Flat, Raceform Ltd, Newbury, RG14 5SJ

2000 - 2001a (Foreign Racing) - See Raceform Interactive

## KREFELD (R-H)

Sunday, April 23

**OFFICIAL GOING: Turf: good**

### 2002a PREIS DER WOHNSTATTE KREFELD WOHNUNGS-AKTIENGESELLSCHAFT - DR. BUSCH-MEMORIAL (GROUP 3) (3YO) (TURF) 1m 110y

**3:35** 3-Y-O **£27,350** (£10,256; £5,128; £2,564; £1,709)

RPR

1 **Dragon Lips (GER)**[184] 3-9-2 0 ........ MarcLerner 8 108+
(Andreas Suborics, Germany) *trckd ldrs: drvn to ld appr 1 1/2f out: styd on strly and wnt clr fnl f: won easing down* **137/10**

2 3 ¼ **Langtang (GER)**[189] 7399 3-9-2 0 ........ JozefBojko 7 101
(A Wohler, Germany) *settled in midfield: clsd to chse ldr 1 1/2f out: kpt on to hold 2nd but no match for wnr* **7/5**[1]

3 ½ **Savile Row (FR)**[24] 1460 3-9-2 0 ........(p) KoenClijmans 11 100
(Frau Erika Mader, Germany) *w.w in rr: swtchd outside and hdwy 2f out: hrd rdn to chse ldrs 1 1/2f out: kpt on at same pce fnl f* **65/1**

4 hd **Colomano**[168] 7842 3-9-2 0 ........ MartinSeidl 6 99
(Markus Klug, Germany) *towards rr: hdwy u.p over 1 1/2f out: styd on fnl f: nvr on terms* **43/10**[3]

5 1 ¼ **Fulminato (GER)**[189] 7399 3-9-2 0 ........ AndraschStarke 10 97
(Andreas Suborics, Germany) *settled in midfield: rdn to cl and chal for 2nd appr 1f out: one pce ins fnl f: fdd late on* **56/10**

6 ½ **Ming Jung (FR)**[189] 7399 3-9-2 0 ........ AndreasHelfenbein 9 96
(Markus Klug, Germany) *hld up towards rr: clsng whn n.m.r over 1 1/2f out: swtchd ins and kpt on at same pce fnl f: nvr in contention* **26/1**

7 1 ¾ **Shinzaro (GER)** 3-9-2 0 ........ OliverWilson 5 92
(D Moser, Germany) *racd keenly: hld up in midfield on outer: dropped into fnl pair bef 1/2-way: hdwy 3f out: c wdst into st and rdn: ended up on stands' rail: bhd fnl 1 1/2f* **76/10**

8 1 ¾ **Kauttio (IRE)** 3-9-2 0 ........ DanielePorcu 2 88
(A Wohler, Germany) *racd v keenly: restrained cl up on inner: hrd rdn and nt qckn 1 1/2f out: sn wknd* **109/10**

9 2 ¼ **Dia Del Sol**[184] 3-9-2 0 ........ AdriedeVries 3 83
(Markus Klug, Germany) *settled towards rr: rdn and no imp fr 2f out: bhd fnl f* **18/5**[2]

10 1 **Edwin**[189] 3-9-2 0 ........ StefanieHofer 4 81
(Mario Hofer, Germany) *plld hrd and led under a tight hold: drvn 2f out: hdd appr fnl 1 1/2f: sn wknd* **29/1**

1m 43.0s (-3.60) **10** Ran SP% **132.8**
PARI-MUTUEL (all including 10 euro stake): WIN 147 PLACE: 25, 15, 43; SF: 679.
**Owner** Stall Lintec **Bred** Stall Parthenaue **Trained** Germany

## 1594 SAINT-CLOUD (L-H)

Sunday, April 23

**OFFICIAL GOING: Turf: good**

### 2003a PRIX PENELOPE (GROUP 3) (3YO FILLIES) (TURF) 1m 2f 110y

**2:45** 3-Y-O **£34,188** (£13,675; £10,256; £6,837; £3,418)

RPR

1 **Sistercharlie (IRE)**[21] 1529 3-9-0 0 ........ MaximeGuyon 7 104+
(H-A Pantall, France) *w.w in rr: began to cl 2 1/2f out: rdn 1 1/2f out: sustained run over 1f out: led fnl 75yds and asserted* **9/2**[3]

2 1 **Listen In (IRE)**[43] 1158 3-9-0 0 ........ AurelienLemaitre 3 102
(F Head, France) *led: drvn and lened 2f out: hdd ins fnl f: rallied to regain ld 110yds out: hdd fnl 75yds: no ex* **7/1**

3 nse **Rythmique (IRE)**[36] 3-9-0 0 ........ ChristopheSoumillon 6 102
(J-C Rouget, France) *dwlt: sn rcvrd to trck ldr: drvn 2f out: styd on to ld narrowly ins fnl f: hdd 110yds out: kpt on gamely* **5/4**[1]

4 snk **Music Lover (FR)**[43] 1158 3-9-0 0 ........ AlexandreRoussel 4 102
(A De Watrigant, France) *chsd ldrs: disp 3rd and drvn 2f out: styd on at same pce fnl f* **12/1**

5 ½ **Palombe (IRE)**[21] 1529 3-9-0 0 ........ Pierre-CharlesBoudot 1 101
(A Fabre, France) *racd keenly: settled cl up on inner: disp 3rd and drvn 2f out: n.m.r ins fnl f: kpt on at same pce* **4/1**[2]

6 1 ¼ **Mademoiselle Marie (FR)**[43] 1158 3-9-0 0 ........ FranckBlondel 5 98
(K Borgel, France) *racd v freely: hld up in fnl pair: drvn and no prog 1 1/2f out: kpt on at same pce fnl f* **7/1**

7 5 **Copying**[41] 3-9-0 0 ........ CristianDemuro 2 89
(C Lerner, France) *racd keenly: hld up in fnl trio: c out wd and drvn 2 1/2f out: no imp on ldrs: bhd whn eased fnl half f* **18/1**

2m 19.06s (-0.54) **7** Ran SP% **120.6**
PARI-MUTUEL (all including 1 euro stake): WIN: 5.10; PLACE: 3.00, 3.70; SF: 24.30.
**Owner** Mme Jacques Cygler **Bred** Ecurie Des Monceaux **Trained** France

**FOCUS**
Plenty of collateral form in this field was rubber-stamed in a tight finish.

## SAN SIRO (R-H)

Sunday, April 23

**OFFICIAL GOING: Turf: good**

### 2004a PREMIO AMBROSIANO (GROUP 3) (4YO+) (TURF) 1m 2f

**3:55** 4-Y-O+ **£27,777** (£12,222; £6,666; £3,333)

RPR

1 **Voice Of Love (IRE)**[168] 7841 4-9-0 0 ........ DarioVargiu 3 107
(Stefano Botti, Italy) *mde all: led: drvn under 2f out: jnd over 1f out: sn rallied and forged ahd: wl on top fnl 75yds* **1/10**[1]

2 1 ½ **Circus Couture (IRE)**[168] 7841 5-8-11 0 ........ FabioBranca 2 101
(Stefano Botti, Italy) *settled cl up on inner: drvn to chse ldr under 2f out: upsides and ev ch over 1f out: sn rdn and one pce* **1/10**[1]

3 snk **Basileus (IRE)**[6] 4-8-11 0 ........ CarloFiocchi 4 101
(Stefano Botti, Italy) *slow to stride and rousted along: racd in fnl pair: clsd to chse ldng pair over 2f out: styd on fnl f: jst missed 2nd* **306/100**[2]

4 1 ¾ **Freedom Beel (IRE)**[21] 4-8-11 0 ........ SilvanoMulas 1 97
(Stefano Botti, Italy) *racd freely: hld up in fnl pair: drvn and clsd 1 1/2f out: kpt on fnl f but nt pce to chal* **1/10**[1]

5 12 **Fico Senza Spine (IRE)**[238] 5944 4-8-11 0 ........ AntonioFresu 5 73
(Luigi Riccardi, Italy) *chsd ldr on outer: rdn and no imp 2 1/2f out: sn lost pl: bhd whn eased fnl f* **218/10**[3]

2m 1.0s (-5.70) **5** Ran SP% **301.7**
PARI-MUTUEL (all including 1 euro stake): WIN 1.10 PLACE 1.43, 1.15 DF 2.02.
**Owner** Scuderia Effevi SRL **Bred** Massimo Parri **Trained** Italy

2005 - 2014a (Foreign Racing) - See Raceform Interactive

## 1792 KEMPTON (A.W) (R-H)

Monday, April 24

**OFFICIAL GOING: Polytrack: standard**
Wind: Slight breeze Weather: Cloudy

### 2015 MATCHBOOK BETTING PODCAST NOVICE AUCTION STKS 5f (P)

**2:10** (2:12) (Class 5) 2-Y-O **£3,234** (£962; £481; £240) **Stalls** Low

Form RPR

1 1 **Corinthia Knight (IRE)**[13] 1694 2-9-4 0 ........ OisinMurphy 3 95+
(Archie Watson) *sn led: shkn up wl over 1f out: drew clr ent fnl f: in n.d wl ins fnl f: rdn out* **4/9**[1]

53 2 7 **Autumn Lodge**[10] 1767 2-8-13 0 ........ ShaneKelly 1 65
(J S Moore) *settled in 3rd on rail: rdn over 1f out: kpt on ent fnl f: one pce and no ch w wnr wl ins fnl f* **8/1**[3]

3 3 **Shesgotthelot** 2-8-8 0 ........ LiamJones 5 49
(J S Moore) *s.s: rn green and 5 l adrift in rr at 1/2-way being pushed along: stl plenty to do whn rdn 2f out: no imp tl styd on strly ins fnl f: snatched 3rd post: bttr for run* **25/1**

2 4 nse **Auntie Pam (IRE)**[16] 1627 2-8-11 0 ........ RichardKingscote 4 52
(Tom Dascombe) *wnt lft s: hased ldr on outer: rdn over 1f out: one pce fr over 1f out: lost 3rd post* **3/1**[2]

5 ¾ **Butterfly Spirit** 2-8-9 0 ........ WilliamCarson 6 47
(Michael Attwater) *t.k.h in 5th: nt clr run between horses and shuffled along fr over 1f out: nvr involved* **66/1**

6 shd **Milchik** 2-8-10 0 ........ KierenFox 2 48
(Michael Attwater) *broke wl: cl up in 4th: pushed along over 1f out: kpt on one pce fnl f* **40/1**

59.88s (-0.62) **Going Correction** -0.075s/f (Stan) **6** Ran SP% **113.1**
Speed ratings (Par 92): **101,89,85,84,83 83**
CSF £4.99 TOTE £1.40: £1.10, £2.80; EX 4.10 Trifecta £28.30.
**Owner** Ontoawinner & Partner **Bred** Tally-Ho Stud **Trained** Upper Lambourn, W Berks

**FOCUS**
There didn't look to be much depth to this race. The winner could be flattered, but this was clearly a very useful effort from the winner.

### 2016 MATCHBOOK BETTING EXCHANGE H'CAP 7f (P)

**2:40** (2:42) (Class 6) (0-60,62) 3-Y-O **£2,264** (£673; £336; £168) **Stalls** Low

Form RPR

11-1 1 **A Sure Welcome**[19] 1564 3-9-7 **59** ........(p) TomMarquand 10 66
(John Spearing) *settled bhd ldr: upsides fr 2f out tl rdn to ld ent fnl f: hrd rdn and kpt on wl ins fnl f: jst hld on* **4/1**[2]

53-3 2 shd **Coverham (IRE)**[18] 1580 3-9-5 **57** ........ RyanTate 11 64+
(James Eustace) *covered up bhd ldrs: rdn 2f out: nt qckn tl kpt on wl ent fnl f: styd on strly nring fin: jst denied* **7/2**[1]

000- 3 1 ¼ **Sweet Pursuit**[224] 6414 3-8-13 **51** ........ OisinMurphy 14 54
(Rod Millman) *pushed along fr wd draw to ld: rdn 2f out: pressed by wnr fr wl over 1f out: hdd ent fnl f: stuck on tl wknd fnl 100yds* **14/1**

003- 4 nk **Varun's Bride (IRE)**[207] 6896 3-9-0 **52** ........ PatDobbs 9 55
(Richard Hannon) *settled in 3rd on inner: rdn over 2f out: drifted to centre fr over 1f out: kpt on tl one pce fnl f* **14/1**

-415 5 3 ¼ **Jack Blane**[19] 1564 3-9-4 **56** ........ GeorgeDowning 2 50
(Daniel Kubler) *chsd ldrs on inner: rdn over 2f out: lft bhd by ldng quartet ent fnl f: one pce after* **5/1**[3]

40-0 6 1 ½ **Sixties Habana**[94] 323 3-9-5 **57** ........ JFEgan 6 47+
(Pat Phelan) *mid-div on outer: racd free on bnd and t.k.h: rdn over 2f out and swtchd wdst sn after: kpt on fr over 1f out: pushed out fnl 100yds: likely improver* **8/1**

-466 7 2 ¼ **Tranquil Tracy**[45] 1123 3-8-7 **45** ........ AdamBeschizza 5 29+
(John Norton) *in rr-div on inner: rdn in centre over 2f out: kpt on one pce fr ovr 1f out* **12/1**

04-6 8 ½ **Venetian Proposal (IRE)**[109] 78 3-9-4 **56** ........ DanielMuscutt 4 38+
(Zoe Davison) *wnt rt s and hmpd rival: in rr: rdn over 2f out: no imp fr over 1f out* **33/1**

-340 9 nk **Sparkling Cossack**[38] 1247 3-8-11 **49** ........ MartinLane 13 30+
(Jeremy Gask) *in rr-divsion on outer: niggled on bnd over 3f out: shkn up over 3f out: rdn over 1f out: styd on one pce: can do bttr* **33/1**

6-40 10 2 **Huddersfilly Town**[40] 1205 3-9-1 **53** ........ SilvestreDeSousa 3 29+
(Ivan Furtado) *in rr: pushed along over 2f out: nt clr run over 1f out: nvr involved* **14/1**

030- 11 ½ **Robin's Purse**[233] 6111 3-9-10 **62** ........ JamieSpencer 7 37
(Charles Hills) *chsd ldrs: rdn over 2f out: no ex fr over 1f out and wknd qckly* **15/2**

45-0 12 5 **The Secrets Out**[19] 1550 3-9-3 **55** ........ RoystonFfrench 12 16+
(Luke Dace) *in rr and t.k.h: rdn over 2f out: wl bhd fr over 1f out* **25/1**

400 13 hd **Raspberry Princess**[18] 1580 3-8-7 **45** ........ RyanPowell 1 6+
(Phil McEntee) *mid-div on inner: rdn over 2f out: no ex and wknd fr over 1f out* **100/1**

0-00 14 28 **Secret Willow**[17] 1597 3-8-10 **48** ........ SamHitchcott 8
(John E Long) *awkward s and pushed along in rr early: lost tch bnd: eased fr wl over 1f out: t.o* **66/1**

1m 26.28s (0.28) **Going Correction** -0.075s/f (Stan) **14** Ran SP% **121.7**
Speed ratings (Par 96): **95,94,93,93,89 87,85,84,84,81 81,75,75,43**
CSF £17.91 CT £163.99 TOTE £4.80: £1.80, £1.80, £4.80; EX 18.20 Trifecta £265.40.
**Owner** Kinnersley Partnership 3 **Bred** Richard Evans Bloodstock **Trained** Kinnersley, Worcs

**FOCUS**
It proved difficult to make up ground, with the first four never far away and finishing clear. Another modest step forward from the winner.

## 2017 BETTER ODDS WITH MATCHBOOK H'CAP (DIV I) 1m (P)
3:15 (3:15) (Class 6) (0-60,61) 3-Y-O £2,264 (£673; £336; £168) Stalls Low

Form RPR
3353 1 **Metronomic (IRE)**17 1597 3-9-4 57 (p) PatDobbs 10 62+
(Richard Hannon) *sn led: briefly hdd over 1f out: sn rdn and led again: kpt on wl ins fnl f* **10/3**1
65-3 2 1 1/4 **Epsom Secret**17 1596 3-9-0 53 JFEgan 8 55+
(Pat Phelan) *taken bk leaving stalls: in rr and t.k.h: shkn up and prog on outer 2f out whilst slowly drifting rt: briefly led over 1f out whn swiftly taken lft and jinked: sn pushed along and kpt on one pce fnl f* **10/1**
2542 3 nk **Masquerade Bling (IRE)**17 1597 3-9-5 58 RobHornby 1 60
(Simon Hodgson) *mid-div on inner: shkn up and prog over 1f out: nt clrest of runs ent fnl f on heels: sn rdn and kpt on one pce* **7/1**
5035 4 shd **De Vegas Kid (IRE)**26 1421 3-9-5 58 GeorgeDowning 9 59
(Tony Carroll) *mid-div on outer: rdn 2f out: swtchd wd over 1f out: kpt on* **6/1**3
440- 5 1/2 **Ocean Temptress**151 8080 3-9-7 60 JosephineGordon 4 60
(John Ryan) *bhd ldrs between horses: rdn 2f out: no ex ent fnl f* **12/1**
00-4 6 1/2 **Plato's Kode (IRE)**52 1000 3-9-8 61 (bt) TomQueally 5 59
(Seamus Durack) *in rr: swtchd out and rdn over 1f out: kpt on wl ent fnl f: nrst fin* **9/2**2
000- 7 1/2 **Delagate This Lord**133 8340 3-9-6 59 LukeMorris 6 56
(Bill Turner) *racd in 2nd on outer: rdn wl over 2f out: no ex and wknd fr over 1f out* **20/1**
-001 8 nse **London Grammar (IRE)**17 1597 3-9-3 56 RyanTate 2 53
(Ralph J Smith) *chsd ldr on inner: tight for room and pushed along to hold pl wl over 3f out: rdn over 2f out and sn began to weaken* **7/1**
5-04 9 2 **Ivor's Magic (IRE)**38 1242 3-9-3 59 TimClark(3) 7 51
(David Elsworth) *in rr: rdn over 2f out wout making any imp on ldrs* **10/1**
6-00 10 4 **Jasmincita (IRE)**14 1685 3-9-4 57 SteveDrowne 3 40
(George Baker) *in rr-div: rdn over 2f out: no imp fr over 1f out* **66/1**
1m 40.46s (0.66) **Going Correction** -0.075s/f (Stan) **10 Ran SP% 112.7**
Speed ratings (Par 96): **93,91,91,91,90 90,89,89,87,83**
CSF £36.14 CT £221.63 TOTE £3.50: £1.30, £3.80, £2.20; EX 26.00 Trifecta £137.30.
**Owner** Middleham Park Racing VIII **Bred** Pier House Stud **Trained** East Everleigh, Wilts

**FOCUS**
A moderate handicap and ordinary form for the grade.

## 2018 BETTER ODDS WITH MATCHBOOK H'CAP (DIV II) 1m (P)
3:45 (3:45) (Class 6) (0-60,61) 3-Y-O £2,264 (£673; £336; £168) Stalls Low

Form RPR
540 1 **Badenscoth**23 1488 3-9-5 61 (h1) JackDuern(3) 6 67+
(Dean Ivory) *in rr: c wdst ent st: sn shkn up: pushed along wl over 1f out to make prog up nrside centre whilst wanting to hang rt: rdn ent fnl f: edgd rt but kpt on wl and led ins fnl f* **12/1**
50-1 2 3/4 **Fleeting Francesca**17 1596 3-9-5 58 DaneO'Neill 7 62
(Chris Gordon) *in rr-div on inner: rdn over 2f out: led ent fnl f: kpt on wl tl hdd wl ins fnl f* **7/2**1
60-0 3 1 1/4 **Mr Mac**82 502 3-8-13 57 (h1) GeorgeWood(5) 4 58
(Peter Hedger) *racd in 4th on outer: rdn over 2f out: kpt on wl and ev ch ent fnl f: kpt on but no ex fnl 110yds* **9/2**3
00-4 4 3/4 **Equal Rights**9 1790 3-9-5 58 JimCrowley 5 57
(Eve Johnson Houghton) *in rr: rdn over 2f out: kpt on ent fnl f* **4/1**2
540- 5 1 1/4 **Power Home (IRE)**151 8082 3-9-2 60 PaddyPilley(5) 8 56
(Denis Coakley) *in rr-div: rdn over 2f out: kpt on one pce fr over 1f out: hands and heels fnl f* **14/1**
0-34 6 2 3/4 **Luduamf (IRE)**19 1564 3-9-6 59 (b1) TomMarquand 9 49
(Richard Hannon) *settled in mid-div: rdn over 3f out: kpt on tl no ex ent fnl f* **7/2**1
056- 7 1 1/2 **Dravid**258 5251 3-9-5 58 RyanTate 1 44
(Rod Millman) *chsd ldrs on inner: rdn over 2f out: kpt on and ev ch on inner ent fnl f: wknd qckly sn after* **7/1**
645- 8 2 **Brexit**261 5165 3-8-10 56 SophieRalston(7) 2 37
(Pat Phelan) *sn led and set str pce: rdn over 2f out: stl there ent fnl f: wknd qckly after* **33/1**
0-00 9 1 1/2 **Follow Me (IRE)**26 1421 3-9-1 54 (h1) JosephineGordon 10 32
(Lee Carter) *in rr: rdn over 2f out: no imp* **16/1**
550 10 3 3/4 **From A Distance (IRE)**28 1401 3-9-0 53 MartinHarley 3 22
(David Simcock) *chsd ldr on outer: rdn over 2f out: kpt on tl wknd fr over 1f out* **16/1**
1m 39.39s (-0.41) **Going Correction** -0.075s/f (Stan) **10 Ran SP% 124.2**
Speed ratings (Par 96): **99,98,97,96,95 92,90,88,87,83**
CSF £57.44 CT £228.92 TOTE £16.20: £4.60, £1.50, £1.90; EX 77.50 Trifecta £519.40.
**Owner** Peter J Skinner **Bred** Peter J Skinner **Trained** Radlett, Herts

**FOCUS**
The time was 1.07sec faster than the first division and the winner came from last. He's the type to find more again.

## 2019 WINNERS ARE WELCOME AT MATCHBOOK MAIDEN FILLIES' STKS 1m (P)
4:20 (4:21) (Class 5) 3-Y-O+ £3,234 (£962; £481; £240) Stalls Low

Form RPR
1 **Time Chaser** 3-9-0 0 JamesDoyle 3 80+
(Roger Charlton) *trckd ldrs on outer: shkn up over 2f out on wd outside: rdn over 1f out: led 100yds out: kpt on strly and nudged out fnl strides: promising* **7/4**1
0- 2 1/2 **Meccabah (FR)**177 7695 3-9-0 0 ThomasBrown 11 79
(Andrew Balding) *hld up in mid-div on outer: rdn over 2f out and c to inner: kpt on wl and ev ch in line of four ent fnl f: sn led: hdd 100yds: kpt on wl* **16/1**
2- 3 1 **Thafeera (USA)**173 7763 3-9-0 0 (h) JimCrowley 13 77
(Charles Hills) *trckd ldr on outer: rdn jst over 2f out: kpt on wl and ev ch in line of four ent fnl f: no ex cl home* **9/4**2
24 4 3 1/2 **First Moon**44 1151 3-9-0 0 (t) JosephineGordon 1 69
(Hugo Palmer) *sn led: rdn over 2f out: kpt on wl and stl ev ch ent fnl f: sn hdd & wknd: pushed out wl ins fnl f* **11/1**
06- 5 1 **Meshaykh (IRE)**173 7763 3-9-0 0 TedDurcan 5 67
(Sir Michael Stoute) *racd in mid-div on inner: rdn over 2f out: kpt on wl wout gng w front four* **7/2**3
6 6 1 1/2 **Al Jawza**28 1401 3-9-0 0 TomMarquand 12 63+
(Richard Hannon) *mid-div on outer: rdn to hold pl wl over 3f out: lft bhd whn pushed along fr over 2f out: gng on encouragingly ins fnl f* **40/1**
00- 7 3/4 **Morello (IRE)**196 7210 3-9-0 0 DaneO'Neill 8 61
(Henry Candy) *mid-div on inner: rdn over 2f out: slighly outpcd: kpt on one pce fr over 1f out* **100/1**
8 4 1/2 **Cape To Cuba** 3-8-9 0 GeorgeWood(5) 9 51+
(James Fanshawe) *s.s: in rr: pushed along fr over 2f out: bttr for run* **50/1**
5- 9 1 **Tremendous (IRE)**224 6414 3-9-0 0 PatDobbs 4 49
(Richard Hannon) *mid-div and t.k.h: rdn over 2f out: no imp on ldrs fr over 1f out* **20/1**
10 1/2 **Sileel (USA)** 3-9-0 0 SilvestreDeSousa 7 48
(Ed Dunlop) *in rr: rdn wl over 3f out: nvr involved* **25/1**
5-3 11 hd **Angel Of Rome (IRE)**32 1333 3-9-0 0 FranBerry 6 47
(Richard Hughes) *in rr-div: rdn over 2f out: no imp on ldrs and pushed out* **20/1**
12 4 **Shamonix (IRE)** 3-9-0 0 SteveDrowne 10 38
(Mark Usher) *in rr: shake up and rdn over 3f out: no ex after* **100/1**
13 17 **Harbouring** 3-9-0 0 RichardKingscote 2
(Jonathan Portman) *racd in mid-div: struggling over 3f out: sn lost pl and wknd: t.o* **66/1**
1m 38.04s (-1.76) **Going Correction** -0.075s/f (Stan) **13 Ran SP% 124.8**
Speed ratings (Par 100): **105,104,103,100,99 97,96,92,91,90 90,86,69**
CSF £32.07 TOTE £2.70: £1.20, £6.20, £1.30; EX 45.00 Trifecta £176.20.
**Owner** K Abdullah **Bred** Juddmonte Farms Ltd **Trained** Beckhampton, Wilts

**FOCUS**
An interesting, useful-looking fillies' maiden. The fourth looks the best initial guide to the form.

## 2020 SMARTER BETS WITH MATCHBOOK BETTING EXCHANGE H'CAP (LONDON MIDDLE DISTANCE SERIES QUALIFIER) 1m 2f 219y(P)
4:50 (4:50) (Class 4) (0-80,82) 4-Y-O+ £4,690 (£1,395; £697; £348) Stalls Low

Form RPR
35-1 1 **Captain Peacock**14 1684 4-9-11 82 (v) JimCrowley 2 90+
(William Knight) *racd in 4th: pushed along 2f out and c to nrside rail: rdn over 1f out w plenty to do: kpt on ent fnl f: pushed along in 3rd fnl 150yds tl flew home nr fin to get up post* **5/4**1
660- 2 hd **Prendergast Hill (IRE)**178 7671 5-9-7 78 HarryBentley 3 85
(Ed de Giles) *led: shkn up ent 2f out: rdn over 1f out: hrd pressed by 3rd and kpt on wl tl jst pipped post* **4/1**3
-150 3 3/4 **Camakasi (IRE)**82 507 6-9-0 71 TomMarquand 1 77
(Ali Stronge) *settled in 3rd: rdn wl over 1f out: kpt on wl and pressed ldr ent fnl f: nt get past and no ex fnl strides* **14/1**
6444 4 2 1/2 **Take Two**23 1498 8-8-12 69 KieranO'Neill 7 71
(Alex Hales) *in rr: rdn over 2f out: no imp ldrs fr over 1f out: kpt on* **12/1**
222- 5 1 3/4 **Wealth Tax**172 7780 4-9-2 73 SilvestreDeSousa 5 72
(Ed Dunlop) *t.k.h and restrained in rr: rdn over 2f out: sn hld* **7/2**2
360- 6 1 1/4 **The New Pharaoh (IRE)**185 7507 6-8-13 73 LouisSteward(3) 6 70
(Chris Wall) *in rr: jinked bnd: rdn over 3f out: no imp on ldr: one pce* **11/1**
504- 7 2 **Woofie (IRE)**248 5607 5-8-12 69 (p) TomQueally 4 63
(Laura Mongan) *racd in 2nd: pushed along over 3f out: no ex and wknd fr 2f out* **40/1**
2m 21.52s (-0.38) **Going Correction** -0.075s/f (Stan) **7 Ran SP% 111.8**
Speed ratings (Par 105): **98,97,97,95,94 93,91**
CSF £6.13 TOTE £2.30: £1.30, £2.10; EX 8.20 Trifecta £45.40.
**Owner** Chasemore Farm **Bred** Chasemore Farm **Trained** Patching, W Sussex

**FOCUS**
A fair handicap. The form is rated around the second.

## 2021 MATCHBOOK CASINO H'CAP 1m 7f 218y(P)
5:20 (5:20) (Class 4) (0-85,82) 4-Y-O+ £4,690 (£1,395; £697; £348) Stalls Low

Form RPR
561- 1 **Next Train's Gone**200 7104 4-8-10 70 RyanTate 5 75+
(James Eustace) *led at slow gallop: injected sme pce fr 4f out: rdn over 2f out: briefly jinked lft and idled ent fnl f w chalrs in bhd: sn gathered up and pushed out ins fnl f: cosily* **3/1**2
306- 2 1 **King Calypso**178 7670 6-9-8 78 TomQueally 4 81
(Denis Coakley) *trckd ldrs in 3rd: rdn over 2f out: one l down whn ldr jinked lft over 1f out: kpt on ins fnl f to take 2nd nr fin: no ch w wnr* **6/1**
436- 3 nk **Chelsea's Boy (IRE)**202 7060 4-9-1 75 FranBerry 7 78
(Ralph Beckett) *settled in 6th: rdn over 2f out: kpt on wl tl lost 2nd nr fin* **2/1**1
/0-0 4 3/4 **Treasure The Ridge (IRE)**35 746 8-9-7 77 (tp) StevieDonohoe 6 79
(Martin Hill) *settled in 5th on rail: rdn over 2f out: rdn over 2f out: kpt on* **12/1**
60-3 5 1 **See And Be Seen**19 1561 7-8-7 68 (p) MitchGodwin(5) 3 69
(Sylvester Kirk) *4th on outer: rdn over 2f out: ch over 1f out: wknd fnl f* **14/1**
24-6 6 nse **Be My Sea (IRE)**53 381 6-9-8 78 GeorgeDowning 2 78
(Tony Carroll) *trckd ldr: rdn over 2f out: one l down whn wnr jinked in front over 1f out: wknd sn after* **5/1**3
15/3 7 6 **Sgt Reckless**19 1555 10-9-12 82 DaneO'Neill 1 75
(Simon Hodgson) *hld up in last: rdn over 2f out: no qckn fr over 1f out* **9/1**
3m 36.16s (6.06) **Going Correction** -0.075s/f (Stan)
**WFA** 4 from 6yo+ 2lb **7 Ran SP% 113.6**
Speed ratings (Par 105): **81,80,80,79,79 79,76**
CSF £20.88 TOTE £3.40: £2.20, £3.30; EX 16.50 Trifecta £69.40.
**Owner** Harold Nass **Bred** Rockville Pike Partnership **Trained** Newmarket, Suffolk

**FOCUS**
The winner got things his own way in this ordinary staying event. The form is rated a little negatively.

## 2022 MATCHBOOK BETTING PODCAST H'CAP 1m 3f 219y(P)
5:50 (5:53) (Class 6) (0-65,67) 4-Y-O+ £2,264 (£673; £336; £168) Stalls Centre

Form RPR
3031 1 **Rail Dancer**19 1556 5-9-3 61 (v) AdamBeschizza 10 72+
(Richard Rowe) *covered up bhd ldrs: travelling strly over 2f out bhd ldrs: rdn to ld ent fnl f: qcknd clr and edgd rt: eased cl home* **9/2**1
10-5 2 2 3/4 **Multigifted**32 290 4-9-0 59 (t) DanielMuscutt 2 63
(Michael Madgwick) *mid-div: rdn 2f out: kpt on wl on inner ins fnl f to take 2nd nr fin: no ch w wnr* **8/1**
5-32 3 1/2 **Halling's Wish**35 1284 7-9-4 65 (b) HectorCrouch(3) 11 68
(Gary Moore) *trckd ldr: rdn over 2f out: kpt on one pce and lost 2nd nring fin* **7/1**2
6233 4 1 1/4 **Bridey's Lettuce (IRE)**48 1072 5-9-8 66 (h) KierenFox 3 67
(John Best) *trckd ldrs on rail: rdn over 2f out: kpt on one pce over 1f out* **15/2**3
3-14 5 1 **Monologue (IRE)**25 1456 4-8-11 56 HarryBentley 6 55
(Simon Hodgson) *chsd ldrs: rdn over 2f out: styd on tl wknd one pce ent fnl f* **9/2**1

216- **6** ½ **Weld Arab (IRE)**[37] 2605 6-9-4 **67**... MitchGodwin(5) 7 65
(Michael Blake) *led: rdn over 2f out: stuck on wl tl hdd ent fnl f: wknd after* **11/1**

-550 **7** 2½ **Alshan Fajer**[13] 1697 7-9-9 **67**... SilvestreDeSousa 4 61
(J R Jenkins) *mid-div on inner: rdn over 2f out: no imp on ldrs* **8/1**

4165 **8** nk **Shining Romeo**[35] 1284 5-9-0 **61**... TimClark(3) 9 55
(Denis Quinn) *s.s and in rr: rdn over 2f out: one pce fr over 1f out* **20/1**

406- **9** 1 **Bergholt (IRE)**[196] 7222 4-9-4 **63**... RyanPowell 1 55
(Tim Vaughan) *in rr-div: pushed along over 2f out: one pce* **16/1**

063- **10** 8 **Sir Pass I Am**[196] 7223 4-9-3 **62**...(h¹) ThomasBrown 12 42
(Andrew Balding) *mid-div on outer: rdn over 2f out: no imp fr over 1f out* **15/2**[3]

0050 **11** 1 **Munsarim (IRE)**[16] 1620 10-8-12 **56**...(b) GeorgeDowning 8 34
(Lee Carter) *in rr: rdn over 2f out: no imp and pushed out fr over 1f out* **50/1**

2m 32.62s (-1.88) **Going Correction** -0.075s/f (Stan) **11** Ran SP% **115.6**
Speed ratings (Par 101): **103,101,100,100,99 99,97,97,96,91 90**
CSF £39.67 CT £248.87 TOTE £4.10: £1.80, £2.70, £2.70; EX 39.60 Trifecta £388.20.
**Owner** Mark Cashmore **Bred** Scuderia Blueberry SRL **Trained** Sullington, W Sussex

**FOCUS**
A modest handicap but the winner had loads in hand. The second and third help pin the level.
T/Plt: £13.60 to a £1 stake. Pool: £54,038.32 - 2,895.19 winning units. T/Qpdt: £8.00 to a £1 stake. Pool: £3,563.19 - 328.55 winning units. **Cathal Gahan**

## 1894 LINGFIELD (L-H)

Monday, April 24

**OFFICIAL GOING: Polytrack: standard**
Wind: light, across in home straight (final 2f) Weather: overcast

### 2023 RACING WELFARE H'CAP 1m 1y(P)
**5:05** (5:05) (Class 6) (0-65,66) 4-Y-0+ **£2,911** (£866; £432; £108; £108) **Stalls** High

Form RPR

25-3 **1** **Rattle On**[12] 1729 4-9-4 **61**... PatCosgrave 5 66
(Jim Boyle) *hld up in tch in midfield: effrt in 3rd jst over 2f out: styd on u.p to ld ins fnl f: drvn out* **11/10**[1]

00B5 **2** nk **Binky Blue (IRE)**[7] 1842 5-8-12 **60**...(h) CharlieBennett(5) 8 64
(Daniel Mark Loughnane) *dwlt: hld up in tch in last pair: effrt on outer jst over 2f out: hdwy u.p 1f out: chsd wnr wl ins fnl f: styd on but nvr quite getting to wnr* **8/1**

0-05 **3** ¾ **Mister Musicmaster**[19] 1553 8-9-5 **62**... LukeMorris 1 64
(Ron Hodges) *broke wl: sn stdd bk into 4th: effrt jst over 2f out: no imp tl hdwy ins fnl f: styd on wl u.p fnl 100yds* **4/1**[2]

3510 **4** 1¼ **Zabdi**[12] 1729 4-9-0 **64**... JoshuaBryan(7) 7 63
(Lee Carter) *sn led: rdn ent fnl 2f: hdd over 1f out: unable qck u.p over 1f out: kpt on same pce ins fnl f* **13/2**[3]

00-0 **4** dht **Cyflymder (IRE)**[75] 614 11-8-0 **50** oh5... DavidEgan(7) 6 49
(David C Griffiths) *chsd ldrs: wnt 2nd over 1f out: rdn to ld on inner over 1f out: hdd ins fnl f: no ex and wknd towards fin* **33/1**

400- **6** 1¾ **Prince Of Cardamom (IRE)**[202] 7035 5-8-6 **56**...(p) JordanUys(7) 3 51
(Jonathan Geake) *stdd after s: hld up in last pair: effrt u.p over 1f out: styd on ins fnl f: nvr trbld ldrs* **14/1**

0-45 **7** 7 **Cleverconversation (IRE)**[23] 1484 4-9-2 **59**...(h) DannyBrock 2 37
(Jane Chapple-Hyam) *taken down early: flashing tail early: sn chsng ldr: drvn 3f out: sn lost pl: bhd over 1f out* **8/1**

1m 36.55s (-1.65) **Going Correction** -0.075s/f (Stan) **7** Ran SP% **112.8**
Speed ratings (Par 101): **105,104,103,102,102 100,93**
CSF £10.52 CT £26.17 TOTE £2.10: £1.50, £2.60; EX 11.00 Trifecta £27.50.
**Owner** Inside Track Racing Club **Bred** New England,Myriad,Stanley House,Wds&cps **Trained** Epsom, Surrey

**FOCUS**
They went a sound pace for this modest contest. The form can't be rated any higher.

### 2024 INJURED JOCKEYS FUND MEDIAN AUCTION MAIDEN STKS 6f 1y(P)
**5:35** (5:35) (Class 6) 4-6-Y-0 **£2,911** (£866; £432; £216) **Stalls** Low

Form RPR

-433 **1** **Frank Cool**[28] 1407 4-9-5 54... LukeMorris 6 54+
(Tony Carroll) *t.k.h: trckd ldrs: effrt over 1f out: led and edgd lft ins fnl f: styd on* **2/1**[2]

3005 **2** 1¼ **Kristoff (IRE)**[26] 1425 4-8-12 44...(p) IsobelFrancis(7) 2 50
(Jim Boyle) *led: rdn over 1f out: sn hdd: edfged rt and styd on same pce ins fnl f* **12/1**

5 **3** nk **Napping**[35] 1287 4-9-0 0... MartinHarley 3 44
(Anabel K Murphy) *pressed ldr: rdn and ev ch over 1f out: led 1f out: hdd and styd on same pce ins fnl f* **6/1**

4200 **4** shd **Arcanista (IRE)**[17] 1603 4-8-7 55...(be) NicolaCurrie(7) 5 44
(Richard Hughes) *t.k.h: hld up wl in tch: dropped to last and pushed along wl over 1f out: hdwy and swtchd rt ins fnl f: kpt on wl towards fin* **9/2**[3]

5404 **5** 2 **Bob Hopeful**[12] 1728 4-9-5 63... PatCosgrave 4 43
(Mike Murphy) *t.k.h: hld up wl in tch: effrt over 1f out: unable qck 1f out: wl hld and kpt on same pce after* **13/8**[1]

00P **R** **Bella's Boy (IRE)**[28] 1406 4-8-12 40...(v¹) JonathanFisher(7) 1
(John Ryan) *ref to r* **66/1**

1m 11.99s (0.09) **Going Correction** -0.075s/f (Stan) **6** Ran SP% **113.1**
Speed ratings: **96,94,93,93,91**
CSF £24.86 TOTE £2.70: £1.10, £5.70; EX 15.80 Trifecta £77.10.
**Owner** Wedgewood Estates **Bred** Wedgewood Estates **Trained** Cropthorne, Worcs

**FOCUS**
A very weak maiden run at a steady pace. The winner only ran to his level.

### 2025 HEART FM H'CAP 5f 6y(P)
**6:05** (6:05) (Class 5) (0-70,69) 4-Y-0+ **£3,234** (£962; £481; £240) **Stalls** High

Form RPR

013 **1** **Dusty Blue**[20] 1547 5-9-1 **63**... LukeMorris 2 72
(David Loughnane) *in tch: swtchd rt and effrt wl over 1f out: hdwy u.p to ld wl ins fnl f: r.o wl* **11/8**[1]

4245 **2** 1½ **Pharoh Jake**[31] 1340 9-8-2 **57**... JaneElliott(7) 3 61
(John Bridger) *led early: sn hdd and chsd ldr: rdn to chal 2f out: led 1f out: hdd and no ex wl ins fnl f* **8/1**

-025 **3** nk **Picansort**[26] 1429 10-9-2 **64**...(b) LiamKeniry 4 68
(Peter Crate) *hld up in rr: clsd to chse ldrs and nt clr run ins fnl f: swtchd rt and styd on fnl 100yds: no threat to wnr* **9/2**[3]

-413 **4** 1¼ **Mossgo (IRE)**[26] 1429 7-9-0 **69**...(t) RossaRyan(7) 6 67
(John Best) *dwlt: pushed along and hdwy to ld over 4f out: rdn over 1f out: hdd and no ex 1f out: wknd wl ins fnl f* **3/1**[2]

-136 **5** ½ **Hot Stuff**[31] 1340 4-8-4 **57**... GeorgiaCox(5) 5 53
(Tony Carroll) *chsd ldrs on outer: effrt over 1f out: no imp and kpt on same pce ins fnl f* **11/2**

58.32s (-0.48) **Going Correction** -0.075s/f (Stan) **5** Ran SP% **111.8**
Speed ratings (Par 103): **100,97,97,95,94**
CSF £12.90 TOTE £2.30: £1.30, £3.80; EX 9.00 Trifecta £23.60.
**Owner** M Chung **Bred** Denford Stud Ltd **Trained** Market Drayton, Shropshire

**FOCUS**
Plenty of course specialists in the field. It was run at a sound pace. The winner is rated close to her old best.

### 2026 TTS NETWORKS H'CAP 1m 1y(P)
**6:35** (6:35) (Class 4) (0-85,86) 4-Y-0+ **£5,175** (£1,540; £769; £384) **Stalls** High

Form RPR

31 **1** **Bouclier (IRE)**[33] 1302 7-9-4 **82**... LukeMorris 2 89
(David Loughnane) *t.k.h: wl in tch in last pair: effrt on outer bnd 2f out: hdwy to chal 1f out: led ins fnl f: r.o wl* **7/1**

325- **2** ¾ **Golden Wedding (IRE)**[164] 7903 5-9-2 **80**... JohnFahy 5 85
(Eve Johnson Houghton) *chsd ldr: rdn and ev ch 2f out: drvn to ld 1f out: hdd and styd on same pce ins fnl f* **9/1**

410- **3** nk **Dream Of Summer (IRE)**[164] 7903 4-9-2 **80**... RobHornby 3 84
(Andrew Balding) *led: rdn over 1f out: hdd and drvn 1f out: kpt on same pce fnl 100yds* **5/1**[3]

051- **4** nk **Shargiah (IRE)**[294] 3951 4-9-3 **81**... AndreaAtzeni 1 84
(Roger Varlan) *trckd ldrs: swtchd lft and effrt on inner over 1f out: styd on same pce fnl f* **5/2**[2]

3214 **5** nse **The Warrior (IRE)**[10] 1766 5-9-8 **86**... JimCrowley 4 89
(Amanda Perrett) *stdd after s: hld up wl in tch in last pair: rdn and clsd to chse ldrs 1f out: styd on same pce fnl 100yds* **5/4**[1]

1m 38.14s (-0.06) **Going Correction** -0.075s/f (Stan) **5** Ran SP% **112.2**
Speed ratings (Par 105): **97,96,95,95,95**
CSF £58.67 TOTE £6.60: £3.80, £3.60; EX 29.40 Trifecta £178.70.
**Owner** M Chung **Bred** Dayton Investments Ltd **Trained** Market Drayton, Shropshire

**FOCUS**
Not a bad contest despite the small field, but ordinary form for the grade. It was run at a steady pace and they finished in a bunch.

### 2027 RETRAINING OF RACEHORSES H'CAP 1m 4f (P)
**7:05** (7:05) (Class 6) (0-60,60) 3-Y-0 **£2,911** (£866; £432; £216) **Stalls** Low

Form RPR

-024 **1** **La Vie En Rose**[74] 637 3-9-7 **60**... JoeFanning 1 65
(Mark Johnston) *chsd ldrs: effrt to chal on inner 2f out: sn led and forged ahd 1f out: styd on wl* **5/1**[3]

4402 **2** 1¾ **Too Many Shots**[16] 1623 3-9-4 **57**... KierenFox 4 59
(John Best) *chsd ldr tl led 3f out: sn rdn and hrd rdn: hdd wl over 1f out: unable qck and kpt on same pce ins fnl f* **4/1**[2]

600- **3** nk **Amadeus Rox (FR)**[203] 7012 3-9-4 **57**... MartinHarley 2 59
(Alan King) *hld up in midfield: swtchd rt and hdwy to join ldrs 3f out: sn rdn and outpcd over 1f out: rallied and kpt on again ins fnl f* **6/1**

600- **4** nse **Curtsy (IRE)**[196] 7210 3-9-6 **59**... LiamKeniry 5 60
(Hughie Morrison) *hld up in midfield: effrt in 5th over 2f out: kpt on ins fnl f: nvr threatening wnr* **12/1**

6061 **5** nk **Bartholomew J (IRE)**[16] 1623 3-8-12 **54**... SimonPearce(3) 9 55+
(Lydia Pearce) *s.i.s: hld up in rr: stl plenty to do and hdwy on inner over 1f out: swtchd rt ins fnl f: r.o strly: nvr gng to rch ldrs* **5/1**[3]

06-5 **6** 1 **Netley Abbey**[12] 1726 3-8-9 **55**... RhiainIngram(7) 8 54
(Harry Dunlop) *chsd ldrs: 4th and unable qck 2f out: kpt on same pce fr over 1f out* **33/1**

600- **7** 2¼ **Nobleman (GER)**[159] 7977 3-9-6 **59**... JimCrowley 7 55
(Hughie Morrison) *t.k.h: hld up in last trio: hung rt bnd 4f out: stl plenty to do and rdn over 1f out: kpt on same pce ins fnl f: nvr trbld ldrs* **3/1**[1]

0406 **8** 2 **Greyjoy (IRE)**[9] 1790 3-8-11 **55**... MitchGodwin(5) 6 48
(Sylvester Kirk) *hld up in last quartet: effrt over 2f out: no imp and styd on same pce fr over 1f out* **14/1**

00-0 **9** 1¾ **Light Gunner (IRE)**[23] 1499 3-9-2 **55**... PatCosgrave 10 45
(Henry Tett) *t.k.h: hld up in last quartet: effrt over 2f out: no imp: nvr trbld ldrs* **25/1**

00-0 **10** 28 **Zipedee**[17] 1596 3-8-0 **46** oh1... JackOsborn(7) 3
(John Ryan) *led tl 3f out: sn dropped out and bhd 2f out: t.o* **66/1**

2m 30.42s (-2.58) **Going Correction** -0.075s/f (Stan) **10** Ran SP% **115.3**
Speed ratings (Par 96): **105,103,103,103,103 102,101,99,98,80**
CSF £24.64 CT £122.44 TOTE £5.30: £1.90, £1.60, £2.50; EX 26.40 Trifecta £158.20.
**Owner** Miss K Rausing **Bred** Miss K Rausing **Trained** Middleham Moor, N Yorks

**FOCUS**
Plenty of unexposed types in the field. It was run at an honest pace and it paid to race handy. Pretty modest form.

### 2028 RACING WELFARE 24 HOUR SUPPORT LINE 08006300443 FILLIES' H'CAP 1m 2f (P)
**7:35** (7:35) (Class 5) (0-75,76) 4-Y-0+ **£3,234** (£962; £481; £240) **Stalls** Low

Form RPR

20-3 **1** **Rum Swizzle**[16] 1630 5-9-1 **69**... LukeMorris 4 74
(Harry Dunlop) *t.k.h: hld up in tch: effrt and rdn to ld 2f out: edgd rt 1f out: hrd drvn and kpt on ins fnl f* **12/1**

06-6 **2** hd **Inke (IRE)**[32] 1323 5-9-8 **76**...(p) PatCosgrave 3 80
(Jim Boyle) *hld up in tch: effrt wl over 1f out: chsd wnr ins fnl f: edgd lft u.p wl ins fnl f: kpt on* **9/2**[3]

235- **3** 1 **Kath's Legacy**[221] 6527 4-9-5 **73**... JimCrowley 6 76
(Ben De Haan) *chsd ldrs tl wnt 2nd 7f out: effrt wl over 1f out: stl pressing ldrs but keeping on same pce whn short of room and snatched up towards fin* **7/2**[2]

2226 **4** ¾ **First Experience**[37] 1261 6-9-1 **76**...(p) JoshuaBryan(7) 1 77
(Lee Carter) *chsd ldr tl 7f out: styd handy: nt clr run 2f out: swtchd lft and effrt to chse wnr 1f out: unable qck and lost 2 pls wl ins fnl f* **12/1**

3112 **5** 4 **Star Of Lombardy (IRE)**[3] 1938 4-9-7 **75**... JoeFanning 5 68
(Mark Johnston) *dwlt: sn rcvrd to ld: hdd and rdn 2f out: no ex and btn 1f out: wknd ins fnl f* **10/11**[1]

2/00 **6** nse **Impressive Day (IRE)**[14] 1687 4-8-13 **70**... NoelGarbutt(3) 2 62
(Gary Moore) *rn in snatches: a rr: nvr trbld ldrs* **25/1**

2m 4.67s (-1.93) **Going Correction** -0.075s/f (Stan) **6** Ran SP% **112.0**
Speed ratings (Par 100): **104,103,103,102,99 99**
CSF £63.05 TOTE £8.90: £3.20, £1.70; EX 34.70 Trifecta £174.30.
**Owner** The Nigel Bennett Partnership **Bred** Granham Farm And P Hearson Bloodstock **Trained** Lambourn, Berks

**FOCUS**
This was competitive enough for the grade, but the pace was muddling. A small pb from the winner.
T/Plt: £340.50 to a £1 stake. Pool: £51,032.21 - 109.40 winning units. T/Qpdt: £63.70 to a £1 stake. Pool: £5,454.98 - 63.37 winning units. **Steve Payne**

# 1700 PONTEFRACT (L-H)
Monday, April 24

**OFFICIAL GOING: Good to firm (good in places) (watered)**
Wind: Light behind, gusting to moderate before 3.35 race, strong for the last two races Weather: Cloudy with sunny periods

## 2029 BANANARAMA AT 80S NIGHT ON 26TH MAY NOVICE STKS — 5f 3y
2:00 (2:00) (Class 5) 2-Y-O £3,234 (£962; £481; £240) Stalls Low

Form RPR
1 **Gisele's Angel** 2-8-11 0 ........ BenCurtis 4 72
(Richard Guest) *qckly away: mde all: rdn clr over 1f out: kpt on strly* **4/1**³
2 1 **Lord Riddiford (IRE)** 2-9-2 0 ........ JasonHart 5 73
(John Quinn) *in tch: hdwy on inner over 2f out: rdn over 1f out: kpt on wl towards fin* **16/1**
3 hd **Sinaloa (IRE)** 2-9-2 0 ........ TonyHamilton 1 73
(Richard Fahey) *dwlt: sn pushed along and hdwy to trck ldrs on inner after 1f: effrt over 2f out: rdn wl over 1f out: styd on fnl f* **2/1**¹
3 4 ¾ **Ventura Knight (IRE)**[18] 1588 2-9-2 0 ........ FrannyNorton 12 70
(Mark Johnston) *prom on outer: rdn along 2f out: drvn over 1f out: kpt on fnl f* **8/1**
5 nk **Collingham Park (IRE)** 2-9-2 0 ........ GrahamLee 10 69+
(Jedd O'Keeffe) *rr: hdwy 2f out: swtchd rt to outer and rdn ent fnl f: kpt on wl: nrst fin* **33/1**
6 ¾ **Palmer (IRE)** 2-9-2 0 ........ ConnorBeasley 2 67
(Bryan Smart) *cl up: pushed along 2f out: rdn over 1f out: wknd fnl f* **3/1**²
7 2 **Queen's Sargent (FR)** 2-9-2 0 ........ ShaneGray 11 59+
(Kevin Ryan) *wnt rt s and towards rr: hdwy over 2f out: sn rdn and no imp* **17/2**
8 2 ¼ **Eyes Of Fire** 2-9-2 0 ........ AndrewMullen 6 51
(Ollie Pears) *dwlt and green: t.k.h and bhd: hdwy 1/2-way: rdn along wl over 1f out: n.d* **25/1**
0 9 9 **Rockesbury**[17] 1604 2-9-2 0 ........ DougieCostello 8 19
(Kevin Frost) *chsd ldrs: rdn along over 2f out: sn wknd* **100/1**
05 10 3 ¼ **Afterthisone**[9] 1792 2-9-2 0 ........ KevinStott 3 7
(Robin Dickin) *chsd ldrs: rdn along over 2f out: sn wknd* **100/1**
1m 3.35s (0.05) **Going Correction** -0.20s/f (Firm) **10 Ran SP% 114.6**
Speed ratings (Par 92): **91,89,89,87,87 86,83,79,65,59**
CSF £61.26 TOTE £4.90: £1.60, £3.80, £1.30; EX 79.90 Trifecta £329.40.
**Owner** Mrs Alison Guest **Bred** Moyns Park Estate And Stud Ltd **Trained** Ingmanthorpe, W Yorks
**FOCUS**
Stalls: Inside all races. This could work out to be a fair 2yo event for the class, rated around the fourth. There are reasons to rate the form cautiously though.

## 2030 LYNSEY BACON MEMORIAL H'CAP — 1m 6y
2:30 (2:30) (Class 4) (0-85,86) 4-Y-O+ £6,469 (£1,925; £962; £481) Stalls Low

Form RPR
33-5 1 **Red Tea**[19] 1562 4-9-5 82 ........ PaulHanagan 2 94+
(Peter Hiatt) *trckd ldrs on inner: swtchd rt and smooth hdwy over 2f out: led over 1f out: rdn clr fnl f: kpt on strly* **4/1**¹
1004 2 2 ¼ **Sands Chorus**[26] 1433 5-9-2 79 ........ JoeDoyle 8 84
(James Given) *trckd ldr: hdwy and cl up 3f out: rdn to chal wl over 1f out: drvn to chse wnr ins fnl f: no imp* **10/1**
000- 3 ½ **Zodiakos (IRE)**[196] 7222 4-9-2 79 ........ TonyHamilton 4 83
(Roger Fell) *trckd ldng pair: hdwy over 2f out: rdn over 1f out: kpt on same pce fnl f* **10/1**
000- 4 1 **Gerry The Glover (IRE)**[240] 5886 5-9-0 77 ........(p) BenCurtis 15 79
(Brian Ellison) *dwlt and swtchd lft to inner s: rr: hdwy 2f out: n.m.r and swtchd markedly rt to outer over 1f out: sn rdn and styd on strly fnl f* **16/1**
03-1 5 1 **Rockwood**[13] 1706 6-8-12 75 ........(v) TomEaves 3 74
(Karen McLintock) *midfield: hdwy over 2f out: rdn along wl over 1f out: kpt on fnl f* **5/1**²
2015 6 ½ **Magic City (IRE)**[18] 1583 8-8-11 77 ........(p) NathanEvans(3) 1 76
(Michael Easterby) *in tch on inner: hdwy 2f out: nt clr run jst over 1f out: swtchd rt and rdn ins fnl f: kpt on* **11/2**³
0130 7 2 ¼ **Alejandro (IRE)**[26] 1422 8-9-9 86 ........ FrannyNorton 10 79
(David Loughnane) *sn led: pushed along 3f out: rdn 2f out: sn drvn: hdd over 1f out and sn wknd* **14/1**
310- 8 hd **Westward Ho (IRE)**[150] 8092 4-9-2 79 ........ PJMcDonald 5 71
(James Bethell) *midfield: effrt and sme hdwy over 2f out: sn rdn along and no imp* **16/1**
00-5 9 1 ¼ **Sunnua (IRE)**[13] 1700 4-8-9 75 ........ SammyJoBell(3) 11 65
(Richard Fahey) *bhd: hdwy over 2f out: sn rdn along and n.d* **14/1**
110- 10 1 ½ **Sovereign Bounty**[240] 5866 5-9-3 80 ........ GrahamLee 16 66
(Jedd O'Keeffe) *hld up: a towards rr* **16/1**
30-0 11 hd **Finn Class (IRE)**[22] 1512 6-9-7 84 ........ PaulMulrennan 14 70
(Michael Dods) *hld up: a towards rr* **20/1**
0-66 12 1 ¼ **Abushamah (IRE)**[14] 1677 6-9-4 81 ........ JamesSullivan 6 64
(Ruth Carr) *a rr* **8/1**
16-0 13 1 ½ **Suitor**[22] 1517 5-8-5 75 ........ BenRobinson(7) 13 54
(Brian Ellison) *dwlt: a rr* **40/1**
1104 14 4 **Shearian**[13] 1700 7-8-5 73 ........ PhilDennis(5) 12 43
(Declan Carroll) *chsd ldrs: rdn along 3f out: sn wknd* **40/1**
100- 15 5 **Lord Franklin**[194] 7287 8-9-6 83 ........ NeilFarley 7 42
(Eric Alston) *chsd ldrs: rdn along 3f out: wknd over 2f out* **66/1**
1m 41.39s (-4.51) **Going Correction** -0.20s/f (Firm) **15 Ran SP% 123.5**
Speed ratings (Par 105): **114,111,111,110,109 108,106,106,105,103 103,102,100,96,91**
CSF £43.73 CT £394.39 TOTE £4.20: £1.60, £4.30, £3.70; EX 46.70 Trifecta £606.40.
**Owner** Ken Read Shelley Tucker Jimmy Cooper **Bred** Sheikh Hamdan Bin Maktoum Al Maktoum **Trained** Hook Norton, Oxon

**FOCUS**
They went a solid pace in this modest handicap and again it paid to be handy. It was a decent winning time and the winner was value for a little further.

## 2031 RIU HOTELS AND RESORTS H'CAP — 5f 3y
3:05 (3:05) (Class 2) (0-100,99) 4-Y-O+
£12,450 (£3,728; £1,864; £932; £466; £234) Stalls Low

Form RPR
-065 1 **Judicial (IRE)**[23] 1501 5-9-5 97 ........(e) JoeDoyle 3 106
(Julie Camacho) *trckd ldrs: hdwy 2f out: rdn to chal whn rdr dropped whip jst ins fnl f: qcknd wl to ld last 75 yds* **10/3**²
20-1 2 1 ½ **Edward Lewis**[5] 1876 4-8-12 95 6ex ........ JoshDoyle(5) 2 99
(David O'Meara) *cl up: rdn to ld over 1f out: drvn and edgd lft ins fnl f: hdd and no ex last 75 yds* **7/4**¹
00-6 3 nk **Northgate Lad (IRE)**[22] 1515 5-8-11 89 ........ BenCurtis 4 92
(Brian Ellison) *chsd ldng pair: hdwy 2f out: rdn over 1f out: drvn and kpt on fnl f* **13/2**³
6503 4 1 ¾ **Line Of Reason (IRE)**[9] 1800 7-9-7 99 ........ PaulMulrennan 5 95
(Paul Midgley) *swtchd lft s and hld up in tch: hdwy over 2f out: rdn to chse ldrs over 1f out: drvn ent fnl f: sn edgd lft and kpt on same pce* **7/1**
60-0 5 1 **Burnt Sugar (IRE)**[5] 1876 5-8-13 91 ........ TonyHamilton 1 84
(Roger Fell) *slt ld: rdn along 2f out: hdd over 1f out: grad wknd* **12/1**
0-11 6 nk **Art Collection (FR)**[10] 1777 4-8-10 88 ........ JamesSullivan 7 85+
(Ruth Carr) *hld up and sn detached in rr: hdwy wl over 1f out: styng on whn nt clr run ins fnl f: no imp after* **10/1**
00-0 7 6 **Another Wise Kid (IRE)**[22] 1515 9-8-9 87 ........ GrahamLee 6 57
(Paul Midgley) *chsd ldrs: rdn along on outer 2f out: sn wknd* **11/1**
1m 0.49s (-2.81) **Going Correction** -0.20s/f (Firm) course record **7 Ran SP% 110.4**
Speed ratings (Par 109): **114,111,111,108,106 106,96**
CSF £8.88 TOTE £4.40: £2.20, £1.50; EX 11.10 Trifecta £45.20.
**Owner** Elite Racing Club **Bred** Elite Racing Club **Trained** Norton, N Yorks
**FOCUS**
This good-quality sprint handicap was run at a decent tempo. Straightforward form, with a small pb from the winner.

## 2032 PONTEFRACT MARATHON H'CAP (ROUND 2 OF THE PONTEFRACT STAYERS CHAMPIONSHIP 2017) — 2m 5f 139y
3:35 (3:36) (Class 5) (0-75,73) 4-Y-O+ £3,234 (£962; £481; £240) Stalls Low

Form RPR
06-2 1 **Tuscan Gold**[13] 1703 10-9-1 60 ........(p) PJMcDonald 10 69
(Micky Hammond) *hld up in rr: stdy hdwy over 5f out: trckd ldrs 3f out: rdn to ld briefly 1 1/2f out: hdd narrowly ent fnl f: sn drvn and rallied gamely to ld again last 100 yds* **6/1**³
00-5 2 nk **Madam Lilibet (IRE)**[13] 1703 8-8-9 54 oh1 ........ JoeyHaynes 6 62
(Sharon Watt) *in tch: pushed along: flashed tail and lost pl after 6f: sn in rr: hdwy 4f out: effrt on outer to chse ldrs 2f out: sn chal: rdn to take narrow ld ent fnl f: sn drvn: hdd last 100 yds: kpt on* **10/1**
30-0 3 8 **Riptide**[13] 1703 11-9-6 65 ........ DougieCostello 5 66
(Michael Scudamore) *hld up in rr: hdwy over 4f out: chsd ldrs over 2f out: sn rdn and kpt on one pce fr over 1f out* **14/1**
000- 4 1 **Waterclock (IRE)**[55] 7158 8-9-8 67 ........(v) TomEaves 1 67
(Micky Hammond) *trckd ldrs: pushed along over 4f out: rdn along and outpcd 3f out: drvn and plugged on fnl 2f* **9/1**
00-6 5 1 ¾ **Gran Paradiso (IRE)**[13] 1703 5-9-6 65 ........(tp) PaulMulrennan 8 63
(Micky Hammond) *towards rr: hdwy and in tch 1/2-way: rdn along over 6f out: drvn over 3f out: one pce* **16/1**
210- 6 1 **La Fritillaire**[181] 7592 5-9-2 61 ........ AndrewMullen 4 58
(James Given) *trckd ldrs: hdwy 5f out: sn cl up: led over 2f out: rdn and hdd 1 1/2f out: sn drvn and wknd* **5/2**¹
320/ 7 5 **Dan Emmett (USA)**[100] 7436 7-9-9 68 ........ GrahamLee 7 61
(Michael Scudamore) *sn led: rdn along over 3f out: drvn over 2f out: sn hdd & wknd* **3/1**²
100- 8 21 **Rock On Bollinski**[192] 7332 7-10-0 73 ........(p) BenCurtis 2 47
(Brian Ellison) *dwlt and rr: hdwy and in tch 1/2-way: rdn along 5f out: wknd over 3f out: sn bhd and eased* **8/1**
005/ 9 16 **Needless Shouting (IRE)**[132] 6424 6-9-3 67 ........ GemmaTutty(5) 3 26
(Joanne Foster) *chsd ldng pair: rdn along 5f out: wknd over 3f out: sn bhd* **20/1**
40-0 10 34 **Duc De Seville (IRE)**[7] 1436 5-8-4 54 oh7 ........ PhilDennis(5) 9
(Michael Chapman) *cl up: rdn along 6f out: wknd 4f out: sn bhd* **150/1**
4m 53.25s (2.25) **Going Correction** -0.20s/f (Firm) **10 Ran SP% 116.0**
Speed ratings (Par 103): **87,86,83,83,82 82,80,73,67,54**
CSF £64.13 CT £805.95 TOTE £6.40: £1.90, £2.90, £4.20; EX 43.30 Trifecta £376.80.
**Owner** Littlethorpe Park Racing 1 **Bred** Mrs James Wigan & London TB Services Ltd **Trained** Middleham, N Yorks
**FOCUS**
An ordinary marathon handicap, run at a routine pace. The first pair were clear but it's hard to be too positive about the form.

## 2033 AWARD WINNING ART OF RACING RACEDAYS MAIDEN STKS — 6f
4:10 (4:11) (Class 5) 3-Y-O+ £3,881 (£1,155; £577; £288) Stalls Low

Form RPR
5- 1 **Black Isle Boy (IRE)**[324] 2913 3-9-3 0 ........ DanielTudhope 3 78
(David O'Meara) *trckd ldng pair: hdwy over 2f out: led wl over 1f out: sn rdn clr: styd on* **5/1**³
20- 2 1 ¾ **Wild Acclaim (IRE)**[146] 8140 3-9-3 0 ........ GrahamLee 2 71
(Ann Duffield) *trckd ldrs on inner: hdwy 2f out: swtchd rt and rdn over 1f out: chsd wnr ins fnl f: no imp* **10/1**
24- 3 ¾ **Undiscovered Angel (FR)**[212] 6762 3-8-9 0 ........ JordanVaughan(3) 9 64
(K R Burke) *trckd ldrs: hdwy on wd outside wl over 1f out: sn rdn and hung rt 1f out: sn one pce* **7/1**
5-23 4 nk **Sheepscar Lad (IRE)**[20] 1543 3-9-3 65 ........ TonyHamilton 8 68
(Nigel Tinkler) *sn slt ld: rdn along over 2f out: hdd wl over 1f out: sn drvn and kpt on same pce* **16/1**
2 5 3 ¾ **Hitchcock**[69] 731 3-9-3 0 ........ TomEaves 6 56
(Kevin Ryan) *in tch on outer: hdwy 2f out: rdn whn carried rt 1f out: sn swtchd lft and one pce* **4/1**²
6 ¾ **Noble Sword** 3-9-3 0 ........ JackGarritty 4 54
(Jedd O'Keeffe) *a towards rr* **33/1**
0 7 3 ¾ **Our Kim (IRE)**[22] 1514 3-9-3 0 ........ PaulMulrennan 5 42
(Mohamed Moubarak) *a rr* **50/1**
8 nk **Snow Excuse** 3-9-3 0 ........(t1) ConnorBeasley 7 41
(Bryan Smart) *dwlt and wnt rt s: green and a rr* **33/1**



The Form Book Flat, Raceform Ltd, Newbury, RG14 5SJ

62- **9** *12* **Star Catch**[213] 6732 3-8-12 0 PaulHanagan 1
(Charles Hills) *cl up on inner: disp ld over 2f out: rdn wl over 1f out: wknd qckly* **5/4**[1]

1m 15.79s (-1.11) **Going Correction** -0.20s/f (Firm) **9** Ran SP% **116.4**
Speed ratings (Par 103): **99,96,95,95,90 89,84,83,67**
CSF £52.86 TOTE £5.90: £1.80, £3.10, £1.70; EX 56.00 Trifecta £293.50.
**Owner** Evan M Sutherland **Bred** Ballyhane Stud **Trained** Upper Helmsley, N Yorks

**FOCUS**
A modest 3yo sprint maiden, the fourth helping with the standard.

## 2034 WALL OF FAME H'CAP 5f 3y
**4:40** (4:40) (Class 5) (0-70,70) 4-Y-0+ **£3,234** (£962; £481; £240) **Stalls** Low

Form RPR

3003 **1** **Oriental Relation (IRE)**[13] 1696 6-9-7 **70** (b) FrannyNorton 12 80
(James Given) *trckd ldr: cl up 1/2-way: rdn to ld wl over 1f out: clr ins fnl f: styd on* **15/2**

03-2 **2** *2 1/4* **Henley**[20] 1547 5-9-6 **69** BenCurtis 10 71
(Tracy Waggott) *trckd ldrs: hdwy 2f out: rdn over 1f out: drvn and kpt on fnl f* **5/1**[3]

054- **3** *hd* **Jack Luey**[125] 8473 10-9-6 **69** (b) PaulHanagan 1 70
(Lawrence Mullaney) *qckly away and led: jnd and rdn over 2f out: hdd wl over 1f out: sn drvn and kpt on same pce* **4/1**[1]

3425 **4** *1* **See Vermont**[12] 1722 9-8-12 **61** (p) DuranFentiman 5 59+
(Rebecca Bastiman) *dwlt and towards rr: swtchd rt to outer and gd hdwy over 1f out: rdn and kpt on fnl f* **20/1**

05-5 **5** *1/2* **Flicka's Boy**[2] 1965 5-9-2 **65** BarryMcHugh 9 61
(Tony Coyle) *chsd ldrs: rdn along wl over 1f out: drvn and edgd lft ins fnl f: no imp* **10/1**

-223 **6** *1/2* **El Principe**[7] 1833 4-9-4 **67** JasonHart 11 61
(Les Eyre) *trckd ldrs on inner: pushed along 2f out: rdn over 1f out: sn drvn and carried hd high: stmbld jst ins fnl f: one pce* **9/2**[2]

0-64 **7** *nk* **Groundworker (IRE)**[19] 1558 6-8-12 **61** (t) PaulMulrennan 2 54
(Paul Midgley) *hld up towards rr: swtchd rt and hdwy wl over 1f out: sn rdn and no imp fnl f* **6/1**

005- **8** *1* **Oriental Splendour (IRE)**[222] 6475 5-9-7 **70** JamesSullivan 7 59
(Ruth Carr) *chsd ldrs:. hdwy 2f out: sn rdn and wknd fnl f* **9/1**

40-4 **9** *1/2* **Gaelic Wizard (IRE)**[18] 1593 9-8-8 **62** (v) GemmaTutty(5) 6 50
(Karen Tutty) *trckd ldrs on inner: effrt 2f out: sn rdn along and wknd* **20/1**

10-0 **10** *2* **Captain Scooby**[112] 21 11-8-8 **57** (v) ConnorBeasley 4 37
(Richard Guest) *a rr* **25/1**

20-0 **11** *7* **Twentysvnthlancers**[9] 1805 4-9-6 **69** GrahamLee 8 24
(Paul Midgley) *dwlt: a rr* **28/1**

1m 1.37s (-1.93) **Going Correction** -0.20s/f (Firm) **11** Ran SP% **116.8**
Speed ratings (Par 103): **107,103,103,101,100 99,99,97,97,93 82**
CSF £42.02 CT £175.87 TOTE £8.30: £3.00, £1.80, £1.60; EX 57.30 Trifecta £193.20.
**Owner** The Cool Silk Partnership **Bred** Brendan Laffan & Michael McCormick **Trained** Willoughton, Lincs

**FOCUS**
A competitive sprint handicap for the class. The winner is worth a bit more at face value.

## 2035 RUGBY LEAGUE EVENING ON MONDAY 12TH JUNE H'CAP (DIV I) 1m 6y
**5:10** (5:11) (Class 5) (0-70,72) 3-Y-0 **£3,234** (£962; £481; £240) **Stalls** Low

Form RPR

50-4 **1** **Alfred Richardson**[31] 1347 3-9-6 **69** PhillipMakin 2 72
(John Davies) *trckd ldng pair: hdwy 2f out: rdn over 1f out: led ins fnl f: drvn out* **11/2**

0-62 **2** *1* **Heir Of Excitement (IRE)**[14] 1678 3-9-9 **72** ShaneGray 7 73
(Kevin Ryan) *cl up: led wl over 1f out: sn rdn: drvn and hdd ins fnl f: kpt on* **7/2**[1]

36-1 **3** *nk* **Copper Baked (FR)**[18] 1589 3-9-7 **70** JoeyHaynes 8 70
(K R Burke) *trckd ldrs: hdwy over 2f out: rdn over 1f out: drvn and kpt on fnl f* **16/1**

505- **4** *hd* **Mister Moosah (IRE)**[212] 6791 3-9-1 **64** PJMcDonald 5 64
(Micky Hammond) *hld up in rr: hdwy 2f out: rdn over 1f out: n.m.r and swtchd lft ins fnl f: kpt on towards fin* **10/1**

-444 **5** *1/2* **Mama Africa (IRE)**[40] 1199 3-9-3 **66** (b[1]) BenCurtis 4 64
(David Barron) *chsd ldrs: rdn along 2f out: drvn over 1f out: kpt on same pce* **8/1**

022- **6** *1/2* **Miss Danby (IRE)**[150] 8087 3-9-5 **68** FrannyNorton 3 65
(Mark Johnston) *led: pushed along over 2f out: rdn wl over 1f out: sn hdd and grad wknd* **6/1**

00-3 **7** *1 1/4* **Sakurajima (IRE)**[14] 1686 3-9-4 **67** (t) PaulHanagan 6 61
(Charles Hills) *hld up in rr: hdwy on outer 1/2-way: chsd ldrs over 2f out: rdn along wl over 1f out: sn drvn and wknd* **4/1**[2]

303- **8** *nse* **Buccaneers Cove (IRE)**[177] 7688 3-9-1 **64** TonyHamilton 10 58
(Richard Fahey) *t.k.h: hld up in tch: effrt 3f out: rdn along 2f out: sn wknd* **5/1**[3]

1m 46.76s (0.86) **Going Correction** -0.20s/f (Firm) **8** Ran SP% **114.6**
Speed ratings (Par 98): **87,86,85,85,85 84,83,83**
CSF £25.15 CT £291.14 TOTE £7.30: £1.70, £1.50, £4.40; EX 30.00 Trifecta £298.70.
**Owner** K Kirkup & J Davies **Bred** J J Davies & K Kirkup **Trained** Piercebridge, Durham

**FOCUS**
There was a bunched finish in this moderate 3yo handicap. The runner-up is the guide to this ordinary form.

## 2036 RUGBY LEAGUE EVENING ON MONDAY 12TH JUNE H'CAP (DIV II) 1m 6y
**5:40** (5:40) (Class 5) (0-70,72) 3-Y-0 **£3,234** (£962; £481; £240) **Stalls** Low

Form RPR

46-1 **1** **Miss Sheridan (IRE)**[14] 1678 3-8-13 **69** HarrisonShaw(7) 8 75
(Michael Easterby) *mde all: rdn over 1f out: hld on gamely towards fin* **7/2**[1]

1-43 **2** *1/2* **Ronnie The Rooster**[51] 1029 3-9-3 **66** BenCurtis 3 71
(David Barron) *chsd wnr: rdn to chal over 1f out: drvn and edgd lft ins fnl f: kpt on towards fin* **4/1**[2]

2413 **3** *1 1/2* **Critical Thinking (IRE)**[41] 1195 3-9-3 **66** DougieCostello 1 68
(Kevin Frost) *in tch: hdwy over 4f out: rdn to chse ldng pair 2f out: drvn over 1f out: kpt on same pce* **12/1**

254- **4** *3* **Miss Bates**[189] 7406 3-9-7 **70** GrahamLee 2 65
(Ann Duffield) *towards rr: hdwy over 3f out: chsd ldrs 2f out: sn rdn and no imp* **15/2**

532- **5** *3 1/2* **Reinstorm**[215] 6681 3-8-9 **58** PaulHanagan 5 45
(Richard Fahey) *chsd ldrs: rdn along over 2f out: sn btn* **4/1**[2]

51- **6** *4* **Showdance Kid**[315] 3208 3-9-4 **72** CliffordLee(5) 4 49
(K R Burke) *chsd ldrs: rdn along 3f out: sn outpcd* **5/1**[3]

016- **7** *13* **Ray Donovan (IRE)**[235] 6045 3-9-1 **64** DanielTudhope 9 12
(David O'Meara) *prom on outer whn carried wd bnd after 1f: bhd after* **20/1**

550- **8** *4 1/2* **Pennington**[177] 7688 3-9-4 **67** FrannyNorton 6 4
(Mark Johnston) *chsd ldrs whn rn wd bnd after 1f: bhd after* **9/1**

1m 43.25s (-2.65) **Going Correction** -0.20s/f (Firm) **8** Ran SP% **113.1**
Speed ratings (Par 98): **105,104,103,100,96 92,79,75**
CSF £17.19 CT £148.61 TOTE £3.90: £1.50, £2.00, £4.00; EX 19.90 Trifecta £113.40.
**Owner** J Blackburn & A Turton & Partner **Bred** Drumlin Bloodstock **Trained** Sheriff Hutton, N Yorks

**FOCUS**
This second division of the 1m 3yo handicap was 3.5secs quicker than the first. The form is rated around the third.
T/Jkpt: Not won. T/Plt: £267.80 to a £1 stake. Pool: £73,701.40 - 200.84 winning units. T/Qpdt: £55.40 to a £1 stake. Pool: £4,894.26 - 65.28 winning units. **Joe Rowntree**

# 1681 WINDSOR (R-H)
Monday, April 24

**OFFICIAL GOING: Good to firm (8.6) (watered)**
Wind: Moderate, behind final 5f Weather: Overcast

## 2037 SKY BET BEST ODDS GUARANTEED FILLIES' NOVICE AUCTION STKS (PLUS 10 RACE) 5f 21y
**4:45** (4:48) (Class 5) 2-Y-0 **£2,911** (£866; £432; £216) **Stalls** Low

Form RPR

0 **1** **Yogi's Girl (IRE)**[16] 1627 2-8-10 0 JFEgan 5 74
(David Evans) *mde virtually all against nr side rail: shkn up 2f out: kpt on wl whn pressed and a holding on* **10/1**

**2** *1/2* **Mother Of Dragons (IRE)** 2-8-10 0 OisinMurphy 7 72
(Joseph Tuite) *pressed wnr: shkn up to chal 2f out: kpt on wl but a hld ins fnl f* **5/1**[3]

3 **3** *1/2* **Aquadabra (IRE)**[16] 1627 2-8-12 0 RobertWinston 1 72
(Mick Channon) *chsd ldng pair against rail: plld out over 1f out: rdn to chal fnl f: styd on but a hld* **7/2**[2]

3 **4** *2 3/4* **Daddies Girl (IRE)**[14] 1681 2-8-11 0 DavidProbert 4 62
(Rod Millman) *chsd ldrs: shkn up and outpcd 2f out: no ch after but kpt on against rail fnl f* **5/2**[1]

**5** *nk* **Gold Filigree (IRE)** 2-9-0 0 ShaneKelly 6 63
(Richard Hughes) *t.k.h: chsd ldrs and in tch: taken out wd and effrt 2f out: nt pce to threaten fnl f* **16/1**

**6** *2 1/4* **Jungle Queen (IRE)** 2-8-11 0 CharlesBishop 9 52
(Eve Johnson Houghton) *spd out wd: shkn up and wknd over 1f out* **16/1**

5 **7** *nk* **Cruel Clever Cat**[23] 1496 2-8-10 0 FergusSweeney 3 50
(John Gallagher) *towards rr: shkn up 2f out: one pce and no real prog* **12/1**

**8** *3/4* **Amazing Alice** 2-8-12 0 JackMitchell 8 50
(Archie Watson) *pushed along towards rr bef 1/2-way: no real prog* **6/1**

**9** *1* **Firenze Rosa (IRE)** 2-8-10 0 WilliamCarson 11 44
(John Bridger) *spd out wd 3f: wknd over 1f out* **100/1**

**10** *7* **Amiirah** 2-8-11 0 MartinDwyer 13 20
(John Gallagher) *a wl in rr: bhd over 1f out* **50/1**

**11** *3/4* **Madam Pomfrey** 2-8-10 0 MartinLane 12 16
(Jonathan Portman) *s.s: a in rr: bhd over 1f out* **28/1**

**12** *16* **Paulamey** 2-8-10 0 SamHitchcott 2
(David Evans) *sn outpcd: t.o* **33/1**

59.48s (-0.82) **Going Correction** -0.15s/f (Firm) **12** Ran SP% **119.6**
Speed ratings (Par 89): **100,99,98,94,93 89,89,88,86,75 74,48**
CSF £58.85 TOTE £12.00: £3.10, £1.50, £1.90; EX 82.10 Trifecta £457.40.
**Owner** A Cooke, K McCabe, Mrs Burns **Bred** Newlands House Stud & Mrs A M Burns **Trained** Pandy, Monmouths

**FOCUS**
The watered ground was given as good to firm (GoingStick: 8.6). The rail on the inner of the straight was dolled out 7yds at 6f and 4yds at the winning line. The rail on the top bend was dolled out 6yds from its normal inner configuration, adding 23yds to race distances of 1m plus. A modest maiden in which the pace held up. The form is rated in line with the race average.

## 2038 SKY BET HORSERACING CASH OUT H'CAP 5f 21y
**5:15** (5:19) (Class 4) (0-85,87) 4-Y-0+ **£4,690** (£1,395; £697; £348) **Stalls** Low

Form RPR

0-24 **1** **Stepper Point**[24] 1465 8-9-10 **86** (p) MartinDwyer 1 93
(William Muir) *racd against nr side rail: disp ld: drvn into narrow ld fnl f: hld on wl* **9/2**[2]

000- **2** *1/2* **Waseem Faris (IRE)**[199] 7124 8-9-7 **83** JFEgan 8 88
(Ken Cunningham-Brown) *trckd ldng pair: chal and tk 2nd ins fnl f: nt qckn last 75yds* **16/1**

030- **3** *1/2* **Stake Acclaim (IRE)**[233] 6114 5-9-10 **86** (p) RobertWinston 2 89
(Dean Ivory) *disp ld: rdn over 1f out: nt qckn and lost 2nd ins fnl f: kpt on* **9/2**[2]

441- **4** *1 1/4* **Dark Shot**[233] 6114 4-9-11 **87** DavidProbert 3 86
(Andrew Balding) *trckd ldng trio: rdn and nt qckn over 1f out: one pce after* **5/2**[1]

326- **5** *1 1/4* **Stormflower**[128] 8429 4-8-7 **69** WilliamCarson 6 63
(John Bridger) *in tch towards rr: rdn and no imp ldrs wl over 1f out* **10/1**[3]

011- **6** *shd* **Secretfact**[210] 6832 4-8-9 **71** JimmyQuinn 9 70+
(Malcolm Saunders) *stdd s: hld up and swtchd fr wd draw: gng wl enough whn nt clr run fr 2f out to ins fnl f: nt rcvr* **16/1**

0-62 **7** *3/4* **Excellent George**[30] 1370 5-9-1 **80** (t) AaronJones(3) 7 71
(Stuart Williams) *chsd ldrs: rdn 2f out: fdd fnl f* **9/2**[2]

0000 **8** *11* **King Of Swing**[35] 1290 4-8-13 **75** (h) ShaneKelly 5 27
(Richard Hughes) *a struggling in rr: bhd fnl 2f* **22/1**

3R0- **9** *99* **Bahamian Heights**[174] 7737 6-8-13 **75** SamHitchcott 4
(Robert Cowell) *reluctant to enter stalls: virtually ref to r: ambled home* **14/1**

58.41s (-1.89) **Going Correction** -0.15s/f (Firm) **9** Ran SP% **115.0**
Speed ratings (Par 105): **109,108,107,105,103 103,102,84,**
CSF £72.18 CT £343.30 TOTE £5.10: £1.60, £4.10, £2.10; EX 67.50 Trifecta £425.10.
**Owner** C L A Edginton **Bred** Whitsbury Manor Stud **Trained** Lambourn, Berks

**FOCUS**
Another sprint in which the pace held up. Pretty ordinary form.

## 2039 GABRIEL AT THE THEATRE ROYAL WINDSOR MAIDEN STKS 1m 1f 194y
**5:45** (5:50) (Class 5) 3-Y-O+ £2,911 (£866; £432; £216) **Stalls** Centre

Form RPR

3-4 **1** **Wasatch Range**[23] 1497 3-8-11 0........................................ RobertTart 12 86+
(John Gosden) *hld up in rr: gd prog on wd outside over 2f out: rdn to chse clr ldng pair wl over 1f out: clsd fnl f: r.o to ld last strides* **4/1**

**2** *shd* **Janszoon** 3-8-11 0........................................................(b[1]) MartinLane 14 85
(Charlie Appleby) *mde most: racd against nr side rail in st: shkn up 3f out: hdd 2f out: led again over 1f out: drvn and kpt on: hdd last strides* **25/1**

3- **3** *1 ½* **Next Challenge (GER)**[175] 7726 3-8-11 0............ JosephineGordon 16 82
(Saeed bin Suroor) *w ldr: clr of rest and gng best 3f out: led 2f out: shkn up and hdd over 1f out: one pce* **10/3**[3]

0/6 **4** *6* **Hawkerland (IRE)**[26] 1420 4-9-7 0.............................. TylerSaunders(7) 9 73+
(Marcus Tregoning) *hld up towards rr: shkn up 3f out: stdy prog 2f out to take 4th fnl f: shaped w promise* **50/1**

2 **5** *3 ¾* **Ply**[19] 1551 3-8-8 0.................................................. KieranShoemark(3) 10 63
(Roger Charlton) *chsd ldrs disputing 5th: rdn over 2f out: no imp ldng pair wl over 1f out: fdd* **3/1**[2]

5- **6** *2 ¼* **Perfect In Pink**[219] 6578 3-8-6 0........................................ JimmyQuinn 8 53+
(Mick Channon) *hld up towards rr: pushed along over 2f out: nvr a factor but kpt on steadily fr over 1f out despite nt clrest of runs: nt disgracd* **33/1**

0- **7** *1 ¼* **Epicurious (IRE)**[233] 6108 3-8-11 0.............................. MartinDwyer 13 56
(Brian Meehan) *in tch in midfield: shkn up wl over 2f out: no prog over 1f out* **80/1**

0-0 **8** *nse* **Marettimo (IRE)**[94] 328 3-8-11 0........................................ DavidProbert 1 55
(Charles Hills) *chsd ldng pair: rdn wl over 2f out: wknd wl over 1f out* **80/1**

2/5- **9** *1* **Silca Star**[369] 1570 4-10-0 0............................................ FergusSweeney 4 56
(Alan King) *uns rdr and cantered off to post: awkward s: t.k.h: hld up in last: nvr a factor but modest late prog* **40/1**

**10** *nk* **Precision** 3-8-11 0.......................................................... OisinMurphy 15 53
(Sir Michael Stoute) *s.i.s: a wl in rr and nvr a factor: modest late prog* **16/1**

0 **11** *1* **C'Est No Mour (GER)**[26] 1420 4-10-0 0........................ CharlesBishop 6 54
(Peter Hedger) *chsd ldng pair: drvn 3f out: wknd 2f out* **100/1**

24- **12** *½* **Swiftsure (IRE)**[185] 7495 3-8-11 0........................................ TedDurcan 7 50
(Sir Michael Stoute) *chsd ldrs disputing 5th: pushed along over 2f out: steadily fdd* **11/4**[1]

22 **13** *1 ½* **Ulysses (GER)**[31] 1342 3-8-11 0............................................ PatDobbs 5 47
(Ralph Beckett) *in tch in abt 8th: shkn up 3f out: no prog over 1f out: fdd over 1f out* **20/1**

**14** *shd* **Orin Swift (IRE)** 3-8-11 0.............................. RichardKingscote 3 47
(Jonathan Portman) *a towards rr: pushed along 3f out: no prog* **100/1**

2m 7.19s (-1.51) **Going Correction** -0.15s/f (Firm)
**WFA** 3 from 4yo 17lb **14** Ran SP% **121.0**
Speed ratings (Par 103): **100,99,98,93,90 89,88,88,87,87 86,85,84,84**
CSF £106.19 TOTE £5.30: £1.70, £6.60, £1.70; EX 130.20 Trifecta £679.00.
**Owner** Rachel Hood & Mrs P Shanahan **Bred** Cheveley Park Stud Ltd **Trained** Newmarket, Suffolk

**FOCUS**
Race distance increased by 23yds. The two Godolphin horses had this between them up front most of the way, but were both collared by the winner, who came from well off the pace. The first three were clear and the form is rated around the third.

## 2040 SKY BET WINDSOR SPRINT SERIES H'CAP (QUALIFIER) 6f 12y
**6:15** (6:21) (Class 3) (0-90,88) 4-Y-O+ £7,439 (£2,213; £1,106; £553) **Stalls** Low

Form RPR

100- **1** **Little Palaver**[197] 7186 5-9-7 88........................................ AdamKirby 8 97
(Clive Cox) *sn wl plcd: trckd ldr over 2f out: led wl over 1f out: drvn clr fnl f: readily* **8/1**

22-2 **2** *2* **Lightning Charlie**[18] 1586 5-9-6 87........................................ PatDobbs 1 90+
(Amanda Perrett) *racd against rail: cl up but trapped bhd ldr: nt clr run fr 2f out and stl trapped: fnlly in the clr last 150yds and r.o to take 2nd fnl strides* **5/1**[3]

-225 **3** *hd* **Pretty Bubbles**[26] 1423 8-9-4 85..............................(v) FergusSweeney 3 87
(J R Jenkins) *hld up in tch: nt clr run 2f out: swtchd lft over 1f out: prog after and styd on to dispute 2nd nr fin: no ch w wnr* **25/1**

000- **4** *1* **Cool Bahamian (IRE)**[135] 8314 6-9-1 85..........(v) EdwardGreatrex(3) 4 84
(Eve Johnson Houghton) *hld up in rr: prog on wd outside 2f out: drvn and kpt on fnl f: nrst fin* **20/1**

321- **5** *shd* **Pettochside**[208] 6883 8-8-10 77............................ JosephineGordon 10 76
(John Bridger) *chsd ldrs towards outer: rdn 2f out: disp 2nd over 1f out: fdd last 150yds* **16/1**

05-0 **6** *shd* **Rio Ronaldo (IRE)**[17] 1606 5-8-13 80.......................... JamieSpencer 5 79+
(Mike Murphy) *s.i.s: hld up in last pair: nt clr run wl over 2f out: looking for room over 1f out but trapped: r.o last 100yds: no ch to threaten* **11/4**[1]

-023 **7** *nk* **Under Siege (IRE)**[33] 1302 5-8-13 83..........................(t) AaronJones(3) 2 81
(Stuart Williams) *chsd ldr to over 2f out: lost pl and btn over 1f out* **8/1**

330- **8** *nk* **Kyllukey**[264] 5034 4-8-12 79........................................ DavidProbert 6 76
(Milton Bradley) *led and grad crossed to nr side rail: rdn and hdd wl over 1f out: wknd fnl f* **66/1**

6240 **9** *nk* **Gold Flash**[13] 1696 5-8-12 79........................................ KieranO'Neill 12 75
(Hugo Froud) *sn in last and pushed along: nvr a factor but kpt on fnl f* **66/1**

31- **10** *1* **Cold Snap (IRE)**[336] 2544 4-9-1 82............................ RobertWinston 11 74
(William Jarvis) *dwlt: hld up in rr: prog on outer 2f out: rdn and no ch w ldrs over 1f out: eased ins fnl f* **3/1**[2]

3005 **11** *shd* **Satchville Flyer**[41] 1184 6-8-9 76........................................ JFEgan 7 68
(David Evans) *chsd ldrs: short of room 1/2-way and lost pl: sn in rr and no ch after* **50/1**

40-0 **12** *9* **Englishman**[10] 1768 7-9-1 82........................................ OisinMurphy 9 45
(Milton Bradley) *chsd ldrs: lost pl sn after 1/2-way: eased whn no ch over 1f out* **12/1**

1m 11.19s (-1.81) **Going Correction** -0.15s/f (Firm) **12** Ran SP% **117.7**
Speed ratings (Par 107): **106,103,103,101,101 101,101,100,100,98 98,86**
CSF £45.42 CT £975.75 TOTE £7.60: £2.80, £1.80, £5.10; EX 43.60 Trifecta £394.20.
**Owner** Trevor Fox **Bred** Mrs Sandra Fox **Trained** Lambourn, Berks

**FOCUS**
A sprint handicap in which it paid to be up there, as more than one of the hold-up horses failed to get a clear run. The winner could be worth more at face value.

## 2041 SKY BET TOP PRICE PROMISE H'CAP 1m 3f 99y
**6:45** (6:48) (Class 4) (0-85,85) 4-Y-O+ £4,690 (£1,395; £697; £348) **Stalls** Centre

Form RPR

31/ **1** **Mr Khalid**[558] 7217 4-9-3 85..........................(h[1]) KieranShoemark(3) 2 91+
(Roger Charlton) *trckd ldrs: clsd to ld 2f out but pressed after: drvn fnl f: hld on* **5/4**[1]

0004 **2** *nk* **Jack Of Diamonds (IRE)**[19] 1562 8-8-7 71 oh3..........(b) JackMitchell 5 76
(Roger Teal) *dwlt: hld up in last: stdy prog on outer over 2f out: tk 2nd and drvn to chal fnl f: outbattled nr fin* **14/1**

644- **3** *1* **Spinners Ball (IRE)**[145] 8161 4-8-9 74............................ TomMarquand 1 77
(Sylvester Kirk) *hld up in tch: effrt over 2f out: drvn to chal ins fnl f: nt qckn last 100yds* **4/1**[2]

3-60 **4** *5* **Cape Discovery**[103] 173 5-9-6 84........................................ ShaneKelly 4 79
(Richard Hughes) *led at gd pce but sn pressed: hdd 6f out: led again over 3f out to 2f out: steadily fdd* **6/1**[3]

03-0 **5** *nk* **Primogeniture (IRE)**[17] 1608 6-9-7 85............................ OisinMurphy 6 80
(Mary Hambro) *chsd ldrs: urged along 5f out: gng bttr whn prog to chal 2f out: sn drvn: lost 2nd and fdd 1f out* **22/1**

066- **6** *21* **Lovely Story (IRE)**[178] 7669 6-8-11 75............................ TomQueally 8 35
(Seamus Durack) *t.k.h: sn pressed ldr: led 6f out to over 3f out: wknd over 2f out: eased and t.o* **13/2**

1-34 **7** *2* **Dream Love**[19] 1555 4-8-10 75........................................ DavidProbert 3 32
(Simon Dow) *taken down early: hld up in tch: urged along 5f out: wknd 3f out: eased 2f out: t.o* **12/1**

2m 26.34s (-3.16) **Going Correction** -0.15s/f (Firm) **7** Ran SP% **110.8**
Speed ratings (Par 105): **104,103,103,99,99 85,84**
CSF £19.42 CT £52.64 TOTE £2.10: £1.30, £6.60; EX 19.70 Trifecta £70.30.
**Owner** Saleh Al Homaizi & Imad Al Sagar **Bred** Saleh Al Homaizi & Imad Al Sagar **Trained** Beckhampton, Wilts

**FOCUS**
Race distance increased by 23yds. This was sound run, to suit those ridden with a bit of patience. The third is the best guide.

## 2042 WINDSOR RACECOURSE ROYAL RUN LOYALTY CARD H'CAP 1m 3f 99y
**7:15** (7:16) (Class 6) (0-65,67) 4-Y-O+ £2,264 (£673; £336; £168) **Stalls** Centre

Form RPR

36-2 **1** **Desert Cross**[19] 1556 4-9-2 61........................................ FranBerry 9 68+
(Jonjo O'Neill) *t.k.h: hld up: prog into midfield 4f out: hdwy to chse ldr over 1f out: shkn up to ld ins fnl f: sn in command: readily* **5/2**[1]

600/ **2** *¾* **Leonardo (GER)**[232] 6171 5-8-7 51 oh2............................ MartinDwyer 8 57
(Mark Pitman) *led: shkn up 2f out: drvn and hdd ins fnl f: kpt on but readily hld* **20/1**

-043 **3** *2* **Party Royal**[19] 1556 7-9-1 59..............................................(p) MartinLane 2 62
(Nick Gifford) *hld up in rr: prog on outer over 2f out: sn rdn: kpt on to take 3rd ins fnl f: nvr able to chal* **10/1**

0-30 **4** *1 ½* **Askari**[61] 856 4-9-6 65........................................................ AdamKirby 3 66
(Tom Clover) *chsd ldr to over 1f out: steadily wknd* **5/1**[2]

-050 **5** *2 ¼* **Goodby Inheritence**[35] 1283 5-9-3 61..........................(bt[1]) TomQueally 5 58
(Seamus Durack) *t.k.h: trckd ldrs: wnt 3rd over 3f out to over 2f out: fdd* **12/1**

-454 **6** *2* **Dakota City**[61] 861 6-9-9 67..........................................(v) AdamBeschizza 6 61
(Julia Feilden) *s.s: hld up in rr: sme prog to chse ldrs over 3f out: wknd 2f out* **8/1**[3]

2204 **7** *1 ¾* **Le Tissier**[23] 1486 4-8-10 55..........................................(p) WilliamCarson 4 46
(Michael Attwater) *mostly chsd ldng pair to over 3f out: lost pl u.p and btn over 2f out* **11/1**

50-6 **8** *nk* **Pretty Jewel**[32] 1334 4-9-3 62........................................ RobertWinston 7 53
(Sarah Hollinshead) *restrained after s and hld up in last: shkn up over 2f out: no prog and nvr involved* **22/1**

343- **9** *½* **Eugenic**[188] 7426 6-8-4 53........................................ LuluStanford(5) 1 43
(Rod Millman) *t.k.h: hld up in tch: wknd 3f out* **5/1**[2]

006- **10** *12* **Ravenswood**[164] 7904 4-8-10 55..............................(p[1]) DavidProbert 10 26
(Jonathan Portman) *chsd ldrs early: lost pl 1/2-way: last and struggling 4f out: sn bhd* **16/1**

2m 30.01s (0.51) **Going Correction** -0.15s/f (Firm) **10** Ran SP% **113.1**
Speed ratings (Par 101): **92,91,90,89,87 86,85,84,84,76**
CSF £56.45 CT £425.60 TOTE £3.40: £1.30, £5.50, £2.20; EX 58.40 Trifecta £413.80.
**Owner** P Hickey **Bred** W T , R T & N S Whittle **Trained** Cheltenham, Gloucs

**FOCUS**
Race distance increased by 23yds. This was steadily run and there's likely more to come from the winner.

## 2043 HOUSEHOLD CAVALRY MOUNTED REGIMENT H'CAP 6f 12y
**7:45** (7:48) (Class 6) (0-65,66) 4-Y-O+ £2,264 (£673; £336; £168) **Stalls** Low

Form RPR

40-1 **1** **Go Amber Go**[12] 1723 5-9-0 63..............................(b[1]) LuluStanford(5) 15 72
(Rod Millman) *wl away and v gd spd to ld on outer: grad tacked across and against nr side rail over 2f out: rdn over 1f out: kpt on wl fnl f* **5/1**[2]

121- **2** *1* **Titus Secret**[292] 3993 5-9-1 59........................................ FergusSweeney 2 65+
(Malcolm Saunders) *prom in chsng gp: rdn 2f out: nt qckn over 1f out: styd on ins fnl f to take 2nd nr fin* **8/1**

153- **3** *¾* **Quite A Story**[144] 8181 5-9-2 65............................ CharlieBennett(5) 10 69
(Patrick Chamings) *prom in chsng gp: rdn to take def 2nd over 1f out and tried to chal: hld ins fnl f and lost 2nd nr fin* **11/2**[3]

2206 **4** *1 ¾* **Spiraea**[20] 1542 7-9-3 66..............................(p[1]) LewisEdmunds(5) 3 65
(Ivan Furtado) *prom in chsng gp: tried to chal 2f out: lost 2nd over 1f out: fdd ins fnl f* **9/2**[1]

105- **5** *1 ½* **Robbie Roo Roo**[188] 7445 4-9-0 58..........(bt[1]) AdamBeschizza 13 52
(Mrs Ilka Gansera-Leveque) *prom in chsng gp on outer: rdn 2f out: fdd over 1f out* **20/1**

530- **6** *1* **Catalinas Diamond (IRE)**[118] 8542 9-8-8 52..............(t) SteveDrowne 6 43+
(Pat Murphy) *outpcd and bhd: rdn over 2f out: kpt on fr over 1f out: nrst fin but n.d* **40/1**

6-46 **7** *hd* **Himalayan Queen**[32] 1326 4-9-2 65........................ SophieKilloran(5) 11 55+
(William Jarvis) *dwlt: bdly outpcd and wl bhd: urged along on wd outside and kpt on fr 2f out: no ch* **20/1**

224- **8** *1 ½* **Concur (IRE)**[179] 7645 4-8-7 51 oh5........................................(t) RyanTate 7 37+
(Rod Millman) *nt on terms w ldrs in midfield: rdn 2f out: kpt on one pce: n.d* **14/1**

4130 **9** *shd* **Nasri**[12] 1723 11-8-12 56..........................................................(v) TomQueally 9 42+
(Emma Owen) *bdly outpcd and bhd: kpt on fnl 2f: no ch* **25/1**

060- **10** 1 1/4 **Flying Sakhee**[131] 8358 4-8-7 **51** oh4 WilliamCarson 1 33+
(John Bridger) *blindfold off late and slowly away: rchd midfield after 2f but nt on terms: no hdwy fnl 2f* **33/1**

-060 **11** 2 **Divine Call**[63] 843 10-9-0 **58** (b) DavidProbert 12 34+
(Milton Bradley) *outpcd and nvr on terms: no real prog fnl 2f* **33/1**

3343 **12** 1/2 **Jack The Laird (IRE)**[11] 1755 4-8-12 **59** (b) JackDuern(3) 4 33
(Dean Ivory) *prom in chsng gp to 2f out: hanging and wknd: eased* **7/1**

00-0 **13** 8 **Secret Look**[35] 1285 7-9-5 **63** (p) TimmyMurphy 14 13
(Richard Phillips) *outpcd and nvr on terms: bhd fnl 2f* **25/1**

2134 **P** **Assertive Agent**[17] 1599 7-9-7 **65** AdamKirby 5 +
(Tony Carroll) *plld and dismntd after 2f* **7/1**

1m 11.8s (-1.20) **Going Correction** -0.15s/f (Firm) **14** Ran SP% **118.5**
Speed ratings (Par 101): **102,100,99,97,95 94,93,91,91,89 87,86,75,**
CSF £39.61 CT £236.41 TOTE £5.50: £2.10, £2.60, £2.40; EX 35.90 Trifecta £197.70.
**Owner** AJ & CS Bricknell-Webb **Bred** Percys (north Harrow) Ltd **Trained** Kentisbeare, Devon

**FOCUS**
The winner got a freebie in front and took full advantage. This was a definite pb from her.
T/Plt: £80.30 to a £1 stake. Pool: £77,806.85 - 706.47 winning units. T/Qpdt: £14.30 to a £1 stake. Pool: £7,413.70 - 381.01 winning units. **Jonathan Neesom**

2044 - 2051a (Foreign Racing) - See Raceform Interactive

# [1785] BRIGHTON (L-H)

Tuesday, April 25

**OFFICIAL GOING: Good to firm (8.3) (watered)**
Wind: Moderate, behind Weather: Sunny and cool

## 2052 TOTEPLACEPOT AT TOTESPORT.COM MAIDEN STKS 5f 60y

**4:50** (4:50) (Class 5) 2-Y-O **£2,911** (£866; £432; £216) **Stalls** Low

Form RPR

5 **1** **Diamond Pursuit**[17] 1627 2-9-0 0 JFEgan 5 70
(Jo Hughes) *pressed ldrs on outer: hung lft wl over 1f out: drvn to dispute ld fnl f: jst prevailed* **3/1**[2]

6 **2** shd **Milton Road**[15] 1681 2-9-5 0 CharlesBishop 2 75
(Mick Channon) *trckd ldrs in 4th: effrt over 1f out: disp ld fnl f: jst denied* **9/2**

4 **3** 1 3/4 **Declarationoflove (IRE)**[15] 1681 2-9-5 0 JackMitchell 3 68
(Tom Clover) *led: hrd rdn and hdd 1f out: one pce* **7/4**[1]

05 **4** 3 1/4 **Controversial Lady (IRE)**[11] 1776 2-8-7 0 GeorgiaDobie(7) 4 52
(J S Moore) *w ldr: hrd rdn and short of room wl over 1f out: sn wknd* **25/1**

**5** 1 1/2 **Global Exceed** 2-9-5 0 JimmyQuinn 6 51
(Ed Dunlop) *dwlt: in rr: rdn over 2f out: nvr able to chal* **7/2**[3]

0 **6** 6 **My Guy (IRE)**[11] 1767 2-9-5 0 LiamKeniry 1 30
(J S Moore) *in tch on inner: rdn over 2f out: sn wknd* **20/1**

1m 2.56s (0.26) **Going Correction** -0.15s/f (Firm) **6** Ran SP% **110.4**
Speed ratings (Par 92): **91,90,88,82,80 70**
CSF £16.05 TOTE £4.30: £1.80, £2.50; EX 16.50 Trifecta £38.00.
**Owner** David Klein & Jo Hughes **Bred** Broughton Bloodstock **Trained** Lambourn. Berks

**FOCUS**
Rail movements increased race distances by 3yds. The going was good to firm (good in places) for the opener, a moderate juvenile maiden in which they went fast from the gate. The form's rated in line with the race averages.

## 2053 TOTEEXACTA AT TOTESPORT.COM H'CAP 6f 210y

**5:20** (5:20) (Class 6) (0-60,61) 4-Y-O+ **£2,264** (£673; £336; £168) **Stalls** Low

Form RPR

0-20 **1** **Tulip Dress**[66] 806 4-9-7 **60** WilliamCarson 5 68
(Anthony Carson) *trckd ldrs: led 2f out: edgd lft over 1f out: rdn clr fnl f* **10/1**

5-4 **2** 2 **Quiet Warrior (IRE)**[33] 1325 6-9-8 **61** (h) JosephineGordon 6 63
(David Loughnane) *led tl 2f out: one pce fnl f* **9/4**[1]

3422 **3** hd **Virile (IRE)**[5] 1898 6-8-11 **57** (bt) FinleyMarsh(7) 7 58
(Sylvester Kirk) *hld up in 5th: hdwy 2f out: edgd lft over 1f out: styd on fnl f* **10/3**[2]

-601 **4** 2 1/4 **Fleeting Glimpse**[20] 1557 4-9-6 **59** (h) DavidProbert 1 54
(Andrew Balding) *dwlt: bhd: sme hdwy and short of room whn hung lft over 1f out: styd on same pce fnl f* **9/2**[3]

0-06 **5** nk **Gypsy Rider**[84] 495 8-8-7 **46** oh1 KieranO'Neill 4 42
(Henry Tett) *towards rr: pushed along 4f out: hdwy on inner 2f out: squeezed through to press ldrs over 1f out: no ex fnl f* **50/1**

-202 **6** 1 3/4 **Hidden Gem**[33] 1325 4-9-2 **58** (vt) AaronJones(3) 8 47
(Stuart Williams) *chsd ldng pair tl wknd over 1f out* **8/1**

0560 **7** 4 1/2 **Indus Valley (IRE)**[20] 1557 10-8-12 **51** (p) KierenFox 3 28
(Lee Carter) *sn outpcd and bhd* **14/1**

5-04 **8** 3 1/2 **Sexton Blake (IRE)**[24] 1484 4-9-6 **59** (b[1]) TimmyMurphy 2 27
(Gary Moore) *dwlt: hdwy to press ldr after 1f: hrd rdn and wknd 2f out* **13/2**

1m 21.82s (-1.28) **Going Correction** -0.15s/f (Firm) **8** Ran SP% **114.2**
Speed ratings (Par 101): **101,98,98,95,95 93,88,84**
CSF £33.17 CT £93.30 TOTE £9.90: £2.80, £1.20, £1.50; EX 30.80 Trifecta £142.20.
**Owner** Hugh & Mindi Byrne & Minster Stud **Bred** Minster Stud **Trained** Newmarket, Suffolk

**FOCUS**
Race distance increased by 3yds. A moderate handicap in which the front-running tactics were overdone, helping set things up for the closers. The winner found 3lb on last year's turf best.

## 2054 TOTEQUADPOT AT TOTESPORT.COM H'CAP 6f 210y

**5:50** (5:50) (Class 4) (0-85,84) 4-Y-O+ **£4,690** (£1,395; £697; £348) **Stalls** Low

Form RPR

323- **1** **Ice Age (IRE)**[198] 7186 4-9-5 **82** RobertWinston 5 93
(Eve Johnson Houghton) *chsd ldr: rdn over 2f out: led ins fnl f: comf* **11/4**[1]

211- **2** 2 1/4 **Coronation Day**[195] 7281 4-9-7 **84** MartinHarley 2 89
(James Tate) *led: rdn over 2f out: hdd ins fnl f: one pce* **9/2**

0440 **3** 1 3/4 **Swiss Cross**[14] 1696 10-8-12 **75** (tp) JosephineGordon 3 75
(Phil McEntee) *chsd ldng pair: rdn over 2f out: styd on fnl f* **22/1**

624- **4** 2 **Fast Dancer (IRE)**[181] 7623 5-9-5 **82** JFEgan 1 77
(Joseph Tuite) *restless and rring in stalls: a 4th: hung lft 2f out: no imp* **4/1**[3]

316- **5** 2 **Tigerwolf (IRE)**[241] 5878 4-9-6 **83** CharlesBishop 6 72
(Mick Channon) *dwlt: bhd: hrd rdn and hung lft fnl 2f: n.d* **10/3**[2]

664- **6** 1/2 **Lyfka**[146] 8158 5-9-6 **83** (bt) DavidProbert 7 71
(Paul Cole) *modest 5th most of way: rdn and n.d fnl 2f* **8/1**

510- **7** 4 **Arlecchino's Leap**[207] 6914 5-9-4 **81** (p) LiamKeniry 4 58
(Mark Usher) *a bhd* **14/1**

1m 20.86s (-2.24) **Going Correction** -0.15s/f (Firm) **7** Ran SP% **110.1**
Speed ratings (Par 105): **106,103,101,99,96 96,91**
CSF £14.16 TOTE £3.40: £1.50, £2.70; EX 10.50 Trifecta £93.90.
**Owner** Eden Racing III **Bred** Piercetown Stud **Trained** Blewbury, Oxon

**FOCUS**
Race distance increased by 3yds. An average handicap in which all bar one were making their reappearance. The runner-up tried to nick it from the front, but paid for going too fast. The winner is rated in line with a better view of his form.

## 2055 TOTETRIFECTA AT TOTESPORT.COM H'CAP 1m 1f 207y

**6:20** (6:21) (Class 5) (0-75,74) 4-Y-O+ **£2,911** (£866; £432; £216) **Stalls** High

Form RPR

560- **1** **Roy Rocket (FR)**[189] 7429 7-9-0 **67** JFEgan 3 75
(John Berry) *rring in stalls: hld up in rr: smooth hdwy over 2f out: led over 1f out: pushed clr: comf* **8/1**

6126 **2** 1 3/4 **Russian Reward (IRE)**[25] 1462 5-9-7 **74** (p) JackMitchell 4 78
(Amanda Perrett) *led for 3f: led 2f out tl over 1f out: one pce* **13/2**[3]

2344 **3** 1 1/2 **Light Of Air (FR)**[15] 1683 4-9-3 **70** (b) TimmyMurphy 5 71
(Gary Moore) *chsd ldng pair: hrd rdn over 1f out: one pce* **3/1**[2]

2105 **4** 4 1/2 **Siouxperhero (IRE)**[8] 1839 8-8-10 **63** (p) DavidProbert 1 55
(William Muir) *in tch: hrd rdn 2f out: hung lft: sn outpcd* **10/1**

513- **5** 2 1/4 **Pack It In (IRE)**[229] 6268 4-9-5 **72** (b) MartinDwyer 8 60
(Brian Meehan) *plld hrd: pressed ldr: led after 3f tl wknd 2f out* **5/2**[1]

0026 **6** 1 3/4 **Solveig's Song**[10] 1789 5-8-6 **66** (p) RossaRyan(7) 7 50
(Steve Woodman) *s.i.s: towards rr: hdwy and in tch 1/2-way: wknd 2f out* **12/1**

16-5 **7** 8 **Becca Campbell (IRE)**[10] 1789 4-8-13 **66** (p) JohnFahy 6 34
(Eve Johnson Houghton) *in tch: rdn 3f out: sn wknd* **7/1**

12-0 **8** 5 **Onehelluvatouch**[10] 1789 4-8-7 **60** oh1 (b) KieranO'Neill 2 18
(Philip Hide) *towards rr: last 5f out: sn struggling* **14/1**

2m 2.17s (-1.43) **Going Correction** -0.15s/f (Firm) **8** Ran SP% **114.0**
Speed ratings (Par 103): **99,97,96,92,91 89,83,79**
CSF £56.15 CT £213.76 TOTE £8.10: £1.90, £2.00, £1.30; EX 42.60 Trifecta £229.40.
**Owner** McCarthy & Berry **Bred** John Berry **Trained** Newmarket, Suffolk

**FOCUS**
Race distance increased by 3yds. A moderate handicap where they again went a good pace, favouring the late-arriving course specialist, Roy Rocket. His best form since last year.

## 2056 @TOTEPOOLRACING FOLLOW US ON TWITTER CLASSIFIED STKS 7f 211y

**6:55** (6:55) (Class 6) 3-Y-O+ **£2,264** (£673; £336; £168) **Stalls** Low

Form RPR

-603 **1** **Andalusite**[10] 1785 4-9-6 52 (v) FergusSweeney 5 62+
(John Gallagher) *chsd ldr: led after 3f: drvn along and in control fnl 2f: styd on wl* **5/1**[2]

000- **2** 3 1/2 **Ettie Hart (IRE)**[194] 7298 4-8-13 54 KeithQuinn(7) 7 54
(Mick Channon) *towards rr: hdwy on inner 3f out: chsd wnr fnl 2f: no imp* **6/1**[3]

56-0 **3** 3 1/2 **Latest Quest (IRE)**[15] 1685 3-8-6 54 JosephineGordon 2 42
(Sylvester Kirk) *prom: wnt 2nd briefly over 2f out: sn outpcd* **13/8**[1]

60-0 **4** 1 1/2 **Rebel Woods (FR)**[48] 1081 4-9-6 46 LiamKeniry 3 42
(Geoffrey Deacon) *niggled along early: mid-div: pushed along 3f out: styd on fnl f* **16/1**

600- **5** 1 3/4 **Dark Phantom (IRE)**[194] 7298 6-9-6 42 JohnFahy 1 38
(Eve Johnson Houghton) *broke wl: chsd ldrs: rdn and btn 2f out* **8/1**

40-0 **6** 4 1/2 **Lemon Drop**[15] 1686 3-8-6 54 SamHitchcott 8 24
(Jim Boyle) *s.i.s: pushed along most of way: a bhd* **5/1**[2]

6-00 **7** 17 **Ormering**[20] 1563 4-8-13 43 (p) FinleyMarsh(7) 9
(Roger Teal) *towards rr: rdn 3f out: sn bhd* **25/1**

4-00 **8** 2 3/4 **Ciel Rouge**[13] 1726 3-8-6 48 (vt[1]) KieranO'Neill 6
(Charlie Wallis) *led for 3f: chsd ldr: hung rt 3f out: wnt bdly lft on camber over 2f out: wknd qckly* **14/1**

1m 35.06s (-0.94) **Going Correction** -0.15s/f (Firm)
**WFA** 3 from 4yo+ 14lb **8** Ran SP% **113.2**
Speed ratings (Par 101): **98,94,91,89,87 83,66,63**
CSF £34.11 TOTE £5.80: £1.80, £2.10, £1.10; EX 27.20 Trifecta £71.20.
**Owner** The LAM Partnership **Bred** Pinnacle Bloodstock Ltd **Trained** Chastleton, Oxon

**FOCUS**
Race distance increased by 3yds. A weak event lacking any depth of worthwhile recent form. The winner pulled herself into the lead, suggesting the pace wasn't overly strong. She bounced back towards her best.

## 2057 TOTEPOOL RACECOURSE APPLE PAY AVAILABLE H'CAP 7f 211y

**7:25** (7:25) (Class 6) (0-60,62) 4-Y-O+ **£2,264** (£673; £336; £168) **Stalls** Low

Form RPR

5-06 **1** **Stormbound (IRE)**[28] 1409 8-9-12 **61** (b) DavidProbert 8 71
(Paul Cole) *hld up in rr: hdwy in centre over 2f out: led over 1f out: pushed clr: comf* **5/2**[1]

505- **2** 4 **Jonnie Skull (IRE)**[254] 5090 11-8-10 **45** (vt) JosephineGordon 5 45
(Phil McEntee) *led tl over 1f out: one pce* **20/1**

4630 **3** 2 3/4 **Lutine Charlie (IRE)**[19] 1587 10-8-10 **45** (p) JFEgan 1 38
(Emma Owen) *chsd ldr: hrd rdn and lost 2nd over 1f out: one pce* **8/1**

-000 **4** 1/2 **Qortaaj**[36] 1285 4-9-6 **62** RossaRyan(7) 7 54
(David Loughnane) *anticipated s and hit gate: dwlt and t.k.h in rr: hrd rdn and sme hdwy 2f out: styd on fnl f* **13/2**

6-02 **5** 3 1/4 **Magic Moments**[29] 1407 4-9-7 **56** MartinHarley 4 41
(Alan King) *plld hrd early: hld up in 5th: short of room and wknd over 2f out* **10/3**[3]

0052 **6** 1/2 **Kristoff (IRE)**[1] 2024 4-8-3 **45** IsobelFrancis(7) 3 31
(Jim Boyle) *chsd ldrs: sltly outpcd whn squeezed out over 2f out: n.d after* **10/1**

40-0 **7** 6 **Live Dangerously**[15] 1683 7-9-6 **55** WilliamCarson 9 25
(John Bridger) *t.k.h: prom tl wknd over 2f out* **3/1**[2]

1m 34.5s (-1.50) **Going Correction** -0.15s/f (Firm) **7** Ran SP% **114.9**
Speed ratings (Par 101): **101,97,94,93,90 90,84**
CSF £50.77 CT £352.49 TOTE £2.90: £2.20, £5.60; EX 45.70 Trifecta £96.00.
**Owner** P F I Cole Ltd **Bred** A Footstep Away Syndicate **Trained** Whatcombe, Oxon
■ Stewards' Enquiry : David Probert three-day ban: guilty of careless riding in that he persisted in pursuing for a gap where there was insufficient room causing knock-on interference (May 9-11)

**FOCUS**
Race distance increased by 3yds. A moderate handicap that turned rough in the straight, and the winner did well to overcome a rough path. He's rated similar to last year's win here.

## 2058 COLLECT TOTEPOOL WINNINGS AT BETFRED SHOPS H'CAP 5f 215y

**7:55** (7:55) (Class 5) (0-70,72) 4-Y-O+ **£2,911** (£866; £432; £216) **Stalls** Low

Form RPR

30- **1** **One Big Surprise**[180] 7644 5-9-7 **70** ShaneKelly 5 78
(Richard Hughes) *prom: drvn to dispute ld fnl f: narrow ld fnl 100yds: all out* **4/1**[2]

114- 2 hd **Bahamian Sunrise**[181] 7626 5-9-4 72....................(p) GeorgeBuckell(5) 2 79
(John Gallagher) *led: jnd ent fnl f: narrowly hdd fnl 100yds: r.o gamely* **5/1**[3]

-332 3 1 1/2 **Captain Bob (IRE)**[27] 1431 6-9-4 67......................(p) MartinHarley 6 69
(Robert Cowell) *hld up in 5th: hdwy and hung lft over 1f out: kpt on fnl f* **5/2**[1]

-666 4 nk **Chetan**[13] 1728 5-9-5 68........................................(tp) WilliamCarson 7 69
(Charlie Wallis) *dwlt: rdn to rcvr: chsd ldr after 1f tl 2f out: kpt on u.p* **12/1**

5434 5 nk **Socialites Red**[13] 1720 4-8-10 59..................................(p) KieranO'Neill 8 60
(Scott Dixon) *chsd ldrs: rdn and short of room over 2f out: nt clr run and swtchd rt wl over 1f out: styd on fnl f* **8/1**

0-56 6 8 **Taajub (IRE)**[27] 1429 10-9-5 68.................................... FergusSweeney 1 42
(Peter Crate) *towards rr: effrt over 2f out: wknd over 1f out* **17/2**

0-50 7 9 **Soaring Spirits (IRE)**[15] 1687 7-9-8 71......................(b) RobertWinston 4 17
(Dean Ivory) *in rr whn sltly hmpd after 1f: sn outpcd and bhd* **4/1**[2]

1m 9.01s (-1.19) **Going Correction** -0.15s/f (Firm) **7** Ran SP% **114.6**
Speed ratings (Par 103): **101,100,98,98,97 87,75**
CSF £24.19 CT £58.92 TOTE £5.00: £2.60, £2.50; EX 21.70 Trifecta £66.30.
**Owner** Withyslade **Bred** Withyslade **Trained** Upper Lambourn, Berks

**FOCUS**
Race distance increased by 3yds. An uncompetitive sprint handicap, but a tight finish, and the first five finished close-up. The winner was basically to form.
T/Jkpt: Not Won. T/Plt: £56.40 to a £1 stake. Pool: £59,980.82 - 776.28 winning units T/Qpdt: £8.80 to a £1 stake. Pool: £5,645.29 - 470.25 winning units **Lee McKenzie**

## 1979 WOLVERHAMPTON (A.W) (L-H)

Tuesday, April 25

**OFFICIAL GOING: Tapeta: standard**
Wind: Fresh across Weather: Cloudy

### 2059 INVEST WOLVERHAMPTON FOR LIFE, WORK & LEARNING H'CAP (FOR GENTLEMAN AMATEUR RIDERS) 2m 120y (Tp)

**6:00** (6:00) (Class 5) (0-75,75) 4-Y-O+ **£2,994** (£928; £464; £232) **Stalls** Low

Form RPR

/6-4 1 **Three Colours Red (IRE)**[7] 1436 5-10-1 62.(p) MrMorganWinstone(7) 5 68
(Robert Stephens) *a.p: jnd ldrs over 3f out: shkn up to ld over 1f out: rdn ins fnl f: jst hld on* **33/1**

3264 2 shd **Icebuster**[11] 1763 9-11-6 74........................................... MrPMillman 3 79
(Rod Millman) *s.s: hld up: racd keenly: hdwy over 2f out: rdn and ev ch ins fnl f: styd on* **11/2**[3]

3230 3 9 **Tingo In The Tale (IRE)**[20] 1556 8-9-11 56 oh1....(tp) SeanHoulihan(5) 1 50
(Sophie Leech) *hld up: pushed along and hdwy over 2f out: rdn over 1f out: sn hung rt and wknd* **10/1**

1621 4 1 1/4 **Bracken Brae**[20] 1561 5-11-7 75........................................ MrSWalker 4 68
(Mark H Tompkins) *chsd ldrs: led over 3f out: rdn and hdd over 1f out: wknd ins fnl f* **1/1**[1]

2/04 5 17 **Bostonian**[18] 1602 7-11-2 75.................................. MrJamesHughes(5) 6 47
(Jo Hughes) *chsd ldr tl led 5f out: hdd over 3f out: rdn and wknd over 1f out* **2/1**[2]

466- 6 15 **Agreement (IRE)**[68] 4816 7-9-13 56 oh1................(b) RichardPatrick(3) 2 10
(Nikki Evans) *led at stdy pce tl hdd 5f out: sn rdn: wknd over 3f out* **50/1**

3m 38.89s (-4.81) **Going Correction** -0.225s/f (Stan) **6** Ran SP% **112.7**
Speed ratings (Par 103): **102,101,97,97,89 82**
CSF £196.72 TOTE £12.20: £4.50, £2.30; EX 37.90 Trifecta £400.20.
**Owner** The Red Partnership **Bred** Liam Delahunty **Trained** Penhow, Newport

**FOCUS**
A shock result with the market 1-2 disappointing. The first two were clear.

### 2060 INVEST WOLVERHAMPTON - CITY OF OPPORTUNITY H'CAP 1m 1f 104y (Tp)

**6:30** (6:32) (Class 6) (0-60,60) 3-Y-O **£1,594** (£1,594; £365; £182) **Stalls** Low

Form RPR

000- 1 dht **London Master**[153] 8073 3-9-7 60................................ AdamBeschizza 6 66+
(Chris Wall) *mid-div: hdwy over 1f out: rdn to join wnr ins fnl f: r.o u.p* **7/4**[1]

5606 1 dht **Log Off (IRE)**[9] 1822 3-9-0 56.................................. HectorCrouch(3) 3 62
(David Evans) *a.p: racd keenly: shkn up to ld over 1f out: rdn and jnd ins fnl f: r.o* **14/1**

365- 3 2 3/4 **All About The Pace**[140] 8235 3-8-10 54........................ RachealKneller(5) 2 54
(Mark Usher) *chsd ldrs: shkn up over 1f out: rdn and edgd lft ins fnl f: styd on same pce* **14/1**

-003 4 3/4 **Love And Be Loved**[20] 1564 3-8-12 51............................. DanielMuscutt 7 50
(John Flint) *hld up: hdwy over 1f out: hmpd sn after: sn rdn: styd on same pce ins fnl f* **10/1**

4-14 5 3/4 **Padleyourowncanoe**[9] 1822 3-9-5 58...................(b[1]) AndrewMullen 13 56
(Daniel Mark Loughnane) *hld up: hdwy u.p over 1f out: nt clr run sn after: styd on: nt rch ldrs* **6/1**[2]

05-0 6 shd **Skilful Lord (IRE)**[18] 1597 3-8-9 48................................(h) BenCurtis 10 45
(Stuart Kittow) *chsd ldrs: rdn over 2f out: edgd lft and styd on same pce fnl f* **10/1**

000- 7 1 1/4 **Size Matters**[136] 8305 3-9-3 56....................................(t[1]) DougieCostello 8 51
(Mark Walford) *sn led: hdd over 6f out: remained handy: led again over 3f out: rdn: hung rt and hdd over 2f out: edgd lft and wknd ins fnl f* **12/1**

-464 8 1 3/4 **Stag Party (IRE)**[63] 848 3-8-2 48............................(t) BenRobinson(7) 4 40
(Julia Brooke) *mid-div: rdn over 2f out: wknd fnl f* **12/1**

0-00 9 2 **Seeing Things (IRE)**[20] 1554 3-9-6 59.....................(t[1]) DanielTudhope 12 50
(Philip McBride) *hld up: hdwy over 1f out: styng on whn hmpd ins fnl f: nvr trbld ldrs* **25/1**

064- 10 1 1/4 **Dyna Might**[206] 6963 3-8-10 49...................................... FrannyNorton 9 35
(Ollie Pears) *s.i.s: sn rcvrd into mid-div: rdn over 3f out: wknd over 2f out* **7/1**[3]

000- 11 3/4 **General Allenby**[227] 6313 3-8-10 49..........................(b[1]) SteveDrowne 5 33
(Henry Tett) *hld up: rdn over 1f out: nvr on terms* **28/1**

0000 12 1/2 **Newton Heath (IRE)**[20] 1564 3-8-6 50..................... CharlieBennett(5) 1 35
(Daniel Mark Loughnane) *w ldr tl led over 6f out: hdd over 3f out: rdn and hdd over 1f out: sn edgd lft: hmpd 1f out: sn wknd* **25/1**

2m 0.35s (-0.45) **Going Correction** -0.225s/f (Stan) **12** Ran SP% **121.2**
Speed ratings (Par 96): **93,93,90,89,89 89,88,86,84,83 82,82**
CSF £14.59 CT £139.52 TOTE £1.30: £1.30, £8.80, £3.90; EX 17.60 Trifecta £118.80.
**Owner** Fung Lok Li **Bred** F L Li **Trained** Newmarket, Suffolk
**Owner** Mrs E Evans **Bred** M A Doyle **Trained** Pandy, Monmouths

**FOCUS**
A moderate but competitive affair, and the judge couldn't split the first two. The dead-heaters had different profiles and the third is the best guide.

### 2061 INVEST CITY OF WOLVERHAMPTON FILLIES' H'CAP 1m 4f 51y (Tp)

**7:05** (7:05) (Class 5) (0-75,77) 4-Y-O+ **£3,234** (£962; £481; £240) **Stalls** Low

Form RPR

50-0 1 **Renfrew Street**[26] 1457 4-9-6 75................................... FrannyNorton 5 83
(Mark Johnston) *s.i.s: sn prom and racd keenly: shkn up to chse ldr over 1f out: rdn and hung lft ins fnl f: styd on to ld post* **9/2**[2]

524- 2 shd **All My Love (IRE)**[29] 6527 5-9-4 72.................................... RobHornby 4 80
(Pam Sly) *hld up: hdwy over 4f out: shkn up to ld over 2f out: rdn over 1f out: hdd post* **9/4**[1]

11-3 3 3 3/4 **Canny Style**[15] 1679 4-8-13 68............................................... KevinStott 8 70+
(Kevin Ryan) *hld up: racd keenly: pushed along over 2f out: hdwy and nt clr run over 1f out: rdn and hung lft ins fnl f: styd on: nt rch ldrs* **11/2**[3]

060- 4 2 **Saumur**[202] 7067 5-9-0 73.................................................. PaddyPilley(5) 1 72
(Denis Coakley) *sn led at stdy pce: hdd over 5f out: rdn over 2f out: nt clr run wl over 1f out: styd on same pce fnl f* **9/2**[2]

0-31 5 nk **Percys Princess**[17] 1630 6-8-0 61 oh1.......................... JaneElliott(7) 6 59
(Michael Appleby) *chsd ldrs: wnt 2nd over 3f out: rdn and ev ch over 2f out: wknd ins fnl f* **13/2**

60-6 6 3/4 **Smart Mover (IRE)**[53] 996 4-8-6 61................................... LukeMorris 7 58
(Nikki Evans) *hld up: rdn over 2f out: no ex fnl f* **40/1**

0P15 7 3/4 **Rowlestone Lass**[29] 1405 7-9-9 77............................. RichardKingscote 2 73
(Richard Price) *chsd ldr tl led over 5f out: hdd over 2f out: wknd ins fnl f* **9/2**[2]

002- 8 10 **Perfect Summer (IRE)**[210] 5642 7-9-1 76....................... LukeCatton(7) 3 56
(Ian Williams) *chsd ldrs tl rdn over 4f out: wknd over 2f out* **40/1**

2m 38.74s (-2.06) **Going Correction** -0.225s/f (Stan) **8** Ran SP% **118.9**
Speed ratings (Par 100): **97,96,94,93,92 92,91,85**
CSF £15.76 CT £56.83 TOTE £6.40: £1.90, £1.20, £2.10; EX 20.60 Trifecta £95.90.
**Owner** Douglas Livingston **Bred** D Curran **Trained** Middleham Moor, N Yorks

**FOCUS**
This was steadily run and developed into a bit of a sprint. The winner's first form on the AW.

### 2062 INVEST CITY OF WOLVERHAMPTON MAIDEN AUCTION FILLIES' STKS 1m 4f 51y (Tp)

**7:40** (7:41) (Class 6) 3-Y-O **£2,522** (£750; £375; £187) **Stalls** Low

Form RPR

2 1 **Stepney**[27] 1424 3-9-0 0............................................................ LukeMorris 3 63+
(Robyn Brisland) *hld up: hdwy over 3f out: shkn up and nt clr run over 1f out: rdn to ld ins fnl f: styd on* **1/1**[1]

00- 2 1/2 **Haldaw**[185] 7548 3-9-0 0............................................................ GrahamLee 1 61
(Mick Channon) *led 1f: chsd ldr tl led again over 1f out: rdn and hdd ins fnl f: styd on same pce* **12/1**

5- 3 3/4 **Pondering**[185] 7548 3-8-11 0.......................................... EdwardGreatrex(3) 5 60+
(Eve Johnson Houghton) *sn prom: pushed along over 3f out: rdn over 2f out: ev ch whn rdr dropped whip ins fnl f: no ex towards fin* **5/4**[2]

56 4 2 1/2 **Cookie's Star**[32] 1342 3-9-0 0...................................... DanielTudhope 4 56
(Philip McBride) *led after 1f: shkn up and hdd over 1f out: hmpd sn after: no ex wl ins fnl f* **10/1**[3]

60 5 14 **Dashanti**[32] 1342 3-8-7 0.......................................... Pierre-LouisJamin(7) 2 34
(Jonathan Portman) *hld up: rdn and wknd over 3f out* **66/1**

2m 39.77s (-1.03) **Going Correction** -0.225s/f (Stan) **5** Ran SP% **112.7**
Speed ratings (Par 93): **94,93,93,91,82**
CSF £13.59 TOTE £2.40: £1.20, £2.40; EX 15.40 Trifecta £24.60.
**Owner** Franconson Partners **Bred** D Curran **Trained** Newmarket, Suffolk

**FOCUS**
An ordinary maiden in which the favourites flip-flopped, and the money proved correct. It was steadily run and the level of the form is fluid.

### 2063 INVEST WOLVERHAMPTON - YOUR NEXT INVESTMENT LOCATION H'CAP 7f 36y (Tp)

**8:10** (8:12) (Class 6) (0-55,55) 4-Y-O+ **£2,458** (£731; £365; £182) **Stalls** High

Form RPR

3212 1 **Prince Of Time**[7] 1868 5-8-13 54......................... CallumRodriguez(7) 11 67+
(Richard Ford) *mid-div: hdwy over 2f out: led over 1f out: pushed out: comf* **5/2**[1]

6-12 2 2 3/4 **Isntshesomething**[12] 1755 5-9-4 52.............................(v) DougieCostello 6 58
(Richard Guest) *a.p: rdn and ev ch over 1f out: edgd lft and styd on same pce ins fnl f* **7/1**[3]

2263 3 1 1/2 **Sheer Intensity (IRE)**[26] 1447 4-9-5 53.............................. DanielTudhope 9 55
(David Evans) *hld up: rdn over 2f out: hdwy over 1f out: styd on to go 3rd towards fin: nt rch ldrs* **8/1**

300 4 1/2 **Moi Aussie**[21] 1544 4-9-2 53..............................(p[1]) AlistairRawlinson(3) 8 54
(Michael Appleby) *chsd ldrs: led wl over 1f out: sn rdn and hdd: styd on same pce ins fnl f* **16/1**

1442 5 1 1/2 **Pick Of Any (IRE)**[31] 1372 4-9-7 55......................................(h) LukeMorris 12 52
(David Loughnane) *s.i.s: hld up: plld hrd: rdn over 2f out: hung lft and styd on ins fnl f: nvr nrr* **7/1**[3]

5003 6 hd **Major Muscari (IRE)**[31] 1359 9-9-7 55..........................(p) GrahamLee 1 52
(Shaun Harris) *s.i.s: hld up: hdwy over 1f out: sn rdn: no ex ins fnl f* **9/1**

0/5- 7 1/2 **Dazeekha**[476] 48 4-9-2 50................................................................ JoeDoyle 2 46
(Michael Herrington) *hld up: hdwy 2f out: nt clr run and stmbld over 1f out: no ex ins fnl f* **20/1**

6500 8 3/4 **City Of Angkor Wat (IRE)**[6] 1887 7-9-6 54..............(p) PaulMulrennan 4 52+
(Conor Dore) *s.i.s: hld up: nt clr run and swtchd rt over 1f out: nvr nr to chal* **7/1**[3]

0400 9 9 **Life Of Fame**[13] 1721 4-9-3 51....................................(tp) BenCurtis 5 23
(Rebecca Menzies) *led: rdn and hdd over 2f out: wknd fnl f* **16/1**

-010 10 1/2 **Locommotion**[26] 1451 5-9-6 54..........................................(bt) FrannyNorton 7 25
(Matthew Salaman) *chsd ldr tl led over 2f out: rdn and hdd wl over 1f out: wknd fnl f* **6/1**[2]

040- 11 4 1/2 **Golden Cape**[286] 4275 4-8-13 52...................................... PhilDennis(5) 3 12
(Michael Mullineaux) *mid-div: drvn along 1/2-way: wknd over 2f out* **50/1**

1m 26.65s (-2.15) **Going Correction** -0.225s/f (Stan) **11** Ran SP% **120.0**
Speed ratings (Par 101): **103,99,98,97,95 95,95,94,83,83 78**
CSF £20.38 CT £126.19 TOTE £3.50: £1.60, £2.10, £2.80; EX 24.90 Trifecta £147.50.
**Owner** B Hartley **Bred** D Curran **Trained** Garstang, Lancs

■ Stewards' Enquiry : Ben Curtis jockey said filly ran too free

**FOCUS**
This was run at a good gallop and the winner did it easily. The runner-up helps set a straightforward level.

## 2064 INVEST WOLVERHAMPTON - WORLD OR INWARD INVESTMENT H'CAP 7f 36y (Tp)
**8:40** (8:40) (Class 5) (0-75,77) 4-Y-0+ **£3,234** (£962; £481; £240) **Stalls** High

Form RPR
3664 **1** **Athassel**[6] 1890 8-9-1 **76** KatherineGlenister(7) 9 84
(David Evans) *hld up in tch: swtchd lft over 1f out: rdn and r.o to ld wl ins fnl f* **12/1**
4124 **2** 1/2 **Wink Oliver**[20] 1553 5-9-1 **69** (p) DougieCostello 1 75
(Jo Hughes) *hld up: hdwy over 1f out: rdn and ev ch ins fnl f: r.o* **16/1**
1031 **3** *shd* **Tavener**[5] 1898 5-8-13 **67** 6ex (p) DavidAllan 11 73
(David C Griffiths) *led: rdn over 1f out: hdd wl ins fnl f* **5/1**[3]
504- **4** *nk* **Haraz (IRE)**[220] 6567 4-9-9 **77** DanielTudhope 4 82
(David O'Meara) *chsd ldr: rdn over 1f out: styd on* **8/1**
4-52 **5** 1 **Capolavoro (FR)**[26] 1450 6-9-6 **74** LukeMorris 2 76
(Robert Cowell) *a.p: rdn wl over 1f out: styd on same pce ins fnl f* **4/1**[2]
1-40 **6** 1/2 **Faintly (USA)**[13] 1717 6-8-11 **65** (b) JackGarritty 6 66
(Ruth Carr) *hld up: hdwy and hung lft fr over 1f out: r.o: nt rch ldrs* **13/2**
3-15 **7** 1 1/2 **Slingsby**[55] 971 6-9-3 **74** (p) NathanEvans(3) 7 71
(Michael Easterby) *chsd ldrs: rdn over 2f out: no ex fnl f* **6/1**
3143 **8** 1 1/4 **Big Amigo (IRE)**[9] 1819 4-9-4 **72** AndrewMullen 3 66
(Daniel Mark Loughnane) *hld up: rdn over 1f out: nvr on terms* **20/1**
0-00 **9** *shd* **Mezmaar**[14] 1696 8-9-7 **75** (h) SteveDrowne 5 68
(Mark Usher) *hld up: rdn over 2f out: a in rr* **25/1**
-006 **10** 2 3/4 **Kingsley Klarion (IRE)**[11] 1778 4-9-9 **77** FrannyNorton 8 63+
(Mark Johnston) *s.i.s: hld up: drvn along 1/2-way: wknd over 1f out* **3/1**[1]

1m 26.42s (-2.38) **Going Correction** -0.225s/f (Stan) **10** Ran SP% **122.6**
Speed ratings (Par 103): **104,103,103,102,101 101,99,98,98,94**
CSF £195.59 CT £1119.81 TOTE £14.00: £2.10, £4.50, £1.80; EX 163.80 Trifecta £1337.20.
**Owner** Mrs E Evans **Bred** Moyns Park Estate And Stud Ltd **Trained** Pandy, Monmouths

**FOCUS**
An open handicap and pretty tight finish. The form seems sound.

## 2065 INVEST CITY OF WOLVERHAMPTON H'CAP 5f 21y (Tp)
**9:10** (9:11) (Class 6) (0-60,64) 3-Y-O **£2,522** (£750; £375; £187) **Stalls** Low

Form RPR
035- **1** **Blue Rocks**[158] 8009 3-9-3 **56** KevinStott 6 61
(Lisa Williamson) *chsd ldrs: rdn over 1f out: r.o to ld towards fin* **10/1**
0-32 **2** 3/4 **Maggi May (IRE)**[9] 1821 3-8-11 **50** PaulMulrennan 4 52
(David Brown) *w ldr: rdn and ev ch fr over 1f out: r.o* **7/1**
3131 **3** 1/2 **Gnaad (IRE)**[9] 1821 3-9-11 **64** 6ex (p) LukeMorris 2 64
(Robert Cowell) *edgd rt s: led: shkn up over 1f out: rdn and hdd towards fin* **11/8**[1]
032 **4** 1 1/4 **Tooty Fruitti**[21] 1543 3-9-7 **60** FrannyNorton 8 57
(Jo Hughes) *hld up: hdwy over 1f out: swtchd lft ins fnl f: no ex towards fin* **6/1**[3]
5-46 **5** *shd* **Coping Stone**[27] 1418 3-9-6 **59** (e[1]) RichardKingscote 7 54
(David Brown) *prom: rdn over 1f out: edgd lft and styd on same pce fnl f* **7/2**[2]
135- **6** *nk* **Rebel Heart**[181] 7615 3-9-0 **58** (v) RyanWhile(5) 1 52
(Bill Turner) *s.i.s: r.o ins fnl f: nvr nrr* **12/1**
-000 **7** 3/4 **Chillililli**[21] 1545 3-8-0 **46** oh1 (p[1]) JaneElliott(7) 5 38
(Michael Appleby) *sn pushed along in rr: r.o ins fnl f: nvr on terms* **50/1**
6450 **8** 6 **Celerity (IRE)**[15] 1688 3-8-2 **48** (b) BenRobinson(7) 3 18
(David Evans) *s.i.s: plld hrd: hdwy over 3f out: rdn over 1f out: wknd fnl f* **12/1**

1m 0.97s (-0.93) **Going Correction** -0.225s/f (Stan) **8** Ran SP% **117.5**
Speed ratings (Par 96): **98,96,96,94,93 93,92,82**
CSF £79.35 CT £157.92 TOTE £14.30: £4.00, £1.50, £1.10; EX 108.90 Trifecta £426.50.
**Owner** E H Jones (paints) Ltd **Bred** David John Brown **Trained** Saighton, Cheshire

**FOCUS**
An ordinary sprint handicap.
T/Plt: £317.00 to a £1 stake. Pool: £68,576.38 - 157.90 winning units T/Qpdt: £12.00 to a £1 stake. Pool: £7,498.74 - 462.25 winning units **Colin Roberts**

# YARMOUTH (L-H)
Tuesday, April 25

**OFFICIAL GOING: Good to firm (good in places; 7.8) (watered)**
Wind: medium, behind in the straight (races up to 1m and final 5f on round course) Weather: overcast, chilly

## 2066 HAVEN SEASHORE HOLIDAY PARK MAIDEN STKS 1m 3y
**1:40** (1:44) (Class 5) 3-Y-O **£3,234** (£962; £481; £240) **Stalls** Centre

Form RPR
**1** **Hakeem** 3-9-5 0 DaneO'Neill 15 79
(William Haggas) *in tch in midfield: effrt 2f out: rdn and hdwy 1f out: styd on to chal 100yds out: led last stride* **12/1**
0- **2** *shd* **Alwahsh (IRE)**[220] 6577 3-9-5 0 PatCosgrave 13 78
(William Haggas) *chsd ldrs: wnt 2nd 1/2-way: rdn 2f out: ev ch ins fnl f: styd on to ld cl home: hdd last strides* **4/1**[2]
56- **3** *nk* **Lady Freyja**[178] 7695 3-9-0 0 StevieDonohoe 11 72
(John Ryan) *led: rdn 2f out: kpt on wl: hrd pressed and drvn ins fnl f: hdd last strides* **150/1**
0- **4** 1/2 **Buxted Dream (USA)**[313] 3315 3-9-5 0 LukeMorris 1 76
(Luca Cumani) *in tch in midfield: effrt and hdwy 2f out: chsd ldrs u.p over 1f out: ev ch ins fnl f: kpt on same pce towards fin* **8/1**
**5** 1 1/4 **Marine One** 3-9-5 0 OisinMurphy 4 73+
(David Simcock) *t.k.h: hld up in tch in midfield: effrt 2f out: hdwy and rdn 1f out: styd on steadily ins fnl f: nvr enough pce to get on terms* **11/4**[1]
**6** *nse* **Mooltazem (IRE)** 3-9-5 0 JimCrowley 8 73+
(John Gosden) *hld up in midfield: nt clr run 2f out: pushed along and hdwy over 1f out: kpt on steadily ins fnl f: nvr threatened ldrs* **9/2**[3]
36- **7** 1 1/2 **Dutch Quality**[194] 7307 3-9-5 0 AndreaAtzeni 2 69
(Marco Botti) *in tch in midfield: effrt 2f out: unable qck over 1f out: styd on same pce ins fnl f* **12/1**
**8** 2 3/4 **Soldier Blue (FR)** 3-9-5 0 (h[1]) MartinLane 12 62
(Charlie Appleby) *chsd ldrs: rdn over 3f out: no ex and btn over 1f out: wknd ins fnl f* **14/1**
**9** 1/2 **Zain Star (IRE)** 3-9-5 0 JamieSpencer 14 61+
(Charlie Fellowes) *stdd s: hld up in rr: swtchd rt: rdn and hdwy into midfield 2f out: no imp and kpt on same pce fr over 1f out* **20/1**
60 **10** 4 1/2 **Chunkyfunkymonkey**[10] 1804 3-9-2 0 (b) LouisSteward(3) 5 50
(John Ryan) *hld up towards rr: rdn ent fnl 2f: sn struggling and wknd over 1f out* **200/1**
00 **11** 4 **Free Forum (IRE)**[14] 1692 3-9-0 0 GeorgeBuckell(5) 9 41
(David Simcock) *hld up in rr: pushed along 1/2-way: rdn jst over 2f out: sn wknd* **100/1**
**12** 1 **Stormy Blues** 3-9-5 0 AdamKirby 10 38
(Charlie Appleby) *wl in tch in midfield: rdn over 2f out: sn struggling and btn over 1f out: fdd* **9/1**
00- **13** 6 **Let's Sway**[195] 7284 3-9-0 0 (h[1]) LemosdeSouza 6 19
(Amy Murphy) *t.k.h: hld up in midfield: rdn and lost pl qckly 2f out: bhd over 1f out* **200/1**
**14** 2 **Lookintomyeyes** 3-8-7 0 (t[1]) MillyNaseb(7) 3 14
(Mrs Ilka Gansera-Leveque) *v.s.a: a towards rr: lost tch over 1f out* **150/1**
0-5 **15** 7 **Piaffe (USA)**[12] 1756 3-9-0 0 DannyBrock 7
(Jane Chapple-Hyam) *chsd ldr tl 1/2-way: sn rdn and steadily lost pl: bhd fnl f* **200/1**

1m 37.48s (-3.12) **Going Correction** -0.525s/f (Hard) **15** Ran SP% **116.6**
Speed ratings (Par 98): **94,93,93,93,91 91,90,87,87,82 78,77,71,69,62**
CSF £57.24 TOTE £15.60: £4.00, £1.60, £22.00; EX 66.30 Trifecta £5410.50 Part won..
**Owner** Hamdan Al Maktoum **Bred** Shadwell Estate Company Limited **Trained** Newmarket, Suffolk

**FOCUS**
There was 3.5mm rain overnight but the ground was on the fast side. The bare form looks just fair but plenty will leave this behind. The third looks the key.

## 2067 JOHN KEMP 4 X 4 SPECIALISTS OF NORWICH MAIDEN AUCTION STKS 1m 3f 104y
**2:10** (2:10) (Class 5) 3-Y-O **£3,234** (£962; £481) **Stalls** Low

Form RPR
3 **1** **Investigation**[20] 1559 3-9-5 0 RobHornby 3 78
(Andrew Balding) *stdd s: t.k.h: hld up in 3rd tl wnt 2nd 6f out: upsides ldr 3f out: rdn 2f out: led 1f out: styd on to assert ins fnl f: eased cl home* **5/2**[2]
-32 **2** 3 1/2 **Testbourne (IRE)**[15] 1675 3-9-0 0 CliffordLee(5) 2 72
(K R Burke) *led: jnd 3f out: shkn up 2f out: drvn and little rspnse over 1f out: hdd 1f out: btn and wknd fnl 100yds* **30/100**[1]
0-00 **3** 46 **Zipedee**[1] 2027 3-8-7 40 JackOsborn(7) 1
(John Ryan) *t.k.h: chsd ldr tl 6f out: rdn over 3f out: sn struggling: t.o over 1f out* **100/1**[3]

2m 29.55s (0.85) **Going Correction** -0.35s/f (Firm) **3** Ran SP% **106.5**
Speed ratings (Par 98): **82,79,46**
CSF £3.80 TOTE £3.00; EX 3.10 Trifecta £2.10.
**Owner** Martin & Valerie Slade & Partner **Bred** Sir Eric Parker **Trained** Kingsclere, Hants

**FOCUS**
Essentially just a two-horse race but the runner-up had shown fair ability and the winner put him away quite well. It was steadily run and ended up a bit of a dash.

## 2068 TED PENNELL 66TH BIRTHDAY H'CAP 1m 2f 23y
**2:45** (2:45) (Class 4) (0-85,84) 4-Y-O+ **£4,690** (£1,395; £697; £348) **Stalls** Low

Form RPR
/26- **1** **Mohatem (USA)**[186] 7512 5-9-6 **83** JimCrowley 2 96
(Owen Burrows) *chsd ldng pair: clsd on bit to join ldr 3f out: rdn to ld over 1f out: asserted ins fnl f and drew clr: styd on* **9/4**[2]
56-1 **2** 3 **Celebration Day (IRE)**[33] 1323 4-8-13 **81** GeorgeWood(5) 7 88
(Simon Crisford) *led: jnd 3f out: rdn 2f out: sn hdd and drvn: no ex and outpcd ins fnl f* **9/2**[3]
/32- **3** 1 **Wapping (USA)**[237] 6032 4-9-7 **84** TomQueally 5 89
(David Lanigan) *hld up off the pce in 5th: clsd 4f out: rdn and edgd lft 2f out: chsd ldng pair jst ins fnl f: kpt on same pce after* **6/1**
020- **4** 2 1/2 **Theydon Grey**[202] 7067 4-9-7 **84** PatCosgrave 6 85
(William Haggas) *hld up in 4th: clsd 4f out: chsd ldrs and rdn 2f out: little rspnse and no imp: 4th and wl hld ins fnl f: eased towards fin* **15/8**[1]
4040 **5** 8 **The Gay Cavalier**[15] 1683 6-8-7 **70** (t) SilvestreDeSousa 4 59
(John Ryan) *stdd s: hld up off the pce in last: effrt and sme hdwy on inner over 2f out: no imp 2f out: wknd over 1f out: eased wl ins fnl f* **14/1**
10-0 **6** 15 **Bertie Moon**[45] 1153 7-8-12 **82** (p) PatrickVaughan(7) 3 36
(Lydia Pearce) *led tl 3f out: sn dropped out u.p: bhd 2f out: sn lost tch* **50/1**

2m 7.07s (-3.43) **Going Correction** -0.35s/f (Firm) **6** Ran SP% **106.6**
Speed ratings (Par 105): **99,96,95,93,87 75**
CSF £11.30 TOTE £3.30: £1.90, £2.40; EX 12.70 Trifecta £44.90.
**Owner** Hamdan Al Maktoum **Bred** W S Farish & Kilroy Thoroughbred Partnership **Trained** Lambourn, Berks

**FOCUS**
This looked a good race for the grade and the form could be worth a bit better..

## 2069 TRAFALGAR RESTAURANT AT YARMOUTH RACECOURSE H'CAP 5f 42y
**3:15** (3:17) (Class 6) (0-60,58) 4-Y-O+ **£2,264** (£673; £336; £168) **Stalls** Centre

Form RPR
3442 **1** **Hurricane Alert**[12] 1759 5-8-6 **50** DavidEgan(7) 7 57
(Mark Hoad) *taken down early: t.k.h: chsd ldrs tl rdn and hdwy to ld over 1f out: clr and in command ins fnl f: styd on: rdn out* **6/1**[2]
3-14 **2** 1 3/4 **Strictly Carter**[31] 1371 4-9-1 **57** GeorgeWood(5) 2 58
(Alan Bailey) *in tch in midfield: effrt 2f out: hdwy to chse ldrs 1f out: wnt 2nd ins fnl f: kpt on but no imp on wnr* **6/1**[2]
0-36 **3** *nk* **Oscars Journey**[42] 1184 7-9-1 **52** (v) SilvestreDeSousa 4 52
(J R Jenkins) *chsd ldr: rdn 2f out: drvn to chse wnr 1f out: 3rd and kpt on same pce fnl 150yds* **5/2**[1]
-454 **4** 1/2 **Chandresh**[71] 722 4-8-8 **45** (b) TomMarquand 8 43
(Robert Cowell) *wl in tch in midfield: effrt 2f out: no imp tl swtchd lft and hdwy ins fnl f: kpt on u.p fnl 100yds: no threat to wnr* **13/2**[3]
0200 **5** 1/2 **Give Us A Belle (IRE)**[42] 1184 8-8-3 **47** (vt) RPWalsh(7) 6 43
(Christine Dunnett) *led: rdn and hdd over 1f out: edgd rt and no ex ins fnl f: wknd towards fin* **20/1**
0005 **6** 2 1/2 **Rojina (IRE)**[10] 1785 4-8-1 **45** JordanUys(7) 3 32
(Lisa Williamson) *in tch in midfield: rdn 2f out: sn outpcd: wl hld and kpt on same pce ins fnl f* **40/1**
-600 **7** *hd* **Humour (IRE)**[71] 724 6-8-13 **50** (b) OisinMurphy 5 37
(Christine Dunnett) *a towards rr of main gp: pushed along 2f out: no hdwy under rdn and kpt on ins fnl f: n.d* **15/2**
0050 **8** 1 1/4 **Only Ten Per Cent (IRE)**[42] 1184 9-9-7 **58** (p) AdamKirby 9 40
(J R Jenkins) *a rr of main gp: effrt 2f out: no imp over 1f out: n.d* **6/1**[2]

0-00 **9** *5* **Edith Weston**[71] [723] 4-8-8 **45**.......................................... TedDurcan 1 9
(Robert Cowell) *v.s.a: nvr on terms* **16/1**
1m 1.17s (-1.53) **Going Correction** -0.525s/f (Hard) **9** Ran SP% **109.6**
Speed ratings (Par 101): **91,88,87,86,86 82,81,79,71**
CSF £38.29 CT £104.11 TOTE £7.70: £2.00, £1.90, £1.50; EX 33.70 Trifecta £130.10.
**Owner** Michael Baldry **Bred** Lady S K Marchwood **Trained** Lewes, E Sussex
**FOCUS**
A moderate sprint handicap in which they raced middle to stands' side. Straightforward, modest form.

## 2070 EASTERN POWER SYSTEMS OF NORWICH H'CAP 1m 3y
**3:50** (3:50) (Class 5) (0-70,72) 4-Y-O+ **£2,911** (£866; £432; £108; £108) **Stalls** Centre

Form RPR
0/1- **1** **Phosphorescence (IRE)**[230] [6231] 7-9-11 **72**.............(b) OisinMurphy 8 79
(George Scott) *mde all: rdn over 1f out: hrd pressed and drvn 1f out: kpt on wl u.pand jst hld on: all out* **7/4**[1]
20-4 **2** *shd* **Harlequin Rock**[18] [1610] 4-8-12 **59**.................................. PatCosgrave 1 65
(Mick Quinn) *hld up in midfield: rdn 3f out: hdwy 1f out: pressed ldrs ins fnl f: styd on and str chal wl ins fnl f: jst failed* **14/1**
-103 **3** *nk* **Ross Raith Rover**[18] [1610] 4-9-3 **64**...........................(b) AndreaAtzeni 7 69
(Robert Eddery) *chsd ldrs: rdn and unable qck over 1f out: looked hld tl rallied u.p ins fnl f: kpt on wl towards fin* **7/2**[2]
0003 **4** *nk* **Flying Fantasy**[5] [1898] 5-9-7 **68**.............................(t) SilvestreDeSousa 2 72
(Stuart Williams) *hld up in tch in midfield: swtchd lft 3f out: edgd lft u.p 2f out: styd on to press ldrs 1f out: kpt on same pce ins fnl f* **9/2**[3]
-060 **4** *dht* **Right Rebel**[39] [1243] 5-9-0 **66**....................................... GeorgeWood(5) 3 70
(Alan Bailey) *in tch in midfield: effrt 2f out: ev ch u.p 1f out: styd on same pce ins fnl f* **20/1**
-110 **6** *1 ¾* **Magic Mirror**[13] [1729] 4-8-8 **55**....................................(v) TomMarquand 5 55
(Mark Rimell) *chsd wnr: rdn 2f out: stl pressing ldrs u.p 1f out: no ex: n.m.r and wknd wl ins fnl f* **9/1**
4123 **7** *1 ¼* **Tee It Up Tommo (IRE)**[20] [1553] 8-9-10 **71**................. StevieDonohoe 4 68
(Daniel Steele) *hld up in last pair: effrt over 1f out: edgd rt u.p 1f out: kpt on same pce ins fnl f* **22/1**
-300 **8** *1* **Tyrsal (IRE)**[75] [636] 6-8-6 **56**........................................ NathanAlison(3) 6 51
(Clifford Lines) *s.i.s: nudged along 2f out: styd on same pce ins fnl f: nvr trbld ldrs* **10/1**
1m 36.68s (-3.92) **Going Correction** -0.525s/f (Hard) **8** Ran SP% **111.6**
Speed ratings (Par 103): **98,97,97,97,97 95,94,93**
CSF £27.18 CT £76.65 TOTE £2.80: £1.20, £2.90, £1.30; EX 27.70 Trifecta £101.40.
**Owner** Niarchos Family **Bred** Niarchos Family **Trained** Newmarket, Suffolk
**FOCUS**
They all followed the front-running winner towards the stands' rail. A bunched finish and ordinary form. The runner-up is rated to last year's C&D mark.

## 2071 WEDDINGS & PRIVATE PARTIES AT YARMOUTH RACECOURSE H'CAP 7f 3y
**4:25** (4:29) (Class 5) (0-75,77) 3-Y-O **£2,911** (£866; £432; £216) **Stalls** Centre

Form RPR
45-3 **1** **Blue On Blue (USA)**[20] [1551] 3-9-7 **74**.............................(h) RobertTart 3 79
(John Gosden) *hld up in tch in midfield: swtchd lft and effrt ent fnl 2f: hdwy and ev ch 1f out: led ins fnl f: hld on wl towards fin* **15/2**[3]
333- **2** *nk* **Glendun (USA)**[194] [7297] 3-9-6 **73**........................................ RyanTate 10 77
(James Eustace) *hld up in tch in midfield: effrt u.p over 1f out: ev ch fnl f: kpt on wl but hld towards fin* **16/1**
012- **3** *shd* **Fire Brigade**[160] [7974] 3-9-4 **71**.................................. JamieSpencer 12 75
(Michael Bell) *dwlt and rousted along early: racd in last trio: rdn and hdwy over 1f out: ev ch ins fnl f: kpt on wl but hld towards fin* **9/1**
0-24 **4** *2 ¼* **Widnes**[17] [1625] 3-9-4 **71**...................................................(b) AdamKirby 1 69
(Alan Bailey) *wl in tch in midfield: effrt 2f out: hdwy u.p to ld over 1f out: hdd ins fnl f: sn btn and wknd fnl 100yds* **16/1**
321- **5** *3 ½* **Getgo**[203] [7032] 3-9-7 **74**................................................(b) TomQueally 11 62
(David Lanigan) *hld up in last trio: swtchd lft and hdwy over 1f out: kpt on but no threat to ldrs ins fnl f* **11/1**
35-1 **6** *nk* **Wurood**[29] [1401] 3-9-10 **77**.................................................... JimCrowley 4 65
(William Haggas) *t.k.h: chsd ldrs tl led ent fnl 2f: rdn and hdd over 1f out: sn btn and wknd ins fnl f* **2/1**[1]
2-65 **7** *3 ¼* **Masonic (IRE)**[12] [1760] 3-9-3 **70**..............................(p[1]) TomMarquand 5 49
(Robyn Brisland) *led for 2f: lost pl u.p over 1f out: wknd fnl f* **14/1**
050- **8** *4* **Seyasah (IRE)**[202] [7071] 3-9-1 **68**...................................... TedDurcan 6 36
(Chris Wall) *stdd s: hld up in last trio: shkn up and effrt whn bmpd over 1f out: no imp after: nvr trbld ldrs* **25/1**
-515 **9** *1* **Porto Ferro (IRE)**[25] [1463] 3-8-12 **70**......................(p) GeorgeWood(5) 2 35
(Dr Jon Scargill) *in tch in midfield: rdn 2f out: sn lost pl and btn: wknd* **50/1**
345- **10** *2 ¾* **Used To Be**[230] [6229] 3-9-2 **74**................................... CliffordLee(5) 8 32
(K R Burke) *t.k.h: pressed ldr tl led 5f out: hdd ent fnl 2f out: lost pl u.p over 1f out: wknd fnl f* **6/1**[2]
000- **11** *1 ¾* **Proud Kate**[152] [8081] 3-8-0 **60** oh15..................................... RPWalsh(7) 9 13
(Christine Dunnett) *chsd ldrs tl 3f out: sn struggling and hung lft: wknd over 1f out and bhd fnl f* **250/1**
1m 23.79s (-2.81) **Going Correction** -0.525s/f (Hard) **11** Ran SP% **102.4**
Speed ratings (Par 98): **95,94,94,91,87 87,83,79,78,75 73**
CSF £92.59 CT £796.74 TOTE £7.60: £2.10, £4.00, £2.60; EX 69.00 Trifecta £617.30.
**Owner** George Strawbridge **Bred** Alberta Davies **Trained** Newmarket, Suffolk
■ Derek Duval was withdrawn. Price at time of withdrawal 13/2. Rule 4 applies to all bets - deduction 10p in the pound.
**FOCUS**
A fair 3yo handicap. Improved form from the winner.

## 2072 ANNUAL BADGES AT YARMOUTH RACECOURSE H'CAP 6f 3y
**5:00** (5:01) (Class 5) (0-75,77) 3-Y-O **£2,911** (£866; £432; £216) **Stalls** Centre

Form RPR
3-26 **1** **Edged In Blue**[61] [875] 3-8-4 **61**.............................. JordanVaughan(3) 10 65
(K R Burke) *w ldrs: rdn over 1f out: sustained effrt u.p to ld towards fin: all out* **25/1**
32-1 **2** *hd* **Comprise**[27] [1432] 3-9-6 **74**........................................... JamieSpencer 8 77
(Michael Bell) *led: rdn over 1f out: hrd pressed and battled on wl ins fnl f: hdd and no ex towards fin* **5/1**[3]
515- **3** *nse* **Trick Of The Light (IRE)**[197] [7217] 3-9-7 **75**.................. AndreaAtzeni 3 78+
(Roger Varian) *trckd ldrs on far rail: gap opened and rdn to chal 1f out: sustained effrt u.p ins fnl f: kpt on but jst hld cl home* **5/2**[1]
332- **4** *1 ¼* **Stanhope**[183] [7574] 3-9-7 **75**........................................... PatCosgrave 6 75
(Mick Quinn) *trckd ldrs: nt clr run and swtchd rt over 1f out: effrt to press ldrs whn squeezed for room: struck twice by rival rdrs whips and snatched up ins fnl f: nt rcvr and one pced after* **9/1**

302- **5** *hd* **Nibras Again**[189] [7424] 3-9-7 **75**...................................... TomMarquand 9 73
(Ismail Mohammed) *t.k.h: hld up wl in tch in midfield: effrt over 1f out: kpt on u.p ins fnl f: nvr quite getting to ldrs* **8/1**
326- **6** *nk* **Etikaal**[199] [7157] 3-9-9 **77**.............................................. JimCrowley 1 74
(Simon Crisford) *w ldr: rdn 2f out: drvn ent fnl f: unable qck and outpcd ins fnl f* **11/4**[2]
044- **7** *1 ¾* **Parys Mountain (IRE)**[188] [7467] 3-9-6 **74**......................... TedDurcan 5 66
(David Brown) *stdd after s: t.k.h: hld up in rr: effrt and wnt lft 1f out: edging lft and no imp ins fnl f: eased towards fin* **17/2**
00-0 **8** *1 ¼* **Percy Toplis**[15] [1688] 3-8-0 **61** oh1............................(p[1]) DavidEgan(7) 11 49
(Christine Dunnett) *t.k.h: hld up in tch: pushed along over 2f out: rdn and kpt on same pce fr over 1f out* **150/1**
233- **9** *nk* **Sitar**[164] [7939] 3-8-13 **67**.................................................. TomQueally 4 54
(James Fanshawe) *stdd after s: t.k.h: hld up in tch in last trio: nt clr run 2f out: effrt over 1f out: no imp* **18/1**
1m 11.85s (-2.55) **Going Correction** -0.525s/f (Hard) **9** Ran SP% **113.3**
Speed ratings (Par 98): **96,95,95,94,93 93,91,89,88**
CSF £142.76 CT £433.98 TOTE £24.20: £4.90, £1.70, £1.10; EX 208.90 Trifecta £1305.60.
**Owner** Mrs Z Wentworth **Bred** Sir P Vela, Norelands & Freynestown **Trained** Middleham Moor, N Yorks
**FOCUS**
A muddling race in which it proved hard to make up significant ground. A length pb from the winner.
T/Plt: £582.20 to a £1 stake. Pool: £52,800.63 - 66.20 winning units T/Qpdt: £17.90 to a £1 stake. Pool: £5,824.55 - 240.77 winning units **Steve Payne**

# 1871 MAISONS-LAFFITTE (R-H)
Tuesday, April 25
**OFFICIAL GOING: Turf: good**

## 2073a PRIX DE RUEIL (CLAIMER) (2YO) (TURF) 5f
**11:40** 2-Y-O **£11,538** (£4,615; £3,461; £2,307; £1,153)

RPR
**1** **Fas Le Fios (IRE)**[11] [1776] 2-8-5 0............................ ClementLecoeuvre(3) 9 66
(J S Moore) *hld up: rdn and hdwy to chal 2f out: led over 1f out: hung lft but r.o fnl f: shade cosily* **30/1**
**2** *snk* **So Sora (FR)**[19] [1594] 2-9-1 0.................................... StephanePasquier 3 72
(P Adda, France) **27/10**[1]
**3** *1 ¼* **Big Words (GER)** 2-8-11 0........................................... AntoineHamelin 7 64
(Matthieu Palussiere, France) **157/10**
**4** *1* **Alets (FR)**[33] [1335] 2-8-11 0.......................................(b) GregoryBenoist 2 60
(C Baillet, France) **41/5**
**5** *hd* **Le Gitan (FR)** 2-9-1 0.................................................. MaximeGuyon 8 63
(M Pimbonnet, France) **19/2**
**6** *1 ¾* **Quick Skips Lad (IRE)**[10] [1792] 2-8-13 0 ow2.. ChristopheSoumillon 10 55
(J S Moore) *midfield: rdn and effrt 2f out: no ex and wknd fnl f* **26/5**
**7** *3* **Scarlett Chope (FR)** 2-8-8 0......................................... ThierryThulliez 5 39
(Y Barberot, France) **49/10**[3]
**8** *2 ½* **Dandies (IRE)** 2-9-1 0................................................ CristianDemuro 1 37
(A Giorgi, Italy) **26/1**
**9** *3* **Norwegian Lord (FR)** 2-9-1 0.......................................(b) JulienAuge 4 26
(C Ferland, France) **3/1**[2]
59.6s **9** Ran SP% **118.4**
PARI-MUTUEL (all including 1 euro stake): WIN 30.60 PLACE 6.20, 1.80, 3.70 DF 48.80 SF 146.40.
**Owner** J S Moore & Partner **Bred** Mattock Stud **Trained** Upper Lambourn, Berks

2074 - 2075a (Foreign Racing) - See Raceform Interactive

# 1715 CATTERICK (L-H)
Wednesday, April 26
**OFFICIAL GOING: Good to firm (8.9) (watered)**
Wind: Moderate against Weather: Cloudy with sunny periods

## 2076 RACING TO SCHOOL H'CAP 5f
**1:50** (1:50) (Class 6) (0-60,60) 4-Y-O+ **£2,264** (£673; £336; £168) **Stalls** Low

Form RPR
-112 **1** **Kinloch Pride**[9] [1828] 5-9-2 **55**.................................(p) GrahamLee 10 64
(Noel Wilson) *in tch: hdwy on outer over 2f out: rdn to chse ldr jst ins fnl f: led last 100 yds: kpt on* **2/1**[1]
03-4 **2** *nk* **The Armed Man**[14] [1722] 4-8-10 **56**.............................. PaulaMuir(7) 8 64
(Chris Fairhurst) *bhd: swtchd rt to outer 2f out: hdwy wl over 1f out: chsd ldrs and hung bdly lft ent fnl f: kpt on towards fin* **4/1**[2]
2015 **3** *1 ¼* **Teepee Time**[27] [1452] 4-8-4 **48**.................................. PhilDennis(5) 2 52
(Michael Mullineaux) *trckd ldrs: hdwy wl over 1f out: sn rdn: kpt on fnl f* **28/1**
4250 **4** *½* **Pearl Noir**[14] [1722] 7-9-7 **60**.........................................(b) DavidAllan 13 62
(Scott Dixon) *qckly away on outer: sn led and swtchd lft towards inner ail: rdn along over 1f out: drvn ins fnl f: hdd & wknd last 100 yds* **20/1**
53-6 **5** *1 ¾* **Searanger (USA)**[14] [1722] 4-9-7 **60**.........................(p) PJMcDonald 4 55
(Rebecca Menzies) *chsd ldrs: rdn along wl over 1f out: n.m.r ins fnl f: kpt on same pce* **6/1**
000- **6** *nk* **Sir Geoffrey (IRE)**[127] [8474] 11-8-7 **46** oh1.....................(b) BenCurtis 5 40
(Scott Dixon) *chsd ldr on inner rail: rdn along wl over 1f out: grad wknd* **33/1**
5533 **7** *¾* **Lizzy's Dream**[27] [1452] 9-8-7 **46**.................................... DuranFentiman 12 38
(Rebecca Bastiman) *towards rr: hdwy wl over 1f out: sn rdn: kpt on fnl f* **25/1**
0-00 **8** *½* **Minty Jones**[103] [216] 8-8-0 **46** oh1..................................(v) AledBeech(7) 7 36
(Michael Mullineaux) *a towards rr* **50/1**
2524 **9** *1 ½* **Culloden**[8] [1869] 5-8-13 **57**........................................ PaddyPilley(5) 6 41
(Shaun Harris) *chsd ldrs: rdn along over 2f out: sn drvn and wknd* **9/2**[3]
0-30 **10** *1 ¼* **Under Approval**[14] [1722] 6-8-5 **49**..........................(b) GemmaTutty(5) 1 29
(Karen Tutty) *a towards rr* **25/1**
0/0- **11** *1* **On The High Tops (IRE)**[209] [6910] 9-8-2 **46** oh1 ow2(p) BenSanderson(7) 9 24
(Colin Teague) *dwlt and towards rr: rdn along and sme hdwy over 2f out: drvn wl over 1f out: sn wknd* **150/1**
-466 **12** *nk* **Fuel Injection**[13] [1759] 6-8-11 **50**.............................(p) JackGarritty 11 25
(Paul Midgley) *prom: rdn along 1/2-way: wknd wl over 1f out* **18/1**
59.73s (-0.07) **Going Correction** -0.025s/f (Good) **12** Ran SP% **112.5**
Speed ratings (Par 101): **99,98,96,95,92 92,91,90,88,86 84,83**
CSF £8.19 CT £163.36 TOTE £2.60: £1.50, £1.60, £6.50; EX 10.00 Trifecta £200.90.

**Owner** G J Paver **Bred** Mrs C K Paver **Trained** Marwood, Co Durham

**FOCUS**

Selective watering and 5mm of rain and hail in the previous 24 hours left the ground Good to Firm (GoingStick: 8.9). All race distances were as advertised. Jockey Graham Lee said the ground was riding good to firm. A fair handicap won by a likeable and improving type.

## 2077 RACINGUK.COM/ANYWHERE 3 DEVICES 1 PRICE H'CAP 7f 6y

**2:20** (2:21) (Class 6) (0-60,60) 3-Y-O **£2,264** (£673; £336; £168) **Stalls** Low

Form RPR

060- **1** **Four Wishes**[239] 6009 3-9-6 **59**............................ DavidAllan 10 65
(Tim Easterby) *rr and sn pushed along: rdn along 3f out: gd hdwy on outer wl over 1f out: rdn ent fnl f: styd on strly to ld last 75 yds* **5/1**[3]

060- **2** ¾ **Hellomoto**[217] 6682 3-9-7 **60**............................(p[1]) TomEaves 1 62
(Kevin Ryan) *towards rr: reminders over 5f out: rdn 3f out: styng on whn n.m.r ent fnl f: sn drvn and kpt on wl towards fin* **8/1**

-355 **3** *nk* **Bismarck The Flyer (IRE)**[61] 903 3-9-5 **58**................ AndrewMullen 8 59
(Ollie Pears) *trckd ldng pair: hdwy and cl up 2f out: rdn over 1f out: drvn and ev ch ent fnl f: kpt on same pce towards fin* **9/1**

00-2 **4** *nk* **A Bit Of Ginger**[19] 1596 3-9-4 **57**............................ ShaneGray 9 57
(Ann Duffield) *trckd ldr: cl up 1/2-way: chal over 2f out: rdn to take slt over 1f out: sn drvn: hdd last 100 yds: kpt on same pce* **8/1**

000- **5** *1* **Urban Spirit (IRE)**[176] 7740 3-8-12 **51**..................... JackGarritty 3 49
(Jedd O'Keeffe) *slt ld: rdn along over 2f out: hdd narrowly over 1f out: cl up: drvn and ev ch ins fnl f: wknd last 100 yds* **10/3**[1]

645- **6** *nk* **Breaking Free**[184] 7571 3-9-0 **53**............................ JasonHart 5 50
(John Quinn) *in tch: pushed along over 3f out: rdn over 2f out: drvn to chse ldrs ent fnl f: kpt on same pce* **4/1**[2]

00-0 **7** ½ **Ching Ching Lor (IRE)**[16] 1680 3-8-12 **51**.................. NeilFarley 7 48
(Declan Carroll) *trckd ldng pair on inner: pushed along over 2f out: rdn wl over 1f out: hld whn n.m.r ins fnl f* **6/1**

606- **8** *1* **Pontecarlo Boy**[201] 7110 3-8-8 **47**............................ CamHardie 2 42
(Richard Whitaker) *chsd ldrs: rdn along over 2f out: sn drvn and wknd* **16/1**

1m 27.44s (0.44) **Going Correction** -0.10s/f (Good) **8** Ran SP% **112.1**
Speed ratings (Par 96): **93,92,91,91,90 89,89,88**
CSF £42.30 CT £348.54 TOTE £5.50: £1.90, £2.80, £2.30; EX 44.10 Trifecta £177.10.
**Owner** Arashan Ali **Bred** Dunchurch Lodge Stud Company **Trained** Great Habton, N Yorks

**FOCUS**

An open-looking handicap which the ears-pricked winner landed comfortably after producing a power-packed run down the outside.

## 2078 BREEDERS BACKING RACING EBF MAIDEN FILLIES' STKS (PLUS 10 RACE) 7f 6y

**2:55** (2:58) (Class 5) 3-Y-O **£3,881** (£1,155; £577; £288) **Stalls** Low

Form RPR

303- **1** **Ghadaayer (IRE)**[175] 7763 3-9-0 75............................ DaneO'Neill 2 78
(Sir Michael Stoute) *led 1f: cl up on inner: pushed along 2f out: rdn to ld again ent fnl f: kpt on wl towards fin* **2/1**[2]

223- **2** 1 ½ **Aimez La Vie (IRE)**[200] 7147 3-9-0 73........................ BarryMcHugh 5 74
(Richard Fahey) *cl up: slt ld after 1f: pushed along wl over 1f out: rdn and hdd ent fnl f: sn drvn and kpt on same pce* **5/4**[1]

3-2 **3** 2 ½ **Castle Hill Cassie (IRE)**[30] 1401 3-9-0 0...................... GrahamLee 8 67
(Ben Haslam) *trckd ldrs: hdwy 2f out: rdn and hung lft ent fnl f: sn drvn and no imp* **8/1**

0 **4** 2 ¼ **Decima (IRE)**[15] 1705 3-8-11 0............................ NathanEvans(3) 10 61
(Michael Easterby) *dwlt: sn trcking ldrs: pushed along over 2f out: rdn over 1f out: n.m.r ent fnl f: one pce* **40/1**

24-0 **5** 1 ¼ **Sue's Angel (IRE)**[14] 1730 3-9-0 0............................ JackGarritty 3 58+
(Richard Fahey) *hld up: hdwy over 2f out: rdn along over 1f out: sn no imp* **20/1**

**6** *2* **Hamster Jam (IRE)** 3-9-0 0............................ JoeFanning 1 52
(Mark Johnston) *trckd ldng pair on inner: pushed along 3f out: rdn over 2f out: grad wknd* **6/1**[3]

**7** *2* **Maid In Brittain** 3-9-0 0............................ CamHardie 9 47
(Antony Brittain) *a rr* **66/1**

6000 **8** 1 ¼ **Red Shanghai (IRE)**[19] 1605 3-8-7 35...................... BenRobinson(7) 4 43
(Charles Smith) *dwlt: a towards rr* **250/1**

**9** *2* **Starboard Watch** 3-9-0 0............................ TomEaves 7 38
(James Given) *dwlt: a towards rr* **28/1**

1m 25.99s (-1.01) **Going Correction** -0.10s/f (Good) **9** Ran SP% **115.7**
Speed ratings (Par 95): **101,99,96,93,92 90,87,86,84**
CSF £4.68 TOTE £3.10: £1.10, £1.40, £1.70; EX 4.70 Trifecta £15.80.
**Owner** Hamdan Al Maktoum **Bred** Shadwell Estate Company Limited **Trained** Newmarket, Suffolk

**FOCUS**

An ordinary fillies' maiden, but the winner is nicely bred and could make up into a useful sort.

## 2079 2017 CATTERICK TWELVE FURLONG SERIES H'CAP (QUALIFIER) 1m 4f 13y

**3:25** (3:25) (Class 5) (0-70,72) 4-Y-O+ **£3,234** (£962; £481; £240) **Stalls** Low

Form RPR

35-4 **1** **Monaco Rose**[16] 1679 4-8-12 **65**...................... AdamMcNamara(3) 2 69
(Richard Fahey) *trckd ldrs on inner: hdwy 2f out: rdn to chal ent fnl f: led last 100 yds: kpt on strly* **5/2**[2]

400- **2** 1 ½ **Fillydelphia (IRE)**[190] 7438 6-8-0 **56**........................ PaulaMuir(7) 3 58
(Patrick Holmes) *hld up: hdwy on outer over 3f out: chal wl over 1f out: rdn and ev ch ent fnl f: sn drvn and kpt on* **28/1**

1044 **3** 1 ¼ **Tred Softly (IRE)**[26] 1469 4-8-8 **58**........................(b) JasonHart 5 58
(John Quinn) *trckd ldrs: hdwy 3f out: rdn to ld wl over 1f out: drvn ent fnl f: hdd last 100 yds: kpt on one pce* **4/1**[3]

**4** 1 ¼ **Star Glitter (FR)**[265] 5093 4-9-4 **68**........................ DanielTudhope 4 66
(David O'Meara) *trckd ldrs: hdwy on outer to ld over 4f out: rdn along 2f out: drvn and hdd wl over 1f out: kpt on one pce* **9/4**[1]

0-50 **5** 1 ½ **Lady Clitico (IRE)**[21] 1560 6-9-1 **64**........................ GrahamLee 10 60
(Rebecca Menzies) *hld up in rr: hdwy 3f out: rdn 2f out: styd on appr fnl f: n.d* **16/1**

00-0 **6** 1 ¼ **Russian Royale**[14] 1716 7-9-4 **67**........................ PJMcDonald 8 61
(Micky Hammond) *hld up towards rr: hdwy 4f out: chsd ldrs over 2f out: sn rdn and no imp* **12/1**

430- **7** 4 ½ **Midnight Warrior**[215] 6738 7-8-7 **56** oh1...................... AndrewMullen 9 42
(Ron Barr) *prom: chsd ldr after 2f: rdn along over 3f out: drvn over 2f out: sn wknd* **20/1**

405- **8** *9* **Cape Love (USA)**[241] 5919 4-9-6 **70**........................ JoeFanning 6 42
(Mark Johnston) *led: pushed along and hdd over 4f out: cl up on inner and rdn over 2f out: drvn and wknd wl over 1f out* **7/1**

2m 37.18s (-1.72) **Going Correction** -0.10s/f (Good) **8** Ran SP% **113.6**
Speed ratings (Par 103): **101,100,99,98,97 96,93,87**
CSF £64.39 CT £272.61 TOTE £2.40: £1.20, £4.90, £1.60; EX 45.00 Trifecta £298.10.
**Owner** Dr Marwan Koukash **Bred** Allan W J Perry **Trained** Musley Bank, N Yorks

**FOCUS**

A moderate handicap which saw the winner wear down her rivals in game fashion.

## 2080 FOLLOW ON TWITTER @CATTERICKRACES H'CAP 5f

**4:00** (4:00) (Class 5) (0-70,72) 3-Y-O **£2,911** (£866; £432; £216) **Stalls** Low

Form RPR

45-3 **1** **Kodicat (IRE)**[54] 1004 3-9-3 **65**............................ TomEaves 1 73
(Kevin Ryan) *rr: hdwy 2f out: rdn over 1f out: chsd clr ldr ins fnl f: kpt on strly to ld towards fin* **6/1**

24-0 **2** 1 ¼ **Flawlessly (FR)**[12] 1782 3-9-0 **62**............................ PJMcDonald 8 65
(James Bethell) *sn led and clr at str pce: rdn and edgd lft over 1f out: drvn ins fnl f: wknd last 100 yds: hdd towards fin* **9/1**

203- **3** 2 ¼ **Dundunah (USA)**[223] 6515 3-9-7 **69**........................ DanielTudhope 6 64
(David O'Meara) *chsd clr ldr: rdn along wl over 1f out: drvn ent fnl f: kpt on same pce* **15/8**[1]

060- **4** 1 ½ **Ventura Secret (IRE)**[172] 7820 3-9-7 **69**...................... DavidAllan 4 59
(Tim Easterby) *trckd ldrs: hdwy 2f out: rdn wl over 1f out: sn no imp* **11/2**[3]

066- **5** 2 ¼ **Mightaswellsmile**[194] 7313 3-9-3 **65**...................... AndrewMullen 3 46
(Ron Barr) *prom on inner: rdn along 2f out: drvn over 1f out: sn wknd* **12/1**

414- **6** *nk* **Hot Hannah**[194] 7313 3-9-0 **69**....................(p[1]) CallumRodriguez(7) 2 49
(Michael Dods) *in tch: rdn along over 2f out: sn drvn and no hdwy* **5/1**[2]

220- **7** 3 ½ **Harbour Lightning**[218] 6641 3-9-3 **65**...................... JoeyHaynes 5 33
(Ann Duffield) *dwlt and towards rr: sme hdwy over 2f out: sn rdn and n.d* **16/1**

2200 **8** *10* **Havelock (IRE)**[11] 1805 3-9-10 **72**............................ JoeFanning 7 4
(Mark Johnston) *prom on wd outside: rdn along 1/2-way: sn wknd* **10/1**

59.63s (-0.17) **Going Correction** -0.025s/f (Good) **8** Ran SP% **113.8**
Speed ratings (Par 98): **100,98,94,92,88 87,82,66**
CSF £57.25 CT £139.19 TOTE £7.00: £1.80, £2.00, £1.90; EX 37.10 Trifecta £297.30.
**Owner** Reilly JDM Holdings Ltd **Bred** Old Carhue Stud **Trained** Hambleton, N Yorks

**FOCUS**

A sprint handicap featuring some unexposed types. The first three look worth following with the second close to her C&D debut figure.

## 2081 BOOK NOW FOR SATURDAY 10TH JUNE H'CAP 7f 6y

**4:35** (4:36) (Class 3) (0-90,88) 4-Y-O+ **£7,762** (£2,310; £1,154; £577) **Stalls** Low

Form RPR

6005 **1** **Luis Vaz De Torres (IRE)**[40] 1238 5-8-10 **77**...........(h) BarryMcHugh 10 84
(Richard Fahey) *trckd ldrs: cl up 1/2-way: rdn to ld appr fnl f: drvn out* **10/1**

**2** *1* **Madroos**[314] 3331 4-8-9 **79**............................ NathanEvans(3) 4 83
(Michael Easterby) *prom: pushed along bef 1/2-way: rdn 2f out: styng on whn n.m.r ins fnl f: kpt on wl towards fin* **12/1**

-011 **3** ½ **Fingal's Cave (IRE)**[14] 1718 5-8-13 **87**...................... JamieGormley(7) 9 90
(Philip Kirby) *towards rr: hdwy on outer to trck ldrs 1/2-way: rdn to chal 2f out: edgd lft ent fnl f: sn drvn and kpt on* **8/1**

36-0 **4** *nse* **Lagenda**[24] 1515 4-9-3 **84**............................(p) KevinStott 13 87+
(Kevin Ryan) *hld up in rr: hdwy 3f out: rdn wl over 1f out: chsd ldrs ins fnl f: kpt on* **15/2**

44-4 **5** 1 ¾ **Ballymore Castle (IRE)**[24] 1512 5-8-12 **82**.......... AdamMcNamara(3) 6 80+
(Richard Fahey) *dwlt and rr: pushed along over 2f out: swtchd rt to outer and rdn over 1f out: styd on wl fnl f: nrst fin* **5/2**[1]

20-5 **6** *hd* **Explain**[33] 1346 5-8-12 **79**............................(p) JackGarritty 8 78+
(Ruth Carr) *chsd ldrs: rdn along over 2f out: drvn over 1f out: no imp fnl f* **9/1**

1614 **7** *nse* **Bint Arcano (FR)**[39] 1261 4-9-3 **84**............................ JoeDoyle 1 81
(Julie Camacho) *chsd ldrs on inner: hdwy over 2f out: rdn and ev ch over 1f out: sn drvn and grad wknd fnl f* **7/1**[3]

100- **8** *nk* **Carnival King (IRE)**[208] 6915 5-9-7 **88**...................... LemosdeSouza 7 84
(Amy Murphy) *in tch on outer: hdwy over 2f out: rdn along wl over 1f out: sn drvn and wknd* **16/1**

402- **9** *1* **Tadaany (IRE)**[128] 8456 5-8-13 **80**........................ DanielTudhope 11 74
(David O'Meara) *led: rdn along over 2f out: drvn over 1f out: sn hdd & wknd* **13/2**[2]

00-0 **10** 3 ½ **Best Trip (IRE)**[6] 1910 10-8-6 **80**....................(t) HarrisonShaw(7) 2 64
(Marjorie Fife) *prom: rdn along over 2f out: drvn wl over 1f out: sn wknd* **33/1**

1m 25.4s (-1.60) **Going Correction** -0.10s/f (Good) **10** Ran SP% **112.9**
Speed ratings (Par 107): **105,103,103,103,101 101,100,100,99,95**
CSF £119.19 CT £1024.46 TOTE £11.20: £3.50, £4.00, £2.00; EX 139.50 Trifecta £598.90.
**Owner** Lets Go Racing 1 **Bred** Peter Molony **Trained** Musley Bank, N Yorks

**FOCUS**

A fair 7f handicap in which it paid to be race handily. The winner's rated close to last year's 6f win here.

## 2082 RACING AGAIN 11TH MAY APPRENTICE H'CAP 7f 6y

**5:05** (5:07) (Class 6) (0-65,71) 4-Y-O+ **£2,264** (£673; £336; £168) **Stalls** Low

Form RPR

504- **1** **Tanawar (IRE)**[202] 7097 7-8-13 **57**............................(b) JoshDoyle 1 63
(Ruth Carr) *trckd ldrs on inner: hdwy 2f out: swtchd rt and effrt over 1f out: sn chsng ldr: rdn ins fnl f: drvn and styd on wl to ld nr fin* **6/1**[3]

14-0 **2** *nk* **Fine Example**[15] 1700 4-9-8 **66**............................(b) LewisEdmunds 3 71
(Kevin Ryan) *trckd ldr: hdwy 3f out: led 2f out: rdn clr over 1f out: drvn ins fnl f: hdd and no ex nr fin* **7/2**[1]

0046 **3** 1 ½ **Masarzain (IRE)**[14] 1720 4-9-2 **63**................(b) CallumRodriguez(3) 6 64
(James Given) *trckd ldrs: hdwy 2f out: rdn to chse ldng pair over 1f out: drvn and kpt on same pce fnl f* **7/1**

60-0 **4** 1 ¾ **In Focus (IRE)**[35] 1312 6-8-11 **60**...................... JamieGormley(5) 9 56+
(Philip Kirby) *hld up: hdwy wl over 2f out: rdn wl over 1f out: kpt on fnl f: nrst fin* **20/1**

1-00 **5** 2 ¼ **Dark Confidant (IRE)**[60] 929 4-8-11 **62**.............. SebastianWoods(7) 4 52
(Richard Fahey) *prom: rdn along over 2f out: drvn wl over 1f out: sn one pce* **16/1**

3030 **6** 1 ½ **Leonard Thomas**[35] 1312 7-8-13 **57**........................(p) RichardOliver 2 43
(Philip Kirby) *dwlt and rr: hdwy over 2f out: rdn along wl over 1f out: kpt on fnl f: n.d* **14/1**

05-1 **7** ¾ **Olympic Duel (IRE)**[19] 1603 4-8-12 **59**...................... BenRobinson(3) 11 43
(Peter Hiatt) *chsd ldrs: rdn along 2f out: grad wknd* **5/1**[2]

-004 **8** ½ **Llewellyn**[14] 1718 9-9-1 **59**............................(v) PhilDennis 13 42
(Declan Carroll) *led: rdn along and hdd 2f out: sn drvn and grad wknd* **12/1**

00-0 **9** 2 ½ **Adiator**[27] 1456 9-8-9 **53** oh3 ow2............................(p) CliffordLee 7 29
(Neville Bycroft) *a towards rr* **20/1**

25-0 **10** *2 ¾* **Grecian King**[42] 1203 4-9-3 **61**......(p) RowanScott 12 30
(David Barron) *midfield: hdwy and in tch 3f out: rdn over 2f out: sn wknd* **28/1**

0010 **11** *nse* **Nelson's Bay**[26] 1473 8-8-8 **57**...... PaulaMuir(5) 8 25
(Wilf Storey) *dwlt: a bhd* **20/1**

300- **12** *2 ¾* **Riponian**[194] 7333 7-8-4 **55**......(t) TheodoreLadd(7) 15 16
(Susan Corbett) *racd wd: chsd ldrs: rdn along: hung rt and wd st: sn wknd* **66/1**

1m 25.75s (-1.25) **Going Correction** -0.10s/f (Good) **12** Ran SP% **105.1**
Speed ratings (Par 101): **103,102,100,98,96 94,93,93,90,87 87,84**
CSF £19.99 CT £109.76 TOTE £6.30: £1.80, £2.00, £2.30; EX 18.20 Trifecta £128.70.
**Owner** G Scruton, D Williamson & R Carr **Bred** J Hanly, Castlemartin Sky & Skymarc Far **Trained** Huby, N Yorks

■ Clergyman was withdrawn. Price at time of withdrawal 7-1. Rule 4 applies to all bets - deduction 10p in the pound.

**FOCUS**
A moderate apprentice handicap which produced a stirring finish and a game winner. There was a decent pace on and the form seems solid.
T/Plt: £66.80 to a £1 stake. Pool: £56,773.71 - 66.80 winning units. T/Qpdt: £12.70 to a £1 stake. Pool: £4,073.18 - 237.02 winning units. **Joe Rowntree**

# EPSOM (L-H)
## Wednesday, April 26

**OFFICIAL GOING: Good (good to firm in places; 7.6)**
Wind: light to medium across Weather: bright spells and a couple of showers

## 2083 INVESTEC ASSET FINANCE H'CAP 5f
**2:10** (2:11) (Class 3) (0-95,90) 4-Y-0+
**£12,450** (£3,728; £1,864; £932; £466; £234) **Stalls** High

Form RPR

00-2 **1** **Majestic Hero (IRE)**[8] 1863 5-9-5 **88**...... JamieSpencer 9 96
(Ronald Harris) *stdd s: hld up in tch in midfield: swtchd lft and clsd over 1f out: shkn up to chal 1f out: led wl ins fnl f: r.o wl under hands and heels riding* **9/2**[2]

35-3 **2** *¾* **Just That Lord**[11] 1793 4-9-1 **84**...... LukeMorris 8 89
(Bill Turner) *led: rdn over 1f out: hdd and styd on same pce wl ins fnl f* **7/1**

0520 **3** *¾* **Normal Equilibrium**[32] 1370 7-8-7 **76** oh3...... FrannyNorton 10 78
(Ivan Furtado) *pressed ldrs: rdn and ev ch over 1f out tl no ex ins fnl f: outpcd towards fin* **9/1**

20-5 **4** *hd* **Pixeleen**[12] 1765 5-9-3 **86**...... OisinMurphy 4 88+
(Malcolm Saunders) *hld up in tch in last trio: effrt over 1f out: swtchd lft and hdwy jst ins fnl f: styd on strly u.p fnl 100yds: nt rch ldrs* **11/2**

-500 **5** *nk* **Shamshon (IRE)**[46] 1152 6-9-7 **90**......(t) AndreaAtzeni 1 91+
(Stuart Williams) *swtg: dropped in bhd after s: hld up in tch in last trio: rdn and hdwy ent fnl f: styd on strly ins fnl f: nt rch ldrs* **5/1**[3]

0502 **6** *1* **Sandfrankskipsgo**[26] 1465 8-8-9 **78**...... ShaneKelly 11 75
(Peter Crate) *hld up in tch in last trio: effrt over 1f out: kpt on ins fnl f: nvr threatened ldrs* **16/1**

06-0 **7** *¾* **Major Pusey**[35] 1302 5-8-6 **80**...... GeorgeBuckell(5) 3 74
(John Gallagher) *in tch in midfield: effrt 2f out: rdn and clsd to chse ldrs 1f out: no ex u.p and wknd wl ins fnl f* **14/1**

560- **8** *1 ½* **Lathom**[249] 5657 4-9-6 **89**...... RyanMoore 7 78
(David O'Meara) *sltly on toes: in tch in midfield: effrt and carried lft over 1f out: hdwy u.p to chse ldrs 1f out: sn struggling and wknd ins fnl f* **4/1**[1]

2641 **9** *1 ¾* **Monumental Man**[26] 1465 8-9-2 **85**......(p) WilliamCarson 6 68
(Michael Attwater) *pressed ldr: rdn over 1f out: no ex 1f out: sn btn and wknd ins fnl f* **14/1**

0031 **10** *4 ½* **Dutiful Son (IRE)**[28] 1423 7-8-12 **81**...... JimCrowley 2 47
(Simon Dow) *in tch in midfield: dropped to rr 2f out: sn btn and bhd ins fnl f* **16/1**

55.69s (-0.01) **Going Correction** +0.175s/f (Good) **10** Ran SP% **117.8**
Speed ratings (Par 107): **107,105,104,104,103 102,101,98,95,88**
CSF £36.52 CT £227.12 TOTE £5.70: £1.60, £2.10, £3.40; EX 29.30 Trifecta £332.90.
**Owner** Mrs Jackie Jarrett & Ridge House Stables **Bred** Mrs Diane Williams **Trained** Earlswood, Monmouths

**FOCUS**
The watered ground was given as good, good to firm in places (GoingStick: 7.6), and although they were taking the top off, the time was just 0.79s slower than standard and Andrea Atzeni said "it's good to firm." The rail on the Derby course was dolled out from 1m2f to the winning post, adding 29yds to all distances except 5f. A competitive sprint which developed along the stands' rail. The winner backed up his recent Newmarket figure.

## 2084 INVESTEC DERBY TRIAL (CONDITIONS RACE) (PLUS 10 RACE) 1m 2f 17y
**2:45** (2:52) (Class 2) 3-Y-0
**£31,125** (£9,320; £4,660; £2,330; £1,165; £585) **Stalls** Low

Form RPR

1- **1** **Cracksman**[189] 7470 3-9-0 92...... FrankieDettori 2 107+
(John Gosden) *q str: dwlt: t.k.h early: rcvrd and wnt 3rd after 2f: trying to switch out rt and nt clr run 3f out: swtchd rt and effrt over 2f out: hdwy to chse ldr over 1f out: rdn and r.o wl fnl f to ld last stride* **4/6**[1]

53-3 **2** *shd* **Permian (IRE)**[12] 1764 3-9-0 101...... FrannyNorton 6 103
(Mark Johnston) *chsd ldrs: clsd 3f out: edging lft and rdn to chal 2f out: led over 1f out: styd on u.p ins fnl f: hdd last stride* **11/2**[3]

000- **3** *1 ¾* **Bay Of Poets (IRE)**[178] 7721 3-9-0 101...... WilliamBuick 4 100+
(Charlie Appleby) *stdd s: hld up in last pair: clsd towards inner whn nt clr run and swtchd rt 2f out: hdwy to chse ldng pair and hanging lft 1f out: kpt on but no imp ins fnl f* **14/1**

1- **4** *3 ½* **Tartini (USA)**[182] 7621 3-9-0 93...... RobertTart 1 93+
(John Gosden) *athletic: hld up in midfield: effrt whn nt clr run and hmpd over 2f out: shifting lft and hdwy jst over 1f out: wnt 4th 150yds out: kpt on but no threat to ldrs* **4/1**[2]

42-2 **5** *2 ¼* **Never Surrender (IRE)**[25] 1497 3-9-0 84...... JamieSpencer 7 88
(Charles Hills) *t.k.h: hld up in tch in last pair: effrt on outer over 2f out a hanging lft down camber after and nvr getting on terms: 5th and plugged on same pce ins fnl f* **20/1**

1- **6** *2 ¼* **Youmkin (USA)**[182] 7622 3-9-0 88......(p[1]) OisinMurphy 3 84
(Saeed bin Suroor) *leggy: bit green: dwlt: sn rcvrd to ld after 1f: rdn over 2f out: hdd over 1f out: 4th and btn 1f out: wknd ins fnl f* **15/2**

41- **7** *nk* **Ahlan Bil Zain (FR)**[190] 7431 3-9-0 83...... JimCrowley 8 84
(David Simcock) *q tall: broke wl and chsng ldrs tl stdd bk into midfield after 1f: effrt over 2f out: no imp over 1f out: btn whn squeezed for room and wknd ins fnl f* **33/1**

04 **8** *7* **Zoffany Bay (IRE)**[14] 1730 3-9-0 0......(h) SilvestreDeSousa 5 69
(George Peckham) *q tall: sltly on toes: led for 1f: chsd ldr tl 3rd and jst getting outpcd whn sltly impeded 2f out: lost pl and wknd over 1f out* **100/1**

2m 10.73s (1.03) **Going Correction** +0.15s/f (Good) **8** Ran SP% **122.5**
Speed ratings (Par 104): **101,100,99,96,94 93,92,87**
CSF £5.50 TOTE £1.60: £1.10, £1.70, £3.70; EX 4.90 Trifecta £36.80.
**Owner** A E Oppenheimer **Bred** Hascombe And Valiant Studs **Trained** Newmarket, Suffolk

**FOCUS**
Race distance increased by 29yds. An interesting Derby trial, but the early gallop wasn't strong and it turned into a test of speed (time was 2.84sec slower than the well-run City And Suburban Handicap later on the card). John Gosden was winning it for the fifth time in the last 11 years. Cracksman is sure to improve and the runner-up is rated to form.

## 2085 INVESTEC CORPORATE BANKING GREAT METROPOLITAN H'CAP 1m 4f 6y
**3:15** (3:22) (Class 3) (0-95,96) 4-Y-0+
**£12,450** (£3,728; £1,864; £932; £466; £234) **Stalls** Centre

Form RPR

-1 **1** **Galapiat**[19] 1608 4-9-11 **96**...... FrannyNorton 9 109+
(Mark Johnston) *str: lw: mde all and set stdy gallop: pushed along and qcknd 3f out: clr over 1f out: r.o strly: readily* **11/10**[1]

461- **2** *4 ½* **Whinging Willie (IRE)**[209] 6892 8-8-8 **78**...... SamHitchcott 5 81
(Gary Moore) *t.k.h: hld up in midfield: dropped bk into last trio 8f out: effrt wd over 3f out: hdwy to go 3rd over 1f out: wnt 2nd 100yds out: styd on but no ch w wnr* **25/1**

300- **3** *1 ¼* **Barwick**[183] 3889 9-9-5 **89**...... FrankieDettori 2 90
(George Baker) *dwlt: hdwy to chse ldrs after 2f: wnt 2nd 3f out and sn rdn: outpcd by wnr but stl clr 2nd 2f out: wl hld 1f out and lost 2nd ins fnl f* **12/1**

64-0 **4** *5* **William Hunter**[25] 1502 5-9-3 **87**...... FergusSweeney 8 80
(Alan King) *lw: t.k.h: chsd ldng trio: effrt but outpcd by ldrs whn shifted lft over 2f out: wl hld 4th over 1f out: plugged on* **7/1**[3]

36-5 **5** *¾* **Sindarban (IRE)**[11] 1802 6-9-7 **91**...... JamieSpencer 4 83
(Keith Dalgleish) *t.k.h: mostly chsd wnr tl 3f out: getting outpcd whn wnt lft over 1f out: wl hld after* **13/2**[2]

626- **6** *1 ½* **Thames Knight**[205] 7015 5-8-10 **80**...... RoystonFfrench 1 69
(Marcus Tregoning) *bit bkwd: t.k.h: hld up in midfield: effrt towards inner over 2f out: pressing for 3rd but no threat to wnr whn pushed lft and hmpd over 1f out: no ch after* **10/1**

201- **7** *2 ½* **Michael's Mount**[183] 7594 4-8-8 **79**......(p) SilvestreDeSousa 3 64
(Ed Dunlop) *t.k.h: w ldrs tl stdd bk into midfield after 1f: shifting lft and effrt over 2f out: no imp whn nt clr run and swtchd rt wl over 1f out: no imp after* **8/1**

5R31 **8** *½* **Royal Marskell**[32] 1361 8-8-5 **82**......(h) DavidEgan(7) 6 67
(Gay Kelleway) *s.i.s: a towards rr: rdn 3f out: sn struggling and wl btn over 1f out* **25/1**

000- **9** *2 ¼* **Ruwasi**[30] 7538 6-9-4 **88**...... RyanMoore 7 69+
(Gary Moore) *hld up in last pair: swtchd lft and effrt jst over 2f out: pressing for 3rd but no threat to wnr whn squeezed for room and bdly hmpd over 1f out: nt rcvrd and eased fnl f* **9/1**

2m 41.79s (2.89) **Going Correction** +0.15s/f (Good) **9** Ran SP% **119.0**
Speed ratings (Par 107): **96,93,92,88,88 87,85,85,83**
CSF £36.63 CT £230.20 TOTE £2.20: £1.10, £5.70, £2.80; EX 47.10 Trifecta £622.20.
**Owner** Miss K Rausing **Bred** Miss K Rausing **Trained** Middleham Moor, N Yorks

**FOCUS**
Race distance increased by 29yds. The favourite enjoyed the run of the race out in front, but he's well regarded and there's a good chance he's a lot better than this lot anyway. The race perhaps lacked depth.

## 2086 INVESTEC CITY AND SUBURBAN H'CAP 1m 2f 17y
**3:50** (3:53) (Class 2) (0-105,102) 4-Y-0+
**£28,012** (£8,388; £4,194; £2,097; £1,048; £526) **Stalls** Low

Form RPR

33-5 **1** **Brorocco**[13] 1757 4-8-4 **85**......(h) JimmyQuinn 10 93+
(Andrew Balding) *stdd s: hld up in rr: swtchd rt and effrt over 2f out: str run over 1f out to ld jst ins fnl f: r.o wl* **7/1**

21-1 **2** *1* **Banditry (IRE)**[57] 963 5-8-10 **91**......(h) StevieDonohoe 11 96
(Ian Williams) *lw: last pair: effrt over 2f out: hdwy on outer over 1f out: styd on wl ins fnl f: wnt 2nd nr fin* **13/2**

2-24 **3** *hd* **Gawdawpalin (IRE)**[25] 1502 4-8-8 **89**...... TomMarquand 5 94
(Sylvester Kirk) *niggled along in midfield: wanting to hang lft down camber and hdwy over 1f out: styd on wl ins fnl f: snatched 3rd cl home* **5/1**[3]

3-40 **4** *nk* **Great Hall**[15] 1704 7-9-7 **102**...... PatCosgrave 12 106
(Mick Quinn) *lw: led for 1f: styd chsng ldrs: effrt to chse clr ldr over 2f out: hung lft but chalng over 1f out: led 1f out: sn hdd and styd on same pce ins fnl f* **20/1**

641- **5** *2* **Speed Company (IRE)**[187] 7499 4-9-4 **99**......(h) RyanMoore 2 99+
(John Quinn) *hld up in midfield: effrt jst over 2f out: no imp tl hdwy jst ins fnl f: styd on wl fnl 100yds: nvr trbld ldrs* **9/2**[2]

6125 **6** *1 ¼* **Dutch Uncle**[39] 1258 5-8-9 **90**...... SilvestreDeSousa 6 88
(Ed Dunlop) *led after 1f: wnt clr over 3f out: rdn jst over 2f out: hdd 1f out: no ex and wknd ins fnl f* **10/1**

10-3 **7** *hd* **Innocent Touch (IRE)**[15] 1704 6-8-13 **94**...... TonyHamilton 4 91
(Richard Fahey) *hld up in midfield: effrt ent fnl 2f: styd on same pce and no imp fr over 1f out* **4/1**[1]

3406 **8** *½* **Eddystone Rock (IRE)**[25] 1494 5-9-4 **99**......(h) KierenFox 3 95
(John Best) *hld up towards rr: effrt whn hmpd 2f out: swtchd rt ent fnl f: kpt on ins fnl f: nvr trbld ldrs* **10/1**

0150 **9** *nse* **Abareeq**[12] 1779 4-8-6 **87**...... FrannyNorton 1 83
(Mark Johnston) *in tch in midfield: clsd on inner whn nt clr run over 2f out: switching rt fr 2f out but stl nt enough room tl 1f out: no threat to ldrs and kpt on same pce after* **10/1**

4330 **10** *7* **Van Huysen (IRE)**[12] 1775 5-8-4 **85**...... JosephineGordon 13 67
(Dominic Ffrench Davis) *chsd ldrs: rdn and outpcd over 2f out: lost pl over 1f out and bhd ins fnl f* **25/1**

5132 **11** *½* **Faithful Creek (IRE)**[19] 1608 5-8-3 **84**......(p) LukeMorris 8 65
(Michael Appleby) *chsd ldrs: rdn over 2f out: unable qck and lost pl over 1f out: bhd ins fnl f* **8/1**

2m 7.89s (-1.81) **Going Correction** +0.15s/f (Good) **11** Ran SP% **127.7**
Speed ratings (Par 109): **113,112,112,111,110 109,109,108,108,103 102**
CSF £56.79 CT £258.76 TOTE £8.20: £2.80, £2.60, £2.50; EX 59.70 Trifecta £385.70.
**Owner** Kingsclere Racing Club **Bred** Kingsclere Stud **Trained** Kingsclere, Hants

**FOCUS**
Race distance increased by 29yds. Dutch Uncle set a decent gallop and the closers came to the fore. The winner resumed his progress.

## 2087 INVESTEC FOREIGN EXCHANGE MAIDEN STKS 1m 113y
4:25 (4:27) (Class 5) 3-4-Y-O £3,881 (£1,155; £577; £288) Stalls Low

Form RPR

6- **1** **Leader's Legacy (USA)**[280] 4533 3-8-13 0..........(t[1]) SilvestreDeSousa 5 89+
(Saeed bin Suroor) *str: lw: chsd ldrs: effrt to chse ldr ent fnl 2f: led over 1f out: sn clr and r.o strly fnl f: readily* **11/8**[1]

534- **2** *4* **Romanor**[204] 7034 3-8-13 75..........(h) ThomasBrown 8 77
(Ed Walker) *w'like: bit bkwd: hld up in midfield: effrt over 2f out: wnt 3rd over 1f out: no ch w wnr but kpt on ins fnl f to go 2nd towards fin* **12/1**

323- **3** *¾* **Carpe Diem Lady (IRE)**[198] 7220 4-9-9 76..........(b) FranBerry 9 73
(Ralph Beckett) *t.k.h: led: wnt clr over 3f out: rdn over 2f out: hdd over 1f out and sn outpcd and kpt on same pce after: lost 2nd towards fin* **5/1**[3]

0-3 **4** *6* **Bahar (USA)**[25] 1485 3-8-13 0.......... FrankieDettori 1 61
(Richard Hannon) *q str: lw: chsd ldr tl over 3f out: urged along over 2f out: outpcd and unbalanced 2f out: changing legs and btn over 1f out: wknd* **7/2**[2]

**5** *3 ¾* **Corredordel Viento (USA)** 3-8-13 0..........(h[1]) JFEgan 3 53
(Simon Dow) *str: bit bkwd: lw: s.i.s and sltly impeded leaving stalls: hld up in last trio: clsd and in tch 5f out: outpcd 3f out: no ch after but plugged on ins fnl f* **14/1**

-343 **6** *3 ¾* **Arnarson**[15] 1692 3-8-13 80.......... RyanMoore 2 44
(Ed Dunlop) *chsd ldrs: wnt 2nd over 3f out tl ent fnl 2f: sn struggling and wl btn over 1f out: eased ins fnl f* **5/1**[3]

060- **7** *5* **Crystal Secret**[190] 7423 3-8-8 50.......... WilliamCarson 6 28
(John Bridger) *sltly on toes: midfield tl dropped to last 5f out: wl bhd and hung lft 2f out* **100/1**

**8** *2 ¼* **Diore Lia (IRE)** 3-8-3 0.......... CharlieBennett(5) 7 23
(Jane Chapple-Hyam) *w'like: bit on the leg: s.i.s: rn green in rr: sme hdwy 5f out: outpcd again 3f out: no ch after* **33/1**

000- **9** *13* **Back To Love (CAN)**[148] 8145 4-9-9 42..........(t[1]) TimmyMurphy 4
(Mark Gillard) *on toes: awkward leaving stalls: midfield: clsd 5f out: struggling and outpcd 3f out: no ch after: t.o* **100/1**

1m 47.06s (0.96) **Going Correction** +0.15s/f (Good) **9** Ran SP% **116.9**
**WFA** 3 from 4yo 15lb
Speed ratings (Par 103): **101,97,96,91,88 84,80,78,66**
CSF £20.98 TOTE £2.40: £1.20, £2.90, £1.60; EX 18.70 Trifecta £83.80.
**Owner** Godolphin **Bred** Ramona S Bass Llc **Trained** Newmarket, Suffolk

**FOCUS**
Race distance increased by 29yds. A comfortable success for the favourite in the end. The form's rated around the runner-up.

## 2088 INVESTEC PRIVATE BANKING H'CAP 1m 113y
5:00 (5:03) (Class 4) (0-80,80) 3-Y-O £5,822 (£1,732; £865; £432) Stalls Low

Form RPR

1-15 **1** **Emenem**[12] 1764 3-9-4 77.......... JFEgan 3 87
(Simon Dow) *chsd ldrs: effrt between rivals to ld 2f out: forged ahd over 1f out: styd on wl: rdn out* **9/1**

2-10 **2** *1 ¾* **Native Prospect**[24] 1518 3-9-7 80.......... OisinMurphy 13 85
(Andrew Balding) *lw; chsd ldrs: wnt 2nd 6f out: ev ch 2f out: shkn up over 1f out: chsd wnr and kpt on same pce ins fnl f* **9/2**[2]

030- **3** *1 ¼* **Star Maker**[175] 7768 3-8-3 69.......... FinleyMarsh(7) 10 71
(Sylvester Kirk) *chsd ldrs: effrt ent fnl 2f: chsd ldng pair 1f out: kpt on same pce u.p ins fnl f* **16/1**

500- **4** *nk* **Fair Power (IRE)**[186] 7549 3-8-9 73.......... MitchGodwin(5) 2 74
(Sylvester Kirk) *wl in tch in midfield: swtchd rt and effrt jst over 2f out: kpt on ins fnl f: nt enough pce to threaten ldrs* **25/1**

-411 **5** *1* **Vantage Point (IRE)**[28] 1434 3-9-7 80..........(p) RyanMoore 4 79+
(Gary Moore) *lw: in tch in midfield: effrt and edgd rt wl over 1f out: kpt on ins fnl f: no threat to ldrs* **7/2**[1]

32-3 **6** *nk* **Quothquan (FR)**[89] 439 3-8-9 73.......... GeorgeWood(5) 7 71
(Michael Madgwick) *hld up in midfield: effrt on outer over 2f out: sme hdwy and edgd lft over 1f out: kpt on ins fnl f: nvr trbld ldrs* **12/1**

106- **7** *1 ¾* **Balgair**[216] 6705 3-9-3 76.......... LukeMorris 1 71+
(Jonathan Portman) *hld up towards rr: effrt over 2f out: sltly impeded and swtchd lft wl over 1f out: kpt on but no imp after* **10/1**

320- **8** *½* **Peloton**[179] 7697 3-8-8 67.......... FrannyNorton 9 60
(Pat Phelan) *swtchd lft after s: hld up in last trio: effrt and hdwy over 2f out: kpt on but no real imp fr over 1f out* **25/1**

505- **9** *2* **Procurator (IRE)**[172] 7820 3-9-7 80.......... TomMarquand 8 69
(Richard Hannon) *t.k.h: chsd ldrs: rdn and unable qck jst over 2f out: wknd ins fnl f* **8/1**

16-1 **10** *½* **Masterofdiscovery**[16] 1685 3-9-2 75..........(b) JohnFahy 5 62
(Clive Cox) *led: jnd over 2f out: sn hdd and rdn: lost pl over 1f out: wknd ins fnl f* **7/1**[3]

10-6 **11** *2 ¼* **Bayston Hill**[16] 1686 3-8-9 68.......... LiamKeniry 16 50
(Mark Usher) *hld up in rr: n.d* **25/1**

120- **12** *1 ¼* **Northdown**[231] 6240 3-9-3 76.......... TomQueally 6 55
(David Lanigan) *s.i.s: a rr* **33/1**

0-1 **13** *hd* **Glorious Power (IRE)**[32] 1358 3-9-7 80.......... DavidProbert 12 59
(Charles Hills) *in tch in midfield: rdn and lost pl 3f out: bhd over 1f out* **16/1**

3-21 **14** *25* **Oud Metha Bridge (IRE)**[42] 1198 3-9-6 79.......... SilvestreDeSousa 11
(Ed Dunlop) *q str: t.k.h: hld up towards rr: swtchd rt over 4f out: bhd hung lft 2f out: sn lost tch and eased ins fnl f* **9/2**[2]

1m 46.69s (0.59) **Going Correction** +0.15s/f (Good) **14** Ran SP% **135.2**
Speed ratings (Par 100): **103,101,100,100,99 98,97,96,95,94 92,91,91,69**
CSF £53.54 CT £696.78 TOTE £11.40: £3.80, £1.50, £5.60; EX 80.00 Trifecta £1606.30.
**Owner** Robert Moss and Christopher Brennan **Bred** D R Tucker **Trained** Ashtead, Surrey

**FOCUS**
Race distance increased by 29yds. A fair handicap in which the pace held up well. The third helps with the standard.
T/Jkpt: Part won. Pool: £5238.79. T/Plt: £52.90 to a £1 stake. Pool: £102,261.03 - 1408.79 winning units. T/Qpdt: £26.10 to a £1 stake. Pool: £5,409.89 - 152.98 winning units.
**Steve Payne**

# [2023] LINGFIELD (L-H)
Wednesday, April 26

**OFFICIAL GOING: Polytrack: standard**
Wind: nil Weather: grey cloud, raining after race 3, bright after race 5

## 2089 RACING WELFARE CLAIMING STKS 7f 1y(P)
4:45 (4:47) (Class 6) 3-Y-O £2,264 (£673; £336; £168) Stalls Low

Form RPR

6024 **1** **Sans Souci Bay**[21] 1554 3-9-10 74..........(b[1]) HollieDoyle(3) 3 77
(Richard Hannon) *t.k.h in rr on outer: shkn up 3f out and swtchd wdst: sn rdn and led 2f out: clr 1f out: rdn out* **11/10**[2]

1500 **2** *3 ½* **Vatican Hill (IRE)**[9] 1841 3-9-13 82.......... AdamKirby 1 68
(Jamie Osborne) *s.s: t.k.h: trckd ldrs in 3rd: shkn up 3f out: sn rdn: no imp on clr ldr over 1f out: pushed out hands and heels ins fnl f* **1/1**[1]

0505 **3** *2* **Lady Volante (IRE)**[19] 1605 3-8-4 54.......... DavidEgan(7) 4 46
(David Evans) *disp ld on outer: rdn over 2f out: dropped to last 2f out: sn hld and pushed out fr over 1f out* **16/1**[3]

-065 **4** *3* **Madam Prancealot (IRE)**[74] 686 3-8-12 51.......... SeanLevey 2 39
(David Evans) *narrow ld on inner: rdn over 2f out: wnr wnt past 2f out: sn hld and pushed out fr over 1f out* **20/1**

1m 26.73s (1.93) **Going Correction** -0.125s/f (Stan) **4** Ran SP% **108.3**
Speed ratings (Par 96): **83,79,76,73**
CSF £2.52 TOTE £1.90; EX 2.60 Trifecta £4.20.
**Owner** J R Shannon **Bred** J R Shannon **Trained** East Everleigh, Wilts
■ Lady Volante was claimed by Miss L. Egerton for £2000

**FOCUS**
Only two mattered in this claimer, which has been given a token rating through the winner.

## 2090 BARBER SHOP FKS HONOR OAK PARK MAIDEN STKS 7f 1y(P)
5:20 (5:23) (Class 5) 3-Y-O £2,911 (£866; £432; £216) Stalls Low

Form RPR

**1** **Casimiro (IRE)** 3-9-2 0.......... KieranShoemark(3) 8 88+
(Roger Charlton) *trckd ldr in 3rd on inner: gng wl and rdn ent fnl f: sn led: rdn clr* **10/1**

0 **2** *3 ¾* **Time's Arrow (IRE)**[25] 1488 3-9-5 0.......... TedDurcan 12 75+
(Sir Michael Stoute) *settled in mid-div: rdn over 1f out: kpt on wl to grab 2nd nr fin* **5/1**[2]

6 **3** *hd* **Tadween (IRE)**[14] 1727 3-9-5 0.......... JimCrowley 10 74
(Richard Hannon) *t.k.h in mid-div: rdn over 1f out: kpt on wl* **6/1**[3]

**4** *hd* **Gustavo Fring (IRE)** 3-9-5 0.......... RobertWinston 11 74
(Richard Spencer) *pressed ldr on outer: rdn wl over 1f out: kpt on wl tl wknd fnl f* **6/1**[3]

0-4 **5** *nk* **Milburn Jack**[18] 1619 3-9-5 0.......... AdamKirby 14 73
(Clive Cox) *early pce to trck ldrs on outer: rdn over 1f out: no imp on wnr: shuffled along on outer ins fnl f* **5/1**[2]

**6** *1* **Balestra** 3-9-5 0.......... RichardKingscote 7 70+
(Charles Hills) *settled in rr-div on outer: rdn wl over 1f out: rn green on outer ent st: kpt on nicely under hands and heels ins fnl f: nvr nrr* **7/2**[1]

**7** *1 ¼* **Be Be King (IRE)** 3-9-2 0.......... HollieDoyle(3) 4 67
(Eve Johnson Houghton) *broke wl and sn led: rdn wl over 1f out: hdd 1f out: no ex and wknd sn after* **14/1**

6 **8** *10* **Clever Lady (IRE)**[12] 1762 3-9-0 0.......... SeanLevey 13 35
(David Evans) *in rr: rdn over 2f out: no ex and pushed along fr over 1f out* **50/1**

00- **9** *2 ¼* **Fox King**[200] 7157 3-9-5 0.......... PatDobbs 9 34
(Ralph Beckett) *fractious s: in rr: pushed along at 1/2-way: rdn over 3f out: no imp* **12/1**

**10** *½* **Symbol In The Sand (NOR)**[241] 3-8-11 0.......... MarcMonaghan(3) 6 28
(Rune Haugen) *trckd ldrs: pushed along on inner fr over 2f out: lft bhd fr over 1f out* **66/1**

6 **11** *2 ¼* **Joy**[19] 1600 3-8-7 0.......... OllieJago(7) 3 21
(Laura Mongan) *in rr-div: niggled along 1/2-way: rdn 3f out: no imp* **66/1**

0-0 **12** *1* **Artsteelwork**[19] 1600 3-8-7 0.......... DarraghKeenan(7) 2 19
(John Butler) *in rr-div: rdn over 3f out: sn hld* **100/1**

**13** *½* **Nevasca (IRE)** 3-9-2 0.......... SimonPearce(3) 5 22
(Lydia Pearce) *in rr: rdn over 2f out: sn hld* **33/1**

**14** *21* **True Gentleman** 3-9-5 0.......... RenatoSouza 1
(Sylvester Kirk) *missed break: detached in rr and pushed along: nvr on terms: no imp* **33/1**

1m 23.31s (-1.49) **Going Correction** -0.125s/f (Stan) **14** Ran SP% **119.4**
Speed ratings (Par 98): **103,98,98,98,97 96,95,83,81,80 78,77,76,52**
CSF £57.36 TOTE £10.70: £2.70, £2.20, £2.00; EX 78.00 Trifecta £484.30.
**Owner** P Inglett & P Hearson **Bred** Ballybrennan Stud **Trained** Beckhampton, Wilts

**FOCUS**
A fair maiden that should produce winners. The front seven were well clear and the form is rated around the fifth.

## 2091 BRIAN HANRAHAN H'CAP 6f 1y(P)
5:50 (5:50) (Class 6) (0-60,61) 3-Y-O+ £2,264 (£673; £336; £168) Stalls Low

Form RPR

60-1 **1** **Termsnconditions (IRE)**[32] 1359 3-9-1 58.......... KieranO'Neill 5 63
(Tim Vaughan) *racd in 3rd: gng wl over 2f out: rdn over 1f out: led 150yds out: hdd nr fin: fought bk and got bk up fnl strides* **9/2**[3]

0364 **2** *nk* **Noble Deed**[28] 1427 7-10-1 61..........(p) AdamBeschizza 4 68
(Michael Attwater) *hld up bhd ldrs: shkn up over 2f out: rdn over 1f out: c between horses and led briefly nr fin: hdd fnl strides* **11/2**

0400 **3** *1* **New Rich**[14] 1723 7-9-12 58..........(b) RobertWinston 3 62
(Eve Johnson Houghton) *in rr: shuffled along by 1/2-way: swtchd to outer over 1f out and hung lft: briefly rdn fnl f: pushed out fnl 100yds: nvr nrr* **3/1**[1]

2324 **4** *¾* **Mr Chuckles (IRE)**[7] 1887 4-9-6 52..........(p) JosephineGordon 8 54
(Daniel Mark Loughnane) *trckd ldr in 2nd: rdn over 2f out: led 1f out: hdd 150yds out: stuck on one pce nr fin: lost shoe* **7/2**[2]

000- **5** *2* **Silver Wings (IRE)**[341] 2435 4-9-7 60.......... DavidEgan(7) 7 56
(David Evans) *trckd ldrs: rdn over 2f out: kpt on one pce* **20/1**

1210 **6** *½* **Krazy Paving**[35] 1304 5-9-11 57..........(b) AdamKirby 1 51
(Anabel K Murphy) *trckd ldrs on inner: rdn wl over 1f out: no imp fnl f* **11/2**

5240 **7** *3* **Justice Rock**[21] 1557 4-8-10 47.......... LuluStanford(5) 9 32
(Phil McEntee) *sn led: rdn ent 2f out: stuck on tl hdd 1f out and wknd* **12/1**

6606 **8** 3¾ **Whaleweigh Station**[35] 1305 6-9-9 **55**....................(v) FergusSweeney 6 29
(J R Jenkins) *s.s: sn racd wd and trckd ldrs: rdn 2f out: no imp and in rr over 1f out: sn hld* **16/1**

1m 11.87s (-0.03) **Going Correction** -0.125s/f (Stan)
**WFA** 3 from 4yo+ 11lb 8 Ran SP% **114.5**
Speed ratings (Par 101): **95,94,93,92,89 88,84,79**
CSF £29.40 CT £85.01 TOTE £5.60: £1.90, £2.20, £1.50; EX 35.80 Trifecta £110.00.
**Owner** T Vaughan **Bred** Tally-Ho Stud **Trained** Aberthin, Vale of Glamorgan

**FOCUS**
This moderate sprint handicap was run at a routine pace. The older horses close up help dictate the level.

## 2092 INJURED JOCKEYS FUND MEDIAN AUCTION MAIDEN STKS 1m 2f (P)
**6:25** (6:28) (Class 6) 3-4-Y-O **£2,264** (£673; £336; £168) **Stalls** Low

Form RPR
242- **1** **Regicide (IRE)**[203] 7063 4-10-0 83.................................... OisinMurphy 6 82+
(James Fanshawe) *t.k.h early: nicely settled in mid-divsion sn after: gng wl whn rdn over 1f out: led ent fnl f: drifted rt to nrside centre: sted up fnl 110yds and led cl home* **2/1**[2]

063- **2** 1 **Kasperenko**[205] 7012 3-8-11 76.................................... TedDurcan 1 79+
(David Lanigan) *trckd ldr on inner: bdly hmpd over 2f out and lost pl: gathered up and rdn bhd ldrs over 1f: picked up wl on inner and led 150yds out: hdd cl home* **7/4**[1]

6-5 **3** nk **Zamalight**[21] 1552 3-8-11 0.................................... JimCrowley 4 76
(Amanda Perrett) *settled in mid-div: shkn up and tk clsr order over 2f out: rdn wl over 1f out: pushed wd by wnr ent fnl f: kpt on* **8/1**

3-2 **4** 2 **Golden Wolf (IRE)**[29] 1410 3-8-11 0.................................... ShaneKelly 7 73
(Richard Hughes) *trckd ldrs on outer: shkn up over 2f out: pushed up to ld and edgd to rail squeezing up two rivals on inner: sn rdn: hdd ent fnl f: no ex* **5/1**

326- **5** 1 **Wordsearch (USA)**[147] 8153 3-8-11 74.................... JosephineGordon 10 73
(Hugo Palmer) *trckd ldr: niggled along over 3f out: upside ldr whn rival edgd to rail over 2f out and got bdly squeezed up: rdn 2f out: kpt on tl wknd ins fnl f* **4/1**[3]

0 **6** 9 **Book Of Dust**[19] 1609 3-8-6 0.................................... LiamJones 5 49
(Giles Bravery) *fractious s: and loaded wout jockey: rdn along over 4f out: hld fr over 2f out* **100/1**

0 **7** 4½ **Luna Bear**[14] 1727 3-8-3 0.................................... NoelGarbutt(3) 3 48+
(Gary Moore) *led: shuffled along whn bdly squeezed up over 2f out: dropped bk through field and eased* **100/1**

**8** 8 **Geordielad** 3-8-11 0.................................... FergusSweeney 2 30
(Jamie Osborne) *s.s: a in rr: rdn wl over 3f out* **33/1**

6 **9** 3¾ **Forestry**[29] 1410 3-8-4 0.................................... Pierre-LouisJamin(7) 8 23
(Jonathan Portman) *a in rr* **100/1**

0- **10** 18 **Masked Bandit**[22] 7219 4-10-0 0....................................(h[1]) DannyBrock 9
(Suzy Smith) *in rr-disvion: rdn along over 4f out: sn lost tch: t.o st* **150/1**

2m 4.62s (-1.98) **Going Correction** -0.125s/f (Stan)
**WFA** 3 from 4yo 17lb 10 Ran SP% **124.0**
Speed ratings (Par 101): **102,101,100,99,98 91,87,81,78,63**
CSF £6.43 TOTE £3.00: £1.20, £1.40, £2.10; EX 8.30 Trifecta £42.80.
**Owner** Chris Van Hoorn Racing **Bred** Flaxman Stables Ireland Ltd **Trained** Newmarket, Suffolk
■ Stewards' Enquiry : Oisin Murphy two-day ban: careless riding (May 10-11)
Jim Crowley two-day ban: guilty of careless riding in that he had allowed his horse to drift right-handed without sufficient correction (May 10-11)
Shane Kelly six-day ban: careless riding (May 10-13, 15-16)

**FOCUS**
A modest maiden, run at a routine pace. A good effort from the winner.

## 2093 HAPPY 60TH BIRTHDAY JACK POWER H'CAP 1m 1y(P)
**6:55** (6:59) (Class 3) (0-95,94) 4-Y-O- **£7,246** (£2,168; £1,084; £542; £270) **Stalls** High

Form RPR
65-4 **1** **Takatul (USA)**[18] 1622 4-8-13 **86**.................................... JimCrowley 2 92+
(Charles Hills) *trckd ldr on inner: shkn up and swtchd off rail to chse ldr over 2f out: rdn wl over 1f out: pressed ldr fnl f tl led cl home* **9/4**[2]

1214 **2** ½ **Take The Helm**[12] 1769 4-9-5 **92**.................................... SeanLevey 1 97
(Brian Meehan) *led: rdn over 2f out: kpt on strly pressed by wnr fnl f: hdd cl home* **11/2**[3]

033- **3** nk **Replenish (FR)**[192] 7383 4-9-2 **94**.................................... GeorgeWood(5) 4 98+
(James Fanshawe) *trckd ldrs: shkn up 2f out: rdn over 1f out: chal between horses ent fnl f: no ex nr fin* **2/1**[1]

6- **4** 1¼ **Chestnut Fire**[61] 905 5-9-5 **92**.................................... AdamKirby 3 93
(Daniel Mark Loughnane) *in rr on inner: rdn over 2f out on inner: kpt on wl tl no ex fnl 110yds* **8/1**

010- **5** ¾ **Noble Peace**[208] 6918 4-8-8 **84**.................................... KieranShoemark(3) 7 84
(Henry Candy) *hld up in last: rdn wl over 1f out: no imp* **8/1**

2036 **6** 1¼ **Bint Dandy (IRE)**[12] 1771 6-9-0 **87**....................................(b) OisinMurphy 5 83
(Chris Dwyer) *trckd ldrs on outer: rdn over 2f out: kpt on tl no imp ent fnl f* **11/1**

00 **7** 11 **Diana Lady (CHI)**[13] 1757 4-8-10 **83**....................................(b[1]) LukeMorris 6 53
(Rune Haugen) *s.s: wnt rt: kpt wd and pressed ldrs: rdn wl over 2f out: sn lost pl ent st and wl hld fr over 1f out* **100/1**

1m 36.21s (-1.99) **Going Correction** -0.125s/f (Stan) 7 Ran SP% **111.0**
Speed ratings (Par 107): **104,103,103,101,101 99,88**
CSF £14.09 TOTE £3.20: £1.80, £2.30; EX 13.20 Trifecta £32.80.
**Owner** Hamdan Al Maktoum **Bred** Shadwell Farm LLC **Trained** Lambourn, Berks

**FOCUS**
This good-quality feature handicap was run at an uneven pace. The first two have some upside.

## 2094 RACING WELFARE 24 HOUR SUPPORT LINE 08006300443 FILLIES' H'CAP 7f 1y(P)
**7:25** (7:26) (Class 5) (0-75,77) 3-Y-O **£2,911** (£866; £432; £216) **Stalls** Low

Form RPR
-431 **1** **Tai Hang Dragon (IRE)**[77] 625 3-9-2 **70**.................................... SeanLevey 9 77+
(Richard Hannon) *trckd ldrs on inner: shkn up over 2f out: rdn over 1f out: no imp on ldr tl styd on strly wl ins fnl f to get up post* **7/1**

6-21 **2** hd **Angel Of Darkness**[15] 1693 3-9-6 **74**.................... SilvestreDeSousa 5 80
(Charles Hills) *led after 1f: rdn over 2f out: kpt on wl and gd ld ent fnl f: hdd fnl stride* **3/1**[2]

503- **3** 2 **The Lacemaker**[214] 6782 3-9-7 **75**.................................... AdamKirby 1 75
(Ed Dunlop) *led: hdd after 1f: trckd ldr on inner: rdn over 2f out: kpt on wl tl no imp fnl f* **6/1**[3]

451- **4** ½ **Miss Laila (IRE)**[230] 6250 3-9-3 **71**.................................... PatCosgrave 11 70
(Tom Clover) *mid-div on outer: rdn over 2f out: kpt on one pce fr over 1f out* **16/1**

-023 **5** ½ **Touch Me (IRE)**[35] 1306 3-8-10 **67**....................(h) JordanVaughan(3) 3 65
(K R Burke) *trckd ldr between horses: gng wl 2f out: tried to switch out over 1f out: sn shuffled along wout being able to qckn: likely improver* **14/1**

536- **6** 1 **Braztime**[222] 6534 3-9-4 **72**.................................... PatDobbs 4 67+
(Richard Hannon) *in rr: shkn up wl over 1f out: rdn and no imp over 1f out* **8/1**

046- **7** nk **Pyjamarama**[186] 7527 3-9-0 **68**.................................... AndreaAtzeni 10 62
(Roger Varian) *in rr: rdn out wd ent st: no imp* **12/1**

1505 **8** ¾ **Pulsating (IRE)**[11] 1786 3-8-9 **63**.................................... StevieDonohoe 7 55
(Daniel Steele) *in rr: rdn over 2f out: no imp* **50/1**

2- **9** 1 **Mad Rose (IRE)**[121] 3-9-4 **72**.................................... RichardKingscote 8 61
(Jonathan Portman) *missed break and wnt rt s: in rr: nvr on terms* **40/1**

61- **10** 8 **Belle Diva (IRE)**[219] 6625 3-9-9 **77**.................................... OisinMurphy 6 45
(Ralph Beckett) *pressed ldr on outer: shkn up to hold pl wl over 3f out: wl btn and eased ent fnl f* **11/4**[1]

1m 23.96s (-0.84) **Going Correction** -0.125s/f (Stan) 10 Ran SP% **114.2**
Speed ratings (Par 95): **99,98,96,95,95 94,93,93,91,82**
CSF £27.65 CT £137.29 TOTE £8.20: £2.10, £1.40, £2.00; EX 19.10 Trifecta £43.50.
**Owner** Rockcliffe Stud **Bred** Lynn Lodge Stud **Trained** East Everleigh, Wilts

**FOCUS**
A modest fillies' handicap. The winner built on her Kempton win.

## 2095 HAPPY ANNIVERSARY JOHN & MARY H'CAP 1m 2f (P)
**7:55** (7:56) (Class 6) (0-60,60) 4-Y-O+ **£2,264** (£673; £336; £168) **Stalls** Low

Form RPR
231- **1** **Victoriously**[151] 8125 5-9-2 **55**....................................(p) MartinLane 7 64+
(Andi Brown) *hld up in rr: shkn up and tk clsr order over 2f out: rdn and swtchd to inner over 2f out: qcknd up wl ent fnl f and led 150yds out: rdn out* **6/1**[2]

3144 **2** 2 **Ixelles Diamond (IRE)**[18] 1618 6-9-3 **56**.................... JosephineGordon 1 61
(Lee Carter) *mid-div on inner: rdn over 2f out: kpt on wl fr over 1f out: one pce ins fnl f* **16/1**

0366 **3** ½ **With Approval (IRE)**[27] 1449 5-9-5 **58**....................(p) PatCosgrave 8 62
(Laura Mongan) *trckd ldr between horses: rdn over 2f out: kpt on on outer fr over 1f out: no imp on wnr ins fnl f* **10/1**

-434 **4** 1½ **Estibdaad (IRE)**[18] 1620 7-9-6 **59**....................(t) DannyBrock 11 60
(Paddy Butler) *led: rdn wl over 2f out: stuck on wl whn chal: hdd over 150yds out: no ex ins fnl f* **8/1**

00-6 **5** ½ **Prince Of Cardamom (IRE)**[2] 2023 5-8-10 **56**...........(p) JordanUys(7) 2 56
(Jonathan Geake) *trckd ldr on inner: shkn up 2f out and gng wl: rdn over 1f out: nt pick up and styd on one pce* **25/1**

5004 **6** 2 **Monna Valley**[30] 1403 5-9-3 **56**.................................... SilvestreDeSousa 3 52
(Stuart Williams) *stelled in mid-div: rdn over 2f out: c wdst st: no imp ent fnl f: hands and heels after* **2/1**[1]

-061 **7** nk **Gunner Moyne**[22] 1544 5-9-4 **60**....................(v) HectorCrouch(3) 12 56
(Gary Moore) *trckd ldr: rdn over 2f out and pressed ldr on outer: kpt on tl wknd ent fnl f* **8/1**

3106 **8** 2½ **Henry Grace (IRE)**[37] 1284 6-8-13 **55**....................(b) HollieDoyle(3) 5 46
(Jimmy Fox) *in rr on inner: rdn over 3f out: kpt on one pce fr over 1f out* **7/1**[3]

0604 **9** hd **Firestorm (GER)**[15] 1695 6-9-3 **56**....................................(e) AdamKirby 6 47
(Michael Attwater) *in rr on outer: rdn on outer and plenty to do over 2f out: mde up grnd being shuffled along fr over 1f out* **10/1**

2600 **10** 3½ **Bassino (USA)**[30] 1406 4-8-9 **53**....................(p[1]) RachealKneller(5) 14 37
(James Bennett) *missed break and wnt rt s: mde up grnd on outer and cl up by 1/2-way: rdn over 2f out: sn wknd* **25/1**

546 **11** 1½ **Marauder**[61] 894 5-9-6 **59**.................................... FergusSweeney 9 40
(Henry Candy) *s.s: in rr: rdn along fr over 3f out: sn hld* **16/1**

/56- **12** 32 **Mette**[243] 5822 4-8-13 **52**.................................... SteveDrowne 10
(Mark Usher) *t.k.h early and racd wdst in mid-div: losing grnd wl over 3f out: sn hld and eased st: t.o* **66/1**

2m 3.97s (-2.63) **Going Correction** -0.125s/f (Stan) 12 Ran SP% **121.5**
Speed ratings (Par 101): **105,103,103,101,101 99,99,97,97,94 93,67**
CSF £98.40 CT £959.02 TOTE £6.40: £1.40, £3.50, £4.30; EX 93.50 Trifecta £608.50.
**Owner** Miss Linsey Knocker **Bred** E I Mack **Trained** Newmarket, Suffolk

**FOCUS**
A weak handicap, run at a fair enough pace. The runner-up sets the level.
T/Plt: £65.50 to a £1 stake. Pool: £56,728.29 - 631.28 winning units. T/Qpdt: £13.70 to a £1 stake. Pool: £7,151.20 - 385.74 winning units. **Cathal Gahan**

2096 - 2103a (Foreign Racing) - See Raceform Interactive

# [1872]BEVERLEY (R-H)
Thursday, April 27

**OFFICIAL GOING: Good to firm (good in places; 7.8)**
Wind: Fresh, against Weather: Heavy grey cloud and showers

## 2104 WESTWOOD H'CAP 5f
**1:40** (1:41) (Class 5) (0-75,76) 3-Y-O+ **£3,780** (£1,131; £565; £283; £141) **Stalls** Low

Form RPR
4-35 **1** **Lydia's Place**[12] 1805 4-9-9 **75**.................................... CliffordLee(5) 7 83
(Richard Guest) *trckd ldr: effrt over 1f out: sn rdn to chal: styd on to ld ins fnl f: drvn out* **13/2**[3]

606 **2** ½ **Bosham**[42] 1222 7-9-9 **73**....................................(bt) NathanEvans(3) 12 79
(Michael Easterby) *rrd s: sn led and swtchd rt to inner rail: pushed along over 1f out: sn jnd and rdn: hdd ins fnl f. kpt on* **8/1**

556- **3** nk **Lawless Louis**[208] 6954 3-8-12 **76**.................................... PatrickVaughan(7) 4 77
(David O'Meara) *trckd ldrs: hdwy 2f out: rdn over 1f out: kpt on fnl f* **8/1**

0-62 **4** hd **Lucky Beggar (IRE)**[10] 1833 7-10-0 **75**.................................... DavidAllan 2 79
(David C Griffiths) *trckd ldrs on inner: effrt and n.m.r over 1f out: swtchd rt and rdn to chse ldng pair ins fnl f: kpt on* **11/4**[1]

6412 **5** ½ **Ticks The Boxes (IRE)**[21] 1592 5-9-12 **73**....................(p) TomEaves 1 75
(John Wainwright) *midfield: hdwy on inner over 1f out: sn rdn and kpt on: nrst fin* **25/1**

1230 **6** hd **Poppy In The Wind**[27] 1475 5-9-10 **76**....................(v) JoshDoyle(5) 6 78
(Alan Brown) *in tch: rdn and hdwy wl over 1f out: drvn and kpt on same pce fnl f* **14/1**

-660 **7** 1¼ **Tarboosh**[10] 1836 4-10-0 **75**....................................(t[1]) PaulMulrennan 3 72
(Paul Midgley) *t.k.h: trckd ldrs: hdwy wl over 1f out: rdn ent fnl f: sn wknd* **16/1**

-303 **8** nk **Compton Park**[5] 1971 10-9-3 **69**.................................... LewisEdmunds(5) 5 65
(Les Eyre) *a towards rr* **9/2**[2]

4212 **9** ¾ **Windforpower (IRE)**[15] 1721 7-9-2 **63**....................................(p) BenCurtis 8 56
(Tracy Waggott) *chsd ldrs on outer: rdn along wl over 1f out: sn drvn and grad wknd* **14/1**

31/- **10** *nk* **Thatcherite (IRE)**[572] 6936 9-9-7 **68**..............................(t) BarryMcHugh 9 60
(Tony Coyle) *a towards rr* **50/1**

031- **11** *4 1/2* **Perfect Symphony (IRE)**[193] 7381 3-9-4 **75**..................(p) KevinStott 13 47
(Kevin Ryan) *a towards rr* **7/1**

305- **12** *7* **Space Artist (IRE)**[208] 6958 7-9-2 **63**.......................... AndrewMullen 10 14
(Nigel Tinkler) *dwlt: a rr* **50/1**

1m 2.11s (-1.39) **Going Correction** -0.20s/f (Firm) **12** Ran SP% **119.9**
**WFA** 3 from 4yo+ 10lb
Speed ratings (Par 103): **103,102,101,101,100 100,98,97,96,96 88,77**
CSF £57.69 CT £432.46 TOTE £7.70: £2.70, £2.90, £2.70; EX 74.50 Trifecta £1075.90.
**Owner** Alfa Site Services Ltd & Partner **Bred** Ashbrittle Stud & Brendan Boyle **Trained** Ingmanthorpe, W Yorks

**FOCUS**
Stalls: inside (all races). This looked competitive but those coming from off the pace were at a definite disadvantage. The time backed up the going description. The winner is rated up slightly on his 2016 peak.

## 2105 IN CELEBRATION OF JILL WILLOWS WOTALASS FILLIES' NOVICE AUCTION STKS (PLUS 10 RACE) 5f

**2:10** (2:14) (Class 5) 2-Y-O **£2,835** (£848; £424; £212; £105) **Stalls** Low

Form RPR

2 **1** **Emilia James**[8] 1872 2-9-0 0.............................................. JoeFanning 5 76
(Mark Johnston) *mde all: rdn and qcknd clr over 1f out: readily* **4/9**[1]

**2** *4* **Miss Bar Beach (IRE)** 2-8-9 0.................................... RowanScott(5) 9 62+
(Keith Dalgleish) *towards rr: hdwy wl over 1f out: sn rdn and styd on strly fnl f* **50/1**

**3** *3/4* **Royal Crown (IRE)** 2-9-0 0.................................... DanielTudhope 8 59
(David O'Meara) *cl up: rdn along 2f out: kpt on same pce* **8/1**[3]

**4** *3 1/4* **Shazzab (IRE)** 2-9-0 0.................................................. TonyHamilton 7 47
(Richard Fahey) *rr: hdwy wl over 1f out: rdn and kpt on fnl f* **6/1**[2]

0 **5** *1* **Hypnotic Dancer (IRE)**[19] 1627 2-9-0 0.......................... PhillipMakin 6 44
(Keith Dalgleish) *trckd ldrs: pushed along over 2f out: sn rdn and wknd over 1f out* **20/1**

**6** *hd* **Plansina** 2-9-0 0........................................................... DuranFentiman 2 43
(Tim Easterby) *in tch: hdwy to chse ldrs 2f out: sn rdn and wknd* **50/1**

0 **7** *2* **Lady Lintera (IRE)**[17] 1673 2-9-0 0.................................... BenCurtis 1 36
(Ann Duffield) *chsd ldng pair: rdn along 2f out: sn wknd* **20/1**

**8** *1* **Monkey Magic** 2-9-0 0.......................................................... TomEaves 10 32
(Nigel Tinkler) *chsd ldrs on outer: rdn along 2f out: sn wknd* **40/1**

**9** *7* **Suanas (IRE)** 2-9-0 0........................................................ JackGarritty 4 7
(Richard Fahey) *a towards rr* **12/1**

**10** *15* **Foxy's Spirit** 2-9-0 0............................................................ DavidAllan 3
(Tim Easterby) *unruly stalls: s.i.s: a bhd* **20/1**

1m 3.41s (-0.09) **Going Correction** -0.20s/f (Firm) **10** Ran SP% **123.0**
Speed ratings (Par 89): **92,85,84,79,77 77,74,72,61,37**
CSF £54.09 TOTE £1.40: £1.10, £8.30, £2.30; EX 32.70 Trifecta £144.50.
**Owner** James Property Ltd **Bred** Red House Stud & Ketton Ashwell Ltd **Trained** Middleham Moor, N Yorks

**FOCUS**
This was one-way traffic as the market predicted. The winner did it in good style but there was probably little depth to this.

## 2106 2017 BERNARD EVANS MEMORIAL H'CAP 7f 96y

**2:45** (2:45) (Class 3) (0-90,88) 3-Y-O

**£7,158** (£2,143; £1,071; £535; £267; £134) **Stalls** Low

Form RPR

322- **1** **Starlight Romance (IRE)**[194] 7356 3-8-5 **75**............. SammyJoBell(3) 6 82
(Richard Fahey) *trckd ldrs: hdwy on inner: 2f out: nt clr run over 1f out: swtchd lft and rdn to chal ent fnl f: led last 75 yds: kpt on wl* **6/1**[3]

553- **2** *1 1/2* **Aardwolf (USA)**[188] 7493 3-9-7 **88**.................................... PJMcDonald 2 91
(Mark Johnston) *chsd ldr: led over 5f out: sn clr: pushed along 2f out: jnd and rdn over 1f out: drvn ent fnl f: hdd and no ex last 75 yds* **5/2**[1]

16-5 **3** *1* **Arc Royal**[16] 1702 3-9-3 **84**........................................ RichardKingscote 1 85
(Tom Dascombe) *led 11/2f: chsd ldr: hdwy 2f out: rdn to chal over 1f out: ev ch tl drvn and edgd lft ent fnl f: kpt on same pce* **5/2**[1]

451- **4** *1 1/4* **Kodiac Khan (IRE)**[134] 8360 3-8-13 **80**.............................. JoeFanning 4 77
(Mark Johnston) *hld up in tch: hdwy on wd outside over 2f out: rdn to chse ldrs over 1f out: sn drvn and no imp* **3/1**[2]

033- **5** *1 3/4* **Fayez (IRE)**[254] 5519 3-9-2 **83**........................................ PhillipMakin 3 76
(David O'Meara) *awkward s: hld up in rr: effrt and sme hdwy 2f out: rdn over 1f out: sn btn* **9/1**

02-0 **6** *3 3/4* **Monks Stand (USA)**[16] 1702 3-9-3 **84**................................(p) DavidAllan 7 68
(Tim Easterby) *chsd ldng pair: hdwy over 2f out: rdn along wl over 1f out: drvn and wknd appr fnl f* **16/1**

1m 31.37s (-2.43) **Going Correction** -0.20s/f (Firm) **6** Ran SP% **112.3**
Speed ratings (Par 102): **105,103,102,100,98 94**
CSF £21.36 TOTE £5.60: £2.40, £2.30; EX 24.20 Trifecta £45.10.
**Owner** Mrs H Steel **Bred** J F Tuthill **Trained** Musley Bank, N Yorks

**FOCUS**
This fair 3yo handicap was run at a sound pace. The winner improved on her consistent 2yo level.

## 2107 DAVID MCGOWAN AND JOHN BINKS MEMORIAL H'CAP 7f 96y

**3:15** (3:16) (Class 5) (0-70,71) 3-Y-O **£3,780** (£1,131; £565; £283; £141) **Stalls** Low

Form RPR

4433 **1** **Atteq**[41] 1244 3-9-4 **70**...............................................(t[1]) AdamMcNamara(3) 1 84
(Richard Fahey) *trckd ldng pair: hdwy over 2f out: cl up over 1f out: rdn to ld appr fnl f: sn clr: readily* **4/1**[2]

6 **2** *7* **Dapper Man (IRE)**[27] 1470 3-9-2 **65**................................ PJMcDonald 2 62
(Roger Fell) *chsd ldr: hdwy over 2f out and sn cl up: rdn to chal over 1f out: ev ch tl drvn ent fnl f and kpt on same pce* **18/1**

050- **3** *hd* **He's A Toff (IRE)**[218] 6681 3-8-8 **57**................................ JasonHart 5 53
(Tim Easterby) *hld up in rr: hdwy on inner 2f out: rdn and n.m.r jst over 1f out: drvn and styd on wl towards fin* **14/1**

1220 **4** *1/2* **Seaview**[14] 1760 3-9-2 **68**...............................................(p[1]) AaronJones(3) 6 63
(David Brown) *led and sn clr: pushed along over 2f out: rdn over 1f out: drvn ent fnl f: kpt on same pce* **14/1**

04-5 **5** *hd* **Our Charlie Brown**[8] 1878 3-9-6 **69**.................................... DavidAllan 9 63
(Tim Easterby) *hld up in tch: hdwy over 2f out: rdn to chse ldrs over 1f out: sn drvn and kpt on same pce* **9/2**[3]

404- **6** *1 3/4* **Fleetfoot Jack (IRE)**[177] 7741 3-9-4 **67**........................ DanielTudhope 4 57
(David O'Meara) *hld up in rr: sme hdwy over 2f out: rdn wl over 1f out: sn drvn and btn* **10/3**[1]

060- **7** *nk* **Pindaric**[177] 7740 3-9-1 **64**.............................................. CamHardie 8 53
(Alan Lockwood) *rr: hdwy over 2f out: sn rdn and kpt on fnl f: nrst fin* **33/1**

604- **8** *2 3/4* **Starlite Sienna (IRE)**[210] 6904 3-9-5 **68**......................... TonyHamilton 3 50
(Richard Fahey) *a towards rr* **8/1**

60-4 **9** *2 3/4* **Geophony (IRE)**[17] 1678 3-9-8 **71**.......................................... JoeFanning 7 46
(Mark Johnston) *chsd ldrs: hdwy on outer over 2f out: rdn wl over 1f out: sn drvn and wknd* **9/2**[3]

1m 30.72s (-3.08) **Going Correction** -0.20s/f (Firm) **9** Ran SP% **112.1**
Speed ratings (Par 98): **109,101,100,100,99 97,97,94,91**
CSF £68.94 CT £909.01 TOTE £4.10: £1.80, £5.10, £4.60; EX 71.80 Trifecta £708.20.
**Owner** Al Shaqab Racing **Bred** Fittocks Stud **Trained** Musley Bank, N Yorks

**FOCUS**
A modest 3yo handicap. There was no hanging around and the principals were always prominent. A surprise winner but no fluke, with a decent time.

## 2108 RAPID LAD H'CAP 1m 1f 207y

**3:50** (3:50) (Class 5) (0-70,70) 4-Y-O+ **£3,780** (£1,131; £565; £283; £141) **Stalls** Low

Form RPR

26-2 **1** **Bit Of A Quirke**[16] 1707 4-8-11 **60**................................ DougieCostello 4 68
(Mark Walford) *trckd ldr: hdwy 3f out and sn cl up: rdn to ld jst over 1f out: sn jnd and drvn ins fnl f: kpt on gamely towards fin* **6/1**[3]

14-4 **2** *nk* **Strummer (IRE)**[36] 1312 4-8-13 **62**....................................(p) KevinStott 7 69
(Kevin Ryan) *hld up towards rr: hdwy 3f out: swtchd lft and effrt 2f out: sn cl up: chal ent fnl f: sn rdn to dispute ld and ev ch tl drvn and kpt on same pce towards fin* **5/1**[2]

23-0 **3** *1 1/4* **Bahamian C**[26] 1498 6-8-10 **62**....................................(t) SammyJoBell(3) 3 66
(Richard Fahey) *trckd ldrs: hdwy over 2f out: rdn over 1f out: drvn to chse ldng pair ins fnl f: kpt on* **8/1**

0-26 **4** *1* **Bling King**[15] 1735 8-8-12 **61**............................................(p) SamJames 5 63
(Geoffrey Harker) *hld up towards rr: hdwy on wd outside over 2f out: rdn over 1f out: styd on fnl f* **8/1**

30-0 **5** *3/4* **Arithmetic (IRE)**[16] 1706 4-9-2 **65**.................................. JackGarritty 9 66
(Ruth Carr) *trckd ldng pair: hdwy and cl up over 2f out: rdn wl over 1f out: drvn appr fnl f: kpt on same pce* **12/1**

5303 **6** *3 1/4* **Ravenhoe (IRE)**[10] 1839 4-9-7 **70**.................................... JoeFanning 1 64
(Mark Johnston) *led: pushed along 3f out and sn jnd: rdn 2f out: drvn over 1f out: hdd appr fnl f: wknd* **9/2**[1]

350- **7** *1 1/4* **Correggio**[180] 7043 7-9-3 **66**........................................ PaulMulrennan 6 58
(Micky Hammond) *hld up: hdwy and in tch 3f out: rdn along 2f out: sn one pce* **14/1**

0230 **8** *4 1/2* **All You (IRE)**[16] 1700 5-9-6 **69**....................................(v) PhillipMakin 8 52
(David O'Meara) *.hld up: a rr* **8/1**

0-00 **9** *4 1/2* **Clayton Hall (IRE)**[16] 1707 4-8-11 **60**..............................(v[1]) TomEaves 10 34
(John Wainwright) *hld up: a rr* **50/1**

214- **10** *1* **Lopito De Vega (IRE)**[270] 4919 5-9-3 **66**............................ DavidAllan 2 38
(David C Griffiths) *t.k.h: trckd ldng pair on inner: hdwy over 3f out: rdn nalong over 2f out: sn wknd* **9/2**[1]

2m 4.94s (-2.06) **Going Correction** -0.20s/f (Firm) **10** Ran SP% **117.0**
Speed ratings (Par 103): **100,99,98,97,97 94,93,90,86,85**
CSF £36.22 CT £243.80 TOTE £5.40: £2.10, £1.60, £2.60; EX 28.20 Trifecta £158.30.
**Owner** A Quirke **Bred** Dr A Gillespie **Trained** Sherriff Hutton, N Yorks

**FOCUS**
This ordinary handicap was run at a sound pace but the form is particularly convincing.

## 2109 ALAN MCGUINNESS AND ROBIN LUNNESS MEMORIAL H'CAP 1m 4f 23y

**4:25** (4:27) (Class 4) (0-85,86) 4-Y-O+ **£5,040** (£1,508; £754; £377; £188) **Stalls** Low

Form RPR

-041 **1** **Be Perfect (USA)**[15] 1719 8-9-7 **82**................................(p) JackGarritty 1 88
(Ruth Carr) *trckd clr ldr: tk clsr order 1/2-way: effrt over 3f out: led on bit wl over 1f out: sn pushed clr: rdn ins fnl f: kpt on strly* **8/1**

1-2 **2** *1 3/4* **Gaelic Tiger**[13] 1781 4-9-10 **86**.................................. DanielTudhope 6 89
(David O'Meara) *hld up: hdwy 3f out and sn pushed along: rdn wl over 1f out: drvn and edgd rt ent fnl f: kpt on towards fin* **6/4**[1]

220- **3** *hd* **Peterhouse (USA)**[188] 7498 5-9-3 **78**.................................... BenCurtis 2 80
(Jason Ward) *hld up in rr: hdwy wl over 2f out: rdn and n.m.r over 1f out: drvn and kpt on same pce fnl f* **6/1**[3]

00-0 **4** *7* **Mysterial**[25] 1517 7-8-8 **74**............................................ PhilDennis(5) 5 65
(Declan Carroll) *rdn along s: sn led and clr: stdd 1/2-way: pushed along and qcknd over 4f out: jnd 3f out and sn rdn: hdd 2f out and sn wknd* **16/1**

112- **5** *3* **Pacharana**[217] 6719 4-9-5 **81**.......................................... JamieSpencer 4 71
(Luca Cumani) *unsettled in stalls: dwlt: hld up in rr: pushed along over 3f out: rdn wl over 2f out: sn wknd and eased* **7/2**[2]

2m 36.37s (-3.43) **Going Correction** -0.20s/f (Firm) **5** Ran SP% **93.5**
Speed ratings (Par 105): **103,101,101,97,95**
CSF £14.64 TOTE £7.60: £2.30, £1.10; EX 13.30 Trifecta £39.60.
**Owner** The Beer Stalkers & Ruth Carr **Bred** Joseph Allen **Trained** Huby, N Yorks
■ Masterpaver was withdrawn. Price at time of withdrawal 7-2. Rule 4 applies to all bets - deduction 20p in the pound.

**FOCUS**
This fair little handicap proved a messy affair and it rather fell apart. The form is rated around the third.

## 2110 BEVERLEY FOLK FESTIVAL HERE IN JUNE MAIDEN AUCTION STKS 1m 100y

**5:00** (5:01) (Class 5) 3-Y-O **£3,780** (£1,131; £565; £283; £141) **Stalls** Low

Form RPR

2 **1** **Rinaria (IRE)**[35] 1333 3-8-11 0................................ JordanVaughan(3) 4 65
(K R Burke) *trckd ldr: hdwy 2f out: rdn to chal jst over 1f out: drvn to dispute ld whn green and edgd lft ins fnl f: sn drvn and edgd rt: kpt on to ld last 100 yds* **5/2**[2]

54-5 **2** *1/2* **Glorvina (IRE)**[10] 1829 3-9-0 0...................................... DanielTudhope 5 64
(David O'Meara) *led: pushed along over 2f out: jnd and rdn jst over 1f out: drvn ins fnl f: edgd lft and hdd last 100 yds: kpt on* **7/2**[3]

0- **3** *1* **Alnasl (IRE)**[244] 5846 3-9-0 0..............................................(h[1]) BenCurtis 3 64+
(Archie Watson) *trckd ldng pair: hdwy over 1f out: effrt whn nt clr run and hmpd ins fnl f: kpt on* **13/8**[1]

0-6 **4** *3 1/4* **Legato (IRE)**[15] 1730 3-9-5 0.................................... RichardKingscote 2 59+
(Tom Dascombe) *dwlt: sn trcking ldrs: rdn along 2f out: sn one pce* **13/2**

0- **5** *3 3/4* **Thomas Crown (IRE)**[230] 6288 3-9-5 0............................ TonyHamilton 1 51
(Roger Fell) *a towards rr* **16/1**

**6** *3 3/4* **High Shaw** 3-9-5 0........................................................... ShaneGray 7 42
(Ann Duffield) *a rr* **12/1**

1m 48.45s (0.85) **Going Correction** -0.20s/f (Firm) **6** Ran SP% **115.8**
Speed ratings (Par 98): **87,86,85,82,78 74**
CSF £12.18 TOTE £2.80: £1.50, £2.10; EX 10.50 Trifecta £19.00.
**Owner** The Mount Racing Club & A Kavanagh **Bred** Rathdown Stud Ltd **Trained** Middleham Moor, N Yorks

**FOCUS**
An ordinary 3yo maiden run at a modest pace. The principals are rated close to their early marks.
T/Plt: £76.00 to a £1 stake. Pool: £63,163.80. 606.57 winning units. T/Qpdt: £14.10 to a £1 stake. Pool: £4,426.14. 230.90 winning units. **Joe Rowntree**

# [1754] CHELMSFORD (A.W) (L-H)

Thursday, April 27

**OFFICIAL GOING: Polytrack: standard**
Wind: light rain Weather: light, across

## 2111 FIRE TECHNOLOGY INTERNATIONAL LTD H'CAP 1m 6f (P)
**5:25** (5:26) (Class 5) (0-70,70) 4-Y-O+ **£5,175** (£1,540; £769; £384) **Stalls** Low

Form RPR

453- **1** **Snowy Dawn**[136] 8339 7-9-6 **67**.................................... AdamBeschizza 1 75
(Steph Hollinshead) *hld up in midfield: cl to trck ldrs and travelling strly over 2f out: nt clr run wl over 1f out: swtchd lft and effrt over 1f out: rdn to ld ins fnl f: styd on: rdn out* **6/1**[3]

2404 **2** ¾ **Bamako Du Chatelet (FR)**[8] 1891 6-9-9 **70**.............(p) StevieDonohoe 3 77
(Ian Williams) *hld up in tch in last quartet: clsd over 3f out: effrt in centre over 1f out: hdwy u.p to chse wnr 100yds out: kpt on wl but nvr getting to wnr* **5/1**[2]

262/ **3** 1 ¾ **Kerrymerry (IRE)**[621] 5398 5-9-7 **68**.................................... LukeMorris 4 73
(Dr Richard Newland) *t.k.h: chsd ldrs: rdn to ld over 1f out: drvn and hdd ins fnl f: no ex and one pced after* **7/2**[1]

2214 **4** 3 ½ **Surround Sound**[15] 1716 7-8-13 **63**...................(t) RachelRichardson(3) 8 63
(Tim Easterby) *s.i.s: plld hrd: hld up in rr: swtchd lft and effrt jst over 1f out: no ch w ldrs but kpt on to snatch 4th on post* **10/1**

5-64 **5** nse **Aumerle**[16] 1697 5-9-5 **66**.................................... JimCrowley 2 66
(Shaun Lycett) *in tch in midfield: clsd to trck ldrs over 2f out: rdn over 1f out: unable qck and wknd ins fnl f* **6/1**[3]

025- **6** 2 ½ **Goldslinger (FR)**[59] 8565 5-9-9 **70**.................................... RobertWinston 10 66
(Dean Ivory) *hdwy to ld after 2f: clr 7f out tl rdn and hdd over 2f out: lost pl over 1f out: wknd ins fnl f* **14/1**

551- **7** 5 **McCools Gold**[197] 7270 4-9-3 **66**.................................... FergusSweeney 9 55
(Alan King) *t.k.h: chsd ldrs tl wnt 2nd after 3f: rdn to ld over 2f out: hdd over 1f out: sn btn and wknd fnl f* **5/1**[2]

06/4 **8** 2 ¼ **Chivers (IRE)**[9] 1870 6-9-2 **70**.................................(t) RossaRyan(7) 5 56
(Daniel Steele) *dwlt: hld up in last pair: rdn 6f out: wknd over 1f out* **50/1**

2652 **9** 2 ¾ **Noguchi (IRE)**[14] 1754 12-9-3 **64**.............................(b) SilvestreDeSousa 7 46
(Chris Dwyer) *hld up in last quartet: effrt on outer over 2f out: no prog: wl btn and eased ins fnl f* **8/1**

22-0 **10** nk **Threediamondrings**[107] 163 4-9-2 **65**.................................(t) FranBerry 6 47
(Brendan Powell) *led for 2f: styd chsng ldrs: rdn 3f out: sn struggling: bhd fnl f* **12/1**

2m 57.49s (-5.71) **Going Correction** -0.375s/f (Stan)
**WFA** 4 from 5yo+ 1lb **10** Ran SP% **120.6**
Speed ratings (Par 103): **101,100,99,97,97 96,93,91,90,90**
CSF £37.47 CT £123.82 TOTE £9.60: £3.30, £1.70, £2.10; EX 43.70 Trifecta £229.90.
**Owner** Mrs Christine Stevenson **Bred** Southcourt Stud **Trained** Upper Longdon, Staffs

**FOCUS**
A modest handicap in which Goldslinger took them along at a decent gallop. The winner has been rated to last year's best.

## 2112 KNIGHT GROUP MAIDEN STKS 6f (P)
**5:55** (5:56) (Class 4) 3-Y-O+ **£8,086** (£2,406; £1,202; £601) **Stalls** Centre

Form RPR

2 **1** **Historic Event (IRE)**[19] 1626 3-8-12 0.................................... PatCosgrave 6 75+
(Saeed bin Suroor) *t.k.h: pressed ldr tl shkn up to ld over 1f out: rn green and drifting rt ins fnl f: styd on: rdn out* **11/10**[1]

**2** ½ **Fair Cop** 3-8-12 0.................................... DavidProbert 4 73+
(Andrew Balding) *t.k.h: hld up in tch: effrt over 1f out: wnt 2nd and pressing wnr u.p ins fnl f: kpt on but hld whn hmpd last strides* **5/2**[2]

552- **3** 2 **Five Star Frank**[129] 8453 3-9-3 73.................................... RobertWinston 3 72
(Eve Johnson Houghton) *plld hrd: trckd ldrs: effrt over 1f out: kpt on same pce u.p ins fnl f* **9/2**[3]

22 **4** ½ **Secret Strategy (IRE)**[12] 1785 3-9-3 0.......................... AdamBeschizza 1 70
(Julia Feilden) *led and set stdy gallop: rdn and qcknd but hung rt over 1f out: sn hdd and outpcd ins fnl f* **6/1**

4-6 **5** 3 ¼ **Double Spin**[38] 1286 3-8-12 0.................................... JimCrowley 7 55
(Robert Cowell) *dwlt: sn rcvrd to chsd ldrs on outer and t.k.h: rdn over 1f out: sn out pced and wknd ins fnl f* **25/1**

00- **6** ½ **Angelical Eve (IRE)**[185] 7574 3-8-12 0.................................... LiamKeniry 5 53
(George Baker) *t.k.h: hld up in tch in last pair: shkn up and outpcd over 1f out: rdn and styd on same pce ins fnl f*

0 **7** ½ **Socks And Shares (IRE)**[8] 1889 4-10-0 0.......................... KierenFox 2 59
(Derek Shaw) *dwlt: t.k.h: hld up in tch in last pair: effrt over 1f out: sn outpcd* **200/1**

1m 12.02s (-1.68) **Going Correction** -0.375s/f (Stan)
**WFA** 3 from 4yo 11lb **7** Ran SP% **114.0**
Speed ratings (Par 105): **96,95,92,92,87 87,86**
CSF £4.06 TOTE £1.80: £1.10, £2.30; EX 5.00 Trifecta £11.90.
**Owner** Godolphin **Bred** Forenaghts Stud **Trained** Newmarket, Suffolk

**FOCUS**
This was steadily run. The fourth has been rated close to form.

## 2113 NATTA BUILDING COMPANY H'CAP 6f (P)
**6:30** (6:30) (Class 3) (0-95,95) 4-Y-O+ **£9,703** (£2,887; £1,443; £721) **Stalls** Centre

Form RPR

404- **1** **Udontdodou**[170] 7858 4-8-10 **84**.................................... ConnorBeasley 1 95
(Richard Guest) *taken down early: hld up in midfield: effrt over 1f out: hdwy u.p 1f out: edgd lft and led 75yds out: r.o* **15/8**[1]

1250 **2** 1 **Zac Brown (IRE)**[13] 1768 6-9-0 **95**.............................(t) JoshuaBryan(7) 7 103
(Charlie Wallis) *led and set str gallop: rdn over 1f out: hdd 75yds out: no ex and styd on same pce after* **20/1**

0-13 **3** 1 ¾ **Alkhor**[7] 1910 4-8-13 **87**.................................... FrankieDettori 8 91
(Richard Hannon) *chsd ldr: rdn over 1f out: stl pressing ldrs in cl 3rd but looked hld whn squeezed for room and hmpd wl ins fnl f* **2/1**[2]

4405 **4** 1 ½ **Golden Amber (IRE)**[25] 1515 6-9-3 **91**.................................... RobertWinston 6 89
(Dean Ivory) *dwlt: hld up in last pair: effrt over 1f out: rdn 1f out: kpt on to go 4th towards fin: no threat to ldrs* **5/1**[3]

56-0 **5** 1 **Flying Pursuit**[25] 1515 4-9-1 **89**.................................(b) AndrewMullen 2 83
(Tim Easterby) *bustled along leaving stalls: chsd ldrs: unable qck u.p over 1f out: wknd ins fnl f* **8/1**

0436 **6** 1 ¾ **Plucky Dip**[43] 1202 6-8-7 **81** oh2.................................... DannyBrock 4 70
(John Ryan) *in tch towards rr: rdn over 2f out: styd on same pce and no imp fr over 1f out* **12/1**

000- **7** 3 ½ **Cincuenta Pasos (IRE)**[173] 7825 6-8-13 **87**...................(t) OisinMurphy 3 65
(Joseph Tuite) *hld up in tch: pushed along 2f out: rdn and little rspnse over 1f out: wknd fnl f* **20/1**

1m 10.17s (-3.53) **Going Correction** -0.375s/f (Stan) **7** Ran SP% **113.1**
Speed ratings (Par 107): **108,106,104,102,101 98,94**
CSF £37.09 CT £80.77 TOTE £2.70: £1.80, £2.70; EX 30.70 Trifecta £89.40.
**Owner** Mrs Alison Guest **Bred** Times Of Wigan Ltd **Trained** Ingmanthorpe, W Yorks

**FOCUS**
Not a bad sprint handicap, and it was run at a pretty good gallop. The runner-up has been rated to form.

## 2114 BUXTED CONSTRUCTION LTD CONDITIONS STKS 6f (P)
**7:05** (7:05) (Class 2) 4-Y-O+
**£18,675** (£5,592; £2,796; £1,398; £699; £351) **Stalls** Centre

Form RPR

363- **1** **Raucous**[208] 6941 4-9-2 105.................................(tp) RyanMoore 2 98
(William Haggas) *t.k.h: trckd ldrs on inner: effrt over 1f out: hdwy to ld jst ins fnl f: drvn to assert 100yds out: r.o wl: rdn out* **5/4**[1]

-605 **2** 1 ¾ **Kadrizzi (FR)**[13] 1769 4-9-6 98.................................(p[1]) RobertWinston 1 96
(Dean Ivory) *sn dropped to last pair and niggled along: swtchd rt and hdwy u.p ins fnl f: styd on wl to snatch 2nd last strides: no threat to wnr* **9/1**

5110 **3** hd **Fujin**[11] 1820 6-9-2 85.................................(v) CharlieBennett 4 91
(Shaun Harris) *w ldr tl led 4f out: rdn over 1f out: drvn and hdd jst ins fnl f: kpt on same pce after: lost 2nd last strides* **50/1**

35-0 **4** hd **Absolutely So (IRE)**[26] 1491 7-9-2 105.......................... OisinMurphy 5 91
(Andrew Balding) *dwlt: hld up in last pair: effrt in centre over 1f out: styd on u.p ins fnl f: no threat to wnr* **5/1**[3]

0021 **5** 2 ½ **Solar Flair**[12] 1794 5-9-6 104.................................... JimCrowley 6 87
(William Knight) *led for 2f: chsd ldr tl unable qck u.p over 1f out: wknd ins fnl f* **11/4**[2]

-000 **6** 7 **Magnus Maximus**[54] 1044 6-9-6 105.................................... LukeMorris 3 72
(Robyn Brisland) *dwlt: sn rcvrd and trckd ldrs: rdn over 1f out: drvn and btn 1f out: bhd and eased ins fnl f* **7/1**

1m 10.0s (-3.70) **Going Correction** -0.375s/f (Stan) course record **6** Ran SP% **112.2**
Speed ratings (Par 109): **109,106,106,106,102 93**
CSF £13.55 TOTE £1.80: £1.10, £4.70; EX 13.10 Trifecta £127.40.
**Owner** Highclere Thoroughbred Racing(Melbourne) **Bred** Saleh Al Homaizi & Imad Al Sagar **Trained** Newmarket, Suffolk

**FOCUS**
With a few not running to their best this may not have been as strong a race as it looked on paper, but the course record was still lowered by 0.16sec. The third is the key to the form, with the runner-up rated close to his recent form.

## 2115 TAMDOWN H'CAP 7f (P)
**7:40** (7:42) (Class 3) (0-95,96) 3-Y-O+ **£16,172** (£4,812; £2,405; £1,202) **Stalls** Low

Form RPR

160- **1** **That Is The Spirit**[161] 7984 6-10-0 **95**.................................... RyanMoore 2 104
(David O'Meara) *mde all: rdn and qcknd over 1f out: drvn ins fnl f: kpt on: drvn out and all out nr fin* **8/1**

20-0 **2** nk **Rusumaat (IRE)**[12] 1801 3-8-11 **91**.................................... JimCrowley 7 94
(Mark Johnston) *chsd ldrs: rdn over 1f out: styd on to chse wnr wl ins fnl f: gng on strly and clsng qckly towards fin* **5/1**[2]

41-0 **3** 1 ¼ **Ower Fly**[25] 1515 4-9-5 **89**.................................... HollieDoyle(3) 5 94
(Richard Hannon) *chsd ldrs: wnt 2nd 2f out: rdn over 1f out: kpt on same pce u.p and lost 2nd wl ins fnl f* **6/1**[3]

62-6 **4** ½ **Viscount Barfield**[19] 1622 4-9-11 **92**.................................(h) OisinMurphy 8 96+
(Andrew Balding) *stdd s: t.k.h: hld up in tch towards rr: effrt over 1f out: kpt on u.p ins fnl f: nvr quite enough pce to rch ldrs* **9/2**[1]

0122 **5** ¾ **Outer Space**[37] 1295 6-9-12 **93**.................................... TimmyMurphy 3 95
(Jamie Osborne) *trckd ldng quartet on inner: nt clr run and hmpd over 1f out: swtchd rt ent fnl f: kpt on same pce ins fnl f* **8/1**

00S- **5** dht **Ghalib (IRE)**[187] 7530 5-9-9 **90**.................................... JamesDoyle 6 92
(Amy Murphy) *in tch in midfield: rdn ent fnl 2f: kpt on u.p ins fnl f: nvr enough pce to threaten wnr* **10/1**

4360 **7** 1 ¼ **Pearl Spectre (USA)**[12] 1794 6-9-7 **88**.......................... JosephineGordon 1 86
(Phil McEntee) *chsd ldr tl 2f out: sn u.p: kpt on same pce and swtchd lft ins fnl f* **16/1**

26-4 **8** hd **Ripoll (IRE)**[5] 1964 4-8-9 **81**.................................(t) MitchGodwin(5) 13 79
(Sylvester Kirk) *hld up in rr: effrt in centre over 1f out: hdwy but wanting to hang lft fr 1f out: wnt lft and kpt on wl ins fnl f: nvr trbld ldrs* **12/1**

2145 **9** 2 ½ **Loyalty**[45] 1177 10-9-9 **90**.................................(v) MartinLane 4 81
(Derek Shaw) *hld up in tch in midfield: effrt and hdwy over 1f out: wl in tch whn nt clr run 1f out: nt rcvr and one pced after* **10/1**

115- **10** ½ **Breakable**[229] 6331 6-9-12 **96**.......................... RachelRichardson(3) 12 86
(Tim Easterby) *hld up in tch in midfield but stuck wd: swtchd rt and effrt over 1f out: no imp and wl hld fnl f* **25/1**

110- **11** ½ **Comedy School (USA)**[187] 7536 3-8-8 **88**.......................... FrannyNorton 11 71
(Mark Johnston) *a towards rr: rdn and struggling over 2f out: nvr trbld ldrs* **8/1**

00-0 **12** 3 **Grand Inquisitor**[19] 1622 5-9-8 **89**.................................(p) StevieDonohoe 10 69
(Ian Williams) *hld up in rr: n.d* **20/1**

000- **13** 3 ½ **Ice Lord (IRE)**[200] 7186 5-9-7 **88**.................................... TedDurcan 9 59
(Chris Wall) *wl in tch in midfield but stuck wd: rdn over 1f out: sn btn and wknd* **20/1**

1m 24.01s (-3.19) **Going Correction** -0.375s/f (Stan)
**WFA** 3 from 4yo+ 13lb **13** Ran SP% **127.6**
Speed ratings (Par 107): **103,102,101,100,99 99,98,98,95,94 94,90,86**
CSF £49.78 CT £269.65 TOTE £9.70: £3.30, £2.70, £2.70; EX 62.40 Trifecta £560.20.
**Owner** F Gillespie **Bred** Cliveden Stud Ltd **Trained** Upper Helmsley, N Yorks

**FOCUS**
This looked wide open beforehand, but the winner faced no competition in front and Ryan Moore took full advantage. The runner-up has been rated to his 2yo form.

## 2116 REDROW PROUDLY SUPPORTING THE J'S HOSPICE H'CAP 1m (P)
**8:15** (8:16) (Class 4) (0-85,87) 4-Y-O+ **£8,086** (£2,406; £1,202; £601) **Stalls** Low

Form RPR

-320 **1** **Pendo**[89] 460 6-9-0 **77**.................................... KierenFox 8 84
(John Best) *chsd ldrs: wnt 2nd 2f out: rdn and ev ch 2f out: sustained effrt u.p to ld 50yds out: styd on: gamely* **20/1**

02-2 **2** ½ **Robero**[9] 1867 5-8-10 **76**.................................... NathanEvans(3) 10 82
(Michael Easterby) *t.k.h: led: jnd and clr w wnr 2f out: drvn over 1f out: kpt on wl u.p tl hdd and no ex 50yds out* **9/2**[2]

2213 **3** *1* **Kenstone (FR)**[35] [1324] 4-8-8 **74**....(p) HollieDoyle(3) 6 78
(Adrian Wintle) *wl in tch in midfield: effrt over 1f out: chsd ldng pair 1f out: kpt on wl ins fnl f* **16/1**

1230 **4** *½* **Tee It Up Tommo (IRE)**[2] [2070] 8-8-8 **71**.... StevieDonohoe 3 74
(Daniel Steele) *stdd after s: hld up in last trio: effrt over 1f out: hdwy under 1f out: styd on wl u.p fnl 110yds: nt rch ldrs* **20/1**

630- **5** *nk* **North Creek**[202] [7108] 4-9-3 **80**.... JamesDoyle 9 82
(Chris Wall) *hld up towards rr: hdwy u.p 1f out: styd on wl ins fnl f: nt rch ldrs* **10/1**

055- **6** *1 ½* **Imperial State**[187] [7540] 4-9-4 **81**....(t) TedDurcan 11 80
(George Scott) *dwlt: hld up in midfield: shkn up 2f out: hdwy jst over 1f out: kpt on under hands and heels ins fnl f: eased towards fin* **20/1**

3440 **7** *1 ¾* **Ice Royal (IRE)**[14] [1757] 4-9-10 **87**....(p) TimmyMurphy 2 82
(Jamie Osborne) *hld up in midfield: effrt over 1f out: drvn 1f out: no imp and one pce fnl f* **10/1**

41-5 **8** *¾* **Tellovoi (IRE)**[10] [1832] 9-8-11 **74**....(h) ConnorBeasley 5 67
(Richard Guest) *rdr late removing hood and v.s.a: t.k.h: hld up in rr: effrt over 1f out: nvr trbld ldrs* **14/1**

-011 **9** *¾* **Welliesinthewater (IRE)**[42] [1224] 7-9-7 **84**....(v) MartinLane 1 75
(Derek Shaw) *stdd after s: hld up in last trio: hung rt and effrt wl over 1f out: stl plenty to do whn n.m.r 1f out: nvr trbld ldrs* **7/1**[3]

10-2 **10** *1* **Shaiyem (IRE)**[9] [1860] 4-9-9 **86**.... FrankieDettori 7 75
(Richard Hannon) *t.k.h: chsd ldr for 2f: styd chsng ldrs: rdn over 1f out: no rspnse and btn 1f out: wknd ins fnl f* **11/8**[1]

4424 **11** *1 ½* **Skidby Mill (IRE)**[7] [1897] 7-8-13 **76**.... PatCosgrave 4 61
(Laura Mongan) *t.k.h: rdn and unable qck over 1f out: wknd ins fnl f* **33/1**

1m 36.62s (-3.28) **Going Correction** -0.375s/f (Stan) **11** Ran SP% **120.7**
Speed ratings (Par 105): **101,100,99,99,98 97,95,94,93,92 91**
CSF £105.98 CT £1517.03 TOTE £22.80: £4.20, £1.80, £3.20; EX 99.90 Trifecta £3915.50.
**Owner** Brett Hopson **Bred** Miss Sue Parkinson **Trained** Oad Street, Kent

**FOCUS**
Nothing was that keen to go on and the two who eventually did went on to dominate the race. The third and fourth help set the standard.

## 2117 EAGLE ROOFING H'CAP — 1m (P)
**8:45** (8:46) (Class 4) (0-85,87) 3-Y-O **£8,086** (£2,406; £1,202; £601) **Stalls** Low

Form RPR

4-1 **1** **Arabian Hope (USA)**[26] [1503] 3-9-7 **84**....(h) JosephineGordon 3 99
(Saeed bin Suroor) *hld up in tch in 4th: wnt 3rd and swtchd rt over 1f out: str chal u.p ins fnl f: r.o wl to ld 50yds out: rdn out* **3/1**[3]

11 **2** *1* **Mystique Moon**[82] [577] 3-9-7 **84**.... WilliamBuick 6 96
(Charlie Appleby) *t.k.h: trckd ldrs: clsd and upsides and stl on bit over 1f out: rdn to ld jst ins fnl f: edgd lft u.p and hdd 50yds out: stl edging lft and one pced after* **9/4**[1]

122- **3** *4 ½* **Inner Circle (IRE)**[205] [7033] 3-9-1 **78**.... JamesDoyle 4 80
(Richard Hannon) *in tch in last pair: effrt in 4th over 1f out: no imp 1f out: wknd but wnt 3rd ins fnl f* **14/1**

3-1 **4** *1 ¼* **Itsakindamagic**[28] [1448] 3-9-10 **87**....(h) OisinMurphy 7 86+
(Andrew Balding) *t.k.h and awkward hd carriage: led: jnd and rdn over 1f out: hdd jst ins fnl f: sn wknd* **11/4**[2]

1- **5** *4 ½* **Ebbesbourne (IRE)**[210] [6897] 3-9-4 **81**.... RyanMoore 8 70
(Sir Michael Stoute) *t.k.h: dropped in bhd ldrs after s: shkn up over 1f out: sn btn and wknd ins fnl f* **7/1**

01- **6** *¾* **Native Soldier (IRE)**[153] [8089] 3-9-3 **80**.... TomQueally 1 67
(William Haggas) *awkward leaving stalls and s.i.s: sn rcvrd and in tch in rr: effrt over 1f out: sn u.p and btn: wknd fnl f* **7/1**

1m 36.54s (-3.36) **Going Correction** -0.375s/f (Stan) **6** Ran SP% **114.1**
Speed ratings (Par 100): **101,100,95,94,89 89**
CSF £10.47 CT £77.83 TOTE £4.00: £2.00, £1.80; EX 13.40 Trifecta £73.30.
**Owner** Godolphin **Bred** Hill 'N' Dale Equine Holdings Inc Et Al **Trained** Newmarket, Suffolk

**FOCUS**
An interesting handicap. All but one of the line-up had won last time out and the first two, both Godolphin horses, drew nicely clear in the closing stages. The level is a bit fluid, with the fourth too keen and the third rated a bit below his 2yo form for now.
T/Plt: £136.40 to a £1 stake. Pool: £71,259.69. 381.13 winning units. T/Qpdt: £60.00 to a £1 stake. Pool: £7,365.57. 90.73 winning units. **Steve Payne**

# [1512] DONCASTER (L-H)
Friday, April 28

**OFFICIAL GOING: Good to firm (good in places; 7.9) (watered)**
Wind: Moderate against veering across for 2.45 race and virtually nil after
Weather: Fine and dry

## 2118 188BET H'CAP — 1m 2f 43y
**1:40** (1:40) (Class 4) (0-80,81) 3-Y-O **£5,175** (£1,540; £769; £384) **Stalls** Low

Form RPR

1- **1** **Eldritch (IRE)**[196] [7318] 3-9-6 **77**.... JimmyFortune 5 85+
(John Gosden) *hld up towards rr: hdwy on outer 3f out: chsd ldrs over 1f out: rdn ins fnl f: led last 100yds: edgd lft last 50yds: kpt on* **15/8**[1]

41- **2** *1 ¾* **Glorious Forever**[207] [7012] 3-9-10 **81**.... ThomasBrown 10 85
(Ed Walker) *trckd ldr: hdwy 3f out: rdn along 2f out: sn cl up: drvn to take narrow ld ent fnl f: hdd and no ex last 100yds* **4/1**[2]

221- **3** *¾* **Whip Nae Nae (IRE)**[189] [7511] 3-9-10 **81**.... KieranO'Neill 7 84
(Richard Hannon) *hld up in rr: hdwy on inner over 2f out: rdn and nt clr run wl over 1f out: sn swtchd rt and rdn: styd on wl fnl f* **9/1**

04-4 **4** *1* **Master Archer (IRE)**[18] [1682] 3-9-1 **77**.... GeorgeWood(5) 1 78
(James Fanshawe) *trckd ldrs on inner: effrt 3f out: rdn along and nt clr run wl over 1f out: drvn and kpt on fnl f* **7/1**[3]

13- **5** *hd* **Pirate Look (IRE)**[151] [8132] 3-9-7 **78**.... TomMarquand 11 78
(Marco Botti) *led: pushed along over 2f out: rdn over 1f out: drvn and hdd ent fnl f: kpt on wl u.p* **11/1**

124- **6** *nse* **Vanity Queen**[227] [6455] 3-9-6 **77**.... LukeMorris 2 77
(Luca Cumani) *trckd ldrs: hdwy 3f out: chsd ldrs over 2f out: rdn to chal over 1f out: ev ch tl drvn and hld whn n.m.r last 50yds* **16/1**

400- **7** *4* **City Dreamer (IRE)**[207] [7016] 3-8-10 **67**.... FergusSweeney 9 65
(Alan King) *hld up: hdwy 3f out: n.m.r and swtchd rt 2f out: chsd ldrs whn hmpd over 1f out: eased after* **20/1**

3-31 **8** *9* **Nick Vedder**[28] [1470] 3-8-11 **73**.... CliffordLee(5) 3 49
(K R Burke) *hld up: a towards rr* **16/1**

331- **9** *2 ¼* **Castellated**[198] [7273] 3-9-2 **73**.... SeanLevey 8 44
(Richard Hannon) *trckd ldrs: pushed along 3f out: sn rdn and wknd* **8/1**

2m 9.64s (0.24) **Going Correction** -0.125s/f (Firm) **9** Ran SP% **113.3**
Speed ratings (Par 100): **94,92,92,91,91 91,87,80,78**
CSF £8.83 CT £51.42 TOTE £2.50: £1.20, £1.60, £2.90; EX 11.10 Trifecta £65.00.
**Owner** George Strawbridge **Bred** Macha Bloodstock & Ptn **Trained** Newmarket, Suffolk

■ Stewards' Enquiry : Kieran O'Neill Kieran O'Neill picked up a two-day careless riding ban (12-13 May) after causing interference when manoeuvring right.

**FOCUS**
Stalls on the inside on the round course and the stands side on the straight course. A bright and sunny afternoon with temperatures of around 12C, and a modest handicap to start with. The top two in the market filled the first two places and the first and third came from well off the pace. Solid form. A pb from the third, with the fifth rated to form.

## 2119 £188 FIRST GOALS WINS AT 188BET H'CAP (DIV I) — 7f 6y
**2:10** (2:13) (Class 5) (0-70,72) 4-Y-O+ **£3,234** (£962; £481; £240) **Stalls** High

Form RPR

5-04 **1** **African Blessing**[6] [1971] 4-9-5 **68**.... PhillipMakin 6 76
(David Barron) *trckd ldrs: hdwy over 2f out: rdn to chal over 1f out: led ins fnl f: drvn out* **4/1**[2]

4532 **2** *nk* **Tadaawol**[16] [1717] 4-9-6 **69**....(p) SilvestreDeSousa 11 76
(Roger Fell) *in tch: hdwy 3f out: pushed along to chse ldrs 2f out: sn chal: rdn to take slt ld jst over 1f out: drvn and hdd ins fnl f: kpt on* **9/4**[1]

2012 **3** *¾* **Lucky Louie**[16] [1729] 4-9-2 **65**....(p) JackMitchell 9 70
(Roger Teal) *hld up towards rr: swtchd rt to stands' rail and hdwy 3f out: cl up 2f out: rdn to dispute ld over 1f out: ev ch tl drvn ins fnl f and kpt on same pce* **8/1**

0-32 **4** *6* **Lucky Lodge**[9] [1890] 7-9-0 **63**....(p) CamHardie 12 52
(Antony Brittain) *towards rr: hdwy over 2f out: rdn wl over 1f out: styd on fnl f: nrst fin* **16/1**

500- **5** *½* **Maureb (IRE)**[211] [6908] 5-9-8 **71**....(p) DuranFentiman 3 58
(Tony Coyle) *t.k.h: trckd ldrs: pushed along wl over 2f out: rdn wl over 1f out: kpt on same pce* **40/1**

322- **6** *2 ½* **Kirkham**[162] [7994] 4-9-4 **67**.... JoeDoyle 2 48
(Julie Camacho) *trckd ldrs: hdwy over 2f out: rdn wl over 1f out: sn no imp* **11/2**[3]

2-10 **7** *½* **First Excel**[28] [1473] 5-8-7 **63**....(v) RPWalsh(7) 4 42
(Roy Bowring) *led: rdn along over 2f out: drvn over 1f out: sn hdd & wknd* **20/1**

530- **8** *1* **By The Law**[258] [5388] 4-9-4 **67**.... DavidAllan 10 44
(Tim Easterby) *dwlt: a towards rr* **33/1**

050- **9** *2 ¼* **Favourite Treat (USA)**[223] [6579] 7-9-9 **72**....(e) JackGarritty 8 43
(Ruth Carr) *dwlt: a towards rr* **12/1**

310- **10** *8* **Reinforced**[196] [7323] 4-9-3 **66**....(p) AndrewMullen 5 15
(Michael Dods) *prom: cl up 1/2-way: rdn along 3f out: sn wknd* **9/1**

2000 **11** *3 ½* **Swiftee (IRE)**[16] [1735] 4-8-8 **57**....(v[1]) LukeMorris 1
(Ivan Furtado) *prom on wd outside: pushed along 1/2-way: sn rdn and wknd wl over 2f out* **33/1**

000- **12** *30* **Just Be Lucky (IRE)**[183] [7644] 5-9-7 **70**....(p) PaulMulrennan 7
(Conor Dore) *towards rr: rdn along bef 1/2-way: sn outpcd and bhd* **66/1**

1m 24.9s (-1.40) **Going Correction** -0.125s/f (Firm) **12** Ran SP% **115.4**
Speed ratings (Par 103): **103,102,101,94,94 91,90,89,87,78 74,39**
CSF £12.27 CT £68.66 TOTE £4.80: £1.60, £1.30, £2.20; EX 15.20 Trifecta £86.00.
**Owner** M Rozenbroek **Bred** Michael Turner **Trained** Maunby, N Yorks

**FOCUS**
Few got into the first division of a modest 7f handicap with a trio drawing well clear of the remainder. Stalls were stands' side but they opted to race down the centre of the track. The form should hold up. The runner-up has been rated to his Catterick latest, with the third building on his recent AW progress.

## 2120 £188 FIRST GOALS WINS AT 188BET H'CAP (DIV II) — 7f 6y
**2:45** (2:46) (Class 5) (0-70,71) 4-Y-O+ **£3,234** (£962; £481; £240) **Stalls** High

Form RPR

356- **1** **Art Echo**[186] [7577] 4-9-5 **67**....(t) BenCurtis 11 75
(John Mackie) *prom: cl up 1/2-way: led over 2f out: rdn over 1f out: drvn and edgd rt ins fnl f: kpt on wl towards fin* **9/1**

0313 **2** *1* **Dark Forest**[12] [1820] 4-9-6 **68**....(p) BarryMcHugh 5 73
(Marjorie Fife) *in tch: hdwy to trck ldrs 3f out: rdn over 1f out: drvn jst ins fnl f: kpt on same pce* **7/1**[2]

0-13 **3** *nse* **Gulland Rock**[16] [1728] 6-9-3 **65**.... WilliamCarson 9 70
(Anthony Carson) *racd nr stands' rail: cl up: rdn along 2f out: ev ch tl drvn ins fnl f and kpt on same pce* **16/1**

50-1 **4** *hd* **Bahamian Bird**[16] [1717] 4-9-6 **71**.... AdamMcNamara(3) 8 75
(Richard Fahey) *slt ld: rdn along and hdd over 2f out: drvn over 1f out: kpt on u.p fnl f* **3/1**[1]

50-0 **5** *1 ¼* **Willsy**[16] [1717] 4-8-13 **66**.... GemmaTutty(5) 4 67
(Karen Tutty) *towards rr: hdwy 2f out: sn rdn and styd on fnl f: nrst fin* **25/1**

3-40 **6** *½* **Athollblair Boy (IRE)**[16] [1735] 4-9-1 **68**.... LewisEdmunds(5) 1 68
(Nigel Tinkler) *hld up in midfield: hdwy over 2f out: rdn to chse ldrs over 1f out: kpt on one pce fnl f* **9/1**

216- **7** *shd* **Mango Chutney**[196] [7334] 4-9-2 **64**....(p) PhillipMakin 6 63
(John Davies) *cl up: rdn along over 2f out: drvn wl over 1f out: grad wknd* **9/1**

-150 **8** *nse* **Tripartite (IRE)**[21] [1606] 4-9-9 **71**.... LukeMorris 10 70
(Jeremy Gask) *in tch: pushed along 3f out: rdn over 2f out: sn one pce* **8/1**[3]

53-0 **9** *1 ½* **Q Cee**[69] [808] 4-8-10 **63**.... LuluStanford(5) 2 58
(Eugene Stanford) *trckd ldrs: hdwy on outer and cl up 3f out: rdn along over 2f out: sn wknd* **12/1**

040- **10** *12* **Cookie Ring (IRE)**[354] [2096] 6-8-0 **55** oh1.... PaulaMuir(7) 3 18
(Patrick Holmes) *s.i.s: a in rr* **100/1**

466- **11** *1 ¼* **Niqnaaqpaadiwaaq**[147] [8188] 5-9-0 **62**.... NeilFarley 12 22
(Eric Alston) *racd nr stands' rail: t.k.h: trckd ldrs: pushed along wl over 2f: sn rdn and wknd* **14/1**

413- **12** *2 ½* **Luang Prabang (IRE)**[213] [6851] 4-9-4 **69**.... LouisSteward(3) 7 22
(Chris Wall) *a in rr* **8/1**[3]

1m 25.68s (-0.62) **Going Correction** -0.125s/f (Firm) **12** Ran SP% **114.8**
Speed ratings (Par 103): **98,96,96,96,95 94,94,94,92,78 77,74**
CSF £68.41 CT £1011.23 TOTE £10.30: £3.20, £2.30, £3.10; EX 88.20 Trifecta £1219.90.
**Owner** Mrs J Mackie **Bred** Follow The Flag Partnership **Trained** Church Broughton , Derbys

**FOCUS**
The second division of a modest handicap. They came up the centre again and the pace was solid enough. The runner-up has been rated close to his recent AW form.

## 2121 188BET.CO.UK MAIDEN FILLIES' STKS — 6f 2y
**3:20** (3:20) (Class 5) 3-Y-O+ **£3,234** (£962; £481; £240) **Stalls** High

Form RPR

2- **1** **Harbour Grey (IRE)**[135] [8361] 3-8-13 0.... SeanLevey 6 79+
(Richard Hannon) *green: t.k.h and hld up: hdwy over 2f out: chsd ldrs over 1f out: rdn to chal ins fnl f: kpt on wl to ld nr fin* **4/1**[2]

2 **2** *nk* **Desert Rain (IRE)**[21] 1600 3-8-13 0 SilvestreDeSousa 11 78
(Saeed bin Suroor) *led: rdn over 1f out: drvn ins fnl f: edgd lft last 100yds: hdd and no ex nr fin* **11/10**[1]

33- **3** *1 ¾* **Beck And Call**[261] 5304 3-8-13 0 DaneO'Neill 8 72
(Henry Candy) *trckd ldrs: hdwy to chse ldr 2f out: rdn to chal over 1f out: ev ch tl drvn and kpt on same pce last 100yds* **9/2**[3]

3 **4** *2* **Art's Desire (IRE)**[32] 1401 3-8-13 0 ThomasBrown 10 66
(Ed Walker) *chsd ldrs: rdn along over 2f out: drvn and one pce fr over 1f out* **7/1**

**5** *3 ¼* **Roubles (USA)** 3-8-8 0 GeorgeWood(5) 1 55+
(James Fanshawe) *green and t.k.h: trckd ldrs on outer: hdwy 1/2-way: rdn along 2f out: grad wknd* **8/1**

-53 **6** *4 ½* **Exquisite Ruby**[20] 1626 3-8-13 0 MartinHarley 9 41
(Charles Hills) *dwlt and t.k.h towards rr: sme hdwy 2f out: nvr nr ldrs* **16/1**

05-0 **7** *½* **Paco Lady**[26] 1514 3-8-8 38 LewisEdmunds(5) 12 39
(Ivan Furtado) *chsd ldr: rdn along wl over 2f out: sn wknd* **125/1**

**8** *hd* **Oriental Lilly** 3-8-13 0 (h1) SamJames 7 39
(Jim Goldie) *s.i.s: a bhd* **80/1**

00- **9** *3* **Kulgri**[196] 7314 3-8-13 0 TomEaves 5 29
(Kevin Ryan) *chsd ldrs: rdn along over 2f out: sn drvn and wknd* **100/1**

**10** *½* **Willow Tiger Lily** 3-8-13 0 TomMarquand 2 27
(J R Jenkins) *a in rr* **100/1**

1m 11.99s (-1.61) **Going Correction** -0.125s/f (Firm) **10** Ran SP% **119.3**
Speed ratings (Par 100): **105,104,102,99,95 89,88,88,84,83**
CSF £9.07 TOTE £5.60: £1.60, £1.10, £1.70; EX 12.20 Trifecta £35.30.
**Owner** Clipper Logistics **Bred** Knocklong House Stud **Trained** East Everleigh, Wilts

**FOCUS**
While a largely uncompetitive fillies' maiden the first three home were the first three in the market and there was not much between them. They came up the centre of the track and veered towards the far side. The form looks decent and this should produce winners. The third has been rated close to her 2yo form.

## 2122 BEST ODDS GUARANTEED AT 188BET H'CAP 6f 2y
**3:55** (3:57) (Class 3) (0-90,86) 3-Y-O **£7,762** (£2,310; £1,154; £577) **Stalls** High

Form RPR

10-2 **1** **Rich And Famous (USA)**[8] 1901 3-9-7 86 JoeFanning 10 93+
(Mark Johnston) *qckly away: mde all: rdn clr wl over 1f out: kpt on strly* **10/3**[1]

21- **2** *1 ½* **Ekhtiyaar**[200] 7224 3-9-6 85 DaneO'Neill 8 88+
(Roger Varian) *trckd ldrs: hdwy over 2f out: rdn to chse wnr over 1f out: drvn ins fnl f: no imp towards fin* **7/2**[2]

21- **3** *¾* **Holmeswood**[162] 7988 3-9-5 84 PaulMulrennan 6 84+
(Michael Dods) *t.k.h: hld up: hdwy 2f out: rdn over 1f out: kpt on fnl f* **5/1**

316- **4** *½* **The Feathered Nest (IRE)**[169] 7893 3-9-2 81 TonyHamilton 9 80
(Richard Fahey) *dwlt and towards rr: hdwy over 2f out: rdn wl over 1f out: kpt on fnl f: nrst fin* **14/1**

121- **5** *nse* **Accidental Agent**[209] 6950 3-9-6 85 CharlesBishop 7 83
(Eve Johnson Houghton) *dwlt and rr: gd hdwy over 2f out: rdn over 1f out: kpt on fnl f: nrst fin* **9/2**[3]

2346 **6** *¾* **Dazacam**[16] 1732 3-9-5 84 RobertWinston 5 80
(Michael Herrington) *hld up and bhd: hdwy on inner 2f out: sn rdn and styd on fnl f: nrst fin* **50/1**

6-26 **7** *¾* **Kamra (USA)**[49] 1124 3-8-13 78 JoeDoyle 11 72
(Michael Herrington) *chsd wnr: pushed along 1/2-way: rdn over 2f out: grad wknd* **80/1**

02-5 **8** *2* **Father McKenzie**[16] 1731 3-8-13 78 RyanTate 13 65
(James Eustace) *chsd ldrs: rdn along over 2f out: sn drvn and grad wknd* **16/1**

41- **9** *½* **Magical Dreamer (IRE)**[212] 6866 3-8-7 77 GeorgeWood(5) 4 63
(James Fanshawe) *swished tail thrght: prom: rdn along over 2f out: wknd wl over 1f out* **20/1**

141- **10** *1 ¼* **Sterling Silva (IRE)**[322] 3093 3-9-7 86 SeanLevey 3 68
(Richard Hannon) *a rr* **11/1**

130- **11** *nse* **Lanjano**[203] 7120 3-8-13 78 KevinStott 12 59
(Kevin Ryan) *chsd ldrs: rdn along 1/2-way: sn wknd* **12/1**

1m 11.73s (-1.87) **Going Correction** -0.125s/f (Firm) **11** Ran SP% **116.7**
Speed ratings (Par 102): **107,105,104,103,103 102,101,98,97,96 96**
CSF £14.74 CT £57.41 TOTE £4.20: £1.90, £1.40, £2.10; EX 12.80 Trifecta £43.50.
**Owner** Sheikh Hamdan bin Mohammed Al Maktoum **Bred** Darley **Trained** Middleham Moor, N Yorks

**FOCUS**
A fair 3yo sprint handicap with an all-the-way winner. As with previous races, they came up the centre. Viable form. A small pb from the winner, with the bare form rated around the sixth for now.

## 2123 BOXING BETTING AT 188BET H'CAP 5f 3y
**4:30** (4:30) (Class 4) (0-85,86) 4-Y-O+ **£5,175** (£1,540; £769; £384) **Stalls** High

Form RPR

660- **1** **Acclaim The Nation (IRE)**[226] 6476 4-8-9 73 JasonHart 2 82
(Eric Alston) *sn led in centre: rdn over 1f out: drvn ins fnl f: hld on gamely* **14/1**

P0-5 **2** *nk* **Bashiba (IRE)**[9] 1876 6-9-7 85 (t) SilvestreDeSousa 13 93
(Nigel Tinkler) *stdd s and sn swtchd lft towards centre: hdwy wl over 1f out: rdn and n.m.r over 1f out: chal ins fnl f: sn drvn and ev ch: nt qckn towards fin* **7/1**

00-0 **3** *¾* **Tylery Wonder (IRE)**[14] 1777 7-9-1 79 (b) MartinHarley 12 84
(Paul Midgley) *racd nr stands rail: cl up rdn and ev ch over 1f out: drvn and edgd lft ins fnl f: kpt on* **14/1**

56-0 **4** *hd* **Laughton**[11] 1831 4-9-4 82 ShaneGray 3 87
(Kevin Ryan) *hld up centre: hdwy to trck ldrs over 2f out: rdn over 1f out: drvn ins fnl f and kpt on same pce* **4/1**[2]

0-01 **5** *nk* **Foxtrot Knight**[8] 1915 5-8-13 77 JackGarritty 11 81
(Ruth Carr) *racwed towards stand side: hld up: hdwy wl over 1f out: sn rdn and kpt on fnl f* **11/2**[3]

30-3 **6** *nk* **Stake Acclaim (IRE)**[4] 2038 5-9-8 86 (p) RobertWinston 4 88
(Dean Ivory) *trckd wnr centre: cl up 2f out: rdn over 1f out: drvn and kpt on same pce fnl f* **5/2**[1]

10-5 **7** *nk* **First Bombardment**[14] 1777 4-8-12 83 PatrickVaughan(7) 10 84
(David O'Meara) *racd towards stands side: chsd ldrs: rdn over 1f out: drvn and no imp fnl f* **22/1**

3342 **8** *1* **Seamster**[14] 1768 10-8-12 83 (t) CameronNoble(7) 5 81
(David Loughnane) *racd centre: chsd ldrs: rdn along wl over 1f out: grad wknd* **10/1**

16-0 **9** *½* **Musharrif**[11] 1831 5-8-12 81 PhilDennis(5) 9 77
(Declan Carroll) *in tch centre: rdn along 2f out: grad wknd* **14/1**

02-0 **10** *½* **Stanghow**[14] 1777 5-9-7 85 (p1) CamHardie 8 79
(Antony Brittain) *chsd ldrs centre: rdn along 2f out: sn drvn and wknd over 1f out* **33/1**

40-0 **11** *nk* **Pea Shooter**[12] 1820 8-9-4 82 BenCurtis 7 75
(Brian Ellison) *chsd ldrs centre: rdn along and edgd rt over 1f out: sn wknd* **33/1**

00-0 **12** *1 ¼* **Secret Missile**[14] 1777 7-8-13 77 (b) DavidAllan 6 66
(David C Griffiths) *in tch centre: rdn along 1/2-way: sn outpcd and bhd* **50/1**

58.64s (-1.86) **Going Correction** -0.125s/f (Firm) **12** Ran SP% **117.7**
Speed ratings (Par 105): **109,108,107,107,106 106,105,103,103,102 101,99**
CSF £104.49 CT £1425.88 TOTE £17.60: £4.60, £2.60, £4.30; EX 153.10 Trifecta £4683.10 Part won..
**Owner** Con Harrington **Bred** Con Harrington **Trained** Longton, Lancs

**FOCUS**
A 5f sprint handicap in which the pace held up, although three of the first five home were all slowly away. The runner-up has been rated close to form.

## 2124 FREE BET AT 188BET FILLIES' H'CAP 6f 2y
**5:05** (5:11) (Class 5) (0-70,72) 4-Y-O+ **£3,234** (£962; £481; £240) **Stalls** High

Form RPR

053- **1** **Shesthedream (IRE)**[196] 7335 4-9-1 63 PhillipMakin 8 71+
(David Barron) *dwlt and towards rr: hdwy and in tch 1/2-way: effrt on outer wl over 1f out: rdn to chal ent fnl f: sn led: drvn and kpt on wl towards fin* **9/1**

00-6 **2** *nk* **French**[16] 1721 4-8-9 57 (p) CamHardie 9 64
(Antony Brittain) *cl up: rdn to ld over 1f out: drvn and hdd ins fnl f: kpt on gamely u.p* **16/1**

40-5 **3** *2* **Meandmyshadow**[6] 1971 9-9-10 72 (b) BenCurtis 4 73
(Alan Brown) *cl up: rdn along 2f out: drvn over 1f out: kpt on same pce ins fnl f* **4/1**[1]

20-0 **4** *hd* **Tigserin (IRE)**[36] 1326 4-9-1 63 KevinStott 3 63
(Giles Bravery) *chsd ldrs: rdn along and outpcd 1/2-way: styd on fr over 1f out* **11/1**

6433 **5** *¾* **Penny Dreadful**[6] 1978 5-8-9 57 (p) DavidAllan 15 55
(Scott Dixon) *cl up: led over 2f out: sn rdn: hdd and drvn over 1f out: grad wknd* **9/2**[2]

104- **6** *nk* **Curious Fox**[190] 7485 4-9-6 68 WilliamCarson 13 65
(Anthony Carson) *rr: rdn along 2f out swtchd lft and hdwy over 1f out: kpt on wl towards fin* **12/1**

30-4 **7** *1 ¾* **Rose Eclair**[11] 1828 4-9-9 71 (b) JasonHart 6 62
(Tim Easterby) *in tch: hdwy 2f out: rdn over 1f out: sn no imp* **8/1**[3]

204- **8** *6* **Penny Pot Lane**[195] 7364 4-9-7 69 PaulMulrennan 5 41
(Richard Whitaker) *rr tl styd on fr over 1f out: n.d* **9/1**

411- **9** *3 ¼* **Spirit Of Rosanna**[286] 4378 5-8-12 60 (tp) AdamBeschizza 14 21
(Steph Hollinshead) *led: rdn along 1/2-way: hdd over 2f out: sn drvn and wknd* **16/1**

140- **10** *2* **Manipura**[225] 6509 4-8-10 58 (p) MartinLane 12 13
(Derek Shaw) *dwlt: a rr* **25/1**

660- **11** *21* **Fever Few**[206] 7059 8-9-5 67 TedDurcan 2
(Chris Wall) *in tch: rdn along after 2f: sn lost pl and bhd* **8/1**[3]

1m 12.42s (-1.18) **Going Correction** -0.125s/f (Firm) **11** Ran SP% **112.0**
Speed ratings (Par 100): **102,101,98,98,97 97,94,86,82,79 51**
CSF £130.19 CT £578.85 TOTE £10.10: £2.80, £4.70, £2.50; EX 189.10 Trifecta £1578.90.
**Owner** Star Alliance 6 - The Orange Brigade **Bred** Ballyreddin Stud **Trained** Maunby, N Yorks
■ Thorntoun Lady was withdrawn. Price at time of withdrawal 14-1. Rule 4 applies to all bets - deduction 5p in the pound.

**FOCUS**
An ordinary fillies' handicap. The second has been rated in line with last year's reappearance run.

## 2125 FREE SPINS AT 188BET H'CAP 2m 109y
**5:40** (5:40) (Class 4) (0-85,85) 4-Y-O+ **£4,851** (£1,443; £721; £360) **Stalls** Low

Form RPR

0/6- **1** **Handiwork**[391] 1209 7-9-5 78 (p) JoeFanning 5 87
(Steve Gollings) *hld up in rr: hdwy on outer wl over 2f out: rdn to ld over 1f out: edgd lft jst ins fnl f: kpt on strly* **9/2**[3]

43-4 **2** *2 ¾* **Fire Jet (IRE)**[32] 1405 4-9-2 79 BenCurtis 6 85
(John Mackie) *trckd ldrs: hdwy 3f out: rdn to take slt advantage 2f: hdd and drvn over 1f out: n.m.r and swtchd rt jst ins fnl f: kpt on* **11/8**[1]

6323 **3** *2 ½* **Ardamir (FR)**[20] 1628 5-9-9 82 (h) FergusSweeney 2 85
(Alan King) *led: pushed along and qcknd over 4f out: rdn along 3f out: hdd 2f out: sn drvn and kpt on same pce* **2/1**[2]

2456 **4** *3 ½* **Jan Smuts (IRE)**[16] 1716 9-8-0 66 oh1 (tp) ConnorMurtagh(7) 3 65
(Wilf Storey) *trckd ldng pair on inner: pushed along whn pce qcknd over 4f out: rdn 3f out: sn drvn and kpt on one pce* **20/1**

060- **5** *7* **Braes Of Lochalsh**[130] 6561 6-9-0 73 SamJames 4 65
(Jim Goldie) *trckd ldr: hdwy over 4f out: rdn along wl over 3f out: sn drvn and wknd* **8/1**

3m 37.02s (-3.38) **Going Correction** -0.125s/f (Firm)
**WFA** 4 from 5yo+ 2lb **5** Ran SP% **109.5**
Speed ratings (Par 105): **102,100,99,97,94**
CSF £11.09 TOTE £6.50: £2.10, £1.20; EX 13.60 Trifecta £20.60.
**Owner** C Johnstone **Bred** The Queen **Trained** Scamblesby, Lincs

**FOCUS**
The gallop was sound and the winner came from the back to win with authority. The winner has been rated close to his old best.
T/Jkpt: Not won. T/Plt: £58.10 to a £1 stake. Pool: £61,350.00 - 1,054.71 winning units. T/Qpdt: £22.30 to a £1 stake. Pool: £4,237.00 - 189.17 winning units. **Joe Rowntree**

# SANDOWN (R-H)
### Friday, April 28

**OFFICIAL GOING: Good (good to firm in places) changing to good after race 3 (2.55)**
Wind: Almost nil Weather: Cloudy

## 2126 BET365 ESHER CUP H'CAP 1m 14y
**1:50** (1:53) (Class 2) (0-100,93) 3-Y-O
**£15,562** (£4,660; £2,330; £1,165; £582; £292) **Stalls** Low

Form RPR

1- **1** **Atty Persse (IRE)**[226] 6480 3-9-1 87 JamesDoyle 1 94+
(Roger Charlton) *athletic: sltly on the leg: chsd ldrs on inner: hrd rdn and nt clr run over 1f out: r.o wl fnl f: led fnl strides* **6/4**[1]

341- **2** *shd* **Fearless Fire (IRE)**[212] 6881 3-8-10 **82**........................ WilliamBuick 7 88
(Andrew Balding) *w'like: bit on the leg: prom: led over 1f out: hung lft ins fnl f: kpt on u.p: hdd fnl strides* **12/1**

10- **3** *nk* **The Grape Escape (IRE)**[188] 7544 3-9-4 **90**........................ PatDobbs 3 95+
(Richard Hannon) *wl made: led for 2f: prom and gng wl whn squeezed for room wl over 1f out: r.o* **11/1**

041- **4** *nk* **Colibri (IRE)**[235] 6183 3-9-6 **92**........................ JimCrowley 13 96
(Hugo Palmer) *q tall: mid-div on outer: gd hdwy over 1f out: chalng whn carried lft ins fnl f: r.o* **14/1**

212- **5** *1* **Juanito Chico (IRE)**[191] 7460 3-8-6 **78**........................(h) MartinDwyer 6 81
(William Jarvis) *bit bkwd: stdd s: t.k.h in rr of midfield: hdwy on inner whn hmpd over 1f out: styd on fnl f* **50/1**

144- **6** *hd* **Contrast (IRE)**[224] 6546 3-9-7 **93**........................ RyanMoore 11 95
(Richard Hannon) *lw: stdd s and dropped in to inner: bhd and sn pushed along: hrd rdn and hdwy over 1f out: kpt on fnl f* **20/1**

242- **7** *¾* **Mister Blue Sky (IRE)**[219] 6664 3-7-10 **75**........................ DavidEgan(7) 5 75
(Sylvester Kirk) *bit bkwd: in tch: squeezed for room after 3f: pressed ldrs over 2f out: hrd rdn over 1f out: styd on same pce* **25/1**

531- **8** *nk* **First Up (IRE)**[219] 6672 3-8-13 **85**........................ JFEgan 9 85+
(Jeremy Noseda) *dwlt: in rr of midfield: rdn and hdwy over 1f out: in tch and styng on whn short of room jst ins fnl f: unable to rcvr* **10/1**[3]

-203 **9** *shd* **Dr Julius No**[13] 1801 3-8-13 **90**........................ PatrickO'Donnell(5) 14 89
(Ralph Beckett) *stdd s: bhd tl styd on fr over 1f out* **16/1**

6-1 **10** *2 ½* **Jupiter Light**[34] 1366 3-8-13 **85**........................ RobertTart 10 78
(John Gosden) *w'like: bit on the leg: towards rr: rdn over 2f out: nvr able to chal* **12/1**

616- **11** *2 ¼* **Rebel De Lope**[203] 7130 3-9-4 **90**........................ JamieSpencer 8 78
(Charles Hills) *prom: led after 2f tl over 1f out: wknd fnl f* **22/1**

34-1 **12** *1* **Cullingworth (IRE)**[13] 1801 3-8-9 **84**........................ SammyJoBell(3) 4 70
(Richard Fahey) *in tch tl wknd over 2f out* **16/1**

1-2 **13** *1 ¾* **Medahim (IRE)**[11] 1841 3-9-1 **87**........................ FrankieDettori 12 69
(Richard Hannon) *athletic: in tch: outpcd 3f out: sn btn* **13/2**[2]

1m 45.39s (2.09) **Going Correction** +0.45s/f (Yiel) **13** Ran SP% **119.5**
Speed ratings (Par 104): **107,106,106,106,105 105,104,104,103,101 99,98,96**
CSF £19.45 CT £155.82 TOTE £2.50: £1.30, £3.70, £3.30; EX 28.20 Trifecta £298.60.

**Owner** Godolphin **Bred** Bjorn Nielsen **Trained** Beckhampton, Wilts

■ Stewards' Enquiry : Pat Dobbs three-day ban: careless riding in that he had switched right when not sufficiently clear (May 12-13, 15)

**FOCUS**
Distance increased by 27yds. James Doyle felt the ground had been "over-watered" and was no quicker than good. Often an interesting handicap and the race should produce its share of winners. The seventh has been rated close to form.

## 2127 BET365 GORDON RICHARDS STKS (GROUP 3) 1m 1f 209y
**2:20** (2:22) (Class 1) 4-Y-O+

**£36,861** (£13,975; £6,994; £3,484; £1,748; £877) **Stalls** Low

Form RPR

124- **1** **Ulysses (IRE)**[174] 7835 4-9-0 116........................ AndreaAtzeni 6 119
(Sir Michael Stoute) *warm: hld up in 6th: smooth hdwy towards centre to ld jst over 1f out: drifted lft: rdn out* **3/1**[2]

13-0 **2** *1* **Deauville (IRE)**[34] 1378 4-9-0 113........................(t) RyanMoore 5 117
(A P O'Brien, Ire) *lw: led: rdn to increase pce ins fnl 3f: hdd jst over 1f out: kpt on wl* **9/2**[3]

554- **3** *3* **My Dream Boat (IRE)**[195] 7353 5-9-0 120........................ AdamKirby 1 111
(Clive Cox) *hld up in rr: rdn over 2f out: no prog tl styd on fr over 1f out: nvr nrr* **11/4**[1]

513- **4** *1 ¾* **Royal Artillery (USA)**[256] 5499 4-9-0 114........................(t) FrankieDettori 8 108
(John Gosden) *lw: sn chsng ldr: chal over 2f out: no ex fnl f* **3/1**[2]

/40- **5** *shd* **Muntazah**[295] 4061 4-9-0 105........................ JimCrowley 4 107
(Owen Burrows) *trckd ldrs: rdn wl over 1f out: one pce* **16/1**

210- **6** *2 ½* **Arthenus**[209] 6973 5-9-0 108........................(p) TomQueally 2 102
(James Fanshawe) *travelled wl in 5th tl wknd 2f out* **20/1**

120- **7** *½* **First Sitting**[216] 6786 6-9-0 105........................ HarryBentley 3 101
(Chris Wall) *hld up in rr: rdn over 2f out: n.d* **33/1**

36-0 **8** *1 ¼* **Restorer**[40] 1271 5-9-0 102........................ MartinDwyer 7 99
(William Muir) *chsd ldrs: rdn 2f out: sn outpcd* **50/1**

2m 14.16s (3.66) **Going Correction** +0.45s/f (Yiel) **8** Ran SP% **110.4**
Speed ratings (Par 113): **103,102,99,98,98 96,95,94**
CSF £15.50 TOTE £4.30: £1.30, £1.50, £1.40; EX 16.10 Trifecta £39.80.

**Owner** Flaxman Stables Ireland Ltd **Bred** Flaxman Stables Ireland Ltd **Trained** Newmarket, Suffolk

**FOCUS**
Distance increased by 27yds. A strong Group 3 and, although they went an unsatisfactory gallop, the right horses came to the fore. The runner-up sets the standard.

## 2128 BET365 CLASSIC TRIAL (GROUP 3) 1m 1f 209y
**2:55** (2:58) (Class 1) 3-Y-O **£36,861** (£13,975; £6,994; £3,484; £1,748) **Stalls** Low

Form RPR

320- **1** **Cunco (IRE)**[180] 7722 3-9-1 104........................ RobertTart 3 105
(John Gosden) *nt grwn: warm: t.k.h in last: rdn over 2f out: hdwy over 1f out: r.o to ld fnl strides* **5/1**[2]

3- **2** *hd* **Intern (IRE)**[266] 5136 3-9-1 0........................ FranBerry 2 104
(Ralph Beckett) *athletic: hld up in 4th: hdwy 2f out: led ins fnl f: kpt on wl u.p: hdd fnl strides* **12/1**

110- **3** *1* **Frankuus (IRE)**[180] 7722 3-9-1 106........................ FrannyNorton 5 102
(Mark Johnston) *lw: trckd ldr: disp ld over 2f out: narrow ld over 1f out tl ins fnl f: kpt on* **6/1**

21-1 **4** *2* **Monarchs Glen**[16] 1725 3-9-1 101........................ FrankieDettori 4 98
(John Gosden) *q tall: led: racd freely and restrained in front: jnd over 2f out: hdd over 1f out: no ex fnl f* **5/6**[1]

1- **5** *hd* **Fierce Impact (JPN)**[200] 7226 3-9-1 81........................ JamieSpencer 1 97
(David Simcock) *athletic: q str: chsd ldng pair: hrd rdn 2f out: one pce* **11/2**[3]

2m 14.33s (3.83) **Going Correction** +0.45s/f (Yiel) **5** Ran SP% **108.6**
Speed ratings (Par 108): **102,101,101,99,99**
CSF £49.61 TOTE £6.10: £2.50, £4.70; EX 49.40 Trifecta £141.70.

**Owner** Stud Haras Don Alberto **Bred** Don Alberto Corporation **Trained** Newmarket, Suffolk

**FOCUS**
Distance increased by 27yds. In truth this was probably an ordinary edition of the race, with the odds-on favourite disappointing having set a steady gallop. It's been rated around the winner and third.

## 2129 BET365 MILE (GROUP 2) 1m 14y
**3:30** (3:32) (Class 1) 4-Y-O+

**£53,874** (£20,425; £10,222; £5,092; £2,555; £1,282) **Stalls** Low

Form RPR

-131 **1** **Sovereign Debt (IRE)**[14] 1773 8-9-1 110........................ JamesSullivan 8 114
(Ruth Carr) *trckd ldr: led wl over 1f out: sn kicked over 2 l ahd: in control nr fin: rdn out* **9/2**[1]

0504 **2** *½* **Gabrial (IRE)**[27] 1494 8-9-1 108........................ FrankieDettori 7 113
(Richard Fahey) *dwlt: bhd tl gd hdwy over 1f out: wnt 2nd and clsd on wnr fnl f: a hld* **10/1**

123- **3** *1 ½* **Jallota**[203] 7115 6-9-1 111........................ JamieSpencer 1 109
(Charles Hills) *chsd ldng pair: rdn and hung lft over 2f out: kpt on fnl f* **10/1**

-210 **4** *nk* **Opal Tiara (IRE)**[34] 1378 4-9-1 111........................ GrahamLee 4 109
(Mick Channon) *hld up disputing 5th: rdn over 2f out: styd on fnl f* **22/1**

205- **5** *1 ¼* **Mitchum Swagger**[170] 7868 5-9-1 110........................ TomQueally 3 106
(David Lanigan) *towards rr: rdn over 2f out: nvr nrr* **14/1**

0-20 **6** *1 ¼* **Cougar Mountain (IRE)**[34] 1378 6-9-4 115........................(tp) RyanMoore 6 106
(A P O'Brien, Ire) *noisy in prelims: lw: hld up disputing 5th: drvn along 2f out: sn outpcd* **5/1**[2]

41-3 **7** *1 ¼* **Dawn Of Hope (IRE)**[27] 1493 4-8-12 110........................ AndreaAtzeni 10 97
(Roger Varian) *sn stdd bk towards rr: abt same pl rest of way: rdn and no hdwy fnl 2f* **5/1**[2]

42-1 **8** *hd* **Kool Kompany (IRE)**[27] 1493 5-9-1 114........................ PatDobbs 5 100
(Richard Hannon) *led tl wl over 1f out: sn wknd* **9/2**[1]

46/- **9** *7* **Tashweeq (IRE)**[544] 7665 4-9-1 106........................ JimCrowley 9 84
(John Gosden) *dwlt: t.k.h in rr: rdn and hung rt over 2f out: little rspnse* **6/1**[3]

1m 44.24s (0.94) **Going Correction** +0.45s/f (Yiel) **9** Ran SP% **113.2**
Speed ratings (Par 115): **113,112,111,110,109 108,106,106,99**
CSF £48.40 TOTE £5.20: £1.70, £2.90, £3.10; EX 43.70 Trifecta £290.90.

**Owner** Lady O'Reilly & Partners **Bred** Yeomanstown Stud **Trained** Huby, N Yorks

**FOCUS**
Distance increased by 27yds. A really open Group 2, they went a good, sound gallop and the two elder statesmen of the field came to the fore, with the winner seeing it out well having pushed the pace throughout. The form isn't strong for the level, though. The winner helps set the standard.

## 2130 BET365.COM H'CAP 5f 10y
**4:05** (4:08) (Class 2) (0-100,93) 3-Y-O

**£12,450** (£3,728; £1,864; £932; £466; £234) **Stalls** Low

Form RPR

26-1 **1** **Jumira Bridge**[13] 1785 3-9-2 **88**........................ AndreaAtzeni 4 96+
(Roger Varian) *str: lw: on toes: dwlt: sn chsng ldrs: led 1f out: drvn out* **11/4**[1]

21-1 **2** *½* **Queen In Waiting (IRE)**[11] 1838 3-9-0 **86** 6ex........................ FrannyNorton 2 92
(Mark Johnston) *athletic: relaxed: narrow ld tl edgd lft and hdd 1f out: kpt on* **11/4**[1]

10-6 **3** *½* **Hyperfocus (IRE)**[21] 1601 3-8-13 **85**........................ JamesDoyle 1 90+
(Hugo Palmer) *early to post: chsd ldrs: fnd gap on far rail and effrt over 1f out: n.m.r ins fnl f: r.o* **8/1**[2]

6013 **4** *½* **Erissimus Maximus (FR)**[16] 1731 3-8-7 **79**........................(b) DavidProbert 3 81
(Chris Dwyer) *sn outpcd in midfield: drvn along and hdwy over 1f out: nrest at fin* **10/1**[3]

10-5 **5** *shd* **Smokey Lane (IRE)**[16] 1732 3-9-7 **93**........................ AdamKirby 8 95
(David Evans) *outpcd and bhd tl gd late hdwy* **25/1**

24 **6** *¾* **Blitz**[16] 1731 3-8-7 **82**........................ HectorCrouch(3) 6 81
(Clive Cox) *lw: w ldr tl no ex ins fnl f* **12/1**

115- **7** *2* **Partitia**[223] 6555 3-9-3 **89**........................ RyanMoore 10 81
(Sir Michael Stoute) *s.s: towards rr: pushed along 2f out: n.d* **10/1**[3]

4-14 **8** *nk* **Just An Idea (IRE)**[100] 291 3-8-10 **82**........................(v) HarryBentley 9 73
(Harry Dunlop) *prom tl wknd over 1f out* **20/1**

10-3 **9** *2 ¼* **Nayyar**[11] 1838 3-9-0 **86**........................ WilliamBuick 7 69
(Charles Hills) *early to post: mid-div: outpcd 1/2-way: n.d fnl 2f* **8/1**[2]

06-5 **10** *2 ¼* **Super Julius**[7] 1940 3-8-9 **81**........................ JohnFahy 5 55
(Eve Johnson Houghton) *outpcd towards rr: n.d fnl 2f* **18/1**

1m 1.02s (-0.58) **Going Correction** 0.0s/f (Good) **10** Ran SP% **115.3**
Speed ratings (Par 104): **104,103,102,101,101 100,97,96,92,89**
CSF £9.09 CT £52.28 TOTE £3.40: £1.40, £1.30, £2.90; EX 11.10 Trifecta £61.60.

**Owner** Sheikh Mohammed Obaid Al Maktoum **Bred** Cheveley Park Stud Ltd **Trained** Newmarket, Suffolk

**FOCUS**
Distance as advertised. A useful 3yo sprint and the right horses came to the fore. The runner-up has been rated simialr to her recent AW win.

## 2131 NORDOFF ROBBINS SIR GEORGE MARTIN MEMORIAL MAIDEN FILLIES' STKS (PLUS 10 RACE) 1m 1f 209y
**4:35** (4:38) (Class 4) 3-Y-O **£6,469** (£1,925; £962; £481) **Stalls** Low

Form RPR

3- **1** **Serenada**[188] 7543 3-9-0 0........................ AndreaAtzeni 2 80
(Roger Varian) *q str: sltly on toes: led for 2f: trckd ldr: rdn to ld in centre 1f out: all out* **2/1**[1]

**2** *shd* **Apphia (IRE)** 3-9-0 0........................ RyanMoore 6 79+
(Hugo Palmer) *q str: towards rr: swtchd alone towards far side and gd hdwy over 1f out: str chal nr fin: jst denied* **12/1**

43- **3** *nk* **So Sleek**[177] 7762 3-9-0 0........................ JamieSpencer 7 78
(Luca Cumani) *q str: prom: led after 2f: wnt to centre in st and hdd 1f out: kpt on wl* **16/1**

**4** *1 ¼* **Symbol** 3-9-0 0........................ TomQueally 4 76+
(James Fanshawe) *q tall: lengthy: green: on toes: hld up in rr: shkn up and hdwy in centre over 1f out: styd on steadily fnl f* **25/1**

03- **5** *1 ¼* **Fashion Theory**[189] 7494 3-9-0 0........................ WilliamBuick 8 73
(Charlie Appleby) *bit bkwd: prom: wnt to centre in st: no ex over 1f out* **6/1**[3]

4-2 **6** *2 ½* **Pure Shores**[15] 1756 3-9-0 0........................ JamesDoyle 9 68+
(Charlie Appleby) *cmpt: mid-div: c wd towards stands' side in st: effrt 2f out: hrd rdn and wknd over 1f out* **15/2**

24- **7** *3 ¼* **Neshmeya**[192] 7441 3-9-0 0........................ JimCrowley 3 62
(Charles Hills) *chsd ldrs: c wd towards stands' side in st: wknd 2f out* **3/1**[2]

0- **8** *4 ½* **Precious Angel (IRE)**[188] 7543 3-9-0 0 PatDobbs 5 53
(Richard Hannon) *q tall: s.s: a in rr: wnt to centre in st: n.d fnl 2f* **40/1**
**9** *9* **Love Conquers (JPN)** 3-9-0 0 FranBerry 1 35
(Ralph Beckett) *athletic: sltly on the leg: missed break and lost 8 l: t.k.h and sn in midfield: wnt to centre in st: wknd 2f out* **9/1**

2m 15.78s (5.28) **Going Correction** +0.45s/f (Yiel) **9** Ran SP% **114.2**
Speed ratings (Par 97): **96,95,95,94,93 91,89,85,78**
CSF £27.53 TOTE £2.80: £2.10, £3.00, £3.40; EX 21.40 Trifecta £303.80.
**Owner** Nurlan Bizakov **Bred** Hesmonds Stud Ltd **Trained** Newmarket, Suffolk

**FOCUS**
Distance increased by 27yds. The runners spread across the track in the straight, with riders looking for better ground, and it was probably just a fair maiden. The winner has been rated to her debut figure.

## 2132 BET365 H'CAP 1m 1f 209y
**5:10** (5:12) (Class 3) (0-95,91) 3-Y-O
**£9,337** (£2,796; £1,398; £699; £349; £175) **Stalls** Low

Form RPR
-116 **1** **Flood Warning**[26] 1518 3-8-13 **83** RyanMoore 4 93
(Clive Cox) *hld up in midfield: hdwy on inner 3f out: led 1f out: drvn out* **16/1**
1-20 **2** *1 ¼* **First Nation**[9] 1886 3-9-7 **91** WilliamBuick 2 98
(Charlie Appleby) *lw: sn chsng ldrs: led 2f out tl 1f out: kpt on u.p* **7/1**
531- **3** *¾* **Century Dream (IRE)**[198] 7283 3-9-2 **86** (t[1]) AndreaAtzeni 3 92
(Simon Crisford) *q str: sltly on toes: t.k.h: led tl 2f out: hrd rdn: kpt on* **7/2**[2]
31- **4** *1 ½* **Naseem (IRE)**[127] 8486 3-9-6 **90** JimCrowley 6 93
(John Gosden) *str: taken wd in bk st: sn prom: rdn 2f out: one pce* **9/4**[1]
21- **5** *1 ½* **Glencadam Glory**[232] 6262 3-9-2 **86** (h[1]) FrankieDettori 8 86+
(John Gosden) *w'like: missed break and lost 12 l: bhd and taken wd in bk st: rdn and struggling 3f out: styd on wl fnl f* **5/1**[3]
600- **6** *4 ½* **Bear Valley (IRE)**[202] 7151 3-9-7 **91** FrannyNorton 1 82
(Mark Johnston) *lw: prom tl wknd 3f out* **33/1**
16-0 **7** *nk* **Gravity Wave (IRE)**[16] 1737 3-8-5 **75** MartinDwyer 7 65
(Sylvester Kirk) *a in rr: rdn and n.d fnl 3f* **40/1**
341- **8** *1 ½* **Anythingtoday (IRE)**[160] 8034 3-8-12 **82** JamesDoyle 5 69
(Hugo Palmer) *lw: in tch tl edgd lft and wknd 2f out* **7/2**[2]

2m 12.92s (2.42) **Going Correction** +0.45s/f (Yiel) **8** Ran SP% **115.6**
Speed ratings (Par 102): **108,107,106,105,104 100,100,98**
CSF £123.14 CT £487.64 TOTE £20.00: £4.80, £3.00, £1.90; EX 120.20 Trifecta £676.50.
**Owner** Cheveley Park Stud **Bred** New England Myriad Stanley & Cheveley Pk **Trained** Lambourn, Berks

**FOCUS**
Distance increased by 27yds. A useful handicap, the runners stayed far side this time but there was a bit of a surprise winner. The third helps set the initial standard.
T/Plt: £114.80 to a £1 stake. Pool: £84,170.00 - 732.85 winning units. T/Qpdt: £70.50 to a £1 stake. Pool: £4,903.00 - 69.52 winning units. **Lee McKenzie**

# 2118 DONCASTER (L-H)
Saturday, April 29
**OFFICIAL GOING: Good to firm (good in places; 8.1) (watered)**
Wind: virtually nil Weather: Cloudy

## 2133 CROWNHOTEL-BAWTRY.COM H'CAP 1m (S)
**4:50** (4:54) (Class 4) (0-80,80) 4-Y-O+ **£4,690** (£1,395; £697; £348) **Stalls** Centre

Form RPR
0-00 **1** **Nicholas T**[19] 1677 5-8-13 **72** FranBerry 15 87
(Jim Goldie) *hld up in rr: swtchd rt to outer and gd hdwy 2f out: rdn and qcknd to ld ins fnl f: sn clr* **16/1**
320- **2** *3 ¼* **Inexes**[206] 7066 5-9-4 **77** BarryMcHugh 16 85
(Marjorie Fife) *hld up towards rr: hdwy over 2f out: rdn over 1f out: kpt on fnl f* **33/1**
06-2 **3** *1 ½* **Desert Ruler**[18] 1700 4-8-13 **72** JackGarritty 14 77
(Jedd O'Keeffe) *hld up in midfield: hdwy over 2f out: swtchd lft and rdn jst over 1f out: kpt on fnl f* **9/2**[1]
66-0 **4** *shd* **Hanseatic**[27] 1517 8-9-2 **75** (t) CamHardie 18 79
(Michael Easterby) *chsd ldrs on outer: hdwy and cl up 2f out: rdn over 1f out: sn drvn and kpt on same pce* **12/1**
40-0 **5** *1 ½* **Pumaflor (IRE)**[12] 1832 5-9-7 **80** ConnorBeasley 1 81
(Richard Whitaker) *hld up: hdwy 2f out: rdn over 1f out: styd on wl fnl f* **25/1**
36-4 **6** *hd* **Frozen Lake (USA)**[44] 1224 5-8-8 **67** HarryBentley 2 67
(Mary Hambro) *cl up: rdn along over 2f out: drvn over 1f out: wknd fnl f* **11/1**
30- **7** *nk* **Midnight Macchiato (IRE)**[245] 5878 4-9-7 **80** AdamKirby 17 80
(David Brown) *cl up on outer: chal over 2f out: rdn wl over 1f out: led appr fnl f: sn hdd and drvn: edgd lft and wknd* **10/1**[3]
50-0 **8** *¾* **Flyboy (IRE)**[19] 1677 4-9-4 **77** (v) DavidNolan 4 75
(David O'Meara) *nvr bttr than midfield* **20/1**
45-1 **9** *nk* **Chaplin Bay (IRE)**[15] 1778 5-9-4 **77** JamesSullivan 6 74
(Ruth Carr) *hld up towards rr: hdwy over 2f out: sn rdn and n.d* **12/1**
1-00 **10** *1 ¼* **Amood (IRE)**[15] 1778 6-9-3 **76** MartinLane 8 70
(Simon West) *bhd: rdn along wl over 1f out: styd on fnl f* **20/1**
45-2 **11** *1 ¾* **Marcano (IRE)**[19] 1687 5-9-3 **76** (t) RyanTate 9 66
(Rod Millman) *chsd ldrs: rdn along over 2f out: sn drvn and wknd* **9/1**[2]
00-5 **12** *hd* **Off Art**[18] 1706 7-8-12 **74** (p) RachelRichardson(3) 11 64
(Tim Easterby) *slt ld: pushed along over 2f out: rdn and hdd wl over 1f out: sn drvn and wknd* **12/1**
4365 **13** *shd* **Boots And Spurs**[27] 1512 8-9-5 **78** (v) JosephineGordon 13 68
(Scott Dixon) *chsd ldrs: rdn along over 2f out: sn drvn and wknd* **20/1**
210- **14** *3* **Tomahawk Kid**[183] 7671 4-9-6 **79** GeorgeDowning 7 62
(Ian Williams) *prom: cl up 1/2-way: rdn to ld wl over 1f out: hdd and drvn ent fnl f: wknd* **14/1**
0-00 **15** *3 ½* **Royal Reserve**[7] 1969 4-8-11 **70** StevieDonohoe 10 45
(Ian Williams) *a bhd* **50/1**
00-0 **16** *1 ½* **Our Boy Jack (IRE)**[22] 1606 8-8-11 **77** (p) CallumRodriguez(7) 5 48
(Conor Dore) *in tch: pushed along over 3f out: rdn wl over 2f out: sn wknd* **100/1**
1/0- **D** *2 ½* **Marylebone**[358] 1992 4-9-7 **80** DougieCostello 3 46
(Ed Walker) *in tch: pushed along 3f out: rdn along over 2f out: sn lost pl: bhd whn eased fnl f* **9/2**[1]

1m 38.36s (-0.94) **Going Correction** -0.05s/f (Good) **17** Ran SP% **123.4**
Speed ratings (Par 105): **102,98,97,97,95 95,95,94,94,92 91,90,90,87,84 82,80**
CSF £479.04 CT £1821.79 TOTE £20.30: £5.20, £7.90, £1.70, £2.90; EX 823.20 Trifecta £3584.40 Part Won..
**Owner** W M Johnstone **Bred** W M Johnstone **Trained** Uplawmoor, E Renfrews
■ Stewards' Enquiry : Dougie Costello 2 day ban (13/15 May) - failed to weigh in

**FOCUS**
A competitive handicap run at a sound pace. It paid to race towards the stands rail with the first four home drawn 15,16,14 and 18. The winner has been rated back to his best.

## 2134 FINE AND COUNTRY "NEWCOMERS" MAIDEN STKS 5f 3y
**5:25** (5:28) (Class 5) 2-Y-O **£2,911** (£866; £432; £216) **Stalls** Centre

Form RPR
**1** **Koditime (IRE)** 2-9-5 0 AdamKirby 6 80
(Clive Cox) *trckd ldrs: hdwy over 1f out: swtchd lft and rdn to chal ent fnl f: kpt on wl to ld last 75 yds* **7/2**[1]
**2** *½* **Dahik (IRE)** 2-9-5 0 JimCrowley 8 78
(Roger Varian) *cl up: led over 2f out: rdn: green and edgd rt jst over 1f out: sn jnd and drvn: hdd and no ex last 75 yds* **5/1**[3]
**3** *1 ¼* **Jellmood** 2-9-5 0 DanielMuscutt 4 74
(Marco Botti) *trckd ldrs: hdwy 2f out: rdn and ev ch over 1f out: kpt on same pce fnl f* **12/1**
**4** *shd* **Central City (IRE)** 2-9-5 0 JosephineGordon 12 73
(Hugo Palmer) *chsd ldrs on outer: hdwy 2f out: rdn over 1f out: kpt on same pce fnl f* **9/2**[2]
**5** *2* **Dontgiveuponbob** 2-9-5 0 DavidNolan 11 66
(Richard Fahey) *towards rr: pushed along and sltly outpcd 1/2-way: hdwy over 1f out: swtchd lft and kpt on wl fnl f* **14/1**
**6** *1* **Funkadelic** 2-9-5 0 PJMcDonald 13 63
(Ben Haslam) *t.k.h: towards rr: hdwy 2f out: rdn and edgd lft ent fnl f: kpt on* **50/1**
**7** *3 ¼* **Angel Force (IRE)** 2-9-0 0 ConnorBeasley 10 46
(David C Griffiths) *dwlt: rr tl hdwy wl over 1f out: kpt on fnl f* **50/1**
**8** *1 ¾* **Levante Player (IRE)** 2-9-5 0 BenCurtis 3 45
(Tom Dascombe) *chsd ldrs: rdn along over 2f out: sn wknd* **11/1**
**9** *¾* **Darkanna (IRE)** 2-9-0 0 PaulHanagan 5 37
(Richard Fahey) *t.k.h: prom: rdn along wl over 1f out: sn wknd* **6/1**
**10** *1* **Shay C** 2-9-5 0 NeilFarley 2 38
(Declan Carroll) *led: rdn along and hdd jst over 2f out: sn wknd* **25/1**
**11** *1* **June Dog** 2-9-5 0 SeanLevey 9 35
(Richard Hannon) *towards rr: effrt and sme hdwy over 2f out: sn rdn and wknd* **13/2**
**12** *½* **Lord Of The Glen** 2-9-5 0 SamJames 1 33
(Jim Goldie) *dwlt: a rr* **50/1**

1m 0.04s (-0.46) **Going Correction** -0.05s/f (Good) **12** Ran SP% **117.1**
Speed ratings (Par 92): **101,100,98,98,94 93,88,85,84,82 80,80**
CSF £19.89 TOTE £4.50: £1.90, £1.90, £3.80; EX 22.50 Trifecta £158.00.
**Owner** Martin McHale & Partner **Bred** Tally-Ho Stud **Trained** Lambourn, Berks

**FOCUS**
An interesting maiden run at a steady pace.

## 2135 CHINA ROSE OF BAWTRY MAIDEN STKS 7f 6y
**6:00** (6:02) (Class 4) 3-Y-O+ **£5,175** (£1,540; £769; £384) **Stalls** Centre

Form RPR
32-3 **1** **Firefright (IRE)**[11] 1862 3-9-1 86 JamesDoyle 5 82
(Jeremy Noseda) *cl up: led 5f out: hdd 2f out and sn pushed along: rdn over 1f out: chal ent fnl f: led last 120 yds: kpt on wl* **5/4**[1]
5-2 **2** *½* **Mountain Angel (IRE)**[112] 127 3-9-1 0 HarryBentley 11 80
(Roger Varian) *in tch on outer: hdwy over 2f out: rdn and ev ch whn n.m.r nr stands rail ent fnl f: kpt on* **9/2**[2]
2 **3** *1* **Made Of Honour (IRE)**[27] 1513 3-8-7 0 JordanVaughan(3) 12 72
(K R Burke) *prom on outer: hdwy to ld 2f out: rdn and edgd rt ent fnl f: drvn and kpt on same pce towards fin* **9/1**
0- **4** *nk* **Mokhalad**[347] 2340 4-10-0 0 JimCrowley 4 81
(Sir Michael Stoute) *led 2f: prom: rdn along 2f out: drvn and kpt on same pce fnl f* **8/1**
**5** *1* **Akdaar** 3-9-1 0 DanielMuscutt 7 73
(Roger Varian) *trckd ldrs: pushed along 2f out: rdn over 1f out: kpt on fnl f* **20/1**
**6** *½* **Gilded Reflection**[347] 2351 4-9-9 84 FranBerry 10 72
(Ralph Beckett) *chsd ldrs: rdn along 2f out: wknd appr fnl f* **5/1**[3]
**7** *5* **Ruled By The Moon** 3-9-3 0 ow2 DavidNolan 1 61
(Ivan Furtado) *dwlt: a towards rr* **100/1**
**8** *2 ¼* **Rubens Dream** 3-9-1 0 PaulHanagan 2 53
(Charles Hills) *in tch: pushed along 3f out: sn rdn and wknd fnl 2f* **14/1**
4 **9** *5* **Kensington Palace (IRE)**[13] 1818 4-10-0 0 BarryMcHugh 6 44
(Marjorie Fife) *t.k.h: trckd ldrs: pushed along over 3f out: sn rdn and outpcd* **100/1**
-5 **10** *10* **Full Tilt Lad (IRE)**[18] 1701 3-9-1 0 BenCurtis 3 12
(Tim Easterby) *dwlt: a bhd* **100/1**

1m 27.66s (1.36) **Going Correction** -0.05s/f (Good)
**WFA** 3 from 4yo+ 13lb **10** Ran SP% **114.8**
Speed ratings (Par 105): **90,89,88,87,86 86,80,77,72,60**
CSF £6.66 TOTE £2.10: £1.10, £2.20, £2.90; EX 8.30 Trifecta £37.90.
**Owner** Mrs Susan Roy **Bred** Mighty Universe Ltd **Trained** Newmarket, Suffolk

**FOCUS**
The pace was steady for this fair maiden. The winner has been rated close to his maiden runs.

## 2136 ZINIZ ITALIAN RESTAURANT OF BAWTRY H'CAP 1m 2f 43y
**6:35** (6:36) (Class 3) (0-95,95) 4-Y-O+ **£7,762** (£2,310; £1,154; £577) **Stalls** Low

Form RPR
145- **1** **Fidaawy**[213] 6884 4-9-6 **94** (h[1]) JimCrowley 2 103+
(Sir Michael Stoute) *set stdy pce: rdn and qcknd clr wl over 1f out: drvn last 100 yds: kpt on* **2/1**[1]
124- **2** *½* **Sam Missile (IRE)**[171] 7869 4-8-13 **87** DanielMuscutt 11 94
(James Fanshawe) *hld up towards rr: hdwy 3f out: rdn along over 1f out: chsd wnr and drvn ins fnl f: kpt on wl towards fin* **3/1**[2]
3/0 **3** *2 ¼* **Ashkoul (FR)**[18] 1704 4-9-4 **92** BenCurtis 3 95
(Michael Appleby) *trckd ldrs: hdwy on inner 3f out: chsd wnr wl over 1f out: sn rdn: drvn and kpt on same pce fnl f* **33/1**
20-0 **4** *1* **Marsh Pride**[17] 1734 5-8-13 **87** PJMcDonald 1 88
(K R Burke) *trckd ldng pair: hdwy to chse wnr 3f out: rdn along over 2f out: drvn wl over 1f out: kpt on same pce* **10/1**
100- **5** *nse* **Banish (USA)**[171] 7869 4-9-3 **91** (bt) JamesDoyle 10 92
(Hugo Palmer) *hld up towards rr: hdwy on inner over 3f out: chsd ldrs over 2f out: sn rdn and kpt on fnl f* **15/2**
024/ **6** *3 ½* **Farquhar (IRE)**[609] 5852 6-9-7 **95** AdamKirby 4 89
(Michael Appleby) *dwlt and racd awkwardly in rr early: sme hdwy wl over 2f out: sn pushed along and n.d* **10/1**

113- **7** *hd* **Just Hiss**[203] 7153 4-8-11 **88**.......... RachelRichardson(3) 6 82
(Tim Easterby) *trckd ldrs: pushed along over 3f out: rdn along wl over 2f out: sn btn* **13/2**[3]

30-0 **8** *3 1/4* **Maraakib (IRE)**[9] 1911 5-8-10 **87**.......... ShelleyBirkett(3) 5 75
(David O'Meara) *chsd wnr: rdn along over 3f out: sn wknd* **16/1**

2m 8.72s (-0.68) **Going Correction** -0.025s/f (Good) **8** Ran SP% **110.4**
Speed ratings (Par 107): **101,100,98,98,97 95,95,92**
CSF £7.35 CT £128.80 TOTE £2.80: £1.10, £1.40, £5.40; EX 9.50 Trifecta £164.10.
**Owner** Hamdan Al Maktoum **Bred** Shadwell Estate Company Limited **Trained** Newmarket, Suffolk

**FOCUS**
A fair handicap run at an even tempo. The third has been rated close to his French form.

## 2137 DELUXE HAIR & BEAUTY LOUNGE H'CAP 1m 3f 197y
**7:05** (7:05) (Class 5) (0-70,71) 3-Y-O **£3,234** (£962; £481; £240) **Stalls** Low

Form RPR

5225 **1** **The Last Debutante**[37] 1331 3-9-2 **64**.......... FrannyNorton 5 70
(Mark Johnston) *sn led: pushed along 3f out: rdn wl over 1f out: jnd and drvn ent fnl f: kpt on gamely towards fin* **9/2**[2]

063 **2** *nse* **Archibelle**[50] 1122 3-8-13 **64**.......... NathanEvans(3) 8 69
(R Mike Smith) *hld up in rr: hdwy wl over 2f out: trckd ldrs wl over 1f out: swtchd lft and rdn to chal ent fnl f: sn disp ld and drvn: ev ch tl no ex nr line* **25/1**

2214 **3** *5* **Moneyoryourlife**[21] 1623 3-9-3 **65**.......... SeanLevey 6 62
(Richard Hannon) *t.k.h: hld up: hdwy to trck ldrs 3f out: rdn 2f out and sn chal: ev ch ent fnl f: sn drvn and kpt on same pce* **7/2**[1]

64-0 **4** *1* **Mr Davies**[28] 1497 3-9-9 **71**.......... AdamKirby 4 66
(David Brown) *hld up in tch: hdwy over 4f out: chsd ldng pair and rdn 2f out: drvn over 1f out: kpt on one pce* **7/2**[1]

23 **5** *nk* **Baltic Eagle (GER)**[10] 1877 3-9-3 **68**.......... MarcMonaghan(3) 7 64
(Rune Haugen) *trckd ldrs: hdwy 4f out: rdn along 2f out: sn drvn and kpt on one pce* **8/1**

500- **6** *1 3/4* **Sheriff Garrett (IRE)**[220] 6681 3-8-7 **58**.......... RachelRichardson(3) 1 50
(Tim Easterby) *chsd ldrs: rdn along over 3f out: wknd wl over 2f out* **14/1**

640- **7** *3/4* **Babalugats (IRE)**[220] 6681 3-8-2 **50** oh4.......... JamesSullivan 2 41
(Tim Easterby) *a rr* **33/1**

60-6 **8** *14* **Delannoy**[24] 1551 3-9-7 **69**.......... CharlesBishop 9 38
(Eve Johnson Houghton) *racd wd and sn chsng wnr: rdn along over 3f out: sn drvn and wknd* **5/1**[3]

056 **9** *15* **Swallow Dancer**[54] 1069 3-8-7 **55**.......... JosephineGordon 3
(Harry Dunlop) *prom: rdn along over 4f out: sn wknd* **9/1**

2m 33.3s (-1.60) **Going Correction** -0.025s/f (Good) **9** Ran SP% **113.9**
Speed ratings (Par 98): **104,103,100,99,99 98,98,88,78**
CSF £104.04 CT £435.46 TOTE £5.30: £2.10, £6.20, £1.30; EX 110.80 Trifecta £324.50.
**Owner** Netherfield House Stud **Bred** Newsells Park Stud **Trained** Middleham Moor, N Yorks

**FOCUS**
Plenty of unexposed runners in this handicap which was run at a steady pace. The third has been rated a bit below his AW form for now.

## 2138 ORIGIN BROADBAND SUPERFAST FILLIES' H'CAP 7f 6y
**7:35** (7:38) (Class 4) (0-80,80) 4-Y-O+ **£5,175** (£1,540; £769; £384) **Stalls** Centre

Form RPR

6-35 **1** **Hells Babe**[35] 1368 4-9-4 **77**.......... AdamKirby 1 87
(Michael Appleby) *mde all: rdn wl over 1f out: drvn and hung rt ins fnl f: kpt on wl towards fin* **8/1**

35-6 **2** *1 1/2* **Florenza**[27] 1512 4-9-7 **80**.......... PJMcDonald 7 86
(Chris Fairhurst) *trckd wnr: hdwy wl over 1f out: sn rdn and ev ch: swtchd lft ins fnl f: kpt on* **6/1**[3]

050- **3** *1* **Company Asset (IRE)**[204] 7108 4-9-4 **77**.......... KevinStott 5 80
(Kevin Ryan) *hld up towards rr: hdwy wl over 2f out: rdn wl over 1f out: sn chsd ldng pair: drvn and kpt on same pce fnl f* **13/2**

51-2 **4** *3/4* **Karisma (IRE)**[9] 1897 4-9-6 **79**.......... JamesDoyle 4 80
(Roger Varian) *trckd ldng pair: hdwy over 2f out: rdn wl over 1f out: drvn and one pce ins fnl f* **2/1**[1]

4-20 **5** *3 1/4* **Invermere**[15] 1766 4-9-7 **80**.......... PaulHanagan 2 73
(Richard Fahey) *trckd ldrs: effrt over 2f out: sn rdn along and no imp* **3/1**[2]

50-0 **6** *3/4* **Rosamaria (IRE)**[10] 1879 4-8-7 **66**.......... JoeDoyle 3 56
(Julie Camacho) *hld up in rr: hdwy 2f out: sn rdn and kpt on fnl f* **25/1**

5100 **7** *1/2* **Lady Lydia (IRE)**[15] 1771 6-9-5 **78**..........(p) DanielMuscutt 6 67
(Gay Kelleway) *dwlt: in tch: rdn along over 2f out: wknd wl over 1f out* **40/1**

600- **8** *3 3/4* **Quick N Quirky (IRE)**[210] 6956 4-9-5 **78**..........(p) DavidAllan 8 57
(Tim Easterby) *trckd ldrs: rdn along 2f out: wknd over 1f out* **12/1**

1m 25.42s (-0.88) **Going Correction** -0.05s/f (Good) **8** Ran SP% **111.0**
Speed ratings (Par 102): **103,101,100,99,95 94,94,89**
CSF £51.71 CT £323.06 TOTE £8.00: £2.80, £1.80, £2.20; EX 46.30 Trifecta £234.80.
**Owner** Mrs Lucinda White **Bred** Mrs Lucinda White (mulbrooke Stud) **Trained** Oakham, Rutland

**FOCUS**
A fair fillies' handicap. It was run at a steady pace and it paid to race handy. It's been rated at face value with the runner-up to form.

## 2139 EASTSIDE MAGAZINE MAIDEN STKS 5f 3y
**8:05** (8:07) (Class 5) 3-Y-O+ **£3,067** (£905; £453) **Stalls** Centre

Form RPR

**1** **Lahore (USA)** 3-9-4 0.......... JamesDoyle 2 82+
(Roger Varian) *dwlt: sn trcking ldrs: green and pushed along over 2f out: swtchd lft and hdwy to chal over 1f out: rdn to ld ins fnl f: edgd rt and kpt on wl* **1/1**[1]

25- **2** *1 3/4* **Liquid (IRE)**[301] 3873 3-9-4 0.......... PhillipMakin 4 75
(David Barron) *cl up: led 3f out: rdn and hung rt ent fnl f: sn hdd: drvn and kpt on wl fnl 100 yds* **5/1**[3]

52- **3** *nse* **Rebecca Rocks**[201] 7216 3-8-13 0.......... DaneO'Neill 3 70
(Henry Candy) *led: hdd 3f out: cl up: rdn wl over 1f out and ev ch: drvn ent fnl f: kpt on* **10/3**[2]

4- **4** *4 1/2* **Primanora**[329] 2886 4-9-9 0.......... AdamKirby 5 58
(Michael Appleby) *chsd ldrs: rdn along 2f out: sn drvn and one pce* **12/1**

**5** *4* **Kodiac Pearl (IRE)** 3-8-13 0.......... LukeMorris 6 39
(Robert Cowell) *green: in tch: rdn along and chsd ldrs over 2f out: sn wknd* **8/1**

60 **6** *6* **Tartufo Classico**[25] 1543 4-9-11 0.......... NathanEvans(3) 1 27
(Derek Shaw) *rr: rdn along bef 1/2-way: sn outpcd and bhd* **100/1**

59.14s (-1.36) **Going Correction** -0.05s/f (Good)
**WFA** 3 from 4yo 10lb **6** Ran SP% **109.5**
Speed ratings (Par 103): **108,105,105,97,91 81**
CSF £6.09 TOTE £2.00: £1.30, £2.30; EX 5.30 Trifecta £13.30.
**Owner** Prince A A Faisal **Bred** Nawara Stud Company Ltd **Trained** Newmarket, Suffolk

**FOCUS**
An interesting sprint maiden. The second and third have been rated close to their 2yo marks.

T/Plt: £130.00 to a £1 stake. Pool: £62,842.70 - 352.72 winning units T/Qpdt: £27.20 to a £1 stake. Pool: £6,203.82 - 168.3 winning units **Joe Rowntree**

# HAYDOCK (L-H)
Saturday, April 29

**OFFICIAL GOING: Good to firm (8.2) (watered)**
Wind: Light breeze, across home straight Weather: Cloudy, sunny spells

## 2140 LIVE CASINO AT 188BET H'CAP 7f 212y
**1:30** (1:32) (Class 5) (0-70,72) 4-Y-O+ **£4,851** (£1,443; £721; £360) **Stalls** Low

Form RPR

400- **1** **La Celebs Ville (IRE)**[185] 7609 4-9-6 **69**..........(p) RichardKingscote 4 80
(Tom Dascombe) *trckd ldrs on inner: plld out to ld 2f out: sn hrd rdn: hld on wl towards fin* **8/1**

260- **2** *1/2* **Whitkirk**[186] 7601 4-9-0 **63**.......... TomQueally 10 73
(Jedd O'Keeffe) *chsd ldr: ev ch 2f out: r.o wl u.p last 2f but nt catch wnr* **14/1**

5566 **3** *nk* **King Oswald (USA)**[24] 1560 4-8-7 **56**..........(p[1]) RyanPowell 13 65
(James Unett) *hld up early: hdwy on outer 4f out: rdn 2f out: ev ch ins fnl f: hld last 100 yds* **25/1**

6021 **4** *nk* **Cosmic Ray**[17] 1735 5-8-11 **60**..........(h) AndrewMullen 1 68
(Les Eyre) *mid-div on inner: rdn over 2f out: nt pce to chal ldrs: but styd on wl* **8/1**

3102 **5** *1 3/4* **Chiswick Bey (IRE)**[18] 1706 9-9-1 **71**.......... ConnorMurtagh(7) 8 75
(Richard Fahey) *mid-div: hdwy 3f out: pushed along and one pce fnl 2f* **15/2**[3]

00-6 **6** *1 3/4* **Crazy Tornado (IRE)**[17] 1717 4-9-4 **67**..........(h) JamieSpencer 2 67
(Keith Dalgleish) *hld up in rr hdwy and nt clr run over 2f out: one pce* **11/2**[1]

0-01 **7** *1/2* **Blue Jacket (USA)**[17] 1721 6-9-0 **63**.......... BarryMcHugh 6 62
(Dianne Sayer) *chsd ldrs: rdn 2f out: no ex fnl f* **12/1**

22-4 **8** *hd* **Someone Exciting**[17] 1717 4-9-0 **63**.......... PatCosgrave 7 61
(David Thompson) *slowly away: keen: hdwy over 1f out: styd on one pce* **9/1**

-064 **9** *5* **Adventureman**[17] 1735 5-8-10 **59**..........(p) JackGarritty 9 46
(Ruth Carr) *led tl rdn and hdd 2f out: wknd* **8/1**

033- **10** *4 1/2* **Energia Flavio (BRZ)**[147] 8206 6-9-4 **67**.......... GrahamLee 3 43
(Patrick Morris) *mid-div: rdn 2f out: fdd* **8/1**

4001 **11** *3 3/4* **Pivotman**[22] 1610 9-9-4 **70**..........(bt) NathanEvans(3) 5 38
(Michael Easterby) *mid-div: short-lived effrt 3f out: rdn and wknd qckly* **13/2**[2]

30-0 **12** *1* **Major Assault**[85] 545 4-9-2 **65**.......... JohnFahy 12 31
(Matthew Salaman) *hld up: nvr nr ldrs* **50/1**

563- **13** *3 1/4* **Captain Peaky**[197] 7327 4-8-13 **62**.......... CamHardie 11 20
(Patrick Holmes) *chse ldrs: rdn and weakend over 2f out* **50/1**

000- **14** *4* **Dutch Barney**[290] 2448 7-8-0 **56** oh11.......... JaneElliott(7) 14 5
(Barry Leavy) *a in rr* **150/1**

1m 40.58s (-3.12) **Going Correction** -0.25s/f (Firm) **14** Ran SP% **117.7**
Speed ratings (Par 103): **105,104,104,103,102 100,99,99,94,90 86,85,82,78**
CSF £110.32 CT £2736.99 TOTE £10.60: £3.60, £6.30, £9.20; EX 164.50 Trifecta £2871.40 Part Won..
**Owner** Newport Rangers **Bred** Bernard Cooke **Trained** Malpas, Cheshire
■ Stewards' Enquiry : Ryan Powell 2 day ban (13/15 May) - used whip above the permitted level

**FOCUS**
The watered ground (5mm on Thursday and 4mm on Friday) was given as good to firm (GoingStick: 8.2). All races run over the Inner Home Straight. Stalls: Inside: 7f and 1m; Centre: 1m2f and 1m4f. Race distance increased by 8yds. A modest handicap. It's been rated around the second and fourth.

## 2141 CHAMPIONS LEAGUE BETTING AT 188BET H'CAP 7f 212y
**2:05** (2:05) (Class 2) (0-105,104) 4-Y-O+
**£20,231** (£6,058; £3,029; £1,514; £757; £380) **Stalls** Low

Form RPR

0-45 **1** **Quixote (GER)**[25] 1546 7-8-6 **89**.......... JosephineGordon 7 98
(David Loughnane) *hld up: hdwy 2f out: qcknd wl to ld ins fnl furong: r.o wl: comf* **11/1**

120- **2** *3 3/4* **Early Morning (IRE)**[227] 6482 6-9-5 **102**.......... JimCrowley 4 102
(Harry Dunlop) *chaaed ldrs: led over 2f out: hdd ins fnal f: styd on but no ch w wnr* **7/2**[2]

200 **3** *nk* **Kyllachy Gala**[65] 888 4-9-2 **104**.......... GeorgeWood(5) 1 104
(Marco Botti) *trckd ldrs: chal 2f out: rdn and one pce fnl f* **20/1**

2-00 **4** *1/2* **Top Notch Tonto (IRE)**[28] 1494 7-8-12 **102**..........(t[1]) BenRobinson(7) 10 101
(Brian Ellison) *slowly away: hdwy 2f out: rdn and styd on wl* **12/1**

0-22 **5** *1/2* **War Glory (IRE)**[15] 1769 4-8-10 **93**.......... PatDobbs 9 90
(Richard Hannon) *mid-div: outpcd appr 2f out: styd on ins fnl f* **11/2**[3]

06-0 **6** *1 1/2* **Poeta Diletto**[28] 1500 4-9-7 **104**.......... AntonioFresu 8 98
(Marco Botti) *trckd ldr: ev ch 2f out: rdn and fdd* **33/1**

5200 **7** *1/2* **Mythical Madness**[15] 1773 6-8-11 **101**..........(p) PatrickVaughan(7) 6 94
(David O'Meara) *mid div: ch 2f out: wknd ins fnl fjurlong* **50/1**

1360 **8** *3/4* **Alfred Hutchinson**[15] 1773 9-8-10 **98**..........(p) JoshDoyle(5) 5 89
(David O'Meara) *a in rr: nvr a factor* **25/1**

40-0 **9** *2 1/4* **Imshivalla (IRE)**[18] 1704 6-8-2 **88**..........(h) SammyJoBell(3) 2 74
(Richard Fahey) *led: hdd over 2f out: wknd qckly* **20/1**

31-3 **10** *5* **El Vip (IRE)**[15] 1766 4-8-11 **94**.......... FrankieDettori 3 68
(Luca Cumani) *keen: in tch tl rdn and weakend 2f out* **5/4**[1]

1m 39.05s (-4.65) **Going Correction** -0.25s/f (Firm) **10** Ran SP% **116.3**
Speed ratings (Par 109): **113,109,108,108,107 106,105,105,102,97**
CSF £46.14 CT £788.77 TOTE £14.30: £3.90, £1.50, £5.10; EX 59.40 Trifecta £1085.50.
**Owner** Weloveracing Ltd **Bred** Siftung Gestut Fahrhof **Trained** Market Drayton, Shropshire

**FOCUS**
Race distance increased by 8yds. The pace picked up a fair way out and the winner came from the back, but it was still eyecatching the way he drew right away in the closing stages. The winner has been rated back to something like his old best, with the second and third a bit off.

## 2142 BEST ODDS GUARANTEED AT 188BET H'CAP 6f 212y
**2:40** (2:40) (Class 2) 4-Y-O+
**£28,012** (£8,388; £4,194; £2,097; £1,048; £526) **Stalls** Low

Form RPR

104- **1** **Afjaan (IRE)**[196] 7354 5-9-1 **100**.......... FrankieDettori 3 111
(William Haggas) *hld up in rr: tk clsr order 3f oiut: shkn up to ld ins fnl f: sn clr: easily* **3/1**[1]

3521 **2** *1 ¾* **Oh This Is Us (IRE)**[15] 1766 4-9-10 **109**.............................. PatDobbs 1 115
(Richard Hannon) *hld up: pushed along and hdwy 3f out: n.m.r 2f out: sn in clr: rdn and r.o wl fnl f* **7/2[2]**

111- **3** *¾* **Fawaareq (IRE)**[295] 4104 4-8-8 **93**.............................. JimCrowley 8 97
(Owen Burrows) *keen in mid-div: pushed along and hdwy to ld appr fnl f: sn rdn and one pce* **11/2**

6-06 **4** *2 ¾* **Calder Prince (IRE)**[72] 775 4-8-7 **92**.................... RichardKingscote 9 89
(Tom Dascombe) *led tl hdd and rdn over 1f out: no ex* **8/1**

-331 **5** *2* **Twin Appeal (IRE)**[14] 1799 6-8-8 **93**..............................(b) BenCurtis 2 84
(David Barron) *keen in mid-div: hdwy on ins 3f out: sn drvn: one pce u.p fnl 2f* **9/2[3]**

00-0 **6** *¾* **Russian Realm**[14] 1799 7-8-3 **88**.............................. CamHardie 4 77
(Paul Midgley) *prom: pushed along and lost pl fr 3f out* **50/1**

1021 **7** *1* **Zoravan (USA)**[27] 1512 4-7-9 **85** oh1....................(v) ShirleyTeasdale(5) 5 71
(Keith Dalgleish) *plld hrd in mid-div: chsng ldrs 3f out: pushed along 2f out: sn rdn and weaknd* **10/1**

010- **8** *nk* **Stamp Hill (IRE)**[224] 6556 4-8-1 **93**.................... ConnorMurtagh(7) 10 79
(Richard Fahey) *w ldrs tl rdn and no ex fr 2f out* **12/1**

01-0 **9** *10* **Penwortham (IRE)**[14] 1799 4-8-0 **88**.................... SammyJoBell(3) 6 47
(Richard Fahey) *prom tl rdn and wknd qckly fr 3f out* **20/1**

1m 26.06s (-4.64) **Going Correction** -0.25s/f (Firm) **9** Ran SP% **115.4**
Speed ratings (Par 109): **116,114,113,110,107 106,105,105,93**
CSF £13.54 CT £54.33 TOTE £4.90: £2.00, £1.30, £1.80; EX 13.40 Trifecta £38.70.
**Owner** Al Shaqab Racing **Bred** Haras Du Logis Saint Germain **Trained** Newmarket, Suffolk

**FOCUS**
Race distance increased by 8yds. The pace was on here and it played into the hands of the hold-up horses, but the form looks strong, with the runner-up coming here off a career-best and the winner and third looking like improvers. The second has been rated as running as well as ever.

## 2143 188BET.CO.UK MAIDEN STKS (PLUS 10 RACE) 1m 3f 140y
**3:15** (3:15) (Class 4) 3-Y-O **£5,822** (£1,732; £865; £432) **Stalls** Centre

Form RPR

2-2 **1** **Maghfoor**[23] 1584 3-9-5 0.............................. JimCrowley 3 86
(Saeed bin Suroor) *trckd ldr gng wl: led appr 2f out: sn chal and rdn: responded to press and hld on wl ins fnl f* **11/8[1]**

**2** *¾* **Humble Hero (IRE)** 3-9-5 0.............................. PatCosgrave 4 85
(William Haggas) *slowly away: hdwy over 3f out: chal fnl f: r.o wl and nt knocked abt: but hld by wnr: promising* **9/4[2]**

3 **3** *2* **Bristol Missile (USA)**[19] 1682 3-9-5 0.............................. PatDobbs 2 82
(Richard Hannon) *trckd ldrs: hdwy 3f out: ev ch 2f out: rdn briefly bef one pce under hands and heels fnl f* **5/2[3]**

4 **4** *11* **Royal Headley (IRE)**[19] 1676 3-9-0 0.............................. JoshDoyle(5) 5 64
(David O'Meara) *led tl hdd bef 2 out: pushed along and wknd* **25/1**

**5** *10* **Striker (IRE)** 3-9-5 0.............................. RichardKingscote 1 48
(Tom Dascombe) *trckd ldrs: lost pl and u.p 3f out: fdd* **16/1**

2m 34.21s (1.21) **Going Correction** -0.25s/f (Firm) **5** Ran SP% **111.2**
Speed ratings (Par 100): **88,87,86,78,72**
CSF £4.85 TOTE £2.20: £1.10, £1.60; EX 4.50 Trifecta £8.90.
**Owner** Godolphin **Bred** Shadwell Estate Company Limited **Trained** Newmarket, Suffolk

**FOCUS**
Race distance reduced by 26yds. This looked a fair maiden but they didn't go that quick early. The winner set the standard and has been rated to the better view of his debut run.

## 2144 188BET EBF STALLIONS MAIDEN FILLIES' STKS (PLUS 10 RACE) 7f 212y
**3:45** (3:46) (Class 5) 3-Y-O **£3,881** (£1,155; £577; £288) **Stalls** Low

Form RPR

**1** **Downton Kitten (USA)** 3-9-0 0.............................. TomQueally 5 74+
(David Lanigan) *4th and keen early stages: hdwy 3f out: pushed along 2f out: rdn appr fnl f: styd on wl u.p to assert last 100 yds* **12/1**

05- **2** *½* **Beyond Recall**[130] 8464 3-9-0 0.............................. JamieSpencer 4 73
(Luca Cumani) *trckd ldr gng wl: hdwy to ld wl over 1f out: rdn appr fnl f: hdd last 100 yds* **6/1**

**3** *1 ¼* **Feint** 3-9-0 0.............................. PatCosgrave 3 70+
(William Haggas) *dwlt at s and lost 5 l: hdwy to chse ldrs over 2f out and received bump: n.m.r whn effrt and crossed 4th appr fnl f: one pce under hands and heels ins last: green* **9/4[2]**

34- **4** *1 ¾* **Nancy Hart**[203] 7157 3-9-0 0..............................(h[1]) RichardKingscote 1 69
(Tom Dascombe) *trckd ldrs: 3rd on inner 4f out: n.m.r and bmpd 3rd wl over 2f out: crossed by 3rd appr fnl f: one pce* **7/4[1]**

3 **5** *2 ¾* **Western Safari (IRE)**[40] 1286 3-9-0 0.............................. PatDobbs 6 59
(Richard Hannon) *led tl pushed along and hdd over 1f out: sn btn* **7/2[3]**

1m 43.62s (-0.08) **Going Correction** -0.25s/f (Firm) **5** Ran SP% **111.3**
Speed ratings (Par 95): **90,89,88,86,83**
CSF £74.51 TOTE £8.80: £2.70, £2.40; EX 60.50 Trifecta £162.50.
**Owner** Kenneth L & Sarah K Ramsey **Bred** Kenneth L Ramsey & Sarah K Ramsey **Trained** Newmarket, Suffolk

**FOCUS**
Race distance increased by 8yds. An ordinary maiden on paper, and things got a bit messy in the closing stages. Muddling form, but the fourth and fifth have been rated close to their previous figures for now.

## 2145 TICKET GIVEAWAYS AT 188BET H'CAP 7f 212y
**4:20** (4:20) (Class 5) (0-75,76) 3-Y-O **£4,851** (£1,443; £721; £360) **Stalls** Low

Form RPR

2532 **1** **Sidewinder (IRE)**[32] 1411 3-9-6 **74**.................... RichardKingscote 4 77
(Tom Dascombe) *hld up: hdwy on outer over 3f out: rdn to chal over 1f out: led ins fnl f: r.o wl u.p* **5/1[2]**

43-3 **2** *nk* **Know Your Limit (IRE)**[19] 1685 3-9-3 **71**.................... ThomasBrown 8 73
(Ed Walker) *prom: pushed along to ld 2f out: rdn over 1f out: hdd ins fnl f: kpt on wl* **9/4[1]**

0-15 **3** *¾* **Fear The Fury (USA)**[71] 788 3-9-8 **76**.................... JamieSpencer 6 76
(K R Burke) *hld up in rr: hdwy to chse ldrs 2f out: pushed along on outer: rdn and r.o fnl f: nrst fin* **8/1**

04-0 **4** *hd* **Lunar Jet**[28] 1497 3-9-1 **69**.............................. GrahamLee 2 69
(John Mackie) *keen on inner early: trckd ldrs fr 3f out: n.m.r 2f out: rdn appr fnl f: r.o wl ins last* **11/1**

2-24 **5** *hd* **Muqaatil (USA)**[33] 1404 3-9-5 **73**.............................. PatDobbs 7 73
(Richard Hannon) *led: hdd and rdn 2f out: kpt on towards fin* **7/1**

026- **6** *1* **Casina Di Notte (IRE)**[183] 7658 3-9-2 **75**.................... GeorgeWood(5) 1 72
(Marco Botti) *hld up inner: pushed along and n.m.r 3f out: chsd ldrs 2f out: rdn and no ex* **6/1[3]**

6-31 **7** *¾* **Cloud Dragon (IRE)**[77] 681 3-9-4 **75**.................... MarcMonaghan(3) 5 70
(Hugo Palmer) *mid-div: pushed along 3f out: sn rdn and no imp* **6/1[3]**

614- **8** *9* **Allux Boy (IRE)**[235] 6213 3-9-4 **72**.............................. AndrewMullen 3 46
(Nigel Tinkler) *plld hrd in 2nd early: chsd ldr tl lost pl: rdn and wknd over 2f out* **25/1**

1m 42.15s (-1.55) **Going Correction** -0.25s/f (Firm) **8** Ran SP% **111.8**
Speed ratings (Par 98): **97,96,95,95,95 94,93,84**
CSF £15.89 CT £86.21 TOTE £5.00: £1.70, £1.40, £2.30; EX 22.70 Trifecta £75.10.
**Owner** The Sidewinder Partnership **Bred** John Hutchinson **Trained** Malpas, Cheshire

**FOCUS**
Race distance increased by 8yds. Following the general pattern for previous races on the card, it paid to be delivered late down the outside. They finished in a bit of a heap. A small pb from the winner.

## 2146 BOXING BETTING AT 188BET H'CAP 1m 2f 42y
**4:55** (4:57) (Class 4) (0-80,82) 4-Y-O+ **£8,086** (£2,406; £1,202; £601) **Stalls** Centre

Form RPR

002- **1** **Caponova (IRE)**[200] 7245 4-9-4 **75**.................... RichardKingscote 6 87+
(Tom Dascombe) *hld up in last: smooth hdwy 3f out: chal over 2f out and sn led: qcknd and wnt clr: v easily* **7/2[2]**

51-1 **2** *3* **Zain Arion (IRE)**[106] 213 4-9-5 **76**.............................. JFEgan 9 80
(John Butler) *mid-div: hdwy 3f out: chal 2f out: sn rdn: r.o wl: but no ch w wnr* **9/1**

3-00 **3** *1 ½* **London Glory**[22] 1610 4-8-8 **65**..............................(b[1]) AndrewMullen 5 66
(David Thompson) *hld up: niggled over 4f out: drvn and hdwy 3f out: r.o last 2f: nrst fin* **20/1**

-613 **4** *¾* **Boycie**[14] 1788 4-8-10 **74**.............................. TinaSmith(7) 1 74+
(Richard Hannon) *hld up inner: pushed along and ct flat footed 3f out: n.m.r on inner tl swtchd and r.o fnl 2f* **7/2[2]**

343- **5** *½* **Panko (IRE)**[194] 7418 4-9-1 **77**.............................. MitchGodwin(5) 8 76
(Ed de Giles) *keen early: trckd ldrs: hdwy to ld briefly over 2f out: rdn and outpcd* **5/2[1]**

1313 **6** *2* **Kingthistle**[18] 1707 4-9-2 **73**.............................. GrahamLee 2 68
(Rebecca Menzies) *trckd ldrs: ch over 2f out: no ex u.p* **5/1[3]**

0-06 **7** *1 ¼* **Framley Garth (IRE)**[18] 1707 5-8-5 **69**.................... PaulaMuir(7) 10 62
(Patrick Holmes) *chsd ldr: ev ch tl rdn and wknd over 2f out* **20/1**

6-0 **8** *3 ¼* **Theodorico (IRE)**[26] 1224 4-9-7 **78**.............................. JohnFahy 7 64
(David Loughnane) *led: hdd over 2f out: pushed along and fdd* **20/1**

2m 10.94s (-1.76) **Going Correction** -0.25s/f (Firm) **8** Ran SP% **114.0**
Speed ratings (Par 105): **108,105,104,103,103 101,100,98**
CSF £32.69 CT £538.48 TOTE £4.80: £1.50, £2.40, £3.50; EX 33.70 Trifecta £479.60.
**Owner** Deva Racing Bushranger Partnership **Bred** Mr & Mrs T O'Brien **Trained** Malpas, Cheshire

**FOCUS**
Race distance reduced by 15yds. Once again the winner was delivered late from behind down the outside, although this one had plenty in hand. It's been rated around the runner-up to the better view of her recent AW form.
T/Plt: £1,045.20 to a £1 stake. Pool: £97,851.39 - 68.35 winning units T/Qpdt: £22.80 to a £1 stake. Pool: £7,322.43 - 237.50 winning units **Keith McHugh**

# 1604 LEICESTER (R-H)
Saturday, April 29

**OFFICIAL GOING: Good (good to firm in places) (watered) changing to good to firm (good in places) after race 1 (2.20)**
Wind: Light behind Weather: Overcast

## 2147 TOTESCOOP6 PLAY TODAY H'CAP 6f
**2:20** (2:20) (Class 4) (0-85,83) 4-Y-O+ **£6,301** (£1,886; £943; £472; £235) **Stalls** High

Form RPR

414- **1** **Time To Exceed (IRE)**[240] 6064 4-9-0 **76**.................... RyanMoore 6 86+
(Henry Candy) *w ldr tl shkn up to ld over 1f out: rdn out* **15/8[1]**

420- **2** *1 ½* **Tanasoq (IRE)**[193] 7433 4-9-1 **77**.............................. DaneO'Neill 5 81
(Owen Burrows) *hld up: hdwy wl over 1f out: rdn and n.m.r 1f out: r.o to go 2nd wl ins fnl f* **4/1[2]**

0-50 **3** *nk* **Highly Sprung (IRE)**[12] 1831 4-9-7 **83**.............................. JoeFanning 2 86
(Mark Johnston) *led: shkn up over 2f out: hdd over 1f out: styd on same pce ins fnl f* **11/2**

60-1 **4** *¾* **Diamond Lady**[9] 1899 6-9-4 **80**.............................. AdamBeschizza 7 81
(William Stone) *chsd ldrs: rdn over 2f out: styd on same pce ins fnl f* **9/2[3]**

1316 **5** *7* **Born To Finish (IRE)**[18] 1696 4-8-12 **79**....................(p) DavidParkes(5) 1 57
(Jeremy Gask) *s.i.s: plld hrd: hdwy over 4f out: rdn over 2f out: wknd fnl f* **10/1**

460- **6** *3 ¼* **Danecase**[169] 7902 4-8-11 **73**.............................. DougieCostello 4 41
(David Dennis) *hld up: plld hrd: hdwy on outer over 2f out: wknd fnl f* **10/1**

42-3 **7** *5* **Sumou (IRE)**[15] 1761 4-9-4 **80**.............................. DavidProbert 3 32
(Milton Bradley) *plld hrd and prom: rdn over 2f out: wknd over 1f out* **16/1**

1m 12.01s (-0.99) **Going Correction** -0.175s/f (Firm) **7** Ran SP% **112.4**
Speed ratings (Par 105): **99,97,96,95,86 81,75**
CSF £9.11 TOTE £2.30: £1.60, £3.10; EX 9.70 Trifecta £35.70.
**Owner** Hunscote Stud **Bred** Hunscote Stud **Trained** Kingston Warren, Oxon

**FOCUS**
After winning the opener Ryan Moore said of the ground: "It's good to firm" and Dane O'Neill's take on it was: "Good fast ground - no jar." There was a slight change to the official description after the first. An ordinary sprint handicap in which the pace was near the stands' rail. The first four came well clear. It's been rated around the runner-up to last year's C&D form.

## 2148 TOTESCOOP6 THE MILLIONAIRE MAKER NOVICE STKS 5f
**2:55** (2:56) (Class 5) 2-Y-O **£3,881** (£1,155; £577; £288) **Stalls** High

Form RPR

2 **1** **Never Back Down (IRE)**[11] 1858 2-9-2 0.................... JamesDoyle 1 84
(Hugo Palmer) *mde all: rdn over 1f out: r.o* **1/3[1]**

**2** *nk* **Haddaf (IRE)** 2-9-2 0.............................. MartinHarley 2 83+
(James Tate) *a.p: chsd wnr over 1f out: sn rdn and ev ch: unable qck nr fin* **6/1[3]**

**3** *2 ½* **Dragons Tail (IRE)** 2-9-2 0.............................. LiamKeniry 6 74+
(Tom Dascombe) *s.i.s: hld up: hdwy 1/2-way: rdn over 1f out: styd on same pce fnl f* **12/1**

6 **4** *3 ¼* **Jedi Master (IRE)**[22] 1604 2-9-2 0.............................. TonyHamilton 5 62
(Richard Fahey) *chsd wnr tl rdn over 1f out: wknd ins fnl f* **5/1[2]**

**5** *3 ¾* **Plundered (IRE)** 2-9-2 0.............................. TedDurcan 7 49
(David Brown) *sn pushed along and prom: rdn 1/2-way: wknd over 1f out: hung rt ins fnl f* **10/1**

**6** *2 ¼* **Misty Breese (IRE)** 2-8-11 0.............................. WilliamCarson 4 36
(Paul D'Arcy) *chsd ldrs tl rdn and wknd over 1f out* **20/1**

0 **7** *½* **Bahuta Acha**[10] 1873 2-9-2 0.............................. DougieCostello 3 39
(David Loughnane) *s.s: bhd: sme hdwy 1/2-way: sn rdn: wknd wl over 1f out* **66/1**

8 2 3/4 **Colorado Dream** 2-9-2 0 ........ SteveDrowne 8 29
(George Baker) *s.i.s: sn pushed along and rn green in rr: wknd 2f out* **25/1**

1m 0.8s (0.80) **Going Correction** -0.175s/f (Firm) 8 Ran SP% **132.9**
Speed ratings (Par 92): **86,85,81,76,70 66,65,61**
CSF £4.26 TOTE £1.20: £1.10, £2.00, £2.90; EX 4.90 Trifecta £25.70.

**Owner** M M Stables **Bred** Cooneen Stud **Trained** Newmarket, Suffolk

**FOCUS**
The winner set a pretty decent standard. The fourth has been rated near his debut form.

## 2149 TOTEPOOLLIVEINFO.COM H'CAP 1m 3f 179y
**3:30** (3:32) (Class 3) (0-95,85) 3-Y-O **£9,451** (£2,829; £1,414; £708) **Stalls** Low

Form RPR
31-4 **1** **Sofia's Rock (FR)**[15] 1764 3-9-7 **85** ........ RyanMoore 2 99
(Mark Johnston) *led after 1f: sn clr: shkn up over 2f out: rdn over 1f out: styd on strly* **5/4**[1]

5-21 **2** 10 **Wefait (IRE)**[28] 1499 3-9-0 **78** ........ JamesDoyle 1 76
(Richard Hannon) *led 1f: chsd wnr tl rdn over 3f out: styd on same pce fnl 2f: wnt 2nd again over 1f out* **5/1**[3]

1- **3** 1 1/2 **Percy's Word**[222] 6623 3-9-7 **85** ........ WilliamBuick 3 81
(Simon Crisford) *chsd ldrs: rdn to chse wnr over 3f out tl over 2f out: styd on same pce* **13/2**

1 **4** 2 **Above Normal**[18] 1701 3-9-7 **85** ........ KevinStott 5 77
(Saeed bin Suroor) *dwlt and wnt lft s: hld up: hdwy to chse wnr over 2f out tl rdn: hung lft and wknd over 1f out: hung rt ins fnl f* **15/8**[2]

2m 31.79s (-2.11) **Going Correction** +0.075s/f (Good) 4 Ran SP% **109.2**
Speed ratings (Par 102): **110,103,102,101**
CSF £7.57 TOTE £2.40; EX 4.30 Trifecta £21.70.

**Owner** Mezzone Family 1 **Bred** Jean-Francois Gribomont **Trained** Middleham Moor, N Yorks

**FOCUS**
Race run over an additional 10yds. An interesting little handicap which saw a nice front-running performance from the favourite. The second and third have been rated a bit below their maiden wins for now.

## 2150 TOTEPOOL EBF STALLIONS KING RICHARD III STKS (LISTED RACE) 7f
**4:05** (4:05) (Class 1) 4-Y-O+ **£28,355** (£10,750; £5,380; £2,680; £1,345) **Stalls** High

Form RPR
220- **1** **Home Of The Brave (IRE)**[175] 7833 5-9-2 113 ........ (t) JamesDoyle 2 117
(Hugo Palmer) *mde all: shkn up over 1f out: rdn ins fnl f: r.o* **5/6**[1]

/10- **2** 1 3/4 **Tasleet**[204] 7115 4-9-2 110 ........ DaneO'Neill 4 112
(William Haggas) *chsd wnr: rdn and edgd rt over 1f out: styd on same pce wl ins fnl f* **5/1**[2]

32-0 **3** 5 **Donjuan Triumphant (IRE)**[15] 1773 4-9-2 110 ........ (t) DavidProbert 1 99
(Andrew Balding) *hld up in tch: plld hrd: shkn up and edgd rt over 2f out: styd on same pce fr over 1f out* **10/1**

1102 **4** 5 **Nimr**[15] 1773 4-9-2 109 ........ TonyHamilton 3 85
(Richard Fahey) *trckd ldrs: rdn over 2f out: wknd over 1f out* **6/1**

430- **5** 37 **So Beloved**[204] 7115 7-9-2 111 ........ RyanMoore 5
(David O'Meara) *racd alone on stands' side fnl 6f: up w the pce tl rdn over 2f out: sn edgd rt: wknd and eased* **11/2**[3]

1m 22.24s (-3.96) **Going Correction** -0.175s/f (Firm) 5 Ran SP% **110.0**
Speed ratings (Par 111): **115,113,107,101,59**
CSF £5.36 TOTE £1.50: £1.10, £2.90; EX 5.00 Trifecta £24.10.

**Owner** Godolphin **Bred** Earl Ecurie Du Grand Chene **Trained** Newmarket, Suffolk

**FOCUS**
Not the strongest renewal of this event, with a couple failing to give their running. The time was quick, 0.46sec inside the standard. The winner has been rated to a similar level as when winning this last year.

## 2151 TOTEEXACTA PICK THE 1ST & 2ND H'CAP 7f
**4:40** (4:43) (Class 5) (0-75,76) 3-Y-O **£3,881** (£1,155; £577; £288) **Stalls** High

Form RPR
1- **1** **Ocean Air (FR)**[247] 5792 3-9-7 **75** ........ MartinHarley 10 83
(James Tate) *racd centre: prom: rdn over 2f out: chsd ldr over 1f out: styd on to ld wl ins fnl f: 1st of 7 in gp* **4/1**[1]

-531 **2** 1 **Traveller (FR)**[60] 962 3-9-6 **74** ........ (t) WilliamBuick 7 79
(Charles Hills) *racd centre: led overall 1f: chsd ldr tl rdn to ld again over 1f out: hdd wl ins fnl f: 2nd of 7 in gp* **17/2**

05-5 **3** 2 1/4 **Navarone (IRE)**[14] 1801 3-9-7 **75** ........ TonyHamilton 5 74
(Richard Fahey) *racd centre: chsd ldrs: rdn over 2f out: edgd lft and no ex ins fnl f: 3rd of 7 in gp* **9/1**

36-2 **4** 1/2 **Favourite Royal (IRE)**[10] 1888 3-9-6 **74** ........ RobertWinston 4 72
(Eve Johnson Houghton) *s.i.s: hld up: racd centre: hdwy 2f out: rdn and hung lft over 1f out: styd on same pce ins fnl f: 4th of 7 in gp* **6/1**[3]

663- **5** 4 **Zebulon (IRE)**[220] 6673 3-9-6 **74** ........ RyanMoore 3 61
(Richard Hannon) *racd centre: plld hrd: led overall 6f out: rdn and hdd over 1f out: wknd ins fnl f: 5th of 7 in gp* **5/1**[2]

3-56 **6** nk **Rapid Rise (IRE)**[57] 1000 3-9-2 **73** ........ AaronJones(3) 1 59
(David Brown) *racd centre: hld up: rdn over 2f out: styd on ins fnl f: nvr nrr: 6th of 7 in gp* **20/1**

440- **7** 1 3/4 **Feel The Vibes**[232] 6289 3-9-0 **68** ........ KieranO'Neill 2 49
(Michael Blanshard) *racd centre: prom: rdn over 2f out: wknd over 1f out: last of 7 in gp* **66/1**

103- **8** 1/2 **Himself**[178] 7764 3-9-8 **76** ........ TomMarquand 9 56
(Richard Hannon) *racd towards stands' side: chsd ldr tl led that trio over 2f out: rdn: hung rt and wknd over 1f out: 1st of 3 in gp* **6/1**[3]

240- **9** 12 **Kody Ridge (IRE)**[245] 5884 3-9-3 **71** ........ (h[1]) TimmyMurphy 13 19
(David Dennis) *racd towards stands' side: hld up: bhd fr 1/2-way: 2nd of 3 in gp* **50/1**

031- **10** 7 **King Of Nepal**[164] 7974 3-9-6 **74** ........ DaneO'Neill 6 3
(Henry Candy) *led trio towards stands' side: rdn and hdd over 2f out: hung rt: wknd and eased over 1f out: last of 3 in gp* **13/2**

1m 24.41s (-1.79) **Going Correction** -0.175s/f (Firm) 10 Ran SP% **107.3**
Speed ratings (Par 98): **103,101,99,98,94 93,91,91,77,69**
CSF £32.81 CT £242.29 TOTE £4.90: £1.70, £2.40, £2.60; EX 33.80 Trifecta £244.00.

**Owner** Saeed Manana **Bred** D R Tucker **Trained** Newmarket, Suffolk

**FOCUS**
An ordinary handicap. The three who raced on the stands' side, separate from the rest, filled the last three places. The level is a bit fluid.

## 2152 TOTETRIFECTA PICK THE 1,2,3 MAIDEN STKS 1m 1f 216y
**5:10** (5:12) (Class 5) 3-Y-O+ **£3,881** (£1,155; £577; £288) **Stalls** Low

Form RPR
2 **1** **Oasis Charm**[9] 1906 3-8-11 0 ........ WilliamBuick 10 90+
(Charlie Appleby) *chsd ldrs: led over 2f out: shkn up over 1f out: pushed out* **2/1**[1]

3- **2** 1 **Mutarabby (IRE)**[173] 7849 3-8-11 0 ........ DaneO'Neill 4 87
(Saeed bin Suroor) *s.i.s: sn prom: chsd wnr 2f out: sn rdn: styd on* **2/1**[1]

54- **3** 7 **Splash Around**[226] 6523 3-8-11 0 ........ RyanMoore 3 73+
(Sir Michael Stoute) *hld up: hdwy over 2f out: shkn up over 1f out: no ex fnl f* **7/2**[2]

**4** hd **Mudajaj (USA)** 3-8-11 0 ........ DavidProbert 6 72
(Charles Hills) *hld up: hdwy over 2f out: sn rdn: no ex fnl f* **10/1**[3]

**5** 1 **Park Paddocks (IRE)** 3-8-11 0 ........ LiamJones 11 70+
(William Haggas) *s.i.s: hld up: styd on fr over 1f out: nt trble ldrs* **20/1**

60- **6** 7 **Nathan Mayer**[169] 7907 3-8-11 0 ........ JoeFanning 1 56+
(Sir Michael Stoute) *hld up: nt clr run over 2f out: nvr nr to chal* **25/1**

64 **7** 2 **Stragar**[35] 1366 3-8-4 0 ........ RayDawson(7) 8 52
(Michael Appleby) *hld up: effrt on outer over 2f out: rdn: hung rt and wknd wl over 1f out* **100/1**

00 **8** 2 1/2 **Somes Sound (IRE)**[17] 1730 3-8-4 0 ........ DavidEgan(7) 12 47
(Jane Chapple-Hyam) *hld up: rdn over 2f out: nvr on terms* **100/1**

**9** nse **Lord Kitten (USA)** 3-8-11 0 ........ MartinHarley 5 47
(David Lanigan) *hld up: bhd and pushed along 1/2-way: effrt on outer over 2f out: wknd wl over 1f out* **33/1**

44 **10** 7 **Pinnata (IRE)**[63] 925 3-8-8 0 ........ (t) AaronJones(3) 7 33
(Stuart Williams) *led: rdn and hdd over 2f out: wknd wl over 1f out* **100/1**

34- **11** 3 1/4 **Caramuru (IRE)**[222] 6623 3-8-11 0 ........ TomMarquand 2 27
(Richard Hannon) *prom: rdn over 3f out: wknd over 2f out* **16/1**

523- **12** 3 **The New Master**[407] 980 4-9-11 75 ........ TimClark(3) 9 24
(David Elsworth) *chsd ldr: ev ch over 2f out: sn rdn and wknd* **33/1**

2m 7.68s (-0.22) **Going Correction** +0.075s/f (Good)
**WFA** 3 from 4yo 17lb 12 Ran SP% **121.3**
Speed ratings (Par 103): **103,102,96,96,95 90,88,86,86,80 78,75**
CSF £5.67 TOTE £3.10: £1.90, £1.50, £1.10; EX 9.50 Trifecta £17.10.

**Owner** Godolphin **Bred** Miss K Rausing & Juddmonte Farms Ltd **Trained** Newmarket, Suffolk

**FOCUS**
Race run over an additional 10yds. This maiden has been won in recent years by Green Moon, who went on to take the Melbourne Cup, and Storm The Stars (in the frame in three Classics), while last year's winner Imperial Aviator added the London Gold Cup and runner-up Ulysses has won a couple of Group 3s. The first two did well to pull clear off what had looked to be an ordinary gallop. The third has been rated as improving a bit on his 2yo form.

## 2153 TOTEPOOL BETTING ON ALL UK RACING H'CAP 1m 1f 216y
**5:45** (5:45) (Class 5) (0-70,70) 4-Y-O+ **£3,881** (£1,155; £577; £288) **Stalls** Low

Form RPR
000- **1** **Angelical (IRE)**[150] 8155 4-8-1 **57** ........ DavidEgan(7) 5 64
(Daniel Mark Loughnane) *hld up: hdwy over 6f out: rdn and hung lft over 1f out: styd on to ld wl ins fnl f* **8/1**

3036 **2** 1 1/2 **Ravenhoe (IRE)**[2] 2108 4-9-7 **70** ........ JoeFanning 1 74
(Mark Johnston) *chsd ldr tl led over 2f out: rdn and edgd lft over 1f out: hdd wl ins fnl f* **9/2**[3]

20-0 **3** nk **Stoneboat Bill**[17] 1735 5-8-8 **62** ........ PhilDennis(5) 3 65
(Declan Carroll) *s.s: hld up: rdn over 1f out: styd on to go 3rd nr fin* **5/2**[1]

2353 **4** nk **Dose**[10] 1879 4-8-13 **62** ........ TonyHamilton 6 64
(Richard Fahey) *prom: plld hrd: lost pl over 6f out: hdwy u.p over 1f out: styd on* **7/2**[2]

0025 **5** hd **Fast And Hot (IRE)**[16] 1758 4-9-4 **67** ........ (b) KieranO'Neill 2 69
(Richard Hannon) *prom: racd keenly: rdn and ev ch whn edgd lft over 1f out: no ex wl ins fnl f* **9/2**[3]

0035 **6** 8 **Playtothewhistle**[7] 1983 6-8-12 **64** ........ (v) AlistairRawlinson(3) 7 50
(Michael Appleby) *led: rdn and hdd over 2f out: wknd fnl f* **8/1**

40-0 **7** 6 **Bohemian Rhapsody (IRE)**[19] 1684 8-9-1 **67** ...... KieranShoemark(3) 8 41
(Brendan Powell) *hld up: pushed along 1/2-way: wknd over 2f out* **20/1**

2m 9.96s (2.06) **Going Correction** +0.075s/f (Good) 7 Ran SP% **114.1**
Speed ratings (Par 103): **94,92,92,92,92 85,80**
CSF £43.22 CT £116.21 TOTE £10.40: £3.80, £2.60; EX 62.00 Trifecta £373.80.

**Owner** Live in Hope Partnership **Bred** Ringfort Stud **Trained** Rock, Worcs

**FOCUS**
Race run over an additional 10yds. Ordinary handicap form, and the first five finished in a bit of a heap. The runner-up has been rated in line with his recent form.
T/Plt: £11.00 to a £1 stake. Pool: £52,717.71 - 3491.3 winning units T/Qpdt: £5.30 to a £1 stake. Pool: £2,753.46 - 380.43 winning units **Colin Roberts**

# 1908 RIPON (R-H)
## Saturday, April 29

**OFFICIAL GOING: Good (good to firm in places in home straight; 8.4) (watered)**
Wind: light half behind, making no material difference Weather: overcast

## 2154 SIS NOVICE AUCTION STKS (PLUS 10 RACE) 5f
**2:10** (2:19) (Class 4) 2-Y-O **£5,175** (£1,540; £769; £384) **Stalls** High

Form RPR
32 **1** **Black Orange**[18] 1694 2-8-10 0 ........ MartinDwyer 7 68
(Gay Kelleway) *mde all: rdn and edgd lft appr fnl f: kpt on wl* **4/1**[2]

0 **2** 3/4 **Rocket Man Dan (IRE)**[28] 1495 2-8-12 0 ........ PhillipMakin 9 67
(Keith Dalgleish) *dwlt sltly: trckd ldrs: racd keenly: bit short of room and swtchd rt appr fnl f: squeezed through gap to chal ins fnl f: rdn and kpt on* **11/8**[1]

**3** 1 3/4 **Aristodemus (IRE)** 2-8-10 0 ........ DuranFentiman 6 59
(Tim Easterby) *prom: rdn 2f out: edgd rt and no ex fnl 75yds* **66/1**

6 **4** 1 1/4 **Revenge**[14] 1803 2-8-12 0 ........ DavidAllan 4 57
(Tim Easterby) *midfield: rdn and hdwy appr fnl f: one pce* **14/1**

0 **5** hd **Kikini Bamalaam (IRE)**[10] 1872 2-8-4 0 ........ RowanScott(5) 8 53
(Keith Dalgleish) *chsd ldrs towards outer: rdn 1/2-way: one pce* **25/1**

**6** 2 1/4 **Mr Wagyu (IRE)** 2-9-2 0 ........ JasonHart 3 52
(John Quinn) *dwlt: hld up: rdn 1/2-way: minor late hdwy: nvr threatened* **9/1**[3]

**7** 1/2 **Kyleque (IRE)** 2-8-12 0 ........ PaulMulrennan 10 46
(Paul Midgley) *in tch: pushed along over 1f out: briefly short of room appr fnl f: wknd ins fnl f* **28/1**

8 *nk* **Faradays Spark (IRE)** 2-8-12 0 PaulHanagan 2 45
(Richard Fahey) *dwlt: sn pushed along and in rr: nvr threatened* **4/1**[2]

9 *½* **Magnus (IRE)** 2-8-12 0 LukeMorris 5 43
(Tom Dascombe) *slowly away: a rr* **9/1**[3]

1m 0.48s (0.48) **Going Correction** -0.275s/f (Firm) **9** Ran SP% **117.6**
Speed ratings (Par 94): **85,83,81,79,78 75,74,73,73**
CSF £9.94 TOTE £4.30: £1.50, £1.10, £10.80; EX 11.70 Trifecta £423.10.
**Owner** Y Pinchen,J Pinchen,J Farley & M Walker **Bred** D R Tucker **Trained** Exning, Suffolk

■ Capla Dancer was withdrawn. Price at time of withdrawal 4/1. Rule 4 applies to bets struck at board prices prior to withdrawal but not to SP bets - deduction 20p in the pound. New market formed.

**FOCUS**
An informative 2yo contest, though it took less winning than expected following the late withdrawal of C&D winner Capla Dancer. A light pb from the winner.

## 2155 RIPONBET PLACE6 LUCKY DIP H'CAP 1m
**2:45** (2:46) (Class 3) (0-90,91) 4-Y-O+ **£9,703** (£2,887; £1,443; £721) **Stalls** Low

Form RPR

00-3 **1** **Gurkha Friend**[14] 1799 5-9-5 **86** TomEaves 6 95
(Karen McLintock) *mde all: rdn over 2f out: kpt on wl* **11/2**[2]

00-6 **2** *1½* **Two For Two (IRE)**[17] 1734 9-9-6 **87** (p) PJMcDonald 9 93
(Roger Fell) *hld up in midfield: rdn over 1f out: kpt on wl fnl f* **8/1**

100- **3** *nk* **Shouranour (IRE)**[130] 8475 7-8-12 **84** (b) LewisEdmunds(5) 2 89
(Alan Brown) *midfield on inner: rdn 2f out: kpt on fnl f* **16/1**

200- **4** *1* **Rousayan (IRE)**[154] 8122 6-9-6 **87** (h) DanielTudhope 7 90
(David O'Meara) *midfield: pushed along and gd hdwy to chse ldr over 1f out: rdn fnl f: no ex fnl 110yds* **7/2**[1]

400- **5** *¾* **Miss Van Gogh**[154] 8122 5-9-3 **84** PaulHanagan 13 85
(Richard Fahey) *swtchd rt s: hld up: pushed along over 2f out: rdn and kpt on fnl f: nrst fin* **14/1**

412- **6** *½* **Dubai's Secret**[280] 4654 4-9-5 **86** SeanLevey 11 86
(David Brown) *trckd ldrs towards outer: rdn 2f out: no ex ins fnl f* **12/1**

063- **7** *1½* **Wilde Inspiration (IRE)**[185] 7623 6-9-0 **81** JoeDoyle 12 77
(Julie Camacho) *racd keenly and sn prom: rdn over 2f out: wknd ins fnl f* **8/1**

-165 **8** *nk* **Worlds His Oyster**[15] 1766 4-9-7 **88** JasonHart 10 84
(John Quinn) *trckd ldrs: rdn over 2f out: wknd ins fnl f* **8/1**

30-0 **9** *1½* **Father Bertie**[28] 1492 5-9-10 **91** (tp) DavidAllan 4 83
(Tim Easterby) *trckd ldrs: rdn over 2f out: wknd fnl f* **6/1**[3]

14-5 **10** *2¾* **Silvery Moon (IRE)**[9] 1911 10-9-0 **88** RobertDodsworth(7) 3 74
(Tim Easterby) *dwlt: hld up: pushed along over 2f out: nvr threatened* **16/1**

4/06 **11** *3* **Mansfield**[31] 1423 4-9-1 **82** ConnorBeasley 1 61
(Michael Wigham) *slowly away: a towards rr* **33/1**

13-0 **12** *nse* **Alexandrakollontai (IRE)**[19] 1677 7-9-3 **84** (b) JamesSullivan 5 63
(Alistair Whillans) *a rr* **50/1**

550- **13** *5* **Le Chat D'Or**[197] 7316 9-9-6 **87** (t) PaulMulrennan 8 54
(Michael Dods) *hld up: rdn over 3f out: sn wknd* **25/1**

1m 38.79s (-2.61) **Going Correction** -0.15s/f (Firm) **13** Ran SP% **120.1**
Speed ratings (Par 107): **107,105,105,104,103 102,101,101,99,96 93,93,88**
CSF £48.65 CT £697.84 TOTE £6.10: £2.50, £3.00, £4.90; EX 55.80 Trifecta £812.00.
**Owner** Self Preservation Society & Don Eddy **Bred** Mrs J Imray **Trained** Ingoe, Northumberland

**FOCUS**
Race distance increased by 12yds. This was run at a good pace throughout and represents solid handicap form for the level. The winner made all. A length pb from the winner.

## 2156 VISIT ATTHERACES.COM H'CAP 6f
**3:20** (3:20) (Class 2) (0-105,105) 4-Y-O+
**£13,695** (£4,100; £2,050; £1,025; £512; £257) **Stalls** High

Form RPR

041- **1** **Intisaab**[203] 7156 6-9-4 **105** (p) ShelleyBirkett(3) 1 114
(David O'Meara) *2nd of 3 far side: led that trio 2f out: sn rdn: overall ldr appr fnl f: kpt on* **17/2**

01-2 **2** *nk* **Muntadab (IRE)**[27] 1515 5-8-11 **95** PJMcDonald 12 103
(Roger Fell) *led stands' side: rdn 2f out: kpt on wl: 1st of 10 in gp* **4/1**[1]

000- **3** *1* **Out Do**[217] 6792 8-9-1 **99** (v) DanielTudhope 9 104
(David O'Meara) *hld up: stands' side: angled rt into clr over 1f out: sn hdwy: rdn and kpt on wl fnl f: 2nd of 10 in gp* **14/1**

501- **4** *shd* **Above The Rest (IRE)**[217] 6764 6-9-3 **101** (h) PhillipMakin 8 105
(David Barron) *midfield stands' side: rdn 2f out: kpt on fnl f: 3rd of 10 in gp* **11/1**

003- **5** *½* **Right Touch**[140] 8311 7-8-12 **99** AdamMcNamara(3) 2 102
(Richard Fahey) *hld up last of 3 far side: rdn over 2f out: kpt on fnl f: 2nd of 3 in gp* **14/1**

200- **6** *¾* **Orion's Bow**[224] 6558 6-9-7 **105** DavidAllan 10 105
(Tim Easterby) *trckd ldrs stands' side: pushed along over 2f out: rdn ent fnl f: no ex fnl 110yds: 4th of 10 in gp* **12/1**

04-0 **7** *¾* **Red Pike (IRE)**[116] 33 6-8-8 **92** ConnorBeasley 3 90
(Bryan Smart) *led trio far side: rdn whn hdd 2f out: wknd ins fnl f: last of 3 in gp* **9/1**

40-3 **8** *nse* **Pipers Note**[28] 1491 7-9-1 **99** JamesSullivan 5 97
(Ruth Carr) *dwlt: sn midfield stands' side: rdn over 2f out: no ex ins fnl f: 5th of 10 in gp* **13/2**[3]

55-0 **9** *nse* **George Bowen (IRE)**[27] 1515 5-8-6 **90** PaulHanagan 7 88
(Richard Fahey) *hld up stands' side: rdn over 2f out: nvr threatened: 6th of 10 in gp* **9/2**[2]

20-5 **10** *1* **Reputation (IRE)**[10] 1880 4-8-8 **92** (v) JasonHart 11 87
(John Quinn) *midfield stands' side: rdn over 2f out: nvr threatened: 7th of 10 in gp* **20/1**

400- **11** *½* **Venturous (IRE)**[273] 4867 4-8-10 **94** PaulMulrennan 6 87
(David Barron) *hld up stands' side: nvr threatened: 8th of 10 in gp* **14/1**

04/0 **12** *nk* **Rasheeq (IRE)**[10] 1876 4-8-7 **91** DuranFentiman 4 83
(Tim Easterby) *prom stands' side: rdn over 2f out: wknd fnl f: 9th of 10 in gp* **66/1**

-552 **13** *11* **Distant Past**[78] 664 6-8-8 **92** ShaneGray 13 49
(Kevin Ryan) *midfield stands' side: rdn and lost pl over 2f out: wknd and eased* **33/1**

1m 10.2s (-2.80) **Going Correction** -0.275s/f (Firm) **13** Ran SP% **117.3**
Speed ratings (Par 109): **107,106,105,105,104 103,102,102,102,101 100,99,85**
CSF £40.84 CT £495.10 TOTE £9.30: £3.70, £1.80, £4.20; EX 61.10 Trifecta £474.60.
**Owner** Stuart Graham **Bred** Shadwell Estate Company Limited **Trained** Upper Helmsley, N Yorks

**FOCUS**
A hotly contested sprint handicap. The first two home came from different sides of the track.

## 2157 DOWNLOAD THE FREE ATTHERACES APP H'CAP 2m
**3:55** (3:56) (Class 2) (0-105,99) 4-Y-O+
**£18,675** (£5,592; £2,796; £1,398; £699; £351) **Stalls** Low

Form RPR

00-0 **1** **My Reward**[14] 1802 5-9-2 **89** DavidAllan 4 96
(Tim Easterby) *led: jnd 12f out: hdd 7f out: remained cl up: rdn to ld again 3f out: styd on wl* **5/1**[2]

00-6 **2** *1* **Sir Chauvelin**[14] 1802 5-9-5 **92** (h) SamJames 6 98
(Jim Goldie) *hld up: rdn over 3f out: hdwy 2f out: wnt 2nd 1f out: styd on* **7/1**[3]

054- **3** *1½* **Yorkidding**[178] 7766 5-9-9 **96** PaulMulrennan 7 100
(Mark Johnston) *trckd ldr: jnd ldr 12f out: led 7f out: pushed along over 4f out: hdd 3f out: sn drvn: plugged on* **8/1**

-410 **4** *1* **Gavlar**[15] 1770 6-9-7 **94** (v) LukeMorris 3 97
(William Knight) *midfield: rdn 3f out: one pce fnl f* **7/1**[3]

1320 **5** *½* **Isharah (USA)**[14] 1802 4-9-4 **95** FrannyNorton 2 97
(Mark Johnston) *trckd ldrs: rdn 3f out: grad wknd fnl f* **8/1**

1-20 **6** *2¾* **Good Run (FR)**[15] 1779 4-9-8 **99** SeanLevey 5 98
(Saeed bin Suroor) *trckd ldrs: rdn 3f out: wknd fnl f* **5/2**[1]

30-1 **7** *5* **Gabrial's King (IRE)**[7] 1976 8-8-13 **89** AdamMcNamara(3) 8 82
(Richard Fahey) *hld up: rdn 3f out: sn wknd* **8/1**

-640 **8** *12* **Intense Tango**[7] 1779 6-9-1 **93** (t) CliffordLee(5) 1 72
(K R Burke) *midfield: rdn and outpcd over 3f out: sn wknd and bhd* **9/1**

3m 27.28s (-4.52) **Going Correction** -0.15s/f (Firm)
**WFA** 4 from 5yo+ 2lb **8** Ran SP% **113.6**
Speed ratings (Par 109): **105,104,103,103,103 101,99,93**
CSF £38.92 CT £273.67 TOTE £6.70: £2.20, £1.70, £2.50; EX 52.30 Trifecta £421.90.
**Owner** M J Macleod **Bred** Millsec Limited **Trained** Great Habton, N Yorks

**FOCUS**
Race distance increased by 12yds. This good quality staying handicap was run at a very steady early pace and former miler My Reward took full advantage. The winner has been rated to a similar level as when runner-up in this race last year.

## 2158 M.C.H. HUTCHINSON MEMORIAL H'CAP 1m 4f 10y
**4:30** (4:30) (Class 2) (0-110,108) 4-Y-O+**£15,562** (£4,660; £2,330; £1,165) **Stalls** Centre

Form RPR

026- **1** **Knights Table**[245] 5879 4-8-8 **96** DavidAllan 1 106+
(James Tate) *trckd ldr: led on bit 2f out: sn pushed clr: v easily* **11/10**[1]

5-60 **2** *5* **Tawdeea**[15] 1779 5-9-3 **104** (p) DanielTudhope 6 105
(David O'Meara) *hld up: rdn over 2f out: wnt 2nd appr fnl f: no ch w wnr* **11/4**[3]

-250 **3** *6* **Fire Fighting (IRE)**[16] 1757 6-9-7 **108** (b) PaulMulrennan 3 99
(Mark Johnston) *led: rdn whn hdd 2f out: lost 2nd appr fnl f and wknd* **5/2**[2]

230 **4** *23* **Vettori Rules**[15] 1770 4-8-12 **100** (h) MartinDwyer 5 55
(Gay Kelleway) *trckd ldr: rdn and lost pl over 4f out: wknd and bhd fnl 2f* **16/1**

2m 32.04s (-4.66) **Going Correction** -0.15s/f (Firm) **4** Ran SP% **108.7**
Speed ratings (Par 109): **109,105,101,86**
CSF £4.43 TOTE £1.90; EX 5.00 Trifecta £9.00.
**Owner** Saeed Manana **Bred** Ashbrittle Stud **Trained** Newmarket, Suffolk

**FOCUS**
Race distance increased by 12yds. An uncompetitive feature handicap and a smooth triumph for the lightly weighted favourite. A step forward from the winner, with the runner-up rated close to form.

## 2159 LADIES DAY 22ND JUNE MAIDEN STKS (PLUS 10 RACE) 1m 1f 170y
**5:05** (5:08) (Class 4) 3-Y-O **£5,175** (£1,540; £769; £384) **Stalls** Low

Form RPR

6 **1** **Daawy (IRE)**[9] 1906 3-9-5 0 DanielTudhope 3 88+
(William Haggas) *mde all: pushed clr over 1f out: easily.* **4/6**[1]

0 **2** *5* **Kilowatt**[28] 1497 3-9-5 0 DavidAllan 2 73
(Tim Easterby) *in tch: pushed along over 2f out: wnt 2nd appr fnl f: kpt on but no ch wnr* **14/1**

62 **3** *¾* **Marqoom**[18] 1701 3-9-5 0 FrannyNorton 4 71
(Mark Johnston) *trckd ldr: rdn along 4f out: one pce* **11/4**[2]

**4** *1* **Thistimenextyear** 3-9-2 0 EdwardGreatrex(3) 5 69
(Richard Spencer) *s.i.s: hld up in rr: pushed along over 2f out: kpt on fnl f: nrst fin* **11/2**[3]

0-5 **5** *5* **Bing Bang Bank (IRE)**[19] 1675 3-9-5 0 PhillipMakin 1 59
(David Barron) *hld up: pushed along 3f out: nvr threatened* **14/1**

**6** *6* **Vindicator (IRE)** 3-9-5 0 PaulMulrennan 8 47
(Michael Dods) *in tch outer: pushed along and lost pl 4f out: wknd over 1f out* **22/1**

0 **7** *6* **Jump Around**[28] 1497 3-8-9 0 CliffordLee(5) 7 29
(K R Burke) *a towards rr* **25/1**

0-5 **8** *1¾* **Kelpie Spirit (IRE)**[19] 1676 3-9-5 0 LukeMorris 6 31
(John Weymes) *in tch: rdn over 3f out: wknd over 2f out* **50/1**

2m 4.48s (-0.92) **Going Correction** -0.15s/f (Firm) **8** Ran SP% **125.5**
Speed ratings (Par 100): **97,93,92,91,87 82,78,76**
CSF £14.72 TOTE £1.80: £1.20, £3.20, £1.10; EX 15.40 Trifecta £42.60.
**Owner** Al Shaqab Racing **Bred** Tinnakill House & Alan Byrne **Trained** Newmarket, Suffolk

**FOCUS**
Race distance increased by 12yds. A straightforward task for the odds-on favourite. The third has been rated a bit below his latest.

## 2160 TRADITIONAL FAMILY FUNDAY SUNDAY 21ST MAY H'CAP 5f
**5:40** (5:42) (Class 4) (0-85,87) 3-Y-O **£7,762** (£2,310; £1,154; £577) **Stalls** High

Form RPR

2103 **1** **Jack Flash (FR)**[7] 1975 3-9-5 **79** (h[1]) JasonHart 4 85
(Les Eyre) *mde all: rdn over 1f out: kpt on* **10/3**[3]

600- **2** *¾* **Copper Knight (IRE)**[287] 4394 3-9-13 **87** DavidAllan 5 90
(Tim Easterby) *trckd ldr: rdn 2f out: kpt on but a hld* **14/1**

0-10 **3** *3* **Logi (IRE)**[9] 1913 3-9-0 **74** (b) PhillipMakin 6 66
(David Barron) *hld up: rdn 1/2-way: kpt on into modest 3rd fnl f* **11/4**[1]

30-2 **4** *2¼* **Yorkshiredebut (IRE)**[14] 1786 3-8-6 **69** EdwardGreatrex(3) 3 53
(Paul Midgley) *j. s: hld up: racd keenly: rdn and hdwy over 1f out: wknd ins fnl f* **6/1**

01- **5** *2¾* **Wadood (IRE)**[207] 7040 3-9-3 **77** LukeMorris 1 51
(Robert Cowell) *trckd ldr: rdn and hung rt 1/2-way: wknd over 1f out: edgd lft ins fnl f* **5/1**

20-6 **6** *5* **Coolfitch (IRE)**[17] 1731 3-9-7 **81** DanielTudhope 2 37
(David O'Meara) *dwlt: hld up: pushed along 2f out: sltly hmpd ins fnl f: nvr threatened* **3/1**[2]

57.5s (-2.50) **Going Correction** -0.275s/f (Firm) **6** Ran SP% **112.4**
Speed ratings (Par 100): **109,107,103,99,95 87**
CSF £43.68 TOTE £5.60: £2.20, £4.70; EX 36.10 Trifecta £107.80.
**Owner** Billy Parker **Bred** S A R L De Chambure Haras D'Etreham **Trained** Catwick, N Yorks

**FOCUS**
An open handicap, despite the relatively small field. The winner was the fifth all-the-way winner on the seven-race card. It's been rated a bit cautiously around the better view of the winner's AW form.
T/Plt: £38.20 to a £1 stake. Pool: £73,992.42 -1411.95 winning units T/Qpdt: £12.00 to a £1 stake. Pool: £4,649.15 - 286.2 winning units **Andrew Sheret**

# 2059 WOLVERHAMPTON (A.W) (L-H)

## Saturday, April 29

**OFFICIAL GOING: Tapeta: standard**
Wind: Almost nil Weather: Overcast

## 2161 BANK'S AMBER BITTER APPRENTICE H'CAP — 6f 20y (Tp)

**5:50** (5:51) (Class 5) (0-75,77) 4-Y-O+ **£3,234** (£962; £481; £240) **Stalls** Low

Form RPR

513- **1** **Compas Scoobie**[166] 7959 4-9-4 **74** CameronNoble(3) 8 85
(Roger Varian) *hld up: gd hdwy 2f out: shkn up to ld ins fnl f: pushed out: comf* **11/4**[1]

3-25 **2** *1 ½* **Cultured Knight**[15] 1768 4-9-5 **77** FinleyMarsh(5) 4 83
(Richard Hughes) *t.k.h early: trckd ldrs: wnt 2nd and gng wl over 1f out: effrt and ev ch briefly ins fnl f: sn edgd rt: one pce* **4/1**[2]

5303 **3** *2 ¾* **Inshaa**[10] 1887 5-8-6 **64** (p) SeamusCronin(5) 1 61+
(Michael Herrington) *s.i.s: bhd and outpcd: gd hdwy appr fnl f: kpt on: nt pce of first two* **7/1**

302 **4** *1* **Bush Warrior (IRE)**[9] 1896 6-8-11 **67** (v) JoshuaBryan(3) 2 61
(Anabel K Murphy) *sn cl up: led over 2f out: rdn and hdd ins fnl f: no ex* **22/1**

00-4 **5** *½* **Dinneratmidnight**[12] 1836 6-9-6 **76** (e) BenRobinson(3) 9 68
(Richard Guest) *trckd ldrs: drvn along over 2f out: one pce fr over 1f out* **9/1**

-150 **6** *½* **Slingsby**[4] 2064 6-9-2 **74** (p) HarrisonShaw(5) 7 65
(Michael Easterby) *sn outpcd and bhd: hdwy fnl f: kpt on: nvr able to chal* **5/1**[3]

3205 **7** *1 ¾* **Curzon Line**[17] 1717 8-9-4 **76** RyanTimby(5) 3 61
(Michael Easterby) *hld up in tch: rdn over 2f out: edgd lft and no imp over 1f out* **6/1**

0320 **8** *2 ¼* **Fleckerl (IRE)**[49] 1140 7-8-13 **71** (p) KatherineGlenister(5) 5 49
(Conor Dore) *s.i.s: bhd and outpcd: nvr on terms* **16/1**

1340 **9** *2* **Elusivity (IRE)**[51] 1109 9-9-5 **72** (p) CharlieBennett 6 44
(Conor Dore) *led to over 2f out: drvn and wknd over 1f out* **40/1**

1m 12.96s (-1.54) **Going Correction** -0.125s/f (Stan) **9** Ran SP% **112.8**
Speed ratings (Par 103): **105,103,99,98,97 96,94,91,88**
CSF £13.19 CT £67.46 TOTE £3.40: £2.00, £1.30, £2.30; EX 12.60 Trifecta £46.90.
**Owner** Michael Hill **Bred** Aston Mullins Stud **Trained** Newmarket, Suffolk

**FOCUS**
A fair apprentice riders' sprint handicap. They went a good gallop on standard Tapeta and the right two horses came to the fore. A length pb from the winner.

## 2162 JENNINGS CUMBERLAND H'CAP — 1m 5f 194y

**6:20** (6:20) (Class 6) (0-65,65) 4-Y-O+ **£2,587** (£770; £384; £192) **Stalls** Low

Form RPR

2 **1** **Temasek Star (IRE)**[22] 1617 6-9-10 **65** (p) ShaneKelly 2 72
(Anthony McCann, Ire) *hld up: smooth hdwy over 2f out: chsng ldrs and hung lft over 1f out: kpt on u.p fnl f to ld cl home* **7/4**[1]

0004 **2** *shd* **With Hindsight (IRE)**[39] 1291 9-9-2 **57** TomEaves 8 64
(Steve Gollings) *chsd ldrs: led after 6f: drvn along over 1f out: kpt on wl fnl f: hdd nr fin* **10/1**

-234 **3** *2* **Captain Swift (IRE)**[80] 616 6-9-9 **64** (p) PatCosgrave 6 68
(John Mackie) *in tch: hdwy to chse ldr over 1f out: sn drvn along: lost 2nd and one pce ins fnl f* **9/4**[2]

3440 **4** *6* **King Julien (IRE)**[12] 1834 4-8-3 **46** oh1 (p) DannyBrock 5 42
(John Ryan) *hld up in tch on ins: nt clr run over 2f out: sn drvn: rallied over 1f out: sn no imp* **11/1**

516- **5** *1* **Want The Fairytale**[12] 6593 4-9-5 **62** FergusSweeney 7 56
(Alan King) *hld up: stdy hdwy on outside 3f out: sn drvn along: hung lft and outpcd over 1f out* **15/2**[3]

**6** *9* **Authorative (IRE)**[8] 1952 7-8-5 **46** oh1 (tp) JimmyQuinn 3 28
(Anthony McCann, Ire) *dwlt: sn pressing ldr: drvn along over 3f out: wknd over 2f out* **16/1**

510- **7** *7* **Kazoey**[219] 6698 4-8-5 **48** DuranFentiman 4 20
(Chris Fairhurst) *led 6f: cl up tl rdn and wknd fr 3f out* **28/1**

30-0 **8** *2 ½* **Rajapur**[29] 1469 4-8-7 **50** JoeyHaynes 1 18
(Philip Kirby) *dwlt: hld up: drvn over 5f out: btn fnl 3f* **14/1**

3m 2.05s (-2.75) **Going Correction** -0.125s/f (Stan)
**WFA** 4 from 6yo+ 1lb **8** Ran SP% **112.3**
Speed ratings (Par 101): **102,101,100,97,96 91,87,86**
CSF £19.58 CT £39.58 TOTE £2.30: £1.10, £3.00, £1.20; EX 17.20 Trifecta £58.10.
**Owner** Miss Rita Shah **Bred** David Reid Scott & Mr A V Nicoll **Trained** Castleblaney, Co. Monaghan

**FOCUS**
A modest staying handicap. They went a muddling gallop, with three different leaders, but the best horse got up late to prevail.

## 2163 WAINWRIGHT GOLDEN BEER H'CAP — 1m 1f 104y (Tp)

**6:50** (6:50) (Class 5) (0-75,77) 4-Y-O+ **£3,234** (£962; £481; £240) **Stalls** Low

Form RPR

306- **1** **Pushaq (IRE)**[24] 1567 4-9-6 **74** (h[1]) ShaneKelly 3 82
(Anthony McCann, Ire) *hld up: smooth hdwy over 2f out: rdn to ld ins fnl f: edgd rt: kpt on wl* **10/1**

441 **2** *¾* **Deep Challenger (IRE)**[12] 1839 5-9-4 **72** FergusSweeney 6 78
(Jamie Osborne) *hld up in tch: effrt and edgd lft over 1f out: drvn and pressed wnr ins fnl f: sn one pce* **7/2**[1]

0403 **3** *¾* **Spes Nostra**[58] 992 9-9-1 **74** (b) LewisEdmunds(5) 11 78
(Iain Jardine) *hld up: rdn along and hdwy over 2f out: kpt on fnl f to take 3rd cl home: nt rch first two* **5/1**[3]

4011 **4** *nk* **Believe It (IRE)**[22] 1598 5-9-2 **77** (b) StephenCummins(7) 7 80
(Richard Hughes) *t.k.h: led: rdn 2f out: hdd ins fnl f: kpt on same pce* **7/1**

4030 **5** *nse* **Yasir (USA)**[58] 990 9-8-2 **63** KatherineGlenister(7) 2 66
(Conor Dore) *hld up towards rr: rdn along and effrt over 2f out: no imp fr over 1f out* **66/1**

610- **6** *3* **Kafoo**[310] 3568 4-8-5 **66** BenRobinson(7) 1 63
(Ed Dunlop) *t.k.h: pressed ldrs: wnt 2nd over 2f out: rdn over 1f out: wknd ins fnl f* **14/1**

15-4 **7** *1 ½* **Drago (IRE)**[37] 1329 5-8-12 **73** (h) PatrickVaughan(7) 4 67
(David O'Meara) *hld up midfield: hdwy to chse ldrs wl over 1f out: sn drvn along: outpcd fnl f* **7/1**

0000 **8** *3 ¼* **Arrowzone**[18] 1706 6-9-6 **74** RyanPowell 10 61
(Kevin Frost) *hld up: rdn along and outpcd over 2f out: n.d after* **50/1**

0301 **9** *nk* **Idol Deputy (FR)**[63] 928 11-9-1 **74** (p) RachealKneller(5) 9 60
(James Bennett) *prom on outside: drvn and outpcd over 2f out: edgd lft and btn over 1f out* **25/1**

1050 **10** *¾* **Fast Play (IRE)**[47] 1175 5-9-0 **73** (b) CharlieBennett(5) 5 58
(Conor Dore) *hld up: drvn along and outpcd over 2f out: btn over 1f out* **33/1**

1303 **11** *10* **Shah Of Armaan (IRE)**[24] 1562 4-9-5 **73** TomEaves 8 37
(Kevin Ryan) *prom tl rdn and wknd fr 2f out* **4/1**[2]

250- **12** *3 ¼* **Street Poet (IRE)**[194] 7408 4-9-7 **75** RobertWinston 12 32
(Michael Herrington) *cl up on outside tl edgd rt and wknd over 1f out* **12/1**

1m 59.37s (-1.43) **Going Correction** -0.125s/f (Stan) **12** Ran SP% **117.6**
Speed ratings (Par 103): **101,100,99,99,96 95,92,92,91 82,79**
CSF £43.55 CT £200.92 TOTE £13.70: £3.90, £1.10, £2.30; EX 66.20 Trifecta £276.50.
**Owner** Miss Rita Shah **Bred** Premier Bloodstock **Trained** Castleblaney, Co. Monaghan

**FOCUS**
A fair handicap. They went a modest gallop. A previous course winner provided a second consecutive victory on the night for Irish trainer Anthony McCann and jockey Shane Kelly. A length pb from the winner.

## 2164 MARSTONS PEDIGREE MAIDEN STKS — 1m 4f 51y (Tp)

**7:20** (7:20) (Class 5) 3-Y-O+ **£3,234** (£962; £481; £240) **Stalls** Low

Form RPR

22-3 **1** **Cape Peninsular**[23] 1583 4-9-7 79 MartinHarley 2 80
(James Tate) *t.k.h: trckd ldrs: hdwy to ld 2f out: drvn clr fnl f* **11/4**[1]

4- **2** *3 ½* **Steaming (IRE)**[185] 7622 3-8-7 0 JFEgan 9 77
(Ralph Beckett) *hld up: hdwy on outside and ev ch 2f out: sn rdn: kpt on same pce fnl f* **11/4**[1]

2-3 **3** *2 ½* **Migyaas (USA)**[19] 1675 3-8-7 0 (p[1]) WilliamCarson 3 73
(Saeed bin Suroor) *cl up: led briefly over 2f out: drvn and outpcd over 1f out* **11/4**[1]

0/5 **4** *7* **Nachi Falls**[7] 1984 4-9-12 0 (t) TomMarquand 1 64
(Nigel Hawke) *hld up on ins: rdn over 2f out: hdwy and edgd lft over 1f out: sn no imp* **50/1**

**5** *1* **I'm Right On Time** 3-8-4 0 JackDuern(3) 8 61
(Dean Ivory) *hld up: drvn along over 3f out: hdwy over 1f out: sn no imp* **80/1**

0 **6** *3 ¼* **I'm Running Late**[31] 1420 3-8-7 0 RobHornby 7 55
(Dean Ivory) *prom on outside: pushed along 5f out: rallied: wknd over 2f out* **66/1**

4 **7** *1 ¼* **Benissimo (IRE)**[7] 1984 7-9-6 0 TobyEley(7) 5 55
(Tony Forbes) *hld up: drvn along over 3f out: nvr on terms* **66/1**

**8** *½* **Red Master (IRE)** 3-8-7 0 AntonioFresu 10 53
(Ed Dunlop) *hld up: drvn and outpcd over 3f out: sn btn* **20/1**[3]

**9** *1 ¼* **Global Empire (IRE)** 3-8-7 0 RyanPowell 4 51
(Simon Crisford) *t.k.h: in tch: drvn and outpcd over 2f out: sn btn* **20/1**[3]

3-2 **10** *1* **Physicist (IRE)**[9] 1900 3-8-7 0 DavidProbert 6 49
(Paul Cole) *led to over 2f out: sn rdn and wknd* **7/2**[2]

2m 37.05s (-3.75) **Going Correction** -0.125s/f (Stan)
**WFA** 3 from 4yo+ 20lb **10** Ran SP% **117.9**
Speed ratings (Par 103): **107,104,103,98,97 95,94,94,93,92**
CSF £10.16 TOTE £3.80: £1.20, £1.40, £1.50; EX 13.00 Trifecta £31.40.
**Owner** Saeed Manana **Bred** Rabbah Bloodstock Limited **Trained** Newmarket, Suffolk

**FOCUS**
A fair middle-distance maiden. They went a respectable gallop and the filly who set the form standard beforehand relished the longer trip. The winner has been rated close to her best and the third close to form.

## 2165 RINGWOOD RAZORBACK H'CAP — 1m 4f 51y (Tp)

**7:50** (7:50) (Class 3) (0-90,92) 4-Y-O **£7,246** (£2,168; £1,084; £542; £270) **Stalls** Low

Form RPR

221- **1** **Gibbs Hill (GER)**[301] 3914 4-9-1 **85** JackMitchell 5 98+
(Roger Varian) *in tch: lost grnd after 5f: smooth hdwy on outside to ld appr fnl f: shkn up and sn qcknd clr: readily* **13/8**[2]

01-2 **2** *2 ½* **Marmajuke Bay**[24] 1555 4-9-1 **85** (p) SteveDrowne 3 89
(Mark Usher) *led: hrd pressed and rdn fr 3f out: hdd appr fnl f: kpt on: no ch w ready wnr* **10/1**

61- **3** *¾* **Amazing Red (IRE)**[367] 1784 4-9-6 **90** PatCosgrave 1 93
(Ed Dunlop) *hld up: stdy hdwy over 2f out: effrt and rdn over 1f out: kpt on same pce fnl f* **6/4**[1]

5231 **4** *2 ¾* **Every Chance (IRE)**[21] 1628 4-9-8 **92** TimmyMurphy 7 90
(Jamie Osborne) *hld up: hdwy and prom after 5f: drvn and outpcd over 2f out: no imp over 1f out* **11/2**[3]

1430 **5** *½* **Ravens Quest**[28] 1504 4-8-6 **76** oh1 DannyBrock 2 74
(John Ryan) *trckd ldrs: rdn 3f out: kpt on same pce fr 2f out* **14/1**

3/ **6** *2 ½* **Tara River (FR)**[63] 8-8-9 **83** (p) RachealKneller(5) 6 77
(Brian Barr) *pressed ldr: ev ch 3f out: rdn and wknd over 1f out* **100/1**

2m 37.41s (-3.39) **Going Correction** -0.125s/f (Stan) **6** Ran SP% **110.2**
Speed ratings (Par 107): **106,104,103,102,101 100**
CSF £16.89 TOTE £2.40: £1.60, £3.10; EX 15.50 Trifecta £29.70.
**Owner** Paul Smith **Bred** Gestut Gorlsdorf **Trained** Newmarket, Suffolk

**FOCUS**
The feature contest was a good middle-distance handicap. They went a respectable gallop, at best, but the winner left a lasting impression. The runner-up has been rated to form.

## 2166 HOBGOBLIN H'CAP — 1m 142y (Tp)

**8:20** (8:21) (Class 6) (0-60,67) 4-Y-O+ **£2,587** (£770; £384; £192) **Stalls** Low

Form RPR

0122 **1** **Lord Murphy (IRE)**[9] 1894 4-9-7 **56** LiamKeniry 6 64
(Daniel Mark Loughnane) *t.k.h: trckd ldrs: effrt and led 1f out: edgd lft: rdn out* **7/4**[1]

06-4 **2** *1 ½* **Stamp Duty (IRE)**[81] 608 9-8-10 **45** TomEaves 8 50
(Suzzanne France) *hld up: rdn and hdwy on outside wl over 1f out: kpt on fnl f: nt rch wnr* **18/1**

2610 3 1 ½ **Vivre La Reve**[33] 1406 5-9-6 **55**....................(h) RyanPowell 10 57
(James Unett) *trckd ldrs: led over 2f out to over 1f out: kpt on same pce ins fnl f* **16/1**

0443 4 1 ½ **Quadriga (IRE)**[13] 1823 7-8-3 **45**....................(b) PaulaMuir(7) 4 44
(Chris Grant) *t.k.h: hld up on outside: hdwy and cl up over 3f out: rdn and one pce over 1f out* **11/1**

4530 5 ½ **Outlaw Torn (IRE)**[16] 1758 8-8-13 **55**....................(e) BenRobinson(7) 11 53
(Richard Guest) *t.k.h: led to over 2f out: drvn and outpcd wl over 1f out* **9/1**[3]

6 1 **Three Majors (IRE)**[36] 1356 4-9-7 **56**....................(tp) ShaneKelly 5 52
(Anthony McCann, Ire) *hld up: stdy hdwy and in tch wl over 1f out: sn rdn and no ex* **7/2**[2]

4005 7 1 ½ **Spirit Of Gondree (IRE)**[38] 1305 9-9-1 **50**....................(b) SteveDrowne 12 43
(Milton Bradley) *hld up: rdn along over 2f out: no imp fr over 1f out* **12/1**

606- 8 1 **Scent Of Power**[179] 7754 5-8-12 **52**.................... GeorgeWood(5) 3 42
(Barry Leavy) *in tch: rdn over 2f out: edgd lft and wknd over 1f out* **33/1**

4000 9 2 **I Can't Stop**[22] 1603 4-8-10 **45**....................(b) DavidProbert 2 31
(Milton Bradley) *hld up on ins: drvn and outpcd over 2f out: btn over 1f out* **33/1**

00-0 10 2 ¼ **Whitchurch**[38] 1312 5-9-2 **51**....................(p) PaddyAspell 1 33
(Philip Kirby) *trckd ldrs tl rdn and wknd over 2f out* **22/1**

5505 11 2 **Commissar**[11] 1864 8-9-3 **52**....................(vt) RobHornby 9 29
(Mandy Rowland) *dwlt and hld up: drvn and outpcd over 2f out: sn btn* **9/1**[3]

1m 49.31s (-0.79) **Going Correction** -0.125s/f (Stan) **11** Ran SP% **116.0**
Speed ratings (Par 101): **98,96,95,94,93 92,91,90,88,86 84**
CSF £36.24 CT £380.18 TOTE £2.60: £1.40, £5.10, £4.20; EX 35.40 Trifecta £279.20.
**Owner** Eclipse Horse Racing **Bred** Nanallac Stud **Trained** Rock, Worcs

**FOCUS**
A modest handicap. They went a muddling gallop, but the clear favourite maintained his good recent form with another cosy victory.

## 2167 LANCASTER BOMBER MAIDEN STKS 1m 142y (Tp)
**8:50** (8:51) (Class 5) 3-Y-O+ **£3,234** (£962; £481; £240) **Stalls** Low

Form RPR

2- 1 **Manchego**[192] 7468 3-8-13 0.................... JackMitchell 10 86
(Hugo Palmer) *mde all: rdn 2f out: hld on wl towards fin* **4/6**[1]

2 hd **Dayking** 3-8-13 0.................... PatCosgrave 6 85
(Saeed bin Suroor) *trckd ldrs: effrt and wnt 2nd over 2f out: sn rdn: kpt on wl fnl f: jst hld* **9/4**[2]

0- 3 7 **Falak (IRE)**[320] 3235 4-9-7 0.................... CameronNoble(7) 4 71
(Roger Varian) *in tch: drvn and outpcd over 2f out: kpt on fnl f: nvr able to chal* **6/1**[3]

4 ½ **Colourful Career (USA)** 3-8-13 0.................... JimmyQuinn 2 67
(Ed Dunlop) *in tch: effrt and rdn over 2f out: no imp fr over 1f out* **12/1**

5 1 ½ **Sir Gnet (IRE)** 3-8-13 0....................(h[1]) AntonioFresu 8 64
(Ed Dunlop) *dwlt: bhd: rdn along 3f out: no imp fr 2f out* **18/1**

0-0 6 4 ½ **Life Of Luxury**[112] 127 4-10-0 0.................... JFEgan 11 56
(Mark Brisbourne) *hld up: drvn and outpcd over 3f out: sn btn* **40/1**

7 ½ **Nazzaa (IRE)** 4-10-0 0.................... TomMarquand 3 55
(Steve Flook) *s.i.s: hld up: struggling over 3f out: sn btn* **50/1**

65 8 hd **Mahna Mahna (IRE)**[31] 1426 3-8-13 0.................... WilliamCarson 7 52
(David W Drinkwater) *plld hrd: pressed wnr to over 2f out: sn rdn and wknd* **66/1**

1m 49.46s (-0.64) **Going Correction** -0.125s/f (Stan)
**WFA** 3 from 4yo+ 15lb **8** Ran SP% **123.9**
Speed ratings (Par 103): **97,96,90,90,88 84,84,84**
CSF £2.70 TOTE £1.70: £1.10, £1.20, £1.80; EX 3.00 Trifecta £8.10.
**Owner** C Humber/D Davidson/Mrs T Brudenell **Bred** Mrs T Brudenell **Trained** Newmarket, Suffolk

**FOCUS**
A fair maiden. The winning time was comparatively the slowest of the night. The winner has been rated as improving on his debut effort.
T/Plt: £11.30 to a £1 stake. Pool: £75,059.37 - 4812.49 winning units T/Qpdt: £8.40 to a £1 stake. Pool: £6,664.16 - 583.48 winning units **Richard Young**

2168 - 2170a (Foreign Racing) - See Raceform Interactive

# SALISBURY (R-H)
Sunday, April 30

**OFFICIAL GOING: Firm (good to firm in places; watered; 9.7)**
Wind: mild against Weather: light rain

## 2171 BETFRED RACING "LIKE US ON FACEBOOK" MAIDEN STKS (DIV I) 6f 213y
**2:00** (2:02) (Class 5) 3-Y-O+ **£3,881** (£1,155; £577; £288) **Stalls** Low

Form RPR

0-2 1 **Sharp Defence (USA)**[15] 1804 3-9-1 **83**.................... TadhgO'Shea 6 84
(John Patrick Shanahan, Ire) *trckd ldrs: rdn to ld wl over 1f out: kpt on wl fnl f* **4/5**[1]

0- 2 2 ¼ **See The Master (IRE)**[239] 6108 3-9-1 0.................... SamHitchcott 2 78
(Clive Cox) *led: rdn and hdd wl over 1f out: kpt on but nt pce of wnr* **5/1**[3]

63- 3 1 ¾ **Eula Varner**[214] 6881 3-8-10 0.................... FergusSweeney 8 68
(Henry Candy) *racd keenly: sn prom: rdn and ev ch 2f out: kpt on same pce* **5/1**[3]

0-6 4 ¾ **Jumira Prince (IRE)**[12] 1862 3-9-1 0.................... JackMitchell 9 71
(Roger Varian) *cl up: edgd rt whn rdn over 1f out: kpt on ins fnl f but nt pce to mount chal* **4/1**[2]

5 7 **Vixen (IRE)** 3-8-10 0.................... TomMarquand 4 47
(Geoffrey Deacon) *awkwardly away: last pair but in tch: rdn over 2f out: nt pce to get involved* **40/1**

-0 6 8 **Charlie Alpha (IRE)**[23] 1600 3-9-1 0.................... KierenFox 1 31
(Roger Ingram) *cl up: rdn 3f out: wknd over 1f out* **100/1**

7 1 ¼ **Love Not War** 3-8-10 0.................... LiamKeniry 10 22
(George Scott) *s.i.s: last pair: effrt over 2f out: wknd over 1f out* **12/1**

0- 8 34 **General Gerrard**[252] 5668 3-8-10 0....................(t[1]) GeorgeWood(5) 7
(Michael Madgwick) *in tch: rdn over 2f out: wknd over 1f out* **100/1**

1m 26.39s (-2.21) **Going Correction** -0.25s/f (Firm)
**WFA** 3 from 4yo 13lb **8** Ran SP% **121.0**
Speed ratings (Par 103): **102,99,97,96,88 79,78,39**
CSF £5.95 TOTE £1.70: £1.02, £2.00, £1.90; EX 6.10 Trifecta £17.00.
**Owner** Thistle Bloodstock Limited **Bred** Donato Lanni **Trained** Kells, Co Kilkenny

**FOCUS**
The watered ground (8mm on Monday and 8mm on Wednesday) was still expected to ride quick. Clerk of the course Jeremy Martin said "We have had no significant rain the last month or so" and the going was given as firm, good to firm in places (GoingStick: 9.7). Stalls: 5f, 6f & 7f - Far side; 1m2f - Inside 1m4f - Stands' side. No more than a fair maiden. The winner has been rated to form.

## 2172 BETFRED RACING "LIKE US ON FACEBOOK" MAIDEN STKS (DIV II) 6f 213y
**2:30** (2:32) (Class 5) 3-Y-O+ **£3,881** (£1,155; £577; £288) **Stalls** Low

Form RPR

00-4 1 **Snow Squaw**[107] 212 3-8-3 67.................... DavidEgan(7) 2 71
(David Elsworth) *trckd ldrs: rdn to chal wl over 1f out: kpt on: led fnl stride* **7/1**

2 2 hd **Del Parco**[18] 1727 3-9-1 0.................... SamHitchcott 10 75
(Clive Cox) *hmpd s: sn upsides ldr: led over 4f out: rdn whn strly chal over 1f out: kpt on: hdd fnl stride* **10/11**[1]

3 4 **Moonwise (IRE)** 3-8-10 0.................... FranBerry 1 60
(Ralph Beckett) *trckd ldrs: swtchd lft over 2f out: sn rdn: kpt on fnl f but nt pce to threaten front pair* **10/3**[2]

0- 4 1 **Zulu**[247] 5820 3-9-1 0.................... RyanTate 9 62
(Rod Millman) *wnt lft s: sn led: hdd over 4f out: chsd ldr tl 2f out: sn rdn: kpt on same pce* **22/1**

34- 5 ½ **Twenty Times (IRE)**[225] 6577 3-8-10 0.................... ShaneKelly 8 56
(Richard Hughes) *hld up in tch: making hdwy whn hmpd over 2f out: rdn over 1f out: kpt on but nt pce to get on terms* **9/2**[3]

6 2 ¾ **Canford Tor (IRE)** 3-9-1 0.................... DaneO'Neill 5 53
(Harry Candy) *s.i.s: last pair but in tch: hdwy whn hmpd over 2f out: sn rdn: nt pce to get on terms: fdd fnl 120yds* **25/1**

7 12 **Babette (IRE)** 3-8-10 0.................... SteveDrowne 3 16
(Tony Newcombe) *last pair but in tch: rdn over 2f out: wknd over 1f out* **66/1**

1m 27.08s (-1.52) **Going Correction** -0.25s/f (Firm)
**WFA** 3 from 4yo 13lb **7** Ran SP% **115.8**
Speed ratings (Par 103): **98,97,93,92,91 88,74**
CSF £14.13 TOTE £10.10: £2.70, £1.40; EX 21.20 Trifecta £54.30.
**Owner** J C Smith **Bred** Littleton Stud **Trained** Newmarket, Suffolk
■ Stewards' Enquiry : Fran Berry two-day ban: guilty of careless riding in that he had switched his mount left-handed when not sufficiently clear (May 15-16)

**FOCUS**
The first two came nicely clear here, but the time was the slower of the two divisions by 0.69sec. The winner has been rated to last year's turf form.

## 2173 BETFRED "HOME OF GOALS GALORE" FILLIES' CONDITIONS STKS (PLUS 10 RACE) 5f
**3:00** (3:03) (Class 3) 2-Y-O **£9,703** (£2,887; £1,443; £721) **Stalls** Low

Form RPR

34 1 **Daddies Girl (IRE)**[6] 2037 2-8-9 0.................... LuluStanford(5) 3 78
(Rod Millman) *prom: led 2f out: kpt on gamely fnl f: rdn out* **7/1**[3]

2 2 ½ **Take Shelter**[11] 1884 2-9-0 0.................... LukeMorris 10 76
(James Tate) *wnt rt s: trckd ldrs: rdn 2f out: kpt on fnl f but a being hld* **1/1**[1]

3 nk **Billesdon Brook** 2-8-11 0.................... SeanLevey 7 72+
(Richard Hannon) *s.i.s: last pair: hdwy over 1f out: r.o wl fnl f: wnt 3rd cl home* **7/1**[3]

0 4 nk **Campion**[22] 1627 2-9-0 0.................... RyanMoore 9 74
(Richard Hannon) *hmpd s: trckd ldrs: rdn 2f out: ev ch ent fnl f: no ex nring fin* **5/1**[2]

5 1 **Di Fede (IRE)** 2-8-11 0.................... FranBerry 1 67
(Ralph Beckett) *mid-div: hdwy over 2f out: rdn over 1f out: kpt on same pce fnl f* **15/2**

6 2 ½ **Highland Mary** 2-8-11 0.................... TomMarquand 8 58+
(Richard Hannon) *hmpd s: mid-div: swtchd lft over 2f out: sn rdn: little imp* **16/1**

7 nse **Hastenplace** 2-8-11 0.................... RyanTate 11 58
(Rod Millman) *mid-div: rdn 2f out: little imp* **40/1**

8 1 ½ **Esther (IRE)** 2-8-11 0.................... ShaneKelly 2 53
(Amy Murphy) *led: rdn and hdd 2f out: wknd ins fnl f* **20/1**

9 2 **Dolly Dagger** 2-8-11 0.................... LiamKeniry 5 45
(Mark Usher) *s.i.s: mid-div: hdwy over 2f out: rdn over 1f out: wknd fnl f* **50/1**

10 4 ½ **Zain Smarts (IRE)** 2-8-11 0.................... JFEgan 6 29
(David Evans) *wnt lft s: prom: rdn over 2f out: sn hld: wknd ent fi al f* **16/1**

1m 0.26s (-0.74) **Going Correction** -0.25s/f (Firm) **10** Ran SP% **124.4**
Speed ratings (Par 93): **95,94,93,93,91 87,87,85,81,74**
CSF £15.18 TOTE £8.30: £2.30, £1.10, £2.40; EX 18.50 Trifecta £101.00.
**Owner** Daddies Girl Partnership **Bred** William Blake **Trained** Kentisbeare, Devon

**FOCUS**
It paid to be up with the gallop in this conditions race. The level is a bit fluid, but it's been rated at the mid point for the race average for now.

## 2174 BETFRED "SUPPORTS JACK BERRY HOUSE" H'CAP 1m 1f 198y
**3:30** (3:31) (Class 4) (0-85,85) 3-Y-O **£5,498** (£1,636; £817; £408) **Stalls** Low

Form RPR

41- 1 **Adamant (GER)**[209] 7013 3-9-3 **81**.................... RyanMoore 2 87
(Sir Michael Stoute) *led: pushed along over 4f out: hdd 3f out: sn rdn: led over 1f out: styd on wl ins fnl f: hld on gamely: drvn rt out* **13/8**[1]

421- 2 nk **Elas Ruby**[171] 7885 3-9-1 **78** ow1.................... JimmyFortune 7 83
(John Gosden) *mid-div: hdwy 3f out: rdn 2f out: styd on wl to press wnr ins fnl f: hld towards fin* **9/2**[2]

00-4 3 1 ½ **Koeman**[25] 1552 3-8-11 **75**.................... JFEgan 6 76
(Mick Channon) *hld up: hdwy over 4f out: rdn over 3f out: chal for 3rd fnl 2f: styd on wl fnl f but hld by front pair* **25/1**

510- 4 ½ **Viking Hoard (IRE)**[207] 7075 3-8-13 **77**.................... JimCrowley 10 77
(Harry Dunlop) *trckd ldrs: led 3f out: rdn and hdd over 1f out: edgd lft and no ex fnl 120yds* **16/1**

6- 5 ½ **Set In Stone (IRE)**[28] 1523 3-8-11 **75**.................... TadhgO'Shea 5 74
(John Patrick Shanahan, Ire) *mid-div: rdn 3f out: hdwy over 1f out: chsd ldrs ent fnl f: styd on* **14/1**

5-15 6 ½ **Earthly (USA)**[34] 1404 3-8-8 **72**.................... RichardKingscote 8 71
(Ralph Beckett) *trckd ldrs: rdn over 3f out: styng on at same pce whn edging sltly rt fnl 100yds* **15/2**

034- 7 hd **Galactic Prince**[207] 7075 3-8-12 **76**.................... DavidProbert 3 74
(Andrew Balding) *trckd ldrs: rdn over 2f out: styng on at same pce whn short of room fnl 100yds* **9/2**[2]

143- 8 3¾ **Haulani (USA)**[198] 7322 3-9-3 **81** FranBerry 9 71
(Philip Hide) *last pair: rdn over 3f out: nvr any imp* **7/1**[3]
2m 8.46s (-1.44) **Going Correction** -0.125s/f (Firm) **8** Ran SP% **115.1**
Speed ratings (Par 100): **100,99,98,98,97 97,97,94**
CSF £9.08 CT £128.33 TOTE £2.50: £1.30, £1.80, £5.00; EX 8.20 Trifecta £158.70.
**Owner** Highclere Thoroughbred Racing - Tennyson **Bred** Mark Johnston Racing Ltd **Trained** Newmarket, Suffolk

**FOCUS**
This was steadily run early on and the winner gradually upped the tempo from the front. They finished in a bit of a heap. The runner-up and third have been rated to their 2yo best.

## 2175 BETFRED "SUPER LEAGUE" EBF STALLIONS MAIDEN STKS 1m 4f 5y
**4:00** (4:00) (Class 5) 3-Y-O **£4,204** (£1,251; £625; £312) **Stalls** Low

Form RPR
42- 1 **Stone The Crows**[158] 8063 3-9-2 0 KieranShoemark(3) 5 81+
(Roger Charlton) *mde all: wandered u.p over 1f out: styd on wl: rdn out* **10/11**[1]
2 3¼ **Nadaitak** 3-9-5 0 JimCrowley 4 76
(Sir Michael Stoute) *trckd ldrs: trckd wnr over 7f out: rdn 2f out: lost 2nd whn hmpd in barging match w 3rd over 1f out: styd on to regain 2nd cl home* **5/2**[2]
3 nk **Unite The Clans (IRE)** 3-9-5 0 TadhgO'Shea 1 75
(John Patrick Shanahan, Ire) *racd keenly: trckd wnr tl over 7f out: rdn 2f out: regained 2nd but hmpd in barging match w runner up over 1f out: a being hld by wnr: no ex whn lost 2nd cl home* **10/1**
4 4 2½ **Turnpike Trip**[100] 328 3-9-5 0 FergusSweeney 3 71
(Henry Candy) *trckd ldrs: rdn 3f out: styd on same pce fnl 2f* **8/1**[3]
5 28 **Hamelin Pool** 3-9-5 0 DaneO'Neill 6 27
(Henry Candy) *trckd ldrs: pushed along 5f out: rdn 3f out: sn wknd* **10/1**
6 30 **Dartmoor Girl (IRE)** 3-9-0 0 TomMarquand 2
(Mark Gillard) *dwlt: racd green: a last: lost tch over 4f out* **66/1**
2m 36.84s (-1.16) **Going Correction** -0.125s/f (Firm) **6** Ran SP% **111.7**
Speed ratings (Par 98): **98,95,95,93,75 55**
CSF £3.32 TOTE £2.10: £1.20, £1.50; EX 3.80 Trifecta £14.80.
**Owner** A E Oppenheimer **Bred** Hascombe And Valiant Studs **Trained** Beckhampton, Wilts

**FOCUS**
A fair maiden. The level is fluid.

## 2176 BETFRED "CITY BOWL" H'CAP 1m 6f 44y
**4:30** (4:31) (Class 3) (0-95,96) 4-Y-O+
**£15,562** (£4,660; £2,330; £1,165; £582; £292)

Form RPR
06-3 1 **The Tartan Spartan (IRE)**[15] 1802 4-9-11 **96** TadhgO'Shea 8 104+
(John Patrick Shanahan, Ire) *hld up: gd hdwy fr 2 out: led fnl 150yds: styd on strly* **3/1**[2]
206- 2 1½ **Sunblazer (IRE)**[134] 8424 7-8-12 **88** (t) JoshuaBryan(7) 2 94
(Kim Bailey) *in tch: hdwy over 2f out: led wl over 1f out: sn rdn: hdd fnl 150yds: styd on but no ex* **20/1**
660- 3 1½ **Paris Protocol**[239] 6110 4-9-3 **88** RyanMoore 3 92
(Richard Hannon) *trckd ldrs: swtchd lft over 2f out: sn rdn: styd on but nt quite pce to chal* **5/4**[1]
50- 4 1¼ **Plymouth Sound**[172] 7869 5-8-8 **77** (v[1]) JohnFahy 4 79
(Eve Johnson Houghton) *racd keenly: hld up: hdwy 3f out: ev ch 2f out: sn rdn: fdd ins fnl f* **12/1**
-014 5 ½ **Cotton Club (IRE)**[73] 759 6-8-5 **74** RyanTate 1 75
(Rod Millman) *in tch: nt clr run over 2f out tl wl over 1f out: sn rdn to chal for 3rd: fdd fnl 150yds* **7/1**[3]
065- 6 shd **Glaring**[30] 6293 6-9-10 **93** JimmyFortune 5 94
(Amanda Perrett) *hld up: shkn up 3f out: rdn 2f out: nvr any imp* **16/1**
/06- 7 3¾ **Mark Hopkins**[317] 3351 5-9-4 **87** ShaneKelly 10 83
(David Elsworth) *led: rdn and hdd wl over 1f out: sn wknd* **11/1**
124- 8 6 **Great And Small**[212] 6917 4-9-2 **87** DavidProbert 11 75
(Andrew Balding) *trckd ldr: struggling to hold pl chsng ldrs whn squeezed up 2f out: sn wknd* **8/1**
3m 6.06s (-1.34) **Going Correction** -0.125s/f (Firm)
**WFA** 4 from 5yo+ 1lb **8** Ran SP% **119.7**
Speed ratings (Par 107): **98,97,96,95,95 95,93,89**
CSF £61.47 CT £112.33 TOTE £4.10: £1.30, £4.50, £1.10; EX 57.90 Trifecta £160.30.
**Owner** Thistle Bloodstock Limited **Bred** Thistle Bloodstock Ltd **Trained** Kells, Co Kilkenny

**FOCUS**
Flag start. A good performance from the winner, who is a stayer on the up. Muddling form. The runner-up has been rated to his turf best for now.

## 2177 BETFRED "FOLLOW US ON TWITTER" FILLIES' H'CAP 6f 213y
**5:00** (5:03) (Class 3) (0-90,87) 3-Y-O+ **£9,703** (£2,887; £1,443; £721) **Stalls** Low

Form RPR
0-12 1 **Cheval Blanche (USA)**[30] 1470 3-8-0 **77** LuluStanford(5) 1 85
(Michael Bell) *racd keenly: led after 1f: kpt on wl to assert ins fnl f: readily* **9/4**[1]
132- 2 3½ **Aristocratic**[200] 7281 4-9-9 **82** (p) RyanMoore 10 86
(Sir Michael Stoute) *led for 1f: trckd wnr: rdn over 2f out: kpt on but nt quite pce to chal: no ex fnl 160yds* **11/4**[2]
2-21 3 nk **Pepita (IRE)**[81] 624 3-8-8 **80** SeanLevey 2 78
(Richard Hannon) *broke wl: trckd ldrs: rdn to press for 2nd 2f out: kpt on but no ex ins fnl f* **11/2**
100/ 4 2½ **Jersey Breeze (IRE)**[555] 7432 4-9-4 **77** GeorgeDowning 5 73
(Mick Channon) *awkwardly away: hld up: rdn over 2f out: no imp tl kpt on into 4th ent fnl f fnl f: nt pce to threaten ldrs* **25/1**
10- 5 ½ **Billesdon Bess**[183] 7698 3-8-9 **81** TomMarquand 8 71
(Richard Hannon) *trckd ldrs: rdn over 2f out: nt pce to threaten: no ex fnl f* **4/1**[3]
-316 6 6 **Mitigate**[12] 1859 3-8-2 **77** HollieDoyle(3) 4 51
(David Elsworth) *in tch: rdn over 2f out: wknd ent fnl f* **8/1**
0-55 7 4 **Here's Two**[10] 1897 4-8-12 **71** LukeMorris 7 39
(Ron Hodges) *in tch: rdn over 2f out: wknd jst over 1f out* **9/1**
1m 25.45s (-3.15) **Going Correction** -0.25s/f (Firm)
**WFA** 3 from 4yo 13lb **7** Ran SP% **117.8**
Speed ratings (Par 104): **108,104,103,100,100 93,88**
CSF £9.14 CT £29.98 TOTE £3.10: £1.70, £1.90; EX 11.20 Trifecta £42.20.
**Owner** The Hon Mrs J M Corbett & C Wright **Bred** Klawervlei Stud **Trained** Newmarket, Suffolk

**FOCUS**
A good performance from the winner here, taking the race apart from the front. The runner-up has been rated to form.

## 2178 BETFRED TV H'CAP (FOR LADY AMATEUR RIDERS) 6f 213y
**5:30** (5:30) (Class 6) (0-65,64) 4-Y-O+ **£3,119** (£967; £483; £242) **Stalls** Low

Form RPR
0425 1 **Almanack**[23] 1603 7-9-12 **55** MissSBrotherton 1 69
(Mark Pattinson) *in tch: hdwy fr 4f out: led 3f out: rdn clr over 1f out: easily* **13/8**[1]
-011 2 6 **Living Leader**[32] 1425 8-9-5 **55** MissCMBerry(7) 6 53
(Grace Harris) *chsd ldrs: sltly outpcd 3f out: hdwy fr 2f out: kpt on to go 2nd fnl f but no ch w wnr* **8/1**
0626 3 1¾ **Mambo Spirit (IRE)**[18] 1723 13-10-0 **62** MissJCooley(5) 5 55
(Tony Newcombe) *t.k.h: hld up: hdwy over 4f out to trck ldrs: rdn over 2f out: sn hld but kpt on to go 3rd fnl f* **16/1**
6406 4 2¾ **Quintus Cerialis (IRE)**[34] 1407 5-9-3 **51** (tp) PoppyBridgwater(5) 2 36
(Karen George) *s.i.s: last: hdwy over 3f out: ev ch 2f out: sn rdn and hld by wnr: no ex and lost 2 pls fnl f* **9/1**
24-0 5 nk **Concur (IRE)**[6] 2043 4-9-7 **50** oh4 (tp) MissJoannaMason 9 34
(Rod Millman) *trckd ldrs: ev ch 3f out: sn rdn: one pce fnl 2f* **7/1**[3]
40-6 6 2¼ **General Brook (IRE)**[94] 421 7-9-7 **50** oh1 (v[1]) MissBrodieHampson 3 28
(John O'Shea) *in tch: outpcd in rr 3f out: sme late prog: n.d* **17/2**
-053 7 ½ **Mister Musicmaster**[6] 2023 8-10-5 **62** BryonyFrost 8 39
(Ron Hodges) *trckd ldr: led over 4f out: hdd 3f out: sn rdn: wknd ent fnl f* **6/1**[2]
0-00 8 1½ **Imperial Link**[67] 865 5-9-10 **53** (p) MissBeckySmith 7 26
(John O'Shea) *led tl over 4f out: rdn 3f out: wknd over 1f out* **20/1**
00-4 9 8 **Knight Of The Air**[45] 1219 5-10-0 **64** MrsCPownall(7) 4 15
(Joseph Tuite) *in tch: rdn over 2f out: wknd over 1f out* **9/1**
1m 27.33s (-1.27) **Going Correction** -0.25s/f (Firm) **9** Ran SP% **117.2**
Speed ratings (Par 101): **97,90,88,85,84 82,81,79,70**
CSF £15.60 CT £157.76 TOTE £2.00: £1.10, £1.60, £3.60; EX 10.90 Trifecta £41.60.
**Owner** M I Pattinson Racing **Bred** Ed's Stud Ltd **Trained** Epsom, Surrey

**FOCUS**
An ordinary heat.
T/Plt: £2.80 to a £1 stake. Pool: £80,031.79 - 20,469.80 winning units. T/Qpdt: £2.10 to a £1 stake. Pool: £6,060.11 - 2,131.68 winning units. **Tim Mitchell**

# 1971 THIRSK (L-H)
Sunday, April 30

**OFFICIAL GOING: Good (good to firm in places; 8.5)**
Wind: Blustery, largely across Weather: Fine

## 2179 THIRSK RACES DISCOVER RACING FAMILY SUNDAY H'CAP 7f
**2:15** (2:16) (Class 6) (0-60,61) 4-Y-O+ **£3,234** (£962; £481; £240) **Stalls** Low

Form RPR
06-0 1 **The Name's Paver**[20] 1680 4-9-5 **58** PaulMulrennan 3 65
(Noel Wilson) *prom: pushed along to ld over 2f out: rdn whn hdd narrowly over 1f out: kpt on: led again towards fin* **11/2**[2]
600- 2 nk **Destination Aim**[177] 7797 10-9-4 **57** GrahamLee 6 63
(Fred Watson) *trckd ldrs: rdn over 1f out: led narrowly appr fnl f: no ex and hdd towards fin* **16/1**
6565 3 1¼ **Cool Strutter (IRE)**[60] 969 5-8-13 **57** GemmaTutty(5) 5 60
(Karen Tutty) *trckd ldrs: rdn over 2f out: kpt on* **17/2**
0014 4 1½ **Bogsnog (IRE)**[18] 1721 7-9-4 **57** JamesSullivan 8 56
(Ruth Carr) *in tch: pushed along to chal over 2f out: rdn over 1f out: sn one pce: edgd lft ins fnl f* **7/2**[1]
0-16 5 1 **Symbolic Star (IRE)**[34] 1408 5-8-8 **54** (p) ConnorMurtagh(7) 9 50+
(Barry Murtagh) *slowly away: hld up on outside: rdn and gd hdwy over 2f out: wknd ins fnl f* **8/1**
0-01 6 2¼ **Luath**[12] 1868 4-9-8 **61** TomEaves 4 51
(Suzzanne France) *midfield on inner: rdn over 2f out: one pce and nvr threatened* **9/1**
250- 7 1¾ **Beverley Bullet**[152] 8145 4-9-1 **57** NathanAlison(3) 7 42+
(Lawrence Mullaney) *slowly away: hld up: rdn over 2f out: nvr threatened ldrs* **13/2**[3]
5050 8 2¼ **Disclosure**[18] 1721 6-8-8 **52** PhilDennis(5) 10 31+
(Declan Carroll) *hld up: tk v str hold and plld way into midfield 1/2-way: rdn to chse ldrs over 2f out: wknd over 1f out* **12/1**
0P50 9 ½ **Devious Spirit (IRE)**[85] 579 5-8-10 **52** AdamMcNamara(3) 1 30+
(Iain Jardine) *hld up: nvr threatened* **12/1**
666- 10 1 **Lukoutoldmakezebak**[229] 6436 4-8-9 **48** JasonHart 2 23
(David Thompson) *led: rdn whn hdd over 2f out: wknd* **33/1**
360 11 hd **Slaying The Dragon (IRE)**[20] 1680 4-8-5 **51** FayeMcManoman(7) 11 26+
(Nigel Tinkler) *stdd s: hld up in midfield: pushed along 3f out: sn btn* **80/1**
000- 12 shd **Saxon Gold (IRE)**[240] 6106 4-9-0 **53** (p) PhillipMakin 12 27
(John Davies) *midfield on outer: lost pl over 3f out: sn bhd* **16/1**
1m 29.57s (2.37) **Going Correction** +0.225s/f (Good) **12** Ran SP% **113.9**
Speed ratings (Par 101): **95,94,93,91,90 87,85,83,82,81 81,81**
CSF £86.47 CT £736.20 TOTE £5.80: £1.80, £4.20, £3.10; EX 90.50 Trifecta £1166.60.
**Owner** G J Paver **Bred** Mrs C K Paver **Trained** Marwood, Co Durham
■ Stewards' Enquiry : Faye McManoman 2 day ban (15-16 May) - guilty of careless riding

**FOCUS**
A moderate handicap, run at a routine sort of pace.

## 2180 VISIT THE START TODAY MAIDEN AUCTION STKS 6f
**2:45** (2:45) (Class 6) 3-Y-O **£3,234** (£962; £481; £240) **Stalls** High

Form RPR
65- 1 **Muscika**[199] 7307 3-9-3 0 DanielTudhope 6 80+
(David O'Meara) *trckd ldrs: briefly short of room over 2f out: rdn and bit outpcd over 1f out: r.o wl fnl 110yds: led towards fin* **15/8**[1]
0 2 ½ **World Power (IRE)**[9] 1947 3-8-13 0 PJMcDonald 4 74
(Paul Cole) *prom: led 3f out: rdn 2f out: hdd appr fnl f: kpt on* **7/1**
0 3 shd **Mabs Cross**[19] 1705 3-8-6 0 ConnorBeasley 5 66
(Michael Dods) *dwlt: sn trckd ldrs: upsides on bit 2f out: rdn to ld narrowly appr fnl f: one pce and hdd towards fin: lost 2nd post* **7/2**[2]
0-4 4 4½ **Angel's Acclaim (IRE)**[16] 1782 3-8-13 0 ShaneGray 11 60
(Kevin Ryan) *midfield: pushed along 2f out: one pce and nvr threatened: wnt 4th post* **11/2**[3]
5 nk **Granny Roz** 3-8-11 0 PhillipMakin 1 57
(David Barron) *wnt lft s: hld up: pushed along and gd hdwy over 1f out: edgd lft and wknd ins fnl f: lost 4th post* **12/1**

2335 **6** *3 ½* **Alfonso Manana (IRE)**[16] 1782 3-9-1 69........................(p) JoeFanning 2 50
(James Given) *chsd ldrs on outer: rdn over 2f out: wknd over 1f out* **7/1**

00- **7** *2 ¾* **Whisper A Word (IRE)**[300] 3947 3-8-4 0............ RachelRichardson(3) 8 34
(Tim Easterby) *midfield: rdn over 2f out: sn wknd* **66/1**

06- **8** *¾* **Vivardia (IRE)**[156] 8087 3-8-11 58........................................ GrahamLee 3 36
(Ben Haslam) *midfield: rdn 3f out: sn wknd* **33/1**

60 **9** *¾* **Nonnie And Norny**[30] 1471 3-8-7 0............................. RoystonFfrench 7 30
(Shaun Harris) *a towards rr* **250/1**

4-0 **10** *17* **Suited**[19] 1705 3-8-11 0........................................................ DavidAllan 12
(Tim Easterby) *led: hdd 3f out: sn wknd* **33/1**

1m 12.75s (0.05) **Going Correction** +0.075s/f (Good) **10** Ran SP% **112.9**
Speed ratings (Par 96): **102,101,101,95,94 90,86,85,84,61**
CSF £14.88 TOTE £2.80: £1.50, £2.10, £1.60; EX 16.80 Trifecta £73.10.
**Owner** Gallop Racing & Dynast Racing **Bred** Dukes Stud & Overbury Stallions Ltd **Trained** Upper Helmsley, N Yorks

**FOCUS**
Not a bad sprint maiden for the class. The second and third have both been rated as improving on their debut efforts.

## 2181 THIRSK RACECOURSE LICENSED FOR WEDDING CEREMONIES H'CAP (DIV I) 6f

**3:15** (3:16) (Class 6) (0-60,64) 3-Y-O **£3,234** (£962; £481; £240) **Stalls** High

Form RPR

00-0 **1** **Kaeso**[28] 1513 3-9-3 56........................................................ TomEaves 8 62
(Nigel Tinkler) *dwlt: midfield on inner: short of room 2f out tl appr fnl f: r.o strly once clr: led post* **11/1**

404- **2** *nk* **Arnold**[197] 7355 3-9-4 57........................................................ JoeyHaynes 1 62
(Ann Duffield) *dwlt: hld up: gd hdwy over 2f out: pushed along to ld over 1f out: rdn ins fnl f: edgd rt fnl 75yds: hdd post* **6/1**[2]

5420 **3** *½* **Scotch Myst**[13] 1835 3-9-2 55........................................... TonyHamilton 9 59
(Richard Fahey) *in tch: ct bhd wkng rival and shuffled bk wl over 1f: rdn and hdwy appr fnl f: kpt on: bit short of room nr fin* **8/1**[3]

43-6 **4** *1 ½* **Paquita Bailarina**[22] 1626 3-9-2 55.................................... JoeFanning 6 54
(James Given) *hld up: racd keenly: hdwy 2f out: rdn to chse ldr appr fnl f: no ex fnl 110yds* **14/1**

533- **5** *1* **Kroy**[247] 5840 3-9-6 59.............................................................. PaulHanagan 10 55
(Ollie Pears) *chsd ldrs: n.m.r 2f out tl jst ins fnl f and lost pl: no ch after but kpt on pushed out* **8/1**[3]

05-2 **6** *½* **Judy Woods (IRE)**[13] 1835 3-9-11 64........................... ConnorBeasley 5 59
(Bryan Smart) *hld up: hdwy on outside over 2f out: rdn to chal over 1f out: hung lft and wknd ins fnl f* **9/2**[1]

00-1 **7** *3 ¾* **See You Mush**[24] 1580 3-9-5 58..........................(bt[1]) AdamBeschizza 13 41
(Mrs Ilka Gansera-Leveque) *prom: rdn over 2f out: wknd fnl f* **8/1**[3]

-300 **8** *4 ½* **Vaux (IRE)**[13] 1835 3-9-4 57........................................(p) GrahamLee 7 27
(Ben Haslam) *hld up: sme hdwy whn hmpd appr fnl f: no ch after* **22/1**

540- **9** *3 ½* **Myllachy**[158] 8072 3-8-11 50.................................................. DavidAllan 4 9
(Tim Easterby) *a towards rr* **14/1**

00-0 **10** *nk* **Zebedee Star**[13] 1835 3-8-9 53................................ GemmaTutty(5) 12 11
(Karen Tutty) *prom: rdn over 2f out: wknd fnl f* **20/1**

325- **11** *1 ¾* **Glyder**[196] 7381 3-9-7 60...................................................... RoystonFfrench 3 13
(John Holt) *chsd ldrs: rdn over 2f out: wknd over 1f out* **14/1**

520- **12** *12* **Equity**[208] 7041 3-9-7 60............................................................ PaulMulrennan 11
(David Brown) *led narrowly: rdn whn hdd over 1f out: wknd* **8/1**[3]

00-0 **13** *3 ½* **Miss Pepper (IRE)**[18] 1715 3-8-7 46 oh1.............................. CamHardie 2
(Paul Midgley) *prom: rdn over 2f out: wknd over 1f out* **100/1**

1m 13.99s (1.29) **Going Correction** +0.075s/f (Good) **13** Ran SP% **115.3**
Speed ratings (Par 96): **94,93,92,90,89 88,83,77,73,72 70,54,49**
CSF £71.53 CT £579.74 TOTE £10.00: £2.90, £2.80, £2.50; EX 143.00 Trifecta £2663.60.
**Owner** M Webb **Bred** Sir Eric Parker **Trained** Langton, N Yorks

**FOCUS**
A moderate sprint handicap.

## 2182 THIRSK RACECOURSE LICENSED FOR WEDDING CEREMONIES H'CAP (DIV II) 6f

**3:45** (3:45) (Class 6) (0-60,62) 3-Y-O **£3,234** (£962; £481; £240) **Stalls** High

Form RPR

0446 **1** **Mr Strutter (IRE)**[51] 1127 3-8-9 55..............................(h) JoshQuinn(7) 11 65
(John Quinn) *mde all: rdn 2 l clr appr fnl f: edgd lft ins fnl f: reduced advantage towards fin but nvr in danger* **8/1**

6-00 **2** *nk* **Majestic Stone (IRE)**[30] 1474 3-8-12 51........................(v[1]) JoeDoyle 5 60
(Julie Camacho) *hld up: rdn 2f out: hdwy appr fnl f: kpt on wl: wnt 2nd 50yds out: gaining at fin* **14/1**

50-3 **3** *1* **Regal Decree**[13] 1835 3-9-1 54............................................ JackGarritty 2 60
(Jedd O'Keeffe) *chsd ldrs: rdn over 2f out: chsd ldr over 1f out: kpt on same pce: lost 2nd 50yds out* **4/1**[1]

4305 **4** *1* **Mimic's Memory**[13] 1835 3-9-4 57........................................ ShaneGray 8 60
(Ann Duffield) *trckd ldrs: rdn over 1f out: one pce* **14/1**

3553 **5** *1 ¾* **Bismarck The Flyer (IRE)**[4] 2077 3-9-5 58.................. AndrewMullen 4 56
(Ollie Pears) *midfield: pushed along over 2f out: rdn over 1f out: one pce* **4/1**[1]

0-33 **6** *¾* **Darvie**[37] 1349 3-9-9 62.......................................................... PhillipMakin 6 58+
(David Barron) *dwlt: hld up: pushed along 2f out: rdn and sme hdwy appr fnl f: one pce and nvr threatened* **7/1**[2]

0-64 **7** *1 ¾* **Ejabah (IRE)**[32] 1432 3-8-9 55...................................... BenRobinson(7) 10 45
(Charles Smith) *midfield: rdn and outpcd over 2f out: no threat after* **12/1**

3-30 **8** *4 ½* **Emerald Secret (IRE)**[13] 1828 3-9-6 59...........................(p) GrahamLee 9 36
(Paul Midgley) *pressed ldr: rdn over 2f out: wknd over 1f out* **11/1**

346- **9** *1 ¾* **Trois Bon Amis (IRE)**[303] 3852 3-9-8 61............................... DavidAllan 3 33
(Tim Easterby) *prom: rdn over 2f out: wknd over 1f out* **9/1**

-512 **10** *3* **Skellig Michael**[58] 1005 3-9-7 60..................................(p) PJMcDonald 12 23+
(Ben Haslam) *prom: rdn over 2f out: wknd over 1f out* **15/2**[3]

600- **11** *2 ½* **I Dare To Dream**[180] 7749 3-8-2 48.................................. JordanUys(7) 1
(Lisa Williamson) *dwlt and wnt lft s: a towards rr* **50/1**

1m 13.46s (0.76) **Going Correction** +0.075s/f (Good) **11** Ran SP% **116.7**
Speed ratings (Par 96): **97,96,95,93,91 90,88,82,79,75 72**
CSF £113.32 CT £524.92 TOTE £9.70: £3.10, £4.70, £1.60; EX 152.50 Trifecta £1049.30.
**Owner** JJ Quinn Racing Ltd **Bred** Wardstown Stud Ltd **Trained** Settrington, N Yorks
■ Stewards' Enquiry : Josh Quinn 4 day ban (15-18 May) - used whip above the permitted level and with his whip arm above shoulder height

**FOCUS**
The second division of the ordinary 6f handicap was 0.53secs quicker than the first.

## 2183 ADVANCE TICKET BOOKING DISCOUNT AT THIRSKRACECOURSE.NET H'CAP 1m 4f 8y

**4:15** (4:15) (Class 6) (0-65,65) 4-Y-O+ **£3,234** (£962; £481; £240) **Stalls** High

Form RPR

-544 **1** **Melabi (IRE)**[19] 1707 4-8-13 65........................ CallumRodriguez(7) 14 73
(Richard Ford) *hld up: rdn and gd hdwy on outside over 2f out: led 1f out: kpt on* **13/2**[3]

-665 **2** *¾* **Mr Sundowner (USA)**[30] 1473 5-8-0 51 oh2.........(t) ConnorMurtagh(7) 8 58
(Wilf Storey) *in tch: wnt prom 5f out: led over 2f out: rdn over 1f out: hdd 1f out: kpt on but a hld* **11/1**

2/32 **3** *1* **Rembrandt**[13] 1834 5-9-7 65...................................................(p) GrahamLee 7 70
(Rebecca Menzies) *in tch: pushed along to chse ldr 2f out: rdn over 1f out: kpt on same pce* **5/1**[2]

00-1 **4** *1 ¾* **Life Knowledge (IRE)**[37] 726 5-8-6 57............................ PaulaMuir(7) 11 59
(Patrick Holmes) *hld up in midfield: rdn and hdwy on outer over 2f out: chsd ldr over 1f out: no ex ins fnl f* **17/2**

1363 **5** *1 ¼* **The Lock Master (IRE)**[26] 1549 10-9-3 64........(p) AlistairRawlinson(3) 1 64
(Michael Appleby) *chsd ldr: rdn 3f out: one pce* **12/1**

56-0 **6** *2 ½* **Steccando (IRE)**[18] 1717 4-9-6 65....................................... JoeFanning 9 61
(Alan Swinbank) *midfield: pushed along over 2f out: rdn over 1f out: one pce* **22/1**

310- **7** *1 ¼* **Pertuis (IRE)**[43] 4409 11-9-5 63........................................... PJMcDonald 12 57
(Micky Hammond) *midfield: rdn over 2f out: one pce* **40/1**

046- **8** *nk* **Mrs Biggs**[138] 8351 5-8-4 53.......................................... PhilDennis(5) 13 47
(Declan Carroll) *in tch: rdn 3f out: wknd fnl f* **10/1**

00-0 **9** *nk* **Moccasin (FR)**[109] 176 8-8-8 52 oh6 ow1......................(v) DavidAllan 10 45
(Geoffrey Harker) *hld up: rdn over 3f out: styd on fnl f: nvr threatened* **20/1**

435- **10** *¾* **Adherence**[188] 7582 4-8-12 57........................................... BarryMcHugh 3 49
(Tony Coyle) *in tch: rdn over 2f out: wknd over 1f out* **14/1**

033- **11** *¾* **Moon Over Rio (IRE)**[95] 6029 6-8-10 59.............. MeganNicholls(5) 15 50+
(Ben Haslam) *hld up: nvr threatened* **20/1**

542- **12** *hd* **Judicious**[263] 5293 10-8-13 57................................................... SamJames 4 48
(Geoffrey Harker) *v.s.a: a towards rr* **20/1**

0-64 **13** *1 ½* **Whitecliff Park (IRE)**[13] 1839 4-8-4 56......................... BenRobinson(7) 6 44
(Brian Ellison) *midfield: rdn over 3f out: sn lost pl and btn* **9/2**[1]

600- **14** *7* **Breton Blues**[177] 7795 7-8-4 51 oh6..............................(p) NathanEvans(3) 5 28
(Fred Watson) *midfield: rdn over 3f out: sn wknd* **50/1**

026- **15** *¾* **King Of Paradise (IRE)**[251] 5718 8-9-2 60.............................. JasonHart 2 36+
(Eric Alston) *led: racd keenly: rdn whn hdd over 2f out: wknd* **22/1**

2m 38.78s (2.58) **Going Correction** +0.225s/f (Good) **15** Ran SP% **117.9**
Speed ratings (Par 101): **100,99,98,97,96 95,94,94,93,93 92,92,91,87,86**
CSF £65.85 CT £390.28 TOTE £7.60: £2.50, £4.30, £1.90; EX 87.60 Trifecta £633.00.
**Owner** J H Chrimes **Bred** Barronstown Stud **Trained** Garstang, Lancs

**FOCUS**
Race distance increased by about 20yds. A weak 1m4f handicap. Straightforward enough form for the class.

## 2184 POMPILIO SAVIGNANO H'CAP 6f

**4:45** (4:47) (Class 4) (0-85,85) 4-Y-O+ **£5,175** (£1,540; £769; £384) **Stalls** High

Form RPR

000- **1** **Zanetto**[173] 7858 7-9-5 83...................................................... JasonHart 8 92+
(John Quinn) *trckd ldrs: briefly had to wait for gap over 1f out: qcknd to ld ins fnl f: rdn and kpt on wl* **8/1**[2]

0-03 **2** *1* **Kalk Bay (IRE)**[16] 1778 10-8-11 82............................(t) HarrisonShaw(7) 2 88
(Michael Easterby) *hld up: gd hdwy on outer 2f out: rdn and ev ch ins fnl f: kpt on* **12/1**

340- **3** *1 ¼* **Rose Marmara**[218] 6793 4-8-13 77...................................(t) BarryMcHugh 7 79
(Brian Rothwell) *chsd ldrs: rdn 2f out: ev ch ins fnl f: one pce* **22/1**

56-U **4** *½* **Casterbridge**[15] 1805 5-8-8 72................................................(h) NeilFarley 6 72
(Eric Alston) *led: rdn 2f out: hdd ins fnl f: no ex* **16/1**

00-3 **5** *¾* **Grandad's World (IRE)**[13] 1831 5-9-2 80.......................... PaulHanagan 9 78
(Richard Fahey) *prom: rdn 2f out: no ex ins fnl f* **2/1**[1]

130- **6** *½* **Market Choice (IRE)**[198] 7325 4-8-10 74............................ PJMcDonald 3 70
(Tracy Waggott) *dwlt: sn in tch on outer: rdn 2f out: no ex ins fnl f* **16/1**

034- **7** *¾* **Duke Cosimo**[166] 7965 7-9-1 79........................................ TomEaves 13 73
(Michael Herrington) *dwlt: hld up: rdn 2f out: nvr threatened* **9/1**[3]

000- **8** *1 ½* **Pomme De Terre (IRE)**[206] 7094 5-9-1 79...........(p) PaulMulrennan 11 68
(Michael Dods) *midfield: rdn 2f out: wknd over 1f out* **8/1**[2]

0-00 **9** *2* **Cosmic Chatter**[13] 1831 7-9-7 85.................................(p) JamesSullivan 4 68
(Ruth Carr) *chsd ldrs: rdn over 2f out: wknd appr fnl f* **8/1**[2]

1- **10** *7* **Oh James**[379] 1494 4-8-11 75............................................ DavidAllan 12 35
(Tim Easterby) *dwlt: hld up: pushed along over 2f out: sn wknd* **8/1**[2]

1m 12.65s (-0.05) **Going Correction** +0.075s/f (Good) **10** Ran SP% **111.6**
Speed ratings (Par 105): **103,101,100,99,98 97,96,94,92,82**
CSF £94.99 CT £2017.39 TOTE £8.50: £2.40, £3.00, £6.40; EX 81.40 Trifecta £1223.20.
**Owner** Malcolm Walker **Bred** Aislabie Bloodstock Ltd **Trained** Settrington, N Yorks

**FOCUS**
Not a bad sprint handicap. The runner-up has been rated in line with his recent form.

## 2185 THIRSK RACECOURSE IDEAL CONFERENCE VENUE MAIDEN STKS 7f 218y

**5:15** (5:18) (Class 5) 3-Y-O **£3,881** (£1,155; £577; £288) **Stalls** Low

Form RPR

**1** **Secret Advisor (FR)** 3-9-5 0................................................... MartinLane 7 77+
(Charlie Appleby) *slowly away: hld up: pushed along and stl plenty to do 2f out: gd hdwy over 1f out: rdn and kpt on wl fnl f: led towards fin* **7/1**[3]

2- **2** *½* **Materialist**[198] 7317 3-9-5 0.............................................(h[1]) AndreaAtzeni 4 76+
(Roger Varian) *early to post: racd keenly: sn led: pushed along over 1f out: rdn ins fnl f: one pce and hdd towards fin* **8/15**[1]

3 **3** *2 ¼* **Born To Boom (IRE)**[18] 1730 3-9-0 0................................ CliffordLee(5) 14 71
(K R Burke) *trckd ldrs: rdn along over 2f out: kpt on same pce* **6/1**[2]

5 **4** *hd* **Give It Some Teddy**[28] 1514 3-9-5 0..................................... NeilFarley 12 70
(Alan Swinbank) *trckd ldrs: rdn over 2f out: kpt on same pce* **20/1**

4- **5** *1 ¼* **Mount Rock**[136] 8384 3-9-2 0........................................ NathanEvans(3) 9 67
(Michael Easterby) *in tch: pushed along over 2f out: rdn appr fnl f: no ex ins fnl f* **10/1**

34 **6** *3 ¼* **Ninepin Bowler**[13] 1829 3-9-5 0...................................... PaulMulrennan 3 59
(Michael Dods) *trckd ldrs: pushed along over 2f out: wknd ins fnl f* **16/1**

00- **7** *1* **Cornerstone Lad**[180] 7740 3-9-5 0......................................... PJMcDonald 10 57
(Micky Hammond) *hld up: sme late hdwy: nvr threatened* **200/1**

**8** *½* **Zone In** 3-9-5 0.............................................................. TonyHamilton 11 56
(Roger Fell) *prom: rdn over 2f out: wknd over 1f out* **66/1**

56- 9 2 **Pioneering (IRE)**[227] 6523 3-9-5 0 DanielTudhope 8 51
(David O'Meara) *midfield: pushed along over 2f out: sn wknd* **22/1**
0 10 2 **Foxy Rebel**[13] 1830 3-9-5 0 JamesSullivan 13 46
(Ruth Carr) *a towards rr* **125/1**
5-0 11 nk **Tread Lightly**[10] 1914 3-9-5 0 DavidAllan 1 45
(Tim Easterby) *dwlt: hld up: nvr threatened* **100/1**
60 12 nk **Rock Island Line**[13] 1829 3-9-5 0 DougieCostello 6 45
(Mark Walford) *midfield: pushed along 3f out: grad wknd* **150/1**
60- 13 26 **Musico (IRE)**[177] 7792 3-9-5 0 JackGarritty 5
(Patrick Holmes) *in tch: rdn over 3f out: wknd* **200/1**
0 14 99 **Tilly Tinker**[20] 1680 3-9-0 0 CamHardie 2
(Michael Easterby) *virtually ref to r and effectively tk no part* **100/1**
1m 41.93s (1.83) **Going Correction** +0.225s/f (Good) **14 Ran SP% 122.0**
Speed ratings (Par 98): **99,98,96,96,94 91,90,90,88,86 85,85,59,**
CSF £11.03 TOTE £8.00: £1.90, £1.10, £1.50; EX 14.70 Trifecta £42.30.
**Owner** Godolphin **Bred** S C E A Haras De Saint Pair **Trained** Newmarket, Suffolk
**FOCUS**
Race distance increased by about 20yds. This wasn't a bad maiden. The third and fifth have been rated close to their debut form.

## 2186 TOTEPOOL THIRSK HUNT CUP THIS SATURDAY H'CAP 7f 218y
**5:45** (5:47) (Class 5) (0-70,71) 3-Y-O **£3,881** (£1,155; £577; £288) **Stalls** Low

Form RPR
00-5 1 **Helovaplan (IRE)**[15] 1804 3-9-6 **68** ConnorBeasley 5 77
(Bryan Smart) *dwlt: hld up: pushed along and hdwy 2f out: rdn to ld 1f out: edgd lft: kpt on* **6/1**[3]
1-6 2 ½ **Lucy's Law (IRE)**[20] 1678 3-9-3 **65** JamesSullivan 2 72
(Tom Tate) *hld up: rdn and hdwy over 1f out: kpt on fnl f* **17/2**
0-36 3 1 **Barwell (IRE)**[16] 1782 3-9-1 **63** PaulMulrennan 3 68
(Michael Dods) *led: hdd over 2f out: sn rdn: kpt on same pce* **8/1**
630- 4 2 **Racemaker**[198] 7319 3-9 7 **69** NeilFarley 6 69
(Andrew Crook) *trckd ldrs: rdn over 2f out: one pce* **33/1**
600- 5 shd **True Romance (IRE)**[188] 7580 3-9-3 **65** TomEaves 4 65
(James Given) *prom: led over 2f out: sn rdn: hdd 1f out: wknd* **10/1**
05-4 6 ½ **Mister Moosah (IRE)**[6] 2035 3-9-2 **64** PJMcDonald 9 63
(Micky Hammond) *midfield: rdn over 2f out: one pce and nvr threatened* **5/1**[2]
330- 7 1½ **Heatongrad (IRE)**[198] 7319 3-9-9 **71** PaulHanagan 7 66
(Richard Fahey) *trckd ldrs: rdn over 2f out: wknd fnl f* **11/4**[1]
545 8 5 **Channel Packet**[24] 1584 3-9-4 **69** AlistairRawlinson(3) 8 53
(Michael Appleby) *in tch on outer: rdn over 2f out: sn wknd* **18/1**
-526 9 1 **Hotfill**[85] 578 3-9-5 **67** PhillipMakin 10 48
(David Barron) *s.i.s: hld up: nvr threatened* **7/1**
00-3 10 11 **Stevie Brown**[24] 1589 3-8-11 **66** KevinLundie(7) 1 22
(David Brown) *midfield on inner: rdn over 2f out: sn wknd* **22/1**
1m 42.1s (2.00) **Going Correction** +0.225s/f (Good) **10 Ran SP% 113.4**
Speed ratings (Par 98): **99,98,97,95,95 94,93,88,87,76**
CSF £54.45 CT £408.00 TOTE £7.90: £3.00, £3.00, £2.30; EX 59.10 Trifecta £757.00.
**Owner** The Smart Set **Bred** Ross Moorhead **Trained** Hambleton, N Yorks
**FOCUS**
Race distance increased by about 20yds. An ordinary 3yo handicap, rated around the runner-up. The runner-up has been rated in line with her Newcastle win.
T/Jkpt: Not Won. T/Plt: £364.40 to a £1 stake. Pool: £95,138.82 - 190.59 winning units. T/Qpdt: £146.20 to a £1 stake. Pool: £6,977.81 - 35.31 winning units. **Andrew Sheret**

2187 - 2200a (Foreign Racing) - See Raceform Interactive

# 1919 CHANTILLY (R-H)
Sunday, April 30
**OFFICIAL GOING: Turf: good; polytrack: standard**

## 2201a PRIX ALLEZ FRANCE (GROUP 3) (4YO+ FILLIES & MARES) (TURF) 1m 2f
**2:45** 4-Y-O+ **£34,188** (£13,675; £10,256; £6,837; £3,418)

RPR
1 **The Black Princess (FR)**[173] 7862 4-8-11 0 FrankieDettori 5 109
(John Gosden) *led: kicked clr fr 1 1/2f out: styd on strly and edgd lft fnl f: a holding runner-up* **11/8**[1]
2 1¼ **Armande (IRE)**[28] 1530 4-8-11 0 Pierre-CharlesBoudot 3 106+
(A Fabre, France) *w.w in midfield between horses: rdn and clsd to chse ldr 1f out: unable to mount a chal* **5/2**[2]
3 ½ **Happy Approach (FR)**[24] 4-8-9 0 GregoryBenoist 1 103
(M Nigge, France) *hld up in midfield on inner: drvn and styd on fr 1 1/2f out: kpt on at same pce fnl f* **12/1**
4 ½ **That Which Is Not (USA)**[28] 1530 4-8-9 0 StephanePasquier 6 102
(F-H Graffard, France) *settled in fnl trio: clsd whn drvn 1 1/2f out: chsd ldrs ins fnl f: nt pce to chal* **7/2**[3]
5 nk **Thank You Bye Bye (FR)**[28] 1530 5-8-11 0 ow2 ChristopheSoumillon 8 103
(J-P Gauvin, France) *w.w in fnl pair: hdwy over 1 1/2f out: sn rdn: styd on fnl f: nt pce to get on terms* **8/1**
6 3 **Olala (GER)**[28] 4-8-9 0 GeraldMosse 2 95
(W Mongil, Germany) *racd a little keenly: hld up on inner bhd ldr: drvn and nt qckn wl over 1f out: one pce fnl f: fdd late on* **25/1**
7 3½ **Flemish Duchesse (FR)**[28] 4-8-9 0 MaximeGuyon 4 88
(Andreas Suborics, Germany) *hld up bhd ldr on outer: drvn and nt qckn wl over 1 1/2f out: wknd fnl f* **25/1**
8 ¾ **Icecapada (IRE)**[196] 7395 5-8-11 0 AlexisBadel 7 89
(Niels Petersen, Norway) *settled in midfield on outer: drvn and short-lived effrt 1 1/2f out: sn btn* **33/1**
9 4½ **Do Re Mi Fa Sol (FR)**[162] 8042 4-8-11 0 FranckBlondel 9 80
(P Decouz, France) *w.w in fnl pair: drvn and no imp fr 2f out: bhd over 1f out* **25/1**
2m 3.26s (-1.54) **9 Ran SP% 126.2**
PARI-MUTUEL (all including 1 euro stake): WIN 2.70 PLACE 1.40, 1.40, 1.70 DF 4.60 SF 8.90.
**Owner** R J H Geffen **Bred** Petra Bloodstock Agency Ltd **Trained** Newmarket, Suffolk
**FOCUS**
The standard is set around the second to the sixth.

## 2202a PRIX DE BARBEVILLE (GROUP 3) (4YO+) (TURF) 1m 7f
**3:30** 4-Y-O+ **£34,188** (£13,675; £10,256; £6,837; £3,418)

RPR
1 **Marmelo**[194] 7456 4-9-0 0 ChristopheSoumillon 6 113+
(Hughie Morrison) *a cl up in main gp on outer: drvn to go 5l 2nd under 2f out: styd on u.p to ld wl over 1f out: sn asserted: won a shade cosily* **11/2**
2 2½ **Bateel (IRE)**[197] 7351 5-8-10 0 Pierre-CharlesBoudot 1 103
(F-H Graffard, France) *w.w in midfield: rdn and hdwy appr 1 1/2f out: chsd ldr 1f out: kpt on at same pce fnl f* **20/1**
3 1 **Travelling Man**[33] 1416 4-8-10 0 AurelienLemaitre 4 105+
(F Head, France) *settled in fnl pair: dropped to last bef 1/2-way: drvn and hdwy over 2f out: styd on wl ins fnl f: nvr on terms* **3/1**[2]
4 3 **Now We Can**[64] 934 8-9-0 0 StephanePasquier 7 102
(N Clement, France) *towards rr: drvn 3f out: hdwy 2f out: styd on u.p fr ins last 1 1/2f: wnt 4th cl home: nrest at fin* **9/1**
5 ¾ **Trip To Rhodos (FR)**[30] 1483 8-9-0 0 MaximeGuyon 5 101
(Pavel Tuma, Czech Republic) *chsd ldrs: 10l 3rd and pushed along 3f out: styd on fr 2 1/2f out: rdn an no further imp 1 1/2f out: kpt on at same pce fnl f* **9/1**
6 ½ **Murafej (IRE)**[40] 5-8-10 0 Francois-XavierBertras 9 97
(F Rohaut, France) *settled in midfield: drvn 2f out: styd on to chse ldrs appr fnl f: nt qckn u.p: fdd last 125yds* **7/2**[3]
7 1 **Cohesion**[16] 1770 4-8-10 0 GeraldMosse 3 99
(David Bridgwater) *pressed ldr on outer (led narrowly and briefly after 3f): jnd ldr 1/2-way and pair 10l clr 3f out: kicked into clr ld 2 1/2f out: hdd wl over 1f out: sn wknd* **20/1**
8 dist **Kloud Gate (FR)**[30] 1483 5-8-10 0 CristianDemuro 8
(Gianluca Bietolini, Italy) *scrubbed along early: in rr: drvn and effrt 2f out: sn btn: bhd whn eased ins fnl f* **20/1**
9 7 **Holdthasigreen (FR)**[30] 1483 5-9-0 0 (p) WilliamsSaraiva 2
(C Le Lay, France) *led on inner (hdd narrowly and briefly after 3f): jnd 1/2-way and pair 10l clr 3f out: hdd 2 1/2f out: sn struggling: wknd 2f out: wl bhd whn eased fnl 1 1/2f* **5/2**[1]
3m 6.89s (-9.21)
**WFA** 4 from 5yo+ 1lb **9 Ran SP% 125.5**
PARI-MUTUEL (all including 1 euro stake): WIN 8.70 PLACE 2.60, 3.70, 2.00 DF 44.00 SF 98.40.
**Owner** The Fairy Story Partnership **Bred** Deepwood Farm Stud **Trained** East Ilsley, Berks

# KYOTO (R-H)
Sunday, April 30
**OFFICIAL GOING: Turf: firm**

## 2203a TENNO SHO (SPRING) (GRADE 1) (4YO+) (TURF) 2m
**7:40** 4-Y-O+ **£1,063,349** (£422,449; £266,588; £159,169; £103,806)

RPR
1 **Kitasan Black (JPN)**[28] 1527 5-9-2 0 YutakaTake 3 119
(Hisashi Shimizu, Japan) **6/5**[1]
2 1¼ **Cheval Grand (JPN)**[42] 5-9-2 0 YuichiFukunaga 6 118
(Yasuo Tomomichi, Japan) **11/1**
3 nk **Satono Diamond (JPN)**[42] 4-9-2 0 Christophe-PatriceLemaire 15 122+
(Yasutoshi Ikee, Japan) **6/4**[2]
4 nk **Admire Deus (JPN)**[36] 6-9-2 0 YasunariIwata 10 117
(Tomoyuki Umeda, Japan) **99/1**
5 3 **Albert (JPN)**[71] 6-9-2 0 YugaKawada 7 114
(Noriyuki Hori, Japan) **214/10**
6 1½ **Dee Majesty (JPN)**[36] 4-9-2 0 MasayoshiEbina 9 116
(Yoshitaka Ninomiya, Japan) **35/1**
7 ¾ **Gold Actor (JPN)**[36] 6-9-2 0 NorihiroYokoyama 12 112
(Tadashige Nakagawa, Japan) **197/10**
8 nk **Tosen Basil (JPN)**[42] 5-9-2 0 HirofumiShii 13 111
(Hideaki Fujiwara, Japan) **79/1**
9 nk **Sciacchetra (JPN)**[36] 4-9-2 0 HironobuTanabe 1 115
(Katsuhiko Sumii, Japan) **89/10**[3]
10 ½ **Fata Morgana (JPN)**[71] 9-9-2 0 SuguruHamanaka 5 110
(Yoshiyuki Arakawa, Japan) **219/1**
11 2 **One And Only (JPN)**[42] 6-9-2 0 RyujiWada 14 108
(Shinsuke Hashiguchi, Japan) **113/1**
12 1¼ **Rainbow Line (JPN)**[36] 4-9-2 0 MircoDemuro 16 111
(Hidekazu Asami, Japan) **222/10**
13 5 **Tamamo Best Play (JPN)**[42] 7-9-2 0 HayatoYoshida 8 101
(Katsumi Minai, Japan) **209/1**
14 ½ **Spirits Minoru (JPN)**[42] 5-9-2 0 HideakiMiyuki 4 101
(Masaru Honda, Japan) **219/1**
15 3 **Yamakatsu Raiden (JPN)**[36] 5-9-2 0 KoheiMatsuyama 17 97
(Kaneo Ikezoe, Japan) **133/1**
16 1¼ **Proletariat (JPN)**[71] 6-8-11 0 (b) MakotoSugihara 11 91
(Shigeyuki Kojima, Japan) **327/1**
17 1½ **Labradorite (JPN)**[71] 8-9-2 0 (b) ManabuSakai 2 94
(Takashi Saito, Japan) **167/1**

PARI-MUTUEL (all including 100 jpy stake): WIN 220; SHOW 110, 160, 110; DF 1040; SF 1430.
**Owner** Ono Shoji **Bred** Yanagawa Bokujo **Trained** Japan

2204 - 2213a (Foreign Racing) - See Raceform Interactive

# 1934 BATH (L-H)
Monday, May 1
**OFFICIAL GOING: Firm (10.6)**
Wind: light half across Weather: cloudy periods

## 2214 MYRACING.COM TIPS FOR EVERY RACE H'CAP 5f 160y
**2:15** (2:16) (Class 6) (0-60,60) 4-Y-O+ **£2,911** (£866; £432; £216) **Stalls** Centre

Form RPR
5603 1 **Kingstreet Lady**[35] 1408 4-8-8 **47** KieranO'Neill 4 54
(Richard Price) *in tch: rdn over 2f out: led jst ins fnl f: kpt on wl: rdn out* **8/1**[3]
05-0 2 1 **Generalyse**[116] 80 8-8-12 **58** (b) RossaRyan(7) 16 62
(Anabel K Murphy) *a.p: rdn for str chal fr 2f out: led briefly jst ins fnl f: kpt on but hld fnl 50yds* **20/1**
3462 3 hd **Compton Prince**[19] 1723 8-8-11 **50** (b) LukeMorris 13 53
(Milton Bradley) *mid-div: hdwy over 1f out: sn rdn: kpt on ins fnl f: wnt 3rd fnl 75yds* **7/1**[2]
0-35 4 1½ **Cee Jay**[84] 604 4-8-11 **55** CharlieBennett(5) 11 53
(Patrick Chamings) *s.i.s: sn pushed along chsng ldrs: rdn over 2f out: kpt on ins fnl f: wnt 4th fnl 50yds* **7/2**[1]

015- **5** *nk* **Captain Ryan**[157] 8094 6-9-7 **60** ........ TimmyMurphy 2 57+
(Geoffrey Deacon) *mid-div: hdwy 3f out: rdn and ev ch over 1f out: fdd fnl 100yds* **10/1**

4421 **6** *hd* **Hurricane Alert**[6] 2069 5-8-10 **56** 6ex ........ DavidEgan(7) 5 52
(Mark Hoad) *mid-div: rdn over 2f out: nt clrest of runs over 1f out: kpt on fnl f but nt pce to get involved* **7/2**[1]

60-0 **7** *1 ¼* **Zophilly (IRE)**[115] 88 4-8-8 **47** oh1 ow1 ........(t) StevieDonohoe 7 39
(Jeremy Gask) *stdd s: hld up: hdwy into midfield over 2f out: sn rdn: no further imp* **50/1**

0504 **8** *hd* **Silver Springs (IRE)**[60] 981 4-8-0 **46** ........ RhiainIngram(7) 1 38
(Roger Ingram) *led: rdn 2f out: hdd jst ins fnl f: fdd* **16/1**

5300 **9** *1 ¼* **Pleadings (USA)**[74] 768 4-8-9 **48** ........(t[1]) WilliamCarson 12 36
(Charlie Wallis) *towards rr: rdn over 2f out: hmpd jst over and jst ins fnl f: kpt on but nvr any threat fnl 120yds* **18/1**

450- **10** *nk* **Wilspa's Magic (IRE)**[313] 3513 4-9-0 **53** ........ DaneO'Neill 10 40
(Ron Hodges) *racd keenly: towards rr: rdn 2f out: bmpd ent fnl f: nvr any imp* **20/1**

060- **11** *nse* **Lucky Clover**[282] 4658 6-9-7 **60** ........ JimmyQuinn 8 46
(Malcolm Saunders) *trckd ldrs: rdn over 2f out: wknd ins fnl f* **10/1**

-440 **12** *1* **Burauq**[94] 438 5-8-10 **49** ........(b) FrannyNorton 3 32
(Milton Bradley) *in tch: rdn over 2f out: wknd ins fnl f* **8/1**[3]

1m 11.19s (-0.01) **Going Correction** -0.25s/f (Firm) **12** Ran SP% **120.0**
Speed ratings (Par 101): **90,88,88,86,86 85,84,83,82,81 81,80**
CSF £161.07 CT £1199.52 TOTE £10.40: £2.70, £6.70, £2.90; EX 213.80 Trifecta £837.90 Part Won..

**Owner** G E Amey **Bred** G E Amey **Trained** Ullingswick, H'fords

**FOCUS**
Stalls: 5f& 5.5f & 2m1f - Centre. 1m5f - Outside. 1m2f, 1m & 1m3f - Inside. This was a weak sprint handicap and it saw a host of chances inside the final furlong.

## 2215 MYRACING.COM H'CAP — 5f 160y
**2:50** (2:50) (Class 4) (0-85,86) 3-Y-O **£5,670** (£1,697; £848; £424; £211) **Stalls** Centre

Form RPR

2313 **1** **Juan Horsepower**[24] 1601 3-9-2 **80** ........(p) KieranO'Neill 6 85
(Richard Hannon) *pushed along early to press ldr: rdn over 2f out: swtchd rt ent fnl f: kpt on fnl 120yds: led towards fin* **10/1**

00-2 **2** *½* **Evergate**[14] 1838 3-9-7 **85** ........ LukeMorris 2 89+
(Robert Cowell) *s.i.s: towards rr: hdwy over 2f out: led over 1f out: sn rdn: kpt on but no ex whn hdd towards fin* **4/1**[2]

010- **3** *1 ¾* **Mutawakked (IRE)**[235] 6260 3-9-5 **83** ........ DaneO'Neill 5 81
(Brian Meehan) *trckd ldrs: rdn 2f out: kpt on to go 3rd ins fnl f but nt quite pce to mount chal* **5/1**[3]

13-2 **4** *shd* **Poet's Society**[114] 125 3-9-8 **86** ........ FrannyNorton 8 84
(Mark Johnston) *sn led: rdn and hdd over 1f out: kpt on same pce ins fnl f* **4/1**[2]

1110 **5** *2 ½* **Dandy Flame (IRE)**[14] 1838 3-8-7 **78** ........ FinleyMarsh(7) 1 67
(Richard Hughes) *in tch: rdn over 2f out: kpt on but nt pce to get on terms* **25/1**

521- **6** *hd* **Sfumato**[243] 6034 3-9-1 **82** ........(h) KieranShoemark(3) 4 71
(Roger Charlton) *trckd ldrs early: rdn in tch over 2f out: nt pce to get on terms* **11/4**[1]

00-0 **7** *4* **Diable D'Or (IRE)**[19] 1731 3-8-13 **77** ........ JimmyQuinn 7 53
(Eve Johnson Houghton) *chsd ldrs: rdn over 2f out: wknd fnl f* **9/1**

31-5 **8** *2* **Big Lachie**[15] 1820 3-9-2 **80** ........ TimmyMurphy 3 49
(Jamie Osborne) *hld up: snatched up whn short of room over 2f out: effrt on outer sn after: wknd fnl f* **12/1**

1m 8.89s (-2.31) **Going Correction** -0.25s/f (Firm) **8** Ran SP% **114.0**
Speed ratings (Par 101): **105,104,102,101,98 98,92,90**
CSF £49.37 CT £228.38 TOTE £10.50: £2.70, £1.50, £2.10; EX 47.40 Trifecta £203.10.

**Owner** Middleham Park Racing LXXXIII **Bred** Max Weston **Trained** East Everleigh, Wilts

**FOCUS**
A good-quality 3yo sprint handicap that saw a tight finish.

## 2216 MYRACING.COM FREE HORSE RACING TIPS H'CAP — 5f 10y
**3:25** (3:26) (Class 5) (0-70,71) 4-Y-O+ **£4,133** (£1,264; £651; £344) **Stalls** Centre

Form RPR

11-6 **1** **Secretfact**[7] 2038 4-9-9 **71** ........ JimmyQuinn 7 79+
(Malcolm Saunders) *hld up 5th: swtchd rt over 1f out: qcknd up wl but drifting lft whn ldng jst ins fnl f: rdn and edgd further lft fnl 100yds: r.o* **5/6**[1]

4515 **2** *1 ¾* **Swendab (IRE)**[19] 1723 9-9-3 **65** ........(v) TimmyMurphy 1 67
(John O'Shea) *led: rdn whn strly chal over 1f out: hdd ins fnl f: keeping on at same pce disputing 2nd whn lft clr 2nd fnl 50yds* **16/1**

1333 **3** *1 ¼* **Frank The Barber (IRE)**[9] 1965 5-8-8 **56** ow1 ........(t) StevieDonohoe 2 57
(Steph Hollinshead) *trckd ldr: rdn for str chal over 1f out: hld by wnr but stl chalng for 2nd whn hmpd fnl 50yds* **9/2**[3]

-404 **4** *1 ¼* **Dodgy Bob**[75] 745 4-9-6 **68** ........(be[1]) FrannyNorton 4 61
(Michael Mullineaux) *trckd ldrs: rdn over 1f out: nt pce to get on terms: lft 4th fnl 50yds* **4/1**[2]

1230 **U** **Powerful Dream (IRE)**[9] 1981 4-9-6 **68** ........(b[1]) LukeMorris 5 71
(Ronald Harris) *trckd ldrs: rdn 2f out: running on but hld by wnr whn bdly hmpd and uns rdr fnl 50yds: probably would have fin 2nd* **6/1**

1m 0.89s (-1.61) **Going Correction** -0.25s/f (Firm) **5** Ran SP% **112.9**
Speed ratings (Par 103): **102,99,97,95,**
CSF £15.45 TOTE £1.60: £1.10, £5.10; EX 15.90 Trifecta £35.50.

**Owner** Premier Conservatory Roofs **Bred** M S Saunders & D Collier **Trained** Green Ore, Somerset

**FOCUS**
This uncompetitive sprint handicap saw late drama. A small pb from the winner, rated around the 3rd to his turf latest.

## 2217 MYRACING.COM NOVICE MEDIAN AUCTION STKS (PLUS 10 RACE) — 5f 10y
**4:00** (4:02) (Class 4) 2-Y-O **£6,921** (£2,059; £1,029; £514) **Stalls** Centre

Form RPR

1 **1** **Rock Of Estonia (IRE)**[21] 1681 2-9-8 0 ........ JamieSpencer 3 82+
(Charles Hills) *mde all: strly pressed fr wl over 1f out: kpt on to assert cl home: drvn out* **30/100**[1]

**2** *¾* **Joe's Spirit (IRE)** 2-8-11 0 ........ LuluStanford(5) 1 73+
(Michael Bell) *trckd ldrs: str chal ent fnl f: kpt on: hld cl home* **8/1**[3]

**3** *hd* **Ghepardo** 2-8-11 0 ........ SeanLevey 6 68+
(Richard Hannon) *trckd wnr: str chal over 1f out: sn rdn: kpt on but hld ins fnl f* **4/1**[2]

**4** *5* **Cranworth Phoenix** 2-8-4 0 ........ GabrieleMalune(7) 2 50+
(Brian Barr) *awkwardly away: chsd ldng trio: rdn 2f out: nt pce to get on terms* **66/1**

1m 1.73s (-0.77) **Going Correction** -0.25s/f (Firm) **4** Ran SP% **109.5**
Speed ratings (Par 95): **96,94,94,86**
CSF £3.51 TOTE £1.20; EX 3.10 Trifecta £3.60.

**Owner** Kangyu Int Racing (HK) Ltd & F Ma **Bred** Colin Kennedy **Trained** Lambourn, Berks

■ Watch Tan was withdrawn. Price at time of withdrawal 25/1. Rule 4 does not apply

**FOCUS**
This could work out to be an above-average novice event for the course.

## 2218 MYRACING.COM FREE BETS AND TIPS H'CAP — 1m 3f 137y
**4:35** (4:35) (Class 4) (0-80,80) 4-Y-O+ **£7,470** (£2,236; £1,118; £559) **Stalls** Low

Form RPR

23-1 **1** **Mornington**[16] 1788 4-9-0 **80** ........ TylerSaunders(7) 1 91+
(Marcus Tregoning) *trckd ldr: led over 2f out: clr ent fnl f: comf* **6/4**[1]

50-4 **2** *2 ¾* **Plymouth Sound**[1] 2176 5-9-4 **77** ........(v) CharlesBishop 4 80
(Eve Johnson Houghton) *trckd ldrs: chal over 2f out: rdn and hld over 1f out: styd on same pce* **3/1**[3]

50-2 **3** *¾* **Sellingallthetime (IRE)**[19] 1719 6-8-9 **73** ........(p) GeorgeBuckell(5) 2 75
(Michael Appleby) *trckd ldr: rdn and ev ch over 2f out: hld over 1f out: styd on same pce* **2/1**[2]

501- **4** *8* **Sunny Future (IRE)**[232] 6362 11-9-3 **76** ........(h) JimmyQuinn 3 65
(Malcolm Saunders) *led tl over 2f out: sn rdn and hld: wknd fnl f* **8/1**

2m 29.24s (-1.36) **Going Correction** +0.025s/f (Good) **4** Ran SP% **109.4**
Speed ratings (Par 105): **105,103,102,97**
CSF £6.29 TOTE £2.30; EX 5.60 Trifecta £8.90.

**Owner** M P N Tregoning **Bred** Dachel Stud **Trained** Whitsbury, Hants

**FOCUS**
This fair little handicap proved a tactical race. Another improved run from the winner.

## 2219 @MYRACINGTIPS JOIN 220,000 RACING FANS H'CAP — 1m 3f 137y
**5:10** (5:10) (Class 6) (0-60,59) 4-Y-O+ **£2,911** (£866; £432; £216) **Stalls** Low

Form RPR

245- **1** **Petrify**[126] 6001 7-9-2 **54** ........(tp) JamieSpencer 4 60
(Bernard Llewellyn) *slowly away: last: rdn over 3f out: no imp tl hdwy jst over 1f out: squeezed through gap fnl 120yds: styd on strly: led cl home* **12/1**

-060 **2** *1 ½* **Golden Muscade (USA)**[42] 1283 4-9-2 **54** ........ StevieDonohoe 5 57
(Brian Barr) *led for 1f: trckd ldr tl rdn over 2f out: styd on ins fnl f: snatched 2nd fnl stride* **12/1**

00-2 **3** *shd* **Hallingham**[20] 1699 7-9-3 **58** ........ HollieDoyle(3) 9 61
(Ken Cunningham-Brown) *sn pushed along: led after 1f: rdn over 1f out: no ex whn hdd cl home: lost 2nd fnl stride* **11/8**[1]

0-06 **4** *1 ¾* **The Quarterjack**[20] 1697 8-8-7 **52** ........ FinleyMarsh(7) 2 52
(Ron Hodges) *trckd ldrs: rdn wl over 2f out: hung lft fnl f: styd on same pce* **10/3**[2]

5000 **5** *½* **Awesome Rock (IRE)**[39] 1322 8-8-7 **45** ........ KieranO'Neill 8 44
(Roger Ingram) *hld up 5th: rdn over 2f out: hdwy ent fnl f: styd on same pce fnl 100yds* **22/1**

05/6 **6** *1 ½* **Eben Dubai (IRE)**[10] 1939 5-9-1 **58** ........ GeorgeWood(5) 3 55
(Tracey Barfoot-Saunt) *racd keenly: trckd ldrs: rdn to chse ldr over 2f out: wknd fnl f* **14/1**

602- **7** *nse* **Moon Arrow (IRE)**[18] 8194 4-8-9 **52** ........(h) MitchGodwin(5) 1 49
(Michael Blake) *hld up: hdwy over 3f out: sn rdn to chse ldrs: no ex fnl 100yds* **4/1**[3]

2m 30.99s (0.39) **Going Correction** +0.025s/f (Good) **7** Ran SP% **111.6**
Speed ratings (Par 101): **99,98,97,96,96 95,95**
CSF £131.17 CT £318.30 TOTE £7.10: £2.90, £7.40; EX 51.70 Trifecta £172.20.

**Owner** G A Security **Bred** Fittocks Stud **Trained** Fochriw, Caerphilly

**FOCUS**
A moderate handicap which saw changing fortunes inside the final furlong. The winner has been rated close to last year's best.

## 2220 @MYRACINGTIPS FOLLOW NOW FOR FREE TIPS CLASSIFIED STKS — 1m 5y
**5:40** (5:41) (Class 5) 3-Y-O **£4,204** (£1,251; £625; £312) **Stalls** Low

Form RPR

03-4 **1** **I'vegotthepower (IRE)**[19] 1737 3-9-0 68 ........(v[1]) JimmyFortune 8 74
(Brian Meehan) *mde virtually all at decent pce: rdn clr ent fnl f: styd on strly: comf* **3/1**[1]

041- **2** *3* **Raj Balaraaj (GER)**[189] 7570 3-9-0 67 ........ SteveDrowne 5 67
(George Baker) *pushed along in tch: hdwy 2f out: sn rdn: styd on to go 2nd ins fnl f: no ch w wnr* **5/1**

2-50 **3** *½* **Challow (IRE)**[12] 1888 3-8-9 69 ........ MitchGodwin(5) 4 66
(Sylvester Kirk) *slowly away: detached in last 1st 3f: hdwy wl over 2f out: sn rdn disputing 3rd: styd on same pce fnl f* **9/2**[3]

353- **4** *nk* **Pacofilha**[201] 7286 3-9-0 69 ........(b[1]) LukeMorris 1 65
(Paul Cole) *racd keenly: trckd wnr: rdn 2f out: styd on same pce fnl f* **4/1**[2]

2-66 **5** *½* **Ocean Promise (USA)**[103] 284 3-8-7 67 ........(p[1]) FinleyMarsh(7) 6 64
(Richard Hughes) *trckd ldrs: rdn over 2f out: sn one pce* **8/1**

004- **6** *3* **Mutineer**[138] 8353 3-9-0 69 ........ GeorgeDowning 2 57
(Daniel Kubler) *trckd ldrs: rdn over 2f out: wknd fnl f* **12/1**

43-3 **7** *6* **Spiritofedinburgh (IRE)**[33] 1426 3-8-11 70 ........ KieranShoemark(3) 3 43
(Brendan Powell) *hld up in tch: effrt 2f out: wknd fnl f* **5/1**

1m 40.72s (-0.08) **Going Correction** +0.025s/f (Good) **7** Ran SP% **115.3**
Speed ratings (Par 99): **101,98,97,97,96 93,87**
CSF £18.59 TOTE £3.20: £2.00, £2.70; EX 19.50 Trifecta £74.40.

**Owner** S E Sangster **Bred** D Farrington, P Gately, T Killarney **Trained** Manton, Wilts

**FOCUS**
A tyically tight 3yo classified stakes on paper, but the winner proved different class. This has been rated around the front two.

T/Plt: £191.20 to a £1 stake. Pool: £65,555.29 - 250.27 winning units. T/Qpdt: £23.10 to a £1 stake. Pool: £3,553.37 - 113.63 winning units. **Tim Mitchell**

# [2104] BEVERLEY (R-H)

## Monday, May 1

**OFFICIAL GOING: Good to firm (good in places; 8.1)**
Wind: Moderate behind Weather: Cloudy with sunny periods

## 2221 MAYDAY RACEDAY NOVICE MEDIAN AUCTION STKS (DIV I) 5f
1:55 (1:56) (Class 6) 2-Y-O £2,587 (£770; £384; £192) Stalls Low

Form RPR
1 **Time Trail** 2-8-11 0 PaulMulrennan 4 69
(Michael Dods) *cl up on inner: slt ld 2f out: rdn jst over 1f out: kpt on wl towards fin* **12/1**
4 2 shd **Noble Manners (IRE)**[12] 1884 2-8-11 0 JoeFanning 7 69+
(Mark Johnston) *sn swtchd lft and trckd ldng pair: hdwy over 1f out: rdn to chal ins fnl f: ev ch: no ex nr fin* **13/8**[1]
3 1 1/4 **Luis Fernandez (USA)** 2-9-2 0 KevinStott 1 69+
(Kevin Ryan) *dwlt and towards rr: hdwy on inner 1/2-way: swtchd lft wl over 1f out: sn rdn and styd on wl fnl f* **12/1**
4 nk **Porchy Party (IRE)** 2-9-2 0 RichardKingscote 8 68+
(Tom Dascombe) *sn trcking ldrs: green and pushed along wl over 1f out: kpt on under hands and heels fnl f* **20/1**
5 1/2 **Highland Bobby** 2-9-2 0 DanielTudhope 9 66
(David O'Meara) *slt ld: pushed along 1/2-way: hdd 2f out: rdn over 1f out: kpt on same pce fnl f* **16/1**
4 6 1/2 **Hot Rock (IRE)**[12] 1873 2-9-2 0 ConnorBeasley 2 64
(Bryan Smart) *chsd ldrs: rdn along wl over 1f out: kpt on u.p fnl f* **3/1**[2]
5 7 1 **Poet's Dawn**[12] 1873 2-9-2 0 DavidAllan 3 61
(Tim Easterby) *chsd ldrs on inner: pushed along over 2f out: rdn over 1f out: wknd fnl f* **12/1**
3 8 1/2 **Crownthorpe**[20] 1694 2-9-2 0 PaulHanagan 10 59
(Richard Fahey) *wnt lft s: in tch on outer: pushed along 1/2-way: sn rdn and wknd* **4/1**[3]
9 6 **Furze Boy** 2-8-13 0 NathanEvans(3) 6 37
(Michael Easterby) *dwlt: green and a rr* **50/1**
10 10 **Archie Perkins (IRE)** 2-9-2 0 TomEaves 5 1
(Nigel Tinkler) *dwlt and wnt lft s: a rr* **66/1**

1m 2.25s (-1.25) **Going Correction** -0.425s/f (Firm) 10 Ran SP% **120.3**
Speed ratings (Par 91): **93,92,90,90,89 88,87,86,76,60**
CSF £32.60 TOTE £15.40: £3.50, £1.10, £3.90; EX 46.00 Trifecta £460.30.
**Owner** M J K Dods **Bred** Kevin Daniel Crabb **Trained** Denton, Co Durham

**FOCUS**
A dry run up to a meeting staged on quick ground. A reasonable gallop and, given the first eight home finished in a bit of a heap, this form is no more than fair. The winner had the run of the race against the far rail.

## 2222 MAYDAY RACEDAY NOVICE MEDIAN AUCTION STKS (DIV II) 5f
2:30 (2:31) (Class 6) 2-Y-O £2,587 (£770; £384; £96; £96) Stalls Low

Form RPR
1 **Havana Star (IRE)** 2-9-2 0 KevinStott 2 72
(Kevin Ryan) *dwlt and wnt lft s: green and sn outpcd in rr: reminders 1/2-way: gd hdwy on inner over 1f out: rdn and kpt on strly to ld ins fnl f: hung bdly lft nr fin* **10/1**
33 2 nk **Rockin Fella (IRE)**[16] 1803 2-9-2 0 PJMcDonald 3 71
(K R Burke) *cl up: effrt and n.m.r on inner over 1f out: sn swtchd lft: rdn to ld narrowly ins fnl f whn hung bdly lft and hdd: kpt on* **9/4**[1]
3 1 **Leeshaan (IRE)** 2-9-2 0 MartinHarley 6 68
(James Tate) *dwlt: hdwy to chse ldrs 1/2-way: effrt on outer and rdn whn sltly hmpd and swtchd rt jst ins fnl f: styng on whn n.m.r cl home* **5/1**
2 4 2 **Thrifty**[17] 1776 2-8-11 0 DavidAllan 4 55
(Tim Easterby) *led: rdn along wl over 1f out: edgd lft ent fnl f: grad wknd* **9/2**[3]
4 dht **Villa Tora** 2-8-11 0 JoeFanning 5 55
(Mark Johnston) *t.k.h early: chsd ldrs on outer: hdwy 2f out: rdn over 1f out and ev ch: kpt on same pce* **8/1**
6 6 3/4 **Ventura Gold (IRE)**[21] 1673 2-9-2 0 PaulHanagan 7 58
(Richard Fahey) *dwlt: green and sn rdn along in rr: styd on fr over 1f out* **3/1**[2]
6 7 1 1/4 **Mount Hellvelyn**[12] 1872 2-9-2 0 JamesSullivan 8 53
(Clive Mulhall) *chsd ldrs: rdn over 1f out: wknd fnl f* **50/1**
0 8 1/2 **Rock On Bertie (IRE)**[12] 1872 2-9-2 0 TomEaves 1 51
(Nigel Tinkler) *chsd ldrs: rdn along wl over 1f out: sn wknd* **16/1**
0 9 7 **St Helens Gate (IRE)**[11] 1908 2-8-11 0 GrahamLee 9 21
(Rebecca Menzies) *dwlt: a rr* **66/1**

1m 2.36s (-1.14) **Going Correction** -0.425s/f (Firm) 9 Ran SP% **120.2**
Speed ratings (Par 91): **92,91,89,86,86 85,83,82,71**
CSF £34.23 TOTE £14.70: £3.10, £1.20, £2.10; EX 42.00 Trifecta £176.40.
**Owner** Hambleton Racing Ltd XXXVIII **Bred** Mubarak Al Naemi **Trained** Hambleton, N Yorks

**FOCUS**
The runner-up has been rated in line with his earlier form.

## 2223 BEVERLEY FOLK FESTIVAL HERE IN JUNE H'CAP 5f
3:05 (3:05) (Class 5) (0-75,76) 3-Y-O £4,410 (£1,320; £660; £330; £164) Stalls Low

Form RPR
60-0 1 **Twizzell**[19] 1731 3-9-7 75 PJMcDonald 1 81
(K R Burke) *slt ld: rdn wl over 1f out: drvn ins fnl f: kpt on wl* **4/1**[3]
60-1 2 3/4 **Stubytuesday**[14] 1835 3-8-7 64 NathanEvans(3) 5 68+
(Michael Easterby) *dwlt and swtchd rt to inner s: sn pushed along in rr: hdwy on inner wl over 1f out: sn rdn and styd on strly fnl f* **11/2**
56-3 3 3/4 **Lawless Louis**[4] 2104 3-9-1 76 PatrickVaughan(7) 9 77
(David O'Meara) *cl up: rdn over 1f out: ev ch tl drvn and kpt on same pce fnl f* **11/4**[1]
66-5 4 nk **Brother McGonagall**[96] 404 3-8-8 62 DavidAllan 8 62
(Tim Easterby) *chsd ldrs: rdn along wl over 1f out: kpt on same pce fnl f* **14/1**
-234 5 1 **Sheepscar Lad (IRE)**[7] 2033 3-8-6 65 LewisEdmunds(5) 3 61
(Nigel Tinkler) *hld up towards rr: hdwy on outer 2f out: rdn over 1f out: styd on fnl f: nrst fin* **10/3**[2]
-002 6 hd **Stringybark Creek**[9] 1970 3-8-10 64 GrahamLee 2 60
(Mick Channon) *chsd ldrs: rdn along wl over 1f out: sn drvn and wknd* **6/1**
405- 7 4 **Whigwham**[229] 6471 3-8-2 63 ConnorMurtagh(7) 7 44
(Richard Fahey) *a towards rr* **16/1**
001- 8 4 1/2 **Newgate Sioux**[229] 6471 3-8-8 62 BarryMcHugh 10 27
(Tony Coyle) *wnt lft s: sn cl up: rdn along wl over 1f out: sn wknd* **40/1**

1m 1.36s (-2.14) **Going Correction** -0.425s/f (Firm) 8 Ran SP% **114.4**
Speed ratings (Par 99): **100,98,97,97,95 95,88,81**
CSF £26.22 CT £69.85 TOTE £5.50: £1.60, £1.90, £1.30; EX 30.30 Trifecta £123.70.
**Owner** John Dance **Bred** Whitsbury Manor Stud **Trained** Middleham Moor, N Yorks

**FOCUS**
A fair handicap in which the gallop was sound throughout, and it has been rated around the 3rd.

## 2224 LYNNE GLENTON H'CAP 7f 96y
3:40 (3:42) (Class 5) (0-70,69) 4-Y-O+ £4,410 (£1,320; £660; £330; £164) Stalls Low

Form RPR
4-02 1 **Fine Example**[5] 2082 4-8-13 66 (b) LewisEdmunds(5) 15 74
(Kevin Ryan) *qckly away and sn swtchd rt to inner rail: mde all: rdn over 1f out: drvn ins fnl f: kpt on gamely* **7/2**[1]
54-4 2 nk **Arcane Dancer (IRE)**[116] 69 4-8-11 59 (p) CamHardie 6 66
(Lawrence Mullaney) *trckd ldrs: hdwy 2f out: rdn over 1f out: drvn and kpt on wl fnl f* **16/1**
4-31 3 shd **Make On Madam (IRE)**[12] 1879 5-9-2 67 NathanEvans(3) 13 74
(Les Eyre) *t.k.h: chsd wnr: rdn wl over 1f out: drvn and kpt on wl fnl f* **11/2**[2]
06-2 4 1 1/2 **I'm Super Too (IRE)**[27] 1544 10-8-8 56 (p[1]) SamJames 5 59+
(Karen Tutty) *in tch on inner: effrt and n.m.r wl over 1f out: sn swtchd lft and rdn: styd on strly fnl f* **12/1**
2300 5 1 **All You (IRE)**[4] 2108 5-9-7 69 (v) DanielTudhope 3 70
(David O'Meara) *trckd ldrs: hdwy over 2f out: rdn over 1f out: kpt on same pce fnl f* **8/1**
0-00 6 shd **First Wheat**[20] 1706 4-8-11 66 (t[1]) HarrisonShaw(7) 12 67
(Michael Easterby) *t.k.h early: chsd ldrs: rdn along wl over 1f out: drvn and one pce fnl f* **25/1**
0665 7 nk **Green Howard**[24] 1610 9-9-3 65 (b) DuranFentiman 1 65
(Rebecca Bastiman) *hld up: hdwy over 2f out: n.m.r and swtchd markedly lft to outer jst over 1f out: sn rdn and kpt on wl towards fin* **12/1**
6033 8 3/4 **So It's War (FR)**[12] 1893 6-9-3 65 (p) PhillipMakin 8 63
(Keith Dalgleish) *trckd ldrs on inner: pushed along 2f out: rdn over 1f out: sn drvn and grad wknd* **7/1**[3]
-406 9 2 1/2 **Faintly (USA)**[6] 2064 6-9-3 65 (b) JamesSullivan 10 57
(Ruth Carr) *hld up towards rr: sme hdwy on wd outside 2f out: sn rdn and no imp fnl f* **9/1**
020- 10 2 1/2 **Talent Scout (IRE)**[214] 6907 11-9-1 68 (p) GemmaTutty(5) 2 53
(Karen Tutty) *rrd s: a rr* **16/1**
000- 11 3 3/4 **Charava (IRE)**[142] 8307 5-8-10 65 PaulaMuir(7) 16 41
(Patrick Holmes) *nvr bttr than midfield* **66/1**
56-0 12 2 **Off The Scale (IRE)**[14] 1833 5-9-4 66 (h) GrahamLee 14 37
(Rebecca Menzies) *a rr* **40/1**
30-0 13 1 1/2 **Red Charmer (IRE)**[20] 1700 7-9-6 68 ShaneGray 9 35
(Ann Duffield) *a towards rr* **12/1**
0-45 14 1/2 **Tafteesh (IRE)**[12] 1890 4-9-4 66 PaulMulrennan 11 32
(Michael Easterby) *hld up: a rr* **8/1**
60-5 15 1 3/4 **Iceaxe**[30] 1489 4-9-6 68 RoystonFfrench 4 30
(John Holt) *midfield: rdn along 3f out: sn wknd* **33/1**

1m 31.61s (-2.19) **Going Correction** -0.425s/f (Firm) 15 Ran SP% **127.9**
Speed ratings (Par 103): **95,94,94,92,91 91,91,90,87,84 80,78,76,75,73**
CSF £65.82 CT £326.77 TOTE £4.50: £2.00, £6.60, £2.30; EX 83.50 Trifecta £600.00.
**Owner** Hambleton Racing Ltd XLIV **Bred** Mrs M E Slade **Trained** Hambleton, N Yorks

**FOCUS**
A modest handicap but one in which an ordinary gallop favoured those right up with the pace.

## 2225 ETTON H'CAP 1m 1f 207y
4:15 (4:15) (Class 4) (0-80,80) 4-Y-O- £7,561 (£2,263; £1,131; £566; £282) Stalls Low

Form RPR
150- 1 **Sunglider (IRE)**[126] 8524 4-9-3 76 DanielTudhope 10 83
(David O'Meara) *trckd ldrs: swtchd outside and hdwy over 2f out: rdn to chal over 1f out: led ent fnl f: drvn and kpt on wl towards fin* **7/2**[3]
3136 2 3/4 **Kingthistle**[2] 2146 4-9-0 73 GrahamLee 3 78
(Rebecca Menzies) *trckd ldng pair on inner: effrt and nt clr run over 1f out: swtchd lft to outer and rdn 1f out: drvn to chal ins fnl f: ev ch: no ex towards fin* **3/1**[2]
3225 3 2 1/2 **Mariee**[39] 1324 4-9-7 80 JoeFanning 1 80
(Mark Johnston) *trckd ldr: hdwy and cl up over 2f out: rdn to dispute ld wl over 1f out: ev ch: drvn ent fnl f: kpt on same pce* **2/1**[1]
406/ 4 5 **Tin Pan Alley**[584] 6713 9-8-8 67 PJMcDonald 6 57
(David C Griffiths) *led: pushed along over 2f out: jnd and rdn wl over 1f out: drvn and hdd ent fnl f: wknd* **20/1**
460- 5 1 1/2 **King Of The Celts (IRE)**[247] 5883 9-8-5 67 RachelRichardson(3) 8 54
(Tim Easterby) *in tch: pushed along 3f out: rdn 2f out: sn drvn and no imp* **9/1**
00-0 6 1/2 **Indian Chief (IRE)**[27] 1549 7-8-12 71 DuranFentiman 4 57
(Rebecca Bastiman) *hld up in rr: sme hdwy over 2f out: sn rdn along and n.d* **18/1**
0-00 7 1 **Save The Bees**[14] 1832 9-9-7 80 NeilFarley 13 64
(Declan Carroll) *hld up: a rr* **11/1**
100- 8 17 **Glance My Way (IRE)**[240] 6128 4-9-2 75 DavidAllan 9 25
(Tim Easterby) *hld up in tch: pushed along over 4f out: rdn wl over 2f out: sn btn* **12/1**

2m 3.48s (-3.52) **Going Correction** -0.425s/f (Firm) 8 Ran SP% **116.6**
Speed ratings (Par 105): **97,96,94,90,89 88,88,74**
CSF £14.80 CT £26.01 TOTE £5.00: £1.70, £1.30, £1.10; EX 17.00 Trifecta £41.80.
**Owner** G Brogan **Bred** Moyglare Stud Farm Ltd **Trained** Upper Helmsley, N Yorks

**FOCUS**
A fair handicap but, although the gallop was no more than fair, the winner looks an improved performer. This has been rated cautiously.

## 2226 BEVERLEY ANNUAL BADGEHOLDERS H'CAP 1m 100y
4:50 (4:50) (Class 4) (0-85,86) 4-Y-O+ £6,301 (£1,886; £943; £353; £353) Stalls Low

Form RPR
1300 1 **Alejandro (IRE)**[7] 2030 8-9-8 86 JosephineGordon 12 96
(David Loughnane) *t.k.h: hld up towards rr: hdwy on outer over 2f out: rdn to chse ldrs over 1f out: drvn to chal ins fnl f: led nr fin* **10/1**
0-02 2 nk **Palmerston**[14] 1832 4-8-13 77 BenCurtis 3 86
(Michael Appleby) *trckd ldr: cl up over 2f out: led wl over 1f out and sn rdn: drvn ins fnl f: hdd and no ex towards fin* **11/2**[2]
0-4 3 3 **Eternal**[16] 1799 5-9-2 85 PhilDennis(5) 10 87
(Declan Carroll) *trckd ldrs: hdwy over 2f out: cl up and rdn over 1f out: drvn and kpt on same pce fnl f* **6/1**[3]
35-0 4 1/2 **Jacbequick**[117] 43 6-9-2 85 (p) JoshDoyle(5) 1 86
(David O'Meara) *trckd ldng pair on inner: effrt over 2f out: rdn wl over 1f out: sn drvn and kpt on same pce* **11/2**[2]
00-5 4 dht **Mon Beau Visage (IRE)**[17] 1778 4-8-12 76 (p) SamJames 8 77
(David O'Meara) *hld up and bhd: hdwy over 2f out: rdn over 1f out: styd on fnl f* **12/1**

25 **6** *7* **Detachment**[17] 1781 4-8-13 **77** JasonHart 4 62+
(Les Eyre) *hld up in tch: hdwy on inner over 2f out: nt clr run and hmpd wl over 1f out: no ch after* **9/1**

01-0 **7** *3/4* **Carnageo (FR)**[29] 1517 4-9-4 **82** PaulHanagan 6 65
(Richard Fahey) *a towards rr* **9/2**[1]

0-01 **8** *1* **Billy Roberts (IRE)**[20] 1700 4-9-0 **78** ConnorBeasley 5 59
(Richard Guest) *stmbld s: a towards rr* **11/2**[2]

100- **9** *1 1/4* **Yorkee Mo Sabee (IRE)**[273] 4946 4-9-2 **80** (h[1]) JoeFanning 7 58
(Mark Johnston) *sn led: rdn along over 2f out: hdd and drvn wl over 1f out: sn wknd* **20/1**

0-04 **10** *shd* **Dubai Dynamo**[14] 1832 12-8-13 **77** JamesSullivan 9 55
(Ruth Carr) *a rr* **14/1**

1m 43.06s (-4.54) **Going Correction** -0.425s/f (Firm) **10** Ran SP% **116.8**
Speed ratings (Par 105): **105,104,101,101,101 94,93,92,91,91**
CSF £64.29 CT £372.47 TOTE £10.80: £3.20, £2.20, £2.70; EX 72.50 Trifecta £646.60.
**Owner** Lydonford Ltd **Bred** Yeomanstown Stud **Trained** Market Drayton, Shropshire

**FOCUS**
A useful-looking handicap but one in which a couple of the market leaders underperformed. The gallop was just an ordinary one. The winner has been rated back to his 2015 form.

## 2227 MAYPOLE DANCERS MAIDEN FILLIES' STKS (PLUS 10 RACE) 1m 1f 207y
**5:25** (5:26) (Class 5) 3-Y-O **£3,780** (£1,131; £565; £283; £141) **Stalls** Low

Form RPR

5- **1** **Coconut Creme**[195] 7441 3-9-0 0 PatCosgrave 5 80
(William Haggas) *trckd ldrs: hdwy over 2f out: rdn to ld appr fnl f: drvn out* **5/4**[1]

4 **2** *1/2* **Extra Mile**[25] 1581 3-9-0 0 (v[1]) JosephineGordon 2 79
(Saeed bin Suroor) *trckd ldng pair on inner: pushed along over 2f out: n.m.r and swtchd lft over 1f out: rdn and ev ch jst ins fnl f whn hung bdly lft: styd on wl towards fin* **5/1**

4-2 **3** *1 1/4* **Mistress Quickly (IRE)**[21] 1682 3-9-0 0 FranBerry 1 76
(Ralph Beckett) *led to 1/2-way: led again 21/2f out and sn pushed along: rdn wl over 1f out: hdd and drvn appr fnl f: kpt on same pce* **5/2**[2]

**4** *3/4* **Nathalie** 3-9-0 0 DanielMuscutt 6 75
(James Fanshawe) *hld up: hdwy on outer 2f out: rdn and ev ch whn sltly hmpd jst ins fnl f: kpt on* **20/1**

353- **5** *14* **Great Court (IRE)**[172] 7885 3-9-0 76 DanielTudhope 3 47
(Luca Cumani) *cl up: led 1/2-way: rdn and hdd 21/2f out: sn drvn and wknd wl over 1f out* **9/2**[3]

46 **6** *11* **Lakeski**[25] 1589 3-9-0 0 DavidAllan 4 25
(Scott Dixon) *a rr: pushed along over 4f out: sn outpcd and bhd* **100/1**

2m 2.69s (-4.31) **Going Correction** -0.425s/f (Firm) **6** Ran SP% **113.6**
Speed ratings (Par 96): **100,99,98,98,86 78**
CSF £8.35 TOTE £2.10: £1.20, £2.50; EX 8.80 Trifecta £25.30.
**Owner** Normandie Stud Ltd **Bred** Normandie Stud Ltd **Trained** Newmarket, Suffolk
■ Stewards' Enquiry : Josephine Gordon two-day ban: careless riding in that she had allowed her mount to drift continually left without sufficient correction (May 15-16)

**FOCUS**
Only fair form but an ordinary gallop didn't really suit many of these and the winner should be able to progress further. This has been rated around the 3rd.

## 2228 WHITE RABBIT APPRENTICE H'CAP 7f 96y
**5:55** (5:57) (Class 6) (0-65,67) 3-Y-O **£2,587** (£770; £384; £192) **Stalls** Low

Form RPR

04-3 **1** **Il Sicario (IRE)**[16] 1790 3-9-12 **67** RichardOliver 7 71
(Mark Johnston) *trckd ldrs: hdwy over 2f out: rdn over 1f out: drvn ins fnl f: led last 80 yds: jst hld on* **3/1**[1]

45-2 **2** *shd* **Golden Guest**[21] 1686 3-9-7 **65** JaneElliott(3) 10 69
(George Margarson) *hld up in rr: hdwy 3f out: chsd ldrs over 1f out: rdn and str run ent fnl f: jst failed* **4/1**[2]

31-0 **3** *nk* **Arthurthedelegator**[26] 1550 3-9-7 **65** MeganNicholls(3) 11 68
(Oliver Greenall) *trckd ldr: cl up 4f out: led 11/2f out and sn rdn: drvn ent fnl f: hdd last 80 yds: no ex towards fin* **8/1**

0000 **4** *2 1/4* **Clean Cut**[27] 1544 3-8-3 **51** oh6 (p[1]) HarrisonShaw(7) 9 49
(Ivan Furtado) *led: rdn along over 2f out: hdd 11/2f out: sn drvn and grad wknd fnl f* **33/1**

3044 **5** *1/2* **Major Cornwallis (IRE)**[14] 1840 3-9-5 **67** SebastianWoods(7) 3 64
(Richard Fahey) *trckd ldrs: hdwy on inner wl over 2f out: rdn wl over 1f out: drvn and wknd fnl f* **11/2**[3]

004 **6** *shd* **Neptune Star**[87] 554 3-8-10 **51** oh3 (h) DavidParkes 6 47
(Jeremy Gask) *bhd: hdwy wl over 2f out: chsd ldrs whn nt clr run and swtchd lft over 1f out: rdn and edgd rt ins fnl f: nrst fin* **25/1**

-030 **7** *2 3/4* **Albizu Campos**[14] 1835 3-8-10 **51** oh3 (p) CliffordLee 12 41
(Lawrence Mullaney) *chsd ldrs: rdn along 2f out: drvn and wknd over 1f out* **20/1**

60-0 **8** *1/2* **Greenview Paradise (IRE)**[11] 1913 3-8-12 **60** ConnorMurtagh(7) 5 49
(Richard Fahey) *a rr* **9/1**

043- **9** *nk* **Bearag**[197] 7380 3-9-9 **64** JoshDoyle 4 52
(David O'Meara) *chsd ldrs: rdn along over 2f out: sn drvn and wknd* **4/1**[2]

321- **10** *1* **Kilbaha Lady (IRE)**[243] 6026 3-9-10 **65** PhilDennis 14 51
(Nigel Tinkler) *chsd ldrs: rdn along over 2f out: sn wknd* **16/1**

1m 32.67s (-1.13) **Going Correction** -0.425s/f (Firm) **10** Ran SP% **118.9**
Speed ratings (Par 97): **89,88,88,85,85 85,82,81,81,80**
CSF £14.86 CT £88.35 TOTE £3.90: £1.70, £1.70, £2.90; EX 17.30 Trifecta £112.70.
**Owner** P D Savill **Bred** Lynn Lodge Stud **Trained** Middleham Moor, N Yorks
■ Stewards' Enquiry : Jane Elliott seven-day ban: used whip above permitted level (May 15-21)

**FOCUS**
An ordinary handicap in which the gallop was reasonable. The winner had to find only a bit of improvement.
T/Jkpt: Not Won. T/Plt: £79.00 to a £1 stake. Pool: £85,975.44 - 793.62 winning units. T/Qpdt: £14.30 to a £1 stake. Pool: £5,569.35 - 286.80 winning units. **Joe Rowntree**

# 2037 WINDSOR (R-H)
Monday, May 1

**OFFICIAL GOING: Good (watered; 8.0)**
Wind: Moderate, against final 5f Weather: Mostly cloudy with drizzle

## 2229 TOTEPLACEPOT RACING'S FAVOURITE BET APPRENTICE TRAINING SERIES H'CAP (RE INITIATIVE) 6f 12y
**2:00** (2:00) (Class 5) (0-70,71) 4-Y-O+ **£3,234** (£962; £481; £240) **Stalls** Low

Form RPR

0630 **1** **Picket Line**[19] 1728 5-9-8 **71** CameronNoble 5 77+
(Geoffrey Deacon) *squeezed out s and then hld up in last: prog out wd fr 1/2-way: rdn to ld ins fnl f: jst hld on* **7/1**[3]

1144 **2** *nse* **Viva Verglas (IRE)**[9] 1980 6-9-2 **70** TobyEley(5) 9 75
(Daniel Mark Loughnane) *trckd ldrs: prog 2f out: led 1f out: hdd ins fnl f: kpt on wl nr fin: jst failed* **8/1**

0-00 **3** *1* **Oeil De Tigre (FR)**[75] 745 6-8-13 **67** NicolaCurrie(5) 6 69
(Tony Carroll) *racd against nr side rail: towards rr: urged along 2f out: prog over 1f out to take 3rd ins fnl f: styd on but unable to chal* **11/2**[2]

5503 **4** *3* **Panther Patrol (IRE)**[16] 1791 7-9-4 **67** (p) SophieKilloran 4 59
(Eve Johnson Houghton) *chsd ldrs: nt qckn and lost pl over 1f out: kpt on same pce fnl f* **11/2**[2]

5104 **5** *1* **Zabdi**[7] 2023 4-9-1 **64** JoshuaBryan 1 53
(Lee Carter) *led against nr side rail: rdn 2f out: hdd & wknd 1f out* **8/1**

10-4 **5** *dht* **Essaka (IRE)**[16] 1791 5-8-7 **59** AledBeech(3) 2 48
(Tony Carroll) *t.k.h: hld up in rr: effrt whn nt clr run over 1f out: kpt on ins fnl f but no ch* **14/1**

02-4 **7** *2 1/4* **Dynamic Girl (IRE)**[11] 1899 4-9-2 **70** (h) StephenCummins(5) 3 52
(Brendan Powell) *trckd ldrs towards nr side rail: rdn to chal over 1f out: wknd qckly fnl f* **9/2**[1]

366- **8** *1/2* **Kinglami**[195] 7430 8-9-5 **68** (p) BenRobinson 11 48
(John O'Shea) *chsd ldr: rdn and wknd over 1f out* **8/1**

35-5 **9** *4 1/2* **Musical Taste**[89] 505 4-8-3 **57** (p[1]) SophieRalston(5) 8 23
(Pat Phelan) *dwlt: racd out wd thrght and nvr able to make much prog* **16/1**

-006 **10** *1* **Flowing Clarets**[75] 735 4-8-13 **67** WilliamCox(5) 7 30
(John Bridger) *chsd ldr to 2f out: wknd qckly* **20/1**

1m 13.53s (0.53) **Going Correction** 0.0s/f (Good) **10** Ran SP% **112.1**
Speed ratings (Par 103): **96,95,94,90,89 89,86,85,79,78**
CSF £59.33 CT £327.83 TOTE £5.80: £2.50, £2.20, £2.40; EX 44.30 Trifecta £355.70.
**Owner** Homegrown Partnership **Bred** Mickley Stud **Trained** Compton, Berks

**FOCUS**
Inner running rail of the home straight was moved to provide fresh racing ground. Inner of straight dolled out 14yds at 6f and 8yds at the winning line. Top bend dolled out 6yds from normal inner configuration, adding 27yds to race distances of 1m-plus. Watering of racing lines was completed at 5pm on Friday, and there was 2mm of rain overnight.

## 2230 TOTEPOOLLIVEINFO.COM FOR RACING RESULTS H'CAP 6f 12y
**2:35** (2:35) (Class 4) (0-85,87) 4-Y-O+ **£5,175** (£1,540; £769; £384) **Stalls** Low

Form RPR

13- **1** **King Of Spin**[233] 6339 4-8-12 **76** ShaneKelly 4 86
(Richard Hughes) *trckd ldrs: led against nr side rail over 2f out: drvn and jnd over 1f out: asserted ins fnl f* **7/1**[3]

055- **2** *1 1/2* **Goring (GER)**[215] 6883 5-9-5 **83** JohnFahy 10 89
(Eve Johnson Houghton) *trckd ldrs: effrt on outer to to take 2nd wl over 1f out and sn upsides wnr: drvn and nt qckn fnl f: eased whn hld last 50yds* **7/2**[1]

/500 **3** *1* **Professor**[30] 1501 7-9-9 **87** AdamBeschizza 1 89
(Michael Attwater) *hld up in last trio: hrd rdn and prog nr side over 1f out: tk 3rd fnl f: nt pce to chal* **15/2**

540- **4** *shd* **Morache Music**[194] 7461 9-9-0 **78** RobertWinston 2 81
(Patrick Chamings) *hld up in last trio: nt clr run over 2f out: last over 1f out: drvn and styd on against nr side ins fnl f: nrly snatched 3rd* **7/1**[3]

2253 **5** *2 3/4* **Pretty Bubbles**[7] 2040 8-9-7 **85** (v) FergusSweeney 8 78
(J R Jenkins) *dwlt: hld up in last trio: prog on outer 2f out: shkn up and one pce jst over 1f out* **8/1**

30-0 **6** *3* **Kyllukey**[7] 2040 4-9-1 **79** DavidProbert 6 62
(Milton Bradley) *trckd ldrs: nt qckn 2f out: lost pl over 1f out: fdd* **16/1**

40-0 **7** *nk* **Tailwind**[117] 45 4-8-10 **74** TomMarquand 9 56
(Richard Hannon) *pressed ldr to 2f out: fdd over 1f out* **13/2**[2]

4-15 **8** *1 1/4* **Artscape**[40] 1302 5-8-6 **73** (h) JackDuern(3) 5 51
(Dean Ivory) *plld hrd: hld up bhd ldng pair: lost pl wl over 1f out: wknd* **17/2**

4202 **9** *3 1/2* **Fairway To Heaven (IRE)**[54] 1087 8-8-11 **75** KierenFox 7 42
(Lee Carter) *led to over 2f out: wknd qckly over 1f out* **7/1**[3]

1m 12.33s (-0.67) **Going Correction** 0.0s/f (Good) **9** Ran SP% **112.3**
Speed ratings (Par 105): **104,102,100,100,96 92,92,90,86**
CSF £30.63 CT £188.71 TOTE £5.90: £1.80, £2.60, £2.60; EX 24.20 Trifecta £251.80.
**Owner** Top Trumps Partnership **Bred** Cheveley Park Stud Ltd **Trained** Upper Lambourn, Berks

**FOCUS**
A fair sprint handicap and improved form from the winner.

## 2231 TOTEQUADPOT INSURE YOUR LAST FOUR MAIDEN STKS 1m 31y
**3:10** (3:11) (Class 5) 3-4-Y-O **£3,234** (£962; £481; £240) **Stalls** Low

Form RPR

0-5 **1** **Desert Dream**[24] 1609 3-9-1 0 PatDobbs 1 79+
(Sir Michael Stoute) *trckd ldrs: plld out and prog 2f out: rdn to ld jst ins fnl f w one rival: styd on to gain upper hand last 100yds* **4/1**[3]

2- **2** *1/2* **Cool Team (IRE)**[213] 6924 3-9-1 0 (t) JamesDoyle 2 78
(Hugo Palmer) *trckd ldr 3f: styd cl up: swtchd arnd rivals fr 2f out and clsd to chal 1f out: w wnr sn after: nt qckn last 100yds* **5/2**[2]

**3** *2 1/2* **Sheila's Rock (IRE)** 3-8-10 0 ShaneKelly 8 67+
(Denis Coakley) *s.s: wl in rr: prog fr 2f out: shkn up and styd on wl to take 3rd nr fin: promising debut* **50/1**

4 **4** *3/4* **Damocles (GER)**[13] 1857 3-9-1 0 (t) RobertTart 10 70
(John Gosden) *trckd ldrs: prog on outer to ld over 1f out: hdd & wknd jst ins fnl f* **5/4**[1]

65 **5** *nk* **Chance To Dream (IRE)**[26] 1551 3-9-1 0 KierenFox 3 69
(John Best) *in tch in midfield: shkn up over 2f out: kpt on u.p fr over 1f out: nrst fin* **40/1**

3- **6** *1* **Lassana Angel**[201] 7285 3-8-5 0 (h) PaddyPilley(5) 5 62+
(Roger Charlton) *hld up towards rr: nudged along and stdy prog fr over 2f out: no hdwy fnl f: likely improver* **9/1**

0-0 **7** *1/2* **Time To Sea (IRE)**[15] 1818 3-9-1 0 LiamKeniry 14 66
(John Butler) *prom: trckd ldr 5f out: chal over 2f out tl fdd over 1f out* **50/1**

60 **8** *3 3/4* **Doodle Dandy (IRE)**[15] 1818 4-9-9 0 TomMarquand 6 55
(David Bridgwater) *led: rdn and hdd over 1f out: wknd* **100/1**

**9** *3 1/2* **Aladdin Sane (IRE)** 3-8-8 0 JordanUys(7) 13 48
(Brian Meehan) *got loose in paddock bef r: v s.i.s: mostly wl in rr: modest late prog* **33/1**

0 **10** *1/2* **Higgy's Heartbeat**[26] 1551 3-8-12 0 JackDuern(3) 4 47
(Dean Ivory) *in tch: effrt on outer over 2f out: wknd over 1f out* **100/1**

00 **11** *1/2* **Garnetta**[30] 1503 3-8-10 0 (p[1]) JackMitchell 7 41
(Amanda Perrett) *trckd ldrs: shkn up over 2f out: wknd wl over 1f out* **100/1**

0- **12** *1/2* **Arquus (IRE)**[273] 4939 4-10-0 0 ThomasBrown 11 48
(Ed de Giles) *sn in last pair and bhd: nvr a factor* **100/1**

0 **13** *1/2* **Mushareefa (IRE)**[24] 1609 3-8-10 0 AntonioFresu 9 39
(Ed Dunlop) *s.i.s: sn in tch: shkn up 4f out: wknd over 2f out* **100/1**

14 8 **Donna Finchella (IRE)** 3-8-10 0 .......... MartinDwyer 12 19
(Brian Meehan) *sed long after rest and lft abt 20 l: nvr able to rcvr* **25/1**

1m 43.54s (-1.16) **Going Correction** 0.0s/f (Good)
**WFA** 3 from 4yo 13lb **14** Ran SP% **121.1**
Speed ratings (Par 103): **105,104,102,101,100 99,99,95,92,91 91,90,90,82**
CSF £14.02 TOTE £5.30: £1.60, £1.40, £8.00; EX 17.50 Trifecta £247.80.
**Owner** Sir Evelyn De Rothschild **Bred** Southcourt Stud **Trained** Newmarket, Suffolk

**FOCUS**
Add 27yds. The bare form looks just fair. The winner progressed, witn the 2nd rated to his debut level.

## 2232 @TOTEPOOLRACING FOR RACING NEWS H'CAP 1m 31y
**3:45** (3:45) (Class 3) (0-95,97) 4-Y-0+ **£8,409** (£2,502; £1,250; £625) **Stalls** Low

Form RPR
00-0 **1** **Secret Art (IRE)**[13] 1860 7-9-7 **92** .......... MartinDwyer 7 97
(William Knight) *trckd ldrs: drvn to cl wl over 1f out: led last 150yds: styd on wl* **9/1**
512/ **2** 1 1/4 **Breden (IRE)**[630] 5215 7-9-5 **90** .......... RobertTart 1 92
(Linda Jewell) *dwlt: hld up in last pair: rdn and prog over 2f out: styd on fnl f to take 2nd last strides* **25/1**
000- **3** *hd* **Medburn Dream**[192] 7505 4-8-12 **83** .......... JFEgan 6 85
(Paul Henderson) *led at gd pce: rdn 2f out: hdd and one pce last 150yds* **5/1[3]**
5-04 **4** 1/2 **Highland Colori (IRE)**[13] 1860 9-9-12 **97** .......... (v) DavidProbert 10 98
(Andrew Balding) *trckd ldr: tried to chal on outer 2f out: nt qckn over 1f out: lost 2 pls fnl f* **9/2[2]**
0540 **5** 3 1/4 **Kingston Kurrajong**[17] 1766 4-9-0 **85** .......... AdamBeschizza 2 78
(Michael Attwater) *in tch: shkn up over 2f out: one pce and no prog after* **13/2**
00-0 **6** 1 1/2 **Winklemann (IRE)**[17] 1766 5-8-11 **82** .......... (t[1]) KierenFox 8 72
(John Flint) *in tch towards rr: urged along over 3f out: struggling after and no imp ldrs* **16/1**
110- **7** 1/2 **Wind In My Sails**[226] 6585 5-9-2 **87** .......... ThomasBrown 11 75
(Ed de Giles) *dwlt: hld up in last pair: taken to outer and shkn up over 2f out: no real prog* **4/1[1]**
603- **8** 11 **Palawan**[213] 6918 4-9-4 **89** .......... DougieCostello 5 52
(Jamie Osborne) *t.k.h: cl up tl wknd 3f out: t.o* **8/1**
360- **9** 9 **Archie (IRE)**[237] 6210 5-9-2 **87** .......... (h) JackMitchell 9 29
(Tom Clover) *taken down early: t.k.h: cl up tl wknd qckly 3f out: t.o* **5/1[3]**

1m 42.82s (-1.88) **Going Correction** 0.0s/f (Good) **9** Ran SP% **115.7**
Speed ratings (Par 107): **109,107,107,107,103 102,101,90,81**
CSF £201.38 CT £1254.14 TOTE £11.30: £3.00, £4.40, £2.10; EX 145.80 Trifecta £1295.80.
**Owner** Art Of Racing **Bred** Grange Stud **Trained** Patching, W Sussex

**FOCUS**
Add 27yds. A useful handicap but mainly exposed sorts. The winner has been rated to last year's best.

## 2233 TOTEPOOL RACECOURSE DEBIT CARD BETTING H'CAP 1m 1f 194y
**4:20** (4:20) (Class 4) (0-85,87) 4-Y-0+ **£5,175** (£1,540; £769; £384) **Stalls** Centre

Form RPR
365- **1** **Solo Hunter**[245] 5964 6-9-2 **86** .......... (b) JoshuaBryan(7) 6 95
(Martyn Meade) *mde virtually all: sent for home over 2f out: drvn and 3 l clr over 1f out: jst hld on* **12/1**
25 **2** *nk* **Getback In Paris (IRE)**[30] 1502 4-9-10 **87** .......... ShaneKelly 8 95
(Richard Hughes) *hld up in last trio: prog over 2f out: rdn to chse wnr over 1f out: clsd ins fnl f: jst too late* **9/2[3]**
565- **3** 3/4 **Biotic**[215] 6870 6-8-10 **73** .......... RyanTate 3 80
(Rod Millman) *hld up in last trio: prog on outer over 2f out: rdn to take 3rd jst over 1f out: clsd on wnr but nt qckn last 75yd* **4/1[2]**
41-2 **4** 8 **Cape Banjo (USA)**[24] 1598 4-9-4 **81** .......... JFEgan 4 72
(Ralph Beckett) *chsd ldrs: shoved along 3f out: no prog 2f out: wknd over 1f out* **3/1[1]**
024- **5** 2 1/2 **Zzoro (IRE)**[192] 7505 4-9-7 **84** .......... PatDobbs 7 70
(Amanda Perrett) *prom: chsd wnr over 3f out to over 1f out: wknd qckly* **5/1**
02-3 **6** *nse* **Cordite (IRE)**[21] 1683 6-8-9 **72** .......... (h) SamHitchcott 5 57
(Jim Boyle) *t.k.h: mostly chsd wnr to over 3f out: sn rdn: wknd wl over 1f out* **11/2**
/4-6 **7** 2 1/4 **Jufn**[42] 1288 4-9-3 **80** .......... LiamKeniry 2 61
(John Butler) *t.k.h: hld up in last trio: rdn and no prog over 2f out: wknd wl over 1f out* **33/1**
22-6 **8** 1 **Archimento**[39] 1324 4-8-12 **75** .......... AntonioFresu 1 54
(Ed Dunlop) *chsd ldrs: shkn up 3f out and no prog: wknd 2f out* **10/1**

2m 7.5s (-1.20) **Going Correction** 0.0s/f (Good) **8** Ran SP% **115.0**
Speed ratings (Par 105): **104,103,103,96,94 94,92,92**
CSF £65.41 CT £258.27 TOTE £12.00: £2.50, £1.50, £1.50; EX 55.90 Trifecta £242.80.
**Owner** The Below Reeve Partnership **Bred** Willie Musson Racing Ltd **Trained** Newmarket, Suffolk
■ Stewards' Enquiry : Joshua Bryan 2 day ban (15-16 May) - used whip above the permitted level

**FOCUS**
Add 27yds. Again, a useful race but a lack of unexposed runners. The winner was close to his 2016 best.

## 2234 COLLECT TOTEPOOL WINNINGS AT BETFRED SHOPS H'CAP 1m 3f 99y
**4:55** (4:55) (Class 4) (0-85,87) 4-Y-0+ **£5,175** (£1,540; £769; £384) **Stalls** Centre

Form RPR
462/ **1** **Sternrubin (GER)**[135] 1960 6-8-13 **77** .......... (h) PatDobbs 3 85+
(Philip Hobbs) *trckd ldr: pushed along over 3f out and looked in trble briefly: drvn to cl fr 2f out: led jst over 1f out: styd on: readily* **5/4[1]**
620- **2** 1 1/2 **Croquembouche (IRE)**[198] 7365 8-9-7 **85** .......... ThomasBrown 4 90
(Ed de Giles) *led: sent for home 3f out: rdn over 2f out: hdd jst over 1f out: one pce* **7/1**
23-5 **3** *nk* **Lime And Lemon (IRE)**[29] 1517 4-8-9 **76** .......... HectorCrouch(3) 5 80
(Clive Cox) *hld up in 3rd: shkn up 3f out: tried to cl fr 2f out: styd on fnl f and nrly snatched 2nd* **13/8[2]**
056- **4** 26 **Stockhill Diva**[189] 7575 7-9-9 **87** .......... LiamKeniry 2 48
(Brendan Powell) *hld up in last: shkn up 3f out: wknd over 2f out: eased and t.o* **5/1[3]**

2m 27.77s (-1.73) **Going Correction** 0.0s/f (Good) **4** Ran SP% **111.7**
Speed ratings (Par 105): **105,104,103,86**
CSF £9.77 TOTE £1.90; EX 7.20 Trifecta £14.40.
**Owner** Terry Warner **Bred** Gestut Karlshof **Trained** Withycombe, Somerset

**FOCUS**
Add 27yds. Only four runners but a fair race. The 2nd has been rated close to last year's form.

## 2235 TOTEPOOL RACECOURSE APPLE PAY BETTING H'CAP 5f 21y
**5:30** (5:32) (Class 5) (0-70,70) 3-Y-0 **£3,234** (£962; £481; £240) **Stalls** Low

Form RPR
0-01 **1** **Fethiye Boy**[81] 638 3-9-5 **68** .......... DavidProbert 13 74
(Ronald Harris) *mde all: darted to far side 1/2-way and clr advantage sn after: drvn over 1f out: hld on to dwindling ld nr fin* **25/1**
35-1 **2** 1/2 **Monteamiata (IRE)**[108] 212 3-9-7 **70** .......... ThomasBrown 2 74+
(Ed Walker) *in tch: rdn and prog 2f out: chsd wnr over 1f out: clsd fnl f: nvr quite got there* **7/1[2]**
21 **3** 1/2 **Midnightly**[39] 1321 3-9-7 **70** .......... AdamBeschizza 12 72
(Rae Guest) *chsd ldrs: rdn over 2f out: disp 2nd over 1f out: clsd on wnr fnl f but a hld* **8/1**
6-35 **4** 1 3/4 **Jashma (IRE)**[63] 956 3-9-0 **63** .......... ShaneKelly 14 59
(Richard Hughes) *dwlt: sn in midfield: followed wnr to far side 2f out but nt on terms: one pce over 1f out* **14/1**
-000 **5** 1 **Lightoller (IRE)**[9] 1970 3-8-6 **62** .......... (v[1]) KeithQuinn(7) 5 55
(Mick Channon) *dwlt: sn in midfield: rdn over 2f out: racd awkwardly after but kpt on ins fnl f: no ch* **33/1**
6301 **6** *hd* **Who Told Jo Jo (IRE)**[21] 1688 3-9-6 **69** .......... LiamKeniry 1 61
(Joseph Tuite) *chsd ldrs: rdn and no prog 2f out: kpt on again ins fnl f* **15/2[3]**
1-3 **7** 3/4 **Team Meeting (USA)**[20] 1693 3-9-7 **70** .......... RobertTart 4 59
(Saeed bin Suroor) *chsd ldrs: rdn over 2f out: nt qckn over 1f out: wl btn after* **7/4[1]**
-603 **8** 1 1/4 **Beach Dancer (IRE)**[21] 1688 3-8-4 **56** oh5 .......... EdwardGreatrex(3) 8 41
(William Knight) *towards rr: followed wnr to far side 2f out but nt on terms: wknd fnl f* **12/1**
4114 **9** 1 1/4 **Roundabout Magic (IRE)**[16] 1786 3-9-4 **67** .......... JFEgan 10 52
(Simon Dow) *chsd wnr: rdn over 2f out in middle of crse: hanging after: lost 2nd over 1f out: wknd and eased* **9/1**
600 **10** 3/4 **Taurean Gold**[24] 1600 3-8-7 **56** oh11 .......... RyanPowell 11 33
(John Bridger) *dwlt: mostly in last pair and off the pce: no real prog fnl 2f* **66/1**
-435 **11** 1 3/4 **Atlanta Belle (IRE)**[20] 1693 3-8-13 **65** .......... LouisSteward(3) 3 36
(Chris Wall) *nvr beyond midfield: rdn and no prog over 2f out* **25/1**
013- **12** 3 1/2 **Silver Penny**[217] 6829 3-9-1 **69** .......... CharlieBennett(5) 9 27
(Jim Boyle) *towards rr: nt clr run over 3f out: sn pushed along and struggling: no ch fnl 2f* **16/1**
2120 **13** 1 **Little Miss Daisy**[16] 1786 3-9-6 **69** .......... MartinDwyer 7 24
(William Muir) *slowly away: nvr able to rcvr and a wl in rr* **14/1**

1m 0.8s (0.50) **Going Correction** 0.0s/f (Good) **13** Ran SP% **120.8**
Speed ratings (Par 99): **96,95,94,91,90 89,88,86,84,83 80,74,73**
CSF £188.94 CT £1601.23 TOTE £22.30: £5.90, £2.40, £2.80; EX 261.40 Trifecta £1673.00.
**Owner** Mrs Ruth M Serrell **Bred** Longdon Stud Ltd **Trained** Earlswood, Monmouths

**FOCUS**
The winner made all and raced towards the far side in the straight, with a few of the others caught out, and the 1-2-3-4 were drawn 13-2-12-14, so the runner-up probably wants noting.
T/Plt: £488.70 to a £1 stake. Pool: £93,338.70 - 139.40 winning units. T/Qpdt: £53.80 to a £1 stake. Pool: £7,182.94 - 98.70 winning units. **Jonathan Neesom**

2236 - 2239a (Foreign Racing) - See Raceform Interactive

# 1650 NAAS (L-H)
Monday, May 1

**OFFICIAL GOING: Good to firm**

## 2240a CAMELOT IRISH EBF MOORESBRIDGE STKS (GROUP 2) 1m 2f
**3:55** (3:55) 4-Y-0+ **£65,555** (£21,111; £10,000; £4,444)

RPR
**1** **Minding (IRE)**[198] 7352 4-9-3 122 .......... RyanMoore 5 122+
(A P O'Brien, Ire) *cl up tl sn disp and led: racd keenly early: over 1 l clr fr 1/2-way: gng best over 2f out: sn drvn clr and styd on wl under hands and heels ins fnl f: easily* **1/3[1]**
**2** 3 1/2 **Moonlight Magic**[212] 6975 4-9-3 116 .......... KevinManning 4 115
(J S Bolger, Ire) *led tl sn jnd and hdd: 2nd 1/2-way: rdn in 2nd over 2f out and sn no imp on easy wnr: kpt on same pce ins fnl f* **6/1[2]**
**3** 2 **Brendan Brackan (IRE)**[36] 1388 8-9-3 112 .......... ColinKeane 3 111
(G M Lyons, Ire) *w.w bhd ldrs in 3rd: pushed along under 2f out and no imp on easy wnr u.p in 3rd 1f out: kpt on same pce ins fnl f to hold 3rd* **12/1**
**4** 3/4 **Johannes Vermeer (IRE)**[205] 7152 4-9-3 109 .......... SeamieHeffernan 2 109
(A P O'Brien, Ire) *hld up in rr: last at 1/2-way: pushed along 1 1/2f out and no imp on easy wnr under hands and heels ins fnl f: kpt on same pce* **8/1[3]**

2m 12.8s (-2.80) **4** Ran SP% **108.1**
CSF £2.76 TOTE £1.10; DF 2.40 Trifecta £6.50.
**Owner** Derrick Smith & Mrs John Magnier & Michael Tabor **Bred** Orpendale, Chelston & Wynatt **Trained** Cashel, Co Tipperary

**FOCUS**
This was all about Minding and she didn't disappoint. The 2nd helps set the level with the winner to par.

## 2241a CANFORD CLIFFS IRISH EBF ATHASI STKS (GROUP 3) (F&M) 7f
**4:30** (4:30) 3-Y-0+
**£40,341** (£12,991; £6,153; £2,735; £1,367; £683)

RPR
**1** **Rehana (IRE)**[23] 1634 3-8-11 107 .......... ShaneFoley 7 105+
(M Halford, Ire) *cl up in 2nd tl sn disp and led after 1f: over 1 l clr bef 1/2-way: pressed fr 1/2-way and jnd briefly over 2f out: regained advantage gng best 1 1/2f out: rdn clr ins fnl f and styd on wl: comf* **6/4[1]**
**2** 2 3/4 **Rose De Pierre (IRE)**[26] 1568 4-9-9 102 .......... PatSmullen 3 101+
(D K Weld, Ire) *broke wl to ld narrowly tl sn jnd and hdd after 1f: impr to dispute ld briefly over 2f out: rdn in cl 2nd 1 1/2f out and no imp on wnr ins fnl f: kpt on same pce* **6/4[1]**
**3** 1 1/4 **Summer Icon**[16] 1795 4-9-9 95 .......... KevinManning 1 98+
(Mick Channon) *chsd ldrs: 3rd 1/2-way: pushed along after 1/2-way and sn no imp on ldrs u.p in 3rd: kpt on same pce ins fnl f: nvr trbld ldrs* **20/1**
**4** 3/4 **Elizabeth Browning (IRE)**[184] 7705 3-8-11 82 .......... (t) RyanMoore 6 92+
(A P O'Brien, Ire) *sn settled in rr: last at 1/2-way: plenty to do under 3f out: pushed along into mod 4th 1 1/2f out and no imp on clr ldrs: rdn and kpt on ins fnl f: nvr trbld ldrs* **16/1**

5 3 **Another Story (IRE)**[52] 1133 4-9-9 95........................ RonanWhelan 5 88
(Ms Sheila Lavery, Ire) *hld up towards rr: pushed along in 5th at 1/2-way and sn no imp on ldrs u.p in rr under 2f out: kpt on one pce in mod 5th ins fnl f* **12/1**[3]
6 4 3/4 **Diamond Fields (IRE)**[22] 1653 4-9-12 106........................ ChrisHayes 2 78
(J A Stack, Ire) *dwlt sltly and in rr early tl impr to sn chse ldrs: 4th 1/2-way: sn pushed along and no ex under 2f out: wknd 1f out* **4/1**[2]

1m 25.2s (-2.30)
**WFA** 3 from 4yo+ 12lb **6** Ran SP% **118.3**
CSF £4.15 TOTE £2.60: £1.10, £1.30; DF 5.20 Trifecta £81.30.
**Owner** H H Aga Khan **Bred** His Highness The Aga Khan's Studs Sc **Trained** Doneany, Co Kildare

**FOCUS**
A straightforward success for the winner, gaining a Group 3-winning bracket after some solid efforts in classier affairs already. While it was slightly surprising that she was re-routed from the English 1,000 Guineas, considering the likelihood of fast ground there, she has enhanced her claims for the Irish equivalent later in the month. The mighty Ridgewood Pearl was the last to do the double in 1995. The 3rd helps set the level.

2242 - 2243a (Foreign Racing) - See Raceform Interactive

# CAPANNELLE (R-H)
Monday, May 1

**OFFICIAL GOING: Turf: good**

## 2244a PREMIO REGINA ELENA DIMENSIONE SUONO2 (GROUP 3) (3YO FILLIES) (TURF) 1m
3:30 3-Y-O **£59,829** (£26,324; £14,358; £7,179)

RPR
1 **Mi Raccomando**[204] 7199 3-8-11 0........................ FabioBranca 2 102
(Stefano Botti, Italy) *a cl up: n.m.r whn stdd and angled out w 3f to run: rdn and hdwy 2f out: led wl over 1f out: r.o gamely fnl f: asserted fnl 50yds* **23/20**[1]
2 snk **Lady Ramon (ITY)** 3-8-11 0........................ LucaManiezzi 5 102
(A Di Dio, Italy) *racd keenly: hld up in midfield: tk clsr order on inner 3f out: chsd ldr 1 1/2f out: sustained chal fnl f: no ex last 50yds* **225/10**
3 3 **Stamp Collecting (IRE)**[22] 3-8-11 0........................ MarioEsposito 8 95
(R Biondi, Italy) *led: kicked for home 3f out: rdn ent fnl 2f: hdd wl over 1f out: one pce u.p fnl f* **13/5**[2]
4 1 1/4 **Sopran Verne (IRE)**[190] 3-8-11 0........................ DarioVargiu 6 92
(Il Cavallo In Testa, Italy) *w.w in tch: 6th and drvn 3f out: styd on u.p fnl f: nt pce to get on terms* **74/10**[3]
5 1/2 **Candy Store (IRE)**[204] 7199 3-8-11 0........................ CristianDemuro 10 91
(Stefano Botti, Italy) *w.w in midfield: drvn and no immediate imp over 2f out: styd on wl u.p fnl f: nvr trbld ldrs* **23/20**[1]
6 shd **Oriental Arrow (IRE)**[263] 3-8-11 0........................ SilvanoMulas 4 91
(Stefano Botti, Italy) *racd in midfield on inner: angled out and drvn 3f out: styd on wl fnl f: nvr nrr* **38/1**
7 1/2 **Alfonsine (IRE)**[176] 3-8-11 0........................ SalvatoreSulas 14 89
(Stefano Botti, Italy) *settled in fnl pair: drvn and began to cl 2 1/2f out: styd on u.p fnl f: nrest at fin* **232/10**
8 nk **Morigane Forlonge (FR)**[205] 7170 3-8-11 0........................ CarloFiocchi 15 89
(Mario Giorgi, Italy) *in rr: hrd rdn and hdwy wl over 2f out: kpt on same pce u.p fnl f* **43/1**
9 1 1/2 **Secret Sharp (IRE)** 3-8-11 0........................ SamueleDiana 7 85
(Ermanno Covone, Italy) *racd in midfield on outer: hrd rdn and styd on wl over 1f out: hld whn n.m.r and eased ins fnl f* **81/1**
10 shd **Fongani (FR)**[171] 7928 3-8-11 0........................ FranckBlondel 12 85
(Simone Brogi, France) *settled towards rr: hdwy 3 1/2f out: styd on to go 8th over 1f out: one pce fnl f* **122/10**
11 1 1/4 **Biri's Angel (IRE)**[190] 3-8-11 0........................ AlessioSatta 9 82
(Simone Langiano, Italy) *towards rr: drvn and sme prog 3f out: kpt on fr over 1f out: nt pce to get involved* **90/1**
12 3 **Movees (IRE)** 3-8-11 0........................ NicolaPinna 1 75
(Stefano Botti, Italy) *prom: cl 4th 1/2-way: rdn to chal for 2nd under 3f out: hrd rdn and no imp 2f out: sn btn* **78/10**
13 2 **Into The Lane (IRE)** 3-8-11 0........................ AndreaAtzeni 3 71
(Stefano Botti, Italy) *sn pressing ldr: drvn and ev ch 2 1/2f out: wkng whn short of room 1 1/2f out* **23/20**[1]
14 1 1/2 **Fataliste (FR)** 3-8-11 0........................ FrankieDettori 11 67
(Endo Botti, Italy) *settled towards rr: effrt on outside 2 1/2f out: sn btn* **79/10**
15 7 **Mon Tresor (FR)**[41] 3-8-11 0........................ PierreBazire 13 51
(Stefano Botti, Italy) *w.w towards rr: hdwy on inner over 3f out: rdn and wknd over 1 1/2f out* **102/10**

1m 36.1s (-3.70) **15** Ran SP% **233.9**
PARI-MUTUEL (all including 1 euro stake): WIN 2.15 PLACE 1.86, 4.70, 1.68 DF 166.40.
**Owner** Scuderia Effevi SRL **Bred** Razza Del Sole Societa Agricola Srl **Trained** Italy

## 2245a PREMIO PARIOLI SISAL MATCHPOINT (GROUP 3) (3YO COLTS) (TURF) 1m
4:50 3-Y-O **£59,829** (£26,324; £14,358; £7,179)

RPR
1 **Anda Muchacho (IRE)**[15] 3-9-2 0........................ DarioVargiu 7 103
(Il Cavallo In Testa, Italy) *chsd ldrs: 3rd and travelling wl over 3f out: drvn to chse ldng pair 2f out: sustained run fnl f: led last stride* **19/10**[2]
2 shd **Patriot Hero (IRE)** 3-9-2 0........................ FrankieDettori 9 103
(Endo Botti, Italy) *a cl up on outer: shkn up to ld 2f out: drvn and styd on fnl f: hdd fnl stride* **21/20**[1]
3 1 1/2 **Amore Hass (IRE)**[29] 3-9-2 0........................ CristianDemuro 1 99
(Stefano Botti, Italy) *settled in midfield on inner: drvn to chse ldrs fr 2 1/2f out: kpt on u.p fnl f: nt pce to chal* **47/10**
4 1 **Aspettatemi (ITY)** 3-9-2 0........................ SalvatoreBasile 5 97
(F Petrazzi, Italy) *led: hdd 2f out: rallied gamely u.p: one pce fnl f* **69/1**
5 4 1/2 **Sun Devil (ITY)**[197] 7401 3-9-2 0........................ AndreaAtzeni 3 87
(Stefano Botti, Italy) *racd in midfield on outer: drvn 2f out: kpt on at same pce: nvr on terms* **17/5**[3]
5 dht **Dulciboy**[15] 3-9-2 0........................ CarloFiocchi 8 87
(Stefano Botti, Italy) *w.w in rr: hdwy 2f out: kpt on fnl f: nrest at fin* **35/1**
7 3 1/2 **Biz Power (IRE)**[29] 3-9-2 0........................ SilvanoMulas 6 79
(Stefano Botti, Italy) *hld up towards rr: rdn 2f out: nvr able to make any imp* **84/10**
8 4 **Together Again**[43] 3-9-2 0........................ FabioBranca 4 69
(Stefano Botti, Italy) *plld v hrd: restrained cl up on inner: lost pl wl over 2f out: sn btn* **17/5**[3]
9 5 **Mister Anthony** 3-9-2 0........................ LucaManiezzi 2 58
(C Impelluso, Italy) *w.w towards rr: rdn and wknd fnl 2 1/2f* **33/1**

1m 36.6s (-3.20) **9** Ran SP% **164.0**
PARI-MUTUEL (all including 1 euro stake): WIN 2.90 PLACE 1.42, 1.28, 1.67 DF 7.77.
**Owner** Scuderia Incolinx & Diego Romeo **Bred** Thomas Hassett **Trained** Italy

# MUNICH (L-H)
Monday, May 1

**OFFICIAL GOING: Turf: soft**

## 2246a WWW.PFERDEWETTEN.DE - BAVARIAN CLASSIC (GROUP 3) (3YO) (TURF) 1m 2f
2:35 3-Y-O **£27,350** (£10,256; £5,128; £2,564; £1,709)

RPR
1 **Warring States (JPN)**[183] 7722 3-9-2 0........................ HarryBentley 3 104
(A Wohler, Germany) *waited towards rr on inner: gd hdwy 2f out: drvn to ld wl over 1f out: hld on gamely u.p fnl 100yds* **11/5**[2]
2 nse **Enjoy Vijay (GER)**[176] 7842 3-9-2 0........................ AndraschStarke 5 104
(P Schiergen, Germany) *w.w towards rr: clsd to chse ldng gp 3f out: rdn and chsd ldr ent fnl f: r.o u.p: jst hld* **11/2**
3 2 1/2 **Kastano (GER)**[176] 7842 3-9-2 0........................ MartinSeidl 6 99
(Markus Klug, Germany) *racd v keenly: led after 2f: drvn and wnt for home 2f out: hdd wl over 1f out: kpt on at one pce* **9/2**
4 1 1/2 **Northsea Star (GER)**[184] 3-9-2 0........................ AdriedeVries 1 96
(Markus Klug, Germany) *led: hdd after 2f: remained cl up: outpcd and rdn 1 1/2f out: kpt on same pce fnl f* **21/10**[1]
5 1 1/2 **Rostam (USA)** 3-9-2 0........................(b) MarcLerner 2 93
(A Wohler, Germany) *chsd ldng trio: hrd rdn but nt qckn 2f out: grad dropped away fnl f* **157/10**
6 1 1/2 **Nerud (USA)**[22] 3-9-2 0........................ JozefBojko 7 90
(A Wohler, Germany) *w.w in rr: rdn and short-lived effrt 1 1/2f out: nvr in contention* **37/10**[3]
7 2 1/2 **Manipur (GER)** 3-9-2 0........................ KoenClijmans 4 85
(Mario Hofer, Germany) *prom on outer: rdn and nt qckn 2f out: sn wknd* **192/10**

2m 14.6s (5.63) **7** Ran SP% **129.3**
PARI-MUTUEL (all including 10 euro stake): WIN 32 PLACE: 24, 30; SF: 301.
**Owner** Qatar Racing Limited **Bred** Shirai Stud Farm **Trained** Germany

2247a (Foreign Racing) - See Raceform Interactive

# 2003 SAINT-CLOUD (L-H)
Monday, May 1

**OFFICIAL GOING: Turf: good to soft**

## 2248a PRIX DU MUGUET (GROUP 2) (4YO+) (TURF) 1m
2:25 4-Y-O+ **£63,333** (£24,444; £11,666; £7,777; £3,888)

RPR
1 **Jimmy Two Times (FR)**[29] 1531 4-9-0 0........................ VincentCheminaud 6 114+
(A Fabre, France) *settled in midfield on outer: 4th and travelling wl under 3f out: drvn to cl 1 1/2f out: led fnl 150yds: r.o* **7/10**[1]
2 1/2 **Kourkan (FR)**[29] 1531 4-9-0 0........................ ChristopheSoumillon 5 113+
(J-M Beguigne, France) *settled in midfield on outer: clsd over 2f out: r.o to go 2nd 50yds out: nvr quite on terms w wnr* **97/10**[3]
3 1 1/4 **Usherette (IRE)**[297] 4107 5-8-10 0........................ MickaelBarzalona 7 106
(A Fabre, France) *hld up in fnl trio: hdwy on outer w 1 1/2f to run: styd on wl fnl f: tk 3rd fnl stride* **181/10**
4 shd **Djiguite (FR)**[29] 1531 5-9-0 0........................ GeraldMosse 2 110+
(D Smaga, France) *w.w in midfield on inner: scrubbed along wl over 2 1/2f out: 5th and n.m.r 2f out: styd on fnl f: nt pce to chal* **147/10**
5 nse **Toscanini (IRE)**[30] 1493 5-9-0 0........................ WilliamBuick 3 110
(Richard Fahey) *led: hdd 150yds out: no ex: lost three pls fnl 50yds* **43/1**
6 shd **Zalamea (IRE)**[55] 1078 4-9-0 0........................ EddyHardouin 8 110
(Carina Fey, France) *slowly away: racd keenly in midfield on inner: kpt on fnl 1 1/2f: nt pce to get on terms w ldrs* **38/1**
7 2 **Attendu (FR)**[29] 1531 4-9-0 0........................ MaximeGuyon 4 105
(C Laffon-Parias, France) *chsd ldng pair: 2nd and drvn 2 1/2f out: no imp whn hrd rdn 1 1/2f out: wknd ins fnl f* **106/10**
8 3/4 **Karar**[177] 7833 5-9-0 0........................ GregoryBenoist 1 103
(F-H Graffard, France) *t.k.h: chsd ldr under restraint: rdn and no imp under 1 1/2f out: grad dropped away fnl f* **16/1**
9 1 1/2 **Spectre (FR)**[177] 7837 4-8-10 0........................ Pierre-CharlesBoudot 9 96
(M Munch, Germany) *racd keenly: hld up in fnl pair: rdn and no imp 2f out: nvr in contention* **99/10**
10 2 **Siyoushake (IRE)**[183] 7723 5-8-10 0........................ StephanePasquier 10 91
(F Head, France) *sn w.w in rr: drvn and no imp 2 1/2f out: bhd fnl 1 1/2f* **9/1**[2]

1m 41.01s (-6.49) **10** Ran SP% **118.3**
PARI-MUTUEL (all including 1 euro stake): WIN 1.50 PLACE 1.10, 1.70, 1.90 DF 9.00 SF 10.10.
**Owner** Godolphin SNC **Bred** F Teboul & J Boniche **Trained** Chantilly, France

## 2249a PRIX GANAY (GROUP 1) (4YO+) (TURF) 1m 2f 110y
3:00 4-Y-O+ **£146,512** (£58,615; £29,307; £14,641; £7,333)

RPR
1 **Cloth Of Stars (IRE)**[22] 1659 4-9-2 0........................ MickaelBarzalona 3 119
(A Fabre, France) *a cl up on inner: drvn to ld ins fnl 1 1/2f: rdn and r.o fnl f: a holding runner-up* **6/5**[1]
2 snk **Zarak (FR)**[37] 1378 4-9-2 0........................ ChristopheSoumillon 2 119+
(A De Royer-Dupre, France) *settled in tch towards rr: rdn and trapped in pocket on rail 2f out: angled out and cl under 1 1/2f out: r.o fnl f: wnt 2nd 100yds out: nvr quite on terms* **12/5**[2]
3 3/4 **Silverwave (FR)**[141] 8329 5-9-2 0........................ Pierre-CharlesBoudot 5 117
(P Bary, France) *w.w in fnl pair: clsd on outer wl over 2f out: styd on to go 2nd 125yds out: nvr able to chal* **84/10**
4 hd **Erupt (IRE)**[155] 8129 5-9-2 0........................ StephanePasquier 8 117
(F-H Graffard, France) *settled in rr: rdn and prog on outer 2f out: styd on fnl f: nt pce to chal* **115/10**

5 2 **Hawkbill (USA)**181 7759 4-9-2 0....(p) WilliamBuick 4 113
(Charlie Appleby) *pressed ldr on outer: rdn to ld narrowly over 1 1/2f out: hdd sn after: styd on at same pce fnl f* **26/1**

6 1 1/2 **Guignol (GER)**181 7759 5-9-2 0.... VincentCheminaud 1 110
(Jean-Pierre Carvalho, Germany) *led: drvn and rallied 3f out: sn rdn: hdd over 1 1/2f out: one pce fnl f* **29/1**

7 1 **Potemkin (GER)**176 7841 6-9-2 0.... GeraldMosse 7 108
(A Wohler, Germany) *racd keenly: hld up in tch on outer: cl 4th and scrubbed along 2 1/2f out: no imp u.p fr 1 1/2f out: dropped away ins fnl f* **42/10**3

2m 11.7s (-7.90) 7 Ran SP% **119.8**
PARI-MUTUEL (all including 1 euro stake): WIN 2.10 PLACE 1.10, 1.20, 1.50 DF 2.80 SF 5.10.
**Owner** Godolphin SNC **Bred** Peter Anastasiou **Trained** Chantilly, France

**FOCUS**
For the second year running this wasn't a deep Prix Ganay on paper. The 3rd-6th help set the level.

## 2250a PRIX DE L'AVRE (LISTED RACE) (3YO) (TURF) 1m 4f
**3:40** 3-Y-O **£23,504** (£9,401; £7,051; £4,700; £2,350)

RPR

1 **Wolf Country**203 7225 3-9-2 0.... WilliamBuick 2 104
(Charlie Appleby) *mde all: sn 2l clr: drvn over 2f out: rdn appr fnl f: styd on wl and a in control: eased cl home* **19/2**

2 3/4 **Falcon Wings**25 1595 3-9-2 0.... StephanePasquier 4 103+
(N Clement, France) **12/5**2

3 1 1/4 **Walsingham (GER)**17 3-9-2 0.... ChristopheSoumillon 6 101
(Waldemar Hickst, Germany) **106/10**

4 3/4 **One One One (FR)**20 3-9-2 0.... Pierre-CharlesBoudot 7 100
(H-A Pantall, France) **19/5**3

5 1 1/4 **Sand Fox (FR)**20 3-9-2 0.... MickaelBarzalona 3 98
(A Fabre, France) *chsd ldr on inner: drvn 2 1/2f out: kpt on wout clsng: dropped away fnl 150yds* **6/4**1

6 hd **Saldier (FR)**15 1826 3-9-2 0.... MaximeGuyon 5 97
(T Castanheira, France) **28/1**

7 4 **Amazing (FR)**15 1826 3-9-2 0.... AntoineHamelin 1 91
(F Vermeulen, France) **121/10**

2m 35.8s (-4.60) 7 Ran SP% **119.5**
PARI-MUTUEL (all including 1 euro stake): WIN 2.00 PLACE 3.10, 2.30, SF 16.20.
**Owner** Godolphin **Bred** Stiftung Gestut Fahrhof **Trained** Newmarket, Suffolk

# 2052 BRIGHTON (L-H)
Tuesday, May 2

**OFFICIAL GOING: Good (good to firm in places)**
Wind: Moderate across, away from stands Weather: Cloudy

## 2251 TOTEPLACEPOT AT TOTESPORT.COM NOVICE AUCTION STKS 5f 60y
**2:00** (2:00) (Class 5) 2-Y-O **£2,911** (£866; £432; £216) **Stalls** Centre

Form RPR

3 1 **Starlight Mystery (IRE)**13 1873 2-8-8 0.... JoeFanning 1 71+
(Mark Johnston) *hld up in 4th: chsd ldr 2f out: led ins fnl f: rdn out* **10/11**1

2 2 **Super Florence (IRE)** 2-8-7 0.... JohnFahy 4 62+
(Eve Johnson Houghton) *dwlt: last tl rdn and hdwy fr over 1f out: r.o to take 2nd ins fnl 100yds* **10/1**3

4 3 1 3/4 **Floss The Hoss (IRE)**13 1872 2-8-10 0.... DavidProbert 2 59
(David Evans) *t.k.h: chsd ldr tl 2f out: one pce* **6/4**2

0 4 nse **Firenze Rosa (IRE)**8 2037 2-8-6 0.... KieranO'Neill 3 55
(John Bridger) *led: rdn 2f out: hdd and no ex ins fnl f* **20/1**

5 nk **Llamrei** 2-8-6 0.... IrineuGoncalves 5 54
(Jo Hughes) *chsd ldrs: rdn and outpcd fnl 2f* **40/1**

1m 2.58s (0.28) **Going Correction** -0.025s/f (Good) 5 Ran SP% **108.7**
Speed ratings (Par 93): **96,92,90,89,89**
CSF £10.34 TOTE £1.60: £1.10, £3.60; EX 6.00 Trifecta £14.20.
**Owner** Ali Saeed **Bred** Rabbah Bloodstock Limited **Trained** Middleham Moor, N Yorks

**FOCUS**
The going was good, good to firm in places. An uncompetitive contest run at a sound pace. Ordinary form rated around the third.

## 2252 HERTZ CAR RENTAL H'CAP 5f 215y
**2:30** (2:30) (Class 5) (0-70,72) 3-Y-O **£2,911** (£866; £432; £216) **Stalls** Centre

Form RPR

242- 1 **Otomo**173 7891 3-9-4 67.... LiamKeniry 6 74
(Philip Hide) *led after 1f: rdn and in control fnl 2f* **10/3**2

36-3 2 3/4 **Raffle King (IRE)**25 1600 3-9-7 70.... CharlesBishop 5 74
(Mick Channon) *sn prom: rdn to chse wnr wl over 1f out: hung lft: kpt on fnl f: a hld* **11/4**1

0-40 3 3 1/2 **Baby Gal**46 1242 3-9-3 66.... WilliamCarson 9 58
(Jim Boyle) *hld up: hdwy and rdn 2f out: one pce* **15/2**

-366 4 1/2 **Hidden Stash**21 1693 3-8-6 62....(v1) WilliamCox(7) 4 53
(Andrew Balding) *in tch on inner: effrt 2f out: no imp* **8/1**

5050 5 1 1/2 **Pulsating (IRE)**6 2094 3-9-0 63.... DannyBrock 7 49
(Daniel Steele) *chsd ldrs on outer tl outpcd 2f out* **12/1**

0243 6 1/2 **Billy's Boots**16 1821 3-8-10 59.... DavidProbert 3 43
(J R Jenkins) *led for 1f: chsd wnr tl wl over 1f out: sn wknd* **20/1**

260- 7 2 **Pastfact**204 7217 3-9-1 64.... FergusSweeney 8 42
(Malcolm Saunders) *outpcd: sn wl bhd: nvr nr ldrs* **16/1**

230- 8 9 **Kiribati**148 8229 3-9-7 70.... JoeFanning 1 19
(Mark Johnston) *lost pl on downhill bnd after 2f: sn bhd* **4/1**3

1m 10.24s (0.04) **Going Correction** -0.025s/f (Good) 8 Ran SP% **111.0**
Speed ratings (Par 99): **98,97,92,91,89 89,86,74**
CSF £12.11 CT £59.41 TOTE £4.50: £1.60, £1.50, £2.50; EX 13.50 Trifecta £92.10.
**Owner** S P C Woods **Bred** D A Yardy **Trained** Findon, W Sussex

**FOCUS**
A strongly run handicap. The winner has ben rated as improving on his 2yo form.

## 2253 ROA/RACING POST OWNERS JACKPOT H'CAP 5f 60y
**3:00** (3:00) (Class 4) (0-85,80) 4-Y-O+ **£4,690** (£1,395; £697; £348) **Stalls** Centre

Form RPR

123- 1 **Cosmopolitan Girl (IRE)**272 5040 4-9-7 80.... JoeFanning 4 91
(Robert Cowell) *sltly missed break and squeezed at s: hdwy to chse ldr after 2f: led ins fnl f: rdn clr* **4/1**2

5026 2 2 1/4 **Sandfrankskipsgo**6 2083 8-9-2 78.... HectorCrouch(3) 1 81
(Peter Crate) *led at gd pce tl ins fnl f: no ex* **4/1**2

4403 3 2 **Swiss Cross**7 2054 10-9-2 75....(tp) DavidProbert 3 71
(Phil McEntee) *short of room at s: outpcd in rr: hdwy on inner 2f out: no imp* **7/1**3

6-54 4 1 3/4 **Emjayem**52 1147 7-9-2 75.... RoystonFfrench 6 65
(John Holt) *wnt lft at s: chsd ldr for 2f: outpcd fnl 2f* **25/1**

22-6 5 2 1/4 **Showmethewayavrilo**15 1836 4-8-7 71.... GeorgiaCox(5) 2 53
(Malcolm Saunders) *short of room at s: 4th most of way tl rdn and btn over 2f out* **15/2**

14-2 6 1 1/2 **Bahamian Sunrise**7 2058 5-8-8 72....(p) GeorgeBuckell(5) 5 49+
(John Gallagher) *short of room: sddle slipped and wnt rt sn after s: n.d fnl 3f* **11/8**1

1m 1.51s (-0.79) **Going Correction** -0.025s/f (Good) 6 Ran SP% **110.2**
Speed ratings (Par 105): **105,101,98,95,91 89**
CSF £19.30 TOTE £2.70: £1.50, £2.50; EX 18.90 Trifecta £49.00.
**Owner** Saleh Al Homaizi & Imad Al Sagar **Bred** Corrin Stud & Dream Ahead Syndicate **Trained** Six Mile Bottom, Cambs

**FOCUS**
They went a strong pace for this fair handicap. The runner-up has been rated to his recent form.

## 2254 EBF STALLIONS BREEDING WINNERS FILLIES' H'CAP 1m 1f 207y
**3:35** (3:35) (Class 3) (0-90,85) 4-Y-O **£9,766** (£2,923; £1,461; £731; £364) **Stalls** High

Form RPR

024- 1 **Singyoursong (IRE)**263 5382 4-9-2 85.... GeorgeBuckell(5) 6 94
(David Simcock) *hld up and bhd: hdwy in centre 2f out: led 1f out: rdn out* **4/1**3

60-1 2 2 1/4 **Pernickety**17 1789 4-8-6 70....(h) JoeFanning 2 75
(Lucy Wadham) *s.i.s: hld up in 5th: hdwy to ld 2f out: hung lft: hdd 1f out: one pce* **3/1**2

432- 3 6 **Lorelina**193 7504 4-9-1 79.... DavidProbert 5 72
(Andrew Balding) *chsd clr ldrs: effrt over 2f out: sn outpcd* **5/4**1

-060 4 3 **Pivotal Flame (IRE)**28 806 4-8-4 68.... KieranO'Neill 4 55
(Pat Phelan) *led at gd pce tl 2f out: wknd 1f out* **40/1**

-512 5 1/2 **Auntie Barber (IRE)**38 1368 4-8-11 78.... AaronJones(3) 1 64
(Stuart Williams) *chsd ldr tl over 2f out: wknd over 1f out* **15/2**

-650 6 1 1/4 **Hawatif (IRE)**73 810 4-9-3 81.... WilliamCarson 3 64
(Anthony Carson) *hld up in 4th: rdn over 2f out: wknd wl over 1f out* **12/1**

2m 2.25s (-1.35) **Going Correction** -0.025s/f (Good) 6 Ran SP% **111.3**
Speed ratings (Par 104): **104,102,97,95,94 93**
CSF £16.04 TOTE £5.00: £2.10, £2.00; EX 18.60 Trifecta £34.50.
**Owner** Saeed Jaber **Bred** Rabbah Bloodstock Limited **Trained** Newmarket, Suffolk

**FOCUS**
This fair handicap was run at a strong pace which suited the closers. It's been rated a bit cautiously.

## 2255 STREAMLINE TAXIS 202020 H'CAP 7f 211y
**4:10** (4:10) (Class 6) (0-55,57) 4-Y-O+ **£2,264** (£673; £336; £168) **Stalls** Centre

Form RPR

000- 1 **Buzz Lightyere**195 7464 4-9-4 51.... LiamKeniry 10 59
(Philip Hide) *chsd ldrs: led wl over 1f out: drvn out* **8/1**3

6-60 2 1 3/4 **Fairy Mist (IRE)**12 1894 10-9-2 49....(v) WilliamCarson 11 53
(John Bridger) *mid-div: hrd rdn over 2f out: styd on to take 2nd nr fin* **16/1**

000- 3 nk **Provoking (USA)**253 5720 4-9-0 52.... CliffordLee(5) 12 55
(David Evans) *prom: hrd rdn over 1f out: kpt on same pce* **16/1**

0-04 4 3/4 **Kafeel (USA)**102 332 6-9-7 57....(p) HectorCrouch(3) 4 59
(Gary Moore) *mid-div: hdwy to chse ldrs over 2f out: one pce fnl f* **7/4**1

0006 5 2 3/4 **Port Lairge**28 1545 7-9-0 52....(v) PhilDennis(5) 2 47
(Michael Chapman) *drvn along most of way: bhd tl styd on wl fnl 2f* **20/1**

00-2 6 2 **Ettie Hart (IRE)**7 2056 4-9-0 54.... KeithQuinn(7) 8 45
(Mick Channon) *towards rr tl styd on u.p fnl 2f* **8/1**3

05-2 7 4 **Jonnie Skull (IRE)**7 2057 11-8-12 45....(vt) DavidProbert 3 26
(Phil McEntee) *led tl wl over 1f out: wknd fnl f* **16/1**

6303 8 3/4 **Lutine Charlie (IRE)**7 2057 10-8-5 45....(p) DavidEgan(7) 9 25
(Emma Owen) *in tch: drvn along over 2f out: btn whn edgd lft over 1f out* **14/1**

3021 9 nse **Sir Jamie**27 1563 4-9-4 51.... GeorgeDowning 7 31
(Tony Carroll) *towards rr: rdn over 2f out: n.d* **6/1**2

500- 10 1 1/2 **Machiavelian Storm (IRE)**127 7299 5-8-7 45.... AliceMills(5) 1 21
(Richard Mitchell) *in tch: bdly hmpd on inner and lost pl 5f out: n.d after* **100/1**

5600 11 2 1/4 **Indus Valley (IRE)**7 2053 10-8-11 51....(b) JaneElliott(7) 6 22
(Lee Carter) *s.i.s: a bhd* **25/1**

12 1 1/2 **Jesse Tree (IRE)**196 7451 4-8-5 45.... WilliamCox(7) 13 17
(John Flint) *w ldr for 3f: wknd 2f out* **16/1**

0/0F 13 66 **Mobley Chaos**74 784 7-8-12 45....(p) FergusSweeney 5
(John Flint) *chsd ldrs: bdly squeezed and lost pl 5f out: bhd whn eased 2f out* **25/1**

1m 34.85s (-1.15) **Going Correction** -0.025s/f (Good) 13 Ran SP% **116.5**
Speed ratings (Par 101): **104,102,101,101,98 96,92,91,91,90 87,86,20**
CSF £120.12 CT £1281.45 TOTE £9.50: £3.30, £3.30, £4.80; EX 141.40 Trifecta £1879.60.
**Owner** Tara Moon Partnership **Bred** M H And Mrs G Tourle **Trained** Findon, W Sussex
■ Stewards' Enquiry : Clifford Lee three-day ban: careless riding (16-18 May)

**FOCUS**
Another strongly run handicap. The winner has been rated within 5lb of his best form.

## 2256 LOVE FAIRS ANTIQUES & COLLECTABLES 7 MAY H'CAP 6f 210y
**4:40** (4:40) (Class 5) (0-75,77) 4-Y-O+ **£2,911** (£866; £432; £216) **Stalls** Centre

Form RPR

510- 1 **Lastmanlastround (IRE)**242 6084 4-10-0 77.... DavidProbert 1 86+
(Rae Guest) *cl up: fnd gap on inner and led 2f out: drvn out* **7/4**2

5-44 2 nk **Duke Of North (IRE)**22 1687 5-8-12 66.... CharlieBennett(5) 4 73
(Jim Boyle) *hld up in handy 5th: rdn into 2nd over 1f out: clsd on wnr fnl f: jst hld* **13/8**1

-050 3 2 1/4 **Corporal Maddox**38 1365 10-9-7 70....(p) RoystonFfrench 5 71
(Ronald Harris) *cl up on outer: hrd rdn wl over 1f out: one pce* **9/1**

041- 4 3/4 **Sarangoo**236 6266 9-9-9 77.... GeorgiaCox(5) 2 76
(Malcolm Saunders) *led tl 2f out: sn hrd rdn and outpcd* **15/2**

-003 5 2 **Air Of York (IRE)**13 1890 5-8-13 62....(p) FergusSweeney 3 56
(John Flint) *pressed ldr tl over 2f out: wknd over 1f out* **6/1**3

1m 23.3s (0.20) **Going Correction** -0.025s/f (Good) 5 Ran SP% **110.5**
Speed ratings (Par 103): **97,96,94,93,90**
CSF £5.02 TOTE £3.00: £1.30, £1.70; EX 5.90 Trifecta £22.60.
**Owner** The Boot Sarratt Racing Syndicate **Bred** Duggan Bloodstock **Trained** Newmarket, Suffolk

**FOCUS**
A truly run handicap. The runner-up has been rated to form.

## 2257 DONATELLO RESTAURANT BRIGHTON APPRENTICE H'CAP 1m 1f 207y
**5:10** (5:10) (Class 6) (0-65,67) 4-Y-O+ **£2,264** (£673; £336; £168) **Stalls** High

Form RPR
363- **1** **Miss Inga Sock (IRE)**[204] 7212 5-8-8 **55**........................ GeorgiaCox(3) 2 61
(Eve Johnson Houghton) *chsd ldr: rdn to dispute ld fr over 1f out: jst prevailed* **6/1**[3]
3400 **2** *hd* **Sir Jack**[33] 1458 4-8-10 **57**................................................ CliffordLee(3) 4 63
(Tony Carroll) *in tch: drvn along over 3f out: edgd lft and styd on to dispute ld fr over 1f out: jst denied* **5/1**[2]
1656 **3** *3* **Hold Firm**[31] 1484 5-8-8 **59**........................................ GabrieleMalune(7) 3 59
(Mark H Tompkins) *prom: lost pl 4f out: rallied on inner and hrd rdn 2f out: one pce fnl f* **8/1**
2340 **4** *shd* **Glenalmond (IRE)**[17] 1788 5-9-9 **67**...............................(p) AaronJones 1 67
(Daniel Steele) *led tl over 1f out: no ex fnl f* **5/1**[2]
-021 **5** *2 ¾* **Victor's Bet (SPA)**[21] 1698 8-9-0 **65**................................ WilliamCox(7) 6 60
(Ralph J Smith) *stdd in rr s: swtchd outside and shkn up over 2f out: no prog tl styd on fnl f* **4/1**[1]
0266 **6** *1* **Solveig's Song**[7] 2055 5-9-1 **66**.....................................(b[1]) RossaRyan(7) 9 59
(Steve Woodman) *hld up: hdwy 5f out: hrd rdn and btn wl over 1f out* **17/2**
050 **7** *¾* **Lord Of The Storm**[31] 1484 9-8-12 **59**........................ DavidParkes(3) 10 50
(Michael Attwater) *towards rr: rdn 3f out: n.d* **12/1**
660- **8** *1 ½* **Ede's The Mover**[323] 3236 4-8-8 **59**........................ SophieRalston(7) 5 48
(Pat Phelan) *mid-div: n.m.r on inner 5f out: sn bhd* **33/1**
100- **9** *16* **Magnificent Madiba**[109] 7421 4-9-6 **64**........................ HectorCrouch 7 22
(George Baker) *t.k.h: trckd ldrs tl wknd qckly over 2f out* **5/1**[2]
2m 3.05s (-0.55) **Going Correction** -0.025s/f (Good) **9** Ran SP% **116.6**
Speed ratings (Par 101): **101,100,98,98,96 95,94,93,80**
CSF £36.41 CT £243.37 TOTE £7.00: £2.00, £2.40, £3.10; EX 34.60 Trifecta £107.60.
**Owner** The Ascot Colts & Fillies Club **Bred** R F Johnson Houghton **Trained** Blewbury, Oxon
**FOCUS**
Not a great race for the grade. The second and third set the level.
T/Plt: £124.60 to a £1 stake. Pool: £55,092.29 - 322.71 winning units. T/Qpdt: £73.40 to a £1 stake. Pool: £3,376.23 - 34.0 winning units. **Lee McKenzie**

# 2111 CHELMSFORD (A.W) (L-H)
Tuesday, May 2

**OFFICIAL GOING: Polytrack: standard**
Wind: virtually nil Weather: overcast

## 2258 TOTEPOOLLIVEINFO.COM VISIT FOR RACING RESULTS FILLIES' NOVICE AUCTION STKS (PLUS 10 RACE) 5f (P)
**6:10** (6:11) (Class 5) 2-Y-O **£4,528** (£1,347; £673; £336) **Stalls** Low

Form RPR
**1** **Blessed To Empress (IRE)** 2-9-0 0........................ LemosdeSouza 5 66
(Amy Murphy) *wnt lft and bmpd s: sn rcvrd to ld and mde rest: rdn over 1f out: kpt on wl and a in command fnl f* **4/1**[1]
**2** *1 ½* **Three Little Birds** 2-8-12 0........................................ SamHitchcott 4 58
(Sylvester Kirk) *wnt rt and bmpd s: hld up in tch: clsd to chse ldrs and swtchd rt wl over 1f out: sn rdn: kpt on u.p ins fnl f: wnt 2nd last stride* **5/1**[3]
**3** *shd* **Princess Lyla (IRE)** 2-8-10 0........................................ RyanTate 3 56
(Richard Hughes) *w wnr tl dropped to 3rd after 1f out: effrt over 1f out: chsd wnr 1f out: styd on same pce after: lost 2nd last stride* **14/1**
**4** *3* **Dorcas** 2-8-12 0............................................................ LukeMorris 7 47
(James Given) *awkward and wnt rt leaving stalls: t.k.h: hdwy to chse wnr after 1f: rdn and unable qck over 1f out: wknd ins fnl f* **4/1**[1]
6 **5** *2 ¼* **Asheena**[13] 1873 2-8-10 0................................................ SeanLevey 2 37
(Paul D'Arcy) *w ldrs early: dropped to 5th but stl in tch after 1f: effrt and swtchd rt over 1f out: no imp: wknd ins fnl f* **9/2**[2]
**6** *7* **Sweet Vixen** 2-8-13 0.................................................. MartinLane 1 15
(Tom Clover) *s.i.s: rdn along and outpcd in rr thrght* **6/1**
**U** **Arabian Jazz (IRE)** 2-8-11 0........................................ DannyBrock 8
(Michael Bell) *awkward leaving stalls and uns rdr* **9/2**[2]
1m 1.51s (1.31) **Going Correction** -0.10s/f (Stan) **7** Ran SP% **114.0**
Speed ratings (Par 90): **85,82,82,77,74 62,**
CSF £23.91 TOTE £5.30: £2.80, £4.40; EX 30.90 Trifecta £310.20.
**Owner** White Diamond Racing Partnership 1 **Bred** Liam Butler & Churchtown House Stud **Trained** Newmarket, Suffolk
**FOCUS**
Probably not the strongest of novice races. It's been rated as ordinary form.

## 2259 TOTEPOOL LIVE INFO DOWNLOAD THE APP H'CAP 1m (P)
**6:40** (6:41) (Class 6) (0-65,67) 3-Y-O **£3,234** (£962; £481; £240) **Stalls** Low

Form RPR
00-4 **1** **Paddy A (IRE)**[27] 1550 3-9-9 **67**........................................ JamesDoyle 3 74
(Philip McBride) *chsd ldr tl pushed into ld 2f out and c centre st: styd on wl u.p ad a doing enough ins fnl f: eased nr fin* **3/1**[1]
23-5 **2** *1* **Orithia (USA)**[17] 1790 3-9-2 **60**......................................(t) DaneO'Neill 8 65
(Seamus Durack) *t.k.h: chsd ldng pair: effrt in centre over 1f out: styd on same pce ins fnl f: wnt 2nd last strides* **12/1**
0-52 **3** *nk* **Power Power (IRE)**[27] 1550 3-9-9 **67**........................ LukeMorris 10 71
(Marco Botti) *dwlt: sn swtchd rt and hdwy on inner to chse ldrs after 2f: nt clrest of runs and swtchd lft over 1f out: chsd wnr and drvn 1f out: kpt on same pce ins fnl f: lost 2nd last strides* **4/1**[2]
632- **4** *2* **Petit Filous**[137] 8404 3-9-7 **65**........................................ AdamKirby 5 64
(Giles Bravery) *in tch in midfield: effrt u.p over 1f out: styd on same pce ins fnl f: nvr trbld ldrs* **7/1**[3]
3531 **5** *¾* **Metronomic (IRE)**[8] 2017 3-9-5 **63** 6ex............................(p) SeanLevey 1 61
(Richard Hannon) *led: hdd 2f out and c centre st: unable qck and 4th 1f out: wknd ins fnl f* **3/1**[1]
140- **6** *1* **Let's Be Happy (IRE)**[187] 7640 3-9-5 **63**........................ JimCrowley 12 58
(Richard Hughes) *stdd s: hld up in tch towards rr: effrt over 1f out: styd on same pce ins fnl f: nvr trbld ldrs* **16/1**
002- **7** *¾* **Buskin River (IRE)**[239] 6191 3-9-8 **66**........................ RyanTate 11 60
(James Eustace) *a towards rr: rdn over 3f out: plugged on fr over 1f out: nvr trbld ldrs* **8/1**
660- **8** *1 ½* **Opening Time**[273] 4981 3-9-7 **65**........................ TimmyMurphy 13 55
(Richard Hannon) *s.i.s: a and nvr gng wl: swtchd rt over 1f out: no imp u.p fnl f* **14/1**
35-0 **9** *¾* **Golden Eye**[22] 1686 3-9-5 **63**........................................ SamHitchcott 2 51
(Sylvester Kirk) *dwlt: hdwy into midfield after 2f: rdn 3f out: struggling and lost pl over 1f out: wknd fnl f* **16/1**
1m 38.94s (-0.96) **Going Correction** -0.10s/f (Stan) **9** Ran SP% **119.7**
Speed ratings (Par 97): **100,99,98,96,95 94,94,92,91**
CSF £42.47 CT £149.47 TOTE £4.40: £1.90, £2.80, £1.70; EX 47.40 Trifecta £161.50.
**Owner** DBAC Syndicate **Bred** Tullpark Ltd **Trained** Newmarket, Suffolk
**FOCUS**
A modest handicap. A minor pb from the second, but the level is a bit fluid.

## 2260 @TOTEPOOLRACING WIN RACING TICKETS ON TWITTER MAIDEN STKS 1m (P)
**7:10** (7:14) (Class 5) 3-Y-O+ **£5,175** (£1,540; £769; £384) **Stalls** Low

Form RPR
54- **1** **Alfarris (FR)**[204] 7226 3-9-1 0........................................ JimCrowley 9 76+
(William Haggas) *dwlt: styd wd early: rcvrd to chse ldrs after 2f: effrt over 1f out: chsd wnr 1f out: styd on wl to ld wl ins fnl f: gng away at fin* **15/8**[1]
03- **2** *1* **Falbon**[138] 8377 3-9-1 0........................................................ LukeMorris 5 74
(Marco Botti) *chsd ldr tl rdn to ld over 1f out: drvn 1f out: hdd and styd on same pce fnl 75yds* **20/1**
06- **3** *nk* **Paradise Lake (IRE)**[178] 7812 3-9-1 0........................ JoeFanning 8 73+
(Sir Michael Stoute) *stdd s: t.k.h: hld up in midfield: n.m.r over 1f out: shkn up and clsd to chse ldrs ins fnl f: nt clrest of runs and swtchd rt 75yds out: kpt on wl under hands and heels riding towards fin* **14/1**
**4** *1* **Mabrook** 3-9-1 0........................................................ DanielMuscutt 4 71+
(Marco Botti) *t.k.h: hld up wl in tch in midfield: effrt over 1f out: 3rd and styd on same pce ins fnl f: lost 3rd towards fin* **3/1**[2]
0 **5** *½* **Al Galayel (IRE)**[20] 1730 3-9-1 0........................................ AdamKirby 7 70
(Luca Cumani) *rn in snatches: in tch in midfield: effrt on inner over 1f out: kpt on ins fnl f: nvr trbld ldrs* **14/1**
**6** *nk* **Abjar** 3-9-1 0........................................................ FrankieDettori 6 69+
(Sir Michael Stoute) *hld up in last trio: hmpd over 6f out: rdn over 3f out: no imp whn rn green and hung lft 1f out: hdwy and swtchd lft ins fnl f: styd on wl fnl 100yds: nt rch ldrs* **10/3**[3]
5- **7** *½* **Ascot Week (USA)**[160] 8073 3-9-1 0........................................ DaneO'Neill 1 68
(Owen Burrows) *led: rdn ent fnl 2f: hdd over 1f out: no ex u.p: wknd wl ins fnl f* **25/1**
**8** *9* **Borntosin (IRE)** 3-8-8 0........................................ JacobMitchell(7) 10 46
(Marco Botti) *v.s.a: in rr: clsd and in tch 5f out: struggling over 2f out: rdn over 1f out: sn wknd* **100/1**
43- **9** *2 ¾* **Accento**[254] 5676 3-9-1 0........................................................ JamesDoyle 2 49
(Hugo Palmer) *t.k.h: chsd ldng pair: swtchd rt and effrt over 1f out: unable qck and btn 1f out: sn wknd and eased ins fnl f* **8/1**
**10** *2 ¼* **Kimene** 3-8-7 0........................................................ HollieDoyle(3) 3 29
(William Stone) *rn green in last trio: wnt rt over 6f out: rdn over 3f out: wknd over 1f out* **100/1**
1m 38.38s (-1.52) **Going Correction** -0.10s/f (Stan) **10** Ran SP% **117.9**
Speed ratings (Par 103): **103,102,101,100,100 99,99,90,87,85**
CSF £46.47 TOTE £3.00: £1.30, £4.60, £3.50; EX 38.30 Trifecta £312.70.
**Owner** Hamdan Al Maktoum **Bred** Ecurie Des Monceaux **Trained** Newmarket, Suffolk
**FOCUS**
This wasn't strongly run and they finished in a bit of a heap, but there were some noteworthy performances. The level is a bit fluid.

## 2261 TOTEPOOL LIKE US ON FACEBOOK H'CAP 1m 2f (P)
**7:40** (7:41) (Class 3) (0-95,95) 4-Y-O+ **£7,158** (£2,143; £1,071; £535; £267) **Stalls** Low

Form RPR
63-6 **1** **Noble Gift**[31] 1502 7-9-6 **94**........................................ JimCrowley 5 100
(William Knight) *taken down early: styd wd early: chsd ldr tl led after 2f: mde rest: rdn over 1f out: hrd pressed and drvn 1f out: styd on wl and asserted wl ins fnl f* **15/8**[1]
4511 **2** *¾* **Ickymasho**[33] 1446 5-9-2 **90**........................................ RichardKingscote 4 95
(Jonathan Portman) *led for 2f: trckd ldng pair fr over 6f out: n.m.r 2f out: swtchd lft and effrt on inner over 1f out: str chal u.p 1f out: kpt on wl but jst outpcd wl ins fnl f* **7/2**[3]
0-51 **3** *1 ¾* **Viewpoint (IRE)**[21] 1695 8-8-7 **81** oh1........................ LukeMorris 1 82
(Michael Appleby) *hld up wl in tch in 4th: effrt over 1f out: drvn to press ldng pair 1f out: unable qck and no ex wl ins fnl f* **8/1**
1023 **4** *¾* **Pactolus (IRE)**[19] 1757 6-9-4 **95**..............................(t) AaronJones(3) 3 95
(Stuart Williams) *stdd s: hld up in tch in rr: effrt on inner over 1f out: chsng ldrs and switching rt ins fnl f: styd on same pce fnl 100yds* **5/1**
0642 **5** *7* **Intrude**[19] 1757 5-9-4 **92**........................................................ SeanLevey 2 81
(Stuart Williams) *chsd ldrs tl wnt 2nd over 6f out: unable qck u.p over 1f out: lost pl 1f out: wknd ins fnl f* **3/1**[2]
2m 5.46s (-3.14) **Going Correction** -0.10s/f (Stan) **5** Ran SP% **109.8**
Speed ratings (Par 107): **108,107,106,105,99**
CSF £8.61 TOTE £2.50: £1.70, £1.50; EX 7.50 Trifecta £28.00.
**Owner** Canisbay Bloodstock **Bred** Theakston Stud **Trained** Patching, W Sussex
**FOCUS**
Not a bad handicap, but most looked handicapped up to their best, the exception being the winner.

## 2262 TOTEPOOL BETTING ON ALL UK RACING H'CAP 5f (P)
**8:10** (8:11) (Class 3) (0-95,95) 4-Y-O+ **£7,439** (£2,213; £1,106; £553) **Stalls** Low

Form RPR
2502 **1** **Zac Brown (IRE)**[5] 2113 6-9-0 **95**..............................(t) JoshuaBryan(7) 3 102
(Charlie Wallis) *mde all: rdn over 1f out: drvn and hrd pressed ins fnl f: hld on wl u.p: gamely* **3/1**[1]
500- **2** *hd* **Exceed The Limit**[269] 5148 4-9-2 **90**........................ LukeMorris 1 96
(Robert Cowell) *t.k.h: chsd ldrs: effrt towards inner over 1f out: hrd drvn and str chal ins fnl f: styd on wl but jst hld towards fin* **8/1**
4333 **3** *1* **Fast Track**[17] 1794 6-9-1 **89**........................................ AdamKirby 7 92
(David Barron) *sn pressing wnr: rdn over 1f out: unable qck jst ins fnl f: styd on same pce fnl 100yds* **3/1**[1]
2055 **4** *½* **Dynamo Walt (IRE)**[47] 1222 6-8-10 **84**........................(v) KierenFox 2 85
(Derek Shaw) *wl in tch in midfield: effrt over 1f out: styd on same pce u.p ins fnl f* **6/1**[3]
60-0 **5** *½* **Lathom**[6] 2083 4-9-1 **89**..............................................(v) JamesDoyle 5 88
(David O'Meara) *wnt rt and bmpd s: sn rcvrd and in tch in midfield on outer: effrt over 1f out: kpt on same pce ins fnl f* **6/1**[3]
6010 **6** *¾* **Top Boy**[47] 1222 7-8-10 **84**..............................................(v) MartinLane 6 81
(Derek Shaw) *broke wl: sn restrained and hld up in last pair: effrt u.p over 1f out: edgd lft u.p and kpt on same pce ins fnl f* **16/1**

00-0 **7** *5* **Independence Day (IRE)**[14] 1863 4-9-3 **91**........................ JimCrowley 4 70
(Robert Cowell) *last pair: effrt ent fnl 2f: no imp u.p over 1f out: wknd ins fnl f* **5/1**[2]

59.05s (-1.15) **Going Correction** -0.10s/f (Stan) **7** Ran SP% **112.2**
Speed ratings (Par 107): **105,104,103,102,101 100,92**
CSF £26.55 TOTE £3.80: £2.00, £4.60; EX 27.10 Trifecta £91.50.
**Owner** Dab Hand Racing **Bred** Tally-Ho Stud **Trained** Ardleigh, Essex

**FOCUS**
A good sprint, and the pace held up. The runner-up has been rated close to his best.

## 2263 COLLECT TOTEPOOL WINNINGS AT BETFRED SHOPS H'CAP 5f (P)
**8:40** (8:40) (Class 6) (0-65,67) 4-Y-O+ **£3,234** (£962; £481; £240) **Stalls** Low

Form RPR

-660 **1** **Classic Pursuit**[10] 1971 6-9-5 **63**..............................(b[1]) RoystonFfrench 2 69+
(Michael Appleby) *s.i.s: wl off the pce in last: rdn over 2f out: hdwy u.p 1f out: str run to chal wl ins fnl f: led on post* **9/4**[1]

2112 **2** *nse* **Roy's Legacy**[10] 1965 8-9-1 **64**.................................. CharlieBennett(5) 10 70
(Shaun Harris) *led: rdn over 2f out: drvn ins fnl f: kpt on gamely u.p: hdd on post* **9/2**

00-6 **3** *1 ¼* **Corridor Kid (IRE)**[16] 1819 4-9-9 **67**...................................(v) KierenFox 8 68
(Derek Shaw) *awkward leaving stalls and s.i.s: off the pce in 5th: hdwy u.p over 1f out: chsd wnr briefly ins fnl f: 3rd and styd on same pce fnl 75yds* **7/1**

2441 **4** *1 ¾* **Borough Boy (IRE)**[14] 1869 7-9-8 **66**..............................(v) MartinLane 9 64
(Derek Shaw) *chsd ldrs tl sltly impeded and dropped to 4th after 1f out: effrt u.p over 1f out: wandered 1f out: no ex and btn ins fnl f: eased towards fin* **7/2**[3]

3114 **5** *1* **Mighty Zip (USA)**[19] 1759 5-8-7 **58**................................(p) JordanUys(7) 1 49
(Lisa Williamson) *bustled along early: chsd ldr after 1f out: rdn over 1f out: unable qck and wknd ins fnl f* **11/4**[2]

500- **6** *3* **Classic Flyer**[200] 7324 5-9-7 **65**..........................................(v) LukeMorris 7 46
(Christine Dunnett) *chsd ldr for 1f: 4th and rdn over 2f out: wknd ins fnl f* **33/1**

1m 0.02s (-0.18) **Going Correction** -0.10s/f (Stan) **6** Ran SP% **113.3**
Speed ratings (Par 101): **97,96,94,92,90 85**
CSF £12.98 CT £59.14 TOTE £3.00: £1.80, £2.60; EX 14.00 Trifecta £61.40.
**Owner** From The Front Racing **Bred** B & B Equine Limited **Trained** Oakham, Rutland
■ Stewards' Enquiry : Charlie Bennett caution; careless riding

**FOCUS**
A modest sprint run at a good gallop.

## 2264 LADIES DAY 22ND JUNE H'CAP 1m 6f (P)
**9:10** (9:11) (Class 5) (0-75,75) 3-Y-O **£5,175** (£1,540; £769; £384) **Stalls** Low

Form RPR

541 **1** **Alabaster**[69] 855 3-9-7 **75**...................................................... LukeMorris 3 86+
(Sir Mark Prescott Bt) *hld up in tch: clsd and rdn over 3f out: rdn to chal over 1f out: wandered and led 1f out: awkward hd carriage and edging lft ins fnl f: kpt on and a doing enough* **6/4**[1]

0-31 **2** *¾* **Look My Way**[16] 1822 3-8-10 **71**.................................... JoshuaBryan(7) 5 80
(Andrew Balding) *t.k.h: led for 2f: chsd ldr tl over 4f out: hemmed in and trcking ldrs over 2f out: gap opened and rdn to press ldrs over 1f out:* **13/2**[3]

45-1 **3** *2 ½* **Addicted To You (IRE)**[60] 1001 3-9-7 **75**............................ JoeFanning 2 80
(Mark Johnston) *chsd ldrs tl wnt 2nd over 4f out: rdn to ld over 1f out: hdd and sltly impeded 1f out: wknd ins fnl f* **5/2**[2]

22-1 **4** *4 ½* **Pete So High (GER)**[106] 265 3-9-7 **75**..............................(p) SeanLevey 1 74
(Richard Hannon) *t.k.h: in tch: rdn over 3f out: outpcd and btn over 1f out: wknd ins fnl f* **5/2**[2]

652 **5** *12* **Gee Sixty Six**[47] 1226 3-9-0 **68**........................................ StevieDonohoe 4 55
(Mark H Tompkins) *stdd after s: plld hrd and chsd ldr tl swtchd rt and led after 2f: rdn and hdd over 1f out: sn btn: wknd and eased wl ins fnl f* **12/1**

-466 **6** *2* **Nothing Compares**[24] 1623 3-8-2 **56** oh2................... RoystonFfrench 6 35
(Mark Johnston) *hld up in rr: rdn over 4f out: lost tch over 1f out* **50/1**

3m 1.27s (-1.93) **Going Correction** -0.10s/f (Stan) **6** Ran SP% **120.1**
Speed ratings (Par 99): **101,100,99,96,89 88**
CSF £13.36 TOTE £2.50: £1.40, £2.30; EX 13.00 Trifecta £30.40.
**Owner** Charles C Walker - Osborne House **Bred** Miss K Rausing **Trained** Newmarket, Suffolk
■ Stewards' Enquiry : Joshua Bryan two-day ban; careless riding (17th-18 May)

**FOCUS**
An interesting staying race for 3yos, and the winner looks the type to progress further. Muddling form.
T/Plt: £33.30 to a £1 stake. Pool: £63,110.79 - 1,381.17 winning units. T/Qpdt: £16.60 to a £1 stake. Pool: £6,788.95 - 301.37 winning units. **Steve Payne**

# 1965 NOTTINGHAM (L-H)
### Tuesday, May 2

**OFFICIAL GOING: Good to firm (good in places; watered; 8.7)**
Wind: Fresh behind Weather: Cloudy

## 2265 32RED CASINO FILLIES' NOVICE STKS (PLUS 10 RACE) 5f 8y
**2:10** (2:13) (Class 5) 2-Y-O **£3,234** (£962; £481; £240) **Stalls** Centre

Form RPR

**1** **Main Desire (IRE)** 2-9-0 0........................................... DanielTudhope 4 84+
(Michael Bell) *racd towards stands' side: trckd ldrs: smooth hdwy 2f out: led over 1f out: pushed out: readily* **7/2**[2]

**2** *1 ¼* **She Believes (IRE)** 2-8-9 0.................................... MitchGodwin(5) 2 76
(Sylvester Kirk) *chsd ldr centre: hdwy 2f out: rdn over 1f out: kpt on wl fnl f* **20/1**

33 **3** *1* **Aquadabra (IRE)**[8] 2037 2-9-0 0.......................................... GrahamLee 3 72
(Mick Channon) *racd centre: led: rdn along 2f out: hdd over 1f out: kpt on same pce* **5/2**[1]

0 **4** *nse* **Mraseel (IRE)**[13] 1884 2-9-0 0......................................... MartinHarley 6 72
(James Tate) *racd cl to stands' rail: cl up: rdn along wl over 1f out: kpt on same pce fnl f* **4/1**[3]

**5** *3 ¾* **Silver Bullet (IRE)** 2-9-0 0........................................ RichardKingscote 1 58
(Tom Dascombe) *wnt lft s: racd centre and towards rr: sme hdwy 2f out: n.d* **20/1**

**6** *1* **Lexington Grace (IRE)** 2-9-0 0....................................... PatDobbs 7 55
(Richard Hannon) *in tch towards stands' side: pushed along over 2f out: sn rdn and outpcd* **8/1**

**7** *1* **Queen Penn** 2-9-0 0........................................................ PaulHanagan 5 51
(Richard Fahey) *racd towards stands' side: dwlt and towards rr: sme hdwy 3f out: pushed along 2f out: sn wknd* **5/1**

**8** *5* **Isoletta** 2-9-0 0............................................................... ThomasBrown 8 33
(Ed Walker) *chsd ldrs stands' side: rdn along over 2f out: sn outpcd and bhd* **33/1**

59.05s (-2.45) **Going Correction** -0.40s/f (Firm) 2y crse rec **8** Ran SP% **111.0**
Speed ratings (Par 90): **103,101,99,99,93 91,90,82**
CSF £66.94 TOTE £4.80: £1.60, £5.40, £1.40; EX 85.20 Trifecta £247.70.
**Owner** Clipper Logistics **Bred** W Maxwell Ervine **Trained** Newmarket, Suffolk

**FOCUS**
They split into two groups, but there was no advantage and the winner would have triumphed no matter where she raced, creating quite a strong impression on debut.

## 2266 32RED.COM MEDIAN AUCTION MAIDEN STKS 1m 72y
**2:40** (2:41) (Class 5) 3-Y-O **£3,881** (£1,155; £577; £288) **Stalls** Centre

Form RPR

0- **1** **Meteor Light (IRE)**[256] 5600 3-9-5 0...........................(h[1]) AdamBeschizza 9 78+
(Ed Vaughan) *hld up: hdwy on outer over 3f out: chsd ldrs 2f out: rdn over 1f out: drvn and styd on to ld wl ins fnl f* **7/2**[2]

3-4 **2** *1 ¼* **Lord Commander**[22] 1675 3-9-5 0....................................... PaulHanagan 5 75
(Richard Fahey) *led: pushed along over 2f out: sn hdd and rdn: cl up and ev ch ent fnl f: sn drvn and no ex last 50 yds* **4/1**[3]

**3** *½* **Khitaamy (IRE)** 3-9-5 0................................................... AntonioFresu 2 74+
(Ed Dunlop) *trckd ldrs on inner: hdwy 3f out: cl up over 2f out: slt ld wl over 1f out and sn rdn: hdd wl ins fnl f: kpt on* **25/1**

-33 **4** *1 ¾* **Desert Explorer (IRE)**[11] 1939 3-9-5 0.......................... RobertWinston 4 70
(Eve Johnson Houghton) *trckd ldrs: hdwy 3f out: rdn to chal 2f out: drvn over 1f out: kpt on same pce* **3/1**[1]

02-3 **5** *1 ½* **Armagnac (IRE)**[35] 1410 3-9-2 70.................................. LouisSteward(3) 3 66
(Michael Bell) *t.k.h: prom: pushed along over 2f out: rdn wl over 1f out: grad wknd* **4/1**[3]

320- **6** *¾* **Harmonise**[206] 7147 3-9-0 70.................................................. GrahamLee 6 60
(Mick Channon) *trckd ldr: cl up 1/2-way: rdn along wl over 2f out: drvn wl over 1f out: grad wknd* **9/2**

**7** *10* **Wicker** 3-9-0 0............................................................................. FranBerry 1 36
(Jane Chapple-Hyam) *dwlt: a rr* **33/1**

5 **8** *12* **La Goulue**[26] 1581 3-9-0 0.................................................. MartinDwyer 7 7
(John Gallagher) *s.i.s: a bhd* **100/1**

1m 44.95s (-4.05) **Going Correction** -0.40s/f (Firm) **8** Ran SP% **113.2**
Speed ratings (Par 99): **104,102,102,100,99 98,88,76**
CSF £17.40 TOTE £5.20: £1.80, £1.30, £5.10; EX 23.60 Trifecta £383.90.
**Owner** Front Runner Racing - I **Bred** Nordkappe Partnership **Trained** Newmarket, Suffolk

**FOCUS**
A fair maiden, no more, and the winner was well backed. It's been rated around the second, third and fourth.

## 2267 32RED ON THE APP STORE H'CAP 1m 72y
**3:10** (3:10) (Class 5) (0-75,76) 4-Y-O+ **£3,881** (£1,155; £577; £288) **Stalls** Centre

Form RPR

-056 **1** **Thaqaffa (IRE)**[21] 1706 4-9-8 **76**.............................. SilvestreDeSousa 6 85
(Amy Murphy) *t.k.h: mde all: qcknd 3f out: rdn along 2f out: styd on strly fnl f* **11/4**[1]

16-2 **2** *1 ½* **Therthaar**[15] 1839 4-9-3 **71**............................................... TomMarquand 1 76
(Ismail Mohammed) *trckd ldrs: hdwy 3f out: sn chsng wnr: rdn wl over 1f out: drvn and kpt on same pce fnl f* **8/1**

20-2 **3** *1 ¼* **Manton Grange**[11] 1939 4-9-7 **75**...................................... SteveDrowne 3 77
(George Baker) *hld up towards rr: hdwy 3f out: chsd ldrs wl over 1f out: rdn and kpt on fnl f* **6/1**[3]

6121 **4** *1 ¼* **Scribner Creek (IRE)**[10] 1983 4-9-1 **69**...................... RobertWinston 11 68
(Daniel Mark Loughnane) *hld up in rr: hdwy on outer 3f out: rdn along 2f out: kpt on u.p fnl f* **7/2**[2]

-000 **5** *½* **Passing Star**[13] 1890 6-9-7 **75**................................(p) RichardKingscote 4 73
(Daniel Kubler) *prom: chsd ldrs 3f out: rdn along over 2f out: drvn and wknd over 1f out* **13/2**

461- **6** *3* **Pacific Salt (IRE)**[159] 8086 4-9-0 **68**............................ PaulMulrennan 5 59
(Pam Sly) *t.k.h: hld up: hdwy on inner over 3f out: chsd ldrs and rdn along over 2f out: sn drvn and wknd* **8/1**

40-0 **7** *shd* **Hijran (IRE)**[106] 267 4-8-10 **64**....................................(p) PaulHanagan 9 54
(Michael Appleby) *trckd wnr: pushed along over 3f out: rdn over 2f out: sn drvn and wknd* **16/1**

1000 **8** *nk* **Pickett's Charge**[21] 1706 4-9-1 **69**............................(h) DougieCostello 7 59
(Richard Guest) *in tch: rdn along over 3f out: sn wknd* **14/1**

1m 46.14s (-2.86) **Going Correction** -0.40s/f (Firm) **8** Ran SP% **111.3**
Speed ratings (Par 103): **98,96,95,94,93 90,90,90**
CSF £23.79 CT £117.50 TOTE £2.80: £1.30, £2.50, £2.10; EX 16.60 Trifecta £70.20.
**Owner** Paul Foster & Friends, Saxtead Livestock **Bred** Incense Partnership **Trained** Newmarket, Suffolk

**FOCUS**
Fair handicap form, there wasn't much pace on and the winner made all. The winner has been rated to his best.

## 2268 32RED.COM EBF STALLIONS BREEDING WINNERS FILLIES' H'CAP 1m 72y
**3:45** (3:46) (Class 3) (0-90,89) 3-Y-O+ **£9,703** (£2,887; £1,443; £721) **Stalls** Centre

Form RPR

443- **1** **Normandie Lady**[164] 8028 4-9-2 **77**.......................................... PaulHanagan 1 86
(Richard Fahey) *trckd ldng pair: smooth hdwy over 2f out: cl up over 1f out: led ent fnl f: sn clr* **4/1**[3]

315- **2** *3 ¾* **Lincoln Rocks**[213] 6947 4-10-0 **89**................................. DanielTudhope 4 89
(David O'Meara) *led and sn clr: pushed along over 2f out: rdn over 1f out: hdd ent fnl f: one pce* **3/1**[2]

5-20 **3** *6* **Stosur (IRE)**[104] 285 6-9-3 **78**..........................................(b) MartinHarley 5 64
(Gay Kelleway) *chsd clr ldr: rdn along over 2f out: drvn wl over 1f out: sn one pce* **12/1**

466- **4** *¾* **Yeah Baby Yeah (IRE)**[126] 8538 4-9-13 **88**..................... MartinDwyer 2 72
(Gay Kelleway) *in tch: rdn along wl over 2f out: n.d* **9/1**

0-11 **5** *3* **La Casa Tarifa (IRE)**[12] 1912 3-8-9 **83**............................ FrannyNorton 3 57
(Mark Johnston) *v s.i.s and lost 15 l s: a bhd* **5/4**[1]

1m 44.04s (-4.96) **Going Correction** -0.40s/f (Firm)
**WFA** 3 from 4yo+ 13lb **5** Ran SP% **107.1**
Speed ratings (Par 104): **108,104,98,97,94**
CSF £15.18 TOTE £5.10: £2.40, £1.80; EX 16.30 Trifecta £78.10.
**Owner** A B Phipps **Bred** A B Phipps **Trained** Musley Bank, N Yorks

**FOCUS**
Little got into this fillies' handicap, the short-price favourite blowing her chance at the start.

## 2269 32RED.COM FILLIES' H'CAP 1m 2f 52y
4:20 (4:22) (Class 5) (0-75,77) 3-Y-O £3,881 (£1,155; £577; £288) Stalls Low

Form RPR
32-6 1 **Mouille Point**13 1885 3-9-6 73 PatDobbs 5 81+
(Richard Hannon) *hld up towards rr: hdwy on outer after 3f: trckd ldr 1/2-way: led over 2f out: rdn wl over 1f out: drvn ins fnl f: hld on gamely* 6/1
1-43 2 hd **Plead**20 1736 3-9-10 77 JackMitchell 4 84
(Archie Watson) *in tch: hdwy on outer 3f out: chsd ldrs 2f out: rdn to chal over 1f out: drvn and ev ch ins fnl f: edgd lft and no ex towards fin* 3/1[1]
-651 3 1 1/2 **Canberra Cliffs (IRE)**10 1968 3-8-12 70 GeorgeWood(5) 6 75
(Don Cantillon) *t.k.h early: trckd ldrs on inner: effrt and nt clr run over 1f out: swtchd rt and rdn to chal ent fnl f: sn drvn and ev ch: hld whn n.m.r towards fin* 7/2[2]
525- 4 1 3/4 **Carol (IRE)**225 6624 3-9-7 74 SilvestreDeSousa 3 75
(Ed Dunlop) *hld up: hdwy over 3f out: rdn along 2f out: kpt on fnl f* 12/1
05-0 5 2 **Kiruna Peak (IRE)**20 1737 3-9-1 68 GrahamLee 8 65
(Mick Channon) *hld up: hdwy over 3f out: rdn along 2f out: sn drvn and no imp* 33/1
6-15 6 1/2 **Nastenka**95 439 3-9-6 73 ThomasBrown 10 69
(Ed Walker) *hld up in rr: hdwy over 2f out: rdn wl over 1f out: n.d* 16/1
40-6 7 nk **Mistress Viz (IRE)**20 1737 3-8-8 61 JamesSullivan 7 56
(John Mackie) *prom: hdwy over 3f out: sn cl up: rdn wl over 1f out: grad wknd* 20/1
54-4 8 2 1/4 **Secret Soul**31 1499 3-9-1 68 (v1) FranBerry 1 59
(Ralph Beckett) *t.k.h: chsd ldrs: rdn along wl over 2f out: sn wknd* 7/1
0-04 9 nk **Patching**10 1968 3-8-12 65 KevinStott 9 56
(Giles Bravery) *a rr* 20/1
442- 10 2 1/4 **Midnight Vixen**234 6336 3-9-7 74 RyanMoore 2 60
(Sir Michael Stoute) *led: rdn along and jnd 3f out: hdd over 2f out: sn drvn and wknd* 5/1[3]

2m 13.19s (-1.11) **Going Correction** -0.40s/f (Firm) 10 Ran SP% 116.7
Speed ratings (Par 96): **88,87,86,85,83 83,83,81,80,79**
CSF £23.71 CT £73.34 TOTE £5.80: £1.60, £1.70, £1.70; EX 23.90 Trifecta £106.80.
**Owner** M J Jooste **Bred** Windmill Farm Partnership **Trained** East Everleigh, Wilts

**FOCUS**
Just a modest handicap, they didn't go overly fast but there were a couple of likeable performances. It's been rated as ordinary form for now.

## 2270 32RED H'CAP 1m 6f
4:50 (4:54) (Class 4) (0-80,78) 4-Y-O+ £6,469 (£1,925; £962; £481) Stalls Low

Form RPR
2212 1 **On Fire**41 1307 4-9-2 71 (p) PaulHanagan 8 77
(James Bethell) *sn trcking ldr: hdwy and cl up over 2f out: rdn to ld wl over 1f: drvn and edgd lft ins fnl f: kpt on* 2/1[1]
3123 2 1/2 **Brigadoon**14 1865 10-9-10 78 RobertWinston 4 83
(Michael Appleby) *led: pushed along and jnd over 2f out: rdn and hdd wl over 1f out: snd riven: nt much on inner ins fnl f: kpt on* 7/1
2-41 3 1/2 **Hallstatt (IRE)**96 423 11-8-9 63 (t) AndrewMullen 5 67
(John Mackie) *trckd ldrs: hdwy over 2f out: rdn wl over 1f out: drvn and kpt on fnl f* 8/1
P150 4 1 3/4 **Rowlestone Lass**7 2061 7-9-6 77 LouisSteward(3) 7 79
(Richard Price) *hld up in tch: swtchd rt wl over 2f out and sn rdn: drvn over 1f out: kpt on same pce* 7/1
6-66 5 3/4 **Excellent Puck (IRE)**96 422 7-9-6 74 GrahamLee 9 75
(Shaun Lycett) *hld up in tch: hdwy on outer wl over 2f out: sn rdn: drvn wl over 1f out: no imp* 16/1
413- 6 1 3/4 **Princess Roania (IRE)**264 4023 6-8-11 72 (tp) JoshuaBryan(7) 2 70
(Peter Bowen) *a rr* 6/1[3]
06-0 7 3/4 **Stanarley Pic**15 1834 6-8-8 62 SilvestreDeSousa 3 59
(Alan Swinbank) *t.k.h: trckd ldrs on inner: pushed along wl over 2f out: rdn wl over 1f out: wknd apporoaching fnl f* 7/2[2]

3m 5.52s (-1.48) **Going Correction** -0.40s/f (Firm) 7 Ran SP% 111.8
Speed ratings (Par 105): **88,87,87,86,86 85,84**
CSF £15.79 CT £89.06 TOTE £2.50: £1.40, £2.40; EX 12.90 Trifecta £46.70.
**Owner** The Hon Mrs C M Holliday **Bred** Cleaboy Farms Co **Trained** Middleham Moor, N Yorks

**FOCUS**
A modest handicap, they didn't go overly quick and it paid to race handy. The runner-up and third have been rated to their recent AW form.

## 2271 32RED.COM H'CAP 5f 8y
5:25 (5:25) (Class 4) (0-80,82) 3-Y-O £6,469 (£1,925; £962; £481) Stalls Centre

Form RPR
01-1 1 **Carlton Frankie**15 1828 3-9-6 82 NathanEvans(3) 8 90+
(Michael Easterby) *qckly away: mde all: shkn up jst over 1f out: kpt on strly* 6/4[1]
2516 2 1 1/2 **Arzaak (IRE)**18 1774 3-9-7 80 (b) SilvestreDeSousa 3 81
(Chris Dwyer) *chsd wnr: rdn and hdwy over 1f out: drvn ins fnl f: no imp* 6/1
0115 3 1 3/4 **Dashing Poet**22 1688 3-8-7 66 (h) AdamBeschizza 2 61
(Jeremy Gask) *chsd ldrs: hdwy 2f out: sn rdn: drvn and kpt on fnl f* 16/1
320- 4 hd **Boundsy (IRE)**213 6950 3-8-10 76 ConnorMurtagh(7) 7 70
(Richard Fahey) *dwlt and towards rr: pushed along over 2f out: rdn wl over 1f out: styd on fnl f* 5/1[3]
1 5 nse **Batten The Hatches**77 731 3-9-7 80 PhillipMakin 4 74
(David Barron) *rr: hdwy 1/2-way: swtchd lft to outer and rdn to chse ldrs over 1f out: green and edgd lft ins fnl f: kpt on* 3/1[2]
00-6 6 6 **Compton Lane**40 1332 3-8-11 73 KieranShoemark(3) 1 46
(Rod Millman) *chsd ldrs: rdn along over 2f out: sn wknd* 20/1
60-4 7 1 **Bellevarde (IRE)**104 288 3-8-8 67 PaulHanagan 6 36
(Richard Price) *a rr: outpcd and bhd fnl 2f* 20/1

57.4s (-4.10) **Going Correction** -0.40s/f (Firm) course record 7 Ran SP% 111.4
Speed ratings (Par 101): **116,113,110,110,110 100,99**
CSF £10.47 CT £96.01 TOTE £2.30: £1.60, £2.90; EX 8.00 Trifecta £33.00.
**Owner** Padgett Hollings Hull Fielding Hoskins **Bred** D Curran **Trained** Sheriff Hutton, N Yorks

**FOCUS**
A fair sprint and a winner firmly on the up. The third has been rated a length off her AW form.
T/Jkpt: £22,771.10 to a £1 stake. Pool: £22,771.10 - 1.0 winning unit. T/Plt: £39.90 to a £1 stake. Pool: £62,344.67 - 1,138.09 winning units. T/Qpdt: £9.90 to a £1 stake. Pool: £4,701.69 - 350.50 winning units. **Joe Rowntree**

# 2161 WOLVERHAMPTON (A.W) (L-H)
Tuesday, May 2

**OFFICIAL GOING: Tapeta: standard**
Wind: Fresh against final 2f Weather: Overcast

## 2272 FCL GLOBAL FORWARDING AMATEUR RIDERS' H'CAP 1m 4f 51y (Tp)
6:00 (6:01) (Class 6) (0-55,55) 4-Y-O+ £2,370 (£735; £367; £183) Stalls Low

Form RPR
0-30 1 **Filament Of Gold (USA)**36 1403 6-10-10 54 (p) RichardPatrick(3) 5 61
(Roy Brotherton) *hld up: hdwy over 5f out: hmpd over 1f out: led 1f out: rdn and edgd lft ins fnl f: styd on u.p* 9/1
0023 2 hd **Senor George (IRE)**10 1985 10-10-0 48 (h) MissHGodfrey(7) 7 55
(Simon Hodgson) *hld up: hdwy on outer over 2f out: hung lft fr over 1f out: sn ev ch: styd on* 9/1
0300 3 3 3/4 **Uphold**45 1257 10-10-13 54 (v) MrRBirkett 2 55
(Gay Kelleway) *chsd ldrs: outpcd over 2f out: rallied over 1f out: sn rdn and ev ch: no ex ins fnl f* 7/1
0000 4 1/2 **Steady Major (IRE)**24 1629 5-10-7 51 (p1) MissBeckyBrisbourne(3) 6 51
(Mark Brisbourne) *prom: racd keenly: chsd ldr 2f out: rdn and ev ch whn hmpd 1f out: no ex ins fnl f* 14/1
0655 5 1 **Cape Spirit (IRE)**19 1754 5-10-6 52 (be1) PoppyBridgwater(5) 11 50
(Andrew Balding) *hld up: pushed along over 2f out: edgd lft and r.o ins fnl f: nvr nrr* 5/1[1]
30-0 6 nk **Cool Music (IRE)**24 1629 7-11-0 55 (p) MissSBrotherton 9 53
(Antony Brittain) *plld hrd: sn led at stdy pce: hdd over 5f out: remained handy: rdn over 1f out: styd on same pce fnl f* 13/2[3]
004 7 hd **L'Ami De Rouge**67 894 4-10-10 54 MrHHunt(3) 3 51
(Ralph J Smith) *hld up in tch: stmbld after 1f: lost pl over 5f out: sn pushed along: rallied over 1f out: styd on same pce fnl f* 18/1
0405 8 nk **Frap**27 1560 4-10-12 53 MrSWalker 1 50
(Ian Williams) *mid-div: outpcd over 2f out: rallied over 1f out: no ex ins fnl f* 11/2[2]
4546 9 hd **Cold Fusion (IRE)**11 1937 4-10-9 50 (p) MissBrodieHampson 10 47
(David Flood) *racd keenly in 2nd pl tl led over 5f out: rdn and hdd 1f out: wknd wl ins fnl f* 16/1
0542 10 1 1/2 **Anton Dolin (IRE)**14 839 9-10-6 52 (be) MrLewisStones(5) 12 46
(Michael Mullineaux) *s.i.s: hld up: hdwy and nt clr run over 1f out: wknd ins fnl f* 9/1
340- 11 1 1/4 **Operateur (IRE)**225 6619 9-10-1 49 MissJPalmer-Kimpton(7) 4 41
(Ben Haslam) *s.i.s: hld up: nvr on terms* 50/1
040- 12 7 **Champagne Rules**218 6840 6-10-9 50 MissCWalton 8 31
(Sharon Watt) *s.i.s: hld up: plld hrd and hdwy over 8f out: chsd ldr over 4f out tl rdn 2f out: wknd over 1f out* 12/1

2m 43.16s (2.36) **Going Correction** -0.075s/f (Stan) 12 Ran SP% 115.3
Speed ratings (Par 101): **89,88,86,86,85 85,85,84,84,83 82,78**
CSF £85.17 CT £602.46 TOTE £11.80: £2.70, £2.80, £3.50; EX 97.30 Trifecta £1279.70.
**Owner** M A Geobey **Bred** Darley **Trained** Elmley Castle, Worcs
■ Stewards' Enquiry : Richard Patrick four-day ban; used whip above the permitted level (27th, 30th May, 14th-15th June)

**FOCUS**
A weak opener for amateur riders, and a messy contest in which the dearth of pace caused more than one coming together early on. The front pair have been rated near their respective bests from the past year.

## 2273 CONTACT US AT FCLGF.COM H'CAP 1m 4f 51y (Tp)
6:30 (6:31) (Class 5) (0-70,72) 3-Y-O £3,234 (£962; £481; £240) Stalls Low

Form RPR
000- 1 **Brimham Rocks**188 7621 3-8-13 62 FranBerry 2 69+
(Ralph Beckett) *hld up in tch: pushed along over 3f out: rdn to ld ins fnl f: edgd lft: styd on wl* 5/4[1]
02-3 2 2 3/4 **Shadow Warrior**20 1737 3-9-7 70 JoeyHaynes 4 71
(Paul D'Arcy) *hld up: hdwy and nt clr run over 1f out: styd on u.p to go 2nd nr fin* 7/2[2]
23-4 3 3/4 **Laureate**49 1190 3-9-6 69 FrannyNorton 5 69
(Mark Johnston) *sn led: rdn over 1f out: hdd ins fnl f: styd on same pce* 15/2[3]
-000 4 nse **Tor**13 1888 3-9-2 65 DavidNolan 6 65
(Iain Jardine) *chsd ldr: rdn and ev ch over 1f out: styd on same pce ins fnl f* 12/1
54-3 5 1 1/4 **Red Caravel (IRE)**41 1300 3-9-9 72 (p1) ShaneKelly 1 70
(Richard Hughes) *chsd ldrs: rdn and hung rt fr over 1f out: no ex ins fnl f* 12/1
4614 6 4 1/2 **Ladofash**26 1591 3-9-2 65 (v) PJMcDonald 3 56
(K R Burke) *s.i.s: hld up: rdn and wknd over 1f out* 7/2[2]

2m 41.36s (0.56) **Going Correction** -0.075s/f (Stan) 6 Ran SP% 116.0
Speed ratings (Par 99): **95,93,92,92,91 88**
CSF £6.22 TOTE £2.00: £1.30, £2.50; EX 7.90 Trifecta £34.50.
**Owner** Mr and Mrs David Aykroyd **Bred** Mr & Mrs David Aykroyd **Trained** Kimpton, Hants

**FOCUS**
A winning time 1.8 seconds quicker than the preceding C&D amateurs' contest, although they still didn't go a mad gallop by any means. Muddling form. The runner-up has been rated to form for now.

## 2274 FCL GLOBAL FORWARDING MAKING LOGISTICS PERSONAL FILLIES' H'CAP 1m 142y (Tp)
7:00 (7:00) (Class 5) (0-70,72) 3-Y-O £3,234 (£962; £481; £240) Stalls Low

Form RPR
256- 1 **Nostalgie**141 8340 3-9-10 72 MartinHarley 2 78+
(James Tate) *led 1f: chsd ldrs: lost pl 1/2-way: pushed along and hdwy over 2f out: led over 1f out: rdn and edgd lft ins fnl f: styd on* 3/1[1]
020- 2 1/2 **Al Nafoorah**210 7049 3-9-5 67 AntonioFresu 1 71+
(Ed Dunlop) *led over 7f out: hdd over 6f out: remained handy: rdn to chse wnr fnl f: styd on* 12/1
40-5 3 1 1/4 **Star Of Bristol (USA)**31 1503 3-9-7 69 ShaneKelly 3 70
(Richard Hughes) *chsd ldrs: led over 6f out: sn stdd pce: qcknd over 2f out: hdd wl over 1f out: styd on same pce ins fnl f* 14/1
5-14 4 3/4 **Elusive Olivia (USA)**32 1470 3-9-6 68 (t) FranBerry 8 67+
(Joseph Tuite) *hld up: shkn up over 1f out: rdn: edgd lft and r.o ins fnl f: nt rch ldrs* 25/1
260- 5 shd **See The Sea (IRE)**273 4975 3-9-7 69 TomMarquand 5 68
(Richard Hannon) *hmpd s: mid-div: hdwy 1/2-way: rdn over 2f out: styd on same pce ins fnl f* 16/1

21-0 **6** *1* **Claire's Secret**[22] 1685 3-9-7 **69** DanielTudhope 9 66
(Philip McBride) *chsd ldrs: wnt 2nd 1/2-way: rdn and ev ch 2f out: no ex ins fnl f* **10/1**

-030 **7** *nk* **Rosemay (FR)**[22] 1680 3-9-4 **66** DavidNolan 10 62
(Iain Jardine) *hld up: rdn over 2f out: nt trble ldrs* **10/1**

321- **8** *hd* **Carducci**[247] 5922 3-9-9 **71** PatDobbs 4 67
(Richard Hannon) *edgd rt s: prom: chsd ldr over 5f out tl 1/2-way: remained handy: rdn over 2f out: styd on same pce fr over 1f out* **13/2**[3]

252 **9** *½* **Wedding Breakfast (IRE)**[15] 1840 3-9-7 **69** (h) JackMitchell 6 63
(Hugo Palmer) *hmpd s: hld up in tch: lost pl over 5f out: n.d after* **10/1**

421- **10** *½* **Three Duchesses**[207] 7107 3-9-4 **71** LuluStanford(5) 7 64
(Michael Bell) *hld up: rdn over 2f out: a in rr* **7/2**[2]

4-00 **11** *8* **Ok By Me (IRE)**[36] 1401 3-8-13 **61** JFEgan 11 36
(David Evans) *hld up: plld hrd: a in rr: eased ins fnl f* **33/1**

1m 50.19s (0.09) **Going Correction** -0.075s/f (Stan) **11** Ran SP% **114.9**
Speed ratings (Par 96): **96,95,94,93,93 92,92,92,91,91 84**
CSF £39.04 CT £353.05 TOTE £4.70: £2.40, £4.10, £3.40; EX 45.00 Trifecta £345.70.
**Owner** Saeed Manana **Bred** Miss K Rausing **Trained** Newmarket, Suffolk

**FOCUS**
A competitive race for the grade run at a decent clip, and a winner back on track. It's been rated around the front-running third to her debut run.

## 2275 FCL GLOBAL FORWARDING MAKING LOGISTICS PERSONAL H'CAP 2m 120y (Tp)
**7:30** (7:30) (Class 5) (0-75,75) 4-Y-O+ **£1,888** (£1,888; £432; £216) **Stalls** Low

Form RPR

4-11 **1** **Masterson (IRE)**[15] 1585 4-9-7 **75** SilvestreDeSousa 5 81
(Mick Channon) *chsd wnr tl led over 2f out: hung lft wl over 1f out: sn rdn: styd on: jnd on line* **11/8**[1]

3-24 **1** *dht* **Denmead**[28] 1548 4-9-1 **69** RobertWinston 3 75
(John Butler) *led at stdy pce: qcknd over 3f out: rdn and hdd over 2f out: hmpd wl over 1f out: rallied and edgd rt ins fnl f: r.o to join wnr on line* **3/1**[2]

6543 **3** *3* **Oratorio's Joy (IRE)**[35] 1412 7-9-6 **71** ShaneKelly 2 73
(Daniel Mark Loughnane) *hld up: rdn over 3f out: hdwy u.p over 2f out: styd on* **7/1**

24-0 **4** *5* **Satish**[20] 1716 4-9-7 **75** (h[1]) DanielTudhope 4 72
(David O'Meara) *hld up: shkn up over 2f out: eased ins fnl f* **7/2**[3]

0-35 **5** *22* **See And Be Seen**[8] 2021 7-8-12 **68** (p) MitchGodwin(5) 1 38
(Sylvester Kirk) *chsd ldrs: rdn over 4f out: wknd wl over 1f out* **9/1**

3m 38.78s (-4.92) **Going Correction** -0.075s/f (Stan)
**WFA** 4 from 7yo 1lb **5** Ran SP% **111.8**
Speed ratings (Par 103): **108,108,106,104,93**
WIN: 2.50D, 1.10M; PL: 2.30 D, 1.10 M; EX: M/D 4.00, D/M 4.60; CSF: M/D 2.94, D/M 3.86; TF: M/D/OJ 7.50, D/M/OJ 17.10;.
**Owner** Box 41 Racing **Bred** Star Pointe Ltd **Trained** West Ilsley, Berks
**Owner** John O'Donnell & Noel Kelly **Bred** J O'Donnell & N Kelly **Trained** Newmarket, Suffolk

**FOCUS**
Only two really ever mattered in this marathon handicap and they ultimately shared the spoils, a decision not without controversy. The third has been rated close to her recent best.

## 2276 FCLGF.COM H'CAP 1m 142y (Tp)
**8:00** (8:00) (Class 6) (0-65,67) 4-Y-O+ **£2,458** (£731; £365; £182) **Stalls** Low

Form RPR

1230 **1** **Gabrial The Thug (FR)**[40] 1334 7-9-5 **62** (t) SilvestreDeSousa 5 69
(Ian Williams) *a.p: shkn up to chse ldr over 2f out: rdn over 1f out: styd on u.p to ld wl ins fnl f* **10/3**[1]

2034 **2** *¾* **Little Choosey**[33] 1449 7-9-3 **60** (bt) JimmyQuinn 2 65
(Roy Bowring) *hld up: hdwy over 1f out: swtchd rt ins fnl f: r.o wl* **12/1**

3-20 **3** *1 ½* **Muzaahim (IRE)**[39] 1338 6-9-1 **58** (h) ShaneKelly 7 60
(Laura Morgan) *hld up: shkn up over 1f out: r.o to go 3rd nr fin: nt rch ldrs* **12/1**

461- **4** *¾* **Russian Ranger (IRE)**[171] 7944 4-9-6 **63** (p) MartinHarley 6 64
(Jonathan Portman) *led: rdn over 1f out: hdd and io ex wl ins fnl f* **4/1**[2]

50-0 **5** *shd* **Mr Cool Cash**[15] 1842 5-9-7 **64** ConnorBeasley 3 64
(Richard Guest) *hld up in tch: rdn over 1f out: styd on* **11/2**

6303 **6** *4 ½* **Hard To Handel**[15] 1932 5-9-7 **64** (b) PaddyAspell 1 55
(Clare Ellam) *hld up: shkn up over 1f out: nt trble ldrs* **9/1**

065- **7** *¾* **Molten Lava (IRE)**[192] 7529 5-9-3 **67** (p[1]) PatrickVaughan(7) 9 56
(Christian Williams) *chsd ldr tl rdn over 2f out: wknd fnl f* **10/1**

05-6 **8** *2 ¼* **Billy Bond**[25] 1610 5-9-5 **62** TonyHamilton 8 47
(Richard Fahey) *chsd ldrs: rdn over 2f out: wknd over 1f out* **5/1**[3]

62/0 **9** *2 ½* **Jeremy's Jet (IRE)**[25] 1610 6-8-8 **58** AledBeech(7) 4 37
(Tony Carroll) *s.i.s: hld up: plld hrd: hdwy over 5f out: pushed along on outer over 2f out: sn wknd* **18/1**

1m 49.77s (-0.33) **Going Correction** -0.075s/f (Stan) **9** Ran SP% **114.9**
Speed ratings (Par 101): **98,97,96,95,95 91,90,88,86**
CSF £43.89 CT £430.84 TOTE £4.50: £1.60, £4.30, £3.40; EX 24.90 Trifecta £170.40.
**Owner** Dr Marwan Koukash **Bred** Alain Plainfosse **Trained** Portway, Worcs

**FOCUS**
An ordinary extended mile event, but a seventh C&D success for the winner. The runner-up has been rated to her best.

## 2277 FCL GLOBAL FORWARDING NOVICE AUCTION STKS 5f 21y (Tp)
**8:30** (8:32) (Class 5) 2-Y-O **£3,234** (£962; £481; £240) **Stalls** Low

Form RPR

**1** **Our Kid (IRE)** 2-9-2 0 TonyHamilton 8 64+
(Richard Fahey) *pushed along and hdwy over 3f out: shkn up to ld and hung lft wl ins fnl f: r.o* **9/4**[1]

6 **2** *¾* **Storm Doris (IRE)**[11] 1934 2-8-11 0 RyanPowell 5 53
(James Unett) *chsd ldr tl led over 1f out: hdd wl ins fnl f* **33/1**

3 **3** *nk* **Shesgotthelot**[8] 2015 2-8-11 0 LiamJones 4 53
(J S Moore) *chsd ldrs: hmpd and lost pl over 3f out: rallied over 1f out: sn hung lft: styd on* **15/2**[3]

**4** *1 ¼* **Data Protection** 2-9-2 0 DougieCostello 1 54+
(William Muir) *in rr: outpcd over 3f out: hdwy and nt clr run fr over 1f out tl wl ins fnl f: r.o: nvr able to chal* **9/2**[2]

0 **5** *shd* **Captain Kissinger**[31] 1496 2-9-2 0 FrannyNorton 2 53
(Jo Hughes) *chsd ldrs: rdn and hmpd over 1f out: styd on same pce ins fnl f* **9/4**[1]

0 **6** *1 ¾* **Mirek (IRE)**[11] 1934 2-9-2 0 (h[1]) PaddyAspell 7 46
(Jonathan Portman) *taken steadily to post: s.s: outpcd: hung lft over 1f out: r.o ins fnl f: nvr nrr* **33/1**

**7** *hd* **Xaar Island** 2-8-11 0 ConnorBeasley 6 40
(David Evans) *sn led: rdn and hdd over 1f out: wknd ins fnl f* **16/1**

**8** *5* **Good Night Out (IRE)** 2-8-11 0 JFEgan 3 22
(David Evans) *sn outpcd: hung lft and eased over 1f out* **8/1**

1m 2.53s (0.63) **Going Correction** -0.075s/f (Stan) **8** Ran SP% **114.4**
Speed ratings (Par 93): **91,89,89,87,87 84,84,76**
CSF £82.36 TOTE £2.60: £1.40, £7.30, £1.60; EX 48.20 Trifecta £462.70.
**Owner** The Market Men **Bred** Patrick Cody **Trained** Musley Bank, N Yorks

**FOCUS**
In all likelihood a moderate auction event, but a pretty taking winner. The level is fluid.

## 2278 FCL PERSONALISED GLOBAL FREIGHT SOLUTIONS H'CAP 7f 36y (Tp)
**9:00** (9:01) (Class 6) (0-60,63) 4-Y-O+ **£2,458** (£731; £365; £182) **Stalls** High

Form RPR

2121 **1** **Prince Of Time**[7] 2063 5-9-4 **63** 6ex CallumRodriguez(7) 8 70
(Richard Ford) *hld up in tch: shkn up over 1f out: led ins fnl f: r.o* **5/2**[2]

0414 **2** *2* **Broughtons Fancy**[41] 1298 4-8-11 **56** BenRobinson(7) 11 58
(Gary Moore) *chsd ldrs: rdn over 2f out: hung lft and styd on to go 2nd nr fin* **9/4**[1]

0500 **3** *½* **Zebelini (IRE)**[10] 1978 5-8-7 **45** JimmyQuinn 10 46
(Roy Bowring) *sn led: rdn over 1f out: hdd ins fnl f: styd on same pce* **50/1**

0440 **4** *1 ½* **Misu Pete**[41] 1298 5-8-4 **49** (v) NicolaCurrie(7) 1 46
(Mark Usher) *hld up: hdwy over 1f out: r.o: nt rch ldrs* **16/1**

-020 **5** *shd* **Free To Roam (IRE)**[41] 1298 4-8-5 **48** LewisEdmunds(5) 2 45
(Luke McJannet) *hld up in tch: rdn over 1f out: styd on same pce ins fnl f* **9/1**

0056 **6** *nk* **Rojina (IRE)**[7] 2069 4-8-2 **47** ow2 GeorgiaDobie(7) 6 43
(Lisa Williamson) *chsd ldr tl rdn over 1f out: hung lft and no ex ins fnl f* **125/1**

6-16 **7** *¾* **Grey Destiny**[16] 1823 7-9-6 **58** DanielTudhope 7 52
(Antony Brittain) *hld up: rdn over 1f out: hung lft and r.o ins fnl f* **13/2**[3]

600- **8** *¾* **Mostashreqah**[225] 6631 4-8-2 **45** LuluStanford(5) 4 38
(Milton Bradley) *prom: rdn over 2f out: wknd wl ins fnl f* **100/1**

0B52 **9** *nk* **Binky Blue (IRE)**[8] 2023 5-9-7 **59** RobertWinston 3 58+
(Daniel Mark Loughnane) *hld up: hdwy over 1f out: running on whn hmpd ins fnl f: eased* **13/2**[3]

05-4 **10** *1* **Bush Beauty (IRE)**[15] 1842 6-9-5 **57** JasonHart 12 46
(Eric Alston) *s.i.s: hld up: rdn and hung lft over 1f out: nvr trbld ldrs* **10/1**

0554 **11** *1 ½* **Rising Sunshine (IRE)**[36] 1408 4-8-9 **47** (bt) FrannyNorton 5 33
(Milton Bradley) *hld up: hdwy over 1f out: styng on same pce whn hmpd ins fnl f: eased* **10/1**

350- **12** *15* **Black Truffle (FR)**[378] 1555 7-9-6 **58** SteveDrowne 9 7
(Mark Usher) *dwlt: hld up: wknd over 2f out* **50/1**

1m 27.46s (-1.34) **Going Correction** -0.075s/f (Stan) **12** Ran SP% **125.8**
Speed ratings (Par 101): **104,101,101,99,99 98,98,97,96,95 94,76**
CSF £9.17 CT £236.64 TOTE £2.90: £1.40, £2.00, £12.20; EX 15.80 Trifecta £495.00.
**Owner** B Hartley **Bred** D Curran **Trained** Garstang, Lancs
■ Stewards' Enquiry : Ben Robinson two-day ban; careless riding (May 16-17)

**FOCUS**
A moderate sprint, in which the early pace appeared strong but didn't collapse. The winner has been rated back to her best.
T/Plt: £80.40 to a £1 stake. Pool: £69,650.84 - 631.83 winning units. T/Qpdt: £12.30 to a £1 stake. Pool: £6,393.26 - 382.30 winning units. **Colin Roberts**

# 2066 YARMOUTH (L-H)
Tuesday, May 2

**OFFICIAL GOING: Good to firm (watered; 7.9)**
Wind: brisk breeze Weather: chilly; 10 degrees

## 2279 HAVEN SEASHORE HOLIDAY PARK MAIDEN STKS (PLUS 10 RACE) 5f 42y
**2:20** (2:20) (Class 4) 2-Y-O **£4,528** (£1,347; £673; £336) **Stalls** Centre

Form RPR

**1** **To Wafij (IRE)** 2-9-5 0 AndreaAtzeni 3 80+
(Roger Varian) *pressed ldr: pushed ahd over 1f out: in command fnl 100yds: readily* **13/8**[1]

4 **2** *1* **Choice Encounter**[10] 1966 2-9-5 0 JamieSpencer 1 76
(Michael Bell) *led narrowly: rdn and hdd over 1f out: outpcd by wnr fnl 100yds but kpt on gamely* **4/1**[3]

**3** *nse* **Validator** 2-9-0 0 PatCosgrave 2 71+
(William Haggas) *missed break: sn rcvrd to chse ldng pair: rdn and edgd rt fnl f: styd on wl cl home and nrly snatched 2nd: promising* **7/2**[2]

**4** *3 ½* **Indian Warrior** 2-9-5 0 JosephineGordon 7 63
(Ed Dunlop) *chsd ldrs: sn pushed along: rdn and no imp wl over 1f out* **12/1**

0 **5** *2 ½* **Contribute**[14] 1858 2-9-5 0 HarryBentley 4 54
(Martyn Meade) *towards rr: rdn over 2f out: nt trble ldrs after* **4/1**[3]

**6** *4* **City Guest (IRE)** 2-9-5 0 TomQueally 5 40
(George Margarson) *missed break: a last: rdn 1/2-way: sn btn* **40/1**

1m 1.57s (-1.13) **Going Correction** -0.525s/f (Hard) **6** Ran SP% **110.4**
Speed ratings (Par 95): **88,86,86,80,76 70**
CSF £8.15 TOTE £2.10: £1.40, £1.50; EX 9.20 Trifecta £19.60.
**Owner** Sheikh Ahmed Al Maktoum **Bred** Tally-Ho Stud **Trained** Newmarket, Suffolk

**FOCUS**
The ground was good to firm (watered). This looked a useful enough 2yo maiden.

## 2280 CONFERENCES AT YARMOUTH RACECOURSE MEDIAN AUCTION MAIDEN STKS 5f 42y
**2:50** (2:54) (Class 6) 3-4-Y-O **£2,587** (£770; £384; £192) **Stalls** Centre

Form RPR

003- **1** **Ocelot**[199] 7356 3-8-9 67 LukeMorris 4 68
(Robert Cowell) *pressed ldr after 1f and t.k.h: drvn ahd over 1f out: clr whn hung rt ins fnl f* **9/4**[2]

4 **2** *3 ¼* **Lambrini Legacy**[17] 1785 3-8-9 0 (h[1]) BenCurtis 7 56
(Lisa Williamson) *taken down early: v keen to post: mounted in stalls: plld hrd: led after 1f: rdn and hdd over 1f out: sn outpcd by wnr but jst clung on to 2nd* **25/1**

20- **3** *nse* **Bequia (IRE)**[196] 7439 3-8-9 0 HarryBentley 1 56
(Martyn Meade) *chsd ldng pair but pushed along after 2f and struggling to keep tabs on them: drvn and kpt on ins fnl f: almost snatched 2nd but no ch w wnr* **4/9**[1]

0- **4** *5* **Sussex Girl**[197] 7407 3-8-9 0 JosephineGordon 5 38
(John Berry) *v awkward to load: chsd ldrs: rdn and wknd over 1f out* **20/1**[3]

6000 **5** *6* **Storming Ambition**[16] 1823 4-9-9 38.........................(t) StevieDonohoe 3 26
(Conrad Allen) *led 1f: pushed along after 2f: sn toiling in rr* **50/1**

1m 0.54s (-2.16) **Going Correction** -0.525s/f (Hard)
**WFA** 3 from 4yo 9lb **5** Ran SP% **110.6**
Speed ratings (Par 101): **96,90,90,82,73**
CSF £34.82 TOTE £3.20: £1.40, £7.00; EX 26.10 Trifecta £32.40.
**Owner** Manor Farm Stud (rutland) **Bred** Manor Farm Stud & Mrs A J Ralli **Trained** Six Mile Bottom, Cambs

**FOCUS**
This didn't look much of a race, but still a likeable performance from the winner. The fourth and fifth highlight the lack of depth to this race.

## 2281 BURLINGTON PALM HOTEL OF GREAT YARMOUTH H'CAP 1m 3f 104y
**3:25** (3:26) (Class 6) (0-55,57) 4-Y-0+ **£2,264** (£673; £336; £168) **Stalls** Low

Form RPR

00-0 **1** **Zubaidah**[27] 1563 5-8-11 **48**.................................(t[1]) EdwardGreatrex(3) 13 54
(Jane Chapple-Hyam) *sn pressing ldr: rdn 3f out: led wl over 1f out: in command ins fnl f* **50/1**

6324 **2** *1 1/4* **Graceful Lady**[27] 1556 4-9-9 **57**....................................... LukeMorris 8 61
(Robert Eddery) *slowly away: bhd: prog 5f out: drvn and outpcd over 3f out: rallied and wnt 4th wl over 1f out: hrd drvn to take 2nd ins fnl f: nt rch wnr* **8/1**

00-0 **3** *1 1/4* **Hint Of Grey (IRE)**[15] 462 4-9-7 **55**............................. JamieSpencer 6 57
(Don Cantillon) *trckd ldrs gng wl: effrt and rdn 3f out: chsd wnr but no imp ins fnl f: lost pl cl to home* **2/1**[1]

133- **4** *1 1/4* **Hope Is High**[221] 6738 4-9-4 **52**.............................. JosephineGordon 11 52
(John Berry) *racd on outside: towards rr: urged along over 2f out: kpt on wout threatening to take 4th ins fnl f* **3/1**[2]

0-00 **5** *3/4* **Sexy Secret**[68] 880 6-9-3 **54**....................................(p) SimonPearce(3) 1 53
(Lydia Pearce) *drvn to ld: urged along 3f out: hdd wl over 1f out: sn lost pl* **16/1**

00-6 **6** *2 1/2* **Sunlit Waters**[20] 1729 4-9-6 **54**.......................................... TomQueally 5 49
(Eve Johnson Houghton) *pressed ldrs: rdn 4f out: no ex over 2f out* **8/1**

000- **7** *shd* **Little Orchid**[133] 8468 4-8-13 **50**............................... ShelleyBirkett(3) 3 45
(Julia Feilden) *pressed ldrs: pushed along over 2f out: one pce and n.d after* **33/1**

-545 **8** *3/4* **Smoky Hill (IRE)**[21] 1698 8-8-11 **52**............................... FinleyMarsh(7) 4 45
(Tony Carroll) *midfield: rdn and struggling fnl 3f* **13/2**[3]

042- **9** *1* **Esspeegee**[242] 6103 4-9-1 **49**..........................................(p) RobertTart 2 41
(Alan Bailey) *towards rr: rdn 5f out: no ch but making modest hdwy whn checked for room ins fnl f* **16/1**

500- **10** *4 1/2* **Beat The Blues**[187] 7646 5-9-0 **48**............................... StevieDonohoe 7 33
(Miss Joey Ellis) *prom: rdn 3f out: sn lost pl: eased ins fnl f* **66/1**

320- **11** *3 1/4* **Shirataki (IRE)**[236] 6256 9-9-0 **55**.................................... MollyKing(7) 12 34
(Peter Hiatt) *stdd s:rdr unbalanced briefly: t.k.h in rr: btn over 3f out* **33/1**

2m 28.22s (-0.48) **Going Correction** -0.15s/f (Firm) **11** Ran SP% **115.0**
Speed ratings (Par 101): **95,94,93,92,91 89,89,89,88,85 82**
CSF £398.33 CT £1194.74 TOTE £28.00: £6.70, £2.60, £1.10; EX 366.50 Trifecta £1728.80.
**Owner** Mrs Jane Chapple-Hyam **Bred** Whatton Manor Stud **Trained** Dalham, Suffolk
■ Stewards' Enquiry : Edward Greatrex two-day ban: used whip above permitted level (16-17 May)

**FOCUS**
Not a bad race of its type. The runner-up has been rated to her Kempton form.

## 2282 WEATHERBYS BANK H'CAP 1m 2f 23y
**4:00** (4:00) (Class 5) (0-70,70) 4-Y-0+ **£2,911** (£866; £432; £216) **Stalls** Low

Form RPR

40-2 **1** **Vernatti**[16] 1818 4-9-2 **65**................................................ RobHornby 1 76+
(Pam Sly) *taken down early: racd enthusiastically: midfield and confidently handled: effrt in 3rd and gng wl over 1f out: rdn and swtchd rt: led ins fnl f and sn strode clr* **11/2**[3]

30-0 **2** *2 1/4* **Longside**[30] 1519 5-9-1 **64**............................................... AndreaAtzeni 8 70
(James Eustace) *cl up: led 6f out: jnd and rdn 3f out: hdd ins fnl f: sn outpcd by wnr* **10/3**[1]

502- **3** *1* **Monsieur Glory**[202] 7274 4-9-7 **70**.................................... PatCosgrave 7 74
(Tom Clover) *rn in snatches: prom tl rdn and lost pl over 5f out: rallied and pressing ldrs over 2f out: nt qckn fnl f* **7/2**[2]

2422 **4** *nk* **Ms Gillard**[17] 1789 4-9-5 **68**.........................................(b) JamieSpencer 6 71
(David Simcock) *dwlt sltly: sn prom: rdn to join ldr 3f out: stl upsides over 1f out: no ex ins fnl f* **7/2**[2]

-000 **5** *1 3/4* **Silver Alliance**[21] 1707 9-8-10 **62**...........................(p) ShelleyBirkett(3) 4 62
(Julia Feilden) *towards rr: rdn and outpcd 3f out: plugged on ins fnl f but no ch* **25/1**

0543 **6** *1/2* **Fantasy Gladiator**[20] 1735 11-9-0 **63**.............................(p) TomQueally 2 62
(Michael Appleby) *last tl over 4f out: nvr on terms but plugged on ins fnl f* **13/2**

0104 **7** *6* **Nouvelle Ere**[21] 1699 6-8-10 **59**.......................................(t) JimmyQuinn 5 46
(Tony Carroll) *led tl 6f out: sn drvn: lost tch 3f out: eased fnl f* **16/1**

0-40 **8** *6* **Sehail (USA)**[10] 1984 4-8-11 **60**..................................(p[1]) HarryBentley 3 35
(George Peckham) *last pair: rdn over 5f out: labouring after: t.o and eased* **14/1**

2m 7.0s (-3.50) **Going Correction** -0.15s/f (Firm) **8** Ran SP% **112.6**
Speed ratings (Par 103): **108,106,105,105,103 103,98,93**
CSF £23.42 CT £72.05 TOTE £7.10: £1.90, £1.40, £1.80; EX 24.70 Trifecta £108.40.
**Owner** Michael H Sly Dr T Davies Mrs Pam Sly **Bred** M H Sly, Dr T Davies & Mrs P Sly **Trained** Thorney, Cambs

**FOCUS**
The winner proved much better than her modest opening mark. The form is a bit muddling, but the runner-up has been rated to his win here last year.

## 2283 KATIES 30TH BIRTHDAY CELEBRATION H'CAP 7f 3y
**4:30** (4:31) (Class 3) (0-95,95) 4-Y-0 **£7,246** (£2,168; £1,084; £542; £270) **Stalls** Centre

Form RPR

355- **1** **Taurean Star (IRE)**[269] 5175 4-9-1 **89**............................ JamieSpencer 4 96
(Michael Bell) *bhd: prog over 2f out: drvn and sustained chal fnl f: led 75yds out: all out* **4/1**[2]

3330 **2** *nk* **Horsted Keynes (FR)**[50] 1177 7-9-2 **90**............................ AndreaAtzeni 2 96
(David Simcock) *last early: stl plenty to do over 2f out: drvn and str run ins fnl f: horse lft it too late and wnr got first run: jst failed* **7/1**

2635 **3** *hd* **Firmdecisions (IRE)**[67] 896 7-9-2 **90**.............................. PatCosgrave 9 95
(Dean Ivory) *led: pushed along over 2f out: hrd rdn and edgd lft 1f out: hdd and no ex fnl 75yds* **20/1**

2006 **4** *1/2* **Realize**[18] 1772 7-8-8 **82**..................................................(t) HarryBentley 1 86
(Stuart Williams) *chsd ldrs: tacked rt after 2f: rdn over 2f out: chal over 1f out: nt qckn fnl 100yds* **9/2**[3]

51-0 **5** *1* **Gothic Empire (IRE)**[24] 1622 5-9-1 **89**.......................... DanielMuscutt 6 90
(James Fanshawe) *slowly away: rdn to trck ldrs after 2f: effrt and n.m.r over 1f out: sn no imp* **5/2**[1]

06-0 **6** *nk* **Georgian Bay (IRE)**[94] 459 7-8-8 **85**..................(v) JordanVaughan(3) 7 86
(K R Burke) *chsd ldrs: drvn to chal over 2f out: n.m.r briefly over 1f out: nt qckn fnl f* **9/1**

00-0 **7** *1 3/4* **Majestic Moon (IRE)**[94] 459 7-8-7 **88**.......................... FinleyMarsh(7) 3 84
(Julia Feilden) *prom and t.k.h: tacked rt after 2f: rdn and ducked rt and lost pl over 1f out* **25/1**

620- **8** *8* **Glory Awaits (IRE)**[227] 6585 7-9-7 **95**...................... JosephineGordon 8 69
(David Simcock) *missed break: towards rr: rdn 1/2-way: sn struggling: eased fnl f* **17/2**

02-3 **9** *3 1/4* **Philba**[121] 5 5-9-3 **91**.......................................................... TomQueally 5 57
(David Lanigan) *sn bhd: drvn and racing awkwardly 3f out: eased fnl f* **20/1**

1m 22.23s (-4.37) **Going Correction** -0.525s/f (Hard) **9** Ran SP% **113.1**
Speed ratings (Par 107): **103,102,102,101,100 100,98,89,85**
CSF £30.15 CT £495.99 TOTE £4.50: £1.60, £2.30, £4.70; EX 23.90 Trifecta £222.10.
**Owner** Brian Goodyear **Bred** Denis McDonnell **Trained** Newmarket, Suffolk

**FOCUS**
A decent handicap. The third has been rated to his winter AW best.

## 2284 TRAFALGAR RESTAURANT AT YARMOUTH RACECOURSE H'CAP 1m 3y
**5:00** (5:03) (Class 4) (0-85,85) 3-Y-O **£4,690** (£1,395; £697; £348) **Stalls** Centre

Form RPR

1- **1** *1 3/4* **Across Dubai**[187] 7649 3-9-6 **84**....................................... PatCosgrave 3 86
(William Haggas) *t.k.h: settled trcking ldrs: rdn to chal over 1f out: limited rspnse and sn outpcd by wnr: almost lost 2nd to hanging rival cl home: fin 2nd: later awrdd the r* **8/13**[1]

10-5 **2** *shd* **Ernststavroblofeld (USA)**[12] 1907 3-9-7 **85**.................. HarryBentley 1 87
(Martyn Meade) *chsd ldrs and sn wanting to hang rt: rdn 3f out: effrt to duel for 2nd 1f out: hung rt but almost secured that position cl home: no match for wnr: fin 3rd: plcd 2nd* **15/2**[2]

156- **3** *1 1/2* **Zymyran**[172] 7909 3-9-6 **84**................................................. AndreaAtzeni 7 82
(David Simcock) *dwlt: t.k.h towards rr early: rdn over 3f out: effrt 2f out: no imp over 1f out: wnt 4th ins fnl f: fin 4th: plcd 3rd* **12/1**

431- **4** *1/2* **X Rated (IRE)**[160] 8074 3-8-9 **78**.................................. RichardOliver(5) 6 75
(Mark Johnston) *led: drvn and hdd over 1f out: kpt on same pce ins fnl f: fin 5th: plcd 4th* **16/1**

2-14 **5** *3 1/4* **Ray's The Money (IRE)**[19] 1760 3-9-1 **79**...............(p[1]) JamieSpencer 2 69
(Michael Bell) *lost grnd at s: tk hold keen and awkward in rr: nvr on terms: eased cl home: fin 6th: plcd 5th* **10/1**[3]

253 **6** *1* **Dubai Waves**[26] 1581 3-8-9 **73**................................... JosephineGordon 5 60
(Hugo Palmer) *prom: rdn 3f out: lost pl 2f out: eased cl home: fin 7th: plcd 6th* **16/1**

121 **D** **Indian Dandy (IRE)**[50] 1176 3-9-5 **83**............................(h) TomQueally 4 89
(Marco Botti) *2nd tl rdn to ld over 1f out: sn asserted: in command fnl 100yds: later disqualified - prohibited substance fnd in sample* **16/1**

1m 35.37s (-5.23) **Going Correction** -0.525s/f (Hard) **7** Ran SP% **108.1**
Speed ratings (Par 101): **103,103,101,101,97 96,105**
CSF £23.80 TOTE £11.70: £3.10, £1.10; EX 27.40 Trifecta £111.80.
**Owner** Sheikh Juma Dalmook Al Maktoum **Bred** Rabbah Bloodstock Limited **Trained** Newmarket, Suffolk

**FOCUS**
A fair 3yo handicap. The fourth and fifth have been rated a bit off their 2yo runs for now.

## 2285 FIRST FURNISHINGS OF GORLESTON FILLIES' H'CAP 7f 3y
**5:30** (5:30) (Class 5) (0-70,71) 4-Y-0+ **£2,911** (£866; £432; £216) **Stalls** Centre

Form RPR

06 **1** **Wahiba (GER)**[61] 986 4-9-0 **61**...................................... AndreaAtzeni 3 73+
(Marco Botti) *mde all: gng best 2f out: 2 l clr and rdn 1f out: cosily* **7/2**[1]

-065 **2** *2 3/4* **Indigo Princess**[33] 1455 4-8-6 **60**................................ RayDawson(7) 2 64
(Michael Appleby) *chsd ldrs: rdn to go 2nd wl over 1f out: kpt on but nt trble ready wnr* **14/1**

010- **3** *2* **Sister Dude**[182] 7743 4-9-7 **68**................................ JosephineGordon 8 67
(Jonathan Portman) *prom: 3rd and rdn 1f out: no imp on ldrs after* **14/1**

55 **4** *hd* **The Yellow Bus**[34] 1419 4-9-10 **71**................................... HarryBentley 1 69
(Michael Wigham) *bhd: rdn and prog 2f out: drvn and chsd ldrs vainly whn duelling for 3rd fnl f* **4/1**[2]

50-3 **5** *3 1/4* **Fantasy Queen**[25] 1603 4-9-2 **63**........................................ TomQueally 4 52
(Eve Johnson Houghton) *last and rdn early: modest effrt over 2f out: nvr on terms* **7/2**[1]

0060 **6** *2 1/2* **Prisom (IRE)**[14] 1868 4-8-1 **55**.................................... RhiainIngram(7) 6 38
(Gay Kelleway) *plld hrd and prom briefly: rdn and ungainly in rr 1/2-way: no ch after* **16/1**

003- **7** *1/2* **Sakhee's Jem**[160] 8064 4-9-4 **65**..........................................(p) BenCurtis 7 46
(Gay Kelleway) *t.k.h chsng ldrs: wnt 2nd 2f out: hrd drvn and lost pl qckly* **6/1**

60-0 **8** *10* **Fidelma Moon (IRE)**[13] 1879 5-9-3 **67**...................... JordanVaughan(3) 5 21
(K R Burke) *pressed wnr tl 1/2-way: rdn and dropped out v tamely and racd awkwardly over 2f out: : t.o* **11/2**[3]

1m 23.56s (-3.04) **Going Correction** -0.525s/f (Hard) **8** Ran SP% **113.3**
Speed ratings (Par 100): **96,92,90,90,86 83,83,71**
CSF £51.17 CT £610.81 TOTE £4.40: £1.50, £4.40, £4.70; EX 64.70 Trifecta £437.10.
**Owner** Gute Freunde Partnership **Bred** Stiftung Gestut Fahrhof **Trained** Newmarket, Suffolk

**FOCUS**
A modest fillies' handicap.
T/Plt: £69.30 to a £1 stake. Pool: £58,183.10 - 612.44 winning units. T/Qpdt: £10.30 to a £1 stake. Pool: £6,881.09 - 493.34 winning units. **Iain Mackenzie**

# ASCOT (R-H)
Wednesday, May 3

**OFFICIAL GOING: Good to firm (firm in places; (str 8.6, rnd 8.1)**
Wind: Moderate, across Weather: Overcast, chilly

## 2286 SODEXO CONDITIONS STKS (PLUS 10 RACE) 5f
**2:00** (2:00) (Class 2) 2-Y-O **£8,715** (£2,609; £1,304; £652; £326) **Stalls** High

Form RPR
0 **1** **Frozen Angel (IRE)**[15] 1858 2-8-11 0 SilvestreDeSousa 2 97+
(Tom Dascombe) *pressed ldr: led 1/2-way: clr and shkn up fnl f: styd on strly* **12/1**
11 **2** 3 ¼ **Corinthia Knight (IRE)**[9] 2015 2-8-11 0 LukeMorris 1 85
(Archie Watson) *athletic: trckd ldng pair: shkn up to chse wnr 2f out: rdn and no imp fr over 1f out* **5/6**[1]
1 **3** 3 **Inviolable Spirit (IRE)**[23] 1673 2-8-11 0 TonyHamilton 5 75
(Richard Fahey) *cmpt: lw: chsd ldrs: shkn up to go 3rd over 1f out: no imp after: one pce* **3/1**[2]
**4** 1 ¾ **Global Tango (IRE)** 2-8-11 0 WilliamBuick 3 68+
(Charles Hills) *tall: pushed along in last: shkn up and outpcd 2f out: no ch after* **8/1**[3]
**5** 1 **Tangled (IRE)** 2-8-11 0 PatDobbs 4 65+
(Richard Hannon) *leggy: athletic: led: jinked rt after 1f: hdd 1/2-way: steadily wknd 2f out* **8/1**[3]

59.76s (-0.74) **Going Correction** -0.025s/f (Good) **5 Ran SP% 109.5**
Speed ratings (Par 99): **104,98,94,91,89**
CSF £22.81 TOTE £10.20: £3.60, £1.10; EX 22.90 Trifecta £57.30.
**Owner** Cleverley, Dance, Mound, Owen **Bred** Yeomanstown Stud **Trained** Malpas, Cheshire

**FOCUS**
The running rail on the Round course was positioned approximately 3yds out from the innermost position from the 1m4f start to the Home straight. Distance of this as advertised. Bit of a turn up here, with the outsider of the five running out a clear winner. The runner-up's Kempton romp always had the chance to flatter him, and this is probably a better guide to his ability.

## 2287 SPINAL INJURIES ASSOCIATION BRITISH EBF FILLIES' CONDITIONS STKS (PLUS 10 RACE) 7f 213y(R)
**2:35** (2:37) (Class 3) 3-Y-O **£9,703** (£2,887; £1,443; £721) **Stalls** Low

Form RPR
1-2 **1** **Prosper**[20] 1760 3-8-12 80 SilvestreDeSousa 9 90
(Roger Varian) *leggy: athletic: lw: trckd ldr: shkn up to ld wl over 1f out: kpt on wl fnl f: jst hld on* **5/1**[2]
1- **2** shd **Icespire**[205] 7210 3-8-12 85 (h) FrankieDettori 7 91+
(John Gosden) *str: t.k.h: hld up in last pair: nt clr run over 2f out: prog w hd at sltly awkward angle jst over 1f out: squeezed through to take 2nd last 100yds: drvn and clsd on wnr: jst failed* **1/1**[1]
324- **3** 1 ¼ **Soldier's Girl (IRE)**[194] 7493 3-8-12 85 PatDobbs 4 86
(Richard Hannon) *lw: trckd ldng pair: rdn to dispute 2nd briefly over 1f out: kpt on same pce fnl f* **14/1**
61- **4** nk **Fleeting Motion**[194] 7494 3-8-12 82 JimCrowley 6 85
(Richard Hannon) *str: lw: hld up in 5th: prog 2f out: rdn to chse wnr jst over 1f out: nt qckn fnl f and lost 2nd last 100yds* **8/1**
16-4 **5** 1 ½ **Blending**[18] 1796 3-8-12 88 JamesDoyle 1 82
(John Gosden) *led: shkn up and hdd wl over 1f out: fdd fnl f* **13/2**[3]
240- **6** 2 **Reachforthestars (IRE)**[198] 7409 3-8-12 94 DanielTudhope 8 77
(David O'Meara) *settled in last pair: urged along 3f out: nt pce to make prog* **10/1**
31- **7** 13 **Cirencester**[223] 6716 3-8-12 78 DaneO'Neill 10 48
(Henry Candy) *unf: pushed up fr wdst draw to chse ldng pair but trapped out wd thrght: wknd over 2f out: t.o* **25/1**

1m 39.45s (-1.25) **Going Correction** 0.0s/f (Good) **7 Ran SP% 110.7**
Speed ratings (Par 100): **106,105,104,104,102 100,87**
CSF £9.73 TOTE £5.90: £2.20, £1.30; EX 11.90 Trifecta £75.60.
**Owner** China Horse Club International Limited **Bred** Newsells Park Stud **Trained** Newmarket, Suffolk

**FOCUS**
Distance increased by 6yds. A couple of key non-runners but still useful form. The favourite got stopped in her run and looked unlucky. It's been rated around the race average and the fifth.

## 2288 LONGINES SAGARO STKS (GROUP 3) 1m 7f 209y
**3:10** (3:10) (Class 1) 4-Y-O+ **£34,026** (£12,900; £6,456; £3,216; £1,614; £810) **Stalls** Low

Form RPR
451- **1** **Sweet Selection**[207] 7150 5-8-13 104 SilvestreDeSousa 8 107
(Hughie Morrison) *trckd ldr in modly run event: pushed along over 3f out: rdn to chal over 2f out: led jst over 1f out: styd on wl* **15/2**
4-35 **2** 1 ½ **Prince Of Arran**[19] 1770 4-8-13 91 StevieDonohoe 2 108
(Charlie Fellowes) *trckd ldng pair in modly run event: rdn over 2f out: no imp tl styd on fr jst over 1f out to take 2nd last 75yds: no ch to chal* **10/1**
135- **3** ¾ **Nearly Caught (IRE)**[200] 7349 7-9-2 114 WilliamBuick 4 107
(Hughie Morrison) *lw: led at mod pce: kicked on 4f out: rdn over 2f out: hdd and one pce jst over 1f out* **7/2**[1]
0-52 **4** 3 ¼ **Maleficent Queen**[18] 1802 5-8-13 105 PhillipMakin 3 100
(Keith Dalgleish) *t.k.h: hld up in 5th in modly run event: poorly plcd whn pce lifted 4f out: rdn over 2f out: tk 4th fnl f but no ch* **10/1**
220- **5** 1 **Pallasator**[192] 7569 8-9-2 113 LukeMorris 5 102
(Sir Mark Prescott Bt) *swtg: walked to post and mounted at s: hld up in 6th in modly run event: poorly plcd whn pce lifted 4f out: hrd rdn over 2f out: hung rt over 1f out: nvr any ch* **7/2**[1]
545- **6** 1 **Battersea**[236] 6283 6-9-2 106 (h) JamesDoyle 1 101
(Roger Varian) *hld up in last in modly run event: poorly plcd whn pce lifted 4f out: rdn over 2f out: one pce and no ch of landing a blow* **4/1**[2]
241- **7** 7 **Harbour Law**[235] 6329 4-9-6 114 TomQueally 6 99
(Laura Mongan) *chsd ldrs in 4th: rdn over 2f out: wkng whn nudged by rival over 1f out: sn bhd* **11/2**[3]

3m 30.23s (1.23) **Going Correction** 0.0s/f (Good)
**WFA** 4 from 5yo+ 1lb **7 Ran SP% 109.8**
Speed ratings (Par 113): **96,95,94,93,92 92,88**
CSF £70.22 TOTE £6.80: £2.70, £5.20; EX 66.70 Trifecta £317.50.
**Owner** Paul Brocklehurst **Bred** S A Douch **Trained** East Ilsley, Berks

**FOCUS**
Distance increased by 18yds. No great gallop here and something of an unsatisfactory race, with little getting into it and the runner-up rated 91. Still, it was another step up the ladder for the highly progressive winner. It's been rated cautiously around the runner-up to his AW form.

## 2289 MERRIEBELLE STABLE PAVILION STKS (GROUP 3) 6f
**3:45** (3:46) (Class 1) 3-Y-O **£45,368** (£17,200; £8,608; £4,288; £2,152; £1,080) **Stalls** High

Form RPR
123- **1** **Blue Point (IRE)**[207] 7149 3-9-1 116 WilliamBuick 6 117
(Charlie Appleby) *lw: dwlt: sn chsd ldng pair in centre: clsd to ld over 1f out: drvn and styd on strly fnl f* **13/8**[1]
21- **2** 1 ½ **Harry Angel (IRE)**[228] 6572 3-9-5 110 AdamKirby 9 116
(Clive Cox) *str: lengthy: plld hrd early: racd towards nr side to 1/2-way: on terms whn gps merged: rdn to chse wnr jst over 1f out: styd on but no imp* **7/2**[2]
010- **3** 1 ½ **Mubtasim (IRE)**[221] 6785 3-9-1 101 PatCosgrave 4 107
(William Haggas) *str: lengthy: swtg: dwlt: hld up in centre: shkn up and prog 2f out: rdn and styd on wl fnl f to take 3rd last 75yds* **10/1**
150- **4** ¾ **Tis Marvellous**[236] 6282 3-9-1 110 (t) LukeMorris 7 105
(Clive Cox) *trckd overall ldr in centre: rdn to chal and upsides over 1f out: outpcd after* **25/1**
006- **5** ¾ **Yalta (IRE)**[208] 7113 3-9-1 106 JamesDoyle 5 102
(Mark Johnston) *overall ldr in centre: hdd and one pce over 1f out* **20/1**
16-5 **6** 1 ½ **Sir Dancealot (IRE)**[14] 1881 3-9-1 108 ShaneKelly 2 98
(David Elsworth) *lw: dwlt: hld up in centre: hrd rdn 2f out: one pce and no prog* **16/1**
10-3 **7** nk **Seven Heavens**[14] 1881 3-9-1 107 FrankieDettori 10 97
(John Gosden) *taken to post v early: racd towards nr side to 1/2-way and led gp: shkn up over 2f out: fdd tamely over 1f out* **7/1**[3]
126- **8** 5 **Mokarris (USA)**[221] 6785 3-9-1 107 JimCrowley 1 81
(Simon Crisford) *chsd ldrs in centre: rdn and nt qckn over 2f out: wknd over 1f out* **7/1**[3]
026- **9** 5 **Legendary Lunch (IRE)**[228] 6572 3-9-1 105 PatDobbs 11 65
(Richard Hannon) *t.k.h: racd towards nr side to 1/2-way: in tch tl wknd over 2f out* **50/1**
411- **10** 3 **Rosie Briar**[193] 7536 3-8-12 96 RobHornby 12 52
(Andrew Balding) *leggy: t.k.h: racd towards nr side to 1/2-way: in tch: wknd over 2f out: sn bhd* **33/1**

1m 11.05s (-3.45) **Going Correction** -0.025s/f (Good) course record **10 Ran SP% 113.8**
Speed ratings (Par 109): **122,120,118,117,116 114,113,106,100,96**
CSF £6.47 TOTE £2.40: £1.10, £1.80, £2.90; EX 9.30 Trifecta £52.80.
**Owner** Godolphin **Bred** Oak Lodge Bloodstock **Trained** Newmarket, Suffolk

**FOCUS**
Distance as advertised. Strong form, with the right two coming to the fore, and it's likely we'll see them back in June as contenders for the Commonwealth Cup. The winner has been rated close to his best.

## 2290 RUNDLE'S PARADISE STKS (LISTED RACE) 1m (S)
**4:20** (4:20) (Class 1) 4-Y-O+ **£20,982** (£7,955; £3,981; £1,983; £995; £499) **Stalls** High

Form RPR
21-2 **1** **Tabarrak (IRE)**[13] 1902 4-9-0 107 JimCrowley 3 114
(Richard Hannon) *trckd ldrs: clsd to ld over 1f out: drvn and pressed after: edgd lft but styd on wl and a holding on* **7/2**[2]
11-4 **2** nk **Ennaadd**[19] 1773 4-9-3 113 SilvestreDeSousa 7 116
(Roger Varian) *trckd ldrs: clsd to chal over 1f out: rdn and pressed wnr after: styd on but a hld* **2/1**[1]
223- **3** 1 ¾ **Firmament**[200] 7354 5-9-0 109 PhillipMakin 6 109
(David O'Meara) *awkward s: hld up in last pair: prog 2f out: swtchd rt and rdn over 1f out: styd on wl to take 3rd last 150yds: no threat to ldng pair* **5/1**[3]
/02- **4** 2 ¼ **Algaith (USA)**[283] 4688 5-9-0 105 FrankieDettori 5 103
(Owen Burrows) *rrd sltly s: w ldrs: led over 2f out to over 1f out: wknd* **16/1**
130- **5** hd **Kaspersky (IRE)**[192] 7565 6-9-0 111 AdamKirby 4 103
(Jane Chapple-Hyam) *str: lw: w ldrs: upsides over 2f out: fdd wl over 1f out* **16/1**
40-0 **6** 2 ¼ **Mondialiste (IRE)**[39] 1378 7-9-0 115 DanielTudhope 2 98
(David O'Meara) *swtg: hld up in last pair: rdn over 2f out: no hdwy and wl btn over 1f out* **7/2**[2]
21/ **7** 7 **Mootaharer (IRE)**[560] 7395 4-9-0 0 DaneO'Neill 1 81
(Charles Hills) *lengthy: mde most to over 2f out: hanging and looked uneasy on grnd: sn wknd* **25/1**

1m 39.44s (-1.36) **Going Correction** -0.025s/f (Good) **7 Ran SP% 110.1**
Speed ratings (Par 111): **105,104,102,100,100 98,91**
CSF £10.06 TOTE £4.40: £2.00, £1.70; EX 11.30 Trifecta £34.80.
**Owner** Hamdan Al Maktoum **Bred** Rathbarry Stud & F & N Woods **Trained** East Everleigh, Wilts

**FOCUS**
Distance as advertised. A decent Listed race with a progressive winner, although the form horse disappointed. The second has been rated as running as well as ever.

## 2291 REDCENTRIC MANNY MERCER APPRENTICE H'CAP 1m (S)
**4:55** (4:55) (Class 4) (0-85,87) 4-Y-O+ **£6,469** (£1,925; £962; £481) **Stalls** High

Form RPR
5261 **1** **Forceful Appeal (USA)**[19] 1769 9-8-12 **76** LouisSteward 9 86
(Simon Dow) *lw: trckd ldr 3f: styd cl up: gng wl 3f out: led 2f out: edgd lft and hrd pressed fnl f: styd on wl* **9/1**
000- **2** nk **Directorship**[187] 7671 11-8-13 **77** HectorCrouch 10 86
(Patrick Chamings) *hld up in last trio: stdy prog nr side over 2f out: rdn to chse wnr over 1f out: chal fnl f: styd on but nt qckn last 150yds* **12/1**
30-1 **3** 3 **Selection (FR)**[28] 1553 4-8-11 **78** GeorgiaCox(3) 5 80
(William Haggas) *trckd ldrs: shkn up wl over 2f out: effrt to chse wnr briefly wl over 1f out: kpt on same pce after* **11/4**[1]
2020 **4** hd **Bunbury**[19] 1766 5-9-2 **87** FinleyMarsh(7) 7 89
(Richard Hughes) *hld up: effrt fr last pl 2f out: prog over 1f out: styd on fnl f and nrly snatched 3rd* **6/1**[3]
/30- **5** 1 ¾ **Cat Silver**[205] 7229 4-8-7 **74** PaddyPilley(3) 4 72
(Roger Charlton) *hld up in last trio: prog on outer 3f out: on terms w ldrs 2f out: fdd over 1f out* **6/1**[3]
00-4 **6** ½ **Gerry The Glover (IRE)**[9] 2030 5-8-8 **77** (p) BenRobinson(5) 6 74
(Brian Ellison) *lw: t.k.h: hld up tl plld way through to press ldr after 3f: led 3f out to 2f out: fdd* **4/1**[2]
2/04 **7** nk **Matravers**[51] 1178 6-8-7 **71** AaronJones 13 67
(Mary Hambro) *trckd ldrs: lost pl over 2f out: no hdwy over 1f out* **16/1**

000- **8** 1 ¼ **Oasis Spear**[203] 7287 5-9-0 **85**............ GabrieleMalune(7) 1 78
(Chris Wall) *t.k.h: wl in tch tl wknd over 2f out* **16/1**
6100 **9** 2 **Lacan (IRE)**[26] 1598 6-9-1 **82**............ DavidParkes(3) 11 71
(Brett Johnson) *lw: t.k.h: led to 3f out: sn wknd* **33/1**
00-0 **10** ¾ **Balmoral Castle**[11] 1964 8-9-2 **87**............ Pierre-LouisJamin(7) 3 74
(Jonathan Portman) *hld up in rr: effrt on outer 3f out: no prog 2f out: wknd* **14/1**
1m 40.46s (-0.34) **Going Correction** -0.025s/f (Good) **10** Ran SP% **114.3**
Speed ratings (Par 105): **100,99,96,96,94 94,93,92,90,89**
CSF £109.04 CT £375.50 TOTE £10.80: £3.20, £3.10, £1.40; EX 97.30 Trifecta £775.40.
**Owner** Mark McAllister **Bred** Juddmonte Farms Inc **Trained** Ashtead, Surrey
**FOCUS**
Distance as advertised. The two eldest runners came away from the favourite late on in this fair handicap.
T/Jkpt: Not won. T/Plt: £70.90 to a £1 stake. Pool: £100,005.31. 1,028.65 winning units. T/Qpdt: £33.00 to a £1 stake. Pool: £7,125.60. 159.76 winning units. **Jonathan Neesom**

# 2251 BRIGHTON (L-H)
## Wednesday, May 3

**OFFICIAL GOING: Good to firm (8.2)**
Wind: Moderate, half behind towards stand Weather: Unsettled

### 2292 EBF NOVICE MEDIAN AUCTION STKS 5f 60y
**5:05** (5:06) (Class 5) 2-Y-O **£3,881** (£1,155; £577; £288) **Stalls** Centre

Form RPR
**1** **Cardsharp** 2-9-2 0............ JoeFanning 5 85+
(Mark Johnston) *mde all: rdn and in control fr over 1f out: comf* **8/11**[1]
62 **2** 3 ½ **Milton Road**[8] 2052 2-9-2 0............ CharlesBishop 6 73
(Mick Channon) *pressed wnr tl outpcd over 1f out* **2/1**[2]
4 **3** ¾ **Felisa**[25] 1627 2-8-11 0............ TomMarquand 2 65
(David Evans) *chsd ldrs: rdn and lost pl 2f out: styd on fnl f* **10/1**[3]
05 **4** 4 ½ **Captain Kissinger**[1] 2277 2-9-2 0............ FranBerry 3 54
(Jo Hughes) *chsd ldrs: hrd rdn 2f out: wknd over 1f out* **20/1**
**5** 2 ¼ **Vegas Boy (IRE)** 2-9-2 0............ TimmyMurphy 1 46
(Jamie Osborne) *outpcd: sn wl bhd* **16/1**
**6** 4 **Red Snapper** 2-8-8 0............ HollieDoyle(3) 4 26
(William Stone) *s.i.s: outpcd: a wl bhd* **50/1**
1m 1.66s (-0.64) **Going Correction** -0.10s/f (Good) **6** Ran SP% **112.9**
Speed ratings (Par 93): **101,95,94,87,83 77**
CSF £2.41 TOTE £1.80: £1.30, £1.10; EX 2.70 Trifecta £6.10.
**Owner** Sheikh Hamdan bin Mohammed Al Maktoum **Bred** Godolphin **Trained** Middleham Moor, N Yorks
**FOCUS**
The ground has quickened through the day and is officially good to firm. All races are 2 yards further than advertised due to rail movements. Gamble landed here with Mark Johnston's winning newcomer looking a useful prospect. It's been rated conservatively for now.

### 2293 TOTEQUADPOT AT TOTESPORT.COM H'CAP 6f 210y
**5:35** (5:35) (Class 5) (0-75,77) 3-Y-O **£3,234** (£962; £481; £240) **Stalls** Centre

Form RPR
-446 **1** **El Torito (IRE)**[21] 1724 3-9-5 **73**............(p[1]) SamHitchcott 4 78
(Jim Boyle) *towards rr: pushed along after 2f: hdwy on inner 3f out: led 2f out: drvn ahd over 1f out: jst hld on* **12/1**
-152 **2** ½ **Spirit Of Sarwan (IRE)**[40] 1343 3-9-4 **75**............ ShelleyBirkett(3) 9 78
(Julia Feilden) *dwlt: bhd and sn rdn along: rapid hdwy fnl f: clsng fast at fin* **8/1**
105- **3** ½ **Miss Icon**[186] 7688 3-9-2 **70**............ DanielMuscutt 8 72
(Patrick Chamings) *mid-div: effrt and nt clr run 2f out: swtchd rt: gd late hdwy* **10/1**
6232 **4** ½ **No Not Again (IRE)**[27] 1580 3-8-7 **64**............ HollieDoyle(3) 2 64
(Richard Hannon) *led tl 2f out: kpt on u.p: lost 2nd fnl 50yds* **7/1**
-246 **5** ¾ **Jumping Jack (IRE)**[20] 1760 3-8-13 **74**............ StephenCummins(7) 6 72
(Richard Hughes) *dwlt: sn trcking ldrs: outpcd 3f out: kpt on fr over 1f out* **8/1**
35-6 **6** 1 ¼ **Teqany (IRE)**[26] 1609 3-9-6 **74**............ FranBerry 7 69
(Owen Burrows) *prom: rdn over 2f out: one pce appr fnl f* **4/1**[2]
000- **7** 1 **Farleigh Mac**[237] 6260 3-9-9 **77**............(h) LiamKeniry 3 69+
(Andrew Balding) *dwlt: plld hrd: trckd ldrs on inner tl wknd 1f out* **7/2**[1]
44-0 **8** 1 ¼ **Fire Palace**[13] 1907 3-9-8 **76**............ PaoloSirigu 5 65
(Robert Eddery) *pressed ldr tl 2f out: wknd over 1f out* **14/1**
40-4 **9** nk **Tawaafoq**[22] 1693 3-9-3 **71**............(h) TomMarquand 11 59
(Richard Hannon) *plld hrd: trckd ldrs on outer tl hrd rdn and wknd over 1f out* **6/1**[3]
430- **10** 3 ¾ **Twiggy**[173] 7898 3-8-11 **65**............(h) StevieDonohoe 10 43
(Jane Chapple-Hyam) *a bhd* **20/1**
1m 21.52s (-1.58) **Going Correction** -0.10s/f (Good) **10** Ran SP% **119.4**
Speed ratings (Par 99): **105,104,103,103,102 101,99,98,98,93**
CSF £106.84 CT £1034.29 TOTE £16.80: £3.90, £2.70, £3.20; EX 159.30 Trifecta £1764.60.
**Owner** The 'In Recovery' Partnership **Bred** Mary F Fogarty **Trained** Epsom, Surrey
**FOCUS**
Add 2yds. The most interesting event on the card was run at a good pace, the winner capitalising on a dream run up the far rail. The runner-up has been rated to his best.

### 2294 OXFAM TRAILWALKER CHALLENGE 29-30 JULY H'CAP 6f 210y
**6:05** (6:05) (Class 6) (0-55,57) 4-Y-O+ **£2,264** (£673; £336; £168) **Stalls** Centre

Form RPR
-065 **1** **Gypsy Rider**[8] 2053 8-8-12 **46** oh1............ StevieDonohoe 6 52
(Henry Tett) *chsd ldrs: rdn 3f out: led over 1f out: drvn out* **12/1**
222 **2** hd **Tidal's Baby**[26] 1603 8-9-9 **57**............ GeorgeDowning 2 62
(Tony Carroll) *towards rr: hrd rdn and hdwy whn edgd lft over 1f out: drew level ins fnl f: outbattled fnl 100yds* **5/2**[1]
500 **3** 2 ¾ **Dr Red Eye**[15] 1868 9-9-2 **50**............(p) JosephineGordon 9 48
(Scott Dixon) *led: rdn over 2f out: hdd over 1f out: kpt on same pce* **5/1**[3]
-030 **4** ½ **The Special One (IRE)**[35] 1425 4-9-6 **54**............(t[1]) TomMarquand 4 50
(Ali Stronge) *mid-div: hrd rdn and hdwy 2f out: one pce fnl f* **6/1**
00-0 **5** 1 **Machiavelian Storm (IRE)**[1] 2255 5-8-7 **46** oh1............ AliceMills(5) 12 40
(Richard Mitchell) *trckd ldrs: chal 2f out: no ex fnl f* **33/1**
-406 **6** 3 **Aye Aye Skipper (IRE)**[105] 293 7-8-12 **46** oh1............(t) SamHitchcott 7 31
(Ken Cunningham-Brown) *bhd: rdn 3f out: hdwy on inner 2f out: no ex fnl f* **9/1**
/0F0 **7** 1 ¼ **Mobley Chaos**[1] 2255 7-8-12 **46** oh1............(p) DanielMuscutt 11 28
(John Flint) *prom tl wknd over 1f out* **14/1**
0064 **8** ¾ **Misu Moneypenny**[35] 1435 4-9-7 **55**............ FranBerry 3 35
(Scott Dixon) *plld hrd in rr: rdn over 2f out: n.d* **12/1**
0/0 **9** 1 ½ **Dragon Khan (IRE)**[26] 1610 8-9-7 **55**............(b) TimmyMurphy 10 31
(John O'Shea) *a towards rr* **4/1**[2]
0000 **10** 13 **Tilly's Bridge**[13] 1894 4-8-12 **46**............(b[1]) LiamKeniry 5
(Steve Woodman) *mid-div: wknd over 2f out: sn bhd* **33/1**
1m 22.12s (-0.98) **Going Correction** -0.10s/f (Good) **10** Ran SP% **117.5**
Speed ratings (Par 101): **101,100,97,97,95 92,91,90,88,73**
CSF £42.50 CT £177.46 TOTE £12.20: £3.70, £1.10, £2.30; EX 45.30 Trifecta £305.70.
**Owner** The Racing 4 Fun Partnership **Bred** Mr And Mrs L Baker **Trained** Lambourn, Berks
**FOCUS**
Add 2yds. A strong pace produced a battling finish between two patiently ridden rivals. The winner was a 54 horse two years ago and he's been rated back to that sort of level.

### 2295 SETYRES H'CAP 1m 3f 198y
**6:35** (6:36) (Class 6) (0-60,58) 4-Y-O+ **£2,587** (£770; £384; £192) **Stalls** High

Form RPR
5-04 **1** **Albert Boy (IRE)**[29] 1545 4-9-4 **55**............ JosephineGordon 5 62
(Scott Dixon) *disp ld: led 3f out tl 2f out: rallied ins fnl f: led nr fin* **10/1**
-604 **2** ½ **Innoko (FR)**[28] 1560 7-9-5 **56**............(h) GeorgeDowning 2 62
(Tony Carroll) *towards rr: hdwy 3f out: led 2f out: drvn 2 l ahd: no ex and hdd nr fin* **15/2**
2325 **3** 1 ¾ **Go On Gal (IRE)**[29] 1548 4-9-4 **58**............ ShelleyBirkett(3) 4 61
(Julia Feilden) *cl up: jnd ldrs 3f out: rdn and styd on same pce fnl 2f* **6/1**
50-1 **4** nk **Avocadeau (IRE)**[12] 1937 6-9-4 **55**............(p) TimmyMurphy 8 58
(Stuart Kittow) *dwlt: sn prom: jnd ldrs 3f out: hrd rdn 2f out: styd on same pce* **9/1**
5013 **5** 2 **Tommys Geal**[18] 1789 5-9-7 **58**............ DanielMuscutt 3 58
(Michael Madgwick) *hld up in 6th: hdwy u.p and in tch 2f out: kpt on same pce fnl f* **7/2**[2]
4002 **6** 5 **Sir Jack**[1] 2257 4-9-6 **57**............ TomMarquand 1 49+
(Tony Carroll) *mid-div: pushed along 5f out: hdwy on inner and hrd rdn over 2f out: wknd over 1f out* **11/4**[1]
0-02 **7** 8 **Cockney Boy**[12] 1937 4-8-12 **54**............ PatrickO'Donnell(5) 9 36
(John Gallagher) *disp ld tl 3f out: wknd over 2f out* **11/2**[3]
360- **8** 22 **Fenner Hill Neasa (IRE)**[254] 5708 4-8-8 **45**............(h) SamHitchcott 6
(Pat Phelan) *s.s: t.k.h in rr: rdn and no ch fnl 3f* **25/1**
2m 33.37s (0.67) **Going Correction** -0.10s/f (Good) **8** Ran SP% **113.3**
Speed ratings (Par 101): **93,92,91,91,89 86,81,66**
CSF £80.05 CT £490.18 TOTE £9.90: £2.70, £2.00, £1.60; EX 79.00 Trifecta £434.70.
**Owner** J Radford **Bred** Clare Castle Farm **Trained** Babworth, Notts
■ Stewards' Enquiry : George Downing four-day ban: used whip above the permitted level (May 17-19, 21)
**FOCUS**
Add 2yds. Low-grade fare but another good finish, the winner battling back well in the final 100 yards. The third pins the level.

### 2296 BRIGHTONGIN.COM MAIDEN AUCTION STKS 1m 1f 207y
**7:05** (7:06) (Class 6) 3-Y-O **£2,587** (£770; £384; £192) **Stalls** High

Form RPR
0-3 **1** **Alnasl (IRE)**[6] 2110 3-8-7 0............(h) EdwardGreatrex(3) 4 65
(Archie Watson) *t.k.h in rr: hdwy on bit over 2f out: shkn up and led over 1f out: carried hd awkwardly: cajoled along and r.o* **4/9**[1]
552- **2** 1 ¾ **Makkadangdang**[189] 7605 3-9-3 74............ LiamKeniry 3 69
(Andrew Balding) *trckd ldr: led over 2f out tl over 1f out: unable qck ins fnl f* **2/1**[2]
040- **3** 17 **Break The Silence**[194] 7496 3-8-13 55............ JosephineGordon 1 31
(Scott Dixon) *chsd ldng pair: niggled along after 2f: wknd over 2f out* **16/1**[3]
000- **4** ¾ **Cadela Rica**[233] 6421 3-8-8 40............ DanielMuscutt 2 25
(Gay Kelleway) *led tl over 2f out: wknd wl over 1f out* **66/1**
2m 2.98s (-0.62) **Going Correction** -0.10s/f (Good) **4** Ran SP% **110.0**
Speed ratings (Par 97): **98,96,83,82**
CSF £1.64 TOTE £1.30; EX 1.90 Trifecta £2.40.
**Owner** K Sohi **Bred** Shadwell Estate Company Limited **Trained** Upper Lambourn, W Berks
**FOCUS**
Add 2yds. No strength in depth in this maiden and the pair with the best form pulled well clear. The winner has been rated a bit below her pre-race mark.

### 2297 COLLECT TOTEPOOL WINNINGS AT BETFRED SHOPS H'CAP 7f 211y
**7:35** (7:35) (Class 5) (0-70,70) 4-Y-O+ **£3,234** (£962; £481; £240) **Stalls** Centre

Form RPR
-013 **1** **Shifting Star (IRE)**[23] 1687 12-8-13 **62**............(vt) WilliamCarson 5 68
(John Bridger) *racd freely: mde all: edgd rt over 2f out: hld on gamely whn chal* **7/2**[3]
-061 **2** ¾ **Stormbound (IRE)**[8] 2057 8-9-4 **67** 6ex............(b) PatCosgrave 3 71
(Paul Cole) *chsd ldng pair: wnt 2nd 5f out: rdn to join wnr over 1f out: kpt on* **13/8**[1]
1242 **3** 3 ¼ **Wink Oliver**[8] 2064 5-9-6 **69**............(p) FranBerry 7 66
(Jo Hughes) *hld up in rr: hdwy over 2f out: rdn to chse ldrs over 1f out: no ex ins fnl f* **3/1**[2]
0035 **4** 3 ½ **Air Of York (IRE)**[1] 2256 5-8-13 **62**............(p) DanielMuscutt 8 50
(John Flint) *hld up in 4th: hrd rdn and wknd over 2f out* **11/2**
35-0 **5** ½ **Tarseekh**[23] 1687 4-8-12 **68**............ FinleyMarsh(7) 6 55
(Chris Gordon) *chsd wnr tl 5f out: wknd over 2f out* **8/1**
1m 35.8s (-0.20) **Going Correction** -0.10s/f (Good) **5** Ran SP% **111.8**
Speed ratings (Par 103): **97,96,93,89,89**
CSF £9.83 TOTE £4.90: £1.90, £1.10; EX 9.70 Trifecta £19.20.
**Owner** Night Shadow Syndicate **Bred** Hardys Of Kilkeel Ltd **Trained** Liphook, Hants
**FOCUS**
Add 2yds. Three non-runners saw some of the interest removed but it still featured some in-form candidates and the veteran winner rolled back the years with a game effort from the front. The runner-up has been rated to his best.

### 2298 COLOUR OBSTACLE RUSH BRIGHTON 6 MAY H'CAP 5f 215y
**8:05** (8:05) (Class 6) (0-55,57) 4-Y-O+ **£2,264** (£673; £336; £168) **Stalls** Centre

Form RPR
00-6 **1** **Sir Geoffrey (IRE)**[7] 2076 11-8-7 **45**............(b) PaddyPilley(5) 7 50
(Scott Dixon) *mde virtually all: hld on gamely fnl f* **11/1**
4223 **2** nk **Virile (IRE)**[8] 2053 6-9-5 **57**............(bt) MitchGodwin(5) 1 61
(Sylvester Kirk) *chsd ldrs: wnt 2nd over 2f out: drew nrly level w wnr ins fnl f: jst hld* **15/8**[1]
3000 **3** 2 **Deer Song**[28] 1557 4-8-12 **45**............ JosephineGordon 6 43
(John Bridger) *prom: rdn over 2f out: kpt on* **7/1**[3]
30P6 **4** ½ **Wedgewood Estates**[28] 1557 6-9-10 **57**............ TomMarquand 8 54
(Tony Carroll) *bhd: hdwy over 2f out: styd on fnl f* **6/1**[2]
-403 **5** 1 **Blistering Dancer (IRE)**[42] 1304 7-9-1 **48**............ GeorgeDowning 3 42
(Tony Carroll) *broke wl: chsd wnr tl over 2f out: one pce* **8/1**

0-00 **6** *nk* **Cooperess**[47] 1246 4-9-7 **54**..........................................(v[1]) TimmyMurphy 2 47
(John O'Shea) *towards rr: bmpd after 1f: styng on at fin* **10/1**
3406 **7** *5* **Great Expectations**[39] 1359 9-9-9 **56**...............................(vt) FranBerry 5 34
(J R Jenkins) *t.k.h towards rr: bmpd after 1f: n.d* **7/1**[3]
0250 **8** *2 ½* **Spowarticus**[39] 1372 8-8-10 **50**...................................(v) FinleyMarsh(7) 9 20
(Scott Dixon) *fair 5th tl wknd over 2f out* **8/1**
1m 9.57s (-0.63) **Going Correction** -0.10s/f (Good) **8** Ran SP% **113.7**
Speed ratings (Par 101): **100,99,96,96,94 94,87,84**
CSF £31.73 CT £159.79 TOTE £12.50: £3.70, £1.10, £2.50; EX 35.80 Trifecta £177.00.
**Owner** General Sir Geoffrey Howlett **Bred** P Rabbitte **Trained** Babworth, Notts
**FOCUS**
Add 2yds. A low-key end to proceedings but another game effort from a front-running veteran.
T/Plt: £60.80 to a £1 stake. Pool: £56,243.67. 675.01 winning units. T/Qpdt: £22.40 to a £1 stake. Pool: £5,348.50. 176.40 winning units. **Lee McKenzie**

## 2029 PONTEFRACT (L-H)
Wednesday, May 3

**OFFICIAL GOING: Good to firm (good in places; 9.1)**
Wind: Strong, against Weather: Cloudy and breezy, sunny periods

### 2299 WILLIAM HILL SUPPORTS THE NORTHERN RACING COLLEGE EBF NOVICE STKS (PLUS 10 RACE) 5f 3y
**2:15** (2:18) (Class 4) 2-Y-O **£4,528** (£1,347; £673; £336) **Stalls** Low

Form RPR
0 **1** **Brandy Station (IRE)**[23] 1673 2-9-2 0.............................. BarryMcHugh 1 76
(Tony Coyle) *qckly away: mde all: rdn over 1f out: kpt on strly* **33/1**
1 **2** *2 ¼* **Jasi (IRE)**[27] 1588 2-9-5 0........................................ AdamMcNamara(3) 8 74
(Richard Fahey) *chsd wnr: rdn along wl over 1f out: drvn and kpt on fnl f* **8/1**
**3** *1 ¼* **Ventura Dragon (IRE)** 2-9-2 0.................................. PaulHanagan 4 64+
(Richard Fahey) *dwlt and green: sn pushed along in rr: hdwy 2f out: kpt on fnl f* **2/1**[1]
**4** *nk* **Armed Response** 2-9-2 0................................................ JackGarritty 5 62
(Jedd O'Keeffe) *chsd ldng pair: rdn along wl over 1f out: kpt on same pce* **11/1**
3 **5** *4* **Marsh Storm (IRE)**[19] 1776 2-8-11 0.................................. PJMcDonald 3 43
(K R Burke) *chsd ldrs on inner: pushed along 3f out: rdn along 2f out: sn one pce* **3/1**[2]
**6** *¾* **Ventura Crest (IRE)** 2-9-2 0............................................. DavidAllan 2 45
(Tim Easterby) *in tch: pushed along 3f out: rdn 2f out: sn wknd* **33/1**
**7** *3* **Admiral Spice (IRE)** 2-9-2 0.................................. RichardKingscote 6 35+
(Tom Dascombe) *green: a towards rr* **7/2**[3]
**8** *6* **Prediction (IRE)** 2-9-2 0...................................................... TomEaves 7 13+
(Kevin Ryan) *dwlt: green: a rr* **8/1**
1m 3.63s (0.33) **Going Correction** -0.10s/f (Good) **8** Ran SP% **117.0**
Speed ratings (Par 95): **93,89,87,86,80 79,74,64**
CSF £277.00 TOTE £27.50: £6.20, £1.70, £1.50; EX 342.30 Trifecta £2339.50.
**Owner** Morecool Racing **Bred** Seamus Finucane **Trained** Norton, N Yorks
**FOCUS**
Probably a fair race to start the meeting off with despite the surprise winner. Two of the three with experience filled the first two positions.

### 2300 TOTEPOOL SUPPORTS THE NRC/BREEDERS BACKING RACING EBF MAIDEN STKS 1m 2f 5y
**2:50** (2:50) (Class 5) 3-Y-O **£4,528** (£1,347; £673; £336) **Stalls** Low

Form RPR
4 **1** **Mudaarab (USA)**[32] 1485 3-9-5 0.............................. RichardKingscote 4 85+
(Sir Michael Stoute) *mde all: jnd and rdn along wl over 1f out: drvn ent fnl f: kpt on wl towards fin* **7/4**[2]
23 **2** *1* **Hold Sway (IRE)**[32] 1497 3-9-5 0...................................... MartinLane 5 83
(Charlie Appleby) *wnt rt s: sn trcking wnr: hdwy and cl up 2f out: rdn to chal over 1f out: drvn and ev ch ins fnl f: rdr dropped whip: kpt on same pce last 100yds* **4/6**[1]
22- **3** *2 ½* **Warm Love**[225] 6640 3-9-0 0............................................. MartinHarley 1 73
(David O'Meara) *trckd ldng pair: effrt over 2f out: sn pushed along and sltly outpcd: rdn over 1f out: kpt on fnl f* **8/1**[3]
0 **4** *26* **Silk Trader (IRE)**[23] 1675 3-9-0 0...................................... PaddyAspell 2 21
(Sharon Watt) *hld up: hdwy to chse ldrs over 3f out: rdn along wl over 2f out: sn outpcd* **100/1**
6 **5** *30* **Company Trader (IRE)**[22] 1701 3-9-5 0.............................. GrahamLee 3
(Sharon Watt) *chsd ldrs: hdwy on wd outside 1/2-way: rdn along 3f out: sn outpcd and bhd* **100/1**
2m 12.95s (-0.75) **Going Correction** -0.10s/f (Good) **5** Ran SP% **109.4**
Speed ratings (Par 99): **99,98,96,75,51**
CSF £3.19 TOTE £2.70: £1.50, £1.10; EX 3.50 Trifecta £4.40.
**Owner** Hamdan Al Maktoum **Bred** Grousemont Farm **Trained** Newmarket, Suffolk
**FOCUS**
Only three of the five made any obvious interest in the betting, and two of them dominated the final stages. The runner-up and third have been rated close to their marks.

### 2301 BETFRED SUPPORTS THE NORTHERN RACING COLLEGE H'CAP 1m 6y
**3:25** (3:26) (Class 5) (0-75,77) 4-Y-O+ **£3,881** (£1,155; £577; £288) **Stalls** Low

Form RPR
0362 **1** **Ravenhoe (IRE)**[4] 2153 4-9-2 **70**..................................... FrannyNorton 1 75
(Mark Johnston) *trckd ldng pair: effrt and nt clr run over v1f out: swtchd to inner ent fnl f: sn rdn and kpt on wl to ld last 100 yds* **11/4**[2]
1-50 **2** *1* **Tellovoi (IRE)**[6] 2116 9-9-6 **74**..................................(h) ConnorBeasley 6 77
(Richard Guest) *trckd ldr: pushed along 3f out: rdn over 2f out: drvn to chal over 1f out: kpt on u.p fnl f* **9/1**
1415 **3** *½* **Celtic Artisan (IRE)**[34] 1449 6-9-2 **70**..............................(bt) NeilFarley 2 72
(Rebecca Menzies) *led: pushed along over 2f out: rdn over 1f out: drvn and edgd rt ins fnl f: hdd last 100 yds: no ex* **16/1**
15-0 **4** *3* **Stanley (GER)**[22] 1700 6-9-8 **76**........................................ GrahamLee 10 71+
(Jonjo O'Neill) *hld up in rr: hdwy on outer 2f out: sn rdn along and kpt on fnl f* **9/1**
5600 **5** *1* **Trinity Star (IRE)**[22] 1700 6-8-13 **67**...........................(p) PaulMulrennan 8 60+
(Michael Dods) *dwlt and rr: hdwy over 2f out: rdn along wl over 1f out: plugged on fnl f* **9/1**
6-05 **6** *1 ¾* **Gambit**[11] 1969 4-9-7 **75**..........................................(t[1]) RichardKingscote 5 64
(Tom Dascombe) *trckd ldrs: effrt over 2f out: sn rdn along and wknd wl over 1f out* **5/2**[1]
0400 **7** *¾* **Hernando Torres**[11] 1969 9-8-5 **66**.............................. HarrisonShaw(7) 7 53
(Michael Easterby) *dwlt: hld up: a rr* **25/1**
645- **8** *2* **Frankster (FR)**[181] 7780 4-8-13 **67**...................................(t) PJMcDonald 4 49
(Micky Hammond) *in tch: rdn along wl over 2f out: sn btn* **20/1**
546- **9** *2 ½* **Popsies Joy (IRE)**[216] 6908 4-8-12 **66**................................... DavidAllan 3 43
(Tim Easterby) *chsd ldrs: rdn along wl over 2f out: sn wknd* **7/1**[3]
1m 44.09s (-1.81) **Going Correction** -0.10s/f (Good) **9** Ran SP% **112.2**
Speed ratings (Par 103): **105,104,103,100,99 97,97,95,92**
CSF £26.69 CT £329.12 TOTE £3.60: £1.30, £3.20, £4.30; EX 29.20 Trifecta £220.60.
**Owner** Kingsley Park 6 **Bred** Miss Linda Lyons **Trained** Middleham Moor, N Yorks
**FOCUS**
A fair handicap and being prominent proved to be an advantage. The runner-up has been rated to last year's turf form.

### 2302 CORAL SUPPORTS THE NORTHERN RACING COLLEGE FILLIES' H'CAP 1m 2f 5y
**4:00** (4:00) (Class 4) (0-85,81) 3-Y-O-**£7,470** (£2,236; £1,118; £559; £279) **Stalls** Low

Form RPR
622- **1** **Melodic Motion (IRE)**[182] 7770 3-8-10 **78**.......................... PaulHanagan 3 84+
(Ralph Beckett) *trckd ldrs: hdwy 2f out: rdn to chse ldng pair over 1f out: styd on wl to ld nr fin* **13/8**[1]
451- **2** *hd* **Celestation**[221] 6762 3-8-7 **75**............................................ FrannyNorton 5 80
(Mark Johnston) *led: jnd and pushed along over 2f out: sn rdn and hdd jst over 1f out: drvn ins fnl f: rallied gamely to ld again last 100 yds:. hdd and no ex nr fin* **9/2**[3]
01- **3** *1 ¼* **Mittens**[188] 7647 3-8-11 **79**.......................................... RichardKingscote 6 82+
(Sir Michael Stoute) *trckd ldr: cl up 3f out: chal 2f out: rdn to ld jst over 1f out: sn drvn and hdd last 100 yds: kpt on same pce* **2/1**[2]
413- **4** *4* **Desert Way (IRE)**[264] 5382 4-10-0 **81**................................ PJMcDonald 2 77
(Rebecca Menzies) *trckd ldng pair on inner: pushed along 3f out: rdn over 2f out: kpt on same pce* **12/1**
120- **5** *¾* **Luna Mare (IRE)**[214] 6951 4-9-8 **78**......................... AdamMcNamara(3) 1 72
(Richard Fahey) *rr: pushed along over 3f out: rdn wl over 2f out: n.d* **7/1**
2m 11.77s (-1.93) **Going Correction** -0.10s/f (Good)
**WFA** 3 from 4yo 15lb **5** Ran SP% **109.8**
Speed ratings (Par 102): **103,102,101,98,98**
CSF £9.17 TOTE £2.50: £1.30, £1.70; EX 8.30 Trifecta £18.10.
**Owner** Qatar Racing Limited **Bred** Old Carhue & Graeng Bloodstock **Trained** Kimpton, Hants
**FOCUS**
An interesting race for fillies, in which the three 3yos dominated. The level is a bit fluid, with the first three all up in trip.

### 2303 TRUSTEES OF THE NORTHERN RACING COLLEGE H'CAP 6f
**4:35** (4:36) (Class 4) (0-80,81) 4-Y-O+ **£5,175** (£1,540; £769; £384) **Stalls** Low

Form RPR
06-1 **1** **Gin In The Inn (IRE)**[16] 1833 4-9-8 **81**.............................. PaulHanagan 2 98
(Richard Fahey) *trckd ldrs: smooth hdwy and cl up wl over 1f out: led appr fnl f: sn qcknd clr: easily* **11/10**[1]
00-0 **2** *6* **Johnny Cavagin**[31] 1512 8-9-8 **81**....................................(t) JimmyQuinn 9 79
(Ronald Thompson) *blind removed late and dwlt: rr: hdwy 2f out: sn rdn: styd on u.p fnl f: no ch w wnr* **10/1**
03-0 **3** *½* **Racquet**[11] 1971 4-8-13 **72**............................................... JamesSullivan 5 68
(Ruth Carr) *set stdy pce: pushed along and qcknd 1/2-way: rdn and hdd 2f out: cl up and drvn over 1f out: kpt on one pce* **25/1**
26-0 **4** *¾* **Mr Orange (IRE)**[21] 1717 4-8-10 **69**...........................(p) DougieCostello 8 63
(Paul Midgley) *chsd ldrs: rdn along 2f out: sn drvn and kpt on one pce* **11/1**
5-44 **5** *1 ½* **Yeeoow (IRE)**[27] 1592 8-9-7 **80**........................................ MartinHarley 11 69
(K R Burke) *trckd ldr: cl up 1/2-way: rdn to ld 2f out: drvn and hdd appr fnl f: sn wknd* **20/1**
00-5 **6** *nk* **Still On Top**[13] 1910 4-8-13 **72**..........................................(h) DavidAllan 10 60
(Tim Easterby) *rr: rdn along 1/2-way: sn drvn and n.d* **7/1**[3]
04-0 **7** *4* **Quick Look**[27] 1586 4-9-3 **79**........................................ NathanEvans(3) 3 54
(Michael Easterby) *chsd ldrs: rdn over 2f out: sn wknd* **3/1**[2]
1m 15.67s (-1.23) **Going Correction** -0.10s/f (Good) **7** Ran SP% **111.2**
Speed ratings (Par 105): **104,96,95,94,92 91,86**
CSF £12.65 CT £164.28 TOTE £2.00: £1.20, £4.20; EX 13.60 Trifecta £153.20.
**Owner** Dean Hardman and Stella Hardman **Bred** Colman O'Flynn **Trained** Musley Bank, N Yorks
**FOCUS**
Four of the declared runners came out during the day, which changed the look of the race, and the favourite won with plenty in hand. The form is all about the winner, and he could be rated a few pounds better at face value.

### 2304 COLONEL AND MRS PADGETT H'CAP 6f
**5:10** (5:10) (Class 5) (0-75,77) 3-Y-O **£3,881** (£1,155; £577; £288) **Stalls** Low

Form RPR
36-2 **1** **Suitcase 'N' Taxi**[13] 1913 3-8-12 **66**..................................... DavidAllan 10 76+
(Tim Easterby) *qckly away: led and sn swtchd lft to inner rail: rdn clr wl over 1f out: strayed on strly* **9/1**
103- **2** *2 ¾* **Springforth**[201] 7330 3-8-12 **66**........................................ JackGarritty 6 66
(Richard Fahey) *trckd ldrs: hdwy and swtchd rt 11/2f out: sn rdn: chsd wnr ins fnl f: no imp* **14/1**
106- **3** *1 ¼* **Halawain (USA)**[202] 7305 3-9-7 **75**...................................... JasonHart 3 71
(John Quinn) *t.k.h early: trckd ldrs on inner: hdwy over 2f out: rdn wl over 1f out: kpt on fnl f* **12/1**
230- **4** *1 ¼* **Mont Royal (FR)**[223] 6712 3-9-3 **71**.................................. MartinHarley 2 63+
(Ollie Pears) *towards rr: hdwy 2f out: n.m.r 11/2f out: sn rdn and kpt on fnl f: nrst fin* **8/1**[3]
240- **5** *1* **Yarmouk (FR)**[179] 7820 3-9-0 **68**....................................... PaulHanagan 5 57
(Richard Fahey) *chsd ldrs on outer: rdn along 2f out: drvn over 1f out: kpt on one pce* **9/2**[2]
1143 **6** *shd* **Intense Romance (IRE)**[13] 1913 3-9-2 **70**.................... PaulMulrennan 9 58
(Michael Dods) *trckd wnr: cl up 1/2-way: rdn 2f out: drvn wl over 1f out: grad wknd fnl f* **8/1**[3]
321- **7** *nk* **Trooper's Gold**[201] 7328 3-9-9 **77**........................................ TomEaves 7 65
(Kevin Ryan) *towards rr: pushed along on outer 1/2-way: rdn and hdwy wl over 1f out: kpt on fnl f: nrst fin* **10/3**[1]
55-4 **8** *1* **Sugar Beach (FR)**[22] 1705 3-9-0 **68**..................................... GrahamLee 4 52
(Ann Duffield) *prom: rdn along 2f out: sn drvn and wknd over 1f out* **12/1**
06-2 **9** *½* **Red Gunner**[102] 356 3-9-4 **77**........................................ JoshDoyle(5) 1 60
(David O'Meara) *dwlt: sn in tch on inner: rdn along 2f out: drvn and wknd over 1f out* **8/1**[3]
340- **10** *1* **Flash Of White**[222] 6743 3-9-3 **71**................................ ConnorBeasley 11 51
(Bryan Smart) *dwlt: a rr* **20/1**
02-0 **11** *13* **Cupid's Arrow (IRE)**[13] 1913 3-8-11 **65**........................ JamesSullivan 8 3
(Ruth Carr) *hmpd sn after s: a rr:rdn 2f out: sn outpcd and eased* **16/1**
1m 15.89s (-1.01) **Going Correction** -0.10s/f (Good) **11** Ran SP% **117.3**
Speed ratings (Par 99): **102,98,96,95,93 93,93,91,91,89 72**
CSF £127.49 CT £1551.41 TOTE £11.10: £2.50, £6.00, £4.80; EX 185.30 Trifecta £2303.30.

**Owner** Ontoawinner 10 & Partner 3 **Bred** Crossfields Bloodstock Ltd **Trained** Great Habton, N Yorks

**FOCUS**

A competitive-looking sprint but it was taken in clear style by the front-running winner. It's been rated around the runner-up to his 2yo form.

## 2305 GO RACING IN YORKSHIRE FUTURE STARS APPRENTICE H'CAP (ROUND 3) 5f 3y

**5:45** (5:45) (Class 5) (0-70,76) 4-Y-0+ **£3,234** (£962; £481; £240) **Stalls** Low

Form RPR

0031 **1** **Oriental Relation (IRE)**[9] 2034 6-9-13 **76** 6ex.......(b) CallumRodriguez 7 79
*(James Given) cl up: led after 1f: jnd and rdn 2f out: drvn and hdd ins fnl f: rallied gamely to ld again last 75 yds: jst hld on* **7/4**[1]

0311 **2** *nse* **Noah Amor (IRE)**[11] 1973 4-9-1 **69**.......ConnorMurtagh(5) 2 72
*(Richard Fahey) qckly away and led 1f: cl up: rdn to chal over 1f out: led ins fnl f: drvn and hdd last 75 yds: rallied towards fin: jst hld* **11/4**[2]

3441 **3** *1 ½* **Space War**[14] 1887 10-9-1 **69**.......(t) RyanTimby(5) 5 67
*(Michael Easterby) hmpd s and bhd: stdy hdwy 1/2-way: rdn wl over 1f out: styd on wl fnl f* **14/1**

2-23 **4** *hd* **Horsforth**[49] 1200 5-8-13 **65**.......(b) BenSanderson(3) 8 62
*(Richard Guest) chsd ldng pair: hdwy over 2f out and sn cl up: rdn to chal over 1f out: drvn ent fnl f: kpt on same pce* **9/1**

10-0 **5** *½* **Bond Bombshell**[16] 1828 4-9-9 **72**.......PatrickVaughan 6 67
*(David O'Meara) chsd ldrs: rdn along 2f out: sn drvn and kpt on fnl f* **25/1**

5025 **6** *hd* **Burtonwood**[14] 1887 5-9-1 **67**.......KieranSchofield(3) 1 61
*(Julie Camacho) dwlt and rr: hdwy 2f out: sn rdn and styd on fnl f* **5/1**[3]

06-6 **7** *7* **Spike (IRE)**[11] 1979 4-8-9 **63**.......SeamusCronin(5) 4 32
*(Donald McCain) in tch: rdn along over 2f out: sn wknd* **25/1**

0-00 **8** *15* **Bop It**[11] 1972 8-8-13 **67**.......(t) HarrisonShaw(5) 3
*(Michael Easterby) chsd ldrs: rdn along wl over 2f out: sn wknd and bhd* **12/1**

1m 3.19s (-0.11) **Going Correction** -0.10s/f (Good) **8** Ran SP% **111.7**
Speed ratings (Par 103): **96,95,93,93,92 92,80,56**
CSF £6.22 CT £45.36 TOTE £2.70: £1.10, £1.30, £2.50; EX 6.80 Trifecta £28.90.
**Owner** The Cool Silk Partnership **Bred** Brendan Laffan & Michael McCormick **Trained** Willoughton, Lincs

**FOCUS**

Just a modest sprint handicap for apprentices. The winner has been rated similar to his C&D latest, with the runner-up to his best.

T/Plt: £82.60 to a £1 stake. Pool: £58,993.17. 521.08 winning units. T/Qpdt: £25.60 to a £1 stake. Pool: £3,901.38. 112.60 winning units. **Joe Rowntree**

# 2272 WOLVERHAMPTON (A.W) (L-H)

Wednesday, May 3

**OFFICIAL GOING: Tapeta: standard**

Wind: Fresh, against final 2f Weather: Overcast

## 2306 BRC ROOFING'S SPRINT SPECTACULAR H'CAP 6f 20y (Tp)

**1:20** (1:20) (Class 6) (0-60,62) 3-Y-0+ **£2,264** (£673; £336; £168) **Stalls** Low

Form RPR

00-0 **1** **Whitecrest**[11] 1965 9-9-9 **60**.......LewisEdmunds(5) 3 68
*(John Spearing) broke wl: nt clr run and lost pl over 5f out: hdwy over 1f out: hung lft and r.o to ld wl ins fnl f* **18/1**

0000 **2** *1 ½* **Insolenceofoffice (IRE)**[37] 1407 9-8-9 **48**.......(v) CallumRodriguez(7) 12 52
*(Richard Ford) prom: chsd ldr 5f out tl led over 1f out: rdn and hdd wl ins fnl f* **22/1**

142 **3** *¾* **Strictly Carter**[8] 2069 4-9-11 **57**.......JimmyFortune 4 61
*(Alan Bailey) hld up: hdwy over 1f out: running on whn rn out of room ins fnl f: wnt 3rd nr fin: nvr able to chal* **4/1**[3]

0-05 **4** *nk* **Dalalah**[11] 1978 4-9-2 **48**.......(v) SeanLevey 9 48
*(Richard Guest) chsd ldrs: edgd lft over 5f out: rdn over 1f out: sn hung lft: styd on same pce ins fnl f* **8/1**

64-5 **5** *½* **Zavikon**[68] 904 3-9-6 **62**.......(h[1]) RyanTate 6 58
*(Richard Hughes) hld up: rdn over 2f out: r.o ins fnl f: nvr nrr* **7/2**[2]

0000 **6** *hd* **Chillililli**[8] 2065 3-7-11 **46** oh1.......(p) JaneElliott(7) 2 41
*(Michael Appleby) sn led: rdn and hdd over 1f out: no ex ins fnl f* **50/1**

3401 **7** *2* **Castlerea Tess**[11] 1979 4-9-12 **58**.......(p) KieranO'Neill 1 50
*(Sarah Hollinshead) chsd ldrs: rdn over 2f out: wknd wl ins fnl f* **11/2**

53-5 **8** *1 ¾* **The Big Short**[11] 1970 3-9-3 **59**.......BenCurtis 7 43
*(Charles Hills) s.i.s: hld up: plld hrd: hung rt fr over 3f out: rdn over 2f out: nvr on terms* **5/2**[1]

1m 14.31s (-0.19) **Going Correction** -0.10s/f (Stan)
**WFA** 3 from 4yo+ 10lb **8** Ran SP% **108.9**
Speed ratings (Par 101): **97,95,94,93,92 92,90,87**
CSF £305.40 CT £1748.38 TOTE £15.10: £5.00, £3.30, £1.70; EX 511.40 Trifecta £1943.40.
**Owner** G M Eales **Bred** J Spearing And Kate Ive **Trained** Kinnersley, Worcs

**FOCUS**

A modest sprint handicap. They went a decent gallop on standard Tapeta into a fresh headwind in the straight. The runner-up has been rated as stepping up on his recent form.

## 2307 HS BUTYL MAIDEN FILLIES' STKS (PLUS 10 RACE) 1m 4f 51y (Tp)

**1:50** (1:51) (Class 5) 3-Y-0 **£3,234** (£962; £481; £240) **Stalls** Low

Form RPR

3 **1** **Pleasant Surprise (IRE)**[14] 1874 3-9-0 0.......JimmyFortune 4 73+
*(Luca Cumani) mde all: set stdy pce tl qckd over 2f out: wnt readily clr fr over 1f out: easily* **4/6**[1]

00- **2** *6* **Plage Depampelonne**[194] 7494 3-9-0 0.......KevinStott 2 60
*(James Bethell) chsd ldrs: rdn over 2f out: styd on same pce fr over 1f out: wnt 2nd wl ins fnl f* **50/1**

6- **3** *1 ½* **Doreen**[203] 7285 3-8-11 0.......KieranShoemark(3) 6 58
*(Sir Michael Stoute) chsd wnr: rdn over 2f out: wkng whn lost 2nd wl ins fnl f* **7/2**[2]

6-0 **4** *¾* **Mirzam (IRE)**[12] 1944 3-9-0 0.......RyanTate 5 57
*(Mick Channon) chsd ldrs: shkn up over 2f out: btn whn hung lft over 1f out* **13/2**

-0 **5** *2 ¼* **Vaudieu**[28] 1552 3-8-11 0.......(b) JackDuern(3) 1 53
*(Dean Ivory) hld up: rdn over 3f out: nvr on terms* **80/1**

00 **6** *nse* **Navajo Grey (IRE)**[11] 1967 3-9-0 0.......LiamJones 8 53
*(Michael Appleby) hld up: rdn over 2f out: sme hdwy over 1f out: wknd fnl f* **66/1**

**7** *1 ½* **Breton Belle (IRE)** 3-9-0 0.......HarryBentley 7 51
*(David Simcock) hld up: shkn up and wknd over 2f out* **6/1**[3]

U- **U** **Asmahan**[140] 8355 3-9-0 0.......RyanPowell 3
*(Simon Crisford) unruly leaving stalls and sn uns rdr* **14/1**

2m 39.98s (-0.82) **Going Correction** -0.10s/f (Stan) **8** Ran SP% **121.2**
Speed ratings (Par 96): **98,94,93,92,91 90,89,**
CSF £51.63 TOTE £1.60: £1.10, £5.80, £1.50; EX 27.50 Trifecta £88.40.
**Owner** Gerry Mordaunt & Partners **Bred** Dreaming Partnership **Trained** Newmarket, Suffolk

**FOCUS**

A fair 3yo middle-distance fillies' maiden. The short-priced favourite proved thoroughly dominant off her own increasing tempo. Muddling form.

## 2308 RINUS ROOFING SUPPLIES H'CAP 1m 4f 51y (Tp)

**2:25** (2:25) (Class 6) (0-65,65) 4-Y-0+ **£1,468** (£1,468; £336; £168) **Stalls** Low

Form RPR

4023 **1** **Pour L'Amour (IRE)**[28] 1560 4-9-0 **63**.......CharlieBennett(5) 4 70
*(Daniel Mark Loughnane) hld up: hdwy over 3f out: wnt 2nd over 1f out: rdn and r.o to join wnr on line* **5/1**[3]

123- **1** *dht* **Reckless Wave (IRE)**[137] 8428 4-9-4 **62**.......ThomasBrown 3 69
*(Ed Walker) hld up in tch: chsd ldr over 3f out tl led wl over 2f out: rdn over 1f out: styd on: jnd on line* **11/4**[1]

5301 **3** *4* **Star Ascending (IRE)**[11] 1985 5-9-0 **58**.......(p) KevinStott 2 59
*(Jennie Candlish) dwlt: hld up: hdwy 2f out: rdn over 1f out: no imp ins fnl f* **9/2**[2]

61-0 **4** *2 ¾* **Infiniti (IRE)**[26] 1610 4-8-4 **55**.......JaneElliott(7) 6 51
*(Barry Leavy) hld up: hdwy on outer over 2f out: rdn over 1f out: no ex fnl f* **50/1**

6/0- **5** *½* **Callaghan (GER)**[153] 2652 4-9-0 **63**.......(t) LewisEdmunds(5) 8 58
*(Tom Gretton) hld up: hdwy 2f out: nt clr run over 1f out: styd on same pce* **40/1**

6-60 **6** *12* **Teak (IRE)**[14] 1891 10-9-0 **65**.......(p) LukeCatton(7) 1 41
*(Ian Williams) sn pushed along to chse ldrs: drvn over 4f out: nt clr run and lost pl over 3f out: sn wknd* **50/1**

4-24 **7** *¾* **Inflexiball**[15] 1864 5-9-0 **58**.......BenCurtis 9 33
*(John Mackie) hld up in tch: rdn over 2f out: wknd over 1f out* **7/1**

0000 **8** *3 ½* **Archipeligo**[14] 1891 6-9-5 **63**.......DavidNolan 5 32
*(Iain Jardine) chsd ldrs: nt clr run over 3f out: lost pl over 2f out* **9/2**[2]

00/2 **9** *28* **Leonardo (GER)**[9] 2042 5-8-7 **51** oh2.......MartinDwyer 7 +
*(Mark Pitman) racd keenly in 2nd pl tl led 10f out: rdn and hdd wl over 2f out: sn wknd* **11/2**

30-0 **10** *59* **Competent**[15] 1864 5-9-0 **63**.......PhilDennis(5) 10 +
*(Tim Fitzgerald) led 2f: chsd ldr: rdn over 6f out: lost 2nd over 3f out: sn wknd and eased* **33/1**

2m 37.85s (-2.95) **Going Correction** -0.10s/f (Stan) **10** Ran SP% **116.9**
Speed ratings (Par 101): **105,105,102,100,100 92,91,89,70,31**
WIN: PL 2.60, RW 2.00; PL: PL 1.60, RW 2.20, SA 1.90; EX: PL-RW 9.20, RW-PL 7.40; CSF: PL-RW 9.42, RW-PL 8.20; TC: PL-RW-SA 32.95, RW-PL-SA 29.60; TF: PL-RW-SA 33.50, RW-PL-SA 25.60.
**Owner** Mrs C Loughnane **Bred** Limestone And Tara Studs **Trained** Rock, Worcs
**Owner** Mrs T Walker **Bred** John Connaughton **Trained** Upper Lambourn, Berks

**FOCUS**

A modest middle-distance handicap. They went a respectable gallop and two of the more likely sorts beforehand still couldn't be separated at the finish. The third has been rated just below his recent effort.

## 2309 POLYROOF ADVANCED LIQUID ROOFING H'CAP 7f 36y (Tp)

**3:00** (3:00) (Class 6) (0-60,63) 3-Y-0 **£2,587** (£770; £384; £192) **Stalls** High

Form RPR

65-0 **1** **Cryptonite (IRE)**[21] 1730 3-9-2 **58**.......AlistairRawlinson(3) 4 62+
*(Michael Appleby) sn led: hdd over 5f out: chsd ldr tl led again 3f out: rdn over 1f out: jst hld on* **5/2**[1]

600- **2** *nk* **Pass The Cristal (IRE)**[210] 7064 3-9-2 **55**.......MartinDwyer 2 59
*(William Muir) hld up: plld hrd: nt clr run wl over 1f out: hdwy sn after: rdn and edgd lft ins fnl f: r.o wl* **10/3**[2]

0440 **3** *nk* **Captain Sedgwick (IRE)**[35] 1428 3-8-1 **47**.......JaneElliott(7) 5 50
*(John Spearing) sn prom: pushed along 1/2-way: rdn over 1f out: nt clr run ins fnl f: r.o* **33/1**

300- **4** *hd* **Bridal March**[203] 7286 3-9-7 **60**.......BenCurtis 9 63
*(John Mackie) chsd ldrs: rdn over 1f out: edgd lft: r.o* **16/1**

1442 **5** *hd* **Viola Park**[28] 1564 3-9-1 **54**.......(b[1]) RyanPowell 8 56
*(Ronald Harris) sn pushed along towards rr: hdwy to ld over 5f out: hdd 3f out: rdn over 1f out: styng on whn hmpd last strides* **11/2**[3]

305- **6** *1 ¼* **Fair Selene**[134] 8467 3-9-1 **59**.......(p) LewisEdmunds(5) 10 58
*(Heather Main) s.i.s: hld up: rdn over 1f out: r.o towards fin: nvr nrr* **7/1**

00-0 **7** *½* **Delagate This Lord**[9] 2017 3-9-6 **59**.......(p[1]) FergusSweeney 1 57
*(Bill Turner) hld up in tch: lost pl over 2f out: r.o ins fnl f* **16/1**

-346 **8** *2 ¾* **Luduamf (IRE)**[9] 2018 3-9-6 **59**.......KieranO'Neill 12 50
*(Richard Hannon) mid-div: pushed along over 4f out: rdn on outer over 2f out: sn lost pl* **13/2**

0620 **9** *2 ¾* **Tink**[28] 1564 3-8-5 **49**.......(p) CharlieBennett(5) 6 33
*(Mark Brisbourne) hld up: plld hrd: hmpd 4f out: sme hdwy over 1f out: sn rdn and hung rt: wknd fnl f* **33/1**

4005 **10** *5* **Mesmeric Moment**[17] 1821 3-8-7 **46** oh1.......(b[1]) RoystonFfrench 3 18
*(Shaun Harris) chsd ldrs: rdn over 2f out: wknd over 1f out* **66/1**

1m 28.97s (0.17) **Going Correction** -0.10s/f (Stan) **10** Ran SP% **112.0**
Speed ratings (Par 97): **95,94,94,94,93 92,91,88,85,79**
CSF £10.03 CT £206.87 TOTE £3.40: £1.30, £1.50, £8.80; EX 13.80 Trifecta £266.80.
**Owner** C L Bacon **Bred** Yeomanstown Stud **Trained** Oakham, Rutland

**FOCUS**

A modest 7f 3yo handicap. The favourite proved a tough customer from a prominent pitch throughout. They finished in a heap.

## 2310 "UP ON THE ROOF" H'CAP 1m 142y (Tp)

**3:35** (3:35) (Class 3) (0-95,95) 4-Y-0 **£7,246** (£2,168; £1,084; £542; £270) **Stalls** Low

Form RPR

54-2 **1** **Ballard Down (IRE)**[35] 1422 4-8-11 **85**.......(v[1]) HarryBentley 6 96
*(William Knight) prom: racd keenly: shkn up to ld and hung lft ins fnl f: r.o wl* **7/2**[3]

102- **2** *3 ¾* **Makzeem**[186] 7699 4-8-11 **88**.......KieranShoemark(3) 3 90
*(Roger Charlton) chsd ldrs: rdn to ld 1f out: sn hdd: and outpcd* **15/8**[1]

4346 **3** *½* **Bold Prediction (IRE)**[19] 1766 7-8-11 **85**.......ThomasBrown 2 86
*(Ed Walker) anticipated the s: led: qcknd over 2f out: rdn and hdd 1f out: styd on same pce* **11/1**

-123 **4** *¾* **Count Montecristo (FR)**[13] 1911 5-8-10 **84**.......KevinStott 4 83
*(Kevin Ryan) racd keenly in 2nd pl: rdn and ev ch over 1f out: no ex ins fnl f* **3/1**[2]

0-00 **5** *2 ¾* **General Macarthur (USA)**[81] 698 4-9-2 **95**.......GeorgeBuckell(5) 5 88
*(David Simcock) hld up: shkn up over 2f out: nt trble ldrs* **7/1**

203- **6** 3 ¼ **Mikmak**140 8356 4-8-10 **84**.............. MartinDwyer 1 69
(William Muir) *hld up: shkn up over 2f out: outpcd over 1f out* **12/1**

1m 47.5s (-2.60) **Going Correction** -0.10s/f (Stan) **6** Ran SP% **110.5**
Speed ratings (Par 107): **107,103,103,102,100 97**
CSF £10.17 TOTE £4.30: £2.30, £1.20; EX 13.70 Trifecta £57.80.
**Owner** Angmering Park Thoroughbreds I **Bred** D Harron, Ederidge Ltd & Glenvale Stud **Trained** Patching, W Sussex

**FOCUS**
The feature contest was a good handicap. They went a respectable gallop and a slightly wayward horse with decent form showed the benefit of first-time headgear. The runner-up has been rated close to form.

## 2311 ROOF CARE (NORTH STAFFS) LTD MAIDEN FILLIES' STKS (PLUS 10 RACE) 1m 142y (Tp)
**4:10** (4:11) (Class 5) 3-Y-O **£3,234** (£962; £481; £240) **Stalls** Low

Form RPR
0-0 **1** **Vice Versa**14 1885 3-8-11 0.............. KieranShoemark(3) 11 78
(Sir Michael Stoute) *w ldr tl led 7f out: rdn over 1f out: styd on gamely* **25/1**
2 **2** *nk* **Jalela**15 1857 3-9-0 0.............. SeanLevey 5 77
(Richard Hannon) *chsd ldrs: rdn over 2f out: ev ch ins fnl f: styd on* **5/6**1
3- **3** 1 ½ **Margherita**233 6414 3-8-7 0.............. DavidEgan(7) 6 74
(Roger Varian) *chsd ldrs: rdn and ev ch over 1f out: styd on same pce ins fnl f* **13/2**3
0- **4** 1 **Melinoe**233 6413 3-9-0 0.............. RyanPowell 3 71+
(Sir Mark Prescott Bt) *hld up: hdwy over 2f out: shkn up and wandered ins fnl f: styd on* **80/1**
2-2 **5** 1 **Spinnaka (IRE)**13 1905 3-9-0 0.............. JimmyFortune 10 69+
(Luca Cumani) *half rrd s: hld up: hdwy on outer over 2f out: shkn up over 1f out: styd on: nt trble ldrs* **9/2**2
0 **6** *hd* **Charming Loza**14 1885 3-9-0 0.............. HarryBentley 7 68
(Charlie Fellowes) *hld up: nt clr run and swtchd rt over 1f out: r.o ins fnl f: nvr nrr* **50/1**
**7** ¾ **Golden State (USA)**189 7632 3-9-0 0.............. BenCurtis 2 67
(Archie Watson) *led: hdd 7f out: chsd wnr tl rdn over 2f out: no ex ins fnl f* **13/2**3
**8** *hd* **Light Of Joy (USA)** 3-9-0 0.............. FergusSweeney 4 66+
(David Lanigan) *s.i.s: rn green in rr: nt clr run over 1f out: r.o towards fin* **33/1**
06- **9** ½ **Moonlight Silver**140 8355 3-9-0 0.............. MartinDwyer 8 65
(William Muir) *hld up in tch: racd keenly: shkn up and nt clr run over 1f out: no ex ins fnl f* **66/1**
6 **10** ½ **Foxy Lass**32 1503 3-9-0 0..............(b1) LiamJones 1 64
(William Haggas) *hld up: sme hdwy u.p over 1f out: no ex fnl f* **22/1**
00- **11** 13 **Piccolino**259 5536 3-8-9 0.............. LewisEdmunds(5) 9 34
(John David Riches) *a in rr: wknd over 2f out* **200/1**

1m 48.84s (-1.26) **Going Correction** -0.10s/f (Stan) **11** Ran SP% **115.7**
Speed ratings (Par 96): **101,100,99,98,97 97,96,96,96,95 84**
CSF £45.08 TOTE £24.60: £5.80, £1.10, £2.00; EX 82.80 Trifecta £517.10.
**Owner** K Abdullah **Bred** Juddmonte Farms Ltd **Trained** Newmarket, Suffolk

**FOCUS**
A decent 3yo fillies' maiden. The much improved winner made all in gutsy fashion here on AW debut from the right horse in second. The runner-up set a good standard, but the pace was ordinary and the field was compressed at the finish, so the level is a bit fluid.

## 2312 21M ENVIROLEAD APPRENTICE H'CAP (DIV I) 1m 142y (Tp)
**4:45** (4:46) (Class 6) (0-55,57) 4-Y-O+ **£2,264** (£673; £336; £168) **Stalls** Low

Form RPR
40-4 **1** **Caribbean Spring (IRE)**13 1894 4-9-3 **54**.............. JaneElliott(3) 6 63
(George Margarson) *hld up: hdwy on outer over 2f out: jnd ldr over 1f out: rdn and edgd lft ins fnl f: r.o to ld post* **8/1**3
04-1 **2** *shd* **Whispered Kiss**13 1894 4-9-0 **55**.............. RossaRyan(7) 2 64
(Mike Murphy) *trckd ldrs: racd keenly: led 2f out: rdn and edgd rt ins fnl f: sn wnt lft: hdd post* **2/1**1
2005 **3** 2 ¾ **Dukes Meadow**21 1729 6-8-13 **50**.............. RhiainIngram(3) 7 53
(Roger Ingram) *hld up: swtchd lft over 1f out: r.o to go 3rd wl ins fnl f: nt rch ldrs* **8/1**3
440- **4** 1 **Sakhalin Star (IRE)**125 8566 6-9-2 **57**..............(e) WilliamCox(7) 3 58
(Richard Guest) *chsd ldrs: rdn over 2f out: styd on same pce ins fnl f* **8/1**3
3550 **5** ½ **Mount Cheiron (USA)**28 1563 6-9-0 **48**..............(b) LewisEdmunds 9 48+
(Richard Ford) *s.s: hld up: edgd lft and r.o ins fnl f: nvr nrr* **6/1**2
4434 **6** 1 **Quadriga (IRE)**4 2166 7-8-7 **46** oh1..............(b) PaulaMuir(5) 4 44
(Chris Grant) *hld up: racd keenly: rdn over 1f out: edgd rt and styd on fnl f: nt trble ldrs* **8/1**3
1360 **7** 1 **Thou Swell (IRE)**15 1864 5-9-8 **56**..............(b) CharlieBennett 11 52
(Shaun Harris) *sn pushed along in mid-div: rdn over 1f out: hmpd ins fnl f: nvr on terms* **16/1**
2004 **8** 3 ½ **Arcanista (IRE)**9 2024 4-9-0 **55**.............. NicolaCurrie(7) 5 43
(Richard Hughes) *hld up: effrt and nt clr run over 1f out: n.d* **11/1**
5000 **9** 6 **City Of Angkor Wat (IRE)**8 2063 7-8-12 **51**...(p) KatherineGlenister(5) 1 27
(Conor Dore) *chsd ldrs: rdn over 2f out: wknd over 1f out* **16/1**
600- **10** ½ **Jon H The Lawman (IRE)**248 5921 4-8-12 **46** oh1.....(v1) LucyKBarry 8 21
(Ronald Thompson) *sn led: rdn and hdd 2f out: wknd fnl f* **100/1**
060- **11** 35 **Trulove**251 5803 4-8-9 **46** oh1.............. MeganNicholls(3) 10
(John David Riches) *chsd ldr: rdn and ev ch over 2f out: wknd over 1f out: hung rt ins fnl f* **150/1**

1m 49.21s (-0.89) **Going Correction** -0.10s/f (Stan) **11** Ran SP% **113.8**
Speed ratings (Par 101): **99,98,96,95,95 94,93,90,84,84 53**
CSF £23.41 CT £135.98 TOTE £11.10: £2.70, £1.30, £2.60; EX 28.40 Trifecta £162.50.
**Owner** Graham Lodge Partnership II **Bred** Rangefield Bloodstock **Trained** Newmarket, Suffolk

**FOCUS**
The first division of a moderate apprentice riders' handicap. They went a respectable gallop and two horses who raced against each other at Lingfield last month dominated the finish. Another step forward by the runner-up.

## 2313 21M ENVIROLEAD APPRENTICE H'CAP (DIV II) 1m 142y (Tp)
**5:15** (5:15) (Class 6) (0-55,57) 4-Y-O+ **£2,264** (£673; £336; £168) **Stalls** Low

Form RPR
0402 **1** **The Dukkerer (IRE)**34 1456 6-9-6 **54**.............. LewisEdmunds 2 63
(James Given) *mid-div: hdwy over 2f out: led over 1f out: rdn and hung lft ins fnl f: jst hld on* **5/2**1
0-44 **2** *hd* **Makhfar (IRE)**21 1729 6-9-0 **55**..............(p) NicolaCurrie(7) 8 64
(Mark Usher) *s.s: hld up: hdwy over 1f out: ev ch wl ins fnl f: r.o* **5/1**2
0500 **3** 5 **Palindrome (USA)**62 988 4-9-2 **50**..............(b) LucyKBarry 1 48
(Ronald Thompson) *prom: rdn over 2f out: styd on same pce fr over 1f out* **10/1**
0-40 **4** 1 ½ **The Greedy Boy**34 1456 4-8-5 **46** oh1..............(bt1) TobyEley(7) 4 41
(Steve Flook) *s.i.s: hld up: styd on fr over 1f out: nt trble ldrs* **33/1**
6310 **5** ½ **Pivotal Dream (IRE)**86 605 4-9-1 **49**.............. CharlieBennett 10 43
(Mark Brisbourne) *chsd ldrs: rdn and nt clr run over 1f out: wknd ins fnl f* **10/1**
5305 **6** 3 ½ **Outlaw Torn (IRE)**4 2166 8-9-7 **55**..............(e) PhilDennis 3 42+
(Richard Guest) *led: hdd over 6f out: led again over 5f out: rdn and hdd over 1f out: wknd ins fnl f* **5/1**2
004 **7** 1 ¾ **Moi Aussie**8 2063 4-9-2 **53**..............(p) RayDawson(3) 9 36
(Michael Appleby) *prom: rdn over 2f out: wknd over 1f out* **7/1**3
0606 **8** 1 ¾ **Gamesters Lad**28 1563 5-8-9 **46** oh1..............(p) MeganNicholls(3) 7 25
(Oliver Greenall) *sn pushed along in rr: nvr on terms* **12/1**
0305 **9** 1 ¼ **Pipers Piping (IRE)**28 1563 11-8-6 **47**.............. WilliamCox(7) 5 24
(Mandy Rowland) *hld up: nvr on terms* **18/1**
-000 **10** 7 **Fishergate**35 1425 4-8-9 **46** oh1..............(b) DavidEgan(3) 11 8+
(Richard Rowe) *s.s: rdn and rushed up to ld over 6f out: hdd over 5f out: chsd ldr: rdn over 3f out: lost 2nd over 2f out: wknd wl over 1f out* **18/1**

1m 48.88s (-1.22) **Going Correction** -0.10s/f (Stan) **10** Ran SP% **113.7**
Speed ratings (Par 101): **101,100,96,95,94 91,89,88,87,81**
CSF £14.08 CT £106.23 TOTE £3.30: £1.70, £2.00, £3.60; EX 16.30 Trifecta £137.00.
**Owner** Andy Clarke **Bred** Mrs Sarah Maccann **Trained** Willoughton, Lincs

**FOCUS**
The second division of a moderate apprentice riders' handicap. The pace collapsed up front but the second wave still managed a slightly quicker winning time. The runner-up has not been rated higher than this for some time.
T/Plt: £42.50 to a £1 stake. Pool: £61,854.92. 1,060.00 winning units. T/Qpdt: £7.50 to a £1 stake. Pool: £5,480.50. 539.64 winning units. **Colin Roberts**

# 2279 YARMOUTH (L-H)
Wednesday, May 3

**OFFICIAL GOING: Good to firm (8.0)**
Wind: medium to strong, across Weather: overcast, chilly

## 2314 MARK SUMNER GOLF PRO SHOPS OF YARMOUTH MAIDEN STKS (PLUS 10 RACE) 1m 3f 104y
**5:20** (5:20) (Class 3) 3-Y-O **£9,451** (£2,829; £1,414; £708; £352) **Stalls** Low

Form RPR
**1** **The Grand Visir** 3-9-5 0.............. RyanMoore 7 86+
(William Haggas) *in tch in midfield: rdn over 3f out: hdwy to chse ldng pair 2f out: chsd clr ldr over 1f out: styd on strly ins fnl f to ld towards fin* **3/1**3
5-3 **2** *nk* **Fibonacci**27 1584 3-9-5 0.............. JackMitchell 1 85+
(Hugo Palmer) *trckd ldrs tl wnt 2nd 4f out: sn upsides ldr and travelling strly: led over 2f out: clr and rdn over 1f out: pressed and drvn ins fnl f: hdd and no ex towards fin* **5/2**2
2 **3** 9 **Orsino (IRE)**11 1984 3-9-5 0.............. DavidProbert 2 70
(Andrew Balding) *stmbld leaving stalls: sn rcvrd and led: jnd and rdn over 3f out: hdd over 2f out: lost 2nd and btn over 1f out: wknd ins fnl f* **15/8**1
5 **4** *nk* **Touwari (IRE)**13 1900 3-9-5 0..............(b) RobertTart 3 70
(John Gosden) *chsd ldr tl over 3f out: sn rdn: outpcd and btn over 1f out: wknd ins fnl f* **7/1**
0 **5** 4 **Air Ministry (IRE)**32 1497 3-8-12 0..............(b) TristanPrice(7) 6 63
(Michael Bell) *hld up in last pair: c towards centre st: rdn 3f out: no imp: wknd over 1f out* **66/1**
**6** 2 ¼ **Dixon** 3-9-5 0.............. JoeyHaynes 5 59
(Mark H Tompkins) *wl in tch in midfield: rdn 3f out: outpcd and btn over 1f out: wknd fnl f* **50/1**
**7** 11 **Stockton (IRE)** 3-9-5 0.............. AdamBeschizza 8 41
(David Simcock) *rn green and a rr: rdn 4f out: lost tch over 2f out* **16/1**

2m 26.79s (-1.91) **Going Correction** -0.175s/f (Firm) **7** Ran SP% **110.2**
Speed ratings (Par 103): **99,98,92,92,89 87,79**
CSF £10.09 TOTE £2.80: £2.00, £2.20; EX 10.10 Trifecta £19.40.
**Owner** Saleh Al Homaizi & Imad Al Sagar **Bred** Qatar B'Stock, Ecurie Monceaux & Skymarc **Trained** Newmarket, Suffolk

**FOCUS**
Stalls: Straight - centre, remainder - inside. Not a bad 3yo maiden. There was a fair pace on and it's form to be positive about. The level is a bit fluid.

## 2315 WEDDINGS & PARTIES AT YARMOUTH RACECOURSE H'CAP 1m 2f 23y
**5:50** (5:50) (Class 6) (0-60,62) 3-Y-O **£2,587** (£770; £384; £192) **Stalls** Low

Form RPR
0615 **1** **Bartholomew J (IRE)**9 2027 3-8-12 **54**.............. SimonPearce(3) 7 66+
(Lydia Pearce) *sn stdd and hld up in rr: shkn up and hdwy ent fnl 2f: rdn to ld 1f out: r.o wl: rdn out* **7/1**3
060- **2** 1 **Solo Mission**189 7622 3-9-9 **62**.............. RyanMoore 6 72+
(William Haggas) *chsd ldr: rdn to ld over 2f out: hdd 1f out: kpt on u.p but a hld ins fnl f* **8/15**1
00-0 **3** 5 **Oceanus (IRE)**103 323 3-9-0 **60**.............. TristanPrice(7) 3 61
(Julia Feilden) *t.k.h: trckd ldrs: clsd to join ldrs 3f out: sn rdn and ev ch tl 3rd and no ex 1f out: wknd ins fnl f* **16/1**
0354 **4** ¾ **De Vegas Kid (IRE)**9 2017 3-9-4 **57**.............. DavidProbert 4 56
(Tony Carroll) *hld up in tch in midfield: effrt to chse ldrs u.p 2f out: unable qck jst over 1f out: wknd ins fnl f* **5/1**2
00-0 **5** 2 ½ **Darcey Lou**28 1552 3-8-11 **50**.............. RobertTart 10 44
(John Best) *stdd and dropped in bhd after s: hld up in rr: effrt over 2f out: no imp u.p over 1f out: wl hld but plugged on to pass btn rivals ins fnl f* **33/1**
06-0 **6** ½ **Casado (IRE)**21 1736 3-9-7 **60**.............. KierenFox 1 53
(John Best) *led: rdn 3f out: sn hdd and drvn: wknd over 1f out: burst blood vessel* **16/1**
0-00 **7** *nk* **Deleyll**76 763 3-8-13 **52**..............(b) RobertWinston 2 45
(John Butler) *t.k.h: hld up in tch in midfield: dropped to rr and u.p over 2f out: wknd over 1f out* **14/1**
0500 **8** 2 ¾ **Seeking Attention (USA)**17 1817 3-9-3 **56**.............. JackMitchell 9 44
(George Scott) *wl in tch: shkn up 2f out: sn u.p and no rspnse: wknd ins fnl f* **16/1**
050- **9** 4 ½ **Maysonri**183 7734 3-8-10 **49**.............. AdamBeschizza 5 28
(Mark Hoad) *dwlt: sn rcvrd and in tch in midfield: lost pl u.p ent fnl 2f: bhd over 1f out* **25/1**

2m 8.74s (-1.76) **Going Correction** -0.175s/f (Firm) **9** Ran SP% **125.5**
Speed ratings (Par 97): **100,99,95,94,92 92,91,89,86**
CSF £12.10 CT £71.46 TOTE £13.20: £2.60, £1.10, £2.00; EX 18.40 Trifecta £130.60.
**Owner** P J Stephenson **Bred** Bernard Colclough **Trained** Newmarket, Suffolk

**FOCUS**
They went a modest pace in this weak handicap and it was another race where two came clear. The third has been rated as finding a bit on his recent AW figures.

## 2316 DRIFTERS FISH AND CHIP SHOP MAIDEN FILLIES' STKS 1m 3y
**6:20** (6:23) (Class 5) 3-4-Y-O £3,234 (£962; £481; £240) **Stalls** Centre

Form RPR

0 **1** **Present Tense**[26] 1609 3-8-13 0 RobertTart 5 88+
(John Gosden) *mde all: rdn over 2f out: clr w runner up 1f out: kpt on u.p: jst hld on* **2/1**[1]

**2** *shd* **Gakku** 3-8-13 0 JackMitchell 8 87+
(Roger Varian) *hld up in tch in midfield: pushed along briefly over 3f out: rdn and hdwy over 2f out: chsd wnr over 1f out: 1 l down 1f out: kpt on wl u.p fnl 100yds: jst failed* **4/1**

0U- **3** *8* **Harba (IRE)**[172] 7939 3-8-13 0 RobertWinston 9 68+
(William Haggas) *stdd s: hld up in last pair: clsd 3f out: effrt in 5th 2f out: no imp on ldng pair over 1f out: kpt on steadily to go modest 3rd cl home* **3/1**[3]

**4** *½* **Frosting** 3-8-13 0 RyanMoore 7 67+
(William Haggas) *w ldrs tl dropped into 4th 5f out: effrt over 2f out: no ex u.p in 4th over 1f out: wnt wl hld 3rd 1f out: plugged on but lost 3rd cl home* **5/2**[2]

6 **5** *3 ½* **Agnethe (IRE)**[25] 1619 3-8-13 0 JoeyHaynes 10 59
(Paul D'Arcy) *w ldrs: rdn and ev ch over 2f out tl 3rd and btn over 1f out: wknd ins fnl f* **66/1**

60 **6** *4* **California Cliffs (IRE)**[26] 1609 3-8-13 0 DavidProbert 2 50
(Rae Guest) *w ldrs: rdn over 2f out: sn struggling and btn 6th over 1f out: wknd* **50/1**

**7** *9* **Shanakill Star (IRE)** 3-8-13 0 JFEgan 3 29
(Miss Joey Ellis) *s.i.s: rn green in rr: lost tch 2f out* **50/1**

**8** *9* **Sunset Bounty** 3-8-13 0 AdamBeschizza 1 9
(Julia Feilden) *a towards rr: reminders over 4f out: lost tch 2f out: t.o* **66/1**

004- **9** *17* **Ronni Layne**[172] 7930 3-8-10 63 MarcMonaghan(3) 4
(Conrad Allen) *taken steadily to post: wl in tch in midfield tl dropped to rr 3f out: bhd 2f out: sn lost tch and eased: t.o* **40/1**

1m 35.62s (-4.98) **Going Correction** -0.50s/f (Hard) 9 Ran SP% **116.3**
Speed ratings (Par 100): **104,103,95,95,91 87,78,69,52**
CSF £10.42 TOTE £3.10: £1.20, £1.70, £1.50; EX 12.90 Trifecta £29.50.
**Owner** K Abdullah **Bred** Juddmonte Farms Ltd **Trained** Newmarket, Suffolk

**FOCUS**
A modest fillies' maiden, but it saw two promising sorts go clear. The level is a bit fluid.

## 2317 VAUXHALL HOLIDAY PARK OF GREAT YARMOUTH H'CAP 1m 3y
**6:50** (6:50) (Class 4) (0-80,80) 4-Y-O+ £4,787 (£1,424; £711; £355) **Stalls** Centre

Form RPR

36-1 **1** **Commodity (IRE)**[23] 1687 4-9-4 77 RyanMoore 4 81+
(Sir Michael Stoute) *t.k.h: led: rdn and hrd pressed 2f out: drvn ins fnl f: hdd towards fin: battled bk u.p to ld again last strides: gamely* **4/9**[1]

006- **2** *hd* **Fashaak (IRE)**[235] 6339 4-9-5 78 JFEgan 3 81
(John Butler) *taken down early: w wnr: pushed along 3f out: drvn and stl ev ch 2f out: battled on gamely to ld towards fin: hdd last strides* **20/1**

220- **3** *nk* **Wings Of Esteem (IRE)**[187] 7671 4-8-10 69 ow1 RobertTart 2 71
(Luke McJannet) *trckd ldrs: effrt to chal 2f out: rdn jst ins fnl f: kpt on wl but jst hld towards fin* **7/1**[3]

0-46 **4** *1 ½* **Kestrel Dot Com**[26] 1598 5-9-4 77 (h) DavidProbert 5 75
(Chris Dwyer) *dwlt: hld up in tch: clsd to trck ldrs 4f out: nt clr run over 2f out: rdn: switching lft and trying to rally over 1f out: kpt on ins fnl f* **11/2**[2]

200- **5** *4 ½* **Dot Green (IRE)**[223] 6710 4-9-7 80 JoeyHaynes 1 68
(Mark H Tompkins) *s.i.s: hld up in rr: effrt and rdn to chal 2f out tl no ex 1f out: wknd ins fnl f* **16/1**

1m 36.25s (-4.35) **Going Correction** -0.50s/f (Hard) 5 Ran SP% **107.8**
Speed ratings (Par 105): **101,100,100,99,94**
CSF £10.23 TOTE £1.20: £1.10, £6.40; EX 10.70 Trifecta £39.40.
**Owner** Highclere T'bred Racing (Wellington) **Bred** Stowell Park Stud **Trained** Newmarket, Suffolk

**FOCUS**
An ordinary handicap that saw a bunched finish.

## 2318 RIVERSIDE RENTALS OF NORFOLK H'CAP 1m 3y
**7:20** (7:21) (Class 6) (0-65,67) 4-Y-O+ £2,587 (£770; £384; £192) **Stalls** Centre

Form RPR

65-2 **1** **Anastazia**[25] 1618 5-9-11 66 JoeyHaynes 7 72
(Paul D'Arcy) *trckd ldrs tl clsd to press ldrs 1/2-way: rdn over 2f out: sustained effrt u.p: led ins fnl f: kpt on* **7/2**[3]

0034 **2** *hd* **Flying Fantasy**[8] 2070 5-9-12 67 (vt¹) DavidProbert 6 73
(Stuart Williams) *stdd after s: hld up in tch in rr: clsd over 2f out: rdn to chse ldrs 2f out: 3rd 1f out: kpt on u.p to chse wnr towards fin: fin wl but nvr quite getting to wnr* **3/1**[2]

0-42 **3** *1* **Harlequin Rock**[8] 2070 4-9-4 59 JFEgan 5 63
(Mick Quinn) *in tch: pushed along 1/2-way: rdn 3f out: kpt on wl ins fnl f: snatched 3rd on post* **11/4**[1]

-050 **4** *nse* **Rustique**[41] 1334 5-9-2 62 (h) JennyPowell(5) 8 66
(Ed Walker) *led: rdn wl over 1f out: kpt on u.p tl hdd ins fnl f: wknd towards fin and lost 2 pls cl home* **4/1**

-060 **5** *3* **Candesta (USA)**[21] 1735 7-9-0 62 JackOsborn(7) 3 59
(Julia Feilden) *pressed ldrs tl rdn 1/2-way: lost pl and swtchd lft over 2f out: kpt on same pce u.p fnl f over 1f out* **12/1**

3400 **6** *11* **Stun Gun**[50] 1186 7-8-12 53 (p) MartinLane 1 26
(Derek Shaw) *pressed ldr: rdn 3f out: lost pl and btn 2f out: wknd fnl f* **16/1**

1m 37.13s (-3.47) **Going Correction** -0.50s/f (Hard) 6 Ran SP% **107.5**
Speed ratings (Par 101): **97,96,95,95,92 81**
CSF £13.06 CT £26.51 TOTE £4.40: £2.20, £1.80; EX 17.00 Trifecta £34.90.
**Owner** K Snell **Bred** K Snell **Trained** Newmarket, Suffolk

**FOCUS**
A tight-looking handicap, run at a routine pace down the middle. Straightforward form rated around the first three.

## 2319 GOLD & SILVER EXCHANGE OF GREAT YARMOUTH H'CAP 7f 3y
**7:50** (7:50) (Class 6) (0-60,62) 4-Y-O+ £2,587 (£770; £384; £192) **Stalls** Centre

Form RPR

-560 **1** **Chelabella**[11] 1983 4-9-1 54 (v) MartinLane 9 61
(Derek Shaw) *mde all: rdn wl over 1f out: forged ahd ins fnl f: clr and styd on strly fnl 100yds: rdn out* **18/1**

4/00 **2** *2* **Swilly Sunset**[34] 1449 4-9-1 57 SimonPearce(3) 1 61+
(Anthony Carson) *dwlt: in rr: pushed along and hdwy jst over 1f out: clsng whn nt clr run jst ins fnl f: swtchd lft 100yds out: r.o strly to go 2nd last strides: no threat to wnr* **11/2**[3]

-255 **3** *nk* **Lunar Deity**[26] 1598 8-8-13 59 MillyNaseb(7) 11 60
(Stuart Williams) *racd nr stands' rail thrght: chsd ldrs: effrt ent fnl 2f: rdn and ev ch over 1f out tl no ex ins fnl f: kpt on same pce after: lost 2nd last strides* **11/4**[1]

1/0- **4** *1 ¼* **Deeds Not Words (IRE)**[189] 7631 6-9-1 57 (p) MarcMonaghan(3) 8 54
(Michael Wigham) *t.k.h: chsd ldrs: effrt 2f out: chsd ldng pair over 1f out: no imp and kpt on same pce ins fnl f* **4/1**[2]

00-5 **5** *½* **Cloud Nine (FR)**[76] 764 4-9-5 58 JoeyHaynes 6 54
(Tony Carroll) *racd in last trio: rdn 1/2-way: hdwy jst over 1f out: styd on wl fnl 100yds: nvr trbld ldrs* **25/1**

14-0 **6** *1 ½* **Intimately**[35] 1427 4-9-4 57 JFEgan 10 49
(Jonathan Portman) *s.i.s: rcvrd and chsd ldrs after 2f: rdn 2f out: unable qck over 1f out: wknd over 1f out* **13/2**

0646 **7** *½* **Cuban Queen (USA)**[14] 1887 4-8-0 46 oh1 DarraghKeenan(7) 2 37
(Julia Feilden) *prom: rdn 2f out: no ex u.p ent fnl 2f: wknd ins fnl f* **25/1**

4250 **8** *1 ½* **Tasaaboq**[14] 1887 6-8-7 51 (t) LuluStanford(5) 3 38
(Phil McEntee) *hld up in last trio: effrt ent fnl 2f: no imp u.p over 1f out: wknd ins fnl f* **7/1**

4115 **9** *15* **Malaysian Boleh**[32] 1487 7-9-7 60 (p) DavidProbert 5 6
(Phil McEntee) *w ldrs tl lost pl u.p jst over 2f out: bhd 1f out: eased wl ins fnl f* **15/2**

1m 24.12s (-2.48) **Going Correction** -0.50s/f (Hard) 9 Ran SP% **112.6**
Speed ratings (Par 101): **94,91,91,89,89 87,87,85,68**
CSF £110.53 CT £361.67 TOTE £19.50: £5.00, £1.90, £1.70; EX 140.40 Trifecta £2327.10.
**Owner** Paddy Barrett **Bred** Mrs F S Williams **Trained** Sproxton, Leics

**FOCUS**
An ordinary handicap. The runners kept more stands' side this time. The winner has been rated to her recent form.

## 2320 NORFOLK CHAMBER OF COMMERCE H'CAP 6f 3y
**8:20** (8:24) (Class 5) (0-75,77) 4-Y-O+ £3,234 (£962; £481; £240) **Stalls** Centre

Form RPR

0-00 **1** **Picture Dealer**[88] 575 8-9-1 72 SimonPearce(3) 2 78
(Lydia Pearce) *sn led: rdn and edgd rt ent fnl f: hld on wl u.p ins fnl f: all out* **25/1**

-325 **2** *½* **Until Midnight (IRE)**[25] 1622 7-8-8 67 LuluStanford(5) 5 71
(Eugene Stanford) *chsd ldrs: effrt 2f out: rdn whn nt clrest of runs and swtchd lft over 1f out: ev ch ins fnl f: kpt on same pce towards fin* **6/1**[2]

120- **3** *nk* **Desert River (IRE)**[205] 7203 4-8-11 65 MartinLane 4 68
(Mark H Tompkins) *in tch in midfield: effrt and hdwy over 1f out: ev ch u.p ins fnl f: unable qck towards fin* **33/1**

-032 **4** *nk* **Gold Club**[25] 1631 6-9-7 75 (p) JackMitchell 8 77
(Tom Clover) *broke wl: restrained to trck ldrs and t.k.h: effrt over 1f out: drvn and styd on same pce ins fnl f* **6/1**[2]

13-1 **5** *nk* **Compas Scoobie**[4] 2161 4-8-13 74 CameronNoble(7) 7 75+
(Roger Varian) *stdd s: hld up in tch in last pair: nt clr run over 1f out tl gap opened 100yds out: r.o strly but nvr able to rch ldrs* **10/11**[1]

6025 **6** *¾* **Out Of The Ashes**[34] 1450 4-9-6 74 (vt) DavidProbert 9 73
(Mohamed Moubarak) *chsd wnr: rdn 2f out: drvn over 1f out: keeping on same pce whn nt clr run ins fnl f: wknd towards fin* **20/1**

0235 **7** *nk* **Rockley Point**[39] 1365 4-9-9 77 JoeyHaynes 6 75
(Paul D'Arcy) *stdd after s: hld up in tch in last pair: nt clr run over 1f out: rdn 1f out: kpt on same pce ins fnl f: nvr able to chal* **16/1**[3]

-654 **8** *½* **Gung Ho Jack**[66] 953 8-9-0 68 KierenFox 3 64
(John Best) *in tch in midfield: effrt 2f out: drvn over 1f out: no ex u.p 1f out: wknd ins fnl f* **20/1**

1m 11.66s (-2.74) **Going Correction** -0.50s/f (Hard) 8 Ran SP% **103.1**
Speed ratings (Par 103): **98,97,96,96,96 95,94,94**
CSF £127.05 CT £3471.99 TOTE £26.20: £4.90, £1.90, £4.80; EX 162.50 Trifecta £1147.00.
**Owner** Killarney Glen **Bred** L Ellinas & Old Mill Stud **Trained** Newmarket, Suffolk

**FOCUS**
Not a bad sprint handicap for the grade. Again they kept more stands' side.
T/Plt: £25.70 to a £1 stake. Pool: £6,3301.37. 1,793.15 winning units. T/Qpdt: £12.90 to a £1 stake. Pool: £6,129.14. 349.34 winning units. **Steve Payne**

# 2201 CHANTILLY (R-H)
Wednesday, May 3

**OFFICIAL GOING: Turf: good to soft; polytrack: standard**

## 2321a PRIX DU VIADUC DE COMMELLES (CLAIMER) (2YO) (TURF) 5f
**11:25** 2-Y-O £9,829 (£3,931; £2,948; £1,965; £982)

RPR

**1** **Canouville (FR)**[27] 1594 2-9-1 0 (p) CristianDemuro 6 82
(P Sogorb, France) **16/5**[2]

**2** *6* **Jurisprudance (FR)**[32] 1496 2-8-11 0 MaximeGuyon 7 56
(George Baker) **9/10**[1]

**3** *3* **Bonjour Baileys (FR)** 2-8-11 0 (b) RonanThomas 5 46
(J-V Toux, France) **34/1**

**4** *½* **Scarlett Chope (FR)**[8] 2073 2-9-1 0 (p) GregoryBenoist 4 48
(Y Barberot, France) **112/10**

**5** *2* **Broadchurch (FR)** 2-8-11 0 FrankPanicucci 1 37
(D Allard, France) **45/1**

**6** *1 ½* **Hurricane Breizh (FR)**[13] 1929 2-8-11 0 (p) MickaelForest 3 31
(W Walton, France) **66/10**[3]

**7** *hd* **Melinoe (FR)** 2-8-8 0 FabriceVeron 8 27
(F-H Graffard, France) **94/10**

**8** *shd* **Acapella Style (FR)**[27] 1594 2-8-5 0 (b¹) ClementLecoeuvre(3) 2 27
(Matthieu Palussiere, France) **168/10**

1m 0.55s (2.25) 8 Ran SP% **118.1**
PARI-MUTUEL (all including 1 euro stake): WIN 4.20 PLACE 1.30, 1.10, 3.10 DF 2.70 SF 8.10.
**Owner** Gerard Augustin-Normand **Bred** Franklin Finance S.A. **Trained** France

2322 - 2329a (Foreign Racing) - See Raceform Interactive

# [2089]LINGFIELD (L-H)

Thursday, May 4

**OFFICIAL GOING: Polytrack: standard**

Wind: light, half against, Weather: overcast

## 2330 INJURED JOCKEYS FUND MEDIAN AUCTION MAIDEN STKS 1m 1y(P)

**2:10** (2:11) (Class 6) 3-Y-O **£2,264** (£673; £336; £168) **Stalls** High

Form RPR

2-5 **1** **Mukalal**[16] 1862 3-9-5 0......................................................(h) JimCrowley 3 82+
(Marcus Tregoning) *taken down early: chsd ldrs: wnt 2nd over 4f out: rdn to ld over 1f out: sn in command and pushed out fnl f* **6/4**[1]

22-6 **2** *3* **Pillar Of Society (IRE)**[14] 1907 3-9-5 80.............................. PatDobbs 4 75
(Richard Hannon) *led: jnd and rdn 2f out: hdd and unable qck over 1f out: kpt on same pce fnl f* **9/4**[2]

3- **3** *2* **Deliberator**[139] 8404 3-9-5 0............................................... MartinHarley 1 71
(William Knight) *chsd ldrs: 3rd and drifted rt bnd 2f out: sn rdn and unable qck: kpt on same pce fnl f* **7/1**

**4** *3 1/4* **Yogiyogiyogi (IRE)** 3-9-0 0............................................ PatCosgrave 8 58
(Denis Coakley) *dwlt: in tch in midfield: effrt in 5th over 2f out: no imp on ldrs over 1f out: wl hld and kpt on same pce fnl f* **20/1**

24-3 **5** *nse* **Fastar (IRE)**[26] 1619 3-9-5 76.......................................... JimmyFortune 5 63
(Brian Meehan) *chsd ldrs tl stdd bk into midfield after 3f: 4th and effrt jst over 2f out: outpcd and btn over 1f out: wl hld and kpt on same pce ins fnl f* **4/1**[3]

**6** *6* **My Illusionist** 3-9-5 0.......................................................... AdamKirby 2 51+
(Harry Dunlop) *v.s.a: rn green in rr and swtchd rt after 1f: clsd onto bk of field 5f out: 6th and outpcd jst over 2f out: wknd over 1f out: eased towards fin* **25/1**

40 **7** *12* **Happy Escape**[33] 1503 3-9-0 0....................................(t) RobertWinston 9 17
(Joseph Tuite) *chsd ldr tl over 4f out: lost pl and towards rr whn wd bnd 2f out: sn wl bhd* **66/1**

50 **8** *3 1/4* **Piccoloro**[24] 1682 3-9-5 0................................................ DanielMuscutt 7 14
(Jonathan Portman) *s.i.s: a towards rr: rdn and struggling over 2f out: sn bhd* **100/1**

5 **9** *18* **Watar Day**[62] 997 3-8-9 0.............................................. AliceMills(5) 10
(Linda Jewell) *in tch: rdn and dropped to rr 1/2-way: lost tch over 2f out: t.o* **100/1**

1m 36.48s (-1.72) **Going Correction** -0.075s/f (Stan) 9 Ran SP% **115.4**
Speed ratings (Par 97): **105,102,100,96,96 90,78,75,57**
CSF £4.85 TOTE £2.10: £1.10, £1.50, £2.30; EX 5.30 Trifecta £17.30.
**Owner** Hamdan Al Maktoum **Bred** Shadwell Estate Company Limited **Trained** Whitsbury, Hants

**FOCUS**
Not a strong maiden but the two market leaders dominated and the unexposed favourite was well on top at the finish. Three's A Crowd got upset in the stalls and was withdrawn.

## 2331 RACING WELFARE CLAIMING STKS 6f 1y(P)

**2:40** (2:40) (Class 6) 3-Y-O+ **£2,264** (£673; £336; £168) **Stalls** Low

Form RPR

5-11 **1** **Flowers On Venus (IRE)**[57] 1087 5-9-9 87..................... MartinHarley 5 88
(Tom Dascombe) *mad all: rdn and readily qcknd clr over 1f out: r.o wl ins fnl f: easily* **4/5**[1]

0601 **2** *3* **Major Crispies**[14] 1896 6-9-7 71......................................(bt) AdamKirby 7 77
(Jeremy Gask) *in tch in 4th: effrt 2f out: no ch w wnr but kpt on u.p ins fnl f to go 2nd last strides* **9/1**

-005 **3** *nk* **Quatrieme Ami**[14] 1915 4-9-11 81...............................(t) DavidProbert 3 80
(Philip McBride) *chsd ldng pair: rdn to chse clr wnr and edgd rt over 1f out: kpt on same pce ins fnl f: lost 2nd last strides* **9/2**[3]

1444 **4** *3/4* **Varsovian**[23] 1696 7-9-8 77................................................ JackDuern(3) 2 78
(Dean Ivory) *hld up in 5th: rdn 2f out: sme hdwy over 1f out: kpt on same pce ins fnl f: nvr trbld ldrs* **4/1**[2]

4450 **5** *2 1/4* **Joyful Dream (IRE)**[27] 1605 3-7-13 53........................(p) HollieDoyle(3) 4 55
(J S Moore) *chsd wnr: rdn over 2f out: lost 2nd and sltly impeded over 1f out: wknd fnl f* **25/1**

4340 **6** *4* **Head Space (IRE)**[15] 1887 9-8-12 61...........................(v) JoshuaBryan(7) 6 53
(Brian Barr) *dwlt: a rr: rdn and no hdwy 2f out: wknd ins fnl f* **66/1**

1m 11.16s (-0.74) **Going Correction** -0.075s/f (Stan)
**WFA** 3 from 4yo+ 10lb 6 Ran SP% **109.1**
Speed ratings (Par 101): **101,97,96,95,92 87**
CSF £8.45 TOTE £1.70: £1.30, £2.40; EX 6.40 Trifecta £15.00.Flowers On Venus was claimed by Mr P Butler for £10,000; Joyful Dream waas claimed by Mr J. Butler for £4,000; Major Crispies was claimed by Mr D. O'Meara for £8,000
**Owner** Owen Promotions Limited **Bred** Mrs A J Donnelly **Trained** Malpas, Cheshire

**FOCUS**
The hot favourite completed a hat-trick with plenty in hand in this claimer.

## 2332 HAPPY BELATED BIRTHDAY AOIFE HEARNE H'CAP 1m 7f 169y(P)

**3:10** (3:11) (Class 6) (0-60,61) 4-Y-O+ **£2,264** (£673; £336; £168) **Stalls** Low

Form RPR

-532 **1** **Night Generation (GER)**[71] 859 5-9-10 61.................(tp) DaneO'Neill 4 69
(Chris Gordon) *t.k.h: swtchd rt and hdwy over 3f out: rdn to chse ldrs 2f out: chal and edgd lft over 1f out: sn led: styd on wl* **9/1**[3]

/310 **2** *1 1/2* **Ascendant**[16] 1870 11-9-7 58........................................... StevieDonohoe 7 64
(Johnny Farrelly) *bustled along early: hdwy to chse ldr after 3f tl 10f out: styd prom: rdn and ev ch over 2f out: led 2f out tl 1f out: styd on same pce u.p ins fnl f* **11/1**

-600 **3** *1 1/2* **Golly Miss Molly**[26] 1620 6-9-7 58.................................(b) MartinLane 6 62
(Jeremy Gask) *hld up in tch in midfield: effrt over 2f out: styd on u.p ins fnl f: wnt 3rd last strides: no threat to ldng pair* **14/1**

0110 **4** *hd* **Briac (FR)**[29] 1556 6-9-2 53........................................... DanielMuscutt 3 57
(Mark Pattinson) *t.k.h: chsd ldrs: rdn over 2f out: styd on same pce fr over 1f out: lost 3rd last strides* **11/2**[2]

4302 **5** *2* **Topalova**[33] 1486 4-8-1 48.............................................. GabrieleMalune(7) 1 50
(Mark H Tompkins) *t.k.h: chsd ldrs: rdn and pressing ldrs ent fnl 2f out: unable qck and outpcd over 1f out: plugged on same pce ins fnl f* **12/1**

0126 **6** *3 3/4* **Par Three (IRE)**[33] 1486 6-9-3 54...................................... AdamKirby 13 51
(Tony Carroll) *hld up in rr: stdy hdwy into midfield 1/2-way: rdn 3f out: wd and lost pl bnd 2f out: no threat to ldrs but kpt on again ins fnl f* **12/1**

2040 **7** *nk* **Le Tissier**[10] 2042 4-9-1 55..........................................(p) WilliamCarson 12 52
(Michael Attwater) *led: rdn and hdd over 2f out: struggling whn n.m.r bnd 2f out: wknd fnl f* **20/1**

4003 **8** *nk* **Movie Magic**[23] 1699 6-8-1 45.......................................(b) DavidEgan(7) 5 42
(Mark Hoad) *t.k.h: hld up in tch in midfield: hdwy to chse ldrs 6f out: rdn and unable qck over 2f out: wknd fnl f* **33/1**

00-2 **9** *shd* **Author's Dream**[40] 1369 4-9-4 58..................................... JimCrowley 9 54+
(William Knight) *s.i.s and sn swiitched lft: last pair and nvr travelled particularly wl: nt clr run and stl bhd bnd 2f out: rdn and sme hdwy ins fnl f: nvr trbld ldrs* **11/8**[1]

46-4 **10** *1/2* **Moon Over Mobay**[13] 1935 4-8-13 53............................. DavidProbert 10 49
(Michael Blanshard) *chsd ldrs tl jnd ldr 10f out: rdn to ld over 2f out: hdd 2f out: sn outpcd: wknd fnl f* **33/1**

0506 **11** *1 3/4* **Ledbury (IRE)**[23] 1698 5-8-8 45................................. JosephineGordon 8 39
(Lee Carter) *t.k.h: hld up towards rr: effrt 2f out: no imp: nvr trbld ldrs* **20/1**

666/ **12** *4 1/2* **Highsalvia Cosmos**[495] 7557 6-9-4 55....................................(t) JFEgan 2 43
(Mark Hoad) *hld up in rr: rdn 2f out: no hdwy and wl bhd fnl f* **50/1**

/00- **13** *9* **Honourable Knight (IRE)**[463] 348 9-8-13 50................. LiamKeniry 14 28
(Mark Usher) *chsd ldrs early: steadily dropped bk into midfield: rdn over 2f out: sn btn: bhd fnl f* **66/1**

3m 24.97s (-0.73) **Going Correction** -0.075s/f (Stan)
**WFA** 4 from 5yo+ 1lb 13 Ran SP% **116.7**
Speed ratings (Par 101): **98,97,96,96,95 93,93,93,93,92 92,89,85**
CSF £93.12 CT £1378.55 TOTE £9.60: £2.50, £2.70, £3.60; EX 62.10 Trifecta £369.60.
**Owner** Party People **Bred** Gestut Etzean **Trained** Morestead, Hampshire

**FOCUS**
They went a steady pace and were tightly bunched turning in but the in-form winner scored with authority in the end and the form looks solid enough.

## 2333 JOIN US FOR LADIES DAY - 12 MAY H'CAP 1m 2f (P)

**3:40** (3:40) (Class 5) (0-75,75) 4-Y-O+ **£2,911** (£866; £432; £216) **Stalls** Low

Form RPR

13-0 **1** **Tom's Rock (IRE)**[24] 1683 4-9-5 73............................. DanielMuscutt 3 83
(John Butler) *t.k.h: hld up in tch in midfield: effrt to press ldrs 2f out: rdn to ld jst ins fnl f: r.o wl: eased towards fin* **8/1**[3]

60-0 **2** *2* **Ataman (IRE)**[23] 1706 5-9-1 72................................. LouisSteward(3) 4 78
(Chris Wall) *trckd ldng pair: wnt 2nd jst over 2f out: rdn and ev ch wl over 1f out: chsd wnr and kpt on same pce ins fnl f* **4/1**[1]

1113 **3** *1 1/4* **Synodic (USA)**[27] 1602 5-9-7 75...............................(t) DaneO'Neill 6 79
(Seamus Durack) *hld up in tch in midfield: hdwy to chse ldrs 2f out: kpt on same pce u.p ins fnl f: wnt 3rd towards fin* **5/1**[2]

036- **4** *shd* **Silver Ghost (IRE)**[199] 7419 4-9-4 72.......................... JimmyFortune 2 75
(Eve Johnson Houghton) *hld up in midfield: rdn and effrt on inner 2f out: swtchd rt jst ins fnl f: styd on wl fnl 100yds: wnt 4th towards fin* **8/1**[3]

1262 **5** *1 1/4* **Russian Reward (IRE)**[9] 2055 5-9-6 74.......................(p) JackMitchell 5 75
(Amanda Perrett) *led for 1f: chsd ldr tl led again over 2f out: rdn and hrd pressed over 1f out: hdd jst ins fnl f: sn btn and wknd wl ins fnl f* **5/1**[2]

0-33 **6** *3* **Bridge Of Sighs**[36] 1430 5-9-6 74.............................. RobertWinston 1 71
(Martin Smith) *stdd after s: hld up in last pair: n.m.r ent fnl 2f: kpt on but no threat to ldrs ins fnl f* **5/1**[2]

250- **7** *3 1/2* **Saga Sprint (IRE)**[206] 7214 4-8-7 68.......................... GinaMangan(7) 8 56
(J R Jenkins) *hld up in last pair: hdwy on outer 5f out: wd and lost pl bnd 2f out: hung lft and wknd 1f out* **100/1**

00-5 **8** *1 1/4* **Theos Lolly (IRE)**[23] 1707 4-9-2 73...................... AdamMcNamara(3) 7 58+
(Richard Fahey) *hld up in last pair: nt clr run and hmpd 2f out: effrt but plenty to do over 1f out: no imp and hmpd again 1f out: nvr trbld ldrs* **5/1**[2]

0/60 **9** *21* **Marmion**[32] 1517 5-9-5 73................................................... AdamKirby 9 16
(Les Eyre) *led after 1f: rdn and hdd over 2f out: losing pl whn squeezed for rom bnd 2f out: bhd and eased ins fnl f* **16/1**

2m 4.18s (-2.42) **Going Correction** -0.075s/f (Stan) 9 Ran SP% **115.8**
Speed ratings (Par 103): **106,104,103,103,102 99,97,96,79**
CSF £40.14 CT £178.38 TOTE £9.90: £2.90, £2.00, £2.00; EX 50.70 Trifecta £435.80.
**Owner** Recycled Products Limited **Bred** R G & T E Levin **Trained** Newmarket, Suffolk
■ Stewards' Enquiry : Gina Mangan caution: careless riding

**FOCUS**
They went a fair pace and the winner produced a surging run to score in good style.

## 2334 #TAKETHEREINS17 H'CAP 7f 1y(P)

**4:10** (4:12) (Class 4) (0-85,86) 3-Y-O **£4,690** (£1,395; £697; £348) **Stalls** Low

Form RPR

3-1 **1** **Horroob**[26] 1619 3-9-9 86............................................... JackMitchell 6 92+
(Roger Varian) *chsd ldr for 1f: stdd bk to trck ldrs: nt clr run ent fnl 2f: gap opened and shkn up over 1f out: qcknd to chal jst ins fnl f: rdn and r.o wl to ld towards fin* **9/4**[1]

10-2 **2** *nk* **Sea Shack**[29] 1554 3-9-0 77................................... SilvestreDeSousa 9 82
(William Knight) *led: rdn ent fnl 2f: hrd pressed 1f out: kpt on gamely u.p tl hdd towards fin* **8/1**

11 **3** *1/2* **Family Fortunes**[27] 1601 3-9-7 84...................................... PatDobbs 7 88+
(Sylvester Kirk) *dwlt: hld up in tch in last pair: swtchd rt and effrt over 1f out: hdwy u.p ins fnl f: r.o strly fnl 100yds: nt quite rch ldrs* **9/1**

12-5 **4** *1/2* **Battered**[23] 1702 3-9-5 82................................................ PatCosgrave 3 85
(William Haggas) *hld up in tch: n.m.r ent fnl 2f: swtchd lft and hdwy over 1f out: chsd ldrs and edgd lft u.p ins fnl f: kpt on same pce fnl 100yds* **7/1**

-221 **5** *1/2* **Tafaakhor (IRE)**[19] 1787 3-9-6 83.................................. JimCrowley 4 84+
(Richard Hannon) *hld up in tch in midfield: n.m.r over 1f out: hdwy ins fnl f: kpt on wl fnl 100yds: nvr quite getting to ldrs* **11/2**[3]

510- **6** *1 1/4* **Angel Down**[259] 5583 3-9-2 79......................................... DaneO'Neill 2 78
(Henry Candy) *hld up in tch: effrt on inner 2f out: hdwy over 1f out to chse ldrs 1f out: keeping on same pce and hld whn n.m.r and eased wl ins fnl f* **33/1**

61- **7** *nk* **Sayem**[141] 8362 3-9-0 77................................................ ThomasBrown 1 74
(Ed Walker) *awkward leaving stalls and slowly away: hld up in tch in rr: effrt on inner over 1f out: swtchd rt and hdwy 1f out: keeping on but nvr any ch of getting to ldrs whn pushed rt towards fin* **33/1**

43-1 **8** *1/2* **Hajjam**[36] 1426 3-8-12 75 ow1..........................................(h) MartinHarley 5 71
(William Knight) *t.k.h early: hld up in tch in midfield: effrt over 2f out: unable qck over 1f out: kpt on same pce ins fnl f* **20/1**

314- **9** *3/4* **Maakaasib**[203] 7305 3-9-7 84........................................ HarryBentley 8 78
(Simon Crisford) *t.k.h: chsd ldrs: wnt 2nd after 1f tl unable qck over 1f out: wknd ins fnl f* **10/1**

1- **10** *1 1/2* **Endless Charm**[155] 8151 3-9-3 80................................... WilliamBuick 10 70+
(Charlie Appleby) *chsd ldrs: ev ch but r awkwardly bnd 2f out: wandered and edgd lft over 1f out: losing pl whn squeezed for room jst ins fnl f: sn wknd* **4/1**[2]

1m 23.48s (-1.32) **Going Correction** -0.075s/f (Stan) 10 Ran SP% **119.5**
Speed ratings (Par 101): **104,103,103,102,101 100,100,99,98,97**
CSF £21.31 CT £137.87 TOTE £2.80: £1.10, £2.30, £2.90; EX 21.00 Trifecta £117.40.
**Owner** Sheikh Ahmed Al Maktoum **Bred** Whitsbury Manor Stud And Mrs M E Slade **Trained** Newmarket, Suffolk
■ Stewards' Enquiry : Dane O'Neill caution: careless riding

**FOCUS**
A fascinating race involving several unexposed last-time-out winners. The pace was steady and there was a tight finish but the well-backed favourite came out on top.

## 2335 WELCOME HOME WILL FILLIES' H'CAP — 6f 1y(P)
**4:40** (4:40) (Class 5) (0-75,75) 4-Y-O+ **£2,911** (£866; £432; £216) **Stalls** Low

Form RPR

0-00 **1** **Sandra's Secret (IRE)**[15] 1876 4-9-7 **75** ........ AdamKirby 3 84
(Les Eyre) *mde all: rdn and kicked clr wl over 1f out: in n.d and rn wl ins fnl f: eased towards fin* **4/1**[3]

1004 **2** 3 ¼ **K'Gari Spirit**[12] 1981 4-8-13 **67** ........(t) MartinLane 5 65
(Jeremy Gask) *hld up in 3rd: clsd to trck ldrs over 3f out: effrt 2f out: outpcd by wnr over 1f out: no ch w wnr but kpt on ins fnl f to go 2nd last strides* **8/1**

356- **3** nk **Welsh Rose**[215] 6960 4-9-3 **71** ........(h) JimCrowley 1 68
(Ed de Giles) *trckd wnr: effrt wl over 1f out: sn outpcd by wnr and btn 1f out: kpt on same pce after: lost 2nd last strides* **9/4**[1]

651- **4** 1 **Wild Dancer**[204] 7267 4-9-3 **74** ........ HectorCrouch[(3)] 4 67
(Patrick Chamings) *stmbld leaving stalls: hld up in rr: effrt over 1f out: sme hdwy u.p but no threat to wnr 1f out: kpt on same pce ins fnl f* **5/2**[2]

0002 **5** nk **Nag's Wag (IRE)**[27] 1599 4-9-4 **72** ........ LiamKeniry 6 64
(George Baker) *s.i.s: effrt and stl plenty to do over 1f out: no imp and kpt on same pce ins fnl f* **5/1**

2400 **6** 4 ½ **Arize (IRE)**[14] 1899 4-8-10 **64** ........ SamHitchcott 2 42
(Jim Boyle) *t.k.h: hld up in midfield: effrt 2f: no imp over 1f out: wknd ins fnl f* **25/1**

1m 11.42s (-0.48) **Going Correction** -0.075s/f (Stan) **6** Ran SP% **111.0**
Speed ratings (Par 100): **100,95,95,93,93 87**
CSF £33.04 TOTE £4.50: £2.50, £2.70; EX 23.50 Trifecta £99.80.
**Owner** Sunpak Potatoes **Bred** Tally-Ho Stud **Trained** Catwick, N Yorks

**FOCUS**
The pace looked decent in this sprint handicap but the winner blitzed her rivals under a front-running ride.

## 2336 RACING WELFARE 24 HOUR SUPPORT LINE 08006300443 H'CAP — 1m 4f (P)
**5:10** (5:11) (Class 5) (0-70,72) 4-Y-O+ **£2,911** (£866; £432; £216) **Stalls** Low

Form RPR

342 **1** **Bosphorus Prince (IRE)**[15] 1892 5-9-8 **71** ........ JohnFahy 3 77+
(Matthew Salaman) *chsd ldr for 2f: styd chsng ldrs: effrt and swtchd lft over 1f out: str chal u.p to ld and edgd rt ins fnl f: r.o* **9/2**[3]

-024 **2** 1 **Bluff Crag**[24] 1684 4-8-13 **69** ........ FinleyMarsh[(7)] 7 73
(Richard Hughes) *stdd after s: t.k.h: hld up in midfield: effrt to chse ldrs over 1f out: rdn and kpt on wl ins fnl f: wnt 2nd towards fin* **7/2**[2]

2343 **3** ½ **Attain**[13] 1937 8-9-4 **70** ........ EdwardGreatrex[(3)] 10 73
(Archie Watson) *chsd ldr after 2f: pressed ldr 7f out: rdn to chal and qcknd jst over 2f out: ev ch after tl unable qck and kpt on same pce fnl 100yds* **10/1**

0050 **4** ¾ **Karam Albaari (IRE)**[40] 1364 9-9-6 **69** ........(v) AdamKirby 1 72
(J R Jenkins) *stdd s: hld up in last pair: clsd over 2f out: rdn and hdwy to chse ldrs 1f out: nt clr run and switching rt ins fnl f: stl n.m.r and kpt on same pce wl ins fnl f* **10/1**

**5** nk **Methag (FR)**[17] 4-9-9 **72** ........ PatCosgrave 5 74
(Alex Hales) *led: rdn and qcknd 2f: hdd whn squeezed for room and hit on nose by winning rdrs whip ins fnl f: no ex after* **25/1**

20-5 **6** nk **Pearly Prince**[40] 1364 5-9-6 **69** ........(h) SilvestreDeSousa 8 70+
(Martin Bosley) *dwlt: shifting lft and hdwy into midfield after 1f: t.k.h: switching rt and effrt bnd 2f out: hdwy and styd on ins fnl f: nt rch ldrs* **7/2**[2]

4042 **7** 1 ¾ **Bamako Du Chatelet (FR)**[7] 2111 6-9-7 **70** ........(v) StevieDonohoe 9 68+
(Ian Williams) *hld up in tch towards rr: effrt and carried wd bnd 2f out: kpt on ins fnl f but nvr threatening ldrs* **11/4**[1]

00- **8** ¾ **The Dancing Lord**[76] 793 8-8-13 **62** ........(t) JFEgan 4 59
(Adam West) *hld up in last pair: effrt 2f out: kpt on same pce and no imp u.p ins fnl f* **33/1**

0 **9** 7 **Sevilla**[120] 47 4-9-5 **68** ........ KieranO'Neill 6 54
(Anabel K Murphy) *t.k.h: hld up in tch in midfield: lost pl over 2f out: bhd over 1f out* **40/1**

2m 34.86s (1.86) **Going Correction** -0.075s/f (Stan) **9** Ran SP% **116.7**
Speed ratings (Par 103): **90,89,89,88,88 88,86,86,81**
CSF £20.54 CT £150.19 TOTE £5.80: £1.80, £1.70, £2.40; EX 30.10 Trifecta £187.40.
**Owner** Mrs D J Hughes **Bred** Serdal Adali **Trained** Tonyrefail, Rhondda Cynon Taff
■ Stewards' Enquiry : Edward Greatrex two-day ban (18-19 May): used whip without giving his mount time to respond

**FOCUS**
They went a steady pace and the first three were always prominent.
T/Jkpt: Part won. Pool: £10,000 - 0.50 winning units. T/Plt: £103.30 to a £1 stake. Pool: £72,030.09 -508.63 winning units. T/Qpdt: £50.20 to a £1 stake. Pool: £4,662.33 - 68.62 winning units. **Steve Payne**

# 1799 MUSSELBURGH (R-H)
Thursday, May 4

**OFFICIAL GOING: Good to firm (good in places)**
Wind: Fresh, half behind in over 3f of home straight Weather: Sunny

## 2337 RACING UK APPRENTICE H'CAP — 5f 1y
**6:10** (6:17) (Class 6) (0-60,57) 4-Y-O+ **£2,587** (£770; £384; £192) **Stalls** High

Form RPR

130- **1** **Longroom**[192] 7584 5-9-7 **57** ........ PhilDennis[(3)] 6 70+
(Noel Wilson) *cl up gng wl: led on bit over 1f out: shkn up and qcknd clr fnl f: readily* **11/10**[1]

5330 **2** 3 ¼ **Lizzy's Dream**[8] 2076 9-8-10 **46** ........ RowanScott[(3)] 3 47
(Rebecca Bastiman) *prom: effrt and pushed along over 1f out: rallied to chse (clr) wnr wl ins fnl f: kpt on: nt pce to chal* **6/1**[3]

150- **3** 1 ¼ **Thornaby Princess**[221] 6813 6-9-3 **50** ........(p) NathanEvans 1 47
(Colin Teague) *led tl rdn and hdd over 1f out: sn no ch w wnr: lost 2nd wl ins fnl f* **12/1**

06-0 **4** 1 ½ **Noodles Blue Boy**[22] 1722 11-9-7 **57** ........(p) LewisEdmunds[(3)] 4 48
(Ollie Pears) *dwlt: hld up in tch on outside: effrt and pushed along 1/2-way: edgd rt and no imp over 1f out* **11/4**[2]

500- **5** 1 ½ **Ss Vega**[233] 6436 4-8-7 **47** ........ KieranSchofield[(7)] 7 33
(Jim Goldie) *hld up: rdn and outpcd 1/2-way: btn over 1f out* **8/1**

-300 **6** 8 **Under Approval**[8] 2076 6-8-10 **49** ........(b) GemmaTutty[(6)] 2 6
(Karen Tutty) *cl up on outside tl rdn and wknd wl over 1f out* **12/1**

58.77s (-1.63) **Going Correction** -0.325s/f (Firm) **6** Ran SP% **115.1**
Speed ratings (Par 101): **100,94,92,90,88 75**
CSF £8.75 TOTE £2.10: £1.30, £2.10; EX 8.30 Trifecta £40.40.
**Owner** Marwood Racing Limited **Bred** Juddmonte Farms Ltd **Trained** Marwood, Co Durham

**FOCUS**
After a warm day the going was changed before the start of racing to good to firm, good in places. A moderate sprint handicap and easy pickings for the favourite. The runner-up helps set a token form standard.

## 2338 RACING UK MAIDEN STKS — 7f 33y
**6:40** (6:40) (Class 5) 3-Y-O+ **£3,234** (£962; £481; £240) **Stalls** Low

Form RPR

525- **1** **Dan Troop**[166] 8033 3-9-2 70 ........ DavidNolan 6 67
(Richard Fahey) *hld up in last pl: effrt and swtchd rt 2f out: rdn to ld ent fnl f: kpt on strly* **4/1**[2]

23-0 **2** 1 ¾ **Valentino Boy (IRE)**[12] 1975 3-9-2 80 ........ TomEaves 7 63
(Brian Ellison) *led: rdn and edgd lft 2f out: hdd ent fnl f: kpt on: nt pce of wnr* **15/2**

5053 **3** hd **Lady Volante (IRE)**[8] 2089 3-8-11 54 ........ NeilFarley 3 57
(Lucinda Egerton) *trckd ldrs: effrt and drvn along 2f out: kpt on same pce ins fnl f* **66/1**

**4** 4 ½ **Don Valentino (IRE)** 3-9-2 0 ........ DanielTudhope 4 50
(David O'Meara) *s.i.s: sn prom: effrt on outside over 2f out: wknd fnl f* **6/1**[3]

022 **5** ¾ **Bonnie Gals**[61] 1033 3-8-6 65 ........ ShirleyTeasdale[(5)] 5 43
(Keith Dalgleish) *pressed ldr: drvn and edgd lft 2f out: wknd over 1f out* **12/1**

**6** ½ **Gloriosus (USA)** 3-9-2 0 ........ JoeFanning 2 46
(Mark Johnston) *slowly away: t.k.h: hld up in tch: rdn and rn green over 2f out: sn outpcd: btn over 1f out* **10/11**[1]

1m 30.07s (1.07) **Going Correction** +0.025s/f (Good) **6** Ran SP% **107.6**
Speed ratings (Par 103): **94,92,91,86,85 85**
CSF £29.53 TOTE £5.50: £2.40, £1.80; EX 20.30 Trifecta £214.90.
**Owner** Mrs Janis Macpherson **Bred** Liam Sheridan **Trained** Musley Bank, N Yorks

**FOCUS**
A fair maiden. The modest standard is set around the winner and the winner and third.

## 2339 RACING UK H'CAP — 1m 2y
**7:10** (7:10) (Class 5) (0-75,77) 4-Y-O+ **£3,881** (£1,155; £577; £288) **Stalls** Low

Form RPR

11-0 **1** **Zeshov (IRE)**[23] 1706 6-9-7 **73** ........ DuranFentiman 2 81
(Rebecca Bastiman) *trckd ldrs: rdn to ld over 1f out: hld on wl fnl f* **11/2**[3]

0-66 **2** ¾ **Crazy Tornado (IRE)**[5] 2140 4-8-10 **67** ........(h) RowanScott[(5)] 4 73
(Keith Dalgleish) *hld up in tch: stdy hdwy against ins rail to chse wnr over 1f out: rdn and veered lft ent fnl f: stened and kpt on fin* **5/2**[1]

340- **3** 3 ½ **Dark Crystal**[205] 7254 6-8-12 **64** ........ GrahamLee 5 62
(Linda Perratt) *fly-jmpd s: hld up in tch on outside: effrt and rdn over 2f out: kpt on fnl f: nt rch first two* **40/1**

00-0 **4** 2 **Ralphy Boy (IRE)**[20] 1778 8-9-7 **73** ........ PJMcDonald 6 67
(Alistair Whillans) *dwlt: hld up: stdy hdwy over 2f out: rdn and no imp whn checked ent fnl f: sn btn* **12/1**

30-0 **5** 1 ¼ **Bernie's Boy**[24] 1677 4-9-11 **77** ........ DougieCostello 1 68
(Roger Fell) *dwel: sn led: rdn and hdd over 1f out: wknd fnl f* **7/1**

310- **6** ¾ **Vizier**[167] 8007 4-9-11 **77** ........ DanielTudhope 7 66
(David O'Meara) *hld up: outpcd after 3f: carried hd high: sme late hdwy: nvr on terms* **4/1**[2]

-000 **7** ¾ **Ellaal**[12] 1969 8-9-3 **69** ........ PaulMulrennan 3 56
(Ruth Carr) *early ldr: pressed ldr: rdn and ev ch over 2f out: edgd lft: wknd over 1f out* **15/2**

520- **8** 2 ¾ **Marbooh (IRE)**[171] 7957 4-9-11 **77** ........ DavidNolan 8 58
(David O'Meara) *prom: rdn over 2f out: wknd over 1f out* **13/2**

1m 40.7s (-0.50) **Going Correction** +0.025s/f (Good) **8** Ran SP% **111.7**
Speed ratings (Par 103): **103,102,98,96,95 94,94,91**
CSF £18.71 CT £482.87 TOTE £6.50: £2.00, £1.40, £5.20; EX 22.60 Trifecta £400.70.
**Owner** Mrs P Bastiman **Bred** Rathbarry Stud **Trained** Cowthorpe, N Yorks

**FOCUS**
A fair, open-looking handicap, in which they went an ordinary pace. The winner has been rated back to his best, with the runner-up to last year's form.

## 2340 RACING UK IN HD H'CAP — 1m 5f 216y
**7:40** (7:40) (Class 6) (0-65,61) 4-Y-O+ **£3,234** (£962; £481; £240) **Stalls** Low

Form RPR

20-1 **1** **Sebastian's Wish (IRE)**[104] 333 4-9-2 **56** ........ JoeFanning 6 66
(Keith Dalgleish) *sn pressing ldr: led over 3f out: rdn fr 2f out: hld on wl fnl f* **2/1**[1]

660- **2** ¾ **Jonny Delta**[12] 7251 10-8-13 **52** ........ SamJames 1 61
(Jim Goldie) *hld up: stdy hdwy and cl up over 2f out: chsd wnr over 1f out: kpt on fnl f: hld nr fin* **13/2**

-010 **3** 3 ¼ **Cosmic Tigress**[36] 1436 6-9-7 **60** ........ JasonHart 5 65
(John Quinn) *t.k.h early: hld up in tch: hdwy to chse wnr over 2f out to over 1f out: kpt on same pce fnl f* **11/2**[2]

0014 **4** hd **Thorntoun Care**[12] 1985 6-9-8 **61** ........(b) TomEaves 7 66
(Iain Jardine) *dwlt: hld up: stdy hdwy whn nt clr run over 3f out to over 2f out: sn swtchd lft and effrt: kpt on same pce fnl f* **6/1**[3]

-302 **5** 9 **The Detainee**[23] 1698 4-9-5 **59** ........ RoystonFfrench 3 52
(Jeremy Gask) *wnt lft s: cl up: drvn and outpcd over 3f out: n.d after* **11/2**[2]

63/0 **6** nk **Jebulani**[38] 1402 7-7-13 **45** ........ ConnorMurtagh[(7)] 2 37
(Barry Murtagh) *trckd ldrs tl rdn and outpcd over 2f out: sn btn* **25/1**

066 **7** 1 ½ **Ibreeq (IRE)**[24] 1675 4-8-10 **50** ........ PJMcDonald 4 40
(Roger Fell) *led to over 3f out: rdn and wknd fnl 2f* **13/2**

3m 4.57s (-0.73) **Going Correction** +0.025s/f (Good) **7** Ran SP% **108.9**
Speed ratings (Par 101): **103,102,100,100,95 95,94**
CSF £13.82 TOTE £2.90: £1.50, £3.20; EX 16.20 Trifecta £85.00.
**Owner** Two Goldfish & A Balloon **Bred** Gestut Schlenderhan **Trained** Carluke, S Lanarks

**FOCUS**
A modest staying handicap, in which the pace was steady, and the winner was up there throughout. Straightforward form, with the winner to his previous best for now.

## 2341 RACING UK DAY PASS JUST £10 H'CAP — 5f 1y
**8:10** (8:10) (Class 4) (0-80,82) 4-Y-O+ **£5,175** (£1,540; £769; £384) **Stalls** High

Form RPR

-401 **1** **Royal Brave (IRE)**[19] 1805 6-9-6 **77** ........ PJMcDonald 4 83
(Rebecca Bastiman) *prom: effrt on outside over 1f out: rdn to ld ent fnl f: drvn out* **4/1**[2]

0606 **2** 3/4 **Silvanus (IRE)**20 1768 12-9-5 **76** GrahamLee 3 85+
(Paul Midgley) *prom: no room at all fr 1/2-way tl swtchd rt and gd hdwy ins fnl f: chsd wnr last 25yds: kpt on: unlucky* **8/1**

-624 **3** nk **Lucky Beggar (IRE)**7 2104 7-9-5 **76** TomEaves 2 78
(David C Griffiths) *slt ld: rdn and hrd pressed fr 1/2-way: hdd ent fnl f: chsd wnr to last 25yds: no ex* **13/2**

46-4 **4** 3/4 **Desert Ace (IRE)**14 1915 6-9-2 **78** (p) CliffordLee(5) 1 77
(Iain Jardine) *cl up: effrt and ev ch over 1f out to ins fnl f: kpt on same pce* **7/2**1

-503 **5** 3/4 **One Boy (IRE)**19 1805 6-9-3 **74** PaulMulrennan 5 71
(Paul Midgley) *in tch: effrt and swtchd rt over 1f out: edgd rt and outpcd ins fnl f* **5/1**3

60-0 **6** 7 **Star Cracker (IRE)**19 1805 5-8-6 **63** (p) SamJames 6 34
(Jim Goldie) *dwlt: bhd: struggling 1/2-way: sn btn* **16/1**

310- **7** 4 1/2 **Alsvinder**335 2863 4-9-11 **82** (h1) DanielTudhope 7 37
(David O'Meara) *w ldrs to 2f out: sn rdn and struggling* **7/2**1

58.05s (-2.35) **Going Correction** -0.325s/f (Firm) 7 Ran SP% **111.4**
Speed ratings (Par 105): **105,103,103,102,100 89,82**
CSF £33.14 TOTE £4.60: £2.10, £3.50; EX 30.90 Trifecta £121.10.
**Owner** James Edgar & William Donaldson **Bred** M Fahy **Trained** Cowthorpe, N Yorks

**FOCUS**
A fair sprint handicap and the pace was ordinary. The winner has been rated back to his old best.

## 2342 RACING UK PROFITS RETURNED TO RACING H'CAP 7f 33y
**8:40** (8:42) (Class 6) (0-60,57) 4-Y-0+ **£2,587** (£770; £384; £192) **Stalls** Low

Form RPR

-122 **1** **Isntshesomething**9 2063 5-9-2 **52** (v) DougieCostello 6 58
(Richard Guest) *hld up in tch: hdwy to ld over 1f out: drvn and kpt on wl fnl f* **9/2**2

00-0 **2** 3/4 **New Abbey Angel (IRE)**55 1125 4-9-2 **57** (v) RowanScott(5) 5 61
(Keith Dalgleish) *s.i.s: hld up: stdy hdwy and carried hd high fr over 2f out: rdn: edgd rt and chsd wnr ins fnl f: kpt on: hld nr fin* **5/1**3

-606 **3** 3 **Harbour Patrol (IRE)**28 1587 5-8-12 **48** (b1) DuranFentiman 1 44
(Rebecca Bastiman) *led: rdn over 2f out: hdd over 1f out: kpt on same pce ins fnl f* **12/1**

0406 **4** 2 1/4 **Jessie Allan (IRE)**40 1372 6-8-9 **45** SamJames 4 35
(Jim Goldie) *cl up: rdn over 2f out: outpcd over 1f out: btn fnl f* **20/1**

04-1 **5** 3/4 **Tanawar (IRE)**8 2082 7-9-7 **57** (b) JamesSullivan 2 45
(Ruth Carr) *t.k.h early: in tch: rdn over 2f out: wknd over 1f out* **5/4**1

00/0 **6** 2 1/4 **Conjuror's Bluff**34 1473 9-8-6 **45** (p) ShelleyBirkett(3) 3 27
(Fred Watson) *hld up midfield: effrt and drvn along over 2f out: no imp fr over 1f out* **66/1**

0-04 **7** 2 1/4 **Cyflymder (IRE)**10 2023 11-8-9 **45** TomEaves 8 21
(David C Griffiths) *chsd ldrs on outside: rdn over 2f out: wknd over 1f out* **10/1**

600- **8** 3/4 **Grandad Chunk (IRE)**244 6100 6-8-10 **46** RoystonFfrench 7 20
(Colin Teague) *stdd s: t.k.h in rr: rdn 2f out: sn wknd* **20/1**

-003 **9** 13 **Little Belter (IRE)**40 1372 5-9-0 **50** (p) JoeFanning 9
(Keith Dalgleish) *hld up on outside: drvn and outpcd over 2f out: sn btn: eased whn no ch ins fnl f* **16/1**

1m 28.86s (-0.14) **Going Correction** +0.025s/f (Good) 9 Ran SP% **113.0**
Speed ratings (Par 101): **101,100,96,94,93 90,88,87,72**
CSF £25.89 CT £250.28 TOTE £4.80: £2.00, £2.20, £3.40; EX 33.60 Trifecta £275.20.
**Owner** Chris Penney **Bred** P Balding **Trained** Ingmanthorpe, W Yorks
■ Stewards' Enquiry : Rowan Scott two-day ban: used whip above permitted level (May 18-19)

**FOCUS**
They went a good pace in this moderate handicap and the two principals pulled clear of the rest. It's been rated around the first three.
T/Plt: £318.20 to a £1 stake. Pool: £57,268.94 - 131.35 winning units. T/Qpdt: £39.00 to a £1 stake. Pool: £4,739.46 - 89.70 winning units. **Richard Young**

# 1828 REDCAR (L-H)
Thursday, May 4

**OFFICIAL GOING: Good to firm (good in places; watered; 8.9)**
Wind: Gusting fresh half against Weather: Cloudy sunny periods

## 2343 ENJOY HOSPITALITY AT REDCAR RACECOURSE (S) STKS 5f
**2:00** (2:01) (Class 6) 2-Y-0 **£2,897** (£855; £427) **Stalls** Centre

Form RPR

055 **1** **Popsi**14 1929 2-8-7 0 (p1) FrannyNorton 5 54
(Jo Hughes) *mde virtually all: rdn and jnd 2f out: drvn ent fnl f: kpt on wl towards fin* **7/2**2

**2** shd **Our Little Pony** 2-8-7 0 PaulHanagan 2 54
(Richard Fahey) *wnt lft s and towards rr: hdwy 2f out: rdn ent fnl f: drvn and ev ch towards fin: jst failed* **15/8**1

0 **3** 3/4 **Placebo Effect (IRE)**15 1873 2-8-12 0 AndrewMullen 3 56
(Ollie Pears) *trckd ldng pair: hdwy 1/2-way: cl up 2f out: sn rdn and disp ld appr fnl f: sn drvn and kpt on same pce fnl 100 yds* **8/1**

6 **4** 1 **Society's Dream (IRE)**14 1908 2-8-7 0 JoeyHaynes 1 47
(K R Burke) *chsd wnr: rdn along 2f out: drvn wl over 1f out: kpt on same pce* **6/1**3

0 **5** 1 1/2 **Tie Em Up Tel (IRE)**23 1694 2-8-12 0 DannyBrock 6 47
(David Evans) *towards rr: rdn along 2f out: kpt on: n.d* **7/2**2

0 **6** 2 3/4 **Paulamey**10 2037 2-8-7 0 RoystonFfrench 4 32
(David Evans) *chsd ldrs: rdn along over 2f out: sn wknd* **50/1**

40 **7** 32 **Glen Valley (IRE)**15 1873 2-8-7 0 (p1) ConnorBeasley 7
(Keith Dalgleish) *dwlt: a towards rr: outpcd and bhd fr 1/2-way* **33/1**

1m 0.61s (2.01) **Going Correction** +0.15s/f (Good) 7 Ran SP% **109.5**
Speed ratings (Par 91): **89,88,87,86,83 79,28**
CSF £9.55 TOTE £3.30: £1.30, £1.80; EX 10.20 Trifecta £29.20.Our Little Pony was bought in for £6000
**Owner** P & L Partners & Jo Hughes **Bred** P & L Partners **Trained** Lambourn. Berks

**FOCUS**
Hard to be certain of the form so early in the season but the highest-rated on RPRs had a mark of 77, suggesting it was a decent event for the level. The winner has been rated around her French form for now.

## 2344 WATCH RACING UK TODAY JUST £10 MAIDEN FILLIES' STKS 5f 217y
**2:30** (2:32) (Class 5) 3-Y-0+ **£3,234** (£962; £481; £240) **Stalls** Centre

Form RPR

35- **1** **Classical Times**188 7667 3-9-0 0 PaulMulrennan 3 83
(Peter Chapple-Hyam) *mde all: pushed clr wl over 1f out: shkn up ent fnl f: sn rdn and kpt on strly* **8/13**1

0-2 **2** 3 1/4 **Excellent Sunset (IRE)**15 1889 3-9-0 0 TomQueally 2 73
(David Lanigan) *trckd ldrs: hdwy over 2f out: sn chsng wnr: rdn and cl up ent fnl f: sn drvn and kpt on same pce* **11/2**3

**3** 2 1/2 **Hindsight** 3-8-11 0 AlistairRawlinson(3) 7 65
(Michael Appleby) *green: trckd ldrs: pushed along 1/2-way: sn hung lft: rdn along 2f out: styd on fnl f* **40/1**

3- **4** 6 **Bella Alissa**250 5869 3-9-0 0 AdamBeschizza 6 46
(Robert Cowell) *trckd ldr: pushed along wl over 2f out: sn rdn and wknd wl over 1f out* **10/3**2

**5** 8 **Les Pecheurs (IRE)** 3-8-7 0 DanielleMooney(7) 1 20
(James Ewart) *chsd ldrs: rdn along 1/2-way: sn outpcd* **100/1**

**6** 12 **Waitomo** 3-9-0 0 JamieSpencer 5
(Charles Hills) *dwlt and green a rr* **20/1**

1m 11.86s (0.06) **Going Correction** +0.15s/f (Good) 6 Ran SP% **108.6**
Speed ratings (Par 100): **105,100,97,89,78 62**
CSF £4.08 TOTE £1.60: £1.10, £2.40; EX 4.50 Trifecta £31.10.
**Owner** Allan Belshaw **Bred** Times Of Wigan Ltd **Trained** Newmarket, Suffolk

**FOCUS**
Using previous renewals as a guide, this will probably be only modest form. It's been rated around the runner-up to the better view of her latest run.

## 2345 RACING UK PROFITS RETURNED TO RACING MAIDEN AUCTION STKS 7f
**3:00** (3:04) (Class 6) 3-Y-0 **£2,897** (£855; £427) **Stalls** Centre

Form RPR

230- **1** **Grinty (IRE)**213 7004 3-9-5 73 PaulMulrennan 7 73
(Michael Dods) *prom: led over 2f out: rdn over 1f out: edgd lft ins fnl f: kpt on wl* **7/4**1

0-2 **2** 1 **Wonder Of Dubai (IRE)**36 1426 3-9-5 0 JamieSpencer 4 70
(Michael Bell) *t.k.h: trckd ldrs: n.m.r and swtchd rt to outer over 1f out: sn rdn and styd on wl towards fin* **15/8**2

**3** hd **Daira Bridge (IRE)** 3-8-12 0 PatrickVaughan(7) 1 70+
(David O'Meara) *cl up: led 3f out: pushed along and hdd over 2f out: rdn wl over 1f out: ev ch and edgd lft ins fnl f: kpt on* **14/1**

**4** hd **Guiding Passion (FR)** 3-8-11 0 JordanVaughan(3) 2 64
(K R Burke) *trckd ldrs ion inner: hdwy and cl up over 2f out: rdn wl over 1f out and ev ch: drvn fnl f and kpt on* **17/2**3

40 **5** hd **Oregon Point (USA)**12 1977 3-9-5 0 DavidAllan 10 69
(Tim Easterby) *wnt rt s: trckd ldrs: pushed along wl over 2f out: cl up and rdn wl over 1f out: kpt on fnl f* **17/2**3

0-5 **6** 4 1/2 **Thomas Crown (IRE)**7 2110 3-9-5 0 TonyHamilton 8 57
(Roger Fell) *towards rr: pushed along and hdwy wl over 2f out: rdn wl over 1f out: no imp fnl f* **25/1**

**7** 1 3/4 **Shevington Moor** 3-9-0 0 ConnorBeasley 5 47
(Bryan Smart) *towards rr: pushed along 1/2-way: hdwy over 2f out: rdn wl over 1f out: sn wknd* **16/1**

00- **8** 3 1/4 **Thornton Mary**139 8397 3-9-0 0 JamesSullivan 9 38
(Brian Rothwell) *wnt rt s: a rr* **200/1**

-50 **9** 15 **Full Tilt Lad (IRE)**5 2135 3-9-5 0 BenCurtis 3 3
(Tim Easterby) *led: rdn along and hdd 3f out: sn wknd* **50/1**

1m 26.81s (2.31) **Going Correction** +0.15s/f (Good) 9 Ran SP% **111.1**
Speed ratings (Par 97): **92,90,90,90,90 85,83,79,62**
CSF £4.85 TOTE £2.30: £1.60, £1.10, £3.70; EX 4.90 Trifecta £37.80.
**Owner** J N Blackburn **Bred** Corrib Racing **Trained** Denton, Co Durham

**FOCUS**
A fair-looking maiden but only the two at the head of the betting were seriously backed.

## 2346 WIN A VIP DAY @ REDCARRACING.CO.UK CLAIMING STKS 7f
**3:30** (3:30) (Class 6) 3-Y-0+ **£2,897** (£855; £427) **Stalls** Centre

Form RPR

-525 **1** **Capolavoro (FR)**9 2064 6-9-5 69 (p) CallumRodriguez(5) 2 72+
(Robert Cowell) *in tch: hdwy to trck ldrs 4f out: effrt 2f out: rdn to chse ldr over 1f out: led jst ins fnl f: hld on wl towards fin* **6/4**1

6402 **2** shd **Cabal**15 1879 10-9-2 63 (b) DavidAllan 1 64+
(Geoffrey Harker) *hld up in rr: hdwy over 2f out: chsd ldrs over 1f out: rdn to chse wnr ins fnl f: sn drvn and kpt on wl: jst hld* **11/4**2

02-6 **3** 1 3/4 **Let's Twist**35 1450 5-9-7 74 ShaneGray 5 64
(Kristin Stubbs) *trckd ldr: effrt over 2f out: rdn along wl over 1f out: drvn appr fnl f: kpt on same pce* **7/1**

4506 **4** nk **Black Dave (IRE)**15 1893 7-9-6 65 SeanLevey 4 62
(David Evans) *led: pushed along 2f out: rdn wl over 1f out: drvn and hdd jst ins fnl f: grad wknd* **9/1**

0300 **5** 3/4 **Sandstream**17 1829 4-9-7 46 (t) RoystonFfrench 3 61
(Tracy Waggott) *trckd ldng pair: pushed along over 2f out: rdn wl over 1f out: drvn and wknd fnl f* **22/1**

106- **6** 3 1/4 **Manatee Bay**139 8402 7-9-10 77 (v) BarryMcHugh 8 55
(Noel Wilson) *t.k.h: hld up in rr: hdwy over 2f out: rdn to chse ldrs over 1f out: edgd lft and wknd fnl f* **6/1**3

-060 **7** 21 **Elements Legacy**64 970 3-8-6 50 FrannyNorton 6
(Tracy Waggott) *in tch: pushed along over 3f out: sn rdn and outpcd* **40/1**

1m 26.31s (1.81) **Going Correction** +0.15s/f (Good)
**WFA** 3 from 4yo+ 12lb 7 Ran SP% **110.2**
Speed ratings (Par 101): **95,94,92,92,91 87,63**
CSF £5.24 TOTE £2.60: £1.70, £1.60; EX 7.30 Trifecta £26.70.
**Owner** Cyril Humphris & Partner **Bred** Cyril Humphris **Trained** Six Mile Bottom, Cambs

**FOCUS**
Quite a competitive race of its type and a tight finish.

## 2347 RACINGUK.COM/DAYPASS H'CAP 1m 1f
**4:00** (4:01) (Class 5) (0-70,72) 3-Y-0 **£3,234** (£721; £721; £240) **Stalls** Low

Form RPR

55-5 **1** **Teodoro (IRE)**48 1244 3-9-7 **69** RichardKingscote 2 76+
(Tom Dascombe) *dwlt and towards rr: hdwy over 4f out: chsd ldrs on inner over 2f out: nt clr run and swtchd rt to outer jst over 1f out: sn rdn: drvn ins fnl f: styd on strly to ld nr line* **7/2**2

-432 **2** hd **Ronnie The Rooster**10 2036 3-9-4 **66** BenCurtis 4 71
(David Barron) *led: rdn along and jnd over 2f out: drvn: edgd lft and hdd narrowly over 1f out: rallied gamely and kpt on wl towards fin* **3/1**1

05-2 **2** dht **Cliff Bay (IRE)**18 1817 3-8-11 **59** (p) PhillipMakin 1 65
(Keith Dalgleish) *trckd ldrs: hdwy 3f out: chal over 2f out: sn rdn and tk slt advantage over 1f out: drvn ins fnl f: hdd nr line* **8/1**

21-0 **4** 3 1/4 **Snookered (IRE)**22 1736 3-8-12 **60** PaulHanagan 7 58
(Richard Fahey) *chsd ldr: rdn along over 2f out: drvn over 1f out: kpt on same pce* **7/1**

00-5 **5** *4* **Breakwater Bay (IRE)**[24] 1678 3-9-0 **62** DavidAllan 9 51
(Tim Easterby) *hld up towards rr: hdwy on inner 3f out: swtchd rt over 2f out and sn rdn: drvn wl over 1f out: sn no imp* **9/1**

115- **6** *1* **Katebird (IRE)**[187] 7697 3-9-9 **71** AndrewMullen 10 58
(Mark Johnston) *hld up: hdwy over 3f out: rdn along to chse ldrs wl over 2f out: sn drvn and no imp* **12/1**

16-0 **7** *8* **Ray Donovan (IRE)**[10] 2036 3-8-11 **64** JoshDoyle(5) 3 33
(David O'Meara) *midfield: rdn along 4f out: drvn wl over 2f out: sn wknd* **66/1**

046- **8** *nk* **Medalla De Oro**[133] 8486 3-9-6 **68** TomMarquand 11 37
(Peter Chapple-Hyam) *trckd ldrs on outer: hdwy to chse ldng pair over 4f out: rdn along over 2f out: sn wknd* **5/1**[3]

000- **9** *5* **Turning Gold**[195] 7495 3-8-10 **58** LukeMorris 8 16
(Sir Mark Prescott Bt) *dwlt: a rr* **16/1**

1m 53.01s (0.01) **Going Correction** +0.15s/f (Good) **9** Ran SP% **112.6**
Speed ratings (Par 99): **105,104,104,101,98 97,90,90,85**
WIN: £4.30; PL: Teodoro £1.60, Ronnie The Rooster £2.00, Cliff Bay £2.70; EX: T/RTR £8.80, T/CB £16.50; CSF: T/RTR £6.98, T/CB £15.29; TC: T/RTR/CB £37.73, T/CB/RTR £45.75; TF: T/RTR/CB £43.90, T/CB/RTR £56.50;.
**Owner** Laurence Bellman & Caroline Ingram **Bred** John Connaughton **Trained** Malpas, Cheshire

**FOCUS**
Probably a decent race for the level. The dead-heating runners-up set the standard.

## 2348 RACINGUK.COM H'CAP 7f
**4:30** (4:31) (Class 4) (0-85,87) 3-Y-O+ **£6,469** (£1,925; £962; £481) **Stalls** Centre

Form RPR

1-11 **1** **Gilgamesh**[54] 1149 3-9-6 **87** JamieSpencer 1 90+
(George Scott) *hld up in tch: hdwy 2f out: swtchd lft and rdn jst over 1f out: drvn ins fnl f: kpt on wl to ld towards fin* **7/4**[1]

51- **2** *nk* **Tai Sing Yeh (IRE)**[189] 7648 3-8-13 **80** (t) RichardKingscote 8 82
(Charles Hills) *led: pushed along 2f out: rdn and hdd narrowly over 1f out: drvn and led again ins fnl f: hdd and no ex towards fin* **9/2**[2]

603- **3** *1 ¼* **Sakhee's Return**[238] 6263 5-9-11 **83** (t) RachelRichardson(3) 9 86
(Tim Easterby) *prom: hdwy and cl up over 2f out: rdn to take slt ld over 1f out: drvn and hdd ins fnl f: no ex last 75 yds* **11/1**

2262 **4** *½* **Tailor's Row (USA)**[69] 902 3-9-0 **81** FrannyNorton 4 79
(Mark Johnston) *prom: rdn along 2f out: ev ch over 1f out: drvn ent fnl f: kpt on same pce* **15/2**

00-6 **5** *½* **Mohab**[17] 1832 4-9-7 **83** SeamusCronin(7) 7 83
(Kevin Ryan) *trckd ldrs: pushed along 2f out: rdn over 1f out: kpt on same pce* **16/1**

066- **6** *2 ¼* **Fieldsman (USA)**[224] 6710 5-10-1 **87** ShelleyBirkett(3) 2 81
(David O'Meara) *trckd ldrs: hdwy over 2f out: cl up wl over 1f out and sn rdn: drvn and wknd ent fnl f* **6/1**[3]

23-4 **7** *2 ½* **Deansgate (IRE)**[20] 1778 4-9-5 **74** (e) JoeDoyle 3 61
(Julie Camacho) *dwlt: a towards rr* **9/1**

5050 **8** *½* **Shamaheart (IRE)**[24] 1677 7-9-12 **81** (p) DavidAllan 6 67
(Geoffrey Harker) *hld up: a towards rr* **12/1**

0-00 **9** *8* **Slemy (IRE)**[22] 1717 6-9-7 **76** JamesSullivan 5 41
(Ruth Carr) *t.k.h: hld up: a towards rr* **33/1**

1m 24.16s (-0.34) **Going Correction** +0.15s/f (Good)
**WFA** 3 from 4yo+ 12lb **9** Ran SP% **115.4**
Speed ratings (Par 105): **107,106,105,104,104 101,98,98,88**
CSF £9.38 CT £65.82 TOTE £2.40: £1.30, £1.80, £3.30; EX 11.70 Trifecta £66.80.
**Owner** Niarchos Family **Bred** Niarchos Family **Trained** Newmarket, Suffolk

**FOCUS**
Despite the favourite going off fairly short, clear of the remainder in the betting, this looked competitive. Two of the three 3yos dominated the finish. The fourth has been rated close to form.

## 2349 REDCAR RACECOURSE CONFERENCE & WEDDING VENUE H'CAP 7f 219y
**5:00** (5:01) (Class 6) (0-60,62) 3-Y-O **£2,897** (£855; £427) **Stalls** Centre

Form RPR

0-54 **1** **Rita's Man (IRE)**[15] 1888 3-9-9 **62** SeanLevey 16 68
(Richard Hannon) *trckd ldrs: hdwy over 2f out: rdn to chal over 1f out: drvn and edgd lft ent fnl f: kpt on wl to ld nr fin* **6/1**[2]

4-54 **2** *hd* **Fairy Lock (IRE)**[101] 376 3-8-11 **50** BenCurtis 2 56
(David Barron) *in tch: hdwy on inner 2f out: rdn over 1f out: led ent fnl f and sn drvn: hdd and no ex nr fin* **10/1**

50-0 **3** *1 ½* **Champion Harbour (IRE)**[12] 1970 3-9-7 **60** PaulHanagan 11 62
(Richard Fahey) *hld up towards rr: hdwy over 2f out: swtchd rt and rdn over 1f out: chsd ldrs ent fnl f: sn drvn and kpt on* **14/1**

000- **4** *½* **Hugging The Rails (IRE)**[162] 8071 3-9-2 **55** (b[1]) JamesSullivan 6 56
(Tim Easterby) *hld up towards rr: hdwy over 2f out: pushed along and n.m.r wl over 1f out: sn rdn and styd on to chse ldrs ent fnl f: drvn and kpt on towards fin* **20/1**

06-6 **5** *1 ½* **Cosmic Sky**[17] 1835 3-9-1 **54** (h) DavidAllan 14 51
(Tim Easterby) *trckd ldrs: cl up 1/2-way: led over 2f out and sn rdn: drvn and hdd ent fnl f: kpt on same pce* **10/1**

00-3 **6** *1 ¼* **American Craftsman (IRE)**[14] 1914 3-9-7 **60** TonyHamilton 3 54
(Roger Fell) *hld up: hdwy over 2f out: rdn along wl over 1f out: no imp fnl f* **7/1**[3]

6-20 **7** *nse* **Kazanan (IRE)**[41] 1348 3-8-6 **50** CallumRodriguez(5) 4 44
(Michael Dods) *hld up in rr: hdwy on inner over 2f out: n.m.r and swtchd rt over 1f out: sn rdn and no imp ins fnl f* **12/1**

0-24 **8** *1 ¼* **A Bit Of Ginger**[8] 2077 3-9-4 **57** ShaneGray 10 48
(Ann Duffield) *chsd ldrs: rdn along wl over 1f out: grad wknd* **12/1**

0300 **9** *1 ¼* **Albizu Campos**[3] 2228 3-8-9 **48** (p) JoeDoyle 7 36
(Lawrence Mullaney) *cl up: disp ld 3f out: rdn along over 2f out: drvn wl over 1f out: grad wknd* **25/1**

4460 **10** *1 ¾* **State Residence (IRE)**[44] 1297 3-9-3 **61** JoshDoyle(5) 5 45
(David O'Meara) *hld up in rr: sme hdwy whn n.m.r and sltly hmpd wl over 1f out: n.d* **10/1**

06-0 **11** *1 ½* **Pontecarlo Boy**[8] 2077 3-8-8 **47** FrannyNorton 15 27
(Richard Whitaker) *hld up towards rr: sme hdwy on outer over 2f out: sn rdn along and n.d* **20/1**

60-0 **12** *4* **Flying Onsite (FR)**[32] 1514 3-9-6 **59** AndrewMullen 13 30
(Nigel Tinkler) *dwlt and bhd: pushed along over 2f out: n.m.r and swtchd lft wl over 1f out: n.d* **20/1**

400- **13** *½* **Parkwarden (IRE)**[251] 5840 3-9-1 **54** JackGarritty 1 23
(Chris Grant) *chsd ldrs: rdn along 3f out: sn wknd* **66/1**

0-03 **14** *hd* **Baker Street**[12] 1968 3-9-8 **61** (p[1]) RichardKingscote 8 30
(Tom Dascombe) *slt ld: rdn along 3f out: hdd over 2f out: sn wknd* **9/2**[1]

500- **15** *3 ¾* **Where's Stewart**[225] 6678 3-8-4 **46** oh1 (t[1]) RachelRichardson(3) 12 6
(Nigel Tinkler) *in tch: rdn along 3f out: sn wknd* **80/1**

5024 **16** *nk* **Stretewise (IRE)**[28] 1589 3-9-9 **62** ConnorBeasley 9 21
(Jason Ward) *chsd ldrs: rdn along wl 3f out: sn wknd* **11/1**

1m 38.47s (1.87) **Going Correction** +0.15s/f (Good) **16** Ran SP% **123.5**
Speed ratings (Par 97): **96,95,94,93,92 91,91,89,88,86 85,81,80,80,76 76**
CSF £60.03 CT £858.18 TOTE £6.80: £1.60, £2.60, £3.30, £5.70; EX 91.10 Trifecta £1177.80.
**Owner** Middleham Park Racing XX **Bred** L White & D McGregor **Trained** East Everleigh, Wilts

**FOCUS**
A competitive moderate contest, in which a few did suffer some traffic problems. Ordinary form.
T/Plt: £4.70 to a £1 stake. Pool: £51,093.05 - 7778.03 winning units. T/Qpdt: £2.30 to a £1 stake. Pool: £3,694.68 - 1139.45 winning units. **Joe Rowntree**

2350 - 2356a (Foreign Racing) - See Raceform Interactive

# CHEPSTOW (L-H)
Friday, May 5

**OFFICIAL GOING: Good to firm (good in places)**
Wind: Blustery Weather: Cloudy

## 2357 COUNTY MARQUEES H'CAP 1m 4f 23y
**1:20** (1:20) (Class 5) (0-75,74) 4-Y-O+ **£4,851** (£1,443; £721; £360) **Stalls** Low

Form RPR

1112 **1** **Moayadd (USA)**[37] 1430 5-9-4 **74** HollieDoyle(3) 3 82+
(Neil Mulholland) *hld up: hdwy over 3f out: led over 1f out: rdn and edgd lft ins fnl f: styd on* **11/4**[1]

0122 **2** *2* **Mazaaher**[16] 1891 7-8-10 **70** (p[1]) KatherineGlenister(7) 1 73
(David Evans) *hld up: hdwy u.p and swtchd rt over 1f out: r.o to go 2nd wl ins fnl f: nt rch wnr* **10/1**

110- **3** *1* **Rosie Royale (IRE)**[208] 7183 5-9-0 **72** GeorgeWood(5) 6 73
(Roger Teal) *chsd ldrs: rdn and nt clr run over 1f out: styd on same pce ins fnl f* **9/1**[3]

204- **4** *shd* **Glens Wobbly**[196] 7508 9-9-3 **73** CallumShepherd(3) 8 74
(Jonathan Geake) *led: rdn and hdd over 1f out: sn edgd lft: no ex ins fnl f* **12/1**

243- **5** *4* **What A Scorcher**[141] 5574 6-9-3 **70** DavidProbert 10 65
(Nikki Evans) *sn prom: chsd ldr 9f out tl rdn over 2f out: no ex fr over 1f out* **7/1**[2]

460- **6** *2 ¾* **Ring Eye (IRE)**[205] 7270 9-8-4 **60** oh4 EdwardGreatrex(3) 9 50
(John O'Shea) *hld up: hdwy over 2f out: shkn up over 1f out: nt trble ldrs* **25/1**

000- **7** *3* **Ma Peek (USA)**[207] 7223 4-9-0 **67** (t) TomMarquand 11 53
(Brian Meehan) *chsd ldrs: lost pl 1/2-way: rdn over 4f out: n.d after* **9/1**[3]

2642 **8** *hd* **Icebuster**[10] 2059 9-9-7 **74** AdamKirby 7 59
(Rod Millman) *s.i.s: wnt prom and racd keenly after 1f: rdn over 3f out: wknd over 1f out: eased* **11/4**[1]

505- **9** *shd* **Barizan (IRE)**[89] 7507 11-9-5 **72** (vt) PatDobbs 5 57
(Brendan Powell) *hld up: rdn over 4f out: a in rr* **20/1**

0-55 **10** *36* **Golden Jubilee (USA)**[34] 1505 8-9-6 **73** (p) StevieDonohoe 2 1
(Nigel Twiston-Davies) *chsd ldrs tl rdn and wknd over 3f out* **18/1**

2m 36.78s (-2.22) **Going Correction** -0.05s/f (Good) **10** Ran SP% **116.5**
Speed ratings (Par 103): **105,103,103,102,100 98,96,96,96,72**
CSF £32.49 CT £220.26 TOTE £3.60: £1.40, £2.70, £2.20; EX 22.40 Trifecta £80.60.
**Owner** P & Mrs K E Malcolm **Bred** Darley **Trained** Limpley Stoke, Wilts
■ Stewards' Enquiry : Katherine Glenister two-day ban (19 & 21 May): careless riding

**FOCUS**
The ground had been watered, with 8mm of irrigation applied on Wednesday and Thursday, and the going description was good to firm, good in places. Stalls: 5f, 6f & 1m - Centre, 1m4f & 2m - Inside. A fair middle-distance handicap run at an even gallop.

## 2358 PTL PORTABLE TOILETS LTD FILLIES' H'CAP 1m 2f 36y
**1:50** (1:52) (Class 5) (0-75,76) 4-Y-O+ **£4,851** (£1,443; £721; £360) **Stalls** Low

Form RPR

13-1 **1** **Perfect Quest**[25] 1683 4-9-9 **76** (t) AdamKirby 1 82
(Clive Cox) *chsd ldr tl shkn up to ld over 2f out: rdn out* **10/11**[1]

0-31 **2** *2* **Rum Swizzle**[11] 2028 5-9-8 **75** 6ex DavidProbert 6 77
(Harry Dunlop) *hld up in tch: chsd wnr over 1f out: sn rdn: styd on same pce ins fnl f* **9/1**[3]

50-6 **3** *1 ½* **Ghinia (IRE)**[25] 1687 6-9-7 **74** RobHornby 2 73
(Pam Sly) *chsd ldrs: shkn up over 2f out: styd on same pce fnl f* **9/4**[2]

460- **4** *1* **Distant High**[121] 7078 6-8-4 **60** oh3 (p) HollieDoyle(3) 5 57
(Richard Price) *s.i.s: hld up: rdn over 2f out: styd on: nvr trbld ldrs* **9/1**[3]

0-66 **5** *½* **Smart Mover (IRE)**[10] 2061 4-8-8 **61** TomMarquand 3 57
(Nikki Evans) *led: rdn and hdd over 2f out: no ex ins fnl f* **33/1**

0-00 **6** *42* **Coup De Vent**[15] 1894 6-8-2 **60** oh15 (b[1]) MitchGodwin(5) 4
(John O'Shea) *s.i.s: plld hrd and hdwy over 8f out: rdn over 2f out: sn wknd and eased* **50/1**

2m 11.68s (1.08) **Going Correction** -0.05s/f (Good) **6** Ran SP% **108.1**
Speed ratings (Par 100): **93,91,90,89,89 55**
CSF £9.31 TOTE £1.70: £1.10, £2.90; EX 6.70 Trifecta £9.60.
**Owner** Hants and Herts **Bred** Mrs S J Walker **Trained** Lambourn, Berks

**FOCUS**
A fair handicap and an improving winner.

## 2359 FEEDER - THE HOMECOMING MAIDEN STKS 1m 2f 36y
**2:20** (2:21) (Class 5) 3-Y-O+ **£4,851** (£1,443; £721; £360) **Stalls** Low

Form RPR

**1** **Laraaib (IRE)** 3-8-12 0 DaneO'Neill 6 81+
(Owen Burrows) *pushed along towards rr early: hdwy over 8f out: chsd ldr fnl f: edgd lft and styd on u.p to ld towards fin* **11/4**[1]

22-5 **2** *¾* **Prerogative (IRE)**[24] 1692 3-8-12 77 (p) PatDobbs 1 79
(Richard Hannon) *led: rdn over 1f out: hdd towards fin* **7/2**[2]

6- **3** *5* **Scales Of Justice (IRE)**[191] 7622 3-8-12 0 SteveDrowne 8 74
(Charles Hills) *chsd ldr: shkn up over 3f out: rdn and ev ch over 1f out: stl cl up tl eased ins fnl f* **7/2**[2]

33 **4** *1 ¾* **Tristram**[15] 1900 3-8-12 0 ShaneKelly 12 66
(Richard Hughes) *hld up in tch: shkn up over 2f out: rdn over 1f out: styd on same pce* **11/1**

5 **5** *5* **Belgravian (FR)**[18] 1830 3-8-12 0 DavidProbert 4 56
(Archie Watson) *trckd ldrs: rdn over 2f out: wknd over 1f out* **4/1**[3]

5-3 **6** *1 ¾* **Pondering**[10] 2062 3-8-4 0 EdwardGreatrex(3) 3 47
(Eve Johnson Houghton) *dwlt: hld up: effrt over 2f out: wknd over 1f out* **14/1**

**7** *1 ½* **High Wells** 3-8-12 0 JohnFahy 11 49
(Seamus Durack) *hld up: rn green: shkn up over 2f out: nvr on terms* **33/1**

**8** *13* **Maitresse (IRE)** 3-8-7 0 RobHornby 7 18
(Seamus Durack) *prom: stdd and lost pl over 8f out: hdwy over 4f out: rdn and wknd over 2f out* **33/1**

9 *18* **Morning Sequel** 4-9-8 0 AdamKirby 10
(Neil Mulholland) *s.i.s: outpcd* **50/1**

2m 7.96s (-2.64) **Going Correction** -0.05s/f (Good)
**WFA** 3 from 4yo 15lb 9 Ran SP% **114.0**
Speed ratings (Par 103): **108,107,103,102,98 96,95,85,70**
CSF £12.14 TOTE £3.50: £1.50, £1.40, £1.60; EX 13.60 Trifecta £44.40.
**Owner** Hamdan Al Maktoum **Bred** Shadwell Estate Company Limited **Trained** Lambourn, Berks
**FOCUS**
A fair maiden and the runner-up helps to set the form.

## 2360 GET THE SKY BET ADVANTAGE VETERANS' H'CAP 5f 16y
**2:50** (2:50) (Class 5) (0-75,75) 6-Y-O+ **£4,851** (£1,443; £721; £360) **Stalls** Centre

Form RPR
1122 **1** **Roy's Legacy**[3] 2263 8-8-5 **64** CharlieBennett(5) 9 71
(Shaun Harris) *chsd ldrs: outpcd over 3f out: hdwy over 1f out: rdn to ld ins fnl f: r.o* **11/4[1]**
104- **2** *3/4* **Silverrica (IRE)**[221] 6831 7-9-2 **75** GeorgiaCox(5) 7 78
(Malcolm Saunders) *stmbld s: outpcd: r.o wl ins fnl f: wnt 2nd nr fin: nt rch wnr* **9/1**
00-0 **3** *1/2* **Babyfact**[21] 1768 6-9-2 **70** PatDobbs 10 71
(Malcolm Saunders) *sn outpcd: hdwy over 1f out: r.o* **11/2[3]**
-000 **4** *nk* **Molly Jones**[62] 1022 8-8-8 **61** oh10 ow1 JohnFahy 5 62?
(Matthew Salaman) *s.i.s and hmpd s: outpcd: r.o wl ins fnl f: nt quite rch ldrs* **66/1**
351- **5** *hd* **Quantum Dot (IRE)**[261] 5546 6-8-5 **62** (b) CallumShepherd(3) 2 61
(Ed de Giles) *chsd ldr who wnt clr over 3f out: tk clsr order over 1f out: rdn and ev ch whn edgd rt ins fnl f: styd on same pce towards fin* **14/1**
5152 **6** *hd* **Swendab (IRE)**[4] 2216 9-8-12 **65** ow1 (b) TimmyMurphy 6 65
(John O'Shea) *chsd ldrs: outpcd over 3f out: hdwy over 1f out: r.o* **15/2**
530- **7** *4 1/2* **Edged Out**[247] 6017 7-9-0 **73** MitchGodwin(5) 8 55
(Christopher Mason) *chsd ldrs: outpcd over 3f out: hdwy over 1f out: wknd wl ins fnl f* **7/1**
530- **8** *1 1/4* **Pour La Victoire (IRE)**[205] 7267 7-9-6 **74** GeorgeDowning 4 52
(Tony Carroll) *edgd rt s: sn outpcd* **7/1**
0423 **9** *4 1/2* **Powerful Wind (IRE)**[17] 1869 8-8-10 **64** (t) KieranO'Neill 1 26
(Charlie Wallis) *led at str pce: clr over 3f out: rdn: edgd rt and c bk to the field over 1f out: wknd and hdd ins fnl f* **9/2[2]**

58.91s (-0.39) **Going Correction** -0.05s/f (Good) 9 Ran SP% **115.2**
Speed ratings: **101,99,99,98,98 97,90,88,81**
CSF £28.51 CT £127.61 TOTE £3.80: £1.40, £2.60, £2.30; EX 33.30 Trifecta £155.10.
**Owner** Notts Racing, S Mohammed & S Rowley **Bred** A Christou **Trained** Carburton, Notts
**FOCUS**
A fair handicap, in which they went a strong pace from the off, and the closers came to the fore late on.

## 2361 WPS EMPLOYEE BENEFITS H'CAP 1m 14y
**3:20** (3:20) (Class 4) (0-80,80) 3-Y-O **£6,469** (£1,925; £962; £481) **Stalls** Centre

Form RPR
-531 **1** **Arctic Sea**[30] 1550 3-8-13 **72** DavidProbert 2 76
(Paul Cole) *s.i.s: hld up: hdwy over 3f out: shkn up to ld over 1f out: rdn out* **9/2[2]**
31- **2** *nk* **War Chief**[207] 7208 3-9-7 **80** FergusSweeney 6 83
(Alan King) *s.i.s: hdwy and hung lft fr over 1f out: r.o* **5/2[1]**
03-0 **3** *shd* **Daimochi (IRE)**[24] 1692 3-8-12 **71** SamHitchcott 4 73
(Clive Cox) *led over 5f: rdn and ev ch fr over 1f out: r.o* **9/1[3]**
066- **4** *1 1/4* **Quandary Peak**[264] 5447 3-9-2 **75** LiamJones 5 74
(J S Moore) *plld hrd and prom: led over 2f out: hdd over 1f out: rdn and edgd rt ins fnl f: styd on same pce* **50/1**
040- **5** *1 3/4* **Fastnet Spin (IRE)**[184] 7764 3-8-11 **77** (v) KatherineGlenister(7) 9 72
(David Evans) *hld up: hdwy over 3f out: rdn over 1f out: carried hd high and hmpd ins fnl f: no ex* **33/1**
-264 **6** *nse* **Hisar (IRE)**[23] 1724 3-9-0 **73** (h) ShaneKelly 3 68
(Ronald Harris) *chsd ldrs: nt clr run over 2f out: sn rdn: no ex ins fnl f* **25/1**
341- **7** *1 3/4* **Habbad (FR)**[156] 8153 3-9-2 **75** TomMarquand 8 66
(Richard Hannon) *hld up in tch: nt clr run fr over 3f out tl over 2f out: sn rdn: no ex fnl f* **5/2[1]**
10- **8** *10* **Gold Award (IRE)**[195] 7544 3-9-4 **77** RobHornby 1 45
(Mick Channon) *chsd ldr tl rdn over 3f out: wknd over 1f out* **9/2[2]**

1m 35.2s (-1.00) **Going Correction** -0.05s/f (Good) 8 Ran SP% **112.3**
Speed ratings (Par 101): **103,102,102,101,99 99,97,87**
CSF £15.50 CT £94.51 TOTE £4.80: £1.70, £1.40, £1.90; EX 17.10 Trifecta £77.80.
**Owner** P F I Cole Ltd **Bred** Waratah Thoroughbreds Pty Ltd **Trained** Whatcombe, Oxon
**FOCUS**
A useful 3yo handicap and the form looks solid.

## 2362 A QUALITY SERVICE LTD (AQS) H'CAP 6f 16y
**3:50** (3:51) (Class 6) (0-60,62) 3-Y-O **£2,587** (£770; £384; £192) **Stalls** Centre

Form RPR
040- **1** **Zambezi Queen (IRE)**[151] 8229 3-9-2 **55** DavidProbert 1 70+
(Paul Cole) *hld up: swtchd rt and hdwy over 3f out: led over 1f out: qcknd clr ins fnl f* **8/1**
0005 **2** *5* **Lightoller (IRE)**[4] 2235 3-9-2 **62** (b[1]) KeithQuinn(7) 3 62
(Mick Channon) *led: rdn and hdd over 1f out: carried hd high: edgd rt and no ex ins fnl f* **8/1**
50-6 **3** *1 1/4* **Everkyllachy (IRE)**[102] 377 3-8-8 **54** (b) GeorgiaDobie(7) 10 50
(J S Moore) *hld up: hdwy over 2f out: rdn over 1f out: styd on same pce ins fnl f* **20/1**
000 **4** *1/2* **Spare Parts (IRE)**[28] 1600 3-8-13 **55** CallumShepherd(3) 15 50
(Charles Hills) *hld up: hdwy over 2f out: rdn over 1f out: styd on same pce fnl f* **14/1**
004- **5** *1 1/4* **Lawfilly**[139] 8425 3-9-2 **55** ShaneKelly 8 46
(Richard Hughes) *hld up: hdwy over 2f out: rdn adn flashed tail fr over 1f out: styd on same pce* **20/1**
4500 **6** *2 1/2* **Celerity (IRE)**[10] 2065 3-8-2 **48** (b) KeelanBaker(7) 5 32
(David Evans) *hld up: hdwy over 2f out: rdn over 1f out: wknd ins fnl f* **33/1**
6030 **7** *hd* **Beach Dancer (IRE)**[4] 2235 3-8-9 **51** EdwardGreatrex(3) 14 34
(William Knight) *chsd ldrs: rdn over 2f out: wknd ins fnl f* **4/1[1]**
305- **8** *1 1/4* **Harlequin Rose (IRE)**[188] 7690 3-8-6 **50** CharlieBennett(5) 2 29
(Patrick Chamings) *chsd ldr tl rdn over 2f out: wknd fnl f* **8/1**
0-03 **9** *nk* **Legendoire (IRE)**[20] 1787 3-9-7 **60** FergusSweeney 13 38
(John Gallagher) *w ldrs: rdn over 1f out: wknd ins fnl f* **5/1[2]**
005- **10** *1* **Lilly Ballerina (IRE)**[309] 3820 3-8-7 **46** oh1 GeorgeDowning 12 21
(Tony Carroll) *hld up: rdn and hung rt over 1f out: nvr on terms* **100/1**
4425 **11** *hd* **Viola Park**[2] 2309 3-9-1 **54** (b) TimmyMurphy 4 29
(Ronald Harris) *s.i.s: sn hung lft and outpcd* **13/2**
00-4 **12** *2 1/2* **Charlie Victor**[36] 1453 3-9-3 **56** AdamKirby 7 29
(Clive Cox) *w ldrs: rdn over 2f out: wkng whn hmpd 1f out* **6/1[3]**
2640 **13** *5* **Glam'Selle**[25] 1688 3-8-8 **47** (p) LiamJones 11
(Ronald Harris) *s.i.s: a in rr: rdn over 2f out: sn wknd* **25/1**

1m 10.42s (-1.58) **Going Correction** -0.05s/f (Good) 13 Ran SP% **121.6**
Speed ratings (Par 97): **108,101,99,99,97 94,93,92,91,90 90,86,80**
CSF £67.43 CT £1293.29 TOTE £10.10: £3.10, £3.30, £7.10; EX 87.70 Trifecta £1914.70.
**Owner** Miss Emily Asprey & Christopher Wright **Bred** Swordlestown Stud **Trained** Whatcombe, Oxon
■ Stewards' Enquiry : Georgia Dobie two-day ban (19&21 May): used whip above permitted level
**FOCUS**
A modest but competitive handicap and an impressive winner.

## 2363 LORD'S TAVERNERS H'CAP (DIV I) 2m 49y
**4:20** (4:20) (Class 6) (0-65,66) 4-Y-O+ **£2,587** (£770; £384; £192) **Stalls** Low

Form RPR
P-02 **1** **Akavit (IRE)**[14] 1935 5-9-6 **64** CallumShepherd(3) 2 69
(Ed de Giles) *mde all: pushed clr 2f out: rdn and edgd rt ins fnl f: styd on wl* **3/1[2]**
0-03 **2** *3* **Riptide**[11] 2032 11-9-7 **65** EdwardGreatrex(3) 3 66
(Michael Scudamore) *s.s: hld up: hdwy over 2f out: sn chsng wnr: rdn over 1f out: no imp fnl f* **7/1[3]**
011- **3** *3 1/4* **Master Dancer**[173] 6256 6-9-6 **66** (p) MitchGodwin(5) 6 63
(Tim Vaughan) *prom: lost pl 9f out: hdwy over 3f out: rdn over 2f out: styd on same pce fr over 1f out* **6/4[1]**
663- **4** *nk* **Taste The Wine (IRE)**[194] 4591 11-8-13 **54** (p) DavidProbert 8 51
(Bernard Llewellyn) *chsd wnr tl rdn over 2f out: styd on same pce fr over 1f out* **20/1**
00-5 **5** *8* **Urban Space**[21] 1763 11-9-8 **63** (t) DanielMuscutt 5 50
(John Flint) *chsd ldrs: rdn over 2f out: hung lft and wknd over 1f out* **8/1**
400- **6** *1* **Sail With Sultana**[36] 946 6-8-2 **48** GeorgeWood(5) 9 34
(Mark Rimell) *s.i.s: hld up: hdwy 9f out: rdn over 3f out: sn wknd* **12/1**
2/0- **7** *9* **Filatore (IRE)**[53] 1523 8-9-5 **60** (b) StevieDonohoe 4 35
(Bernard Llewellyn) *chsd ldrs: rdn over 5f out: wknd over 2f out* **7/1[3]**

3m 37.16s (-1.74) **Going Correction** -0.05s/f (Good) 7 Ran SP% **113.6**
Speed ratings (Par 101): **102,100,98,98,94 94,89**
CSF £23.59 CT £41.78 TOTE £3.80: £1.90, £3.40; EX 21.30 Trifecta £50.10.
**Owner** Simon Treacher & Partner **Bred** Tenuta Genzianella Di Manuela Martinelli **Trained** Ledbury, H'fords
**FOCUS**
A modest staying handicap.

## 2364 LORD'S TAVERNERS H'CAP (DIV II) 2m 49y
**4:50** (4:51) (Class 6) (0-65,65) 4-Y-O+ **£2,587** (£770; £384; £192) **Stalls** Low

Form RPR
046- **1** **Kashgar**[278] 4912 8-9-10 **65** StevieDonohoe 2 70
(Bernard Llewellyn) *hld up: hdwy over 2f out: rdn to ld over 1f out: jst hld on* **9/1[3]**
5460 **2** *nk* **Cold Fusion (IRE)**[3] 2272 4-8-3 **50** (t[1]) HollieDoyle(3) 3 55
(David Flood) *prom: chsd wnr fnl f: sn rdn and edgd lft: styd on wl* **9/1[3]**
004- **3** *3 3/4* **Powderonthebonnet (IRE)**[202] 7367 9-8-4 **50** (p[1]) GeorgeWood(5) 7 50
(Sam Thomas) *w ldr: rdn to ld over 2f out: hdd over 1f out: styd on same pce ins fnl f* **7/2[2]**
2-32 **4** *3 1/4* **Thomas Blossom (IRE)**[93] 508 7-9-8 **63** (t) TomMarquand 6 59
(Ali Stronge) *hld up: hdwy u.p: nt clr run and swtchd rt over 1f out: no ex wl ins fnl f* **7/2[2]**
060- **5** *1* **Sigurd (GER)**[26] 5183 5-8-8 **49** (p) FergusSweeney 1 44
(Jonjo O'Neill) *trckd ldrs: plld hrd: rdn over 1f out: styd on same pce* **15/8[1]**
50-0 **6** *2 3/4* **Rob's Legacy**[18] 1834 4-8-2 **46** oh1 RoystonFfrench 8 38
(Shaun Harris) *hld up: rdn over 3f out: nt trble ldrs* **25/1**
020/ **7** *2 1/4* **Taroum (IRE)**[7] 8261 10-9-0 **55** (bt) DanielMuscutt 4 44
(John Flint) *led: rdn and hdd over 2f out: wknd ins fnl f* **16/1**
500/ **8** *26* **L Frank Baum (IRE)**[53] 5997 10-9-10 **65** (b) AdamKirby 5 23
(Bernard Llewellyn) *hld up: hdwy over 11f out: rdn and wknd over 2f out: eased* **20/1**

3m 43.45s (4.55) **Going Correction** -0.05s/f (Good)
**WFA** 4 from 5yo+ 1lb 8 Ran SP% **113.7**
Speed ratings (Par 101): **86,85,83,82,81 80,79,66**
CSF £84.51 CT £337.84 TOTE £7.10: £2.30, £3.00, £1.80; EX 63.90 Trifecta £289.50.
**Owner** Alex James **Bred** J L C Pearce **Trained** Fochriw, Caerphilly
**FOCUS**
They went a steady gallop in the second division of the staying handicap, and the time was 6.29sec slower than the first leg.
T/Jkpt: Not won. T/Plt: £122.10 to a £1 stake. Pool: £57,281.00 - 468.86 winning units. T/Qpdt: £44.30 to a £1 stake. Pool: £4,522.00 - 101.95 winning units. **Colin Roberts**

# 2330 LINGFIELD (L-H)
Friday, May 5

**OFFICIAL GOING: Polytrack: standard**
Wind: light half against Weather: cloudy

## 2365 JOIN US FOR COUNTRYSIDE DAY - 3RD JUNE (S) STKS 1m 1y(P)
**2:10** (2:10) (Class 6) 3-Y-O+ **£2,264** (£673; £336; £168) **Stalls** High

Form RPR
-600 **1** **Chelwood Gate (IRE)**[23] 1728 7-9-10 70 (v) JosephineGordon 3 74
(Patrick Chamings) *hld up: hdwy 2f out: led jst over 1f out: qcknd readily clr* **4/1[3]**
01-5 **2** *3 3/4* **Isis Blue**[25] 1683 7-10-1 65 RyanTate 6 69
(Rod Millman) *trckd ldr: led over 2f out: rdn and hdd jst over 1f out: kpt on but sn outpcd by wnr* **7/2[2]**
5553 **3** *1* **Dana's Present**[13] 1982 8-10-1 70 (p[1]) LiamKeniry 5 67
(Tom Dascombe) *travelled wl: trckd ldr: trckd ldr jst over 2f out: rdn over 1f out: fnd little and sn hld* **8/1**
051 **4** *4* **Willwams (IRE)**[49] 1238 3-8-4 75 RossaRyan(7) 1 49
(Richard Hannon) *hld up: rdn into 4th 2f out: nt pce to get on terms w ldrs* **7/4[1]**
244- **5** *6* **Brasted (IRE)**[149] 8252 5-9-8 70 JoshuaBryan(7) 2 43
(Lee Carter) *hld up: short of room and clipped heels on bnd 2f out: sn rdn: nvr threatened* **6/1**

-525 6 34 **Gaelic Silver (FR)**$^{24}$ 1695 11-9-7 69......................(p) HectorCrouch$^{(3)}$ 4
(Gary Moore) *led tl rdn over 2f out: sn wknd* **10/1**

1m 37.46s (-0.74) **Going Correction** +0.05s/f (Slow)
**WFA** 3 from 5yo+ 13lb **6** Ran SP% **113.1**
Speed ratings (Par 101): **105,101,100,96,90 56**
CSF £18.49 TOTE £5.30: £2.20, £2.30; EX 20.30 Trifecta £105.50.There was no bid for the winner
**Owner** P R Chamings **Bred** Jusoor Syndicate **Trained** Baughurst, Hants

**FOCUS**
A modest heat. The wind was half across, 45 degrees from behind the stands.

## 2366 HAPPY BIRTHDAY MARY BRENNAN MAIDEN STKS 7f 1y(P)
**2:40** (2:42) (Class 5) 3-Y-O+ **£2,911** (£866; £432; £216) **Stalls** Low

Form RPR
0- **1** **Silent Echo**$^{333}$ 2976 3-9-0 0................................ JamesDoyle 3 88+
(Roger Charlton) *mde all: r.o wl to assert fnl f: rdn out* **2/1**$^{2}$

02 **2** 1 ¼ **Time's Arrow (IRE)**$^{9}$ 2090 3-9-0 0........................ SilvestreDeSousa 10 84
(Sir Michael Stoute) *trckd wnr: chal over 2f out: rdn and ev ch wl over 1f out: kpt on but a being hld fnl f* **8/11**$^{1}$

300- **3** 7 **Vigee Le Brun (IRE)**$^{195}$ 7547 3-8-2 72......................... JordanUys$^{(7)}$ 5 60
(Brian Meehan) *trckd ldrs: rdn over 2f out: kpt on to chse ldng pair jst over 1f out but nvr gng pce to get on terms* **10/1**$^{3}$

0- **4** 4 ½ **Primadonia**$^{242}$ 6189 3-8-9 0.......................................... JimmyQuinn 6 48
(Richard Hughes) *mid-div: rdn over 2f out: kpt on fnl f but n.d: snatched 4th fnl stride* **50/1**

50- **5** shd **Sattar (IRE)**$^{176}$ 7891 3-8-11 0....................................... NoelGarbutt$^{(3)}$ 9 53
(Luke McJannet) *in tch: rdn to chse ldng pair over 2f out: nt pce to get on terms: fdd fnl f* **66/1**

**6** 4 ½ **Know The Truth** 3-8-9 0................................................ ThomasBrown 1 36+
(Andrew Balding) *dwlt: racd green: towards rr: sme minor late prog: n.d* **20/1**

0-0 **7** shd **Nigh Or Never (IRE)**$^{23}$ 1730 3-9-0 0............................ FrannyNorton 7 40+
(Tom Dascombe) *towards rr: sme minor late prog: nvr any threat* **16/1**

60 **8** 1 ½ **Joy**$^{9}$ 2090 3-8-9 0............................................................ JosephineGordon 2 31
(Laura Mongan) *trckd ldrs: rdn over 2f out: wknd over 1f out* **100/1**

04- **9** ¾ **Punkawallah**$^{202}$ 7366 3-9-0 0.................................. RichardKingscote 8 34+
(Tom Dascombe) *a towards rr* **16/1**

0 **10** 1 **Espresso Martini**$^{13}$ 1962 3-9-0 0................................ JimmyFortune 4 31+
(Brian Meehan) *a towards rr* **33/1**

1m 24.33s (-0.47) **Going Correction** +0.05s/f (Slow) **10** Ran SP% **124.2**
Speed ratings (Par 103): **104,102,94,89,89 84,84,82,81,80**
CSF £3.93 TOTE £3.10: £1.80, £1.02, £2.50; EX 4.70 Trifecta £21.30.
**Owner** K Abdullah **Bred** Juddmonte Farms Ltd **Trained** Beckhampton, Wilts

**FOCUS**
As the betting suggested beforehand, this proved a match.

## 2367 ROY GALPIN MEMORIAL H'CAP 6f 1y(P)
**3:10** (3:10) (Class 6) (0-65,65) 4-Y-O+ **£2,264** (£673; £336; £168) **Stalls** Low

Form RPR
310- **1** **Mad Endeavour**$^{213}$ 7059 6-9-7 65..................................(b) MartinLane 1 71
(Stuart Kittow) *s.i.s: sn rousted along to ld: drvn whn strly chal over 1f out: briefly hdd fnl 120yds: hld on: all out* **9/2**$^{3}$

3642 **2** hd **Noble Deed**$^{9}$ 2091 7-9-3 61...................................(p) AdamBeschizza 8 66
(Michael Attwater) *in tch:hdwy over 2f out: rdn for str chal over 1f out: ev ch thrght fnl f: kpt on wl: jst hld* **7/2**$^{2}$

0234 **3** nk **Bookmaker**$^{15}$ 1898 7-8-6 57......................................(p) JaneElliott$^{(7)}$ 2 62
(John Bridger) *trckd ldr: rdn for str chal over 1f out: ev ch thrght fnl f: hld cl home* **7/2**$^{2}$

60-5 **4** 5 **Staffa (IRE)**$^{30}$ 1557 4-8-9 53...................................... SilvestreDeSousa 6 43
(Denis Coakley) *hld up: rdn in 5th over 1f out: sn one pce: hmpd whn lft 4th fnl 120yds* **5/2**$^{1}$

0510 **5** nk **Autumn Tonic (IRE)**$^{22}$ 1759 5-8-12 56......................... WilliamCarson 5 45
(Charlie Wallis) *hld up: sme prog 2f out: sn rdn: nt pce to threaten* **20/1**

1020 **6** 1 ¼ **Encapsulated**$^{23}$ 1723 7-8-6 57....................................... RhiainIngram$^{(7)}$ 3 42
(Roger Ingram) *in tch: rdn to chse ldrs over 1f out: wknd ins fnl f* **10/1**

40-0 **7** 3 ¾ **Perfect Pastime**$^{15}$ 1898 9-8-7 58............................(h) IsobelFrancis$^{(7)}$ 4 32
(Jim Boyle) *slowly away: nvr travelling in detached last* **16/1**

0004 **8** ¾ **Rigolleto (IRE)**$^{23}$ 1723 9-9-4 62............................(p) JosephineGordon 7 33+
(Anabel K Murphy) *trckd ldr: rdn over 1f out: narrow advantage whn lost action bdly and immediately eased fnl 120yds* **14/1**

1m 12.38s (0.48) **Going Correction** +0.05s/f (Slow) **8** Ran SP% **117.6**
Speed ratings (Par 101): **98,97,97,90,90 88,83,82**
CSF £21.32 CT £61.97 TOTE £5.80: £1.90, £1.40, £1.60; EX 23.20 Trifecta £71.90.
**Owner** Reg Gifford **Bred** S R Hope **Trained** Blackborough, Devon

**FOCUS**
It paid to be close to the pace here.

## 2368 GREATER LONDON PROPERTIES H'CAP 5f 6y(P)
**3:40** (3:41) (Class 4) (0-85,87) 4-Y-O+ **£4,690** (£1,395; £697; £348) **Stalls** High

Form RPR
-000 **1** **Brother Tiger**$^{18}$ 1833 8-8-13 77................................ SilvestreDeSousa 2 84+
(David C Griffiths) *trckd ldrs: shkn up ent fnl f: r.o wl to ld fnl 120yds: readily* **10/3**$^{1}$

-503 **2** 1 **Highly Sprung (IRE)**$^{6}$ 2147 4-9-5 83.............................. FrannyNorton 6 86+
(Mark Johnston) *hmpd s: sn rousted along in midfield: last pair and drvn turning in: r.o strly ins fnl f: wnt 2nd cl home* **4/1**$^{2}$

1642 **3** hd **The Big Lad**$^{18}$ 1836 5-8-6 77.................................(be) NicolaCurrie$^{(7)}$ 9 79+
(Richard Hughes) *s.i.s: rdn in last pair over 1f out: r.o strly ins fnl f: wnt 3rd cl home* **15/2**

4610 **4** hd **Dungannon**$^{17}$ 1863 10-9-2 87...................................(b) JoshuaBryan$^{(7)}$ 3 89
(Andrew Balding) *mid-div: rdn and hdwy ent fnl f: wnt 2nd fnl 100yds: kpt on but no ex whn lost 2 pls cl home* **13/2**

26-5 **5** hd **Stormflower**$^{11}$ 2038 4-8-7 71 oh2.......................................... LukeMorris 8 72
(John Bridger) *little slowly away: sn chsng ldrs: rdn 2f out: kpt on fnl f* **20/1**

320- **6** nk **Flying Bear (IRE)**$^{136}$ 8463 6-9-0 78.................................... MartinLane 7 78
(Jeremy Gask) *s.i.s and hmpd s: bhd: hdwy ent fnl f where nt best of runs: r.o fnl 120yds* **16/1**

4134 **7** shd **Mossgo (IRE)**$^{11}$ 2025 7-8-7 71 oh2.................................(t) KierenFox 5 71
(John Best) *wnt rt s: led: jnd over 2f out: sn rdn: hdd fnl 120yds: kpt on but no ex* **20/1**

6410 **8** hd **Monumental Man**$^{9}$ 2083 8-9-7 85...............................(p) WilliamCarson 4 84
(Michael Attwater) *hmpd s: sn prom: disp ld over 2f out: sn rdn: hdd fnl 120yds: hld whn short of room cl home* **13/2**

2534 **9** ½ **Vimy Ridge**$^{29}$ 1586 5-8-8 72......................................... JosephineGordon 1 71
(Alan Bailey) *in tch: hdwy on inner turning in: rdn in cl 4th whn nt clr run ent fnl f: fdd towards fin* **9/2**$^{3}$

59.31s (0.51) **Going Correction** +0.05s/f (Slow) **9** Ran SP% **115.1**
Speed ratings (Par 105): **97,95,95,94,94 93,93,93,92**
CSF £16.57 CT £90.48 TOTE £4.20: £1.80, £2.00, £2.10; EX 20.50 Trifecta £138.50.
**Owner** Norcroft Park Stud **Bred** Norcroft Park Stud **Trained** Bawtry, S Yorks

**FOCUS**
They finished in a heap behind the cosy winner.

## 2369 CONGRATULATIONS ON YOUR ENGAGEMENT EILEEN & JP H'CAP 1m 1y(P)
**4:10** (4:10) (Class 5) (0-75,75) 4-Y-O+ **£2,911** (£866; £432; £216) **Stalls** High

Form RPR
1660 **1** **Berrahri (IRE)**$^{25}$ 1687 6-9-2 70................................... JosephineGordon 2 77
(John Best) *led for 1f: trckd ldr: rdn over 2f out: carried sltly rt ent fnl f: kpt on fnl 120yds: led fnl stride* **5/1**$^{3}$

43-6 **2** shd **Handytalk (IRE)**$^{28}$ 1606 4-9-2 75.................................. LuluStanford$^{(5)}$ 5 82
(Rod Millman) *plld hrd: led after 1f: rdn 2f out: drifted sltly rt ent fnl f: kpt on: hdd fnl stride* **11/4**$^{1}$

0-30 **3** 1 ½ **Thundering Blue (USA)**$^{13}$ 1969 4-9-7 75.................... JimmyFortune 4 78+
(David Menuisier) *hld up: pushed along in last turning in: sn rdn: r.o strly fnl f: wnt 3rd fnl 50yds* **7/2**$^{2}$

53/6 **4** 1 **Bumptious**$^{18}$ 1830 4-9-7 75.................................................. SeanLevey 1 76
(Ismail Mohammed) *trckd ldrs: rdn over 2f out: kpt on same pce fnl f* **11/2**

10P- **5** ½ **Frank Bridge**$^{239}$ 6266 4-9-5 73........................................ CharlesBishop 9 73
(Eve Johnson Houghton) *hld up: rdn 2f out: kpt on ins fnl f but nt pave to get involved* **33/1**

4405 **6** 1 **Fire Diamond**$^{23}$ 1728 4-9-1 69.....................................(p) FrannyNorton 3 67
(Tom Dascombe) *awkward leaving stalls: racd keenly: hld up: rdn into 4th turning in: nt pce to get on terms: fdd fnl 100yds* **7/2**$^{2}$

5630 **7** 3 ¾ **Archangel Raphael (IRE)**$^{20}$ 1788 5-9-4 75.....(e$^{1}$) KieranShoemark$^{(3)}$ 7 64
(Amanda Perrett) *trckd ldrs: rdn 2f out: wknd fnl f* **12/1**

1m 37.33s (-0.87) **Going Correction** +0.05s/f (Slow) **7** Ran SP% **113.8**
Speed ratings (Par 103): **106,105,104,103,102 101,98**
CSF £18.96 CT £53.50 TOTE £5.80: £2.30, £2.50; EX 20.90 Trifecta £86.80.
**Owner** White Turf Racing Uk **Bred** Kilnamoragh Stud **Trained** Oad Street, Kent
■ Stewards' Enquiry : Lulu Stanford 2 day ban (19/21 May) - guilty of careless riding in that she allowed her mount to drift right-handed over a considerable distance

**FOCUS**
They didn't go much of a gallop here, and the pace held up.

## 2370 INJURED JOCKEYS FUND H'CAP 5f 6y(P)
**4:45** (4:46) (Class 6) (0-60,62) 4-Y-O+ **£2,264** (£673; £252; £252) **Stalls** High

Form RPR
0-00 **1** **Frangarry (IRE)**$^{41}$ 1372 5-9-5 55.............................. JosephineGordon 6 63
(Alan Bailey) *pressed ldr: led over 1f out: rdn clr: comf* **9/1**

1005 **2** 1 ½ **Dandilion (IRE)**$^{13}$ 1980 4-9-6 56.......................................(t) LukeMorris 8 59
(Alex Hales) *mid-div: hdwy 2f out: sn rdn: kpt on to chse wnr ins fnl f but a being hld* **5/1**$^{2}$

5026 **3** 2 ¼ **Vale Of Flight (IRE)**$^{13}$ 1981 4-9-5 62........................... BenRobinson$^{(7)}$ 9 57
(Luke McJannet) *trckd ldrs: rdn whn c wd ent st: kpt on ins fnl f* **8/1**

0020 **3** dht **Camino**$^{22}$ 1759 4-8-4 45............................................... LuluStanford$^{(5)}$ 3 40
(Andi Brown) *chsd ldrs: rdn over 2f out: chsd wnr ent fnl f: kpt on same pce* **7/1**

2452 **5** 1 **Pharoh Jake**$^{11}$ 2025 9-9-0 57........................................... JaneElliott$^{(7)}$ 5 48
(John Bridger) *trckd ldrs: rdn over 2f out: sn one pce* **5/1**$^{2}$

3000 **6** hd **Barnsdale**$^{22}$ 1759 4-8-2 45...................................... MeganEllingworth$^{(7)}$ 7 35
(John Holt) *mid-div on outer: rdn 2f out: kpt on same pce fnl f* **50/1**

52-0 **7** nk **Foxford**$^{30}$ 1557 6-8-13 54.................................................. PaddyPilley$^{(5)}$ 10 43
(Patrick Chamings) *racd keenly: in tch on outer: dropped to last trio over 2f out: sn rdn: no threat after* **11/1**

4-20 **8** ½ **Eland Ally**$^{109}$ 270 9-8-7 50..........................................(p) RossaRyan$^{(7)}$ 2 37
(Anabel K Murphy) *s.i.s: last pair: rdn over 1f out: nvr any imp* **20/1**

0-02 **9** 2 ¾ **Bubbly Bailey**$^{30}$ 1221 7-8-10 46..........................(v) SilvestreDeSousa 4 23
(J R Jenkins) *short of room sn after s and dropped to last pair: rdn 2f out: no imp* **6/1**$^{3}$

4-03 **10** nk **Wattaboutsteve**$^{44}$ 1305 6-8-9 45...................................... FrannyNorton 1 21
(Ralph J Smith) *led: rdn and hdd over 1f out: sn wknd* **7/2**$^{1}$

59.56s (0.76) **Going Correction** +0.05s/f (Slow) **10** Ran SP% **118.5**
Speed ratings (Par 101): **95,92,89,89,87 87,86,85,81,80**
Place: Vale Of Flight £1.40, Camino £1.50; Tricast: Frangarry, Dandilion, Vale Of Flight £191.29, Frangarry, Dandilion, Camino £173.98; TC: 4-3-9 191.29, 173.98; Tote Trifecta: 4-3-1 £184.90 4-3-9 £286.90 CSF £54.51 TOTE £10.80: £2.60, £1.90; EX 69.70.
**Owner** Dr S P Hargreaves **Bred** Carrigbeg Stud & David Powell **Trained** Newmarket, Suffolk

**FOCUS**
A moderate sprint handicap.

## 2371 RACING WELFARE H'CAP 1m 4f (P)
**5:20** (5:20) (Class 6) (0-65,67) 3-Y-O **£2,264** (£673; £336; £168) **Stalls** Low

Form RPR
50-1 **1** **Arab Moon**$^{23}$ 1726 3-9-9 67.................................... SilvestreDeSousa 10 77+
(William Knight) *hld up bhd: hdwy 2f out: c wdst ent st: str run ent fnl f: led fnl 120yds: eased towards fin* **2/1**$^{1}$

005- **2** 1 ¾ **Starshell (IRE)**$^{202}$ 7366 3-9-2 60........................................ LukeMorris 4 65+
(Sir Mark Prescott Bt) *s.i.s: last trio: hdwy over 3f out: rdn to chse ldrs ent st: ev ch briefly fnl 120yds: sn outpcd by easy wnr* **2/1**$^{1}$

560 **3** 1 **The Raven Master (IRE)**$^{30}$ 1551 3-9-4 65............... LouisSteward$^{(3)}$ 7 69
(Michael Bell) *trckd ldr: led over 2f out: rdn over 1f out: hdd fnl 120yds: no ex* **10/1**

006- **4** 2 ¾ **Russian Regard (IRE)**$^{163}$ 8074 3-9-6 64.................. RichardKingscote 6 63
(Jonathan Portman) *mid-div: rdn and hdwy over 1f out: kpt on same pce fnl f* **20/1**

63-6 **5** nk **Pentito Rap (USA)**$^{28}$ 1597 3-8-5 49.................................. RyanTate 1 48
(Rod Millman) *trckd ldrs: rdn over 2f out: kpt on same pce fnl f* **8/1**$^{3}$

00-0 **6** 2 ½ **General Allenby**$^{10}$ 2060 3-8-5 49........................... JosephineGordon 5 44
(Henry Tett) *sn struggling in last: nvr travelling: styd on fnl f: nvr any threat* **33/1**

00-4 **7** ¾ **Curtsy (IRE)**$^{11}$ 2027 3-9-1 59................................................ LiamKeniry 9 53
(Hughie Morrison) *mid-div: hdwy 4f out: rdn and ev ch over 2f out: wknd fnl f* **6/1**$^{2}$

000- **8** ½ **Bed Of Diamonds**$^{170}$ 7976 3-8-0 47................................ NoelGarbutt$^{(3)}$ 2 40
(Adam West) *trckd ldrs: rdn over 2f out: sn wknd* **66/1**

-650 **9** 3 **Affair**$^{43}$ 1331 3-7-13 50............................................... TheodoreLadd$^{(7)}$ 8 38
(Hughie Morrison) *led: rdn and hdd over 2f out: wknd fnl f* **50/1**

00-0 **10** *31* **Caspian Gold (IRE)**[20] 1790 3-9-4 **62**.............................. JimmyQuinn 3
(Richard Hughes) *mid-div: rdn 4f out: wknd over 2f out: t.o* **20/1**
2m 31.12s (-1.88) **Going Correction** +0.05s/f (Slow) **10** Ran SP% **117.1**
Speed ratings (Par 97): **108,106,106,104,104 102,101,101,99,78**
CSF £5.31 CT £30.49 TOTE £2.80: £1.30, £1.30, £3.30; EX 7.60 Trifecta £46.20.
**Owner** Angmering Park Thoroughbreds Iv **Bred** Genesis Green Stud Ltd **Trained** Patching, W Sussex

**FOCUS**
The leader picked up the gallop heading out on the final circuit and the first two came from off the pace. The race is likely to throw up some winners.
T/Plt: £51.30 to a £1 stake. Pool: £53,785.00 - 1,048.06 winning units. T/Qpdt: £15.40 to a £1 stake. Pool: £4,393.00 - 284.94 winning units. **Tim Mitchell**

# 2337 MUSSELBURGH (R-H)

Friday, May 5

**OFFICIAL GOING: Good to firm (7.3)**
Wind: Fresh, half behind in over 3f of home straight Weather: Sunny

## 2372 CORE (OIL AND GAS) H'CAP 5f 1y
**2:00** (2:00) (Class 6) (0-65,67) 3-Y-O **£2,587** (£770; £384; £192) **Stalls** High

| Form | | | | RPR |
|---|---|---|---|---|
| 3624 | **1** | | **Lady Cristal (IRE)**[14] 1940 3-9-4 **66**............................(p) CliffordLee(5) 4<br>(K R Burke) *cl up on outside: effrt and rdn over 1f out: led ins fnl f: kpt on strly* **7/2**[2] | 72 |
| 4-02 | **2** | *1 1/4* | **Flawlessly (FR)**[9] 2080 3-9-5 **62**.................................. PJMcDonald 7<br>(James Bethell) *led at decent gallop: rdn over 1f out: hdd ins fnl f: kpt on same pce* **9/4**[1] | 64 |
| 00-4 | **3** | *shd* | **Hamidans Girl (IRE)**[25] 1688 3-9-10 **67**.......................... PhillipMakin 3<br>(Keith Dalgleish) *dwlt: bhd: rdn and hdwy over 1f out: kpt on fnl f: nrst fin* **13/2** | 68 |
| 16-4 | **4** | *3 1/4* | **Jorvik Prince**[23] 1715 3-8-12 **60**.............................. GemmaTutty(5) 5<br>(Karen Tutty) *loose in preliminaries: prom: rdn over 2f out: one pce fr over 1f out* **14/1** | 49 |
| 0-04 | **5** | *1 1/4* | **La Haule Lady**[18] 1835 3-8-12 **55**..............................(p) PaulMulrennan 8<br>(Paul Midgley) *prom against stands' rail: drvn and outpcd over 1f out: n.d after* **16/1** | 40 |
| 4133 | **6** | *1* | **Royal Celebration**[77] 787 3-9-0 **57**............................ ConnorBeasley 2<br>(Bryan Smart) *sn outpcd and bhd: effrt on outside 1/2-way: no further imp over 1f out: btn fnl f* **9/1** | 38 |
| 3305 | **7** | *1/2* | **Prazeres**[15] 1913 3-9-7 **64**...............................................(t) JasonHart 6<br>(Les Eyre) *prom: drvn and outpcd 1/2-way: btn over 1f out* **4/1**[3] | 44 |
| 00-0 | **8** | *1 3/4* | **Henrietta's Dream**[49] 1244 3-8-2 **45**..........................(v[1]) JamesSullivan 1<br>(John Wainwright) *dwlt: bhd and a struggling: nvr on terms* **150/1** | 18 |

59.0s (-1.40) **Going Correction** -0.425s/f (Firm) **8** Ran SP% **109.5**
Speed ratings (Par 97): **94,92,91,86,84 83,82,79**
CSF £10.73 CT £42.57 TOTE £3.70: £1.50, £1.30, £1.90; EX 12.70 Trifecta £34.70.
**Owner** Champagne Charlies Club & Mrs E Burke **Bred** Knocktoran Stud And Carrigbeg Stud **Trained** Middleham Moor, N Yorks

**FOCUS**
A 46-55 5f handicap for three-year-olds, but a fair race for the grade with several coming into it in decent form. The pace was strong.

## 2373 WEATHERBYS BANK BRITISH STALLION STUDS EBF MAIDEN STKS 5f 1y
**2:30** (2:31) (Class 5) 2-Y-O **£3,234** (£962; £481; £240) **Stalls** High

| Form | | | | RPR |
|---|---|---|---|---|
| 62 | **1** | | **Faithful Promise**[15] 1909 2-9-0 0...................................... JoeFanning 4<br>(Mark Johnston) *mde all: rdn and edgd lft wl over 1f out: kpt on strly fnl f* **2/1**[2] | 76 |
| 6 | **2** | *2 1/4* | **Shobrom (IRE)**[17] 1858 2-9-5 0.................................... PaulHanagan 2<br>(Richard Fahey) *chsd ldng pair: rdn along 1/2-way: hdwy to chse wnr ins fnl f: edgd lft: kpt on: nt pce to chal* **4/6**[1] | 73 |
| | **3** | *4 1/2* | **Shanghai Elastic** 2-9-0 0........................................... PhillipMakin 6<br>(David Barron) *t.k.h early: w wnr: rdn whn checked wl over 1f out: outpcd fnl f* **11/1**[3] | 52 |
| 05 | **4** | *1* | **Hypnotic Dancer (IRE)**[8] 2105 2-8-9 0......................... RowanScott(5) 1<br>(Keith Dalgleish) *dwlt: sn pushed along in rr: shortlived effrt wl over 1f out: sn btn* **40/1** | 48 |
| | **5** | *6* | **Holmfirst** 2-9-5 0........................................................ PaulMulrennan 5<br>(Paul Midgley) *dwlt: outpcd and bhd: no ch fr 1/2-way* **50/1** | 32 |

58.8s (-1.60) **Going Correction** -0.425s/f (Firm) **5** Ran SP% **106.1**
Speed ratings (Par 93): **95,91,84,82,73**
CSF £3.36 TOTE £2.60: £1.30, £1.10; EX 3.70 Trifecta £5.80.
**Owner** Saeed Manana **Bred** Petches Farm Ltd **Trained** Middleham Moor, N Yorks

**FOCUS**
They finished well strung out in this novice event which featured a well-supported favourite who was beaten on merit. The time was marginally faster than the preceding handicap for three-year-olds so the form should be fair at least. The winner has been rated as improving slightly.

## 2374 JACKSON BOYD LAWYERS H'CAP 7f 33y
**3:00** (3:00) (Class 4) (0-80,82) 3-Y-O **£5,175** (£1,540; £769; £384) **Stalls** Low

| Form | | | | RPR |
|---|---|---|---|---|
| 1F-3 | **1** | | **Thomas Cranmer (USA)**[31] 1546 3-9-11 **82**.................... JoeFanning 5<br>(Mark Johnston) *dwlt: sn led: mde rest: jnd over 2f out: rdn and edgd lft wl over 1f out: hld on wl fnl f* **13/2** | 91 |
| 4331 | **2** | *nk* | **Atteq**[8] 2107 3-9-5 **76** 6ex.............................................(t) PaulHanagan 3<br>(Richard Fahey) *early ldr: pressed ldr: disp ld over 2f out: rdn over 1f out: kpt on fnl f: hld nr fin* **6/5**[1] | 84 |
| 03-1 | **3** | *2 3/4* | **Proud Archi (IRE)**[16] 1878 3-9-10 **81**.......................... PaulMulrennan 8<br>(Michael Dods) *hld up: smooth hdwy to trck ldrs over 2f out: rdn over 1f out: sn one pce* **11/2**[3] | 82 |
| 46-4 | **4** | *3* | **Seduce Me**[24] 1702 3-9-7 **78**.......................................(p) JoeyHaynes 1<br>(K R Burke) *s.i.s: hld up on ins: effrt and rdn 2f out: no imp fnl f* **5/1**[2] | 71 |
| 4445 | **5** | *hd* | **Mama Africa (IRE)**[11] 2035 3-8-9 **66**..................................(b) BenCurtis 2<br>(David Barron) *in tch on ins: rdn over 2f out: no imp over 1f out* **16/1** | 58 |
| 33-6 | **6** | *3/4* | **Mr Coco Bean (USA)**[25] 1680 3-9-1 **72**........................ ShaneGray 6<br>(Ann Duffield) *s.i.s: hld up in last pl: drvn along over 2f out: nvr able to chal* **20/1** | 62 |
| 62 | **7** | *3 3/4* | **Dapper Man (IRE)**[8] 2107 3-8-2 **65** ow1...................... BenSanderson(7) 7<br>(Roger Fell) *t.k.h early: cl up: hdwy and ev ch over 2f out: wknd over 1f out* **14/1** | 46 |
| -455 | **8** | *1/2* | **The Bard's Advice**[56] 1127 3-8-1 **63**.......................... RowanScott(5) 4<br>(Keith Dalgleish) *in tch: hung lft bnd over 4f out: rdn and wknd fr over 2f out* **40/1** | 42 |

1m 28.95s (-0.05) **Going Correction** -0.025s/f (Good) **8** Ran SP% **110.6**
Speed ratings (Par 101): **99,98,95,92,91 91,86,86**
CSF £13.72 CT £42.83 TOTE £5.20: £2.00, £1.10, £2.00; EX 16.00 Trifecta £35.00.
**Owner** Sheikh Hamdan bin Mohammed Al Maktoum **Bred** Darley **Trained** Middleham Moor, N Yorks

**FOCUS**
Quite a competitive 7f handicap for three-year-olds featuring the seemingly well-handicapped Atteq who was 4lb well in with his penalty for his wide-margin win at Beverley the previous week. The pace was ordinary and the first two had the run of the race. It's been rated around the winner.

## 2375 WEATHERBYS PRIVATE BANK H'CAP 1m 4f 104y
**3:30** (3:30) (Class 4) (0-85,87) 4-Y-O+ **£6,469** (£1,925; £962; £481) **Stalls** Low

| Form | | | | RPR |
|---|---|---|---|---|
| 400- | **1** | | **Corton Lad**[147] 8283 7-9-7 **81**.......................................(tp) PhillipMakin 2<br>(Keith Dalgleish) *pressed ldr: led gng wl over 2f out: sn rdn: kpt on wl fnl f* **11/4**[3] | 89 |
| 3423 | **2** | *3/4* | **Go George Go (IRE)**[23] 1716 4-8-12 **72**......................... JoeFanning 3<br>(Alan Swinbank) *trckd ldrs: smooth hdwy and ev ch over 2f out: rdn over 1f out: kpt on same pce wl ins fnl f* **2/1**[1] | 78 |
| 5025 | **3** | *5* | **Falcon's Fire (IRE)**[16] 1891 4-8-10 **75**....................... RowanScott(5) 5<br>(Keith Dalgleish) *hld up in tch: hdwy to chse ldrs over 2f out: rdn and edgd rt over 1f out: sn outpcd* **11/2** | 74 |
| 00-4 | **4** | *4 1/2* | **Green Light**[13] 1976 6-9-13 **87**........................................... TomEaves 4<br>(Brian Ellison) *hld up in tch: pushed along briefly 5f out: drvn over 2f out: wknd wl over 1f out* **5/2**[2] | 78 |
| 0 | **5** | *40* | **Fisherman's Blues (IRE)**[34] 1498 4-8-6 **66**.................. PaulHanagan 1<br>(Peter Niven) *t.k.h: led to over 2f out: sn rdn and wknd: eased whn btn fnl f* **25/1** | |

2m 42.44s (0.44) **Going Correction** -0.025s/f (Good) **5** Ran SP% **107.8**
Speed ratings (Par 105): **97,96,93,90,63**
CSF £8.27 TOTE £3.70: £1.40, £1.50; EX 8.30 Trifecta £22.60.
**Owner** J Hutton **Bred** Frank Brady And Brian Scanlon **Trained** Carluke, S Lanarks

**FOCUS**
Not strong race for the money on offer and the pace was ordinary. The winner has been rated close to his best, with a small pb from the runner-up.

## 2376 CRUDEN GROUP H'CAP 1m 208y
**4:00** (4:00) (Class 4) (0-80,81) 3-Y-O **£5,175** (£1,540; £769; £384) **Stalls** Low

| Form | | | | RPR |
|---|---|---|---|---|
| 126- | **1** | | **Euro Nightmare (IRE)**[200] 7409 3-9-6 **76**.................... PhillipMakin 3<br>(Keith Dalgleish) *hld up in tch: niggled along 1/2-way: effrt over 2f out: led ins fnl f: styd on strly* **6/1**[2] | 83+ |
| 00-3 | **2** | *1 1/2* | **Jamacho**[13] 1977 3-9-0 **70**............................................... BenCurtis 6<br>(Brian Ellison) *led at ordinary gallop: rdn and hdd over 2f out: rallied and ev ch briefly ins fnl f* **14/1** | 74 |
| 11-2 | **3** | *3/4* | **Election Day**[16] 1875 3-9-11 **81**...................................... JoeFanning 4<br>(Mark Johnston) *pressed ldr: led over 2f out: rdn and edgd lft over 1f out: edgd rt and hdd ins fnl f: one pce* **4/5**[1] | 83 |
| 155- | **4** | *5* | **Davy's Dilemma**[218] 6903 3-9-6 **76**............................ PaulMulrennan 1<br>(Michael Dods) *hld up: pushed along 1/2-way: drvn and no imp fr 2f out* **10/1** | 68 |
| 30-4 | **5** | *1 1/2* | **George Reme (IRE)**[16] 1878 3-9-7 **77**...........................(p[1]) JasonHart 2<br>(John Quinn) *trckd ldrs tl rdn and wknd fr 2f out* **7/1**[3] | 66 |
| 230- | **6** | *6* | **Kuraka**[203] 7329 3-8-11 **72**........................................... CliffordLee(5) 5<br>(K R Burke) *hld up in tch on outside: rdn over 3f out: wknd over 2f out* **7/1**[3] | 48 |

1m 52.94s (-0.96) **Going Correction** -0.025s/f (Good) **6** Ran SP% **110.6**
Speed ratings (Par 101): **103,101,101,96,95 89**
CSF £73.00 TOTE £5.20: £2.10, £3.30; EX 61.50 Trifecta £138.70.
**Owner** J S Morrison **Bred** Miss Annmarie Burke **Trained** Carluke, S Lanarks

**FOCUS**
Quite an interesting handicap but the pace was no more than fair. The winner showed a good turn of foot. A pb from the runner-up.

## 2377 BAM CONSTRUCTION H'CAP 7f 33y
**4:30** (4:30) (Class 5) (0-75,77) 4-Y-O+ **£3,234** (£962; £481; £240) **Stalls** Low

| Form | | | | RPR |
|---|---|---|---|---|
| 0313 | **1** | | **Tavener**[10] 2064 5-9-2 **70**.............................................(p) DavidAllan 2<br>(David C Griffiths) *mde all: rdn along 2f out: hld on wl fnl f* **6/1**[3] | 77 |
| 5322 | **2** | *1/2* | **Tadaawol**[7] 2119 4-9-1 **69**..........................................(p) TonyHamilton 9<br>(Roger Fell) *prom: effrt and rdn over 2f out: kpt on wl to take 2nd nr fin* **6/4**[1] | 74 |
| -633 | **3** | *1/2* | **Vallarta (IRE)**[29] 1586 7-9-4 **72**................................ JamesSullivan 4<br>(Ruth Carr) *pressed wnr: rdn along 2f out: kpt on ins fnl f: hld nr fin* **11/2**[2] | 76 |
| 20P- | **4** | *1 1/2* | **Flinty Fell (IRE)**[185] 7743 4-9-2 **70**...............................(h) PhillipMakin 8<br>(Keith Dalgleish) *hld up in tch: effrt and rdn 2f out: kpt on same pce fnl f* **9/1** | 70 |
| 20-0 | **5** | *2 3/4* | **Short Work**[21] 1778 4-9-4 **77**....................................(p) JoshDoyle(5) 7<br>(David O'Meara) *s.i.s: hld up: effrt and rdn over 2f out: outpcd over 1f out* **16/1** | 70 |
| 226- | **6** | *3/4* | **Fidra Bay (IRE)**[350] 2422 4-9-0 **68**................................ JoeFanning 3<br>(Alan Swinbank) *stdd s: hld up: pushed along over 2f out: wknd over 1f out* **16/1** | 59 |
| 650- | **7** | *nk* | **Donnelly's Rainbow (IRE)**[185] 7743 4-9-3 **71**............ DuranFentiman 6<br>(Rebecca Bastiman) *hld up: rdn and hdwy on outside over 2f out: wknd wl over 1f out* **16/1** | 61 |
| 00-0 | **8** | *10* | **Shootingsta (IRE)**[57] 1105 5-9-7 **75**.........................(b[1]) ConnorBeasley 1<br>(Bryan Smart) *t.k.h: trckd ldrs tl rdn and wknd fr over 2f out: eased whn btn ins fnl f* **6/1**[3] | 38 |

1m 28.38s (-0.62) **Going Correction** -0.025s/f (Good) **8** Ran SP% **111.6**
Speed ratings (Par 103): **102,101,100,99,96 95,94,83**
CSF £14.65 CT £50.72 TOTE £5.60: £1.70, £1.10, £1.70; EX 13.70 Trifecta £46.10.
**Owner** Baker, Hensby, Longden, Baker **Bred** Car Colston Hall Stud **Trained** Bawtry, S Yorks

**FOCUS**
Exposed sorts in this handicap in which the winner dictated matters and few featured. The second and third have been rated close to their recent efforts.

## 2378 RACINGUK.COM H'CAP 1m 208y
**5:00** (5:03) (Class 6) (0-60,61) 4-Y-O+ **£2,587** (£770; £384; £192) **Stalls** Low

| Form | | | | RPR |
|---|---|---|---|---|
| 0214 | **1** | | **Cosmic Ray**[6] 2140 5-9-7 **60**..........................................(h) JoeFanning 6<br>(Les Eyre) *pressed ldr: led gng wl over 2f out: rdn and clr w runner-up over 1f out: kpt on wl fnl f* **5/4**[1] | 70 |

0640 **2** *1 ½* **Adventureman**[6] 2140 5-9-6 **59**....................(p) JamesSullivan 7 66
(Ruth Carr) *led: rdn and hdd over 2f out: rallied and clr of rest over 1f out: kpt on same pce ins fnl f* **6/1**[2]

5221 **3** *6* **Kerry Icon**[25] 1679 4-8-8 **52**....................(h) RichardOliver[(5)] 3 47
(Iain Jardine) *prom: effrt and rdn over 1f out: edgd lft and sn outpcd by first two* **6/1**[2]

606 **4** *½* **Tambour**[20] 1804 4-9-3 **61**.................... RowanScott[(5)] 1 55
(Keith Dalgleish) *rrd in stalls: slowly away: hld up: pushed along and effrt over 2f out: no imp fr over 1f out* **11/1**

00-0 **5** *4 ½* **Let Right Be Done**[121] 44 5-8-12 **51**....................(p[1]) PaulMulrennan 8 36
(Linda Perratt) *trckd ldrs on outside: rdn over 2f out: wknd over 1f out* **16/1**

0100 **6** *4 ½* **Nelson's Bay**[9] 2082 8-8-11 **57**.................... PaulaMuir[(7)] 9 33
(Wilf Storey) *s.i.s: hld up: pushed along over 3f out: no imp fr 2f out* **20/1**

11-0 **7** *8* **Scruffy McGuffy**[13] 1983 4-9-8 **61**.................... ShaneGray 2 21
(Ann Duffield) *hld up: drvn and outpcd 3f out: btn fnl 2f* **16/1**

100- **8** *nk* **Eeny Mac (IRE)**[249] 5980 10-8-3 **47**....................(p) ShirleyTeasdale[(5)] 5 6
(John Wainwright) *hld up: rdn along 3f out: wknd 2f out* **66/1**

0230 **9** *52* **A Boy Named Sue**[44] 1298 4-8-6 **48**....................(v) NathanEvans[(3)] 4
(Peter Niven) *in tch: drvn and outpcd over 3f out: wknd over 2f out: t.o* **7/1**[3]

1m 53.11s (-0.79) **Going Correction** -0.025s/f (Good) **9 Ran SP% 111.9**
Speed ratings (Par 101): **102,100,95,94,90 86,79,79,33**
CSF £8.43 CT £31.73 TOTE £1.80: £1.10, £2.30, £1.70; EX 10.60 Trifecta £25.10.
**Owner** Over The Moon Racing III **Bred** Winterbeck Manor Stud **Trained** Catwick, N Yorks

**FOCUS**
A low-grade handicap with exposed sorts and the form is likely to be weak. It was run at a modest gallop and few got involved.
T/Plt: £17.50 to a £1 stake. Pool: £44,351.00 - 2,522.29 winning units. T/Qpdt: £12.60 to a £1 stake. Pool: £2,489.00 - 197.44 winning units. **Richard Young**

2379 - 2380a (Foreign Racing) - See Raceform Interactive

## [2133]DONCASTER (L-H)

Saturday, May 6

**OFFICIAL GOING: Good to firm (good in places; watered; 8.3)**
Wind: Fresh behind Weather: Cloudy

### 2381 BLACK AND VEATCH H'CAP — 6f 2y
**5:15** (5:19) (Class 3) (0-90,90) 4-Y-O+ **£7,762** (£2,310; £1,154; £577) **Stalls** Low

Form RPR

020- **1** **The Commendatore**[252] 5878 4-8-12 **81**.................... PhillipMakin 15 90
(David Barron) *in tch in wd outside: hdwy over 2f out: rdn to chal ent fnl f: styd on wl to ld last 100 yds* **8/1**[2]

-104 **2** *½* **Jaywalker (IRE)**[19] 1831 6-9-4 **87**.................... DuranFentiman 7 94
(Rebecca Bastiman) *trckd ldrs: hdwy over 2f out: rdn to ld over 1f out: jnd and drvn ent fnl f: hdd and no ex last 100 yds* **9/1**[3]

4111 **3** *1 ¼* **Foolaad**[14] 1971 6-9-0 **83**....................(t) BenCurtis 4 86
(Roy Bowring) *trckd ldrs: hdwy on inner 3f out: rdn to chse ldng pair over 1f out: drvn ent fnl: kpt on same pce* **4/1**[1]

-116 **4** *hd* **Art Collection (FR)**[12] 2031 4-9-2 **85**.................... JamesSullivan 1 87
(Ruth Carr) *dwlt and rr: hdwy wl over 2f out: rdn along wl over 1f out: styd on fnl f: nrst fin* **11/1**

011- **5** *nk* **Classic Seniority**[232] 6539 5-9-7 **90**.................... DanielTudhope 8 91
(Marjorie Fife) *hld up: hdwy wl over 2f out: rdn to chse ldrs over 1f out: no imp ins fnl f* **12/1**

36-6 **6** *hd* **Qeyaadah (IRE)**[16] 1902 4-9-2 **88**.................... AlistairRawlinson[(3)] 10 89
(Michael Appleby) *in tch on outer: hdwy over 2f out: rdn along wl over 1f out: kpt on fnl f: nrst fin* **12/1**

0-05 **7** *½* **Burnt Sugar (IRE)**[12] 2031 5-8-11 **87**.................... BenSanderson[(7)] 9 86
(Roger Fell) *hld up in midfield: hdwy wl over 2f out: rdn and n.m.r over 1f out: kpt on fnl f* **10/1**

-105 **8** *1 ½* **Handsome Dude**[19] 1831 5-9-2 **85**....................(b) AndrewMullen 13 79
(David Barron) *midfield: hdwy over 2f out: rdn along wl over 1f out: n.d* **8/1**[2]

011- **9** *½* **Syrian Pearl**[220] 6878 6-9-4 **87**.................... AdamBeschizza 12 80+
(Chris Wall) *dwlt and bhd: hdwy over 2f out: rdn over 1f out: kpt on fnl f* **25/1**

60-0 **10** *1 ½* **My Name Is Rio (IRE)**[34] 1515 7-9-4 **87**.................... ConnorBeasley 11 75
(Michael Dods) *a towards rr* **16/1**

50-5 **11** *nk* **Related**[115] 170 7-9-7 **90**....................(b) LukeMorris 3 77
(Paul Midgley) *cl up: led wl over 2f out: rdn and hdd over 1f out: sn wknd* **12/1**

3030 **12** *1 ¾* **Tatlisu (IRE)**[41] 1385 7-9-3 **89**.................... AdamMcNamara[(3)] 14 70
(Richard Fahey) *dwlt: a rr* **14/1**

11-0 **13** *¾* **Munfallet (IRE)**[19] 1831 6-9-7 **90**.................... PatCosgrave 6 69
(David Brown) *chsd ldrs: rdn along wl over 2f out: sn wknd* **16/1**

1-00 **14** *3* **Kenny The Captain (IRE)**[19] 1831 6-8-8 **84**........ RobertDodsworth[(7)] 5 53
(Tim Easterby) *a towards rr* **40/1**

00-0 **15** *2* **B Fifty Two (IRE)**[21] 1799 8-9-7 **90**.................... BarryMcHugh 2 53
(Marjorie Fife) *led: pushed along 1/2-way: sn rdn and hdd: wknd wl over 1f out* **25/1**

1m 10.11s (-3.49) **Going Correction** -0.125s/f (Firm) **15 Ran SP% 121.3**
Speed ratings (Par 107): **118,117,115,115,115 114,114,112,111,109 109,106,105,101,99**
CSF £76.72 CT £344.15 TOTE £10.50: £3.70, £2.90, £2.00; EX 96.70 Trifecta £1893.60.
**Owner** Ron Hull **Bred** J K Beckitt & Son **Trained** Maunby, N Yorks
■ Stewards' Enquiry : Phillip Makin £650 fine: attempted to weigh out without a safety vest

**FOCUS**
After 5mm of water was applied to the straight course on Friday the going was officially described as good to firm, good in places. Stalls - Inside. Races 6 & 7 increased by 12yds. A competitive sprint for the grade and solid form. It paid to race handily. Straightforward form. A clear pb from the winner, with the runner-up helping to set the level.

### 2382 MOTT MACDONALD BENTLEY NOVICE STKS — 5f 3y
**5:50** (5:52) (Class 5) 2-Y-O **£3,234** (£962; £481; £240) **Stalls** Low

Form RPR

1 **1** **Mutanaaseq (IRE)**[15] 1934 2-9-6 0.................... DaneO'Neill 2 86
(Richard Hannon) *trckd ldr: cl up 1/2-way: chal over 1f out: rdn to take narrow advantage jst ins fnl f: drvn last 100 yds: edgd lft and kpt on wl towards fin* **11/8**[1]

1 **2** *hd* **Bengali Boys (IRE)**[17] 1873 2-9-3 0.................... AdamMcNamara[(3)] 1 85
(Richard Fahey) *led: pushed along 2f out: rdn over 1f out: edgd lft and hdd jst ins fnl f: rallied gamely and disp ld last 100 yds: no ex towards fin* **3/1**[3]

**3** *2 ¼* **Story Minister (IRE)** 2-9-2 0.................... PJMcDonald 3 73+
(Tom Dascombe) *dwlt: sn trcking ldng pair: pushed along 2f out: sn rdn and kpt on same pce fnl f* **14/1**

6 **4** *1 ¾* **Jim Rockford**[15] 1941 2-9-2 0.................... DanielTudhope 4 67
(Ralph Beckett) *t.k.h: trckd ldrs: pushed along 2f out: sn rdn and no imp* **11/4**[2]

3 **5** *5* **Sinaloa (IRE)**[12] 2029 2-9-2 0.................... TonyHamilton 5 49
(Richard Fahey) *t.k.h: trckd ldrs: pushed along over 2f out: rdn wl over 1f out: sn outpcd* **7/1**

1m 0.39s (-0.11) **Going Correction** -0.125s/f (Firm) **5 Ran SP% 112.9**
Speed ratings (Par 93): **95,94,91,88,80**
CSF £6.02 TOTE £2.20: £1.10, £2.20; EX 5.30 Trifecta £29.90.
**Owner** Hamdan Al Maktoum **Bred** Patrick F Kelly **Trained** East Everleigh, Wilts

**FOCUS**
An interesting little novice and the two previous winners fought out a close finish. They went steady and it turned into a 2f sprint. The level is a bit fluid.

### 2383 MORGAN SINDALL SWECO MAIDEN STKS — 6f 2y
**6:20** (6:20) (Class 5) 3-4-Y-O **£3,234** (£962; £481; £240) **Stalls** Low

Form RPR

**1** **Desert Frost (IRE)** 3-9-2 0.................... PatCosgrave 3 79+
(Saeed bin Suroor) *t.k.h early: trckd ldrs: hdwy to ld 2f out: rdn over 1f out: kpt on wl fnl f* **8/11**[1]

4- **2** *1 ¼* **Crafty Madam (IRE)**[194] 7574 3-8-11 0.................... LukeMorris 1 70+
(Clive Cox) *prom on inner: cl up 1/2-way: chal 2f out: sn rdn and ev ch: kpt on same pce fnl f* **7/2**[2]

**3** *1 ½* **Dirchill (IRE)** 3-9-2 0.................... AndrewMullen 9 70
(David Barron) *t.k.h in rr: hdwy over 2f out: rdn and green over 1f out: chsd ldng pair and edgd lft ins fnl f: kpt on* **14/1**

**4** *2* **Summerghand (IRE)** 3-9-2 0.................... DanielTudhope 6 64
(David O'Meara) *trckd ldrs: hdwy and cl up over 2f out: rdn wl over 1f out: grad wknd* **9/2**[3]

0- **5** *1 ½* **Shelneverwalkalone**[334] 2970 3-8-11 0.................... TomEaves 5 54
(Ivan Furtado) *led: rdn along and hdd 2f out: sn drvn and wknd* **50/1**

0- **6** *nk* **Harwood**[245] 6129 3-9-2 0.................... ConnorBeasley 4 58
(David O'Meara) *prom: rdn along over 2f out: sn wknd* **16/1**

**7** *1* **Jessinamillion** 3-9-2 0.................... PJMcDonald 2 55
(James Bethell) *trckd ldrs: hdwy and cl up 1/2-way: rdn along over 2f out: sn wknd* **20/1**

0 **8** *7* **Ruled By The Moon**[7] 2135 3-9-2 0.................... DavidNolan 7 32
(Ivan Furtado) *a rr* **25/1**

1m 11.95s (-1.65) **Going Correction** -0.125s/f (Firm) **8 Ran SP% 121.4**
Speed ratings (Par 103): **106,104,102,99,97 97,95,86**
CSF £3.81 TOTE £1.50: £1.10, £1.20, £4.40; EX 3.90 Trifecta £21.90.
**Owner** Godolphin **Bred** Marathon Bloodstock **Trained** Newmarket, Suffolk

**FOCUS**
Little depth to this maiden and the odds-on newcomer did it nicely. The pace picked up from halfway. Ordinary form.

### 2384 WATER AID H'CAP — 7f 6y
**6:50** (6:51) (Class 2) (0-105,100) 3-Y-O+
**£12,450** (£3,728; £1,864; £932; £466; £234) **Stalls** Low

Form RPR

53-2 **1** **Aardwolf (USA)**[9] 2106 3-8-5 **89**.................... PJMcDonald 2 92
(Mark Johnston) *set stdy pce: qcknd 3f out: rdn along wl over 1f out: drvn and hld on wl fnl f* **7/2**[1]

06-1 **2** *½* **Gallipoli (IRE)**[29] 1606 4-9-3 **89**.................... DavidNolan 4 95
(Richard Fahey) *t.k.h: trckd ldng pair: hdwy over 2f out: rdn to chal over 1f out: drvn ins fnl f: kpt on* **4/1**[2]

110- **3** *¾* **Alnashama**[246] 6082 5-9-2 **88**.................... DaneO'Neill 8 92
(Charles Hills) *trckd wnr: rdn along wl over 1f out: drvn and kpt on fnl f* **11/1**

640- **4** *½* **Truth Or Dare**[218] 6915 6-9-2 **88**.................... JamieSpencer 10 91+
(James Bethell) *hld up in rr: swtchd rt to outer and effrt over 2f out: rdn to chse ldrs over 1f out: edgd lft and no imp ins fnl f* **10/1**

0-06 **5** *1 ¼* **Russian Realm**[7] 2142 7-8-13 **85**.................... CamHardie 7 84
(Paul Midgley) *t.k.h: trckd ldrs: pushed along over 2f out: rdn wl over 1f out: kpt on one pce* **25/1**

202- **6** *½* **Get Knotted (IRE)**[197] 7497 5-10-0 **100**....................(p) PaulMulrennan 9 98
(Michael Dods) *trckd ldrs: hdwy over 2f out:: rdn wl over 1f out: sn drvn and no imp* **11/2**[3]

3315 **7** *½* **Twin Appeal (IRE)**[7] 2142 6-9-7 **93**....................(b) PhillipMakin 1 90
(David Barron) *trckd ldrs: hdwy over 2f out: rdn along wl over 1f out: sn drvn and kpt on one pce* **4/1**[2]

0000 **8** *¾* **Steel Train (FR)**[22] 1773 6-9-6 **99**.................... PatrickVaughan[(7)] 3 94
(David O'Meara) *s.i.s: a rr* **11/1**

110- **9** *3 ½* **Orewa (IRE)**[217] 6954 3-8-6 **90**.................... BenCurtis 5 71
(Brian Ellison) *in tch: pushed along wl over 2f out: sn rdn and wknd* **10/1**

1m 24.67s (-1.63) **Going Correction** -0.125s/f (Firm)
**WFA** 3 from 4yo+ 12lb **9 Ran SP% 116.3**
Speed ratings (Par 109): **104,103,102,102,100 100,99,98,94**
CSF £17.67 CT £139.74 TOTE £4.30: £1.60, £1.70, £3.10; EX 13.70 Trifecta £101.50.
**Owner** Sheikh Hamdan bin Mohammed Al Maktoum **Bred** Darley **Trained** Middleham Moor, N Yorks

**FOCUS**
A good handicap but not the strongest for the level, with the topweight rated 5lb below the ceiling. The winner has been rated to the better view of his form.

### 2385 STONBURY H'CAP — 1m (S)
**7:20** (7:22) (Class 3) (0-90,90) 3-Y-O **£7,762** (£2,310; £1,154; £577) **Stalls** Low

Form RPR

210- **1** **City Of Joy**[196] 7544 3-9-1 **84**.................... DanielTudhope 6 88
(Sir Michael Stoute) *hld up in rr: hdwy on outer over 3f out: chse ldrs 2f out: rdn to chal over 1f out: drvn and ev ch whn carried rt ins last 100 yds: kpt on wl to ld nr fin* **4/1**[3]

31-1 **2** *hd* **Mustarrid (IRE)**[30] 1582 3-9-7 **90**.................... DaneO'Neill 5 93
(Richard Hannon) *trckd ldrs: hdwy 3f out: qckn to ld over 2f out: rdn over 1f out: jnd and drvn ins fnl f: edgd rt last 100 yds: hdd and no ex nr fin* **3/1**[2]

21 **3** *1* **Bless Him (IRE)**[35] 1485 3-8-13 **82**.................... JamieSpencer 2 83
(David Simcock) *stdd s and hld up in rr taking t.k.h: hdwy on inner to trck ldrs 3f out: rdn along wl over 1f out: drvn ent fnl f: no imp towards fin* **9/4**[1]

51-3 **4** *1 ¼* **In First Place**[16] 1912 3-8-11 **80**.................... TonyHamilton 1 78
(Richard Fahey) *in tch: pushed along over 3f out: rdn and outpcd 2f out: kpt on u.p fnl f* **12/1**

-313 **5** *nk* **Glorious Artist (IRE)**$^{24}$ 1724 3-9-0 **83** LukeMorris 7 80
(Charles Hills) *trckd ldrs: rdn along over 2f out: drvn wl over 1f out: kpt on same pce* **20/1**

212- **6** *hd* **Mister Belvedere**$^{233}$ 6499 3-9-4 **87** PaulMulrennan 4 84
(Michael Dods) *trckd ldng pair: pushed along 3f out: rdn over 2f out: drvn wl over 1f out: kpt on one pce* **9/1**

0-1 **7** *nk* **Flashy Snapper**$^{20}$ 1818 3-9-4 **90** EdwardGreatrex$^{(3)}$ 3 86
(Simon Crisford) *.t.k.h: set stdy pce: qcknd over 3f out: rdn along and hdd over 2f out: sn drvn: wknd over 1f out* **11/2**

1m 39.27s (-0.03) **Going Correction** -0.125s/f (Firm) **7** Ran SP% **113.6**
Speed ratings (Par 103): **95,94,93,92,92 92,91**
CSF £16.19 TOTE £5.30: £2.10, £1.90; EX 18.70 Trifecta £54.50.
**Owner** Saeed Suhail **Bred** Hascombe And Valiant Studs **Trained** Newmarket, Suffolk

**FOCUS**
An interesting 3yo handicap and form to keep an eye on, with the three market leaders coming to the fore. The pace was moderate until halfway. The third has been rated to his maiden figure.

## 2386 CAPGEMINI H'CAP — 1m 6f 115y
**7:50** (7:51) (Class 4) (0-85,86) 4-Y-0+ **£5,175** (£1,540; £769; £384) **Stalls** Low

Form RPR

1321 **1** **Midtech Star (IRE)**$^{22}$ 1763 5-8-7 **66** (v) LukeMorris 4 72
(Ian Williams) *hld up: hdwy over 3f out: chsd ldrs 2f out: rdn along wl over 1f out: styd on strly ins fnl f: led towards fin* **7/1**$^{3}$

1134 **2** *nk* **Codeshare**$^{22}$ 1781 5-9-10 **83** PJMcDonald 6 88
(Alan Swinbank) *in tch: hdwy 4f out: trckd ldrs over 2f out: rdn to ld wl over 1f out: drvn ent fnl f: hdd and no ex towards fin* **13/2**$^{2}$

555- **3** *3/4* **Waiting For Richie**$^{224}$ 6795 4-8-7 **68** AndrewMullen 3 72
(Tom Tate) *chsd clr ldr: tk clsr order over 4f out: rdn along wl over 2f out: drvn wl over 1f out: kpt on wl u.p fnl f* **16/1**

0-04 **4** *1/2* **Mysterial**$^{9}$ 2109 7-8-8 **72** PhilDennis$^{(5)}$ 9 75
(Declan Carroll) *led and sn clr: pushed along 3f out: rdn over 2f out: hdd wl over 1f out and sn drvn: kpt on same pce fnl f* **25/1**

234- **5** *nk* **New World Power (JPN)**$^{239}$ 6294 4-9-6 **81** JamieSpencer 7 84
(David Simcock) *stdd s: hld up and bhd: hdwy over 3f out: chsd ldrs 2f out: sn rdn: cl up and drvn over 1f out: kpt on same pce fnl f* **11/8**$^{1}$

4121 **6** *6* **Royal Flag**$^{34}$ 1519 7-9-0 **73** TomEaves 8 67
(Brian Ellison) *hld up towards rr: sme hdwy 4f out: rdn along wl over 2f out: sn outpcd* **13/2**$^{2}$

0000 **7** *11* **Buthelezi (USA)**$^{29}$ 1608 9-8-10 **69** BenCurtis 5 48
(Brian Ellison) *dwlt: a rr: rdn along wl over 3f out: sn outpcd* **16/1**

0411 **8** *6* **Be Perfect (USA)**$^{9}$ 2109 8-9-13 **86** (p) JamesSullivan 2 57
(Ruth Carr) *trckd ldng pair: hdwy 5f out: rdn along over 3f out: sn drvn and wknd* **8/1**

040- **9** *3/4* **Stormin Tom (IRE)**$^{166}$ 8051 5-9-0 **76** RachelRichardson$^{(3)}$ 1 46
(Tim Easterby) *chsd ldrs: rdn along wl over 3f out: sn wknd* **16/1**

3m 9.15s (1.75) **Going Correction** +0.275s/f (Good) **9** Ran SP% **113.9**
Speed ratings (Par 105): **106,105,105,105,105 101,95,92,92**
CSF £51.03 CT £700.03 TOTE £5.60: £1.80, £2.30, £4.70; EX 42.30 Trifecta £483.80.
**Owner** Midtech **Bred** Denis McDonnell **Trained** Portway, Worcs

**FOCUS**
Race distance increased by 12yds. A decent staying handicap and they finished in a bit of a heap.

## 2387 YORKSHIRE WATER FILLIES' H'CAP — 1m 3f 197y
**8:20** (8:20) (Class 4) (0-85,83) 4-Y-0+ **£5,175** (£1,540; £769; £384) **Stalls** Low

Form RPR

31- **1** **Vuela**$^{180}$ 7848 4-9-4 **80** JamieSpencer 3 86+
(Luca Cumani) *trckd ldng pair: hdwy 4f out: cl up 3f out: chal 2f out and sn rdn: drvn to take slt ld jst ins fnl f: kpt on wl towards fin* **11/10**$^{1}$

1125 **2** *1/2* **Star Of Lombardy (IRE)**$^{12}$ 2028 4-8-13 **75** PJMcDonald 5 80
(Mark Johnston) *led: pushed along 3f out: jnd and rdn 2f out: drvn and hdd narrowly ins fnl f: kpt on gamely* **15/2**

355- **3** *nk* **Turning The Table (IRE)**$^{217}$ 6951 4-9-5 **81** TomEaves 1 85
(David Simcock) *hld up in rr: hdwy on inner over 3f out: chsd ldng pair 2f out and sn rdn: drvn to chal jst over 1f out: disp ld and v ch ins fnl f tl no ex last 75 yds* **9/2**$^{3}$

564- **4** *2 1/2* **Jelly Monger (IRE)**$^{154}$ 5240 5-9-7 **83** PaulMulrennan 2 83
(Dominic Ffrench Davis) *trckd ldrs: hdwy over 4f out: cl up 3f out: sn rdn along: drvn 2f out: grad wknd appr fnl f* **7/1**

/031 **5** *6* **Langlauf (USA)**$^{73}$ 856 4-8-12 **79** (p) LuluStanford$^{(5)}$ 4 69
(Rod Millman) *trckd ldr: hdwy over 4f out: pushed along over 3f out: sn rdn along wknd fnl 2f* **7/2**$^{2}$

2m 36.83s (1.93) **Going Correction** +0.275s/f (Good) **5** Ran SP% **112.3**
Speed ratings (Par 102): **104,103,103,101,97**
CSF £10.18 TOTE £1.80: £1.20, £3.40; EX 7.80 Trifecta £26.60.
**Owner** S Stuckey **Bred** Stuart Stuckey **Trained** Newmarket, Suffolk

**FOCUS**
Race distance increased by 12yds. A useful handicap, run at an ordinary pace, and an unexposed winner. The third has been rated to last year's C&D form.
T/Plt: £23.40 to a £1 stake. Pool: £71,566.92 - 2,229.09 winning units. T/Qpdt: £7.60 to a £1 stake. Pool: £7,678.89 - 740.84 winning units. **Joe Rowntree**

# GOODWOOD (R-H)
Saturday, May 6

**OFFICIAL GOING: Straight course - good; round course - good to firm (good in places; watered; 7.4)**
Wind: Fresh, across (towards stands) Weather: Fine

## 2388 BETFRED "FOLLOW US ON TWITTER" H'CAP — 1m 6f
**1:35** (1:36) (Class 5) (0-75,75) 4-Y-0+ **£5,175** (£1,540; £769; £384) **Stalls** Low

Form RPR

043- **1** **October Storm**$^{190}$ 7670 4-9-6 **72** GrahamLee 12 81
(Mick Channon) *hld up in last pair: nt clr run 3f out to 2f out: gd prog on outer wl over 1f out: swept into the ld 150yds out: sn clr* **8/1**$^{3}$

5114 **2** *3* **Ayr Of Elegance**$^{35}$ 1505 5-9-8 **73** LiamKeniry 6 78
(Philip Hide) *hld up in last pair: stdy prog on outer over 2f out: wnr wnt past 1f out: styd on to take 2nd nr fin* **16/1**

-241 **3** *3/4* **Denmead**$^{4}$ 2275 4-9-9 **75** 6ex RobertWinston 4 79
(John Butler) *led: had most in trble over 2f out: hdd and outpcd last 150yds* **5/1**$^{1}$

041- **4** *2 1/4* **Art Of Swing (IRE)**$^{178}$ 7870 5-9-6 **71** TomQueally 2 72
(Gary Moore) *trckd ldrs: wnt 2nd jst over 2f out and sn rdn: fdd fnl f* **12/1**

400- **5** *1* **Fitzwilly**$^{237}$ 6362 7-9-5 **70** JimmyFortune 7 69
(Mick Channon) *hld up in rr: stl there and pushed along on inner over 2f out: styd on fr over 1f out: nvr nrr but nt pce to threaten* **14/1**

54-5 **6** *1/2* **Mazalto (IRE)**$^{29}$ 1602 4-9-5 **71** ShaneKelly 5 70
(Pat Phelan) *prom: chsd ldr 6f out to jst over 2f out: steadily wknd* **10/1**

02-0 **7** *shd* **Perfect Summer (IRE)**$^{11}$ 2061 7-9-10 **75** (p) StevieDonohoe 8 74
(Ian Williams) *lost pl after 6f: dropped to rr and rdn 3f out: stl in last pair over 1f out: kpt on late on outer* **25/1**

455- **8** *hd* **Ivanhoe**$^{51}$ 7625 7-9-2 **67** (b) TomMarquand 13 65
(Michael Blanshard) *hld up towards rr: rdn 3f out: plugged on fr over 1f out: n.d* **20/1**

54-0 **9** *1/2* **Onorina (IRE)**$^{25}$ 1697 5-9-3 **68** SamHitchcott 9 66
(Jim Boyle) *t.k.h: hld up: wd bnd 12f out: prog to chse ldrs 6f out: wd bnd sn after: stl in chsng gp 2f out: wknd over 1f out* **12/1**

4604 **10** *1 1/4* **Spiritoftomintoul**$^{34}$ 1519 8-8-10 **66** CliffordLee$^{(5)}$ 3 62
(Tony Carroll) *hld up in midfield: rdn wl over 2f out: no prog and wknd over 1f out* **6/1**$^{2}$

3- **11** *3 3/4* **Three Star General**$^{34}$ 5620 4-9-8 **74** (p) PatDobbs 10 65
(David Pipe) *hld up towards rr: waiting for room 3f out: rdn and no prog over 2f out: wknd* **16/1**

3242 **12** *2 3/4* **Miss Tiger Lily**$^{25}$ 1697 7-9-7 **72** HarryBentley 14 59
(Harry Dunlop) *chsd ldr to 6f out: wknd fr 3f out* **8/1**$^{3}$

06-0 **13** *1* **Maestro Mac (IRE)**$^{29}$ 1602 4-9-3 **74** (t$^{1}$) CharlieBennett$^{(5)}$ 1 59
(Hughie Morrison) *in tch on inner: wknd fr over 2f out* **8/1**$^{3}$

500- **14** *4 1/2* **Tobouggaloo**$^{246}$ 6090 6-9-2 **67** MartinDwyer 11 46
(Stuart Kittow) *t.k.h: trckd ldrs: rdn and stl in tch jst over 2f out: wknd qckly* **16/1**

3m 2.56s (-1.04) **Going Correction** -0.075s/f (Good) **14** Ran SP% **121.7**
Speed ratings (Par 103): **99,97,96,95,95 94,94,94,94,93 91,89,89,86**
CSF £131.19 CT £715.42 TOTE £9.20: £3.00, £5.10, £2.90; EX 170.60 Trifecta £820.80.
**Owner** Jon and Julia Aisbitt **Bred** Meon Valley Stud **Trained** West Ilsley, Berks

**FOCUS**
First two furlongs of One Mile course dolled out 6yds, increasing distances of 7f and 1m races by 10yds. Clifford Lee described the going as "good to firm, on the the fast side." No great gallop on here in what appeared an open handicap, but a clear-cut winner who needs his effort upgrading considering he came from off the pace. Ordinary form.

## 2389 BETFRED TV EBF STALLIONS DAISY WARWICK STKS (LISTED RACE) (F&M) — 1m 3f 218y
**2:05** (2:09) (Class 1) 4-Y-0+ **£23,680** (£8,956; £4,476; £2,236) **Stalls** High

Form RPR

20-1 **1** **Ajman Princess (IRE)**$^{36}$ 1468 4-9-0 107 FranBerry 1 107+
(Roger Varian) *trckd ldr: led over 2f out: shkn up and drew clr over 1f out: flashed tail whn rdn fnl f but in n.d* **6/1**

100- **2** *5* **Elysian Fields (GR)**$^{164}$ 8068 6-9-0 95 KieranShoemark 9 98
(Amanda Perrett) *hld up in last trio: pushed along 3f out: prog 2f out: short of room briefly wl over 1f out: rdn and kpt on wl after to take 2nd nr fin* **20/1**

101- **3** *nk* **Dance The Dream**$^{214}$ 7060 4-9-0 93 MartinDwyer 8 98
(Marcus Tregoning) *humoured along in last and nt gng that wl: rdn 3f out: prog 2f out: wanting to hang but kpt on u.p fnl f to take 3rd last strides* **9/2**$^{3}$

100- **4** *nk* **Colonial Classic (FR)**$^{217}$ 6951 4-9-0 89 DanielMuscutt 6 97
(James Fanshawe) *trckd ldng pair: chsd wnr 2f out: outpcd over 1f out: lost 2 pls nr fin* **9/1**

146- **5** *1 3/4* **Moorside**$^{206}$ 7271 4-9-0 95 HarryBentley 4 94
(Charles Hills) *hld up in midfield: shkn up and prog over 3f out to press ldrs over 2f out: hanging rt u.p wl over 1f out: outpcd after* **13/2**

115- **6** *4 1/2* **Dubka**$^{206}$ 7271 4-9-0 99 PatDobbs 2 87+
(Sir Michael Stoute) *trckd ldng pair: pushed along and nt qckn over 2f out: already btn whn impeded wl over 1f out: wknd* **11/4**$^{1}$

\- **7** *2* **Chinoiseries**$^{565}$ 7339 4-9-0 89 ShaneKelly 3 84
(David Simcock) *t.k.h: hld up: dropped to last and cajoled along 2f out: taken fr inner to outer after: keeping on whn eased last strides: nt disgraced* **25/1**

01-1 **8** *7* **Alf Guineas (IRE)**$^{30}$ 1583 4-9-0 85 TomQueally 7 73
(John Gosden) *sn led: hdd and pushed along over 2f out: wknd rapidly over 1f out* **7/2**$^{2}$

2m 34.75s (-3.65) **Going Correction** -0.075s/f (Good) **8** Ran SP% **113.3**
Speed ratings (Par 111): **109,105,105,105,104 101,99,95**
CSF £109.21 TOTE £5.00: £1.70, £4.40, £1.50; EX 89.40 Trifecta £394.50.
**Owner** Sheikh Mohammed Obaid Al Maktoum **Bred** Darley **Trained** Newmarket, Suffolk

**FOCUS**
Distance as advertised. A couple of the fancied runners disappointed, so this didn't take as much winning as expected, but even so a taking effort from Ajman Princess, who overcame a market drift. Small personal bests from the third and fourth.

## 2390 BETFRED "TREBLE ODDS ON LUCKY 15'S" H'CAP — 7f
**2:40** (2:43) (Class 2) (0-100,99) 4-Y-0+ **£32,345** (£9,625; £4,810; £2,405) **Stalls** Low

Form RPR

5113 **1** **Gossiping**$^{38}$ 1422 5-8-7 **85** ShaneKelly 14 93
(Gary Moore) *trckd ldrs: gaps appeared and clsd to chal jst over 1f out: edgd lft but led ins fnl f: drvn out* **25/1**

0514 **2** *1/2* **Make Music**$^{22}$ 1771 4-8-10 **88** RobHornby 6 94
(Andrew Balding) *trckd ldng pair: led over 1f out: drvn and hdd ins fnl f: kpt on* **16/1**

2145 **3** *shd* **The Warrior (IRE)**$^{12}$ 2026 5-8-8 **86** (e) FrannyNorton 7 92
(Amanda Perrett) *hld up towards rr: nvr clrest of runs fr 3f out: stl waiting for room over 1f out: weaved through fnl f and fin strly: nrly snatched 2nd* **12/1**

23-1 **4** *3/4* **Ice Age (IRE)**$^{11}$ 2054 4-8-8 **86** HarryBentley 9 90
(Eve Johnson Houghton) *trckd ldrs: rdn to chal jst over 1f out: sltly impeded jst ins fnl f: styd on same pce* **11/2**$^{2}$

2-22 **5** *3/4* **Lightning Charlie**$^{12}$ 2040 5-8-6 **87** KieranShoemark$^{(3)}$ 4 89
(Amanda Perrett) *hld up in midfield: nt clr run wl over 1f out and angled lft: drvn to chse ldrs fnl f and sltly impeded: styd on* **7/1**

00-3 **6** *1* **Medburn Dream**$^{5}$ 2232 4-8-0 **85** oh2 DavidEgan$^{(7)}$ 3 84
(Paul Henderson) *led at str pce but pressed: hdd over 1f out: fdd ins fnl f* **17/2**

560- **7** *shd* **Fox Trotter (IRE)**$^{194}$ 7573 5-8-10 **88** KierenFox 10 87+
(Brian Meehan) *hld up in rr: rdn 3f out: no prog and stl wl in rr over 1f out: styd on strly last 150yds: gng on at fin* **20/1**

115- **8** *shd* **Baron Bolt**$^{208}$ 7213 4-9-1 **93** JimmyFortune 13 92
(Paul Cole) *hld up but sn in midfield: rdn on outer 2f out: cl enough but no imp ldrs over 1f out: one pce* **33/1**

4/05 **9** *nse* **Eltezam (IRE)**$^{21}$ 1794 4-9-5 **97** (h) PatDobbs 2 96
(Richard Hannon) *trckd ldrs on inner: shkn up 2f out: nt qckn over 1f out: one pce after* **6/1**$^{3}$

01-3 **10** *1 ¼* **Charles Molson**[22] 1769 6-8-13 **94**.......................... HectorCrouch(3) 15 89
(Patrick Chamings) *hld up fr wd draw: shkn up on outer 2f out: nvr pce to make meaningful prog* **14/1**

115- **11** *3 ½* **Zwayyan**[231] 6585 4-8-9 **87**.......................................... FranBerry 5 77
(William Haggas) *hld up in midfield: shkn up and nt qckn 2f out: no hdwy after: eased last 75yds* **7/2**[1]

12-0 **12** *2 ¾* **Roll On Rory**[21] 1799 4-9-1 **93**..........................................(b) GrahamLee 1 71
(Jason Ward) *w ldr at str pce to 2f out: wknd qckly* **12/1**

0-34 **13** *¾* **Fiftyshadesofgrey (IRE)**[71] 896 6-8-11 **89**.................. SteveDrowne 16 65
(George Baker) *hld up wl in rr fr wd draw: shkn up and no prog over 2f out: no ch after* **33/1**

-516 **14** *2* **Suzi's Connoisseur**[22] 1769 6-9-7 **99**......................(vt) DanielMuscutt 8 70
(Stuart Williams) *hld up wl in rr: shkn up and no prog over 2f out* **16/1**

420- **15** *1* **Show Stealer**[233] 6518 4-9-3 **95**....................................... MartinDwyer 12 63
(Rae Guest) *dropped in fr wd draw and hld up: t.k.h: no prog on inner over 2f out* **33/1**

1m 24.11s (-2.89) **Going Correction** -0.075s/f (Good) **15** Ran SP% **126.2**
Speed ratings (Par 109): **113,112,112,111,110 109,109,109,109,107 103,100,99,97,96**
CSF £377.63 CT £5079.69 TOTE £32.70: £6.90, £5.40, £4.10; EX 741.10 Trifecta £4567.90.

**Owner** G L Moore & Partner **Bred** Darley **Trained** Lower Beeding, W Sussex

**FOCUS**
Distance increased by 10yds. A couple of the outsiders came to the fore in this useful handicap, with the favourite disappointing. They went a good gallop. It's been rated around the winner, the runner-up and fourth.

## 2391 BETFRED "SUPPORTS JACK BERRY HOUSE" H'CAP 5f
**3:15** (3:15) (Class 3) (0-95,94) 4-Y-O+ **£9,703** (£2,887; £1,443; £721) **Stalls** High

Form RPR

20-6 **1** **Vibrant Chords**[18] 1863 4-9-3 **90**.................................... TomMarquand 4 101
(Henry Candy) *chsd ldrs: swtchd to outer and rdn over 1f out: styd on fnl f to ld last 75yds: readily* **5/1**[2]

60-1 **2** *¾* **A Momentofmadness**[21] 1793 4-9-0 **90**............(h) CallumShepherd(3) 2 98
(Charles Hills) *dwlt: t.k.h and sn rcvrd to dispute ld: led on outer 1/2-way: rdn over 1f out: hdd last 75yds: inclined hd towards wnr sn after* **8/1**

41-4 **3** *¾* **Dark Shot**[12] 2038 4-8-7 **87**.................................... JoshuaBryan(7) 6 93
(Andrew Balding) *chsd ldrs: drvn over 1f out: styd on to take 3rd fnl f: nvr quite able to chal* **4/1**[1]

30-3 **4** *nk* **Gamesome (FR)**[17] 1876 6-9-6 **93**.................................... GrahamLee 10 98
(Paul Midgley) *in tch: shkn up over 1f out and squeezed through rivals sn after: rdn and styd on to press for 3rd nr fin* **8/1**

1244 **5** *2 ½* **Kasbah (IRE)**[35] 1501 5-9-7 **94**.......................................... JackMitchell 5 90
(Amanda Perrett) *disp ld to 1/2-way: styd pressing ldrs tl wknd ins fnl f* **8/1**

00-2 **6** *1 ¼* **Waseem Faris (IRE)**[12] 2038 8-8-4 **84**........................ FinleyMarsh(7) 8 75
(Ken Cunningham-Brown) *disp ld to 1/2-way: nt qckn wl over 1f out: fdd* **16/1**

1336 **7** *½* **Just Us Two (IRE)**[21] 1793 5-8-9 **82**............................(p) HarryBentley 3 71
(Robert Cowell) *racd on outer: disp ld to 1/2-way: chsd ldr after tl wknd fnl f* **11/1**

-241 **8** *3* **Stepper Point**[12] 2038 8-9-2 **89**.......................................(p) MartinDwyer 7 67
(William Muir) *disp ld to 1/2-way: wknd wl over 1f out* **8/1**

246- **9** *1* **Boy In The Bar**[182] 7821 6-9-0 **87**................................ StevieDonohoe 1 62
(Ian Williams) *outpcd and a bhd* **8/1**

5-32 **10** *nk* **Just That Lord**[10] 2083 4-8-12 **85**.................................. RobertWinston 9 59
(Bill Turner) *racd towards nr side rail: w ldrs to 1/2-way: wknd 2f out* **7/1**[3]

56.53s (-3.67) **Going Correction** -0.55s/f (Hard) **10** Ran SP% **118.9**
Speed ratings (Par 107): **107,105,104,104,100 98,97,92,90,90**
CSF £45.70 CT £177.83 TOTE £5.20: £1.80, £2.90, £1.70; EX 43.40 Trifecta £148.60.

**Owner** Paul G Jacobs **Bred** Moyns Park Estate And Stud Ltd **Trained** Kingston Warren, Oxon

**FOCUS**
A useful sprint and a winner firmly on the up. It's been rated slightly positively, with the fourth close to his latest.

## 2392 BETFRED "WATCH SKY SPORTS IN OUR SHOPS" CONQUEROR STKS (LISTED RACE) (F&M) 1m
**3:50** (3:53) (Class 1) 3-Y-O+
**£22,684** (£8,600; £4,304; £2,144; £1,076; £540) **Stalls** Low

Form RPR

21-5 **1** **Laugh Aloud**[21] 1795 4-9-10 108....................................(t) JimmyFortune 7 112
(John Gosden) *mde all: stretched clr 2f out: in n.d after: styd on strly* **3/1**[2]

331- **2** *3 ¼* **Intimation**[202] 7392 5-9-10 104........................................ PatDobbs 3 105
(Sir Michael Stoute) *trckd ldrs: shkn up to take 2nd wl over 1f out: already outpcd whn hung bdly lft sn after: kpt on but no ch w wnr* **9/4**[1]

52-0 **3** *1 ¾* **Desert Haze**[21] 1795 4-9-7 98........................................ FranBerry 5 98
(Ralph Beckett) *hld up in last pair: rdn and prog on outer wl over 1f out: styd on to take 3rd ins fnl f: no threat* **10/1**

26-0 **4** *1 ¼* **Crowning Glory (FR)**[21] 1795 4-9-7 93........................ StevieDonohoe 2 95
(Ralph Beckett) *chsd ldrs: rdn over 2f out: no prog and btn wl over 1f out: kpt on ins fnl f* **16/1**

-000 **5** *nk* **Epsom Icon**[63] 1046 4-9-7 100.......................................... GrahamLee 9 94
(Mick Channon) *wl in tch: shkn up 2f out: prog and tk 3rd briefly 1f out: one pce after* **18/1**

0-00 **6** *¾* **Lucy The Painter (IRE)**[21] 1795 5-9-7 94........................ HarryBentley 8 92
(Ed de Giles) *towards rr: rdn wl over 2f out: nt clr run wl over 1f out: nvr a threat but plugged on fnl f* **16/1**

05-2 **7** *nk* **Materialistic**[21] 1795 4-9-7 97........................................... ShaneKelly 1 92
(Luca Cumani) *cl up on inner: shkn up and outpcd 2f out: fdd fnl f* **4/1**[3]

03-3 **8** *1 ¼* **Zest (IRE)**[21] 1795 4-9-7 97.......................................... TomQueally 4 89
(James Fanshawe) *hld up in last pair: shkn up on inner 2f out: nt qckn and no prog* **15/2**

120/ **9** *3 ¼* **Uele River**[598] 6444 5-9-7 89.......................................... TomMarquand 6 81
(Henry Candy) *chsd wnr: rdn wl over 2f out: lost 2nd and wknd qckly wl over 1f out* **33/1**

1m 36.28s (-3.62) **Going Correction** -0.075s/f (Good) **9** Ran SP% **116.6**
Speed ratings (Par 111): **115,111,110,108,108 107,107,106,102**
CSF £10.29 TOTE £3.40: £1.30, £1.40, £2.40; EX 11.20 Trifecta £60.50.

**Owner** Godolphin **Bred** Darley **Trained** Newmarket, Suffolk

**FOCUS**
Distance increased by 10yds. Run at a sound gallop, the two previous winners at this level came to the fore, with the winner stealing away off the front. The third and fourth help set the standard.

## 2393 BETFRED MOBILE MEDIAN AUCTION MAIDEN STKS 7f
**4:25** (4:26) (Class 5) 3-Y-O **£5,175** (£1,540; £769; £384) **Stalls** Low

Form RPR

662- **1** **Queen Of Time**[189] 7695 3-8-11 80.......................... KieranShoemark(3) 6 74
(Henry Candy) *blindfold off sltly late and dwlt: hld up in 5th: prog on outer 3f out: shkn up to ld over 1f out: styd on and a readily holding runner-up* **4/5**[1]

5 **2** *1 ¼* **Patchwork**[24] 1727 3-9-5 0.............................................. ShaneKelly 2 76
(Richard Hughes) *t.k.h: cl up on inner: waiting for a gap fr 3f out tl swtchd lft to outer 2f out: rdn to chse wnr 1f out: styd on but bird had flown* **4/1**[2]

462- **3** *3 ¼* **Harry Beau**[194] 7571 3-9-5 63.............................................. PatDobbs 3 67
(Richard Hannon) *led: rdn and hdd over 1f out: hanging lft and outpcd after* **9/2**[3]

5 **4** *6* **Tenby Two**[15] 1948 3-9-0 0.............................................. GrahamLee 8 46
(Mick Channon) *mostly in last pair: pushed along and racd awkwardly fr 1/2-way: lft bhd over 2f out: tk remote 4th nr fin* **6/1**

5-5 **5** *nk* **Delahay**[22] 1761 3-9-0 0............................................ TomMarquand 7 45
(Michael Blanshard) *t.k.h: pressed ldr to 2f out: wknd qckly* **40/1**

**6** *shd* **Fivos** 3-9-0 0.......................................................... GeorgeWood(5) 9 50
(David Bridgwater) *restless stalls: rn green in last pair: lft bhd over 2f out* **33/1**

60-0 **7** *3 ½* **Crystal Secret**[10] 2087 3-8-9 50.................................... MitchGodwin(5) 4 35
(John Bridger) *pressed for ld early but rousted along and lost pl bef 1/2-way: wknd over 2f out* **33/1**

1m 27.12s (0.12) **Going Correction** -0.075s/f (Good) **7** Ran SP% **116.3**
Speed ratings (Par 99): **96,94,90,84,83 83,79**
CSF £4.50 TOTE £1.70: £1.10, £2.30; EX 4.90 Trifecta £11.30.

**Owner** First Of Many **Bred** Shortgrove Manor Stud **Trained** Kingston Warren, Oxon

■ Stewards' Enquiry : Kieran Shoemark caution: careless riding

**FOCUS**
Distance increased by 10yds. A pretty ordinary maiden, but it's likely the winner is useful. The third is the key to the form.

## 2394 BETFRED CELEBRATING 50 YEARS OF SUCCESS H'CAP (DIV I) 1m 1f 197y
**5:00** (5:04) (Class 5) (0-70,72) 3-Y-O **£5,175** (£1,540; £769; £384) **Stalls** Low

Form RPR

5-45 **1** **Road To Dubai (IRE)**[24] 1736 3-9-2 **70**........................ GeorgeWood(5) 7 78+
(George Scott) *trckd ldrs: prog to chse ldr 2f out: hanging rt rest of way but clsd to ld jst ins fnl f: urged along and steadily asserted* **11/2**[3]

2143 **2** *¾* **Moneyoryourlife**[7] 2137 3-9-2 **65**.............................. KieranO'Neill 13 71
(Richard Hannon) *trckd ldr: led wl over 2f out and sent for home: hdd jst ins fnl f: styd on but hld last 100yds* **7/1**

45-0 **3** *1 ¼* **Chaparrachik (IRE)**[24] 1736 3-9-6 **72**.................. KieranShoemark(3) 10 75
(Amanda Perrett) *t.k.h: trckd ldrs: rdn to dispute 2nd briefly 2f out: nt qckn and chsd ldng pair after: styd on but unable to cl* **11/1**

0-60 **4** *3 ½* **Delannoy**[7] 2137 3-9-4 **67**..........................................(p[1]) CharlesBishop 2 63
(Eve Johnson Houghton) *chsd ldrs: rdn over 2f out: 4th over 1f out but lft bhd by ldng trio after* **25/1**

46-5 **5** *¾* **Fields Of Fortune**[26] 1685 3-9-4 **70**.............................. HollieDoyle(3) 8 65+
(Richard Hannon) *dwlt: t.k.h: hld up in last pair: stl last of main gp 2f out and long way off the pce: styd on after: nrst fin but no ch* **9/2**[2]

621- **6** *nk* **Dominating (GER)**[178] 7866 3-9-4 **67**............................ FrannyNorton 6 61
(Mark Johnston) *trckd ldrs: lost pl bdly 3f out: struggling and wl in rr 2f out: plugged on again fnl f* **7/2**[1]

-450 **7** *1* **Malt Teaser (FR)**[31] 1550 3-9-1 **64**.................................. MartinDwyer 1 56
(John Best) *s.i.s: rchd midfield bef 1/2-way: in tch over 2f out: pushed along and steadily lft bhd* **20/1**

50-3 **8** *1 ¼* **Percy Thrower (IRE)**[30] 1591 3-9-0 **66**.................. CallumShepherd(3) 5 55
(Charles Hills) *hld up in rr: effrt on inner 3f out: one pce and nvr able to threaten* **25/1**

06-0 **9** *nse* **Ashazuri**[31] 1550 3-8-9 **65**..................................(h[1]) Pierre-LouisJamin(7) 12 54
(Jonathan Portman) *led to wl over 2f out: wknd wl over 1f out* **50/1**

-430 **10** *2 ½* **Rock N Roll Global (IRE)**[16] 1907 3-9-5 **68**.................. ShaneKelly 14 52
(Richard Hughes) *nvr bttr than midfield: outpcd over 2f out: edgd rt over 1f out: fdd* **8/1**

60-0 **11** *2 ¼* **Mr Scaff (IRE)**[26] 1686 3-8-13 **62**.......................................... GrahamLee 9 42
(Paul Henderson) *nvr beyond midfield: shkn up and no prog wl over 2f out: sn btn* **20/1**

1616 **12** *11* **Oberyn (IRE)**[86] 647 3-9-3 **66**................................................ PatDobbs 4 24
(Sylvester Kirk) *hld up in midfield: shkn up and no prog 3f out: wl btn after: hmpd over 1f out and wknd* **20/1**

046- **13** *83* **Duchess Of Fife**[177] 7885 3-9-2 **65**..................................(h[1]) FranBerry 11
(William Knight) *reluctant to go to post: awkward s: reluctant to exert herself and t.o fr 4f out* **12/1**

2m 7.7s (-0.40) **Going Correction** -0.075s/f (Good) **13** Ran SP% **119.4**
Speed ratings (Par 99): **98,97,96,93,93 92,91,90,90,88 87,78,11**
CSF £38.89 CT £415.87 TOTE £6.10: £2.30, £2.00, £3.60; EX 41.30 Trifecta £831.20.

**Owner** Mohammed Al Nabouda **Bred** Rabbah Bloodstock Limited **Trained** Newmarket, Suffolk

**FOCUS**
Distance as advertised. Division one of a modest handicap, the front two in the market disappointed. The third has been rated in line with the better view of his maiden form.

## 2395 BETFRED CELEBRATING 50 YEARS OF SUCCESS H'CAP (DIV II) 1m 1f 197y
**5:30** (5:36) (Class 5) (0-70,73) 3-Y-O **£5,175** (£1,540; £769; £384) **Stalls** Low

Form RPR

40-1 **1** **Darkroom Angel**[21] 1790 3-9-5 **71**.............................. HectorCrouch(3) 6 78
(Philip Hide) *led 3f: dropped to 3rd 4f out but stl gng strly: chsd ldr again 2f out: rdn to chal fnl f: styd on to ld last 75yds* **6/1**[3]

-442 **2** *½* **Alexander M (IRE)**[30] 1591 3-9-3 **66**.............................. FrannyNorton 11 72
(Mark Johnston) *led after 3f: rdn 2f out: edgd lft fnl f: styd on but hdd last 75yds* **9/1**

31-4 **3** *1 ¾* **Glenys The Menace (FR)**[26] 1685 3-9-3 **66**................(h) MartinDwyer 5 68
(John Best) *wl in tch: rdn over 2f out: styd on fr over 1f out to take 3rd fnl f: nvr able to chal* **9/1**

45-0 **4** *½* **Amelia Dream**[16] 1907 3-9-7 **70**.......................................... GrahamLee 13 71
(Mick Channon) *towards rr: shkn up 3f out: prog 2f out: styd on to take 4th fnl f* **20/1**

0-11 **5** *1 ¾* **Arab Moon**[1] 2371 3-9-7 **73** 6ex.............................. CallumShepherd(3) 14 71+
(William Knight) *in tch in midfield on outer: rdn over 2f out: kpt on same pce and nvr able to threaten* **11/4**[1]

5-05 **6** 1/2 **Meteoric Riser (USA)**28 1619 3-9-2 **65**............................ ShaneKelly 4 62
(Richard Hughes) *pushed along early then settled in rr: pushed along 3f out: kpt on steadily fr 2f out but nvr nr enough to be involved* **18/1**
30-3 **7** 1 1/4 **Star Maker**10 2088 3-9-6 **69**.............................................. PatDobbs 12 63
(Sylvester Kirk) *swift move to trck ldrs after 2f: wnt 2nd 4f out to 2f out: shkn up and wknd jst over 1f out* **11/2**2
0-32 **8** 2 1/2 **Dream Magic (IRE)**92 552 3-8-13 **67**...................... CharlieBennett(5) 1 56
(Daniel Mark Loughnane) *t.k.h: trckd ldrs: steadily wknd fr over 2f out* **10/1**
00-0 **9** nse **Nobleman (GER)**12 2027 3-8-9 **58**................................(h1) LiamKeniry 2 47
(Hughie Morrison) *t.k.h: trckd ldrs: rdn over 2f out: wknd over 1f out* **10/1**
500 **10** 7 **Hippocampus (IRE)**14 1961 3-9-0 **66**.................. HollieDoyle(3) 10 41
(Richard Hannon) *dropped qckly to last over 8f out: nt gng wl after and bhd fr 1/2-way* **22/1**
63-0 **11** 1 1/2 **Exspectation (IRE)**26 1686 3-8-13 **62**........................ TomMarquand 3 34
(Michael Blanshard) *dwlt: a in rr: pushed along and struggling by 1/2-way: bhd fnl 3f* **33/1**
643 **12** 3 1/4 **Magic Pass**20 1818 3-9-1 **64**......................................(h) ThomasBrown 7 29
(Andrew Balding) *a in rr and pushed along bef 1/2-way: brief effrt 3f out: sn wknd* **8/1**

2m 7.57s (-0.53) **Going Correction** -0.075s/f (Good) **12** Ran SP% **122.9**
Speed ratings (Par 99): **99,98,97,96,95 95,94,92,91,86 85,82**
CSF £59.93 CT £495.36 TOTE £6.90: £1.90, £3.00, £2.90; EX 62.80 Trifecta £540.50.
**Owner** The Perfect Smiths **Bred** David Jamison Bloodstock **Trained** Findon, W Sussex

**FOCUS**
Distance as advertised. This looked the lesser of the two divisions. The third helps with the standard, with the fourth to her maiden form.
T/Plt: 177.20 to a £1 stake. Pool: £116,906.93 - 481.37 winning units T/Qpdt: £26.70 to a £1 stake. Pool: £7,676.45 - 212.30 winning units **Jonathan Neesom**

# 1901 NEWMARKET (R-H)
## Saturday, May 6

**OFFICIAL GOING: Good to firm (watered; 8.4; far side: 8.3, centre: 8.5, stands' side: 8.4)**
Wind: light, half against, of no consequence Weather: overcast

## 2396 SPRING LODGE STKS (H'CAP) (FORMERLY THE SUFFOLK STAKES) 1m 1f
**1:50** (1:51) (Class 2) 3-Y-0+
**£31,125** (£9,320; £4,660; £2,330; £1,165; £585) **Stalls** High

Form RPR
110- **1** **Playful Sound**211 7119 4-8-12 **93**.................................. WilliamBuick 5 103
(Sir Michael Stoute) *swtg: chsd ldr tl rdn to ld 2f out: hdd ent fnl f: battled bk gamely u.p to ld wl ins fnl f: styd on* **10/1**
20-1 **2** 1 1/4 **Next Stage**18 1860 4-9-1 **96**.......................................... JimCrowley 8 103
(Saeed bin Suroor) *lw: stdd s: hld up in tch in midfield: clsd to join ldrs and travelling strly 2f out: rdn to ld and edgd lft ent fnl f: drvn ins fnl f: hdd wl ins fnl f: wkng towards fin* **2/1**1
413- **3** 1/2 **Central Square (IRE)**153 7154 5-9-9 **104**...................... AndreaAtzeni 6 110+
(Roger Varian) *swtg: stdd s: hld up in last pair: rdn 3f out: swtchd rt over 1f out: hdwy 1f out: styd on to go 3rd ins fnl f: nvr getting on terms w ldrs but gng on wl at fin* **7/1**3
1500 **4** 1 1/2 **Abareeq**10 2086 4-8-6 **87**................................................ JoeFanning 2 90
(Mark Johnston) *stdd s: t.k.h: hld up in tch in midfield: effrt over 2f out: hdwy to chse ldrs u.p over 1f out: edgd lft and no imp 1f out: kpt on same pce ins fnl f* **12/1**
12-1 **5** 2 1/2 **Ballet Concerto**35 1492 4-9-7 **102**................................... RyanMoore 9 99
(Sir Michael Stoute) *hld up in tch in midfield: effrt over 2f out: unable qck and changing legs on downhill run over 1f out: sltly impeded and swtchd rt ent fnl f: kpt on same pce ins fnl f* **11/4**2
-404 **6** shd **Great Hall**10 2086 7-9-7 **102**.......................................... PatCosgrave 7 99
(Mick Quinn) *led: rdn and hdd 2f out: unable qck and lost pl over 1f out: wknd ins fnl f* **25/1**
00-3 **7** 1 1/4 **Bancnuanaheireann (IRE)**80 744 10-8-10 **94**.. AlistairRawlinson(3) 1 88
(Michael Appleby) *chsd ldrs: rdn ent fnl 2f: unable qck and lost pl over 1f out: wknd ins fnl f* **33/1**
02-2 **8** nk **Grapevine (IRE)**14 1964 4-8-9 **90**................................. JamieSpencer 3 84
(Charles Hills) *stdd s: t.k.h: hld up in tch in rr: effrt and switching lft over 1f out: no imp and wl hld wen swtchd rt ins fnl f* **17/2**
15-5 **9** 11 **Dolphin Vista (IRE)**35 1494 4-9-4 **99**........................... PaulHanagan 10 69
(Richard Fahey) *t.k.h: trckd ldrs: rdn 3f out: sn struggling and lost pl: bhd ins fnl f* **12/1**

1m 51.91s (0.21) **Going Correction** +0.10s/f (Good) **9** Ran SP% **114.3**
Speed ratings (Par 109): **103,101,101,100,97 97,96,96,86**
CSF £30.04 CT £152.73 TOTE £10.70: £2.80, £1.30, £2.40; EX 37.90 Trifecta £242.20.
**Owner** Newsells Park Stud **Bred** Newsells Park Stud **Trained** Newmarket, Suffolk

**FOCUS**
Just 2mm of water was applied to the course on Thursday night, and it had been dry since, so the going was given as good to firm (GoingStick: 8.4 (Stands' side 8.4; Centre 8.5; Far side 8.3). Clerk of the course Michael Prosser said that the breeze was across and that there was a slight headwind as well. The false rail was up on the stands' side of the course from the 1m2f start to the 2.5 furlong point (the bushes). The re-positioning of the bend into the home straight increased the distance of the 1m4f race by 9yds. This looked a good handicap, but the early pace wasn't strong and the time was 4.11sec outside standard. The level is a bit fluid.

## 2397 LONGHOLES PALACE HOUSE STKS (GROUP 3) 5f
**2:20** (2:22) (Class 1) 3-Y-0+
**£34,026** (£12,900; £6,456; £3,216; £1,614; £810) **Stalls** High

Form RPR
521- **1** **Marsha (IRE)**216 6990 4-9-7 111......................................... LukeMorris 12 118+
(Sir Mark Prescott Bt) *lw: hld up towards rr: clsd into midfield and travelling strly 1/2-way: swtchd lft 2f out: rdn and qcknd to ld ent fnl f: edging rt but hld on wl u.p ins fnl f: gamely* **8/1**
20-0 **2** nk **Washington DC (IRE)**12 2046 4-9-3 111......................(t) RyanMoore 11 113
(A P O'Brien, Ire) *lw: hld up in tch: pushed along and clsd 2f out: rdn to chal ent fnl f: drvn and ev ch fnl f: r.o but a jst hld* **10/3**1
306- **3** 1 **Goldream**197 7520 8-9-3 110.......................................(p) MartinHarley 14 109
(Robert Cowell) *hld up in tch: clsd to chse ldrs and rdn over 1f out: kpt on but unable qck u.p fnl f* **12/1**
600- **4** 1 1/2 **Kachy**245 6120 4-9-3 110............................................. RichardKingscote 8 104
(Tom Dascombe) *in rr: rdn and hdwy over 1f out: styd on ins fnl f: nvr trbld ldrs* **25/1**
41-1 **5** shd **Priceless**15 1936 4-9-0 107................................................. AdamKirby 10 101
(Clive Cox) *t.k.h: chsd ldr tl led over 1f out: rdn and hdd ent fnl f: no ex and wknd ins fnl f* **5/1**2
22-2 **6** shd **Ornate**16 1903 4-9-3 110.................................................. FrankieDettori 6 103
(Robert Cowell) *chsd ldrs: rdn and ev ch over 1f out tl no ex jst ins fnl f: wknd fnl 100yds* **12/1**
6-11 **7** 1 1/4 **Kimberella**22 1772 7-9-3 110.............................................. PaulHanagan 4 99
(Richard Fahey) *lw: hld up in tch towards rr: clsd to chse ldrs and rdn 2f out: unable qck and no imp over 1f out: wknd ins fnl f* **12/1**
112- **8** nse **Alpha Delphini**231 6574 6-9-3 110............................(p) ConnorBeasley 2 99
(Bryan Smart) *stuck out wd towards centre: in tch in midfield overall: effrt 2f out: unable qck over 1f out: wknd ins fnl f* **16/1**
010- **9** 3/4 **Cotai Glory**216 6990 5-9-6 112...................................... JamieSpencer 9 99+
(Charles Hills) *taken down early: stmbld bdly leaving stalls and in rr: swtchd lft over 1f out: racing awkwardly 1f out: hdwy ins fnl f: styd on fnl 100yds: nvr trbld ldrs* **20/1**
4442 **10** 1/2 **Gracious John (IRE)**22 1772 4-9-3 108.............................. JFEgan 16 94
(David Evans) *chsd ldrs: rdn 2f out: unable qck and sn struggling: wknd ins fnl f* **33/1**
110- **11** 1/2 **Dancing Star**245 6120 4-9-0 108.................................... DavidProbert 7 89
(Andrew Balding) *swtg: niggled along in midfield: lost pl and dropped towards rr 1/2-way: rallied 1f out and kpt on ins fnl f: nvr trbld ldrs* **12/1**
3-1 **12** 2 **Muthmir (IRE)**22 1765 7-9-3 110........................................ JimCrowley 5 85
(William Haggas) *lw: hld up in tch in midfield: effrt 2f out: no imp u.p over 1f out: wknd ins fnl f* **6/1**3
0310 **13** 2 1/4 **Royal Birth**22 1772 6-9-3 95.............................................(t) AaronJones 15 77
(Stuart Williams) *hld up in tch in midfield: effrt but unbalanced and lost pl over 1f out: towards rr and sltly impeded sn after: wknd ins fnl f* **66/1**
252- **14** 7 **Thesme**241 6230 5-9-0 109.............................................. AndreaAtzeni 3 49
(Nigel Tinkler) *taken down early: stuck out wd towards centre: chsd ldrs tl rdn and lost pl qckly over 1f out: fdd ins fnl f* **33/1**
310- **15** 1/2 **Just Glamorous (IRE)**216 6990 4-9-6 114........................ TomEaves 13 53
(Ronald Harris) *led tl over 1f out: sn rdn and lost pl: wknd fnl f* **40/1**

58.18s (-0.92) **Going Correction** +0.10s/f (Good) **15** Ran SP% **120.2**
Speed ratings (Par 113): **111,110,108,106,106 106,104,104,102,102 101,98,94,83,82**
CSF £32.02 TOTE £8.90: £2.60, £1.40, £4.20; EX 44.30 Trifecta £481.80.
**Owner** Elite Racing Club **Bred** Elite Racing Club **Trained** Newmarket, Suffolk

**FOCUS**
It was disappointing that Profitable, who won this last year, was a non-runner, but still a good race and it produced the same one-two as the 2016 Group 1 Prix de l'Abbaye, with the 2015 winner of this (who subsequently bagged two Group 1s) in third. They raced middle to stands' side. The runner-up has been rated to form.

## 2398 DUNADEN JOCKEY CLUB STKS (GROUP 2) 1m 4f
**2:55** (2:58) (Class 1) 4-Y-0+ **£56,710** (£21,500; £10,760; £5,360; £2,690) **Stalls** Centre

Form RPR
54-2 **1** **Seventh Heaven (IRE)**42 1379 4-9-1 114........................ RyanMoore 2 120
(A P O'Brien, Ire) *swtg: hld up mainly in 4th: clsd to go 3rd 3f out: rdn to chal 2f out: led over 1f out and sn in command: clr and styd on strly ins fnl f* **4/7**1
13-0 **2** 5 **One Foot In Heaven (IRE)**27 1659 5-9-1 113................. JimCrowley 3 112
(A De Royer-Dupre, France) *squeezed for room leaving stalls: hld up in rr: pushed along to cl 3f out: rdn and unbalanced on downhill run over 1f out: hdwy to chse clr wnr ins fnl f: kpt on but no ch w wnr* **7/2**2
-120 **3** 1 3/4 **Pinzolo**22 1770 6-9-1 102............................................ SilvestreDeSousa 5 109
(Ismail Mohammed) *swtg: t.k.h: chsd ldr tl led after 2f: clr 8f out: rdn and hrd pressed over 2f out: hdd over 1f out: nt pce of wnr and one pced after: lost 2nd ins fnl f* **25/1**
-11 **4** 1 1/2 **Galapiat**10 2085 4-9-1 107.................................................. JoeFanning 1 107
(Mark Johnston) *led for 2f: chsd ldr: clsd 3f out: rdn and ev ch over 2f out tl 3rd and unable qck over 1f out: wl hld and plugged on same pce ins fnl f* **5/1**3
413- **5** 25 **Cleonte (IRE)**244 6176 4-9-1 101.................................... WilliamBuick 4 78
(Andrew Balding) *cmpt: chsd ldng pair after 2f: rdn 3f out: sn struggling and dropped to rr 2f out: wl bhd and eased ins fnl f* **25/1**

2m 34.39s (2.39) **Going Correction** +0.10s/f (Good) **5** Ran SP% **110.2**
Speed ratings (Par 115): **96,92,91,90,73**
CSF £2.90 TOTE £1.50: £1.10, £1.90; EX 3.20 Trifecta £14.00.
**Owner** Derrick Smith & Mrs John Magnier & Michael Tabor **Bred** La Traviata Syndicate **Trained** Cashel, Co Tipperary

**FOCUS**
Race distance increased by 9yds. There wasn't much strength in depth to this Group 2, but the winner is a bona fide Group 1 performer and she got the job done in straightforward fashion. The winner has been rated to form.

## 2399 QIPCO 2000 GUINEAS STKS (GROUP 1) (BRITISH CHAMPIONS SERIES) (C&F) 1m
**3:35** (3:39) (Class 1) 3-Y-O
**£283,550** (£107,500; £53,800; £26,800; £13,450; £6,750) **Stalls** High

Form RPR
111- **1** **Churchill (IRE)**210 7149 3-9-0 122................................... RyanMoore 3 122+
(A P O'Brien, Ire) *lw: trckd ldrs: moved lft to r against stands' rail 1/2-way effrt 2f out: rdn to ld over 1f out: styd on wl u.p and a doing enough ins fnl f: rdn out* **6/4**1
1-1 **2** 1 **Barney Roy**14 1959 3-9-0 115.......................................... JamesDoyle 5 119+
(Richard Hannon) *lw: t.k.h: midfield: swtchd lft and effrt 2f out: stmbld bdly and unbalanced on downhill run over 1f out: swtchd rt and hdwy ent fnl f: styd on u.p to chse wnr wl ins fnl f: no imp* **7/2**2
1-1 **3** nk **Al Wukair (IRE)**26 1689 3-9-0 113.............................. GregoryBenoist 7 118+
(A Fabre, France) *lengthy: stdd s: t.k.h: hld up in tch in last trio: swtchd rt and effrt over 1f out: r.o wl u.p ins fnl f to go 3rd towards fin: nvr getting on terms w wnr* **11/2**
22-4 **4** hd **Lancaster Bomber (USA)**42 1375 3-9-0 117......... DonnachaO'Brien 4 117
(A P O'Brien, Ire) *lw: led and set stdy gallop: pushed along 2f out: hdd and rdn over 1f out: kpt on wl u.p but nvr quite matching pce of wnr: lost 2 pls wl ins fnl f* **14/1**
12 **5** 1 3/4 **Dream Castle**14 1959 3-9-0 110..........................(h1) SilvestreDeSousa 10 114+
(Saeed bin Suroor) *stdd s: t.k.h: hld up in tch in last pair: nt clr run and hmpd 2f out: swtchd rt and then bk lft over 1f out: hdwy u.p ins fnl f: styd on: nvr trbld ldrs* **8/1**
1-1 **6** nk **Eminent (IRE)**16 1904 3-9-0 111.................................... JimCrowley 2 112
(Martyn Meade) *hld up in tch in midfield: effrt and rdn in 4th 3f out: stl chsng ldrs but unable qck whn nudged rt ent fnl f: keeping on same pce and hld whn n.m.r wl ins fnl f* **5/1**3

3110 **7** *nk* **Top Score**[42] [1375] 3-9-0 108 ........ JoeFanning 9 111
(Saeed bin Suroor) *stdd s: t.k.h: hld up in tch in rr: swtchd lft and effrt 2f out: sme hdwy u.p jst over 1f out: kpt on same pce and no imp ins fnl f* **100/1**

12-0 **8** *1 ½* **Spirit Of Valor (USA)**[42] [1375] 3-9-0 102 ........(bt) SeamieHeffernan 8 108
(A P O'Brien, Ire) *chsd ldr for 3f: stdd bk into midfield 1/2-way: effrt and shkn up over 1f out: sn hung rt and no imp: kpt on same pce fnl f* **33/1**

31-5 **9** *3 ¾* **Larchmont Lad (IRE)**[16] [1904] 3-9-0 110 ........ WilliamBuick 6 99
(Richard Hannon) *lw: hld up in tch in midfield: rdn 3f out: sn struggling and lost pl 2f out: bhd 1f out* **33/1**

3-13 **10** *hd* **Law And Order (IRE)**[18] [1861] 3-9-0 104 ........ MartinHarley 1 98
(James Tate) *chsd ldrs tl wnt 2nd after 3f: ev ch 3f out: sn rdn: outpcd and btn over 1f out: wknd fnl f* **100/1**

1m 36.61s (-1.99) **Going Correction** +0.10s/f (Good) **10** Ran SP% **119.9**
Speed ratings (Par 113): **113,112,111,111,109 109,109,107,103,103**
CSF £6.93 CT £23.14 TOTE £2.70: £1.30, £1.40, £1.90; EX 8.60 Trifecta £27.60.
**Owner** Michael Tabor & Derrick Smith & Mrs John Magnier **Bred** Liberty Bloodstock **Trained** Cashel, Co Tipperary
■ Stewards' Enquiry : James Doyle two-day ban: careless riding (May 21-22)

**FOCUS**
The first seven were covered by just under 4l at the line and things got a bit messy for some of the beaten runners, so it's hard to get that excited by the bare form. However, the winner is rarely spectacular in the way he goes about things - he's just a professional who knows how to get the job done - and the second, third and fifth all look to have improvement in them. The winner and fourth almost reproduced their Dewhurst form and set the standard.

## 2400 HOT STREAK H'CAP 6f
**4:10** (4:15) (Class 2) (0-100,100) 3-Y-O **£12,938** (£3,850; £1,924; £962) **Stalls** High

Form RPR

120- **1** **Danielsflyer (IRE)**[261] [5583] 3-9-0 93 ........ SilvestreDeSousa 6 103
(David Barron) *hld up in last pair: swtchd rt and effrt jst over 2f out: rdn to chal ent fnl f: led ins f: r.o wl: eased nr fin* **25/1**

32-3 **2** *½* **Eqtiraan (IRE)**[28] [1621] 3-9-7 100 ........ JimCrowley 4 108
(Richard Hannon) *tall: stdd s: t.k.h: hld up in midfield: clsd to join ldrs and travelling strly over 2f out: rdn to ld and edgd lft over 1f out: sn hrd pressed and hdd ins fnl f: kpt on wl but a hld after* **8/1**

0-21 **3** *2* **Mostahel**[19] [1837] 3-9-0 93 ........ FrankieDettori 3 95
(Richard Hannon) *str: lw: keen to post: pressed ldr: rdn and ev ch jst over 2f out: edgd lft and unable qck over 1f out: kpt on same pce ins fnl f* **7/2**[2]

1-12 **4** *nk* **Queen In Waiting (IRE)**[8] [2130] 3-8-10 89 ........ JoeFanning 1 90
(Mark Johnston) *t.k.h: led: rdn 2f out: hdd and unable qck whn edgd lft over 1f out: styd on same pce u.p ins fnl f* **10/1**

31-4 **5** *nse* **Mazyoun**[21] [1801] 3-8-10 89 ........(b) JosephineGordon 9 90
(Hugo Palmer) *t.k.h: trckd ldrs: rdn: edgd lft and unable qck over 1f out: kpt on same pce ins fnl f* **12/1**

153- **6** *¾* **The Wagon Wheel (IRE)**[217] [6954] 3-8-6 85 ........ PaulHanagan 2 83
(Richard Fahey) *lw: chsd ldrs: rdn 2f out: outpcd whn short of room over 1f out: kpt on same pce ins fnl f* **7/1**[3]

0-55 **7** *1* **Smokey Lane (IRE)**[8] [2130] 3-9-0 93 ........ AdamKirby 5 88
(David Evans) *hld up in tch: rdn over 2f out: no imp whn nt clrest of runs over 1f out: kpt on same pce and no threat to ldrs after* **16/1**

31-1 **8** *½* **Victory Angel (IRE)**[16] [1901] 3-8-13 92 ........ AndreaAtzeni 10 86
(Roger Varian) *lw: t.k.h: early: hld up in tch: effrt over 1f out: no imp and btn whn nt clr run and swtchd rt jst ins fnl f* **13/8**[1]

10- **9** *½* **Exmouth**[225] [6748] 3-8-13 92 ........ RyanMoore 8 84+
(Sir Michael Stoute) *stdd s: t.k.h: hld up in tch in last: effrt on stands' rail over 1f out: stl plenty to do whn nt clr run and hmpd jst ins fnl f: swtchd rt and no imp after* **16/1**

1m 11.86s (-0.34) **Going Correction** +0.10s/f (Good) **9** Ran SP% **116.3**
Speed ratings (Par 105): **106,105,102,102,102 101,99,99,98**
CSF £212.10 CT £884.16 TOTE £40.60: £7.20, £2.30, £1.20; EX 308.00 Trifecta £2298.80.
**Owner** Elliott Brothers And Peacock **Bred** Michael McGlynn **Trained** Maunby, N Yorks

**FOCUS**
A good sprint handicap which should throw up winners. The fourth and fifth have been rated close to form.

## 2401 HAVANA GOLD NEWMARKET STKS (LISTED RACE) (C&G) 1m 2f
**4:45** (4:46) (Class 1) 3-Y-O **£22,684** (£8,600; £4,304; £2,144; £1,076) **Stalls** High

Form RPR

3-32 **1** **Permian (IRE)**[10] [2084] 3-9-0 101 ........ RyanMoore 2 109
(Mark Johnston) *chsd clr ldr: clsd ent fnl 2f: rdn to ld over 1f out: clr 1f out and styd on strly ins fnl f: rdn out* **5/2**[2]

-121 **2** *4 ½* **Speedo Boy (FR)**[58] [1114] 3-9-3 95 ........ SilvestreDeSousa 1 103
(Ian Williams) *str: hld up in 4th: wnt 3rd 4f out: rdn ent fnl 2f: drvn to go 2nd but wnr gng clr 1f out: kpt on same pce and no imp after* **20/1**

1-31 **3** *1 ½* **Khalidi**[18] [1861] 3-9-3 110 ........ FrankieDettori 4 100
(John Gosden) *hld up in 3rd tl 4f out: rdn and clsd over 2f out: swtchd lft 2f out: unable qck u.p and unbalanced over 1f out: wnt 3rd and kpt on same pce ins fnl f: eased nr fin* **11/10**[1]

54-5 **4** *3 ¼* **Majoris (IRE)**[28] [1621] 3-9-0 97 ........(t) JamesDoyle 5 90
(Hugo Palmer) *t.k.h: led and sn clr: reduced advantage and rdn 2f out: hdd over 1f out and no ex: lost 2nd 1f out and wknd ins fnl f* **16/1**

1 **5** *22* **Night Circus (IRE)**[18] [1857] 3-9-0 0 ........ WilliamBuick 3 46
(Charlie Appleby) *lw: stdd s: hld up in rr: clsd and rdn over 2f out: btn over 1f out: heavily eased ins fnl f* **3/1**[3]

2m 3.66s (-2.14) **Going Correction** +0.10s/f (Good) **5** Ran SP% **111.8**
Speed ratings (Par 107): **112,108,107,104,87**
CSF £38.35 TOTE £3.00: £1.30, £4.00; EX 19.70 Trifecta £47.90.
**Owner** Sheikh Hamdan bin Mohammed Al Maktoum **Bred** Darley **Trained** Middleham Moor, N Yorks

**FOCUS**
This race fell apart somewhat with the third, fourth and fifth not giving their true running, and the winner was left to beat the outsider of the field (who had a penalty), but still a smart enough performance. The runner-up went some way to confirming his latest soft ground French form.

## 2402 QIPCO RACING WELFARE H'CAP 1m
**5:20** (5:22) (Class 2) (0-105,102) 3-Y-O **£12,938** (£3,850; £1,924; £962) **Stalls** High

Form RPR

310- **1** **Ronald R (IRE)**[260] [5595] 3-8-7 88 ........ JoeFanning 5 99
(Michael Bell) *t.k.h: hld up in tch towards rr: hdwy over 2f out: rdn to chal over 1f out: led and edgd lft ins fnl f: hld on cl home: all out* **14/1**

1-1 **2** *hd* **Son Of The Stars**[23] [1760] 3-8-8 89 ........ SeanLevey 6 99
(Richard Hannon) *str: too t.k.h: hld up in tch in midfield: clsd to trck ldrs 3f out: led and travelling strly 2f out: rdn and unbalanced on downhill run over 1f out: hdd ins fnl f: edging lft but battled bk wl towards fin: jst hld* **5/2**[1]

1-55 **3** *2 ¾* **High Acclaim (USA)**[19] [1841] 3-8-6 87 ........ SilvestreDeSousa 9 91
(Roger Teal) *t.k.h: hld up in tch in midfield: effrt 2f out: chsd clr ldng pair jst over 1f out: kpt on but no imp ins fnl f* **33/1**

5642 **4** *2 ¼* **Grey Britain**[21] [1801] 3-9-4 99 ........ AdamKirby 7 98
(John Ryan) *chsd ldrs tl lost pl 3f out: bhd and nt clr run 2f out: swtchd lft over 1f out and rallied u.p 1f out: styd on wl to snatch 4th last strides: no threat to ldrs* **10/1**

112- **5** *hd* **Andok (IRE)**[196] [7541] 3-8-6 87 ........ PaulHanagan 8 85
(Richard Fahey) *lengthy: hld up in last pair: rdn over 2f: swtchd rt and hdwy over 1f out: no imp and edgd lft 1f out: wknd ins fnl f and lost 4th last strides* **9/2**[3]

4-46 **6** *4* **Sea Fox (IRE)**[14] [1959] 3-9-5 100 ........ JFEgan 3 89
(David Evans) *chsd ldrs: rdn 3f out: outpcd and btn over 1f out: wknd ins fnl f* **22/1**

10- **7** *½* **Seniority**[259] [5646] 3-8-7 88 ........ LiamJones 10 76
(William Haggas) *stdd s: t.k.h: hld up in tch in rr: effrt 2f out: sme hdwy over 1f out but nvr getting on terms w ldrs: wknd ins fnl f* **20/1**

31-5 **8** *5* **Via Serendipity**[14] [1959] 3-8-11 92 ........(t) JosephineGordon 2 69
(Hugo Palmer) *t.k.h: hld up in tch in midfield: hdwy to chse ldrs 1/2-way: wnt 2nd briefly wl over 2f out: sn u.p and struggling: wknd fnl f* **15/2**

5-1 **9** *1 ½* **Eagle Creek (IRE)**[25] [1692] 3-9-0 95 ........ AndreaAtzeni 1 68+
(Simon Crisford) *lengthy: wnt rt s: t.k.h: hdwy to ld after 1f: hdd 2f out: sn rdn: unbalanced and btn over 1f out: wknd fnl f* **11/4**[2]

215- **10** *15* **Medieval (IRE)**[198] [7491] 3-9-7 102 ........ FrankieDettori 4 41
(Paul Cole) *led for 1f: styd pressing ldr tl wl over 2f out: lost pl and bhd whn unbalnaced on downhill run over 1f out: eased fnl f* **16/1**

1m 37.64s (-0.96) **Going Correction** +0.10s/f (Good) **10** Ran SP% **118.9**
Speed ratings (Par 105): **108,107,105,102,102 98,98,93,91,76**
CSF £49.05 CT £1179.80 TOTE £16.80: £4.30, £1.50, £7.20; EX 64.20 Trifecta £1494.30.
**Owner** W J and T C O Gredley **Bred** M Morrissey **Trained** Newmarket, Suffolk

**FOCUS**
An interesting handicap. The early pace wasn't that strong an several raced keenly, but a couple of lightly raced, unexposed colts came clear, and there are reasons to be positive about both. The time was 1.03sec slower than the Guineas. The fourth has been rated to the balance of his form.
T/Jkpt: Not Won. T/Plt: £98.50 to a £1 stake. Pool: £214,991.95 - 1,593.05 winning units. T/Qpdt: £19.10 to a £1 stake. Pool: £10,840.22 - 419.35 winning units. **Steve Payne**

# 2179 THIRSK (L-H)
### Saturday, May 6

**OFFICIAL GOING: Good to firm (watered; 8.7)**
Wind: fresh across Weather: overcast

## 2403 TOTESCOOP6 PLAY FOR JUST £2 TODAY NOVICE AUCTION STKS 5f
**1:55** (1:56) (Class 5) 2-Y-O **£3,234** (£962; £481; £240) **Stalls** High

Form RPR

**1** **Guzman (IRE)** 2-9-2 0 ........ TonyHamilton 6 72
(Richard Fahey) *in tch towards outer: pushed along and hdwy over 1f out: led narrowly ins fnl f: rdn and kpt on fnl 110yds* **5/2**[1]

**2** *nk* **Trusting Friend (USA)** 2-9-2 0 ........ KevinStott 4 71
(Kevin Ryan) *trckd ldr: rdn 2f out: ev ch ins fnl f: kpt on* **7/1**

**3** *½* **Seen The Lyte (IRE)** 2-8-11 0 ........ JasonHart 9 64
(John Quinn) *led: racd keenly: hdd 2f out: pushed along over 1f out: kpt on fnl f* **9/1**

**4** *nk* **Danehill Desert (IRE)** 2-8-13 0 ........ SammyJoBell[(3)] 5 70+
(Richard Fahey) *squeezed out s: hld up: stmbld 3f out: pushed along over 1f out: r.o wl fnl 110yds* **11/1**

03 **5** *½* **Just For The Craic (IRE)**[17] [1872] 2-9-2 0 ........ JamesSullivan 11 66
(Ruth Carr) *trckd ldr: rdn to ld 2f out: hdd ins fnl f: no ex* **9/2**[2]

**6** *2 ¼* **Super Major (IRE)** 2-9-2 0 ........ AndrewMullen 8 58
(Michael Dods) *in tch: rdn to chse ldrs over 1f out: wknd ins fnl f* **6/1**

**7** *¾* **Chatburn (IRE)** 2-9-2 0 ........ DanielTudhope 7 55
(David O'Meara) *in tch: pushed along over 1f out: wknd ins fnl f* **11/2**[3]

**8** *5* **Orient Princess** 2-8-11 0 ........ PaulMulrennan 10 32
(Paul Midgley) *dwlt: a towards rr* **25/1**

0 **9** *4 ½* **Progressive Jazz (IRE)**[17] [1872] 2-9-2 0 ........ BenCurtis 3 21
(K R Burke) *reminder leaving stalls: chsd ldrs on outer: lost pl 3f out: sn bhd* **25/1**

1m 1.18s (1.58) **Going Correction** +0.125s/f (Good) **9** Ran SP% **114.9**
Speed ratings (Par 93): **92,91,90,90,89 85,84,76,69**
CSF £20.38 TOTE £3.00: £1.50, £2.50, £2.60; EX 13.90 Trifecta £175.50.
**Owner** Merchants and Missionaries **Bred** Casablanca Jewel Partnership **Trained** Musley Bank, N Yorks

**FOCUS**
Rail movements: add 20yds to Races 4 and 6. A fair juvenile novice contest. They went a respectable gallop, at best, on good to firm ground that had been heavily watered. The winning time reflected that irrigation. The winner was backed heavily just before the off. It's been rated around the race average for recent years. It's been rated around the race average.

## 2404 TOTEPOOLLIVEINFO.COM H'CAP 6f
**2:30** (2:30) (Class 4) (0-80,85) 4-Y-O+ **£6,469** (£1,925; £962; £481) **Stalls** High

Form RPR

0-32 **1** **Art Obsession (IRE)**[66] [971] 6-9-2 75 ........ PaulMulrennan 4 83
(Paul Midgley) *in tch: pushed along and hdwy over 1f out: rdn to ld jst ins fnl f: edgd rt: kpt on* **10/1**

32-1 **2** *1 ½* **Magical Effect (IRE)**[16] [1910] 5-9-7 80 ........ JamesSullivan 3 83
(Ruth Carr) *prom: pushed along over 1f out: rdn appr fnl f: kpt on* **15/8**[1]

/0-0 **3** *nk* **Taskeen (IRE)**[16] [1910] 4-9-1 74 ........ TonyHamilton 1 76
(Roger Fell) *hld up: rdn over 1f out: kpt on fnl f* **16/1**

3436 **4** *hd* **Suqoor**[17] [1880] 4-9-7 80 ........(p) DavidAllan 6 81
(Chris Dwyer) *w ldr: rdn to ld narrowly wl over 1f out: hdd jst ins fnl f: one pce* **8/1**[3]

232- **5** *1 ¾* **My Dad Syd (USA)**[142] [8389] 5-9-1 74 ........ GeorgeDowning 2 71
(Ian Williams) *hld up: rdn and sme hdwy appr fnl f: no ex fnl 110yds and eased* **11/1**

04-6 **6** *1 ½* **Wilde Extravagance (IRE)**[14] [1972] 4-8-9 68 ........ JoeDoyle 7 59
(Julie Camacho) *trckd ldrs: racd keenly: rdn over 1f out: wknd ins fnl f* **12/1**

3-04 **7** *3 ¾* **Bogart**[17] [1876] 8-9-4 82 ........(p) LewisEdmunds[(5)] 8 61
(Kevin Ryan) *led narrowly: pushed along whn hdd wl over 1f out: sn rdn: wknd fnl f* **5/2**[2]

6-32 **8** *16* **Geoff Potts (IRE)**[77] 808 4-8-9 **73**............................(h) DavidParkes(5) 9 1
(Jeremy Gask) *dwlt: sn trckd ldrs: drvn over 1f out: wknd* **14/1**
1m 12.53s (-0.17) **Going Correction** +0.125s/f (Good) **8** Ran SP% **112.1**
Speed ratings (Par 105): **106,104,103,103,101 99,94,72**
CSF £28.06 CT £300.45 TOTE £9.10: £2.80, £1.10, £4.20; EX 30.90 Trifecta £602.10.
**Owner** Pee Dee Tee Syndicate & T W Midgley **Bred** Lynch Bages Ltd & Camas Park Stud **Trained** Westow, N Yorks

**FOCUS**
A fair sprint handicap. They went a decent gallop and a horse in good form when last seen on the AW in March came through to prevail in taking fashion on the heavily watered surface. The winner has been rated to last year's form.

## 2405 TOTESCOOP6 RACING'S MILLIONAIRE MAKER MAIDEN STKS 5f
**3:05** (3:08) (Class 4) 3-Y-O+ **£5,175** (£1,540; £769; £384) **Stalls** High

Form RPR
030- **1** **Savannah's Dream**[232] 6538 3-9-0 **83**............................ DanielTudhope 1 73
(David O'Meara) *pressed ldr: pushed along 2f out: led 1f out: rdn and kpt on* **10/11**[1]
25-2 **2** *½* **Liquid (IRE)**[7] 2139 3-9-5 **75**.............................. PhillipMakin 4 75
(David Barron) *led narrowly: pushed along 2f out: drvn appr fnl f: sn hdd: one pce fnl 110yds* **Evs**[2]
**3** *8* **Yorkshire Rover** 3-8-12 **0**.............................. KevinLundie(7) 2 46
(David Brown) *hld up: pushed along 1/2-way: wknd over 1f out* **16/1**[3]
0- **4** *8* **Sniper Viper**[209] 7184 3-9-0 **0**.............................(b) TonyHamilton 3 12
(Daniel Kubler) *dwlt: hld up: outpcd 1/2-way: sn bhd* **40/1**
1m 0.43s (0.83) **Going Correction** +0.125s/f (Good) **4** Ran SP% **110.7**
Speed ratings (Par 105): **98,97,84,71**
CSF £2.18 TOTE £1.70; EX 2.40 Trifecta £3.30.
**Owner** Roger Peel **Bred** Mrs Mary Taylor **Trained** Upper Helmsley, N Yorks

**FOCUS**
A fairly decent little maiden sprint. The right two horses came clear of the third off a respectable gallop. The runner-up has been rated to form for now.

## 2406 TOTEPOOL THIRSK HUNT CUP H'CAP 7f 218y
**3:40** (3:43) (Class 2) (0-100,99) 4-Y-O+ **£16,172** (£4,812; £1,803; £1,803) **Stalls** Low

Form RPR
4-05 **1** **Cote D'Azur**[25] 1704 4-9-1 **93**.............................. PJMcDonald 17 101
(Les Eyre) *out sharply fr wd stall and mde most: pushed along over 2f out: rdn over 1f out: kpt on* **8/1**
0-62 **2** *½* **Two For Two (IRE)**[7] 2155 9-8-9 **87**............................(p) TonyHamilton 15 94
(Roger Fell) *hld up in midfield on outer: rdn over 2f out: hdwy over 1f out: wnt 2nd ins fnl f: kpt on wl* **12/1**
60-0 **3** *2* **Stipulate**[21] 1802 8-8-10 **93**.............................. MeganNicholls(5) 12 95
(Brian Ellison) *dwlt: hld up: pushed along and hdwy 2f out: kpt on wl fnl f* **33/1**
23-5 **3** *dht* **Spring Offensive (IRE)**[41] 1388 5-8-8 **93**............... ConnorMurtagh(7) 9 95
(Richard Fahey) *midfield towards outer: rdn and hdwy over 2f out: chsd ldr over 1f out: one pce fnl f* **13/2**[1]
00-4 **5** *nk* **Rousayan (IRE)**[7] 2155 6-8-6 **87**.............................. ShelleyBirkett(3) 8 89
(David O'Meara) *trckd ldrs: pushed along 2f out: rdn appr fnl f: one pce* **15/2**[3]
-505 **6** *2* **God Willing**[21] 1799 6-8-12 **90**..............................(b[1]) NeilFarley 2 87
(Declan Carroll) *prom: rdn over 2f out: wknd ins fnl f* **20/1**
000- **7** *nk* **Sound Advice**[211] 7121 8-9-1 **98**.............................. RowanScott(5) 5 94
(Keith Dalgleish) *in tch: rdn over 2f out: one pce* **33/1**
-500 **8** *nk* **Mutarakez (IRE)**[18] 1860 5-8-11 **89**.............................. PaulMulrennan 18 89+
(Brian Meehan) *hld up: pushed along 2f out: bit short of room ent fnl f: kpt on* **15/2**[3]
610- **9** *½* **Moonlightnavigator (USA)**[182] 7825 5-8-10 **88**............ JackGarritty 14 83
(John Quinn) *trckd ldrs on outer: rdn over 2f out: wknd ins fnl f* **20/1**
22-0 **10** *1 ½* **Briyouni (FR)**[18] 1860 4-8-9 **87**.............................. KevinStott 7 78
(Kevin Ryan) *hld up in midfield: rdn over 2f out: nvr threatened* **16/1**
4-50 **11** *nse* **Silvery Moon (IRE)**[7] 2155 10-8-6 **87**.................. RachelRichardson(3) 6 78
(Tim Easterby) *hld up: nvr threatened* **33/1**
01-2 **12** *½* **Heir To A Throne (FR)**[26] 1677 4-8-9 **87**.......................... ShaneGray 10 77
(Kevin Ryan) *trckd ldrs: rdn over 2f out: wknd fnl f* **10/1**
0-43 **13** *shd* **Hidden Rebel**[19] 1832 5-8-8 **86**..............................(h) JoeDoyle 3 76
(Alistair Whillans) *midfield: rdn over 2f out: wknd fnl f* **25/1**
1650 **14** *shd* **Worlds His Oyster**[7] 2155 4-8-7 **85**..............................(p) JasonHart 13 74
(John Quinn) *hld up in midfield: rdn over 2f out: nvr threatened* **12/1**
0-00 **15** *2 ¼* **Dream Walker (FR)**[35] 1494 8-9-0 **99**........................ BenRobinson(7) 11 83
(Brian Ellison) *a towards rr* **50/1**
0-02 **16** *1 ¼* **Lat Hawill (IRE)**[21] 1799 6-9-1 **93**..............................(v) PhillipMakin 1 74
(Keith Dalgleish) *dwlt: sn in tch on inner: rdn over 2f out: wknd fnl f* **7/1**[2]
50-1 **17** *3 ¾* **Reaver (IRE)**[14] 1969 4-8-7 **85** oh1.............................. BenCurtis 4 58
(Eve Johnson Houghton) *midfield on inner: rdn over 2f out: sn wknd* **7/1**[2]
1m 38.87s (-1.23) **Going Correction** +0.15s/f (Good) **17** Ran SP% **127.5**
Speed ratings (Par 109): **112,111,109,109,109 107,106,106,106,104 104,104,103,103,101 100,96**
WIN: 11.40 Cote d'Azur; PL: 9.20 Stipulate, 2.40 Spring Offensive, 2.90 Cote d'Azur, 2.20 Two For Two; EX: 54.30; CSF: 96.26; TC: 917.02, 351.38; TF: 957.70, 725.50;.
**Owner** Billy Parker & Steven Parker **Bred** W N Greig **Trained** Catwick, N Yorks
■ Stewards' Enquiry : Ben Curtis £290 fine: in breach of Rule (D)47.5

**FOCUS**
Race distance increased 20yds. The feature contest was a good quality 1m handicap won by the high-class Farhh on his seasonal reappearance as a 4yo in 2012. Today's 4yo winner stays further and made this a proper test from the front. It's been rated around the winner to his Silver Cambridgeshire run, with the runner-up close to last year's best.

## 2407 TOTEPOOL RACECOURSE DEBIT CARD BETTING AVAILABLE FILLIES' H'CAP 5f
**4:15** (4:17) (Class 4) (0-85,88) 3-Y-O+ **£6,469** (£1,925; £962; £481) **Stalls** High

Form RPR
10-6 **1** **Rose Berry**[19] 1838 3-8-10 **76**..............................(h) DavidAllan 1 83
(Chris Dwyer) *in tch outer: rdn to chse ldr over 1f out: led 110yds out: kpt on* **13/2**
650- **2** *1* **Midnight Malibu (IRE)**[211] 7124 4-9-8 **82**........... RachelRichardson(3) 5 89
(Tim Easterby) *led: rdn over 1f out: edgd lft ins f: hdd 110yds out: one pce* **11/2**[3]
16-0 **3** *1* **Miningold**[19] 1828 4-8-7 **69**.............................. CallumRodriguez(5) 3 72
(Michael Dods) *hld up in tch: rdn to chse ldr over 1f out: one pce* **12/1**
40-4 **4** *¾* **Southern Belle (IRE)**[21] 1793 4-9-9 **87**...................... BenRobinson(7) 7 88
(Robert Cowell) *chsd ldr: rdn 2f out: no ex fnl f* **11/4**[2]
22-0 **5** *1 ¾* **Jumping Around (IRE)**[19] 1838 3-8-13 **79**........................ ShaneGray 2 69
(Ian Williams) *dwlt: hld up: pushed along over 1f out: minor late hdwy: nvr threatened* **14/1**
016- **6** *1 ¼* **Compton Poppy**[233] 6507 3-8-11 **77**.............................. GeorgeDowning 8 63
(Tony Carroll) *hld up in tch: rdn 2f out: wknd ins fnl f* **14/1**
60-4 **7** *2 ¼* **Olivia Fallow (IRE)**[18] 1863 5-10-0 **85**.............................. PaulMulrennan 4 67
(Paul Midgley) *chsd ldr: pushed along 2f out: wknd fnl f* **2/1**[1]
59.55s (-0.05) **Going Correction** +0.125s/f (Good)
**WFA** 3 from 4yo+ 9lb **7** Ran SP% **109.7**
Speed ratings (Par 102): **105,103,101,100,97 95,92**
CSF £38.05 CT £386.15 TOTE £8.90: £3.10, £2.50; EX 45.80 Trifecta £323.40.
**Owner** Strawberry Fields Stud **Bred** Aljw Bloodstock **Trained** Newmarket, Suffolk

**FOCUS**
A decent fillies' sprint handicap. They went a proper gallop and the heavily watered ground has negated any stands' side draw bias in the shorter races on this card. The runner-up has been rated to form.

## 2408 @TOTEPOOLRACING WIN RACING TICKETS ON TWITTER MAIDEN STKS 1m 4f 8y
**4:50** (4:50) (Class 5) 3-4-Y-O **£3,234** (£962; £481; £240) **Stalls** High

Form RPR
20 **1** **Globetrotter (IRE)**[16] 1906 3-8-9 **0**.............................. DavidAllan 9 82+
(James Tate) *sn prom: led over 3f out: sn pushed along: rdn and jnd over 1f out: hdd ins fnl f: rallied to ld again towards fin* **15/8**[1]
0 **2** *hd* **Key Bid**[26] 1682 3-8-9 **0**.............................. MartinLane 5 81+
(Charlie Appleby) *trckd ldrs: pushed along over 4f out: rdn and hdwy to join ldr over 1f out: led narrowly ins fnl f: one pce and hdd towards fin* **11/4**[3]
5 **3** *11* **Sunrize (IRE)**[17] 1874 3-8-6 **0**.............................. ShelleyBirkett(3) 6 63
(David O'Meara) *trckd ldrs: rdn over 3f out: grad wknd* **16/1**
4-33 **4** *nk* **The Grey Warrior (IRE)**[26] 1676 3-8-9 **74**.......................... KevinStott 4 63
(Kevin Ryan) *midfield: rdn and rn wd on bnd 4f out: drvn over 2f out: no imp* **5/2**[2]
**5** *¾* **Montanna** 3-8-10 **0** ow1.............................. JackGarritty 1 62
(Jedd O'Keeffe) *midfield: rdn over 3f out: plugged on* **14/1**
00- **6** *2 ½* **New Society (IRE)**[218] 6924 3-8-10 **0** ow1........................ PaulMulrennan 8 58
(James Bethell) *sn led: rdn whn hdd over 3f out: wknd fnl 2f* **50/1**
**7** *10* **Donnachies Girl (IRE)**[30] 4-9-9 **0**.............................. JoeDoyle 2 38
(Alistair Whillans) *a rr* **20/1**
**8** *33* **Red Ochre**[46] 4-10-0 **0**.............................. JasonHart 3
(John Quinn) *hld up: rdn over 3f out: sn wknd* **22/1**
00 **9** *33* **Jump Around**[7] 2159 3-8-4 **0**.............................. JoeyHaynes 7
(K R Burke) *hld up: rdn over 3f out: sn wknd and bhd* **33/1**
2m 39.15s (2.95) **Going Correction** +0.15s/f (Good)
**WFA** 3 from 4yo 19lb **9** Ran SP% **115.8**
Speed ratings (Par 103): **96,95,88,88,87 86,79,57,35**
CSF £6.90 TOTE £2.30: £1.10, £1.60, £4.20; EX 8.80 Trifecta £57.70.
**Owner** Saeed Manana **Bred** Rabbah Bloodstock Limited **Trained** Newmarket, Suffolk
■ Stewards' Enquiry : Martin Lane two-day ban: used whip above permitted level (May 21-22)

**FOCUS**
Race distance increased 20yds. An ordinary middle-distance maiden. The winning time was modest on the heavily watered ground. The level is fluid.

## 2409 COLLECT TOTEPOOL WINNINGS AT BETFRED SHOPS H'CAP 5f
**5:25** (5:25) (Class 4) (0-85,86) 4-Y-O+ **£6,469** (£1,925; £962; £481) **Stalls** High

Form RPR
00-3 **1** **Excessable**[22] 1777 4-9-0 **78**..............................(t) DavidAllan 7 87
(Tim Easterby) *dwlt: sn in tch: pushed along and qcknd to ld appr fnl f: kpt on: shade cosily* **7/2**[1]
0026 **2** *1* **Orient Class**[22] 1777 6-8-13 **84**.............................. ConnorMurtagh(7) 3 89
(Paul Midgley) *hld up in tch: smooth hdwy 2f out: pushed along to chal appr fnl f: rdn and kpt on* **10/1**
214- **3** *1 ½* **Fruit Salad**[206] 7288 4-8-7 **74**.............................. NathanEvans(3) 5 74
(James Bethell) *in tch: rdn 2f out: briefly bit short of room over 1f out: kpt on fnl f* **7/2**[1]
3420 **4** *1* **Seamster**[8] 2123 10-8-11 **82**..............................(t) CameronNoble(7) 1 78
(David Loughnane) *chsd ldrs on outer: rdn 2f out: no ex ins fnl f* **8/1**
16-0 **5** *3 ¼* **Singeur (IRE)**[17] 1876 10-9-3 **86**.............................. RowanScott(5) 2 70
(Rebecca Bastiman) *dwlt: sn pushed along towards rr: minor late hdwy: nvr threatened* **14/1**
0-50 **6** *1* **First Bombardment**[8] 2123 4-8-13 **82**.............................. JoshDoyle(5) 6 63
(David O'Meara) *prom: rdn 2f out: wknd fnl f* **13/2**[2]
0-00 **7** *hd* **Pea Shooter**[8] 2123 8-8-8 **79**.............................. BenRobinson(7) 9 59
(Brian Ellison) *hld up: rdn 1/2-way: edgd lft to outside over 1f out: nvr threatened* **11/1**
20-0 **8** *shd* **Kibaar**[17] 1876 5-9-7 **85**.............................. JoeDoyle 4 65
(Kevin Ryan) *pressed ldr: led 1/2-way: sn rdn: hdd appr fnl f: wknd* **8/1**
6-00 **9** *7* **Musharrif**[8] 2123 5-9-1 **79**.............................. NeilFarley 8 33
(Declan Carroll) *led narrowly: rdn whn hdd 1/2-way: wknd over 1f out* **7/1**[3]
58.57s (-1.03) **Going Correction** +0.125s/f (Good) **9** Ran SP% **116.6**
Speed ratings (Par 105): **113,111,109,107,102 100,100,100,88**
CSF £40.55 CT £132.71 TOTE £5.80: £1.70, £3.40, £1.80; EX 42.70 Trifecta £367.30.
**Owner** B Guerin & Habton Farms **Bred** Whitsbury Manor Stud **Trained** Great Habton, N Yorks
■ Stewards' Enquiry : Ben Robinson two-day ban (21-22 May): used whip without giving his mount time to respond

**FOCUS**
A decent sprint handicap. The winner recorded comparatively the best winning time on the card by a clear margin. The runner-up has been rated to form.
T/Plt: £197.70 to a £1 stake. Pool: £56,719.39 - 209.34 winning units. T/Qpdt: £53.90 to a £1 stake. Pool: £2,904.80 - 39.85 winning units. **Andrew Sheret**

2410 - 2419a (Foreign Racing) - See Raceform Interactive

# 2379 CHURCHILL DOWNS (L-H)
Saturday, May 6

**OFFICIAL GOING: Dirt: sloppy changing to wet fast after 6.55pm; turf: good**

## 2420a KENTUCKY DERBY PRESENTED BY YUM! BRANDS (GRADE 1) (3YO) (DIRT) 1m 2f (D)
**11:46** 3-Y-O **£1,329,918** (£325,203; £162,601; £81,300; £48,780)

RPR
**1** **Always Dreaming (USA)**[35] 1507 3-9-0 **0**................ JohnRVelazquez 5 124+
(Todd Pletcher, U.S.A) *trckd ldr: led 1/2-way: rdn and styd on strly to draw clr fnl f: readily* **47/10**[1]
**2** *2 ¾* **Lookin At Lee (USA)**[20] 1827 3-9-0 **0**........................(b) CoreyJLanerie 1 119
(Steven Asmussen, U.S.A) *hld up: gd hdwy on ins over 2f out: rdn and chsd (clr) wnr ins fnl f: kpt on: nt pce to chal* **33/1**

3 5 **Battle Of Midway (USA)**[28] 1649 3-9-0 0 FlavienPrat 11 109
(Jerry Hollendorfer, U.S.A) *trckd ldrs: effrt and wnt cl 2nd 2f out to ins fnl f: sn outpcd* **40/1**

4 1 **Classic Empire (USA)**[20] 1827 3-9-0 0 (b) JulienRLeparoux 14 107
(Mark Casse, Canada) *hld up: pushed along and gd hdwy on outside over 2f out: rdn and kpt on fr over 1f out: no imp* **68/10**[3]

5 3/4 **Practical Joke (USA)**[28] 1643 3-9-0 0 JoelRosario 19 105
(Chad C Brown, U.S.A) *t.k.h early: hld up in tch: rdn over 2f out: effrt and angled rt over 1f out: sn no imp: btn ins fnl f* **28/1**

6 3/4 **Tapwrit (USA)**[28] 1643 3-9-0 0 (b) JoseLOrtiz 16 104
(Todd Pletcher, U.S.A) *t.k.h early: hld up: rdn 3f out: hdwy over 1f out: no imp fnl f* **27/1**

7 3 **Gunnevera (USA)**[35] 1507 3-9-0 0 (b) JavierCastellano 10 98
(Antonio Sano, U.S.A) *hld up on outside: rdn and effrt bnd over 2f out: no imp wl over 1f out: btn fnl f* **10/1**

8 hd **McCraken (USA)**[28] 1643 3-9-0 0 BrianJosephHernandezJr 15 97
(Ian Wilkes, U.S.A) *t.k.h early: hld up midfield: rdn and hdwy over 2f out: outpcd whn checked over 1f out: sn btn* **69/10**

9 1 **Gormley (USA)**[28] 1649 3-9-0 0 VictorEspinoza 18 95
(John Shirreffs, U.S.A) *in tch on outside: hdwy over 2f out: rdn and hung lft over 1f out: sn wknd* **223/10**

10 2 1/4 **Irish War Cry (USA)**[28] 1640 3-9-0 0 RajivMaragh 17 91
(H Graham Motion, U.S.A) *cl up: wnt 2nd over 4f out to 2f out: rdn and wknd over 1f out* **48/10**[2]

11 2 **Hence (USA)**[40] 3-9-0 0 FlorentGeroux 8 87
(Steven Asmussen, U.S.A) *midfield on outside: drvn along over 4f out: wknd over 2f out* **15/1**

12 3/4 **Untrapped (USA)**[20] 1827 3-9-0 0 RicardoSantanaJr 4 85
(Steven Asmussen, U.S.A) *midfield on ins: struggling over 3f out: btn fnl 2f* **58/1**

13 hd **Girvin (USA)**[35] 1506 3-9-0 0 MikeESmith 7 85
(Joe Sharp, U.S.A) *hld up on ins: pushed along fr 1/2-way: struggling 3f out: sn btn* **221/10**

14 1 1/2 **Patch (USA)**[35] 1506 3-9-0 0 TylerGaffalione 20 82
(Todd Pletcher, U.S.A) *hld up midfield on outside: struggling over 3f out: sn wknd* **141/10**

15 2 **J Boys Echo (USA)**[28] 1643 3-9-0 0 LuisSaez 13 78
(Dale Romans, U.S.A) *hld up: rdn along 4f out: sn n.d: btn over 2f out* **47/1**

16 3 1/4 **Sonneteer (USA)**[20] 1827 3-9-0 0 KentJDesormeaux 12 71
(J Keith Desormeaux, U.S.A) *bhd and sn pushed along: drvn and no imp fr over 4f out: nvr on terms* **40/1**

17 2 1/2 **Fast And Accurate (USA)**[42] 3-9-0 0 (b) ChanningHill 3 66
(Michael J Maker, U.S.A) *prom: rdn and lost pl over 3f out: struggling whn hmpd over 2f out* **42/1**

18 12 **Irap (USA)**[28] 1643 3-9-0 0 MarioGutierrez 9 42
(Doug O'Neill, U.S.A) *hld up bhd ldng gp: drvn along over 3f out: wknd over 2f out* **41/1**

19 5 **State Of Honor (CAN)**[35] 1507 3-9-0 0 JoseLezcano 6 32
(Mark Casse, Canada) *led to 1/2-way: cl up tl rdn and wknd qckly over 2f out* **54/1**

P **Thunder Snow (IRE)**[42] 1375 3-9-0 0 ChristopheSoumillon 2
(Saeed bin Suroor) *s.i.s: bucking and kicking and immediately unrideable: p.u after 1f* **164/10**

2m 3.59s (2.40) **20** Ran SP% **121.7**
PARI-MUTUEL (all including 2 usd stake): WIN 11.40; PLACE (1-2) 7.20, 26.60; SHOW (1-2-3) 5.80, 15.20, 20.80; SF 336.20.
**Owner** MeB Racing, Brooklyn Boyz Et Al **Bred** Santa Rosa Partners **Trained** USA

**FOCUS**
The track had dried out to an official description of wet-fast (sealed). There were two notable absentees, the now retired Not This Time, who was made a 14-1 shot straight after his close second in last year's Breeders' Cup Juvenile, and Mastery, who had earned a 105 Beyer speed figure when winning the Grade 2 San Felipe at Santa Anita in March but who finished that race with an injury. None of this lot had fully convinced through the trials and at this stage they don't look a particularly good bunch. The pace was strong on a tiring track and they finished slowly: 22.70 (2f), 23.83 (4f), 24.59 (6f), 26.15 (8f), 26.32 (line), with the winner earning a provisional Beyer speed figure of 102. It should again be noted the race was won by the favourite - that's five straight now since the qualifying criteria changed (from Graded-stakes earnings to points picked up in prep races) ahead of the 2013 edition.

2421 - 2423a (Foreign Racing) - See Raceform Interactive

# HAMILTON (R-H)
Sunday, May 7

**OFFICIAL GOING: Good to firm (8.3)**
Wind: Breezy, half against Weather: Cloudy, bright

## 2424 TOTEPLACEPOT SIX PLACES IN SIX RACES H'CAP 5f 7y
**1:35** (1:35) (Class 5) (0-70,72) 4-Y-0+ **£4,528** (£1,347; £673; £336) **Stalls** Centre

Form RPR

2612 1 **Spirit Of Wedza (IRE)**[62] 1062 5-9-7 **67** JoeDoyle 6 73
(Julie Camacho) *mde all: rdn over 1f out: kpt on wl fnl f* **2/1**[1]

1150 2 1 1/4 **Top Of The Bank**[15] 1972 4-9-12 **72** (p) TonyHamilton 5 73
(Kristin Stubbs) *pressed wnr: rdn along over 1f out: kpt on ins fnl f* **10/1**

5-55 3 shd **Flicka's Boy**[13] 2034 5-9-3 **63** (v) BarryMcHugh 3 64
(Tony Coyle) *trckd ldrs: rdn and edgd rt over 1f out: kpt on ins fnl f* **4/1**[2]

630- 4 nk **Insurplus (IRE)**[243] 6215 4-9-2 **62** (v) SamJames 7 62
(Jim Goldie) *in tch: rdn and outpcd 2f out: kpt on ins fnl f: nt pce to chal* **6/1**

4450 5 2 1/4 **Ambitious Icarus**[15] 1965 8-9-4 **64** (e) ConnorBeasley 4 55
(Richard Guest) *taken early to post: hld up in tch: rdn over 2f out: edgd rt and no imp over 1f out* **11/2**

0620 6 1 **Salvatore Fury (IRE)**[17] 1910 7-9-11 **71** (v) GrahamLee 1 59
(Keith Dalgleish) *hld up: pushed along over 2f out: sn outpcd: n.d after* **9/2**[3]

59.17s (-0.83) **Going Correction** -0.275s/f (Firm) **6** Ran SP% **110.3**
Speed ratings (Par 103): **95,93,92,92,88 87**
CSF £21.56 TOTE £3.20: £1.70, £4.60; EX 19.50 Trifecta £52.90.
**Owner** Owners Group 005 **Bred** N Hartery **Trained** Norton, N Yorks

**FOCUS**
An ordinary sprint handicap in which they went a good pace but the positions hardly changed throughout.

## 2425 TOTEPOOL TANGERINE TREES CONDITIONS STKS (PLUS 10 RACE) 5f 7y
**2:05** (2:05) (Class 2) 3-Y-0 **£18,675** (£5,592; £2,796; £1,398; £699) **Stalls** Centre

Form RPR

36-4 1 **Equimou**[23] 1765 3-9-1 100 PhillipMakin 4 100
(Robert Eddery) *in tch: smooth hdwy over 2f out: shkn up to ld over 1f out: pushed out fnl f* **9/2**[3]

P22- 2 3/4 **Dream Of Dreams (IRE)**[211] 7155 3-9-2 105 KevinStott 6 98+
(Kevin Ryan) *slowly away: nt handle trck and bdly outpcd: rdn and hdwy whn rdr dropped whip over 1f out: edgd rt: chsd wnr wl ins fnl f: kpt on: nt pce to chal* **1/1**[1]

2125 3 3/4 **Sutter County**[23] 1774 3-9-6 103 JoeFanning 2 100
(Mark Johnston) *chsd clr ldng pair: clsd 1/2-way: effrt and ev ch briefly over 1f out: one pce and lost 2nd wl ins fnl f* **5/2**[2]

3-30 4 4 **Plata O Plomo**[15] 1975 3-9-2 85 BarryMcHugh 5 81
(Tony Coyle) *led: hung rt thrght: rdn and hdd over 1f out: sn wknd* **22/1**

-324 5 1 1/4 **Merry Banter**[25] 1732 3-9-4 84 PaulMulrennan 1 79
(Paul Midgley) *pressed ldr: swtchd lft 1/2-way: rdn and wknd over 1f out* **20/1**

58.37s (-1.63) **Going Correction** -0.275s/f (Firm) **5** Ran SP% **105.9**
Speed ratings (Par 105): **102,100,99,93,91**
CSF £8.79 TOTE £4.10: £2.20, £1.10; EX 9.80 Trifecta £16.90.
**Owner** Edwin S Phillips **Bred** Stratford Place Stud & Minster Stud **Trained** Newmarket, Suffolk

**FOCUS**
The feature contest and a decent conditions event for 3yos. The time was 0.8 secs faster than the opening handicap.

## 2426 TOTEPOOL BUTTONHOOK H'CAP 1m 5f 16y
**2:35** (2:35) (Class 3) (0-95,93) 4-Y-0+
**£12,450** (£3,728; £1,864; £932; £466; £234) **Stalls** High

Form RPR

00-1 1 **Corton Lad**[2] 2375 7-8-10 **87** 6ex (tp) RowanScott(5) 6 95
(Keith Dalgleish) *mde all: 4 l clr to 1/2-way: rdn 2f out: hld on wl cl home* **8/1**[3]

3-1 2 hd **Kensington Star**[27] 1676 4-8-6 **78** (p) JasonHart 5 86
(Keith Dalgleish) *dwlt: hld up: pushed along and rn green 3f out: hdwy to chse wnr 2f out: sn rdn and edgd rt: kpt on wl towards fin: jst hld* **9/2**[2]

5-11 3 2 3/4 **Monjeni**[40] 1412 4-8-2 **74** oh1 (p) JamesSullivan 4 78
(Ian Williams) *t.k.h early: prom: effrt and rdn 2f out: kpt on same pce fnl f* **8/1**[3]

-223 4 3/4 **Busy Street**[25] 1719 5-8-7 **79** PJMcDonald 1 81
(Alan Swinbank) *hld up in last pl: effrt whn nt clr run and swtchd lft 2f out: rdn and no imp appr fnl f* **6/4**[1]

0-01 5 2 1/4 **Renfrew Street**[12] 2061 4-8-8 **80** JoeFanning 3 79
(Mark Johnston) *trckd ldrs: effrt and rdn over 2f out: wknd over 1f out* **9/2**[2]

5530 6 nk **Sennockian Star**[36] 1502 7-9-7 **93** AndrewMullen 2 92
(Mark Johnston) *chsd (clr) wnr tl clsd 1/2-way: rdn over 2f out: wknd over 1f out* **8/1**[3]

2m 46.24s (-7.66) **Going Correction** -0.275s/f (Firm) **6** Ran SP% **109.7**
Speed ratings (Par 107): **112,111,110,109,108 108**
CSF £40.76 TOTE £10.40: £3.90, £2.70; EX 53.40 Trifecta £482.50.
**Owner** J Hutton **Bred** Frank Brady And Brian Scanlon **Trained** Carluke, S Lanarks

**FOCUS**
This decent middle-distance handicap was run at what looked a stop-start pace, but the time was under standard.

## 2427 TOTEEXACTA PICK THE 1ST & 2ND H'CAP 1m 3f 15y
**3:10** (3:10) (Class 5) (0-70,69) 4-Y-0+ **£4,528** (£1,347; £673; £336) **Stalls** High

Form RPR

-13P 1 **Genres**[82] 727 5-9-6 **68** JoeFanning 5 73
(Alan Swinbank) *trckd ldrs: smooth hdwy to ld over 2f out: hrd pressed and rdn over 1f out: hld on wl fnl f* **5/1**[3]

0-14 2 1 **Life Knowledge (IRE)**[7] 2183 5-8-2 **57** PaulaMuir(7) 2 60
(Patrick Holmes) *missed break: hld up: hdwy over 2f out: rdn and ev ch over 1f out to ins fnl f: kpt on same pce nr fin* **4/1**[2]

0020 3 1 1/4 **Restive (IRE)**[66] 992 4-9-7 **69** (h) TomEaves 1 70
(Iain Jardine) *prom: effrt and rdn over 2f out: kpt on same pce ins fnl f* **11/2**

4 4 1 1/2 **Star Glitter (FR)**[11] 2079 4-8-13 **68** PatrickVaughan(7) 7 67
(David O'Meara) *prom: stdy hdwy and cl up over 2f out: rdn and edgd rt over 1f out: outpcd fnl f* **5/1**[3]

566- 5 9 **Celtic Power**[230] 6619 5-8-2 **57** (v[1]) SeanMooney(7) 4 40
(Jim Goldie) *w ldr led over 3f out: hdd over 2f out: rdn and wknd over 1f out* **14/1**

252- 6 4 1/2 **Nanny Makfi**[229] 6654 4-8-6 **54** (p[1]) JasonHart 3 30
(Keith Dalgleish) *t.k.h: led to over 3f out: rallied: rdn and wknd wl over 1f out* **15/8**[1]

056- 7 41 **Recognition (IRE)**[65] 3728 4-8-11 **66** (p) ConnorMurtagh(7) 6
(Barry Murtagh) *hld up: pushed along 1/2-way: struggling wl over 2f out: sn btn: t.o* **66/1**

2m 21.24s (-4.36) **Going Correction** -0.275s/f (Firm) **7** Ran SP% **111.7**
Speed ratings (Par 103): **104,103,102,101,94 91,61**
CSF £23.93 TOTE £5.30: £2.40, £2.30; EX 24.10 Trifecta £119.10.
**Owner** Brian Valentine **Bred** Millsec Limited **Trained** Melsonby, N Yorks

**FOCUS**
A modest but fairly competitive handicap, the early pace was modest and the time was the slowest of the day comparatively, but the principals came from off the gallop.

## 2428 TOTETRIFECTA PICK THE 1, 2, 3 H'CAP 6f 6y
**3:45** (3:46) (Class 4) (0-80,80) 4-Y-0+ **£6,469** (£1,925; £962; £481) **Stalls** Centre

Form RPR

1312 1 **Zylan (IRE)**[15] 1971 5-9-4 **77** TonyHamilton 5 89+
(Roger Fell) *hld up: smooth hdwy over 2f out: shkn up to ld over 1f out: pushed out fnl f: comf* **15/8**[1]

50-0 2 1 1/4 **Portland Street (IRE)**[20] 1833 4-8-7 **66** (b[1]) ConnorBeasley 7 71
(Bryan Smart) *trckd ldrs: rdn and led briefly over 1f out: kpt on same pce ins fnl f* **7/2**[2]

5656 3 2 3/4 **Buccaneers Vault (IRE)**[20] 1833 5-9-2 **75** (p) PaulMulrennan 3 71
(Paul Midgley) *hld up in tch: rdn over 2f out: effrt over 1f out: edgd rt: kpt on ins fnl f: nt rch wnr* **6/1**[3]


The Form Book Flat, Raceform Ltd, Newbury, RG14 5SJ

00-5 **4** *2 ¼* **Maureb (IRE)**[9] 2119 5-8-10 **69**....................(p) BarryMcHugh 2 58
(Tony Coyle) *hld up in tch: rdn over 2f out: no imp fr over 1f out* **9/1**

215- **5** *3 ¼* **Picks Pinta**[223] 6836 6-8-0 **66**....................ConnorMurtagh(7) 1 45
(John David Riches) *sn chsng ldr: rdn over 2f out: wknd over 1f out* **25/1**

-000 **6** *1 ¾* **Foresight (FR)**[15] 1972 4-8-11 **70**....................(p[1]) TomEaves 4 43
(Kevin Ryan) *led tl rdn and hdd over 1f out: sn wknd* **16/1**

00-0 **7** *1 ¼* **Khelman (IRE)**[35] 1512 7-9-4 **80**....................AdamMcNamara(3) 6 49
(Richard Fahey) *dwlt: bhd and nvr gng wl: nvr on terms* **7/2**[2]

1m 10.07s (-2.13) **Going Correction** -0.275s/f (Firm) 7 Ran SP% **113.2**
Speed ratings (Par 105): **103,101,97,94,90 88,86**
CSF £8.42 CT £31.16 TOTE £2.20: £1.90, £1.70; EX 7.90 Trifecta £32.70.
**Owner** R G Fell **Bred** Philip And Mrs Jane Myerscough **Trained** Nawton, N Yorks

**FOCUS**
A number with questions to answer in this fair sprint handicap, but the well backed favourite scored like an improving type.

## 2429 TOTEPOOL SUPPORTING #MHAW17 8TH-14TH MAY 2017 MAIDEN STKS 1m 68y
**4:20** (4:20) (Class 5) 3-5-Y-O **£4,528** (£1,347; £673; £336) **Stalls** Low

Form RPR

**1** **What Wonders Weave (IRE)**[16] 1953 3-8-10 0....................PhillipMakin 9 71
(John Patrick Shanahan, Ire) *cl up: rdn to ld over 1f out: kpt on wl fnl f* **10/3**[2]

6 **2** *1 ¼* **Hamster Jam (IRE)**[11] 2078 3-8-10 0....................JoeFanning 4 68
(Mark Johnston) *led: rdn and hdd over 1f out: rallied: kpt on same pce last 100yds* **16/1**

32-0 **3** *¾* **Somnambulist**[22] 1801 3-9-1 74....................(h) JasonHart 1 71
(Keith Dalgleish) *trckd ldrs: effrt and rdn 2f out: kpt on ins fnl f* **7/2**[3]

4 **4** *4 ½* **El Nino Sea (IRE)**[17] 1914 3-9-1 0....................TonyHamilton 6 61
(Richard Fahey) *hld up midfield: effrt and rdn over 2f out: no imp over 1f out* **12/1**

4 **5** *½* **Last Chance Paddy (USA)**[59] 1111 3-9-1 0....................NeilFarley 5 60
(Alan Swinbank) *prom: drvn along over 2f out: outpcd over 1f out* **33/1**

6 **6** *1 ¼* **Senatus (FR)**[20] 1829 5-10-0 0....................(h) GrahamLee 10 60+
(Karen McLintock) *missed break: hld up: pushed along over 3f out: no imp fr 2f out* **11/1**

3 **7** *nk* **Mellor Brook (IRE)**[20] 1829 3-9-1 0....................ConnorBeasley 2 56
(Bryan Smart) *s.i.s: hld up on outside: stmbld bnd over 5f out: stdy hdwy on outside over 3f out: rdn and wknd 2f out* **6/4**[1]

060- **8** *8* **Diamond Avalanche (IRE)**[181] 7850 4-10-0 50...(h[1]) DougieCostello 11 41
(Patrick Holmes) *s.i.s: hld up : rdn along over 3f out: wknd 2f out* **100/1**

0 **9** *½* **Acid Test**[20] 1829 3-9-1 0....................JackGarritty 8 36
(Jedd O'Keeffe) *stdd bhd ldng gp: rdn over 3f out: wknd 2f out* **66/1**

**10** *8* **Sindarin**[44] 4-10-0 0....................SamJames 7 21
(Jim Goldie) *hld up: rdn along over 3f out: wknd over 2f out* **80/1**

**11** *2 ½* **Bajan Beacon** 4-10-0 0....................TomEaves 3 15
(Iain Jardine) *s.i.s: t.k.h: hld up: rdn and outpcd over 3f out: wknd over 2f out* **33/1**

1m 46.22s (-2.18) **Going Correction** -0.275s/f (Firm)
**WFA** 3 from 4yo+ 13lb 11 Ran SP% **116.8**
Speed ratings (Par 103): **99,97,97,92,92 90,90,82,81,73 71**
CSF £52.12 TOTE £3.80: £1.60, £3.70, £1.40; EX 31.50 Trifecta £95.60.
**Owner** Thistle Bloodstock Limited **Bred** Thistle Bloodstock Limited **Trained** Kells, Co Kilkenny

**FOCUS**
Limited experience generally in this maiden, and those with ratings set just an ordinary standard. The fillies had the finish between them.

## 2430 COLLECT TOTEPOOL WINNINGS AT BETFRED SHOPS H'CAP 1m 68y
**4:55** (4:55) (Class 5) (0-70,72) 4-Y-O+ **£4,528** (£1,347; £673; £336) **Stalls** Low

Form RPR

2- **1** **Try Again (IRE)**[32] 1569 4-9-3 **66**....................BenCurtis 10 74
(Paul W Flynn, Ire) *hld up in tch on outside: rdn and hdwy to ld over 1f out: kpt on wl fnl f* **7/2**[1]

01-0 **2** *¾* **Be Kool (IRE)**[27] 1677 4-9-9 **72**....................(v) CamHardie 11 78
(Brian Ellison) *hld up in midfield: rdn and hung rt over 2f out: hdwy to press wnr ins fnl f: kpt on: hld nr fin* **12/1**

0330 **3** *nk* **So It's War (FR)**[6] 2224 6-8-11 **65**....................(p) RowanScott(5) 6 70
(Keith Dalgleish) *s.i.s: hld up: rdn and hdwy 3f out: kpt on ins fnl f: nrst fin* **4/1**[2]

333- **4** *¾* **Fivehundredmiles (IRE)**[120] 128 4-9-8 **71**....................PhillipMakin 4 75
(John Patrick Shanahan, Ire) *trckd ldrs: effrt and drvn along 2f out: kpt on same pce ins fnl f* **7/2**[1]

16-0 **5** *¾* **Amy Blair**[21] 1823 4-8-7 **56**....................(h) ConnorBeasley 7 58
(Keith Dalgleish) *led: qcknd 1/2-way: rdn over 2f out: hdd over 1f out: no ex ins fnl f* **16/1**

000- **6** *3 ¾* **Indian Giver**[223] 6839 9-8-0 **56** oh1....................ConnorMurtagh(7) 5 49
(John David Riches) *hld up: drvn and outpcd over 2f out: kpt on ins fnl f: nvr able to chal* **40/1**

212- **7** *1 ¼* **Jordan James (IRE)**[205] 7333 4-9-0 **70**....................KieranSchofield(7) 12 60
(Brian Ellison) *s.i.s: hld up on outside: rdn over 2f out: kpt on fnl f: nvr able to chal* **11/1**

000- **8** *1* **Auxiliary**[201] 7435 4-9-5 **68**....................DougieCostello 2 56
(Patrick Holmes) *s.i.s: hld up: drvn and outpcd over 3f out: sme late hdwy: nvr rchd ldrs* **16/1**

10-5 **9** *nse* **Beadlam (IRE)**[18] 1879 4-9-1 **64**....................TonyHamilton 8 52
(Roger Fell) *chsd ldr: drvn over 2f out: wknd over 1f out* **10/1**[3]

20-5 **10** *1* **Al Hawraa**[53] 1201 4-9-0 **63**....................KevinStott 9 49
(Kevin Ryan) *in tch: drvn and outpcd over 2f out: sn wknd* **16/1**

350- **11** *2 ½* **Stardrifter**[198] 7500 5-9-7 **70**....................GrahamLee 1 50
(Linda Perratt) *hld up: pushed along and checked bnd over 5f out: rdn and outpcd over 3f out: sn btn* **18/1**

30/6 **12** *hd* **Cline**[51] 1243 4-8-13 **62**....................ShaneGray 3 41
(Kevin Ryan) *hld up in midfield: drvn and struggling 3f out: btn fnl f* **25/1**

1m 44.2s (-4.20) **Going Correction** -0.275s/f (Firm) 12 Ran SP% **118.8**
Speed ratings (Par 103): **110,109,108,108,107 103,102,101,101,100 97,97**
CSF £46.84 CT £180.11 TOTE £5.10: £1.60, £2.90, £2.20; EX 47.00 Trifecta £306.10.
**Owner** C Munnelly & Partners Partnership **Bred** T A Killoran **Trained** Colehill, Co Longford

**FOCUS**
Quite a few returning from breaks, but this modest handicap was run faster than the preceding maiden, according to hand timing.
T/Plt: £137.40 to a £1 stake. Pool: £56,674.00 - 412.46 winning units T/Qpdt: £37.40 to a £1 stake. Pool: £4,389.00 - 117.30 winning units **Richard Young**

# [2396] NEWMARKET (R-H)
Sunday, May 7

**OFFICIAL GOING: Good to firm (overall 8.8, stands' side 8.9, centre 8.7, far side 8.8)**
Wind: medium, half behind Weather: light cloud, bright spells later

## 2431 QATAR RACING H'CAP 1m 4f
**1:50** (1:54) (Class 2) (0-105,101) 4-Y-O+
**£31,125** (£9,320; £4,660; £2,330; £1,165; £585) **Stalls** Centre

Form RPR

16-4 **1** **Frontiersman**[35] 1516 4-9-10 **101**....................WilliamBuick 1 116+
(Charlie Appleby) *lw: hld up in wl in tch in midfield: clsd to chse ldrs and nt clr run 2f out: swtchd lft and chsd ldr 2f out: rdn to ld over 1f out: hung rt but styd on strly ins fnl f: readily* **5/2**[1]

030- **2** *2 ½* **Top Tug (IRE)**[50] 5655 6-9-7 **98**....................AdamKirby 7 107
(Alan King) *hld up in tch in midfield: rdn 3f out: swtchd lft and hdwy u.p over 1f out: styd on strly ins fnl f to go 2nd fnl 50yds: no threat to wnr* **25/1**

222- **3** *nk* **Mainstream**[233] 6545 4-9-5 **96**....................(h) RyanMoore 8 105+
(Sir Michael Stoute) *swtg: stdd s: t.k.h in rr: clsd: swtchd rt and nt clr run over 2f out: swtchd lft 2f out and hdwy over 1f out: styd on strly ins fnl f: wnt 3rd towards fin: no threat to wnr* **6/1**[3]

11 **4** *1* **Big Country (IRE)**[36] 1502 4-9-3 **94**....................SilvestreDeSousa 3 101
(Michael Appleby) *tall: lengthy: chsd ldr tl led over 3f out: hdd and drvn over 1f out: unable to match pce of wnr ins fnl f: wknd wl ins fnl f and lost 2 pls fnl 50yds* **7/2**[2]

02U2 **5** *½* **Final**[17] 1911 5-9-2 **93**....................RichardKingscote 10 99
(Mark Johnston) *lw: wl in tch in midfield: nt clr run over 2f out: swtchd rt and effrt u.p 2f out: hdwy to chse ldrs jst over 1f out: styd on same pce ins fnl f* **10/1**

1-12 **6** *3 ½* **Banditry (IRE)**[11] 2086 5-9-1 **92**....................(v) StevieDonohoe 13 93
(Ian Williams) *taken down early: stdd s: t.k.h: hld up in last trio: hdwy over 2f out: chsd ldrs but no ex u.p over 1f out: wknd ins fnl f* **10/1**

202- **7** *2* **Cosmeapolitan**[144] 8123 4-9-4 **95**....................FergusSweeney 2 92
(Alan King) *hld up in tch in midfield: clsd to chse ldrs 4f out: effrt jst over 2f out: unable qck and btn over 1f out: wknd ins fnl f* **14/1**

113- **8** *4* **Beardwood**[153] 8231 5-9-0 **91**....................(p) JamesDoyle 11 82
(Mark Johnston) *hld up in tch in midfield: clsd to trck ldrs 3f out: rdn and unable qck 2f out: lost pl over 1f out: wknd ins fnl f* **18/1**

231- **9** *4* **Going Up (IRE)**[163] 8096 4-8-8 **85**....................DavidProbert 12 70
(Rae Guest) *chsd ldrs tl wnt 2nd wl over 2f out tl 2f out: sn lost pl u.p: wknd fnl f* **16/1**

-243 **10** *1 ¾* **Lord Napier (IRE)**[36] 1505 4-8-2 **79**....................(p) JosephineGordon 9 61
(John Ryan) *t.k.h: hld up in tch in midfield: dropped to last trio and rdn 3f out: wknd over 1f out* **50/1**

23-0 **11** *19* **Mustajeer**[23] 1779 4-9-7 **98**....................JimCrowley 4 49
(Owen Burrows) *swtg: t.k.h: led and nvr totally settled: hdd over 3f out: lost pl and bhd 2f out: bhd and eased ins fnl f: t.o* **9/1**

/460 **12** *6* **Warrior Of Light (IRE)**[16] 1942 6-9-2 **93**....................ShaneKelly 6 35
(Brendan Powell) *swtg: hld up in last trio: shkn up over 2f out: sn btn: wl bhd and eased ins fnl f: t.o* **66/1**

2m 32.96s (0.96) **Going Correction** +0.05s/f (Good) 12 Ran SP% **118.4**
Speed ratings (Par 109): **98,96,96,95,95 92,91,88,86,84 72,68**
CSF £73.13 CT £350.47 TOTE £3.50: £1.70, £4.30, £2.00; EX 62.80 Trifecta £187.80.
**Owner** Godolphin **Bred** Stanley Estate And Stud Co **Trained** Newmarket, Suffolk

**FOCUS**
The false rail was utilised on the stands' side of the course for both days of the Qipco Guineas Festival and it ran from the 1m2f start to the 2.5 furlong point (the bushes). The re-positioning of the bend into the home straight increased this race by 9yds. A cracking start to the day's racing, which produced a taking winner.

## 2432 CHARM SPIRIT DAHLIA STKS (GROUP 2) (F&M) 1m 1f
**2:20** (2:27) (Class 1) 4-Y-O+
**£51,039** (£19,350; £9,684; £4,824; £2,421; £1,215) **Stalls** High

Form RPR

21-2 **1** **Somehow (IRE)**[7] 2190 4-9-0 113....................(v) RyanMoore 1 115+
(A P O'Brien, Ire) *lw: stdd s: hld up in tch in last trio: clsd and nt clr run over 2f out: squeezed through to chse ldrs 2f out: rdn and chalng over 1f out: led 1f out: styd on strly and drew away ins fnl f: readily* **13/8**[1]

3-14 **2** *3 ¼* **Elbereth**[23] 1775 6-9-0 100....................DavidProbert 7 107
(Andrew Balding) *led: shifted lft to rail and rdn 2f out: drvn and hdd 1f out: outpcd by wnr but kpt on for clr 2nd ins fnl f* **25/1**

10-0 **3** *4 ½* **Aim To Please (FR)**[35] 1531 4-9-0 106....................GeraldMosse 4 97
(F Doumen, France) *t.k.h: hld up in tch in last trio: nt clr run over 2f out: effrt 2f out: no ch w ldng pair but styd on ins fnl f to go 3rd last strides* **14/1**

3332 **4** *nk* **Muffri'Ha (IRE)**[23] 1771 5-9-0 107....................PatCosgrave 3 96
(William Haggas) *t.k.h: trckd ldrs: rdn 2f out: edging lft and outpcd over 1f out: wl hld and plugged on same pce ins fnl f* **9/2**[2]

40-1 **5** *¾* **Aljazzi**[22] 1795 4-9-0 102....................(h) FrankieDettori 8 95
(Marco Botti) *wl in tch in midfield: effrt 2f out: 3rd and outpcd u.p over 1f out: wknd ins fnl f and lost 2 pls fnl 75yds* **10/1**

1-44 **6** *1* **Silver Step (FR)**[80] 771 4-9-0 107....................(h) JamesDoyle 6 92
(Mme Pia Brandt, France) *w'like: hld up in rr: rdn 3f out: no imp and no ch w ldrs and swtchd rt over 1f out: plugged on* **16/1**

153- **7** *17* **Skiffle**[252] 5939 4-9-0 103....................WilliamBuick 2 79
(Charlie Appleby) *lw: hit nose on stall gate: wnt rt s: sn chsng ldr: rdn and jst beginning to struggle whn nudged rt 2f out: dropped to rr and unbalanced on downhill run over 1f out: bhd and eased ins fnl f: fin lame* **8/1**[3]

1m 49.19s (-2.51) **Going Correction** +0.05s/f (Good) 7 Ran SP% **92.9**
Speed ratings (Par 115): **113,110,106,105,105 104,89**
CSF £27.70 TOTE £1.80: £1.40, £6.90; EX 26.80 Trifecta £183.60.
**Owner** Michael Tabor & Derrick Smith & Mrs John Magnier **Bred** Orpendale, Chelston & Wynatt **Trained** Cashel, Co Tipperary

■ Nezwaah was withdrawn. Price at time of withdrawal 9/2. Rule 4 applies to all bets - deduction 15p in the pound.

**FOCUS**
Not the strongest Group 2 on paper, and it was weakened further when Nezwaah burst the gates and had to be withdrawn. That said, it was a bit of a tactical affair and the winner impressed in coming from behind and drawing clear. The winner has been rated close to form.

## 2433 LONGHOLES H'CAP 6f
**2:55** (2:58) (Class 2) 4-Y-0+
**£31,125** (£9,320; £4,660; £2,330; £1,165; £585) **Stalls** High

Form RPR
50-2 **1** **Mr Lupton (IRE)**[23] 1765 4-9-9 **107**.................................. GeraldMosse 4 116
(Richard Fahey) *hw: hld up in tch towards rr of main gp: clsd to trck ldrs whn nt clr run wl over 1f out: gap opened and rdn to chal 1f out: led ins fnl f: qcknd and r.o strly: readily* **10/1**

0003 **2** *1 ¼* **Eastern Impact (IRE)**[57] 1152 6-9-4 **102**........................ PaulHanagan 6 107
(Richard Fahey) *trckd ldrs: effrt to chal 2f out: rdn to ld over 1f out: drvn and hdd ins fnl f: unable qck w wnr and styd on same pce after* **7/1**[2]

4100 **3** *¾* **Go Far**[22] 1794 7-8-6 **97**..............................................(v) JoshuaBryan[(7)] 16 100
(Alan Bailey) *trckd ldrs: rdn to chal 2f out: unable qck u.p jst ins fnl f: styd on same pce fnl 100yds* **50/1**

20-2 **4** *½* **East Street Revue**[18] 1876 4-8-10 **94**........................(b) DuranFentiman 2 95
(Tim Easterby) *in tch in midfield : effrt 2f out: rdn and ev ch over 1f out tl no ex jst ins fnl f: styd on same pce fnl 100yds* **12/1**

41-1 **5** *¾* **Intisaab**[8] 2156 6-9-7 **108**..........................................(p) ShelleyBirkett[(3)] 15 107
(David O'Meara) *hld up wl in tch in midfield: effrt over 1f out: kpt on same pce u.p and no imp ins fnl f* **10/1**

453- **6** *1* **Projection**[267] 5409 4-9-5 **103**........................................... JamesDoyle 12 98
(Roger Charlton) *taken down early: hld up in tch in midfield: effrt over 1f out: unable qck u.p 1f out and kpt on same pce ins fnl f* **4/1**[1]

4-01 **7** *shd* **Gunmetal (IRE)**[18] 1880 4-8-10 **94**................................ AndreaAtzeni 8 89+
(Charles Hills) *hld up wl in tch in midfield: nt clr run 2f out: shuffled bk over 1f out: swtchd rt and rdn 1f out: styd on wl ins fnl f: unable to rcvr and no ch of rching ldrs* **4/1**[1]

000- **8** *½* **Clear Spring (IRE)**[198] 7497 9-8-11 **95**........................ TomMarquand 1 88
(John Spearing) *in tch in midfield: rdn over 2f out: hdwy u.p to chal wl over 1f out: no ex jst ins fnl f: wknd fnl 100yds* **50/1**

32-5 **9** *nse* **Seeking Magic**[19] 1863 9-8-7 **94**..............................(t) HectorCrouch[(3)] 14 87
(Clive Cox) *taken down early: led rdn ent fnl 2f: hdd over 1f out: lost pl and btn 1f out: wknd ins fnl f* **20/1**

3150 **10** *shd* **Poyle Vinnie**[16] 1946 7-9-1 **102**..........................(p) AlistairRawlinson[(3)] 9 95
(Michael Appleby) *taken down early: t.k.h: s.i.s: hld up in rr of main gp: hdwy to chse ldrs 2f out: rdn and pressing ldrs over 1f out tl no ex jst ins fnl f: wknd fnl 100yds* **66/1**

02-2 **11** *¾* **Big Time (IRE)**[107] 326 6-9-4 **102**.............................(v) MartinHarley 13 93
(Kevin Ryan) *hld up in tch in rr of main gp: effrt 2f out: swtchd lft and rdn over 1f out: no imp and kpt on same pce ins fnl f: nvr trbld ldrs* **12/1**

1-00 **12** *7* **Swift Approval (IRE)**[36] 1491 5-8-12 **96**............................(t) FranBerry 7 64
(Stuart Williams) *pressed ldr: rdn and ev ch 2f out: losing pl whn sltly impeded over 1f out: wknd fnl f* **50/1**

00-2 **13** *22* **Captain Colby (USA)**[36] 1491 5-9-2 **100**....................(b) WilliamBuick 11
(Ed Walker) *wnt sharply rt s: hld up in rr of main gp: swtchd rt and effrt ent fnl 2f: no imp and btn over 1f out: wl btn and heavily eased ins fnl f* **7/1**[2]

-110 **14** *3 ½* **Hakam (USA)**[23] 1769 5-8-9 **93**................................ SilvestreDeSousa 10
(Michael Appleby) *hw: s.i.s: a detached in last: bhd and heavily eased ins fnl f: t.o: burst blood vessel* **8/1**[3]

1m 10.63s (-1.57) **Going Correction** +0.05s/f (Good) **14** Ran SP% **121.8**
Speed ratings (Par 109): **112,110,109,108,107 106,106,105,105,105 104,95,65,61**
CSF £76.84 CT £3452.82 TOTE £12.50: £3.50, £2.60, £12.00; EX 85.50 Trifecta £2778.00.
**Owner** N D Kershaw & Partner **Bred** Ms E O'Neill **Trained** Musley Bank, N Yorks

**FOCUS**
Some quality types have taken this down the years like Goldream (2014) and Maarek (2012) among plenty of other smart sprinters, so this should be a race to follow. The runner-up has been rated close to last year's form.

## 2434 QIPCO 1000 GUINEAS STKS (GROUP 1) (BRITISH CHAMPIONS SERIES) (FILLIES) 1m
**3:35** (3:38) (Class 1) 3-Y-0
**£283,550** (£107,500; £53,800; £26,800; £13,450; £6,750) **Stalls** High

Form RPR
2 **1** **Winter (IRE)**[29] 1634 3-9-0 106........................................ WayneLordan 7 117
(A P O'Brien, Ire) *tall: str: swtg: squeezed for room sn after s: hld up wl in tch in midfield: pushed along to ld 2f out: in command and styd on strly ins fnl f: rdn out* **9/1**

131- **2** *2* **Rhododendron (IRE)**[212] 7116 3-9-0 116........................ RyanMoore 9 115+
(A P O'Brien, Ire) *hw: hld up in tch in midfield: trckd ldrs whn nt clr run over 2f out: stl no room and getting squeezed out whn swtchd sharply lft over 1f out: hdwy 1f out: styd on wl u.p to go 2nd last strides: nvr getting to wnr* **5/4**[1]

1-1 **3** *nk* **Daban (IRE)**[18] 1883 3-9-0 108........................................ FrankieDettori 1 111
(John Gosden) *hw: wnt rt leaving stalls: stdd and dropped in bhd: hld up in rr: clsd over 2f out: rdn to chse ldrs over 1f out: chsd wnr jst over 1f out: styd on but no imp ins fnl f: lost 2nd last strides* **5/1**[2]

1- **4** *1 ¼* **Talaayeb**[225] 6782 3-9-0 94................................................ JimCrowley 11 108
(Owen Burrows) *str: hld up in tch in midfield: clsd and nt clrest of runs over 2f out: swtchd lft and effrt 2f out: hdwy and edgd lft over 1f out: chsd ldng pair 1f out: kpt on same pce and lost 3rd ins fnl f* **11/1**

132- **5** *2 ¼* **Fair Eva**[226] 6748 3-9-0 110............................................. JamesDoyle 3 103
(Roger Charlton) *swtg: stdd s: hld up in tch towards rr: clsd over 2f out: chsd ldrs and rdn over 1f out: unable qck and btn 1f out: 5th and kpt on same pce ins fnl f* **8/1**[3]

23-2 **6** *5* **Unforgetable Filly**[18] 1883 3-9-0 105............................ WilliamBuick 8 91
(Hugo Palmer) *trckd ldrs: effrt to chal over 2f out: chsd wnr but unable qck whn edgd rt over 1f out: sn lost pl and btn 1f out: wknd ins fnl f* **25/1**

11-3 **7** *1 ¼* **Poet's Vanity**[18] 1883 3-9-0 104.................................... DavidProbert 14 89
(Andrew Balding) *hw: t.k.h: trckd ldrs: effrt to chse ldrs 2f out: 3rd and unable qck u.p over 1f out: sn struggling and wknd ins fnl f* **20/1**

13-2 **8** *¾* **Urban Fox**[15] 1958 3-9-0 104.......................................... MartinHarley 4 87
(James Tate) *hld up in tch towards rr: clsd and nt clr run ent fnl 2f: midfield and no imp whn impeded and swtchd lft over 1f out: no imp and wknd ins fnl f* **50/1**

14-5 **9** *1 ½* **Queen Kindly**[15] 1958 3-9-0 112.................................... GeraldMosse 13 83
(Richard Fahey) *hw: hld up in tch in midfield: swtchd lft and effrt 2f out: no imp u.p over 1f out: wknd fnl f* **33/1**

20-1 **10** *½* **Hydrangea (IRE)**[29] 1634 3-9-0 111.................................... PBBeggy 6 82
(A P O'Brien, Ire) *hw: led: rdn over 2f out: hdd 2f out: unable qck whn edgd lft u.p over 1f out: sn btn and wknd fnl f* **9/1**

10-6 **11** *2 ½* **Kilmah**[18] 1883 3-9-0 100........................................ RichardKingscote 12 77
(Mark Johnston) *pressed ldrs: ev ch 3f out: shkn up over 2f out: sn rdn and no rspnse: lost pl and btn over 1f out: wknd* **100/1**

10-4 **12** *8* **Intricately (IRE)**[29] 1634 3-9-0 112............................ DonnachaO'Brien 5 58
(Joseph Patrick O'Brien, Ire) *str: pressed ldr: rdn and ev ch over 2f out tl outpcd 2f out: lost pl u.p over 1f out: wknd* **20/1**

1-0 **13** *2 ¼* **Ce La Vie**[42] 1387 3-9-0 87.............................................. TomQueally 2 53
(Keith Dalgleish) *stdd s: t.k.h: hld up in rr: rdn over 3f out: sn struggling and bhd* **150/1**

0 **14** *30* **Dream Start**[19] 1857 3-9-0 0..................................(t[1]) JosephineGordon 10
(John Ryan) *a towards rr: rdn over 3f out: sn struggling and bhd: t.o and virtually p.u ins fnl f* **200/1**

1m 35.66s (-2.94) **Going Correction** +0.05s/f (Good) **14** Ran SP% **121.0**
Speed ratings (Par 110): **116,114,113,112,110 105,103,103,101,101 98,90,88,58**
CSF £19.50 CT £70.33 TOTE £10.40: £3.10, £1.10, £2.10; EX 22.40 Trifecta £167.60.
**Owner** Mrs John Magnier & Michael Tabor & Derrick Smith **Bred** Laddies Poker Two Syndicate **Trained** Cashel, Co Tipperary

**FOCUS**
Another Ballydoyle domination of a Classic, the first two being sired by Galileo and essentially outstaying their rivals in what was a well-run Guineas. The time was good and it looks form to be positive about. It's been rated slighly above the Guineas winning average.

## 2435 HAVANA GOLD MAIDEN STKS (PLUS 10 RACE) 5f
**4:10** (4:12) (Class 4) 2-Y-0 **£6,469** (£1,925; £962; £481) **Stalls** High

Form RPR
**1** **Way Of Wisdom** 2-9-5 0................................................ WilliamBuick 1 83+
(Charlie Appleby) *cmpt: pressed ldng pair: shkn up over 1f out: rdn jst over 1f out: styd on to ld 100yds out: kpt on wl and a holding chalr after* **5/1**[3]

**2** *nk* **Kit Marlowe** 2-9-5 0...................................................... JamesDoyle 5 82+
(Mark Johnston) *lengthy: lw: pressed ldr: ev ch: shkn up and rn green on downhill run over 1f out: rdn jst over 1f out: led ins fnl f: sn hdd: kpt on wl but a jst hld after* **7/4**[2]

4 **3** *1 ¼* **Qaaraat**[16] 1941 2-9-5 0................................................. JimCrowley 4 77
(Ed Dunlop) *str: lw: led: shkn up over 1f out: rdn ent fnl f: hdd ins fnl f: no ex and wknd towards fin* **13/8**[1]

**4** *1* **Red Roman** 2-9-5 0......................................................... JamieSpencer 2 73+
(Charles Hills) *str: wl in tch in midfield: effrt to press ldrs whn rn green: edgd rt and impeded over 1f out: sn wandered and outpcd: kpt on same pce ins fnl f* **16/1**

**5** *6* **De Bruyne Horse** 2-9-5 0.............................................. RyanMoore 3 52
(Richard Hannon) *cmpt: dwlt: rn green in last pair: rdn ent fnl 2f: outpcd and unbalanced on downhill run over 1f out: wknd fnl f* **8/1**

**6** *1* **Solid Man (JPN)** 2-9-5 0................................................ FranBerry 6 48
(Ralph Beckett) *cmpt: dwlt: rn green in last pair: effrt 2f out: outpcd: unbalanced and drifting rt over 1f out: wknd fnl f* **14/1**

1m 0.54s (1.44) **Going Correction** +0.05s/f (Good) **6** Ran SP% **114.8**
Speed ratings (Par 95): **90,89,87,85,76 74**
CSF £14.42 TOTE £5.70: £2.30, £1.50; EX 16.70 Trifecta £40.70.
**Owner** Godolphin **Bred** Godolphin **Trained** Newmarket, Suffolk

**FOCUS**
Winners of this have a mixed record, so it remains to be seen how good this one is. Not much separated the first three home. The opening level is fluid.

## 2436 TWEENHILLS PRETTY POLLY STKS (LISTED RACE) (FILLIES) 1m 2f
**4:45** (4:45) (Class 1) 3-Y-0
**£22,684** (£8,600; £4,304; £2,144; £1,076; £540) **Stalls** High

Form RPR
41- **1** **Horseplay**[207] 7285 3-9-0 95.......................................... DavidProbert 6 100
(Andrew Balding) *neat: stdd s: t.k.h: hld up in tch in 4th: clsd to press ldrs 3f out: rdn and ev ch ent fnl 2f: stl chalng whn edgd rt 1f out: led ins fnl f: styd on wl: gamely* **11/2**[2]

1- **2** *¾* **Isabel De Urbina (IRE)**[229] 6648 3-9-0 80......................... FranBerry 1 98
(Ralph Beckett) *leggy: athletic: hld up in tch in last pair: clsd to press ldrs 3f out: rdn ent fnl 2f: wnt 2nd and pressing wnr 100yds out: kpt on but a hld after* **9/1**

1- **3** *1 ½* **Astronomy's Choice**[212] 7118 3-9-0 86......................... FrankieDettori 3 95
(John Gosden) *tall: lengthy: lw: trckd ldrs tl wnt 2nd 4f out: rdn and ev ch 3f out: stl pressing ldrs but unable qck over 1f out: 3rd and kpt on same pce fnl 100yds* **4/6**[1]

30-0 **4** *1 ¾* **Miss Infinity (IRE)**[18] 1881 3-9-0 101.............................. RyanMoore 2 92
(Mark Johnston) *led: rdn 2f out: edgd rt 1f out: hdd ins fnl f: no ex and wknd fnl 100yds* **16/1**

135- **5** *½* **Teofonic (IRE)**[190] 7698 3-9-0 90................................... FrannyNorton 5 91
(Mark Johnston) *chsd ldr tl 4f out: dropped to last 3f out: no imp and drifting rt over 1f out: styd on ins fnl f: no threat to ldrs* **16/1**

42-0 **6** *2* **Kazimiera**[18] 1883 3-9-0 90.......................................... WilliamBuick 4 88
(Charlie Appleby) *stdd s: t.k.h early: hld up in tch: effrt in 5th wl over 2f out: no imp and wandering rt on downhill run over 1f out: no imp and eased towards fin* **7/1**[3]

2m 4.6s (-1.20) **Going Correction** +0.05s/f (Good) **6** Ran SP% **109.6**
Speed ratings (Par 104): **106,105,104,102,102 100**
CSF £47.72 TOTE £6.00: £2.30, £3.20; EX 52.50 Trifecta £136.80.
**Owner** Cliveden Stud **Bred** Cliveden Stud **Trained** Kingsclere, Hants

**FOCUS**
In the last four years this race has been won by two subsequent Oaks winners (Talent and Taghrooda) and last year the third, Even Song, went on to win the Ribblesdale. The early pace wasn't that strong and it developed into a bit of a dash, with the field fairly well bunched at the finish. Nevertheless, the winner could be an interesting candidate for Epsom, having now shown she's not just a soft-ground filly, and with her stamina for 1m4f not in doubt on breeding.

## 2437 QIPCO SUPPORTING BRITISH RACING H'CAP 1m 2f
**5:20** (5:20) (Class 3) (0-95,93) 3-Y-0 **£9,703** (£2,887; £1,443; £721) **Stalls** High

Form RPR
21-0 **1** **Leshlaa (USA)**[23] 1780 3-9-4 **90**..............................(h[1]) JamieSpencer 4 106
(Saeed bin Suroor) *lengthy: stdd s: hld ip in rr: clsd and pushed along 3f out: swtchd rt and effrt jst over 2f out: wnt 2nd and hung lft u.p over 1f out: hrd drvn to chal 1f out: led wl ins fnl f: styd on* **16/1**

22-1 **2** *nk* **Dubai Horizon (IRE)**[29] 1624 3-8-13 **85**.................. SilvestreDeSousa 3 100
(Saeed bin Suroor) *athletic: lw: t.k.h: chsd ldr tl led jst over 2f out: wnt lft u.p over 1f out: hrd pressed 1f out: hdd wl ins fnl f: kpt on u.p but hld towards fin* **15/2**

62-6 **3** *8* **Society Red**[22] 1801 3-8-7 **79** PaulHanagan 2 78
(Richard Fahey) *t.k.h early: hld up in tch in midfield: effrt to chse ldrs 2f out: 3rd and jst getting outpcd whn carried lft and sltly impeded over 1f out: 3rd and btn 1f out: outpcd but stl clr 3rd fnl f* **33/1**

0-13 **4** *9* **Bin Battuta**[18] 1886 3-9-7 **93** JimCrowley 8 74
(Saeed bin Suroor) *hld up in last trio: effrt ent fnl 2f: outpcd over 1f out and wl hld 4th 1f out: wknd fnl f* **9/4**[1]

21-4 **5** *1* **Wahash (IRE)**[18] 1886 3-9-4 **90** FrankieDettori 9 69
(Richard Hannon) *swtg: t.k.h: hld up wl in tch in midfield: effrt jst over 2f out: sn struggling and outpcd: wknd fnl f* **11/1**

21 **6** *nk* **Oasis Charm**[8] 2152 3-9-4 **90** WilliamBuick 5 68
(Charlie Appleby) *lw: hld up in midfield: effrt 3f out: no imp 2f out and outpcd whn drifted rt over 1f out: wknd fnl f* **6/1**[3]

5221 **7** *2* **Specialist (IRE)**[52] 1226 3-8-5 **77** FrannyNorton 1 51
(Mark Johnston) *leggy: chsd ldrs tl rdn and lost pl over 3f out: outpcd and btn over 1f out: wknd fnl f* **33/1**

13 **8** *1 1/4* **Harlow**[31] 1582 3-8-12 **84** JosephineGordon 10 56
(Hugo Palmer) *taken down early: stdd s: hld up in last trio: rdn 3f out: no imp and outpcd whn hmpd jst over 2f out: wknd over 1f out* **11/1**

21-2 **9** *8* **Mister Manduro (FR)**[23] 1764 3-9-0 **86** RyanMoore 7 42
(Mark Johnston) *str: led: rdn 3f out: hdd jst over 2f out: unbalanced and lost pl over 1f out: eased fnl f* **3/1**[2]

2m 3.63s (-2.17) **Going Correction** +0.05s/f (Good) **9** Ran SP% **110.3**
Speed ratings (Par 103): **110,109,103,96,95 95,93,92,86**
CSF £118.05 CT £3309.24 TOTE £19.00: £4.60, £2.00, £7.00; EX 130.80 Trifecta £3026.30.
**Owner** Godolphin **Bred** Darley **Trained** Newmarket, Suffolk
■ Count Calabash was withdrawn. Price at time of withdrawal 14-1. Rule 4 applies to all bets - deduction 5p in the pound.

**FOCUS**
A decent handicap which was full of useful types. It would be surprising if a few winners don't emerge from this, some well above average. To illustrate that point, Prize Money was second in this last year, and he's now won at Group 2 level. The opening level is fluid but the first two are bred to be smart.
T/Jkpt: Not won. T/Plt: £206.70 to a £1 stake. Pool: £158,693.00 - 767.74 winning units T/Qpdt: £39.10 to a £1 stake. Pool: £7,827.00 - 199.77 winning units **Steve Payne**

2438 - 2439a (Foreign Racing) - See Raceform Interactive

## 1632 LEOPARDSTOWN (L-H)

Sunday, May 7

**OFFICIAL GOING: Good to firm changing to good to firm (firm in places) after race 6 (3.55)**

### 2440a ARD GLEN CONSTRUCTION AMETHYST STKS (GROUP 3) 1m

**2:10** (2:10) 3-Y-0+

**£31,794** (£10,256; £4,871; £2,179; £1,102; £564)

RPR

**1** **Custom Cut (IRE)**[15] 1974 8-9-9 108 (p) DanielTudhope 1 110
(David O'Meara) *mde all: almost 2 l clr at 1/2-way: rdn 2f out and strly pressed over 1f out: kpt on wl u.p far side ins fnl f* **9/2**[2]

**2** *1/2* **Raymonda (USA)**[301] 4178 4-9-6 101 PatSmullen 2 106
(D K Weld, Ire) *trckd ldr: gng wl under 2f out and clsr in 2nd over 1f out where rdn: kpt on wl wout matching wnr ins fnl f* **5/1**[3]

**3** *nse* **Cougar Mountain (IRE)**[9] 2129 6-10-0 113 (tp) SeamieHeffernan 5 114+
(A P O'Brien, Ire) *hld up bhd ldrs: last fr 1/2-way: stl gng wl in rr into st: tk clsr order in 5th under 2f out: sn rdn and r.o wl nr side into 3rd wl ins fnl f: nrst fin* **9/4**[1]

**4** *3/4* **Gordon Lord Byron (IRE)**[28] 1653 9-10-0 103 WJLee 3 112
(T Hogan, Ire) *dwlt and in rr early tl impr to sn chse ldrs in 3rd: pushed along 2f out and no imp on ldrs u.p in 3rd ent fnl f: kpt on same pce ins fnl f where dropped to 4th* **16/1**

**5** *1 1/4* **Tribal Beat (IRE)**[239] 6353 4-9-12 115 (p) KevinManning 4 107
(J S Bolger, Ire) *dwlt and towards rr early tl impr to chse ldrs in 4th: rdn in 4th under 3f out and no ex u.p over 1f out: kpt on one pce in 5th wl ins fnl f* **9/4**[1]

**6** *1 1/2* **Elleval (IRE)**[22] 1811 7-9-9 101 (p) ColmO'Donoghue 6 101
(David Marnane, Ire) *chsd ldrs briefly tl sn settled in rr: 5th fr 1/2-way: pushed along and dropped to rr under 2f out: one pce fnl f* **12/1**

1m 44.17s (2.97) **Going Correction** +0.325s/f (Good) **6** Ran SP% **110.0**
Speed ratings: **98,97,97,96,95 93**
CSF £25.38 TOTE £4.20: £2.30, £1.90; DF 26.20 Trifecta £83.30.
**Owner** Frank Gillespie & Pat Breslin **Bred** Moyglare Stud Farm Ltd **Trained** Upper Helmsley, N Yorks
■ Stewards' Enquiry : Daniel Tudhope caution: used whip with arm above shoulder height

**FOCUS**
A familiar British-trained raider proved too sprightly for the home-team, and the lightly raced runner-up made a fine start to the season, but this turned into a sprint.

### 2441a DERRINSTOWN STUD 1,000 GUINEAS TRIAL (GROUP 3) (FILLIES) 1m

**2:45** (2:45) 3-Y-0

**£30,256** (£9,743; £4,615; £2,051; £1,025; £512)

RPR

**1** **Bean Feasa**[7] 2189 3-9-0 99 (t[1]) KevinManning 6 104+
(J S Bolger, Ire) *chsd ldrs early tl impr into 2nd after 1f: rdn 2f out and styd on wl to ld ins fnl f: extended advantage clsng stages* **10/3**[1]

**2** *2 3/4* **Asking (IRE)**[16] 1954 3-9-0 88 (tp) AnaO'Brien 2 97
(A P O'Brien, Ire) *sn led: over 2 l clr fr 1/2-way: stl gng wl into st: rdn over 1f out and reduced advantage: hdd u.p ins fnl f and no imp on wnr clsng stages* **9/2**[3]

**3** *1 1/2* **Shes Ranger (IRE)**[14] 1998 3-9-0 94 RobsonAguiar 1 93+
(Adrian Murray, Ire) *prom tl sn settled bhd ldrs: 3rd 1/2-way: rdn 2f out and no imp on ldrs u.p in 3rd ins fnl f where edgd sltly lft: kpt on same pce* **7/1**

**4** *2 1/4* **Perle De La Mer (IRE)**[224] 6815 3-9-0 93 WJLee 3 88+
(W McCreery, Ire) *sn trckd ldr in 2nd briefly tl dropped to 4th after 1f: racd keenly early: rdn over 2f out and no imp on ldrs u.p in 5th 1 1/2f out: kpt on one pce ins fnl f and wnt 4th clsng stages* **9/2**[3]

**5** *1 1/2* **Holy Cat (IRE)**[225] 6784 3-9-0 94 PatSmullen 5 85+
(M D O'Callaghan, Ire) *w.w and settled towards rr: last at 1/2-way: rdn bef st and no imp u.p in rr under 2f out: kpt on one pce ins fnl f and wnt 5th cl home* **4/1**[2]

**6** *1/2* **Elizabeth Browning (IRE)**[6] 2241 3-9-0 93 (t) SeamieHeffernan 4 92+
(A P O'Brien, Ire) *dwlt and pushed along in rr early: 5th 1/2-way: rdn into 4th 2f out and no imp on wnr u.p in 4th whn bdly hmpd and checked on inner ins fnl 100yds: eased and lost two pls cl home* **4/1**[2]

1m 42.06s (0.86) **Going Correction** +0.325s/f (Good) **6** Ran SP% **111.9**
Speed ratings: **108,105,103,101,100 99**
CSF £18.28 TOTE £3.00: £1.60, £1.90; DF 16.40 Trifecta £78.90.
**Owner** Godolphin **Bred** Darley **Trained** Coolcullen, Co Carlow
■ Stewards' Enquiry : Robson Aguiar two-day ban: careless riding

**FOCUS**
An ordinary race for this level. Victory went to a maiden, though at least some credibility can be accorded the form on the basis she was the highest-rated runner in the field.

### 2442a DERRINSTOWN STUD DERBY TRIAL STKS (GROUP 3) 1m 2f

**3:20** (3:20) 3-Y-0

**£50,427** (£16,239; £7,692; £3,418; £1,709)

RPR

**1** **Douglas Macarthur (IRE)**[29] 1636 3-9-3 110 EmmetMcNamara 6 112
(A P O'Brien, Ire) *led: 1 l clr bef 1/2-way: rdn and jnd briefly into st: regained narrow advantage under 2f out: kpt on wl far side ins fnl f* **7/1**

**2** *hd* **Yucatan (IRE)**[29] 1636 3-9-3 111 SeamieHeffernan 2 112+
(A P O'Brien, Ire) *w.w towards rr: 5th 1/2-way: impr into 4th after 1/2-way: swtchd rt under 2f out: sn rdn and kpt on wl nr side ins fnl f to chal clsng stages: jst hld* **13/8**[1]

**3** *shd* **Capri (IRE)**[29] 1636 3-9-3 113 ColmO'Donoghue 1 111
(A P O'Brien, Ire) *cl up bhd ldr in 2nd: rdn on terms briefly into st: hdd narrowly under 2f out: kpt on wl wout matching wnr ins fnl f: denied 2nd fnl strides* **9/4**[2]

**4** *1 3/4* **Insayshable (IRE)**[32] 1565 3-9-3 0 ColinKeane 3 108
(G M Lyons, Ire) *chsd ldrs: 3rd 1/2-way: pushed along bhd ldrs into st: rdn in 3rd 1 1/2f out and clsd u.p to chal briefly ins fnl f: no ex clsng stages where dropped to 4th* **5/1**[3]

**5** *7* **Dubai Sand (IRE)**[29] 1636 3-9-3 104 KevinManning 5 95
(J S Bolger, Ire) *hld up in 5th: racd keenly early: rdn in 5th under 4f out and sn wknd to rr* **10/1**

**P** **Naturalist (IRE)**[32] 1565 3-9-3 0 WJLee 4
(W McCreery, Ire) *w.w in rr: last at 1/2-way: clsr in 5th over 3f out: hung rt into st and eased 2f out: p.u qckly: lame* **14/1**

2m 9.5s (1.30) **Going Correction** +0.325s/f (Good) **6** Ran SP% **113.8**
Speed ratings: **107,106,106,105,99**
CSF £19.33 TOTE £7.10: £2.60, £1.40; DF 21.80 Trifecta £39.10.
**Owner** M J Jooste & Mrs Magnier & M Tabor & D Smith **Bred** Lodge Park Stud **Trained** Cashel, Co Tipperary

**FOCUS**
A clean sweep for Ballydoyle with three admirable colts, if a little short of the standard likely to be required to win a Derby, whether at Epson or the Curragh. Ultimately, the runner-up may prove the pick of them. The winner has been rated in line with his Ballysax form.

2443 - 2446a (Foreign Racing) - See Raceform Interactive

## 2321 CHANTILLY (R-H)

Sunday, May 7

**OFFICIAL GOING: Turf: soft; polytrack: standard**

### 2447a PRIX DE LA SEINE (LISTED RACE) (3YO FILLIES) (TURF) 1m 3f

**3:25** 3-Y-0

**£23,504** (£9,401; £7,051; £4,700; £2,350)

RPR

**1** **Musawaah (USA)**[13] 3-8-13 0 AurelienLemaitre 4 101+
(F Head, France) **12/5**[1]

**2** *2* **Kitesurf**[30] 3-8-13 0 MickaelBarzalona 5 97
(A Fabre, France) *a cl up: 3rd and drvn 2f out: hrd rdn to chse ldr 1 1/2f out: styd on fnl f: nt pce of wnr* **41/10**[2]

**3** *1 1/2* **Lady Paname (FR)**[26] 3-8-13 0 TonyPiccone 6 94+
(E Lellouche, France) **81/10**

**4** *1* **Szolnok (USA)**[28] 1657 3-8-13 0 CristianDemuro 2 92
(S Cerulis, France) **269/10**

**5** *nse* **Site Seeing (FR)**[17] 3-8-13 0 StephanePasquier 7 92
(N Clement, France) **73/10**

**6** *1 3/4* **Muthla (FR)**[57] 1158 3-8-13 0 TheoBachelot 3 89
(J-M Beguigne, France) **26/5**

**7** *snk* **Meisho Felicity (FR)**[82] 3-8-13 0 GregoryBenoist 9 89
(S Kobayashi, France) **128/10**

**8** *8* **Hessoesse (FR)** 3-8-13 0 IoritzMendizabal 1 74
(Pavel Tuma, Czech Republic) **56/1**

**9** *dist* **Agathonia (USA)**[17] 1900 3-8-13 0 (p) Pierre-CharlesBoudot 8
(Charlie Appleby) *hld up in fnl trio on outer: tk clsr order 1/2-way: drvn in midfield on outer 3f fr home: lost pl and last 2f out: wl hld whn eased* **49/10**[3]

2m 23.4s (143.40) **9** Ran SP% **117.7**
PARI-MUTUEL (all including 1 euro stake): WIN: 3.40; PLACE: 1.40, 1.60, 2.30; DF: 7.50; SF: 12.50.
**Owner** Hamdan Al Maktoum **Bred** Shadwell Farm LLC **Trained** France

### 2448a PRIX DE GUICHE (GROUP 3) (3YO COLTS & GELDINGS) (TURF) 1m 1f

**4:10** 3-Y-0

**£34,188** (£13,675; £10,256; £6,837; £3,418)

RPR

**1** **Phelps Win (FR)**[28] 1658 3-9-2 0 Pierre-CharlesBoudot 3 112+
(H-A Pantall, France) *trckd ldr: shkn up to ld 2f out: drvn out fnl f: readily* **31/10**[3]

**2** *3 1/2* **Plumatic**[45] 3-9-2 0 MaximeGuyon 5 105
(A Fabre, France) *settled in 3rd: scrubbed along 2f out: rdn to chse ldr over 1f out: kpt on but no imp on wnr: eased late on* **4/5**[1]

**3** *1* **Stunning Spirit**[21] 1824 3-9-2 0 AurelienLemaitre 4 103
(F Head, France) *racd keenly: hld up in fnl pair: rdn and effrt 1 1/2f out: kpt on at same pce fnl f: nvr trbld ldrs* **5/2**[2]

**4** *2* **Phoceen (FR)**[12] 2074 3-9-2 0 (b) IoritzMendizabal 2 98
(F Chappet, France) *hld up in rr: tk clsr order 1 1/2f out: one pce fnl f: nvr in contention* **198/10**

**5** *4* **Saglawy (FR)**[12] 2074 3-9-2 0 StephanePasquier 1 91
(N Clement, France) *led field in single file: drvn 2 1/2f out: hdd 2f out: sn rdn: wknd over 1f out* **199/10**

1m 55.53s (4.43) **5** Ran SP% **118.1**
PARI-MUTUEL (all including 1 euro stake): WIN: 4.10; PLACE: 1.60, 1.10; SF: 12.30.
**Owner** Mme Nadine Chiari **Bred** Mme N Chiari **Trained** France

2449 - (Foreign Racing) - See Raceform Interactive

# 1846 COLOGNE (R-H)

Sunday, May 7

**OFFICIAL GOING: Turf: good**

## 2450a GERLING-PREIS (GROUP 2) (4YO+) (TURF) 1m 4f
3:40 4-Y-0+ £34,188 (£13,247; £6,837; £3,418; £2,136)

RPR
1 **Dschingis Secret (GER)**[197] 7555 4-9-0 0 AdriedeVries 4 115+
(Markus Klug, Germany) **9/5**[1]
2 6 **Sirius (GER)**[18] 6-9-0 0 AndraschStarke 7 103+
(Andreas Suborics, Germany) **11/5**[2]
3 ½ **Kasalla (GER)**[189] 7720 4-8-10 0 MartinSeidl 3 99
(Markus Klug, Germany) **16/5**[3]
4 hd **Tres Rock Glory (IRE)**[19] 1871 4-8-10 0 LudovicBoisseau 6 98+
(F Head, France) **59/10**
5 3 **Nepal (GER)**[343] 2730 4-8-10 0 MichaelCadeddu 2 93
(Dr A Bolte, Germany) **57/10**
6 16 **Kashmar (GER)**[21] 4-8-10 0 MarcLerner 8 68
(Werner Glanz, Germany) **44/5**

2m 29.47s (-3.43) **6 Ran SP% 130.4**
PARI-MUTUEL (all including 10 euro stake): WIN 28 PLACE: 18, 18; SF: 63.
**Owner** Horst Pudwill **Bred** Gestut Park Wiedingen **Trained** Germany

2451 - VOID

# AYR (L-H)

Monday, May 8

**OFFICIAL GOING: Good to firm (good in places; 8.6)**
Wind: Breezy, half against Weather: Sunny

## 2452 SUMMER WEDDINGS AT WESTERN HOUSE HOTEL NOVICE STKS 5f
2:00 (2:00) (Class 5) 2-Y-O £3,234 (£962; £481; £240) Stalls High

Form RPR
2 1 **Havana Grey**[16] 1966 2-9-2 0 PJMcDonald 4 83+
(K R Burke) *t.k.h: pressed ldr: shkn up to ld 1f out: rdn: edgd lft and qcknd clr: readily* **4/7**[1]
0 2 5 **Shay C**[9] 2134 2-9-2 0 DanielTudhope 7 65
(Declan Carroll) *t.k.h: led against stands' rail: rdn and hdd 1f out: kpt on: no ch w ready wnr* **33/1**
5 3 ½ **Collingham Park (IRE)**[14] 2029 2-9-2 0 GrahamLee 1 64+
(Jedd O'Keeffe) *trckd ldrs on outside: shkn up whn vaulted plastic bag 2f out: sn rdn: kpt on fnl f: nvr able to chal* **4/1**[2]
4 hd **Go Now Go Now (IRE)** 2-9-2 0 JoeFanning 6 62+
(Mark Johnston) *trckd ldrs: rdn and outpcd wl over 1f out: kpt on fnl f: no imp* **14/1**
4 5 4 **Che Bella (IRE)**[18] 1908 2-8-11 0 PhillipMakin 3 43
(Keith Dalgleish) *dwlt: t.k.h: hld up: pushed along and edgd lft whn hmpd over 1f out: sn n.d* **8/1**[3]
0 6 ½ **Lord Of The Glen**[9] 2134 2-9-2 0 SamJames 5 46
(Jim Goldie) *hld up in tch: pushed along and outpcd 2f out: n.d after* **100/1**
7 6 **Sam James (IRE)** 2-9-2 0 TomEaves 2 24
(Iain Jardine) *dwlt: hld up: pushed along and outpcd 1/2-way: btn over 1f out* **16/1**

58.46s (-0.94) **Going Correction** -0.55s/f (Hard) **7 Ran SP% 111.2**
Speed ratings (Par 93): **85,77,76,75,69 68,59**
CSF £23.41 TOTE £1.30: £1.10, £8.90; EX 16.00 Trifecta £52.00.
**Owner** Global Racing Club & Mrs E Burke **Bred** Mickley Stud & Lady Lonsdale **Trained** Middleham Moor, N Yorks

**FOCUS**
Track on innermost line - distances as advertised. This was all the about the winner and he didn't disappoint. He can rate higher than the bare form.

## 2453 BOOK DIRECT AT WESTERN HOUSE HOTEL H'CAP 5f
2:30 (2:31) (Class 6) (0-60,57) 4-Y-0+ £2,587 (£770; £384; £192) Stalls High

Form RPR
30-1 1 **Longroom**[4] 2337 5-9-7 57 GrahamLee 3 78+
(Noel Wilson) *mde all: qcknd clr on bit over 1f out: v easily* **1/4**[1]
006- 2 3½ **Cheeni**[214] 7093 5-8-9 45 (p) SamJames 4 46
(Jim Goldie) *tk t.k.h: hld up on outside: hdwy to chse (clr) wnr ent fnl f: kpt on but flattered by proximity to v easy wnr* **16/1**
/0-0 3 4½ **On The High Tops (IRE)**[12] 2076 9-8-9 45 (t[1]) JamesSullivan 1 30
(Colin Teague) *awkward s: hld up in tch on outside: hdwy to chse wnr over 2f out: rdn and drifted rt over 1f out: lost 2nd 1f out: sn outpcd* **66/1**
000- 4 1¾ **Another Desperado (IRE)**[256] 5803 4-8-9 45 PJMcDonald 7 24
(Rebecca Bastiman) *prom: drvn along over 2f out: wknd over 1f out* **25/1**
5-00 5 2¾ **Grecian King**[12] 2082 4-9-7 57 (b[1]) PhillipMakin 5 26
(David Barron) *hld up in tch: rdn and outpcd over 2f out: btn over 1f out* **12/1**[3]
0153 6 2¾ **Teepee Time**[12] 2076 4-8-12 48 TomEaves 2 7
(Michael Mullineaux) *missed break: hld up: rdn over 2f out: sn no imp and btn* **8/1**[2]
600- 7 24 **Lowrie**[221] 6910 4-8-7 50 ConnorMurtagh[(7)] 6
(John David Riches) *pressed wnr: drvn and outpcd over 2f out: lost tch over 1f out: t.o* **22/1**

58.2s (-1.20) **Going Correction** -0.55s/f (Hard) **7 Ran SP% 114.4**
Speed ratings (Par 101): **87,81,74,71,67 62,24**
CSF £5.94 TOTE £1.20: £1.02, £5.90; EX 6.30 Trifecta £86.40.
**Owner** Marwood Racing Limited **Bred** Juddmonte Farms Ltd **Trained** Marwood, Co Durham

**FOCUS**
Another sprint that proved one-way traffic as expected. Another step forward from the winner.

## 2454 FOLLOW @RACING_UK ON TWITTER H'CAP 6f
3:00 (3:02) (Class 6) (0-60,62) 4-Y-0+ £2,587 (£770; £384; £192) Stalls High

Form RPR
554- 1 **Duncan Of Scotland (IRE)**[263] 5578 4-8-11 50 (b) PaulMulrennan 6 60
(Lee Smyth, Ire) *mde all: set decent gallop: clr over 1f out: kpt on wl fnl f: unchal* **11/1**
5510 2 1 **Sea Of Green**[16] 1978 5-8-10 49 (p) PJMcDonald 17 56
(Jim Goldie) *hld up: rdn along and hdwy over 2f out: kpt on wl to take 2nd nr fin: no ch w wnr* **12/1**
40-2 3 ¾ **Our Place In Loule**[16] 1978 4-8-11 50 TomEaves 14 55
(Noel Wilson) *prom on nr side of gp: effrt and chsd (clr) wnr over 1f out: edgd lft and kpt on fnl f: lost 2nd towards fin* **6/1**[1]
0-50 4 1 **Secret City (IRE)**[16] 1978 11-8-3 47 (b) RowanScott[(5)] 13 49
(Rebecca Bastiman) *midfield: rdn and outpcd over 2f out: rallied fnl f: kpt on: nt pce to chal* **11/1**
500- 5 hd **Perfect Words (IRE)**[204] 7386 7-9-7 60 DanielTudhope 3 61
(Marjorie Fife) *in tch: rdn and hdwy over 1f out: no imp ins fnl f* **7/1**[2]
4064 6 1¼ **Jessie Allan (IRE)**[4] 2342 6-8-7 46 oh1 JamesSullivan 10 43
(Jim Goldie) *hld up: hdwy on far side of gp over 1f out: rdn and no imp fnl f* **16/1**
0654 7 2 **Silhuette (IRE)**[16] 1973 4-9-7 60 (p) PhillipMakin 1 51
(Colin Teague) *awkward s: in tch on far side of gp: rdn 2f out: wknd fnl f* **20/1**
100- 8 1½ **Dutch Dream**[188] 7747 4-8-11 50 GrahamLee 16 37
(Linda Perratt) *bhd and sn pushed along: outpcd 1/2-way: kpt on fnl f: nvr on terms* **25/1**
0402 9 ¾ **National Service (USA)**[21] 1931 6-8-7 46 (tp) JoeFanning 12 31
(Clare Ellam) *fly-jmpd s: bhd: rdn over 2f out: sme late hdwy: nvr on terms* **16/1**
6/5- 10 1½ **Modern Tutor**[23] 1812 8-8-12 51 (p[1]) DougieCostello 11 31
(Miss Nicole McKenna, Ire) *dwlt: hld up: rdn over 2f out: sn no imp* **20/1**
4/0- 11 3¼ **Little Cupcake**[59] 1129 6-8-7 46 oh1 (b[1]) JoeyHaynes 8 16
(Paul W Flynn, Ire) *chsd clr ldng pair to 1/2-way: rdn and wknd wl over 1f out* **7/1**[2]
10-4 12 ½ **Goninodaethat**[23] 1805 9-9-5 58 SamJames 2 27
(Jim Goldie) *racd on far side of gp: chsd wnr tl rdn and wknd over 1f out* **10/1**[3]
200- 13 11 **Spoken Words**[231] 6615 8-8-0 46 oh1 (p) ConnorMurtagh[(7)] 15
(John David Riches) *midfield on nr side of gp: drvn over 2f out: wknd wl over 1f out* **50/1**
0-00 14 37 **Poor Duke (IRE)**[39] 1456 7-9-1 54 JasonHart 9
(Michael Mullineaux) *bhd and sn struggling: no ch fr 1/2-way: eased whn no ch over 1f out* **11/1**
00/0 15 2¾ **New Decade**[16] 1978 8-8-7 46 oh1 PaulHanagan 7
(Jim Goldie) *blindfold slow to remove and slowly away: a bhd: struggling bef 1/2-way: eased whn no ch over 1f out* **7/1**[2]

1m 9.95s (-2.45) **Going Correction** -0.55s/f (Hard) **15 Ran SP% 120.7**
Speed ratings (Par 101): **94,92,91,90,90 88,85,83,82,80 76,75,61,11,8**
CSF £129.71 CT £895.89 TOTE £10.20: £4.00, £4.00, £2.30; EX 123.00 Trifecta £604.00.
**Owner** Joseph Swanson **Bred** Premier Bloodstock **Trained** Magheralin, Co Down

**FOCUS**
They were well strung out down the centre in this moderate sprint and the winner dominated. He's rated back towards his better 2yo form.

## 2455 TENNENT'S H'CAP 7f 50y
3:30 (3:32) (Class 6) (0-60,60) 3-Y-O £2,587 (£770; £384; £192) Stalls High

Form RPR
0-00 1 **Ching Ching Lor (IRE)**[12] 2077 3-8-11 50 TomEaves 2 57
(Declan Carroll) *trckd ldrs: rdn over 2f out: hdwy over 1f out: led wl ins fnl f: styd on strly* **15/2**[3]
5260 2 ½ **Hollywood Harry (IRE)**[21] 1835 3-9-3 56 (p) PhillipMakin 6 62
(Keith Dalgleish) *in tch on outside: hdwy to chse ldr over 2f out: led and drifted lft over 1f out: hdd and no ex wl ins fnl f* **9/1**
545 3 3½ **Play With Me**[30] 1626 3-9-0 53 JoeFanning 10 50
(Keith Dalgleish) *hld up midfield: drvn along over 2f out: hdwy and drifted lft over 1f out: kpt on fnl f: nt rch first two* **16/1**
04-2 4 1 **Arnold**[8] 2181 3-9-4 57 JoeyHaynes 8 51+
(Ann Duffield) *s.i.s: hld up: hdwy on outside over 2f out: rdn and edgd lft over 1f out: sn no imp* **13/8**[1]
000- 5 3¼ **Mr Enthusiastic**[191] 7690 3-8-10 49 PaulHanagan 1 35
(Noel Wilson) *t.k.h: led: rdn and hdd over 1f out: wknd ins fnl f* **14/1**
0-50 6 1 **Kelpie Spirit (IRE)**[9] 2159 3-9-2 55 DanielTudhope 4 38
(John Weymes) *dwlt: t.k.h: hld up: rdn over 2f out: hdwy over 1f out: sn no imp* **14/1**
501- 7 ½ **Peny Arcade**[185] 7792 3-9-3 56 PaulMulrennan 9 38
(Alistair Whillans) *t.k.h: hld up: drvn and outpcd over 2f out: n.d after* **8/1**
04- 8 ½ **Guiding Star**[14] 2047 3-8-13 52 (p) DougieCostello 11 33
(Patrick J McKenna, Ire) *hld up: stdy hdwy over 2f out: rdn over 1f out: sn wknd* **33/1**
004- 9 hd **Good Boy Jasper**[209] 7247 3-9-7 60 GrahamLee 5 40
(Linda Perratt) *plld hrd: hld up in midfield: drvn and outpcd over 2f out: n.d after* **20/1**
45-6 10 ¾ **Breaking Free**[12] 2077 3-8-13 52 (v) JasonHart 3 30
(John Quinn) *missed break: t.k.h and sn midfield: drvn along and outpcd over 2f out: btn over 1f out* **6/1**[2]
200- 11 ½ **Warleggan (FR)**[234] 6534 3-8-7 46 PJMcDonald 7 23
(Linda Perratt) *chsd ldr to over 2f out: rdn and wknd wl over 1f out* **33/1**

1m 29.87s (-3.53) **Going Correction** -0.575s/f (Hard) **11 Ran SP% 115.1**
Speed ratings (Par 97): **97,96,92,91,87 86,85,85,85,84 83**
CSF £69.91 CT £1052.98 TOTE £9.00: £2.80, £2.20, £3.90; EX 71.40 Trifecta £950.40.
**Owner** C H Stephenson & David Tate **Bred** Michael G Daly **Trained** Malton, N Yorks

**FOCUS**
An ordinary 3yo handicap, run at a fair pace. The first pair were clear, the winner obviously not flattered by his Redcar run.

## 2456 BOBBY'S BAR H'CAP 1m 5f 26y
4:00 (4:00) (Class 5) (0-70,71) 4-Y-0+ £3,234 (£962; £481; £240) Stalls Low

Form RPR
60-2 1 **Jonny Delta**[4] 2340 10-8-3 52 JamesSullivan 3 59
(Jim Goldie) *prom: effrt and rdn 2f out: led ins fnl f: edgd lft: rdn out* **5/2**[1]
50-0 2 ¾ **Ice Galley (IRE)**[37] 1498 4-9-5 68 GrahamLee 5 74
(Philip Kirby) *trckd ldr: led and rdn 3f out: hdd ins fnl f: kpt on: hld nr fin* **5/2**[1]
2040 3 6 **Magistral**[12] 1716 7-9-1 71 (p) ConnorMurtagh[(7)] 1 68
(Iain Jardine) *trckd ldrs: effrt and ev ch 2f out: sn rdn: outpcd fnl f* **11/2**[3]
44 4 7 **Star Glitter (FR)**[1] 2427 4-9-5 68 DanielTudhope 2 57
(David O'Meara) *hld up in tch: effrt and pushed along over 2f out: wknd over 1f out* **11/4**[2]
043/ 5 10 **Cadore (IRE)**[45] 3238 9-8-3 55 (p) SammyJoBell[(3)] 4 26
(Lucy Normile) *s.i.s: hld up: rdn along and struggling over 3f out: sn btn* **50/1**

523- **6** *13* **Hayward Field (IRE)**[326] 3323 4-9-7 **70**........................ PaulMulrennan 7 22
(Noel Wilson) *led at modest gallop: rdn and hdd 3fd out: wknd fr 2f out* **12/1**

2m 50.16s (-3.84) **Going Correction** -0.575s/f (Hard) **6** Ran SP% **108.8**
Speed ratings (Par 103): **88,87,83,79,73 65**
CSF £8.46 TOTE £3.20: £1.80, £1.90; EX 10.70 Trifecta £38.80.
**Owner** Johnnie Delta Racing **Bred** Miss Gill Quincey **Trained** Uplawmoor, E Renfrews

**FOCUS**
They went a routine sort of pace in this modest staying handicap. The front pair were clear but there were doubts over what they beat.

## 2457 BOOK YOUR CELEBRATION AT WESTERN HOUSE HOTEL H'CAP 1m
**4:30** (4:33) (Class 3) (0-95,93) 4-Y-O+ **£7,762** (£2,310; £1,154; £577) **Stalls** Low

Form RPR
124- **1** **Sophie P**[213] 7126 4-8-13 **85**............................................. PJMcDonald 4 93
(R Mike Smith) *trckd ldrs: rdn to ld over 1f out: hld on wl cl home* **9/1**
-001 **2** *shd* **Nicholas T**[9] 2133 5-8-8 **80**................................................... SamJames 7 91+
(Jim Goldie) *dwlt: hld up in last pl: hdwy on outside over 2f out: sn rdn: edgd lft and kpt on wl fnl f: jst hld* **9/2**[2]
0113 **3** *1 3/4* **Fingal's Cave (IRE)**[12] 2081 5-9-1 **87**......................... DougieCostello 9 91
(Philip Kirby) *led: rdn and hdd over 1f out: kpt on same pce ins fnl f* **25/1**
5112 **4** *3/4* **Inaam (IRE)**[24] 1778 4-8-11 **83**......................................... PaulHanagan 1 85
(Richard Fahey) *hld up in tch: rdn over 2f out: hung lft: kpt on same pce fr over 1f out* **10/1**
60-5 **5** *1 1/4* **King's Pavilion (IRE)**[26] 1734 4-9-0 **86**............................ PhillipMakin 6 85
(David Barron) *trckd ldrs: rdn and outpcd 2f out: no imp fnl f* **4/1**[1]
213- **6** *2 1/4* **Hibou**[212] 7159 4-9-4 **90**.......................................................(b) TomEaves 5 84
(Iain Jardine) *hld up: stdy hdwy over 2f out: rdn and wknd over 1f out* **8/1**[3]
0210 **7** *3 1/2* **Zoravan (USA)**[9] 2142 4-8-12 **84**.......................................(v) JoeFanning 3 69
(Keith Dalgleish) *t.k.h: prom: rdn over 2f out: wknd wl over 1f out* **9/2**[2]

1m 38.24s (-5.56) **Going Correction** -0.575s/f (Hard) **7** Ran SP% **90.4**
Speed ratings (Par 107): **104,103,102,101,100 97,94**
CSF £29.88 CT £408.47 TOTE £9.90: £4.20, £2.20; EX 34.90 Trifecta £315.60.
**Owner** Smith, Matheson, Stewart **Bred** New Hall Stud **Trained** Galston, E Ayrshire
■ Kharbetation was withdrawal. Price at time of withdrawal 3-1. Rule 4 applies to all bets - deduction 25p in the pound.

**FOCUS**
This good-quality handicap was run at an average pace and is rated around the front-running third. The winner improved again.

## 2458 RACINGUK.COM AMATEUR RIDERS' H'CAP 1m
**5:00** (5:00) (Class 5) (0-75,74) 4-Y-O+ **£3,119** (£967; £483; £242) **Stalls** Low

Form RPR
5030 **1** **Testa Rossa (IRE)**[38] 1472 7-10-5 **72**..............................(b) MissRHill(7) 6 85
(Jim Goldie) *hld up on outside: smooth hdwy to ld over 3f out: clr wl over 1f out: edgd lft: pushed out fnl f: unchal* **10/1**
0-34 **2** *6* **Forever A Lady (IRE)**[19] 1879 4-10-10 **70**........................ MrsCBartley 4 69
(Keith Dalgleish) *led to 3f out: pushed along 2f out: kpt on fnl f: no imp* **4/1**[2]
-140 **3** *2 1/4* **Rebel State (IRE)**[95] 516 4-9-9 **62**............................ MissACawley(7) 3 56
(Jedd O'Keeffe) *in tch: hdwy and edgd lft over 1f out: kpt on same pce fnl f* **7/1**
000- **4** *3/4* **Gworn**[125] 7141 7-10-5 **70**..........................................(p) MrRyanNichol(5) 1 62
(R Mike Smith) *cl up: pushed along over 2f out: outpcd fr over 1f out* **11/2**
20-0 **5** *2* **Jabbaar**[27] 1706 4-11-0 **74**.........................................(b) MissSBrotherton 7 62
(David Barron) *t.k.h early: hld up in tch: drvn and outpcd over 2f out: n.d after* **11/4**[1]
33-0 **6** *1 1/4* **Mustaqbal (IRE)**[28] 1677 5-10-6 **73**..........................(p) MissSEDods(7) 2 65
(Michael Dods) *s.i.s: hld up in tch: pushed along over 2f out: 4th and no imp whn n.m.r: hmpd and stmbld bdly appr fnl f: sn btn* **5/1**[3]
1434 **7** *1 1/2* **Kiwi Bay**[27] 1706 12-9-13 **66**.......................................... MissCADods(7) 5 47
(Michael Dods) *t.k.h: cl up: tl rdn and wknd wl over 1f out* **8/1**

1m 39.76s (-4.04) **Going Correction** -0.575s/f (Hard) **7** Ran SP% **111.4**
Speed ratings (Par 103): **97,91,88,88,86 84,83**
CSF £46.85 TOTE £8.50: £3.90, £1.50; EX 50.10 Trifecta £359.00.
**Owner** Mr & Mrs Gordon Grant **Bred** Hugo Merry And Khalid Al-Mudhaf **Trained** Uplawmoor, E Renfrews

**FOCUS**
A modest handicap, confined to amateur riders. The winner at least matched his AW form.
T/Plt: £199.40 to a £1 stake. Pool: £43,126.00 - 216.22 winning units T/Qpdt: £108.60 to a £1 stake. Pool: £2,890.00 - 26.60 winning units **Richard Young**

# 2258 CHELMSFORD (A.W) (L-H)
Monday, May 8

**OFFICIAL GOING: Polytrack: standard**
Wind: light to medium, half against Weather: bright spells, light cloud

## 2459 BET TOTEPLACEPOT AT TOTESPORT.COM NOVICE STKS (PLUS 10 RACE) 5f (P)
**5:40** (5:41) (Class 4) 2-Y-O **£5,822** (£1,732; £865; £432) **Stalls** Low

Form RPR
**1** **Denaar (IRE)** 2-9-2 0.......................................................... FrankieDettori 1 86+
(Richard Hannon) *broke wl: sn hdd but styd pressing ldr on inner: shkn up to ld over 1f out: qcknd clr and r.o strly ins fnl f: eased towards fin: easily* **10/11**[1]
03 **2** *2 3/4* **Poignant**[16] 1966 2-9-2 0.................................................... JackMitchell 3 72
(Archie Watson) *trckd ldrs: effrt over 1f out: chsd clr wnr 150yds out: no imp but kpt on for clr 2nd* **7/2**[3]
4 **3** *2* **Kodiac Express (IRE)**[23] 1792 2-8-11 0............................ JimCrowley 4 60
(Mike Murphy) *sn led: rdn and hdd over 1f out: sn outpcd and lost 2nd 150yds out: wl hld and plugged on same pce after* **16/1**
**4** *3 1/2* **Mimram** 2-8-8 0........................................................................ JackDuern(3) 5 47
(Dean Ivory) *s.i.s: rn green and bustled along in detached last: clsd and hung rt bnd 2f out: sn rdn and outpcd: wnt wl hld 4th jst ins fnl f* **33/1**
**5** *2 3/4* **Budgie** 2-9-2 0......................................................................... MartinLane 2 42
(Mark H Tompkins) *rdn and outpcd after 1f out: sme hdwy over 2f out: struggling and wnt lft over 1f out: wl btn whn nt clr run and hmpd ins fnl f* **28/1**
**6** *2* **Branscombe** 2-9-2 0............................................................ FrannyNorton 6 35
(Mark Johnston) *rn green: chsd ldrs: outpcd over 1f out: wkng whn hung lft 1f out: bhd ins fnl f* **3/1**[2]

1m 0.28s (0.08) **Going Correction** -0.15s/f (Stan) **6** Ran SP% **111.9**
Speed ratings (Par 95): **93,88,85,79,75 72**
CSF £4.40 TOTE £1.60: £1.10, £2.00; EX 4.70 Trifecta £14.10.
**Owner** Al Shaqab Racing **Bred** Gerry Burke **Trained** East Everleigh, Wilts

**FOCUS**
Much to like about the performance of the favourite, though a suspicion that this lacked depth. The winner's pretty useful.

## 2460 BET TOTETRIFECTA AT TOTESPORT.COM H'CAP 1m 5f 66y(P)
**6:10** (6:10) (Class 6) (0-65,65) 4-Y-O+ **£3,234** (£962; £481; £240) **Stalls** Low

Form RPR
430/ **1** **Mishko (IRE)**[971] 6239 6-9-6 **64**.............................................. JimCrowley 4 71
(Steve Gollings) *sn led and mde rest: rdn ent 2f out: drvn over 1f out: kpt on u.p and a holding runner-up ins fnl f* **2/1**[1]
2334 **2** *1/2* **Bridey's Lettuce (IRE)**[14] 2022 5-9-7 **65**.............................(h) KierenFox 1 71
(John Best) *hld up in tch in midfield: effrt in 3rd on inner over 1f out: drvn and pressing wnr 1f out: ev ch ins fnl f: drvn and a hld fnl 150yds* **4/1**[3]
233 **3** *2 1/4* **Marshall Aid (IRE)**[27] 1697 4-9-7 **65**..............................(p) KieranO'Neill 8 68
(Mark Usher) *in tch in midfield: effrt on outer over 3f out: rdn to press wnr ent fnl 2f: unable qck over 1f out: 3rd and kpt on same pce ins fnl f* **8/1**
32-4 **4** *2 3/4* **The Juggler**[25] 1754 4-8-9 **53**.............................................. JimmyQuinn 2 52
(William Knight) *taken down early: led: sn hdd and chsd ldng pair: wnt 2nd briefly wl over 2f out: sn rdn: 4th and unable qck over 1f out: wl hld and kpt on same pce ins fnl f* **5/1**
4433 **5** *3 1/4* **Wordiness**[17] 1935 9-9-6 **64**........................................ SilvestreDeSousa 3 58
(David Evans) *stdd and short of room leaving stalls: hld up in rr: effrt over 2f out: nt clr run on inner over 1f out: sn swtchd rt: no ch w ldrs and kpt on same pce ins fnl f* **7/2**[2]
0305 **6** *3 3/4* **Yasir (USA)**[9] 2163 9-8-12 **63**............................... KatherineGlenister(7) 6 52
(Conor Dore) *sn dropped to rr and hld up in rr: sme hdwy 4f out: effrt and rdn wl over 1f out: sn outpcd and btn: wknd fnl f* **16/1**
040- **7** *1/2* **Astrosecret**[222] 6886 4-8-13 **64**..................................... GabrieleMalune(7) 7 52
(Mark H Tompkins) *hld up in tch: effrt over 2f out: no imp and hung lft u.p over 1f out: wknd fnl f* **25/1**
4536 **8** *11* **Oyster Card**[20] 1870 4-8-7 **51** oh6....................................(p) LukeMorris 5 23
(Michael Appleby) *chsd wnr: shkn up 6f out: rdn over 4f out: struggling u.p and lost pl wl over 2f out: bhd and eased ins fnl f* **20/1**

2m 51.64s (-1.96) **Going Correction** -0.15s/f (Stan) **8** Ran SP% **117.8**
Speed ratings (Par 101): **100,99,98,96,94 92,92,85**
CSF £10.60 CT £52.98 TOTE £2.70: £1.30, £1.60, £2.20; EX 11.70 Trifecta £55.20.
**Owner** Lloyd Martell **Bred** Kabansk Ltd & Rathbarry Stud **Trained** Scamblesby, Lincs

**FOCUS**
A weak staying handicap, in which the favourite landed some tidy bets on his return from a 971-day break. The second and third help set a straightforward level.

## 2461 BET TOTEQUADPOT AT TOTESPORT.COM H'CAP 1m 6f (P)
**6:40** (6:40) (Class 3) (0-90,87) 4-Y-O+ **£7,623** (£2,398; £1,290) **Stalls** Low

Form RPR
311- **1** **Cartwright**[221] 6906 4-9-9 **87**...................................................(p) LukeMorris 4 101
(Sir Mark Prescott Bt) *mde all: qcknd gallop 6f out: clr and shkn up 2f out: in n.d after: eased wl ins fnl f: easily: unchal* **3/1**[2]
41-4 **2** *8* **Velvet Revolution**[23] 1798 4-9-7 **85**.................................. MartinHarley 1 87
(Marco Botti) *trckd wnr: rdn and clsd on ldr but hung rt 3f out: stl hanging and struggling 2f out: wl hld and drifted bk lft 1f out* **1/1**[1]
4546 **3** *8* **Dakota City**[14] 2042 6-8-4 **70**.......................................(b[1]) ShelleyBirkett(3) 2 61
(Julia Feilden) *lft 3rd after 1f: rdn over 3f out: sn struggling: wl btn 2f out* **12/1**[3]
1-12 **P** **Lost The Moon**[65] 1027 4-8-8 **79**................................ GabrieleMalune(7) 3
(Mark H Tompkins) *stmbld bdly leaving stalls and rdr lost off side iron: kicked foot out of nr side iron sn after and p.u after 1f* **3/1**[2]

3m 0.43s (-2.77) **Going Correction** -0.15s/f (Stan) **4** Ran SP% **107.7**
Speed ratings (Par 107): **101,96,91,**
CSF £6.45 TOTE £3.50; EX 4.50 Trifecta £17.40.
**Owner** Exors Of The Late J L C Pearce **Bred** Meon Valley Stud **Trained** Newmarket, Suffolk

**FOCUS**
A disappointing turnout numerically for this staying handicap, though it featured a hugely progressive winner. Hard form to gauge.

## 2462 BET TOTEEXACTA AT TOTESPORT.COM H'CAP 6f (P)
**7:10** (7:10) (Class 4) (0-85,85) 4-Y-O+ **£6,469** (£1,925; £962; £481) **Stalls** Centre

Form RPR
4366 **1** **Plucky Dip**[11] 2113 6-9-0 **78**................................................. JimCrowley 7 85
(John Ryan) *stdd s and sn dropped in: hld up in rr: effrt on inner over 1f out: styd on wl to chal wl ins fnl f: led towards fin* **8/1**
2351 **2** *hd* **Dark Side Dream**[16] 1980 5-8-9 **73**............................ SilvestreDeSousa 2 79
(Chris Dwyer) *chsd ldr: effrt ent fnl 2f: drvn over 1f out: kpt on u.p and ev ch wl ins fnl f: wnt 2nd again last strides* **11/4**[1]
2210 **3** *hd* **Fredricka**[17] 1936 6-8-13 **77**...............................................(v) RenatoSouza 1 82
(Jose Santos) *t.k.h: trckd ldrs: effrt over 1f out: drvn ent fnl f: wnt 2nd ins fnl f and ev ch fnl 75yds: kpt on u.p but lost 2nd last strides* **10/1**
1103 **4** *nk* **Fujin**[11] 2114 6-9-2 **85**..................................................(v) CharlieBennett(5) 3 89
(Shaun Harris) *led and crossed to inner: c centre and rdn wl over 1f out: edgd rt ent fnl f: hdd and no ex towards fin* **9/2**[2]
0-43 **5** *1 3/4* **Parkour (IRE)**[45] 1346 4-9-1 **79**...........................................(b) LukeMorris 5 78
(Marco Botti) *stdd s: hld up in tch: effrt over 1f out: rdn ent fnl f: kpt on same pce ins fnl f* **7/1**
4-20 **6** *3/4* **Mutamid**[24] 1778 5-9-5 **83**.................................................. TomMarquand 4 79
(Ismail Mohammed) *in tch in midfield: shkn up 3f out: rdn over 1f out: kpt on same pce and no imp ins fnl f* **9/2**[2]
1211 **7** *4 1/2* **Treaty Of Rome (USA)**[22] 1820 5-8-11 **75**..................(v) TonyHamilton 6 57
(Derek Shaw) *t.k.h: hld up in tch in midfield but stuck wd: effrt ent fnl 2f: lost pl and bhd over 1f out: wknd fnl f* **5/1**[3]

1m 11.74s (-1.96) **Going Correction** -0.15s/f (Stan) **7** Ran SP% **112.4**
Speed ratings (Par 105): **107,106,106,106,103 102,96**
CSF £29.22 TOTE £10.50: £4.30, £2.10; EX 36.50 Trifecta £273.80.
**Owner** Byron, Lavallin & Donnison **Bred** Cheveley Park Stud Ltd **Trained** Newmarket, Suffolk

**FOCUS**
Three of these had won their last AW start, so this should be reliable form. It was sound run.

## 2463 TOTEPOOL BETTING AT TOTESPORT.COM MAIDEN FILLIES' STKS 7f (P)
**7:40** (7:41) (Class 4) 3-Y-O+ **£5,822** (£1,732; £865; £432) **Stalls** Low

Form RPR
2 **1** **Alnaas**[17] 1948 3-9-0 0........................................................(t) JimCrowley 5 81+
(John Gosden) *sn led and mde rest: rdn over 1f out: fnd ex and asserted 1f out: in command and kpt on wl under hands and heels riding ins fnl f* **10/11**[1]

52-3 **2** *1 1/2* **Isabel's On It**[18] 1905 3-9-0 77 PatCosgrave 1 77+
(William Haggas) *trckd ldrs: nt clr run and trying to switch rt fr wl over 1f out: eventually got out and rdn 150yds: styd on under to chse wnr wl ins fnl f: no threat to wnr* **7/4**[2]

**3** *1 1/4* **Karijini (GER)** 3-9-0 0 SilvestreDeSousa 3 71
(Simon Crisford) *chsd ldr: rdn and ev ch ent fnl 2f: unable qck w wnr 1f out: kpt on same pce and lost 2nd towards fin* **14/1**

3 **4** *3* **Omneeya**[17] 1947 3-9-0 0 TomMarquand 4 63
(Marco Botti) *chsd ldng trio: effrt to press ldrs u.p over 1f out: no ex whn nudged rt 150yds out: wknd fnl 100yds* **5/1**[3]

00- **5** *10* **Cool Breeze (IRE)**[237] 6454 3-8-9 0 SophieKilloran(5) 2 36
(David Simcock) *stdd s: t.k.h: hld up in 5th: pushed along ent fnl 2f: sn outpcd and wl btn 1f out* **100/1**

60 **6** *3 1/4* **Clever Lady (IRE)**[12] 2090 3-8-7 0 KatherineGlenister(7) 7 27
(David Evans) *stdd and awkward leaving stalls: hld up in last trio: pushed along over 2f out: sn outpcd and wl btn over 1f out* **100/1**

3/0 **7** *2* **Flower Cup**[21] 1837 4-9-12 0 (h) IrineuGoncalves 6 25
(Chris Dwyer) *stdd s: hld up in detached last: struggling over 2f out: swtchd rt over 1f out: n.d* **100/1**

1m 24.9s (-2.30) **Going Correction** -0.15s/f (Stan)
**WFA** 3 from 4yo 12lb **7** Ran SP% **115.1**
Speed ratings (Par 102): **107,105,103,100,89 85,83**
CSF £2.79 TOTE £1.90: £1.20, £1.30; EX 3.40 Trifecta £10.70.
**Owner** Hamdan Al Maktoum **Bred** Shadwell Estate Company Limited **Trained** Newmarket, Suffolk

**FOCUS**
A fair fillies' maiden, in which the favourite set the standard judged on last month's Newbury second. She's rated similar to her debut effort.

## 2464 TOTEPOOL BETTING ON ALL UK RACING H'CAP 7f (P)

**8:10** (8:16) (Class 5) (0-70,75) 4-Y-0+ **£5,175** (£1,540; £769; £384) **Stalls** Low

Form RPR

-023 **1** **Lucymai**[88] 641 4-9-3 **66** RobertWinston 9 74
(Dean Ivory) *chsd ldng trio: effrt over 1f out: hdwy u.p ins fnl f: styd on strly to ld fnl 50yds* **6/1**[3]

3131 **2** *1* **Tavener**[3] 2377 5-9-5 **75** 6ex (p) FinleyMarsh(7) 2 80
(David C Griffiths) *t.k.h: led: rdn over 1f out: drvn ins fnl f: hdd and no ex 50yds out* **4/1**[2]

0402 **3** *3/4* **Miss Goldsmith (IRE)**[21] 1842 4-8-12 **61** (h) TonyHamilton 8 64
(Richard Fahey) *t.k.h: hld up in tch in midfield: effrt over 1f out: edgd lft u.p 1f out: hdwy ins fnl f: kpt on wl to go 3rd cl home* **14/1**

2610 **4** *1/2* **Hipz (IRE)**[20] 1868 6-9-2 **65** (p) IrineuGoncalves 6 67
(Ivan Furtado) *t.k.h: chsd ldr: effrt over 1f out: ev ch ins fnl f: stl ev ch but looking hld whn squeezed for room 50yds: no ex and lost 3rd cl home* **14/1**

2015 **5** *nse* **Foie Gras**[19] 1893 7-9-7 **70** (p) SilvestreDeSousa 4 71
(Chris Dwyer) *hld up in tch in midfield: effrt and awkward hd carriage bnd 2f out: swtchd lft over 1f out: hdwy u.p ins fnl f: styd on wl: nt rch ldrs* **7/1**

0006 **6** *1/2* **Newstead Abbey**[19] 1890 7-9-7 **70** JimCrowley 3 70
(Michael Herrington) *chsd ldrs: effrt over 1f out: pressing ldrs u.p 1f out: kpt on same pce ins fnl f* **15/8**[1]

6322 **7** *1* **East Coast Lady (IRE)**[37] 1489 5-9-3 **69** HollieDoyle(3) 1 66
(William Stone) *s.i.s: toook t.k.h: hld up in last pair: effrt over 1f out: kpt on u.p ins fnl f: nvr threatened ldrs* **6/1**[3]

03-0 **8** *2 3/4* **The Firm (IRE)**[25] 1755 8-8-13 **62** JimmyQuinn 7 52
(J R Jenkins) *stdd s: hld up in last pair: pushed along over 1f out: kpt on same pce and no imp under hands and heels riding ins fnl f* **66/1**

4-05 **9** *1* **Torment**[18] 1898 4-9-4 **67** WilliamCarson 10 54
(Charlie Wallis) *stdd s: in tch in last trio: rdn over 2f out: no imp: wl hld and kpt on same pce fr over 1f out* **12/1**

1m 25.54s (-1.66) **Going Correction** -0.15s/f (Stan) **9** Ran SP% **118.4**
Speed ratings (Par 103): **103,101,101,100,100 99,98,95,94**
CSF £28.38 CT £250.39 TOTE £7.50: £2.20, £1.50, £2.90; EX 33.60 Trifecta £310.10.
**Owner** Roger S Beadle **Bred** Richard Kent **Trained** Radlett, Herts

**FOCUS**
A strongly run and competitive handicap. The winner was close to her best and the second better than ever, taking into account the rider's claim.

## 2465 SHIRES PLAY HERE ON 7TH JULY H'CAP 1m (P)

**8:40** (8:48) (Class 6) (0-65,65) 4-Y-0+ **£3,234** (£962; £481; £240) **Stalls** Low

Form RPR

6563 **1** **Hold Firm**[6] 2257 5-8-8 **59** GabrieleMalune(7) 1 65
(Mark H Tompkins) *hld up in 4th: effrt to chse ldng pair and edging lft over 1f out: hdwy to chse wnr and clsng ent fnl f: led 100yds out: rdn out* **10/3**[2]

4430 **2** *1 1/4* **Greyfriarschorista**[39] 1449 10-8-9 **60** (vt) KatherineGlenister(7) 8 63
(David Evans) *bustled up to ld and sn clr: shkn up ent fnl 2f: rdn over 1f out: hdd and no ex fnl 100yds* **20/1**

2022 **3** *hd* **Mowhoob**[37] 1484 7-8-8 **52** LukeMorris 3 55
(Brian Barr) *s.i.s: hld up in last pair: effrt over 2f out: hdwy u.p ent fnl f: kpt on wl and pressing for 2nd towards fin: nvr getting to wnr* **5/1**[3]

2534 **4** *3 1/4* **Freddy With A Y (IRE)**[45] 1338 7-9-5 **63** JimmyQuinn 5 58
(J R Jenkins) *hld up in midfield: shkn up wl over 1f out: sme hdwy jst over 1f out: 4th and kpt on same pce ins fnl f* **7/1**

0230 **5** *3 1/2* **Pool House**[37] 1484 6-8-13 **57** (b) RobertWinston 4 44
(Mike Murphy) *hld up in last pair: effrt u.p over 1f out: no imp and wl hld fnl f* **7/1**

0-50 **6** *2 1/2* **Win Lose Draw (IRE)**[97] 501 5-9-4 **62** (p) SilvestreDeSousa 6 43
(Michael Appleby) *chsd ldng pair: pushed along to chse clr ldr 3f out: no imp u.p over 1f out: wknd fnl f* **7/4**[1]

4006 **7** *3/4* **Stun Gun**[5] 2318 7-9-4 **62** (p) TonyHamilton 2 42
(Derek Shaw) *chsd clr ldr tl 3 out: rdn lost pl over 1f out: bhd ins fnl f* **10/1**

1m 38.55s (-1.35) **Going Correction** -0.15s/f (Stan) **7** Ran SP% **115.0**
Speed ratings (Par 101): **100,98,98,95,91 89,88**
CSF £61.95 CT £330.33 TOTE £4.40: £2.30, £5.60; EX 76.80 Trifecta £250.70.
**Owner** Raceworld **Bred** Richard W Farleigh **Trained** Newmarket, Suffolk

■ Kafoo was withdrawn. Price at time of withdrawal 5-1. Rule 4 applies bets placed prior to withdrawal, but not to SP bet - deduction 15p in the pound.

**FOCUS**
This was strongly run and few got involved. A small step up from the winner on recent efforts.
T/Plt: £73.30 to a £1 stake. Pool: £43,166.00 - 588.89 winning units T/Qpdt: £26.60 to a £1 stake. Pool: £2,930.00 - 109.92 winning units **Steve Payne**

# 1864 SOUTHWELL (L-H)

Monday, May 8

**OFFICIAL GOING: Fibresand: standard**
Wind: Strong across Weather: Overcast

## 2466 BLOOMFIELDS HORSEBOXES H'CAP 1m 13y(F)

**2:10** (2:11) (Class 5) (0-75,75) 4-Y-0+ **£2,911** (£866; £432; £216) **Stalls** Low

Form RPR

5123 **1** **Alpha Tauri (USA)**[76] 850 11-9-1 **74** LewisEdmunds(5) 9 83
(Charles Smith) *qckly away and sn slt ld: rdn clr over 2f out: rdn over 1f out: styd on strly* **6/1**[3]

1420 **2** *4 1/2* **Muqarred (USA)**[27] 1700 5-9-7 **75** (p) TonyHamilton 2 74
(Roger Fell) *cl up: pushed along 3f out: rdn over 2f out: drvn wl over 1f out: kpt on* **6/1**[3]

-326 **3** *2* **Secret Glance**[26] 1718 5-8-6 **63** HollieDoyle(3) 3 57
(Adrian Wintle) *rr and rdn along after 3f: swtchd rt over 3f out: hdwy on wd outside home turn: sn rdn: chsd ldrs and edgd lft ent fnl f: sn drvn and kpt on same pce* **11/2**[2]

3602 **4** *1/2* **Warfare**[54] 1201 8-9-5 **73** BarryMcHugh 1 66
(Tim Fitzgerald) *trckd ldrs: pushed along over 3f out: sn rdn and sltly outpcd: kpt on u.p fr wl over 1f out* **20/1**

3650 **5** *1 3/4* **Boots And Spurs**[9] 2133 8-9-0 **68** (v) DavidAllan 4 57
(Scott Dixon) *towards rr: pushed along 3f out: rdn and hdwy 2f out: sn drvn and no imp* **11/2**[2]

1040 **6** *3/4* **Shearian**[14] 2030 7-9-0 **73** PhilDennis(5) 7 60
(Declan Carroll) *in tch: hdwy to chse ldrs over 3f out: rdn to chse wnr over 2f out: drvn wl over 1f out and sn one pce* **10/1**

12-0 **7** *9* **Eium Mac**[20] 1868 8-8-7 **61** oh8 (b) JoeDoyle 8 27
(Neville Bycroft) *dwlt: sn chsng ldrs on outer: cl up over 5f out: rdn along 3f out: sn wknd* **12/1**

-224 **8** *2 1/4* **Swansway**[19] 1893 4-8-9 **66** NathanEvans(3) 6 27
(Michael Easterby) *hld up: effrt and sme hdwy wl over 3f out: sn rdn along and outpcd fnl 2f* **4/1**[1]

0-05 **9** *8* **Mr Cool Cash**[6] 2276 5-8-10 **64** ConnorBeasley 5 7
(Richard Guest) *chsd ldrs: rdn along over 3f out: sn drvn and wknd* **8/1**

1m 45.1s (1.40) **Going Correction** +0.25s/f (Slow) **9** Ran SP% **112.0**
Speed ratings (Par 103): **103,98,96,96,94 93,84,82,74**
CSF £40.06 CT £208.35 TOTE £5.60: £1.80, £2.20, £1.60; EX 35.70 Trifecta £128.80.
**Owner** J R Theaker **Bred** Flaxman Holdings Ltd **Trained** Temple Bruer, Lincs

**FOCUS**
A fair handicap. They went a respectable gallop and a course specialist won readily. The winning time suggests the track was riding on the slow side. The winner is rated back to his old best.

## 2467 BOOKIES.COM FREE BETS MAIDEN STKS 1m 13y(F)

**2:40** (2:41) (Class 5) 3-Y-0+ **£2,911** (£866; £432; £216) **Stalls** Low

Form RPR

3 **1** **Mark Of Approval (USA)**[20] 1857 3-9-1 0 JamesDoyle 7 91+
(John Gosden) *dwlt and racd wd: in tch: hdwy and cl up 1/2-way: led jst over 3f out: sn jnd and rdn along wl over 2f out: styd on wl appr fnl f: readily* **1/9**[1]

**2** *5* **Maratha (IRE)** 3-9-1 0 (v1) SilvestreDeSousa 1 77
(Simon Crisford) *trckd ldrs on inner: hdwy jst over 3f out and sn chal: disp ld wl over 2f out: sn rdn and ev ch tl edgd lft jst over 1f out and kpt on same pce* **4/1**[2]

66 **3** *17* **Albert's Back**[22] 1818 3-8-12 0 NathanEvans(3) 6 37
(Michael Easterby) *rr: wd st and sn rdn: swtchd rt to stands rail and drvn wl over 1f out: plugged on to take remote 3rd nr fin* **14/1**[3]

50- **4** *1/2* **Jethro (IRE)**[15] 2260 6-9-7 0 BenRobinson(7) 2 39
(Brian Ellison) *towards rr: hdwy to chse ldrs over 3f out: rdn along wl over 2f out: sn wknd* **40/1**

06/ **5** *nse* **Mesti Boleh**[683] 3567 6-9-11 0 HollieDoyle(3) 4 39
(Michael Scudamore) *cl up: pushed along 1/2-way: wknd over 3f out* **100/1**

60- **6** *13* **Austerity (IRE)**[356] 2349 4-10-0 0 NeilFarley 3 9
(Alan Swinbank) *led: rdn along over 3f out: sn hdd and grad wknd* **33/1**

0 **7** *1 1/2* **Tawfeer**[19] 1889 3-9-1 0 RyanPowell 5 3
(James Unett) *chsd ldrs: rdn along wl over 3f out: sn outpcd* **125/1**

1m 44.23s (0.53) **Going Correction** +0.25s/f (Slow)
**WFA** 3 from 4yo+ 13lb **7** Ran SP% **123.8**
Speed ratings (Par 103): **107,102,85,84,84 71,69**
CSF £1.43 TOTE £1.10: £1.10, £1.50; EX 1.90 Trifecta £4.00.
**Owner** Godolphin **Bred** Keithshire Farm **Trained** Newmarket, Suffolk

**FOCUS**
A thoroughly uncompetitive maiden. They went a respectable gallop and the long odds-on winner came clear of the second favourite from over 1f out. The rest showed bery little.

## 2468 BOOKMAKERS.CO.UK FREE BETS MEDIAN AUCTION MAIDEN STKS 1m 3f 23y(F)

**3:10** (3:10) (Class 5) 3-5-Y-0 **£3,881** (£1,155; £577; £288) **Stalls** Low

Form RPR

2-24 **1** **Pealer (GER)**[18] 1906 3-8-11 83 (t) JamesDoyle 5 88
(John Gosden) *sn led: pushed clr 3f out: cruised home: unchal* **2/7**[1]

00- **2** *19* **Meyandi**[187] 7769 3-8-11 0 LiamKeniry 3 56
(Andrew Balding) *prom: chsd wnr after 2f: pushed along 4f out: rdn over 3f out: plugged on one pce* **7/2**[2]

**3** *29* **Bishop Of Bling (IRE)**[117] 6863 4-10-0 0 LouisSteward 2 7
(Chris Wall) *chsd wnr 2f: prom on inner: rdn along over 5f out: sn wknd and bhd fnl 3f* **5/1**[3]

0 **4** *42* **Cecilator**[17] 1944 3-8-6 0 NeilFarley 1
(Noel Williams) *a rr: outpcd and bhd fr 4f out* **80/1**

660- **P** **Alidara (IRE)**[194] 7627 5-9-9 35 (h) TonyHamilton 4
(Emma Owen) *rr: pushed along after 4f: sn outpcd and bhd 5f out: t.o and p.u 3f: dismntd* **100/1**

2m 28.35s (0.35) **Going Correction** +0.25s/f (Slow)
**WFA** 3 from 4yo+ 17lb **5** Ran SP% **118.9**
Speed ratings (Par 103): **108,94,73,42,**
CSF £2.11 TOTE £1.20: £1.10, £1.70; EX 2.00 Trifecta £2.80.
**Owner** Emma Capon, A Lloyd Webber & Rachel Hood **Bred** Stiftung Gestut Fahrhof **Trained** Newmarket, Suffolk

**FOCUS**
The feature contest was a thoroughly uncompetitive middle-distance maiden. They went a respectable gallop and the odds-on favourite came well clear of the second favourite in the straight. The winner is given a bit of credit despite doubts over what he beat.

## 2469 MANSFIELD SAND H'CAP 6f 16y(F)
**3:40** (3:41) (Class 5) (0-70,71) 4-Y-O+ **£2,911** (£866; £432; £216) **Stalls** Low

Form RPR
41-0 **1** **Tricky Dicky**[21] 1833 4-9-4 **67** .......... DuranFentiman 6 78
(Olly Williams) *mde virtually all: rdn wl over 1f out: drvn ins fnl f: kpt on strly towards fin* **8/1**
3323 **2** *2* **Captain Bob (IRE)**[13] 2058 6-8-13 **67** ..........(p) CallumRodriguez(5) 5 72
(Robert Cowell) *trckd ldrs: hdwy 3f out: effrt to chal wl over 1f out: sn rdn and edgd lft: drvn ins fnl f: kpt on same pce* **9/4**[1]
2504 **3** *1 ¼* **Monsieur Jimmy**[20] 1868 5-8-9 **58** .......... BarryMcHugh 9 59
(Declan Carroll) *rr on outer: wd st: hdwy over 2f out:: rdn and edgd lft over 1f out: kpt on u.p fnl f* **7/1**[3]
0625 **4** *1* **All Or Nothin (IRE)**[16] 1979 8-8-0 **56** oh3 .......... DavidEgan(7) 7 54
(Paddy Butler) *cl up: pushed along 3f out: rdn over 2f out: drvn over 1f out: grad wknd* **20/1**
0162 **5** *½* **Jacob's Pillow**[20] 1869 6-8-10 **66** ..........(p) BenRobinson(7) 3 62
(Rebecca Bastiman) *cl up on inner: disp ld over 2f out: sn rdn and ev ch: drvn and wknd over 1f out* **12/1**
1430 **6** *4 ½* **Big Amigo (IRE)**[13] 2064 4-9-8 **71** .......... AndrewMullen 1 53
(Daniel Mark Loughnane) *towards rr: effrt on inner and sme hdwy over 2f out: sn rdn and n.d* **10/1**
1442 **7** *shd* **Viva Verglas (IRE)**[7] 2229 6-9-0 **70** .......... TobyEley(7) 4 51
(Daniel Mark Loughnane) *dwlt: a towards rr* **10/3**[2]
3400 **8** *7* **Elusivity (IRE)**[9] 2161 9-9-7 **70** ..........(p) RobertWinston 2 29
(Conor Dore) *chsd ldrs on inner: rdn along wl over 2rf out: sn drvn and wknd* **20/1**
3661 **9** *nk* **Fortinbrass (IRE)**[22] 1823 7-8-8 **62** .......... LewisEdmunds(5) 8 20
(John Balding) *in tch: rdn along 1/2-way: sn drvn and wknd fnl 2f* **8/1**
1m 17.45s (0.95) **Going Correction** +0.25s/f (Slow) **9** Ran SP% **114.9**
Speed ratings (Par 103): **103,100,98,97,96 90,90,81,80**
CSF £26.21 CT £133.17 TOTE £10.50: £2.80, £1.10, £2.80; EX 33.90 Trifecta £235.30.
**Owner** Eight Gents and a Lady **Bred** Onslow, Stratton & Parry **Trained** Market Rasen, Lincs
**FOCUS**
A modest handicap. They went a respectable gallop and an AW newcomer took to the Fibresand like a duck to water. He recorded a clear pb.

## 2470 HILLTOP EQUESTRIAN CENTRE AVAILABLE TO RENT H'CAP 7f 14y(F)
**4:10** (4:10) (Class 6) (0-60,64) 3-Y-O **£2,264** (£673; £336; £168) **Stalls** Low

Form RPR
3054 **1** **Mimic's Memory**[8] 2182 3-9-4 **57** .......... ShaneGray 5 63
(Ann Duffield) *prom: cl up 2f out: rdn wl over 1f out: led ent fnl f: sn drvn and kpt on wl towards fin* **10/1**
63-5 **2** *¾* **Eponina (IRE)**[54] 1199 3-9-9 **62** .......... CamHardie 6 66
(Ben Haslam) *towards rr: hdwy on outer 2f out: rdn to chse ldrs over 1f out: chal ins fnl f: sn drvn and ev ch tl no ex towards fin* **20/1**
000- **3** *2* **Treagus**[179] 7883 3-9-7 **60** .......... JosephineGordon 2 59
(Charlie Fellowes) *cl up: led 3f out: rdn along over 2f out: hdd over 1f out: kpt on u.p fnl f* **9/4**[2]
0000 **4** *1 ½* **Red Shanghai (IRE)**[12] 2078 3-8-4 **46** oh1 .......... NoelGarbutt(3) 1 41
(Charles Smith) *in tch: hdwy on inner 3f out: sn chsng ldrs: rdn 2f out: led briefly over 1f out: sn hdd & wknd ins fnl f* **100/1**
6-30 **5** *½* **Tea El Tee (IRE)**[28] 1688 3-8-6 **52** .......... DavidEgan(7) 7 45
(Gay Kelleway) *in tch: hdwy on outer 3f out: chsd ldrs 2f out: rdn wl over 1f out: drvn and one pce fnl f* **7/1**[3]
5-01 **6** *3 ½* **Cryptonite (IRE)**[5] 2309 3-9-8 **64** 6ex .......... AlistairRawlinson(3) 3 48
(Michael Appleby) *t.k.h: trckd ldrs: effrt wl over 2f out: rdn wl over 1f out: sn drvn and btn* **5/4**[1]
444- **7** *14* **Smiley Riley (IRE)**[252] 5974 3-9-3 **56** .......... DuranFentiman 8
(Tony Coyle) *chsd ldrs on outer: rdn along 3f out: sn wknd* **25/1**
300- **8** *5* **Nellie's Dancer**[179] 7891 3-9-8 **61** .......... DavidAllan 4
(Scott Dixon) *led: rdn along and hdd 3f out: sn wknd* **16/1**
66-0 **9** *4* **Born To Boogie**[59] 1123 3-8-7 **46** oh1 .......... AndrewMullen 9
(Chris Grant) *dwlt: a rr* **20/1**
1m 33.46s (3.16) **Going Correction** +0.25s/f (Slow) **9** Ran SP% **117.0**
Speed ratings (Par 97): **91,90,87,86,85 81,65,59,55**
CSF £183.53 CT £612.35 TOTE £10.40: £2.90, £4.80, £1.40; EX 115.20 Trifecta £1059.70.
**Owner** Peter Wilson & Partner **Bred** Llety Farms **Trained** Constable Burton, N Yorks
**FOCUS**
A modest 3yo handicap and these young horses found it tough on the slow-running Fibresand, with the first wave of pace collapsing to a degree. The fourth seemingly highlights the limitations of the form.

## 2471 BOOKIES.COM FREE BETS H'CAP 1m 4f 14y(F)
**4:40** (4:40) (Class 5) (0-70,72) 4-Y-O+ **£2,911** (£866; £432; £216) **Stalls** Low

Form RPR
3635 **1** **The Lock Master (IRE)**[8] 2183 10-9-3 **69** .........(p) AlistairRawlinson(3) 3 77
(Michael Appleby) *in tch: hdwy 1/2-way: led 4f out: rdn clr wl over 2f out: drvn over 1f out: kpt on wl towards fin* **5/1**
/4-2 **2** *1 ¼* **Serenity Now (IRE)**[67] 526 9-9-2 **72** .......... BenRobinson(7) 4 78
(Brian Ellison) *hld up in rr: hdwy 5f out: chsd wnr wl over 2f out: rdn and ch whn edgd lft wl over 1f out: drvn and edgd lft again ent fnl f: no imp towards fin* **4/1**[2]
4-13 **3** *7* **Deep Resolve (IRE)**[36] 1519 6-9-7 **70** .......... RobertWinston 2 65
(Alan Swinbank) *hld up in tch: hdwy 4f out: chsd ldng pair 3f out: sn rdn: drvn over 2f out: sn one pce* **2/1**[1]
5500 **4** *8* **Alshan Fajer**[14] 2022 7-8-9 **65** .......... GinaMangan(7) 1 47
(J R Jenkins) *hld up in rr: sme hdwy over 3f out: sn rdn along: plodded on fnl 2f* **33/1**
3-43 **5** *nk* **Vercingetorix (IRE)**[25] 325 6-9-7 **70** ..........(b) DavidNolan 8 52
(Harriet Bethell) *cl up: led over 5f out: rdn along 4f out: wknd over 3f out* **12/1**
40-6 **6** *9* **Patent**[60] 1101 4-8-9 **58** ..........(be[1]) AndrewMullen 5 25
(Peter Niven) *chsd ldrs: rdn along 3f out: sn drvn and wknd* **12/1**
013/ **7** *13* **Rolling Dice**[833] 7514 6-9-7 **70** .......... LiamKeniry 7 16
(Dominic Ffrench Davis) *cl up: rdn along 4f out: sn wknd* **10/1**
5213 **8** *38* **What Usain**[19] 1892 5-9-8 **71** ..........(h) LiamJones 6
(Michael Appleby) *set str gallop: rdn along and hdd over 5f out: wknd qckly and sn bhd* **9/2**[3]
2m 45.3s (4.30) **Going Correction** +0.25s/f (Slow) **8** Ran SP% **115.6**
Speed ratings (Par 103): **95,94,89,84,83 77,69,43**
CSF £25.61 CT £52.59 TOTE £6.50: £2.10, £1.60, £1.30; EX 26.90 Trifecta £61.40.
**Owner** K G Kitchen **Bred** Patrick F Kelly **Trained** Oakham, Rutland

**FOCUS**
An ordinary middle-distance handicap. They went a muddling gallop, strong initially and then a more conservative pace down the back, but the right three horses still came to the fore. The winner's best effort since last spring.

## 2472 COMPARE HORSE RACING ODDS @ BOOKIES.COM H'CAP 4f 214y(F)
**5:10** (5:11) (Class 6) (0-55,55) 4-Y-O+ **£2,264** (£673; £336; £168) **Stalls** Centre

Form RPR
0040 **1** **Llewellyn**[12] 2082 9-9-2 **55** ..........(v) PhilDennis(5) 5 65
(Declan Carroll) *cl up centre: rdn to ld appr fnl f: drvn out* **4/1**[2]
0-36 **2** *2 ¼* **Kodimoor (IRE)**[84] 722 4-8-9 **50** ..........(bt) DavidEgan(7) 7 52
(Christopher Kellett) *racd centre: in tch: rdn along over 2f out: hdwy over 1f out:. drvn and styd on wl fnl f* **9/2**[3]
0-61 **3** *shd* **Sir Geoffrey (IRE)**[5] 2298 11-9-2 **55** 6ex ..........(b) PaddyPilley(5) 6 57
(Scott Dixon) *racd towards stands side: slt ld: rdn along 2f out: hdd appr fnl f: sn drvn and edgd rt: kpt on same pce* **3/1**[1]
00-6 **4** *nse* **Excellent World (IRE)**[16] 1977 4-9-5 **53** .......... BarryMcHugh 8 54+
(Tony Coyle) *racd towards stands side: sn rdn along and wl outpcd in rr: rdn along and bhd 1/2-way: gd hdwy over 1f out: styng on whn swtchd lft ins fnl f: kpt on strly towards fin* **12/1**
-006 **5** *2 ¾* **Toni's A Star**[41] 1413 5-9-1 **54** ..........(b) GeorgiaCox(5) 4 45
(Tony Carroll) *racd towards far side: cl up: rdn along 2f out: ev ch tl drvn and wknd appr fnl f* **4/1**[2]
606 **6** *½* **Tartufo Classico**[9] 2139 4-8-9 **46** oh1 .......... NathanEvans(3) 3 36
(Derek Shaw) *racd towards far side: chsd ldrs: rdn along and outpcd 1/2-way: sme late hdwy* **25/1**
3266 **7** *7* **Red Flute**[39] 1452 5-8-12 **46** oh1 ..........(v) LiamKeniry 1 10
(Denis Quinn) *racd towards far side: prom: rdn over 2f out: sn drvn and wknd* **5/1**
000 **8** *2 ¼* **Slipalongtrevaskis**[34] 1543 4-8-5 **46** oh1 .......... GinaMangan(7) 2 2
(J R Jenkins) *racd towards far side: prom: rdn over 2f out: sn drvn and wknd* **20/1**
1m 1.0s (1.30) **Going Correction** +0.30s/f (Slow) **8** Ran SP% **116.1**
Speed ratings (Par 101): **101,97,97,97,92 91,80,77**
CSF £22.75 CT £61.11 TOTE £4.10: £1.30, £1.50, £1.60; EX 23.50 Trifecta £79.80.
**Owner** Mrs Sarah Bryan **Bred** Elite Racing Club **Trained** Malton, N Yorks
**FOCUS**
A moderate sprint handicap. They went a proper gallop and a previously decent 7f Fibresand performer won decisively right back in trip. The form could feasilby be rated 4lb better.
T/Plt: £16.70 to a £1 stake. Pool: £41,456.00 - 2,469.20 winning units T/Qpdt: £7.70 to a £1 stake. Pool: £2,582.00 - 333.89 winning units **Joe Rowntree**

# [2229]WINDSOR (R-H)
Monday, May 8

**OFFICIAL GOING: Good to firm (8.3)**
Wind: Almost nil Weather: Cloudy, chilly

## 2473 BRITISH STALLION STUDS EBF NOVICE STKS (PLUS 10 RACE) 5f 21y
**5:50** (5:51) (Class 4) 2-Y-O **£4,592** (£1,366; £683; £341) **Stalls** Low

Form RPR
43 **1** **Declarationoflove (IRE)**[13] 2052 2-9-2 0 .......... AndreaAtzeni 3 80
(Tom Clover) *chsd ldng pair: plld out over 2f out: clsd over 1f out: pushed firmly into the ld ins fnl f: styd on wl* **5/1**[3]
5 **2** *1 ¼* **Spoof**[17] 1941 2-9-2 0 .......... JamieSpencer 10 76
(Charles Hills) *racd wd: w ldr: led 2f out: rdn and hdd ins fnl f: one pce* **9/4**[1]
24 **3** *2 ½* **The Love Doctor (IRE)**[20] 1858 2-9-2 0 .......... JFEgan 4 67
(David Evans) *led against nr side rail: hdd 2f out: fdd fnl f but hld on for 3rd* **11/4**[2]
**4** *shd* **Dutch Stranger** 2-8-11 0 .......... DavidProbert 1 61
(Harry Dunlop) *chsd ldrs: prog into 4th wl over 1f out: kpt on fnl f to chal for 3rd nr fin* **28/1**
**5** *½* **Starboy (IRE)** 2-9-2 0 .......... OisinMurphy 2 64
(George Scott) *dwlt: wl off the pce in 8th: prog 2f out: rdn and styd on fnl f to press for 3rd nr fin* **8/1**
**6** *7* **Haven's View** 2-9-2 0 .......... ShaneKelly 9 39
(Richard Hughes) *dwlt: spd to chse ldrs to 1/2-way: sn wknd* **18/1**
**7** *2 ½* **Merchant Marine (IRE)** 2-9-2 0 .......... FranBerry 5 30
(Ralph Beckett) *dwlt: nvr beyond midfield and nvr on terms w ldrs: fdd 2f out* **15/2**
**8** *1 ¾* **Spring Romance (IRE)** 2-9-2 0 .......... AdamKirby 7 24
(Dean Ivory) *dwlt and s.i.s: mostly in last pair and a bhd* **20/1**
**9** *1* **Saria** 2-8-11 0 .......... RyanPowell 8 15
(Daniel Mark Loughnane) *dwlt: outpcd in last and rn green: a bhd* **50/1**
0 **10** *1 ¼* **Mullion Star**[28] 1681 2-9-2 0 .......... DanielMuscutt 6 16
(Michael Madgwick) *sn in midfield and nt on terms w ldrs: wknd 2f out* **250/1**
1m 0.62s (0.32) **Going Correction** +0.15s/f (Good) **10** Ran SP% **112.8**
Speed ratings (Par 95): **103,101,97,96,96 84,80,78,76,74**
CSF £15.62 TOTE £5.70: £2.00, £1.20, £1.10; EX 17.50 Trifecta £38.20.
**Owner** Ian Barratt, Stephen Short & Adam Signy **Bred** Liam Butler & Churchtown House Stud **Trained** Newmarket, Suffolk
■ Tom Clover's first winner.
**FOCUS**
Inner of straight was dolled out 14yds at 6f and 8yds at the winning line. Top bend was dolled out 6yds from normal inner configuration, adding 27yds to race distances of 1m+. Not much got involved in this opening novice race, but the first three had already shown a fair level of ability.

## 2474 ALFINI H'CAP 6f 12y
**6:20** (6:22) (Class 5) (0-70,70) 3-Y-O **£2,911** (£866; £432; £216) **Stalls** Low

Form RPR
-343 **1** **Hart Stopper**[19] 1888 3-9-7 **70** .......... JamieSpencer 12 81+
(Michael Bell) *awkward s: racd in last trio tl gd prog fr 2f out: racd sltly awkwardly but squeezed through to ld jst over 1f out: drvn out and styd on wl* **5/1**[1]
2132 **2** *1 ¼* **Delfie Lane**[28] 1685 3-9-6 **69** ..........(p) ShaneKelly 1 72
(Richard Hughes) *trckd ldng pair: waiting for a gap against nr side rail 2f out: swtchd lft wl over 1f out and sn clsd to chal: outpcd by wnr fnl f* **8/1**[3]
340- **3** *hd* **Inlawed**[244] 6213 3-9-3 **66** .......... RichardKingscote 7 68+
(Ed Walker) *hld up towards rr: prog nr side 2f out but wnr already overtaken him: r.o fnl f and nrly snatched 2nd* **15/2**[2]
45-2 **4** *¾* **Always Thankful**[27] 1705 3-9-6 **69** .......... SeanLevey 3 69
(Ismail Mohammed) *cl up bhd ldrs: rdn to chal and upsides over 1f out: one pce fnl f* **15/2**[2]

04-1 **5** ¾ **Daring Guest (IRE)**[65] 1024 3-8-12 **68**............................ JaneElliott[(7)] 4 65
(George Margarson) *t.k.h: chsd ldrs: rdn to cl over 1f out: one pce fnl f*
**10/1**

5014 **6** *nk* **Brother In Arms (IRE)**[32] 1580 3-9-2 **65**.................. GeorgeDowning 2 61
(Tony Carroll) *wl in tch in midfield: pushed along 2f out: nt qckn over 1f out: shkn up and kpt on fnl f*
**25/1**

0052 **7** 1 ¼ **Lightoller (IRE)**[3] 2362 3-8-13 **62**.................(b) CharlesBishop 13 54
(Mick Channon) *mde most to jst over 1f out: wknd*
**15/2**[2]

020- **8** *hd* **Herm (IRE)**[211] 7185 3-9-5 **68**.............................................. JFEgan 11 60
(David Evans) *hld up wl in rr: effrt on wd outside over 2f out: one pce and nvr rchd ldrs*
**12/1**

03-2 **9** 1 **Bahamian Paradise**[24] 1762 3-9-1 **64**........................... OisinMurphy 15 52
(Hughie Morrison) *hld up towards rr: nt clr run over 1f out: nt rcvr and no real prog after*
**8/1**[3]

0-00 **10** 1 ¼ **Bobby Vee**[33] 1554 3-9-2 **65**............................................ DaneO'Neill 6 49
(Dean Ivory) *w ldr to wl over 1f out: wknd*
**50/1**

641- **11** 2 **Odelouca (IRE)**[186] 7776 3-9-5 **68**................................. FranBerry 9 46
(Brendan Powell) *restrained after s and sn in last: pushed along and no prog 2f out: shkn up and plugged on fnl f: nvr involved*
**25/1**

**12** *nk* **Beast**[205] 7373 3-9-2 **65**............................................ AdamBeschizza 10 42
(Lee Carter) *c out of stalls slowest: a wl in rr: pushed along over 2f out: nvr involved*
**25/1**

-202 **13** ½ **Met By Moonlight**[28] 1688 3-9-2 **65**................................ DavidProbert 5 40
(Ron Hodges) *chsd ldrs: rdn and wknd qckly over 1f out*
**8/1**[3]

3-4P **14** ¾ **Three C's (IRE)**[24] 1761 3-9-7 **70**.............................(t[1]) TimmyMurphy 14 43
(David Dennis) *racd on outer: nvr bttr than midfield: wknd over 1f out* **66/1**

2-0 **15** 14 **Mad Rose (IRE)**[12] 2094 3-9-2 **70**.................................. GeorgeWood[(5)] 8
(Jonathan Portman) *chsd ldrs 2f: sn u.p and wknd: t.o*
**33/1**

1m 12.74s (-0.26) **Going Correction** +0.15s/f (Good) **15** Ran SP% **120.0**
Speed ratings (Par 99): **107,105,105,104,103 102,101,100,99,97 95,94,94,93,74**
CSF £40.44 CT £308.90 TOTE £4.00: £1.80, £2.90, £3.30; EX 36.40 Trifecta £609.80.
**Owner** Christopher Wright **Bred** Manor Farm Stud (rutland) **Trained** Newmarket, Suffolk

**FOCUS**
A competitive 3yo sprint handicap and it looked a fair race for the grade. Sound form, rated around the runner-up.

## 2475 ROYAL WINDSOR RACECOURSE MONDAY NIGHT RACING MAIDEN STKS 1m 31y

**6:50** (6:53) (Class 5) 3-Y-O **£2,911** (£866; £432; £216) **Stalls** Low

Form RPR

4 **1** **Rumpole**[16] 1961 3-9-5 0.................................................. AdamKirby 14 80
(Hughie Morrison) *led after 1f and mde rest: stretched on over 3f out: pushed along and wl in command over 1f out*
**10/3**[3]

63- **2** 2 **Daira Prince (IRE)**[187] 7769 3-9-5 0............................... AndreaAtzeni 10 75
(Roger Varian) *prom: chsd wnr after 3f: shkn up 2f out: no imp fr over 1f out: kpt on*
**7/4**[1]

**3** 1 ¼ **Noble Conquest (FR)** 3-9-5 0...................................(h[1]) OisinMurphy 6 72+
(Sir Michael Stoute) *sn in midfield: pushed along and prog 3f out: disp 2nd 2f out: shkn up briefly over 1f out: no imp on wnr*
**3/1**[2]

**4** 2 ½ **Near Kettering** 3-9-5 0................................................. JamieSpencer 11 66
(Luca Cumani) *rn green but chsd ldrs: shkn up wl over 2f out: rchd 4th wl over 1f out but no imp on ldrs after*
**14/1**

0- **5** 2 **Red Emperor (IRE)**[227] 6750 3-9-5 0........................ RichardKingscote 5 62
(Amanda Perrett) *chsd ldrs: pushed along fr 3f out and steadily outpcd*
**50/1**

**6** *nse* **Harbour Force (FR)** 3-9-5 0........................................... MartinDwyer 3 62
(William Muir) *towards rr: sme prog 1/2-way: shkn up in 7th over 3f out: one pce and no imp on ldrs*
**25/1**

0 **7** 2 **Donna Finchella (IRE)**[7] 2231 3-9-0 0.......................... JimmyFortune 7 52
(Brian Meehan) *led 1f: chsd wnr to 5f out: fdd over 2f out*
**66/1**

40- **8** *hd* **Babamunchkin**[180] 7865 3-9-0 0...................................... LouisSteward 4 52
(Michael Bell) *wl in rr: sme limited prog 3f out: no hdwy fnl 2f*
**33/1**

02- **9** 1 **Footman (GER)**[145] 8354 3-9-5 0...................................... ShaneKelly 9 54+
(Richard Hughes) *hld up in midfield: abt 9th whn stl appeared green 4f out and restrained: no prog after: likely to do bttr*
**16/1**

**10** ¾ **Tidal Watch (IRE)** 3-9-5 0............................................... FranBerry 13 53
(Jonjo O'Neill) *restless stalls: slowly away: mostly in last tl 2f out: sme late hdwy but nvr involved*
**66/1**

5- **11** 2 ¾ **Wootyhoot (FR)**[229] 6672 3-9-5 0.................................... TomQueally 1 46
(James Fanshawe) *rn green and wl in rr: rdn and no prog over 2f out* **16/1**

**12** ¾ **Upended** 3-9-5 0........................................................... AdamBeschizza 2 45
(Chris Wall) *difficult to load into stall: a wl in rr: pushed along and no prog over 2f out*
**100/1**

**13** 15 **Lifeboat Lad (USA)** 3-9-5 0....................................(h[1]) SteveDrowne 12 10
(Dean Ivory) *racd wd: in tch to over 3f out: wknd: eased over 1f out: t.o*
**100/1**

1m 47.77s (3.07) **Going Correction** +0.15s/f (Good) **13** Ran SP% **116.6**
Speed ratings (Par 99): **90,88,86,84,82 82,80,80,79,78 75,74,59**
CSF £8.94 TOTE £4.20: £1.40, £1.20, £1.60; EX 11.50 Trifecta £27.70.
**Owner** M Kerr-Dineen, M Hughes & W Eason **Bred** Brightwalton Bloodstock Ltd **Trained** East Ilsley, Berks

**FOCUS**
Add 27yds. The winner got his own way in front and few seriously threatened, but probably a fair enough maiden. The form is rated around the eunner-up but will take time to unravel.

## 2476 ROYAL RUN LOYALTY CARD MAIDEN STKS 1m 2f

**7:20** (7:22) (Class 5) 3-Y-O+ **£2,911** (£866; £432; £216) **Stalls** Centre

Form RPR

**1** **Silken Dancer** 3-8-13 0................................................ WilliamBuick 2 83
(Charlie Appleby) *wl in tch: trckd ldr 4f out: shkn up to ld wl over 1f out: stydd on wl fnl f: tk several fs to pull up*
**8/1**

5- **2** 2 **Cross Step (USA)**[172] 7982 3-9-0 0 ow1.....................(p[1]) AdamKirby 4 80+
(Charlie Appleby) *led 4f: cl 2nd whn carried lft 5f out and dropped to 5th: effrt again over 2f out: chsd wnr fnl f: styd on but no imp*
**9/1**

**3** ¾ **Sea Sovereign (IRE)**[31] 4-10-0 0.................................. TimmyMurphy 12 78
(Mark Pitman) *cl up: lft in ld briefly 5f out: nudged along and stl cl up on inner 2f out: light reminders and styd on same pce: promising effrt* **100/1**

**4** *nse* **Marie Josephe** 3-8-8 0.................................................. ShaneKelly 10 72+
(Richard Hughes) *free to post: hld up towards rr: pushed along over 2f out: styd on steadily fr over 1f out and nrly snatched 3rd: shaped w promise*
**66/1**

0- **5** 1 ½ **Clemento (IRE)**[222] 6881 3-8-13 0.................................. AndreaAtzeni 5 74
(Roger Charlton) *chsd ldrs: shkn up 3f out: one pce and no imp after* **5/2**[2]

**6** *nk* **Qaviy Cash** 3-8-13 0..............................................(t) JosephineGordon 7 73+
(Hugo Palmer) *dwlt: in rr: shkn up wl over 2f out: kpt on steadily fr over 1f out*
**12/1**

**7** 1 ¼ **Casement (IRE)** 3-8-10 0...................................... KieranShoemark[(3)] 6 71+
(Roger Charlton) *dwlt: t.k.h in rr and rn green: stl wl in rr 3f out: kpt on steadily fnl 2f: nt disgracd*
**20/1**

5- **8** 1 ¼ **Sea Skimmer**[199] 7501 3-8-13 0...................................(v[1]) OisinMurphy 13 68
(Saeed bin Suroor) *free to post: restless in stalls: cl up: led over 4f out: hdd & wknd wl over 1f out*
**9/4**[1]

**9** 1 **Murchison River** 3-8-13 0................................................ DaneO'Neill 8 66
(Henry Candy) *chsd ldrs but rn green and reminder after 4f: lost pl 4f out: kpt on again fr 2f out*
**33/1**

**10** 2 ½ **Kings City (IRE)** 3-8-13 0............................................. JamieSpencer 16 61
(Luca Cumani) *dwlt: hld up in rr: pushed along 3f out: one pce and n.d*
**25/1**

04- **11** 7 **Lisp (IRE)**[206] 7318 3-8-13 0........................................... DavidProbert 14 47
(Charles Hills) *t.k.h: hld up in rr: hanging lft bnd 6f out to 5f out: rn green and no prog*
**33/1**

0- **12** 6 **Niseko**[187] 7770 3-8-13 0................................................... MartinDwyer 15 35
(William Muir) *in rr: hanging lft bnd 6f out to 5f out: sharp reminders 4f out: wknd*
**100/1**

**13** 51 **Inch Wing (IRE)**[22] 9-9-9 0............................................ AdamBeschizza 1
(Mark Hoad) *s.s: sn t.o*
**250/1**

32- **P** **Chiefofchiefs**[255] 5850 4-10-0 0.................................. StevieDonohoe 3
(Charlie Fellowes) *w ldr: led after 4f: hung v bdly lft bnd 5f out and ref to r properly after: p.u*
**7/1**[3]

2m 8.87s (0.17) **Going Correction** +0.15s/f (Good)
**WFA** 3 from 4yo+ 15lb **14** Ran SP% **119.0**
Speed ratings (Par 103): **105,103,102,102,101 101,100,99,98,96 90,86,45,**
CSF £72.65 TOTE £7.10: £2.60, £2.90, £11.70; EX 75.90 Trifecta £4167.40.
**Owner** Godolphin **Bred** Darley **Trained** Newmarket, Suffolk

**FOCUS**
Add 27yds. This form has a muddling feel to it but a few shaped as though they can do better. A 1-2 for Charlie Appleby.

## 2477 HAPPY 60TH BIRTHDAY SUE HARLOW H'CAP 1m 2f

**7:50** (7:50) (Class 4) (0-80,81) 4-Y-O+ **£4,690** (£1,395; £697; £348) **Stalls** Centre

Form RPR

51-4 **1** **Shargiah (IRE)**[14] 2026 4-9-8 **81**.................................... AndreaAtzeni 3 88+
(Roger Varian) *trckd ldr to 1/2-way: styd in 3rd: shkn up over 2f out: rdn to cl over 1f out: styd on wl to ld last 80yds*
**4/1**[3]

1 **2** 1 **Eskendash (USA)**[40] 1420 4-9-4 **77**................................. AdamKirby 7 82+
(Pam Sly) *s.s: t.k.h and sn in tch: waiting for room over 3f out: shkn up over 2f out: prog over 1f out: drvn and styd on to take 2nd last strides*
**3/1**[2]

60-2 **3** *nk* **Prendergast Hill (IRE)**[14] 2020 5-9-7 **80**....................... HarryBentley 9 84
(Ed de Giles) *led: shkn up and sent for home over 2f out: jnd and hrd rdn over 1f out: hdd and one pce last 80yds*
**11/4**[1]

6-40 **4** *hd* **Ripoll (IRE)**[11] 2115 4-9-5 **78**.......................................(t) OisinMurphy 4 82
(Sylvester Kirk) *prom: trckd ldr 1/2-way: shkn up over 2f out: drvn and upsides over 1f out: hanging and nt qckn after: lost pls nr fin*
**8/1**

-215 **5** 1 ½ **Captain Courageous (IRE)**[38] 1462 4-9-2 **75**........ RichardKingscote 1 76
(Ed Walker) *in tch: shkn up in 5th over 2f out: no imp ldrs over 1f out: kpt on*
**11/2**

400- **6** 2 **Sark (IRE)**[164] 8100 4-8-11 **70**............................................ JFEgan 5 67
(David Evans) *hld up and last after 3f: reminder over 2f out: pushed along and kpt on steadily fr over 1f out: nt disgracd*
**12/1**

06-0 **7** *nse* **Best Example (USA)**[107] 349 5-9-2 **75**........................ AdamBeschizza 2 72
(Julia Feilden) *chsd ldrs: drvn in 4th over 2f out: fdd over 1f out* **33/1**

-216 **8** 1 ¾ **Choral Clan (IRE)**[31] 1602 6-9-1 **74**............................ JackMitchell 8 67
(Brendan Powell) *t.k.h: hld up: rdn in 6th over 2f out: no prog and wknd over 1f out*
**25/1**

2m 11.84s (3.14) **Going Correction** +0.15s/f (Good) **8** Ran SP% **112.6**
Speed ratings (Par 105): **93,92,91,91,90 89,88,87**
CSF £15.91 CT £37.04 TOTE £4.10: £1.60, £1.30, £1.20; EX 15.20 Trifecta £34.80.
**Owner** Saif Ali **Bred** Rabbah Bloodstock Limited **Trained** Newmarket, Suffolk

**FOCUS**
Add 27yds. A fair handicap but rather muddling. The third looks the best guide.

## 2478 IRISH NIGHT ON 12TH JUNE H'CAP 1m 3f 99y

**8:20** (8:21) (Class 4) (0-80,82) 4-Y-O+ **£4,690** (£1,395; £697; £348) **Stalls** Centre

Form RPR

44-3 **1** **Spinners Ball (IRE)**[14] 2041 4-8-11 **75**.......................... MitchGodwin[(5)] 9 82
(Sylvester Kirk) *trckd ldr: rdn over 2f out: clsd to chal over 1f out: styd on u.p to ld last strides*
**10/3**[2]

240- **2** *shd* **The Otmoor Poet**[21] 7215 4-9-3 **76**..............................(p[1]) DavidProbert 3 83
(Alex Hales) *led: rdn over 2f out: kpt on u.p fr over 1f out: hdd last strides*
**20/1**

351- **3** 2 ½ **Hepplewhite**[131] 8554 4-8-13 **72**..................................(p) MartinDwyer 6 75
(William Muir) *in tch: rdn to chse ldng pair over 2f out: no imp fnl f* **6/1**

10-2 **4** ¾ **Hermann**[118] 163 4-9-8 **81**.............................................. SeanLevey 7 82
(Richard Hannon) *mostly trckd ldng pair to over 2f out: nt qckn and btn over 1f out: kpt on*
**9/4**[1]

260- **5** 2 ¾ **Giveaway Glance**[39] 7220 4-9-6 **79**............................... FergusSweeney 1 76
(Alan King) *hld up in last pair: rdn and no real prog over 2f out* **8/1**

0042 **6** *nse* **Jack Of Diamonds (IRE)**[14] 2041 8-9-1 **74**..................(b) JackMitchell 5 71
(Roger Teal) *hld up in tch: cajoled along wl over 2f out: rdn and no rspnse wl over 1f out: wl btn after*
**5/1**[3]

10-5 **7** ½ **Syncopate**[26] 1719 8-9-7 **80**............................................ RobHornby 8 76
(Pam Sly) *hld up in last pair: rdn 3f out: no prog*
**13/2**

2m 30.65s (1.15) **Going Correction** +0.15s/f (Good) **7** Ran SP% **114.0**
Speed ratings (Par 105): **101,100,99,98,96 96,96**
CSF £60.93 CT £383.47 TOTE £4.60: £2.00, £8.20; EX 58.50 Trifecta £520.50.
**Owner** E McCay **Bred** Lynch-Bages Ltd **Trained** Upper Lambourn, Berks

**FOCUS**
Add 27yds. The one-two raced two-one for most of the way. A small pb from the winner.

T/Jkpt: Part won. T/Plt: £87.90 to a £1 stake. Pool: £68,727.00 - 781.65 winning units T/Qpdt: £18.80 to a £1 stake. Pool: £4,894.00 - 258.95 winning units **Jonathan Neesom**

2479-2482a (Foreign Racing) - See Raceform Interactive

## 2247 SAINT-CLOUD (L-H)
Monday, May 8

**OFFICIAL GOING: Turf: very soft**

### 2483a PRIX GREFFULHE (GROUP 2) (3YO COLTS & FILLIES) (TURF) 1m 2f
1:35 3-Y-O £63,333 (£24,444; £11,666; £7,777; £3,888)

RPR
1 **Recoletos (FR)**36 1528 3-9-2 0 OlivierPeslier 4 114+
(C Laffon-Parias, France) *settled next to last: clsd over 2f out: shkn up to ld wl over 1f out: drvn out fnl f: readily* 9/2[3]
2 2 1/2 **Waldgeist**190 7722 3-9-2 0 Pierre-CharlesBoudot 2 108
(A Fabre, France) *chsd ldr on outer: drvn to ld ent last 2f: hdd sn after: kpt on u.p fnl f: jst hld on for 2nd* 4/5[1]
3 hd **Akihiro (JPN)**22 1826 3-9-2 0 MaximeGuyon 3 108
(A Fabre, France) *hld up in rr: last and drvn wl over 1f out: styd on ins fnl f: jst missed 2nd* 2/1[2]
4 1 3/4 **Monreal (IRE)**21 3-9-2 0 MickaelBarzalona 1 104
(Jean-Pierre Carvalho, Germany) *led: hdd after 1f: chsd ldr on inner: rdn to chal 2f out: kpt on at same pce* 20/1
5 2 1/2 **Saldier (FR)**7 2250 3-9-2 0 GeraldMosse 5 99
(T Castanheira, France) *led after 1f: kicked for home appr 2 1/2f out: hdd under 2f out: grad dropped away fnl f* 22/1

2m 13.97s (-2.03) 5 Ran SP% 116.2
PARI-MUTUEL (all including 1 euro stake): WIN 4.50 PLACE 1.60, 1.40; SF 9.30.
**Owner** Sarl Darpat France **Bred** Sarl Darpat France **Trained** Chantilly, France

### 2484a PRIX DU BEL AIR (H'CAP) (3YO) (TURF) 1m
2:15 3-Y-O
£22,094 (£8,931; £6,581; £4,230; £2,585; £1,645)

RPR
1 **Roc Angel (FR)**35 3-9-4 0 TonyPiccone 15 96
(F Chappet, France) 18/1
2 3/4 **Touching The Sky (IRE)**133 8532 3-9-2 0 OlivierPeslier 6 92
(Alex Fracas, France) 269/10
3 1 1/2 **Cheries Amours (FR)**20 3-8-11 0 JeromeMoutard 11 84
(T Castanheira, France) 168/10
4 1 3/4 **Chiarush (IRE)**35 3-8-8 0 StephanePasquier 1 77
(G Botti, France) 73/10[3]
5 snk **Argentic (FR)**35 3-9-1 0 MaximeGuyon 13 83
(F Head, France) 51/10[2]
6 3/4 **Tresor (IRE)**38 3-8-10 0 CristianDemuro 8 76
(Y Barberot, France) 19/2
7 hd **Arpani (FR)**38 3-8-8 0 (p) AntoineHamelin 3 74
(T Castanheira, France) 35/1
8 1 **Cry Baby (IRE)**35 3-9-1 0 TheoBachelot 9 79
(Y Barberot, France) 213/10
9 1 1/4 **Rebecca (FR)**38 3-9-0 0 MickaelBarzalona 12 75
(H-A Pantall, France) 15/1
10 snk **Sugar Bay**35 3-8-11 0 JulienAuge 14 71
(C Ferland, France) 104/10
11 1 1/4 **Streets Of Rio (FR)**35 3-9-1 0 Pierre-CharlesBoudot 2 73
(H-A Pantall, France) 42/10[1]
12 3/4 **Jeannajonh (FR)**35 3-9-0 0 MickaelForest 7 70
(W Walton, France) 217/10
13 8 **Brise De Mer (FR)**40 3-8-11 0 (p) GeraldMosse 5 48
(George Baker) *chsd ldrs: cl 4th and racd keenly bef 1/2-way: rdn and lost pl over 2f out: dropped away appr fnl f* 27/1
14 hd **Melissa Jane**35 3-9-0 0 GregoryBenoist 10 51
(Y Barberot, France) 96/10
15 1 3/4 **Ucel (IRE)**18 3-8-13 0 (b) IoritzMendizabal 4 46
(F Chappet, France) 146/10

1m 43.93s (-3.57) 15 Ran SP% 117.8
PARI-MUTUEL (all including 1 euro stake): WIN 8.60 PLACE 4.90, 8.40, 5.80 DF 169.00 SF 259.40.
**Owner** Antoine Gilibert **Bred** Deln Ltd & Howard Kaskel **Trained** France

### 2485a PRIX D'HEDOUVILLE (GROUP 3) (4YO+) (TURF) 1m 4f
3:20 4-Y-O+ £34,188 (£13,675; £10,256; £6,837; £3,418)

RPR
1 **Tiberian (FR)**41 1416 5-9-0 0 OlivierPeslier 2 112+
(Alain Couetil, France) *w.w in tch: cl 3rd travelling wl 3f out: clsd to join ldr ins fnl f: led 100yds out: pushed out: cosily* 11/4[2]
2 1 **Talismanic**20 1871 4-8-11 0 MickaelBarzalona 1 107
(A Fabre, France) *led: rdn 1 1/2f out: hdd 100yds out: no ex* 10/11[1]
3 1 3/4 **Way To Paris**29 4-8-11 0 Pierre-CharlesBoudot 6 105+
(Antonio Marcialis, Italy) *hld up next to last: drvn over 2f out: styd on at same pce fnl f* 15/2
4 hd **Matchwinner (GER)**32 6-8-11 0 AntoineHamelin 3 104+
(A Kleinkorres, Germany) *w.w in rr: rousted along 1 1/2f out: kpt on at same pce fnl f* 16/1
5 nse **Cafe Royal (GER)**29 1659 6-9-0 0 GregoryBenoist 5 107+
(A Schutz, France) *settled bhd ldng pair: 4th and pushed along 3f out: kpt on at one pce* 16/1
6 7 **Moonshiner (GER)**219 6971 4-9-2 0 MaximeGuyon 4 98+
(Jean-Pierre Carvalho, Germany) *trckd ldr on outer: drvn along and no imp 2 1/2f out: wknd ins fnl f* 5/1[3]

2m 35.44s (-4.96) 6 Ran SP% 119.2
PARI-MUTUEL (all including 1 euro stake): WIN 3.80 PLACE 1.50, 1.30, SF 6.50.
**Owner** Earl Haras Du Logis, Heiko Volz & Stefan Falk **Bred** H Volz , J Ince & S Falk **Trained** France

2486 - 2491a (Foreign Racing) - See Raceform Interactive

## 2204 SHA TIN (R-H)
Sunday, May 7

**OFFICIAL GOING: Turf: good to firm**

### 2492a CHAMPIONS MILE (GROUP 1) (3YO+) (COURSE A+3) (TURF) 1m
9:00 3-Y-O+
£952,978 (£367,816; £167,189; £95,297; £55,172; £33,437)

RPR
1 **Contentment (AUS)**28 1670 6-9-0 0 (e) BrettPrebble 1 119
(J Size, Hong Kong) *led: hdd 4 1/2f out: rdn to ld narrowly 2f out: hdd 1 1/2f out: rallied to ld again 100yds out: drvn out* 25/1
2 nk **Beauty Only (IRE)**28 1670 6-9-0 0 (t) ZacPurton 2 118+
(A S Cruz, Hong Kong) *in tch: rdn 2f out: kpt on wl fr over 1f out: nrst fin* 12/5[2]
3 3/4 **Helene Paragon (FR)**28 1670 5-9-0 0 TommyBerry 4 116
(John Moore, Hong Kong) *midfield: dropped towards rr 5f out: hdwy on outer fr 3f out: rdn 2f out: led 1 1/2f out: hdd 100yds out: no ex clsng stages* 79/10[3]
4 1 1/2 **Circuit Land (USA)**28 1670 6-9-0 0 (t) HughBowman 3 113
(C S Shum, Hong Kong) *chsd ldr: dropped to 3rd 4 1/2f out: rdn 2f out: briefly evey ch under 2f out: kpt on same pce* 31/1
5 2 **Stormy Antarctic**36 1493 4-9-0 0 (b) KarisTeetan 7 108
(Ed Walker) *plld hrd: towards rr tl rapid hdwy to ld 4 1/2f out: rdn and hdd 2f out: wknd over 1f out* 28/1
6 5 **Convey**23 1775 5-9-0 0 OlivierPeslier 6 97
(Sir Michael Stoute) *hld up towards rr: rdn and outpcd fr 2 1/2f out: wknd ins fnl f* 52/1
P **Rapper Dragon (AUS)**28 1670 4-9-0 0 (h) JoaoMoreira 5
(John Moore, Hong Kong) *hld up towards rr: rdn and struggling 4f out: sn p.u* 2/5[1]

1m 35.23s (0.53) 7 Ran SP% 124.4
PARI-MUTUEL (all including 10 hkd stake): WIN 260.00; PLACE 28.00, 11.00, 16.50; DF 353.00.
**Owner** Benson Lo Tak Wing **Bred** P J Favretto **Trained** Hong Kong

2493 - 2494a (Foreign Racing) - See Raceform Interactive

## 2452 AYR (L-H)
Tuesday, May 9

**OFFICIAL GOING: Good to firm (good in places; watered; 8.7)**
Wind: Breezy, half against Weather: Cloudy, bright

### 2495 BOOK NOW FOR QTS LADIES NIGHT MEDIAN AUCTION MAIDEN STKS 6f
2:00 (2:01) (Class 5) 3-5-Y-O £3,234 (£962; £481; £240) Stalls High

Form RPR
34- 1 **Dalton**341 2830 3-9-4 0 DanielTudhope 2 84+
(David O'Meara) *prom: shkn up and hdwy to ld over 1f out: pushed out fnl f: readily* 5/2[2]
226- 2 3 3/4 **Hee Haw (IRE)**210 7248 3-9-4 69 JoeFanning 4 72
(Keith Dalgleish) *led: rdn and hdd over 1f out: drifted lft: kpt on fnl f: nt pce of wnr* 10/1
-22 3 6 **Poet's Reward**25 1782 3-9-4 0 PhillipMakin 6 53
(David Barron) *trckd ldrs: pushed along and outpcd 2f out: sn no imp* 13/8[1]
56 4 2 1/2 **England Expects**28 1705 3-8-8 0 CliffordLee(5) 1 40
(K R Burke) *w ldr: rdn over 2f out: edgd lft and wknd over 1f out* 10/3[3]
0- 5 17 **Miss Quick**221 6925 3-8-13 0 (t[1]) ShaneGray 5
(Ann Duffield) *dwlt: in tch: drvn and struggling over 3f out: lost tch over 2f out* 100/1

1m 12.76s (0.36) **Going Correction** 0.0s/f (Good) 5 Ran SP% 99.8
Speed ratings (Par 103): **97,92,84,80,58**
CSF £19.34 TOTE £3.20: £1.40, £2.70; EX 19.80 Trifecta £26.70.
**Owner** David W Armstrong **Bred** Cheveley Park Stud Ltd **Trained** Upper Helmsley, N Yorks
■ Calypso Jo was withdrawn. Price at time of withdrawal 9/1. Rule 4 applies to all bets - deduction 10p in the pound.

**FOCUS**
The watered ground was given as good to firm, good in places (GoingStick: 8.7). The rail was on its innermost line and distances were as advertised. Jockeys variously described the ground as "quite quick" and "on the fast side of good." An ordinary maiden with a disappointing favourite. The form is rated around the runner-up.

### 2496 WEDDINGS AT WESTERN HOUSE HOTEL MAIDEN STKS 1m 2f
2:30 (2:30) (Class 5) 3-Y-O+ £3,234 (£962; £481; £240) Stalls Low

Form RPR
1 **Paddyplex**46 4-10-0 0 PhillipMakin 7 83
(Keith Dalgleish) *hld up in tch: smooth hdwy to chse ldr over 2f out: sn rdn: led ins fnl f: kpt on strly* 14/1
3235 2 1 **Fiendish (USA)**18 1939 3-8-8 75 JoeFanning 9 75
(Mark Johnston) *t.k.h early: led: rdn over 1f out: edgd lft: hdd ins fnl f: kpt on same pce nr fin* 15/8[2]
0632 3 9 **Archibelle**10 2137 3-8-5 69 NathanEvans(3) 8 57
(R Mike Smith) *chsd ldr: drvn and outpcd over 2f out: no imp over 1f out* 7/4[1]
4 3 1/4 **Leven (IRE)**15 2049 3-8-13 0 TomEaves 1 56
(John Patrick Shanahan, Ire) *chsd ldrs: drvn and outpcd over 2f out: n.d after* 10/3[3]
5 2 3/4 **Hugoigo** 3-8-6 0 SeanMooney(7) 4 50
(Jim Goldie) *s.i.s: bhd: pushed along and hdwy 2f out: sn no imp* 50/1
6 1 1/2 **Nuova Scuola** 4-9-9 0 SamJames 2 43
(Jim Goldie) *hld up: pushed along over 3f out: nvr on terms* 33/1
040- 7 3 1/2 **Newspeak (IRE)**207 7323 5-10-0 51 (p) GrahamLee 5 41
(Fred Watson) *hld up in midfield: stdy hdwy 3f out: rdn and wknd 2f out* 100/1
0 8 13 **Wemyss Point**17 1984 5-10-0 0 PaddyAspell 11 15
(Philip Kirby) *s.i.s: hld up: drvn and struggling over 3f out: sn btn* 18/1

2m 9.78s (-2.22) **Going Correction** -0.45s/f (Firm)
**WFA** 3 from 4yo+ 15lb 8 Ran SP% 112.0
Speed ratings (Par 103): **90,89,82,79,77 76,73,62**
CSF £39.19 TOTE £12.20: £2.50, £1.40, £1.10; EX 44.80 Trifecta £85.00.
**Owner** G & J Park **Bred** Jill Park **Trained** Carluke, S Lanarks

**FOCUS**
An ordinary maiden rated around the front-running second. The first pair were clear.

## 2497 SPRING PROMOTION AT WESTERN HOUSE HOTEL H'CAP 1m 2f
**3:00** (3:00) (Class 4) (0-85,83) 4-Y-O+ **£5,822** (£1,732; £865; £432) **Stalls** Low

Form RPR
6-00 **1** **Euchen Glen**[48] 1307 4-9-7 **83** SamJames 4 91+
(Jim Goldie) *hld up on ins: smooth hdwy and poised to chal over 1f out: shkn up and led ins fnl f: qcknd: readily* **13/2**[3]

500- **2** *1 1/4* **Royal Regent**[172] 8007 5-8-9 **74** SammyJoBell(3) 3 76
(Lucy Normile) *trckd ldrs: hdwy to ld over 1f out: hdd ins fnl f: kpt on: hld nr fin* **16/1**

100- **3** *shd* **Warp Factor (IRE)**[17] 1989 4-9-2 **78** (b) DanielTudhope 1 80
(John Patrick Shanahan, Ire) *trckd ldrs: smooth hdwy to chal over 1f out: rdn to ld briefly ins fnl f: sn one pce* **6/4**[1]

100- **4** *shd* **Archie's Advice**[227] 6772 6-9-2 **78** JoeFanning 7 80
(Keith Dalgleish) *t.k.h: hld up in tch: hdwy and prom whn hung lft over 1f out: kpt on ins fnl f* **9/1**

16-0 **5** *3* **Eez Eh (IRE)**[29] 1683 4-8-11 **73** (p) PhillipMakin 5 69
(Keith Dalgleish) *sn pressing ldr: rdn to ld over 2f out: hdd over 1f out: wknd ins fnl f* **9/1**

5-65 **6** *7* **Pullman Brown (USA)**[29] 1677 5-8-13 **75** PaddyAspell 2 57
(Philip Kirby) *s.i.s: hld up: effrt on outside 3f out: edgd lft and wknd wl over 1f out* **9/2**[2]

050- **7** *3 1/2* **Intiwin (IRE)**[213] 7159 5-8-9 **71** GrahamLee 6 46
(Linda Perratt) *hld up in tch: rdn along over 2f out: wknd wl over 1f out* **20/1**

4033 **8** *2 3/4* **Spes Nostra**[10] 2163 9-8-12 **74** (b) PaulHanagan 8 43
(Iain Jardine) *led to over 2f out: rdn and wknd wl over 1f out* **10/1**

2m 7.66s (-4.34) **Going Correction** -0.45s/f (Firm) **8 Ran SP% 111.3**
Speed ratings (Par 105): **99,98,97,97,95 89,87,84**
CSF £94.90 CT £227.33 TOTE £7.30: £2.00, £4.90, £1.10; EX 89.20 Trifecta £461.50.
**Owner** W M Johnstone **Bred** W M Johnstone **Trained** Uplawmoor, E Renfrews

**FOCUS**
A nice performance from the winner, who not for the first time showed off a turn of foot. He could improve again.

## 2498 BELHAVEN FOR MACMILLAN MAY H'CAP 1m 2f
**3:30** (3:30) (Class 6) (0-65,65) 4-Y-O+ **£2,587** (£770; £384; £192) **Stalls** Low

Form RPR
443- **1** **Visitant**[151] 8286 4-9-7 **65** AndrewMullen 9 76
(David Thompson) *hld up on outside: effrt and shkn up over 2f out: edgd lft and hdwy to ld over 1f out: sn qcknd clr: readily* **10/1**

0-03 **2** *5* **Stoneboat Bill**[10] 2153 5-9-4 **62** DanielTudhope 5 63
(Declan Carroll) *hld up on ins: stdy hdwy over 2f out: stdy hdwy over 1f out: rdn and kpt on to take 2nd cl home: no ch w wnr* **3/1**[1]

0-05 **3** *nk* **Arithmetic (IRE)**[12] 2108 4-9-6 **64** JamesSullivan 1 64
(Ruth Carr) *early ldr: cl up: hdwy to ld over 2f out to over 1f out: sn drvn and one pce* **8/1**

511/ **4** *2 1/4* **Six Silver Lane**[18] 1952 9-9-7 **65** (b) DavidNolan 11 61
(John James Feane, Ire) *hld up in tch on outside: hdwy over 2f out: rdn and edgd lft wl over 1f out: sn outpcd* **13/2**[3]

405- **5** *2 3/4* **Picture Painter (IRE)**[29] 5923 4-8-9 **60** (h) SeanMooney(7) 8 51
(Jim Goldie) *hld up: pushed along and outpcd over 3f out: rallied over 1f out: kpt on: nt pce to chal* **16/1**

06-0 **6** *1/2* **Maskoon**[37] 1519 6-9-0 **58** PaddyAspell 6 48
(Philip Kirby) *hld up on ins: effrt and drvn 3f out: wknd fr 2f out* **10/1**

500- **7** *4* **Black Agnes (IRE)**[18] 1952 4-9-7 **65** (b) PaulMulrennan 2 47+
(Lee Smyth, Ire) *t.k.h: trckd ldrs: led over 3f out to over 2f out: wknd over 1f out* **7/1**

4-42 **8** *3 1/4* **Strummer (IRE)**[12] 2108 4-9-7 **65** (p) KevinStott 7 41
(Kevin Ryan) *in tch: effrt and rdn 2f out: wknd fnl f* **4/1**[2]

434- **9** *14* **Remember Rocky**[244] 6221 8-8-13 **60** (b) AdamMcNamara(3) 12 10
(Lucy Normile) *pressed ldr: led over 3f out to over 2f out: sn lost pl* **16/1**

0660 **10** *26* **Scannermandango**[39] 1473 4-8-7 **51** oh5 SamJames 4
(Jim Goldie) *dwlt: sn led: hdd over 4f out: wknd fr 3f out: t.o* **50/1**

2m 7.09s (-4.91) **Going Correction** -0.45s/f (Firm) **10 Ran SP% 113.9**
Speed ratings (Par 101): **101,97,96,94,92 92,89,86,75,54**
CSF £39.14 CT £255.05 TOTE £11.00: £3.20, £1.50, £2.40; EX 41.90 Trifecta £385.60.
**Owner** N Park **Bred** Cheveley Park Stud Ltd **Trained** Bolam, Co Durham

**FOCUS**
This was run at a good gallop and it suited those ridden with patience. The form is rated around the runner-up.

## 2499 AYRHIRE MAGAZINE H'CAP 6f
**4:00** (4:00) (Class 5) (0-75,76) 3-Y-O **£3,234** (£962; £481; £240) **Stalls** High

Form RPR
00-6 **1** **Burrishoole Abbey (IRE)**[22] 1841 3-9-3 **76** CliffordLee(5) 2 82
(K R Burke) *mde all: rdn 2f out: hld on gamely fnl f* **7/2**[2]

1-43 **2** *1 1/2* **El Hombre**[31] 1625 3-9-7 **75** JoeFanning 4 76
(Keith Dalgleish) *dwlt: t.k.h: sn chsng ldrs: rdn and chsd wnr over 1f out: edgd lft: kpt on same pce ins fnl f* **11/2**[3]

-103 **3** *1/2* **Logi (IRE)**[10] 2160 3-9-4 **72** (b) PhillipMakin 9 72
(David Barron) *hld up in tch: effrt and hdwy over 1f out: edgd lft: kpt on fnl f: nt pce to chal* **7/2**[2]

1246 **4** *1* **Right Action**[19] 1913 3-9-3 **71** PaulHanagan 1 67
(Richard Fahey) *pressed ldr: rdn over 2f out: lost 2nd over 1f out: outpcd fnl f* **11/4**[1]

052- **5** *4* **Savannah Moon (IRE)**[237] 6477 3-8-13 **67** TomEaves 5 51
(Kevin Ryan) *plld hrd: hld up: drvn along over 2f out: no imp wl over 1f out: sn btn* **20/1**

0-66 **6** *2 3/4* **Lady Molly (IRE)**[22] 1828 3-8-2 **61** oh2 (p) RowanScott(5) 6 36
(Keith Dalgleish) *trckd ldrs: rdn over 2f out: wknd over 1f out* **16/1**

041- **7** *3/4* **Desperados Destiny**[210] 7259 3-9-7 **75** PaulMulrennan 7 47
(Michael Dods) *in tch: drvn along over 2f out: wknd wl over 1f out* **11/2**[3]

1m 11.64s (-0.76) **Going Correction** 0.0s/f (Good) **7 Ran SP% 112.5**
Speed ratings (Par 99): **105,103,102,101,95 92,91**
CSF £22.07 CT £70.31 TOTE £3.70: £2.30, £2.80; EX 23.80 Trifecta £121.70.
**Owner** Mrs M Gittins **Bred** Grange Stud **Trained** Middleham Moor, N Yorks

**FOCUS**
The class-dropping winner dictated matters here. He's rated close to his 2yo form.

## 2500 QTS H'CAP 7f 50y
**4:30** (4:30) (Class 4) (0-85,87) 4-Y-O+ **£5,822** (£1,732; £865; £432) **Stalls** High

Form RPR
06-4 **1** **Tommy G**[22] 1833 4-8-12 **74** SamJames 4 81
(Jim Goldie) *hld up: hdwy on outside over 2f out: rdn over 1f out: led ins fnl f: kpt on strly* **5/1**

130- **2** *1* **Glengarry**[234] 6560 4-9-10 **86** PhillipMakin 9 90+
(Keith Dalgleish) *t.k.h: pressed ldr: led 1/2-way: rdn and hdd ins fnl f: kpt on same pce nr fin* **7/2**[1]

41-0 **3** *1/2* **Ionization (IRE)**[24] 1799 4-9-11 **87** DanielTudhope 6 90
(John Patrick Shanahan, Ire) *trckd ldrs: effrt and wnt 2nd briefly over 1f out: hung lft and hmpd appr fnl f: rallied nr fin* **4/1**[2]

0-40 **4** *nk* **Character Onesie (IRE)**[17] 1969 5-8-12 **74** PaulHanagan 2 76
(Richard Fahey) *hld up in tch: drvn and outpcd over 2f out: rallied over 1f out: kpt on ins f* **9/2**[3]

5-10 **5** *1/2* **Chaplin Bay (IRE)**[10] 2133 5-9-1 **77** JamesSullivan 5 78
(Ruth Carr) *hld up: rdn over 2f out: sn hung lft: kpt on fnl f: nvr able to chal* **7/2**[1]

000- **6** *13* **Royal Duchess**[236] 6501 7-8-10 **72** JoeDoyle 7 39
(Lucy Normile) *cl up: wnt 2nd over 2f out to over 1f out: sn wknd* **20/1**

0060 **7** *5* **Kingsley Klarion (IRE)**[14] 2064 4-8-13 **75** JoeFanning 8 29
(Mark Johnston) *t.k.h: led to 1/2-way: rdn and wknd over 2f out* **10/1**

1m 29.03s (-4.37) **Going Correction** -0.45s/f (Firm) **7 Ran SP% 113.1**
Speed ratings (Par 105): **106,104,104,103,103 88,82**
CSF £22.27 CT £75.53 TOTE £5.70: £2.90, £2.00; EX 23.40 Trifecta £58.80.
**Owner** Johnnie Delta Racing **Bred** Jim Goldie **Trained** Uplawmoor, E Renfrews
■ Stewards' Enquiry : Sam James two-day ban; careless riding (May23-24)

**FOCUS**
An open handicap. The form is rated around the third and fourth.

## 2501 CONFERENCE AND EVENTS AT AYR RACECOURSE APPRENTICE H'CAP 1m
**5:00** (5:00) (Class 6) (0-60,61) 4-Y-O+ **£2,587** (£770; £384; £192) **Stalls** Low

Form RPR
6-0 **1** **Not A Bad Oul Day (IRE)**[9] 2193 5-9-4 **59** 6ex DavidEgan(3) 3 69
(John James Feane, Ire) *mde virtually all: hrd pressed over 2f out to over 1f out: edgd rt and drew clr fnl f* **6/4**[1]

0-02 **2** *3* **New Abbey Angel (IRE)**[5] 2342 4-9-5 **57** (v) RowanScott 4 60
(Keith Dalgleish) *pressed wnr: clr of rest 1/2-way: chal over 2f out: sn rdn: carried hd high and hung lft: no ex appr fnl f* **3/1**[2]

400- **3** *1 3/4* **Joyful Star**[237] 6478 7-9-1 **53** LewisEdmunds 9 52
(Fred Watson) *t.k.h early: hld up: pushed along over 2f out: hdwy over 1f out: kpt on: nt* **11/1**

610- **4** *1* **Rioja Day (IRE)**[71] 7602 7-8-13 **56** (b) SeanMooney(5) 8 52
(Jim Goldie) *chsd ldrs: drvn and outpcd wl over 2f out: kpt on fnl f: no imp* **25/1**

0-04 **5** *1 3/4* **In Focus (IRE)**[13] 2082 6-9-4 **59** PatrickVaughan(3) 7 51
(Philip Kirby) *prom: rdn over 2f out: no imp wl over 1f out* **8/1**[3]

460- **6** *1 1/4* **Gone With The Wind (GER)**[172] 8011 6-9-6 **61** MeganNicholls(3) 2 50
(Rebecca Bastiman) *t.k.h: rdn and effrt on wd outside wl over 2f out: sn no imp* **12/1**

010- **7** *1/2* **Norville (IRE)**[123] 108 10-8-5 **46** (b) CallumRodriguez(3) 5 34
(Lee Smyth, Ire) *hld up: rdn along over 3f out: wknd fr wl over 1f out* **9/1**

0-00 **8** *15* **Rajapur**[10] 2162 4-8-9 **47** PhilDennis 1
(Philip Kirby) *t.k.h: hld up: drvn along 3f out: sn no imp: btn fnl 2f* **33/1**

1m 40.15s (-3.65) **Going Correction** -0.45s/f (Firm) **8 Ran SP% 108.9**
Speed ratings (Par 101): **100,97,95,94,92 91,90,75**
CSF £5.25 CT £28.44 TOTE £2.70: £1.10, £1.70, £3.50; EX 6.60 Trifecta £38.10.
**Owner** D A Lynch **Bred** Barnane Stud **Trained** Curragh, Co Kildare

**FOCUS**
Only two ever mattered here. Weak form.
T/Plt: £67.60 to a £1 stake. Pool: £70,945.57 - 765.27 winning units T/Qpdt: £21.60 to a £1 stake. Pool: £4,963.65 - 169.3 winning units **Richard Young**

# 2147 LEICESTER (R-H)
Tuesday, May 9

**OFFICIAL GOING: Good to firm (good in places; watered; 8.8)**
Wind: Light behind Weather: Cloudy

## 2502 BEEBY MAIDEN AUCTION FILLIES' STKS (PLUS 10 RACE) 5f
**6:00** (6:02) (Class 5) 2-Y-O **£3,234** (£962; £481; £240) **Stalls** High

Form RPR
**1** **Marchingontogether** 2-8-6 0 SilvestreDeSousa 6 73+
(Ivan Furtado) *sn pushed along in mid-div: hdwy u.p over 1f out: led wl ins fnl f: sn clr* **14/1**

U **2** *2 1/4* **Arabian Jazz (IRE)**[7] 2258 2-8-8 0 DannyBrock 8 67
(Michael Bell) *mid-div: pushed along 1/2-way: hdwy over 1f out: r.o to go 2nd wl ins fnl f* **12/1**

5 **3** *1/2* **Queen Of Kalahari**[20] 1884 2-8-10 0 JimCrowley 5 67+
(Charles Hills) *chsd ldr tl led 2f out: rdn: edgd lft and hdd over 1f out: ev ch ins fnl f: styd on same pce* **9/4**[1]

**4** *1 1/2* **Magic Applause (IRE)** 2-8-12 0 JamieSpencer 1 64
(George Scott) *hld up: hdwy over 1f out: styd on same pce wl ins fnl f* **12/1**

**5** *nse* **Nampara** 2-8-8 0 JoeyHaynes 3 59+
(Paul D'Arcy) *mid-div: hdwy 1/2-way: rdn to ld and hung lft over 1f out: hdd and no ex wl ins fnl f* **50/1**

6 **6** *1/2* **Jungle Queen (IRE)**[15] 2037 2-8-8 0 JohnFahy 2 58
(Eve Johnson Houghton) *sn pushed along towards rr: hdwy 2f out: rdn over 1f out: no ex wl ins fnl f* **11/1**[3]

**7** *2 1/2* **Hope And Glory (IRE)** 2-8-8 0 FrannyNorton 4 49+
(Tom Dascombe) *prom: pushed along and nt clr run 2f out: wknd over 1f out* **20/1**

**8** *nk* **Grandma Tilly** 2-8-12 0 RoystonFfrench 10 52
(Steph Hollinshead) *prom: rdn 1/2-way: wknd over 1f out* **33/1**

**9** *1 1/2* **Pursuing The Dream (IRE)** 2-8-12 0 DougieCostello 12 46
(Jamie Osborne) *hld up: plld hrd: shkn up over 2f out: nt trble ldrs* **22/1**

**10** *1/2* **Elixsoft (IRE)** 2-8-8 0 ConnorBeasley 7 40
(Roger Fell) *s.i.s: hung rt ins fnl f: nvr on terms* **16/1**

**11** *1* **Katherine Place** 2-8-6 0 SamHitchcott 9 35+
(Sylvester Kirk) *led 3f: wknd fnl f* **14/1**

12 *hd* **Terri Rules (IRE)** 2-8-7 0 ShelleyBirkett(3) 15 38
(Julia Feilden) *rn green and hung rt in rr: nvr on terms* **100/1**

13 *2 ½* **Cove Beach** 2-8-12 0 (t¹) LukeMorris 11 31
(Paul Cole) *chsd ldrs: rdn 1/2-way: wknd wl over 1f out* **20/1**

3 14 *4 ½* **Ghepardo**[8] 2217 2-8-10 0 SeanLevey 13 13
(Richard Hannon) *s.i.s: hdwy over 3f out: wknd wl over 1f out* **3/1**[2]

0 15 *13* **Dark Hedges**[20] 1873 2-8-8 0 DuranFentiman 14
(Olly Williams) *prom: lost pl over 3f out: bhd fr 1/2-way* **100/1**

1m 1.59s (1.59) **Going Correction** +0.025s/f (Good) **15** Ran SP% **119.5**
Speed ratings (Par 90): **88,84,83,81,81 80,76,75,73,72 71,70,66,59,38**
CSF £158.67 TOTE £11.00: £4.40, £3.90, £1.30; EX 174.90 Trifecta £2744.50.
**Owner** Bgc Racing & Partner **Bred** Whatcote Farm Stud **Trained** Wiseton, Nottinghamshire

**FOCUS**
There was a false rail from the top of the hill on the back straight all the way to the winning line, increasing distances on the round course by approximately 10yds. This looked just an ordinary maiden auction for fillies, and they were spread across the track, with the winner and second challenging up the middle. Questionable depth to the race.

## 2503 RIVER SOAR FILLIES' H'CAP 6f
**6:30** (6:30) (Class 5) (0-75,76) 3-Y-O **£3,881** (£1,155; £577; £288) **Stalls** High

Form RPR

0-60 **1** **Quench Dolly**[27] 1731 3-9-5 **73** FergusSweeney 3 95
(John Gallagher) *mde virtually all: pushed clr fr over 1f out: easily* **20/1**

160- **2** *8* **The Stalking Moon (IRE)**[232] 6630 3-9-2 **70** JasonHart 2 66
(John Quinn) *mid-div: sn pushed along: hdwy 2f out: rdn to chse wnr over 1f out: styd on same pce* **13/2**

353- **3** *2 ¼* **Island Cloud**[146] 8352 3-9-2 **70** TomMarquand 1 59
(Heather Main) *w ldrs: rdn over 2f out: wknd ins fnl f* **25/1**

4311 **4** *2 ¼* **Tai Hang Dragon (IRE)**[13] 2094 3-9-7 **75** SeanLevey 4 57
(Richard Hannon) *prom: rdn over 1f out: wknd fnl f* **6/1**[3]

-213 **5** *4* **In The Spotlight (IRE)**[96] 522 3-9-2 **70** LouisSteward 5 39
(Henry Spiller) *hld up: hdwy over 1f out: wknd fnl f* **14/1**

04-0 **6** *1* **Chicago Star**[28] 1705 3-8-13 **67** TonyHamilton 9 33
(Mick Channon) *hld up: nvr on terms* **16/1**

50-3 **7** *6* **Kachess**[22] 1828 3-9-8 **76** RichardKingscote 10 23
(Tom Dascombe) *hld up: shkn up 1/2-way: wknd over 2f out* **7/2**[1]

242 **8** *1 ¼* **Global Alexander (IRE)**[25] 1761 3-9-7 **75** AdamKirby 8 18
(Clive Cox) *w ldrs tl rdn over 2f out: wknd wl over 1f out* **9/2**[2]

100- **9** *hd* **Santafiora**[212] 7185 3-9-2 **73** (h) KieranShoemark(3) 7 15
(Roger Charlton) *hld up: shkn up whn nt clr run wl over 1f out: sn wknd: eased ins fnl f* **8/1**

000- **10** *½* **Limelite (IRE)**[199] 7549 3-9-1 **72** HollieDoyle(3) 11 13
(Richard Hannon) *chsd ldrs: rdn over 2f out: wkng whn hung lft over 1f out* **12/1**

0235 **11** *6* **Touch Me (IRE)**[13] 2094 3-8-9 **66** (h) JordanVaughan(3) 6
(K R Burke) *chsd ldrs: pushed along over 4f out: wknd over 2f out* **16/1**

1m 11.47s (-1.53) **Going Correction** +0.025s/f (Good) **11** Ran SP% **113.9**
Speed ratings (Par 96): **111,100,97,94,89 87,79,78,77,77 69**
CSF £140.38 CT £2112.62 TOTE £23.30: £6.10, £2.40, £6.90; EX 200.60 Trifecta £3720.40.
**Owner** Quench Racing Partnership **Bred** Mrs R J Gallagher **Trained** Chastleton, Oxon

**FOCUS**
The first five finishers came from the bottom five stalls, with the middle of the track again looking the place to be. This doesn't look form to believe in, with the winner's effort very much out of line with her profile.

## 2504 KIRBY MALLORY H'CAP 1m 2f
**7:00** (7:01) (Class 4) (0-85,84) 4-Y-O+ **£5,175** (£1,540; £769; £384) **Stalls** Low

Form RPR

132- **1** **Burguillos**[200] 7499 4-9-7 **84** JimmyFortune 2 96+
(Alan King) *hld up in tch: racd keenly: led on bit ins fnl f: edgd rt: sn clr: comf* **7/4**[1]

32-3 **2** *1 ½* **Wapping (USA)**[14] 2068 4-9-7 **84** (b¹) TomQueally 3 88
(David Lanigan) *s.i.s: hld up: rdn and hung rt fr over 2f out: hdwy over 1f out: styd on to go 2nd nr fin: no ch w wnr* **4/1**[3]

240- **3** *nk* **Compton Mill**[174] 7980 5-8-11 **79** (t) CharlieBennett(5) 6 82
(Hughie Morrison) *chsd ldr tl wnt upsides over 3f out: rdn to ld over 1f out: hdd ins fnl f: styd on same pce* **6/1**

3-05 **4** *3 ½* **Primogeniture (IRE)**[15] 2041 6-9-6 **83** (b) RichardKingscote 5 79
(Mary Hambro) *led: qcknd 4f out: jnd over 3f out: rdn and hdd over 1f out: no ex ins fnl f* **10/1**

2253 **5** *2 ½* **Mariee**[8] 2225 4-9-3 **80** SilvestreDeSousa 1 71
(Mark Johnston) *chsd ldrs: rdn over 3f out: wknd fnl f* **5/2**[2]

266- **6** *7* **Art Scholar (IRE)**[383] 1588 10-8-2 **65** oh1 RoystonFfrench 4 42
(Michael Appleby) *hld up: rdn over 3f out: n.d* **50/1**

2m 10.68s (2.78) **Going Correction** +0.025s/f (Good) **6** Ran SP% **110.3**
Speed ratings (Par 105): **89,87,87,84,82 77**
CSF £8.77 TOTE £2.30: £1.80, £2.00; EX 7.90 Trifecta £22.10.
**Owner** Hunscote Stud **Bred** Minster Stud And Mrs H Dalgety **Trained** Barbury Castle, Wilts

**FOCUS**
Add 10yds. Some of these are unconvincing types but the winner had loads in hand. He improved in line with his 3yo form.

## 2505 VIS-A-VIS SYMPOSIUMS H'CAP 1m 53y
**7:30** (7:30) (Class 4) (0-85,84) 3-Y-O+ **£5,175** (£1,540; £769; £384) **Stalls** Low

Form RPR

421- **1** **Naval Warfare (IRE)**[235] 6534 3-9-1 **84** DavidProbert 1 97
(Andrew Balding) *mde all: qcknd 1/2-way: rdn over 1f out: styd on: edgd lft towards fin* **15/8**[1]

4-1 **2** *1 ¼* **Sabador (FR)**[48] 1299 3-8-10 **79** ThomasBrown 3 89
(Ed Walker) *hld up: plld hrd: rdn over 2f out: hdwy over 1f out: chsd wnr ins fnl f: styd on* **4/1**[3]

56-1 **3** *3* **Art Echo**[11] 2120 4-9-1 **71** (t) BenCurtis 2 77
(John Mackie) *s.i.s: sn chsng ldrs: rdn over 2f out: chsd wnr over 1f out tl no ex ins fnl f* **11/2**

522- **4** *3 ¾* **Rotherwick (IRE)**[193] 7666 5-10-0 **84** LukeMorris 4 81
(Paul Cole) *w wnr tl settled into 2nd pl after 1f: rdn and lost 2nd over 2f out: no ex fr over 1f out* **5/2**[2]

/43- **5** *25* **Ski Blast**[360] 2256 6-9-5 **75** SilvestreDeSousa 5 15
(Ivan Furtado) *hld up: rdn over 3f out: wknd and eased over 2f out* **10/1**

1m 45.76s (0.66) **Going Correction** +0.025s/f (Good)
**WFA** 3 from 4yo+ 13lb **5** Ran SP% **107.8**
Speed ratings (Par 105): **97,95,92,89,64**
CSF £9.15 TOTE £3.20: £1.70, £1.80; EX 9.80 Trifecta £23.20.
**Owner** Qatar Racing Limited **Bred** Rathasker Stud **Trained** Kingsclere, Hants

**FOCUS**
Add 10yds. It's possible neither of the unexposed first two were seen at their best and they may rate higher in due course.

## 2506 ROTHWELL H'CAP 7f
**8:00** (8:12) (Class 4) (0-80,82) 3-Y-O **£5,175** (£1,540; £769; £384) **Stalls** High

Form RPR

61- **1** **Mickey Rich**[132] 8557 3-9-6 **77** AdamKirby 6 88
(Hughie Morrison) *led: hdd over 5f out: remained w ldr tl shkn up to ld again over 2f out: hrd rdn and edgd rt fr over 1f out: styd on gamely* **15/2**[3]

42-1 **2** *1 ½* **Ejaaby**[20] 1889 3-9-11 **82** JimCrowley 2 89
(Roger Varian) *hld up: hdwy over 2f out: chsd wnr over 1f out: rdn and ev ch ins fnl f: no ex towards fin* **6/4**[1]

4-31 **3** *3* **Il Sicario (IRE)**[8] 2228 3-8-10 **67** SilvestreDeSousa 1 66
(Mark Johnston) *w ldrs: rdn and ev ch wl over 1f out: nt clr run sn after: edgd rt and no ex ins fnl f* **3/1**[2]

10-0 **4** *1 ¾* **Abiento (IRE)**[22] 1841 3-9-5 **76** TonyHamilton 3 70
(Richard Fahey) *prom: racd keenly: shkn up over 1f out: no ex fnl f* **14/1**

405- **5** *nk* **Dourado (IRE)**[202] 7467 3-9-4 **75** TomMarquand 10 68
(Patrick Chamings) *chsd ldrs: rdn over 2f out: styd on same pce fr over 1f out* **8/1**

10-5 **6** *5* **Giennah (IRE)**[82] 765 3-9-7 **78** ShaneKelly 8 58
(Daniel Mark Loughnane) *hld up: rdn over 1f out: nvr on terms* **33/1**

323- **7** *1* **Kings Academy**[159] 8175 3-9-4 **75** LukeMorris 7 52
(Paul Cole) *w ldr tl led over 5f out: rdn and hdd over 2f out: wknd over 1f out* **10/1**

66-0 **8** *6* **Spun Gold**[28] 1692 3-8-11 **68** JamieSpencer 4 29
(Luca Cumani) *hld up: shkn up over 2f out: wknd over 1f out* **10/1**

1m 24.81s (-1.39) **Going Correction** +0.025s/f (Good) **8** Ran SP% **115.7**
Speed ratings (Par 101): **108,106,102,100,100 94,93,86**
CSF £19.46 CT £42.51 TOTE £7.80: £2.80, £1.10, £1.50; EX 24.90 Trifecta £72.50.
**Owner** Kerr-Dineen, Eason, Rothwell & Malpas **Bred** New England Stud, Myriad & T Vestey **Trained** East Ilsley, Berks

■ Pennsylvania Dutch was withdrawn. Price at time of withdrawal 10/3. Rule 4 applies to bets struck at board prices prior to withdrawal but not to SP bets - deduction 20p in the pound. New market formed.

**FOCUS**
A delay of almost 13 minutes after Pennsylvania Dutch went down in his stall - and the others were removed from the gates - but thankfully the horse got back up. The main action unfolded middle to far side, with the four horses who raced closest to the stands' side for most of the way filling the last four places. The unexposed 1-2 both improved.

## 2507 SHEARSBY H'CAP 7f
**8:30** (8:40) (Class 6) (0-60,60) 3-Y-O **£3,234** (£962; £481; £240) **Stalls** High

Form RPR

00-0 **1** **Pursuing Steed**[27] 1727 3-8-13 **57** CharlieBennett(5) 12 75+
(Hughie Morrison) *hld up: hdwy over 1f out: r.o to ld wl ins fnl f* **14/1**

3-32 **2** *2 ½* **Coverham (IRE)**[15] 2016 3-9-7 **60** RyanTate 2 71
(James Eustace) *hld up in tch: rdn to chse ldr and hung lft over 1f out: ev ch ins fnl f: styd on same pce* **3/1**[1]

0-00 **3** *1* **Delagate This Lord**[6] 2309 3-9-4 **57** (p) LukeMorris 5 65
(Bill Turner) *s.i.s: hdwy over 4f out: led 1/2-way: rdn over 1f out: hdd and no ex wl ins fnl f* **14/1**

0-44 **4** *1 ¼* **Luxford**[32] 1597 3-8-7 **46** SilvestreDeSousa 4 51
(John Best) *hld up in tch: hmpd and lost pl over 2f out: hdwy over 1f out: styd on same pce wl ins fnl f* **7/1**[2]

3115 **5** *2* **Tigerfish (IRE)**[40] 1451 3-8-11 **53** (p) HollieDoyle(3) 15 53+
(William Stone) *stmbld s: hld up: hdwy over 1f out: nt trble ldrs* **11/1**[3]

004- **6** *½* **Banta Bay**[187] 7776 3-9-3 **56** KierenFox 1 54
(John Best) *chsd ldrs: rdn over 2f out: no ex ins fnl f* **12/1**

000- **7** *1* **Lesanti**[164] 8118 3-8-13 **55** CallumShepherd(3) 9 50+
(Ed de Giles) *hld up in tch: rdn and hung lft over 1f out: no ex ins fnl f* **12/1**

0-40 **8** *¾* **African Girl**[45] 1371 3-8-10 **52** SimonPearce(3) 6 45
(Lydia Pearce) *chsd ldrs: rdn over 2f out: wknd ins fnl f* **33/1**

650 **9** *8* **Mahna Mahna (IRE)**[10] 2167 3-9-5 **58** WilliamCarson 10 30
(David W Drinkwater) *chsd ldrs: rdn over 2f out: wknd over 1f out* **40/1**

0-44 **10** *½* **Equal Rights**[15] 2018 3-9-5 **58** (p¹) JohnFahy 18 29
(Eve Johnson Houghton) *hld up: rdn 1/2-way: n.d* **14/1**

56-0 **11** *¾* **Dravid**[15] 2018 3-8-11 **55** (b¹) LuluStanford(5) 11 23
(Rod Millman) *hld up: plld hrd: rdn over 2f out: nvr on terms* **14/1**

005- **12** *6* **Rakematiz**[275] 5202 3-9-6 **59** AdamKirby 17 11
(Brett Johnson) *chsd ldrs: rdn over 2f out: sn wknd* **12/1**

0000 **13** *2 ½* **Newton Heath (IRE)**[14] 2060 3-8-9 **48** ow1 ShaneKelly 16
(Daniel Mark Loughnane) *chsd ldrs: lost pl over 4f out: wknd over 2f out* **66/1**

0-00 **14** *2 ¼* **Unzipped**[17] 1968 3-9-1 **54** CamHardie 7
(Stuart Edmunds) *led to 1/2-way: rdn over 2f out: wknd wl over 1f out:* **25/1**

000- **15** *2 ¾* **Shakabula (IRE)**[214] 7109 3-9-7 **60** BenCurtis 14
(Brian Ellison) *s.i.s: a in rr* **25/1**

5-05 **16** *2 ½* **Circuit**[90] 615 3-8-11 **50** JamieSpencer 8
(Mick Quinn) *s.i.s: sn swtchd rt: a in rr* **25/1**

352F **17** *21* **Champagne Queen**[22] 1835 3-8-11 **50** (t) DavidProbert 3
(Rae Guest) *w ldrs to 1/2-way: rdn over 2f out: sn wknd* **12/1**

1m 25.72s (-0.48) **Going Correction** +0.025s/f (Good) **17** Ran SP% **121.7**
Speed ratings (Par 97): **103,100,99,97,95 94,93,92,83,83 82,75,72,69,66 63,39**
CSF £51.39 CT £646.49 TOTE £18.50: £4.10, £1.50, £3.80, £1.80; EX 85.70 Trifecta £1361.20.
**Owner** Caveat Emptor Partnership **Bred** A E Smith And Co **Trained** East Ilsley, Berks

**FOCUS**
Again, middle to far side was the place to be. The winner improved on his handicap debut.

T/Jkpt: Not Won. T/Plt: £208.80 to a £1 stake. Pool: £83,479.03 - 291.73 winning units T/Qpdt: £3.70 to a £1 stake. Pool: £8,526.56 - 1672.32 winning units **Colin Roberts**

## 2214 BATH (L-H)

Wednesday, May 10

**OFFICIAL GOING: Firm (11.4)**

Wind: Almost nil Weather: Fine

### 2508 PERFECT DYNAMICS H'CAP — 5f 10y

5:35 (5:35) (Class 5) (0-75,74) 3-Y-O — **£2,911** (£866; £432) **Stalls** Centre

Form — RPR

21-4 **1** **Desert Sport (USA)**[18] 1970 3-9-7 **74** .......... JimmyFortune 3 79
(Robert Cowell) *trckd ldrs: wnt 2nd wl over 1f out: led 1f out: shkn up: edgd lft and r.o wl: comf* **6/5**[1]

52-6 **2** 2 ½ **Fabric**[18] 1970 3-9-6 **73** .......... PatDobbs 2 69
(Richard Hannon) *chsd ldr tl led over 3f out: edgd lft wl over 1f out: hdd 1f out: sn outpcd* **6/5**[1]

-063 **3** 4 ½ **Prancelina (IRE)**[25] 1786 3-8-8 **61** .......... JosephineGordon 1 41
(Phil McEntee) *led: hdd over 3f out: nt clr run wl over 1f out: sn btn* **5/1**[2]

1m 0.9s (-1.60) **Going Correction** -0.20s/f (Firm) **3** Ran SP% **107.6**
Speed ratings (Par 99): **104,100,92**
CSF £2.94 TOTE £2.00; EX 2.60 Trifecta £2.50.
**Owner** Mohammed Al Shafar **Bred** Greenwood Lodge Farm Inc **Trained** Six Mile Bottom, Cambs

**FOCUS**
The going was firm and there were plenty of non-runners on the card. The stalls were in the centre for the sprint races and on the inside for the other three events. There were only three runners in this opening contest but the pace was decent and the winner forged clear. The time was 0.40 seconds slower than standard. The winner confirmed Nottingham form with the second.

### 2509 ALIDE HIRE SERVICES H'CAP — 5f 160y

6:05 (6:05) (Class 6) (0-60,60) 4-Y-0+ — **£2,264** (£673; £336; £168) **Stalls** Centre

Form — RPR

4623 **1** **Compton Prince**[9] 2214 8-8-11 **50** .......... (b) RobertWinston 1 57
(Milton Bradley) *chsd ldrs: hmpd and lost pl over 4f out: hdwy over 2f out: nt clr run over 1f out: r.o to ld post* **3/1**[2]

15-5 **2** hd **Captain Ryan**[9] 2214 6-9-7 **60** .......... JosephineGordon 4 66
(Geoffrey Deacon) *hld up: plld hrd: hdwy over 3f out: shkn up to ld over 1f out: rdn and edgd lft ins fnl f: hdd post* **5/2**[1]

03 **3** 2 **Louis Vee (IRE)**[20] 1896 9-8-3 **46** ow3 .......... (b[1]) BenRobinson(7) 8 48
(John O'Shea) *s.i.s: sn rcvrd to ld: edgd lft over 4f out: rdn and hdd over 1f out: no ex wl ins fnl f* **16/1**

4400 **4** nse **Burauq**[9] 2214 5-8-7 **49** .......... (b) HectorCrouch(3) 3 48
(Milton Bradley) *chsd ldrs: rdn over 2f out: styd on* **14/1**

30-6 **5** ½ **Catalinas Diamond (IRE)**[16] 2043 9-8-11 **50** .......... (t) SteveDrowne 5 48
(Pat Murphy) *hld up: hdwy over 2f out: rdn over 1f out: styd on same pce ins fnl f* **9/1**

00-5 **6** 1 ½ **Silver Wings (IRE)**[14] 2091 4-8-12 **58** .......... DavidEgan(7) 10 51
(David Evans) *sn chsng ldr: rdn and ev ch over 1f out: no ex ins fnl f* **4/1**[3]

-006 **7** 3 ½ **Jeanie's Place**[39] 1490 4-9-2 **55** .......... (t) WilliamCarson 2 36
(Charlie Wallis) *broke wl: sn lost pl: n.d after* **8/1**

0-00 **8** 3 **Zophilly (IRE)**[9] 2214 4-8-7 **46** oh1 .......... (t) KieranO'Neill 9 17
(Jeremy Gask) *in rr: drvn along over 3f out: no rspnse* **14/1**

5040 **9** 5 **Silver Springs (IRE)**[9] 2214 4-8-0 **46** .......... RhiainIngram(7) 6
(Roger Ingram) *chsd ldrs: hmpd over 4f out: lost pl over 3f out: sn rdn: wknd 2f out* **16/1**

1m 9.93s (-1.27) **Going Correction** -0.20s/f (Firm) **9** Ran SP% **119.8**
Speed ratings (Par 101): **100,99,97,97,96 94,89,85,79**
CSF £11.44 CT £104.69 TOTE £4.30: £1.60, £1.20, £6.00; EX 10.80 Trifecta £155.70.
**Owner** E A Hayward **Bred** Whitsbury Manor Stud **Trained** Sedbury, Gloucs
■ Stewards' Enquiry : Ben Robinson four-day ban; careless riding (24-27 May)

**FOCUS**
The winner overcame trouble to narrowly deny the favourite in this minor sprint handicap. The form is rated around the second.

### 2510 WEATHERBYS BANK MAIDEN STKS — 5f 160y

6:35 (6:36) (Class 4) 3-Y-0+ — **£5,166** (£1,546; £773; £387) **Stalls** Centre

Form — RPR

63-5 **1** **Zebulon (IRE)**[11] 2151 3-9-4 72 .......... PatDobbs 4 73
(Richard Hannon) *broke wl: sn outpcd: rdn over 1f out: r.o wl ins fnl f to ld last strides* **7/2**[2]

2 **2** nk **Fair Cop**[13] 2112 3-8-13 0 .......... DavidProbert 3 67
(Andrew Balding) *led early: settled to chse ldr tl led again over 2f out: rdn ins fnl f: hdd last strides* **4/11**[1]

20- **3** nk **Gloriux**[172] 8027 3-9-1 0 .......... (h[1]) CallumShepherd(3) 1 71
(Charles Hills) *free to post: chsd ldrs: pushed along and outpcd 1/2-way: rdn over 1f out: r.o ins fnl f* **7/1**[3]

0/5 **4** nk **Under The Covers**[21] 1889 4-9-9 0 .......... CharlesBishop 2 68
(Ronald Harris) *s.i.s: sn rcvrd to ld: rdn and hdd over 2f out: ev ch ins fnl f: styd on* **33/1**

1m 9.14s (-2.06) **Going Correction** -0.20s/f (Firm)
**WFA** 3 from 4yo 10lb **4** Ran SP% **111.0**
Speed ratings (Par 105): **105,104,104,103**
CSF £5.48 TOTE £5.40; EX 5.90 Trifecta £9.80.
**Owner** Mrs J Wood **Bred** Kevin & Meta Cullen **Trained** East Everleigh, Wilts

**FOCUS**
There was little separating the four runners at the finish in this maiden and the odds-on favourite was turned over. The winner is rated to his 2yo form.

### 2511 WEATHERBYS BANK H'CAP — 1m

7:05 (7:05) (Class 5) (0-70,70) 4-Y-0+ **£4,568** (£1,367; £683; £342; £170) **Stalls** Low

Form — RPR

0530 **1** **Mister Musicmaster**[10] 2178 8-8-13 **62** .......... DavidProbert 7 71
(Ron Hodges) *hld up: hdwy over 2f out: led ins fnl f: r.o wl* **5/1**

365- **2** 4 **Hot Mustard**[205] 7417 7-9-2 **65** .......... JosephineGordon 6 65
(William Muir) *chsd ldr who wnt clr 7f out: shkn up and tk clsr order over 2f out: ev ch over 1f out: styd on same pce ins fnl f* **11/4**[2]

3-41 **3** 1 ½ **Caledonia Laird**[23] 1842 6-9-0 **63** .......... IrineuGoncalves 3 59
(Jo Hughes) *hld up: hdwy 6f out: rdn to ld over 1f out: hdd and no ex ins fnl f* **15/8**[1]

6031 **4** 2 ¼ **Andalusite**[15] 2056 4-8-8 **57** .......... (v) FergusSweeney 4 48
(John Gallagher) *led: racd keenly: clr 7f out tl over 2f out: rdn and hdd over 1f out: wknd ins fnl f* **4/1**[3]

452- **5** 20 **Gannicus**[116] 6889 6-9-2 **70** .......... (tp) JennyPowell(5) 1 15
(Brendan Powell) *pushed along to chse ldrs: lost pl 6f out: rdn and wknd over 2f out: eased over 1f out* **5/1**

1m 37.81s (-2.99) **Going Correction** -0.20s/f (Firm) **5** Ran SP% **114.8**
CSF £19.64 TOTE £5.80: £2.60, £2.20; EX 18.20 Trifecta £74.70.
**Owner** Mrs L Sharpe & Mrs S G Clapp **Bred** Mrs J Fuller And S Dutfield **Trained** Charlton Mackrell, Somerset

**FOCUS**
The breakaway leader faded and the winner scored with authority in this handicap. However, none of these had the most compelling profiles.

### 2512 ROYDS WITHY KING H'CAP — 1m 2f 37y

7:35 (7:35) (Class 5) (0-75,77) 4-Y-0+ — **£2,911** (£866; £432; £216) **Stalls** Low

Form — RPR

3433 **1** **Attain**[6] 2336 8-8-7 **63** .......... EdwardGreatrex(3) 4 69
(Archie Watson) *chsd ldrs: wnt 2nd over 8f out: ldr wnt clr over 7f out: tk clsr order 2f out: rdn and edgd lft over 1f out: sn led: styd on: eased nr fin* **3/1**[3]

04-4 **2** 1 ½ **Glens Wobbly**[5] 2357 9-8-13 **73** .......... JordanUys(7) 2 76
(Jonathan Geake) *pushed along to ld: wnt clr over 7f out: c bk to the field 2f out: rdn and hdd 1f out: no ex ins fnl f* **10/3**

336- **3** hd **East India**[20] 7500 5-9-4 **74** .......... (h) HectorCrouch(3) 5 77
(George Baker) *pushed along early in rr: wnt 3rd over 3f out: rdn over 2f out: cl up and nt clr run over 1f out: styd on* **2/1**[1]

13-5 **4** 11 **Pack It In (IRE)**[15] 2055 4-9-5 **72** .......... JimmyFortune 8 62
(Brian Meehan) *plld hrd in 2nd tl over 8f out: racd in 3rd pl tl rdn over 3f out: wknd and eased over 1f out* **5/2**[2]

2m 8.22s (-2.78) **Going Correction** -0.20s/f (Firm) **4** Ran SP% **110.0**
Speed ratings (Par 103): **103,101,101,92**
CSF £12.61 TOTE £5.60; EX 10.50 Trifecta £32.70.
**Owner** Boadicea Bloodstock **Bred** Millsec Limited **Trained** Upper Lambourn, W Berks

**FOCUS**
This was weakened by four withdrawals but they went a good pace and an in-form runner came out on top. The runner-up is rated to his best 1m2f form.

### 2513 RAINBOW CASINOS H'CAP — 1m 2f 37y

8:05 (8:05) (Class 5) (0-75,77) 3-Y-O — **£2,911** (£866; £432; £216) **Stalls** Low

Form — RPR

554- **1** **Quloob**[180] 7907 3-9-3 **71** .......... DaneO'Neill 6 79
(Owen Burrows) *trckd ldrs: lost pl 5f out: hdwy over 2f out: r.o u.p to ld nr fin* **9/4**[2]

3-41 **2** nk **I'vegotthepower (IRE)**[9] 2220 3-9-6 **74** 6ex .......... (v) JimmyFortune 4 81
(Brian Meehan) *disp ld tl wnt on over 8f out: hdd over 5f out: chsd ldr: drvn to ld ins fnl f: hung rt and hdd nr fin* **9/4**[2]

51-2 **3** 2 ¼ **Celestation**[7] 2302 3-9-7 **75** .......... AndrewMullen 7 78
(Mark Johnston) *disp ld tl settled into 2nd over 8f out: led over 5f out: qcknd over 2f out: rdn and hdd ins fnl f: styd on same pce* **11/8**[1]

-000 **4** 9 **Sublime**[78] 848 3-8-2 **56** oh11 .......... KieranO'Neill 3 41
(Rod Millman) *hld up: racd keenly: hdwy 5f out: rdn over 2f out: hung rt over 1f out: sn hung lft and wknd* **25/1**[3]

2m 8.64s (-2.36) **Going Correction** -0.20s/f (Firm) **4** Ran SP% **107.5**
Speed ratings (Par 99): **101,100,98,91**
CSF £7.47 TOTE £3.50; EX 5.80 Trifecta £10.80.
**Owner** Hamdan Al Maktoum **Bred** Shadwell Estate Company Limited **Trained** Lambourn, Berks

**FOCUS**
Not many runners but an unexposed type finished well to beat two in-form rivals and the form looks solid. A clear pb from the winner.

### 2514 M J CHURCH H'CAP — 5f 160y

8:35 (8:35) (Class 5) (0-75,77) 4-Y-0+ — **£2,911** (£866; £432; £216) **Stalls** Centre

Form — RPR

230U **1** **Powerful Dream (IRE)**[9] 2216 4-9-6 **68** .......... (p) DavidProbert 3 75
(Ronald Harris) *chsd ldrs: rdn to ld ins fnl f: r.o* **7/2**[3]

1/0- **2** 1 ½ **Harrison Stickle**[373] 1928 5-9-2 **64** .......... FergusSweeney 5 66
(John Gallagher) *rrd s: bhd: rdn over 1f out: r.o wl to go 2nd nr fin: no ch w wnr* **9/2**

1526 **3** hd **Swendab (IRE)**[5] 2360 9-8-10 **65** .......... (b) BenRobinson(7) 7 66
(John O'Shea) *w ldr tl rdn to ld over 1f out: edgd lft: hdd ins fnl f: no ex towards fin* **9/2**

6664 **4** 2 ¼ **Chetan**[15] 2058 5-9-5 **67** .......... (tp) WilliamCarson 1 61
(Charlie Wallis) *sn led: rdn and hdd over 1f out: no ex ins fnl f* **9/4**[1]

556- **5** 10 **Vincentti (IRE)**[197] 7591 7-9-7 **76** .......... (h) DavidEgan(7) 2 37
(Ronald Harris) *dwlt: sn pushed along in rr: rdn 1/2-way: edgd rt and wknd over 1f out* **3/1**[2]

1m 9.55s (-1.65) **Going Correction** -0.20s/f (Firm) **5** Ran SP% **114.4**
Speed ratings (Par 103): **103,101,100,97,84**
CSF £19.44 TOTE £4.90: £2.80, £2.00; EX 20.80 Trifecta £48.80.
**Owner** Ridge House Stables Ltd **Bred** Ballyhane Stud **Trained** Earlswood, Monmouths

**FOCUS**
This set up for the closers but the winner scored with authority and the runner-up can be marked up because he missed the break. Weak form though, with doubts over the field.
T/Plt: £665.70 to a £1 stake. Pool: £53,578.15 - 58.75 winning units T/Qpdt: £111.20 to a £1 stake. Pool: £4,045.82 - 26.90 winning units **Colin Roberts**

## 2459 CHELMSFORD (A.W) (L-H)

Wednesday, May 10

**OFFICIAL GOING: Polytrack: standard**

Wind: virtually nil Weather: sunny

### 2515 TOTEPLACEPOT RACING'S FAVOURITE MAIDEN FILLIES' STKS — 1m 5f 66y(P)

5:55 (5:56) (Class 5) 3-Y-0+ — **£5,175** (£1,540; £769; £384) **Stalls** Low

Form — RPR

442 **1** **Utopian Dream**[43] 1414 3-8-8 74 .......... (b) RobertTart 3 85
(John Gosden) *mde all: clr and gng best whn shkn up 3f out: in command 2f out: styd on: eased towards fin: unchal* **9/4**[2]

4-3 **2** 5 **Inconceivable (IRE)**[19] 1944 3-8-8 0 .......... JoeFanning 2 77
(Ralph Beckett) *t.k.h to post: t.k.h: trckd ldrs tl wnt 2nd over 6f out: rdn over 3f out: no imp: wl hld and plugged on same pce after* **10/11**[1]

0- **3** ¾ **Munstead Star**[200] 7543 3-8-8 0 .......... RobHornby 7 76
(Andrew Balding) *hld up in last pair: hdwy 6f out: wnt 3rd and clr of field 4f out: effrt wl over 2f out: no threat to wnr and kpt on same pce fnl 2f* **9/1**

-05 **4** 47 **Vaudieu**[7] 2307 3-8-5 0 .......... (b) JackDuern(3) 8 5
(Dean Ivory) *a towards rr: rdn 7f out: lost tch 4f out: t.o but plugged on to pass wl btn rivals fr 3f out* **66/1**

25-4 **5** 2 **Tuolumne Meadows**[19] 1938 4-10-0 77 .......... AdamKirby 1
(Paul Cole) *midfield: swtchd rt and sme hdwy u.p over 5f out: 4th and btn 4f out: lost tch and t.o fnl 2f* **9/2**[3]

00-2 **6** *15* **Haldaw**[15] 2062 3-8-9 67 ow1 GrahamLee 5
(Mick Channon) *t.k.h: chsd wnr for 3f: chsd ldrs after: rdn and struggling 5f out: lost tch 3f out: t.o* **16/1**

000- **7** *1 ½* **Theydon Girls**[354] 2483 4-9-9 0 GeorgeWood(5) 4
(Peter Charalambous) *t.k.h to post: t.k.h: chsd ldr after 3f: rdn over 6f out: lost 2nd over 5f out and sn struggling: t.o over 2f out* **66/1**

**8** *1 ¾* **Astroshadow** 3-8-1 0 GabrieleMalune(7) 6
(Mark H Tompkins) *t.k.h to post: stdd and dropped in after s: hld up in last pair: rdn 6f out: sn struggling: lost tch 4f out: t.o* **50/1**

2m 49.79s (-3.81) **Going Correction** -0.20s/f (Stan)
**WFA** 3 from 4yo 20lb **8** Ran SP% **122.2**
Speed ratings (Par 100): **103,99,99,70,69 60,59,58**
CSF £5.03 TOTE £3.50: £1.30, £1.10, £2.70; EX 5.80 Trifecta £24.60.
**Owner** Helena Springfield Ltd **Bred** Meon Valley Stud **Trained** Newmarket, Suffolk

**FOCUS**
An ordinary fillies' maiden. They went steady but still finished well strung out. The winner backed up her latest Wolverhampton form.

## 2516 @TOTEPOOLRACING WIN RACING TICKETS ON TWITTER H'CAP 5f (P)

**6:25** (6:26) (Class 4) (0-85,84) 4-Y-O+ **£8,086** (£2,406; £1,202; £601) **Stalls** Low

Form RPR

0554 **1** **Dynamo Walt (IRE)**[8] 2262 6-9-7 **84** (v) KierenFox 1 89
(Derek Shaw) *t.k.h: hld up in tch in rr: effrt over 1f out: str run u.p ins fnl f to ld nr fin* **10/3**[2]

-252 **2** *½* **Cultured Knight**[11] 2161 4-8-9 **79** FinleyMarsh(7) 2 82
(Richard Hughes) *stdd s: t.k.h: trckd ldrs: rdn and hdwy to chal ent fnl f: styd on u.p to ld 75yds out: hdd and no ex nr fin* **11/4**[1]

5032 **3** *shd* **Highly Sprung (IRE)**[5] 2368 4-9-6 **83** JoeFanning 3 86+
(Mark Johnston) *dwlt: in tch: effrt to chse ldrs and nt clrest of runs 1f out: gap opened and drvn ins fnl f: styd on wl fnl 75yds* **11/4**[1]

-064 **4** *shd* **Saved My Bacon (IRE)**[48] 1326 6-8-10 **73** (h) RobertTart 6 76
(Chris Dwyer) *taken down early: hld up in tch: in last pair: effrt in centre over 1f out: hdwy 1f out: styd on wl u.p fnl 100yds* **16/1**

0106 **5** *hd* **Top Boy**[8] 2262 7-9-7 **84** (v) MartinLane 4 86
(Derek Shaw) *t.k.h: sn chsng ldr: drvn and ev ch over 1f out: unable qck and styd in same pce ins fnl f* **6/1**[3]

0-06 **6** *shd* **Kyllukey**[9] 2230 4-8-9 **77** GeorgeWood(5) 8 79
(Milton Bradley) *led: rdn over 1f out: hdd 75yds out: no ex* **33/1**

5203 **7** *2 ¾* **Normal Equilibrium**[14] 2083 7-8-7 **75** LewisEdmunds(5) 7 68
(Ivan Furtado) *chsd ldrs on outer: rdn over 1f out: lost pl and bhd 1f out: wknd ins fnl f* **7/1**

59.62s (-0.58) **Going Correction** -0.20s/f (Stan) **7** Ran SP% **112.0**
Speed ratings (Par 105): **96,95,95,94,94 94,90**
CSF £12.38 CT £26.90 TOTE £5.00: £3.10, £1.20; EX 14.50 Trifecta £43.40.
**Owner** Brian Johnson (Northamptonshire) **Bred** Dan Major **Trained** Sproxton, Leics

**FOCUS**
A bunch finish in this typical 0-85 sprint handicap, off an ordinary pace. The winner is rated in line with his winter form.

## 2517 TOTEQUADPOT FOUR PLACES IN FOUR RACES FILLIES' H'CAP 1m (P)

**6:55** (6:56) (Class 3) (0-90,85) 3-Y-O **£12,938** (£3,850; £1,924; £962) **Stalls** Low

Form RPR

1- **1** **Pavillon**[161] 8152 3-9-1 **79** AdamKirby 6 87+
(Clive Cox) *hld up towards rr: effrt 2f out: swtchd rt and hdwy u.p over 1f out: styd on strly u.p ins fnl f to ld on post* **9/2**[2]

10- **2** *nse* **Salamah (IRE)**[228] 6787 3-8-12 **76** SilvestreDeSousa 7 83
(Simon Crisford) *chsd ldrs: effrt 2f out: styd on u.p to ld 100yds out: kpt on wl: hdd on post* **6/1**

10-3 **3** *2* **Illaunmore (USA)**[27] 1760 3-9-4 **82** RobertTart 3 84
(John Gosden) *chsd ldrs: clsd and upsides on inner ent fnl 2f: rdn to ld over 1f out: drvn 1f out: hdd 100yds out and styd on same pce after* **3/1**[1]

01- **4** *¾* **Rely On Me (IRE)**[186] 7818 3-8-13 **77** OisinMurphy 2 77+
(Andrew Balding) *hld up in last trio: n.m.r sn after s: effrt 2f out: swtchd rt over 1f out: edging lft and hdwy ins fnl f: kpt on wl wout threatening ldrs* **10/1**

-213 **5** *2* **Pepita (IRE)**[10] 2177 3-9-2 **80** SeanLevey 9 76
(Richard Hannon) *led: jnd and rdn and hdd over 1f out: no ex 1f out: wknd ins fnl f* **12/1**

412- **6** *1 ¼* **Flying North**[214] 7147 3-9-4 **82** TimmyMurphy 1 75
(Richard Hannon) *rousted along leaving stalls: in tch in midfield: pushed along over 3f out: no imp u.p over 1f out: plugged on same pce ins fnl f* **5/1**[3]

24-5 **7** *nk* **Storm Cry**[20] 1901 3-9-6 **84** JoeFanning 8 76
(Mark Johnston) *t.k.h: hld up in tch in midfield: hmpd over 6f out: effrt in 4th over 2f out: no imp over 1f out* **12/1**

001- **8** *1 ¼* **Textured (IRE)**[177] 7956 3-9-3 **81** RyanMoore 5 70
(Sir Michael Stoute) *sn dropped to rr and nvr travelling wl: no imp u.p over 1f out: n.d* **7/1**

3-14 **9** *6* **Millie's Kiss**[47] 1343 3-8-9 **73** LukeMorris 4 48
(Philip McBride) *chsd ldrs: rdn over 3f out: struggling u.p and lost pl over 1f out: bhd ins fnl f* **16/1**

1m 37.69s (-2.21) **Going Correction** -0.20s/f (Stan) **9** Ran SP% **117.0**
Speed ratings (Par 100): **103,102,100,100,98 96,96,95,89**
CSF £32.11 CT £94.45 TOTE £5.30: £1.60, £2.10, £2.00; EX 34.50 Trifecta £111.60.
**Owner** Mondial Racing & Robert Haim **Bred** J Bernstein & R Haim **Trained** Lambourn, Berks

**FOCUS**
A 3yo fillies' handicap at this time of the year with this sort of prize money should work out to be decent form. It's rated around the third and fifth.

## 2518 TOTEPOOL SUPPORTING MENTAL HEALTH AWARENESS WEEK H'CAP 7f (P)

**7:25** (7:27) (Class 2) (0-100,99) 4-Y-O+ **£19,407** (£5,775; £2,886; £1,443) **Stalls** Low

Form RPR

0110 **1** **Welliesinthewater (IRE)**[13] 2116 7-8-7 **85** oh1 (v) KierenFox 1 92
(Derek Shaw) *chsd ldr tl 3f out: effrt over 1f out: styd on u.p to chal ins fnl f: led wl ins fnl f: rdn out* **14/1**

4-53 **2** *¾* **Mount Tahan (IRE)**[18] 1974 5-8-13 **91** KevinStott 5 96
(Kevin Ryan) *t.k.h: chsd ldrs tl wnt 2nd 3f out: rdn to ld over 1f out: kpt on u.p and maintained narrow ld tl hdd and no ex wl ins fnl f* **5/1**[3]

60-1 **3** *½* **That Is The Spirit**[13] 2115 6-9-7 **99** DanielTudhope 8 103
(David O'Meara) *sn led: rdn and hdd over 1f out: kpt on u.p and stl v ch tl no ex and one pced fnl 100yds* **9/2**[2]

2-64 **4** *½* **Viscount Barfield**[13] 2115 4-8-13 **91** (h) OisinMurphy 4 93
(Andrew Balding) *trckd ldrs: effrt over 1f out: drvn and pressing ldrs ins fnl f: styd on same pce fnl 100yds* **3/1**[1]

1450 **5** *nse* **Loyalty**[13] 2115 10-8-11 **89** (v) MartinLane 2 91
(Derek Shaw) *hld up in tch: hdwy to chse ldrs and swtchd rt jst ins fnl f: chal and n.m.r sn after: jst outpcd towards fin* **14/1**

40-6 **6** *5* **Basil Berry**[25] 1794 6-9-0 **92** (b) SilvestreDeSousa 7 81
(Chris Dwyer) *dropped in after s: hld up in rr of main gp: effrt over 1f out: sme hdwy 1f out: kpt on same pce ins fnl f* **8/1**

1225 **7** *2* **Outer Space**[13] 2115 6-9-0 **92** TimmyMurphy 9 75
(Jamie Osborne) *in tch in midfield on outer: rdn over 1f out: little rspnse and sn btn: wknd ins fnl f* **14/1**

4054 **8** *4 ½* **Golden Amber (IRE)**[13] 2113 6-8-7 **90** LuluStanford(5) 3 61
(Dean Ivory) *v.s.a: n.d* **7/1**

1114 **9** *5* **Hammer Gun (USA)**[33] 1598 4-8-7 **85** (v) LukeMorris 6 43
(Derek Shaw) *t.k.h: hld up in tch: rdn over 1f out: sn btn: bhd and eased ins fnl f* **7/1**

1m 24.35s (-2.85) **Going Correction** -0.20s/f (Stan) **9** Ran SP% **116.0**
Speed ratings (Par 109): **108,107,106,106,105 100,97,92,87**
CSF £82.77 CT £375.08 TOTE £15.30: £3.50, £1.70, £2.00; EX 110.50 Trifecta £667.80.
**Owner** Shawthing Racing Partnership **Bred** Brendan Ryan **Trained** Sproxton, Leics

**FOCUS**
Four of these were re-opposing after contesting a C&D handicap at the end of April, but they could only manage third, fourth, fifth and seventh, with the winner causing a bit of an upset. He's been awarded a surprise pb.

## 2519 TOTEPOOLLIVEINFO.COM FOR RACING RESULTS CONDITIONS STKS 1m 6f (P)

**7:55** (7:55) (Class 2) 4-Y-O+ **£19,407** (£5,775; £2,886; £1,443) **Stalls** Low

Form RPR

046- **1** **Harrison**[242] 6329 4-9-3 103 GrahamLee 1 108
(Mick Channon) *chsd ldr: rdn ent fnl 3f: ev ch 2f out: kpt on u.p to ld 1f out: wnt clr ins fnl f: styd on wl: readily* **5/1**

130- **2** *2 ¼* **St Michel**[214] 7150 4-9-10 112 (p) LukeMorris 2 112
(Sir Mark Prescott Bt) *hld up in tch in 4th: effrt and swtchd rt wl over 1f oiut: sn edging lft and no imp: kpt on to chse wnr 75yds out: nvr enough pce to chal* **15/8**[1]

2350 **3** *1* **Dylan Mouth (IRE)**[18] 1957 6-9-4 110 AndreaAtzeni 4 103
(Marco Botti) *trckd ldng pair: rdn over 3f out: keeping on same pce in 4th whn nt clr run and swtchd rt ins fnl f: kpt on to go 3rd towards fin: no threat to wnr* **10/3**[3]

1-34 **4** *¾* **Fabricate**[26] 1779 5-9-8 102 (p) RyanMoore 3 106
(Michael Bell) *led: rdn ent fnl 2f: hdd 1f out: no ex and one pced after: lost 2 pls fnl 75yds* **9/4**[2]

0-50 **5** *8* **Ballynanty (IRE)**[26] 1779 5-9-4 97 OisinMurphy 5 91
(Andrew Balding) *stdd and dropped in bhd after s: hld up in rr: effrt over 1f out: no imp and wknd ins fnl f* **14/1**

2m 57.96s (-5.24) **Going Correction** -0.20s/f (Stan) **5** Ran SP% **112.0**
Speed ratings (Par 109): **106,104,104,103,99**
CSF £15.08 TOTE £6.10: £3.00, £1.70; EX 18.00 Trifecta £68.20.
**Owner** T Radford **Bred** Mike Channon Bloodstock Ltd **Trained** West Ilsley, Berks

**FOCUS**
Despite the small field this was a high-class conditions race with four of the field possessing three-figure official ratings. Harrison looks improved, the second and fourth helping with the standard.

## 2520 TOTEPOOL BETTING ON ALL UK RACING H'CAP 1m 2f (P)

**8:25** (8:29) (Class 2) (0-100,95) 3-Y-O **£16,172** (£4,812; £2,405; £1,202) **Stalls** Low

Form RPR

16-2 **1** **Drochaid**[34] 1582 3-8-7 **81** ow1 OisinMurphy 5 89
(Andrew Balding) *t.k.h: chsd ldr for 1f: styd chsng ldrs: rdn to ld 2f out: hrd pressed wl ins fnl f: jst hld on: all out* **5/1**[2]

21-0 **2** *shd* **Zumurudee (USA)**[67] 1040 3-9-2 **90** DanielMuscutt 2 97+
(Marco Botti) *wnt rt leaving stalls: hld up in tch in last trio: hdwy u.p over 1f out: chsd wnr 1f out: styd on and str chal towards fin: jst hld* **5/1**[2]

101- **3** *4 ½* **Total Star**[224] 6868 3-9-7 **95** LukeMorris 4 93
(Luca Cumani) *hld up in last trio: hdwy u.p over 1f out: chsd clr ldng pair wl ins fnl f: kpt on but no threat to ldrs* **10/1**

52-0 **4** *1* **Ghayyar (IRE)**[74] 933 3-8-12 **86** SeanLevey 3 82
(Richard Hannon) *hld up in tch in midfield: effrt in centre over 1f out: kpt on to go 4th wl ins fnl f: no threat to ldrs* **25/1**

31-0 **5** *1 ¾* **Elucidation (IRE)**[21] 1886 3-9-0 **88** RyanMoore 7 81
(Sir Michael Stoute) *led: tl 7f out: chsd ldr tl rdn to chal 2f out tl over 1f out: 3rd and no ex 1f out: wknd and lost 2 pls wl ins fnl f* **11/8**[1]

65-4 **6** *1* **Red Ensign (IRE)**[25] 1797 3-9-0 **88** AndreaAtzeni 1 79
(Simon Crisford) *t.k.h: hld up in tch in midfield: effrt on inner over 1f out: drvn and no imp 1f out: wl hld fnl f* **9/1**[3]

20-1 **7** *2 ½* **Curlew River**[27] 1756 3-8-7 **81** JoeFanning 9 67
(Mark Johnston) *chsd ldr and t.k.h: after 1f tl dropped to 3rd over 7f out: rdn and unable qck over 2f out: lost pl over 1f out: wknd fnl f* **14/1**

015- **8** *½* **Plant Pot Power (IRE)**[180] 7909 3-8-8 **85** HollieDoyle(3) 6 70
(Richard Hannon) *t.k.h: chsd ldrs: swtchd rt 8f out: hdwy to ld 7f out tl rdn and hdd 2f out: struggling whn impeded over 1f out: wknd fnl f* **25/1**

-21 **9** *7* **Solajan (IRE)**[63] 1089 3-8-3 **77** (h) SilvestreDeSousa 8 48
(Ed Dunlop) *t.k.h: hld up in midfield: hmpd and stmbld after 2f: in rr after: swtchd rt and effrt over 2f out: no imp and hung lft over 1f out: eased fnl f* **9/1**[3]

2m 3.83s (-4.77) **Going Correction** -0.20s/f (Stan) **9** Ran SP% **118.9**
Speed ratings (Par 105): **111,110,107,106,105 104,102,101,96**
CSF £31.20 CT £240.30 TOTE £6.90: £2.30, £2.80, £3.60; EX 40.80 Trifecta £205.20.
**Owner** Mick and Janice Mariscotti **Bred** Meon Valley Stud **Trained** Kingsclere, Hants

**FOCUS**
Unexposed 3yos from big stables in this handicap and, despite the well-backed favourite disappointing, it's form that it should pay to be positive about. The winner improved.

## 2521 UB40 PLAY HERE ON 12TH AUGUST MEDIAN AUCTION MAIDEN STKS 1m 2f (P)

**8:55** (9:00) (Class 5) 3-5-Y-O **£5,175** (£1,540; £769; £384) **Stalls** Low

Form RPR

63-2 **1** **Kasperenko**[14] 2092 3-8-13 80 TomQueally 7 87
(David Lanigan) *chsd ldrs: hdwy to chse wnr 4f out: rdn over 1f out: styd on to ld 1f out: sn in command: styd on* **2/1**[2]

5 **2** *2 ¾* **Grieg Hall**[20] 1906 3-8-13 0 JamesDoyle 4 81
(John Gosden) *led: pushed along ent fnl 2f out: hdd 1f out: sn btn and one pced fnl f* **8/11**[1]

0 **3** *2 ¾* **Zack Mayo**[22] 1857 3-8-13 0 OisinMurphy 5 76
(Philip McBride) *chsd ldrs on inner: 3rd and pushed along ent fnl 2f: outpcd and btn whn swtchd rt over 1f out: clr 3rd and kpt on same pce ins fnl f* **20/1**

0- **4** *11* **Arcadian Sea (IRE)**[196] 7621 3-8-13 0................(h[1]) SilvestreDeSousa 8 54
(William Jarvis) *chsd ldr tl 4f out: 4th and outpcd over 2f out: wknd over 1f out* **20/1**

00 **5** *1 ½* **Incredible Dream (IRE)**[84] 747 4-9-11 0...................... JackDuern(3) 2 52
(Dean Ivory) *s.i.s and wnt lft s: hld up in rr: n.d: swtchd rt and sltly impeded wl over 1f out: no ch but passed btn rivals ins fnl f* **66/1**

**6** *2 ¾* **Toronto Sound** 3-8-13 0.............................................. LukeMorris 9 45
(Sir Mark Prescott Bt) *wnt bdly rt s: sn swtchd lft and a rr: rdn over 2f out: sn struggling: wknd over 1f out* **8/1**[3]

0 **7** *3 ¾* **Borntosin (IRE)**[8] 2260 3-8-8 0........................ GeorgeWood(5) 6 38
(Marco Botti) *short of room leaving stalls: in tch in midfield: 5th and outpcd u.p over 2f out: wknd over 1f out* **33/1**

0 **8** *3* **Red Master (IRE)**[11] 2164 3-8-13 0................................ JimmyQuinn 1 32
(Ed Dunlop) *hld up in 6th: nvr on terms w ldrs: rdn over 2f out: outpcd and btn 2f out: sn wknd* **20/1**

2m 5.3s (-3.30) **Going Correction** -0.20s/f (Stan)
**WFA** 3 from 4yo 15lb **8** Ran SP% **121.1**
Speed ratings (Par 103): **105,102,100,91,90 88,85,83**
CSF £3.81 TOTE £3.00: £1.10, £1.10, £4.40; EX 4.00 Trifecta £18.60.
**Owner** Ms Delaney, Black & Middleham Park L **Bred** Hillwood Thoroughbred Breeding Ltd **Trained** Newmarket, Suffolk
■ Clearance was withdrawn. Price at time of withdrawal 40/1. Rule 4 does not apply.

**FOCUS**
Despite the decent prize on offer this was an uncompetitive maiden and the first three pulled well clear of the rest. The winner is going the right way.
T/Plt: £42.20 to a £1 stake. Pool: £77,840.69 - 1,344.46 winning units T/Qpdt: £23.20 to a £1 stake. Pool: £6,141.26 - 195.09 winning units **Steve Payne**

# CHESTER (L-H)
Wednesday, May 10

**OFFICIAL GOING: Good (good to firm in places; watered; 7.9)**
Wind: Light, against Weather: Sunny

## 2522 STELLAR GROUP LILY AGNES CONDITIONS STKS (PLUS 10 RACE) 5f 15y
**1:50** (1:53) (Class 2) 2-Y-O

**£12,450** (£3,728; £1,864; £932; £466; £234) **Stalls** Low

Form RPR

01 **1** **Yogi's Girl (IRE)**[16] 2037 2-8-11 0.............................................. JFEgan 3 81
(David Evans) *mde all: rdn over 1f out: strly pressed ins fnl f: hld on gamely* **4/1**[2]

321 **2** *nse* **Black Orange**[11] 2154 2-9-2 0.................................. MartinDwyer 4 86
(Gay Kelleway) *racd keenly: sn w wnr: rdn 2f out: str chal ins fnl f: r.o for press: jst denied* **12/1**

4 **3** *2 ¼* **Central City (IRE)**[11] 2134 2-9-2 0................................... JamesDoyle 8 78
(Hugo Palmer) *in tch on inner: effrt 2f out: swtchd rt ins fnl f: styd on: nt pce of front pair* **11/2**

21 **4** *½* **Emilia James**[13] 2105 2-8-11 0........................................ FrannyNorton 9 71
(Mark Johnston) *midfield: hdwy 1/2-way: effrt to chse ldrs 2f out: kpt on ins fnl f: nt pce to chal* **5/1**[3]

43 **5** *3 ½* **Felisa**[7] 2292 2-8-11 0.................................................. ConnorBeasley 7 58
(David Evans) *s.i.s: outpcd and bhd: styd on fnl f: nvr nrr* **33/1**

**6** *1 ¼* **The Golden Cue** 2-9-2 0.............................................. RoystonFfrench 1 59
(Steph Hollinshead) *hld up: outpcd 3f out: kpt on ins fnl f: nvr able to trble ldrs* **66/1**

12 **7** *1* **Requinto Dawn (IRE)**[25] 1803 2-9-2 0............................ TonyHamilton 5 55+
(Richard Fahey) *broke wl: trckd ldrs tl rdn and wknd over 1f out* **2/1**[1]

62 **8** *3 ¼* **Storm Doris (IRE)**[8] 2277 2-8-11 0................................... RyanPowell 6 39
(James Unett) *no bttr than midfield: outpcd 1/2-way: c wd ent st wl over 1f out: nvr a threat* **66/1**

2 **9** *1 ½* **Big Time Maybe (IRE)**[19] 1934 2-9-2 0................ RichardKingscote 10 38+
(Tom Dascombe) *racd on outer: chsd ldrs tl wknd 2f out* **5/1**[3]

**10** *17* **Sir Walter (IRE)** 2-9-2 0................................................... JasonHart 11
(Eric Alston) *missed break: rn v green: bdly outpcd and a wl bhd* **50/1**

1m 0.41s (-0.59) **Going Correction** -0.125s/f (Firm) **10** Ran SP% **117.6**
Speed ratings (Par 99): **99,98,95,94,88 86,85,80,77,50**
CSF £49.81 TOTE £4.70: £2.60, £3.20, £1.90; EX 47.80 Trifecta £297.60.
**Owner** A Cooke, K McCabe, Mrs A M Burns **Bred** Newlands House Stud & Mrs A M Burns **Trained** Pandy, Monmouths

**FOCUS**
Race distances as advertised. The ground was given as good, good to firm in places before the start of the meeting and had been watered with 3mm on each of Saturday, Monday and Tuesday. Clerk of the course Andrew Morris said: "We've had no rain since May 1 and have watered in the build-up to the meeting. The track is in great condition with lots of moisture this morning. With this beautiful weather it will be drying out all the time and we're expecting good, fast ground." The opener was the usual speed test for juveniles. Eight of the ten had a previously run, with four of them having a win in their profiles. Speed proveed crucial with the first two always 1-2.

## 2523 ARKLE FINANCE CHESHIRE OAKS (FOR THE ROBERT SANGSTER MEMORIAL CUP) (LISTED RACE) 1m 3f 75y
**2:25** (2:27) (Class 1) 3-Y-O

**£34,026** (£12,900; £6,456; £3,216; £1,614; £810) **Stalls** Low

Form RPR

1-3 **1** **Enable**[19] 1943 3-9-0 102.................................................. FrankieDettori 3 112+
(John Gosden) *racd keenly: trckd ldr: led 3f out: qcknd up over 2f out: rdn and nrly 3 l clr over 1f out: eased towards fin* **2/1**[2]

**2** *1 ¾* **Alluringly (USA)**[20] 1916 3-9-0 0.......................................... RyanMoore 2 109+
(A P O'Brien, Ire) *trckd ldrs: rdn to go 2nd over 2f out: nt qckn over 1f out: kpt on ins fnl f: no imp on wnr* **1/1**[1]

13- **3** *9* **Tansholpan**[193] 7698 3-9-0 89........................................... AndreaAtzeni 4 94
(Roger Varian) *hld up in tch: rdn 3f out: wnt 3rd over 2f out: kpt on one pce fnl f: no ch w front two* **8/1**[3]

140- **4** *6* **Rich Legacy (IRE)**[192] 7722 3-9-5 105.............................. OisinMurphy 7 89
(Ralph Beckett) *hld up: effrt 3f out: no imp on ldrs: wknd over 1f out* **14/1**

10-6 **5** *1 ¾* **Hidden Steps**[25] 1796 3-9-0 87...................................(h) DavidProbert 1 81
(Andrew Balding) *racd keenly: hld up in tch: pushed along and outpcd over 2f out: wl btn* **33/1**

310- **6** *4* **Argenterie**[229] 6748 3-9-0 92............................................ MartinDwyer 6 74
(Marcus Tregoning) *in rr: rdn over 5f out: outpcd whn wnt wd ent st wl over 1f out: nvr a threat* **16/1**

506- **7** *9* **Erica Bing**[195] 7655 3-9-0 88............................................. FrannyNorton 5 59
(Jo Hughes) *led: hdd 3f out: wknd over 2f out* **66/1**

2m 23.8s (-1.00) **Going Correction** -0.125s/f (Firm) **7** Ran SP% **111.4**
Speed ratings (Par 107): **98,96,90,85,84 81,75**
CSF £4.06 TOTE £2.60: £1.50, £1.20; EX 4.40 Trifecta £15.40.
**Owner** K Abdullah **Bred** Juddmonte Farms Ltd **Trained** Newmarket, Suffolk

**FOCUS**
They didn't go that quick and it developed into a bit of a dash, but the market leaders drew clear of some useful rivals and it looks decent form, rated on the positive side.

## 2524 BOODLES DIAMOND H'CAP 5f 15y
**3:00** (3:02) (Class 2) (0-105,103) 4-Y-O+

**£18,675** (£5,592; £2,796; £1,398; £699; £351) **Stalls** Low

Form RPR

10-1 **1** **El Astronaute (IRE)**[22] 1863 4-8-8 **90**................................. JasonHart 1 96
(John Quinn) *mde all: rdn over 1f out: hld on wl nr fin* **2/1**[1]

-004 **2** *nk* **Taexali (IRE)**[16] 2046 4-8-11 **93**.............................(b) SilvestreDeSousa 2 98
(John Patrick Shanahan, Ire) *in tch on inner: effrt over 1f out: r.o ins fnl f: clsd on wnr nr fin* **4/1**[2]

025- **3** *¾* **Confessional**[200] 7537 10-8-10 **92**.................................(e) DavidAllan 6 94
(Tim Easterby) *chsd ldrs: rdn to go 2nd over 1f out: no real imp on wnr: hld nr fin* **10/1**

21-3 **4** *½* **Spring Loaded (IRE)**[119] 170 5-8-13 **95**........................ JoeyHaynes 5 95
(Paul D'Arcy) *hld up: rdn and hdwy over 1f out: r.o ins fnl f: nt quite pce of ldrs* **9/2**[3]

10-0 **5** *3* **Bossipop**[23] 1831 4-8-3 **85**............................................(b) CamHardie 13 75
(Tim Easterby) *bhd: pushed along over 1f out: styd on ins fnl f: nt rch ldrs* **50/1**

4204 **6** *hd* **Seamster**[4] 2409 10-7-13 **84** oh2.......................................(t) HollieDoyle(3) 9 73
(David Loughnane) *chsd ldrs: rdn over 1f out: kpt on same pce ins fnl f* **16/1**

3060 **7** *5* **Ballesteros**[29] 1696 8-8-3 **85**............................................ PaulHanagan 10 56
(Richard Fahey) *racd off pce: pushed along over 2f out: nvr a threat* **33/1**

00-0 **8** *hd* **Blithe Spirit**[19] 1936 6-8-8 **90**............................................ NeilFarley 8 60
(Eric Alston) *w ldr: rdn 2f out: wknd over 1f out* **12/1**

0-21 **9** *10* **Majestic Hero (IRE)**[14] 2083 5-8-10 **92**........................ JamieSpencer 7 26
(Ronald Harris) *s.i.s: racd off the pce: rn wd 2f out: lft bhd after* **11/2**

59.17s (-1.83) **Going Correction** -0.125s/f (Firm) **9** Ran SP% **114.5**
Speed ratings (Par 109): **109,108,107,106,101 101,93,93,77**
CSF £9.78 CT £62.45 TOTE £2.80: £1.30, £1.50, £2.70; EX 12.10 Trifecta £72.40.
**Owner** Ross Harmon **Bred** T Jones **Trained** Settrington, N Yorks

**FOCUS**
The runners that were due to be housed in stalls 3 and 4 were taken out earlier in the day, along with stalls 11 and 12, so that shifted the field down a bit. However, that made little difference as the horse in stall 1 got a flyer and made every yard. He's rated in line with his Newmarket win.

## 2525 188BET CHESTER CUP H'CAP 2m 2f 140y
**3:35** (3:36) (Class 2) 4-Y-O+

**£73,908** (£22,248; £11,124; £5,544; £2,784; £1,404) **Stalls** High

Form RPR

200- **1** **Montaly**[186] 7824 6-9-6 **99**.................................................. OisinMurphy 2 106
(Andrew Balding) *trckd ldrs early: sn in midfield: hdwy over 1f out: str run fnl 75yds to ld cl home* **16/1**

54-3 **2** *nk* **Yorkidding**[11] 2157 5-9-3 **96**..................................... RichardKingscote 3 102
(Mark Johnston) *led for 3f: trckd ldrs after: rdn to go 2nd over 1f out: led ins fnl f: hdd and hld towards fin* **9/1**

303- **3** *¾* **Fun Mac (GER)**[205] 7411 6-9-9 **102**................................(t) JimCrowley 13 107
(Hughie Morrison) *trckd ldrs: effrt 2f out: rdn to chal ins fnl f: wanted to lug lft: hld nr fin* **25/1**

135- **4** *½* **Who Dares Wins (IRE)**[56] 6545 5-8-13 **92**................(p) TomMarquand 7 97+
(Alan King) *midfield: hdwy 2f out: plld out to the rt whn nt clr run ins fnl f: styd on: gng on at the fin* **5/1**[2]

43-5 **5** *¾* **Magic Circle (IRE)**[25] 1798 5-9-5 **98**................................. FranBerry 18 102
(Ralph Beckett) *midfield: swtchd rt and hdwy over 2f out: fairly wd ent st wl over 1f out: styd on: nt quite get to ldrs* **25/1**

3112 **6** *½* **Watersmeet**[26] 1770 6-9-8 **101**........................................ FrannyNorton 6 104
(Mark Johnston) *prom: led wl over 2f out: rdn over 1f out: hdd ins fnl f: no ex fnl 50yds* **8/1**[3]

0-62 **7** *3 ½* **Sir Chauvelin**[11] 2157 5-8-13 **92**....................................... SamJames 11 91+
(Jim Goldie) *hld up: nt clr run over 1f out: styd on ins fnl f: nrst fin* **14/1**

30-4 **8** *nse* **Angel Gabrial (IRE)**[25] 1802 8-9-3 **96**........................... PaulHanagan 19 95
(Richard Fahey) *prom: led after 3f: hdd wl over 2f out: stl there 1f out: wknd fnl 100yds* **25/1**

60-0 **9** *hd* **Suegioo (FR)**[25] 1802 8-9-6 **102**.....................(p) AdamMcNamara(3) 16 101+
(Richard Fahey) *rdn s: in rr: nt a travelling wl: rdn over 2f out: styd on ins fnl f: nrst fin* **40/1**

202- **10** *3 ¼* **Nakeeta**[193] 7708 6-9-10 **103**......................................(h) JamieSpencer 10 99
(Iain Jardine) *racd keenly: hld up: rdn over 2f out: sme hdwy over 1f out: nvr able to get gng* **16/1**

-310 **11** *1* **First Mohican**[26] 1770 9-9-4 **100**...............................(h) HollieDoyle(3) 17 94
(Alan King) *s.i.s: t.k.h: in rr div: in midfield on outer 7f out: outpcd over 2f out: nvr a threat* **33/1**

16-1 **12** *nk* **Blakeney Point**[25] 1798 4-8-9 **95**.......................(p) KieranShoemark(3) 1 89
(Roger Charlton) *trckd ldrs: rdn 2f out: nt qckn over 1f out: eased whn hld ins fnl f* **4/1**[1]

5/0- **13** *½* **Duke Of Clarence (IRE)**[371] 1967 8-9-4 **97**................... JamesDoyle 15 91
(Ian Williams) *chsd ldrs: 5 wd on first bnd after 2f: effrt over 2f out: wknd over 1f out* **50/1**

551- **14** *shd* **Golden Spear**[22] 7708 6-9-1 **94**...................................(t) RyanMoore 12 87
(A J Martin, Ire) *midfield early: hld up: nvr able to get competitive* **10/1**

50/ **15** *1* **Good Tradition (IRE)**[25] 4851 6-9-0 **93**........................ PaulMulrennan 9 85
(Donald McCain) *midfield tl rdn and wknd over 2f out* **50/1**

324- **16** *2 ¾* **The Cashel Man (IRE)**[214] 7150 5-8-13 **92**..................(b) WilliamBuick 8 81
(David Simcock) *in rr: hdwy over 3f out: rdn on outer over 2f out whn no imp: wknd wl over 1f out* **9/1**

253- **17** *12* **Sea Of Heaven (IRE)**[214] 7150 5-9-4 **97**........................ LukeMorris 14 73
(Sir Mark Prescott Bt) *midfield: effrt on wd outside over 2f out: sn lost pl: pushed wd over 1f out: bhd after: eased whn btn appr fnl f* **9/1**

4m 3.37s (-1.43) **Going Correction** -0.125s/f (Firm)
**WFA** 4 from 5yo+ 1lb **17** Ran SP% **126.1**
Speed ratings (Par 109): **98,97,97,97,97 96,95,95,95,93 93,93,93,93,92 91,86**
CSF £148.26 CT £3603.00 TOTE £26.00: £4.80, £2.50, £6.50, £1.90; EX 255.70 Trifecta £9416.10.
**Owner** Farleigh Racing **Bred** Farleigh Court Racing Partnership **Trained** Kingsclere, Hants

**FOCUS**
A highly competitive handicap, but as is always the case around here, run of the race proved paramount, and the first two enjoyed rail-hugging runs in the first half of the field. Ordinary form for the grade, the winner posting a small pb.

## 2526 SPORTING INDEX H'CAP 1m 4f 63y
4:05 (4:06) (Class 3) (0-90,90) 3-Y-O

£9,960 (£2,982; £1,491; £745; £372; £187) Stalls Low

| Form | | | | RPR |
|---|---|---|---|---|
| 213 | 1 | | **Here And Now**28 1725 3-8-8 77 PaulHanagan 1 (Ralph Beckett) *chsd ldrs: rdn and nt clr run over 1f out: plld to out ins fnl f: r.o strly to ld nr fin* 15/2[3] | 88+ |
| 41-1 | 2 | ½ | **Stradivarius (IRE)**21 1875 3-9-7 90 FrankieDettori 6 (John Gosden) *prom: rdn and edgd lft over 1f out: led ins fnl f: hdd and hld nr fin* 1/1[1] | 100 |
| 36-1 | 3 | 2¼ | **Jukebox Jive (FR)**35 1559 3-9-0 83 JFEgan 4 (Anthony Honeyball) *led: rdn over 1f out: hdd ins fnl f: no ex fnl 75yds* 12/1 | 89 |
| 5-51 | 4 | 3 | **Teodoro (IRE)**6 2347 3-8-6 75 6ex FrannyNorton 2 (Tom Dascombe) *racd keenly: in tch: rdn and outpcd over 2f out: kpt on ins fnl f: nvr able to chal* 8/1 | 76 |
| 2-1 | 5 | ½ | **Al Zaman (IRE)**18 1984 3-9-1 84 (t) JimCrowley 5 (Simon Crisford) *in tch: effrt 3f out: outpcd over 1f out: no imp after* 11/2[2] | 84 |
| 21-3 | 6 | 4 | **Whip Nae Nae (IRE)**12 2118 3-9-1 84 RyanMoore 8 (Richard Hannon) *swtchd lft s: hld up: rdn 2f out: no imp* 8/1 | 78 |
| 2-12 | 7 | 5 | **The Blues Master (IRE)**21 1877 3-8-8 77 (p[1]) PJMcDonald 3 (Mark Johnston) *hld up: pushed along over 4f out: lft bhd over 1f out* 25/1 | 63 |
| 3211 | 8 | 7 | **Global Revival (IRE)**21 1877 3-8-9 78 SilvestreDeSousa 7 (Ed Dunlop) *hld up: rdn over 2f out: wknd over 1f out* 18/1 | 53 |

2m 35.05s (-3.45) **Going Correction** -0.125s/f (Firm) 8 Ran SP% **116.2**
Speed ratings (Par 103): **106,105,104,102,101 99,95,91**
CSF £15.72 CT £93.00 TOTE £7.80: £2.40, £1.10, £3.70; EX 20.60 Trifecta £147.40.
**Owner** J H Richmond-Watson **Bred** Lawn Stud **Trained** Kimpton, Hants

**FOCUS**
The first three home were in the first three throughout, so it's hard to think this is reliable form, although the first two will surely hold their own in similar races in the short term. The time was decent.

## 2527 DEEPBRIDGE CAPITAL MAIDEN STKS (PLUS 10 RACE) 1m 2f 70y
4:35 (4:38) (Class 3) 3-Y-O

£8,715 (£2,609; £1,304; £652; £326; £163) Stalls High

| Form | | | | RPR |
|---|---|---|---|---|
| 2-25 | 1 | | **Never Surrender (IRE)**14 2084 3-9-5 88 JamieSpencer 3 (Charles Hills) *mde all: rdn over 1f out: sn pressed: r.o and in command fnl 100yds* 2/1[1] | 81+ |
| 33 | 2 | 1¾ | **Bristol Missile (USA)**11 2143 3-9-5 0 TomMarquand 4 (Richard Hannon) *midfield: clsd over 3f out: wnt 2nd 2f out: rdn to chal 1f out: nt qckn ins fnl f: no imp on wnr fnl 100yds* 9/2[3] | 78+ |
| 0-2 | 3 | 3 | **Meccabah (FR)**16 2019 3-9-0 0 WilliamBuick 5 (Andrew Balding) *prom: chalng 3f out: rdn and nt qckn 2f out: styd on same pce fnl f* 11/4[2] | 67+ |
| 46- | 4 | 3½ | **Solar Cross**189 7769 3-9-2 0 KieranShoemark(3) 10 (Roger Charlton) *hld up in rr: rdn 3f out: hdwy 2f out: kpt on ins fnl f: nvr able to trble ldrs* 8/1 | 65+ |
| 3 | 5 | ¾ | **Unite The Clans (IRE)**10 2175 3-9-5 0 JimCrowley 2 (John Patrick Shanahan, Ire) *hld up: outpcd over 2f out: kpt on fnl f: no imp* 7/1 | 63 |
| -030 | 6 | ½ | **Baker Street**6 2349 3-9-5 61 (p) BenCurtis 9 (Tom Dascombe) *sn chsd ldrs: rdn over 3f out: outpcd over 2f out: one pce fnl f* 50/1 | 62 |
| 0-64 | 7 | hd | **Legato (IRE)**13 2110 3-9-5 66 FrannyNorton 1 (Tom Dascombe) *hld up: rdn and outpcd over 2f out: swtchd rt ins fnl f: kpt on: nvr able to get competitive* 25/1 | 62 |
| 6-5 | 8 | 15 | **Katmandoo (USA)**18 1967 3-9-5 0 RichardKingscote 8 (Tom Dascombe) *midfield: rdn 4f out: wknd 3f out: wl bhd over 2f out* 20/1 | 32 |
| 0- | 9 | 99 | **Poetic Voice**301 4270 3-9-5 0 JasonHart 7 (Eric Alston) *chsd wnr tl pushed along 5f out: wknd over 3f out: t.o: b.b.v* 66/1 | |

2m 10.85s (-0.35) **Going Correction** -0.125s/f (Firm) 9 Ran SP% **113.9**
Speed ratings (Par 103): **96,94,92,89,88 88,88,76,**
CSF £10.71 TOTE £3.10: £1.30, £1.50, £1.10; EX 11.30 Trifecta £28.20.
**Owner** D M James, Cavendish Inv Ltd, B W Hills **Bred** Lynch Bages Ltd **Trained** Lambourn, Berks

**FOCUS**
A fairly decent maiden and the first four are all likely to prove better than the bare form.

## 2528 ADARIS GLOBAL FOREIGN EXCHANGE H'CAP 7f 1y
5:05 (5:09) (Class 4) (0-85,87) 4-Y-O+

£7,470 (£2,236; £1,118; £559; £279; £140) Stalls Low

| Form | | | | RPR |
|---|---|---|---|---|
| 2464 | 1 | | **Russian Soul (IRE)**60 1152 9-9-4 82 DougieCostello 8 (Jamie Osborne) *hld up: hdwy whn nt clr run over 2f out: nt clr run again over 1f out: burst through between horses ins fnl f: str chal: led narrowly towards fin* 14/1 | 91+ |
| 6-11 | 2 | shd | **Gin In The Inn (IRE)**7 2303 4-9-9 87 6ex PaulHanagan 6 (Richard Fahey) *midfield: nt clr run over 2f out: hdwy over 1f out: led narrowly ins fnl f: hdd narrowly towards fin* 15/8[1] | 95+ |
| 6-04 | 3 | 1¾ | **Lagenda**14 2081 4-9-6 84 (p) ShaneGray 1 (Kevin Ryan) *trckd ldrs: rdn over 1f out: chalng ins fnl f: hld in 3rd whn squeezed out nr fin* 6/1[3] | 88 |
| 6 | 4 | ½ | **Mulligatawny (IRE)**20 1911 4-9-7 85 TonyHamilton 14 (Roger Fell) *towards rr: nt clr run over 1f out: swtchd rt and gd prog ins fnl f: fin strly* 28/1 | 87 |
| 2-10 | 5 | nk | **Twin Point**75 896 6-9-3 81 (t) StevieDonohoe 2 (Charlie Fellowes) *chsd ldrs: rdn over 1f out: ch ins fnl f: styd on same pce towards fin* 5/1[2] | 82 |
| 24-4 | 6 | ½ | **Fast Dancer (IRE)**15 2054 5-9-2 80 FrannyNorton 11 (Joseph Tuite) *hld up towards rr: hdwy whn nt clr run over 1f out: r.o: gng on at fin* 10/1 | 85+ |
| 1112 | 7 | 1 | **Call Out Loud**36 1546 5-9-0 81 (vt) AlistairRawlinson(3) 12 (Michael Appleby) *chsd ldr: upsides 2f out: rdn over 1f out: stl chalng ins fnl f: no ex fnl 100yds* 25/1 | 78 |
| 6-00 | 8 | 1¼ | **Gabrial The Tiger (IRE)**20 1910 5-9-1 82 AdamMcNamara(3) 9 (Richard Fahey) *led: rdn over 1f out: hdd ins fnl f: fdd fnl 100yds* 22/1 | 76 |
| 360- | 9 | nk | **Zapper Cass (FR)**151 8308 4-9-5 83 TomEaves 4 (Tony Coyle) *in tch: rdn whn chsng ldrs and nt much ent fnl f: hmpd and sn lost pl: no imp after* 20/1 | 76 |
| 56-0 | 10 | 1 | **Eqleem**33 1606 4-9-4 82 JFEgan 13 (David Evans) *hld up: rdn over 1f out: kpt on ins fnl f: nvr able to trble ldrs* 100/1 | 72 |
| 1340 | 11 | 1½ | **Sir Billy Wright (IRE)**38 1515 6-9-1 84 CliffordLee(5) 7 (David Evans) *midfield: rdn over 2f out: outpcd over 1f out* 16/1 | 70 |
| 0-00 | 12 | 17 | **Dark Defender**21 1880 4-9-6 84 (v) JimCrowley 3 (Keith Dalgleish) *chsd ldrs tl rdn and wknd over 1f out* 11/1 | 24 |
| 061- | 13 | 29 | **Skeaping**110 338 4-9-2 80 (b) JamieSpencer 10 (Gordon Elliott, Ire) *sed awkwardly: sooon outpcd: a bhd: t.o* 25/1 | |

1m 25.37s (-1.13) **Going Correction** -0.125s/f (Firm) 13 Ran SP% **116.9**
Speed ratings (Par 105): **101,100,98,98,97 97,96,94,94,93 91,72,39**
CSF £36.42 CT £189.12 TOTE £13.30: £3.60, £1.20, £3.20; EX 48.80 Trifecta £234.10.
**Owner** Mrs A G Kavanagh **Bred** Societe Civile De L'Ecurie De Meautry **Trained** Upper Lambourn, Berks

**FOCUS**
The pace seemed sound early but the finish turned out to be slightly messy, with a few horses needing room when none was available. The first two are both a bit better than the bare form.
T/Jkpt: Not Won. T/Plt: £25.70 to a £1 stake. Pool: £196,898.00 - 5,576.56 winning units T/Qpdt: £5.80 to a £1 stake. Pool: £13,102.95 - 1,660.21 winning units **Darren Owen**

2529 - 2535a (Foreign Racing) - See Raceform Interactive

# 2446 CHANTILLY (R-H)
Wednesday, May 10

**OFFICIAL GOING: Polytrack: standard; turf: good to soft**

## 2536a PRIX CHEMIN DU ROI (CLAIMER) (3YO) (POLYTRACK) 7f
2:50 3-Y-O £9,829 (£3,931; £2,948; £1,965; £982)

| | | | RPR |
|---|---|---|---|
| 1 | | **Island In The Sky (IRE)**10 3-8-6 0 (p) JeromeMoutard(5) 5 (R Le Gal, France) 16/1 | 74 |
| 2 | 1¼ | **If I Say So**10 3-8-13 0 ow2 (p) GeraldMosse 4 (M Boutin, France) 19/1 | 73 |
| 3 | 1¼ | **Sirma Traou Land (FR)**10 3-8-11 0 (p) ChristopheSoumillon 3 (R Le Gal, France) 7/2[2] | 68 |
| 4 | ¾ | **Stormy (FR)**75 3-9-4 0 (b) AurelienLemaitre 12 (S Cerulis, France) 10/1 | 73 |
| 5 | 1¾ | **Allegheny Bay (IRE)**40 1463 3-8-11 0 TonyPiccone 6 (J S Moore) *led: rdn and hdd 2f out: steadily fdd* 6/1[3] | 61 |
| 6 | 1¼ | **Buttonwood** 3-8-11 0 AlexisBadel 9 (Antonio Marcialis, Italy) 30/1 | 58 |
| 7 | 3½ | **Douceur D'Antan (FR)**20 3-8-11 0 MickaelBarzalona 11 (P Adda, France) 8/1 | 48 |
| 8 | nk | **Trapped (FR)**33 3-8-8 0 VincentCheminaud 2 (F Belmont, France) 69/1 | 44 |
| 9 | snk | **Fils De L'Air (FR)**154 3-9-4 0 Pierre-CharlesBoudot 8 (P Sogorb, France) 23/10[1] | 54 |
| 10 | 3 | **Lucky Mistake (IRE)**58 3-9-1 0 CristianDemuro 1 (J Reynier, France) 15/2 | 43 |
| 11 | 5 | **Panos (FR)**15 3-9-1 0 AntoineHamelin 7 (Henk Grewe, Germany) 49/1 | 29 |
| 12 | 1¾ | **Kassiani (IRE)** 3-8-8 0 (p) ClementLecoeuvre(3) 10 (X Thomas-Demeaulte, France) 44/1 | 21 |

PARI-MUTUEL (all including 1 euro stake): WIN 3.60 (coupled with Sirma Traou Land); PLACE 3.10, 4.40, 2.00; DF 75.40; SF 131.30.
**Owner** Marc-Elie Uzan **Bred** Max Morris **Trained** France

2537 - 2544a (Foreign Racing) - See Raceform Interactive

# 2076 CATTERICK (L-H)
Thursday, May 11

**OFFICIAL GOING: Good to firm (8.9)**
Wind: light behind in home straight, making no material difference Weather: Warm and sunny

## 2545 ANNUAL BADGE HOLDER'S GUEST DAY FILLIES' NOVICE AUCTION STKS (PLUS 10 RACE) 5f
2:05 (2:08) (Class 5) 2-Y-O £2,911 (£866; £432; £216) Stalls Low

| Form | | | | RPR |
|---|---|---|---|---|
| | 1 | | **Izzy Bizu (IRE)** 2-9-0 0 PJMcDonald 8 (Mark Johnston) *dwlt and wnt rt s: sn in tch: rdn and hdwy over 1f out: kpt on to ld towards fin* 7/2[2] | 70 |
| 2 | 2 | 1¼ | **Three Little Birds**9 2258 2-8-9 0 MitchGodwin(5) 6 (Sylvester Kirk) *trckd ldr: pushed along 1/2-way: rdn to chal over 1f out: led jst ins fnl f: one pce and hdd towards fin* 4/1[3] | 66 |
| 0 | 3 | 1½ | **Nsnas Alward**27 1776 2-9-0 0 TomEaves 7 (Kevin Ryan) *sn led: rdn 2f out: hdd jst ins fnl f: one pce: hld in 3rd whn short of room towards fin* 15/2 | 60 |
| | 4 | 1½ | **Seaella (IRE)** 2-9-0 0 CamHardie 4 (John Quinn) *hld up in tch: pushed along 1/2-way: kpt on ins fnl f: nrst fin* 11/1 | 55 |
| | 5 | 2¾ | **Lady Anjorica (IRE)** 2-8-9 0 RowanScott(5) 2 (Keith Dalgleish) *slowly away: hld up in rr: rdn over 2f out: sme late hdwy: nvr threatened* 8/1 | 45 |
| 3 | 6 | 1¼ | **Royal Crown (IRE)**14 2105 2-9-0 0 DanielTudhope 1 (David O'Meara) *trckd ldr: rdn 1/2-way: wknd over 1f out* 2/1[1] | 40 |
| 0 | 7 | 16 | **Suanas (IRE)**14 2105 2-9-0 0 TonyHamilton 5 (Richard Fahey) *slowly into strinde: sn outpcd in rr: a bhd* 20/1 | |

59.29s (-0.51) **Going Correction** -0.35s/f (Firm) 7 Ran SP% **111.5**
Speed ratings (Par 90): **90,88,85,83,78 76,51**
CSF £16.91 TOTE £4.40: £2.30, £1.90; EX 18.50 Trifecta £98.80.
**Owner** Lowther Racing & P D Savill **Bred** Mark Salmon **Trained** Middleham Moor, N Yorks

**FOCUS**
All race distances as advertised. A warm and sunny afternoon at the Yorkshire track and the potential for the official good to firm ground to dry out even further. A couple of key morning withdrawals meant this novice stakes took a lot less winning than was originally expected and the form is fairly modest.

## 2546 RACING UK ANYWHERE AVAILABLE NOW CLAIMING STKS 1m 4f 13y
2:35 (2:35) (Class 6) 4-Y-0+ £2,264 (£673; £336; £168) Stalls Low

Form RPR
-315 1 **Percys Princess**[16] 2061 6-8-3 60 JaneElliott(7) 2 62+
(Michael Appleby) *trckd ldrs: rdn to ld wl over 2f out: styd on to draw clr fnl f* 7/2[2]
002- 2 6 **San Quentin (IRE)**[154] 8282 6-9-2 73 JoshDoyle(5) 5 63
(Tony Coyle) *hld up: pushed along and hdwy over 2f out: rdn to chse ldr over 1f out: sn one pce: eased towards fin* 5/1
4140 3 ¾ **Retrieve (AUS)**[48] 1341 9-9-8 96 (t) LucyKBarry(5) 3 68
(Jamie Osborne) *trckd ldr: led over 7f out: rdn whn hdd wl over 2f out: sn one pce: lost 2nd over 1f out* 1/1[1]
-435 4 hd **Vercingetorix (IRE)**[3] 2471 6-9-5 70 (b) GrahamLee 6 60
(Harriet Bethell) *in tch: hdwy to briefly join ldr over 3f out: rdn and outpcd over 2f out: plugged on fnl f* 9/2[3]
0-00 5 3½ **Moccasin (FR)**[11] 2183 8-8-13 42 (v) PhillipMakin 1 48
(Geoffrey Harker) *dwlt: sn pushed along to ld: hdd over 7f out: rdn over 3f out: wknd over 1f out* 100/1
200- 6 1¼ **Chauvelin**[219] 7044 6-9-3 54 (v) AndrewMullen 4 50
(Nigel Tinkler) *hld up in tch: rdn over 2f out: nvr threatened* 33/1

2m 36.32s (-2.58) **Going Correction** -0.125s/f (Firm) 6 Ran SP% 111.0
Speed ratings (Par 101): **103,99,98,98,96 95**
CSF £20.36 TOTE £2.80: £1.60, £2.00; EX 20.80 Trifecta £37.40.San Quentin was claimed by Dr R. D. P. Newland for £9000. Also, Vercingetorix was claimed by Mr I. J. Jardine for £8000.
**Owner** C A Blyth **Bred** Norman A Blyth **Trained** Oakham, Rutland

**FOCUS**
A weak claimer, in which the odds-on favourite was well beaten and is clearly nowhere near the force of his current handicap mark. The fifth highlights the limitations.

## 2547 BOOK NOW FOR 10TH JUNE MAIDEN STKS 7f 6y
3:10 (3:11) (Class 5) 3-Y-0+ £2,911 (£866; £432; £216) Stalls Low

Form RPR
3-62 1 **Armandihan (IRE)**[24] 1829 3-9-2 79 KevinStott 4 82+
(Kevin Ryan) *mde all: pushed clr over 1f out: rdn ins fnl f: eased towards fin* 11/10[1]
0-4 2 1½ **Mokhalad**[12] 2135 4-10-0 0 DaneO'Neill 2 79
(Sir Michael Stoute) *dwlt: sn trckd ldrs: rdn 2f out: kpt on to go 2nd ins fnl f but no threat wnr* 5/4[2]
30 3 1¾ **The Eagle's Nest (IRE)**[46] 1389 3-9-2 0 TonyHamilton 9 70
(Richard Fahey) *prom: rdn 2f out: one pce: lost 2nd ins fnl f* 13/2[3]
0- 4 5 **Almunther (IRE)**[204] 4-10-0 0 PJMcDonald 6 61
(Micky Hammond) *midfield: pushed along over 2f out: rdn over 2f out: kpt on* 20/1
4 5 2¼ **Yorkshire Pudding**[19] 1977 3-8-8 0 RachelRichardson(3) 3 46
(Tim Easterby) *trckd ldrs: rdn over 2f out: sn wknd* 20/1
6 3½ **Pastime** 3-9-2 0 MartinDwyer 8 41
(Gay Kelleway) *v.s.a and bhd: minor late hdwy* 20/1
0-0 7 ½ **Zaytoon (IRE)**[24] 1829 4-10-0 30 TomEaves 1 44
(Micky Hammond) *midfield: rdn over 2f out: wknd over 1f out* 150/1
04 8 ½ **Decima (IRE)**[15] 2078 3-8-4 0 HarrisonShaw(7) 10 34
(Michael Easterby) *a towards rr* 33/1
- 9 3¼ **Starfall**[41] 4-9-9 0 RowanScott(5) 5 34
(Christopher Wilson) *s.i.s: a rr* 150/1

1m 26.67s (-0.33) **Going Correction** -0.125s/f (Firm)
**WFA** 3 from 4yo 12lb 9 Ran SP% 123.9
Speed ratings (Par 103): **96,94,92,86,84 80,79,78,75**
CSF £2.81 TOTE £2.10: £1.02, £1.10, £2.00; EX 3.20 Trifecta £8.00.
**Owner** T A Rahman **Bred** Agricola Del Parco **Trained** Hambleton, N Yorks

**FOCUS**
This maiden lacked depth and revolved around the first two in the betting. The winner can do better again if putting it all together.

## 2548 CATTERICKBRIDGE.CO.UK FILLIES' H'CAP 7f 6y
3:45 (3:48) (Class 4) (0-85,85) 4-Y-0+ £6,469 (£1,925; £962; £481) Stalls Low

Form RPR
0-14 1 **Bahamian Bird**[13] 2120 4-8-8 72 PJMcDonald 7 81
(Richard Fahey) *trckd ldr: rdn 2f out: led over 1f out: kpt on wl to draw clr ins fnl f* 7/4[2]
20-0 2 4 **Courier**[27] 1778 5-9-7 85 BarryMcHugh 3 83
(Marjorie Fife) *trckd ldr: rdn over 2f out: swtchd rt ins fnl f: kpt on to go 2nd towards fin: no ch wnr* 13/2[3]
20-6 3 ¾ **Alpine Dream (IRE)**[19] 1971 4-8-8 72 (b) CamHardie 8 68
(Tim Easterby) *hld up in tch: rdn 2f out: kpt on wl fnl f: wnt 3rd towards fin* 17/2
11-2 4 ½ **Coronation Day**[16] 2054 4-9-6 84 LukeMorris 1 79
(James Tate) *led: rdn 2f out: hdd over 1f out: edgd lft ins fnl f: wknd and lost 2 pls towards fin* 11/8[1]
5360 5 nk **Be Royale**[22] 1890 7-7-9 66 oh1 (t[1]) JaneElliott(7) 5 60
(Michael Appleby) *in tch: rdn 2f out: one pce* 16/1
06/ 6 12 **Sexy Legs**[729] 2198 5-8-11 75 NeilFarley 2 36
(Lucinda Egerton) *dwlt: hld up in tch: rdn over 2f out: wknd over 1f out* 50/1

1m 25.54s (-1.46) **Going Correction** -0.125s/f (Firm) 6 Ran SP% 110.2
Speed ratings (Par 102): **103,98,97,97,96 82**
CSF £12.81 CT £68.57 TOTE £3.20: £2.20, £3.20; EX 13.50 Trifecta £42.50.
**Owner** Lady Juliet Tadgell **Bred** Lady Juliet Tadgell **Trained** Musley Bank, N Yorks

**FOCUS**
An uncompetitive fillies' handicap proved easy pickings for last month's C&D winner. There's a bit of doubt over the strength of this C&D form.

## 2549 GO RACING IN YORKSHIRE H'CAP 1m 7f 189y
4:15 (4:16) (Class 6) (0-65,63) 4-Y-0+ £2,264 (£673; £336; £168) Stalls Low

Form RPR
-505 1 **Lady Clitico (IRE)**[15] 2079 6-9-8 61 (p) GrahamLee 3 67
(Rebecca Menzies) *hld up: pushed along and gd hdwy 2f out: rdn to ld appr fnl f: styd on wl* 15/2
-460 2 3¼ **Crakehall Lad (IRE)**[43] 1436 6-8-6 45 (h) NeilFarley 4 46
(Andrew Crook) *dwlt: hld up: hdwy on outer 3f out: rdn 2f out: styd on: wnt 2nd 110yds out* 14/1
1504 3 1 **Dream Serenade**[30] 1703 4-8-13 55 (h) LukeMorris 6 55
(Michael Appleby) *led: drvn over 2f out: hdd appr fnl f: one pce: lost 2nd 110yds out* 11/4[2]
0631 4 1¾ **Cavalieri (IRE)**[24] 1834 7-9-9 62 (tp) KevinStott 10 60
(Philip Kirby) *in tch: rdn over 2f out: one pce* 9/4[1]
-506 5 nk **Adrakhan (FR)**[24] 1834 6-8-6 45 CamHardie 11 42
(Wilf Storey) *trckd ldrs: rdn to chal over 2f out: wknd ins fnl f* 10/1
625- 6 8 **Kisumu**[97] 5758 5-9-10 63 PJMcDonald 8 51
(Micky Hammond) *hld up: rdn over 2f out: sn wknd* 7/1[3]
30-0 7 nse **Midnight Warrior**[15] 2079 7-9-1 54 (t[1]) AndrewMullen 7 42
(Ron Barr) *trckd ldr: rdn over 2f out: wknd over 1f out* 9/1
5-00 8 21 **Wayside Magic**[58] 1188 4-8-6 48 JoeDoyle 1 11
(Neville Bycroft) *trckd ldr: lost pl over 3f out: rdn over 2f out: wknd over 1f out: eased fnl f* 16/1

3m 34.46s (2.46) **Going Correction** -0.125s/f (Firm)
**WFA** 4 from 5yo+ 1lb 8 Ran SP% 113.3
Speed ratings (Par 101): **88,86,85,85,84 80,80,70**
CSF £101.14 CT £358.38 TOTE £9.40: £2.20, £3.50, £1.20; EX 110.50 Trifecta £470.90.
**Owner** The Extra Time Partnership **Bred** Tally-Ho Stud **Trained** Mordon, Durham

**FOCUS**
They only started racing in the final half-mile in this poor staying handicap and that paved the way for Lady Clitico to gain a first win over 2m. The second and third anchor the form.

## 2550 CATTERICK VETERANS' H'CAP 5f 212y
4:45 (4:45) (Class 5) (0-75,75) 6-Y-0+ £3,881 (£1,155; £577; £288) Stalls Low

Form RPR
6333 1 **Vallarta (IRE)**[6] 2377 7-9-4 72 JackGarritty 6 79
(Ruth Carr) *chsd ldr: led over 2f out: sn pushed along: rdn over 1f out: kpt on* 3/1[1]
3320 2 ¾ **Meshardal (GER)**[24] 1833 7-8-11 65 (p[1]) JamesSullivan 2 70
(Ruth Carr) *hld up in midfield: pushed along and hdwy over 2f out: rdn to chse ldr over 1f out: kpt on* 7/2[2]
0000 3 shd **Extrasolar**[24] 1833 7-9-3 71 PhillipMakin 4 75
(Geoffrey Harker) *dwlt: hld up: pushed along and hdwy over 1f out: kpt on wl fnl f* 6/1
-602 4 ½ **Willbeme**[19] 1972 9-8-6 67 RayDawson(7) 3 70
(Neville Bycroft) *in tch: rdn 2f out: one pce* 4/1[3]
2120 5 1 **Windforpower (IRE)**[14] 2104 7-8-9 63 (p) ConnorBeasley 7 62
(Tracy Waggott) *midfield: rdn over 2f out: in tch appr fnl f: one pce* 16/1
0-53 6 1 **Meandmyshadow**[13] 2124 9-9-3 71 (b) BenCurtis 5 67
(Alan Brown) *chsd ldr: rdn and outpcd over 2f out: no threat after* 6/1
0-00 7 4 **Secret Missile**[13] 2123 7-9-4 72 PJMcDonald 1 55
(David C Griffiths) *dwlt: hld up: pushed along whn short of room on rail over 1f out: nt rcvr* 16/1
0-00 8 6 **Best Trip (IRE)**[15] 2081 10-9-0 75 (t[1]) HarrisonShaw(7) 8 39
(Marjorie Fife) *led: rdn whn hdd over 2f out: sn wknd* 12/1

1m 12.43s (-1.17) **Going Correction** -0.125s/f (Firm) 8 Ran SP% 115.3
Speed ratings: **102,101,100,100,98 97,92,84**
CSF £13.78 CT £58.65 TOTE £4.50: £1.40, £1.40, £3.20; EX 11.70 Trifecta £88.30.
**Owner** Douglas Renton **Bred** Frank O'Meara **Trained** Huby, N Yorks

**FOCUS**
Recent winning form was thin on the ground in this handicap, which was only open to 6yos and above. Ordinary form, the winner close to last year's best.

## 2551 RACING AGAIN 25TH MAY H'CAP 5f
5:15 (5:16) (Class 5) (0-75,77) 4-Y-0+ £2,911 (£866; £432; £216) Stalls Low

Form RPR
062 1 **Bosham**[14] 2104 7-9-3 74 (bt) NathanEvans(3) 1 81
(Michael Easterby) *mde all: pushed along 2f out: rdn over 1f out: kpt on wl* 11/4[1]
6062 2 1 **Silvanus (IRE)**[7] 2341 12-9-8 76 GrahamLee 3 79
(Paul Midgley) *chsd ldrs: rdn 2f out: kpt on: wnt 2nd nr fin* 3/1[2]
0311 3 hd **Oriental Relation (IRE)**[8] 2305 6-9-3 76 (b) CallumRodriguez(5) 7 79
(James Given) *prom: rdn 2f out: one pce: lost 2nd nr fin* 11/4[1]
-666 4 ¾ **Compton River**[36] 1558 5-9-0 68 ConnorBeasley 5 68
(Bryan Smart) *chsd ldrs: rdn 2f out: one pce fnl f* 12/1
200- 5 ¾ **Pearl Acclaim (IRE)**[146] 8403 7-9-7 75 (p) DanielTudhope 6 72
(David O'Meara) *chsd ldrs: rdn 2f out: no ex fnl f* 9/2[3]
30-4 6 95 **Flash City (ITY)**[25] 1819 9-9-1 69 (e[1]) JamesSullivan 2
(Ruth Carr) *hld up: eased over 1f out: p.u ins fnl f and walked across line* 14/1

57.61s (-2.19) **Going Correction** -0.35s/f (Firm) 6 Ran SP% 110.9
Speed ratings (Par 103): **103,101,101,99,98**
CSF £11.00 TOTE £3.60: £2.80, £1.60; EX 10.40 Trifecta £19.20.
**Owner** Peter Easterby **Bred** Rabbah Bloodstock Limited **Trained** Sheriff Hutton, N Yorks

**FOCUS**
They dipped under the Racing Post standard time in this competitive sprint handicap. The winner made all and is rated to form.
T/Plt: £74.30 to a £1 stake. Pool: £50,212.40 - 493.33 winning units. T/Qpdt: £9.40 to a £1 stake. Pool: £3,578.86 - 281.72 winning units. **Andrew Sheret**

# 2522 CHESTER (L-H)
Thursday, May 11

**OFFICIAL GOING: Good (good to firm in places; watered; 7.8)**
Wind: Light, behind in straight of just over 1f Weather: Sunny

## 2552 GATELEY PLC CHANGING THE LEGAL LANDSCAPE H'CAP 1m 2f 70y
1:50 (1:51) (Class 2) (0-105,105) 4-Y-0+
£18,675 (£5,592; £2,796; £1,398; £699; £351) Stalls High

Form RPR
211- 1 **Khairaat (IRE)**[244] 6286 4-8-7 91 JimCrowley 1 106+
(Sir Michael Stoute) *mde all: drew clr ins fnl f: pushed out: comf* 10/11[1]
3-51 2 4½ **Brorocco**[15] 2086 4-8-5 89 (h) JimmyQuinn 8 95+
(Andrew Balding) *hld up in rr: hdwy on outer over 2f out: chsd ldrs over 1f out: styd on to take 2nd ins fnl f: no ch w wnr* 4/1[2]
-642 3 2 **Mistiroc**[27] 1779 6-9-1 99 (v) JasonHart 7 101
(John Quinn) *chsd wnr: ev ch 3f out: rdn 2f out: outpcd by wnr over 1f out: lost 2nd ins fnl f: no ex towards fin* 11/1
50- 4 1¾ **Berkshire (IRE)**[180] 7934 6-9-7 105 JamieSpencer 4 104
(Paul Cole) *trckd ldrs: pushed along and nt qckn over 2f out: kpt on same pce ins fnl f: no imp* 7/1[3]

5306 **5** *hd* **Sennockian Star**[4] 2426 7-8-9 **93** FrannyNorton 6 91
(Mark Johnston) *in tch: pushed along and outpcd over 2f out: kpt on u.p ins fnl f: nvr able to trble ldrs* **12/1**

0-10 **6** *½* **Gabrial's King (IRE)**[12] 2157 8-8-5 **89** PaulHanagan 5 86
(Richard Fahey) *hld up: pushed along and outpcd over 2f out: kpt on ins fnl f: nvr able to trble ldrs* **20/1**

/0-0 **7** *2 ¾* **Parish Boy**[26] 1148 5-8-9 **93** JosephineGordon 3 85
(David Loughnane) *hld up in tch: pushed along 3f out: outpcd over 2f out: bhd fnl f* **40/1**

2m 11.18s (-0.02) **Going Correction** +0.025s/f (Good) 7 Ran SP% **108.1**
Speed ratings (Par 109): **101,97,95,94,94 93,91**
CSF £4.04 CT £17.55 TOTE £1.60: £1.10, £2.60; EX 4.50 Trifecta £19.40.
**Owner** Hamdan Al Maktoum **Bred** Shadwell Estate Company Limited **Trained** Newmarket, Suffolk

**FOCUS**
The ground was officially good, good to firm in places and clerk of the course Andrew Morris said: "We put 2mm of water on last night and we have moved the rails from the six to the one and a half marker and I am really pleased with the ground. It is very similar to how it was yesterday before racing. The times yesterday were not that rapid." After riding in the opener Jamie Spencer said: "It is nice fast ground" and Jimmy Quinn said: "It is fast." This actual race distance was 1m 2f 84y (+14y) after the aforementioned rail movements. A decent race to start the second day of the May meeting, that was taken apart by the winner. The form is rated at something like face value.

## 2553 SPORTINGBET.COM HUXLEY STKS (GROUP 3) 1m 2f 70y
**2:25** (2:25) (Class 1) 4-Y-O+

**£42,532** (£16,125; £8,070; £4,020; £2,017; £1,012) **Stalls** High

Form RPR

3-02 **1** **Deauville (IRE)**[13] 2127 4-9-0 113 (t) RyanMoore 4 116
(A P O'Brien, Ire) *mde all: rdn and qcknd over 1f out: r.o and edgd rt ins fnl f: hld on wl nr fin* **6/4**[1]

12-1 **2** *nk* **Poet's Word (IRE)**[28] 1757 4-9-0 111 AndreaAtzeni 5 115
(Sir Michael Stoute) *in tch: impr over 1f out: wnt 2nd ins fnl f: r.o and clsd nr fin: a hld* **4/1**[3]

2122 **3** *2 ¾* **Folkswood**[22] 1882 4-9-0 113 (p) WilliamBuick 2 110
(Charlie Appleby) *racd keenly: prom: wnt 2nd 2f out: nt pce of wnr over 1f out: lost 2nd ins fnl f: kpt on same pce fnl 100yds* **10/3**[2]

5042 **4** *2* **Gabrial (IRE)**[13] 2129 8-9-0 113 PaulHanagan 3 106
(Richard Fahey) *hld up in rr: rdn over 2f out: kpt on u.p clsng stages: nt pce to trble ldrs* **16/1**

10-1 **5** *hd* **Snoano**[30] 1704 5-9-0 102 DavidAllan 1 106
(Tim Easterby) *hld up: effrt on inner to chse ldrs over 1f out: no ex ins fnl f* **25/1**

13-4 **6** *23* **Royal Artillery (USA)**[13] 2127 4-9-0 114 (t) FrankieDettori 6 60
(John Gosden) *sn chsd ldr: effrt upsides over 3f out tl over 2f out: sn lost 2nd: wknd wl over 1f out: eased whn wl btn ins fnl f* **5/1**

2m 10.22s (-0.98) **Going Correction** +0.025s/f (Good) 6 Ran SP% **109.5**
Speed ratings (Par 113): **104,103,101,99,99 81**
CSF £7.36 TOTE £2.30: £1.40, £2.40; EX 8.30 Trifecta £18.30.
**Owner** Mrs F Hay/M Tabor/Mrs J Magnier/D Smith **Bred** Mrs F H Hay **Trained** Cashel, Co Tipperary

**FOCUS**
The rail between the 6f and 1 1/2f point was moved out 3 yards after racing on Wednesday. This actual race distance was 1m 2f 84y(+14y). The right two came to the fore late on, with the winning favourite always doing enough having very much had the run of the race. The runner-up may be the one to take from the contest moving forward. Deauville is rated to form and Poet's Word continues to progress.

## 2554 BOODLES DIAMOND H'CAP 7f 127y
**3:00** (3:04) (Class 2) (0-100,100) 3-Y-O

**£18,675** (£5,592; £2,796; £1,398; £699; £351) **Stalls** Low

Form RPR

31-2 **1** **Mutawatheb (IRE)**[61] 1142 3-9-3 **96** JimCrowley 5 102
(Richard Hannon) *in tch: impr to go 2nd over 1f out: r.o to ld fnl 150yds: in control nr fin* **7/2**[1]

0640 **2** *1 ¼* **Masham Star (IRE)**[27] 1780 3-9-7 **100** FrannyNorton 2 103
(Mark Johnston) *led: rdn and qcknd nrly 3 l clr over 1f out: hdd fnl 150yds: outpcd by wnr nr fin* **9/1**

21-2 **3** *shd* **Areen Heart (FR)**[22] 1878 3-8-7 **86** oh2 PaulHanagan 6 89
(Richard Fahey) *t.k.h: midfield: rdn and hdwy over 1f out: hung rt ins fnl f: r.o and clsd towards fin* **8/1**[3]

51-3 **4** *2 ¾* **Via Egnatia (USA)**[23] 1859 3-9-6 **99** FrankieDettori 1 95
(John Gosden) *t.k.h: hld up: rdn and carried hd to one side over 1f out: styd on ins fnl f: nvr able to trble ldrs* **7/2**[1]

0-21 **5** *hd* **Sharp Defence (USA)**[11] 2171 3-8-10 **89** 6ex WayneLordan 4 89+
(John Patrick Shanahan, Ire) *chsd ldrs: n.m.r and lost pl 2f out: nt clr run over 1f out: rallied ins fnl f: styd on: no imp on front three* **6/1**[2]

6020 **6** *3 ½* **Letmestopyouthere (IRE)**[27] 1774 3-8-10 **89** JFEgan 3 76
(David Evans) *towards rr: nt clr run 2f out: rdn over 1f out: kpt on ins fnl f: nt trbld ldrs* **25/1**

1210 **7** *hd* **Mailshot (USA)**[26] 1801 3-9-3 **96** JoeFanning 11 82
(Mark Johnston) *hld up: pushed along over 1f out: nvr able to get competitive* **25/1**

6-53 **8** *1 ¾* **Arc Royal**[14] 2106 3-8-4 **86** oh3 SammyJoBell(3) 8 68
(Tom Dascombe) *missed break: in rr: rdn over 1f out: nvr a threat* **14/1**

64-1 **9** *4 ½* **Aventinus (IRE)**[21] 1895 3-8-7 **86** WilliamBuick 10 57
(Hugo Palmer) *mainly trckd ldrs: wnt 2nd over 2f out: rdn and lost 2nd over 1f out: wknd ins fnl f* **11/1**

16-0 **10** *10* **Rebel De Lope**[13] 2126 3-8-9 **88** JamieSpencer 7 34+
(Charles Hills) *checked early on: racd on wd outer: chsd ldr 6f out: rdn and lost 2nd over 2f out: wknd over 1f out: eased whn btn ins fnl f* **9/1**

1m 33.58s (-0.22) **Going Correction** +0.025s/f (Good) 10 Ran SP% **112.5**
Speed ratings (Par 105): **102,100,100,97,97 94,94,92,87,77**
CSF £34.49 CT £231.06 TOTE £4.10: £1.40, £3.00, £2.30; EX 36.70 Trifecta £264.60.
**Owner** Hamdan Al Maktoum **Bred** Rosetown Bloodstock **Trained** East Everleigh, Wilts

**FOCUS**
The actual race distance for this smart handicap was 7f 127y(+13y). The betting was quite open for this and it's likely to be good form, although some do emerge with excuses. Progress again from the winer, with a small pb for the second.

## 2555 MBNA CHESTER VASE STKS (GROUP 3) 1m 4f 63y
**3:35** (3:36) (Class 1) 3-Y-O

**£42,532** (£16,125; £8,070; £4,020; £2,017; £1,012) **Stalls** Low

Form RPR

**1** **Venice Beach (IRE)**[21] 1917 3-9-0 0 (tp) RyanMoore 3 108+
(A P O'Brien, Ire) *broke wl: led early: sn trckd ldrs: led jst over 1f out: r.o ins fnl f: drvn out* **5/2**[1]

40- **2** *1 ¼* **Wings Of Eagles (FR)**[193] 7722 3-9-0 101 SeamieHeffernan 4 106+
(A P O'Brien, Ire) *hld up towards rr: hdwy 2f out: rdn and disorganised over 1f out: r.o ins fnl f: clsd nr fin to take 2nd* **8/1**

230- **3** *nse* **The Anvil (IRE)**[41] 1481 3-9-0 109 DonnachaO'Brien 1 106
(A P O'Brien, Ire) *pushed along s: sn led: rdn over 2f out: hdd jst over 1f out: kpt on u.p: nt pce of wnr wl ins fnl f: lost 2nd fin* **7/1**

3-1 **4** *1* **Tamleek (USA)**[21] 1906 3-9-0 93 JimCrowley 2 104
(Saeed bin Suroor) *hld up in tch: effrt over 2f out: on inner and chsd ldrs over 1f out: one pce fnl 150yds* **11/4**[2]

3-1 **5** *2 ¾* **Count Octave**[44] 1414 3-9-0 86 DavidProbert 5 100
(Andrew Balding) *taken bk early on: hld up: rdn 3f out: outpcd over 2f out: kpt on ins fnl f: nvr able to trble ldrs* **9/1**

20-1 **6** *½* **Cunco (IRE)**[13] 2128 3-9-0 104 FrankieDettori 6 99
(John Gosden) *broke wl: prom: racd bhd ldrs after 2f: effrt to chse ldr over 3f out: ev ch sn after: rdn and lost 2nd wl over 1f out: wknd ins fnl f* **5/1**[3]

00- **7** *8* **Finn McCool (IRE)**[201] 7539 3-9-0 101 (p[1]) WayneLordan 7 86
(A P O'Brien, Ire) *hld up: rdn wl over 2f out: lft bhd over 1f out* **20/1**

**8** *34* **Druids Cross (IRE)**[183] 7872 3-9-0 90 ColmO'Donoghue 8 32
(Joseph Patrick O'Brien, Ire) *broke wl: chsd ldr after 2f: pushed along 4f out: lost 2nd over 3f out: wknd qckly* **40/1**

2m 35.84s (-2.66) **Going Correction** +0.025s/f (Good) 8 Ran SP% **112.7**
Speed ratings (Par 109): **109,108,108,107,105 105,99,77**
CSF £22.36 TOTE £2.90: £1.30, £2.70, £1.60; EX 23.20 Trifecta £81.90.
**Owner** Smith/Mrs Magnier/Tabor/Flaxman Stables **Bred** Orpendale, Chelston & Wynatt **Trained** Cashel, Co Tipperary

**FOCUS**
The rail between the 6f and 1 1/2f point will be moved out 3 yards after racing on Wednesday. This actual race distance was 1m 4f 83y(+20y). The O'Brien runners dominated, the trainer responsible for the first three home, but it's doubtful any of these will be having a significant impact at Epsom next month. The form is rated around the avergae for placed horses in this race. Venice Beach is rated just below a typical Vase winner.

## 2556 ENGLISH FINE COTTONS EBF MAIDEN STKS (PLUS 10 RACE) 5f 15y
**4:05** (4:07) (Class 3) 2-Y-O

**£8,715** (£2,609; £1,304; £652; £326; £163) **Stalls** Low

Form RPR

3 **1** **Dragons Tail (IRE)**[12] 2148 2-9-5 0 RichardKingscote 2 85
(Tom Dascombe) *disp ld: def advantage 2f out: rdn clr ins fnl f: r.o wl* **3/1**[2]

24 **2** *4 ½* **Auntie Pam (IRE)**[17] 2015 2-9-0 0 (p[1]) FrannyNorton 1 64
(Tom Dascombe) *trckd ldrs: rdn to take 2nd wl over 1f out: nt pce of wnr and no ch ins fnl f* **6/1**[3]

622 **3** *1 ¼* **Milton Road**[8] 2292 2-9-5 0 JFEgan 7 64
(Mick Channon) *rdn early: in tch: rdn and outpcd over 1f out: prog ins fnl f: styd on fnl 150yds: gng on at fin but no ch* **12/1**

2 **4** *hd* **Dahik (IRE)**[12] 2134 2-9-5 0 JimCrowley 3 64
(Roger Varian) *trckd ldrs: effrt to chal for 2nd 1f out: no ch w wnr: kpt on same pce fnl 100yds* **4/6**[1]

**5** *2 ¼* **Haveoneyerself (IRE)** 2-8-12 0 DarraghKeenan(7) 8 55
(John Butler) *missed break: in rr: rdn over 1f out: sme prog ins fnl f: nvr able to trble ldrs* **33/1**

40 **6** *¾* **Nobrassnolass (IRE)**[21] 1909 2-9-0 0 (v[1]) DavidProbert 10 48
(Tom Dascombe) *disp ld to 2f out: rdn and lost 2nd wl over 1f out: sn wknd* **50/1**

**7** *1* **Rusty Blade (IRE)** 2-9-0 0 CharlieBennett(5) 4 49
(Daniel Mark Loughnane) *towards rr: sn pushed along: nvr able to get to ldrs: wl btn ins fnl f* **100/1**

1m 1.62s (0.62) **Going Correction** +0.025s/f (Good) 7 Ran SP% **112.9**
Speed ratings (Par 97): **96,88,86,86,82 81,80**
CSF £20.14 TOTE £4.00: £2.40, £3.40; EX 21.20 Trifecta £92.30.
**Owner** Goss Hyden Jones Owen **Bred** Old Carhue Stud **Trained** Malpas, Cheshire

**FOCUS**
The rail movement meant the actual race distance was 5f 25y(+10y). Six non-runners didn't necessarily weaken this juvenile maiden by a lot, as the most likely contenders for success remained. The winner was quite impressive but the worth of the form is open to doubt.

## 2557 T&L LEASING H'CAP 6f 17y
**4:35** (4:39) (Class 3) (0-90,89) 3-Y-O

**£9,960** (£2,982; £1,491; £745; £372; £187) **Stalls** Low

Form RPR

5305 **1** **Zamjar**[20] 1945 3-8-12 **80** (b) AndreaAtzeni 1 83
(Ed Dunlop) *pushed along early: chsd ldrs: rdn over 1f out: r.o ins fnl f: led fnl 75yds* **11/4**[1]

1-51 **2** *nk* **Turin Redstar**[89] 678 3-9-6 **88** (p) FranBerry 10 93+
(Ralph Beckett) *hld up in rr: rdn and hdwy on inner over 1f out: running on whn nt clr run and hmpd wl ins fnl f: fin strly* **11/1**

0-43 **3** *nk* **Sayesse**[20] 1940 3-9-4 **86** JFEgan 4 87
(Mick Channon) *no bttr than midfield early: hdwy over 1f out: sn swtchd to inner rail: chalng ins fnl f: hld nr fin* **5/1**[2]

3-24 **4** *½* **Poet's Society**[10] 2215 3-9-4 **86** FrannyNorton 7 85
(Mark Johnston) *broke wl: prom: led after 1f: rdn over 1f out: hdd fnl 75yds: no ex nr fin: n.m.r post* **11/2**[3]

5-15 **5** *1 ½* **Full Intention**[24] 1838 3-9-0 **82** RichardKingscote 6 78+
(Tom Dascombe) *prom: rdn over 1f out: keeping on jst over 1 l down but hld whn clipped heels towards fin* **5/1**[2]

**6** *½* **Impart**[146] 8412 3-9-3 **85** DavidNolan 8 78
(David O'Meara) *midfield: outpcd over 2f out: hdwy ins fnl f: styd on towards fin: nt rch ldrs* **33/1**

01-0 **7** *hd* **Awesome Allan (IRE)**[29] 1731 3-8-12 **80** (t) DavidAllan 2 72
(David Evans) *broke wl: led: hdd after 1f: n.m.r sn after: rdn over 1f out: chalng wl ins fnl f: nt qckning whn n.m.r sn after: no ex towards fin* **10/1**

450- **8** *1 ½* **Kreb's Cycle (IRE)**[210] 7305 3-9-1 **83** JamieSpencer 5 75+
(Ian Williams) *hld up: hdwy over 1f out: rdn whn nt clr run ins fnl f: allowed to coast home after* **8/1**

100- **9** *1 ½* **The Amber Fort (USA)**[201] 7549 3-8-7 **78** ShelleyBirkett(3) 3 60
(David O'Meara) *chsd ldrs: rdn 2f out: wknd over 1f out: wl btn whn checked ins fnl f* **16/1**

520- **10** *3 ¾* **Turanga Leela**[187] 7820 3-8-11 **79** StevieDonohoe 12 49
(Ian Williams) *in tch: sn pushed along: outpcd fnl 2f: bhd ins fnl f* **25/1**

1m 14.7s (0.90) **Going Correction** +0.025s/f (Good) 10 Ran SP% **116.6**
Speed ratings (Par 103): **95,94,94,93,91 90,90,88,86,81**
CSF £35.03 CT £149.16 TOTE £3.80: £1.30, £2.70, £2.00; EX 33.20 Trifecta £151.50.
**Owner** Abdullah Saeed Al Naboodah **Bred** Manor Farm Stud (rutland) **Trained** Newmarket, Suffolk
■ Stewards' Enquiry : J F Egan caution; careless riding

**FOCUS**
The rail between the 6f and 1 1/2f point was moved out 3 yards after racing on Wednesday. This actual race distance was 6f 30y(+13y). A competitive sprint run at a fast pace and the gamble came off, although there were a couple of hard-luck stories. The winner improved a bit further and the second looked unlucky.

## 2558 VIRGIN ATLANTIC H'CAP — 1m 2f 70y
5:05 (5:06) (Class 3) (0-90,90) 4-Y-0+
£9,960 (£2,982; £1,491; £745; £372; £187) Stalls High

Form / RPR
6132 1 **Storm King**[37] 1549 8-8-11 **80** ... DavidAllan 8 87
(David C Griffiths) *mde all: rdn 1f out: kpt on wl: edgd rt towards fin* **8/1**
41-2 2 ¾ **Kapstadt (FR)**[55] 798 7-9-4 **87** ... StevieDonohoe 1 92
(Ian Williams) *a.p: rdn over 1f out: tried to chal ins fnl f: kpt on u.p: hld towards fin* **10/3**[2]
0-51 3 hd **Energia Fox (BRZ)**[93] 609 6-8-12 **81** ... PaulHanagan 7 86
(Richard Fahey) *chsd ldrs: effrt on outer over 2f out: tried to chal ins fnl f: sltly checked whn hld towards fin* **9/2**[3]
00-0 4 3½ **Outback Blue**[31] 1683 4-8-7 **76** oh3 ... (t[1]) JFEgan 3 73
(David Evans) *s.i.s: hld up: rdn and hdwy over 1f out: chsd ldrs ins fnl f: no imp fnl 100yds* **12/1**
00-5 5 ½ **Banish (USA)**[12] 2136 4-9-7 **90** ... (bt) RyanMoore 5 86
(Hugo Palmer) *hld up: rdn over 1f out: no imp* **10/3**[2]
02-1 6 1¼ **Caponova (IRE)**[12] 2146 4-9-0 **83** ... RichardKingscote 2 77
(Tom Dascombe) *missed break: in rr: outpcd 2f out: nvr able to get on terms* **3/1**[1]
00-0 7 5 **Lord Franklin**[17] 2030 8-8-11 **80** ... JasonHart 6 64
(Eric Alston) *prom: pushed along 3f out: rdn and wknd over 1f out* **22/1**

2m 11.67s (0.47) **Going Correction** +0.025s/f (Good) 7 Ran SP% **112.5**
Speed ratings (Par 107): **99,98,98,95,95 94,90**
CSF £33.57 CT £134.50 TOTE £9.80: £4.00, £2.20; EX 31.80 Trifecta £248.40.
**Owner** Eros Bloodstock **Bred** Norcroft Park Stud And D Laidlaw **Trained** Bawtry, S Yorks
■ Stewards' Enquiry : David Allan caution; careless riding.

**FOCUS**
The actual race distance for the finale was 1m 2f 84y(+14y) due to rail movements. Amazingly stall 8 managed to get over from a really wide position on the track (stalls positioned close to the outside rail at this distance) and lead, so this may not be the most reliable of results all things considered. The winner is rated to his recent AW form.
T/Jkpt: £2,450.50 to a £1 stake. Pool: £44,109.86 - 18.0 winning units. T/Plt: £42.70 to a £1 stake. Pool: £183,506.98 - 3,135.74 winning units. T/Qpdt: £20.00 to a £1 stake. Pool: £10,468.17 - 386.90 winning units. **Darren Owen**

# LYON PARILLY (R-H)
Thursday, May 11
**OFFICIAL GOING: Turf: soft**

## 2559a PRIX BEDEL (LISTED RACE) (4YO+) (TURF) — 1m 4f
4:40 4-Y-0+ £22,222 (£8,888; £6,666; £4,444; £2,222)

RPR
1 **Mille Et Mille**[41] 1483 7-9-0 0 ... FranckBlondel 6 108
(C Lerner, France) **5/1**
2 ¾ **Apilobar (FR)**[23] 1871 4-9-0 0 ... CristianDemuro 5 107
(F Vermeulen, France) **3/1**[1]
3 2½ **Pump Pump Palace (FR)**[53] 4-9-0 0 ... Pierre-CharlesBoudot 7 103
(J-P Gauvin, France) **9/2**
4 1¼ **Tawdeea**[12] 2158 5-9-0 0 ... (p) TonyPiccone 1 101
(David O'Meara) *hld up in rr: rdn 3f out: plugged on for 4th in st but nvr able to chal* **17/2**
5 7½ **Thurgovia (IRE)**[388] 4-8-10 0 ... Francois-XavierBertras 3 85
(D Smaga, France) **17/1**
6 9½ **Zemindari (FR)**[23] 1871 5-9-0 0 ... AlexisBadel 4 74
(H-F Devin, France) **43/10**[3]
7 14 **Launched (IRE)**[23] 1871 5-9-0 0 ... StephanePasquier 2 51
(P Bary, France) **33/10**[2]

2m 40.23s (6.72) 7 Ran SP% **118.1**

**Owner** Nicolas Saltiel **Bred** Haras De La Perelle **Trained** France

# 2421 MAISONS-LAFFITTE (R-H)
Thursday, May 11
**OFFICIAL GOING: Turf: good to soft**

## 2560a PRIX MATCHEM (LISTED RACE) (3YO) (ROUND) (TURF) — 1m 1f
12:10 3-Y-0 £23,504 (£9,401; £7,051; £4,700; £2,350)

RPR
1 **Uni**[32] 1657 3-8-10 0 ... MaximeGuyon 4 98
(F Chappet, France) *led til hdd after 1f: trckd ldr: led again after 3f: drvn whn chal and hdd narrowly under 1 1/2f out: led again wl over 1f out: styd on: readily* **114/10**
2 ¾ **Franz Schubert**[32] 1658 3-9-0 0 ... MickaelBarzalona 3 100+
(A Fabre, France) *w.w wl in tch: drvn to chse ldng pair 1 1/2f out: styd on u.p fnl f: nvr on terms* **2/5**[1]
3 snk **Temple Church (IRE)**[20] 1943 3-9-0 0 ... IoritzMendizabal 1 100
(Hughie Morrison) *wnt rt leaving stalls: racd keenly: hld up bhd ldng pair: drvn and styd on fnl f: nt pce to chal* **15/2**
4 snk **Executive Force**[26] 1797 3-9-0 0 ... ChristopheSoumillon 5 99
(William Haggas) *rrd leaving stalls: sn rcvrd to ld after 1f: hdd after 3f: chsd ldr: drvn to chal and led narrowly under 1 1/2f out: hdd appr fnl f: same pce u.p* **48/10**[2]
5 4 **Prinz Hlodowig (FR)**[32] 1658 3-9-0 0 ... VincentCheminaud 2 91
(M Delzangles, France) *racd keenly: hld up in rr: rdn and no imp 1 1/2f out: wl hld fnl f* **36/5**[3]

1m 58.0s (3.30) 5 Ran SP% **120.7**
PARI-MUTUEL (all including 1 euro stake): WIN 12.40; PLACE 1.50, 1.10; SF 29.30.
**Owner** Haras D'Etreham & S Kumin **Bred** Haras D'Etreham **Trained** France

## 2561a PRIX TEXANITA (GROUP 3) (3YO) (TURF) — 5f 110y
1:50 3-Y-0 £34,188 (£13,675; £10,256; £6,837; £3,418)

RPR
1 **Aladdine**[20] 3-8-10 0 ... AurelienLemaitre 9 107+
(F Head, France) *mde all: led: rdn appr fnl f: r.o: readily* **9/2**[3]
2 2 **City Light (FR)**[20] 3-9-0 0 ... ChristopheSoumillon 8 105
(S Wattel, France) *racd keenly: hld up in tch: drvn to chse ldr over 1f out: styd on u.p: no match for wnr* **89/10**
3 ¾ **Straight Right (FR)**[31] 1689 3-9-0 0 ... OlivierPeslier 5 102
(C Ferland, France) *racd in fnl trio: clsd wl over 1 1/2f out: chsd ldrs into fnl f: kpt on at same pce* **5/2**[1]
4 1¼ **Clem Fandango (FR)**[216] 7113 3-8-10 0 ... GregoryBenoist 1 94
(Keith Dalgleish) *w.w in tch: cl 4th and drvn 2f out: rdn and no imp 1 1/2f out: one pce fnl f* **17/5**[2]
5 ¾ **Spanish Fly (IRE)**[32] 1660 3-8-10 0 ... VincentCheminaud 7 91
(M Delcher Sanchez, France) *racd in fnl trio: rowed along and began to cl over 1 1/2f out: one pce fnl f: nvr trbld ldrs* **116/10**
6 snk **Becquamis (FR)**[177] 7972 3-9-0 0 ... AntoineWerle 6 95
(T Lemer, France) *trckd ldr: rdn and no imp 1 1/2f out: grad dropped away* **39/1**
7 ¾ **Greyway (FR)**[25] 1824 3-9-0 0 ... IoritzMendizabal 2 93
(J-M Lefebvre, France) *hld up in rr: hrd rdn over 1 1/2f out: passed btn rivals ins fnl f: nvr in contention* **146/10**
8 1¾ **Afandem (IRE)**[216] 7113 3-9-2 0 ... MaximeGuyon 3 89
(Hugo Palmer) *chsd ldng gp: outpcd and lost pl 1 1/2f out: wl hld fnl f* **5/1**
9 ½ **Capchop (FR)**[32] 1660 3-9-0 0 ... (b) Jean-BernardEyquem 4 85
(P Sogorb, France) *chsd ldrs: 3rd whn rdn and no imp under 2f out: sn btn: wl hld and eased fnl f* **176/10**

1m 3.03s (-4.27) 9 Ran SP% **118.5**
PARI-MUTUEL (all including 1 euro stake): WIN 5.50; PLACE 1.80, 2.40, 1.50; DF 15.90; SF 33.40.
**Owner** Mme Frederic Head **Bred** Ian Fair **Trained** France

# 2286 ASCOT (R-H)
Friday, May 12
**OFFICIAL GOING: Good to firm (watered; str 8.4, rnd 7.8)**
Wind: Almost nil Weather: Fine but cloudy

## 2562 WOOD & WOOD SIGNS APPRENTICE H'CAP — 1m 7f 209y
5:35 (5:35) (Class 3) (0-90,91) 4-Y-0+ £7,762 (£2,310; £1,154; £577) Stalls Low

Form / RPR
223- 1 **Graceland (FR)**[196] 7669 5-9-8 **82** ... LouisSteward 2 89
(Michael Bell) *hld up in 6th: smooth prog to ld 2f out and sn 2 l clr: edgd lft fnl f: rdn out and hld on* **9/2**[2]
-055 2 ¾ **Oceane (FR)**[21] 1942 5-10-3 **91** ... (p) HollieDoyle 9 97
(Alan King) *hld up in 8th: prog over 2f out: rdn to chse wnr jst over 1f out: edgd rt but styd on and clsd nr fin: a hld* **11/2**[3]
3-33 3 3¾ **Swashbuckle**[21] 1942 4-9-5 **87** ... JoshuaBryan(5) 8 89
(Andrew Balding) *sltly on toes: led at fair pce: edgd lft and hdd 2f out: nt qckn and sn outpcd: kpt on again fnl f* **9/4**[1]
302- 4 1¼ **Medburn Cutler**[203] 7507 7-8-10 **77** ... (p) TylerSaunders(7) 7 77
(Paul Henderson) *trckd ldng pair: nt qckn 2f out and lost pl: kpt on same pce fnl f* **16/1**
-355 5 hd **See And Be Seen**[10] 2275 7-8-6 **69** oh2 ... (p) MitchGodwin(3) 6 69
(Sylvester Kirk) *trckd ldng trio: moved up to chal jst over 2f out but sn outpcd by wnr: chsng after tl fdd fnl f* **25/1**
060- 6 1 **Hatsaway (IRE)**[224] 6919 6-9-0 **77** ... CharlieBennett(3) 10 76
(Pat Phelan) *hld up in last pair: effrt over 2f out: one pce and no imp ldrs over 1f out* **20/1**
214- 7 ¾ **Arthur Mc Bride (IRE)**[203] 7498 8-9-11 **85** ... (t) MarcMonaghan 5 83
(Nigel Twiston-Davies) *s.s: hld up in 7th: shkn up on outer over 2f out: no prog and btn wl over 1f out* **12/1**
/6-1 8 ½ **Handiwork**[14] 2125 7-9-2 **83** ... (p) FinleyMarsh(7) 1 80
(Steve Gollings) *hld up in 5th: gng wl enough over 2f out: shkn up and limited rspnse over 1f out: no hdwy after* **9/2**[2]
4-56 9 1 **Daisy Boy (IRE)**[100] 507 6-8-5 **72** ... (t) MillyNaseb(7) 3 68
(Stuart Williams) *t.k.h: chsd ldr and clr of rest early: chal over 2f out: sing to lost pl whn squeezed out sn after: wknd* **12/1**
R310 10 9 **Royal Marskell**[16] 2085 8-8-12 **79** ... (h) TristanPrice(7) 4 64
(Gay Kelleway) *s.s: t.k.h: hld up in last: rdn and wknd over 2f out* **28/1**

3m 31.37s (2.37) **Going Correction** +0.20s/f (Good)
**WFA** 4 from 5yo+ 1lb 10 Ran SP% **115.8**
Speed ratings (Par 107): **102,101,99,99,99 98,98,97,97,92**
CSF £28.46 CT £69.56 TOTE £5.20: £1.80, £2.20, £1.30; EX 27.70 Trifecta £83.70.
**Owner** The Chriselliam Partnership **Bred** Capital Pur Sang & Mr Francois Drion **Trained** Newmarket, Suffolk
■ Stewards' Enquiry : Tristan Price five-day ban; used his whip when out of contention (26th, 27th, 29th-31st May)
Joshua Bryan caution; careless riding

**FOCUS**
The running rail on the round course is positioned approximately 3 yards out from its innermost position from the 1m4f start to the home straight, increasing distances as follows: Race 1 18yds and race 3 12yds. A decent apprentice riders' staying handicap. They went a modest gallop on good to firm ground but the right two horses still came to the fore. The winner has been rated close to her best, and the third close to form.

## 2563 GODFREY TABINER BRITISH EBF MAIDEN FILLIES' STKS (PLUS 10 RACE) — 5f
6:05 (6:10) (Class 4) 2-Y-0 £5,175 (£1,540; £769; £384) Stalls High

Form / RPR
1 **Mrs Gallagher** 2-9-0 0 ... SilvestreDeSousa 8 82
(William Jarvis) *athletic: lw: gd spd to ld: hdd over 1f out: kpt on wl to ld again nr fin: jst hld on* **12/1**
2 nse **Ertiyad** 2-9-0 0 ... PatCosgrave 2 82
(William Haggas) *leggy: athletic: in tch: pushed along 2f out: prog jst over 1f out: styd on wl fnl f: tk 2nd last stride and jst failed* **9/2**[2]
3 nse **Out Of The Flames** 2-9-0 0 ... RyanMoore 1 82
(Richard Hannon) *cmpt: lw: in tch: prog on outer over 2f out: narrow ld over 1f out: kpt on fnl f: hdd nr fin* **7/2**[1]

4 3 **Cardaw Lily (IRE)** 2-9-0 0 JamieSpencer 10 71
(Richard Hughes) *w'like: q cl-cpld: s.i.s: racd in last trio tl prog jst over 2f out: tk 4th fnl f: one pce and no imp after* **33/1**

5 ½ **Madeline (IRE)** 2-9-0 0 AndreaAtzeni 3 69+
(Roger Varian) *w'like: chsd ldrs: pushed along 2f out: kpt on but nvr pce to threaten* **11/2**[3]

3 6 1¾ **Ziarah (IRE)**[23] 1884 2-9-0 0 (h) WilliamBuick 6 63
(James Tate) *chsd ldrs: shkn up and no prog wl over 1f out: n.d after* **11/2**[3]

2 7 1½ **Angel Of The South (IRE)**[32] 1681 2-9-0 0 RobertWinston 7 57
(Dean Ivory) *q str: w ldr to wl over 1f out: wknd qckly fnl f* **6/1**

8 1½ **Charming Guest (IRE)** 2-9-0 0 GrahamLee 4 52
(Mick Channon) *leggy: slowly away: mostly in last trio: nvr a factor* **16/1**

9 ½ **Awesome** 2-9-0 0 AdamKirby 5 50
(Clive Cox) *q str: prom: chsd ldng pair after 2f to wl over 1f out: wknd qckly* **7/1**

10 ¾ **Lady Alavesa** 2-9-0 0 MartinDwyer 11 47
(Gay Kelleway) *q tall: s.i.s: a in last trio: struggling fr 1/2-way* **66/1**

11 27 **Comselle** 2-8-11 0 KieranShoemark(3) 9
(Stuart Kittow) *q str: chsd ldng pair 2f: sn wknd: eased over 1f out: t.o* **66/1**

1m 0.74s (0.24) **Going Correction** -0.10s/f (Good) **11** Ran SP% **117.5**
Speed ratings (Par 92): **94,93,93,89,88 85,83,80,79,78 35**
CSF £64.89 TOTE £14.20: £3.30, £1.80, £1.70; EX 97.10 Trifecta £466.70.

**Owner** Ms E L Banks **Bred** Ors Bloodstock & Stanley House Stud **Trained** Newmarket, Suffolk

**FOCUS**
A decent juvenile fillies' maiden won by Clive Brittain's subsequent Queen Mary, Moyglare Stud, and Coronation Stakes winner Rizeena on her second start in 2013. They went a decent gallop and three promisingly-bred newcomers produced a thrilling three-way photo finish.

## 2564 CHAMPAGNE BOLLINGER MAIDEN FILLIES' STKS 1m 1f 212y
**6:40** (6:43) (Class 4) 3-Y-0+ **£5,175** (£1,540; £769; £384) **Stalls** Low

Form RPR

5 1 **Mori**[21] 1944 3-8-12 0 RyanMoore 7 92
(Sir Michael Stoute) *medium-sized: q str: pressed ldr: rdn over 2f out: sustained chal to ld jst over 1f out: drvn and asserted last 150yds* **5/4**[1]

4 2 1¾ **Glittering Jewel (USA)**[23] 1885 3-8-12 0 WilliamBuick 2 88
(Charlie Appleby) *lw: led: shkn up over 2f out: drvn and hdd jst over 1f out: kpt on same pce after* **5/2**[2]

0 3 7 **Tranquil Star (IRE)**[23] 1885 3-8-12 0 GeraldMosse 5 74
(Jeremy Noseda) *hld up in 6th: rdn 3f out: prog 2f out: styd on to take modest 3rd ins fnl f* **6/1**[3]

6-4 4 2 **Cubswin (IRE)**[21] 1944 3-8-9 0 KieranShoemark(3) 3 70
(Roger Charlton) *unf: sltly on toes; racd in 5th: outpcd 4f out: wnt 4th over 3f out to over 1f out: wknd* **10/1**

24-3 5 hd **Getna (USA)**[41] 1503 3-8-12 75 TomMarquand 1 70
(Richard Hannon) *leggy: chsd ldng pair: urged along 3f out but clr of rest: drvn and lft bhd wl over 1f out: lost 3rd and wknd ins fnl f* **10/1**

6 ½ **Stylish Dancer** 3-8-12 0 JamieSpencer 9 69
(Luca Cumani) *str: v relaxed: s.s: rn green in last: pushed along 1/2-way: lft bhd over 3f out: kpt on fnl f* **14/1**

50- 7 1½ **Darwasl**[302] 4298 3-8-12 0 JimCrowley 8 66
(Brian Meehan) *unf: chsd ldng trio: urged along 1/2-way: lost 4th and wknd over 3f out* **40/1**

8 17 **Quay Point (IRE)** 4-9-13 0 PatCosgrave 6 33
(Laura Mongan) *q str: a in last pair: wknd rapidly over 2f out: t.o* **100/1**

2m 8.03s (0.63) **Going Correction** +0.20s/f (Good)
**WFA** 3 from 4yo 15lb **8** Ran SP% **115.6**
Speed ratings (Par 102): **105,103,98,96,96 95,94,81**
CSF £4.52 TOTE £2.00: £1.10, £1.40, £2.30; EX 4.80 Trifecta £14.20.

**Owner** K Abdullah **Bred** Juddmonte Farms Ltd **Trained** Newmarket, Suffolk

**FOCUS**
Race distance increased 12yds. A fairly decent fillies' maiden won by Sir Michael Stoute's subsequent York Listed Galtres Stakes winner Abingdon on her second start and seasonal reappearance in 2016. The same trainer was responsible for another progressive winner here off a respectable, at best, gallop. The level is a bit fluid.

## 2565 AGV H'CAP 7f
**7:15** (7:17) (Class 2) (0-105,103) 3-Y-0
**£18,675** (£5,592; £2,796; £1,398; £699; £351) **Stalls** Centre

Form RPR

-143 1 **Winning Ways (IRE)**[21] 1945 3-8-3 85 oh1 ow1 (t) JFEgan 5 98
(Jeremy Noseda) *coltish: trckd ldrs gng wl: shkn up to ld 2f out: clr whn edgd rt then lft: readily* **7/2**[2]

0-02 2 3¾ **Rusumaat (IRE)**[15] 2115 3-8-12 94 JimCrowley 7 97
(Mark Johnston) *mde most to 2f out: no ch w wnr sn after but kpt on to retain 2nd* **8/1**

60-1 3 1½ **Bacchus**[21] 1945 3-9-1 97 (p) WilliamBuick 2 98
(Brian Meehan) *racd on outer: in tch: effrt over 2f out: rdn to dispute 2nd jst over 1f out: nt qckn after* **8/1**

0-24 4 1½ **Berkshire Boy (IRE)**[25] 1841 3-8-3 85 oh2 ow1 (b) RobHornby 6 80
(Andrew Balding) *s.s: mostly in last: rdn over 2f out: kpt on fr over 1f out: nvr nrr but n.d* **20/1**

34-1 5 3¼ **Khafoo Shememi (IRE)**[27] 1797 3-9-7 103 RyanMoore 1 89
(Richard Hannon) *lw: racd on outer: w ldr to over 2f out: sn rdn and btn: fdd* **5/1**[3]

41-1 6 2 **Original Choice (IRE)**[25] 1841 3-8-4 86 SilvestreDeSousa 4 67
(William Haggas) *cl up: ch and rdn jst over 2f out: wknd over 1f out* **10/3**[1]

21-5 7 1¼ **Accidental Agent**[14] 2122 3-8-3 85 JosephineGordon 3 62
(Eve Johnson Houghton) *s.s: mostly in rr: drvn and in tch jst over 2f out: sn wknd* **8/1**

2-31 8 nse **Jewel House**[24] 1862 3-8-5 90 ow1 KieranShoemark(3) 8 67
(John Gosden) *wl on terms to over 2f out: sn rdn and wknd* **6/1**

124- 9 ½ **Mutahaady (IRE)**[176] 7989 3-8-8 90 JoeyHaynes 9 66
(K R Burke) *in tch: rdn and wknd over 2f out* **33/1**

1m 25.88s (-1.72) **Going Correction** -0.10s/f (Good) **9** Ran SP% **117.3**
Speed ratings (Par 105): **105,100,99,97,93 91,89,89,89**
CSF £32.21 CT £212.82 TOTE £4.20: £1.70, £2.60, £2.10; EX 36.40 Trifecta £162.40.

**Owner** P Makin **Bred** Swordlestown Stud **Trained** Newmarket, Suffolk

**FOCUS**
The feature contest was a good quality 3yo handicap. They went a decent gallop and a well-treated young horse finished strongly to win from just off the pace. The third has been rated close to form.

## 2566 MONTFORT H'CAP 6f
**7:50** (7:51) (Class 3) (0-95,96) 4-Y-0+ **£7,762** (£2,310; £1,154; £577) **Stalls** Centre

Form RPR

10-2 1 **Normandy Barriere (IRE)**[23] 1880 5-9-9 96 WilliamBuick 5 103
(Nigel Tinkler) *trckd ldrs: coaxed along over 2f out: shkn up to cl over 1f out: led jst ins fnl f and sn in command: rdn out* **3/1**[1]

0003 2 ¾ **Moonraker**[23] 1880 5-9-2 89 GrahamLee 1 93
(Mick Channon) *t.k.h: hld up bhd ldrs: clsd over 2f out: rdn to chal and upsides over 1f out: styd on ins fnl f but readily hld by wnr* **4/1**[3]

00-1 3 ½ **Little Palaver**[18] 2040 5-9-5 92 AdamKirby 2 94
(Clive Cox) *lw: trckd ldr: chal and upsides fr 2f out to jst ins fnl f: styd on same pce after* **7/1**

5045 4 1½ **Watchable**[27] 1793 7-9-9 96 (p) RyanMoore 3 93
(David O'Meara) *mde most: jnd and rdn 2f out: hdd and fdd jst ins fnl f* **7/1**

0610 5 2¼ **Sign Of The Kodiac (IRE)**[28] 1772 4-9-4 91 JimCrowley 4 81
(James Given) *trckd ldng pair: cl up 2f out: rdn and nt qckn over 1f out: fdd* **8/1**

431- 6 ½ **Mazzini**[192] 7737 4-9-4 91 TomQueally 6 79
(James Fanshawe) *fractious paddock: dwlt: hld up in last pair: tried to cl on ldrs over 1f out: sn shkn up and no rspnse* **7/2**[2]

00-0 7 ½ **Venturous (IRE)**[13] 2156 4-9-5 92 SilvestreDeSousa 7 79
(David Barron) *hld up in last pair: shkn up and no rspnse over 1f out: wl btn after* **6/1**

1m 14.45s (-0.05) **Going Correction** -0.10s/f (Good) **7** Ran SP% **117.6**
Speed ratings (Par 107): **96,95,94,92,89 88,88**
CSF £15.98 TOTE £3.80: £1.90, £2.30; EX 17.00 Trifecta £99.40.

**Owner** Eddie Carswell **Bred** Tinnakill Bloodstock & L Cantillon **Trained** Langton, N Yorks

**FOCUS**
A good handicap. They went an, at best, respectable gallop. The first two have been rated similar to their Newmarket latest.

## 2567 MITIE TOTAL SECURITY H'CAP 1m (S)
**8:20** (8:23) (Class 4) (0-85,86) 3-Y-0 **£5,175** (£1,540; £769; £384) **Stalls** Low

Form RPR

42-3 1 **Hajaj (IRE)**[93] 626 3-8-12 76 StevieDonohoe 10 82
(Charlie Fellowes) *hld up in midfield: prog over 2f out: drvn over 1f out: r.o fnl f to ld last 50yds: hld on wl* **33/1**

11-6 2 shd **Graphite Storm**[21] 1945 3-9-8 86 RyanMoore 17 92
(Clive Cox) *hld up in last: swtchd to nr side and rapid prog 2f out: drvn to chal last 100yds: jst pipped last strides* **6/1**[2]

12-5 3 hd **Juanito Chico (IRE)**[14] 2126 3-9-0 78 (h) SilvestreDeSousa 11 83+
(William Jarvis) *dwlt: hld up wl in rr: swtchd to outer and prog over 2f out: rdn to ld over 1f out: drvn and kpt on but hdd last 50yds* **8/1**[3]

52-1 4 hd **Multi Facets (IRE)**[128] 48 3-9-4 82 JamieSpencer 14 87+
(David Simcock) *athletic: lw: stdd s: hld up in last pair: nt clr run wl over 1f out: gd prog after: gng on at fin: nt rch ldrs* **10/1**

05-0 5 1¼ **Procurator (IRE)**[16] 2088 3-8-11 78 HollieDoyle(3) 4 80
(Richard Hannon) *pressed ldrs: rdn and tried to chal over 1f out: one pce fnl f* **25/1**

1 6 ¾ **Yamarhaba Malayeen (IRE)**[30] 1727 3-9-4 82 AndreaAtzeni 15 82
(Simon Crisford) *lengthy: in tch: rdn over 2f out: no prog tl styd on wl fnl f: nrst fin* **9/2**[1]

30-2 7 ½ **Endless Gold**[30] 1730 3-8-12 76 WilliamBuick 6 75
(Charlie Appleby) *lw: prom: rdn and nt qckn over 1f out: one pce after* **12/1**

0-53 8 1¼ **Ernststavroblofeld (USA)**[10] 2284 3-9-7 85 OisinMurphy 2 81
(Martyn Meade) *trckd ldr: led 2f out to over 1f out: wknd ins fnl f* **11/1**

1130 9 ¾ **Poetic Force (IRE)**[28] 1764 3-9-3 81 (t) GeorgeDowning 5 75
(Tony Carroll) *wl in tch in midfield: rdn and no prog over 2f out: n.d after* **80/1**

22-3 10 2½ **Inner Circle (IRE)**[15] 2117 3-9-0 78 TomMarquand 3 66
(Richard Hannon) *noisy in paddock: trckd ldrs on outer: chal and upsides 2f out to over 1f out: wknd* **40/1**

110- 11 1 **Tara Celeb**[216] 7147 3-9-1 79 GrahamLee 12 65
(Mick Channon) *hld up wl in rr: pushed along over 2f out: one pce and no imp ldrs whn shkn up over 1f out* **25/1**

6-10 12 nk **Jupiter Light**[14] 2126 3-9-2 83 KieranShoemark(3) 7 68
(John Gosden) *chsd ldrs: rdn over 2f out: wknd over 1f out* **10/1**

31-0 13 9 **First Up (IRE)**[14] 2126 3-9-7 85 JFEgan 16 48
(Jeremy Noseda) *lw: chsd ldrs: u.p and losing pl 1/2-way: bhd over 1f out* **6/1**[2]

0-15 14 1¼ **Cinque Port**[22] 1895 3-9-1 79 JimCrowley 8 39
(Richard Hughes) *led to 2f out: eased once btn* **25/1**

52-1 15 3½ **International Law**[21] 1939 3-9-3 81 (p) JimmyFortune 13 33
(Brian Meehan) *chsd ldrs tl wknd over 2f out: bhd and eased over 1f out* **20/1**

1- P **Come On Come On (IRE)**[225] 6888 3-9-5 83 AdamKirby 1
(Clive Cox) *q str: lost action and p.u after 1f* **12/1**

1m 41.34s (0.54) **Going Correction** -0.10s/f (Good) **16** Ran SP% **122.7**
Speed ratings (Par 101): **93,92,92,92,91 90,90,88,88,85 84,84,75,73,70**
CSF £211.51 CT £1849.22 TOTE £54.70: £7.90, £2.20, £2.20, £2.60; EX 510.80 Trifecta £2053.80.

**Owner** Khalifa Bin Hamad Al Attiyah **Bred** Lismacue Mare Syndicate **Trained** Newmarket, Suffolk

**FOCUS**
A decent 3yo handicap. They went an, at best, respectable gallop and the race developed towards the stands' side. The first four horses home all came from that, high side of the draw. The fifth has been rated close to form.

T/Plt: £27.30 to a £1 stake. Pool: £92,877.44 - 2477.87 winning units. T/Qpdt: £10.10 to a £1 stake. Pool: £6725.35 - 491.88 winning units. **Jonathan Neesom**

# 2552 CHESTER (L-H)

Friday, May 12

**OFFICIAL GOING: Good to firm (good in places) changing to good after race 2 (2.25)**

Wind: Light, behind in straight of over 1f Weather: Rain early on

## 2568 CRABBIE'S EARL GROSVENOR H'CAP 7f 127y

**1:50** (1:54) (Class 2) (0-105,105) 4-Y-0+

**£18,675** (£5,592; £2,796; £1,398; £699; £351) **Stalls** Low

Form RPR

00-0 **1** **Sound Advice**[6] 2406 8-9-0 **98**.......... DougieCostello 8 108
(Keith Dalgleish) *hld up: rdn and hdwy over 1f out: quickned to ld ins fnl f: sn edgd lft: r.o wl* **12/1**

20-6 **2** *1 ¼* **El Hayem (IRE)**[20] 1960 4-8-6 **90**.......... AndreaAtzeni 2 99+
(Sir Michael Stoute) *missed break: midfield: nt clr run fr 2f out tl hdwy over 1f out: chalng ins fnl f: nt pce of wnr towards fin* **13/8**[1]

04-0 **3** *2 ¼* **Ice Slice (IRE)**[30] 1734 6-8-9 **93**.......... RyanTate 4 94
(James Eustace) *chsd ldrs: dropped to midfield 4f out: nt qckn over 1f out: hdwy on outer sn after: styd on to take 3rd wl ins fnl f: nt pce to rch front two* **4/1**[2]

23-0 **4** *1 ¼* **Fuwairt (IRE)**[41] 1492 5-8-7 **91**.......... JFEgan 13 89+
(Roger Fell) *hld up: hdwy 4f out: chsd ldrs over 2f out: sn chalng: rdn to ld over 1f out: hdd ins fnl f: no ex whn changed legs fnl 75yds* **16/1**

550- **5** *shd* **Michele Strogoff**[142] 8478 4-8-4 **88**.......... DuranFentiman 1 86
(Tony Coyle) *chsd ldrs: rdn and ev ch over 1f out: stl chalng ins fnl f: styd on same pce fnl 75yds* **14/1**

0-42 **6** *1 ½* **Tribal Path (IRE)**[33] 1652 7-8-2 **86**..........(t) ConorHoban 10 80
(Damian Joseph English, Ire) *w ldr: rdn and chalng fr over 1f out: no ex fnl 150yds: eased whn hld towards fin* **33/1**

-020 **7** *¾* **Lat Hawill (IRE)**[6] 2406 6-8-4 **93**..........(v) RowanScott(5) 12 91+
(Keith Dalgleish) *missed break: in rr: pushed along over 3f out: rdn 2f out: hdwy on inner for press over 1f out: styng on whn nt clr run and snatched up ins fnl f: nt rcvr* **16/1**

-064 **8** *nk* **Calder Prince (IRE)**[13] 2142 4-8-6 **90**.......... FrannyNorton 14 82
(Tom Dascombe) *chsd ldrs: rdn and chalng over 1f out: one pce ins fnl f* **16/1**

103- **9** *1 ¾* **Hillbilly Boy (IRE)**[176] 7997 7-9-7 **105**.......... RichardKingscote 11 92
(Tom Dascombe) *led: rdn whn hdd over 1f out: wknd fnl 150yds: eased* **10/1**

06-0 **10** *1 ½* **Gabrial's Kaka (IRE)**[41] 1492 7-8-9 **93**.......... PaulHanagan 3 76
(Richard Fahey) *towards rr: pushed along: rdn 2f out: nvr able to get on terms* **17/2**[3]

2250 **11** *13* **Intransigent**[28] 1769 8-8-7 **91**.......... OisinMurphy 9 42
(Andrew Balding) *midfield: effrt over 2f out: wknd over 1f out: eased whn btn ins fnl f* **16/1**

1m 33.76s (-0.04) **Going Correction** +0.15s/f (Good) **11** Ran SP% **118.5**
Speed ratings (Par 109): **106,104,102,101,101 99,98,98,96,95 82**
CSF £32.01 CT £97.90 TOTE £16.30: £3.60, £1.30, £1.60; EX 46.60 Trifecta £278.00.
**Owner** A R M Galbraith **Bred** G L S Partnership **Trained** Carluke, S Lanarks
■ Stewards' Enquiry : Duran Fentiman caution; careless riding

**FOCUS**
Rail movements meant that the actual race distance was 7f 151yds. Light rain was falling on ground which had 2mm of water added to it after racing on Thursday. After the first race, the jockeys said the ground was loose on top but quick underneath. This decent handicap was fast and furious, and run in a time 2.56sec slower than standard. The winner is rated to his best.

## 2569 HOMESERVE DEE STKS (LISTED RACE) (C&G) 1m 2f 70y

**2:25** (2:26) (Class 1) 3-Y-0

**£42,532** (£16,125; £8,070; £4,020; £2,017; £1,012) **Stalls** High

Form RPR

**1** **Cliffs Of Moher (IRE)**[195] 7704 3-9-0 0..........(t) RyanMoore 7 108+
(A P O'Brien, Ire) *sn prom: pushed along whn chsng ldr over 3f out: rdn over 1f out: edgd lft sltly whn led ins fnl f: r.o strly towards fin* **4/5**[1]

00-3 **2** *1 ½* **Bay Of Poets (IRE)**[16] 2084 3-9-0 101.......... WilliamBuick 1 105
(Charlie Appleby) *in tch: effrt and hdwy 2f out: styng on whn wanting to lug lft wl ins fnl f: tk 2nd nr fin: nt pce to trble wnr* **5/1**[3]

13-4 **3** *¾* **Max Zorin (IRE)**[24] 1861 3-9-0 95.......... DavidProbert 8 103
(Andrew Balding) *racd keenly: led: rdn over 1f out: hdd ins fnl f: no ex towards fin* **25/1**

1- **4** *1 ¼* **Mirage Dancer**[203] 7496 3-9-0 87.......... OisinMurphy 6 101+
(Sir Michael Stoute) *swtchd lft jst after s: racd keenly: hld up: pushed along over 2f out: hdwy on inner over 1f out: styd on towards fin: nt rch ldrs: can improve* **7/2**[2]

12-6 **5** *4* **Al Hamdany (IRE)**[24] 1861 3-9-0 97.......... HarryBentley 9 93
(Marco Botti) *hld up in rr: rdn to go pce over 2f out: styd on to take 5th ins fnl f: nvr able to trble ldrs* **33/1**

125- **6** *3* **Star Of Rory (IRE)**[229] 6801 3-9-0 98.......... RichardKingscote 4 87
(Tom Dascombe) *racd keenly: prom: pushed along over 2f out: sn outpcd by ldrs: rdn and wknd 1f out* **16/1**

23-1 **7** *6* **Fujaira Bridge (IRE)**[22] 1914 3-9-0 81.......... AndreaAtzeni 5 75
(Roger Varian) *racd keenly: chsd ldrs: rdn 2f out: wknd over 1f out* **12/1**

14-6 **8** *6* **Majeste**[23] 1881 3-9-0 101.......... TomMarquand 3 63
(Richard Hannon) *no bttr than midfield: niggled along over 5f out: rdn over 3f out: wknd over 2f out* **25/1**

2m 10.85s (-0.35) **Going Correction** +0.15s/f (Good) **8** Ran SP% **118.7**
Speed ratings (Par 107): **107,105,105,104,101 98,93,89**
CSF £5.44 TOTE £1.70: £1.02, £1.80, £7.00; EX 6.50 Trifecta £45.40.
**Owner** Mrs John Magnier **Bred** Wave Syndicate **Trained** Cashel, Co Tipperary

**FOCUS**
Actual race distance 1m 2f 96yds. A fascinating renewal of this Listed Derby Trial, which had thrown up two Epsom Derby winners in its recent history - Oath in 1999 and Kris Kin in 2003. Aidan O'Brien, who had won four of the previous ten runnings (five in total), including with subsequent Irish 2,000 winner and Breeders' Cup Turf winner Magician (2013), continued his stranglehold on the race. The form is a bit below the race standard, with the third the key. Cliffs Of Moher is capable of better.

## 2570 SUSTAINABLE GROUP (UK) LTD H'CAP 5f 15y

**3:00** (3:02) (Class 2) (0-105,99) 3-Y-0

**£18,675** (£5,592; £2,796; £1,398; £699; £351) **Stalls** Low

Form RPR

00-2 **1** **Copper Knight (IRE)**[13] 2160 3-8-9 **87**.......... DavidAllan 4 100
(Tim Easterby) *mde all: rdn clr ent fnl f: r.o wl: eased towards fin* **7/1**

0-22 **2** *2 ¼* **Evergate**[11] 2215 3-8-7 **85**.......... JoeFanning 3 90
(Robert Cowell) *chsd wnr thrght: ev ch over 2f out: rdn and hung lft whn nt qckn over 1f out: no imp on wnr fnl f* **7/2**[2]

45-5 **3** *2* **Megan Lily (IRE)**[20] 1975 3-8-8 **86**.......... PaulHanagan 2 84
(Richard Fahey) *racd keenly: chsd ldrs: rdn over 1f out: kpt on same pce and no imp fnl f* **10/1**

15-0 **4** *1 ½* **Partitia**[14] 2130 3-8-9 **87**.......... AndreaAtzeni 6 79
(Sir Michael Stoute) *in rr: pushed along whn n.m.r jst over 1f out: styd on ins fnl f: nt trble ldrs* **13/2**

3133 **5** *¾* **Tomily (IRE)**[28] 1774 3-9-7 **99**.......... RyanMoore 5 89
(Richard Hannon) *midfield: rdn and hung lft whn outpcd by ldrs over 1f out: wl hld after* **5/1**[3]

251- **6** *2 ¾* **Rosabelle**[230] 6763 3-8-12 **90**.......... DavidProbert 1 70
(Alan Bailey) *hld up: pushed along 2f out: effrt over 1f out but no imp: hung rt and bmpd sn after: wl btn ins fnl f* **3/1**[1]

0-21 **7** *6* **Rich And Famous (USA)**[14] 2122 3-9-1 **93**.......... FrannyNorton 8 51
(Mark Johnston) *chsd ldrs: rdn and wknd 2f out: bhd over 1f out* **11/2**

1m 0.88s (-0.12) **Going Correction** +0.15s/f (Good) **7** Ran SP% **114.2**
Speed ratings (Par 105): **106,102,99,96,95 91,81**
CSF £31.49 CT £245.22 TOTE £8.50: £3.70, £2.40; EX 37.40 Trifecta £294.00.
**Owner** A Denham & Partner **Bred** Wardstown Stud Ltd **Trained** Great Habton, N Yorks

**FOCUS**
Actual race distance 5f 35yds. The official going was changed to good all round before this race. There were three absentees from this decent 5f dash, drawn in stalls 10, 9 and 7. The first three filled those positions virtually throughout and the form could be rated a bit higher.

## 2571 BOODLES DIAMOND ORMONDE STKS (GROUP 3) 1m 5f 84y

**3:35** (3:35) (Class 1) 4-Y-0+

**£42,532** (£16,125; £8,070; £4,020; £2,017; £1,012) **Stalls** Low

Form RPR

451- **1** **Western Hymn**[191] 7766 6-9-0 110..........(p[1]) FrankieDettori 3 112
(John Gosden) *tucked in to trck ldrs after 1f: rdn 2f out: wnt 2nd ins fnl f: styd on towards fin: led post* **7/2**[2]

20-3 **2** *shd* **US Army Ranger (IRE)**[33] 1654 4-9-0 117.......... RyanMoore 9 112
(A P O'Brien, Ire) *trckd ldrs: wnt 2nd after 3f: rdn 2f out: led jst over 1f out: all out towards fin: hdd post* **2/1**[1]

251- **3** *¾* **Duretto**[202] 7545 5-9-3 112.......... DavidProbert 4 114
(Andrew Balding) *midfield: nt clr run 3f out: pushed along and hdwy 2f out: rdn whn chsng ldrs but no real imp over 1f out: styd on towards fin* **15/2**

1-62 **4** *¾* **Wall Of Fire (IRE)**[30] 1733 4-9-0 107..........(b) WilliamBuick 5 110+
(Hugo Palmer) *hld up: rdn 2f out: hdwy over 1f out: styd on to chse ldrs after: one pce fnl strides* **12/1**

1-21 **5** *2* **Winning Story**[28] 1770 4-9-0 108..........(p) JoeFanning 8 107
(Saeed bin Suroor) *w ldr: led after 1f: rdn 2f out: hdd jst over 1f out: no ex fnl 100yds* **9/1**

642- **6** *7* **Red Verdon (USA)**[302] 4332 4-9-0 113.......... PatSmullen 11 96
(Ed Dunlop) *racd keenly in midfield: pushed along 3f out: rdn and no imp over 1f out: one pce after* **8/1**

4501 **7** *12* **Carbon Dating (IRE)**[27] 1802 5-9-0 107.......... TadhgO'Shea 7 78
(John Patrick Shanahan, Ire) *hld up: rdn and outpcd over 2f out: nvr a threat* **20/1**

3P1- **8** *6* **Diamonds Pour Moi**[175] 8024 4-8-11 105.......... OisinMurphy 1 66
(Ralph Beckett) *led for 1f: trckd ldrs after 3f: rdn whn hmpd jst over 2f out: lost pl qckly and wknd: eased fnl f* **13/2**[3]

5 **9** *9* **Culmination**[30] 1733 5-9-0 0.......... PaulHanagan 2 56
(Donald McCain) *s.i.s: bhd: struggling to keep up 4f out: lost tch fr 3f out* **100/1**

2m 52.69s (-0.01) **Going Correction** +0.15s/f (Good) **9** Ran SP% **115.2**
Speed ratings (Par 113): **106,105,105,105,103 99,92,88,82**
CSF £10.86 TOTE £4.40: £1.40, £1.20, £2.50; EX 12.70 Trifecta £88.90.
**Owner** RJH Geffen and Rachel Hood **Bred** Newsells Park Stud **Trained** Newmarket, Suffolk

**FOCUS**
Actual race distance 1m 5f 124yds. A good-quality renewal of this Group 3 feature, despite the absence of Midterm, with all eyes on last year's Epsom Derby runner-up US Army Ranger. They went quickly early on and it served up a dramatic finish. Western Hymn was close to his best but some of his rivals weren't.

## 2572 TMT GROUP MAIDEN FILLIES' STKS (PLUS 10 RACE) 7f 1y

**4:05** (4:05) (Class 4) 3-Y-0

**£7,470** (£2,236; £1,118; £559; £279; £140) **Stalls** Low

Form RPR

2- **1** **Gymnaste (IRE)**[165] 8131 3-9-0 0.......... FrankieDettori 4 87+
(John Gosden) *bmpd s: trckd ldrs: led 1f out: qcknd clr ins fnl f: sn edgd lft: comf* **11/8**[1]

430- **2** *2 ¼* **Highland Pass**[217] 7118 3-9-0 79..........(h[1]) DavidProbert 3 77
(Andrew Balding) *bmpd s: towards rr: hdwy on inner over 1f out: sn cl up chsng ldrs: styd on to take 2nd under 100yds out: no ch w wnr* **7/2**[2]

54- **3** *½* **Cheerfilly (IRE)**[181] 7939 3-9-0 0.......... RichardKingscote 1 75
(Tom Dascombe) *led: rdn over 1f out: sn hdd: outpcd by wnr ins fnl f: lost 2nd under 100yds out: styd on same pce* **8/1**

6-5 **4** *1 ¼* **Set In Stone (IRE)**[12] 2174 3-9-0 75.......... TadhgO'Shea 6 72
(John Patrick Shanahan, Ire) *hld up: pushed along 3f out: effrt and hdwy on outer 2f out: hung lft for press whn chsng ldrs over 1f out: no imp fnl 75yds: nt pce to chal* **8/1**

22 **5** *1 ¼* **Desert Rain (IRE)**[14] 2121 3-9-0 0.......... JFEgan 7 69
(Saeed bin Suroor) *trckd ldrs: effrt 2f out: chsd ldrs over 1f out: one pce ins fnl f* **5/1**[3]

**6** *6* **Princess Ophelia** 3-8-11 0.......... AlistairRawlinson(3) 5 52
(Michael Appleby) *bmpd s: in rr: outpcd and lft bhd over 2f out: hung lft u.p over 1f out: nvr a threat* **80/1**

0- **7** 2 ¾ **Alniyat**[191] 7763 3-9-0 0 .......... PatSmullen 2 45
(Ed Dunlop) *chsd ldr: rdn and lost 2nd wl over 1f out: sn wknd* **14/1**
1m 27.72s (1.22) **Going Correction** +0.15s/f (Good) 7 Ran SP% **111.1**
Speed ratings (Par 98): **99,96,95,94,93 86,83**
CSF £5.88 TOTE £2.10: £1.20, £2.70; EX 6.70 Trifecta £28.30.

**Owner** Cheveley Park Stud **Bred** Pontchartrain Stud **Trained** Newmarket, Suffolk

**FOCUS**
Actual race distance 7f 25yds. This was probably just a fair maiden, but the winner is undeniably promising. The second and fourth set the standard.

## 2573 LDF CONDITIONS STKS 5f 15y
**4:35** (4:36) (Class 3) 3-Y-O+
**£9,960** (£2,982; £1,491; £745; £372; £187) **Stalls** Low

Form RPR
0651 **1** **Judicial (IRE)**[18] 2031 5-9-8 102 .......... (e) JoeDoyle 3 111
(Julie Camacho) *chsd ldrs: effrt on wd outside over 1f out led ins fnl f: r.o strly to draw clr ins fnl 75yds: readily* **6/4**[1]

04-5 **2** 4 **Double Up**[21] 1946 6-9-8 101 .......... (t) HarryBentley 2 96
(Roger Varian) *a.p: effrt to ld over 1f out: hdd ins fnl f: outpcd by wnr after* **11/4**[2]

360- **3** ¾ **Canny Kool**[332] 3250 5-9-4 99 .......... DougieCostello 1 90
(Brian Ellison) *in tch: effrt to chse ldrs over 1f out: kpt on u.p ins fnl f: nt pce of wnr* **12/1**

66-6 **4** ¾ **Duke Of Firenze**[21] 1946 8-9-8 103 .......... DavidAllan 4 91
(David C Griffiths) *s.i.s and bmpd s: hld up: nt clr run and swtchd lft over 1f out: proging whn nt clr run ins fnl f: styd on towards fin* **13/2**[3]

5330 **5** 1 ¾ **Caspian Prince (IRE)**[69] 1044 8-9-11 107 .......... (t) TomEaves 10 88
(Tony Coyle) *gd spd and led: rdn and hdd over 1f out: fdd fnl 100yds* **20/1**

250- **6** ½ **Reflektor (IRE)**[314] 3890 4-9-4 96 .......... RichardKingscote 5 79
(Tom Dascombe) *prom: rdn over 1f out: wknd ins fnl f* **8/1**

0042 **7** ¾ **Taexali (IRE)**[2] 2524 4-9-4 93 .......... (b) TadhgO'Shea 7 76
(John Patrick Shanahan, Ire) *midfield and sn pushed along: hdwy on outer over 2f out: outpcd over 1f out: nt clr run whn swtchd lft ins fnl f: eased whn no ch fnl 75yds* **9/1**

0665 **8** 2 **Secret Asset (IRE)**[25] 1836 12-9-1 65 .......... (v) JordanUys(7) 6 73?
(Lisa Williamson) *sed awkwardly and bmpd: towards rr: rdn over 1f out: no imp* **125/1**

1-4 **9** 4 **Dandyman Port (IRE)**[19] 1997 3-8-4 0 .......... JoeFanning 8 46
(Des Donovan, Ire) *s.i.s and wnt rt s: bhd: outpcd over 2f out: nvr a threat* **50/1**

1m 0.92s (-0.08) **Going Correction** +0.15s/f (Good)
**WFA** 3 from 4yo+ 9lb 9 Ran SP% **116.3**
Speed ratings (Par 107): **106,99,98,97,94 93,92,89,82**
CSF £5.59 TOTE £2.60: £1.10, £1.40, £4.20; EX 7.20 Trifecta £39.70.

**Owner** Elite Racing Club **Bred** Elite Racing Club **Trained** Norton, N Yorks

**FOCUS**
Actual race distance 5f 35yds. A furiously run conditions event and a taking performance from the highly progressive winner. The proximity of the eighth rather limits the form.

## 2574 DW SPORTS APPRENTICE H'CAP 1m 4f 63y
**5:05** (5:05) (Class 4) (0-85,85) 4-Y-O+
**£9,337** (£2,796; £1,398; £699; £349; £175) **Stalls** Low

Form RPR
524- **1** **St Mary's**[223] 6951 4-8-9 78 .......... WilliamCox(7) 11 86+
(Andrew Balding) *taken bk s: hld up: hdwy over 2f out: rdn on outer over 1f out: r.o to ld ins fnl f: in command towards fin* **14/1**

00-3 **2** 1 ½ **Warp Factor (IRE)**[3] 2497 4-8-13 78 .......... CliffordLee(3) 1 83
(John Patrick Shanahan, Ire) *chsd ldrs: rdn to ld 1f out: hdd ins fnl f: nt pce of wnr towards fin* **9/4**[1]

0163 **3** ¾ **Modernism**[78] 884 8-9-1 80 .......... (p) LewisEdmunds(3) 8 84
(Ian Williams) *midfield: hdwy over 3f out: rdn to ld 2f out: hdd 1f out: stl ev ch wl ins fnl f: no ex towards fin* **10/1**

00-1 **4** ½ **Archippos**[40] 1517 4-9-2 83 .......... DavidEgan(5) 3 86+
(Philip Kirby) *struggled to hold position early: no bttr than midfield: nvr really travelling: lost pl 4f out: nt clr run 2f out: outpcd and c wd outer over 1f out: styd on ins fnl f: gng on at fin* **4/1**[2]

01-0 **5** 1 ¾ **Michael's Mount**[16] 2085 4-9-0 79 .......... (p) GeorgeWood(3) 2 79
(Ed Dunlop) *midfield: lost pl 3f out: rallied to chse ldrs over 1f out: one pce fnl 100yds* **7/1**[3]

22/0 **6** 2 **Tobacco Road (IRE)**[35] 1608 7-9-4 80 .......... (h) AlistairRawlinson 6 77
(David Pipe) *racd keenly: hld up: hdwy on outer over 3f out: ev ch 2f out: rdn over 1f out: one pce ins fnl f* **28/1**

20-2 **7** ½ **Croquembouche (IRE)**[11] 2234 8-9-9 85 .......... AaronJones 4 81
(Ed de Giles) *led: rdn and hdd 2f out: stl there and ev ch over 1f out: wknd fnl 150yds* **8/1**

500- **8** shd **Gabrial's Star**[203] 7498 8-9-8 84 .......... (b) AdamMcNamara 10 80
(Richard Fahey) *missed break: in rr: hdwy over 3f out: rdn to chse ldrs 2f out: one pce and no imp over 1f out* **17/2**

050- **9** 2 ¾ **Nabhan**[23] 4920 5-8-11 78 .......... BenRobinson(5) 7 70
(Bernard Llewellyn) *chsd ldrs: lost pl 3f out: sn in rr: u.p wl over 1f out: plugged on but n.d ins fnl f* **25/1**

230/ **10** 14 **Subcontinent (IRE)**[100] 6734 5-9-3 84 .......... CallumRodriguez(5) 5 53
(Venetia Williams) *w ldr tl rdn over 2f out: sn wknd* **10/1**

2m 40.07s (1.57) **Going Correction** +0.15s/f (Good) 10 Ran SP% **117.0**
Speed ratings (Par 105): **100,99,98,98,97 95,95,95,93,84**
CSF £45.89 CT £343.55 TOTE £26.60: £4.70, £1.10, £4.00; EX 69.00 Trifecta £835.30.

**Owner** Kingsclere Racing Club **Bred** Kingsclere Stud **Trained** Kingsclere, Hants

**FOCUS**
Actual race distance 1m 4f 101yds. Not a strong handicap for the meeting. The third has been rated in line with his winter AW form.

T/Jkpt: Part won. T/Plt: £11.30 to a £1 stake. Pool: £133,635.00 - 11,732.81 winning units. T/Qpdt: £8.80 to a £1 stake. Pool: £6,450.00 - 726.29 winning units. **Darren Owen**

# 2365 LINGFIELD (L-H)
Friday, May 12

**OFFICIAL GOING: Good to soft (good in places; 7.4)**
Wind: medium, behind on straight course Weather: overcast

## 2575 50 SHADES & THE DREAM GIRLS FILLIES' H'CAP 1m 2f
**1:40** (1:40) (Class 4) (0-85,80) 4-Y-O+ **£4,690** (£1,395; £697) **Stalls** Low

Form RPR
214- **1** **Kullu (IRE)**[203] 7504 4-9-2 75 .......... (h) StevieDonohoe 1 84
(Charlie Fellowes) *t.k.h: mde all: shkn up over 2f out: rdn and fnd ex 2f out: styd on and in command fnl f: pushed out: comf* **4/6**[1]

6-62 **2** 5 **Inke (IRE)**[18] 2028 5-9-5 78 .......... PatCosgrave 3 80
(Jim Boyle) *stdd s: hld up in 3rd: effrt to chse wnr over 2f out: no imp u.p over 1f out: hld and eased wl ins fnl f* **9/2**[3]

21-1 **3** 35 **Princess Nia (IRE)**[21] 1938 4-9-7 80 .......... MartinDwyer 2 9
(Brian Meehan) *t.k.h: trckd wnr: shkn up 4f out: rdn and dropped to 3rd over 2f out: sn wl beatem virtually p.u ins fnl f: t.o* **11/4**[2]

2m 12.16s (1.66) **Going Correction** +0.30s/f (Good) 3 Ran SP% **104.8**
Speed ratings (Par 102): **105,101,73**
CSF £3.57 TOTE £1.60; EX 3.70 Trifecta £3.80.

**Owner** A E Oppenheimer **Bred** Hascombe Stud **Trained** Newmarket, Suffolk

**FOCUS**
Watering until the day before racing was followed by 5mm of rain overnight and 3mm in the morning to leave the going as Good to Soft, Good in places. Stevie Donohoe, winning jockey in the first race, said: "It's lovely," while second-placed Pat Cosgrave remarked: "It's on the slow side of good." All distances were as advertised. Stalls: Straight, Centre, Round: Inside. 1m3f+: Outside. A disappointing turn-out numerically for this fillies' handicap, but it produced a winner who looks worth following. The runner-up has been rated to her recent AW form.

## 2576 7TH BARRY GURR MEMORIAL MAIDEN STKS 1m 3f 133y
**2:15** (2:15) (Class 5) 3-Y-O **£2,911** (£866; £432; £216) **Stalls** High

Form RPR
2 **1** **Janszoon**[18] 2039 3-9-5 0 .......... JamesDoyle 6 88
(Charlie Appleby) *trckd ldrs tl stdd bk into midfield 8f out: effrt in 3rd 2f out: hdwy to ld over 1f out: styd on strly: readily* **11/4**[2]

0-5 **2** 3 ½ **UAE King**[20] 1963 3-9-5 0 .......... SilvestreDeSousa 3 82
(Roger Varian) *led: edgd rt: drvn and hdd over 1f out: kpt on one pced for clr 2nd ins fnl f* **4/1**[3]

5-2 **3** 4 **Karawaan (IRE)**[20] 1963 3-9-5 0 .......... JimCrowley 4 75
(Sir Michael Stoute) *chsd ldr tl 8f out: wnt 2nd again 3f out: rdn ent fnl 2f out: 3rd and no imp over 1f out: wknd ins fnl f* **10/11**[1]

5-6 **4** 1 **Perfect In Pink**[18] 2039 3-9-0 0 .......... GrahamLee 5 69
(Mick Channon) *hld up in tch in midfield: effrt to chse ldng trio ent fnl 2f: no threat to wnr but kpt on steadily ins fnl f* **50/1**

0 **5** 10 **Diore Lia (IRE)**[16] 2087 3-8-9 0 .......... CharlieBennett(5) 7 52
(Jane Chapple-Hyam) *stdd after s: hld up in last pair: pushed along 3f out: sn outpcd: wl btn over 1f out: wknd fnl f* **100/1**

**6** ½ **Dreamtide** 3-8-11 0 .......... KieranShoemark(3) 1 51
(Amanda Perrett) *dwlt: hld up in last pair: pushed along 3f out: sn btn* **25/1**

0-0 **7** 3 ¼ **Epicurious (IRE)**[18] 2039 3-9-5 0 .......... MartinDwyer 2 51
(Brian Meehan) *in tch in midfield: effrt over 2f out: sn struggling and wknd 2f out* **66/1**

3- **8** 86 **Emirates Flight**[174] 8034 3-9-0 0 .......... (t[1]) JosephineGordon 8
(Saeed bin Suroor) *t.k.h: hld up in midfield but nvr settled: hdwy to press ldr 8f out tl lost pl qckly 3f out: bhd and eased fnl 2f: t.o* **9/1**

2m 36.22s (4.72) **Going Correction** +0.30s/f (Good) 8 Ran SP% **117.3**
Speed ratings (Par 99): **96,93,91,90,83 83,81,23**
CSF £14.33 TOTE £3.50: £1.40, £1.60, £1.02; EX 15.50 Trifecta £17.70.

**Owner** Godolphin **Bred** Andrew Rosen **Trained** Newmarket, Suffolk

**FOCUS**
A decent-looking maiden in which several leading stables were represented. The winner was well on top at the line and looked to relish the rain-softened ground. The runner-up has been rated to her latest form.

## 2577 EUROPEAN BREEDERS FUND (EBF) NOVICE STKS (PLUS 10 RACE) 4f 217y
**2:45** (2:46) (Class 4) 2-Y-O **£6,301** (£1,886; £943; £472; £235) **Stalls** Centre

Form RPR
**1** **One Minute (IRE)** 2-8-11 0 .......... PatCosgrave 7 84+
(William Haggas) *chsd ldrs: swtchd lft 1/2-way: effrt to chal whn rn green: edgd lft and bumping w rival over 1f out: led jst ins fnl f: styd on strly and drew clr after: readily* **8/1**

1 **2** 3 ¾ **To Wafij (IRE)**[10] 2279 2-9-8 0 .......... SilvestreDeSousa 6 81
(Roger Varian) *led and c to r towards stands' rail: rdn 2f out: edgd lft u.p and hrd pressed over 1f out: edgd bk rt and hdd jst ins fnl f: sn outpcd and wknd towards fin* **10/11**[1]

0 **3** ¾ **Demons Rock (IRE)**[28] 1767 2-9-2 0 .......... JamesDoyle 5 72
(Tom Dascombe) *pressed ldrs: effrt to chal and bumping w wnr over 1f out: no ex and outpcd jst ins fnl f: wknd towards fin* **7/1**[3]

**4** 1 ¼ **Elysium Dream** 2-8-8 0 .......... HollieDoyle(3) 1 63+
(Richard Hannon) *wnt lft s: rn green and wl outpcd in last pair: switching rt after 2f: hdwy over 1f out: no threat to wnr but styd on strly ins fnl f* **20/1**

**5** 3 ¼ **Tadbir (IRE)** 2-9-2 0 .......... JimCrowley 4 56
(Brian Meehan) *chsd ldrs: shkn up 2f out: rn green and sn btn: wknd fnl f* **5/2**[2]

**6** 2 ¾ **Erastus** 2-9-2 0 .......... GrahamLee 3 46
(Mick Channon) *midfield but nvr on terms w ldrs: outpcd 1/2-way: no ch after* **25/1**

**7** 17 **Sir Hector (IRE)** 2-9-2 0 .......... RobHornby 2
(Charlie Wallis) *sn dropped to rr and wl outpcd* **66/1**

59.82s (1.62) **Going Correction** +0.10s/f (Good) 7 Ran SP% **114.7**
Speed ratings (Par 95): **91,85,83,81,76 72,45**
CSF £15.92 TOTE £7.60: £4.20, £1.10; EX 13.70 Trifecta £73.70.

**Owner** Abdulla Al Mansoori **Bred** Mubarak Al Naemi **Trained** Newmarket, Suffolk

**FOCUS**
Some well thought-of colts contested this, but it was a filly which crept under the radar who prevailed in style and looks a fine prospect.

## 2578 MORGAN CASS H'CAP 4f 217y
3:20 (3:20) (Class 3) (0-95,96) 4-Y-O **£7,246** (£2,168; £1,084; £542; £270) **Stalls** Centre

Form RPR
0-12 1 **Edward Lewis**[18] 2031 4-9-5 **96** ........ JoshDoyle(5) 6 106
(David O'Meara) *hld up in tch in midfield: smooth hdwy to join ldr over 1f out: led 1f out: sn shkn up and asserted: styd on wl: rdn out* **9/4**[1]
600- 2 1 1/4 **Orvar (IRE)**[202] 7537 4-9-6 **92** ........ JimCrowley 4 97
(Robert Cowell) *chsd ldrs: effrt u.p over 1f out: chsd wnr jst ins fnl f: kpt on wl u.p but nvr getting on terms w wnr* **3/1**[2]
5520 3 2 3/4 **Distant Past**[13] 2156 6-9-2 **88** ........(p) KevinStott 1 83
(Kevin Ryan) *chsd ldr: rdn ent fnl 2f out: lost 2nd and unable qck over 1f out: wknd ins fnl f* **6/1**
2410 4 *nse* **Stepper Point**[6] 2391 8-9-3 **89** ........(v[1]) MartinDwyer 5 84
(William Muir) *led: jnd and rdn over 1f out: hdd jst ins fnl f: no ex and wknd fnl 100yds* **6/1**
42-3 5 4 1/2 **Oh So Sassy**[24] 1863 7-9-4 **90** ........ LouisSteward 3 74
(Chris Wall) *hld up in tch: effrt 2f out: rdn and no imp over 1f out: wknd ins fnl f: eased towards fnl* **9/2**[3]
000- 6 21 **Union Rose**[223] 6944 5-9-7 **93** ........(p) JamesDoyle 2
(Ronald Harris) *sn dropped to rr and struggling: rdn 3f out: lost tch 2f out* **8/1**

59.15s (0.95) **Going Correction** +0.10s/f (Good) 6 Ran SP% **113.6**
Speed ratings (Par 107): **96,94,89,89,82 48**
CSF £9.43 TOTE £3.40: £1.60, £1.60; EX 9.90 Trifecta £39.60.
**Owner** Akela Construction Ltd **Bred** Pantile Stud **Trained** Upper Helmsley, N Yorks

**FOCUS**
What looked a tight sprint on paper resulted in a confortable success for the progressive winner, who foiled a gamble on the runner-up. The runner-up has been rated as running his best race since moving to Britain.

## 2579 AIREY MILLER H'CAP 6f
3:55 (3:56) (Class 4) (0-85,84) 3-Y-O **£4,690** (£1,395; £697; £348) **Stalls** Centre

Form RPR
-601 1 **Quench Dolly**[3] 2503 3-8-11 **79** 6ex........ GeorgeBuckell(5) 2 94
(John Gallagher) *dwlt: sn rcvrd to ld and mde rest: pushed along and qcknd over 1f out: clr and styd on strly fnl f: easily* **5/2**[2]
2-50 2 6 **Father McKenzie**[14] 2122 3-8-13 **76**........ PatCosgrave 4 72
(James Eustace) *chsd wnr: rdn 2f out: outpcd u.p over 1f out: no ch w wnr but battled on to hold 2nd ins fnl f* **17/2**
15-3 3 *hd* **Trick Of The Light (IRE)**[17] 2072 3-8-13 **76**........ SilvestreDeSousa 8 71
(Roger Varian) *t.k.h: hld up in tch in midfield: effrt to chse ldrs ent fnl 2f: drvn and outpcd over 1f out: no ch w wnr and battling for placings fnl f: kpt on same pce* **9/4**[1]
62-0 4 1/2 **Kings Heart (IRE)**[21] 1940 3-7-9 **65** oh3........ JaneElliott(7) 3 59
(Mark Usher) *in tch in midfield: effrt in 4th 2f out: outpcd over 1f out: no ch w wnr and battling for placing fnl f: flashed tail u.p and kpt on same pce* **33/1**
1110 5 10 **Lord Cooper**[20] 1959 3-9-1 **78**........(tp) JimmyFortune 5 40
(Jose Santos) *hld up in tch: effrt over 2f out: no imp and wknd over 1f out* **14/1**
001- 6 1 3/4 **Open Wide (USA)**[214] 7216 3-8-13 **79**........ KieranShoemark(3) 6 35
(Amanda Perrett) *t.k.h: hld up in last pair: stmbld bdly after 1f out: effrt ent fnl 2f: sn struggling and wknd over 1f out* **10/1**
411- 7 1 1/4 **Thammin**[239] 6507 3-9-7 **84**........(h[1]) JimCrowley 9 36
(Owen Burrows) *dwlt: hld up in tch in midfield: clsd to trck ldrs over 3f out tl jst over 2f out: sn shkn up and no rspnse: wknd over 1f out* **5/1**[3]
6-32 8 44 **Raffle King (IRE)**[10] 2252 3-8-7 **70**........ GeorgeDowning 7
(Mick Channon) *keen to post: chsd ldrs tl lost pl u.p over 3f out: lost tch 2f out and eased ins fnl f: t.o* **9/1**

1m 11.53s (0.33) **Going Correction** +0.10s/f (Good) 8 Ran SP% **115.2**
Speed ratings (Par 101): **101,93,92,92,78 76,74,16**
CSF £24.26 CT £53.93 TOTE £3.90: £1.60, £2.50, £1.10; EX 27.30 Trifecta £73.70.
**Owner** Quench Racing Partnership **Bred** Mrs R J Gallagher **Trained** Chastleton, Oxon

**FOCUS**
This looked to be a competitive sprint on paper, but it turned out to be a procession for the winner, who was completing a demolition job for the second time in the space of three days. She's been rated similar to her previous win.

## 2580 HAROLD SIMMONS MEMORIAL MAIDEN STKS (DIV I) 7f
4:25 (4:29) (Class 5) 3-Y-O+ **£2,911** (£866; £432; £216) **Stalls** Centre

Form RPR
244- 1 **Zefferino**[182] 7906 3-9-0 83........ JamesDoyle 2 69
(Roger Charlton) *chsd ldng trio: effrt u.p over 1f out: led jst ins fnl f: styd on wl: eased cl home* **13/8**[2]
00 2 1 1/2 **Luna Bear**[16] 2092 3-8-6 0........ NoelGarbutt(3) 10 59
(Gary Moore) *racd along on stands' rail: overall ldr: rdn ent fnl 2f: hdd jst ins fnl f: kpt on same pce after* **50/1**
0-32 3 1/2 **Mr Tyrrell (IRE)**[34] 1619 3-9-0 80........ JimCrowley 6 63
(Richard Hannon) *chsd ldrs: effrt ent fnl 2f: drvn and ev ch over 1f out: styd on same pce ins fnl f* **5/4**[1]
3400 4 3 3/4 **Sparkling Cossack**[18] 2016 3-8-9 46........(p[1]) RobHornby 3 48
(Jeremy Gask) *hld up in midfield: effrt ent fnl 2f: drvn over 1f out: no imp on ldrs: wnt 4th ins fnl f* **66/1**
0 5 1 **Golden Cannon**[27] 1787 6-9-7 0........ StevieDonohoe 8 49?
(Sheena West) *led main gp and pressing overall ldr: rdn ent fnl 2f: no ex over 1f out: wknd ins fnl f* **100/1**
6 11 **African Quest** 3-8-6 0........ ShelleyBirkett(3) 1 16
(Gary Moore) *s.i.s: a towards rr: struggling 1/2-way: plugged on to pass btn rivals over 1f out: n.d* **50/1**
7 1 3/4 **Bringit (IRE)** 3-9-0 0........ TimmyMurphy 5 16
(Jamie Osborne) *awkward leaving stalls and s.i.s: a rr: n.d* **12/1**
50- 8 2 1/2 **Piccola Poppy**[198] 7616 4-9-7 0........ JosephineGordon 9 8
(John Bridger) *midfield: rdn 1/2-way: sn struggling: wl btn fnl 2f* **66/1**
0/ 9 12 **Rip N Roar (IRE)**[765] 1276 5-9-12 0........ JimmyFortune 7
(Tom Clover) *s.i.s: a wl bhd: t.o* **20/1**
10 52 **Noble Masterpiece** 3-8-11 0........ KieranShoemark(3) 4
(Sir Michael Stoute) *bolted to post: s.i.s: hld up in rr of main gp: lost pl and eased after 3f: t.o* **3/1**[3]

1m 25.67s (2.37) **Going Correction** +0.10s/f (Good)
**WFA** 3 from 4yo+ 12lb 10 Ran SP% **127.9**
Speed ratings (Par 103): **90,88,87,83,82 69,67,64,51,**
CSF £94.91 TOTE £2.60: £1.10, £11.00, £1.10; EX 85.60 Trifecta £253.50.
**Owner** Saleh Al Homaizi & Imad Al Sagar **Bred** Saleh Al Homaizi & Imad Al Sagar **Trained** Beckhampton, Wilts

**FOCUS**
With the well-touted newcomer boiling over and running a stinker, this was not the strongest of maidens, but the winner did it well and looks progressive. The fourth anchors the form.

## 2581 HAROLD SIMMONS MEMORIAL MAIDEN STKS (DIV II) 7f
4:55 (4:57) (Class 5) 3-Y-O+ **£2,911** (£866; £432; £216) **Stalls** Centre

Form RPR
1 **Express Lady (IRE)** 3-8-9 0........ JosephineGordon 8 77
(Hugo Palmer) *t.k.h: hld up in tch in midfield: clsd to trck ldrs 3f out: clr w wnr and shkn up to ld over 1f out: rn green but a doing enough ins fnl f* **11/4**[2]
0-4 2 1 **Buxted Dream (USA)**[17] 2066 3-9-0 0........ JimmyFortune 9 79
(Luca Cumani) *led: rdn 2f out: clr w wnr whn hdd and rdn over 1f out: kpt on but a hld ins fnl f* **1/2**[1]
00- 3 7 **Mordoree (IRE)**[195] 7696 3-8-9 0........ SamHitchcott 4 55
(Clive Cox) *rr of main gp: pushed along over 1f out: sme hdwy 2f out: chsd clr ldng pair over 1f out: no imp but kpt on for clr 2nd* **14/1**
0 4 5 **Hell Of A Lady**[30] 1727 3-8-9 0........ RobHornby 3 42
(Michael Attwater) *chsd ldr tl over 2f out: sn struggling u.p: wknd over 1f out* **66/1**
5 1 1/2 **Pride Of Angels** 4-9-7 0........ TimmyMurphy 1 42
(Gary Moore) *wnt lft s and s.i.s: rcvrd to chse ldrs after 2f: rdn ent fnl 2f: sn struggling and wknd over 1f out* **10/1**[3]
00- 6 1 1/2 **Kuiper Belt (USA)**[182] 7908 3-9-0 0........ TomQueally 6 39
(David Lanigan) *in tch towards rr of main gp: shkn up and rn green ent fnl 2f: no hdwy and wknd over 1f out* **10/1**[3]
065- 7 11 **Links Bar Marbella (IRE)**[261] 5775 4-9-12 44........ JohnFahy 5 13
(Eric Wheeler) *hld up in rr: lost tch 5f out: n.d* **66/1**
00 8 2 1/4 **Mister Chow**[24] 1862 3-8-11 0........ NoelGarbutt(3) 7 3
(Gary Moore) *s.i.s: a wl bhd* **33/1**
005- 9 2 1/2 **Dance With Kate**[17] 5256 6-9-2 34........ RyanWhile(5) 2
(Bill Turner) *chsd ldrs: rdn 1/2-way: sn lost pl: wl bhd fnl f* **50/1**

1m 24.66s (1.36) **Going Correction** +0.10s/f (Good)
**WFA** 3 from 4yo+ 12lb 9 Ran SP% **126.1**
Speed ratings (Par 103): **96,94,86,81,79 77,65,62,59**
CSF £4.88 TOTE £3.80: £1.40, £1.02, £3.60; EX 5.20 Trifecta £22.50.
**Owner** Dr Ali Ridha **Bred** Rabbah Bloodstock Limited **Trained** Newmarket, Suffolk

**FOCUS**
Not the strongest of maidens, but the winning debutant did it well and can climb the ladder. The level is fluid.

## 2582 SILK SERIES LADY RIDERS' H'CAP 7f
5:30 (5:31) (Class 4) (0-80,80) 4-Y-O+ **£6,469** (£1,925; £962; £481) **Stalls** Centre

Form RPR
-442 1 **Duke Of North (IRE)**[10] 2256 5-9-2 **66**........ IsobelFrancis(5) 6 73
(Jim Boyle) *hld up in rr: effrt 2f out: clsd on clr ldng pair over 1f out: led ins fnl f: r.o wl* **7/2**[3]
25-2 2 1 3/4 **Golden Wedding (IRE)**[18] 2026 5-10-7 **80**........ GeorgiaCox 8 82
(Eve Johnson Houghton) *taken down early: midfield: effrt ent fnl 2f: edging lft u.p and clsd on clr ldng pair over 1f out: chsd wnr ins fnl f: kpt on* **11/4**[1]
6641 3 1/2 **Athassel**[17] 2064 8-10-0 **78**........ MissEMacKenzie(5) 7 79
(David Evans) *hld up in midfield: shkn up ent fnl 2f: clsd on clr ldng pair over 1f out: styd on to go 3rd ins fnl f: no threat to wnr* **12/1**
-320 4 4 1/2 **Flexible Flyer**[35] 1606 8-10-1 **79**........(h) MissEBushe(5) 5 68
(Chris Dwyer) *t.k.h: w ldr and wnt clr after 2f: pushed along and led over 1f out: hdd ins fnl f: sn wknd* **9/1**
1312 5 *nse* **Tavener**[4] 2464 5-10-2 **75** 6ex........(p) SammyJoBell 1 64
(David C Griffiths) *led and wnt clr w rival after 2f: rdn and hdd over 1f out: no ex and wknd ins fnl f* **9/2**
0441 6 2 **Anonymous John (IRE)**[23] 1890 5-10-2 **75**........ JosephineGordon 3 58
(Dominic Ffrench Davis) *taken down early: chsd ldng pair: rdn over 2f out: no imp u.p and lost pl over 1f out: wknd ins fnl f* **3/1**[2]
0-60 7 13 **Veeraya**[59] 1186 7-9-6 **65**........(t) ShelleyBirkett 2 13
(Julia Feilden) *midfield: dropped to rr and rdn 3f out: wl btn fnl 2f* **16/1**

1m 26.22s (2.92) **Going Correction** +0.10s/f (Good) 7 Ran SP% **115.6**
Speed ratings (Par 105): **87,85,84,79,79 76,62**
CSF £13.92 CT £102.27 TOTE £4.70: £2.20, £1.50; EX 15.10 Trifecta £90.50.
**Owner** The Paddock Space Partnership **Bred** Kenilworth Partnership **Trained** Epsom, Surrey

**FOCUS**
The two leaders went off too quickly and set it up for the held-up winner, whose jockey was enjoying her first success under Rules. The runner-up has been rated close to his turf best.
T/Plt: £8.70 to a £1 stake. Pool: £25,305.00 - 2,903.34 winning units. T/Qpdt: £3.50 to a £1 stake. Pool: £2,425.00 - 675.70 winning units. **Steve Payne**

# 2265 NOTTINGHAM (L-H)
Friday, May 12

**OFFICIAL GOING: Good changing to good (good to soft in places) after race 3 (6.15)**
Wind: Light behind Weather: Cloudy with heavy shower

## 2583 JUST JANE FILLIES' NOVICE MEDIAN AUCTION STKS (PLUS 10 RACE) 5f 8y
5:10 (5:21) (Class 5) 2-Y-O **£3,234** (£962; £481; £240) **Stalls** High

Form RPR
5 1 **Neola**[20] 1966 2-9-0 0........ BenCurtis 9 88
(Mick Channon) *in tch on outer: hdwy over 2f out: led wl over 1f out: sn rdn and edgd rt: clr ins fnl f* **8/1**[3]
6 2 7 **Lexington Grace (IRE)**[10] 2265 2-9-0 0........ CamHardie 10 63
(Richard Hannon) *trckd ldrs: pushed along 1/2-way: hdwy wl over 1f out: rdn and kpt on fnl f* **14/1**
6 3 3/4 **Mocead Cappall**[20] 1966 2-9-0 0........ RoystonFfrench 2 60
(John Holt) *uns rdr and bolted bef s: t.k.h: cl up: led after 1f: rdn along and hdd wl over 1f out: kpt on same pce* **66/1**
4 2 1/4 **Shania Says (IRE)** 2-9-0 0........ WilliamCarson 7 52
(Tony Carroll) *chsd ldrs: pushed along and sltly outpcd 1/2-way: rdn wl over 1f out: kpt on fnl f* **8/1**[3]
3 5 1/2 **Under Offer (IRE)**[22] 1908 2-9-0 0........ LukeMorris 8 50
(James Tate) *trckd ldrs: hdwy and cl up 1/2-way: rdn along 2f out: sn btn* **9/4**[1]

6 3 1/4 **Wings Of The Rock (IRE)** 2-9-0 0.................................. RyanPowell 6 39
(Scott Dixon) *dwlt: hdwy and cl up on outer over 3f out: rdn along 2f out: sn wknd* **3/1**[2]
7 nk **Mops Tango** 2-9-0 0.......................................................... LiamJones 1 37
(Michael Appleby) *sn outpcd and a rr* **66/1**
8 1 1/4 **Sandkissed (IRE)** 2-9-0 0........................................... LemosdeSouza 4 33
(Amy Murphy) *qckly away and led 1f: prom: rdn along bef 1/2-way: sn wknd* **25/1**

59.62s (-1.88) **Going Correction** -0.55s/f (Hard) 8 Ran SP% **91.5**
Speed ratings (Par 90): **93,81,80,77,76 71,70,68**
CSF £63.13 TOTE £8.50: £1.60, £2.70, £8.80; EX 60.90 Trifecta £949.80.
**Owner** Bastian Family **Bred** E & R Bastian **Trained** West Ilsley, Berks
■ Enrolment was withdrawn. Price at time of withdrawal 3-1. Rule 4 applies to all bets - deduction 25p in the pound.

**FOCUS**
All races on outer track and distances as advertised. Rain before racing caused the ground to be changed to good. Not a bad juvenile fillies' median auction on paper, but a delayed start and the withdrawal of one of the market leaders limited interest. The winner scored emphatically. The second and third will be the key to the level.

## 2584 WILDMAN MAIDEN STKS 1m 2f 50y
5:45 (5:47) (Class 5) 3-Y-O £3,234 (£962; £481; £240) Stalls Low

Form RPR
56-2 1 **Okool (FR)**[20] 1967 3-9-5 81.................................................. SeanLevey 2 79
(Owen Burrows) *t.k.h: trckd ldr: effrt and cl up 3f out: rdn to ld 11/2f out: jnd and drvn ent fnl f: kpt on wl last 100 yds* **7/4**[1]
-6 2 1 1/4 **Chief Craftsman**[20] 1967 3-9-5 0........................................ LukeMorris 12 76
(Luca Cumani) *trckd ldng trio: hdwy on outer 3f out: rdn over 1f out: sn chal: disp ld ent fnl f: ev ch tl drvn and no ex last 100yds* **18/1**
23- 3 1 1/2 **Flaming Marvel (IRE)**[160] 8208 3-9-5 0.................................. DanielMuscutt 5 73
(James Fanshawe) *t.k.h: trckd ldng pair. hdwy on inner whn n.m.r 2f out: rdn along and squeezed through over 1f out: sn drvn and kpt on same pce* **5/2**[2]
05- 4 1 3/4 **William Booth (IRE)**[136] 8537 3-9-5 0.................................. FranBerry 1 69
(Daniel Mark Loughnane) *set stdy pce: qcknd over 3f out: rdn along over 2f out: hdd 11/2f out: sn drvn and grad wknd* **33/1**
0- 5 4 **Uptown Funk (IRE)**[203] 7501 3-9-5 0.................................. RobertTart 3 61+
(John Gosden) *dwlt and towards rr: hdwy on inner over 3f out: rdn along over 2f out: kpt on fnl f* **3/1**[3]
5 6 4 **Circling Vultures**[49] 1347 3-9-5 0........................................ CamHardie 6 53
(Antony Brittain) *in tch: rdn along over 3f out: drvn 2f out: sn one pce* **100/1**
0 7 nk **Wasm**[30] 1730 3-9-5 0.........................................................(t) RyanPowell 8 52+
(Simon Crisford) *rr: hdwy wl over 2f out: styd on appr fnl f* **12/1**
05 8 2 **Air Ministry (IRE)**[9] 2314 3-9-5 0....................................(b) DannyBrock 4 48
(Michael Bell) *towards rr: hdwy on outer 3f out: rdn along over 2f out: sn no imp* **50/1**
5 9 2 3/4 **Hamelin Pool**[12] 2175 3-9-5 0..........................................(b[1]) BenCurtis 11 43
(Henry Candy) *in tch: rdn along over 3f out: sn drvn and wknd* **66/1**
10 2 1/2 **Sputnik Planum (USA)** 3-9-5 0........................................ MartinLane 9 38
(David Lanigan) *dwlt: a rr* **25/1**
6 11 7 **Forward Contract (USA)**[22] 1900 3-9-5 0........................ LiamKeniry 10 24
(Hughie Morrison) *in tch: rdn along over 3f out: sn wknd* **50/1**
12 7 **Volturnus** 3-9-5 0............................................................... LiamJones 13 10
(Jamie Osborne) *a rr* **80/1**
0 13 nk **Geordielad**[16] 2092 3-9-0 0.............................................. LucyKBarry[(5)] 7 9
(Jamie Osborne) *a rr* **100/1**

2m 13.6s (-0.70) **Going Correction** -0.375s/f (Firm) 13 Ran SP% **118.3**
Speed ratings (Par 99): **87,86,84,83,80 77,76,75,72,70 65,59,59**
CSF £35.64 TOTE £3.50: £1.50, £1.70, £1.30; EX 20.60 Trifecta £41.40.
**Owner** Hamdan Al Maktoum **Bred** Madame Maja Sundstrom **Trained** Lambourn, Berks

**FOCUS**
An interesting maiden with several well-bred types representing major yards. The pace was steady and the first four held those positions throughout. The fourth is the key to the form.

## 2585 GOLDEN FLEECE MAIDEN FILLIES' STKS (PLUS 10 RACE) 1m 75y
6:15 (6:19) (Class 5) 3-Y-O £3,234 (£962; £481; £240) Stalls Centre

Form RPR
1 **Maid To Remember** 3-9-0 0................................................ FranBerry 10 84+
(Ralph Beckett) *green and towards rr: hdwy and swtchd lft over 3f out: chsd ldrs and swtchd rt wl over 1f out: rdn and str run ent fnl f: edgd lft and led nr fin* **5/1**[3]
6- 2 nk **Sasini**[307] 4147 3-8-11 0............................................... CallumShepherd[(3)] 6 78
(Charles Hills) *in tch: hdwy 3f out: rdn over 1f out: chal ent fnl f: drvn to ld last 100 yds: hdd and no ex nr fin* **16/1**
40- 3 1 3/4 **Alouja (IRE)**[191] 7763 3-9-0 0........................................... DaneO'Neill 13 74
(Hugo Palmer) *prom: cl up 1/2-way: rdn to ld 2f out: drvn and jnd ent fnl f: hdd last 100 yds: kpt on same pce* **8/1**
62- 4 2 1/4 **Music Lesson**[191] 7761 3-9-0 0............................................ LukeMorris 3 69
(Hughie Morrison) *trckd ldrs: hdwy 3f out: rdn along 2f out: drvn over 1f out: kpt on one pce* **9/2**[2]
3 5 1 1/2 **Feint**[13] 2144 3-9-0 0.............................................................. BenCurtis 9 65
(William Haggas) *in tch: pushed along 3f out: rdn over 2f out: sn no imp* **9/4**[1]
66 6 1 **Al Jawza**[18] 2019 3-9-0 0.................................................. SeanLevey 11 63
(Richard Hannon) *trckd ldrs: pushed along 3f out: rdn 2f out: sn one pce* **20/1**
4- 7 2 1/4 **Dancing Dragon (IRE)**[242] 6404 3-9-0 0............................. LiamKeniry 1 58
(George Baker) *chsd ldrs: rdn along 3f out: sn drvn and wknd* **66/1**
0-5 8 3 **Cribbs Causeway (IRE)**[30] 1730 3-9-0 0............................ FergusSweeney 4 51+
(Roger Charlton) *dwlt: a towards rr* **20/1**
9 1 1/4 **Exacting** 3-9-0 0.................................................................... SteveDrowne 8 48
(Daniel Kubler) *s.i.s: green and bhd tl sme late hdwy* **66/1**
10 1 1/2 **Street Marie (USA)** 3-9-0 0................................................ RobertTart 14 45
(John Gosden) *s.i.s: green and a towards rr* **7/1**
2-6 11 3 **Fairy Lights**[36] 1581 3-9-0 0.............................................. JackMitchell 2 38
(Roger Varian) *led: rdn along 3f out: hdd 2f out and sn wknd* **14/1**
00 12 3 **Mushareefa (IRE)**[11] 2231 3-9-0 0.................................... AntonioFresu 7 31
(Ed Dunlop) *a rr* **100/1**
00- 13 13 **Angel In Disguise (IRE)**[169] 8082 3-9-0 0......................... DanielMuscutt 5
(Philip McBride) *t.k.h in midfield: rdn along over 3f out: sn wknd* **66/1**
0 14 34 **Maid In Brittain**[16] 2078 3-9-0 0.....................................(t[1]) CamHardie 12
(Antony Brittain) *midfield: rdn along on outer over 3f out: sn wknd* **100/1**

1m 45.7s (-3.30) **Going Correction** -0.375s/f (Firm) 14 Ran SP% **117.8**
Speed ratings (Par 96): **101,100,98,96,95 94,91,88,87,86 83,80,67,33**
CSF £76.00 TOTE £6.00: £2.30, £5.50, £3.00; EX 117.00 Trifecta £1814.90.
**Owner** Normandie Stud Ltd **Bred** R Shaykhutdinov **Trained** Kimpton, Hants

**FOCUS**
A fair looking 3yo fillies' maiden with a number of top yards represented. The pace looked reasonable and the winner came from well back. The form makes sense rated around the third, fourth and sixth, and it fits the race standard.

## 2586 49 SQUADRON H'CAP 1m 75y
6:50 (6:52) (Class 4) (0-80,81) 4-Y-O+ £5,175 (£1,540; £769; £384) Stalls Centre

Form RPR
12-0 1 **Zlatan (IRE)**[20] 1969 4-9-1 77.................................(p) CallumShepherd[(3)] 3 83
(Ed de Giles) *trckd ldrs: hdwy 3f out: swtchd lft 2f out: rdn to chal over 1f out: led ent fnl f: sn drvn and edgd rt: hld on wl towards fin* **6/1**[2]
0-05 2 nk **Pumaflor (IRE)**[13] 2133 5-9-6 79........................................(p) JasonHart 7 84
(Richard Whitaker) *trckd ldng pair: cl up 3f out: led 2f out and sn rdn: hdd narrowly ent fnl f: sn drvn and carried rt: ev ch tl no ex nr fin* **7/1**[3]
0156 3 shd **Magic City (IRE)**[18] 2030 8-8-10 76........................... HarrisonShaw[(7)] 1 81
(Michael Easterby) *awkward and stmbld shortly after s: towards rr: hdwy on inner 3f out: trckd ldrs 2f out: rdn over 1f out: chsd ldng pair ins fnl f: sn drvn and kpt on wl towards fin* **7/1**[3]
04-4 4 2 1/4 **Haraz (IRE)**[17] 2064 4-8-11 77..............................(v[1]) PatrickVaughan[(7)] 8 77
(David O'Meara) *t.k.h: chsd ldrs: led over 6f out: rdn along 3f out: hdd 2f out: sn drvn and kpt on same pce fnl f* **10/1**
-660 5 1/2 **Abushamah (IRE)**[18] 2030 6-9-7 80................................ JamesSullivan 9 78
(Ruth Carr) *trckd ldrs: hdwy 3f out: rdn along 2f out: drvn over 1f out: no imp fnl f* **8/1**
00-0 6 2 1/2 **Invictus (GER)**[23] 1323 5-8-9 75...............................(h) CameronNoble[(7)] 5 68
(David Loughnane) *led: hdd over 6f out: trckd ldr: pushed along over 3f out: rdn wl over 2f out: grad wknd* **25/1**
000- 7 1/2 **Saxo Jack (FR)**[153] 8319 7-9-0 78...............................(t) SophieKilloran[(5)] 6 70
(Sophie Leech) *s.i.s and bhd: hdwy 3f out: rdn along whn n.m.r and swtchd rt over 1f out: kpt on fnl f* **50/1**
230- 8 shd **Topology**[188] 7813 4-9-3 76................................................ LiamKeniry 11 67
(Joseph Tuite) *towards rr: sme hdwy on outer over 3f out: rdn along wl over 2f out: sn hung lft and wknd* **12/1**
55-6 9 1/2 **Imperial State**[15] 2116 4-9-8 81...........................................(t) LukeMorris 2 71
(George Scott) *towards rr: hdwy over 3f out: rdn along wl over 2f out: sn drvn and no imp* **3/1**[1]
5530 10 3 1/4 **House Of Commons (IRE)**[20] 1969 4-9-4 77.................. LiamJones 4 60
(Michael Appleby) *in tch: rdn along on outer 3f out: sn drvn and wknd 2f out* **7/1**[3]
043- 11 7 **Pirate's Treasure**[291] 4720 4-9-7 80..............................(h[1]) DavidNolan 10 47
(Jennie Candlish) *rr whn n.m.r and unbalanced after 1f: a rr after* **22/1**

1m 44.83s (-4.17) **Going Correction** -0.375s/f (Firm) 11 Ran SP% **114.8**
Speed ratings (Par 105): **105,104,104,102,101 99,98,98,98,95 88**
CSF £45.43 CT £304.85 TOTE £6.50: £2.00, £2.40, £2.60; EX 41.30 Trifecta £531.80.
**Owner** Gwyn Powell & Richard Meakes **Bred** Roundhill Stud **Trained** Ledbury, H'fords

**FOCUS**
The going was changed to Good, good to soft in places before this race. The feature contest and a fair mile handicap which was run 0.87 secs faster than the preceding maiden. It produced a good finish. The third has been rated close to his AW form.

## 2587 RUBUS FILLIES' H'CAP 1m 75y
7:25 (7:26) (Class 5) (0-70,72) 3-Y-O+ £3,234 (£962; £481; £240) Stalls Centre

Form RPR
36-6 1 **Braztime**[16] 2094 3-9-3 72................................................ SeanLevey 3 78+
(Richard Hannon) *trckd ldr: cl up 3f out: led 2f out: rdn over 1f out: drvn clr ins fnl f: kpt on strly* **13/2**[2]
20-2 2 1 **Al Nafoorah**[10] 2274 3-8-12 67........................................ AntonioFresu 10 70
(Ed Dunlop) *trckd ldrs: hdwy 3f out: n.m.r 2f out: sn rdn: chsd wnr ent fnl f: sn drvn and kpt on* **9/2**[1]
0-00 3 1 1/4 **Hijran (IRE)**[10] 2267 4-9-1 64........................................(p) RayDawson[(7)] 5 67
(Michael Appleby) *midfield: hdwy over 3f out: chsd ldng pair 2f out and sn rdn: drvn and kpt on fnl f* **16/1**
30-4 4 nk **Singing Sands (IRE)**[32] 1686 3-9-3 72.........................(t) FergusSweeney 7 71+
(Seamus Durack) *dwlt and rr: hdwy over 2f out: sn rdn: styd on wl appr fnl f: nrst fin* **10/1**
30-0 5 3 **Beatbybeatbybeat**[30] 1717 4-10-0 70................................(v) CamHardie 1 65
(Antony Brittain) *t.k.h: chsd ldrs on inner: pushed along over 2f out: rdn wl over 1f out: grad wknd* **16/1**
06-0 6 3/4 **Miss Ranger (IRE)**[23] 1879 5-9-11 67.................................. BenCurtis 9 61
(Brian Ellison) *dwlt and rr: hdwy on outer over 2f out: rdn along wl over 1f out: kpt on fnl f: nrst fin* **14/1**
-144 7 3/4 **Elusive Olivia (USA)**[10] 2274 3-8-13 68...........................(t) FranBerry 8 57
(Joseph Tuite) *towards rr: hdwy 3f out: rdn along over 2f out: n.d* **12/1**
-201 8 2 1/4 **Tulip Dress**[17] 2053 4-9-8 64........................................ WilliamCarson 12 51
(Anthony Carson) *hld up: hdwy 4f out: chsd ldrs 3f out: rdn over 2f out: sn wknd* **11/1**
46-0 9 2 1/4 **Pyjamarama**[16] 2094 3-8-11 66........................................ JackMitchell 6 45
(Roger Varian) *trckd ldrs on inner: pushed along 4f out: rdn 3f out: sn drvn and wknd* **8/1**
0-26 10 2 3/4 **Pobbles**[107] 392 3-9-1 70.................................................(p) LukeMorris 2 42
(George Scott) *led: rdn along over 3f out: hdd 2f out and sn wknd* **10/1**
34-4 11 6 **Nancy Hart**[13] 2144 3-9-0 69............................................... JasonHart 4 27
(Tom Dascombe) *t.k.h: prom: rdn along 3f out: wknd over 2f out* **10/1**
2-34 12 2 **Do You Know (IRE)**[107] 392 3-8-10 65.......................... DanielMuscutt 11 19
(Marco Botti) *a towards rr* **7/1**[3]

1m 46.69s (-2.31) **Going Correction** -0.375s/f (Firm)
**WFA** 3 from 4yo+ 13lb 12 Ran SP% **116.9**
Speed ratings (Par 100): **96,95,93,93,90 89,88,86,84,81 75,73**
CSF £35.24 CT £458.73 TOTE £8.40: £2.40, £2.10, £6.20; EX 56.50 Trifecta £684.50.
**Owner** Chris Giles **Bred** Mr & Mrs G Middlebrook **Trained** East Everleigh, Wilts

**FOCUS**
This modest fillies' handicap was run 1.86 secs slower than the faster of the two earlier races over the distance, suggesting the rain was having an effect. The runner-up has been rated to her AW latest.

## 2588 SMOKEY JOE H'CAP 1m 2f 50y
8:00 (8:01) (Class 5) (0-75,77) 3-Y-O £3,234 (£962; £481; £240) Stalls Low

Form RPR
60-6 1 **Nathan Mayer**[13] 2152 3-9-1 68........................................ FranBerry 6 75+
(Sir Michael Stoute) *trckd ldrs: hdwy on outer 3f out: rdn and cl up over 1f out: drvn ins fnl f: kpt on wl to ld nr fin* **10/1**
4-04 2 nk **Lunar Jet**[13] 2145 3-9-2 69................................................ BenCurtis 2 75+
(John Mackie) *dwlt and hld up towards rr: stdy hdwy over 4f out: trckd ldrs over 2f out: chal over 1f out: rdn to take narrow ld ent fnl f: sn drvn: hdd and no ex nr fin* **3/1**[2]

4422 **3** ¾ **Alexander M (IRE)**[6] 2395 3-8-13 **66** FrannyNorton 11 70
(Mark Johnston) *prom: hdwy 3f out: cl up 2f out: sn rdn to chal and ev ch: drvn ins fnl f: kpt on* **11/4**[1]

14-0 **4** ½ **See The City (IRE)**[30] 1737 3-9-7 **74** RyanTate 10 77
(James Eustace) *led 1f: chsd ldrs: cl up 3f out: led over 2f out: rdn wl over 1f out: drvn and hdd ent fnl f: kpt on same pce towards fin* **22/1**

00-0 **5** 1½ **City Dreamer (IRE)**[14] 2118 3-8-12 **65** FergusSweeney 5 69+
(Alan King) *hld up in rr: hdwy 3f out: rdn wl over 1f out: styd on fnl f: nrst fin* **6/1**[3]

620 **6** 8 **Zehrah (IRE)**[21] 1944 3-9-6 **73** MartinLane 7 57
(Simon Crisford) *chsd ldrs: rdn along wl 3f out: drvn over 2f out: sn wknd* **16/1**

4-52 **7** 1¼ **Glorvina (IRE)**[15] 2110 3-9-0 **67** DavidNolan 1 49
(David O'Meara) *led: rdn along 3f out: hdd over 2f out: sn drvn and grad wknd* **14/1**

553- **8** 1¾ **Chocolate Box (IRE)**[199] 7598 3-9-7 **74** LukeMorris 4 52
(Luca Cumani) *towards rr: rdn along over 3f out: n.d* **8/1**

0-10 **9** 1¼ **Glorious Power (IRE)**[16] 2088 3-9-10 **77** DavidProbert 3 53
(Charles Hills) *trckd ldr: hdwy over 3f out: rdn along wl over 2f out: grad wknd* **16/1**

-503 **10** 1¾ **Challow (IRE)**[11] 2220 3-9-2 **69** LiamKeniry 9 41
(Sylvester Kirk) *dwlt: a rr* **16/1**

344- **11** 5 **Solent Meads (IRE)**[151] 8340 3-9-6 **73** (b) DaneO'Neill 8 35
(Daniel Kubler) *midfield: rdn along over 3f out: sn outpcd* **33/1**

2m 11.77s (-2.53) **Going Correction** -0.375s/f (Firm) 11 Ran SP% **117.8**
Speed ratings (Par 99): **95,94,94,93,92 86,85,83,82,81 77**
CSF £40.12 CT £108.15 TOTE £9.60: £3.10, £1.80, £1.50; EX 47.80 Trifecta £193.70.
**Owner** Sir Evelyn De Rothschild **Bred** Southcourt Stud **Trained** Newmarket, Suffolk

**FOCUS**
An ordinary but competitive handicap which was run 1.83 secs faster than the earlier maiden over the trip. It produced another close finish. The third has been rated close to his Goodwood latest.

## 2589 WITHAM SHIELD H'CAP 6f 18y
**8:30** (8:34) (Class 6) (0-60,60) 4-Y-0+ **£2,587** (£770; £384; £192) **Stalls** High

Form RPR

4345 **1** **Socialites Red**[17] 2058 4-8-13 **59** (p) RPWalsh(7) 1 70
(Scott Dixon) *cl up centre: led 1/2-way: rdn 2f out: edgd rt to stands' rail ent fnl f: kpt on wl* **14/1**

/0-4 **2** 2 **Deeds Not Words (IRE)**[9] 2319 6-9-4 **57** (p) DavidProbert 7 62
(Michael Wigham) *in tch: hdwy in centre over 2f out: rdn to chse wnr over 1f out: drvn ins fnl f: no imp towards fin* **4/1**[2]

3330 **3** ¾ **Loumarin (IRE)**[29] 1759 5-8-7 **53** (p) RayDawson(7) 2 56
(Michael Appleby) *cl up centre: chsd wnr 1/2-way: rdn along 2f out: drvn and edgd rt to stands' rail ent fnl f: kpt on* **16/1**

0144 **4** 1 **Bogsnog (IRE)**[12] 2179 7-9-4 **57** JamesSullivan 12 57
(Ruth Carr) *trckd ldrs centre: hdwy over 2f out: rdn wl over 1f out: drvn and kpt on same pce fnl f* **8/1**

0550 **5** nk **Multi Quest**[36] 1593 5-8-12 **51** (b) FrannyNorton 17 50+
(John E Long) *racd nr stands' rail: in tch: hdwy 2f out: rdn and styng on whn nt clr run jst ins fnl f: swtchd lft and kpt on: nrst fin* **14/1**

21-2 **6** ½ **Titus Secret**[18] 2043 5-9-7 **60** FergusSweeney 5 57
(Malcolm Saunders) *racd wd: in tch: hdwy to chse ldrs centre 2f out and sn rdn: drvn ent fnl f: one pce* **3/1**[1]

40-0 **7** 1¾ **Manipura**[14] 2124 4-9-2 **55** (p) RyanPowell 13 47
(Derek Shaw) *dwlt and hmpd s: in rr and sn swtchd rt to stands' rail: hdwy over 2f out: swtchd lft and rdn over 1f out: kpt on fnl f* **40/1**

0-00 **8** ¾ **Captain Scooby**[18] 2034 11-9-2 **55** (b) SeanLevey 9 45
(Richard Guest) *bhd centre: hdwy 2f out: sn rdn and styd on fnl f* **25/1**

3640 **9** 1¾ **Keene's Pointe**[50] 1325 7-9-3 **56** DannyBrock 6 41
(Steph Hollinshead) *in tch centre: rdn along jst over 2f out: sn drvn and grad wknd* **16/1**

-500 **10** 1 **Clon Rocket (IRE)**[20] 1965 4-8-7 **46** LiamJones 11 28
(John Holt) *chsd ldrs nr stands' rail: rdn along over 2f out: sn wknd* **33/1**

2232 **11** ¾ **Virile (IRE)**[9] 2298 6-9-4 **57** (bt) LukeMorris 10 36
(Sylvester Kirk) *dwlt and bhd in centre: sn rdn along: nvr a factor* **15/2**[3]

04-0 **12** 3¼ **Goadby**[36] 1593 6-8-11 **50** (p) RoystonFfrench 4 20
(John Holt) *narrow ld centre: hdd 1/2-way: sn rdn along and wknd fnl 2f* **22/1**

500- **13** 3¼ **Diminutive (IRE)**[184] 7863 5-9-0 **53** (p) DanielMuscutt 14 13
(Grace Harris) *hmpd s: in tch towards stands' side: rdn along over 2f out: sn wknd* **40/1**

4-03 **14** 27 **Spellmaker**[30] 1723 8-9-4 **57** MartinLane 15
(Tony Newcombe) *hmpd s: chsd ldrs stands' side: rdn along over 2f out: sn wknd* **12/1**

03-0 **15** nk **Jazz Legend (USA)**[24] 1869 4-9-6 **59** (p) BenCurtis 16
(Mandy Rowland) *wnt lft s: racd nr stands' rail: cl up: rdn along wl over 2f out: sn drvn and wknd* **40/1**

1m 13.1s (-1.60) **Going Correction** -0.55s/f (Hard) 15 Ran SP% **119.1**
Speed ratings (Par 101): **88,85,84,83,82 81,79,78,76,74 73,69,65,29,28**
CSF £63.55 CT £916.90 TOTE £13.70: £3.70, £1.70, £6.10; EX 96.00 Trifecta £1610.40.
**Owner** J Melo Racing **Bred** Selwood, Hoskins & Trickledown **Trained** Babworth, Notts

**FOCUS**
A big field for this low-grade sprint handicap and something of a surprise winner. The winner has been rated back to something like last year's better turf form.
T/Plt: £593.80 to a £1 stake. Pool: £46,392.85 - 57.03 winning units. T/Qpdt: £73.00 to a £1 stake. Pool: £3,581.29 - 36.30 winning units. **Joe Rowntree**

# 2154 RIPON (R-H)
Friday, May 12

**OFFICIAL GOING: Good to firm (good in places; watered; 8.3)**
Wind: light half behind Weather: Overcast

## 2590 SIS TRADING SERVICES NOVICE AUCTION STKS 5f
**6:00** (6:02) (Class 5) 2-Y-0 **£3,881** (£1,155; £577; £288) **Stalls** High

Form RPR

31 **1** **Starlight Mystery (IRE)**[10] 2251 2-9-1 **0** PaulMulrennan 3 68
(Mark Johnston) *dwlt: sn chsd ldrs: pushed along 1/2-way: rdn to chal strly fnl f: kpt on: led post* **2/1**[1]

00 **2** hd **Bahuta Acha**[13] 2148 2-8-10 **0** SamJames 1 62
(David Loughnane) *sn led: rdn 2f out: strly pressed fnl f: kpt on but hdd post* **25/1**

**3** shd **Star Of Zaam (IRE)** 2-8-12 **0** JordanVaughan(3) 6 67+
(K R Burke) *s.i.s: hld up and rn green: rdn and hdwy on outer 2f out: chsd ldrs 1f out: kpt on: rdr dropped rein and briefly stopped riding 25yds out* **7/2**[3]

0 **4** 1½ **Faradays Spark (IRE)**[13] 2154 2-8-13 **0** TonyHamilton 8 60+
(Richard Fahey) *outpcd towards rr tl kpt on wl fnl f* **9/1**

5 **5** hd **Highland Bobby**[11] 2221 2-9-2 **0** DanielTudhope 2 62
(David O'Meara) *prom: rdn and bit outpcd over 1f out: one pce fnl f* **11/4**[2]

0 **6** 2¼ **Monkey Magic**[15] 2105 2-8-9 **0** AndrewMullen 7 47
(Nigel Tinkler) *trckd ldrs: bit short of room on rail and lost pl appr fnl f: no threat after* **33/1**

3 **7** nk **Aristodemus (IRE)**[13] 2154 2-8-11 **0** DuranFentiman 5 48
(Tim Easterby) *trckd ldrs: rdn 2f out: wknd ins fnl f* **11/2**

59.84s (-0.16) **Going Correction** -0.275s/f (Firm) 7 Ran SP% **114.4**
Speed ratings (Par 93): **90,89,89,87,86 83,82**
CSF £50.87 TOTE £3.20: £1.60, £8.40; EX 43.90 Trifecta £203.80.
**Owner** Ali Saeed **Bred** Rabbah Bloodstock Limited **Trained** Middleham Moor, N Yorks

**FOCUS**
The going was good to firm, good in places, and the rail on the bend from the back straight to home straight was dolled out by 6 yards adding approximately 12 yard to races on the round course. There was a tight finish in this opening novice event and a last-time-out winner just prevailed. It's been rated around the ordinary race average.

## 2591 SPORTS INFORMATION SERVICES (S) STKS 1m 1f 170y
**6:30** (6:30) (Class 6) 3-4-Y-0 **£3,234** (£962; £481; £240) **Stalls** Low

Form RPR

5315 **1** **Metronomic (IRE)**[10] 2259 3-8-7 **60** RossaRyan(7) 2 62+
(Richard Hannon) *chsd ldr: racd keenly: pushed along to ld over 2f out: sn rdn: drvn and kpt on fnl f* **5/4**[1]

0243 **2** 1½ **Crindle Carr (IRE)**[76] 925 3-8-9 **67** AndrewMullen 5 54
(David Barron) *midfield: rdn over 3f out: hdwy to chse ldr over 1f out: styd on but a hld* **9/4**[2]

460- **3** 2¼ **Calypso Delegator (IRE)**[211] 7044 4-9-10 **47** (p[1]) PJMcDonald 6 51
(Micky Hammond) *midfield: rdn over 3f out: hdwy to chse ldr over 1f out: wknd fnl 75yds* **28/1**

3600 **4** 2½ **Slaying The Dragon (IRE)**[12] 2179 4-9-10 **51** TonyHamilton 1 46
(Nigel Tinkler) *hld up: rdn over 3f out: minor late hdwy: nvr threatened* **50/1**

-000 **5** nse **Clayton Hall (IRE)**[15] 2108 4-9-10 **55** (t[1]) PaulMulrennan 7 46
(John Wainwright) *chsd ldrs: rdn over 3f out: hung repeatedly rt: wknd over 1f out* **14/1**

-050 **6** 2½ **Never Say (IRE)**[72] 969 4-9-2 **42** JordanVaughan(3) 3 36
(Jason Ward) *dwlt: hld up: nvr threatened* **9/1**

6-00 **7** 11 **Ray Donovan (IRE)**[8] 2347 3-8-9 **64** (v[1]) SamJames 4 19
(David O'Meara) *led: sn clr: reduced advantage over 3f out: rdn whn hdd over 2f out: wknd* **5/1**[3]

2m 4.99s (-0.41) **Going Correction** -0.15s/f (Firm)
**WFA** 3 from 4yo 15lb 7 Ran SP% **114.0**
Speed ratings (Par 101): **95,93,92,90,89 87,79**
CSF £4.19 TOTE £2.20: £1.10, £1.40; EX 6.00 Trifecta £49.20.Crindle Carr was claimed by Mr J L Flint for for £6,000
**Owner** Middleham Park Racing VIII **Bred** Pier House Stud **Trained** East Everleigh, Wilts

**FOCUS**
Race distance increased by 12yds. The favourite scored with authority in this weak seller.

## 2592 SIS TRUSTED DELIVERY PARTNER H'CAP 6f
**7:05** (7:06) (Class 4) (0-85,87) 4-Y-0 **£7,561** (£2,263; £1,131; £566; £282) **Stalls** High

Form RPR

0-56 **1** **Explain**[16] 2081 5-9-0 **78** (p) JackGarritty 4 86
(Ruth Carr) *s.i.s: hld up in tch: rdn over 2f out: hdwy appr fnl f: kpt on: led towards fin* **6/1**

42-2 **2** ½ **Straightothepoint**[22] 1910 5-9-6 **84** ConnorBeasley 3 90
(Bryan Smart) *led narrowly: rdn 2f out: kpt on: hdd towards fin* **2/1**[1]

0-02 **3** ¾ **Johnny Cavagin**[9] 2303 8-9-3 **81** (t) AndrewMullen 7 85
(Ronald Thompson) *s.i.s: sn in tch: rdn 2f out: chal ins fnl f: kpt on* **10/1**

00-4 **4** 2½ **Honeysuckle Lil (IRE)**[22] 1910 5-8-10 **77** (p) RachelRichardson(3) 9 73
(Tim Easterby) *chsd ldrs: swtchd rt 2f out: rdn to chal appr fnl f: wknd fnl 110yds* **17/2**

0-03 **5** ½ **Taskeen (IRE)**[6] 2404 4-8-10 **74** TonyHamilton 1 68
(Roger Fell) *dwlt: hld up: outpcd in rr 1/2-way: sme late hdwy: nvr threatened* **9/2**[2]

0-05 **6** 1¾ **Lathom**[10] 2262 4-9-9 **87** (v) DanielTudhope 11 75
(David O'Meara) *prom: rdn 2f out: wknd ins fnl f* **5/1**[3]

3-00 **7** 4 **Mishaal (IRE)**[27] 1799 7-9-7 **85** PaulMulrennan 5 61
(Michael Herrington) *chsd ldrs: rdn over 2f out: wknd appr fnl f* **8/1**

1m 10.6s (-2.40) **Going Correction** -0.275s/f (Firm) 7 Ran SP% **113.2**
Speed ratings (Par 105): **105,104,103,100,99 97,91**
CSF £18.07 CT £116.90 TOTE £8.10: £4.40, £1.30; EX 24.00 Trifecta £121.20.
**Owner** The Beer Stalkers & Ruth Carr **Bred** Tibthorpe Stud **Trained** Huby, N Yorks

**FOCUS**
This was weakened by several withdrawals but it still looked competitive and the winner finished well to deny the favourite. The runner-up has been rated to his C&D latest.

## 2593 SIS CELEBRATING 30 YEARS IN HORSERACING H'CAP 1m 1f 170y
**7:40** (7:40) (Class 3) (0-90,92) 4-Y-0+
**£12,450** (£3,728; £1,864; £932; £466; £234) **Stalls** Low

Form RPR

0042 **1** **Sands Chorus**[18] 2030 5-8-11 **79** PaulMulrennan 1 86
(James Given) *mde all: pushed along 3f out: rdn fnl f: hld on towards fin* **9/2**[2]

60-0 **2** hd **Dance King**[22] 1911 7-8-11 **79** (tp) DavidAllan 2 85
(Tim Easterby) *slowly away: hld up: pushed along over 2f out: hdwy over 1f out: angled lft to outer appr fnl f: rdn and kpt on wl* **9/2**[2]

-414 **3** 1½ **Swift Emperor (IRE)**[41] 1492 5-9-10 **92** PhillipMakin 5 95
(David Barron) *midfield: stdy hdwy 3f out: pushed along 2f out: rdn to chal appr fnl f: one pce* **3/1**[1]

15-2 **4** 3½ **Lincoln Rocks**[10] 2268 4-9-7 **89** DanielTudhope 3 84
(David O'Meara) *trckd ldr: rdn over 2f out: wknd ins fnl f* **9/2**[2]

0-00 **5** 2¼ **Imshivalla (IRE)**[13] 2141 6-9-4 **86** (h) PaulHanagan 6 77
(Richard Fahey) *hld up: rdn along over 2f out: nvr threatened* **20/1**

226- **6** hd **Rainbow Rebel (IRE)**[203] 7499 4-9-6 **88** PJMcDonald 7 78
(Mark Johnston) *in tch: rdn over 2f out: wknd fnl f* **9/2**[2]

052 **7** 16 **Hail Clodius (IRE)**[40] 1517 5-9-3 **85** (h[1]) TonyHamilton 4 43
(Roger Fell) *trckd ldr: lost pl qckly 3f out: sn bhd* **8/1**[3]

2m 2.01s (-3.39) **Going Correction** -0.15s/f (Firm) 7 Ran SP% **113.6**
Speed ratings (Par 107): **107,106,105,102,101 100,88**
CSF £24.52 TOTE £3.90: £2.50, £3.00; EX 28.90 Trifecta £113.00.

**Owner** The Cool Silk Partnership **Bred** Worksop Manor Stud **Trained** Willoughton, Lincs

**FOCUS**

Race distance increased by 12yds. There was an open market in this handicap and the winner made all and held off a strong finisher. The winner has been rated to his AW form.

## 2594 ROA/RACING POST OWNERS' JACKPOT H'CAP 2m

**8:15** (8:15) (Class 5) (0-75,72) 4-Y-0+ **£3,881** (£1,155; £577; £288) **Stalls** High

| Form | | | | RPR |
|---|---|---|---|---|
| 10-6 | 1 | | **La Fritillaire**[18] 2032 5-8-13 **61**........ AndrewMullen 6<br>(James Given) *midfield: pushed along over 3f out: rdn and hdwy 2f out: led ins fnl f: styd on wl* **5/1** | 66 |
| /323 | 2 | 3/4 | **Rembrandt**[12] 2183 5-9-3 **65**........(t[1]) DougieCostello 8<br>(Rebecca Menzies) *chsd clr ldr: clsd over 3f out: rdn to ld narrowly over 2f out: hdd ins fnl f: kpt on* **9/2** | 69 |
| 4564 | 3 | 2 1/4 | **Jan Smuts (IRE)**[14] 2125 9-8-8 **63**........(tp) ConnorMurtagh(7) 7<br>(Wilf Storey) *s.i.s: hld up: hdwy and in tch 7f out: rdn over 2f out: one pce* **10/1** | 64 |
| -044 | 4 | 1/2 | **Mysterial**[6] 2386 7-9-5 **72**........ PhilDennis(5) 1<br>(Declan Carroll) *led: sn clr: reduced advantage over 3f out: rdn whn hdd over 2f out: no ex ins fnl f* **3/1[1]** | 73 |
| 100- | 5 | 4 | **Medina Sidonia (IRE)**[196] 7670 5-9-10 **72**........(p) DavidAllan 3<br>(Tim Easterby) *hld up: pushed along over 4f out: rdn over 3f out: nvr threatened* **7/2[2]** | 68 |
| 31-0 | 6 | 15 | **Wishing Well**[30] 1719 5-9-9 **71**........ PJMcDonald 4<br>(Micky Hammond) *hld up: rdn over 3f out: sn wknd* **4/1[3]** | 49 |

3m 30.9s (-0.90) **Going Correction** -0.15s/f (Firm) **6 Ran SP% 111.2**

Speed ratings (Par 103): **96,95,94,94,92 84**

CSF £26.56 CT £206.97 TOTE £4.40: £2.90, £4.20; EX 12.70 Trifecta £79.80.

**Owner** Ingram Racing **Bred** Mrs P M Ignarski **Trained** Willoughton, Lincs

**FOCUS**

Race distance increased by 12yds. They went a good pace and the winner returned to form to strike back at 2m. The third has been rated to his recent form.

## 2595 SIS STREAMING CONTENT GLOBALLY MAIDEN STKS 6f

**8:45** (8:48) (Class 5) 3-Y-O **£3,881** (£1,155; £577; £288) **Stalls** High

| Form | | | | RPR |
|---|---|---|---|---|
| 32- | 1 | | **Yalawin (IRE)**[193] 7726 3-9-5 0........(h[1]) HarryBentley 6<br>(Roger Varian) *trckd ldrs on outer: led on bit appr fnl f: nudged clr: easily* **4/9[1]** | 86+ |
| 6- | 2 | 4 1/2 | **Black Salt**[200] 7578 3-9-5 0........ PhillipMakin 5<br>(David Barron) *in tch: pushed along to chse ldrs over 1f out: kpt on: wnt 2nd nr fin* **14/1** | 69 |
| 20-2 | 3 | 1/2 | **Wild Acclaim (IRE)**[18] 2033 3-9-5 72........ PaulHanagan 2<br>(Ann Duffield) *in tch towards outer: pushed along to chse ldr appr fnl f: rdn ins fnl f: one pce and lost 2nd nr fin* **4/1[2]** | 67 |
| 460- | 4 | 5 | **Silk Mill Blue**[192] 7749 3-9-0 59........ PhilDennis(5) 11<br>(Richard Whitaker) *led narrowly: rdn over 2f out: hdd appr fnl f: wknd ins fnl f* **33/1** | 51 |
| 0- | 5 | 1 1/4 | **Poet's Time**[386] 1583 3-9-0 0........ DavidAllan 3<br>(Tim Easterby) *dwlt: sn outpcd in rr: sme hdwy over 1f out: nvr threatened* **33/1** | 42 |
| 0 | 6 | 1 3/4 | **Zone In**[12] 2185 3-9-5 0........ TonyHamilton 7<br>(Roger Fell) *w ldr: pushed along over 2f out: wknd over 1f out* **20/1** | 41 |
| 6 | 7 | 1/2 | **Noble Sword**[18] 2033 3-9-5 0........ JackGarritty 9<br>(Jedd O'Keeffe) *w ldr: rdn over 2f out: sn wknd* **25/1** | 40 |
| 25 | 8 | 1/2 | **Hitchcock**[18] 2033 3-9-5 0........ TomEaves 10<br>(Kevin Ryan) *trckd ldrs: rdn over 2f out: wknd over 1f out* **7/1[3]** | 38 |

1m 12.5s (-0.50) **Going Correction** -0.275s/f (Firm) **8 Ran SP% 122.9**

Speed ratings (Par 99): **92,86,85,78,77 74,74,73**

CSF £9.41 TOTE £1.30: £1.10, £2.70, £1.50; EX 8.30 Trifecta £30.10.

**Owner** Sheikh Ahmed Al Maktoum **Bred** Rockfield Farm **Trained** Newmarket, Suffolk

■ Kings Will Dream was withdrawn. Price at time of withdrawal 25-1. Rule 4 does not apply.

**FOCUS**

The hot favourite surged clear to get off the mark at the third attempt. Kings Will Dream gave trouble at the start and was withdrawn. The third has been rated a bit below his latest, with the runner-up a big improver on his debut effort.

T/Plt: £51.90 to a £1 stake. Pool: £52,129.89 - 732.16 winning units. T/Qpdt: £21.60 to a £1 stake. Pool: £4520.87 - 154.32 winning units. **Andrew Sheret**

2596 - 2602a (Foreign Racing) - See Raceform Interactive

# 2562 ASCOT (R-H)

Saturday, May 13

**OFFICIAL GOING: Good to firm (watered; str 8.5; rnd 7.9)**

Wind: Light, against in home straight Weather: Fine but cloudy

## 2603 ROSLING KING H'CAP 1m 3f 211y

**2:15** (2:15) (Class 3) (0-95,96) 4-Y-0+ **£9,703** (£2,887; £1,443; £721) **Stalls** Low

| Form | | | | RPR |
|---|---|---|---|---|
| 103- | 1 | | **Appeared**[233] 6709 5-9-4 **91**........ AndreaAtzeni 8<br>(Roger Varian) *trckd ldr 2f then settled in 4th: prog over 2f out: led wl over 1f out: jinked briefly lft 1f out but styd on strly and clr fnl f* **9/4[1]** | 108+ |
| /13- | 2 | 4 1/2 | **Batts Rock (IRE)**[364] 2252 4-8-10 **83**........ JamieSpencer 5<br>(Michael Bell) *dwlt: prog to trck ldr after 2f: rdn to chal 2f out but looking arnd: nt qckn and qckly outpcd by wnr sn after: kpt on to take 2nd fnl f* **8/1** | 91 |
| 10-3 | 3 | 3/4 | **Lord George (IRE)**[29] 1779 4-9-4 **96**........ GeorgeWood(5) 4<br>(James Fanshawe) *chsd ldng pair after 2f: rdn 3f out: kpt on u.p but nvr pce to threaten* **9/2[3]** | 103 |
| 06-0 | 4 | shd | **Mark Hopkins**[13] 2176 5-8-4 **84**........ DavidEgan(7) 2<br>(David Elsworth) *nt that wl away: pushed up to ld then t.k.h: rdn and hdd wl over 1f out: one pce* **20/1** | 91 |
| 4-04 | 5 | 1/2 | **William Hunter**[17] 2085 5-8-10 **86**........ KieranShoemark(3) 9<br>(Alan King) *hld up in last: stl there over 2f out: rdn and sme prog to chse ldrs over 1f out but no ch w wnr* **6/1** | 92 |
| 40-5 | 6 | 2 | **Fleeting Visit**[21] 1964 4-8-10 **83**........ JohnFahy 10<br>(Eve Johnson Houghton) *hld up in 5th: rdn over 2f out: hanging rt and no prog* **10/1** | 86 |
| 26-1 | 7 | 2 1/4 | **Mohatem (USA)**[18] 2068 5-9-3 **90**........ JimCrowley 7<br>(Owen Burrows) *t.k.h: hld up in last trio: shkn up over 2f out: no prog and wl btn over 1f out* **3/1[2]** | 89 |

2m 32.95s (0.45) **Going Correction** +0.175s/f (Good) **7 Ran SP% 113.2**

Speed ratings (Par 107): **105,102,101,101,101 99,98**

CSF £20.42 CT £73.79 TOTE £3.00: £1.90, £3.30; EX 20.20 Trifecta £101.60.

**Owner** Sheikh Mohammed Obaid Al Maktoum **Bred** Darley **Trained** Newmarket, Suffolk

**FOCUS**

After the first jockeys variously reported the ground good and on the faster side of good. There was a loose patch of ground in Swinley Bottom where a sprinkler had been accidentally set off. Rail movements added 12yds to the distance of the first race, which was hit by non-runners. They went an uneven gallop and the winner proved a class apart.

## 2604 CAREY GROUP BUCKHOUNDS STKS (LISTED RACE) 1m 3f 211y

**2:50** (2:50) (Class 1) 4-Y-0+

**£25,519** (£9,675; £4,842; £2,412; £1,210; £607) **Stalls** Low

| Form | | | | RPR |
|---|---|---|---|---|
| 132- | 1 | | **Desert Encounter (IRE)**[245] 6321 5-9-0 102........(h) SeanLevey 5<br>(David Simcock) *t.k.h: hld up in 8th: waiting for a gap 2f out tl swtchd rt and swift prog to ld over 1f out: sn rdn clr: decisively* **8/1** | 112+ |
| 204- | 2 | 2 3/4 | **Star Storm (IRE)**[143] 8479 5-9-0 107........ TomQueally 2<br>(James Fanshawe) *hld up in 6th: prog over 2f out: rdn to chal and edgd lft over 1f out: wnr sn shot past: kpt on same pce after* **12/1** | 105 |
| 6-00 | 3 | hd | **Restorer**[15] 2127 5-9-0 102........ MartinDwyer 10<br>(William Muir) *t.k.h: hld up in last: rdn over 2f out: prog on outer jst over 1f out: r.o wl fnl f and nrly snatched 2nd* **40/1** | 105 |
| 26-1 | 4 | 3/4 | **Knights Table**[14] 2158 4-9-0 104........ DavidAllan 3<br>(James Tate) *hld up in midfield: rdn over 2f out: trying to cl but wouldn't have won whn impeded over 1f out: styd on again ins fnl f* **6/1[3]** | 105+ |
| 16-1 | 5 | 2 1/2 | **UAE Prince (IRE)**[23] 1911 4-9-0 97........ AndreaAtzeni 8<br>(Roger Varian) *trckd ldr: rdn to chal over 2f out: outpcd over 1f out: fdd* **9/4[1]** | 100 |
| 1-21 | 6 | hd | **Wild Hacked (USA)**[29] 1779 4-9-0 106........ DanielMuscutt 9<br>(Marco Botti) *cl up on outer: rdn over 2f out: fdd over 1f out* **9/2[2]** | 99 |
| 40-5 | 7 | 3/4 | **Muntazah**[15] 2127 4-9-0 105........ JimCrowley 6<br>(Owen Burrows) *led: drvn and edgd lft over 2f out: hdd & wknd over 1f out* **6/1[3]** | 98 |
| 2503 | 8 | 2 3/4 | **Fire Fighting (IRE)**[14] 2158 6-9-0 106........(b) MartinHarley 4<br>(Mark Johnston) *plld hrd early: hld up in last trio: rdn over 2f out: trying to make an effrt whn impeded over 1f out: wknd* **12/1** | 97+ |
| 256- | 9 | 16 | **Carntop**[232] 6752 4-9-0 105........ FranBerry 1<br>(Ralph Beckett) *trckd ldng pair: styd alone against inner rail in st: wknd qckly over 2f out: t.o* **11/1** | 68 |

2m 33.38s (0.88) **Going Correction** +0.175s/f (Good) **9 Ran SP% 114.8**

Speed ratings (Par 111): **104,102,102,101,99 99,99,97,86**

CSF £97.69 TOTE £6.20: £2.30, £3.30, £9.30; EX 95.80 Trifecta £3370.80.

**Owner** Abdulla Al Mansoori **Bred** Tally-Ho Stud **Trained** Newmarket, Suffolk

■ Stewards' Enquiry : Tom Queally three-day ban: careless riding (May 27, 29-30)

**FOCUS**

Race run over 12yds further than advertised. This decent Listed race was run at what appeared to be an initial steady gallop, before picking up by halfway. The first three home came from the rear four positions in a race which became messy in the home straight. The third has been rated to last year's best (AW) form.

## 2605 CLUB GODOLPHIN EBF "BREEDERS' SERIES" FILLIES' H'CAP 1m (S)

**3:25** (3:27) (Class 2) 3-Y-0+

**£28,012** (£8,388; £4,194; £2,097; £1,048; £526) **Stalls** Centre

| Form | | | | RPR |
|---|---|---|---|---|
| 1110 | 1 | | **Tisbutadream (IRE)**[70] 1026 3-7-7 **86** oh2........ DavidEgan(7) 2<br>(David Elsworth) *pressed ldr: led 3f out: rdn 2f out: looked vulnerable fnl f but styd on wl last 100yds* **11/1** | 96 |
| 500- | 2 | 1 | **Permission**[232] 6746 4-9-1 **88**........(h) DanielMuscutt 9<br>(James Fanshawe) *t.k.h: hld up in rr: prog over 2f out: sn rdn: chsd wnr 1f out and threatened to cl: no imp last 100yds* **11/2[3]** | 98 |
| 24-1 | 3 | 2 3/4 | **Singyoursong (IRE)**[11] 2254 4-9-3 **90**........ JamieSpencer 5<br>(David Simcock) *stdd s: hld up in last pair: prog 3f out: hrd rdn to try to cl 2f out: disp 2nd 1f out: kpt on same pce* **7/2[1]** | 94 |
| 0005 | 4 | 1 | **Epsom Icon**[7] 2392 4-9-10 **97**........ JimCrowley 4<br>(Mick Channon) *wl in tch: rdn to chse wnr over 2f out to 1f out: fdd* **15/2** | 99 |
| 10-2 | 5 | 3/4 | **Raven's Lady**[28] 1796 3-8-0 **86** oh1........ JimmyQuinn 8<br>(Marco Botti) *stdd s: hld up in last pair: prog 3f out: rdn and looking unlikely to win whn short of room over 1f out: one pce after* **11/2[3]** | 83 |
| 32-2 | 6 | 3 3/4 | **Aristocratic**[13] 2177 4-8-9 **82**........(p) AndreaAtzeni 3<br>(Sir Michael Stoute) *led to 3f out: lost 2nd over 2f out: wknd u.p* **9/2[2]** | 73 |
| 250- | 7 | 6 | **Sagely (IRE)**[254] 6069 4-9-8 **95**........ AntonioFresu 6<br>(Ed Dunlop) *chsd ldng pair: rdn over 3f out: sn lost 3rd: fdd steadily tl wknd and eased fnl f* **16/1** | 73 |
| 4-10 | 8 | 3 1/2 | **Ejayteekay**[23] 1897 4-8-2 **75**........ JosephineGordon 7<br>(Hughie Morrison) *chsd ldrs to over 3f out: sn wknd and bhd* **12/1** | 45 |
| 32-1 | 9 | 16 | **Tegara**[23] 1897 4-7-11 **75**........ SophieKilloran(5) 1<br>(David Simcock) *t.k.h: chsd ldng pair to over 3f out: sn wknd: t.o* **10/1** | 8 |

1m 42.42s (1.62) **Going Correction** +0.075s/f (Good)

**WFA** 3 from 4yo 13lb **9 Ran SP% 113.9**

Speed ratings (Par 96): **94,93,90,89,88 84,78,75,59**

CSF £69.28 CT £258.98 TOTE £13.30: £3.50, £2.00, £1.50; EX 87.60 Trifecta £1071.10.

**Owner** Mrs Anne Coughlan & Ten Green Bottles **Bred** J F Tuthill **Trained** Newmarket, Suffolk

■ Stewards' Enquiry : Jimmy Quinn caution: careless riding

**FOCUS**

Race run over an extra 12yds. A good-quality and tight-looking fillies' handicap. Those waited with seemed at a disadvantage. A pb from the runner-up.

## 2606 TOTESCOOP6 VICTORIA CUP (HERITAGE H'CAP) 7f

**4:00** (4:02) (Class 2) 4-Y-0+

**£65,362** (£19,572; £9,786; £4,893; £2,446; £1,228) **Stalls** Centre

| Form | | | | RPR |
|---|---|---|---|---|
| 14-3 | 1 | | **Fastnet Tempest (IRE)**[21] 1960 4-8-5 **89**........(p) JosephineGordon 18<br>(William Haggas) *t.k.h: hld up in midfield gng wl: prog 2f out: gap appeared 1f out and sn chalng: rdn to ld last 100yds: styd on wl* **5/1[1]** | 98+ |
| 1-14 | 2 | 3/4 | **George William**[21] 1960 4-8-11 **95**........ SeanLevey 23<br>(Richard Hannon) *hld up in midfield: prog 2f out: jst bhd wnr whn nt clr run briefly 1f out: r.o wl fnl f to take 2nd last strides* **8/1[3]** | 102+ |
| -400 | 3 | shd | **Zhui Feng (IRE)**[21] 1960 4-9-0 **98**........(p[1]) MartinDwyer 11<br>(Amanda Perrett) *led and crossed to nr side rail: def advantage 3f out: pressed wl over 1f out: kpt on wl but hdd and outpcd last 100yds* **25/1** | 104 |
| 40-0 | 4 | 1 | **Shady McCoy (USA)**[31] 1734 7-8-5 **89**........ JimmyQuinn 26<br>(Ian Williams) *t.k.h: hld up wl in rr: prog 2f out: threaded through fr over 1f out: nt clr run and swtchd ins fnl f: r.o to snatch 4th last stride* **33/1** | 92 |
| 1-30 | 5 | shd | **Charles Molson**[7] 2390 6-8-3 **92**........ CharlieBennett(5) 20<br>(Patrick Chamings) *t.k.h: hld up towards rr: prog 2f out: nt clr run briefly over 1f out: r.o fnl f: nrst fin* **16/1** | 95 |

2300 **6** *nse* **Holiday Magic (IRE)**[29] 1769 6-8-3 94 HarrisonShaw(7) 27 97
(Michael Easterby) *t.k.h: chsd ldr: clsd over 1f out: lost 2nd and one pce fnl f* **50/1**

00-5 **7** *hd* **Bossy Guest (IRE)**[21] 1960 5-9-5 103 WilliamBuick 24 105
(Mick Channon) *racd against rail: in tch: rdn over 2f out: styd on fnl f: nrst fin but nvr able to chal* **12/1**

1453 **8** *nk* **The Warrior (IRE)**[7] 2390 5-7-13 88 (e) GeorgeWood(5) 25 90
(Amanda Perrett) *prom: rdn over 2f out: on terms w ldrs jst over 1f out: one pce fnl f* **12/1**

-232 **9** *1 1/4* **Hors De Combat**[29] 1766 6-9-5 103 JimCrowley 22 101
(Denis Coakley) *hld up wl in rr: prog against nr side rail jst over 1f out: styd on but nvr a threat* **10/1**

502- **10** *hd* **Remarkable**[210] 7354 4-9-4 105 (b) KieranShoemark(3) 13 103+
(John Gosden) *hmpd s: mostly in midfield: rdn and styd on fr 2f out: n.d but did best of those forced to r on outer* **15/2**[2]

050- **11** *1* **Outback Traveller (IRE)**[182] 7932 6-9-7 105 MartinHarley 19 100+
(Robert Cowell) *hld up wl in rr: pushed along and passed several rivals fr 2f out but nvr threatened to be involved* **33/1**

20-0 **12** *nk* **Withernsea (IRE)**[42] 1494 6-8-12 96 BarryMcHugh 2 90
(Richard Fahey) *plld hrd out wd early: settled bttr by 1/2-way in midfield: rdn and no prog 2f out* **33/1**

0-00 **13** *hd* **Heaven's Guest (IRE)**[29] 1766 7-8-9 96 SammyJoBell(3) 14 90
(Richard Fahey) *wnt rt s: chsd ldrs: stl cl up jst over 1f out: wknd* **20/1**

20-4 **14** *1* **Miracle Of Medinah**[21] 1974 6-8-5 94 LuluStanford(5) 16 85
(Mark Usher) *chsd ldng pair: rdn over 2f out: clsd to chal over 1f out: wknd fnl f* **40/1**

01-4 **15** *1 1/4* **Above The Rest (IRE)**[14] 2156 6-9-3 101 (h) FranBerry 5 89
(David Barron) *racd out wd: nvr on terms w ldrs: no ch over 1f out* **12/1**

55-1 **16** *1 3/4* **Taurean Star (IRE)**[11] 2283 4-8-8 92 ow1 JamieSpencer 7 75
(Michael Bell) *s.s: hld up in last: styd on fr over 1f out: nvr a ch* **8/1**[3]

400- **17** *1 1/4* **Gm Hopkins**[210] 7354 6-9-10 108 TomQueally 10 87
(John Gosden) *rrd bdly s: wl in rr and racd on outer: nvr a factor* **25/1**

10-5 **18** *nk* **Noble Peace**[17] 2093 4-7-9 84 RichardOliver(5) 12 63
(Henry Candy) *t.k.h: prom tl wknd 2f out* **50/1**

6-4 **19** *nse* **Chestnut Fire**[17] 2093 5-8-8 92 WilliamCarson 8 70
(Daniel Mark Loughnane) *awkward s: racd on outer and nvr on terms* **33/1**

2-06 **20** *1 3/4* **Bertiewhittle**[28] 1799 9-8-2 91 RowanScott(5) 15 65
(David Barron) *a towards rr and towards outer: pushed along and no prog 2f out* **50/1**

0000 **21** *1/2* **Steel Train (FR)**[7] 2384 6-8-9 96 ShelleyBirkett(3) 17 68
(David O'Meara) *nvr beyond midfield: wknd over 1f out* **40/1**

10-0 **22** *nse* **Stamp Hill (IRE)**[14] 2142 4-8-9 93 TonyHamilton 1 65
(Richard Fahey) *racd on outer and nvr on terms w ldrs* **50/1**

443- **23** *1* **Squats (IRE)**[224] 6942 5-9-1 104 GeorgiaCox(5) 6 74
(William Haggas) *racd wdst of all and nvr on terms* **16/1**

6052 **24** *3* **Kadrizzi (FR)**[16] 2114 4-9-0 98 (p) RobertWinston 3 59
(Dean Ivory) *racd on outer: nvr on terms: rdn over 2f out: eased whn no ch fnl f* **25/1**

1m 27.14s (-0.46) **Going Correction** +0.075s/f (Good) **24** Ran SP% **135.4**
Speed ratings (Par 109): **105,104,104,102,102 102,102,102,100,100 99,99,98,97,96 94,92,92,92,90 89,89,88,85**
CSF £38.25 CT £966.09 TOTE £5.70: £2.00, £2.50, £6.40, £9.30; EX 47.20 Trifecta £1732.80.
**Owner** O T I Racing & Partner **Bred** Rockhart Trading Ltd **Trained** Newmarket, Suffolk

**FOCUS**
Another competitive edition of this historic handicap. The whole field congregated towards the stands' side and those who raced out towards the centre weren't seen to best effect. High numbers came out on top for the fourth year running, the winner coming from 18 and the seven horses from stalls 20 or higher all finishing in the first nine. The race provided a boost to the form of Newbury's Spring Cup, won by Banksea. The third helps set the standard.

## 2607 TOTEPOOLLIVEINFO.COM NOVICE STKS (PLUS 10 RACE) 5f
**4:35** (4:35) (Class 3) 2-Y-O **£7,762** (£2,310; £1,154; £577) **Stalls** High

Form RPR

**1** **Aqabah (USA)** 2-9-2 0 WilliamBuick 1 88
(Charlie Appleby) *off the pce in last trio: pushed along and at least 3 l bhd ldng trio jst over 1f out: reminder and styd on wl fnl f to ld last strides: shade cleverly* **9/4**[1]

3 **2** *hd* **Jellmood**[14] 2134 2-9-2 0 AndreaAtzeni 4 87
(Marco Botti) *pressed ldng pair: chal 2f out: rdn to take narrow ld ins fnl f: hdd last strides* **5/1**[3]

2 **3** *hd* **Haddaf (IRE)**[14] 2148 2-9-2 0 MartinHarley 2 87
(James Tate) *pressed ldr: led narrowly 2f out: sn rdn: hrd pressed after: hdd ins fnl f: kpt on* **9/4**[1]

1 **4** *3/4* **Cardsharp**[10] 2292 2-9-8 0 FranBerry 3 90
(Mark Johnston) *led to 2f out: styd pressing ldrs tl no ex ins fnl f* **7/2**[2]

**5** *9* **Zabaletaswansong (GER)** 2-9-2 0 SeanLevey 6 51
(Richard Hannon) *a in last trio: wknd 2f out* **14/1**

**6** *hd* **Carouse (IRE)** 2-9-2 0 LiamKeniry 5 51
(Andrew Balding) *a in last trio: wknd 2f out* **16/1**

1m 0.48s (-0.02) **Going Correction** +0.075s/f (Good) **6** Ran SP% **113.0**
Speed ratings (Par 97): **103,102,102,101,86 86**
CSF £14.15 TOTE £2.90: £1.90, £2.20; EX 12.70 Trifecta £44.60.
**Owner** Godolphin **Bred** Glendalough Llc **Trained** Newmarket, Suffolk

**FOCUS**
There was a very tight finish to this fair novice event.

## 2608 WINNING POST BOOKMAKERS BRISTOL H'CAP 6f
**5:10** (5:12) (Class 4) (0-80,82) 4-Y-O+ **£6,469** (£1,925; £962; £481) **Stalls** Centre

Form RPR

2-22 **1** **Robero**[16] 2116 5-9-7 80 WilliamBuick 22 94
(Michael Easterby) *racd clsr to nr side than rivals: mde all: drew clr over 1f out: rdn out: unchal* **7/2**[1]

0-65 **2** *2 3/4* **Red Tycoon (IRE)**[32] 1696 5-9-4 80 KieranShoemark(3) 21 85
(Ken Cunningham-Brown) *racd clsr to nr side than rivals: chsd wnr: rdn and styd on fr over 1f out: nvr able to chal* **20/1**

060- **3** *hd* **War Whisper (IRE)**[191] 7781 4-9-4 80 HollieDoyle(3) 8 84+
(Richard Hannon) *hld up wl in rr: prog on wd outside fr 2f out: r.o to chal for 2nd whn hung lft nr fin* **7/1**[3]

0621 **4** *1 1/2* **Nezar (IRE)**[35] 1631 6-9-5 78 RobertWinston 16 78
(Dean Ivory) *hld up in midfield gng wl: nt clr run and lost pl wl over 1f out: rdn and r.o wl fnl f: nvr able to chal* **8/1**

104- **5** *1* **Storm Melody**[192] 7772 4-9-2 75 JimCrowley 2 71
(Jonjo O'Neill) *chsd ldrs on outer: drvn 2f out: pressed for a pl fr over 1f out: kpt on* **8/1**

/02- **6** *1 1/4* **Dark Alliance (IRE)**[38] 1570 6-9-6 79 SteveDrowne 12 71
(Adrian Paul Keatley, Ire) *dwlt: wl in rr: drvn 2f out: styd on fnl f: n.d* **20/1**

21-5 **7** *nse* **Pettochside**[19] 2040 8-9-4 77 JosephineGordon 14 69
(John Bridger) *on terms w wnr to 2f out: one pce fr over 1f out* **16/1**

6540 **8** *1/2* **Gung Ho Jack**[10] 2320 8-8-7 66 KierenFox 13 57
(John Best) *taken down early but reluctant to go to post tl others c on the trck: prom: drvn 2f out: one pce over 1f out* **33/1**

3165 **9** *nk* **Born To Finish (IRE)**[14] 2147 4-9-4 77 (p) MartinHarley 20 67
(Jeremy Gask) *dwlt: wl in rr: rdn 2f out: styd on fnl f: n.d* **25/1**

5-06 **10** *1 1/4* **Rio Ronaldo (IRE)**[19] 2040 5-9-7 80 AndreaAtzeni 17 66
(Mike Murphy) *dwlt: hld up in midfield: nt clr run briefly wl over 1f out: no prog after* **5/1**[2]

4503 **11** *hd* **Hamish McGonagain**[21] 1980 4-8-12 71 (p) AdamBeschizza 5 56
(Jeremy Gask) *prom on outer: drvn and lost pl wl over 1f out: no hdwy after* **33/1**

1003 **12** *nk* **Among Angels**[25] 1867 5-8-13 77 CharlieBennett(5) 9 61
(Daniel Mark Loughnane) *racd on outer: nvr beyond midfield: no prog over 1f out* **25/1**

6301 **13** *3/4* **Picket Line**[12] 2229 5-8-8 74 CameronNoble(7) 3 56
(Geoffrey Deacon) *prom on outer: drvn 2f out: wknd over 1f out* **16/1**

-020 **14** *2* **Bahamian Dollar**[60] 1185 4-8-12 78 KatherineGlenister(7) 25 53
(David Evans) *taken down early: racd towards nr side but nvr on terms w pair that fin 1st and 2nd* **33/1**

2020 **15** *1* **Fairway To Heaven (IRE)**[12] 2230 8-8-10 74 JennyPowell(5) 19 46
(Lee Carter) *dwlt: nvr beyond midfield: rdn and no prog 2f out: wknd over 1f out* **33/1**

600 **16** *1 1/4* **Equally Fast**[72] 989 5-9-2 75 (h) LiamKeniry 1 43
(Peter Hiatt) *dwlt: hld up in last trio: gng wl whn nt clr run over 2f out to 1f out: rdn and no prog whn in the clr* **33/1**

/1-4 **17** *nk* **Moondyne Joe (IRE)**[109] 387 4-9-7 80 DanielMuscutt 4 47
(Mark Pattinson) *prom on outer: wknd 2f out* **33/1**

30-0 **18** *hd* **Pour La Victoire (IRE)**[8] 2360 7-8-13 72 GeorgeDowning 18 38
(Tony Carroll) *s.v.s: a wl in rr* **33/1**

0003 **19** *4 1/2* **Very Honest (IRE)**[23] 1899 4-9-7 80 (v) SeanLevey 15 32
(Brett Johnson) *taken down early: prom on outer 4f: wknd qckly* **33/1**

6206 **20** *11* **Salvatore Fury (IRE)**[6] 2424 7-8-12 71 (p) FranBerry 23
(Keith Dalgleish) *hld up wl in rr: struggling over 2f out: t.o* **14/1**

1m 13.64s (-0.86) **Going Correction** +0.075s/f (Good) **20** Ran SP% **132.8**
Speed ratings (Par 105): **108,104,104,102,100 99,99,98,97,96 96,95,94,91,90 88,88,88,82,67**
CSF £81.98 CT £468.17 TOTE £4.30: £1.70, £6.10, £2.40, £2.30; EX 95.70 Trifecta £1139.90.
**Owner** Alan Zheng **Bred** Mrs P C Burton & Mr R J Lampard **Trained** Sheriff Hutton, N Yorks

**FOCUS**
Ordinary handicap form for the track. They raced further from the rail than in the Victoria Cup but again high numbers emerged on top. The runner-up has been rated close to form.
T/Jkpt: Not Won. T/Plt: £294.10 to a £1 stake. Pool: £205,781.27 - 510.64 winning units T/Qpdt: £19.00 to a £1 stake. Pool: £15,595.77 - 605.35 winning units **Jonathan Neesom**

# 2140 HAYDOCK (L-H)
Saturday, May 13

**OFFICIAL GOING: Jumps course - good (good to soft in places; 7.4) flat course - good to firm changing to good after race 2 (14:35)**
Wind: Moderate, half against in home straight of about 4f Weather: Fine

## 2609 PERTEMPS NETWORK STAYERS' H'CAP 1m 6f
**2:35** (2:35) (Class 4) (0-85,85) 4-Y-O+ **£6,469** (£1,925; £962; £481) **Stalls** Low

Form RPR

-113 **1** **Monjeni**[6] 2426 4-8-11 73 (p) PaulHanagan 6 83
(Ian Williams) *racd keenly: hld up: pushed along over 3f out: hdwy over 2f out: led jst over 1f out: edgd lft fnl 150yds: r.o wl to draw away fnl 75yds* **3/1**[3]

240- **2** *1 3/4* **Jaameh (IRE)**[266] 5653 4-9-7 83 DaneO'Neill 2 91+
(Mark Johnston) *led: pressed 2f ut: rdn and hdd jst over 1f out: outpcd by wnr fnl 75yds* **9/4**[1]

156- **3** *4 1/2* **Zenafire**[35] 7625 8-8-5 66 (p) FrannyNorton 7 68
(Sarah Hollinshead) *hld up: niggled along 7f out: rdn over 2f out: hdwy over 1f out: styd on ins fnl f: tk 3rd ins fnl 75yds: nt pce to trble front two* **11/2**

34-2 **4** *1 1/4* **Lexington Law (IRE)**[44] 1457 4-9-9 85 TomMarquand 5 85
(Alan King) *trckd ldrs: effrt on inner over 2f out: sn n.m.r and hmpd whn chalng: no ex ins fnl f* **11/4**[2]

60-5 **5** *1 3/4* **Braes Of Lochalsh**[15] 2125 6-8-10 71 (p) SamJames 4 69
(Jim Goldie) *prom: pushed along 3f out: rdn and outpcd 2f out: kpt on one pce whn n.d ins fnl f* **14/1**

4/5- **6** *3 3/4* **Fantasy King**[257] 2439 11-8-9 70 TomEaves 3 62
(James Moffatt) *hld up in rr: rdn over 2f out: sme hdwy over 1f out: no imp on ldrs: wknd ins fnl f* **25/1**

40-6 **7** *nk* **Togetherness (IRE)**[29] 1763 4-9-1 77 DavidProbert 8 69
(Harry Dunlop) *dwlt: chsd ldr after nrly 2f: rdn and lost 2nd over 2f out: wknd over 1f out* **16/1**

3m 7.87s **Going Correction** -0.275s/f (Firm) **7** Ran SP% **114.2**
Speed ratings (Par 105): **72,71,68,67,66 64,64**
CSF £10.18 CT £33.77 TOTE £3.90: £2.00, £1.80; EX 9.30 Trifecta £30.20.
**Owner** Ian Williams **Bred** The Kathryn Stud **Trained** Portway, Worcs

**FOCUS**
Flat races on the Inner Home Straight. Distance increased by 74yds. The right two came clear in what was a useful handicap.

## 2610 PERTEMPS NETWORK SPRING TROPHY STKS (LISTED RACE) 6f 212y
**3:45** (3:46) (Class 1) 3-Y-O+
**£20,982** (£7,955; £3,981; £1,983; £995; £499) **Stalls** Low

Form RPR

5212 **1** **Oh This Is Us (IRE)**[14] 2142 4-9-7 110 TomMarquand 5 115+
(Richard Hannon) *racd keenly: in tch: nt clr run fr over 2f out tl fnd gap ins fnl f: r.o to ld towards fin* **9/4**[1]

5-04 **2** *nk* **Absolutely So (IRE)**[16] 2114 7-9-7 102 DavidProbert 1 113
(Andrew Balding) *chsd ldrs: n.m.r and lost pl 2f out: rallied ins fnl f: r.o to ld fnl 110yds: hdd and hld towards fin* **7/1**

30-5 **3** *1* **So Beloved**[14] 2150 7-9-7 109 DanielTudhope 2 110
(David O'Meara) *hld up: hdwy on outer over 2f out: led over 1f out: hdd fnl 110yds: styd on same pce towards fin* **6/1**[3]

124- **4** *1* **Certificate**[218] 7115 6-9-7 110 PaulMulrennan 3 108
(Roger Varian) *racd keenly: trckd ldrs: rdn to chal fr over 1f out: no ex fnl 75yds* **9/4**[1]

233- **5** *2* **Von Blucher (IRE)**[231] 6788 4-9-7 99 (t) PJMcDonald 8 102
(Rebecca Menzies) *chsd ldr: rdn to chal over 1f out: one pce fnl 100yds* **18/1**

56-0 **6** *1 ¾* **Birchwood (IRE)**[42] 1491 4-9-7 108 PaulHanagan 4 97
(Richard Fahey) *led: rdn and hdd over 1f out: wknd fnl 100yds* **11/2**[2]

**7** *3 ¾* **Mutamaded (IRE)**[568] 4-9-7 0 DaneO'Neill 7 87
(Brian Meehan) *hld up in rr: pushed along over 2f out: outpcd over 1f out: nvr a threat* **20/1**

1m 28.12s (-2.58) **Going Correction** -0.275s/f (Firm) 7 Ran SP% **113.7**
Speed ratings (Par 111): **115,114,113,112,110 108,103**
CSF £18.91 TOTE £3.10: £1.70, £3.60; EX 15.90 Trifecta £63.60.
**Owner** Team Wallop **Bred** Herbertstown House Stud **Trained** East Everleigh, Wilts

**FOCUS**
Distance increased by 28yds. Sound form for the level, with a progressive winner who overcame trouble. The runner-up is the key to the form, with the fifth rated close to his best.

## 2611 PERTEMPS NETWORK CONDITIONS STKS 6f
**4:20** (4:20) (Class 2) 3-Y-O+
**£12,450** (£3,728; £1,864; £932; £466; £234) **Stalls** High

Form RPR

-625 **1** **Mythmaker**[29] 1772 5-9-5 101 ConnorBeasley 5 108
(Bryan Smart) *w ldr: led 2f out: hdd briefly over 1f out: r.o gamely whn continually pressed ins fnl f: a doing enough towards fin* **9/2**[3]

26-6 **2** *nk* **Aeolus**[23] 1903 6-9-5 107 ThomasBrown 3 107
(Ed Walker) *trckd ldrs: rdn to ld briefly over 1f out: continued to chal ins fnl f: r.o u.p: hld towards fin* **4/1**[2]

-040 **3** *1* **Amazour (IRE)**[29] 1769 5-9-9 99 TomMarquand 7 108
(Ismail Mohammed) *dwlt: hld up: rdn wl over 1f out: swtchd lft whn hdwy ent fnl f: styd on wl towards fin* **25/1**

00-6 **4** *hd* **Orion's Bow**[14] 2156 6-9-9 104 AndrewMullen 1 107
(Tim Easterby) *led: hdd 2f out: continued to chal: no ex fnl 50yds* **13/2**

055- **5** *1 ½* **George Dryden (IRE)**[251] 6161 5-9-5 101 PaulHanagan 9 98
(Ann Duffield) *racd keenly: trckd ldrs: rdn and hung lft over 1f out: one pce ins fnl f* **14/1**

350- **6** *hd* **Waady (IRE)**[308] 4151 5-9-5 109 (h) DaneO'Neill 6 98
(John Gosden) *racd keenly: midfield: rdn over 1f out: kpt on ins fnl f: nt pce of ldrs* **2/1**[1]

0650 **7** *4 ½* **Naadirr (IRE)**[63] 1150 6-9-5 102 TomEaves 4 83
(Kevin Ryan) *stdd s: hld up in rr: rdn over 1f out: sn outpcd: nvr a threat* **10/1**

000- **8** *6* **Jack Dexter**[210] 7350 8-9-5 99 SamJames 2 64
(Jim Goldie) *in rr: outpcd wl over 1f out: lft bhd fnl f* **10/1**

1m 11.34s (-2.46) **Going Correction** -0.275s/f (Firm) 8 Ran SP% **113.5**
Speed ratings (Par 109): **105,104,103,103,101 100,94,86**
CSF £22.49 TOTE £5.60: £1.80, £1.80, £5.20; EX 23.30 Trifecta £570.00.
**Owner** Crossfields Racing **Bred** Crossfields Bloodstock Ltd **Trained** Hambleton, N Yorks

**FOCUS**
Distance as advertised. Little got into this, with the favourite disappointing. The third is the key to the level. The winner has been rated close to his AW best.

## 2612 PERTEMPS NETWORK H'CAP 7f 212y
**5:25** (5:25) (Class 3) (0-95,91) 3-Y-O **£9,703** (£2,887; £1,443; £721) **Stalls** Low

Form RPR

6-1 **1** **Leader's Legacy (USA)**[17] 2087 3-9-5 **89** (t) DaneO'Neill 3 99+
(Saeed bin Suroor) *chsd ldr: led over 1f out: rdn and r.o wl fnl f* **2/1**[1]

10-3 **2** *1 ½* **The Grape Escape (IRE)**[15] 2126 3-9-7 **91** TomMarquand 5 98
(Richard Hannon) *racd keenly: hld up in tch: effrt over 2f out: styd on to take 2nd wl ins fnl f: nt pce of wnr: no imp towards fin* **9/4**[2]

3-31 **3** *½* **Carigrad (IRE)**[26] 1829 3-8-9 **79** DavidProbert 1 85
(Hugo Palmer) *led after 1f: rdn and hdd over 1f out: styd on same pce fnl 100yds* **9/2**[3]

40-6 **4** *3 ¾* **Reachforthestars (IRE)**[10] 2287 3-9-6 **90** PaulHanagan 2 87
(David O'Meara) *in tch: rdn over 1f out: one pce and no imp ins fnl f* **16/1**

5-02 **5** *shd* **Devil's Bridge (IRE)**[23] 1912 3-8-10 **87** RossaRyan[(7)] 4 84
(Richard Hannon) *led for 1f: prom: rdn 2f out: hung lft and one pce over 1f out: n.d after* **6/1**

31-5 **6** *9* **X Rated (IRE)**[11] 2284 3-8-7 **77** FrannyNorton 7 53
(Mark Johnston) *in rr after 1f: swtchd to inner rail after 2f: outpcd over 3f out: rdn and hung lft over 2f out: nvr a threat* **10/1**

1m 41.08s (-2.62) **Going Correction** -0.275s/f (Firm) 6 Ran SP% **111.5**
Speed ratings (Par 103): **107,105,105,101,101 92**
CSF £6.69 TOTE £3.30: £1.80, £1.60; EX 6.20 Trifecta £23.00.
**Owner** Godolphin **Bred** Ramona S Bass Llc **Trained** Newmarket, Suffolk

**FOCUS**
Distance increased by 28yds. The right two came to the fore and the form looks good. The runner-up has been rated to his Sandown latest, with a small pb from the third.

# 2575 LINGFIELD (L-H)
### Saturday, May 13

**OFFICIAL GOING: Good (good to soft in places; 7.7)**
Wind: strong, behind on straight course Weather: cloud, bright spells

## 2613 BETFRED MOBILE OAKS TRIAL FILLIES' STKS (LISTED RACE) 1m 3f 133y
**1:55** (1:57) (Class 1) 3-Y-O
**£22,684** (£8,600; £4,304; £2,144; £1,076; £540) **Stalls** High

Form RPR

1-32 **1** **Hertford Dancer**[31] 1736 3-9-0 76 FrankieDettori 1 98
(John Gosden) *in tch: trckd ldng pair 6f out: effrt on inner and hit rail 3f out: rdn to chse wnr 2f out: sn swtchd rt: styd on to chal 1f out: led ins fnl f: gng away and eased towards fin* **8/1**

5-4 **2** *1 ½* **Pocketfullofdreams (FR)**[20] 1998 3-9-0 99 (h) RyanMoore 3 96
(A P O'Brien, Ire) *led tl 10f out: chsd ldr after tl led again travelling strly over 2f out: rdn wl over 1f out: hrd pressed and drvn 1f out: hdd ins fnl f: no ex* **15/8**[2]

1 **3** *6* **The Sky Is Blazing (IRE)**[43] 1471 3-9-0 82 PatCosgrave 5 86
(William Haggas) *trckd ldng pair tl 6f out: rdn 3f out: outpcd by ldng pair 2f out: wnt 3rd over 1f out: no threat to ldrs and kpt on same pce after* **11/8**[1]

41- **4** *3 ¾* **Camerone (IRE)**[221] 7034 3-9-0 80 WilliamBuick 6 80
(Ralph Beckett) *t.k.h: led 10f out tl rdn and hdd over 2f out: sn swtchd rt and outpcd in 3rd: wknd over 1f out* **7/1**[3]

1-65 **5** *3* **Mary Anne Evans**[31] 1737 3-9-0 69 (p[1]) JimmyFortune 2 75?
(John Gosden) *hld up in last pair: effrt 3f out: sn struggling and outpcd 2f out: wl btn after* **33/1**

-231 **6** *½* **Flight Of Fantasy**[36] 1607 3-9-0 77 RichardKingscote 4 74
(Harry Dunlop) *s.i.s: hld up in rr: pushed along 3f out: sn struggling and outpcd: wl btn fnl 2f* **9/1**

2m 32.07s (0.57) **Going Correction** +0.175s/f (Good) 6 Ran SP% **113.4**
Speed ratings (Par 104): **105,104,100,97,95 95**
CSF £23.93 TOTE £8.50: £2.80, £1.40; EX 23.60 Trifecta £60.40.
**Owner** 5 Hertford Street Racing Club **Bred** Highclere Stud **Trained** Newmarket, Suffolk

**FOCUS**
Race distances as advertised. Following an early morning shower, the going was good to soft (good in places), accompanied with a strong headwind in the home straight. Not a reliable trial for the Oaks, and the last to triumph at Epsom was Ramruma in 1999, and this year's winner doesn't hold an entry. They went a fair gallop and the first two came clear. The runner-up has been rated to form for now.

## 2614 BETFRED DERBY TRIAL STKS (LISTED RACE) (C&G) 1m 3f 133y
**2:30** (2:31) (Class 1) 3-Y-O
**£34,026** (£12,900; £6,456; £3,216; £1,614; £810) **Stalls** High

Form RPR

2-40 **1** **Best Solution (IRE)**[91] 697 3-9-5 113 PatCosgrave 6 113
(Saeed bin Suroor) *trckd ldrs and clr in ldng quartet: pushed into ld over 2f out: sn rdn and readily wnt clr: 4 l clr 1f out: styd on wl: eased clsd home* **7/1**[3]

21-5 **2** *3 ¼* **Glencadam Glory**[15] 2132 3-9-0 86 (h) JimmyFortune 4 102
(John Gosden) *led to s: s.i.s: hld up off the pce in last pair: effrt and clsd over 2f out: swtchd rt and styd on u.p to chse clr wnr ins fnl f: kpt on wl for clr 2nd but no threat to wnr* **16/1**

1-4 **3** *3* **Tartini (USA)**[17] 2084 3-9-0 93 FrankieDettori 5 97
(John Gosden) *t.k.h early: chsd ldr tl 9f out: styd handy in ldng quartet: effrt over 2f out: sn drvn to chse clr wnr: kpt on same pce and no imp on wnr: lost 2nd ins fnl f* **5/1**[2]

10-3 **4** *½* **Frankuus (IRE)**[15] 2128 3-9-5 104 JoeFanning 8 101
(Mark Johnston) *chsd ldrs and clr in ldng quartet: hdwy to chse ldr 9f out tl over 2f out: sn swtchd rt and rdn: 3rd and no imp u.p 2f out: plugged on same pce and lost 3rd ins fnl f* **14/1**

14-5 **5** *3 ¼* **Apex King (IRE)**[25] 1861 3-9-0 97 GrahamLee 7 91
(Ed Dunlop) *dwlt: hld up off the pce in last pair: effrt jst over 2f out: sme prog but nvr on terms w wnr: 5th and wl hld over 1f out: wknd fnl f* **25/1**

**6** *6* **Sir John Lavery (IRE)**[207] 7447 3-9-0 0 RyanMoore 3 81
(A P O'Brien, Ire) *stdd s: hld up off the pce in 6th: sme prog 5f out: effrt over 2f out: no imp: wl btn 6th over 1f out: wknd fnl f* **11/8**[1]

1-41 **7** *2 ¾* **Sofia's Rock (FR)**[14] 2149 3-9-0 98 RichardKingscote 1 77
(Mark Johnston) *led: wnt clr 8f out: rdn and hdd over 2f out: no ex u.p: lost pl and bhd over 1f out* **7/1**[3]

1 **P** **Zamfir**[36] 1609 3-9-0 90 WilliamBuick 2
(Charlie Appleby) *off the pce in midfield: lost pl on downhill run and dropped to last 4f out: sn lost tch: t.o whn p.u and dismntd ins fnl f* **7/1**[3]

2m 31.84s (0.34) **Going Correction** +0.175s/f (Good) 8 Ran SP% **112.7**
Speed ratings (Par 107): **105,102,100,100,98 94,92,**
CSF £104.37 TOTE £7.90: £2.70, £4.90, £1.80; EX 121.50 Trifecta £469.20.
**Owner** Godolphin **Bred** Cecil & Martin McCracken **Trained** Newmarket, Suffolk

**FOCUS**
The last winner of the Lingfield Derby Trial that won at Epsom was High-Rise in 1998, though this year's winner goes there with as a live each-way chance. They went a good gallop, making it a good test at the distance. It's been rated around the winner to his best, and the fourth as close to form.

## 2615 BETFRED "FOLLOW US ON TWITTER" H'CAP 1m 2f
**3:05** (3:06) (Class 6) (0-65,65) 4-Y-O+ **£2,264** (£673; £336; £168) **Stalls** Low

Form RPR

6-50 **1** **Becca Campbell (IRE)**[18] 2055 4-9-4 **65** (p) EdwardGreatrex[(3)] 3 73+
(Eve Johnson Houghton) *hld up in last quartet: rdn and hdwy 2f out: clsng to chse ldrs whn swtchd rt and bmpd rival 1f out: wnt 2nd and rdr lost whip ins fnl f: r.o wl to ld towards fin* **12/1**

00-0 **2** *½* **Poppy Time**[31] 1735 4-9-2 **60** RyanTate 5 67
(James Eustace) *chsd ldr: rdn to ld ent fnl 2f: drvn ins fnl f: kpt on wl tl hdd and no ex towards fin* **10/1**

0-40 **3** *3 ¼* **Weardiditallgorong**[28] 1789 5-9-0 **58** (b) RobHornby 6 59
(Des Donovan, Ire) *hld up in midfield: hdwy over 2f out: drvn to chse ldrs over 1f out: kpt on same pce ins fnl f* **17/2**[3]

5-31 **4** *½* **Rattle On**[19] 2023 4-9-6 **64** PatCosgrave 2 64
(Jim Boyle) *hld up in midfield: effrt to chse clr ldng pair 2f out: clsng to chse ldrs whn bmpd 1f out: kpt on same pce ins fnl f* **7/2**[1]

640- **5** *1 ¾* **Kerrera**[171] 8075 4-9-2 **60** GrahamLee 10 57
(Paul Webber) *hld up in last trio: swtchd lft: rdn and hdwy but stl plenty to do over 1f out: styd on strly ins fnl f: wnt 5th last strides: nvr trbld ldrs* **16/1**

440- **6** *nk* **Megalala (IRE)**[206] 7464 16-8-0 **51** oh1 JaneElliott[(7)] 14 47
(John Bridger) *led: rdn and hdd ent fnl 2f: kpt on gamely and stl pressing ldr tl 1f out: no ex and wknd ins fnl f* **33/1**

-304 **7** *6* **Askari**[19] 2042 4-9-6 **64** JimmyFortune 12 49
(Tom Clover) *hld up in last quintet: effrt and hdwy into midfield: 2f out: no imp over 1f out: nvr trbld ldrs* **7/1**[2]

2666 **7** *dht* **Solveig's Song**[11] 2257 5-9-6 **64** (b) JackMitchell 4 49
(Steve Woodman) *in tch in midfield: no hdwy u.p over 2f out: wknd over 1f out* **16/1**

0610 **9** *½* **Gunner Moyne**[17] 2095 5-8-13 **60** (v) HectorCrouch[(3)] 9 44
(Gary Moore) *in tch in midfield: effrt over 2f out: sn u.p and unable qck: wknd over 1f out* **17/2**[3]

-431 **10** *nk* **Embankment**[35] 1620 8-9-2 **60** KierenFox 13 44
(Michael Attwater) *chsd ldrs: rdn and unable qck over 2f out: wknd fnl f* **7/1**[2]

1605 **11** *6* **Runaiocht (IRE)**[35] 1620 7-9-5 **63** (b) LiamKeniry 11 36
(Paul Burgoyne) *taken down early: hld up in rr: short lived effrt 2f out: sn btn and wknd* **16/1**

2030 **12** *½* **Cat Royale (IRE)**[31] 1729 4-9-0 **65** (p) DarraghKeenan[(7)] 7 37
(John Butler) *chsd ldrs: rdn and no rspnse over 2f out: sn lost pl: wknd over 1f out* **7/1**[2]

0-35 **13** *5* **Frankie**[66] 1082 6-8-0 **51** oh6 TinaSmith[(7)] 8 13
(Jimmy Fox) *a towards rr and niggled along early: lost tch u.p 2f out* **14/1**

2m 11.87s (1.37) **Going Correction** +0.175s/f (Good) 13 Ran SP% **124.8**
Speed ratings (Par 101): **101,100,98,97,96 95,91,91,90,90 85,85,81**
CSF £132.51 CT £1097.46 TOTE £17.30: £3.90, £3.80, £3.30; EX 188.20 Trifecta £2230.80.
**Owner** Eden Racing Club **Bred** Lynn Lodge Stud **Trained** Blewbury, Oxon
■ Stewards' Enquiry : Tina Smith five-day ban: used whip when out of contention (27 May-1 June)

**FOCUS**
A modest handicap in which a fair pace was set by Megalala.

## 2616 BETFRED "SUPPORTS JACK BERRY HOUSE" CHARTWELL FILLIES' STKS (GROUP 3) 7f
**3:40** (3:44) (Class 1) 3-Y-O+

**£34,026** (£12,900; £6,456; £3,216; £1,614; £810) **Stalls** Centre

Form RPR

40-1 **1** **Mix And Mingle (IRE)**[23] 1902 4-9-4 106........................ RyanMoore 11 111
(Chris Wall) *racd alone nr stands' rail: in tch in midfield overall: j. path over 5f out: rdn to ld over 1f out: edgd lft 1f out: clr and r.o wl ins fnl f* **9/2**[2]

113- **2** *2 ¼* **Qemah (IRE)**[245] 6352 4-9-4 115........................ FrankieDettori 3 105
(J-C Rouget, France) *t.k.h: hld up in tch in midfield: bmpd ent fnl 2f: swtchd lft and effrt over 1f out: hdwy to chse clr wnr ins fnl f: nvr any ch of getting on terms: pushed along and kpt on same pce after* **1/1**[1]

352- **3** *1 ½* **Pirouette**[232] 6746 4-9-4 103........................ JimmyFortune 10 101
(Hughie Morrison) *chsd ldrs: upsides ldr: effrt and edgd lft ent fnl 2f: sn rdn to chal and wandered: unable qck w wnr over 1f out: kpt on same pce ins fnl f* **8/1**[3]

-061 **4** *shd* **Realtra (IRE)**[29] 1771 5-9-4 107........................(b) JackMitchell 6 101
(Roger Varian) *chsd ldr: upsides ent 2f out: rdn and unable qck over 1f out: styd on same pce ins fnl f* **8/1**[3]

0-13 **5** *1 ¾* **Ashadihan**[29] 1771 4-9-4 105........................(b[1]) KevinStott 8 96
(Kevin Ryan) *led: rdn and hdd over 1f out: no ex u.p 1f out: wknd ins fnl f* **10/1**

3003 **6** *1 ¼* **Summer Icon**[12] 2241 4-9-4 95........................ GrahamLee 9 93
(Mick Channon) *stdd s: t.k.h: hld up in last trio: effrt over 2f out: 6th and no imp over 1f out: kpt on same pce fnl f* **40/1**

1-0 **7** *8* **Narnia Dawn (IRE)**[41] 1531 4-9-4 90........................(t[1]) PatCosgrave 5 71
(F-H Graffard, France) *t.k.h: hld up in last trio: outpcd and pushed along 2f out: swtchd rt over 1f out: no ch but kpt on past btn horses ins fnl f* **33/1**

31- **8** *2 ¼* **Eartha Kitt**[211] 7314 3-8-6 84........................ RichardKingscote 4 61
(Tom Dascombe) *stdd s: hld up in rr: outpcd and rdn 2f out: wl btn over 1f out: wknd* **16/1**

50- **9** *hd* **Rien Que Pour Toi (FR)**[19] 4-9-4 99........................ ThomasHuet 2 72
(T Castanheira, France) *in tch in midfield: swtchd lft and effrt over 2f out: no imp and btn over 1f out: eased fnl f* **66/1**

00-4 **10** *4 ½* **Blue Bayou**[42] 1491 4-9-4 102........................ KierenFox 7 52
(Brian Meehan) *hld up in tch in midfield: rdn wl over 2f out: sn struggling and wl btn over 1f out: wknd fnl f* **20/1**

24-4 **11** *3 ¼* **Robanne**[28] 1795 4-9-4 97........................ EdwardGreatrex 1 43
(William Knight) *chsd ldrs: rdn 3f out: sn struggling and lost pl ent fnl 2f: bhd fnl f* **25/1**

1m 22.31s (-0.99) **Going Correction** +0.175s/f (Good)
**WFA** 3 from 4yo+ 12lb 11 Ran SP% **120.9**
Speed ratings (Par 110): **112,109,107,107,105 104,95,92,92,87 83**
CSF £9.15 TOTE £5.70: £1.50, £1.10, £3.00; EX 11.90 Trifecta £64.90.
**Owner** Ms Aida Fustoq **Bred** Deerfield Farm **Trained** Newmarket, Suffolk
■ Stewards' Enquiry : Jimmy Fortune caution: careless riding

**FOCUS**
A fair renewal of this Group 3 event in which the favourite became only the second 115-rated runner in the race. Ryan Moore showed good awareness in racing alone on the stands' rail. The winner has been rated to the better view of her Newmarket latest.

## 2617 BETFRED "RACING'S BIGGEST SUPPORTER" H'CAP 7f 135y
**4:15** (4:17) (Class 3) (0-95,89) 4-Y-O **£7,246** (£2,168; £1,084; £542; £270) **Stalls** Centre

Form RPR

0-20 **1** **Shaiyem (IRE)**[16] 2116 4-9-7 **89**........................ FrankieDettori 3 97
(Richard Hannon) *t.k.h: trckd ldr tl led 2f out: shkn and asserted over 1f out: pressed but a doing enough ins fnl f: r.o: pushed out* **2/1**[1]

0S-5 **2** *1 ¼* **Ghalib (IRE)**[16] 2115 5-9-6 **88**........................ PatCosgrave 7 93
(Amy Murphy) *taken down early: trckd ldrs: swtchd lft over 2f out: effrt to press ldr u.p over 1f out: kpt on but a hld by wnr: eased towards fin* **7/2**[3]

60-0 **3** *2 ½* **Fox Trotter (IRE)**[7] 2390 5-9-4 **86**........................ JimmyFortune 1 85
(Brian Meehan) *stdd s: hld up in last pair: pushed along over 1f out: kpt on to go 3rd last strides: nvr trbld ldrs* **10/3**[2]

100- **4** *hd* **Ravenous**[208] 7015 6-8-13 **81**........................ KieranO'Neill 2 79
(Luke Dace) *rrd as stalls opened and slowly away: hdwy to chse ldrs 1/2-way: effrt u.p to press ldrs over 1f out: no ex and btn 3rd 1f out: wknd ins fnl f: lost 3rd last strides* **25/1**

10-3 **5** *5* **Dream Of Summer (IRE)**[19] 2026 4-8-12 **80**........................ RyanMoore 6 66
(Andrew Balding) *led: hdd and rdn 2f out: lost pl and btn 5th 1f out: wknd ins fnl f* **4/1**

0-10 **6** *6* **In The Red (IRE)**[21] 1960 4-9-5 **87**........................(p[1]) GrahamLee 4 58
(Martin Smith) *in tch in midfield: pushed along over 2f out: sn struggling: bhd over 1f out* **10/1**

1m 32.28s (-0.02) **Going Correction** +0.175s/f (Good) 6 Ran SP% **111.6**
Speed ratings (Par 107): **107,105,103,103,98 92**
CSF £9.15 TOTE £2.40: £1.30, £2.30; EX 9.70 Trifecta £27.70.
**Owner** Al Shaqab Racing **Bred** Ellen O'Neill **Trained** East Everleigh, Wilts

**FOCUS**
Not the strongest of handicaps for the grade, and the race was won up the advantageous stands' rail. They didn't go a great pace. The fourth has been rated as running close to his best form over a mile.

## 2618 BETFRED.COM H'CAP 7f
**4:50** (4:51) (Class 4) (0-85,85) 4-Y-O+ **£4,690** (£1,395; £697; £348) **Stalls** Centre

Form RPR

03-0 **1** **Black Bess**[52] 1301 4-9-7 **85**........................ PatCosgrave 7 93
(Jim Boyle) *t.k.h: chsd ldr tl led 2f out: rdn over 1f out: styd on wl and a doing enough ins fnl f* **4/1**[2]

506- **2** *¾* **Pastoral Player**[189] 7825 10-9-7 **85**........................ JohnFahy 2 90
(Hughie Morrison) *taken down early: stdd and dropped in bhd after s: hld up in rr: rdn and hdwy ent fnl f: clsng but flashed tail u.p ins fnl f: swtchd lft towards fin and wnt 2nd last strides* **8/1**

40-4 **3** *nk* **Morache Music**[12] 2230 9-8-13 **77**........................ RobHornby 4 81
(Patrick Chamings) *in tch in midfield: rdn over 2f out: hdwy u.p to chse wnr over 1f out: kpt on but a hld ins fnl f: lost 2nd last strides* **9/2**[3]

00-4 **4** *1 ¾* **Cool Bahamian (IRE)**[19] 2040 6-9-7 **85**........................(v) RyanMoore 3 84
(Eve Johnson Houghton) *hld up in tch: effrt to chse ldrs and rdn over 1f out: no imp ins fnl f: eased towards fin* **6/1**

100- **5** *2 ½* **Big Chill (IRE)**[197] 7671 5-8-9 **73**........................ KieranO'Neill 6 66
(Patrick Chamings) *chsd ldrs: rdn ent fnl 2f: 5th and no ex u.p over 1f out: wknd ins fnl f* **12/1**

00/4 **6** *1* **Jersey Breeze (IRE)**[13] 2177 4-8-10 **74**........................ GrahamLee 1 64
(Mick Channon) *hld up in tch: pushed along ent fnl 2f: rdn and no imp over 1f out: wknd ins fnl f* **7/1**

-452 **7** *36* **Evening Attire**[36] 1606 6-9-4 **82**........................ RichardKingscote 5
(William Stone) *led: hung lft and hdd 2f out: sn lost pl: bhd and eased fnl f: t.o: burst blood vessel* **9/4**[1]

1m 23.42s (0.12) **Going Correction** +0.175s/f (Good) 7 Ran SP% **114.5**
Speed ratings (Par 105): **106,105,104,102,99 98,57**
CSF £35.10 TOTE £4.00: £2.20, £3.80; EX 38.00 Trifecta £238.00.
**Owner** The Clean Sweep Partnership **Bred** Paddock Space **Trained** Epsom, Surrey

**FOCUS**
A moderate handicap and they once again headed for the stands' rail. There was a solid gallop. A pb from the winner.

## 2619 BETFRED "WATCH SKY SPORTS IN OUR SHOPS" MAIDEN FILLIES' STKS (PLUS 10 RACE) 6f
**5:20** (5:20) (Class 5) 3-Y-O **£2,911** (£866; £432; £108; £108) **Stalls** Centre

Form RPR

**1** **Yaraki** 3-9-0 0........................ PatCosgrave 4 80+
(William Haggas) *chsd ldr tl led 2f out: hrd pressed and rdn over 1f out: styd on wl and a doing enough ins fnl f: rdn out* **6/4**[1]

234- **2** *nk* **Dealer's Choice (IRE)**[165] 8140 3-8-7 77........................(h[1]) DavidEgan(7) 3 79
(Roger Varian) *hld up in tch: hdwy to press ldrs 2f out: rdn and ev ch over 1f out: kpt on u.p but a jst hld ins fnl f* **7/1**

02-0 **3** *1 ½* **Think Fashion (IRE)**[21] 1958 3-9-0 85........................ GrahamLee 6 74
(Brian Meehan) *t.k.h: hld up wl in tch in midfield: swtchd rt and effrt u.p to press ldrs over 1f out: no ex and outpcd fnl 100yds* **7/2**[2]

**4** *4 ½* **Fortitude (IRE)** 3-9-0 0........................ RyanMoore 7 60
(Hugo Palmer) *trckd ldrs: nt clr run: lost pl and swtchd lft jst over 2f out: 5th and pushed along over 1f out: no threat to ldrs and kpt on same pce fnl f* **6/1**

2 **4** *dht* **May Sky**[22] 1947 3-9-0 0........................ JimmyFortune 2 60
(John Gosden) *hld up in tch: clsd to press ldrs 2f out: pushed along: rn green and edging lft over 1f out: sn btn and wknd ins fnl f* **4/1**[3]

5-0 **6** *1 ½* **Tremendous (IRE)**[19] 2019 3-9-0 0........................ KieranO'Neill 1 55
(Richard Hannon) *led: rdn and hdd 2f out: lost pl u.p over 1f out: wknd ins fnl f* **25/1**

0 **7** *11* **Willow Tiger Lily**[15] 2121 3-8-7 0........................ GinaMangan(7) 5 20
(J R Jenkins) *hld up in rr: in tch: rdn over 2f out: sn struggling: bhd over 1f out* **100/1**

1m 11.62s (0.42) **Going Correction** +0.175s/f (Good) 7 Ran SP% **113.8**
Speed ratings (Par 96): **104,103,101,95,95 93,78**
CSF £12.91 TOTE £2.50: £1.30, £3.30; EX 10.30 Trifecta £33.10.
**Owner** Lael Stable **Bred** Lael Stables **Trained** Newmarket, Suffolk

**FOCUS**
An average maiden and a treble on the card for Pat Cosgrave, who steered home the Frankel debutant. The runner-up helps set the standard.
T/Plt: £295.80 to a £1 stake. Pool: £63,139.00 - 213.40 winning units. T/Qpdt: £40.80 to a £1 stake. Pool: £3,876.00 - 94.90 winning units. **Steve Payne**

# 2583 NOTTINGHAM (L-H)
Saturday, May 13

**OFFICIAL GOING: Good (good to soft in places; 7.9)**
Wind: Moderate against Weather: Cloudy

## 2620 GENTING CASINO NOTTINGHAM 10 YEAR ANNIVERSARY MAIDEN STKS 6f 18y
**2:05** (2:11) (Class 5) 3-Y-O+ **£3,234** (£962; £481; £240) **Stalls** Centre

Form RPR

02-2 **1** **Merlin**[26] 1830 3-9-2 79........................ SilvestreDeSousa 9 77+
(Michael Bell) *mde most: rdn over 1f out: kpt on strly* **1/1**[1]

**2** *2* **Hollander** 3-9-2 0........................ PhillipMakin 8 69
(William Muir) *trckd ldrs: hdwy over 2f out: green and pushed along wl over 1f out: swtchd lft and rdn ent fnl f: kpt on* **4/1**[3]

**3** *½* **Razzmatazz** 3-8-11 0........................ SamHitchcott 5 62
(Clive Cox) *t.k.h: hld up in tch: hdwy over 2f out: swtchd lft and rdn to chse ldrs over 1f out: kpt on wl fnl f* **14/1**

4-4 **4** *hd* **Primanora**[14] 2139 4-9-7 0........................ AdamKirby 2 64
(Michael Appleby) *cl up: rdn along 2f out: drvn over 1f out: kpt on same pce* **14/1**

32-4 **5** *2* **Stanhope**[18] 2072 3-9-2 75........................ OisinMurphy 6 60
(Mick Quinn) *chsd ldrs: rdn along 2f out: wknd over 1f out* **5/2**[2]

0-4 **6** *hd* **Primadonia**[8] 2366 3-8-11 0........................ FergusSweeney 1 54
(Richard Hughes) *t.k.h: in tch: chsd ldrs over 2f out: rdn along wl over 1f out: grad wknd* **40/1**

**7** *1 ¾* **D'Waterside** 3-9-2 0........................ DougieCostello 7 54
(David Loughnane) *dwlt: green and a towards rr* **50/1**

0 **8** *nk* **Babette (IRE)**[13] 2172 3-8-11 0........................ JasonHart 4 48
(Tony Newcombe) *a towards rr* **100/1**

1m 14.0s (-0.70) **Going Correction** -0.15s/f (Firm)
**WFA** 3 from 4yo 10lb 8 Ran SP% **117.3**
Speed ratings (Par 103): **98,95,94,94,91 91,89,88**
CSF £5.66 TOTE £1.80: £1.10, £1.50, £2.40; EX 6.40 Trifecta £48.80.
**Owner** The Queen **Bred** The Queen **Trained** Newmarket, Suffolk
■ Rivas Rose Marie was withdrawn. Price at time of withdrawal 33/1. Rule 4 does not apply

**FOCUS**
All races were on the outer track. The rail was set out two yards on the home bend, adding six yards to races 3, 5, 6 and 7. A fair maiden. They went a decent gallop on ground officially described as good, good to soft in places. The level is a bit fluid.

## 2621 FIRST PAST THE POST DG CARS H'CAP (A JOCKEY CLUB GRASSROOTS SPRINT SERIES QUALIFIER) 5f 8y
**2:40** (2:43) (Class 5) (0-75,75) 4-Y-O+ **£3,234** (£962; £481; £240) **Stalls** Centre

Form RPR

1145 **1** **Mighty Zip (USA)**[11] 2263 5-8-0 **61** oh9........................(p) JordanUys(7) 1 68
(Lisa Williamson) *racd centre: chsd ldrs: hdwy over 2f out: rdn over 1f out: cl up ins fnl f: kpt on wl to ld nr fin* **50/1**

6601 **2** *hd* **Classic Pursuit**[11] 2263 6-8-13 **67**........................(b) RoystonFfrench 3 73
(Michael Appleby) *hmpd s and rr: hdwy on outer over 2f out: rdn along to chse ldrs over 1f out: drvn to chal ins fnl f: ev ch tl no ex nr line* **8/1**

111 **3** *nse* **Major Valentine**[21] 1965 5-8-9 **70** BenRobinson(7) 12 76
(John O'Shea) *racd towards stands rail: cl up: led 3f out: rdn along and hdd over 1f out: drvn and rallied ins fnl f: slt ld last 50 yds: hdd nr line* **6/1**[3]

5021 **4** *nk* **Zac Brown (IRE)**[11] 2262 6-9-0 **75** (t) JoshuaBryan(7) 4 80
(Charlie Wallis) *hmpd s: in tch centre: hdwy over 2f out: rdn to take slt ld jst over 1f out: sn drvn: hdd last 50 yds: kpt on* **6/1**[3]

6-U4 **5** *1 ½* **Casterbridge**[13] 2184 5-9-3 **71** (h) NeilFarley 8 70
(Eric Alston) *racd centre: led 2f: cl up: rdn along wl over 1f out: drvn and kpt on same pce fnl f* **7/1**

5020 **6** *2 ½* **Steelriver (IRE)**[26] 1833 7-9-3 **71** BenCurtis 11 61
(David Barron) *s.i.s and bhd: sn swtchd lft to r centre: rdn along 1/2-way: hdwy wl over 1f out: styd on fnl f: nrst fin* **5/1**[2]

00-6 **7** *¾* **Classic Flyer**[11] 2263 5-8-8 **62** (v) JFEgan 7 50
(Christine Dunnett) *hmpd s: in tch centre: rdn along 1/2-way: grad wknd* **100/1**

-544 **8** *nk* **Emjayem**[11] 2253 7-9-4 **72** LiamJones 9 59
(John Holt) *a towards rr* **33/1**

0053 **9** *1 ¼* **Quatrieme Ami**[9] 2331 4-9-5 **73** (t) SilvestreDeSousa 6 55
(Philip McBride) *hmpd s: a rr* **7/2**[1]

362- **10** *3 ½* **John Joiner**[192] 7774 5-8-4 **63** MitchGodwin(5) 5 32
(Peter Hedger) *hmpd s and twoards rr: rdn along and sme hdwy 1/2-way: sn wknd* **10/1**

04-2 **10** *dht* **Silverrica (IRE)**[8] 2360 7-9-7 **75** LukeMorris 2 44
(Malcolm Saunders) *wnt rt s: chsd ldrs centre: rdn along over 2f out: sn drvn and wknd* **12/1**

2005 **12** *1 ¾* **Give Us A Belle (IRE)**[18] 2069 8-8-0 **61** oh15 (tp) RPWalsh(7) 10 24
(Christine Dunnett) *racd towards stands side: cl up: rdn along over 2f out: sn drvn and wknd* **100/1**

1m 0.8s (-0.70) **Going Correction** -0.15s/f (Firm) **12** Ran SP% **114.7**
Speed ratings (Par 103): **99,98,98,98,95 91,90,90,88,82 82,79**
CSF £400.36 CT £2803.15 TOTE £48.80: £6.50, £2.90, £2.10; EX 934.40 TRIFECTA Not Won..
**Owner** Heath House Racing **Bred** Dr Catherine Wills **Trained** Saighton, Cheshire

**FOCUS**
A fair sprint handicap. They went a decent gallop and it produced a thrilling four-way photo-finish, three of whom were drawn 1, 3 and 4, including the shock 50-1 winner. The runner-up has been rated close to last year's C&D form.

## 2622 BEST BET DG CARS 01159500500 H'CAP 1m 6f
**3:15** (3:16) (Class 4) (0-80,80) 4-Y-0+ **£5,175** (£1,540; £769; £384) **Stalls** Low

Form RPR

3-42 **1** **Fire Jet (IRE)**[15] 2125 4-9-8 **79** BenCurtis 6 88+
(John Mackie) *hld up in rr: smooth hdwy 4f out: trckd ldrs over 2f out: cl up wl over 1f out: rdn to ld ent fnl f: styd on strly* **3/1**[1]

52-4 **2** *2 ¼* **Corpus Chorister (FR)**[43] 1466 4-9-9 **80** HarryBentley 8 85
(David Menuisier) *led: pushed along 3f out: rdn 2f out: sn jnd and drvn: hdd ent fnl f: kpt on same pce last 150 yds* **7/2**[2]

1232 **3** *1* **Brigadoon**[11] 2270 10-9-5 **78** AlistairRawlinson(3) 3 81
(Michael Appleby) *trckd ldr: hdwy over 3f out: cl up over 2f out: sn rdn: drvn appr fnl f and kpt on same pce* **10/1**

4335 **4** *nk* **Wordiness**[5] 2460 9-8-8 **64** JFEgan 11 67
(David Evans) *stdd s and swtchd lft to inner: hld up and bhd: stdy hdwy over 4f out: chsd ldrs 2f out: sn rdn: drvn and kpt on fnl f* **16/1**

-111 **5** *3 ¾* **Masterson (IRE)**[11] 2275 4-9-7 **78** SilvestreDeSousa 7 75
(Mick Channon) *trckd ldrs: hdwy 4f out: rdn along over 2f out: drvn wl over 1f out: one pce appr fnl f* **5/1**[3]

036- **6** *¾* **Daghash**[305] 4230 8-9-3 **73** OisinMurphy 5 69
(Stuart Kittow) *t.k.h: in tch: hdwy 4f out: chsd ldrs 3f out: rdn along over 2f out: drvn wl over 1f out: no imp* **8/1**

60-6 **7** *2 ¾* **The New Pharaoh (IRE)**[19] 2020 6-9-3 **73** LouisSteward 4 65
(Chris Wall) *hld up towards rr: hdwy 5f out: chsd ldrs on outer 4f out: rdn along over 3f out: wknd over 2f out* **16/1**

45-0 **8** *1* **Itlaaq**[31] 1719 11-9-4 **77** (t) NathanEvans(3) 1 68
(Michael Easterby) *trckd ldrs on inner: hdwy 4f out: rdn along wl over 2f out: sn drvn and wknd* **14/1**

0665 **9** *shd* **Al Khafji**[33] 1684 4-8-9 **66** (p[1]) StevieDonohoe 10 57
(Jeremy Gask) *prom: rdn along over 4f out: wknd over 3f out* **11/1**

333- **10** *41* **Chebsey Beau**[161] 6519 7-9-0 **70** JasonHart 9 3
(John Quinn) *in tch: pushed along over 4f out: rdn along 4f out: sn outpcd and bhd* **14/1**

3m 3.79s (-3.21) **Going Correction** -0.15s/f (Firm) **10** Ran SP% **117.5**
Speed ratings (Par 105): **103,101,101,100,98 98,96,96,96,72**
CSF £13.50 CT £93.22 TOTE £4.80: £1.50, £1.90, £2.50; EX 17.60 Trifecta £104.30.
**Owner** Ladas **Bred** Ladas **Trained** Church Broughton , Derbys

**FOCUS**
Race distance increased by 6yds. A fair staying handicap. They went a decent gallop and the favourite won readily. The third and fourth have been rated close to their recent form.

## 2623 EBF WEATHERBYS GENERAL STUD BOOK ONLINE KILVINGTON STKS (LISTED RACE) (F&M) 6f 18y
**3:50** (3:51) (Class 1) 3-Y-0+
**£22,684** (£8,600; £4,304; £2,144; £1,076; £540) **Stalls** Centre

Form RPR

**1** **Artistica (GER)**[26] 3-8-7 0 SamHitchcott 11 97
(D Moser, Germany) *wnt rt and bmpd s: bhd centre and rdn along over 2f out: sn swtchd rt to stands rail and gd hdwy wl over 1f out: str run ent fnl f: edgd lft and styd on strly to ld towards fin* **33/1**

00-2 **2** *½* **Futoon (IRE)**[22] 1936 4-9-3 89 JoeDoyle 17 98
(Kevin Ryan) *prom: cl up 1/2-way: led wl over 1f out and sn rdn: drvn ins fnl f: hdd and no ex towards fin* **20/1**

/33- **3** *hd* **Bounce**[310] 4062 4-9-3 92 FergusSweeney 12 97
(Henry Candy) *bmpd s and rr centre: hdwy over 2f out: rdn over 1f out: styd on wl fnl f* **9/1**

0-54 **4** *¾* **Pixeleen**[17] 2083 5-9-3 86 PhillipMakin 9 95
(Malcolm Saunders) *racd centre: hld up: hdwy wl over 1f out: rdn to chse ldrs ent fnl f: sn drvn and kpt on wl* **25/1**

6060 **5** *nk* **Buying Trouble (USA)**[22] 1936 4-9-3 96 JFEgan 3 95
(David Evans) *racd centre: hld up: hdwy wl over 1f out: rdn and n.m.r ent fnl f: sn drvn and kpt on wl towards fin* **20/1**

0-36 **6** *1 ½* **Iseemist (IRE)**[22] 1936 6-9-3 92 JoeyHaynes 10 89
(John Gallagher) *prom centre: rdn and cl up 2f out: drvn over 1f out: grad wknd* **25/1**

22-0 **7** *1 ½* **Glitter Girl**[21] 1958 3-8-7 100 BenCurtis 2 81
(William Haggas) *hld up centre: hdwy on wd outside over 2f out: rdn to chse ldrs over 1f out: drvn and wknd ins fnl f* **9/2**[2]

03-5 **8** *½* **Evil Spell**[22] 1936 5-9-3 99 OisinMurphy 14 83
(Robert Cowell) *racd towards stands side: chsd ldrs: rdn along wl over 1f out: hld whn sltly hmpd ent fnl f* **20/1**

110- **9** *½* **Rural Celebration**[184] 7892 6-9-3 84 (v) DavidNolan 6 81
(Kevin Ryan) *qckly away and led in centre: rdn along over 2f out: hdd and drvn wl over 1f out: wknd* **50/1**

63-6 **10** *1 ¼* **Mystic Dawn (IRE)**[21] 1958 3-8-7 100 LukeMorris 13 74
(David Simcock) *racd towards stands side: in tch: rdn along over 2f out: sn wknd* **8/1**

00-4 **11** *1 ¼* **Belledesert**[22] 1936 4-9-3 85 RoystonFfrench 7 73
(Steph Hollinshead) *sltly hmpd s: a towards rr centre* **50/1**

06-3 **12** *1 ¾* **Imtiyaaz (IRE)**[22] 1936 5-9-3 89 MartinLane 5 68
(Roger Varian) *chsd ldrs centre: rdn along 2f out: sn drvn and wknd appr fnl f* **18/1**

10-3 **13** *1 ¼* **Lady Macapa**[22] 1946 4-9-3 97 AdamKirby 8 64
(Clive Cox) *cl up centre: pushed along over 2f out: sn rdn and edgd lft: wknd wl over 1f out* **3/1**[1]

211- **14** *1* **Tropical Rock**[240] 6525 3-8-7 85 SilvestreDeSousa 16 57
(Ralph Beckett) *racd towards stands rail: in tch: rdn along 2f out: sn wknd* **6/1**[3]

03-0 **15** *1* **Pichola Dance (IRE)**[21] 1958 3-8-7 93 (b[1]) HarryBentley 1 54
(Roger Varian) *chsd ldrs centre: rdn along wl over 2f out: sn wknd* **20/1**

143- **16** *19* **Spring Fling**[177] 7990 6-9-3 94 TimmyMurphy 15
(Henry Candy) *racd tiowards stands rail: in tch: pushed along over 2f out: rdn wl over 1f out: sn wknd and bhd whn eased ins fnl f* **20/1**

1m 13.13s (-1.57) **Going Correction** -0.15s/f (Firm)
**WFA** 3 from 4yo+ 10lb **16** Ran SP% **122.2**
Speed ratings (Par 111): **104,103,103,102,101 99,97,97,96,94 93,90,89,87,86 61**
CSF £556.11 TOTE £23.30: £8.90, £5.90, £3.00; EX 657.40 Trifecta £1959.70.
**Owner** Gestut Brummerhof **Bred** Snc Lagardere Elevage **Trained** Germany

**FOCUS**
A good quality Listed contest for fillies and mares. They went a decent gallop and the race developed middle to stands' side with horses drawn 11, 17 and 12 filling the first three places.

## 2624 GENTING CASINO AT THE CORNERHOUSE H'CAP (JOCKEY CLUB GRASSROOTS MIDDLE DISTANCE SERIES QUALIFIER) 1m 2f 50y
**4:25** (4:29) (Class 4) (0-80,80) 4-Y-0+ **£5,175** (£1,540; £769; £384) **Stalls** Low

Form RPR

314- **1** **Toulson**[220] 7077 4-9-5 **78** CharlesBishop 10 91
(Eve Johnson Houghton) *prom: trckd ldr 1/2-way: hdwy over 2f out: cl up over 1f out: rdn to ld ins fnl f: kpt on strly* **5/1**[2]

10-0 **2** *1 ¾* **Tomahawk Kid**[14] 2133 4-9-6 **79** SilvestreDeSousa 3 88
(Ian Williams) *trckd ldng pair whn hmpd after 1f and sn pulling hrd: cl up after 3f: led 1/2-way: rdn clr over 2f out: jnd and drvn over 1f out: hdd ins fnl f: kpt on same pce last 100 yds* **5/1**[2]

43-5 **3** *4 ½* **Panko (IRE)**[14] 2146 4-9-1 **77** CallumShepherd(3) 4 77
(Ed de Giles) *dwlt and rr: hdwy on inner 3f out: rdn along to chse ldrs 2f out: drvn over 1f out: kpt on fnl f* **8/1**[3]

05-2 **4** *¾* **Wannabe Friends**[21] 1969 4-9-6 **79** LukeMorris 9 78
(Luca Cumani) *t.k.h: trckd ldrs: hdwy to chse ldng pair over 2f out and sn rdn: drvn over 1f out: sn one pce* **11/8**[1]

50-1 **5** *2 ¼* **Sunglider (IRE)**[12] 2225 4-9-7 **80** DavidNolan 5 75
(David O'Meara) *hld up towards rr: hdwy 4f out in tch over 3f out: rdn along over 2f out: sn one pce* **10/1**

10-0 **6** *shd* **Westward Ho (IRE)**[19] 2030 4-9-1 **77** NathanEvans(3) 8 72
(James Bethell) *hld up: hdwy and in tch 4f out: rdn along 3f out: sn one pce* **16/1**

2-0 **7** *6* **Cornborough**[32] 1706 6-8-11 **70** JasonHart 6 53+
(Mark Walford) *towards rr: pushed along wl over 3f out: sn rdn and wknd over 2f out* **10/1**

0-00 **8** *2 ¼* **Lord Franklin**[2] 2558 8-9-7 **80** NeilFarley 7 59
(Eric Alston) *led: slipped and stmbld after 1f: hdd 1/2-way: cl up: rdn along 4f out: sn wknd* **28/1**

40/4 **9** *5* **No Win No Fee**[21] 1982 7-8-9 **68** JFEgan 1 37
(Barry Leavy) *chsd ldrs: pushed along over 4f out: rdn wl over 3f out: sn wknd* **50/1**

2m 10.55s (-3.75) **Going Correction** -0.15s/f (Firm) **9** Ran SP% **116.0**
Speed ratings (Par 105): **109,107,104,103,101 101,96,94,90**
CSF £30.36 CT £197.60 TOTE £6.30: £1.90, £1.50, £2.10; EX 35.00 Trifecta £187.70.
**Owner** Mrs Virginia Neale **Bred** Cherry Park Stud **Trained** Blewbury, Oxon

**FOCUS**
Race distance increased by 6yds. A fair handicap. They went a decent gallop and a few of these were tightened up quite badly down the back, including the favourite who got lit up for a spell and failed to fire thereafter. The runner-up has been rated as running a length pb.

## 2625 DOWNLOAD THE APP DG CARS H'CAP 1m 75y
**5:00** (5:08) (Class 5) (0-75,77) 3-Y-0 **£3,234** (£962; £481; £240) **Stalls** Centre

Form RPR

42-0 **1** **Mister Blue Sky (IRE)**[15] 2126 3-9-2 **75** MitchGodwin(5) 6 82+
(Sylvester Kirk) *trckd ldrs: hdwy and cl up over 2f out: rdn over 1f out: led jst ins fnl f: drvn and edgd lft towards fin: hld on wl* **7/2**[1]

343 **2** *nk* **Arsenio Lupin**[66] 1089 3-9-7 **75** (t) OisinMurphy 10 80+
(Denis Quinn) *hld up in rr: hdwy wl over 2f out: swtchd rt and rdn over 1f out: fin strly: jst hld* **16/1**

556- **3** *nk* **Suspect Package (USA)**[144] 8466 3-9-4 **72** (h[1]) TimmyMurphy 2 76
(James Fanshawe) *t.k.h: trckd ldrs: pushed along and sltly outpcd 2f out: rdn over 1f out: styd on strly fnl f* **8/1**[3]

03-3 **4** *1 ½* **Miss Osier**[114] 310 3-8-5 **62** NoelGarbutt(3) 1 65+
(Rae Guest) *set stdy pce: pushed along and jnd 3f out: rdn and qcknd wl over 2f out: drvn over 1f out: hdd jst ins fnl f: hld whn n.m.r towards fin* **50/1**

30-0 **5** *1* **Heatongrad (IRE)**[13] 2186 3-9-2 **70** JackGarritty 7 68
(Richard Fahey) *t.k.h: in tch: hdwy over 3f out: chsd ldrs over 2f out: sn rdn: drvn over 1f out: no imp fnl f* **16/1**

60-5 **6** *½* **Whiteley (IRE)**[33] 1686 3-8-8 **62** SilvestreDeSousa 5 61+
(Mick Channon) *in tch: hdwy on inner to trck ldrs 4f out: effrt over 2f out: rdn and ev ch over 1f out: drvn and wknd ent fnl f* **7/1**[2]

1522 **7** *nk* **Spirit Of Sarwan (IRE)**[10] 2293 3-9-2 **77** (p[1]) MillyNaseb(7) 3 73
(Julia Feilden) *t.k.h: chsd ldrs: rdn along wl over 2f out: sn drvn and kpt on one pce* **8/1**[3]

25-6 **8** *½* **Tagur (IRE)**[50] 1348 3-8-12 **66** (p) ShaneGray 4 61
(Kevin Ryan) *t.k.h: cl up: jnd ldr 3f out: rdn along over 2f out: ev ch tl drvn appr fnl f and wknd* **16/1**

50-0 **9** *¾* **Aelius**[41] 1513 3-8-10 **67** (t[1]) NathanEvans(3) 8 60
(Michael Easterby) *hld up towards rr: hdwy on inner 3f out: nt clr run and rdn along over 2f out: sn drvn and btn* **7/1**[2]

2465 **10** *shd* **Jumping Jack (IRE)**[10] 2293 3-8-13 **74**........................ FinleyMarsh(7) 14 67
(Richard Hughes) *a rr* **10/1**

21-5 **11** *½* **Getgo**[18] 2071 3-9-5 **73**..................................................(b) StevieDonohoe 13 65
(David Lanigan) *dwlt: a rr* **12/1**

03-3 **12** *4½* **The Lacemaker**[17] 2094 3-9-7 **75**....................................... AdamKirby 11 57
(Ed Dunlop) *t.k.h: hld up: hdwy and in tch over 3f out: sn rdn along and wknd 2f out* **12/1**

553 **13** *3¾* **Trade Route (IRE)**[77] 916 3-9-5 **73**......................................(p) JFEgan 9 46
(David Elsworth) *towards rr: hdwy on outer and in tch over 3f out: sn rdn and wknd* **8/1[3]**

1m 46.16s (-2.84) **Going Correction** -0.15s/f (Firm) **13** Ran SP% **124.6**
Speed ratings (Par 99): **108,107,107,105,104 104,104,103,102,102 102,97,94**
CSF £68.22 CT £452.26 TOTE £4.50: £2.00, £5.70, £3.30; EX 82.20 Trifecta £902.50.
**Owner** Deauville Daze Partnership 1 **Bred** Shadwell Estate Company Limited **Trained** Upper Lambourn, Berks

■ Stewards' Enquiry : Mitch Godwin four-day ban: careless riding (May 27, 29-31)

**FOCUS**
Race distance increased by 6yds. A fair 3yo handicap. They went a muddling gallop but the favourite ground out a deserved second career victory. It's been rated around the third back to his debut form.

## 2626 LEXUS NOTTINGHAM APPRENTICE H'CAP (PART OF THE RACING EXCELLENCE INITIATIVE) 1m 75y
**5:35** (5:36) (Class 6) (0-60,63) 4-Y-0+ **£2,587** (£770; £384; £192) **Stalls** Centre

Form RPR

0652 **1** **Indigo Princess**[11] 2285 4-9-10 **63**.................................... RayDawson 14 70
(Michael Appleby) *trckd ldrs: hdwy over 2f out: rdn over 1f out: led jst ins fnl f: drvn out* **9/2[2]**

0342 **2** *½* **Little Choosey**[11] 2276 7-9-3 **61**......................(bt) StephenCummins(5) 13 67
(Roy Bowring) *trckd ldrs on outer: hdwy 2f out: rdn to chal over 1f out: ev ch ins fnl f: kpt on* **7/2[1]**

0-00 **3** *2¼* **Tom's Anna (IRE)**[47] 1407 7-8-4 **46** oh1.................. GabrieleMalune(3) 7 47
(Sean Regan) *trckd ldrs: hdwy over 3f out: led over 2f out: rdn wl over 1f out: drvn and hdd jst ins fnl f: kpt on same pce* **20/1**

2633 **4** *3* **Sheer Intensity (IRE)**[18] 2063 4-8-6 **52**........................ KeelanBaker(7) 8 46
(David Evans) *dwlt and bhd: hdwy over 3f out: rdn over 1f out: kpt on appr fnl f* **9/1**

5040 **5** *¾* **Sarakova (IRE)**[38] 1563 4-8-4 **46** oh1..........................(b) AledBeech(3) 12 38
(Kevin Frost) *in tch: rdn along: lost pl and bhd 3f out: styd on u.p fr over 1f out* **16/1**

1-00 **6** *2¼* **Walking In Rhythm (IRE)**[21] 1983 4-8-13 **57**.................... TobyEley(5) 5 44
(Barry Leavy) *in tch: hdwy to chse ldrs 3f out: rdn along over 2f out: drvn and wkng whn hung lft 1f out* **16/1**

0004 **7** *3¼* **Qortaaj**[18] 2057 4-9-7 **60**.................................................. BenRobinson 3 40
(David Loughnane) *chsd ldr: rdn along over 3f out: sn drvn and wknd* **15/2**

0-60 **8** *3¼* **Ada Misobel (IRE)**[39] 1544 4-8-7 **49**......................(b) BenSanderson(3) 6 21+
(Roy Bowring) *awkward: v s.i.s and lost many l s: detached tl hdwy to join field 4f out: rdn along and n.m.r 3f out: sn wknd* **9/1**

050- **9** *4* **Tatawu (IRE)**[249] 6212 5-9-2 **60**....................................... MollyKing(5) 11 23
(Peter Hiatt) *dwlt: a rr* **11/2[3]**

600- **10** *1¼* **Tamarin**[445] 682 5-8-4 **46** oh1........................................(p) JordanUys(3) 4 6
(Lisa Williamson) *led: rdn along over 3f out: hdd over 2f out: sn wknd* **33/1**

6220 **11** *¾* **Cahar Fad (IRE)**[47] 1402 5-8-4 **46**..............................(bt) MillyNaseb(3) 9 4
(Steph Hollinshead) *chsd ldr on outer: rdn along over 3f out: sn wknd* **15/2**

1m 46.69s (-2.31) **Going Correction** -0.15s/f (Firm) **11** Ran SP% **118.8**
Speed ratings (Par 101): **105,104,102,99,98 96,93,89,85,84 83**
CSF £20.85 CT £294.71 TOTE £5.30: £1.70, £1.60, £4.60; EX 19.70 Trifecta £488.10.
**Owner** Philip A Jarvis **Bred** Philip A Jarvis **Trained** Oakham, Rutland

**FOCUS**
Race distance increased by 6yds. A modest apprentice riders' handicap. They went a strong gallop and two more patiently ridden horses at the head of the betting came through to fight it out.
T/Plt: £602.00 to a £1 stake. Pool: £54,816.94 - 66.47 winning units T/Qpdt: £86.40 to a £1 stake. Pool: £2,907.82 - 24.9 winning units **Joe Rowntree**

# 2403 THIRSK (L-H)
Saturday, May 13

**OFFICIAL GOING: Good to firm (8.7)**
Wind: Virtually nil Weather: Fine

## 2627 ABF THE SOLDIERS' CHARITY (S) STKS 6f
**5:45** (5:46) (Class 6) 3-5-Y-0 **£2,587** (£770; £384; £192) **Stalls** High

Form RPR

3112 **1** **Noah Amor (IRE)**[10] 2305 4-9-8 71................................ ConnorMurtagh(7) 5 72+
(Richard Fahey) *mde all: pushed along over 1f out: edgd lft: rdn and kpt on wl fnl f: comf* **1/1[1]**

3334 **2** *2¾* **Hadley**[21] 1978 4-9-6 50..............................................(p) DougieCostello 4 53
(Tracy Waggott) *chsd ldr: rdn over 2f out: one pce fnl f* **9/1**

1603 **3** *hd* **Roaring Rory**[21] 1973 4-9-7 63..................................(p) LewisEdmunds(5) 3 58
(Ollie Pears) *chsd ldr: rdn over 1f out: one pce fnl f* **11/2**

5043 **4** *1¾* **Monsieur Jimmy**[5] 2469 5-9-12 47.......................................... DanielTudhope 1 53
(Declan Carroll) *chsd ldr: rdn over 2f out: wknd ins fnl f* **9/2[2]**

-055 **5** *2¼* **Silver Bid (USA)**[25] 1869 5-9-1 59...................................... GemmaTutty(5) 7 40
(Karen Tutty) *chsd ldr: rdn over 2f out: wknd appr fnl f* **5/1[3]**

/-60 **6** *32* **Ivy Matilda**[92] 655 4-9-1 38............................................ JamesSullivan 6
(Colin Teague) *s.i.s: a in rr: t.o fnl 2f* **250/1**

1m 12.8s (0.10) **Going Correction** -0.05s/f (Good) **6** Ran SP% **110.6**
Speed ratings (Par 101): **97,93,93,90,87 45**
CSF £10.74 TOTE £1.80: £1.10, £4.60; EX 9.70 Trifecta £32.30.Winner was bought by Gallop Racing for £9,000
**Owner** Middleham Park Racing XVI & Partner **Bred** Mrs Claire Doyle **Trained** Musley Bank, N Yorks

**FOCUS**
They were racing on watered ground to maintain the surface. The rail was re-aligned on both bends adding 30 yards to races over 1m, and 40 yards to the 1m4f event. A low-grade contest to start with the favourite doing enough. The form is arguable. Straightforward form, with the runner-up rated to his mark.

## 2628 ALEXANDER KETTLEWELL STAG PARTY H'CAP 5f
**6:15** (6:15) (Class 6) (0-60,62) 4-Y-0+ **£3,234** (£962; £481; £240) **Stalls** High

Form RPR

1121 **1** **Kinloch Pride**[17] 2076 5-9-3 **61**......................................(p) PhilDennis(5) 12 72
(Noel Wilson) *chsd ldrs towards stands' side: rdn to ld over 1f out: kpt on wl* **4/1[1]**

2504 **2** *2* **Pearl Noir**[17] 2076 7-9-6 **59**..................................................(b) LouisSteward 3 61
(Scott Dixon) *racd towards far side: w ldr: rdn over 2f out: one pce* **10/1**

5240 **3** *nk* **Culloden**[17] 2076 5-8-12 **56**........................................(v[1]) PaddyPilley(5) 16 57
(Shaun Harris) *racd towards stands' side: led narrowly: rdn over 2f out: hdd over 1f out: one pce* **9/1**

-530 **4** *2¾* **Storm Trooper (IRE)**[21] 1971 6-9-6 **62**....................(p[1]) AaronJones(3) 13 53
(Marjorie Fife) *chsd ldrs towards stands' side: rdn over 2f out: one pce* **13/2[2]**

50-3 **5** *shd* **Thornaby Princess**[9] 2337 6-8-11 **50**......................(p) RoystonFfrench 10 41
(Colin Teague) *chsd ldrs towards stands' side: rdn over 2f out: one pce* **14/1**

5506 **6** *¾* **Ryedale Rio (IRE)**[25] 1869 4-8-13 **55**..............(b[1]) RachelRichardson(3) 2 43
(Tim Easterby) *dwlt: sn chsd ldrs towards far side: rdn over 2f out: one pce* **14/1**

-640 **7** *1¼* **Groundworker (IRE)**[19] 2034 6-9-7 **60**........................(t) PaulMulrennan 9 43
(Paul Midgley) *chsd ldrs centre: rdn over 2f out: wknd fnl f* **9/1**

3-65 **8** *½* **Searanger (USA)**[17] 2076 4-9-5 **58**..............................(t[1]) PJMcDonald 11 40
(Rebecca Menzies) *hld up towards stands' side: rdn 1/2-way: nvr threatened* **13/2[2]**

5250 **9** *shd* **Novabridge**[25] 1869 9-8-7 **46**..................................................(b) JoeDoyle 14 27
(Karen Tutty) *hld up towards stands' side: nvr threatened* **14/1**

-030 **10** *2* **A J Cook (IRE)**[21] 1978 7-8-9 **48**........................................ CamHardie 15 22
(Ron Barr) *dwlt: hld up stands' side: nvr threatened* **20/1**

4254 **11** *1¼* **See Vermont**[19] 2034 9-9-7 **60**......................................(p) DanielTudhope 6 30
(Rebecca Bastiman) *dwlt: a towards rr centre* **7/1[3]**

0000 **12** *1* **Rat Catcher (IRE)**[44] 1452 7-8-1 **47** oh1 ow1..........(b) GeorgiaDobie(7) 8 13
(Lisa Williamson) *in tch centre: rdn 1/2-way: wknd over 1f out* **66/1**

3006 **13** *2* **Under Approval**[9] 2337 6-8-7 **46** oh1..................................(p) JoeyHaynes 4 5
(Karen Tutty) *in tch towards far side: rdn 1/2-way: wknd over 1f out* **50/1**

/00- **14** *8* **Good Move (IRE)**[277] 5278 5-8-7 **46** oh1...................(t[1]) JamesSullivan 5
(Brian Rothwell) *hld up towards far side: rdn 1/2-way: sn wknd* **100/1**

58.96s (-0.64) **Going Correction** -0.05s/f (Good) **14** Ran SP% **117.5**
Speed ratings (Par 101): **103,99,99,94,94 93,91,90,90,87 85,83,80,67**
CSF £42.19 CT £351.58 TOTE £4.40: £1.90, £4.10, £3.10; EX 40.90 Trifecta £456.80.
**Owner** G J Paver **Bred** Mrs C K Paver **Trained** Marwood, Co Durham

■ Another Desperado was withdrawn. Price at time of withdrawal 50/1. Rule 4 does not apply

**FOCUS**
A modest sprint handicap which very few got into. The first three were always in the front rank, but the winner did it nicely. Fair form for the grade.

## 2629 CLIFF STUD REARING WINNERS H'CAP 1m 4f 8y
**6:45** (6:45) (Class 4) (0-80,82) 4-Y-0+ **£5,175** (£1,540; £769; £384) **Stalls** High

Form RPR

420- **1** **Mutadaffeq (IRE)**[187] 7847 4-9-2 **73**............................ DanielTudhope 11 86+
(David O'Meara) *trckd ldrs: pushed along to ld 2f out: rdn clr over 1f out: kpt on pushed out fnl f: comf* **7/2[1]**

640- **2** *3¼* **Throckley**[208] 7412 6-9-7 **78**.................................................(t[1]) SamJames 1 84
(John Davies) *hld up in midfield: hdwy 3f out: pushed along to chse ldr over 1f out: rdn fnl f: kpt on but no ch w wnr* **9/1**

-003 **3** *2¼* **London Glory**[14] 2146 4-8-8 **65**......................................(b) AndrewMullen 7 67
(David Thompson) *midfield: rdn and hdwy to chse ldrs 2f out: styd on same pce* **14/1**

20-3 **4** *1½* **Peterhouse (USA)**[16] 2109 5-9-7 **78**...................................... BenCurtis 6 78
(Jason Ward) *v.s.a: hld up: rdn and hdwy on outer over 2f out: styd on same pce fr over 1f out* **5/1[2]**

420- **5** *nk* **Age Of Elegance (IRE)**[155] 8283 5-9-7 **78**.................. ConnorBeasley 5 78
(Roger Fell) *led: rdn whn hdd 2f out: no ex* **15/2**

-005 **6** *1¾* **Top Of The Glas (IRE)**[21] 1976 6-9-2 **78**............. MeganNicholls(5) 10 75
(Brian Ellison) *hld up in midfield: rdn 3f out: no imp* **7/1[3]**

1-02 **7** *2½* **Airton**[21] 1976 4-9-5 **76**...................................................... PJMcDonald 13 69
(James Bethell) *hld up: rdn over 3f out: nvr threatened* **5/1[2]**

0-00 **8** *¾* **Sikandar (IRE)**[21] 1976 5-9-2 **73**..............................(tp) DougieCostello 12 65
(Brian Ellison) *dwlt: sn prom: rdn over 3f out: wknd fnl 2f* **28/1**

110- **9** *6* **Transpennine Star**[199] 7624 4-9-7 **78**..................... PaulMulrennan 3 60
(Michael Dods) *trckd ldrs: rdn over 3f out: sn wknd* **12/1**

50-0 **10** *2¼* **Wotabreeze (IRE)**[31] 1719 4-9-5 **76**...................................... JasonHart 4 54
(John Quinn) *midfield: pushed along over 3f out: wknd over 2f out* **16/1**

2m 37.77s (1.57) **Going Correction** +0.275s/f (Good) **10** Ran SP% **113.5**
Speed ratings (Par 105): **105,102,101,100,100 98,97,96,92,91**
CSF £34.54 CT £388.19 TOTE £4.20: £1.40, £2.90, £4.00; EX 41.70 Trifecta £500.40.
**Owner** The Get Round The Back Syndicate **Bred** Shadwell Estate Company Limited **Trained** Upper Helmsley, N Yorks

**FOCUS**
The alignment of the rail on both bends added 40 yards to the distance. A fairly competitive handicap for the grade and while the early pace was slow and the race was almost six seconds slower than standard, the winner may well be ahead of the game. The runner-up has been rated to his York September form.

## 2630 DICK PEACOCK SPRINT H'CAP 6f
**7:15** (7:15) (Class 5) (0-75,77) 3-Y-0 **£3,881** (£1,155; £577; £288) **Stalls** High

Form RPR

00-4 **1** **Scofflaw**[23] 1913 3-9-5 **76**.......................................... AdamMcNamara(3) 2 82+
(Richard Fahey) *midfield: pushed along and hdwy over 2f out: rdn to ld narrowly over 1f out: edgd rt: strly pressed ins fnl f: hld on wl* **9/2[2]**

21 **2** *nk* **Historic Event (IRE)**[16] 2112 3-9-2 **75**..........(p[1]) CallumRodriguez(5) 15 80+
(Saeed bin Suroor) *in tch towards inner: pushed along and hdwy 2f out: rdn to chal strly ins fnl f: kpt on but a jst hld* **3/1[1]**

3356 **3** *1¼* **Alfonso Manana (IRE)**[13] 2180 3-8-13 **67**.........................(b[1]) JoeFanning 7 68
(James Given) *dwlt: hld up: hung lft to outside over 1f out: sn gd hdwy: rdn and kpt on fnl f* **20/1**

2-00 **4** *¾* **Cupid's Arrow (IRE)**[10] 2304 3-8-9 **63**.............................. JamesSullivan 3 62
(Ruth Carr) *hld up towards outer: pushed along and hdwy over 1f out: rdn and kpt on fnl f* **28/1**

200- **5** ¾ **Little Miss Lola**[276] 5289 3-8-9 **63** ........ NeilFarley 8 59
(Alan Swinbank) *dwlt: midfield: rdn over 2f out: kpt on wl fnl f* **66/1**

0-12 **6** ½ **Stubytuesday**[12] 2223 3-8-12 **66** ........ CamHardie 6 61
(Michael Easterby) *midfield: rdn over 2f out: chsd ldrs over 1f out: one pce fnl f* **10/1**

6-54 **7** 3 ½ **Brother McGonagall**[12] 2223 3-8-8 **62** ........ DavidAllan 16 45
(Tim Easterby) *midfield on inner: outpcd and dropped towards rr over 2f out: angled lft over 1f out: kpt on ins fnl f* **7/1**[3]

14-6 **8** 6 **Hot Hannah**[17] 2080 3-9-0 **68** ........(p) ConnorBeasley 5 32
(Michael Dods) *led: rdn over 2f out: hdd over 1f out: wknd* **33/1**

03-3 **9** *hd* **Dundunah (USA)**[17] 2080 3-9-1 **69** ........ DanielTudhope 12 33
(David O'Meara) *prom: rdn over 2f out: wknd over 1f out* **10/1**

-060 **10** 1 ¼ **Trick Of The Lyte (IRE)**[23] 1913 3-8-9 **63** ........ JasonHart 13 23
(John Quinn) *hld up: pushed along over 2f out: nvr threatened* **25/1**

6011 **11** 1 **Man About Town (IRE)**[50] 1348 3-8-9 **68** ........ CliffordLee(5) 11 24
(K R Burke) *dwlt: sn prom: rdn over 2f out: wknd over 1f out* **9/1**

5-31 **12** 4 **Kodicat (IRE)**[17] 2080 3-9-4 **72** ........ TomEaves 9 16
(Kevin Ryan) *chsd ldrs: rdn over 2f out: wknd over 1f out* **15/2**

031- **D** ¾ **Man Of Verve (IRE)**[210] 7355 3-9-0 **77** ........ JoshQuinn(7) 10
(John Quinn) *prom: rdn and lost pl over 2f out: wknd over 1f out: fin last: disqualified after rdr failed to weigh in* **16/1**

1m 12.34s (-0.36) **Going Correction** -0.05s/f (Good) **13** Ran SP% **118.0**
Speed ratings (Par 99): **100,99,97,96,95 95,90,82,82,80 79,74,73**
CSF £16.94 CT £254.94 TOTE £5.30: £1.90, £1.90, £5.20; EX 22.20 Trifecta £392.20.
**Owner** P Timmins & A Rhodes Haulage **Bred** Mrs M E Slade **Trained** Musley Bank, N Yorks
■ Stewards' Enquiry : Josh Quinn one-day ban: weighed in light (27 May)

**FOCUS**
The pace failed to hold up in this modest sprint handicap and the first three came from off the pace. The third has been rated to form.

## 2631 ELWICK STUD FILLIES' H'CAP 5f
**7:45** (7:45) (Class 5) (0-75,76) 3-Y-0+ **£3,881** (£1,155; £577; £288) **Stalls** High

Form RPR

0-24 **1** **Yorkshiredebut (IRE)**[14] 2160 3-8-11 **69** ........ PaulMulrennan 7 76
(Paul Midgley) *chsd ldrs: rdn to ld ent fnl f: edgd rt: kpt on wl* **9/2**[2]

2306 **2** 2 ¼ **Poppy In The Wind**[16] 2104 5-9-12 **75** ........(v) BenCurtis 1 78+
(Alan Brown) *slowly away: bdly outpcd in rr tl kpt on wl fr over 1f out: wnt 2nd 110yds out: no ch w wnr* **9/2**[2]

4335 **3** 1 ½ **Penny Dreadful**[15] 2124 5-8-12 **61** oh4........(b) DavidAllan 3 59
(Scott Dixon) *led: rdn over 1f out: hdd ent fnl f: no ex* **11/2**[3]

0-40 **4** ½ **Rose Eclair**[15] 2124 4-9-6 **69** ........(b) JasonHart 4 65
(Tim Easterby) *hld up: rdn along 3f out: kpt on ins fnl f: nvr threatened* **13/2**

03-1 **5** 1 ¾ **Ocelot**[11] 2280 3-8-9 **67** ........ LukeMorris 5 53
(Robert Cowell) *chsd ldrs: rdn 1/2-way: wknd ins fnl f* **5/2**[1]

520- **6** 1 ¼ **My Cherry Blossom**[211] 7313 3-8-0 **61** oh1........ RachelRichardson(3) 2 42
(Tim Easterby) *chsd ldrs: rdn 1/2-way: wknd fnl f* **14/1**

131- **7** 2 **Broadhaven Honey (IRE)**[215] 7217 3-9-4 **76** ........ AndrewMullen 9 50
(Tony Carroll) *prom: rdn 1/2-way: wknd over 1f out* **10/1**

060- **8** 14 **Birdcage**[231] 6770 4-9-9 **75** ........ AdamMcNamara(3) 6 2
(Patrick Morris) *slowly away: hld up: rdn 3f out: wknd and bhd fnl 2f* **40/1**

58.82s (-0.78) **Going Correction** -0.05s/f (Good)
**WFA** 3 from 4yo+ 9lb **8** Ran SP% **111.8**
Speed ratings (Par 100): **104,100,98,97,94 92,89,66**
CSF £23.87 CT £111.84 TOTE £6.20: £2.10, £1.60, £1.80; EX 25.40 Trifecta £111.00.
**Owner** Taylor's Bloodstock Ltd **Bred** Yasmeena Partnership **Trained** Westow, N Yorks

**FOCUS**
Probably no more than a ordinary fillies' sprint handicap for the grade.

## 2632 JW 4X4 NORTHALLERTON MAIDEN STKS 7f 218y
**8:15** (8:19) (Class 5) 3-Y-0+ **£3,881** (£1,155; £577; £288) **Stalls** Low

Form RPR

4 **1** **Afaak**[25] 1862 3-9-1 0 ........ DaneO'Neill 2 81+
(Charles Hills) *trckd ldr: rdn along and briefly outpcd in 3rd over 3f out: clsd 2f out: led 1f out: kpt on* **8/15**[1]

**2** 2 ½ **Tribal Conquest (IRE)** 3-9-1 0 ........ MartinLane 8 75
(Charlie Appleby) *slowly away: sn trckd ldr: pushed along to ld over 1f out: hdd 1f out: rdn and one pce* **11/4**[2]

**3** 1 ¾ **Tinker Tailor (IRE)** 4-9-9 0 ........(t[1]) PaulMulrennan 9 69
(Denis Quinn) *slowly away: sn midfield: pushed along over 2f out: kpt on wl: wnt 3rd ins fnl f* **33/1**

3- **4** 3 ¼ **Different Journey**[312] 3981 4-9-7 0 ........ RyanTimby(7) 12 66
(Michael Easterby) *led: pushed along and brielfy clr over 2f out: hdd over 1f out: wknd fnl f* **14/1**

6 **5** 1 ¼ **Competition**[21] 1984 5-10-0 0........(t) JamesSullivan 13 63
(Brian Rothwell) *hld up: pushed along and sme late hdwy: nvr threatened* **50/1**

4 **6** 2 **Triangulate**[26] 1830 5-10-0 0 ........ PJMcDonald 6 58
(Micky Hammond) *midfield: pushed along over 2f out: no imp* **18/1**

5- **7** 5 **Sir Runs A Lot**[452] 600 5-10-0 0 ........ PhillipMakin 4 46
(David Barron) *hld up: pushed along over 2f out: nvr threatened* **10/1**[3]

45 **8** 8 **Last Chance Paddy (USA)**[6] 2429 3-9-1 0 ........ NeilFarley 7 24
(Alan Swinbank) *a towards rr* **16/1**

6 **9** 4 ½ **High Shaw**[16] 2110 3-9-1 0 ........ ShaneGray 1 13
(Ann Duffield) *a towards rr* **50/1**

1m 41.55s (1.45) **Going Correction** +0.275s/f (Good)
**WFA** 3 from 4yo+ 13lb **9** Ran SP% **125.7**
Speed ratings (Par 103): **103,100,98,95,94 92,87,79,74**
CSF £2.54 TOTE £1.50: £1.10, £1.30, £5.70; EX 3.00 Trifecta £62.70.
**Owner** Hamdan Al Maktoum **Bred** Shadwell Estate Company Limited **Trained** Lambourn, Berks

**FOCUS**
The alignment of the rail on the bend added 30 yards to the official distance. Not a strong maiden but the market spoke with the two well-backed Newmarket raiders coming clear. The level is a bit fluid.

## 2633 THIRSK RACECOURSE - THE PERFECT WEDDING VENUE H'CAP 6f
**8:45** (8:48) (Class 6) (0-60,61) 4-Y-0+ **£3,234** (£962; £481; £240) **Stalls** High

Form RPR

3-42 **1** **The Armed Man**[17] 2076 4-8-13 **59** ........ PaulaMuir(7) 20 68
(Chris Fairhurst) *prom towards stands' side: pushed along to ld appr fnl f: edgd lft towards far rail: kpt on* **8/1**

2001 **2** 1 ½ **Kyllach Me (IRE)**[21] 1978 5-9-5 **58** ........(v) ConnorBeasley 4 63
(Bryan Smart) *prom towards far side: rdn over 2f out: kpt on* **7/1**[3]

5653 **3** ½ **Cool Strutter (IRE)**[13] 2179 5-9-4 **57** ........ SamJames 18 60
(Karen Tutty) *hld up towards stands' side: rdn and hdwy over 1f out: kpt on fnl f* **10/1**

0-23 **4** *nse* **Our Place In Loule**[5] 2454 4-8-11 **50** ........ PJMcDonald 1 53
(Noel Wilson) *dwlt: sn chsd ldrs towards far side: rdn 2f out: kpt on* **9/2**[2]

-005 **5** 1 ¾ **Dark Confidant (IRE)**[17] 2082 4-9-1 **61** ........ ConnorMurtagh(7) 6 59
(Richard Fahey) *in tch centre: rdn over 2f out: kpt on same pce* **20/1**

34-6 **6** ¾ **Young Tiger**[21] 1978 4-9-4 **57** ........ AndrewMullen 12 52
(Tom Tate) *racd towards stands' side: led: rdn and edgd lft 2f out: hdd appr fnl f: sltly hmpd ins fnl f: wknd fnl 110yds* **9/1**

0-40 **7** 1 ½ **Gaelic Wizard (IRE)**[19] 2034 9-9-2 **60** ........(v) GemmaTutty(5) 8 51
(Karen Tutty) *midfield centre: rdn over 2f out: one pce* **16/1**

60-0 **8** *hd* **Whipphound**[128] 80 9-9-2 **55** ........(p) JackGarritty 3 45
(Ruth Carr) *hld up in tch towards far side: pushed along over 2f out: rdn over 1f out: nvr threatened* **33/1**

00-5 **9** *nk* **Perfect Words (IRE)**[5] 2454 7-9-7 **60** ........ DanielTudhope 14 49
(Marjorie Fife) *chsd ldrs towards stands' side: rdn over 2f out: grad wknd over 1f out* **11/1**

2-40 **10** 3 **Someone Exciting**[14] 2140 4-9-3 **61** ........ CallumRodriguez(5) 10 41
(David Thompson) *dwlt: sn midfield centre: rdn over 2f out: wknd fnl f* **4/1**[1]

41-6 **11** 1 ¾ **Chip Or Pellet**[21] 1965 4-8-10 **49** ........ TomEaves 11 24
(Nigel Tinkler) *chsd ldrs towards stands' side: rdn over 2f out: wknd over 1f out* **16/1**

-054 **12** 1 **Dalalah**[10] 2306 4-8-8 **47** ........(v) JasonHart 9 19
(Richard Guest) *midfield centre: rdn 1/2-way: wknd over 1f out* **20/1**

4425 **13** 2 **Pick Of Any (IRE)**[18] 2063 4-9-2 **55** ........(h) LukeMorris 15 21
(David Loughnane) *a towards rr* **16/1**

-000 **14** 2 **Hab Reeh**[21] 1978 9-8-7 **46** oh1........(p) JamesSullivan 2 6
(Ruth Carr) *chsd ldrs far side: rdn over 2f out: wknd* **33/1**

40-0 **15** ½ **Cookie Ring (IRE)**[15] 2120 6-8-13 **52** ........(p[1]) DougieCostello 17 11
(Patrick Holmes) *dwlt: a towards rr* **40/1**

004- **16** 4 **Mercers Row**[186] 7860 10-9-5 **58** ........ JoeDoyle 19 5
(Michael Herrington) *a towards rr* **40/1**

0566 **17** 2 ½ **Rojina (IRE)**[11] 2278 4-8-0 **46** oh1........ GeorgiaDobie(7) 7
(Lisa Williamson) *chsd ldrs centre: rdn over 2f out: wknd* **66/1**

06-6 **18** 4 ½ **Kingfisher Girl**[114] 309 4-8-7 **46** oh1........(p) RoystonFfrench 5
(Michael Appleby) *in tch towards far side: rdn and lost pl over 3f out: sn bhd* **50/1**

1m 12.58s (-0.12) **Going Correction** -0.05s/f (Good) **18** Ran SP% **130.6**
Speed ratings (Par 101): **98,96,95,95,92 91,89,89,89,85 82,81,78,76,75 70,66,60**
CSF £61.69 CT £607.93 TOTE £10.20: £2.30, £2.60, £3.20, £1.40; EX 82.30 Trifecta £892.90.
**Owner** Mrs C A Arnold **Bred** C W Fairhurst **Trained** Middleham, N Yorks
■ Stewards' Enquiry : Paula Muir caution: guilty of careless riding

**FOCUS**
A big field for this modest sprint handicap and they mainly came up the centre, with the winner drifting from one side of the track to the other. Fair form for the grade.
T/Plt: £71.70 to a £1 stake. Pool: £61,775.69 - 628.38 winning units T/Qpdt: £16.60 to a £1 stake. Pool: £5,481.68 - 244.03 winning units **Andrew Sheret**

2634 - 2636a (Foreign Racing) - See Raceform Interactive

# CURRAGH (R-H)
Saturday, May 13

**OFFICIAL GOING: Good (good to yielding in places on the straight course)**

## 2637a IRISH STALLION FARMS EBF BLUE WIND STKS (GROUP 3) (F&M) 1m 2f
**3:55** (3:59) 3-Y-0+
**£37,820** (£12,179; £5,769; £2,564; £1,282; £641)

RPR

**1** **Turret Rocks (IRE)**[13] 2190 4-9-9 104 ........ KevinManning 6 106+
(J S Bolger, Ire) *chsd ldrs in 4th: pushed along over 2f out: gd hdwy to press ldrs in 3rd ent fnl f: kpt on wl to ld fnl 50yds* **6/1**[3]

**2** ¾ **Laganore (IRE)**[13] 2190 5-9-9 109 ........ PatSmullen 5 104+
(A J Martin, Ire) *racd in mid-div: clsr to chse ldrs 2f out: on terms ent fnl f and led fnl 100yds: strly pressed and hdd fnl 50yds* **7/4**[1]

**3** 1 **Creggs Pipes (IRE)**[13] 2190 5-9-9 105 ........ WJLee 2 102
(Andrew Slattery, Ire) *led: strly pressed ent fnl f: hdd fnl 100yds: no ex w principals clsng stages* **7/1**

**4** 1 ¾ **Beautiful Morning**[13] 2190 4-9-9 102 ........ ColmO'Donoghue 7 99+
(Mrs John Harrington, Ire) *bit slowly away and racd towards rr: rdn 3f out: prog ent fnl f in 6th: styd on strly into 4th clsng stages: nrst fin* **9/2**[2]

**5** ½ **Key To My Heart (IRE)**[20] 1998 3-8-9 90 ........(b) AnaO'Brien 9 98
(A P O'Brien, Ire) *trckd ldr in 2nd: rdn and nt qckn in 4th ent fnl f: sn one pce and dropped to 5th cl home* **12/1**

**6** 3 **Butterflies (IRE)**[20] 1998 3-8-9 96 ........ MichaelHussey 4 92
(A P O'Brien, Ire) *chsd ldrs in 3rd: rdn and nt qckn under 2f out in 5th: dropped to 6th ins fnl f* **14/1**

**7** 6 ½ **Flying Fairies (IRE)**[38] 1568 4-9-9 98 ........ DeclanMcDonogh 8 79
(John M Oxx, Ire) *checked leaving stalls: racd in mid-div: rdn and no imp over 2f out: sn one pce* **8/1**

**8** 13 **Cirin Toinne (IRE)**[48] 1387 4-9-9 94 ........(t[1]) RonanWhelan 1 53
(J S Bolger, Ire) *racd in rr of mid-div: t.k.h: rdn 3f out: no imp and detached 2f out: eased* **25/1**

**9** 33 **Chilli Spice (IRE)**[13] 2190 4-9-9 85 ........ ConnorKing 3
(J P Murtagh, Ire) *slowly away: racd in rr thrght: nvr a factor: eased under 2f out* **50/1**

2m 8.58s (-0.72) **Going Correction** +0.225s/f (Good)
**WFA** 3 from 4yo+ 15lb **9** Ran SP% **112.6**
Speed ratings: **111,110,109,108,107 105,100,89,63**
CSF £16.36 TOTE £6.20: £1.50, £1.20, £2.40; DF 18.10 Trifecta £106.90.
**Owner** Mrs June Judd **Bred** J S Bolger **Trained** Coolcullen, Co Carlow

**FOCUS**
A group three which amongst others things, threw up a rematch of the second-fourth-fifth and sixth from a Listed affair at Gowran thirteen days earlier, and they raced on genuinely good ground on the round course, which came into use for the time during the afternoon.

2638 - 2640a (Foreign Racing) - See Raceform Interactive

# BELMONT PARK (L-H)

Saturday, May 13

**OFFICIAL GOING: Dirt: sloppy (sealed), turf: yielding**

## 2641a MAN O' WAR STKS (GRADE 1) (4YO+) (TURF) 1m 3f (T)

10:13 4-Y-0+ £195,121 (£65,040; £32,520; £16,260; £9,756)

RPR

1 **Zhukova (IRE)**[28] 1808 5-8-2 0 ow2 JohnRVelazquez 4 115+
(D K Weld, Ire) *trckd ldr: rdn to ld early in st: styd on strly and forged clr: easily* 9/10[1]

2 6 **Tagh1eeb (USA)**[42] 6-8-9 0 (b) JoseLOrtiz 5 111
(Michael J Maker, U.S.A) *in tch: rdn 3f out: kpt on and jst hld 2nd: no ch w wnr* 102/10

3 nse **Sadler's Joy (USA)**[42] 4-8-5 0 JulienRLeparoux 1 107+
(Thomas Albertrani, U.S.A) *hld up in tch on inner: had to wait for run early in st: rdn 2f out: angled out and kpt on fnl f: jst missed 2nd: no ch w wnr* 7/2[3]

4 3/4 **Charming Kitten (USA)**[21] 7-8-3 0 (b) IradOrtizJr 2 104
(Michael J Maker, U.S.A) *led: rdn and hdd early in st: no ex w wnr after: lost 3rd cl home* 91/10

5 6 1/2 **Wake Forest (GER)**[70] 7-8-9 0 JavierCastellano 3 98
(Chad C Brown, U.S.A) *hld up in tch: rdn into st: sn outpcd and btn: wknd* 27/10[2]

2m 25.31s (10.26) **5** Ran SP% **120.7**

PARI-MUTUEL (all including 2 usd stake): WIN 3.80; PLACE (1-2) 3.40, 6.10; SHOW (1-2-3) 2.40, 3.60, 3.00; SF 28.20.

**Owner** John D Murrell **Bred** Mrs C L Weld **Trained** Curragh, Co Kildare

# 1077 DEAUVILLE (R-H)

Saturday, May 13

**OFFICIAL GOING: Turf: very soft; polytrack: standard**

## 2642a PRIX RMC (CLAIMER) (2YO) (TURF) 5f

12:35 2-Y-0 £11,538 (£4,615; £3,461; £2,307; £1,153)

RPR

1 **Lamchope (FR)**[25] 2-8-8 0 (p) MaximeGuyon 1 77
(C Escuder, France) 13/5[2]

2 3 **So Sora (FR)**[18] 2073 2-8-11 0 StephanePasquier 4 70
(P Adda, France) 23/10[1]

3 2 1/2 **Jurisprudance (FR)**[10] 2321 2-8-11 0 (p) MickaelBarzalona 7 61
(M Boutin, France) 67/10

4 1 1/4 **Quick Skips Lad (IRE)**[18] 2073 2-8-13 0 ow2(p) ChristopheSoumillon 2 58
(J S Moore) *racd in fnl pair: shkn up and clsd wl over 1 1/2f out: chsd ldng trio into fnl f: kpt on at one pce: nvr on terms* 77/10

5 2 1/2 **Some Nights (FR)**[7] 2-9-1 0 (b) AntoineHamelin 8 51
(Matthieu Palussiere, France) 56/10[3]

6 1 **Uchronique (FR)**[51] 1335 2-9-1 0 AlexisBadel 3 47
(M Boutin, France) 112/10

7 hd **Jasmine A La Plage (FR)**[14] 2-8-8 0 EddyHardouin 6 40
(Matthieu Palussiere, France) 154/10

8 4 1/2 **Sorina (GER)** 2-8-11 0 TheoBachelot 5 26
(Henk Grewe, Germany) 146/10

59.37s (1.87) **8** Ran SP% **118.4**

PARI-MUTUEL (all including 1 euro stake): WIN 3.60 PLACE 1.30, 1.30, 1.80 DF 3.90 SF 9.50.

**Owner** Patrick Dreux **Bred** A Chopard **Trained** France

## 2643a PRIX DE SAINT-GEORGES (GROUP 3) (3YO+) (TURF) 5f

2:35 3-Y-0+ £34,188 (£13,675; £10,256; £6,837; £3,418)

RPR

1 **Signs Of Blessing (IRE)**[153] 8330 6-9-11 0 StephanePasquier 3 123
(F Rohaut, France) *mde all: travelled strly: drvn and r.o fnl f: readily* 4/1[2]

2 2 **Profitable (IRE)**[223] 6990 5-9-0 0 JamesDoyle 8 105
(Clive Cox) *chsd ldr on outer in 2nd and drvn over 1 1/2f out: styd on at same pce fnl f: nvr on terms w wnr* 13/8[1]

3 3/4 **Finsbury Square (IRE)**[49] 1376 5-9-6 0 (b) ChristopheSoumillon 6 108
(F Chappet, France) *settled in fnl trio: tk clsr order 1 1/2f out: drvn and styd on fnl f: nvr trbld ldrs* 5/1[3]

4 nk **Son Cesio (FR)**[223] 6990 6-9-0 0 Pierre-CharlesBoudot 5 101
(H-A Pantall, France) *chsd ldr: rdn and no imp 1 1/2f out: one pce fnl f* 11/2

5 3/4 **Rangali**[44] 1461 6-9-0 0 (b) MickaelBarzalona 10 98
(D Guillemin, France) *stdd leaving stalls: w.w in rr: styd on fr over 1f out: nvr in contention* 10/1

6 2 1/2 **Largent Du Bonheur (FR)**[18] 2075 4-9-0 0 VincentCheminaud 4 89
(M Delzangles, France) *racd in midfield: 5th and niggled along 1 1/2f out: no imp: rdn and btn fnl f* 25/1

7 3 **Love Spirit**[44] 1461 7-9-0 0 MaximeGuyon 7 78
(Louis Baudron, France) *settled in midfield: rdn and nt qckn wl over 1 1/2f out: sn wknd* 12/1

8 nk **Eskimo Point (IRE)**[18] 2075 5-9-0 0 TonyPiccone 1 77
(Mario Hofer, Germany) *chsd ldr on inner: outpcd and drvn wl over 1 1/2f out: wknd fnl f* 25/1

9 8 **City Money (IRE)**[18] 2075 5-9-0 0 OlivierPeslier 2 49
(M Delcher Sanchez, France) *w.w in fnl trio: scrubbed along over 2f out: sn bhd* 12/1

57.34s (-0.16) **9** Ran SP% **122.3**

PARI-MUTUEL (all including 1 euro stake): WIN 4.70 PLACE 1.50, 1.40, 1.60 DF 6.90 SF 15.00.

**Owner** Mme Isabelle Corbani **Bred** S Boucheron **Trained** Sauvagnon, France

**FOCUS**

A smart performance from the winner. The third and fifth help set the standard.

## 2644a ABU DHABI POULE D'ESSAI DES POULICHES (GROUP 1) (3YO FILLIES) (STRAIGHT) (TURF) 1m (R)

3:15 3-Y-0 £244,188 (£97,692; £48,846; £24,401; £12,222)

RPR

1 **Precieuse (IRE)**[34] 1660 3-9-0 0 OlivierPeslier 3 113
(F Chappet, France) *chsd ldrs nr side: gd prog 1 1/2f out: r.o u.p to ld fnl 125yds: drifted rt: drvn out* 33/1

2 1 3/4 **Sea Of Grace (IRE)**[24] 1883 3-9-0 0 ChristopheSoumillon 11 109
(William Haggas) *w.w towards rr in centre: hdwy on outer 2 1/2f out: led ent fnl f: hdd 125yds out: styd on but nt pce of wnr* 6/1[3]

3 3/4 **Heuristique (IRE)**[55] 1270 3-9-0 0 Pierre-CharlesBoudot 18 107
(F-H Graffard, France) *towards rr in centre: midfield whn gps merged bef 1/2-way: clsd to chse front rnk 2f out: n.m.r tl drvn between horses 1 1/2f out: styd on u.p fnl f: nt pce to chal* 22/1

4 snk **Wajnah (FR)**[69] 3-9-0 0 GregoryBenoist 5 107
(F Rohaut, France) *a cl up towards nr side: drvn wl over 2f out: styd on fnl f: could nvr muster pce to get on terms* 14/1

5 1 1/4 **Rain Goddess (IRE)**[21] 1958 3-9-0 0 WayneLordan 7 104
(A P O'Brien, Ire) *prom towards nr side: pushed along under 2f out but nt qckn: rdn 1 1/2f out: styd on fnl f: tk 5th post: nvr trbld ldrs* 14/1

6 nse **Roly Poly (USA)**[24] 1883 3-9-0 0 (p) DonnachaO'Brien 16 104
(A P O'Brien, Ire) *midfield in centre: wl in tch 3f out: rdn to press ldrs under 2f out: led 1 1/2f out: hdd ent fnl f: no ex: lost 5th post* 18/1

7 3/4 **Via Ravenna (IRE)**[33] 1690 3-9-0 0 VincentCheminaud 2 102
(A Fabre, France) *midfield nr side: hdwy and followed eventual wnr 1 1/2f out: outpcd and rdn over 1f out: kpt on at same pce fnl f* 7/2[2]

8 1 3/4 **Cristal Fizz (IRE)**[203] 7547 3-9-0 0 GeraldMosse 8 98
(William Haggas) *towards rr in centre: drvn and nt clr run wl over 2f out: swtchd stands' side and hrd rdn 1 1/2f out: styd on fnl f: nvr nrr* 16/1

9 hd **Gokena (FR)**[14] 2170 3-9-0 0 JulienAuge 9 98
(P Sogorb, France) *towards rr: clsd into midfield over 2f out: sn rdn and no imp: wl hld fnl f* 66/1

10 1 3/4 **Thais (FR)**[33] 1690 3-9-0 0 MaximeGuyon 17 94
(P Bary, France) *cl up in centre: 3rd and ev ch appr 2f out: sn rdn and nt qckn: wknd ins fnl f* 28/1

11 1/2 **Senga (USA)**[27] 1825 3-9-0 0 StephanePasquier 14 93
(P Bary, France) *prom in centre: drvn to chse ldrs over 2f out: sn rdn: wknd fnl f* 10/3[1]

12 4 **Asidious Alexander (IRE)**[218] 7114 3-9-0 0 ....(b[1]) MickaelBarzalona 12 83
(Simon Crisford) *midfield in centre: n.m.r and bmpd 2 1/2f out: rdn and no imp 1 1/2f out: sn wknd: wl hld fnl f* 40/1

13 3/4 **Amaani (FR)**[55] 3-9-0 0 TonyPiccone 10 82
(G E Mikhalides, France) *led nr side gp of ten: gps merged after 3f and disp ld: drvn and hdd wl over 2f out: sn wknd* 80/1

14 3/4 **Toulifaut (IRE)**[27] 1825 3-9-0 0 CristianDemuro 4 80
(J-C Rouget, France) *missed break: in rr: prog into midfield over 2f out: rdn and btn ins fnl 1 1/2f: wl hld whn eased ins fnl f* 12/1

15 3 **Charm Appeal (FR)**[7] 2421 3-9-0 0 AlexisBadel 15 73
(H-F Devin, France) *led centre gp of eight: disp ld whn gps merged after 3f: hdd 1 1/2f out: wknd* 22/1

16 3 1/2 **Delectation**[26] 1846 3-9-0 0 EduardoPedroza 6 65
(A Wohler, Germany) *towards rr early: in midfield bef 1/2-way: rdn and n.m.r 2f out: sn btn: eased ins fnl f* 13/2

17 2 **Festive (FR)**[25] 3-9-0 0 (p) TheoBachelot 13 60
(Eric Saint-Martin, France) *chsd ldrs centre gp: rdn and wknd 2f out* 80/1

18 7 **Smoulder**[3] 2532 3-9-0 0 PBBeggy 1 44
(A P O'Brien, Ire) *a towards rr: rdn and lost tch over 2f out: sn wl bhd* 40/1

1m 37.69s (-3.11) **18** Ran SP% **129.0**

PARI-MUTUEL (all including 1 euro stake): WIN 29.00 PLACE 7.00, 3.50, 4.90 DF 146.50 SF 360.20.

**Owner** Mme Anne-Marie Hayes **Bred** Knocktoran Stud **Trained** France

**FOCUS**

An extremely well subscribed edition of the French 1000 Guineas, with some strength in depth. The runners merged mid-track from halfway and the form is best rated around the fourth. The third, fourth and fifth have been rated to the better view of their form, with the ninth to her best.

2645 - 2655a (Foreign Racing) - See Raceform Interactive

# 2634 CURRAGH (R-H)

Sunday, May 14

**OFFICIAL GOING: Good (good to yielding in places on the straight course)**

## 2656a PG DUFFY & SONS CITROEN H'CAP 5f

2:25 (2:25) (45-75,75) 3-Y-0+ £5,791 (£1,795; £855; £385; £150)

RPR

1 **Gopsies Daughter (IRE)**[2] 2602 6-8-4 **51** oh3 MartinDwyer 6 57
(Denis Gerard Hogan, Ire) *mid-div: hdwy far side fr under 2f out: rdn to ld narrowly ins fnl f where edgd sltly lft: kpt on wl clsng stages where strly pressed to jst hold on: all out* 16/1

2 nse **Palavicini Run (IRE)**[8] 2410 4-9-7 **73** (b) DonaghO'Connor(5) 14 79
(J F Levins, Ire) *mid-div: rdn after 1/2-way and hdwy over 1f out where swtchd rt: r.o wl to chal ins fnl f where sltly impeded: kpt on wl in 2nd clsng stages: jst failed* 20/1

3 3/4 **A Few Dollars More (IRE)**[13] 2239 5-10-0 **75** (b) DeclanMcDonogh 17 78
(Andrew Slattery, Ire) *pushed along early to chse ldrs: effrt under 2f out: no imp on ldrs wl ins fnl f: kpt on same pce* 9/2[1]

4 1/2 **Blairmayne (IRE)**[13] 2239 4-10-0 **75** ShaneFoley 11 77
(Miss Natalia Lupini, Ire) *mid-div: 9th bef 1/2-way: rdn after 1/2-way and clsd u.p nr side ins fnl f: nrst fin* 8/1

5 nk **Accalia (IRE)**[217] 7192 4-10-0 **75** (v) ColinKeane 10 75
(J C Hayden, Ire) *chsd ldrs: rdn to ld briefly over 1f out: hdd ins fnl f and no ex clsng stages* 7/1[3]

6 hd **Pillar**[2] 2602 4-8-10 **57** RonanWhelan 1 57
(Adrian McGuinness, Ire) *hld up towards rr: swtchd rt 1 1/2f out and sme late hdwy far side fr over 1f out: swtchd lft wl ins fnl f and kpt on wl clsng stages: nvr nrr* 12/1

7 nk **Fast Kar (IRE)**[23] 1955 3-7-11 **60** oh10 AndrewBreslin(7) 5 55
(Barry John Murphy, Ire) *in rr of mid-div: hdwy after 1/2-way to chse ldrs wl ins fnl f: kpt on same pce clsng stages: nvr nrr* 40/1

8 1 **Sweetest Taboo (IRE)**[13] 2239 6-9-0 **61** (h) WJLee 2 56
(W McCreery, Ire) *hld up towards rr: prog after 1/2-way: kpt on u.p far side ins fnl f: nvr nrr* 11/2[2]

9 *hd* **Molans Mare (IRE)**[20] 2047 7-7-11 **51** oh6................. DamienMelia(7) 3 45
(Keith Henry Clarke, Ire) *hld up towards rr: sme late hdwy fr over 1f out. nvr nrr* **25/1**
10 *shd* **Rattling Jewel**[13] 2239 5-9-12 **73**................................ WayneLordan 18 67
(Miss Nicole McKenna, Ire) *in rr of mid-div: kpt on one pce ins fnl f: nvr nrr* **11/1**
11 *hd* **Piazzini (IRE)**[21] 1996 4-8-13 **65**................................ MarkFlanagan(5) 21 58
(Gerard Keane, Ire) *sn led narrowly nr side: rdn 2f out and jnd: hdd over 1f out: wknd* **33/1**
12 *hd* **One Boy (IRE)**[10] 2341 6-9-13 **74**........................................ PatSmullen 4 67
(Paul Midgley) *chsd ldrs far side: rdn under 2f out and no ex ent fnl f: wknd* **10/1**
13 *1* **Battleroftheboyne (IRE)**[32] 1740 8-8-10 **60**................ GaryHalpin(3) 19 49
(Eamonn O'Connell, Ire) *hld up in tch nr side: rdn under 2f out and sn no ex: one pce ins fnl f* **14/1**
14 *3/4* **Strategic Force (IRE)**[13] 2239 6-10-0 **75**...................(bt) NGMcCullagh 8 61
(Gerard O'Leary, Ire) *in tch far side: rdn under 2f out and sn no ex: wknd ins fnl f* **20/1**
15 *2* **Dewpoint (IRE)**[21] 1996 3-8-6 **62**................................ MichaelHussey 7 37
(Patrick Tallis, Ire) *s.i.s and in rr early: tk clsr order towards rr bef 1/2-way: kpt on one pce fnl 2f: nvr a factor* **33/1**
16 *shd* **Jenniechild (IRE)**[233] 6754 4-9-6 **67**................................ ChrisHayes 12 46
(Peter Fahey, Ire) *chsd ldrs: 5th 1/2-way: rdn under 2f out and sn no ex: wknd fnl f* **14/1**
17 *1/2* **Times In Anatefka (IRE)**[88] 742 7-8-0 **52**.........(tp) KillianLeonard(5) 20 29
(Adrian Brendan Joyce, Ire) *prom tl sn settled bhd ldr: rdn after 1/2-way and sn wknd* **20/1**
18 *2 1/2* **Idlers Dream (IRE)**[20] 2047 4-7-13 **56**................. ScottMcCullagh(10) 13 24
(Damian Joseph English, Ire) *mid-div: rdn and wknd fr 1/2-way* **40/1**
19 *3 1/2* **Blue Bounty**[29] 1812 6-7-11 **51** oh5................................ SeanDavis(7) 9 6
(J H Culloty, Ire) *dwlt sltly: pushed along to sn chse ldrs: pushed along in 6th bef 1/2-way and no ex u.p under 2f out: wknd and eased ins fnl f* **25/1**
20 *24* **Dunleer (IRE)**[128] 103 3-8-4 **60** oh15................................ RoryCleary 15
(Donal Kinsella, Ire) *in tch: 8th bef 1/2-way: rdn and wknd after 1/2-way: eased in rr 1 1/2f out* **50/1**

1m 1.98s (-0.92) **Going Correction** -0.075s/f (Good)
**WFA** 3 from 4yo+ 9lb **20** Ran SP% **136.2**
Speed ratings: **104,103,102,101,101 101,100,99,98,98 98,97,96,95,91 91,90,86,81,42**
CSF £321.17 CT £1746.48 TOTE £25.80: £3.90, £5.50, £1.60, £2.30; DF 679.10 Trifecta £3963.60.
**Owner** W G Reardon **Bred** William Reardon **Trained** Cloughjordan, Co Tipperary

**FOCUS**
A competitive sprint handicap which presented tangled form-lines and produced a very tight finish. Four of the first five (the exception being the winner) were drawn high. The runner-up has been rated to the best view of her form, with the third and fourth to their latest.

## 2657a SOLE POWER SPRINT STKS (LISTED RACE) 5f
**2:55** (2:56) 4-Y-O+
**£25,213** (£8,119; £3,846; £1,709; £854; £427)

RPR
1 **Acapulco (USA)**[190] 7829 4-9-0 107........................(t[1]) DonnachaO'Brien 6 107+
(A P O'Brien, Ire) *chsd ldrs: hdwy in 4th under 2f out to chal over 1f out: rdn to ld ins fnl f and kpt on wl clsng stages: readily* **11/8**[1]
2 *1/2* **Ardhoomey (IRE)**[20] 2046 5-9-10 112................................(t) ColinKeane 7 114+
(G M Lyons, Ire) *hooded to load: w.w towards rr: gng wl after 1/2-way: pushed along over 1f out where nt clr run briefly: r.o wl ins fnl f into 2nd cl home: nt trble wnr* **7/2**[2]
3 *1/2* **Willytheconqueror (IRE)**[30] 1765 4-9-5 104................. MartinDwyer 11 107
(William Muir) *chsd ldrs nr side: rdn 1 1/2f out and no imp on wnr disputing 2nd wl ins fnl f: kpt on same pce in 3rd clsng stages* **12/1**
4 *1* **Spirit Quartz (IRE)**[20] 2046 9-9-8 103................................ ChrisHayes 2 107
(Barry John Murphy, Ire) *chsd ldrs: pushed along under 2f out: sn rdn and n.m.r between horses disputing 2nd briefly ins fnl f: no ex clsng stages where dropped to 4th* **33/1**
5 *hd* **Ostatnia (IRE)**[23] 1936 5-9-0 90................................................(v) WJLee 3 98
(W McCreery, Ire) *broke wl to ld briefly tl sn hdd and settled bhd ldr: rdn in 2nd over 1f out and sn no ex: one pce ins fnl f where dropped to 5th* **20/1**
6 *1 1/4* **Sir Robert Cheval**[23] 1946 6-9-5 101........................... AdamBeschizza 5 99
(Robert Cowell) *s.i.s and pushed along in rr early: tk clsr order in 8th bef 1/2-way: rdn under 2f out and sme hdwy to chse ldrs: swtchd lft over 1f out and sn no ex in 5th: one pce ins fnl f* **10/1**
7 *1 1/2* **Monsieur Joe (IRE)**[29] 1800 10-9-5 109............................ PatSmullen 8 93
(Paul Midgley) *chsd ldrs nr side: rdn 2f out and sn no ex: wknd between horses 1f out* **14/1**
8 *nk* **Primo Uomo (IRE)**[20] 2046 5-9-5 104.........................(t) NGMcCullagh 12 92
(Gerard O'Leary, Ire) *dwlt sltly: towards rr thrght: pushed along 2f out and sn no ex: one pce fnl f* **6/1**[3]
9 *shd* **Just Glamorous (IRE)**[8] 2397 4-9-8 110....................... KevinManning 1 95
(Ronald Harris) *sn led: pushed along far side and pressed under 2f out: rdn over 1f out and sn hdd: wknd ins fnl f* **14/1**

1m 0.33s (-2.57) **Going Correction** -0.075s/f (Good) **9** Ran SP% **116.4**
Speed ratings: **117,116,115,113,113 111,109,108,108**
CSF £6.09 TOTE £1.90: £1.02, £1.60, £3.40; DF 6.50 Trifecta £37.80.
**Owner** Mrs John Magnier & Michael Tabor & Derrick Smith **Bred** Dr Charles Giles **Trained** Cashel, Co Tipperary

**FOCUS**
A good race for this level, seeing that the winner was such a high-achieving juvenile in 2015 and that the second was a Group 2 winner last term. These Listed Irish sprint often provide good picking for British raiders, but the home defence was strong in this instance. The standard is set by the third, fourth and fifth.

2658 - 2662a (Foreign Racing) - See Raceform Interactive

# 2244 CAPANNELLE (R-H)
Sunday, May 14
**OFFICIAL GOING: Turf: good**

## 2663a PREMIO DELLA REPUBBLICA - GBI RACING (GROUP 2) (4YO+) (TURF) 1m 1f
**4:25** 4-Y-O+ **£78,632** (£34,598; £18,871; £9,435)

RPR
1 **Time To Choose**[35] 4-9-2 0............................................. FabioBranca 2 109+
(Stefano Botti, Italy) *racd keenly: hld up in fnl pair: clsd over 2f out: sustained run u.p fnl f: led cl home* **6/5**[1]
2 *nk* **Greg Pass (IRE)**[7] 5-9-2 0................................................. DarioVargiu 5 108
(Il Cavallo In Testa, Italy) *trckd ldr: rdn to chal under 2f out: led appr fnl f: styd on gamely: hdd cl home* **9/5**[3]
3 *3 1/2* **Voice Of Love (IRE)**[21] 2004 4-9-2 0............................ AntonioFresu 3 101
(Stefano Botti, Italy) *led: kicked for home over 2 1/2f out: hdd appr fnl f: no ex* **6/5**[1]
4 *6 1/2* **Basileus (IRE)**[21] 2004 4-9-2 0........................................ CarloFiocchi 4 89
(Stefano Botti, Italy) *hld up in rr: drvn 3f out: kpt on at one pce: nvr trbld ldrs* **101/10**
5 *9* **Per Un Dixir (IRE)**[13] 4-9-2 0...................................... SalvatoreSulas 1 76
(Stefano Botti, Italy) *racd keenly: chsd ldng pair: rdn and no imp 2 1/2f out: wknd u.p ins fnl 2f: eased whn wl hld last 200yds* **31/20**[2]

1m 48.2s (-6.50) **5** Ran SP% **174.8**
PARI-MUTUEL (all including 1 euro stake): WIN 2.18 PLACE 2.12, 2.16 DF 9.00.
**Owner** Scuderia Effevi SRL **Bred** Razza Del Velino Srl **Trained** Italy

# 2642 DEAUVILLE (R-H)
Sunday, May 14
**OFFICIAL GOING: Turf: soft; polytrack: standard**

## 2664a PRIX DE MONDOVI (MAIDEN) (2YO) (TURF) 5f
**1:35** 2-Y-O **£11,538** (£4,615; £3,461; £2,307; £1,153)

RPR
1 **Warren (FR)** 2-8-11 0....................................................... TheoBachelot 7 78
(Y Barberot, France) **19/2**
2 *3* **White Feather**[24] 1919 2-9-2 0.................................. MickaelBarzalona 6 72
(Jo Hughes) *w ldrs: sltly outpcd and drvn 2f out: rdn and styd on fnl f: no ch w wnr* **22/5**[3]
3 *1 1/4* **We Ride The World (IRE)**[19] 2-9-2 0.................... ThibaultSpeicher 10 68
(Louis Baudron, France) **127/10**
4 *1/2* **Cristot (FR)** 2-8-11 0...................................................... CristianDemuro 1 61
(J-C Rouget, France) **21/10**[1]
5 *hd* **Zone Regard (IRE)**[24] 1919 2-8-13 0......................... StephanePasquier 2 62
(M Delcher Sanchez, France) **187/10**
6 *1 1/2* **Reboot (IRE)** 2-9-2 0...................................................... AntoineHamelin 8 60
(Matthieu Palussiere, France) **137/10**
7 *3* **Marvellous Night (FR)** 2-8-5 0........................... ClementLecoeuvre(3) 4 41
(H De Nicolay, France) **38/1**
8 *5* **Vanturi (IRE)**[14] 2-9-2 0................................................(b[1]) CesarPasserat 3 31
(J-V Toux, France) **71/1**
9 *3* **French King** 2-8-11 0.......................................... Pierre-CharlesBoudot 9 15
(H-A Pantall, France) **5/2**[2]
10 *3 1/2* **Meran (FR)** 2-8-13 0 ow2.................................... ChristopheSoumillon 5 5
(M Nigge, France) **135/10**

59.43s (1.93) **10** Ran SP% **118.9**
PARI-MUTUEL (all including 1 euro stake): WIN 10.50 PLACE 2.70, 2.10, 3.20 DF 21.30 SF 34.90.

**Owner** Ecurie Des Monnaies & Ecurie Bred To Win Sc **Bred** Gestut Zur Kuste Ag **Trained** France

## 2665a THE GURKHA COOLMORE PRIX SAINT-ALARY (GROUP 1) (3YO FILLIES) (TURF) 1m 2f
**2:35** 3-Y-O **£122,094** (£48,846; £24,423; £12,200; £6,111)

RPR
1 **Sobetsu**[219] 7116 3-9-0 0................................................ WilliamBuick 11 109+
(Charlie Appleby) *trckd ldr on outer: led 2f out: drvn over 1 1/2f out: wnt clr ent fnl f: v readily* **14/1**
2 *3* **Vue Fantastique (FR)**[35] 1657 3-9-0 0............................ OlivierPeslier 1 103
(F Chappet, France) *chsd ldng pair on inner: nt clr run 1 1/2f out: rdn and styd on to go 2nd fnl 125yds: no ch w wnr* **25/1**
3 *1 3/4* **Coronet**[218] 7151 3-9-0 0................................................ FrankieDettori 10 100+
(John Gosden) *w.w in rr: hdwy on outer 2f out: styd on ins fnl f: tk 3rd fnl stride: nvr plcd to chal* **5/2**[1]
4 *shd* **Hebah (IRE)**[35] 1657 3-9-0 0................................. ChristopheSoumillon 7 99+
(J-C Rouget, France) *racd keenly: hld up in midfield on outer: bmpd over 1 1/2f out: drvn and styd on ins fnl f: nvr able to chal* **4/1**[3]
5 *shd* **Gold Luck (FR)**[35] 1657 3-9-0 0.......................................... MaximeGuyon 3 99
(F Head, France) *chsd ldng pair on outer: rdn to chse ldr 1 1/2f out: one pce u.p fnl f* **3/1**[2]
6 *1/2* **Lady Frankel**[28] 1825 3-9-0 0................................ Pierre-CharlesBoudot 6 98
(A Fabre, France) *rrd leaving stalls: racd in midfield on inner: shkn up and effrt appr 1 1/2f out but n.m.r: styd on same pce fnl f* **9/2**
7 *1 3/4* **Body Sculpt (FR)**[7] 3-9-0 0.......................................... GregoryBenoist 9 95
(S Kobayashi, France) *racd in fnl trio: tk clsr order 2f out: nt clr run 1 1/2f out: nvr able to get involved* **50/1**
8 *snk* **Peace In Motion (USA)**[27] 1846 3-9-0 0......................... MarcLerner 4 94
(Waldemar Hickst, Germany) *a towards rr: rdn 2f out but no imp: one pce fnl f* **28/1**
9 *4* **Asking (IRE)**[7] 2441 3-9-0 0................................................(p) RyanMoore 2 88
(A P O'Brien, Ire) *racd in midfield between horses: drvn and no imp 2f out: n.m.r and bmpd over 1 1/2f out: wl hld fnl f* **12/1**
10 *7* **Estelle Ma Belle (FR)**[24] 3-9-0 0........................................ GeraldMosse 8 74
(T Castanheira, France) *led on inner: hdd 2f out: wknd more than 1 1/2f out* **50/1**

11 8 **Monroe Bay (IRE)**[35] 1657 3-9-0 0 VincentCheminaud 5 56
(P Bary, France) *w.w towards rr: lost pl sn after 1/2-way: adrift in last and wl btn fnl 2f* **11/1**

2m 5.92s (-4.28) **11** Ran SP% **125.7**
PARI-MUTUEL (all including 1 euro stake): WIN 21.20 PLACE 5.80, 5.20, 2.30 DF 108.70 SF 290.30.
**Owner** Godolphin **Bred** Darley **Trained** Newmarket, Suffolk

**FOCUS**
This early Group 1 for 3yo fillies looked competitive, but the winner proved a class apart and the second was nicely clear too.

## 2666a ABU DHABI POULE D'ESSAI DES POULAINS (GROUP 1) (3YO COLTS) (STRAIGHT) (TURF) 1m (R)
3:15 3-Y-O £293,025 (£117,230; £58,615; £29,282; £14,666)

RPR
1 **Brametot (IRE)**[28] 1824 3-9-2 0 CristianDemuro 3 118
(J-C Rouget, France) *4th early on in stands' side gp of five: in fnl trio whn gps merged in centre bef 1/2-way: hdwy 2f out: chal appr fnl f: r.o wl u.p: led fnl stride* **4/1**[2]

2 shd **Le Brivido (FR)**[40] 3-9-2 0 Pierre-CharlesBoudot 13 118
(A Fabre, France) *chsd ldrs in centre gp of eight: drvn to cl over 1 1/2f out: led appr fnl f: r.o wl u.p: hdd fnl stride* **16/1**

3 3 **Rivet (IRE)**[24] 1904 3-9-2 0 FrankieDettori 8 111+
(William Haggas) *led gp of eight in centre: hdd appr 1/2-way: sn regained ld: rdn 1 1/2f out: hdd appr fnl f: styd on but no match for front two* **9/2**[3]

4 6 **Spotify (FR)**[28] 1824 3-9-2 0 MaximeGuyon 11 97
(C Ferland, France) *trckd ldr in centre: rowed along but nt qckn over 2f out: sn outpcd by ldrs: kpt on u.p ins fnl f* **25/1**

5 nse **Orderofthegarter (IRE)**[36] 1633 3-9-2 0 SeamieHeffernan 2 97
(A P O'Brien, Ire) *led stands' side gp of five: chsd ldng pair whn gps merged in centre bef 1/2-way: drvn 3f out: a little outpcd whn rdn over 2f out: styd on u.p fnl f* **4/1**[2]

6 nk **Inns Of Court (IRE)**[33] 3-9-2 0 MickaelBarzalona 7 96
(A Fabre, France) *chsd ldrs in centre: led appr 1/2-way: sn hdd: grad dropped away ins fnl 1 1/2f* **10/1**

7 3 **African Ride**[34] 1689 3-9-2 0 OlivierPeslier 5 89
(C Laffon-Parias, France) *chsd ldr stands' side: midfield whn gp merged bef 1/2-way: rdn over 1 1/2f out: one pce u.p fnl f: fdd late on* **33/1**

8 1 3/4 **Mankib**[26] 3-9-2 0 AurelienLemaitre 1 85
(F Head, France) *racd 3rd in stands' side gp: towards rr whn gps merged: rdn and no imp wl over 1 1/2f out: kpt on past btn horses fnl f* **28/1**

9 1 **Kings Gift (IRE)**[22] 1959 3-9-2 0 PaulMulrennan 10 83
(Michael Dods) *towards rr in centre gp: rdn and no hdwy 2f out: wl hld fnl f* **50/1**

10 shd **Peace Envoy (FR)**[13] 2242 3-9-2 0 RyanMoore 6 83
(A P O'Brien, Ire) *in rr centre gp: rdn and no imp 1 1/2f out: bhd fnl f* **11/1**

11 shd **South Seas (IRE)**[30] 1780 3-9-2 0 OisinMurphy 4 83
(Andrew Balding) *settled 5th in stands' side gp: towards rr whn gps merged: nvr able to get involved* **16/1**

12 1/2 **Salsabeel (IRE)**[26] 1859 3-9-2 0 WilliamBuick 12 82
(Charlie Appleby) *cl up in centre gp: drvn to chse ldrs 2f out: sn btn: wknd fnl f* **28/1**

13 12 **National Defense**[34] 1689 3-9-2 0 ChristopheSoumillon 9 54
(Mme C Head-Maarek, France) *racd freely: hld up bhd front rnk centre gp: drvn and lost pl ins last 2f: wknd wl over 1f out* **7/2**[1]

1m 36.82s (-3.98) **13** Ran SP% **125.2**
PARI-MUTUEL (all including 1 euro stake): WIN 6.00 PLACE 2.30, 4.10, 2.50 DF 34.80 SF 35.00.
**Owner** Al Shaqab Racing & Gerard Augustin-Normand **Bred** H Cardemil **Trained** Pau, France

**FOCUS**
As was the case in the previous day's Pouliches, the runners merged mid-track after a couple of furlong and kicked up the turf. The principals had it to themselves from a fair way out and it's form to be positive about.

# HOPPEGARTEN (R-H)
Sunday, May 14

**OFFICIAL GOING: Turf: good**

## 2667a COMER GROUP INTERNATIONAL OLEANDER-RENNEN (GROUP 2) (4YO+) (TURF) 2m
3:50 4-Y-O+ £34,188 (£13,247; £6,837; £3,418; £2,136)

RPR
1 **Red Cardinal (IRE)**[231] 6822 5-9-2 0 EduardoPedroza 11 106+
(A Wohler, Germany) *settled in fnl 3rd: tk clsr order 4f out: 6th and styng on 3f out: rdn to chal 1 1/2f out: led appr fnl f: styd on wl* **16/5**[2]

2 1 1/4 **Nearly Caught (IRE)**[11] 2288 7-9-4 0 AdamKirby 10 107
(Hughie Morrison) *trckd ldr: drvn over 2 1/2f out and styd on: led over 1 1/2f out: hdd appr fnl f: kpt on at same pce* **19/10**[1]

3 nse **San Salvador (GER)**[49] 4-9-2 0 AlexanderPietsch 3 108+
(Andreas Suborics, Germany) *chsd ldrs: 4th and a little outpcd 2 1/2f out: styd on u.p fnl f: jst failed to snatch 2nd* **127/10**

4 2 1/4 **Iraklion (GER)**[28] 5-9-2 0 MichaelCadeddu 14 102
(Christian Sprengel, Germany) *w.w in fnl pair: began to cl over 3f out: styd on u.p: tk 4th cl home: nvr nrr* **247/10**

5 1/2 **Summershine (IRE)**[28] 6-8-13 0 BayarsaikhanGanbat 2 99
(Frau Anna Schleusner-Fruhriep, Germany) *cl up on inner: 3rd and drvn 3f out: styd on at same pce u.p* **114/1**

6 hd **Near England (IRE)**[238] 6610 4-8-13 0 AdriedeVries 7 102
(Markus Klug, Germany) *led: kicked for home 3f out: hdd 1 1/2f out: no ex* **31/5**[3]

7 1 3/4 **Son Macia (GER)**[27] 4-8-13 0 DanielePorcu 9 100
(Andreas Suborics, Germany) *w.w in midfield: 5th and drvn 3f out: styd on at one pce fnl f* **217/10**

8 1 3/4 **Caccini (FR)**[28] 4-9-2 0 TomLukasek 5 101
(Adam Wyrzyk, Poland) *w.w in midfield: rdn and no imp 3f out: one pce* **103/10**

9 1 3/4 **Carpathian (FR)**[44] 1483 4-9-2 0 FilipMinarik 1 99
(Jean-Pierre Carvalho, Germany) *settled towards rr: tk clsr order 3f out: styd on at same pce* **151/10**

10 11 **Apoleon (GER)**[28] 7-9-2 0 BauyrzhanMurzabayev 13 84
(Frau Anna Schleusner-Fruhriep, Germany) *towards rr: rdn and no imp fnl half m: nvr in contention* **49/1**

11 5 **Be Famous (GER)**[44] 1483 5-9-2 0 MickaelBerto 12 78
(Frau S Steinberg, Germany) *hld up in midfield: rdn and wknd fr 2 1/2f out* **77/10**

12 1 3/4 **Seismos (IRE)**[28] 9-9-2 0 IoannisPoullis 16 76
(Henk Grewe, Germany) *sn chsng ldrs: outpcd and rdn along 3 1/2f out: sn wknd* **36/1**

13 6 **Niron (GER)**[28] 8-9-2 0 KevinWoodburn 15 70
(M Mayer, Germany) *w.w in rr: wl hld fr 3f out* **126/1**

14 2 3/4 **Bebe Cherie (FR)**[42] 5-8-13 0 MartinSeidl 4 64
(Markus Klug, Germany) *settled in midfield on inner: wknd u.p fr 3f out* **33/1**

15 3 3/4 **Rock Of Romance (IRE)**[28] 7-9-2 0 StephenHellyn 8 63
(A Wohler, Germany) *chsd ldng gp: rdn and no imp 3f out: sn wknd* **33/1**

16 nk **Fields Of Athenry (IRE)**[245] 6390 5-9-2 0 OliverWilson 6 62
(Flemming Velin, Denmark) *w.w in midfield: rdn and effrt after 1/2-way: sn btn: wknd ins fnl 3f* **51/1**

3m 33.9s
**WFA** 4 from 5yo+ 1lb **16** Ran SP% **128.5**
PARI-MUTUEL (all including 10 euro stake): WIN 42 PLACE: 14, 15, 22, 33; SF: 83.
**Owner** Australian Bloodstock Stable **Bred** Lynch Bages Ltd **Trained** Germany

# 1930 LES LANDES
Sunday, May 14

**OFFICIAL GOING: Good (good to soft in places)**
Wind: Light, across towards viewing area Weather: Fine

## 2669a JT REWARDS H'CAP SPRINT (TURF) 5f 100y
3:05 (3:14) 3-Y-O+ £1,780 (£640; £380)

RPR
1 **Purley Queen (IRE)**[331] 8-9-13 0 AliceMills 51
(Mrs C Gilbert, Jersey) *prom: rdn to chal fr 2f out: led wl ins fnl f: drvn out* **4/1**[3]

2 3/4 **Country Blue (FR)**[27] 1931 8-10-11 0 (p) MattieBatchelor 60
(Mrs A Malzard, Jersey) *broke best: led tl wl ins fnl f: no ex* **6/4**[1]

3 nk **National Service (USA)**[6] 2454 6-9-7 0 (tp) PaddyAspell 41
(Clare Ellam) *broke wl: trckd ldr: drvn and nt clr run 2f out: kpt on one pce* **5/1**

4 1 3/4 **It Must Be Faith**[44] 1475 7-10-12 0 MissSBrotherton 54
(Michael Appleby) *trckd ldrs: 5th into st: kpt on one pce* **15/8**[2]

5 2 1/2 **Ron's Ballad**[27] 1933 4-8-13 0 AndrewElliott 19
(K Kukk, Jersey) *outpcd: last into st: kpt on past btn rivals* **20/1**

6 1 1/2 **Honcho (IRE)**[27] 1932 5-10-5 0 MrFTett 34
(Mrs A Malzard, Jersey) *sn outpcd* **16/1**

7 3 **First Cat**[27] 1931 10-9-0 0 PhilipPrince 5
(K Kukk, Jersey) *outpcd: nvr able to chal* **6/1**

8 7 **My Meteor**[27] 1931 10-10-1 0 ow3 MarkQuinlan
(Natalie Lloyd-Beavis) *broke wl: trckd ldr tl wknd rapidly ent st* **8/1**

9 3 **Spanish Bounty**[258] 12-9-9 0 ow4 VictoriaMalzard
(Mrs A Malzard, Jersey) *s.s: outpcd thrght* **16/1**

**Owner** Manor Farm Racing **Bred** Mark & Pippa Hackett **Trained** Jersey

## 2670a LA VERTE RUE ASSOCIATES 2017 JERSEY GUINEAS (CONDITIONS) (TURF) 1m 100y
3:40 (3:46) 3-Y-O+ £2,380 (£860; £510)

RPR
1 **Black Night (IRE)**[85] 817 5-10-5 0 PhilipPrince 77+
(J Moon, Jersey) *trckd ldrs: shkn up and hdwy 3 wd to ld 3f out: rdn clr fr over 1f out* **2/5**[1]

2 7 **Hard To Handel**[12] 2276 5-10-5 0 (b) PaddyAspell 62
(Clare Ellam) *t.k.h trcking ldrs: kpt on to take 2nd ins fnl f: no ch w wnr* **5/1**[3]

3 3 **Flutterbee**[27] 1932 5-10-2 0 MattieBatchelor 52
(Mrs A Malzard, Jersey) *hld up: 5th into st: kpt on to take 3rd nr fin* **7/2**[2]

4 nse **Princess Kodia (IRE)**[27] 1931 4-10-2 0 MrFTett 52
(Mrs A Malzard, Jersey) *led tl 3f out: wknd ins fnl f* **14/1**

5 3 **Chapeau Bleu (IRE)**[258] 5-10-2 0 AliceMills 45
(Mrs C Gilbert, Jersey) *hld up: nvr able to chal* **12/1**

6 1 1/2 **Gabster (IRE)**[27] 1932 4-10-2 0 MarkQuinlan 42
(K Kukk, Jersey) *trckd ldr tl drvn and weakeed fr over 2f out* **14/1**

7 7 **Mendacious Harpy (IRE)**[27] 1931 6-10-2 0 VictoriaMalzard 27
(Mrs A Malzard, Jersey) *nvr on terms* **10/1**

8 2 1/2 **Benoordenhout (IRE)**[27] 1931 6-10-5 0 AndrewElliott 24
(T Le Brocq, Jersey) *racd wd in mid-div: rdn and struggling fr 4f out* **5/1**[3]

9 8 **Diamond Penny (IRE)**[701] 3219 9-10-5 0 (p) ThomasMarett 6
(Mrs A Corson, Jersey) *mid-div: rdn and wknd fr 3f out* **20/1**

**Owner** Mrs Anne Moon **Bred** Manister House Stud **Trained** St-Martin, Jersey

## 2671a ROCQUETTE CIDER H'CAP (TURF) 1m 4f
4:15 (4:15) 3-Y-O+ £1,460 (£525; £315)

RPR
1 **Aussie Lyrics (FR)**[258] 7-10-10 0 AliceMills 67
(Mrs C Gilbert, Jersey) *trckd ldrs in 4th: smooth hdwy to go 2nd over 3f out: led 2f out: idled in front: pushed out* **3/1**[2]

2 2 **Rainbow Lad (IRE)**[27] 1930 4-10-12 0 MissSBrotherton 66
(Michael Appleby) *trckd ldrs in 3rd: hdwy to ld over 4f out: hdd 2f out: no ex* **4/9**[1]

3 4 **Hawaiian Freeze**[27] 1930 8-9-1 0 RyanWhile 35
(J Moon, Jersey) *hld up: rdn to go mod 3rd wl over 2f out: nvr trbld ldrs* **9/2**[3]

4 7 **Mr Opulence**[27] 1930 8-9-5 0 AndrewElliott 27
(T Le Brocq, Jersey) *hld up: drvn along fr over 3f out: last into st: nvr able to chal* **6/1**

5 15 **Frivolous Prince (IRE)**[27] 1930 4-9-10 0 (tp) PhilipPrince 8
(K Kukk, Jersey) *led at decent pce: rn wd on bnd 6f out: sn rdn along and hdd over 4f out: wknd* **8/1**

6 *10* **Spring Dixie (IRE)**[27] 1930 5-8-9 0................................(h) MissMHooper
(Mrs A Malzard, Jersey) *trckd ldr tl wknd fr 3f out* **15/2**

**Owner** White Spot Racing **Bred** Hugh Hogg **Trained** Jersey

## 2672a LIBERATION BREWERY H'CAP (TURF) 1m 1f
**4:50** (4:50) (0-55,0) 3-Y-0+ **£1,780** (£640; £380)

RPR

1 **Captain James (FR)**[27] 7-8-13 0........................................ PaddyAspell 43
(Mrs C Gilbert, Jersey) *hld up: hdwy 4 wd to chal fr 3f out: led 2f out and hung lft: drvn out* **9/2**[3]

2 *3* **Lucifers Shadow (IRE)**[27] 1933 8-10-0 0...........................(v) AliceMills 52
(Mrs C Gilbert, Jersey) *hld up: hdwy on inner to chal fr 3f out: ev ch whn n.m.r and bmpd over 1f out: no ex* **11/8**[1]

3 *3* **Brown Velvet**[27] 1931 5-9-5 0..........................................(p) AndrewElliott 37
(K Kukk, Jersey) *racd keenly: disp ld tl 2f out: ch whn n.m.r and bmpd over 1f out: no ex* **10/1**

4 *3* **Caius College Girl (IRE)**[53] 1298 5-10-12 0................ MattieBatchelor 52
(Natalie Lloyd-Beavis) *racd keenly trcking ldrs: ch over 2f out: kpt on one pce* **5/2**[2]

5 *1* **Ocean Crystal**[27] 1933 5-9-5 0.................................................... MrFTett 29
(Mrs A Malzard, Jersey) *shkn up s to dispute ld: hdd & wknd 2f out* **5/1**

6 *½* **Grey Panel (FR)**[27] 1932 9-9-9 0.............................................. RyanWhile 32
(T Le Brocq, Jersey) *trckd ldrs: rdn and swtchd 5 wd to chal fr 3f out: sn wknd* **5/2**[2]

7 *1 ½* **Carrera**[27] 1933 7-9-7 0.................................................... VictoriaMalzard 27
(Mrs A Malzard, Jersey) *slowest away: sn trcking ldrs: wknd fr wl over 1f out* **14/1**

8 *½* **Lady Petrus**[245] 12-8-5 0 oh7............................................... PhilipPrince 10
(K Kukk, Jersey) *racd wd: prom: lost pl 6f out: nvr able to get bk on terms* **12/1**

9 *9* **Grey Gem (IRE)**[27] 1933 6-10-0 0....................................... MarkQuinlan 15
(K Kukk, Jersey) *trckd ldrs: drvn and wknd fr 3f out* **9/1**

**Owner** Crystal Racing **Bred** R Marot **Trained** Jersey

2673 - (Foreign Racing) - See Raceform Interactive

# [2292] BRIGHTON (L-H)
## Monday, May 15

**OFFICIAL GOING: Good (good to soft in places)**
Wind: fresh, medium to strong, against, hard work for all Weather: light cloud

## 2674 TOTEPLACEPOT AT TOTESPORT.COM MAIDEN STKS 5f 60y
**2:10** (2:12) (Class 5) 3-Y-0+ **£2,911** (£866; £432; £216) **Stalls** Centre

Form RPR

224 1 **Secret Strategy (IRE)**[18] 2112 3-9-3 74..................... AdamBeschizza 1 72
(Julia Feilden) *trckd ldrs on inner: pushed into ld 2f out: 2 l clr and drvn over 1f out: styd on wl and a in command fnl f* **13/8**[2]

42 2 *2 ¾* **Lambrini Legacy**[13] 2280 3-8-12 0...................................... KieranO'Neill 5 57
(Lisa Williamson) *taken down early: sn led: hdd and rdn 2f out: styd on same pce fnl f* **14/1**[3]

322- 3 *½* **Golden Easter (USA)**[280] 5242 3-8-12 72......................... LukeMorris 3 55
(Robert Cowell) *broke wl: sn stdd to chse ldr and t.k.h: effrt wl over 1f out: 3rd and styd on same pce u.p ins fnl f* **8/13**[1]

0-0 4 *3* **General Gerrard**[15] 2171 3-8-12 0.............................(t) GeorgeWood(5) 4 50
(Michael Madgwick) *chsd ldrs on outer: rdn over 2f out: c centre to stands' side 2f out: unable qck and outpcd over 1f out: wl hld and kpt on same pce fnl f* **100/1**

00- 5 *7* **Ballysampson**[185] 7900 3-9-0 0.......................................... HectorCrouch(3) 2 25
(Simon Dow) *taken down early: hld up wl in tch in rr: shkn up over 1f out: sn unbalanced and btn: wknd fnl f* **25/1**

1m 4.21s (1.91) **Going Correction** +0.20s/f (Good) 5 Ran SP% **111.5**
Speed ratings (Par 103): **92,87,86,82,70**
CSF £21.26 TOTE £2.30: £1.10, £3.70; EX 12.90 Trifecta £22.90.
**Owner** The Strategists **Bred** Tom And Hazel Russell **Trained** Exning, Suffolk

**FOCUS**
A fair maiden. They went a decent gallop on ground officially described as good, good to soft in places. The jockeys concurred with that description. The favourite disappointed but the first two ran to form.

## 2675 RETRAINING OF RACEHORSES ROR H'CAP 5f 215y
**2:40** (2:40) (Class 6) (0-65,67) 4-Y-0+ **£2,264** (£673; £336; £168) **Stalls** Centre

Form RPR

0-01 1 **Whitecrest**[12] 2306 9-9-7 65.................................................. LukeMorris 5 70
(John Spearing) *broke v qckly: sn stdd and hld up in midfield: effrt and drvn to chse ldrs over 1f out chsd ldr 1f out: styd on strly u.p to ld last stride* **5/1**[2]

3244 2 *shd* **Mr Chuckles (IRE)**[19] 2091 4-8-0 51 oh2..................(be[1]) DavidEgan(7) 4 56
(Daniel Mark Loughnane) *trckd ldrs: clsd to join ldr ent fnl 2f: rdn to ld over 1f out: drvn ins fnl f: hrd pressed 100yds out: kpt on: hdd last stride* **3/1**[1]

4142 3 *2 ¼* **Broughtons Fancy**[13] 2278 4-9-4 62..................................... TimmyMurphy 1 63
(Gary Moore) *taken down early: trckd ldrs: nt clr run and swtchd rt over 2f out: hdwy to chse ldrs and swtchd rt jst over 1f out: ev ch ins fnl f: squeezed for room and snatched up wl ins fnl f: nt rcvr* **3/1**[1]

0526 4 *3* **Kristoff (IRE)**[20] 2057 4-8-0 51...................................(p) IsobelFrancis(7) 8 39
(Jim Boyle) *led tl over 4f out: pressed ldr tl jst over 1f out: rdn and outpcd over 1f out: 5th and wl hld 1f out: plugged on same pce after* **16/1**

-050 5 *1 ¼* **Torment**[7] 2464 4-9-9 67.........................................(p[1]) SilvestreDeSousa 7 52
(Charlie Wallis) *sn w ldr: led over 4f out: rdn 2f out: hdd over 1f out: 4th and no ex u.p 1f out: wknd ins fnl f* **3/1**[1]

1150 6 *3 ¼* **Malaysian Boleh**[12] 2319 7-8-7 58...........................(v) JacobMitchell(7) 3 32
(Phil McEntee) *s.i.s: hld up in last pair: c centre 1/2-way: rdn and struggling ent fnl 2f: wknd over 1f out* **10/1**[3]

046- 7 *6* **The Perfect Show**[212] 7362 4-9-4 62............................ RobertWinston 2 18
(Milton Bradley) *dwlt: hld up in last pair: effrt ent fnl 2f: sn struggling: bhd over 1f out* **20/1**

30-0 8 *2 ½* **Bushwise (IRE)**[122] 217 4-8-11 55...............................(p) DavidProbert 6 3
(Milton Bradley) *in tch in midfield: rdn ent fnl 2f: sn struggling: wknd over 1f out* **25/1**

1m 11.21s (1.01) **Going Correction** +0.20s/f (Good) 8 Ran SP% **115.2**
Speed ratings (Par 101): **101,100,97,93,92 87,79,76**
CSF £20.59 CT £52.94 TOTE £6.20: £1.50, £1.50, £1.20; EX 23.70 Trifecta £60.50.

**Owner** G M Eales **Bred** J Spearing And Kate Ive **Trained** Kinnersley, Worcs

■ Stewards' Enquiry : Luke Morris caution: future conduct in races

David Egan two-day ban: used whip above permitted level (29-30 May)

**FOCUS**
A modest sprint handicap. They went a decent gallop and it is sound form, if very ordinary.

## 2676 TOTEQUADPOT AT TOTESPORT.COM H'CAP 6f 210y
**3:15** (3:15) (Class 5) (0-75,74) 4-Y-0+ **£2,911** (£866; £432; £216) **Stalls** Centre

Form RPR

100- 1 **In Ken's Memory**[215] 7272 4-8-13 66....................... SilvestreDeSousa 5 74
(Michael Appleby) *mde all: rdn 2f out: forged ahd u.p ins fnl f: in command 100yds out: styd on wl* **7/4**[1]

-116 2 *2* **Murdanova (IRE)**[62] 1189 4-9-4 71................................ RobertWinston 2 73
(Daniel Mark Loughnane) *trckd ldng pair: effrt on inner over 1f out: chsd wnr 100yds out: styd on same pce u.p after* **9/1**

-103 3 *1 ½* **Black Caesar (IRE)**[100] 570 6-9-3 70................................ HarryBentley 4 68
(Philip Hide) *chsd ldr: effrt u.p over 1f out: no ex and lost 2nd 100yds out: kpt on same pce after* **5/2**[3]

30-1 4 *1 ¼* **One Big Surprise**[20] 2058 5-9-7 74........................................ FranBerry 3 69
(Richard Hughes) *stdd after s: trckd ldng trio: effrt over 1f out: sn rdn and no imp: wl hld and kpt on same pce fnl f* **2/1**[2]

000- 5 *2 ½* **Popeswood (IRE)**[147] 8458 5-8-10 63......................... AdamBeschizza 1 51
(Lee Carter) *taken down early: hld up in rr: effrt u.p over 1f out: no imp: n.d* **20/1**

1m 23.62s (0.52) **Going Correction** +0.20s/f (Good) 5 Ran SP% **113.0**
Speed ratings (Par 103): **105,102,101,99,96**
CSF £17.26 TOTE £2.60: £1.50, £4.80; EX 15.30 Trifecta £59.50.

**Owner** Greenstead Hall Racing Ltd **Bred** Greenstead Hall Racing Ltd **Trained** Oakham, Rutland

**FOCUS**
A fair handicap. The well-backed favourite was a confirmed front-runner and she made all in game fashion down in trip. This wasn't a strong race but the winner may do better.

## 2677 FXELECTRICAL.COM H'CAP 7f 211y
**3:50** (3:50) (Class 4) (0-80,82) 3-Y-0+ **£4,690** (£1,395; £697; £348) **Stalls** High

Form RPR

22-1 1 **Morning Suit (USA)**[128] 114 3-9-3 82..................... SilvestreDeSousa 7 89
(Mark Johnston) *hld up in last pair: rdn ent fnl 3f: hdwy: shifting lft but qckd to ld over 1f out: sn clr and in command fnl f: eased towards fin: comf* **4/1**

21-4 2 *2 ¼* **Munawer**[25] 1907 3-8-10 78........................................ MarcMonaghan(3) 1 79
(Hugo Palmer) *dwlt: hld up in tch in last pair: clsd and nt clr run over 2f out: sn swtchd rt: effrt and squeezed through over 1f out: chsd clr wnr 1f out: clr 2nd and kpt on after: no ch w wnr* **5/2**[1]

0131 3 *2 ¾* **Shifting Star (IRE)**[12] 2297 12-9-0 66 oh1................(vt) WilliamCarson 6 64
(John Bridger) *t.k.h: led for 1f: styd chsng ldr: rdn to ld over 1f out: sn hdd and carried lft: 3rd and no ex 1f out: plugged on same pce ins fnl f* **16/1**

23-4 4 *2 ½* **Radjash**[35] 1682 3-8-12 77..................................................(p) MartinLane 2 66
(Charlie Appleby) *in tch in midfield: nt clr run and swtchd rt jst over 2f out: pressing ldrs whn squeezed for room over 1f out: sn outpcd and wl hld fnl f* **3/1**[3]

501- 5 *¾* **Diamond Bear (USA)**[214] 7297 3-8-11 76......................... LukeMorris 5 64
(Sir Mark Prescott Bt) *t.k.h: wl in tch in midfield: rdn ent fnl 2f: squeezed for room wl over 1f out: no threat to ldrs after* **11/4**[2]

10-6 6 *9* **British Embassy (IRE)**[23] 1969 5-9-8 79.....................(h) RyanWhile(5) 4 53+
(Bill Turner) *led rdrless to post: t.k.h: chsd ldr tl led after 1f: hdd over 1f out: squeezed for room and dropped to rr 1f out: sn eased: rein broke* **14/1**

1m 36.45s (0.45) **Going Correction** +0.20s/f (Good)
**WFA** 3 from 4yo+ 13lb 6 Ran SP% **112.8**
Speed ratings (Par 105): **105,102,100,97,96 87**
CSF £14.55 TOTE £4.20: £2.00, £2.30; EX 16.30 Trifecta £75.40.

**Owner** Sheikh Hamdan bin Mohammed Al Maktoum **Bred** Darley **Trained** Middleham Moor, N Yorks

**FOCUS**
The feature contest was a fairly decent handicap. They went a respectable gallop and once again the form should hold up to scrutiny. A clear pb from the winner.

## 2678 LABYRINTH CHALLENGE 18-20 AUGUST H'CAP 1m 3f 198y
**4:20** (4:20) (Class 5) (0-70,70) 4-Y-0+ **£2,911** (£866; £432; £216) **Stalls** High

Form RPR

3443 1 **Light Of Air (FR)**[20] 2055 4-9-7 70................................ TimmyMurphy 3 79
(Gary Moore) *chsd ldr tl 7f out: styd chsng ldrs tl wnt 2nd again over 3f out: led 2f out: edgd lft u.p ent fnl f: r.o wl and drew clr ins fnl f* **5/2**[2]

5441 2 *5* **Melabi (IRE)**[15] 2183 4-9-0 68.................................. CallumRodriguez(5) 5 69
(Richard Ford) *stdd s: hld up in last: clsd to trck rivals over 2f out: effrt to chse wnr and drvn over 1f out: edging lft and no imp 1f out: wknd ins fnl f* **4/5**[1]

0340 3 *3 ¼* **Tempuran**[18] 1369 8-8-11 60.............................................(v[1]) JimmyQuinn 1 56
(David Bridgwater) *led tl over 4f out: lost pl u.p 3f out: 5th and wl hld 1f out: plugged on u.p to go 3rd 100yds out* **10/1**

0-00 4 *2* **Live Dangerously**[20] 2057 7-8-7 56 oh3......................... WilliamCarson 2 49
(John Bridger) *stdd s: t.k.h: hld up in 3rd tl wnt 2nd 7f out: led over 4f out tl hdd 2f out: sn drifted rt u.p and wknd over 1f out* **14/1**

1254 5 *nse* **Spirit Of The Vale (IRE)**[24] 1937 4-8-7 56...................(t) ShaneGray 6 49
(Oliver Greenall) *taken down early: hld up in 4th: effrt in 3rd over 2f out: no imp and outpcd over 1f out: wknd ins fnl f* **9/1**[3]

2m 34.83s (2.13) **Going Correction** +0.20s/f (Good) 5 Ran SP% **109.9**
Speed ratings (Par 103): **100,96,94,93,93**
CSF £4.88 TOTE £3.50: £1.70, £1.10; EX 5.60 Trifecta £16.90.

**Owner** R E Anderson **Bred** Rabbah Bloodstock Limited **Trained** Lower Beeding, W Sussex

**FOCUS**
A modest middle-distance handicap. They went a respectable gallop and the second-favourite, and top-weight, decisively made the most of this drop into a 0-70. It's hard to be positive about this form.

## 2679 HACIENDA CLASSICAL HERE 9 SEPT CLASSIFIED STKS 1m 1f 207y
4:50 (4:51) (Class 6) 3-Y-O+ £2,264 (£673; £336; £168) Stalls High

Form RPR

5225 **1** **Av A Word**[37] 1623 3-8-6 55 (p) LukeMorris 15 60
(Daniel Kubler) *hld up in midfield: rdn 4f out: swtchd rt and hdwy 3f out: chal over 1f out: sn led: hung lft onto inner rail ins fnl f: hrd pressed towards fin: all out* **6/1**[3]

3406 **2** *nk* **Betsalottie**[40] 1556 4-9-7 52 WilliamCarson 11 61
(John Bridger) *hld up in midfield: hdwy 3f out: rdn to chse ldrs over 2f out: led over 1f out: sn hdd and drifted lft ent fnl f: swtchd rt ins fnl f: rallied strly towards fin: nvr quite getting up* **3/1**[2]

0-06 **3** *8* **Lemon Drop**[20] 2056 3-7-13 52 (b[1]) IsobelFrancis(7) 5 44
(Jim Boyle) *taken down early: t.k.h: hld up in rr: c centre but stl bhd 3f out: hdwy ent fnl f: r.o strly to pass btn rivals ins fnl f: wnt 3rd 50yds out: nvr trbld ldrs* **25/1**

00-0 **4** *1½* **Let's Sway**[20] 2066 3-8-6 55 (h) LemosdeSouza 4 41
(Amy Murphy) *hld up in midfield: clsd to chse ldrs whn swtchd lft over 2f out: drvn and no imp over 1f out: wnt modest 3rd ins fnl f: plugged on but lost 3rd 50yds out* **20/1**

000- **5** *2* **Lady Of York**[159] 8246 3-8-6 46 JoeyHaynes 12 37
(Alan Bailey) *led and racd keenly: rdn ent fnl 2f: hdd over 1f out: sn btn: wknd ins fnl f* **25/1**

500 **6** *2¾* **Lord E (IRE)**[27] 1862 3-8-3 55 (v[1]) NoelGarbutt(3) 1 32
(Gary Moore) *chsd clr ldng trio: rdn 4f out: unable qck and outpcd over 2f out: wknd over 1f out* **14/1**

000- **7** *7* **Suzi Icon**[296] 4640 5-9-7 45 (p[1]) SilvestreDeSousa 6 20
(Michael Appleby) *t.k.h: led for 1f: chsd ldrs after: rdn ent fnl 2f: btn and hung lft over 1f out: eased ins fnl f* **6/1**[3]

6060 **8** *2¼* **Gamesters Lad**[12] 2313 5-9-7 42 (p) ShaneGray 8 15
(Oliver Greenall) *s.i.s and early reminder: hld up in rr: clsd whn nt clr run 3f out: swtchd rt over 2f out: sn rdn and outpcd: wknd over 1f out* **25/1**

6-56 **9** *5* **Netley Abbey**[21] 2027 3-7-13 53 RhiainIngram(7) 14 5
(Harry Dunlop) *hld up in midfield: lost pl and dropped to last trio over 4f out: no ch after* **7/1**

-046 **10** *1½* **Hi There Silver (IRE)**[33] 1726 3-8-6 44 (p[1]) KieranO'Neill 10 2
(Michael Madgwick) *prom in main gp: rdn 6f out: lost pl over 2f out: sn wknd* **33/1**

03-4 **11** *8* **Varun's Bride (IRE)**[21] 2016 3-8-3 52 HollieDoyle(3) 3
(Richard Hannon) *hld up in midfield: effrt over 2f out: sn btn and wknd: t.o* **11/4**[1]

050- **12** *24* **Royal Sentiment (IRE)**[152] 8355 3-8-6 53 (v[1]) DannyBrock 2
(Mark Usher) *t.k.h: chsd ldr tl jst over 2f out: sn dropped out and eased over 1f out: t.o* **25/1**

36-0 **13** *12* **Cranwell**[68] 1081 5-9-7 51 (h[1]) FergusSweeney 7
(George Baker) *hld up in last quartet: struggling 3f out: sn wl btn: t.o and virtually p.u fnl f* **10/1**

00-0 **14** *12* **Back To Love (CAN)**[19] 2087 4-9-4 42 (p[1]) CallumShepherd(3) 9
(Mark Gillard) *awkward leaving stalls: s.i.s: a rr: lost tch 3f: t.o and virtually p.u fnl f: bit slipped through mouth* **66/1**

2m 4.36s (0.76) **Going Correction** +0.20s/f (Good)
**WFA** 3 from 4yo+ 15lb **14** Ran SP% **133.1**
Speed ratings (Par 101): **104,103,97,96,94 92,86,84,80,79 73,54,44,34**
CSF £25.07 TOTE £6.80: £2.00, £2.40, £7.60; EX 28.30 Trifecta £721.70.
**Owner** Peter Onslow & Kevin Nash **Bred** Peter Onslow **Trained** Lambourn, Berks

**FOCUS**
A moderate Classified Stakes contest. Two of the horses towards the head of the betting came through to fight this out off a decent gallop, with a break back to the third. The runner-up is key to this low-grade form.

## 2680 COLLECT TOTEPOOL WINNINGS AT BETFRED SHOPS H'CAP 5f 60y
5:25 (5:25) (Class 5) (0-75,77) 4-Y-O+ £2,911 (£866; £432; £216) Stalls Centre

Form RPR

-566 **1** **Taajub (IRE)**[20] 2058 10-9-2 **65** FergusSweeney 1 74
(Peter Crate) *mde all: rdn and kicked 2 l clr 2f out: r.o wl ins fnl f: rdn out* **7/2**[3]

6423 **2** *2* **The Big Lad**[10] 2368 5-9-7 **77** (b) NicolaCurrie(7) 5 79
(Richard Hughes) *t.k.h: hld up in tch in 4th: effrt to chse wnr and hung lft over 1f out: kpt on but no imp ins fnl f* **11/8**[1]

3456 **3** *6* **Billyoakes (IRE)**[84] 844 5-9-5 **68** (p) LukeMorris 4 49
(Charlie Wallis) *trckd ldng pair: rdn over 2f out: drvn to chse clr wnr briefly over 1f out: 3rd and btn 1f out: wknd ins fnl f* **5/2**[2]

53-0 **4** *3¾* **Cherry Kool**[47] 1429 4-9-2 **68** (t[1]) AaronJones(3) 2 36
(Stuart Williams) *t.k.h: w wnr tl ent fnl 2f: rdn and dropped to rr over 1f out: wknd ins fnl f* **9/2**

1m 3.22s (0.92) **Going Correction** +0.20s/f (Good) **4** Ran SP% **111.1**
Speed ratings (Par 103): **100,96,87,81**
CSF £8.98 TOTE £6.10; EX 7.20 Trifecta £18.90.
**Owner** Peter Crate **Bred** Rabbah Bloodstock Limited **Trained** Newdigate, Surrey

**FOCUS**
A fair little sprint handicap. A particularly well-treated veteran rolled back the years with a dominant victory. The second is rated to recent AW form.
T/Plt: £62.90 to a £1 stake. Pool: £52,199.00 - 829.24 winning units T/Qpdt: £17.80 to a £1 stake. Pool: £3,158.00 - 176.75 winning units **Steve Payne**

# WETHERBY (L-H)
Monday, May 15

**OFFICIAL GOING: Good (good to firm in places; 8.9) changing to good after race 3 (2.50)**
Wind: Moderate across Weather: Overcast with showers

## 2681 YORKSHIRE POST LADIES DAY - TUESDAY 6TH JUNE MAIDEN STKS 1m 2f
1:50 (1:50) (Class 5) 3-Y-O £2,911 (£866; £432; £216) Stalls Centre

Form RPR

0- **1** **Shymkent**[194] 7770 3-9-5 0 DanielTudhope 2 86
(David O'Meara) *trckd ldrs on inner: hdwy over 3f out: n.m.r and swtchd rt over 2f out: sn chal: led 11/2f out: sn jnd and rdn: hdd ins fnl f: drvn and rallied to ld again towards fin* **50/1**

**2** *hd* **Born To Be Alive (IRE)** 3-9-0 0 CliffordLee(5) 3 85
(K R Burke) *hld up in tch: smooth hdwy on outer 21/2f out: chal 11/2f out: sn rdn and tk slt advantage ins fnl f: drvn: hdd and no ex towards fin* **15/2**

5 **3** *4½* **Pilgrim's Treasure (USA)**[25] 1914 3-9-5 0 KevinStott 9 76
(Charlie Appleby) *dwlt and rr: hdwy 3f out: pushed along over 2f out: rdn wl over 1f out: kpt on fnl f* **7/1**[3]

0-2 **4** *2½* **Alwahsh (IRE)**[20] 2066 3-9-5 0 JimCrowley 11 71
(William Haggas) *racd wd and prom: swtchd lft towards inner after 4f: cl up: led over 3f out: rdn along and jnd 2f out: sn hdd and drvn: wknd appr fnl f* **10/11**[1]

**5** *¾* **Uber Cool (IRE)** 3-9-5 0 PaulMulrennan 1 69
(Jane Chapple-Hyam) *trckd ldrs on inner: hdwy over 4f out: sn cl up on inner: rdn along over 2f out: grad wknd* **40/1**

**6** *5* **Powderhouse (IRE)** 3-9-5 0 PhillipMakin 8 59+
(Charlie Appleby) *dwlt and rr: hdwy over 3f out: chsd ldrs 2f out: sn rdn and no imp* **14/1**

5 **7** *3½* **Dawaaleeb (USA)**[27] 1857 3-9-5 0 DaneO'Neill 10 52
(Charles Hills) *prom: pushed along 3f out: rdn over 2f out: sn drvn and wknd* **4/1**[2]

**8** *5* **Mod** 3-9-0 0 DanielMuscutt 5 37
(James Fanshawe) *a towards rr* **20/1**

04 **9** *3¼* **Silk Trader (IRE)**[12] 2300 3-8-9 0 PhilDennis(5) 6 31
(Sharon Watt) *a rr* **125/1**

**10** *1¾* **Bicolour (USA)** 3-9-0 0 JoeFanning 4 27
(Mark Johnston) *led: pushed along and hdd over 3f out: rdn along wl over 2f out: sn wknd* **20/1**

00 **11** *24* **Foxy Rebel**[15] 2185 3-9-5 0 JamesSullivan 7
(Ruth Carr) *plld hrd: chsd ldrs: rdn along over wl over 3f out: sn wknd* **125/1**

2m 8.91s (-0.09) **Going Correction** +0.25s/f (Good) **11** Ran SP% **118.8**
Speed ratings (Par 99): **110,109,106,104,103 99,96,92,90,88 69**
CSF £377.52 TOTE £65.50: £12.20, £2.20, £2.70; EX 738.70 Trifecta £1954.10.
**Owner** Nurlan Bizakov **Bred** Hesmonds Stud Ltd **Trained** Upper Helmsley, N Yorks

**FOCUS**
The morning rain had visibly got into the ground through this fair 3yo maiden, in which two came nicely clear at the finish. The jockeys afterwards reported it rode like the easy side of good underfoot. Big improvement from the winner buit the two market leaders didn't run their races.

## 2682 RACING UK NOW LIVE ON YOUVIEW 231 MAIDEN AUCTION STKS 7f
2:20 (2:22) (Class 5) 3-Y-O £2,911 (£866; £432; £216) Stalls Low

Form RPR

42 **1** **Komodo (IRE)**[23] 1977 3-9-0 0 JackGarritty 3 77
(Jedd O'Keeffe) *trckd ldrs: pushed along over 2f out: rdn wl over 1f out: styd on strly u.p fnl f to ld nr fin* **5/1**[3]

3 **2** *½* **Hindsight**[11] 2344 3-8-7 0 PaulHanagan 7 68
(Michael Appleby) *trckd ldng pair: hdwy over 2f out: chal over 1f out: rdn to take slt ld jst ins fnl f: sn drvn: hdd and no ex nr fin* **14/1**

22-2 **3** *hd* **Benjamin Thomas (IRE)**[35] 1680 3-9-0 75 JasonHart 5 74
(John Quinn) *trckd ldr on inner: hdwy and cl up over 2f out: rdn wl over 1f out: drvn and ev ch ent fnl f tl no ex towards fin* **15/8**[2]

23-3 **4** *5* **Red Royalist**[23] 1961 3-9-0 80 MartinDwyer 1 61
(Marcus Tregoning) *hld up in rr: pushed along and hdwy on inner over 2f out: swtchd markedly rt to outer wl over 1f out: sn drvn and kpt on fnl f: nvr nr ldrs* **11/10**[1]

-220 **5** *½* **Rag Tatter**[25] 1913 3-9-0 74 KevinStott 8 59
(Kevin Ryan) *led: pushed along wl over 2f out: rdn wl over 1f out: drvn and hdd jst ins fnl f: wknd qckly* **14/1**

**6** *2¾* **Powercell (IRE)** 3-8-8 0 ow1 DavidAllan 6 46
(Tim Easterby) *dwlt: a towards rr* **40/1**

05 **7** *14* **New Tale**[23] 1977 3-9-0 0 DuranFentiman 9 14
(Olly Williams) *wnt rt s: a towards rr: rdn along wl over 2f out: sn outpcd* **66/1**

066- **8** *¾* **Orientelle**[210] 7407 3-8-7 45 CamHardie 4 5
(Richard Whitaker) *plld hrd early: in tch: rdn along 3f out: sn wknd* **100/1**

1m 29.26s (2.26) **Going Correction** +0.25s/f (Good) **8** Ran SP% **117.3**
Speed ratings (Par 99): **97,96,96,90,89 86,70,69**
CSF £69.32 TOTE £7.00: £1.80, £3.40, £1.10; EX 73.20 Trifecta £290.60.
**Owner** Geoff & Sandra Turnbull **Bred** Irish National Stud **Trained** Middleham Moor, N Yorks

**FOCUS**
A modest 3yo maiden that saw a tight finish. The second and third set the level.

## 2683 WATCH RACING UK ON BT TV H'CAP 5f 110y
2:50 (2:51) (Class 4) (0-80,80) 4-Y-O+ £5,822 (£1,732; £865; £432) Stalls High

Form RPR

6243 **1** **Lucky Beggar (IRE)**[11] 2341 7-9-2 **76** DavidAllan 6 86
(David C Griffiths) *trckd ldr: cl up 2f out: rdn to ld 11/2f out: kpt on strly fnl f* **11/4**[1]

0-03 **2** *2½* **Tylery Wonder (IRE)**[17] 2123 7-9-6 **80** (b) PaulMulrennan 2 82
(Paul Midgley) *led: pushed along and qcknd over 2f out: rdn and hdd 11/2f out: sn drvn and kpt on same pce fnl f* **11/4**[1]

4-06 **3** *1½* **Landing Night (IRE)**[122] 219 5-9-3 **77** (t) PJMcDonald 4 74
(Rebecca Menzies) *hld up: hdwy on outer over 2f out: rdn to chse ldrs over 1f out: drvn and kpt on fnl f* **10/1**

10-3 **4** *½* **Appleberry (IRE)**[41] 1542 5-9-2 **79** (h) AlistairRawlinson(3) 10 74
(Michael Appleby) *trckd ldrs: pushed along over 2f out: sn rdn: drvn and kpt on fnl f* **14/1**

0565 **5** *nk* **Aguerooo (IRE)**[46] 1454 4-9-6 **80** (p) AndrewMullen 8 74
(Ollie Pears) *dwlt: sn trcking ldrs: effrt 2f out: rdn over 1f out: drvn and one pce fnl f* **11/1**

40-3 **6** *½* **Rose Marmara**[15] 2184 4-9-3 **77** (t[1]) BarryMcHugh 1 70
(Brian Rothwell) *trckd ldng pair on inner: pushed along over 2f out: sn rdn: drvn wl over 1f out: one pce* **6/1**[2]

-015 **7** *½* **Foxtrot Knight**[17] 2123 5-9-6 **80** JamesSullivan 9 73
(Ruth Carr) *s.i.s: a rr* **7/1**[3]

5230 **8** *1¼* **Sophisticated Heir (IRE)**[47] 1423 7-9-5 **79** (b) JoeFanning 3 66
(Michael Herrington) *chsd ldrs: rdn along over 2f out: sn wknd* **11/1**

1m 7.51s (1.51) **Going Correction** +0.25s/f (Good) **8** Ran SP% **112.5**
Speed ratings (Par 105): **99,95,93,93,92 91,91,89**
CSF £9.41 CT £62.09 TOTE £3.80: £1.50, £1.40, £2.40; EX 12.10 Trifecta £90.70.
**Owner** David Kilpatrick **Bred** Mrs Cherry Faeste **Trained** Bawtry, S Yorks



The Form Book Flat, Raceform Ltd, Newbury, RG14 5SJ

**FOCUS**
Not a bad sprint handicap. It paid to be handy but it's hard to be positive about the form given the 1-2 were always on the pace.

## 2684 RACING UK NOW ON TALK TALK TV H'CAP 7f
3:25 (3:25) (Class 4) (0-80,79) 4-Y-0+ £5,822 (£1,732; £865; £432) Stalls Low

Form RPR
6-00 1 **Theodorico (IRE)**$^{16}$ [2146] 4-9-2 **74**........ PJMcDonald 14 85+
(David Loughnane) *in tch: gd hdwy over 2f out: rdn over 1f out: led ins fnl f: drvn out* **22/1**
-000 2 1 1/4 **Like No Other**$^{31}$ [1778] 4-9-1 **73**........(b$^{1}$) JoeFanning 4 79
(Les Eyre) *hld up towards rr: swtchd rt and hdwy over 2f out: rdn wl over 1f out: drvn and styd on strly fnl f* **12/1**
2346 3 1 1/4 **Intensical (IRE)**$^{27}$ [1867] 6-9-4 **76**........(p) DavidNolan 12 79
(Ivan Furtado) *towards rr: hdwy over 2f out: rdn to chse ldrs over 1f out: styng on whn n.m.r ins fnl f: swtchd rt and drvn: kpt on wl towards fin* **20/1**
0-00 4 nk **Royal Connoisseur (IRE)**$^{25}$ [1910] 6-9-7 **79**........ PaulHanagan 9 81
(Richard Fahey) *trckd ldrs: hdwy 2f out: rdn and ev ch over 1f out: drvn ent fnl f: kpt on same pce* **12/1**
-502 5 1/2 **Tellovoi (IRE)**$^{12}$ [2301] 9-9-3 **75**........(v$^{1}$) ConnorBeasley 3 75
(Richard Guest) *trckd ldng pair: hdwy and cl up over 2f out: rdn along wl over 1f out: drvn and ev ch ent fnl f: wknd towards fin* **10/1**
-445 6 3/4 **Enjoy Life (IRE)**$^{28}$ [1833] 4-9-3 **75**........(p) TomEaves 13 73
(Kevin Ryan) *cl up: chal 2f out: rdn to ld wl over 1f out: sn drvn: hdd ins fnl f: wknd towards fin* **10/1**
00-3 7 nk **Dutch Artist (IRE)**$^{33}$ [1717] 5-8-13 **76**........ JoshDoyle$^{(5)}$ 8 74
(David O'Meara) *hld up in midfield: hdwy over 2f out: rdn along wl over 1f out: kpt on fnl f* **11/2$^{2}$**
30-0 8 1/2 **Steal The Scene (IRE)**$^{38}$ [1606] 5-8-13 **71**........ RichardKingscote 6 68+
(Kevin Frost) *hld up in midfield: hdwy over 2f out: chsd ldrs over 1f out: rdn and nt clr run ins fnl f: no imp* **20/1**
-000 9 1 1/2 **Amood (IRE)**$^{16}$ [2133] 6-9-3 **75**........(p) JasonHart 11 67+
(Simon West) *stdd s and swtchd lft to inner: hld up in rr: hdwy 2f out: rdn over 1f out: no imp fnl f* **14/1**
00-3 10 1 **Zodiakos (IRE)**$^{21}$ [2030] 4-9-7 **79**........ TonyHamilton 7 69
(Roger Fell) *slt ld: pushed along over 2f out: rdn and hdd wl over 1f out: sn drvn and wknd* **5/1$^{1}$**
-216 11 nk **Cliff (IRE)**$^{104}$ [501] 7-8-8 **71**........ LewisEdmunds$^{(5)}$ 16 60
(Nigel Tinkler) *a towards rr* **25/1**
0-04 12 3/4 **Specialv (IRE)**$^{23}$ [1972] 4-8-11 **69**........(p) BenCurtis 10 56
(Brian Ellison) *hld up: a towards rr* **14/1**
-000 13 4 **Slemy (IRE)**$^{11}$ [2348] 6-9-2 **74**........ JamesSullivan 5 50
(Ruth Carr) *dwlt: a rr* **14/1**
00-0 14 2 **Le Roi Du Temps (USA)**$^{38}$ [1606] 4-9-3 **75**........ AndrewMullen 15 45
(Tom Tate) *a towards rr* **33/1**
22-6 15 5 **Kirkham**$^{17}$ [2119] 4-8-7 **65**........ JoeDoyle 2 22
(Julie Camacho) *chsd ldrs on inner: rdn along 2f out: sn wknd* **15/2$^{3}$**
060- 16 11 **Redvers (IRE)**$^{296}$ [4627] 9-9-1 **73**........(b) PaulMulrennan 1
(Noel Wilson) *in tch: hdwy over 2f out: rdn to chse ldrs and n.m.r over 1f out: sn drvn and wknd* **25/1**

1m 28.59s (1.59) **Going Correction** +0.25s/f (Good) 16 Ran SP% **121.9**
Speed ratings (Par 105): **100,98,97,96,96 95,95,94,92,91 91,90,85,83,77 65**
CSF £246.09 CT £5533.06 TOTE £28.60: £4.30, £3.30, £4.10, £3.20; EX 312.40 Trifecta £5507.60.
**Owner** Mike And Eileen Newbould **Bred** J S Bolger & John Corcoran **Trained** Market Drayton, Shropshire

**FOCUS**
There was a brisk early pace on in this open-looking handicap. The winner is rated back to something like his best.

## 2685 RACING UK NOW LIVE ON YOUVIEW 231 H'CAP 1m
4:00 (4:01) (Class 5) (0-75,75) 4-Y-0+ £2,911 (£866; £432; £216) Stalls Low

Form RPR
35 1 **Fire Tree (IRE)**$^{33}$ [1735] 4-9-2 **70**........ JimCrowley 11 84
(Charlie Fellowes) *trckd ldrs: hdwy on outer over 2f out: rdn to ld over 1f out: clr ins fnl f: kpt on strly* **10/3$^{1}$**
6-23 2 3 **Desert Ruler**$^{16}$ [2133] 4-9-4 **72**........ JackGarritty 12 79
(Jedd O'Keeffe) *midfield: hdwy over 2f out: chsd ldrs over 1f out: rdn to chse wnr ins fnl f: sn drvn and no imp* **9/2$^{2}$**
6601 3 1 3/4 **Berrahri (IRE)**$^{10}$ [2369] 6-9-6 **74**........ MartinDwyer 13 77
(John Best) *dwlt and towards rr: pushed along 3f out: hdwy 2f out: sn rdn: styd on strly fnl f: nrst fin* **20/1**
0-54 4 1 **Mon Beau Visage (IRE)**$^{14}$ [2226] 4-9-7 **75**........(p) PhillipMakin 6 76+
(David O'Meara) *t.k.h: trckd ldrs: hdwy 2f out: n.m.r jst over 1f out: swtchd rt ins fnl f: kpt on wl towards fin* **7/1$^{3}$**
01-3 5 1 1/2 **Bollihope**$^{131}$ [42] 5-9-5 **73**........ ConnorBeasley 8 70+
(Richard Guest) *towards rr: hdwy over 2f out: rdn over 1f out: kpt on fnl f* **20/1**
655- 6 hd **Auspicion**$^{171}$ [8092] 5-9-4 **72**........ JamesSullivan 15 69
(Tom Tate) *trckd ldrs on outer: hdwy and cl up over 2f out: rdn to dispute ld and ev ch jst over 1f out: sn drvn and kpt on same pce* **12/1**
5630 7 2 3/4 **Captain Revelation**$^{40}$ [1562] 5-9-7 **75**........ RichardKingscote 14 65
(Tom Dascombe) *cl up: chal over 2f out: rdn to dispute over 1f out: ev ch tl drvn and wknd ins fnl f* **20/1**
-313 8 2 **Make On Madam (IRE)**$^{14}$ [2224] 5-9-1 **69**........ PJMcDonald 1 55
(Les Eyre) *chsd ldng pair on inner: pushed along over 2f out: rdn wl over 1f out: sn drvn and grad wknd* **12/1**
3222 9 1/2 **Tadaawol**$^{10}$ [2377] 4-9-4 **72**........(p) TonyHamilton 9 57
(Roger Fell) *in tch: rdn along wl over 2f out: grad wknd* **7/1$^{3}$**
1202 10 1/2 **Barwah (USA)**$^{67}$ [1104] 6-9-2 **70**........ AndrewMullen 4 54
(Peter Niven) *in tch on inner: pushed along over 2f out: rdn and n.m.r over 1f out: sn drvn and wknd* **40/1**
26-6 11 1 3/4 **Fidra Bay (IRE)**$^{10}$ [2377] 4-8-13 **67**........ JoeFanning 5 47
(Alan Swinbank) *t.k.h: hld up towards rr: n.d* **20/1**
012- 12 2 1/4 **Totally Magic (IRE)**$^{202}$ [7601] 5-8-13 **67**........ CamHardie 16 41
(Richard Whitaker) *stdd and swtchd lft s: a rr* **40/1**
010- 13 nk **Nonno Giulio (IRE)**$^{188}$ [7857] 6-9-2 **75**........ JoshDoyle$^{(5)}$ 3 49
(Tony Coyle) *t.k.h: in tch: pushed along over 2f out: sn rdn and wknd* **20/1**
3030 14 1/2 **Shah Of Armaan (IRE)**$^{16}$ [2163] 4-9-5 **73**........(p$^{1}$) TomEaves 2 46
(Kevin Ryan) *slt ld: rdn along over 2f out: drvn and hdd over 1f out: wknd* **33/1**
0010 15 4 1/2 **Pivotman**$^{16}$ [2140] 9-8-13 **70**........(bt) NathanEvans$^{(3)}$ 10 32
(Michael Easterby) *trckd ldrs: rdn along wl over 2f out: sn wknd* **20/1**
0-0P 16 2 1/4 **Cambodia (IRE)**$^{60}$ [1224] 4-9-3 **71**........(h) DavidAllan 7 28
(Chris Wall) *unruly stalls: s.i.s: a rr* **14/1**

1m 41.86s (0.86) **Going Correction** +0.25s/f (Good) 16 Ran SP% **124.7**
Speed ratings (Par 103): **105,102,100,99,97 97,94,92,92,91 90,87,87,87,82 80**
CSF £14.66 CT £230.42 TOTE £4.10: £1.50, £1.40, £4.20, £2.00; EX 21.40 Trifecta £316.60.
**Owner** Never So Bold **Bred** Peter Reynolds & Robert Dore **Trained** Newmarket, Suffolk

**FOCUS**
Another well-subscribed handicap. It was run at an average pace and rates fair form. A step up from the winner on his Irish level.

## 2686 RACING UK PROFITS RETURNED TO RACING H'CAP 1m 6f
4:30 (4:31) (Class 5) (0-70,70) 3-Y-O £2,911 (£866; £432; £216) Stalls Low

Form RPR
-343 1 **Cray (IRE)**$^{34}$ [1701] 3-9-7 **70**........ PJMcDonald 1 75
(James Bethell) *trckd ldr: reminders 1/2-way: rdn along over 4f out: hdwy to ld 3f out: drvn along wl over 1f out: edgd lft ins fnl f: kpt on gamely* **7/2$^{2}$**
0-40 2 1/2 **Padrinho (IRE)**$^{33}$ [1737] 3-8-13 **62**........ KierenFox 7 66
(John Best) *hld up in rr: hdwy over 3f out: chsd ldrs 2f out: effrt to chal over 1f out: sn rdn and ev ch ins fnl f: drvn and no ex towards fin* **9/2**
5-05 3 2 3/4 **Kiruna Peak (IRE)**$^{13}$ [2269] 3-9-3 **66**........ GrahamLee 6 66
(Mick Channon) *prom: trckd ldr 1/2-way: cl up over 4f out: rdn to dispute ld 3f out: drvn along wl over 1f out: kpt on same pce fnl f* **15/2**
00-6 4 4 1/2 **Sheriff Garrett (IRE)**$^{16}$ [2137] 3-8-7 **56**........ DavidAllan 2 50
(Tim Easterby) *trckd ldrs: hdwy over 3f out: rdn along over 2f out: sn drvn and one pce* **4/1$^{3}$**
5600 5 10 **Naupaka**$^{23}$ [1968] 3-8-9 **58**........(h$^{1}$) TomEaves 3 38
(Brian Ellison) *hld up and bhd: hdwy 5f out: chsd ldrs 3f out: swtchd lft wl over 1f out: sn drvn and btn* **12/1**
-050 6 1 **Costa Percy**$^{33}$ [1736] 3-8-13 **62**........(p$^{1}$) BenCurtis 5 40
(K R Burke) *in tch: hdwy over 4f out: rdn along 3f out: sn drvn and wknd* **12/1**
000- 7 1/2 **Newt**$^{206}$ [7494] 3-9-1 **64**........ PaulMulrennan 4 42
(Sir Mark Prescott Bt) *led: pushed along and jnd over 4f out: rdn and hdd 3f out: sn drvn and wknd over 2f out* **3/1$^{1}$**

3m 6.16s (1.16) **Going Correction** +0.25s/f (Good) 7 Ran SP% **112.6**
Speed ratings (Par 99): **106,105,104,101,95 95,95**
CSF £18.88 TOTE £4.50: £2.30, £2.80; EX 23.10 Trifecta £109.70.
**Owner** J Carrick&Clarendon Thoroughbred Racing **Bred** Churchtown House Stud **Trained** Middleham Moor, N Yorks

**FOCUS**
There was no hanging around in this moderate 3yo staying handicap. They kept to the centre down the home straight and the form is rated around the third.

## 2687 GO RACING IN YORKSHIRE FUTURE STARS APPRENTICE H'CAP (DIV I) 1m 2f
5:00 (5:02) (Class 6) (0-60,60) 4-Y-0+ £2,587 (£770; £384; £192) Stalls Centre

Form RPR
6652 1 **Mr Sundowner (USA)**$^{15}$ [2183] 5-8-8 **52**........(t) ConnorMurtagh$^{(5)}$ 7 60
(Wilf Storey) *trckd ldrs: hdwy 3f out: led over 1f out: sn rdn and kpt on wl fnl f* **9/2$^{2}$**
1022 2 2 3/4 **Hannington**$^{32}$ [1758] 6-9-4 **60**........(t) RayDawson$^{(3)}$ 2 63
(Michael Appleby) *in tch: hdwy 3f out: rdn to chse ldrs wl over 1f out: kpt on u.p fnl f: nrst fin* **4/1$^{1}$**
3056 3 1/2 **Outlaw Torn (IRE)**$^{12}$ [2313] 8-8-10 **54**........(e) WilliamCox$^{(5)}$ 10 56
(Richard Guest) *trckd ldrs on inner: hdwy 3f out: rdn along wl over 1f pout: drvn and kpt on same pce fnl f* **16/1**
00-2 4 1 1/4 **Fillydelphia (IRE)**$^{19}$ [2079] 6-8-13 **57**........ PaulaMuir$^{(5)}$ 4 57
(Patrick Holmes) *hld up in rr: hdwy on wd outside over 2f out: rdn over 1f out: kpt on strly fnl f: nrst fin* **7/1$^{3}$**
2213 5 3/4 **Kerry Icon**$^{10}$ [2378] 4-8-8 **52**........(h) JamieGormley$^{(5)}$ 9 51
(Iain Jardine) *cl up: led after 3f: pushed along over 2f out: sn rdn: hdd over 1f out: wknd fnl f* **7/1$^{3}$**
6-24 6 3/4 **I'm Super Too (IRE)**$^{14}$ [2224] 10-9-3 **56**........(p) GemmaTutty 3 53
(Karen Tutty) *in tch: hdwy 3f out: rdn along 2f out: no imp appr fnl f* **12/1**
06-0 7 1 1/4 **Scent Of Power**$^{16}$ [2166] 5-8-11 **50**........ LuluStanford 11 45
(Barry Leavy) *trckd ldng pair: hdwy 3f out: rdn along over 2f out: sn drvn and grad wknd* **12/1**
6-06 8 3 **First Summer**$^{93}$ [689] 5-9-5 **58**........ CharlieBennett 8 48
(Shaun Harris) *a towards rr* **16/1**
300- 9 3/4 **Diamond Runner (IRE)**$^{213}$ [7336] 5-8-9 **53**........(e$^{1}$) BenSanderson$^{(5)}$ 6 41
(Lawrence Mullaney) *a towards rr* **11/1**
0306 10 1 **Leonard Thomas**$^{19}$ [2082] 7-8-13 **55**........(p) PatrickVaughan$^{(3)}$ 1 41
(Philip Kirby) *hld up in tch: effrt and sme hdwy on inner 3f out: rdn along over 2f out: sn wknd* **10/1**
10-3 11 2 **Lean On Pete (IRE)**$^{27}$ [1864] 8-9-7 **60**........ JoshDoyle 5 43
(Ollie Pears) *led 3f: cl up: rdn along wl over 2f out: sn wknd* **8/1**

2m 11.82s (2.82) **Going Correction** +0.25s/f (Good) 11 Ran SP% **118.9**
Speed ratings (Par 101): **98,95,95,94,93 93,92,89,89,88 86**
CSF £23.14 CT £268.52 TOTE £4.90: £1.60, £1.40, £5.60; EX 21.60 Trifecta £433.00.
**Owner** W Storey **Bred** Hunter Valley Farm Et Al **Trained** Muggleswick, Co Durham

**FOCUS**
This ordinary handicap for apprentice riders was run at a fair pace. Straightforward form, the winner close to his latest.

## 2688 GO RACING IN YORKSHIRE FUTURE STARS APPRENTICE H'CAP (DIV II) 1m 2f
5:35 (5:36) (Class 6) (0-60,60) 4-Y-0+ £2,587 (£770; £384; £192) Stalls Centre

Form RPR
46-0 1 **Mrs Biggs**$^{15}$ [2183] 5-8-11 **50**........ PhilDennis 2 58
(Declan Carroll) *.led: hdd over 3f out: cl up: rdn along 2f out: drvn to ld again ent fnl f: kpt on gamely* **7/1**
-264 2 1 **Bling King**$^{18}$ [2108] 8-9-7 **60**........(p) CliffordLee 3 66
(Geoffrey Harker) *trckd ldrs: cl up 3f out: effrt and ev ch whn n.m.r wl over 1f out: sn rdn: drvn and kpt on same pce fnl f* **9/4$^{1}$**
40-4 3 1/2 **Sakhalin Star (IRE)**$^{12}$ [2312] 6-8-12 **56**........(e) BenSanderson$^{(5)}$ 11 61
(Richard Guest) *sn prom: cl up on outer 1/2-way: slt ld 3f out: rdn along 2f out: drvn over 1f out: hdd ent fnl f: kpt on same pce* **6/1$^{3}$**
-640 4 1 **Whitecliff Park (IRE)**$^{15}$ [2183] 4-8-8 **52**........ KieranSchofield$^{(5)}$ 4 55+
(Brian Ellison) *dwlt and rr: hdwy and in tch over 4f out: pushed along on outer 3f out: rdn to chse ldrs 2f out: sn drvn and kpt on same pce fnl f* **8/1**
/6-0 5 1/2 **Druid's Diamond**$^{35}$ [1676] 4-8-10 **54**........ ConnorMurtagh$^{(5)}$ 1 56
(Mark Walford) *trckd ldrs: hdwy on inner 3f out: rdn and cl up 2f out: drvn appr fnl f: wknd* **20/1**
4021 6 3/4 **The Dukkerer (IRE)**$^{12}$ [2313] 6-9-6 **59**........ LewisEdmunds 8 60
(James Given) *prom: rdn along wl over 2f out: drvn over 1f out: grad wknd* **9/2$^{2}$**

420- **7** *6* **Shift On Sheila**[206] 7516 4-8-13 **57** WilliamCox(5) 10 47
(Pam Sly) *a rr* **16/1**

400 **8** *7* **Dan's Hopeforglory**[28] 1829 5-8-8 **52** JonathanFisher(5) 9 30
(Peter Niven) *dwlt: a rr* **66/1**

26-0 **9** *½* **King Of Paradise (IRE)**[15] 2183 8-9-5 **58** RowanScott 7 35
(Eric Alston) *cl up: rdn along wl over 3f out: sn wknd* **22/1**

33-0 **10** *27* **Midlight**[27] 1868 5-9-2 **55** (t) JoshDoyle 5
(Ruth Carr) *t.k.h: a towards rr: bhd fnl 2f* **7/1**

2m 12.13s (3.13) **Going Correction** +0.25s/f (Good) **10** Ran SP% **115.8**
Speed ratings (Par 101): **97,96,95,95,94 94,89,83,83,61**
CSF £22.48 CT £101.68 TOTE £7.30: £2.50, £1.10, £2.40; EX 21.90 Trifecta £166.70.
**Owner** The Deeciders I **Bred** Martin Percival **Trained** Malton, N Yorks

**FOCUS**
The second division of the ordinary apprentice riders' handicap. There was an uneven pace on. The form is rated around the runner-up to last year's level.
T/Jkpt: Not won. T/Plt: £1,522.90 to a £1 stake. Pool: £54,628.00 - 35.87 winning units T/Qpdt: £67.30 to a £1 stake. Pool: £4,380.00 - 65.05 winning units **Joe Rowntree**

## 2473 WINDSOR (R-H)

Monday, May 15

**OFFICIAL GOING: Good (good to firm in places) meeting abandoned after race 4 (6.50) due to slippery bends**
Wind: Moderate, across Weather: Overcast with drizzle

### 2689 SPORTING LIFE PICK 7 MEDIAN AUCTION MAIDEN STKS — 1m 2f
5:20 (5:22) (Class 5) 3-5-Y-O — £2,911 (£866; £432; £216) Stalls Centre

Form RPR

32-P **1** **Chiefofchiefs**[7] 2476 4-10-0 0 StevieDonohoe 4 80
(Charlie Fellowes) *covered up bhd ldrs: prog 2f out and swtchd to nr side rail: shkn up to ld ins fnl f: won w bit in hand* **5/1**

46- **2** *¾* **Jake's Hill**[196] 7726 3-8-13 0 CharlesBishop 7 78
(Eve Johnson Houghton) *wl in tch: pushed along and prog 3f out: led over 1f out: hdd ins fnl f: kpt on wl but readily hld* **17/2**

344- **3** *1 ¾* **See Of Rome**[206] 7501 3-8-13 76 FranBerry 13 74
(Richard Hughes) *sweating: prom: upsides wl over 1f out: shkn up and nt qckn sn after: kpt on* **7/2**[3]

0 **4** *2 ¼* **Orin Swift (IRE)**[21] 2039 3-8-8 0 MitchGodwin(5) 8 70
(Jonathan Portman) *towards rr but in tch: prog over 2f out: rdn to chse ldrs over 1f out: no imp after* **150/1**

34-2 **5** *hd* **Romanor**[19] 2087 3-8-13 80 (h) WilliamBuick 6 69
(Ed Walker) *t.k.h: hld up in tch: prog on outer over 2f out: hanging and fnd nil over 1f out* **3/1**[2]

00 **6** *shd* **C'Est No Mour (GER)**[21] 2039 4-10-0 0 TomMarquand 10 70
(Peter Hedger) *towards rr but in tch: prog wl over 1f out: rdn and styd on fnl f: nvr nrr* **200/1**

2- **7** *2 ¾* **Bullington Bear (FR)**[394] 1479 4-10-0 0 (p[1]) OisinMurphy 14 64
(Jane Chapple-Hyam) *trckd ldr: upsides 3f out to over 1f out: wknd* **33/1**

6- **8** *1* **Lady Bergamot (FR)**[194] 7762 3-8-3 0 GeorgeWood(5) 5 56
(James Fanshawe) *trckd ldrs: urged along 3f out: hanging and wknd fr 2f out* **20/1**

**9** *2* **Sparte Quercus (IRE)** 4-10-0 0 AdamKirby 2 58
(Ed Dunlop) *cl up bhd ldrs tl wknd jst over 2f out* **50/1**

**10** *nk* **Star Gypsy (FR)** 3-8-13 0 JamieSpencer 15 57
(Luca Cumani) *s.s: mostly in last and detached 4f out: passed a few late on* **33/1**

**11** *1 ¼* **Desert Song** 3-8-13 0 JFEgan 11 54
(Pat Phelan) *stdd s and hld up in last pair: hld up in last pair: pushed along 4f out: passed a few late on* **100/1**

00 **12** *½* **Theglasgowwarrior**[23] 1967 3-8-13 0 LouisSteward 16 53
(Michael Bell) *a in last quartet: pushed along and detached fr main field 3f out* **100/1**

0-2 **13** *2 ¼* **Highland Cradle**[44] 1485 3-8-13 0 RyanMoore 3 49
(Sir Michael Stoute) *coltish preliminaries: sweating: led: hrd rdn over 2f out: hdd & wknd rapidly over 1f out* **9/4**[1]

0 **14** *1* **King Kevin**[23] 1967 3-8-13 0 AntonioFresu 9 47
(Ed Dunlop) *in tch: urged along 4f out: wknd over 2f out* **150/1**

**15** *30* **Tiger Khan** 3-8-13 0 PatCosgrave 1
(Harry Dunlop) *a wl in rr: t.o* **100/1**

2m 9.79s (1.09) **Going Correction** -0.025s/f (Good)
**WFA** 3 from 4yo 15lb **15** Ran SP% **122.6**
Speed ratings (Par 103): **94,93,92,90,90 89,87,86,85,85 84,83,81,81,57**
CSF £45.96 TOTE £6.90: £2.00, £3.00, £1.60; EX 56.40 Trifecta £268.10.
**Owner** Mervyn Ayers **Bred** Executive Bloodlines **Trained** Newmarket, Suffolk

**FOCUS**
Rail movements added 31yds to all races of a mile and over. Times suggested that the ground was riding on the quick side, but there was concern that it was rather slippery with a horse losing his footing in the 5.50, and for the second year running the meeting was abandoned before the Listed Royal Windsor Stakes could be run. This opening auction maiden was probably a modest event. The first three are rated to form, but the fourth and sixth cast some doubt.

### 2690 SKY BET TOP PRICE PROMISE H'CAP — 1m 2f
5:50 (5:53) (Class 4) (0-85,85) 3-Y-O — £4,690 (£1,395; £697; £348) Stalls Centre

Form RPR

331- **1** **Crowned Eagle**[194] 7769 3-9-7 **85** FrankieDettori 5 102+
(John Gosden) *mde all: pushed clr over 2f out: in n.d after: eased fnl 100yds* **6/4**[1]

1 **2** *1* **Secret Advisor (FR)**[15] 2185 3-9-3 **81** WilliamBuick 9 92+
(Charlie Appleby) *hld up: impeded bnd 6f out and dropped to last pair: gd prog on outer over 2f out: pushed along and r.o to take 2nd ins fnl f: clsd on eased down wnr nr fin* **10/3**[2]

2-00 **3** *2 ½* **Western Duke (IRE)**[26] 1886 3-9-7 **85** FranBerry 13 91
(Ralph Beckett) *chsd wnr 3f and again over 2f out but sn outpcd: lost 2nd ins fnl f* **16/1**

14- **4** *6* **Tamayef (IRE)**[213] 7322 3-9-0 **78** JamesDoyle 2 72
(Hugo Palmer) *trckd ldrs: rdn over 2f out: nt qckn and outpcd sn after: one pce over 1f out* **33/1**

1 **5** *3 ½* **Comrade Conrad (IRE)**[35] 1682 3-9-3 **81** HarryBentley 11 68+
(Roger Charlton) *wl in tch: slipped bnd over 5f out: shkn up and effrt over 3f out: nvr rchd ldrs after* **12/1**

00-1 **6** *1 ¾* **Lightly Squeeze**[28] 1840 3-8-11 **75** (p) OisinMurphy 12 59
(Philip Hide) *s.i.s: rapid prog to press wnr after 3f to over 2f out: steadily wknd* **50/1**

10 **7** *4* **Mori Yoshinari (IRE)**[33] 1736 3-8-13 **77** TomMarquand 7 53
(Richard Hannon) *in tch: drvn and no prog wl over 2f out: wknd* **40/1**

4115 **8** *6* **Vantage Point (IRE)**[19] 2088 3-9-2 **80** (p) RyanMoore 6 44
(Gary Moore) *in tch: shkn up 3f out: sn no prog and wknd* **25/1**

1-3 **9** *4* **Manangatang (IRE)**[26] 1875 3-8-12 **76** JamieSpencer 3 32+
(Luca Cumani) *in tch: pushed along firmly 3f out and no prog: wknd and heavily eased fnl f* **13/2**[3]

51- **10** *1 ¾* **Rosarno (IRE)**[206] 7501 3-9-5 **83** (t[1]) AndreaAtzeni 8 35
(Charles Hills) *a towards rr and nvr a real factor: heavily eased fnl f* **12/1**

51- **11** *19* **Buzz (FR)**[152] 8355 3-9-0 **78** LiamKeniry 4 +
(Hughie Morrison) *hld up: t.k.h after 2f: stmbld bnd 6f out and dropped to rr: nvr gng wl after* **16/1**

40-5 **12** *33* **Fastnet Spin (IRE)**[10] 2361 3-8-11 **75** (b[1]) JFEgan 1
(David Evans) *chsd ldrs to 4f out: wknd rapidly 3f out: eased and t.o* **100/1**

2m 8.68s (-0.02) **Going Correction** -0.025s/f (Good) **12** Ran SP% **115.7**
Speed ratings (Par 101): **99,98,96,91,88 87,84,79,76,74 59,33**
CSF £5.61 CT £54.83 TOTE £2.20: £1.20, £2.30, £3.50; EX 7.30 Trifecta £81.30.
**Owner** Lady Bamford **Bred** Lady Bamford **Trained** Newmarket, Suffolk

**FOCUS**
Rail run over an additional 31yds. A warm handicap with all the dozen runners having won previously, but the pace slowed going to the far bend and there was some scrimmaging. The winner impressed and the first two look worth following.

### 2691 WEATHERBYS RACING BANK NOVICE STKS (PLUS 10 RACE) — 5f 21y
6:20 (6:21) (Class 3) 2-Y-O — £6,469 (£1,925; £962; £481) Stalls Low

Form RPR

**1** **Last Voyage (USA)** 2-9-2 0 WilliamBuick 5 76+
(Charlie Appleby) *dwlt sltly: sn chsd ldrs: shkn up to chal over 1f out: narrow ld ins fnl f: pushed out last 50yds and jst hld on* **11/10**[1]

42 **2** *shd* **Choice Encounter**[13] 2279 2-9-2 0 JamieSpencer 2 76
(Michael Bell) *dwlt but qckly rcvrd to ld: rdn over 1f out: hdd ins fnl f: kpt on wl nr fin: jst denied* **7/2**[2]

4 **3** *½* **Indian Warrior**[13] 2279 2-9-2 0 JamesDoyle 4 74
(Ed Dunlop) *w ldr and racd against rail: rdn and stl upsides 1f out: styd on same pce* **14/1**

5 **4** *4 ½* **Straight Ash (IRE)**[38] 1604 2-9-2 0 TomMarquand 1 58
(Richard Hannon) *chsd ldrs: rdn 2f out: steadily fdd over 1f out* **9/1**

**5** *1* **Wildnightinvegas (IRE)** 2-9-2 0 SeanLevey 7 54
(Richard Hannon) *dwlt sltly: sn in tch: pushed along 2f out: steadily fdd* **10/1**

**6** *6* **Bond Angel** 2-8-11 0 TomQueally 3 28
(David Evans) *a in rr: pushed along 2f out: bhd over 1f out* **50/1**

**7** *1 ¼* **Following Breeze (IRE)** 2-8-11 0 DavidProbert 8 23
(Jim Boyle) *s.i.s: a in rr: bhd over 1f out* **40/1**

22 **U** **Last Page**[31] 1767 2-9-2 0 JFEgan 6
(David Evans) *bucking violently and uns rdr after 50yds* **9/2**[3]

1m 0.06s (-0.24) **Going Correction** -0.025s/f (Good) **8** Ran SP% **118.2**
Speed ratings (Par 97): **100,99,99,91,90 80,78,**
CSF £5.34 TOTE £1.90: £1.10, £1.60, £3.10; EX 4.60 Trifecta £30.30.
**Owner** Godolphin **Bred** Team Valor Llc & Gaynor Rupert **Trained** Newmarket, Suffolk

**FOCUS**
Race distance as advertised. A fair little novice event in which the winner was value for a wider margin of victory. The second and third ran in keeping with their Yarmouth form.

### 2692 SKY BET ROYAL WINDSOR SPRINT SERIES H'CAP (QUALIFIER) — 6f 12y
6:50 (6:51) (Class 3) (0-90,90) 3-Y-O+ — £7,439 (£2,213; £1,106; £553) Stalls Low

Form RPR

0-00 **1** **Englishman**[21] 2040 7-9-4 **80** DavidProbert 1 87
(Milton Bradley) *mde virtually all: drvn and edgd lft off nr side rail over 1f out: hld on nr fin* **33/1**

14-1 **2** *shd* **Time To Exceed (IRE)**[16] 2147 4-9-5 **81** RyanMoore 6 88
(Henry Candy) *chsd ldrs: pushed along over 2f out: swtchd rt to r against rail 1f out: drvn and r.o to take 2nd nr fin: jst failed* **7/2**[1]

-133 **3** *¾* **Alkhor**[18] 2113 4-9-11 **87** FrankieDettori 3 92
(Richard Hannon) *w wnr: stl nrly upsides fnl f: hld last 100yds and lost 2nd pl sn after* **6/1**[3]

31-0 **4** *nk* **Gulliver**[25] 1904 3-9-4 **90** (bt) AndreaAtzeni 5 91+
(Hugo Palmer) *s.s and early reminder off the pce in last: prog on outer over 2f out: drvn and kpt on fnl f: nrst fin* **5/1**[2]

55-2 **5** *¾* **Goring (GER)**[14] 2230 5-9-9 **85** JohnFahy 9 86
(Eve Johnson Houghton) *chsd ldrs: effrt on outer 2f out: rdn and ch 1f out: one pce after* **8/1**

41 **6** *1 ¼* **Sparkalot**[38] 1600 3-8-5 **77** oh1 ow1 JFEgan 7 71
(Simon Dow) *pressed ldrs: shkn up and no rspnse 2f out: fdd fnl f* **7/2**[1]

4-13 **7** *3 ¼* **Sword Exceed (GER)**[25] 1895 3-8-9 **81** OisinMurphy 4 65
(Ivan Furtado) *trckd ldrs: nudged along 2f out: lost grnd over 1f out: nvr on terms after* **8/1**

5/0- **8** *13* **Lawmaking**[173] 8069 4-10-0 **90** LiamKeniry 2 35
(Henry Spiller) *sn outpcd: bhd fr 1/2-way: t.o* **80/1**

1-2 **9** *2 ½* **Don't Blame Me**[45] 1467 4-9-0 **76** AdamKirby 8 13
(Clive Cox) *pressed ldrs to 1/2-way: wknd over 2f out: eased and t.o* **8/1**

1m 11.36s (-1.64) **Going Correction** -0.025s/f (Good)
**WFA** 3 from 4yo+ 10lb **9** Ran SP% **112.9**
Speed ratings (Par 107): **109,108,107,107,106 104,100,83,79**
CSF £142.63 CT £814.47 TOTE £44.40: £8.60, £1.60, £1.90; EX 301.70 Trifecta £2134.60.
**Owner** E A Hayward **Bred** Peter Winkworth **Trained** Sedbury, Gloucs

**FOCUS**
Race distance as advertised. Fair sprint handicap form, the winner bouncing back off his reduced mark. The runner-up found a bit on her bare Leicester form.

### 2693 SKY BET ROYAL WINDSOR STKS (LISTED RACE) (C&G) — 1m 31y
(7:20) (Class 1) 3-Y-O+ — £

### 2694 SKY BET BEST ODDS GUARANTEED H'CAP — 1m 31y
(7:50) (Class 5) (0-70,) 3-Y-O — £

### 2695 SKY BET HORSERACING CASH OUT H'CAP — 1m 3f 99y
(8:20) (Class 5) (0-75,) 3-Y-O — £

T/Plt: £13.40 to a £1 stake. Pool: £71,986.00 - 5,362.55 winning units T/Qpdt: £2.60 to a £1 stake. Pool: £5,527.00 - 2,103.61 winning units **Jonathan Neesom**

## 2483 SAINT-CLOUD (L-H)

Monday, May 15

**OFFICIAL GOING: Turf: soft**

### 2696a PRIX D'ALSACE (H'CAP) (4YO+) (TURF) 7f

12:47 4-Y-0+

**£20,888** (£8,444; £6,222; £4,000; £2,444; £1,555)

RPR

1 **Borsakov (IRE)**[41] 5-9-6 **0** .... TheoBachelot 13 87
(V Luka Jr, Czech Republic) **145/10**

2 1/2 **Crepusculedesdieux (FR)**[15] 6-9-13 **0** ....(p) GeraldMosse 2 93
(C Boutin, France) **29/1**

3 hd **Rakhsh (FR)**[43] 1531 5-9-7 **0** .... EddyHardouin 5 86
(Carina Fey, France) **153/10**

4 nk **Yume (FR)**[15] 6-9-4 **0** ....(b) AntoineHamelin 1 83
(C Lerner, France) **57/10**[1]

5 snk **Lefortovo (FR)**[25] 1920 4-9-11 **0** .... MickaelBarzalona 7 89
(Jo Hughes) *a cl up: drvn to chal 2f out: virtually upsides ldr fr 1 1/2f out: styd on u.p: no ex fnl 75yds: dropped fr 2nd to 5th cl home* **77/10**

6 snk **Risk Major (FR)**[27] 4-9-1 **0** ....(b) MaximeGuyon 11 79
(V Luka Jr, Czech Republic) **26/1**

7 snk **Comedia Eria (FR)**[35] 5-9-1 **0** .... FabriceVeron 3 78
(P Monfort, France) **73/10**[3]

8 3/4 **Moonlight Gambler (FR)**[25] 1920 8-9-6 **0** .... AurelienLemaitre 16 81
(N Caullery, France) **36/1**

9 2 **Nisham (IRE)**[48] 5-9-6 **0** ....(p) FranckBlondel 10 76
(J Phelippon, France) **146/10**

10 1 **Line Drummer (FR)**[35] 1691 7-9-8 **0** .... CristianDemuro 6 75
(J Reynier, France) **122/10**

11 snk **Cap Rocat (FR)**[62] 4-9-8 **0** .... Pierre-CharlesBoudot 14 75
(F-H Graffard, France) **63/10**[2]

12 1 3/4 **Pont Neuilly (FR)**[14] 7-9-1 **0** ....(p) VincentCheminaud 4 63
(Yves de Nicolay, France) **29/1**

13 3/4 **Enjoy The Silence (FR)**[14] 4-9-2 **0** .... TonyPiccone 15 62
(C Boutin, France) **192/10**

14 3/4 **Grey Caviar (FR)**[14] 4-9-0 **0** .... FabienLefebvre 8 58
(M Le Forestier, France) **46/1**

15 1 **Mr Splendid (FR)**[27] 8-9-5 **0** .... AlexisBadel 12 60
(G Doleuze, France) **117/10**

16 4 **Furious Des Aigles (FR)**[41] 5-9-0 **0** .... RonanThomas 9 45
(Mme C Barande-Barbe, France) **41/5**

1m 28.01s (-4.19) **16** Ran SP% **117.6**

PARI-MUTUEL (all including 1 euro stake): WIN 15.50; PLACE 5.40, 9.40, 6.20; DF 321.80; SF 667.60.

**Owner** Partyday Cz **Bred** Niarchos Family **Trained** Czech Republic

### 2697a PRIX DE GARCHES (CLAIMER) (3YO) (TURF) 1m

1:50 3-Y-0 **£11,538** (£4,615; £3,461; £2,307; £1,153)

RPR

1 **Tap Tap Boom**[48] 1417 3-8-11 0 .... TheoBachelot 2 79
(George Baker) *mde all: broke wl and led: pushed along over 2f out: drvn wl over 1f out: styd on wl fnl f* **142/10**

2 1 1/4 **Frosty Bay (FR)**[22] 3-8-11 0 .... AurelienLemaitre 3 76
(N Caullery, France) **111/10**

3 1 1/2 **Vecellio (IRE)**[29] 3-8-7 0 .... AlexandreChesneau[(8)] 1 77
(G Botti, France) **225/10**

4 snk **La Fibrossi (FR)**[26] 3-8-6 0 .... TristanBaron[(5)] 8 72
(H-A Pantall, France) **17/5**[1]

5 shd **Deimos (FR)**[57] 3-9-4 0 .... FranckBlondel 7 79
(K Borgel, France) **41/10**[2]

6 1 3/4 **A Magic Man (IRE)**[211] 7401 3-9-1 0 .... MaximeGuyon 4 72
(Henk Grewe, Germany) **98/10**

7 2 1/2 **Wootalove (FR)**[201] 3-8-11 0 .... MickaelBarzalona 5 62
(Mme Pia Brandt, France) **197/10**

8 1 **Sublissimo (FR)**[20] 3-9-1 0 .... Pierre-CharlesBoudot 12 64
(J Phelippon, France) **67/10**

9 2 **Beauregard**[35] 3-8-11 0 .... StephanePasquier 11 55
(N Clement, France) **9/2**[3]

10 hd **Sabree**[14] 2247 3-9-1 0 .... GeraldMosse 6 59
(F-H Graffard, France) **132/10**

11 1 1/4 **Marcoussis**[14] 2247 3-8-8 0 .... ClementLecoeuvre[(3)] 10 52
(C Laffon-Parias, France) **236/10**

1m 42.54s (-4.96) **11** Ran SP% **117.8**

PARI-MUTUEL (all including 1 euro stake): WIN 15.20; PLACE 4.90, 4.30, 6.80; DF 65.00; SF 141.20.

**Owner** Steve & Jolene De'Lemos **Bred** London Thoroughbred Services Ltd **Trained** Manton, Wilts

## 2221 BEVERLEY (R-H)

Tuesday, May 16

**OFFICIAL GOING: Good (7.4)**

Wind: Fresh half against Weather: Heavy cloud and showers

### 2698 RACING UK NOW IN HD NOVICE STKS 5f

**2:00** (2:00) (Class 5) 2-Y-0 **£3,780** (£1,131; £565; £283; £141) **Stalls** Low

Form RPR

2 1 **Lord Riddiford (IRE)**[22] 2029 2-9-2 0 .... JasonHart 11 77
(John Quinn) *.cl up: led jst over 1f out: rdn and hung lft ins fnl f: kpt on wl towards fin* **8/1**

4 2 1 3/4 **Porchy Party (IRE)**[15] 2221 2-9-2 0 .... RichardKingscote 7 71
(Tom Dascombe) *trckd ldng pair: hdwy and cl up over 1f out: effrt whn swtchd rt jst ins fnl f: sn rdn and kpt on* **9/2**[2]

52 3 1 1/4 **Spoof**[8] 2473 2-8-13 0 ....(h[1]) CallumShepherd[(3)] 2 66
(Charles Hills) *t.k.h: trckd ldrs on inner: nt clr run and swtchd lft over 1f out: sn rdn and ev ch ins fnl f: kpt on same pce* **2/1**[1]

4 shd **The Right Choice (IRE)** 2-9-2 0 .... PaulHanagan 4 66+
(Richard Fahey) *dwlt and towards rr: hdwy 3f out: sn in tch: rdn wl over 1f out: kpt on fnl f: nrst fin* **9/2**[2]

0 5 shd **Magic Jazz (IRE)**[27] 1872 2-9-2 0 .... KevinStott 1 65
(Kevin Ryan) *in tch on inner: hdwy 2f out: sn rdn and kpt on fnl f* **12/1**

6 2 3/4 **Skyva** 2-9-2 0 .... TomEaves 8 56
(Brian Ellison) *in tch on outer: hdwy over 2f out: rdn over 1f out: kpt on same pce* **33/1**

4 7 shd **Go Now Go Now (IRE)**[8] 2452 2-9-2 0 .... JoeFanning 5 55
(Mark Johnston) *dwlt: sn chsng ldrs: pushed along over 2f out: rdn wl over 1f out: sn one pce* **7/1**[3]

0 8 5 **Archie Perkins (IRE)**[15] 2221 2-9-2 0 .... AndrewMullen 9 37
(Nigel Tinkler) *a towards rr* **100/1**

9 nk **Reinbeau Prince** 2-9-2 0 .... TonyHamilton 12 36
(Richard Fahey) *dwlt and hmpd sn after s: sn swtchd rt to inner: green and t.k.h after: a rr* **25/1**

10 4 1/2 **Laith Alareen** 2-9-2 0 .... PhillipMakin 6 20
(David O'Meara) *qckly away and led: pushed along 2f out: rdn and hdd over 1f out: sn wknd* **14/1**

11 7 **Haafdasee** 2-9-2 0 .... DavidAllan 3
(Tim Easterby) *green: sn rdn along and a towards rr* **50/1**

1m 4.55s (1.05) **Going Correction** +0.15s/f (Good) **11** Ran SP% **117.4**

Speed ratings (Par 93): **97,94,92,92,91 87,87,79,78,71 60**

CSF £42.89 TOTE £8.10: £2.40, £1.80, £1.40; EX 56.80 Trifecta £150.40.

**Owner** The Jam Partnership **Bred** Malachy M Harney **Trained** Settrington, N Yorks

**FOCUS**

There was 2mm of rainfall in the morning and the going was given as good (GoingStick: 7.4). The early pace wasn't that strong and the principals raced prominently. The first two both progressed.

### 2699 VERY BRITISH RACEDAY SATURDAY 10 JUNE (S) STKS 5f

**2:30** (2:30) (Class 6) 3-Y-0 **£2,587** (£770; £384; £192) **Stalls** Low

Form RPR

4461 1 **Mr Strutter (IRE)**[16] 2182 3-9-2 61 ....(h) JasonHart 5 65
(John Quinn) *qckly away: mde all: rdn and kpt on strly fnl f* **11/10**[1]

05-0 2 2 3/4 **Whigwham**[15] 2223 3-8-6 60 .... PaulHanagan 8 45
(Richard Fahey) *trckd ldrs: hdwy to chse wnr wl over 1f out: sn rdn: drvn and no imp fnl f* **11/4**[2]

3000 3 3 1/2 **Vaux (IRE)**[16] 2181 3-8-11 54 ....(p) GrahamLee 4 38
(Ben Haslam) *towards rr: hdwy over 2f out: rdn to chse ldrs over 1f out: kpt on fnl f* **9/2**[3]

000- 4 hd **Tess Graham**[255] 6129 3-8-6 35 ....(p[1]) JamesSullivan 3 32
(Sarah Hollinshead) *rr: hdwy 1/2-way: chsd ldrs wl over 1f out: sn rdn and kpt on same pce* **28/1**

0-00 5 5 **Henrietta's Dream**[11] 2372 3-8-3 25 ....(v) NathanEvans[(3)] 7 14
(John Wainwright) *prom: pushed along 1/2-way: rdn 2f out: sn drvn and wknd* **100/1**

0- 6 3 **Digital Revolution**[349] 2793 3-8-6 0 .... CamHardie 6
(Antony Brittain) *in tch on outer: rdn along 2f out: sn btn* **40/1**

30-0 7 shd **Precious Skye (IRE)**[24] 1973 3-8-6 49 .... JoeDoyle 2
(Ronald Thompson) *a rr* **40/1**

00-0 8 5 **Melaniemillie**[26] 1913 3-8-6 57 ....(p[1]) AndrewMullen 1
(Ollie Pears) *cl up on inner: pushed along after 2f: rdn 1/2-way: hld whn sltly hmpd wl over 1f out: sn wknd* **11/2**

1m 4.56s (1.06) **Going Correction** +0.15s/f (Good) **8** Ran SP% **117.2**

Speed ratings (Par 97): **97,92,87,86,78 73,73,65**

CSF £4.39 TOTE £2.10: £1.10, £1.50, £1.70; EX 5.30 Trifecta £12.80.

**Owner** JJ Quinn Racing Ltd **Bred** Wardstown Stud Ltd **Trained** Settrington, N Yorks

**FOCUS**

A straightforward success for the short-priced favourite in this low-grade race with no depth.

### 2700 ANNIE OXTOBY MEMORIAL H'CAP 5f

**3:00** (3:01) (Class 5) (0-70,72) 4-Y-0+ **£3,780** (£1,131; £565; £283; £141) **Stalls** Low

Form RPR

3-22 1 **Henley**[22] 2034 5-9-6 **69** .... BenCurtis 3 78
(Tracy Waggott) *qckly away: mde all: rdn over 1f out: drvn and hld on wl towards fin* **11/4**[1]

5340 2 3/4 **Vimy Ridge**[11] 2368 5-9-0 **70** ....(t[1]) JoshuaBryan[(7)] 4 76
(Alan Bailey) *in tch: hdwy to chse ldrs 2f out: sn rdn: drvn ent fnl f: styd on wl towards fin* **5/1**[2]

3451 3 shd **Socialites Red**[4] 2589 4-8-9 **65** 6ex ....(p) RPWalsh[(7)] 8 71
(Scott Dixon) *chsd wnr: rdn over 1f out: drvn ent fnl f: styd on* **13/2**

0-00 4 1 3/4 **Twentysvnthlancers**[22] 2034 4-9-4 **67** .... GrahamLee 11 66+
(Paul Midgley) *t.k.h: hld up in rr: hdwy on inner wl over 1f out: rdn ent fnl f: styd on wl: nrst fin* **40/1**

1/-0 5 hd **Thatcherite (IRE)**[19] 2104 9-9-2 **65** ....(t) BarryMcHugh 5 64
(Tony Coyle) *midfield: hdwy 2f out: rdn to chse ldrs over 1f out: drvn and kpt on fnl f* **14/1**

4125 6 1 **Ticks The Boxes (IRE)**[19] 2104 5-9-6 **72** ....(p) NathanEvans[(3)] 12 67
(John Wainwright) *hld up and bhd: hdwy 2f out: rdn and n.m.r jst over 1f out: styd on fnl f: nrst fin* **14/1**

500- 7 shd **Total Power**[327] 3568 4-9-4 **67** .... TomEaves 9 62
(Brian Ellison) *rr: hdwy 2f out: rdn to chse ldrs and edgd rt jst over 1f out: sn drvn and no imp* **25/1**

54-3 8 5 **Jack Luey**[22] 2034 10-9-6 **69** ....(b) PaulHanagan 7 46
(Lawrence Mullaney) *in tch on outer: pushed along over 2f out: sn rdn and wknd over 1f out* **6/1**[3]

0-05 9 4 1/2 **Bond Bombshell**[13] 2305 4-9-0 **70** .... PatrickVaughan[(7)] 2 30
(David O'Meara) *chsd ldrs on inner: rdn along wl over 1f out: drvn: edgd lft and bmpd jst over 1f out: sn wknd* **7/1**

05-0 10 1 1/2 **Oriental Splendour (IRE)**[22] 2034 5-9-6 **69** .... JamesSullivan 13 24
(Ruth Carr) *towards rr: sme hdwy over 2f out: sn rdn and n.d* **18/1**

20-0 11 5 **Tinsill**[24] 1978 6-8-0 **56** oh6 .... RobertDodsworth[(7)] 14
(Nigel Tinkler) *a towards rr* **50/1**

353- 12 9 **Point Of Woods**[216] 7267 4-9-6 **69** .... JackGarritty 1
(Tina Jackson) *chsd ldrs on inner: nt clr run and swtchd lft 1 1/2f out: rdn and hmpd appr fnl f: wknd and eased* **12/1**

0601 13 4 1/2 **Red Invader (IRE)**[53] 1340 7-9-1 **64** ....(p) LiamKeniry 6
(John Butler) *chsd ldrs: rdn along over 2f out: sn wknd* **22/1**

1m 4.42s (0.92) **Going Correction** +0.15s/f (Good) **13** Ran SP% **122.3**

Speed ratings (Par 103): **98,96,96,93,93 91,91,83,76,74 66,51,44**

CSF £15.45 CT £85.20 TOTE £3.50: £1.50, £1.80, £2.60; EX 16.40 Trifecta £80.40.

**Owner** David Tate **Bred** Dandy's Farm **Trained** Spennymoor, Co Durham

**FOCUS**
A competitive sprint on paper, but the well-backed winner had them all in trouble from an early stage. A small pb from him, with the second close to form.

## 2701 HAVE YOUR BIRTHDAY MESSAGE HERE H'CAP — 1m 100y
**3:30** (3:30) (Class 4) (0-85,86) 4-Y-0+ **£6,301** (£1,886; £943; £472; £235) **Stalls** Low

Form — RPR

0-43 **1** **Eternal**[15] 2226 5-9-7 **85** ........ TonyHamilton 6 — 92
(Declan Carroll) *.trckd ldr: effrt and cl up 2f out: rdn ent fnl f: sn drvn: led last 75 yds: jst hld on* — **5/1**[3]

0-65 **2** *nse* **Mohab**[12] 2348 4-9-4 **82** ........ TomEaves 9 — 88
(Kevin Ryan) *hld up in rr: hdwy over 2f out: swtchd lft towards pouter and rdn over 1f out: drvn ins fnl f: fin strly: jst failed* — **14/1**

0-46 **3** *shd* **Gerry The Glover (IRE)**[13] 2291 5-8-11 **75** ........ (p) BenCurtis 4 — 81+
(Brian Ellison) *hld up in rr: hdwy on outer over 1f out: rdn ins fnl f: fin strly: jst hld* — **9/2**[2]

00-0 **4** *1 ½* **Yorkee Mo Sabee (IRE)**[15] 2226 4-8-11 **75** ........ (h) JoeFanning 1 — 77
(Mark Johnston) *set gd pce: pushed along over 1f out: rdn ent fnl f: hdd last 75 yds: no ex* — **20/1**

10-0 **5** *½* **Sovereign Bounty**[22] 2030 5-9-1 **79** ........ GrahamLee 7 — 80
(Jedd O'Keeffe) *chsd ldng pair: pushed along wl over 1f out: sn rdn and kpt on same pce fnl f* — **12/1**

-000 **6** *1 ½* **Save The Bees**[15] 2225 9-8-10 **79** ........ (b) PhilDennis(5) 2 — 77
(Declan Carroll) *hld up towards rr: hdwy on inner wl over 1f out: rdn and styd on wl fnl f* — **33/1**

5-04 **7** *½* **Jacbequick**[15] 2226 6-9-3 **84** ........ (v) JoshDoyle(3) 3 — 81
(David O'Meara) *stmbld s: in tch: hdwy on outer over 2f out: rdn along wl over 1f out: drvn and wknd fnl f* — **7/1**

0-45 **8** *7* **Rousayan (IRE)**[10] 2406 6-9-8 **86** ........ (v) DanielTudhope 5 — 66
(David O'Meara) *plld hrd: chsd ldrs: rdn along wl over 1f out: sn drvn and wknd* — **9/4**[1]

256 **9** *6* **Detachment**[15] 2226 4-8-11 **75** ........ PJMcDonald 8 — 42
(Les Eyre) *trckd ldrs: hdwy over 2f out: rdn wl over 1f out: drvn and wknd appr fnl f* — **5/1**[3]

1m 46.57s (-1.03) **Going Correction** +0.025s/f (Good) — **9** Ran SP% **116.8**
Speed ratings (Par 105): **106,105,105,104,103 102,101,94,88**
CSF £72.40 CT £342.37 TOTE £5.20: £1.60, £4.50, £1.80; EX 68.90 Trifecta £440.70.
**Owner** Steve Ryan **Bred** Nawara Stud Co Ltd **Trained** Malton, N Yorks

**FOCUS**
There was a tight finish to this handicap. The winner's best form in Britain.

## 2702 RACING AGAIN ON WEDNESDAY 31 MAY H'CAP (DIV I) — 1m 1f 207y
**4:00** (4:00) (Class 5) (0-70,72) 3-Y-0 **£3,780** (£1,131; £565; £283; £141) **Stalls** Low

Form — RPR

6513 **1** **Canberra Cliffs (IRE)**[14] 2269 3-9-4 **72** ........ GeorgeWood(5) 7 — 79
(Don Cantillon) *trckd ldrs: smooth hdwy over 2f out: rdn to ld appr fnl f: kpt on wl* — **11/4**[1]

00-0 **2** *¾* **Size Matters**[21] 2060 3-8-2 **54** ........ NathanEvans(3) 8 — 58
(Mark Walford) *led: pushed along over 2f out: rdn wl over 1f out: hdd and drvn appr fnl f: kpt on wl u.p* — **16/1**

00-5 **3** *¾* **True Romance (IRE)**[16] 2186 3-9-2 **65** ........ TomEaves 10 — 67
(James Given) *sn trcking ldr: effrt 2f out and sn rdn: drvn appr fnl f: kpt on* — **17/2**

20-0 **4** *2 ½* **Conistone**[36] 1678 3-8-12 **61** ........ PJMcDonald 2 — 58
(James Bethell) *trckd ldrs on inner: hdwy over 2f out: rdn along over 1f out: drvn and kpt on same pce fnl f* — **14/1**

0-36 **5** *¾* **American Craftsman (IRE)**[12] 2349 3-8-9 **58** ........ (p) ConnorBeasley 6 — 54
(Roger Fell) *hld up in tch: hdwy on outer over 2f out: rdn along to chse ldrs over 1f out: drvn and kpt on one pce fnl f* — **6/1**[3]

15-6 **6** *2* **Katebird (IRE)**[12] 2347 3-9-7 **70** ........ JoeFanning 3 — 62
(Mark Johnston) *.trckd ldrs: effrt over 2f out: rdn along wl over 1f out: sn drvn and wknd* — **5/1**[2]

04-0 **7** *2 ½* **Starlite Sienna (IRE)**[19] 2107 3-9-3 **66** ........ PaulHanagan 5 — 53
(Richard Fahey) *a rr* — **14/1**

54-4 **8** *½* **Miss Bates**[22] 2036 3-9-5 **68** ........ (t[1]) GrahamLee 4 — 54
(Ann Duffield) *hld up in rr: sme hdwy 3f out: rdn along over 2f out: n.d* **8/1**

50-3 **9** *8* **He's A Toff (IRE)**[19] 2107 3-8-8 **57** ........ JasonHart 1 — 27
(Tim Easterby) *hld up: a towards rr* — **7/1**

415- **10** *1 ¾* **Ode To Glory**[209] 7471 3-9-5 **68** ........ MartinHarley 9 — 34
(Rae Guest) *dwlt: sn chsng ldrs on outer: rdn along 2½f out: drvn wl over 1f out: sn wknd* — **11/1**

2m 6.81s (-0.19) **Going Correction** +0.025s/f (Good) — **10** Ran SP% **119.3**
Speed ratings (Par 99): **101,100,99,97,97 95,93,93,86,85**
CSF £52.17 CT £341.52 TOTE £3.80: £1.50, £5.50, £3.10; EX 56.40 Trifecta £418.50.
**Owner** Mrs Catherine Reed **Bred** Barry Davis **Trained** Newmarket, Suffolk

**FOCUS**
A good performance from the winner, who is very much on the up. Again pace dominated, with little making ground from the rear.

## 2703 RACING AGAIN ON WEDNESDAY 31 MAY H'CAP (DIV II) — 1m 1f 207y
**4:30** (4:30) (Class 5) (0-70,72) 3-Y-0 **£3,780** (£1,131; £565; £283; £141) **Stalls** Low

Form — RPR

32-5 **1** **Reinstorm**[22] 2036 3-8-9 **58** ........ PaulHanagan 1 — 65
(Richard Fahey) *trckd ldrs on inner: hdwy 2f out: cl up over 1f out: rdn and n.m.r ins fnl f: led last 100 yds* — **8/1**

0-32 **2** *½* **Jamacho**[11] 2376 3-9-9 **72** ........ BenCurtis 5 — 78
(Brian Ellison) *trckd ldr: cl up 1/2-way: rdn to chal 2f out: drvn to take slt ld and edgd rt jst over 1f out: drvn and edgd rt ins fnl f: hdd and no ex last 100 yds* — **9/2**[2]

5603 **3** *5* **The Raven Master (IRE)**[11] 2371 3-9-2 **65** ........ LouisSteward 3 — 61
(Michael Bell) *led: jnd and rdn 2f out: drvn and hdd whn n.m.r and hmpd appr fnl f: sn one pce* — **11/2**[3]

6-13 **4** *¾* **Copper Baked (FR)**[22] 2035 3-9-6 **69** ........ JoeyHaynes 4 — 64
(K R Burke) *hld up towards rr: hdwy over 2f out: rdn to chse ldrs whn n.m.r and swtchd lft over 1f out: sn drvn and no imp* — **12/1**

00-4 **5** *¾* **Hugging The Rails (IRE)**[12] 2349 3-8-4 **53** ........ JamesSullivan 6 — 46
(Tim Easterby) *hld up in tch: hdwy on outer over 2f out: rdn along over 1f out: no imp fnl f* — **9/1**

-440 **6** *2 ½* **Tewafeedj**[24] 1968 3-9-1 **64** ........ KevinStott 9 — 52
(Kevin Ryan) *chsd ldrs: rdn along over 2f out: sn drvn and wknd* — **9/1**

4322 **7** *nk* **Ronnie The Rooster**[12] 2347 3-9-7 **70** ........ PhillipMakin 2 — 57
(David Barron) *trckd ldrs: swtchd lft to outer and effrt over 2f out: rdn wl over 1f out: sn drvn and btn* — **9/4**[1]

60-0 **8** *shd* **Pindaric**[19] 2107 3-8-12 **61** ........ CamHardie 8 — 48
(Alan Lockwood) *dwlt: a rr* — **20/1**

0-40 **9** *10* **Geophony (IRE)**[19] 2107 3-9-6 **69** ........ JoeFanning 7 — 36
(Mark Johnston) *a rr* — **12/1**

2m 7.11s (0.11) **Going Correction** +0.025s/f (Good) — **9** Ran SP% **115.6**
Speed ratings (Par 99): **100,99,95,95,94 92,92,92,84**
CSF £43.92 CT £216.96 TOTE £8.20: £2.80, £1.50, £2.00; EX 50.60 Trifecta £408.20.
**Owner** Mrs H Steel **Bred** Mrs H Steel **Trained** Musley Bank, N Yorks

**FOCUS**
The slower of the two divisions by 0.3sec. Again pace held up well, and the winner improved up in trip.

## 2704 RACING UK DAY PASS JUST £10 MAIDEN STKS — 7f 96y
**5:00** (5:02) (Class 5) 3-Y-O **£3,780** (£1,131; £565; £283; £141) **Stalls** Low

Form — RPR

5-22 **1** **Mountain Angel (IRE)**[17] 2135 3-9-5 80 ........ AndreaAtzeni 6 — 84+
(Roger Varian) *t.k.h: trckd ldr: cl up 2f out: led over 1f out: sn rdn clr: readily* — **8/11**[1]

**2** *4 ½* **Liquid Gold (IRE)** 3-9-0 0 ........ PaulHanagan 5 — 67+
(Richard Fahey) *trckd ldrs: hdwy 2f out: green and pushed along 1 1/2f out: styd to chse wnr ins fnl f* — **4/1**[3]

**3** *2 ¾* **Inshiraah (FR)** 3-9-0 0 ........ AndrewMullen 2 — 60
(George Peckham) *chsd ldrs: pushed along over 2f out: rdn and green over 1f out: kpt on same pce* — **25/1**

06 **4** *2* **Zone In**[4] 2595 3-9-5 0 ........ TonyHamilton 3 — 60
(Roger Fell) *led: pushed along over 2f out: sn rdn and hdd over 1f out: sn drvn and one pce* — **50/1**

6 **5** *3* **Gloriosus (USA)**[12] 2338 3-9-5 0 ........ JoeFanning 1 — 52+
(Mark Johnston) *t.k.h: chsd ldng pair effrt wl over 2f out: sn rdn along: green and outpcd fr over 1f out* — **3/1**[2]

**6** *6* **Super Ruby** 3-9-0 0 ........ BenCurtis 4 — 32
(K R Burke) *s.i.s: hld up towards rr: effrt and sme hdwy on outer 2 1/2f out: sn pushed along and n.d* — **20/1**

00- **7** *15* **Zarkavon**[327] 3561 3-9-0 0 ........ TomEaves 7
(John Wainwright) *a rr: outpcd and bhd fnl 3f* — **150/1**

1m 34.69s (0.89) **Going Correction** +0.025s/f (Good) — **7** Ran SP% **114.1**
Speed ratings (Par 99): **95,89,86,84,81 74,57**
CSF £3.97 TOTE £1.70: £1.30, £1.60; EX 4.80 Trifecta £31.10.
**Owner** Ziad A Galadari **Bred** Yeomanstown Stud **Trained** Newmarket, Suffolk

**FOCUS**
This proved an easy task for the odds-on favourite. He's given credit for this win, but the overall form is modest.

## 2705 BEVERLEY MIDDLE DISTANCE SERIES H'CAP — 1m 4f 23y
**5:35** (5:37) (Class 6) (0-60,60) 3-Y-O **£2,587** (£770; £384; £192) **Stalls** Low

Form — RPR

64-0 **1** **Dyna Might**[21] 2060 3-8-10 **49** ........ (p[1]) AndrewMullen 2 — 55
(Ollie Pears) *sltly hmpd and reminders s: trckd ldng pair on inner: pushed along over 2f out: rdn and n.m.r over 1f out: swtchd lft and drvn to chal ent fnl f: kpt on wl to ld last 75 yds* — **33/1**

0-55 **2** *½* **Breakwater Bay (IRE)**[12] 2347 3-9-7 **60** ........ DavidAllan 1 — 65
(Tim Easterby) *wnt lft s: led: pushed along 2f out: rdn over 1f out: sn jnd: drvn ent fnl f: hdd and no ex last 75 yds* — **4/1**[3]

4666 **3** *1 ¼* **Nothing Compares**[14] 2264 3-8-11 **50** ........ JoeFanning 3 — 53
(Mark Johnston) *trckd ldr: effrt and cl up over 2f out: rdn wl over 1f out: sn drvn and ev ch tl kpt on same pce ins fnl f* — **10/1**

00-3 **4** *1* **Amadeus Rox (FR)**[22] 2027 3-9-4 **57** ........ MartinHarley 4 — 59
(Alan King) *trckd ldrs on inner: hdwy 2f out: effrt and nt clr run over 1f out: sn rdn and kpt on fnl f* — **9/4**[1]

4022 **5** *½* **Too Many Shots**[22] 2027 3-9-5 **58** ........ KierenFox 6 — 59
(John Best) *trckd ldrs: hdwy over 2f out: rdn and ch over 1f out: sn drvn and kpt on same pce* — **7/2**[2]

560- **6** *shd* **Silver Gleam (IRE)**[172] 8087 3-9-0 **53** ........ JasonHart 11 — 54+
(Chris Fairhurst) *hld up in rr: hdwy 3f out: rdn along 2f out: drvn along on inner over 1f out: kpt on fnl f* — **40/1**

-335 **7** *nk* **Spirit Of Rome (IRE)**[27] 1877 3-9-6 **59** ........ PJMcDonald 8 — 59
(James Bethell) *chsd ldrs: hdwy over 2f out: rdn along wl over 1f out: sn drvn and kpt on same pce fnl f* — **8/1**

4640 **8** *2* **Stag Party (IRE)**[21] 2060 3-8-2 **46** ........ (t[1]) RowanScott(5) 5 — 43+
(Julia Brooke) *hld up in midfield: hdwy on inner over 3f out: rdn along to chse ldrs 2f out: sn drvn and no imp* — **22/1**

6-05 **9** *hd* **Diamante (IRE)**[49] 1410 3-8-13 **52** ........ GeorgeDowning 12 — 49+
(Daniel Kubler) *towards rr: hdwy on outer over 5f out: chsd ldrs 3f out: rdn along 2f out: sn drvn and grad wknd* — **40/1**

4600 **10** *1 ½* **Navajo Star (IRE)**[24] 1968 3-8-11 **50** ........ BenCurtis 9 — 44+
(Michael Appleby) *a towards rr* — **14/1**

40-0 **11** *nk* **Babalugats (IRE)**[17] 2137 3-8-7 **46** ........ DuranFentiman 10 — 40+
(Tim Easterby) *a rr* — **25/1**

560 **12** *6* **Mount Cleshar**[62] 1205 3-8-9 **48** ........ LiamKeniry 7 — 32+
(John Butler) *a rr* — **25/1**

2m 43.43s (3.63) **Going Correction** +0.025s/f (Good) — **12** Ran SP% **119.7**
Speed ratings (Par 97): **88,87,86,86,85 85,85,84,84,83 82,78**
CSF £154.30 CT £1457.38 TOTE £30.20: £6.30, £1.90, £3.40; EX 228.90 Trifecta £4778.10 Part won..
**Owner** Ownaracehorse Ltd (ownaracehorse.co.uk) **Bred** Northmore Stud **Trained** Norton, N Yorks

**FOCUS**
Not for the first time on the card, it paid to race prominently, the first three just swapping places in the closing stages. Ordinary form, with 9lb improvement from the winner.
T/Jkpt: Not won. T/Plt: £62.30 to a £1 stake. Pool: £76,751.11 - 898.05 winning units. T/Qpdt: £39.60 to a £1 stake. Pool: £4,605.36 - 4605.36 winning units. **Joe Rowntree**

# 2357 CHEPSTOW (L-H)
Tuesday, May 16

**OFFICIAL GOING: Good to soft**
Wind: only slight, partly behind them in the straight Weather: rain, easing through evening

## 2706 BEST ODDS GUARANTEED AT 188BET NOVICE AUCTION STKS — 5f 16y
**5:40** (5:40) (Class 5) 2-Y-O **£3,234** (£962; £481; £240) **Stalls** Centre

Form — RPR

**1** **Debutante's Ball (IRE)** 2-8-11 0 ........ LiamJones 8 — 72
(J S Moore) *s.i.s: towards rr: pushed along to cl 3f out: sn chsng ldrs: drvn 1f out: r.o to ld fnl 50 yds* — **25/1**

5 **2** *1 ¼* **May Remain**[36] 1681 2-9-2 0 ........ OisinMurphy 4 — 72
(Paul Cole) *racd keenly: cl up: drvn to ld ent fnl f: hdd fnl 50 yds* — **6/5**[1]

6 **3** *2* **Billiebrookedit (IRE)**[45] 1495 2-9-2 0 ........ RobertWinston 3 65
(Steph Hollinshead) *led: rdn and hdd ent fnl f: hung sltly rt and unable qck* **8/1**

4 **4** *3 1/2* **Data Protection**[14] 2277 2-9-2 0 ........ MartinDwyer 2 52
(William Muir) *prom: rdn 2f out: outpcd by ldrs fnl f* **13/2**[3]

**5** *3/4* **Holdenhurst** 2-8-11 0 ........ MitchGodwin(5) 1 50
(Sylvester Kirk) *cl up 1f: chsd ldrs after: rdn 1/2-way: grad wknd fnl f* **16/1**

**6** *2 3/4* **Major Peirson (IRE)** 2-9-2 0 ........ JFEgan 7 40
(Jo Hughes) *dwlt: pushed along in rr: rdn over 1f out: kpt on but no real imp* **16/1**

2 **7** *11* **Super Florence (IRE)**[14] 2251 2-8-11 0 ........ CharlesBishop 6
(Eve Johnson Houghton) *awkward leaving stalls: chsd ldrs: rdn and no rspnse 1/2-way: sn wknd* **3/1**[2]

1m 1.12s (1.82) **Going Correction** +0.225s/f (Good) **7** Ran SP% **110.5**
Speed ratings (Par 93): **94,92,88,83,82 77,60**
CSF £52.36 TOTE £15.20: £7.40, £1.50; EX 112.10 Trifecta £616.80.
**Owner** Mrs Wendy Jarrett & J S Moore **Bred** Hyde Park Stud & Roger O'Callaghan **Trained** Upper Lambourn, Berks

**FOCUS**
Ground on the slow side after 7mm of rain the previous day. They raced up the middle of the track in this ordinary-looking novice event. The runner-up looks the best guide.

## 2707 LIVE CASINO AT 188BET MAIDEN AUCTION STKS 1m 14y
**6:10** (6:12) (Class 6) 3-Y-O **£2,587** (£770; £384; £192) **Stalls** Centre

Form RPR

2- **1** **Evening Hill**[196] 7733 3-9-5 0 ........ PatDobbs 7 75+
(Richard Hughes) *chsd ldrs: pushed along and wnt 2nd 3f out where ldr was 5 l clr: clsd to ld 1f out: sn c clr: comf* **5/2**[2]

34- **2** *3* **Valley Of Rocks (IRE)**[217] 7243 3-9-5 0 ........ FrannyNorton 6 66
(Mark Johnston) *t.k.h: led: clr after 2f: stl 5 l up 3f out: drvn and hdd 1f out: no ex* **2/1**[1]

0-4 **3** *1* **Zulu**[16] 2172 3-9-5 0 ........ RyanTate 5 64
(Rod Millman) *cl up 2f: outpcd by ldr after 2f: rdn and lost 2nd 3f out: kpt on: one pce fnl f* **10/1**

**4** *8* **Sonnetist** 3-9-5 0 ........ TomMarquand 2 46+
(Richard Hannon) *green in preliminaries: s.i.s: in rr: drvn over 3f out: hung rt and wnt modest 4th over 1f out* **4/1**[3]

**5** *11* **Queen Moon (IRE)** 3-9-0 0 ........ OisinMurphy 4 17
(Andrew Balding) *s.s: sn in tch w main body: wknd over 2f out: lost modest 4th over 1f out* **8/1**

**6** *3 3/4* **Act Swiftly (IRE)** 3-9-5 0 ........ LiamJones 3 14
(J S Moore) *s.i.s and chsd along in rr: drvn after 3f: bhd fr 1/2-way* **25/1**

**7** *9* **Kyshoni (IRE)** 3-9-0 0 ........ TomQueally 1
(Mike Murphy) *s.s: sn in tch w main body: rdn 3f out: wknd qckly* **18/1**

1m 38.64s (2.44) **Going Correction** +0.225s/f (Good) **7** Ran SP% **111.2**
Speed ratings (Par 97): **96,93,92,84,73 69,60**
CSF £7.45 TOTE £3.40: £1.80, £1.60; EX 7.20 Trifecta £33.50.
**Owner** The Heffer Syndicate **Bred** Natton House Thoroughbreds **Trained** Upper Lambourn, Berks

**FOCUS**
Not much depth to this maiden and the favourite did too much early running. They raced middle to stands' side. The form is rated a shade negatively.

## 2708 188BET H'CAP 1m 14y
**6:40** (6:42) (Class 5) (0-75,77) 4-Y-O+ **£3,234** (£962; £481; £240) **Stalls** Centre

Form RPR

5431 **1** **Roman De Brut (IRE)**[27] 1893 5-8-11 **70** ........ CharlieBennett(5) 13 82
(Daniel Mark Loughnane) *one of 3 to r stands' side: prom overall: drvn over 2f out: sn hung rt: led 1f out: kpt on wl to pull clr fnl f* **7/1**

1500 **2** *3 1/4* **Tripartite (IRE)**[18] 2120 4-9-1 **69** ........ MartinLane 1 75
(Jeremy Gask) *prom: rdn to go 2nd 3f out: led 2f out: sn edgd rt: hdd 1f out: no ex fnl f* **7/1**

214- **3** *2 3/4* **Barista (IRE)**[173] 8086 9-8-7 **64** ........ HollieDoyle(3) 8 63
(Brian Forsey) *s.i.s: in rr: drvn and hdwy over 2f out: styd on to go 3rd ins fnl f* **14/1**

0050 **4** *2 1/4* **Satchville Flyer**[22] 2040 6-9-6 **74** ........ JFEgan 12 68
(David Evans) *hld up and t.k.h: hdwy 3f out: sn drvn: styd on fnl f to go hld 4th nr fin* **16/1**

60-0 **5** *nk* **My Lucille (IRE)**[39] 1606 4-9-7 **75** ........ AdamBeschizza 10 68
(Chris Wall) *led tl rdn and hdd 2f out: wknd and lost 2 pls ins fnl f* **9/1**

-006 **6** *1 3/4* **Raashdy (IRE)**[103] 527 4-8-9 **63** ........ LukeMorris 14 52
(Peter Hiatt) *one of 3 to r stands' side: towards rr overall: rdn 1/2-way: styd on fnl 2f: unable to trble ldrs* **20/1**

466- **7** *1/2* **Zaria**[239] 6635 6-8-1 **62** ........(p) WilliamCox(7) 11 50
(Richard Price) *in tch: racd w main body in centre tl swtchd to r w 2 other stands' side 1/2-way: rdn 3f out: wknd over 1f out* **16/1**

-665 **8** *4 1/2* **Smart Mover (IRE)**[11] 2358 4-8-7 **61** oh3 ........ RyanTate 6 38
(Nikki Evans) *chsd ldrs: rdn and lost pl 3f out: wknd over 1f out* **20/1**

00-4 **9** *nk* **Overhaugh Street**[46] 1473 4-8-6 **63** ........ CallumShepherd(3) 3 40
(Ed de Giles) *prom tl rdn and lost pl over 3f out: grad wknd* **6/1**[3]

000- **10** *2* **Fit For The Job (IRE)**[233] 6821 5-9-6 **74** ........ TimmyMurphy 2 46
(Jonjo O'Neill) *trckd ldrs: shkn up and unable qck 2f out: wknd 1f out* **9/2**[1]

41-4 **11** *1 1/4* **Sarangoo**[14] 2256 9-9-4 **77** ........ RyanWhile(5) 9 46
(Malcolm Saunders) *cl up: rdn and lost 2nd over 3f out: wknd over 1f out* **20/1**

3621 **12** *10* **Ravenhoe (IRE)**[13] 2301 4-9-5 **73** ........ FrannyNorton 7 19
(Mark Johnston) *chsd ldrs: rdn 3f out: wknd 2f out: eased fnl f* **5/1**[2]

1m 37.09s (0.89) **Going Correction** +0.225s/f (Good) **12** Ran SP% **116.9**
Speed ratings (Par 103): **104,100,98,95,95 93,93,88,88,86 85,75**
CSF £52.70 CT £669.74 TOTE £8.20: £2.60, £3.00, £4.40; EX 70.00 Trifecta £784.50.
**Owner** Phil Slater **Bred** Tinnakill Bloodstock **Trained** Rock, Worcs

**FOCUS**
The winner was one of only two horses who raced stands' side throughout, with the others middle to far side. A clear pb from the winner, but the form isn't taken too literally.

## 2709 188BET.CO.UK H'CAP 6f 16y
**7:10** (7:13) (Class 5) (0-70,70) 4-Y-O+ **£3,234** (£962; £481; £240) **Stalls** Centre

Form RPR

0402 **1** **Indian Affair**[24] 1980 7-8-12 **61** ........(bt) RobertWinston 11 68
(Milton Bradley) *trckd ldrs: rdn over 1f out: r.o to ld jst ins fnl f: drvn out* **9/2**[1]

11-0 **2** *3/4* **Spirit Of Rosanna**[18] 2124 5-8-10 **59** ........(tp) AdamBeschizza 6 64
(Steph Hollinshead) *led: rdn 2f out: hdd jst ins fnl f: r.o* **9/2**[1]

5-40 **3** *1 3/4* **Kaaber (USA)**[116] 332 6-8-0 **56** oh5 ........(b) DavidEgan(7) 8 55
(Roy Brotherton) *chsd ldrs: rdn 3f out: over 2f out: swtchd lft over 1f out: carried further lft ins fnl f: kpt on to take 3rd nr fin* **12/1**

200- **4** *hd* **Jaganory (IRE)**[216] 7268 5-8-2 **56** oh1 ........(p) LuluStanford(5) 4 55
(Christopher Mason) *midfield: clsd 3f out: drvn over 2f out: sn ev ch: edgd rt over 1f out: hung lft and no ex ins fnl f: lost 3rd nr fin* **25/1**

0600 **5** *2 3/4* **Divine Call**[22] 2043 10-8-8 **57** ........(b) DavidProbert 10 47
(Milton Bradley) *s.i.s: towards rr: hdwy over 2f out: drvn and r.o fnl f* **16/1**

0000 **6** *nk* **King Of Swing**[22] 2038 4-9-7 **70** ........(h) PatDobbs 9 59+
(Richard Hughes) *sed awkwardly: hld up: pushed along over 2f out: no imp tl r.o fnl f* **10/1**

64-1 **7** *1 1/4* **Bonjour Steve**[134] 20 6-8-13 **62** ........(p) KieranO'Neill 3 47
(Richard Price) *t.k.h: trckd ldrs: rdn 3f out: wknd fnl f* **7/1**[2]

0-00 **8** *1* **Major Assault**[17] 2140 4-8-12 **61** ........ JohnFahy 13 43
(Matthew Salaman) *towards rr: rdn 2f out: no real imp* **14/1**

560- **9** *4* **Fantasy Justifier (IRE)**[203] 7590 6-9-4 **67** ........ LukeMorris 2 36
(Ronald Harris) *t.k.h: cl up: rdn and little rspnse 2f out: wknd fnl f* **8/1**[3]

2-65 **10** *2 3/4* **Showmethewayavrilo**[14] 2253 4-9-5 **68** ........ OisinMurphy 7 28+
(Malcolm Saunders) *rrd s: in rr: rdn 1/2-way: no real imp* **9/2**[1]

00/0 **11** *1/2* **A Definite Diamond**[34] 1729 4-8-4 **56** oh11 ........ AaronJones(3) 1 15
(Grace Harris) *midfield on outer: rdn 1/2-way: wknd 2f out* **100/1**

630- **12** *7* **Donttouchthechips (IRE)**[260] 5953 4-9-0 **63** ........ StevieDonohoe 12
(Nikki Evans) *cl up: drvn 3f out: sn wknd: bhd fnl f* **14/1**

1m 12.92s (0.92) **Going Correction** +0.225s/f (Good) **12** Ran SP% **119.0**
Speed ratings (Par 103): **102,101,98,98,94 94,92,91,86,82 81,72**
CSF £23.34 CT £234.80 TOTE £6.00: £1.90, £1.70, £5.10; EX 25.10 Trifecta £463.20.
**Owner** J M Bradley **Bred** Mette Campbell-Andenaes **Trained** Sedbury, Gloucs

**FOCUS**
They all raced stands' side to begin with, before a few of them drifted out under pressure, and the rail again looked the place to be. The winner is rated to his latter 2016 turf form.

## 2710 FOLLOW US ON TWITTER AT 188BET FILLIES' H'CAP 1m 2f
**7:40** (7:41) (Class 5) (0-70,69) 4-Y-O+ **£3,234** (£962; £481; £240) **Stalls** Low

Form RPR

63-1 **1** **Miss Inga Sock (IRE)**[14] 2257 5-8-6 **59** ........ GeorgiaCox(5) 10 66
(Eve Johnson Houghton) *trckd ldrs in steadily run r: rdn over 2f out: led narrowly 1f out: asserted fnl 75 yds: pushed out* **3/1**[2]

605- **2** *1/2* **Dora's Field (IRE)**[200] 7669 4-9-7 **69** ........ OisinMurphy 3 75
(Stuart Kittow) *s.i.s: sn trcking ldr in steadily run r: chal 3f out: rdn 2f out: ev ch tl unable qck fnl 75 yds* **4/1**[3]

00-1 **3** *3/4* **Angelical (IRE)**[17] 2153 4-8-5 **60** ........ DavidEgan(7) 8 64+
(Daniel Mark Loughnane) *plld hrd: trckd ldrs in steadily run r: drvn 3f out: swtchd rt over 1f out: styd on u.p fnl f* **11/4**[1]

-550 **4** *1* **Here's Two**[16] 2177 4-9-7 **69** ........ LukeMorris 5 71
(Ron Hodges) *t.k.h: led and set stdy pce: jnd 3f out and sn increased tempo: rdn 2f out: hdd 1f out: one pce and lost 3rd towards fin* **7/1**

4-04 **5** *2* **Dizzey Heights (IRE)**[31] 526 5-9-2 **67** ........ ShelleyBirkett(3) 6 65
(Stuart Kittow) *dwlt sltly: hld up in steadily run r: hdwy 3f out: sn drvn: outpcd by ldrs over 1f out: keeping on towards fin* **8/1**

0-24 **6** *3* **Pensax Lady (IRE)**[71] 1067 4-8-4 **57** ........ CharlieBennett(5) 9 49
(Daniel Mark Loughnane) *t.k.h towards rr in steadily run r: rdn and outpcd over 2f out: no ch after* **13/2**

50-0 **7** *hd* **Saga Sprint (IRE)**[12] 2333 4-8-10 **65** ........ GinaMangan(7) 7 57
(J R Jenkins) *hld up in last in steadily run r: rdn and outpcd over 2f out: no ch after* **25/1**

2m 16.67s (6.07) **Going Correction** +0.25s/f (Good) **7** Ran SP% **112.5**
Speed ratings (Par 100): **85,84,84,83,81 79,79**
CSF £14.86 CT £34.98 TOTE £3.70: £1.40, £2.40; EX 19.00 Trifecta £41.20.
**Owner** The Ascot Colts & Fillies Club **Bred** R F Johnson Houghton **Trained** Blewbury, Oxon

**FOCUS**
The first race of the night on the round course. They went slow early, so it proved hard to make up ground, and the winner challenged more towards the middle than the next four finishers, who raced more far side. The winner got back towards her 3yo form.

## 2711 DAILY RACING SPECIALS AT 188BET H'CAP 1m 4f
**8:10** (8:15) (Class 6) (0-65,67) 3-Y-O **£2,587** (£770; £384; £192) **Stalls** Low

Form RPR

6-04 **1** **Mirzam (IRE)**[13] 2307 3-9-7 **65** ........ CharlesBishop 12 75
(Mick Channon) *trckd ldrs: rdn 2f out: led over 1f out: styd on wl* **12/1**

000- **2** *1* **Knight Destroyer (IRE)**[234] 6777 3-9-5 **63** ........ TimmyMurphy 1 71
(Jonjo O'Neill) *midfield: impr gng wl whn briefly nt clr run over 2f out: swtchd rt over 1f out: r.o wl fnl f: tk 2nd cl home* **16/1**

034- **3** *hd* **Eolian**[216] 7286 3-9-5 **63** ........ OisinMurphy 5 71
(Andrew Balding) *a.p: rdn to ld over 2f out: kpt on u.p: lost 2nd cl home* **9/2**[1]

0-46 **4** *3 1/2* **Plato's Kode (IRE)**[22] 2017 3-9-2 **60** ........(tp) TomQueally 6 62
(Seamus Durack) *chsd ldrs: rdn and sltly outpcd 2f out: styd on fnl f* **16/1**

00-1 **5** *2 3/4* **London Master**[21] 2060 3-9-7 **65** ........ AdamBeschizza 11 63
(Chris Wall) *s.i.s: hld up: rdn and hdwy 3f out: styd on same pce fnl 2f* **5/1**[2]

00-0 **6** *1 1/2* **Bed Of Diamonds**[11] 2371 3-8-4 **51** oh6 ........ NoelGarbutt(3) 10 46
(Adam West) *s.s: racd keenly towards rr: rdn 3f out: styd on fr over 1f out* **66/1**

-116 **7** *2 1/2* **Daily Trader**[34] 1736 3-9-9 **67** ........ DavidProbert 13 58
(David Evans) *hld up: hdwy on outer over 3f out: rdn over 2f out: wknd fnl f* **9/2**[1]

050- **8** *1/2* **Cape Cruiser (USA)**[153] 8355 3-9-6 **64** ........ PatDobbs 2 54
(Ralph Beckett) *led tl rdn and hdd over 2f out: wknd fnl f* **14/1**

0-30 **9** *1* **Hot Lick**[82] 881 3-8-6 **55** ........(t[1]) MeganNicholls(5) 4 44
(Dan Skelton) *t.k.h: chsd ldrs tl lost pl 5f out: styd on fnl f* **25/1**

025- **10** *1 3/4* **Bianca Minola (FR)**[218] 7209 3-9-7 **65** ........ TomMarquand 14 51
(David Menuisier) *prom: trckd ldr after 2f: lost 2nd and rdn over 3f out: wknd 2f out: gng on again fnl f* **20/1**

00-3 **11** *2* **Black Prince (FR)**[34] 1726 3-8-9 **53** ........ JFEgan 7 36
(Anthony Honeyball) *towards rr: hdwy on outer 4f out: rdn 3f out: wknd fnl f* **7/1**[3]

66-3 **12** *1 1/4* **Mystical Nelly**[48] 1424 3-9-1 **59** ........ LukeMorris 9 40
(Jonathan Portman) *cl up 1f: midfield after tl hdwy to chse ldrs 4f out: rdn over 2f out: wknd over 1f out* **40/1**

0-10 **13** *17* **American Patrol (IRE)**[104] 502 3-9-2 **60** ........ FrannyNorton 3 14
(Neil Mulholland) *hld up and a last: rdn and no rspnse 3f out: t.o fnl 2f* **9/1**

2m 42.02s (3.02) **Going Correction** +0.25s/f (Good) **13** Ran SP% **114.2**
Speed ratings (Par 97): **99,98,98,95,94 93,91,91,90,89 87,87,75**
CSF £165.92 CT £867.04 TOTE £12.40: £3.70, £4.40, £1.90; EX 236.30 Trifecta £1192.00.
**Owner** Box 41 Racing **Bred** J K Thoroughbreds **Trained** West Ilsley, Berks
■ Perla Blanca was withdrawn. Price at time of withdrawal 12-1. Rule 4 applies to all bets - deduction 5p in the pound

**FOCUS**
A modest handicap run at a steady pace. It has been rated in line with the race averages.

## 2712 TICKET GIVEAWAYS AT 188BET H'CAP 2m
**8:40** (8:42) (Class 6) (0-60,60) 4-Y-O+ **£2,587** (£577; £577; £192) **Stalls** Low

Form RPR

63-0 **1** **Sir Pass I Am**[22] 2022 4-9-5 **60**.......... OisinMurphy 7 72+
(Andrew Balding) *trckd ldrs: rdn to ld 2f out: styd on strly: 10 l clr whn heavily eased fnl 75yds: pack clsd and line jst c in time* **3/1**[1]

00-0 **2** *nk* **My Mo (FR)**[23] 1758 5-8-9 **55**..........(p) DavidEgan(7) 5 55
(David Dennis) *a.p: rdn to ld 3f out: sn hdd and qckly outpcd: kpt on same pce but clsd on heavily eased wnr towards fin: jnd for 2nd post* **8/1**[3]

4602 **2** *dht* **Cold Fusion (IRE)**[11] 2364 4-8-7 **51**..........(tp) HollieDoyle(3) 1 51
(David Flood) *t.k.h in midfield: lost pl 7f out: hdwy on outer over 2f out: styd on fnl f: clsd on heavily eased wnr towards fin: tk share of 2nd post* **10/1**

311- **4** *2* **Work (IRE)**[15] 7532 4-9-5 **60**..........(t) PatDobbs 2 57
(David Pipe) *hld up: hdwy into midfield after 6f: rdn 3f out: kpt on same pce fnl 2f* **16/1**

63-4 **5** *1/2* **Taste The Wine (IRE)**[11] 2363 11-8-13 **52**.......... DavidProbert 6 49
(Bernard Llewellyn) *towards rr: rdn over 3f out: styd on fnl f* **14/1**

0/6- **6** *nse* **Aristocracy**[426] 957 6-9-0 **53**.......... TimmyMurphy 3 50
(Fergal O'Brien) *prom: rdn 3f out: styd on same pce* **10/1**

-064 **7** *nse* **The Quarterjack**[15] 2219 8-8-12 **51**.......... LukeMorris 8 48
(Ron Hodges) *hld up: rdn and hdwy over 3f out: disputing 2nd but nowhere nr wnr whn hmpd over 1f out: one pce after* **7/1**[2]

2303 **8** *3/4* **Tingo In The Tale (IRE)**[21] 2059 8-9-1 **54**..........(tp) TomMarquand 4 50
(Sophie Leech) *midfield: rdn over 3f out: styd on fnl f* **20/1**

0-52 **9** *2 3/4* **Madam Lilibet (IRE)**[22] 2032 8-9-5 **58**.......... PaddyAspell 11 50
(Sharon Watt) *chsd ldrs tl rel to r and dropped to detached last after 3f: styd on u.p fnl 2f* **8/1**[3]

4-02 **10** *4 1/2* **The Lampo Genie**[40] 1585 5-9-5 **58**..........(b) StevieDonohoe 9 45
(Johnny Farrelly) *hld up: hdwy 1/2-way: drvn 3f out: sn wknd* **8/1**[3]

3-00 **11** *9* **Tarakkom (FR)**[69] 1082 5-8-12 **51**.......... TomQueally 12 27
(Peter Hiatt) *led: clr after 2f tl after 5f: drvn and hdd 3f out: wknd wl over 1f out* **8/1**[3]

/0-5 **12** *6* **Idle Talker (IRE)**[117] 315 5-9-7 **60**.......... MartinLane 10 29
(Nick Gifford) *prom: rdn 3f out: wknd 2f out* **16/1**

3m 44.3s (5.40) **Going Correction** +0.25s/f (Good)
**WFA** 4 from 5yo+ 1lb **12** Ran SP% **123.3**
Speed ratings (Par 101): **96,95,95,94,94 94,94,94,92,90 86,83**
WIN: £4.20; PL: Sir Pass I Am £1.70, My Mo £3.10, Cold Fusion £2.30; EX: SP/MM £20.70, SP/CF £24.40; CSF: SP/MM £13.93, SP/CF £17.71; TC: SP/MM/CF £111.54, SP/CF/MM £114.12; TF: SP/MM/CF £154.00, SP/CF/MM £137.90;.
**Owner** Mrs Sandie Newton **Bred** Mrs J S Newton **Trained** Kingsclere, Hants

**FOCUS**
The bare result doesn't tell anything like the full story in this low-grade staying handicap. The heavily eased winner took a clear step forward.
T/Plt: £599.30 to a £1 stake. Pool: £69,390.45 - 84.51 winning units. T/Qpdt: £154.60 to a £1 stake. Pool: £6,976.09 - 33.38 winning units. **Richard Lowther**

2713-2719a (Foreign Racing) - See Raceform Interactive

# 2508 BATH (L-H)
## Wednesday, May 17

**OFFICIAL GOING: Good (good to soft in places) changing to soft (good to soft in places) after race 2 (17:55)**
Wind: mild breeze against Weather: light rain

## 2720 SIS H'CAP 5f 10y
**5:20** (5:23) (Class 5) (0-70,72) 3-Y-O **£3,234** (£962; £481; £240) **Stalls** Centre

Form RPR

-354 **1** **Jashma (IRE)**[16] 2235 3-9-0 **62**.......... ShaneKelly 5 73
(Richard Hughes) *chsd ldr: edgd lft whn rdn over 1f out: led ins fnl f: r.o wl* **6/1**[3]

003- **2** *2* **Secret Agent**[146] 8494 3-8-12 **65**.......... GeorgeWood(5) 3 69
(William Muir) *chsd ldr: rdn oer 2f out: kpt on ins fnl f: wnt 2nd towards fin* **13/2**

011 **3** *1/2* **Fethiye Boy**[16] 2235 3-9-5 **72**.......... MitchGodwin(5) 4 74
(Ronald Harris) *led: sn pressed by loose horse: rdn 2f out: hdd ins fnl f: no ex* **9/2**[1]

60-0 **4** *1* **Pastfact**[15] 2252 3-8-13 **61**.......... JosephineGordon 6 59
(Malcolm Saunders) *sn pushed along: mid-div: hdwy 2f out: kpt on same pce fnl f* **17/2**

2020 **5** *1 1/4* **Met By Moonlight**[9] 2474 3-9-3 **65**.......... RichardKingscote 2 59
(Ron Hodges) *mid-div: sn pushed along : hdwy 2f out: nt clr run briefly wl over 1f out: kpt on ins fnl f but nt pce to threaten* **13/2**

1153 **6** *1* **Dashing Poet**[15] 2271 3-9-3 **65**..........(h) MartinLane 1 55
(Jeremy Gask) *racd keenly early: trckd ldrs: rdn wl over 2f out: fdd ins fnl f* **7/1**

0324 **7** *1 1/2* **Tooty Fruitti**[22] 2065 3-8-11 **59**.......... FrannyNorton 9 44
(Jo Hughes) *v bdly hmpd leaving stalls: a last pair: nvr rcvrd* **8/1**

40-0 **8** *15* **Kody Ridge (IRE)**[18] 2151 3-9-7 **69**..........(h) TimmyMurphy 11
(David Dennis) *v s.i.s: a detached in last* **16/1**

0520 **U** **Lightoller (IRE)**[9] 2474 3-8-7 **62**..........(b) KeithQuinn(7) 8
(Mick Channon) *veered bdly rt leaving stalls and uns rdr* **5/1**[2]

1m 3.25s (0.75) **Going Correction** +0.40s/f (Good) **9** Ran SP% **115.8**
Speed ratings (Par 99): **110,106,106,104,102 100,98,74,**
CSF £44.75 CT £192.64 TOTE £7.30: £2.40, £2.40, £1.40; EX 51.10 Trifecta £158.30.
**Owner** M Clarke, S Geraghty, J Jeffries **Bred** Jonathan David Clague **Trained** Upper Lambourn, Berks

**FOCUS**
Some starts have been moved at this track following remeasuring, so some races will not have speed figures until there is sufficient data to calculate updated median times. Not a bad sprint handicap run at a sound pace. It paid to race handy and the winner reversed Windsor form with the favourite..

## 2721 BRITISH STALLION STUDS EBF MAIDEN STKS 1m 3f 137y
**5:55** (5:55) (Class 4) 3-4-Y-O **£4,690** (£1,395; £697; £348) **Stalls** Low

Form RPR

34-4 **1** **Nathania**[39] 1624 3-8-7 **79** ow1.......... ShaneKelly 8 75
(Richard Hughes) *mid-div: hdwy over 3f out: rdn to ld jst over 1 out: kpt on wl* **9/2**[3]

035- **2** *1 1/2* **Beach Break**[187] 7908 3-8-11 77..........(b[1]) FranBerry 9 76
(Ralph Beckett) *trckd ldr: chal over 2f out: rdn and ev ch ent fnl f: kpt on but no ex* **4/1**[2]

2-34 **3** *hd* **Sufi**[40] 1607 3-8-11 78.......... PatDobbs 4 76
(Richard Hannon) *led: rdn whn chal over 2f out: hdd jst over 1f out: kpt on but no ex* **3/1**[1]

5 **4** *2* **Park Paddocks (IRE)**[18] 2152 3-8-11 0.......... LiamJones 6 73
(William Haggas) *mid-div: hdwy over 2f out: sn rdn: kpt on same pce fr over 1f out: wnt 4th jst ins fnl f* **9/2**[3]

50 **5** *1 3/4* **Akamanto (IRE)**[25] 1963 3-8-11 0.......... RichardKingscote 7 70
(Richard Hannon) *trckd ldrs: rdn over 2f out: sn one pce* **7/1**

4 **6** *1 3/4* **Mudajaj (USA)**[18] 2152 3-8-11 0.......... GavinLerena 1 67+
(Charles Hills) *hld up: effrt over 2f out: nt pce to get on terms* **9/2**[3]

**7** *3/4* **Dance Rock** 4-10-0 0.......... TrevorWhelan 10 67
(Neil Mulholland) *dwlt: last pair: hdwy on outer over 3f out: sn rdn to chse ldrs: one pce fnl 2f* **50/1**

0 **8** *3 1/4* **Nazzaa (IRE)**[18] 2167 4-10-0 0.......... TimmyMurphy 2 61
(Steve Flook) *in tch: snatched up whn short of room on inner 3f out and lost pl: sn rdn: nvr bk on terms* **100/1**

0 **9** *21* **Morning Sequel**[12] 2359 4-9-9 0.......... LiamKeniry 3 22
(Neil Mulholland) *mid-div: clipped heels and dropped to last pair over 5f out: nvr travelling after: wknd over 2f out* **80/1**

2m 36.98s (6.38) **Going Correction** +0.425s/f (Yiel)
**WFA** 3 from 4yo 17lb **9** Ran SP% **116.2**
Speed ratings (Par 105): **95,94,93,92,91 90,89,87,73**
CSF £23.01 TOTE £4.50: £2.00, £1.50, £1.60; EX 23.50 Trifecta £58.10.
**Owner** Harvey Rosenblatt & Friends **Bred** Newsells Park Stud **Trained** Upper Lambourn, Berks

**FOCUS**
Visibility had deteriorated badly prior to the second race. Some big stables in opposition for this maiden which was run at a steady pace. Ordinary form, rated around the principals.

## 2722 CREST NICHOLSON BATH RIVERSIDE H'CAP 1m 2f 37y
**6:25** (6:25) (Class 5) (0-70,69) 4-Y-O+ **£2,911** (£866; £432; £216) **Stalls** Low

Form RPR

00-6 **1** **Berkeley Vale**[25] 1983 6-9-5 **64**..........(b) RobertWinston 7 68
(Roger Teal) *trckd ldr: rdn 2f out: led over 1f out: kpt on wl* **11/4**[2]

4331 **2** *1 1/4* **Attain**[7] 2512 8-9-7 **69** 6ex.......... EdwardGreatrex(3) 3 71
(Archie Watson) *led: rdn 2f out: hdd over 1f out: kpt on but no ex fnl f* **15/8**[1]

5/66 **3** *3/4* **Eben Dubai (IRE)**[16] 2219 5-8-5 **55**.......... GeorgeWood(5) 5 55
(Tracey Barfoot-Saunt) *plld hrd: trckd ldrs: rdn to chse ldng pair over 2f out: kpt on same pce fnl f* **8/1**

604- **4** *shd* **Saint Helena (IRE)**[138] 8144 9-9-7 **66**..........(b) FranBerry 4 66
(Mark Gillard) *hld up last but in tch: rdn and hdwy over 2f out: sn chsng ldng trio: swtchd lft over 1f out: styd on same pce fnl f* **7/1**

00-0 **5** *9* **Henryhudsonbridge (USA)**[117] 333 5-8-8 **60**..........(t[1]) WilliamCox(7) 1 44
(John Flint) *trckd ldrs: rdn over 3f out: sn hld: wknd over 1f out* **10/1**

-516 **6** *12* **Kay Sera**[60] 1256 9-8-11 **56**.......... MartinDwyer 6 18
(Tony Newcombe) *last pair but in tch: rdn over 3f out: wknd over 2f out* **9/2**[3]

2m 14.54s (3.54) **Going Correction** +0.425s/f (Yiel) **6** Ran SP% **112.3**
Speed ratings (Par 103): **102,101,100,100,93 83**
CSF £8.36 TOTE £4.00: £1.90, £1.10; EX 10.50 Trifecta £57.90.
**Owner** Mrs Muriel Forward & Dr G C Forward **Bred** Edward Hyde **Trained** Great Shefford, Berks

**FOCUS**
The going was eased to soft, good to soft in places, prior to the third race. A weak race for the grade, run at a steady pace. The winner only needed to match last summer's form.

## 2723 RAINBOW CASINOS BRISTOL FILLIES' H'CAP 1m 5f 11y
**6:55** (6:55) (Class 5) (0-75,77) 4-Y-O+ **£3,465** (£1,037; £518; £259) **Stalls** High

Form RPR

222- **1** **Admiral's Sunset**[191] 7848 4-9-2 **74**.......... CharlieBennett(5) 4 86
(Hughie Morrison) *trckd ldr: led over 2f out: pushed clr: comf* **5/4**[1]

10-3 **2** *7* **Rosie Royale (IRE)**[12] 2357 5-9-0 **72**.......... GeorgeWood(5) 3 73
(Roger Teal) *trckd ldr: pushed along 4f out: rdn to ld briefly wl over 2f out: kpt on but sn hld by wnr* **3/1**[2]

1252 **3** *4* **Star Of Lombardy (IRE)**[11] 2387 4-9-9 **76**.......... FrannyNorton 8 69
(Mark Johnston) *led: rdn and hdd wl over 2f out: sn one pce* **7/2**[3]

-313 **4** *hd* **Iona Island**[56] 1303 4-8-11 **64**.......... FranBerry 5 57
(Peter Hiatt) *trckd ldrs: wnt 2nd over 5f out: chal 3f out: sn rdn and hld: one pce fnl 2f* **9/2**

2m 56.04s (4.04) **Going Correction** +0.425s/f (Yiel) **4** Ran SP% **109.8**
Speed ratings (Par 100): **104,99,97,97**
CSF £5.32 TOTE £2.70; EX 6.20 Trifecta £11.30.
**Owner** A N Solomons **Bred** Lakin Bloodstock, Hillard Bloodstock & Trading Ltd **Trained** East Ilsley, Berks

**FOCUS**
Four withdrawals took some interest out of this handicap. It was run at an honest pace and the winner did it easily. It was rated in line with her 3yo best.

## 2724 ALPHA PORTFOLIO MANAGEMENT H'CAP 5f 160y
**7:25** (7:25) (Class 6) (0-55,55) 4-Y-O+ **£2,264** (£673; £336; £168) **Stalls** Centre

Form RPR

-000 **1** **Zophilly (IRE)**[7] 2509 4-8-12 **46** oh1..........(t) MartinLane 3 53
(Jeremy Gask) *s.i.s: towards rr: rdn and hdwy fr 2f out: led ins fnl f: r.o strly* **20/1**

5000 **2** *1 1/4* **Diamond Vine (IRE)**[53] 1359 9-8-12 **46** oh1..........(p) FrannyNorton 16 49
(Ronald Harris) *mid-div on outer: pushed along over 3f out: hdwy 2f out: ev ch jst ins fnl f: outpcd by wnr cl home* **20/1**

030- **3** *1 1/4* **Majestic Girl (IRE)**[202] 7641 4-8-10 **49**.......... GeorgeWood(5) 13 48
(Steve Flook) *towards rr of mid-div: pushed along over 3f out: rdn and hdwy fr 2f out: r.o wl fnl f: wnt 3rd cl home* **16/1**

0-65 **4** *hd* **Catalinas Diamond (IRE)**[7] 2509 9-9-2 **50**..........(t) ShaneKelly 14 48
(Pat Murphy) *hld up towards rr: prog 2f out: swtchd rt and rdn ent fnl f: r.o wl* **7/1**[3]

4004 **5** *shd* **Burauq**[7] 2509 5-8-11 **48**..........(b) HectorCrouch(3) 4 46
(Milton Bradley) *mid-div: rdn and hdwy 2f out: chsng ldrs whn squeezed up ent fnl f: kpt on* **7/1**[3]

00-0 **6** *3/4* **Mostashreqah**[15] 2278 4-8-7 **46** oh1.......... LuluStanford(5) 8 41+
(Milton Bradley) *prom: rdn over 2f out: led over 1f out: hdd ins fnl f: no ex* **10/1**

0006 **7** *2 3/4* **Arizona Snow**[69] 1112 5-8-12 **46** oh1..........(p) CharlesBishop 17 32+
(Ronald Harris) *prom: rdn and ev ch fr over 2f out tl ent fnl f: fdd* **16/1**

0/00 **8** *shd* **My Meteor**[3] 2669 10-8-10 **49**.......... PaddyPilley(5) 10 35+
(Natalie Lloyd-Beavis) *led: rdn whn strly pressed fr over 2f out: hdd over 1f out: fdd fnl f* **50/1**

4000 **9** *2½* **Royal Normandy**[84] 854 5-8-12 **46** oh1....................(b) StevieDonohoe 5 24
(Grace Harris) *mid-div: rdn and hdwy 2f out: chsng ldrs whn squeezed out jst over 1f out: no threat after* **14/1**

-354 **10** *4* **Cee Jay**[16] 2214 4-9-2 **55**.......................................... CharlieBennett(5) 11 20
(Patrick Chamings) *towards rr of midfield: struggling fr over 3f out: nvr threatened* **10/3**[1]

00-0 **11** *7* **Angelito**[100] 602 8-9-6 **54**.............................................. RobertWinston 6
(Tony Newcombe) *awkwardly away: sn drvn along in rr: nvr any danger* **9/2**[2]

000- **12** *5* **Sabato (IRE)**[261] 5958 4-9-1 **49**.................................... TimmyMurphy 15
(Fergal O'Brien) *mid-div: rdn over 2f out: wknd over 1f out* **12/1**

50-0 **13** *12* **Wilspa's Magic (IRE)**[16] 2214 4-9-2 **50**................... RichardKingscote 7
(Ron Hodges) *in tch: rdn 3f out: sn wknd* **10/1**

1m 13.64s (2.44) **Going Correction** +0.40s/f (Good) **13** Ran SP% **126.8**
Speed ratings (Par 101): **99,97,95,95,95 94,90,90,87,81 72,65,49**
CSF £366.78 CT £6626.40 TOTE £27.50: £5.70, £4.90, £4.60; EX 532.40.
**Owner** Horses First Partners **Bred** John Martin McLoughney **Trained** Stockbridge, Hants

**FOCUS**
A modest contest, albeit with a number a potentially well-handicapped runners in the field. The pace was sound and it suited the closers. The form is rated around the runner-up.

## 2725 KERSFIELD FILLIES' H'CAP 5f 160y
**7:55** (7:57) (Class 5) (0-70,74) 3-Y-O+ **£3,752** (£1,116; £557; £278) **Stalls** Centre

Form RPR

0-03 **1** **Babyfact**[12] 2360 6-10-0 **69**........................................ JosephineGordon 4 76
(Malcolm Saunders) *prom: disp ld over 2f out: rdn into v narrow advantage jst over 1f out: strly pressed thrght fnl f: hld on* **5/1**[3]

50-5 **2** *hd* **Incentive**[36] 1705 3-8-12 **62**............................................. LiamKeniry 3 66
(Stuart Kittow) *led: jnd over 2f out: rdn whn edgd lft and hdd jst over 1f out: kpt on w ev ch: jst hld* **10/1**

5-12 **3** *½* **Monteamiata (IRE)**[16] 2235 3-9-8 **72**......................... ThomasBrown 10 74
(Ed Walker) *uns rdr in parade ring: unsettled stalls: hld up: hdwy over 2f out: sn rdn to chse ldng pair: ch ent fnl f: kpt on but no ex* **5/4**[1]

6031 **4** *1½* **Kingstreet Lady**[16] 2214 4-8-11 **52**............................... KieranO'Neill 1 51
(Richard Price) *chsd ldrs: drvn over 2f out: nt best f runs and swtchd lft over 1f out: kpt on but nt pce to chal* **10/1**

33-0 **5** *1¼* **Sitar**[22] 2072 3-8-10 **65**................................................... GeorgeWood(5) 7 58
(James Fanshawe) *in tch: rdn to chse ldrs over 2f out: nt pce to chal: fdd fnl 100yds* **9/2**[2]

30U1 **6** *1* **Powerful Dream (IRE)**[7] 2514 4-10-5 **74** 6ex..................(p) ShaneKelly 5 66
(Ronald Harris) *s.i.s: last but wl in tch: hdwy 2f out: sn rdn: nt pce to chal: fdd fnl 120yds* **9/1**

13-0 **7** *8* **Silver Penny**[16] 2235 3-8-13 **68**.................................. CharlieBennett(5) 2 32
(Jim Boyle) *trckd ldrs: rdn over 2f out: hung rt over 1f out: wknd ins fnl f* **14/1**

1m 13.06s (1.86) **Going Correction** +0.40s/f (Good)
**WFA** 3 from 4yo+ 9lb **7** Ran SP% **114.1**
Speed ratings (Par 100): **103,102,102,100,98 97,86**
CSF £51.50 CT £98.18 TOTE £6.10: £2.40, £4.60; EX 52.70 Trifecta £134.50.
**Owner** Mrs Ginny Nicholas **Bred** M S Saunders And Chris Scott **Trained** Green Ore, Somerset
■ Stewards' Enquiry : Thomas Brown four-day ban; used whip above the permitted level (May 31, Jun 1, 5-6)

**FOCUS**
Not a great race for the grade.

## 2726 DU PONT H'CAP 1m
**8:25** (8:25) (Class 6) (0-60,60) 3-Y-O **£2,264** (£673; £336; £168) **Stalls** Low

Form RPR

60-5 **1** **Waves (IRE)**[49] 1432 3-9-4 **60**.................................... EdwardGreatrex(3) 1 72
(Eve Johnson Houghton) *hld up in last trio: hdwy over 2f out: rdn to ld wl over 1f out: sn clr: styd on strly* **16/1**

**2** *4½* **Secret Memories (IRE)**[17] 2191 3-8-13 **57**.........(t[1]) KillianHennessy(5) 2 59
(Miss Katy Brown, Ire) *trckd ldrs: rdn 2f out: ev ch whn rdr dropped whip sn after: kpt on same pce* **11/1**

4250 **3** *hd* **Viola Park**[12] 2362 3-9-1 **54**.......................................(p) FrannyNorton 10 56
(Ronald Harris) *trckd ldrs: rdn 2f out: ev ch whn hanging lft wl over 1f out: kpt on same pce fnl f* **10/1**

260- **4** *2* **Royal Melody**[182] 7974 3-9-0 **58**..............................(p) GeorgeWood(5) 12 55
(Heather Main) *mid-div: hdwy on outer over 3f out: rdn over 2f out: ev ch wl over 1f out: kpt on same pce fnl f* **16/1**

05-0 **5** *1¾* **Holyroman Princess**[25] 1968 3-8-12 **56**..................(b[1]) LuluStanford(5) 9 49
(Rod Millman) *towards rr of midfield: drvn along fr over 3f out: kpt on fnl 2f but nvr threatened to get on terms* **8/1**

0-51 **6** *1½* **Crucial Moment**[31] 1817 3-9-0 **58**................................... RyanWhile(5) 16 48
(Bill Turner) *towards rr of midfield: hdwy on outer over 3f out: rdn over 2f out: kpt on same pce fr over 1f out* **6/1**[2]

0353 **7** *1½* **Hold Me Tight (IRE)**[49] 1428 3-8-9 **55**..................(b) GeorgiaDobie(7) 15 42
(J S Moore) *disp ld tl clr ldr over 5f out: rdn and hdd wl over 1f out: sn hld: wknd fnl f* **8/1**

000- **8** *½* **Champagne Reign (IRE)**[152] 8404 3-9-1 **54**.................... LiamJones 11 40
(J S Moore) *s.i.s: in last pair: drvn along 3f out: sme minor late prog: nvr any danger* **33/1**

4060 **9** *½* **Greyjoy (IRE)**[23] 2027 3-8-9 **53**...................................... MitchGodwin(5) 6 38
(Sylvester Kirk) *s.i.s: in last pair: rdn wl over 2f out: sme minor late prog: nvr any danger* **8/1**

000- **10** *1* **Henry Did It (IRE)**[218] 7244 3-9-2 **55**................................ ShaneKelly 14 37
(Tony Carroll) *trckd ldrs: rdn over 2f out: wknd ent fnl f* **12/1**

60-0 **11** *1* **Opening Time**[15] 2259 3-9-7 **60**.........................................(b[1]) PatDobbs 3 40
(Richard Hannon) *disp ld tl over 5f out: chsd ldr: rdn wl over 2f out: wknd jst over 1f out* **5/1**[1]

6430 **12** *1¾* **Toolatetodelegate**[40] 1596 3-9-3 **56**............................ StevieDonohoe 7 32
(Brian Barr) *mid-div: effrt wl over 2f out: wknd jst over 1f out* **25/1**

4205 **13** *17* **Never Folding (IRE)**[42] 1550 3-9-7 **60**.........................(t) RobertWinston 5
(Seamus Durack) *mid-div: rdn over 2f out: wknd over 1f out: eased whn btn* **13/2**[3]

1m 42.37s (1.57) **13** Ran SP% **121.3**
CSF £184.36 CT £1924.07 TOTE £13.00: £4.60, £4.20, £2.70; EX 116.50 Trifecta £1471.50.
**Owner** BP McNamee & RL Maynard **Bred** Mary & Michael Kelly **Trained** Blewbury, Oxon
■ Stewards' Enquiry : Lulu Stanford two-day ban; used whip above the permitted level (31st May - 1st June)

**FOCUS**
The pace was honest for this modest handicap. The form is best rated around the third.
T/Plt: £2482.00 to a £1 stake. Pool: £57,834.22 - 17.01 winning units T/Qpdt: £270.50 to a £1 stake. Pool: £5,118.87 - 14 winning units **Tim Mitchell**

# 2314 YARMOUTH (L-H)
Wednesday, May 17

**OFFICIAL GOING: Good (watered; 8.0)**
Wind: light, half against, of no consequence Weather: light cloud, bright spells later

## 2727 AKS SKIPS OF NORWICH MAIDEN STKS 6f 3y
**1:40** (1:43) (Class 5) 3-Y-O+ **£3,557** (£1,058; £529; £264) **Stalls** Centre

Form RPR

4-22 **1** **Farook (IRE)**[30] 1837 3-9-3 79............................................ DaneO'Neill 9 71+
(Charles Hills) *trckd ldng trio: clsd to join ldrs over 2f out: rdn to ld over 1f out: kpt on and a doing enough ins fnl f: rdn out* **4/9**[1]

530- **2** *¾* **Peace Dreamer (IRE)**[189] 7867 3-8-12 0............................... LukeMorris 2 63
(Robert Cowell) *w ldr tl led 1/2-way: rdn and hung lft 2f out: sn hdd: kpt on wl u.p after for clr 2nd : a jst hld ins fnl f* **7/1**

00 **3** *3¾* **Higgy's Heartbeat**[16] 2231 3-9-0 0................................. JackDuern(3) 5 56
(Dean Ivory) *hld up in tch: effrt 2f out: hdwy over 1f out: chsd clr ldng pair jst ins fnl f: styd on but nvr threatening ldrs* **28/1**

0 **4** *½* **Shyarch**[29] 1857 3-9-3 0...................................................... RyanPowell 6 54+
(George Margarson) *s.i.s: bustled along in rr: hdwy u.p to pass btn rivals over 1f out: kpt on ins fnl f: nvr trbld ldrs* **20/1**

**5** *1½* **Deciding Vote** 3-8-12 0........................................................ LouisSteward 3 44
(Chris Wall) *in tch in midfield: effrt to chse ldrs and hung lft over 1f out: no imp 1f out: wknd ins fnl f* **5/1**[3]

3000 **6** *nk* **Pleadings (USA)**[16] 2214 4-9-7 46.......................(tp) LewisEdmunds(5) 8 50
(Charlie Wallis) *in tch in midfield: effrt 2f out: unable qck over 1f out: wl hld and kpt on same pce ins fnl f* **50/1**

240- **7** *1½* **Jack Nevison**[217] 7268 4-9-5 74.................................... BenRobinson(7) 7 45
(John O'Shea) *led: sn restrained to trck ldrs: clsd and ev ch over 2f out: sn rdn and unable qck: wknd fnl f* **4/1**[2]

00 **8** *4* **Socks And Shares (IRE)**[20] 2112 4-9-12 0......................... KierenFox 4 33
(Derek Shaw) *taken down early: s.i.s: hld up in rr: struggling over 2f out: bhd over 1f out* **50/1**

00-0 **9** *3½* **Proud Kate**[22] 2071 3-8-5 42............................................ JacobMitchell(7) 1 14
(Christine Dunnett) *sn led: hdd and rdn 1/2-way: steadily lost pl: bhd fnl f* **125/1**

1m 12.89s (-1.51) **Going Correction** -0.275s/f (Firm)
**WFA** 3 from 4yo 9lb **9** Ran SP% **131.3**
Speed ratings (Par 103): **99,98,93,92,90 89,87,82,77**
CSF £5.68 TOTE £1.30: £1.02, £1.90, £8.20; EX 5.50 Trifecta £91.40.
**Owner** Hamdan Al Maktoum **Bred** J Hanly, A Stroud & Castlemartin Sky **Trained** Lambourn, Berks

**FOCUS**
Before racing got underway, there were a couple of changes to the going. It was given as good (called good to firm, watered at the overnight stage) following 15mm of rain falling after that original description was given. Those who had official figures suggested this race was a fair contest, but time may tell this is just modest form. The second seems the best guiide.

## 2728 BURLINGTON PALM HOTEL OF GREAT YARMOUTH H'CAP 1m 3f 104y
**2:10** (2:11) (Class 5) (0-75,77) 4-Y-O+ **£3,234** (£962; £481; £240) **Stalls** Low

Form RPR

**1** **Sean O'Casey (IRE)**[226] 7024 4-9-7 **75**...................... SilvestreDeSousa 8 85+
(Michael Appleby) *t.k.h: chsd ldr tl led 8f out: rdn ent fnl 3f: clr 2f out: styd on wl and totally in command after* **13/8**[1]

1/6- **2** *3¼* **Stoney Broke**[277] 5415 4-9-5 **73**...................................... DanielMuscutt 4 76
(James Fanshawe) *hld up in tch in midfield: hdwy 4f out: chsd wnr and rdn over 2f out: no imp but kpt on to hold on to 2nd ins fnl f* **5/1**[3]

/5-0 **3** *nk* **Silca Star**[23] 2039 4-9-7 **75**................................................ MartinHarley 6 78
(Alan King) *stdd s: hld up in last pair: hdwy 4f out: sn chsng ldrs: rdn ent fnl 2f: 3rd and no imp over 1f out: kpt on same pce ins fnl f* **11/2**

40-0 **4** *hd* **Hard Toffee (IRE)**[40] 1602 6-9-3 **71**................................... RobertTart 2 73
(Conrad Allen) *hld up in pair: effrt 3f out: sme hdwy u.p over 1f out: kpt on ins fnl f: nvr a threat to wnr* **10/1**

0-02 **5** *1¼* **Longside**[15] 2282 5-8-11 **65**.................................................. RyanTate 3 65
(James Eustace) *wl in tch in midfield: swtchd rt and effrt over 2f out: no imp and kpt on same pce fr over 1f out* **3/1**[2]

40-0 **6** *19* **Astrosecret**[9] 2460 4-8-3 **64**...................................... GabrieleMalune(7) 5 33
(Mark H Tompkins) *t.k.h: chsd ldng pair tl wnt 2nd wl over 3f out tl lost 2nd over 2f out: sn lost pl and wknd over 1f out* **25/1**

/055 **7** *22* **Instill**[28] 1892 5-8-11 **70**............................................(v[1]) LewisEdmunds(5) 7 2
(Mandy Rowland) *t.k.h: led tl 8f out: chsd wnr tl wl over 3f out: sn dropped out and bhd 3f out: t.o fnl f* **20/1**

2m 25.88s (-2.82) **Going Correction** -0.275s/f (Firm) **7** Ran SP% **112.8**
Speed ratings (Par 103): **99,96,96,96,95 81,65**
CSF £9.92 CT £34.90 TOTE £2.20: £1.10, £3.60; EX 10.60 Trifecta £35.80.
**Owner** C L Bacon **Bred** Western Bloodstock **Trained** Oakham, Rutland

**FOCUS**
A few of these were below par when last seen, so this may not be particularly strong form. The race is rated around the second and third.

## 2729 READE CATERING HOGG ROASTS AT YARMOUTH RACECOURSE H'CAP 1m 2f 23y
**2:45** (2:45) (Class 6) (0-60,61) 4-Y-O+ **£2,264** (£673; £336; £168) **Stalls** Low

Form RPR

0201 **1** **Street Art (IRE)**[55] 1322 5-8-9 **51**.................................(bt) HollieDoyle(3) 3 59
(Mike Murphy) *trckd ldrs and travelled strly: swtchd rt 2f out: rdn to ld ent fnl f: styd on wl: rdn out* **16/1**

3000 **2** *1¼* **Tyrsal (IRE)**[22] 2070 6-9-2 **55**............................................. RobertTart 7 63
(Clifford Lines) *hld up in last pair: clsd 4f out: trcking ldrs on inner: nt clr run 2f out: forced to swtchd arnd 4 rivals fr over 1f out: fnlly in the clr and hdwy ins fnl f: wnt 2nd wl ins fnl f: nvr getting to wnr* **8/1**

0060 **3** *½* **Stun Gun**[9] 2465 7-8-12 **51**...............................................(p) KierenFox 9 56
(Derek Shaw) *hld up in last pair: effrt 2f out: hdwy u.p over 1f out: styd on wl ins fnl f to go 3rd wl ins fnl f: nvr getting to wnr* **40/1**

0-02 **4** *1* **Poppy Time**[4] 2615 4-9-7 **60**................................................ RyanTate 8 63
(James Eustace) *t.k.h: trckd ldrs: clsd to join ldrs and stl on bridle over 2f out: rdn to ld over 1f out: sn hdd and one pced fnl f: lost 2 pls wl ins fnl f* **9/4**[1]

-005 **5** *nse* **Sexy Secret**[15] 2281 6-8-11 **53**.................................(p) SimonPearce(3) 2 56
(Lydia Pearce) *rousted along to ld: rdn and hdd over 2f out: styd on same pce u.p fr over 1f out* **12/1**

2065 **6** *2* **Moving Robe (IRE)**[55] 1322 4-8-7 **46** oh1 LukeMorris 13 45
(Conrad Allen) *t.k.h: hld up in tch in midfield: shuffled bk towards rr 4f out: swtchd rt and rallied over 2f out: drvn to chse ldrs over 1f out: no ex 1f out: wknd ins fnl f* **33/1**

50-2 **7** *6* **Young Tom**[29] 1864 4-9-8 **61** SilvestreDeSousa 11 50
(Michael Appleby) *chsd ldr: rdn to ld over 2f out tl hdd and unable qck over 1f out: btn jst ins fnl f: sn eased* **5/2**[2]

-423 **8** *1 3/4* **Harlequin Rock**[14] 2318 4-9-7 **60** PatCosgrave 6 45
(Mick Quinn) *hld up in midfield: swtchd rt 7f out: hdwy u.p over 2f out: no imp over 1f out: wknd fnl f* **7/1**[3]

0005 **9** *4* **Silver Alliance**[15] 2282 9-9-0 **60** (p) TristanPrice(7) 1 38
(Julia Feilden) *s.i.s and wnt bdly rt s: rcvrd and in midfield after 2f: rdn over 2f out: son struggling: wknd over 1f out* **18/1**

0003 **10** *7* **Haabis (USA)**[36] 1695 4-8-6 **52** (h) DavidEgan(7) 4 18
(George Peckham) *t.k.h: hld up in tch in midfield: lost pl u.p 3f out: bhd over 1f out* **25/1**

060- **11** *3* **Icons Image**[228] 6966 4-8-2 **46** oh1 RichardOliver(5) 5 6
(Alan Bailey) *s.i.s: rousted along early: hdwy into midfield and t.k.h: struggling 3f out: bhd over 1f out* **33/1**

5050 **12** *1* **Commissar**[18] 2166 8-8-12 **51** (tp) RobHornby 12 9
(Mandy Rowland) *chsd ldrs tl lost pl over 3f out: bhd over 1f out* **50/1**

2m 8.54s (-1.96) **Going Correction** -0.275s/f (Firm) 12 Ran SP% **115.9**
Speed ratings (Par 101): **96,95,94,93,93 92,87,85,82,77 74,73**
CSF £128.92 CT £4960.12 TOTE £12.30: £3.90, £2.90, £9.50; EX 144.40 Trifecta £1092.40.
**Owner** Ms Denise Tibbett **Bred** Minch Bloodstock **Trained** Westoning, Beds

**FOCUS**
This featured confirmed moderate performers, in which a couple dominated the betting. The winner built slightly on his recent victory.

## 2730 JOHN CORNELL MEMORIAL H'CAP 1m 3y
**3:20** (3:21) (Class 4) (0-85,87) 4-Y-0+ **£5,175** (£1,540; £769; £384) **Stalls** Centre

Form RPR

-464 **1** **Kestrel Dot Com**[14] 2317 5-8-12 **75** (b1) SilvestreDeSousa 7 87
(Chris Dwyer) *t.k.h: hld up in tch: effrt to chal 2f out: led and hung lft over 1f out: clr and r.o strly ins fnl f: readily* **11/4**[1]

6425 **2** *3 3/4* **Intrude**[15] 2261 5-9-2 **79** (p1) MartinHarley 5 82
(Stuart Williams) *hld up in tch in rr: nt clr run ent fnl 2f: swtchd rt and effrt over 1f out: hdwy to chse ldng pair 1f out: styd on to go 2nd cl home: no threat to wnr* **9/1**

60-0 **3** *1/2* **Archie (IRE)**[16] 2232 5-9-7 **84** PatCosgrave 1 86
(Tom Clover) *hld up in tch: effrt and hdwy 2f out: chsd wnr over 1f out: sn carried lft and no ex jst ins fnl f: wknd wl ins fnl f and lost 2nd cl home* **20/1**

6-06 **4** *2* **Georgian Bay (IRE)**[15] 2283 7-9-4 **84** (v) JordanVaughan(3) 3 82
(K R Burke) *trckd ldrs: moved lft 1/2-way: effrt and ev ch u.p 2f out tl unable qck and btn 4th 1f out: wknd ins fnl f* **5/1**[3]

6-66 **5** *nk* **Qeyaadah (IRE)**[11] 2381 4-9-7 **87** AlistairRawlinson(3) 8 84
(Michael Appleby) *hld up in tch: effrt to chse ldrs and rdn 2f out: no imp and btn whn hung lft 1f out: wknd ins fnl f* **5/1**[3]

06-2 **6** *1/2* **Fashaak (IRE)**[14] 2317 4-8-8 **78** DavidEgan(7) 4 74
(John Butler) *taken down early: w ldr tl led over 2f out: rdn and hdd over 1f out: no ex and wknd ins fnl f* **11/2**

3201 **7** *5* **Pendo**[20] 2116 6-9-4 **81** KierenFox 2 65
(John Best) *taken down early: led tl over 2f out: sn u.p and struggling: bhd and wl btn whn nt clr run jst ins fnl f: eased wl ins fnl f* **4/1**[2]

1m 36.65s (-3.95) **Going Correction** -0.275s/f (Firm) 7 Ran SP% **110.1**
Speed ratings (Par 105): **108,104,103,101,101 100,95**
CSF £25.79 CT £378.23 TOTE £3.10: £1.90, £3.50; EX 22.50 Trifecta £118.70.
**Owner** Mrs Nicola Thorne **Bred** Shadwell Estate Company Limited **Trained** Newmarket, Suffolk
■ Dot Green was withdrawn. Price at time of withdrawal 25/1. Rule 4 does not apply

**FOCUS**
Probably not a strong race for the level even though a couple of them arrived in okay form. The winner is rated to form.

## 2731 GROSVENOR CASINO OF GREAT YARMOUTH H'CAP 1m 3y
**3:50** (3:53) (Class 6) (0-65,66) 4-Y-0+ **£2,264** (£673; £336; £168) **Stalls** Centre

Form RPR

1033 **1** **Ross Raith Rover**[22] 2070 4-9-6 **64** (p) PaoloSirigu 7 72
(Robert Eddery) *chsd ldr early: sn stdd to trck ldng pair: lost pl 3f out: swtchd lft and effrt 2f out: hdwy u.p ent fnl f: str chal ins fnl f: styd on wl to ld towards fin* **9/2**[2]

0504 **2** *hd* **Rustique**[14] 2318 5-9-3 **61** (h) LukeMorris 3 68
(Ed Walker) *t.k.h: sn chsng ldr: effrt to chal wl over 1f out: rdn to ld jst over 1f out: drvn ins fnl f: hdd and no ex towards fin* **7/2**[1]

356- **3** *1 1/2* **Castle Talbot (IRE)**[271] 5610 5-9-7 **65** PatCosgrave 4 68
(Tom Clover) *hld up in tch: effrt ent fnl 2f: drvn to chse ldrs over 1f out: styd on same pce ins fnl f* **11/1**

4001 **4** *3/4* **Samphire Coast**[46] 1484 4-9-4 **62** (v) KierenFox 6 63
(Derek Shaw) *stdd s: t.k.h: hld up in tch in rr: swtchd rt over 2f out: effrt u.p to chse ldrs over 1f out: styd on same pce ins fnl f* **5/1**[3]

-133 **5** *2 3/4* **Gulland Rock**[19] 2120 6-9-8 **66** WilliamCarson 10 61
(Anthony Carson) *led: rdn ent fnl 2f: hdd jst over 1f out: wknd ins fnl f* **6/1**

254- **6** *1* **Tommy's Secret**[149] 8458 7-9-5 **63** MartinHarley 11 56
(Jane Chapple-Hyam) *chsd ldrs: rdn 3f out: outpcd over 2f out: hung lft u.p and no imp over 1f out: wknd ins fnl f* **7/1**

-406 **7** *1 1/2* **Atholblair Boy (IRE)**[19] 2120 4-9-8 **66** SilvestreDeSousa 9 55
(Nigel Tinkler) *t.k.h: hld up in tch: swtchd lft over 3f out: effrt u.p over 2f out: no imp and btn over 1f out: wknd ins fnl f* **9/2**[2]

1m 38.15s (-2.45) **Going Correction** -0.275s/f (Firm) 7 Ran SP% **110.4**
Speed ratings (Par 101): **101,100,99,98,95 94,93**
CSF £19.08 CT £150.43 TOTE £4.80: £2.60, £2.30; EX 20.50 Trifecta £178.90.
**Owner** Mrs Pamela Aitken & Ian Anderson **Bred** Shadwell Estate Company Limited **Trained** Newmarket, Suffolk

**FOCUS**
Four runners came out but none of them looked like being strongly fancied in the betting, so all the leading candidates from the entries stage remained. The early gallop wasn't strong. The second and third set a straightofrward level.

## 2732 WEDDINGS & PRIVATE PARTIES AT YARMOUTH RACECOURSE H'CAP (DIV I) 7f 3y
**4:25** (4:27) (Class 6) (0-60,62) 3-Y-0+ **£2,264** (£673; £336; £168) **Stalls** Centre

Form RPR

-025 **1** **Magic Moments**[22] 2057 4-9-11 **56** MartinHarley 10 63
(Alan King) *racd towards stands' side: mde virtually all: rdn wl over 1f out: kpt on wl ins fnl f* **9/2**[2]

262- **2** *1* **Tennessee Rose (IRE)**[228] 6963 3-9-6 **62** AntonioFresu 9 62
(Luke McJannet) *stdd after s: t.k.h: hld up in tch in midfield: effrt ent fnl f: drvn to chse wnr over 1f out: styd on same pce ins fnl f* **13/2**[3]

000- **3** *2 1/4* **Cainhoe Star**[403] 1337 4-9-10 **55** WilliamCarson 8 54
(Anthony Carson) *hld up in tch in rr: effrt over 2f out: hdwy u.p over 1f out: battling for 3rd and hung lft 1f out: no imp and kpt on same pce ins fnl f* **8/1**

0004 **4** *1/2* **Clean Cut**[16] 2228 3-8-6 **48** (p) SilvestreDeSousa 6 41
(Ivan Furtado) *w wnr: rdn ent fnl 2f: 3rd and outpcd over 1f out: kpt on same pce ins fnl f* **4/1**[1]

3430 **5** *1 3/4* **Jack The Laird (IRE)**[23] 2043 4-9-11 **59** (p) JackDuern(3) 2 52
(Dean Ivory) *trckd ldrs: effrt 2f out: unable qck u.p and styd on same pce fr over 1f out* **13/2**[3]

5-00 **6** *1/2* **The Secrets Out**[23] 2016 3-8-10 **52** (h1) RoystonFfrench 3 39
(Luke Dace) *taken down early: hld up in tch: rdn over 2f out: sme hdwy u.p over 1f out: wl hld 6th and kpt on same pce ins fnl f* **12/1**

033 **7** *1 1/4* **Louis Vee (IRE)**[7] 2509 9-8-8 **46** (b) BenRobinson(7) 11 34
(John O'Shea) *racd towards stands' side: wl in tch in midfield: effrt ent fnl 2f: unable qck qckn and btn over 1f out: plugged on same pce fnl f* **12/1**

1544 **8** *7* **Little Indian**[42] 1557 7-9-7 **52** PaddyAspell 5 22
(J R Jenkins) *hld up in tch towards rr: effrt ent fnl: no hdwy: wknd over 1f out* **14/1**

30-0 **9** *3* **Robin's Purse**[23] 2016 3-9-3 **59** DaneO'Neill 4 25
(Charles Hills) *s.i.s: sn rcvrd and t.k.h in midfield: effrt to chse ldrs 2f out: no ex and btn over 1f out: eased ins fnl f* **9/1**

0000 **10** *2 3/4* **I Can't Stop**[18] 2166 4-9-0 **45** LukeMorris 1
(Milton Bradley) *chsd ldrs: drvn and unable qck over 2f out: sn struggling: wknd over 1f out* **16/1**

006- **11** *5* **Ripper Street (IRE)**[175] 8072 3-8-13 **62** (h1) DavidEgan(7) 7
(Christine Dunnett) *s.i.s: hld up in tch in rr: rdn over 3f out: sn strugglingd: bhd over 1f out* **33/1**

1m 24.79s (-1.81) **Going Correction** -0.275s/f (Firm)
**WFA** 3 from 4yo+ 11lb 11 Ran SP% **116.8**
Speed ratings (Par 101): **99,97,95,94,92 92,90,82,79,76 70**
CSF £33.70 CT £192.17 TOTE £5.10: £1.90, £2.00, £3.40; EX 36.20 Trifecta £453.90.
**Owner** Ray Bailey **Bred** Peter & Tony Hockenhull **Trained** Barbury Castle, Wilts

**FOCUS**
The betting suggested this was an open contest at a moderate level, but the winner did it nicely. The form is taken at face value around the second and third.

## 2733 WEDDINGS & PRIVATE PARTIES AT YARMOUTH RACECOURSE H'CAP (DIV II) 7f 3y
**4:55** (4:58) (Class 6) (0-60,59) 3-Y-0+ **£2,264** (£673; £336; £168) **Stalls** Centre

Form RPR

040 **1** **Moi Aussie**[14] 2313 4-9-6 **51** SilvestreDeSousa 5 58
(Michael Appleby) *mde all: rdn ent fnl 2f: forged ahd jst ins fnl f: styd on wl: eased towards fin* **10/3**[2]

20-0 **2** *1 1/2* **How's Lucy**[40] 1596 3-8-9 **51** DannyBrock 4 50
(Jane Chapple-Hyam) *chsd ldrs tl wnt 2nd 1/2-way: effrt and pressing wnr 2f out: no ex jst ins fnl f: outpcd fnl 100yds: jst hld 2nd cl home* **13/2**[3]

04-5 **3** *hd* **Lawfilly**[12] 2362 3-8-10 **52** RyanTate 9 51+
(Richard Hughes) *bmpd s: hld up in rr: swtchd lft and hdwy over 1f out: kpt on wl ins fnl f: pressing for 2nd towards fin: no threat to wnr* **8/1**

/002 **4** *1 1/4* **Swilly Sunset**[14] 2319 4-10-0 **59** WilliamCarson 10 58
(Anthony Carson) *hld up in last trio: swtchd lft and effrt over 2f out: hdwy u.p 1f out: styd on ins fnl f: snatched 4th last strides* **2/1**[1]

00-5 **5** *hd* **Pitch High (IRE)**[41] 1589 3-9-1 **57** RoystonFfrench 6 52
(Julia Feilden) *chsd wnr tl 4f out: rdn and outpcd over 2f out: rallied over 1f out: kpt on ins fnl f w threatening wnr* **22/1**

6000 **6** *3* **Humour (IRE)**[22] 2069 6-8-10 **48** (v) DavidEgan(7) 3 39
(Christine Dunnett) *chsd ldrs: rdn wl over 2f out: 3rd and outpcd over 1f out: wknd ins fnl f* **16/1**

-006 **7** *1* **Cooperess**[14] 2298 4-9-0 **52** (v) BenRobinson(7) 11 40
(John O'Shea) *hld up in tch in midfield: rdn over 2f out: drifting lft and no hdwy over 1f out: wknd ins fnl f* **9/1**

0300 **8** *3 3/4* **Chandrayaan**[70] 1084 10-8-7 **45** (v) GinaMangan(7) 2 24
(John E Long) *in tch in midfield: rdn wl over 2f out: no imp and btn over 1f out: wknd ins fnl f* **66/1**

4060 **9** *3 1/2* **Great Expectations**[14] 2298 9-9-8 **53** (t) PaddyAspell 1 23
(J R Jenkins) *hld up in tch in last trio: swtchd rt after 1f out: effrt ent fnl 2f: sn struggling and bhd over 1f out* **50/1**

5540 **10** *3 1/4* **Rising Sunshine (IRE)**[15] 2278 4-9-2 **47** (bt) LukeMorris 8 8
(Milton Bradley) *wnt rt and bmpd s: hld up in tch: shkn up ent fnl f: wknd over 1f out* **12/1**

1m 24.78s (-1.82) **Going Correction** -0.275s/f (Firm)
**WFA** 3 from 4yo+ 11lb 10 Ran SP% **112.2**
Speed ratings (Par 101): **99,97,97,95,95 91,90,86,82,78**
CSF £23.87 CT £156.89 TOTE £4.30: £1.50, £2.30, £2.20; EX 26.90 Trifecta £149.70.
**Owner** The Horse Watchers **Bred** The C H F Partnership **Trained** Oakham, Rutland

**FOCUS**
A weak race where it appeared to favour those both prominent and close to the stands' rail. The second helps with the level.

## 2734 RACING WELFARE H'CAP 6f 3y
**5:25** (5:27) (Class 6) (0-60,61) 3-Y-O **£2,264** (£673; £336; £168) **Stalls** Centre

Form RPR

0-63 **1** **Everkyllachy (IRE)**[12] 2362 3-8-11 **53** (b) HollieDoyle(3) 4 59
(J S Moore) *bustled along in midfield: hdwy to chse ldrs and swtchd rt over 1f out: ev ch ins fnl f: styd on wl to ld last strides* **13/2**

000- **2** *nk* **Wotadoll**[168] 8152 3-8-10 **52** JackDuern(3) 10 57
(Dean Ivory) *bmpd s: hld up in tch: hdwy 2f out: rdn and ev ch 2f out: led 1f out: kpt on wl u.p: hdd last strides* **18/1**

4-55 **3** *nk* **Zavikon**[14] 2306 3-9-7 **60** (h) RyanTate 12 64
(Richard Hughes) *taken down early: stdd and hmpd s: hld up in rr: clsd in centre 2f out: shkn up to chse ldrs 1f out: drvn and ev ch wl ins fnl f: kpt on* **11/2**[2]

000- **4** *1 1/4* **Sadierosecliﬀord (IRE)**[207] 7528 3-8-6 **52** RayDawson(7) 14 52
(Giles Bravery) *chsd ldr: rdn and ev ch over 1f out tl no ex ins fnl f: wknd towards fin* **18/1**

00-5 **5** *1 1/2* **Defining Moment**[136] 1 3-9-4 **57** MartinHarley 15 53
(Rae Guest) *hld up in tch: clsd to trck ldrs 2f out: rdn and ev ch over 1f out tl no ex ins fnl f: wknd fnl 50yds* **12/1**

-305 **6** *3 1/4* **Tea El Tee (IRE)**[9] 2470 3-8-6 **52** (p) DavidEgan(7) 2 38
(Gay Kelleway) *hld up in tch in midfield: effrt 2f out: no imp u.p over 1f out: wknd ins fnl f* **9/1**

1240 7 1 ¾ **Popsilca**[53] 1363 3-9-1 **54** PatCosgrave 7 35
(Mick Quinn) *led: rdn wl over 1f out: hdd 1f out: no ex and wknd ins fnl f* **14/1**

3-64 8 1 **Paquita Bailarina**[17] 2181 3-9-2 **55** LukeMorris 5 33
(James Given) *in tch in midfield: rdn 1/2-way: outpcd u.p over 1f out: wknd ins fnl f* **9/2**[1]

6-36 9 ½ **Camaradorie (IRE)**[90] 763 3-9-4 **60** SimonPearce[(3)] 1 36
(Lydia Pearce) *in tch in midfield but stuck in centre: effrt 2f out: unable qck and btn over 1f out: wknd ins fnl f* **17/2**

0-00 10 nk **Percy Toplis**[22] 2072 3-9-4 **57** (p) KierenFox 9 33
(Christine Dunnett) *bmpd s: in tch in midfield: rdn over 2f out: keeping on same pce whn sltly impeded over 1f out: wknd ins fnl f* **25/1**

0006 11 4 **Chillililli**[14] 2306 3-8-0 **46** oh1 (p) RPWalsh[(7)] 11 10
(Michael Appleby) *bmpd s and slowly away: a rr: n.d* **40/1**

50-5 12 8 **Sattar (IRE)**[12] 2366 3-9-2 **55** (b[1]) AntonioFresu 16
(Luke McJannet) *t.k.h: hld up in tch in midfield: effrt 2f out: no ex u.p over 1f out: sn wknd* **6/1**[3]

000- 13 4 ½ **Compton Brave**[212] 7414 3-8-7 **46** oh1 SilvestreDeSousa 8
(J R Jenkins) *wnt rt s: chsd ldrs tl 2f out: sn lost pl u.p: bhd fnl f* **22/1**

040- 14 5 **Embleton**[188] 7884 3-8-13 **57** LewisEdmunds[(5)] 6
(Charlie Wallis) *chsd ldrs tl 1/2-way: sn dropped out: wl bhd fnl f* **33/1**

1m 12.0s (-2.40) **Going Correction** -0.275s/f (Firm) **14** Ran SP% **120.2**
Speed ratings (Par 97): **105,104,104,102,100 96,93,92,91,91 86,75,69,62**
CSF £112.52 CT £709.41 TOTE £9.80: £2.90, £6.70, £1.80; EX 161.50 Trifecta £1872.50.
**Owner** Ever Equine & J S Moore **Bred** Mrs T Mahon **Trained** Upper Lambourn, Berks

**FOCUS**
This looked impossible to break down before the off, with so many angles to approach the race from, but it was one of the exposed ones that proved successful. The form is rated slightly positively.
T/Plt: £186.40 to a £1 stake. Pool: £62,984.37 - 246.66 winning units T/Qpdt: £129.10 to a £1 stake. Pool: £4,065.60 - 23.3 winning units **Steve Payne**

# YORK (L-H)
## Wednesday, May 17

**OFFICIAL GOING: Soft**
Wind: Virtually nil Weather: Persistent rain

## 2735 SKY BET FIRST RACE SPECIAL H'CAP — 1m 2f 56y
**2:20** (2:22) (Class 2) (0-100,100) 4-Y-0+
**£15,562** (£4,660; £2,330; £1,165; £582; £292) **Stalls** Low

Form RPR

6-00 1 **Master Carpenter (IRE)**[25] 1960 6-9-2 **95** PhillipMakin 5 108
(Rod Millman) *hld up in tch: smooth hdwy to trck ldrs over 2f out: swtchd rt and effrt over 1f out: rdn to ld appr fnl f: sn clr: styd on strly* **12/1**

014- 2 5 **Al Neksh**[208] 7499 4-8-12 **91** FrankieDettori 3 95+
(William Haggas) *lw: hld up towards rr: gd hdwy on inner 3f out: chsd ldrs 2f out: rdn and ev ch over 1f out: drvn and kpt on same pce fnl f* **7/1**[2]

0-05 3 1 ½ **Oasis Fantasy (IRE)**[104] 542 6-9-4 **97** JamieSpencer 6 98
(David Simcock) *prom: sn trcking clr ldr: hdwy 3f out: slt ld 2f out and sn rdn: hdd appr fnl f: sn drvn and kpt on same pce* **20/1**

062- 4 ¾ **Awake My Soul (IRE)**[197] 7744 8-9-1 **94** JamesSullivan 19 93
(Tom Tate) *sn led: pushed along 3f out: rdn and hdd 2f out: drvn over 1f out: kpt on same pce* **25/1**

0- 5 nk **Qassem (IRE)**[193] 7824 4-9-1 **94** JamesDoyle 4 93
(Hugo Palmer) *trckd ldrs: hdwy over 3f out and sn cl up: rdn to dispute ld 2f out and ev ch tl drvn and appr fnl f and kpt on same pce* **11/1**

0-30 6 1 **Innocent Touch (IRE)**[21] 2086 6-9-0 **93** PaulHanagan 8 90
(Richard Fahey) *trckd ldrs: hdwy 3f out: rdn along 2f out: sn drvn and grad wknd* **20/1**

2U25 7 hd **Final**[10] 2431 5-9-0 **93** JoeFanning 13 89+
(Mark Johnston) *towards rr: hdwy wl over 2f out: sn rdn: styd on wl fnl f* **25/1**

530- 8 1 **Not So Sleepy**[175] 8068 5-9-7 **100** (t) AdamKirby 2 94
(Hughie Morrison) *hld up in rr: hdwy on inner 3f out: rdn along 2f out: sn drvn and no imp* **16/1**

02-6 9 nk **Erik The Red (FR)**[33] 1779 5-9-6 **99** KevinStott 12 93
(Kevin Ryan) *chsd ldrs: rdn along over 2f out: drvn and wknd over 1f out* **8/1**[3]

02-6 10 ½ **Saunter (FR)**[37] 1691 4-9-6 **99** JimmyFortune 7 92
(David Menuisier) *hld up: hdwy over 3f out: in tch and rdn along over 2f out: sn no imp* **11/1**

41-5 11 hd **Speed Company (IRE)**[21] 2086 4-9-6 **99** (h) RyanMoore 14 92
(John Quinn) *stdd and swtchd lft s: hld up towards rr: effrt 3f out: sn rdn along and n.d* **12/1**

13-0 12 3 ½ **Beardwood**[10] 2431 5-8-12 **91** (p) AndreaAtzeni 11 77
(Mark Johnston) *hld up: hdwy over 3f out: rdn along over 2f out: n.d* **25/1**

5-54 13 3 **Lustrous Light (IRE)**[24] 1999 4-9-7 **100** OisinMurphy 15 80
(Ralph Beckett) *a towards rr* **25/1**

-622 14 1 ¼ **Two For Two (IRE)**[11] 2406 9-8-12 **91** (p) TonyHamilton 1 69
(Roger Fell) *towards rr: hdwy 3f out: rdn along and tch 2f out: sn drvn and wknd* **25/1**

156- 15 ¾ **Shabeeb (USA)**[237] 6715 4-9-7 **100** JimCrowley 17 76
(Roger Varian) *lw: hld up: a rr* **14/1**

6 16 6 **Repercussion**[29] 1860 4-9-2 **95** (h) StevieDonohoe 9 60
(Charlie Fellowes) *lw: chsd ldrs: rdn along 3f out: wknd 2f out* **10/1**

02-0 17 4 **Cosmeapolitan**[10] 2431 4-9-2 **95** FergusSweeney 18 52
(Alan King) *a towards rr* **16/1**

2000 18 ¾ **Mythical Madness**[18] 2141 6-9-5 **98** (p) DanielTudhope 16 54
(David O'Meara) *in tch: hdwy 4f out: rdn along over 3f out: sn wknd* **50/1**

50-5 19 3 ¼ **Kentuckyconnection (USA)**[25] 1974 4-9-4 **97** ConnorBeasley 20 47
(Bryan Smart) *a rr* **50/1**

/20- 20 4 ½ **Lovell**[335] 3300 4-9-0 **93** WilliamBuick 10 34
(Charlie Appleby) *trckd ldng pair: pushed along over 3f out: rdn wl over 2f out: sn wknd* **6/1**[1]

2m 12.71s (0.21) **Going Correction** +0.525s/f (Yiel) **20** Ran SP% **130.1**
Speed ratings (Par 109): **120,116,114,114,113 113,113,112,111,111 111,108,106,105,104 99,96,96,93,89**
CSF £85.22 CT £1714.25 TOTE £15.60: £3.80, £2.20, £5.90, £8.60; EX 156.40 Trifecta £6001.60 Part Won..
**Owner** David Little The Links Partnership **Bred** Naiff Sa & Newtown Stud **Trained** Kentisbeare, Devon

**FOCUS**
Stalls inside rail, race distance +32yds to 1m2f88yds. Persistent rain turned the ground soft ahead of the first race of the 2017 Dante Festival. This looked a wide-open handicap beforehand but nothing could live with the winner, who's rated close to last year's best. The action unfolded up the middle in the straight.

## 2736 INFINITY TYRES H'CAP — 6f
**2:55** (2:58) (Class 2) (0-105,102) 4-Y-0+
**£15,562** (£4,660; £2,330; £1,165; £582; £292) **Stalls** Centre

Form RPR

3/0- 1 **Al Qahwa (IRE)**[288] 5000 4-8-13 **94** DanielTudhope 8 103
(David O'Meara) *prom: rdn to chal strly over 1f out: kpt on: led towards fin* **25/1**

1-22 2 nk **Muntadab (IRE)**[18] 2156 5-9-2 **97** TonyHamilton 2 105
(Roger Fell) *lw: led narrowly: rdn over 1f out: kpt on: hdd towards fin* **6/1**[1]

00-0 3 1 ¼ **Lincoln (IRE)**[45] 1515 6-8-12 **93** GrahamLee 18 97+
(Mick Channon) *hld up: rdn and hdwy over 1f out: kpt on wl* **14/1**

0-63 4 ½ **Northgate Lad (IRE)**[23] 2031 5-8-8 **89** BenCurtis 1 91
(Brian Ellison) *half-rrd s: sn in tch: rdn 2f out: kpt on* **8/1**[3]

6-05 5 nk **Flying Pursuit**[20] 2113 4-8-6 **87** (b) DuranFentiman 3 88
(Tim Easterby) *chsd ldrs: rdn 2f out: kpt on same pce* **10/1**

5-00 6 1 **George Bowen (IRE)**[18] 2156 5-8-7 **88** (h[1]) PaulHanagan 13 86
(Richard Fahey) *prom: pushed along over 1f out: rdn ins fnl f: wknd fnl 50yds* **8/1**[3]

0120 7 nse **King Robert**[28] 1880 4-8-12 **93** (v) ConnorBeasley 19 91
(Bryan Smart) *dwlt: sn pushed along in rr: kpt on ins fnl f: nvr threatened* **20/1**

04-1 8 ½ **Udontdodou**[20] 2113 4-8-7 **88** JoeFanning 16 84
(Richard Guest) *dwlt: hld up: rdn over 1f out: sme late hdwy: nvr threatened* **7/1**[2]

00-0 9 1 **Toofi (FR)**[45] 1515 6-8-11 **92** JFEgan 14 85
(John Butler) *midfield: rdn over 2f out: one pce* **25/1**

-011 10 hd **Wentworth Falls**[30] 1831 5-9-1 **96** PhillipMakin 7 89
(Geoffrey Harker) *dwlt: hld up in midfield: rdn over 1f out: no imp* **6/1**[1]

5036 11 1 ½ **Ninjago**[30] 1831 7-8-10 **91** (b) OisinMurphy 9 79
(Paul Midgley) *midfield: rdn over 2f out: wknd fnl 110yds* **14/1**

5005 12 3 ½ **Shamshon (IRE)**[21] 2083 6-8-8 **89** (t) PJMcDonald 11 66
(Stuart Williams) *hld up: rdn over 2f out: wknd over 1f out* **16/1**

0-00 13 nk **Ride Like The Wind (IRE)**[46] 1491 5-9-7 **102** (h) JamieSpencer 12 86
(Kevin Ryan) *dwlt: hld up in rr: stl on bit over 1f out: pushed along and sme hdwy ent fnl f: eased fnl 50yds* **12/1**

1-00 14 2 ¾ **Giant Spark**[45] 1520 5-8-12 **93** PaulMulrennan 10 60
(Paul Midgley) *prom: rdn over 2f out: wknd over 1f out* **16/1**

0-50 15 shd **Reputation (IRE)**[18] 2156 4-8-9 **90** JasonHart 6 57
(John Quinn) *w ldr: rdn over 2f out: wknd over 1f out* **25/1**

0-50 16 3 ½ **Related**[11] 2381 7-8-6 **87** CamHardie 5 42
(Paul Midgley) *midfield: rdn 1/2-way: wknd fnl 2f* **25/1**

1m 12.83s (0.93) **Going Correction** +0.525s/f (Yiel) **16** Ran SP% **125.3**
Speed ratings (Par 109): **114,113,111,111,110 109,109,108,107,107 105,100,100,96,96 91**
CSF £163.76 CT £2274.37 TOTE £41.90: £8.00, £1.80, £2.90, £2.30; EX 266.40 Trifecta £1435.50.
**Owner** Gallop Racing **Bred** Rathasker Stud **Trained** Upper Helmsley, N Yorks

**FOCUS**
Stalls centre. Not the greatest surprise that this competitive heat on softish ground produced a big-priced winner who produced a pb. The race developed up the centre of the track.

## 2737 DUKE OF YORK CLIPPER LOGISTICS STKS (GROUP 2) — 6f
**3:30** (3:31) (Class 1) 3-Y-0+
**£70,887** (£26,875; £13,450; £6,700; £3,362; £1,687) **Stalls** Centre

Form RPR

10-2 1 **Tasleet**[18] 2150 4-9-8 **110** (p[1]) JimCrowley 9 118
(William Haggas) *hld up: hdwy 2f out: swtchd lft and rdn over 1f out: qcknd to ld ent fnl f: edgd rt and kpt on wl towards fin* **14/1**

400- 2 2 ½ **Magical Memory (IRE)**[256] 6120 5-9-8 **114** FrankieDettori 12 110
(Charles Hills) *in tch on outer: hdwy 2f out: chal over 1f out: rdn and ev ch ent fnl f: sn edgd lft and kpt on same pce* **14/1**

-142 3 1 ½ **Comicas (USA)**[53] 1377 4-9-8 **113** (b) JamesDoyle 3 105
(Charlie Appleby) *prom: hdwy to ld 2f out: rdn over 1f out: hdd 1f out: sn drvn and hld whn n.m.r ins fnl f* **25/1**

66-0 4 1 ½ **Mobsta (IRE)**[46] 1491 5-9-8 **106** AndreaAtzeni 11 100
(Mick Channon) *in rr: rdn along and outpcd 1/2-way: hdwy wl over 1f out: kpt on u.p fnl f* **20/1**

121- 5 ¾ **The Tin Man**[214] 7350 5-9-13 **117** TomQueally 1 103
(James Fanshawe) *chsd ldrs on inner: hdwy over 2f out: rdn wl over 1f out: grad wknd appr fnl f* **5/1**[2]

0041 6 2 **Tupi (IRE)**[46] 1491 5-9-8 **109** RyanMoore 5 92
(Richard Hannon) *in rr: outpcd 1/2-way: swtchd rt and rdn 2f out: styd on appr fnl f* **12/1**

210- 7 ½ **Growl**[157] 8330 5-9-8 **114** (p) GrahamLee 10 90
(Richard Fahey) *chsd ldrs: hdwy and cl up 2f out: sn rdn and hld whn sltly hmpd appr fnl f* **14/1**

433- 8 3 ½ **Suedois (FR)**[227] 6991 6-9-8 **114** DanielTudhope 4 79
(David O'Meara) *cl up: rdn along 2f out: drvn and edgd appr fnl f: sn wknd* **11/2**[3]

2214 9 3 **Jungle Cat (IRE)**[53] 1376 5-9-8 **113** (p) WilliamBuick 7 69
(Charlie Appleby) *chsd ldrs: rdn along over 2f out: sn drvn and wknd* **8/1**

06-5 10 1 ¼ **Nameitwhatyoulike**[46] 1491 8-9-8 **105** ConnorBeasley 6 65
(Bryan Smart) *led: rdn along and hdd 2f out: sn wknd* **25/1**

-120 11 4 **Baccarat (IRE)**[53] 1376 8-9-8 **111** AdamKirby 2 52
(Charlie Appleby) *towards rr: hdwy and in tch 1/2-way: sn rdn and wknd* **20/1**

13-1 12 11 **Brando**[27] 1903 5-9-8 **116** TomEaves 8 17
(Kevin Ryan) *lw: trckd ldrs: effrt over 2f out: sn rdn and wknd qckly: bhd and eased fnl f* **5/2**[1]

1m 12.74s (0.84) **Going Correction** +0.525s/f (Yiel) **12** Ran SP% **116.6**
Speed ratings (Par 115): **115,111,109,107,106 104,103,98,94,93 87,73**
CSF £180.64 TOTE £17.40: £4.30, £3.60, £7.50; EX 206.90 Trifecta £8491.20.
**Owner** Hamdan Al Maktoum **Bred** Whitsbury Manor Stud **Trained** Newmarket, Suffolk

**FOCUS**
Stalls centre. This looked well up to standard, although the time was only 0.09sec faster than the handicap 35min earlier on the card (rain was still falling). With ground conditions deteriorating, how reliable a form guide this will prove come Royal Ascot remains to be seen. The form has been rated at face value, Tasleet in line with the race's better unpenalised winners.

## 2738 TATTERSALLS MUSIDORA STKS (GROUP 3) (FILLIES) 1m 2f 56y
4:05 (4:05) (Class 1) 3-Y-O £56,710 (£21,500; £10,760; £5,360; £2,690) Stalls Low

Form RPR
1-1 1 **Shutter Speed**[26] 1943 3-9-0 108 FrankieDettori 1 105+
(John Gosden) *tall: str: t.k.h: trckd ldng pair: hdwy 3f out: led over 2f out: pushed along wl over 1f out: rdn and kpt on fnl f* **4/7**[1]
1- 2 1 3/4 **Vintage Folly**[170] 8131 3-9-0 76 JamesDoyle 5 100
(Hugo Palmer) *lengthy: racd wd early: trckd ldr: hdwy and cl up 3f out: rdn along to chse wnr 2f out: drvn and kpt on fnl f* **12/1**
3-1 3 1 **Serenada**[19] 2131 3-9-0 82 AndreaAtzeni 3 98
(Roger Varian) *trckd ldrs: hdwy 3f out: chsd ldng pair wl over 1f out: sn rdn and no imp fnl f* **15/2**[3]
0 4 2 1/2 **Vociferous Marina (IRE)**[24] 1998 3-9-0 102 (t) KevinManning 4 93
(J S Bolger, Ire) *unf: hld up in rr: hdwy 3f out: chsd ldrs 2f out: sn rdn and kpt on same pce* **4/1**[2]
0-04 5 22 **Miss Infinity (IRE)**[10] 2436 3-9-0 101 RyanMoore 2 52
(Mark Johnston) *set stdy pce: pushed along and qcknd over 3f out: rdn and hdd 2f out: sn wknd* **16/1**

2m 18.62s (6.12) **Going Correction** +0.525s/f (Yiel) **5 Ran SP% 109.0**
Speed ratings (Par 106): **96,94,93,91,74**
CSF £8.22 TOTE £1.40: £1.10, £3.70; EX 7.40 Trifecta £22.50.
**Owner** K Abdullah **Bred** Juddmonte Farms Ltd **Trained** Newmarket, Suffolk

**FOCUS**
Stalls inside rail, race distance +32yds to 1m2f88yds. Probably a good running of a race that can be a key Oaks trial, although this year's winner is heading to France rather than Epsom. They raced middle to far side in the straight.

## 2739 CONUNDRUM HR CONSULTING H'CAP 7f
4:35 (4:38) (Class 3) (0-95,91) 3-Y-O

£12,450 (£3,728; £1,864; £932; £466; £234) Stalls High

Form RPR
2-54 1 **Battered**[13] 2334 3-8-13 83 RyanMoore 6 100
(William Haggas) *hld up in midfield: pushed along and hdwy over 2f out: rdn to ld ins fnl f: edgd lft: kpt on wl* **4/1**[1]
4-13 2 2 1/2 **Lualiwa**[28] 1878 3-8-9 79 KevinStott 10 89
(Kevin Ryan) *racd keenly: pressed ldr: led over 3f out: rdn 2f out: edgd rt appr fnl f: hdd ins fnl f: sn sltly hmpd by wnr: no ex fnl 50yds* **16/1**
22-1 3 nse **Starlight Romance (IRE)**[20] 2106 3-8-7 80 SammyJoBell(3) 17 90
(Richard Fahey) *trckd ldrs: rdn to chal over 1f out: sltly hmpd and swtchd lft appr fnl f: kpt on* **9/1**
301- 4 1 3/4 **Golden Apollo**[193] 7820 3-8-11 81 DavidAllan 13 86
(Tim Easterby) *midfield: rdn over 2f out: kpt on* **16/1**
110- 5 1 1/4 **Simply Brilliant**[250] 6285 3-9-7 91 PaulHanagan 18 93+
(Richard Fahey) *lw: dwlt: midfield on outside: pushed along and lost pl over 2f out: kpt on ins fnl f* **10/1**
1-45 6 3/4 **Mazyoun**[11] 2400 3-9-4 88 (b) FrankieDettori 3 88
(Hugo Palmer) *dwlt: hld up in rr: pushed along and hdwy over 1f out: kpt on ins fnl f: nvr threatened ldrs* **7/1**[3]
1 7 nk **Sir Reginald Brown**[37] 1680 3-7-12 75 ConnorMurtagh(7) 16 74
(Richard Fahey) *leggy: scope: trckd ldrs: rdn over 2f out: wknd ins fnl f* **5/1**[2]
65-1 8 1 3/4 **Muscika**[17] 2180 3-8-9 79 HarryBentley 14 74
(David O'Meara) *cmpt: dwlt: hld up in midfield: rdn over 2f out: no imp* **14/1**
2-1 9 2 3/4 **Harbour Grey (IRE)**[19] 2121 3-8-9 79 TomMarquand 8 67
(Richard Hannon) *trckd ldrs: rdn over 2f out: wknd fnl f* **12/1**
10-0 10 nse **Orewa (IRE)**[11] 2384 3-9-4 88 BenCurtis 11 76
(Brian Ellison) *hld up: nvr threatened* **16/1**
610- 11 8 **Tawny Port**[228] 6954 3-9-1 85 TomEaves 5 52
(James Given) *hld up: rdn along and bhd fr over 3f out* **16/1**
0-10 12 11 **Flashy Snapper**[11] 2385 3-9-4 88 OisinMurphy 9 26
(Simon Crisford) *midfield: rdn over 2f out: wknd over 1f out and eased* **16/1**
423- 13 7 **Parnassian (IRE)**[181] 7989 3-9-5 89 JoeyHaynes 1 9
(K R Burke) *in tch inner: rdn over 3f out: wknd fnl 2f: eased* **20/1**
2-06 14 27 **Monks Stand (USA)**[20] 2106 3-8-12 82 (b[1]) JasonHart 2
(Tim Easterby) *wnt rt s: led narrowly: hdd over 3f out: wknd over 2f out: eased* **50/1**

1m 28.18s (2.88) **Going Correction** +0.525s/f (Yiel) **14 Ran SP% 118.8**
Speed ratings (Par 103): **104,101,101,99,97 96,96,94,91,91 82,69,61,30**
CSF £68.81 CT £564.61 TOTE £4.80: £2.20, £5.20, £3.20; EX 76.00 Trifecta £491.90.
**Owner** B Haggas **Bred** Coln Valley Stud **Trained** Newmarket, Suffolk

**FOCUS**
Stalls far-side rail. A useful 3yo handicap. They raced middle to far side in the straight and the form is rated through the second.

## 2740 BRITISH STALLION STUDS EBF NOVICE STKS (PLUS 10 RACE) 5f
5:05 (5:06) (Class 3) 2-Y-O

£12,450 (£3,728; £1,864; £932; £466; £234) Stalls High

Form RPR
1 1 **Santry (IRE)**[46] 1495 2-9-8 0 JimCrowley 5 92
(Declan Carroll) *str: t.k.h early: trckd ldrs: hdwy 2f out: rdn to ld ins fnl f: kpt on strly* **9/4**[1]
2 2 1/4 **Consequences (IRE)** 2-9-2 0 DanielTudhope 2 78+
(David O'Meara) *str: wnt sltly lft s: prom: hdwy to ld 2f out: rdn ent fnl f: sn edgd lft and hdd: kpt on same pce* **4/1**[3]
6 3 1 1/4 **Palmer (IRE)**[23] 2029 2-9-2 0 ConnorBeasley 1 73
(Bryan Smart) *w'like: in tch: chsd ldrs 2f out: rdn along and sltly outpcd over 1f out: kpt on u.p fnl f* **12/1**
4 nse **It Dont Come Easy (IRE)** 2-9-2 0 PaulHanagan 10 73+
(Richard Fahey) *cmpt: trckd ldrs: hdwy 2f out: rdn over 1f out: kpt on same pce fnl f* **10/3**[2]
5 nk **Savalas (IRE)** 2-9-2 0 TomEaves 11 72+
(Kevin Ryan) *w'like: bit bkwd: prom: cl up 2f out: rdn and ev ch over 1f out: kpt on same pce fnl f* **15/2**
02 6 5 **Rocket Man Dan (IRE)**[18] 2154 2-9-2 0 DougieCostello 9 54
(Keith Dalgleish) *leggy: awkward s: in tch: hdwy over 2f out: rdn along wl over 1f out: sn drvn and wknd* **9/1**
7 1 1/4 **Knockout Blow** 2-9-2 0 RyanMoore 7 49
(Mark Johnston) *str: led: pushed along 1/2-way: rdn and hdd 2f out: sn wknd* **10/1**
0 8 1 1/4 **Furze Boy**[16] 2221 2-8-13 0 NathanEvans(3) 8 45
(Michael Easterby) *leggy: chsd ldrs: rdn along over 2f out: sn wknd* **66/1**

1m 1.87s (2.57) **Going Correction** +0.525s/f (Yiel) **8 Ran SP% 113.9**
Speed ratings (Par 97): **100,96,94,94,93 85,83,81**
CSF £11.31 TOTE £3.30: £1.50, £1.50, £2.90; EX 13.70 Trifecta £80.30.
**Owner** Ray Flegg, John Bousfield & Steve Ryan **Bred** Peter Molony **Trained** Malton, N Yorks

**FOCUS**
Stalls stands' side rail. There was money about for one or two of the newcomers and the penalised favourite was well supported near the off, suggesting this might have been a fair novice. The first three raced furthest away from the stands' rail but this was agood effort from the winner however viewed.

## 2741 YORK DATA SERVICES INTERNET CLOUD SOLUTIONS H'CAP 1m 3f 188y
5:35 (5:37) (Class 4) (0-85,85) 4-Y-O+

£12,450 (£3,728; £1,864; £932; £466; £234) Stalls Centre

Form RPR
1-12 1 **Zain Arion (IRE)**[18] 2146 4-8-13 77 JFEgan 10 87
(John Butler) *trckd ldng pair on inner: hdwy to chse ldr over 4f out: led wl over 3f out: rdn clr over 2f out: kpt on strly fnl f* **20/1**
010- 2 1 1/2 **Purple Rock (IRE)**[163] 8231 5-9-0 81 (t) NathanEvans(3) 2 88
(Michael Easterby) *in tch on inner: hdwy 4f out: chsd wnr over 2f out: rdn wl over 1f out: drvn fnl f: no imp towards fin* **14/1**
000- 3 6 **Tapis Libre**[204] 7594 9-8-7 78 HarrisonShaw(7) 18 75
(Jacqueline Coward) *rr: hdwy 3f out: rdn along 2f out: kpt on appr fnl f* **50/1**
20-4 4 2 1/4 **Theydon Grey**[22] 2068 4-9-5 83 RyanMoore 5 77
(William Haggas) *hld up towards rr: hdwy on inner over 4f out: chsd ldrs over 2f out: sn rdn and kpt on fnl f* **6/1**[2]
0-30 5 nk **Chancery (USA)**[27] 1911 9-9-7 85 (p) DanielTudhope 14 78
(David O'Meara) *trckd ldrs: hdwy over 4f out: rdn along 3f out: drvn 2f out and kpt on one pce* **11/1**
2123 6 1 1/2 **Lac Leman (GER)**[33] 1781 6-9-2 80 (h) GrahamLee 20 71
(Pauline Robson) *swtg: swtchd lft s and hld up towards rr: hdwy 3f out: rdn over 2f out: drvn wl over 1f out: kpt on: n.d* **12/1**
340- 7 1 3/4 **Red Rannagh (IRE)**[189] 7869 4-9-7 85 JamieSpencer 3 73
(David Simcock) *lw: awkward s and slowly away: t.k.h in rr: sltly hmpd after 1 1/2f and sn plld hrd: hdwy: hanging and reminders over 4f out: drvn along and in tch 3f out: plugged on u.p fnl 2f* **11/2**[1]
0-00 8 1/2 **Maraakib (IRE)**[18] 2136 5-9-4 85 JoshDoyle(3) 4 72
(David O'Meara) *trckd ldrs: hdwy and cl up 4f out: rdn along 3f out: drvn 2f out and sn one pce* **12/1**
143- 9 6 **Island Flame (IRE)**[138] 8584 4-8-12 76 PaulHanagan 8 54
(Richard Fahey) *hld up towards rr: hdwy 3f out: rdn along over 2f out: n.d* **12/1**
140- 10 8 **Carthage (IRE)**[251] 6267 6-8-9 73 BenCurtis 9 38
(Brian Ellison) *midfield: pushed along 5f out: in tch and rdn 4f out: sn wknd* **25/1**
0-60 11 4 1/2 **Mukhayyam**[25] 1976 5-9-5 83 (p) DavidAllan 6 41
(Tim Easterby) *trckd ldr: rdn along over 4f out: sn wknd* **8/1**[3]
1-22 12 2 3/4 **Marmajuke Bay**[18] 2165 4-9-7 85 (p) SteveDrowne 15 38
(Mark Usher) *chsd ldrs on outer: rdn along over 4f out: sn wknd* **9/1**
2234 13 1 3/4 **Busy Street**[10] 2426 5-9-1 79 JoeFanning 17 30
(Alan Swinbank) *in tch on outer: rdn along 4f out: sn wknd* **10/1**
00-0 14 3/4 **Glance My Way (IRE)**[16] 2225 4-8-9 73 (b[1]) JasonHart 11 22
(Tim Easterby) *prom: rdn along 4f out: drvn 3f out: grad wknd* **33/1**
2-11 15 1 1/4 **Samtu (IRE)**[64] 1182 6-9-6 84 BarryMcHugh 1 31
(Marjorie Fife) *led: pushed along 5f out: rdn over 4f out: hdd wl over 3f out and sn wknd* **14/1**
26-6 16 3 1/2 **Thames Knight**[21] 2085 5-8-6 77 TylerSaunders(7) 16 19
(Marcus Tregoning) *lw: a towards rr* **11/1**

2m 40.9s (7.70) **Going Correction** +0.525s/f (Yiel) **16 Ran SP% 126.5**
Speed ratings (Par 105): **95,94,90,88,88 87,86,85,81,76 73,71,70,69,69 66**
CSF £278.40 CT £13027.16 TOTE £26.70: £4.20, £4.40, £7.20, £1.70; EX 416.30 Trifecta £7628.40 Part Won..
**Owner** Asaad Al Banwan **Bred** Lynch Bages & Camas Park Stud **Trained** Newmarket, Suffolk

**FOCUS**
Stalls centre, race distance +32yds to 1m4f. A bit of a slog for most, but the first two coped well, drawing clear of the rest. The form isn't taken too literally but the winner continues to progress.
T/Jkpt: Not Won T/Plt: £310.30 to a £1 stake. Pool: £240,064.56 - 564.6 winning units T/Qpdt: £51.80 to a £1 stake. Pool: £15,775.12 - 225.22 winning units **Joe Rowntree/Andrew Sheret**

2742 - 2749a (Foreign Racing) - See Raceform Interactive

# 2431 NEWMARKET (R-H)
Thursday, May 18

**OFFICIAL GOING: Good to soft (6.8) changed to soft after race 2 (6.20)**
Wind: virtually nil Weather: light rain

## 2750 FEDERATION OF BLOODSTOCK AGENTS NOVICE AUCTION STKS (PLUS 10 RACE) 6f
5:50 (5:51) (Class 4) 2-Y-O £4,204 (£1,251; £625; £312) Stalls Low

Form RPR
4 1 **Red Roman**[11] 2435 2-9-2 0 SilvestreDeSousa 12 87
(Charles Hills) *mde all: rdn and fnd ex over 1f out: clr and in command ins fnl f: r.o wl: eased towards fin: comf* **2/1**[1]
2 2 1/2 **Initiative (IRE)** 2-9-0 0 DaneO'Neill 7 78+
(Henry Spiller) *stdd s and slowly away: t.k.h: hld up towards rr: hdwy into midfield 1/2-way: effrt and rn green wl over 1f out: hdwy whn nt clr run and swtchd lft over 1f out: r.o wl ins fnl f: wnt 2nd last strides* **20/1**
5 3 nk **Gold Filigree (IRE)**[24] 2037 2-8-11 0 ShaneKelly 9 74
(Richard Hughes) *t.k.h: chsd ldrs tl wnt 2nd 4f out: rdn and pressing wnr 2f out: unable qck over 1f out: styd on same pce ins fnl f: lost 2nd last strides* **6/1**[2]
054 4 3 1/2 **Controversial Lady (IRE)**[23] 2052 2-8-5 0 LiamJones 4 57
(J S Moore) *in tch in midfield: rdn over 2f out: sn outpcd: rallied 1f out: styd on steadily ins fnl f: no threat to ldrs* **33/1**
5 1 **Iconic Sunset** 2-9-0 0 LukeMorris 5 63+
(James Tate) *hld up in rr: rdn over 2f out: hdwy ent fnl f: swtchd lft and kpt on ins fnl f: nvr trbld ldrs* **12/1**
6 1 1/4 **Simply Breathless** 2-8-7 0 SamHitchcott 11 52
(Clive Cox) *chsd ldrs: rdn over 2f out: outpcd and lost pl wl over 1f out: wknd fnl f* **8/1**

5 7 1 **Nampara**[9] 2502 2-8-7 0 JoeyHaynes 10 49
(Paul D'Arcy) *t.k.h: chsd wnr tl over 4f out: wnt 3rd and rdn ent fnl 2f: sn outpcd: wknd fnl f* **25/1**

0 8 1 **Terri Rules (IRE)**[9] 2502 2-8-9 0 AdamBeschizza 8 48
(Julia Feilden) *restless in stalls: chsd ldrs: rdn 2f out: sn outpcd and struggling: wknd fnl f* **66/1**

0 9 ½ **Amazing Alice**[24] 2037 2-8-9 0 JackMitchell 3 47
(Archie Watson) *in tch in midfield: rdn over 2f out: no imp and kpt on same pce after: nvr trbld ldrs* **16/1**

10 1 ¼ **Cent Flying** 2-9-2 0 MartinDwyer 2 50
(William Muir) *t.k.h: hld up in rr: pushed along 2f out: kpt on same pce and no imp fr over 1f out: nvr trbld ldrs* **14/1**

0 11 1 ¾ **Mysaan (IRE)**[27] 1941 2-9-2 0 TomQueally 1 45
(Brian Meehan) *chsd ldrs: rdn and lost pl 1/2-way: wknd over 1f out* **7/1**[3]

12 ½ **Aldbury Lass (IRE)** 2-8-6 0 ShelleyBirkett(3) 6 36
(Julia Feilden) *hld up towards rr: rdn jst over 2f out: sn struggling and wknd over 1f out* **66/1**

13 7 **If We Can Can** 2-8-10 0 JoeFanning 13 16
(Mark Johnston) *v.s.a and wnt lft s: hdwy into midfield after 2f: rdn over 2f out: lost pl and btn over 1f out: wknd fnl f* **8/1**

1m 15.49s (3.29) **Going Correction** +0.475s/f (Yiel) **13** Ran SP% **117.1**
Speed ratings (Par 95): **97,93,93,88,87 85,84,82,82,80 78,77,68**
CSF £50.86 TOTE £2.70: £1.40, £7.00, £2.00; EX 59.20 Trifecta £296.80.
**Owner** John C Grant & The Hon R J Arculli **Bred** Mrs F S Williams **Trained** Lambourn, Berks

**FOCUS**
Stands' side course used, with stalls far side except 1m4f: centre. A damp and gloomy evening on the Rowley Mile. An ordinary juvenile event for the track, though encouragement to be taken from the first three home. An improved effort from the winner.

## 2751 EBF STALLIONS FRIENDS OF RACING WELFARE MAIDEN STKS (PLUS 10 RACE) 1m 2f
**6:20** (6:23) (Class 4) 3-Y-O **£5,175** (£1,540; £769; £384) **Stalls** Low

Form RPR
232 1 **Hold Sway (IRE)**[15] 2300 3-9-5 84 (p[1]) WilliamBuick 3 90
(Charlie Appleby) *mde all: rdn over 2f out: clr w runner up over 1f out: asserted u.p ins fnl f: styd on wl* **11/4**[2]

4- 2 1 **Zenon (IRE)**[287] 5073 3-9-5 0 AdamKirby 2 88
(John Gosden) *chsd ldng pair: effrt to chse wnr jst over 2f out: sn chalng and clr w wnr: kpt on but jst outpcd ins fnl f* **8/1**[3]

3-2 3 2 **Mutarabby (IRE)**[19] 2152 3-9-5 0 DaneO'Neill 5 84+
(Saeed bin Suroor) *awkward as stalls opened and s.i.s: t.k.h: hld up in last pair: effrt over 3f out: carried lft and impeded over 2f out: chsd clr ldng pair over 1f out: edging rt but kpt on wl ins fnl f* **9/4**[1]

5 4 8 **Marine One**[23] 2066 3-9-5 0 OisinMurphy 8 68
(David Simcock) *t.k.h: hld up in tch in midfield: rdn over 3f out: 4th and getting outpcd whn wnt rt wl over 1f out: wl hld and plugged on same pce after* **11/4**[2]

0 5 5 **Buldan**[30] 1857 3-9-5 0 JoeFanning 7 58
(Sir Michael Stoute) *t.k.h: hld up in tch in rr: swtchd lft and clsd 4f out: rdn wl over 2f out: getting outpcd whn sltly impeded and tk false step and wnt rt over 2f out: wl hld after* **14/1**

0 6 7 **Aladdin Sane (IRE)**[17] 2231 3-8-12 0 JordanUys(7) 6 44
(Brian Meehan) *hld up in tch in midfield: dropped to last: rdn and struggling over 3f out: n.d after* **100/1**

63-2 7 8 **King Of Paris**[33] 1787 3-9-5 78 JackMitchell 9 28
(Roger Varian) *t.k.h: chsd ldr tl lost 2nd and wnt lft over 2f out: btn whn unbalanced and wnt rt downhill run wl over 1f out: bhd and eased ins fnl f* **8/1**[3]

2m 9.68s (3.88) **Going Correction** +0.475s/f (Yiel) **7** Ran SP% **114.0**
Speed ratings (Par 101): **103,102,100,94,90 84,78**
CSF £24.42 TOTE £4.00: £1.60, £3.20; EX 23.20 Trifecta £78.10.
**Owner** Godolphin **Bred** Merry Fox Stud Limited **Trained** Newmarket, Suffolk

**FOCUS**
This fair maiden was run at a leisurely early tempo and that did little to help a number of these. The first three were clear and the winner is rated to a better view of his Doncaster run.

## 2752 SUFFOLK CHAMBER OF COMMERCE H'CAP 1m 4f
**6:50** (6:54) (Class 4) (0-85,86) 4-Y-0+ **£7,762** (£2,310; £1,154; £577) **Stalls** Centre

Form RPR
0-24 1 **Hermann**[10] 2478 4-9-5 81 SeanLevey 11 87
(Richard Hannon) *mde all: battled on wl u.p fr over 1f out: all out: v gamely* **11/2**[3]

2462 2 hd **Alcatraz (IRE)**[31] 1932 5-9-2 78 (p) TrevorWhelan 3 83
(George Baker) *hld up in tch: hdwy to chse ldng trio and shifted lft 2f out: hanging lft but lft 3rd 1f out: styd on wl to go 2nd cl home: nt quite rch wnr* **16/1**

20-0 3 ½ **Against The Odds**[33] 1798 4-9-6 82 (t[1]) AdamKirby 5 86
(Paul Cole) *chsd wnr: drvn and str chal fr wl over 1f out: kpt on wl but a jst hld ins fnl f: lost 2nd cl home* **13/2**

0-06 4 4 ½ **Bertie Moon**[23] 2068 7-8-13 80 (p) CharlieBennett(5) 1 77
(Lydia Pearce) *in rr: rdn and struggling 5f out: hdwy to pass btn horses over 1f out: styd on ins fnl f to snatch 4th last strides: nvr trbld ldrs* **40/1**

-665 5 hd **Excellent Puck (IRE)**[16] 2270 7-8-10 72 LukeMorris 7 69
(Shaun Lycett) *chsd ldrs: rdn and outpcd over 2f out: no imp and kpt on same pce fr over 1f out: lost 4th last strides* **22/1**

103- 6 3 ¼ **Opposition**[299] 4628 4-9-7 83 SilvestreDeSousa 12 74
(Ed Dunlop) *chsd ldrs: struggling u.p whn nudged lft 2f out: wknd over 1f out* **9/2**[1]

-066 7 1 ¼ **Zamperini (IRE)**[41] 1608 5-9-5 81 (v) MartinDwyer 9 70
(Mike Murphy) *hld up in rr: effrt 4f out: awkward hd carriage and hanging rt after: midfield and no hdwy over 1f out: stl hanging and plugging on same pce ins fnl f* **10/1**

5-11 8 nk **Captain Peacock**[24] 2020 4-9-10 86 (v) OisinMurphy 10 75+
(William Knight) *hld up in tch: effrt 4f out: 3rd and pressing ldrs 2f out: hung violently lft over 1f out and lost pl: wknd ins fnl f* **5/1**[2]

40-4 9 9 **Duke Of Diamonds**[41] 1608 5-8-8 73 ShelleyBirkett(3) 8 48
(Julia Feilden) *hld up in midfield: struggling 4f out: wl btn and eased fnl f* **13/2**

/505 10 16 **Lanceur (FR)**[43] 1555 8-9-5 81 AdamBeschizza 6 30
(William Stone) *midfield: rdn and dropped to rr 4f out: wl bhd and eased over 1f out: t.o* **33/1**

-604 11 13 **Cape Discovery**[24] 2041 5-9-6 82 ShaneKelly 4 10
(Richard Hughes) *hld up in tch in midfield: lost pl 3f out: t.o and eased over 1f out: t.o* **8/1**

2m 39.15s (7.15) **Going Correction** +0.475s/f (Yiel) **11** Ran SP% **112.7**
Speed ratings (Par 105): **95,94,94,91,91 89,88,88,82,71 62**
CSF £83.40 CT £579.29 TOTE £6.30: £1.90, £3.60, £2.40; EX 79.00 Trifecta £555.50.

**Owner** Michael Kerr-Dineen & Martin Hughes **Bred** Compagnia Generale Srl **Trained** East Everleigh, Wilts

**FOCUS**
Race distance increased by 12yds. This took plenty of getting in the deteriorating ground and they finished well spaced out behind the three principals. The winner was the least exposed and found a bit of improvement.

## 2753 32RED.COM MAIDEN FILLIES' STKS (PLUS 10 RACE) 7f
**7:25** (7:26) (Class 5) 3-Y-O **£3,881** (£1,155; £577; £288) **Stalls** Low

Form RPR
22 1 **Jalela**[15] 2311 3-9-0 0 FrankieDettori 6 83
(Richard Hannon) *racd keenly: rdn over 1f out: almost 2 l clr 1f out: tiring u.p wl ins fnl f: all out and jst hld on* **5/4**[1]

34- 2 nse **Shaaqaaf (IRE)**[203] 7647 3-9-0 0 DaneO'Neill 8 82
(John Gosden) *stdd s: sn in tch in midfield: effrt to chse ldrs 3f out: wnt 2nd over 2f out: rdn over 1f out: styd on steadily and grad clsd fnl 75yds: jst failed* **9/2**[3]

0 3 10 **Dr Goodhead (FR)**[27] 1948 3-9-0 0 GavinLerena 3 56
(Charles Hills) *chsd ldr tl over 2f out: sn outpcd and wl hld 3rd over 1f out: wknd* **20/1**

4 1 ¼ **Velvet Charm** 3-9-0 0 (h[1]) MartinHarley 5 53
(Rae Guest) *stdd s: hld up in tch in rr: effrt and pushed along over 3f out: 5th and outpcd whn rn green on downhill run over 1f out: wl btn after: wnt 4th ins fnl f* **25/1**

5 2 ¾ **Lightning Mark (IRE)** 3-9-0 0 WilliamBuick 4 45
(John Gosden) *in tch in midfield: effrt in 4th 3f out: outpcd 2f out: sn wl btn: wknd fnl f* **9/4**[2]

6 5 **Quinquereme** 3-9-0 0 SilvestreDeSousa 1 32
(Michael Bell) *in tch in midfield: rdn over 2f out: sn struggling and outpcd: wknd wl over 1f out* **10/1**

60- 7 27 **Denver Spirit (IRE)**[187] 7939 3-8-7 0 GabrieleMalune(7) 9
(Luca Cumani) *chsd ldrs: sddle slipped after 2f: dropped to rr 4f out: lost tch 2f out and eased: t.o* **40/1**

1m 28.56s (3.16) **Going Correction** +0.475s/f (Yiel) **7** Ran SP% **113.5**
Speed ratings (Par 96): **100,99,88,87,83 78,47**
CSF £7.20 TOTE £2.00: £1.40, £2.20; EX 7.50 Trifecta £46.70.
**Owner** Al Shaqab Racing **Bred** The Pocock Family **Trained** East Everleigh, Wilts

**FOCUS**
The first two pulled clear in this fillies' maiden as many failed to handle the worsening track conditions. The winner set the standard and is rated close to form.

## 2754 REWARDS4RACING.COM FILLIES' H'CAP (A JOCKEY CLUB GRASSROOTS MIDDLE DISTANCE SERIES QUALIFIER) 1m
**8:00** (8:02) (Class 5) (0-75,77) 3-Y-O **£3,881** (£1,155; £577; £288) **Stalls** Low

Form RPR
20-6 1 **Harmonise**[16] 2266 3-9-2 70 SilvestreDeSousa 1 78
(Mick Channon) *niggled along towards rr: rdn and hdwy chse ldrs 3f out: chsd ldr wl over 1f out: ev ch 1f out: led ins fnl f: styd on wl* **6/1**[2]

21-0 2 1 **Carducci**[16] 2274 3-9-3 71 SeanLevey 6 76
(Richard Hannon) *chsd ldr tl led over 2f out: rdn over 1f out: hdd and styd on same pce ins fnl f* **12/1**

53-4 3 1 **Pacofilha**[17] 2220 3-9-0 68 LukeMorris 9 71
(Paul Cole) *t.k.h: hld up in tch in midfield: rdn to chse ldr briefly 2f out: 3rd and styd on same pce u.p fr over 1f out* **10/1**

1- 4 1 ¼ **Tribute Act**[218] 7278 3-9-7 75 TomQueally 12 75+
(James Fanshawe) *s.i.s: hld up in rr: hdwy u.p over 2f out: chsd ldng trio over 1f out: styd on same pce ins fnl f* **5/1**[1]

51-4 5 10 **Miss Laila (IRE)**[22] 2094 3-9-3 71 PatCosgrave 3 48
(Tom Clover) *short of room leaving stalls: in tch in midfield: rdn to chse ldrs 3f out: outpcd wl over 1f out: wknd fnl f* **12/1**

403- 6 2 ¾ **Funky Footsteps (IRE)**[213] 7416 3-9-5 73 CharlesBishop 7 44
(Eve Johnson Houghton) *chsd ldrs: rdn 3f out: rdn and struggling to qckn 3f out: outpcd and btn 2f out: wknd over 1f out* **16/1**

56-1 7 2 ¼ **Nostalgie**[16] 2274 3-9-9 77 MartinHarley 5 43+
(James Tate) *hld up in tch in last quartet: hdwy to chse ldrs 4f out: rdn and chsng ldrs 3f out: struggling 2f out: sn outpcd and wknd over 1f out* **7/1**[3]

60-5 8 1 ¼ **See The Sea (IRE)**[16] 2274 3-9-1 69 TomMarquand 4 32
(Richard Hannon) *chsd ldrs: lost pl u.p 3f out: no ch fnl 2f* **16/1**

221- 9 3 ¼ **Conqueress (IRE)**[267] 5772 3-9-5 73 AdamKirby 8 28
(Tom Dascombe) *flashing tail at times: led tl rdn and hdd over 2f out: lost pl 2f out: wknd over 1f out* **16/1**

06-0 10 5 **Moonlight Silver**[15] 2311 3-9-0 68 MartinDwyer 2 12
(William Muir) *hld up in tch in midfield: rdn over 2f out: sn btn: eased ins fnl f* **25/1**

21 11 3 ¾ **Rinaria (IRE)**[21] 2110 3-9-0 71 JordanVaughan(3) 14 6
(K R Burke) *t.k.h: hld up in tch in last quartet: rdn 3f out: sn bhd* **14/1**

0-41 12 5 **Snow Squaw**[18] 2172 3-8-11 72 DavidEgan(7) 11
(David Elsworth) *t.k.h: t.k.h: hld up in midfield: rdn and lost pl 3f out: wl bhd fnl 2f: t.o* **10/1**

4-26 13 15 **Pure Shores**[20] 2131 3-9-8 76 WilliamBuick 10
(Charlie Appleby) *t.k.h: hld up in midfield: hdwy to chse ldrs 5f out: lost pl qckly 3f out: bhd and eased over 1f out: t.o* **7/1**[3]

1m 42.43s (3.83) **Going Correction** +0.475s/f (Yiel) **13** Ran SP% **117.7**
Speed ratings (Par 96): **99,98,97,95,85 83,80,79,76,71 67,62,47**
CSF £75.01 CT £734.35 TOTE £6.10: £2.40, £4.50, £3.40; EX 96.70 Trifecta £698.70.
**Owner** Wood Street Syndicate II **Bred** J Repard & S Dibb **Trained** West Ilsley, Berks

**FOCUS**
This featured some promising sorts and may prove a decent race for the grade. They got racing from an early stage and the winner came from last. The first four were nicely clear and the winner is rated close to last September's nursery second..

## 2755 RACING UK NOW LIVE ON YOUVIEW 231 H'CAP 1m
**8:30** (8:36) (Class 4) (0-85,85) 3-Y-O **£7,762** (£2,310; £1,154; £577) **Stalls** Low

Form RPR
12-3 1 **Fire Brigade**[23] 2071 3-8-9 73 SilvestreDeSousa 7 79+
(Michael Bell) *dwlt: sn rcvrd and travelled strly in midfield: clsd to join ldrs ent fnl 2f: rdn and ev ch over 1f out: led 1f out: styd on wl* **7/2**[2]

510- 2 ½ **Trading Punches (IRE)**[235] 6800 3-9-5 83 PatCosgrave 6 88
(David Brown) *chsd ldr tl led over 2f out: sn rdn: hdd 1f out: kpt on wl but a jst hld ins fnl f* **16/1**

3-16 3 3 ¼ **Doctor Bartolo (IRE)**[34] 1764 3-9-1 79 LukeMorris 5 77
(Charles Hills) *led: rdn and hdd over 2f out: stl pressing ldrs in 3rd but unable qck over 1f out: outpcd ins fnl f* **11/1**

41-0 **4** *5* **Warrior's Spirit (IRE)**[27] 1945 3-9-3 **81**.............................. SeanLevey 2 67
(Richard Hannon) *t.k.h: trckd ldrs: clsd and upsides over 2f out: drvn and unable qck over 1f out: wknd ins fnl f* **5/2**[1]

41-0 **5** *2 ½* **Sterling Silva (IRE)**[20] 2122 3-9-6 **84**.......................... TomMarquand 4 64
(Richard Hannon) *t.k.h: chsd ldrs: rdn 3f out: outpcd u.p over 2f out: wl hld 2f out: plugged on* **33/1**

11-0 **6** *9* **Rashford's Double (IRE)**[33] 1801 3-9-5 **83**.................(p[1]) DavidNolan 9 43
(Richard Fahey) *in tch in midfield: u.p and tried to cl 3f out: sn struggling and outpcd: wknd over 1f out* **16/1**

1-1 **7** *nk* **Ocean Air (FR)**[19] 2151 3-9-3 **81**.................................... MartinHarley 10 40
(James Tate) *hld up in tch: effrt to chse ldrs 3f out: unable qck and no imp 2f out: wknd over 1f out* **5/2**[1]

01-6 **8** *25* **Native Soldier (IRE)**[21] 2117 3-9-1 **79**.............................. TomQueally 1
(William Haggas) *taken down early: a rr: rdn 1/2-way: sn struggling: wl bhd fnl 2f: t.o* **20/1**

61-4 **9** *3 ¾* **Fleeting Motion**[15] 2287 3-9-7 **85**.................................... WilliamBuick 3
(Richard Hannon) *chsd ldrs tl 3f out: sn lost pl: bhd and eased ins fnl f* **9/1**[3]

1m 42.93s (4.33) **Going Correction** +0.475s/f (Yiel) **9** Ran SP% **117.2**
Speed ratings (Par 101): **97,96,93,88,85 76,76,51,47**
CSF £58.20 CT £564.16 TOTE £4.60: £1.80, £4.40, £2.50; EX 62.20 Trifecta £484.30.
**Owner** The Fitzrovians **Bred** Stowell Hill Ltd **Trained** Newmarket, Suffolk

**FOCUS**
This competitive affair was run in near darkness on tiring ground. The winner probably has more to offer yet.
T/Plt: £379.00 to a £1 stake. Pool: £70,132.12 - 135.06 winning units T/Qpdt: £103.50 to a £1 stake. Pool: £6,520.56 - 46.59 winning units **Steve Payne**

## 2171 SALISBURY (R-H)
### Thursday, May 18

**OFFICIAL GOING: Good to soft (soft in places; 7.3) changed to good to soft after race 1 (1.40)**
Wind: virtually nil Weather: showers

### 2756 SIMON & NERYS DUTFIELD MEMORIAL NOVICE STKS (PLUS 10 RACE) 5f
**1:40** (1:42) (Class 4) 2-Y-O **£4,043** (£1,203; £601; £300) **Stalls** High

Form RPR

**1** **Youkan (IRE)** 2-9-2 0.......................................................... MartinLane 12 76+
(Stuart Kittow) *travelled wl: in tch: led over 1f out: pushed clr: readily* **20/1**

**2** *2 ¼* **Joegogo (IRE)** 2-9-2 0............................................................ JFEgan 5 68+
(David Evans) *s.i.s: bhd: swtchd to center 3f out: rdn and hdwy over 1f out: drifted rt but rn wl ins fnl f: wnt 2nd fnl 120yds: a being hld:* **14/1**

**3** *¾* **Luna Eclipse (IRE)** 2-9-2 0................................................ LiamKeniry 2 65+
(Andrew Balding) *mid-div: sn pushed along: rdn 2f out: kpt on wl ins fnl f: wnt 3rd towards fin* **15/2**[3]

**4** *nk* **Gaelic Spirit (IRE)** 2-8-11 0.................................... JosephineGordon 6 59+
(Joseph Tuite) *led: rdn over 2f out: hdd over 1f out: kpt on but no ex ins fnl f* **3/1**[1]

64 **5** *¾* **Jim Rockford**[12] 2382 2-9-2 0............................................... FranBerry 7 63
(Ralph Beckett) *hld up: hdwy over 2f out: sn rdn: hung rt over 1f out: kpt on same pce fnl f* **3/1**[1]

**6** *nk* **Reverberation** 2-8-11 0...................................... MitchGodwin[(5)] 9 62+
(Sylvester Kirk) *mid-div: rdn over 2f out: nt clrest of runs over 1f out: kpt on fnl 120yds* **25/1**

**7** *nk* **Bodybuilder** 2-9-2 0............................................................... PatDobbs 11 59
(Richard Hannon) *mid-div: rdn over 2f out: kpt on same pce* **7/2**[2]

0 **8** *¾* **Hastenplace**[18] 2173 2-8-11 0............................................ RyanTate 8 52
(Rod Millman) *trckd ldrs: rdn over 2f out: wknd fnl f* **8/1**

**9** *½* **Devil Or Angel** 2-8-11 0.................................................. JimmyQuinn 1 50
(Bill Turner) *pressed ldr: rdn over 2f out: wknd ins fnl f* **40/1**

4 **10** *nk* **Cranworth Phoenix**[17] 2217 2-8-12 0 ow1................ StevieDonohoe 10 50
(Brian Barr) *mid-div: rdn 2f out: nvr threatened: wknd ins fnl f* **66/1**

**11** *½* **Cabanon Bay** 2-9-2 0.......................................................... JohnFahy 14 52
(Malcolm Saunders) *s.i.s: a towards rr* **20/1**

1m 2.64s (1.64) **Going Correction** +0.325s/f (Good) **11** Ran SP% **119.1**
Speed ratings (Par 95): **99,95,94,93,92 92,91,90,89,89 88**
CSF £259.11 TOTE £26.50: £5.90, £3.40, £2.50; EX 257.90 Trifecta £1618.80.
**Owner** Mrs Linda Francis **Bred** Martin Francis Ltd **Trained** Blackborough, Devon

**FOCUS**
There was 5mm of rain on Tuesday night and a further 26mm of rain the previous day, resulting in the going description being very different from declaration time. The going was given as good to soft, soft in places (GoingStick: 7.3), but soon changed to good to soft all round when jockeys returning after the first race reported that it was just on the easy side. A fair maiden in which racing away from the inside rail looked no bad thing. They finished compressed behind the winner and the form is rated a fraction under the race average.

### 2757 LASCAR RUBY ANNIVERSARY H'CAP 6f
**2:10** (2:10) (Class 5) (0-75,77) 3-Y-O **£3,396** (£1,010; £505; £252) **Stalls** High

Form RPR

315- **1** **Scorching Heat**[208] 7549 3-9-1 **76**.............................. JoshuaBryan[(7)] 3 84+
(Andrew Balding) *trckd ldr: led 2f out: kpt on wl: rdn out* **5/2**[1]

0-10 **2** *1 ¼* **Glory Of Paris (IRE)**[27] 1945 3-9-7 **75**................................ RyanTate 4 78
(Rod Millman) *mid-div: hdwy after swtchd lft 2f out: sn rdn: r.o t go 2nd fnl 120yds: a being hld* **4/1**[2]

1105 **3** *¾* **Dandy Flame (IRE)**[17] 2215 3-9-2 **77**....................... FinleyMarsh[(7)] 15 78
(Richard Hughes) *hld up: pushed along and hdwy 2f out: r.o wl fnl f: wnt 3rd fnl 100yds: clsng on ldrs at fin* **22/1**

041- **4** *1* **Coastal Cyclone**[168] 8175 3-9-8 **76**...................................... FranBerry 1 74
(Harry Dunlop) *s.i.s: sn mid-div: rdn over 2f out: kpt on to go 3rd briefly fnl 120yds: nt pce to get on terms* **9/1**

4-21 **5** *½* **Red Alert**[84] 878 3-9-4 **72**...................................... JosephineGordon 16 68
(Joseph Tuite) *led: rdn and hdd 2f out: kpt on tl no ex fnl 120yds* **12/1**

35-6 **6** *½* **Rebel Heart**[23] 2065 3-8-7 **61** oh4.......................................(v) JimmyQuinn 9 56
(Bill Turner) *s.i.s: towards rr: rdn over 2f out: kpt on ins fnl f: nvr trbld ldrs* **25/1**

23-0 **7** *1 ¾* **Kings Academy**[9] 2506 3-9-7 **75**................................ DougieCostello 5 64
(Paul Cole) *hld up: rdn 2f out: kpt on ins fnl f: nvr trbld ldrs* **16/1**

421- **8** *nk* **Foxcatcher**[213] 7414 3-9-1 **72**.................................(b) HectorCrouch[(3)] 13 60
(Clive Cox) *trckd ldr: rdn wl over 2f out: wknd ent fnl f* **6/1**[3]

0026 **9** *1 ¼* **Stringybark Creek**[17] 2223 3-8-10 **64**.......................................... JFEgan 14 48
(Mick Channon) *mid-div on outer: rdn over 2f out: sn btn* **14/1**

3-1 **10** *¾* **Qatari Riyals (IRE)**[40] 1626 3-9-7 **75**..................................... PatDobbs 7 57
(Richard Hannon) *mid-div: rdn 3f out: sn hld: nt best of runs in last over 1f out: wknd fnl f* **6/1**[3]

1m 15.32s (0.52) **Going Correction** +0.325s/f (Good) **10** Ran SP% **115.6**
Speed ratings (Par 99): **109,107,106,105,104 103,101,100,99,98**
CSF £11.98 CT £179.28 TOTE £4.00: £2.00, £1.70, £5.50; EX 14.30 Trifecta £177.10.
**Owner** Qatar Racing Limited **Bred** Dukes Stud & Overbury Stallions Ltd **Trained** Kingsclere, Hants

**FOCUS**
A fair handicap, if ordinary for the grade, with an improved winner.

### 2758 PRIORITY MAILING & DIGITAL PRINT CLAIMING STKS 6f 213y
**2:45** (2:46) (Class 5) 3-Y-O **£3,396** (£1,010; £505; £252) **Stalls** High

Form RPR

0241 **1** **Sans Souci Bay**[22] 2089 3-9-4 75.................................(b) HollieDoyle[(3)] 8 83
(Richard Hannon) *in tch: hdwy to ld 2f out: sn clr: easily* **6/4**[1]

0654 **2** *8* **Madam Prancealot (IRE)**[22] 2089 3-8-0 51...............(v[1]) KieranO'Neill 9 41
(David Evans) *dwlt: last pair: pushed along and stdy prog fr 4f out: disp hld 3rd over 1f out: wnt 2nd ent fnl f: no ch w wnr* **12/1**

033- **3** *2 ¼* **Black Bubba (IRE)**[152] 8425 3-8-11 65..................................... JFEgan 1 46
(David Evans) *last trio: pushed along over 3f out: rdn to dispute hld 3rd 2f out: no ex ins fnl f* **5/1**[3]

000- **4** *4* **Jenji (IRE)**[260] 6035 3-7-11 39.......................................... NoelGarbutt[(3)] 6 25
(David Evans) *chsd ldrs: rdn wl over 2f out: sn one pce* **66/1**

400- **5** *¾* **Jackman**[254] 6208 3-8-5 46................................................... JimmyQuinn 5 28
(Tony Carroll) *in tch: rdn wl over 2f out: pressed for hld 4th over 1f out: nvr threatened ldrs* **25/1**

0-66 **6** *8* **Compton Lane**[16] 2271 3-9-1 71............................................ RyanTate 7 17
(Rod Millman) *racd keenly: prom: led 3f out: rdn and hdd 2f out: wknd ent fnl f* **3/1**[2]

6-00 **7** *7* **Dravid**[9] 2507 3-8-2 55.................................................. LuluStanford[(5)] 4
(Rod Millman) *led tl 3f out: wknd 2f out: eased whn btn* **11/1**

3460 **8** *2 ½* **Luduamf (IRE)**[15] 2309 3-9-0 57..................................(b) RossaRyan[(7)] 2
(Richard Hannon) *s.i.s: a last* **9/1**

1m 29.37s (0.77) **Going Correction** +0.325s/f (Good) **8** Ran SP% **113.0**
Speed ratings (Par 99): **108,98,96,91,90 81,73,70**
CSF £21.07 TOTE £2.60: £1.10, £3.70, £1.80; EX 15.90 Trifecta £65.50.The winner was the subject of a friendly claim by Mr Richard Hannon for £12,000.
**Owner** J R Shannon **Bred** J R Shannon **Trained** East Everleigh, Wilts

**FOCUS**
The Rod Millman-trained pair Compton Lane and Dravid took each other on in front, going a strong gallop, and that set things up nicely for the favourite. A decent effort from him in an otherwise weak race.

### 2759 SMITH & WILLIAMSON MAIDEN FILLIES' STKS (DIV I) 1m 1f 201y
**3:20** (3:20) (Class 5) 3-Y-O+ **£3,881** (£1,155; £577; £288) **Stalls** Low

Form RPR

0- **1** **Fleur Forsyte**[197] 7761 3-9-0 0.................................... DanielMuscutt 6 81+
(James Fanshawe) *trckd ldrs: chal gng wl 3f out: led 2f out: edgd lft ent fnl f: styd on wl* **3/1**[1]

**2** *nk* **Lightening Dance** 3-9-0 0.................................... JosephineGordon 10 80
(Amanda Perrett) *s.i.s: towards rr: hdwy fr 3f out: rdn to dispute 2nd whn sltly hmpd ent fnl f: styd on wl: clsng on wnr at fin* **11/2**[3]

0-6 **3** *1 ¾* **Trilliant (IRE)**[28] 1905 3-9-0 0........................................ ThomasBrown 3 76
(Ed Walker) *trckd ldrs: swtchd lft 2f out: sn rdn: disputing cl 2nd whn hmpd ent fnl f: styd on same pce* **11/2**[3]

06- **4** *6* **Star Of Doha**[197] 7761 3-9-0 0............................................. FranBerry 9 64
(Ralph Beckett) *led: rdn and hdd 2f out: wknd ins fnl f* **9/2**[2]

54 **5** *2 ½* **Tenby Two**[12] 2393 3-9-0 0...................................................... JFEgan 1 59
(Mick Channon) *in last trio: rdn 3f out: nvr gng pce to get on terms* **12/1**

**6** *hd* **Shanandoa**[332] 6-9-9 0.........................................(h[1]) RachealKneller[(5)] 2 60
(Brian Barr) *s.i.s: last: drifted lft into center fr over 2f out: nvr threatened to get on terms* **66/1**

**7** *shd* **Lupin (USA)** 3-9-0 0........................................................... PatDobbs 7 58
(Sir Michael Stoute) *trckd ldrs: chal 3f out: sn rdn: wknd over 1f out* **3/1**[1]

00 **8** *7* **Donna Finchella (IRE)**[10] 2475 3-9-0 0........................ TomMarquand 8 44
(Brian Meehan) *in tch: pushed along over 4f out: wknd 2f out* **33/1**

**9** *8* **Performance Art (IRE)**[160] 8292 3-9-0 0........................ SteveDrowne 5 28
(Seamus Mullins) *mid-div tl wknd over 2f out* **40/1**

2m 11.55s (1.65) **Going Correction** +0.325s/f (Good)
**WFA** 3 from 6yo 14lb **9** Ran SP% **113.5**
Speed ratings (Par 100): **106,105,104,99,97 97,97,91,85**
CSF £19.35 TOTE £4.10: £1.70, £2.10, £1.80; EX 22.20 Trifecta £114.70.
**Owner** Normandie Stud Ltd **Bred** Normandie Stud Ltd **Trained** Newmarket, Suffolk

**FOCUS**
This was the stronger run of the two divisions and much the quicker, by 5.38sec. The first three were clear and the form is rated around the race averages.

### 2760 SMITH & WILLIAMSON MAIDEN FILLIES' STKS (DIV II) 1m 1f 201y
**3:55** (3:55) (Class 5) 3-Y-O+ **£3,881** (£1,155; £577; £288) **Stalls** Low

Form RPR

**1** **Mam'Selle (IRE)** 3-9-0 0.................................................. RobertWinston 8 69+
(William Haggas) *trckd ldrs: rdn over 2f out: kpt on wl to ld ins fnl f: fnd more whn strly chal fnl 100yds: hld on: all out* **4/1**[3]

**2** *nse* **Circulation** 3-9-0 0............................................................... FranBerry 1 68+
(Ralph Beckett) *s.i.s: last pair: swtchd lft over 3 out: u.p but making gd hdwy whn hmpd 2f out: str run to press wnr ins fnl f: kpt on wl: jst hld* **11/4**[2]

0-0 **3** *1 ½* **Precious Angel (IRE)**[20] 2131 3-9-0 0.................................. PatDobbs 6 65
(Richard Hannon) *slowly away: hdwy to ld after 1f: rdn whn strly pressed fr wl over 2f out: led ins fnl f: kpt on but no ex* **28/1**

04 **4** *1 ¾* **Cecilator**[10] 2468 3-9-0 0................................................ DougieCostello 7 61?
(Noel Williams) *trckd ldrs: rdn for str chal over 2f out: ev ch over 1f out: no ex ent fnl f* **150/1**

3-6 **5** *hd* **Lassana Angel**[17] 2231 3-8-9 0.................................(h) PaddyPilley[(5)] 9 61+
(Roger Charlton) *led for 1f: trckd ldrs: racd keenly 5f out: chal 3f out: rdn and ev ch whn hung bdly lft 2f out: hld after: kpt on same pce* **5/1**

3-3 **6** *nk* **Nurse Nightingale**[129] 144 3-9-0 0.............................. JosephineGordon 2 60
(Hugo Palmer) *hld up: rdn over 2f out: styd on fnl f but nt pce to get on terms* **15/8**[1]

06 **7** *3* **Charming Loza**[15] 2311 3-9-0 0........................................ StevieDonohoe 4 54
(Charlie Fellowes) *in tch: hdwy fr 4f out to chal 3f out: sn rdn and hld: wknd jst over 1f out* **10/1**

0 **8** *8* **Harbouring**[24] 2019 3-8-9 0 MitchGodwin(5) 3 38
(Jonathan Portman) *broke wl: stdd after 1f: in tch: rdn 3f out: wknd over 1f out* **100/1**

2m 16.93s (7.03) **Going Correction** +0.325s/f (Good) **8** Ran SP% **112.3**
Speed ratings (Par 100): **84,83,82,81,81 80,78,72**
CSF £14.83 TOTE £5.70: £1.40, £1.30, £4.00; EX 18.80 Trifecta £136.10.
**Owner** Highclere Thoroughbred Racing - TS Eliot **Bred** Roundhill Stud & C & M Murphy **Trained** Newmarket, Suffolk

**FOCUS**
This was steadily run and developed into a sprint. The time was a mammoth 5.38sec slower than the first division and the form is rated cautiously.

## 2761 BRITISH STALLION STUDS EBF FILLIES' H'CAP 1m 1f 201y
**4:25** (4:28) (Class 4) (0-85,82) 3-Y-O **£7,762** (£2,310; £1,154; £577) **Stalls** Low

Form RPR

21- **1** **White Chocolate (IRE)**[211] 7465 3-9-1 **76** DanielMuscutt 6 83+
(David Simcock) *trckd ldrs: rdn to ld over 1f out: kpt on wl: rdn out* **7/2**[2]

10-5 **2** *1 ¼* **Billesdon Bess**[18] 2177 3-9-1 **79** HollieDoyle(3) 4 83
(Richard Hannon) *racd keenly: led tl 3f out: sn rdn: stl ev ch over 1f out: kpt on but nt pce of wnr fnl f* **11/2**

32-2 **3** *shd* **Pattie**[131] 115 3-8-11 **72** JFEgan 10 76
(Mick Channon) *s.i.s: last pair: hdwy 3f out: rdn 2f out: ev ch over 1f out: kpt on same pce fnl furlng* **5/1**[3]

100- **4** *1 ¼* **Cotinga**[197] 7768 3-8-11 **72** FranBerry 11 74
(Ralph Beckett) *hld up: hdwy 3f out: sn rdn: kpt on same pce ins fnl f* **11/2**

60-5 **5** *¾* **Duke's Girl**[49] 1448 3-8-0 **66** (h) LuluStanford(5) 9 67
(Michael Bell) *trckd ldr: led 3f out: sn rdn: hdd over 1f out: fdd fnl 120yds* **14/1**

-156 **6** *4 ½* **Nastenka**[16] 2269 3-8-11 **72** ThomasBrown 5 63
(Ed Walker) *trckd ldrs: rdn 3f out: wknd over 1f out* **10/1**

24-6 **7** *3 ½* **Vanity Queen**[20] 2118 3-9-2 **77** JosephineGordon 3 61
(Luca Cumani) *veered lft leaving stalls and rdr briefly lost iron: hld up: hdwy 5f out to trck ldrs: rdn over 2f out: wknd over 1f out* **11/4**[1]

2m 14.08s (4.18) **Going Correction** +0.325s/f (Good) **7** Ran SP% **112.1**
Speed ratings (Par 98): **96,95,94,93,93 89,86**
CSF £21.89 CT £93.47 TOTE £3.20: £2.00, £2.60; EX 17.90 Trifecta £63.00.
**Owner** The Rumble Racing Club **Bred** Scuderia Waldeck Srl **Trained** Newmarket, Suffolk

**FOCUS**
A competitive handicap despite the recduced field. The winner has the scope to do better.

## 2762 SHADWELL STUD RACING EXCELLENCE APPRENTICE H'CAP (DIV I) 6f 213y
**4:55** (4:59) (Class 5) (0-70,72) 4-Y-O+ **£4,528** (£1,347; £673; £336) **Stalls** High

Form RPR

4-06 **1** **Intimately**[15] 2319 4-8-6 **56** Pierre-LouisJamin(5) 1 61
(Jonathan Portman) *slowly away: bhd: swtchd to center 3f out: hdwy 2f out: rdn to chal jst over 1f out: kpt on wl: led fnl stride* **10/1**

60-6 **2** *shd* **Danecase**[19] 2147 4-9-8 **72** RossaRyan(5) 5 76
(David Dennis) *hld up: hdwy over 2f out: chal wl over 1f out: rdn to ld jst ins fnl f: hdd fnl stride* **6/1**[2]

165- **3** *½* **Frantical**[282] 5264 5-8-8 **56** AledBeech(3) 4 59
(Tony Carroll) *mid-div: hdwy over 2f out: sn swtchd rt: str run on far rail to hold ev ch jst ins fnl f: kpt on but no ex cl home* **12/1**

0100 **4** *¾* **Locommotion**[23] 2063 5-8-5 **55** oh2 StephenCummins(5) 6 56
(Matthew Salaman) *plld hrd: trckd ldr: rdn and ev ch over 1f out: no ex fnl 75yds* **11/1**

123- **5** *1* **Edge (IRE)**[217] 7299 6-8-5 **57** (b) KeelanBaker(7) 2 55
(Bernard Llewellyn) *hld up: hdwy 3f out: rdn over 1f out: ev ch ent fnl f: kpt on same pce* **6/1**[2]

-335 **6** *nk* **Rafaaf (IRE)**[49] 1456 9-8-9 **59** MollyKing(5) 10 57
(Peter Hiatt) *mid-div: effrt over 2f out: kpt on ins fnl f* **10/1**

60-0 **7** *¾* **Flying Sakhee**[24] 2043 4-8-5 **55** oh8 SophieRalston(5) 12 51
(John Bridger) *led: pushed along 3f out: hdd jst ins fnl f: fdd fnl 100yds* **33/1**

5034 **8** *5* **Panther Patrol (IRE)**[17] 2229 7-9-1 **65** (p) TylerSaunders(5) 7 48
(Eve Johnson Houghton) *trckd ldrs: rdn 2f out: wknd ent fnl f* **6/1**[2]

0-00 **9** *3* **Pc Dixon**[51] 1409 4-8-8 **60** LenkaHelmecka(7) 9 35
(Mick Channon) *in tch: effrt over 2f out: wknd over 1f out* **12/1**

3-06 **10** *1 ½* **Mezzotint (IRE)**[117] 349 8-9-8 **67** JoshuaBryan 11 38
(Lee Carter) *racd keenly: trckd ldrs: effrt over 2f out: wknd over 1f out* **5/1**[1]

-600 **11** *1 ¾* **Gatillo**[47] 1498 4-9-4 **66** (t[1]) FinleyMarsh(3) 3 32
(Julia Feilden) *mid-div tl dropped rr 3f out: n.d after* **7/1**[3]

1m 31.83s (3.23) **Going Correction** +0.325s/f (Good) **11** Ran SP% **116.9**
Speed ratings (Par 103): **94,93,93,92,91 90,90,84,80,79 77**
CSF £68.49 CT £736.14 TOTE £11.50: £2.90, £1.70, £4.60; EX 83.30 Trifecta £1179.00.
**Owner** Whitcoombe Park Racing **Bred** S Emmet And Miss R Emmet **Trained** Upper Lambourn, Berks

**FOCUS**
There was a tight finish to this apprentice race. Modest form for the grade.

## 2763 SHADWELL STUD RACING EXCELLENCE APPRENTICE H'CAP (DIV II) 6f 213y
**5:25** (5:30) (Class 5) (0-70,71) 4-Y-O+ **£4,528** (£1,347; £673; £336) **Stalls** High

Form RPR

250- **1** **Many Dreams (IRE)**[176] 8064 4-9-2 **66** JasonWatson(7) 8 74
(Gary Moore) *rrd leaving stalls: sn mid-div: hung lft whn shkn up 2f out: hdwy over 1f out: kpt on wl to ld towards fin: pushed out* **7/1**

0123 **2** *hd* **Lucky Louie**[20] 2119 4-9-5 **67** (p) RossaRyan(5) 5 74
(Roger Teal) *s.i.s: towards rr: swtchd to center 3f out: hdwy 2f out: led jst ins fnl f: kpt on: hdd towards fin* **11/4**[1]

20-5 **3** *2 ¾* **Bella's Venture**[28] 1899 4-9-4 **61** JoshuaBryan 7 61
(John Gallagher) *trckd ldr: rdn 2f out: ev ch ent fnl f: kpt on but no ex fnl 80yds* **16/1**

4302 **4** *¾* **Greyfriarschorista**[10] 2465 10-8-8 **54** (vt) KatherineGlenister(3) 1 52
(David Evans) *led: 5 l clr 3f out: rdn and hdd jst ins fnl f: no ex* **10/1**

0-55 **5** *½* **Cloud Nine (FR)**[15] 2319 4-8-10 **56** MillyNaseb(3) 11 53
(Tony Carroll) *hld up: swtchd to center 3f out: sn rdn: kpt on ins fnl f* **14/1**

155- **6** *hd* **Vincenzo Coccotti (USA)**[150] 8456 5-9-9 **71** (p) NicolaCurrie(5) 6 67
(Ken Cunningham-Brown) *in tch: effrt 2f out: kpt on same pce fnl f* **11/1**

2320 **7** *shd* **Virile (IRE)**[6] 2589 6-8-13 **59** (bt) FinleyMarsh(3) 10 55
(Sylvester Kirk) *mid-div: swtchd to center 3f out: hdwy 2f out: drifted rt sn after: kpt on same pce* **12/1**

536- **8** *3* **Captain Marmalade (IRE)**[203] 7642 5-8-10 **56** AledBeech(3) 9 44
(Jimmy Fox) *mid-div: effrt 2f out: wknd fnl f* **11/2**[3]

04-6 **9** *1 ½* **Bingo George (IRE)**[129] 139 4-8-9 **57** (h) WilliamCox(5) 4 41
(Andrew Balding) *racd keenly: trckd ldrs: rdn 2f out: wknd ent fnl f* **5/1**[2]

4064 **10** *6* **Quintus Cerialis (IRE)**[18] 2178 5-8-5 **53** oh2 (tp) TylerSaunders(5) 2 22
(Karen George) *awkwardly away: a towards rr* **11/1**

1m 31.43s (2.83) **Going Correction** +0.325s/f (Good) **10** Ran SP% **117.2**
Speed ratings (Par 103): **96,95,92,91,91 90,90,87,85,78**
CSF £26.70 CT £303.04 TOTE £7.90: £2.60, £1.10, £4.70; EX 32.50 Trifecta £404.00.
**Owner** Bryan Fry **Bred** Tally-Ho Stud **Trained** Lower Beeding, W Sussex

**FOCUS**
This was run at a good pace thanks to Greyfriarschorista. It was the quicker of the two divisions by 0.40sec but the form is just modest.
T/Plt: £379.40 to a £1stake. Pool: £56,396.63 - 108.50 winning units T/Qpdt: £26.30 to a £1 stake. Pool: £5,064.32 - 142.0 winning units **Tim Mitchell**

# 2735 YORK (L-H)
### Thursday, May 18

**OFFICIAL GOING: Soft (good to soft in places; 6.2) changed to good to soft (soft in places) after race 1 (2.20)**
Wind: Moderate across Weather: Cloudy with sunny periods Rails: innermost position; no changes to advertised race distances

## 2764 BETFRED "SUPPORTS JACK BERRY HOUSE" H'CAP 5f
**2:20** (2:20) (Class 2) (0-105,103) 4-Y-O+
**£15,562** (£4,660; £2,330; £1,165; £582; £292) **Stalls** Centre

Form RPR

6-64 **1** **Duke Of Firenze**[6] 2573 8-9-7 **103** DavidAllan 11 112
(David C Griffiths) *lw: hld up: swtchd rt and hdwy wl over 1f out: rdn to ld jst ins fnl f: edgd lft and kpt on wl* **13/2**[2]

4/00 **2** *nk* **Rasheeq (IRE)**[19] 2156 4-8-2 **87** RachelRichardson(3) 16 95
(Tim Easterby) *hld up: hdwy on outer wl over 1f out: rdn ent fnl f: styd on strly* **12/1**

1500 **3** *1 ½* **Poyle Vinnie**[11] 2433 7-9-3 **102** (p) AlistairRawlinson(3) 8 105
(Michael Appleby) *hld up: hdwy 2f out: swtchd lft and rdn to chal over 1f out: disp ld and ev ch ent fnl f: sn rdn and kpt on same pce* **10/1**

0262 **4** *1* **Orient Class**[12] 2409 6-8-3 **85** CamHardie 12 84
(Paul Midgley) *lw: cl up: rdn wl over 1f out: narrow led briefly ent fnl f: sn hdd and drvn: kpt on same pce* **9/1**

00-6 **5** *¾* **Union Rose**[6] 2578 5-8-11 **93** (p) OisinMurphy 4 90
(Ronald Harris) *swtg: led: rdn along wl over 1f out: drvn and hdd ent fnl f: grad wknd* **14/1**

060- **6** *½* **Tumblewind**[342] 3116 7-8-3 **85** FrannyNorton 15 80
(Richard Whitaker) *cl up: rdn along wl over 1f out: wknd appr fnl f* **25/1**

01-4 **7** *½* **Soie D'Leau**[27] 1946 5-9-2 **98** TonyHamilton 17 91
(Kristin Stubbs) *swtg: cl up: rdn along 2f out: wknd over 1f out* **8/1**

0132 **8** *½* **Robot Boy (IRE)**[33] 1793 7-9-6 **102** PhillipMakin 9 93
(David Barron) *prom: cl up 2f out: rdn to dispute ld over 1f out: ev ch tl drvn and hld whn n.m.r jst ins fnl f* **7/1**[3]

600- **9** *1 ¼* **Snap Shots (IRE)**[222] 7156 5-8-9 **91** BarryMcHugh 6 78
(Tony Coyle) *dwlt: sn chsng ldrs: rdn along 2f out: sn wknd* **16/1**

000- **10** *2 ¼* **Move In Time**[250] 6327 9-9-4 **100** DanielTudhope 5 79
(David O'Meara) *towards rr: pushed along 1/2-way: rdn wl over 1f out: sn outpcd* **17/2**

0-04 **11** *3* **Mont Kiara (FR)**[29] 1880 4-8-7 **89** (h[1]) HarryBentley 10 57
(Kevin Ryan) *dwlt: chsd ldrs: rdn along 2f out: sn wknd* **6/1**[1]

-260 **12** *2 ¼* **Justice Good (IRE)**[47] 1501 5-8-11 **100** DavidEgan(7) 1 60
(David Elsworth) *dwlt: sn trcking ldrs on outer: rdn along 2f out: sn wknd* **15/2**

59.83s (0.53) **Going Correction** +0.35s/f (Good) **12** Ran SP% **116.7**
Speed ratings (Par 109): **109,108,106,104,103 102,101,100,98,95 90,86**
CSF £80.81 CT £788.25 TOTE £7.10: £2.40, £4.60, £3.10; EX 110.50 Trifecta £1380.00.
**Owner** Adlam,Damary-Thompson,Wilson,Griffiths **Bred** Cheveley Park Stud Ltd **Trained** Bawtry, S Yorks

**FOCUS**
Race distances as advertised. The ground had dried out a little and after the first the views of the jockeys included "It's not as bad as I thought it would be," "They are getting through it at the moment but it will be quite sticky by the end of the day," "It is a little bit more holding than yesterday," and "It is typical drying ground, tacky." There was a going change following the first. Five non-runners in this, but still a warm sprint handicap. It looked to be riding quicker on the stands' side than down the middle, and the first three came from the rear.

## 2765 BETFRED MIDDLETON STKS (GROUP 2) (F&M) 1m 2f 56y
**2:55** (2:55) (Class 1) 4-Y-O+ **£70,887** (£26,875; £13,450; £6,700) **Stalls** Low

Form RPR

210- **1** **Blond Me (IRE)**[207] 7566 5-9-0 106 OisinMurphy 2 111
(Andrew Balding) *t.k.h: trckd ldng pair: hdwy 2f out: swtchd rt and rdn ent fnl f: styd on wl to ld last 75 yds* **11/1**

31-1 **2** *1 ¼* **The Black Princess (FR)**[18] 2201 4-9-0 105 FrankieDettori 1 109
(John Gosden) *led: pushed along and jnd over 2f out: rdn wl over 1f out: drvn ent fnl f: hdd and no ex last 75 yds* **11/8**[1]

\- **3** *nk* **Smart Call (SAF)**[474] 5-9-3 119 JimCrowley 5 111
(Sir Michael Stoute) *str: lw: hld up in rr: hdwy wl over 1f out: rdn ent fnl f: styd on wl towards fin* **5/1**[3]

331- **4** *1 ½* **Queen's Trust**[194] 7831 4-9-3 118 RyanMoore 3 109
(Sir Michael Stoute) *trckd ldr: hdwy 3f out: sn cl up: chal 2f out: rdn to dispute over 1f out and ev ch: wknd ins fnl f* **6/4**[2]

2m 9.76s (-2.74) **Going Correction** 0.0s/f (Good) **4** Ran SP% **107.1**
Speed ratings (Par 115): **110,109,108,107**
CSF £26.20 TOTE £10.00; EX 27.90 Trifecta £99.60.
**Owner** Mrs Barbara M Keller **Bred** Wardstown Stud Ltd **Trained** Kingsclere, Hants

**FOCUS**
Distance as advertised. Two non-runners, including a key one in So Mi Dar, but still a quality contest. There was a bit of a turn-up, though, the outsider of the quartet coming through to win with a bit in hand. They went an ordinary gallop courtesy of the runner-up, who's rated similar to her recent French form.

## 2766 BETFRED DANTE STKS (GROUP 2) 1m 2f 56y
**3:30** (3:31) (Class 1) 3-Y-O

**£105,310** (£39,925; £19,981; £9,953; £4,995; £2,506) **Stalls** Low

Form RPR

-321 **1** **Permian (IRE)**[12] 2401 3-9-0 106 FrannyNorton 7 114
(Mark Johnston) *trckd ldrs: hdwy on inner wl over 2f out: rdn to chal wl over 1f out: led 1f out: sn edgd lft: drvn and edgd rt ;last 100 yds: kpt on strly* **10/1**

13 **2** ¾ **Benbatl**[28] 1904 3-9-0 106 PatCosgrave 8 112
(Saeed bin Suroor) *prom: trckd ldr over 4f out: cl up wl over 2f out: rdn to ld narrowly and briefly appr fnl f: sn hdd and drvn: kpt on* **4/1**[1]

2-1 **3** ½ **Crystal Ocean**[26] 1967 3-9-0 89 AndreaAtzeni 2 111
(Sir Michael Stoute) *athletic: trckd ldrs: hdwy over 2f out: rdn over 1f out: styd on to chse ldng pair ins fnl f: sn edgd lft and kpt on wl towards fin* **8/1**

0-1 **4** 2 **Rekindling**[40] 1636 3-9-0 109 DonnachaO'Brien 1 107
(Joseph Patrick O'Brien, Ire) *leggy: swtg: hld up in tch: hdwy wl over 2f out: rdn to chse ldrs wl over 1f out: drvn and kpt on fnl f* **9/2**[2]

61-1 **5** 1½ **Wolf Country**[17] 2250 3-9-0 99 WilliamBuick 4 104
(Charlie Appleby) *cmpt: set sound gallop. pushed along over 2f out: sn jnd and rdn: hdd appr fnl f: grad wknd* **6/1**[3]

13-1 **6** 3¾ **Forest Ranger (IRE)**[34] 1780 3-9-0 106 TonyHamilton 9 97
(Richard Fahey) *str: lengthy: lw: hld up towards rr: hdwy over 3f out: rdn along over 2f out: sn no imp* **8/1**

11-2 **7** 2 **Syphax (USA)**[34] 1780 3-9-0 110 JamieSpencer 6 93
(Kevin Ryan) *dwlt: sn niggled along in rr and rn in snatches: sme hdwy over 3f out: sn rdn along and n.d* **12/1**

3- **8** 5 **Exemplar (IRE)**[235] 6817 3-9-0 110 (t) RyanMoore 3 84
(A P O'Brien, Ire) *cmpt: hld up towards rr: sme hdwy 3f out: rdn along over 2f out: n.d* **6/1**[3]

01- **9** 1¼ **Swiss Storm**[243] 6570 3-9-0 89 JimCrowley 10 82
(David Elsworth) *lw: t.k.h: sn prom on outer: chsd ldr after 2f: rdn along over 4f out: wknd 3f out* **16/1**

10-4 **10** 4½ **Contrapposto (IRE)**[28] 1904 3-9-0 99 JimmyFortune 11 73
(David Menuisier) *in tch: sme hdwy 4f out: rdn along over 3f out: sn wknd* **25/1**

2m 8.4s (-4.10) **Going Correction** 0.0s/f (Good) **10** Ran SP% **115.5**
Speed ratings (Par 111): **116,115,115,113,112 109,107,103,102,99**
CSF £49.34 TOTE £11.20: £2.90, £2.10, £2.20; EX 53.10 Trifecta £435.90.
**Owner** Sheikh Hamdan bin Mohammed Al Maktoum **Bred** Darley **Trained** Middleham Moor, N Yorks

**FOCUS**
The last horse to complete the Dante-Derby double was Golden Horn in 2015 but Cracksman, who has the same connections, was an absentee because of the ground. His Derby chances received a boost from the winner. The race didn't shed a great deal of light on the murky Derby picture, but it was run at what appeared to be a good tempo and the time was only 1.4sec outside standard. Wednesday's Musidora, incidentally, was run over 32yds further. Not the strongest renewal but Permian franked his Epsom form.

## 2767 BETFRED TV HAMBLETON H'CAP (LISTED RACE) 7f 192y
**4:05** (4:06) (Class 1) (0-110,109) 4-Y-0+

**£28,355** (£10,750; £5,380; £2,680; £1,345; £675) **Stalls** Low

Form RPR

104- **1** **Here Comes When (IRE)**[183] 7978 7-9-1 103 (h) OisinMurphy 12 114
(Andrew Balding) *trckd ldrs: hdwy and cl up 2f out: rdn to ld over 1f out: clr ins fnl f: kpt on strly* **10/1**

21-P **2** 2¼ **Chelsea Lad (IRE)**[26] 1960 4-8-8 96 RichardKingscote 1 102
(Martyn Meade) *swtg: trckd ldrs on inner: hdwy over 2f out: rdn to chse wnr ent fnl f: sn drvn and no imp* **11/2**[1]

164- **3** nk **Victory Bond**[330] 3543 4-8-12 100 PatCosgrave 9 105
(William Haggas) *lw: in tch: hdwy wl over 2f out: rdn over 1f out: drvn and kpt on fnl f* **8/1**[3]

02 **4** 2¼ **Another Touch**[26] 1960 4-8-9 97 PaulHanagan 13 97
(Richard Fahey) *hld up: hdwy 3f out and sn pushed along: chsd ldrs and swtchd lft to inner over 1f out: drvn and kpt on wl fnl f* **11/1**

02-6 **5** shd **Get Knotted (IRE)**[12] 2384 5-8-12 100 (p) PaulMulrennan 18 100
(Michael Dods) *midfield: hdwy wl over 2f out: rdn along to chse ldrs whn n.m.r and swtchd rt over 1f out: kpt on u.p fnl f* **25/1**

-051 **6** nk **Cote D'Azur**[12] 2406 4-8-9 97 PJMcDonald 10 96
(Les Eyre) *led: qcknd over 3f out: jnd and rdn 2f out: hdd and drvn over 1f out: grad wknd* **20/1**

00-0 **7** 2¼ **Instant Attraction (IRE)**[47] 1494 6-8-9 97 JackGarritty 7 91
(Jedd O'Keeffe) *prom: trckd ldr over 4f out: rdn along wl over 2f out: drvn over 1f out: wknd* **10/1**

4-10 **8** ½ **Bravery (IRE)**[29] 1882 4-9-3 105 DanielTudhope 11 98
(David O'Meara) *hld up towards rr: hdwy over 3f out: rdn along and in tch over 2f out: drvn wl over 1f out and no imp* **20/1**

/66- **9** ½ **White Lake**[320] 3910 5-9-1 103 (b[1]) AndreaAtzeni 5 95
(Roger Varian) *trckd ldrs: hdwy on inner 3f out: rdn along 2f out: sn drvn and wknd* **11/1**

215- **10** nk **Thikriyaat (IRE)**[264] 5873 4-9-7 109 JimCrowley 15 100
(Sir Michael Stoute) *hld up: a towards rr* **13/2**[2]

23-0 **11** 1 **Home Cummins (IRE)**[26] 1960 5-8-7 95 oh1 (p) SammyJoBell 17 84
(Richard Fahey) *a towards rr* **25/1**

-004 **12** 1¾ **Top Notch Tonto (IRE)**[19] 2141 7-8-13 101 (t) BenCurtis 20 86
(Brian Ellison) *hld up towards rr: hdwy on wd outside 4f out: rdn along wl over 2f out: sn wknd* **16/1**

50-0 **13** nse **Havre De Paix (FR)**[26] 1960 5-8-7 95 oh3 FrannyNorton 14 79
(David Menuisier) *chsd ldrs: rdn along wl over 3f out: sn wknd* **50/1**

20-0 **14** nk **Glory Awaits (IRE)**[16] 2283 7-8-7 95 oh2 (b) HarryBentley 19 79
(David Simcock) *a towards rr* **33/1**

110- **15** 1¾ **Murad Khan (FR)**[201] 7701 4-8-11 99 WilliamBuick 3 79
(Hugo Palmer) *swtg: trckd ldr: pushed along over 3f out: rdn wl over 2f out: sn drvn and wknd* **9/1**

4-30 **16** 1½ **Donncha (IRE)**[26] 1960 6-8-12 100 PatSmullen 8 76
(Robert Eddery) *hld up: a bhd* **13/2**[2]

6-60 **17** ½ **Strong Steps**[30] 1860 5-8-7 95 oh5 (p) AndrewMullen 6 70
(Roger Fell) *a bhd* **50/1**

1m 35.96s (-3.04) **Going Correction** 0.0s/f (Good) **17** Ran SP% **128.0**
Speed ratings (Par 111): **115,112,112,110,110 109,107,107,106,106 105,103,103,103,101 99,99**
CSF £61.73 CT £495.20 TOTE £13.80: £3.10, £2.30, £2.50, £3.00; EX 110.60 Trifecta £654.20.
**Owner** Mrs Fitri Hay **Bred** Old Carhue & Graeng Bloodstock **Trained** Kingsclere, Hants
■ Stewards' Enquiry : Andrea Atzeni caution; careless riding

**FOCUS**
Distance as advertised. Run at a sound gallop, the field was strung out fairly early and the form looks strong. The winner is rated back to something like his best.

## 2768 BRITISH STALLION STUDS EBF WESTOW STKS (LISTED RACE) 5f
**4:35** (4:35) (Class 1) 3-Y-O **£28,355** (£10,750; £5,380; £2,680; £1,345) **Stalls** Centre

Form RPR

215- **1** **Fashion Queen**[273] 5584 3-8-11 98 DanielTudhope 3 101
(David O'Meara) *racd towards centre: led: jnd and rdn wl over 1f out: hdd narrowly and drvn ins fnl f: rallied gamely to ld again nr line* **20/1**

12-1 **2** hd **Kyllang Rock (IRE)**[36] 1732 3-9-2 91 MartinHarley 1 105
(James Tate) *lw: trckd wnr towards centre: hdwy to dispute ld over 1f out: sn rdn and tk narrow advantage ins fnl f: drvn and edgd lft last 75 yds: hdd nr line* **9/1**

6-11 **3** 8 **Jumira Bridge**[20] 2130 3-9-2 93 AndreaAtzeni 4 76
(Roger Varian) *trckd ldng pair towards centre: hdwy 2f out: rdn over 1f out: sn drvn and kpt on one pce* **5/1**[3]

010- **4** 5 **Ardad (IRE)**[228] 6990 3-9-7 108 FrankieDettori 7 63
(John Gosden) *racd nr stands rail: cl up: rdn along over 2f out: sn wknd* **3/1**[2]

11-1 **5** 8 **Brian The Snail (IRE)**[37] 1702 3-9-2 102 WilliamBuick 6 30
(Richard Fahey) *racd towards stands rail: trckd ldrs: rdn along over 2f out: sn edgd lft and wknd* **5/6**[1]

1m 0.17s (0.87) **Going Correction** +0.35s/f (Good) **5** Ran SP% **111.0**
Speed ratings (Par 107): **107,106,93,85,73**
CSF £157.76 TOTE £16.10: £3.70, £3.10; EX 52.80 Trifecta £263.20.
**Owner** Clipper Logistics **Bred** Bolton Grange **Trained** Upper Helmsley, N Yorks

**FOCUS**
A rather unsatisfactory race with the two market leaders failing to give their running. They raced nearest the stands' side while the first two, who came well clear, raced out in the centre. The first two are both rated as improving.

## 2769 STRATFORD PLACE STUD BREEDS GROUP WINNERS EBFSTALLIONS.COM MAIDEN STKS (PLUS 10 RACE) 6f
**5:05** (5:07) (Class 2) 2-Y-O

**£12,450** (£3,728; £1,864; £932; £466; £234) **Stalls** High

Form RPR

**1** **Zap** 2-9-5 0 PaulHanagan 6 77+
(Richard Fahey) *str: swtg: trckd ldrs: hdwy over 1f out: rdn to ld ins fnl f: kpt on wl* **5/1**[3]

**2** 1 **Red Force One** 2-9-5 0 RichardKingscote 10 74+
(Tom Dascombe) *tall: racd nr stands rail: cl up: effrt wl over 1f out: sn rdn: styd on u.p fnl f* **10/1**

**3** nk **Makanah** 2-9-5 0 JimCrowley 9 73
(Simon Crisford) *athletic: lw: cl up: rdn along over 1f out: kpt on u.p ins fnl f* **9/2**[2]

5 **4** nse **Dontgiveuponbob**[19] 2134 2-9-5 0 TonyHamilton 4 73
(Richard Fahey) *leggy: slt ld: rdn over 1f out: hdd ins fnl f: sn edgd lft and kpt on* **8/1**

**5** 2¾ **Vj Day (USA)** 2-9-5 0 JamieSpencer 8 65+
(Kevin Ryan) *lengthy: str: dwlt: trckd ldrs: pushed along over 2f out: rdn wl over 1f out: green and sn wknd* **7/2**[1]

4 **6** 1 **Global Tango (IRE)**[15] 2286 2-9-5 0 AndreaAtzeni 2 62
(Charles Hills) *trckd ldrs on outre: cl up 1/2-way: rdn along 2f out: sn wknd* **7/1**

**7** nk **New Empire** 2-9-5 0 JimmyFortune 7 61+
(Peter Chapple-Hyam) *w'like: green and wnt bdly lft s: a rr* **12/1**

**8** 9 **Taifbalady (IRE)** 2-9-5 0 RyanMoore 3 34
(Mark Johnston) *lengthy: chsd ldrs: rdn along bef 1/2-way: wknd over 2f out: sn bhd* **9/2**[2]

1m 16.16s (4.26) **Going Correction** +0.35s/f (Good) **8** Ran SP% **115.6**
Speed ratings (Par 99): **85,83,83,83,79 78,77,65**
CSF £53.66 TOTE £6.10: £2.20, £2.80, £1.90; EX 64.10 Trifecta £282.00.
**Owner** Peter Timmins **Bred** Cheveley Park Stud Ltd **Trained** Musley Bank, N Yorks

**FOCUS**
Distance as advertised. A useful little maiden that should produce winners, with the fourth likely to pin the form eventually. They raced centre-to-stands' side.

## 2770 INVESTEC WEALTH H'CAP 2m 56y
**5:35** (5:35) (Class 3) (0-90,90) 4-Y-0+

**£12,450** (£3,728; £1,864; £932; £466; £234) **Stalls** Low

Form RPR

00-0 **1** **Injam (IRE)**[57] 1309 4-8-12 80 GrahamLee 17 90
(Jedd O'Keeffe) *prom: slt ld 3f out: rdn and hdd wl over 1f out: cl up: drvn ent fnl f: styd on wl to ld last 75 yds* **20/1**

23-1 **2** 1 **Graceland (FR)**[6] 2562 5-9-2 82 LouisSteward 12 91
(Michael Bell) *hld up in rr: hdwy 4f out: chsd ldrs over 2f out: rdn to take slt ld over 1f out: drvn ins fnl f: hdd and no ex fnl 75 yds* **4/1**[1]

040- **3** 1½ **Blue Hussar (IRE)**[25] 7359 6-8-11 77 (p) PJMcDonald 3 84
(Micky Hammond) *hld up in midfield: gd hdwy on inner over 3f out: clsd up 2f out: sn rdn and ev ch tl drvn ins fnl f and kpt on same pce last 100 yds* **14/1**

11-6 **4** 1¼ **Silva Eclipse**[57] 1309 4-8-12 80 JackGarritty 2 86
(Jedd O'Keeffe) *trckd ldrs: pushed along and sltly outpcd over 2f out: sn rdn and kpt on to chal appr fnl f: sn drvn and kpt on same pce* **10/1**

2121 **5** 3¼ **On Fire**[16] 2270 4-8-6 74 (p) PaulHanagan 15 76
(James Bethell) *lw: hld up and bhd: hdwy over 3f out: rdn along 2f out: styd on u.p fnl f* **9/1**

04-1 **6** ½ **Grumeti**[52] 1405 9-9-4 84 FergusSweeney 5 85
(Alan King) *in tch: hdwy to chse ldrs 4f out: rdn along over 2f out: sn drvn and kpt on one pce* **9/1**

41/0 **7** 1 **Mr Cripps**[41] 1608 5-9-5 85 RichardKingscote 14 85
(Ralph Beckett) *in tch: hdwy to chse ldrs over 3f out: rdn along over 2f out: drvn wl over 1f out: sn one pce* **8/1**[3]

13-1 **8** 2¾ **Kajaki (IRE)**[36] 1716 4-8-9 77 (p) KevinStott 4 74
(Kevin Ryan) *trckd ldng pair: pushed along over 3f out: rdn over 2f out: sn drvn and grad wknd* **9/1**

1-22 **9** 3/4 **Gaelic Tiger**21 2109 4-9-4 **86**........ DanielTudhope 7 82
(David O'Meara) *trckd ldrs: rdn along over 3f out: drvn over 2f out: sn wknd* **5/1**2

06-0 **10** 1/2 **Saved By The Bell (IRE)**26 1976 7-8-12 **85**........ PatrickVaughan(7) 1 80
(David O'Meara) *hld up: effrt and sme hdwy 4f out: sn rdn along and n.d* **16/1**

1011 **11** 3 **Tatting**30 1865 8-9-1 **81**........ PaulMulrennan 8 72
(Lawrence Mullaney) *hld up: a rr* **33/1**

00-0 **12** hd **Buonarroti (IRE)**46 1517 6-9-3 **83**........ TomEaves 6 74
(Declan Carroll) *in tch: hdwy to chse ldrs over 4f out: rdn along 3f out: drvn over 2f out and sn wknd* **14/1**

0-02 **13** 3 3/4 **Ice Galley (IRE)**10 2456 4-8-3 **71** oh3........ FrannyNorton 16 58
(Philip Kirby) *lw: led: rdn along 4f out: hdd 3f out: sn wknd* **11/1**

3m 37.5s (3.00) **Going Correction** 0.0s/f (Good)
**WFA** 4 from 5yo+ 1lb **13** Ran SP% **122.1**
Speed ratings (Par 107): **92,91,90,90,88 88,87,86,86,85 84,84,82**
CSF £100.56 CT £1200.12 TOTE £23.20: £6.50, £1.80, £3.90; EX 145.50 Trifecta £2212.70.
**Owner** Miss S Long **Bred** John M Weld **Trained** Middleham Moor, N Yorks

**FOCUS**
A fair staying handicap. They went what appeared a fairly steady gallop and there were plenty still involved inside the final two furlongs. The form is rated around the runner-up.
T/Jkpt: Not Won. T/Plt: £10,865.10 to a £1 stake. Pool: £240,223.92 - 16.14 winning units
T/Qpdt: £478.90 to a £1 stake. Pool: £18,897.94 - 29.20 winning units **Joe Rowntree**

## 2424 HAMILTON (R-H)

Friday, May 19

**OFFICIAL GOING: Good to firm (good in places; 8.3)**
Wind: Almost nil Weather: Overcast, dry

### 2771 BB FOODSERVICE EBF NOVICE STKS (PLUS 10 RACE) (A £20,000 BB FOODSERVICE 2YO SERIES QUALIFIER) 5f 7y
**5:55** (5:56) (Class 4) 2-Y-O **£5,175** (£1,540; £769; £384) **Stalls** High

Form RPR

5 **1** **Unfortunately (IRE)**31 1858 2-8-11 0........ CliffordLee(5) 8 88+
(K R Burke) *trckd ldrs: shkn up to ld over 1f out: qcknd clr fnl f: readily* **13/8**1

5 **2** 3 **Marnie James**39 1673 2-9-2 0........ TomEaves 7 75
(Iain Jardine) *dwlt: t.k.h: hld up bhd ldng gp: n.m.r briefly over 4f out: hdwy over 1f out: chsd (clr) wnr ent fnl f: kpt on: no imp* **15/2**

4 **3** 3 3/4 **Armed Response**16 2299 2-9-2 0........ JackGarritty 3 62
(Jedd O'Keeffe) *trckd ldrs on outside: rdn and outpcd wl over 1f out: rallied fnl f: nt rch first two* **15/2**

3 **4** 1 **Story Minister (IRE)**13 2382 2-9-2 0........ PJMcDonald 6 58
(Tom Dascombe) *t.k.h: led: rdn over 1f out: hdd ent fnl f: sn outpcd* **4/1**2

06 **5** nk **Lord Of The Glen**11 2452 2-8-9 0........(p1) SeanMooney(7) 2 57
(Jim Goldie) *midfield on outside: rdn over 2f out: kpt on fnl f: nt pce to chal* **80/1**

**6** 1 1/2 **Crown Of Cortez** 2-8-13 0........ TonyHamilton 10 53+
(Richard Fahey) *s.i.s: rn green in rr: kpt on fnl f: nvr able to chal* **6/1**3

**7** 1 1/2 **Jive Lady (IRE)** 2-8-8 0........ JoeFanning 4 38+
(Mark Johnston) *trckd ldr tl rdn and wknd over 1f out* **14/1**

**8** 5 **Bertie Wallace (IRE)** 2-8-8 0........ RowanScott(5) 9 25
(Keith Dalgleish) *s.i.s: rn green in rr and sn outpcd: struggling over 2f out: sn btn* **18/1**

**9** 3 1/4 **Oriental Power** 2-8-13 0........ SamJames 5 13
(Jim Goldie) *s.i.s: rn green in rr: nvr on terms* **33/1**

**10** 3 3/4 **Acromatic (IRE)** 2-8-13 0........ CamHardie 1 +
(John Quinn) *wnt bdly rt s: a outpcd and wl bhd* **18/1**

58.41s (-1.59) **Going Correction** -0.20s/f (Firm) **10** Ran SP% **117.3**
Speed ratings (Par 95): **104,99,93,91,91 88,86,78,73,67**
CSF £14.70 TOTE £2.70: £1.50, £2.20, £2.50; EX 18.60 Trifecta £73.10.
**Owner** J Laughton & Mrs E Burke **Bred** Tally-Ho Stud **Trained** Middleham Moor, N Yorks

**FOCUS**
All distances as advertised. After a dry few days, the going is Good to firm (good in places, 8.3). This novice stakes went to the favourite who did everything right. The runner-up has been rated as improving a bit on his debut effort.

### 2772 RACINGUK.COM H'CAP 1m 68y
**6:25** (6:26) (Class 4) (0-85,87) 4-Y-O+ **£5,175** (£1,540; £769; £384) **Stalls** Low

Form RPR

3-15 **1** **Rockwood**25 2030 6-8-12 **75**........(v) GrahamLee 1 82
(Karen McLintock) *trckd ldrs: rdn and ev ch fr over 1f out: led ins fnl f: hld on gamely* **3/1**2

1-03 **2** nk **Ionization (IRE)**10 2500 4-9-10 **87**........ TadhgO'Shea 7 93
(John Patrick Shanahan, Ire) *led at slow pce: rdn and hrd pressed whn faltered over 1f out: drifted lft and hdd ins fnl f: kpt on: jst hld* **7/1**

0012 **3** shd **Nicholas T**11 2457 5-9-3 **80**........ SamJames 8 86+
(Jim Goldie) *hld up in last pl in slowly run r: stdy hdwy on outside over 2f out: rdn over 1f out: kpt on fnl f: hld nr fin* **15/8**1

102 **4** 1 1/2 **Safe Voyage (IRE)**78 989 4-9-7 **84**........ JackGarritty 5 87
(John Quinn) *trckd ldrs: rdn over 2f out: kpt on same pce fnl f* **9/1**

2-04 **5** 3/4 **Brilliant Vanguard (IRE)**27 1969 4-9-2 **79**........ TomEaves 6 80
(Kevin Ryan) *trckd ldrs: effrt and rdn whn n.m.r briefly over 1f out: sn outpcd: no imp fnl f* **11/2**3

00-4 **6** 1 3/4 **Archie's Advice**10 2497 6-9-1 **78**........ JoeFanning 4 75
(Keith Dalgleish) *dwlt: hld up in tch: pushed along over 2f out: no imp fr over 1f out* **11/2**3

1m 50.08s (1.68) **Going Correction** -0.20s/f (Firm) **6** Ran SP% **113.1**
Speed ratings (Par 105): **83,82,82,81,80 78**
CSF £23.67 CT £47.88 TOTE £4.70: £2.40, £2.40; EX 33.20 Trifecta £80.90.
**Owner** I R Clements & Dr L G Parry **Bred** Norcroft Park Stud **Trained** Ingoe, Northumberland

**FOCUS**
A small field for this 1m 1/2f Class 4 handicap. There wasn't much pace on and it was a sprint finish.

### 2773 RACING TOGETHER H'CAP 1m 68y
**7:00** (7:00) (Class 5) (0-70,78) 4-Y-O+ **£3,881** (£1,155; £577; £288) **Stalls** Low

Form RPR

33-4 **1** **Fivehundredmiles (IRE)**12 2430 4-9-9 **71**........(b1) TadhgO'Shea 3 80
(John Patrick Shanahan, Ire) *chsd clr ldr: rdn and effrt over 2f out: led over 1f out: hld on wl fnl f* **9/2**2

6-05 **2** shd **Amy Blair**12 2430 4-8-8 **56**........(h) PJMcDonald 1 64
(Keith Dalgleish) *led and sn clr: rdn over 2f out: hdd over 1f out: rallied and renewed chal ins fnl f: jst hld* **11/2**3

5-60 **3** 2 1/2 **Billy Bond**17 2276 5-8-12 **60**........ TonyHamilton 2 62
(Richard Fahey) *prom: pushed along and effrt over 2f out: kpt on ins fnl f: nt rch first two* **17/2**

0203 **4** nk **Restive (IRE)**12 2427 4-9-7 **69**........(h) TomEaves 6 70
(Iain Jardine) *hld up: stdy hdwy over 2f out: rdn and kpt on same pce ins fnl f* **11/2**3

-662 **5** 3 1/4 **Crazy Tornado (IRE)**15 2339 4-9-4 **71**........(h) RowanScott(5) 8 65
(Keith Dalgleish) *hld up in tch: rdn and outpcd over 2f out: drifted lft and no imp fr over 1f out* **9/2**2

0301 **6** 1 3/4 **Testa Rossa (IRE)**11 2458 7-9-13 **78** 6ex........(b) NathanEvans(3) 10 68
(Jim Goldie) *hld up: rdn along over 5f out: sn outpcd: no imp fr over 2f out* **10/3**1

500- **7** 3 3/4 **The Lynch Man**164 8240 4-9-2 **64**........(v) CamHardie 9 45
(John Quinn) *hld up: rdn and struggling over 2f out: sn btn* **16/1**

05-0 **8** 10 **Cape Love (USA)**23 2079 4-9-5 **67**........ JoeFanning 4 25
(Mark Johnston) *cl up in chsng gp tl rdn and wknd qckly over 2f out* **14/1**

1m 44.2s (-4.20) **Going Correction** -0.20s/f (Firm) **8** Ran SP% **113.3**
Speed ratings (Par 103): **113,112,110,110,106 105,101,91**
CSF £28.76 CT £173.07 TOTE £5.00: £2.00, £1.50, £2.90; EX 32.70 Trifecta £145.20.
**Owner** Thistle Bloodstock Limited **Bred** Thistle Bloodstock Ltd **Trained** Kells, Co Kilkenny

**FOCUS**
A competitive class 5 run at a strong pace where the leaders never came back. The fourth has been rated close to his recent form.

### 2774 PDM MAINS TO DRAINS BRAVEHEART H'CAP 1m 4f 15y
**7:30** (7:30) (Class 3) (0-95,96) 4-Y-O+ **£16,172** (£4,812; £2,405; £1,202) **Stalls** Low

Form RPR

-620 **1** **Sir Chauvelin**9 2525 5-9-7 **94**........ SamJames 6 102+
(Jim Goldie) *in tch: effrt whn nt clr run over 2f out to over 1f out: rdn and kpt on wl to ld towards fin* **7/1**

3-12 **2** shd **Kensington Star**12 2426 4-8-2 **78**........(p) NathanEvans(3) 8 86+
(Keith Dalgleish) *hld up on outside: pushed along over 2f out: hdwy over 1f out: kpt on wl u.p fnl f: jst hld* **3/1**1

4-32 **3** nse **Yorkidding**9 2525 5-9-9 **96**........ JoeFanning 1 103
(Mark Johnston) *cl up: led over 2f out: sn rdn: drifted lft ins fnl f: hdd towards fin* **4/1**2

24-2 **4** 2 **Sam Missile (IRE)**20 2136 4-9-3 **90**........ DanielMuscutt 3 94
(James Fanshawe) *trckd ldrs: rdn and ev ch whn hung rt over 1f out: no ex ins fnl f* **3/1**1

0-11 **5** 1 1/4 **Corton Lad**12 2426 7-8-13 **91** 6ex........(tp) RowanScott(5) 5 93
(Keith Dalgleish) *led: rdn and hdd over 2f out: rallied: outpcd fnl f* **14/1**

61-3 **6** 1/2 **Amazing Red (IRE)**20 2165 4-9-2 **89**........ GrahamLee 9 90
(Ed Dunlop) *trckd ldrs: pushed along and outpcd over 2f out: no imp fr over 1f out* **6/1**3

1334 **7** 6 **Footlight**29 1911 4-8-5 **78**........ BarryMcHugh 4 69
(Richard Fahey) *trckd ldrs: drvn along over 2f out: wknd over 1f out* **16/1**

45-0 **8** 1 1/2 **Master Of Irony (IRE)**37 1719 5-8-13 **86**........(b) CamHardie 7 75
(John Quinn) *dwlt: hld up: pushed along over 4f out: wknd over 2f out* **22/1**

2m 34.81s (-3.79) **Going Correction** -0.20s/f (Firm) **8** Ran SP% **113.7**
Speed ratings (Par 107): **104,103,103,102,101 101,97,96**
CSF £27.98 CT £95.41 TOTE £7.60: £2.20, £1.60, £1.60; EX 30.70 Trifecta £97.50.
**Owner** J Fyffe **Bred** W M Johnstone **Trained** Uplawmoor, E Renfrews

**FOCUS**
An interesting feature middle-distance handicap with a thrilling finish. The third has been rated to her Chester Cup figure.

### 2775 SODEXO WILLIAM WALLACE H'CAP 6f 6y
**8:05** (8:06) (Class 4) (0-85,83) 3-Y-O **£6,469** (£1,925; £962; £481) **Stalls** Centre

Form RPR

5-1 **1** **Black Isle Boy (IRE)**25 2033 3-9-2 **78**........ SamJames 7 85
(David O'Meara) *trckd ldrs: rdn to ld over 1f out: kpt on strly fnl f* **5/1**3

03-2 **2** 1 **Springforth**16 2304 3-8-1 **66**........ NathanEvans(3) 5 70
(Richard Fahey) *in tch: rdn and edgd rt over 2f out: effrt and swtchd lft over 1f out: chsd wnr wl ins fnl f: r.o* **5/1**3

40-1 **3** nk **Dandy Highwayman (IRE)**29 1913 3-9-4 **80**........ TomEaves 6 83
(Ollie Pears) *led: rdn and hdd over 1f out: kpt on same pce ins fnl f* **15/2**

-215 **4** nse **Sharp Defence (USA)**8 2554 3-9-7 **83**........ TadhgO'Shea 3 86
(John Patrick Shanahan, Ire) *cl up: drvn along over 2f out: kpt on same pce ins fnl f* **13/8**1

021- **5** 1 3/4 **Saint Equiano**225 7090 3-9-7 **83**........(h) JoeFanning 1 80
(Keith Dalgleish) *prom on outside: pushed along and hung rt over 2f out: outpcd fr over 1f out: no imp and eased ins fnl f* **5/2**2

1m 11.41s (-0.79) **Going Correction** -0.20s/f (Firm) **5** Ran SP% **111.8**
Speed ratings (Par 101): **97,95,95,95,92**
CSF £28.58 TOTE £6.20: £2.90, £2.90; EX 22.70 Trifecta £87.10.
**Owner** Evan M Sutherland **Bred** Ballyhane Stud **Trained** Upper Helmsley, N Yorks

**FOCUS**
A decent 3yo sprint handicap with a taking performance from a progressive winner. The runner-up has been rated to a small pb, and the third to his Ripon win.

### 2776 PATERSONS OF GREENOAKHILL H'CAP 6f 6y
**8:40** (8:40) (Class 5) (0-75,76) 3-Y-O+ **£3,881** (£1,155; £577; £288) **Stalls** Centre

Form RPR

-432 **1** **El Hombre**10 2499 3-9-0 **75**........ RowanScott(5) 11 89
(Keith Dalgleish) *dwlt: hdwy to ld after 2f: rdn and edgd rt over 1f out: kpt on strly to draw clr fnl f* **11/4**2

0-02 **2** 6 **Portland Street (IRE)**12 2428 4-9-5 **66**........(b) ConnorBeasley 8 63
(Bryan Smart) *led 2f: pressed wnr: rdn over 2f out: effrt and edgd rt over 1f out: one pce fnl f* **13/8**1

536- **3** 2 **Love Oasis**215 7381 3-8-12 **68**........ JoeFanning 12 56
(Mark Johnston) *chsd ldrs on nr side of gp: drvn along over 2f out: edgd lft and outpcd fr over 1f out* **12/1**

4044 **4** 4 1/2 **Dodgy Bob**18 2216 4-9-5 **66**........(p) TomEaves 5 42
(Michael Mullineaux) *dwlt: hld up: rdn over 2f out: rallied over 1f out: no imp fnl f* **20/1**

6-33 **5** nk **Lawless Louis**18 2223 3-8-13 **76**........ PatrickVaughan(7) 2 49
(David O'Meara) *chsd ldrs: rdn over 2f out: wknd over 1f out* **8/1**

30-4 **6** shd **Insurplus (IRE)**12 2424 4-9-1 **62**........(v) SamJames 3 37
(Jim Goldie) *hld up: drvn and struggling wl over 2f out: nvr on terms* **9/1**

00-0 **7** 2 **Avenue Of Stars**49 1472 4-9-13 **74**........(b1) GrahamLee 6 42
(Karen McLintock) *cl up tl rdn and wknd over 1f out* **15/2**3

545- 8 *17* **Bunce (IRE)**[220] 7252 9-9-2 **63**.......................................... PJMcDonald 9
(Linda Perratt) *hld up: struggling 1/2-way: sn btn: t.o* **33/1**

1m 10.21s (-1.99) **Going Correction** -0.20s/f (Firm)
**WFA** 3 from 4yo+ 9lb **8** Ran SP% **113.0**
Speed ratings (Par 103): **105,97,94,88,87 87,85,62**
CSF £7.40 CT £41.75 TOTE £3.90: £1.30, £1.60, £3.40; EX 8.90 Trifecta £80.40.
**Owner** Weldspec Glasgow Limited **Bred** Mrs J McMahon **Trained** Carluke, S Lanarks

**FOCUS**
A modest enough sprint handicap won in spectacular style by a 3yo going places. The runner-up has been rated a stone off his C&D latest.

## 2777 ASPIN GROUP MCGRATTAN PILING H'CAP 5f 7y
**9:10** (9:10) (Class 6) (0-65,63) 4-Y-0+ **£3,234** (£962; £481; £240) **Stalls** High

Form RPR
-400 1 **Nuala Tagula (IRE)**[27] 1978 4-8-13 **55**.............................(t) JackGarritty 5 62
(John Quinn) *t.k.h early: pressed ldr: effrt and rdn over 1f out: led ent fnl f: drvn out* **3/1**[2]
130- 2 *shd* **Bronze Beau**[219] 7290 10-9-7 **63**..................................(tp) TonyHamilton 3 70
(Kristin Stubbs) *led: rdn along wl over 1f out: hdd ent fnl f: kpt on: hld nr fin* **6/1**
06-2 3 *1 1/4* **Cheeni**[11] 2453 5-8-0 **45**...............................................(p) NathanEvans(3) 9 47
(Jim Goldie) *sn in tch: effrt and rdn 2f out: edgd rt ins fnl f: kpt on same pce* **9/2**[3]
500 4 *hd* **Very First Blade**[66] 1184 8-8-2 **49**.................................. RowanScott(5) 4 50
(Michael Mullineaux) *dwlt: bhd and outpcd: hdwy on outside 1/2-way: effrt and rdn over 1f out: one pce ins fnl f* **12/1**
5102 5 *1 1/2* **Sea Of Green**[11] 2454 5-8-7 **49**.........................................(p) SamJames 6 45
(Jim Goldie) *t.k.h: sn prom: effrt and drvn along 2f out: outpcd whn checked ins fnl f* **2/1**[1]
00-0 6 *1 1/2* **Dutch Dream**[11] 2454 4-8-9 **51** ow1........................................ GrahamLee 7 42
(Linda Perratt) *chsd ldrs: drvn and outpcd over 2f out: sme late hdwy: n.d* **13/2**

59.4s (-0.60) **Going Correction** -0.20s/f (Firm) **6** Ran SP% **111.8**
Speed ratings (Par 101): **96,95,93,93,91 88**
CSF £20.54 CT £77.19 TOTE £3.40: £1.70, £2.00; EX 18.80 Trifecta £73.50.
**Owner** Mrs S Quinn **Bred** Miss S Von Schilcher **Trained** Settrington, N Yorks

**FOCUS**
A low-key finale that seemed to emphasise there was an advantage up the rail. The winner has been rated near her AW best.
T/Plt: £121.20 to a £1 stake. Pool: £60,639.45 - 365.17 winning units T/Qpdt: £21.70 to a £1 stake. Pool: £4,245.69 - 144.55 winning units **Richard Young**

# [1957]NEWBURY (L-H)
Friday, May 19

**OFFICIAL GOING: Soft (good to soft in places; 4.9)**
Wind: virtually nil Weather: overcast

## 2778 COOLMORE STUD MAIDEN STKS (PLUS 10 RACE) (DIV I) 7f (S)
**1:30** (1:32) (Class 4) 3-Y-0 **£6,469** (£1,925; £962; £481) **Stalls** Centre

Form RPR
0- 1 **Almoreb (IRE)**[212] 7470 3-9-5 0.......................................... DaneO'Neill 9 78+
(Richard Hannon) *led: hdd over 2f out: rdn whn carried sltly lft over 1f out: led fnl 100yds: kpt on wl* **8/1**[3]
4 2 *1/2* **Highway One (USA)**[28] 1947 3-9-0 0.......................... FrankieDettori 2 71
(George Baker) *trckd ldrs: rdn to chse ldng pair over 1f out: kpt on ins fnl f: snatched 2nd cl home* **12/1**
2-2 3 *hd* **Top Mission**[31] 1862 3-9-5 0.......................................... WilliamCarson 12 76+
(Saeed bin Suroor) *trckd ldr: led over 2f out: drifted lft wl over 1f out: drifted rt u.p jst bef fnl f: hdd fnl 100yds: no ex* **6/5**[1]
4 *2 1/4* **Addeybb (IRE)** 3-9-5 0.......................................... MartinHarley 3 70+
(William Haggas) *hld up towards rr: rdn over 1f out: r.o wl ins fnl f: wnt 4th cl home* **8/1**[3]
5 *nse* **Rigoletto (SWI)** 3-9-5 0.......................................... JimmyFortune 1 70+
(Luca Cumani) *hld up towards rr: shkn up in last pair over 1f out: rdn and r.o wl fnl f but no threat to ldrs* **20/1**
2646 6 *nk* **Hisar (IRE)**[14] 2361 3-9-5 70.......................................... ShaneKelly 8 69
(Ronald Harris) *mid-div: hdwy 2f out: sn rdn: kpt on same pce fnl f* **66/1**
05- 7 *1/2* **Bois D'Ebene (IRE)**[184] 7977 3-9-0 0.......................... HarryBentley 11 63
(Roger Charlton) *racd keenly in midfield: trckd ldrs 2f out: sn rdn to chse ldng trio: no ex and lost 3 pls towards fin* **20/1**
0-2 8 *1/2* **See The Master (IRE)**[19] 2171 3-9-5 0.......................... AdamKirby 7 66
(Clive Cox) *in tch: rdn 2f out: sn oe pce* **7/2**[2]
9 *3/4* **Mulsanne Chase** 3-9-5 0.......................................... SteveDrowne 4 64
(Brian Barr) *hld up towards rr: rdn and sme prog over 1f out: nt pce to get involved* **200/1**
000 10 *nk* **Mister Chow**[7] 2581 3-9-2 0.......................................... HectorCrouch(3) 10 64
(Gary Moore) *slowly away: sn mid-div: one pce fnl 2f* **200/1**
11 *1* **Right About Now (IRE)** 3-9-5 0.......................................... SeanLevey 5 61
(Ismail Mohammed) *prom: rdn 2f out: wknd ent fnl f* **20/1**
12 *13* **Waitingforachance** 3-9-0 0.......................................... JFEgan 6 22
(Mick Channon) *dwlt: a towards rr: wknd 2f out* **50/1**

1m 30.98s (5.28) **Going Correction** +0.625s/f (Yiel) **12** Ran SP% **116.3**
Speed ratings (Par 101): **94,93,93,90,90 90,89,89,88,87 86,71**
CSF £90.14 TOTE £9.90: £3.10, £3.50, £1.10; EX 99.30 Trifecta £450.80.
**Owner** Hamdan Al Maktoum **Bred** Stowell Park Stud **Trained** East Everleigh, Wilts

**FOCUS**
Rails position increases race distances 16 yards for Races 4, 6, 7 and 8. The first division of a fairly decent 3yo maiden. They went a sensible gallop on testing ground, officially soft, good to soft in places.

## 2779 WELCOME TO THE STARLIGHT RACEDAY MAIDEN STKS (PLUS 10 RACE) 6f
**2:00** (2:02) (Class 4) 2-Y-0 **£6,469** (£1,925; £962; £481) **Stalls** Centre

Form RPR
1 **Nebo (IRE)** 2-9-2 0.......................................... CallumShepherd(3) 4 88+
(Charles Hills) *mid-div: hdwy over 2f out: led over 1f out: edgd rt ent fnl f: sn rdn: r.o strly: readily* **25/1**
2 *2 1/4* **Westerland** 2-9-5 0.......................................... FrankieDettori 3 81+
(John Gosden) *hld up: hdwy whn bmpd over 2f out: sn rdn: kpt o ins fnl f: wnt 2nd fnl 70yds: nt pce of wnr* **15/8**[1]
3 *nk* **George (IRE)** 2-9-5 0.......................................... PatDobbs 6 80
(Sylvester Kirk) *trckd ldrs: led briefly 2f out: sn rdn: outpcd by wnr ent fnl f: no ex whn lost 2nd fnl 70yds* **20/1**
4 *1 1/2* **Grand Koonta (IRE)** 2-9-5 0.......................................... AdamKirby 13 76
(Clive Cox) *trckd ldrs: rdn to chal for 2nd over 1f out: kpt on but no ex fnl f* **6/1**
5 *3* **Liva (IRE)** 2-9-5 0.......................................... JimmyFortune 9 67
(David Evans) *led tl rdn 2f out: sn hld: kpt on same pce fnl f* **33/1**
6 *1 1/4* **Billy Dylan (IRE)** 2-9-5 0.......................................... SeanLevey 10 63+
(Richard Hannon) *nvr bttr than mid-div* **9/2**[2]
7 *nk* **Like Lightning (IRE)** 2-9-5 0.......................................... LiamJones 1 62
(J S Moore) *mid-div: swtchd lft over 2f out: sn rdn: nvr any imp* **100/1**
8 *1 3/4* **Tadleel** 2-9-5 0.......................................... AntonioFresu 8 57
(Ed Dunlop) *trckd ldrs: rdn over 2f out: wknd over 1f out* **20/1**
9 *nk* **Mafeking** 2-9-5 0.......................................... MartinHarley 5 56
(Harry Dunlop) *towards rr: sme minor late hdwy: n.d* **33/1**
10 *shd* **Mr Top Hat** 2-9-5 0.......................................... JFEgan 11 56
(David Evans) *trckd ldrs: rdn 2f out: sn wknd* **50/1**
11 *5* **Gravina** 2-9-0 0.......................................... FergusSweeney 7 36
(Alan King) *a towards rr* **25/1**
12 *1 1/2* **Aiya (IRE)** 2-9-5 0.......................................... ThomasBrown 12 36
(Andrew Balding) *s.i.s: mid-div: rdn 2f out: sn wknd* **9/1**
13 *4* **Enjazaat** 2-9-5 0.......................................... DaneO'Neill 2 24
(Owen Burrows) *wnt lft leaving stalls: towards rr: hdwy over 2f out: rdn wl over 1f out: sn wknd* **5/1**[3]

1m 16.44s (3.44) **Going Correction** +0.625s/f (Yiel) **13** Ran SP% **120.0**
Speed ratings (Par 95): **102,99,98,96,92 90,90,88,87,87 81,79,73**
CSF £67.99 TOTE £37.20: £8.30, £1.20, £5.10; EX 112.20 Trifecta £2057.60.
**Owner** Mrs Julie Martin And David R Martin **Bred** Select Bloodstock & Melchior Bloodstock **Trained** Lambourn, Berks

**FOCUS**
A decent juvenile maiden made up entirely of well-bred newcomers. They went a sensible gallop on the soft ground and it produced some encouraging displays, including a taking winner. It's been rated around the solid race average.

## 2780 STARLIGHT H'CAP 6f
**2:35** (2:37) (Class 2) (0-100,100) 4-Y-0+**£19,407** (£5,775; £2,886; £1,443) **Stalls** Centre

Form RPR
020- 1 **Blaine**[210] 7497 7-9-1 **94**...........................................(b) FrankieDettori 11 104
(Brian Barr) *mid-div: hdwy 2f out: led over 1f out: edgd lft: r.o wl* **25/1**
3-14 2 *1 1/2* **Ice Age (IRE)**[13] 2390 4-8-7 **86**.......................................... HarryBentley 1 91
(Eve Johnson Houghton) *trckd ldr: led briefly over 1f out: sn rdn: kpt on w ev ch tl no ex fnl 100yds* **3/1**[1]
46-0 3 *hd* **Boy In The Bar**[13] 2391 6-8-7 **86**..............................(b) JosephineGordon 7 91
(Ian Williams) *travelled wl: trckd ldr: rdn and ev ch briefly over 1f out: kpt on again fnl 100yds: nrly snatched 2nd cl home* **10/1**
00-0 4 *3* **Clear Spring (IRE)**[12] 2433 9-9-2 **95**.......................................... MartinHarley 12 90
(John Spearing) *mid-div: hdwy over 1f out: sn rdn: kpt on ins fnl f but nt gng pce to get on terms* **6/1**[3]
1300 5 *1/2* **Eljaddaaf (IRE)**[34] 1794 6-8-11 **90**..............................(h) RobertWinston 4 83
(Dean Ivory) *little slowly away: towards rr: rdn oer 1f out: r.o fnl f: nvr trbld ldrs* **20/1**
-010 6 *1 1/2* **Gunmetal (IRE)**[12] 2433 4-8-12 **94**.......................................... CallumShepherd(3) 5 90+
(Charles Hills) *sddle slipped leaving stalls: trckd ldrs: rdn 2f out: sn hld: eased whn sddle slipped again fnl 120yds* **5/1**[2]
060- 7 *2 1/2* **Shared Equity**[210] 7497 6-9-4 **97**.......................................... JimmyFortune 13 78
(Jedd O'Keeffe) *hld up: rdn over 1f out: kpt on fnl f but nt gng pce to get on terms* **7/1**
020- 8 *nk* **Ashpan Sam**[242] 6633 8-8-12 **91**...........................................(p) WilliamCarson 10 71
(David W Drinkwater) *led: rdn and hdd over 1f out: wknd fnl f* **50/1**
00-2 9 *1/2* **Exceed The Limit**[17] 2262 4-8-13 **92**.......................................... PatDobbs 2 70
(Robert Cowell) *prom: rdn 2f out: sn hld: wknd fnl f* **14/1**
0-20 10 *1 1/4* **Captain Colby (USA)**[12] 2433 5-9-7 **100**..............................(b) ThomasBrown 6 74
(Ed Walker) *dwlt bdly: a in rr* **11/1**
1-00 11 *10* **Scrutineer (IRE)**[48] 1491 4-9-5 **98**.......................................... JFEgan 14 40
(Mick Channon) *mid-div: effrt over 1f out: sn wknd* **8/1**

1m 13.97s (0.97) **Going Correction** +0.625s/f (Yiel) **11** Ran SP% **114.2**
Speed ratings (Par 109): **118,116,115,111,111 109,105,105,104,103 89**
CSF £94.78 CT £836.15 TOTE £15.50: £5.10, £1.40, £3.00; EX 112.80 Trifecta £705.10.
**Owner** The Golden Horse Racing Club & Hitchins **Bred** Toby Barker **Trained** Longburton, Dorset

**FOCUS**
The feature contest was a good sprint handicap. They went a decent gallop on the testing surface and it proved hard to make up ground from a far side, low draw. The runner-up has been rated to form.

## 2781 STARLIGHT WISHES H'CAP 1m 4f
**3:05** (3:06) (Class 5) (0-70,72) 4-Y-0+ **£4,528** (£1,347; £673; £336) **Stalls** Low

Form RPR
0-52 1 **Multigifted**[25] 2022 4-8-6 **60**...........................................(t) GeorgeWood(5) 4 67
(Michael Madgwick) *trckd ldr: rdn over 2f out: led fnl 150yds: styd on gamely: drvn out* **10/1**
5 2 *1 1/4* **Methag (FR)**[15] 2336 4-9-9 **72**.......................................... FergusSweeney 20 77
(Alex Hales) *trckd ldr: rdn to chal over 2f out tl ent fnl f: styd on* **20/1**
41-4 3 *2* **Art Of Swing (IRE)**[13] 2388 5-9-4 **70**.......................................... HectorCrouch(3) 18 72
(Gary Moore) *led: rdn whn strly chal over 2f out: hdd fnl 150yds: no ex* **8/1**
60-4 4 *nk* **Saumur**[24] 2061 5-9-9 **72**.......................................... MartinHarley 10 74
(Denis Coakley) *mid-div: hdwy fr 4f out: rdn whn swtchd rt to chse ldng trio over 1f out: styd on fnl f but nt pce to threaten* **8/1**
55-0 5 *3/4* **Ivanhoe**[13] 2388 7-9-2 **65**...........................................(b) DaneO'Neill 7 65
(Michael Blanshard) *in tch: rdn wl over 2f out: styd on same pce* **12/1**
0-45 6 *1 1/4* **Rahmah (IRE)**[47] 1519 5-9-4 **67**.......................................... TimmyMurphy 2 65+
(Geoffrey Deacon) *v awkwardly away: bhd: hdwy fr 4f out: rdn in midfield over 2f out: styd on same pce* **12/1**
3342 7 *1/2* **Bridey's Lettuce (IRE)**[11] 2460 5-9-2 **65**..............................(h) KierenFox 6 67+
(John Best) *hld up bhd: pushed along whn nt clr run twice over 2f out: hdwy whn short of room and hmpd jst over 1f out: no ch after* **13/2**[2]
23-1 8 *hd* **Reckless Wave (IRE)**[16] 2308 4-9-3 **66**.......................................... ThomasBrown 12 63
(Ed Walker) *towards rr of mid-div: rdn wl over 2f out: sme minor late prog: n.d* **9/2**[1]
31/6 9 *1 1/4* **Rocky Elsom (USA)**[27] 1092 10-8-6 **62** ow1.............. RossaRyan(7) 11 57
(Sophie Leech) *hld up towards rr: rdn over 1f out: last ent fnl f: styd on but nvr any ch* **25/1**
045- 10 *2* **Mr Caffrey**[22] 1253 5-9-2 **65**...........................................(b) TrevorWhelan 19 57
(John Flint) *mid-div: rdn over 3f out: wknd over 1f out* **40/1**
0231 11 *nk* **Pour L'Amour (IRE)**[16] 2308 4-9-4 **67**.......................................... RobertWinston 17 59
(Daniel Mark Loughnane) *trckd ldrs: rdn over 2f out: hld whn sltly hmpd over 1f out: wknd fnl f* **14/1**



The Form Book Flat, Raceform Ltd, Newbury, RG14 5SJ

6-21 **12** *shd* **Desert Cross**[25] 2042 4-9-4 **67**........................ ShaneKelly 3 58
(Jonjo O'Neill) *mid-div: rdn over 2f out: no imp: wknd ins fnl f* **7/1**[3]
00-6 **13** *7* **Sark (IRE)**[11] 2477 4-9-7 **70**........................ JFEgan 1 50
(David Evans) *hld up towards rr: midfield u.p 2f out: wknd ent fnl f* **12/1**
3025 **14** *1 ½* **The Detainee**[15] 2340 4-8-10 **59**........................(p) LiamJones 13 37
(Jeremy Gask) *in tch: pushed along over 7f out: drvn over 3f out: wknd over 1f out* **28/1**

2m 44.2s (8.70) **Going Correction** +0.60s/f (Yiel) **14** Ran SP% **119.6**
Speed ratings (Par 103): **95,94,92,92,92 91,90,90,90,88 88,88,83,82**
CSF £200.66 CT £1684.84 TOTE £11.00: £3.40, £6.80, £2.30; EX 309.00 Trifecta £5029.00.
**Owner** Mrs L N Harmes **Bred** Mrs L N Harmes **Trained** Denmead, Hants

**FOCUS**
Race distance increased 16 yards. An ordinary middle-distance handicap. They went a respectable gallop in testing conditions. A pb from the winner, but the race has been rated a bit cautiously.

## 2782 COOLMORE STUD MAIDEN STKS (PLUS 10 RACE) (DIV II) 7f (S)
**3:40** (3:41) (Class 4) 3-Y-O **£6,469** (£1,925; £962; £481) **Stalls** Centre

Form RPR
2- **1** **Mutoondresdashorse**[372] 2173 3-9-5 0........................ AdamKirby 9 77
(Paul Cole) *mid-div: hdwy 2f out: led over 1f out: drifted lft: r.o wl: rdn out* **7/2**[2]
5 **2** *¾* **Alqalsar (IRE)**[27] 1961 3-9-5 0........................ DaneO'Neill 3 74
(Brian Meehan) *mid-div: hdwy over 2f out: rdn to chse wnr over 1f out: kpt on but a being hld ins fnl f* **7/2**[2]
0 **3** *¾* **Tidal Watch (IRE)**[11] 2475 3-9-5 0........................ ShaneKelly 8 72
(Jonjo O'Neill) *stdd s: last: pushed along 3f out: rdn and hdwy over 1f out: edgd lft whn chsng ldng pair ent fnl f: kpt on wl* **50/1**
34 **4** *5* **Art's Desire (IRE)**[21] 2121 3-9-0 0........................ ThomasBrown 12 54
(Ed Walker) *pressed ldr: led 2f out: sn rdn and hdd: no ex ins fnl f* **7/1**[3]
5 **5** *1 ½* **Vixen (IRE)**[19] 2171 3-8-9 0........................ PaddyPilley(5) 7 50
(Geoffrey Deacon) *racd keenly: mid-div: rdn 2f out: nt pce to get involved* **33/1**
0-5 **6** *nk* **Red Emperor (IRE)**[11] 2475 3-9-5 0........................ PatDobbs 10 54
(Amanda Perrett) *mid-div: rdn over 2f out: nvr any imp* **20/1**
0 **7** *1 ¾* **Lifeboat Lad (USA)**[11] 2475 3-9-5 0........................(h) SteveDrowne 6 50
(Dean Ivory) *mid-div: struggling in rr 3f out: nvr any danger after* **66/1**
6 **8** *3 ¼* **Balestra**[23] 2090 3-9-5 0........................ FrankieDettori 4 41
(Charles Hills) *prom: rdn over 2f out: wknd over 1f out* **2/1**[1]
6 **9** *8* **Canford Tor (IRE)**[19] 2172 3-9-5 0........................ FergusSweeney 1 21
(Henry Candy) *prom: rdn 2f out: wknd over 1f out* **20/1**
**10** *¾* **Captive (FR)** 3-9-5 0........................ SeanLevey 2 19
(Richard Hannon) *chsd ldrs: struggling 3f out: wknd over 1f out* **8/1**
00- **11** *7* **Sixties Symphony**[268] 5771 3-9-0 0........................ TrevorWhelan 5
(John Flint) *led tl rdn 2f out: sn wknd* **200/1**

1m 31.56s (5.86) **Going Correction** +0.625s/f (Yiel) **11** Ran SP% **117.8**
Speed ratings (Par 101): **91,90,89,83,81 81,79,75,66,65 57**
CSF £15.22 TOTE £4.50: £1.50, £1.40, £9.40; EX 15.30 Trifecta £440.80.
**Owner** 9.36 from Paddington **Bred** Robert Pocock **Trained** Whatcombe, Oxon

**FOCUS**
The second division of a fairly decent 3yo maiden. It was run in a time over half-a-second slower on the testing ground. It's been rated slightly higher than the first division.

## 2783 MARTIN GRAY MEMORIAL EBF STALLIONS MAIDEN STKS (PLUS 10 RACE) 1m 2f
**4:15** (4:17) (Class 4) 3-Y-O **£6,469** (£1,925; £962; £481) **Stalls** Low

Form RPR
**1** **Dubai Thunder** 3-9-5 0........................ AdamKirby 10 102+
(Saeed bin Suroor) *trckd ldr: led over 2f out: rdn clr over 1f out: styd on strly: impressive* **7/2**[2]
3- **2** *10* **Hawridge Flyer**[210] 7503 3-9-5 0........................ PatDobbs 2 80
(Stuart Kittow) *mid-div: hmpd bnd 7f out: pushed along wl over 3f out: hdwy 2f out: sn rdn: styd on wl to snatch 2nd fnl strides but nvr any ch w wnr* **9/1**
**3** *nk* **Dark Pearl (IRE)** 3-9-5 0........................ JimmyQuinn 14 79
(Ed Walker) *towards rr on outer: hdwy 3f out: rdn 2f out: styd on to go 2nd fnl 120yds but no ch w wnr: lost 2nd fnl strides* **50/1**
0- **4** *3* **Tuff Rock (USA)**[198] 7769 3-9-5 0........................ ThomasBrown 17 74
(Ed Walker) *led: rdn and hdd over 2f out: sn hld by wnr: no ex fnl 120yds* **33/1**
4 **5** *1 ½* **Mabrook**[17] 2260 3-9-5 0........................(h[1]) MartinHarley 6 71
(Marco Botti) *in tch: hdwy 3f out: rdn to chse ldng pair 2f out: styd on same pce fnl f* **9/1**
**6** *2 ½* **Peterport** 3-9-5 0........................ FrankieDettori 8 66+
(John Gosden) *hld up towards rr: hdwy over 4f out: rdn in 4th 2f out: fdd ins fnl f* **11/4**[1]
6 **7** *½* **Qaviy Cash**[11] 2476 3-9-5 0........................(t) JosephineGordon 12 65
(Hugo Palmer) *mid-div: rdn wl over 2f out: nvr threatened: styd on same pce* **16/1**
-3 **8** *hd* **Nathan**[27] 1967 3-9-5 0........................ JimmyFortune 15 65
(Simon Crisford) *trckd ldrs: rdn over 2f out: sn one pce* **4/1**[3]
6 **9** *nk* **Magellan**[27] 1962 3-9-5 0........................ HarryBentley 4 64
(Roger Charlton) *mid-div: rdn wl over 2f out: styd on same pce* **20/1**
**10** *½* **Amber Morning** 3-8-9 0........................ PaddyPilley(5) 9 58
(Roger Charlton) *hld up towards rr: rdn over 2f out: no imp tl styd on fnl f* **40/1**
0 **11** *1 ½* **Unit Of Assessment (IRE)**[31] 1857 3-9-5 0........................ ShaneKelly 16 60
(William Knight) *mid-div: rn wd on bnd 7f out: rdn over 3f out: nvr any imp* **150/1**
00 **12** *shd* **Espresso Martini**[14] 2366 3-9-5 0........................ KierenFox 5 60
(Brian Meehan) *towards rr of mid-div: rdn over 3f out: nvr any imp* **150/1**
25 **13** *1* **Ply**[25] 2039 3-9-2 0........................ KieranShoemark(3) 20 58
(Roger Charlton) *hld up towards rr: rdn into midfield over 2f out: no further imp: wknd fnl f* **16/1**
5 **14** *15* **Corredordel Viento (USA)**[23] 2087 3-9-5 0........................ JFEgan 7 30
(Simon Dow) *mid-div tl wknd over 2f out* **50/1**
0-0 **15** *20* **About Glory**[29] 1906 3-9-5 0........................ SeanLevey 18
(Richard Hannon) *mid-div on outer: carried wd on bnd 7f out: drvn 3f out: wknd 2f out* **100/1**
6- **16** *nk* **Royal Sunday (FR)**[198] 7770 3-9-5 0........................ FergusSweeney 1
(Alan King) *stdd s: a towards rr* **40/1**
5 **17** *1* **Sir Gnet (IRE)**[20] 2167 3-9-5 0........................(h) AntonioFresu 19
(Ed Dunlop) *trckd ldr tl rdn over 3f out: sn wknd* **50/1**
0 **18** *22* **Murchison River**[11] 2476 3-9-2 0........................ HectorCrouch(3) 13
(Henry Candy) *mid-div tl wknd over 2f out: eased whn btn* **50/1**

2m 13.34s (4.54) **Going Correction** +0.625s/f (Yiel) **18** Ran SP% **123.4**
Speed ratings (Par 101): **106,98,97,95,94 92,91,91,91,90 89,89,88,76,60 60,59,42**
CSF £32.71 TOTE £4.30: £1.90, £2.60, £24.30; EX 34.50 Trifecta £1997.20.
**Owner** Godolphin **Bred** Darley **Trained** Newmarket, Suffolk

**FOCUS**
Race distance increased 16 yards. A decent 1m2f 3yo maiden won by the progressive dual Group 3 winner Ulysses in 2016. They went a decent gallop on the testing ground and it produced a winning performance full of future promise. The form could be rated 3lb higher.

## 2784 JOHN SUNLEY MEMORIAL H'CAP 1m 3f
**4:45** (4:46) (Class 4) (0-85,87) 3-Y-O **£6,469** (£1,925; £962; £481) **Stalls** Low

Form RPR
421- **1** **Mount Moriah**[214] 7406 3-9-3 **81**........................ HarryBentley 8 98
(Ralph Beckett) *w ldr: led wl over 1f out: rdn clr: eased towards fin* **8/1**
54-3 **2** *3 ¾* **Splash Around**[20] 2152 3-8-10 **74**........................ PatDobbs 6 84+
(Sir Michael Stoute) *mid-div: hdwy fr 2f out: sn rdn: chsd wnr ent fnl f but nvr any threat* **15/2**
03-1 **3** *5* **Outcrop (IRE)**[37] 1737 3-8-12 **76**........................ RobertWinston 1 77
(Hughie Morrison) *racd keenly: led: rdn and hdd wl oer 1f out: sn hld by wnr: no ex ins fnl f* **14/1**
4-21 **4** *1* **Blushing Red (FR)**[70] 1122 3-8-11 **75**........................ AntonioFresu 11 74
(Ed Dunlop) *hld up: hdwy 3f out: sn rdn: styd on same pce* **25/1**
-231 **5** *4 ½* **Mullarkey**[37] 1736 3-8-10 **74**........................ KierenFox 9 66
(John Best) *hld up: rdn over 2f out: styd on into hld 5th over 1f out: nvr threatened to get involved* **12/1**
1-36 **6** *8* **Whip Nae Nae (IRE)**[9] 2526 3-9-6 **84**........................ SeanLevey 2 62
(Richard Hannon) *trckd ldrs: rdn over 2f out: wknd over 1f out* **13/2**[2]
14 **7** *20* **Above Normal**[20] 2149 3-9-5 **83**........................(p[1]) DaneO'Neill 5 27
(Saeed bin Suroor) *trckd ldrs: rdn over 2f out: sn wknd* **20/1**
3-41 **8** *2* **Wasatch Range**[25] 2039 3-9-7 **85**........................ FrankieDettori 4 26
(John Gosden) *hld up: rdn 3f out: nvr any imp: wknd 2f out* **5/2**[1]
41-6 **9** *3* **Azam**[30] 1886 3-9-9 **87**........................(p) RobertTart 3 23
(John Gosden) *mid-div tl wknd 2f out* **7/1**[3]
2-1 **10** *34* **Manchego**[20] 2167 3-9-6 **84**........................ JosephineGordon 7
(Hugo Palmer) *trckd ldrs: rdn over 3f out: wknd 2f out* **13/2**[2]

2m 26.82s (5.62) **Going Correction** +0.625s/f (Yiel) **10** Ran SP% **113.6**
Speed ratings (Par 101): **104,101,97,96,93 87,73,71,69,44**
CSF £64.88 CT £823.88 TOTE £10.40: £3.20, £2.10, £4.20; EX 79.70 Trifecta £960.60.
**Owner** Norman Brunskill **Bred** Lady Bland And Newsells Park Stud Ltd **Trained** Kimpton, Hants

**FOCUS**
Race distance increased 16 yards. A decent middle-distance 3yo handicap where an ability to cope with the soft ground was at a premium.

## 2785 SUNSEEKER APPRENTICE H'CAP 1m 2f
**5:20** (5:20) (Class 5) (0-70,72) 4-Y-O+ **£4,528** (£1,347; £673; £336) **Stalls** Low

Form RPR
0255 **1** **Fast And Hot (IRE)**[20] 2153 4-8-13 **67**........................(b) RossaRyan(5) 12 80
(Richard Hannon) *trckd ldr: led over 2f out: clr over 1f out: pushed out: easily* **11/2**[3]
6060 **2** *4 ½* **Essenaitch (IRE)**[39] 1687 4-9-2 **68**........................ KatherineGlenister(3) 14 73
(David Evans) *trckd ldrs: rdn over 2f out: chal for 2nd wl over 1f out: wnt clr 2nd ent fnl f but no ch w wnr* **17/2**
4444 **3** *4 ½* **Take Two**[25] 2020 8-9-0 **68**........................ WilliamCox(5) 15 65
(Alex Hales) *mid-div: hdwy 3f out: sn rdn: pressed for hld 2nd over 1f out: styd on same pce fnl f* **3/1**[1]
2-53 **4** *nk* **Maroc**[39] 1684 4-9-7 **70**........................(p) CameronNoble 7 66
(Nikki Evans) *led: rdn and hdd 2f out: styd on same pce* **12/1**
00-0 **5** *5* **Della Valle (GER)**[39] 1683 4-9-4 **67**........................ MeganNicholls 3 54
(Mike Murphy) *trckd ldrs: rdn over 2f out: wknd over 1f out* **20/1**
6050 **6** *4* **Runaiocht (IRE)**[6] 2615 7-9-0 **63**........................(b) JordanUys 2 43
(Paul Burgoyne) *hld up: rdn into 6th over 2f out: no further imp fr over 1f out* **25/1**
22-5 **7** *2 ¼* **Wealth Tax**[25] 2020 4-9-6 **72**........................ JoshQuinn(3) 8 48
(Ed Dunlop) *in tch: rdn 3f out: sn btn* **17/2**
504- **8** *¾* **Pink Ribbon (IRE)**[184] 7973 5-9-1 **69**........................ TinaSmith(5) 11 44
(Sylvester Kirk) *mid-div: rdn wl over 2f out: nvr any imp: wknd fnl f* **12/1**
0405 **9** *6* **The Gay Cavalier**[24] 2068 6-8-13 **67**........................(t) JackOsborn(5) 13 31
(John Ryan) *slowly away: a bhd* **14/1**
0242 **10** *4* **Bluff Crag**[15] 2336 4-9-4 **70**........................ FinleyMarsh(3) 6 27
(Richard Hughes) *a towards rr* **10/3**[2]
333- **11** *37* **Lady Nahema (IRE)**[310] 4257 4-8-6 **60**........................ MollyKing(5) 5
(Martin Bosley) *mid-div: struggling and lost pl over 3f out: sn wknd: t.o* **33/1**

2m 14.34s (5.54) **Going Correction** +0.625s/f (Yiel) **11** Ran SP% **118.1**
Speed ratings (Par 103): **102,98,94,94,90 87,85,84,80,76 47**
CSF £50.57 CT £167.61 TOTE £6.00: £1.60, £3.80, £1.60; EX 71.10 Trifecta £269.20.
**Owner** Derek And Jean Clee **Bred** D D & Mrs J P Clee **Trained** East Everleigh, Wilts

**FOCUS**
Race distance increased 16 yards. An ordinary apprentice riders' handicap on testing ground which produced a commanding winner. The winner has been rated in line with his best.
T/Plt: £274.80 to a £1 stake. Pool: £60,677.00 - 220.74 winning units T/Qpdt: £58.80 to a £1 stake. Pool: £4,236.00 - 72.02 winning units **Tim Mitchell**

# 1776 NEWCASTLE (A.W) (L-H)
Friday, May 19

**OFFICIAL GOING: Tapeta: standard**
Wind: Virtually Nil Weather: Overcast

## 2786 TARMAC TRADING NOVICE STKS (PLUS 10 RACE) 6f (Tp)
**5:45** (5:47) (Class 4) 2-Y-O **£7,115** (£2,117; £1,058; £529) **Stalls** Centre

Form RPR
**1** **Rajasinghe (IRE)** 2-9-2 0........................ StevieDonohoe 4 89+
(Richard Spencer) *prom: led over 2f out: rdn and qcknd clr appr fnl f: edgd rt towards fin: impressive* **9/1**[3]
**2** *4* **Indomeneo** 2-9-2 0........................ PaulHanagan 6 77
(Richard Fahey) *midfield: pushed along over 2f out: hdwy over 1f out: kpt on to go 2nd 110yds out: no ch w wnr* **16/1**
**3** *½* **Move It Move It** 2-9-2 0........................ DougieCostello 12 76+
(Keith Dalgleish) *hld up in rr: rdn and gd hdwy over 1f out: styd on wl: wnt 3rd towards fin* **25/1**
**4** *½* **Rufus King** 2-9-2 0........................ LukeMorris 10 74
(Mark Johnston) *prom: rdn over 2f out: edgd rt and no ex ins fnl f* **25/1**
1 **5** *½* **Gold Town**[28] 1941 2-9-8 0........................ PhillipMakin 3 79
(Charlie Appleby) *prom: rdn over 2f out: outpcd by wnr over 1f out: no ex ins fnl f* **8/13**[1]
**6** *1 ¾* **Fink Hill (USA)** 2-9-2 0........................ ConnorBeasley 2 67
(Richard Guest) *dwlt: sn midfield: rdn 2f out: wknd ins fnl f* **7/2**[2]

7 nk **Gangland** 2-9-2 0 (h[1]) DavidNolan 5 66
(Richard Fahey) *dwlt: hld up: pushed along 1/2-way: kpt on ins fnl f* **50/1**
8 2 1/4 **Shaheen (IRE)** 2-9-2 0 JasonHart 13 60
(John Quinn) *midfield: rdn and outpcd 1/2-way: kpt on ins fnl f* **14/1**
9 1 1/4 **Far Dawn** 2-9-2 0 KieranO'Neill 11 56
(Simon Crisford) *racd keenly: trckd ldrs: rdn over 2f out: wknd* **20/1**
00 10 2 3/4 **Rock On Bertie (IRE)**[18] 2222 2-8-13 0 RachelRichardson(3) 9 48
(Nigel Tinkler) *led narrowly: rdn whn hdd over 2f out: wknd* **100/1**
11 4 **Admiral Rooke (IRE)** 2-9-2 0 AndrewMullen 14 36
(Michael Dods) *midfield: rdn 1/2-way: wknd over 1f out* **66/1**
12 6 **Cheers Monsieur** 2-9-2 0 DuranFentiman 7 18
(Tim Easterby) *hld up: rdn and bhd fr 1/2-way* **66/1**
5 13 1 **I Am Dandy (IRE)**[34] 1803 2-9-2 0 JoeyHaynes 1 15
(James Ewart) *chsd ldrs: rdn 1/2-way: wknd over 1f out* **33/1**

1m 12.09s (-0.41) **Going Correction** +0.225s/f (Slow) 13 Ran SP% **128.0**
Speed ratings (Par 95): **111,105,105,104,103 101,100,97,96,92 87,79,77**
CSF £138.26 TOTE £13.60: £2.90, £4.10, £7.30; EX 190.30 Trifecta £1874.20.
**Owner** Rebel Racing **Bred** James & Geoff Mulcahy **Trained** Newmarket, Suffolk

**FOCUS**
Going: Standard. Stalls: Straight: Centre. 1m2f and 1m4f: Far side. 2m: Inside. Some nicely-bred and quite expensive juveniles were on show and the race produced a really nice prospect in the winning debutant. The level is a bit fluid, but it's likely to prove at least as good as rated.

## 2787 O'BRIEN H'CAP 1m 2f 42y (Tp)
6:15 (6:15) (Class 4) (0-85,84) 4-Y-0+ £7,762 (£2,310; £1,154; £577) Stalls High

Form RPR
0330 1 **Spes Nostra**[10] 2497 9-8-11 74 (b) DougieCostello 6 81
(Iain Jardine) *midfield: pushed along and hdwy to chse ldr over 1f out: rdn and kpt on fnl f: led towards fin* **10/1**
0-50 2 1/2 **Theos Lolly (IRE)**[15] 2333 4-8-9 72 PaulHanagan 5 78
(Richard Fahey) *trckd ldr: racd keenly: pushed along to ld over 2f out: rdn appr fnl f: kpt on: led towards fin* **5/1**[3]
0-40 3 2 1/2 **Navajo War Dance**[27] 1964 4-9-5 82 JoeyHaynes 7 83
(K R Burke) *midfield: pushed along to chse ldrs over 2f out: rdn and one pce fr appr fnl f* **5/1**[3]
120- 4 nse **Al Destoor**[153] 7744 7-9-7 84 (t) DavidNolan 3 85
(Jennie Candlish) *trckd ldr: rdn 2f out: one pce fnl f* **5/2**[1]
50/0 5 1/2 **Belle De Lawers**[35] 1781 6-9-5 82 PhillipMakin 8 82
(James Bethell) *hld up: pushed along and sme hdwy over 1f out: rdn and one pce fnl f* **11/2**
6024 6 1 3/4 **Warfare**[11] 2466 8-8-5 73 PhilDennis(5) 1 69
(Tim Fitzgerald) *slowly away: hld up: pushed along over 2f out: nvr threatened* **12/1**
53-5 7 1/2 **Taper Tantrum (IRE)**[57] 1323 5-9-3 80 (v) LukeMorris 4 75
(Michael Bell) *led at stdy pce: rdn whn hdd over 2f out: grad wknd over 1f out* **7/2**[2]
/060 8 8 **Masterful Act (USA)**[35] 1781 10-8-7 70 oh5 AndrewMullen 2 49
(John Balding) *hld up: rdn over 2f out: sn wknd and bhd* **100/1**

2m 13.54s (3.14) **Going Correction** +0.225s/f (Slow) 8 Ran SP% **117.3**
Speed ratings (Par 105): **96,95,93,93,93 91,91,84**
CSF £60.61 CT £284.77 TOTE £11.50: £3.10, £1.90, £2.20; EX 63.80 Trifecta £554.50.
**Owner** James A Cringan **Bred** James A Cringan **Trained** Carruthertown, D'fries & G'way

**FOCUS**
An ordinary handicap which saw the winner end a lengthy losing run. The winner has been rated to last autumn's form.

## 2788 NEWCASTLE INTERNATIONAL AIRPORT H'CAP 2m 56y (Tp)
6:50 (6:50) (Class 3) (0-95,94) 4-Y-0+ £12,938 (£3,850; £1,924; £962) Stalls Low

Form RPR
161- 1 **Flymetothestars**[223] 7139 4-9-3 91 LukeMorris 4 104+
(Sir Mark Prescott Bt) *trckd ldrs: pushed along to ld over 1f out: edgd lft 1f out: rdn and styd on wl* **5/4**[1]
3-13 2 2 **Endless Acres (IRE)**[34] 1798 4-9-3 91 (v) StevieDonohoe 2 101
(Charlie Fellowes) *prom: led 3f out: rdn whn hdd over 1f out: checked sltly by wnr 1f out and swtchd rt: styd on but a hld* **5/2**[2]
16-2 3 7 **Champagne Champ**[28] 1942 5-9-7 93 PhillipMakin 3 95
(Rod Millman) *led: hdd 3f out: sn rdn: readily outpcd by ldng pair fnl 2f* **8/1**
5/0- 4 2 3/4 **Excellent Result (IRE)**[32] 6118 7-9-7 93 PaulHanagan 6 92
(Richard Spencer) *midfield: rdn over 3f out: plugged on: nvr threatened* **20/1**
2261 5 2 1/4 **Zakatal**[77] 1002 11-9-0 86 DougieCostello 5 82
(Rebecca Menzies) *midfield: rdn over 2f out: no imp* **25/1**
461 6 2 **Uncle Bernie (IRE)**[38] 1703 7-8-8 80 oh6 (p) AndrewMullen 8 74
(Sarah Hollinshead) *hld up: nvr threatened* **40/1**
4104 7 4 1/2 **Gavlar**[20] 2157 6-9-8 94 (v) BenCurtis 10 82
(William Knight) *hld up: rdn over 3f out: sn wknd* **5/1**[3]
3205 8 19 **Isharah (USA)**[20] 2157 4-9-6 94 JasonHart 1 59
(Mark Johnston) *fly leapt s and rdr lost iron: sn trckd ldrs: rdn over 3f out: sn wknd: eased* **10/1**

3m 35.78s (0.58) **Going Correction** +0.225s/f (Slow)
**WFA** 4 from 5yo+ 1lb 8 Ran SP% **120.9**
Speed ratings (Par 107): **107,106,102,101,100 99,96,87**
CSF £4.75 CT £17.76 TOTE £2.00: £1.20, £1.40, £2.40; EX 5.40 Trifecta £25.40.
**Owner** Mpr Lii, Mrs Jones & Osborne House **Bred** Lady Bamford **Trained** Newmarket, Suffolk

**FOCUS**
This was an above-average race of its type given the front two are progressive and dominated the finish. It's been rated around the third.

## 2789 RUTHERFORD WILKINSON FILLIES' H'CAP 1m 5y (Tp)
7:20 (7:21) (Class 3) (0-95,89) 4-Y-0+ £11,644 (£3,465; £1,731; £865) Stalls Centre

Form RPR
40-5 1 **Prying Pandora (FR)**[42] 1606 4-8-8 76 PaulHanagan 1 86
(Richard Fahey) *trckd ldr: pushed along to ld over 1f out: rdn and kpt on fnl f* **6/4**[1]
3-00 2 2 1/2 **Alexandrakollontai (IRE)**[20] 2155 7-9-0 82 (b) DougieCostello 4 86
(Alistair Whillans) *in tch: chsd ldr 1/2-way: rdn over 2f out: drvn and one pce ins fnl f* **5/1**
5-24 3 2 **Lincoln Rocks**[7] 2593 4-9-7 89 PhillipMakin 3 88
(David O'Meara) *led: rdn and edgd lft 2f out: sn hdd: no ex fnl f* **5/2**[2]
30-1 4 1 1/4 **Toboggan's Fire**[55] 1368 4-9-1 83 JoeyHaynes 2 80
(Ann Duffield) *rrd s and slowly away: hld up: in tch 1/2-way: rdn over 2f out: sn btn* **3/1**[3]

1m 39.45s (0.85) **Going Correction** +0.225s/f (Slow) 4 Ran SP% **110.2**
Speed ratings (Par 104): **104,101,99,98**
CSF £8.97 TOTE £2.00; EX 9.20 Trifecta £32.90.
**Owner** Middleham Park Racing X **Bred** Francis Montauban **Trained** Musley Bank, N Yorks

**FOCUS**
Not the most competitve handicap numerically and the winner made the most of a fairly lenient mark. The third has been rated around her recent form.

## 2790 ADVANTEX H'CAP 1m 5y (Tp)
7:55 (7:56) (Class 6) (0-60,62) 3-Y-0 £3,234 (£962; £481; £240) Stalls Centre

Form RPR
0-03 1 **Champion Harbour (IRE)**[15] 2349 3-9-7 59 PaulHanagan 3 65
(Richard Fahey) *hld up: pushed along and gd hdwy 2f out: briefly short of room bhd ldrs appr fnl f and swtchd rt: rdn and kpt on: led towards fin* **4/1**[1]
0541 2 hd **Mimic's Memory**[11] 2470 3-9-10 62 6ex ShaneGray 1 67
(Ann Duffield) *prom: rdn over 2f out: drvn to ld appr fnl f: kpt on: hdd towards fin* **14/1**
00-0 3 shd **Turning Gold**[15] 2347 3-9-5 57 (b[1]) LukeMorris 5 62
(Sir Mark Prescott Bt) *led: rdn over 2f out: drvn over 1f out: hdd appr fnl f: rallied towards fin: jst hld* **8/1**[3]
-542 4 1 1/2 **Fairy Lock (IRE)**[15] 2349 3-9-0 52 AndrewMullen 10 53
(David Barron) *dwlt: sn midfield: rdn over 2f out: hdwy to chse ldrs over 1f out: edgd rt ins fnl f and one pce* **5/1**[2]
-400 5 3/4 **Huddersfilly Town**[25] 2016 3-9-1 53 DavidNolan 11 53
(Ivan Furtado) *trckd ldrs: rdn over 3f out: no ex fnl 110yds* **33/1**
01-0 6 3 3/4 **Peny Arcade**[11] 2455 3-9-4 56 PaulMulrennan 14 52
(Alistair Whillans) *hld up: racd keenly: rdn and hdwy over 1f out: sltly impeded ins fnl f: eased fnl 50yds* **14/1**
46-0 7 3 1/4 **Trois Bon Amis (IRE)**[19] 2182 3-9-7 59 JasonHart 6 43
(Tim Easterby) *trckd ldrs: rdn over 2f out: wknd fnl f* **25/1**
605- 8 1/2 **Miss Monro (IRE)**[340] 3222 3-9-6 58 BenCurtis 8 41
(Brian Ellison) *midfield: rdn over 2f out: wknd over 1f out* **20/1**
4600 9 hd **State Residence (IRE)**[15] 2349 3-9-7 59 PhillipMakin 9 42
(David O'Meara) *hld up: pushed along 3f out: nvr threatened* **8/1**[3]
3345 10 2 1/4 **Beauchamp Opal**[50] 1445 3-9-7 59 (p[1]) StevieDonohoe 12 37
(Charlie Fellowes) *in tch: rdn over 2f out: wknd fnl f* **4/1**[1]
000- 11 4 **Coachella (IRE)**[207] 7574 3-9-3 55 JoeyHaynes 2 24
(Ed de Giles) *trckd ldrs: rdn over 2f out: wknd appr fnl f* **16/1**
300- 12 14 **Tael O' Gold**[161] 8284 3-8-8 53 JamieGormley(7) 13
(Iain Jardine) *midfield: rdn over 3f out: sn wknd and bhd* **25/1**
004- 13 3/4 **Breathoffreshair**[196] 7792 3-9-5 57 DougieCostello 4
(Richard Guest) *a rr: bhd fnl 2f* **8/1**[3]

1m 40.76s (2.16) **Going Correction** +0.225s/f (Slow) 13 Ran SP% **124.6**
Speed ratings (Par 97): **98,97,97,96,95 91,88,87,87,85 81,67,66**
CSF £62.09 CT £349.70 TOTE £5.10: £1.80, £3.50, £3.30; EX 42.90 Trifecta £378.60.
**Owner** Mike Browne & Mrs Dee Howe **Bred** Gurpreet Singh **Trained** Musley Bank, N Yorks

**FOCUS**
A fair handicap which produced a thrilling finish. The winner shrugged off a slightly troubled passage.

## 2791 DISCOVER DUBAI MEDIAN AUCTION MAIDEN STKS 7f 14y (Tp)
8:30 (8:31) (Class 4) 3-5-Y-0 £7,115 (£2,117; £1,058; £529) Stalls Centre

Form RPR
1 **Hugin (IRE)**[406] 1327 3-9-0 0 JamieSpencer 10 86+
(David Simcock) *in tch: pushed along and qcknd to ld appr fnl f: edgd lft: rdn and kpt on wl* **11/10**[1]
5 2 3 1/4 **Bob Maxwell (IRE)**[47] 1513 3-9-0 0 PhillipMakin 2 77
(David Barron) *midfield: rdn and hdwy over 1f out: wnt 2nd 1f out: kpt on but no ch wnr* **9/1**
5-53 3 1 3/4 **Navarone (IRE)**[20] 2151 3-9-0 75 PaulHanagan 4 72
(Richard Fahey) *midfield: pushed along and hdwy appr fnl f: rdn and one pce ins fnl f* **5/1**[3]
3-40 4 2 1/4 **Deansgate (IRE)**[15] 2348 4-9-11 73 (e) JoeDoyle 6 70
(Julie Camacho) *in tch: rdn to chse ldr appr fnl f: wknd fnl 110yds* **5/1**[3]
5 1/2 **Mio Ragazzo** 3-9-0 0 LukeMorris 3 65
(Marco Botti) *s.i.s: hld up: pushed along and hdwy over 1f out: no ex ins fnl f* **3/1**[2]
4-00 6 5 **Suited**[19] 2180 3-9-0 60 DuranFentiman 7 51
(Tim Easterby) *led: rdn whn hdd appr fnl f: wknd* **66/1**
65 7 1/2 **Competition**[6] 2632 5-9-8 0 (t) SammyJoBell(3) 1 54
(Brian Rothwell) *prom: pushed along 2f out: wknd appr fnl f* **50/1**
0 8 11 **Bajan Beacon**[12] 2429 4-9-11 0 DougieCostello 5 24
(Iain Jardine) *s.i.s: rdn over 3f out: sn btn and bhd* **66/1**

1m 26.54s (0.34) **Going Correction** +0.225s/f (Slow)
**WFA** 3 from 4yo+ 11lb 8 Ran SP% **120.9**
Speed ratings (Par 105): **107,103,101,98,98 92,91,79**
CSF £13.83 TOTE £1.90: £1.10, £3.30, £1.90; EX 16.40 Trifecta £78.30.
**Owner** Steffen Norris **Bred** Glenvale Stud **Trained** Newmarket, Suffolk

**FOCUS**
An ordinary maiden which produced an impressive winner who should rate much higher in time. The third and fourth set the standard.

## 2792 DISCOVER BERLIN CLASSIFIED STKS 7f 14y (Tp)
9:00 (9:01) (Class 6) 3-Y-0+ £3,105 (£924; £461; £230) Stalls Centre

Form RPR
0-44 1 **Rey Loopy (IRE)**[42] 1596 3-8-10 51 PaulMulrennan 8 67+
(Ben Haslam) *hld up in midfield: smooth hdwy 2f out: led over 1f out: pushed clr: eased towards fin* **11/2**[3]
4005 2 3 1/2 **Highly Focussed (IRE)**[65] 1204 3-8-10 55 PaulHanagan 14 56+
(Ann Duffield) *hld up in rr: gd hdwy on bit 2f out: pushed along appr fnl f: kpt on: wnt 2nd towards fin* **4/1**[2]
000- 3 1/2 **My Girl Maisie (IRE)**[330] 3561 3-8-10 50 DougieCostello 2 55
(Richard Guest) *hld up: gd hdwy 2f out: rdn to go 2nd appr fnl f: sn no ch w wnr: no ex and lost 2nd towards fin* **10/1**
00-0 4 7 **Lesanti**[10] 2507 3-8-10 55 JoeyHaynes 12 37
(Ed de Giles) *midfield: rdn and sme hdwy 2f out: wknd ins fnl f* **7/2**[1]
66-0 5 1 **Lukoutoldmakezebak**[19] 2179 4-9-4 45 AdamMcNamara(3) 4 39
(David Thompson) *led: hdd over 4f out: chsd ldr: rdn over 2f out: wknd fnl f* **66/1**
6-65 6 nk **Cosmic Sky**[15] 2349 3-8-10 51 (h) JasonHart 13 34
(Tim Easterby) *trckd ldrs: rdn 2f out: wknd ins fnl f* **8/1**
0-00 7 3/4 **Flying Onsite (FR)**[15] 2349 3-8-10 54 AndrewMullen 10 32
(Nigel Tinkler) *hld up: rdn and sme hdwy over 1f out: sltly hmpd ins fnl f: eased fnl 75yds* **14/1**
4004 8 nk **Sparkling Cossack**[7] 2580 3-8-10 46 (p) RoystonFfrench 5 31
(Jeremy Gask) *midfield: rdn over 2f out: already wkng whn sltly short of room over 1f out* **14/1**
00-0 9 nk **Pipe Dreamer**[126] 221 3-8-10 50 (b[1]) ShaneGray 3 31
(Kevin Ryan) *s.i.s: a towards rr* **14/1**

0-60 **10** *nk* **King Otto**[72] 1083 3-8-10 55 LukeMorris 7 30
(Phil McEntee) *chsd ldrs: rdn over 2f out: sn wknd* **8/1**

555 **11** *8* **Seneca Chief**[50] 1453 3-8-10 53 (h[1]) BenCurtis 6 10
(Daniel Kubler) *hld up: racd keenly and plld way into ld over 4f out: rdn over 2f out: hdd over 1f out: wknd* **14/1**

0-20 **12** *13* **Sir Harry Collins (IRE)**[51] 1418 3-8-10 55 (p[1]) StevieDonohoe 1
(Richard Spencer) *trckd ldrs: rdn over 2f out: wknd and eased* **9/1**

1m 27.69s (1.49) **Going Correction** +0.225s/f (Slow)
**WFA** 3 from 4yo 11lb 12 Ran SP% **127.1**
Speed ratings (Par 101): **100,96,95,87,86 85,85,84,84,84 74,60**
CSF £29.94 TOTE £6.60: £2.20, £2.10, £4.30; EX 40.60 Trifecta £877.70.
**Owner** Daniel Shapiro **Bred** Worldwide Partners **Trained** Middleham Moor, N Yorks

**FOCUS**
This looked competitive on paper, but the winner was in a different league to his rivals.
T/Plt: £432.90 to a £1 stake. Pool: £44,323.00 - 102.38 winning units T/Qpdt: £9.10 to a £1 stake. Pool: £4,171.00 - 454.92 winning units **Andrew Sheret**

## 2750 NEWMARKET (R-H)
### Friday, May 19

**OFFICIAL GOING: Soft (6.1)**
Wind: light, across, of no consequence Weather: overcast

## 2793 JOHN TANNER H'CAP (DIV I) 1m
**1:40** (1:42) (Class 5) (0-70,72) 3-Y-O **£3,881** (£1,155; £577; £288) **Stalls** Low

Form RPR

364- **1** **Keepup Kevin**[204] 7640 3-9-6 67 JohnFahy 7 75
(Pam Sly) *travelled strly: pressed ldrs tl led 3f out: rdn clr 2f out: styd on wl and a in command ins fnl f: readily* **10/1**

0-22 **2** *2* **Wonder Of Dubai (IRE)**[15] 2345 3-9-11 72 LouisSteward 12 74
(Michael Bell) *hld up in tch: effrt and hdwy to chse wnr 2f out: swtchd rt over 1f out: kpt on same pce ins fnl f* **12/1**

204- **3** *hd* **Dance Teacher (IRE)**[233] 6880 3-9-7 68 GeraldMosse 3 70+
(Ralph Beckett) *t.k.h: hld up in tch in midfield: effrt jst over 2f out: chsd ldng pair: kpt on steadily ins fnl f: nvr enough pce to threaten wnr* **11/4[1]**

0-41 **4** *2* **Paddy A (IRE)**[17] 2259 3-9-11 72 SilvestreDeSousa 6 69
(Philip McBride) *hld up in tch in midfield: effrt over 2f out: 5th and no imp whn edging rt 1f out: styd on same pce ins fnl f* **5/1[2]**

443- **5** *nk* **Broughtons Knight**[202] 7697 3-9-10 71 PatCosgrave 8 67
(Henry Spiller) *stdd s: t.k.h: hld up in tch in rr: hdwy 3f out: rdn to chse ldrs over 1f out: kpt on same pce and no imp fnl f* **8/1**

32-4 **6** *1* **Petit Filous**[17] 2259 3-8-11 65 DavidEgan(7) 1 59
(Giles Bravery) *hld up in tch: swtchd rt and effrt over 1f out: kpt on same pce and no imp fr over 1f out* **11/1**

0505 **7** *5* **Pulsating (IRE)**[17] 2252 3-8-10 60 AaronJones(3) 11 42
(Daniel Steele) *t.k.h: hld up in rr: effrt over 2f out: hdwy into midfield but nt on terms w ldrs over 1f out: kpt on same pce after* **66/1**

245- **8** *2 ¼* **Flood Defence (IRE)**[204] 7640 3-9-2 63 AdamBeschizza 4 40
(Chris Wall) *hld up in tch towards rr: rdn and no imp over 1f out: wknd over 1f out* **16/1**

1- **9** *4* **Scots Piper**[236] 6808 3-9-10 71 FrannyNorton 5 39
(Mark Johnston) *led tl 3f out: sn u.p and struggling: wknd over 1f out* **15/2[3]**

5-22 **10** *¾* **Golden Guest**[18] 2228 3-9-6 67 RyanPowell 2 33
(George Margarson) *t.k.h: pressed ldr tl 3f out: sn lost pl u.p: wknd over 1f out* **12/1**

4-04 **11** *17* **Eburaci (IRE)**[31] 1866 3-9-3 64 (v) TomQueally 10
(Charlie Fellowes) *wl in tch in midfield: rdn over 2f out: sn struggling: wknd qckly over 1f out* **12/1**

1m 43.04s (4.44) **Going Correction** +0.55s/f (Yiel) 11 Ran SP% **114.1**
Speed ratings (Par 99): **99,97,96,94,94 93,88,86,82,81 64**
CSF £120.15 CT £428.43 TOTE £11.20: £3.00, £3.60, £1.20; EX 146.40 Trifecta £1030.50.
**Owner** Mrs P M Sly **Bred** Mrs P M Sly **Trained** Thorney, Cambs
■ Stewards' Enquiry : Louis Steward 2 day ban - used whip above the permitted level (5/6 June)

**FOCUS**
Stands' side course used, with stalls on far side except 1m6f: centre. There was overnight rain and intermittent showers prior to racing. The ground officially given as soft and after the first, Silvestre de Sousa stated that it was "proper soft ground, a bit on the heavy side". Only a modest 3yo handicap but a few of these might be able to improve on the bare form. The second has been rated as running a small pb.

## 2794 JOHN TANNER H'CAP (DIV II) 1m
**2:10** (2:13) (Class 5) (0-70,72) 3-Y-O **£3,881** (£1,155; £577; £288) **Stalls** Low

Form RPR

561- **1** **Rake's Progress**[199] 7734 3-9-3 64 GeraldMosse 11 78+
(Heather Main) *chsd ldr for 3f: styd chsng ldrs tl wnt 2nd again 3f out: rdn and ev ch 2f out: led over 1f out: asserted ins fnl f: styd on strly* **12/1**

16-4 **2** *2* **Bruny Island (IRE)**[119] 323 3-8-7 54 MartinLane 1 64
(Charlie Fellowes) *t.k.h: hld up in tch in midfield: clsd to press ldrs over 2f out: rdn and ev ch over 1f out: no ex and outpcd ins fnl f* **11/4[1]**

000- **3** *4* **Oh It's Saucepot**[202] 7695 3-8-13 60 AdamBeschizza 4 60
(Chris Wall) *stdd and short of room sn after s: hld up in tch in rr: pushed along and hdwy over 2f out: 4th over 1f out: kpt on steadily to go 3rd ins fnl f: no threat to ldng pair* **25/1**

1-06 **4** *2 ¾* **Claire's Secret**[17] 2274 3-8-13 67 DavidEgan(7) 9 60
(Philip McBride) *chsd ldrs: wnt 2nd 5f out tl led over 3f out: rdn and hrd pressed ent fnl f: hdd over 1f out and btn 3rd 1f out wknd ins fnl f* **14/1**

3-1 **5** *4* **Passcode**[31] 1866 3-9-3 71 JoshuaBryan(7) 8 55
(Andrew Balding) *hld up in tch in midfield: effrt 3f out: nt clrest of runs jst over 2f out: no imp and wl hld over 1f out* **10/3[2]**

4-23 **6** *1 ¾* **Still Waiting**[126] 210 3-9-2 63 CharlesBishop 12 43
(William Jarvis) *stdd and dropped in bhd after s: effrt over 2f out: sn no imp: wl hld over 1f out* **15/2**

050- **7** *shd* **Lady Kaviar (IRE)**[241] 6655 3-9-5 66 RyanPowell 2 46
(George Margarson) *hld up in tch: rdn over 2f out: unable qck and outpcd sn after: wknd over 1f out* **33/1**

4-30 **8** *½* **Al Mansor (IRE)**[30] 1888 3-9-7 68 TomMarquand 3 47
(Richard Hannon) *t.k.h: sn led: hdd and rdn over 3f out: lost pl and btn 2f out: sn wknd* **9/2[3]**

5450 **9** *42* **Channel Packet**[19] 2186 3-9-6 67 SilvestreDeSousa 10
(Michael Appleby) *nvr travelling wl in rr: lost tch 2f: t.o* **10/1**

20-0 **10** *1 ¼* **Northdown**[23] 2088 3-9-11 72 TomQueally 7
(David Lanigan) *chsd ldrs tl lost pl qckly over 3f out: wl bhd 2f out: t.o* **20/1**

1m 42.53s (3.93) **Going Correction** +0.55s/f (Yiel) 10 Ran SP% **114.7**
Speed ratings (Par 99): **102,100,96,93,89 87,87,86,44,43**
CSF £43.40 CT £846.00 TOTE £14.40: £3.90, £1.80, £5.50; EX 59.70 Trifecta £1075.90.
**Owner** Coxwell Partnership **Bred** Mr & Mrs A E Pakenham **Trained** Kingston Lisle, Oxon

**FOCUS**
Half a second quicker than the first division, but not many got involved in this modest handicap. It's been rated slightly positively.

## 2795 CHEMTEST H'CAP 7f
**2:45** (2:48) (Class 4) (0-80,82) 4-Y-O+ **£5,175** (£1,540; £769; £384) **Stalls** Low

Form RPR

6-13 **1** **Art Echo**[10] 2505 4-8-12 71 (t) PatCosgrave 2 78
(John Mackie) *trckd ldrs tl wnt 2nd over 5f out: upsides ldr 2f out: rdn to ld but unbalanced on downhill run over 1f out: styd on wl ins fnl f: drvn out* **2/1[2]**

5220 **2** *1 ¼* **Lexington Times (IRE)**[84] 896 5-9-7 80 JamesSullivan 8 84
(Ruth Carr) *stdd and squeezed for room leaving stalls: hld up in tch in rr: clsd to trck ldrs 2f out: effrt ent fnl f: drvn to chse wnr ins fnl f: kpt on same pce after* **9/2[3]**

30-0 **3** *1 ¾* **Midnight Macchiato (IRE)**[20] 2133 4-9-5 78 SilvestreDeSousa 3 78
(David Brown) *taken down early: chsd ldr tl led over 5f out: rdn and hdd over 1f out: cl 3rd and keeping on same pce whn short of room 1f out: kpt on same pce ins fnl f* **13/8[1]**

505- **4** *shd* **Another Boy**[210] 7506 4-8-11 75 (p) GeorgiaCox(5) 10 74
(Ralph Beckett) *hld up in tch in 4th: clsd to chse ldng pair over 2f out: rdn 2f out: chsd wnr jst over 1f out: lost 2nd ins fnl f: wknd towards fin* **13/2**

021- **5** *6* **Venutius**[276] 5521 10-9-3 76 GavinLerena 9 60
(Charles Hills) *led tl over 5f out: rdn and dropped to last 3f out: bhd over 1f out* **11/1**

1m 28.82s (3.42) **Going Correction** +0.55s/f (Yiel) 5 Ran SP% **111.3**
Speed ratings (Par 105): **102,100,98,98,91**
CSF £11.24 TOTE £2.80: £1.40, £1.90; EX 11.80 Trifecta £21.00.
**Owner** Annwell Inn Syndicate **Bred** Follow The Flag Partnership **Trained** Church Broughton , Derbys

**FOCUS**
A race hit by six non-runners and its only modest form as a result. The runner-up has been rated close to form.

## 2796 MCCULLOUGHS AIR-CONDITIONING AND VENTILATION H'CAP 1m 2f
**3:20** (3:22) (Class 3) (0-90,89) 4-Y-O+ **£7,762** (£2,310; £1,154; £577) **Stalls** Low

Form RPR

24-5 **1** **Zzoro (IRE)**[18] 2233 4-9-1 83 GavinLerena 2 91
(Amanda Perrett) *w ldr tl led over 3f out: rdn over 1f out: edgd lft ins fnl f: asserted and styd on wl fnl 100yds* **7/2[3]**

30-0 **2** *2* **Interconnection**[37] 1734 6-9-7 89 (p) AdamBeschizza 1 93
(Ed Vaughan) *trckd ldrs: upsides wnr and wnt clr 2f out: rdn over 1f out: no ex and outpcd ins fnl f* **7/4[2]**

2121 **3** *13* **Mr Red Clubs (IRE)**[27] 1982 8-8-3 78 (p) RayDawson(7) 5 56
(Michael Appleby) *hld up in tch: clsd and nt clr run 4f out: rdn 3f out: outpcd and btn 2f out: wknd* **14/1**

21/5 **4** *6* **Sky Cape**[90] 809 5-9-3 85 TomMarquand 3 51
(Heather Main) *led tl over 3f out: sn rdn: outpcd and btn 2f out: wknd* **16/1**

0-13 **5** *21* **Selection (FR)**[16] 2291 4-8-10 78 PatCosgrave 4 2
(William Haggas) *trckd ldrs: rdn over 3f out: btn over 2f out: eased over 1f out: t.o* **13/8[1]**

2m 8.38s (2.58) **Going Correction** +0.55s/f (Yiel) 5 Ran SP% **109.2**
Speed ratings (Par 107): **111,109,99,94,77**
CSF £9.91 TOTE £4.60: £2.40, £1.70; EX 10.10 Trifecta £49.60.
**Owner** Mr & Mrs F Cotton, Mr & Mrs P Conway **Bred** Hatta Bloodstock **Trained** Pulborough, W Sussex

**FOCUS**
No more than fair form. In two groups early, they seemed to go a decent pace and finished well strung out. The winner has been rated to the better view of his form.

## 2797 EDMONDSON HALL SOLICITORS & SPORTS LAWYERS H'CAP 1m 6f
**3:55** (3:57) (Class 2) (0-105,103) 4-Y-O+ **£18,675** (£5,592; £2,796; £1,398; £699) **Stalls** Centre

Form RPR

53-2 **1** **Saigon City**[47] 1516 7-8-11 93 PatCosgrave 3 101
(Declan Carroll) *trckd ldrs: rdn 3f out: swtchd lft u.p over 2f out: led over 1f out: kpt on wl ins fnl f: rdn out* **9/4[2]**

105- **2** *2 ¼* **Oriental Fox (GER)**[149] 8479 9-9-7 103 FrannyNorton 2 108
(Mark Johnston) *led for 2f: chsd ldr tl led again over 2f out: drvn and hdd over 1f out: kpt on same pce ins fnl f* **12/1**

24/6 **3** *5* **Farquhar (IRE)**[20] 2136 6-8-13 95 (h[1]) SilvestreDeSousa 5 93
(Michael Appleby) *t.k.h: stdd s and styd wd early: led after 2f: rdn and hdd over 2f out: 3rd and no ex over 1f out: wknd ins fnl f* **5/1**

413- **4** *1* **Cape Cova (IRE)**[195] 7824 4-9-5 101 TomQueally 4 97
(John Gosden) *hld up in rr: rdn 5f out: sn struggling and no threat to ldrs after: plugged on ins fnl f* **15/8[1]**

11-1 **5** *4 ½* **Cartwright**[11] 2461 4-8-11 93 6ex (p) RyanPowell 1 83
(Sir Mark Prescott Bt) *hld up in tch: clsd to trck 5f out: chsd ldrs and rdn 3f out: sn outpcd: wknd over 1f out* **9/2[3]**

3m 2.03s (5.03) **Going Correction** +0.55s/f (Yiel) 5 Ran SP% **108.1**
Speed ratings (Par 109): **107,105,102,102,99**
CSF £23.96 TOTE £3.10: £1.60, £4.00; EX 24.20 Trifecta £61.10.
**Owner** C H Stephenson,Tate,Flegg & Bousfield **Bred** Martin Percival **Trained** Malton, N Yorks

**FOCUS**
Despite the small field this had the look of a decent staying handicap that was extended by 9yds. The runner-up has been rated to form.

## 2798 MUSEUM OF THE YEAR FINALIST MAIDEN STKS 1m
**4:25** (4:30) (Class 5) 3-Y-O **£3,881** (£1,155; £577; £288) **Stalls** Low

Form RPR

6- **1** **Music Seeker (IRE)**[219] 7283 3-9-5 0 RyanTate 6 85
(James Eustace) *chsd ldr: rdn to ld over 1f out: clr and styd on strly ins fnl f: readily* **14/1**

63 **2** *3* **Tadween (IRE)**[23] 2090 3-9-5 0 TomMarquand 1 78
(Richard Hannon) *hld up in tch in midfield: nt clr run over 2f out: sn rdn and hdwy 2f out: chsd ldrs over 1f out: kpt on to go 2nd ins fnl f: nvr enough pce to threaten wnr* **4/1[3]**

2-3 **3** *1 ½* **Thafeera (USA)**[25] 2019 3-9-0 0....................................(h) GavinLerena 8 70
(Charles Hills) *t.k.h: led: rdn and hdd over 1f out: sn unable qck: lost 2nd and kpt on same pce ins fnl f* **2/1**[1]

**4** *1 ¾* **Warsaw Road (IRE)** 3-8-12 0............................... GabrieleMalune(7) 10 71+
(Luca Cumani) *in tch in midfield: effrt over 2f out: rn green on downhill run over 1f out: kpt on same pce ins fnl f* **25/1**

**5** *1 ¼* **La Rav (IRE)** 3-9-5 0.......................................................... PatCosgrave 3 68+
(Luca Cumani) *in tch in midfield: effrt over 2f out: 4th and unable qck over 1f out: wknd ins fnl f* **8/1**

0 **6** *3 ½* **Upended**[11] 2475 3-9-5 0................................................ AdamBeschizza 9 60
(Chris Wall) *stdd and dropped in bhd after s: hld up in rr: no imp under pressed 2f out :sme hdwy but no threat to ldrs ins fnl f* **66/1**

**7** *2 ¼* **Jus Pires (USA)** 3-9-5 0................................................ GeraldMosse 7 54+
(Jeremy Noseda) *t.k.h: chsd ldrs: rdn over 2f out: outpcd whn hung rt on downhill run wl over 1f out: wknd fnl f* **3/1**[2]

0 **8** *2 ¾* **Tallulah's Quest (IRE)**[31] 1857 3-8-11 0................... ShelleyBirkett(3) 5 43
(Julia Feilden) *hld up in tch: effrt over 2f out: unable qck and carried rt wl over 1f out: sn btn: fdd ins fnl f* **100/1**

0 **9** *25* **Nevasca (IRE)**[23] 2090 3-9-2 0.................................... SimonPearce(3) 2
(Lydia Pearce) *midfield : rdn and lost pl 5f out: lost tch over 2f out: t.o* **100/1**

**10** *½* **Good Business (IRE)** 3-9-0 0................................ SilvestreDeSousa 4
(Jeremy Noseda) *t.k.h: hld up in tch in midfield: lost pl and rdn 3f out: sn lost tch: t.o* **8/1**

1m 42.72s (4.12) **Going Correction** +0.55s/f (Yiel) 10 Ran SP% **114.5**
Speed ratings (Par 99): **101,98,96,94,93 90,87,85,60,59**
CSF £67.49 TOTE £14.60: £3.30, £1.50, £1.30; EX 89.80 Trifecta £241.30.
**Owner** J C Smith **Bred** P J Connolly **Trained** Newmarket, Suffolk

**FOCUS**
This wouldn't be a strong 3yo maiden by the track's usual standard, but the winner did it well. The time compared favourably to both divisions of the 0-70 handicaps for the same age group. The runner-up has been rated as progressing from his AW latest.

## 2799 DISCOVER NEWMARKET H'CAP 1m
**4:55** (5:00) (Class 3) (0-95,94) 4-Y-0+ **£7,762** (£2,310; £1,154; £577) **Stalls** Low

Form RPR

50-2 **1** **G K Chesterton (IRE)**[37] 1734 4-9-2 **89**.............................. MartinLane 2 101+
(Charlie Appleby) *mde all and set stdy gallop: rdn and qcknd ent fnl f: 2 l clr whn ducked ins fnl f: styd on wl: rdn out* **5/2**[2]

10-0 **2** *2* **Moonlightnavigator (USA)**[13] 2406 5-9-1 **88**......... SilvestreDeSousa 3 93
(John Quinn) *t.k.h: pressed wnr: rdn over 2f out: lost 2nd and unable qck u.p over 1f out: chsd clr wnr again ins fnl f: kpt on but no imp* **11/2**[3]

40-4 **3** *1 ¼* **Truth Or Dare**[13] 2384 6-9-1 **88**........................................ GeraldMosse 4 90
(James Bethell) *t.k.h: hld up in rr: rdn over 2f out: styd on u.p ins fnl f: wnt 3rd wl ins fnl f: no threat to wnr* **12/1**

24-0 **4** *¾* **Storm Ahead (IRE)**[27] 1960 4-9-5 **92**................................ PatCosgrave 1 92
(Marcus Tregoning) *t.k.h: trckd ldng pair: effrt over 2f out: chsd wnr and edgd lft over 1f out: lost 2nd and wknd ins fnl f* **7/4**[1]

5-41 **5** *2 ¼* **Takatul (USA)**[23] 2093 4-9-1 **88**........................................ GavinLerena 5 83
(Charles Hills) *t.k.h: hld up in tch: pushed along 3f out: rdn to chse ldrs but unable qck over 1f out: wknd ins fnl f* **8/1**

33-3 **6** *11* **Replenish (FR)**[23] 2093 4-9-7 **94**...................................... TomQueally 7 64
(James Fanshawe) *t.k.h: in tch in midfield: rdn over 2f out: unable qck and dropped to rr over 1f out: bhd and eased ins fnl f* **9/1**

1m 42.76s (4.16) **Going Correction** +0.55s/f (Yiel) 6 Ran SP% **109.1**
Speed ratings (Par 107): **101,99,97,97,94 83**
CSF £15.34 CT £120.54 TOTE £2.60: £1.50, £2.40; EX 12.70 Trifecta £73.30.
**Owner** Godolphin **Bred** Darley **Trained** Newmarket, Suffolk

**FOCUS**
Despite the small-field this had the look of an above average race, although it probably proved advantageous to be on the pace and not all of them handled the ground. The runner-up has been rated to form.

## 2800 32RED.COM "HANDS AND HEELS" APPRENTICE SERIES APPRENTICE H'CAP 6f
**5:30** (5:34) (Class 5) (0-75,76) 4-Y-0+ **£3,881** (£1,155; £577; £288) **Stalls** Low

Form RPR

3232 **1** **Captain Bob (IRE)**[11] 2469 6-8-12 **67**....................(p) JonathanFisher(3) 7 74
(Robert Cowell) *pressed ldr tl led over 2f out: rdn over 1f out: kpt on wl and a holding runner up ins fnl f* **4/1**[2]

53-1 **2** *½* **Ancient Astronaut**[27] 1972 4-9-10 **76**..............................(h) DavidEgan 3 81
(John Quinn) *in tch in ldng quintet: pushed along over 2f out: rdn to press ldr over 1f out: ev ch fnl f: kpt on but a jst hld* **5/4**[1]

3220 **3** *nk* **East Coast Lady (IRE)**[11] 2464 5-9-3 **69**.......................... GabrieleMalune 5 73
(William Stone) *chsd ldng pair: rdn over 2f out: unable qck and outpcd over 1f out: rallied ins fnl f: pressing ldng pair wl ins fnl f: kpt on* **8/1**[3]

-000 **4** *1* **Secret Missile**[8] 2550 7-9-3 **72**.............................. StephenCummins(3) 2 73+
(David C Griffiths) *sn dropped to 6th and lost tch w ldrs: shkn up over 1f out: hdwy ins fnl f: r.o v strly fnl 100yds: nt rch ldrs* **8/1**[3]

0000 **5** *2 ¼* **Something Lucky (IRE)**[56] 1339 5-8-8 **60**................. KieranSchofield 8 54
(Daniel Steele) *in tch in ldng quintet: rdn 2f out: flashing tail and kpt on same pce fr over 1f out* **25/1**

0256 **6** *1* **Out Of The Ashes**[16] 2320 4-9-4 **73**....................(vt) DarraghKeenan(3) 4 63
(Mohamed Moubarak) *led tl over 2f out: rdn and lost 2nd over 1f out: wknd ins fnl f* **10/1**

0600 **7** *1* **Great Expectations**[2] 2733 9-8-1 **59** oh6....................(t) GinaMangan(6) 6 46
(J R Jenkins) *restless in stalls: sn wl off the pce in last pair: styd on ins fnl f: nvr trbld ldrs* **33/1**

2350 **8** *12* **Rockley Point**[16] 2320 4-9-2 **76**.................................... OliverDaykin(8) 1 25
(Paul D'Arcy) *v.s.a: a off the pce in rr: n.d* **8/1**[3]

1m 15.61s (3.41) **Going Correction** +0.55s/f (Yiel) 8 Ran SP% **113.7**
Speed ratings (Par 103): **99,98,97,96,93 92,90,74**
CSF £9.25 CT £36.38 TOTE £5.20: £1.70, £1.10, £2.50; EX 11.60 Trifecta £37.50.
**Owner** The Cool Silk Partnership **Bred** Martyn J McEnery **Trained** Six Mile Bottom, Cambs

**FOCUS**
An apprentice 'hands and heels' race for riders who hadn't ridden more than 10 winners prior to April 16th. It's modest form. The runner-up has been rated to his latest, with the third close to her recent AW form.

T/Plt: £72.20 to a £1 stake. Pool: £47,044.00 - 651.53 winning units T/Qpdt: £11.00 to a £1 stake. Pool: £3,096.00 - 280.00 winning units **Steve Payne**

# 2764 YORK (L-H)
### Friday, May 19

**OFFICIAL GOING: Soft (good to soft in places; overall 5.9; farside 5.7, centre 5.7, stands' side 5.9)**
Wind: Moderate against Weather: Overcast and showers

## 2801 LANGLEYS SOLICITORS BRITISH EBF MARYGATE FILLIES' STKS (LISTED) 5f
**2:20** (2:21) (Class 1) 2-Y-O
**£28,355** (£10,750; £5,380; £2,680; £1,345; £675) **Stalls** High

Form RPR

1 **1** **Main Desire (IRE)**[17] 2265 2-8-12 0............................ DanielTudhope 9 94+
(Michael Bell) *leggy: athletic: trckd ldrs towards stands rail: hdwy 2f out: effrt ent fnl f: sn rdn: kpt on wl to ld last 75 yds* **4/1**[1]

51 **2** *½* **Neola**[7] 2583 2-8-12 0.......................................................... GrahamLee 2 92+
(Mick Channon) *str: racd centre: prom: hdwy to ld wl over 1f out: rdn ent fnl f: hdd and no ex last 75 yds* **4/1**[1]

5 **3** *1 ½* **Mistress Of Venice**[30] 1872 2-8-12 0.................................. LukeMorris 7 87
(James Given) *athletic: lw: overall ldr nr stands rail: rdn along and hdd wl over 1f out: kpt on u.p fnl f* **16/1**

1 **4** *1 ¾* **Maggies Angel (IRE)**[29] 1908 2-8-12 0........................... PaulHanagan 4 81
(Richard Fahey) *leggy: in tch towards stands side: pushed along and sltly outpcd over 2f out: rdn over 1f out: styd on wl fnl f* **6/1**[2]

341 **5** *½* **Daddies Girl (IRE)**[19] 2173 2-8-12 0............................... AndreaAtzeni 8 79
(Rod Millman) *leggy: towards rr stands side: rdn along over 2f out: styd on fnl f* **9/1**[3]

21 **6** *1 ¼* **Get Even**[41] 1627 2-8-12 0............................................... JamieSpencer 15 75
(Jo Hughes) *unf: stdd s and sn swtchd lft: hld up in rr: hdwy over 1f out: sn rdn and kpt on fnl f* **20/1**

1 **7** *hd* **Kentish Waltz (IRE)**[29] 1919 2-8-12 0........................... FabriceVeron 14 73
(E J O'Neill, France) *leggy: scope: prom nr stands rail: rdn along wl over 1f out: wknd fnl f* **6/1**[2]

2 **8** *¾* **Mount Victoria (IRE)**[29] 1908 2-8-12 0.......................... PaulMulrennan 3 71
(James Given) *unf: racd centre: chsd ldrs: rdn along 2f out: sn wknd* **25/1**

45 **9** *3 ½* **Che Bella (IRE)**[11] 2452 2-8-12 0.................................... DougieCostello 5 58
(Keith Dalgleish) *racd towards centre: towards rr: rdn along 1/2-way: sn outpcd* **66/1**

621 **10** *nse* **Faithful Promise**[14] 2373 2-8-12 0..................................... JoeFanning 1 58
(Mark Johnston) *cmpt: wnt lft s: racd centre: prom: rdn along over 2f out: sn wknd* **9/1**[3]

1 **11** *1 ¼* **Izzy Bizu (IRE)**[8] 2545 2-8-12 0.................................... PJMcDonald 10 54
(Mark Johnston) *leggy: dwlt: sn trcking ldrs nr stands rail: effrt 2f out: sn rdn and hld whn n.m.r over 1f out: wknd* **11/1**

0 **12** *1* **Dolly Dagger**[19] 2173 2-8-12 0.......................................... RobHornby 6 50
(Mark Usher) *leggy: racd towards centre: a rr* **100/1**

1 **13** *¾* **Blessed To Empress (IRE)**[17] 2258 2-8-12 0.......... LemosdeSouza 11 47
(Amy Murphy) *str: in tch stands side: rdn along over 2f out: sn wknd* **25/1**

1m 1.7s (2.40) **Going Correction** +0.50s/f (Yiel) 13 Ran SP% **117.7**
Speed ratings (Par 98): **100,99,96,94,93 91,90,89,84,84 82,80,79**
CSF £17.46 TOTE £4.40: £1.70, £1.90, £4.50; EX 20.30 Trifecta £189.60.
**Owner** Clipper Logistics **Bred** W Maxwell Ervine **Trained** Newmarket, Suffolk

**FOCUS**
The rails were at their innermost position on the round course, so no alteration to official race distances as per stalls section. There was 5mm of overnight rain and it was a dreary day leading up to racing. This was a deep edition of this sometimes lukewarm Listed prize for 2yo fillies and it's worth being positive about the form. It's been rated around the race average.

## 2802 LONGINES IRISH CHAMPIONS WEEKEND FILLIES' STKS (REGISTERED AS THE MICHAEL SEELY MEMORIAL) (LISTED) 7f 192y
**2:55** (2:56) (Class 1) 3-Y-O
**£28,355** (£10,750; £5,380; £2,680; £1,345; £675) **Stalls** Low

Form RPR

4-1 **1** **Tomyris**[29] 1905 3-9-0 82...................................................... AndreaAtzeni 2 104+
(Roger Varian) *hld up: hdwy over 2f out: rdn to ld jst over 1f out: drvn ins fnl f: kpt on wl towards fin* **5/1**

113- **2** *¾* **On Her Toes (IRE)**[286] 5172 3-9-0 97.............................. RyanMoore 5 102
(William Haggas) *lw: hld up: pushed along over 2f out: swtchd lft and hdwy over 1f out: rdn to chse wnr ins fnl f: sn drvn to chal and ev ch tl no ex towards fin* **5/2**[2]

1-1 **3** *2 ½* **Sibilance**[34] 1796 3-9-0 93..................................................... FranBerry 8 96
(Ralph Beckett) *w'like: t.k.h: led: c wd home turn to stands rail: pushed along over 2f out: rdn wl over 1f out: hdd appr fnl f: kpt on same pce* **4/1**[3]

35-1 **4** *3 ¼* **Classical Times**[15] 2344 3-9-0 96................................ PaulMulrennan 1 89
(Peter Chapple-Hyam) *str: t.k.h: hdwy and cl up 3f out: rdn along wl over 1f out: sn drvn and grad wknd* **8/1**

1 **5** *1 ¼* **Mulhimatty**[28] 1947 3-9-0 0.................................................. JimCrowley 7 86
(Charles Hills) *unf: scope: hld up in rr: hdwy on outer 3f out: chsd ldrs over 2f out: sn rdn and wknd* **20/1**

-1 **6** *1* **Dancing Breeze (IRE)**[30] 1885 3-9-0 87.......................... WilliamBuick 6 84
(John Gosden) *lw: plld hrd: chsd ldrs: sn cl up: pushed along 3f out: rdn over 2f out: wknd wl over 1f out* **9/4**[1]

1m 41.01s (2.01) **Going Correction** +0.40s/f (Good) 6 Ran SP% **111.9**
Speed ratings (Par 104): **105,104,101,98,97 96**
CSF £17.75 TOTE £6.00: £2.60, £1.70; EX 17.90 Trifecta £93.20.
**Owner** Nurlan Bizakov **Bred** Hesmonds Stud Ltd **Trained** Newmarket, Suffolk

**FOCUS**
This Listed prize has been won in recent seasons by fillies like Chachamaidee, Laugh Out Loud and Nemoralia, all of whom went on to make their mark at the top level. They went an ordinary gallop and the field came over to race on the stands' side once in line for home. The time was just under five seconds outside standard. A below-standard renewal rated around the second and third.

## 2803 BETWAY YORKSHIRE CUP (GROUP 2) (BRITISH CHAMPIONS SERIES) 1m 5f 188y
**3:30** (3:31) (Class 1) 4-Y-O+
**£93,571** (£35,475; £17,754; £8,844; £4,438; £2,227) **Stalls** Low

Form RPR

322- **1** **Dartmouth**[215] 7405 5-9-1 118............................................... RyanMoore 3 114
(Sir Michael Stoute) *trckd ldrs: hdwy over 2f out: sn swtchd rt towards stands side: rdn over 1f out: styd on strly nr stands rail ins fnl f to ld nr fin* **11/4**[1]



The Form Book Flat, Raceform Ltd, Newbury, RG14 5SJ

013- **2** *nk* **Simple Verse (IRE)**[216] 7349 5-9-1 113............................ OisinMurphy 4 113
(Ralph Beckett) *trckd ldrs: hdwy on inner 3f out: cl up wl over 1f out: sn rdn: styd on to ld ins fnl f: sn drvn: hdd and no ex nr line* **13/2**

124/ **3** *nk* **High Jinx (IRE)**[747] 1934 9-9-1 102........................................ DavidAllan 2 112
(Tim Easterby) *sn led and clr: pushed along 3f out: rdn and hdd over 2f out: cl up: drvn and ev ch ins fnl f: no ex towards fin* **40/1**

022- **4** *hd* **Endless Time (IRE)**[208] 7569 5-8-12 114......................... WilliamBuick 6 109
(Charlie Appleby) *trckd ldrs: hdwy over 3f out: cl up 2f out: sn rdn: led jst over 1f out: sn drvn and hdd ins fnl f: kpt on* **5/1**[3]

32-1 **5** *¾* **Marmelo**[19] 2202 4-9-1 110................................................ AndreaAtzeni 1 111
(Hughie Morrison) *lw: trckd ldr: hdwy 3f out: led over 2f out and sn rdn: drvn and hdd over 1f out: kpt on same pce u.p fnl f* **5/1**[3]

050- **6** *1* **Clever Cookie**[252] 6284 9-9-1 109..............................(p) DanielTudhope 8 109
(Peter Niven) *hld up in rr: hdwy 3f out: rdn along over 2f out: kpt on fnl f* **10/1**

4-31 **7** *26* **Muntahaa (IRE)**[27] 1957 4-9-1 113...................................... JimCrowley 5 73
(John Gosden) *hld up towards rr: hdwy 4f out: rdn along 3f : sn drvn and wknd* **9/2**[2]

11-4 **8** *12* **Crimean Tatar (TUR)**[27] 1957 4-9-1 109........................... JackMitchell 7 56
(Hugo Palmer) *a rr: rdn along 3f out: sn outpcd* **9/1**

3m 1.9s (1.70) **Going Correction** +0.40s/f (Good) **8** Ran SP% **113.0**
Speed ratings (Par 115): **111,110,110,110,110 109,94,87**
CSF £20.56 TOTE £3.00: £1.40, £2.30, £6.40; EX 20.00 Trifecta £333.30.

**Owner** The Queen **Bred** Darley **Trained** Newmarket, Suffolk

■ Stewards' Enquiry : David Allan four-day ban: used whip above permitted level (Jun 5-8)

**FOCUS**
A strong Yorkshire Cup. There was a sound pace on and it threw up a thrilling finish with the runners spread across the track. It's been rated around the runner-up and fifth.

## 2804 BETWAY JORVIK H'CAP 1m 3f 188y
**4:05** (4:06) (Class 2) 4-Y-O+

**£31,125** (£9,320; £4,660; £2,330; £1,165; £585) **Stalls** Centre

Form RPR

020- **1** **Lord Yeats**[224] 7117 4-8-9 88........................................... PaulMulrennan 6 102
(Jedd O'Keeffe) *mde all: wd home turn and led field towards stands rail: rdn over 2f out: clr over 1f out: styd on strly* **12/1**

32-1 **2** *6* **Burguillos**[10] 2504 4-8-11 90 6ex.................................. RyanMoore 4 94
(Alan King) *trckd ldrs: hdwy 3f out: rdn wl over 1f out: sn chsng wnr: drvn and no imp fnl f* **3/1**[2]

21-1 **3** *nk* **Gibbs Hill (GER)**[20] 2165 4-9-1 94.................................... AndreaAtzeni 1 98
(Roger Varian) *lw: hld up in tch: hdwy 3f out: rdn along to chse ldng pair wl over 1f out: drvn and kpt on same pce fnl f* **15/8**[1]

15-0 **4** *1 ¼* **Southdown Lad (IRE)**[48] 1502 4-9-1 94.......................... OisinMurphy 5 96
(William Knight) *hld up in rr: hdwy over 3f out: rdn along over 2f out: styd on appr fnl f: nrst fin* **9/2**[3]

4-6 **5** *shd* **Cymro (IRE)**[38] 1704 5-9-7 100................................ RichardKingscote 3 102
(Tom Dascombe) *trckd ldng pair: hdwy to chse wnr 3f out: rdn along 2f out: sn drvn and kpt on one pce* **6/1**

10-0 **6** *8* **Soldier In Action (FR)**[34] 1802 4-9-10 103........................... FranBerry 7 92
(Mark Johnston) *chsd wnr: pushed along 4f out: sn rdn and wknd* **14/1**

3/03 **7** *2 ¼* **Ashkoul (FR)**[20] 2136 4-8-13 92.......................................... BenCurtis 9 77
(Michael Appleby) *trckd ldrs: hdwy to chse wnr over 3f out: rdn along over 2f out: sn drvn and btn* **16/1**

**8** *6* **Song Of Love (IRE)**[70] 1134 5-7-10 82............................. RPWalsh(7) 8 58
(Shaun Harris) *a towards rr* **50/1**

2m 33.46s (0.26) **Going Correction** +0.40s/f (Good) **8** Ran SP% **114.5**
Speed ratings (Par 109): **115,111,110,109,109 104,103,99**
CSF £48.14 CT £99.60 TOTE £13.70: £3.30, £1.40, £1.10; EX 58.20 Trifecta £181.60.

**Owner** Geoff & Sandra Turnbull **Bred** Geoff & Sandra Turnbull **Trained** Middleham Moor, N Yorks

**FOCUS**
Good handicap form, with a dominant display from Lord Yeats who brought the field over to the stands' side in the straight. The 2014 winner Arab Spring landed the Duke of Edinburgh Stakes at Royal Ascot next time. The second, third and fourth have been rated close to form.

## 2805 IRISH EBF FRANK WHITTLE PARTNERSHIP FILLIES' H'CAP 7f
**4:35** (4:36) (Class 3) (0-90,88) 4-Y-O+

**£12,450** (£3,728; £1,864; £932; £466; £234) **Stalls** Low

Form RPR

-351 **1** **Hells Babe**[20] 2138 4-8-11 81................................. AlistairRawlinson(3) 2 95
(Michael Appleby) *mde all: wd home turn and led field to stands rail: rdn wl over 1f out: drvn and kpt on wl fnl f* **4/1**[1]

5-62 **2** *2* **Florenza**[20] 2138 4-8-13 80................................................... JimCrowley 8 89
(Chris Fairhurst) *prom: rdn to chse wnr 2f out: drvn over 1f out: kpt on fnl f* **5/1**[2]

50-3 **3** *½* **Company Asset (IRE)**[20] 2138 4-8-9 76............................. KevinStott 6 84
(Kevin Ryan) *lw: hld up towards rr: hdwy over 2f out: rdn wl over 1f out: styd on fnl f: nrst fin* **8/1**

6140 **4** *3 ¼* **Bint Arcano (FR)**[23] 2081 4-9-0 81........................................ JoeDoyle 9 80
(Julie Camacho) *lw: in tch: hdwy to chse ldrs 3f out: rdn along over 2f out: drvn wl over 1f out: sn one pce* **9/1**

243- **5** *1* **Dark Intention (IRE)**[192] 7857 4-8-9 76 ow2............... PaulMulrennan 1 73
(Lawrence Mullaney) *chsd ldrs: rdn along wl over 2f out: drvn wl over 1f out: grad wknd* **11/2**[3]

-110 **6** *6* **Carolinae**[35] 1771 5-9-7 88.................................................. RyanMoore 4 69
(Charlie Fellowes) *towards rr: effrt 3f out: sn rdn along and nvr a factor* **5/1**[2]

-000 **7** *2 ½* **Nouvelli Dancer (IRE)**[43] 1586 4-8-10 77............................. DavidAllan 5 52
(David C Griffiths) *dwlt: a rr* **20/1**

3615 **8** *1 ¾* **Shypen**[35] 1771 4-9-0 88........................................... ConnorMurtagh(7) 10 58
(Richard Fahey) *sn chsng wnr: cl up 1/2-way: rdn wl over 2f out: sn wknd* **14/1**

500- **9** *26* **Lil Sophella (IRE)**[155] 8385 8-8-13 80............................ DanielTudhope 3
(Patrick Holmes) *hld up: hdwy on outer over 3f out: sn chsng ldrs: rdn along over 2f out: sn drvn and wknd* **7/1**

1m 28.06s (2.76) **Going Correction** +0.40s/f (Good) **9** Ran SP% **113.8**
Speed ratings (Par 104): **100,97,97,93,92 85,82,80,50**
CSF £23.41 CT £151.52 TOTE £4.80: £1.70, £1.90, £2.80; EX 28.10 Trifecta £164.30.

**Owner** Mrs Lucinda White **Bred** Mrs Lucinda White (mulbrooke Stud) **Trained** Oakham, Rutland

**FOCUS**
A fair fillies' handicap. They went an average pace with the stands' side again favoured off the home bend. Straightforward form.

## 2806 YORKSHIRE EQUINE PRACTICE H'CAP 5f
**5:05** (5:11) (Class 3) (0-90,89) 3-Y-O

**£12,450** (£3,728; £1,864; £932; £466; £234) **Stalls** Centre

Form RPR

0-66 **1** **Coolfitch (IRE)**[20] 2160 3-8-9 80...................................... JoshDoyle(3) 10 89
(David O'Meara) *swtg: hld up: hdwy to trck ldrs and n.m.r over 1f out: rdn to ld ins fnl f: kpt on strly* **16/1**

5-53 **2** *1 ½* **Megan Lily (IRE)**[7] 2570 3-9-1 86.............................. AdamMcNamara(3) 1 90
(Richard Fahey) *cl up: led over 2f out: rdn over 1f out: drvn and hdd ins fnl f: kpt on same pce* **14/1**

1212 **3** *½* **Major Jumbo**[37] 1732 3-9-2 89.................................. LewisEdmunds(5) 14 91
(Kevin Ryan) *chsd ldrs: rdn along 2f out: drvn over 1f out: kpt on fnl f* **7/1**

0-01 **4** *shd* **Twizzell**[18] 2223 3-8-11 79.......................................... RichardKingscote 8 81
(K R Burke) *cl up: rdn to dispute ld wl over 1f out: drvn and kpt on same pce fnl f* **12/1**

030- **5** *½* **Stoneyford Lane (IRE)**[228] 7004 3-8-8 76.................. RoystonFfrench 2 76
(Steph Hollinshead) *towards rr: rdn along and outpcd 1/2-way: hdwy over 1f out: kpt on wl towards fin* **20/1**

30-1 **6** *nk* **Savannah's Dream**[13] 2405 3-9-1 83............................... DanielTudhope 7 82
(David O'Meara) *lw: chsd ldrs: rdn along wl over 1f out: sn drvn and grad wknd* **9/1**

20-4 **7** *1 ¼* **Boundsy (IRE)**[17] 2271 3-8-4 75.................................. SammyJoBell(3) 3 69
(Richard Fahey) *lw: cl up: rdn along 2f out: sn drvn and wknd* **10/1**

01-2 **8** *5* **Computable**[27] 1975 3-8-13 81............................................. DavidAllan 11 57
(Tim Easterby) *swtg: t.k.h and towards rr: effrt 1/2-way: rdn along wl over 1f out: n.d* **8/1**

13-1 **9** *1* **Justanotherbottle (IRE)**[37] 1731 3-9-4 86........................ RyanMoore 12 59
(Declan Carroll) *lw: t.k.h: trckd ldrs: pushed along 1/2-way: sn rdn and wknd wl over 1f out* **9/2**[1]

1031 **10** *2 ½* **Jack Flash (FR)**[20] 2160 3-8-7 82.........................(h) ConnorMurtagh(7) 13 46
(Les Eyre) *led: rdn along 1/2-way: sn hdd & wknd over 1f out* **5/1**[2]

2-12 **11** *21* **Comprise**[24] 2072 3-8-2 75............................................... LuluStanford(5) 5
(Michael Bell) *s.i.s: a bhd* **13/2**[3]

260- **12** *nk* **Angel Meadow**[209] 7536 3-9-2 84...................................... JimCrowley 15
(Micky Hammond) *in tch: rdn along over 2f out: sn wknd* **16/1**

1m 1.36s (2.06) **Going Correction** +0.50s/f (Yiel) **12** Ran SP% **121.8**
Speed ratings (Par 103): **103,100,99,99,98 98,96,88,86,82 49,48**
CSF £228.13 CT £1747.97 TOTE £24.30: £6.40, £4.40, £2.60; EX 417.50 Trifecta £6950.40.

**Owner** W Hoffman Racing **Bred** P Kelly **Trained** Upper Helmsley, N Yorks

**FOCUS**
This race has thrown up several subsequent Group performers, including 2014 winner G Force who added the Haydock Sprint Cup later in the year. Those who raced away from the stands's rail appeared to be favoured. It's been rated slightly positively, with the fifth getting back towards the level of his 2yo form.

## 2807 7IM SUPPORTS CYSTIC FIBROSIS CARE STKS (H'CAP) 1m 3f 188y
**5:40** (5:41) (Class 4) (0-80,79) 3-Y-O

**£12,450** (£3,728; £1,864; £932; £466; £234) **Stalls** Centre

Form RPR

432- **1** **Alqamar**[207] 7580 3-9-4 76.............................................(p[1]) WilliamBuick 7 88
(Charlie Appleby) *trckd ldrs: hdwy and wd st: led 3f out and edgd rt to stands rail: rdn 2f out: drvn clr appr fnl f* **14/5**[1]

53-4 **2** *5* **Lester Kris (IRE)**[30] 1877 3-9-1 73................................ AndreaAtzeni 10 77
(Richard Hannon) *prom: rdn along 3f out: drvn to chse wnr wl over 1f out: kpt on same pce fnl f:* **16/1**

4-05 **3** *½* **Sue's Angel (IRE)**[23] 2078 3-8-0 65......................... ConnorMurtagh(7) 2 68
(Richard Fahey) *hld up in rr: hdwy wl over 2f out: rdn wl over 1f out: kpt on appr fnl f: nrst fin* **25/1**

65-2 **4** *1 ½* **Bedouin (IRE)**[37] 1737 3-9-3 75.................................(b) JamieSpencer 4 76
(Luca Cumani) *dwlt and rr: hdwy over 4f out: chsd ldrs wl over 2f out: sn rdn and kpt on same pce* **9/1**

501- **5** *2 ½* **Nordic Combined (IRE)**[258] 6130 3-8-10 68.......................... DavidAllan 1 65
(Brian Ellison) *towards rr: scrubbed along 5f out: rdn and hdwy on inner over 2f out: sn drvn and wknd over 1f out* **20/1**

00-1 **6** *¾* **Brimham Rocks**[17] 2273 3-8-11 69......................................... FranBerry 5 65
(Ralph Beckett) *in tch: hdwy to trck ldrs and wd st: cl up whn hmpd 3f out: sn chsng wnr and rdn 2f out: sn drvn and wknd* **10/3**[2]

24-0 **7** *3 ½* **Swiftsure (IRE)**[25] 2039 3-9-7 79........................................ RyanMoore 3 69
(Sir Michael Stoute) *hld up in rr: hdwy 3f out: rdn 2f out: n.d* **6/1**[3]

21-6 **8** *3 ¾* **Dominating (GER)**[13] 2394 3-8-9 67................................ OisinMurphy 6 51
(Mark Johnston) *chsd ldrs: rdn along over 3f out: drvn and wknd over 2f out* **16/1**

31 **9** *4 ½* **Investigation**[24] 2067 3-9-6 78............................................ RobHornby 9 55
(Andrew Balding) *t.k.h: racd wd and prom: rapid hdwy to ld after 2f and sn clr: pushed along 4f out: rdn and hdd 3f out: sn wknd* **10/1**

05-1 **10** *20* **Taxmeifyoucan (IRE)**[43] 1591 3-9-2 74.........................(p) JimCrowley 8 19+
(Keith Dalgleish) *hld up: smooth hdwy on outer 4f out: cl up whn bdly hmpd on stands rail 3f out: no ch after and eased* **10/1**

3-42 **11** *2 ¾* **Lord Commander**[17] 2266 3-9-2 77..................... AdamMcNamara(3) 11 17
(Richard Fahey) *led 2f: chsd ldr: rdn along over 3f out: sn drvn and wknd* **16/1**

2m 35.63s (2.43) **Going Correction** +0.40s/f (Good) **11** Ran SP% **118.1**
Speed ratings (Par 101): **107,103,103,102,100 100,97,95,92,79 77**
CSF £50.06 CT £945.86 TOTE £3.40: £1.60, £4.40, £4.50; EX 54.90 Trifecta £749.40.

**Owner** Godolphin **Bred** Darley **Trained** Newmarket, Suffolk

**FOCUS**
A decent 3yo handicap for the class. A small pb from the runner-up.

T/Jkpt: Not won. T/Plt: £106.10 to a £1 stake. Pool: £174,967.00 - 1,648.06 winning units
T/Qpdt: £21.10 to a £1 stake. Pool: £10,064.00 - 475.78 winning units **Joe Rowntree**

2808 - 2814a (Foreign Racing) - See Raceform Interactive

2381 # DONCASTER (L-H)

Saturday, May 20

**OFFICIAL GOING: Soft changing to heavy after race 2 (6.20)**

Wind: Moderate against Weather: Overcast with heavy showers

## 2815 CROWNHOTEL-BAWTRY.COM APPRENTICE H'CAP 1m 3f 197y

5:50 (5:50) (Class 5) (0-70,72) 4-Y-0+ £3,234 (£962; £481; £240) Stalls Low

Form RPR

5-41 1 **Monaco Rose**24 2079 4-9-2 69 SebastianWoods(7) 5 79
(Richard Fahey) *trckd ldrs: hdwy on inner over 2f out: led over 1f out: rdn and kpt on wl fnl f* 11/2[3]

224- 2 2 **Arrowtown**258 6163 5-9-5 70 (h) HarrisonShaw(5) 8 77+
(Michael Easterby) *trckd ldrs: hdwy on bit 3f out: cl up 2f out: shkn up over 1f out: sn rdn and kpt on fnl f* 11/4[1]

1-33 3 nk **Canny Style**25 2061 4-9-8 68 LewisEdmunds 4 74
(Kevin Ryan) *hld up: in tch: hdwy over 4f out: chsd ldrs 3f out: cl up 2f out: sn rdn and kpt on same pce fnl f* 11/2[3]

14-0 4 1 1/4 **Lopito De Vega (IRE)**23 2108 5-9-0 65 FinleyMarsh(5) 3 69
(David C Griffiths) *hld up in rr: stdy hdwy 4f out: rdn to chse ldrs wl over 1f out: kpt on u.p fnl f: nrst fin* 8/1

-041 5 2 1/4 **Albert Boy (IRE)**17 2295 4-8-12 58 PaddyPilley 6 59
(Scott Dixon) *trckd ldr: cl up 1/2-way: led wl over 3f out: jnd and rdn 2f out: drvn and hdd over 1f out: wknd fnl f* 10/1

/31- 6 8 **Our Kylie (IRE)**297 4489 5-8-12 61 BenRobinson(3) 7 49
(Brian Ellison) *rr: pushed along bef 1/2-way: rdn along over 4f out: nvr a factor* 7/2[2]

50-0 7 23 **Street Poet (IRE)**21 2163 4-9-7 72 SeamusCronin(5) 2 23
(Michael Herrington) *led: rdn along 4f out: sn hdd & wknd qckly* 25/1

1116 8 4 **Smiley Bagel (IRE)**31 1891 4-9-10 70 JennyPowell 10 15
(Ed Walker) *trckd ldrs: pushed along over 3f out: rdn wl over 2f out: drvn and wknd qckly wl over 1f out: sn bhd and heavily eased* 10/1

3600 9 11 **Thou Swell (IRE)**17 2312 5-8-5 56 oh1 (v) BenSanderson(5) 9
(Shaun Harris) *a towards rr: rdn along over 4f out: wknd 3f out: sn bhd* 25/1

2m 45.85s (10.95) **Going Correction** +0.75s/f (Yiel) 9 Ran SP% 116.6

Speed ratings (Par 103): **93,91,91,90,89 83,68,65,58**

CSF £21.24 CT £85.80 TOTE £6.20: £1.90, £1.50, £1.90; EX 27.30 Trifecta £85.80.

**Owner** Dr Marwan Koukash **Bred** Allan W J Perry **Trained** Musley Bank, N Yorks

**FOCUS**

Add 12yds to race distance. Soft ground for this seven-race card, with 41mm of rain having fallen on the track in the last seven days. This open looking apprentice riders' handicap was run at what looked an even gallop but the time was some 17secs slower than standard, suggesting conditions were every bit as testing as officially described.

## 2816 HOWCROFT INDUSTRIAL SUPPLIES LTD NOVICE AUCTION STKS 5f 3y

6:20 (6:20) (Class 5) 2-Y-O £3,234 (£962; £481; £240) Stalls High

Form RPR

1 **Holy Tiber (IRE)** 2-8-11 0 StevieDonohoe 10 73+
(George Scott) *hld up in tch: smooth hdwy over 2f out: rdn jst over 1f out: led ins fnl f: kpt on strly* 20/1

64 2 1/2 **Jedi Master (IRE)**21 2148 2-8-13 0 AdamMcNamara(3) 5 76
(Richard Fahey) *in tch: pushed along and outpcd 1/2-way: rdn 2f out: styd on appr fnl f: fin wl* 9/1

5 3 1 1/4 **Zabaletaswansong (GER)**7 2607 2-9-2 0 SeanLevey 7 72
(Richard Hannon) *prom: cl up and rdn along over 1f out: ev ch whn sltly hmpd ins fnl f: kpt on* 13/2[3]

4 nk **Alaska (IRE)** 2-8-9 0 MitchGodwin(5) 9 68
(Sylvester Kirk) *chsd ldrs: hdwy 2f out: rdn to ld over 1f out: edgd lft and hdd ins fnl f: kpt on wl* 9/1

5 1/2 **Mabo** 2-9-2 0 KevinStott 8 69
(Richard Fahey) *dwlt and rr: green: pushed along and outpcd 1/2-way: hdwy wl over 1f out: rdn and edgd rt appr fnl f: kpt on wl* 8/1

4 6 3/4 **Our Man In Havana**39 1694 2-9-0 0 JimCrowley 4 64
(Tom Dascombe) *trckd ldrs: pushed along wl over 1f out: sn rdn and kpt on same pce* 9/4[1]

002 7 3/4 **Bahuta Acha**8 2590 2-8-12 0 PJMcDonald 2 59
(David Loughnane) *racd towards far side: chsd ldrs: hdwy to chse ldr 2f out: rdn wl over 1f out: grad wknd* 15/2

3 8 1/2 **Flo's Melody**30 1909 2-8-11 0 TonyHamilton 6 56
(Richard Fahey) *a towards rr* 9/2[2]

0 9 9 **Kyleque (IRE)**21 2154 2-8-12 0 GrahamLee 3 25
(Paul Midgley) *led: rdn along and edgd lft towards far rail 2f out: hdd over 1f out: wknd qckly* 25/1

10 2 **El Bertie (IRE)** 2-8-12 0 AndrewMullen 1 18+
(Tim Easterby) *dwlt and wnt lft s: green and a bhd* 25/1

1m 3.5s (3.00) **Going Correction** +0.75s/f (Yiel) 10 Ran SP% 117.6

Speed ratings (Par 93): **106,105,103,102,101 100,99,98,84,81**

CSF £186.02 TOTE £30.50: £5.80, £2.60, £2.20; EX 377.20 Trifecta £2261.60.

**Owner** Matt Bartram **Bred** Quiet Waters Syndicate **Trained** Newmarket, Suffolk

**FOCUS**

Despite the stalls being on the stands' side, they came down the middle and were fanned right across the track in the final furlong. Those with previous experience didn't set a particularly high standard but a few of these look interesting going forward. The level is a bit fluid.

## 2817 EBF BREEDERS' SERIES CHASE MEDICAL FILLIES' H'CAP (TBA BONUS RACE) 1m 2f 43y

6:50 (6:51) (Class 3) (0-95,92) 3-Y-0+ £12,938 (£3,850; £1,924; £962) Stalls Low

Form RPR

641- 1 **Indulged**190 7901 4-9-1 84 GeorgeWood(5) 1 94
(James Fanshawe) *t.k.h: prom: hdwy 3f out: led wl over 1f out: rdn and hung bdly rt to stands rail jst over 1f out: drvn out* 10/3[2]

311- 2 1 1/4 **High Hopes**251 6378 4-9-8 86 JimCrowley 7 93
(David Simcock) *hld up in rr: hdwy wl over 3f out: rdn to chse ldrs wl over 1f out: chsd wnr and drvn ins fnl f: no imp towards fin* 15/8[1]

414- 3 2 1/4 **Berengaria (IRE)**273 5632 3-8-6 84 PJMcDonald 3 86
(Mark Johnston) *set stdy pce: pushed along and qcknd 3f out: rdn over 2f out: hdd wl over 1f pout: sn drvn and kpt on same pce fnl f* 7/1

1-00 4 3 3/4 **Ce La Vie**13 2434 3-8-9 87 JoeFanning 5 81
(Keith Dalgleish) *t.k.h: trckd ldrs: hdwy 4f out: cl up over 2f out: sn rdn: drvn over 1f out: sn one pce* 15/2

-005 5 5 **Imshivalla (IRE)**8 2593 6-9-5 83 TonyHamilton 2 68
(Richard Fahey) *plld hrd: hld up in tch: effrt over 3f out: rdn along over 2f out: sn btn* 13/2[3]

1-31 6 19 **Vogueatti (USA)**92 781 4-9-1 79 GrahamLee 4 26
(Marco Botti) *prom: trckd ldr after 3f: cl up 4f out: rdn along 3f out: sn drvn and wknd* 10/1

100/ 7 14 **Lahayeb**534 8093 5-10-0 92 (h[1]) SilvestreDeSousa 6 11
(Michael Appleby) *hld up: a rr* 16/1

2m 19.34s (9.94) **Going Correction** +0.75s/f (Yiel)

**WFA** 3 from 4yo+ 14lb 7 Ran SP% 110.4

Speed ratings (Par 104): **90,89,87,84,80 65,53**

CSF £9.28 TOTE £4.10: £2.10, £1.70; EX 11.20 Trifecta £43.70.

**Owner** Cheveley Park Stud **Bred** Cheveley Park Stud Ltd **Trained** Newmarket, Suffolk

**FOCUS**

Add 12yds to race distance. The going was changed to heavy before this race. Not a particularly deep 0-95 fillies' handicap with only one horse rated above 87 and the early gallop looked very steady, but several of these have the potential to do better this year.

## 2818 SUNBETS.CO.UK H'CAP 7f 213y(R)

7:20 (7:22) (Class 3) (0-95,93) 3-Y-O £7,762 (£2,310; £1,154; £577) Stalls Low

Form RPR

41-4 1 **Me Too Nagasaki (IRE)**44 1582 3-8-8 80 JFEgan 7 89
(Jeremy Noseda) *trckd ldrs: hdwy on outer over 3f out: chsd ldng pair 2f out: rdn to chal ent fnl f: ev ch whn hung rt wl ins fnl f: drvn and rallied to ld nr line* 5/1

1-45 2 hd **Wahash (IRE)**13 2437 3-9-3 89 SeanLevey 1 97
(Richard Hannon) *led: qcknd wl over 2f out and sn pushed along: rdn over 1f out: drvn ins fnl f: hdd nr fin* 9/2[3]

-553 3 3 **High Acclaim (USA)**14 2402 3-9-1 87 (p[1]) SilvestreDeSousa 5 88
(Roger Teal) *trckd ldr: hdwy and cl up 3f out: chal over 2f out: rdn and ev ch whn n.m.r ent fnl f: sn drvn and kpt on same pce* 11/4[2]

41-0 4 11 **Ahlan Bil Zain (FR)**24 2084 3-8-11 83 JimCrowley 4 59
(David Simcock) *hld up in tch: hdwy over 3f out: rdn along to chse ldrs 2f out: sn drvn and btn over 1f out* 5/1

61- 5 1 1/2 **Mandarin (GER)**232 6924 3-9-0 86 DanielMuscutt 3 58
(Marco Botti) *trckd ldng pair: pushed along wl over 2f out: sn rdn and wknd wl over 1f out* 2/1[1]

1m 44.56s (4.86) **Going Correction** +0.75s/f (Yiel) 5 Ran SP% 111.5

Speed ratings (Par 103): **105,104,101,90,89**

CSF £26.52 TOTE £6.00: £2.50, £2.40; EX 23.50 Trifecta £68.20.

**Owner** C Fox, B Wilson & R Levitt **Bred** Kevin Walsh **Trained** Newmarket, Suffolk

■ Stewards' Enquiry : Sean Levey 2 day ban - used whip above the permitted level (5/6 June)

**FOCUS**

This was weakened by the withdrawal of two of the most interesting runners but it produced a cracking finish and the winner might be value for more than the wining margin given he still looks quite green.

## 2819 SUN BETS DOWNLOAD THE APP MAIDEN STKS 6f 2y

7:50 (7:51) (Class 5) 3-Y-O+ £3,234 (£962; £481; £240) Stalls High

Form RPR

1 **Alaadel** 4-9-12 0 JimCrowley 6 84+
(William Haggas) *hld up in rr: smooth hdwy wl over 2f out: chal over 1f out: rdn to take slt ld appr fnl f: green and wandered ins last 100 yds: kpt on* 11/10[1]

2 nk **Ptarmigan Ridge** 3-9-3 0 DanielMuscutt 1 75+
(James Fanshawe) *dwlt and hld up in rr: hdwy wl over 2f out: cl up whn green: rdn and outpcd over 1f out: r.o ins fnl f: fin strly* 5/1[3]

3 3 3/4 **Dirchill (IRE)**14 2383 3-9-3 0 AndrewMullen 8 73
(David Barron) *chsd ldng pair: tk clsr order over 2f out: rdn to ld over 1f out: green: sn jnd and hdd appr fnl f: kpt on wl towards fin* 9/4[2]

0-5 4 6 **Shelneverwalkalone**14 2383 3-8-12 0 TomEaves 3 50
(Ivan Furtado) *led and sn clr: pushed along over 2f out: rdn wl over 1f out: sn hdd and drvn: grad wknd* 18/1

40 5 3 3/4 **Kensington Palace (IRE)**21 2135 4-9-12 0 JamesSullivan 2 46
(Marjorie Fife) *towards rr: rdn along wl over 2f out: sn outpcd and bhd* 20/1

- 6 nk **Fille The Force** 3-8-12 0 DavidAllan 7 38
(Scott Dixon) *chsd ldr: rdn along over 2f out: drvn wl over 1f out: sn wknd* 12/1

1m 16.83s (3.23) **Going Correction** +0.75s/f (Yiel)

**WFA** 3 from 4yo 9lb 6 Ran SP% 112.8

Speed ratings (Par 103): **108,107,106,98,93 93**

CSF £7.28 TOTE £2.10: £1.30, £2.60; EX 7.20 Trifecta £11.30.

**Owner** Hamdan Al Maktoum **Bred** Cheveley Park Stud Ltd **Trained** Newmarket, Suffolk

**FOCUS**

Not a deep maiden by any stretch but the winner could be smart - he's certainly bred to be, and the two in behind him shouldn't be long in winning races.

## 2820 SUNBETS.CO.UK BET £5 & GET £10 H'CAP 7f 6y

8:20 (8:23) (Class 4) (0-85,84) 3-Y-O £5,175 (£1,540; £769; £384) Stalls High

Form RPR

41-0 1 **Mjjack (IRE)**39 1702 3-8-10 78 CliffordLee(5) 5 85
(K R Burke) *trckd ldrs: pushed along on outer 2f out: rdn over 1f out: styd on ent fnl f: sn edgd rt: led last 100 yds* 9/2[2]

10- 2 hd **Musawaat**210 7544 3-9-7 84 JimCrowley 12 90
(Charles Hills) *prom: cl up 1/2-way: slt ld wl over 1f out and sn rdn: drvn ent fnl f: hdd last 100 yds: kpt on* 9/2[2]

421- 3 1 1/4 **Shenanigans (IRE)**172 8139 3-9-4 81 SilvestreDeSousa 11 84
(Roger Varian) *trckd ldrs: hdwy over 2f out: rdn to chse ldr over 1f out: ev ch ent fnl f: sn drvn and kpt on same pce* 3/1[1]

445- 4 1 **Hernandes (FR)**234 6881 3-8-6 74 JennyPowell(5) 13 74+
(Ed Walker) *hld up: hdwy over 2f out: rdn to chse ldrs over 1f out: drvn ent fnl f: kpt on same pce* 14/1

005- 5 2 1/2 **Lady In Question (IRE)**231 6954 3-8-13 76 TonyHamilton 9 70
(Richard Fahey) *.hld up in rr: hdwy 3f out: chsd ldrs and rdn wl over 1f out: drvn whn n.m.r and hld ent fnl f: one pce* 6/1[3]

2540 6 1 1/2 **Party Tiger**55 1386 3-8-10 73 KevinStott 4 63
(Richard Fahey) *set stdy pce: qcknd over 2f out: rdn and hdd wl over 1f out: sn drvn and wknd* 14/1

21-0 7 3/4 **Trooper's Gold**17 2304 3-9-0 77 TomEaves 8 65
(Kevin Ryan) *t.k.h: hld up in rr: hdwy 1/2-way: rdn to chse ldrs over 2f out: sn drvn and wknd* 10/1

160- 8 2 3/4 **Haworth**225 7120 3-8-9 72 PJMcDonald 1 53
(James Bethell) *in tch: rdn along 3f out: wknd over 2f out* 10/1

31-0 9 11 **Chipping (IRE)**39 1702 3-8-12 75 PaulMulrennan 6 27
(Michael Dods) *t.k.h: prom: rdn along over 2f out: sn wknd* 17/2

1m 30.92s (4.62) **Going Correction** +0.75s/f (Yiel) 9 Ran SP% 117.7

Speed ratings (Par 101): **103,102,101,100,97 95,94,91,79**

CSF £25.63 CT £71.03 TOTE £5.70: £2.10, £1.60, £1.50; EX 31.70 Trifecta £135.30.

**Owner** Mrs M Gittins **Bred** Derrymore House Syndicate **Trained** Middleham Moor, N Yorks

**FOCUS**
Not a bad 3yo handicap and no surprise if a few of the beaten horses prove better than their current marks. The winner had a recent run under his belt, unlike the next four home and that may have been a crucial factor. The early gallop looked fairly steady.

## 2821 BET & WATCH AT SUNBETS.CO.UK H'CAP 6f 2y
**8:50** (8:53) (Class 4) (0-80,81) 4-Y-O+ **£5,175** (£1,540; £769; £384) **Stalls** High

Form RPR

0-00 **1** **Khelman (IRE)**$^{13}$ 2428 7-9-3 **79**........................ AdamMcNamara$^{(3)}$ 12 88
(Richard Fahey) *hld up towards rr: hdwy 1/2-way: swtchd rt to stands' rail 2f out: rdn to chse ldrs over 1f out: squeezed through on rail to ld ins fnl f: styd on* **12/1**

-023 **2** ½ **Johnny Cavagin**$^{8}$ 2592 8-9-7 **80**........................(t) AndrewMullen 1 87
(Ronald Thompson) *dwlt and in rr: stdy hdwy wl over 2f out: chsd ldrs on wd outside over 1f out: rdn and edgd rt ins fnl f: kpt on* **$7/1^{3}$**

454- **3** 1¼ **Dandyleekie (IRE)**$^{207}$ 7590 5-9-6 **79**........................ DanielTudhope 14 82
(David O'Meara) *trckd ldrs nr stands' rail: hdwy over 2f out: chsd ldr over 1f out: swtchd lft and rdn to chal ent fnl f: sn drvn and kpt on same pce* **$7/2^{1}$**

500- **4** 1¼ **Signore Piccolo**$^{217}$ 7360 6-9-4 **77**........................(h) SamJames 3 77
(David Loughnane) *racd towards centre: trckd ldrs: hdwy wl over 1f out: cl up and rdn ent fnl f: sn drvn and kpt on same pce* **14/1**

1315 **5** ½ **Dream Farr (IRE)**$^{50}$ 1467 4-9-3 **76**........................(t) ThomasBrown 13 74
(Ed Walker) *racd towards stands' rail: trckd ldrs: hdwy 2f out: rdn over 1f out: drvn and kpt on same pce fnl f* **12/1**

22-4 **6** hd **Manshood (IRE)**$^{35}$ 1804 4-8-13 **72**........................(b) MartinLane 16 69
(Paul Midgley) *racd in rr on stands' rail: led: rdn wl over 1f out: drvn and hdd ins fnl f: grad wknd* **14/1**

0-34 **7** 6 **Appleberry (IRE)**$^{5}$ 2683 5-9-6 **79**........................(h) SilvestreDeSousa 9 58
(Michael Appleby) *in tch: pushed along wl over 2f out: sn rdn and wknd wl over 1f out* **$9/2^{2}$**

3-00 **8** 2 **He's My Cracker**$^{43}$ 1606 4-9-5 **78**........................ SamHitchcott 5 51
(Clive Cox) *in tch: rdn along 1/2-way: wknd over 2f out* **14/1**

0-64 **9** 1¾ **Money Team (IRE)**$^{36}$ 1777 6-9-5 **78**........................ PhillipMakin 4 46
(David Barron) *a towards rr* **$7/1^{3}$**

3-03 **10** hd **Racquet**$^{17}$ 2303 4-8-12 **71**........................ JamesSullivan 2 39
(Ruth Carr) *chsd ldrs on wd outside: rdn along wl over 2f out: sn wknd* **20/1**

00-0 **11** 3¼ **Etienne Gerard**$^{28}$ 1972 5-8-6 **72**........................ FayeMcManoman$^{(7)}$ 11 30
(Nigel Tinkler) *prom towards centre: rdn along over 2f out: sn wknd* **40/1**

/06- **12** ¾ **Star Citizen**$^{317}$ 4032 5-9-6 **79**........................ GrahamLee 10 35
(Fred Watson) *a in rr* **40/1**

0-30 **13** 2 **Van Gerwen**$^{36}$ 1777 4-9-8 **81**........................(h) PJMcDonald 6 31
(Les Eyre) *prom towards centre: rdn along 2f out: sn drvn and wknd over 1f out* **20/1**

1-0 **14** 9 **Oh James**$^{20}$ 2184 4-9-0 **73**........................($h^{1}$) DavidAllan 15
(Tim Easterby) *rrd s: a bhd* **20/1**

1m 17.37s (3.77) **Going Correction** +0.75s/f (Yiel) **14** Ran SP% **120.0**
Speed ratings (Par 105): **104,103,101,100,99 99,91,88,86,85 81,80,77,65**
CSF £86.80 CT £370.41 TOTE £14.90: £4.20, £2.30, £1.60; EX 128.50 Trifecta £475.90.
**Owner** S & G Clayton **Bred** Oghill House Stud & Jimmy Hyland **Trained** Musley Bank, N Yorks

**FOCUS**
A wide-open handicap run at what looked a decent gallop set by Manshood.
T/Plt: £170.80 to a £1 stake. Pool: £84,539.17 - 361.32 winning units T/Qpdt: £16.60 to a £1 stake. Pool: £7,876.79 - 350.22 winning units **Joe Rowntree**

# 2778 NEWBURY (L-H)
Saturday, May 20

**OFFICIAL GOING: Soft (good to soft in places; 5.1)**
Wind: mild breeze half against Weather: showers

## 2822 AL RAYYAN STKS (REGISTERED AS THE ASTON PARK STAKES) (GROUP 3) 1m 4f
**1:50** (1:50) (Class 1) 4-Y-O+
**£56,710** (£21,500; £10,760; £5,360; £2,690; £1,350) **Stalls** Low

Form RPR

03-5 **1** **Hawkbill (USA)**$^{19}$ 2249 4-9-0 117........................(p) WilliamBuick 6 119
(Charlie Appleby) *sweating: mde all: racd clst to far rails home st: clr 3f out: in command fnl 2f: rdn out* **$3/1^{1}$**

54-3 **2** 2 **My Dream Boat (IRE)**$^{22}$ 2127 5-9-0 117........................ AdamKirby 4 116
(Clive Cox) *swtg: hld up 6th: rdn over 3f out: no imp tl hdwy over 1f out: chsd wnr ent fnl f: drifted lft: kpt on but a being hld* **$4/1^{3}$**

20-5 **3** 2 **Midterm**$^{28}$ 1957 4-9-0 115........................($v^{1}$) RyanMoore 2 113
(Sir Michael Stoute) *trckd ldrs: rdn 3f out: sn chsng wnr: nt pce to get on terms: no ex fnl f* **$7/2^{2}$**

11-0 **4** ½ **To Be Wild (IRE)**$^{36}$ 1779 4-9-0 104........................ JosephineGordon 5 112
(Hugo Palmer) *pressed wnr for 5f: trckd wnr: rdn 3f out: kpt on but nt pce to chal fnl 2f* **16/1**

013- **5** 8 **Across The Stars (IRE)**$^{276}$ 5557 4-9-0 113........................ FrankieDettori 3 99
(Sir Michael Stoute) *t.k.h: trckd ldrs: rdn over 2f out: nvr threatened wnr: wknd fnl f* **6/1**

2-12 **6** 19 **Chemical Charge (IRE)**$^{28}$ 1957 5-9-0 111........................($v^{1}$) OisinMurphy 1 69
(Ralph Beckett) *swtg: hld up 5th: rdn 3f out: nvr threatened: wknd 2f out: eased whn btn* **$7/2^{2}$**

2m 42.75s (7.25) **Going Correction** +0.90s/f (Soft) **6** Ran SP% **109.6**
Speed ratings (Par 113): **111,109,108,108,102 90**
CSF £14.42 TOTE £3.30: £1.80, £2.10; EX 13.90 Trifecta £28.00.
**Owner** Godolphin **Bred** Helen K Groves Revokable Trust **Trained** Newmarket, Suffolk
■ Stewards' Enquiry : Adam Kirby two-day ban: used whip above permitted level (Jun 5-6)

**FOCUS**
Some starts have been moved at this track following remeasuring, so some races will not have speed figures until there is sufficient data to calculate updated median times. Senior riders in the first agreed that the ground was riding soft. The rail on the 7f and 5f bends had been moved out 9yds off the inside rail to provide fresh ground, and the opener was run over an additional 28yds. It was only the second running of this event since it was promoted from Listed status, and was a hot Group 3 on paper. There are doubts over the form, however, given the winner had the run of the race, but the first two were the top candidates on pre-race figures. The time was almost 14sec slower than standard. The winner has been rated back to something like his Eclipse form.

## 2823 SHALAA CARNARVON STKS (LISTED RACE) 6f
**2:20** (2:23) (Class 1) 3-Y-O
**£39,697** (£15,050; £7,532; £3,752; £1,883; £945) **Stalls** Centre

Form RPR

312 **1** **Visionary (IRE)**$^{36}$ 1774 3-9-0 101........................ JamieSpencer 4 95
(Robert Cowell) *lw: racd center: hld up: pushed along 3f out: hdwy 2f out: drvn to ld ent fnl f: hld on* **$4/1^{2}$**

201- **2** hd **Simmie (IRE)**$^{186}$ 7972 3-8-12 99........................ RichardKingscote 5 92
(K R Burke) *racd center: hld up: hdwy 2f out: sn rdn and drifted to stands' side: kpt on wl ins fnl f: wnt 2nd fnl 120yds: jst hld* **7/1**

**3** 1½ **Florida Times (IRE)**$^{33}$ 1844 3-8-9 0........................ AndreaAtzeni 1 85
(David O'Meara) *racd center: trckd ldr: rdn and ev ch ent fnl f tl no ex fnl 120yds* **11/1**

-140 **4** ½ **Just An Idea (IRE)**$^{22}$ 2130 3-9-0 79........................ JosephineGordon 2 88
(Harry Dunlop) *racd center: led: rdn over 1f out: hdd ent fnl f: no ex fnl 120yds* **40/1**

234- **5** 1 **Perfect Angel (IRE)**$^{204}$ 7667 3-8-9 100........................ OisinMurphy 3 80
(Andrew Balding) *racd center: trckd ldr: chal 2f out: sn rdn: ev ch ent fnl f: no ex fnl 120yds* **$5/2^{1}$**

416- **6** 5 **Barrington (IRE)**$^{317}$ 4060 3-9-0 99........................($t^{1}$) FrankieDettori 6 69
(Charles Hills) *racd keenly on stands' side: sn prom: rdn over 1f out: wknd ent fnl f* **15/2**

250- **7** 4½ **Koropick (IRE)**$^{218}$ 7347 3-9-0 105........................ WilliamBuick 8 54
(Hugo Palmer) *racd stands' side: hld up: effrt over 2f out: wknd over 1f out* **8/1**

01-4 **8** 11 **Private Matter**$^{31}$ 1881 3-9-3 106........................ RyanMoore 7 22
(Richard Fahey) *lw: stmbld leaving stalls: racd stands' side: trckd ldr: effrt over 2f out: sn btn* **$9/2^{3}$**

1m 16.27s (3.27) **8** Ran SP% **112.9**
CSF £31.02 TOTE £4.70: £1.50, £2.10, £3.10; EX 32.40 Trifecta £200.50.
**Owner** Khalifa Dasmal **Bred** K A Dasmal **Trained** Six Mile Bottom, Cambs

**FOCUS**
There were two groups early and the five who raced towards the middle filled the first five places, while those who filled the last three places raced more towards the stands' side. The bare form looks ordinary for the grade. The form has been rated a bit cautiously, but could be rated 6lb higher.

## 2824 AL ZUBARAH LONDON GOLD CUP H'CAP 1m 2f
**2:55** (2:57) (Class 2) 3-Y-O
**£43,575** (£13,048; £6,524; £3,262; £1,631; £819) **Stalls** Low

Form RPR

120- **1** **Defoe (IRE)**$^{224}$ 7151 3-9-0 **88**........................ AndreaAtzeni 1 104
(Roger Varian) *trckd ldrs: rdn over 2f out: chal ent fnl f: led fnl 120yds: styd on wl: rdn out* **8/1**

41-2 **2** 1¼ **Fearless Fire (IRE)**$^{22}$ 2126 3-8-11 **85**........................ OisinMurphy 7 99
(Andrew Balding) *lw: racd keenly: led: chal over 2f out: rdn over 1f out: drifted lft: hdd fnl 120yds: styd on but no ex* **$7/2^{1}$**

121- **3** 3¼ **Time To Study (FR)**$^{184}$ 7982 3-9-0 **88**........................ FrannyNorton 12 95+
(Mark Johnston) *lw: in tch: hdwy hld up towards rr: hdwy 4f out: nt clr run over 3f out: rdn over 2f out: wnt 3rd ins fnl f: styd on* **9/1**

31-3 **4** 1 **Century Dream (IRE)**$^{22}$ 2132 3-8-13 **87**........................(t) HarryBentley 11 92
(Simon Crisford) *in tch: hdwy over 3f out: rdn to chal 2f out: sn hld: styd on same pce* **$6/1^{2}$**

001 **5** 1¼ **Duke Of Bronte**$^{28}$ 1962 3-8-9 **83**........................ RyanTate 5 86
(Rod Millman) *w'like: mid-div: hdwy fr 4f out: rdn wl over 2f out: styd on same pce* **16/1**

11-5 **6** 12 **Count Calabash (IRE)**$^{31}$ 1886 3-9-1 **89**........................ AdamKirby 9 68
(Paul Cole) *mid-divison: clipped rails on bnd 7f out: hdwy over 4f out: rdn over 2f out: nvr threatened: wknd over 1f out* **14/1**

44-6 **7** 9 **Contrast (IRE)**$^{22}$ 2126 3-9-5 **93**........................ RyanMoore 10 54
(Richard Hannon) *slowly away: sn drvn in last: nvr any threat* **14/1**

214 **8** hd **Bush House (IRE)**$^{48}$ 1518 3-8-7 **81**........................(b) JosephineGordon 8 41
(Hugo Palmer) *w'like: trckd ldrs: effrt over 3f out: wknd over 2f out* **14/1**

56-4 **9** nk **Zymyran**$^{18}$ 2284 3-8-9 **83**........................ TomMarquand 14 43
(David Simcock) *s.i.s: a towards rr* **50/1**

2-65 **10** 9 **Al Hamdany (IRE)**$^{8}$ 2569 3-9-7 **95**........................($p^{1}$) FrankieDettori 6 37
(Marco Botti) *swtg: mid-div: hdwy over 6f out: rdn to chse ldrs over 3f out: wknd over 2f out* **16/1**

-412 **11** 7 **I'vegotthepower (IRE)**$^{10}$ 2513 3-8-3 **77**........................(v) KierenFox 3 5
(Brian Meehan) *trckd ldr: rdn 4f out: wknd 3f out* **33/1**

41-2 **12** 2 **Glorious Forever**$^{22}$ 2118 3-8-11 **85**........................ JamieSpencer 13 9
(Ed Walker) *str: stdd s: towards rr: sme prog over 3f out: sn rdn: wknd over 2f out* **$13/2^{3}$**

12-5 **13** 10 **Andok (IRE)**$^{14}$ 2402 3-8-13 **87**........................ PaulHanagan 4
(Richard Fahey) *trckd ldrs early: in tch whn hmpd on bnd 7f out: mid-div: rdn over 3f out: sn wknd* **8/1**

2m 14.57s (5.77) **Going Correction** +0.90s/f (Soft) **13** Ran SP% **118.7**
Speed ratings (Par 105): **112,111,108,107,106 97,89,89,89,82 76,75,67**
CSF £35.73 CT £263.77 TOTE £9.60: £3.30, £1.70, £2.90; EX 40.80 Trifecta £519.20.
**Owner** Sheikh Mohammed Obaid Al Maktoum **Bred** Darley **Trained** Newmarket, Suffolk
■ Stewards' Enquiry : Andrea Atzeni two-day ban: used whip in an incorrect place (Jun 5-6)

**FOCUS**
Race run over an additional 28yds. This is usually a red-hot handicap, with Green Moon (later won a Melbourne Cup) beating Monterosso (Dubai World Cup) in 2010 and subsequent Group scorers Al Kazeem, Cannock Chase and Time Test winning it since. They finished strung out behind the first five, who finished well clear, with the first two ending up on the far rail. It's been rated as a strong race, and the winner, third and fourth could back it being rated a bit better still.

## 2825 AL SHAQAB LOCKINGE STKS (GROUP 1) (BRITISH CHAMPIONS SERIES) 1m (S)

**3:30** (3:38) (Class 1) 4-Y-0+

**£198,485** (£75,250; £37,660; £18,760; £9,415; £4,725) **Stalls** Centre

Form RPR

12-3 **1** **Ribchester (IRE)**[56] 1378 4-9-0 122 ........ WilliamBuick 5 126
(Richard Fahey) *lw: mde all: drifted rt over 1f out to fin racing on stands' rail fnl f: kpt on strly: rdn out* **7/4**[1]

013- **2** *3 ¾* **Lightning Spear**[217] 7352 6-9-0 120 ........ OisinMurphy 4 117
(David Simcock) *lw: trckd ldrs: rdn to chse wnr over 2f out: nt quite pce to chal but kpt on wl* **9/2**[3]

510- **3** *2 ½* **Breton Rock (IRE)**[217] 7352 7-9-0 112 ........ AndreaAtzeni 9 112
(David Simcock) *hld up: rdn and hdwy wl over 1f out: kpt on into 3rd fnl f but no threat to ldrs* **25/1**

1-21 **4** *¾* **Somehow (IRE)**[13] 2432 4-8-11 114 ........(v) RyanMoore 1 107
(A P O'Brien, Ire) *trckd ldrs: rdn over 2f out: styd on into 4th fnl f but nvr gng pce to threaten* **10/3**[2]

205- **5** *3* **Galileo Gold**[217] 7352 4-9-0 121 ........ FrankieDettori 7 103
(Hugo Palmer) *lw: racd keenly: racd alone nrest stands' side: prom: rdn over 2f out: sn hung lft and hld: wknd ins fnl f* **9/2**[3]

111- **6** *3* **Aclaim (IRE)**[225] 7115 4-9-0 114 ........(t) JamieSpencer 2 96
(Martyn Meade) *hld up: effrt over 2f out: nvr threatened: wknd jst over 1f out* **9/1**

05-5 **7** *¾* **Mitchum Swagger**[22] 2129 5-9-0 110 ........ TomQueally 3 94
(David Lanigan) *lw: trckd ldrs: rdn over 2f out: wknd over 1f out* **25/1**

0-45 **8** *4 ½* **Toscanini (IRE)**[19] 2248 5-9-0 112 ........ PaulHanagan 8 84
(Richard Fahey) *s.i.s: a last* **50/1**

1m 43.0s (3.30) **Going Correction** +0.90s/f (Soft) **8** Ran SP% **115.5**
Speed ratings (Par 117): **119,115,112,112,109 106,105,100**
CSF £9.92 CT £143.87 TOTE £2.40: £1.20, £1.80, £4.60; EX 12.60 Trifecta £123.90.

**Owner** Godolphin **Bred** A Thompson & M O'Brien **Trained** Musley Bank, N Yorks

**FOCUS**
This didn't unfold as expected from a tactical point of view, with the apparent intended pacemaker Toscanini missing the break, but it was clear William Buick intended to be positive anyway on the winner, who put up a high-class performance from the front. A slightly improved effort from the winner.

## 2826 OLYMPIC GLORY CONDITIONS STKS (PLUS 10 RACE) 6f

**4:05** (4:08) (Class 2) 2-Y-0 **£32,345** (£9,625; £4,810; £2,405) **Stalls** Centre

Form RPR

1 **1** **Denaar (IRE)**[12] 2459 2-9-5 0 ........ FrankieDettori 4 93+
(Richard Hannon) *leggy: athletic: a.p: led 2f out: sn strly chal and rdn: kpt on wl to assert fnl 100yds* **2/1**[1]

311 **2** *¾* **Starlight Mystery (IRE)**[8] 2590 2-9-0 0 ........ FrannyNorton 8 85
(Mark Johnston) *trckd ldrs: rdn 2f out: running on whn swtchd lft ent fnl f: kpt on but a being hld clsng stages* **20/1**

1 **3** *1 ½* **Koditime (IRE)**[21] 2134 2-9-5 0 ........ AdamKirby 6 85+
(Clive Cox) *cmpt: travelled wl trcking ldrs: str chal 2f out: rdn ent fnl f: nt qckn: no ex fnl 120yds* **13/5**[3]

**4** *½* **Rogue** 2-9-2 0 ........ TomMarquand 2 81+
(Richard Hannon) *str: hmpd s: trckd ldrs: rdn and ev ch wl over 2f out: sn hld: kpt on same pce fnl f* **16/1**

2 **5** *½* **Kit Marlowe**[13] 2435 2-9-5 0 ........ WilliamBuick 3 82
(Mark Johnston) *stmbld and wnt lft leaving stalls: prom: rdn and ev ch whn hung lft over 2f out: kpt on same pce* **5/2**[2]

243 **6** *26* **The Love Doctor (IRE)**[12] 2473 2-9-5 0 ........ JamieSpencer 1 19+
(David Evans) *led: rdn and hdd whn carried sltly lft 2f out: sn wknd: eased fnl f* **8/1**

1m 17.86s (4.86) **6** Ran SP% **111.4**
CSF £37.79 TOTE £2.40: £1.50, £3.70; EX 19.90 Trifecta £51.20.

**Owner** Al Shaqab Racing **Bred** Gerry Burke **Trained** East Everleigh, Wilts

**FOCUS**
The third running of this race, and the first two winners were subsequently successful at up to Group 2. All of these started off up the middle but the first three finishers raced slightly more towards the stands' side than the others, before drifting onto the near rail in the closing stages. The other three all had excuses. A step up from the runner-up.

## 2827 HARAS DE BOUQUETOT FILLIES' TRIAL STKS (LISTED RACE) 1m 2f

**4:40** (4:40) (Class 1) 3-Y-0

**£39,697** (£15,050; £7,532; £3,752; £1,883; £945) **Stalls** Low

Form RPR

2 **1** **Natavia**[31] 1885 3-9-0 0 ........ RyanMoore 4 101+
(Roger Charlton) *lw: trckd ldrs: led 2f out: sn pushed clr: comf* **9/4**[2]

1161 **2** *3 ¾* **Flood Warning**[22] 2132 3-9-0 88 ........ AdamKirby 5 93
(Clive Cox) *trckd ldrs: rdn to ld 3f out: edgd lft: hdd 2f out: kpt on but sn hld by wnr* **15/2**

1- **3** *3 ¾* **Aljezeera**[280] 5387 3-9-0 81 ........ FrankieDettori 2 86
(Luca Cumani) *tall: led tl 3f out: sn rdn and outpcd by front pair: kpt on ins fnl f but no threat after* **7/2**[3]

0-1 **4** *12* **Gracious Diana**[29] 1944 3-9-0 88 ........ WilliamBuick 6 62
(John Gosden) *lengthy: lw: trckd ldr: rdn w ch 3f out: sn hld: wknd over 1f out* **2/1**[1]

-432 **5** *1* **Plead**[18] 2269 3-9-0 81 ........(b[1]) OisinMurphy 1 60
(Archie Watson) *awkwardly away: last but in tch: hdwy 3f out: rdn over 2f out: wknd over 1f out* **14/1**

1-21 **6** *10* **Prosper**[17] 2287 3-9-0 89 ........ AndreaAtzeni 3 40
(Roger Varian) *trckd ldr: rdn over 2f out: sn wknd* **8/1**

2m 17.08s (8.28) **Going Correction** +0.90s/f (Soft) **6** Ran SP% **115.9**
Speed ratings (Par 104): **102,99,96,86,85 77**
CSF £19.72 TOTE £3.00: £1.70, £2.90; EX 16.30 Trifecta £85.20.

**Owner** K Abdullah **Bred** Newsells Park Stud **Trained** Beckhampton, Wilts

**FOCUS**
Race run over an additional 28yds. Eswarah won this event and the Oaks in 2005, and the 2014 winner, Volume, was third at Epsom. A year earlier Winsili won this and the Nassau Stakes, while Queen's Trust, only fourth last year, won at the Breeders' Cup later. Four of these hold Oaks entries, including the emphatic winner. The time was 2.5sec slower than the earlier London Gold Cup. The runner-up has been rated to her handicap latest.

## 2828 TORONADO H'CAP 1m (S)

**5:10** (5:14) (Class 2) (0-105,104) 4-Y-0+

**£24,900** (£7,456; £3,728; £1,864; £932; £468) **Stalls** Centre

Form RPR

0-00 **1** **Withernsea (IRE)**[7] 2606 6-8-10 93 ........ PaulHanagan 12 103+
(Richard Fahey) *racd center: hld up: rdn and hdwy over 2f out: chal jst ins fnl f: led fnl 90yds: drvn out* **12/1**

24-5 **2** *nk* **Brigliadoro (IRE)**[32] 1860 6-8-7 90 ........ TomMarquand 8 98
(Philip McBride) *s.i.s: racd center: towards rr: hdwy over 2f out: sn rdn: lft in ld ent fnl f: hdd fnl 90yds: kpt on* **20/1**

5000 **3** *1 ¼* **Mutarakez (IRE)**[14] 2406 5-8-4 87 ........ KierenFox 15 92+
(Brian Meehan) *racd center: hld up towards rr: hdwy over 2f out: led over 1f out: rdn whn veered bdly rt and hdd ent fnl f: keeping on but hld whn drifted lft towards fin* **10/1**

200- **4** *4 ½* **Dark Red (IRE)**[238] 6786 5-8-13 96 ........ RyanMoore 4 91
(Ed Dunlop) *racd far side: chsd ldrs: kpt on same pce fnl 2f* **12/1**

0-36 **5** *4 ½* **Medburn Dream**[14] 2390 4-7-11 85 oh2 ........ RichardOliver[(5)] 7 70
(Paul Henderson) *racd center: led: rdn and drifted lft over 2f out: hdd over 1f out: no ex fnl f* **20/1**

0-00 **6** *nk* **Grand Inquisitor**[23] 2115 5-8-3 86 ........ FrannyNorton 14 70
(Ian Williams) *racd center: hld up towards rr: hdwy 3f out: sn rdn: styd on but nt pce to get on terms* **14/1**

26-2 **7** *5* **Sinfonietta (FR)**[49] 1492 5-8-9 92 ........ HarryBentley 2 65
(David Menuisier) *racd far side but drifted to center over 3f out: in tch: rdn wl over 2f out: sn one pce* **3/1**[1]

00-1 **8** *1 ¼* **Calvados Spirit**[45] 1562 4-8-6 89 ........ MartinDwyer 11 59
(William Muir) *racd center: a mid-div* **25/1**

2-01 **9** *¾* **Zlatan (IRE)**[8] 2586 4-7-13 85 oh6 ........(p) NoelGarbutt[(3)] 5 53
(Ed de Giles) *racd center: nvr bttr than mid-div* **16/1**

3463 **10** *¾* **Bold Prediction (IRE)**[17] 2310 7-8-2 85 ........ LiamJones 10 51
(Ed Walker) *racd center: trckd ldr: rdn over 3f out: grad fdd* **50/1**

0-62 **11** *2 ¼* **El Hayem (IRE)**[8] 2568 4-8-9 92 ........ AndreaAtzeni 13 53
(Sir Michael Stoute) *lw: racd center: mid-div: rdn wl over 2f out: nvr any imp: wknd over 1f out* **4/1**[2]

24-3 **12** *1* **Top Beak (IRE)**[28] 1964 4-8-4 90 ........(t) CharlieBennett[(3)] 6 49
(Hughie Morrison) *racd center: mid-div: rdn 3f out: wknd over 1f out* **9/1**

30-3 **13** *5* **Candelisa (IRE)**[49] 1492 4-8-11 94 ........(p) JackGarritty 9 41
(Jedd O'Keeffe) *racd center: mid-div: rdn over 2f out: wknd over 1f out* **7/1**[3]

6300 **14** *20* **Brex Drago (ITY)**[32] 1860 5-9-1 98 ........ AntonioFresu 1
(Marco Botti) *racd far side: mid-div: rdn 3f out: sn wknd* **33/1**

10-P **15** *2* **Raising Sand**[49] 1492 5-8-11 94 ........ DougieCostello 3
(Jamie Osborne) *racd far side: mid-div: rdn over 3f out: sn wknd* **16/1**

1m 45.1s (5.40) **Going Correction** +0.90s/f (Soft) **15** Ran SP% **128.7**
Speed ratings (Par 109): **109,108,107,102,98 98,93,91,91,90 88,87,82,62,60**
CSF £246.89 CT £2561.92 TOTE £12.30: £3.80, £6.70, £3.20; EX 322.60 Trifecta £2683.00.
**Owner** Tiffin Sandwiches Limited & Partner **Bred** Yeomanstown Stud **Trained** Musley Bank, N Yorks

**FOCUS**
The runners were spread all over the place, with the first three drifting to the stands' side in the closing stages. The winner has been rated to his best.
T/Jkpt: £10,850.20. Pool: £65,102.00 - 6 winning units. T/Plt: £131.40 to a £1 stake. Pool: £186,132.31 - 1033.89 winning units T/Qpdt: £21.10 to a £1 stake. Pool: £10,451.54 - 366.29 winning units **Tim Mitchell**

# 2793 NEWMARKET (R-H)

Saturday, May 20

**OFFICIAL GOING: Good to soft (6.7)**
Wind: medium, across Weather: cloudy with bright spells and showers

## 2829 BETWAY FAIRWAY STKS (LISTED RACE) 1m 2f

**2:05** (2:06) (Class 1) 3-Y-0 **£20,982** (£7,955; £3,981; £1,983; £995) **Stalls** High

Form RPR

6424 **1** **Grey Britain**[14] 2402 3-9-3 99 ........ GeraldMosse 5 103
(John Ryan) *mde all: jnd and rdn ent fnl 2f: battled on wl to fight off chalrs ins fnl f: all out: gamely* **10/1**

011- **2** *nse* **Desert Skyline (IRE)**[213] 7471 3-9-3 94 ........ FranBerry 4 102
(David Elsworth) *stdd s: hld up in tch in last pair: clsd and shkn up to chal 2f out: sn rdn: maintained effrt and battled w wnr ins fnl f: jst hld* **7/1**

1 **3** *1 ¾* **Call To Mind**[28] 1961 3-9-3 82 ........ JimCrowley 6 98
(William Haggas) *trckd ldng pair: clsd and rdn to chal jst over 2f out: drvn over 1f out: stl ev ch but jst beginning to get outpcd whn short of room wl ins fnl f* **11/4**[2]

1-01 **4** *5* **Leshlaa (USA)**[13] 2437 3-9-3 103 ........(h) SilvestreDeSousa 3 88
(Saeed bin Suroor) *hld up in last pair: effrt wl over 2f out: rdn to chal ent fnl 2f: drvn over 1f out: outpcd and btn jst ins fnl f: wknd fnl 100yds* **11/8**[1]

1-02 **5** *4 ½* **Zumurudee (USA)**[10] 2520 3-9-3 96 ........ MartinHarley 1 79
(Marco Botti) *trckd wnr: rdn to chal over 2f out: drvn over 1f out: 5th and outpcd ent fnl f: wknd ins fnl f* **11/2**[3]

2m 8.44s (2.64) **Going Correction** +0.45s/f (Yiel) **5** Ran SP% **105.7**
Speed ratings (Par 107): **107,106,105,101,97**
CSF £63.79 TOTE £10.70: £2.80, £2.70; EX 47.10 Trifecta £163.20.
**Owner** G Smith-Bernal **Bred** D R Tucker **Trained** Newmarket, Suffolk

**FOCUS**
Stands' side course used, with stalls on far side, except 1m4f: centre. A blustery day with a strong crosswind towards the stands' rail. After the first rider Fran Berry claimed the ground was 'tacky'. They went a routine pace on this ordinary Listed race for 3yos and there was a tight finish.

## 2830 BETWAY KING CHARLES II STKS (LISTED RACE) 7f

**2:40** (2:40) (Class 1) 3-Y-0

**£20,982** (£7,955; £3,981; £1,983; £995; £499) **Stalls** High

Form RPR

15-4 **1** **Taamol (IRE)**[36] 1780 3-9-0 95 ........ JimCrowley 6 105
(Sir Michael Stoute) *dwlt and short of room leaving stalls: travelled strly and trckd ldrs: effrt jst over 2f out: drvn and str chal jst over 1f out: led ins fnl f: hld on wl* **15/8**[1]

1-50 **2** *hd* **Larchmont Lad (IRE)**[14] 2399 3-9-5 108 ................................ PatDobbs 5 109
(Richard Hannon) *trckd ldrs: effrt ent fnl 2f: drvn to press ldng pair ent fnl f: wnt 2nd and ev ch wl ins fnl f: styd on wl* **7/2**[2]

0-30 **3** *½* **Seven Heavens**[17] 2289 3-9-0 107 ................................ RobertTart 7 103
(John Gosden) *led to post: led: rdn 2f out: sn edgd rt: drvn over 1f out: hdd ins fnl f: kpt on but no ex wl ins fnl f* **7/2**[2]

10-0 **4** *1 ¾* **Solomon's Bay (IRE)**[29] 1945 3-9-0 87 .................... SilvestreDeSousa 1 98
(Roger Varian) *stdd and dropped in bhd after s: hld up in tch in rr: swtchd rt and effrt ent fnl 2f: drvn over 1f out: 4th: hung lft and kpt on same pce ins fnl f* **14/1**

6402 **5** *2 ½* **Masham Star (IRE)**[9] 2554 3-9-0 101 ................................ JoeFanning 4 92
(Mark Johnston) *t.k.h early: trckd ldr: effrt to chal ent fnl 2f: squeezed out and lost pl wl over 1f out: no threat to ldrs and styd on same pce after* **8/1**

1 **6** *2 ½* **Desert Frost (IRE)**[14] 2383 3-9-0 0 ................................ PatCosgrave 2 85
(Saeed bin Suroor) *trckd ldrs: effrt to chal ent fnl 2f: sn edgd lft u.p: unable qck and outpcd ent fnl f: wknd ins fnl f* **13/2**[3]

1m 26.68s (1.28) **Going Correction** +0.45s/f (Yiel) **6** Ran SP% **110.3**
Speed ratings (Par 107): **110,109,109,107,104 101**
CSF £8.29 TOTE £2.40: £1.70, £1.90; EX 9.40 Trifecta £24.70.
**Owner** Hamdan Al Maktoum **Bred** Derek Gibbons, Tomas Kerin & Ann Gibbons **Trained** Newmarket, Suffolk
■ Stewards' Enquiry : Pat Dobbs four-day ban: used whip above permitted level (Jun 5-8)

**FOCUS**
An up-to-scratch edition of this 3yo Listed contest, run at a fair enough pace.

## 2831 BETWAY SPRINT TROPHY H'CAP 6f
**3:15** (3:15) (Class 2) (0-105,105) 3-Y-O

**£28,012** (£8,388; £4,194; £2,097; £1,048; £526) **Stalls** High

Form RPR

21-2 **1** **Ekhtiyaar**[22] 2122 3-8-5 89 ................................ SilvestreDeSousa 6 98+
(Roger Varian) *chsd ldrs: effrt in 3rd 2f out: short of room: impeded and swtchd rt over 1f out: drvn and rallied to ld 100yds out: styd on wl* **3/1**[1]

20-0 **2** *hd* **Poet's Princess**[28] 1958 3-8-0 84 ................................ KieranO'Neill 7 91
(Hughie Morrison) *chsd ldrs: wnt 2nd 3f out: rdn to press ldr 2f out: getting short of room and swtchd rt over 1f out: drvn and pressing wnr 100yds out: kpt on wl* **16/1**

6011 **3** *1* **Quench Dolly**[8] 2579 3-8-8 92 ................................ FergusSweeney 5 96
(John Gallagher) *led: rdn and hung lft over 1f out: drvn 1f out: hdd 100yds out: no ex* **13/2**

21-3 **4** *8* **Holmeswood**[22] 2122 3-8-1 85 ................................ (p[1]) LukeMorris 4 63+
(Michael Dods) *in tch: effrt over 2f out: wnt 4th whn stmbld bdly wl over 1f out: no imp and wl hld over 1f out: kpt on to hold 4th ins fnl f* **6/1**[3]

10-3 **5** *1* **Mutawakked (IRE)**[19] 2215 3-8-0 84 oh1 ................................ JimmyQuinn 2 59
(Brian Meehan) *in tch in midfield: rdn and outpcd over 2f out: no ch w ldrs and plugged on same pce fr over 1f out* **16/1**

50-0 **6** *2* **Kreb's Cycle (IRE)**[9] 2557 3-8-0 84 oh2 ................................ RyanPowell 3 53
(Ian Williams) *in tch in last pair: effrt towards centre over 2f out: no imp and wl btn over 1f out* **11/1**

00-1 **7** *2 ½* **Nautical Haven**[86] 877 3-7-11 84 oh2 ................................ HollieDoyle(3) 10 45
(Kevin Ryan) *in tch in midfield: rdn over 2f out: sn outpcd: wknd over 1f out* **11/1**

3144 **8** *¾* **Wick Powell**[36] 1774 3-8-11 95 ................................ AndrewMullen 1 53
(David Barron) *chsd ldr tl 3f out: lost pl u.p 2f out: sn wknd* **12/1**

2-32 **9** *nk* **Eqtiraan (IRE)**[14] 2400 3-9-7 105 ................................ JimCrowley 8 62
(Richard Hannon) *hld up in tch in rr: hdwy into midfield 1/2-way: sn rdn and no imp: wknd over 1f out* **9/2**[2]

62-1 **10** *¾* **Esprit De Corps**[36] 1761 3-7-10 87 ................................ DavidEgan(7) 9 42
(Roger Charlton) *in tch: rdn 3f out: no imp whn nt clr run wl over 1f out: sn swtchd rt and no hdwy: bhd ins fnl f* **10/1**

1m 12.82s (0.62) **Going Correction** +0.45s/f (Yiel) **10** Ran SP% **116.0**
Speed ratings (Par 105): **113,112,111,100,99 96,93,92,92,91**
CSF £53.67 CT £293.29 TOTE £3.50: £1.40, £5.20, £2.60; EX 57.50 Trifecta £293.10.
**Owner** Hamdan Al Maktoum **Bred** James Ortega Bloodstock **Trained** Newmarket, Suffolk

**FOCUS**
A hot 3yo sprint handicap, run in driving rain. Top form with the principals coming clear.

## 2832 BETWAY EBF FILLIES' NOVICE STKS (PLUS 10 RACE) 6f
**3:50** (3:52) (Class 4) 2-Y-O **£4,528** (£1,347; £673; £336) **Stalls** High

Form RPR

**1** **Tajaanus (IRE)** 2-9-0 0 ................................ JimCrowley 7 75+
(Richard Hannon) *s.i.s: in tch in rr: pushed along 2f out: hdwy to chse wnr whn swtchd rt and rn green ent fnl f: rn to ld ins fnl f: styd on wl* **7/2**[3]

0 **2** *½* **Queen Penn**[18] 2265 2-8-11 0 ................................ SammyJoBell(3) 1 74
(Richard Fahey) *chsd ldrs: rdn over 1f out: styd on and drvn to press ldrs ins fnl f: kpt on wl to go 2nd on post* **9/1**

4 **3** *nse* **Villa Tora**[19] 2222 2-9-0 0 ................................ JoeFanning 6 73
(Mark Johnston) *t.k.h: led: rdn over 2f out: hdd ins fnl f: kpt on but a jst hld after: lost 2nd on post* **7/1**

**4** *1 ¼* **Sultanaa** 2-9-0 0 ................................ SilvestreDeSousa 8 70
(Ismail Mohammed) *hld up in tch: effrt 2f out: bmpd over 1f out: swtchd rt ent fnl f: kpt on ins fnl f: 4th and no imp whn short of room towards fin* **11/4**[2]

**5** *1 ¾* **Atalanta Queen** 2-9-0 0 ................................ FranBerry 10 64
(Brian Meehan) *in tch in midfield: rdn over 2f out: n.m.r and trying to switch rt over 1f out swtchd lft 1f out: kpt on same pce ins fnl f* **20/1**

22 **6** *4* **Take Shelter**[20] 2173 2-9-0 0 ................................ MartinHarley 9 52
(James Tate) *chsd ldr: rdn over 1f out: sn hanging rt and lost 2nd: wknd ins fnl f* **5/2**[1]

0 **7** *22* **Cherubic**[31] 1884 2-9-0 0 ................................ LukeMorris 4
(Charles Hills) *s.i.s: in tch in last pair: rdn 1/2-way: bhd 2f out: sn lost tch* **12/1**

1m 16.26s (4.06) **Going Correction** +0.45s/f (Yiel) **7** Ran SP% **112.4**
Speed ratings (Par 92): **90,89,89,87,85 79,50**
CSF £32.71 TOTE £4.10: £1.80, £4.80; EX 36.00 Trifecta £284.90.
**Owner** Hamdan Al Maktoum **Bred** Shadwell Estate Company Limited **Trained** East Everleigh, Wilts

**FOCUS**
A fair fillies' novice event and the winner could be going places. It's been rated in line with the recent race average.

## 2833 BETWAY DOWNLOAD THE APP H'CAP 7f
**4:25** (4:25) (Class 3) (0-95,97) 4-Y-O+ **£7,762** (£2,310; £1,154; £577) **Stalls** High

Form RPR

333- **1** **Ifwecan**[265] 5934 6-9-3 91 ................................ RobertWinston 3 99
(Martin Smith) *chsd ldr tl led jst over 2f out: edging lft to stand' rail 2f out: rdn over 1f out: forged ahd ins fnl f: jst hld on* **16/1**

00-0 **2** *nse* **Ice Lord (IRE)**[23] 2115 5-8-12 86 ................................ FranBerry 9 94+
(Chris Wall) *stdd and throw hd in air leaving stalls: hld up in rr: stl last whn swtchd rt over 1f out: chsd clr ldng pair 150yds: r.o v strly u.p after: jst failed* **20/1**

15-0 **3** *2* **Baron Bolt**[14] 2390 4-9-3 91 ................................ (p) LukeMorris 4 93
(Paul Cole) *hld up in tch in midfield: clsd to trck ldrs 3f out: wnt 2nd 2f out: drvn and 1 l down jst over 1f out: styd on same pce after ad lost 2nd wl ins fnl f* **5/1**[2]

0-00 **4** *2 ¾* **London Protocol (FR)**[28] 1960 4-9-3 91 ................................ (p) MartinHarley 11 86
(K R Burke) *trckd ldng trio: wnt 3rd whn squeezed for room and wnt lft 2f out: 3rd and no imp u.p over 1f out: 4th and kpt on same pce ins fnl f* **7/2**[1]

/050 **5** *1 ½* **Eltezam (IRE)**[14] 2390 4-9-7 95 ................................ (h) PatDobbs 1 86
(Richard Hannon) *hld up in last pair: swtchd rt and effrt 2f out: flashed tail u.p and no imp jst over 1f out: wl hld and plugged on same pce fnl f* **5/1**[2]

4-45 **6** *¾* **Ballymore Castle (IRE)**[24] 2081 5-8-4 81 ................................ SammyJoBell(3) 14 70
(Richard Fahey) *hld up in tch in midfield: nt clr and swtchd rt 2f out: midfield and stl plenty whn nt clr run again ent fnl f: styd on same pce after* **7/2**[1]

560- **7** *2 ½* **Scottish Glen**[189] 7933 11-9-3 94 ................................ HectorCrouch(3) 12 76
(Patrick Chamings) *hld up in midfield: effrt whn nt clr run and hmpd 2f out: no imp over 1f out: nvr trbld ldrs* **20/1**

01-0 **8** *½* **King Of Naples**[48] 1512 4-8-10 84 ................................ DanielMuscutt 10 65
(James Fanshawe) *in tch in midfield: swtchd rt and effrt ent fnl 2f: no imp u.p over 1f out: wknd ins fnl f* **13/2**[3]

00-0 **9** *½* **Carnival King (IRE)**[24] 2081 5-8-13 87 ................................ LemosdeSouza 8 67
(Amy Murphy) *chsd ldrs: rdn over 2f out: outpcd and btn whn nt clr run and swtchd rt over 1f out: wknd ins fnl f* **16/1**

0-00 **10** *2 ¼* **Majestic Moon (IRE)**[18] 2283 7-8-11 85 ................................ RoystonFfrench 6 58
(Julia Feilden) *led tl over 2f out: sn rdn and struggling whn bdly hmpd 2f out: bhd and nt rcvr after* **25/1**

1m 27.07s (1.67) **Going Correction** +0.45s/f (Yiel) **10** Ran SP% **116.2**
Speed ratings (Par 107): **108,107,105,102,100 99,97,96,95,93**
CSF £294.60 CT £1832.35 TOTE £11.50: £3.00, £4.60, £2.20; EX 237.90 Trifecta £829.40.
**Owner** Henry & Jade Syndicate **Bred** P T Tellwright **Trained** Newmarket, Suffolk

**FOCUS**
They went a sound pace in this good-quality handicap and it's solid form.

## 2834 BETWAY MAIDEN FILLIES' STKS (PLUS 10 RACE) 1m 4f
**5:00** (5:05) (Class 5) 3-Y-O **£3,881** (£1,155; £577; £288) **Stalls** Centre

Form RPR

45-2 **1** **Star Rock**[29] 1944 3-9-0 80 ................................ RobertWinston 1 82
(Hughie Morrison) *t.k.h: chsd ldr tl led over 3f out: rdn over 1f out: styd on and hld on wl ins fnl f: rdn out* **15/8**[1]

33- **2** *½* **God Given**[214] 7441 3-9-0 0 ................................ LukeMorris 8 81
(Luca Cumani) *chsd ldrs tl wnt 2nd 3f out: rdn to press ldr 2f out: drvn over 1f out: kpt on ins fnl f but a jst hld* **15/8**[1]

4-4 **3** *1 ¼* **Really Super**[28] 1963 3-9-0 0 ................................ FranBerry 7 79+
(Ralph Beckett) *hld up in tch: clsd to trck ldrs 4f out: effrt in 3rd 2f out: ev ch u.p over 1f out: no ex and outpcd fnl 100yds* **3/1**[2]

4 **4** *20* **Marie Josephe**[12] 2476 3-9-0 0 ................................ ShaneKelly 3 47
(Richard Hughes) *t.k.h: hld up in tch in midfield: rdn over 3f out: outpcd over 2f out: 4th and wl btn over 1f out: wknd* **8/1**[3]

0 **5** *2 ¾* **Miss Liguria**[29] 1944 3-9-0 0 ................................ MartinHarley 9 43
(Ed Walker) *styd wd early: chsd ldrs: rdn and lost pl whn edgd rt 3f out: outpcd and wl btn 2f out: wknd* **20/1**

0- **6** *3 ¾* **Lagertha (IRE)**[214] 7441 3-9-0 0 ................................ JackMitchell 4 37
(Hugo Palmer) *led tl rdn and hdd over 3f out: 4th and outpcd over 2f out: wknd and wl btn over 1f out* **33/1**

0 **7** *23* **Breton Belle (IRE)**[17] 2307 3-9-0 0 ................................ PatCosgrave 2
(David Simcock) *hld up in last pair: rdn 4f out: sn struggling: t.o fnl 2f* **20/1**

0 **8** *3 ¼* **Kimene**[18] 2260 3-8-11 0 ................................ HollieDoyle(3) 6
(William Stone) *hld up in last pair: rdn over 6f out: lost tch 3f out: t.o* **66/1**

2m 38.11s (6.11) **Going Correction** +0.45s/f (Yiel) **8** Ran SP% **119.6**
Speed ratings (Par 96): **97,96,95,82,80 78,62,60**
CSF £5.63 TOTE £2.60: £1.10, £1.50, £1.50; EX 5.80 Trifecta £12.90.
**Owner** Ben & Sir Martyn Arbib **Bred** Arbib Bloodstock Partnership **Trained** East Ilsley, Berks

**FOCUS**
Race distance increased by 9yds. Not a bad 3yo fillies' maiden. The market principals came clear.

## 2835 BETWAY H'CAP 5f
**5:35** (5:37) (Class 4) (0-85,86) 4-Y-O+ **£5,175** (£1,540; £769; £384) **Stalls** High

Form RPR

04-2 **1** **Paddy Power (IRE)**[36] 1777 4-8-10 75 ................................ SammyJoBell(3) 2 85
(Richard Fahey) *niggled along and off the pce in midfield: clsd to chsd ldrs over 1f out: nt clr run ent fnl f: gap opened and hdwy ins fnl f: led 100yds out: r.o wl* **11/4**[1]

0-36 **2** *¾* **Stake Acclaim (IRE)**[22] 2123 5-9-10 86 ................................ (p) RobertWinston 10 93
(Dean Ivory) *chsd ldr and clr in ldng trio: led over 1f out: sn rdn: hdd and styd on same pce ins fnl f* **3/1**[2]

354- **3** *1 ¾* **Justice Lady (IRE)**[257] 6195 4-9-3 79 ................................ ShaneKelly 7 80
(David Elsworth) *stdd and swtchd lft after s: hld up in midfield: clsd to trck ldrs 2f out: swtchd rt and rdn to chse ldr jst over 1f out: no ex and outpcd fnl 100yds* **8/1**

03-6 **4** *½* **Racing Angel (IRE)**[30] 1899 5-8-2 69 ................................ LuluStanford(5) 8 68
(Mick Quinn) *off the pce in midfield: rdn 1/2-way: hdwy to chse ldrs and drvn over 1f out: no ex and one pced ins fnl f* **12/1**

2046 **5** *2 ¼* **Seamster**[10] 2524 10-8-12 81 ................................ (t) CameronNoble(7) 9 72
(David Loughnane) *pressed ldrs and clr in ldng trio: rdn 2f out: drvn over 1f out: wknd ins fnl f* **17/2**

60-1 **6** *2 ¾* **Acclaim The Nation (IRE)**[22] 2123 4-9-0 76 ................................ JasonHart 11 57
(Eric Alston) *led tl rdn and hdd over 1f out: sn outpcd u.p: wknd ins fnl f* **11/2**[3]

113- **7** *2 ½* **Royal Mezyan (IRE)**[155] 8403 6-8-12 79 ................................ GeorgiaCox(5) 6 51
(Henry Spiller) *sn outpcd in rr: swtchd rt over 1f out: nvr on terms* **12/1**

0100 **8** *2 ¾* **Foxy Forever (IRE)**[32] 1863 7-9-6 82 ................................ (t) FranBerry 1 44
(Michael Wigham) *hld up wl off the pce in rr and styd wd early: drifting lft 2f out: nvr on terms* **20/1**

41-6 **9** *shd* **Consulting**[134] 93 4-9-4 80 ................................ (t[1]) MartinHarley 4 42
(Stuart Williams) *sn outpcd in last trio: nvr on terms* **16/1**

1m 1.2s (2.10) **Going Correction** +0.45s/f (Yiel) **9** Ran SP% **114.7**
Speed ratings (Par 105): **101,99,97,96,92 88,84,79,79**
CSF £11.02 CT £57.19 TOTE £3.80: £1.50, £1.80, £2.10; EX 12.50 Trifecta £64.40.
**Owner** M Scaife & R A Fahey **Bred** Yeguada De Milagro Sa **Trained** Musley Bank, N Yorks

**FOCUS**
A fair sprint handicap and there was no hanging around.

T/Plt: £395.10 to a £1 stake. Pool: £128,667.70 - 237.69 winning units T/Qpdt: £45.10 to a £1 stake. Pool: £8,904.33 - 146 winning units **Steve Payne**

## 2627THIRSK (L-H)
Saturday, May 20

**OFFICIAL GOING: Soft (good to soft in places; 6.8)**
Wind: light across, making no material difference Weather: overcast, odd shower, steady rain 5th to 7th

### 2836 IRISH STALLION FARMS EBF MAIDEN FILLIES' STKS (PLUS 10 RACE) 5f
**1:40** (1:43) (Class 4) 2-Y-0 **£4,528** (£1,347; £673; £336) **Stalls** Centre

Form RPR
3 1 **Validator**18 2279 2-9-0 0 BenCurtis 11 77+
(William Haggas) *mde all: pushed along over 1f out: kpt on wl: comf* **1/1**1
2 2¼ **Ajwan** 2-9-0 0 TonyHamilton 10 67
(Richard Fahey) *chsd ldr: pushed along over 1f out: kpt on but a hld* **6/1**2
3 1 **Donny Belle** 2-9-0 0 TomEaves 2 63
(David Brown) *in tch: pushed along 1/2-way: rdn over 1f out: kpt on fnl f* **33/1**
4 ½ **Twentytwowontdo (IRE)** 2-9-0 0 DanielTudhope 3 62
(David O'Meara) *chsd ldr: pushed along over 2f out: rdn over 1f out: no ex ins fnl f* **16/1**
5 nse **Dubai Classic (IRE)** 2-9-0 0 JoeyHaynes 4 61+
(K R Burke) *hld up: pushed along 1/2-way: kpt on ins fnl f: nrst fin* **25/1**
6 3½ **Benaras (USA)** 2-9-0 0 DavidAllan 13 49
(Tim Easterby) *dwlt: sn chsd ldr: rdn over 2f out: wknd fnl f* **6/1**2
7 ½ **Lil Gem (IRE)** 2-9-0 0 PJMcDonald 6 47
(Keith Dalgleish) *midfield: sn pushed along: nvr threatened* **25/1**
8 1¼ **Mecca's Minstrel (IRE)** 2-9-0 0 PaulMulrennan 7 42
(Michael Dods) *hld up: pushed along 1/2-way: nvr threatened* **11/1**3
9 4 **Foxxy Brown** 2-8-11 0 AdamMcNamara(3) 5 28
(Richard Fahey) *hld up: nvr threatened* **16/1**
10 2 **French Silk** 2-9-0 0 DuranFentiman 8 21
(Chris Fairhurst) *slowly away: a rr* **100/1**
11 18 **Your Just Desserts (IRE)** 2-9-0 0 GrahamLee 1
(Micky Hammond) *v.s.a: a wl bhd* **33/1**

1m 0.67s (1.07) **Going Correction** +0.225s/f (Good) **11 Ran SP% 113.2**
Speed ratings (Par 92): **100,96,94,94,93 88,87,85,79,75 47**
CSF £6.11 TOTE £1.70: £1.10, £1.50, £9.10; EX 6.90 Trifecta £127.30.
**Owner** Cheveley Park Stud **Bred** Cheveley Park Stud Ltd **Trained** Newmarket, Suffolk

**FOCUS**
The going was soft, good to soft in places. An interesting maiden run at an honest pace with the field racing mainly up the centre.

### 2837 JACKIE'S 50TH CELEBRATION H'CAP 5f
**2:10** (2:11) (Class 4) (0-80,82) 4-Y-0+ **£4,851** (£1,443; £721; £360) **Stalls** Centre

Form RPR
0-40 1 **Elysian Flyer (IRE)**72 1103 5-9-4 77 GrahamLee 4 88
(Paul Midgley) *chsd ldrs: pushed along to ld over 1f out: rdn and kpt on fnl f* **16/1**
2431 2 1¼ **Lucky Beggar (IRE)**5 2683 7-9-9 82 6ex DavidAllan 6 88
(David C Griffiths) *chsd ldrs: rdn over 2f out: kpt on fnl f: wnt 2nd nr fin* **10/3**2
-040 3 nk **Bogart**14 2404 8-9-7 80 (t1) TomEaves 5 85
(Kevin Ryan) *prom: pushed along over 2f out: rdn over ev ch over 1f out: one pce fnl f: lost 2nd nr fin* **14/1**
4-00 4 ½ **Quick Look**17 2303 4-9-1 77 NathanEvans(3) 8 80
(Michael Easterby) *dwlt: hld up: rdn over 2f out: kpt on fr appr fnl f* **14/1**
-221 5 ¾ **Henley**4 2700 5-9-2 75 6ex BenCurtis 11 75
(Tracy Waggott) *dwlt but sn led: rdn whn hdd over 1f out: no ex fnl f* **3/1**1
00-5 6 ½ **Pearl Acclaim (IRE)**9 2551 7-9-0 73 (p) DanielTudhope 13 72
(David O'Meara) *chsd ldrs towards stands' side: rdn 1/2-way: one pce* **6/1**3
6-00 7 hd **Major Pusey**24 2083 5-9-5 78 JoeyHaynes 10 76
(John Gallagher) *chsd ldrs: rdn over 2f out: one pce* **7/1**
2-30 8 2¾ **Sumou (IRE)**21 2147 4-9-4 77 TonyHamilton 3 65
(Milton Bradley) *hld up in tch: pushed along and dropped to rr 2f out: no threat after* **25/1**
5-50 9 shd **Swirral Edge**33 1828 4-9-1 74 PhillipMakin 9 62
(David Brown) *hld up: rdn 2f out: nvr threatened* **10/1**
0-45 10 nk **Dinneratmidnight**21 2161 6-9-1 74 (e) ConnorBeasley 12 61
(Richard Guest) *midfield: sn pushed along: rdn over 2f out: wknd over 1f out* **12/1**
000- 11 hd **Lexi's Hero (IRE)**238 6793 9-9-1 77 (v) AdamMcNamara(3) 1 63
(Patrick Morris) *midfield: rdn over 2f out: wknd fnl f* **40/1**

59.94s (0.34) **Going Correction** +0.225s/f (Good) **11 Ran SP% 117.1**
Speed ratings (Par 105): **106,104,103,102,101 100,100,96,95,95 95**
CSF £68.60 CT £787.53 TOTE £20.90: £4.50, £1.70, £4.00; EX 91.10 Trifecta £1870.50.
**Owner** Robert And Sheila Bradley **Bred** Tom Shirley **Trained** Westow, N Yorks

**FOCUS**
Plenty of pace for this open sprint handicap. The runner-up has been rated to the better view of his recent form.

### 2838 MARION GIBSON BROWN MEMORIAL H'CAP 7f 218y
**2:45** (2:48) (Class 4) (0-85,85) 4-Y-0+ **£4,851** (£1,443; £721; £360) **Stalls** Low

Form RPR
0-00 1 **Finn Class (IRE)**26 2030 6-9-4 82 PaulMulrennan 8 91
(Michael Dods) *hld up: pushed along and gd hdwy on outer over 2f out: rdn to chal strly ins fnl f: kpt on: led nr fin* **11/1**
6505 2 shd **Boots And Spurs**12 2466 8-8-11 75 (v) TomEaves 11 83
(Scott Dixon) *trckd ldr: led 2f out: sn rdn: strly pressed ins fnl f: kpt on but hdd nr fin* **28/1**
64 3 ½ **Mulligatawny (IRE)**10 2528 4-9-7 85 TonyHamilton 10 92
(Roger Fell) *midfield on inner: rdn and gd hdwy appr fnl f: kpt on wl* **9/1**3
1-00 4 1½ **Carnageo (FR)**19 2226 4-9-0 81 AdamMcNamara(3) 15 84+
(Richard Fahey) *hld up: pushed along over 2f out: bit short of room over 1f out and angled rt to outside: sn rdn and hdwy: kpt on ins fnl f* **10/1**
63-0 5 shd **Wilde Inspiration (IRE)**21 2155 6-9-2 80 JoeDoyle 6 83
(Julie Camacho) *trckd ldrs: rdn 2f out: one pce* **6/1**1
064- 6 2¼ **Madrinho (IRE)**252 6338 4-9-5 83 BarryMcHugh 18 81
(Tony Coyle) *hld up: rdn over 2f out: hdwy and in tch over 1f out: no ex ins fnl f* **50/1**
0-50 7 ½ **Off Art**21 2133 7-8-8 72 (p) DavidAllan 5 69
(Tim Easterby) *sn led: rdn whn hdd 2f out: wknd ins fnl f* **9/1**3
6605 8 2 **Abushamah (IRE)**8 2586 6-9-0 78 (p1) JamesSullivan 16 70
(Ruth Carr) *prom: rdn over 2f out: wknd ins fnl f* **9/1**3
00-3 9 ½ **Shouranour (IRE)**21 2155 7-9-3 84 (b) JoshDoyle(3) 13 75
(Alan Brown) *midfield on outer: rdn over 2f out: wknd fnl f.* **10/1**
66-6 10 3½ **Fieldsman (USA)**16 2348 5-9-7 85 DanielTudhope 9 68+
(David O'Meara) *trckd ldrs: bit short of room and lost room over 2f out: wknd over 1f out* **7/1**2
02-0 11 ¾ **Tadaany (IRE)**24 2081 5-8-8 79 (p) PatrickVaughan(7) 7 60
(David O'Meara) *prom: rdn over 2f out: wknd over 1f out* **28/1**
/060 12 1½ **Mansfield**21 2155 4-9-1 79 AdamBeschizza 12 57
(Michael Wigham) *dwlt: a towards rr* **66/1**
2-00 13 2¼ **Briyouni (FR)**14 2406 4-9-7 85 KevinStott 14 58
(Kevin Ryan) *midfield: rdn over 2f out: wknd over 1f out* **16/1**
104- 14 5 **Run To The Hills (USA)**190 7902 4-9-7 85 StevieDonohoe 3 46
(George Peckham) *dwlt: a towards rr* **10/1**

1m 44.05s (3.95) **Going Correction** +0.625s/f (Yiel) **14 Ran SP% 108.6**
Speed ratings (Par 105): **105,104,104,102,102 100,100,98,97,94 93,91,89,84**
CSF £244.49 CT £2116.55 TOTE £10.50: £3.00, £6.40, £3.20; EX 188.00 Trifecta £1772.90.
**Owner** M D Pearson **Bred** Rabbah Bloodstock Limited **Trained** Denton, Co Durham
■ Torrid was withdrawn. Price at time of withdrawal 7-1. Rule 4 applies to all bets - deduction 10p in the pound.

**FOCUS**
Add 30yds due to rail movement. The pace was sound for this open handicap. The third has been rated to his best.

### 2839 CONSTANT SECURITY SERVICES H'CAP 5f
**3:20** (3:20) (Class 2) (0-100,101) 4-Y-0+ **£12,938** (£3,850; £1,924; £962) **Stalls** Centre

Form RPR
500- 1 **Kickboxer (IRE)**245 6556 6-9-2 95 BenCurtis 2 101+
(Michael Appleby) *dwlt sltly: sn chsd ldrs: pushed along to ld over 1f out: rdn and kpt on wl fnl f* **6/1**
400- 2 2 **Ladweb**217 7358 7-8-7 86 oh4 JoeyHaynes 1 85
(John Gallagher) *w ldr: rdn to ld 2f out: hdd over 1f out: kpt on but sn no ch w wnr* **20/1**
0-30 3 1¾ **Pipers Note**21 2156 7-9-5 98 JamesSullivan 4 91
(Ruth Carr) *chsd ldrs: rdn over 2f out: one pce* **8/1**
-121 4 hd **Edward Lewis**8 2578 4-9-5 101 JoshDoyle(3) 7 93
(David O'Meara) *hld up in tch: pushed along and sme hdwy over 1f out: one pce fnl f* **2/1**1
2624 5 shd **Orient Class**2 2764 6-8-0 86 oh1 ConnorMurtagh(7) 6 77
(Paul Midgley) *chsd ldrs: rdn over 2f out: one pce* **11/4**2
00-0 6 1¼ **Jack Dexter**7 2611 8-9-2 95 SamJames 5 82
(Jim Goldie) *hld up: rdn 2f out: nvr threatened* **11/2**3
0-00 7 1¼ **Independence Day (IRE)**18 2262 4-8-9 88 (p) TonyHamilton 3 70
(Robert Cowell) *led narrowly: rdn whn hdd 2f out: wknd fnl f* **12/1**

1m 0.01s (0.41) **Going Correction** +0.225s/f (Good) **7 Ran SP% 113.2**
Speed ratings (Par 109): **105,101,99,98,98 96,94**
CSF £103.33 TOTE £7.90: £3.10, £7.20; EX 95.00 Trifecta £526.60.
**Owner** Craig Buckingham & Martyn Elvin **Bred** Rathasker Stud **Trained** Oakham, Rutland

**FOCUS**
A decent handicap despite the small field. It was run at an even tempo and the two who raced away from the stands rail dominated. The winner has been rated back to something like his best, with the runner-up limiting the form.

### 2840 UKINSURANCENET H'CAP 6f
**3:55** (3:59) (Class 3) (0-90,90) 4-Y-0+ **£7,762** (£2,310; £1,154; £577) **Stalls** Centre

Form RPR
01-4 1 **Naggers (IRE)**48 1515 6-9-2 85 PaulMulrennan 1 103+
(Paul Midgley) *trckd ldrs far side: pushed along to ld over 1f out: kpt on strly to draw clr fnl f: v easily* **3/1**1
1050 2 3½ **Handsome Dude**14 2381 5-8-7 83 (b) ConnorMurtagh(7) 20 90+
(David Barron) *led stands' side gp: rdn over 2f out: kpt on wl but no ch w wnr fnl f: 1st of 10 in gp* **11/1**
1113 3 2¼ **Foolaad**14 2381 6-9-0 83 (t) BenCurtis 4 83
(Roy Bowring) *dwlt: hld up far side: rdn and hdwy 2f out: kpt on: 2nd of 9 in gp* **7/1**3
40-0 4 nk **Eccleston**48 1515 6-9-6 89 (v) DanielTudhope 10 88
(David O'Meara) *dwlt: hld up far side: rdn and hdwy 2f out: kpt on: 3rd of 9 in gp* **6/1**2
1-00 5 1½ **Munfallet (IRE)**14 2381 6-9-5 88 PhillipMakin 3 82
(David Brown) *led far side: rdn whn hdd over 1f out: sn outpcd: plugged on ins fnl f: 4th of 9 in gp* **33/1**
11-5 6 1½ **Classic Seniority**14 2381 5-9-7 90 BarryMcHugh 11 79
(Marjorie Fife) *chsd ldrs stands' side: rdn over 2f out: one pce: 2nd of 10 in gp* **14/1**
5056 7 1½ **God Willing**14 2406 6-9-0 88 PhilDennis(5) 8 73
(Declan Carroll) *hld up far side: rdn and sme hdwy 2f out: nvr threatened: 5th of 9 in gp* **12/1**
-000 8 1¼ **Kenny The Captain (IRE)**14 2381 6-8-8 80 RachelRichardson(3) 13 61
(Tim Easterby) *prom stands' side: rdn over 2f out: wknd over 1f out: 3rd of 10 in gp* **33/1**
-000 9 shd **Cosmic Chatter**20 2184 7-8-13 82 (p) JamesSullivan 9 62
(Ruth Carr) *swtchd rt s to r stands' side: hld up: rdn over 2f out: nvr threatened: 4th of 10 in gp* **33/1**
0-40 10 2½ **Intense Style (IRE)**48 1515 5-9-4 87 (b) PJMcDonald 2 59
(Les Eyre) *chsd ldrs far side: rdn over 2f out: wknd over 1f out: 6th of 9 in gp* **11/1**
110/ 11 nk **Roaring Forties (IRE)**640 5533 4-9-6 89 DuranFentiman 16 60
(Rebecca Bastiman) *hld up stands' side: nvr threatened: 5th of 10 in gp* **66/1**
0-00 12 ¾ **My Name Is Rio (IRE)**14 2381 7-8-11 85 CallumRodriguez(5) 15 54
(Michael Dods) *chsd ldrs stands' side: rdn over 2f out: wknd over 1f out: 6th of 10 in gp* **20/1**
3121 13 nk **Zylan (IRE)**13 2428 5-9-2 85 TonyHamilton 17 53
(Roger Fell) *midfield stands' side: rdn over 2f out: wknd over 1f out: 7th of 10 in gp* **12/1**
031- 14 hd **Jameerah**222 7206 4-8-13 82 ConnorBeasley 14 49
(Bryan Smart) *in tch stands' side: rdn 2f out: sn wknd: 8th of 10 in gp* **20/1**
6-04 15 hd **Laughton**22 2123 4-8-13 82 ShaneGray 7 49
(Kevin Ryan) *in tch far side: rdn 2f out: sn wknd: 7th of 9 in gp* **20/1**
2-00 16 ½ **Roll On Rory**14 2390 4-9-7 90 (v) GrahamLee 18 55
(Jason Ward) *chsd ldr stands' side: reminders early: weakend fnl 2f: 9th of 10 in gp* **20/1**

140- **17** 4 1/2 **Harwoods Volante (IRE)**[193] 7858 6-9-2 **88**................ JoshDoyle(3) 12 39
(David O'Meara) *a towards rr stands' side: hld up last of 10 in gp* **40/1**
-000 **18** 2 **Mishaal (IRE)**[8] 2592 7-9-1 **84**.................... TomEaves 6 28
(Michael Herrington) *midfield far side: wknd and bhd fr over 2f out: 8th of 9 in gp* **50/1**
00-0 **19** 22 **See The Sun**[33] 1831 6-9-2 **85**.................... DavidAllan 5
(Tim Easterby) *prom far side: rdn over 2f out: wknd and eased* **28/1**
1m 12.79s (0.09) **Going Correction** +0.225s/f (Good) **19** Ran SP% **127.7**
Speed ratings (Par 107): **108,103,100,99,97 95,93,92,92,88 88,87,87,86,86 85,79,77,47**
CSF £31.43 CT £232.95 TOTE £3.40: £1.40, £3.30, £2.50, £2.00; EX 44.00 Trifecta £301.20.
**Owner** Taylor's Bloodstock Ltd **Bred** Azienda Agricola Rosati Colarieti **Trained** Westow, N Yorks
**FOCUS**
They went a sound pace for this competitive handicap with the field splitting into two groups. They finished well strung out and the winner was most impressive. A clear pb from the winner.

## 2841 WHARTON CONSTRUCTION MAIDEN STKS (DIV I) 1m 4f 8y
**4:30** (4:30) (Class 5) 3-Y-O+ **£3,881** (£1,155; £577; £288) **Stalls** High

Form RPR
02 **1** **Key Bid**[14] 2408 3-8-11 0.................... (p[1]) MartinLane 6 81
(Charlie Appleby) *trckd ldr: jnd ldr 6f out: led over 3f out: rdn and strly pressed fr 2f out: kpt on gamely: asserted towards fin* **6/4**[2]
4-2 **2** 1/2 **Steaming (IRE)**[21] 2164 3-8-11 0.................... JFEgan 9 80
(Ralph Beckett) *in tch: trckd ldrs over 3f out: rdn to join ldr 2f out: kpt on: hld towards fin* **10/11**[1]
50 **3** 9 **Hurricane Hollow**[28] 1984 7-10-0 0.................... PhillipMakin 2 67
(David Barron) *hld up: hdwy to trck ldrs 3f out: rdn 2f out: sn outpcd by ldng pair and hld in 3rd* **6/1**[3]
5 **4** 8 **Toast Of London**[32] 1866 4-9-9 0.................... CamHardie 3 49
(Antony Brittain) *midfield: pushed along and lost pl over 4f out: dropped to rr bef plugging on fnl 2f* **50/1**
-0 **5** 1/2 **Sambuca Nera**[39] 1701 3-8-6 0.................... JoeDoyle 10 47
(James Given) *led: jnd 6f out: hdd over 3f out: wknd over 2f out* **25/1**
6 **6** 3 3/4 **Nuova Scuola**[11] 2496 4-9-9 0.................... SamJames 7 42
(Jim Goldie) *hld up: rdn over 3f out: sn btn* **25/1**
65 **7** 3/4 **Company Trader (IRE)**[17] 2300 3-8-11 0.................... PaddyAspell 5 45
(Sharon Watt) *trckd ldrs: rdn over 3f out: wknd* **66/1**
0- **8** 4 **Unblinking**[68] 7627 4-9-11 0.................... JoshDoyle(3) 8 39
(Nigel Twiston-Davies) *a rr* **16/1**
6 **9** 11 **Nightdress (IRE)**[40] 1676 3-8-6 0.................... DuranFentiman 4 16
(Tony Coyle) *racd keenly in midfield: rdn over 3f out: wknd 2f out and bhd* **25/1**
2m 49.47s (13.27) **Going Correction** +0.625s/f (Yiel)
**WFA** 3 from 4yo+ 17lb **9** Ran SP% **127.5**
Speed ratings (Par 103): **91,90,84,79,79 76,76,73,66**
CSF £3.47 TOTE £2.40: £1.10, £1.02, £2.20; EX 3.70 Trifecta £9.10.
**Owner** Godolphin **Bred** Aldridge Racing Partnership **Trained** Newmarket, Suffolk
**FOCUS**
Add 40yds due to rail movement. An uncompetitive maiden with the market leaders dominating. The third has been rated up a bit on his previous Flat form.

## 2842 WHARTON CONSTRUCTION MAIDEN STKS (DIV II) 1m 4f 8y
**5:05** (5:26) (Class 5) 3-Y-O+ **£3,881** (£1,155; £577; £288) **Stalls** High

Form RPR
**1** **Ottonian** 3-8-11 0.................... MartinLane 6 80+
(Charlie Appleby) *trckd ldr: led over 8f out: jnd over 2f out: rdn 2f out: styd on wl: pushed out and in command fnl 75yds* **2/1**[1]
02 **2** 1 1/2 **Kilowatt**[21] 2159 3-8-11 0.................... DavidAllan 4 78
(Tim Easterby) *prom: jnd ldr over 2f out: sn pushed along: rdn ent fnl f: no ex fnl 75yds* **2/1**[1]
**3** 6 **Relevant (IRE)** 3-8-6 0.................... JoeyHaynes 9 63
(K R Burke) *hld up in tch: rdn along over 3f out: hdwy to go 3rd ent fnl f: kpt on: no threat ldng pair* **20/1**
0- **4** nk **Inspector (IRE)**[178] 8063 3-8-11 0.................... (t) TomEaves 5 68
(Hugo Palmer) *trckd ldrs: rdn over 2f out: sn outpcd by ldng pair: lost 3rd ent fnl f: one pce* **12/1**
5 **5** 8 **Hugoigo**[11] 2496 3-8-4 0.................... SeanMooney(7) 2 55
(Jim Goldie) *hld up in tch: rdn over 3f out: sn wknd* **40/1**
53 **6** 1 **Sunrize (IRE)**[14] 2408 3-8-8 0.................... ShelleyBirkett(3) 8 54
(David O'Meara) *led: hdd over 8f out: trckd ldr: rdn over 3f out: wknd fnl 2f* **9/1**[3]
0 **7** 36 **Sindarin**[13] 2429 4-10-0 0.................... (h[1]) SamJames 7
(Jim Goldie) *hld up: rdn over 4f out: sn wknd and bhd* **100/1**
55 **U** **Belgravian (FR)**[15] 2359 3-8-11 0.................... BenCurtis 3
(Archie Watson) *restless in stall: fly leapt s and uns rdr* **11/4**[2]
2m 52.84s (16.64) **Going Correction** +0.625s/f (Yiel)
**WFA** 3 from 4yo+ 17lb **8** Ran SP% **119.2**
Speed ratings (Par 103): **86,85,81,80,75 74,50,**
CSF £6.43 TOTE £3.10: £1.70, £1.10, £4.20; EX 7.20 Trifecta £100.50.
**Owner** Godolphin **Bred** Darley **Trained** Newmarket, Suffolk
**FOCUS**
Add 40yds due to rail movement. An ordinary maiden in which the market leaders finished a long way clear. It's been rated around the runner-up.

## 2843 BOOK FOR LADIES' DAY - SATURDAY 9TH SEPTEMBER H'CAP 6f
**5:40** (5:58) (Class 6) (0-65,65) 4-Y-O+ **£3,234** (£962; £481; £240) **Stalls** Centre

Form RPR
0-62 **1** **French**[22] 2124 4-9-3 **61**.................... (p) CamHardie 7 70
(Antony Brittain) *chsd ldrs: rdn to ld over 1f out: kpt on wl* **6/1**[3]
00-0 **2** 3 **Show Palace**[28] 1965 4-9-6 **64**.................... DavidNolan 6 64
(Jennie Candlish) *dwlt: hld up in midfield racing keenly: smooth hdwy to trck ldr over 1f out: rdn and one pce fnl f* **16/1**
4505 **3** 1/2 **Ambitious Icarus**[13] 2424 8-9-4 **62**.................... (e) ConnorBeasley 9 61
(Richard Guest) *hld up: sn pushed along: hdwy over 1f out: kpt on fnl f: wnt 3rd fnl 50yds* **9/1**
-450 **4** 3/4 **Tafteesh (IRE)**[19] 2224 4-9-4 **65**.................... NathanEvans(3) 5 61
(Michael Easterby) *midfield: rdn along 1/2-way: kpt on fnl f* **11/2**[2]
-010 **5** 1 **Blue Jacket (USA)**[21] 2140 6-9-5 **63**.................... PaulMulrennan 4 56
(Dianne Sayer) *led narrowly: rdn over 2f out: hdd over 1f out: wknd ins fnl f* **5/1**[1]
140- **6** 2 1/4 **Full Of Promise**[182] 8031 4-9-1 **65**.................... ShelleyBirkett(3) 3 49
(Richard Fahey) *chsd ldrs: rdn over 2f out: wknd fnl f* **10/1**
0401 **7** shd **Llewellyn**[12] 2472 9-8-11 **60**.................... (b) PhilDennis(5) 2 46
(Declan Carroll) *prom: rdn over 2f out: wknd over 1f out* **15/2**
3-30 **8** 3 3/4 **Tango Sky (IRE)**[105] 583 8-8-11 **62**.................... ConnorMurtagh(7) 12 37
(Paul Midgley) *hld up: nvr threatened* **9/1**
225- **9** 4 1/2 **Exotic Guest**[325] 3777 7-9-6 **64**.................... (p) JamesSullivan 8 25
(Ruth Carr) *half rrd s and slowly away: hld up: nvr threatened* **16/1**
10-0 **10** 7 **Reinforced**[22] 2119 4-9-2 **65**.................... (p) CallumRodriguez(5) 10 5
(Michael Dods) *midfield: rdn 1/2-way: sn wknd and bhd* **7/1**
0-06 **11** hd **Star Cracker (IRE)**[16] 2341 5-9-3 **61**.................... (p) SamJames 1 1
(Jim Goldie) *pressed ldr: rdn over 2f out: wknd over 1f out: eased* **14/1**
140- **12** 33 **Reflation**[218] 7334 5-9-0 **65**.................... PaulaMuir(7) 11
(Patrick Holmes) *sn pushed along in rr: t.o 1/2-way* **33/1**
1m 14.15s (1.45) **Going Correction** +0.225s/f (Good) **12** Ran SP% **121.1**
Speed ratings (Par 101): **99,95,94,93,92 89,88,83,77,68 68,24**
CSF £100.24 CT £871.27 TOTE £7.00: £2.40, £4.80, £3.70; EX 113.60 Trifecta £2297.30.
**Owner** Antony Brittain **Bred** Northgate Lodge Stud Ltd **Trained** Warthill, N Yorks
**FOCUS**
This was competitive enough for the grade.
T/Plt: £351.30 to a £1 stake. Pool: £78,961.20 - 164.05 winning units T/Qpdt: £114.50 to a £1 stake. Pool: £5,386.70 - 34.80 winning units **Andrew Sheret**

2844 - 2850a (Foreign Racing) - See Raceform Interactive

# PIMLICO (L-H)
Saturday, May 20
**OFFICIAL GOING: Dirt: standard changing to fast after 8.27pm; turf: good**

## 2851a PREAKNESS STKS (GRADE 1) (3YO) (DIRT) 1m 1f 110y(D)
**11:48** 3-Y-O **£731,707** (£243,902; £134,146; £73,170; £36,585)

RPR
**1** **Cloud Computing (USA)**[42] 1640 3-9-0 0.................... JavierCastellano 2 118
(Chad C Brown, U.S.A) *trckd ldrs: rdn under 3f out: styd on to ld narrowly 100yds out: rdn out* **134/10**
**2** hd **Classic Empire (USA)**[14] 2420 3-9-0 0.................... (b) JulienRLeparoux 5 118
(Mark Casse, Canada) *w ldr: led over 3f out: rdn 2 1/2f out: hdd 100yds out: kpt on* **11/5**[2]
**3** 4 3/4 **Senior Investment (USA)**[35] 3-9-0 0.................... ChanningHill 8 108
(Kenneth McPeek, U.S.A) *hld up towards rr: rdn 3f out: drvn under 2f out: styd on fnl f: nrst fin* **32/1**
**4** 1/2 **Lookin At Lee (USA)**[14] 2420 3-9-0 0.................... (b) CoreyJLanerie 9 107
(Steven Asmussen, U.S.A) *hld up in rr: stdy hdwy fr 3 1/2f out: rdn 3f out: kpt on: nvr gng pce to rch ldrs* **19/2**[3]
**5** nse **Gunnevera (USA)**[14] 2420 3-9-0 0.................... (b) MikeESmith 6 107
(Antonio Sano, U.S.A) *midfield: rdn 3 1/2f out: hdwy appr fnl f: no ex ins fnl f* **112/10**
**6** nk **Multiplier (USA)**[27] 3-9-0 0.................... JoelRosario 1 106
(Brendan P Walsh, U.S.A) *hld up towards rr: rdn and kpt on steadily fr under 3f out: nt clr run over 1f out: n.d* **196/10**
**7** 3/4 **Conquest Mo Money (USA)**[34] 1827 3-9-0 0.................... JorgeCarreno 10 105
(Miguel L Hernandez, U.S.A) *in tch in midfield: rdn 3 1/2f out: hrd drvn under 2f out: wknd ins fnl f* **107/10**
**8** 7 1/2 **Always Dreaming (USA)**[14] 2420 3-9-0 0.................... JohnRVelazquez 4 89
(Todd Pletcher, U.S.A) *led: hdd over 3f out: rdn 3f out: wknd 1 1/2f out* **6/5**[1]
**9** 3/4 **Hence (USA)**[14] 2420 3-9-0 0.................... FlorentGeroux 3 88
(Steven Asmussen, U.S.A) *hld up towards rr: rdn and sme hdwy 3 1/2f out: wknd 1 1/2f out* **224/10**
**10** 1 1/4 **Term Of Art (USA)**[42] 1649 3-9-0 0.................... (b[1]) JoseLOrtiz 7 85
(Doug O'Neill, U.S.A) *trckd ldrs: rdn 4f out: lost pl 2 1/2f out: sn struggling* **47/1**
1m 55.98s (0.39) **10** Ran SP% **124.2**
PARI-MUTUEL (all including 2 usd stake): WIN 28.80; PLACE (1-2) 8.60, 4.40; SHOW (1-2-3) 6.00, 4.00, 10.20; SF 98.40.
**Owner** Klaravich Stables Inc & William H Lawrence **Bred** Hill 'N' Dale Equine Holdings Inc & Stretch Run Ve **Trained** USA
**FOCUS**
This year's Kentucky Derby didn't look a good race and the Preakness doesn't seem anything out of the ordinary either. It did go to a newcomer to the Triple Crown series, who just edged out last year's Champion 2yo, with the pair clear, but the Derby winner flopped and, like at Churchill Downs, the time was nothing special. The splits were 23.16 (2f), 23.65 (4f), 24.19 (6f), 25.63 (8f), 19.35 (line). The third and sixth help set the standard.

# 2590 RIPON (R-H)
Sunday, May 21
**OFFICIAL GOING: Good (good to soft in places; 7.8)**
Wind: light half behind Weather: overcast

## 2852 PREMEX SERVICES SUPPORTING WOODEN SPOON CHARITY NOVICE STKS 6f
**2:00** (2:01) (Class 5) 2-Y-O **£3,234** (£962; £481; £240) **Stalls** High

Form RPR
5 **1** **De Bruyne Horse**[14] 2435 2-9-2 0.................... SilvestreDeSousa 8 94+
(Richard Hannon) *mde all: pushed along: kpt on strly to draw clr fnl f: easily* **11/2**[2]
1 **2** 7 **Way Of Wisdom**[14] 2435 2-9-9 0.................... WilliamBuick 1 83
(Charlie Appleby) *trckd ldrs: pushed along to chse ldr 2f out: rdn over 1f out: sn no imp and btn in 2nd: edgd rt towards fin* **1/2**[1]
**3** 5 **Weellan** 2-9-2 0.................... PhillipMakin 5 58+
(John Quinn) *in tch: pushed along over 2f out: rdn and rn green over 1f out: bit short of room and swtchd rt 1f out: kpt on to go 3rd fnl 75yds* **8/1**[3]
6 **4** 1 3/4 **Ventura Crest (IRE)**[18] 2299 2-9-2 0.................... DuranFentiman 2 53
(Tim Easterby) *trckd ldr: rdn over 2f out: wknd ins fnl f* **66/1**
**5** 3 3/4 **Musbaq (USA)** 2-9-2 0.................... DaneO'Neill 7 42
(Mark Johnston) *s.i.s: hld up: pushed along and bit clsr 1/2-way: wknd over 1f out* **9/1**
**6** 2 **Reel Mr Bond** 2-9-2 0.................... ShaneGray 3 36
(Kevin Ryan) *dwlt: hld up: rdn over 3f out: sn bhd* **25/1**
**7** 4 **Lever Du Soleil (FR)** 2-9-2 0.................... DavidAllan 6 24
(Tim Easterby) *trckd ldrs: pushed along 1/2-way: wknd fnl 2f* **25/1**
1m 12.01s (-0.99) **Going Correction** -0.10s/f (Good) **7** Ran SP% **112.3**
Speed ratings (Par 93): **102,92,86,83,78 76,70**
CSF £8.39 TOTE £9.00: £3.30, £1.10; EX 10.90 Trifecta £32.20.
**Owner** Middleham Park Racing Lxv & K Sohi **Bred** Frazer Hood **Trained** East Everleigh, Wilts

**FOCUS**
After riding in the opener Phillip Makin said: "The ground is on the slow side of good" and Shane Gray said: "It is on the easy side of good". This was a fair novice event.

## 2853 CALDER CABINS FLAT CAPS SUPPORTING SPOON H'CAP 6f
2:35 (2:37) (Class 6) (0-60,61) 3-Y-O £3,234 (£962; £481; £240) Stalls High

Form RPR
4-24 1 **Arnold**[13] 2455 3-9-7 **60** JoeyHaynes 7 67+
(Ann Duffield) *in tch racing keenly: pushed along to ld over 1f out: rdn ins fnl f: kpt on wl* **9/2**[2]
-410 2 1 3/4 **Little Kingdom (IRE)**[34] 1835 3-9-4 **57** BenCurtis 2 59
(Tracy Waggott) *chsd ldrs on outside: rdn over 2f out: wnt 2nd ins fnl f: kpt on but no threat wnr* **18/1**
-540 3 3/4 **Brother McGonagall**[8] 2630 3-9-8 **61** DavidAllan 1 61
(Tim Easterby) *chsd ldrs towards outer: rdn and lost pl 2f out: kpt on ins fnl f* **4/1**[1]
00-5 4 nk **Urban Spirit (IRE)**[25] 2077 3-8-11 **50** JackGarritty 3 49
(Jedd O'Keeffe) *midfield: pushed along 1/2-way: kpt on fnl 110yds: nrst fin* **7/1**
0-11 5 1/2 **Termsnconditions (IRE)**[25] 2091 3-9-6 **59** KieranO'Neill 6 56
(Tim Vaughan) *prom: rdn over 2f out: edgd rt over 1f out: wknd fnl 110yds* **9/2**[2]
-46 6 1 1/2 **Stopdworldnletmeof**[47] 1543 3-8-0 **46** oh1 DavidEgan(7) 8 39
(David Flood) *led: rdn whn hdd over 1f out: wknd fnl f* **11/1**
-640 7 3 **Ejabah (IRE)**[21] 2182 3-8-7 **51** LewisEdmunds(5) 9 35
(Charles Smith) *hld up: rdn over 2f out: nvr threatened* **8/1**
33-5 8 1 1/2 **Kroy**[21] 2181 3-9-5 **58** PaulHanagan 10 37
(Ollie Pears) *chsd ldrs: pushed along and lost pl over 3f out: no threat after* **5/1**[3]
00-0 9 5 **Clear As A Bell (IRE)**[34] 1835 3-9-2 **55** (b1) DuranFentiman 4 19
(Tim Easterby) *s.i.s: hld up on outer: rdn 1/2-way: wknd over 1f out* **33/1**
000- 10 shd **Equipe**[219] 7331 3-8-9 **48** CamHardie 5 12
(Richard Whitaker) *dwlt: a towards rr* **66/1**

1m 13.08s (0.08) **Going Correction** -0.10s/f (Good) **10** Ran SP% **114.7**
Speed ratings (Par 97): **95,92,91,91,90 88,84,82,75,75**
CSF £80.04 CT £356.99 TOTE £4.10: £1.60, £4.60, £2.50; EX 63.70 Trifecta £265.70.
**Owner** D J & S A Shewring, D Marshall, B Craig **Bred** Tirnaskea Stud **Trained** Constable Burton, N Yorks

**FOCUS**
An ordinary 3yo sprint handicap. The balance of the second, third and fourth back this level.

## 2854 VW VAN CENTRE (WEST YORKSHIRE) H'CAP 1m 1f 170y
3:10 (3:10) (Class 4) (0-80,80) 3-Y-O £6,469 (£1,925; £962; £481) Stalls Low

Form RPR
-541 1 **Rita's Man (IRE)**[17] 2349 3-8-6 **65** SilvestreDeSousa 4 75+
(Richard Hannon) *hld up in midfield: swtchd to outer and gd hdwy over 2f out: rdn to ld over 1f out: kpt on wl: comf* **11/4**[1]
1-62 2 4 **Lucy's Law (IRE)**[21] 2186 3-8-10 **69** JamesSullivan 7 70
(Tom Tate) *hld up in rr: rdn over 2f out: angled rt towards inner and hdwy appr fnl f: squeezed through gap ins fnl f: kpt on wl: wnt 2nd nr fin* **9/1**
30-4 3 nk **Racemaker**[21] 2186 3-8-10 **69** NeilFarley 1 69
(Andrew Crook) *led: rdn over 2f out: hdd over 1f out: one pce: lost 2nd nr fin* **28/1**
34-3 4 nk **Golconda Prince (IRE)**[41] 1678 3-8-5 **64** PaulHanagan 8 64
(Richard Fahey) *midfield: hdwy to chse ldr over 3f out: rdn over 2f out: one pce* **6/1**
526- 5 2 1/2 **Powerful Love (IRE)**[212] 7511 3-9-1 **74** JoeFanning 6 69
(Mark Johnston) *hld up: hdwy to chse ldr over 3f out: sn rdn: wknd ins fnl f* **10/1**
053- 6 4 **Alshibaa (IRE)**[190] 7940 3-8-12 **71** DaneO'Neill 9 57
(William Haggas) *dwlt: sn trckd ldr: rdn over 2f out: wknd over 1f out* **3/1**[2]
22-3 7 2 **Warm Love**[18] 2300 3-9-0 **73** DanielTudhope 2 55
(David O'Meara) *trckd ldr: rdn over 2f out: wknd over 1f out* **9/2**[3]
1225 8 6 **Good Time Ahead (IRE)**[68] 1195 3-8-9 **68** PaddyAspell 3 38
(Philip Kirby) *in tch: racd keenly: rdn over 3f out: sn wknd and bhd* **18/1**

2m 5.1s (-0.30) **Going Correction** 0.0s/f (Good) **8** Ran SP% **111.9**
Speed ratings (Par 101): **101,97,97,97,95 92,90,85**
CSF £26.68 CT £555.01 TOTE £4.10: £1.60, £2.00, £6.10; EX 19.90 Trifecta £433.90.
**Owner** Middleham Park Racing XX **Bred** L White & D McGregor **Trained** East Everleigh, Wilts

**FOCUS**
Distance increased by 12yds. A modest 3yo handicap, run at a strong pace. Straightforward enough form.

## 2855 RIPON, YORKSHIRE'S GARDEN RACECOURSE H'CAP 1m 1f
3:40 (3:42) (Class 2) (0-105,102) 4-Y-O+
£14,317 (£4,287; £2,143; £1,071; £535; £269) Stalls Low

Form RPR
0-31 1 **Gurkha Friend**[22] 2155 5-8-9 **90** SilvestreDeSousa 6 97
(Karen McLintock) *mde all: rdn over 2f out: strly pressed over 1f out: hld on gamely* **2/1**[1]
-561 2 nk **Briardale (IRE)**[37] 1781 5-8-9 **90** PJMcDonald 8 96
(James Bethell) *in tch: racd quite keenly: rdn to chal strly over 1f out: kpt on: a jst hld* **15/2**
204- 3 1 **Knight Owl**[209] 7573 7-8-7 **93** GeorgeWood(5) 1 97
(James Fanshawe) *midfield on inner: angled lft and forced way into clr on outer 2f out: sn rdn to chse ldrs: kpt on* **7/1**
26-6 4 nse **Rainbow Rebel (IRE)**[9] 2593 4-8-6 **87** JoeFanning 4 91
(Mark Johnston) *trckd ldrs: rdn over 2f out: kpt on* **8/1**
531- 5 3/4 **Empress Ali (IRE)**[216] 7408 6-8-9 **90** JamesSullivan 10 92
(Tom Tate) *prom: rdn over 2f out: one pce* **22/1**
00-5 6 3/4 **Miss Van Gogh**[22] 2155 5-8-2 **83** PaulHanagan 7 83
(Richard Fahey) *hld up: pushed along over 2f out: rdn over 1f out: kpt on fnl f: nvr threatened* **13/2**[3]
0-15 7 hd **Snoano**[10] 2553 5-9-7 **102** DavidAllan 2 102
(Tim Easterby) *dwlt: hld up in midfield: rdn over 2f out: sltly hmpd 2f out: one pce* **4/1**[2]
-500 8 4 **Silvery Moon (IRE)**[15] 2406 10-8-2 **86** RachelRichardson(3) 3 77
(Tim Easterby) *midfield on outer: rdn over 2f out: wknd over 1f* **25/1**
-600 9 4 **Strong Steps**[3] 2767 5-8-9 **90** (p) TonyHamilton 5 72
(Roger Fell) *hld up in rr: rdn 3f out: wknd over 1f out* **16/1**

1m 53.89s (-0.81) **Going Correction** 0.0s/f (Good) **9** Ran SP% **116.1**
Speed ratings (Par 109): **103,102,101,101,101 100,100,96,93**
CSF £17.86 CT £89.58 TOTE £2.90: £1.60, £2.40, £2.10; EX 20.90 Trifecta £115.00.
**Owner** Self Preservation Society & Don Eddy **Bred** Mrs J Imray **Trained** Ingoe, Northumberland
■ Stewards' Enquiry : George Wood four-day ban: careless riding (5-8 June)

**FOCUS**
Distance increased by 12yds. It paid to be handy in this feature handicap.

## 2856 WILMOT-SMITH MEMORIAL EBF "BREEDERS SERIES' FILLIES" H'CAP 6f
4:10 (4:12) (Class 3) (0-95,87) 3-Y-O+
£12,450 (£3,728; £1,864; £932; £466; £234) Stalls High

Form RPR
0-44 1 **Southern Belle (IRE)**[15] 2407 4-9-12 **85** JoeFanning 7 93+
(Robert Cowell) *s.i.s: sn midfield: rdn and gd hdwy appr fnl f: led ins fnl f: edgd rt: kpt on* **13/2**[2]
16-4 2 1/2 **The Feathered Nest (IRE)**[23] 2122 3-8-13 **81** PaulHanagan 1 85+
(Richard Fahey) *1 of 2 who racd far side: in tch w main gp: pushed along over 2f out: rdn over 1f out: r.o wl* **9/4**[1]
60-6 3 1 1/4 **Tumblewind**[3] 2764 7-9-12 **85** FrannyNorton 5 87
(Richard Whitaker) *chsd ldrs: rdn over 2f out: kpt on: carried rt by wnr fnl 110yds* **10/1**
66-5 4 1 1/2 **Perfect Madge (IRE)**[36] 1796 3-9-5 **87** KevinStott 8 82
(Kevin Ryan) *rrd s and slowly away: hld up: rdn and hdwy appr fnl f: edgd rt but kpt on: nrst fin* **10/1**
0-44 5 1/2 **Honeysuckle Lil (IRE)**[9] 2592 5-8-13 **75** (p) RachelRichardson(3) 4 71
(Tim Easterby) *midfield: on outer: rdn over 2f out: one pce* **8/1**[3]
-001 6 nk **Sandra's Secret (IRE)**[17] 2335 4-9-5 **81** NathanEvans(3) 11 76
(Les Eyre) *led narrowly: rdn 2f out: hdd ins fnl f: wknd* **9/1**
14-0 7 2 3/4 **Savannah Slew**[39] 1731 3-8-10 **78** (h) AndrewMullen 2 62
(James Given) *slowly away: hld up: rdn over 2f out: nvr threatened* **10/1**
0-36 8 1/2 **Rose Marmara**[6] 2683 4-9-1 **77** (t) AdamMcNamara(3) 3 61
(Brian Rothwell) *1 of 2 who racd far side: in tch w main gp: rdn over 2f out: wknd fnl f* **20/1**
0-00 9 hd **Blithe Spirit**[11] 2524 6-9-9 **87** PhilDennis(5) 6 71
(Eric Alston) *w ldr: rdn over 2f out: wknd fnl f* **25/1**
136- 10 1/2 **Love Island**[239] 6793 8-9-9 **82** (h) PaulMulrennan 9 64
(Richard Whitaker) *chsd ldrs: rdn over 2f out: wknd fnl f* **11/1**
260- 11 7 **Groupie**[226] 7114 3-9-3 **85** JamesSullivan 10 43
(Tom Tate) *chsd ldrs: rdn 1/2-way: sn wknd and bhd* **20/1**

1m 11.69s (-1.31) **Going Correction** -0.10s/f (Good)
**WFA** 3 from 4yo+ 9lb **11** Ran SP% **114.2**
Speed ratings (Par 107): **104,103,101,99,99 98,94,94,94,93 84**
CSF £20.10 CT £147.72 TOTE £6.90: £2.50, £1.60, £3.40; EX 27.10 Trifecta £295.10.
**Owner** Ahmed Jaber **Bred** Rabbah Bloodstock Limited **Trained** Six Mile Bottom, Cambs

**FOCUS**
Not a bad fillies' sprint handicap.

## 2857 PATRICIA CHEAL CELEBRATION MAIDEN STKS 1m 1f
4:40 (4:42) (Class 5) 3-Y-O £3,234 (£962; £481; £240) Stalls Low

Form RPR
2-2 1 **Materialist**[21] 2185 3-9-5 0 (h) AndreaAtzeni 3 83
(Roger Varian) *racd keenly in tch: trckd ldrs over 4f out: pushed along over 2f out: rdn over 1f out: led 75yds out: kpt on* **11/8**[1]
43- 2 nk **Another Eclipse (IRE)**[212] 7511 3-9-5 0 TomEaves 7 82
(David Simcock) *midfield: rdn along over 3f out: in tch in 4th over 1f out: styd on wl fnl 110yds* **10/1**
02-2 3 1 **Mathix (FR)**[40] 1692 3-9-5 80 SilvestreDeSousa 5 80
(William Haggas) *dwlt: sn trckd ldr: pressed ldr 2f out: rdn to ld 2f out: hdd 75yds out: no ex* **5/2**[2]
5-32 4 shd **Lamloom (IRE)**[31] 1914 3-9-5 78 DanielTudhope 9 80
(David O'Meara) *racd keenly and sn led: jnd 3f out: sn pushed along: hdd 2f out: rdn and one pce* **4/1**[3]
5 5 2 **Montanna**[15] 2408 3-9-5 0 JackGarritty 4 75
(Jedd O'Keeffe) *in tch: rdn and outpcd 3f out: styd on fnl f* **66/1**
04 6 8 **Immortalised**[29] 1967 3-9-5 0 PJMcDonald 6 58
(K R Burke) *trckd ldr: rdn 4f out: wknd over 2f out* **10/1**
44 7 3 3/4 **El Nino Sea (IRE)**[14] 2429 3-9-5 0 PaulHanagan 8 49
(Richard Fahey) *hld up: nvr threatened* **28/1**
8 1/2 **Delegation** 3-9-5 0 DavidAllan 1 48
(Tim Easterby) *midfield: rdn 3f out: wknd over 1f out* **66/1**
00- 9 2 **Mr C (IRE)**[334] 3477 3-9-5 0 AndrewMullen 2 44
(Ollie Pears) *a towards rr* **100/1**

1m 54.68s (-0.02) **Going Correction** 0.0s/f (Good) **9** Ran SP% **116.3**
Speed ratings (Par 99): **100,99,98,98,96 89,86,86,84**
CSF £16.84 TOTE £2.20: £1.10, £3.60, £1.20; EX 16.70 Trifecta £41.90.
**Owner** Sheikh Mohammed Obaid Al Maktoum **Bred** Darley **Trained** Newmarket, Suffolk

**FOCUS**
Distance increased by 12yds. A fair 3yo maiden.

## 2858 MIDDLEHAM TRAINERS ASSOCIATION APPRENTICE H'CAP 5f
5:10 (5:10) (Class 5) (0-70,70) 4-Y-O+ £3,881 (£1,155; £577; £288) Stalls High

Form RPR
5042 1 **Pearl Noir**[8] 2628 7-8-11 **60** (b) PaddyPilley(3) 5 67
(Scott Dixon) *mde all: rdn over 1f out: kpt on* **7/2**[1]
3522 2 1 **Entertaining Ben**[29] 1981 4-9-0 **67** FinleyMarsh(7) 7 70
(Amy Murphy) *chsd ldr: rdn over 1f out: kpt on* **4/1**[2]
1451 3 1 1/2 **Mighty Zip (USA)**[8] 2621 5-8-11 **62** (p) JordanUys(5) 3 60
(Lisa Williamson) *chsd ldr: rdn over 1f out: one pce* **13/2**
1221 4 1/2 **Roy's Legacy**[16] 2360 8-9-7 **67** CharlieBennett 8 63
(Shaun Harris) *chsd ldr: rdn over 1f out: edgd rt and one pce: no ex towards fin* **6/1**[3]
U40- 5 3/4 **Mitchum**[257] 6216 8-9-4 **67** LewisEdmunds(5) 1 60
(Ron Barr) *midfield: rdn 1/2-way: one pce and nvr threatened* **10/1**
-620 6 1/2 **Sarabi**[122] 303 4-9-5 **65** (p) AlistairRawlinson 4 56
(Scott Dixon) *hld up: rdn and kpt on ins fnl f: nvr threatened* **12/1**
6-03 7 1 **Miningold**[15] 2407 4-9-4 **69** (p) CallumRodriguez(5) 6 57
(Michael Dods) *midfield: rdn 2f out: wknd ins fnl f* **4/1**[2]
600- 8 6 **Sir Domino (FR)**[188] 7959 5-9-3 **70** PaulaMuir(7) 2 36
(Patrick Holmes) *hld rrd s and s.i.s: hld up: rdn 1/2-way: sn bhd: hung rt ins fnl f* **12/1**

59.07s (-0.93) **Going Correction** -0.10s/f (Good) **8** Ran SP% **114.3**
Speed ratings (Par 103): **103,101,99,98,97 96,94,85**
CSF £17.59 CT £86.37 TOTE £4.60: £1.70, £2.70, £2.00; EX 22.70 Trifecta £94.90.
**Owner** P J Dixon & Partners **Bred** Mrs Yvette Dixon **Trained** Babworth, Notts

**FOCUS**
Solid sprinting form for the class.
T/Jkpt: Not won. T/Plt: £26.60 to a £1 stake. Pool: £69,177.00 - 2,598.90 winning units T/Qpdt: £7.90 to a £1 stake. Pool: £3,406.00 - 430.40 winning units **Andrew Sheret**

2859 - 2860a (Foreign Racing) - See Raceform Interactive

## [2236]NAAS (L-H)

Sunday, May 21

**OFFICIAL GOING: Good to yielding**

### 2861a COOLMORE WAR COMMAND ROCHESTOWN STKS (LISTED RACE) 5f

**3:15** (3:17) 2-Y-O

**£32,777** (£10,555; £5,000; £2,222; £1,111; £555)

RPR

1 **True Blue Moon (IRE)**[39] [1738] 2-9-3 0.................... DonnachaO'Brien 5 94
(Joseph Patrick O'Brien, Ire) *chsd ldrs: 4th 1/2-way: rdn in 5th over 1f out and r.o wl to ld wl ins fnl f* **8/1**

2 ½ **Verhoyen**[8] [2634] 2-9-3 0.............................................(h[1]) NGMcCullagh 4 92
(M C Grassick, Ire) *late to post: w.w in rr: pushed along after 1/2-way: rdn in 6th ent fnl f and r.o wl into 2nd wl ins fnl f: nt rch wnr* **20/1**

3 ¾ **Simmy's Copshop**[29] [1966] 2-9-3 0.......................... DeclanMcDonogh 6 90
(Richard Fahey) *hld up bhd ldrs: 3rd 1/2-way: tk clsr order nr side after 1/2-way: rdn almost on terms ent fnl f: no ex wl ins fnl f where dropped to 3rd: kpt on same pce* **3/1**[2]

4 ½ **T For Tango (IRE)**[42] [1650] 2-9-3 0.................................... PatSmullen 2 88
(J A Nash, Ire) *settled bhd ldrs: 5th 1/2-way: hdwy after 1/2-way gng wl far side to ld over 1f out where rdn: hdd wl ins fnl f and wknd cl home* **8/1**

5 ½ **Mamba Noire (FR)**[15] [2412] 2-8-12 0.................................. ShaneFoley 3 84
(K J Condon, Ire) *cl up and sn disp ld: hdd 2f out: rdn almost on terms ins fnl f and sn no ex between horses where n.m.r: wknd ane eased clsng stages* **4/1**[3]

6 ½ **Sirici (IRE)**[30] [1949] 2-8-12 0.......................................... ChrisHayes 7 79
(J A Stack, Ire) *w.w towards rr: pushed along in 6th after 1/2-way and dropped to rr u.p ent fnl f: kpt on same pce in 6th wl ins fnl f: nvr trbld ldrs* **14/1**

7 3 ¾ **Dali (USA)**[20] [2238] 2-9-3 0..................................................(t) RyanMoore 1 71
(A P O'Brien, Ire) *sn led narrowly tl sn jnd and disp ld: led narrowly 2f out: sn rdn and hdd between horses over 1f out: no ex whn checked in 4th ins fnl f: sn dropped to rr and eased* **7/4**[1]

1m 2.0s **7 Ran SP% 115.0**
CSF £139.02 TOTE £8.60: £4.00, £7.80; DF 161.60 Trifecta £648.60.
**Owner** Brian Dolan **Bred** Brian Dolan **Trained** Owning Hill, Co Kilkenny

**FOCUS**
Several strong lines of two-year-old form represented here, with the winner confirming his superiority over the favourite, who was fancied to turn around their Dundalk placings. Not strong form for the grade.

### 2862a COOLMORE STUD IRISH EBF FILLIES' SPRINT STKS (LISTED RACE) 6f

**3:45** (3:47) 2-Y-O **£32,777** (£10,555; £5,000; £2,222; £1,111)

RPR

1 **Alpha Centauri (IRE)**[20] [2236] 2-9-0 0...................... ColmO'Donoghue 5 102+
(Mrs John Harrington, Ire) *sltly awkward s: settled bhd ldrs tl wnt 2nd after 1f: disp fr 1/2-way and sn led narrowly: pushed along and pressed briefly 1 1/2f out: sn qcknd clr and in command: easily* **8/11**[1]

2 5 **Actress (IRE)**[7] [2655] 2-9-0 0................................................ RyanMoore 2 87
(A P O'Brien, Ire) *trckd ldrs: pushed along 2f out and brief effrt in cl 2nd nr side 1 1/2f out: sn rdn briefly and no imp on easy wnr: kpt on same pce ins fnl f* **9/4**[2]

3 1 **Shapes (IRE)**[20] [2236] 2-9-0 0.............................................. ColinKeane 4 84
(G M Lyons, Ire) *broke wl to ld narrowly tl jnd fr 1/2-way and sn hdd narrowly: rdn 2f out and sn no imp on easy wnr u.p in 3rd: kpt on same pce ins fnl f* **8/1**[3]

4 5 **Moonlight Bay**[56] [1383] 2-9-0 0.......................................... ChrisHayes 1 69
(Kevin Prendergast, Ire) *cl up far side early tl sn settled in rr: tk clsr order in 4th fr bef 1/2-way: rdn and no ex under 2f out: one pce after* **8/1**[3]

5 4 ½ **Camacho Dancer (IRE)**[7] [2655] 2-9-0 0....................... RobbieDowney 3 56
(Keith Henry Clarke, Ire) *chsd ldrs in 4th and racd keenly early: pushed along in rr fr bef 1/2-way and no imp after* **66/1**

1m 13.53s (0.33) **5 Ran SP% 112.4**
CSF £2.70 TOTE £1.50: £1.02, £1.70; DF 2.70 Trifecta £5.60.
**Owner** Niarchos Family **Bred** Niarchos Family **Trained** Moone, Co Kildare

**FOCUS**
The same result as the maiden in which the front three filled the exact placings over this C&D earlier this month. All three fillies seem to have improved since but the winner is something special and confirmed herself as a cut above her rivals. The third has been rated as improving a bit, but the form could could easily be rated higher.

### 2863a EMS COPIERS LACKEN STKS (GROUP 3) 6f

**4:15** (4:15) 3-Y-O

**£32,777** (£10,555; £5,000; £2,222; £1,111; £555)

RPR

1 **Caravaggio (USA)**[287] [5212] 3-9-6 116.............................. RyanMoore 7 121+
(A P O'Brien, Ire) *dwlt and towards rr early: 5th bef 1/2-way: gng wl under 2f out and pushed along into 3rd over 1f out: r.o strly to ld ins fnl f where sn clr and in command: easily* **8/15**[1]

2 4 ¾ **Psychedelic Funk**[28] [1997] 3-9-3 103................................. ColinKeane 9 103
(G M Lyons, Ire) *chsd ldrs: pushed along in 3rd 2f out: sn rdn and lost pl briefly 1f out: no imp on easy wnr in 3rd ins fnl f: kpt on u.p into 2nd clsng stages* **10/1**[3]

3 1 ¾ **Mr Scarlet**[28] [1997] 3-9-3 96............................................. RonanWhelan 8 97
(Ms Sheila Lavery, Ire) *w.w in rr: rdn in 6th 1 1/2f out and r.o u.p ins fnl f into nvr threatening 3rd fnl strides: nt trble easy wnr* **25/1**

4 hd **Gorane (IRE)**[28] [1997] 3-9-0 100.......................... DeclanMcDonogh 6 94
(Henry De Bromhead, Ire) *wnt lft s and bmpd rival: led: stl gng wl over 1 l clr at 1/2-way: rdn 1 1/2f out and hdd u.p ins fnl f: no ch w easy wnr and wknd into 3rd clsng stages: denied 3rd fnl strides* **14/1**

5 hd **Khukri (IRE)**[28] [1997] 3-9-3 107.......................... ColmO'Donoghue 2 96
(Mrs John Harrington, Ire) *wnt sltly lft s: chsd ldrs: pushed along in 4th 2f out: rdn over 1f out and no imp on easy wnr u.p in 4th ins fnl f: kpt on one pce clsng stages where dropped to 5th* **10/3**[2]

6 1 ¾ **Pedestal (IRE)**[341] [3247] 3-9-3 95...........................(t[1]) SeamieHeffernan 4 91
(A P O'Brien, Ire) *settled bhd ldrs: pushed along in 6th bef 1/2-way and no imp u.p in rr 1 1/2f out: kpt on again ins fnl f into mod 6th: nvr trbld ldrs* **16/1**

7 4 ¾ **Mister Trader**[341] [3247] 3-9-3 103.................................(t[1]) PatSmullen 5 75
(D J Bunyan, Ire) *bmpd at s: cl up bhd ldr: 2nd 1/2-way: pushed along 2f out and no ex u.p over 1f out: wknd and eased ins fnl f* **40/1**

1m 12.33s (-0.87) **7 Ran SP% 116.2**
CSF £7.70 TOTE £1.40: £1.02, £3.80; DF 9.50 Trifecta £104.40.
**Owner** Mrs John Magnier & Michael Tabor & Derrick Smith **Bred** Windmill Manor Farms Inc Et Al **Trained** Cashel, Co Tipperary

**FOCUS**
A straightforward success from a horse in which Aidan O'Brien has described as one of the fastest he has ever seen. The standard is set around the second and sixth.

2864 - 2865a (Foreign Racing) - See Raceform Interactive

## [2663]CAPANNELLE (R-H)

Sunday, May 21

**OFFICIAL GOING: Turf: soft**

### 2866a PREMIO CARLO D'ALESSIO (GROUP 3) (4YO+) (TURF) 1m 4f

**1:30** 4-Y-0+ **£27,777** (£12,222; £6,666; £3,333)

RPR

1 **Full Drago (ITY)**[217] [7402] 4-9-0 0.............................. CristianDemuro 2 109
(Stefano Botti, Italy) *mde all: rdn along 2f out: forged clr fnl f: wl on top fin* **1/3**[1]

2 4 **Refuse To Bobbin (IRE)**[20] 7-8-9 0......................... GermanoMarcelli 3 98
(M Narduzzi, Italy) *w.w in fnl pair: prog 3f out: chsd ldr wl over 2f out: styd on at same pce* **131/10**

3 ½ **Time Chant**[42] 5-8-9 0........................................................... DarioVargiu 4 97
(Stefano Botti, Italy) *chsd ldr: drvn and no imp 3f out: styd on ins fnl f: nt quite rch runner-up* **9/2**[3]

4 hd **Quelindo (GER)**[49] 5-8-9 0.............................................. AlbertoSanna 1 97
(Gabor Maronka, Hungary) *chsd ldng pair: angled out and rdn 2 1/2f out: no immediate imp: styd on u.p fnl f* **61/20**[2]

5 12 **Multicolours** 6-8-9 0........................................ PierantonioConvertino 6 78
(Iacopo Bindi, Italy) *racd in rr wl off pce: clsd 1/2-way to join bkmarkers: no further imp 3f out: wl hld whn eased 1 1/2f out* **193/10**

2m 28.9s (1.70) **5 Ran SP% 129.9**
PARI-MUTUEL (all including 1 euro stake): WIN 1.33 PLACE 1.09, 2.24 DF 8.51.
**Owner** Dioscuri Srl **Bred** Massimo Dragoni **Trained** Italy

### 2867a PREMIO TUDINI - IITRIS (GROUP 3) (3YO+) (TURF) 6f

**3:45** 3-Y-0+ **£27,777** (£12,222; £6,666; £3,333)

RPR

1 **Trust You**[28] 5-9-0 0.......................................................... SilvanoMulas 10 102
(Endo Botti, Italy) *racd in midfield on outer: rdn and gd hdwy fr over 2f out: led 1 1/2f out: kpt on wl: drvn out* **17/2**

2 1 ¼ **Pensierieparole**[118] [384] 5-9-0 0........................................ DarioVargiu 8 98
(Il Cavallo In Testa, Italy) *hld up in rr: gd hdwy on outer fr over 2f out: rdn over 1f out: kpt on wl: no imp on wnr last 100yds* **112/10**

3 1 **Penalty (ITY)**[238] 3-8-7 0..................................................... FabioBranca 1 95
(Stefano Botti, Italy) *hld up in midfield: rdn and kpt on fr over 2f out: nrst fin* **67/10**

4 1 ¼ **Plusquemavie (IRE)**[28] 6-9-0 0.............................. GianpasqualeFois 3 91
(V Fazio, Italy) *hld up towards rr: rdn and hdwy fr under 2f out: no ex last 100yds* **6/4**[1]

5 nk **Dutch Breeze**[330] [3645] 6-9-0 0.............................. GiuseppeCannarella 7 90
(S Cannavo, Italy) *led: rdn 2f out: hdd 1 1/2f out: no ex ins fnl f* **212/10**

6 1 ¼ **Harlem Shake (IRE)**[196] [7840] 6-9-0 0............................ LucaManiezzi 2 86
(Marco Gasparini, Italy) *hld up towards rr: rdn and kpt on steadily fr 2f out: n.d* **114/10**

7 3 **Kathy Dream (IRE)**[196] [7840] 5-8-10 0...................... SalvatoreBasile 11 72
(Luigi Biagetti, Italy) *trckd ldrs on outer: rdn under 2f out: wknd ins fnl f: eased last 75yds* **43/10**[2]

8 nse **Zapel**[28] 4-9-0 0.................................................................. CristianDemuro 6 76
(Stefano Botti, Italy) *trckd ldrs: rdn over 2f out: wknd fnl f* **59/10**[3]

9 7 **Last Gift (IRE)**[34] 5-8-10 0................................................ CarloFiocchi 9 50
(M Narduzzi, Italy) *prom: rdn 2f out: sn outpcd and btn: eased fnl f* **179/10**

10 3 ½ **Swallow Street (IRE)**[234] [6895] 3-8-5 0............ PierantonioConvertino 4 40
(M Bebbu, Italy) *in tch: rdn over 2f out: wknd over 1f out: eased ins fnl f* **59/10**[3]

11 4 **Lohit**[51] 6-9-0 0.................................................................. GermanoMarcelli 5 30
(Luis Alberto Acuna, Italy) *in tch: rdn and unable qck appr 2f out: sn btn and eased* **30/1**

1m 7.9s (-2.40)
**WFA** 3 from 4yo+ 9lb **11 Ran SP% 140.6**
PARI-MUTUEL (all including 1 euro stake): WIN 9.45 PLACE 3.23, 3.52, 2.86 DF 162.20.
**Owner** Antonio Rizzo **Bred** Mrs A R Ruggles **Trained** Italy

### 2868a DERBY ITALIANO - SISAL MATCHPOINT (GROUP 2) (3YO) (TURF) 1m 3f

**5:00** 3-Y-O **£273,504** (£120,341; £65,641; £32,820)

RPR

1 **Mac Mahon (ITY)**[28] 3-9-2 0.......................................... CristianDemuro 5 112+
(Stefano Botti, Italy) *waited in midfield: dropped towards rr wl bef 1/2-way: gd hdwy on outer 3f out: led 2f out: powered clr over 1f out: won easing down* **37/10**

2 5 **Back On Board (IRE)**[20] 3-9-2 0...................................... AntonioFresu 11 103
(Stefano Botti, Italy) *led after 1f: 5l clr bef 1/2-way: drvn for home 3f out: hdd 2f out: rallied gamely u.p to hold 2nd* **5/2**[2]

3 hd **Anda Muchacho (IRE)**[20] [2245] 3-9-2 0.......................... DarioVargiu 10 103
(Il Cavallo In Testa, Italy) *chsd ldng trio: rdn and nt qckn 2f out: kpt on u.p fnl f: jst hld for 2nd* **341/100**[3]

4 2 **Amore Hass (IRE)**[20] [2245] 3-9-2 0............................ VincentCheminaud 8 99
(Stefano Botti, Italy) *w.w in midfield: tk clsr order 2 1/2f out: styd on at one pce fnl f* **118/10**

5 3 ½ **Patriot Hero (IRE)**[20] [2245] 3-9-2 0......................... MickaelBarzalona 7 93
(Endo Botti, Italy) *plld hrd: restrained in fnl trio: hrd rdn and hdwy over 2f out: kpt on but nvr in contention* **76/10**

6 ¾ **Ground Rules (ITY)**[20] 3-9-2 0.............................................. FabioBranca 3 91
(Stefano Botti, Italy) *w.w in fnl trio: hdwy on inner under 3f out: nt clr run and hmpd 2f out: one pce fnl f* **5/2**[2]

7 2 1/2 **Diditi** 3-9-2 0 PierantonioConvertino 1 87
(Il Cavallo In Testa, Italy) *led: hdd after 1f: chsd ldr: rdn and wakened 1 1/2f out* **74/1**
8 4 1/2 **Menuhin (ITY)** 3-9-2 0 LucaManiezzi 6 79
(Stefano Botti, Italy) *last away: sn rushed up to r in midfield: rdn and wknd under 2f out* **141/10**
9 2 1/2 **Fortissimo (GER)** 3-9-2 0 CarloFiocchi 2 74
(R Rohne, Germany) *racd keenly: hld up in tch: lost pl 2 1/2f out: sn btn* **229/10**
10 1 **Kensai (FR)**[42] 1658 3-9-2 0 FrankieDettori 4 72
(Simone Brogi, France) *settled in midfield: clsd 3f out: rdn and wknd ins fnl 2f* **12/5**[1]
11 4 **Aethos (IRE)**[20] 3-9-2 0 SilvanoMulas 9 65
(Stefano Botti, Italy) *racd keenly: hld up in fnl trio: rdn and no imp 2 1/2f out: wl hld fnl 2f* **12/5**[1]

2m 16.5s **11** Ran SP% **191.5**
PARI-MUTUEL (all including 1 euro stake): WIN 2.18 PLACE 2.12, 2.16 DF 9.00.
**Owner** Takaya Shimakawa **Bred** Massimiliano Porcelli **Trained** Italy

## 2450 COLOGNE (R-H)
Sunday, May 21

**OFFICIAL GOING: Turf: good**

### 2869a MEHL-MULHENS-RENNEN - GERMAN 2000 GUINEAS (GROUP 2) (3YO COLTS & FILLIES) (TURF) 1m
**4:05** 3-Y-0 **£85,470** (£25,641; £11,111; £5,982; £2,564)

RPR
1 **Poetic Dream (IRE)**[33] 3-9-2 0 EduardoPedroza 4 108+
(A Wohler, Germany) *hld up in midfield: short of room on inner appr 2f out: sn rdn: styd on wl fr over 1f out: led cl home: drvn out* **61/10**
2 nk **Lockheed**[225] 7148 3-9-2 0 PatCosgrave 2 107
(William Haggas) *led: rdn and strly pressed fr 2f out: kpt on wl: hdd clsng stages* **9/5**[1]
3 shd **Empire Of The Star (FR)**[14] 3-9-2 0 MaximeGuyon 8 107
(A Wohler, Germany) *chsd ldr: rdn and pressed ldr strly fr 2f out: kpt on wl but a jst hld: dropped to 3rd clsng stages* **47/10**[3]
4 2 **Dragon Lips (GER)**[28] 2002 3-9-2 0 AndraschStarke 3 102
(Andreas Suborics, Germany) *in tch: t.k.h fr 4f out: rdn and kpt on same pce fr 2 1/2f out* **14/5**[2]
5 3/4 **Savile Row (FR)**[28] 2002 3-9-2 0 (p) KoenClijmans 7 101+
(Frau Erika Mader, Germany) *hld up in rr: rdn 2 1/2f out: styd on ins fnl f: nrst fin* **38/1**
6 2 **Fulminato (GER)**[28] 2002 3-9-2 0 FilipMinarik 5 96
(Andreas Suborics, Germany) *hld up towards rr: rdn and kpt on steadily fr 2 1/2f out* **12/1**
7 nk **Shinzaro (GER)**[28] 2002 3-9-2 0 OliverWilson 1 95
(D Moser, Germany) *hld up towards rr of midfield: rdn and no imp fr 2 1/2f out* **115/10**
8 5 **Dia Del Sol**[28] 2002 3-9-2 0 IoritzMendizabal 6 84
(Markus Klug, Germany) *in tch in midfield: rdn 2 1/2f out: wknd over 1f out: eased last 100yds* **6/1**
9 3 **Rostam (USA)**[20] 2246 3-9-2 0 (b) JozefBojko 9 77
(A Wohler, Germany) *trckd ldrs: rdn 2 1/2f out: wknd under 2f out: eased last 100yds* **246/10**

1m 34.83s (-3.56) **9** Ran SP% **130.1**
PARI-MUTUEL (all including 10 euro stake): WIN 71 PLACE: 20, 18, 21; SF: 287.
**Owner** Jaber Abdullah **Bred** Rabbah Bloodstock Limited **Trained** Germany

2870 - 2880a (Foreign Racing) - See Raceform Interactive

## 2696 SAINT-CLOUD (L-H)
Friday, May 19

**OFFICIAL GOING: Turf: very soft**

### 2881a PRIX DE LA MONTAGNE SAINTE-GENEVIEVE (CONDITIONS) (2YO) (TURF) 6f
**12:45** 2-Y-0 **£11,111** (£4,444; £3,333; £2,222; £1,111)

RPR
1 **Dann (FR)**[29] 1929 2-9-2 0 AlexandreGavilan 2 84
(D Guillemin, France) **13/5**[2]
2 1 1/4 **La Canche (FR)**[29] 1919 2-8-7 0 EddyHardouin 6 71
(T Clout, France) **12/5**[1]
3 hd **Sedary (FR)**[24] 2-8-5 0 MlleZoePfeil(10) 8 79
(H-F Devin, France) **16/5**[3]
4 shd **Hautot (FR)**[29] 1919 2-8-10 0 CristianDemuro 9 73
(P Sogorb, France) **11/2**
5 2 **Sens Des Affaires (FR)** 2-8-10 0 TheoBachelot 5 67
(Y Barberot, France) **9/1**
6 3 **Saint Nicolas (FR)**[29] 1919 2-8-10 0 (p) MaximeGuyon 3 58
(C & Y Lerner, France) **216/10**
7 1 1/4 **Fancy Dresser (FR)**[29] 1929 2-8-10 0 (b1) AntoineHamelin 1 55
(Matthieu Palussiere, France) **194/10**
8 8 **Pif D'Avril (FR)**[45] 2-8-7 0 AurelienLemaitre 7 28
(F-X De Chevigny, France) **55/1**

1m 17.91s (1.11) **8** Ran SP% **117.5**
PARI-MUTUEL (all including 1 euro stake): WIN 3.60 PLACE 1.30, 1.30, 1.30 DF 5.80 SF 13.60.
**Owner** Ecurie Jarlan **Bred** Ecurie Jarlan **Trained** France

## CARLISLE (R-H)
Monday, May 22

**OFFICIAL GOING: Good to firm (good in places; 7.6)**
Wind: Breezy, half against in over 2f of home straight Weather: Fine, dry

### 2882 BRITISH STALLION STUDS EBF NOVICE STKS (PLUS 10 RACE) 5f
**2:20** (2:22) (Class 4) 2-Y-0 **£6,469** (£1,925; £962; £481) **Stalls** Low

Form RPR
3 1 **Ventura Dragon (IRE)**[19] 2299 2-9-2 0 TonyHamilton 1 72+
(Richard Fahey) *t.k.h: hld up on ins: checked and pushed along after 1f: rdn and hdwy over 1f out: kpt on wl fnl f to ld post* **5/4**[1]
2 nse **Seyaady** 2-9-2 0 FrannyNorton 3 72+
(Mark Johnston) *trckd ldrs: effrt and rn green 2f out: led wl ins fnl f: kpt on: hdd post* **10/1**
3 shd **Magic Mark** 2-8-11 0 CliffordLee(5) 10 71+
(K R Burke) *hld up on outside: effrt and pushed along 2f out: hdwy and ev ch wl ins fnl f: jst hld* **9/2**[3]
4 2 1/4 **Life For Rent** 2-9-2 0 JasonHart 2 63+
(Tim Easterby) *missed break: rn green in rr: hdwy and edgd rt over 1f out: kpt on fnl f: bttr for r* **66/1**
02 5 3/4 **Shay C**[14] 2452 2-9-2 0 NeilFarley 9 61
(Declan Carroll) *pressed ldr: led over 2f out: rdn and edgd rt over 1f out: hdd wl ins fnl f: no ex* **14/1**
6223 6 2 3/4 **Milton Road**[11] 2556 2-9-2 0 GrahamLee 6 51
(Mick Channon) *prom: rdn and outpcd 2f out: edgd rt and sn no imp* **7/2**[2]
0 7 3 1/4 **Albarino**[37] 1803 2-9-2 0 TomEaves 7 39+
(Kevin Ryan) *unruly and uns rdr bef s: led to over 2f out: rdn and wknd over 1f out* **10/1**
6 8 6 **Heavenly Pulse (IRE)**[37] 1792 2-9-2 0 ShaneGray 5 17
(Ann Duffield) *hld up in tch: rdn and outpcd over 2f out: wknd wl over 1f out* **66/1**

1m 4.14s (3.34) **Going Correction** +0.30s/f (Good) **8** Ran SP% **112.7**
Speed ratings (Par 95): **85,84,84,81,79 75,70,60**
CSF £15.04 TOTE £2.30: £1.10, £2.80, £1.80; EX 14.70 Trifecta £73.50.
**Owner** Middleham Park Racing XLII & Partner **Bred** Laurence & Carla Sheedy **Trained** Musley Bank, N Yorks

**FOCUS**
Carlisle's opening Flat fixture of the season. After the first, winning rider Tony Hamilton said: "It's good ground, just on the quick side." A tight finish to this novice event, which should produce winners, although it's not easy form to assess. The pace rather collapsed and the principals came from the rear.

### 2883 RACING UK IN HD H'CAP (A JOCKEY CLUB GRASSROOTS SPRINT SERIES QUALIFIER) 5f 193y
**2:50** (2:51) (Class 4) (0-80,80) 4-Y-0+ **£5,498** (£1,636; £817; £408) **Stalls** Low

Form RPR
6040 1 **Merdon Castle (IRE)**[81] 989 5-9-2 75 (e) JamesSullivan 4 82
(Ruth Carr) *hld up in last pl: pushed along 1/2-way: hdwy over 1f out: led wl ins fnl f: r.o* **4/1**[3]
04-0 2 1/2 **Penny Pot Lane**[24] 2124 4-8-9 68 FrannyNorton 3 73
(Richard Whitaker) *cl up: led over 4f out: rdn over 1f out: edgd lft and hdd wl ins fnl f: kpt on: hld nr fin* **7/2**[2]
5655 3 2 1/4 **Aguerooo (IRE)**[7] 2683 4-9-7 80 (p) AndrewMullen 8 78
(Ollie Pears) *prom: effrt and pushed along 2f out: keeping on whn checked briefly ins fnl f: nt rch first two* **6/1**
6-04 4 3/4 **Mr Orange (IRE)**[19] 2303 4-8-9 68 (p) CamHardie 7 63
(Paul Midgley) *led 2f: cl up: rdn over 2f out: outpcd ins fnl f* **4/1**[3]
-445 5 3/4 **Yeeoow (IRE)**[19] 2303 8-8-13 77 (p) CliffordLee(5) 6 70
(K R Burke) *hld up in tch: effrt on outside 2f out: outpcd ins fnl f* **3/1**[1]
0-00 6 9 **Shootingsta (IRE)**[17] 2377 5-8-13 72 (p) TomEaves 1 36
(Bryan Smart) *t.k.h: trckd ldrs: swtchd lft over 3f out: rdn and wknd fr 2f out* **9/1**

1m 15.1s (1.40) **Going Correction** +0.30s/f (Good) **6** Ran SP% **111.5**
Speed ratings (Par 105): **102,101,98,97,96 84**
CSF £17.95 CT £79.24 TOTE £4.00: £2.60, £1.90; EX 15.50 Trifecta £65.20.
**Owner** Mrs Ruth A Carr **Bred** Littleton Stud **Trained** Huby, N Yorks

**FOCUS**
A modest handicap, lacking in-form contenders. The runner-up has been rated to last year's C&D run.

### 2884 HIGH DEFINITION RACING UK H'CAP 7f 173y
**3:20** (3:21) (Class 4) (0-85,87) 4-Y-0+ **£5,498** (£1,636; £817; £408) **Stalls** Low

Form RPR
144- 1 **Pensax Boy**[299] 4776 5-9-3 80 AndrewMullen 8 87
(Daniel Mark Loughnane) *midfield: rdn along over 3f out: hdwy over 1f out: kpt on fnl f to ld towards fin* **16/1**
50-5 2 nk **Michele Strogoff**[10] 2568 4-9-10 87 TomEaves 3 93
(Tony Coyle) *prom: effrt and rdn 2f out: led wl ins fnl f: no ex and hdd nr fin* **7/1**
-064 3 1 **Georgian Bay (IRE)**[5] 2730 7-9-2 84 (p) CliffordLee(5) 6 88
(K R Burke) *hld up: rdn along over 2f out: hdwy over 1f out: kpt on ins fnl f: nvr able to chal* **4/1**[1]
-430 4 nk **Hidden Rebel**[16] 2406 5-9-7 84 GrahamLee 1 87
(Alistair Whillans) *hld up in tch: pushed along over 2f out: effrt and flashed tail repeatedly fr over 1f out: kpt on ins fnl f* **13/2**[3]
-052 5 hd **Pumaflor (IRE)**[10] 2586 5-8-12 80 (p) PhilDennis(5) 9 83
(Richard Whitaker) *t.k.h: led: rdn and edgd lft over 1f out: hdd and no ex wl ins fnl f* **6/1**[2]
00-0 6 1 1/2 **Quick N Quirky (IRE)**[23] 2138 4-8-9 75 (tp) RachelRichardson(3) 4 74
(Tim Easterby) *hld up on ins: pushed along over 2f out: hdwy over 1f out: kpt on fnl f: no imp* **25/1**
1-20 7 3/4 **Heir To A Throne (FR)**[16] 2406 4-9-9 86 ShaneGray 11 83
(Kevin Ryan) *pressed ldr: rdn along over 2f out: edgd rt over 1f out: outpcd ins fnl f* **15/2**
6210 8 1 3/4 **Ravenhoe (IRE)**[6] 2708 4-8-10 73 FrannyNorton 7 66
(Mark Johnston) *hld up: rdn over 2f out: hdwy and angled lft over 1f out: no imp fnl f* **12/1**
0-02 9 nk **Courier**[11] 2548 5-9-7 84 CamHardie 10 77
(Marjorie Fife) *prom: rdn along over 3f out: wknd over 1f out* **16/1**
1133 10 1 **Fingal's Cave (IRE)**[14] 2457 5-9-3 87 JamieGormley(7) 2 77+
(Philip Kirby) *s.s: bhd: rdn 3f out: nvr on terms* **10/1**

-010 **11** *4* **Billy Roberts (IRE)**[21] 2226 4-9-1 **78**.................................... JasonHart 5 59
(Richard Guest) *dwlt: t.k.h and prom on outside after 2f: rdn over 2f out: wknd fnl f: eased whn btn* **14/1**

1m 41.05s (1.05) **Going Correction** +0.30s/f (Good) **11** Ran SP% **110.9**
Speed ratings (Par 105): **106,105,104,104,104 102,101,100,99,98 94**
CSF £116.93 CT £531.29 TOTE £16.70: £4.70, £2.10, £1.70; EX 129.20 Trifecta £975.20.
**Owner** S & A Mares **Bred** C A Cyzer **Trained** Rock, Worcs

**FOCUS**
Race run over an extra 8yds. Something of a blanket finish to this fair handicap, which was run at a good gallop. A length pb from the winner, with the runner-up helping to set the standard.

## 2885 WATCH RACING UK IN HD H'CAP (DIV I) 6f 195y
**3:50** (3:51) (Class 5) (0-70,72) 3-Y-O **£3,396** (£1,010; £505; £252) **Stalls** Low

Form RPR
-622 **1** **Heir Of Excitement (IRE)**[28] 2035 3-9-9 **72**........................ ShaneGray 8 80
(Kevin Ryan) *mde virtually all: rdn and edgd rt 2f out: hdd briefly ins fnl f: hld on wl cl home* **9/2**[2]

4-55 **2** *nk* **Our Charlie Brown**[25] 2107 3-9-4 **67**............................. JamesSullivan 3 74
(Tim Easterby) *trckd ldrs: effrt whn hmpd wl over 1f out: rcvrd and led briefly ins fnl f: no ex and hld cl home* **7/1**[3]

21 **3** *shd* **Acadian Angel (IRE)**[41] 1705 3-9-8 **71**................................ JasonHart 2 78+
(John Quinn) *t.k.h: hld up on ins: rdn and effrt over 1f out: kpt on ins fnl f: hld cl home* **9/2**[2]

4-06 **4** *nk* **Chicago Star**[13] 2503 3-9-2 **65**........................................ GrahamLee 7 71
(Mick Channon) *dwlt: hld up: hdwy on outside over 2f out: rdn and kpt on ins fnl f* **10/1**

-313 **5** *2 ¾* **Il Sicario (IRE)**[13] 2506 3-9-7 **70**....................................... FrannyNorton 6 69
(Mark Johnston) *trckd ldrs: effrt and rdn 2f out: wknd ins fnl f* **7/2**[1]

620 **6** *1 ½* **Dapper Man (IRE)**[17] 2374 3-8-7 **63**.....................(p[1]) BenSanderson(7) 1 58
(Roger Fell) *hld up bhd ldng gp: rdn over 2f out: no imp over 1f out* **14/1**

40-5 **7** *¾* **Yarmouk (FR)**[19] 2304 3-9-4 **67**.................................... TonyHamilton 10 60
(Richard Fahey) *trckd ldr: j. path after 2f: rdn over 2f out: wknd appr fnl f* **9/2**[2]

106- **8** *3* **Uncle Charlie (IRE)**[172] 8174 3-9-2 **65**................................. TomEaves 4 50
(Ann Duffield) *t.k.h: in tch: rdn over 2f out: wknd over 1f out* **14/1**

1m 29.41s (2.31) **Going Correction** +0.30s/f (Good) **8** Ran SP% **111.7**
Speed ratings (Par 99): **98,97,97,97,94 92,91,88**
CSF £33.95 CT £146.84 TOTE £4.20: £1.40, £2.60, £1.60; EX 38.50 Trifecta £180.80.
**Owner** STS Racing Limited **Bred** Mr And Mrs P & S Martin **Trained** Hambleton, N Yorks

**FOCUS**
Race run over an additional 8yds. A four-way finish to this modest handicap, which was run just over half a second quicker than division two. The result stood after a lengthy stewards' enquiry. Straightforward form.

## 2886 WATCH RACING UK IN HD H'CAP (DIV II) 6f 195y
**4:20** (4:21) (Class 5) (0-70,72) 3-Y-O **£3,396** (£1,010; £505; £252) **Stalls** Low

Form RPR
2464 **1** **Right Action**[13] 2499 3-9-10 **71**........................................ TonyHamilton 5 74
(Richard Fahey) *hld up towards rr: rdn and hdwy over 1f out: led and edgd lft ins fnl f: kpt on wl towards fin* **4/1**[1]

1-03 **2** *½* **Arthurthedelegator**[21] 2228 3-9-6 **67**.......................... JamesSullivan 1 69
(Oliver Greenall) *t.k.h: pressed ldr: rdn and edgd lft fr over 1f out: kpt on fnl f to take 2nd cl home* **9/2**[2]

5-60 **3** *nse* **Tagur (IRE)**[9] 2625 3-9-3 **64**..............................................(p) TomEaves 3 66
(Kevin Ryan) *led: rdn over 1f out: edgd lft and hdd ins fnl f: rallied: hld nr fin* **9/2**[2]

60-1 **4** *¾* **Four Wishes**[26] 2077 3-9-3 **64**............................................ CamHardie 2 64
(Tim Easterby) *trckd ldrs: effrt and drvn along 2f out: kpt on same pce ins fnl f* **5/1**[3]

5260 **5** *5* **Hotfill**[22] 2186 3-9-4 **65**.......................................................... PhillipMakin 4 51
(David Barron) *prom: drvn and outpcd 2f out: n.d after* **9/1**

04-6 **6** *1 ¼* **Mutineer**[21] 2220 3-9-7 **68**............................................... ThomasBrown 8 51
(Daniel Kubler) *hld up: rdn over 2f out: sn outpcd: n.d after* **11/1**

463- **7** *1 ½* **Peach Pavlova (IRE)**[223] 7248 3-9-6 **67**............................ GrahamLee 7 46
(Ann Duffield) *hld up in tch: rdn and outpcd over 2f out: sn btn* **16/1**

00-4 **8** *¾* **Bridal March**[19] 2309 3-8-13 **60**...................................... FrannyNorton 6 37
(John Mackie) *dwlt and veered lft s: bhd: struggling over 2f out: sn btn* **6/1**

1m 29.93s (2.83) **Going Correction** +0.30s/f (Good) **8** Ran SP% **111.5**
Speed ratings (Par 99): **95,94,94,93,87 86,84,83**
CSF £20.88 CT £81.26 TOTE £4.30: £1.50, £1.50, £1.80; EX 16.10 Trifecta £97.40.
**Owner** Middleham Park Racing LVII & Partner **Bred** Aunty Ifl **Trained** Musley Bank, N Yorks
■ Stewards' Enquiry : James Sullivan two-day ban (5-6 Jun): used whip above permitted level

**FOCUS**
Race run over an extra 8yds. Ordinary handicap form, and the slower division by half a second. The third has been rated close to his best.

## 2887 DURDAR MAIDEN STKS 6f 195y
**4:55** (5:01) (Class 5) 3-5-Y-O **£3,396** (£1,010; £505; £252) **Stalls** Low

Form RPR
3 **1** **Moonwise (IRE)**[22] 2172 3-8-12 0.................................... PhillipMakin 3 78
(Ralph Beckett) *t.k.h: mde all: rdn over 1f out: kpt on fnl f: jst lasted* **10/11**[1]

**2** *hd* **Peach Melba** 3-8-12 0.............................................. FrannyNorton 9 77
(Mark Johnston) *trckd ldrs: stdy hdwy to chse wnr over 1f out: shkn up: green and drifted lft over 1f out: kpt on wl fnl f: jst hld: bttr for r* **9/1**[3]

**3** *9* **Raselasad (IRE)** 3-9-3 0.................................................. JasonHart 2 58
(Tracy Waggott) *hld up in tch: effrt 2f out: chsd clr ldng pair 1f out: kpt on: no imp* **50/1**

66 **4** *¾* **Senatus (FR)**[15] 2429 5-10-0 0..........................................(h) GrahamLee 4 60+
(Karen McLintock) *hld up: shkn up and stdy hdwy wl over 1f out: kpt on fnl f: nvr nr ldrs* **6/1**[2]

**5** *¾* **Infamous Lawman (IRE)** 3-9-3 0..................................... TomEaves 11 54
(Brian Ellison) *in tch: effrt and rdn over 2f out: wknd ent fnl f* **25/1**

40- **6** *2 ¼* **Great Return**[381] 2008 4-9-7 0.................................... JordanUys(7) 10 52
(Lisa Williamson) *t.k.h: hld up: shkn up whn checked 2f out: sn outpcd: n.d after* **66/1**

3-4 **7** *shd* **Different Journey**[9] 2632 4-9-7 0................................ RyanTimby(7) 12 52
(Michael Easterby) *hld up: pushed along whn checked 2f out: sn rdn and no imp* **12/1**

0 **8** *1 ¼* **Donnachies Girl (IRE)**[16] 2408 4-9-4 0......................... RowanScott(5) 8 43
(Alistair Whillans) *towards rr: drvn and outpcd over 2f out: n.d after* **50/1**

**9** *4* **Jennies Gem** 4-10-0 0............................................... AndrewMullen 7 38
(Ollie Pears) *hld up in tch: rdn over 2f out: wknd 1f out* **100/1**

**10** *2* **Hamriyah** 3-9-3 0..............................................................(h[1]) CamHardie 1 28
(Tim Easterby) *reluctant to enter stalls: hld up: rdn and outpcd 3f out: btn fnl 2f* **33/1**

00- **11** *32* **With Intent**[251] 6446 3-9-3 0..........................................(p[1]) JamesSullivan 6
(Ollie Pears) *pressed ldr to over 2f out: sn rdn and wknd: eased* **150/1**

1m 28.3s (1.20) **Going Correction** +0.30s/f (Good)
**WFA** 3 from 4yo+ 11lb **11** Ran SP% **98.2**
Speed ratings (Par 103): **105,104,94,93,92 90,90,88,84,81 45**
CSF £5.64 TOTE £1.80: £1.10, £2.10, £7.10; EX 7.30 Trifecta £169.90.
**Owner** Tullpark Limited **Bred** Tullpark Ltd **Trained** Kimpton, Hants
■ Daira Bridge was withdrawn. Price at time of withdrawal 7-2. Rule 4 applies to all bets - deduction 20p in the pound.

**FOCUS**
Race run over an extra 8yds. The race was delayed by several minutes as second favourite Daira Bridge (withdrawn) refused to enter the stalls. There was no depth to this and the first two, the only 3yo fillies in the field, fought out the finish, well clear of the rest and wide apart from each other. The level is fluid.

## 2888 RACINGUK.COM H'CAP 6f 195y
**5:25** (5:26) (Class 5) (0-75,75) 4-Y-O+ **£3,396** (£1,010; £505; £252) **Stalls** Low

Form RPR
-342 **1** **Forever A Lady (IRE)**[14] 2458 4-9-1 **69**............................ GrahamLee 9 78
(Keith Dalgleish) *dwlt: bhd and pushed along: plenty to do 3f out: hdwy on outside over 1f out: led ins fnl f: pushed out* **12/1**

44-0 **2** *1* **Little Miss Kodi (IRE)**[33] 1890 4-9-0 **75**......................... TobyEley(7) 11 81
(Daniel Mark Loughnane) *hld up: pushed along and hdwy 2f out: chsd wnr ins fnl f: r.o* **16/1**

0-00 **3** *1* **Flyboy (IRE)**[23] 2133 4-9-7 **75**.....................................(b[1]) TonyHamilton 3 79
(Richard Fahey) *n.m.r s: hld up: hdwy whn nt clr run wl over 1f out: angled rt and kpt on wl fnl f: nt rch first two* **6/1**[3]

-021 **4** *¾* **Fine Example**[21] 2224 4-8-11 **70**...............................(b) LewisEdmunds(5) 2 72+
(Kevin Ryan) *trckd ldrs: effrt and ev ch over 1f out to ins fnl f: kpt on same pce* **7/2**[2]

-041 **5** *1 ¾* **African Blessing**[24] 2119 4-9-4 **72**.................................... PhillipMakin 4 69
(David Barron) *hld up: rdn and hdwy over 1f out: kpt on same pce ins fnl f* **13/5**[1]

0-04 **6** *hd* **Ralphy Boy (IRE)**[18] 2339 8-9-3 **71**................................ JamesSullivan 7 67
(Alistair Whillans) *hld up midfield: hdwy to ld over 1f out: hdd ins fnl f: sn btn* **20/1**

0-04 **7** *2 ¼* **Yorkee Mo Sabee (IRE)**[6] 2701 4-9-7 **75**...................(h) FrannyNorton 6 65
(Mark Johnston) *hld up midfield: hdwy and ev ch over 1f out: wknd ins fnl f* **13/2**

0-54 **8** *1 ¼* **Maureb (IRE)**[15] 2428 5-8-13 **67**......................................(p) ShaneGray 12 54
(Tony Coyle) *chsd clr ldng pair: stdy hdwy and ev ch over 1f out: rdn and wknd fnl f* **16/1**

5025 **9** *12* **Tellovoi (IRE)**[7] 2684 9-9-7 **75**.............................................(v) JasonHart 5 29
(Richard Guest) *pressed ldr and sn clr of rest: led over 2f out to over 1f out: sn wknd* **11/1**

0-05 **10** *11* **Bernie's Boy**[18] 2339 4-9-7 **75**.............................................(p) TomEaves 1
(Roger Fell) *led at str gallop: hdd over 2f out: sn hmpd and wknd* **22/1**

1m 28.27s (1.17) **Going Correction** +0.30s/f (Good) **10** Ran SP% **114.5**
Speed ratings (Par 103): **105,103,102,101,99 99,97,95,81,69**
CSF £183.49 CT £1294.34 TOTE £13.00: £3.30, £5.60, £1.90; EX 226.50 Trifecta £2278.70.
**Owner** Ken McGarrity **Bred** Mick McGinn **Trained** Carluke, S Lanarks

**FOCUS**
Race run over an extra 8yds. It was the quickest of the four C&D races on the card. The pace collapsed, with the two who'd disputed it finishing out the back and the first three home all racing in the rear quartet. The winner has been rated back to her best.

## 2889 RACING UK DAY PASS H'CAP 2m 1f 47y
**6:00** (6:00) (Class 5) (0-70,72) 4-Y-O+ **£3,396** (£1,010; £505; £252) **Stalls** Low

Form RPR
134- **1** **Frederic**[206] 5856 6-10-0 **72**........................................... GrahamLee 5 84+
(Keith Dalgleish) *hld up: smooth hdwy 3f out: led on bit over 1f out: shkn up and qcknd clr fnl f: readily* **5/2**[1]

-606 **2** *4 ½* **Teak (IRE)**[19] 2308 10-9-4 **62**....................................(tp) FrannyNorton 10 66
(Ian Williams) *trckd ldrs: effrt and wnt 2nd over 3f out: led briefly wl over 1f out: kpt on fnl f: no ch w wnr* **11/4**[2]

0-61 **3** *6* **La Fritillaire**[10] 2594 5-9-5 **63**.................................... AndrewMullen 9 60
(James Given) *chsd ldr: led over 3f out to wl over 1f out: sn outpcd* **7/2**[3]

-032 **4** *1 ½* **Riptide**[17] 2363 11-9-5 **63**............................................. PhillipMakin 8 59
(Michael Scudamore) *hld up on outside: drvn and outpcd over 3f out: rallied 2f out: sn no imp* **10/1**

5643 **5** *2 ¼* **Jan Smuts (IRE)**[10] 2594 9-8-11 **62**.....................(tp) ConnorMurtagh(7) 4 55
(Wilf Storey) *prom: rdn along over 3f out: wknd over 1f out* **12/1**

00-5 **6** *4 ½* **Medina Sidonia (IRE)**[10] 2594 5-9-10 **71**........(p) RachelRichardson(3) 7 60
(Tim Easterby) *hld up: drvn and outpcd over 3f out: btn fnl 2f* **9/1**

305- **7** *34* **Omid**[226] 7138 9-8-6 **50**.............................................(tp) JamesSullivan 3 5
(Kenneth Slack) *led: drvn and hdd over 3f out: sn wknd: t.o* **12/1**

501- **8** *42* **La Bacouetteuse (FR)**[223] 7251 12-9-9 **67**.........................(p) TomEaves 2
(Iain Jardine) *hld up: drvn along 5f out: wknd over 3f out: t.o* **40/1**

3m 53.24s (0.24) **Going Correction** +0.30s/f (Good) **8** Ran SP% **114.4**
Speed ratings (Par 103): **111,108,106,105,104 102,86,66**
CSF £9.60 CT £22.91 TOTE £2.90: £1.10, £1.70, £1.30; EX 13.50 Trifecta £44.70.
**Owner** Paul & Clare Rooney **Bred** Fittocks Stud **Trained** Carluke, S Lanarks

**FOCUS**
Race run over an extra 8yds. A modest staying handicap with an easy winner. The winner improved and the third has been rated a bit below her latest.
T/Plt: £37.10 to a £1 stake. Pool: £43,558.00 - 1,172.20 winning units T/Qpdt: £10.10 to a £1 stake. Pool: £3,210.00 - 316.41 winning units **Richard Young**

# 2502 LEICESTER (R-H)
## Monday, May 22

**OFFICIAL GOING: Soft (5.1)**
Wind: Light behind Weather: Fine

## 2890 SARTORIUS NOVICE AUCTION STKS (PLUS 10 RACE) 5f
**6:05** (6:06) (Class 4) 2-Y-O **£4,528** (£1,347; £673; £336) **Stalls** High

Form RPR
53 **1** **Queen Of Kalahari**[13] 2502 2-8-11 0.................................. JimCrowley 4 69
(Charles Hills) *chsd ldr: rdn to ld over 1f out: r.o* **5/2**[2]

0 **2** *1* **Lady Alavesa**[10] 2563 2-8-11 0.......................................... MartinDwyer 5 66+
(Gay Kelleway) *hld up: hdwy 2f out: rdn to chse wnr and hung lft ins fnl f: r.o* **16/1**

0 **3** 1 ½ **Time For Treacle**[38] 1776 2-8-6 0............................ RobJFitzpatrick(5) 1 60
(Ben Haslam) *sn chsng ldrs: rdn over 1f out: styd on same pce wl ins fnl f* **50/1**

6 **4** ½ **The Golden Cue**[12] 2522 2-9-2 0................................ RoystonFfrench 2 64
(Steph Hollinshead) *led: rdn and hdd over 1f out: styd on same pce ins fnl f* **10/1**

4 **5** 1 ¼ **Danehill Desert (IRE)**[16] 2403 2-8-13 0.............. AdamMcNamara(3) 6 59
(Richard Fahey) *sn pushed along and prom: rdn 1/2-way: styd on same pce fnl f* **9/4**[1]

1 **6** 1 ¼ **Capla Dancer (IRE)**[32] 1909 2-8-10 0....................(h[1]) RussellHarris(7) 7 56
(K R Burke) *dwlt: hld up: hung lft fr 1/2-way: rdn over 1f out: nvr on terms* **5/1**[3]

**7** 8 **Rio Santos** 2-9-2 0............................................................... RyanTate 3 26
(Rod Millman) *chsd ldrs: pushed along and lost pl over 3f out: wknd 1/2-way* **14/1**

64 **8** 3 ¾ **Revenge**[23] 2154 2-8-13 0................................................ HollieDoyle(3) 9 12
(Tim Easterby) *sn pushed along and prom: rdn and wknd wl over 1f out* **10/1**

0 **9** ¾ **Abu Dhabi Doo**[33] 1873 2-8-6 0.............................. MeganNicholls(5) 8 5
(K R Burke) *sn pushed along in rr: bhd fr 1/2-way* **20/1**

1m 2.29s (2.29) **Going Correction** +0.275s/f (Good) **9 Ran SP% 113.5**
Speed ratings (Par 95): **92,90,88,87,85 83,70,64,63**
CSF £41.00 TOTE £2.80: £1.10, £3.90, £8.00; EX 14.20 Trifecta £594.10.
**Owner** Mrs J K Powell **Bred** Minster Stud **Trained** Lambourn, Berks

**FOCUS**
Some starts have been moved at this track following remeasuring, so some races will not have speed figures until there is sufficient data to calculate updated median times. Few could be seriously fancied in this juvenile contest beforehand and, with the second and third home having shown little on their debuts, it's probably form to be dubious about. The winner found a bit on his previous efforts.

## 2891 JAMES WARD (S) STKS — 1m 3f 179y
**6:35** (6:35) (Class 5) 4-Y-0+ **£3,234** (£962; £481; £240) **Stalls** Low

Form RPR

1403 **1** **Retrieve (AUS)**[11] 2546 9-9-4 90.......................(t) DougieCostello 8 66
(Jamie Osborne) *a.p: chsd ldr 10f out: rdn to ld and hung lft fr wl over 1f out: styd on* **1/2**[1]

33-0 **2** 1 ¼ **Moon Over Rio (IRE)**[22] 2183 6-8-4 57................... MeganNicholls(5) 7 55
(Ben Haslam) *hld up: hdwy over 2f out: jnd wnr over 1f out: stl ev ch whn carried lft ins fnl f: no ex towards fin* **3/1**[2]

0-60 **3** 8 **Mr Standfast**[71] 636 4-9-0 47............................................... KierenFox 2 47
(Alan Phillips) *led at stdy pce tl pushed along and qcknd over 3f out: rdn and hdd wl over 1f out: wknd fnl f* **25/1**

-404 **4** *shd* **The Greedy Boy**[19] 2313 4-8-8 43 ow1....................(bt) JoshuaBryan(7) 3 48
(Steve Flook) *chsd ldr 2f: remained handy: rdn over 2f out: hung lft over 1f out: wknd fnl f* **12/1**[3]

0-00 **5** 12 **Whitchurch**[23] 2166 5-9-0 49...........................................(p) PaddyAspell 6 28
(Philip Kirby) *hld up: rdn over 2f out: wknd wl over 1f out* **16/1**

**6** 2 ½ **Optical High**[55] 8-8-7 0...............................................(p) AledBeech(7) 4 24
(Tony Forbes) *s.s: a in rr: pushed along over 5f out: lost tch over 3f out* **33/1**

2m 43.27s (9.37) **Going Correction** +0.70s/f (Yiel) **6 Ran SP% 112.0**
Speed ratings (Par 103): **96,95,89,89,81 80**
CSF £2.23 TOTE £1.40: £1.02, £2.00; EX 2.40 Trifecta £13.70.
**Owner** Melbourne 10 Racing **Bred** Darley **Trained** Upper Lambourn, Berks

**FOCUS**
Race run over an extra 10yds. This weak seller revolved around the odds-on favourite, who was a mile clear on ratings. The standard is set around the third and fourth.

## 2892 HENRY ALKEN H'CAP — 1m 3f 179y
**7:05** (7:06) (Class 5) (0-70,70) 3-Y-0 **£3,234** (£962; £481; £240) **Stalls** Low

Form RPR

04-0 **1** **King Of Scotland (FR)**[138] 48 3-8-10 62.............. CharlieBennett(3) 1 68
(Hughie Morrison) *chsd ldrs: led over 8f out: rdn and hung lft wl over 1f out: styd on wl* **16/1**

0-30 **2** 1 ¼ **Star Maker**[16] 2395 3-9-0 68........................................ MitchGodwin(5) 3 72
(Sylvester Kirk) *hld up in tch: nt clr run fr over 2f out tl over 1f out: rdn to chse wnr ins fnl f: sn ev ch: no ex towards fin* **11/2**[2]

0-00 **3** 2 ½ **Mr Scaff (IRE)**[16] 2394 3-8-8 57........................................ MartinDwyer 4 57
(Paul Henderson) *sn pushed along to chse ldrs: led over 10f out tl over 8f out: chsd wnr: rdn and ev ch over 2f out: lost 2nd over 1f out: styd on same pce fnl f* **10/1**

5-36 **4** ¾ **Pondering**[17] 2359 3-9-2 68.................................. EdwardGreatrex(3) 6 67
(Eve Johnson Houghton) *hld up: hdwy over 3f out: rdn over 2f out: chsd wnr and hung rt over 1f out: wknd wl ins fnl f* **16/1**

34-3 **5** 1 ½ **Eolian**[6] 2711 3-8-7 63................................................... JoshuaBryan(7) 5 60
(Andrew Balding) *chsd ldrs: rdn over 3f out: no ex fnl f* **1/1**[1]

0-26 **6** *shd* **Haldaw**[12] 2515 3-9-4 67................................................ CharlesBishop 8 63
(Mick Channon) *broke wl: lost pl after 1f: hld up: rdn over 2f out: nt trble ldrs* **33/1**

3-43 **7** 29 **Laureate**[20] 2273 3-9-5 68................................................ JimCrowley 7 18
(Mark Johnston) *led: hdd over 10f out: remained handy tl pushed along over 2f out: sn wknd and eased* **9/1**

4-04 **8** 35 **Mr Davies**[23] 2137 3-9-7 70.........................................(t[1]) AdamKirby 2
(David Brown) *prom: lost pl over 10f out: pushed along and wknd over 4f out* **13/2**[3]

2m 40.38s (6.48) **Going Correction** +0.70s/f (Yiel) **8 Ran SP% 112.5**
Speed ratings (Par 99): **106,105,103,103,102 101,82,59**
CSF £97.53 CT £930.65 TOTE £16.70: £4.50, £1.80, £2.40; EX 122.30 Trifecta £1302.30.
**Owner** The Caledonian Racing Society **Bred** Ennistown Stud **Trained** East Ilsley, Berks

**FOCUS**
Race run over an extra 10yds. This handicap featured no former winners from a combined 43 starts. The winner was one of the least exposed of the party and was making its handicap and turf debuts. The runner-up has been rated to form.

## 2893 J.F. HERRING H'CAP — 1m 2f
**7:35** (7:35) (Class 4) (0-80,82) 4-Y-0+ **£5,175** (£1,540; £769; £384) **Stalls** Low

Form RPR

60-5 **1** **Giveaway Glance**[14] 2478 4-9-4 77................................ FergusSweeney 4 85
(Alan King) *hld up: racd keenly: nt clr run and lost pl wl over 2f out: hdwy over 1f out: r.o to ld towards fin* **14/1**

03-6 **2** ¾ **Mikmak**[19] 2310 4-9-9 82.................................................(p) MartinDwyer 6 88
(William Muir) *hld up: racd keenly: hdwy over 2f out: rdn to ld ins fnl f: edgd lft and hdd towards fin* **14/1**

40-3 **3** ¾ **Compton Mill**[13] 2504 5-9-3 79...............................(t) CharlieBennett(3) 10 83
(Hughie Morrison) *chsd ldr tl led 3f out: rdn and hdd over 1f out: styd on* **9/2**[2]

4-60 **4** 1 **Jufn**[21] 2233 4-9-3 76......................................................(h[1]) TrevorWhelan 1 78
(John Butler) *led 7f: sn hrd rdn: rallied to ld over 1f out: hdd ins fnl f: no ex towards fin* **33/1**

556- **5** 1 ¼ **Indy (IRE)**[202] 7744 6-9-2 75................................................ JackGarritty 8 75
(John Quinn) *plld hrd and prom: rdn over 2f out: sn outpcd: swtchd lft over 1f out: styd on ins fnl f* **13/2**

12 **6** ¾ **Eskendash (USA)**[14] 2477 4-9-5 78........................................ AdamKirby 7 76
(Pam Sly) *hld up: hdwy over 2f out: rdn over 1f out: no ex ins fnl f* **2/1**[1]

00-6 **7** *nk* **Swaheen**[30] 1976 5-9-2 80...................................... GeorgeWood(5) 9 77
(Julie Camacho) *chsd ldrs: rdn over 2f out: styd on same pce fnl f* **6/1**[3]

0/0- **8** ½ **Hidden Oasis (IRE)**[250] 6496 6-9-2 75.................................. FranBerry 5 71
(Jonjo O'Neill) *hld up: racd keenly: shkn up over 2f out: edgd rt fr over 1f out: no ex ins fnl f* **16/1**

2400 **9** 14 **Gold Flash**[28] 2040 5-8-13 77................................................ RyanWhile(5) 3 45
(Hugo Froud) *chsd ldrs: rdn over 2f out: wknd wl over 1f out* **66/1**

40-0 **10** 4 **High Draw (FR)**[41] 1700 4-9-2 75........................................ JimCrowley 2 35
(K R Burke) *hld up: swtchd lft over 3f out: rdn over 2f out: sn wknd* **8/1**

2m 11.68s (3.78) **Going Correction** +0.525s/f (Yiel) **10 Ran SP% 113.9**
Speed ratings (Par 105): **105,104,103,103,102 101,101,100,89,86**
CSF £189.03 CT £1024.33 TOTE £17.50: £3.50, £3.40, £1.80; EX 107.20 Trifecta £1905.10.
**Owner** Mrs K Holmes **Bred** Pitchall Stud **Trained** Barbury Castle, Wilts

**FOCUS**
Race run over an extra 10yds. Only a couple of these arrived here in any kind of form. The fourth has been rated to his penultimate AW form.

## 2894 JOHN FERNELEY H'CAP — 1m 53y
**8:05** (8:07) (Class 4) (0-80,80) 3-Y-0 **£5,175** (£1,540; £769; £384) **Stalls** Low

Form RPR

30-2 **1** **On To Victory**[40] 1724 3-9-3 76..................................(h) TomMarquand 5 91
(Eve Johnson Houghton) *hld up: pushed along over 4f out: hdwy over 2f out: edgd rt over 1f out: rdn to ld ins fnl f: styd on wl* **4/1**[2]

030- **2** 2 ¼ **Black Trilby (IRE)**[276] 5615 3-9-6 79.............................. AdamKirby 10 89+
(Clive Cox) *trckd ldrs: racd keenly: rdn to ld and hung rt over 1f out: hdd ins fnl f: styd on same pce* **3/1**[1]

141- **3** 8 **Hersigh**[192] 7898 3-9-4 80......................................(p) AdamMcNamara(3) 8 72
(Saeed bin Suroor) *s.i.s: sn pushed along to chse ldrs: led 6f out: clr 5f out tl c bk to the field over 2f out: rdn and hdd over 1f out: wknd ins fnl f* **11/2**[3]

661- **4** ¾ **Subatomic**[230] 7056 3-9-5 78................................................ FranBerry 7 68
(Ralph Beckett) *sn led: hdd 6f out: chsd ldr who wnt clr 5f out: tk clsr order over 2f out: rdn over 1f out: wknd fnl f* **17/2**

06-0 **5** 1 **Balgair**[26] 2088 3-8-11 75............................................ MitchGodwin(5) 9 63
(Jonathan Portman) *hld up in tch: rdn over 2f out: wknd over 1f out* **6/1**

-413 **6** 12 **Revel**[55] 1411 3-9-1 77................................................(t) AaronJones(3) 4 37
(Stuart Williams) *s.i.s: hld up: rdn over 3f out: nvr on terms* **10/1**

-210 **7** 8 **Oud Metha Bridge (IRE)**[26] 2088 3-9-6 79........................ JimCrowley 3 21
(Ed Dunlop) *hld up: rdn 1/2-way: a in rr* **8/1**

10-0 **8** 13 **Gold Award (IRE)**[17] 2361 3-9-2 75............................(v[1]) CharlesBishop 1
(Mick Channon) *hld up: rdn over 3f out: sn wknd* **22/1**

2352 **9** 6 **Fiendish (USA)**[13] 2496 3-9-2 75........................................ JoeFanning 6
(Mark Johnston) *chsd ldrs tl rdn adn wknd over 2f out: eased* **16/1**

1m 46.97s (1.87) **Going Correction** +0.275s/f (Good) **9 Ran SP% 115.6**
Speed ratings (Par 101): **101,98,90,90,89 77,69,56,50**
CSF £16.45 CT £66.02 TOTE £5.60: £2.20, £1.60, £1.50; EX 21.50 Trifecta £87.50.
**Owner** HP Racing On To Victory **Bred** The Aston House Stud **Trained** Blewbury, Oxon

**FOCUS**
Race run over an extra 10yds. An informative 3yo handicap, which had been won in 2015 by subsequent Cambridgeshire winner Third Time Lucky. The level is a bit fluid.

## 2895 BRITISH STALLION STUDS EBF MAIDEN STKS — 7f
**8:35** (8:38) (Class 5) 3-Y-0 **£4,528** (£1,347; £673; £336) **Stalls** High

Form RPR

5-2 **1** **To Dibba**[50] 1514 3-9-5 0................................................ AndreaAtzeni 1 83+
(Roger Varian) *led 1f: remained handy: led again 2f out: pushed out* **4/5**[1]

3-4 **2** 2 ½ **Loujain (IRE)**[50] 1514 3-9-5 0........................................(b[1]) JimCrowley 6 76
(John Gosden) *s.i.s: hld up: plld hrd: hdwy 4f out: rdn and ev ch over 1f out: styd on same pce ins fnl f* **13/2**

22 **3** 1 ¼ **Del Parco**[22] 2172 3-9-5 0................................................ AdamKirby 5 73
(Clive Cox) *plld hrd: trckd ldrs: led 5f out: hdd 3f out: sn rdn and hung rt: no ex ins fnl f* **3/1**[2]

00- **4** 9 **Tally's Son**[222] 7269 3-9-5 0........................................ DougieCostello 9 50
(Grace Harris) *w ldr: led 6f out tl 5f out: chsd ldr tl 3f out: sn rdn and outpcd* **200/1**

0- **5** 2 ¾ **Coral Caye**[198] 7818 3-9-0 0.....................................(h[1]) RoystonFfrench 2 37
(Steph Hollinshead) *prom: lost pl after 1f: outpcd over 4f out: n.d after* **200/1**

**6** 4 ½ **Mark Of Excellence (IRE)** 3-9-5 0........................................ JoeFanning 3 31
(Saeed bin Suroor) *s.s: hld up: hdwy over 2f out: wknd wl over 1f out* **4/1**[3]

-244 **7** 7 **Widnes**[27] 2071 3-9-5 70................................................(b) RobertTart 8 13
(Alan Bailey) *chsd ldrs tl rdn and wknd over 2f out* **16/1**

1m 26.81s (0.61) **Going Correction** +0.275s/f (Good) **7 Ran SP% 120.8**
Speed ratings (Par 99): **107,104,102,92,89 84,76**
CSF £7.96 TOTE £1.60: £1.20, £2.80; EX 6.90 Trifecta £15.40.
**Owner** Sheikh Ahmed Al Maktoum **Bred** Darley **Trained** Newmarket, Suffolk

■ Here I Go Again and Wannabe Like You were withdrawn. Prices at time of withdrawal 200-1 and 20-1. Rule 4 does not apply

**FOCUS**
This had the look of an above-average maiden, the favourite having chased home subsequent 2,000 Guineas fifth Dream Castle on his seasonal reappearance. The first three drew well clear. The runner-up has been rated to his debut form.

T/Plt: £181.60 to a £1 stake. Pool: £46,520.00 - 256.11 winning units T/Qpdt: £83.10 to a £1 stake. Pool: £4,034.00 - 48.50 winning units **Colin Roberts**

## [2343] REDCAR (L-H)
Monday, May 22

**OFFICIAL GOING: Good to firm (good in places; 8.7)**
Wind: light behind Weather: Fine

### 2896 RACINGUK.COM NOVICE AUCTION STKS 5f 217y
**2:10** (2:11) (Class 5) 2-Y-O **£3,234** (£962; £481; £240) **Stalls** Centre

Form RPR
3 **1** **Luis Fernandez (USA)**[21] 2221 2-9-2 0 KevinStott 5 78+
(Kevin Ryan) *prom: kpt on pushed out to ld towards fin* **9/4**[1]
0 **2** *hd* **Chatburn (IRE)**[16] 2403 2-9-2 0 DanielTudhope 12 77
(David O'Meara) *sn led: rdn appr fnl f: edgd sltly lft ins fnl f: kpt on but hdd towards fin* **11/1**
**3** *3 1/4* **We Are The World** 2-9-2 0 BenCurtis 6 72+
(Archie Watson) *prom: rdn over 2f out: l down whn hmpd ins fnl f: nt rcvr* **14/1**
3 **4** *3/4* **Benadalid**[51] 1495 2-9-2 0 RoystonFfrench 8 65
(Chris Fairhurst) *chsd ldrs: rdn along 1/2-way: kpt on same pce* **7/2**[2]
4 **5** *hd* **Shazzab (IRE)**[25] 2105 2-8-11 0 JackGarritty 13 59+
(Richard Fahey) *outpcd in rr tl kpt on wl fr appr fnl f* **12/1**
0 **6** *nk* **Magnus (IRE)**[23] 2154 2-9-2 0 RichardKingscote 9 63
(Tom Dascombe) *midfield: pushed along 1/2-way: edgd lft over 1f out: kpt on ins fnl f: nvr threatened ldrs* **20/1**
50 **7** *3/4* **Poet's Dawn**[21] 2221 2-9-2 0 DavidAllan 4 61
(Tim Easterby) *in tch: rdn over 2f out: one pce* **16/1**
60 **8** *1* **Mount Hellvelyn**[21] 2222 2-8-13 0 NathanEvans(3) 2 57
(Clive Mulhall) *prom: rdn over 2f out: wknd fnl f* **125/1**
**9** *1/2* **Arcavallo (IRE)** 2-9-2 0 PaulMulrennan 7 56
(Michael Dods) *slowly away: sn midfield: pushed along over 2f out: wknd ins fnl f* **12/1**
**10** *1* **Laydee Victoria (IRE)** 2-8-11 0 JoeDoyle 11 51+
(Ollie Pears) *hld up: sn pushed along: sme late hdwy: nvr threatened* **100/1**
46 **11** *2 1/4* **Hot Rock (IRE)**[21] 2221 2-9-2 0 ConnorBeasley 1 45
(Bryan Smart) *hld up: nvr threatened* **8/1**[3]
**12** *2 3/4* **Emerald Rocket (IRE)** 2-8-13 0 JordanVaughan(3) 10 37
(K R Burke) *hld up: sn pushed along: a towards rr* **16/1**
0 **13** *3/4* **Elixsoft (IRE)**[13] 2502 2-8-11 0 SilvestreDeSousa 14 29
(Roger Fell) *a towards rr* **20/1**
6 **14** *1 3/4* **Plansina**[25] 2105 2-8-11 0 DuranFentiman 3 24
(Tim Easterby) *midfield: rdn over 2f out: wknd over 1f out* **100/1**

1m 10.15s (-1.65) **Going Correction** -0.20s/f (Firm) **14 Ran SP% 118.5**
Speed ratings (Par 93): **103,102,98,97,97 96,95,94,93,92 89,85,84,82**
CSF £26.74 TOTE £2.70: £1.20, £4.30, £3.50; EX 30.50 Trifecta £271.70.
**Owner** Mrs R G Hillen **Bred** Castleton Lyons & Kilboy Estate **Trained** Hambleton, N Yorks

**FOCUS**
It was dry over the weekend and race day was dry as well, so the ground was good to firm, good in places (watered). This looked a fair novice race. It's been rated as modest form.

### 2897 WATCH RACING UK IN HD H'CAP 5f
**2:40** (2:43) (Class 6) (0-60,62) 3-Y-O **£2,749** (£818; £408; £204) **Stalls** Centre

Form RPR
506 **1** **Ebitda**[87] 904 3-8-7 46 oh1 LukeMorris 3 53
(Scott Dixon) *trckd ldrs: rdn over 2f out: led 100yds out: kpt on* **25/1**
25-0 **2** *1 1/4* **Glyder**[22] 2181 3-9-5 58 RoystonFfrench 17 61
(John Holt) *prom: rdn to ld appr fnl f: hdd 110yds out: one pce* **25/1**
6-44 **3** *nk* **Jorvik Prince**[17] 2372 3-9-4 57 SamJames 1 58
(Karen Tutty) *led narrowly: rdn over 2f out: hdd appr fnl f: kpt on same pce* **7/1**[3]
6-02 **4** *3/4* **Mr Skinnylegs**[30] 1973 3-8-12 58 KieranSchofield(7) 7 57
(Brian Ellison) *in tch: rdn over 2f out: edgd rt fnl f: kpt on wl fnl 110yds* **9/2**[1]
00-3 **5** *2 1/2* **Flashing Light**[40] 1715 3-9-5 58 DavidAllan 4 48
(Tim Easterby) *w ldr: rdn over 2f out: wknd ins fnl f* **9/1**
01-0 **6** *hd* **Newgate Sioux**[21] 2223 3-9-6 59 DuranFentiman 10 48
(Tony Coyle) *chsd ldrs: rdn over 2f out: no ex ins fnl f* **50/1**
6330 **7** *1/2* **Backinanger**[35] 1835 3-9-2 55 (b[1]) KevinStott 9 42
(Kevin Ryan) *chsd ldrs: rdn over 2f out: no ex fnl f* **14/1**
00-0 **8** *1/2* **Pavers Pride**[38] 1782 3-9-7 60 DanielTudhope 8 48
(Noel Wilson) *midfield: rdn over 2f out: no imp* **10/1**
0-00 **9** *shd* **Miss Pepper (IRE)**[22] 2181 3-8-4 46 oh1 (h[1]) SammyJoBell(3) 11 37
(Paul Midgley) *midfield: pushed along over 1f out: short of room ent fnl f and again 110yds out: no ch after* **100/1**
-045 **10** *1/2* **La Haule Lady**[17] 2372 3-9-1 54 (p) PaulMulrennan 12 37
(Paul Midgley) *a midfield* **14/1**
430- **11** *1* **Foxy Boy**[226] 7143 3-9-4 62 CallumRodriguez(5) 2 42
(Michael Dods) *v.s.a: a rr* **6/1**[2]
-336 **12** *nk* **Darvie**[22] 2182 3-9-6 59 JosephineGordon 13 38
(David Barron) *dwlt: a outpcd in rr* **15/2**
20-0 **13** *hd* **Equity**[22] 2181 3-9-5 58 (v[1]) DaneO'Neill 15 36
(David Brown) *hld up: rdn over 2f out: nvr threatened* **20/1**
00-0 **14** *1* **Kulgri**[24] 2121 3-8-7 46 oh1 JoeDoyle 14 20
(Kevin Ryan) *midfield: rdn over 2f out: wknd over 1f out* **33/1**
00-0 **15** *hd* **Nyx**[40] 1715 3-8-7 46 oh1 (h) ConnorBeasley 6 20
(Richard Guest) *a rr* **40/1**
00-5 **16** *3* **Nifty Niece (IRE)**[40] 1715 3-8-11 50 (p[1]) JoeyHaynes 16 13
(Ann Duffield) *hld up: rdn over 2f out: sn wknd* **28/1**

57.57s (-1.03) **Going Correction** -0.20s/f (Firm) **16 Ran SP% 113.4**
Speed ratings (Par 97): **100,98,97,96,92 92,91,90,90,89 87,87,87,85,85 80**
CSF £468.00 CT £4285.74 TOTE £28.10: £5.10, £4.60, £2.10, £1.60; EX 817.70 Trifecta £4084.40 Part won..
**Owner** Chesterfield Estates **Bred** Selwood, Hoskins & Trickledown **Trained** Babworth, Notts

■ Paco Lady was withdrawn. Price at time of withdrawal 12-1. Rule 4 applies to all bets - deduction 5p in the pound.
■ Stewards' Enquiry : Kieran Schofield caution: future conduct in races

**FOCUS**
A moderate 3yo sprint handicap. The runner-up has been rated to her best.

### 2898 PAT AND LES HOLMES CELEBRATION MAIDEN FILLIES' STKS 7f
**3:10** (3:11) (Class 5) 3-Y-O+ **£3,234** (£962; £481; £240) **Stalls** Centre

Form RPR
0 **1** **Golden State (USA)**[19] 2311 3-9-0 0 DanielTudhope 1 77
(Archie Watson) *trckd ldr: racd keenly: rdn over 1f out: led ins fnl f: kpt on* **13/2**
2-25 **2** *1* **Spinnaka (IRE)**[19] 2311 3-9-0 78 LukeMorris 3 74
(Luca Cumani) *trckd ldr: rdn to ld over 1f out: hdd ins fnl f: one pce* **2/1**[1]
**3** *hd* **UAE Queen** 3-9-0 0 AndreaAtzeni 12 74
(Roger Varian) *in tch: pushed along over 2f out: rdn to chse ldr over 1f out: kpt on* **5/2**[2]
**4** *1/2* **Caridade (USA)** 3-9-0 0 KevinStott 2 72
(Kevin Ryan) *midfield: rdn and hdwy over 1f out: kpt on fnl f* **33/1**
0 **5** *1/2* **Lyric Harmony (IRE)**[32] 1905 3-9-0 0 SamJames 8 71
(Giles Bravery) *hld up in midfield: rdn over 1f out: kpt on wl fnl f* **18/1**
2- **6** *2 1/2* **Lovely Acclamation (IRE)**[287] 5237 3-9-0 0 SilvestreDeSousa 10 64
(Ismail Mohammed) *hld up in midfield: rdn and hdwy over 1f out: wknd ins fnl f* **4/1**[3]
5 **7** *1/2* **Granny Roz**[22] 2180 3-9-0 0 JosephineGordon 6 63
(David Barron) *led: rdn whn hdd over 1f out: wandered lft and rt and wknd ins fnl f* **33/1**
**8** *4* **New Delhi (IRE)** 3-9-0 0 JoeFanning 5 52
(Mark Johnston) *midfield: rdn over 2f out: wknd over 1f out* **16/1**
006- **9** *3 3/4* **Tweetheart**[268] 5889 4-9-8 49 (h) NathanEvans(3) 13 46
(Ron Barr) *prom: rdn over 2f out: wknd over 1f outr* **200/1**
0-5 **10** *3/4* **Poet's Time**[10] 2595 3-9-0 0 DavidAllan 4 40
(Tim Easterby) *hld up: nvr threatened* **125/1**
6- **11** *3 1/4* **Harbour Belle**[343] 3208 3-9-0 0 PaulMulrennan 9 31
(Michael Dods) *hld up: nvr threatened* **50/1**
00- **12** *29* **Shannah Bint Eric**[243] 6679 3-9-0 0 JoeDoyle 11
(Kevin Ryan) *trckd ldr: rdn over 3f out: sn wknd and eased* **150/1**

1m 22.29s (-2.21) **Going Correction** -0.20s/f (Firm)
**WFA** 3 from 4yo 11lb **12 Ran SP% 116.2**
Speed ratings (Par 100): **104,102,102,102,101 98,98,93,89,88 84,51**
CSF £19.23 TOTE £8.20: £1.90, £1.20, £1.40; EX 23.20 Trifecta £68.20.
**Owner** Nick Bradley Racing 6 & Partners **Bred** Burleson Farm & Mike Burleson **Trained** Upper Lambourn, W Berks

**FOCUS**
A fair fillies' maiden. The first two have been rated a bit below their best for now.

### 2899 RACINGUK.COM/DAYPASS H'CAP 5f
**3:40** (3:40) (Class 3) (0-90,87) 3-Y-O+ **£7,762** (£2,310; £1,154; £577) **Stalls** Centre

Form RPR
0-31 **1** **Excessable**[16] 2409 4-9-7 83 (t) DavidAllan 8 93
(Tim Easterby) *trckd ldrs: pushed along over 1f out: led ins fnl f: rdn and kpt on wl* **9/2**[2]
05-1 **2** *1* **Dakota Gold**[30] 1975 3-9-3 87 ConnorBeasley 6 90
(Michael Dods) *dwlt: hld up: pushed along and hdwy 2f out: rdn and kpt on wl fnl f* **5/2**[1]
0-40 **3** *nk* **Olivia Fallow (IRE)**[16] 2407 5-9-9 85 PaulMulrennan 5 90
(Paul Midgley) *hld up: rdn and hdwy over 1f out: kpt on wl fnl f: edgd lft 75yds out* **14/1**
00-6 **4** *1 3/4* **Lexington Place**[33] 1876 7-9-7 83 JackGarritty 3 82
(Ruth Carr) *s.i.s: hld up: pushed along and stl plenty to do over 1f out: r.o wl fnl f* **10/1**
134- **5** *nk* **Hilary J**[212] 7537 4-9-6 82 JoeyHaynes 9 80
(Ann Duffield) *prom: rdn to ld over 1f out: hdd ins fnl f: wknd fnl 75yds* **12/1**
0-52 **6** *1 1/4* **Bashiba (IRE)**[24] 2123 6-9-11 87 (t) SilvestreDeSousa 2 80
(Nigel Tinkler) *hld up: rdn and sme hdwy over 1f out: one pce whn sltly hmpd 75yds out* **7/1**[3]
-056 **7** *3/4* **Lathom**[10] 2592 4-9-9 85 (v) DanielTudhope 4 76
(David O'Meara) *chsd ldrs: rdn 1/2-way: wknd fnl f* **10/1**
50-2 **8** *1 1/4* **Midnight Malibu (IRE)**[16] 2407 4-9-5 84 NathanEvans(3) 11 70
(Tim Easterby) *led narrowly: rdn 2f out: hdd over 1f out: wknd* **18/1**
351 **9** *1* **Lydia's Place**[25] 2104 4-9-2 78 BenCurtis 1 61
(Richard Guest) *chsd ldrs: rdn 1/2-way: wknd fnl f* **12/1**
03-0 **10** *nk* **Bapak Asmara (IRE)**[38] 1777 5-9-6 82 JoeDoyle 10 64
(Kevin Ryan) *prom: rdn 1/2-way: wknd appr fnl f* **25/1**
011- **11** *7* **Fast Act (IRE)**[224] 7202 5-9-10 86 KevinStott 7 42
(Kevin Ryan) *prom: rdn and lost pl 1/2-way: wknd over 1f out* **20/1**

56.27s (-2.33) **Going Correction** -0.20s/f (Firm)
**WFA** 3 from 4yo+ 8lb **11 Ran SP% 113.4**
Speed ratings (Par 107): **110,108,107,105,104 102,101,99,97,97 86**
CSF £15.42 CT £142.39 TOTE £5.90: £2.60, £1.40, £4.80; EX 21.10 Trifecta £180.20.
**Owner** B Guerin & Habton Farms **Bred** Whitsbury Manor Stud **Trained** Great Habton, N Yorks

**FOCUS**
A decent sprint handicap. The runner-up has been rated similar to his Thirsk effort.

### 2900 RACING UK STRAIGHT MILE SERIES FILLIES' H'CAP (RACING UK STRAIGHT MILE SERIES QUALIFIER) 7f 219y
**4:10** (4:10) (Class 5) (0-70,72) 3-Y-O+ **£3,234** (£962; £481; £240) **Stalls** Centre

Form RPR
1- **1** **Khamaary (IRE)**[220] 7331 3-9-3 71 DaneO'Neill 3 93+
(Mark Johnston) *mde all: pushed clr fnl 2f: eased towards fin: impressive* **1/1**[1]
4455 **2** *7* **Mama Africa (IRE)**[17] 2374 3-8-10 64 BenCurtis 8 66
(David Barron) *hld up: rdn and hdwy to go 2nd 1f out: kpt on wl but no ch w wnr* **12/1**
4022 **3** *1 1/4* **Cabal**[18] 2346 10-9-7 63 (b) DavidAllan 5 65
(Geoffrey Harker) *hld up: rdn 2f out: kpt on fnl f* **12/1**
0-06 **4** *1 1/4* **Rosamaria (IRE)**[23] 2138 4-9-7 63 PaulMulrennan 2 62
(Julie Camacho) *hld up in rr: rdn 2f out: kpt on fnl f: nvr threatened* **16/1**
0-04 **5** *nk* **Tigserin (IRE)**[24] 2124 4-9-6 62 KevinStott 6 60
(Giles Bravery) *trckd ldrs: rdn over 2f out: one pce* **12/1**
244 **6** *hd* **First Moon**[28] 2019 3-9-4 72 (t) JosephineGordon 11 67
(Hugo Palmer) *trckd ldrs: rdn over 2f out: wknd ins fnl f* **8/1**[2]
404- **7** *2 3/4* **One Too Many (IRE)**[244] 6658 3-8-12 66 SilvestreDeSousa 7 54
(David Brown) *hld up: racd keenly: rdn and sme hdwy 2f out: wknd fnl f* **11/1**[3]
0-50 **8** *1/2* **Sunnua (IRE)**[28] 2030 4-9-9 72 SebastianWoods(7) 10 62
(Richard Fahey) *midfield: rdn over 2f out: wknd over 1f out* **11/1**[3]

10-0 **9** *nk* **Graceful Act**42 1679 9-8-9 **51** oh5 JoeDoyle 4 40
(Ron Barr) *trckd ldr: rdn over 2f out: wknd over 1f out* **100/1**
0-53 **10** *2* **Star Of Bristol (USA)**20 2274 3-9-2 **70** (p1) ShaneKelly 9 51
(Richard Hughes) *trckd ldrs: rdn over 2f out: wknd over 1f out.* **16/1**
605- **11** *2 1/4* **Fleurtille**353 2855 8-9-3 **59** ConnorBeasley 1 38
(Ray Craggs) *trckd ldrs: rdn over 2f out: wknd* **80/1**
1m 35.72s (-0.88) **Going Correction** -0.20s/f (Firm)
**WFA** 3 from 4yo+ 12lb 11 Ran SP% **114.8**
Speed ratings (Par 100): **96,89,87,86,86 86,83,82,82,80 78**
CSF £13.89 CT £96.47 TOTE £1.90: £1.10, £3.90, £3.70; EX 16.10 Trifecta £89.50.
**Owner** Hamdan Al Maktoum **Bred** Shadwell Estate Company Limited **Trained** Middleham Moor, N Yorks

**FOCUS**
The winner had the run of things in front whilst a few in behind raced keenly, but even so she was clearly much better than this level. The second and third have been rated to their recent form.

## 2901 RACING UK PROFITS RETURNED TO RACING MEDIAN AUCTION MAIDEN STKS 7f 219y
**4:40** (4:40) (Class 6) 3-5-Y-O **£2,897** (£855; £427) **Stalls** Centre

Form RPR
52 **1** **Patchwork**16 2393 3-9-2 0 ShaneKelly 2 80
(Richard Hughes) *trckd ldr: qcknd to ld ent fnl f: kpt on pushed out* **1/2**1
042- **2** *1 1/2* **Nuncio**145 8560 3-9-2 73 JosephineGordon 4 74
(Daniel Kubler) *trckd ldr: racd keenly: rdn to ld over 1f out: hdd ent fnl f: one pce* **4/1**2
6523 **3** *4 1/2* **Eddiebet**34 1866 3-9-2 72 DanielTudhope 1 66
(David O'Meara) *led: rdn whn hdd over 1f out: wknd and eased ins fnl f* **4/1**2
1m 37.14s (0.54) **Going Correction** -0.20s/f (Firm)
**WFA** 3 from 4yo 12lb 3 Ran SP% **106.7**
Speed ratings (Par 101): **89,87,83**
CSF £2.72 TOTE £1.50; EX 2.60 Trifecta £3.00.
**Owner** The Queen **Bred** The Queen **Trained** Upper Lambourn, Berks

**FOCUS**
An uncompetitive maiden. It's been given a token rating through the runner-up.

## 2902 RACINGUK.COM H'CAP (DIV I) 1m 2f 1y
**5:10** (5:11) (Class 6) (0-60,62) 3-Y-O **£2,897** (£855; £427) **Stalls** Low

Form RPR
6-45 **1** **Shambra (IRE)**36 1817 3-9-2 **55** SilvestreDeSousa 11 67
(Roger Fell) *trckd ldrs: racd keenly: led 7f out: rdn 3 out: strly pressed ent fnl f: hld on gamely* **7/2**1
5-00 **2** *nk* **Tread Lightly**22 2185 3-9-8 **61** DavidAllan 3 72
(Tim Easterby) *midfield: pushed along to chse ldr 3f out: rdn to chal strly ent fnl f: kpt on but a jst hld* **6/1**3
0-03 **3** *14* **Dreamofdiscovery (IRE)**52 1470 3-9-6 **59** JoeDoyle 9 44
(Julie Camacho) *midfield: rdn over 3f out: plugged on into poor 3rd over 1f out* **13/2**
0360 **4** *3 3/4* **Panther In Pink (IRE)**62 1297 3-8-7 **46** oh1 (p1) JoeyHaynes 7 24
(Ann Duffield) *trckd ldrs: racd keenly: rdn over 3f out: wknd over 1f out* **33/1**
40-3 **5** *2 3/4* **Midnight Man (FR)**54 1434 3-9-6 **62** JordanVaughan(3) 8 34
(K R Burke) *hld up: rdn and sme hdwy on outer 3f out: wknd fnl 2f* **4/1**2
002- **6** *3 1/2* **Chaucer's Tale**199 7792 3-9-4 **60** (t1) NathanEvans(3) 4 26
(Michael Easterby) *led: hdd 7f out: trckd ldr: rdn over 3f out: sn wknd* **4/1**2
00-0 **7** *1/2* **Thornton Mary**18 2345 3-8-5 **47** SammyJoBell(3) 1 12
(Brian Rothwell) *dwlt: hld up: nvr threatened* **66/1**
0005 **8** *3 1/4* **River Warrior**62 1297 3-8-7 **46** oh1 (b) ConnorBeasley 6 5
(Richard Fahey) *midfield: rdn over 4f out: sn wknd* **11/1**
-200 **9** *nk* **Kazanan (IRE)**18 2349 3-8-5 **49** CallumRodriguez(5) 5 7
(Michael Dods) *s.i.s: sn midfield: rdn over 3f out: wknd* **8/1**
2m 5.58s (-1.52) **Going Correction** -0.225s/f (Firm) 9 Ran SP% **113.7**
Speed ratings (Par 97): **97,96,85,82,80 77,77,74,74**
CSF £24.38 CT £129.01 TOTE £4.10: £1.30, £2.60, £2.00; EX 26.30 Trifecta £159.90.
**Owner** R G Fell **Bred** John O'Kelly Bloodstock Services **Trained** Nawton, N Yorks
■ Stewards' Enquiry : David Allan two-day ban: used whip above permitted level (9-10 June)

**FOCUS**
Not much depth to this race but the time was 0.27sec faster than the second division.

## 2903 RACINGUK.COM H'CAP (DIV II) 1m 2f 1y
**5:40** (5:40) (Class 6) (0-60,62) 3-Y-O **£2,897** (£855; £427) **Stalls** Low

Form RPR
602- **1** **Clenymistra (IRE)**214 7482 3-9-3 **56** DanielTudhope 11 65
(David O'Meara) *trckd ldr on outer: jnd ldr 8f out: pushed along to ld over 2f out: rdn over 2f out: kpt on: hld on towards fin* **6/1**2
005- **2** *1/2* **Single Estate**290 5120 3-8-7 **46** oh1 JoeDoyle 7 54
(Simon Waugh) *hld up in rr: rdn and gd hdwy on outer over 3f out: chsd wnr ins fnl f: styd on* **40/1**
00-0 **3** *2 3/4* **Regal Mirage (IRE)**42 1680 3-8-8 **47** DavidAllan 6 50
(Tim Easterby) *trckd ldrs: rdn along 4f out: no ex ins fnl f* **13/2**3
0-00 **4** *1* **Nigh Or Never (IRE)**17 2366 3-9-7 **60** RichardKingscote 9 61
(Tom Dascombe) *dwlt: midfield: rdn and hdwy to chse ldrs over 2f out: no ex fnl f* **2/1**1
0-03 **5** *nk* **Oceanus (IRE)**19 2315 3-9-0 **60** MillyNaseb(7) 10 60
(Julia Feilden) *in tch: rdn and outpcd over 3f out: styd on fnl f* **12/1**
600- **6** *1 1/2* **Permanent**202 7749 3-9-5 **58** JosephineGordon 2 56
(Daniel Kubler) *trckd ldrs: rdn over 2f out: wknd fnl f* **10/1**
00-5 **7** *3/4* **Steel Helmet (IRE)**33 1875 3-9-9 **62** BenCurtis 4 58
(Brian Ellison) *led: jnd 8f out: rdn whn hdd over 2f out: wknd over 1f out* **7/1**
000- **8** *6* **Hazy Manor (IRE)**223 7244 3-9-0 **53** PaulMulrennan 1 42+
(Julia Brooke) *midfield on inner: n.m.r 2f out: wknd fnl f* **25/1**
00-0 **9** *1* **Sai Kung Star**32 1914 3-8-4 **46** oh1 NathanEvans(3) 3 29
(Nigel Tinkler) *dwlt: a towards rr* **20/1**
2-15 **10** *2 1/4* **Beepeecee**54 1428 3-9-9 **62** (p) ShaneKelly 8 41
(Richard Hughes) *hld up: rdn over 2f out: wknd* **7/1**
2m 5.85s (-1.25) **Going Correction** -0.225s/f (Firm) 10 Ran SP% **113.8**
Speed ratings (Par 97): **96,95,93,92,92 91,90,85,84,83**
CSF £220.87 CT £1594.86 TOTE £6.80: £1.90, £7.90, £2.40; EX 215.10 Trifecta £2178.60.
**Owner** Hambleton Racing Ltd XXVII **Bred** Mrs E Fitzsimons **Trained** Upper Helmsley, N Yorks

**FOCUS**
A slightly slower time than the first leg. It's been rated in line with the first division.
T/Jkpt: Not won. T/Plt: £17.20 to a £1 stake. Pool: £50,392.00 - 2,927.14 winning units T/Qpdt: £4.20 to a £1 stake. Pool: £2,860.00 - 679.42 winning units **Andrew Sheret**

# 2689 WINDSOR (R-H)
Monday, May 22

**OFFICIAL GOING: Good (good to firm in places; 7.1)**
Wind: Almost nil Weather: Fine, very warm

## 2904 THAMES VALLEY AIR AMBULANCE FILLIES' NOVICE STKS (PLUS 10 RACE) 5f 21y
**5:55** (5:56) (Class 4) 2-Y-O **£3,946** (£1,174; £586; £293) **Stalls** Low

Form RPR
3 **1** **Out Of The Flames**10 2563 2-9-0 0 OisinMurphy 3 82+
(Richard Hannon) *chsd ldng pair and immediately clr of rest: rdn to ld over 1f out: steadily drew clr but had to be kpt up to work* **2/7**1
4 **2** *3* **Listen Alexander (IRE)**32 1909 2-9-0 0 JFEgan 9 71
(David Evans) *led and immediately clr w two others: rdn and hdd over 1f out: kpt on one pce* **12/1**
43 **3** *3/4* **Kodiac Express (IRE)**14 2459 2-9-0 0 RobertWinston 1 69
(Mike Murphy) *pressed ldr in clr ldng trio to over 1f out: one pce* **14/1**
**4** *6* **Ellthea (IRE)** 2-9-0 0 PJMcDonald 5 47+
(K R Burke) *s.i.s: outpcd along w five others: shkn up 2f out: kpt on to take modest 4th fnl f* **6/1**2
**5** *1 1/4* **Hollie's Dream** 2-9-0 0 SeanLevey 2 42+
(David Evans) *chsd ldng trio but outpcd by them fr the s: no imp 2f out: lost 4th fnl f* **20/1**
0 **6** *2 3/4* **Darkanna (IRE)**23 2134 2-9-0 0 PaulHanagan 10 33+
(Richard Fahey) *disp 4th pl to 1/2-way but outpcd by ldng trio fr the s: wknd over 1f out* **7/1**3
**7** *1/2* **Roses In June (IRE)** 2-9-0 0 LiamJones 7 31+
(J S Moore) *outpcd along w five others: nvr a factor* **40/1**
**8** *1/2* **Rue Cambon (IRE)** 2-9-0 0 StevieDonohoe 6 29+
(George Peckham) *dwlt: outpcd in last and a bhd* **20/1**
**9** *6* **Sunset Flyer** 2-9-0 0 LemosdeSouza 4 7+
(Amy Murphy) *s.i.s: outpcd along w five others: effrt fr rr of that gp 2f out: wknd qckly over 1f out* **33/1**
59.9s (-0.40) **Going Correction** -0.05s/f (Good) 9 Ran SP% **133.8**
Speed ratings (Par 92): **101,96,95,85,83 79,78,77,67**
CSF £7.25 TOTE £1.30: £1.02, £2.60, £3.90; EX 6.90 Trifecta £32.50.
**Owner** Qatar Racing Limited **Bred** Gary Hodson & Peter Moule **Trained** East Everleigh, Wilts

**FOCUS**
Inner of straight dolled out 2yds at 6f and 1yd at the winning line. Top bend dolled out 4yds from normal inner configuration, adding 14yds to race distances of 1m plus. The distance of this was as advertised. Little got into this, those with previous experience dominating.

## 2905 BRITISH STALLION STUDS EBF FILLIES' NOVICE STKS (PLUS 10 RACE) 6f 12y
**6:25** (6:27) (Class 4) 2-Y-O **£6,469** (£1,925; £962; £481) **Stalls** Low

Form RPR
4 **1** **Elysium Dream**10 2577 2-9-0 0 RyanMoore 3 75
(Richard Hannon) *chsd ldrs: lost pl 1/2-way and pushed along in last trio over 2f out: taken to outer and prog over 1f out: drvn and r.o fnl f to ld last stride* **9/4**1
20 **2** *shd* **Angel Of The South (IRE)**10 2563 2-9-0 0 RobertWinston 5 75
(Dean Ivory) *trckd ldng pair gng wl: shkn up to ld over 1f out: rdn and kpt on fnl f: hdd last stride* **7/1**
**3** *2* **Not After Midnight (IRE)** 2-9-0 0 GeorgeDowning 4 69+
(Daniel Kubler) *s.i.s: mostly in last tl shkn up and prog over 2f out: rdn and styd on fr over 1f out to take 3rd ins fnl f* **66/1**
**4** *1/2* **Reflect Alexander (IRE)** 2-9-0 0 JFEgan 2 68
(David Evans) *pressed ldr: upsides over 1f out and against nr side rail: one pce after* **16/1**
**5** *1 3/4* **Angel Islington (IRE)** 2-9-0 0 OisinMurphy 1 62
(Andrew Balding) *wl in tch: lost pl 2f out: n.d after: kpt on ins fnl f* **10/1**
4 **6** *3/4* **Cardaw Lily (IRE)**10 2563 2-9-0 0 JamieSpencer 8 60
(Richard Hughes) *stdd s but sn cl up: pushed along 2f out: wknd 1f out* **7/2**3
**7** *1/2* **Dathanna (IRE)** 2-9-0 0 WilliamBuick 7 64
(Charlie Appleby) *free to post: t.k.h: led to over 1f out: fdd and eased* **5/2**2
**8** *1 1/2* **Little Miss Lilly** 2-9-0 0 SamHitchcott 6 54
(Clive Cox) *a in last trio: struggling over 2f out* **14/1**
1m 13.03s (0.03) **Going Correction** -0.05s/f (Good) 8 Ran SP% **117.2**
Speed ratings (Par 92): **97,96,94,93,91 90,89,87**
CSF £19.33 TOTE £3.40: £1.40, £2.10, £10.40; EX 17.70 Trifecta £392.20.
**Owner** The Racing Cricketers **Bred** Bolton Grange **Trained** East Everleigh, Wilts

**FOCUS**
Distance as advertised. As in the first race those with experience came to the fore. The runner-up has been rated in line with her debut effort.

## 2906 GREEN PARLOUR FILLIES' H'CAP 1m 3f 99y
**6:55** (6:57) (Class 3) (0-95,92) 4-Y-O+ **£7,439** (£2,213; £1,106; £553) **Stalls** Centre

Form RPR
55-3 **1** **Turning The Table (IRE)**16 2387 4-8-10 **81** JamieSpencer 3 92+
(David Simcock) *stdd s: hld up in last: smooth prog over 3f out: nudged into ld ins fnl f: sn clr* **4/1**3
3-11 **2** *4 1/2* **Perfect Quest**17 2358 4-8-9 **80** (t) WilliamBuick 6 83
(Clive Cox) *chsd clr ldr: pushed along to cl 3f out: led 2f out: rdn and hdd ins fnl f: sn outpcd* **3/1**2
32-3 **3** *1 1/2* **Lorelina**20 2254 4-8-8 **79** OisinMurphy 1 79
(Andrew Balding) *chsd ldng pair: pushed along 3f out: tried to cl 2f out: edgd lft u.p over 1f out: one pce* **2/1**1
0-04 **4** *1* **Marsh Pride**23 2136 5-9-1 **86** PJMcDonald 2 85
(K R Burke) *led and clr after 3f: c bk to field 3f out: rdn and hdd 2f out: wknd* **9/2**
20-5 **5** *4 1/2* **Luna Mare (IRE)**19 2302 4-8-7 **78** oh2 (p1) PaulHanagan 4 69
(Richard Fahey) *hld up in 5th: pushed along over 4f out: no prog and wl btn 2f out* **12/1**
232- **6** *17* **Mighty Lady**295 4919 4-8-7 **78** JimmyQuinn 7 40
(Robyn Brisland) *t.k.h: hld up in 4th: pushed along 3f out: wknd 2f out: eased* **10/1**
2m 26.64s (-2.86) **Going Correction** -0.05s/f (Good) 6 Ran SP% **113.3**
Speed ratings (Par 104): **108,104,103,102,99 87**
CSF £16.61 TOTE £5.10: £2.40, £1.90; EX 17.40 Trifecta £40.40.
**Owner** Mrs Doreen Tabor **Bred** John O'Connor **Trained** Newmarket, Suffolk


The Form Book Flat, Raceform Ltd, Newbury, RG14 5SJ

**FOCUS**
Distance increased by 14yds. They were soon quite well strung out, with the fourth opening up a clear lead, and the winner came from off the pace. Fair form. The runner-up has been rated to form.

## 2907 WEATHERBYS PRIVATE BANK LEISURE STKS (LISTED RACE) 6f 12y
**7:25** (7:26) (Class 1) 3-Y-0+

**£20,982** (£7,955; £3,981; £1,983; £995; £499) **Stalls** Low

Form RPR

020- **1** **Perfect Pasture**[186] 7997 7-9-0 107 ........(v) SeanLevey 4 112
(Michael Easterby) *trckd ldr: led wl over 1f out: drvn out and hld on wl fnl f* **25/1**

10-0 **2** *nk* **Dancing Star**[16] 2397 4-8-9 108 ........ OisinMurphy 3 106
(Andrew Balding) *trckd ldng pair: rdn to take 2nd against rail over 1f out: drvn to chal last 150yds: styd on but a jst hld* **3/1**[3]

0-21 **3** *¾* **Mr Lupton (IRE)**[15] 2433 4-9-0 113 ........ PaulHanagan 7 109
(Richard Fahey) *hld up disputing 5th: rdn and tried to cl fr 2f out: n.m.r over 1f out: styd on fnl f to take 3rd last 75yds: nvr able to chal* **9/4**[1]

63-1 **4** *1* **Raucous**[25] 2114 4-9-0 105 ........(tp) RyanMoore 5 106
(William Haggas) *trckd ldrs: rdn to dispute 2nd over 1f out: nt qckn and lost grnd fnl f* **11/4**[2]

1-15 **5** *hd* **Intisaab**[15] 2433 6-9-0 108 ........(p) ShelleyBirkett 8 106
(David O'Meara) *hld up disputing 5th: shkn up over 2f out: trying to cl whn no room over 1f out: kpt on same pce fnl f but nvr a threat after* **11/1**

025/ **6** *3 ¾* **Tropics (USA)**[660] 4858 9-9-0 111 ........(h) RobertWinston 9 96
(Dean Ivory) *hld up in 7th fr wd draw: effrt on outer 2f out: no prog 1f out: wknd* **8/1**

000- **7** *½* **Johnny Barnes (IRE)**[213] 7497 5-9-0 104 ........ WilliamBuick 6 94
(John Gosden) *dwlt: mostly in last and nvr really gng* **12/1**

0-00 **8** *nse* **Emell**[51] 1494 7-9-0 97 ........(v[1]) KieranO'Neill 1 94
(Tim Vaughan) *fast away: led: rdn 3f out: hdd wl over 1f out: sn wknd* **80/1**

1m 10.71s (-2.29) **Going Correction** -0.05s/f (Good) **8** Ran SP% **114.7**
Speed ratings (Par 111): **113,112,111,110,110 105,104,104**
CSF £99.41 TOTE £16.90: £5.40, £1.40, £1.20; EX 151.10 Trifecta £1552.20.
**Owner** S Hull, S Hollings & D Swales **Bred** Mrs Jean Turpin **Trained** Sheriff Hutton, N Yorks
■ Stewards' Enquiry : Paul Hanagan caution: careless riding

**FOCUS**
Distance as advertised. Bit of a turn up in this Listed sprint, but the form looks sound enough with the right horses finishing immediately in behind. The runner-up has been rated a bit below her Goodwood form, with the third to his non-handicap best.

## 2908 STOKE PARK MAIDEN FILLIES' STKS 1m 31y
**7:55** (7:59) (Class 5) 3-Y-0+ **£2,911** (£866; £432; £216) **Stalls** Low

Form RPR

3 **1** **Tirania**[31] 1948 3-9-0 0 ........ PatCosgrave 12 84+
(William Haggas) *mde all: pushed clr fr 2f out: in n.d after: comf* **4/6**[1]

**2** *3 ¾* **Euqranian (USA)** 3-9-0 0 ........(h[1]) JFEgan 11 75
(Jeremy Noseda) *chsd wnr: rdn over 2f out: sn outpcd: kpt on* **5/1**[3]

3- **3** *¾* **Italian Heiress**[230] 7055 3-9-0 0 ........ PaulHanagan 2 73
(Clive Cox) *cl up: pushed along 3f out: no ch w wnr but tk 3rd fnl f and kpt on* **4/1**[2]

5- **4** *1 ¼* **Paradise Cove**[215] 7465 3-9-0 0 ........ LiamJones 1 70
(William Haggas) *trckd ldrs: pushed along 3f out: nvr any ch but kpt on fnl f to take 4th last strides* **8/1**

**5** *hd* **Characterized** 3-9-0 0 ........ TimmyMurphy 4 69
(Geoffrey Deacon) *trckd ldng pair: stl gng wl enough over 2f out: shkn up over 1f out: one pce and lost 3rd fnl f: shaped w promise* **66/1**

**6** *2 ½* **Celtik Secret** 3-9-0 0 ........ RobertWinston 13 63
(Hughie Morrison) *in tch in midfield: rchd 6th 2f out: no hdwy or imp ldrs after* **20/1**

0 **7** *1 ½* **Wicker**[20] 2266 3-9-0 0 ........ StevieDonohoe 8 60
(Jane Chapple-Hyam) *a in midfield: pushed along and no prog 3f out: one pce after* **66/1**

6 **8** *¾* **Know The Truth**[17] 2366 3-9-0 0 ........ LiamKeniry 9 58
(Andrew Balding) *plld hrd and hld up towards rr: taken to outer over 2f out: kpt on same pce fr over 1f out: n.d* **25/1**

**9** *2 ¾* **Kalani Rose** 3-9-0 0 ........ JackMitchell 5 51
(Ben De Haan) *hld up in rr: nvr on terms: taken to outer over 1f out and kpt on nr fin* **66/1**

54- **10** *3 ¼* **Annoushka**[237] 6855 4-9-12 0 ........ AdamBeschizza 14 47
(Mrs Ilka Gansera-Leveque) *t.k.h: hld up in last trio: awkward bnd 5f out: nvr a factor* **66/1**

0 **11** *1 ¾* **Shamonix (IRE)**[28] 2019 3-9-0 0 ........ RobHornby 6 39
(Mark Usher) *prom: pushed along over 3f out: wknd over 2f out* **100/1**

**12** *hd* **Queen Beatrice** 3-9-0 0 ........ SamHitchcott 10 39
(William Muir) *dwlt: mostly in last: pushed along 3f out: no prog* **50/1**

**13** *2 ¼* **Shujaha (AUS)** 4-9-9 0 ........(h[1]) HectorCrouch(3) 3 37
(Pat Murphy) *dwlt: t.k.h: a towards rr: wknd over 2f out* **100/1**

1m 45.6s (0.90) **Going Correction** -0.05s/f (Good)
**WFA** 3 from 4yo 12lb **13** Ran SP% **126.3**
Speed ratings (Par 100): **93,89,88,87,87 84,83,82,79,76 74,74,72**
CSF £4.59 TOTE £1.70: £1.02, £2.10, £1.60; EX 6.10 Trifecta £15.00.
**Owner** Miss Yvonne Jacques **Bred** Mill House Stud & Cheveley Park Stud Ltd **Trained** Newmarket, Suffolk

**FOCUS**
Distance increased by 14yds. One-way traffic in this fillies' maiden, the favourite winning readily from the front. The winner has been rated as fitting the usual standard for this race.

## 2909 SOLENT FORTS H'CAP 1m 2f
**8:25** (8:28) (Class 5) (0-70,72) 4-Y-0+ **£2,911** (£866; £432; £216) **Stalls** Centre

Form RPR

2551 **1** **Fast And Hot (IRE)**[3] 2785 4-8-11 67 ........(b) RossaRyan(7) 12 74
(Richard Hannon) *racd wd: trckd ldrs: prog on outer 3f out: rdn to ld over 1f out: jnd fnl f: drvn and jst prevailed* **6/5**[1]

0602 **2** *shd* **Essenaitch (IRE)**[3] 2785 4-9-5 68 ........ JFEgan 5 74
(David Evans) *hld up in midfield: swift move on inner to ld wl over 2f out and grabbed rail: edgd lft and hdd over 1f out: rallied to join wnr ins fnl f: jst pipped* **7/2**[2]

105- **3** *1 ½* **Hearty (IRE)**[216] 7425 4-9-2 65 ........ AdamBeschizza 9 68+
(Richard Rowe) *hld up and sn detached in last pair: clsd on main gp 5f out: gd prog fr over 3f out: rdn and styd on wl fr over 1f out to take 3rd nr fin* **28/1**

00-0 **4** *¾* **Loving Your Work**[124] 290 6-8-8 60 ........ HectorCrouch(3) 8 62
(Ken Cunningham-Brown) *hld up in rr of main gp: shkn up and prog fr 3f out: styd on to take 3rd ins fnl f tl nr fin* **14/1**

0/ **5** *nk* **Iniesta (IRE)**[546] 6777 6-9-9 72 ........ TimmyMurphy 4 73
(Fergal O'Brien) *hld up in last of main gp: stdy prog against rail over 2f out: shkn up over 1f out: kpt on fnl f: nvr able to chal but nrst fin* **22/1**

5-01 **6** *5* **Ebbisham (IRE)**[40] 1729 4-9-7 70 ........(p) PatCosgrave 6 61
(Jim Boyle) *prom: rdn to chal wl over 2f out: chsd ldng pair after but lft bhd by them: lost 3rd and wknd fnl f* **8/1**[3]

63-0 **7** *2 ½* **Spinart**[42] 1683 4-9-5 68 ........ RobHornby 1 54
(Pam Sly) *cl up bhd ldrs: lost pl wl over 2f out: no hdwy over 1f out: wknd* **8/1**[3]

04-0 **8** *3 ½* **Woofie (IRE)**[28] 2020 5-9-3 66 ........(p) OisinMurphy 7 45
(Laura Mongan) *pressed ldr to 3f out: sn lost pl and btn* **20/1**

0/20 **9** *30* **Leonardo (GER)**[19] 2308 5-8-7 56 oh2 ........ JimmyQuinn 2
(Mark Pitman) *mde most to wl over 2f out: wknd rapidly and t.o* **16/1**

56-0 **10** *93* **Mette**[26] 2095 4-8-7 56 oh6 ........(h[1]) KieranO'Neill 11
(Mark Usher) *stdd s: t.k.h and hld up in last pair: sn detached: clsd briefly 5f out: wknd rapidly 4f out: t.o and virtually p.u* **100/1**

13/0 **11** *13* **Rolling Dice**[14] 2471 6-9-4 67 ........ LiamKeniry 3
(Dominic Ffrench Davis) *prom: wknd rapidly over 4f out: sn t.o and virtually p.u 2f out* **33/1**

0000 **12** *1 ½* **Genuine Approval (IRE)**[58] 1364 4-9-2 65 ........ RobertWinston 10
(John Butler) *w ldng pair to over 3f out: wknd rapidly and t.o 2f out: poor 10th whn virtually p.u ins fnl f* **16/1**

2m 9.33s (0.63) **Going Correction** -0.05s/f (Good) **12** Ran SP% **124.8**
Speed ratings (Par 103): **95,94,93,93,92 88,86,84,60, ,**
CSF £5.08 CT £83.55 TOTE £2.40: £1.10, £1.60, £7.20; EX 6.40 Trifecta £105.10.
**Owner** Derek And Jean Clee **Bred** D D & Mrs J P Clee **Trained** East Everleigh, Wilts

**FOCUS**
Distance increased by 14yds. The market leaders came to the fore in this modest handicap, with the favourite following up his recent Newbury win, which was also gained at the expense of today's runner-up. The winner has been rated close to his winter AW form.
T/Plt: £8.70 to a £1 stake. Pool: £65,764.00 - 7,494.61 winning units T/Qpdt: £3.60 to a £1 stake. Pool: £4,499.00 - 1,240.01 winning units **Jonathan Neesom**

# 2674 BRIGHTON (L-H)
Tuesday, May 23

**OFFICIAL GOING: Good (good to firm in places; 8.2)**
Wind: light breeze against Weather: sunny with mist moving in at 5.00pm

## 2910 TOTEPLACEPOT AT TOTESPORT.COM MAIDEN AUCTION STKS 5f 215y
**2:20** (2:22) (Class 5) 2-Y-0 **£2,911** (£866; £432; £216) **Stalls** Low

Form RPR

5 **1** **Holdenhurst**[7] 2706 2-9-0 0 ........ MitchGodwin(5) 4 71
(Sylvester Kirk) *trckd ldr: rdn over 1f out: kpt on to ld jst ins fnl f: a holding on* **12/1**

**2** *½* **Hateya (IRE)** 2-9-0 0 ........ PatCosgrave 3 64
(Jim Boyle) *little slowly away: racd keenly: sn mid-div: rdn and hdwy fr 2f out: kpt on wl fnl f: clsng on wnr at fin* **16/1**

U2 **3** *hd* **Arabian Jazz (IRE)**[14] 2502 2-9-0 0 ........ DannyBrock 9 64
(Michael Bell) *trckd ldrs: rdn over 1f out: kpt on ins fnl f: clsng on wnr at fin* **15/8**[1]

0 **4** *1 ½* **Move To The Front (IRE)**[52] 1496 2-9-5 0 ........(b[1]) AdamKirby 1 66
(Clive Cox) *trckd ldrs: rdn over 2f out: kpt on same pce fnl f* **9/4**[2]

3 **5** *¾* **Princess Lyla (IRE)**[21] 2258 2-9-0 0 ........ ShaneKelly 2 57
(Richard Hughes) *broke wl: set decent pce: rdn and hdd jst ins fnl f: fdd fnl 100yds* **5/1**[3]

**6** *½* **Safe Waters** 2-9-0 0 ........ CharlesBishop 6 55
(Eve Johnson Houghton) *sn outpcd towards rr: hdwy over 1f out: kpt on ins fnl f* **14/1**

**7** *hd* **Disapproval (IRE)** 2-9-0 0 ........ GeorgeDowning 5 54
(Daniel Kubler) *mid-div: rdn 2f out: no imp tl kpt on ins fnl f* **33/1**

**8** *1 ¾* **Fusion Central (IRE)** 2-9-0 0 ........ TomMarquand 8 49
(Richard Hannon) *s.i.s: towards rr: outpcd 3f out: nvr threatened* **12/1**

06 **9** *9* **Mirek (IRE)**[21] 2277 2-9-5 0 ........(h) PaddyAspell 11 25
(Jonathan Portman) *s.i.s: midfield 3f out: wknd over 1f out* **50/1**

**10** *7* **Raven's Girl** 2-9-0 0 ........ LiamKeniry 7
(Michael Madgwick) *s.i.s: a towards rr* **33/1**

1m 11.46s (1.26) **Going Correction** +0.075s/f (Good) **10** Ran SP% **118.0**
Speed ratings (Par 93): **94,93,93,91,90 89,89,86,74,65**
CSF £183.95 TOTE £12.10: £3.30, £5.00, £1.10; EX 208.70 Trifecta £1249.50.
**Owner** Ansells Of Watford **Bred** Southill Stud **Trained** Upper Lambourn, Berks

**FOCUS**
Rail movements added 4yds to all race distances. Drying conditions. This looked a modest maiden. The third has been rated close to her Leicester form.

## 2911 TRAILWALKER 100KM CHALLENGE 29-30 JULY H'CAP 6f 210y
**2:50** (2:50) (Class 6) (0-60,60) 3-Y-0 **£2,264** (£673; £336; £168) **Stalls** Low

Form RPR

00-2 **1** **Pass The Cristal (IRE)**[20] 2309 3-9-3 56 ........ DougieCostello 16 62+
(William Muir) *hld up towards rr: rdn and hdwy over 1f out: r.o strly fnl f: led cl home: drvn rt out* **7/1**[2]

05-6 **2** *nk* **Fair Selene**[20] 2309 3-9-5 58 ........(v[1]) GavinLerena 7 63
(Heather Main) *hld up towards rr: hdwy over 1f out: sn rdn and drifted lft: r.o wl to ld fnl 70yds: hdd cl home* **10/1**

050- **3** *½* **Fanfair**[280] 5528 3-8-12 54 ........ HollieDoyle(3) 5 58
(Richard Hannon) *mid-div: rdn 2f out: hdwy over 1f out: ev ch fnl 70yds: kpt on* **14/1**

00-3 **4** *½* **Sweet Pursuit**[29] 2016 3-8-12 51 ........ WilliamCarson 15 53+
(Rod Millman) *trckd ldrs: rdn to ld wl over 1f out: drifted sltly lft ins fial f: hdd fnl 70yd: no ex and hld whn short of room cl homen* **6/1**[1]

60-0 **5** *1 ¼* **Aberdonian**[136] 126 3-8-7 49 ........ HectorCrouch(3) 10 48
(Jeremy Gask) *mid-div: rdn 2f out: kpt on ins fnl f but nt pce to get on terms* **33/1**

5-00 **6** *nk* **Golden Eye**[21] 2259 3-9-1 59 ........ MitchGodwin(5) 13 57
(Sylvester Kirk) *mid-div: dropped to rr whn outpcd 2f out: kpt on wl again ins fnl f* **10/1**

3526 **7** *nk* **Whatalove**[46] 1596 3-8-8 47 ........ TomMarquand 4 44
(Martin Keighley) *w ldr: rdn and ev ch over 2f out: sltly hmpd ent fnl f: no ex* **8/1**[3]

0-06 **8** *1* **Sixties Habana**[29] 2016 3-9-2 55 ........ JFEgan 8 50
(Pat Phelan) *broke wl: racd keenly: sn stdd bk towards rr: rdn 2f out: kpt on fnl f but nt pce to get involved* **9/1**

3664 **9** *nk* **Hidden Stash**[21] 2252 3-9-0 60 ........(v) WilliamCox(7) 14 54
(Andrew Balding) *mid-div: drvn 2f out: sme minor late prog: n.d* **8/1**[3]

066- **10** 1 ¼ **Iron Lady (IRE)**[223] 7279 3-8-11 **50**.......... JosephineGordon 3 43
(William Muir) *led: rdn and hdd wl over 1f out: ev ch whn sltly hmpd ent fnl f: fdd fnl 120yds* **16/1**

0-50 **11** 1 **Shouldertoshoulder**[46] 1600 3-9-1 **54**.......... HarryBentley 1 42
(Stuart Williams) *chsd ldrs: rdn over 2f out: wknd ent fnl f* **11/1**

0046 **12** ¾ **Neptune Star**[22] 2228 3-8-10 **49**..........(h) RobHornby 9 35
(Jeremy Gask) *hld up towards rr: making sme hdwy on far rails whn denied clr run over 1f out: no ch after* **12/1**

4-60 **13** 1 **Venetian Proposal (IRE)**[29] 2016 3-8-13 **52**..........(p) LiamKeniry 2 35
(Zoe Davison) *hld up towards rr of midfield: rdn 2f out: hmpd ent fnl f: little imp after* **25/1**

600 **14** 2 ¼ **Joy**[18] 2366 3-8-4 **46** oh1.......... CharlieBennett(3) 6 23
(Laura Mongan) *chsd ldrs: rdn over 2f out: wknd over 1f out* **33/1**

6000 **15** 2 ¼ **Taurean Gold**[22] 2235 3-8-7 **46** oh1.......... RyanPowell 12 17
(John Bridger) *chsd ldrs: rdn over 2f out: wknd over 1f out* **33/1**

1m 24.07s (0.97) **Going Correction** +0.075s/f (Good) **15** Ran SP% **118.4**
Speed ratings (Par 97): **97,96,96,95,94 93,93,92,91,90 89,88,87,84,82**
CSF £70.71 CT £963.30 TOTE £6.10: £2.70, £3.90, £5.10; EX 55.30 Trifecta £1729.70.
**Owner** O'Mulloy, Schwartz **Bred** Grangecon Stud **Trained** Lambourn, Berks
■ Stewards' Enquiry : Gavin Lerena caution: careless riding
William Carson two-day ban (6-7 Jun): careless riding

**FOCUS**
Add 4yds. A moderate handicap that set up for the closers. It's been rated as very ordinary form.

## 2912 STREAMLINE TAXIS 202020 FILLIES' H'CAP 6f 210y
**3:20** (3:21) (Class 4) (0-85,87) 4-Y-0+ **£4,690** (£1,395; £697) **Stalls** Low

Form RPR

0020 **1** **Staintondale Lass (IRE)**[39] 1771 4-9-7 **85**.......... HarryBentley 4 91
(Ed Vaughan) *trckd ldr: rdn to chal over 2f out: led ent fnl f: kpt on wl: drvn rt out* **3/1**[3]

3-01 **2** nk **Black Bess**[10] 2618 4-9-9 **87**.......... PatCosgrave 1 92
(Jim Boyle) *led: rdn over 2f out: hdd ent fnl f: kpt on gamely: hld cl home* **11/10**[1]

64-6 **3** 3 ½ **Lyfka**[28] 2054 5-9-3 **81**..........(tp) AdamKirby 3 77
(Paul Cole) *trckd ldrs: rdn to chal over 2f out tl edgd lft over 1f out: no ex fnl f* **2/1**[2]

1m 23.67s (0.57) **Going Correction** +0.075s/f (Good) **3** Ran SP% **106.0**
Speed ratings (Par 102): **99,98,94**
CSF £6.46 TOTE £2.90; EX 3.10 Trifecta £6.20.
**Owner** A M Pickering **Bred** Ringfort Stud **Trained** Newmarket, Suffolk

**FOCUS**
Add 4yds. A poor turnout numerically but not a bad race. The winner has been rated to form.

## 2913 STREAMLINE TAXIS SUPPORTS THE MARTLETS HOSPICE H'CAP 1m 1f 207y
**3:50** (3:50) (Class 5) (0-75,77) 4-Y-0+ **£2,911** (£866; £432; £216) **Stalls** High

Form RPR

/006 **1** **Impressive Day (IRE)**[29] 2028 4-8-12 **67**..........(p[1]) HectorCrouch(3) 9 77
(Gary Moore) *hld up mid-div: hdwy over 2f out: rdn to ld jst over 1f out: styd on wl to draw clr: rdn out* **25/1**

4412 **2** 4 **Deep Challenger (IRE)**[24] 2163 5-9-7 **73**.......... DougieCostello 6 75+
(Jamie Osborne) *led after 1f tl over 5f out: rdn to chal wl over 2f out: led wl over 1f out: hdd jst bef fnl f: sn hld: kpt on same pce* **4/1**[1]

-336 **3** nk **Bridge Of Sighs**[19] 2333 5-9-7 **73**.......... PatCosgrave 7 74
(Martin Smith) *hld up mid-div: rdn and hdwy fr 2f out: pressed for hld 2nd ins fnl f: kpt on same pce fnl 120yds* **4/1**[1]

130- **4** nk **Rubensian**[214] 7499 4-9-6 **77**.......... GeorgeBuckell(5) 4 78
(David Simcock) *v.s.a: detached in last wl off pce: hdwy fr 3f out: pressed for hld 2nd fnl 120yds: kpt on same pce* **6/1**[3]

60-1 **5** 2 ½ **Roy Rocket (FR)**[28] 2055 7-9-7 **73**.......... JFEgan 1 69
(John Berry) *hld up towards rr: stdy prog fr over 2f out: styd on fnl f but nt pce to get on terms* **5/1**[2]

22-0 **6** 1 ½ **Galinthias**[122] 354 5-8-10 **69**.......... DavidEgan(7) 2 62
(Simon Dow) *trckd ldrs: led over 5f out: rdn whn jnd over wl 2f out: hdd over 1f out: wknd ins fnl f* **16/1**

-501 **7** ½ **Becca Campbell (IRE)**[10] 2615 4-9-1 **70**..........(p) EdwardGreatrex(3) 8 62
(Eve Johnson Houghton) *hld up mid-div: rdn over 2f out: nt pce to get involved* **5/1**[2]

52-5 **8** 1 **Gannicus**[13] 2511 6-9-3 **69**..........(vt) ShaneKelly 3 59
(Brendan Powell) *led for 1f: chsd ldrs: rdn 3f out: wknd jst over 1f out* **25/1**

0-06 **9** 3 ¼ **Invictus (GER)**[11] 2586 5-9-6 **72**..........(h) JosephineGordon 10 55
(David Loughnane) *sn prom: rdn wl over 2f out: sn wknd* **9/1**

0-56 **10** 2 **Ban Shoof**[120] 380 4-9-6 **72**.......... TimmyMurphy 5 51
(Gary Moore) *a towards rr* **18/1**

2m 3.31s (-0.29) **Going Correction** +0.075s/f (Good) **10** Ran SP% **116.5**
Speed ratings (Par 103): **104,100,100,100,98 97,96,95,93,91**
CSF £122.63 CT £494.02 TOTE £25.70: £7.50, £1.70, £1.50; EX 186.30 Trifecta £1033.20.
**Owner** Power Geneva Ltd **Bred** Darley **Trained** Lower Beeding, W Sussex

**FOCUS**
Add 4yds. The runners were soon spread out, with four of these racing clear of the others for a long way and they finished second, sixth, eighth and ninth. The winner has been rated back to her 2yo Godolphin level.

## 2914 LABYRINTH CHALLENGE 18 AUG H'CAP 1m 1f 207y
**4:20** (4:21) (Class 6) (0-60,60) 4-Y-0+ **£2,264** (£673; £336; £168) **Stalls** High

Form RPR

0601 **1** **Master Of Heaven**[73] 1146 4-9-0 **53**..........(p) PatCosgrave 3 58
(Jim Boyle) *mde all: jst hld on: all out* **10/1**

0135 **2** shd **Tommys Geal**[20] 2295 5-9-4 **57**.......... JosephineGordon 5 62
(Michael Madgwick) *mid-div: hdwy fr 2f out: sn rdn: kpt on wl ins fnl f: jst failed* **9/2**[1]

0026 **3** 2 ¼ **Sir Jack**[20] 2295 4-9-4 **60**.......... HollieDoyle(3) 12 63
(Tony Carroll) *hld up towards rr: rdn and gd hdwy over 1f out: chsng ldng pair whn hung lft ent fnl f: no further imp* **11/2**[2]

-004 **4** 1 ¼ **Live Dangerously**[8] 2678 7-9-0 **53**.......... WilliamCarson 4 51
(John Bridger) *mid-div: rdn and hdwy fr 2f out: chsd ldrs ent fnl f: styd on same pce* **10/1**

063- **5** 2 **Fitzwilliam**[329] 3737 5-8-9 **48**.......... JFEgan 13 42
(Mick Channon) *trckd ldrs: racd keenly: sn rdn: kpt on same pce* **14/1**

40-0 **6** 2 ¾ **Funny Oyster (IRE)**[49] 1544 4-8-13 **52**.......... SamHitchcott 11 41
(Chris Gordon) *hld up towards rr: rdn and hdwy fr over 2f out: styd on but nt pce to get involved* **20/1**

00-3 **7** 1 ½ **Provoking (USA)**[21] 2255 4-8-8 **50**.......... NoelGarbutt(3) 16 36
(David Evans) *racd keenly towards rr of mid-div: rdn over 2f out: nvr threatened to get on terms* **7/1**[3]

40-6 **8** ½ **Megalala (IRE)**[10] 2615 16-8-3 **49**.......... JaneElliott(7) 14 34
(John Bridger) *chsd wnr tl rdn over 2f out: fdd fnl f* **16/1**

60-0 **9** shd **Fenner Hill Neasa (IRE)**[20] 2295 4-8-4 **46** oh1.....(h) CharlieBennett(3) 8 31
(Pat Phelan) *hld up towards rr: sme late prog: n.d* **33/1**

650- **10** ½ **Its A Sheila Thing**[268] 5923 4-8-9 **48**..........(h) GeorgeDowning 9 32
(Tony Carroll) *racd keenly in rr: mid-div whn rdn 2f out: sn wknd* **16/1**

400 **11** ½ **Dalavand (IRE)**[42] 1697 4-8-9 **48**.......... RobHornby 15 31
(Laura Mongan) *mid-div: rdn over 2f out: wknd ent fnl f* **12/1**

0000 **12** 2 **Fishergate**[20] 2313 4-8-13 **59**.......... DavidEgan(7) 7 38
(Richard Rowe) *a towards rr* **33/1**

0605 **13** 3 ½ **Just Fred (IRE)**[45] 1629 4-8-8 **47**..........(tp) TomMarquand 6 20
(Neil Mulholland) *a towards rr* **14/1**

0120 **14** 3 **Etaad (USA)**[43] 1683 6-9-4 **60**..........(b) HectorCrouch(3) 2 27
(Gary Moore) *trckd ldrs: rdn 2f out: sn wknd* **8/1**

2m 4.36s (0.76) **Going Correction** +0.075s/f (Good) **14** Ran SP% **118.8**
Speed ratings (Par 101): **99,98,97,96,94 92,91,90,90,90 89,88,85,83**
CSF £52.60 CT £276.80 TOTE £8.00: £2.60, £2.20, £2.60; EX 29.70 Trifecta £139.30.
**Owner** Maid In Heaven Partnership **Bred** Qatar Bloodstock Ltd **Trained** Epsom, Surrey

**FOCUS**
Add 4yds. A moderate handicap.

## 2915 LOVEFAIRS VINTAGE FAIR 27 AUG H'CAP (DIV I) 7f 211y
**4:50** (4:50) (Class 6) (0-60,61) 4-Y-0+ **£2,264** (£673; £336; £168) **Stalls** Low

Form RPR

6334 **1** **Sheer Intensity (IRE)**[10] 2626 4-9-0 **51**.......... JFEgan 12 57
(David Evans) *hld up: rdn and hdwy over 1f out: drifted lft ent fnl f: led fnl 120yds: r.o wl* **4/1**[3]

145- **2** 1 ¾ **World Record (IRE)**[187] 7986 7-9-7 **58**.......... PatCosgrave 3 60+
(Mick Quinn) *trckd ldrs: rdn for str chal over 2f out: ev ch ent fnl f: no ex towards fin* **3/1**[1]

0-26 **3** nk **Ettie Hart (IRE)**[21] 2255 4-9-1 **52**.......... CharlesBishop 10 53
(Mick Channon) *led: rdn whn strly chal 2f out: hdd fnl 120yds: no ex cl home* **7/2**[2]

0-05 **4** 1 ¼ **Machiavelian Storm (IRE)**[20] 2294 5-8-8 **45**.......... JosephineGordon 6 43
(Richard Mitchell) *mid-div: rdn over 2f out: kpt on to go 4th ins fnl f but nt pce to get on terms* **10/1**

000- **5** 1 **Alketios (GR)**[280] 5509 6-9-5 **56**.......... SamHitchcott 9 52
(Chris Gordon) *mid-div: hdwy over 2f out: sn rdn: wnt 4th ent fnl f: no ex fnl 100yds* **14/1**

200- **6** 3 ¼ **Golden Isles (IRE)**[203] 7754 4-9-6 **57**.......... GavinLerena 11 48
(Heather Main) *trckd ldrs: rdn over 2f out: fdd fnl 120yds* **4/1**[3]

50-0 **7** 6 **Piccola Poppy**[11] 2580 4-8-8 **45**..........(v[1]) WilliamCarson 7 20
(John Bridger) *mid-div: rdn over 2f out: wknd ent fnl f* **25/1**

4/6- **8** 3 **Max Beddow (IRE)**[466] 544 4-9-3 **54**.......... TimmyMurphy 13 22
(Geoffrey Deacon) *prom tl rdn 3f out: wknd jst over 1f out* **40/1**

6-00 **9** 5 **Zebedee's Son (IRE)**[62] 1298 4-8-1 **45**..........(b[1]) RhiainIngram(7) 2
(Roger Ingram) *a towards rr* **22/1**

1m 37.19s (1.19) **Going Correction** +0.075s/f (Good) **9** Ran SP% **113.6**
Speed ratings (Par 101): **97,95,94,93,92 89,83,80,75**
CSF £15.75 CT £45.02 TOTE £4.80: £1.50, £1.50, £1.40; EX 19.90 Trifecta £40.70.
**Owner** Mrs E Evans **Bred** Ms V Vartanov **Trained** Pandy, Monmouths

**FOCUS**
Add 4yds. Four non-runners including the first two in the betting forecast, Kafeel and Freddy With A Y. The time was 1.13sec slower than the second division. Straightforward form.

## 2916 LOVEFAIRS VINTAGE FAIR 27 AUG H'CAP (DIV II) 7f 211y
**5:20** (5:20) (Class 6) (0-60,58) 4-Y-0+ **£2,264** (£673; £336; £168) **Stalls** Low

Form RPR

3300 **1** **Suitsus**[41] 1729 6-9-6 **57**..........(t) TimmyMurphy 2 67
(Geoffrey Deacon) *hld up towards rr: rdn and hdwy over 1f out: str run ent fnl f despite hanging bdly lft: sn bmpd the 3rd: led fnl 100yds: r.o* **16/1**

3663 **2** 2 **With Approval (IRE)**[27] 2095 5-9-7 **58**..........(p) PatCosgrave 7 63
(Laura Mongan) *chsd ldr: rdn over 2f out: led ent fnl f: hdd fnl 100yds: no ex* **7/1**[2]

00-1 **3** 1 ¼ **Buzz Lightyere**[21] 2255 4-9-3 **54**.......... LiamKeniry 12 59
(Philip Hide) *chsd ldrs: keeping on in cl 3rd whn taking a hefty knock ins fnl f: kpt on but nt time to rcvr* **11/8**[1]

1106 **4** 1 ½ **Magic Mirror**[28] 2070 4-9-2 **53**..........(p[1]) TomMarquand 4 52
(Mark Rimell) *led: rdn 2f out: hdd ent fnl f: no ex fnl 120yds* **8/1**[3]

5-50 **5** ½ **Musical Taste**[22] 2229 4-9-4 **55**..........(v[1]) JFEgan 10 53
(Pat Phelan) *hld up towards rr: rdn 2f out: little imp tl r.o wl fnl f: nvr threatened to get involved* **50/1**

-602 **6** nk **Fairy Mist (IRE)**[21] 2255 10-8-11 **48**..........(v) WilliamCarson 3 45
(John Bridger) *in tch: rdn over 2f out: kpt on ins fnl f* **10/1**

3633 **7** 1 **Bold Max**[54] 1451 6-8-8 **45**..........(p) SamHitchcott 8 40
(Zoe Davison) *mid-div: rdn and hdwy over 1f out: chalng for 3rd ent fnl f: fdd fnl 100yds* **25/1**

3024 **8** 4 **Greyfriarschorista**[5] 2763 10-9-3 **54**..........(vt) AdamKirby 11 40
(David Evans) *nvr bttr than mid-div* **7/1**[2]

6000 **9** nse **Bassino (USA)**[27] 2095 4-8-9 **51**..........(p) RachealKneller(5) 6 37
(James Bennett) *chsd ldrs: rdn over 2f out: wknd fnl f* **33/1**

3030 **10** nk **Lutine Charlie (IRE)**[21] 2255 10-8-1 **45**..........(p) DavidEgan(7) 1 30
(Emma Owen) *mid-div: rdn over 2f out: wknd ent fnl f* **33/1**

0-00 **11** 5 **Back To Love (CAN)**[8] 2679 4-8-5 **45**..........(h) NoelGarbutt(3) 9 18
(Mark Gillard) *mid-div: rdn wl over 2f out: wknd over 1f out* **50/1**

0040 **12** 58 **Qortaaj**[10] 2626 4-9-6 **57**..........(h[1]) JosephineGordon 5 +
(David Loughnane) *rrd bdly leaving stall and blindfold removed late: a wl detached in last* **9/1**

1m 36.06s (0.06) **Going Correction** +0.075s/f (Good) **12** Ran SP% **116.8**
Speed ratings (Par 101): **102,100,98,97,96 96,95,91,91,91 86,28**
CSF £116.87 CT £260.37 TOTE £20.30: £4.60, £2.20, £1.20; EX 148.90 Trifecta £391.40.
**Owner** Suitsus Partnership **Bred** Mrs Susan Cole & Miss Lesley McGrath **Trained** Compton, Berks
■ Stewards' Enquiry : Liam Keniry two-day ban: careless riding (Jun 6-7)

**FOCUS**
Add 4yds. Reduced visibility due to fog. The time was 1.13sec quicker than the first division. The runner-up helps set the level.

## 2917 HUMAN LEAGUE HERE 8TH SEPT H'CAP 5f 215y
**5:50** (5:51) (Class 5) (0-70,71) 4-Y-0+ **£2,911** (£866; £432; £216) **Stalls** Low

Form RPR

0-00 **1** **Perfect Pastime**[18] 2367 9-8-13 **62**..........(p) PatCosgrave 7 70
(Jim Boyle) *in tch: ldng whn bk in view ins fnl f: r.o: rdn out* **16/1**

1033 **2** ¾ **Black Caesar (IRE)**[8] 2676 6-9-7 **70**.......... LiamKeniry 4 75
(Philip Hide) *trckd ldr: chsng wnr whn bk in view ins fnl f: kpt on but hld towards fin* **7/2**[3]

0/46 **3** *nk* **Jersey Breeze (IRE)**[10] 2618 4-9-8 **71**.................................... JFEgan 5 75
(Mick Channon) *led: chalng for 2nd whn bk in view ins fnl f: kpt on but no ex cl home* **10/3**[2]
-500 **4** *3 1/4* **Soaring Spirits (IRE)**[28] 2058 7-9-2 **68**........................(b) JackDuern(3) 3 62
(Dean Ivory) *trckd ldrs: 4th whn bk in view ins fnl f: kpt on same pce fnl 120yds* **12/1**
4-60 **5** *shd* **Bingo George (IRE)**[5] 2763 4-8-8 **57**.................................. RobHornby 2 50
(Andrew Balding) *hld up last pair: 5th whn bk in view ins fnl f: styd on but nt pce to get on terms* **13/2**
4421 **6** *1 3/4* **Duke Of North (IRE)**[11] 2582 5-9-4 **70**...................... CharlieBennett(3) 6 58
(Jim Boyle) *trckd ldrs: already wknd into 6th whn bk in view ins fnl f* **9/4**[1]
0-45 **7** *6* **Essaka (IRE)**[22] 2229 5-8-2 **58**........................................ AledBeech(7) 1 27
(Tony Carroll) *a last pair: sddle looked to have slipped whn bk in view ins fnl f* **10/1**

(-70.20) **Going Correction** +0.075s/f (Good) course record **7** Ran SP% **112.1**
CSF £68.15 TOTE £9.30: £5.40, £1.60; EX 61.50 Trifecta £310.30.
**Owner** The Paddock Space Partnership 2 **Bred** R G & T E Levin **Trained** Epsom, Surrey

**FOCUS**
Add 4yds. Thick fog reduced visibility down to about the last half-furlong in the closing stages. The runner-up has been rated to form. No winning time was recorded.
T/Jkpt: Not Won. T/Plt: £75.60 to a £1 stake. Pool: £75,846.72 - 731.59 winning units T/Qpdt: £12.80 to a £1 stake. Pool: £4,536.04 - 261.80 winning units **Tim Mitchell**

# 2786 NEWCASTLE (A.W) (L-H)
## Tuesday, May 23

**OFFICIAL GOING: Tapeta: standard**
Wind: Fresh, against on straight course and in over 3f of home straight on round course Weather: Fine, dry

## 2918 TECH TALENT H'CAP (DIV I) 1m 5y (Tp)
**2:10** (2:11) (Class 6) (0-60,62) 4-Y-0+ **£2,587** (£770; £384; £192) **Stalls** Centre

Form RPR
-165 **1** **Symbolic Star (IRE)**[23] 2179 5-8-8 **54**..................(p) ConnorMurtagh(7) 1 60
(Barry Murtagh) *dwlt: sn in tch: smooth hdwy to ld over 1f out: sn pushed along: hld on wl towards fin* **8/1**
-160 **2** *hd* **Grey Destiny**[21] 2278 7-9-5 **58**............................................ CamHardie 3 64
(Antony Brittain) *t.k.h: hld up: hdwy over 2f out: chsd wnr fnl f: kpt on: hld cl home* **11/1**
-016 **3** *1* **Luath**[23] 2179 4-9-8 **61**.......................................................... TomEaves 12 64
(Suzzanne France) *dwlt: hld up: pushed along over 2f out: hdwy over 1f out: kpt on fnl f: nt pce to chal* **8/1**
50-0 **4** *2 3/4* **Beverley Bullet**[23] 2179 4-9-3 **56**.................................. DanielTudhope 2 53
(Lawrence Mullaney) *led at ordinary gallop: rdn and hdd over 1f out: outpcd fnl f* **7/1**[3]
300- **5** *2 3/4* **Thornaby Nash**[224] 7253 6-9-2 **60**............................... GemmaTutty(5) 8 51
(Karen Tutty) *cl up: drvn over 2f out: outpcd over 1f out: n.d after* **14/1**
-203 **6** *3/4* **Muzaahim (IRE)**[21] 2276 6-9-5 **58**...............................(h) TrevorWhelan 5 53
(Laura Morgan) *rrd and lost several l s: hld up: rdn over 2f out: effrt over 1f: sn no imp* **5/1**[2]
6-01 **7** *nk* **The Name's Paver**[23] 2179 4-9-9 **62**........................... PaulMulrennan 11 51
(Noel Wilson) *prom: rdn over 2f out: wknd over 1f out* **3/1**[1]
1006 **8** *3/4* **Nelson's Bay**[18] 2378 8-8-9 **55**..................................... PaulaMuir(7) 7 42
(Wilf Storey) *t.k.h: hld up: rdn over 2f out: sn no imp* **16/1**
000- **9** *shd* **Ivors Involvement (IRE)**[164] 8307 5-8-7 **49**.................. NathanEvans(3) 4 36
(Tina Jackson) *t.k.h: cl up tl rdn and wknd over 1f out* **14/1**
30-0 **10** *hd* **Ginger Charlie**[49] 1545 4-8-9 **48**................................ JamesSullivan 10 35
(Ruth Carr) *dwlt: hld up: rdn over 2f out: sn no imp: btn over 1f out* **20/1**
000- **11** *1 1/2* **Hellavashock**[144] 8587 4-9-0 **58**................................. RowanScott(5) 9 41
(Alistair Whillans) *midfield: drvn and outpcd over 2f out: sn btn* **16/1**
000- **12** *11* **The King's Steed**[214] 7513 4-8-11 **50**............................ GrahamLee 6 9
(Micky Hammond) *hld up bhd ldng gp: rdn and outpcd over 2f out: sn wknd* **16/1**

1m 43.8s (5.20) **Going Correction** +0.50s/f (Slow) **12** Ran SP% **120.5**
Speed ratings (Par 101): **94,93,92,90,87 86,86,85,85,85 83,72**
CSF £94.54 CT £746.71 TOTE £9.50: £2.70, £2.60, £2.70; EX 92.50 Trifecta £508.10.
**Owner** Murtagh, O'Rourke & Trinders **Bred** Darley **Trained** Low Braithwaite, Cumbria

**FOCUS**
The first division of a modest handicap. They went a sedate gallop and the winner grabbed an advantage over 1f out. Straightforward form rated around the runner-up to last year's best.

## 2919 TECH TALENT H'CAP (DIV II) 1m 5y (Tp)
**2:40** (2:42) (Class 6) (0-60,62) 4-Y-0+ **£2,587** (£770; £384; £192) **Stalls** Centre

Form RPR
-150 **1** **Table Manners**[69] 1203 5-9-2 **58**................................ NathanEvans(3) 10 66
(Wilf Storey) *hld up: hdwy over 2f out: led ent fnl f: edgd lft: rdn out* **10/1**
4060 **2** *2 1/4* **Faintly (USA)**[22] 2224 6-9-8 **61**...............................(b) JamesSullivan 8 64
(Ruth Carr) *hld p: hdwy and hung lft fr over 2f out: kpt on fnl f to take 2nd cl home: no ch w wnr* **5/2**[1]
50-2 **3** *shd* **Broctune Papa Gio**[122] 361 10-9-0 **58**..............(b) LewisEdmunds(5) 11 61
(Gillian Boanas) *led: rdn: edgd lft and hdd ent fnl f: kpt on same pce: lost 2nd nr fin* **8/1**
3436 **4** *2 1/2* **Lord Rob**[53] 1469 6-8-9 **48**..........................................(p) AndrewMullen 7 45
(David Thompson) *prom: effrt and wnt 2nd over 2f out to over 1f out: sn no ex* **10/1**
-645 **5** *1* **Lozah**[105] 609 4-9-9 **62**............................................... TonyHamilton 6 57
(Roger Fell) *hld up: pushed along and hdwy over 2f out: kpt on fnl f: nvr able to chal* **8/1**
00/3 **6** *4 1/2* **Geordie George (IRE)**[35] 1868 5-9-7 **60**........................(t[1]) GrahamLee 2 45
(Rebecca Menzies) *chsd ldrs: drvn and outpcd over 2f out: sn btn* **13/2**[3]
6 **7** *4* **Three Majors (IRE)**[24] 2166 4-9-2 **55**.......................(tp) LukeMorris 12 31
(Anthony McCann, Ire) *in tch: drvn along over 2f out: wknd wl over 1f out* **11/2**[2]
225- **8** *3* **Affectionate Lady (IRE)**[309] 4445 6-9-0 **53**....................(b) TomEaves 1 23
(Paul Collins) *dwlt: hld up: rdn along over 3f out: btn fnl 2f* **20/1**
-000 **9** *1* **Torch**[69] 1210 4-9-5 **58**...........................................(p) DanielMuscutt 5 26
(John Butler) *hld up midfield: drvn and struggling over 3f out: sn btn* **20/1**
-246 **10** *1* **I'm Super Too (IRE)**[8] 2687 10-8-12 **56**..................(p) GemmaTutty(5) 4 21
(Karen Tutty) *hld up: rdn along 3f out: sn wknd* **16/1**
00-0 **11** *1/2* **Mayfield Boy**[57] 1403 6-8-11 **50**.................................. CamHardie 3 14
(Antony Brittain) *pressed ldr: drvn and struggling over 2f out: sn btn* **28/1**

000/ **12** *5* **Crossley**[664] 4762 8-8-0 **46** oh1................................(p) KieranSchofield(7) 9
(Neville Bycroft) *t.k.h: hld up in tch: drvn and struggling wl over 2f out: sn wknd* **50/1**

1m 42.27s (3.67) **Going Correction** +0.50s/f (Slow) **12** Ran SP% **118.5**
Speed ratings (Par 101): **101,98,98,96,95 90,86,83,82,81 81,76**
CSF £33.62 CT £218.08 TOTE £11.10: £3.00, £1.90, £2.80; EX 48.20 Trifecta £353.30.
**Owner** Geegeez.co.uk 1 **Bred** Raymond Clive Tooth **Trained** Muggleswick, Co Durham

**FOCUS**
The second division of a modest handicap. They went a more respectable gallop and the winning time was about 1.5 seconds quicker.

## 2920 GOSPELWARE APP TECHNOLOGY H'CAP 1m 2f 42y (Tp)
**3:10** (3:10) (Class 4) (0-85,84) 4-Y-0+ **£5,045** (£1,501; £750; £375) **Stalls** High

Form RPR
1-41 **1** **Shargiah (IRE)**[15] 2477 4-9-7 **84**.................................. AndreaAtzeni 6 94+
(Roger Varian) *trckd ldrs: shkn up to ld over 1f out: pushed along and edgd lft ins fnl f: comf* **9/4**[1]
06-1 **2** *1 1/2* **Pushaq (IRE)**[24] 2163 4-9-1 **78**...............................(h) LukeMorris 1 85
(Anthony McCann, Ire) *in tch: rdn over 2f out: chsd wnr ins fnl f: kpt on: nt pce to chal* **7/1**
3-01 **3** *shd* **Tom's Rock (IRE)**[19] 2333 4-9-3 **80**............................... DanielMuscutt 2 87
(John Butler) *trckd ldrs: effrt and hdwy to chal over 1f out: kpt on same pce ins fnl f* **9/2**[2]
00-0 **4** *5* **Oasis Spear**[20] 2291 5-9-6 **83**............................................. DavidAllan 7 80
(Chris Wall) *t.k.h: trckd ldrs: led after 3f: rdn and hdd over 1f out: kpt on same pce fnl f* **6/1**[3]
1-35 **5** *4* **Bollihope**[8] 2685 5-8-10 **73**........................................ ConnorBeasley 3 62
(Richard Guest) *dwlt: hld up: rdn along and hdwy over 2f out: edgd lft: no imp over 1f out* **6/1**[3]
0056 **6** *1/2* **Top Of The Glas (IRE)**[10] 2629 6-8-13 **76**.......................... TomEaves 8 64
(Brian Ellison) *hld up: rdn and outpcd 3f out: no imp fr 2f out* **14/1**
13P1 **7** *13* **Genres**[16] 2427 5-8-8 **71**.................................................. JoeFanning 5 33
(Sally Haynes) *led 3f: cl up tl wknd fr 2f out* **8/1**
4202 **8** *4* **Muqarred (USA)**[15] 2466 5-8-11 **74**.........................(p) TonyHamilton 4 28
(Roger Fell) *hld up: rdn and outpcd 3f out: sn wknd* **25/1**

2m 14.41s (4.01) **Going Correction** +0.50s/f (Slow) **8** Ran SP% **111.6**
Speed ratings (Par 105): **103,101,101,97,94 94,83,80**
CSF £17.55 CT £62.83 TOTE £2.60: £1.30, £1.90, £1.90; EX 18.70 Trifecta £55.80.
**Owner** Saif Ali **Bred** Rabbah Bloodstock Limited **Trained** Newmarket, Suffolk

**FOCUS**
A decent handicap. They went a muddling gallop with the pace only lifting about 5f out. The second and third have been rated to the better view of their recent wins.

## 2921 GO REBOOT MAIDEN STKS 1m 2f 42y (Tp)
**3:40** (3:43) (Class 5) 3-Y-0 **£3,557** (£1,058; £529; £264) **Stalls** High

Form RPR
4-3 **1** **Master Singer (USA)**[31] 1963 3-9-5 0............................ AndreaAtzeni 1 95+
(John Gosden) *prom: smooth hdwy to ld 3f out: shkn up and qcknd clr fnl 2f: v easily* **8/15**[1]
400- **2** *16* **Moonlight Blue (IRE)**[249] 6534 3-9-5 69...................... PaulMulrennan 7 60
(Michael Dods) *hld up midfield: rdn along over 2f out: hdwy to chse (clr) wnr over 1f out: kpt on fnl f: no imp* **50/1**
0-4 **3** *1 1/4* **Melinoe**[20] 2311 3-9-0 0................................................... LukeMorris 3 53
(Sir Mark Prescott Bt) *trckd ldrs: rdn and ev ch briefly 3f out: edgd lft and one pce fnl 2f* **7/2**[2]
0- **4** *1 1/2* **Two Dollars (IRE)**[202] 7769 3-9-5 0............................... TrevorWhelan 6 55
(William Jarvis) *hld up: drvn and outpcd over 4f out: plugged on fr over 1f out: nvr able to chal* **66/1**
56 **5** *2 1/4* **Circling Vultures**[11] 2584 3-9-5 0...................................... CamHardie 5 50
(Antony Brittain) *dwlt: hld up: effrt and rdn over 3f out: no imp fr 2f out* **100/1**
3-3 **6** *2 3/4* **Fortuities (IRE)**[53] 1471 3-9-0 0.................................. JackGarritty 12 40+
(Jedd O'Keeffe) *pressed ldr: carried rt over 3f out: drvn and outpcd fr 2f out* **9/2**[3]
**7** *shd* **Point Of Discovery** 3-9-5 0.......................................... DanielMuscutt 8 44
(Marco Botti) *hld up: pushed along and green over 4f out: struggling over 2f out* **8/1**
00- **8** *11* **Satis House**[164] 8305 3-9-0 0.................................... RoystonFfrench 4 17
(Susan Corbett) *prom tl rdn and wknd over 2f out* **150/1**
**9** *4* **Rip Van Go** 3-9-5 0......................................................... NeilFarley 11 14
(Sally Haynes) *bhd: pushed along 1/2-way: struggling fnl 3f* **50/1**
**10** *3 1/2* **Parasail** 3-9-0 0............................................................. JoeFanning 9 2
(Mark Johnston) *t.k.h: led: hung rt bnd over 3f out: sn hdd: continued to hang rt and sn eased* **16/1**

2m 11.28s (0.88) **Going Correction** +0.50s/f (Slow) **10** Ran SP% **129.7**
Speed ratings (Par 99): **116,103,102,101,99 97,96,88,84,82**
CSF £56.27 TOTE £1.50: £1.10, £7.00, £1.50; EX 32.40 Trifecta £127.70.
**Owner** Teneri Farms Inc **Bred** Teneri Farm Inc & Bernardo A Calderon **Trained** Newmarket, Suffolk

**FOCUS**
A fairly decent 3yo maiden, which fell apart in behind the form horse, who won by a wide margin with any amount in hand off a respectable gallop.

## 2922 SUNDERLAND SOFTWARE CITY H'CAP 7f 14y (Tp)
**4:10** (4:11) (Class 3) (0-95,92) 3-Y-0+ **£9,703** (£2,887; £1,443; £721) **Stalls** Centre

Form RPR
21-4 **1** **Omran**[32] 1945 3-9-0 **89**............................................... AndreaAtzeni 9 98+
(Marco Botti) *awkward and rdr lost iron briefly s: sn rcvrd and trckd ldrs: led gng wl over 1f out: pushed out fnl f: readily* **4/5**[1]
4211 **2** *3* **Custard The Dragon**[35] 1867 4-9-7 **85**............................(p) BenCurtis 1 89
(John Mackie) *pressed ldr: ev ch over 2f out to over 1f out: sn chsng wnr: kpt on fnl f: nt pce to chal* **12/1**
0000 **3** *shd* **Amood (IRE)**[8] 2684 6-9-0 **78** oh3.................................(p) JasonHart 5 82
(Simon West) *hld up: stdy hdwy over 2f out: effrt and rdn over 1f out: kpt on fnl f: nt pce to chal* **20/1**
1124 **4** *nk* **Inaam (IRE)**[15] 2457 4-9-4 **82**........................................ PaulHanagan 4 85
(Richard Fahey) *in tch: rdn along over 2f out: kpt on same pce fnl f* **6/1**[2]
-400 **5** *shd* **Young John (IRE)**[108] 581 4-9-3 **81**................................ JackGarritty 7 84
(Richard Fahey) *t.k.h: in tch: rdn along 2f out: one pce fnl f* **16/1**
3150 **6** *4* **Twin Appeal (IRE)**[17] 2384 6-9-7 **92**...................(b) ConnorMurtagh(7) 2 87
(David Barron) *led: rdn and hdd over 1f out: wknd fnl f* **9/1**[3]
2-11 **7** *nk* **Morning Suit (USA)**[8] 2677 3-8-13 **88** 6ex........................ JoeFanning 3 79
(Mark Johnston) *t.k.h: trckd ldrs: outpcd over 2f out: btn fnl f* **6/1**[2]
000- **8** *1* **Majdool (IRE)**[322] 3980 4-9-9 **87**..................................... GrahamLee 6 80
(Noel Wilson) *hld up: rdn along over 2f out: sn n.d: btn over 1f out* **66/1**

4505 **9** 1 3/4 **Loyalty**[13] 2518 10-9-11 **89**....................(v) TonyHamilton 8 78
(Derek Shaw) *hld up: rdn over 2f out: wknd fnl f* **33/1**
1m 28.69s (2.49) **Going Correction** +0.50s/f (Slow)
**WFA** 3 from 4yo+ 11lb **9** Ran SP% **116.9**
Speed ratings (Par 107): **105,101,101,101,101 96,96,94,92**
CSF £12.12 CT £118.76 TOTE £1.70: £1.10, £3.60, £5.60; EX 14.60 Trifecta £147.10.
**Owner** H E Sherida Al-Kaabi **Bred** Bugley Stud & D B Clark **Trained** Newmarket, Suffolk

**FOCUS**
The feature contest was a good handicap. They went a respectable gallop and the particularly strong market leader won this pretty much as he liked. The runner-up has been rated a bit below his Southwell form.

## 2923 DIGITAL SKILLS SUMMIT H'CAP 6f (Tp)
**4:40** (4:41) (Class 5) (0-70,72) 4-Y-0+ **£3,234** (£962; £481; £240) **Stalls** Centre

Form RPR
-421 **1** **The Armed Man**[10] 2633 4-8-8 **64**.................... PaulaMuir(7) 14 75
(Chris Fairhurst) *mde virtually all: rdn 2f out: styd on wl fnl f* **11/2**[2]
0256 **2** 1 3/4 **Burtonwood**[20] 2305 5-8-11 **65**.................... CallumRodriguez(5) 1 70
(Julie Camacho) *trckd ldrs on outside: effrt and chal over 1f out: kpt on same pce ins fnl f* **8/1**
101- **3** 3/4 **Danish Duke (IRE)**[294] 4970 6-9-9 **72**....................(p) JamesSullivan 11 75
(Ruth Carr) *trckd ldrs: effrt and pushed along 2f out: kpt on same pce fnl f* **25/1**
2236 **4** shd **El Principe**[29] 2034 4-9-4 **67**....................(h) JasonHart 13 69
(Les Eyre) *w wnr to 1/2-way: drvn and outpcd wl over 1f out: one pce after* **6/1**[3]
341- **5** 1 **Caeser The Gaeser (IRE)**[197] 7852 5-8-13 **67**........ LewisEdmunds(5) 8 66
(Nigel Tinkler) *s.i.s: sn pushed along in rr: hdwy over 1f out: kpt on fnl f: nvr able to chal* **8/1**
1-60 **6** 1 **Chip Or Pellet**[10] 2633 4-8-7 **56** oh3....................(b[1]) TomEaves 10 52
(Nigel Tinkler) *hld up on ins: drvn along over 2f out: kpt on same pce fr over 1f out* **20/1**
3033 **7** 3/4 **Inshaa**[24] 2161 5-8-8 **64**....................(p) SeamusCronin(7) 4 57
(Michael Herrington) *in tch: drvn along over 2f out: outpcd appr fnl f* **10/1**
1256 **8** nk **Ticks The Boxes (IRE)**[7] 2700 5-9-6 **72**....................(p) NathanEvans(3) 3 65
(John Wainwright) *in tch: drvn and outpcd over 2f out: n.d after* **14/1**
3-15 **9** 1 1/4 **Epeius (IRE)**[31] 1972 4-9-2 **65**.................... GrahamLee 7 54+
(Ben Haslam) *hld up: pushed along 1/2-way: sme hdwy whn nt clr run fr over 1f out: no imp fnl f* **7/1**
6012 **10** 1 1/2 **Major Crispies**[19] 2331 6-9-1 **71**....................(vt) TommyO'Connor(7) 12 55
(David O'Meara) *sn rdn along in rr: struggling 1/2-way: nvr on terms* **10/1**
314- **11** hd **Gun Case**[207] 7662 5-9-2 **70**.................... RowanScott(5) 9 53
(Alistair Whillans) *towards rr and sn drvn along: struggling over 2f out: sn btn* **4/1**[1]
-040 **12** 10 **Presto Boy**[88] 899 5-8-7 **56** oh11.................... JoeDoyle 2 7
(John Balding) *midfield on outside: drvn along over 2f out: wknd over 1f out* **33/1**
1m 15.23s (2.73) **Going Correction** +0.50s/f (Slow) **12** Ran SP% **120.8**
Speed ratings (Par 103): **101,98,97,97,96 94,93,93,91,89 89,76**
CSF £48.91 CT £1046.46 TOTE £5.00: £1.90, £3.20, £4.70; EX 55.20 Trifecta £865.50.
**Owner** Mrs C A Arnold **Bred** C W Fairhurst **Trained** Middleham, N Yorks

**FOCUS**
An ordinary handicap. Most of the field came over to race up the stands' side rail but the winning time was modest. The runner-up has been rated to form.

## 2924 BYTENIGHT MAIDEN STKS 5f (Tp)
**5:10** (5:10) (Class 5) 3-Y-O **£3,557** (£1,058; £529; £264) **Stalls** Centre

Form RPR
03 **1** **Mabs Cross**[23] 2180 3-9-0 0.................... PaulMulrennan 2 74
(Michael Dods) *trckd ldrs gng wl in centre: smooth hdwy to ld over 1f out: shkn up and qcknd clr fnl f: readily* **3/1**[2]
4-65 **2** 3 3/4 **Double Spin**[26] 2112 3-9-0 65.................... DanielTudhope 1 60
(Robert Cowell) *slt ld in centre tl rdn and hdd over 1f out: kpt on same pce fnl f* **10/1**
020- **3** 3/4 **Gaval**[234] 6950 3-9-5 65.................... PhillipMakin 6 62
(David Barron) *w ldrs in centre to over 1f out: drvn and one pce fnl f* **4/1**[3]
05- **4** 1/2 **Metisian**[274] 5713 3-9-5 0.................... GrahamLee 4 61
(Jedd O'Keeffe) *bhd and pushed along centre: hdwy over 1f out: rdn and no imp fnl f* **16/1**
3 **5** 4 **Yorkshire Rover**[17] 2405 3-8-12 0.................... KevinLundie(7) 9 46
(David Brown) *chsd ldrs on nr side of gp: drvn over 2f out: wknd over 1f out* **25/1**
60 **6** 3/4 **Noble Sword**[11] 2595 3-9-5 0.................... JackGarritty 3 43
(Jedd O'Keeffe) *bhd and drvn along centre : no imp fr 2f out* **50/1**
0-43 **7** 2 3/4 **Hamidans Girl (IRE)**[18] 2372 3-9-0 69.................... JoeFanning 5 29
(Keith Dalgleish) *t.k.h early: w ldrs to 2f out: sn rdn and wknd* **7/4**[1]
5 **8** 3 1/2 **Kodiac Pearl (IRE)**[24] 2139 3-9-0 0.................... LukeMorris 8 16
(Robert Cowell) *cl up on nr side of gp: struggling over 2f out: sn wknd* **7/1**
0 **9** 10 **Catskill**[122] 357 3-8-11 0.................... NathanEvans(3) 7
(Wilf Storey) *in tch on nr side of gp: drvn along over 2f out: sn wknd* **66/1**
1m 1.52s (2.02) **Going Correction** +0.50s/f (Slow) **9** Ran SP% **116.1**
Speed ratings (Par 99): **103,97,95,95,88 87,83,77,61**
CSF £32.52 TOTE £3.50: £1.40, £2.30, £1.60; EX 24.10 Trifecta £121.20.
**Owner** David W Armstrong **Bred** Highfield Farm Llp **Trained** Denton, Co Durham

**FOCUS**
An ordinary 3yo sprint maiden. The winning filly arrived on the up, and really appreciated the drop back to 5f here on Tapeta, producing a thoroughly convincing first victory.

## 2925 DIGITAL CATAPULT NORTH EAST & TEES VALLEY FILLIES' H'CAP 5f (Tp)
**5:40** (5:40) (Class 5) (0-70,70) 3-Y-O+ **£3,557** (£1,058; £529; £264) **Stalls** Centre

Form RPR
1436 **1** **Intense Romance (IRE)**[20] 2304 3-8-13 **70**.................... CallumRodriguez(5) 1 77
(Michael Dods) *prom on outside: effrt and rdn over 1f out: led ins fnl f: kpt on wl* **7/2**[2]
02-1 **2** 1/2 **Marseille (IRE)**[39] 1782 3-9-4 **70**.................... JoeDoyle 8 75
(Julie Camacho) *t.k.h: cl up: effrt over 1f out: drvn to chal ins fnl f: kpt on: hld cl home* **2/1**[1]
3-30 **3** nk **Dundunah (USA)**[10] 2630 3-9-0 **66**.................... DanielTudhope 6 70
(David O'Meara) *led: rdn along over 1f out: hdd ins fnl f: kpt on same pce: lost 2nd nr fin* **9/1**
-234 **4** 1/2 **Horsforth**[20] 2305 5-9-6 **64**....................(b) ConnorBeasley 5 69
(Richard Guest) *in tch: rdn and effrt 2f out: kpt on same pce ins fnl f* **7/2**[2]
134- **5** 3 1/4 **Roys Dream**[217] 7440 3-9-4 **70**.................... TonyHamilton 4 60
(Paul Collins) *cl up: rdn over 2f out: wknd over 1f out* **16/1**

0-00 **6** 1 **Manipura**[11] 2589 4-8-11 **58**....................(p) NathanEvans(3) 3 48
(Derek Shaw) *slowly away: hld up: rdn over 2f out: wknd over 1f out* **14/1**
4102 **7** 4 1/2 **Little Kingdom (IRE)**[2] 2853 3-8-5 **57**.................... RoystonFfrench 7 28
(Tracy Waggott) *prom: drvn along over 2f out: wknd over 1f out* **6/1**[3]
1m 1.83s (2.33) **Going Correction** +0.50s/f (Slow)
**WFA** 3 from 4yo+ 8lb **7** Ran SP% **114.6**
Speed ratings (Par 100): **101,100,99,98,93 92,84**
CSF £11.01 CT £56.07 TOTE £5.20: £2.90, £1.70; EX 11.40 Trifecta £111.60.
**Owner** Hugh Malcolm Linsley **Bred** John O'Connor **Trained** Denton, Co Durham

**FOCUS**
A modest fillies' sprint handicap. They went a respectable gallop and another previous C&D winner came to the fore. The fourth has been rated to her latest C&D effort.
T/Plt: £39.20 to a £1 stake. Pool: £66,245.34 - 1,232.20 winning units T/Qpdt: £5.70 to a £1 stake. Pool: £5,629.48 - 724.30 winning units **Richard Young**

# 2620 NOTTINGHAM (L-H)
Tuesday, May 23

**OFFICIAL GOING: Soft (good to soft places; 6.4) changed to good to soft (soft in places) after race 3 (3.00)**
Wind: Moderate half against Weather: Fine & dry

## 2926 BETTINGGODS.COM QUENTIN FRANKS RACING EBF NOVICE STKS 6f 18y
**2:00** (2:01) (Class 5) 2-Y-O **£3,234** (£962; £481; £240) **Stalls** High

Form RPR
0 **1** **Green Power**[31] 1966 2-9-2 0.................... MartinDwyer 1 85
(John Gallagher) *wnt lft s: sn cl up: led after 1f: pushed along and qcknd 2f out: rdn ent fnl f: drvn and hld on wl towards fin* **10/1**
**2** nk **Raydiance** 2-9-2 0.................... PJMcDonald 5 84
(K R Burke) *trckd ldrs: hdwy to chse wnr over 2f out: rdn over 1f out: styd on to chal ins fnl f: drvn and kpt on wl towards fin: jst hld* **8/1**
5 **3** 9 **Global Exceed**[28] 2052 2-9-2 0.................... JamieSpencer 2 57
(Ed Dunlop) *wnt lft s: trckd: ldrs: pushed along and hdwy 2f out: sn rdn and kpt on same pce* **6/1**
2 **4** 3 **Zain Flash**[46] 1604 2-9-2 0.................... SeanLevey 7 48
(David Evans) *led 1f: prom: edgd lft wl over 2f out and sn rdn along: outpcd fr wl over 1f out* **3/1**[2]
**5** nk **Master Grey (IRE)** 2-9-2 0.................... OisinMurphy 4 47
(Rod Millman) *green and sn outpcd in rr tl sme late hdwy* **4/1**[3]
**6** 5 **Panophobia** 2-8-13 0.................... AdamMcNamara(3) 6 32
(Richard Fahey) *chsd ldrs: pushed along and edgd lft after 2f: lost pl bef 1/2-way: sn rdn and bhd* **11/4**[1]
**7** 28 **Macho Guest (IRE)** 2-9-2 0.................... TomQueally 3 +
(George Margarson) *dwlt: hdwy to chse ldrs on outer whn bmpd after 2f: sn pushed along: lost pl 1/2-way: sn bhd and eased* **12/1**
1m 16.33s (1.63) **Going Correction** +0.05s/f (Good) **7** Ran SP% **113.8**
Speed ratings (Par 93): **91,90,78,74,74 67,30**
CSF £83.41 TOTE £14.00: £5.20, £5.70; EX 97.60 Trifecta £362.80.
**Owner** Nino's Partnership **Bred** Crossfields Bloodstock Ltd **Trained** Chastleton, Oxon

**FOCUS**
There had been 45mm of rain the previous week, and although it had been dry since Sunday the going remained on the easy side, being given as soft, good to soft in places (GoingStick: 6.4). The Outer track was in use, with the rail out 4yds, which added 12yds to races 4, 5 and 6, and 24yds to Race 3. The first two came well clear in this novice event.

## 2927 BETTINGGODS.COM MASTER RACING TIPSTER H'CAP (A JOCKEY CLUB GRASSROOTS SPRINT SERIES QUALIFIER) 6f 18y
**2:30** (2:33) (Class 5) (0-75,76) 3-Y-O **£3,234** (£962; £481; £240) **Stalls** High

Form RPR
02-3 **1** **Fantasy Keeper**[103] 638 3-8-11 **65**.................... OisinMurphy 8 76+
(Michael Appleby) *trckd ldrs: hdwy over 2f out: swtchd lft to outer and rdn jst over 1f out: led ent fnl f: kpt on strly* **8/1**
2204 **2** 2 **Seaview**[26] 2107 3-8-10 **67**.................... AaronJones(3) 7 70
(David Brown) *qckly away and cl up: led after 2f: jnd and pushed along 2f out: rdn and edgd sltly lft over 1f out: drvn: hung lft and hdd ent fnl f: kpt on same pce* **14/1**
-502 **3** nk **Father McKenzie**[11] 2579 3-9-7 **75**.................... RyanTate 6 77
(James Eustace) *trckd ldrs: cl up 1/2-way: chal 2f out: sn rdn and ev ch: drvn ins fnl f: kpt on same pce* **3/1**[1]
0-04 **4** 1 **Abiento (IRE)**[14] 2506 3-9-3 **74**.................... AdamMcNamara(3) 13 73+
(Richard Fahey) *towards rr: hdwy 1/2-way: pushed along over 2f out: rdn wl over 1f out: kpt on u.p fnl f* **5/1**[2]
0-40 **5** 1/2 **Bellevarde (IRE)**[21] 2271 3-8-10 **64**.................... KieranO'Neill 12 61
(Richard Price) *slt ld nr stands rail: hdd after 2f : trckd ldrs: rdn along over 1f out: kpt on one pce fnl f* **33/1**
1232 **6** 2 1/2 **Cappananty Con**[61] 1332 3-9-8 **76**....................(t[1]) RobertWinston 11 65
(Dean Ivory) *rr: hdwy over 2f out: rdn over 1f out: kpt on fnl f: nvr rch ldrs* **8/1**
540- **7** 1 1/2 **Captain Hawk**[199] 7818 3-9-7 **75**.................... StevieDonohoe 3 59
(Ian Williams) *sltly hmpd s: a towards rr* **20/1**
34-3 **8** 3 1/4 **Glacier Point**[39] 1762 3-9-5 **73**.................... JohnFahy 1 47
(Clive Cox) *stmbld s: sn prom: pushed along over 2f out: rdn wl over 1f out: sn wknd* **12/1**
44-0 **9** 2 1/2 **Vintage Dream (IRE)**[43] 1678 3-8-9 **63**.................... KevinStott 5 29
(Noel Wilson) *cl up: rdn along over 2f out: sn drvn and wknd* **16/1**
602- **10** 3 3/4 **Angel Palanas**[211] 7579 3-8-8 **65**.................... JordanVaughan(3) 2 19
(K R Burke) *chsd ldrs on outer: rdn along over 2f out: sn wknd* **12/1**
2-04 **11** 1 1/2 **Kings Heart (IRE)**[11] 2579 3-8-8 **62**....................(p[1]) MartinDwyer 10 11
(Mark Usher) *rrd s: a rr* **7/1**[3]
1344 **12** 3 **Tranquil Daze (IRE)**[62] 1306 3-9-0 **68**.................... SeanLevey 9 8
(David Brown) *midfield: rdn along wl over 2f out: sn wknd* **20/1**
1m 15.03s (0.33) **Going Correction** +0.05s/f (Good) **12** Ran SP% **116.8**
Speed ratings (Par 99): **99,96,95,94,93 90,88,84,80,75 73,69**
CSF £109.52 CT £413.61 TOTE £10.30: £2.80, £4.50, £1.80; EX 155.00 Trifecta £585.70.
**Owner** The Fantasy Fellowship B **Bred** Cheveley Park Stud Ltd **Trained** Oakham, Rutland

**FOCUS**
An ordinary sprint won by a handicap debutant. The runner-up has been rated to her AW form, with the third close to form.

## 2928 BETTINGGODS.COM VALUE RACING TIPS H'CAP 2m
**3:00** (3:00) (Class 5) (0-75,77) 4-Y-O+ **£3,234** (£962; £481; £240) **Stalls** Low

Form RPR
532- **1** **Coeur De Lion**[67] 7624 4-9-6 **73**.................................. FergusSweeney 2 82+
(Alan King) *.trckd ldrs: hdwy to chse ldr 4f out: chal 3f out: rdn to ld over 2f out: drvn and styd on wl fnl f* **1/1**[1]
51-0 **2** *3* **McCools Gold**[26] 2111 4-8-13 **66**..................................(p) MartinHarley 9 71
(Alan King) *trckd ldrs: rapid hdwy to ld over 7f out and qcknd pce: pushed along over 3f out: hdd and rdn over 2f out: drvn over 1f out: kpt on same pce* **6/1**[3]
05-0 **3** *1 1/4* **Barizan (IRE)**[18] 2357 11-9-2 **67**..................................(bt) MartinDwyer 7 70
(Brendan Powell) *trckd ldrs: pushed along over 4f out: rdn along 3f out: drvn wl over 1f out: plugged on one pce* **20/1**
20/0 **4** *2* **Dan Emmett (USA)**[29] 2032 7-9-1 **66**.................................. JimCrowley 4 67
(Michael Scudamore) *set stdy pce: hdd over 7f out: cl up: pushed along over 4f out: rdn 3f out: drvn fnl 2f and kpt on one pce* **7/1**
00-6 **5** *1/2* **Sail With Sultana**[18] 2363 6-8-5 **56** oh11........................ FrannyNorton 6 56?
(Mark Rimell) *chsd ldrs: rdn along wl over 2f out: sn drvn and one pce* **33/1**
340- **6** *2 3/4* **Aramist (IRE)**[158] 8399 7-9-12 **77**.................................. JamieSpencer 5 74
(Sally Haynes) *hld up in rr: effrt and sme hdwy 3f out: rdn along over 2f out: nvr a factor* **12/1**
36-3 **7** *1 3/4* **Chelsea's Boy (IRE)**[29] 2021 4-9-8 **75**.................................. FranBerry 3 70
(Ralph Beckett) *in tch: pushed along over 3f out: rdn wl over 2f out: sn drvn and btn* **5/1**[2]
00-0 **8** *1/2* **Rock On Bollinski**[29] 2032 7-9-0 **72**........................(p) BenRobinson(7) 1 66
(Brian Ellison) *s.i.s and lost several l s: jnd rr of field after 6f: rdn along 4f out: nvr a factor* **20/1**

3m 37.46s (2.96) **Going Correction** -0.05s/f (Good)
**WFA** 4 from 6yo+ 1lb **8 Ran SP% 113.6**
Speed ratings (Par 103): **90,88,87,86,86 85,84,84**
CSF £7.04 CT £71.45 TOTE £1.60: £1.10, £2.20, £4.70; EX 7.70 Trifecta £78.20.
**Owner** The Barbury Lions 2 **Bred** Mr & Mrs R Kelvin-Hughes **Trained** Barbury Castle, Wilts

**FOCUS**
Race distance increased by 24yds. The early pace wasn't that strong but it picked up down the back. It paid to race prominently. The runner-up has been rated as improving.

## 2929 BETTINGGODS.COM SPORTS GURU BRITISH EBF FILLIES' H'CAP 1m 2f 50y
**3:30** (3:30) (Class 4) (0-80,78) 3-Y-O **£6,469** (£1,925; £962; £481) **Stalls** Low

Form RPR
44-0 **1** **Harebell (IRE)**[32] 1944 3-9-0 **71**..................................(h[1]) FranBerry 6 77+
(Ralph Beckett) *hld up in rr: hdwy 4f: green and rdn along wl over 2f out: styd on wl appr fnl f: led nr fin* **7/1**
25-4 **2** *1* **Carol (IRE)**[21] 2269 3-9-3 **74**.................................. OisinMurphy 7 78
(Ed Dunlop) *sn trcking ldr: cl up over 3f out: led over 2f out: sn rdn: drvn ins fnl f: hdd and no ex towards fin* **5/1**[3]
43-6 **3** *nk* **Canterbury Quad (FR)**[54] 1459 3-9-6 **77**........................ LouisSteward 5 80
(Henry Spiller) *in tch: gd hdwy 3f out: cl up 2f out: sn chal: drvn and ev ch ent fnl f: no ex last 50 yds* **20/1**
21-0 **4** *2 1/2* **Three Duchesses**[21] 2274 3-9-0 **71**.................................. JamieSpencer 4 69
(Michael Bell) *hld up in tch: hdwy 4f: chsd ldrs wl over 2f out: sn rdn and no imp* **12/1**
1- **5** *nk* **Di Alta (IRE)**[213] 7548 3-9-6 **77**..................................(h) ThomasBrown 1 75
(Ed Walker) *s.i.s and lost several l at s: sn w field: rr: hdwy over 4f out: chsd ldrs over 3f out: rdn over 2f and sn no imp* **5/1**[3]
41-0 **6** *3* **Marilyn**[33] 1907 3-9-1 **72**.................................. JimCrowley 3 64
(Chris Wall) *chsd ldng pair: rdn along 3f out and sn edgd lft: drvn 2f out: grad wknd* **3/1**[1]
50-4 **7** *1 1/2* **Prize Diva**[94] 814 3-8-9 **66**.................................. PJMcDonald 2 55
(David Elsworth) *chsd ldrs on inner: rdn along wl over 3f out: sn wknd* **8/1**
1-23 **8** *2* **Celestation**[13] 2513 3-9-7 **78**.................................. FrannyNorton 8 63
(Mark Johnston) *sn led: pushed along 4f out: rdn 3f out: hdd over 2f out: sn drvn and wknd wl over 1f out* **4/1**[2]

2m 14.26s (-0.04) **Going Correction** -0.05s/f (Good) **8 Ran SP% 114.4**
Speed ratings (Par 98): **98,97,96,94,94 92,91,89**
CSF £41.74 CT £667.15 TOTE £9.30: £2.40, £1.90, £5.00; EX 49.40 Trifecta £932.90.
**Owner** J H Richmond-Watson **Bred** J H Richmond-Watson **Trained** Kimpton, Hants

**FOCUS**
Race distance increased by 12yds. They went a decent gallop and that set things up for a closer.

## 2930 BETTINGGODS.COM FREE RACING TIPS BRITISH EBF MAIDEN STKS 1m 75y
**4:00** (4:01) (Class 5) 3-Y-O **£3,881** (£1,155; £577; £288) **Stalls** Centre

Form RPR
05- **1** **Envoy**[209] 7622 3-9-5 0.................................. RyanTate 10 82
(James Eustace) *t.k.h: prom: cl up 4f out: led wl over 2f out: jnd and rdn 2f out: slt ld and drvn ent fnl f: kpt on strly* **9/1**
2 **2** *2 3/4* **Maratha (IRE)**[15] 2467 3-9-5 0..................................(v) OisinMurphy 3 76
(Simon Crisford) *prom on inner: cl up over 3f out: rdn along 2f out: sn outpcd: styd on wl u.p fnl f* **9/4**[2]
3 **3** *shd* **Stararchitecture (IRE)**[54] 1448 3-9-5 0......................(t) JamieSpencer 8 76
(William Haggas) *trckd ldrs: hdwy on outer 3f out: cl up 2f out: sn rdn and edgd lft: ev ch ent fnl f: sn drvn and kpt on same pce* **9/2**[3]
2- **4** *nk* **Sporting Times**[259] 6211 3-9-5 0.................................. FranBerry 9 75
(Ed Dunlop) *trckd ldrs: hdwy 3f: chal 2f out: rdn and ev ch whn n.m.r over 1f out: drvn ins fnl f: kpt on same pce* **13/8**[1]
**5** *6* **Long Socks** 3-9-5 0.................................. MartinHarley 5 61
(Alan King) *in tch: pushed along over 3f: rdn over 2f out: sn no imp* **25/1**
6 **6** *11* **Harbour Force (FR)**[15] 2475 3-9-5 0.................................. MartinDwyer 7 36
(William Muir) *t.k.h: chsd ldrs 3f: sn lost pl* **14/1**
0 **7** *1 1/2* **Three's A Crowd (IRE)**[41] 1727 3-9-2 0................ CallumShepherd(3) 2 33
(Ed de Giles) *hld up: a towards rr* **100/1**
0 **8** *3* **Starboard Watch**[27] 2078 3-9-0 0.................................. JimCrowley 4 21
(James Given) *sn led: rdn along over 3f out: hdd wl over 2f out: sn wknd* **33/1**
**9** *1 3/4* **Bombero (IRE)** 3-9-5 0.................................. ThomasBrown 6 22
(Ed de Giles) *dwlt: a in rr* **50/1**
**10** *hd* **Dutch Melody** 3-9-0 0.................................. AdamBeschizza 1 16
(Chris Wall) *towards rr: rdn along over 3f out: n.d* **33/1**

1m 48.1s (-0.90) **Going Correction** -0.05s/f (Good) **10 Ran SP% 116.4**
Speed ratings (Par 99): **102,99,99,98,92 81,80,77,75,75**
CSF £28.72 TOTE £11.80: £2.40, £1.70, £1.50; EX 45.30 Trifecta £178.20.
**Owner** H R Moszkowicz **Bred** Henry And Mrs Rosemary Moszkowicz **Trained** Newmarket, Suffolk

■ Stewards' Enquiry : Adam Beschizza £140 fine: weighed in with excess chamois leather

**FOCUS**
Race distance increased by 12yds. A fair maiden. The runner-up has been rated to his fluid Southwell debut figure.

## 2931 BETTINGGODS.COM BIG RACE BOOKIE BUSTERS CLASSIFIED STKS 1m 75y
**4:30** (4:32) (Class 5) 3-Y-O **£3,234** (£962; £481; £240) **Stalls** Centre

Form RPR
6-63 **1** **Dragons Voice**[76] 1083 3-9-0 70.................................. FranBerry 3 75
(Philip Hide) *prom: racd keenly: cl up and rdn 2f out: sn drvn and kpt on gamely fnl f to ld last 75 yds* **8/1**
0-22 **2** *3/4* **Al Nafoorah**[11] 2587 3-9-0 70.................................. AntonioFresu 4 73
(Ed Dunlop) *t.k.h: trckd ldrs: swtchd rt and hdwy over 2f out: rdn to ld wl over 1f out: sn drvn and edgd consistently lft: hdd and no ex last 75 yds* **4/1**[1]
10 **3** *hd* **Musikel (IRE)**[33] 1907 3-8-11 70..........................(p[1]) JordanVaughan(3) 9 72
(K R Burke) *in tch: hdwy 3f out: sn chsng ldrs: edgd lft and rdn 2f out: kpt on u.p fnl f* **8/1**
2-35 **4** *1 1/2* **Armagnac (IRE)**[21] 2266 3-9-0 70.................................. JamieSpencer 7 69
(Michael Bell) *hld up in rr: hdwy 3f: trckd ldrs 2f out: rdn and n.m.r whn swtchd lft over 1f out: drvn and kpt on fnl f* **7/1**
0-00 **5** *3* **Time To Sea (IRE)**[22] 2231 3-9-0 68.................................. RobertWinston 2 62
(John Butler) *led: rdn along and hdd over 4f out: wknd fnl 2f* **6/1**[3]
560- **6** *hd* **Junoesque**[249] 6535 3-9-0 63.................................. MartinDwyer 6 62
(John Gallagher) *prom: led over 4f out: rdn over 2f out: hdd wl over 1f: sn drvn and grad wknd* **33/1**
-650 **7** *4 1/2* **Masonic (IRE)**[28] 2071 3-9-0 67.................................. MartinHarley 10 51
(Robyn Brisland) *hld up: effrt and sme hdwy down outside over 3f: rdn along over 2f: sn wknd* **12/1**
10 **8** *3 3/4* **Broad Appeal**[43] 1686 3-9-0 69.................................. MartinLane 5 43
(Jonathan Portman) *midfield: hdwy and in tch over 3f: rdn along wl over 2f: sn wknd* **14/1**
-566 **9** *1* **Rapid Rise (IRE)**[24] 2151 3-8-11 70........................ KieranShoemark(3) 8 40
(David Brown) *a rr* **7/1**
450- **10** *1/2* **Mach One**[202] 7770 3-9-0 65..................................(b[1]) OisinMurphy 1 39
(Clive Cox) *dwlt: sn rdn along to chse ldrs: effrt over 3f out: sn drvn and wknd* **9/2**[2]

1m 47.97s (-1.03) **Going Correction** -0.05s/f (Good) **10 Ran SP% 117.0**
Speed ratings (Par 99): **103,102,102,100,97 97,92,89,88,87**
CSF £40.19 TOTE £8.40: £2.60, £2.00, £2.70; EX 32.50 Trifecta £264.80.
**Owner** Heart Of The South Racing **Bred** Parry, Stratton, Steele-Mortimer **Trained** Findon, W Sussex

**FOCUS**
Race distance increased by 12yds. A modest but competitive heat. The runner-up has been rated similar to her recent efforts.

## 2932 BETTINGGODS.COM FREE BETTING TIPS H'CAP 5f 8y
**5:00** (5:03) (Class 5) (0-75,70) 4-Y-O+ **£3,234** (£962; £481; £240) **Stalls** High

Form RPR
650- **1** **Rainbow Orse**[218] 7413 5-9-6 **69**..................................(p) JimCrowley 9 76
(Robert Cowell) *racd nr stands rail: prom: rdn wl over 1f out: styd on ent fnl f: led last 50 yds* **2/1**[1]
4414 **2** *nk* **Borough Boy (IRE)**[21] 2263 7-9-2 **65**..............................(v) MartinLane 2 71
(Derek Shaw) *racd towards centre: trckd ldrs: hdwy wl over 1f out: rdn to ld jst ins fnl f: sn drvn: hdd and no ex last 50 yds* **10/1**
4-10 **3** *3/4* **Bonjour Steve**[7] 2709 6-8-13 **62**..................................(p) KieranO'Neill 3 65
(Richard Price) *trckd ldrs towards centre: hdwy 2f out: rdn to ld wl over 1f out: drvn and hdd jst ins fnl f: kpt on* **8/1**
-150 **4** *nk* **Artscape**[22] 2230 5-9-7 **70**..................................(h) RobertWinston 4 72
(Dean Ivory) *in tch: pushed along 1/2-way: rdn 2f out: kpt on u.p fnl f* **9/2**[2]
0-63 **5** *1/2* **Corridor Kid (IRE)**[21] 2263 4-9-4 **67**..................................(v) KierenFox 6 67+
(Derek Shaw) *blind removed late: dwlt and towards rr: hdwy 2f out: rdn wl over 1f out: styd on wl fnl f: nrst fin* **8/1**
4000 **6** *2* **Elusivity (IRE)**[15] 2469 9-9-6 **69**..................................(p) MartinHarley 1 62
(Conor Dore) *racd centre: cl up: rdn along over 2f out: grad wknd* **20/1**
-000 **7** *1* **Coiste Bodhar (IRE)**[35] 1869 6-9-2 **70**........................ PaddyPilley(5) 8 60
(Scott Dixon) *led: rdn along over 2f out: hdd and drvn wl over 1f out: grad wknd* **8/1**
0030 **8** *1* **Miracle Garden**[59] 1370 5-9-7 **70**.................................. StevieDonohoe 7 56
(Ian Williams) *a rr: outpcd and bhd 1/2-way: sme late hdwy* **5/1**[3]

1m 1.15s (-0.35) **Going Correction** +0.05s/f (Good) **8 Ran SP% 115.4**
Speed ratings (Par 103): **104,103,102,101,101 97,96,94**
CSF £23.80 CT £134.48 TOTE £2.70: £1.30, £2.20, £2.50; EX 13.40 Trifecta £52.00.
**Owner** G Johnson **Bred** D R Botterill **Trained** Six Mile Bottom, Cambs

**FOCUS**
A modest sprint won by a real course specialist. The runner-up has been rated to his recent AW form.
T/Plt: £672.70 to a £1 stake. Pool: £54,127.02 - 58.73 winning units T/Qpdt: £13.90 to a £1 stake. Pool: £5,406.66 - 286.03 winning units **Joe Rowntree**

2933 - 2940a (Foreign Racing) - See Raceform Interactive

# JAGERSRO (R-H)
Tuesday, May 23

**OFFICIAL GOING: Dirt: standard**

## 2941a KVALLSPOSTENLOPET (H'CAP) (4YO+) (DIRT) 1m 143y(D)
**5:59** 4-Y-O+
**£4,255** (£2,127; £1,063; £709; £443; £265)

RPR
**1** **Well Tried**[660] 7-10-1 **0**.................................. AndreasTapiaDalbark(5) 3
(Vanja Sandrup, Sweden) **132/10**
**2** *4* **Nanodes (SWE)** 4-9-13 **0**..................................(b) JacobJohansen 2
(Lennart Reuterskiold Jr, Sweden) **13/5**[2]
**3** *7* **Mustajjid**[1123] 1725 6-9-13 **0**.................................. Jan-ErikNeuroth 6
(Wido Neuroth, Norway) **13/2**
**4** *2* **Viewpoint (IRE)**[21] 2261 8-10-1 **0**.................................. SilvestreDeSousa 5
(Michael Appleby) *hld up: rdn and hdwy after 1/2-way: no ex in st* **8/5**[1]
**5** *hd* **Whatdoesthefoxsay (NOR)**[296] 5-9-11 **0**.................................. ElioneChaves 1
(Dina Danekilde, Sweden) **7/2**[3]
**6** *5* **Lord Of Persia (USA)**[2395] 7272 9-9-6 **0**.................................. JosefinLandgren(5) 4
(Peter Jardby, Sweden) **164/10**

7 3 **Great Soprano (USA)**[1316] 7286 8-9-8 0 ShaneKarlsson 8
(Hans-Inge Larsen, Sweden) **74/10**
1m 47.8s **7** Ran SP% **126.5**

**Owner** Sven Olof Gotthardsson **Bred** Juddmonte Farms **Trained** Sweden

## 2942a PRAMMS MEMORIAL (LISTED RACE) (4YO+) (DIRT) 1m 143y(D)
7:09 4-Y-0+ **£62,056** (£22,163; £11,524; £7,092; £3,546)

RPR

1 **Brownie (FR)**[254] 5-9-4 0 OliverWilson 4
(Bent Olsen, Denmark) **27/10**[2]
2 4 **Silver Ocean (USA)**[205] 9-9-4 0 CarlosLopez 1
(Niels Petersen, Norway) **32/5**
3 1 ¼ **Gunvald (USA)** 4-9-4 0 (b) ElioneChaves 6
(Fredrik Reuterskiold, Sweden) **26/5**[3]
4 6 **Mrs Loreen (SWE)** 5-9-1 0 Per-AndersGraberg 3
(Lennart Reuterskiold Jr, Sweden) **7/1**
5 2 ½ **Hurricane Red (IRE)**[229] 7-9-4 0 JacobJohansen 2
(Lennart Reuterskiold Jr, Sweden) **8/5**[1]
6 9 **Appelina (DEN)**[313] 4-9-1 0 (p) Jan-ErikNeuroth 5
(Wido Neuroth, Norway) **156/10**
7 dist **Tap For Me (ARG)** 4-9-4 0 ValmirDeAzeredo 7
(Peter Jardby, Sweden) **35/1**
8 1 **Supersta**[39] 1773 6-9-4 0 (p) SilvestreDeSousa 8
(Michael Appleby) *prom on outer: rdn and lost pl bef 1/2-way: eased and wl btn ent st: t.o* **44/5**
1m 45.7s **8** Ran SP% **126.6**

**Owner** Lone Kaj-Nielsen **Bred** Mme Sylviane Jeffroy **Trained** Denmark

## 2943a LANWADES STUD JAGERSRO SPRINT (LISTED RACE) (3YO+) (DIRT) 6f (D)
8:15 3-Y-0+ **£17,730** (£8,865; £4,255; £2,836; £1,773)

RPR

1 **Spykes Bay (USA)**[254] 8-9-6 0 MartinRodriguez 10
(Vanja Sandrup, Sweden) **77/10**
2 ½ **Breakdancer (FR)**[101] 694 4-9-6 0 (b) ElioneChaves 11
(Fredrik Reuterskiold, Sweden) **66/10**[3]
3 nk **No Comment (DEN)**[254] 4-9-6 0 NelsonDeSouza 3
(Bent Olsen, Denmark) **40/1**
4 hd **Hakam (USA)**[16] 2433 5-9-6 0 SilvestreDeSousa 6
(Michael Appleby) *racd towards rr: kpt on u.p in st: fin quite wl but nt pce to chal* **43/5**
5 nse **Only Bacan (CHI)**[243] 3-9-6 0 (b) AlexandreDosSantos 9
(Francisco Castro, Sweden) **179/10**
6 nk **Over The Ocean (USA)**[292] 5098 7-9-6 0 Per-AndersGraberg 7
(Niels Petersen, Norway) **6/5**[1]
7 1 ¼ **Captain America (SWE)**[19] 7-9-6 0 (b) OliverWilson 1
(Annike Bye Hansen, Norway) **13/2**[2]
8 nk **Ikc Dragon Heart (USA)**[338] 7-9-6 0 (b) JacobJohansen 12
(Lennart Reuterskiold Jr, Sweden) **138/10**
9 2 **Free Zone**[109] 551 8-9-6 0 (b) RebeccaColldin 2
(Claes Bjorling, Sweden) **102/10**
10 3 ½ **Freemanip (ARG)** 5-9-6 0 ValmirDeAzeredo 4
(Peter Jardby, Sweden) **206/10**
11 dist **Beat Baby (IRE)**[593] 10-9-6 0 FaustoHenrique 8
(Niels Petersen, Norway) **198/10**
1m 12.6s
**WFA** 3 from 4yo+ 9lb **11** Ran SP% **126.7**

**Owner** Lars Malm & Susanne & Paul Tengquist **Bred** Brylynn Farm Inc **Trained** Sweden

# 2881 SAINT-CLOUD (L-H)
Tuesday, May 23

**OFFICIAL GOING: Turf: good**

## 2944a PRIX DE PONTARME (LISTED RACE) (3YO) (TURF) 1m
12:10 3-Y-0 **£23,504** (£9,401; £7,051; £4,700)

RPR

1 **Trais Fluors**[29] 3-9-0 0 VincentCheminaud 3 108+
(A Fabre, France) **9/2**[3]
2 1 ½ **D'bai (IRE)**[205] 7722 3-9-4 0 (p) WilliamBuick 2 108
(Charlie Appleby) *led: rdn 2f out: kpt on but hdd wl ins fnl f and no ex w wnr after* **9/2**[3]
3 ¾ **Ratiocination (IRE)**[13] 3-9-0 0 StephanePasquier 1 102
(P Bary, France) **4/5**[1]
4 2 ½ **Veranda (FR)**[35] 3-9-0 0 Pierre-CharlesBoudot 4 97
(A Fabre, France) **13/5**[2]
1m 44.8s (-2.70) **4** Ran SP% **119.7**
PARI-MUTUEL (all including 1 euro stake): WIN 5.50 PLACE 2.70, 3.00, SF 17.50.
**Owner** Scea Haras De Saint Pair **Bred** Scea Haras De Saint Pair **Trained** Chantilly, France

## 2945a PRIX CLEOPATRE (GROUP 3) (3YO FILLIES) (TURF) 1m 2f 110y
1:20 3-Y-0 **£34,188** (£13,675; £10,256; £6,837; £3,418)

RPR

1 **Terrakova (IRE)**[195] 3-8-11 0 MaximeGuyon 1 104+
(F Head, France) *trckd ldr: nt clr run early in st: rdn to chal over 1f out: led fnl f: styd on* **17/10**[1]
2 ¾ **Panthelia (FR)**[24] 2168 3-8-11 0 Jean-BernardEyquem 5 103+
(P Sogorb, France) *prom: rdn to chal 2f out: styd on and up for 2nd towards fin: nt pce of wnr* **232/10**
3 1 **Penny Lane (GER)**[44] 1657 3-8-11 0 Pierre-CharlesBoudot 8 101+
(F-H Graffard, France) *sn trcking ldr: rdn to chal 2f out: led over 1f out: hdd fnl f: no ex and dropped to 3rd towards fin* **36/5**[3]
4 ½ **Rythmique (IRE)**[30] 2003 3-8-11 0 ChristopheSoumillon 7 100
(J-C Rouget, France) *hld up: rdn and effrt on wd outside 2f out: styd on same pce fnl f* **3/1**[2]
5 1 ¼ **Mademoiselle Marie (FR)**[30] 2003 3-8-11 0 FranckBlondel 3 98+
(K Borgel, France) *midfield: rdn 2f out: sn outpcd* **126/10**

6 snk **Pink Paint (FR)**[24] 3-8-11 0 VincentCheminaud 4 97
(M Delcher Sanchez, France) *midfield: rdn 2f out: outpcd and fdd fnl f* **37/1**
7 1 ¾ **Terre (FR)**[20] 3-8-11 0 AlexisBadel 2 94
(Mme C Head-Maarek, France) *led: rdn and strly pressed 2f out: hdd over 1f out: wknd fnl f* **3/1**[2]
8 1 ½ **Limited Edition (FR)**[44] 3-8-11 0 TonyPiccone 6 91
(E Lellouche, France) *hld up in rr: no imp st* **212/10**
2m 16.32s (-3.28) **8** Ran SP% **117.9**
PARI-MUTUEL (all including 1 euro stake): WIN 2.70 PLACE 1.50, 4.10, 2.10 DF 25.20 SF 39.10.
**Owner** Wertheimer & Frere **Bred** Wertheimer Et Frere **Trained** France

## 2946a PRIX CORRIDA (GROUP 2) (4YO+ FILLIES & MARES) (TURF) 1m 2f 110y
1:50 4-Y-0+ **£63,333** (£24,444; £11,666; £7,777; £3,888)

RPR

1 **Armande (IRE)**[23] 2201 4-8-11 0 Pierre-CharlesBoudot 2 111+
(A Fabre, France) *midfield on inner: rdn to chal and led 2f out: styd on and asserted: readily* **5/2**[2]
2 3 **That Which Is Not (USA)**[23] 2201 4-8-11 0 StephanePasquier 8 105+
(F-H Graffard, France) *hld up in rr: rdn into st: swtchd rt appr fnl f: styd on and up for 2nd cl home: no ch w wnr* **61/10**[3]
3 ¾ **Haggle**[16] 2449 4-8-11 0 WilliamBuick 5 104
(H-F Devin, France) *trckd ldr: rdn to chal 2f out: sn outpcd by wnr: kpt on but wl hld: lost 2nd cl home* **19/2**
4 2 **Rosental**[193] 7929 5-8-11 0 ChristopheSoumillon 4 100
(Luca Cumani) *midfield: rdn on outer into st: outpcd fnl f* **67/10**
5 snk **Saimaa (IRE)**[25] 4-8-11 0 AlexisBadel 3 99
(H-F Devin, France) *trckd ldr: shuffled bk whn rdn into st: outpcd fnl f* **174/10**
6 2 **Left Hand**[233] 6989 4-9-4 0 (p) MaximeGuyon 6 102
(C Laffon-Parias, France) *hld up: no imp u.p in st: nvr a factor* **6/4**[1]
7 shd **Redcold (FR)**[44] 4-8-11 0 FrankPanicucci 7 95
(C Laffon-Parias, France) *led: rdn and hdd 2f out: sn wknd* **205/10**
8 ¾ **Glade**[24] 2169 4-8-11 0 JulienAuge 1 94
(C Ferland, France) *hld up: rdn and effrt on inner early in st: no ex fnl f: eased and dropped to last cl home* **222/10**
2m 16.69s (-2.91) **8** Ran SP% **119.6**
PARI-MUTUEL (all including 1 euro stake): WIN 3.50 PLACE 1.70, 2.30, 2.80 DF 7.10 SF 11.50.
**Owner** Lady O'Reilly & Baron Edouard De Rothschild **Bred** Petra Bloodstock & Ecurie De Meautry **Trained** Chantilly, France

## 2947a PRIX DU LYS (GROUP 3) (3YO) (TURF) 1m 4f
3:00 3-Y-0 **£34,188** (£13,675; £10,256; £6,837; £3,418)

RPR

1 **Called To The Bar (IRE)**[20] 3-9-2 0 MickaelBarzalona 4 111+
(Mme Pia Brandt, France) *mde all: rdn over 1f out: styd on and a doing enough: pushed out: cosily* **6/1**
2 2 **Ice Breeze**[22] 3-9-2 0 VincentCheminaud 2 107
(P Bary, France) *cl up: rdn 2f out: styd on wout matching wnr fnl f* **9/2**[3]
3 1 **Shakeel (FR)**[33] 3-9-2 0 ChristopheSoumillon 6 106
(A De Royer-Dupre, France) *in tch: rdn and effrt over 1f out: styd on wout matching wnr fnl f* **2/1**[1]
4 1 ½ **Falcon Wings**[22] 2250 3-9-2 0 StephanePasquier 3 103
(N Clement, France) *hld up: rdn over 2f out: outpcd: jst prevailed for 4th* **21/10**[2]
5 hd **Merikha**[29] 3-9-2 0 MaximeGuyon 1 103
(A Fabre, France) *hld up: rdn early in st: outpcd fnl 2f: jst missed out for 4th* **57/10**
6 1 ¼ **Walsingham (GER)**[22] 2250 3-9-2 0 MarcLerner 5 101
(Waldemar Hickst, Germany) *trckd wnr: rdn and brief effrt 2f out: sn no ex: wknd: dropped to last cl home* **169/10**
2m 35.74s (-4.66) **6** Ran SP% **118.6**
PARI-MUTUEL (all including 1 euro stake): WIN 7.00 PLACE 3.40, 2.30, SF 38.00.
**Owner** Fair Salinia Ltd **Bred** Fair Salinia Ltd **Trained** France

# 2495 AYR (L-H)
Wednesday, May 24

**OFFICIAL GOING: Good (good to firm in places; 8.1)**
Wind: Breezy, half against Weather: Overcast

## 2948 EBF STALLIONS APPLETISER NOVICE STKS (PLUS 10 RACE) 6f
2:20 (2:21) (Class 4) 2-Y-0 **£4,269** (£1,270; £634; £317) **Stalls High**

Form RPR

1 **Chookie Dunedin** 2-9-2 0 DougieCostello 8 82
(Keith Dalgleish) *mde all: rdn over 1f out: edgd lft ins fnl f: kpt on wl* **10/1**
2 hd **Bustam (IRE)** 2-9-2 0 (h[1]) JasonHart 9 81+
(John Quinn) *dwlt: hld up: pushed along over 2f out: hdwy on nr side of gp over 1f out: hung lft and chsd wnr ins fnl f: kpt on* **7/2**[1]
3 1 ½ **Columbia Kid (IRE)**[23] 2236 2-8-8 0 ShaneBKelly(3) 1 72
(Lee Smyth, Ire) *hld up on far side of gp: pushed along and hdwy over 2f out: kpt on ins fnl f: nt rch first two* **14/1**
4 hd **Mont Kinabalu (IRE)** 2-9-2 0 KevinStott 3 76+
(Kevin Ryan) *pressed wnr: rdn over 2f out: one pce and lost two pls ins fnl f* **9/2**[3]
5 1 ¼ **Myboyhenry (IRE)** 2-8-11 0 CliffordLee(5) 4 73
(K R Burke) *in tch: rdn and rn green over 2f out: rallied over 1f out: no imp fnl f* **4/1**[2]
42 6 hd **Noble Manners (IRE)**[23] 2221 2-8-11 0 JoeFanning 11 67
(Mark Johnston) *in tch on nr side of gp: drvn along over 2f out: one pce fr over 1f out* **7/2**[1]
7 3 **John Kirkup** 2-9-2 0 PaulMulrennan 2 63
(Michael Dods) *prom: drvn along over 2f out: wknd appr fnl f* **18/1**
8 1 ½ **Jackontherocks** 2-8-11 0 CallumRodriguez(5) 5 59
(Michael Dods) *hld up: shkn up over 2f out: no imp fr over 1f out* **16/1**
0 9 3 **Sam James (IRE)**[16] 2452 2-9-2 0 TomEaves 6 50
(Iain Jardine) *missed break: bhd: struggling over 2f out: nvr on terms* **28/1**
0 10 nk **Primo's Comet**[53] 1495 2-9-2 0 (p[1]) SamJames 10 49
(Jim Goldie) *t.k.h: cl up: rdn over 2f out: wknd over 1f out* **80/1**

0 **11** *2 ¾* **Sir Walter (IRE)**[14] 2522 2-9-2 0 ... NeilFarley 7 40
(Eric Alston) *dwlt: hld up: rdn over 2f out: sn btn* **33/1**
1m 13.28s (0.88) **Going Correction** +0.025s/f (Good) 11 Ran SP% **117.2**
Speed ratings (Par 95): **95,94,92,92,90 90,86,84,80,80 76**
CSF £44.31 TOTE £14.10: £3.00, £1.40, £6.10; EX 46.90 Trifecta £849.90.
**Owner** Raeburn Brick Limited **Bred** D And J Raeburn **Trained** Carluke, S Lanarks

**FOCUS**
Track on innermost line - distances as advertised. Jockeys riding in the first race reported the ground to be on the fast side.\n\x\x They kept to the centre in this interesting novice event and went an average pace. It could prove useful form. It's been rated as an ordinary renewal.

## 2949 WHYTE & MACKAY H'CAP (DIV I) 6f
**2:50** (2:50) (Class 6) (0-60,62) 3-Y-O+ **£2,587** (£770; £384; £192) **Stalls** High

Form RPR
0-40 **1** **Goninodaethat**[16] 2454 9-9-8 **57** ... NathanEvans(3) 6 62
(Jim Goldie) *prom: rdn over 2f out: led ent fnl f: hld on wl cl home* **14/1**
00-5 **2** *nse* **Ss Vega**[20] 2337 4-8-13 **45** ... SamJames 2 50
(Jim Goldie) *dwlt: hld up on far side of gp: rdn and hdwy over 1f out: edgd rt and kpt on wl cl home: jst hld* **14/1**
04-0 **3** *1* **Guiding Star**[16] 2455 3-8-7 **48** ...(p) ConnorBeasley 9 48
(Patrick J McKenna, Ire) *trckd ldrs: led gng wl over 2f out: rdn and hdd ent fnl f: sn one pce* **28/1**
3302 **4** *1 ½* **Lizzy's Dream**[20] 2337 9-9-0 **46** ... DuranFentiman 11 43
(Rebecca Bastiman) *in tch on nr side of gp: rdn and edgd lft over 1f out: kpt on ins fnl f* **16/1**
0/00 **5** *nk* **New Decade**[16] 2454 8-8-6 **45** ... SeanMooney(7) 10 41
(Jim Goldie) *dwlt: bhd: rdn and hung lft over 2f out: kpt on fnl f: nvr able to chal* **33/1**
00-0 **6** *hd* **Spoken Words**[16] 2454 8-8-6 **45** ...(p) ConnorMurtagh(7) 4 41
(John David Riches) *hld up in tch: effrt and drvn along 2f out: kpt on same pce fnl f* **50/1**
54-1 **7** *1 ½* **Duncan Of Scotland (IRE)**[12] 2602 4-9-13 **62** ...(b) ShaneBKelly(3) 5 56
(Lee Smyth, Ire) *cl up: drvn and ev ch over 2f out: wknd fnl f* **6/5**[1]
00-0 **8** *1 ½* **Warleggan (FR)**[16] 2455 3-8-4 **45** ... ShaneGray 7 30+
(Linda Perratt) *dwlt: bhd: rdn and flashed tail fr 2f out: kpt on fnl f: nvr rchd ldrs* **100/1**
3300 **9** *1 ¼* **Backinanger**[2] 2897 3-9-0 **55** ...(b) KevinStott 3 36
(Kevin Ryan) *led to over 2f out: rallied: wknd appr fnl f* **12/1**[3]
4203 **10** *2 ¼* **Scotch Myst**[24] 2181 3-9-3 **58** ... PaulHanagan 1 32
(Richard Fahey) *in tch on far side of gp: drvn along over 2f out: edgd lft and wknd over 1f out* **9/4**[2]
0030 **11** *15* **Little Belter (IRE)**[20] 2342 5-9-3 **49** ...(p) JoeFanning 8
(Keith Dalgleish) *missed break: hld up towards rr: struggling over 2f out: sn wknd* **14/1**
1m 12.77s (0.37) **Going Correction** +0.025s/f (Good)
**WFA** 3 from 4yo+ 9lb 11 Ran SP% **119.1**
Speed ratings (Par 101): **98,97,96,94,94 93,91,89,88,85 65**
CSF £190.09 CT £5437.50 TOTE £15.70: £4.10, £4.30, £8.30; EX 198.90 Trifecta £4117.90.
**Owner** G E Adams & J S Goldie **Bred** W G H Barrons **Trained** Uplawmoor, E Renfrews
■ Stewards' Enquiry : Sean Mooney two-day ban; used whip above the permitted level (Jun 7-8)

**FOCUS**
A weak sprint handicap. Again the runners kept more towards the middle before drifting far side and there was a strong pace on. The first two have been rated near their marks.

## 2950 WHYTE & MACKAY H'CAP (DIV II) 6f
**3:20** (3:21) (Class 6) (0-60,59) 3-Y-O+ **£2,587** (£770; £384; £192) **Stalls** High

Form RPR
**1** **Polly Douglas (IRE)**[180] 8109 4-8-5 **45** ... AndrewBreslin(7) 4 57+
(Kieran P Cotter, Ire) *chsd ldr: led and rdn over 2f out: 3 l clr over 1f out: kpt on fnl f* **3/1**[1]
6-23 **2** *1 ½* **Cheeni**[5] 2777 5-8-12 **45** ...(p) SamJames 7 52
(Jim Goldie) *in tch: hdwy to chse wnr over 1f out: sn rdn and edgd lft: kpt on ins fnl f: nt pce to chal* **8/1**
1025 **3** *2 ¾* **Sea Of Green**[5] 2777 5-9-4 **51** ...(p) FranBerry 5 49+
(Jim Goldie) *missed break and rrd s: wl bhd: stdy hdwy whn nt clr run 2f out: angled rt and kpt on wl fnl f: nt rch first two* **3/1**[1]
-504 **4** *½* **Secret City (IRE)**[16] 2454 11-8-13 **46** ...(b) DuranFentiman 2 43
(Rebecca Bastiman) *hld up: rdn over 2f out: hdwy over 1f out: kpt on fnl f: nvr able to chal* **11/2**[2]
0-00 **5** *½* **Whipphound**[11] 2633 9-9-6 **53** ...(p) JamesSullivan 8 48
(Ruth Carr) *hld up: stdy hdwy 1/2-way: rdn and kpt on same pce fnl f* **7/1**[3]
60-0 **6** *3* **Trulove**[21] 2312 4-8-5 **45** ... ConnorMurtagh(7) 3 31
(John David Riches) *in tch: drvn over 2f out: wknd over 1f out* **40/1**
0-06 **7** *1 ½* **Dutch Dream**[5] 2777 4-9-1 **48** ... GrahamLee 10 30
(Linda Perratt) *in tch: rdn along over 2f out: wknd over 1f out* **16/1**
604- **8** *3 ¾* **Bahamian Sunshine**[117] 453 4-9-1 **51** ...(b) ShaneBKelly(3) 6 22
(Lee Smyth, Ire) *led to over 2f out: rdn and wknd over 1f out* **8/1**
0-60 **9** *12* **Davinci Dawn**[38] 1818 3-8-5 **47** ...(p[1]) ShaneGray 9
(Ann Duffield) *dwlt: bhd: struggling over 2f out: sn btn* **18/1**
1m 12.1s (-0.30) **Going Correction** +0.025s/f (Good)
**WFA** 3 from 4yo+ 9lb 9 Ran SP% **113.7**
Speed ratings (Par 101): **103,101,97,96,96 92,90,85,69**
CSF £27.55 CT £76.64 TOTE £4.00: £1.80, £1.80, £1.50; EX 26.00 Trifecta £94.20.
**Owner** D J Mooney **Bred** David Mooney **Trained** Portarlington, Co Laois

**FOCUS**
This second division of the weak sprint handicap was 0.61secs quicker than the first. The runner-up has been rated a bit better than her recent runs here and at Hamilton.

## 2951 GUINNESS H'CAP 5f
**3:50** (3:50) (Class 3) (0-90,84) 4-Y-O+ **£7,762** (£2,310; £1,154; £577) **Stalls** High

Form RPR
4011 **1** **Royal Brave (IRE)**[20] 2341 6-9-3 **80** ... PJMcDonald 2 86
(Rebecca Bastiman) *hld up: hdwy over 1f out: sn rdn: kpt on wl fnl f to ld towards fin* **5/1**[3]
3210 **2** *hd* **Aprovado (IRE)**[40] 1777 5-9-0 **82** ...(p) CallumRodriguez(5) 5 87
(Michael Dods) *led to over 3f out: regained ld over 2f out: rdn over 1f out: kpt on fnl f: hdd towards fin* **14/1**
2201 **3** *½* **Invincible Ridge (IRE)**[37] 1836 9-9-3 **80** ... NeilFarley 4 83
(Eric Alston) *prom: effrt and drvn along over 1f out: edgd lft: kpt on same pce ins fnl f* **14/1**
6-41 **4** *½* **Tommy G**[15] 2500 4-9-0 **77** ... SamJames 1 78+
(Jim Goldie) *dwlt: bhd and outpcd: hdwy and edgd lft over 1f out: kpt on fnl f: nvr able to chal* **3/1**[2]
-032 **5** *½* **Tylery Wonder (IRE)**[9] 2683 7-9-3 **80** ...(b) PaulMulrennan 8 79
(Paul Midgley) *wnt rt s: cl up: led over 3f out to over 2f out: rallied: kpt on same pce ins fnl f* **11/2**

2-22 **6** *nk* **Straightothepoint**[12] 2592 5-9-7 **84** ... ConnorBeasley 7 82
(Bryan Smart) *prom: effrt and rdn over 2f out: edgd lft over 1f out: kpt on same pce fnl f* **11/8**[1]
58.72s (-0.68) **Going Correction** +0.025s/f (Good) 6 Ran SP% **112.5**
Speed ratings (Par 107): **106,105,104,104,103 102**
CSF £63.57 CT £908.03 TOTE £4.70: £2.20, £5.50; EX 40.80 Trifecta £185.80.
**Owner** James Edgar & William Donaldson **Bred** M Fahy **Trained** Cowthorpe, N Yorks

**FOCUS**
A good sprint handicap. As expected there was a frantic pace on down the centre. The runner-up has been rated to his best.

## 2952 ROA/RACING POST OWNERS' JACKPOT H'CAP 1m
**4:20** (4:20) (Class 4) (0-85,86) 4-Y-O+ **£5,498** (£1,636; £817; £408) **Stalls** Low

Form RPR
0123 **1** **Nicholas T**[5] 2772 5-9-5 **83** ... SamJames 7 92+
(Jim Goldie) *s.i.s: hld up: smooth hdwy on outside to ld over 2f out: sn rdn: edgd lft over 1f out: drvn out fnl f* **5/2**[1]
20-2 **2** *1 ¼* **Inexes**[25] 2133 5-8-13 **77** ... PhillipMakin 11 83
(Marjorie Fife) *hld up: stdy hdwy over 2f out: rdn and chsd wnr 1f out: edgd lft: kpt on same pce last 100yds* **7/2**[2]
300- **3** *¾* **Royal Shaheen (FR)**[204] 7744 4-9-3 **81** ... PJMcDonald 9 85
(Alistair Whillans) *prom: rdn over 2f out: effrt and cl up whn checked appr fnl f: r.o* **25/1**
0-30 **4** *hd* **Zodiakos (IRE)**[9] 2684 4-9-1 **79** ... TonyHamilton 6 83
(Roger Fell) *.pressed ldr: ev ch over 2f out to wl over 1f out: kpt on same pce fnl f* **9/1**
6 **5** *1 ½* **Gilded Reflection**[25] 2135 4-9-2 **80** ... FranBerry 5 80
(Ralph Beckett) *hld up bhd ldng gp: stdy hdwy 3 out: rdn and sltly outpcd whn checked over 1f out: rallied ins fnl f: r.o* **5/1**
-043 **6** *2 ¾* **Lagenda**[14] 2528 4-9-1 **84** ...(p) LewisEdmunds(5) 4 78
(Kevin Ryan) *trckd ldrs: n.m.r over 2f out: rdn and wknd over 1f out* **9/2**[3]
6625 **7** *1 ¾* **Crazy Tornado (IRE)**[5] 2773 4-8-7 **71** ... JoeFanning 10 61
(Keith Dalgleish) *t.k.h: led: rdn and hdd over 2f out: wknd over 1f out* **8/1**
1m 38.85s (-4.95) **Going Correction** -0.425s/f (Firm) 7 Ran SP% **110.6**
Speed ratings (Par 105): **107,105,105,104,103 100,98**
CSF £10.56 CT £158.07 TOTE £3.20: £1.60, £2.20; EX 12.40 Trifecta £126.10.
**Owner** W M Johnstone **Bred** W M Johnstone **Trained** Uplawmoor, E Renfrews
■ Stewards' Enquiry : Sam James caution; careless riding

**FOCUS**
This was hit by four defectors but it was still run to suit the closers. The second to the fifth have all been rated close to form.

## 2953 JACK DANIEL'S H'CAP 1m 2f
**4:50** (4:50) (Class 5) (0-75,79) 4-Y-O+ **£3,234** (£962; £481; £240) **Stalls** Low

Form RPR
00-4 **1** **Gworn**[16] 2458 7-9-0 **68** ... PJMcDonald 8 81
(R Mike Smith) *in tch: drvn and outpcd over 2f out: rallied over 1f out: led wl ins fnl f: kpt on wl* **8/1**
6005 **2** *hd* **Trinity Star (IRE)**[21] 2301 6-8-11 **65** ...(b) PaulMulrennan 14 77
(Michael Dods) *hld up: pushed along and effrt over 2f out: kpt on to take 2nd cl home: jst hld* **14/1**
00-2 **3** *nk* **Royal Regent**[15] 2497 5-9-3 **74** ... SammyJoBell(3) 11 85
(Lucy Normile) *hld up: gd hdwy on outside over 2f out: drifted lft and led over 1f out: hdd wl ins fnl f: no ex* **8/1**
30-0 **4** *2* **Miningrocks (FR)**[53] 1498 5-8-6 **65** ... PhilDennis(5) 13 72
(Declan Carroll) *led: rdn and qcknd clr over 2f out: hdd over 1f out: outpcd fnl f* **18/1**
6-21 **5** *4* **Bit Of A Quirke**[27] 2108 4-8-10 **64** ... DougieCostello 9 63
(Mark Walford) *trckd ldrs: effrt and rdn over 2f out: edgd lft over 1f out: sn btn* **6/1**[2]
6-05 **6** *1 ¾* **Eez Eh (IRE)**[15] 2497 4-8-12 **71** ...(p) RowanScott(5) 2 67
(Keith Dalgleish) *s.i.s: hld up on ins: rdn and edgd lft over 2f out: sn no imp* **14/1**
2034 **7** *¾* **Restive (IRE)**[5] 2773 4-8-10 **69** ...(h) CliffordLee(5) 5 63
(Iain Jardine) *prom: rdn along over 2f out: wknd wl over 1f out* **7/2**[1]
-053 **8** *nse* **Arithmetic (IRE)**[15] 2498 4-8-10 **64** ... JamesSullivan 4 58
(Ruth Carr) *hld up on outside: drvn along over 2f out: wknd over 1f out* **13/2**[3]
20-5 **9** *¾* **Age Of Elegance (IRE)**[11] 2629 5-9-9 **77** ...(p) TonyHamilton 10 69
(Roger Fell) *pressed ldr to over 2f out: rdn and wknd over 1f out* **8/1**
3301 **10** *1* **Spes Nostra**[5] 2787 9-9-4 **79** 6ex ...(b) JamieGormley(7) 6 69
(Iain Jardine) *bhd and sn outpcd: struggling 1/2-way: sme late hdwy: nvr on terms* **20/1**
50-0 **11** *½* **Stardrifter**[17] 2430 5-8-13 **67** ... GrahamLee 1 56
(Linda Perratt) *hld up midfield: drvn and outpcd over 2f out: n.d after* **66/1**
-420 **12** *1 ¾* **Strummer (IRE)**[15] 2498 4-8-11 **65** ...(p) KevinStott 7 51
(Kevin Ryan) *in tch: hdwy to chse clr ldr over 2f out to over 1f out: sn wknd* **12/1**
2m 6.17s (-5.83) **Going Correction** -0.425s/f (Firm) 12 Ran SP% **115.7**
Speed ratings (Par 103): **106,105,105,104,100 99,98,98,98,97 96,95**
CSF £111.95 CT £925.86 TOTE £8.90: £2.90, £3.80, £2.70; EX 139.80 Trifecta £1264.10.
**Owner** R Gibson **Bred** Azienda Agricola F Lli Nencini **Trained** Galston, E Ayrshire

**FOCUS**
This modest handicap was run at a solid pace and the principals came clear. The third appears the best guide to the level.

## 2954 TENNENT'S BRITISH STALLION STUDS EBF ROTHESAY STKS (LISTED RACE) (F&M) 1m 2f
**5:20** (5:24) (Class 1) 4-Y-O+ **£28,355** (£10,750; £5,380; £2,680; £1,345) **Stalls** Low

Form RPR
520- **1** **Nezwaah**[220] 7404 4-9-0 108 ... AndreaAtzeni 3 109+
(Roger Varian) *trckd ldrs: stdy hdwy whn nt clr run and angled rt over 1f out: led on bit 1f out: shkn up and sn qcknd clr: v readily* **1/2**[1]
24-1 **2** *3 ¾* **Sophie P**[16] 2457 4-9-0 89 ... PJMcDonald 5 96
(R Mike Smith) *hld up: hdwy on outside over 2f out: led briefly over 1f out: kpt on fnl f: no ch w wnr* **20/1**
-524 **3** *nse* **Maleficent Queen**[21] 2288 5-9-0 105 ... JoeFanning 1 96
(Keith Dalgleish) *t.k.h: led: rdn and hdd over 1f out: rallied: kpt on same pce fnl f* **11/2**[2]
103- **4** *¾* **Pure Art**[229] 7119 4-9-0 99 ... FranBerry 4 94
(Ralph Beckett) *hld up in tch: effrt and drvn along over 2f out: kpt on fnl f: nvr able to chal* **6/1**[3]

5 ¾ **Elm Grove (IRE)**[20] 2352 5-9-0 89 ........ WJLee 2 93
(W McCreery, Ire) *slowly away: sn chsng ldr: rdn and outpcd over 2f out: n.d after* **11/1**

2m 8.25s (-3.75) **Going Correction** -0.425s/f (Firm) **5** Ran SP% **109.4**
Speed ratings (Par 111): **98,95,94,94,93**
CSF £11.80 TOTE £1.40: £1.10, £6.10; EX 10.50 Trifecta £27.10.
**Owner** Sheikh Ahmed Al Maktoum **Bred** Darley **Trained** Newmarket, Suffolk

**FOCUS**
Thankfully this was a solid test and the winner proved in a different league. The fourth helps put it into perspective. The level is fluid, with the second and fifth running above themselves at face value.

## 2955 FRANKLIN & SONS PREMIUM TONIC APPRENTICE H'CAP 1m 1f 20y
**5:55** (5:56) (Class 6) (0-65,66) 4-Y-0+ **£2,587** (£770; £384; £192) **Stalls** Low

Form RPR

4340 **1** **Kiwi Bay**[16] 2458 12-9-10 **66** ........ CallumRodriguez 12 72
(Michael Dods) *hld up: hdwy over 2f out: led over 1f out: r.o wl fnl f* **16/1**

-032 **2** ½ **Stoneboat Bill**[15] 2498 5-9-3 **62** ........ GerO'Neill(3) 5 67
(Declan Carroll) *hld up: stdy hdwy on outside over 2f out: rdn and chsd wnr ins fnl f: r.o* **5/2**[1]

34-0 **3** 1 **Remember Rocky**[15] 2498 8-8-13 **58** ........(b) KieranSchofield(3) 8 61
(Lucy Normile) *in tch: drvn and outpcd over 2f out: rallied fnl f: nt rch first two* **16/1**

202- **4** ½ **Penelope Pitstop**[168] 8260 5-8-0 **49** oh1 ........ CharlotteMcFarland(7) 11 51
(Lee Smyth, Ire) *t.k.h: led and sn clr w sddle gng sltly forward: c wd bnd ent st: hdd over 1f out: sn btn* **20/1**

**5** nse **Colour Contrast (IRE)**[221] 7377 4-8-13 **60** ........ JamieGormley(5) 10 62
(Iain Jardine) *cl up : effrt over 2f out: ev ch wl over 1f out: outpcd fnl f* **7/1**[3]

12 **6** nk **Lucent Dream (IRE)**[57] 1409 6-9-2 **63** ........(t) HarrisonShaw(5) 1 64
(John C McConnell, Ire) *hld up: pushed along and effrt 2f out: no imp appr fnl f* **7/2**[2]

40-3 **7** 1 **Dark Crystal**[20] 2339 6-9-4 **63** ........ ConnorMurtagh(3) 3 62
(Linda Perratt) *in tch: effrt and rdn over 2f out: outpcd fnl f* **10/1**

6-05 **8** ¾ **Druid's Diamond**[9] 2688 4-8-9 **54** ........ JoshQuinn(3) 7 52
(Mark Walford) *hld up midfield: rdn and outpcd over 2f out: no imp over 1f out* **14/1**

**9** shd **Ebony Princess (IRE)**[39] 1812 7-8-2 **49** ........ AndrewBreslin(5) 4 48
(Kieran P Cotter, Ire) *s.i.s: t.k.h in rr: rdn over 2f out: wknd over 1f out* **10/1**

1-00 **10** 4 **Scruffy McGuffy**[19] 2378 4-9-4 **60** ........(p[1]) MeganNicholls 2 50
(Ann Duffield) *midfield: stdy hdwy over 3f out: wknd over 2f out* **25/1**

10-4 **11** nse **Rioja Day (IRE)**[15] 2501 7-8-7 **54** ........(b) SeanMooney(5) 9 44
(Jim Goldie) *chsd ldr: drvn along over 2f out: sn wknd* **20/1**

0-05 **12** 7 **Let Right Be Done**[19] 2378 5-8-4 **49** oh1 ........(p) PaulaMuir(3) 6 25
(Linda Perratt) *hld up bhd ldng gp: struggling over 2f out: sn wknd* **16/1**

1m 54.77s (-2.73) **Going Correction** -0.425s/f (Firm) **12** Ran SP% **119.2**
Speed ratings (Par 101): **95,94,93,93,93 92,92,91,91,87 87,81**
CSF £54.69 CT £681.70 TOTE £14.70: £4.00, £2.40, £4.10; EX 47.80 Trifecta £556.80.
**Owner** Kiwi Racing **Bred** Templeton Stud **Trained** Denton, Co Durham

**FOCUS**
A competitive handicap for the class, run at a strong pace, that saw a bunched finish. The balance of the third and fourth set an ordinary level.
T/Plt: £8,132.90 to a £1 stake. Pool: £73,531.15. 6.60 winning units. T/Qpdt: £38.60 to a £1 stake. Pool: £5,443.52. 104.15 winning units. **Richard Young**

# 2015 KEMPTON (A.W) (R-H)
Wednesday, May 24

**OFFICIAL GOING: Polytrack: standard to slow**
Wind: nil Weather: Warm, light cloud

## 2956 100% PROFIT BOOST AT 32REDSPORT.COM APPRENTICE H'CAP 2f 219y(P)
**6:10** (6:10) (Class 5) (0-70,71) 4-Y-0+ **£3,234** (£962; £481; £240) **Stalls** Low

Form RPR

0311 **1** **Rail Dancer**[30] 2022 5-9-4 **70** ........(v) DavidEgan(3) 9 78+
(Richard Rowe) *settled in mid-div: travelling best bhd ldrs wl over 1f out: shkn up and upsides ent fnl f where rdn and led: sn clr and drifted rt: pushed out fnl 110yds* **2/1**[1]

1125 **2** 1 ½ **Boychick (IRE)**[53] 1498 4-9-5 **68** ........ JennyPowell 3 71
(Ed Walker) *settled bhd ldr on outer: rdn over 2f out: upsides ent fnl f: kpt on ins fnl f but nvr getting to wnr* **9/4**[2]

00-5 **3** ¾ **Dark Phantom (IRE)**[29] 2056 6-8-7 **56** oh11 ........ PaddyPilley 2 58
(Eve Johnson Houghton) *led: rdn over 2f out: hdd over 1f out: almost upsides ent fnl f: kpt on but no imp on wnr* **20/1**

6660 **4** 1 ¼ **Solveig's Song**[11] 2615 5-8-10 **62** ........(p) JoshuaBryan(3) 10 61
(Steve Woodman) *settled in mid-div on outer: rdn wl over 2f out: kpt on one pce fr over 1f out* **16/1**

-360 **5** 1 ¼ **Rightway (IRE)**[49] 1553 6-8-12 **66** ........ AledBeech(5) 1 63
(Tony Carroll) *t.k.h bhd ldr on inner: settled bttr after 5f: rdn over 2f out: led over 1f out: hdd ent fnl f and wknd after* **20/1**

243- **6** 2 **Transmitting**[214] 7531 4-9-1 **67** ........ CameronNoble(3) 8 60
(Ed Vaughan) *missed break: sn settled in rr: rdn over 2f out: no imp over 1f out* **7/2**[3]

00 **7** 2 **Sevilla**[20] 2336 4-8-8 **62** ........ DarraghKeenan(5) 7 51
(Anabel K Murphy) *slow s: settled in last: plenty to do ent st: rdn wl over 2f out: kpt on one pce fr over 1f out* **66/1**

0500 **8** 5 **Fast Play (IRE)**[25] 2163 5-9-8 **71** ........(b) GeorgeWood 6 51
(Conor Dore) *settled bhd ldrs on outer: tk clsr over and almost upsides ent st: rdn out wd over 2f out: wknd over 1f out* **33/1**

50-0 **9** 4 ½ **Tatawu (IRE)**[11] 2626 5-8-4 **58** ........ MollyKing(5) 5 29
(Peter Hiatt) *in rr: nudged along ent st to hold pl: rdn wl over 2f out: lft bhd wl over 1f out: no ex* **16/1**

2m 26.45s (4.55) **Going Correction** +0.075s/f (Slow) **9** Ran SP% **112.0**
Speed ratings (Par 103): **86,84,84,83,82 81,79,76,72**
CSF £6.10 CT £61.54 TOTE £3.10: £1.80, £1.10, £4.80; EX 8.00 Trifecta £65.20.
**Owner** Mark Cashmore **Bred** Scuderia Blueberry SRL **Trained** Sullington, W Sussex

**FOCUS**
A modest apprentice riders' handicap. They went a sedate gallop on standard to slow Polytrack and it helped to race prominently, although that shouldn't be allowed to detract from the winner's ready victory. The second, third and fourth help set the level.

## 2957 32RED CASINO MEDIAN AUCTION MAIDEN STKS 7f (P)
**6:40** (6:41) (Class 6) 3-4-Y-0 **£2,587** (£770; £384; £192) **Stalls** Low

Form RPR

**1** **Chatting (IRE)** 3-8-12 0 ........ JosephineGordon 2 66+
(Hugo Palmer) *hld up in rr gp: way bhd ent st whn shkn up: began to pass btn horses fr over 2f out: angled out wd and pushed along: clsng on ldrs and 6 l to find ent fnl f: str run 100yds out and led post* **7/1**

550- **2** hd **Wigan Warrior**[191] 7956 3-9-3 69 ........ SeanLevey 7 70
(David Brown) *bhd ldrs in chsng gp: rdn over 2f out: ev ch in line of four ins fnl f: stuck on wl: jst ct cl home* **5/1**[2]

3-3 **3** nk **Margherita**[21] 2311 3-8-5 0 ........ DavidEgan(7) 9 64
(Roger Varian) *bhd ldrs in chsng gp: rdn over 2f out: briefly led ent fnl f: ev ch in line of four after: stuck on wl: jst hld post* **6/5**[1]

6 **4** hd **My Illusionist**[20] 2330 3-9-3 0 ........ LukeMorris 4 69
(Harry Dunlop) *bhd clr ldr ldng chsng gp: rdn over 2f out: kpt on wl and upsides ent fnl f where jinked sltly rt: stuck on wl and ev ch in four way fin fnl f: jst hld post* **12/1**

0- **5** hd **Madeleine Bond**[321] 4054 3-8-12 0 ........ DaneO'Neill 6 63
(Henry Candy) *bhd ldr in chsng gp on outer: rdn over 2f out: prog and upsides ent fnl f: kpt on wl in four way fin fnl f: jst hld post* **13/2**[3]

0300 **6** 3 ¼ **Beach Dancer (IRE)**[19] 2362 3-9-0 50 ........ EdwardGreatrex(3) 1 59
(William Knight) *clr ldr and set str gallop: rdn over 2f out: stl 3 l up over 1f out w chsng gp clsng: hdd ent fnl f and wknd fnl 150yds* **16/1**

40 **7** 2 ½ **Accomplice**[77] 1083 3-8-12 0 ........ DavidProbert 3 48
(Michael Blanshard) *bhd ldr in chsng gp: rdn over 2f out: kpt on wl tl wknd over 1f out* **20/1**

00 **8** 3 ½ **Geordielad**[12] 2584 3-9-3 0 ........ FergusSweeney 12 43
(Jamie Osborne) *in rr gp clst to the pce: rdn and no imp fr over 2f out* **150/1**

**9** nk **Columbian Cartel** 4-10-0 0 ........ LiamJones 11 46
(J S Moore) *s.s: in rr gp: rdn over 2f out: nvr involved* **100/1**

**10** ½ **Allofmelovesallofu** 3-9-3 0 ........ PatDobbs 8 41
(Ken Cunningham-Brown) *in rr gp: rdn over 2f out: one pce after* **33/1**

6 **11** 3 ½ **Fivos**[18] 2393 3-8-12 0 ........ GeorgeWood(5) 5 32
(David Bridgwater) *bhd ldr in chsng gp: rdn over 2f out where edgd rt: sn wknd* **66/1**

0 **12** 8 **Our Ruth**[105] 624 4-9-9 0 ........ KieranO'Neill 13 9
(Jimmy Fox) *in rr of chsng gp: rdn wl over 3f out: wknd qckly after* **150/1**

0 **13** 59 **True Gentleman**[28] 2090 3-8-12 0 ........ MitchGodwin(5) 10
(Sylvester Kirk) *rn green and rdn along leaving stalls: sn detached and nvr involved: t.o* **33/1**

1m 26.51s (0.51) **Going Correction** +0.075s/f (Slow)
**WFA** 3 from 4yo 11lb **13** Ran SP% **116.0**
Speed ratings (Par 101): **100,99,99,99,98 95,92,88,88,87 83,74,6**
CSF £39.24 TOTE £8.60: £2.50, £2.10, £1.10; EX 45.50 Trifecta £107.50.
**Owner** Diana, Countess Of Wilton & Partners **Bred** Successori del Marchese G Guglielmi **Trained** Newmarket, Suffolk

**FOCUS**
An ordinary maiden. They went a decent gallop and it produced an exciting five-way photo-finish.

## 2958 BRITISH STALLION STUDS EBF FILLIES' NOVICE STKS (PLUS 10 RACE) 6f (P)
**7:10** (7:11) (Class 4) 2-Y-0 **£4,592** (£1,366; £683; £341) **Stalls** Low

Form RPR

5 **1** **Di Fede (IRE)**[24] 2173 2-9-0 0 ........ RichardKingscote 3 74
(Ralph Beckett) *pressed ldr on outer: rdn along 2f out: kpt on wl to chal ent fnl f: str drive nr fin and jst led post* **7/4**[1]

04 **2** nse **Mraseel (IRE)**[22] 2265 2-9-0 0 ........(p[1]) MartinHarley 1 74
(James Tate) *sn led: rdn 2f out: briefly hdd over 1f out: led again ent fnl f where pressed by wnr tl hdd cl home* **8/1**[3]

**3** ¾ **Klosters (IRE)** 2-8-11 0 ........ KieranShoemark(3) 5 72
(Roger Charlton) *settled in mid-div on inner: rdn 2f out bhd ldrs: kpt on wl and tk 3rd post* **11/1**

**4** ½ **Miss Mo Brown Bear (IRE)** 2-9-0 0 ........ PatDobbs 9 70
(Richard Hannon) *chsd ldrs on outer: rdn along in centre 2f out: kpt on wl ent fnl f: jst lost 3rd post* **12/1**

**5** hd **Flirtare (IRE)** 2-9-0 0 ........ GavinLerena 11 70
(Amanda Perrett) *settled in mid-div: rdn 2f out: kpt on one pce fr over 1f out* **10/1**

**6** 1 **Hello Girl** 2-9-0 0 ........ RobertWinston 8 68
(Dean Ivory) *mid-div on outer: rdn 2f out: kpt on one pce fr over 1f out* **50/1**

**7** 1 ¼ **Special Mission** 2-9-0 0 ........ LukeMorris 7 63+
(Sir Mark Prescott Bt) *in rr-div on inner: rdn 2f out: no imp tl styd on strly ins fnl f* **20/1**

**8** ¾ **Sensory (IRE)** 2-9-0 0 ........ RobertTart 6 61
(John Gosden) *in rr: pushed along bnd ent st: rdn 2f out: no imp on ldrs and pushed out ent fnl f: bttr for run* **10/1**

**9** nk **Song Of Summer** 2-9-0 0 ........ OisinMurphy 4 60
(Archie Watson) *in rr-div: effrt 2f out: kpt on one pce* **16/1**

**10** 1 ¼ **Scandaleuse (USA)** 2-9-0 0 ........ RyanMoore 10 56+
(Sir Michael Stoute) *wnt lft s: swtchd bk to rail and in rr: swtchd to outer ent st: sn rdn: no picked up and pushed out on outer fr over 1f out* **3/1**[2]

**11** nse **Hunni** 2-9-0 0 ........ JosephineGordon 2 56
(Tom Clover) *settled bhd ldrs on rail: rdn 2f out: led over 1f out: hdd & wknd qckly ent fnl f* **25/1**

1m 14.08s (0.98) **Going Correction** +0.075s/f (Slow) **11** Ran SP% **123.1**
Speed ratings (Par 92): **96,95,94,94,94 92,91,90,89,87 87**
CSF £17.31 TOTE £3.00: £1.30, £2.80, £3.50; EX 18.90 Trifecta £112.70.
**Owner** Robert Ng **Bred** Robert Ng **Trained** Kimpton, Hants

**FOCUS**
A fair juvenile fillies' novice contest. They went a respectable gallop and the only two horses with prior form could barely be separated at the line.

## 2959 32RED H'CAP (LONDON MIDDLE DISTANCE SERIES QUALIFIER) 1m 2f 219y(P)
7:40 (7:40) (Class 3) (0-95,96) 4-Y-0+
£7,470 (£2,236; £1,118; £559; £279; £140) Stalls Low

Form RPR
11- 1 **Wadigor**[208] 7666 4-9-10 96 HarryBentley 2 108+
(Roger Varian) *hld up in 4th on outer: shkn up 2f out: rdn over 1f out: led 100yds out: easily* 4/5[1]
42-1 2 1 1/2 **Regicide (IRE)**[28] 2092 4-8-11 83 OisinMurphy 1 90+
(James Fanshawe) *hld up in 5th on inner: rdn 2f out on inner: led over 1f out: kpt on wl tl hdd 100yds out: no ex cl home* 5/1[2]
0-11 3 1 3/4 **Jacob Cats**[49] 1555 8-9-7 93 (v) RyanMoore 7 97
(William Knight) *hld up in last: rdn 2f out: kpt on for 3rd fr over 1f out but no threat to ldng pair* 16/1
252 4 hd **Getback In Paris (IRE)**[23] 2233 4-9-3 89 ShaneKelly 4 92
(Richard Hughes) *settled in 3rd on inner: rdn 2f out: ev ch over 1f out: kpt on in dual for 3rd ent fnl f: one pce fnl f* 7/1
31/1 5 3 1/2 **Mr Khalid**[30] 2041 4-9-0 89 (h) KieranShoemark(3) 8 86
(Roger Charlton) *pressed ldr on outer: rdn along 2f out: sn wknd* 6/1[3]
0-0 6 12 **Storm Rock**[53] 1502 5-9-4 90 DavidProbert 5 65
(Harry Dunlop) *led: rdn 2f out: sn hdd & wknd qckly* 25/1
2m 21.47s (-0.43) **Going Correction** +0.075s/f (Slow) 6 Ran SP% 108.7
Speed ratings (Par 107): **104,102,101,101,98 90**
CSF £4.73 CT £27.59 TOTE £1.70: £1.20, £2.10; EX 5.00 Trifecta £34.30.
**Owner** Sheikh Ahmed Al Maktoum **Bred** Panda Bloodstock **Trained** Newmarket, Suffolk
**FOCUS**
The feature contest was a good handicap. They went a modest gallop, but the strong favourite still showed his class by remaining unbeaten with another fluent victory.

## 2960 32RED.COM H'CAP (LONDON MILE SERIES QUALIFIER) 1m (P)
8:10 (8:10) (Class 4) (0-85,86) 4-Y-0+ £5,175 (£1,540; £769; £384) Stalls Low

Form RPR
6-11 1 **Commodity (IRE)**[21] 2317 4-9-2 78 RyanMoore 13 86
(Sir Michael Stoute) *c across fr wd draw and sn led stdd pce ent st: shkn up 2f out: rdn over 1f out: kpt on wl ins fnl f: snug* 7/2[1]
5-22 2 1 **Golden Wedding (IRE)**[12] 2582 5-9-4 80 CharlesBishop 6 85
(Eve Johnson Houghton) *chsd ldr: rdn over 1f out: kpt on ent fnl f: nvr getting to wnr ins fnl f* 15/2
1-00 3 1 1/4 **Glorious Poet**[47] 1606 4-8-13 75 AndrewMullen 1 77
(Tony Carroll) *settled in mid-div on rail: rdn 2f out: kpt on wl fr over 1f out: tk 3rd post* 8/1
30-0 4 hd **Harlequin Striker (IRE)**[65] 1288 5-9-6 82 (h) RobertWinston 3 84
(Dean Ivory) *briefly led: pressed wnr after: rdn over 1f out: kpt on tl no ex ins fnl f* 33/1
1-24 5 nse **Cape Banjo (USA)**[23] 2233 4-9-4 80 PatDobbs 2 82
(Ralph Beckett) *uns rdr on way to s: settled bhd ldr: rdn over 1f out: kpt on tl no ex fnl 150yds* 6/1[3]
30-5 6 1/2 **North Creek**[27] 2116 4-9-4 80 LukeMorris 10 80
(Chris Wall) *in rr on rail: rdn 2f out: nt clr run over 1f out: kpt on one pce ins fnl f* 5/1[2]
0-06 7 1 **Winklemann (IRE)**[23] 2232 5-9-2 78 (p) DanielMuscutt 11 76
(John Flint) *in rr: rdn 2f out: kpt on fr over 1f out: no imp on ldrs* 16/1
0 8 hd **Golden Raven (IRE)**[47] 1598 5-9-7 83 TimmyMurphy 4 81
(Jamie Osborne) *in rr-div on rail: briefly shkn up over 1f out: nvr involved after* 16/1
10-0 9 nk **Wind In My Sails**[23] 2232 5-9-7 86 (h) CallumShepherd(3) 8 83
(Ed de Giles) *a in rr: no imp over 1f out* 20/1
0310 10 nk **Dutiful Son (IRE)**[28] 2083 7-8-12 81 DavidEgan(7) 7 77
(Simon Dow) *missed break and lost several l: settled in rr: sddle slipped in bkst: rdn over 1f out: no imp* 25/1
12-6 11 hd **Dubai's Secret**[25] 2155 4-9-10 86 SeanLevey 5 82
(David Brown) *bhd ldrs on outer: rdn 2f out: sn lft bhd* 7/1
30-5 12 1 **Cat Silver**[21] 2291 4-8-10 72 HarryBentley 9 66
(Roger Charlton) *in rr-div on outer: rdn 2f out: no imp after and kpt on one pce* 7/1
1m 39.66s (-0.14) **Going Correction** +0.075s/f (Slow) 12 Ran SP% 124.4
Speed ratings (Par 105): **103,102,100,100,100 100,99,98,98,98 98,97**
CSF £30.84 CT £207.66 TOTE £6.80: £1.60, £2.80, £6.20; EX 25.30 Trifecta £291.20.
**Owner** Highclere T'bred Racing (Wellington) **Bred** Stowell Park Stud **Trained** Newmarket, Suffolk
**FOCUS**
A decent handicap. They went a proper gallop and the favourite made most of the running in resolute fashion from a poor draw.

## 2961 32RED ON THE APP STORE H'CAP 7f (P)
8:40 (8:40) (Class 6) (0-65,65) 4-Y-0+ £2,587 (£770; £384; £192) Stalls Low

Form RPR
40-5 1 **Helfire**[41] 1755 4-9-3 64 CharlieBennett(3) 7 74
(Hughie Morrison) *settled in mid-div on inner: angled to centre over 2f out: shkn up and smooth prog: rdn over 1f out: drifted rt: kpt on wl and led jst ins fnl f: rdn out and only jst hld off late chal post* 7/2[1]
0354 2 shd **Air Of York (IRE)**[21] 2297 5-9-2 60 (p) DanielMuscutt 9 70
(John Flint) *in rr-div on rail: rdn 2f out: prog and kpt on strly fr over 1f out: fin fast last 50yds and jst denied post* 12/1
500- 3 3 1/2 **Royal Caper**[274] 5734 7-8-11 55 StevieDonohoe 11 56
(Miss Joey Ellis) *chsd ldrs: rdn over 2f out: kpt on one pce fr over 1f out* 28/1
1045 4 1/2 **Zabdi**[23] 2229 4-8-11 62 JoshuaBryan(7) 4 61
(Lee Carter) *led: rdn over 2f out: kpt on wl tl wknd jst ins fnl f and hdd: no ex after* 10/1[3]
600 5 3/4 **Doodle Dandy (IRE)**[23] 2231 4-8-13 62 GeorgeWood(5) 3 59
(David Bridgwater) *chsd ldrs: rdn wl over 1f out: kpt on one pce after* 16/1
50-0 6 hd **Black Truffle (FR)**[22] 2278 7-8-4 55 NicolaCurrie(7) 5 52
(Mark Usher) *in rr: rdn over 2f out: kpt on wl fr over 1f out: nrst fin* 50/1
6400 7 1/2 **Keene's Pointe**[12] 2589 7-8-3 54 DavidEgan(7) 10 50
(Steph Hollinshead) *hld up in rr: rdn over 2f out: kpt on wl fr over 1f out: nrst fin* 16/1
050 8 3/4 **Spirit Of Gondree (IRE)**[25] 2166 9-8-7 51 oh3 (b) RobHornby 1 45
(Milton Bradley) *in rr-div: rdn over 2f out: no imp over 1f out* 16/1
1423 9 4 **Broughtons Fancy**[9] 2675 4-8-12 56 ShaneKelly 6 39
(Gary Moore) *rrd s and missed break: hld up in last: rdn over 2f out: no imp after* 4/1[2]
-002 10 2 3/4 **Evanescent (IRE)**[56] 1427 8-9-3 61 RobertWinston 2 37
(Tony Carroll) *tk fierce hold early bhd ldrs: swtchd off rail ent bnd and settled bttr: rdn 2f out: sn hld* 12/1
65-0 11 3 3/4 **Molten Lava (IRE)**[22] 2276 5-9-0 65 (p) PatrickVaughan(7) 12 31
(Christian Williams) *mid-div: rdn 2f out: sn lft bhd* 20/1
5-10 12 shd **Olympic Duel (IRE)**[28] 2082 4-9-1 59 LukeMorris 8 25
(Peter Hiatt) *in rr-div: rdn over 2f out: nt qckn and pushed out after* 7/2[1]
5264 13 10 **Kristoff (IRE)**[9] 2675 4-8-0 51 IsobelFrancis(7) 13
(Jim Boyle) *cl up on outer: rdn over 2f out: wknd qckly after: t.o* 25/1
1m 25.86s (-0.14) **Going Correction** +0.075s/f (Slow) 13 Ran SP% 120.6
Speed ratings (Par 101): **103,102,98,98,97 97,96,95,91,88 83,83,72**
CSF £45.09 CT £1035.85 TOTE £4.30: £1.80, £4.00, £7.80; EX 52.90 Trifecta £1183.00.
**Owner** Deborah Collett & M J Watson **Bred** M J Watson **Trained** East Ilsley, Berks
**FOCUS**
A modest handicap. They went a decent gallop, though, and the joint-favourite produced the quickest comparative wining time on the night so far. The winner has been rated to last year's best.

## 2962 RACING UK IN STUNNING HD H'CAP 6f (P)
9:10 (9:11) (Class 6) (0-65,65) 4-Y-0+ £2,587 (£770; £384; £192) Stalls Low

Form RPR
0-42 1 **Deeds Not Words (IRE)**[12] 2589 6-9-0 58 (p) DavidProbert 2 65
(Michael Wigham) *cl up bhd ldrs: rdn over 1f out: kpt on wl ins fnl f: got up post* 5/2[1]
442- 2 hd **Arctic Angel (IRE)**[153] 8496 4-9-7 65 (h[1]) TomQueally 5 71
(James Fanshawe) *hld up in mid-div on inner: prog 2f out: rdn and led ent fnl f: kpt on wl tl hdd post* 3/1[2]
05-5 3 2 1/4 **Robbie Roo Roo**[30] 2043 4-9-0 58 (bt) AdamBeschizza 8 58
(Mrs Ilka Gansera-Leveque) *cl up: shkn up over 2f out: rdn over 1f out: kpt on ins fnl f to take 3rd post: no imp on ldng pair* 12/1
5-02 4 1/2 **Generalyse**[23] 2214 8-8-5 56 (b) RossaRyan(7) 3 54
(Anabel K Murphy) *led: rdn 2f out: kpt on tl hdd ent fnl f and wknd after and jst lost 3rd post* 16/1
53-0 5 3 1/4 **Forever Yours (IRE)**[98] 734 4-9-4 65 JackDuern(3) 9 53
(Dean Ivory) *hmpd s and in rr-div: wnt wdst in st and carried lft 2f out: stened up and kpt on nicely ins fnl f: can do bttr* 16/1
6422 6 1 3/4 **Noble Deed**[19] 2367 7-9-3 61 KierenFox 1 44+
(Michael Attwater) *awkward s and almost unshipped jockey: rdr lost iron: sn sorted and hld up in rr: rdn 2f out: kpt on: nvr nrr* 3/1[2]
46-0 7 shd **The Perfect Show**[9] 2675 4-9-4 62 LukeMorris 11 45
(Milton Bradley) *bhd ldr: rdn wl over 1f out: sn no imp and wknd ent fnl f* 50/1
0065 8 3/4 **Toni's A Star**[16] 2472 5-8-0 51 (b) AledBeech(7) 10 32
(Tony Carroll) *t.k.h on outer of mid-div: drifted lft 2f out: rdn over 1f out: kpt on one pce* 40/1
4006 9 2 1/4 **Arize (IRE)**[20] 2335 4-9-3 61 SamHitchcott 6 35
(Jim Boyle) *t.k.h in rr-div: rdn and n.m.r over 2f out: no imp after* 25/1
6231 10 1/2 **Compton Prince**[14] 2509 8-9-4 62 (b) RobertWinston 7 34
(Milton Bradley) *wnt lft s: t.k.h in mid-div on outside: rdn 2f out: sn hld* 9/1[3]
0000 11 3/4 **Waneen (IRE)**[38] 1819 4-8-11 62 DarraghKeenan(7) 4 32
(John Butler) *in rr on inner: rdn and no imp fr 2f out* 20/1
1m 13.21s (0.11) **Going Correction** +0.075s/f (Slow) 11 Ran SP% 121.0
Speed ratings (Par 101): **102,101,98,98,93 91,91,90,87,86 85**
CSF £9.96 CT £78.88 TOTE £3.60: £1.50, £1.80, £3.40; EX 15.30 Trifecta £123.00.
**Owner** D Hassan **Bred** B Holland, S Hillen & J Cullinan **Trained** Newmarket, Suffolk
**FOCUS**
A modest handicap. They went a proper gallop and two heavily-backed horses fought out a thrilling final furlong. Another small step up from the winner.
T/Plt: £25.00 to a £1 stake. Pool: £73,244.43. 2,135.06 winning units. T/Qpdt: £13.20 to a £1 stake. Pool: £5,404.65. 302.8 winning units. **Cathal Gahan**

# 2613 LINGFIELD (L-H)
Wednesday, May 24

**OFFICIAL GOING: Good (good to firm in places, good to soft 1st 2f of straight course; 7.7)**
Wind: Almost nil Weather: Fine, very warm

## 2963 NEWSTEAM GROUP MAIDEN STKS 1m 3f 133y
2:10 (2:11) (Class 5) 3-Y-0+ £2,911 (£866; £432; £216) Stalls High

Form RPR
5-2 1 **Cross Step (USA)**[16] 2476 3-8-11 0 (p) WilliamBuick 12 82
(Charlie Appleby) *trckd ldr: shkn up to ld 2f out: drvn fnl f: jst hld on* 12/1
2 2 shd **Humble Hero (IRE)**[25] 2143 3-8-11 0 RyanMoore 10 82+
(William Haggas) *s.i.s: hld up in 8th: urged along and little prog wl over 2f out: rdn and fnlly r.o over 1f out: fin strly to take 2nd nr fin: jst failed* 1/1[1]
-3 3 1/2 **Glassy Waters (USA)**[47] 1607 3-8-11 0 JosephineGordon 8 81
(Saeed bin Suroor) *trckd ldrs: clsd over 2f out: swtchd ins to chse wnr over 1f out: str chal fnl f: hd high and nt qckn after: lost 2nd nr fin* 11/4[2]
0 4 5 **Kazawi**[32] 1963 3-8-8 0 KieranShoemark(3) 2 73
(Roger Charlton) *led: rdn and hdd 2f out: steadily fdd* 7/1[3]
3 5 shd **Sea Sovereign (IRE)**[16] 2476 4-10-0 0 TimmyMurphy 6 74
(Mark Pitman) *trckd ldng pair: chal 3f out: rdn 2f out: steadily fdd over 1f out* 28/1
6 1/2 **Mancini** 3-8-11 0 RichardKingscote 5 72
(Jonathan Portman) *s.s: hld up in last quartet: pushed along 3f out: stdy prog 2f out: rdn and kpt on fnl f: nrst fin* 100/1
7 nse **War Drums** 3-8-11 0 LukeMorris 1 72
(Luca Cumani) *trckd ldrs in 5th: pushed along fr 1/2-way at times and rn green: no imp on ldrs 2f out: kpt on* 33/1
4-6 8 1 1/2 **Lethal Impact (JPN)**[32] 1963 3-8-11 0 OisinMurphy 9 69
(David Simcock) *hld up in 7th: shkn up over 2f out: no real prog but nt disgracd* 8/1
24 9 2 1/4 **Tapdanceallthewaÿ**[34] 1900 3-8-6 0 FrannyNorton 11 60
(Amanda Perrett) *trckd ldrs in 6th: outpcd 3f out: pushed along and threatened to stay on 2f out: fdd fnl f* 66/1
10 20 **Iley Boy** 3-8-11 0 MartinDwyer 3 32
(John Gallagher) *s.s: mostly in last pair: t.o* 100/1
0 11 7 **Stockton (IRE)**[21] 2314 3-8-11 0 FergusSweeney 7 21
(David Simcock) *a in rr: urged along 5f out: t.o* 100/1
12 15 **Ruby Taylor** 5-9-2 0 (h[1]) JordanUys(7) 4
(Nick Lampard) *s.v.s: a detached in last: t.o 4f out* 200/1
2m 30.98s (-0.52) **Going Correction** +0.025s/f (Good)
**WFA** 3 from 4yo+ 17lb 12 Ran SP% 119.3
Speed ratings (Par 103): **102,101,101,98,98 97,97,96,95,82 77,67**
CSF £24.53 TOTE £10.70: £3.10, £1.10, £1.60; EX 22.70 Trifecta £69.20.

**Owner** Godolphin **Bred** Blackstone Farm Llc **Trained** Newmarket, Suffolk

**FOCUS**

The official going was good, good to firm in places, while it was good to soft in places from 7.5f to 5.5f on the straight course. All distances as advertised. An interesting maiden with the future in mind and the three principles were clear of the rest.

## 2964 MENZIES DISTRIBUTION LTD H'CAP 1m 3f 133y

2:40 (2:40) (Class 6) (0-60,59) 4-Y-O+ £2,264 (£673; £336; £168) Stalls High

Form RPR

0433 1 **Party Royal**[30] 2042 7-9-7 59 ............(p) MartinLane 8 65
(Nick Gifford) *s.i.s: sn trckd ldrs on outer: prog gng wl 3f out: led 2f out: rdn and edgd lft: kpt on* **8/1**

6042 2 ¾ **Innoko (FR)**[21] 2295 7-9-6 58 ............(h) GeorgeDowning 1 63
(Tony Carroll) *hld up in last pair: prog on outer 3f out: rdn and styd on to take 2nd last 100yds: nt rch wnr* **8/1**

2424 3 ¾ **Powered (IRE)**[43] 1698 4-9-3 55 ............ SeanLevey 2 60+
(David Evans) *hld up in last pair: tried to make prog on inner wl over 2f out and nt clr run: swtchd out wd over 1f out: r.o fnl f to take 3rd last strides* **10/1**

33-4 4 hd **Hope Is High**[22] 2281 4-9-0 52 ............ JosephineGordon 11 57
(John Berry) *trckd ldrs: chal 2f out: chsd wnr after: hld whn sltly short of room on inner fnl f: lost 2 pls last 100yds* **11/4**[1]

430- 5 1 ¼ **Hermarna (IRE)**[27] 7425 4-9-6 58 ............ TrevorWhelan 7 59
(Neil King) *chsd ldrs: urged along fr 1/2-way: plugged on fnl 2f* **12/1**

/444 6 ¾ **Money Talks**[23] 1303 7-8-13 56 ............(p) GeorgeWood(5) 6 56
(Michael Madgwick) *hld up in rr: rdn over 2f out: plugged on but nvr a threat* **7/1**

55 7 2 **Brooke's Point**[58] 1402 4-8-8 46 ............(p) LukeMorris 12 43
(Neil Mulholland) *trckd ldr: led 3f out to 2f out: sn wknd* **4/1**[2]

3253 8 2 ¾ **Go On Gal (IRE)**[21] 2295 4-8-12 57 ............ FinleyMarsh(7) 4 49
(Julia Feilden) *hld up in midfield: rdn wl over 2f out: one pce and n.d* **6/1**[3]

0030 9 6 **Movie Magic**[20] 2332 6-8-0 45 ............(b) DavidEgan(7) 3 27
(Mark Hoad) *t.k.h: trckd ldrs: rdn 3f out: sn wknd* **33/1**

-060 P **Race Time (USA)**[71] 1186 4-8-7 45 ............(p) MartinDwyer 9
(Zoe Davison) *led to 3f out: wknd rapidly: p.u over 1f out: dismntd* **100/1**

2m 33.48s (1.98) **Going Correction** +0.025s/f (Good) **10 Ran SP% 116.4**

Speed ratings (Par 101): **94,93,93,92,92 91,90,88,84,**

CSF £70.26 CT £650.26 TOTE £5.00: £1.90, £2.70, £3.20; EX 29.50 Trifecta £210.30.

**Owner** Coldunell Limited **Bred** Old Mill Stud & S Williams & J Parry **Trained** Findon, W Sussex

**FOCUS**

A moderate handicap. The runner-up has been rated a fraction up on his latest effort.

## 2965 SUPPORT YOUR LOCAL INDEPENDENT RETAILER H'CAP 1m 3f 133y

3:10 (3:11) (Class 4) (0-80,80) 4-Y-O+ £4,690 (£1,395; £697; £348) Stalls High

Form RPR

3-53 1 **Panko (IRE)**[11] 2624 4-9-0 76 ............ CallumShepherd(3) 3 84
(Ed de Giles) *mde all: sent for home over 2f out: hrd pressed fnl f: fnd ex to hold on nr fin* **6/1**[3]

24-2 2 hd **All My Love (IRE)**[29] 2061 5-9-3 76 ............ RobHornby 6 83
(Pam Sly) *hld up in midfield: prog over 2f out: rdn to chse wnr over 1f out: str chal fnl f: kpt on but jst hld nr fin* **10/1**

1 3 2 **Rosa Damascena (FR)**[74] 1143 4-9-2 75 ............ MartinHarley 4 78
(Alan King) *chsd ldng pair: nt qckn and dropped to 4th over 2f out: kpt on to take 3rd again fnl f: unable to chal* **6/1**[3]

316- 4 1 ¾ **West Drive (IRE)**[249] 6581 4-9-0 80 ............ CameronNoble(7) 2 80
(Roger Varian) *hld up in last pair: shkn up wl over 2f out: nvr pce to threaten but plugged on* **2/1**[1]

033- 5 2 **Blaze Of Hearts (IRE)**[210] 7627 4-9-5 78 ............ RobertWinston 5 75
(Dean Ivory) *chsd wnr: rdn and nt qckn wl over 2f out: lost 2nd and fdd over 1f out* **8/1**

0-02 6 hd **Takbeer (IRE)**[68] 1248 5-9-1 74 ............(p) DavidProbert 1 71
(Nikki Evans) *t.k.h: hld up in tch: rdn over 2f out: no prog* **20/1**

22-6 7 ½ **Under Attack (IRE)**[32] 1964 4-9-4 80 ............(h) KieranShoemark(3) 7 79
(Roger Charlton) *restless stalls: dwlt: hld up in last pair: shkn up over 2f out: trying to make prog but stl in last pair whn repeatedly denied a run fr over 1f out* **4/1**[2]

353- 8 ¾ **Milrow (IRE)**[202] 729 4-9-1 74 ............(tp) LukeMorris 8 69
(Dr Richard Newland) *dwlt: sn chsd ldrs: rdn 3f out: fdd fr 2f out* **16/1**

2m 32.51s (1.01) **Going Correction** +0.025s/f (Good) **8 Ran SP% 112.8**

Speed ratings (Par 105): **97,96,95,94,93 92,92,92**

CSF £61.31 CT £372.59 TOTE £6.70: £1.80, £2.70, £1.80; EX 48.40 Trifecta £102.00.

**Owner** Simon Treacher & Partner **Bred** Jennifer & Evelyn Cullen **Trained** Ledbury, H'fords

**FOCUS**

A useful handicap and solid form.

## 2966 TELEGRAPH H'CAP 1m 6f

3:40 (3:40) (Class 5) (0-70,72) 4-Y-O+ £2,911 (£866; £432; £216) Stalls Low

Form RPR

0006 1 **Dovils Date**[60] 1364 8-9-0 62 ............ DavidProbert 4 68
(Tim Vaughan) *mde all: rdn 2f out: jnd fnl f: hld on wl* **12/1**

62/3 2 shd **Kerrymerry (IRE)**[27] 2111 5-9-6 68 ............ LukeMorris 5 73
(Dr Richard Newland) *trckd ldng trio: wnt 2nd wl over 2f out: hrd rdn to chal over 1f out: w wnr fnl f: nt go past nr fin* **7/2**[2]

51-3 3 1 ½ **Hepplewhite**[16] 2478 4-9-10 72 ............ MartinDwyer 1 75
(William Muir) *n.m.r sn after s: hld up in rr: prog on outer 3f out: rdn to take 3rd jst over 1f out: kpt on but unable to chal* **7/1**[3]

00-5 4 1 ¼ **Fitzwilly**[18] 2388 7-9-7 69 ............ CharlesBishop 6 70
(Mick Channon) *hld up in midfield: prog over 2f out to dispute 3rd over 1f out: one pce after* **10/1**

053- 5 3 ¼ **Incus**[214] 7532 4-7-9 50 oh4............ DavidEgan(7) 9 47
(Ed de Giles) *hld up in rr: rdn over 2f out: fdd over 1f out* **25/1**

240/ 6 ¾ **Wintour Leap**[580] 8193 6-8-13 61 ............ LiamKeniry 8 57
(Robert Stephens) *chsd wnr to wl over 2f out: steadily wknd* **80/1**

3-01 7 2 ¼ **Sir Pass I Am**[8] 2712 4-9-4 66 6ex............ OisinMurphy 3 58
(Andrew Balding) *n.m.r after s: sn chsd ldng pair: shkn up 3f out: sn lost pl and btn* **10/11**[1]

66/0 8 1 **Highsalvia Cosmos**[20] 2332 6-8-4 52 ............(t) FrannyNorton 7 43
(Mark Hoad) *hld up in rr: rdn and no prog over 2f out* **50/1**

333 9 ¾ **Marshall Aid (IRE)**[16] 2460 4-9-2 64 ............(p) KieranO'Neill 11 54
(Mark Usher) *hld up in last pair: outpcd 4f out: no ch after* **14/1**

00-0 10 10 **Honourable Knight (IRE)**[20] 2332 9-7-13 50 oh3....... HollieDoyle(3) 12 26
(Mark Usher) *hld up in last pair: outpcd 4f out: no ch after* **66/1**

3m 5.59s (-4.41) **Going Correction** +0.025s/f (Good) **10 Ran SP% 119.1**

Speed ratings (Par 103): **113,112,112,111,109 109,107,107,106,101**

CSF £54.33 CT £327.39 TOTE £16.10: £3.40, £1.60, £2.30; EX 66.60 Trifecta £442.00.

**Owner** Itsfuninit **Bred** Cranford Stud **Trained** Aberthin, Vale of Glamorgan

■ Stewards' Enquiry : Luke Morris two-day ban; careless riding (7th-8th June)

**FOCUS**

A fair handicap and it paid to race prominently.

## 2967 NEWSTRAID CHARITY RACEDAY H'CAP 4f 217y

4:10 (4:11) (Class 5) (0-70,71) 4-Y-O+ £2,911 (£866; £432; £216) Stalls Centre

Form RPR

534 1 **Zipedeedodah (IRE)**[40] 1768 5-9-5 66............(t) OisinMurphy 1 75
(Joseph Tuite) *racd centre: prom: led over 1f out: styd on wl* **11/4**[1]

5661 2 1 ¼ **Taajub (IRE)**[9] 2680 10-9-10 71 6ex............ FergusSweeney 4 75
(Peter Crate) *prom in centre: nt qckn 2f out: chsd wnr over 1f out: kpt on but unable to chal* **6/1**[3]

513- 3 1 **Prominna**[426] 1059 7-9-1 62............ GeorgeDowning 2 62+
(Tony Carroll) *awkward s and slowly away: wl in rr: prog in centre 1/2-way: rdn and styd on fnl f to take 3rd nr fin* **25/1**

4525 4 nk **Pharoh Jake**[19] 2370 9-8-9 56............ WilliamCarson 7 55
(John Bridger) *towards rr: rdn 2f out: styd on wl fnl f: nrst fin* **12/1**

4230 5 1 **Powerful Wind (IRE)**[19] 2360 8-9-2 63............(t) RobertWinston 8 59
(Charlie Wallis) *fast away: led and crossed to nr side rail over 3f out: hdd and fdd over 1f out* **8/1**

0-60 6 1 ½ **Classic Flyer**[11] 2621 5-8-12 59............(v) FrannyNorton 3 49
(Christine Dunnett) *nvr bttr than midfield: rdn and no prog wl over 1f out* **33/1**

42-5 7 nk **Kiringa**[32] 1981 4-9-0 61............ LukeMorris 5 50
(Robert Cowell) *prom: rdn 2f out: wknd fnl f* **5/1**[2]

6-20 8 ¾ **Fly True**[109] 573 4-9-7 68............(h) MartinLane 12 55+
(Jeremy Gask) *s.v.s and lost all ch: bhd tl kpt on fnl f* **8/1**

0165 9 nk **Archimedes (IRE)**[92] 851 4-9-6 67............(tp) JosephineGordon 11 52
(David C Griffiths) *racd against rail early and chsd ldrs: struggling fr 1/2-way* **7/1**

51-5 10 2 **Quantum Dot (IRE)**[19] 2360 6-8-11 61............(b) CallumShepherd(3) 6 39
(Ed de Giles) *prom tl wknd over 1f out: eased* **8/1**

0050 11 4 ½ **Give Us A Belle (IRE)**[11] 2621 8-8-7 54 oh8............(vt) KierenFox 10 16
(Christine Dunnett) *racd against rail: struggling in rr bef 1/2-way* **66/1**

58.38s (0.18) **Going Correction** +0.025s/f (Good) **11 Ran SP% 119.4**

Speed ratings (Par 103): **99,97,95,94,93 90,90,89,88,85 78**

CSF £19.19 CT £299.22 TOTE £3.60: £1.60, £2.10, £4.30; EX 22.30 Trifecta £427.00.

**Owner** D M Synergy & Mark Wellbelove **Bred** Tally-Ho Stud **Trained** Lambourn, Berks

**FOCUS**

A modest handicap run at a good pace.

## 2968 DAILY MAIL CLAIMING STKS 7f 135y

4:40 (4:40) (Class 6) 3-Y-O+ £2,264 (£673; £336; £168) Stalls Centre

Form RPR

5064 1 **Black Dave (IRE)**[20] 2346 7-8-12 64............ KatherineGlenister(7) 3 64
(David Evans) *racd centre: trckd ldrs: led 2f out: hrd pressed fnl f: hld on wl* **8/1**

6001 2 nk **Chelwood Gate (IRE)**[19] 2365 7-9-7 67............(v) JosephineGordon 5 65
(Patrick Chamings) *hld up in rr and racd against rail: swtchd out wd 1/2-way and prog: tk 2nd ins fnl f: kpt on: jst hld* **9/2**[3]

503 3 2 **Corporal Maddox**[22] 2256 10-9-7 68............(p) LukeMorris 2 60
(Ronald Harris) *dwlt: racd centre: hld up: prog 3f out: chal over 1f out: one pce fnl f* **10/1**

4305 4 3 **Jack The Laird (IRE)**[7] 2732 4-9-8 59............ JackDuern(3) 8 57
(Dean Ivory) *hld up in centre: nt qckn 2f out: no imp after: tk 4th last strides* **16/1**

1004 5 hd **Locommotion**[6] 2762 5-10-0 53............ JohnFahy 10 60
(Matthew Salaman) *t.k.h: led after 1f against rail: hdd 2f out: hanging and wknd fnl f* **33/1**

600 6 3 **Beach Bar (IRE)**[60] 891 6-10-0 92............(h) SamHitchcott 7 53
(Brendan Powell) *prom towards nr side: rdn sn after 1/2-way: steadily lft bhd* **3/1**[2]

4600 7 1 **Luduamf (IRE)**[6] 2758 3-8-10 57............ HollieDoyle(3) 9 44
(Richard Hannon) *racd towards nr side: sn lost pl: struggling fr 1/2-way* **10/1**

-040 8 1 **Ivor's Magic (IRE)**[30] 2017 3-8-0 57............ AaronJones(3) 1 32
(David Elsworth) *hld up in centre: shkn up and no prog over 2f out* **14/1**

3146 9 8 **Regarde Moi**[72] 1177 9-9-2 85............ JacobMitchell(7) 12 24
(Marco Botti) *racd against rail: led 1f: struggling fr 1/2-way* **5/2**[1]

1m 30.68s (-1.62) **Going Correction** +0.025s/f (Good)

**WFA** 3 from 4yo+ 12lb **9 Ran SP% 116.5**

Speed ratings (Par 101): **109,108,106,103,103 100,99,98,90**

CSF £44.30 TOTE £9.30: £2.50, £2.30, £2.50; EX 48.40 Trifecta £371.70.Chelwood Gate was claimed by Conor Dore for £8,000.

**Owner** Mrs E Evans & J Smith **Bred** Richard Frayne **Trained** Pandy, Monmouths

**FOCUS**

A claimer in which the two market leaders underperformed. The form has been rated conservatively.

## 2969 SMITHS NEWS FILLIES' H'CAP 6f

5:10 (5:13) (Class 6) (0-65,71) 4-Y-O+ £2,911 (£866; £432; £216) Stalls Centre

Form RPR

-011 1 **Whitecrest**[9] 2675 9-9-13 71 6ex............ LukeMorris 1 78
(John Spearing) *racd towards nr side rail: pressed ldr after 2f: led 2f out: hrd pressed fnl f: hld on wl* **8/1**[3]

0-00 2 nk **Flying Sakhee**[6] 2762 4-8-3 52 oh4 ow1............ MitchGodwin(5) 6 58
(John Bridger) *hld up in rr: prog in centre 1/2-way: rdn to chal and w wnr fnl f: nt qckn nr fin* **10/1**

0P64 3 3 **Wedgewood Estates**[21] 2298 6-8-11 55............ KierenFox 14 52
(Tony Carroll) *hld up in rr: swtchd to outer 1/2-way: prog over 1f out: kpt on to take 3rd last strides* **10/1**

0004 4 hd **Molly Jones**[19] 2360 8-8-11 55 ow1............ JohnFahy 2 52
(Matthew Salaman) *hld up in centre: prog 1/2-way: rdn to chal over 1f out: fdd fnl f: lost 3rd last strides* **25/1**

2-00 5 nk **Foxford**[19] 2370 6-8-8 52............ JosephineGordon 5 48
(Patrick Chamings) *led against rail: hdd 2f out: fdd* **8/1**[3]

6014 6 ¾ **Fleeting Glimpse**[29] 2053 4-9-1 59............(h) DavidProbert 4 52
(Andrew Balding) *awkward s and slowly away: t.k.h: hld up wl in rr: kpt on fr over 1f out: no ch* **4/1**[1]

00-4 7 shd **Refuse Colette (IRE)**[60] 1359 8-9-2 60............ JimCrowley 9 53
(Mick Quinn) *pressed ldrs: nt qckn 2f out: fdd over 1f out* **6/1**[2]

0060 8 nk **Flowing Clarets**[23] 2229 4-9-4 62............ WilliamCarson 13 54
(John Bridger) *chsd ldrs: rdn 2f out: fdd over 1f out* **20/1**

-460 9 1 **Himalayan Queen**[30] 2043 4-9-0 63............ SophieKilloran(5) 8 53
(William Jarvis) *dwlt: hld up in last pair: nt clr run over 2f out: no great prog after* **10/1**

5505 **10** *nse* **Multi Quest**[12] 2589 5-8-7 **51** oh1 ................(b) SamHitchcott 11 40
(John E Long) *pressed ldr 2f: sn lost pl: struggling fr 1/2-way* **10/1**
3/00 **11** *nk* **Flower Cup**[16] 2463 4-9-4 **62** ................(h) IrineuGoncalves 7 50
(Chris Dwyer) *dwlt: wl in rr: effrt out wd 1/2-way: sn no prog* **40/1**
0060 **12** *1* **Jeanie's Place**[14] 2509 4-8-5 **52** ................(t) HollieDoyle(3) 15 37
(Charlie Wallis) *reluctant to go bhd stalls: racd towards nr side rail: struggling fr 1/2-way* **14/1**
03-0 **13** *1 ½* **Sakhee's Jem**[22] 2285 4-9-5 **63** ................(p) MartinDwyer 10 44
(Gay Kelleway) *dwlt: a in rr: pushed along and no prog 2f out* **10/1**
1m 10.74s (-0.46) **Going Correction** +0.025s/f (Good) **13** Ran SP% **119.7**
Speed ratings (Par 98): **104,103,99,99,98 97,97,97,96,96 95,94,92**
CSF £83.86 CT £843.61 TOTE £6.80: £2.40, £4.50, £3.80; EX 120.50 Trifecta £1286.60.
**Owner** G M Eales **Bred** J Spearing And Kate Ive **Trained** Kinnersley, Worcs

**FOCUS**
A modest handicap and the two principles fought out a tight finish, clear of the remainder. A pb from the runner-up.
T/Jkpt: Not won. T/Plt: £112.30 to a £1 stake. Pool: £70,704.38. 459.25 winning units. T/Qpdt: £50.70 to a £1 stake. Pool: £4,891.75. 71.30 winning units. **Jonathan Neesom**

## 2727 YARMOUTH (L-H)
Wednesday, May 24

**OFFICIAL GOING: Good to firm (good in back straight; 7.8)**
Wind: fresh, behind Weather: sunny

### 2970 HOLIDAYS ON THE NORFOLK BROADS MEDIAN AUCTION MAIDEN STKS 6f 3y
**2:00** (2:01) (Class 5) 3-5-Y-O **£3,234** (£962; £481; £240) **Stalls** Centre

Form RPR
2- **1** **Cartographer**[196] 7867 3-9-0 **0** ................ JamieSpencer 5 84+
(Martyn Meade) *trckd ldrs: nudged into ld jst over 1f out: sn clr: nt extended* **4/9**[1]
6 **2** *4* **Pastime**[13] 2547 3-9-5 **0** ................ DanielMuscutt 3 71
(Gay Kelleway) *s.i.s: midfield: rdn over 2f out: sn outpcd: rallied and kpt on ins fnl f to go 2nd towards fin: no ch w wnr* **100/1**
65 **3** *1* **Agnethe (IRE)**[21] 2316 3-9-0 **0** ................ JoeyHaynes 2 63
(Paul D'Arcy) *chsd ldr: rdn and ev ch 2f out tl brushed aside by wnr 1f out: wnt 2nd briefly ins fnl f: kpt on on same pce* **50/1**
3-00 **4** *nk* **Kings Academy**[6] 2757 3-9-5 **73** ................(t[1]) SilvestreDeSousa 4 67
(Paul Cole) *led: rdn 2f out: hdd jst over 1f out and sn outpcd: lost 2 pls wl ins fnl f* **4/1**[2]
24 **5** *¾* **May Sky**[11] 2619 3-9-0 **0** ................ RobertTart 7 60
(John Gosden) *stdd s: hld up: effrt over 2f out: kpt on same pce fr over 1f out* **6/1**[3]
04 **6** *12* **Shyarch**[7] 2727 3-8-12 **0** ................ JaneElliott(7) 1 26
(George Margarson) *s.i.s: outpcd in rr: n.d* **33/1**
1m 9.14s (-5.26) **Going Correction** -0.725s/f (Hard) course record **6** Ran SP% **109.4**
Speed ratings (Par 103): **106,100,99,98,97 81**
CSF £63.41 TOTE £1.40: £1.10, £8.60; EX 40.50 Trifecta £195.20.
**Owner** The Snailwell Stud Limited **Bred** Bearstone Stud Ltd **Trained** Newmarket, Suffolk

**FOCUS**
Not much of a maiden but a taking effort from the red-hot favourite. The level is a bit fluid.

### 2971 CONGRATULATIONS MR & MRS SMITH H'CAP 1m 3f 104y
**2:30** (2:30) (Class 5) (0-70,72) 4-Y-O+ **£2,911** (£866; £432; £216) **Stalls** Low

Form RPR
**1** **Adjective**[316] 4-9-7 **69** ................ DanielMuscutt 4 75
(James Fanshawe) *pressed ldr tl led 2f: sn edgd rt over 1f out: styd on wl ins fnl f: rdn out* **2/1**[1]
0002 **2** *1* **Tyrsal (IRE)**[7] 2729 6-8-7 **55** ................(p) RobertTart 3 59
(Clifford Lines) *hld up in tch in last pair: hdwy on inner over 2f out: effrt to chse ldrs over 1f out: chsd wnr and kpt on same pce ins fnl f* **2/1**[1]
1503 **3** *nk* **Camakasi (IRE)**[30] 2020 6-9-10 **72** ................ TomMarquand 1 76
(Ali Stronge) *chsd ldrs: effrt and swtchd rt 2f out: nt clr run and swtchd lft over 1f out: kpt on same pce u.p ins fnl f* **5/1**[2]
6-00 **4** *1 ½* **Best Example (USA)**[16] 2477 5-9-6 **71** ................ ShelleyBirkett(3) 7 73
(Julia Feilden) *in tch in midfield: effrt to press ldrs 2f out: unable qck u.p over 1f out: styd on same pce ins fnl f* **10/1**
0504 **5** *3 ¾* **Karam Albaari (IRE)**[20] 2336 9-9-7 **69** ................(v) AdamKirby 5 64
(J R Jenkins) *stdd and dropped in bhd: effrt 2f out: no imp: nvr trbld ldrs* **14/1**
2130 **6** *nse* **What Usain**[16] 2471 5-9-6 **71** ................(p) AlistairRawlinson(3) 2 66
(Michael Appleby) *led tl over 1f out: sn outpcd: wknd ins fnl f* **7/1**[3]
2m 29.31s (0.61) **Going Correction** -0.05s/f (Good) **6** Ran SP% **111.6**
Speed ratings (Par 103): **95,94,94,92,90 90**
CSF £5.87 TOTE £2.90: £2.60, £1.10; EX 6.30 Trifecta £18.80.
**Owner** Glentree Pastoral Pty Ltd **Bred** Juddmonte Farms Ltd **Trained** Newmarket, Suffolk

**FOCUS**
A modest handicap and they didn't go much of a gallop early, but a winner capable of rating higher. The third has been rated to form for now.

### 2972 FAT LARRY'S BURGERS AT GREAT YARMOUTH RACECOURSE H'CAP 1m 6f 17y
**3:00** (3:01) (Class 6) (0-60,62) 4-Y-O+ **£2,264** (£673; £336; £168) **Stalls** High

Form RPR
3242 **1** **Graceful Lady**[22] 2281 4-9-6 **58** ................ JFEgan 12 63
(Robert Eddery) *hld up in rr: hdwy 4f out: chsd ldrs over 1f out: styd on wl to ld towards fin* **4/1**[2]
5043 **2** *¾* **Dream Serenade**[13] 2549 4-9-2 **54** ................(h) SilvestreDeSousa 13 58
(Michael Appleby) *chsd ldrs: clsd and upsides over 3f out: rdn to ld over 2f out: battled on wl u.p tl hdd and no ex towards fin* **3/1**[1]
0042 **3** *¾* **With Hindsight (IRE)**[25] 2162 9-9-4 **59** ................ AdamMcNamara(3) 9 62
(Steve Gollings) *led: jnd over 3f out: hdd over 2f out: kpt on wl u.p and stl ev ch tl unable qck and kpt on same pce fnl f* **9/2**[3]
00-0 **4** *1 ¾* **Little Orchid**[22] 2281 4-8-7 **48** ................ ShelleyBirkett(3) 2 49
(Julia Feilden) *hld up in last quartet: effrt in centre 3f out: hdwy over 1f out: kpt on wl ins fnl f: snatched 4th last stride* **22/1**
42-0 **5** *shd* **Esspeegee**[22] 2281 4-8-10 **48** ................(p) RobertTart 8 49
(Alan Bailey) *in tch in midfield on outer: hdwy to chse ldrs 4f out: unable qck u.p over 1f out: kpt on same pce fnl f* **16/1**
1266 **6** *2 ¾* **Par Three (IRE)**[20] 2332 6-8-10 **53** ................(p) GeorgiaCox(5) 1 50
(Tony Carroll) *in rr: rdn over 3f out: hdwy ent fnl f: styd on: nvr trbld ldrs* **12/1**
046/ **7** *1 ¾* **Kalimantan (IRE)**[600] 6899 7-9-4 **56** ................ DanielMuscutt 6 51
(Tim Vaughan) *chsd ldrs: u.p and unable qck over 2f out: lost pl and kpt on same pce fr over 1f out* **8/1**
4005 **8** *¾* **Azamesse (IRE)**[97] 762 5-8-7 **52** ................ GinaMangan(7) 4 46
(J R Jenkins) *hld up in last quartet: effrt over 2f out: nvr trbld ldrs* **50/1**
5450 **9** *nse* **Smoky Hill (IRE)**[22] 2281 8-8-12 **50** ................ JoeyHaynes 11 44
(Tony Carroll) *chsd ldrs: unable qck over 2f out: wknd over 1f out* **14/1**
-324 **10** *hd* **Thomas Blossom (IRE)**[19] 2364 7-9-10 **62** ................(tp) TomMarquand 7 55
(Ali Stronge) *in tch in midfield: lost pl u.p 2f out: wl btn 1f out* **9/1**
000- **11** *nk* **Maison Brillet (IRE)**[161] 8359 10-9-3 **55** ................(p) JackMitchell 5 48
(Clive Drew) *in tch in midfield: rdn over 3f out: wknd over 1f out* **40/1**
3m 3.47s (-4.13) **Going Correction** -0.05s/f (Good) **11** Ran SP% **113.3**
Speed ratings (Par 101): **109,108,108,107,107 105,104,104,104,103 103**
CSF £15.41 CT £54.59 TOTE £4.50: £1.50, £1.60, £2.10; EX 13.80 Trifecta £50.70.
**Owner** Graham & Lynn Knight **Bred** J C Sillett **Trained** Newmarket, Suffolk

**FOCUS**
Sound form for the level, with the right horses coming to the fore.

### 2973 JOHN KEMP 4 X 4 CENTRES OF NORWICH FILLIES' H'CAP 1m 3y
**3:30** (3:30) (Class 4) (0-85,82) 4-Y-O+ **£4,690** (£1,395; £697; £348) **Stalls** Centre

Form RPR
0366 **1** **Bint Dandy (IRE)**[28] 2093 6-9-3 **78** ................(b) AdamBeschizza 3 87
(Chris Dwyer) *trckd ldrs: upsides ldr and travelling strly 2f out: rdn to ld over 1f out: gng clr whn rdr dropped whip jst ins fnl f: r.o wl* **15/2**[3]
3450 **2** *2 ½* **Rebel Surge (IRE)**[40] 1771 4-9-7 **82** ................(p) StevieDonohoe 2 85
(Richard Spencer) *t.k.h: hld up in tch in last pair: effrt to press ldrs 2f out: drvn to chse wnr 1f out: no imp: kpt on* **15/2**[3]
-203 **3** *2 ½* **Stosur (IRE)**[22] 2268 6-9-1 **76** ................(b) JamieSpencer 1 74
(Gay Kelleway) *led: rdn and hdd over 1f out: sn hung lft and lost 2nd 1f out: wknd ins fnl f* **11/1**
00-1 **4** *¾* **In Ken's Memory**[9] 2676 4-8-11 **72** 6ex ................ SilvestreDeSousa 5 68
(Michael Appleby) *chsd ldr: rdn ent fnl 2f: outpcd u.p and btn over 1f out: wknd ins fnl f* **5/4**[1]
536- **5** *15* **Blind Faith (IRE)**[215] 7504 4-9-4 **79** ................ AdamKirby 4 40
(Luca Cumani) *hld up in tch in rr: shkn up over 2f out: sn struggling: wknd over 1f out* **2/1**[2]
1m 34.13s (-6.47) **Going Correction** -0.725s/f (Hard) **5** Ran SP% **109.6**
Speed ratings (Par 102): **103,100,98,97,82**
CSF £54.21 TOTE £11.30: £4.70, £4.70; EX 46.20 Trifecta £157.30.
**Owner** M M Foulger **Bred** Ballyhane Stud **Trained** Newmarket, Suffolk

**FOCUS**
Bit of a turn up here with the two clear market leaders disappointing. Not form to put much faith in. The winner has been rated in line with last year's turf best, and the runner-up to her recent AW form.

### 2974 PLEASURE WOOD HILLS THEME PARK H'CAP 1m 3y
**4:00** (4:00) (Class 5) (0-70,70) 4-Y-O+ **£2,911** (£866; £432; £216) **Stalls** Centre

Form RPR
663 **1** **King Oswald (USA)**[25] 2140 4-8-7 **56** ................(p) RyanPowell 9 67
(James Unett) *hld up in tch in last pair: smooth hdwy to trck ldr over 1f out: rdn hands and heels and qcknd to ld ins fnl f: stormed clr: easily* **4/1**[3]
3605 **2** *4* **Be Royale**[13] 2548 7-9-1 **64** ................(t) SilvestreDeSousa 7 66
(Michael Appleby) *in tch in midfield: hdwy to ld 2f out: sn rdn: hdd ins fnl f: sn brushed aside by wnr: kpt on for clr 2nd* **8/1**
20-3 **3** *6* **Wings Of Esteem (IRE)**[21] 2317 4-9-5 **68** ................ StevieDonohoe 5 56
(Luke McJannet) *taken down early: in tch in midfield: effrt ent fnl 2f: 3rd and unable qck over 1f out: wknd ins fnl f* **2/1**[1]
5-21 **4** *½* **Anastazia**[21] 2318 5-9-5 **68** ................ JoeyHaynes 2 55
(Paul D'Arcy) *pressed ldr: effrt ent fnl 2f: no ex and outpcd over 1f out: wknd ins fnl f* **7/2**[2]
-014 **5** *9* **Admirable Art (IRE)**[56] 1419 7-9-5 **68** ................ AdamKirby 3 34
(Tony Carroll) *led: rdn and hdd 2f out: sn lost pl and wknd over 1f out* **6/1**
6000 **6** *¾* **Gatillo**[6] 2762 4-9-3 **66** ................ AdamBeschizza 1 30
(Julia Feilden) *racd alone middle to far side: w ldrs: rdn over 2f out: lost pl qckly over 1f out: sn wknd* **25/1**
-000 **7** *9* **Red Cossack (CAN)**[9] 1683 6-8-11 **65** ................(t) GeorgiaCox(5) 8 9
(Paul Webber) *hld up in rr: rdn over 2f out: sn btn and bhd* **14/1**
1m 34.09s (-6.51) **Going Correction** -0.725s/f (Hard) **7** Ran SP% **111.5**
Speed ratings (Par 103): **103,99,93,92,83 82,73**
CSF £33.16 CT £78.71 TOTE £5.00: £2.10, £3.30; EX 29.70 Trifecta £116.50.
**Owner** M Watkinson & P Steadman **Bred** Darley **Trained** Wolverhampton, West Midlands

**FOCUS**
The first two came clear in what was a modest handicap, with it setting up for the closers. The winner has been rated to his AW form and the runner-up to her recent level.

### 2975 FOLLOW US ON FACEBOOK AT YARMOUTH RACECOURSE H'CAP 7f 3y
**4:30** (4:31) (Class 4) (0-80,82) 4-Y-O+ **£4,690** (£1,395; £697; £348) **Stalls** Centre

Form RPR
0064 **1** **Realize**[22] 2283 7-9-8 **81** ................ JamieSpencer 6 89
(David Simcock) *trckd ldng pair: effrt to chal over 1f out: rdn to ld jst ins fnl f: r.o wl* **11/8**[1]
3/64 **2** *¾* **Bumptious**[19] 2369 4-9-1 **74** ................ StevieDonohoe 4 79
(Ismail Mohammed) *led and set stdy gallop: rdn 2f out: hrd drvn and edgd lft ent fnl f: sn hdd and kpt on same pce after* **14/1**
5-60 **3** *1* **Imperial State**[12] 2586 4-9-6 **79** ................(t[1]) TomMarquand 5 81
(George Scott) *chsd ldr: drvn and ev ch over 1f out: no ex and outpcd ins fnl f* **8/1**[3]
4364 **4** *hd* **Suqoor**[18] 2404 4-9-6 **79** ................(p) SilvestreDeSousa 9 80
(Chris Dwyer) *hld up in rr: effrt u.p over 1f out: styd on strly ins fnl f: nt rch ldrs* **3/1**[2]
2/1- **5** *5* **Song Of Shadows**[153] 8496 4-9-9 **82** ................(t[1]) AdamBeschizza 3 70
(Michael Wigham) *s.i.s: t.k.h in midfield: rdn 2f out: sn outpcd: wknd fnl f* **16/1**
3252 **6** *5* **Until Midnight (IRE)**[21] 2320 7-8-4 **68** ................ LuluStanford(5) 1 42
(Eugene Stanford) *hld up in tch in last pair: effrt 2f out: sn outpcd: wknd fnl f* **8/1**[3]
661 **7** *4 ½* **Plucky Dip**[16] 2462 6-9-7 **80** ................ AdamKirby 8 42
(John Ryan) *in tch in midfield: u.p and unable qck over 2f out: wknd over 1f out* **8/1**[3]
1m 23.93s (-2.67) **Going Correction** -0.725s/f (Hard) **7** Ran SP% **113.0**
Speed ratings (Par 105): **86,85,84,83,78 72,67**
CSF £22.00 CT £114.28 TOTE £2.60: £1.30, £6.20; EX 22.40 Trifecta £110.40.
**Owner** Tick Tock Partnership **Bred** M J Watson **Trained** Newmarket, Suffolk

**FOCUS**
Ordinary handicap form. The winner has been rated to his turf form.

## 2976 BBC RADIO NORFOLK H'CAP 7f 3y
**5:00** (5:00) (Class 6) (0-60,60) 4-Y-O+ **£2,264** (£673; £336; £168) **Stalls** Centre

Form RPR
0401 1 **Moi Aussie**[7] 2733 4-9-4 57 6ex SilvestreDeSousa 8 64
(Michael Appleby) *mde all: rdn 2f out: kpt on wl u.p fnl f: eased nr fin* **6/4**[1]
0-35 2 1 ½ **Rosie Crowe (IRE)**[62] 1325 5-8-11 **50** (v) RoystonFfrench 5 52
(Shaun Harris) *chsd wnr: rdn 2f out: kpt on same pce u.p ins fnl f* **12/1**
0024 3 ½ **Swilly Sunset**[7] 2733 4-9-3 **59** (h[1]) SimonPearce(3) 9 60
(Anthony Carson) *hld up in rr: effrt u.p over 2f out: hdwy 1f out: wnt 3rd wl ins fnl f: nvr threatened wnr* **11/4**[2]
4/56 4 1 ½ **Monsieur Royale**[98] 739 7-8-8 **47** JackMitchell 1 44
(Clive Drew) *in tch in last pair: effrt over 2f out: styd on to chse ldrs over 1f out: no ex and styd on same pce ins fnl f* **22/1**
-0 5 hd **The Happy Hammer (IRE)**[83] 984 11-8-5 **49** LuluStanford(5) 6 45
(Eugene Stanford) *in tch in midfield: effrt over 2f out: drvn and clsd to chse ldrs over 1f out: no ex and one pce ins fnl f* **25/1**
0304 6 5 **The Special One (IRE)**[21] 2294 4-9-0 **53** (t) TomMarquand 4 36
(Ali Stronge) *in tch in midfield: rdn 2f out: unable qck over 1f out: wknd ins fnl f* **12/1**
0-41 7 ½ **Caribbean Spring (IRE)**[21] 2312 4-9-0 **60** JaneElliott(7) 2 41
(George Margarson) *in tch in midfield: rdn 3f out: unable qck over 1f out: wknd ins fnl f* **15/2**[3]
-506 8 3 ¾ **Win Lose Draw (IRE)**[16] 2465 5-9-0 **60** (p) RayDawson(7) 7 31
(Michael Appleby) *chsd ldrs: lost pl over 1f out: bhd ins fnl f* **15/2**[3]

1m 23.06s (-3.54) **Going Correction** -0.725s/f (Hard) **8** Ran SP% **113.8**
Speed ratings (Par 101): **91,89,88,87,86 81,80,76**
CSF £21.17 CT £46.25 TOTE £2.10: £1.10, £3.30, £1.20; EX 21.20 Trifecta £87.80.
**Owner** The Horse Watchers **Bred** The C H F Partnership **Trained** Oakham, Rutland
■ Stewards' Enquiry : Lulu Stanford four-day ban; used whip above the permitted level (Jun 7-10)

**FOCUS**
A moderate handicap, although the the first and third ran up to last week's C&D form.
T/Plt: £85.10 to a £1 stake. Pool: £58,696.08. 503.28 winning units. T/Qpdt: £39.90 to a £1 stake. Pool: £3,791.10. 70.17 winning units. **Steve Payne**

2977 - (Foreign Racing) - See Raceform Interactive

# 2560 MAISONS-LAFFITTE (R-H)
Wednesday, May 24

**OFFICIAL GOING: Turf: good to soft**

## 2978a PRIX DE LA MADELEINE (CONDITIONS) (3YO FILLIES) (ROUND) (TURF) 1m 2f (S)
**2:05** 3-Y-O
**£14,059** (£5,683; £4,188; £2,692; £1,645; £1,047)

RPR
1 **Golden Legend (FR)**[212] 7586 3-8-13 0 AlexisBadel 2 90
(H-F Devin, France) **57/10**
2 shd **Golden Attitude (USA)**[25] 2168 3-8-13 0 AurelienLemaitre 1 90
(F Head, France) **6/4**[1]
3 hd **Viola Da Terra (FR)**[71] 3-8-13 0 Pierre-CharlesBoudot 10 90
(F-H Graffard, France) **13/2**
4 snk **Gipoia (FR)**[18] 3-8-13 0 VincentCheminaud 6 89
(M Delzangles, France) **11/2**[3]
5 4 **Orrery (USA)**[36] 3-8-9 0 StephanePasquier 5 77
(P Bary, France) **11/1**
6 ½ **Belleire (FR)**[17] 3-8-9 0 CristianDemuro 9 76
(M Nigge, France) **24/1**
7 5 ½ **Fuenteesteis (FR)**[25] 2168 3-9-0 0 ow1 ChristopheSoumillon 4 70
(R Avial Lopez, Spain) **48/10**[2]
8 snk **Assanilka (FR)**[39] 1796 3-8-13 0 GeraldMosse 3 69
(Harry Dunlop) *prom: rdn over 2f out: sn no ex and btn: wknd* **18/1**
9 ¾ **Nest Love (FR)**[21] 3-8-9 0 JeromeClaudic 7 64
(J-P Gallorini, France) **70/1**

2m 5.2s (2.80) **9** Ran SP% **119.9**
PARI-MUTUEL (all including 1 euro stake): WIN 6.70; PLACE 1.80, 1.30, 1.90; DF 6.60; SF 18.20.
**Owner** Mme Henri Devin **Bred** Mme H Devin **Trained** France

2979-2986a (Foreign Racing) - See Raceform Interactive

# 2545 CATTERICK (L-H)
Thursday, May 25

**OFFICIAL GOING: Good to firm (9.1)**
Wind: light behind Weather: Sunny

## 2987 EBF FILLIES' NOVICE STKS (PLUS 10 RACE) (DIV I) 5f
**1:50** (1:50) (Class 5) 2-Y-O **£2,911** (£866; £432; £216) **Stalls** Low

Form RPR
1 1 **Time Trail**[24] 2221 2-9-4 0 PaulMulrennan 1 76
(Michael Dods) *mde all: racd keenly: pushed along and edgd lft appr fnl f: strly pressed fnl 75yds: jst hld on* **7/4**[1]
5 2 hd **Lady Anjorica (IRE)**[14] 2545 2-9-0 0 TonyHamilton 5 71+
(Keith Dalgleish) *midfield on inner: rdn and hdwy over 1f out: chal strly fnl 75yds: kpt on: jst hld* **10/1**
62 3 2 ¼ **Lexington Grace (IRE)**[13] 2583 2-9-0 0 KieranO'Neill 9 63
(Richard Hannon) *chsd ldr: rdn 1/2-way: kpt on same pce* **3/1**[2]
0 4 1 ¼ **Zain Smarts (IRE)**[25] 2173 2-8-7 0 DavidEgan(7) 10 59
(David Evans) *chsd ldr on outer: rdn 1/2-way: edgd lft 1f out: one pce* **20/1**
5 hd **Moonlit Sands (IRE)** 2-9-0 0 TomEaves 8 58
(Brian Ellison) *slowly away: rn green in rr tl kpt on ins fnl f* **20/1**
6 2 **Silver Starlight** 2-9-0 0 DavidAllan 6 51
(Tim Easterby) *s.i.s: hld up: pushed along 1/2-way: nvr threatened* **18/1**
3 7 hd **Seen The Lyte (IRE)**[19] 2403 2-9-0 0 JasonHart 3 50
(John Quinn) *chsd ldr: rdn 1/2-way: wknd fnl f* **7/2**[3]
0 8 ¾ **Hope And Glory (IRE)**[16] 2502 2-9-0 0 BenCurtis 7 48
(Tom Dascombe) *chsd ldrs: rdn 1/2-way: already wknd whn hmpd jst ins fnl f* **18/1**
0 9 nk **Mops Tango**[13] 2583 2-8-7 0 RayDawson(7) 4 46
(Michael Appleby) *a outpcd in rr* **50/1**

58.54s (-1.26) **Going Correction** -0.375s/f (Firm) **9** Ran SP% **114.7**
Speed ratings (Par 90): **95,94,91,89,88 85,85,84,83**
CSF £20.13 TOTE £2.60: £1.20, £2.60, £1.20; EX 20.30 Trifecta £57.60.
**Owner** M J K Dods **Bred** Kevin Daniel Crabb **Trained** Denton, Co Durham

**FOCUS**
The watered ground (8mm Monday/Tuesday) was described as good to firm. Races 3, 4, 5 & 7 increased by 6yds. They went a good pace and the first two fought out a close finish. The third has been rated to her latest form.

## 2988 EBF FILLIES' NOVICE STKS (PLUS 10 RACE) (DIV II) 5f
**2:20** (2:21) (Class 5) 2-Y-O **£2,911** (£866; £432; £216) **Stalls** Low

Form RPR
1 **Rebel Assault (IRE)** 2-9-0 0 JasonHart 6 92+
(Mark Johnston) *mde all: pushed clr fr over 1f out: v easily* **5/2**[1]
4 2 8 **Magic Applause (IRE)**[16] 2502 2-9-0 0 BenCurtis 10 63
(George Scott) *chsd ldr: rdn 1/2-way: one pce and no ch w easy wnr fr over 1f out* **7/2**[3]
00 3 5 **Dark Hedges**[16] 2502 2-9-0 0 DuranFentiman 1 45
(Olly Williams) *hld up: rdn 1/2-way: kpt on to go remote 3rd ins fnl f* **150/1**
0 4 3 ¼ **Angel Force (IRE)**[26] 2134 2-9-0 0 TonyHamilton 5 33
(David C Griffiths) *chsd ldr: rdn 1/2-way: wknd fnl f* **6/1**
5 1 ¾ **Mable Lee (IRE)** 2-9-0 0 TomEaves 4 27
(Iain Jardine) *outpcd in rr tl sme late hdwy* **25/1**
24 6 ½ **Thrifty**[24] 2222 2-9-0 0 DavidAllan 9 25
(Tim Easterby) *midfield: stmbld 1/2-way: sn outpcd and nvr threatened* **11/4**[2]
05 7 ¾ **Kikini Bamalaam (IRE)**[26] 2154 2-8-9 0 RowanScott(5) 7 23
(Keith Dalgleish) *a outpcd in rr* **14/1**
8 14 **Cathie's Dream (USA)** 2-9-0 0 PaulMulrennan 11
(Noel Wilson) *dwlt: a in rr* **16/1**

57.91s (-1.89) **Going Correction** -0.375s/f (Firm) **8** Ran SP% **108.8**
Speed ratings (Par 90): **100,87,79,74,71 70,69,46**
CSF £10.33 TOTE £3.00: £1.50, £1.30, £8.70; EX 11.40 Trifecta £439.30.
**Owner** Mrs Christine E Budden & Partners **Bred** Christine E Budden & Partners **Trained** Middleham Moor, N Yorks
■ Orient Princess (50-1) was withdrawn not under orders. Rule 4 does not apply.

**FOCUS**
The second division was run 1.03secs quicker than the first leg and an impressive all-the-way winner. It was a card on which pace dominated.

## 2989 SUPPORT LOCAL BUSINESS (S) STKS 5f 212y
**2:55** (2:55) (Class 6) 3-4-Y-O **£2,264** (£673; £336; £168) **Stalls** Low

Form RPR
-650 1 **Searanger (USA)**[12] 2628 4-9-4 56 RowanScott(5) 2 63
(Rebecca Menzies) *dwlt: sn midfield: pushed along and hdwy 2f out: short of room in bhd ldrs over 1f out: swtchd rt 1f out: kpt on: led post* **7/1**
33-3 2 hd **Black Bubba (IRE)**[7] 2758 3-8-10 65 BenCurtis 1 56
(David Evans) *led: rdn over 2f out: kpt on: hdd nr fin* **3/1**[2]
00-0 3 2 **Carlovian**[33] 1978 4-9-5 44 (p) KieranO'Neill 4 52
(Christopher Kellett) *prom: rdn wl over 2f out: kpt on same pce* **28/1**
6-60 4 shd **Spike (IRE)**[22] 2305 4-9-5 60 (b[1]) PaulMulrennan 3 52
(Donald McCain) *chsd ldr: rdn over 2f out: kpt on same pce* **12/1**
5-02 5 2 **Whigwham**[9] 2699 3-8-5 60 PaulHanagan 5 38
(Richard Fahey) *midfield: pushed along and outpcd 1/2-way: nvr threatened* **7/2**[3]
000- 6 3 ½ **Deben**[212] 7604 4-9-2 56 DanielleMooney(7) 6 38
(John Weymes) *sn in tch: rdn over 2f out: wknd over 1f out* **25/1**
4611 7 3 ¾ **Mr Strutter (IRE)**[9] 2699 3-9-4 61 (h) JasonHart 11 28
(John Quinn) *dwlt sltly: hld up: pushed along 1/2-way: no imp: btn whn short of room and swtchd lft over 1f out* **2/1**[1]
00-0 8 3 **Where's Stewart**[21] 2349 3-8-10 35 (t[1]) AndrewMullen 9 10
(Nigel Tinkler) *s.i.s: a in rr* **125/1**
0-00 9 3 ½ **Zebedee Star**[25] 2181 3-8-5 49 (b[1]) JamesSullivan 10
(Karen Tutty) *chsd ldrs on outside: rdn over 2f out: wknd over 1f out* **22/1**

1m 11.8s (-1.80) **Going Correction** -0.375s/f (Firm)
**WFA** 3 from 4yo 9lb **9** Ran SP% **113.2**
Speed ratings (Par 101): **97,96,94,93,91 86,81,77,72**
CSF £26.77 TOTE £8.20: £2.30, £1.20, £5.70; EX 27.70 Trifecta £661.70.Carlovian was sold to Mr M T Walford for £7000.
**Owner** ICM Racing & John Dance **Bred** Phoenix Rising Farms **Trained** Mordon, Durham

**FOCUS**
Race distance increased by 6yds. A modest seller. The third is among those who set the level.

## 2990 RDA RICHMOND AND CATTERICK GROUP H'CAP 5f 212y
**3:30** (3:30) (Class 5) (0-70,72) 4-Y-O+ **£2,911** (£866; £432; £216) **Stalls** Low

Form RPR
3202 1 **Meshardal (GER)**[14] 2550 7-9-7 **65** (p) JamesSullivan 4 72
(Ruth Carr) *midfield: pushed along and hdwy over 1f out: rdn to ld 110yds out: kpt on* **3/1**[1]
0003 2 ½ **Extrasolar**[14] 2550 7-10-0 **72** PhillipMakin 1 77
(Geoffrey Harker) *dwlt: sn trckd ldrs on inner: pushed along over 1f out: rdn and ev ch ins fnl f: kpt on* **7/2**[2]
30 3 hd **Lackaday**[33] 1978 5-9-0 **58** (p) PaulHanagan 2 62
(Noel Wilson) *led: rdn over 2f out: hdd 110yds out: one pce: lost 2nd post* **8/1**
33-0 4 1 ¾ **Bold Spirit**[43] 1720 6-8-11 **60** (t) PhilDennis(5) 5 59
(Declan Carroll) *chsd ldrs: rdn over 2f out: one pce* **11/1**
0004 5 6 **Secret Missile**[6] 2800 7-10-0 **72** DavidAllan 6 52
(David C Griffiths) *midfield: rdn and outpcd over 2f out: nvr threatened* **13/2**
1502 6 1 ¼ **Top Of The Bank**[18] 2424 4-10-0 **72** (p) TonyHamilton 3 48
(Kristin Stubbs) *prom: rdn over 2f out: wknd fnl f* **10/1**
1-01 7 1 ¾ **Tricky Dicky**[17] 2469 4-10-0 **72** DuranFentiman 7 42
(Olly Williams) *hld up: rdn 1/2-way: sn wknd* **9/2**[3]
1205 8 8 **Windforpower (IRE)**[14] 2550 7-9-4 **62** (p) BenCurtis 9 6
(Tracy Waggott) *a in rr* **20/1**

1m 11.2s (-2.40) **Going Correction** -0.375s/f (Firm) **8** Ran SP% **112.0**
Speed ratings (Par 103): **101,100,100,97,89 88,85,75**
CSF £12.98 CT £72.79 TOTE £3.80: £1.50, £1.90, £2.30; EX 14.90 Trifecta £90.60.
**Owner** The Hollinbridge Partnership & Ruth Carr **Bred** Gestut Hofgut Heymann **Trained** Huby, N Yorks

**FOCUS**
Race distance increased by 6yds. A fair handicap and solid form for the level.

## 2991 LESLIE PETCH H'CAP (2017 CATTERICK TWELVE FURLONG SERIES QUALIFIER) 1m 4f 13y
**4:05** (4:06) (Class 5) (0-70,70) 3-Y-O **£3,234** (£962; £481; £240) **Stalls** Low

Form RPR
0241 **1** **La Vie En Rose**[31] 2027 3-9-2 **65**.................................... FrannyNorton 2 73+
(Mark Johnston) *trckd ldrs: pushed along over 2f out: led ins fnl f: kpt on wl pushed out* **3/1**[2]
-552 **2** 2 1/4 **Breakwater Bay (IRE)**[9] 2705 3-8-11 **60**.............................. DavidAllan 5 64
(Tim Easterby) *led: rdn over 2f out: hdd ins fnl f: one pce* **7/2**[3]
40-6 **3** 3 3/4 **Zamadance**[33] 1968 3-9-0 **63**.......................................... AntonioFresu 6 61
(Ed Dunlop) *hld up in midfield: racd quite keenly: pushed along over 2f out: rdn over 1f out: kpt on to go modest 3rd nr fin* **12/1**
30-6 **4** 3/4 **Kuraka**[20] 2376 3-9-4 **70**............................................ JordanVaughan(3) 9 67
(K R Burke) *prom: rdn over 2f out: wknd ins fnl f: lost 3rd nr fin* **22/1**
650- **5** 2 1/2 **Veiled Secret (IRE)**[201] 7812 3-9-5 **68**............................... LukeMorris 8 61
(Sir Mark Prescott Bt) *dwlt: hld up: pushed along 8f out: midfield on outside 6f out: drvn over 2f out: sn no imp* **9/4**[1]
006 **6** 1 3/4 **Navajo Grey (IRE)**[22] 2307 3-8-8 **57**.............................. AndrewMullen 1 47
(Michael Appleby) *s.i.s: hld up: hdwy into midfield 6f out: rdn over 2f out: wknd ins fnl f* **16/1**
6061 **7** 2 1/4 **Log Off (IRE)**[30] 2060 3-8-12 **61**.................................... KieranO'Neill 7 47
(David Evans) *hld up: rdn over 2f out: nvr threatened* **14/1**
0-50 **8** 4 1/2 **Steel Helmet (IRE)**[3] 2903 3-8-13 **62**..............................(v[1]) BenCurtis 4 41
(Brian Ellison) *trckd ldrs: rdn over 2f out: wknd over 1f out* **9/1**
2m 34.64s (-1.26) **Going Correction** -0.375s/f (Firm) **8** Ran SP% **112.6**
Speed ratings (Par 99): **99,97,95,94,92 91,90,87**
CSF £13.49 CT £105.65 TOTE £4.10: £1.40, £1.20, £3.40; EX 13.10 Trifecta £65.20.
**Owner** Miss K Rausing **Bred** Miss K Rausing **Trained** Middleham Moor, N Yorks

**FOCUS**
Race distance increased by 6yds. A fair handicap won in good style by a filly on the up.

## 2992 RACING UK PROFITS RETURNED TO RACING H'CAP 5f
**4:40** (4:40) (Class 4) (0-85,85) 3-Y-O **£6,469** (£1,925; £962; £481) **Stalls** Low

Form RPR
5162 **1** **Arzaak (IRE)**[23] 2271 3-9-4 **82**...........................................(b) DavidAllan 7 87
(Chris Dwyer) *chsd ldr towards outer: rdn over 2f out: kpt on: led towards fin* **9/2**[2]
3245 **2** *nk* **Merry Banter**[18] 2425 3-9-6 **84**.......................................... PaulMulrennan 3 88
(Paul Midgley) *led: rdn 2f out: kpt on but hdd towards fin* **12/1**
544- **3** 1 3/4 **The Nazca Lines (IRE)**[230] 7120 3-8-12 **76**........................ JasonHart 2 74
(John Quinn) *chsd ldr: rdn and outpcd 1/2-way: kpt on fnl f: wnt 3rd towards fin* **11/1**
0-04 **4** 1/2 **Tahoo (IRE)**[33] 1975 3-9-6 **84**............................................. BenCurtis 5 80
(K R Burke) *chsd ldr: rdn 1/2-way: kpt on same pce* **11/1**
3131 **5** 1/2 **Juan Horsepower**[24] 2215 3-9-6 **84**...............................(p) KieranO'Neill 4 78
(Richard Hannon) *outpcd in rr tl kpt on fnl f: nrst fin* **5/1**[3]
2-00 **6** *nk* **Blue Suede (IRE)**[33] 1975 3-8-12 **76**................................ PaulHanagan 6 69
(Richard Fahey) *chsd ldr: rdn 1/2-way: no ex ins fnl f* **11/2**
-126 **7** *nk* **Scuzeme**[33] 1975 3-9-2 **80**................................................ PhillipMakin 8 72
(David Barron) *dwlt: hld up: pushed along 1/2-way: rdn over 1f out: no imp* **8/1**
-244 **8** *nk* **Poet's Society**[14] 2557 3-9-7 **85**........................................ FrannyNorton 1 76+
(Mark Johnston) *hld up in tch: pushed along 1/2-way: sme hdwy ent fnl f: n.m.r fnl 150yds and nvr able to chal* **3/1**[1]
57.49s (-2.31) **Going Correction** -0.375s/f (Firm) **8** Ran SP% **110.7**
Speed ratings (Par 101): **103,102,99,98,98 97,97,96**
CSF £52.18 CT £533.45 TOTE £5.60: £1.60, £2.70, £3.60; EX 53.80 Trifecta £733.20.
**Owner** M M Foulger **Bred** Gerard Kerin **Trained** Newmarket, Suffolk

**FOCUS**
A useful sprint and they went flat out from the off. A length pb from the winner.

## 2993 HAPPY 80TH BIRTHDAY MICHAEL RYAN RATING RELATED MAIDEN STKS 7f 6y
**5:15** (5:15) (Class 6) 3-Y-O+ **£2,264** (£673; £336; £168) **Stalls** Low

Form RPR
4204 **1** **Dusky Maid (IRE)**[55] 1471 3-9-0 65.................................... JoeDoyle 2 66
(James Given) *prom: rdn over 2f out: led 75yds out: kpt on* **8/1**
0-00 **2** 1 1/4 **Greenview Paradise (IRE)**[24] 2228 3-9-0 58............... TonyHamilton 5 63
(Richard Fahey) *prom: rdn over 2f out: kpt on* **40/1**
32-0 **3** 1/2 **Chickenfortea (IRE)**[38] 1835 3-9-0 60............................. JasonHart 8 61
(Eric Alston) *led: rdn over 2f out: hdd 75yds out: no ex* **14/1**
-004 **4** 1 1/4 **Cupid's Arrow (IRE)**[12] 2630 3-9-0 62........................... JamesSullivan 7 58+
(Ruth Carr) *midfield: pushed along 2f out: rdn and kpt on fnl f* **7/2**[1]
**5** 1/2 **Eadaoins Pet (IRE)**[255] 6429 4-9-4 63..................... DMSimmonson(7) 1 61
(John James Feane, Ire) *stmbld sltly s: in tch on inner: rdn 2f out: one pce* **4/1**[2]
002- **6** 3/4 **Halinka (IRE)**[183] 8072 3-9-0 64.................................... PaulMulrennan 10 55+
(Roger Varian) *dwlt: hld up in rr: stl plenty to do whn angled to outer over 1f out: rdn and kpt on fnl f: nrst fin* **13/2**[3]
43-0 **7** 2 **Bearag**[24] 2228 3-8-7 63.............................................. PatrickVaughan(7) 6 49
(David O'Meara) *trckd ldrs: rdn over 2f out: wknd ins fnl f* **22/1**
6-45 **8** 1 1/2 **Langham**[100] 729 4-9-4 65........................................(p[1]) RayDawson(7) 13 49
(Michael Appleby) *midfield: rdn over 2f out: nvr threatened* **12/1**
0445 **9** 3/4 **Major Cornwallis (IRE)**[24] 2228 3-9-0 65...................... PaulHanagan 12 43+
(Richard Fahey) *hld up in midfield: rdn over 2f out: nvr threatened* **13/2**[3]
336- **10** 1 1/4 **Mayleen (IRE)**[234] 7003 3-9-0 64...................................... JoeyHaynes 14 40+
(Ann Duffield) *hld up on outer: nvr threatened* **33/1**
00-0 **11** 1/2 **Decadent Times (IRE)**[35] 1913 3-9-0 61............................. PhillipMakin 9 38+
(Marjorie Fife) *hld up in midfield: rdn over 2f out: wknd* **9/1**
000- **12** 8 **Daring Knight**[33] 6510 4-9-11 64..................................(b) PaddyAspell 3 21+
(Clare Ellam) *dwlt: a in rr* **125/1**
1m 25.66s (-1.34) **Going Correction** -0.375s/f (Firm)
**WFA** 3 from 4yo 11lb **12** Ran SP% **114.9**
Speed ratings (Par 101): **92,90,90,88,88 87,84,83,82,80 80,71**
CSF £294.73 TOTE £8.80: £2.90, £4.80, £4.30; EX 212.50 Trifecta £4086.70.
**Owner** The Cool Silk Partnership **Bred** L O'Donovan **Trained** Willoughton, Lincs

**FOCUS**
Race distance increased by 6yds. An ordinary maiden and it paid to race handily, the first three home being prominent throughout.

## 2994 RACING AGAIN 2ND JUNE APPRENTICE H'CAP 5f
**5:45** (5:45) (Class 6) (0-55,54) 4-Y-O+ **£2,264** (£673; £336; £168) **Stalls** Low

Form RPR
-362 **1** **Kodimoor (IRE)**[17] 2472 4-9-3 **50**...........................(bt) RobJFitzpatrick 2 62
(Christopher Kellett) *chsd ldrs: rdn to ld 2f out: kpt on wl* **7/1**
-613 **2** 2 3/4 **Sir Geoffrey (IRE)**[17] 2472 11-9-1 **48**...........................(b) PaddyPilley 11 50
(Scott Dixon) *led: rdn whn hdd 2f out: kpt on same pce* **8/1**
3303 **3** 3/4 **Loumarin (IRE)**[13] 2589 5-9-0 **53**..............................(p) RayDawson(6) 1 52
(Michael Appleby) *prom: rdn and outpcd 1/2-way: kpt on fnl f* **11/4**[1]
0060 **4** *shd* **Under Approval**[12] 2628 6-8-9 **45**.............................(p) GemmaTutty(3) 10 44
(Karen Tutty) *s.i.s: hld up: rdn and sme hdwy over 1f out: kpt on* **20/1**
000- **5** 1 3/4 **Hit The Lights (IRE)**[170] 8242 7-9-7 **54**.....................(p) RowanScott 8 47
(Marjorie Fife) *hld up: rdn 1/2-way: nvr threatened* **5/1**[2]
-000 **6** 1/2 **Minty Jones**[29] 2076 8-8-12 **45**.....................................(v) LuluStanford 4 36
(Michael Mullineaux) *midfield: rdn 1/2-way: nvr threatened* **16/1**
0-35 **7** 3/4 **Thornaby Princess**[12] 2628 6-9-2 **49**.........................(p) LewisEdmunds 6 37
(Colin Teague) *hld up: rdn 1/2-way: nvr threatened* **11/2**[3]
4544 **8** 3/4 **Chandresh**[30] 2069 4-8-9 **45**..................................(b) CallumRodriguez(3) 3 31
(Robert Cowell) *midfield: rdn 1/2-way: wknd over 1f out* **6/1**
0-03 **9** 2 1/2 **On The High Tops (IRE)**[17] 2453 9-8-7 **45**.........(p) ConnorMurtagh(5) 7 22
(Colin Teague) *chsd ldrs: rdn 1/2-way: wknd over 1f out* **50/1**
30-0 **10** 2 1/4 **Caymus**[38] 1828 4-8-10 **46**..........................................(t) PatrickVaughan(3) 9 14
(Tracy Waggott) *s.i.s: a in rr* **25/1**
58.23s (-1.57) **Going Correction** -0.375s/f (Firm) **10** Ran SP% **113.1**
Speed ratings (Par 101): **97,92,91,91,88 87,86,85,81,77**
CSF £58.31 CT £194.01 TOTE £7.70: £2.50, £2.30, £1.60; EX 44.00 Trifecta £168.10.
**Owner** Blythe Stables Llp **Bred** Tally-Ho Stud **Trained** Lathom, Lancs

**FOCUS**
A moderate handicap and again nothing could get competitive from off the pace. A clear step up on his recent AW form by the winner.
T/Plt: £63.30 to a £1 stake. Pool: £58,865.67 - 678.63 winning units. T/Qpdt: £27.30 to a £1 stake. Pool: £3,709.44 - 100.54 winning units. **Andrew Sheret**

# [2515]CHELMSFORD (A.W) (L-H)
Thursday, May 25

**OFFICIAL GOING: Polytrack: standard**
Wind: virtually nil Weather: sunny and warm

## 2995 TOTEPLACEPOT AT BETFRED.COM H'CAP 5f (P)
**5:50** (5:52) (Class 6) (0-60,62) 4-Y-O+ **£3,234** (£962; £481; £240) **Stalls** Low

Form RPR
4513 **1** **Mighty Zip (USA)**[4] 2858 5-8-11 **57**...............................(p) JordanUys(7) 5 66
(Lisa Williamson) *sn led and mde rest: rdn over 1f out: kpt on wl: rdn over 1f out: kpt on wl ins fnl f* **2/1**[1]
6020 **2** 3/4 **Doctor Parkes**[33] 1965 11-9-0 **60**.................................... MillyNaseb(7) 2 66
(Stuart Williams) *broke wl: sn restrained to chse wnr: effrt over 1f out: sn drvn: swtchd rt ins fnl f: styd on wl towards fin* **11/4**[2]
1365 **3** 3/4 **Hot Stuff**[31] 2025 4-9-3 **56**..........................................(p[1]) DavidProbert 3 60
(Tony Carroll) *hld up in tch in 5th: effrt and hdwy over 1f out: 4th and kpt on same pce ins fnl f* **5/1**
3333 **4** 1/2 **Frank The Barber (IRE)**[24] 2216 5-9-7 **60**.................(t) RobertWinston 4 62
(Steph Hollinshead) *hld up in tch in midfield: effrt over 1f out: styd on same pce and no imp ins fnl f* **7/2**[3]
6263 **5** 3 1/4 **Mambo Spirit (IRE)**[25] 2178 13-9-9 **62**............................. MartinLane 8 52
(Tony Newcombe) *hld up in rr: shkn up over 1f out: no imp: n.d* **12/1**
0006 **6** 2 1/2 **Barnsdale**[20] 2370 4-8-0 **46** oh1............................ MeganEllingworth(7) 7 27
(John Holt) *chsd ldrs on outer: lost pl u.p wl over 1f out: bhd ins fnl f* **25/1**
1m 0.74s (0.54) **Going Correction** -0.075s/f (Stan) **6** Ran SP% **110.4**
Speed ratings (Par 101): **92,90,89,88,83 79**
CSF £7.46 CT £20.63 TOTE £2.20: £1.50, £2.40; EX 8.80 Trifecta £31.20.
**Owner** Heath House Racing **Bred** Dr Catherine Wills **Trained** Saighton, Cheshire
■ Rat Catcher (25-1) was withdrawn not under orders. Rule 4 does not apply.

**FOCUS**
A straightforward success for the favourite, who got an uncontested lead. Straightforward form.

## 2996 TOTEEXACTA AT BETFRED.COM H'CAP 1m (P)
**6:20** (6:24) (Class 5) (0-70,71) 4-Y-O+ **£5,175** (£1,540; £769; £384) **Stalls** Low

Form RPR
2304 **1** **Tee It Up Tommo (IRE)**[28] 2116 8-9-5 **71**...................... HollieDoyle(3) 3 79
(Daniel Steele) *dwlt: hld up in last pair: hdwy and squeezed through over 1f out: chsd clr wnr and hung lft 1f out: styd on wl to ld towards fin* **5/1**[3]
0314 **2** 3/4 **Andalusite**[15] 2511 4-8-7 **56**....................................(v) RoystonFfrench 1 62
(John Gallagher) *led: 5 l clr 1/2-way: rdn over 1f out: hdd towards fin* **12/1**
0155 **3** 2 1/2 **Foie Gras**[17] 2464 7-9-7 **70**.............................................(p) TrevorWhelan 7 71
(Chris Dwyer) *in tch in midfield early: niggled along and dropped towards rr: effrt on outer over 1f out: styd on strly ins fnl f: snatched 3rd on post: nvr trbld ldrs* **14/1**
63-0 **4** *nse* **Captain Peaky**[26] 2140 4-8-8 **57**...................................... JoeFanning 10 57
(Patrick Holmes) *hld up in midfield: clsd whn nt clr run and swtchd rt over 1f out: squeezed for room 1f out: wnt 3rd and kpt on ins fnl f: nvr getting to ldrs and lost 3rd on post* **25/1**
5631 **5** 1/2 **Hold Firm**[17] 2465 5-8-13 **62**.......................................... StevieDonohoe 6 61
(Mark H Tompkins) *prom in chsng gp: effrt u.p ent fnl 2f: keeping on but nt getting on terms w wnr whn squeezed for room jst ins fnl f: kpt on fnl 100yds: nvr enough pce to chal* **10/1**
1214 **6** 3 1/4 **Scribner Creek (IRE)**[23] 2267 4-9-6 **69**......................... RobertWinston 2 61
(Daniel Mark Loughnane) *hld up in tch towards rr on inner: nt clr run and forced to switch rt over 1f out: nvr any ch and kpt on same pce ins fnl f* **2/1**[1]
0014 **7** 1 **Samphire Coast**[8] 2731 4-8-13 **62**.....................................(v) KierenFox 5 51
(Derek Shaw) *fly j. as stalls opened and slowly away: t.k.h: hld up in rr on outer: hdwy to go prom in chsng gp over 2f out: no imp u.p over 1f out: wknd ins fnl f* **11/4**[2]
0406 **8** 1 1/4 **Shearian**[17] 2466 7-9-8 **71**............................................. TomEaves 8 58
(Declan Carroll) *chsd clr ldr tl unable qck u.p over 1f out: wknd ins fnl f* **25/1**
61-4 **9** 1 1/2 **Russian Ranger (IRE)**[23] 2276 4-9-0 **63**......................(p) DavidProbert 9 46
(Jonathan Portman) *prom in chsng gp: effrt over 2f out: chsd clr wnr over 1f out: no imp and lost 2nd 1f out: losing pl whn squeezed out sn after: sn wknd* **12/1**

44-5 **10** *5* **Brasted (IRE)**[20] 2365 5-8-12 **68**..............................(t) JoshuaBryan(7) 11 40
(Lee Carter) *in tch in midfield on outer: lost pl u.p over 2f out: bhd fnl f* **20/1**

1m 39.44s (-0.46) **Going Correction** -0.075s/f (Stan) **10** Ran SP% **120.3**
Speed ratings (Par 103): **99,98,95,95,95 91,90,89,88,83**
CSF £63.18 CT £807.03 TOTE £5.90: £2.10, £4.50, £3.30; EX 86.30 Trifecta £1447.50.
**Owner** Vectis Racing **Bred** Oghill House Stud **Trained** Henfield, W Sussex

**FOCUS**
A modest handicap run at a good pace. The first two came from the rear and the runner-up is the best guide.

## 2997 TOTEQUADPOT AT BETFRED.COM MAIDEN STKS 1m (P)
**6:55** (6:58) (Class 4) 3-Y-O+ **£8,086** (£2,406; £1,202; £601) **Stalls** Low

Form RPR

4 **1** **Archetype (FR)**[33] 1962 3-9-2 0.......................................... MartinLane 10 79
(Simon Crisford) *chsd ldrs: effrt over 2f out: drvn and stdy on to chse ldr 150yds out: kpt on wl u.p to ld last stride* **9/2**[3]

2-2 **2** *shd* **Cool Team (IRE)**[24] 2231 3-9-2 0..........................................(t) JoeFanning 3 78
(Hugo Palmer) *led: rdn and forged ahd over 1f out: kpt on u.p ins fnl f: hdd last stride* **3/1**[2]

0 **3** *nk* **Najashee (IRE)**[33] 1961 3-9-2 0.......................................... DaneO'Neill 8 77+
(Owen Burrows) *s.i.s: hld up: hdwy into midfield after 2f: rdn and effrt in 6th over 2f out: c wd st: rn green but steadily clsd tl styd on strly wl ins fnl f: wnt 3rd last stride: nvr quite getting to ldrs* **8/1**

0 **4** *shd* **Star Gypsy (FR)**[10] 2689 3-8-11 0.............................. GeorgeWood(5) 9 77+
(Luca Cumani) *in tch in 5th: effrt ent fnl 2f: styd on wl ins fnl f: wnt 3rd towards fin: kpt on but nvr quite getting to ldrs: lost 3rd last stride* **50/1**

3 **5** *1 1/4* **Noble Conquest (FR)**[17] 2475 3-9-2 0.......................................... OisinMurphy 7 74
(Sir Michael Stoute) *chsd ldr: rdn over 1f out: unable qck u.p and lost 2nd 150yds out: kpt on same pce after and lost 2 pls towards fin* **11/10**[1]

0-3 **6** *8* **Falak (IRE)**[26] 2167 4-10-0 0.......................................... DanielMuscutt 13 59
(Roger Varian) *dropped in bhd after s: hld up in last trio: hdwy into midfield and swtchd rt over 1f out: nvr threatened ldrs but kpt on ins fnl f* **16/1**

0-4 **7** *1 1/2* **Aware (IRE)**[34] 1939 3-8-13 0.............................. CallumShepherd(3) 12 52
(Charles Hills) *stdd s: hld up in rr: sme hdwy but nt on terms w ldrs whn swtchd rt over 1f out: wl hld but kpt on ins fnl f* **33/1**

0-4 **8** *1* **Arcadian Sea (IRE)**[15] 2521 3-8-9 0.............................. AarronMiller(7) 14 50
(William Jarvis) *hld up in midfield on outer: effrt and no imp over 1f out: wl hld whn hung lft 1f out* **100/1**

00 **9** *1/2* **Red Master (IRE)**[15] 2521 3-9-2 0.......................................... TomEaves 5 49
(Ed Dunlop) *chsd ldrs: rdn and outpcd over 2f out: wl hld and plugged on same pce fr over 1f out* **100/1**

6 **10** *3/4* **Toronto Sound**[15] 2521 3-9-2 0.......................................... RyanPowell 6 47
(Sir Mark Prescott Bt) *midfield: rdn and dropped towards rr over 2f out: no ch over 1f out* **50/1**

00 **11** *1 1/2* **Our Kim (IRE)**[31] 2033 3-8-9 0.......................................... DavidEgan(7) 1 44
(Mohamed Moubarak) *t.k.h: hld up in tch in midfield: no hdwy u.p over 1f out: wl btn whn nt clr run ins fnl f* **100/1**

00 **12** *2 1/4* **King Kevin**[10] 2689 3-8-13 0.......................................... NathanAlison(3) 4 39
(Ed Dunlop) *t.k.h: hld up in tch in midfield: pushed along and outpcd over 2f out: wl btn over 1f out* **100/1**

03- **13** *5* **Glassalt**[156] 8464 3-8-11 0.......................................... DavidProbert 11 22
(Michael Bell) *s.i.s: a bhd* **25/1**

1m 39.24s (-0.66) **Going Correction** -0.075s/f (Stan)
**WFA** 3 from 4yo 12lb **13** Ran SP% **122.5**
Speed ratings (Par 105): **100,99,99,99,98 90,88,87,87,86 85,82,77**
CSF £18.43 TOTE £7.30: £2.20, £1.20, £2.80; EX 23.40 Trifecta £110.90.
**Owner** Highclere Thoroughbred Racing-Wordsworth **Bred** E A R L Ecurie Du Grand Chene Haras **Trained** Newmarket, Suffolk

**FOCUS**
A fair maiden. The first five finished well clear of the rest and the form is rated around the runner-up.

## 2998 TOTETRIFECTA AT BETFRED.COM H'CAP 1m 2f (P)
**7:25** (7:27) (Class 4) (0-80,79) 3-Y-O **£8,086** (£2,406; £1,202; £601) **Stalls** Low

Form RPR

051- **1** **Melting Dew**[191] 7963 3-9-4 **76**.......................................... DavidProbert 2 84+
(Sir Michael Stoute) *in tch in midfield: effrt to chse ldrs and swtchd rt 1f out: edgd lft u.p but styd on wl to ld last stride* **6/1**[3]

54-1 **2** *shd* **Alfarris (FR)**[23] 2260 3-9-6 **78**.......................................... DaneO'Neill 1 85+
(William Haggas) *chsd ldr for 2f: styd chsng ldrs: effrt over 1f out: led under jst ins fnl f: kpt on u.p ins fnl f: hdd last stride* **1/1**[1]

34-0 **3** *3* **Galactic Prince**[25] 2174 3-9-3 **75**.......................................... OisinMurphy 4 76
(Andrew Balding) *led: rdn over 1f out: hdd jst ins fnl f: no ex and outpcd fnl 100yds* **9/2**[2]

13-5 **4** *1* **Pirate Look (IRE)**[27] 2118 3-9-6 **78**.......................................... DanielMuscutt 5 77
(Marco Botti) *t.k.h: hld up wl in tch in midfield: effrt over 1f out: 4th and no imp 1f out: kpt on same pce ins fnl f* **9/2**[2]

6525 **5** *2 1/4* **Gee Sixty Six**[23] 2264 3-8-9 **67**.......................................... StevieDonohoe 3 62
(Mark H Tompkins) *stdd and dropped in bhd after s: hld up on rr: effrt over 1f out: kpt on u.p ins fnl f: nvr trbld ldrs* **25/1**

-100 **6** *3/4* **Glorious Power (IRE)**[13] 2588 3-9-2 **77**................. CallumShepherd(3) 8 70
(Charles Hills) *stdd and dropped in bhd after s: hld up in last pair: effrt over 1f out: sn drvn and no imp fnl f* **25/1**

16 **7** *4* **Villette (IRE)**[43] 1725 3-9-7 **79**.......................................... RobertWinston 7 64
(Dean Ivory) *t.k.h: chsd ldrs 8f out tl over 1f out: sn outpcd u.p: wknd ins fnl f* **25/1**

43-0 **8** *nk* **Haulani (USA)**[25] 2174 3-9-7 **79**..........................................(t[1]) TomEaves 6 63
(Philip Hide) *dropped in sn after s: hld up in midfield: rdn over 2f out: lost pl over 1f out: bhd ins fnl f* **14/1**

2m 6.97s (-1.63) **Going Correction** -0.075s/f (Stan) **8** Ran SP% **118.9**
Speed ratings (Par 101): **103,102,100,99,97 97,94,93**
CSF £12.74 CT £28.62 TOTE £6.40: £1.90, £1.10, £1.80; EX 13.80 Trifecta £41.10.
**Owner** K Abdullah **Bred** Juddmonte Farms Ltd **Trained** Newmarket, Suffolk

**FOCUS**
An interesting contest, and the first two, both handicap debutants, look capable of better.

## 2999 TOTEWIN AT BETFRED.COM H'CAP 1m 2f (P)
**8:00** (8:04) (Class 2) (0-105,105) 4-Y-O+**£22,641** (£6,737; £3,367; £1,683) **Stalls** Low

Form RPR

1660 **1** **Fanciful Angel (IRE)**[33] 1960 5-9-7 **105**.......................................... DanielMuscutt 5 112+
(Marco Botti) *restless in stalls: s.i.s: t.k.h: hld up in rr: stuck bhd a wall of horses over 2f out: hdwy to chse ldrs ent fnl f: r.o wl u.p to ld cl home* **9/2**[2]

3-61 **2** *hd* **Noble Gift**[23] 2261 7-8-11 **98**.......................................... CallumShepherd(3) 4 104
(William Knight) *rousted along early to ld over 8f out: rdn over 1f out: hrd pressed and kpt on wl u.p ins fnl f: hdd cl home* **8/1**

2136 **3** *nk* **Qaffaal (USA)**[42] 1757 6-8-4 **91**.......................................... NathanEvans(3) 3 96
(Michael Easterby) *hld up in tch in midfield: swtchd rt and hdwy over 1f out: drvn to chal 1f out: kpt on wl but unable qck towards fin* **9/2**[2]

00-4 **4** *4* **Dark Red (IRE)**[5] 2828 5-8-12 **96**.......................................... PatCosgrave 10 93
(Ed Dunlop) *hld up in tch in midfield: effrt over 1f out: hung lft 1f out: no threat to ldng trio after: kpt on under hands and heels riding ins fnl f to go 4th cl home* **10/3**[1]

140- **5** *nk* **Capricious Cantor (IRE)**[343] 3297 4-9-0 **98**.......................................... LukeMorris 1 95
(Ed Dunlop) *chsd ldrs: effrt to go 2nd 2f out tl over 1f out: 4th and outpcd 1f out: wknd ins fnl f: lost 4th cl home* **25/1**

2003 **6** *1 1/4* **Kyllachy Gala**[26] 2141 4-9-1 **104**.......................................... GeorgeWood(5) 6 98+
(Marco Botti) *hld up in midfield: hmpd and dropped towards rr after 2f: clsd but nt clr run over 1f out: rdn and hdwy 1f out: swtchd lft ins fnl f: kpt on: no threat to ldrs* **12/1**

60 **7** *nk* **Repercussion**[8] 2735 4-8-11 **95**..........................................(h) StevieDonohoe 2 89
(Charlie Fellowes) *hld up in tch in midfield: effrt on inner over 1f out: styd on same pce and no imp u.p fnl f* **7/1**[3]

5004 **8** *7* **Abareeq**[19] 2396 4-9-3 **101**.......................................... JoeFanning 12 81
(Mark Johnston) *t.k.h: chsd ldrs: unable qck u.p over 1f out: wknd fnl f* **16/1**

341- **9** *nk* **What About Carlo (FR)**[162] 7546 6-9-2 **100**.......................................... CharlesBishop 9 79
(Eve Johnson Houghton) *in tch in midfield on outer: rdn ent fnl 2f: outpcd and btn over 1f out: wknd ins fnl f* **14/1**

3300 **10** *hd* **Van Huysen (IRE)**[29] 2086 5-7-9 **86** oh1.......................................... DavidEgan(7) 7 65
(Dominic Ffrench Davis) *t.k.h gng to post: hld up in last trio: wknd over 1f out* **25/1**

0-30 **11** *3 3/4* **Bancnuanaheireann (IRE)**[19] 2396 10-8-10 **97**.. AlistairRawlinson(3) 8 68
(Michael Appleby) *niggled along in last pair: no hdwy u.p over 1f out: sn wknd* **20/1**

-155 **12** *1/2* **Hamelin (IRE)**[41] 1779 7-9-0 **98**.......................................... OisinMurphy 11 68
(George Scott) *led for 2f: chsd ldr tl 2f out: losing pl whn impeded over 1f out: sn wknd* **14/1**

2m 4.24s (-4.36) **Going Correction** -0.075s/f (Stan) **12** Ran SP% **122.4**
Speed ratings (Par 109): **114,113,113,110,110 109,108,103,103,102 99,99**
CSF £40.83 CT £173.45 TOTE £6.50: £3.10, £2.10, £2.50; EX 51.50 Trifecta £236.70.
**Owner** Touch Gold Racing (Fanciful) **Bred** Berjis Desai **Trained** Newmarket, Suffolk

**FOCUS**
A good handicap, but the pace wasn't strong and it turned into a relative test of speed in the straight. The winner confirmed his Dubai form.

## 3000 TOTEPLACE AT BETFRED.COM H'CAP 7f (P)
**8:30** (8:35) (Class 5) (0-75,81) 3-Y-O **£5,175** (£1,540; £769; £384) **Stalls** Low

Form RPR

26-6 **1** **Etikaal**[30] 2072 3-9-7 **75**..........................................(p[1]) DaneO'Neill 1 85
(Simon Crisford) *rousted along early: hdwy to ld after 1f: mde rest: rdn over 1f out: styd on wl and a in command ins fnl f: rdn out* **8/1**

03-2 **2** *2 1/4* **Falbon**[23] 2260 3-9-3 **76**.......................................... GeorgeWood(5) 3 80
(Marco Botti) *chsd ldrs: effrt u.p to chse wnr over 1f out: clr 2nd but kpt on same pce ins fnl f* **9/2**[3]

33-2 **3** *3* **Glendun (USA)**[30] 2071 3-9-7 **75**.......................................... RyanTate 5 71
(James Eustace) *hld up in midfield: effrt over 1f out: styd on ins fnl f to go 3rd fnl 75yds: no threat to ldng pair* **4/1**[2]

445- **4** *3/4* **Swag (IRE)**[233] 7033 3-9-1 **72**..........................................(t) NathanEvans(3) 8 66
(Michael Easterby) *hld up in tch in last pair: effrt on inner over 1f out: kpt on ins fnl f to go 4th towards fin: no threat to ldrs* **12/1**

2411 **5** *1/2* **Sans Souci Bay**[7] 2758 3-9-10 **81** 6ex..........................................(b) HollieDoyle(3) 4 74
(Richard Hannon) *in tch in midfield: effrt over 1f out: drifted rt and no imp over 1f out: kpt on same pce ins fnl f* **7/2**[1]

00-0 **6** *1/2* **Farleigh Mac**[22] 2293 3-9-7 **75**..........................................(h) OisinMurphy 2 66
(Andrew Balding) *t.k.h: led for 1f: chsd ldr: rdn and lost 2nd over 1f out: 3rd and outpcd whn edgd rt 1f: wknd ins fnl f* **7/1**

3-13 **7** *2 3/4* **Gala Celebration (IRE)**[50] 1554 3-9-1 **69**.......................................... JoeFanning 9 53
(John Gallagher) *t.k.h: chsd ldng trio: effrt over 1f out: sn btn and wknd fnl f* **6/1**

110- **8** *8* **Iftitah (IRE)**[208] 7688 3-8-13 **67**..........................................(t) StevieDonohoe 7 29
(George Peckham) *hld up in last pair: no hdwy over 1f out: bhd whn eased wl ins fnl f* **25/1**

05-3 **9** *2* **Miss Icon**[22] 2293 3-9-3 **71**.......................................... DavidProbert 6 28
(Patrick Chamings) *rrd as stalls opened and short of room sn after s: hld up in midfield: rdn over 1f out: sn dropped to rr: bhd and eased wl ins fnl f* **16/1**

1m 25.07s (-2.13) **Going Correction** -0.075s/f (Stan) **9** Ran SP% **115.7**
Speed ratings (Par 99): **109,106,103,102,101 101,97,88,86**
CSF £43.97 CT £168.19 TOTE £9.60: £2.50, £1.90, £1.50; EX 34.80 Trifecta £312.90.
**Owner** Hamdan Al Maktoum **Bred** Shadwell Estate Company Limited **Trained** Newmarket, Suffolk

**FOCUS**
The pace was controlled by the winner and few got involved. The third could prove the best guide.

## 3001 LADIES DAY 22ND JUNE WITH BLUE H'CAP 7f (P)
**9:00** (9:04) (Class 6) (0-55,55) 4-Y-O+ **£3,234** (£962; £481; £240) **Stalls** Low

Form RPR

00-0 **1** **Suzi Icon**[10] 2679 5-8-12 **46** oh1..........................................(p) LiamJones 7 52
(Michael Appleby) *in tch in midfield: hdwy u.p on inner over 1f out: str chal ins fnl f: r.o wl to ld towards fin* **20/1**

4404 **2** *nk* **Misu Pete**[23] 2278 5-9-0 **48**.......................................... OisinMurphy 6 53
(Mark Usher) *chsd ldrs: swtchd rt and chal u.p over 1f out: led ins fnl f: hdd and no ex wl ins fnl f* **9/2**[2]

0006 **3** *3* **Humour (IRE)**[8] 2733 6-9-0 **48**..........................................(v) KierenFox 9 46
(Christine Dunnett) *sn dropped to rr: hdwy u.p in centre over 1f out: styd on strly ins fnl f: snatched 3rd last stride: nvr trbld ldrs* **10/1**

5430 **4** *hd* **Caledonian Gold**[35] 1894 4-9-7 **55**.......................................... JoeyHaynes 14 52
(Paul D'Arcy) *taken down early: in tch in midfield: clsd on outer to chse ldrs 2f out: rdn over 1f out: drvn to chse ldrs 1f out: styd in same pce u.p ins fnl f* **12/1**

30-3 **5** *1 1/4* **Majestic Girl (IRE)**[8] 2724 4-8-12 **49**.......................................... HollieDoyle(3) 11 44
(Steve Flook) *dwlt: in rr: hdwy whn nt clr run and hmpd over 1f out: hdwy ent fnl f: styd on wout any ch of rching ldrs* **12/1**

000- **6** *1 1/2* **Ashford Island**[227] 7231 4-8-12 **46** oh1..................(b[1]) RoystonFfrench 8 38
(Adam West) *hld up in midfield: nt clr run on inner and hmpd over 1f out: rdn and sme hdwy 1f out: kpt on ins fnl f: nvr trbld ldrs* **50/1**

2323 **7** *shd* **Home Again**[35] 1894 4-8-11 **52**.......................................... JoshuaBryan(7) 1 41
(Lee Carter) *w ldr tl led 1/2-way: rdn over 1f out: hdd and no ex ins fnl f: wknd fnl 100yds* **4/1**[1]

0/00 **8** *4* **Deftera Fantutte (IRE)**[99] 739 6-8-5 **46** oh1................ DavidEgan(7) 15 25
(Natalie Lloyd-Beavis) *led tl 4f out: unable qck over 1f out: wknd fnl f* **33/1**

5105 **9** *2½* **Autumn Tonic (IRE)**[20] 2367 5-9-6 **54**.........................(p1) LukeMorris 10 26
(Charlie Wallis) *hld up in midfield: nt clr run over 2f out: swtchd rt and effrt over 1f out: wknd fnl f* **20/1**

0-00 **10** *1¼* **Shamlan (IRE)**[63] 1334 5-9-7 **55**..............................(bt1) StevieDonohoe 2 24
(Johnny Farrelly) *s.i.s: nvr gng wl in rr: n.d* **6/1**[3]

0-00 **11** *1¼* **Cookie Ring (IRE)**[12] 2633 6-8-13 **54**...........................(v) PaulaMuir(7) 3 20+
(Patrick Holmes) *v.s.a and lost many l: rdn over 2f out: kpt on to pass btn horses ins fnl f: n.d* **12/1**

0500 **12** *8* **Disclosure**[25] 2179 6-9-2 **50**............................................... TomEaves 13
(Declan Carroll) *in tch in midfield: outpcd and swtchd rt over 1f out: sn btn and wknd ins fnl f* **8/1**

0-60 **13** *11* **Daydream (IRE)**[128] 273 4-8-11 **50**..........................(t) GeorgeWood(5) 5
(Tony Newcombe) *t.k.h: chsd ldrs: rdn 3f out: bhd and eased ins fnl f* **6/1**[3]

6060 **14** *7* **Whaleweigh Station**[29] 2091 6-9-6 **54**...........................(v) JoeFanning 4
(J R Jenkins) *chsd ldrs: losing pl whn hmpd over 1f out: sn eased: t.o* **20/1**

1m 26.85s (-0.35) **Going Correction** -0.075s/f (Stan) **14** Ran SP% **129.2**
Speed ratings (Par 101): **99,98,95,95,93 91,91,87,84,82 81,72,59,51**
CSF £109.62 CT £1001.51 TOTE £19.50: £6.50, £2.00, £2.70; EX 123.60 Trifecta £1786.60.
**Owner** Greenstead Hall Racing Ltd **Bred** Greenstead Hall Racing Ltd **Trained** Oakham, Rutland

**FOCUS**
A very moderate heat run at a good gallop. The winner looks well treated now she's revitalised.
T/Plt: £60.70 to a £1 stake. Pool: £72,842.79 - 875.02 winning units. T/Qpdt: £7.80 to a £1 stake. Pool: £8,000.74 - 751.80 winning units. **Steve Payne**

## 2388 GOODWOOD (R-H)
Thursday, May 25

**OFFICIAL GOING: Good (7.5)**
Wind: virtually nil Weather: sunny/warm

### 3002 MATCHBOOK BETTING EXCHANGE EBF NOVICE STKS (PLUS 10 RACE) 6f
**2:00** (2:00) (Class 4) 2-Y-O **£6,469** (£1,925; £962; £481) **Stalls** High

Form RPR

**1** **Masar (IRE)** 2-9-2 0.......................................................... WilliamBuick 5 85+
(Charlie Appleby) *athletic: s.i.s: in last pair: hdwy but nt clrest of runs over 1f out: swtchd rt ent fnl f: r.o wl: led fnl strides* **5/2**[1]

**2** *shd* **Invincible Army (IRE)** 2-9-2 0........................................ MartinHarley 9 85+
(James Tate) *str: slowly away: in last trio: hdwy over 2f out: led over 1f out: strly pressed fnl 80yds: kpt on: hdd fnl strides* **7/2**[2]

**3** *3¼* **Bartholomeu Dias** 2-9-2 0............................................... GavinLerena 1 75
(Charles Hills) *str: trckd ldrs: rdn 2f out: kpt on but nt pce of front pair ins fnl f* **14/1**

**4** *nse* **Folk Tale (IRE)** 2-9-2 0.................................................... MartinLane 4 75
(Charlie Appleby) *str: s.i.s: in last pair: hdwy over 2f out: kpt on but nt pce of front pair fnl f* **9/1**

**5** *2¼* **Montague (IRE)** 2-9-2 0................................................... OisinMurphy 8 68
(Jamie Osborne) *w'like: in tch: effrt 2f out: hmpd ent fnl f: kpt on same pce* **25/1**

1 **6** *nk* **Kick On Kick On**[48] 1604 2-9-8 0........................................ AdamKirby 3 73
(Clive Cox) *w'like: led: rdn and hdd over 1f out: no ex ins fnl f* **7/1**

**7** *¾* **Tathmeen (IRE)** 2-9-2 0.................................................... JimCrowley 2 67
(Richard Hannon) *tall: lw: trckd ldr: rdn 2f out: hld in 4th whn edgd rt ent fnl f: kpt on same pce* **5/1**[3]

**8** *nk* **Another Day Of Sun (IRE)** 2-9-2 0......................... SilvestreDeSousa 6 64
(Mick Channon) *tall: trckd ldrs: rdn 2f out: keeping on at same pce disputing hld 5th whn squeezed out ent fnl f* **10/1**

**9** *10* **Masked Defender (USA)** 2-9-2 0........................................ PatDobbs 7 34
(Amanda Perrett) *unf: bit bkwd: in tch: rdn over 2f out: wknd over 1f out* **20/1**

**10** *7* **Hornby** 2-9-2 0.............................................................. AdamBeschizza 10 13
(Michael Attwater) *unf: chsd ldrs tl wknd 2f out* **100/1**

1m 11.32s (-0.88) **Going Correction** -0.025s/f (Good) **10** Ran SP% **115.3**
Speed ratings (Par 95): **104,103,99,99,96 96,95,94,81,72**
CSF £10.70 TOTE £3.50: £1.30, £1.60, £3.70; EX 13.90 Trifecta £167.60.
**Owner** Godolphin **Bred** Godolphin **Trained** Newmarket, Suffolk

**FOCUS**
Only the second running of this novice contest, which had been won last season by subsequent Group 3 Molecomb Stakes Yalta. This renewal looked well up to scratch. The starting point is fluid.

### 3003 MOLECOMB BLUE H'CAP 7f
**2:35** (2:35) (Class 2) (0-105,102) 4-Y-O+**£16,172** (£4,812; £2,405; £1,202) **Stalls** Low

Form RPR

1131 **1** **Gossiping**[19] 2390 5-8-7 **88**................................................ ShaneKelly 4 98+
(Gary Moore) *swtg: in tch: hdwy over 1f out: led ent fnl f: rdn clr: readily* **7/2**[1]

4530 **2** *1¾* **The Warrior (IRE)**[12] 2606 5-8-7 **88**..........................(v1) TomMarquand 3 93
(Amanda Perrett) *lw: mid-div: hdwy over 1f out: sn rdn: kpt on ins fnl f: snatched 2nd cl home* **8/1**

3302 **3** *hd* **Horsted Keynes (FR)**[23] 2283 7-8-10 **91**.......................... AndreaAtzeni 6 95
(David Simcock) *hld up: hdwy over 1f out: kpt on to chse wnr fnl 120yds but a being hld: lost 2nd cl home* **10/1**

0-04 **4** *nk* **Shady McCoy (USA)**[12] 2606 7-8-8 **89**..................... SilvestreDeSousa 8 93+
(Ian Williams) *slowly away: in last pair: rdn and gd hdwy over 1f out: r.o strly ins fnl f: wnt 4th cl home* **5/1**[2]

0-03 **5** *nk* **Castle Harbour**[35] 1902 4-9-7 **102**...........................(p1) FrankieDettori 1 105
(John Gosden) *trckd ldrs: rdn and ev ch ent fnl f: no ex fnl 120yds* **7/2**[1]

-406 **6** *2* **Mutawathea**[91] 892 6-9-0 **100**............................(p) GeorgeWood(5) 2 97
(Simon Crisford) *led: rdn and hdd whn drifted lft ent fnl f: fdd* **6/1**[3]

003 **7** *nk* **Professor**[24] 2230 7-8-5 **86**........................................ JosephineGordon 9 83
(Michael Attwater) *mid-div: rdn over 2f out: nt pce to threaten but keeping on whn squeezed out jst onside fnl f* **33/1**

33-5 **8** *nk* **Accession (IRE)**[35] 1902 8-9-3 **98**.................................... MartinLane 10 94
(Charlie Fellowes) *prom: disp over 2f out tl rdn wl over 1f out: carried lft ent fnl f: fdd* **25/1**

4-40 **9** *1¼* **Robanne**[12] 2616 4-9-2 **97**................................................ JimCrowley 7 89
(William Knight) *hld up in last pair: rdn 2f out: nvr any imp* **16/1**

1-03 **10** *hd* **Ower Fly**[28] 2115 4-8-5 **89**............................................ HollieDoyle(3) 5 81
(Richard Hannon) *trckd ldrs: rdn over 2f out: outpcd over 1f out* **12/1**

1m 25.79s (-1.21) **Going Correction** -0.025s/f (Good) **10** Ran SP% **116.0**
Speed ratings (Par 109): **105,103,102,102,102 99,99,99,97,97**
CSF £31.99 CT £256.36 TOTE £4.60: £1.70, £2.30, £3.10; EX 35.60 Trifecta £274.50.
**Owner** G L Moore & Partner **Bred** Darley **Trained** Lower Beeding, W Sussex

**FOCUS**
Add 15 yards to the race distance. A competitive handicap and a fifth win of the year for the highly progressive Gossiping, who quickened best off a steady pace. He continues to progress.

### 3004 THREE FRIDAY NIGHTS H'CAP 2m
**3:10** (3:10) (Class 4) (0-85,85) 4-Y-O+ **£6,469** (£1,925; £962; £481) **Stalls** Low

Form RPR

0-05 **1** **Chartbreaker (FR)**[55] 1466 6-9-3 **78**..............................(p) PatCosgrave 1 84
(Chris Gordon) *slowly away: sn trcking ldrs: rdn over 2f out: led fnl 100yds: styd on: drvn out* **16/1**

02-4 **2** *¾* **Medburn Cutler**[13] 2562 7-9-1 **76**..........................(p) SilvestreDeSousa 2 81
(Paul Henderson) *lw: trckd ldr: rdn 2f out: led ent fnl f: hdd fnl 100yds: styd on but no ex* **7/2**[2]

43-1 **3** *½* **October Storm**[19] 2388 4-9-0 **77**........................................ GrahamLee 9 81+
(Mick Channon) *hld up in last pair: nt clr run 3f out tl swtchd out over 1f out: sn rdn and hdwy: styd on wl fnl f: wnt 3rd towards fin: nt rch ldrs* **9/4**[1]

-021 **4** *¾* **Akavit (IRE)**[20] 2363 5-8-5 **69** ow1.............................. CallumShepherd(3) 5 73
(Ed de Giles) *lw: led: qcknd pce over 4f out: rdn 2f out: hdd ent fnl f: kpt on w ev ch tl no ex fnl 120yds* **7/1**

1142 **5** *3¼* **Ayr Of Elegance**[19] 2388 5-8-10 **74**............................ HectorCrouch(3) 7 74
(Philip Hide) *mid-div: rdn over 2f out: nt pce to mount chal* **5/1**[3]

-121 **6** *8* **Amanto (GER)**[44] 1697 7-9-0 **75**..................................(t) TomMarquand 4 65
(Ali Stronge) *mid-div: rdn over 2f out: nt pce to get on terms: fdd fnl f* **10/1**

0145 **7** *2¾* **Cotton Club (IRE)**[25] 2176 6-8-11 **72**................................ OisinMurphy 10 59
(Rod Millman) *hld up in last pair: rdn over 2f out: nvr any imp: wknd over 1f out* **13/2**

05/ **8** *9* **One Pursuit (IRE)**[741] 2231 9-9-5 **85**............................ MeganNicholls(5) 8 61
(Charlie Mann) *trckd ldrs: rdn over 2f out: sn hld: wknd over 1f out* **50/1**

3m 31.14s (2.14) **Going Correction** -0.025s/f (Good)
**WFA** 4 from 5yo+ 1lb **8** Ran SP% **112.4**
Speed ratings (Par 105): **93,92,92,92,90 86,85,80**
CSF £68.99 CT £176.63 TOTE £19.10: £4.20, £1.70, £1.10; EX 80.70 Trifecta £243.90.
**Owner** Mrs Kate Digweed **Bred** Hans Wirth **Trained** Morestead, Hampshire

**FOCUS**
Add 10 yards to the race distance. A messy staying affair and a nightmare for the backers of the favourite, who was repeatedly stopped in his run. The first two are rated to form.

### 3005 CIGALUS GERARD BERTRAND WINES H'CAP 1m 1f 11y
**3:45** (3:46) (Class 4) (0-85,86) 3-Y-O
**£6,225** (£1,864; £932; £466; £233; £117) **Stalls** Low

Form RPR

440- **1** **Eynhallow**[226] 7243 3-8-9 **73**........................................ JamieSpencer 3 87
(Roger Charlton) *hld up detached in last pair: tk clsr order 4f out: gd hdwy fr 2f out: led ent fnl f: styd on strly: asserting nr fin* **20/1**

12 **2** *½* **Secret Advisor (FR)**[10] 2690 3-9-3 **81**.......................... WilliamBuick 7 94
(Charlie Appleby) *str: lw: trckd ldrs: rdn to ld over 1f out: hdd ent fnl f: kpt on w ev ch tl no ex cl home* **11/8**[1]

31-2 **3** *3½* **War Chief**[20] 2361 3-9-3 **81**....................................(h1) FergusSweeney 9 86
(Alan King) *s.i.s: detached in last: tk clsr order over 4f out: hdwy over 1f out: styd on fnl f but nt pce of front pair* **14/1**

-102 **4** *2¼* **Native Prospect**[29] 2088 3-9-3 **81**.................................... OisinMurphy 10 81
(Andrew Balding) *lw: led: jnd 3f out: sn rdn: hdd over 1f out: kpt on same pce* **14/1**

1-1 **5** *2* **Eldritch (IRE)**[27] 2118 3-9-8 **86**....................................... FrankieDettori 8 82
(John Gosden) *athletic: s.i.s: detached in last trio: hdwy 5f out: effrt over 2f out: nt pce to get on terms* **10/3**[2]

06-3 **6** *2¼* **Paradise Lake (IRE)**[23] 2260 3-8-12 **76**............................. RyanMoore 1 67
(Sir Michael Stoute) *lw: cl up: effrt 2f out: sn hung lft and hld* **7/1**

2-36 **7** *hd* **Quothquan (FR)**[29] 2088 3-8-4 **73**.............................. GeorgeWood(5) 5 64
(Michael Madgwick) *in tch: rdn 3f out: nt pce to chal: fdd fnl f* **33/1**

3-03 **8** *1* **Daimochi (IRE)**[20] 2361 3-8-8 **72**.................................. SamHitchcott 6 60
(Clive Cox) *prom early: trckd ldrs after 2f: rdn over 2f out: fdd fnl f* **33/1**

2-21 **9** *nk* **Maghfoor**[26] 2143 3-9-7 **85**............................................ JimCrowley 2 73
(Saeed bin Suroor) *str: prom: led 3f out: rdn and hdd over 1f out: wknd fnl f* **6/1**[3]

1m 54.67s (-1.63) **Going Correction** -0.025s/f (Good) **9** Ran SP% **115.9**
Speed ratings (Par 101): **106,105,102,100,98 96,96,95,95**
CSF £47.47 CT £418.88 TOTE £25.60: £5.30, £1.10, £4.10; EX 60.20 Trifecta £1723.10.
**Owner** Exors Of The Late Rj McCreery & Partners **Bred** Stowell Hill Ltd & D Ludlow **Trained** Beckhampton, Wilts

**FOCUS**
Add 15 yards to the race distance. An informative 3yo handicap, in which the first and third home came from a long way back. Big improvement from the winner on his handicap debut, with the runner-up to his mark.

### 3006 MARKEL HEIGHT OF FASHION STKS (LISTED RACE) (FILLIES) 1m 1f 197y
**4:20** (4:21) (Class 1) 3-Y-O **£23,680** (£8,956; £4,476; £2,236) **Stalls** Low

Form RPR

51 **1** **Mori**[13] 2564 3-9-0 88............................................................ RyanMoore 2 94
(Sir Michael Stoute) *lw: trckd ldr: shkn up over 2f out: led over 1f out: kpt up to work fnl f: readily* **15/8**[1]

5-1 **2** *1¾* **Coconut Creme**[24] 2227 3-9-0 80.................................. PatCosgrave 6 90
(William Haggas) *tall: led: rdn and hdd over 1f out: kpt on but hld fnl f* **7/1**

21-3 **3** *nk* **Indian Blessing**[40] 1796 3-9-0 87.................................... JamieSpencer 3 89
(Ed Walker) *hld up: hdwy 3f out: rdn 2f out: r.o ins fnl f: clsng on 2nd at fin* **16/1**

21-2 **4** *½* **Elas Ruby**[25] 2174 3-9-0 82................................................ WilliamBuick 7 88
(John Gosden) *trckd ldrs: rdn over 2f out: r.o w 3rd ins fnl f: clsng on 2nd towards fin* **10/1**

2 **5** *7* **Gakku**[22] 2316 3-9-0 0...................................................... AndreaAtzeni 1 74
(Roger Varian) *w'like: trcking ldrs whn short of room and snatched up after 1f: rdn over 2f out: wknd jst over 1f out* **13/2**[3]

1 **6** *hd* **Falcon Cliffs (IRE)**[92] 862 3-9-0 76................................. OisinMurphy 4 74
(Joseph Tuite) *leggy: hld up last: rdn 2f out: nt pce to get involved* **40/1**

1-2 **7** *nk* **Icespire**[22] 2287 3-9-0 90.....................................(h) FrankieDettori 5 73
(John Gosden) *racd too keenly: trckd ldrs: rdn over 2f out: wknd jst over 1f out* **2/1**[2]

2m 6.4s (-1.70) **Going Correction** -0.025s/f (Good) **7** Ran SP% **111.4**
Speed ratings (Par 104): **105,103,103,102,97 97,96**
CSF £14.67 TOTE £2.50: £1.40, £2.50; EX 14.70 Trifecta £136.80.
**Owner** K Abdullah **Bred** Juddmonte Farms Ltd **Trained** Newmarket, Suffolk
■ Stewards' Enquiry : William Buick two-day ban; used whip above the permitted level (Jun 8-9)

**FOCUS**
Add 10 yards to the race distance. The 46th running of this Listed feature, which had been won by the brilliant Snow Fairy in 2010 prior to her subsequent Epsom Oaks/Irish Oaks victories. Mori provided Sir Michael Stoute with his fifth win in the race. The first two dominated. An ordinary renewal despite four pulling clear.

## 3007 ORIENS AVIATION EBF MAIDEN FILLIES' STKS (PLUS 10 RACE) 1m 1f 197y
4:55 (4:55) (Class 5) 3-Y-O **£2,937** (£2,937; £673; £336) **Stalls** Low

Form RPR
2 **1** **Apphia (IRE)**[27] 2131 3-9-0 0 WilliamBuick 1 81
(Hugo Palmer) *trckd ldrs: led over 1f out: rdn whn strly chal ins fnl f: sn disputing: kpt on wl* **2/1**[1]
4-0 **1** *dht* **Hadeeqa (IRE)**[36] 1885 3-9-0 0 JimCrowley 11 81+
(Simon Crisford) *hld up towards rr: hdwy over 2f out: rdn for str chal ins fnl f: sn disputing: kpt on wl* **7/1**[3]
**3** *1 ¾* **Sugardrop** 3-9-0 0 PatDobbs 9 78
(Amanda Perrett) *athletic: tall: mid-div: hdwy over 2f out: rdn over 1f out: kpt on but nt pce of front pair fnl f* **14/1**
4 **4** *1 ¼* **Persistence (IRE)**[127] 283 3-9-0 0 FranBerry 8 75
(Ralph Beckett) *cmpt: trckd ldrs: rdn 2f out: kpt on but nt pce to get on terms* **9/1**
3- **5** *1 ½* **Angel's Quest (FR)**[210] 7647 3-9-0 0 ShaneKelly 10 72
(Richard Hughes) *str: mid-div: hdwy 3f out: rdn to chse ldrs 2f out: no ex ins fnl f* **17/2**
**6** *¾* **Paris Rooftops (IRE)** 3-9-0 0 JamieSpencer 7 71+
(Luca Cumani) *athletic: s.i.s: in last pair: hdwy fr 2f out: kpt on but nvr gng pce to get involved* **10/1**
6- **7** *8* **Button Up (IRE)**[169] 8246 3-9-0 0 RyanMoore 5 55
(Sir Michael Stoute) *str: lw: trckd ldrs: effrt over 2f out: wknd over 1f out* **7/2**[2]
0 **8** *1 ¼* **Street Marie (USA)**[13] 2585 3-8-11 0 KieranShoemark(3) 4 52
(John Gosden) *w'like: led: rdn and hdd over 1f out: sn wknd* **25/1**
0-00 **9** *6* **Crystal Secret**[19] 2393 3-8-9 50 MitchGodwin(5) 6 40
(John Bridger) *a towards rr* **200/1**
**10** *¾* **Estrellada** 3-9-0 0 GrahamLee 2 39
(Mick Channon) *leggy: s.i.s: sn mid-div: pushed along over 3f out: wknd 2f out* **16/1**
**11** *3 ¼* **Sampaquita (FR)** 3-8-11 0 HectorCrouch(3) 3 32
(Gary Moore) *tall: mid-div: rdn 3f out: wknd 2f out* **40/1**

2m 8.94s (0.84) **Going Correction** -0.025s/f (Good) **11** Ran SP% **117.0**
Speed ratings (Par 96): **95,95,93,92,91 90,84,83,78,78 75**
WIN: 1.50 Apphia, 3.70 Hadeeqa; PL: 1.10 Apphia, 2.40 Hadeeqa, 3.80 Sugardrop; EX: 11.40, 8.20, 11.40; CSF: 8.10, 10.50; TC: ; TF: 152.70, 90.70, 152.70;.
**Owner** Hamdan Al Maktoum **Bred** Shadwell Estate Company Limited **Trained** Newmarket, Suffolk
**Owner** The Mixed Blessing Partnership **Bred** Lynch Bages, Camas Park & Brittas House **Trained** Newmarket, Suffolk

**FOCUS**
Add 10 yards to the race distance. This maiden had been won by subsequent dual Group 1 winner Speedy Boarding in 2015. The judge was unable to split the first two home after a lengthy photo finish. Apphia set a good standard and the form is rated around that.

## 3008 WRIGHT JOINERY APPRENTICE H'CAP 6f
5:25 (5:25) (Class 5) (0-70,72) 4-Y-O+ **£4,528** (£1,347; £673; £336) **Stalls** High

Form RPR
0-62 **1** **Danecase**[7] 2762 4-9-5 72 RossaRyan(7) 1 78
(David Dennis) *lw: trckd ldrs: rdn to chal ent fnl f: led fnl 50yds: kpt on* **9/4**[1]
0003 **2** *hd* **Deer Song**[22] 2298 4-8-7 56 oh11 JaneElliott(3) 2 61
(John Bridger) *led: rdn 2f out: hdd fnl 50yds: kpt on* **25/1**
5-52 **3** *1 ½* **Captain Ryan**[15] 2509 6-9-1 61 HectorCrouch 9 62
(Geoffrey Deacon) *trckd ldrs: rdn over 1f out: ev ch ins fnl f: no ex fnl 75yds* **7/1**[3]
53-3 **4** *2* **Quite A Story**[31] 2043 5-9-4 64 CharlieBennett 5 58
(Patrick Chamings) *lw: in tch: rdn 2f out: nt pce to threaten* **11/4**[2]
3200 **5** *nk* **Virile (IRE)**[7] 2763 6-8-12 58 (bt) MitchGodwin 3 51
(Sylvester Kirk) *trckd ldrs: rdn 2f out: kpt on same pce fnl f* **9/1**
0-00 **6** *½* **Pour La Victoire (IRE)**[12] 2608 7-9-7 72 (b) AledBeech(5) 10 64
(Tony Carroll) *hld up: rdn over 1f out: kpt on fnl f but nt pce to get on terms* **12/1**
000- **7** *¾* **Easy Code**[271] 5881 4-9-12 72 GeorgiaCox 8 61
(William Haggas) *s.i.s: in last pair: sme hdwy u.p over 2f out: nvr threatened ldrs* **10/1**
00-5 **8** *2* **Monarch Maid**[48] 1599 6-9-1 68 MollyKing(7) 4 51
(Peter Hiatt) *trckd ldrs: rdn over 2f out: wknd over 1f out* **9/1**
020- **9** *29* **Keep It Dark**[171] 8234 8-8-5 58 AbbieWibrew(7) 7
(William Knight) *a towards rr* **28/1**

1m 11.08s (-1.12) **Going Correction** -0.025s/f (Good) **9** Ran SP% **114.0**
Speed ratings (Par 103): **106,105,103,101,100 100,99,96,57**
CSF £59.51 CT £345.46 TOTE £3.40: £1.40, £3.90, £2.00; EX 54.70 Trifecta £446.10.
**Owner** Favourites Racing (Syndication) Ltd 6 **Bred** D D & Mrs J P Clee **Trained** Hanley Swan, Worcestershire
■ Stewards' Enquiry : Jane Elliott seven-day ban; used whip above the permitted level (8th-14th June)

**FOCUS**
A moderate apprentice handicap, in which the runner-up, a 30-race maiden, was racing from well out of the weights. The form is rated cautiously.
T/Jkpt: Not Won. T/Plt: £47.40 to a £1 stake. Pool: £98,469.56 - 1,514.51 winning units. T/Qpdt: £9.40 to a £1 stake. Pool: £6,060.13 - 473.49 winning units. **Tim Mitchell**

# 2126 SANDOWN (R-H)
Thursday, May 25

**OFFICIAL GOING: Good to firm**
Wind: Light, behind in home straight, opposite to usual prevailing direction
Weather: Sunny, hot

## 3009 MATCHBOOK BETTING EXCHANGE H'CAP (A JOCKEY CLUB GRASSROOTS MIDDLE DISTANCE SERIES QUALIFIER) 1m 1f 209y
6:00 (6:02) (Class 5) (0-75,75) 4-Y-O+ **£3,881** (£1,155; £577; £288) **Stalls** Low

Form RPR
6134 **1** **Boycie**[26] 2146 4-8-13 74 TinaSmith(7) 10 85
(Richard Hannon) *hld up in rr: stdy prog on inner fr 3f out: rdn to trck ldr jst over 1f out: rdr dropped whip but pushed into the ld 140yds out: styd on wl* **7/1**[3]
36-4 **2** *½* **Silver Ghost (IRE)**[21] 2333 4-9-1 72 EdwardGreatrex(3) 7 82
(Eve Johnson Houghton) *led: rdn over 2f out: kpt on wl after: hdd last 150yds: clr of rest but readily hld by wnr* **5/1**[2]
0-63 **3** *4 ½* **Ghinia (IRE)**[20] 2358 6-9-4 72 RobHornby 3 73
(Pam Sly) *hld up towards rr: rdn and prog over 2f out: drvn and in tch over 1f out: kpt on but outpcd by ldng pair* **15/2**
245- **4** *1* **The Major**[259] 6268 4-8-11 72 TristanPrice(7) 1 71
(Michael Bell) *cl up: rdn to chse ldr 2f out to jst over 1f out: one pce* **20/1**
2-36 **5** *3 ¼* **Cordite (IRE)**[24] 2233 6-9-3 71 (h) TomQueally 13 64
(Jim Boyle) *trckd ldr: rdn wl over 2f out: produced half-hearted effrt and lost 2nd 2f out: immediately btn* **10/1**
0426 **6** *1 ¾* **Jack Of Diamonds (IRE)**[17] 2478 8-9-5 73 (b) JackMitchell 16 62
(Roger Teal) *hld up in last pair: hrd rdn 2f out: one pce and no threat to ldrs* **14/1**
0-12 **7** *1* **Pernickety**[23] 2254 4-9-3 71 (h) RichardKingscote 15 58
(Lucy Wadham) *s.i.s: rushed up into midfield: chsd ldrs and u.p 2f out: wknd over 1f out* **9/2**[1]
0-02 **8** *5* **Ataman (IRE)**[21] 2333 5-9-6 74 LouisSteward 5 51
(Chris Wall) *hld up in midfield: rdn and no prog over 2f out: wknd over 1f out* **15/2**
331- **9** *10* **Graceful James (IRE)**[168] 8282 4-9-7 75 SamHitchcott 17 32
(Jimmy Fox) *rdn in last by 1/2-way: sn bhd* **20/1**
30-0 **10** *9* **Topology**[13] 2586 4-9-7 75 JosephineGordon 11 14
(Joseph Tuite) *t.k.h: trckd ldrs: wknd jst over 2f out: eased* **16/1**
253- **11** *34* **Nucky Thompson**[49] 6242 4-9-6 74 (h) SilvestreDeSousa 14
(Richard Spencer) *trckd ldrs but trapped out wd: wknd over 2f out w rdr looking down: eased and t.o* **7/1**[3]

2m 7.14s (-3.36) **Going Correction** 0.0s/f (Good) **11** Ran SP% **114.5**
Speed ratings (Par 103): **111,110,107,106,103 102,101,97,89,82 55**
CSF £40.76 CT £267.82 TOTE £7.10: £2.90, £1.30, £3.30; EX 29.00 Trifecta £159.70.
**Owner** Mrs V Hubbard & K T Ivory **Bred** Highclere Stud **Trained** East Everleigh, Wilts

**FOCUS**
Some starts have been moved at this track following remeasuring, so some races will not have speed figures until there is sufficient data to calculate updated median times. Round Course was on outer/April meeting configuration, adding 29yds to all Round Course distances. Silvestre de Sousa described the ground as "good" while Sam Hitchott said, "It's nice but the further you go the quicker it gets." It was changed to good to firm all over following this contest. The right two came to the fore in a fair handicap. The winner built on his Doncaster win.

## 3010 BETTER ODDS WITH MATCHBOOK NATIONAL STKS (LISTED RACE) 5f 10y
6:30 (6:30) (Class 1) 2-Y-O **£14,744** (£5,590; £2,797; £1,393; £699) **Stalls** Low

Form RPR
21 **1** **Havana Grey**[17] 2452 2-9-3 0 PJMcDonald 1 100
(K R Burke) *mde all against rail: 2 l clr over 1f out and had rest hrd at work: drvn fnl f: ld dwindled nr fin but nvr under serious threat* **5/1**[3]
01 **2** *1* **Frozen Angel (IRE)**[22] 2286 2-9-3 0 RichardKingscote 2 97+
(Tom Dascombe) *racd in 4th: rdn over 2f out and dropped to last: rallied over 1f out: n.m.r ins fnl f: tk 2nd last 100yds and clsd on wnr nr fin* **7/4**[1]
23 **3** *nk* **Haddaf (IRE)**[12] 2607 2-9-3 0 MartinHarley 5 95
(James Tate) *nt pce to compensate for wdst draw and hld up in last: rdn and effrt 2f out: styng on to dispute 2nd whn impeded ins fnl f: nrst fin* **10/1**
1 **4** *1 ½* **Sound And Silence**[37] 1858 2-9-3 0 WilliamBuick 4 90
(Charlie Appleby) *racd off the rail: trckd ldng pair: chsd wnr wl over 1f out but sn rdn and no imp: lost 2nd last 100yds* **2/1**[2]
1 **5** *½* **Chagatai (IRE)**[41] 1767 2-9-3 0 AdamKirby 3 88
(Clive Cox) *chsd wnr to wl over 1f out: hanging bdly and racd awkwardly after: one pce fnl f* **6/1**

59.93s (-1.67) **Going Correction** -0.30s/f (Firm) **5** Ran SP% **109.7**
Speed ratings (Par 101): **101,99,98,96,95**
CSF £14.12 TOTE £6.10: £2.30, £1.70; EX 15.10 Trifecta £52.80.
**Owner** Global Racing Club & Mrs E Burke **Bred** Mickley Stud & Lady Lonsdale **Trained** Middleham Moor, N Yorks

**FOCUS**
Distance as advertised. A good little juvenile sprint, and everything went right for the winner, who made all against the favoured rail. Perhaps not the deepest renewal.

## 3011 MATCHBOOK VIP HENRY II STKS (GROUP 3) 2m 50y
7:05 (7:05) (Class 1) 4-Y-O+
**£36,861** (£13,975; £6,994; £3,484; £1,748; £877) **Stalls** Centre

Form RPR
30-4 **1** **Big Orange**[61] 1374 6-9-2 117 (p) FrankieDettori 1 116
(Michael Bell) *mde all at decent pce: stretched on fr 3f out: sn clr: galloped on relentlessly: unchal* **4/5**[1]
21-2 **2** *5* **Higher Power**[40] 1798 5-9-2 103 TomQueally 6 110
(James Fanshawe) *chsd wnr after 3f: rdn over 2f out: kpt on but no imp at all* **7/1**[3]
201- **3** *2* **She Is No Lady**[232] 7088 5-8-13 101 FranBerry 2 105
(Ralph Beckett) *awkward s: in tch: 5th after 4f: rdn 3f out: kpt on to take 3rd wl over 1f out: no threat* **17/2**
/00- **4** *5* **Vent De Force**[278] 5655 6-9-2 102 RyanMoore 5 102
(Hughie Morrison) *chsd wnr 3f: racd in 3rd after: rdn and no imp over 2f out: lost 3rd wl over 1f out: fdd* **16/1**
403- **5** *1 ¾* **Berghain (IRE)**[39] 4-9-0 103 JackMitchell 3 100
(J Hirschberger, Germany) *mostly in last pair and nvr in the hunt: rdn and no prog 3f out* **50/1**
00-1 **6** *1 ¾* **Elidor**[43] 1733 7-9-2 108 SilvestreDeSousa 4 97
(Mick Channon) *restrained s: hld up in last: rdn and no prog 3f out* **12/1**
12-0 **7** *7* **Quest For More (IRE)**[61] 1374 7-9-9 117 (b) JamieSpencer 7 96
(Roger Charlton) *stdd s: hld up but chsd ldng trio after 4f: rdn 3f out: looked ill at ease on grnd and sn wknd* **9/2**[2]

3m 32.67s (-6.03) **Going Correction** 0.0s/f (Good)
**WFA** 4 from 5yo+ 1lb **7** Ran SP% **112.3**
Speed ratings (Par 113): **113,110,109,107,106 105,101**
CSF £6.80 TOTE £1.70: £1.20, £3.00; EX 7.00 Trifecta £27.00.
**Owner** W J and T C O Gredley **Bred** Stetchworth & Middle Park Studs **Trained** Newmarket, Suffolk

**FOCUS**
Distance increased by 29yds. A race that revolved around the favourite and it spelt trouble for his rivals once he got his own way in front. He never looked in any danger and was chased home by a progressive pair. Big Orange is rated close to his best.

## 3012 MATCHBOOK BRIGADIER GERARD STKS (GROUP 3) 1m 1f 209y
7:35 (7:37) (Class 1) 4-Y-0+

£36,861 (£13,975; £6,994; £3,484; £1,748; £877) Stalls Low

Form RPR
01-6 1 **Autocratic**$^{36}$ 1882 4-9-0 102 ........ RyanMoore 3 115
(Sir Michael Stoute) *hld up in 5th: shkn up and prog over 2f out: looked to want to hang in bhd rivals over 1f out but forced through to cl: drvn to ld last 150yds: r.o wl* **8/1**
016- 2 1 ¼ **Algometer**$^{205}$ 7759 4-9-3 112 ........ JimCrowley 6 115
(David Simcock) *hld up in last pair: rdn over 2f out: prog on outer wl over 1f out: styd on wl to take 2nd last 100yds but nt pce of wnr* **4/1**$^{2}$
50-1 3 1 **Calderon (IRE)**$^{36}$ 1882 4-9-3 114 ........ PatDobbs 8 113
(Richard Hannon) *sn trckd ldr: shkn up over 2f out: pushed into the ld jst over 1f out to last 150yds: outpcd after* **4/1**$^{2}$
0-06 4 1 ½ **Mondialiste (IRE)**$^{22}$ 2290 7-9-0 113 ........ DanielTudhope 1 107
(David O'Meara) *stdd s: hld up in last pair: rdn over 2f out: no prog and stl in last over 1f out: styd on fnl f to take 4th nr fin* **9/1**
42-6 5 nk **Red Verdon (USA)**$^{13}$ 2571 4-9-0 113 ........ AdamKirby 5 106
(Ed Dunlop) *sn in 4th: first one rdn 3f out: styd cl up tl outpcd fr over 1f out* **11/2**$^{3}$
511- 6 ¾ **Chain Of Daisies**$^{271}$ 5893 5-8-11 110 ........ FergusSweeney 7 102
(Henry Candy) *led: rdn over 2f out: hdd & wknd jst over 1f out* **11/4**$^{1}$
110- 7 2 ¼ **Baydar**$^{208}$ 7700 4-9-0 105 ........ WilliamBuick 2 100
(Hugo Palmer) *clup in 3rd: steadily lost pl fr over 2f out: fdd fnl f* **9/1**

2m 7.1s (-3.40) **Going Correction** 0.0s/f (Good) 7 Ran SP% **113.2**
Speed ratings (Par 113): **111,110,109,108,107 107,105**
CSF £38.86 TOTE £5.30: £3.10, £2.90; EX 43.10 Trifecta £124.70.
**Owner** Cheveley Park Stud **Bred** Cheveley Park Stud Ltd **Trained** Newmarket, Suffolk

**FOCUS**
Distance increased by 29yds. A race weakened by the defection of So Mi Dar but still smart form with two progressive types coming to the fore late on. The third helps set the standard.It was run at a decent gallop.

## 3013 MATCHBOOK TRADERS CONFERENCE HERON STKS (LISTED RACE) 1m
8:10 (8:10) (Class 1) 3-Y-0

£20,982 (£7,955; £3,981; £1,983; £995; £499) Stalls Low

Form RPR
4-15 1 **Khafoo Shememi (IRE)**$^{13}$ 2565 3-9-0 100 ........ RyanMoore 6 108
(Richard Hannon) *mde all: shkn up 2f out: jnd 100yds out and drvn: lifted home fnl strides* **5/1**$^{2}$
110- 2 nk **Escobar (IRE)**$^{245}$ 6707 3-9-0 106 ........ WilliamBuick 3 107
(Hugo Palmer) *dwlt: hld up in last pair: prog on outer 2f out: tk 2nd fnl f: edgd lft but str chal and w wnr last 100yds: jst denied* **11/2**$^{3}$
12-3 3 2 ¼ **Zainhom (USA)**$^{33}$ 1959 3-9-0 109 ........ JimCrowley 2 102
(Sir Michael Stoute) *trckd ldng pair: waiting for a gap 2f out: rdn to chse wnr over 1f out to fnl f: one pce* **5/6**$^{1}$
-130 4 ¾ **Law And Order (IRE)**$^{19}$ 2399 3-9-3 103 ........ MartinHarley 5 103
(James Tate) *trckd ldrs in 4th: rdn 2f out: disp 2nd jst over 1f out: one pce fnl f* **8/1**
00-2 5 6 **Rodaini (USA)**$^{36}$ 1881 3-9-3 106 ........ (v) FrankieDettori 4 89
(Simon Crisford) *t.k.h: mostly chsd wnr: rdn over 2f out: lost 2nd and wknd over 1f out* **8/1**
30-0 6 ½ **Baileys Showgirl (FR)**$^{47}$ 1621 3-8-9 99 ........ SilvestreDeSousa 1 80
(Mark Johnston) *dwlt: a in last pair: rdn over 2f out: lost tch over 1f out* **33/1**

1m 42.61s (-0.69) **Going Correction** 0.0s/f (Good) 6 Ran SP% **111.8**
Speed ratings (Par 107): **103,102,100,99,93 93**
CSF £31.19 TOTE £6.20: £2.10, £2.40; EX 23.20 Trifecta £50.60.
**Owner** Saeed Suhail **Bred** Mrs M McWey **Trained** East Everleigh, Wilts

**FOCUS**
Distance increased by 29yds. Debatable how strong a race this was, with the favourite a tad disappointing, and the winner making all under a good ride. The fourth helps the standard.

## 3014 MATCHBOOK BETTING PODCAST WHITSUN CUP H'CAP 1m
8:40 (8:41) (Class 3) (0-95,95) 4-Y-0+

£9,337 (£2,796; £1,398; £699; £349; £175) Stalls Low

Form RPR
211- 1 **Laidback Romeo (IRE)**$^{291}$ 5206 5-9-4 92 ........ AdamKirby 3 101
(Clive Cox) *in tch in midfield: rdn and prog fr 2f out: drvn to ld 150yds out and edgd lft: styd on wl* **8/1**
/41- 2 1 **Greenside**$^{208}$ 7699 6-9-3 91 ........ TomMarquand 12 98
(Henry Candy) *dwlt: hld up in last pair: prog over 2f out: hanging whn drvn jst over 1f out: r.o to take 2nd last strides* **6/1**$^{3}$
0-00 3 nk **Sir Roderic (IRE)**$^{33}$ 1960 4-9-5 93 ........ DanielTudhope 4 99
(Rod Millman) *hld up in last quarter: smooth prog on outer 2f out: rdn jst over 1f out: chsd wnr ins fnl f: kpt on one pce and lost 2nd last strides* **9/1**
00-4 4 2 ½ **Midhmaar**$^{43}$ 1734 4-9-1 89 ........ JimCrowley 2 89
(Owen Burrows) *disp ld 3f: styd cl up: rdn 2f out: one pce and lft bhd fnl f* **11/2**$^{2}$
1-30 5 1 ½ **Timeless Art (IRE)**$^{37}$ 1860 4-8-8 85 ow2 ........ CliffordLee$^{(5)}$ 10 84
(K R Burke) *in tch in midfield: rdn and clsd on ldrs fr 2f out: no imp jst over 1f out: fdd* **11/2**$^{2}$
3001 6 hd **Alejandro (IRE)**$^{24}$ 2226 8-9-2 90 ........ JosephineGordon 8 86
(David Loughnane) *t.k.h: cl up: plld way into ld after 3f: rdn and hdd 2f out: steadily wknd* **16/1**
12-0 7 2 **Mountain Rescue (IRE)**$^{33}$ 1960 5-9-1 89 ........ HarryBentley 5 81
(Chris Wall) *trckd ldrs: rdn 2f out: hanging and nt qckn over 1f out: wknd fnl f* **17/2**
02-2 8 hd **Makzeem**$^{22}$ 2310 4-9-0 88 ........ (p$^{1}$) RyanMoore 7 79
(Roger Charlton) *disp ld 3f: trckd ldr: led again 2f out gng easily: shkn up over 1f out: hdd and folded tamely 150yds out* **5/1**$^{1}$
20-0 9 nk **Cricklewood Green (USA)**$^{131}$ 235 6-8-3 82 ........ MitchGodwin$^{(5)}$ 13 73
(Sylvester Kirk) *mostly in last pair: rdn over 2f out: plugged on fnl f: nvr in it* **66/1**
0-01 10 1 **Secret Art (IRE)**$^{24}$ 2232 7-9-7 95 ........ MartinDwyer 11 83
(William Knight) *trckd ldrs but trapped out wd: lost pl 2f out: sn wknd* **16/1**
2611 11 4 **Forceful Appeal (USA)**$^{22}$ 2291 9-8-5 82 ........ EdwardGreatrex$^{(3)}$ 1 61
(Simon Dow) *a in last quartet: rdn and no prog over 2f out: sn bhd* **25/1**
0- 12 5 **Munaashid (USA)**$^{240}$ 6864 4-8-10 84 ........ SilvestreDeSousa 6 52
(Ed Dunlop) *a towards rr: no prog over 2f out: wknd and eased over 1f out* **10/1**

1m 42.57s (-0.73) **Going Correction** 0.0s/f (Good) 12 Ran SP% **119.6**
Speed ratings (Par 107): **103,102,101,99,97 97,95,95,95,94 90,85**
CSF £55.93 CT £455.43 TOTE £9.20: £2.50, £2.60, £3.30; EX 72.30 Trifecta £616.40.
**Owner** Alan G Craddock **Bred** Mrs B Gardiner **Trained** Lambourn, Berks

**FOCUS**
Distance increased by 29yds. Good handicap form, the race set up for the closers. The winner continues to progress.
T/Plt: £773.30 to a £1 stake. Pool: £96,215.93 - 90.82 winning units. T/Qpdt: £80.10 to a £1 stake. Pool: £6,031.52 - 55.66 winning units. **Jonathan Neesom**

3015 - 3018a (Foreign Racing) - See Raceform Interactive

# BADEN-BADEN (L-H)
Thursday, May 25

**OFFICIAL GOING: Turf: good**

## 3019a 39TH BADENER MEILE POWERED BY DSV DEUTSCHER SPORTVERLAG (GROUP 2) (3YO+) (TURF) 1m
3:35 3-Y-0+ £34,188 (£13,247; £6,837; £3,418; £2,136)

RPR
1 **Palace Prince (GER)**$^{18}$ 5-9-2 0 ........ (p) FilipMinarik 3 111
(Jean-Pierre Carvalho, Germany) *chsd ldrs on inner: drvn to ld wl over 1 1/2f out: styd on wl fnl f* **13/2**
2 1 **Degas (GER)**$^{18}$ 4-9-2 0 ........ AndraschStarke 6 109
(Markus Klug, Germany) *chsd ldr on outer: cl 3rd and rdn along 1 1/2f out: styd on fnl f: a hld by wnr* **56/10**
3 hd **Wonnemond (GER)**$^{18}$ 4-9-2 0 ........ BayarsaikhanGanbat 4 108+
(S Smrczek, Germany) *racd in 4th: drvn along 2 1/2f out: styd on fnl f: nt pce to chal* **13/10**$^{1}$
4 ¾ **Diplomat (GER)**$^{46}$ 1661 6-9-2 0 ........ StephenHellyn 1 107
(Mario Hofer, Germany) *w.w in fnl pair on inner: styd on for press wl over 1f out: nvr able to chal* **26/5**$^{3}$
5 3 **A Raving Beauty (GER)**$^{24}$ 4-8-13 0 ........ (b) GeraldMosse 2 97
(Andreas Suborics, Germany) *w.w in fnl pair on outer: rdn and no imp over 1 1/2f out: sn btn* **31/5**
6 2 **El Loco (GER)**$^{39}$ 4-9-2 0 ........ AdriedeVries 5 95
(Markus Klug, Germany) *led: rdn whn pressed ins fnl 2f: hdd wl over 1 1/2f out: sn wknd* **5/2**$^{2}$

1m 36.38s (-2.73) 6 Ran SP% **130.6**
PARI-MUTUEL (all including 10 euro stake): WIN 75 PLACE: 30, 32 SF 346.
**Owner** Gestut Hony-Hof **Bred** Gestut Hony-Hof **Trained** Germany

3020 - (Foreign Racing) - See Raceform Interactive

# 2720 BATH (L-H)
Friday, May 26

**OFFICIAL GOING: Firm (good to firm in places; 10.3)**
Wind: Fresh behind Weather: Fine

## 3021 TMGROUP WHO CARES WINS H'CAP 5f 160y
1:40 (1:40) (Class 5) (0-75,76) 4-Y-0+ £2,911 (£866; £432; £216) Stalls Centre

Form RPR
0U16 1 **Powerful Dream (IRE)**$^{9}$ 2725 4-9-3 71 ........ (p) LukeMorris 2 76
(Ronald Harris) *s.i.s: sn pushed along in rr: hdwy 2f out: chsd ldr fnl f: r.o u.p to ld post* **7/1**$^{3}$
4-20 2 shd **Silverrica (IRE)**$^{13}$ 2621 7-9-1 74 ........ GeorgiaCox$^{(5)}$ 3 78
(Malcolm Saunders) *chsd ldrs: led over 1f out: sn rdn: hdd post* **7/1**$^{3}$
-066 3 2 **Kyllukey**$^{16}$ 2516 4-9-8 76 ........ DaneO'Neill 8 73
(Milton Bradley) *w ldrs: led 4f out: hdd over 2f out: sn rdn: styd on same pce wl ins fnl f* **12/1**
6650 4 2 ½ **Secret Asset (IRE)**$^{14}$ 2573 12-8-4 65 ........ (v) JordanUys$^{(7)}$ 1 54
(Lisa Williamson) *hld up: swtchd rt over 1f out: r.o ins fnl f: nt rch ldrs* **8/1**
3024 5 ¾ **Bush Warrior (IRE)**$^{27}$ 2161 6-8-3 62 oh1 ow1 ........ (b) MitchGodwin$^{(5)}$ 5 49
(Anabel K Murphy) *led: hdd 4f out: remained handy tl rdn over 1f out: styd on same pce* **11/1**
0-11 6 ¾ **Go Amber Go**$^{32}$ 2043 5-8-8 67 ........ (b) LuluStanford$^{(5)}$ 4 51
(Rod Millman) *s.i.s: hdwy over 3f out: led over 2f out: rdn: hung rt and hdd over 1f out: wknd ins fnl f* **7/4**$^{1}$
4-26 7 15 **Bahamian Sunrise**$^{24}$ 2253 5-9-7 75 ........ (p) MartinDwyer 7 10
(John Gallagher) *chsd ldr: pushed along 3f out: wknd over 1f out: eased ins fnl f* **3/1**$^{2}$

1m 9.0s (-2.20) **Going Correction** -0.625s/f (Hard) 7 Ran SP% **113.5**
Speed ratings (Par 103): **89,88,86,82,81 80,60**
CSF £52.91 CT £575.95 TOTE £7.70: £2.80, £3.30; EX 39.20 Trifecta £373.30.
**Owner** Ridge House Stables Ltd **Bred** Ballyhane Stud **Trained** Earlswood, Monmouths

**FOCUS**
A bright and sunny afternoon with a tailwind in the straight. The ground had officially been changed to firm from good to firm earlier in the day and it was lightening quick. They went fast up front here and the race collapsed in the final furlong. The runner-up is a solid guide.

## 3022 EBF STALLIONS FILLIES' NOVICE STKS (PLUS 10 RACE) (DIV I) 5f 10y
2:10 (2:12) (Class 4) 2-Y-0 £4,528 (£1,347; £673; £336) Stalls Centre

Form RPR
04 1 **Campion**$^{26}$ 2173 2-9-0 0 ........ PatDobbs 2 76
(Richard Hannon) *mde virtually all: shkn up ins fnl f: r.o: edgd rt towards fin* **8/13**$^{1}$
0 2 ¾ **Awesome**$^{14}$ 2563 2-9-0 0 ........ AdamKirby 6 73
(Clive Cox) *chsd wnr: rdn and ev ch over 1f out: r.o* **7/2**$^{2}$
3 2 ¾ **So Hi Society (IRE)** 2-9-0 0 ........ LukeMorris 7 63
(Archie Watson) *chsd ldrs: pushed along 1/2-way: styd on same pce ins fnl f* **11/2**$^{3}$
4 1 ¼ **Jo's Girl (IRE)** 2-9-0 0 ........ TimmyMurphy 4 58
(Jamie Osborne) *green to post: prom: shkn up 1/2-way: styd on same pce fnl f* **16/1**
5 5 2 ½ **Llamrei**$^{24}$ 2251 2-8-7 0 ........ FinleyMarsh$^{(7)}$ 1 49
(Jo Hughes) *s.i.s: sn pushed along in rr: nvr trbld ldrs* **33/1**

6 *84* **Glamorous Rocket (IRE)** 2-9-0 0 ShaneKelly 9
(Ronald Harris) *s.s: outpcd* **16/1**

1m 0.41s (-2.09) **Going Correction** -0.625s/f (Hard) **6** Ran SP% **114.2**
Speed ratings (Par 92): **91,89,85,83,79**
CSF £3.20 TOTE £1.70: £1.40, £1.50; EX 3.40 Trifecta £8.30.
**Owner** Rockcliffe Stud **Bred** Rockcliffe Stud **Trained** East Everleigh, Wilts

**FOCUS**
A weak fillies' juvenile race, in which the market proved invaluable. The order barely changed and the form will take time to work out.

## 3023 EBF STALLIONS FILLIES' NOVICE STKS (PLUS 10 RACE) (DIV II) 5f 10y
**2:45** (2:46) (Class 4) 2-Y-O **£4,528** (£1,347; £673; £336) **Stalls** Centre

Form RPR

1 **Heartache** 2-9-0 0 AdamKirby 7 92+
(Clive Cox) *chsd ldrs: rdn to ld over 1f out: r.o wl* **7/2[2]**

2 *6* **Fab (IRE)** 2-9-0 0 TimmyMurphy 6 70
(Jamie Osborne) *sn led: hdd 2f out: rdn and ev ch over 1f out: styd on same pce ins fnl f* **16/1**

3 *1* **Lynn's Memory**[12] 2655 2-9-0 0 PatDobbs 3 66
(Joseph Patrick O'Brien, Ire) *hld up in tch: rdn and hung lft over 1f out: styd on same pce: wnt 3rd nr fin* **9/1**

53 4 *nk* **Gold Filigree (IRE)**[8] 2750 2-9-0 0 ShaneKelly 4 65
(Richard Hughes) *chsd ldr tl led 2f out: rdn and hdd over 1f out: edgd lft and no ex ins fnl f* **15/8[1]**

6 5 *8* **Bond Angel**[11] 2691 2-9-0 0 TomQueally 5 35
(David Evans) *s.i.s: hld up: hung rt over 3f out: nvr on terms* **20/1**

5 6 *3/4* **Atalanta Queen**[6] 2832 2-9-0 0 MartinDwyer 1 33
(Brian Meehan) *s.i.s: hld up: shkn up 2f out: nvr on terms* **6/1**

7 *1 3/4* **Axe Cap (IRE)** 2-9-0 0 LukeMorris 2 26
(Archie Watson) *free to post: prom: pushed along 1/2-way: wknd wl over 1f out* **5/1[3]**

0 8 *1 1/4* **Esther (IRE)**[26] 2173 2-9-0 0 (h[1]) DanielMuscutt 9 22
(Amy Murphy) *stdd s: hld up: a in rr* **12/1**

59.58s (-2.92) **Going Correction** -0.625s/f (Hard) **8** Ran SP% **116.3**
Speed ratings (Par 92): **98,88,86,86,73 72,69,67**
CSF £57.05 TOTE £5.00: £2.10, £5.20, £3.00; EX 71.90 Trifecta £282.90.
**Owner** The Hot To Trot Syndicate **Bred** Whitsbury Manor Stud **Trained** Lambourn, Berks

**FOCUS**
This looked the stronger of the two divisions and produced an impressive winner in a fast time.

## 3024 C W ACCOUNTANCY SERVICES H'CAP 1m 2f 37y
**3:20** (3:21) (Class 6) (0-65,67) 3-Y-O **£2,264** (£673; £336; £168) **Stalls** Low

Form RPR

0-60 1 **Bayston Hill**[30] 2088 3-9-7 **65** DanielMuscutt 3 71
(Mark Usher) *hld up: hdwy over 6f out: shkn up and nt clr run over 1f out: rdn to ld ins fnl f: r.o wl* **9/1**

0004 2 *2* **Sublime**[16] 2513 3-8-2 **46** oh1 (p[1]) KieranO'Neill 12 48
(Rod Millman) *led: hdd over 8f out: chsd ldr who wnt clr over 7f out: tk clsr order over 4f out: led over 2f out: rdn and hung lft over 1f out: hdd ins fnl f: styd on same pce* **25/1**

56-0 3 *1* **Famous Dynasty (IRE)**[51] 1550 3-9-4 **62** DaneO'Neill 10 62
(Michael Blanshard) *sn pushed along and prom: rdn over 1f out: styd on to go 3rd nr fin* **10/1**

600- 4 *nk* **Born To Please**[188] 8025 3-8-2 **50** ow3 (p) SophieScardifield[(7)] 4 53
(Mark Usher) *plld hrd and prom: led over 8f out: clr over 7f out: c bk to the field over 4f out: hdd over 2f out: nt clr run over 1f out: no ex wl ins fnl f* **66/1**

0-50 5 *3 1/4* **Cribbs Causeway (IRE)**[14] 2585 3-9-6 **64** FergusSweeney 6 58
(Roger Charlton) *hld up: styd on fnl 2f: nvr nrr* **13/2[3]**

-516 6 *nse* **Crucial Moment**[9] 2726 3-8-9 **58** MitchGodwin[(5)] 1 51
(Bill Turner) *hld up: hdwy over 6f out: rdn over 2f out: no ex ins fnl f* **12/1**

3-65 7 *3 1/2* **Pentito Rap (USA)**[21] 2371 3-8-4 **48** RyanTate 13 35
(Rod Millman) *hld up: plld hrd: shkn up and nt clr run wl over 1f out: nvr rchd ldrs* **5/1[2]**

666 8 *3/4* **Al Jawza**[14] 2585 3-9-9 **67** PatDobbs 2 52
(Richard Hannon) *s.i.s: hld up: pushed along over 3f out: nvr on terms* **5/1[2]**

5000 9 *2 1/2* **Hippocampus (IRE)**[20] 2395 3-8-11 **62** RossaRyan[(7)] 5 43
(Richard Hannon) *prom: lost pl over 6f out: hdwy over 2f out: wknd over 1f out* **20/1**

-056 10 *3 3/4* **Meteoric Riser (USA)**[20] 2395 3-9-6 **64** ShaneKelly 7 38
(Richard Hughes) *hld up: rdn over 3f out: wknd 2f out* **4/1[1]**

55-0 11 *1/2* **Kitsey (IRE)**[34] 1968 3-9-2 **63** HollieDoyle[(3)] 9 36
(Richard Hannon) *mid-div: lost pl over 6f out: rdn over 4f out: bhd fnl 3f* **10/1**

006- 12 *3* **Garth Rockett**[254] 6481 3-8-7 **56** JennyPowell[(5)] 14 23
(Brendan Powell) *hld up: rdn over 3f out: n.d* **33/1**

50-0 13 *1 3/4* **Pennington**[32] 2036 3-9-6 **64** LukeMorris 8 28
(Mark Johnston) *chsd ldrs: rdn over 3f out: wknd over 2f out* **16/1**

2m 9.5s (-1.50) **Going Correction** -0.30s/f (Firm) **13** Ran SP% **121.5**
Speed ratings (Par 97): **94,92,91,91,88 88,85,85,83,80 79,77,76**
CSF £224.00 CT £2299.02 TOTE £11.30: £3.20, £7.60, £3.10; EX 379.80 Trifecta £5329.30.
**Owner** High Five Racing and Partners **Bred** Selwood Bloodstock & Mrs S Read **Trained** Upper Lambourn, Berks

**FOCUS**
Few featured in this low-grade handicap, in which the first four pulled clear. The winner has been rated to his 2yo level.

## 3025 BRITISH STALLION STUDS EBF NOVICE STKS (PLUS 10 RACE) 5f 160y
**3:55** (3:57) (Class 3) 2-Y-O **£6,469** (£1,925; £962; £481) **Stalls** Centre

Form RPR

1 **Prince Of The Dark** 2-9-2 0 AdamKirby 2 87+
(Clive Cox) *sn prom: chsd ldr over 2f out: rdn to ld ins fnl f: r.o wl* **7/4[1]**

22U 2 *2 1/4* **Last Page**[11] 2691 2-9-2 0 TomQueally 5 80
(David Evans) *led: rdn over 1f out: hdd ins fnl f: styd on same pce* **11/2[3]**

43 3 *3 1/4* **Qaaraat**[19] 2435 2-9-2 0 DaneO'Neill 6 69
(Ed Dunlop) *chsd ldrs: rdn over 1f out: wknd ins fnl f* **11/4[2]**

51 4 *3/4* **Diamond Pursuit**[31] 2052 2-8-10 0 FinleyMarsh[(7)] 7 68
(Jo Hughes) *chsd ldr 3f: sn rdn: wknd ins fnl f* **16/1**

5 *2 1/4* **Sunbreak (IRE)** 2-9-2 0 LukeMorris 9 59
(Mark Johnston) *sn pushed along in rr: hung lft and rdn over 1f out: n.d* **8/1**

6 6 *1 1/4* **Erastus**[14] 2577 2-9-2 0 CharlesBishop 8 55
(Mick Channon) *chsd ldrs: rdn and edgd rt over 1f out: wknd fnl f* **33/1**

7 *5* **Bin Daahir** 2-8-13 0 CallumShepherd[(3)] 3 39
(Charles Hills) *hld up: pushed along and wknd over 2f out* **8/1**

1m 9.02s (-2.18) **Going Correction** -0.625s/f (Hard) **7** Ran SP% **109.5**
Speed ratings (Par 97): **89,86,81,80,77 76,69**
CSF £10.79 TOTE £3.20: £1.90, £2.30; EX 11.50 Trifecta £27.30.
**Owner** Alan G Craddock **Bred** Alan & Robin Craddock **Trained** Lambourn, Berks
■ City Gent was withdrawn. Price at time of withdrawal 12/1. Rule 4 applies to all bets - deducation 5p in the pound.

**FOCUS**
An informative affair and the second impressive juvenile winner on the card for a Clive Cox-trained newcomer. The winner has been useful and the runner-up has been rated to form.

## 3026 E&H DRYLINING H'CAP 1m 5f 11y
**4:30** (4:30) (Class 6) (0-60,61) 4-Y-O+ **£2,264** (£673; £336; £168) **Stalls** High

Form RPR

-065 1 **Gambol (FR)**[22] 924 7-9-5 **57** (v[1]) AdamKirby 7 64
(Ian Williams) *hld up: hdwy over 2f out: rdn to ld ins fnl f: edgd lft: styd on* **5/1[1]**

-121 2 *2* **Willyegolassiego**[45] 1699 4-9-9 **61** LiamKeniry 3 65
(Neil Mulholland) *hld up: hdwy over 2f out: rdn to chse wnr ins fnl f: styd on same pce towards fin* **5/1[1]**

000- 3 *2 1/2* **Wassail**[205] 7767 4-8-6 **47** ow2 CallumShepherd[(3)] 2 47
(Ed de Giles) *chsd ldrs: wnt 2nd over 2f out: rdn to ld over 1f out: hdd and no ex ins fnl f* **12/1**

0602 4 *2 1/4* **Golden Muscade (USA)**[25] 2219 4-9-2 **54** LukeMorris 9 50
(Brian Barr) *sn led: hdd over 10f out: chsd ldr who sn wnt clr: tk clsr order over 3f out: led over 2f out: rdn and hdd over 1f out: wknd ins fnl f* **6/1[2]**

0005 5 *1/2* **Awesome Rock (IRE)**[25] 2219 8-8-7 **45** KieranO'Neill 5 40
(Roger Ingram) *hld up: hdwy over 2f out: nt clr run wl over 1f out: sn rdn: wknd ins fnl f* **40/1**

0640 6 *1 1/4* **The Quarterjack**[10] 2712 8-8-6 **51** (p) FinleyMarsh[(7)] 1 44
(Ron Hodges) *hld up in tch: rdn over 2f out: wknd fnl f* **6/1[2]**

5-1 7 *2 1/2* **Petrify**[25] 2219 7-9-1 **58** (tp) MitchGodwin[(5)] 8 47
(Bernard Llewellyn) *hld up: rdn over 4f out: nvr nrr* **8/1[3]**

35-5 8 *4* **Skylark Lady (IRE)**[86] 39 4-9-0 **59** (p) RossaRyan[(7)] 6 42
(Nikki Evans) *plld hrd and prom: pushed along and lost pl over 5f out: rdn over 2f out: sn wknd* **16/1**

006- 9 *3 3/4* **Magnus Romeo**[135] 5473 6-8-12 **50** (t) MartinDwyer 10 27
(Johnny Farrelly) *chsd ldrs: rdn over 3f out: wknd over 2f out* **16/1**

60-6 10 *hd* **Ring Eye (IRE)**[21] 2357 9-9-1 **56** EdwardGreatrex[(3)] 12 33
(John O'Shea) *hld up: rdn over 4f out: a in rr* **12/1**

066/ 11 *1 1/2* **Vexillum (IRE)**[227] 5256 8-8-7 **45** (p) SamHitchcott 11 19
(Neil Mulholland) *plld hrd and prom: led over 10f out: sn clr: c bk to the field over 3f out: hdd over 2f out: wknd wl over 1f out* **16/1**

6555 12 *1/2* **Cape Spirit (IRE)**[24] 2272 5-8-5 **50** (be) MichaelColes[(7)] 4 23
(Andrew Balding) *s.i.s: hld up and a in rr* **8/1[3]**

2m 50.21s (-1.79) **Going Correction** -0.30s/f (Firm) **12** Ran SP% **119.6**
Speed ratings (Par 101): **93,91,90,88,88 87,86,83,81,81 80,80**
CSF £29.25 CT £290.19 TOTE £5.60: £2.00, £2.00, £4.50; EX 28.90 Trifecta £652.20.
**Owner** Eventmasters Racing **Bred** Baron Georg Von Ullmann **Trained** Portway, Worcs

**FOCUS**
This was strongly run and represents solid form for this grade. The winner has been rated in line with his better jumping form.

## 3027 M J CHURCH H'CAP 1m 2f 37y
**5:05** (5:05) (Class 4) (0-85,84) 4-Y-O+ **£5,175** (£1,540; £769) **Stalls** Low

Form RPR

2-32 1 **Wapping (USA)**[17] 2504 4-9-7 **84** (b) TomQueally 2 91
(David Lanigan) *w ldr tl settled into 2nd pl over 8f out: shkn up and hung lft fr over 2f out: led over 1f out: sn rdn: styd on u.p* **8/11[1]**

0-23 2 *3/4* **Prendergast Hill (IRE)**[18] 2477 5-9-0 **80** (p) CallumShepherd[(3)] 1 85
(Ed de Giles) *led: qcknd over 3f out: rdn and hdd over 1f out: hmpd sn after: rallied and ev ch ins fnl f: styd on same pce towards fin* **11/8[2]**

0-60 3 *16* **Togetherness (IRE)**[13] 2609 4-8-10 **73** (p[1]) PatDobbs 4 46
(Harry Dunlop) *w ldrs tl settled into 3rd over 8f out: rdn over 3f out: wknd over 2f out* **12/1[3]**

2m 8.72s (-2.28) **Going Correction** -0.30s/f (Firm) **3** Ran SP% **107.7**
Speed ratings (Par 105): **97,96,83**
CSF £2.04 TOTE £1.70; EX 1.90 Trifecta £2.00.
**Owner** Lord Lloyd-Webber **Bred** W S Farish & Watership Down Stud **Trained** Newmarket, Suffolk

**FOCUS**
Only three runners, but they got racing from an early stage and came home in market order. The second is the best guide.

## 3028 HAPPY 65TH BIRTHDAY BRIAN PERRY H'CAP 1m 2f 37y
**5:35** (5:37) (Class 6) (0-65,67) 4-Y-O+ **£2,264** (£673; £336; £168) **Stalls** Low

Form RPR

4550 1 **Mamnoon (IRE)**[51] 1556 4-8-7 **53** (b[1]) HollieDoyle[(3)] 10 61
(Roy Brotherton) *mde all: rdn over 1f out: clr ins fnl f: styd on* **14/1**

-000 2 *2 1/4* **St Andrews (IRE)**[41] 1603 4-8-8 **51** (t) GeorgeDowning 1 55
(Ian Williams) *chsd ldrs: rdn and outpcd over 1f out: rallied ins fnl f: r.o* **7/1**

3312 3 *nse* **Attain**[9] 2722 8-9-6 **66** EdwardGreatrex[(3)] 7 70
(Archie Watson) *hld up: hdwy over 2f out: rdn over 1f out: r.o* **11/4[1]**

65-2 4 *3/4* **Hot Mustard**[16] 2511 7-9-7 **64** MartinDwyer 3 66
(William Muir) *plld hrd and prom: rdn to chse wnr over 1f out: no ex wl ins fnl f* **4/1[2]**

43-0 5 *2 1/2* **Eugenic**[32] 2042 6-8-4 **52** LuluStanford[(5)] 5 49
(Rod Millman) *hld up: racd keenly: rdn over 2f out: styd on fr over 1f out: nvr nrr* **6/1[3]**

062- 6 *nk* **Bob's Boy**[25] 7421 4-9-3 **60** (p) LiamKeniry 9 57
(Warren Greatrex) *chsd wnr: rdn over 2f out: lost 2nd over 1f out: wknd fnl f* **10/1**

25- 7 *2 1/4* **Patanjali (IRE)**[254] 6485 4-9-0 **57** JohnFahy 2 50
(Eve Johnson Houghton) *prom: racd keenly: stdd and lost pl over 8f out: rdn over 2f out: btn over 1f out* **7/1**

2430 8 *3/4* **Jazri**[64] 1322 6-8-7 **50** oh2 (b) LukeMorris 4 41
(Milton Bradley) *s.i.s: hld up: effrt over 2f out: nt trble ldrs* **25/1**

456- 9 *3/4* **Whitstable Pearl (IRE)**[53] 7987 4-8-6 **51** ow1 CallumShepherd[(3)] 11 42
(Sophie Leech) *s.s: a in rr* **33/1**

0/6- 10 *64* **Touched By Love (USA)**[163] 8366 4-9-7 **64** DaneO'Neill 6
(Ismail Mohammed) *hdwy over 7f out: rdn over 3f out: sn wknd and eased* **10/1**

2m 9.22s (-1.78) **Going Correction** -0.30s/f (Firm) **10** Ran SP% **117.6**
Speed ratings (Par 101): **95,93,93,92,90 90,88,87,87,36**
CSF £109.40 CT £354.84 TOTE £16.10: £3.90, £2.80, £1.30; EX 157.10 Trifecta £781.30.

**Owner** M A Geobey **Bred** Shadwell Estate Company Limited **Trained** Elmley Castle, Worcs

**FOCUS**
A moderate handicap. The third has been rated just off his recent form.
T/Plt: £1,495.80 to a £1 stake. Pool: £45,802.00 - 30.62 winning units T/Qpdt: £204.40 to a £1 stake. Pool: £4,109.00 - 20.10 winning units **Colin Roberts**

# 3002 GOODWOOD (R-H)
## Friday, May 26

**OFFICIAL GOING: Good (good to firm in places on round course; watered; 7.7)**
Wind: light, behind Weather: sunny and warm

### 3029 MATCHBOOK BETTING EXCHANGE NOVICE AUCTION STKS 5f
**2:00** (2:02) (Class 5) 2-Y-O **£4,528** (£1,347; £673; £336) **Stalls** High

Form RPR
52 **1** **May Remain**[10] 2706 2-9-2 0 JamieSpencer 8 77
(Paul Cole) *w'like: t.k.h: hld up in tch in midfield: effrt to chal between rivals 1f out: rdn to ld 100yds out: r.o wl* **2/1**[2]
2 **2** ¾ **Mother Of Dragons (IRE)**[32] 2037 2-8-11 0 OisinMurphy 7 69
(Joseph Tuite) *cmpt: sn led: rdn over 1f out: hdd and one pced fnl 100yds* **4/5**[1]
04 **3** *hd* **Firenze Rosa (IRE)**[24] 2251 2-8-11 0 JosephineGordon 6 68
(John Bridger) *leggy: pressed ldr: rdn and ev ch over 1f out: unable qck and kpt on same pce fnl 100yds* **25/1**
0 **4** 1 ¼ **Pursuing The Dream (IRE)**[17] 2502 2-8-11 0 DougieCostello 1 64+
(Jamie Osborne) *str: stdd after s: hld up in tch in last pair: clsng whn cannoned into and pushed rt ent fnl 2f: shkn up and hdwy to chse ldng trio 1f out: kpt on same pce ins fnl f* **12/1**
0 **5** 1 **Devil Or Angel**[8] 2756 2-8-8 0 CharlieBennett(3) 9 60
(Bill Turner) *leggy: chsd ldrs: rdn 2f out: outpcd u.p over 1f out: rallied and kpt on again ins fnl f: no threat to ldrs* **16/1**
**6** ½ **Alaskan Star (IRE)** 2-9-2 0 GavinLerena 3 63
(Amanda Perrett) *athletic: taken steadily to s: in tch in midfield: shkn up and clsd to chse ldrs over 1f out: lost 4th 1f out and kpt on same pce ins fnl f* **9/1**[3]
**7** ½ **Wild State (IRE)** 2-9-2 0 LiamJones 2 62
(J S Moore) *str: dwlt: sn rcvrd and in tch in midfield: rdn whn swtchd sharply rt and cannoned into rival ent fnl 2f: outpcd over 1f out: kpt on same pce ins fnl f* **20/1**
5 **8** 1 ¼ **Butterfly Spirit**[32] 2015 2-8-11 0 WilliamCarson 4 52+
(Michael Attwater) *w'like: hld up in tch in last pair: effrt over 1f out: no imp whn nt clr run jst ins fnl f: nvr trbld ldrs* **40/1**
6 **9** *nse* **Milchik**[32] 2015 2-8-11 0 KierenFox 5 52
(Michael Attwater) *w'like: chsd ldrs: rdn ent fnl 2f: lost pl over 1f out: wknd ins fnl f* **33/1**

58.95s (-1.25) **9** Ran SP% **126.5**
CSF £4.21 TOTE £3.20: £1.20, £1.02, £5.00; EX 4.70 Trifecta £39.80.
**Owner** PJL Racing Wright Asprey Meyrick Wilcock **Bred** The Ultimate Best Partnership **Trained** Whatcombe, Oxon

**FOCUS**
Some starts have been moved at this track following remeasuring, so some races will not have speed figures until there is sufficient data to calculate updated median times. The first 2f of the mile course was dolled out 5yds, the top bend was out 3yds and the lower bend was out 6yds from the 6f marker to the 2f marker in the straight. A warm, sunny day and the ground was watered to an official description of good (good to firm in places on the round course). Probably a fair novice race.

### 3030 CALA HOMES H'CAP 7f
**2:35** (2:37) (Class 4) (0-85,87) 4-Y-O+ **£6,469** (£1,925; £962; £481) **Stalls** Low

Form RPR
0-50 **1** **Noble Peace**[13] 2606 4-9-3 **81** HarryBentley 2 90
(Henry Candy) *lw: chsd ldng trio: effrt over 1f out: drvn and styd on to chal ins fnl f: led 75yds out: hld on wl after* **6/1**[2]
06-2 **2** *hd* **Pastoral Player**[13] 2618 10-9-4 **85** CharlieBennett(3) 6 93
(Hughie Morrison) *taken down early: hld up in midfield: clsd and effrt over 1f out: hdwy to chal ins fnl f: kpt on but a jst hld* **6/1**[2]
3-62 **3** 1 ¼ **Handytalk (IRE)**[21] 2369 4-9-0 **78** OisinMurphy 5 83
(Rod Millman) *t.k.h: chsd ldr: swtchd ins at cutaway 2f out and sn chalng: rdn to ld 1f out: rdr dropped reins briefly and edgd lft: sn drvn and hdd 75yds out: no ex* **15/2**[3]
365 **4** *nk* **Medburn Dream**[6] 2828 4-8-12 **83** DavidEgan(7) 10 87
(Paul Henderson) *chsd ldng pair: effrt u.p over 1f out: styd on same pce ins fnl f* **15/2**[3]
-000 **5** *nk* **Majestic Moon (IRE)**[6] 2833 7-9-7 **85** AdamBeschizza 7 88
(Julia Feilden) *led: rdn over 1f out: hdd 1f out: no ex and outpcd fnl 100yds* **25/1**
4641 **6** 2 ¾ **Russian Soul (IRE)**[16] 2528 9-9-9 **87** DougieCostello 3 83
(Jamie Osborne) *hld up in midfield: effrt over 1f out: styd on same pce ins fnl f: nvr enough pce to threaten ldrs* **11/2**[1]
0-03 **7** ¾ **Fox Trotter (IRE)**[13] 2617 5-9-6 **84** JamieSpencer 12 78
(Brian Meehan) *lw: stdd fr wd draw and dropped into last quartet: clsng whn hmpd on inner ay cutaway 2f out: swtchd lft and hdwy jst over 1f out: kpt on u.p ins fnl f: no threat to ldrs* **6/1**[2]
60-3 **8** 2 ¼ **War Whisper (IRE)**[13] 2608 4-9-5 **83** TomMarquand 13 70
(Richard Hannon) *hld up in last quartet: sme hdwy u.p over 1f out: no imp ins fnl f: nvr trbld ldrs* **8/1**
00-0 **9** ½ **Good Luck Charm**[46] 1687 8-8-5 **72** NoelGarbutt(3) 1 58
(Gary Moore) *hld up in last quartet: effrt u.p on inner over 1f out: nvr trbld ldrs* **16/1**
0-66 **10** 2 ¾ **British Embassy (IRE)**[11] 2677 5-8-10 **79** (h) RyanWhile(5) 8 58
(Bill Turner) *taken down early and led to post: stdd and awkward leaving stalls: t.k.h on outer in midfield: rdn and no rspnse over 2f out: wknd over 1f out* **50/1**
1000 **11** 2 ¼ **Lacan (IRE)**[23] 2291 6-9-0 **78** (v[1]) JackMitchell 9 51
(Brett Johnson) *stdd s: t.k.h: hld up off the pce in rr: swtchd lft and effrt over 2f out: no hdwy: n.d* **50/1**
2-30 **12** 8 **Philba**[24] 2283 5-9-7 **85** (tp) StevieDonohoe 11 36
(David Lanigan) *hld up in midfield: rdn over 2f out: sn struggling: bhd ins fnl f* **50/1**

1m 26.0s (-1.00) **Going Correction** -0.125s/f (Firm) **12** Ran SP% **108.5**
Speed ratings (Par 105): **100,99,98,98,97 94,93,91,90,87 84,75**
CSF £35.40 CT £231.68 TOTE £6.60: £2.40, £2.20, £2.50; EX 43.50 Trifecta £305.30.
**Owner** One Too Many & Candy **Bred** The Pocock Family **Trained** Kingston Warren, Oxon
■ Arlecchino's Leap was withdrawn. Price at time of withdrawal 14/1. Rule 4 applies to all bets - decuction 5p in the pound.

**FOCUS**
Add 15yds. This looked a competitive handicap but not many got seriously involved. The runner-up is a solid guide.

### 3031 BRENDA HAMILTON FILLIES' H'CAP 1m
**3:10** (3:10) (Class 4) (0-80,82) 3-Y-O
**£6,225** (£1,864; £932; £466; £233; £117) **Stalls** Low

Form RPR
62-1 **1** **Queen Of Time**[20] 2393 3-9-3 **79** KieranShoemark(3) 1 90
(Henry Candy) *hld up in tch in midfield: nt clr run briefly jst over 2f out: swtchd rt and qcknd over 1f out: rdn to ld and drifted lft jst ins fnl f: r.o strly: readily* **11/2**[3]
521- **2** 2 ½ **Panova**[222] 7380 3-9-7 **80** OisinMurphy 10 86
(Sir Michael Stoute) *hld up in tch in last trio: clsd and swtchd lft over 2f out: nt clr run 2f out: swtchd lft and effrt over 1f out: hdwy u.p to chse clr wnr ins fnl f: kpt on for clr 2nd but no threat to wnr* **6/1**
641- **3** 2 **Dellaguista (IRE)**[159] 8443 3-9-2 **75** PatCosgrave 3 76
(William Haggas) *chsd ldrs: rdn to chse ldr wl over 1f out: unable qck and styd on same pce ins fnl f* **5/1**[2]
21 **4** ¾ **Alnaas**[18] 2463 3-9-6 **79** (t) FrankieDettori 4 78
(John Gosden) *athletic: t.k.h: led and nvr really settled: rdn over 1f out: hdd jst ins fnl f: no ex and outpcd fnl 150yds* **2/1**[1]
00-3 **5** *nse* **Vigee Le Brun (IRE)**[21] 2366 3-8-10 **69** KierenFox 5 68
(Brian Meehan) *hld up in last pair: swtchd rt and effrt u.p over 1f out: hdwy and swtchd lft ins fnl f: r.o strly fnl 100yds: nvr trbld ldrs* **33/1**
241- **6** 3 ¼ **Syndicate**[171] 8237 3-9-4 **77** FranBerry 8 69
(Ralph Beckett) *chsd ldrs: effrt 2f out: unable qck u.p over 1f out: wknd ins fnl f* **10/1**
0-12 **7** 3 ¼ **Fleeting Francesca**[32] 2018 3-8-2 **61** JosephineGordon 7 45
(Chris Gordon) *in tch in midfield: rdn over 2f out: sn outpcd: wknd over 1f out* **16/1**
6-61 **8** ¾ **Braztime**[14] 2587 3-9-5 **78** TomMarquand 11 60
(Richard Hannon) *str: chsd ldr: rdn over 2f out: drvn and lost 2nd wl over 1f out: sn lost pl and wknd fnl f* **16/1**
12-6 **9** 11 **Flying North**[16] 2517 3-9-9 **82** JamieSpencer 6 39
(Richard Hannon) *hld up in last pair: swtchd lft and shkn up over 2f out: sn btn: bhd fnl f* **8/1**
3166 **10** 4 **Mitigate**[26] 2177 3-8-9 **75** DavidEgan(7) 9 23
(David Elsworth) *midfield but nvr travelling wl: lost pl u.p over 2f out: bhd fnl f* **50/1**

1m 37.89s (-2.01) **Going Correction** -0.125s/f (Firm) **10** Ran SP% **116.5**
Speed ratings (Par 98): **105,102,100,99,99 96,93,92,81,77**
CSF £38.49 CT £180.23 TOTE £6.60: £2.00, £1.90, £1.70; EX 37.60 Trifecta £185.10.
**Owner** First Of Many **Bred** Shortgrove Manor Stud **Trained** Kingston Warren, Oxon

**FOCUS**
Add 15yds. This looked a good race for the grade and the form is rated on the positive side.

### 3032 EBF STALLIONS COCKED HAT STKS (LISTED RACE) (C&G) 1m 3f 44y
**3:45** (3:45) (Class 1) 3-Y-O
**£22,684** (£8,600; £4,304; £2,144; £1,076; £540) **Stalls** High

Form RPR
-313 **1** **Khalidi**[20] 2401 3-9-3 109 FrankieDettori 3 112+
(John Gosden) *hld up off the pce in last trio: rdn 4f out: hdwy to chse clr ldr and drifting rt over 2f out: clsd and hanging rt over 1f out: sn led: clr ins fnl f: styd on wl: eased nr fin* **10/3**[2]
1-5 **2** 5 **Fierce Impact (JPN)**[28] 2128 3-9-0 92 OisinMurphy 1 99
(David Simcock) *lw: s.i.s: hld up off the pce in rr: effrt over 2f out: swtchd towards inner 2f out: hdwy u.p and swtchd rt again jst over 1f out: kpt on to go 2nd wl ins fnl f: no ch w wnr* **10/1**
14-2 **3** ½ **Raheen House (IRE)**[35] 1943 3-9-0 110 JamieSpencer 5 98
(Brian Meehan) *racd off the pce in 3rd: effrt over 2f out: swtchd lft over 1f out: styd on same pce and nvr a threat to wnr after* **6/4**[1]
1-14 **4** 1 ¼ **Monarchs Glen**[28] 2128 3-9-0 101 (p[1]) RobertTart 4 96
(John Gosden) *taken down early: sn led and wnt clr: 8 l clr 4f out: rdn over 2f out: hdd and wandered rt over 1f out: sn btn: wknd and lost 2 pls wl ins fnl f* **11/2**
0-1 **5** 6 **Shymkent**[11] 2681 3-9-0 86 HarryBentley 2 86
(David O'Meara) *w'like: chsd ldr tl over 2f out: sn drvn and no hdwy: bhd and wknd over 1f out* **40/1**
1 **6** 3 ¼ **The Grand Visir**[23] 2314 3-9-0 87 PatCosgrave 6 80
(William Haggas) *lengthy: hld up off the pce in last trio: rdn 3f out: sn struggling: bhd fnl f* **4/1**[3]

2m 22.77s (-3.73) **Going Correction** -0.125s/f (Firm) course record **6** Ran SP% **110.0**
Speed ratings (Par 107): **108,104,104,103,98 96**
CSF £32.45 TOTE £3.70: £2.10, £5.00; EX 30.00 Trifecta £72.00.
**Owner** Nizar Anwar **Bred** Aston House Stud **Trained** Newmarket, Suffolk

**FOCUS**
Add 15yds. Troy in 1979 was the last horse to win this and follow up in the Derby, but recent winners include Rewilding (2010) and Storm The Stars (2015), who both then ran third at Epsom, and Masked Marvel (2011), who landed the St Leger. Just last year Prize Money was runner-up and later landed a Meydan Group 2. This year's race fell apart a bit, with the favourite disappointing and the fourth doing too much early running in a clear lead, but still smart stuff from the winner, who lowered the course record. He's rated to a better view of his Newmarket win.

### 3033 EBF "BREEDERS SERIES" FILLIES' H'CAP 1m 3f 218y
**4:20** (4:20) (Class 3) (0-90,86) 3-Y-O+ **£12,938** (£3,850; £1,924; £962) **Stalls** High

Form RPR
22-1 **1** **Melodic Motion (IRE)**[23] 2302 3-8-7 **82** OisinMurphy 6 90+
(Ralph Beckett) *tall: t.k.h: in tch in 4th: pushed along and effrt over 1f out: rdn to ld jst ins fnl f: forged ahd wl ins fnl f: hld on wl* **11/8**[1]
64-4 **2** *nk* **Jelly Monger (IRE)**[20] 2387 5-9-9 **81** RobertWinston 2 89
(Dominic Ffrench Davis) *t.k.h: hld up in last trio: swtchd lft and effrt over 2f out: hdwy u.p over 1f out: ev ch ins fnl f: pressing wnr and kpt on wl towards fin* **22/1**
511- **3** ¾ **Notice (IRE)**[253] 6527 4-9-5 **77** JamieSpencer 3 84
(David Simcock) *stdd s: hld up in rr: rdn and hdwy over 1f out: drvn and ev ch ins fnl f: unable qck and one pced wl ins fnl f* **7/1**
-411 **4** *nk* **Monaco Rose**[6] 2815 4-8-11 **69** DougieCostello 4 75
(Richard Fahey) *chsd ldrs: swtchd lft to chse ldr and effrt jst over 2f out: drvn and ev ch 1f out: unable qck and one pced wl ins fnl f* **11/2**[3]
12-5 **5** 4 ½ **Pacharana**[29] 2109 4-9-8 **80** PatCosgrave 1 79
(Luca Cumani) *hld up in midfield: swtchd lft and effrt over 2f out: no imp u.p and edgd rt over 1f out: wknd ins fnl f* **16/1**

0-11 **6** *hd* **Darkroom Angel**[20] 2395 3-8-2 **77**............................ JosephineGordon 8 75
(Philip Hide) *led: rdn ent fnl 2f: drvn over 1f out: hdd jst ins fnl f: sn btn and wknd* **4/1**[2]

60/6 **7** 1 1/2 **Allumage**[79] 1079 5-9-13 **85**............................ TomMarquand 5 81
(Sylvester Kirk) *hld up in last pair: effrt on inner over 2f out: no imp and hung lft ent fnl f: sn wknd* **25/1**

10-0 **8** 16 **Comedy School (USA)**[29] 2115 3-8-11 **86**.................. HarryBentley 7 56
(Mark Johnston) *chsd ldr tl jst over 2f out: sn lost pl: bhd fnl f* **17/2**

2m 37.43s (-0.97) **Going Correction** -0.125s/f (Firm)
**WFA** 3 from 4yo+ 17lb **8** Ran SP% **114.6**
Speed ratings (Par 104): **98,97,97,97,94 93,92,82**
CSF £37.02 CT £164.30 TOTE £2.10: £1.10, £4.40, £2.20; EX 29.40 Trifecta £190.80.
**Owner** Qatar Racing Limited **Bred** Old Carhue & Graeng Bloodstock **Trained** Kimpton, Hants
■ Stewards' Enquiry : Robert Winston two-day ban; used whip in an incorrect place (Jun 9-10)

**FOCUS**
Add 10yds. The pace looked modest and there was a bunched finish. There's more to come from the winner.

## 3034 SOUTHERN CRANES H'CAP 6f
**4:55** (4:56) (Class 2) (0-105,98) 3-Y-0+
**£15,562** (£4,660; £2,330; £1,165; £582; £292) **Stalls** High

Form RPR

6-03 **1** **Boy In The Bar**[7] 2780 6-9-2 **86**...................(v) JosephineGordon 4 96
(Ian Williams) *hld up in tch in midfield: swtchd lft and effrt ent fnl f: r.o wl to ld wl ins fnl f: gng away at fin* **6/1**[2]

0-61 **2** 1 **Vibrant Chords**[20] 2391 4-9-10 **94**........................ TomMarquand 7 101
(Henry Candy) *lw: hld up in tch in midfield: effrt to chse ldrs and nt clrest of run over 1f out: sn swtchd lft and rdn: r.o wl ins fnl f to go 2nd towards fin* **5/1**[1]

1003 **3** 1/2 **Go Far**[19] 2433 7-9-7 **98**............................(v) JoshuaBryan(7) 10 103
(Alan Bailey) *sn w ldr: rdn 2f out: edging rt ent fnl f: led but stl shifting rt ins fnl f: hdd and lost 2 pls wl ins fnl f* **20/1**

-124 **4** 3/4 **Queen In Waiting (IRE)**[20] 2400 3-8-10 **89**................ OisinMurphy 14 90
(Mark Johnston) *led: rdn and edgd rt over 1f out: hdd and one pced ins fnl f* **8/1**[3]

0-32 **5** 3/4 **Stellarta**[41] 1794 6-9-11 **95**.............................. HarryBentley 3 95
(Michael Blanshard) *in tch in midfield: clsd to chse ldrs over 2f out: rdn and ev ch whn carried rt ins fnl f: no ex and wknd towards fin* **12/1**

0520 **6** nk **Kadrizzi (FR)**[13] 2606 4-9-13 **97**......................(p) PatCosgrave 2 96
(Dean Ivory) *in tch in midfield: hdwy over 2f out: rdn and ev ch over 1f out tl no ex ins fnl f: wknd fnl 100yds* **12/1**

0-04 **7** 1 **Clear Spring (IRE)**[7] 2780 9-9-9 **93**...................... LiamJones 9 89
(John Spearing) *chsd ldrs: rdn and ev ch over 1f out: carried rt 1f out: no ex and squeezed for room jst ins fnl f: wknd fnl 100yds* **25/1**

31-6 **8** nse **Mazzini**[14] 2566 4-9-1 **90**.............................. GeorgeWood(5) 1 86
(James Fanshawe) *broke in midfield but stdd bk to last trio after 1f: swtchd rt and effrt u.p over 1f out: no imp ins fnl f: wknd fnl 100yds* **5/1**[1]

111- **9** shd **Upstaging**[206] 7752 5-9-10 **94**............................ JamieSpencer 6 90
(Paul Cole) *hld up in last trio: clsd and nt clr run 1f out: switching lft ins fnl f: nvr getting enough room and no imp* **16/1**

0032 **10** 3/4 **Moonraker**[14] 2566 5-9-6 **90**.............................. FranBerry 11 83
(Mick Channon) *stdd s: t.k.h in midfield: swtchd lft and effrt over 1f out: no imp ins fnl f* **10/1**

0-00 **11** nk **Toofi (FR)**[9] 2736 6-9-8 **92**.............................. RobertWinston 5 84
(John Butler) *hld up in rr: effrt jst over 1f out: nt clr run and swtchd lft ins fnl f: nvr trbld ldrs* **11/1**

2-50 **12** 1 **Seeking Magic**[19] 2433 9-9-2 **93**....................(t) WilliamCox(7) 12 82
(Clive Cox) *chsd ldrs: rdn over 2f out: lost pl over 1f out: bhd ins fnl f* **20/1**

2445 **13** 1/2 **Kasbah (IRE)**[20] 2391 5-9-8 **92**.......................... GavinLerena 13 79
(Amanda Perrett) *chsd ldrs: rdn over 1f out: sn struggling: wknd ins fnl f* **16/1**

1m 9.61s (-2.59) **Going Correction** -0.125s/f (Firm)
**WFA** 3 from 4yo+ 9lb **13** Ran SP% **116.7**
Speed ratings (Par 109): **112,110,110,109,108 107,106,106,106,105 104,103,102**
CSF £34.00 CT £567.36 TOTE £6.70: £2.30, £1.80, £5.90; EX 40.10 Trifecta £813.90.
**Owner** Sovereign Racing **Bred** Brinkley Stud S R L **Trained** Portway, Worcs
■ Stewards' Enquiry : Joshua Bryan caution: careless riding

**FOCUS**
A decent sprint handicap with the winner rated back to his old best.

## 3035 VEOLIA H'CAP 5f
**5:25** (5:25) (Class 5) (0-70,71) 3-Y-0 **£4,528** (£1,347; £673; £336) **Stalls** High

Form RPR

52-3 **1** **Rebecca Rocks**[27] 2139 3-9-7 **70**.......................... PatCosgrave 8 78
(Henry Candy) *lw: mde all: rdn over 1f out: styd on strly to assert ins fnl f: gng away at fin* **3/1**[1]

520U **2** 1 **Lightoller (IRE)**[9] 2720 3-8-12 **61**.....................(b) GavinLerena 7 65
(Mick Channon) *chsd wnr: rdn and pressing wnr over 1f out: no ex and styd on same pce fnl 100yds* **15/2**

3541 **3** 3/4 **Jashma (IRE)**[9] 2720 3-9-5 **68** 6ex.......................... ShaneKelly 2 69+
(Richard Hughes) *stdd and bmpd s: hld up in last pair: effrt over 1f out: hdwy to chse ldrs and drvn ins fnl f: styd on same pce fnl 100yds* **3/1**[1]

-213 **4** 1 1/2 **Mercers**[79] 1088 3-9-1 **64**.............................. JamieSpencer 1 60
(Peter Crate) *taken down early: stdd and bmpd s: hld up in rr: shkn up and clsd 2f out: rdn to chse ldrs 1f out: sn no imp: wknd fnl 100yds* **4/1**[3]

213 **5** 1 1/2 **Midnightly**[25] 2235 3-9-8 **71**.............................. AdamBeschizza 3 62
(Rae Guest) *hld up in tch in midfield: clsd to chse ldrs and rdn 2f out: edgd lft and no ex ent fnl f: wknd ins fnl f* **7/2**[2]

4500 **6** 3 3/4 **Grecian Divine (IRE)**[44] 1731 3-9-7 **70**.................. OisinMurphy 4 47
(Joseph Tuite) *chsd ldrs tl 2f out: sn rdn and lost pl: wknd ins fnl f* **16/1**

0000 **7** 1/2 **Taurean Gold**[3] 2911 3-8-7 **56** oh11...................... JosephineGordon 6 31
(John Bridger) *in tch in midfield: rdn ent fnl 2f: outpcd and btn over 1f out: wknd ins fnl f* **25/1**

57.9s (-2.30) **7** Ran SP% **113.7**
CSF £25.53 CT £71.78 TOTE £4.10: £2.10, £3.40; EX 23.30 Trifecta £68.60.
**Owner** Hunscote Stud **Bred** Hunscote Stud **Trained** Kingston Warren, Oxon

**FOCUS**
The first two finishers filled the top two spots throughout. Improvement from the winner.
T/Plt: £73.60 to a £1 stake. Pool: £74,488.00 - 1,010.90 winning units T/Qpdt: £32.10 to a £1 stake. Pool: £4,369.00 - 136.0 winning units **Steve Payne**

# 2609 HAYDOCK (L-H)
Friday, May 26

**OFFICIAL GOING: Good to firm (watered; 8.6)**
Wind: Moderate, half behind Weather: Hot & Sunny

## 3036 RACINGUK.COM H'CAP 1m 2f 42y
**2:20** (2:20) (Class 5) (0-75,77) 4-Y-0+ **£3,557** (£1,058; £529; £264) **Stalls** Centre

Form RPR

2155 **1** **Captain Courageous (IRE)**[18] 2477 4-9-7 **74**........ RichardKingscote 4 88
(Ed Walker) *mde all: rdn over 1f out: r.o wl to draw clr fnl f* **9/2**[2]

6-22 **2** 6 **Therthaar**[24] 2267 4-9-7 **74**.............................. SilvestreDeSousa 6 76
(Ismail Mohammed) *prom: rdn over 2f out: tk 2nd over 1f out: unable to go w wnr fnl f* **5/2**[1]

00-0 **3** 1 1/4 **Saxo Jack (FR)**[14] 2586 7-9-10 **77**......................(t) SeanLevey 10 77+
(Sophie Leech) *in rr: swtchd rt 3f out: hdwy over 2f out: styd on towards fin: nt rch ldrs* **25/1**

11-1 **4** 3/4 **Estrella Eria (FR)**[43] 1758 4-9-5 **72**..................(h) AndrewMullen 2 70
(George Peckham) *racd keenly: trckd ldrs: pushed along over 3f out: nt pce of wnr over 1f out: no ex fnl f* **9/1**

4-04 **5** 1 1/4 **Satish**[24] 2275 4-9-5 **72**..............................(v[1]) DanielTudhope 11 68
(David O'Meara) *hld up in rr: hdwy over 2f out: one pce fnl f* **14/1**

0064 **6** 1 1/2 **False Id**[43] 1758 4-8-12 **65**.............................. CamHardie 8 58
(Marjorie Fife) *plld hrd: hld up: hdwy to go prom after 3f: rdn over 2f out: wknd over 1f out* **10/1**

3-03 **7** 1/2 **Bahamian C**[29] 2108 6-8-6 **62**.......................(t) SammyJoBell(3) 7 54
(Richard Fahey) *racd keenly: trckd ldrs: lost pl after 2f: rdn over 2f out: sn edgd lft: kpt on u.p and no imp fr over 1f out* **10/1**

1222 **8** hd **Mazaaher**[21] 2357 7-9-0 **72**........................(p) CliffordLee(5) 9 63
(David Evans) *hld up: rdn 3f out: no imp* **8/1**[3]

0/40 **9** 2 1/2 **No Win No Fee**[13] 2624 7-8-4 **64**...................... JaneElliott(7) 5 50
(Barry Leavy) *midfield: rdn and wknd 2f out* **100/1**

-000 **10** 6 **Royal Reserve**[27] 2133 4-8-9 **65**....................(t[1]) AdamMcNamara(3) 1 39
(Ian Williams) *midfield: rdn and wknd over 2f out* **9/2**[2]

2m 10.48s (-2.22) **Going Correction** -0.55s/f (Hard) **10** Ran SP% **115.7**
Speed ratings (Par 103): **86,81,80,79,78 77,77,76,74,70**
CSF £15.99 CT £251.24 TOTE £6.30: £2.40, £1.30, £5.00; EX 21.60 Trifecta £477.60.
**Owner** Laurence Bellman **Bred** Edgeridge & Glenvale **Trained** Upper Lambourn, Berks

**FOCUS**
All races run over the Inner Home Straight. A fair handicap. They went, at best, a respectable gallop on good to firm ground. The winner had an uncontested lead but the form is rated at face value.

## 3037 BRITISH STALLION STUDS EBF NOVICE STKS (PLUS 10 RACE) 6f
**2:55** (2:57) (Class 4) 2-Y-O **£4,592** (£1,366; £683; £341) **Stalls** Centre

Form RPR

**1** **Finniston Farm** 2-9-2 0.............................. RichardKingscote 6 84+
(Tom Dascombe) *a.p: led over 2f out: rdn over 1f out: r.o wl towards fin* **10/1**

**2** 1 1/2 **Mutakatif (IRE)** 2-9-2 0.............................. JimCrowley 2 79+
(Charles Hills) *hld up: hdwy over 2f out: chalng over 1f out: no ex nr fin* **2/1**[1]

**3** 3/4 **Learn By Heart** 2-9-2 0.............................. DanielTudhope 7 77+
(William Haggas) *coltish in paddock: hld up: hdwy over 1f out: styd on towards fin: nt quite pce of front two* **6/1**

**4** 1 **Hard Graft** 2-9-2 0.............................. SeanLevey 11 74
(David Brown) *a.p: rdn 2f out: nt qckn over 1f out: styd on same pce ins fnl f* **33/1**

**5** 1/2 **Al Fujairah** 2-9-2 0.............................. SilvestreDeSousa 1 72
(Richard Hannon) *coltish in paddock: racd keenly: in tch: rdn and chalng over 1f out: no ex fnl 100yds* **9/2**[3]

**6** 1 3/4 **Ferik (IRE)** 2-9-2 0.............................. AndrewMullen 9 66+
(David Evans) *midfield: rdn over 1f out: kpt on same pce fnl f* **50/1**

**7** 1 1/2 **Game Player (IRE)** 2-9-2 0.............................. AndreaAtzeni 5 62
(Roger Varian) *chsd ldrs: rdn and hung lft fr 2f out: one pce fr over 1f out* **7/2**[2]

**8** 1 1/4 **Dichato (USA)** 2-9-2 0.............................. WilliamBuick 3 58
(John Gosden) *towards rr: sn pushed along: plugged on fr 1f out: nt pce to trble ldrs* **9/1**

**9** 1/2 **Mountain Approach (IRE)** 2-9-2 0.......................... TonyHamilton 10 56
(Richard Fahey) *racd keenly: led: hdd over 2f out: wknd over 1f out* **25/1**

**10** 4 1/2 **Brockey Rise (IRE)** 2-8-11 0.............................. CliffordLee(5) 4 42
(David Evans) *a in rr: sn pushed along: wl bhd fnl f* **40/1**

**11** 5 **Snoop** 2-8-11 0.............................. PJMcDonald 8 21
(David Loughnane) *missed break: in rr: lft bhd fnl f* **100/1**

1m 11.22s (-2.58) **Going Correction** -0.55s/f (Hard) **11** Ran SP% **119.3**
Speed ratings (Par 95): **95,93,92,90,90 87,85,84,83,77 70**
CSF £30.03 TOTE £14.00: £2.90, £1.50, £2.00; EX 44.70 Trifecta £280.60.
**Owner** The Famous Five Partnership **Bred** Stetchworth & Middle Park Studs Ltd **Trained** Malpas, Cheshire

**FOCUS**
A fascinating juvenile novice contest with a field made up entirely by newcomers. The winner is held in high regard at home and produced a thoroughly professional performance. It is above-average juvenile form off a decent gallop.

## 3038 RACING UK IN HD H'CAP 6f
**3:30** (3:31) (Class 4) (0-80,82) 3-Y-O **£5,822** (£1,732; £865; £432) **Stalls** Centre

Form RPR

4321 **1** **El Hombre**[7] 2776 3-9-4 **82** 6ex.......................... RowanScott(5) 5 91
(Keith Dalgleish) *in tch: rdn over 2f out: r.o to ld fnl 150yds: in command towards fin* **9/2**[2]

-155 **2** 1 **Full Intention**[15] 2557 3-9-7 **80**.......................... PJMcDonald 13 86
(Tom Dascombe) *chsd ldrs: rdn to ld wl over 1f out: hdd fnl 150yds: no ex nr fin* **12/1**

01-6 **3** 1/2 **Open Wide (USA)**[14] 2579 3-9-6 **79**...................... PaulMulrennan 8 83+
(Amanda Perrett) *racd keenly in midfield: hdwy over 1f out: hung lft ins fnl f: r.o towards fin* **16/1**

15 **4** 2 1/4 **Batten The Hatches**[24] 2271 3-9-6 **79**.................. PhillipMakin 1 76
(David Barron) *a.p: rdn and chalng over 1f out: styd on same pce ins fnl f* **14/1**

02-5 **5** 1 **Nibras Again**[31] 2072 3-9-1 **74**.......................... SilvestreDeSousa 4 70+
(Ismail Mohammed) *midfield: swtchd lft and hdwy over 1f out: kpt on ins fnl f: nt quite pce to chal* **7/1**

2-16 **6** *1 ¾* **Ashwaq**[35] 1940 3-9-2 **75** SeanLevey 10 63
(Richard Hannon) *chsd ldrs: rdn over 2f out: one pce ins fnl f and no imp* **25/1**

00-0 **7** *hd* **The Amber Fort (USA)**[15] 2557 3-8-13 **75** ShelleyBirkett(3) 14 63
(David O'Meara) *midfield: rdn over 1f out: one pce ins fnl f: nvr able to trble ldrs* **100/1**

0-61 **8** *½* **Burrishoole Abbey (IRE)**[17] 2499 3-9-3 **81** CliffordLee(5) 9 67
(K R Burke) *chsd ldrs: rdn over 2f out: fdd ins fnl f* **8/1**

6-21 **9** *12* **Suitcase 'N' Taxi**[23] 2304 3-9-1 **74** DavidAllan 11 22
(Tim Easterby) *led: rdn and hdd wl over 1f out: sn wknd* **6/1**[3]

40-3 **10** *9* **Inlawed**[18] 2474 3-8-9 **68** RichardKingscote 12
(Ed Walker) *sn outpcd towards rr: wl bhd 1/2-way* **11/1**

34-1 **11** *2 ½* **Dalton**[17] 2495 3-9-8 **81** DanielTudhope 7
(David O'Meara) *sn outpcd and bhd: eased whn wl btn over 1f out: lame* **4/1**[1]

031- **12** *7* **Dagonet (IRE)**[220] 7424 3-9-9 **82** (h[1]) JimCrowley 3
(Roger Charlton) *hld up: rdn over 2f out: sn wknd* **12/1**

1- **13** *16* **Sumner Beach**[396] 1706 3-9-8 **81** WilliamBuick 6
(Brian Ellison) *a outpcd and wl bhd* **20/1**

1m 10.39s (-3.41) **Going Correction** -0.55s/f (Hard) **13** Ran SP% **121.9**
Speed ratings (Par 101): **100,98,98,95,93 91,91,90,74,62 59,49,28**
CSF £58.02 CT £839.28 TOTE £5.70: £1.90, £3.70, £5.90; EX 74.20 Trifecta £1675.60.
**Owner** Weldspec Glasgow Limited **Bred** Mrs J McMahon **Trained** Carluke, S Lanarks

**FOCUS**
A fairly decent 3yo sprint handicap. They went a proper gallop and the in-form winner was the first horse to dip under a standard winning time on this quick ground. The winner confirmed his wide-margin Hamilton win.

## 3039 GEORGE FORMBY BIRTHDAY MAIDEN FILLIES' STKS (PLUS 10 RACE) 7f 212y
**4:05** (4:05) (Class 5) 3-Y-O **£3,557** (£1,058; £529; £264) **Stalls** Low

Form RPR

0- **1** **Smart Together (USA)**[244] 6782 3-9-0 0 WilliamBuick 8 78+
(John Gosden) *hld up: on wd outer on bnd over 5f out: hdwy over 2f out: rdn over 1f out: r.o ins fnl f to ld cl home* **8/1**

6-2 **2** *hd* **Sasini**[14] 2585 3-9-0 0 DavidProbert 1 77
(Charles Hills) *prom: led after 1f: rdn wl over 1f out: hdd cl home* **7/4**[1]

40-3 **3** *½* **Alouja (IRE)**[14] 2585 3-9-0 78 AndreaAtzeni 3 76
(Hugo Palmer) *racd keenly: trckd ldrs: rdn 2f out: chalng fr over 1f out: hld nr fin* **9/4**[2]

6-5 **4** *¾* **Polly Glide (IRE)**[37] 1885 3-9-0 0 JimCrowley 4 74+
(Luca Cumani) *stdd early: hld up: rdn and hdwy over 1f out: styd on towards fin* **11/2**[3]

62 **5** *2* **Hamster Jam (IRE)**[19] 2429 3-9-0 0 FrannyNorton 5 69
(Mark Johnston) *led for 1f: remained prom: rdn and nt qckn over 1f out: styd on same pce fnl 150yds* **22/1**

**6** *1 ½* **Labhay (IRE)** 3-9-0 0 RichardKingscote 2 65
(William Haggas) *racd keenly: trckd ldrs: effrt on inner wl over 1f out: one pce ins fnl f* **15/2**

**7** *3 ¼* **Master Me (IRE)** 3-8-9 0 CliffordLee(5) 7 58
(K R Burke) *midfield: rdn over 2f out: wknd over 1f out* **40/1**

**8** *hd* **Best Of My Love (IRE)** 3-9-0 0 SilvestreDeSousa 6 57
(Mick Channon) *hld up: rdn 2f out: outpcd whn hung lft over 1f out: nvr a threat* **25/1**

1m 39.41s (-4.29) **Going Correction** -0.55s/f (Hard) **8** Ran SP% **116.0**
Speed ratings (Par 96): **99,98,98,97,95 94,90,90**
CSF £22.46 TOTE £9.30: £2.40, £1.20, £1.10; EX 30.50 Trifecta £127.20.
**Owner** George Strawbridge **Bred** Augustin Stable **Trained** Newmarket, Suffolk

**FOCUS**
A fair 3yo fillies' maiden. They went a respectable gallop and the form horse got collared in the closing stages. The form is rated around the second and third.

## 3040 WIGAN WARRIORS BUSINESS CLUB H'CAP 7f 212y
**4:40** (4:40) (Class 4) (0-80,80) 3-Y-O **£5,822** (£1,732; £865; £432) **Stalls** Low

Form RPR

5321 **1** **Sidewinder (IRE)**[27] 2145 3-9-4 **77** RichardKingscote 4 83
(Tom Dascombe) *chsd ldrs: rdn to go 2nd over 1f out: r.o ins fnl f: led cl home* **11/2**[2]

2-30 **2** *nk* **Inner Circle (IRE)**[14] 2567 3-9-4 **77** SeanLevey 1 82
(Richard Hannon) *led: rdn over 2f out: hdd cl home* **8/1**

31 **3** *1* **Excel Again**[98] 777 3-9-4 **77** DavidAllan 10 80
(James Tate) *towards rr: rdn and hdwy 2f out: nt clr run briefly sn after: r.o ins fnl f: nt quite pce of front two* **9/2**[1]

-146 **4** *¾* **Ray's The Money (IRE)**[24] 2284 3-9-5 **78** (v) LouisSteward 12 79
(Michael Bell) *missed break: in rr: rdn and hdwy over 2f out: styd on u.p ins fnl f: no further imp towards fin* **12/1**

3-13 **5** *3 ¼* **Proud Archi (IRE)**[21] 2374 3-9-7 **80** PaulMulrennan 6 74
(Michael Dods) *trckd ldrs: rdn 2f out: one pce fnl f* **11/2**[2]

1-34 **6** *nk* **In First Place**[20] 2385 3-9-3 **79** SammyJoBell(3) 5 72
(Richard Fahey) *in tch: rdn over 2f out: one pce fnl f* **8/1**

31-6 **7** *5* **Thaaqib**[36] 1895 3-9-6 **79** JimCrowley 3 60
(Charles Hills) *prom: rdn over 2f out: wknd over 1f out* **11/2**[2]

04-0 **8** *4* **Go On Mayson**[44] 1730 3-9-0 **73** AndrewMullen 2 45
(David Evans) *in rr: u.p over 2f out: nvr a threat* **40/1**

14 **9** *1* **Cyrus Dallin**[90] 927 3-9-5 **78** AndreaAtzeni 14 48
(William Muir) *hld up: rdn over 3f out: no imp u.p 2f out: wknd over 1f out* **20/1**

-153 **10** *½* **Fear The Fury (USA)**[27] 2145 3-8-12 **76** CliffordLee(5) 9 45
(K R Burke) *edgey in stalls: midfield: rdn 3f out: wknd 2f out* **6/1**[3]

1m 37.8s (-5.90) **Going Correction** -0.55s/f (Hard) course record **10** Ran SP% **115.7**
Speed ratings (Par 101): **107,106,105,104,101 101,96,92,91,90**
CSF £48.61 CT £220.08 TOTE £6.50: £1.80, £2.90, £2.10; EX 44.20 Trifecta £316.10.
**Owner** The Sidewinder Partnership **Bred** John Hutchinson **Trained** Malpas, Cheshire

**FOCUS**
A fairly decent 3yo handicap. They went a proper gallop and the long-time leader got collared late into the action by a previous C&D winner under Richard Kingscote, who completed a treble on the card. Further improvement from the winner.

## 3041 ALBERT BROWN MEMORIAL H'CAP (A JOCKEY CLUB GRASSROOTS MIDDLE DISTANCE SERIES QUALIFIER) 1m 2f 42y
**5:10** (5:12) (Class 5) (0-70,71) 3-Y-O **£3,557** (£1,058; £529; £264) **Stalls** Centre

Form RPR

000- **1** **Dream Machine (IRE)**[191] 7976 3-9-4 **67** LouisSteward 5 75
(Michael Bell) *prom: rdn to ld 2f out: edgd lft wl ins fnl f: hld on wl* **8/1**

6151 **2** *¾* **Bartholomew J (IRE)**[23] 2315 3-8-10 **62** SimonPearce(3) 7 68+
(Lydia Pearce) *s.i.s: in rr: swtchd rt over 2f out: hdwy over 1f out: r.o ins fnl f: fin wl* **17/2**

4223 **3** *1 ½* **Alexander M (IRE)**[14] 2588 3-9-7 **70** FrannyNorton 1 73
(Mark Johnston) *a.p: led 3f out: hdd 2f out: rdn and stl ev ch 1f out: no ex towards fin* **11/4**[1]

1432 **4** *¾* **Moneyoryourlife**[20] 2394 3-9-5 **68** SeanLevey 8 70
(Richard Hannon) *hld up: hdwy 2f out: angled rt for run over 1f out: styd on ins fnl f: nt quite pce of ldrs* **5/1**[3]

4133 **5** *1* **Critical Thinking (IRE)**[32] 2036 3-8-12 **66** CliffordLee(5) 4 66
(Kevin Frost) *midfield: effrt 2f out: chsd ldrs for press over 1f out: styd on same pce fnl 100yds* **14/1**

44-0 **6** *3 ¼* **Solent Meads (IRE)**[14] 2588 3-9-8 **71** (b) RobHornby 2 64
(Daniel Kubler) *midfield: rdn over 2f out: no imp over 1f out: one pce ins fnl f* **50/1**

0-45 **7** *12* **Hugging The Rails (IRE)**[10] 2703 3-8-4 **53** (b) AndrewMullen 6 22
(Tim Easterby) *prom: rdn 3f out: wknd over 1f out* **16/1**

0306 **8** *nk* **Baker Street**[16] 2527 3-8-12 **61** RichardKingscote 10 29
(Tom Dascombe) *led: rdn and hdd 3f out: wknd over 2f out: eased whn wl btn over 1f out* **13/2**

36-0 **9** *36* **Dutch Quality**[31] 2066 3-9-7 **70** AndreaAtzeni 9
(Marco Botti) *hld up: rdn over 4f out: no imp 3f out: eased whn wl btn over 1f out* **4/1**[2]

2m 8.08s (-4.62) **Going Correction** -0.55s/f (Hard) **9** Ran SP% **112.8**
Speed ratings (Par 99): **96,95,94,93,92 90,80,80,51**
CSF £68.46 CT £205.06 TOTE £8.70: £2.50, £2.40, £1.20; EX 65.50 Trifecta £379.50.
**Owner** J Barnett & Timmy Hyde **Bred** Keatly Overseas Ltd **Trained** Newmarket, Suffolk
■ Fleetfoot Jack was withdrawn. Price at time of withdrawal 16/1. Rule 4 applies to all bets - deduction 5p in the pound.

**FOCUS**
A modest 3yo handicap. They went a respectable gallop and the closing second didn't get out in time. The form is rated around the third and fourth.

## 3042 WATCH RACING UK ON BT TV H'CAP 1m 2f 42y
**5:40** (5:41) (Class 3) (0-95,95) 3-Y-O **£7,439** (£2,213; £1,106; £553) **Stalls** Centre

Form RPR

1 **1** **Laraaib (IRE)**[21] 2359 3-8-9 **83** JimCrowley 5 93+
(Owen Burrows) *chsd ldr: led over 2f out: rdn over 1f out: r.o and in command wl ins fnl f* **4/1**[3]

1-1 **2** *1 ¾* **Atty Persse (IRE)**[28] 2126 3-9-3 **91** WilliamBuick 6 97
(Roger Charlton) *broke wl: sn hld up in rr: hdwy over 2f out: sn wnt 2nd: rdn whn chalng 1f out: edgd rt and unable qck ins fnl f: hld after* **1/1**[1]

4-1 **3** *½* **Weekender**[50] 1584 3-8-11 **85** AndreaAtzeni 7 90
(John Gosden) *hld up: pushed along 3f out: rdn whn chsng ldrs over 1f out: kpt on ins fnl f: unable to mount serious chal* **11/4**[2]

25-6 **4** *3 ¼* **Star Of Rory (IRE)**[14] 2569 3-9-7 **95** RichardKingscote 1 93
(Tom Dascombe) *prom: rdn and outpcd over 2f out: no imp after* **18/1**

01-3 **5** *2 ¼* **Total Star**[16] 2520 3-9-7 **95** DavidProbert 2 89
(Luca Cumani) *led: rdn and hdd over 2f out: wknd over 1f out* **12/1**

2m 7.25s (-5.45) **Going Correction** -0.55s/f (Hard) course record **5** Ran SP% **109.6**
Speed ratings (Par 103): **99,97,97,94,92**
CSF £8.45 TOTE £5.00: £2.40, £1.10; EX 8.00 Trifecta £18.90.
**Owner** Hamdan Al Maktoum **Bred** Shadwell Estate Company Limited **Trained** Lambourn, Berks

**FOCUS**
The feature contest was a good 3yo handicap which produced the quickest of the three 1m2f races on the day off a respectable gallop. The first three were unexposed and all are potentially better than this.
T/Jkpt: Not won. T/Plt: £37.80 to a £1 stake. Pool: £58,897.00 - 1,555.66 winning units T/Qpdt: £13.00 to a £1 stake. Pool: £4,398.00 - 336.60 winning units **Darren Owen**

# 2372 MUSSELBURGH (R-H)
Friday, May 26

**OFFICIAL GOING: Good to firm (watered; 6.7)**
Wind: Slight, half against in over 3f of home straight Weather: Sunny, hot

## 3043 RACING UK NOW IN HD H'CAP 1m 4f 104y
**6:40** (6:40) (Class 6) (0-65,64) 4-Y-O+ **£3,234** (£962; £481; £240) **Stalls** Low

Form RPR

0-11 **1** **Sebastian's Wish (IRE)**[22] 2340 4-9-7 **64** JoeFanning 5 76+
(Keith Dalgleish) *mde all at ordinary gallop: pushed clr fr over 2f out: eased ins fnl f* **5/2**[1]

2144 **2** *7* **Surround Sound**[29] 2111 7-9-3 **63** (t) RachelRichardson(3) 7 66
(Tim Easterby) *missed break: hld up: effrt and rdn over 2f out: hung rt over 1f out: chsd (clr) wnr ins fnl f: kpt on: no imp* **7/1**

6-01 **3** *1* **Mrs Biggs**[11] 2688 5-8-2 **50** PhilDennis(5) 8 49
(Declan Carroll) *chsd wnr to 4f out: sn drvn along: rallied and regained 2nd over 2f out to ins fnl f: no ex* **6/1**[3]

0443 **4** *1 ¼* **Tred Softly (IRE)**[30] 2079 4-9-1 **58** (b) JackGarritty 4 55
(John Quinn) *trckd ldrs: rdn and wnt 2nd 4f out to over 2f out: edgd rt and outpcd over 1f out* **10/1**

6521 **5** *hd* **Mr Sundowner (USA)**[11] 2687 5-8-2 **52** (t) ConnorMurtagh(7) 6 49
(Wilf Storey) *hld up: rdn and hdwy on outside over 2f out: edgd rt and outpcd over 1f out* **9/2**[2]

3013 **6** *1 ½* **Star Ascending (IRE)**[23] 2308 5-9-1 **58** (p) JoeDoyle 1 53
(Jennie Candlish) *in tch: rdn and hung rt over 2f out: no imp over 1f out* **8/1**

3/06 **7** *1 ¼* **Jebulani**[22] 2340 7-7-13 **45** (p) NathanEvans(3) 2 38
(Barry Murtagh) *hld up in tch on ins: drvn and struggling over 2f out: btn over 1f out* **80/1**

0-24 **8** *1* **Fillydelphia (IRE)**[11] 2687 6-8-7 **57** PaulaMuir(7) 10 48
(Patrick Holmes) *hld up in tch: effrt and rdn 3f out: wknd over 1f out* **28/1**

0144 **9** *2* **Thorntoun Care**[22] 2340 6-9-4 **61** (b) TomEaves 9 49
(Iain Jardine) *s.i.s: hld up: stdy hdwy 3f out: rdn and wknd over 1f out* **10/1**

66-5 **10** *4 ½* **Celtic Power**[19] 2427 5-8-12 **55** SamJames 3 36
(Jim Goldie) *hld up: drvn along 3f out: wknd fnl 2f* **20/1**

2m 44.23s (2.23) **Going Correction** +0.10s/f (Good) **10** Ran SP% **112.3**
Speed ratings (Par 101): **96,91,90,89,89 88,87,87,85,82**
CSF £18.97 CT £92.65 TOTE £2.60: £1.40, £2.50, £1.50; EX 23.20 Trifecta £88.80.
**Owner** Two Goldfish & A Balloon **Bred** Gestut Schlenderhan **Trained** Carluke, S Lanarks
■ Stewards' Enquiry : Connor Murtagh two-day ban: failed to obtain best possible placing (Jun 9-10)

**FOCUS**
Add 10yds to race distance. The going was good to firm after a drying day. They went an even tempo for this open handicap.

## 3044 RACINGUK.COM MAIDEN STKS 7f 33y
7:10 (7:11) (Class 5) 3-Y-0+ £3,234 (£962; £481; £240) Stalls Low

Form RPR
23-2 1 **Aimez La Vie (IRE)**30 2078 3-8-12 73 PaulHanagan 4 76
(Richard Fahey) *trckd ldrs: effrt and plld out over 1f out: sn drvn along: kpt on wl to ld cl home* 11/10[1]
54-3 2 shd **Cheerfilly (IRE)**14 2572 3-8-12 77 BenCurtis 2 75
(Tom Dascombe) *t.k.h early: led at ordinary gallop: hung lft bnd over 3f out: rdn and hrd pressed fr 2f out: edgd lft and kpt on fnl f: hdd cl home* 2/1[2]
24-3 3 1 ¼ **Undiscovered Angel (FR)**32 2033 3-8-9 73 JordanVaughan(3) 1 71
(K R Burke) *trckd ldr: chal gng wl over 2f out: rdn and edgd lft over 1f out: one pce whn n.m.r cl home* 11/4[3]
4 13 **Palace Ball** 3-8-12 0 TomEaves 3 36
(Stuart Coltherd) *.dwlt: bhd: outpcd and hung rt over 2f out: sn wknd* 33/1
1m 30.74s (1.74) **Going Correction** +0.10s/f (Good) 4 Ran SP% 110.6
Speed ratings (Par 103): **94,93,92,77**
CSF £3.72 TOTE £1.80; EX 3.40 Trifecta £3.90.
**Owner** Mr & Mrs N Wrigley **Bred** Lynn Lodge Stud And Foxtale Farm **Trained** Musley Bank, N Yorks

**FOCUS**
Add 10yds to race distance. Not a bad maiden despite the small field. It was run at a steady pace and produced an exciting finish. The winner is rated to a better view of his form.

## 3045 SHAWBROOK BANK H'CAP 7f 33y
7:40 (7:40) (Class 3) (0-90,88) 3-Y-0+ £12,938 (£3,850; £1,924; £962) Stalls Low

Form RPR
0051 1 **Luis Vaz De Torres (IRE)**30 2081 5-9-7 81 (h) PaulHanagan 6 88
(Richard Fahey) *in tch: stdy hdwy on outside over 2f out: chsd ldr: edgd rt and drvn over 1f out: led wl ins fnl f: r.o* 6/1
30-2 2 ¾ **Glengarry**17 2500 4-9-12 86 TomEaves 2 91
(Keith Dalgleish) *t.k.h: led: qcknd 3f out: sn rdn along: hdd wl ins fnl f: no ex* 7/2[2]
-105 3 1 ½ **Chaplin Bay (IRE)**17 2500 5-9-2 76 JamesSullivan 4 77
(Ruth Carr) *dwlt: hld up: effrt and hdwy 2f out: kpt on same pce ins fnl f* 11/2[3]
4-50 4 3 ½ **Storm Cry**16 2517 3-8-5 81 RichardOliver(5) 1 68
(Mark Johnston) *t.k.h: trckd ldrs tl rdn and wknd over 1f out* 7/1
F-31 5 1 **Thomas Cranmer (USA)**21 2374 3-9-3 88 JoeFanning 3 73
(Mark Johnston) *chsd ldr: drvn along over 2f out: wknd wl over 1f out* 6/4[1]
-046 6 6 **Ralphy Boy (IRE)**4 2888 8-8-11 71 JoeDoyle 5 44
(Alistair Whillans) *hld up: pushed along whn checked wl over 2f out: sn rdn: wknd wl over 1f out* 14/1
1m 28.48s (-0.52) **Going Correction** +0.10s/f (Good)
**WFA** 3 from 4yo+ 11lb 6 Ran SP% 111.1
Speed ratings (Par 107): **106,105,103,99,98 91**
CSF £26.34 TOTE £7.00: £2.40, £2.30; EX 25.00 Trifecta £89.00.
**Owner** Lets Go Racing 1 **Bred** Peter Molony **Trained** Musley Bank, N Yorks

**FOCUS**
Add 10yds to race distance. A fair handicap run at a sound pace. The form's rated a bit cautiously.

## 3046 DAIKIN APPLIED (UK) LTD H'CAP 1m 5f 216y
8:10 (8:11) (Class 4) (0-80,81) 4-Y-0+ £7,762 (£2,310; £1,154; £577) Stalls Low

Form RPR
04-6 1 **Great Fighter**13 991 7-9-4 73 (v) SamJames 9 84
(Jim Goldie) *dwlt: hld up: stdy hdwy over 2f out: rdn to ld appr fnl f: kpt on strly to draw clr* 11/4[2]
0103 2 4 ½ **Cosmic Tigress**22 2340 6-8-5 60 JamesSullivan 5 64
(John Quinn) *hld up: hdwy on outside over 2f out: drvn and chsd (clr) wnr ins fnl f: kpt on: nt pce to chal* 16/1
0253 3 nse **Falcon's Fire (IRE)**21 2375 4-9-5 74 PaulHanagan 4 78
(Keith Dalgleish) *prom: hdwy to ld over 2f out: rdn and hdd appr fnl f: no ex and lost 2nd ins fnl f* 9/1
2523 4 3 **Star Of Lombardy (IRE)**9 2723 4-9-7 76 JoeFanning 10 75
(Mark Johnston) *cl up: rdn and ev ch over 2f out: edgd rt and outpcd fr over 1f out* 7/1[3]
26- 5 ¾ **Maoi Chinn Tire (IRE)**218 5061 10-9-7 76 (p) JoeDoyle 7 74
(Jennie Candlish) *hld up: pushed along and effrt over 2f out: outpcd fr over 1f out* 18/1
/0-0 6 ¾ **Buyer Beware (IRE)**29 1719 5-9-4 73 JackGarritty 2 70
(Patrick Holmes) *trckd ldrs: drvn and outpcd over 2f out: n.d after* 66/1
-064 7 hd **Card High (IRE)**44 1719 7-8-11 73 (t) ConnorMurtagh(7) 6 70
(Wilf Storey) *t.k.h: hld up: hdwy and cl up after 6f: rdn and wknd over 1f out* 9/1
40-0 8 1 ¼ **Stormin Tom (IRE)**20 2386 5-9-2 74 RachelRichardson(3) 3 69
(Tim Easterby) *led: rdn and hdd over 2f out: sn wknd* 16/1
10-2 9 2 **Purple Rock (IRE)**9 2741 5-9-9 81 (t) NathanEvans(3) 8 73
(Michael Easterby) *hld up: drvn and outpcd 3f out: btn fnl 2f* 7/4[1]
3m 2.17s (-3.13) **Going Correction** +0.10s/f (Good) 9 Ran SP% 114.1
Speed ratings (Par 105): **112,109,109,107,107 106,106,106,104**
CSF £45.08 CT £348.61 TOTE £4.00: £1.40, £2.80, £2.10; EX 45.10 Trifecta £333.50.
**Owner** J Fyffe **Bred** Darley **Trained** Uplawmoor, E Renfrews
■ Stewards' Enquiry : Joe Fanning caution; careless riding

**FOCUS**
Add 10yds to race distance. This was competitive enough and they went an honest pace. The winner carried his jumps improvement over.

## 3047 CENTRAL TAXIS FASTER GREENER SAFER H'CAP 7f 33y
8:40 (8:41) (Class 5) (0-70,68) 3-Y-0 £5,175 (£1,540; £769; £384) Stalls Low

Form RPR
-552 1 **Our Charlie Brown**4 2885 3-9-6 67 JamesSullivan 1 77+
(Tim Easterby) *t.k.h: trckd ldrs: smooth hdwy to ld over 1f out: rdn out* 6/4[1]
425- 2 2 **Vaulted**223 7355 3-9-7 68 PaulHanagan 2 71
(Richard Fahey) *hld up: stdy hdwy over 2f out: effrt and swtchd lft over 1f out: sn chsng wnr: kpt on fnl f: nt pce to chal* 4/1[2]
0-00 3 shd **Aelius**13 2625 3-9-1 65 (t) NathanEvans(3) 8 68
(Michael Easterby) *dwlt: hld up: rdn and hdwy over 2f out: kpt on ins fnl f* 9/2[3]
504- 4 nk **Pepys**189 8009 3-9-2 63 TomEaves 3 65
(Bryan Smart) *hld up towards rr: rdn over 2f out: keeping on whn checked over 1f out: kpt on: no imp* 10/1
2602 5 6 **Hollywood Harry (IRE)**18 2455 3-8-7 59 (p) RowanScott(5) 6 45
(Keith Dalgleish) *pressed ldr: led 1/2-way to over 1f out: wknd fnl f* 8/1
30-0 6 7 **Kiribati**24 2252 3-9-7 68 JoeFanning 4 35
(Mark Johnston) *led to 1/2-way: cl up tl rdn and wknd over 1f out: eased* 14/1
-666 7 4 ½ **Lady Molly (IRE)**17 2499 3-8-10 57 SamJames 7 12
(Keith Dalgleish) *hld up: drvn and struggling over 2f out: sn wknd* 20/1
20-0 8 3 ¼ **Harbour Lightning**30 2080 3-8-11 63 PhilDennis(5) 5 9
(Noel Wilson) *prom: rdn over 2f out: wknd over 1f out* 33/1
1m 29.24s (0.24) **Going Correction** +0.10s/f (Good) 8 Ran SP% 112.8
Speed ratings (Par 99): **102,99,99,99,92 84,79,75**
CSF £7.23 CT £20.87 TOTE £2.00: £1.10, £2.10, £1.80; EX 8.60 Trifecta £48.80.
**Owner** Ontoawinner, SDH Project Services Ltd 2 **Bred** North Bradon Stud & D R Tucker **Trained** Great Habton, N Yorks

**FOCUS**
Add 10yds to race distance. A strongly run handicap with the front four finishing clear. The second and third help the standard.

## 3048 PAY FOR RACING UK VIA PHONE BILL H'CAP 1m 2y
9:10 (9:10) (Class 6) (0-65,67) 4-Y-0+ £3,234 (£962; £481; £240) Stalls Low

Form RPR
2141 1 **Cosmic Ray**21 2378 5-9-12 67 (h) JoeFanning 5 75
(Les Eyre) *t.k.h: trckd ldrs: shkn up to ld over 1f out: kpt on wl fnl f* 9/4[1]
6402 2 2 **Adventureman**21 2378 5-9-7 62 (p) JamesSullivan 7 65
(Ruth Carr) *t.k.h: led: rdn: edgd lft and hdd over 1f out: rallied: kpt on same pce ins fnl f* 6/1[3]
-050 3 ½ **Let Right Be Done**2 2955 5-8-7 48 (p) JoeDoyle 3 50
(Linda Perratt) *hld up: rdn along and hdwy over 2f out: kpt on ins fnl f: nvr able to chal* 25/1
0000 4 nk **Ellaal**22 2339 8-9-5 67 ConnorMurtagh(7) 4 68
(Ruth Carr) *t.k.h: in tch: rdn and effrt over 2f out: kpt on same pce ins fnl f* 9/1
4023 5 1 **Miss Goldsmith (IRE)**18 2464 4-9-5 60 (h) PaulHanagan 2 59
(Richard Fahey) *hld up: rdn over 2f out: hdwy over 1f out: edgd lft: kpt on same pce fnl f* 6/1[3]
-040 6 1 **Cyflymder (IRE)**22 2342 11-8-4 48 oh3 RachelRichardson(3) 9 44
(David C Griffiths) *in tch: rdn along over 2f out: wknd over 1f out* 33/1
-052 7 ¾ **Amy Blair**7 2773 4-8-9 55 (h) RowanScott(5) 6 50
(Keith Dalgleish) *t.k.h: pressed ldr: drvn over 2f out: wknd over 1f out* 7/2[2]
0-40 8 12 **Catastrophe**125 361 4-9-3 58 JackGarritty 1 24
(John Quinn) *prom: drvn and outpcd over 2f out: sn wknd* 10/1
34-0 9 10 **Silver Duke (IRE)**142 44 6-9-3 58 (b) SamJames 10
(Jim Goldie) *s.i.s: sn pushed along in rr: struggling wl over 2f out: sn btn* 18/1
1m 41.59s (0.39) **Going Correction** +0.10s/f (Good) 9 Ran SP% 112.7
Speed ratings (Par 101): **102,100,99,99,98 97,96,84,74**
CSF £15.57 CT £260.35 TOTE £3.70: £1.20, £1.60, £5.10; EX 12.00 Trifecta £255.40.
**Owner** Over The Moon Racing III **Bred** Winterbeck Manor Stud **Trained** Catwick, N Yorks

**FOCUS**
Add 10yds to race distance. A moderate handicap.
T/Plt: £61.30 to a £1 stake. Pool: £37,574.00 - 612.86 winning units T/Qpdt: £17.80 to a £1 stake. Pool: £2,854.00 - 160.33 winning units **Richard Young**

# 2299 PONTEFRACT (L-H)
Friday, May 26

**OFFICIAL GOING: Good (good to firm in places; watered; 8.8)**
Wind: Light across Weather: Fine & dry

## 3049 RUGBY LEAGUE EVENING ON 12TH JUNE H'CAP 1m 6y
6:30 (6:30) (Class 5) (0-75,76) 4-Y-0+ £3,234 (£962; £481; £240) Stalls Low

Form RPR
-544 1 **Mon Beau Visage (IRE)**11 2685 4-9-7 75 (p) DanielTudhope 2 84
(David O'Meara) *in tch: hdwy to trck ldrs 3f out: effrt on outer and cl up 2f out: led appr fnl f: sn rdn and styd on* 11/4[1]
6-04 2 1 ½ **Hanseatic**27 2133 8-9-0 75 (t) HarrisonShaw(7) 3 80
(Michael Easterby) *trckd ldrs on inner: effrt and nt clr run wl over 1f out: rdn and hdwy ent fnl f: sn chsng wnr: drvn and no imp towards fin* 11/4[1]
1025 3 nk **Chiswick Bey (IRE)**27 2140 9-9-0 71 AdamMcNamara(3) 13 75
(Richard Fahey) *rr: hdwy 3f out: rdn wl over 1f out: styd on appr fnl f* 16/1
60-2 4 4 **Whitkirk**27 2140 4-8-10 64 TonyHamilton 9 59
(Jedd O'Keeffe) *sn trcking ldr: hdwy and cl up 3f out: rdn to ld briefly wl over 1f out: sn hdd and drvn: wknd ins fnl f* 7/1[2]
-02 5 3 **Be Kool (IRE)**19 2430 4-9-5 73 (v) CamHardie 11 61
(Brian Ellison) *t.k.h: hld up in midfield: hdwy on outer over 2f out: rdn along wl over 1f out: n.d* 12/1[3]
20-0 6 1 ¼ **Talent Scout (IRE)**25 2224 11-8-7 66 (p) GemmaTutty(5) 8 51
(Karen Tutty) *led: pushed along over 2f out: rdn and hdd wl over 1f out: sn wknd* 33/1
10-0 7 ½ **Nonno Giulio (IRE)**11 2685 6-9-4 75 JoshDoyle(3) 5 59
(Tony Coyle) *chsd ldrs: rdn along 3f out: sn drvn and wknd* 25/1
0000 8 1 ¼ **Swiftee (IRE)**28 2119 4-8-0 61 oh7 (b[1]) JaneElliott(7) 7 42
(Ivan Furtado) *dwlt: a towards rr* 40/1
045- 9 12 **Interlink (USA)**157 8473 4-9-3 71 SilvestreDeSousa 6 24
(Michael Appleby) *in tch: hdwy to chse ldrs 3f out: rdn along over 2f out: sn drvn and wknd* 11/4[1]
0-05 10 14 **Willsy**28 2120 4-8-11 65 ShaneGray 4
(Karen Tutty) *blind removed late: s.i.s: a detached* 25/1
1m 45.3s (-0.60) **Going Correction** +0.05s/f (Good) 10 Ran SP% 119.1
Speed ratings (Par 103): **105,103,103,99,96 94,94,93,81,67**
CSF £9.73 CT £104.88 TOTE £3.70: £1.30, £1.70, £3.90; EX 13.00 Trifecta £98.50.
**Owner** The Pink Pot Partnership LLP **Bred** Stephanie Hanly **Trained** Upper Helmsley, N Yorks

**FOCUS**
A strongly-run handicap and most convincing performance by the winner in a race in which the first three were clear. The winner is rated to his AW best.

## 3050 CONSTANT SECURITY SERVING YORKSHIRE RACECOURSES H'CAP 1m 4f 5y
**7:00** (7:00) (Class 4) (0-80,82) 4-Y-0+ **£5,175** (£1,540; £769; £384) **Stalls** Low

Form RPR
20-1 **1** **Mutadaffeq (IRE)**[13] 2629 4-9-9 **82**................................ DanielTudhope 8 93+
(David O'Meara) *hld up: stdy hdwy over 4f out: trckd ldrs 3f out: rdn to ld jst over 1f out: drvn ins fnl f: kpt on wl towards fin* **3/1**[1]
5-00 **2** *1 ½* **Itlaaq**[13] 2622 11-8-11 **75**.....................................(t) MeganNicholls[(5)] 6 83
(Michael Easterby) *hld up in rr: stdy hdwy on outer over 4f out: trckd ldrs over 2f out: rdn over 1f out: chsd wnr ins fnl f: sn drvn and ch tl no ex last 100 yds* **25/1**
140- **3** *2 ¼* **Pumblechook**[234] 7060 4-9-4 **77**........................................ PJMcDonald 9 81
(Mark Johnston) *trckd ldrs: hdwy 3f out: rdn along wl over 1f out: kpt on fnl f* **8/1**
10-0 **4** *3 ¼* **Torremar (FR)**[66] 1292 4-9-1 **74**.........................................(p) KevinStott 2 73
(Kevin Ryan) *chsd ldr 1f: prom: hdwy and cl up over 3f out: led wl over 2f out: rdn along and hdd wl over 1f out: sn drvn and kpt on one pce* **16/1**
1-54 **5** *2 ¼* **Western Prince**[122] 389 4-9-5 **78**.......................(h) SilvestreDeSousa 10 73
(Michael Appleby) *hld up: hdwy over 4f out: rdn along to chse ldrs over 2f out: drvn wl over 1f out: no imp* **7/1**[3]
0-06 **6** *1* **Indian Chief (IRE)**[25] 2225 7-8-10 **69**............................ DuranFentiman 4 63
(Rebecca Bastiman) *dwlt and rr: hdwy on outer over 2f out: rdn along wl over 1f out: kpt on: n.d* **25/1**
0444 **7** *hd* **Mysterial**[14] 2594 7-8-7 **71**............................................ LewisEdmunds[(5)] 3 64
(Declan Carroll) *led: jnd and pushed along 4f out: rdn and hdd wl over 2f out: sn drvn and wknd* **4/1**[2]
030- **8** *9* **Ingleby Hollow**[200] 7846 5-8-12 **74**................................... JoshDoyle[(3)] 5 53
(David O'Meara) *trckd ldrs: hdwy 4f out: rdn along over 2f out: sn drvn and wknd* **14/1**
050- **9** *½* **Hernandoshideaway**[251] 6561 5-9-2 **80**..........(p) CallumRodriguez[(5)] 11 58
(Michael Dods) *t.k.h: help up in midfield: pushed along 4f out: rdn wl over 2f out: sn btn* **12/1**
22-0 **10** *22* **Tamayuz Magic (IRE)**[54] 1517 6-9-2 **82**...............(b) HarrisonShaw[(7)] 12 25
(Michael Easterby) *prom: chsd ldr after 1f: rdn along 3f out: sn wknd* **8/1**
452- **11** *25* **Scottish Summit (IRE)**[317] 4272 4-9-1 **74**........................... DavidAllan 1
(Geoffrey Harker) *midfield: rdn along over 3f out: sn wknd* **14/1**
063/ **12** *19* **Sheriff Of Nawton (IRE)**[543] 8056 6-9-3 **76**.................. TonyHamilton 7
(Roger Fell) *a towards rr* **50/1**

2m 36.82s (-3.98) **Going Correction** +0.05s/f (Good) 12 Ran SP% **116.3**
Speed ratings (Par 105): **115,114,112,110,108 108,108,102,101,87 70,57**
CSF £85.26 CT £551.33 TOTE £3.90: £1.70, £6.10, £3.00; EX 50.10 Trifecta £2215.80.
**Owner** The Get Round The Back Syndicate **Bred** Shadwell Estate Company Limited **Trained** Upper Helmsley, N Yorks

**FOCUS**
A strongly-run handicap in which the first two both came from off the pace. The winner confirmed the good impression from Thirsk.

## 3051 EBF STALLIONS YOUNGSTERS CONDITIONS STKS (PLUS 10 RACE) 6f
**7:30** (7:35) (Class 2) 2-Y-0 **£12,450** (£3,728; £1,864; £932) **Stalls** Low

Form RPR
4 **1** **Rufus King**[7] 2786 2-9-2 0................................................... PJMcDonald 5 89
(Mark Johnston) *trckd ldng pair: lft in slt ld over 4f out: pushed along 2f out: rdn over 1f out: kpt on strly fnl f* **2/1**[1]
13 **2** *6* **Inviolable Spirit (IRE)**[23] 2286 2-9-6 0.......................... TonyHamilton 6 75
(Richard Fahey) *cl up whn carried bdly rt after 1f: trckd ldng pair after: hdwy 2f out: rdn to chse wnr over 1f out: drvn ent fnl f: kpt on same pce* **7/2**[3]
1 **3** *1* **Havana Star (IRE)**[25] 2222 2-9-6 0...................................... KevinStott 4 72
(Kevin Ryan) *slt ld whn hung bdly rt after 1f: sn corrected and cl up: rdn along and hung rt home turn 2f out: sn drvn and kpt on same pce* **11/4**[2]
**4** *25* **Situation** 2-8-13 0.................................................................. ShaneGray 7
(Richard Guest) *green: sn outpcd and a bhd* **25/1**

1m 19.04s (2.14) **Going Correction** +0.05s/f (Good) 4 Ran SP% **86.1**
Speed ratings (Par 99): **87,79,77,44**
CSF £5.36 TOTE £2.10; EX 4.30 Trifecta £4.70.
**Owner** Garrett J Freyne Racing **Bred** Newsells Park Stud **Trained** Middleham Moor, N Yorks
■ Jasi and Squirrelheed were withdrawn. Price at time of withdrawal 3/1 and 20/1 respectively. Rule 4 applies to all bets - deduction 25p in the pound.

**FOCUS**
A race reduced to four runners and though the winner is a likeable sort who should progress it is hard to know what the form is worth. The second is rated near his pre-race mark.

## 3052 CONSTANT SECURITY SERVICES H'CAP 5f 3y
**8:00** (8:01) (Class 4) (0-85,85) 4-Y-0+ **£5,175** (£1,540; £769; £384) **Stalls** Low

Form RPR
0-63 **1** **Tumblewind**[5] 2856 7-9-2 **85**........................................ LewisEdmunds[(5)] 3 95+
(Richard Whitaker) *trckd ldrs: effrt whn nt clr run and hmpd 1 1/2f out: n.m.r: swtchd rt and hmpd again 1f out: rdn to chal jst ins fnl f: kpt on wl to ld last 100 yds* **7/2**[1]
0622 **2** *1* **Silvanus (IRE)**[15] 2551 12-9-0 **78**...................................... GrahamLee 11 83
(Paul Midgley) *hld up in rr: hdwy 2f out: rdn to chse ldrs over 1f out: chal and ev ch ent fnl f: sn drvn and kpt on same towards fin* **16/1**
123 **3** *½* **Escalating**[58] 1423 5-9-5 **83**....................................(t) SilvestreDeSousa 12 86
(Michael Appleby) *hld up towards rr: hdwy over 2f out: rdn over 1f out: kpt on wl fnl f* **8/1**
2-00 **4** *1 ¼* **Stanghow**[28] 2123 5-9-5 **83**................................................. CamHardie 10 82
(Antony Brittain) *in tch: hdwy over 2f out: rdn to ld 1 1/2f out and sn hung lft: drvn and edgd lft ent fnl f: hdd last 100 yds: one pce* **20/1**
0-00 **5** *1 ½* **B Fifty Two (IRE)**[20] 2381 8-9-7 **85**...................................(t) PhillipMakin 5 78
(Marjorie Fife) *in tch: hdwy 2f out: rdn over 1f out: no imp fnl f* **14/1**
-000 **6** *nk* **Musharrif**[20] 2409 5-8-12 **76**............................................... TonyHamilton 2 68
(Declan Carroll) *led: rdn along 2f out: hdd 1 1/2f out: sn drvn and grad wknd* **10/1**
-506 **7** *1* **First Bombardment**[20] 2409 4-9-3 **81**.........................(h) DanielTudhope 1 69
(David O'Meara) *chsd ldrs: rdn along on inner 2f out: drvn over 1f out: grad wknd* **7/1**[3]
0-35 **8** *hd* **Grandad's World (IRE)**[26] 2184 5-8-13 **80**........... AdamMcNamara[(3)] 6 68
(Richard Fahey) *a towards rr* **13/2**[2]
0323 **9** *1 ½* **Highly Sprung (IRE)**[16] 2516 4-9-5 **83**............................ FrannyNorton 4 65+
(Mark Johnston) *.a towards rr* **7/1**[3]
20-1 **10** *1 ¾* **Black Grass**[36] 1915 4-8-10 **81**.................................(v[1]) HarrisonShaw[(7)] 9 57
(Michael Easterby) *cl up: rdn along to dispute ld 2f out: drvn and n.m.r over 1f out: hld whn hmpd ent fnl f* **10/1**
3113 **11** *2 ¼* **Oriental Relation (IRE)**[15] 2551 6-9-1 **79**.................(b) PaulMulrennan 7 47
(James Given) *chsd ldng pair: rdn along whn hmpd and bmpd 1 1/2f out: drvn and hmpd again 1f out: wknd* **9/1**
443- **12** *¾* **Astrophysics**[189] 8010 5-8-9 **73**........................................... PaddyAspell 8 38
(Lynn Siddall) *dwlt: a rr* **33/1**

1m 3.23s (-0.07) **Going Correction** +0.05s/f (Good) 12 Ran SP% **120.1**
Speed ratings (Par 105): **102,100,99,97,95 94,93,92,90,87 84,82**
CSF £65.33 CT £434.30 TOTE £3.80: £1.60, £4.40, £2.50; EX 73.90 Trifecta £639.60.
**Owner** R M Whitaker **Bred** Hellwood Stud Farm **Trained** Scarcroft, W Yorks

**FOCUS**
A run-of-the-mill sprint handicap in which the well-backed winner did well to overcome trouble in running. He looks back to his best, albeit helped by a 5lb claim.

## 3053 BANANARAMA LIVE AFTER THE LAST RACE FILLIES' H'CAP 1m 2f 5y
**8:30** (8:30) (Class 5) (0-70,69) 3-Y-0+ **£3,234** (£962; £481; £240) **Stalls** Low

Form RPR
-232 **1** **Bonnie Arlene (IRE)**[44] 1726 3-8-9 **64**............................ FrannyNorton 6 70
(Mark Johnston) *trckd ldr: hdwy and cl up over 2f out: rdn to ld 1 1/2f out: drvn ins fnl f: kpt on wl* **10/3**[2]
-466 **2** *1 ¾* **Livella Fella (IRE)**[37] 1879 4-10-0 **69**......................... SilvestreDeSousa 2 72
(Keith Dalgleish) *led: jnd over 2f out: rdn and hdd 1 1/2f out: sn drvn: kpt on same pce fnl f* **7/4**[1]
136- **3** *shd* **Rubis**[147] 8586 4-9-3 **58**....................................................... TonyHamilton 3 61
(Richard Fahey) *hld up in rr: hdwy over 2f out: rdn along wl over 1f out: styd on fnl f* **9/2**[3]
40-0 **4** *1 ¼* **Babamunchkin**[18] 2475 3-8-10 **65**..................................... PaulMulrennan 5 65
(Michael Bell) *dwlt and rr: hdwy on outer wl over 1f out: rdn and kpt on fnl f* **7/1**
006- **5** *shd* **Navajo Thunder (IRE)**[256] 6421 3-8-1 **56**......................... AndrewMullen 7 55
(Michael Appleby) *t.k.h: trckd ldng pair: hdwy 2f out: rdn and hung lft over 1f out: sn drvn and one pce* **14/1**
-240 **6** *1 ¼* **Inflexiball**[23] 2308 5-9-2 **57**................................................... GrahamLee 4 55
(John Mackie) *trckd ldng pair on inner: hdwy 3f out: rdn along wl over 1f out: sn drvn and grad wknd* **8/1**
625- **7** *1 ½* **La Havrese (FR)**[151] 8527 6-9-6 **61**..................................... PaddyAspell 1 56
(Lynn Siddall) *t.k.h: in tch: pushed along wl over 2f out: rdn and wknd over 1f out* **16/1**

2m 12.71s (-0.99) **Going Correction** +0.05s/f (Good)
**WFA** 3 from 4yo+ 14lb 7 Ran SP% **113.8**
Speed ratings (Par 100): **105,103,103,102,102 101,100**
CSF £9.50 CT £24.95 TOTE £3.50: £1.70, £1.80; EX 8.10 Trifecta £30.20.
**Owner** Paul Dean & Ron Priestley **Bred** Tinnakill Bloodstock **Trained** Middleham Moor, N Yorks

**FOCUS**
An ordinary fillies' handicap in which the pace was moderate and few featured. It's not the most convincing form.

## 3054 KEN SUTTON 70TH BIRTHDAY MAIDEN STKS 6f
**9:00** (9:02) (Class 5) 3-Y-0+ **£3,234** (£962; £481; £240) **Stalls** Low

Form RPR
3-23 **1** **Castle Hill Cassie (IRE)**[30] 2078 3-9-0 71........................ GrahamLee 4 72
(Ben Haslam) *cl up: rdn to ld ent fnl f: sn edgd lft: drvn and hung lft last 100 yds: jst hld on* **9/2**[2]
2-23 **2** *shd* **Benjamin Thomas (IRE)**[11] 2682 3-9-5 75........................... JasonHart 6 76
(John Quinn) *trckd ldng pair: hdwy to chse wnr jst ins fnl f: sn drvn and ev ch: jst failed* **7/4**[1]
0 **3** *¾* **Jessinamillion**[20] 2383 3-9-5 0........................................... PJMcDonald 5 73
(James Bethell) *hld up towards rr: gd hdwy over 1f out: rdn and styd on strly fnl f* **20/1**
06- **4** *1 ¼* **Equiano Springs**[255] 6447 3-9-5 0..................................... AndrewMullen 3 74+
(Tom Tate) *trckd ldng pair on inner: hdwy wl over 1f out: rdn ent fnl f: styng on along inner whn hmpd and snatched up ins last 100 yds: nt rcvr* **25/1**
0-6 **5** *2 ¾* **Harwood**[20] 2383 3-9-5 0.................................................. DanielTudhope 2 60
(David O'Meara) *slt ld: rdn along wl over 1f out: hdd ent fnl f: hld whn n.m.r and sltly hmpd wl ins fnl f* **7/1**[3]
00 **6** *3* **Tilly Tinker**[26] 2185 3-9-0 0.................................................. CamHardie 7 46
(Michael Easterby) *a rr* **33/1**
P6 **P** **Avago Josh**[38] 1866 3-8-12 0.............................................. JaneElliott[(7)] 8
(Ivan Furtado) *dwlt and bhd: rdn along and outpcd 1/2-way: lost action and detached whn p.u wl over 1f out* **50/1**

1m 16.97s (0.07) **Going Correction** +0.05s/f (Good) 7 Ran SP% **80.6**
Speed ratings (Par 103): **101,100,99,98,94 90,**
CSF £6.00 TOTE £3.70: £1.70, £1.10; EX 5.60 Trifecta £33.80.
**Owner** Ontoawinner Trojan Horse J Pak & Partner **Bred** Yeomanstown Stud **Trained** Middleham Moor, N Yorks
■ Stewards' Enquiry : Graham Lee caution; careless riding

**FOCUS**
Not a strong maiden particularly after the withdrawal at the start of the market leader. The winner is rated to form with the winner a bit below.
T/Plt: £16.20 to a £1 stake. Pool: £76,240.97 - 3,424.74 winning units T/Qpdt: £5.70 to a £1 stake. Pool: £4,525.39 - 578.60 winning units **Joe Rowntree**

3055-3056a (Foreign Racing) - See Raceform Interactive

# 2438 LEOPARDSTOWN (L-H)
Friday, May 26
**OFFICIAL GOING: Good to firm (good in places)**

## 3057a SEAMUS & ROSEMARY MCGRATH MEMORIAL SAVAL BEG STKS (LISTED RACE) 1m 6f
**7:05** (7:05) 4-Y-0+ **£25,213** (£8,119; £3,846; £1,709; £854)

RPR
**1** **Order Of St George (IRE)**[33] 1999 5-9-12 120................. RyanMoore 1 120+
(A P O'Brien, Ire) *w.w bhd ldrs in 4th: pushed along in 4th into st and prog on outer to ld gng best over 1f out: kpt on wl to assert under hands and heels ins fnl f: comf* **4/11**[1]
**2** *2 ¼* **Twilight Payment (IRE)**[33] 1999 4-9-8 108.................(t) KevinManning 2 112
(J S Bolger, Ire) *prom tl sn settled bhd ldrs in 3rd: pushed along in 3rd 3f out and impr u.p to chal briefly on terms over 1f out: sn hdd and no imp on easy wnr ins fnl f: kpt on same pce* **4/1**[2]

3 3 3/4 **Motherland (IRE)**[36] 1918 4-9-5 104........................ DonnachaO'Brien 3 104
(Joseph Patrick O'Brien, Ire) *sn led: over 1 l clr at 1/2-way: pushed along into st and hdd u.p over 1f out: no imp on ldrs disputing 3rd ins fnl f: kpt on one pce in 3rd clsng stages: jst hld 3rd* **8/1**[3]

4 shd **Stars Over The Sea (USA)**[20] 7058 6-9-5 100............. WayneLordan 4 103
(Henry De Bromhead, Ire) *trckd ldr in 2nd: pushed along into st and no imp on ldrs u.p disputing 3rd ins fnl f: kpt on one pce in 4th clsng stages: jst hld for 3rd* **33/1**

5 8 **Carbon Dating (IRE)**[14] 2571 5-9-5 107.......................... ChrisHayes 5 92
(John Patrick Shanahan, Ire) *in rr thrght: rdn into st and no imp on ldrs under 2f out: eased ins fnl f* **16/1**

3m 3.28s (2.28) **Going Correction** +0.475s/f (Yiel) **5** Ran SP% **113.2**
Speed ratings: **112,110,108,108,103**
CSF £2.36 TOTE £1.20: £1.02, £1.90; DF 2.20 Trifecta £5.20.
**Owner** M Tabor/D Smith/Mrs Magnier/L J Williams **Bred** Paget Bloodstock **Trained** Cashel, Co Tipperary

**FOCUS**
A straightforward success for Order Of St George, who will come on plenty for this and he should be hard to beat as he attempts to win back-to-back Ascot Gold Cups. The runner-up has been rated as running a pb.

3058 - 3061a (Foreign Racing) - See Raceform Interactive

# 2568 CHESTER (L-H)
## Saturday, May 27

**OFFICIAL GOING: Good to firm (good in places; watered; 7.9)**
Wind: Breezy, behind in straight Weather: Sultry, cloudy

## 3062 STELLAR GROUP MAIDEN STKS 7f 127y
**1:55** (1:56) (Class 4) 3-Y-0+
**£6,225** (£1,864; £932; £466; £233; £117) **Stalls** Low

Form RPR

30-2 1 **Highland Pass**[15] 2572 3-8-11 78..............................(h) DavidProbert 7 76
(Andrew Balding) *trckd ldrs: 3rd 2f out: pushed along to ld ins fnl f: rdn and r.o wl* **9/4**[2]

-323 2 1 1/4 **Mr Tyrrell (IRE)**[15] 2580 3-9-2 80............................... TimmyMurphy 10 78
(Richard Hannon) *trckd ldrs: pushed along 2f out: hdwy on outer over 1f out: rdn and r.o wl ins fnl f* **7/1**[3]

2 3 1/2 **Musical Terms**[35] 1962 3-9-2 0...................................... PatCosgrave 9 77
(William Haggas) *racd in 2nd: gng wl: pushed along to ld over 1f out: rdn and hdd ins fnl f: one pce* **11/10**[1]

5-0 4 1/2 **Ascot Week (USA)**[25] 2260 3-9-2 0................................. DaneO'Neill 6 76
(Owen Burrows) *led: pushed along and hdd over 1f out: rdn and one pce* **20/1**

43- 5 3 1/4 **Aldrin (FR)**[244] 6805 4-10-0 0.......................................(t) JFEgan 2 71
(David Pipe) *mid-div: briefly rdn over 1f out: eased whn btn* **8/1**

6 2 1/4 **Mac O'Polo (IRE)** 3-9-2 0................................................ BenCurtis 5 63
(Tom Dascombe) *slowly away: in rr: pushed along 3f out: rdn over 2f out: sme late hdwy* **10/1**

40-6 7 2 1/4 **Great Return**[5] 2887 4-9-7 0......................................... JordanUys[(7)] 3 61
(Lisa Williamson) *hld up in rr: pushed along over 2f out: nvr a factor* **50/1**

5660 8 3 1/4 **Rojina (IRE)**[14] 2633 4-9-4 41................................ RobJFitzpatrick[(5)] 4 48?
(Lisa Williamson) *mid-div: pushed along 3f out: drvn over 2f out: grad lost tch* **150/1**

00-0 9 17 **Tamarin**[14] 2626 5-9-9 42................................................(p) KevinStott 1 9
(Lisa Williamson) *t.k.h early: struggling fr 3f out: rdn over 2f out: fdd* **150/1**

1m 35.68s (1.88) **Going Correction** +0.375s/f (Good)
**WFA** 3 from 4yo+ 12lb **9** Ran SP% **119.1**
Speed ratings (Par 105): **105,103,103,102,99 97,95,91,74**
CSF £18.77 TOTE £3.00: £1.50, £2.20, £1.02; EX 17.40 Trifecta £29.90.
**Owner** Kingsclere Racing Club **Bred** Kingsclere Stud **Trained** Kingsclere, Hants

**FOCUS**
The watered ground was given as good to firm, good in places (GoingStick: 7.9). The entire length of the rail was out by between 3yds and 9yds. Race distance increased by 40yds. A fair maiden in which the form trip finished 1-2-3. The winner didn't need to match her best.

## 3063 CORINTHIAN SPORTS FILLIES' H'CAP 6f 17y
**2:30** (2:30) (Class 4) (0-85,84) 3-Y-0+ **£8,086** (£2,406; £1,202; £601) **Stalls** Low

Form RPR

20-0 1 **Turanga Leela**[16] 2557 3-8-12 77..............................(v[1]) PhillipMakin 2 84
(Ian Williams) *qckly away: mde all: kicked clr over 1f out: rdn and hld on wl ins fnl f* **4/1**[1]

4513 2 1 1/2 **Socialites Red**[11] 2700 4-8-3 66...................................(p) RPWalsh[(7)] 6 70
(Scott Dixon) *mid-div: hdwy 2f out: pushed along over 1f out: rdn and r.o wl ins fnl f: nvr nrr* **15/2**

0-61 3 nk **Rose Berry**[21] 2407 3-9-2 81..................................(h) AdamBeschizza 5 86+
(Chris Dwyer) *mid-div: prog to trck ldrs 3f out: bmpd and hit rail 2f out: lost pl briefly: rdn and r.o appr fnl f: fin wl* **9/2**[2]

36-0 4 1 **Love Island**[6] 2856 8-9-7 82.................................(h) LewisEdmunds[(5)] 8 82+
(Richard Whitaker) *hld up in last: hdwy 3f out: n.m.r over 2f out: rdn and r.o wl fnl 2 fs: tk 4th cl home* **7/1**

0016 5 nk **Sandra's Secret (IRE)**[6] 2856 4-9-11 81..................... FrannyNorton 10 80
(Les Eyre) *broke wl: chsd ldr 2f out: rdn and weakend ins fnl f: lost 4th cl home* **9/1**

2535 6 1 3/4 **Pretty Bubbles**[26] 2230 8-10-0 84..............................(v) DavidProbert 9 77
(J R Jenkins) *hld up: effrt u.p on outer over 2f out: no imp* **16/1**

-540 7 nk **Maureb (IRE)**[5] 2888 5-8-11 67...................................... BenCurtis 7 59
(Tony Coyle) *mid-div early: trckd ldrs 3f out: rdn over 2f out: grad wknd* **9/1**

8 1/2 **Nudge**[6] 2864 4-9-4 74...................................................(b) TimmyMurphy 1 65
(Mrs A M O'Shea, Ire) *hld up and a struggling to go pce: nvr a factor* **8/1**

44-1 9 1/2 **Moonshine Dancer**[142] 75 3-8-6 71 ow1............................ JFEgan 3 58
(Christian Williams) *mid-div: pushed along 2f out: sn rdn: no imp* **5/1**[3]

-334 10 27 **Bithynia (IRE)**[129] 288 3-7-11 65.............................(t[1]) NathanAllison[(3)] 4
(Christopher Kellett) *broke wl: racd w ldrs: pushed along and losing pl whn bmpd 3rd 2f out: rdn and wknd: heavily eased fnl f* **33/1**

1m 15.48s (1.68) **Going Correction** +0.375s/f (Good)
**WFA** 3 from 4yo+ 9lb **10** Ran SP% **119.0**
Speed ratings (Par 102): **103,101,100,99,98 96,96,95,94,58**
CSF £35.06 CT £142.52 TOTE £5.70: £1.10, £3.60, £2.20; EX 38.40 Trifecta £187.50.
**Owner** Eventmasters Racing **Bred** Chasemore Farm **Trained** Portway, Worcs

**FOCUS**
Race distance increased by 40yds. A typical Chester sprint, where early speed from the gate proved crucial. She backed up last year's C&D win.

## 3064 MBNA H'CAP 7f 127y
**3:05** (3:06) (Class 2) (0-105,105) 4-Y-0+
**£28,012** (£8,388; £4,194; £2,097; £1,048; £526) **Stalls** Low

Form RPR

4-31 1 **Fastnet Tempest (IRE)**[14] 2606 4-8-10 94.................(p) FrannyNorton 1 106+
(William Haggas) *slowly away: in rr and plenty to do over 2f out: shot through gap on rail to make rapid hdwy ent fnl f: r.o wl under presure to ld cl home* **5/6**[1]

1-00 2 nk **Penwortham (IRE)**[28] 2142 4-8-3 87..........................(h[1]) CamHardie 5 95
(Richard Fahey) *hld up: hdwy on outer over 2f out: rdn and gd hdwy to ld ins fnl f: r.o wl: ct last 25yds* **50/1**

3-04 3 1 3/4 **Fuwairt (IRE)**[15] 2568 5-8-6 90...................................... JFEgan 9 94
(Roger Fell) *trckd ldrs: pushed along over 2f out: rdn and led briefly ent fnl f: r.o one pce* **12/1**

1-40 4 hd **Above The Rest (IRE)**[14] 2606 6-9-3 101..................(h) PhillipMakin 10 104+
(David Barron) *trckd ldrs: gng wl: n.m.r over 1f out: sn rdn and one pce* **16/1**

0200 5 3/4 **Lat Hawill (IRE)**[15] 2568 6-8-4 93..........................(v) RowanScott[(5)] 12 94
(Keith Dalgleish) *in rr: rdn over 2f out: hdwy u.p on outer ent fnl f: r.o wl: nvr nrr* **28/1**

-644 6 3/4 **Viscount Barfield**[17] 2518 4-8-7 91............................(h) DavidProbert 11 90
(Andrew Balding) *t.k.h: mid-div on outer: effrt 2f out: rdn and no ex ent fnl f* **11/1**

1160 7 1 3/4 **My Target (IRE)**[43] 1773 6-8-13 97............................ AdamBeschizza 2 92
(Michael Wigham) *mid-div: pushed along fr 3f out: no imp* **12/1**

6-00 8 nse **Gabrial's Kaka (IRE)**[15] 2568 7-8-0 91...................... ConnorMurtagh[(7)] 3 86
(Richard Fahey) *trckd ldrs: pushed along over 2f out: sn rdn and one pce* **20/1**

4-03 9 1/2 **Ice Slice (IRE)**[15] 2568 6-8-9 93........................................ RyanTate 7 87
(James Eustace) *led: hdd 3f out: regained ld over 1f out: rdn: sn hdd & wknd fnl f* **6/1**[2]

0-01 10 6 **Sound Advice**[15] 2568 8-9-5 103.................................... DougieCostello 6 82
(Keith Dalgleish) *broke wl: racd in 2nd tl led 3f out: hdd over 1f out: no ex* **8/1**[3]

1m 33.87s (0.07) **Going Correction** +0.375s/f (Good) **10** Ran SP% **119.7**
Speed ratings (Par 109): **114,113,111,111,111 110,108,108,107,101**
CSF £71.15 CT £357.25 TOTE £1.50: £1.10, £8.00, £2.30; EX 35.70 Trifecta £733.10.
**Owner** O T I Racing & Partner **Bred** Rockhart Trading Ltd **Trained** Newmarket, Suffolk

**FOCUS**
Race distance increased by 40yds. This was run at a good gallop and a couple of those held up towards the back came through to fight it out. The winner continues on the upgrade.

## 3065 CALDWELL CONSTRUCTION H'CAP 1m 2f 70y
**3:40** (3:41) (Class 4) (0-85,87) 4-Y-0+
**£6,225** (£1,864; £932; £466; £233; £117) **Stalls** High

Form RPR

-513 1 **Energia Fox (BRZ)**[16] 2558 6-9-0 81....................... AdamMcNamara[(3)] 6 88
(Richard Fahey) *racd in 3rd: gng wl: qckndto ld on ins over 1f out: rdn and responded whn chal: hld on wl* **11/2**[3]

1-22 2 hd **Kapstadt (FR)**[16] 2558 7-9-9 87.................................... FrannyNorton 8 93
(Ian Williams) *trckd ldrs: hdwy on outer over 1f out: rdn and chal wnr ins fnl f: r.o wl but jst hld* **5/1**[2]

6500 3 2 1/4 **Worlds His Oyster**[21] 2406 4-9-5 83.............................. PhillipMakin 2 85
(John Quinn) *mid-div: hdwy into 4th 2f out: styd on u.p fnl f: nt pce of front two* **5/1**[2]

43-5 4 1 3/4 **Dark Intention (IRE)**[8] 2805 4-8-10 74.....................(h[1]) CamHardie 9 72
(Lawrence Mullaney) *hld up: pushed along 1/2-way: effrt on outside over 1f out: hrd rdn: styd on wl to take 4th cl home* **14/1**

4-46 5 nk **Fast Dancer (IRE)**[17] 2528 5-9-0 78............................ DougieCostello 7 75
(Joseph Tuite) *hld up: pushed along and effrt 2f out: hrd rdn ent fnl f: r.o one pce: pipped for 4th nr fining line* **10/1**

0421 6 1 1/4 **Sands Chorus**[15] 2593 5-9-5 83........................................ KevinStott 1 78
(James Given) *led: rdn and hdd over 1f out: no ex u.p fnl f* **2/1**[1]

5-40 7 6 **Drago (IRE)**[28] 2163 5-8-9 73.......................................(h) BenCurtis 3 56
(David O'Meara) *racd in 2nd: pushed along 2f out: sn rdn and wknd* **16/1**

210- 8 3 **Mubajal**[254] 6517 4-9-7 85.............................................. DaneO'Neill 5 62
(Owen Burrows) *mid-div: rdn over 2f out: no rspnse and eased* **8/1**

0-00 9 47 **Glance My Way (IRE)**[10] 2741 4-8-7 71.................(b) AdamBeschizza 4
(Tim Easterby) *hld up in last: hrd rdn 4f out: sn lost tch* **40/1**

2m 12.55s (1.35) **Going Correction** +0.375s/f (Good) **9** Ran SP% **117.2**
Speed ratings (Par 105): **109,108,107,105,105 104,99,97,59**
CSF £33.68 CT £147.64 TOTE £5.40: £1.50, £1.90, £2.20; EX 26.40 Trifecta £163.90.
**Owner** Dr Marwan Koukash **Bred** Haras Estrela Energia **Trained** Musley Bank, N Yorks

**FOCUS**
Race distance increased by 42yds. The first two met here earlier in the month, and once again there was little between them at the finish. The race lacked a bit of depth.

## 3066 BRITISH STALLION STUDS EBF MAIDEN STKS (PLUS 10 RACE) 6f 17y
**4:15** (4:17) (Class 2) 2-Y-0
**£12,450** (£3,728; £1,864; £932; £466; £234) **Stalls** Low

Form RPR

2 1 **Headway**[36] 1941 2-9-5 0.................................................. KevinStott 4 81+
(William Haggas) *trckd ldrs: circled front two and qcknd wl to ld over 1f out: rdn briefly: sn clr: easily* **4/5**[1]

0 2 3 **Knockout Blow**[10] 2740 2-9-5 0...................................... FrannyNorton 8 72
(Mark Johnston) *led: hdd over 1f out: rdn and r.o one pce fnl f* **10/1**

0 3 1 1/2 **Levante Player (IRE)**[28] 2134 2-9-5 0.............................. BenCurtis 6 68
(Tom Dascombe) *trckd ldrs: hit flat spot over 2f out: rallied u.p fnl f: fin wl to take 3rd* **10/1**

4 1/2 **Yafta** 2-9-5 0.................................................................. DaneO'Neill 9 66+
(Richard Hannon) *trckd ldr: pushed along over 1f out: sn lft bhd by front two: r.o one pce under hand riding: lost 3rd last 75yds* **9/2**[2]

5 1 1/4 **Chai Chai (IRE)** 2-9-5 0................................................ DavidProbert 2 62+
(Andrew Balding) *mid-div: effrt 2f out: one pce u.p fr over 1f out* **7/1**[3]

435 6 3/4 **Felisa**[17] 2522 2-9-0 0...................................................... JFEgan 5 55
(David Evans) *slowly away: hdwy on outer over 2f out: pushed along wl over 1f out: rdn ent fnl f: no ex* **20/1**

43 7 4 1/2 **Floss The Hoss (IRE)**[25] 2251 2-9-0 0............................. PhillipMakin 7 42
(David Evans) *mid-div on outer: pushed along 1/2-way: effrt 2f out but no imp: eased* **25/1**

8 9 **Renton** 2-9-5 0 DougieCostello 3 20
(Tony Coyle) *in rr: drvn over 2f out: no imp* **50/1**
9 16 **Kathy** 2-9-0 0 AdamBeschizza 1
(Scott Dixon) *rn green in rr: bhd and lost tch fr 2f out* **25/1**
1m 16.74s (2.94) **Going Correction** +0.375s/f (Good) **9** Ran SP% **118.8**
Speed ratings (Par 99): **95,91,89,88,86 85,79,67,46**
CSF £9.92 TOTE £1.60: £1.10, £2.30, £2.90; EX 10.50 Trifecta £47.90.
**Owner** The Royal Ascot Racing Club **Bred** Whatton Manor-Global Equine-L Stratton **Trained** Newmarket, Suffolk

**FOCUS**
Race distance increased by 40yds. A nice performance from the winner, who likely has Royal Ascot on his agenda now. He's rated to his debut level but should have more to offer.

## 3067 MIONETTO PROSECCO H'CAP 1m 5f 84y
**4:50** (4:51) (Class 3) (0-90,90) 4-Y-0+
**£14,006** (£4,194; £2,097; £1,048; £524; £263) **Stalls** Low

Form RPR
40-2 1 **Jaameh (IRE)**[14] 2609 4-9-3 **86** DaneO'Neill 7 99+
(Mark Johnston) *hld up: smooth hdwy to take clsr order over 2f out: qcknd to ld over 1f out: rdn clr: comf* **11/2**[2]
1504 2 3 **Rowlestone Lass**[25] 2270 7-8-6 **75** JFEgan 2 79
(Richard Price) *mid-div: hdwy on inner 2f out: briefly n.m.r: fnd gap and drvn along ent fnl f: r.o wl but no ch w wnr* **20/1**
-106 3 ¾ **Gabrial's King (IRE)**[16] 2552 8-9-3 **89** AdamMcNamara(3) 8 92
(Richard Fahey) *v.s.a: sn mde up lost grnd but remained in rr: hdwy u.p on outer over 2f out: r.o strly ins fnl f* **16/1**
156- 4 hd **Emperor Napoleon**[280] 5653 4-9-5 **88** DavidProbert 4 91
(Andrew Balding) *t.k.h early: led: rdn and hdd over 1f out: one pce ins fnl f* **5/2**[1]
210- 5 ½ **Sir Valentine (GER)**[232] 7117 4-9-5 **88** DougieCostello 9 90
(Alan King) *chsd ldr: pushed along 3f out: rdn over 1f out: wknd* **7/1**[3]
50-0 6 1 **Nabhan**[15] 2574 5-8-7 **76** (p[1]) AdamBeschizza 10 76
(Bernard Llewellyn) *hld up: effrt and nt clr run over 2f out: rdn and sme hdwy fr over 1f out* **40/1**
-124 7 ½ **Byron Flyer**[50] 1309 6-9-4 **87** FrannyNorton 3 91+
(Ian Williams) *mid-div: drvn and n.m.r wl over 1f out: nt rcvr: eased* **5/2**[1]
06-2 8 nk **Sunblazer (IRE)**[27] 2176 7-9-0 **90** (t) JoshuaBryan(7) 6 89
(Kim Bailey) *hld up: hdwy over 2f out: sn drvn along: rdn and no ex fnl f* **16/1**
53-1 9 2 **Snowy Dawn**[30] 2111 7-8-2 **71** oh1 RoystonFfrench 1 67
(Steph Hollinshead) *trckd ldrs: pushed along 2f out: rdn and wknd wl over 1f out* **11/1**
40-2 10 4 **The Otmoor Poet**[19] 2478 4-8-9 **78** (p) BenCurtis 5 68
(Alex Hales) *trckd ldrs: rdn and wknd over 2f out* **16/1**
2m 55.66s (2.96) **Going Correction** +0.375s/f (Good) **10** Ran SP% **118.2**
Speed ratings (Par 107): **105,103,102,102,102 101,101,101,99,97**
CSF £109.32 CT £1661.65 TOTE £4.50: £2.70, £6.40, £4.60; EX 78.80 Trifecta £562.40.
**Owner** Hamdan Al Maktoum **Bred** Peter & Hugh McCutcheon **Trained** Middleham Moor, N Yorks

**FOCUS**
Race distance increased by 76yds. A bit of a stop-start gallop, and with the field bunching up on the turn in the race developed into a bit of a sprint-off. The impressive winner built on his reappearance promise.

## 3068 ROSIES AFTER PARTY H'CAP 1m 4f 63y
**5:20** (5:25) (Class 4) (0-85,83) 3-Y-0 **£6,225** (£1,864; £932; £466) **Stalls** Low

Form RPR
63-1 1 **Atkinson Grimshaw (FR)**[89] 959 3-9-0 **76** DavidProbert 5 83+
(Andrew Balding) *led at modest gallop: qcknd tempo over 3f out: sn 3 l clr: rdn over 1f out and extended advantage: 5 l clr ins fnl f: nvr threatened* **9/2**[3]
0-43 2 2½ **Koeman**[27] 2174 3-9-0 **76** JFEgan 2 77
(Mick Channon) *hld up: pushed along over 3f out: 4th 2f out: r.o u.p to go 2nd ent fnl f: no ch w wnr* **7/1**
1 3 4 **Voski (USA)**[64] 1342 3-9-7 **83** FrannyNorton 3 78
(Mark Johnston) *trckd ldr: ct flat footed whn pce qcknd over 3f out: hrd rdn over 2f out: one pce and lost 2nd ent fnl f* **1/1**[1]
6-21 4 1¼ **Okool (FR)**[15] 2584 3-9-5 **81** DaneO'Neill 4 74
(Owen Burrows) *hld up: t.k.h 1/2-way: pushed along whn pce qcknd over 3f out: rdn over 2f out: no ex* **2/1**[2]
2m 44.96s (6.46) **Going Correction** +0.375s/f (Good) **4** Ran SP% **114.0**
Speed ratings (Par 101): **93,91,88,87**
CSF £28.93 TOTE £4.40; EX 22.50 Trifecta £101.10.
**Owner** David Brownlow **Bred** Ali Alqama **Trained** Kingsclere, Hants

**FOCUS**
Race distance increased by 64yds. A tactical affair in which the winner dictated a pace to suit himself. It's hard to be sure of this form given the race's tactical nature.
T/Plt: £15.10 to a £1 stake. Pool: £74,835.01 - 3,604.77 winning units T/Qpdt: £6.50 to a £1 stake. Pool: £3,662.74 - 410.92 winning units **Keith McHugh**

# 3029 GOODWOOD (R-H)
### Saturday, May 27
**OFFICIAL GOING: Straight course - good; round course - good to firm (watered; 7.8)**
Wind: light across Weather: overcast

## 3069 MATCHBOOK BETTING EXCHANGE FESTIVAL STKS (LISTED RACE) 1m 1f 197y
**2:00** (2:02) (Class 1) 4-Y-0+
**£28,355** (£10,750; £5,380; £2,680; £1,345; £675) **Stalls** Low

Form RPR
20-0 1 **First Sitting**[29] 2127 6-9-0 105 GeraldMosse 2 112
(Chris Wall) *t.k.h: trckd ldr tl 1/2-way: clsd on inner to join ldr 3f out: sn led: rdn and qcknd over 1f out: 3 l clr 1f out: jst hld on* **16/1**
41-3 2 nse **Spark Plug (IRE)**[38] 1882 6-9-0 112 (p) JamieSpencer 7 112+
(Brian Meehan) *hld up in tch: stl travelling strly 2f out: swtchd lft and effrt over 1f out: rdn to chse wnr and 3 l down 1f out: drvn and r.o strly ins fnl f: jst failed: too much to do* **4/1**[3]
613- 3 3½ **Mount Logan (IRE)**[248] 6666 6-9-0 109 AndreaAtzeni 3 105
(Roger Varian) *taken down early: trckd ldng pair: wnt 2nd 1/2-way tl 3f out: rdn over 2f out: unable qck u.p over 1f out: 3rd and kpt on same pce fnl f* **2/1**[1]
20-5 4 ½ **Tullius (IRE)**[56] 1493 9-9-0 110 (v) LiamKeniry 4 104
(Andrew Balding) *t.k.h: hld up in tch in midfield: effrt on inner over 2f out: 4th and styd on same pce ins fnl f* **15/2**
50-4 5 2 **Berkshire (IRE)**[16] 2552 6-9-0 102 LukeMorris 5 100
(Paul Cole) *led and set stdy gallop: jnd and rdn 3f out: sn hdd: outpcd over 1f out: wknd ins fnl f* **12/1**
34-4 6 2¼ **Abdon**[38] 1882 4-9-0 109 FrankieDettori 1 95
(Sir Michael Stoute) *s.i.s: t.k.h: hld up in tch in last pair: effrt and nt clr run ent fnl 2f: swtchd lft over 1f out: sn rdn and no imp: wknd ins fnl f* **3/1**[2]
444- 7 9 **Tony Curtis**[233] 7101 4-9-0 105 SeanLevey 6 77
(Richard Hannon) *t.k.h: hld up in last pair: rdn over 2f out: no imp and hung rt over 1f out: bhd fnl f* **10/1**
2m 9.06s (0.96) **Going Correction** +0.25s/f (Good) **7** Ran SP% **112.8**
Speed ratings (Par 111): **106,105,103,102,101 99,92**
CSF £76.06 TOTE £21.80: £6.60, £2.00; EX 96.20 Trifecta £304.30.
**Owner** Bringloe & Clarke **Bred** Juddmonte Farms Ltd **Trained** Newmarket, Suffolk

**FOCUS**
Opening race run over an extra 10yds. Some starts have been moved at this track following remeasuring, so some races will not have speed figures until there is sufficient data to calculate updated median times. The cutaway was taken away for this card. A blustery afternoon and the wind was slightly in the faces of the runners coming up the straight. A good quality Listed contest in which the front two pulled clear and it threw up a slightly surprising winner. He's rated to a better view of his form.

## 3070 BASKETMAKERS COMPANY CELEBRATION EBF FILLIES' NOVICE STKS (PLUS 10 RACE) 6f
**2:35** (2:36) (Class 4) 2-Y-0 **£6,469** (£1,925; £962; £481) **Stalls** High

Form RPR
5 1 **Madeline (IRE)**[15] 2563 2-9-0 0 AndreaAtzeni 5 86
(Roger Varian) *trckd ldrs tl led over 2f out: pushed along and edgd rt over 1f out: r.o wl and a doing enough ins the fnl f: rdn out* **7/2**[2]
3 2 1 **Billesdon Brook**[27] 2173 2-9-0 0 SeanLevey 2 83
(Richard Hannon) *trckd ldrs: clsd and upsides ldr 2f out: sn rdn and edgd rt ent fnl f: kpt on wl for clr 2nd but a hld* **6/4**[1]
3 4 **Elizabeth Bennet (IRE)** 2-8-11 0 CallumShepherd(3) 3 71
(Charles Hills) *hld up in tch towards rr: hdwy over 2f out: chsd ldrs and rdn over 1f out: 3rd and no imp fnl f* **16/1**
4 1½ **Silca Mistress** 2-9-0 0 CharlesBishop 1 67+
(Mick Channon) *s.i.s: in tch in last trio: swtchd rt and effrt 2f out: hdwy over 1f out: kpt on steadily ins fnl f to go 4th nr fin: nvr trbld ldrs* **16/1**
5 ½ **Missy Mischief (USA)** 2-9-0 0 GeraldMosse 4 65
(Jeremy Noseda) *in tch in midfield: effrt ent fnl 2f: 4th and no imp over 1f out: wknd wl ins fnl f and lost 4th nr fin* **7/1**[3]
6 5 **Sardenya (IRE)** 2-9-0 0 JosephineGordon 7 50
(Roger Charlton) *s.i.s: sn detached in last and rn green: clsd and travelling bttr 3f out: outpcd 2f out: swtchd rt and kpt on to pass btn rivals ins fnl f: nvr trbld ldrs* **16/1**
7 ½ **Salty Sugar** 2-9-0 0 JoeFanning 8 49+
(John Gosden) *in tch in midfield: shkn up 2f out: sn outpcd and wknd over 1f out* **8/1**
8 hd **Laura Knight (IRE)** 2-8-11 0 HectorCrouch(3) 10 48
(Gary Moore) *flashing tail leaving stalls: led tl rdn and hdd 1/2-way: lost pl and wknd over 1f out* **25/1**
9 2¼ **Summer Thunder (USA)** 2-9-0 0 JamieSpencer 6 41
(Paul Cole) *chsd ldr tl 1/2-way: sn rdn and struggling: btn over 1f out: fdd fnl f* **16/1**
10 ¾ **Shimmy Shoes (IRE)** 2-8-11 0 EdwardGreatrex(3) 9 39
(Archie Watson) *in tch in midfield: rdn over 2f out: sn struggling and wknd over 1f out* **16/1**
1m 13.09s (0.89) **Going Correction** +0.25s/f (Good) **10** Ran SP% **119.1**
Speed ratings (Par 92): **104,102,97,95,94 88,87,87,84,83**
CSF £9.32 TOTE £3.70: £1.70, £1.10, £5.10; EX 9.70 Trifecta £72.50.
**Owner** Sheikh Mohammed Obaid Al Maktoum **Bred** Manfred Wurtenberger **Trained** Newmarket, Suffolk

**FOCUS**
Several interesting newcomers on show here but it was the two with experience that ended up dominating.

## 3071 WINNERS ARE WELCOME AT MATCHBOOK H'CAP 7f
**3:10** (3:10) (Class 2) 3-Y-0 **£64,690** (£19,250; £9,620; £4,810) **Stalls** Low

Form RPR
1253 1 **Sutter County**[20] 2425 3-9-0 **103** AndreaAtzeni 3 110
(Mark Johnston) *mde all: rdn 2f out: edgd lft briefly ins fnl f: pressed and hld on wl towards fin: gamely* **9/1**
1-20 2 ½ **Medahim (IRE)**[29] 2126 3-7-13 **91** HollieDoyle(3) 7 96
(Richard Hannon) *t.k.h: hld up in tch in last trio: switching lft 3f out: clsng whn nt clr run and swtchd rt over 1f out: chsng ldrs ins fnl f: running on wl whn swtchd rt towards fin: snatched 2nd last strides* **10/1**
361- 3 hd **Hyde Park**[218] 7495 3-8-4 **93** JosephineGordon 10 97
(John Gosden) *chsd ldrs: effrt to chse wnr over 1f out: hanging rt after: styd on and clsd to press wnr wl ins fnl f: kpt on: lost 2nd last strides* **15/2**[3]
3-11 4 1¼ **Horroob**[23] 2334 3-7-8 **90** DavidEgan(7) 12 91
(Roger Varian) *t.k.h: hld up in tch in midfield: effrt 2f out: chsd ldrs and rdn over 1f out: kpt on u.p ins fnl f: nvr enough pce to rch ldrs* **4/1**[2]
213 5 nk **Bless Him (IRE)**[21] 2385 3-7-12 **90** oh5 ow1 (h[1]) AaronJones(3) 4 93+
(David Simcock) *t.k.h: hld up in midfield: shuffled bk to rr over 2f out: hdwy and nt clr run over 1f out: sn swtchd lft: stl shifting lft but styd on wl ins fnl f: nvr gng to rch ldrs* **17/2**
1100 6 ½ **Top Score**[21] 2399 3-9-2 **110** (p) GeorgeWood(5) 6 109
(Saeed bin Suroor) *hld up in tch in rr: swtchd lft over 2f out: hdwy u.p over 1f out: kpt on ins fnl f: nvr enough pce to get on terms* **3/1**[1]
1-36 7 3½ **Volatile**[43] 1780 3-8-9 **98** LukeMorris 1 87
(James Tate) *dwlt: hdwy to trck ldrs after 2f: rdn ent fnl 2f: unable qck over 1f out: switching lft and wknd u.p ins fnl f* **10/1**
212- 8 1 **Town Charter (USA)**[296] 5058 3-7-10 **90** ow1 RichardOliver(5) 8 76
(Mark Johnston) *t.k.h: hld up in tch in last trio: swtchd lft over 3f out: rdn 2f out: no imp and struggling whn hung rt and hmpd over 1f out: wknd ins fnl f* **16/1**
53-6 9 1 **The Wagon Wheel (IRE)**[21] 2400 3-8-0 **89** oh5 JoeyHaynes 5 73
(Richard Fahey) *t.k.h: chsd ldrs: rdn ent fnl 2f: unable qck and beginning to struggle whn squeezed for room and hmpd over 1f out: no ch after* **16/1**

3-21 **10** 4 ½ **Aardwolf (USA)**[21] 2384 3-8-4 **93** JoeFanning 11 65
(Mark Johnston) *chsd wnr tl over 1f out: sn btn and fdd ins fnl f* **8/1**
1m 27.47s (0.47) **Going Correction** +0.25s/f (Good) **10** Ran SP% **118.3**
Speed ratings (Par 105): **107,106,106,104,104 103,99,98,97,92**
CSF £96.71 CT £733.96 TOTE £9.70: £2.90, £3.30, £2.40; EX 93.70 Trifecta £1685.70.
**Owner** Sheikh Hamdan bin Mohammed Al Maktoum **Bred** Darley **Trained** Middleham Moor, N Yorks

**FOCUS**
Race run over an extra 12yds. A valuable and competitive 3yo handicap in which there was a fair amount of trouble in behind the leader. The pace looked pretty steady and it was one by one of the most exposed runners in the field, so this is form to have doubts about. The winner gave the seventh a much bigger beating than in Lingfield's Spring Cup.

## 3072 SMARTER BETS AT MATCHBOOK TAPSTER STKS (LISTED RACE) 1m 3f 218y
**3:45** (3:45) (Class 1) 4-Y-0+ **£29,600** (£11,195; £5,595; £2,795) **Stalls** High

Form RPR
34-3 **1** **Second Step (IRE)**[35] 1957 6-9-0 110 JamieSpencer 3 111
(Roger Charlton) *hld up in tch in 4th: effrt over 2f out: rdn and chal over 1f out: led jst ins fnl f: hld on wl: rdn out* **7/2**[2]
32-1 **2** ½ **Desert Encounter (IRE)**[14] 2604 5-9-3 108 (h) SeanLevey 4 113
(David Simcock) *stdd and awkward leaving stalls: t.k.h: hld up in tch in rr: effrt over 1f out: rdn to chal 1f out: kpt on wl u.p: hld towards fin* **2/1**[1]
212- **3** 1 ¼ **Barsanti (IRE)**[246] 6752 5-9-0 109 AndreaAtzeni 1 108
(Roger Varian) *chsd ldr tl led 6f out: rdn over 2f out: hdd jst ins fnl f: no ex and outpcd fnl 75yds* **2/1**[1]
-114 **4** 1 ¼ **Galapiat**[21] 2398 4-9-0 105 JoeFanning 2 106
(Mark Johnston) *led and set stdy gallop: hdd 6f out: rdn over 2f out: ev ch after tl unable qck 1f out: wknd ins fnl f* **9/2**[3]
-003 **5** hd **Restorer**[14] 2604 5-9-0 102 MartinDwyer 5 106
(William Muir) *chsd ldrs: effrt ent fnl 2f out: unable qck over 1f out: kpt on same pce ins fnl f* **18/1**
2m 39.64s (1.24) **Going Correction** +0.25s/f (Good) **5** Ran SP% **112.3**
Speed ratings (Par 111): **105,104,103,103,102**
CSF £11.17 TOTE £3.90: £2.10, £1.60; EX 12.00 Trifecta £17.50.
**Owner** Merry Fox Stud Limited **Bred** Merry Fox Stud Limited **Trained** Beckhampton, Wilts

**FOCUS**
Race run over an extyra 10yds. A reasonable Listed race on paper and all five held some sort of chance entering the final two furlongs. The winner, the highest rated runner in here, looks back to near his best again now. Pretty straightforward form.

## 3073 GENTLEMAN'S MEASURE IN MEMORY OF PHIL WIGGINS H'CAP 1m 6f
**4:20** (4:20) (Class 2) (0-105,103) 4-Y-0+ **£16,172** (£4,812; £2,405; £1,202) **Stalls** Low

Form RPR
30-2 **1** **Top Tug (IRE)**[20] 2431 6-9-4 **100** AndreaAtzeni 9 108+
(Alan King) *hld up in last quartet: clsd and travelling strly whn nt clr run 2f out tl swtchd lft over 1f out: pushed along and qcknd to ld ins fnl f: r.o wl: comf* **10/3**[1]
405/ **2** 1 ¾ **High Secret (IRE)**[14] 7341 6-8-8 **95** MeganNicholls(5) 11 100
(Paul Nicholls) *t.k.h: chsd ldrs tl hdwy to ld 9f out: rdn 2f out: battled wl tl hdd and outpcd ins fnl f* **20/1**
24-0 **3** nk **The Cashel Man (IRE)**[17] 2525 5-8-7 **92** (b) EdwardGreatrex(3) 6 96
(David Simcock) *stdd s: hld up in rr: hdwy and n.m.r jst over 2f out: hdwy u.p over 1f out: kpt on wl ins fnl f: no threat to wnr* **8/1**
6-10 **4** 2 **Blakeney Point**[17] 2525 4-8-13 **95** (p) JamieSpencer 10 96
(Roger Charlton) *chsd ldr tl 10f out: styd in tch: clsd and travelled wl to join ldrs 2f out: rdn over 1f out: unable qck 1f out: outpcd ins fnl f* **7/1**[3]
05-2 **5** 1 ¼ **Oriental Fox (GER)**[8] 2797 9-9-7 **103** JoeFanning 7 103
(Mark Johnston) *chsd ldr: wnt 2nd 3f out: rdn and ev ch 2f out tl unable qck 1f out: wknd ins fnl f* **15/2**
0-40 **6** 1 ¾ **Angel Gabrial (IRE)**[17] 2525 8-8-12 **94** PatDobbs 4 91
(Richard Fahey) *stdd s: hld up in rr: effrt ent fnl 2f: styd on to pass btn rivals ins fnl f: nvr trbld ldrs* **7/1**[3]
13-2 **7** nk **Batts Rock (IRE)**[14] 2603 4-8-2 **84** JosephineGordon 3 85+
(Michael Bell) *hld up in tch in last quartet: clsd and wl in tch whn clipped heels and stmbld jst over 2f out: effrt over 1f out: no imp ins fnl f* **9/2**[2]
10-2 **8** hd **Manjaam (IRE)**[63] 1361 4-9-1 **97** LukeMorris 1 93
(Ed Dunlop) *hld up in tch in midfield: edgd lft jst over 2f out: effrt on inner to chse ldrs over 1f out: sn drvn and unable qck: wknd ins fnl f* **9/1**
65-6 **9** 1 ¾ **Glaring**[27] 2176 6-8-4 **91** (p[1]) GeorgeWood(5) 8 85
(Amanda Perrett) *t.k.h: hld up in tch in midfield: effrt over 2f out: no imp u.p whn nudged lft over 1f out: wknd fnl f* **14/1**
**10** 2 ¾ **Cosmelli (ITY)**[216] 4-9-7 **103** (b) MartinDwyer 5 93
(Gay Kelleway) *led tl 9f out: chsd ldr tl 3f out: sn u.p: wknd over 1f out* **33/1**
-505 **11** 19 **Ballynanty (IRE)**[17] 2519 5-8-8 **90** (p[1]) LiamKeniry 2 54
(Andrew Balding) *wl in tch in midfield: wnt 4th 5f out: shkn up ent fnl 2f: sn btn: bhd and eased ins fnl f* **33/1**
3m 6.59s (2.99) **11** Ran SP% **116.4**
CSF £74.48 CT £491.55 TOTE £4.00: £1.70, £5.60, £2.70; EX 91.40 Trifecta £762.90.
**Owner** Elite Racing Club **Bred** Wretham Stud **Trained** Barbury Castle, Wilts
■ Stewards' Enquiry : Luke Morris three-day ban: careless riding (Jun 10-12)

**FOCUS**
Race run over an extra 10yds. A wide open staying handicap on paper and the gallop look sound. The winner, a 130-rated hurdler, won with a bit in hand and isn't fully exposed over staying trips on the Flat. The form is rated around the third and fourth.

## 3074 BETTER ODDS WITH MATCHBOOK VETERANS' H'CAP 6f
**4:55** (4:56) (Class 4) (0-80,83) 6-Y-0+ **£6,469** (£1,925; £962; £481) **Stalls** High

Form RPR
244- **1** **Joe Packet**[229] 7221 10-8-10 **76** Pierre-LouisJamin(7) 5 83
(Jonathan Portman) *in tch in midfield: clsd to press ldr over 1f out: shkn up to ld 1f out: styd on and forged ahd ins fnl f: jst hld on* **25/1**
0-43 **2** nse **Morache Music**[14] 2618 9-9-3 **76** (p) LiamKeniry 10 83+
(Patrick Chamings) *stdd s: hld up in last trio: swtchd lft ent fnl f: hdwy and edging rt ins fnl f: drvn and r.o strly fnl 100yds: jst failed* **15/2**
1-50 **3** 1 ¼ **Pettochside**[14] 2608 8-9-4 **77** JosephineGordon 3 80
(John Bridger) *sn prom: led after 1f: rdn over 1f out: hdd 1f out: no ex and btn 100yds out: kpt on same pce after* **5/2**[1]
-001 **4** 1 ¼ **Englishman**[12] 2692 7-9-10 **83** JoeFanning 9 82
(Milton Bradley) *hld up in tch in midfield: rdn and hdwy to chse ldrs over 1f out: unable qck 1f out and styd on same pce ins fnl f* **8/1**
0-14 **5** nk **Diamond Lady**[28] 2147 6-9-4 **80** HollieDoyle(3) 6 78
(William Stone) *pressed ldrs: rdn 2f out: unable qck over 1f and kpt on same pce ins fnl f* **6/1**[3]
0324 **6** 1 **Gold Club**[24] 2320 6-9-2 **75** (p) AndreaAtzeni 4 70
(Tom Clover) *pressed ldrs: rdn 2f out: unable qck and outpcd over 1f out: kpt on same pce ins fnl f* **9/2**[2]
400- **7** ¾ **Gold Hunter (IRE)**[239] 6914 7-9-3 **76** LiamJones 2 68
(Steve Flook) *s.i.s: in tch in last trio: hdwy 2f out: rdn over 1f out: no imp 1f out: wknd wl ins fnl f* **14/1**
-001 **8** 4 **Picture Dealer**[24] 2320 8-8-13 **75** SimonPearce(3) 1 54
(Lydia Pearce) *wnt rt s: sn rcvrd and in tch in midfield: rdn 2f out: sn struggling and lost pl over 1f out: wknd fnl f* **8/1**
510- **9** 1 ¼ **He's My Boy (IRE)**[221] 7430 6-8-6 **70** GeorgeWood(5) 8 45
(James Fanshawe) *stdd s: hld up in tch in last trio: effrt over 1f out: drvn and no imp ent fnl f: sn wknd* **10/1**
1m 12.32s (0.12) **Going Correction** +0.25s/f (Good) **9** Ran SP% **114.6**
Speed ratings: **109,108,107,105,105 103,102,97,95**
CSF £198.73 CT £647.91 TOTE £19.00: £4.50, £2.40, £1.60; EX 129.20 Trifecta £866.20.
**Owner** J G B Portman **Bred** Stuart McPhee Bloodstock Ltd **Trained** Upper Lambourn, Berks

**FOCUS**
A reasonably competitive sprint handicap won by last year's runner-up. Marginally the winner's best form since 2014.

## 3075 MATCHBOOK BETTING PODCAST EBF MAIDEN FILLIES' STKS (PLUS 10 RACE) 7f
**5:25** (5:28) (Class 5) 3-Y-O **£4,980** (£1,491; £745; £372; £186) **Stalls** Low

Form RPR
425- **1** **Contentment**[215] 7574 3-9-0 77 (t[1]) PatDobbs 3 77+
(William Haggas) *mde all: gng best 2f out: pushed along and fnd ex over 1f out: in command fnl f: eased towards fin: comf* **9/4**[2]
62-4 **2** 1 ½ **Music Lesson**[15] 2585 3-9-0 77 JosephineGordon 5 71
(Hughie Morrison) *in tch in last pair: shkn up 3f out: sn rdn: chsd wnr 1f out: styd on but nvr threatening wnr* **5/2**[3]
**3** 1 ¼ **Deleyla** 3-9-0 0 AndreaAtzeni 1 68
(Roger Varian) *dwlt: t.k.h: sn trcking ldrs: rdn ent fnl 2f: unable qck over 1f out: wknd ins fnl f* **13/8**[1]
0-4 **4** 1 ¼ **Sussex Girl**[25] 2280 3-8-11 0 SimonPearce(3) 2 64
(John Berry) *t.k.h: trckd wnr tl 1/2-way: effrt on inner 2f out: unable qck over 1f out: wknd ins fnl f* **33/1**
0- **5** 11 **Forever Excel (IRE)**[245] 6782 3-9-0 0 SteveDrowne 4 35
(Charles Hills) *stdd and dropped in bhd after s: hld up in rr: rdn over 2f out: no imp: wknd over 1f out* **9/1**
1m 29.2s (2.20) **Going Correction** +0.25s/f (Good) **5** Ran SP% **110.4**
Speed ratings (Par 96): **97,95,93,92,79**
CSF £8.28 TOTE £3.40: £1.70, £1.50; EX 7.30 Trifecta £10.90.
**Owner** Highclere T'Bred Racing-Edward Lear **Bred** Mrs F S Williams **Trained** Newmarket, Suffolk

**FOCUS**
A modest little fillies' maiden dominated from the front by Contentment who finally delivered on the promise of her debut fourth at Newbury last summer. The runner-up is the best guide.
T/Plt: £209.90 to a £1 stake. Pool: £106,230.77 - 369.28 winning units T/Qpdt: £35.00 to a £1 stake. Pool: £6,665.82 - 140.7 winning units **Steve Payne**

# 3036 HAYDOCK (L-H)
Saturday, May 27

**OFFICIAL GOING: Firm (good to firm in places; watered; 9.8)**
Wind: Fresh across Weather: Cloudy with sunny spells

## 3076 AMIX READY MIXED CONCRETE H'CAP 2m 45y
**2:20** (2:21) (Class 2) (0-100,100) 4-Y-O+ **£12,938** (£3,850; £1,924; £962) **Stalls** Low

Form RPR
-323 **1** **Yorkidding**[8] 2774 5-9-8 **98** RichardKingscote 8 104
(Mark Johnston) *hld up: hdwy over 2f out: sn rdn: led 1f out: styd on gamely* **3/1**[2]
0-00 **2** hd **Suegioo (FR)**[17] 2525 8-9-10 **100** (p) TonyHamilton 6 105
(Richard Fahey) *s.i.s: hld up: pushed along over 4f out: hdwy over 1f out: rdn and ev ch wl ins fnl f: styd on* **10/1**
60-3 **3** shd **Paris Protocol**[27] 2176 4-8-10 **88** JimCrowley 5 93
(Richard Hannon) *chsd ldrs: rdn and ev ch fr over 1f out: styd on* **9/2**[3]
14-0 **4** 1 ¼ **Arthur Mc Bride (IRE)**[15] 2562 8-8-8 **84** (t) RobHornby 1 87
(Nigel Twiston-Davies) *led: qcknd over 3f out: rdn and hung rt over 2f out: hdd 1f out: styd on same pce wl ins fnl f* **14/1**
126- **5** ½ **Parliamentarian (IRE)**[229] 7215 4-8-12 **90** MartinLane 3 92
(Charlie Appleby) *a.p: rdn over 2f out: sn hung rt: ev ch over 1f out: no ex wl ins fnl f* **11/4**[1]
023/ **6** 1 ¼ **Cool Sky**[41] 6749 8-8-8 **84** AndrewMullen 9 85
(Ian Williams) *hld up: rdn over 2f out: hdwy over 1f out: styd on* **20/1**
-333 **7** nk **Swashbuckle**[15] 2562 4-8-9 **87** (p[1]) OisinMurphy 2 88
(Andrew Balding) *chsd ldr tl rdn over 2f out: styd on same pce fr over 1f out* **9/2**[3]
1-42 **8** nk **Velvet Revolution**[19] 2461 4-8-7 **85** (p) DanielMuscutt 10 85
(Marco Botti) *hld up: hdwy over 2f out: rdn and ev ch over 1f out: wknd wl ins fnl f* **11/1**
3m 36.66s (2.36) **Going Correction** -0.30s/f (Firm)
**WFA** 4 from 5yo+ 1lb **8** Ran SP% **116.9**
Speed ratings (Par 109): **82,81,81,81,80 80,80,80**
CSF £33.54 CT £134.69 TOTE £3.90: £1.50, £3.30, £1.70; EX 31.10 Trifecta £195.80.
**Owner** Paul Robert York **Bred** Bluehills Racing Limited **Trained** Middleham Moor, N Yorks

**FOCUS**
All races were run over the stands' side in the home straight. Allowing for rail movements, the actual race distance of this was 2m 69yds. There was rain before racing and after riding in the opener Tony Hamilton said of the ground: "The rain has taken the jar out" while Martin Lane said: "It is good to firm ground, they have just taken the top off a little." No great gallop on here, all the runners were still in with a chance 2f out and they finished in a bit of a heap. Ordinary form for the grade.

## 3077 AMIX SILVER BOWL H'CAP 1m 37y
**2:55** (2:56) (Class 2) 3-Y-O
**£37,350** (£11,184; £5,592; £2,796; £1,398; £702) **Stalls** Low

Form RPR
-022 **1** **Rusumaat (IRE)**[15] 2565 3-9-3 **97** RichardKingscote 5 108
(Mark Johnston) *mde all: rdn over 1f out: r.o wl: eased nr fin* **11/2**[2]
211 **2** 2 ½ **Indian Dandy (IRE)**[25] 2284 3-8-9 **89** (h) DanielMuscutt 1 94
(Marco Botti) *a.p: chsd wnr over 2f out: rdn and hung lft fr over 1f out: styd on same pce ins fnl f* **11/2**[2]

4025 **3** 2 3/4 **Masham Star (IRE)**[7] 2830 3-9-7 **101**................................. AdamKirby 2 100
(Mark Johnston) *chsd wnr over 3f : remained handy: rdn over 2f out: no ex ins fnl f* **14/1**

2-31 **4** 1 1/4 **Fire Brigade**[9] 2755 3-8-0 **80**........................................... KieranO'Neill 11 76+
(Michael Bell) *s.i.s: hld up: pushed along over 3f out: nt clr run and swtchd rt over 1f out: r.o ins fnl f: nt rch ldrs* **12/1**

1-12 **5** hd **Mustarrid (IRE)**[21] 2385 3-9-0 **94**....................................... JimCrowley 6 89
(Richard Hannon) *hld up: hdwy over 2f out: rdn and hung lft fr over 1f out: no ex ins fnl f* **7/2[1]**

1-00 **6** 1/2 **First Up (IRE)**[15] 2567 3-8-3 **83**.....................................(b[1]) JimmyQuinn 9 77
(Jeremy Noseda) *s.i.s: sn pushed along in rr: hdwy over 2f out: rdn and hung lft over 1f out: no ex* **16/1**

1-62 **7** 2 **Graphite Storm**[15] 2567 3-8-8 **88**................................. SamHitchcott 12 78
(Clive Cox) *s.i.s: hld up: effrt over 2f out: nvr on terms* **15/2[3]**

61-1 **8** 1/2 **Mickey Rich**[18] 2506 3-8-2 **85**.................................. CharlieBennett(3) 10 73
(Hughie Morrison) *chsd ldrs: wnt 2nd over 4f out tl rdn over 2f out: hung rt over 1f out: sn wknd* **11/2[2]**

2100 **9** 1 1/4 **Mailshot (USA)**[16] 2554 3-9-0 **94**..................................... HarryBentley 4 80
(Mark Johnston) *prom: rdn over 3f out: wknd over 1f out* **20/1**

4-10 **10** 3/4 **Cullingworth (IRE)**[29] 2126 3-8-1 **84**......................... SammyJoBell(3) 7 68
(Richard Fahey) *s.i.s: hld up: shkn up over 2f out: nvr on terms* **20/1**

2-63 **11** 4 **Society Red**[20] 2437 3-8-0 **80** oh1.................................. AndrewMullen 3 55
(Richard Fahey) *s.i.s: sn prom and plld hrd: stdd and lost pl over 6f out: rdn over 2f out: wknd over 1f out* **9/1**

1m 40.41s (-4.29) **Going Correction** -0.30s/f (Firm) **11** Ran SP% **119.9**
Speed ratings (Par 105): **109,106,103,102,102 101,99,99,98,97 93**
CSF £36.64 CT £401.72 TOTE £5.90: £2.40, £1.90, £4.20; EX 35.30 Trifecta £557.30.
**Owner** Hamdan Al Maktoum **Bred** J C Bloodstock **Trained** Middleham Moor, N Yorks
■ Stewards' Enquiry : Jimmy Quinn caution: careless riding

**FOCUS**
Actual race distance 1m 50yds. Good handicap form, they appeared to go a sound gallop and little got into it. The race standard suggests the form's worth a chance at that level.

## 3078 ARMSTRONG AGGREGATES SANDY LANE STKS (GROUP 2) 6f

**3:30** (3:32) (Class 1) 3-Y-O

**£51,039** (£19,350; £9,684; £4,824; £2,421; £1,215) **Stalls** Centre

Form RPR

21-2 **1** **Harry Angel (IRE)**[24] 2289 3-9-0 114.................................. AdamKirby 1 122
(Clive Cox) *mde all: racd keenly: shkn up and qcknd over 1f out: sn clr: impressive* **5/6[1]**

-111 **2** 4 1/2 **Second Thought (IRE)**[43] 1774 3-9-0 105.................. RobertWinston 6 108
(William Haggas) *hld up: shkn up over 1f out: r.o to go 2nd wl ins fnl f: no ch w wnr* **7/2[2]**

10-3 **3** 1 3/4 **Mubtasim (IRE)**[24] 2289 3-9-0 107.................................. PatCosgrave 2 102
(William Haggas) *prom: rdn and edgd lft over 1f out: no ex ins fnl f* **5/1[3]**

1-30 **4** 1 3/4 **Poet's Vanity**[20] 2434 3-8-11 104...................................... OisinMurphy 3 93
(Andrew Balding) *chsd wnr: rdn over 1f out: wknd ins fnl f* **11/1**

330- **5** 1 3/4 **Medicine Jack**[245] 6785 3-9-0 104..................................(b[1]) GaryCarroll 5 91
(G M Lyons, Ire) *hld up in tch: hmpd after 1f: rdn over 2f out: wknd over 1f out* **25/1**

1-15 **6** 3/4 **Brian The Snail (IRE)**[9] 2768 3-9-0 102......................... TonyHamilton 7 88
(Richard Fahey) *chsd ldrs tl rdn and wknd over 1f out* **14/1**

**7** 4 **Alphabet**[14] 2636 3-8-11 95...............................................(t) WayneLordan 4 73
(A P O'Brien, Ire) *s.i.s: hld up: wknd wl over 1f out* **33/1**

1m 8.56s (-5.24) **Going Correction** -0.50s/f (Hard) course record **7** Ran SP% **115.2**
Speed ratings (Par 111): **114,108,105,103,101 100,94**
CSF £4.07 TOTE £1.70: £1.30, £2.10; EX 4.90 Trifecta £11.80.
**Owner** Peter Ridgers **Bred** Cbs Bloodstock **Trained** Lambourn, Berks

**FOCUS**
Distance as advertised. A good little race and an impressive winner, who made all and smashed the course record. The form could rate higher at face value.

## 3079 ARMSTRONG AGGREGATES TEMPLE STKS (GROUP 2) 5f

**4:05** (4:07) (Class 1) 3-Y-O+

**£56,710** (£21,500; £10,760; £5,360; £2,690; £1,350) **Stalls** Centre

Form RPR

1-15 **1** **Priceless**[21] 2397 4-9-1 107.................................................. AdamKirby 6 112
(Clive Cox) *chsd ldrs: shkn up to ld over 1f out: drvn out* **11/2[3]**

06-3 **2** 1/2 **Goldream**[21] 2397 8-9-4 110...........................................(p) PatCosgrave 9 113
(Robert Cowell) *s.i.s: hld up: swtchd rt and hdwy over 1f out: rdn and hung lft ins fnl f: r.o* **10/1**

12-0 **3** nk **Alpha Delphini**[21] 2397 6-9-4 110..............................(p) ConnorBeasley 7 112
(Bryan Smart) *edgd rt s: chsd ldrs: pushed along 1/2-way: rdn over 1f out: r.o: n.m.r towards fin* **14/1**

3150 **4** 1 1/2 **Final Venture**[63] 1376 5-9-4 111.....................................(h) OisinMurphy 4 107
(Paul Midgley) *w ldrs: rdn and ev ch over 1f out: styd on same pce ins fnl f* **20/1**

00-4 **5** 1/2 **Kachy**[21] 2397 4-9-4 110.............................................. RichardKingscote 8 105
(Tom Dascombe) *edgd rt s: sn chsng ldrs: rdn over 1f out: styd on same pce ins fnl f* **6/1**

0-02 **6** 1/2 **Washington DC (IRE)**[21] 2397 4-9-4 111....................(t) WayneLordan 1 103
(A P O'Brien, Ire) *hld up: hdwy over 1f out: sn rdn: hung lft ins fnl f: no ex* **3/1[1]**

360- **7** 1/2 **Take Cover**[237] 6990 10-9-4 112........................................ DavidAllan 5 101
(David C Griffiths) *led: rdn and hdd over 1f out: no ex ins fnl f* **11/1**

513 **8** 1/2 **Encore D'Or**[43] 1772 5-9-4 103...................................... HarryBentley 3 100
(Robert Cowell) *hdwy over 3f out: rdn over 1f out: no ex fnl f* **33/1**

50-6 **9** nk **Waady (IRE)**[14] 2611 5-9-4 107.......................................(h) JimCrowley 11 98
(John Gosden) *hld up: pushed along 1/2-way: rdn and edgd lft over 1f out: nt trble ldrs* **14/1**

310- **10** 3/4 **Quiet Reflection**[224] 7350 4-9-6 116................................ MartinHarley 10 98
(K R Burke) *s.i.s and n.m.r after s: in rr: shkn up and edgd lft fr over 1f out: nvr on terms* **4/1[2]**

10-0 **11** 1/2 **Cotai Glory**[21] 2397 5-9-4 112........................................ GavinLerena 12 94
(Charles Hills) *edgd rt s: sn pushed along towards rr: n.d* **10/1**

52-0 **12** 5 **Thesme**[21] 2397 5-9-1 106................................................ AndrewMullen 2 73
(Nigel Tinkler) *racd keenly: w ldrs 3f: sn rdn: hung lft and wknd over 1f out* **50/1**

57.55s (-3.25) **Going Correction** -0.50s/f (Hard) **12** Ran SP% **124.2**
Speed ratings (Par 115): **106,105,104,102,101 100,99,99,98,97 96,88**
CSF £61.51 TOTE £6.20: £2.10, £3.20, £4.40; EX 65.50 Trifecta £758.50.
**Owner** A D Spence **Bred** Biddestone Stud Ltd **Trained** Lambourn, Berks

**FOCUS**
Distance as advertised. A couple of the fancied runners disappointed and the main action late on unfolded more towards the stands' side, but a progressive winner. Not the strongest renewal, but the first three are rated within a couple of pounds of their marks.

## 3080 EBF STALLIONS CECIL FRAIL STKS (SPONSORED BY ARMSTRONG AGGREGATES) (LISTED RACE) (F&M) 6f

**4:35** (4:39) (Class 1) 3-Y-O+

**£26,653** (£10,105; £5,057; £2,519; £1,264; £634) **Stalls** Centre

Form RPR

0605 **1** **Buying Trouble (USA)**[14] 2623 4-9-3 93...................... AndrewMullen 14 102
(David Evans) *s.i.s: hld up: swtchd to r stands' side over 4f out: hdwy 2f out: rdn to ld 1f out: r.o: 1st of 4 in gp* **14/1**

33-3 **2** 1/2 **Bounce**[14] 2623 4-9-3 92............................................. FergusSweeney 10 100
(Henry Candy) *chsd ldrs: swtchd to racd stands' side over 4f out: led wl over 1f out: hdd 1f out: r.o: 2nd of 4 in gp* **3/1[2]**

0-22 **3** 1/2 **Futoon (IRE)**[14] 2623 4-9-3 92........................................ JoeDoyle 2 99
(Kevin Ryan) *overall ldr in centre: hdd over 3f out: stl led that gp whn rdn and ev ch wl over 1f out: 1st of 6 that gp* **7/1[3]**

43-0 **4** 3/4 **Spring Fling**[14] 2623 6-9-3 94........................................ MartinHarley 6 96+
(Henry Candy) *racd centre: hld up: hdwy whn hmpd over 2f out: r.o: 2nd of 6 in gp* **16/1**

3-60 **5** 1 1/4 **Mystic Dawn (IRE)**[14] 2623 3-8-8 98........................... HarryBentley 5 90
(David Simcock) *racd centre: chsd ldrs: rdn over 1f out: styd on same pce ins fnl f: 3rd of 6 in gp* **9/1**

**6** 2 1/2 **Sugar Free (GER)**[26] 4-9-3 100.................................... OliverWilson 4 84
(D Moser, Germany) *stmbld s: racd centre: hld up: effrt over 1f out: wknd ins fnl f: 4th of 6 in gp* **10/1**

40-5 **7** hd **Mayfair Lady**[37] 1903 4-9-3 100...................................... TonyHamilton 7 84
(Richard Fahey) *w ldr centre: rdn whn hmpd over 1f out: wknd fnl f: 5th of 6 in gp* **16/1**

112- **8** 3 1/2 **Gravity Flow (IRE)**[231] 7146 4-9-3 99............................. PatCosgrave 9 73
(William Haggas) *w ldrs tl swtchd to racd centre over 4f out: overall ldr over 3f out: rdn and hung lft fr over 2f out: hdd wl over 1f out: wknd fnl f: 3rd of 4 in gp* **7/4[1]**

4114 **9** 5 **Veena (FR)**[84] 1030 4-9-3 78............................................. DanielMuscutt 8 57
(David Simcock) *hld up: swtchd to racd stands' side over 4f out: hdwy to chse ldr over 3f out: rdn and hung lft over 2f out: wknd over 1f out: last of 4 in gp* **50/1**

110- **10** nse **Go On Go On Go On**[262] 6230 4-9-3 97............................ AdamKirby 3 56
(Clive Cox) *racd centre: prom: pushed along over 2f out: hung lft and wknd over 1f out: last of 6 in gp* **8/1**

1m 10.8s (-3.00) **Going Correction** -0.50s/f (Hard)
**WFA** 3 from 4yo+ 9lb **10** Ran SP% **124.5**
Speed ratings (Par 111): **100,99,98,97,96 92,92,87,81,81**
CSF £59.76 TOTE £20.40: £3.70, £1.60, £2.50; EX 91.40 Trifecta £643.30.
**Owner** Mrs I M Folkes **Bred** Flaxman Holdings Limited **Trained** Pandy, Monmouths
■ Stewards' Enquiry : Pat Cosgrave caution: future conduct in races

**FOCUS**
Distance as advertised. The front two came home against the stands' rail, helped by the favourite hanging out into the centre of the course and hampering several of the other runners. Not the strongest of Listed races, with the winner's best effort since her standout Newmarket run.

## 3081 AMIX H'CAP 1m 3f 175y

**5:10** (5:10) (Class 3) (0-95,94) 3-Y-O

**£9,337** (£2,796; £1,398; £699; £349; £175) **Stalls** Centre

Form RPR

-410 **1** **Sofia's Rock (FR)**[14] 2614 3-9-7 **94**.................................. JimCrowley 6 103
(Mark Johnston) *mde all: rdn and hung rt fr over 2f out: styd on* **7/2[3]**

42-1 **2** 3 **Stone The Crows**[27] 2175 3-8-9 **85**........................ KieranShoemark(3) 1 89
(Roger Charlton) *hld up: hdwy on bit 3f out: nt clr run over 2f out: sn rdn to chse wnr: hung lft over 1f out: edgd rt and styd on same pce ins fnl f* **8/1**

-212 **3** 1 3/4 **Wefait (IRE)**[28] 2149 3-8-7 **80** oh2.................................... KieranO'Neill 3 81
(Richard Hannon) *chsd wnr 4f: remained handy: rdn and hung lft over 4f out: outpcd over 3f out: rallied over 1f out: no ex ins fnl f* **25/1**

2-21 **4** hd **Face The Facts (IRE)**[35] 1963 3-8-13 **86**......................... RobertTart 5 87
(John Gosden) *hld up: pushed along over 4f out: sn outpcd: styd on ins fnl f: nt trble ldrs* **2/1[1]**

2-15 **5** 5 **Al Zaman (IRE)**[17] 2526 3-8-10 **83**...............................(t[1]) OisinMurphy 4 76
(Simon Crisford) *s.i.s: hdwy over 10f out: chsd wnr 8f out: rdn over 3f out: hung rt and lost 2nd over 2f out: wknd fnl f* **5/1**

21 **6** 3/4 **Janszoon**[15] 2576 3-9-3 **90**................................................... MartinLane 2 81
(Charlie Appleby) *hld up: pushed along and hdwy over 3f out: sn rdn: rdr dropped whip over 2f out: wknd fnl f* **5/2[2]**

2m 30.59s (-3.21) **Going Correction** -0.30s/f (Firm) **6** Ran SP% **115.8**
Speed ratings (Par 103): **98,96,94,94,91 90**
CSF £31.05 TOTE £4.90: £2.20, £2.80; EX 26.20 Trifecta £172.80.
**Owner** Mezzone Family 1 **Bred** Jean-Francois Gribomont **Trained** Middleham Moor, N Yorks
■ Stewards' Enquiry : Jim Crowley caution: careless riding

**FOCUS**
An interesting 3yo handicap. Actual distance 1m3f 164yds. The winner and third are rated similar to their Leicester run.

## 3082 ARMSTRONG FAMILY SUPPORT THE ABF H'CAP 7f 37y

**5:40** (5:40) (Class 3) (0-95,90) 3-Y-O **£9,703** (£2,887; £1,443; £721) **Stalls** Low

Form RPR

0-1 **1** **Silent Echo**[22] 2366 3-9-2 **85**.............................................. HarryBentley 1 94+
(Roger Charlton) *s.i.s: hld up: racd keenly: hdwy over 2f out: led on bit over 1f out: rdn out* **9/1[3]**

1-2 **2** nk **Chessman (IRE)**[36] 1945 3-9-7 **90**...................................... RobertTart 2 98+
(John Gosden) *hld up: nt clr run over 2f out: shkn up: nt clr run and swtchd rt over 1f out: r.o wl to go 2nd nr fin: nt rch wnr* **4/5[1]**

31- **3** 1/2 **Mojito (IRE)**[211] 7658 3-9-0 **83**......................................... PatCosgrave 3 89
(William Haggas) *s.i.s: plld hrd and sn prom: shkn up to ld over 1f out: sn hdd: styd on same pce towards fin* **9/4[2]**

-530 **4** 4 **Arc Royal**[16] 2554 3-9-0 **83**........................................ RichardKingscote 8 78
(Tom Dascombe) *led: qcknd 3f out: rdn and hdd over 1f out: no ex fnl f* **11/1**

51-2 **5** 2 1/2 **Tai Sing Yeh (IRE)**[23] 2348 3-9-2 **85**..............................(t) GavinLerena 6 73
(Charles Hills) *chsd ldr: rdn and ev ch over 1f out: hung lft and wknd ins fnl f* **10/1**

1m 29.01s (-3.69) **Going Correction** -0.30s/f (Firm) **5** Ran SP% **113.7**
Speed ratings (Par 103): **109,108,108,103,100**
CSF £17.67 TOTE £7.40: £2.70, £1.10; EX 18.70 Trifecta £45.60.
**Owner** K Abdullah **Bred** Juddmonte Farms Ltd **Trained** Beckhampton, Wilts

**FOCUS**
Actual distance 7f 50yds. A good-quality little handicap that proved something of a messy affair. The first three should prove better than the bare form.
T/Jkpt: Not Won. T/Plt: £446.90 to a £1 stake. Pool: £152,392.42 - 248.88 winning units T/Qpdt: £53.10 to a £1 stake. Pool: £7,975.74 - 111.1 winning units **Colin Roberts**

## [2756]SALISBURY (R-H)
### Saturday, May 27

**OFFICIAL GOING: Good to firm (good in places; 8.5)**
Wind: light against Weather: overcast but warm

## 3083 BATHWICK TYRES EBF NOVICE STKS (PLUS 10 RACE) 5f
**5:45** (5:48) (Class 4) 2-Y-O **£4,043** (£1,203; £601; £300) **Stalls** Low

Form RPR

1 **Nine Below Zero** 2-9-2 0 ShaneKelly 5 81+
(Ralph Beckett) *wnt lft and slowly away: sn travelling strly bhd ldrs: shkn up to ld jst ins fnl f: r.o wl* **7/1**[3]

2 1 ½ **Mokaatil** 2-9-2 0 JackMitchell 3 76
(Owen Burrows) *s.i.s: sn travelling strly bhd ldrs: led over 1f out: rdn and hdd jst ins fnl f: kpt on but nt pce of wnr* **5/1**[2]

2 3 1 **Joegogo (IRE)**[9] 2756 2-8-13 0 HectorCrouch(3) 7 72
(David Evans) *trckd ldrs: rdn 2f out: kpt on same pce fnl f* **5/2**[1]

4 1 **Midsummer Knight** 2-9-2 0 CharlesBishop 8 68
(Mick Channon) *hld up bhd ldrs: effrt 2f out: kpt on but nt pce to threaten fnl f* **12/1**

0 5 ½ **Bodybuilder**[9] 2756 2-9-2 0 SeanLevey 2 67
(Richard Hannon) *led: rdn and hdd over 1f out: no ex fnl f* **5/1**[2]

0 6 2 **Cabanon Bay**[9] 2756 2-9-2 0 JohnFahy 4 59
(Malcolm Saunders) *racd keenly: pressed ldr: rdn and ev ch 2f out: wknd fnl f* **33/1**

7 19 **Lord Del Boy** 2-8-11 0 RyanWhile(5) 6
(Bill Turner) *s.i.s: a outpcd in last* **33/1**

1m 1.25s (0.25) **Going Correction** -0.10s/f (Good) **7 Ran SP% 88.0**
Speed ratings (Par 95): **94,91,90,88,87 84,54**
CSF £21.74 TOTE £7.20: £2.50, £2.70; EX 28.20 Trifecta £69.70.
**Owner** P K Gardner **Bred** Springcombe Park Stud **Trained** Kimpton, Hants
■ Gotti was withdrawn. Price at time of withdrawal 7/4f. Rule 4 applies to all bets - deduction 35p in the pound.

**FOCUS**
Rail erected up to 14ft off permanent far side rail between 6F and 2F. There was a tight finish to this fair-looking novice event. The third sets the level.

## 3084 BATHWICK TYRES ANDOVER H'CAP 6f
**6:15** (6:16) (Class 6) (0-65,67) 4-Y-O+ **£3,234** (£962; £481; £240) **Stalls** Low

Form RPR

316- 1 **Swanton Blue (IRE)**[168] 8316 4-9-6 **64** ThomasBrown 12 72
(Ed de Giles) *led after 1f: kpt on strly: rdn out* **12/1**

50-4 2 2 ¼ **Langley Vale**[35] 1979 8-9-4 **62** (v) JackMitchell 1 63
(Roger Teal) *hld up: hdwy over 1f out: sn rdn: r.o wl fnl f: snatched 2nd fnl stride* **6/1**[3]

1-26 3 hd **Titus Secret**[15] 2589 5-9-2 **60** (h[1]) JohnFahy 5 61
(Malcolm Saunders) *led for 1f: chsd wnr: rdn and drifted lft over 1f out: kpt on but a being hld fnl f: lot 2nd fnl stride* **11/4**[1]

6644 4 2 **Chetan**[17] 2514 5-9-8 **66** (tp) LouisSteward 10 61
(Charlie Wallis) *chsd ldrs: rdn 2f out: kpt on same pce fnl f* **8/1**

4003 5 nk **New Rich**[31] 2091 7-8-13 **57** (v) CharlesBishop 6 51
(Eve Johnson Houghton) *mid-div: rdn over 2f out: kpt on ent fnl f but nt pce to get involved* **7/1**

4021 6 ¾ **Indian Affair**[11] 2709 7-9-4 **65** (bt) HectorCrouch(3) 14 57
(Milton Bradley) *mid-div: hdwy 3f out: sn rdn: one pce fnl 2f* **13/2**

0000 7 1 ¼ **Royal Normandy**[10] 2724 5-8-7 **51** oh6 (b) MartinDwyer 13 39
(Grace Harris) *hld up towards rr: rdn and prog into midfield 2f out: no further imp fnl f* **25/1**

3020 8 1 **Light From Mars**[45] 1728 12-9-9 **67** (p) LukeMorris 2 52
(Ronald Harris) *mid-div: rdn 3f out: nvr any imp* **14/1**

6005 9 2 ¼ **Divine Call**[11] 2709 10-8-11 **55** (b) ShaneKelly 4 33
(Milton Bradley) *s.i.s: towards rr: rdn in midfield 2f out: fdd fnl f* **25/1**

005/ 10 2 ¾ **Thewestwalian (USA)**[647] 5507 9-8-1 **52** MollyKing(7) 11 22
(Peter Hiatt) *slowly away: towards rr: rdn 2f out: wknd jst over 1f out* **33/1**

0/00 11 7 **A Definite Diamond**[11] 2709 4-8-4 **51** oh6 AaronJones(3) 9
(Grace Harris) *chsd ldrs tl wknd 2f out* **100/1**

335- 12 2 ¼ **Champagne Bob**[250] 6636 5-8-12 **59** EdwardGreatrex(3) 3
(Richard Price) *mid-div for over 3f: wknd over 1f out* **5/1**[2]

1m 13.52s (-1.28) **Going Correction** -0.10s/f (Good) **12 Ran SP% 120.5**
Speed ratings (Par 101): **104,101,100,98,97 96,95,93,90,87 77,74**
CSF £81.37 CT £264.96 TOTE £14.70: £3.60, £2.80, £1.40; EX 101.00 Trifecta £276.00.
**Owner** E B De Giles **Bred** Tally-Ho Stud **Trained** Ledbury, H'fords

**FOCUS**
This moderate sprint handicap proved uneventful.

## 3085 BATHWICK TYRES SALISBURY MAIDEN STKS 6f
**6:45** (6:46) (Class 5) 3-Y-O+ **£3,881** (£1,155; £577; £288) **Stalls** Low

Form RPR

4-2 1 **Crafty Madam (IRE)**[21] 2383 3-9-0 0 LukeMorris 7 70
(Clive Cox) *in tch: tk clsr order over 2f out: rdn to take narrow advantage jst over 1f out: hld on: drvn out* **5/2**[1]

2 hd **Cobalty Isle (IRE)** 3-9-2 0 HectorCrouch(3) 2 74
(Henry Candy) *in tch: swtchd rt and hdwy 2f out: str chal thrght fnl f: jst hld* **16/1**

-003 3 ¾ **Delagate This Lord**[18] 2507 3-8-12 57 (p) DavidEgan(7) 4 72
(Bill Turner) *prom: rdn to ld 2f out: narrowly hdd jst over 1f out: kpt on w ev ch: no ex towards fin* **25/1**

0-40 4 2 ½ **Tawaafoq**[24] 2293 3-9-5 70 (h) SeanLevey 13 64
(Richard Hannon) *hld up: hdwy over 1f out: sn rdn: wnt 4th ent fnl f: styd on but nt pce to get on terms* **12/1**

222- 5 3 **Port Isaac (IRE)**[205] 7782 4-9-7 78 TylerSaunders(7) 5 56
(Marcus Tregoning) *mid-div: outpcd over 2f out: kpt on fr over 1f out: wnt 5th cl home* **8/1**

2 6 nk **Hollander**[14] 2620 3-9-5 0 MartinDwyer 6 53
(William Muir) *led tl rdn 2f out: wknd ins fnl f* **7/2**[3]

20-3 7 nk **Gloriux**[17] 2510 3-9-2 73 (h) CallumShepherd(3) 3 52
(Charles Hills) *mid-div: rdn over 3f out: nvr any imp* **14/1**

00 8 shd **Babette (IRE)**[14] 2620 3-9-0 0 JackMitchell 11 47
(Tony Newcombe) *towards rr: sme late prog: nvr any danger* **100/1**

-320 9 ¾ **Raffle King (IRE)**[15] 2579 3-9-5 74 CharlesBishop 12 50
(Mick Channon) *hld up towards rr: sme minor late prog: nvr any danger* **16/1**

440- 10 hd **Tesko Fella (IRE)**[225] 7319 3-9-5 69 JoeyHaynes 1 49
(Luke McJannet) *trckd ldrs: rdn over 2f out: wknd over 1f out* **50/1**

6- 11 2 ¾ **Clip Art**[339] 3511 3-9-0 0 ShaneKelly 8 35
(Jamie Osborne) *a towards rr* **50/1**

222- 12 ½ **Subjective**[228] 7259 3-9-5 74 JamieSpencer 9 39
(David Simcock) *trckd ldrs tl rdn over 2f out: grad fdd: eased whn btn ins fnl f* **3/1**[2]

1m 13.84s (-0.96) **Going Correction** -0.10s/f (Good)
**WFA** 3 from 4yo 9lb **12 Ran SP% 121.8**
Speed ratings (Par 103): **102,101,100,97,93 93,92,92,91,91 87,86**
CSF £45.97 TOTE £3.30: £1.10, £4.10, £6.20; EX 55.60 Trifecta £667.20.
**Owner** Con Harrington **Bred** Con Harrington **Trained** Lambourn, Berks

**FOCUS**
A modest sprint maiden in which the principals came clear.

## 3086 BATHWICK TYRES H'CAP 1m 6f 44y
**7:15** (7:15) (Class 4) (0-85,85) 4-Y-O+ **£7,762** (£2,310; £1,154; £577) **Stalls** Far side

Form RPR

6-04 1 **Mark Hopkins**[14] 2603 5-8-12 **83** DavidEgan(7) 3 95
(David Elsworth) *mde all: drifted sltly lft but styd on strly to assert fnl f: rdn out* **7/2**[2]

0/3 2 3 ½ **Volpone Jelois (FR)**[30] 1498 4-8-4 **73** (p) MeganNicholls(5) 7 80
(Paul Nicholls) *trckd ldrs: rdn to chse wnr fr 2f out: styd on tl no ex fnl 120yds* **4/1**[3]

31-0 3 7 **Going Up (IRE)**[20] 2431 4-9-7 **85** JamieSpencer 1 82
(Rae Guest) *hld up: hdwy over 2f out: rdn to chse ldng pair over 1f out: nt pce to get on terms: jst hld on for 3rd* **5/1**

0-42 4 nse **Plymouth Sound**[26] 2218 5-8-13 **77** (p) JohnFahy 5 74
(Eve Johnson Houghton) *hld up: rdn over 2f out: no imp tl hdwy ent fnl f: styd on to nrly snatch 3rd fnl stride* **6/1**

420- 5 1 ¼ **Harry Hunt**[22] 8250 10-9-4 **82** LiamKeniry 9 77
(Graeme McPherson) *chsd ldrs: pushed along over 5f out: rdn 3f out: one pce fnl 2f* **25/1**

112- 6 3 **High Command (IRE)**[166] 8339 4-9-0 **85** CameronNoble(7) 8 76
(Roger Varian) *trckd ldrs: rdn 3f out: wknd ent fnl f* **11/4**[1]

01-4 7 15 **Sunny Future (IRE)**[26] 2218 11-8-11 **75** (h) MartinDwyer 6 56
(Malcolm Saunders) *hld up: hdwy into 5th u.p 2f out: wknd over 1f out: eased ins fnl f* **10/1**

13/- P **Stock Hill Fair**[652] 5335 9-9-1 **79** PatDobbs 4
(Brendan Powell) *trckd ldr tl rdn over 2f out: sn wknd: p.u over 1f out* **20/1**

3m 2.25s (-5.15) **Going Correction** -0.10s/f (Good) **8 Ran SP% 117.5**
Speed ratings (Par 105): **110,108,104,103,103 101,92,**
CSF £18.53 CT £70.14 TOTE £4.40: £1.50, £1.40, £1.90; EX 20.50 Trifecta £123.90.
**Owner** Exors Of The Late R J McCreery **Bred** Stowell Hill Ltd **Trained** Newmarket, Suffolk

**FOCUS**
Few landed a blow in this fair staying handicap.

## 3087 BATHWICK TYRES BOURNEMOUTH H'CAP 1m 4f 5y
**7:45** (7:48) (Class 6) (0-65,72) 3-Y-O **£3,234** (£962; £481; £240) **Stalls** Low

Form RPR

600- 1 **Pow Wow**[198] 7883 3-9-3 **61** JamieSpencer 13 70+
(Roger Charlton) *mid-div: lost pl in last pair over 6f out: hdwy 3f out: rdn to ld ent fnl f: styd on: drvn out* **2/1**[1]

-041 2 1 **Mirzam (IRE)**[11] 2711 3-9-7 **72** DavidEgan(7) 4 78+
(Mick Channon) *mid-div: hdwy 3f out: chal 2f out: rdn and ev ch ent fnl f: styd on but no ex* **3/1**[2]

0-00 3 4 **Light Gunner (IRE)**[33] 2027 3-8-5 **52** EdwardGreatrex(3) 6 52
(Henry Tett) *wnt lft s: hld up: rdn whn swtchd lft 2f out: hdwy over 1f out: styd on wl to snatch 2nd fnl stride* **25/1**

06-5 4 shd **Magic Beans**[35] 1968 3-9-1 **62** (p[1]) CharlieBennett(3) 11 61
(Hughie Morrison) *led: rdn whn chal over 2f out: hdd ent fnl f: kpt on same pce: lost 3rd fnl stride* **6/1**[3]

0-30 5 2 **Percy Thrower (IRE)**[21] 2394 3-9-2 **63** CallumShepherd(3) 3 59
(Charles Hills) *mid-div: hdwy 3f out: rdn and ev ch whn edgd rt 2f out: one pce after* **10/1**

45-5 6 ½ **Charlie Rascal (FR)**[124] 378 3-9-3 **61** LukeMorris 1 56
(Peter Chapple-Hyam) *nvr bttr than mid-div* **16/1**

6160 7 hd **Oberyn (IRE)**[21] 2394 3-9-8 **66** RenatoSouza 12 61+
(Sylvester Kirk) *trckd ldrs: looked to hit rails over 3f out: sn rdn: one pce fnl 2f* **25/1**

5-05 8 1 ½ **Holyroman Princess**[10] 2726 3-8-5 **54** (b) LuluStanford(5) 9 47
(Rod Millman) *trckd ldr tl 4f out: sn rdn: nvr bk on terms: fdd fnl f* **16/1**

06-4 9 1 ½ **Russian Regard (IRE)**[22] 2371 3-9-0 **63** GeorgeWood(5) 5 53
(Jonathan Portman) *trckd ldrs: rdn whn hmpd over 2f out: wknd ent fnl f* **11/1**

00-0 10 3 **Noble Behest**[35] 1962 3-9-2 **60** MartinDwyer 8 46
(Marcus Tregoning) *hmpd leaving stalls: mid-div: rdn over 3f out: nvr threatened: wknd fnl f* **8/1**

50-0 11 5 **Royal Sentiment (IRE)**[12] 2679 3-8-9 **53** SteveDrowne 2 31
(Mark Usher) *a in rr* **66/1**

2m 38.41s (0.41) **Going Correction** -0.10s/f (Good) **11 Ran SP% 122.1**
Speed ratings (Par 97): **94,93,90,90,89 88,88,87,86,84 81**
CSF £8.00 CT £118.42 TOTE £3.40: £1.60, £1.40, £6.50; EX 11.70 Trifecta £195.90.
**Owner** Philip Newton **Bred** Philip Newton **Trained** Beckhampton, Wilts

**FOCUS**
There was a messy pace on in this 3yo handicap, but the runner-up still gives it a fair look.

## 3088 BATHWICK TYRES FERNDOWN CLASSIFIED STKS 1m 1f 201y
**8:15** (8:18) (Class 5) 3-Y-O **£3,396** (£1,010; £505; £252) **Stalls** Low

Form RPR

-550 1 **Cartavio (IRE)**[101] 737 3-9-0 68 LiamKeniry 5 72
(Andrew Balding) *a.p: led over 2f out: rdn over 1f out: hung rt ins fnl f: styd on: drvn out* **10/1**

12-0 2 1 ¼ **Phoenix Dawn**[45] 1736 3-9-0 68 (p) MartinDwyer 3 70
(Brendan Powell) *led: rdn 5f out: hdd over 2f out: rallying in cl 2nd whn squeezed out fnl 140yds: swtchd lft: kpt on again to regain 2nd whn clr run fnl 60yds* **16/1**

6-55 3 hd **Fields Of Fortune**[21] 2394 3-8-11 69 (h[1]) HollieDoyle(3) 4 70
(Richard Hannon) *mid-div: pushed along 5f out: hdwy over 2f out: mounting chal ins fnl f whn squeezed up on rails fnl 140yds: no ex whn lost 2nd cl home* **5/2**[1]

5-04 4 ¾ **Amelia Dream**[21] 2395 3-8-7 70 DavidEgan(7) 7 67
(Mick Channon) *trckd ldrs: rdn over 2f out: kpt on same pce* **11/2**[3]

62-3 **5** *1 1/4* **Harry Beau**[21] 2393 3-9-0 70 PatDobbs 9 65
(Richard Hannon) *mid-div: rdn over 2f out: styd on fnl f but nt pce to get on terms* **12/1**

-061 **6** *nk* **Kyllachys Tale (IRE)**[95] 848 3-9-0 70 JackMitchell 8 64
(Roger Teal) *trckd ldrs: edgd lft u.p over 1f out: kpt on tl no ex fnl 120yds* **20/1**

0-31 **7** *2 3/4* **Alnasl (IRE)**[24] 2296 3-8-11 70 (h) EdwardGreatrex(3) 6 59
(Archie Watson) *hld up last pair: effrt over 2f out: wknd fnl f* **5/1**[2]

454 **8** *1/2* **Gunmaker (IRE)**[38] 1889 3-9-0 70 JamieSpencer 1 58
(David Simcock) *hld up: swtchd out for effrt 2f out: sn rdn: nvr any imp* **5/2**[1]

2m 10.77s (0.87) **Going Correction** -0.10s/f (Good) **8** Ran SP% **116.6**
Speed ratings (Par 99): **92,91,90,90,89 89,86,86**
CSF £153.34 TOTE £13.40: £3.30, £3.50, £1.30; EX 154.30 Trifecta £640.10.
**Owner** Mick and Janice Mariscotti **Bred** Thomas G Cooke **Trained** Kingsclere, Hants
■ Stewards' Enquiry : Liam Keniry three-day ban: careless riding (Jun 10-12)

**FOCUS**
An ordinary classified event for 3yos.
T/Plt: £245.50 to a £1 stake. Pool: £63,981.94 - 190.19 winning units T/Qpdt: £14.10 to a £1 stake. Pool: £6,399.38 - 334.1 winning units **Tim Mitchell**

## 2801 YORK (L-H)
### Saturday, May 27

**OFFICIAL GOING: Good to firm (good in places) changing to good after race 3 (3:15)**
Wind: Moderate behind Weather: Sunny with cloudy periods and thunder showers

## 3089 CONSTANT SECURITY STKS (H'CAP) 7f
**2:10** (2:10) (Class 2) (0-110,113) 3-Y-0+
**£18,675** (£5,592; £2,796; £1,398; £699; £351) **Stalls** Low

Form RPR

056- **1** **Golden Stunner (IRE)**[200] 7861 4-9-1 96 FranBerry 5 107
(Ralph Beckett) *awkward and wnt rt s: sn led: rdn wl over 1f out: clr ent fnl f: kpt on strly* **7/1**

23-3 **2** *2* **Firmament**[24] 2290 5-10-0 109 DanielTudhope 2 115
(David O'Meara) *trckd ldrs: hdwy over 2f out: rdn to chse wnr ent fnl f: sn drvn and no imp* **7/4**[1]

2-65 **3** *1 1/2* **Get Knotted (IRE)**[9] 2767 5-9-5 100 (p) PaulMulrennan 6 102
(Michael Dods) *slt bump s: trckd ldrs: hdwy over 2f out: rdn over 1f out: drvn and kpt on same pce fnl f* **7/2**[2]

-225 **4** *3/4* **War Glory (IRE)**[28] 2141 4-9-0 95 oh2 TomMarquand 7 95
(Richard Hannon) *trckd wnr: pushed along 3f out: cl up and rdn 2f out: sn drvn and wknd appr fnl f* **8/1**

03-5 **5** *1 3/4* **Right Touch**[28] 2156 7-9-4 99 PaulHanagan 1 94
(Richard Fahey) *trckd ldng pair: hdwy over 2f out: rdn along wl over 1f out: sn drvn and one pce* **8/1**

022- **6** *6* **Danzeno**[243] 6837 6-9-7 105 AlistairRawlinson(3) 3 84
(Michael Appleby) *dwlt: hld up: a rr* **4/1**[3]

1m 23.57s (-1.73) **Going Correction** +0.30s/f (Good) **6** Ran SP% **113.3**
Speed ratings (Par 109): **121,118,117,116,114 107**
CSF £20.11 TOTE £6.90: £2.80, £1.50; EX 21.40 Trifecta £84.00.
**Owner** Sutong Pan **Bred** Fergus Cousins **Trained** Kimpton, Hants

**FOCUS**
Races 2, 3 & 6 increased by 39yds. The going was good to firm (good in places) prior to the opener, a decent handicap in which the winner dictated at an ordinary gallop. Fran Berry said that it was "good, fast ground". The winner picked up on her 3yo progress.

## 3090 WEDDINGMATES.CO.UK GRAND CUP STKS (LISTED RACE) 1m 5f 188y
**2:40** (2:41) (Class 1) 4-Y-0+
**£28,355** (£10,750; £5,380; £2,680; £1,345; £675) **Stalls** Low

Form RPR

31-6 **1** **Dal Harraild**[35] 1957 4-9-3 109 PaulHanagan 13 115
(William Haggas) *hld up in tch: hdwy over 3f out: chsd ldrs over 2f out: rdn to ld 11/2f out: styd on strly fnl f* **3/1**[1]

02-0 **2** *3 1/2* **Nakeeta**[17] 2525 6-9-0 102 (h) PaulMulrennan 14 107
(Iain Jardine) *hld up in rr: hdwy 3f out: chsd ldrs 2f out: swtchd rt to outer and rdn wl over 1f out: styd on fnl f* **14/1**

522- **3** *1 1/2* **Seamour (IRE)**[247] 6708 6-9-0 104 TomEaves 4 105
(Brian Ellison) *in tch: hdwy 4f out: chsd ldng pair 3f out: rdn over 2f out: drvn to chse wnr over 1f out: kpt on same pce fnl f* **14/1**

46-1 **4** *hd* **Harrison**[17] 2519 4-9-0 109 GrahamLee 9 105
(Mick Channon) *trckd ldr: hdwy and cl up 5f out: led wl over 3f out: rdn along over 2f out: hdd 11/2f out and sn drvn: kpt on same pce* **7/1**[2]

6-31 **5** *2 1/4* **The Tartan Spartan (IRE)**[27] 2176 4-9-0 102 TadhgO'Shea 7 101
(John Patrick Shanahan, Ire) *in tch: hdwy 4f out: chsd ldrs over 2f out: sn rdn along and kpt on one pce* **11/1**

3-00 **6** *nk* **Curbyourenthusiasm (IRE)**[114] 540 6-9-0 108 TomMarquand 5 101
(David Simcock) *dwlt and towards rr: hdwy over 4f out: rdn along 3f out: drvn 2f out and no imp* **8/1**[3]

3503 **7** *6* **Dylan Mouth (IRE)**[17] 2519 6-9-0 106 AntonioFresu 2 93
(Marco Botti) *chsd ldng pair: rdn along 4f out: drvn 3f out: sn wknd* **16/1**

054- **8** *14* **Goldmember**[247] 6708 4-9-0 102 StevieDonohoe 6 73
(David Simcock) *a rr: bhd fr over 3f out* **12/1**

50-6 **9** *7* **Clever Cookie**[8] 2803 9-9-0 109 (p) DanielTudhope 3 63
(Peter Niven) *sn led: pushed along over 4f out: hdd and rdn over 3f out: drvn over 2f out: sn wknd and eased* **3/1**[1]

101- **10** *3 1/2* **Alyssa**[239] 6917 4-8-12 102 FranBerry 12 56
(Ralph Beckett) *racd wd early: prom: pushed along 5f out: rdn over 4f out: sn wknd* **7/1**[2]

3m 2.72s (2.52) **Going Correction** +0.30s/f (Good) **10** Ran SP% **121.4**
Speed ratings (Par 111): **104,102,101,101,99 99,96,88,84,82**
CSF £52.56 TOTE £3.50: £1.50, £4.70, £4.10; EX 50.10 Trifecta £678.60.
**Owner** St Albans Bloodstock Limited **Bred** St Albans Bloodstock Llp **Trained** Newmarket, Suffolk

**FOCUS**
Race distance increased by 39yds. There was heavy rain and thunderstorms before and during this decent Listed staying event, in which they went only a slow pace. The winner progressed last year and is still unexposed as a stayer.

## 3091 JOIN CLUB GODOLPHIN H'CAP 1m 3f 188y
**3:15** (3:17) (Class 3) (0-90,89) 4-Y-0+ **£9,703** (£2,887; £1,443; £721) **Stalls** Centre

Form RPR

0-44 **1** **Theydon Grey**[10] 2741 4-8-9 82 GeorgiaCox(5) 10 90
(William Haggas) *racd wd early: trckd ldr: hdwy and cl up 3f out: slt ld 2f out and sn pushed along: strly chal over 1f out and ins fnl f: carried hd high and cajoled along: kpt on wl towards fin* **5/1**[2]

-305 **2** *nk* **Chancery (USA)**[10] 2741 9-9-2 84 (p) DanielTudhope 5 91
(David O'Meara) *hld up towards rr: hdwy wl over 2f out: chsd ldrs and rdn over 1f out: swtchd lft ent fnl f: styd on strly towards fin* **8/1**

0-32 **3** *nk* **Warp Factor (IRE)**[15] 2574 4-8-11 79 TadhgO'Shea 8 86
(John Patrick Shanahan, Ire) *trckd ldrs: hdwy over 3f out: rdn to chal 2f out: drvn and ev ch ent fnl f: no ex towards fin* **7/1**

0-02 **4** *3/4* **Dance King**[15] 2593 7-9-0 82 (tp) PaulMulrennan 3 87
(Tim Easterby) *trckd ldrs: hdwy on inner 3f out: cl up 2f out: sn chal: rdn and ev ch ent fnl f tl no ex towards fin* **6/1**[3]

1 **5** *3 1/4* **Sean O'Casey (IRE)**[10] 2728 4-9-0 82 StevieDonohoe 6 82
(Michael Appleby) *trckd ldng pair: hdwy on outer 3f out: rdn along 2f out: drvn and ev ch ent fnl f: kpt on same pce* **5/1**[2]

521- **6** *8* **St Malo (USA)**[214] 7597 4-9-0 82 WilliamBuick 1 77
(Roger Varian) *trckd ldng pair on inner: hdwy 4f out: cl up 3f out: rdn along 2f out: sn drvn and wknd* **2/1**[1]

0-00 **7** *3* **Havana Beat (IRE)**[36] 1942 7-9-7 89 GeorgeDowning 7 72
(Tony Carroll) *hld up towards rr: hdwy 3f out: rdn along over 2f out: sn drvn and btn* **25/1**

453 **8** *1/2* **Dolphin Village (IRE)**[35] 1976 7-9-0 82 (h) TomEaves 9 64
(Shaun Harris) *hld up: a rr* **22/1**

4110 **9** *5* **Be Perfect (USA)**[21] 2386 8-9-4 86 (p) JamesSullivan 4 60
(Ruth Carr) *led: pushed along over 3f out: rdn and hdd 2f out: sn drvn and wknd* **16/1**

2m 35.07s (1.87) **Going Correction** +0.30s/f (Good) **9** Ran SP% **118.6**
Speed ratings (Par 107): **105,104,104,104,101 96,94,94,90**
CSF £45.81 CT £284.06 TOTE £5.80: £1.90, £2.80, £2.50; EX 46.10 Trifecta £442.30.
**Owner** The Going Grey Partnership **Bred** Pinnacle Bloodstock Ltd **Trained** Newmarket, Suffolk

**FOCUS**
Races distance increased by 39yds. A fair middle-distance handicap in which the last two winners of the race scored again during their next two outings. They went only a fair gallop and there was a bunched finish. A small pb from the winner.

## 3092 UNIBET SPRINT STKS (H'CAP) 5f
**3:50** (3:51) (Class 2) (0-105,105) 3-Y-0+
**£31,125** (£9,320; £4,660; £2,330; £1,165; £585) **Stalls** Centre

Form RPR

0-21 **1** **Copper Knight (IRE)**[15] 2570 3-8-3 95 RachelRichardson(3) 5 104
(Tim Easterby) *racd towards far side: mde all: rdn clr over 1f out: drvn out* **5/1**[1]

/002 **2** *1 1/4* **Rasheeq (IRE)**[9] 2764 4-8-9 90 JasonHart 15 97
(Tim Easterby) *racd towards centre: hld up: hdwy on outer wl over 1f out: sn rdn: styd on wl fnl f* **20/1**

0454 **3** *3/4* **Watchable**[15] 2566 7-8-7 95 (v) PatrickVaughan(7) 19 99
(David O'Meara) *racd centre: prom: rdn along 2f out: drvn and edgd lft ins fnl f: kpt on* **33/1**

-200 **4** *shd* **Harry Hurricane**[100] 773 5-9-3 98 (b) WilliamBuick 3 102+
(George Baker) *hld up towards far side: hdwy 2f out: rdn to chse ldrs over 1f out: n.m.r and swtchd rt jst insiode fnl f: styd on towards fin* **9/1**

1-40 **5** *1/2* **Scie D'Leau**[9] 2764 5-8-12 96 NathanEvans(3) 2 98
(Kristin Stubbs) *racd towards far side: chsd wnr: rdn along wl over 1f out: drvn and kpt on same pce fnl f* **10/1**

0-34 **6** *1/2* **Gamesome (FR)**[21] 2391 6-8-11 92 GrahamLee 9 92
(Paul Midgley) *midfield centre: hdwy wl over 1f out: rdn and styng on whn n.m.r ins fnl f: nrst fin* **8/1**[3]

5034 **7** *3/4* **Line Of Reason (IRE)**[33] 2031 7-9-2 97 (p) PaulMulrennan 1 98+
(Paul Midgley) *racd towards far side: trckd ldrs: hdwy over 1f out: rdn whn n.m.r ins fnl f: nt rcvr* **8/1**[3]

0-65 **8** *3/4* **Union Rose**[9] 2764 5-8-9 90 TomMarquand 12 85
(Ronald Harris) *racd centre: towards rr and rdn along 1/2-way: styd on appr fnl f* **33/1**

3305 **9** *3/4* **Caspian Prince (IRE)**[15] 2573 8-9-10 105 (t) TomEaves 7 97
(Tony Coyle) *racd centre: prom: rdn along 2f out: drvn over 1f out: grad wknd* **25/1**

-303 **10** *nk* **Pipers Note**[7] 2839 7-9-2 97 JamesSullivan 11 88
(Ruth Carr) *racd centre: midfield: rdn along and hdwy whn n.m.r over 1f out: n.d* **12/1**

0420 **11** *hd* **Taexali (IRE)**[15] 2573 4-9-0 95 (b) AntonioFresu 13 85
(John Patrick Shanahan, Ire) *racd towards stands side early: bhd tl styd on fr wl over 1f out* **25/1**

0-24 **12** *shd* **East Street Revue**[20] 2433 4-8-13 94 (b) DuranFentiman 8 84
(Tim Easterby) *racd centre: nvr bttr than midfield* **8/1**[3]

25-3 **13** *hd* **Confessional**[17] 2524 10-8-11 92 (e) JackGarritty 16 81
(Tim Easterby) *chsd ldrs centre: rdn along wl over 1f out: grad wknd* **33/1**

0-1 **14** *1 1/4* **Love On The Rocks (IRE)**[43] 1768 4-8-7 88 (h) PaulHanagan 17 73
(Charles Hills) *racd centre: chsd ldrs: rdn along 2f out: grad wknd* **10/1**

5003 **15** *1 1/4* **Poyle Vinnie**[9] 2764 7-9-7 102 (p) StevieDonohoe 14 82
(Michael Appleby) *racd towards stands side: towards rr: hdwy 2f out: sn rdn and n.d* **25/1**

0-00 **16** *hd* **Venturous (IRE)**[15] 2566 4-8-8 89 SamJames 10 69
(David Barron) *racd towards stands side: a towards rr* **25/1**

00-3 **17** *3/4* **Out Do**[28] 2156 8-9-4 99 (v) DanielTudhope 6 89+
(David O'Meara) *racd towards far side: chsd ldrs: rdn over 1f out: wknd ent fnl f: sn eased* **11/2**[2]

-210 **18** *2 1/4* **Rich And Famous (USA)**[15] 2570 3-8-4 93 PJMcDonald 18 59
(Mark Johnston) *racd towards stands side: chsd ldrs on outer: rdn along over 2f out: sn wknd* **16/1**

57.51s (-1.79) **Going Correction** -0.05s/f (Good)
**WFA** 3 from 4yo+ 8lb **18** Ran SP% **134.3**
Speed ratings (Par 109): **112,110,108,108,107 107,105,104,103,102 102,102,102,100,98 97,96,93**
CSF £114.44 CT £3132.51 TOTE £5.60: £2.00, £4.70, £8.80, £2.70; EX 127.20 Trifecta £5061.60 Part Won..
**Owner** A Denham & Partner **Bred** Wardstown Stud Ltd **Trained** Great Habton, N Yorks

**FOCUS**
A valuable, competitive sprint handicap in which the action developed down the far side. There was another downpour before and during the race, resulting in the ground being eased to good. The third looks the best guide.

## 3093 YORKSHIRE REGIMENT BRITISH EBF NOVICE MEDIAN AUCTION STKS (PLUS 10 RACE) 6f
**4:25** (4:26) (Class 3) 2-Y-O **£7,762** (£2,310; £1,154; £577) **Stalls** High

Form RPR
1 **Zaman** 2-9-2 0 WilliamBuick 4 80
(Charlie Appleby) *prom: rdn 2f out: slt ld ent fnl f: sn drvn and kpt on wl towards fin* **2/1**[1]
2 1 **Royal Household** 2-9-2 0 TomMarquand 9 77+
(Richard Hannon) *trckd ldrs on outer: hdwy and cl up 1/2-way: rdn to chal 2f out and sn edgd lft: ev ch ent fnl f: sn drvn and edgd lft: kpt on* **16/1**
0 3 shd **Queen's Sargent (FR)**[33] 2029 2-9-2 0 ShaneGray 2 77
(Kevin Ryan) *trckd ldrs on outer: cl up over 3f out: slt ld over 2f out: rdn wl over 1f out: hdd ent fnl f: ev ch tl no ex last 75 yds* **8/1**
4 2 1/4 **Move Over** 2-9-2 0 PaulMulrennan 7 70+
(Richard Hannon) *cl up: slt ld halfwasy: hdd over 2f out and sn rdn: drvn appr fnl and kpt on same pce* **8/1**
5 2 **Northern Law (IRE)** 2-9-2 0 JasonHart 8 64
(John Quinn) *slt ld: hdd 1/2-way: rdn along whn n.m.r wl over 1f out: sn wknd* **8/1**
6 4 **Harvest Day** 2-8-4 0 (t[1]) HarrisonShaw(7) 11 47
(Michael Easterby) *dwlt and rr: hdwy over 2f out: rdn along wl over 1f out: n.d* **40/1**
7 nk **Jazz Magic (IRE)** 2-9-2 0 NeilFarley 3 51
(Sally Haynes) *a towards rr* **20/1**
8 1 1/4 **Mashaheer** 2-9-2 0 GrahamLee 5 47
(William Haggas) *hld up towards rr: sme hdwy over 2f out: sn rdn and wknd* **3/1**[2]
9 shd **Lyrical Pursuit** 2-8-8 0 NathanEvans(3) 6 42
(Michael Easterby) *chsd ldrs: rdn along over 2f out: grad wknd* **33/1**
10 3 1/4 **Peter Leonard** 2-9-2 0 PaulHanagan 1 37
(Richard Fahey) *t.k.h: chsd ldrs: rdn along 1/2-way: sn wknd* **6/1**[3]

1m 12.53s (0.63) **Going Correction** -0.05s/f (Good) **10 Ran SP% 122.0**
Speed ratings (Par 97): **93,91,91,88,85 80,80,78,78,74**
CSF £38.54 TOTE £2.50: £1.20, £4.90, £2.50; EX 37.30 Trifecta £196.80.
**Owner** Godolphin **Bred** Laundry Cottage Stud Farm **Trained** Newmarket, Suffolk

**FOCUS**
The 2016 winner, Packing Stones, was a decent juvenile, and this year's winner also looks a classy act.

## 3094 INFINITY TYRES BRITISH EBF FILLIES' H'CAP 1m 2f 56y
**5:00** (5:01) (Class 3) (0-90,86) 3-Y-O **£8,086** (£2,406; £1,202; £601) **Stalls** Low

Form RPR
1-5 1 **Ebbesbourne (IRE)**[30] 2117 3-9-1 **80** (h[1]) WilliamBuick 6 92+
(Sir Michael Stoute) *trckd ldrs: effrt 2f out: rdn and n.m.r over 1f out: styd on to ld ins fnl f: drvn out* **12/1**
210- 2 3/4 **Appointed**[238] 6954 3-9-6 **85** JasonHart 9 95
(Tim Easterby) *hld up in rr: hdwy 2f out: rdn over 1f out: styd on wl fnl f* **25/1**
5131 3 1 3/4 **Canberra Cliffs (IRE)**[11] 2702 3-8-11 **76** FranBerry 7 83
(Don Cantillon) *trckd ldrs: hdwy over 2f out: sn chal: rdn to take slt ld jst over 1f out: hdd and drvn ins fnl f: kpt on same pce* **5/1**[3]
13 4 3/4 **The Sky Is Blazing (IRE)**[14] 2613 3-9-7 **86** GrahamLee 2 92
(William Haggas) *trckd ldr: cl up 3f out: rdn to ld 2f out: drvn and hdd jst over 1f out: grad wknd* **3/1**[1]
50-3 5 1 3/4 **Crimson Rosette (IRE)**[38] 1885 3-8-13 **78** StevieDonohoe 5 80+
(Charlie Fellowes) *dwlt and t.k.h whn hmpd after 150 yds: rr: hdwy on inner over 2f out: swtchd rt and effrt to chse ldrs over 1f out: sn rdn and no imp* **10/3**[2]
6-11 6 2 1/2 **Miss Sheridan (IRE)**[33] 2036 3-8-6 **74** NathanEvans(3) 4 72
(Michael Easterby) *led: pushed along and qcknd over 3f out: rdn and hdd 2f out: sn wknd* **6/1**
6-54 7 2 1/2 **Set In Stone (IRE)**[15] 2572 3-8-10 **75** TadhgO'Shea 10 68
(John Patrick Shanahan, Ire) *trckd ldrs: hdwy 3f out: rdn over 2f out: drvn and wknd over 1f out* **12/1**
246- 8 22 **Clef**[218] 7493 3-9-2 **81** PaulHanagan 3 32
(Richard Fahey) *trckd ldrs whn hmpd after 150 yds: in tch: hdwy over 3f out: in tch and rdn along whn n.m.r and hmpd wl over 1f out: sn wknd and eased* **8/1**
1 9 4 1/2 **Ice Dancing (IRE)**[77] 1151 3-8-12 **77** PaulMulrennan 1 19
(Michael Bell) *t.k.h early: trckd ldng pair on inner: effrt and n.m.r 3f out: rdn along over 2f out: sn wknd* **12/1**
14- 10 3 1/2 **Desert Water (IRE)**[253] 6548 3-9-1 **80** TomMarquand 8 16
(Richard Hannon) *rr whn hmpd after 150 yds: hld up: pushed along 4f out: rdn over 3f out: sn outpcd and bhd* **33/1**

2m 15.06s (2.56) **Going Correction** +0.30s/f (Good) **10 Ran SP% 120.0**
Speed ratings (Par 100): **101,100,99,98,97 95,93,75,71,69**
CSF £276.39 CT £1702.11 TOTE £13.30: £3.60, £8.30, £2.20; EX 221.70 Trifecta £1500.30.
**Owner** James Wigan **Bred** J Wigan & London Thoroughbred Services **Trained** Newmarket, Suffolk

**FOCUS**
Race run over an extra 39yds. An interesting middle-distance handicap for 3yo fillies. They went only a modest tempo. A slightly positive view has been taken of the form.

## 3095 JOHN WRIGHT ELECTRICAL H'CAP (FOR GENTLEMAN AMATEUR RIDERS) 7f
**5:30** (5:33) (Class 4) (0-80,80) 4-Y-O+ **£7,486** (£2,322; £1,160; £580) **Stalls** Low

Form RPR
-001 1 **Theodorico (IRE)**[12] 2684 4-11-1 **79** MrPJCawley(5) 9 95
(David Loughnane) *cl up: led 1/2-way: rdn clr 2f out: kpt on strly* **9/1**
443- 2 6 **Destroyer**[240] 6899 4-11-1 **79** MrBJames(5) 4 79
(Tom Tate) *trckd ldrs: rdn along over 2f out: chsd wnr over 1f out: drvn ins fnl f: no imp* **14/1**
2 3 1 **Madroos**[31] 2081 4-11-7 **80** MrWEasterby 2 77
(Michael Easterby) *trckd ldrs on inner: hdwy over 2f out: sn rdn and kpt on u.p fnl f* **5/1**[1]
0-63 4 1/2 **Alpine Dream (IRE)**[16] 2548 4-10-6 **70** (b) HenryMorshead(5) 20 66
(Tim Easterby) *t.k.h: in tch ion outer: hdwy over 2f out: rdn over 1f out: edgd lft and kpt on same pce fnl f* **16/1**
6563 5 shd **Buccaneers Vault (IRE)**[20] 2428 5-11-1 **74** MrSWalker 14 70
(Paul Midgley) *awkward and hmpd s: midfield: hdwy on outer wl over 2f out: rdn wl over 1f out: kpt on fnl f* **8/1**[3]
0-05 6 1/2 **Short Work**[22] 2377 4-11-2 **75** (p) ThomasGreatrex 6 70
(David O'Meara) *chsd ldrs: rdn along 2f out: drvn over 1f out: one pce* **14/1**
0250 7 2 **Tellovoi (IRE)**[5] 2888 9-10-10 **74** (h) MrTGreenwood(5) 1 63
(Richard Guest) *slt ld: hdd 1/2-way: rdn over 2f out: drvn wl over 1f out: grad wknd* **20/1**
-141 8 1/2 **Bahamian Bird**[16] 2548 4-11-2 **80** MrBillyGarritty(5) 18 68
(Richard Fahey) *chsd ldrs: rdn along over 2f out: drvn wl over 1f out: sn one pce* **7/1**[2]
2160 9 nk **Cliff (IRE)**[12] 2684 7-10-8 **67** (p) MrAlexFerguson 10 54
(Nigel Tinkler) *.towards rr: hdwy over 2f out: swtchd rt and rdn over 1f out: kpt on fnl f* **20/1**
2350 10 1 **King Of Dreams**[42] 1788 4-10-7 **73** MrMSJohnson(7) 8 58
(David Simcock) *towards rr: hdwy 3f out: swtchd lft to inner and rdn wl over 1f out: kpt on fnl f* **12/1**
6413 11 1 **Athassel**[15] 2582 8-11-0 **78** MrJFlook(5) 15 60
(David Evans) *hmpd s and towards rr: swtchd lft to inner and hdwy 3f out: rdn over 2f out: drvn and no imp fr over 1f out* **25/1**
-561 12 3/4 **Explain**[15] 2592 5-11-2 **80** (p) MrWillPettis(5) 17 60
(Ruth Carr) *in tch on outer: sltly hmpd over 5f out: rdn along 3f out: sn no hdwy* **11/1**
0-4 13 hd **Almunther (IRE)**[16] 2547 4-10-9 **71** MrJoeWright(3) 16 51
(Micky Hammond) *wnt lft s: a towards rr* **50/1**
06-6 14 hd **Manatee Bay**[23] 2346 7-10-12 **76** (v) MrBLynn(5) 7 55
(Noel Wilson) *in tch: rdn along over 2f out: sn drvn and wknd* **28/1**
465- 15 1 1/4 **Tukhoom (IRE)**[236] 7005 4-11-3 **79** MrHHunt(3) 19 55
(Michael Herrington) *chsd ldrs: rdn along 3f out: wknd over 2f out* **8/1**[3]
235 16 2 1/4 **Order Of Service**[18] 1867 7-10-9 **73** (e) MrJamesKendrick(5) 5 43
(Shaun Harris) *s.i.s: a rr* **33/1**
-000 17 2 1/4 **Best Trip (IRE)**[16] 2550 10-10-13 **72** (t) MrJohnDawson 11 36
(Marjorie Fife) *t.k.h: in tch: rdn along wl over 2f out: sn wknd* **33/1**
-122 18 4 1/2 **Rock Warbler (IRE)**[115] 513 4-11-1 **74** (t) MrEGlassonbury 3 26
(Oliver Greenall) *in tch on inner: pushed along over 3f out: rdn over 2f out: sn wknd* **14/1**
3132 19 7 **Dark Forest**[29] 2120 4-10-10 **69** (p) MrRBirkett 13 3
(Marjorie Fife) *wnt rt s: in tch whn stmbld over 5f out: sn towards rr* **10/1**

1m 25.73s (0.43) **Going Correction** +0.30s/f (Good) **19 Ran SP% 137.0**
Speed ratings (Par 105): **109,102,101,100,100 99,97,96,96,95 94,93,93,92,91 88,86,81,73**
CSF £132.10 CT £745.69 TOTE £12.60: £2.80, £3.90, £2.10, £3.90; EX 179.40 Trifecta £1785.10.
**Owner** Mike And Eileen Newbould **Bred** J S Bolger & John Corcoran **Trained** Market Drayton, Shropshire

**FOCUS**
A competitive handicap for amateurs, but the winner turned it into a procession. They didn't go that fast, and the winner was up there throughout. The form could rate higher at face value.
T/Plt: £569.10 to a £1 stake. Pool: £95,205.00 - 167.29 winning units T/Qpdt: £117.30 to a £1 stake. Pool: £5,150.00 - 43.90 winning units **Joe Rowntree**

3096 - 3097a (Foreign Racing) - See Raceform Interactive

# 2655 CURRAGH (R-H)
Saturday, May 27

**OFFICIAL GOING: Straight course - good to yielding; round course - good changing to straight course - yielding to soft; round course - yielding after race 1 (1.50)**

## 3098a COLD MOVE IRISH EBF MARBLE HILL STKS (LISTED RACE) 6f
**3:00** (3:01) 2-Y-O
**£30,256** (£9,743; £4,615; £2,051; £1,025; £512)

RPR
1 **Brother Bear (IRE)**[20] 2438 2-9-3 0 ColmO'Donoghue 2 103
(Mrs John Harrington, Ire) *broke wl to ld early far side tl sn hdd and settled bhd ldr: 2nd 1/2-way: led gng best 1 1/2f out: sn rdn and edgd lft u.p ins fnl f: styd on wl nr side to assert clsng stages* **2/1**[1]
2 3 **Would Be King (IRE)**[14] 2634 2-9-3 0 ColinKeane 5 94
(G M Lyons, Ire) *chsd ldrs: 3rd 1/2-way: rdn 2f out and no imp on wnr u.p in 2nd wl ins fnl f: kpt on same pce* **7/1**
3 1 3/4 **U S Navy Flag (USA)**[14] 2635 2-9-3 0 (t) SeamieHeffernan 4 89
(A P O'Brien, Ire) *chsd ldrs early tl sn led: rdn and hdd 1 1/2f out: no imp on wnr wl ins fnl f where dropped to 3rd* **14/1**
4 1/2 **Aqabah (USA)**[14] 2607 2-9-3 0 PatSmullen 7 87
(Charlie Appleby) *w.w towards rr early: 6th 1/2-way: pushed along after 1/2-way: rdn nr side under 2f out and no ex u.p in 4th wl ins fnl f* **3/1**[2]
5 nk **Gold Town**[8] 2786 2-9-3 0 (p[1]) ChristopheSoumillon 3 86
(Charlie Appleby) *chsd ldrs: 5th 1/2-way: tk clsr order bhd ldrs gng wl far side 2f out: rdn over 1f out and no imp ins fnl f: one pce in 5th clsng stages* **10/1**
6 2 1/2 **Sioux Nation (USA)**[8] 2808 2-9-3 0 RyanMoore 1 79
(A P O'Brien, Ire) *s.i.s and in rr: last at 1/2-way: pushed along nr side 2f out and no ex ins fnl f where rdn briefly: one pce under hands and heels clsng stages* **9/2**[3]
7 nse **Mount Wellington (IRE)**[36] 1949 2-9-3 0 DonnachaO'Brien 6 79
(A P O'Brien, Ire) *chsd ldrs: 4th 1/2-way: rdn 2f out and no ex u.p over 1f out: wknd and eased ins fnl f* **10/1**

1m 16.51s (1.01) **Going Correction** +0.15s/f (Good) **7 Ran SP% 113.9**
Speed ratings: **99,95,92,92,91 88,88**
CSF £16.51 TOTE £2.50: £1.70, £4.00; DF 14.30 Trifecta £142.30.
**Owner** Mill House LLC **Bred** Martin White **Trained** Moone, Co Kildare

**FOCUS**
A proper race this, won by a colt of some quality and how far he can go will be very interesting to see.

## 3099a WEATHERBYS IRELAND GREENLANDS STKS (GROUP 2) 6f
**3:35** (3:35) 4-Y-O+
**£60,512** (£19,487; £9,230; £4,102; £2,051; £1,025)

RPR
1 **Gordon Lord Byron (IRE)**[20] 2440 9-9-3 110 ChrisHayes 3 115
(T Hogan, Ire) *trckd ldrs early tl sn settled in 2nd: led narrowly fr 1/2-way: pushed along fr 2f out: rdn over 1f out and kpt on wl u.p to assert clsng stages* **20/1**
2 1 1/2 **Only Mine (IRE)**[55] 1520 4-9-0 105 SeamieHeffernan 2 107
(Joseph G Murphy, Ire) *sn disp and led narrowly: hdd narrowly fr 1/2-way and sn pushed along: no imp on wnr u.p in 2nd far side ins fnl f: kpt on same pce* **14/1**

3 ½ **Suedois (FR)**[10] 2737 6-9-3 114 ColinKeane 4 108
(David O'Meara) *broke wl to ld briefly tl sn hdd and settled bhd ldrs in 3rd: gng wl in 3rd after 1/2-way: rdn over 1f out and sn no imp on wnr u.p in 3rd nr side: kpt on same pce* **9/4**[1]

4 ½ **Downforce (IRE)**[33] 2046 5-9-3 111 WJLee 7 107
(W McCreery, Ire) *w.w: 5th 1/2-way: gng wl bhd ldrs nr side after 1/2-way: swtchd lft and rdn over 1f out: no imp on wnr u.p in 5th ins fnl f: kpt on into 4th cl home* **3/1**[3]

5 *nk* **Mobsta (IRE)**[10] 2737 5-9-3 106 RonanWhelan 6 106
(Mick Channon) *dwlt: sn chsd ldrs: 4th 1/2-way: pushed along after 1/2-way and no imp on wnr u.p in 4th ins fnl f: one pce clsng stages where dropped to 5th* **9/2**

6 3 ½ **Blue De Vega (GER)**[48] 1653 4-9-3 105 (t¹) PatSmullen 5 95
(M D O'Callaghan, Ire) *w.w: last at 1/2-way: pushed along fr 2f out and no ex u.p ent fnl f: one pce after* **11/4**[2]

1m 15.15s (-0.35) **Going Correction** +0.15s/f (Good) **6** Ran SP% **112.0**
Speed ratings: **108,106,105,104,104 99**
CSF £232.27 TOTE £13.40: £4.00, £5.00; DF 60.00 Trifecta £336.10.

**Owner** Dr Cyrus Poonawalla & Morgan J Cahalan **Bred** Roland H Alder **Trained** Nenagh, Co Tipperary

**FOCUS**
The absence of Acapulco looked likely to have a detrimental effect on this race, but not a bit of it as it turned out. Gordon Lord Byron is rated closer to last season's peak.

## 3100a TATTERSALLS IRISH 2,000 GUINEAS (GROUP 1) (ENTIRE COLTS & FILLIES) 1m
**4:10** (4:10) 3-Y-O
**£146,153** (£48,717; £23,076; £10,256; £5,128; £2,564)

RPR

1 **Churchill (IRE)**[21] 2399 3-9-0 122 RyanMoore 6 125+
(A P O'Brien, Ire) *w.w: 5th 1/2-way: prog on outer into 3rd fr 2f out and impr gng best to ld over 1f out: rdn and extended advantage ins fnl f where edgd sltly rt: kpt on wl* **4/9**[1]

2 2 ½ **Thunder Snow (IRE)**[21] 2420 3-9-0 118 ChristopheSoumillon 2 119
(Saeed bin Suroor) *prom tl sn settled bhd ldr: disp 2nd at 1/2-way: gng wl in 2nd over 2f out and led briefly under 2f out: sn rdn and hdd over 1f out: no imp on wnr ins fnl f where swtchd lft: kpt on same pce* **5/1**[2]

3 4 ½ **Exultant (IRE)**[13] 2661 3-9-0 105 ShaneFoley 5 109+
(M Halford, Ire) *hld up in rr: last at 1/2-way: pushed along over 3f out and clsd u.p on outer into 3rd over 1f out: hung sltly rt ins fnl f where no imp on clr ldrs: kpt on one pce* **7/1**[3]

4 4 **Glastonbury Song (IRE)**[36] 1954 3-9-0 105 ColinKeane 4 100
(G M Lyons, Ire) *hld up bhd ldrs: rdn in 4th under 2f out and no imp on ldrs u.p over 1f out: one pce in 4th ins fnl f* **20/1**

5 1 **Lancaster Bomber (USA)**[21] 2399 3-9-0 117 DonnachaO'Brien 1 97
(A P O'Brien, Ire) *sn led: over 1 l clr at 1/2-way: pushed along over 2f out and sn hdd u.p: wknd over 1f out* **11/1**

6 26 **Spirit Of Valor (USA)**[21] 2399 3-9-0 106 (bt) SeamieHeffernan 3 38
(A P O'Brien, Ire) *chsd ldrs: disp 2nd at 1/2-way: rdn in 3rd under 3f out and sn no ex: wknd to rr 2f out: eased fnl f* **33/1**

1m 40.46s (-5.54) **Going Correction** -0.325s/f (Firm) **6** Ran SP% **114.5**
Speed ratings: **114,111,107,103,102 76**
CSF £3.30 TOTE £1.40: £1.02, £1.90; DF 3.10 Trifecta £8.60.

**Owner** Michael Tabor & Derrick Smith & Mrs John Magnier **Bred** Liberty Bloodstock **Trained** Cashel, Co Tipperary

**FOCUS**
Another routine day at the office for the brilliant 2000 Guineas winner, becoming the ninth horse to complete the Guineas double, following in the footsteps of such standout colts as Rodrigo de Triano, Tirol and Don't Forget Me, and alongside fellow Ballydoyle luminaries as Gleneagles, Henrythenavigator and Rock of Gibraltar. While Churchill did all that was required of him here, it was disappointing that neither of the colts (Barney Roy or Al Wukair) that followed him home at Newmarket took up the challenge today, for all that their connections were ruing the lack of a true pace that day. This was a missed chance to prove a point. We will probably have to wait for the St James's Palace Stakes for that. Churchill is rated up 4lb on his Newmarket form and just below the best recent winners of this race.

## 3101a LANWADES STUD STKS (GROUP 2) (F&M) 1m
**4:45** (4:46) 4-Y-O+ **£60,512** (£19,487; £9,230; £4,102; £2,051)

RPR

1 **Creggs Pipes (IRE)**[14] 2637 5-9-0 105 DeclanMcDonogh 2 110+
(Andrew Slattery, Ire) *broke wl to ld and mde all: narrow advantage at 1/2-way: stl gng wl 2f out where pressed clly: rdn ins fnl f and styd on strly to extend advantage: comf* **3/1**[2]

2 3 ¾ **Opal Tiara (IRE)**[29] 2129 4-9-0 111 RonanWhelan 3 101
(Mick Channon) *trckd ldr: cl 2nd at 1/2-way: pushed along almost on terms over 2f out: sn rdn in 2nd and no imp on wnr u.p ins fnl f: kpt on same pce* **5/2**[1]

3 1 ½ **Turret Rocks (IRE)**[14] 2637 4-9-0 109 KevinManning 4 98
(J S Bolger, Ire) *trckd ldrs: 3rd 1/2-way: pushed along 3f out and no imp on wnr u.p in 3rd fr under 2f out: kpt on same pce* **5/2**[1]

4 8 ½ **Raymonda (USA)**[20] 2440 4-9-0 104 PatSmullen 1 78
(D K Weld, Ire) *jinked lft and uns rdr on way to s: w.w towards rr: 4th 1/2-way: pushed along under 2f out and no imp on ldrs: one pce ins fnl f* **7/2**[3]

5 12 **Zest (IRE)**[21] 2392 4-9-0 96 TomQueally 5 50
(James Fanshawe) *hooded to load: in rr thrght: pushed along 3f out and sn wknd* **12/1**

1m 41.16s (-4.84) **Going Correction** -0.325s/f (Firm) **5** Ran SP% **112.1**
Speed ratings: **111,107,105,97,85**
CSF £11.07 TOTE £4.60: £1.70, £1.60; DF 10.90 Trifecta £26.90.

**Owner** Delphi Six Syndicate **Bred** John Hayes **Trained** Thurles, Co Tipperary

■ Stewards' Enquiry : Ronan Whelan caution: hit horse with excessive force and in an area other than on the hind quarters or down the shoulder

**FOCUS**
A first Group-race win for this admirable front-running mare, whose chance increased with every drop of rain that fell on the course. She still had to go and get the job done, which she did in style. A pb from Creggs Pipes.

3102 - (Foreign Racing) - See Raceform Interactive

# BORDEAUX LE BOUSCAT (R-H)
Saturday, May 27

**OFFICIAL GOING: Turf: good to soft**

## 3103a 161ST DERBY DU MIDI (LISTED RACE) (3YO) (TURF) 1m 1f 110y
**12:50** 3-Y-O **£23,504** (£9,401; £7,051; £4,700; £2,350)

RPR

1 **Mask Of Time (IRE)**[17] 3-9-0 0 ow1 Pierre-CharlesBoudot 6 104
(A Fabre, France) **15/2**

2 *nk* **Troarn (FR)**[29] 3-8-10 0 ow1 CristianDemuro 5 99
(J-C Rouget, France) **67/10**[3]

3 3 ½ **Dream Awhile (USA)**[51] 1595 3-8-10 0 ow1 HugoJourniac 3 92
(J-C Rouget, France) **9/10**[1]

4 *nk* **Vert Diamand (FR)** 3-9-0 0 ow1 Jean-BernardEyquem 4 96
(T De Lauriere, France) **51/1**

5 ¾ **Ajmal (IRE)**[47] 1689 3-9-0 0 ow1 VincentCheminaud 1 94
(A Fabre, France) **73/10**

6 *snk* **Allons Y (FR)**[77] 1158 3-8-10 0 ow1 Francois-XavierBertras 8 90
(F Rossi, France) **188/10**

7 4 ½ **Fazendera (IRE)**[28] 2170 3-8-10 0 ow1 IoritzMendizabal 2 81
(D Guillemin, France) **162/10**

8 5 **Livrable**[28] 2170 3-9-0 0 ow1 MaximeGuyon 7 74
(C Ferland, France) **56/10**[2]

2m 3.83s **8** Ran SP% **117.4**
PARI-MUTUEL (all including 1 euro stake): WIN: 4.20 (coupled with Ajmal); PLACE: 1.40, 1.40, 1.10; DF: 16.70; SF: 41.00.
**Owner** Ballymore Thoroughbred Ltd **Bred** Dayton Investments (breeding) Limited **Trained** Chantilly, France

## 3104a 95TH GRAND PRIX DE BORDEAUX (LISTED RACE) (4YO+) (TURF) 1m 1f 110y
**1:50** 4-Y-O+ **£25,641** (£10,256; £7,692; £5,128; £2,564)

RPR

1 **Chiverny (FR)**[28] 2169 5-9-0 0 ow1 Jean-BernardEyquem 3 107+
(F Chappet, France) **91/10**

2 1 ½ **Primero (FR)**[69] 1271 4-9-0 0 ow1 MaximeGuyon 5 104
(C Ferland, France) **43/5**[3]

3 *nse* **Best Fouad (FR)**[28] 2169 6-9-6 0 ow1 Pierre-CharlesBoudot 7 110
(F Rohaut, France) **4/5**[1]

4 *snk* **Qurbaan (USA)**[43] 1773 4-9-6 0 ow1 Francois-XavierBertras 6 110+
(F Rohaut, France) **18/5**[2]

5 3 ½ **Instant De Reve (FR)**[12] 4-9-0 0 ow1 ThierryThulliez 1 96+
(Mme C Barande-Barbe, France) **87/10**

6 *nse* **Bharuch (IRE)**[35] 5-9-0 0 ow1 MickaelForest 8 96
(P Aragoni, Italy) **108/10**

7 1 ½ **Landym (FR)**[47] 1691 6-9-3 0 ow1 MickaelBarzalona 2 96
(H-A Pantall, France) **40/1**

2m 4.2s **7** Ran SP% **118.8**
PARI-MUTUEL (all including 1 euro stake): WIN: 10.10; PLACE: 1.60, 1.80, 1.10; DF: 30.60; SF 85.50.
**Owner** Eddir Loungar **Bred** Bloodstock Agency Ltd & M-F Mathet **Trained** France

# 3019 BADEN-BADEN (L-H)
Saturday, May 27

**OFFICIAL GOING: Turf: good**

## 3105a WACKENHUT MERCEDES-BENZ SILBERNE PEITSCHE (GROUP 3) (3YO+) (TURF) 6f
**4:00** 3-Y-O+ **£27,350** (£10,256; £5,128; £2,564; £1,709)

RPR

1 **Artistica (GER)**[14] 2623 3-8-8 0 WladimirPanov 7 103+
(D Moser, Germany) *w.w wl in tch: shkn up to chal over 2f out: rdn appr 1f out: led ins fnl f: drvn out* **43/10**

2 ¾ **Millowitsch (GER)**[20] 4-9-6 0 AndreasHelfenbein 5 106
(Markus Klug, Germany) *chsd ldng pair: sltly outpcd 1/2-way: hrd rdn 2f out: styd on fnl f: wnt 2nd fnl 50yds: nt rch wnr* **5/2**[2]

3 ½ **Mc Queen (FR)**[218] 7525 5-9-6 0 StephenHellyn 3 104
(Yasmin Almenrader, Germany) *w.w in fnl pair: rdn 2f out: hdwy appr fnl f: styd on u.p: nvr nrr* **138/10**

4 1 **Donnerschlag**[272] 5943 7-9-6 0 (b) FilipMinarik 8 101
(Jean-Pierre Carvalho, Germany) *broke wl and led: drvn 1/2-way: rallied whn chal over 2f out: hdd ins fnl f: no ex: dropped two pls fnl 50yds* **21/10**[1]

5 2 ½ **Schang (GER)**[26] 4-9-6 0 MichaelCadeddu 6 93
(P Vovcenko, Germany) *settled towards rr: 5th and drvn 1/2-way but no imp: one pce u.p fnl 1 1/2f* **22/5**

6 1 ¼ **Sunny Belle (IRE)**[27] 3-8-8 0 AndraschStarke 1 84
(P Schiergen, Germany) *chsd ldr: 3rd and nt qckn whn rdn 1 1/2f out: dropped away ins fnl f* **4/1**[3]

7 4 ½ **Muharaaj (IRE)**[272] 5949 6-9-6 0 (p) KoenClijmans 2 75
(Frau Erika Mader, Germany) *outpcd in fnl pair: adrift in last 1/2-way: rdn and clsd 2f out: nvr able to get in contention* **199/10**

1m 7.83s (-2.46)
**WFA** 3 from 4yo+ 9lb **7** Ran SP% **129.8**
PARI-MUTUEL (all including 10 euro stake): WIN 53 PLACE: 18, 17, 24; SF: 223.
**Owner** Gestut Brummerhof **Bred** Snc Lagardere Elevage **Trained** Germany

3106-3107a (Foreign Racing) - See Raceform Interactive

## 3096 CURRAGH (R-H)

Sunday, May 28

**OFFICIAL GOING: Yielding (good to yielding on round course)**

### 3108a TATTERSALLS GOLD CUP (GROUP 1) 1m 2f 110y
2:20 (2:21) 4-Y-0+

**£151,282** (£48,717; £23,076; £10,256; £5,128; £2,564)

RPR

1 **Decorated Knight**[64] 1378 5-9-3 113 AndreaAtzeni 1 117
(Roger Charlton) *trckd ldrs in 4th: 3rd after 4f: travelled wl into 2nd under 2f out: led appr fnl f: kpt on wl* **7/2**[1]

2 1 1/4 **Somehow (IRE)**[8] 2825 4-9-0 114 (v) SeamieHeffernan 3 113+
(A P O'Brien, Ire) *racd towards rr: prog whn short of room 2f out: swtchd rt over 1f out in 4th: swtchd lft in 3rd ins fnl f: styd on strly in to 2nd fnl 75yds: nt rch wnr* **4/1**[2]

3 2 1/4 **Deauville (IRE)**[17] 2553 4-9-3 114 RyanMoore 8 111
(A P O'Brien, Ire) *trckd ldr in 2nd: dropped to 4th after 4f: rdn into 3rd over 1f out: no imp in 4th ins fnl f: kpt on same pce into 3rd clsng stages* **4/1**[2]

4 3/4 **Success Days (IRE)**[49] 1654 5-9-3 114 ShaneFoley 5 109
(K J Condon, Ire) *led: rdn 2f out: strly pressed and hdd appr fnl f: wknd ins fnl 100yds* **9/2**[3]

5 shd **Johannes Vermeer (IRE)**[27] 2240 4-9-3 109 DonnachaO'Brien 7 109
(A P O'Brien, Ire) *racd in mid-div: pushed along in 6th 3f out: 5th ent fnl f: kpt on same pce: nvr on terms* **8/1**

6 1 3/4 **Reckless Gold (IRE)**[299] 5000 4-9-3 96 WayneLordan 2 106
(Joseph Patrick O'Brien, Ire) *racd in mid-div: pushed along 4f out: kpt on same pce ins fnl f: nvr nrr* **50/1**

7 hd **Moonlight Magic**[27] 2240 4-9-3 116 KevinManning 4 105
(J S Bolger, Ire) *trckd ldrs in 3rd: wnt 2nd after 4f: rdn and nt qckn in 4th under 2f out: sn no ex* **11/2**

8 6 **Gentil J (IRE)**[5] 2938 4-9-0 84 (t) ChrisHayes 6 90
(H Rogers, Ire) *racd in rr thrght: nvr a factor: rdn and detached appr fnl f* **100/1**

2m 18.03s (-1.97) **Going Correction** +0.25s/f (Good) **8** Ran SP% **109.9**
Speed ratings: **117,116,114,113,113 112,112,108**
CSF £16.22 CT £52.12 TOTE £3.90: £1.40, £1.40, £1.10; DF 15.50 Trifecta £62.80.
**Owner** Saleh Al Homaizi & Imad Al Sagar **Bred** Saleh Al Homaizi & Imad Al Sagar **Trained** Beckhampton, Wilts

**FOCUS**
Not a very strong Group 1 contest. The winner did it well under an uncomplicated ride, and is rated to his best, while the runner-up struggled to get a clear passage.

### 3109a AIRLIE STUD GALLINULE STKS (GROUP 3) 1m 2f
2:50 (2:54) 3-Y-0

**£32,777** (£10,555; £5,000; £2,222; £1,111; £555)

RPR

1 **Homesman (USA)**[14] 2661 3-9-3 93 (b[1]) RyanMoore 8 101+
(A P O'Brien, Ire) *hld up in 5th: pushed along in 5th under 3f out: clsr in 3rd 1f out: styd on wl to press ldr ins fnl f: led fnl 100yds: kpt on wl* **5/1**[2]

2 hd **Perfect To Play (IRE)**[43] 1806 3-9-3 0 GaryCarroll 9 101
(Joseph G Murphy, Ire) *chsd ldrs in 4th: pushed along in 3rd 3f out: wnt 2nd under 2f out: led 1f out: strly pressed fnl f and hdd fnl 100yds: kpt on* **9/1**

3 2 **Finn McCool (IRE)**[8] 2847 3-9-3 97 (b) DonnachaO'Brien 2 97
(A P O'Brien, Ire) *sn led: rdn under 2f out: hdd 1f out: no ex w principals in 3rd ins fnl 100yds: kpt on same pce* **8/1**

4 shd **Twin Star (IRE)**[8] 2848 3-9-3 0 RonanWhelan 5 97+
(Ms Sheila Lavery, Ire) *racd towards rr: rdn and prog 2f out: wnt 5th 1f out: kpt on wl clsng stages into 4th cl home* **22/1**

5 nk **Red Label (IRE)**[28] 2191 3-9-3 105 ColmO'Donoghue 1 96
(Mrs John Harrington, Ire) *chsd ldrs in 3rd: pushed along in 4th under 3f out: nt qckn appr fnl f: swtchd lft and kpt on same pce* **2/1**[1]

6 1 1/2 **Utah (IRE)**[238] 6987 3-9-3 94 SeamieHeffernan 6 93
(A P O'Brien, Ire) *racd in rr tl rdn and sme hdwy on outer over 2f out: kpt on wl fnl f: nvr nrr* **16/1**

7 shd **Act Of Valour**[20] 2479 3-9-3 0 (b) PatSmullen 7 93
(M D O'Callaghan, Ire) *sn trckd ldr in 2nd: rdn and nt qckn over 1f out: wknd ins fnl f* **13/2**[3]

8 2 1/4 **Angel Island (IRE)**[12] 2714 3-9-0 92 ChrisHayes 4 86
(J A Stack, Ire) *racd in mid-div on inner: rdn and no imp under 2f out: squeezed for room and checked 1f out: no ex* **16/1**

9 hd **Vociferous Marina (IRE)**[11] 2738 3-9-0 102 (t) KevinManning 3 85
(J S Bolger, Ire) *a towards rr: pushed along under 3f out: no imp appr fnl f: nvr on terms* **13/2**[3]

2m 12.63s (3.33) **Going Correction** +0.25s/f (Good) **9** Ran SP% **113.9**
Speed ratings: **96,95,94,94,93 92,92,90,90**
CSF £48.38 TOTE £5.20: £1.70, £2.70, £2.40; DF 43.80 Trifecta £415.20.
**Owner** Mrs J Magnier & M Tabor & D Smith & J Allen LLC **Bred** Joseph Allen Llc **Trained** Cashel, Co Tipperary

**FOCUS**
This has to go down as a weak Group 3, won by a 93-rated colt from a maiden.

### 3110a TATTERSALLS IRISH 1,000 GUINEAS (GROUP 1) (FILLIES) 1m
3:25 (3:29) 3-Y-0

**£146,153** (£48,717; £23,076; £10,256; £5,128; £2,564)

RPR

1 **Winter (IRE)**[21] 2434 3-9-0 116 RyanMoore 4 119+
(A P O'Brien, Ire) *chsd ldrs in 4th: gd hdwy to press ldrs 2f out and sn led: clr appr fnl f: styd on wl: easily* **8/13**[1]

2 4 3/4 **Roly Poly (USA)**[15] 2644 3-9-0 110 (p) SeamieHeffernan 7 108+
(A P O'Brien, Ire) *racd in rr: prog under 2f out: wnt 4th 1f out: kpt on wl into 2nd fnl strides: nt trble wnr* **14/1**

3 hd **Hydrangea (IRE)**[21] 2434 3-9-0 110 (p[1]) PBBeggy 3 108
(A P O'Brien, Ire) *led for 2f: pressed ldr in 2nd: nt qckn w wnr over 1f out: kpt on same pce fnl f: ct for 2nd fnl strides* **7/1**[3]

4 nse **Intricately (IRE)**[21] 2434 3-9-0 110 DonnachaO'Brien 5 108
(Joseph Patrick O'Brien, Ire) *hld up in 7th: clsr 2f out to chse ldrs: wnt 3rd ins fnl f: kpt on same pce: dropped to 4th fnl strides* **14/1**

5 1 1/4 **Bean Feasa**[21] 2441 3-9-0 103 KevinManning 1 83
(J S Bolger, Ire) *trckd ldrs in 3rd whn squeezed for room on inner after 2f: pushed along over 3f out: wknd under 2f out: no ex - fin 6th but promoted to 5th* **20/1**

6 11 **Rehana (IRE)**[27] 2241 3-9-0 107 PatSmullen 6 83
(M Halford, Ire) *pressed ldr in 2nd tl led after 2f: hdd 2f out: sn no ex -demoted to 6th* **6/1**[2]

7 1/2 **Aneen (IRE)**[230] 7232 3-9-0 0 ChrisHayes 8 79
(Kevin Prendergast, Ire) *hld up in 6th: rdn and nt qckn over 1f out: sn no ex* **10/1**

8 2 **Asking (IRE)**[14] 2665 3-9-0 97 (tp) AnaO'Brien 2 74
(A P O'Brien, Ire) *settled off ldrs in 5th: rdn and nt qckn over 1f out: sn wknd* **50/1**

1m 39.78s (-6.22) **Going Correction** -0.375s/f (Firm) **8** Ran SP% **117.9**
Speed ratings: **116,111,111,111,98 100,98,96**
CSF £12.08 CT £39.05 TOTE £1.40: £1.02, £2.80, £1.90; DF 10.40 Trifecta £34.70.
**Owner** Mrs John Magnier & Michael Tabor & Derrick Smith **Bred** Laddies Poker Two Syndicate **Trained** Cashel, Co Tipperary

**FOCUS**
A strikingly impressive performance by the winner to complete the Guineas double without having anything like hard race. Overall, a triumph for Aidan O'Brien, responsible for the first three. Winter is rated up 2lb on Newmarket, and one of the best recent winners of this.

3111 - 3114a (Foreign Racing) - See Raceform Interactive

## 3105 BADEN-BADEN (L-H)

Sunday, May 28

**OFFICIAL GOING: Turf: good**

### 3115a ITTLINGEN DERBY TRIAL - FRUHJAHRS-PREIS (GROUP 3) (3YO) (TURF) 1m 2f
1:40 3-Y-0

**£27,350** (£10,256; £5,128; £2,564; £1,709)

RPR

1 **Langtang (GER)**[35] 2002 3-9-2 0 EduardoPedroza 2 102+
(A Wohler, Germany) *led: hdd after 2 1/2f and chsd ldr: drvn to cl over 2 1/2f out: rdn and led appr 1 1/2f out: styd on fnl f: drvn out* **6/4**[1]

2 1 1/4 **Rebello (FR)**[56] 1528 3-9-2 0 MarcLerner 1 100
(D & P Prod'Homme, France) *chsd ldr on inner: cl 3rd and rdn 2f out: styd on u.p fnl f: led cl home: unable to chal wnr* **134/10**

3 nk **Kastano (GER)**[27] 2246 3-9-2 0 AndreasHelfenbein 4 99
(Markus Klug, Germany) *racd keenly: chsd ldr between horses: allowed to stride on and led after 2 1/2f: rdn 2f out: hdd appr 1 1/2f out: kpt on at same pce* **23/5**

4 1 1/4 **Ming Jung (FR)**[35] 2002 3-9-2 0 MartinSeidl 3 96
(Markus Klug, Germany) *hld up in fnl quartet: rdn and nt qckn 1 1/2f out: styd on at same pce* **153/10**

5 nse **Real Value (FR)**[21] 3-9-2 0 StephenHellyn 5 96
(Mario Hofer, Germany) *chsd ldr on outer: dropped into fnl pair 1/2-way: plugged on fnl 1 1/2f: nt pce to get on terms* **173/10**

6 hd **Enjoy Vijay (GER)**[27] 2246 3-9-2 0 AndraschStarke 7 96
(P Schiergen, Germany) *settled in fnl quartet: drvn and short-lived effrt over 1 1/2f out: one pce fnl f* **14/5**[3]

7 3/4 **Instigator (GER)**[21] 3-9-2 0 FilipMinarik 6 94
(Jean-Pierre Carvalho, Germany) *settled in fnl pair: scrubbed along to hold pl sn after 1/2-way: kpt on at same pce: nvr in contention* **27/10**[2]

2m 2.38s (-2.61) **7** Ran SP% **129.7**
PARI-MUTUEL (all including 10 euro stake): WIN 25 PLACE: 16, 37; SF: 300.
**Owner** Klaus Allofs & Stiftung Gestut Fahrhof **Bred** Stiftung Gestut Fahrhof **Trained** Germany

### 3116a GROSSER PREIS DER BADISCHEN WIRTSCHAFT (GROUP 2) (4YO+) (TURF) 1m 3f
3:25 4-Y-0+

**£34,188** (£13,247; £6,837; £3,418; £2,136)

RPR

1 **Guignol (GER)**[27] 2249 5-9-6 0 FilipMinarik 2 116
(Jean-Pierre Carvalho, Germany) *led: grad increased tempo fr 4f out: rdn wl over 2 1/2f out: styd on gamely u.p: jst hld on* **58/10**

2 nk **Iquitos (GER)**[182] 8129 5-9-6 0 AndraschStarke 5 115+
(H-J Groschel, Germany) *w.w in fnl pair on inner: clsd u.p 2f out: chsd ldr fr 1f out: styd on but wl u.p: nt quite get up* **3/1**[3]

3 4 **Wai Key Star (GER)**[237] 7028 4-9-0 0 EduardoPedroza 1 102
(A Wohler, Germany) *racd keenly: hld up in midfield on inner: rdn and kpt on same pce fr 1 1/2f out: no match for front two* **13/5**[2]

4 1 1/4 **Devastar (GER)**[203] 7843 5-9-0 0 MartinSeidl 3 100
(Markus Klug, Germany) *chsd ldr: rdn and no imp wl over 1 1/2f out: grad dropped away* **104/10**

5 hd **Dschingis Secret (GER)**[21] 2450 4-9-3 0 DanielePorcu 6 103
(Markus Klug, Germany) *racd keenly: hld up in fnl pair on outer: rdn and c wd into st: no imp fnl 2f* **21/10**[1]

6 1/2 **Va Bank (IRE)**[42] 5-9-0 0 Per-AndersGraberg 4 99
(M Janikowski, Poland) *racd keenly: hld up in midfield on outer: effrt u.p wl over 1 1/2f out: sn btn* **18/5**

2m 15.64s (-3.63) **6** Ran SP% **130.3**
PARI-MUTUEL (all including 10 euro stake): WIN 68 PLACE: 29, 23; SF: 224.
**Owner** Stall Ullmann **Bred** Stall Ullmann **Trained** Germany

3117 - (Foreign Racing) - See Raceform Interactive

## 2536 CHANTILLY (R-H)

Sunday, May 28

**OFFICIAL GOING: Turf: good**

### 3118a PRIX D'ISPAHAN (GROUP 1) (4YO+) (TURF) 1m 1f
3:25 4-Y-0+

**£122,094** (£48,846; £24,423; £12,200; £6,111)

RPR

1 **Mekhtaal**[49] 1659 4-9-2 0 GregoryBenoist 6 116+
(J-C Rouget, France) *trckd ldr: rdn appr 1f out: sustained chal fnl f: led cl home* **7/2**[2]

2 nk **Robin Of Navan (FR)**[49] 1659 4-9-2 0 CristianDemuro 1 115
(Harry Dunlop) *led: drvn 1 1/2f out: rallied gamely fnl f: hdd cl home* **18/1**

3 1/2 **Usherette (IRE)**[27] 2248 5-8-13 0 MickaelBarzalona 3 111+
(A Fabre, France) *hld up in fnl trio on inner: drvn to chse ldng pair into fnl f: n.m.r: styd on but nt pce to get on terms* **7/2**[2]

4 5 **Dicton**[28] 2211 4-9-2 0 OlivierPeslier 5 103
(Gianluca Bietolini, Italy) *racd keenly: hld up in rr: rdn and nt qckn 1 1/2f out: one pce fnl f: nvr in contention* **12/1**[3]

5 5 **Zarak (FR)**[27] 2249 4-9-2 0 ChristopheSoumillon 4 93
(A De Royer-Dupre, France) *hld up in fnl trio on outer: shkn up and nt qckn 1 1/2f out: wl hld fnl f* **4/5**[1]

1m 49.92s (-1.18) **5** Ran SP% **113.0**
PARI-MUTUEL (all including 1 euro stake): WIN: 3.30; PLACE: 2.20, 5.00; SF: 39.10.
**Owner** Al Shaqab Racing **Bred** Haras Du Mezeray And Skymarc Farm **Trained** Pau, France

**FOCUS**
This is usually taken by good horses with the likes of Goldikova, Cirrus Des Aigles, Solow and A Shin Hikari all recent winners, the last-named by a whopping margin. None of the 2017 field, however, looked quite in the class of those aforementioned names, so it remains to be seen how solid this form is for the level. Mekhtaal won with a bit to spare.

## 3119a PRIX VICOMTESSE VIGIER (GROUP 2) (4YO+) (TURF) 1m 7f
3:55 4-Y-0+ **£63,333** (£24,444; £11,666; £7,777; £3,888)

RPR

1 **Vazirabad (FR)**[64] 1374 5-9-4 0 ChristopheSoumillon 3 111+
(A De Royer-Dupre, France) *racd keenly: led reluctantly: hdd after 1 1/2f and trckd ldr: led again over 4f out: drvn 2f out: hdd 1 1/2f out: rallied to regain ld ent fnl f: styd on: a holding runner-up* **2/11**[1]

2 snk **Sirius (GER)**[21] 2450 6-9-0 0 MaximeGuyon 1 106
(Andreas Suborics, Germany) *racd keenly: led after 1 1/2f and set stdy pce: hdd over 4f out: chsd ldr tl rdn and styd on to ld 1 1/2f out: hdd ent fnl f: styd on: a hld by wnr* **14/1**[3]

3 1 ½ **Travelling Man**[28] 2202 4-9-0 0 (b[1]) AurelienLemaitre 4 105
(F Head, France) *racd keenly: restrained in 3rd: drvn to chse ldrs 1 1/2f out: styd on at same pce fnl f* **11/2**[2]

3m 37.11s (21.01) **3** Ran SP% **106.7**
PARI-MUTUEL (all including 1 euro stake): WIN: 1.20; SF: 3.30.
**Owner** H H Aga Khan **Bred** Haras De Son Altesse L'Aga Khan Scea **Trained** Chantilly, France

**FOCUS**
This was very slowly run with a sprint finish.

# 2004 SAN SIRO (R-H)
Sunday, May 28

**OFFICIAL GOING: Turf: good**

## 3120a PREMIO CARLO VITTADINI (GROUP 3) (3YO+) (TURF) 1m
4:25 3-Y-0+ **£31,196** (£13,726; £7,487; £3,743)

RPR

1 **Circus Couture (IRE)**[27] 5-9-5 0 FabioBranca 3 104
(Stefano Botti, Italy) *racd keenly: hld up in fnl pair: clsd wl over 1f out: sustained run to ld 75yds out: cosily* **27/20**[2]

2 1 **Father Frost (IRE)**[287] 5453 5-9-5 0 CarloFiocchi 5 102
(Josef Vana, Czech Republic) *w.w in rr: drvn to cl over 1 1/2f out: chal u.p 1f out: led fnl 125yds: hdd 75yds out: no match for wnr* **27/4**

3 ½ **Greg Pass (IRE)**[14] 2663 5-9-5 0 DarioVargiu 1 101
(Il Cavallo In Testa, Italy) *led: drvn 2f out: rdn 1f out: hdd fnl 125yds: styd on* **4/5**[1]

4 ½ **Azzeccagarbugli (IRE)**[21] 4-9-5 0 AntonioFresu 2 99
(Stefano Botti, Italy) *racd keenly: hld up bhd ldr on inner: rdn appr 1f out: styd on fnl f* **27/20**[2]

5 ¾ **Justice Well**[197] 5-9-5 0 GiuseppeCannarella 4 98
(Luciano Vitabile, Italy) *racd keenly: hld up bhd ldr on outer: drvn to chse ldrs over 1f out: kpt on at same pce u.p* **87/20**[3]

1m 36.8s (-5.30) **5** Ran SP% **172.3**
PARI-MUTUEL (all including 1 euro stake): WIN 2.33 PLACE 1.71, 3.58 DF 34.26.
**Owner** Scuderia Effevi SRL **Bred** Azienda Agricola Marriano **Trained** Italy

## 3121a OAKS D'ITALIA (GROUP 2) (3YO FILLIES) (TURF) 1m 3f
5:05 3-Y-0 **£158,119** (£69,572; £37,948; £18,974)

RPR

1 **Folega** 3-8-11 0 NicolaPinna 4 105
(Stefano Botti, Italy) *w.w towards rr: moved into midfield bef 1/2-way: swtchd outside and styd on fr 1 1/2f out: sustained run u.str.p to ld fnl 75yds: all out* **66/10**

2 ½ **Paiardina (IRE)**[43] 3-8-11 0 MarcoMonteriso 9 104
(Stefano Botti, Italy) *led: 3l clr 3 1/2f out: rdn and styd on fnl f: hdd 75yds out: no ex* **109/10**

3 4 **Alambra (IRE)**[21] 3-8-11 0 IoritzMendizabal 3 97
(Stefano Botti, Italy) *hld up in rr: gd hdwy 3 1/2f out: styd on to chse ldr appr fnl f: kpt on at same pce* **96/10**

4 1 ½ **Stamp Collecting (IRE)**[27] 2244 3-8-11 0 MarioEsposito 8 94
(R Biondi, Italy) *settled in midfield: drvn and prog on outer 3f out: chsd ldrs over 1f out: one pce fnl f* **103/20**[3]

5 ½ **Candy Store (IRE)**[27] 2244 3-8-11 0 AntonioFresu 7 93
(Stefano Botti, Italy) *w.w towards rr: hdwy 2f out: styd on fnl f: nvr in contention* **11/5**[1]

6 2 ½ **La Gommeuse (IRE)**[21] 3-8-11 0 DarioVargiu 5 89
(Il Cavallo In Testa, Italy) *racd in midfield: rdn and no imp 2f out: kpt on at same pce* **53/20**[2]

7 hd **Lunastorta (USA)**[63] 3-8-11 0 CarloFiocchi 2 89
(Agostino Affe', Italy) *hld up in midfield on inner: outpcd and drvn after 1/2-way: last and u.p 4f out: styd on fr 1 1/2f out: nt trble ldrs* **87/10**

8 6 **Mi Raccomando**[27] 2244 3-8-11 0 FabioBranca 6 78
(Stefano Botti, Italy) *racd keenly: hld up in tch: chsd ldr u.p 2f out: wkng whn hmpd 1 1/2f out: wl hld whn eased fnl f* **11/5**[1]

9 6 **Windjammer (GER)**[217] 7563 3-8-11 0 JozefBojko 10 67
(A Wohler, Germany) *chsd ldr: rdn and nt qckn 3f out: wknd ins fnl 1 1/2f* **68/10**

10 5 **Great Aventura (IRE)**[21] 3-8-11 0 SilvanoMulas 1 58
(Cristiano Davide Fais, Italy) *racd keenly: restrained cl up on inner: 3rd and hrd rdn over 3f out: sn btn and dropped away: wl hld whn eased fnl f* **23/1**

2m 13.7s (-4.90) **10** Ran SP% **164.4**
PARI-MUTUEL (all including 1 euro stake): WIN 7.56 PLACE 2.71, 3.85, 3.38 DF 42.73.
**Owner** Scuderia Rencati Srl **Bred** Azienda Agricola Francesca Srl **Trained** Italy

3122-3128a (Foreign Racing) - See Raceform Interactive

# 2870 SHA TIN (R-H)
Sunday, May 28

**OFFICIAL GOING: Turf: good to firm**

## 3129a STANDARD CHARTERED CHAMPIONS & CHATER CUP (GROUP 1) (3YO+) (COURSE A) (TURF) 1m 4f
9:05 3-Y-0+
**£595,611** (£229,885; £104,493; £59,561; £34,482; £20,898)

RPR

1 **Werther (NZ)**[28] 2211 5-9-0 126 HughBowman 1 120+
(John Moore, Hong Kong) *trckd ldrs: prom 2 1/2f out: rdn to ld 2f out: kpt on strly and drew clr fnl f: comf* **41/20**[2]

2 3 **Blazing Speed**[28] 2211 8-9-0 125 (t) NeilCallan 5 115
(A S Cruz, Hong Kong) *chsd ldr: led narrowly appr 2f out: rdn and hdd 2f out: outpcd by wnr fnl f: no ex clsng stages: jst hld 2nd* **81/10**

3 shd **Eagle Way (AUS)**[28] 2209 4-9-0 107 (b) JoaoMoreira 7 115
(John Moore, Hong Kong) *hld up in rr: hdwy into midfield 5f out: rdn and kpt on fr 2f out: nvr gng pce to chal: nrly snatched 2nd cl home* **1/1**[1]

4 4 **Helene Charisma (FR)**[28] 2209 4-9-0 100 (t) DouglasWhyte 4 109
(John Moore, Hong Kong) *hld up towards rr: rdn and kpt on steadily fr 2f out: n.d* **57/10**[3]

5 ½ **Gold Mount**[28] 2209 4-9-0 95 (t) SilvestreDeSousa 3 108
(A S Cruz, Hong Kong) *racd in midfield: rdn under 3f out: edgd lft on home turn: sn no imp* **81/10**

6 4 **Basic Trilogy (NZ)**[28] 2209 5-9-0 101 (b) KCLeung 2 101
(John Moore, Hong Kong) *led: wnt clr 7f out: hdd appr 2f out: sn rdn: wknd 1 1/2f out* **145/1**

6 dht **Designs On Rome (IRE)**[28] 2211 7-9-0 119 (b) SamClipperton 6 101
(John Moore, Hong Kong) *hld up towards rr: rdn 3f out: wknd 1 1/2f out* **73/1**

2m 29.26s (1.06) **7** Ran SP% **121.7**
PARI-MUTUEL (all including 10 hkd stake): WIN 30.50; PLACE 13.00, 19.50, 11.00; DF 88.50.
**Owner** Johnson Chen **Bred** C D Allison, C V & J A Barnao et al **Trained** Hong Kong

3130 - 3133a (Foreign Racing) - See Raceform Interactive

# CHATEAUBRIANT (L-H)
Saturday, May 27

**OFFICIAL GOING: Turf: soft**

## 3134a PRIX MAREDSOUS (MAIDEN) (3YO FILLIES) (TURF) 1m 1f 165y
6:50 3-Y-0 **£9,401** (£3,760; £2,820; £1,880; £940)

RPR

1 **Queen Boudica**[32] 3-8-10 0 NicolasBarzalona(6) 5
(A Fabre, France) *sn prom: rdn to chal and led early in st: styd on: drew clr: readily* **7/10**[1]

2 6 **Maklau (FR)** 3-9-2 0 ChristopherGrosbois 13
(J Boisnard, France) **24/1**

3 ¾ **Vision Rebelle (FR)**[39] 3-8-8 0 EmmanuelEtienne(3) 7
(Mme S Adet, France) **58/1**

4 ¼ **Sapotille (FR)**[39] 3-8-11 0 JeromeClaudic 4
(E Libaud, France) **94/1**

5 nse **Pelagie (FR)**[196] 3-8-6 0 TristanBaron(5) 2
(H-A Pantall, France) **10/1**[3]

6 3 ½ **Vila Gracinda (FR)** 3-8-11 0 SoufianeSaadi 14
(H-A Pantall, France) **53/1**

7 nk **Yanling (FR)**[12] 3-8-2 0 MlleVictoriaSanchez(9) 9
(Matthieu Palussiere, France) **52/1**

8 2 ½ **Anse De Bel'Amande (FR)** 3-8-11 0 LudovicBoisseau 16
(F Lemercier, France) **133/1**

9 nse **Strawberry Thief**[24] 3-8-11 0 RaphaelMarchelli 3
(F-H Graffard, France) **16/1**

10 3 **Ipazia**[39] 3-8-8 0 MllePaulineDominois(3) 8
(Mme A Fabre, France) **15/2**[2]

11 ¾ **Domacasi (FR)** 3-8-13 0 ow2 AlexandreRoussel 6
(S Renaud, France) **77/1**

12 3 ½ **Money In My Pocket (IRE)**[212] 7640 3-8-11 0 (p) AntoineHamelin 1
(Harry Dunlop) *led: rdn and hdd home bnd: no ex: wknd* **12/1**

13 ½ **Soleimana (FR)**[39] 3-9-2 0 SebastienMartino 10
(Freddy Grizon, France) **12/1**

14 5 ½ **Earth (FR)**[54] 3-8-11 0 (p) FabienLefebvre 15
(H De Nicolay, France) **44/1**

15 ¾ **Devon Finestra** 3-8-11 0 MathieuAndrouin 12
(T Poche, France) **21/1**

16 7 **Lindikova (FR)** 3-8-11 0 MickaelBerto 11
(R Rohne, Germany) **79/1**

**Owner** Godolphin SNC **Bred** Darley **Trained** Chantilly, France

# 2995 CHELMSFORD (A.W) (L-H)
Monday, May 29

**OFFICIAL GOING: Polytrack: standard**
Wind: light, across Weather: bright spells, overcast later

## 3135 TOTEPLACEPOT CHELMSFORD CITY'S 1000TH RACE NOVICE MEDIAN AUCTION STKS 6f (P)
1:55 (1:57) (Class 5) 2-Y-0 **£4,528** (£1,347; £673; £336) **Stalls** Low

Form RPR

2 1 **Joe's Spirit (IRE)**[28] 2217 2-9-2 0 FrannyNorton 10 80
(Michael Bell) *mde all: rdn over 1f out: sustained battle w runner-up after: styd on and hld on wl ins fnl f: gamely* **10/3**[1]

5 2 hd **Tangled (IRE)**[26] 2286 2-9-2 0 TomMarquand 11 79
(Richard Hannon) *w wnr: rdn and hung lft over 1f out: drvn and sustained chal u.p fnl f: jst hld* **5/1**[2]

3 1 ½ **Bath And Tennis (IRE)** 2-8-11 0 .................................... LukeMorris 1 70
(Sir Mark Prescott Bt) *chsd ldrs: rdn and flashed tail u.p over 1f out: wnt 3rd ins fnl f: kpt on but nvr getting on terms w ldrs* **10/3[1]**

4 ¾ **Armum (IRE)** 2-8-12 0 ow1 .................................... DougieCostello 4 69
(Jamie Osborne) *chsd ldrs: 3rd and swtchd rt over 1f out: sn rdn: lost 3rd and kpt on same pce ins fnl f* **8/1**

5 1 **Shawwal** 2-9-2 0 .................................... DaneO'Neill 6 72
(John Gosden) *hld up in tch towards rr of main gp: effrt to chse ldrs over 1f out: kpt on same pce ins fnl f: eased towards fin* **8/1**

6 2 ¾ **Olive Mabel** 2-8-11 0 .................................... RyanPowell 3 56
(Dean Ivory) *hld up in rr of main gp: sme hdwy into 6th over 1f out: kpt on steadily but no imp on ldrs* **25/1**

7 6 **Cromer (IRE)** 2-9-2 0 .................................... (h[1]) JackMitchell 2 43+
(Martyn Meade) *v restless in stalls and rring: v.s.a: detached in last tl passed btn horses ins fnl f: n.d* **10/1**

4 8 ¾ **Mimram**[21] 2459 2-8-8 0 .................................... JackDuern(3) 5 36
(Dean Ivory) *wnt rt and awkward leaving stalls: chsd ldrs early: shuffled bk towards rr whn rdn and swtchd rt wl over 1f out: sn outpcd: bhd fnl f* **33/1**

9 ½ **Wiff Waff** 2-8-13 0 .................................... AaronJones(3) 8 40
(Stuart Williams) *t.k.h: hld up in midfield on outer: hung rt bnd 3f out: lost pl and btn over 1f out: bhd fnl f* **25/1**

5 10 7 **Starboy (IRE)**[21] 2473 2-9-2 0 .................................... PatCosgrave 9 19
(George Scott) *chsd ldrs: rdn and struggling over 2f out: lost pl over 1f out: fdd fnl f* **6/1[3]**

1m 13.43s (-0.27) **Going Correction** -0.025s/f (Stan) 10 Ran SP% **119.1**
Speed ratings (Par 93): **100,99,97,96,95 91,83,82,82,72**
CSF £20.00 TOTE £3.90: £1.60, £2.10, £1.70; EX 17.30 Trifecta £60.50.
**Owner** Middleham Park Racing XCI & Partner **Bred** S Gorman **Trained** Newmarket, Suffolk

**FOCUS**
Previous experience told here.

## 3136 TOTEEXACTA CLASSIFIED CLAIMING STKS 6f (P)
**2:30** (2:30) (Class 6) 4-Y-O+ **£3,234** (£962; £481; £240) **Stalls** Low

Form RPR

0005 1 **Passing Star**[27] 2267 6-9-7 73 .................................... (t[1]) GeorgeDowning 4 77
(Daniel Kubler) *routed along early: off the pce towards rr: hdwy to chse clr ldng pair wl over 1f out: styd on u.p to chse ldr 100yds: sustained run to ld towards fin* **3/1[1]**

0-56 2 ½ **Pearl Acclaim (IRE)**[9] 2837 7-9-4 72 .................................... (p) JoshDoyle(3) 7 76
(David O'Meara) *racd keenly: w ldr and sn clr of field: led ent fnl 2f: rdn over 1f out: drvn and forged ahd ins fnl f: hdd and no ex towards fin* **4/1[3]**

0120 3 1 ¾ **Major Crispies**[6] 2923 6-9-0 71 .................................... (vt) PatrickVaughan(7) 5 70
(David O'Meara) *s.i.s: bhd and rdn along: hdwy into 4th but stl nt on terms w ldrs wl over 1f out: high hd carriage but kpt on to go 3rd wl ins fnl f* **9/2**

0-06 4 2 ¼ **Mostashreqah**[12] 2724 4-8-3 42 .................................... (p) FrannyNorton 6 46
(Milton Bradley) *led and clr w rival: hdd ent fnl 2f: rdn and stl ev ch over 1f out tl no ex ins fnl f: lost 2nd 100yds out: wknd towards fin* **25/1**

600- 5 ¾ **Take A Note**[209] 7738 8-8-6 69 .................................... (v) CharlieBennett(3) 8 49
(Patrick Chamings) *dwlt and rousted along early: midfield but nt on terms w ldrs: dropped to rr 2f out: kpt on ins fnl f: nvr trbld ldrs* **6/1**

4250 6 ½ **Pick Of Any (IRE)**[16] 2633 4-8-4 53 .................................... (h) CameronNoble(7) 3 50
(David Loughnane) *a towards rr: dropped to last and u.p 3f out: hung lft and kpt on ins fnl f: nvr trbld ldrs* **8/1**

56-5 7 hd **Vincentti (IRE)**[19] 2514 7-9-3 75 .................................... (p) LukeMorris 2 55
(Ronald Harris) *chsd clr ldng pair tl 5th and rdn wl over 2f out: little rspnse and btn over 1f out: lost 2 pls ins fnl f* **7/2[2]**

1m 13.23s (-0.47) **Going Correction** -0.025s/f (Stan) 7 Ran SP% **114.6**
Speed ratings (Par 101): **102,101,99,96,95 94,94**
CSF £15.36 TOTE £4.60: £3.00, £2.80; EX 21.00 Trifecta £50.30.
**Owner** Alan Bell **Bred** Whitsbury Manor Stud & A W M Christie-Miller **Trained** Lambourn, Berks

**FOCUS**
Pearl Acclaim and Mostashreqah took each other on up front and that set things up for a closer. The fourth limits the form.

## 3137 TOTEQUADPOT H'CAP 1m (P)
**3:05** (3:08) (Class 7) (0-50,50) 4-Y-O+ **£2,911** (£866; £432; £216) **Stalls** Low

Form RPR

0000 1 **Just Fab (IRE)**[67] 1325 4-8-13 **45** .................................... (b) CharlieBennett(3) 11 55
(Lee Carter) *in tch in midfield: swtchd rt over 2f out: effrt to chse clr ldng quartet wl over 1f out: styd on wl u.p to ld 100yds: sn in command and gng away at fin* **16/1**

-606 2 2 ¾ **Emily Goldfinch**[116] 521 4-9-7 **50** .................................... DannyBrock 10 53
(Phil McEntee) *chsd ldrs: clsd and ev ch over 2f out: drvn over 1f out: led ins fnl f: sn hdd and kpt on same pce fnl 100yds* **25/1**

0205 3 1 **Free To Roam (IRE)**[27] 2278 4-8-11 **47** .................................... BenRobinson(7) 9 48
(Luke McJannet) *chsd ldr tl led 2f out: sn drvn: hdd ins fnl f: no ex and one pce after* **14/1**

5400 4 ½ **Rising Sunshine (IRE)**[12] 2733 4-9-2 **45** .................................... (bt) RobertWinston 7 45
(Milton Bradley) *chsd ldrs: hmpd sn after s: 4th and rdn 2f out: drvn over 1f out: kpt on ins fnl f but nvr matching pce of wnr* **20/1**

0-0 5 3 ½ **Thatsthewaytodoit (IRE)**[138] 176 4-9-5 **48** .................................... GeorgeDowning 2 39
(Daniel Mark Loughnane) *led: hdd 2f out: unable qck u.p over 1f out: wknd ins fnl f* **6/1[2]**

60-0 6 1 ½ **Fire Empress**[112] 605 4-9-4 **47** .................................... (h) RyanPowell 16 35
(James Unett) *s.i.s: wl off the pce in rr: gd hdwy on outer 3f out: no imp over 1f out and kpt on same pce after* **66/1**

05-0 7 hd **Waggle (IRE)**[100] 807 4-9-2 **45** .................................... AdamBeschizza 8 32
(Michael Wigham) *in tch in midfield: rdn 4f out: outpcd over 1f out: rallied and sme hdwy u.p 1f out: no threat to ldrs* **10/1**

0-35 8 2 **Majestic Girl (IRE)**[4] 3001 4-9-3 **49** .................................... HollieDoyle(3) 5 32
(Steve Flook) *s.i.s: sn in midfield but nt on terms w ldrs: nt clrest of runs on inner over 2f out: effrt wl over 1f out: no imp* **6/1[2]**

3105 9 ½ **Pivotal Dream (IRE)**[26] 2313 4-9-5 **48** .................................... DougieCostello 13 29
(Mark Brisbourne) *routed along early: in midfield: n.m.r over 2f out: sn swtchd rt: u.p and plugged on same pce fr over 1f out* **12/1**

0205 10 ¾ **Mulled Wine**[39] 1894 4-9-7 **50** .................................... PatCosgrave 4 30
(John Best) *hmpd sn after s: wl off the pce in rr: rdn over 3f out: sme hdwy but nt on terms over 1f out: nvr trbld ldrs* **4/1[1]**

2346 11 hd **General Tufto**[41] 1868 12-9-7 **50** .................................... (b) JoeyHaynes 14 29
(Charles Smith) *towards rr: rdn 5f out: nvr trbld ldrs* **16/1**

050- 12 1 **Star Links (USA)**[158] 8500 11-9-2 **45** .................................... (be[1]) LukeMorris 15 22
(John Butler) *midfield: hmpd and swtchd lft after 1f: struggling u.p over 2f out: wknd over 1f out* **10/1**

0053 13 2 **Dukes Meadow**[26] 2312 6-9-0 **50** .................................... RhiainIngram(7) 12 22
(Roger Ingram) *hld up off the pce towards rr: effrt and swtchd lft over 1f out: nvr trbld ldrs* **7/1[3]**

00-6 14 7 **Ashford Island**[4] 3001 4-8-13 **45** .................................... (b) NoelGarbutt(3) 6
(Adam West) *hmpd sn after s: t.k.h: hld up in rr: n.d* **20/1**

-600 15 7 **Ada Misobel (IRE)**[16] 2626 4-9-3 **49** .................................... (p) AlistairRawlinson(3) 3
(Roy Bowring) *taken down early: chsd ldrs tl lost pl over 2f out: wknd over 1f out: wl bhd ins fnl f* **16/1**

000 16 19 **Zerafino (BEL)**[70] 1287 4-9-2 **45** .................................... DaneO'Neill 1
(Jimmy Fox) *a in rr: eased 3f out: t.o* **33/1**

1m 40.35s (0.45) **Going Correction** -0.025s/f (Stan) **16** Ran SP% **129.1**
Speed ratings (Par 97): **96,93,92,91,88 86,86,84,84,83 83,82,80,73,66 47**
CSF £390.29 CT £5664.15 TOTE £32.50: £6.20, £5.90, £3.30, £5.00; EX 524.60.
**Owner** Mrs S A Pearson **Bred** Michael Egan **Trained** Epsom, Surrey

■ Stewards' Enquiry : Charlie Bennett two-day ban: used whip above the permitted level (Jun 12-13)

Adam Beschizza two-day ban: guilty of careless riding in that he allowed his mount to drift left-handed without correction (Jun 12-13)

**FOCUS**
A low grade but competitive handicap. The winner has been rated back to the level she showed last October.

## 3138 TOTETRIFECTA H'CAP 2m (P)
**3:40** (3:40) (Class 4) (0-85,86) 4-Y-O+ **£8,086** (£2,406; £1,202; £601) **Stalls** Low

Form RPR

61-1 1 **Next Train's Gone**[35] 2021 4-9-1 **73** .................................... RyanTate 6 87+
(James Eustace) *mde all: gng best over 2f out: rdn and readily asserted over 1f out: eased towards fin: unchal* **10/11[1]**

3-50 2 9 **Taper Tantrum (IRE)**[10] 2787 5-9-7 **77** .................................... (v) PatCosgrave 1 79
(Michael Bell) *t.k.h early: hld up in tch in 3rd: reminders over 4f out: rdn to chse wnr over 3f out: hrd drvn and btn over 2f out: wl btn but clr 2nd over 1f out* **7/2[2]**

6062 3 9 **Teak (IRE)**[7] 2889 10-8-6 **62** .................................... (v) LukeMorris 5 53
(Ian Williams) *chsd ldr: rdn over 4f out: dropped to last and wl btn 3f out: wnt modest 3rd ins fnl f* **5/1[3]**

-12P 4 3 ¾ **Lost The Moon**[21] 2461 4-9-7 **79** .................................... JoeyHaynes 2 66
(Mark H Tompkins) *hld up in tch in 4th: swtchd rt 4f out: 3rd and no imp u.p over 2f out: wknd over 1f out* **7/2[2]**

3m 27.58s (-2.42) **Going Correction** -0.025s/f (Stan)
**WFA** 4 from 5yo+ 1lb 4 Ran SP% **113.5**
Speed ratings (Par 105): **105,100,96,94**
CSF £4.72 TOTE £1.60; EX 6.00 Trifecta £11.70.
**Owner** Harold Nass **Bred** Rockville Pike Partnership **Trained** Newmarket, Suffolk

**FOCUS**
This proved straightforward for the favourite.

## 3139 TOTEWIN FILLIES' H'CAP 7f (P)
**4:15** (4:16) (Class 5) (0-70,70) 4-Y-O+ **£5,175** (£1,540; £769; £384) **Stalls** Low

Form RPR

2203 1 **East Coast Lady (IRE)**[10] 2800 5-9-3 **69** .................................... HollieDoyle(3) 5 77
(William Stone) *sn pushed up to ld and mde rest: rdn over 1f out: styd on wl and a dong enough ins fnl f* **6/1[2]**

0231 2 1 ¼ **Lucymai**[21] 2464 4-9-7 **70** .................................... RobertWinston 6 75+
(Dean Ivory) *in tch in midfield on outer: clsd to chse wnr ent fnl 2f: sn rdn: kpt on but a hld ins fnl f* **6/4[1]**

-045 3 3 ½ **Tigserin (IRE)**[7] 2900 4-9-5 **68** .................................... PatCosgrave 1 63
(Giles Bravery) *chsd ldr for 1f: settled bk and wl in tch in midfield: effrt to chse ldrs over 1f out: no imp: wl hld but kpt on to hold 3rd ins fnl f* **6/1[2]**

2010 4 ½ **Tulip Dress**[17] 2587 4-9-1 **64** .................................... DaneO'Neill 7 58
(Anthony Carson) *dwlt: hld up in tch in last pair: pushed rt after 2f: sn dropped bk in again: swtchd rt wl over 1f out: swtchd bk lft and hdwy u.p over 1f out: kpt on ins fnl f: no threat to ldng pair* **12/1**

6104 5 1 **Hipz (IRE)**[21] 2464 6-8-10 **64** .................................... (p) GeorgeWood(5) 3 55
(Ivan Furtado) *wl in tch in midfield: off side cheek piece fell off after 1f: effrt over 1f out: no threat to ldng pair and kpt on same pce ins fnl f* **6/1[2]**

553- 6 3 ¼ **Loveatfirstsight**[151] 8570 4-8-13 **62** .................................... AdamBeschizza 8 44
(Michael Attwater) *dwlt: rcvrd to chse ldr after 1f: drvn and lost 2nd ent fnl 2f: lost pl and btn over 1f out: wknd ins fnl f* **12/1**

1221 7 2 ¼ **Isntshesomething**[25] 2342 5-8-12 **61** ow3 .................................... (v) DougieCostello 2 37
(Richard Guest) *hld up in tch: effrt over 1f out: no imp and sn btn: wknd ins fnl f* **7/1[3]**

0/54 8 6 **Under The Covers**[19] 2510 4-9-3 **66** .................................... LukeMorris 4 26
(Ronald Harris) *taken down early: stdd s: t.k.h: hld up in last pair: swtchd rt and hdwy 5f out: sn pressing ldrs: losing pl whn sltly impeded over 1f out: wknd fnl f* **11/1**

1m 25.96s (-1.24) **Going Correction** -0.025s/f (Stan) **8** Ran SP% **119.1**
Speed ratings (Par 100): **106,104,100,100,98 95,92,85**
CSF £16.15 CT £58.94 TOTE £8.50: £2.10, £1.10, £1.80; EX 18.70 Trifecta £94.20.
**Owner** Miss Caroline Scott **Bred** Mountarmstrong Stud **Trained** West Wickham, Cambs

**FOCUS**
A modest event decided by contrasting trips for the first two. The runner-up has been rated to her latest form.

## 3140 TOTEPLACE H'CAP 7f (P)
**4:50** (4:50) (Class 5) (0-75,77) 4-Y-O+ **£5,175** (£1,540; £769; £384) **Stalls** Low

Form RPR

3512 1 **Dark Side Dream**[21] 2462 5-9-7 **74** .................................... AdamBeschizza 5 82
(Chris Dwyer) *mde all: rdn over 1f out: wandered rt 1f out: drvn and hld on wl ins fnl f: rdn out* **3/1[1]**

0600 2 ½ **Kingsley Klarion (IRE)**[20] 2500 4-9-10 **77** .................................... DaneO'Neill 1 83
(Mark Johnston) *in tch in midfield: effrt on inner to chse wnr over 1f out: drvn and chal ins fnl f: r.o but a jst hld* **6/1[3]**

20-0 3 2 **Marbooh (IRE)**[25] 2339 4-9-9 **76** .................................... (t[1]) PatCosgrave 2 77
(David O'Meara) *t.k.h: hld up in tch in midfield: effrt over 1f out: hdwy u.p to chse ldng pair jst ins fnl f: kpt on but nvr enough pce to chal* **9/2[2]**

4444 4 hd **Varsovian**[25] 2331 7-9-9 **76** .................................... RobertWinston 3 76
(Dean Ivory) *hld up in tch in last pair: effrt 2f out: hdwy and edgd lft u.p ins fnl f: kpt on but nvr enough pce to threaten ldrs* **3/1[1]**

-060 5 1 **Mezzotint (IRE)**[11] 2762 8-9-6 **76** .................................... CharlieBennett(3) 4 73
(Lee Carter) *stdd and dropped in bhd after s: hld up in rr: effrt on inner over 1f out: kpt on same pce u.p ins fnl f* **14/1**

3463 6 1 ½ **Intensical (IRE)**[14] 2684 6-9-4 **76** .................................... (p) GeorgeWood(5) 7 69
(Ivan Furtado) *t.k.h: pressed ldng pair on outer: rdn and unable qck over 1f out: btn whn bmpd ins fnl f: wknd fnl 100yds* **9/2[2]**



The Form Book Flat, Raceform Ltd, Newbury, RG14 5SJ

4563 7 3 3/4 **Billyoakes (IRE)**[14] 2680 5-9-0 67 ......(p) LukeMorris 6 50
(Charlie Wallis) *t.k.h: chsd wnr tl over 1f out: sn u.p and unable qck: wknd ins fnl f* **12/1**

1m 26.89s (-0.31) **Going Correction** -0.025s/f (Stan) 7 Ran SP% **115.0**
Speed ratings (Par 103): **100,99,97,96,95 94,89**
CSF £21.72 TOTE £3.20: £2.00, £3.30; EX 23.00 Trifecta £150.70.
**Owner** M M Foulger **Bred** Newsells Park Stud **Trained** Newmarket, Suffolk

**FOCUS**
A fair handicap. The runner-up has been rated to his April figure at Newcastle.

## 3141 THE SHIRES LIVE HERE ON 7TH JULY H'CAP 5f (P)
**5:25** (5:26) (Class 6) (0-55,54) 3-Y-O **£3,234** (£962; £481; £240) **Stalls** Low

Form RPR
5550 1 **Seneca Chief**[10] 2792 3-9-6 **53** ......(h) GeorgeDowning 5 65
(Daniel Kubler) *stdd s: t.k.h: hld up in last trio: clsng and swtchd rt jst over 1f out: str run to ld ins fnl f: sn clr and gng rt away at fin: readily* **12/1**

-000 2 4 1/2 **Percy Toplis**[12] 2734 3-9-6 **53** ......(v[1]) AdamBeschizza 7 49
(Christine Dunnett) *chsd ldrs: effrt in 3rd 2f out: pressing ldrs 1f out: totally outpcd by wnr fnl 100yds but kpt on to go 2nd towards fin* **9/2**[2]

00-4 3 1 1/4 **Sadieroseclifford (IRE)**[12] 2734 3-9-0 **52** ...... GeorgeWood(5) 12 44
(Giles Bravery) *chsd ldrs: wnt 2nd over 2f out: rdn over 1f out: styd on and pressing ldr 1f out tl totally outpcd by wnr fnl 100yds: lost 2nd towards fin* **6/1**[3]

6400 4 1 **Glam'Selle**[24] 2362 3-8-13 **46** ......(p) LukeMorris 6 34
(Ronald Harris) *s.i.s: hld up in rr: hdwy and swtchd lft jst over 1f out: styd on ins fnl f: no ch w wnr* **8/1**

6-06 5 1/2 **Sweet Amazement**[42] 1837 3-9-3 **50** ...... SteveDrowne 8 36
(Mark Usher) *in tch in midfield: effrt over 1f out: kpt on same pce ins fnl f* **20/1**

-652 6 1 1/2 **Joysunny**[47] 1715 3-8-13 **49** ...... NathanEvans(3) 4 30
(Michael Easterby) *v free to post and rdr wout irons: led for 1f: chsd ldrs tl rdn and struggling over 2f out: wknd ins fnl f* **15/8**[1]

-200 7 hd **Sir Harry Collins (IRE)**[10] 2792 3-9-7 **54** ......(p) RobertWinston 1 34
(Richard Spencer) *hld up in tch in midfield: effrt and trying to switch out rt over 1f out: styd on same pce and no imp ins fnl f* **9/2**[2]

0-00 8 1/2 **Artsteelwork**[33] 2090 3-8-5 **45** ...... DarraghKeenan(7) 2 23
(John Butler) *midfield tl dropped towards rr 1/2-way: rdn over 1f out: no imp and btn whn sltly impeded ins fnl f* **16/1**

0050 9 1 3/4 **Mesmeric Moment**[26] 2309 3-8-9 **45** ......(b) CharlieBennett(3) 3 17+
(Shaun Harris) *hdwy to ld after 1f and sn clr: rdn ent fnl f: hdd ins fnl f: sn btn and wknd qckly* **14/1**

1m 0.87s (0.67) **Going Correction** -0.025s/f (Stan) 9 Ran SP% **121.5**
Speed ratings (Par 97): **93,85,83,82,81 79,78,77,75**
CSF £68.72 CT £371.07 TOTE £15.00: £3.80, £1.50, £1.90; EX 87.50 Trifecta £376.60.
**Owner** Mr & Mrs G Middlebrook **Bred** Mr & Mrs G Middlebrook **Trained** Lambourn, Berks

**FOCUS**
A moderate sprint run at a good pace.
T/Plt: £249.70 to a £1 stake. Pool: £61,013.36 - 178.32 winning units T/Qpdt: £123.00 to a £1 stake. Pool: £4,321.81 - 26.0 winning units **Steve Payne**

# 2890 LEICESTER (R-H)
Monday, May 29

**OFFICIAL GOING: Good changing to good to soft after race 3 (3.15)**
Wind: Light across Weather: Light rain turning heavier through the afternoon

## 3142 TOTEPLACEPOT AT BETFRED.COM FILLIES' H'CAP 1m 53y
**2:05** (2:06) (Class 5) (0-70,72) 3-Y-O+ **£3,881** (£1,155; £577; £288) **Stalls** Low

Form RPR
06-5 1 **Meshaykh (IRE)**[35] 2019 3-9-2 **70** ...... FrankieDettori 10 79+
(Sir Michael Stoute) *led 1f: chsd ldr tl led again wl over 2f out: rdn over 1f out: styd on* **15/8**[1]

30-0 2 1 **Twiggy**[26] 2293 3-8-7 **64** ow2 ...... KieranShoemark(3) 1 68
(Jane Chapple-Hyam) *hld up in tch: racd keenly: effrt and nt clr run over 1f out: chsd wnr ins fnl f: r.o* **20/1**

0-50 3 1 1/4 **Fastnet Spin (IRE)**[14] 2690 3-9-4 **72** ......(v) JimCrowley 8 73
(David Evans) *hld up: swtchd lft over 1f out: r.o ins fnl f: nt rch ldrs* **14/1**

0-56 4 1/2 **Whiteley (IRE)**[16] 2625 3-8-9 **63** ow1 ...... GrahamLee 9 63
(Mick Channon) *hld up: hdwy over 2f out: nt clr run and lost pl over 1f out: r.o ins fnl f* **8/1**

0-51 5 hd **Waves (IRE)**[12] 2726 3-8-12 **69** ...... EdwardGreatrex(3) 6 69
(Eve Johnson Houghton) *hld up: pushed along and hdwy over 2f out: rdn and edgd rt over 1f out: styd on* **6/1**[3]

0-44 6 1 1/4 **Singing Sands (IRE)**[17] 2587 3-9-4 **72** ......(t) OisinMurphy 3 69
(Seamus Durack) *chsd ldrs: chsd wnr over 2f out: rdn over 1f out: no ex ins fnl f* **3/1**[2]

-000 7 nk **Imperial Link**[29] 2178 5-8-7 **56** oh6 ......(p) FinleyMarsh(7) 7 55
(John O'Shea) *led after 1f: hdd wl over 2f out: rdn: hung rt and outpcd over 1f out: styd on towards fin* **50/1**

10-3 8 3/4 **Sister Dude**[27] 2285 4-9-12 **68** ...... MartinHarley 5 65
(Jonathan Portman) *prom: rdn over 2f out: edgd rt and no ex ins fnl f* **18/1**

460- 9 4 1/2 **Sandwood Bay**[229] 7286 3-8-13 **67** ......(e[1]) ThomasBrown 4 51
(Mark H Tompkins) *hld up: hdwy u.p over 2f out: wknd fnl f* **33/1**

52-5 10 3 1/4 **Savannah Moon (IRE)**[20] 2499 3-8-12 **66** ...... KevinStott 13 42
(Kevin Ryan) *hld up: rdn over 2f out: nvr on terms* **25/1**

05-0 11 nk **Miss Monro (IRE)**[10] 2790 3-7-11 **58** oh1 ow2 ...... KieranSchofield(7) 11 34
(Brian Ellison) *hld up: pushed along 5f out: a in rr* **50/1**

000- 12 15 **Delirium (IRE)**[214] 7647 3-8-5 **59** ...... RobHornby 12
(Ed de Giles) *prom: rdn over 2f out: sn edgd rt and wknd* **25/1**

1m 45.9s (0.80) **Going Correction** +0.30s/f (Good)
**WFA** 3 from 4yo+ 12lb 12 Ran SP% **116.4**
Speed ratings (Par 100): **108,107,105,105,105 103,103,102,98,95 94,79**
CSF £48.21 CT £417.42 TOTE £2.70: £1.40, £7.90, £3.40; EX 47.20 Trifecta £375.10.
**Owner** Al Shaqab Racing **Bred** Jim McCormack **Trained** Newmarket, Suffolk

**FOCUS**
A modest handicap and it went to the one with most potential. Those who chased her home all came from off the pace. The second and fourth help set the standard.

## 3143 BET TOTEEXACTA AT BETFRED.COM (S) STKS 1m 2f
**2:40** (2:42) (Class 5) 3-5-Y-O **£3,234** (£962; £481; £240) **Stalls** Low

Form RPR
0263 1 **Sir Jack**[6] 2914 4-9-2 60 ...... CliffordLee(5) 8 66
(Tony Carroll) *chsd ldr 4f: remained handy: shkn up to ld 2f out: rdn and lost off hind plate over 1f out: c clr fnl f* **13/8**[1]

4243 2 5 **Powered (IRE)**[5] 2964 4-9-7 55 ...... JimCrowley 4 56
(David Evans) *prom: rdn over 2f out: chsd wnr ins fnl f: styd on same pce* **5/2**[2]

6-00 3 1 1/4 **Scent Of Power**[14] 2687 5-8-13 48 ......(t[1]) JaneElliott(7) 1 53
(Barry Leavy) *chsd ldrs: wnt 2nd 6f out tl led 3f out: hdd 2f out: no ex ins fnl f* **10/1**

0610 4 1 1/2 **Log Off (IRE)**[4] 2991 3-8-3 61 ...... FinleyMarsh(7) 2 53
(David Evans) *hld up: effrt whn nt clr run wl over 1f out: sn rdn and hung lft: nt trble ldrs* **11/2**[3]

4-00 5 5 **Woofie (IRE)**[7] 2909 5-9-7 66 ...... GrahamLee 7 41
(Laura Mongan) *hld up: rdn and carried hd high over 2f out: no rspnse* **6/1**

6 1/2 **Mizpah (IRE)**[653] 5400 5-8-9 45 ...... TobyEley(7) 5 35
(Ken Wingrove) *s.i.s: hld up: pushed along over 4f out: a in rr* **100/1**

-020 7 16 **Cockney Boy**[26] 2295 4-9-4 54 ...... EdwardGreatrex(3) 6 8
(John Gallagher) *sn pushed along to ld: rdn and hdd 3f out: wknd wl over 1f out* **16/1**

2m 10.32s (2.42) **Going Correction** +0.30s/f (Good)
**WFA** 3 from 4yo+ 14lb 7 Ran SP% **112.3**
Speed ratings (Par 103): **102,98,97,95,91 91,78**
CSF £5.61 TOTE £3.20: £2.00, £1.10; EX 4.90 Trifecta £23.70.There was no bid for the winner.
**Owner** Shropshire Wolves **Bred** Aislabie Bloodstock Ltd **Trained** Cropthorne, Worcs

**FOCUS**
A seller dominated by the favourite. The second and third help set the level.

## 3144 BET TOTEQUADPOT AT BETFRED.COM H'CAP 1m 53y
**3:15** (3:15) (Class 4) (0-80,82) 4-Y-O+ **£6,469** (£1,925; £962; £481) **Stalls** Low

Form RPR
0P-5 1 **Frank Bridge**[24] 2369 4-8-13 **72** ...... PatDobbs 1 79
(Eve Johnson Houghton) *racd keenly: w ldrs tl settled into 2nd pl over 6f out: shkn up to ld over 1f out: edgd rt ins fnl f: rdn out* **16/1**

00-2 2 1 1/2 **Directorship**[26] 2291 11-9-9 **82** ...... OisinMurphy 2 86
(Patrick Chamings) *a.p: rdn over 1f out: hung lft ins fnl f: r.o to go 2nd nr fin* **6/1**

4311 3 nk **Roman De Brut (IRE)**[13] 2708 5-9-4 **77** ...... WilliamBuick 9 80
(Daniel Mark Loughnane) *w ldr tl led 7f out: qcknd over 3f out: rdn and hdd over 1f out: styd on same pce ins fnl f: lost 2nd nr fin* **10/3**[1]

5052 4 hd **Boots And Spurs**[9] 2838 8-9-5 **78** ......(v) FranBerry 6 81
(Scott Dixon) *led 1f: remained handy: rdn over 2f out: hmpd ins fnl f: r.o* **4/1**[3]

-404 5 1/2 **Character Onesie (IRE)**[20] 2500 5-8-13 **72** ...... TonyHamilton 5 74
(Richard Fahey) *hld up: rdn over 2f out: r.o towards fin: nt rch ldrs* **5/1**

2013 6 nk **Showboating (IRE)**[75] 1208 9-8-11 **75** ...... LewisEdmunds(5) 4 76
(John Balding) *s.i.s: hld up: racd keenly: rdn over 2f out: r.o: nt trble ldrs* **9/1**

4303 7 2 1/4 **Mister Music**[52] 1606 8-9-2 **80** ...... CliffordLee(5) 10 76
(Tony Carroll) *hld up: rdn over 2f out: nvr on terms* **7/2**[2]

342- 8 nse **Peak Storm**[258] 6442 8-9-3 **79** ...... EdwardGreatrex(3) 8 75
(John O'Shea) *hld up: nt clr run over 2f out: swtchd lft and nt clr run wl over 1f out: n.d* **28/1**

1m 46.97s (1.87) **Going Correction** +0.30s/f (Good) 8 Ran SP% **115.6**
Speed ratings (Par 105): **102,100,100,100,99 99,96,96**
CSF £108.96 CT £407.00 TOTE £16.90: £3.70, £2.50, £1.30; EX 126.60 Trifecta £424.50.
**Owner** John Dyer **Bred** Catherine Dyer **Trained** Blewbury, Oxon

**FOCUS**
A fair handicap and it paid to race prominently. The runner-up has been rated to his latest form.

## 3145 BET TOTETRIFECTA AT BETFRED.COM EBF MAIDEN FILLIES' STKS 1m 3f 179y
**3:50** (3:50) (Class 4) 3-Y-O+ **£6,301** (£1,886; £943; £472; £235) **Stalls** Low

Form RPR
5-64 1 **Perfect In Pink**[17] 2576 3-8-10 73 ...... GrahamLee 8 78
(Mick Channon) *hld up: hdwy 1/2-way: outpcd 3f out: rallied over 1f out: r.o to ld towards fin* **7/1**

0-3 2 1 1/4 **Munstead Star**[19] 2515 3-8-10 0 ...... OisinMurphy 5 76
(Andrew Balding) *disp ld: rdn over 1f out: edgd rt ins fnl f: hdd nr fin* **9/2**[2]

43-3 3 1/2 **So Sleek**[31] 2131 3-8-10 80 ...... WilliamBuick 1 75
(Luca Cumani) *disp ld: rdn over 2f out: edgd lft ins fnl f: hdd and unable qck towards fin* **4/6**[1]

4 12 **Sure To Explore (IRE)** 3-8-10 0 ...... SamHitchcott 3 56
(William Muir) *s.i.s: in rr: pushed along 5f out: nvr on terms* **20/1**

0 5 7 **Quay Point (IRE)**[17] 2564 4-9-13 0 ...... JimCrowley 2 46
(Laura Mongan) *prom: rdn over 2f out: wknd wl over 1f out* **50/1**

6 6 1 1/4 **Dreamtide**[17] 2576 3-8-10 0 ...... PatDobbs 7 43
(Amanda Perrett) *prom: pushed along over 5f out: wknd over 3f out* **16/1**

0- 7 hd **Franny Nisbet**[175] 8227 3-8-10 0 ...... RobHornby 9 42
(William Muir) *s.s: a in rr* **50/1**

0 8 3/4 **Astroshadow**[19] 2515 3-8-10 0 ...... ThomasBrown 4 41
(Mark H Tompkins) *hld up: wknd 4f out* **100/1**

6-3 9 22 **Doreen**[26] 2307 3-8-7 0 ...... KieranShoemark(3) 6 6
(Sir Michael Stoute) *trckd ldrs: rdn over 3f out: wknd and eased over 2f out* **11/2**[3]

2m 35.79s (1.89) **Going Correction** +0.30s/f (Good)
**WFA** 3 from 4yo 17lb 9 Ran SP% **121.6**
Speed ratings (Par 102): **105,104,103,95,91 90,90,89,75**
CSF £39.63 TOTE £10.00: £2.00, £1.90, £1.02; EX 41.50 Trifecta £80.20.
**Owner** George Materna **Bred** Ashbrittle Stud **Trained** West Ilsley, Berks

**FOCUS**
Three came clear in this fair fillies' maiden and the winner deserves plenty of credit, coming from much further back than the front pair who had the run of it. The runner-up has been rated to the better view of her Chelmsford form.

## 3146 @TOTEPOOLRACING FOLLOW US ON TWITTER H'CAP 6f
**4:25** (4:26) (Class 3) (0-95,92) 3-Y-O
**£12,450** (£3,728; £1,864; £932; £466; £234) **Stalls** High

Form RPR
-550 1 **Smokey Lane (IRE)**[23] 2400 3-9-7 **92** ...... FranBerry 3 101
(David Evans) *hld up: hdwy 2f out: led over 1f out: rdn and edgd lft ins fnl f: r.o wl* **12/1**

15-1 2 2 3/4 **Scorching Heat**[11] 2757 3-8-11 **82** ...... OisinMurphy 2 82
(Andrew Balding) *w ldrs: rdn and ev ch over 1f out: styd on same pce ins fnl f* **3/1**[2]

2-12 3 1/2 **Ejaaby**[20] 2506 3-9-2 **87** ...... JimCrowley 1 86
(Roger Varian) *w ldr tl led over 2f out: rdn and hdd over 1f out: styd on same pce ins fnl f* **9/4**[1]

1-0 **4** shd **Sumner Beach**[3] 3038 3-8-10 **81** ....(t[1]) MartinLane 5 79
(Brian Ellison) *hld up: hdwy u.p over 1f out: styd on* **80/1**
01-3 **5** 1 ½ **Parfait (IRE)**[42] 1841 3-9-1 **86** .... WilliamBuick 11 79
(John Gosden) *prom: shkn up over 2f out: no ex ins fnl f* **5/1**[3]
21-6 **6** 1 ¼ **Sfumato**[28] 2215 3-8-7 **81** ....(h) KieranShoemark(3) 8 70
(Roger Charlton) *trckd ldrs: racd keenly: shkn up and nt clr run over 2f out: no ex fnl f* **16/1**
0134 **7** 1 ¼ **Erissimus Maximus (FR)**[31] 2130 3-8-5 **79** ....(b) EdwardGreatrex(3) 6 64
(Chris Dwyer) *led: rdn: edgd lft and hdd over 2f out: wknd ins fnl f* **12/1**
-433 **8** 1 ¼ **Sayesse**[18] 2557 3-9-1 **86** .... GrahamLee 7 67
(Mick Channon) *prom: lost pl wl over 4f out: n.d after* **14/1**
1315 **9** hd **Juan Horsepower**[4] 2992 3-8-13 **84** ....(p) PatDobbs 10 65
(Richard Hannon) *prom: rdn over 2f out: wknd over 1f out* **16/1**
0-41 **10** ½ **Scofflaw**[16] 2630 3-8-11 **82** .... TonyHamilton 9 61
(Richard Fahey) *hld up: shkn up over 2f out: nvr on terms* **10/1**

1m 12.06s (-0.94) **Going Correction** +0.30s/f (Good) **10** Ran SP% **116.6**
Speed ratings (Par 103): **118,114,113,113,111 109,108,106,106,105**
CSF £48.03 CT £113.55 TOTE £15.20: £3.30, £1.60, £1.20; EX 61.90 Trifecta £274.10.
**Owner** Walters Plant Hire P T Civil Engineering **Bred** Miss Philippa Proctor Quinn **Trained** Pandy, Monmouths

**FOCUS**
A useful sprint handicap but bit of a surprise winner. The form has been rated at face value for now, with the second and third close to their latest.

## 3147 TOTEPOOLLIVEINFO.COM FILLIES' H'CAP 7f
**5:00** (5:00) (Class 4) (0-85,82) 4-Y-0+ **£6,469** (£1,925; £962; £481) **Stalls** High

Form RPR
4502 **1** **Rebel Surge (IRE)**[5] 2973 4-9-7 **82** ....(p) GrahamLee 2 88
(Richard Spencer) *chsd ldr to 1/2-way: remained handy: rdn to ld ins fnl f: r.o: hung rt towards fin* **2/1**[2]
6521 **2** 1 ½ **Indigo Princess**[16] 2626 4-7-11 **65** .... JaneElliott(7) 4 67
(Michael Appleby) *s.i.s: racd keenly and sn prom: wnt 2nd 1/2-way: rdn to ld over 1f out: hdd ins fnl f: styd on same pce* **6/4**[1]
-622 **3** 1 ¼ **Amber Mystique**[73] 1245 4-9-0 **75** .... TonyHamilton 1 74
(Kristin Stubbs) *led: qcknd over 2f out: rdn and hdd over 1f out: edgd rt and no ex wl ins fnl f* **7/2**[3]
5-40 **4** ¾ **Bush Beauty (IRE)**[27] 2278 6-7-13 **67** .... PaulaMuir(7) 5 64
(Eric Alston) *hld up: plld hrd: pushed along and outpcd over 2f out: r.o towards fin* **8/1**

1m 27.57s (1.37) **Going Correction** +0.30s/f (Good) **4** Ran SP% **106.7**
Speed ratings (Par 102): **104,102,100,100**
CSF £5.26 TOTE £3.70; EX 5.60 Trifecta £11.70.
**Owner** Rebel Racing III **Bred** Tally-Ho Stud **Trained** Newmarket, Suffolk

**FOCUS**
Modest handicap form. The winner has been rated to the better view of her winter AW form.

## 3148 COLLECT TOTEPOOL WINNINGS AT BETFRED SHOPS APPRENTICE H'CAP 1m 3f 179y
**5:35** (5:35) (Class 6) (0-65,65) 4-Y-0+ **£3,234** (£962; £481; £240) **Stalls** Low

Form RPR
0415 **1** **Albert Boy (IRE)**[9] 2815 4-9-0 **58** .... FinleyMarsh(3) 7 68
(Scott Dixon) *led: hdd over 10f out: chsd ldr tl over 2f out: rdn to go 2nd again over 1f out: led ins fnl f: drvn clr* **4/1**[3]
20-0 **2** 5 **Shirataki (IRE)**[27] 2281 9-8-5 **54** ....(h) MollyKing(8) 8 56
(Peter Hiatt) *led over 10f out: sn clr: c bk to the field over 2f out: shkn up over 1f out: hdd and no ex ins fnl f* **28/1**
3151 **3** ½ **Percys Princess**[18] 2546 6-9-10 **65** .... JaneElliott 1 66
(Michael Appleby) *prom: chsd ldr over 2f out: rdn and hung rt fr over 1f out: styd on same pce fnl f* **7/2**[2]
0-13 **4** ¾ **Angelical (IRE)**[13] 2710 4-8-12 **61** .... TobyEley(8) 4 61
(Daniel Mark Loughnane) *s.i.s: hld up: hdwy over 4f out: rdn over 2f out: styd on same pce fnl f* **5/2**[1]
43-6 **5** 2 ¼ **Lady Of Yue**[140] 141 7-9-9 **64** ....(p) JoshuaBryan 2 60
(Eugene Stanford) *s.i.s: hdwy over 8f out: nt clr run over 4f out: rdn over 2f out: styd on same pce fr over 1f out* **9/2**
6351 **6** 18 **The Lock Master (IRE)**[21] 2471 10-9-6 **64** ....(p) RayDawson(3) 6 32
(Michael Appleby) *chsd ldrs: lost pl over 8f out: rdn over 3f out: wknd over 2f out* **5/1**
40-0 **7** 2 ¾ **Golden Cape**[34] 2063 4-8-7 **51** oh2 .... AledBeech(3) 5 14
(Michael Mullineaux) *broke wl: plld hrd: sn stdd and lost pl: bhd and pushed along over 5f out: sn wknd* **25/1**

2m 39.44s (5.54) **Going Correction** +0.30s/f (Good) **7** Ran SP% **112.9**
Speed ratings (Par 101): **93,89,89,88,87 75,73**
CSF £90.81 CT £424.86 TOTE £5.00: £2.10, £6.60; EX 88.90 Trifecta £219.80.
**Owner** J Radford **Bred** Clare Castle Farm **Trained** Babworth, Notts

**FOCUS**
Moderate handicap form but a clear-cut winner. Straightforward form, wth the second, third and fourth helping to cement the level.
T/Plt: £21.90 to a £1 stake. Pool: £57,957.37 - 1,926.89 winning units T/Qpdt: £9.00 to a £1 stake. Pool: £5,040.19 - 413.39 winning units **Colin Roberts**

# 2896 REDCAR (L-H)
Monday, May 29

**OFFICIAL GOING: Good (good to firm in places; watered; 8.4)**
Wind: Virtually nil Weather: Heavy cloud

## 3149 WATCH RACING UK TODAY JUST £10 NOVICE AUCTION STKS 5f
**12:45** (12:47) (Class 5) 2-Y-0 **£3,234** (£962; £481; £240) **Stalls** Centre

Form RPR
02 **1** **Chatburn (IRE)**[7] 2896 2-8-13 0 .... TomEaves 8 80
(David O'Meara) *mde all: rdn wl over 1f out: drvn ins fnl f: kpt on wl towards fin* **7/2**[3]
12 **2** ¾ **Bengali Boys (IRE)**[23] 2382 2-9-5 0 .... PaulHanagan 5 84+
(Richard Fahey) *t.k.h: prom: effrt 2f out: rdn over 1f out: ev ch whn hung lft ins fnl f: kpt on* **5/2**[1]
2 **3** 2 **Wahoo**[40] 1873 2-9-0 0 .... PaulMulrennan 2 72
(Michael Dods) *wnt lft at s: trckd ldrs: hdwy 2f out: rdn over 1f out: cl up and rdn whn carried lft ins fnl f: sn swtchd rt and kpt on* **3/1**[2]
**4** ½ **Global Academy (IRE)** 2-9-2 0 .... MartinDwyer 10 72
(Gay Kelleway) *trckd ldrs: hdwy and cl up over 2f out: rdn and ev ch over 1f out: kpt on same pce fnl f* **8/1**
3 **5** ¾ **Star Of Zaam (IRE)**[17] 2590 2-8-12 0 .... JordanVaughan(3) 1 68
(K R Burke) *sltly hmpd and wnt lft s: in tch: hdwy over 2f out: chsd ldrs over 1f out: sn rdn and kpt on fnl f* **6/1**
6 **6** 1 ½ **Funkadelic**[30] 2134 2-9-2 0 .... PJMcDonald 11 64
(Ben Haslam) *in tch: rdn along 2f out: no imp appr fnl f* **20/1**
**7** 2 ¼ **Burns Supper (IRE)** 2-9-0 0 .... JasonHart 9 54
(James Ewart) *chsd ldrs: rdn along wl over 1f out: sn edgd lft and wknd* **100/1**
55 **8** nse **Highland Bobby**[17] 2590 2-9-2 0 .... PhillipMakin 3 55
(David O'Meara) *towards rr: pushed along 1/2-way: rdn 2f out: n.d* **25/1**
**9** 1 ¾ **Bad Dog** 2-8-8 0 .... HarrisonShaw(7) 7 48
(Michael Easterby) *dwlt: bhd tl sme late hdwy* **66/1**
6 **10** ½ **Super Major (IRE)**[23] 2403 2-9-0 0 .... AndrewMullen 12 45
(Michael Dods) *in tch on outer: rdn along over 2f out: sn wknd* **25/1**
**11** 12 **Mendali** 2-8-11 0 .... DavidAllan 6
(David C Griffiths) *a in rr* **100/1**

59.04s (0.44) **Going Correction** -0.025s/f (Good) **11** Ran SP% **117.1**
Speed ratings (Par 93): **95,93,90,89,88 86,82,82,79,78 59**
CSF £11.91 TOTE £4.00: £1.80, £1.10, £1.60; EX 13.90 Trifecta £35.30.
**Owner** David W Armstrong **Bred** Thomas Hassett **Trained** Upper Helmsley, N Yorks

**FOCUS**
An above-average race for the track staged on ground that the jockeys described as good and just on the easy side. The gallop was reasonable and this race should throw up winners.

## 3150 RACINGUK.COM/DAYPASS MEDIAN AUCTION MAIDEN STKS 5f 217y
**1:15** (1:16) (Class 5) 3-Y-0 **£3,234** (£962; £481; £240) **Stalls** Centre

Form RPR
6-2 **1** **Black Salt**[17] 2595 3-9-5 0 .... PhillipMakin 9 73
(David Barron) *cl up: slt ld 4f out: rdn over 1f out: drvn and edgd lft ins fnl f: kpt on wl towards fin* **5/2**[2]
45 **2** 1 ¼ **Yorkshire Pudding**[18] 2547 3-8-11 0 .... RachelRichardson(3) 8 63
(Tim Easterby) *chsd ldrs on outer: hdwy over 2f out: rdn wl over 1f out: kpt on wl fnl f* **33/1**
4 **3** nse **Don Valentino (IRE)**[25] 2338 3-9-5 0 .... PaulMulrennan 3 68
(David O'Meara) *prom: cl up 1/2-way: rdn to chal over 1f out: drvn ins fnl f: no ex towards fin* **8/1**[3]
**4** 1 ¾ **Melrose Girl** 3-9-0 0 .... ConnorBeasley 2 57
(Bryan Smart) *dwlt: sn in tch: trckd ldrs 1/2-way: rdn along over 2f out: kpt on fnl f* **18/1**
34-2 **5** ¾ **Valley Of Rocks (IRE)**[13] 2707 3-9-5 **75** .... JoeFanning 6 60
(Mark Johnston) *slt ld 2f: cl up: rdn 2f out: sn drvn and wknd appr fnl f* **1/1**[1]
06- **6** 2 ½ **Arabela Dawn (IRE)**[215] 7605 3-9-0 0 .... JasonHart 4 47
(John Quinn) *a towards rr* **40/1**
**7** 2 ¾ **Pipers Way** 3-9-5 0 .... PaulHanagan 5 43
(Richard Fahey) *dwlt: sn rdn along: green and bhd: kpt on u.p fnl 2f* **9/1**
**8** ¾ **Foxtrix** 3-8-11 0 ow2 .... CallumRodriguez(5) 7 38
(Michael Dods) *chsd ldrs: rdn along bef 1/2-way: sn outpcd* **16/1**

1m 11.94s (0.14) **Going Correction** -0.025s/f (Good) **8** Ran SP% **116.2**
Speed ratings (Par 99): **98,96,96,93,92 89,85,84**
CSF £75.72 TOTE £3.70: £1.30, £4.80, £1.60; EX 57.10 Trifecta £469.50.
**Owner** All About York II & Partner **Bred** D R Tucker **Trained** Maunby, N Yorks

**FOCUS**
With the market leader disappointing this race didn't take as much winning as had previously sseemed likely. The gallop was reasonable. The winner has been rated to his latest form.

## 3151 CONGRATULATIONS GOLDEN TICKET WINNER (S) STKS 7f
**1:50** (1:52) (Class 6) 3-5-Y-0 **£2,749** (£818; £408; £204) **Stalls** Centre

Form RPR
-260 **1** **Pobbles**[17] 2587 3-8-5 **68** ....(v[1]) PaulHanagan 9 50
(George Scott) *towards rr: hdwy 3f out: swtchd rt to outer and rdn to chse ldrs over 1f out: chal ent fnl f: sn drvn and edgd lft: led last 75yds* **11/4**[2]
0434 **2** 2 ¼ **Monsieur Jimmy**[16] 2627 5-9-6 **47** .... GerO'Neill(7) 11 59
(Declan Carroll) *hld up in tch: smooth hdwy over 3f out: slt ld wl over 1f out: jnd and rdn ent fnl f: sn carried lft: hdd and no ex last 75yds* **8/1**
0-00 **3** nk **Fidelma Moon (IRE)**[27] 2285 5-9-2 **65** .... JordanVaughan(3) 3 50
(K R Burke) *led: pushed along over 2f out: rdn and hdd wl over 1f out: drvn and kpt on same pce fnl f* **7/2**[3]
6000 **4** 2 **State Residence (IRE)**[10] 2790 3-8-7 **56** ....(p[1]) ShelleyBirkett(3) 7 43
(David O'Meara) *in tch: hdwy over 2f out: rdn along wl over 1f out: chsd ldrs ent fnl f: kpt on* **9/1**
-000 **5** 3 ¾ **Ray Donovan (IRE)**[17] 2591 3-8-13 **59** ....(v) PhillipMakin 10 36
(David O'Meara) *trckd ldrs: hdwy and cl up over 3f out: rdn along over 2f out: drvn and wknd over 1f out* **22/1**
0-54 **6** 1 ¼ **Urban Spirit (IRE)**[8] 2853 3-8-10 **50** .... PaulMulrennan 1 29
(Jedd O'Keeffe) *trckd ldrs: cl up 1/2-way: rdn along over 2f out: drvn wl over 1f out: sn wknd* **5/2**[1]
4100 **7** 5 **Oakley Pride (IRE)**[61] 1421 3-8-13 **60** ....(bt) MartinDwyer 8 19
(Gay Kelleway) *v s.i.s and lost several l s: rdn along and jnd field 4f out: outpcd fr wl over 2f out* **14/1**
0-00 **8** ½ **Slave To Freedom**[47] 1718 3-8-5 **48** ....(p[1]) JoeFanning 2 9
(Ann Duffield) *trckd ldrs: cl up 1/2-way: rdn along wl over 2f out: sn wknd* **66/1**
00 **9** 15 **Bajan Beacon**[10] 2791 4-9-7 0 .... TomEaves 5
(Iain Jardine) *a towards rr* **66/1**
60 **10** 8 **High Shaw**[16] 2632 3-8-10 0 ....(v[1]) ShaneGray 6
(Ann Duffield) *cl up: rdn along 1/2-way: sn wknd* **66/1**

1m 25.34s (0.84) **Going Correction** -0.025s/f (Good)
**WFA** 3 from 4yo+ 11lb **10** Ran SP% **114.1**
Speed ratings (Par 101): **94,91,91,88,84 83,77,76,59,50**
CSF £23.80 TOTE £3.50: £1.40, £2.30, £2.10; EX 24.60 Trifecta £130.40.
**Owner** Matt Bartram **Bred** D J And Mrs Deer **Trained** Newmarket, Suffolk
■ Stewards' Enquiry : Paul Hanagan 2 day ban - used whip above the permitted level (12-13 June)

**FOCUS**
An uncompetitive event in which the winner didn't have to better the pick of her AW form to get off the mark on only this second turf start. The gallop was reasonable and there was no bid for the winner. The runner-up is the key to the form.

## 3152 RACING UK PROFITS RETURNED TO RACING H'CAP 5f
**2:25** (2:26) (Class 5) (0-75,77) 3-Y-0 **£3,234** (£962; £481; £240) **Stalls** Centre

Form RPR
1- **1** **Storm Over (IRE)**[294] 5244 3-9-6 **74** .... JoeFanning 9 90+
(Robert Cowell) *bmpd and wnt lft s: in tch: edgd lft to far rail 1/2-way and sn trcking ldrs: hdwy to chse ldr 2f out: rdn to ld jst over 1f out: kpt on strly* **11/2**[2]
0-40 **2** 2 ¾ **Boundsy (IRE)**[10] 2806 3-9-5 **73** .... PaulHanagan 8 78
(Richard Fahey) *racd centre: in tch: pushed along and hdwy 2f out: rdn over 1f out: styd on to chse wnr ins fnl f: no imp* **9/2**[1]

-022 **3** 1 3/4 **Flawlessly (FR)**24 2372 3-8-10 64 PJMcDonald 1 63
(James Bethell) *racd towards far side: sn led and set brisk pce: rdn and hdd over 1f out: kpt on same pce fnl f* **8/13**

-260 **4** 1 3/4 **Kamra (USA)**31 2122 3-9-9 77 (p1) TomEaves 5 69
(Michael Herrington) *racd towards centre: chsd ldrs: rdn along wl over 1f out: drvn and kpt on same pce fnl f* **25/1**

-241 **5** 1 1/2 **Yorkshiredebut (IRE)**16 2631 3-9-7 75 PaulMulrennan 7 62
(Paul Midgley) *racd towards centre: chsd ldrs: rdn along over 1f out: sn drvn and wknd* **11/22**

60-4 **6** nk **Ventura Secret (IRE)**33 2080 3-9-0 68 DavidAllan 10 54
(Tim Easterby) *wnt lft s: racd centre: towards rr: hdwy 2f out: sn rdn: styd on fnl f: nrst fin* **16/1**

6241 **7** 1 **Lady Cristal (IRE)**24 2372 3-9-1 72 (p) JordanVaughan(3) 2 54
(K R Burke) *racd towards far side: chsd ldr: rdn along 2f out: sn drvn and wknd* **8/13**

13 **8** nse **Suwaan (IRE)**37 1970 3-9-3 71 JamesSullivan 11 53
(Ruth Carr) *dwlt: racd centre: a towards rr* **9/21**

-223 **9** 3/4 **Poet's Reward**20 2495 3-9-0 75 ConnorMurtagh(7) 3 54
(David Barron) *racd towards far side: chsd ldrs: rdn along over 2f out: sn wknd* **12/1**

000- **10** 6 **Princeofthequeen (USA)**248 6743 3-8-13 67 (h1) PhillipMakin 6 25
(David O'Meara) *dwlt: a towards rr* **22/1**

66-5 **11** 1 **Mightaswellsmile**33 2080 3-8-9 63 AndrewMullen 4 17
(Ron Barr) *in tch: rdn along 1/2-way: sn wknd* **33/1**

57.65s (-0.95) **Going Correction** -0.025s/f (Good) 11 Ran SP% **114.1**
Speed ratings (Par 99): **106,101,98,96,93 93,91,91,90,80 79**
CSF £28.73 CT £199.47 TOTE £6.30: £2.80, £2.70, £2.00; EX 32.80 Trifecta £237.90.
**Owner** Abdulla Al Mansoori **Bred** J Dorrian **Trained** Six Mile Bottom, Cambs

**FOCUS**
A competitive handicap run at a strong gallop and one won in fine style by Storm Over, who looks the sort to remain ahead of his mark for some time. The runner-up has been rated close to form.

## 3153 MARKET CROSS JEWELLERS H'CAP 1m 2f 1y
**3:00** (3:01) (Class 4) (0-80,79) 4-Y-0+ **£5,175** (£1,540; £769; £384) **Stalls Low**

Form RPR

-00 **1** **Cornborough**16 2624 6-8-12 70 (p) JasonHart 3 77
(Mark Walford) *trckd ldng pair: hdwy over 2f out: rdn to dispute ld over 1f out: drvn to ld ins fnl f: kpt on gamely towards fin* **7/1**

0-05 **2** 1/2 **Jabbaar**21 2458 4-9-0 72 PhillipMakin 2 78
(David Barron) *trckd ldr: hdwy and cl up over 3f out: rdn to ld wl over 1f out: jnd and drvn ent fnl f: sn hdd: kpt on wl u.p towards fin* **15/2**

0006 **3** 1 1/4 **Save The Bees**13 2701 9-9-1 78 PhilDennis(5) 1 81
(Declan Carroll) *led: pushed along and qcknd over 3f out: rdn over 2f out: hdd and drvn over 1f out: kpt on wl u.p fnl f* **8/1**

43-1 **4** nse **Visitant**20 2498 4-9-3 75 AndrewMullen 8 80+
(David Thompson) *awkward s: sn swtchd to inner: t.k.h in rr: no room and edgd rt on home turn: swtchd to inner and hdwy to trck ldrs 3f out: nt clr run over 1f out: swtchd rt and rdn ent fnl f: n.m.r: kpt o* **2/11**

0-34 **5** 1/2 **Peterhouse (USA)**16 2629 5-9-5 77 (p) BenCurtis 7 79
(Jason Ward) *trckd ldrs: pushed along 3f out: rdn wl over 1f out: drvn and kpt on same pce fnl f* **5/13**

00-3 **6** 1 **Tapis Libre**12 2741 9-8-13 78 HarrisonShaw(7) 6 78
(Jacqueline Coward) *hld up in rr: hdwy 2f out: sn rdn: kpt on wl fnl f* **16/1**

0-15 **7** 1 1/4 **Sunglider (IRE)**16 2624 4-9-7 79 AndreaAtzeni 4 76
(David O'Meara) *hld up in tch: hdwy on outer over 3f out: chsd ldrs 2f out: rdn and ch over 1f out: sn drvn and wknd ins fnl f* **4/12**

0/50 **8** 4 **Deinonychus**47 1716 6-9-0 72 (h) RoystonFfrench 5 61
(Michael Appleby) *hld up towards rr: hdwy 4f out: pushed along 3f out: rdn 2f out: wknd over 1f out* **50/1**

2m 5.72s (-1.38) **Going Correction** -0.025s/f (Good) 8 Ran SP% **113.2**
Speed ratings (Par 105): **104,103,102,102,102 101,100,97**
CSF £56.62 CT £427.04 TOTE £11.20: £3.10, £1.80, £2.20; EX 58.90 Trifecta £581.70.
**Owner** Cornborough Racing Club **Bred** Mr & Mrs A E Pakenham **Trained** Sherriff Hutton, N Yorks

**FOCUS**
A fair handicap but a muddling gallop and a race in which it paid to race up with the pace. The eyecatcher was Visitant, who would almost certainly have won granted a clear passage. The winner has been rated to form.

## 3154 RACING UK ZETLAND GOLD CUP H'CAP 1m 2f 1y
**3:35** (3:37) (Class 2) (0-105,102) 3-Y-0+ **£16,172** (£4,812; £2,405; £1,202) **Stalls Low**

Form RPR

5612 **1** **Briardale (IRE)**8 2855 5-9-2 90 PaulHanagan 8 104
(James Bethell) *t.k.h: sn led: rdn and qcknd clr wl over 1f out: readily* **6/1**

6-64 **2** 6 **Rainbow Rebel (IRE)**8 2855 4-8-13 87 PJMcDonald 10 89
(Mark Johnston) *prom: hdwy to chse wnr over 2f out: rdn wl over 1f out: kpt on: no ch w wnr* **9/1**

-001 **3** 1 1/2 **Euchen Glen**20 2497 4-9-0 88 SamJames 7 87
(Jim Goldie) *hld up in rr: hdwy over 3f out: rdn to chse ldrs wl over 1f out: sn drvn and kpt on same pce* **10/1**

-126 **4** nk **Banditry (IRE)**22 2431 5-9-3 91 (h) StevieDonohoe 2 89
(Ian Williams) *trckd ldrs: pushed along 3f out: rdn and sltly outpcd 2f out: kpt on u.p fnl f* **11/41**

3-00 **5** 1 1/4 **Beardwood**12 2735 5-9-1 89 (p) JoeFanning 5 85
(Mark Johnston) *hld up in tch: hdwy on outer 3f out: rdn to chse ldrs wl over 1f out: sn drvn and no imp ent fnl f* **12/1**

13-6 **6** 3/4 **Hibou**21 2457 4-9-2 90 (b) TomEaves 4 84
(Iain Jardine) *dwlt and hld up towards rr: hdwy 3f out: chsd ldrs 2f out: sn rdn and wknd over 1f out* **10/1**

00-0 **7** 2 1/2 **King Bolete (IRE)**86 1042 5-10-0 102 AndreaAtzeni 6 91
(Roger Varian) *in tch: hdwy to chse ldrs on outer 4f out: rdn along wl over 2f out: sn drvn and wknd* **5/13**

4143 **8** 2 **Swift Emperor (IRE)**17 2593 5-9-4 92 PhillipMakin 1 77
(David Barron) *trckd wnr: pushed along 3f out: rdn over 2f out: sn drvn and wknd* **9/22**

/030 **9** 2 1/2 **Ashkoul (FR)**10 2804 4-9-3 91 (b1) BenCurtis 3 71
(Michael Appleby) *bmpd at s: hld up: hdwy to chse ldrs 4f out: rdn along 3f out: sn drvn and wknd* **25/1**

2m 3.72s (-3.38) **Going Correction** -0.025s/f (Good) 9 Ran SP% **115.5**
Speed ratings (Par 109): **112,107,106,105,104 104,102,100,98**
CSF £58.54 CT £531.76 TOTE £6.60: £1.70, £3.00, £2.80; EX 55.80 Trifecta £535.60.
**Owner** J Carrick&Clarendon Thoroughbred Racing **Bred** Rabbah Bloodstock Limited **Trained** Middleham Moor, N Yorks

**FOCUS**
A competitive handicap on paper was turned into a procession by the winner, who had the run of the race but who turned in a much-improved effort. The level is a bit fluid.

## 3155 COME RACING AGAIN TOMORROW H'CAP 1m 5f 218y
**4:10** (4:12) (Class 6) (0-65,64) 4-Y-0+ **£2,749** (£818; £408; £204) **Stalls Low**

Form RPR

0-55 **1** **Miss Tree**138 174 6-8-8 51 JasonHart 2 59
(John Quinn) *set stdy gallop: pushed along and qcknd wl over 2f out: rdn wl over 1f out: kpt on strly* **11/41**

0-00 **2** 1 3/4 **Midnight Warrior**18 2549 7-8-9 52 (t) DavidAllan 8 57
(Ron Barr) *trckd wnr: effrt 3f out: rdn along over 2f out: drvn over 1f out: no imp ins fnl f* **8/1**

5065 **3** 1 3/4 **Adrakhan (FR)**18 2549 6-8-0 45 ow1 SammyJoBell(3) 1 49
(Wilf Storey) *trckd ldrs on inner: hdwy over 3f out: rdn along 2f out: drvn over 1f out: kpt on same pce fnl f* **15/2**

4034 **4** 1/2 **Major Rowan**42 1834 6-9-2 59 PhillipMakin 9 61+
(John Davies) *hld up towards rr: hdwy and in tch 5f out: effrt to chse ldrs over 2f out: rdn wl over 1f out: drvn and no imp fnl f* **13/23**

244- **5** 2 **Jan De Heem**196 7955 7-9-3 60 JamesSullivan 3 61
(Tina Jackson) *hld up towards rr: hdwy 4f out: in tch and rdn over 2f out: sn drvn and no imp fnl f* **14/1**

0-33 **6** nk **Percy Verence**95 880 4-8-12 55 RoystonFfrench 4 54
(Tracy Waggott) *trckd ldng pair: pushed along 3f out: rdn 2f out: sn drvn and kpt on one pce* **16/1**

14-5 **7** nk **Question Of Faith**42 1834 6-8-9 52 PaulHanagan 12 50
(Martin Todhunter) *in tch: pushed along and hdwy on outer over 3f out: rdn to chse ldrs over 2f out: sn drvn and no imp* **5/12**

35-0 **8** 1 **Adherence**29 2183 4-8-12 55 DuranFentiman 10 52
(Tony Coyle) *hld up: a towards rr* **20/1**

00-6 **9** 1 3/4 **Chauvelin**18 2546 6-8-11 54 (v) AndrewMullen 11 48
(Nigel Tinkler) *in tch: pushed along 4f out: rdn on inner 3f out: sn drvn and wknd* **28/1**

3043 **10** 1 1/4 **Thackeray**61 1436 10-8-2 45 JoeFanning 5 37
(Chris Fairhurst) *hld up: a in rr* **16/1**

0-06 **11** 3 1/2 **Russian Royale**33 2079 7-9-7 64 PJMcDonald 7 51
(Micky Hammond) *chsd ldrs: rdn along over 3f out: sn wknd* **11/1**

3m 6.01s (1.31) **Going Correction** -0.025s/f (Good) 11 Ran SP% **114.5**
Speed ratings (Par 101): **95,94,93,92,91 91,91,90,89,88 86**
CSF £24.08 CT £147.40 TOTE £5.00: £2.00, £2.60, £2.70; EX 31.50 Trifecta £212.30.
**Owner** Trainers House Enterprises Ltd **Bred** Trainers House Enterprises Limited **Trained** Settrington, N Yorks

**FOCUS**
A moderate handicap in which the wnner was allowed an uncontested lead. The winner has been rated back to her best.

T/Jkpt: Not Won. T/Plt: £246.10 to a £1 stake. Pool: £65,689.72 - 194.85 winning units T/Qpdt: £59.10 to a £1 stake. Pool: £4,153.26 - 52.0 winning units **Joe Rowntree**

# 2904 WINDSOR (R-H)
Monday, May 29

**OFFICIAL GOING: Good to soft (6.5)**
Wind: virtually nil Weather: overcast/showers Rails: (Rail movements: R3, 5, 7 & 8 +14yds)

## 3156 ROYAL RUN LOYALTY CARD NOVICE AUCTION STKS 6f 12y
**1:45** (1:45) (Class 5) 2-Y-0 **£3,557** (£1,058; £529; £264) **Stalls Low**

Form RPR

**1** **Optimum Time (IRE)** 2-8-12 0 CharlesBishop 2 79+
(Eve Johnson Houghton) *trckd ldrs: swtchd out over 1f out: led ins fnl f: r.o wl: readily* **9/23**

53 **2** 3 1/2 **Zabaletaswansong (GER)**9 2816 2-9-2 0 SeanLevey 9 71
(Richard Hannon) *trckd ldr: rdn to ld over 1f out: hdd ins fnl f: nt pce of wnr* **11/42**

532 **3** 2 3/4 **Autumn Lodge**35 2015 2-8-12 0 ShaneKelly 5 59
(J S Moore) *broke sharply: led: rdn and hdd over 1f out: no ex ins fnl f: jst hld on for 3rd* **10/1**

**4** hd **Groundnut** 2-8-12 0 RichardKingscote 8 58+
(Jonathan Portman) *little slowly away: towards rr: hdwy 4f out: rdn over 2f out: kpt on ins fnl f: nrly snatched 3rd fnl stride* **16/1**

**5** 4 1/2 **Dreamboat Annie** 2-8-7 0 KieranO'Neill 11 40
(Mark Usher) *chsd ldrs: rdn over 2f out: fdd ins fnl f* **100/1**

**6** 3 1/2 **Rampant Lion (IRE)** 2-9-2 0 JamesDoyle 6 38
(Mark Johnston) *sn pushed along towards rr: rdn 3f out: nvr gng pce to get involved* **5/21**

**7** 2 3/4 **Lastoneforthecraic (IRE)** 2-8-7 0 ow3 HectorCrouch(3) 3 24
(David Evans) *in tch: rdn 3f out: wknd over 1f out* **33/1**

**8** 1 **Hemingford (IRE)** 2-9-0 0 DavidProbert 7 25
(Charlie Fellowes) *sn outpcd: a towards rr* **14/1**

**9** 3 1/4 **Barbarianatthegate** 2-9-2 0 KierenFox 4 17
(Brian Meehan) *sn pushed along: a towards rr* **9/1**

**10** 3 1/2 **Maveway (IRE)** 2-8-7 0 JFEgan 1
(David Evans) *s.i.s: a towards rr* **20/1**

1m 14.82s (1.82) **Going Correction** +0.275s/f (Good) 10 Ran SP% **113.8**
Speed ratings (Par 93): **98,93,89,89,83 78,75,73,69,64**
CSF £16.52 TOTE £5.10: £1.90, £1.30, £2.30; EX 16.70 Trifecta £89.30.
**Owner** The Picnic Partnership **Bred** A Kirwan **Trained** Blewbury, Oxon

**FOCUS**
Some starts have been moved at this track following remeasuring, so some races will not have speed figures until there is sufficient data to calculate updated median times. All rail movements as per last meeting: Inner of straight dolled out 2yds at 6f and 1yd at the winning line. Top bend dolled out 4yds from normal inner configuration, adding 14yds to race distances of 1m+. There was a light shower the previous day and 8.7mm of rain overnight, turning the watered ground good to soft. There was further rain around during the meeting. This looked a fair novice race but it proved hard to make up significant ground. They stayed near side.

## 3157 MPM FLOORING LTD MAIDEN STKS 5f 21y
**2:20** (2:21) (Class 5) 3-Y-0+ **£3,493** (£1,039; £519; £259) **Stalls Low**

Form RPR

22 **1** **Fair Cop**19 2510 3-9-0 0 DavidProbert 5 81
(Andrew Balding) *mde all: drifted lft whn rdn over 1f out: kpt on wl: rdn out* **9/41**

33-3 **2** 1 3/4 **Beck And Call**31 2121 3-9-0 75 FergusSweeney 10 75
(Henry Candy) *prom: rdn 2f out: carried sltly lft over 1f out: kpt on but hld fnl 120yds* **4/12**

2-03 **3** 2 1/4 **Think Fashion (IRE)**[16] 2619 3-9-0 82 ........ JamesDoyle 6 67
(Brian Meehan) *trckd ldrs: rdn over 1f out: kpt on same pce fnl f* **9/4**[1]

5 **4** 3/4 **Pride Of Angels**[17] 2581 4-9-8 0 ........ TimmyMurphy 2 67
(Gary Moore) *trckd ldrs: rdn over 1f out: kpt on but nt pce to chal* **50/1**

65- **5** 1 1/2 **Eskimo Bay (IRE)**[262] 6295 3-9-2 0 ........ HectorCrouch(3) 4 64
(Clive Cox) *chsd ldrs: rdn over 2f out: sn one pce* **5/1**[3]

52-3 **6** 1 1/2 **Five Star Frank**[32] 2112 3-9-5 73 ........ CharlesBishop 8 58
(Eve Johnson Houghton) *trckd ldrs: rdn 2f out: nt pce to get on terms: fdd ins fnl f* **11/1**

0-04 **7** 7 **General Gerrard**[14] 2674 3-9-5 0 ........(t) LiamKeniry 9 33
(Michael Madgwick) *in tch: rdn over 2f out: wknd over 1f out* **100/1**

4/ **8** 2 **Paradise Found**[858] 246 6-9-8 0 ........ JFEgan 3 24
(Emma Owen) *s.i.s: a towards rr* **100/1**

**9** 10 **Texas Wedge** 3-9-5 0 ........ JosephineGordon 7
(William Muir) *s.i.s: a bhd* **22/1**

1m 2.07s (1.77) **Going Correction** +0.275s/f (Good)
**WFA** 3 from 4yo+ 8lb **9** Ran SP% **114.8**
Speed ratings (Par 103): **96,93,89,88,86 83,72,69,53**
CSF £11.39 TOTE £3.00: £1.40, £1.50, £1.10; EX 11.90 Trifecta £26.70.
**Owner** J C Smith **Bred** Littleton Stud **Trained** Kingsclere, Hants

**FOCUS**
A fair sprint maiden. They raced middle to stands' side. The runner-up has been rated to form.

## 3158 SKY BET FILLIES' H'CAP — 1m 3f 99y
**2:55** (2:55) (Class 4) (0-85,87) 4-Y-0+ **£4,851** (£1,443; £721; £360) **Stalls** Centre

Form RPR

2-00 **1** **Perfect Summer (IRE)**[23] 2388 7-8-13 73 ........(v) RichardKingscote 2 80
(Ian Williams) *pushed along early: sn led: hdd over 5f out: rdn and sltly outpcd 3f out: rallied over 1f out: led ins fnl f: styd on strly* **9/1**

3-53 **2** 1 1/2 **Lime And Lemon (IRE)**[28] 2234 4-8-13 76 ........ HectorCrouch(3) 5 80
(Clive Cox) *trckd ldrs: rdn to ld over 2f out: hdd ins fnl f: no ex* **7/2**[2]

21-3 **3** 1 3/4 **Apres Midi (IRE)**[38] 1938 4-9-7 81 ........ JamesDoyle 3 82
(K R Burke) *trckd ldr: led over 5f out: rdn and hdd over 2f out: sn hung lft u.p: styd on same pce in fnl f* **11/2**[3]

5-31 **4** 6 **Turning The Table (IRE)**[7] 2906 4-9-13 87 6ex ........ JamieSpencer 4 83
(David Simcock) *dwlt: detached in 4th tl hdwy 3f out: chal 2f out: sn rdn: wknd fnl f* **4/6**[1]

2m 31.36s (1.86) **Going Correction** +0.30s/f (Good) **4** Ran SP% **107.6**
Speed ratings (Par 102): **105,103,102,98**
CSF £35.82 TOTE £10.50; EX 29.40 Trifecta £56.80.
**Owner** The Ferandlin Peaches **Bred** John O'Connor **Trained** Portway, Worcs

**FOCUS**
Add 14yds. The favourite bombed out and the form is not obviously strong. They raced far side in the straight. The runner-up has been rated to her C&D latest.

## 3159 SKY BET WINDSOR SPRINT SERIES H'CAP (QUALIFIER) — 5f 21y
**3:30** (3:30) (Class 2) (0-105,105) 3-Y-0 **£12,938** (£3,850; £1,924; £962) **Stalls** Low

Form RPR

-222 **1** **Evergate**[17] 2570 3-8-3 87 ........ KieranO'Neill 5 96
(Robert Cowell) *a.p: hung lft early: rdn to ld over 1f out: drifted lft towards fin: kpt on wl: rdn out* **4/1**[2]

32-1 **2** 1 **Yalawin (IRE)**[17] 2595 3-8-4 88 ........ HarryBentley 3 93
(Roger Varian) *trckd ldrs: rdn wl over 1f out: kpt on to go 2nd ins fnl f but nt pce to threaten wnr* **5/4**[1]

3-10 **3** 3/4 **Justanotherbottle (IRE)**[10] 2806 3-8-2 86 ........ JoeDoyle 1 88
(Declan Carroll) *led: rdn and hdd over 1f out: kpt on same pce fnl f* **15/2**

14-6 **4** 3/4 **Castleacre**[39] 1901 3-8-7 91 ........ JosephineGordon 4 90
(Hugo Palmer) *last but in tch: rdn over 2f out: no imp tl r.o ins fnl f: clsng on ldrs nring fin* **10/1**

1335 **5** 1/2 **Tomily (IRE)**[17] 2570 3-9-1 99 ........ SeanLevey 2 97
(Richard Hannon) *trckd ldrs: rdn 2f out: kpt on but nt pce to mount chal* **13/2**[3]

2-11 **6** 6 **Ascot Day (IRE)**[131] 291 3-8-3 87 ........ JimmyQuinn 6 63
(David Simcock) *chsd ldrs: rdn 2f out: wknd fnl f* **8/1**

1m 1.7s (1.40) **Going Correction** +0.275s/f (Good) **6** Ran SP% **109.7**
Speed ratings (Par 105): **99,97,96,95,94 84**
CSF £9.01 TOTE £5.50: £2.40, £1.20; EX 12.10 Trifecta £50.30.
**Owner** The Ever Hopefuls **Bred** V I Araci **Trained** Six Mile Bottom, Cambs

**FOCUS**
Only six runners but a decent 3yo sprint handicap. The action unfolded middle to stands' side. It's been rated slightly positively.

## 3160 SKY BET TOP PRICE PROMISE H'CAP — 1m 2f
**4:05** (4:05) (Class 3) (0-95,92) 4-Y-0+ **£7,439** (£2,213; £1,106; £553) **Stalls** Centre

Form RPR

14-1 **1** **Toulson**[16] 2624 4-9-0 85 ........ CharlesBishop 4 94
(Eve Johnson Houghton) *trckd ldrs: chal over 3f out: rdn to ld wl over 1f out: drifted rt fnl 120yds: hld on: all out* **6/4**[1]

2524 **2** shd **Getback In Paris (IRE)**[5] 2959 4-9-4 89 ........ ShaneKelly 6 97
(Richard Hughes) *hld up: hdwy over 2f out: rdn for str chal jst over 1f out: kpt on: jst hld* **5/1**[3]

124- **3** 3 3/4 **Indira**[325] 4078 6-9-7 92 ........ JosephineGordon 7 93
(John Berry) *trckd ldrs: chal over 3f out: sn rdn: drifted lft but stl ev ch ent fnl f: no ex fnl 150yds* **25/1**

12/2 **4** 3 1/2 **Breden (IRE)**[28] 2232 7-9-5 90 ........(h) RobertTart 5 84
(Linda Jewell) *s.i.s: last: rdn over 2f out: no imp tl hdwy over 1f out: styd on fnl f: wnt 4th cl home* **14/1**

0-02 **5** nk **Tomahawk Kid**[16] 2624 4-8-11 82 ........ DavidProbert 1 75
(Ian Williams) *hld up: hdwy to ld wl over 2f out: rdn and hdd wl over 1f out: no ex fnl f* **5/1**[3]

-431 **6** 4 1/2 **Eternal**[13] 2701 5-9-1 86 ........ JoeDoyle 2 70
(Declan Carroll) *led: sn clr: rdn and hdd wl over 2f out: wknd over 1f out* **9/2**[2]

5112 **7** 16 **Ickymasho**[27] 2261 5-9-7 92 ........ RichardKingscote 8 44
(Jonathan Portman) *chsd clr ldr: chal over 3f out: sn rdn: wknd over 1f out: eased* **12/1**

2m 11.17s (2.47) **Going Correction** +0.30s/f (Good) **7** Ran SP% **109.7**
Speed ratings (Par 107): **102,101,98,96,95 92,79**
CSF £8.40 CT £112.63 TOTE £2.40: £2.30, £2.40; EX 9.10 Trifecta £82.90.
**Owner** Mrs Virginia Neale **Bred** Cherry Park Stud **Trained** Blewbury, Oxon

**FOCUS**
Add 14yds. A decent handicap. The action unfolded up the middle in the straight.

## 3161 FAMOUS MONDAY NIGHT RACING H'CAP — 6f 12y
**4:40** (4:40) (Class 4) (0-85,86) 4-Y-0+ **£4,851** (£1,443; £721; £360) **Stalls** Low

Form RPR

-000 **1** **Major Pusey**[9] 2837 5-8-13 76 ........ FergusSweeney 8 89
(John Gallagher) *racd in centre: mde all: drifted lft fnl f: kpt on wl: rdn out* **10/1**[3]

0200 **2** 2 1/4 **Bahamian Dollar**[16] 2608 4-8-7 77 ........ KatherineGlenister(7) 9 83
(David Evans) *racd in centre: chsd ldrs: rdn to chse wnr 2f out: kpt on but a being hld fnl f* **20/1**

-060 **3** 2 1/4 **Rio Ronaldo (IRE)**[16] 2608 5-9-1 78 ........ JamesDoyle 11 77
(Mike Murphy) *racd in centre: hld up: hdwy 2f out: sn rdn: kpt on fnl f but nt gng pce to get on terms* **7/2**[2]

3-1 **4** nk **King Of Spin**[28] 2230 4-9-5 82 ........ ShaneKelly 10 80
(Richard Hughes) *racd in centre: mid-div: hdwy over 2f out: sn rdn: kpt on fnl f but nt gng pce to get involved* **5/2**[1]

0-44 **5** 3 **Cool Bahamian (IRE)**[16] 2618 6-9-7 84 ........(v) JohnFahy 1 72
(Eve Johnson Houghton) *mid-div: lost pl whn rdn and swtchd to r stands' side 3f out: kpt on again fnl f but no ch* **11/1**

500- **6** shd **Field Of Vision (IRE)**[209] 7737 4-9-3 80 ........ JosephineGordon 2 68
(Joseph Tuite) *s.i.s: towards rr: struggling whn swtchd to r stands' side 3f out: kpt on ins fnl f but no ch* **20/1**

060- **7** 1 **Monteverdi (FR)**[303] 4867 4-9-9 86 ........ JamieSpencer 12 71
(Jamie Osborne) *racd alone on far side rails fr 3f out: mid-div: effrt 3f out: wknd ent fnl f* **7/2**[2]

3400 **8** 1 1/2 **Sir Billy Wright (IRE)**[19] 2528 6-9-3 83 ........ HectorCrouch(3) 7 63
(David Evans) *racd in centre: chsd wnr: rdn over 2f out: wknd over 1f out* **10/1**[3]

406- **9** 5 **Wiley Post**[272] 6000 4-8-13 76 ........(b) TomMarquand 3 40
(Tony Carroll) *racd in centre: mid-div: hdwy 3f out: wknd over 1f out* **33/1**

-300 **10** 1 1/4 **Sumou (IRE)**[9] 2837 4-8-11 74 ........ DavidProbert 5 34
(Milton Bradley) *racd in centre: chsd ldrs: rdn over 2f out: wknd over 1f out* **40/1**

1m 12.49s (-0.51) **Going Correction** +0.275s/f (Good) **10** Ran SP% **114.4**
Speed ratings (Par 105): **114,111,108,107,103 103,102,100,93,91**
CSF £188.45 CT £838.32 TOTE £15.30: £3.50, £5.50, £1.20; EX 199.40 Trifecta £959.50.
**Owner** C R Marks (banbury) **Bred** C R Marks (Banbury) **Trained** Chastleton, Oxon

**FOCUS**
A useful sprint handicap but the runners were spread out all over the place. The winner has ben rated back to his best, and the runner-up close to form.

## 3162 CARIBBEAN NIGHT 5TH JUNE H'CAP (DIV I) — 1m 31y
**5:15** (5:15) (Class 5) (0-70,72) 3-Y-0 **£3,557** (£1,058; £529; £264) **Stalls** Low

Form RPR

655 **1** **Chance To Dream (IRE)**[28] 2231 3-9-8 71 ........ KierenFox 13 78
(John Best) *racd centre fnl 3f: s.i.s: towards rr: pushed along 3f out: hdwy 2f out: str run ent fnl f: led fnl 100yds: styd on wl* **9/1**[3]

5401 **2** 1/2 **Badenscoth**[35] 2018 3-9-0 66 ........(h) JackDuern(3) 8 71+
(Dean Ivory) *racd centre fnl 3f: s.i.s: towards rr: hdwy fr 4f out: rdn to ld 2f out: kpt on but no ex whn hdd fnl 100yds* **11/1**

5411 **3** 1 **Rita's Man (IRE)**[8] 2854 3-9-1 71 6ex ........ RossaRyan(7) 6 74+
(Richard Hannon) *racd centre fnl 3f: keen early: trckd ldrs: rdn over 2f out: ev ch over 1f out: kpt on same pce ins fnl f* **2/1**[1]

62-2 **4** 2 1/4 **Tennessee Rose (IRE)**[12] 2732 3-9-0 63 ........ JamesDoyle 11 61
(Luke McJannet) *led tl over 4f out: trcking ldrs whn kpt to stands' side rails 3f out: sn rdn: drifted lft over 1f out: styd on fnl f* **6/1**[2]

066- **5** shd **Hawridge Glory (IRE)**[283] 5594 3-8-9 58 ........ DavidProbert 1 56
(Rod Millman) *racd centre fnl 3f: hld up: rdn and stdy prog fr over 2f out: styd on fnl f* **16/1**

5030 **6** nk **Challow (IRE)**[17] 2588 3-9-4 67 ........ LiamKeniry 2 64
(Sylvester Kirk) *racd stands' side 3f out: mid-div: rdn over 2f out: drifted lft ent fnl f: kpt on but no threat* **20/1**

3530 **7** 4 1/2 **Hold Me Tight (IRE)**[12] 2726 3-8-7 56 oh2 ........(b) LiamJones 12 43
(J S Moore) *racd centre fnl 3f: mid-div: rdn 3f out: nvr threatened* **25/1**

0-30 **8** 2 1/4 **Sakurajima (IRE)**[35] 2035 3-9-0 66 ........(t) CallumShepherd(3) 7 48
(Charles Hills) *kpt to stands' side 3f out: mid-div: rdn 3f out: nvr any imp* **14/1**

6-16 **9** 3/4 **Alemaratalyoum (IRE)**[54] 1550 3-9-9 72 ........ JamieSpencer 3 52
(Ed Dunlop) *kpt stands' side fnl 3f: racd keenly in tch: hdwy to ld over 4f out: rdn and hdd 2f out: sn wknd* **6/1**[2]

000- **10** 10 **Gaia Princess (IRE)**[217] 7571 3-8-12 61 ........ SeanLevey 5 18
(Gary Moore) *racd centre fnl 3f: racd keenly: trckd ldrs: rdn over 2f out: wknd over 1f out* **40/1**

00-0 **11** 20 **Morello (IRE)**[35] 2019 3-9-2 65 ........ FergusSweeney 10
(Henry Candy) *racd centre fnl 3f: sn prom: rdn over 2f out: wknd over 1f out* **16/1**

040 **12** nk **Zoffany Bay (IRE)**[33] 2084 3-9-7 70 ........ JosephineGordon 4
(George Peckham) *racd centre fnl 3f: in tch: rdn over 3f out: wknd 2f out* **12/1**

1m 47.11s (2.41) **Going Correction** +0.30s/f (Good) **12** Ran SP% **117.4**
Speed ratings (Par 99): **99,98,97,95,95 94,90,88,87,77 57,57**
CSF £100.59 CT £282.01 TOTE £12.10: £2.90, £3.50, £1.30; EX 136.80 Trifecta £311.10.
**Owner** Mr & Mrs H Jarvis And & Mrs S Malcolm **Bred** Ballylinch Stud **Trained** Oad Street, Kent

**FOCUS**
Add 14yds. Again, the runners were all over the place in the straight. The fourth helps set the initial standard.

## 3163 CARIBBEAN NIGHT 5TH JUNE H'CAP (DIV II) — 1m 31y
**5:50** (5:50) (Class 5) (0-70,72) 3-Y-0 **£3,557** (£1,058; £529; £264) **Stalls** Low

Form RPR

-116 **1** **Sir Plato (IRE)**[40] 1875 3-9-8 71 ........ WilliamCarson 8 77+
(Rod Millman) *sn led: rdn 2f out: jnd cl home: all out: jst hld on* **5/2**[1]

20-0 **2** shd **Peloton**[33] 2088 3-9-2 65 ........ KieranO'Neill 10 70
(Pat Phelan) *racd keenly in tch: rdn over 2f out: str run ent fnl f: pressed wnr cl home: jst failed* **11/2**[2]

6-00 **3** 1 1/4 **Ashazuri**[23] 2394 3-8-5 61 ........(h) Pierre-LouisJamin(7) 2 63
(Jonathan Portman) *trckd ldrs: rdn to chse wnr over 2f out: wandered u.p over 1f out: kpt on cl home* **16/1**

0-43 **4** 1/2 **It's How We Roll (IRE)**[75] 1205 3-9-4 67 ........(b) TomMarquand 6 68
(John Spearing) *mid-div: rdn over 2f out: hdwy over 1f out: kpt on ins fnl f* **8/1**

405- **5** 3 3/4 **Ingleby Mackenzie**[227] 7319 3-9-4 67 ........ CharlesBishop 1 59
(Mick Channon) *in tch tl lost pl u.p over 3f out: styd on again fnl f but n.d* **8/1**

-113 **6** 3/4 **Dangerous Ends**[96] 864 3-9-0 **63**.........................(v) JosephineGordon 4 54
(Brett Johnson) *trckd ldrs: rdn to dispute cl 2nd over 2f out: wknd ins fnl f* **11/2**[2]

-000 **7** 3 1/2 **Ok By Me (IRE)**[27] 2274 3-8-8 **57**.........................(v[1]) JFEgan 11 40
(David Evans) *towards rr: sme minor late prog: nvr any threat to ldrs* **16/1**

000- **8** 1/2 **Vibes (IRE)**[166] 8352 3-9-8 **71**......................... JamesDoyle 12 52
(Jamie Osborne) *hld up: carried wd on bnd over 5f out: rdn and sme prog over 2f out: wknd over 1f out* **7/1**[3]

060- **9** 17 **Socrates**[187] 8066 3-9-3 **66**......................... RichardKingscote 7 8
(Daniel Kubler) *a towards rr* **16/1**

3-30 **10** 6 **Spiritofedinburgh (IRE)**[28] 2220 3-9-2 **70**......................... JennyPowell(5) 5
(Brendan Powell) *broke wl: trckd wnr: rdn 3f out: wknd 2f out* **25/1**

1m 47.31s (2.61) **Going Correction** +0.30s/f (Good) 10 Ran SP% **115.6**
Speed ratings (Par 99): **98,97,96,96,92 91,88,87,70,64**
CSF £15.64 CT £184.02 TOTE £3.10: £1.10, £2.20, £4.00; EX 14.50 Trifecta £367.00.
**Owner** The Sir Plato Partnership **Bred** Noel Finegan **Trained** Kentisbeare, Devon

**FOCUS**
Add 14yds. The second division of a modest handicap. The action was up the middle in the straight. The fourth has been rated to the better view of his form.
T/Plt: £231.10 to a £1 stake. Pool: £62,752.00 - 271.45 winning units T/Qpdt: £171.80 to a £1 stake. Pool: £3,163.00 - 18.40 winning units **Tim Mitchell**

## 3142 LEICESTER (R-H)
### Tuesday, May 30

**OFFICIAL GOING: Good to soft (7.1)**
Wind: Light behind Weather: Overcast

## 3164 BRITISH STALLION STUDS EBF MAIDEN STKS (PLUS 10 RACE) (DIV I) 6f
**1:50** (1:50) (Class 4) 2-Y-O **£5,175** (£1,540; £769; £384) **Stalls** High

Form RPR

2 **1** **Westerland**[11] 2779 2-9-5 0......................... FrankieDettori 6 86+
(John Gosden) *hld up: hdwy over 2f out: shkn up over 1f out: sn ev ch: rdn and edgd rt ins fnl f: r.o to ld post* **8/15**[1]

**2** nse **Hey Gaman** 2-9-5 0......................... MartinHarley 2 86+
(James Tate) *a.p: shkn up to ld over 1f out: r.o: hdd post* **6/1**[3]

**3** 1 3/4 **Match Maker (IRE)** 2-9-5 0......................... RyanMoore 3 81+
(Simon Crisford) *hld up: swtchd rt and hdwy over 1f out: r.o: nt rch ldrs* **9/2**[2]

**4** 1 1/2 **Fighting Irish (IRE)** 2-9-5 0......................... AdamKirby 4 76+
(Harry Dunlop) *w ldr tl led over 3f out: shkn up hdd over 1f out: edgd rt and styd on same pce ins fnl f* **66/1**

3 **5** 4 **George (IRE)**[11] 2779 2-9-5 0......................... PatDobbs 11 64
(Sylvester Kirk) *hld up: swtchd rt and hdwy over 1f out: nt trble ldrs* **9/1**

**6** 2 3/4 **Rhosneigr (IRE)** 2-9-5 0......................... WilliamBuick 8 56
(Charles Hills) *s.i.s: in rr and pushed along over 3f out: hdwy over 1f out: wknd fnl f* **33/1**

0 **7** 1 **Admiral Spice (IRE)**[27] 2299 2-9-5 0......................... RichardKingscote 1 53
(Tom Dascombe) *led over 2f: remained handy: rdn over 2f out: edgd rt over 1f out: sn wknd* **22/1**

6 **8** nse **City Guest (IRE)**[28] 2279 2-9-5 0......................... DanielMuscutt 7 53
(George Margarson) *prom: shkn up over 1f out: wknd ins fnl f* **100/1**

**9** 2 3/4 **Moakkad** 2-9-5 0......................... JimCrowley 5 45+
(Mark Johnston) *trckd ldrs: shkn up over 2f out: wknd over 1f out* **20/1**

**10** 4 **Vice Marshal (IRE)** 2-9-5 0......................... StevieDonohoe 9 33
(Charlie Fellowes) *s.i.s: sn pushed along in rr: wknd over 2f out* **66/1**

1m 12.26s (-0.74) **Going Correction** -0.125s/f (Firm) 10 Ran SP% **123.7**
Speed ratings (Par 95): **99,98,96,94,89 85,84,84,80,75**
CSF £4.48 TOTE £1.50: £1.02, £2.00, £1.90; EX 5.60 Trifecta £19.10.
**Owner** K Abdullah **Bred** Juddmonte Farms Ltd **Trained** Newmarket, Suffolk

**FOCUS**
Some starts have been moved at this track following remeasuring, so some races will not have speed figures until there is sufficient data to calculate updated median times. Race distances as advertised. Easier ground than for the previous day's fixture, Frankie Dettori calling it "loose" after winning the first, but the times suggested it wasn't far off being good. This maiden has produced some smart horses, including 2014 winner Toormore. The two divisions last year went to recent Irish Guineas runner-up Thunder Snow and Listed scorer Rodaini. Winners should emerge from this division, which was 0.85sec quicker than the other. The level will take time to settle.

## 3165 BRITISH STALLION STUDS EBF MAIDEN STKS (PLUS 10 RACE) (DIV II) 6f
**2:20** (2:23) (Class 4) 2-Y-O **£5,175** (£1,540; £769; £384) **Stalls** High

Form RPR

0 **1** **June Dog**[31] 2134 2-9-5 0......................... SeanLevey 6 78
(Richard Hannon) *mde all: rdn and hung lft ins fnl f: jst hld on* **8/1**[3]

**2** hd **Prince Ahwahnee** 2-9-5 0......................... AdamKirby 2 77+
(Clive Cox) *s.i.s: pushed along in rr early: swtchd lft 2f out: hdwy over 1f out: r.o* **4/1**[2]

**3** 3/4 **James Garfield (IRE)** 2-9-5 0......................... OisinMurphy 5 75+
(George Scott) *s.s: hld up: hdwy over 1f out: r.o* **14/1**

3 **4** 1 **Leeshaan (IRE)**[29] 2222 2-9-5 0......................... MartinHarley 4 73
(James Tate) *trckd ldrs: rdn over 1f out: nt clr run ins fnl f: styd on same pce* **5/2**[1]

6 **5** 6 **Solid Man (JPN)**[23] 2435 2-9-5 0......................... FranBerry 10 54
(Ralph Beckett) *s.i.s: hld up: hdwy over 2f out: rdn over 1f out: edgd rt and wknd ins fnl f* **5/2**[1]

0 **6** 1 **Owen The Law**[39] 1941 2-9-5 0......................... JFEgan 3 51
(David Evans) *chsd ldrs: rdn over 1f out: wknd fnl f* **33/1**

**7** 3/4 **Austin Powers (IRE)** 2-9-5 0......................... JoeFanning 8 49
(Mark Johnston) *prom: rdn over 2f out: wknd over 1f out* **20/1**

**8** 3/4 **Free Spirited** 2-9-5 0......................... TonyHamilton 1 47
(Richard Fahey) *hld up: racd keenly: rdn over 2f out: wknd over 1f out* **14/1**

5 **9** 6 **Budgie**[22] 2459 2-9-5 0......................... StevieDonohoe 7 29
(Mark H Tompkins) *chsd ldr tl rdn over 2f out: wknd over 1f out* **50/1**

**10** 3 1/2 **General Zoff** 2-9-5 0......................... MartinDwyer 9 18
(William Muir) *s.s: sn pushed along in rr: wknd over 2f out* **25/1**

1m 13.11s (0.11) **Going Correction** -0.125s/f (Firm) 10 Ran SP% **115.1**
Speed ratings (Par 95): **94,93,92,91,83 82,81,80,72,67**
CSF £37.93 TOTE £8.50: £2.20, £1.90, £3.20; EX 46.90 Trifecta £629.60.
**Owner** Sullivan Bloodstock Limited **Bred** L J Vaessen **Trained** East Everleigh, Wilts

**FOCUS**
This looked the weaker division of what is often a good race and the time was 0.85sec slower. The first four finished clear. The fourth helps set the opening level.

## 3166 STATHERN CLAIMING STKS 7f
**2:50** (2:52) (Class 5) 3-Y-O **£3,881** (£1,155; £577; £288) **Stalls** High

Form RPR

4204 **1** **Jet Setter (IRE)**[53] 1605 3-9-1 62......................... GeorgeDowning 3 69
(Tony Carroll) *hld up: hdwy 2f out: led ins fnl f: pushed clr* **10/1**

3-32 **2** 3 1/2 **Black Bubba (IRE)**[5] 2989 3-8-6 62 ow1......................... JFEgan 5 51
(David Evans) *hld up in tch: n.m.r and shkn up over 1f out: styd on same pce ins fnl f* **5/2**[1]

4225 **3** 2 1/4 **Allegheny Bay (IRE)**[20] 2536 3-9-1 63......................... LiamJones 6 54
(J S Moore) *led: rdn and hung lft over 2f out: hdd and no ex ins fnl f* **7/1**

564 **4** 2 3/4 **Cookie's Star**[35] 2062 3-8-4 60......................... JosephineGordon 1 36
(Philip McBride) *sn outpcd: r.o u.p ins fnl f: nvr nrr* **8/1**

2205 **5** 2 1/2 **Rag Tatter**[15] 2682 3-9-1 72.........................(p[1]) KevinStott 8 40
(Kevin Ryan) *trckd ldrs: hmpd over 2f out: rdn over 1f out: wknd ins fnl f* **7/2**[2]

-004 **6** 1 3/4 **Kings Academy**[6] 2970 3-9-4 72.........................(t) PaulStJohn-Dennis(7) 2 46
(Paul Cole) *prom: shkn up over 1f out: hung lft and wknd fnl f* **9/2**[3]

000- **7** 1 3/4 **She's Rosanna**[209] 7768 3-8-1 45 ow1......................... RoystonFfrench 7 17
(Steph Hollinshead) *hld up in tch: hmpd over 2f out: wknd over 1f out* **66/1**

-050 **8** 9 **Trust The Indian**[127] 377 3-8-7 45 ow3.........................(p) RyanWhile(5) 4 5
(Bill Turner) *racd keenly: prom: rdn whn n.m.r and wknd over 1f out* **50/1**

0-30 **9** 7 **Stevie Brown**[30] 2186 3-8-11 65.........................(p[1]) OisinMurphy 9
(David Brown) *prom: racd alone tl hung rt 4f out: rdn and wknd over 2f out* **16/1**

1m 25.68s (-0.52) **Going Correction** -0.125s/f (Firm) 9 Ran SP% **111.0**
Speed ratings (Par 99): **97,93,90,87,84 82,80,70,62**
CSF £33.27 TOTE £11.40: £2.30, £1.80, £1.70; EX 46.10 Trifecta £313.90.No claims for this race
**Owner** Last Day Racing Partnership **Bred** Thomas Bergin **Trained** Cropthorne, Worcs

**FOCUS**
The whole field were maidens in this weak claimer. The winner has been rated back to his 2yo best.

## 3167 CORONATION FILLIES' H'CAP 7f
**3:20** (3:21) (Class 4) (0-85,87) 3-Y-O **£6,469** (£1,925; £962; £481) **Stalls** High

Form RPR

563- **1** **Bahamadam**[244] 6882 3-9-5 **83**......................... RobertWinston 13 91
(Eve Johnson Houghton) *hld up: hdwy over 1f out: rdn ins fnl f: r.o to ld nr fin* **33/1**

01-4 **2** nk **Rely On Me (IRE)**[20] 2517 3-8-13 **77**......................... OisinMurphy 11 84
(Andrew Balding) *trckd ldrs: led over 1f out: rdn and hung rt ins fnl f: hdd nr fin* **8/1**[3]

21- **3** 2 3/4 **Cashla Bay**[213] 7695 3-9-3 **81**......................... FrankieDettori 7 81+
(John Gosden) *plld hrd: w ldr tl swtchd rt and led over 5f out: shkn up and hdd over 1f out: styd on same pce ins fnl f* **1/1**[1]

2-21 **4** 1 3/4 **Rutherford (IRE)**[82] 1102 3-8-13 **77**......................... KevinStott 10 72
(Kevin Ryan) *led: hdd over 5f out: remained handy: rdn and ev ch over 1f out: edgd rt and no ex ins fnl f* **25/1**

61-0 **5** 1/2 **Sayem**[26] 2334 3-8-13 **77**......................... ThomasBrown 9 71
(Ed Walker) *hld up: pushed along and hdwy over 2f out: edgd rt and styd on same pce fnl f* **16/1**

-503 **6** 2 1/2 **Fastnet Spin (IRE)**[1] 3142 3-8-8 **72**.........................(v) JFEgan 5 59
(David Evans) *hld up: pushed along and hdwy 3f out: rdn over 1f out: wknd ins fnl f* **16/1**

51- **7** 3/4 **Phalaborwa**[260] 6414 3-9-1 **79**......................... HarryBentley 8 64
(Ed Vaughan) *s.i.s and n.m.r s: in rr and rdn over 2f out: sn hung rt: n.d* **12/1**

0-20 **8** 1 **Jule In The Crown**[39] 1945 3-9-8 **86**......................... JimCrowley 4 69
(Mick Channon) *hld up: hdwy over 2f out: rdn and ev ch wl over 1f out: wknd fnl f* **11/1**

21-6 **9** 4 1/2 **Brogan**[41] 1878 3-9-1 **79**......................... RichardKingscote 2 50
(Tom Dascombe) *chsd ldrs: rdn over 2f out: wknd over 1f out* **7/1**[2]

60-0 **10** 6 **Arwa (IRE)**[38] 1958 3-9-9 **87**......................... WilliamBuick 6 42
(Charles Hills) *mid-div: hdwy 1/2-way: rdn over 2f out: wknd over 1f out* **16/1**

1m 24.31s (-1.89) **Going Correction** -0.125s/f (Firm) 10 Ran SP% **114.1**
Speed ratings (Par 98): **105,104,101,99,98 96,95,94,88,82**
CSF £271.45 CT £540.35 TOTE £30.80: £8.70, £2.60, £1.02; EX 363.40 Trifecta £1519.90.
**Owner** J P Repard **Bred** J P Repard **Trained** Blewbury, Oxon

**FOCUS**
They initially split into two groups in this fair fillies' handicap and although they merged by halfway, the winner and second came from the stands'-side bunch.

## 3168 FOREST H'CAP 1m 2f
**3:50** (3:50) (Class 4) (0-80,78) 4-Y-O+ **£6,301** (£1,886; £943; £472; £235) **Stalls** Low

Form RPR

0-21 **1** **Vernatti**[28] 2282 4-9-2 **73**......................... RobHornby 3 83+
(Pam Sly) *prom: led over 8f out: qcknd over 3f out: rdn over 1f out: styd on wl* **11/8**[1]

-000 **2** 3 1/2 **Lord Franklin**[17] 2624 8-9-6 **77**......................... NeilFarley 5 80
(Eric Alston) *led: hdd over 8f out: chsd wnr: rdn over 2f out: styd on same pce fnl f* **14/1**

-055 **3** 3/4 **Craftsmanship (FR)**[45] 1788 6-9-6 **77**.........................(p) PaoloSirigu 7 79
(Robert Eddery) *s.i.s: hld up and bhd: swtchd lft and hdwy over 2f out: rdn to go 3rd over 1f out: no imp fnl f* **11/2**

4052 **4** 1 1/2 **Anton Chigurh**[10] 1695 8-9-0 **71**......................... RichardKingscote 1 70
(Nikki Evans) *hld up in tch: rdn over 2f out: styd on same pce fr over 1f out* **40/1**

10-6 **5** 21 **Vizier**[26] 2339 4-9-5 **76**......................... JimCrowley 2 33
(David O'Meara) *chsd ldrs: rdn over 3f out: wknd wl over 1f out* **5/1**[3]

05-2 **6** 4 **Dora's Field (IRE)**[14] 2710 4-9-0 **71**......................... OisinMurphy 4 20
(Stuart Kittow) *s.i.s: hld up: rdn and wknd over 2f out* **11/4**[2]

2m 9.23s (1.33) 6 Ran SP% **109.9**
CSF £20.63 TOTE £2.80: £1.40, £5.20; EX 18.50 Trifecta £73.80.
**Owner** Michael H Sly Dr T Davies Mrs Pam Sly **Bred** M H Sly, Dr T Davies & Mrs P Sly **Trained** Thorney, Cambs

**FOCUS**
The only race on the card on the round course, this modest handicap was dominated by the winner. Her two closest market rivals failed to give their running.

## 3169 BRITISH STALLION STUDS EBF NOVICE STKS (PLUS 10 RACE) 5f
**4:20** (4:25) (Class 4) 2-Y-O **£6,469** (£1,925; £962; £481) **Stalls** High

Form RPR

1 **Roussel (IRE)** 2-9-2 0 WilliamBuick 10 77+
(Charlie Appleby) *sn prom: led wl over 1f out: sn shkn up and edgd rt: pushed out* **4/5**[1]

03 2 ¾ **Demons Rock (IRE)**[18] 2577 2-9-2 0 RichardKingscote 5 74
(Tom Dascombe) *trckd ldrs: shkn up over 1f out: hmpd ins fnl f: r.o to go 2nd nr fin* **15/2**[3]

4 3 nk **Alaska (IRE)**[10] 2816 2-9-2 0 OisinMurphy 1 73
(Sylvester Kirk) *chsd ldrs: pushed along 1/2-way: styd on* **11/2**[2]

4 1 ¼ **Catapult** 2-9-2 0 PaoloSirigu 4 69
(Robert Eddery) *w ldr tl pushed along 3f out: rdn over 1f out: styd on same pce ins fnl f* **100/1**

5 shd **Onefootinparadise** 2-8-11 0 JosephineGordon 2 63
(Philip McBride) *s.s: pushed along early in rr: then racd keenly over 3f out: hdwy over 1f out: sn ev ch: styd on same pce wl ins fnl f* **40/1**

6 1 ½ **Sienna Says** 2-8-11 0 GeorgeDowning 3 58
(Tony Carroll) *trckd ldrs: racd keenly: pushed along and lost pl over 3f out: hdwy over 1f out: styd on same pce ins fnl f* **100/1**

7 ¾ **Quayside** 2-9-2 0 TonyHamilton 8 60+
(Richard Fahey) *green to post: sn pushed along in rr: r.o ins fnl f: nvr nrr* **10/1**

0 8 2 ½ **Jive Lady (IRE)**[11] 2771 2-8-11 0 JoeFanning 7 46
(Mark Johnston) *led: rdn and hdd wl over 1f out: nt clr run 1f out: sn edgd lft and wknd* **16/1**

9 2 ¼ **Charnock Richard** 2-9-2 0 AdamKirby 9 43
(David Brown) *chsd ldr: pushed along 1/2-way: sn lost pl* **16/1**

10 ½ **Mutabaahy (IRE)** 2-9-2 0 JimCrowley 11 41
(Ed Dunlop) *s.s: outpcd* **20/1**

1m 1.42s (1.42) **Going Correction** -0.125s/f (Firm) **10** Ran SP% **112.7**
Speed ratings (Par 95): **83,81,81,79,79 76,75,71,67,67**
CSF £6.68 TOTE £1.70: £1.10, £1.80, £2.50; EX 7.20 Trifecta £19.40.
**Owner** Godolphin **Bred** Tom Darcy And Vincent McCarthy **Trained** Newmarket, Suffolk
■ Mocead Cappall was withdrawn. Price at time of withdrawal 33/1. Rule 4 does not apply

**FOCUS**
The winner will surely step up on this bare form. The second and third have been rated near their pre-race marks.

## 3170 OADBY H'CAP 5f
**4:50** (4:50) (Class 5) (0-75,76) 4-Y-O+ **£3,881** (£1,155; £577; £288) **Stalls** High

Form RPR

-U45 1 **Casterbridge**[17] 2621 5-9-2 **70** NeilFarley 5 80
(Eric Alston) *mde all: rdn and hung rt ins fnl f: styd on u.p* **9/2**[3]

00-4 2 1 **Signore Piccolo**[10] 2821 6-9-1 **76** (h) RossaRyan(7) 8 82
(David Loughnane) *chsd wnr to 1/2-way: rdn and hung rt fr over 1f out: r.o to go 2nd nr fin* **9/4**[1]

2562 3 ½ **Burtonwood**[7] 2923 5-8-7 **66** ow1 (p) CallumRodriguez(5) 1 70
(Julie Camacho) *prom: chsd wnr 1/2-way: rdn and ev ch fr over 1f out tl no ex towards fin* **4/1**[2]

4142 4 2 ¾ **Borough Boy (IRE)**[7] 2932 7-8-11 **65** (v) TonyHamilton 7 59
(Derek Shaw) *trckd ldrs: rdn over 1f out: styd on same pce ins fnl f* **8/1**

R0-0 5 1 ¾ **Bahamian Heights**[36] 2038 6-9-7 **75** (h) GeorgeDowning 3 63
(Robert Cowell) *awkward s: pushed along in rr: rdn over 1f out: edgd rt ins fnl f: nvr trbld ldrs* **18/1**

62-0 6 nk **John Joiner**[17] 2621 5-8-8 **62** JoeFanning 2 49
(Peter Hedger) *hld up: effrt over 1f out: no ex ins fnl f* **9/1**

2566 7 2 ¾ **Out Of The Ashes**[11] 2800 4-9-2 **70** (bt[1]) JimCrowley 6 47
(Mohamed Moubarak) *prom: lost pl 1/2-way: wknd fnl f* **9/1**

6206 8 1 **Sarabi**[9] 2858 4-8-11 **65** (p) FranBerry 9 38
(Scott Dixon) *s.i.s: hld up: rdn 1/2-way: wknd over 1f out* **16/1**

1m 0.05s (0.05) **Going Correction** -0.125s/f (Firm) **8** Ran SP% **111.2**
Speed ratings (Par 103): **94,92,91,87,84 83,79,77**
CSF £14.18 CT £41.29 TOTE £5.20: £1.90, £1.10, £2.10; EX 16.80 Trifecta £55.80.
**Owner** Liam & Tony Ferguson **Bred** Liam & Tony Ferguson **Trained** Longton, Lancs
■ Stewards' Enquiry : Neil Farley 2 day ban - used whip down the shoulder in the forehand (13-14 June)

**FOCUS**
An ordinary sprint handicap short on in-form runners.

## 3171 SAFFRON 3-Y-O FILLIES' H'CAP 6f
**5:20** (5:20) (Class 5) (0-75,77) 3-Y-O **£4,528** (£1,347; £673; £336) **Stalls** High

Form RPR

41-0 1 **Magical Dreamer (IRE)**[32] 2122 3-9-7 **75** (h[1]) DanielMuscutt 10 85
(James Fanshawe) *flashed tail. mde all: shkn up and edgd rt fr over 1f out: styd on* **16/1**

555- 2 1 ¼ **Bassmah**[298] 5119 3-9-5 **73** StevieDonohoe 1 79
(Ismail Mohammed) *chsd wnr: rdn and ev ch over 1f out: styd on same pce wl ins fnl f* **16/1**

11-5 3 nse **Ventura Blues (IRE)**[53] 1601 3-9-9 **77** PatDobbs 4 83
(Richard Hannon) *hld up: swtchd rt and hdwy over 1f out: r.o: nt rch ldrs* **13/2**

60-2 4 4 **The Stalking Moon (IRE)**[21] 2503 3-9-2 **70** FranBerry 12 63
(John Quinn) *hld up: pushed along over 2f out: hung rt and r.o ins fnl f: nvr nrr* **4/1**[2]

5-16 5 nk **Wurood**[35] 2071 3-9-8 **76** (t[1]) JimCrowley 5 68
(William Haggas) *s.i.s: sn mid-div: hdwy over 2f out: rdn over 1f out: styd on same pce* **7/2**[1]

-631 6 4 **Everkyllachy (IRE)**[13] 2734 3-8-2 **56** (b) LiamJones 13 35
(J S Moore) *hld up: rdn over 2f out: nvr nrr* **12/1**

303- 7 1 ½ **Twilight Spirit**[249] 6732 3-8-9 **63** GeorgeDowning 9 38
(Tony Carroll) *prom: rdn over 2f out: wknd over 1f out* **20/1**

050- 8 1 ¼ **Our Greta (IRE)**[239] 7004 3-8-9 **70** RayDawson(7) 6 41
(Michael Appleby) *prom: rdn and edgd lft over 2f out: wknd over 1f out* **20/1**

00-5 9 hd **Little Miss Lola**[17] 2630 3-8-7 **61** NeilFarley 2 31
(Sally Haynes) *plld hrd and prom: sddle slipped sn after s: wknd over 1f out* **22/1**

203- 10 7 **Norwegian Highness (FR)**[197] 7956 3-9-1 **74** LewisEdmunds(5) 7 22
(Kevin Ryan) *hld up in tch: plld hrd: lost pl 1/2-way: nt clr run over 2f out: wknd over 1f out* **11/2**[3]

2-62 11 shd **Fabric**[20] 2508 3-8-11 **72** RossaRyan(7) 11 19
(Richard Hannon) *trckd ldrs: plld hrd: pushed along over 2f out: wknd over 1f out* **10/1**

1m 11.62s (-1.38) **Going Correction** -0.125s/f (Firm) **11** Ran SP% **113.4**
Speed ratings (Par 96): **104,102,102,96,96 91,89,87,87,77 77**
CSF £230.24 CT £1857.22 TOTE £19.10: £4.50, £4.80, £2.10; EX 205.80 Trifecta £1003.20.
**Owner** Fred Archer Racing - Ladylove **Bred** Rockfield Farm **Trained** Newmarket, Suffolk

**FOCUS**
An ordinary fillies' handicap in which the first three, all of whom raced on the far side of the group, finished clear. The 1-2 were up there throughout.
T/Plt: £20.50 to a £1 stake. Pool: £62,647.74 -2221.54 winning units T/Qpdt: £3.20 to a £1 stake. Pool: £4,689.68 - 1069.12 winning units **Colin Roberts**

# 2963 LINGFIELD (L-H)
## Tuesday, May 30

**OFFICIAL GOING: Polytrack: standard**
Wind: Moderate, across (towards stands) Weather: Cloudy

## 3172 CASH OUT AT BET365 H'CAP 1m 1y(P)
**2:10** (2:11) (Class 6) (0-65,64) 4-Y-O+ **£2,264** (£673; £336; £168) **Stalls** High

Form RPR

4-12 1 **Whispered Kiss**[27] 2312 4-9-3 **60** ShaneKelly 7 67
(Mike Murphy) *led 1f then t.k.h bhd ldrs: gap available on inner and pushed through to ld over 2f out: drvn over 1f out: kpt on wl* **2/1**[2]

0223 2 1 **Mowhoob**[22] 2465 7-8-9 **52** LukeMorris 6 57
(Brian Barr) *chsd ldrs but pushed along early: rdn 2f out: styd on fr over 1f out to chse wnr ins fnl f: unable to chal* **9/1**

60-0 3 1 ¾ **Ede's The Mover**[28] 2257 4-8-12 **55** KieranO'Neill 9 55
(Pat Phelan) *trckd ldr after 2f: led 3f out to over 2f out: chsd wnr after: drvn and hld over 1f out: lost 2nd and one pce ins fnl furl* **25/1**

-314 4 ½ **Rattle On**[17] 2615 4-9-7 **64** PatCosgrave 8 63
(Jim Boyle) *awkward s: sn in midfield: rdn wl over 2f out: tried to make prog over 1f out but kpt on at same pce only to take 4th fnl f* **7/4**[1]

B520 5 1 ¾ **Binky Blue (IRE)**[28] 2278 5-9-5 **62** DaneO'Neill 10 57
(Daniel Mark Loughnane) *awkward s and slowest away: hld up in 10th: stl there 2f out: pushed along and kpt on steadily fr over 1f out: nvr nr ldrs* **8/1**[3]

500 6 1 **Blackthorn Stick (IRE)**[53] 1603 8-8-10 **53** (p) JimmyQuinn 2 46
(Paul Burgoyne) *wl in tch: effrt on inner 2f out: no prog fnl f* **14/1**

33-0 7 nse **Lady Nahema (IRE)**[11] 2785 4-9-0 **57** TomMarquand 5 49
(Martin Bosley) *hld up towards rr: rdn over 2f out: no prog tl styd on ins fnl f* **25/1**

-060 8 1 ¾ **Palace Moon**[62] 1425 12-8-7 **50** oh2 (t) AdamBeschizza 4 38
(Michael Attwater) *nvr bttr than midfield: shkn up and no prog over 2f out: nvr a factor* **25/1**

0-0 9 ½ **The Dancing Lord**[26] 2336 8-8-13 **59** (t) NoelGarbutt(3) 3 46
(Adam West) *sn outpcd in last: rdn over 3f out: no great prog* **33/1**

-000 10 ¾ **Herculian Prince**[108] 690 5-8-12 **55** LiamKeniry 12 40
(Conor Dore) *spd fr wd draw to ld after 1f: hdd 3f out: wknd 2f out* **100/1**

0-00 11 4 ½ **Our Boy Jack (IRE)**[31] 2133 8-8-9 **59** (p) KatherineGlenister(7) 11 33
(Conor Dore) *t.k.h: chsd ldrs but trapped out wd: wknd qckly over 2f out* **33/1**

1m 37.87s (-0.33) **Going Correction** -0.05s/f (Stan) **11** Ran SP% **115.9**
Speed ratings (Par 101): **99,98,96,95,94 93,92,91,90,89 85**
CSF £18.07 CT £347.45 TOTE £3.20: £1.50, £2.70, £6.60; EX 16.90.
**Owner** D Ellison, B Olkowicz, C Speller **Bred** T Ellison, B Olkowicz And C Speller **Trained** Westoning, Beds

**FOCUS**
A moderate handicap. The runner-up and third help set the level.

## 3173 CASINO AT BET365 H'CAP 7f 1y(P)
**2:40** (2:40) (Class 5) (0-70,72) 3-Y-O **£2,911** (£866; £432; £216) **Stalls** Low

Form RPR

1-30 1 **Team Meeting (USA)**[29] 2235 3-9-7 **70** (h[1]) SilvestreDeSousa 5 79
(Saeed bin Suroor) *mde virtually all: clr w runner-up wl over 1f out: hrd pressed fnl f: jst prevailed* **13/8**[1]

6-41 2 nse **Mulzim**[41] 1888 3-9-9 **72** DaneO'Neill 6 81
(Ed Dunlop) *t.k.h: trckd wnr after 3f: rdn to chal over 1f out: sustained effrt fnl f: jst pipped* **7/2**[2]

3-16 3 3 ¾ **Altiko Tommy (IRE)**[41] 1888 3-9-5 **68** LiamKeniry 3 67
(George Baker) *t.k.h: trckd ldrs: nudged by rival after 2f: rdn and outpcd over 2f out: kpt on u.p to take 3rd nr fin* **7/1**

0-26 4 ¾ **Royal Peace (IRE)**[41] 1889 3-8-13 **65** HollieDoyle(3) 2 62
(Richard Hannon) *trckd wnr 3f: chsd ldng pair after: rdn and nt on terms fr 2f out: lost 3rd nr fin* **12/1**

00-0 5 1 ½ **Santafiora**[21] 2503 3-9-4 **70** KieranShoemark(3) 4 63
(Roger Charlton) *hld up in rr: rchd 5th over 2f out but nowhere nr ldrs: pushed along and no imp after* **20/1**

4-15 6 ½ **Daring Guest (IRE)**[22] 2474 3-8-11 **67** JaneElliott(7) 9 59
(George Margarson) *hld up in rr: outpcd wl over 2f out: no ch after: kpt on ins fnl f* **12/1**

1-11 7 ¾ **A Sure Welcome**[36] 2016 3-9-0 **63** (p) TomMarquand 7 53
(John Spearing) *hld up in rr: rdn and outpcd over 2f out: no ch after: kpt on ins fnl f* **6/1**[3]

0 8 10 **Beast**[22] 2474 3-8-13 **62** AdamBeschizza 8 25
(Lee Carter) *stdd s: hld up in last: nvr involved and bhd over 2f out* **66/1**

60-6 9 13 **Harbour Town**[101] 813 3-8-13 **62** LukeMorris 1
(Harry Dunlop) *cl up whn hmpd on inner after 2f: rdn and wknd 3f out: eased over 1f out: t.o* **25/1**

1m 24.36s (-0.44) **Going Correction** -0.05s/f (Stan) **9** Ran SP% **112.6**
Speed ratings (Par 99): **100,99,95,94,93 92,91,80,65**
CSF £6.74 CT £29.03 TOTE £2.50: £1.10, £1.60, £1.90; EX 8.60 Trifecta £33.20.
**Owner** Godolphin **Bred** Darley **Trained** Newmarket, Suffolk

**FOCUS**
The first two home were dominant and will likely be capable of mixing it in a slightly better grade.

## 3174 BET365 EBF FILLIES' NOVICE STKS (PLUS 10 RACE) 6f 1y(P)
**3:10** (3:11) (Class 5) 2-Y-O **£2,911** (£866; £432; £216) **Stalls** Low

Form RPR

1 **Dotted Swiss (IRE)** 2-9-0 0 TomMarquand 5 71+
(Richard Hannon) *chsd ldng pair: urged along 2f out: clsd on inner to chal jst over 1f out: led ins fnl f: kpt on wl* **9/4**[1]

00 2 ½ **Amazing Alice**[12] 2750 2-9-0 0 LukeMorris 1 70
(Archie Watson) *led: rdn 2f out: hdd ins fnl f: kpt on* **8/1**[2]

33 **3** *2 1/4* **Shesgotthelot**[28] 2277 2-9-0 0 ........ LiamKeniry 6 63
(J S Moore) *pressed ldr: rdn and nt qckn over 1f out: sn lost 2nd and one pce after* **8/1**[2]
**4** *1 1/4* **Inuk (IRE)** 2-9-0 0 ........ ShaneKelly 9 59
(Richard Hughes) *chsd ldrs: urged along over 2f out: outpcd sn after: one pce over 1f out* **20/1**
**5** *nse* **Gigi (IRE)** 2-9-0 0 ........ GavinLerena 4 59+
(Charles Hills) *green to post: hld up in midfield: outpcd and rn green over 2f out: n.d after but kpt on fnl f* **10/1**[3]
**6** *3 1/4* **Star Of Vendome (FR)** 2-9-0 0 ........ PatCosgrave 3 51+
(Harry Dunlop) *s.s: jst in tch at bk of main gp: outpcd over 2f out* **12/1**
**7** *1 1/2* **Zoraya (FR)** 2-9-0 0 ........ DavidProbert 7 45
(Paul Cole) *racd on outer: in tch tl wknd over 2f out* **16/1**
**8** *1/2* **Sorority** 2-9-0 0 ........ SilvestreDeSousa 2 43
(Mark Johnston) *green to post: sn in 7th and rn green: no prog over 2f out: wknd on inner after* **9/4**[1]
**9** *10* **Gower Gold** 2-8-9 0 ........ GeorgeBuckell(5) 8 13
(John Gallagher) *sn outpcd and bhd: t.o* **33/1**

1m 13.23s (1.33) **Going Correction** -0.05s/f (Stan) **9 Ran SP% 114.1**
Speed ratings (Par 90): **89,88,85,83,83 79,77,76,63**
CSF £21.38 TOTE £3.80: £1.70, £2.20, £2.30; EX 23.70 Trifecta £100.70.
**Owner** Merriebelle Irish Farm Limited **Bred** Sean Gorman **Trained** East Everleigh, Wilts

**FOCUS**
An informative fillies' novice event, though probably form to be dubious about given the proximity of the runner-up, who'd been well beaten in two previous turf runs. The level is fluid.

## 3175 BET365 MAIDEN AUCTION STKS 1m 2f (P)
**3:40** (3:40) (Class 5) 3-Y-O **£2,911** (£866; £432; £216) **Stalls** Low

Form RPR
06 **1** **I'm Running Late**[31] 2164 3-9-5 0 ........ PatCosgrave 1 71
(Dean Ivory) *chsd ldng pair: rdn over 2f out: clsd qckly jst over 1f out to ld 150yds out: sn clr* **8/1**
-320 **2** *3 1/2* **Dream Magic (IRE)**[24] 2395 3-9-5 65 ........ LukeMorris 4 64
(Daniel Mark Loughnane) *trckd ldr: rdn to chal over 2f out: eventually forced way past over 1f out: hdd and readily outpcd last 150yds* **6/4**[1]
-520 **3** *1 3/4* **Glorvina (IRE)**[18] 2588 3-8-11 67 ........ JoshDoyle(3) 5 56
(David O'Meara) *hld up in 4th: rdn over 2f out: nt qckn and no imp tl kpt on to take 3rd nr fin* **11/4**[3]
0- **4** *1 1/4* **Autumn Glow**[223] 7465 3-9-0 0 ........ AdamBeschizza 6 53
(Miss Joey Ellis) *s.s: hld up in last: rdn and no prog over 2f out: kpt on to take 4th last strides* **25/1**
3-34 **5** *shd* **Miss Osier**[17] 2625 3-8-11 63 ........ NoelGarbutt(3) 2 53
(Rae Guest) *led: rdn and jnd 2f out: hdd & wknd qckly over 1f out* **5/2**[2]

2m 6.03s (-0.57) **Going Correction** -0.05s/f (Stan) **5 Ran SP% 110.2**
Speed ratings (Par 99): **100,97,95,94,94**
CSF £20.64 TOTE £7.50: £2.40, £1.10; EX 17.20 Trifecta £46.20.
**Owner** Wood Hall Stud Limited **Bred** Wood Hall Stud **Trained** Radlett, Herts

**FOCUS**
With the favourite rated only 65, this maiden took little winning. Not solid form, but it's been rated around the runner-up for now.

## 3176 BET365 H'CAP 5f 6y(P)
**4:10** (4:12) (Class 4) (0-80,81) 4-Y-O+ **£4,690** (£1,395; £697; £348) **Stalls** High

Form RPR
0-00 **1** **Tailwind**[29] 2230 4-8-11 72 ........ (b[1]) HollieDoyle(3) 1 81
(Richard Hannon) *mde all: clr 1/2-way: rdn over 1f out: stl 3 l ahd fnl f: jst clung on* **4/1**[2]
1211 **2** *shd* **Menelik (IRE)**[29] 2239 8-9-5 77 ........ (bt) DavidProbert 5 85
(Des Donovan, Ire) *slowly away: racd in 5th and outpcd by wnr fr 1/2-way: prog 2f out: drvn to take 2nd last 75yds: clsd nr fin: jst failed* **9/1**
0262 **3** *1 1/2* **Sandfrankskipsgo**[28] 2253 8-9-2 77 ........ HectorCrouch(3) 6 79
(Peter Crate) *chsd wnr: outpcd 1/2-way: no imp over 1f out: lost 2nd last 75yds: kpt on* **8/1**
43 **4** *1* **Rosealee (IRE)**[46] 1768 4-9-4 76 ........ AdamBeschizza 3 75
(Jeremy Gask) *chsd ldng pair: outpcd by wnr 1/2-way: lost pl over 1f out: one pce after* **9/2**[3]
0001 **5** *nk* **Brother Tiger**[25] 2368 8-9-9 81 ........ SilvestreDeSousa 2 79
(David C Griffiths) *chsd ldrs: outpcd 1/2-way: wd bnd 2f out and no ch after: kpt on ins fnl f* **2/1**[1]
0443 **6** *shd* **Come On Dave (IRE)**[43] 1836 8-9-3 75 ........ (b) LiamKeniry 7 72
(John Butler) *s.i.s: mostly in last pair: outpcd fr 1/2-way: no ch after: kpt on ins fnl f* **16/1**
2522 **P** **Cultured Knight**[20] 2516 4-9-7 79 ........ (b[1]) ShaneKelly 4
(Richard Hughes) *s.s: last tl broke down and p.u 2f out* **11/2**

58.11s (-0.69) **Going Correction** -0.05s/f (Stan) **7 Ran SP% 113.9**
Speed ratings (Par 105): **103,102,100,98,98 98,**
CSF £38.14 TOTE £6.00: £2.80, £3.90; EX 44.20 Trifecta £222.80.
**Owner** R Barnett **Bred** W And R Barnett Ltd **Trained** East Everleigh, Wilts

**FOCUS**
A fair sprint handicap and a significant gamble landed by the front-running Tailwind. The winner has been rated back to his best, with the third close to form.

## 3177 POKER AT BET365 H'CAP 6f 1y(P)
**4:40** (4:45) (Class 5) (0-70,73) 4-Y-O+ **£2,911** (£866; £432; £216) **Stalls** Low

Form RPR
04-6 **1** **Curious Fox**[32] 2124 4-9-5 68 ........ DavidProbert 6 80
(Anthony Carson) *pressed ldr: rdn to chal 2f out: led 1f out: r.o wl and drew clr: readily* **7/1**[3]
0006 **2** *2 1/2* **King Of Swing**[14] 2709 4-8-13 62 ........ ShaneKelly 4 66
(Richard Hughes) *t.k.h: trckd ldng trio: rdn and nt qckn 2f out: styd on fnl f to take 2nd last strides: no ch w wnr* **11/4**[2]
5026 **3** *nk* **Top Of The Bank**[5] 2990 4-9-9 72 ........ (p) SilvestreDeSousa 5 75
(Kristin Stubbs) *led: rdn 2f out: hdd 1f out: one pce and no ch w wnr after: lost 2nd last strides* **7/4**[1]
5030 **4** *2 1/4* **Hamish McGonagain**[17] 2608 4-9-8 71 ........ (p) AdamBeschizza 9 67+
(Jeremy Gask) *hld up in last pair: stl there and no ch whn nt clr run jst over 1f out: styd on fnl 150yds: nvr nrr* **8/1**
3200 **5** *nse* **Fleckerl (IRE)**[31] 2161 7-9-7 70 ........ LiamKeniry 3 66
(Conor Dore) *dwlt: hld up in last pair: rdn and sme prog into midfield 1f out: nvr a threat* **12/1**
0042 **6** *1 1/4* **K'Gari Spirit**[26] 2335 4-9-4 67 ........ (t) MartinLane 1 59
(Jeremy Gask) *t.k.h: trckd ldng trio on inner: nt qckn 2f out: fdd over 1f out* **10/1**
0111 **7** *nk* **Whitecrest**[6] 2969 9-9-10 73 6ex ........ LukeMorris 7 64
(John Spearing) *trckd ldng trio but trapped wd: lost grnd over 2f out: no ch whn nt clr run jst over 1f out* **9/1**
0505 **8** *1 3/4* **Torment**[15] 2675 4-8-7 63 ........ (p) JoshuaBryan(7) 8 48
(Charlie Wallis) *t.k.h: pressed ldng pair on outer tl wknd 2f out* **20/1**

1m 10.82s (-1.08) **Going Correction** -0.05s/f (Stan) **8 Ran SP% 118.2**
Speed ratings (Par 103): **105,101,101,98,98 96,96,93**
CSF £27.59 CT £49.32 TOTE £7.90: £2.10, £1.40, £1.30; EX 34.30 Trifecta £123.60.
**Owner** Carson, Francis, Ghauri & Percy **Bred** Minster Stud **Trained** Newmarket, Suffolk

**FOCUS**
Few got involved in this sprint handicap and the first three pulled clear.

## 3178 BET365.COM H'CAP 1m 4f (P)
**5:10** (5:10) (Class 5) (0-70,71) 3-Y-O **£2,911** (£866; £432; £216) **Stalls** Low

Form RPR
-156 **1** **Earthly (USA)**[30] 2174 3-9-9 71 ........ DavidProbert 4 81+
(Ralph Beckett) *hld up in midfield: waiting for room over 3f out: prog to chse ldr over 2f out: forced to come wd in st to chal over 1f out: drvn ahd ins fnl f* **11/4**[2]
05-2 **2** *3/4* **Starshell (IRE)**[25] 2371 3-9-0 62 ........ LukeMorris 3 71
(Sir Mark Prescott Bt) *trckd ldr 2f: styd cl up: led wl over 2f out and sent for home: racd awkwardly and wd off bnd wl over 1f out: hdd and nt qckn ins fnl f* **13/8**[1]
-302 **3** *nk* **Star Maker**[8] 2892 3-9-1 68 ........ GeorgiaCox(5) 1 76+
(Sylvester Kirk) *trckd ldrs: waiting for room on inner 3f out to over 2f out: prog to chal over 1f out: upsides fnl f: styd on* **9/2**[3]
1-43 **4** *7* **Glenys The Menace (FR)**[24] 2395 3-9-5 67 ........ (h) SteveDrowne 7 64+
(John Best) *hld up in last pair: pushed along 4f out: effrt whn stmbld over 2f out: prog to take 4th 1f out: no ch w ldng trio but kpt on* **12/1**
50-0 **5** *3 1/4* **Penny Red**[50] 1682 3-9-3 68 ........ KieranShoemark(3) 6 60
(William Knight) *sn hld up in last pair: pushed along and waiting for room 3f out: outpcd over 2f out: nt clr run briefly over 1f out: one pce after* **14/1**
5-30 **6** *1 3/4* **Angel Of Rome (IRE)**[36] 2019 3-9-7 69 ........ ShaneKelly 5 58
(Richard Hughes) *hld up in midfield: rdn and outpcd over 2f out: wknd over 1f out* **28/1**
0-00 **7** *6* **Marettimo (IRE)**[36] 2039 3-9-5 67 ........ GavinLerena 2 46
(Charles Hills) *led to over 3f out: wknd qckly and sn bhd* **16/1**
5-66 **8** *3 3/4* **Katebird (IRE)**[14] 2702 3-9-6 68 ........ PatCosgrave 8 41
(Mark Johnston) *trckd ldr after 2f: led over 3f out to wl over 2f out: wknd rapidly* **12/1**

2m 30.66s (-2.34) **Going Correction** -0.05s/f (Stan) **8 Ran SP% 114.3**
Speed ratings (Par 99): **105,104,104,99,97 96,92,89**
CSF £7.60 CT £18.00 TOTE £3.70: £1.30, £1.20, £1.40; EX 8.20 Trifecta £27.80.
**Owner** K Abdullah **Bred** Juddmonte Farms Inc **Trained** Kimpton, Hants

**FOCUS**
This was steadily run and only developed in the final half-mile. The first three finished a long way clear. The third has been rated to form.
T/Plt: £92.90 to a £1 stake. Pool: £64,831.65 - 509.08 winning units T/Qpdt: £39.10 to a £1 stake. Pool: £4,011.46 - 75.9 winning units **Jonathan Neesom**

# 3149 REDCAR (L-H)
## Tuesday, May 30

**OFFICIAL GOING: Good (good to firm in places; watered; 8.4)**
Wind: Moderate, across in Straight Mile ( run-in 5f from Round Course) Weather: OVERCAST

## 3179 LONGINES IRISH CHAMPION WEEKEND EBF FILLIES' NOVICE MEDIAN AUCTION STKS (PLUS 10 RACE) 5f 217y
**2:00** (2:02) (Class 5) 2-Y-O **£3,881** (£1,155; £577; £288) **Stalls** Centre

Form RPR
**1** **Dance Diva** 2-9-0 0 ........ PaulHanagan 8 73+
(Richard Fahey) *rn green: in tch: effrt 2f out: led ent fnl f: changed legs cl home: r.o* **11/8**[1]
**2** *1/2* **Miss Dd (IRE)** 2-9-0 0 ........ BenCurtis 5 70
(Tom Dascombe) *a.p: rdn over 2f out: chalng ins fnl f: hld nr fin* **14/1**
**3** *2* **Astraea** 2-8-11 0 ........ NathanEvans(3) 10 64
(Michael Easterby) *w ldr: rdn over 2f out: stl ev ch ent fnl f: unable qck* **20/1**
0 **4** *1/2* **Dyson's Girl**[41] 1872 2-9-0 0 ........ ConnorBeasley 12 62
(Bryan Smart) *led: rdn 2f out: hdd ent fnl f: styd on same pce* **25/1**
**5** *3/4* **Paco Bleue** 2-9-0 0 ........ DavidAllan 4 60
(Tim Easterby) *in tch: rdn over 2f out: one pce ins fnl f* **16/1**
**6** *nk* **Patty Patch** 2-9-0 0 ........ (h[1]) GrahamLee 11 61+
(Richard Spencer) *towards rr: pushed along 1/2-way: green and hung lft whn effrt over 1f out: styd on: nt pce to chal* **10/1**
4 **7** *1 3/4* **Seaella (IRE)**[19] 2545 2-9-0 0 ........ JasonHart 2 54
(John Quinn) *sed awkwardly: towards rr: outpcd over 2f out: styd on u.p ins fnl f: nvr able to trble ldrs* **17/2**[3]
**8** *1/2* **Miss Van Winkle** 2-9-0 0 ........ FrannyNorton 6 52
(Mark Johnston) *w ldrs: rdn over 2f out: losing pl whn hmpd over 1f out: wknd after* **7/1**[2]
**9** *1* **Milan Reef (IRE)** 2-9-0 0 ........ SamJames 9 49
(David Loughnane) *dwlt: sn in midfield: rdn and wknd over 2f out* **66/1**
**10** *1/2* **Deauville Society (IRE)** 2-9-0 0 ........ RyanPowell 1 48+
(Sir Mark Prescott Bt) *hmpd s: a in rr: sn outpcd: nvr a threat* **14/1**
03 **11** *11* **Nsnas Alward**[19] 2545 2-9-0 0 ........ TomEaves 7 15
(Kevin Ryan) *restless in stalls: midfield: rdn and wknd over 2f out* **14/1**
**12** *2* **Tweeting** 2-9-0 0 ........ JackGarritty 3 9
(John Quinn) *green: a outpcd and bhd* **25/1**

1m 11.46s (-0.34) **Going Correction** 0.0s/f (Good) **12 Ran SP% 114.1**
Speed ratings (Par 90): **102,101,98,98,97 96,94,93,92,91 76,74**
CSF £20.06 TOTE £2.00: £1.20, £4.20, £5.60; EX 22.50 Trifecta £315.00.
**Owner** Cheveley Park Stud **Bred** Cheveley Park Stud Ltd **Trained** Musley Bank, N Yorks

**FOCUS**
There was 2mm of rain during racing the previous day and 1mm of rain overnight, but drying conditions on race day. The bare form of this fillies' novice event is probably just ordinary, but the winner made a good impression. The form will take time to settle.

## 3180 HIGH DEFINITION RACING UK MAIDEN H'CAP 1m 5f 218y
**2:30** (2:31) (Class 6) (0-65,65) 3-Y-O **£2,897** (£855; £427) **Stalls** Low

Form RPR
00-6 **1** **New Society (IRE)**[24] 2408 3-9-4 62 ........ PJMcDonald 3 72
(James Bethell) *a.p: rdn to ld over 1f out: r.o wl to draw clr ins fnl f: comf* **8/1**[3]

0-64 2 3 **Sheriff Garrett (IRE)**[15] 2686 3-8-10 **54** DavidAllan 8 59
(Tim Easterby) *led: jinked rt on bnd after jst over 1f: rdn and edgd rt 2f out: hdd over 1f out: kpt on same pce and unable to go w wnr ins fnl f* **5/1**[2]

0-40 3 ½ **Curtsy (IRE)**[25] 2371 3-8-11 **58** CharlieBennett(3) 5 62
(Hughie Morrison) *midfield: rdn over 3f out: hdwy 2f out: styd on ins fnl f: gng on at fin* **7/2**[1]

053- 4 1 **Bodacious Name (IRE)**[197] 7954 3-8-10 **54** JasonHart 10 57
(John Quinn) *racd keenly: midfield: u.p 4f out: hdwy on inner over 1f out: n.m.r and hmpd ins fnl f: styd on* **16/1**

0-06 5 1 **General Allenby**[25] 2371 3-8-2 **46** (be¹) AndrewMullen 4 47
(Henry Tett) *trckd ldrs: effrt over 2f out: outpcd by ldrs over 1f out: kpt on ins fnl f* **20/1**

60-2 6 ½ **Dirty Randy (IRE)**[44] 1822 3-9-3 **61** (p) DougieCostello 9 62
(Keith Dalgleish) *prom: forced sltly wd on bnd after jst over 1f: rdn over 2f out: edgd lft over 1f out: no ex fnl 100yds* **8/1**[3]

60-6 7 1 **Silver Gleam (IRE)**[14] 2705 3-8-9 **53** PaulHanagan 1 52+
(Chris Fairhurst) *in rr: u.p 5f out: hdwy over 3f out: styd on ins fnl f: nvr able to trble ldrs* **9/1**

6-50 8 3½ **Katmandoo (USA)**[20] 2527 3-9-7 **65** BenCurtis 7 59
(Tom Dascombe) *hld up: rdn and hdwy over 3f out: no imp on ldrs: one pce ins fnl f* **10/1**

6663 9 1 **Nothing Compares**[14] 2705 3-8-7 **51** FrannyNorton 6 43
(Mark Johnston) *in tch: pushed along over 4f out: rdn over 3f out: wknd 2f out* **8/1**[3]

545 10 ¾ **Tenby Two**[12] 2759 3-9-6 **64** GrahamLee 12 55
(Mick Channon) *hld up: u.p over 3f out: nvr a threat* **9/1**

60-0 11 ¾ **Mystic Maeve (IRE)**[139] 175 3-8-3 **47** JamesSullivan 2 37
(Roger Fell) *midfield: rdn and wknd 2f out* **50/1**

-500 12 47 **Full Tilt Lad (IRE)**[26] 2345 3-8-2 **46** oh1 DuranFentiman 11
(Tim Easterby) *dwlt: midfield: lost pl after 6f: u.p in rr 5f out: t.o* **33/1**

3m 4.53s (-0.17) **Going Correction** -0.025s/f (Good) **12 Ran SP% 116.9**
Speed ratings (Par 97): **99,97,97,96,95 95,95,93,92,92 91,64**
CSF £46.16 CT £167.53 TOTE £10.00: £3.20, £2.30, £1.50; EX 56.30 Trifecta £238.70.
**Owner** John Dance **Bred** Desert Star Phoenix Jvc **Trained** Middleham Moor, N Yorks

**FOCUS**
A moderate race in which it proved hard to make up ground, but a likeable performance from the winner.

## 3181 BRITISH RACING SCHOOL CHARITY CYCLE RIDE H'CAP 7f 219y
**3:00** (3:01) (Class 5) (0-70,70) 4-Y-O+ **£3,234** (£962; £481; £240) **Stalls** Centre

Form RPR

2423 1 **Wink Oliver**[27] 2297 5-9-6 **69** (p) DougieCostello 10 76
(Jo Hughes) *stdd s: hld up in rr: smooth hdwy travelling wl 3f out: produced to chal ins fnl f: styd on to ld fnl 50yds: gd ride* **16/1**

00-5 2 hd **Thornaby Nash**[7] 2918 6-8-11 **60** TomEaves 11 66
(Karen Tutty) *prom: rdn to ld over 1f out: pressed ins fnl f: hdd fnl 50yds: kpt on* **20/1**

0223 3 1¾ **Cabal**[8] 2900 10-9-0 **63** (b) DavidAllan 8 65
(Geoffrey Harker) *in tch: rdn over 2f out: ev ch over 1f out: styd on same pce wl ins fnl f* **11/2**[2]

6455 4 ½ **Lozah**[7] 2919 4-8-13 **62** ConnorBeasley 13 63
(Roger Fell) *hld up: hdwy over 1f out: styd on ins fnl f: nvr able to chal* **12/1**

2050 5 3 **Curzon Line**[31] 2161 8-9-4 **70** NathanEvans(3) 9 64
(Michael Easterby) *led: rdn over 2f out: hdd over 1f out: no ex fnl 100yds* **9/2**[1]

-050 6 1½ **Willsy**[4] 3049 4-8-11 **65** GemmaTutty(5) 6 55
(Karen Tutty) *midfield: rdn over 2f out: one pce ins fnl f* **20/1**

12-0 7 nse **Jordan James (IRE)**[23] 2430 4-9-7 **70** BenCurtis 4 60
(Brian Ellison) *prom: rdn over 2f out: wknd over 1f out* **11/2**[2]

4313 8 1½ **Newmarket Warrior (IRE)**[50] 1677 6-9-0 **70** (p) JamieGormley(7) 3 57
(Iain Jardine) *in rr: rdn over 2f out: kpt on fnl f: nvr able to trble ldrs: lame* **9/2**[1]

105- 9 ½ **Im Dapper Too**[217] 7601 6-8-11 **60** SamJames 2 46
(John Davies) *in tch: rdn over 2f out: wknd over 1f out* **6/1**[3]

3/0- 10 3¾ **Dylan's Storm (IRE)**[14] 3002 5-8-13 **62** (p) PaulMulrennan 7 39
(Peter Niven) *in tch: rdn and wknd 2f out* **66/1**

503- 11 2½ **Quoteline Direct**[210] 7755 4-9-0 **63** (h) PJMcDonald 1 34
(Micky Hammond) *midfield: rdn 2f out: wknd over 1f out* **14/1**

30-0 12 1½ **By The Law**[32] 2119 4-9-2 **65** DuranFentiman 5 33
(Tim Easterby) *hld up: rdn over 3f out: sn outpcd: nvr a threat* **33/1**

1m 36.1s (-0.50) **Going Correction** 0.0s/f (Good) **12 Ran SP% 115.6**
Speed ratings (Par 103): **102,101,100,99,96 95,95,93,93,89 86,85**
CSF £299.50 CT £1981.92 TOTE £12.60: £4.00, £6.50, £2.20; EX 290.00 Trifecta £2887.70.
**Owner** P & L Partners **Bred** Norman Court Stud **Trained** Lambourn, Berks

**FOCUS**
A modest handicap.

## 3182 RACING UK HD ON SKY432 MEDIAN AUCTION MAIDEN STKS 1m 2f 1y
**3:30** (3:30) (Class 5) 3-5-Y-O **£3,234** (£962; £481; £240) **Stalls** Low

Form RPR

4 1 **Near Kettering**[22] 2475 3-9-0 0 JamieSpencer 3 79+
(Luca Cumani) *racd in 2nd pl: led over 2f out: hdd narrowly jst over 1f out: bmpd ins fnl f: regained ld fnl 110yds: kpt on gamely* **2/1**[2]

2-23 2 hd **Pattie**[12] 2761 3-8-9 73 GrahamLee 6 73
(Mick Channon) *hld up: hdwy over 2f out: sn chalng: led narrowly jst over 1f out: lent on rival ins fnl f: hdd fnl 110yds: kpt on: jst hld* **2/1**[2]

3- 3 5 **Bolder Bob (IRE)**[218] 7580 3-9-0 0 PhillipMakin 1 68
(David Barron) *led: rdn and hdd over 2f out: no ex ins fnl f: outpcd by front two fnl 150yds* **7/4**[1]

4 ¾ **Count Simon (IRE)** 3-9-0 0 PJMcDonald 5 67
(Andrew Balding) *chsd ldrs: rdn over 4f out: outpcd over 1f out: green and kpt on ins fnl f* **12/1**[3]

66 5 14 **Nuova Scuola**[10] 2841 4-9-9 0 SamJames 4 35
(Jim Goldie) *in rr: rdn over 4f out: lft bhd fnl 3f* **66/1**

2m 6.73s (-0.37) **Going Correction** -0.025s/f (Good)
**WFA** 3 from 4yo 14lb **5 Ran SP% 112.2**
Speed ratings (Par 103): **100,99,95,95,84**
CSF £6.57 TOTE £2.90: £1.30, £1.30; EX 5.90 Trifecta £8.80.
**Owner** Mrs A Silver & C Bloor **Bred** Michael E Broughton **Trained** Newmarket, Suffolk

**FOCUS**
A fair maiden.

## 3183 RACING UK IN GLORIOUS HD H'CAP 5f
**4:00** (4:01) (Class 4) (0-85,87) 4-Y-O+ **£6,469** (£1,925; £962; £481) **Stalls** Centre

Form RPR

510 1 **Lydia's Place**[8] 2899 4-8-13 **78** CliffordLee(5) 1 84
(Richard Guest) *led main gp: overall ld 2f out: rdn and edgd rt over 1f out: r.o ins fnl f* **11/2**[3]

010- 2 ½ **Economic Crisis (IRE)**[262] 6324 8-9-1 **75** PaulMulrennan 6 79
(Colin Teague) *a.p: effrt whn checked over 1f out: r.o ins fnl f: hld nr fin* **33/1**

0150 3 nk **Foxtrot Knight**[15] 2683 5-9-5 **79** JamesSullivan 9 82
(Ruth Carr) *dwlt: in rr: swtchd lft and hdwy over 1f out: r.o ins fnl f: no ex fnl strides* **8/1**

0-10 4 hd **Black Grass**[4] 3052 4-9-4 **81** NathanEvans(3) 11 83
(Michael Easterby) *in tch: rdn over 1f out: r.o towards fin* **9/2**[2]

0032 5 1¼ **Extrasolar**[5] 2990 7-8-12 **72** (p) PhillipMakin 10 70
(Geoffrey Harker) *midfield: hdwy over 1f out: styd on ins fnl f: nt quite pce of ldrs* **7/2**[1]

3360 6 shd **Just Us Two (IRE)**[24] 2391 5-9-6 **80** (p) DavidAllan 8 78
(Robert Cowell) *prom: rdn over 1f out: no ex fnl 100yds* **13/2**

5060 7 ¾ **First Bombardment**[4] 3052 4-9-0 **81** (t¹) PatrickVaughan(7) 5 76
(David O'Meara) *in tch: rdn 1/2-way one pce ins fnl f* **10/1**

6-44 8 1½ **Desert Ace (IRE)**[26] 2341 6-9-3 **77** (b¹) DougieCostello 2 66
(Iain Jardine) *swtchd lft s: racd alone far side: overall ld tl 2f out: rdn over 1f out: wknd fnl f* **8/1**

523- 9 1½ **Rosina**[209] 7772 4-9-7 **81** JoeyHaynes 4 65
(Ann Duffield) *in rr: rdn over 1f out: nvr able to trble ldrs* **9/1**

58.33s (-0.27) **Going Correction** 0.0s/f (Good) **9 Ran SP% 113.4**
Speed ratings (Par 105): **102,101,100,100,98 98,97,94,92**
CSF £156.32 CT £1438.77 TOTE £6.30: £2.00, £7.10, £2.90; EX 189.50 Trifecta £1312.20.
**Owner** Alfa Site Services Ltd & Partner **Bred** Ashbrittle Stud & Brendan Boyle **Trained** Ingmanthorpe, W Yorks

**FOCUS**
A fair, competitive sprint handicap.

## 3184 RACING UK PROFITS RETURNED TO RACING H'CAP 5f 217y
**4:30** (4:33) (Class 5) (0-70,72) 3-Y-O **£3,234** (£962; £481; £240) **Stalls** Centre

Form RPR

0-01 1 **Kaeso**[30] 2181 3-9-0 **62** TomEaves 7 74
(Nigel Tinkler) *hld up in rr: hdwy over 2f out: led wl over 1f out: r.o wl to draw clr ins fnl f* **7/2**[2]

1033 2 3 **Logi (IRE)**[21] 2499 3-9-10 **72** PhillipMakin 1 74
(David Barron) *upset in stalls: in tch: effrt 2f out: wnt 2nd 1f out: no ch w wnr ins fnl f* **5/2**[1]

-016 3 2¼ **Cryptonite (IRE)**[22] 2470 3-8-12 **60** (p¹) BenCurtis 6 55
(Michael Appleby) *led: rdn and hdd wl over 1f out: kpt on same pce ins fnl f* **6/1**

5611 4 2¾ **Endeavour (IRE)**[45] 1786 3-9-4 **66** JamesSullivan 10 52
(Marjorie Fife) *w ldr: ev ch 2f out: rdn and nt qckn over 1f out: fdd ins fnl f* **12/1**

3-20 5 1¾ **Bahamian Paradise**[22] 2474 3-8-12 **63** CharlieBennett(3) 8 43
(Hughie Morrison) *midfield: hmpd over 2f out: sn rdn: nvr able to trble ldrs* **7/1**

30-3 6 1 **Eltanin (IRE)**[46] 1782 3-9-7 **69** JasonHart 5 46
(John Quinn) *in rr: pushed along 1/2-way: rdn and and no imp 2f out: nvr a threat* **11/2**[3]

00-5 7 hd **Bay Station**[109] 657 3-9-1 **68** CliffordLee(5) 3 45
(Jason Ward) *trckd ldrs: swtchd rt over 2f out: wknd over 1f out* **33/1**

0441 8 nk **Night Shadow**[77] 1193 3-9-1 **63** PaulMulrennan 11 39
(Alan Brown) *midfield: losing pl whn hmpd over 2f out: n.d after* **22/1**

5-26 9 ½ **Judy Woods (IRE)**[30] 2181 3-9-2 **64** ConnorBeasley 4 38
(Bryan Smart) *in rr: outpcd 1/2-way: nvr a threat* **9/1**

1m 11.43s (-0.37) **Going Correction** 0.0s/f (Good) **9 Ran SP% 117.9**
Speed ratings (Par 99): **102,98,95,91,89 87,87,87,86**
CSF £13.00 CT £51.31 TOTE £4.30: £1.60, £2.10, £1.80; EX 16.90 Trifecta £102.90.
**Owner** M Webb **Bred** Sir Eric Parker **Trained** Langton, N Yorks
■ Stewards' Enquiry : Clifford Lee 2 day ban - guilty of careless riding in that he had allowed his mount to drift right without sufficient correction (13/14 June)

**FOCUS**
An ordinary race but a winner to keep on side.

## 3185 FOLLOW REDCARRACING ON FACEBOOK & TWITTER AMATEUR RIDERS' MAIDEN H'CAP 5f 217y
**5:00** (5:02) (Class 6) (0-65,57) 4-Y-O+ **£2,799** (£861; £430) **Stalls** Centre

Form RPR

4-05 1 **Concur (IRE)**[30] 2178 4-10-3 **46** (tp) MrPMillman 10 52
(Rod Millman) *hld up in midfield: rdn and hdwy over 2f out: led over 1f out: styd on ins fnl f* **8/1**

405 2 1¼ **Kensington Palace (IRE)**[10] 2819 4-11-0 **57** (p¹) MissBeckySmith 11 59
(Marjorie Fife) *bhd: rdn 2f out: hdwy 2f out: r.o towards fin: nt rch wnr* **6/1**[3]

-605 3 nk **Bingo George (IRE)**[7] 2917 4-10-4 **52** PoppyBridgwater(5) 2 53
(Andrew Balding) *in tch: prom 1/2-way: rdn 2f out: ev ch ins fnl f: nt qckn: no ex nr fin* **9/2**[2]

0646 4 1 **Jessie Allan (IRE)**[22] 2454 6-9-11 **45** MissRHill(5) 5 43
(Jim Goldie) *midfield: hdwy over 1f out: chsd ldrs ins fnl f: kpt on* **9/1**

5066 5 ¾ **Ryedale Rio (IRE)**[17] 2628 4-10-10 **53** (b) MrWEasterby 4 49
(Tim Easterby) *chsd ldrs: rdn 2f out: nt qckn over 1f out: styd on same pce ins fnl f* **10/1**

/00- 6 hd **Shudbeme**[351] 3224 4-10-2 **45** (p) MissCWalton 7 41+
(Neville Bycroft) *bhd: rdn and edgd lft whn hdwy over 1f out: styd on ins fnl f: nvr able to trble ldrs* **66/1**

-234 7 1½ **Our Place In Loule**[17] 2633 4-10-7 **50** (p¹) MissSBrotherton 1 41
(Noel Wilson) *unruly bef r: led: rdn and hdd over 1f out: fdd ins fnl f* **7/4**[1]

00-0 8 5 **Grandad Chunk (IRE)**[26] 2342 6-9-11 **45** MrBLynn(5) 9 21
(Colin Teague) *hld up: rdn 1/2-way: rdn 2f out: wknd ent fnl f* **22/1**

400- 9 6 **Jacksonfire**[197] 7960 5-10-2 **45** (p) MissMMullineaux 8 3
(Michael Mullineaux) *towards rr: pushed long bef 1/2-way: nvr able to get on terms w ldrs* **33/1**

06-0 10 nse **Tweetheart**[8] 2898 4-10-6 **49** (h) MissEmmaSayer 6 7
(Ron Barr) *sed awkwardly: in rr: plugged on fnl f: nvr a threat* **28/1**

0540 11 ¾ **Dalalah**[17] 2633 4-10-3 **46** (b¹) MissJoannaMason 12 2
(Richard Guest) *sed awkwardly: sn chsd ldrs: rdn and wknd over 1f out* **16/1**

000- **12** ½ **Kylla**294 5270 4-10-2 **45**..........(v¹) MissAWaugh 3
(Shaun Harris) *prom tl rdn and wknd 2f out* **100/1**

1m 12.75s (0.95) **Going Correction** 0.0s/f (Good) **12** Ran SP% **118.1**
Speed ratings (Par 101): **93,91,90,89,88 88,86,79,71,71 70,69**
CSF £52.96 CT £248.72 TOTE £9.30: £2.70, £2.40, £1.40; EX 67.10 Trifecta £344.40.
**Owner** Miss Gloria Abbey **Bred** Miss Annmarie Burke **Trained** Kentisbeare, Devon

**FOCUS**
A moderate race and the first two came from off what looked a strong pace, and like a couple of other winners on the card they challenged towards the stands' rail.
T/Jkpt: Not Won. T/Plt: £375.30 to a £1 stake. Pool: £62,470.79 - 121.51 winning units T/Qpdt: £89.20 to a £1 stake. Pool: £4,146.65 - 34.37 winning units **Darren Owen**

## 2306 WOLVERHAMPTON (A.W) (L-H)
### Tuesday, May 30

**OFFICIAL GOING: Tapeta: standard**
Wind: Light breeze Weather: Warm, sunny intervals

## 3186 JOIN THE BLACK COUNTRY CHAMBER OF COMMERCE H'CAP 5f 21y (Tp)
**6:10** (6:10) (Class 6) (0-65,65) 3-Y-O+ **£2,264** (£673; £336; £168) **Stalls** Low

Form RPR

44-3 **1** **Absolutely Awesome**129 357 3-9-3 **64**.......... JFEgan 9 68
(John Butler) *trckd ldrs: hdwy into 2nd over 2f out: rdn over 1f out: led last 100yds: on top nr fin* **3/1**¹

2010 **2** ½ **Cruise Tothelimit (IRE)**48 1722 9-9-3 **63**..........(bt¹) ConnorMurtagh(7) 3 68
(Patrick Morris) *led: 3 l clr 2f out: rdn appr fnl f: hdd last 100yds* **9/1**

0052 **3** nk **Dandilion (IRE)**25 2370 4-9-0 **56**..........(t) CallumShepherd(3) 5 60
(Alex Hales) *hld up: hdwy on outer over 2f out: rdn and r.o strly fnl f* **7/2**²

4010 **4** 3 **Llewellyn**10 2843 9-9-2 **60**..........(v) PhilDennis(5) 1 53
(Declan Carroll) *trckd ldrs on inner: pushed along 2f out: rdn over 1f out: one pce* **11/1**

-001 **5** hd **Frangarry (IRE)**25 2370 5-9-7 **60**.......... JosephineGordon 8 52
(Alan Bailey) *mid-div: rdn along 2f out: no imp* **7/1**

-000 **6** 2¾ **Bop It**27 2305 8-9-4 **64**..........(t) HarrisonShaw(7) 6 47
(Michael Easterby) *mid-div: u.p over 2f out: one pce* **12/1**

00-0 **7** 1¼ **Total Power**14 2700 4-9-5 **65**.......... BenRobinson(7) 7 43
(Brian Ellison) *hld up: drvn over 2f out: rdn appr fnl f: no imp* **13/2**³

600- **8** shd **Your Gifted (IRE)**318 4378 10-9-2 **62**..........(v) JordanUys(7) 2 40
(Lisa Williamson) *in rr: drvn over 2f out: nvr a factor* **40/1**

6504 **9** ¾ **Archie Stevens**40 1896 7-9-4 **62**.......... PaddyPilley(5) 11 37
(Clare Ellam) *hld up: effrt on outer over 2f out: rdn and no rspnse* **25/1**

6-00 **10** ¾ **The Perfect Show**6 2962 4-9-5 **58**.......... RobertWinston 4 30
(Milton Bradley) *prom: 2nd 1/2-way: lost 2nd wl over 2f out: sn rdn and wknd* **12/1**

1m 1.63s (-0.27) **Going Correction** 0.0s/f (Stan)
**WFA** 3 from 4yo+ 8lb **10** Ran SP% **113.1**
Speed ratings (Par 101): **102,101,100,95,95 91,89,89,87,86**
CSF £29.56 CT £99.28 TOTE £4.60: £1.70, £2.60, £1.40; EX 31.80 Trifecta £102.50.
**Owner** Mark McKay **Bred** Willie McKay **Trained** Newmarket, Suffolk
■ Stewards' Enquiry : J F Egan 2 day ban - guilty of careless riding in that he allowed his mount to drift left-handed towards the rail when insufficiently clear (13/14 June)

**FOCUS**
A moderate sprint to open the card and very few got into contention from off the pace. The runner-up has been rated to his recent C&D form.

## 3187 INVEST CITY OF WOLVERHAMPTON NOVICE STKS (PLUS 10 RACE) 6f 20y (Tp)
**6:40** (6:41) (Class 4) 2-Y-O **£3,946** (£1,174; £586; £293) **Stalls** Low

Form RPR

**1** **Awsaaf** 2-9-2 0.......... AdamKirby 10 76
(Simon Crisford) *broke wl: led: kicked on 2f out: rdn over 1f out: edgd rt and rn green ins fnl f but a in control: comf* **3/1**¹

46 **2** 2¼ **Our Man In Havana**10 2816 2-9-2 0.......... RichardKingscote 6 69
(Tom Dascombe) *mid-div on outer: prog over 2f out: pushed along ent fnl f: r.o wl* **6/1**³

30 **3** shd **Crownthorpe**29 2221 2-8-13 0.......... SammyJoBell(3) 11 69
(Richard Fahey) *hld up: hdwy over 2f out: pushed along inide fnl f: r.o wl* **14/1**

20 **4** ¾ **Kheleyf's Girl**46 1776 2-8-11 0.......... JFEgan 2 62
(David Evans) *chsd ldr: stl 2nd and rdn over 1f out: one pce ent fnl f* **22/1**

53 **5** 1¾ **Global Exceed**7 2926 2-9-2 0.......... JimmyQuinn 5 62
(Ed Dunlop) *trckd ldrs: 3rd 2f out: rdn over 1f out: wknd ins fnl f* **16/1**

4 **6** 1¾ **Shania Says (IRE)**18 2583 2-8-11 0.......... WilliamCarson 13 51+
(Tony Carroll) *hld up: pushed along and r.o one pce fnl 2 fs* **28/1**

**7** nk **Jaalboot** 2-9-2 0.......... DaneO'Neill 3 55
(Owen Burrows) *mid-div: pushed along 2f out: rdn over 1f out: styd on one pce* **5/1**²

**8** 1¾ **Mr Carbonator** 2-8-13 0.......... AdamMcNamara(3) 9 50
(Richard Fahey) *in rr: pushed along over 2f out: one pce under hand riding fnl f* **33/1**

0 **9** 1 **Tony Soprano (IRE)**39 1941 2-9-2 0.......... HarryBentley 8 47
(Martyn Meade) *hld up: hrd rdn over 2f out: no imp* **15/2**

**10** 1¾ **Puramente** 2-9-2 0.......... AndrewMullen 4 42
(Jo Hughes) *slowly away: a in rr* **50/1**

2 **11** 2 **Trusting Friend (USA)**24 2403 2-9-2 0.......... KevinStott 7 36
(Kevin Ryan) *trckd ldrs: rdn and lost pl appr 2f out: wknd* **3/1**¹

1m 15.43s (0.93) **Going Correction** 0.0s/f (Stan) **11** Ran SP% **118.0**
Speed ratings (Par 95): **93,90,89,88,86 84,83,81,80,77 75**
CSF £20.56 TOTE £3.80: £1.40, £1.80, £3.90; EX 24.40 Trifecta £274.20.
**Owner** Hamdan Al Maktoum **Bred** Lordship Stud **Trained** Newmarket, Suffolk

**FOCUS**
Some speedily bred juveniles on show in this novice stakes and one of the newcomers was too good for more experienced rivals.

## 3188 UNIVERSITY OF WOLVERHAMPTON RACING MAIDEN STKS 7f 36y (Tp)
**7:10** (7:13) (Class 5) 3-Y-O **£3,234** (£962; £481; £240) **Stalls** High

Form RPR

23 **1** **Dhalam (USA)**38 1962 3-9-5 0..........(t¹) FrankieDettori 8 81
(John Gosden) *prom: trckd ldrs: wnt 2nd 3f out: pushed along 2f out: rdn and led ins fnl f: pushed out to maintain dwindling advantage: jst hld on* **2/5**¹

63- **2** nse **Narjes**232 7209 3-8-9 0..........(h¹) GeorgeWood(5) 7 76
(James Fanshawe) *mid-div: pushed along 2f out: rdn appr fnl f: r.o strly and clsd on wnr ins fnl f: jst failed* **12/1**³

3 **3** nse **Inshiraah (FR)**14 2704 3-9-0 0.......... AndrewMullen 3 76
(George Peckham) *trckd ldrs: effrt over 2f out: rdn and r.o wl ins fnl f* **50/1**

**4** ¾ **Tamih (IRE)** 3-9-5 0.......... JackMitchell 1 79
(Roger Varian) *mid-div: prog 2f out: rdn over 1f out: r.o ins fnl f* **25/1**

- **5** 2¾ **Plutonian (IRE)** 3-9-2 0.......... CallumShepherd(3) 4 71
(Charles Hills) *trckd ldrs: pushed along over 2f out: rdn over 1f out: one pce* **20/1**

3 **6** ¾ **Karijini (GER)**22 2463 3-9-0 0.......... DaneO'Neill 10 64
(Simon Crisford) *led: rdn and hdd ins fnl f: wknd* **4/1**²

2-0 **7** 1½ **Natajack**58 1513 3-9-2 0.......... AdamMcNamara(3) 9 65
(Richard Fahey) *hld up: rdn 2f out: one pce* **16/1**

**8** nse **Blazed (IRE)** 3-9-5 0.......... FranBerry 5 65
(Roger Charlton) *hld up: effrt over 2f out: rdn and one pce fnl f* **16/1**

**9** 11 **Wolfcatcherjack (IRE)** 3-9-5 0.......... RyanPowell 12 35
(Sir Mark Prescott Bt) *hld up in last: drvn over 2f out: no imp* **50/1**

**10** 1¾ **Emilene** 3-9-0 0..........(h¹) WilliamCarson 11 26
(Mark Brisbourne) *hld up on outer: effrt 1/2-way and sn pushed along: grad lost tch* **200/1**

4 **11** 2 **Mystery Of War (IRE)**111 615 3-8-12 0.......... FletcherYarham(7) 2 25
(George Scott) *slowly away: a in rr* **66/1**

1m 28.43s (-0.37) **Going Correction** 0.0s/f (Stan) **11** Ran SP% **125.4**
Speed ratings (Par 99): **102,101,101,101,97 97,95,95,82,80 78**
CSF £7.45 TOTE £1.40: £1.02, £2.70, £10.00; EX 8.70 Trifecta £76.90.
**Owner** Abdullah Saeed Al Naboodah **Bred** Waymore Llc **Trained** Newmarket, Suffolk

**FOCUS**
An inexperienced bunch in this 3yo maiden but with a number of major yards represented it could prove a fair contest of its type. It's been rated around the winner.

## 3189 AT THE RACES VIRGIN 535 FILLIES' H'CAP 1m 142y (Tp)
**7:40** (7:42) (Class 5) (0-75,77) 3-Y-O+ **£3,072** (£914; £456; £228) **Stalls** Low

Form RPR

6-24 **1** **Favourite Royal (IRE)**31 2151 3-9-0 **74**.......... RobertWinston 5 80
(Eve Johnson Houghton) *hld up in 5th: swished tail 3f out: hdwy over 2f out: chal between front two ent fnl f: rdn to ld fnl 150yds: r.o wl* **5/2**²

03-1 **2** hd **Ghadaayer (IRE)**34 2078 3-9-3 **77**.......... JimCrowley 7 82
(Sir Michael Stoute) *trckd ldr: led 2f out: briefly hdd over 1f out: sn regained ld u.p: passed again 150yds out: r.o but jst hld* **1/1**¹

6-10 **3** 2 **Nostalgie**12 2754 3-9-3 **77**.......... MartinHarley 8 78
(James Tate) *trckd ldrs: chsd 2nd 2f out: rdn and led briefly over 1f out: sn lost advantage and wknd wl ins fnl f* **9/2**³

0-05 **4** 2 **Beatbybeatbybeat**18 2587 4-9-10 **71**..........(v) CamHardie 6 69
(Antony Brittain) *hld up in last: effrt over 2f out: rdn and r.o one pce fnl f* **33/1**

46-0 **5** 6 **Duchess Of Fife**24 2394 3-8-5 **65**.......... JosephineGordon 4 47
(William Knight) *chsd ldrs: bmpd along 5f out and 3f out: drvn over 2f out: wknd* **12/1**

24-3 **6** 1½ **Royal Icon**50 1680 3-8-5 **65**.......... JoeDoyle 3 44
(Kevin Ryan) *led: hdd and pushed along 2f out: sn rdn and wknd* **16/1**

1m 49.71s (-0.39) **Going Correction** 0.0s/f (Stan)
**WFA** 3 from 4yo 13lb **6** Ran SP% **113.3**
Speed ratings (Par 100): **101,100,99,97,91 90**
CSF £5.47 CT £8.82 TOTE £3.90: £1.50, £1.40; EX 6.50 Trifecta £13.40.
**Owner** J Cross,M Duckham,L Godfrey,P Wollaston **Bred** Emma Capon Bloodstock **Trained** Blewbury, Oxon

**FOCUS**
This modest fillies' handicap was run at a steady pace early and developed into something of a sprint in the straight. The third and fourth help set the level.

## 3190 INVEST CITY OF WOLVERHAMPTON H'CAP 2m 120y (Tp)
**8:10** (8:11) (Class 4) (0-85,86) 4-Y-O+ **£4,851** (£1,443; £721; £360) **Stalls** Low

Form RPR

00-0 **1** **Gabrial's Star**18 2574 8-9-4 **83**..........(p) AdamMcNamara(3) 5 89
(Richard Fahey) *hld up: hdwy on outer over 2f out: rdn and qcknd to ld ins fnl f: comf* **3/1**²

110- **2** 2 **Little Stampy (IRE)**20 2535 6-8-7 **69** oh1..........(p) ShaneGray 1 72
(D Broad, Ire) *trckd ldrs: drvn 2f out: ev ch whn rdn over 1f out: pushed along and tk 2nd last 100yds* **5/1**³

1115 **3** nk **Masterson (IRE)**17 2622 4-9-0 **78**.......... SilvestreDeSousa 3 81
(Mick Channon) *led: qcknd pce 4f out: kicked on over 2f out: rdn over 1f out: hdd ins fnl f: one pce* **6/5**¹

55-0 **4** 1¾ **Lady Makfi (IRE)**64 1405 5-9-0 **76**.......... StevieDonohoe 4 77
(Johnny Farrelly) *hld up: last 2f out: briefly rdn and wnt 4th over 1f out: one pce* **8/1**

615 **5** 1½ **Zakatal**11 2788 11-9-10 **86**.......... DougieCostello 2 85
(Rebecca Menzies) *racd in 2nd: pushed along over 2f out: lost position over 1f out: wknd* **8/1**

3m 43.92s (0.22) **Going Correction** 0.0s/f (Stan)
**WFA** 4 from 5yo+ 1lb **5** Ran SP% **109.3**
Speed ratings (Par 105): **99,98,97,97,96**
CSF £17.15 TOTE £4.00: £1.70, £2.60; EX 16.50 Trifecta £30.10.
**Owner** Dr Marwan Koukash **Bred** Miss K Rausing **Trained** Musley Bank, N Yorks

**FOCUS**
The feature race and a fair contest despite the small field. They seemed to go an even gallop but it went to the horse with the best turn of pace. A small pb from the runner-up, with the third rated to form.

## 3191 INVEST WOLVERHAMPTON - WORLD OR INWARD INVESTMENT H'CAP 1m 142y (Tp)
**8:40** (8:42) (Class 6) (0-60,60) 3-Y-O **£2,264** (£673; £336; £168) **Stalls** Low

Form RPR

-001 **1** **Ching Ching Lor (IRE)**22 2455 3-9-1 **54**.......... TomEaves 7 65
(Declan Carroll) *trckd ldrs: reminders 3f out: drvn 2f out: rdn and hdwy to ld ins fnl f: on top last 100yds* **11/2**³

3-40 **2** ¾ **Varun's Bride (IRE)**15 2679 3-8-13 **52**.......... SilvestreDeSousa 6 61
(Richard Hannon) *racd in 2nd: led over 2f out: hrd rdn over 1f out: hdd ins fnl f: no ex* **5/1**²

1-04 **3** ¾ **Snookered (IRE)**26 2347 3-9-4 **60**.......... AdamMcNamara(3) 5 68
(Richard Fahey) *t.k.h early: mid-div: rdn over 2f out: hdwy and r.o wl ins fnl f* **11/4**¹

0034 **4** ½ **Love And Be Loved**35 2060 3-8-12 **51**.......... DanielMuscutt 10 58
(John Flint) *led tl hdd after 2f: remained prom: pushed along 2f out: 3rd and rdn over 1f out: one pce fnl f* **14/1**

-240 **5** 4 **A Bit Of Ginger**26 2349 3-9-3 **56**.......... ShaneGray 2 54
(Ann Duffield) *mid-div: effrt 2f out: rdn over 1f out: styd on ins fnl f* **12/1**

5000 **6** *nk* **Seeking Attention (USA)**27 2315 3-9-0 **53**...............(b1) OisinMurphy 4 51
(George Scott) *slowly away: racd rnd field to ld after 2 fs: rdn and hdd over 2f out: wknd* **16/1**
0-46 **7** *1 1/4* **Primadonia**17 2620 3-9-7 **60**.................................... FranBerry 9 55
(Richard Hughes) *mid-div: pushed along 3f out: drvn 2f out: one pce* **16/1**
0600 **8** *1 1/2* **Greyjoy (IRE)**13 2726 3-8-10 **49**.................................... RobHornby 1 41
(Sylvester Kirk) *hld up: effrt 2f out: rdn over 1f out: no imp* **10/1**
40-0 **9** *nk* **Embleton**13 2734 3-8-8 **52**.................................... LewisEdmunds(5) 3 43
(Charlie Wallis) *hld up: drvn and swtchd to outer wl over 1f out: one pce* **66/1**
00-0 **10** *nse* **Peking Flyer (IRE)**52 1619 3-8-13 **52**...............(t1) RichardKingscote 12 43
(Ed Walker) *hld up in last: nvr a threat* **7/1**
**11** *1/2* **Mick The Poser (IRE)**351 3237 3-8-7 **46** oh1.............. AndrewMullen 8 36
(Jennie Candlish) *mid-div: rdn 3f out: no rspnse* **33/1**
-000 **12** *3 1/4* **Seeing Things (IRE)**35 2060 3-9-5 **58**...............(t) JosephineGordon 11 41
(Philip McBride) *hld up: rowed along over 2f out: no imp* **12/1**

1m 51.67s (1.57) **Going Correction** 0.0s/f (Stan) **12** Ran SP% **118.6**
Speed ratings (Par 97): **93,92,91,91,87 87,86,84,84,84 84,81**
CSF £33.14 CT £92.84 TOTE £6.60: £2.30, £2.00, £1.30; EX 42.00 Trifecta £97.90.
**Owner** C H Stephenson & David Tate **Bred** Michael G Daly **Trained** Malton, N Yorks

**FOCUS**
The time of this moderate handicap was 1.96 secs slower than the earlier fillies' race over the trip. The form looks fair for the grade, though. The runner-up helps set the opening level.

## 3192 INVEST WOLVERHAMPTON - CITY OF OPPORTUNITY H'CAP 1m 4f 51y (Tp)
**9:10** (9:10) (Class 6) (0-60,58) 4-Y-0+ **£2,264** (£673; £336; £168) **Stalls** Low

Form RPR
1-04 **1** **Infiniti (IRE)**27 2308 4-8-10 **54**.................................... JaneElliott(7) 7 61
(Barry Leavy) *trckd ldrs: hdwy to ld over 2f out: sn kicked 2 l clr: rdn over 1f out: r.o strly ins fnl f: readily* **5/1**2
2/0- **2** *1* **Sir Dylan**20 684 8-8-13 **50**..............................(h) RobertWinston 11 55
(Polly Gundry) *mid-div: hdwy to trck ldr over 2f out: rdn over 1f out: r.o wl but nvr catching wnr* **7/1**
0-06 **3** *3/4* **Cool Music (IRE)**28 2272 7-9-2 **53**..............................(p) CamHardie 9 57
(Antony Brittain) *hld up: hdwy on outer over 3f out: 4th 2f out: hrd rdn to take 3rd over 1f out: r.o* **10/1**
0-60 **4** *3 1/4* **Pretty Jewel**36 2042 4-9-7 **58**..............................(h1) RobHornby 10 57
(Kevin Frost) *hld up: hdwy over 2f out: hrd rdn and r.o fnl 2 fs* **12/1**
6066 **5** *1* **Yul Finegold (IRE)**109 661 7-9-6 **57**.................... JosephineGordon 1 54
(Conor Dore) *mid-div: drvn 2f out: hrd rdn wl over 1f out: one pce* **14/1**
6404 **6** *1/2* **Whitecliff Park (IRE)**15 2688 4-9-0 **58**...................(p1) BenRobinson(7) 3 55
(Brian Ellison) *slowly away: hld up: sme hdwy fnl 2 fs: but nvr a threat* **2/1**1
4260 **7** *4* **Dove Mountain (IRE)**74 1249 6-9-0 **58**...............(tp) JoshuaBryan(7) 12 48
(Anabel K Murphy) *hld up in last: mod hdwy last 2 fs* **14/1**
4050 **8** *14* **Frap**28 2272 4-8-13 **50**.................................... StevieDonohoe 2 18
(Ian Williams) *trckd ldrs: bmpd along 3f out: sn rdn and wknd* **6/1**3
/06- **9** *1* **Sailor Malan**356 3041 5-9-7 **58**..............................(h1) DannyBrock 6 24
(Suzy Smith) *racd in 2nd: led 3f out: pushed along and hdd 2f out: rdn and wknd* **25/1**
-000 **10** *16* **Speculator**85 1067 5-9-6 **57**..............................(p) AdamKirby 4
(John Butler) *led and looked difficult ride: cocked jaw 7f out: niggled and hdd 3f out: bmpd along and no rspnse* **10/1**

2m 38.0s (-2.80) **Going Correction** 0.0s/f (Stan) **10** Ran SP% **119.8**
Speed ratings (Par 101): **109,108,107,105,105 104,102,92,92,81**
CSF £41.17 CT £343.45 TOTE £5.80: £2.00, £3.10, £2.80; EX 41.60 Trifecta £198.80.
**Owner** Frank Dronzek & Mrs Susan Ashford **Bred** Allevamento Ficomontanino Srl **Trained** Forsbrook, Staffs

**FOCUS**
A low-grade middle distance handicap in which they finished fairly strung out. The winner proved the most straightforward. The runner-up has been rated in line with his old Flat form, but his hurdle form suggests higher is possible.
T/Plt: £23.40 to a £1 stake. Pool: £76,287.81 - 2377.16 winning units T/Qpdt: £5.50 to a £1 stake. Pool: £6,934.61 - 929.63 winning units **Keith McHugh**

# 2948 AYR (L-H)
## Wednesday, May 31
**OFFICIAL GOING: Good (good to firm in places; 8.3)**
Wind: Light, half against Weather: Overcast

## 3193 RACING UK H'CAP (FOR LADY AMATEUR RIDERS) 1m 5f 26y
**6:10** (6:10) (Class 6) (0-65,64) 4-Y-0+ **£2,495** (£774; £386; £193) **Stalls** Low

Form RPR
**1** **High Expectations (FR)**54 7167 6-9-2 **45**...................... MsLO'Neill 11 54+
(Gordon Elliott, Ire) *t.k.h: trckd ldrs: hdwy to ld over 2f out: hrd pressed fr over 1f out: kpt on wl fnl f* **7/2**1
051- **2** *1* **Buzz Boy (ITY)**88 7746 4-9-3 **53**..............(b) MissESmith-Chaston(7) 1 61
(Adrian Paul Keatley, Ire) *hld up: hdwy on outside over 2f out: rdn to chal over 1f out: edgd rt: kpt on same pce wl ins fnl f* **12/1**
0-21 **3** *4* **Jonny Delta**23 2456 10-9-8 **56**.................................... MissRHill(5) 10 58
(Jim Goldie) *s.i.s: hld up: pushed along over 2f out: hdwy to chse (clr) ldng pair over 1f out: sn no imp* **6/1**2
1440 **4** *hd* **Thorntoun Care**5 3043 6-10-4 **61**..............................(b) MrsCBartley 3 62
(Iain Jardine) *hld up: hdwy over 2f out: kpt on fnl f: nvr able to chal* **11/1**3
0-52 **5** *1* **Nafaath (IRE)**59 1519 11-10-0 **62**..............................(p) MissAMcCain(5) 4 62
(Donald McCain) *hld up bhd ldng gp: hdwy to ld after 4f: rdn and hdd over 2f out: outpcd fr over 1f out* **11/1**3
10/0 **6** *1/2* **Sergeant Pink (IRE)**14 1519 11-9-10 **53**.............(b) MissEmmaSayer 6 52
(Dianne Sayer) *led 4f: cl up: ev ch over 3f out to over 2f out: rdn and wknd over 1f out* **40/1**
**7** *1 1/4* **Ripped (IRE)**12 2814 5-9-6 **49**..............................(tp) MissCWalton 2 46
(Gavin Cromwell, Ire) *t.k.h: prom: effrt and ev ch over 2f out: wknd over 1f out* **7/2**1
0/0- **8** *2* **Meadow Cross (IRE)**12 2814 5-9-4 **50**..............(b) MissEEasterby(3) 5 45
(Denis Gerard Hogan, Ire) *hld up: stdy hdwy over 2f out: sn pushed along and no imp* **6/1**2
005/ **9** *1/2* **Mallory Heights (IRE)**39 1992 7-9-6 **49**...........(t1) MissJoannaMason 7 43
(Garvan Donnelly, Ire) *in tch: drvn and outpcd over 2f out: sn n.d: btn over 1f out* **11/1**3
35-0 **10** *11* **Match My Fire (IRE)**60 1498 4-10-0 **64**...................(p) MissSEDods(7) 9 42
(Michael Dods) *prom on outside: rdn over 3f out: wknd over 2f out* **16/1**

2m 50.48s (-3.52) **Going Correction** -0.675s/f (Hard) **10** Ran SP% **114.0**
Speed ratings (Par 101): **83,82,79,79,79 78,78,76,76,69**
CSF £46.82 CT £243.00 TOTE £3.90: £1.80, £3.60, £2.10; EX 51.70 Trifecta £188.40.
**Owner** M J Wasylocha **Bred** Martin Wasylocha **Trained** Longwood, Co Meath

**FOCUS**
Inner most rail in 2yds. They went an uneven pace in this moderate handicap, confined to lady amateurs. Race distance increased 12yds. It's been rated at face value.

## 3194 WEDDINGS AT WESTERN HOUSE HOTEL MAIDEN FILLIES' STKS 6f
**6:40** (6:42) (Class 5) 3-Y-0+ **£3,881** (£1,155; £577; £288) **Stalls** Centre

Form RPR
23 **1** **Made Of Honour (IRE)**32 2135 3-8-9 0.......................... CliffordLee(5) 1 77
(K R Burke) *pressed ldr: rdn to ld over 1f out: edgd rt ins fnl f: kpt on wl* **5/4**1
0-22 **2** *3 1/4* **Excellent Sunset (IRE)**27 2344 3-9-0 73.................... PaulMulrennan 2 67
(David Lanigan) *led: rdn over 2f out: hdd over 1f out: kpt on same pce fnl f* **6/4**2
0 **3** *1 3/4* **Oriental Lilly**33 2121 3-9-0 0.................................... SamJames 7 61
(Jim Goldie) *dwlt: t.k.h: in tch: pushed along over 2f out: effrt over 1f out: kpt on same pce fnl f* **28/1**
65-0 **4** *13* **Connacht Girl (IRE)**31 2188 3-9-0 86..........................(b1) ShaneFoley 6 20
(Adrian Paul Keatley, Ire) *in tch: drvn and outpcd over 2f out: sn wknd* **7/2**3

1m 10.98s (-1.42) **Going Correction** -0.15s/f (Firm) **4** Ran SP% **110.1**
Speed ratings (Par 100): **103,98,96,79**
CSF £3.53 TOTE £1.50; EX 3.80 Trifecta £12.80.
**Owner** Ontoawinner, D Mackay & Mrs E Burke **Bred** Limetree Stud **Trained** Middleham Moor, N Yorks
■ Fintry Flyer was withdrawn. Price at time of withdrawal 40-1. Rule 4 does not apply.

**FOCUS**
Straightforward fillies' maiden form.

## 3195 CONFERENCES AT AYR RACECOURSE H'CAP 6f
**7:10** (7:12) (Class 4) (0-80,82) 3-Y-0+ **£5,822** (£1,732; £865; £432) **Stalls** Centre

Form RPR
5-11 **1** **Black Isle Boy (IRE)**12 2775 3-9-6 **82**.................................... SamJames 7 89+
(David O'Meara) *t.k.h early: trckd ldrs: rdn to ld over 1f out: edgd lft ins fnl f: jst hld on* **2/1**1
0- **2** *shd* **The Mcgregornator (IRE)**44 1843 3-8-11 **73**...............(t1) ShaneFoley 3 79
(Adrian Paul Keatley, Ire) *trckd ldrs: drvn along over 2f out: rallied over 1f out: chsd wnr ins fnl f: kpt on: jst hld* **6/1**
4455 **3** *1 1/2* **Yeeoow (IRE)**9 2883 8-9-5 **74**..............................(p) CliffordLee(5) 8 80
(K R Burke) *prom: effrt and rdn over 1f out: kpt on same pce ins fnl f* **14/1**
3331 **4** *shd* **Vallarta (IRE)**20 2550 7-9-7 **74**.................................... JamesSullivan 5 77
(Ruth Carr) *led: rdn and hdd over 1f out: kpt on same pce ins fnl f* **4/1**3
-321 **5** *1 1/2* **Art Obsession (IRE)**25 2404 6-9-12 **79**.................... PaulMulrennan 4 77
(Paul Midgley) *hld up: rdn and hdwy over 1f out: kpt on same pce ins fnl f* **7/2**2
200- **6** *7* **Dawoodi**242 6954 3-8-13 **75**.................................... PJMcDonald 6 49
(Linda Perratt) *hld up: rdn over 2f out: wknd over 1f out* **33/1**
60-0 **7** *2 3/4* **Zapper Cass (FR)**21 2528 4-10-1 **82**.................................... TomEaves 1 49
(Tony Coyle) *in tch: rdn over 2f out: sn wknd* **6/1**

1m 10.77s (-1.63) **Going Correction** -0.15s/f (Firm)
**WFA** 3 from 4yo+ 9lb **7** Ran SP% **113.7**
Speed ratings (Par 105): **104,103,101,101,99 90,86**
CSF £14.45 CT £129.40 TOTE £3.20: £1.70, £3.50; EX 15.00 Trifecta £129.50.
**Owner** Evan M Sutherland **Bred** Ballyhane Stud **Trained** Upper Helmsley, N Yorks

**FOCUS**
A competitive sprint handicap, run at a solid pace.

## 3196 BOOK DIRECT AT WESTERN HOUSE HOTEL H'CAP 1m
**7:40** (7:42) (Class 6) (0-60,60) 3-Y-0+ **£2,587** (£770; £384; £192) **Stalls** Low

Form RPR
3-00 **1** **Midlight**16 2688 5-9-7 **53**..............................(t) JamesSullivan 1 60
(Ruth Carr) *pressed ldr and sn clr of rest: led 3f out: clr over 1f out: hld on wl fnl f* **10/1**
3604 **2** *1/2* **Panther In Pink (IRE)**9 2902 3-7-13 **46** oh1.......(h1) SammyJoBell(3) 11 49
(Ann Duffield) *hld up in tch: rdn over 2f out: hdwy on outside over 1f out: chsd wnr ins fnl f: kpt on fin* **25/1**
3-04 **3** *1 1/4* **Captain Peaky**6 2996 4-9-11 **57**.................................... PhillipMakin 2 60
(Patrick Holmes) *prom: effrt and pushed along over 2f out: chsd wnr over 1f out to ins fnl f: kpt on same pce* **9/2**2
00-3 **4** *2* **Joyful Star**22 2501 7-9-7 **53**.................................... PaulMulrennan 9 51
(Fred Watson) *hld up: rdn and hdwy 2f out: no imp fnl f* **5/1**3
504 **5** *hd* **Coral Princess (IRE)**83 1102 3-8-9 **53**.................................... JasonHart 7 48
(Keith Dalgleish) *midfield: drvn and outpcd over 2f out: n.d after* **16/1**
-022 **6** *1* **New Abbey Angel (IRE)**22 2501 4-9-9 **60**...................(v) RowanScott(5) 8 55
(Keith Dalgleish) *s.i.s: hld up: pushed along and carried hd high over 2f out: kpt on fnl f: nvr able to chal* **10/3**1
**7** *1 1/4* **Cosy Club (IRE)**31 2199 3-9-2 **60**..............................(b) ShaneFoley 4 49
(Adrian Paul Keatley, Ire) *led at decent gallop: hdd 3f out: wknd wl over 1f out* **13/2**
0-40 **8** *nse* **Rioja Day (IRE)**7 2955 7-9-1 **54**..............................(b) SeanMooney(7) 5 46
(Jim Goldie) *hld up towards rr: drvn and struggling over 2f out: kpt on fnl f: no imp* **14/1**
0503 **9** *1 1/2* **Let Right Be Done**5 3048 5-8-13 **48**...............(p) AdamMcNamara(3) 10 36
(Linda Perratt) *prom: rdn over 2f out: edgd lft over 1f out: wknd fnl f* **10/1**
6600 **10** *2 1/2* **Scannermandango**22 2498 4-8-9 **46**...................... CallumRodriguez(5) 3 28
(Jim Goldie) *dwlt: bhd: drvn along and outpcd over 2f out: sn btn* **40/1**
/005 **11** *1 3/4* **New Decade**7 2949 8-9-0 **46** oh1.................................... SamJames 6 24
(Jim Goldie) *hld up midfield: drvn and struggling over 2f out: sn btn* **14/1**
0-00 **12** *36* **Warleggan (FR)**7 2949 3-8-4 **48** oh1 ow2...................... ShaneGray 12
(Linda Perratt) *dwlt: bhd: lost tch fr 1/2-way: t.o* **40/1**

1m 38.06s (-5.74) **Going Correction** -0.675s/f (Hard)
**WFA** 3 from 4yo+ 12lb **12** Ran SP% **117.4**
Speed ratings (Par 101): **101,100,99,97,97 96,94,94,93,90 89,53**
CSF £235.99 CT £1296.88 TOTE £12.60: £3.20, £6.00, £2.50; EX 308.90 Trifecta £2204.70.
**Owner** Cragg Wood Racing **Bred** Sheikh Sultan Bin Khalifa Al Nayhan **Trained** Huby, N Yorks

**FOCUS**
Race distance increased by 6yds. They went hard up front in this weak handicap. The runner-up has been rated to her best.

## 3197 WESTERN HOUSE HOTEL COASTAL GETAWAY H'CAP 1m 2f
**8:10** (8:11) (Class 5) (0-75,76) 4-Y-0+ **£3,234** (£962; £481; £240) **Stalls** Low

Form RPR
0-41 **1** **Gworn**7 2953 7-9-6 **74** 6ex.................................... PJMcDonald 2 81+
(R Mike Smith) *prom: shkn up over 1f out: led ins fnl f: pushed out: comf* **11/4**2

0-64 **2** 1 1/2 **Dovil's Duel (IRE)**[20] 690 6-8-9 **63**.................................... ShaneGray 1 67
(Gavin Cromwell, Ire) *led at stdy pce: rdn over 2f out: hdd ins fnl f: kpt on same pce* **9/1**

205- **3** *hd* **Maulesden May (IRE)**[139] 8480 4-8-10 **69**.................. RowanScott(5) 6 72
(Keith Dalgleish) *trckd ldrs on outside: rdn over 2f out: rallied over 1f out: kpt on ins fnl f* **11/1**

034- **4** *nse* **Tectonic (IRE)**[167] 8387 8-8-12 **66**....................................(p) JasonHart 5 69
(Keith Dalgleish) *t.k.h early: in tch: effrt whn n.m.r briefly over 1f out: kpt on ins fnl f: no imp* **14/1**

0052 **5** *shd* **Trinity Star (IRE)**[7] 2953 6-8-11 **65**..........................(b) PaulMulrennan 8 68+
(Michael Dods) *dwlt: hld up on ins: effrt and swtchd rt wl over 1f out: kpt on fnl f: nvr able to chal* **5/4**[1]

\- **6** 2 1/4 **Carrigeen Prince (IRE)**[21] 2531 5-8-13 **67**........................ ShaneFoley 4 65
(Garvan Donnelly, Ire) *pressed ldr: rdn over 2f out: outpcd fnl f* **15/2**[3]

50-0 **7** 8 **Intiwin (IRE)**[22] 2497 5-8-12 **69**........................... AdamMcNamara(3) 7 51
(Linda Perratt) *rrd s: bhd: outpcd over 2f out: hung lft over 1f out: sn btn* **25/1**

2m 4.33s (-7.67) **Going Correction** -0.675s/f (Hard) 7 Ran SP% **111.7**
Speed ratings (Par 103): **103,101,101,101,101 99,93**
CSF £25.73 CT £228.27 TOTE £3.30: £1.70, £3.50; EX 22.30 Trifecta £142.50.
**Owner** R Gibson **Bred** Azienda Agricola F Lli Nencini **Trained** Galston, E Ayrshire

**FOCUS**
Race distance increased by 6yds. This proved a messy handicap due to a stop-start pace.

## 3198 WESTERN HOUSE HOTEL SUMMER WEDDING PACKAGE H'CAP 7f 50y
**8:40** (8:40) (Class 6) (0-65,65) 4-Y-O+ **£2,587** (£770; £384; £192) **Stalls** High

Form RPR

/1-1 **1** **Burren View Lady (IRE)**[12] 2809 7-9-2 **60**...................(bt) ShaneFoley 3 67
(Denis Gerard Hogan, Ire) *prom: effrt over 2f out: rallied and led 1f out: edgd lft and hld on wl cl home* **11/4**[2]

-010 **2** *hd* **The Name's Paver**[8] 2918 4-9-4 **62**.................................... TomEaves 4 69
(Noel Wilson) *led at modest gallop: rdn along 2f out: hdd 1f out: rallied: hld whn blkd nr fin* **5/1**[3]

0-52 **3** 3 1/4 **Ss Vega**[7] 2949 4-8-7 **51** oh6................................................ SamJames 6 49
(Jim Goldie) *hld up in tch: pushed along 2f out: kpt on to chse ldng pair ins fnl f: r.o* **6/1**

4-15 **4** 3/4 **Tanawar (IRE)**[27] 2342 7-9-4 **62**..................................(b) JamesSullivan 8 59
(Ruth Carr) *cl up: rdn and edgd lft over 1f out: sn outpcd* **15/2**

3303 **5** *nk* **So It's War (FR)**[24] 2430 6-9-2 **65**...............................(p) RowanScott(5) 7 61
(Keith Dalgleish) *dwlt: t.k.h in rr: hdwy and cl up over 4f out: rdn and outpcd over 1f out: sn btn* **9/4**[1]

330- **6** 1 3/4 **Diamonds A Dancing**[254] 6636 7-9-4 **62**.......................(h) ShaneGray 11 53
(Donald McCain) *prom: drvn and outpcd 2f out: n.d after* **14/1**

00-0 **7** 8 **Charava (IRE)**[30] 2224 5-9-4 **62**.......................................(p) PhillipMakin 2 33
(Patrick Holmes) *hld up: drvn and outpcd over 2f out: sn btn* **16/1**

1m 30.12s (-3.28) **Going Correction** -0.675s/f (Hard) 7 Ran SP% **112.7**
Speed ratings (Par 101): **91,90,87,86,85 83,74**
CSF £16.34 CT £73.99 TOTE £3.50: £1.50, £2.80; EX 15.60 Trifecta £57.30.
**Owner** Is That All Syndicate **Bred** L Mulryan **Trained** Cloughjordan, Co Tipperary

**FOCUS**
Race distance increased by 6yds. An ordinary handicap, hit by non-runners. It's been rated around the second and third.

## 3199 BOOK THE AWARD WINNING WESTERN HOUSE HOTEL H'CAP 7f 50y
**9:10** (9:10) (Class 4) (0-85,87) 3-Y-O+ **£5,822** (£1,732; £865; £432) **Stalls** High

Form RPR

4-12 **1** **Sabador (FR)**[22] 2505 3-9-3 **85**......................................... PJMcDonald 8 93
(Ed Walker) *hld up midfield: effrt and plld out 2f out: led appr fnl f: edgd lft and sn pushed clr: readily* **9/4**[1]

00-0 **2** 3 1/4 **Jay Kay**[43] 1867 8-8-12 **74**.............................................(h) CliffordLee(5) 2 78
(K R Burke) *chsd clr ldr: rdn over 2f out: chsd wnr ins fnl f: kpt on: no imp* **14/1**

33-5 **3** 1 1/2 **Fayez (IRE)**[34] 2106 3-9-0 **82**............................................. PhillipMakin 7 78
(David O'Meara) *slowly away: bhd: rdn and hdwy over 1f out: kpt on fnl f: nvr able to chal* **11/1**

6-60 **4** *hd* **Fieldsman (USA)**[11] 2838 5-9-6 **84**........................ PatrickVaughan(7) 10 84
(David O'Meara) *hld up in tch: drvn along over 2f out: kpt on same pce ins fnl f* **9/1**

3125 **5** 3/4 **Tavener**[19] 2582 5-9-6 **77**.................................................(p) ConnorBeasley 1 75
(David C Griffiths) *t.k.h: led and sn clr: hdd 1f out: sn outpcd* **22/1**

2100 **6** 1 **Zoravan (USA)**[23] 2457 4-9-7 **83**.....................................(v) RowanScott(5) 3 78
(Keith Dalgleish) *in tch: rdn over 2f out: no ex fnr over 1f out* **17/2**

331- **7** 1 1/4 **Makkaar (IRE)**[215] 7665 3-9-2 **84**........................................ JasonHart 9 72
(Mark Johnston) *s.i.s: bhd: struggling 1/2-way: hdwy over 1f out: kpt on fnl f: nvr able to chal* **4/1**[2]

0-52 **8** 3 3/4 **Michele Strogoff**[9] 2884 4-10-2 **87**...................................... TomEaves 5 69
(Tony Coyle) *trckd ldrs: rdn over 2f out: wknd over 1f out* **13/2**[3]

20-0 **9** 1 3/4 **Dragon King (IRE)**[41] 1910 5-9-9 **83**................(h[1]) AdamMcNamara(3) 6 60
(Iain Jardine) *hld up: pushed along over 2f out: sn no imp: btn over 1f out* **20/1**

-065 **10** 1 3/4 **Russian Realm**[25] 2384 7-9-12 **83**.................................... PaulMulrennan 11 56
(Paul Midgley) *hld up: drvn along over 2f out: wknd wl over 1f out* **9/1**

1m 26.54s (-6.86) **Going Correction** -0.675s/f (Hard) course record
**WFA** 3 from 4yo+ 11lb 10 Ran SP% **118.7**
Speed ratings (Par 105): **112,108,106,106,105 104,102,98,96,94**
CSF £37.53 CT £301.93 TOTE £3.50: £1.02, £5.00, £4.10; EX 36.30 Trifecta £476.00.
**Owner** P K Siu **Bred** Guy Pariente Holding Sprl **Trained** Upper Lambourn, Berks

**FOCUS**
Race distance increased by 6yds. A fair handicap, run at a strong pace.
T/Plt: £470.50 to a £1 stake. Pool: £66,579.38. 103.29 winning units. T/Qpdt: £62.50 to a £1 stake. Pool: £5,447.83. 64.50 winning units. **Richard Young**

# 2698 BEVERLEY (R-H)
Wednesday, May 31

**OFFICIAL GOING: Good to firm (8.0)**
Wind: Light, across Weather: Fine & dry

## 3200 ETTON CLAIMING STKS 5f
**2:00** (2:00) (Class 6) 2-Y-O **£2,587** (£770; £384; £192) **Stalls** Low

Form RPR

2 **1** **Our Little Pony**[27] 2343 2-8-6 0.......................................... PaulHanagan 2 60
(Richard Fahey) *trckd ldr on inner: nt clr run and swtchd lft over 1f out: sn rdn to chal: styd on to ld ins fnl f* **7/4**[1]

0551 **2** 1 1/4 **Popsi**[27] 2343 2-8-1 0................................................(p) NathanEvans(3) 5 54
(Jo Hughes) *sn cl up: rdn to take slt ld jst over 1f out: drvn and hdd ins fnl f: kpt on* **4/1**[3]

64 **3** 2 **Society's Dream (IRE)**[27] 2343 2-8-7 0.............................. JoeyHaynes 1 49
(K R Burke) *chsd ldrs: pushed along 1/2-way: hdwy wl over 1f out: sn rdn and kpt on fnl f* **8/1**

035 **4** 1 **Just For The Craic (IRE)**[25] 2403 2-9-1 0....................... JackGarritty 7 54
(Ruth Carr) *sn led: rdn along 2f out: hdd jst over 1f out: grad wknd* **9/4**[2]

5 **5** 1/2 **Holmfirst**[26] 2373 2-8-11 0.................................................. GrahamLee 8 48
(Paul Midgley) *sn pushed along and outpcd in rr: hdwy 2f out: styd on appr fnl f* **25/1**

5 **6** 6 **Autumn Belle**[41] 1908 2-8-12 0....................................... AndrewMullen 3 27
(Ollie Pears) *n.m.r after s: trckd ldrs: effrt on outer 2f out: rdn over 1f out: sn wknd* **10/1**

**7** 9 **Christmas Night** 2-8-11 0...................................................... JoeDoyle 4
(Ollie Pears) *a rr* **33/1**

1m 4.01s (0.51) **Going Correction** -0.075s/f (Good) 7 Ran SP% **114.1**
Speed ratings (Par 91): **92,90,86,85,84 74,60**
CSF £9.17 TOTE £1.90: £1.10, £3.80; EX 7.10 Trifecta £24.40.The winner was claimed by Mr L. A. Mullaney for £8,000. Popsi was claimed by Mrs Marjorie Fife for £7,000.
**Owner** Mel Roberts & Ms Nicola Meese 1 **Bred** Mel Roberts & Ms Nicola Meese **Trained** Musley Bank, N Yorks

**FOCUS**
Light watering took place overnight (2mm) and the going was given as good to firm (GoingStick: 8.0). The rail around the bottom bend was out 2yds to its narrowest position, adding 7yds to all races over 7F plus. Three of the first four had met at Redcar last time, but the weights were slightly different here and the positions changed. Straightforward form.

## 3201 RACING UK NOW IN HD H'CAP (DIV I) 5f
**2:30** (2:39) (Class 6) (0-65,70) 3-Y-O+ **£2,587** (£770; £384; £192) **Stalls** Low

Form RPR

1625 **1** **Jacob's Pillow**[23] 2469 6-9-12 **65**................................(p) DanielTudhope 4 73
(Rebecca Bastiman) *trckd ldrs: hdwy 2f out: rdn to ld appr fnl f: sn drvn and kpt on wl* **5/1**

4211 **2** 1 **The Armed Man**[8] 2923 4-9-10 **70** 6ex.............................. PaulaMuir(7) 11 74
(Chris Fairhurst) *racd wd: chsd ldrs: hdwy 2f out: rdn over 1f out: chsd wnr ins fnl f: no imp towards fin* **10/3**[2]

1650 **3** 1/2 **Archimedes (IRE)**[7] 2967 4-10-0 **67**...............................(p) DavidAllan 2 70
(David C Griffiths) *chsd ldrs: hdwy over 1f out: sn rdn and kpt on* **9/1**

5465 **4** 1 1/2 **David's Beauty (IRE)**[67] 1372 4-9-6 **59**.........................(p) GrahamLee 1 56
(Brian Baugh) *led: pushed along 2f out: sn rdn: hdd and drvn appr fnl f: grad wknd* **11/1**

-600 **5** 1/2 **George Bailey (IRE)**[39] 1973 5-8-9 **51** oh6.............(b[1]) NathanEvans(3) 3 46
(Suzzanne France) *in tch: hdwy wl over 1f out: sn rdn and kpt on same pce fnl f* **16/1**

1506 **6** 3/4 **Malaysian Boleh**[16] 2675 7-8-10 **56**............................ JacobMitchell(7) 9 49
(Phil McEntee) *sltly hmpd s and bhd: hdwy 2f out: sn rdn and kpt on fnl f* **33/1**

0006 **7** *nk* **Minty Jones**[6] 2994 8-8-7 **51** oh6.................................(v) PhilDennis(5) 10 43
(Michael Mullineaux) *bhd: hdwy on outer wl over 1f out: sn rdn and no imp* **50/1**

/-05 **8** 1 3/4 **Thatcherite (IRE)**[15] 2700 9-9-10 **63**...........................(t) PaulHanagan 6 53
(Tony Coyle) *sn outpcd: rdn along and detached 1/2-way: sme hdwy u.p over 1f out: n.d* **4/1**[3]

0-00 **9** *hd* **Tinsill**[15] 2700 6-8-12 **51** oh3.........................................(p) AndrewMullen 5 36
(Nigel Tinkler) *dwlt and wnt lft s. a rr* **33/1**

0036 **10** 2 1/4 **Major Muscari (IRE)**[36] 2063 9-8-12 **54**................(p) CharlieBennett(3) 7 31
(Shaun Harris) *in tch: rdn along 2f out: sn wknd* **25/1**

0421 **11** 1 **Pearl Noir**[10] 2858 7-9-2 **60**...........................................(b) PaddyPilley(5) 8 33+
(Scott Dixon) *wnt lft s: sn cl up: rdn along 2f out: sn drvn and wknd* **11/4**[1]

1m 2.95s (-0.55) **Going Correction** -0.075s/f (Good) 11 Ran SP% **122.3**
Speed ratings (Par 101): **101,99,98,96,95 94,93,90,90,87 85**
CSF £22.34 CT £153.78 TOTE £6.10: £1.50, £2.80, £2.60; EX 24.00 Trifecta £147.80.
**Owner** Miss Rebecca Bastiman **Bred** Lael Stables **Trained** Cowthorpe, N Yorks

**FOCUS**
A modest sprint handicap but the two leaders set a decent gallop.

## 3202 RACING UK NOW IN HD H'CAP (DIV II) 5f
**3:00** (3:04) (Class 6) (0-65,67) 3-Y-O+ **£2,587** (£770; £384; £192) **Stalls** Low

Form RPR

1516 **1** **Crosse Fire**[45] 1820 5-9-12 **63**............................................. DavidAllan 9 70
(Scott Dixon) *prom on outer: hdwy over 1f out: rdn to chal ent fnl f: drvn to ld last 75 yds* **5/1**[2]

-303 **2** 1/2 **Dundunah (USA)**[8] 2925 3-9-7 **66**................................(t[1]) DanielTudhope 1 69
(David O'Meara) *trckd ldrs on inner: swtchd lft and hdwy whn hmpd jst over 1f out: sn rdn and styd on to chal last 100 yds: no ex nr fin* **11/4**[1]

6033 **3** *nse* **Roaring Rory**[18] 2627 4-9-5 **61**..................................(p) LewisEdmunds(5) 7 66
(Ollie Pears) *trckd ldrs: pushed along 2f out: rdn and edgd rt over 1f out: nt clr run and swtchd rt ent fnl f: fin strly* **12/1**

-100 **4** 2 1/2 **First Excel**[33] 2119 5-9-1 **59**.........................................(b) BenSanderson(7) 8 55
(Roy Bowring) *cl up: rdn to take slt ld whn hung bdly lft 1f out: hdd last 100 yds: hld whn rdr dropped rein and wknd* **12/1**

0-00 **5** 2 **Kestrel Call (IRE)**[44] 1833 4-10-2 **67**................................(t) BenCurtis 5 56
(Michael Appleby) *chsd ldrs: rdn along wl over 1f out: drvn and no imp fnl f* **25/1**

-606 **6** 1/2 **Chip Or Pellet**[8] 2923 4-8-12 **49** oh2...............................(b) PaulHanagan 3 36
(Nigel Tinkler) *sltly hmpd s: in tch: hdwy 2f out: sn rdn and no imp* **7/1**[3]

4-66 **7** *hd* **Young Tiger**[18] 2633 4-9-4 **55**........................................ AndrewMullen 2 41
(Tom Tate) *led: rdn along 2f out: hdd jst over 1f out: sn wknd* **11/4**[1]

0606 **8** *hd* **Whispering Wolf**[39] 1973 4-8-9 **49** oh4.......................... NathanEvans(3) 10 35
(Suzzanne France) *a rr* **33/1**

-004 **9** 2 3/4 **Twentysvnthlancers**[15] 2700 4-10-2 **67**.............................. GrahamLee 6 43
(Paul Midgley) *a towards rr* **8/1**

000- **10** 6 **Knockamany Bends (IRE)**[166] 8409 7-9-1 **52**............(tp) PaddyAspell 4 6
(John Wainwright) *t.k.h early: chsd ldrs: rdn along 2f out: sn wknd* **33/1**

1m 3.2s (-0.30) **Going Correction** -0.075s/f (Good)
**WFA** 3 from 4yo+ 8lb 10 Ran SP% **118.7**
Speed ratings (Par 101): **99,98,98,94,90 90,89,89,85,75**
CSF £19.18 CT £159.68 TOTE £5.30: £1.60, £2.20, £3.10; EX 21.50 Trifecta £159.00.
**Owner** Paul J Dixon & Darren Lucas **Bred** Dr A Gillespie **Trained** Babworth, Notts
■ Stewards' Enquiry : Lewis Edmunds 2 day ban - guilty of careless riding, in that he manoeuvred right when insufficiently clear (14/15 June)

**FOCUS**
The slower of the two divisions by 0.25sec. The winner has been rated to his turf best, with the second, third and fourth near their respective levels.

## 3203 BRITISH RACING SCHOOL CHARITY CYCLE RIDE H'CAP 7f 96y
**3:30** (3:31) (Class 5) (0-70,75) 4-Y-O+ **£3,780** (£1,131; £565; £283; £141) **Stalls** Low

Form RPR

0-06 **1** **Talent Scout (IRE)**[5] 3049 11-8-13 **66**......................(p) GemmaTutty(5) 6 73
(Karen Tutty) *mde all: rdn wl over 1f out: drvn and edgd lft ins fnl f: hld on gamely* **12/1**

3130 **2** ½ **Make On Madam (IRE)**[16] 2685 5-9-7 **69**.................... JoeFanning 9 75
(Les Eyre) *a cl up: rdn to chal wl over 1f out: drvn and ev ch ins fnl f: kpt on* **6/1**[2]

2460 **3** ¾ **I'm Super Too (IRE)**[8] 2919 10-8-7 **55**....................(p) RoystonFfrench 2 59
(Karen Tutty) *hld up: hdwy on inner wl over 1f out: rdn ent fnl f: styd on wl towards fin* **16/1**

4-42 **4** ¾ **Arcane Dancer (IRE)**[30] 2224 4-8-13 **61**......................(p) PaulHanagan 1 63
(Lawrence Mullaney) *trckd ldrs: hdwy over 2f out: rdn to chse ldng pair over 1f out: sn drvn and kpt on same pce* **5/2**[1]

46-0 **5** ½ **Popsies Joy (IRE)**[28] 2301 4-9-3 **65**.................................. DavidAllan 10 66
(Tim Easterby) *dwlt and bhd: hdwy wl over 2f out: in tch and nt clr run 11/2f out: sn rdn and styd on wl fnl f. nrst fin* **10/1**

0-05 **6** ½ **Danot (IRE)**[45] 1823 5-9-0 **62**.......................................(p[1]) JackGarritty 14 61+
(Jedd O'Keeffe) *hld up towards rr: hdwy over 2f out: n.m.r over 1f out: sn rdn: styd on fnl f: nrst fin* **20/1**

4231 **7** nk **Wink Oliver**[1] 3181 5-9-13 **75** 6ex...........................(p) AndrewMullen 5 73+
(Jo Hughes) *dwlt and rr: hdwy on inner 2f out: rdn over 1f out: kpt on fnl f: nrst fin* **7/1**[3]

-003 **8** 1 ½ **Hijran (IRE)**[19] 2587 4-8-9 **64**.......................................(p) RayDawson(7) 4 59
(Michael Appleby) *hld up: hdwy on outer over 2f out: rdn to chse ldrs over 1f out: sn drvn and no imp* **8/1**

0444 **9** nk **Dodgy Bob**[12] 2776 4-8-11 **64**.......................................(p) PhilDennis(5) 3 58
(Michael Mullineaux) *chsd ldrs: rdn 2f out: drvn over 1f out: wknd fnl f* **20/1**

400- **10** nk **Pennine Warrior**[202] 7896 6-8-4 **57**............................(p) PaddyPilley(5) 12 50
(Scott Dixon) *prom on outer: hdwy wl over 2f out: rdn wl over 1f out: drvn and wknd ent fnl f* **25/1**

-040 **11** 1 ¼ **Specialv (IRE)**[16] 2684 4-9-6 **68**.......................................(p) BenCurtis 13 58
(Brian Ellison) *hld up in rr: pushed along over 2f out: rdn wl over 1f out: n.d* **16/1**

0-00 **12** ½ **Steal The Scene (IRE)**[16] 2684 5-9-7 **69**........................ RyanPowell 11 57
(Kevin Frost) *midfield: hdwy on outer 1/2-way: rdn along to chse ldrs wl over 1f out: sn drvn and wknd* **12/1**

060- **13** 4 ½ **Relight My Fire**[240] 7010 7-9-1 **66**....................(p) RachelRichardson(3) 7 43
(Tim Easterby) *a towards rr* **16/1**

1m 33.48s (-0.32) **Going Correction** -0.075s/f (Good) **13** Ran SP% **122.0**
Speed ratings (Par 103): **98,97,96,95,95 94,94,92,92,91 90,89,84**
CSF £81.81 CT £1218.40 TOTE £16.10: £4.00, £2.00, £5.20; EX 103.90 Trifecta £1347.90.
**Owner** Thoroughbred Homes Ltd **Bred** Johnston King **Trained** Osmotherley, N Yorks

**FOCUS**
Race distance increased by 7yds. This was dominated by the winner and it proved hard to make up ground.

## 3204 DR EDDIE MOLL H'CAP 1m 100y
**4:00** (4:00) (Class 4) (0-80,82) 4-Y-O+ **£5,040** (£1,508; £754; £377; £188) **Stalls** Low

Form RPR

-022 **1** **Palmerston**[30] 2226 4-9-7 **80**.................................................. BenCurtis 6 86
(Michael Appleby) *trckd ldng pair: hdwy 2f out: rdn to ld ent fnl f: sn jnd and drvn: kpt on wl towards fin* **5/2**[1]

4-44 **2** ¾ **Haraz (IRE)**[19] 2586 4-9-3 **76**.......................................(v) DanielTudhope 2 80
(David O'Meara) *trckd ldrs on inner: smooth hdwy whn nt clr run over 1f out: squeezed through ent fnl f: sn rdn to chal and ev ch tl drvn and no ex towards fin* **7/2**[3]

000- **3** nk **Altharoos (IRE)**[167] 8385 7-9-2 **75**.................................... GrahamLee 1 78
(Micky Hammond) *hld up: hdwy over 2f out: swtchd lft wl over 1f out: n.m.r appr fnl f: sn rdn and kpt on wl towards fin* **11/1**

-304 **4** 1 ½ **Zodiakos (IRE)**[7] 2952 4-9-4 **77**...................................... PaulHanagan 4 77+
(Roger Fell) *hld up in rr: hdwy 2f out: swtchd lft and hdwy over 1f out: sn rdn and kpt on fnl f* **11/4**[2]

6050 **5** 1 ¾ **Abushamah (IRE)**[11] 2838 6-9-3 **76**..............................(p) JackGarritty 7 72
(Ruth Carr) *t.k.h: trckd ldrs: hdwy on outer over 2f out: rdn over 1f out: drvn and wknd ins fnl f* **9/1**

-040 **6** 2 **Jacbequick**[15] 2701 6-9-6 **82**...........................................(p) JoshDoyle(3) 8 74
(David O'Meara) *clsd up: rdn to take slt ld 11.2f out: hdd and drvn ent fnl f: sn wknd* **6/1**

0100 **7** 8 **Pivotman**[16] 2685 9-8-7 **69**..........................................(bt) NathanEvans(3) 5 43
(Michael Easterby) *led: pushed along 3f out: rdn over 2f out: drvn and hdd 11/2f out: sn wknd* **25/1**

1m 44.26s (-3.34) **Going Correction** -0.075s/f (Good) **7** Ran SP% **113.9**
Speed ratings (Par 105): **113,112,111,110,108 106,98**
CSF £11.51 CT £78.45 TOTE £3.00: £1.70, £2.50; EX 11.60 Trifecta £55.50.
**Owner** Infinity Racing & Craig Buckingham **Bred** Carwell Equities Ltd **Trained** Oakham, Rutland

**FOCUS**
Race distance increased by 7yds. A fair handicap run at a good gallop.

## 3205 HULL FC H'CAP 1m 1f 207y
**4:30** (4:30) (Class 5) (0-70,72) 4-Y-O+ **£3,780** (£1,131; £565; £283; £141) **Stalls** Low

Form RPR

02-0 **1** **Bromance**[130] 360 4-8-7 **56** oh1........................................(p) JoeFanning 9 65
(Peter Niven) *hld up in rr: hdwy on outer over 2f out: chsd ldrs over 1f out: rdn to ld and hung bdly rt ent fnl f: drvn out* **12/1**

3005 **2** 2 ½ **All You (IRE)**[30] 2224 5-9-4 **67**...................................(v) DanielTudhope 11 71
(David O'Meara) *stmbld s: hld up in rr: hdwy over 2f out: swtchd lft to outer and rdn over 1f out: fin strly* **5/1**[2]

005- **3** nse **Dream Free**[303] 4942 4-8-11 **63**................................... NathanEvans(3) 7 67
(Mark Walford) *trckd ldrs: effrt 2f out and sn pushed along: rdn over 1f out: styng on whn hmpd ent fnl f: kpt on wl towards fin* **11/2**[3]

02-3 **4** shd **Monsieur Glory**[29] 2282 4-9-7 **70**..............................(v) PaulHanagan 4 77+
(Tom Clover) *hld up in tch: hdwy on inner over 1f out: swtchd lft and effrt whn hmpd ent fnl f: sn rdn and styd on wl towards fin* **9/4**[1]

0-30 **5** nse **Lean On Pete (IRE)**[16] 2687 8-8-10 **59**........................ AndrewMullen 10 63
(Ollie Pears) *set gd pce: pushed along over 2f out: rdn wl over 1f out: drvn and hdd ent fnl f: kpt on same pce* **20/1**

60-5 **6** 1 ¼ **King Of The Celts (IRE)**[30] 2225 9-8-13 **65**........ RachelRichardson(3) 8 66
(Tim Easterby) *trckd ldng pair: hdwy 2f out: rdn over 1f out: drvn and one pce fnl f* **9/1**

00-0 **7** 1 ¼ **Auxiliary**[24] 2430 4-9-3 **66**.............................................(p) JackGarritty 3 65
(Patrick Holmes) *trckd ldrs: pushed along 2f out: rdn over 1f out: wkng whn n.m.r ent fnl f* **16/1**

26-6 **8** 2 ¾ **Rockliffe**[50] 1700 4-8-11 **60**................................................ GrahamLee 2 53
(Micky Hammond) *hld up: a towards rr* **10/1**

06/4 **9** 3 ½ **Tin Pan Alley**[30] 2225 9-9-2 **65**............................................ DavidAllan 6 51
(David C Griffiths) *trckd ldr: hdwy and cl up 3f out: rdn to chal 2f out: drvn over 1f out: wkng whn n.m.r ent fnl f* **5/1**[2]

2m 5.04s (-1.96) **Going Correction** -0.075s/f (Good) **9** Ran SP% **116.9**
Speed ratings (Par 103): **104,102,101,101,101 100,99,97,94**
CSF £71.77 CT £374.42 TOTE £10.90: £3.20, £1.50, £2.10; EX 72.10 Trifecta £467.20.
**Owner** The SB Club **Bred** Bearstone Stud Ltd **Trained** Barton-le-Street, N Yorks
■ Stewards' Enquiry : Joe Fanning 3 day ban - guilty of careless riding in that he allowed his mount to hang right without sufficient correction (14-16 June)

**FOCUS**
Race distance increased by 7yds. There was a good pace on here.

## 3206 SKIDBY MAIDEN STKS 7f 96y
**5:00** (5:00) (Class 5) 3-Y-O+ **£3,780** (£1,131; £565; £283; £141) **Stalls** Low

Form RPR

65 **1** **Gloriosus (USA)**[15] 2704 3-9-2 0.................................... JoeFanning 2 78
(Mark Johnston) *mde all: jnd and rdn wl over 1f out: drvn ins fnl f: hld on gamely towards fin* **8/1**[3]

022 **2** nse **Time's Arrow (IRE)**[26] 2366 3-9-2 81........................ DanielTudhope 5 78
(Sir Michael Stoute) *trckd ldng pair: smooth hdwy to trck wnr over 2f out: chal over 1f out: rdn to dispute ld ent fnl f: sn drvn and ev ch: jst hld* **4/11**[1]

345- **3** 4 ½ **Doctor Cross (IRE)**[250] 6741 3-9-2 70............................ PaulHanagan 3 66
(Richard Fahey) *hld up in tch: hdwy 3f out: chsd ldng pair: 2f out: sn rdn and no imp* **3/1**[2]

06- **4** nk **Princess Nearco (IRE)**[291] 5414 3-8-11 0........................ JackGarritty 6 61
(Patrick Holmes) *dwlt and rr: hdwy over 2f out: rdn wl over 1f out: kpt on same pce* **50/1**

60 **5** 13 **Nightdress (IRE)**[11] 2841 3-8-11 0................................ DuranFentiman 4 27
(Tony Coyle) *chsd wnr: awkward and pushed along 3f out: rdn over 2f out: sn drvn and wknd* **66/1**

**6** 22 **Snow Blaze** 3-8-4 0........................................................ RayDawson(7) 1
(Michael Appleby) *dwlt: sn chsng ldrs: rdn along wl over 2f out: sn outpcd* **33/1**

1m 33.13s (-0.67) **Going Correction** -0.075s/f (Good) **6** Ran SP% **115.8**
Speed ratings (Par 103): **100,99,94,94,79 54**
CSF £12.14 TOTE £7.10: £3.30, £1.10; EX 15.70 Trifecta £19.20.
**Owner** Sheikh Hamdan bin Mohammed Al Maktoum **Bred** Darley **Trained** Middleham Moor, N Yorks

**FOCUS**
Race distance increased by 7yds. There was a turn-up in this maiden.

## 3207 COTTINGHAM H'CAP (BEVERLEY MIDDLE DISTANCE SERIES) 1m 4f 23y
**5:30** (5:30) (Class 6) (0-60,59) 3-Y-O **£2,587** (£770; £384; £192) **Stalls** Low

Form RPR

-365 **1** **American Craftsman (IRE)**[15] 2702 3-9-4 **56**..........(p) DanielTudhope 3 64
(Roger Fell) *set stdy pce: j. path after 11/2f: qcknd 4f out: pushed along wl over 2f out: rdn along wl over 1f: jnd and drvn ent fnl f: kpt on wl u.p towards fin* **2/1**[1]

4-01 **2** ½ **Dyna Might**[15] 2705 3-9-2 **54**.........................................(p) AndrewMullen 6 61
(Ollie Pears) *hld up in tch: hdwy on outer 3f out: rdn to chse wnr and edgd rt over 1f out: drvn to chal ent fnl f: ev ch tl no ex towards fin* **8/1**

0-04 **3** 7 **Conistone**[15] 2702 3-9-7 **59**.................................................. PaulHanagan 7 55
(James Bethell) *t.k.h: trckd wnr: pushed along 3f out: rdn 2f out: sn drvn and kpt on one pce* **4/1**[2]

00-0 **4** 2 ¼ **Bollin Ted**[41] 1914 3-8-9 **47**.................................................. DavidAllan 5 39
(Tim Easterby) *t.k.h early: trckd ldrs: pushed along and lost pl over 3f out: plugged on one pce fnl 2f* **13/2**

0-00 **5** 4 **Chionodoxa**[41] 1914 3-8-4 **45**.................................. RachelRichardson(3) 1 31
(Tim Easterby) *hld up in rr: effrt and sme hdwy 3f out: sn rdn along and n.d* **16/1**

05-2 **6** 2 **Single Estate**[9] 2903 3-8-7 **45**.................................................. JoeDoyle 9 28
(Simon Waugh) *trckd ldrs on outer: pushed along 3f out: rdn over 2f out: sn wknd* **11/2**[3]

000 **7** ¾ **Somes Sound (IRE)**[32] 2152 3-8-7 **52**............................ DavidEgan(7) 4 33
(Jane Chapple-Hyam) *trckd wnr on inner: pushed along over 3f out: rdn wl over 2f out: sn wknd* **7/1**

000- **8** 19 **Jupiter Ascending**[230] 7306 3-8-2 **47** ow2..............(bt[1]) RayDawson(7) 2
(Michael Appleby) *plld hrd: hld up towards rr: effrt over 3f out: sn rdn along and wknd* **25/1**

2m 40.31s (0.51) **Going Correction** -0.075s/f (Good) **8** Ran SP% **115.4**
Speed ratings (Par 97): **95,94,90,88,85 84,84,71**
CSF £19.20 CT £59.02 TOTE £2.90: £1.20, £2.20, £1.70; EX 18.00 Trifecta £45.10.
**Owner** Geoff & Sandra Turnbull **Bred** Sweetmans Bloodstock **Trained** Nawton, N Yorks

**FOCUS**
Race distance increased by 7yds. The gallop was a steady one, dictated by the winner. The form could be rated a bit better, but the race lacked depth.
T/Plt: £251.80 to a £1 stake. Pool: £74,373.60. 215.55 winning units. T/Qpdt: £89.00 to a £1 stake. Pool: £4,752.70. 39.50 winning units. **Joe Rowntree**

# 2956 KEMPTON (A.W) (R-H)
### Wednesday, May 31

**OFFICIAL GOING: Polytrack: standard to slow**
Wind: Nil Weather: Fine, bright and sunny

## 3208 RACING UK IN STUNNING HD APPRENTICE H'CAP 1m 2f 219y(P)
**6:20** (6:21) (Class 6) (0-65,65) 4-Y-O+ **£2,587** (£770; £384; £192) **Stalls** Low

Form RPR

0215 **1** **Victor's Bet (SPA)**[29] 2257 8-9-7 **65**........................ MeganNicholls 14 73
(Ralph J Smith) *slow s: hld up in last: tk clsr order over 3f out: swtchd to inner over 2f out and rdn: led ent fnl f: rdn out* **12/1**

1352 **2** 1 ¾ **Tommys Geal**[8] 2914 5-8-13 **57**........................................ JaneElliott 7 62
(Michael Madgwick) *settled in rr-div on inner: shkn up and prog on inner 2f out: ev ch over 1f out and rdn: wnr wnt past on ins: kpt on but no ch* **11/2**[3]

-323 **3** 1 **Halling's Wish**[26] 2022 7-9-7 **65**....................................(b) BenRobinson 2 68
(Gary Moore) *chsd ldrs: shkn up and ev ch over 1f in firing line: rdn and kpt on one pce fnl f* **5/1**[2]

1040 **4** 1 1/4 **Nouvelle Ere**[29] 2282 6-8-11 **58**......(t) RossaRyan(3) 3 59
(Tony Carroll) *led for 2f: remained bhd ldr after: shkn up 2f out and sn led: rdn wl over 1f out: hdd ent fnl f: no ex fnl 150yds* **12/1**

2-44 **5** 3/4 **The Juggler**[23] 2460 4-8-0 **51**...... AbbieWibrew(7) 10 51
(William Knight) *led after 2f: shkn up 2f out and hdd: nudged along after: kpt on again ins fnl f* **10/1**

123- **6** *nse* **Iballisticvin**[197] 7969 4-9-2 **65**...... JasonWatson(5) 5 65
(Gary Moore) *chsd ldrs: rdn wl over 1f out: kpt on between horses fr over 1f out: kpt on one pce* **4/1**[1]

-620 **7** 1 **The Ginger Berry**[48] 1758 7-9-6 **64**......(h) JoshuaBryan 8 62
(Dr Jon Scargill) *in rr-div: smooth prog over 2f out: travelling wl over 1f out in centre: rdn and nt picked up: kpt on one pce after* **10/1**

0506 **8** 2 **Runaiocht (IRE)**[12] 2785 7-9-4 **62**......(b) JordanUys 4 57
(Paul Burgoyne) *plld hrd chsng ldrs on inner: particularly on bnd: bhd ldrs ent st: rdn 2f out: one pce after* **20/1**

006- **9** 1/2 **Lady Lunchalot (USA)**[200] 7936 7-8-5 **56**......(p) TheodoreLadd(7) 13 50
(Polly Gundry) *in rr-div: rdn over 1f out: kpt on one pce fnl f* **25/1**

6-40 **10** 3/4 **Moon Over Mobay**[27] 2332 4-8-2 **51**...... NicolaCurrie(5) 9 44
(Michael Blanshard) *settled in mid-div: rdn over 1f out: one pce after* **25/1**

5004 **11** *nk* **Alshan Fajer**[23] 2471 7-9-0 **63**......(vt[1]) GinaMangan(5) 11 55
(J R Jenkins) *wnt sharply to rail and hmpd rival sn after s: in rr-div: rdn 2f out: no imp fr over 1f out* **33/1**

4310 **12** 2 1/2 **Embankment**[18] 2615 8-9-2 **60**...... RhiainIngram 12 48
(Michael Attwater) *mid-div on outer: rdn out 1f out: no imp on ldrs* **25/1**

340- **13** 7 **Classic Mission**[244] 6892 6-9-1 **64**......(b) Pierre-LouisJamin(5) 1 41
(Jonathan Portman) *missed break: hmpd sn after: c wd ent st: no imp whn rdn over 1f out* **16/1**

0300 **14** 5 **Cat Royale (IRE)**[18] 2615 4-8-13 **62**......(p) DarraghKeenan(5) 6 31
(John Butler) *cl up on outer of ldrs: rdn over 2f out: wknd sn after* **16/1**

2m 22.15s (0.25) **Going Correction** 0.0s/f (Stan) **14** Ran SP% **116.6**
Speed ratings (Par 101): **99,97,97,96,95 95,94,93,92,92 92,90,85,81**
CSF £68.85 CT £379.30 TOTE £10.40: £3.40, £1.80, £2.60; EX 85.40 Trifecta £508.10.
**Owner** Homecroft Wealth Racing & Kevin Old **Bred** Jose Simo Vazquez **Trained** Epsom, Surrey

**FOCUS**
Moderate fare in the opener. The track had been watered and was officially given as standard to slow. Straightforward form rated around the second and third.

## 3209 32RED ON THE APP STORE MAIDEN STKS 1m 3f 219y(P)
**6:50** (6:56) (Class 5) 3-Y-O+ **£3,234** (£962; £481; £240) **Stalls** Centre

Form RPR

**1** **Zubayr (IRE)**[18] 5-9-9 0...... MeganNicholls(5) 2 86+
(Paul Nicholls) *settled in rr-div: mid-div on outer over 4f out: shkn up 3f out and smooth prog: sn upsides and rdn: led 2f out: clr ld over 1f out: idled ins fnl f and kpt up to work* **7/1**[3]

44 **2** 2 1/4 **Turnpike Trip**[31] 2175 3-8-11 0...... DaneO'Neill 7 79
(Henry Candy) *settled in mid-div: shkn up fr wl over 3f out and making prog: rdn over 2f out w plenty to do: kpt on wl fr over 1f out: tk 2nd ins fnl f: nvr nrr* **25/1**

2 **3** 1/2 **Nadaitak**[31] 2175 3-8-11 0...... OisinMurphy 8 78
(Sir Michael Stoute) *hld up in rr-div: plenty to do whn rdn over 1f out on inner: styd on wl ins fnl f but too late to make any imp on wnr: tk 3rd nr fin: nvr nrr* **5/1**[2]

6 **4** 2 1/2 **Peterport**[12] 2783 3-8-11 0...... WilliamBuick 14 74+
(John Gosden) *reluctant to load: chsd ldr: upsides over 2f out: sn rdn: kpt on wl tl wknd nr fin and lost 3rd nr fin* **13/8**[1]

**5** 2 1/2 **Distant (USA)** 3-8-6 0...... JFEgan 5 65+
(Roger Charlton) *in last: shkn up and began passing rivals out wd on bnd over 4f out: rdn over 2f out: kpt on wl fr over 1f out: likely improver* **14/1**

23 **6** 5 **Orsino (IRE)**[28] 2314 3-8-11 0...... DavidProbert 11 62+
(Andrew Balding) *chsd clr ldr: led over 3f out: rdn over 2f out: hdd 2f out: kpt on one pce after* **7/1**[3]

0 **7** 7 **Kings City (IRE)**[23] 2476 3-8-11 0...... LukeMorris 4 51
(Luca Cumani) *chsd ldrs: rdn wl over 4f out fr pack to try cl on ldrs: 3rd ent st: kpt on tl one pce fr over 1f out* **50/1**

6-3 **8** 1/2 **Scales Of Justice (IRE)**[26] 2359 3-8-11 0...... GavinLerena 13 50
(Charles Hills) *slow away and green: given a few reminder after sed: in rr: rdn over 2f out: nvr involved* **16/1**

00 **9** 4 **Nazzaa (IRE)**[14] 2721 4-10-0 0...... TimmyMurphy 3 45
(Steve Flook) *chsd ldrs: nudged along and no imp fr wl over 1f out* **200/1**

0 **10** 1 1/4 **Amber Morning**[12] 2783 3-8-3 0...... EdwardGreatrex(3) 1 37
(Roger Charlton) *in rr: pushed along fr over 2f out: nvr involved* **50/1**

**11** *nk* **Raining Stars** 3-8-6 0...... GeorgeWood(5) 12 41
(James Fanshawe) *settled in mid-div: rdn wl over 2f out: no imp* **40/1**

00 **12** 12 **Stockton (IRE)**[7] 2963 3-8-11 0...... AdamBeschizza 6 22
(David Simcock) *in rr: rdn over 2f out: nvr involved* **200/1**

4 **13** 15 **Thistimenextyear**[32] 2159 3-8-11 0...... StevieDonohoe 9
(Richard Spencer) *coltish in paddock: got warm and reluctant to load: s.s: settled in rr-div: rdn over 2f out: sn no rspnse: t.o* **7/1**[3]

5 **P** **I'm Right On Time**[32] 2164 3-8-8 0...... JackDuern(3) 10
(Dean Ivory) *led and wnt clr: spent force by 5f out: hdd wl over 3f out: t.o over 2f out: sn p.u* **100/1**

2m 32.04s (-2.46) **Going Correction** 0.0s/f (Stan)
**WFA** 3 from 4yo+ 17lb **14** Ran SP% **117.0**
Speed ratings (Par 103): **108,106,106,104,102 99,94,94,91,91 90,82,72,**
CSF £170.98 TOTE £8.70: £2.50, £8.10, £1.70; EX 251.30 Trifecta £1120.70.
**Owner** P J Vogt **Bred** His Highness The Aga Khan's Studs S C **Trained** Ditcheat, Somerset

**FOCUS**
A messy race with \bI'm Right On Time\p tearing off from the front and they were all well strung out from an early stage.

## 3210 FOLLOW @RACING_UK ON TWITTER FILLIES' NOVICE AUCTION STKS (PLUS 10 RACE) 6f (P)
**7:20** (7:27) (Class 5) 2-Y-O **£3,234** (£962; £481; £240) **Stalls** Low

Form RPR

**1** **Electric Landlady (IRE)** 2-8-8 0...... JackDuern(3) 2 77
(Denis Coakley) *settled in mid-div on inner: shkn up over 2f out and angled to outside: clsng on ldrs gng wl 2f out: rdn over 1f out and qcknd up: edgd rt and led 150yds out: kpt on* **20/1**

6 **2** 2 **Hello Girl**[7] 2958 2-8-11 0...... RobertWinston 5 71
(Dean Ivory) *racd in mid-div on inner: n.m.r on heels turning in where shkn up: stuck to inner and niggled along to cl on ldrs over 1f out: rdn ent fnl f: no imp on ldr cl home* **7/2**[2]

4 **3** 3 **Jonnysimpson (IRE)**[47] 1767 2-8-11 0...... SilvestreDeSousa 3 62
(Brendan Powell) *sn led and set str pce: rdn over 2f out: kpt on wl: hdd 150yds out and wknd* **5/1**

0 **4** 4 1/2 **Fusion Central (IRE)**[8] 2910 2-8-12 0...... TomMarquand 7 50
(Richard Hannon) *restless in stalls: settled in rr-div: rdn over 2f out w plenty to do: kpt on wl fr over 1f out: nudged out fnl f* **14/1**

02 **5** 1 3/4 **Lady Alavesa**[9] 2890 2-8-11 0...... MartinDwyer 6 43
(Gay Kelleway) *pressed ldr: rdn over 2f out: wknd over 1f out* **9/2**[3]

**6** 2 **Headline Act** 2-8-13 0...... OisinMurphy 1 39
(Archie Watson) *mid-div on rail: rdn over 2f out: no imp after* **11/4**[1]

**7** *hd* **Show Of Force** 2-8-13 0...... LukeMorris 11 39
(Jonathan Portman) *in rr: rdn ent st and c wd into bnd: pushed along fr over 1f out* **25/1**

**8** 4 1/2 **Kentucky Blueblood (USA)** 2-8-11 0...... JFEgan 10 23
(Richard Guest) *in last and pushed along early: rdn over 2f out: nvr gng pce* **10/1**

**9** *shd* **Anna Briggs** 2-8-11 0...... DavidProbert 4 23
(Michael Blanshard) *chsd ldrs: rdn over 2f out: no imp after and wknd* **50/1**

0 **10** *nk* **Amiirah**[37] 2037 2-8-6 0...... GeorgeWood(5) 9 22
(John Gallagher) *wnt lft ss: pushed along to hold pl fr over 3f out: nvr gng pce* **66/1**

**11** 6 **Mrs Teasdale** 2-8-9 0...... EdwardGreatrex(3) 8 5
(Archie Watson) *in rr: struggling over 2f out: nvr involved* **20/1**

1m 12.94s (-0.16) **Going Correction** 0.0s/f (Stan) **11** Ran SP% **116.3**
Speed ratings (Par 90): **101,98,94,88,86 83,83,77,76,76 68**
CSF £84.44 TOTE £25.30: £5.50, £1.50, £1.80; EX 111.80 Trifecta £823.00.
**Owner** Pmc Syndicate **Bred** Samuel William Ormsby **Trained** West Ilsley, Berks

**FOCUS**
Just a modest maiden, but the winner took it well.

## 3211 32RED CASINO H'CAP 7f (P)
**7:50** (7:54) (Class 4) (0-85,87) 3-Y-O **£5,175** (£1,540; £769; £384) **Stalls** Low

Form RPR

50-1 **1** **Keyser Soze (IRE)**[39] 1977 3-9-7 **83**...... StevieDonohoe 12 92
(Richard Spencer) *edgy in paddock: hld up in rr: shkn up and prog wdst of all over 2f out: rdn over 1f out: qcknd up wl and led 1f out: sn clr and pushed out* **16/1**

2-1 **2** 2 1/4 **Gymnaste (IRE)**[19] 2572 3-9-11 **87**...... WilliamBuick 4 93+
(John Gosden) *hld up in mid-div on rail: swtchd to centre over 2f out: gng wl whn nt clr run over 1f out: waited for gap and rdn ent fnl f: wnr had gone: pushed out for 2nd* **5/2**[1]

0-10 **3** *hd* **Abatement**[40] 1945 3-9-4 **83**...... KieranShoemark(3) 11 85
(Roger Charlton) *in rr on inner: shkn up and prog over 1f out: sn rdn and kpt on wl fnl f* **33/1**

431- **4** 3/4 **Al Reeh (IRE)**[189] 8066 3-9-4 **80**...... LukeMorris 1 80+
(Marco Botti) *chsd ldr on inner: rdn over 1f out: sn led and instantly drifted lft across rivals: sn hdd: kpt on again at one pce fnl f* **11/2**[2]

2215 **5** 2 1/2 **Tafaakhor (IRE)**[27] 2334 3-9-7 **83**...... JimCrowley 3 76
(Richard Hannon) *chsd ldr: rdn over 1f out: sltly hmpd ent fnl f: kpt on one pce after* **6/1**[3]

0-22 **6** 3/4 **Sea Shack**[27] 2334 3-9-4 **80**...... SilvestreDeSousa 9 71
(William Knight) *settled bhd ldr: rdn over 2f out: sltly hmpd ent fnl f: kpt on* **6/1**[3]

10-6 **7** 1 1/4 **Angel Down**[27] 2334 3-9-3 **79**...... DaneO'Neill 6 67
(Henry Candy) *in rr-div: rdn over 2f out: kpt on one pce* **14/1**

2-1 **8** 1/2 **Mutoondresdashorse**[12] 2782 3-9-2 **78**...... AdamKirby 7 64
(Paul Cole) *in rr-div: shkn up and prog on inner over 2f out: kpt on wl tl wknd fnl f* **6/1**[3]

3-1 **9** *nk* **Dubai Art**[147] 34 3-9-2 **78**...... DavidNolan 10 64
(Richard Fahey) *hld up in rr-div: rdn over 1f out: nt picked up* **33/1**

3133 **10** 5 **Blaze Of Glory (FR)**[103] 788 3-9-10 **86**...... DougieCostello 5 58
(Jamie Osborne) *led: rdn wl over 1f out: hdd sn after and wknd qckly* **40/1**

41-4 **11** *nk* **Coastal Cyclone**[13] 2757 3-8-13 **75**...... DavidProbert 13 46
(Harry Dunlop) *a in rr* **20/1**

2-12 **12** 5 **Archer's Arrow (USA)**[41] 1895 3-9-6 **82**......(p[1]) OisinMurphy 8 40
(Saeed bin Suroor) *chsd ldrs: rdn 2f out: sn wknd* **10/1**

1m 24.86s (-1.14) **Going Correction** 0.0s/f (Stan) **12** Ran SP% **121.5**
Speed ratings (Par 101): **106,103,103,102,99 98,97,96,96,90 90,84**
CSF £55.60 CT £1390.45 TOTE £21.80: £4.60, £1.50, £8.00; EX 113.30 Trifecta £2497.40.
**Owner** Rebel Racing (2) **Bred** J Hanly **Trained** Newmarket, Suffolk

**FOCUS**
A typically competitive 3yo handicap for the time of year and it looks to be fair form. It favoured those who were ridden patiently, with the pace collapsing.

## 3212 100% PROFIT BOOST AT 32REDSPORT.COM H'CAP (LONDON MILE SERIES QUALIFIER) 1m (P)
**8:20** (8:20) (Class 3) (0-90,92) 4-Y-O+
**£7,470** (£2,236; £1,118; £559; £279; £140) **Stalls** Low

Form RPR

-404 **1** **Ripoll (IRE)**[23] 2477 4-8-11 **79**......(t) PatDobbs 5 88+
(Sylvester Kirk) *hld up in last: shkn up over 2f out: prog on heels over 1f out: passing rivals and swtchd to inner ent fnl f: sn rdn and kpt on strly wl ins fnl f: got up nr fin* **9/1**

10-1 **2** *nk* **Lastmanlastround (IRE)**[29] 2256 4-8-11 **79**...... DavidProbert 2 87
(Rae Guest) *settled bhd ldr on rail: shkn up over 2f out: sn rdn and led ent fnl f: kpt on wl tl hdd cl home* **12/1**

10-3 **3** 1 **Alnashama**[25] 2384 5-9-7 **89**...... JimCrowley 7 95
(Charles Hills) *settled bhd ldr on outer: shkn up over 2f out: sn rdn: ev ch ent fnl f: stuck on: no ex nr fin* **7/1**[3]

0-10 **4** 1 1/4 **Reaver (IRE)**[25] 2406 4-9-2 **84**...... CharlesBishop 11 87
(Eve Johnson Houghton) *in rr-div: shkn up over 2f out: rdn 2f out: kpt on one pce after* **8/1**

4-21 **5** *nk* **Ballard Down (IRE)**[28] 2310 4-9-10 **92**......(v) HarryBentley 1 94
(William Knight) *.mid-div on inner: rdn over 2f out: kpt on one pce fr over 1f out* **11/4**[1]

431- **6** 1/2 **Dark Devil (IRE)**[234] 7189 4-9-4 **86**...... DavidNolan 8 87
(Richard Fahey) *chsd ldrs: shkn up over 2f out: sn rdn: kpt on tl no ex ent fnl f* **7/1**[3]

4641 **7** *shd* **Kestrel Dot Com**[14] 2730 5-9-1 **83**......(b) SilvestreDeSousa 10 84
(Chris Dwyer) *settled bhd ldrs on outer: shkn up over 2f out: rdn between horses over 1f out: pushed out fnl f* **11/2**[2]

5405 **8** 1/2 **Kingston Kurrajong**[30] 2232 4-9-1 **83**...... AdamBeschizza 4 83
(Michael Attwater) *led: shkn up over 2f out: sn rdn: kpt on wl tl hdd ent fnl f: wknd qckly after* **14/1**

03-0 **9** 1/2 **Palawan**[30] 2232 4-9-5 **87**...... DougieCostello 3 85
(Jamie Osborne) *s.s: in rr: rdn over 2f out: kpt on one pce fr over 1f out* **33/1**

130- **10** *38* **Unforgiving Minute**[174] 8279 6-9-5 **87**.............................. AdamKirby 6
(John Butler) *t.k.h in rr-div: shkn up over 2f out and emptied qckly: t.o* **12/1**

1m 39.61s (-0.19) **Going Correction** 0.0s/f (Stan) **10** Ran SP% **113.2**
Speed ratings (Par 107): **100,99,98,97,97 96,96,96,95,57**
CSF £107.94 CT £814.57 TOTE £11.00: £2.90, £3.90, £2.30; EX 99.20 Trifecta £299.50.

**Owner** David Harding & Peter Reglar **Bred** Mrs Bridget Delaney **Trained** Upper Lambourn, Berks

**FOCUS**
An open older horse handicap. It was yet another winner on the night to score from off the pace.

## 3213 32RED.COM H'CAP 1m 7f 218y(P)
**8:50** (8:51) (Class 4) (0-85,87) 4-Y-O+ **£5,175** (£1,540; £769; £384) **Stalls** Low

Form RPR

06-2 **1** **King Calypso**[37] 2021 6-9-7 **78**.............................. OisinMurphy 9 86
(Denis Coakley) *in rr: shkn up and prog over 3f out: rdn over 2f out: kpt on wl and led wl ins fnl f: pushed out* **13/2**[3]

2-41 **2** *1 ¼* **Charismatic Man (IRE)**[75] 1248 4-9-9 **87**.................... GeorgiaCox(5) 5 93
(Ralph Beckett) *chsd ldr: shkn up over 2f out: kpt on wl and rdn over 1f out: ev ch ins fnl f: briefly led ins fnl f: sn hdd and no ex* **2/1**[1]

122- **3** *1 ¼* **Tyrell (IRE)**[174] 7223 4-8-13 **72**..............................(v[1]) FergusSweeney 4 77
(Alan King) *clr ldr: roughly 7 l clr after first circ: c bk to field in bk st on fnl circ: shkn up over 2f out: kpt on wl tl hdd ins fnl f* **3/1**[2]

3555 **4** *3 ¾* **See And Be Seen**[19] 2562 7-8-9 **66**..............................(p) LukeMorris 6 66
(Sylvester Kirk) *chsd ldr on outer: rdn over 2f out: kpt on one pce fr over 1f out* **16/1**

60-6 **5** *1 ¼* **Hatsaway (IRE)**[19] 2562 6-8-10 **67**.............................. JFEgan 8 66
(Pat Phelan) *in rr: rdn over 2f out: kpt on fr over 1f out: nt gng pce to chal* **8/1**

-303 **6** *3 ¼* **Tetradrachm**[75] 1248 4-9-3 **81**.............................. GeorgeBuckell(5) 1 76
(David Simcock) *chsd ldrs on inner: rdn over 2f out: kpt on one pce fr over 1f out* **15/2**

-550 **7** *4* **Golden Jubilee (USA)**[26] 2357 8-8-10 **70**..........(p) KieranShoemark(3) 7 60
(Nigel Twiston-Davies) *in rr-div: rdn along over 2f out: kpt on one pce after* **33/1**

0-0 **8** *8* **Foresee (GER)**[59] 1517 4-9-4 **77**.............................. AdamKirby 2 57
(Tony Carroll) *mid-div on inner: rdn over 2f out: sn no ex* **12/1**

212/ **9** *7* **Dire Straits (IRE)**[636] 8164 6-9-1 **72**..............................(t[1]) DavidProbert 3 44
(Stuart Kittow) *awkward s: hld up in rr: rdn over 2f out: no prog after* **20/1**

3m 32.29s (2.19) **Going Correction** 0.0s/f (Stan)
**WFA** 4 from 6yo+ 1lb **9** Ran SP% **115.8**
Speed ratings (Par 105): **94,93,92,90,90 88,86,82,79**
CSF £19.95 CT £47.55 TOTE £7.60: £2.40, £1.10, £1.50; EX 23.30 Trifecta £68.50.

**Owner** Pearlygems **Bred** Miss K Rausing **Trained** West Ilsley, Berks

**FOCUS**
Only two horses with ratings in the 80s took their chance and it's not strong form for the grade.

## 3214 32RED H'CAP 7f (P)
**9:20** (9:20) (Class 4) (0-80,82) 4-Y-O+ **£5,175** (£1,540; £769; £384) **Stalls** Low

Form RPR

4130 **1** **Athassel**[4] 3095 8-8-12 **78**.............................. KatherineGlenister(7) 6 88
(David Evans) *hld up in rr: shkn up over 2f out: pushed along and angled to outer: rdn over 1f out: kpt on wl and led 150yds out: rdn out* **12/1**

-206 **2** *1 ½* **Mutamid**[23] 2462 5-9-9 **82**.............................. SilvestreDeSousa 7 88
(Ismail Mohammed) *hld up in mid-div on rail: rdn in centre 2f out: kpt on wl and led over 1f out: kpt on tl hdd 150yds out* **7/2**[2]

4416 **3** *2* **Anonymous John (IRE)**[19] 2582 5-8-13 **75**.......... KieranShoemark(3) 5 76
(Dominic Ffrench Davis) *in rr: rdn over 2f out: kpt on wl fr over 1f and ev ch ent fnl f: no ex cl home* **16/1**

-000 **4** *1 ½* **Mezmaar**[36] 2064 8-8-12 **71**..............................(h) SteveDrowne 13 68
(Mark Usher) *chsd ldr on outer: rdn over 2f out: kpt on one pce fr over 1f out* **20/1**

00-1 **5** *1* **Nightingale Valley**[54] 1599 4-9-2 **75**.............................. OisinMurphy 10 71
(Stuart Kittow) *settled in mid-div between horse: stuck bhd wall of horses travelling wl fr wl over 1f out: gap appeared ent fnl f: c across horse in bhd and clipped heels resulting in a fall: pushed out after* **16/1**

-222 **6** *1 ¾* **Golden Wedding (IRE)**[7] 2960 5-9-7 **80**.................... CharlesBishop 8 69
(Eve Johnson Houghton) *chsd ldrs on outer: rdn over 2f out: kpt on tl one pce ent fnl f* **4/1**[3]

0030 **7** *2* **Among Angels**[18] 2608 5-9-1 **77**.............................. CharlieBennett(3) 3 61
(Daniel Mark Loughnane) *in rr on inner: rdn over 2f out: wknd fr over 1f out* **20/1**

115- **8** *3* **Toriano**[297] 5199 4-9-8 **81**.............................. AdamKirby 12 57
(James Eustace) *in rr: rdn over 2f out: no ex over 1f out: pushed out after* **2/1**[1]

540- **9** *7* **Posh Bounty**[211] 7738 6-9-0 **73**..............................(h[1]) JimmyQuinn 4 30
(Paul Burgoyne) *chsd ldrs on inner: rdn over 2f out: struggling after and pushed out fr over 1f out* **50/1**

104- **10** *4 ½* **Multitask**[181] 8178 7-9-2 **75**.............................. TimmyMurphy 1 20
(Gary Moore) *led: rdn over 2f out: kpt on tl hdd & wknd qckly fr over 1f out* **14/1**

421/ **F** **Porta Rosa (USA)**[546] 8073 4-9-9 **82**.............................. JFEgan 2
(Mohamed Moubarak) *pressed ldr: rdn over 2f out and stuck on: began to wknd over 1f out: rival c across and clipped heels ent fnl f where fell* **20/1**

1m 25.47s (-0.53) **Going Correction** 0.0s/f (Stan) **11** Ran SP% **117.9**
Speed ratings (Par 105): **103,101,99,97,96 94,91,88,80,75**
CSF £51.37 CT £691.84 TOTE £13.00: £3.20, £2.30, £4.40; EX 57.80 Trifecta £658.30.

**Owner** Mrs E Evans **Bred** Moyns Park Estate And Stud Ltd **Trained** Pandy, Monmouths

■ Stewards' Enquiry : Oisin Murphy seven-day ban: careless riding in that at the time he manoeuvred right to make his run there was insufficient room (Jun 14-20)

**FOCUS**
Some interesting contenders in a fair closing race, but once again being held up proved advantageous.

T/Jkpt: Not won. T/Plt: £135.60 to a £1 stake. Pool: £73,545.99. 395.90 winning units. T/Qpdt: £20.60 to a £1 stake. Pool: £6,725.48. 240.65 winning units. **Cathal Gahan**

2926

# NOTTINGHAM (L-H)
Wednesday, May 31

**OFFICIAL GOING: Good (good to firm in places; 7.8)**
Wind: Light, against Weather: Sunny spells

## 3215 TOTEPLACEPOT SIX PLACES IN SIX RACES EBF MAIDEN FILLIES' STKS (PLUS 10 RACE) 5f 8y
**2:20** (2:25) (Class 5) 2-Y-O **£3,234** (£962; £481; £240) **Stalls** High

Form RPR

6 **1** **Wings Of The Rock (IRE)**[19] 2583 2-9-0 0.............................. LukeMorris 8 74
(Scott Dixon) *w ldr tl led 2f out: sn rdn and hung lft: styd on* **16/1**

3 **2** *1* **Donny Belle**[11] 2836 2-9-0 0.............................. JimCrowley 4 70
(David Brown) *prom: pushed along 1/2-way: chsd wnr ins fnl f: r.o* **5/1**[3]

**3** *nse* **Tulip Fever** 2-9-0 0.............................. PatCosgrave 2 70+
(William Haggas) *mid-div: hdwy over 1f out: r.o* **4/1**[1]

**4** *1 ½* **Alba Del Sole (IRE)** 2-9-0 0.............................. SeanLevey 6 65
(John Gosden) *hld up: hdwy over 1f out: nt rch ldrs* **10/1**

4 **5** *¾* **Gaelic Spirit (IRE)**[13] 2756 2-9-0 0.............................. FranBerry 9 62
(Joseph Tuite) *led 3f: sn rdn and hung lft: no ex ins fnl f* **6/1**

406 **6** *2* **Nobrassnolass (IRE)**[20] 2556 2-9-0 0................(v) RichardKingscote 11 55
(Tom Dascombe) *chsd ldrs: pushed along 1/2-way: wknd fnl f* **16/1**

0 **7** *1 ¾* **Saria**[23] 2473 2-9-0 0.............................. TomMarquand 1 49
(Daniel Mark Loughnane) *sn pushed along in rr: nvr on terms* **100/1**

**8** *nk* **One For June (IRE)** 2-9-0 0.............................. LiamJones 7 47
(William Haggas) *sn pushed along in rr: n.d* **9/2**[2]

**9** *shd* **Marilyn M (IRE)** 2-9-0 0.............................. SilvestreDeSousa 10 47
(George Scott) *s.i.s: sn pushed along in rr: nvr on terms* **8/1**

**10** *3 ¾* **Elusive Bird** 2-9-0 0.............................. KevinStott 12 34
(Giles Bravery) *s.i.s: outpcd* **25/1**

**11** *5* **Peas On Earth** 2-9-0 0.............................. KierenFox 3 16
(Derek Shaw) *wnt lft s and hung lft almost throuhgout sn bhd* **100/1**

1m 0.47s (-1.03) **Going Correction** -0.225s/f (Firm) **11** Ran SP% **106.9**
Speed ratings (Par 90): **99,97,97,94,93 90,87,87,87,81 73**
CSF £77.19 TOTE £13.30: £4.00, £2.20, £1.40; EX 109.80 Trifecta £648.20.

**Owner** The Cool Silk Partnership **Bred** Tom & Alex Frost **Trained** Babworth, Notts

■ Mnemonic Alexander was withdrawn. Price at time of withdrawal 15-2. Rule 4 applies to all bets - deduction 10p in the pound.

**FOCUS**
Some starts have been moved at this track following remeasuring, so some races will not have speed figures until there is sufficient data to calculate updated median times. Outer track. Rail set out 6yds on the home bend and 4yds on the stands' bend. Drying ground on a warm, sunny day. Few got seriously involved in this race but it looked a fair enough fillies' maiden. The race has been rated below the race average.

## 3216 TOTEPOOLLIVEINFO.COM VISIT FOR RACING RESULTS FILLIES' H'CAP 6f 18y
**2:50** (2:52) (Class 5) (0-75,76) 4-Y-O+ **£3,234** (£962; £481; £240) **Stalls** High

Form RPR

5132 **1** **Socialites Red**[4] 3063 4-8-10 **66**..............................(p) RPWalsh(7) 6 74
(Scott Dixon) *mde all: rdn and hung lft over 1f out: jst hld on* **4/1**[2]

-621 **2** *shd* **French**[11] 2843 4-9-4 **67**..............................(p) CamHardie 3 74
(Antony Brittain) *hld up in tch: lost pl over 3f out: rallied over 2f out: rdn to chse wnr ins fnl f: sn ev ch: styd on* **7/1**

211- **3** *2 ½* **Roman Holiday (IRE)**[225] 7430 4-9-13 **76**....................(p) HarryBentley 1 75
(Ed Vaughan) *s.i.s: pushed along in rr: hdwy and hung lft over 2f out: sn rdn: no ex ins fnl f* **6/1**[3]

4-44 **4** *nk* **Primanora**[18] 2620 4-9-3 **66**.............................. SilvestreDeSousa 8 64
(Michael Appleby) *chsd ldr: rdn over 1f out: edgd lft: no ex ins fnl f* **4/1**[2]

0-50 **5** *3 ½* **Monarch Maid**[6] 3008 6-9-5 **68**.............................. TomMarquand 5 55
(Peter Hiatt) *chsd ldrs: pushed along over 3f out: outpcd over 2f out: n.d after* **18/1**

61 **6** *½* **Wahiba (GER)**[29] 2285 4-9-6 **69**.............................. JimCrowley 7 54
(Marco Botti) *s.i.s: hdwy over 3f out: shkn up and wknd over 1f out* **5/2**[1]

-536 **7** *½* **Meandmyshadow**[20] 2550 9-9-7 **70**..............................(b) LukeMorris 4 53
(Alan Brown) *prom: pushed along over 3f out: lost pl over 2f out* **12/1**

1m 13.44s (-1.26) **Going Correction** -0.225s/f (Firm) **7** Ran SP% **108.3**
Speed ratings (Par 100): **99,98,95,95,90 89,89**
CSF £28.02 CT £144.46 TOTE £3.70: £1.60, £4.90; EX 25.10 Trifecta £172.60.

**Owner** J Melo Racing **Bred** Selwood, Hoskins & Trickledown **Trained** Babworth, Notts

**FOCUS**
A modest fillies' handicap.

## 3217 EBF TOTEQUADPOT INSURE YOUR PLACEPOT LAST FOUR FILLIES' H'CAP 1m 75y
**3:20** (3:20) (Class 4) (0-80,80) 3-Y-O **£6,469** (£1,925; £962; £481) **Stalls** Centre

Form RPR

1-02 **1** **Carducci**[13] 2754 3-9-1 **74**.............................. SeanLevey 3 77
(Richard Hannon) *hld up: hdwy over 2f out: sn rdn: led over 1f out: styd on* **15/8**[1]

6-44 **2** *½* **Seduce Me**[26] 2374 3-9-4 **77**..............................(p) MartinHarley 5 79
(K R Burke) *hld up: swtchd rt over 1f out: sn rdn: r.o ins fnl f: wnt 2nd nr fin* **6/1**

63-3 **3** *nk* **Eula Varner**[31] 2171 3-8-8 **67**.............................. FergusSweeney 2 68
(Henry Candy) *plld hrd: led 7f out: shkn up over 2f out: hdd over 1f out: styd on same pce wl ins fnl f* **9/2**[3]

-040 **4** *2 ¼* **Patching**[29] 2269 3-8-4 **63**.............................. LiamJones 1 59
(Giles Bravery) *chsd ldrs: rdn whn nt clr run over 2f out: styd on same pce ins fnl f* **16/1**

0-01 **5** *2 ½* **Vice Versa**[28] 2311 3-9-7 **80**.............................. RyanMoore 4 70
(Sir Michael Stoute) *led 1f: remained handy and racd keenly: rdn and ev ch over 1f out: eased whn btn ins fnl f* **2/1**[2]

1m 46.87s (-2.13) **Going Correction** -0.225s/f (Firm) **5** Ran SP% **106.5**
Speed ratings (Par 98): **101,100,100,97,95**
CSF £12.05 TOTE £2.50: £1.50, £3.30; EX 10.40 Trifecta £29.80.

**Owner** Sultan Ali **Bred** Seamus Burns Esq **Trained** East Everleigh, Wilts

**FOCUS**
Add 18yds. Probably not form to be positive about. The pace looked steady and the front-running third wasn't beaten far despite having pulled hard, and the fifth/last filly home was disappointing.

## 3218 TOTEPOOL RACECOURSE DEBIT CARD BETTING AVAILABLE H'CAP 1m 75y
3:50 (3:52) (Class 2) (0-110,109) 3-Y-O+£16,172 (£4,812; £2,405; £1,202) Stalls Centre

Form RPR
024 1 **Another Touch**[13] 2767 4-9-3 98 TonyHamilton 2 108
(Richard Fahey) *chsd ldrs: nt clr run over 2f out: led over 1f out: shkn up ins fnl f: r.o: comf* 9/4[1]
30-5 2 2 ½ **Kaspersky (IRE)**[28] 2290 6-10-0 109 MartinHarley 8 113
(Jane Chapple-Hyam) *s.i.s: rcvrd to ld 7f out: rdn and hdd over 1f out: styd on same pce ins fnl f* 6/1
-650 3 2 ¼ **Dragon Mall (USA)**[97] 888 4-9-7 102 (h) JamieSpencer 5 101
(David Simcock) *hld up: hdwy over 1f out: r.o to go 3rd post: nt trble ldrs* 9/2[2]
02-4 4 hd **Algaith (USA)**[28] 2290 5-9-10 105 JimCrowley 1 103
(Owen Burrows) *led 1f: chsd ldr: rdn over 2f out: no ex ins fnl f: b.b.v* 5/1[3]
0-00 5 1 ¼ **Big Baz (IRE)**[39] 1960 7-9-7 102 MartinDwyer 7 97
(William Muir) *prom: outpcd over 3f out: rallied over 2f out: no ex fnl f* 5/1[3]
6-06 6 13 **Poeta Diletto**[32] 2141 4-9-5 100 TomMarquand 3 66
(Marco Botti) *plld hrd and prom: rdn over 3f out: wknd over 2f out* 20/1
466- 7 21 **One Word More (IRE)**[236] 7121 7-9-0 95 (h) DavidNolan 4 12
(Tim Easterby) *hld up: rdn over 3f out: wknd wl over 1f out: b.b.v* 6/1
1m 44.13s (-4.87) **Going Correction** -0.225s/f (Firm) 7 Ran SP% **115.6**
Speed ratings (Par 109): **115,112,110,110,108 95,74**
CSF £16.69 CT £56.03 TOTE £2.90: £1.60, £2.90; EX 13.90 Trifecta £43.90.
**Owner** Nicholas Wrigley & Kevin Hart **Bred** Shadwell Estate Co Ltd **Trained** Musley Bank, N Yorks
**FOCUS**
Add 18yds. A straightforward race to assess.

## 3219 BRITISH EBF TOTEPOOL NOTTINGHAMSHIRE OAKS STKS (LISTED RACE) (F&M) 1m 2f 50y
4:20 (4:21) (Class 1) 4-Y-O+
£22,684 (£8,600; £4,304; £2,144; £1,076; £540) Stalls Low

Form RPR
200- 1 **Wilamina (IRE)**[250] 6746 4-9-0 97 AndreaAtzeni 10 102
(Martyn Meade) *chsd ldr 9f out: tl led over 1f out: rdn out* 11/1
4-13 2 1 **Singyoursong (IRE)**[18] 2605 4-9-0 90 (h[1]) JamieSpencer 7 100+
(David Simcock) *s.i.s: hld up and bhd: swtchd rt over 1f out: rdn: edgd lft and r.o wl ins fnl f: nt rch wnr: too much to do* 16/1
116- 3 1 ¼ **Entsar (IRE)**[207] 7823 4-9-0 95 PatCosgrave 8 97
(William Haggas) *trckd ldrs: rdn over 2f out: chsd wnr fnl f: no ex towards fin* 7/2[2]
00-2 4 ½ **Permission**[18] 2605 4-9-0 93 (h) DanielMuscutt 3 96
(James Fanshawe) *s.i.s: hld up: rdn over 2f out: r.o towards fin: nt trble ldrs* 8/1
-006 5 nse **Lucy The Painter (IRE)**[25] 2392 5-9-0 93 HarryBentley 2 96
(Ed de Giles) *hld up: rdn over 2f out: styng on whn nt clr run wl ins fnl f* 16/1
60-4 6 nk **Very Dashing**[60] 1500 4-9-0 96 FranBerry 4 95
(Ralph Beckett) *plld hrd: trckd ldrs: rdn over 1f out: no ex wl ins fnl f* 6/1[3]
10-1 7 1 ½ **Playful Sound**[25] 2396 4-9-0 99 RyanMoore 5 92
(Sir Michael Stoute) *sn led: qcknd over 2f out: rdn and hdd over 1f out: no ex ins fnl f* 13/8[1]
1-10 8 27 **Alf Guineas (IRE)**[25] 2389 4-9-0 85 JamesDoyle 6 38
(John Gosden) *hld up: plld hrd: rdn over 2f out: wknd wl over 1f out* 14/1
2m 9.67s (-4.63) **Going Correction** -0.225s/f (Firm) 8 Ran SP% **112.5**
Speed ratings (Par 111): **109,108,107,106,106 106,105,83**
CSF £159.73 TOTE £14.90: £3.20, £3.40, £1.50; EX 161.40 Trifecta £1232.50.
**Owner** The Snailwell Stud Limited **Bred** John Boden And Willie Kane **Trained** Newmarket, Suffolk
**FOCUS**
Add 18yds. The bare form doesn't look that strong, with the runner-up officially rated just 90, the third, fourth and sixth having excuses, and the favourite bombing out completely.

## 3220 TOTEPOOL BETTING ON ALL UK RACING H'CAP 1m 6f
4:50 (4:50) (Class 5) (0-70,70) 3-Y-O £3,234 (£962; £481; £240) Stalls Low

Form RPR
1-60 1 **Dominating (GER)**[12] 2807 3-9-2 65 FrannyNorton 4 74+
(Mark Johnston) *led 1f: chsd ldrs: lost grnd on ldng pair 10f out: tk clsr order over 3f out: chsd ldr over 2f out: rdn to ld over 1f out: styd on wl* 2/1[1]
00-2 2 4 **Plage Depampelonne**[28] 2307 3-9-3 66 JamieSpencer 2 69
(James Bethell) *hld up: hdwy u.p over 2f out: edgd lft fr over 1f out: styd on to go 2nd wl ins fnl f: no imp on wnr* 7/1
0-34 3 nk **Amadeus Rox (FR)**[15] 2705 3-8-8 57 FergusSweeney 7 59
(Alan King) *chsd ldr after 1f: lost grnd on ldr who wnt clr over 11f out: tk clsr order over 3f out: sn swtchd lft: led over 2f out: rdn and hdd over 1f out: no ex ins fnl f* 11/4[2]
064 4 7 **Astrostorm**[64] 1414 3-8-2 54 NoelGarbutt[(3)] 6 46
(Mark H Tompkins) *hld up: pushed along 6f out: hdwy to go 4th and hung lft over 1f out: nvr trbld ldrs* 25/1
4-35 5 7 **Red Caravel (IRE)**[29] 2273 3-9-7 70 (b[1]) ShaneKelly 1 53
(Richard Hughes) *hld up: hdwy u.p over 2f out: wknd wl over 1f out* 11/1
6146 6 14 **Ladofash**[29] 2273 3-8-11 63 (v) JordanVaughan[(3)] 5 26
(K R Burke) *pushed along leaving stalls: led after 1f: wnt clr over 11f out: c bk to the field over 3f out: hdd & wknd over 2f out* 8/1
640 7 66 **Stragar**[32] 2152 3-8-7 56 SilvestreDeSousa 3
(Michael Appleby) *hld up: disp 3rd 8f out: rdn over 5f out: wknd 3f out* 5/1[3]
3m 3.41s (-3.59) 7 Ran SP% **112.5**
CSF £16.04 TOTE £3.30: £1.30, £3.00; EX 19.40 Trifecta £43.10.
**Owner** A D Spence **Bred** Gestut Etzean **Trained** Middleham Moor, N Yorks
**FOCUS**
Add 30yds. A 3yo staying handicap run at a good pace.

## 3221 COLLECT TOTEPOOL WINNINGS AT BETFRED SHOPS "HANDS AND HEELS" APPRENTICE H'CAP 1m 2f 50y
5:20 (5:20) (Class 6) (0-65,65) 4-Y-O+ £2,587 (£770; £384; £192) Stalls Low

Form RPR
0-04 1 **Miningrocks (FR)**[7] 2953 5-9-12 65 GerO'Neill 6 73+
(Declan Carroll) *led at stdy pce 3f: plld hrd in 2nd pl tl led again over 2f out: sn pushed along: styd on: comf* 15/8[1]
5436 2 1 ¼ **Fantasy Gladiator**[29] 2282 11-9-9 62 (p) ConnorMurtagh 4 68
(Michael Appleby) *chsd ldrs: shkn up over 2f out: chsd wnr ins fnl f: no ex nr fin* 3/1[2]
65-3 3 2 ¼ **Frantical**[13] 2762 5-9-4 57 AledBeech 3 58+
(Tony Carroll) *hld up in tch: plld hrd: lost pl over 7f out: pushed along and hdwy over 2f out: styd on to go 3rd wl ins fnl f* 5/1[3]
0-02 4 1 ¼ **Shirataki (IRE)**[2] 3148 9-8-12 54 (h) MollyKing[(3)] 2 53
(Peter Hiatt) *s.i.s: hld up: hdwy to ld 7f out: pushed along and hdd over 2f out: no ex ins fnl f* 12/1
-060 5 4 ½ **First Summer**[16] 2687 5-9-3 56 (p) FinleyMarsh 5 46
(Shaun Harris) *chsd ldrs: pushed along over 3f out: styd on same pce fnl 2f* 8/1
000- 6 1 **Heat Storm (IRE)**[150] 7231 6-8-7 46 oh1 (v) MillyNaseb 1 35
(James Unett) *s.s: hld up: pushed along over 3f out: n.d* 14/1
-246 7 ½ **Pensax Lady (IRE)**[15] 2710 4-8-13 55 TobyEley[(3)] 7 43
(Daniel Mark Loughnane) *hld up: pushed along over 3f out: nvr on terms* 10/1
2m 16.72s (2.42) **Going Correction** -0.225s/f (Firm) 7 Ran SP% **111.0**
Speed ratings (Par 101): **81,80,78,77,73 72,72**
CSF £7.08 TOTE £2.50: £1.40, £2.00; EX 8.00 Trifecta £20.60.
**Owner** Mrs Sarah Bryan **Bred** M Daguzan-Garros & Rolling Hills Farm **Trained** Malton, N Yorks
**FOCUS**
Add 18yds. A weak race run at a slow pace early on. Straightforward form.
T/Plt: £158.70 to a £1 stake. Pool: £60,419.36. 277.87 winning units. T/Qpdt: £24.50 to a £1 stake. Pool: £3,803.20. 114.80 winning units. **Colin Roberts**

3222 - 3229a (Foreign Racing) - See Raceform Interactive

# 3135 CHELMSFORD (A.W) (L-H)
Thursday, June 1

**OFFICIAL GOING: Polytrack: standard (9.10 abandoned due to power failure)**
Wind: light, across Weather: sunny and warm

## 3230 TOTEPLACEPOT AT TOTESPORT.COM NOVICE AUCTION STKS (PLUS 10 RACE) 5f (P)
6:10 (6:12) (Class 4) 2-Y-O £7,115 (£2,117; £1,058; £529) Stalls Low

Form RPR
214 1 **Emilia James**[22] 2522 2-9-3 0 RyanMoore 1 84
(Mark Johnston) *mde all: rdn over 1f out: asserting 1f out: styd on strly and drew wl clr ins fnl f: comf* 8/13[1]
531 2 3 ¼ **Queen Of Kalahari**[10] 2890 2-9-3 0 JimCrowley 3 72
(Charles Hills) *pressed wnr: rdn to chal over 1f out: unable qck w wnr 1f out: clr 2nd and styd on same pce ins fnl f* 3/1[2]
22 3 2 ¼ **Three Little Birds**[21] 2545 2-8-4 0 DavidEgan[(7)] 5 58
(Sylvester Kirk) *wl in tch in 4th: effrt over 1f out: 3rd and unable qck 1f out: wknd ins fnl f* 5/1[3]
10 4 2 **Blessed To Empress (IRE)**[13] 2801 2-9-3 0 LemosdeSouza 4 57
(Amy Murphy) *swtchd lft sn after s: t.k.h: trckd ldng pair: rdn over 1f out: 4th and outpcd 1f out: wknd ins fnl f* 12/1
5 32 **Monsieur Renard** 2-9-2 0 AdamBeschizza 2
(Charlie Wallis) *s.i.s: rn v green and sn rdn along: t.o after 2f* 100/1
1m 1.12s (0.92) **Going Correction** -0.025s/f (Stan) 5 Ran SP% **112.3**
Speed ratings (Par 95): **91,85,82,79,27**
CSF £2.88 TOTE £1.40: £1.10, £2.80; EX 2.60 Trifecta £4.20.
**Owner** James Property Ltd **Bred** Red House Stud & Ketton Ashwell Ltd **Trained** Middleham Moor, N Yorks
**FOCUS**
This was steadily run and dominated by the odds-on favourite. The runner-up has been rated to her pre-race mark.

## 3231 TOTEEXACTA AT TOTESPORT.COM H'CAP 5f (P)
6:40 (6:40) (Class 3) (0-90,91) 4-Y-O+ £9,703 (£2,887; £1,443; £721) Stalls Low

Form RPR
4104 1 **Stepper Point**[20] 2578 8-9-7 88 (v) MartinDwyer 6 97
(William Muir) *mde all and sn clr: rdn over 1f out: nvr gng to be ct: pushed out fnl 100yds* 5/2[2]
-620 2 1 ¼ **Excellent George**[38] 2038 5-8-12 79 (t) HarryBentley 2 83
(Stuart Williams) *chsd wnr: rdn over 1f out: kpt on u.p and clsd ins fnl f: nvr getting to wnr* 7/4[1]
0644 3 1 **Saved My Bacon (IRE)**[22] 2516 6-8-6 73 (h) AdamBeschizza 9 73
(Chris Dwyer) *taken down early: stdd and dropped in bhd after s: hld up off the pce in rr: hdwy and swtchd lft over 1f out: 3rd and styd on wl ins fnl f: nvr getting to wnr* 8/1
5541 4 1 ¼ **Dynamo Walt (IRE)**[22] 2516 6-9-5 86 (v) KierenFox 8 82
(Derek Shaw) *t.k.h: hld up in midfield: effrt u.p over 1f out: kpt on ins fnl f: nvr threatening wnr* 10/3[3]
0600 5 2 ½ **Ballesteros**[22] 2524 8-8-2 72 SammyJoBell[(3)] 5 59
(Richard Fahey) *3rd but nt on terms w wnr: rdn over 1f out: lost 3rd and no imp 1f out: plugged on* 9/1
4-00 6 2 **Seve**[111] 664 5-9-2 83 TimmyMurphy 7 63
(Karen George) *taken down early: squeezed for room sn after s: t.k.h: hld up off the pce in midfield: effrt over 1f out: no imp: n.d* 33/1
59.66s (-0.54) **Going Correction** -0.025s/f (Stan) 6 Ran SP% **112.1**
Speed ratings (Par 107): **103,101,99,97,93 90**
CSF £7.27 CT £27.14 TOTE £3.60: £2.50, £1.40; EX 9.10 Trifecta £32.40.
**Owner** C L A Edginton **Bred** Whitsbury Manor Stud **Trained** Lambourn, Berks
**FOCUS**
They gave the winner too much rope here.

## 3232 TOTEQUADPOT AT TOTESPORT.COM H'CAP 1m (P)
7:10 (7:13) (Class 2) (0-100,99) 3-Y-O £19,407 (£5,775; £2,886; £1,443) Stalls Low

Form RPR
10-1 1 **City Of Joy**[26] 2385 3-8-11 89 RyanMoore 4 97+
(Sir Michael Stoute) *sn dropped to rr and niggled along early: travelling bk on bridle after 1f: rdn and hdwy over 1f out: chsng ldrs and swtchd rt ent fnl f: led 100yds out: styd on wl: rdn out* 10/3[2]
2111 2 ¾ **Tricorn (IRE)**[42] 1907 3-9-4 96 JamesDoyle 5 102+
(John Gosden) *hld up in last pair: effrt over 1f out: hdwy u.p ins fnl f: pressing ldrs and styd on wl u.p fnl 100yds: wnt 2nd last strides* 2/1[1]
51-0 3 hd **Intimate Art (IRE)**[41] 1945 3-7-9 80 oh1 DavidEgan[(7)] 8 85
(Andrew Balding) *dwlt: rcvrd to chse ldr 6f out: rdn and ev ch over 1f out: led 1f out: edgd rt and hdd 100yds: kpt on same pce after: lost 2nd last strides* 16/1
1-23 4 2 ½ **Election Day**[27] 2376 3-8-4 82 FrannyNorton 2 81
(Mark Johnston) *chsd ldr for 2f: styd chsng ldrs: effrt on inner over 1f out: hung rt and no imp jst ins fnl f: wknd fnl 100yds* 6/1[3]

61-5 **5** 1 **Mandarin (GER)**[12] 2818 3-8-8 **86**........ DanielMuscutt 7 83
(Marco Botti) *led: rdn over 1f out: hdd 1f out: no ex and wknd fnl 100yds* **20/1**

1-23 **6** ¾ **Areen Heart (FR)**[21] 2554 3-8-9 **87**........ JimCrowley 3 82
(Richard Fahey) *t.k.h: hld up in tch in midfield: rdn over 1f out: unable qck and btn 1f out: wknd ins fnl f* **10/3**[2]

163- **7** ¾ **Sultan Baybars**[201] 7930 3-9-3 **95**........ AndreaAtzeni 1 88
(Roger Varian) *hld up in tch in midfield: effrt over 1f out: unable qck and wknd ins fnl f* **9/1**

1m 37.79s (-2.11) **Going Correction** -0.025s/f (Stan) **7 Ran SP% 114.4**
Speed ratings (Par 105): **109,108,108,105,104 103,103**
CSF £10.46 CT £89.42 TOTE £4.00: £1.40, £1.80; EX 10.10 Trifecta £94.70.
**Owner** Saeed Suhail **Bred** Hascombe And Valiant Studs **Trained** Newmarket, Suffolk

**FOCUS**
A decent handicap, and the first three are all capable of winning more races.

## 3233 TOTETRIFECTA AT TOTESPORT.COM FILLIES' H'CAP 1m (P)
7:40 (7:42) (Class 2) (0-100,96) 3-Y-O+ **£19,407** (£5,775; £2,886; £1,443) **Stalls** Low

Form RPR

315- **1** **Amabilis**[236] 7147 3-8-6 **85**........ JosephineGordon 1 96+
(Ralph Beckett) *trckd ldng pair: effrt on inner and rdn to chal over 1f out: led 1f out: r.o strly and drew clr ins fnl f: eased towards fin* **9/4**[1]

0-33 **2** 3 ¾ **Illaunmore (USA)**[22] 2517 3-7-10 **82**........ DavidEgan(7) 2 83
(John Gosden) *t.k.h: led and set stdy gallop: pushed along and qcknd jst over 2f out: rdn over 1f out: hdd 1f out: outpcd by wnr but hld on to 2nd ins fnl f* **11/4**[2]

43-1 **3** nk **Normandie Lady**[30] 2268 4-8-12 **83**........ SammyJoBell(3) 4 86
(Richard Fahey) *stdd s: t.k.h: hld up in tch in rr: effrt on inner over 1f out: rdn and styd on ins fnl f to press for 2nd towards fin: no ch w wnr* **5/1**[3]

2-10 **4** 1 ¼ **Tegara**[19] 2605 4-8-6 **77** oh3........ HollieDoyle(3) 3 77
(David Simcock) *chsd ldr: rdn over 2f out: 3rd and unable qck over 1f out: wl hld 4th and kpt on same pce ins fnl f* **9/1**

216- **5** 1 ¾ **Spatial**[237] 7116 3-9-3 **96**........ RyanMoore 5 89
(Sir Michael Stoute) *stdd s: t.k.h: hld up in tch in last pair: effrt over 1f out: no imp: wl hld 5th and one pced ins fnl f: eased towards fin* **11/4**[2]

1m 39.27s (-0.63) **Going Correction** -0.025s/f (Stan)
**WFA** 3 from 4yo 11lb **5 Ran SP% 110.8**
Speed ratings (Par 96): **102,98,97,96,94**
CSF £8.77 TOTE £3.10: £1.20, £1.50; EX 7.70 Trifecta £23.20.
**Owner** K Abdullah **Bred** Juddmonte Farms Ltd **Trained** Kimpton, Hants

**FOCUS**
This was steadily run and turned into a dash up the straight.

## 3234 TOTEWIN AT TOTESPORT.COM MAIDEN STKS (PLUS 10 RACE) 7f (P)
8:10 (8:11) (Class 4) 3-Y-O **£8,086** (£2,406; £1,202; £601) **Stalls** Low

Form RPR

2-23 **1** **Top Mission**[13] 2778 3-9-5 85........(p[1]) JosephineGordon 1 83+
(Saeed bin Suroor) *mde virtually all: rdn: ducked lft and hit rail jst over 1f out: asserted jst ins fnl f: hrd pressed towards fin: hld on* **10/11**[1]

0-42 **2** nk **Buxted Dream (USA)**[20] 2581 3-9-5 76........ AndreaAtzeni 6 82+
(Luca Cumani) *dwlt: sn in midfield: clsd and swtchd rt over 1f out: hdwy to chse wnr 100yds: hung lft but str chal towards fin: jst hld* **11/4**[2]

2 **3** 1 ½ **Peach Melba**[10] 2887 3-9-0 0........ FrannyNorton 5 73+
(Mark Johnston) *chsd ldrs: nt clr run: swtchd rt and rdr got whip stuck in nk strap fr over 1f out: chsng ldrs but rdr unable to offer much assistance and hung lft ins fnl f: eased towards fin* **4/1**[3]

0 **4** 2 **Saaheq**[40] 1962 3-9-5 0........ JimCrowley 7 72
(Brian Meehan) *chsd ldrs: effrt to chse wnr over 1f tl 100yds out: wknd towards fin* **16/1**

36- **5** 3 **Malcolm The Pug (IRE)**[320] 4390 3-9-5 0........ TomMarquand 3 64
(Richard Hannon) *w ldr: rdn 2f out: lost 2nd and unable qck over 1f out: wknd ins fnl f* **7/1**

**6** 1 **Pioneertown (IRE)** 3-9-5 0........ RyanPowell 2 61+
(Sir Mark Prescott Bt) *sn outpcd and bustled along in last trio: clsd 3f out: rdn and outpcd over 1f out: wknd fnl f* **50/1**

**7** ¾ **Miss Pacific** 3-9-0 0........ DavidProbert 8 54
(William Jarvis) *s.i.s: off the pce in rr and rdn along: clsd and in tch 3f out: wknd fnl f* **50/1**

**8** 7 **Hanningfield** 3-9-5 0........ DannyBrock 4 40
(Michael Bell) *sn rdn along in last trio: clsd and in tch 3f out: wknd over 1f out* **66/1**

1m 25.73s (-1.47) **Going Correction** -0.025s/f (Stan) **8 Ran SP% 122.8**
Speed ratings (Par 101): **107,106,104,102,99 98,97,89**
CSF £4.06 TOTE £1.90: £1.02, £1.60, £1.40; EX 5.30 Trifecta £11.20.
**Owner** Godolphin **Bred** Darley **Trained** Newmarket, Suffolk

**FOCUS**
A fair maiden.

## 3235 TOTEPLACE AT TOTESPORT.COM H'CAP 1m 2f (P)
8:40 (8:47) (Class 4) (0-85,83) 4-Y-O+ **£8,086** (£2,406; £1,202; £601) **Stalls** Low

Form RPR

6-12 **1** **Celebration Day (IRE)**[37] 2068 4-9-7 **83**........ RyanPowell 2 90
(Simon Crisford) *mde all: rdn over 1f out: styd on wl ins fnl f: rdn out* **5/2**[2]

2/06 **2** ½ **Tobacco Road (IRE)**[20] 2574 7-9-1 **77**........(t[1]) TomMarquand 3 83
(David Pipe) *taken down early: chsd wnr tl 7f out: styd chsng ldrs: effrt on inner over 1f out: pressing wnr ins fnl f: kpt on but hld towards fin* **8/1**

2-31 **3** 1 **Cape Peninsular**[33] 2164 4-9-4 **80**........ MartinHarley 6 84
(James Tate) *chsd wnr 7f out: rdn over 1f out: awkward hd carriage and unable qck: lost 2nd and kpt on same pce ins fnl f* **15/8**[1]

3041 **4** 2 ½ **Tee It Up Tommo (IRE)**[7] 2996 8-8-12 **77** 6ex........ HollieDoyle(3) 1 76
(Daniel Steele) *s.i.s: wl off the pce in last: clsd and in tch 1/2-way: effrt over 1f out: kpt on ins fnl f but nvr threatened ldrs* **5/1**[3]

3-62 **5** ¾ **Mikmak**[10] 2893 4-9-6 **82**........(p) MartinDwyer 5 80
(William Muir) *hld up off the pce in 5th: clsd and in tch 1/2-way: effrt over 1f out: 4th and no imp 1f out: wknd ins fnl f* **5/1**[3]

213 **6** 3 ½ **Mr Red Clubs (IRE)**[13] 2796 8-8-9 **78**........(p) RayDawson(7) 4 69
(Michael Appleby) *chsd ldrs: rdn over 2f out: lost pl and dropped to rr over 1f out: wknd fnl f* **20/1**

2m 6.13s (-2.47) **Going Correction** -0.025s/f (Stan) **6 Ran SP% 112.6**
Speed ratings (Par 105): **108,107,106,104,104 101**
CSF £21.97 TOTE £3.20: £1.70, £3.50; EX 23.50 Trifecta £89.70.
**Owner** Mohammed Al Nabouda **Bred** Rabbah Bloodstock Limited **Trained** Newmarket, Suffolk

**FOCUS**
There was a power cut at the track prior to this race, which meant the floodlights could not be switched on, so the final race on the card was abandoned. They didn't go a great gallop early on.

## 3236 CCR LADIES DAY 22ND JUNE H'CAP 1m 6f (P)
(9:10) (Class 6) (0-65,) 4-Y-O+ £

T/Plt: £12.20 to a £1 stake. Pool: £52,369.84 - 3121.75 winning units. T/Qpdt: £7.20 to a £1 stake. Pool: £4,127.13 - 421.35 winning units. **Steve Payne**

# 2771 HAMILTON (R-H)
Thursday, June 1

**OFFICIAL GOING: Good (6.8)**
Wind: Breezy, half behind in sprints and in 5f of home straight on round course
Weather: Overcast

## 3237 BB FOODSERVICE NOVICE AUCTION STKS (PLUS 10 RACE) (A £20,000 BB FOODSERVICE 2YO SERIES QUALIFIER) 5f 7y
2:00 (2:01) (Class 4) 2-Y-O **£5,175** (£1,540; £769; £384) **Stalls** High

Form RPR

43 **1** **Villa Tora**[12] 2832 2-8-7 0........ JoeFanning 5 70+
(Mark Johnston) *t.k.h early: mde all against stands' rail: shkn up over 1f out: kpt on wl fnl f: comf* **2/5**[1]

**2** 1 ¼ **Eva Docc (IRE)** 2-8-6 0........ ConnorBeasley 3 65
(Keith Dalgleish) *trckd ldng pair: effrt and pressed wnr over 1f out: kpt on ins fnl f* **28/1**

**3** 3 **Medici Oro** 2-8-12 0........ PaulMulrennan 1 60
(David Brown) *pressed wnr tl rdn and outpcd over 1f out: kpt on ins fnl f: no imp* **17/2**[3]

**4** nse **Double Reflection** 2-8-6 0........ JoeyHaynes 4 54
(K R Burke) *dwlt: sn in tch: pushed along and effrt over 2f out: one pce fr over 1f out* **11/1**

**5** 3 ¾ **Ty Rock Brandy (IRE)** 2-8-6 0........ ShaneGray 6 40
(Lee Smyth, Ire) *slowly away: bhd and outpcd: hdwy over 2f out: rdn and wknd over 1f out* **50/1**

04 **6** 4 ½ **Faradays Spark (IRE)**[20] 2590 2-8-13 0........ PaulHanagan 7 31
(Richard Fahey) *s.i.s: a outpcd and bhd: no ch fr 1/2-way* **7/1**[2]

**Going Correction** -0.20s/f (Firm) **6 Ran SP% 108.2**
Speed ratings (Par 95): **92,90,85,85,79 71**
CSF £13.26 TOTE £1.30: £1.10, £8.10; EX 12.90 Trifecta £42.20.
**Owner** Kingsley Park 6 **Bred** D R Botterill **Trained** Middleham Moor, N Yorks

**FOCUS**
Some starts have been moved at this track following remeasuring, so some races will not have speed figures until there is sufficient data to calculate updated median times. The going was good. An uncompetitive maiden run at an honest pace. It'll take a bit of time for the true worth of the form to become clear.

## 3238 DICK BIRKETT MEMORIAL H'CAP 5f 7y
2:30 (2:30) (Class 5) (0-75,72) 4-Y-O+ **£5,175** (£1,540; £769; £384) **Stalls** High

Form RPR

30-2 **1** **Bronze Beau**[13] 2777 10-8-13 **64**........(tp) ShaneGray 5 71
(Kristin Stubbs) *mde virtually all: rdn over 1f out: hld on gamely cl home* **9/2**[3]

4-30 **2** shd **Jack Luey**[16] 2700 10-9-4 **69**........(b) PaulHanagan 2 76
(Lawrence Mullaney) *disp ld thrght: rdn over 1f out: kpt on wl fnl f: jst hld* **5/2**[2]

45-0 **3** 4 **Bunce (IRE)**[13] 2776 9-8-11 **62**........ PJMcDonald 7 54
(Linda Perratt) *outpcd and bhd: rdn and hdwy over 1f out: kpt on fnl f: nvr able to chal* **12/1**

1121 **4** ½ **Noah Amor (IRE)**[19] 2627 4-8-13 **71**........ PatrickVaughan(7) 1 61
(David O'Meara) *trckd ldrs on outside: rdn over 2f out: edgd lft and wknd ins fnl f* **2/1**[1]

40-5 **5** 2 ¼ **Mitchum**[11] 2858 8-9-0 **65**........(p) DavidAllan 3 47
(Ron Barr) *flyj. s: bhd and outpcd: shortlived effrt 2f out: sn btn* **11/2**

/50- **6** 6 **First Rate**[367] 2742 4-9-2 **67**........ DanielTudhope 4 28
(Marjorie Fife) *t.k.h: in tch on outside: rdn over 2f out: wknd over 1f out* **12/1**

59.12s (-0.88) **Going Correction** -0.20s/f (Firm) **6 Ran SP% 110.9**
Speed ratings (Par 103): **99,98,92,91,88 78**
CSF £15.72 TOTE £4.10: £2.00, £1.90; EX 14.50 Trifecta £87.60.
**Owner** G J Daly & Kristin Stubbs **Bred** Meon Valley Stud **Trained** Norton, N Yorks

**FOCUS**
Not a great race for the grade. A strongly run handicap in which it paid to race handy.

## 3239 DM HALL H'CAP 6f 6y
3:00 (3:03) (Class 5) (0-70,76) 3-Y-O+ **£5,175** (£1,540; £769; £384) **Stalls** Centre

Form RPR

512- **1** **Control Centre (IRE)**[243] 6961 3-9-3 **67**........ DanielTudhope 10 78
(Marjorie Fife) *in tch on nr side of gp: effrt and pushed along over 2f out: led over 1f out: kpt on wl* **8/1**

36-3 **2** ½ **Love Oasis**[13] 2776 3-9-3 **67**........ JoeFanning 4 76
(Mark Johnston) *s.i.s: bhd and sn swtchd to nr side of gp: effrt and edgd to stands' rail wl over 1f out: sn chsng wnr: kpt on fnl f* **11/2**[2]

34-5 **3** 3 ¾ **Roys Dream**[9] 2925 3-9-6 **70**........ TonyHamilton 9 67
(Paul Collins) *in tch: drvn along over 2f out: hdwy over 1f out: kpt on fnl f: nt rch first two* **11/1**

0045 **4** 1 ¼ **Secret Missile**[7] 2990 7-10-2 **72**........(p) DavidAllan 7 67
(David C Griffiths) *bhd and sn pushed along: hdwy over 1f out: kpt on fnl f: no imp* **7/1**

U451 **5** nk **Casterbridge**[2] 3170 5-10-6 **76** 6ex........ NeilFarley 8 70
(Eric Alston) *led: rdn: edgd rt and hdd over 1f out: wknd ins fnl f* **2/1**[1]

0-46 **6** hd **Reckless Serenade (IRE)**[47] 1805 3-9-0 **69**........ RowanScott(5) 1 61
(Keith Dalgleish) *t.k.h: cl up on far side of gp: rdn over 2f out: wknd over 1f out* **14/1**

15-5 **7** 3 ½ **Picks Pinta**[25] 2428 6-9-2 **65**........(p) ConnorMurtagh(7) 6 48
(John David Riches) *cl up: ev ch over 2f out to over 1f out: sn wknd* **6/1**[3]

00-0 **8** 12 **Sir Domino (FR)**[11] 2858 5-10-0 **70**........(p) JackGarritty 2 14
(Patrick Holmes) *flyj. s: bhd on far side of gp: struggling over 2f out: sn wknd* **33/1**

0-53 **8** *12* **Dark Phantom (IRE)**[8] 2956 6-8-7 **46** oh1 PaddyPilley(5) 8
(Eve Johnson Houghton) *led but pressed: hdd & wknd 3f out: eased whn no ch over 1f out* **7/2**[2]
000 **9** *76* **Dalavand (IRE)**[9] 2914 4-8-7 **48** (p[1]) OllieJago(7) 1
(Laura Mongan) *shoved along to get gng early: in tch in last trio to 4f out: wknd rapidly: t.o whn virtually p.u fnl 2f* **25/1**
2m 31.48s (-0.02) **Going Correction** -0.05s/f (Good) **9** Ran SP% **113.2**
Speed ratings (Par 101): **98,97,96,96,91 87,83,75,25**
CSF £14.38 CT £55.75 TOTE £3.90: £1.50, £1.90, £1.40; EX 15.40 Trifecta £58.10.
**Owner** Mrs Jane Chapple-Hyam **Bred** Whatton Manor Stud **Trained** Dalham, Suffolk
**FOCUS**
Lowly handicap form.
T/Plt: £717.70 to a £1 stake. Pool: £56,944.62 - 57.92 winning units. T/Qpdt: £240.20 to a £1 stake. Pool: £4,114.30 - 12.67 winning units. **Jonathan Neesom**

# 2918 NEWCASTLE (A.W) (L-H)
Thursday, June 1

**OFFICIAL GOING: Tapeta: standard**
Wind: light half against Weather: Fine

## 3252 TRANSFLEX VEHICLE HIRE H'CAP 1m 2f 42y (Tp)
**6:20** (6:20) (Class 5) (0-70,70) 4-Y-O+ **£5,175** (£1,540; £769; £384) **Stalls** High

Form RPR
55-6 **1** **Auspicion**[17] 2685 5-9-4 **67** AndrewMullen 9 76
(Tom Tate) *hld up: pushed along and hdwy on outer over 2f out: rdn to ld appr fnl f: edgd lft: kpt on wl* **7/2**[2]
2-34 **2** *1 3/4* **Henpecked**[14] 1345 7-9-6 **69** (p) PaulMulrennan 6 74
(Alistair Whillans) *trckd ldrs: led over 2f out: sn rdn: hdd appr fnl f: kpt on same pce* **12/1**
400- **3** *1 1/2* **Yensir**[302] 5027 4-9-4 **67** PaddyAspell 1 69
(Grant Tuer) *trckd ldrs: rdn 2f out: kpt on same pce* **14/1**
0-22 **4** *nk* **Highway Robber**[114] 607 4-8-0 **52** oh1 ow1 RachelRichardson(3) 2 53
(Wilf Storey) *prom: rdn and lost 2f out: kpt on ins fnl f* **20/1**
0033 **5** *shd* **London Glory**[19] 2629 4-8-10 **64** (b) LewisEdmunds(5) 4 65
(David Thompson) *midfield: hdwy 3f out: rdn to chal 2f out: no ex fnl 110yds* **11/4**[1]
545- **6** *shd* **Omotesando**[320] 4377 7-9-2 **65** KevinStott 7 66+
(Oliver Greenall) *hld up in midfield: rdn and n.m.r 2f out: styd on ins fnl f* **8/1**
**7** *2 1/2* **Apalis (FR)**[70] 5-9-2 **68** NathanEvans(3) 8 64
(Michael Easterby) *hld up in midfield on outer: rdn and sme hdwy over 2f out: wknd ins fnl f* **8/1**
100- **8** *5* **Almutamarred (USA)**[228] 7385 5-8-13 **65** AdamMcNamara(3) 3 51
(David Brown) *dwlt: midfield: rdn 2f out: wknd fnl f* **6/1**[3]
34/0 **9** *3* **Sandgate**[16] 1469 5-8-2 **54** NathanAlison(3) 5 34
(Kenny Johnson) *a towards rr* **150/1**
0-40 **10** *9* **Overhaugh Street**[16] 2708 4-8-10 **62** CallumShepherd(3) 10 24
(Ed de Giles) *led: rdn whn hdd over 2f out: sn wknd: eased* **12/1**
2m 14.17s (3.77) **Going Correction** +0.325s/f (Slow) **10** Ran SP% **112.9**
Speed ratings (Par 103): **97,95,94,94,94 94,92,88,85,78**
CSF £43.47 CT £516.94 TOTE £4.70: £1.60, £2.40, £3.30; EX 42.10 Trifecta £676.00.
**Owner** David Storey **Bred** Lael Stables **Trained** Tadcaster, N Yorks
**FOCUS**
An ordinary 55-70 handicap featuring mainly exposed sorts. The pace was just fair and the winner was the only one of the principals to come from off the pace.

## 3253 ROGER RICHFIELD MEMORIAL FILLIES' H'CAP 6f (Tp)
**6:50** (6:51) (Class 4) (0-85,82) 4-Y-O+ **£7,956** (£2,367; £1,183; £591) **Stalls** Centre

Form RPR
6-04 **1** **Love Island**[5] 3063 8-9-2 **82** (h) LewisEdmunds(5) 3 89
(Richard Whitaker) *chsd ldrs: rdn and briefly outpcd in 4th 2f out: jocked dropped whip ins fnl f: r.o: led post* **13/8**[1]
2103 **2** *hd* **Fredricka**[24] 2462 6-9-3 **78** (p) RenatoSouza 2 84
(Chris Dwyer) *led: rdn over 1f out: edgd lft ins fnl f: hdd post* **15/8**[2]
020 **3** *1 3/4* **New Road Side**[48] 1777 4-9-3 **78** PaulMulrennan 4 78
(Richard Guest) *pressed ldr: rdn 2f out: one pce and hld in 3rd fnl 110yds* **11/2**
-324 **4** *3/4* **Palenville (IRE)**[107] 729 4-8-13 **74** PaddyAspell 6 72
(Grant Tuer) *dwlt: trckd ldrs: rdn and outpcd in 4th appr fnl f: no threat after* **9/2**[3]
1m 14.73s (2.23) **Going Correction** +0.325s/f (Slow) **4** Ran SP% **106.4**
Speed ratings (Par 102): **98,97,95,94**
CSF £4.82 TOTE £3.50; EX 2.10 Trifecta £11.50.
**Owner** R M Whitaker **Bred** Hellwood Farm And J B Pemberton **Trained** Scarcroft, W Yorks
**FOCUS**
Just four runners in this sprint and a game effort by the winner.

## 3254 BRITISH STALLION STUDS EBF NOVICE STKS (PLUS 10 RACE) 5f (Tp)
**7:20** (7:22) (Class 4) 2-Y-O **£6,469** (£1,925; £962; £481) **Stalls** Centre

Form RPR
**1** **Pilkington** 2-9-2 **0** DanielTudhope 7 76
(David O'Meara) *trckd ldrs: led gng wl over 1f out: rdn ins fnl f: edgd lft and hld on towards fin* **11/1**
**2** *nk* **Sosian** 2-8-11 **0** PaulHanagan 5 70
(Richard Fahey) *dwlt: hld up and sn pushed along: stl only 6th appr fnl f: r.o wl* **12/1**
**3** *3/4* **Global Humor (USA)** 2-9-2 **0** PaulMulrennan 2 72
(Ed Dunlop) *trckd ldrs: pushed along over 1f out: chal ent fnl f: rdn and wandered ins fnl f: one pce fnl 75yds* **11/8**[1]
**4** *1 1/4* **Big Les (IRE)** 2-9-2 **0** GrahamLee 4 68
(Karen McLintock) *hld up in tch: pushed along 2f out: rdn and kpt on ins fnl f* **33/1**
6 **5** *2 3/4* **Branscombe**[24] 2459 2-9-2 **0** PJMcDonald 3 58
(Mark Johnston) *led narrowly: rdn whn hdd over 1f out: wknd ins fnl f* **6/1**[3]
41 **6** *2 1/4* **Almane (IRE)**[43] 1872 2-9-2 **0** AdamMcNamara(3) 1 53
(Richard Fahey) *fly leapt s: sn prom: hung repeatedly lft: rdn 2f out: wknd fnl f* **2/1**[2]
1m 1.58s (2.08) **Going Correction** +0.325s/f (Slow) **6** Ran SP% **108.7**
Speed ratings (Par 95): **96,95,94,92,87 84**
CSF £112.36 TOTE £10.70: £7.60, £3.80; EX 33.40 Trifecta £244.40.
**Owner** David W Armstrong **Bred** Highfield Farm Llp **Trained** Upper Helmsley, N Yorks
**FOCUS**
Four newcomers filled the frame in this juvenile novice and is is hard to know the value of the form. The form will take time to settle.

## 3255 KPMG CUTTING THROUGH COMPLEXITY H'CAP 1m 5y (Tp)
**7:50** (7:53) (Class 3) (0-95,94) 4-Y-O+ **£9,703** (£2,887; £1,443; £721) **Stalls** Centre

Form RPR
1-30 **1** **El Vip (IRE)**[33] 2141 4-9-7 **94** JamieSpencer 3 107+
(Luca Cumani) *stdd s: hld up in rr: swtchd rt to stands' rail 1/2-way: nudged along and hdwy 2f out: qcknd through gap to ld ins fnl f: pushed clr: easily* **2/1**[1]
02-1 **2** *2 1/4* **Torrid**[52] 1677 6-8-6 **82** NathanEvans(3) 10 87
(Michael Easterby) *trckd ldrs: pushed along over 2f out: rdn to ld over 1f out: hdd ins fnl f: kpt on but no ch w wnr* **13/2**[3]
6-40 **3** *1 1/4* **Chestnut Fire**[19] 2606 5-9-3 **90** DanielTudhope 8 92
(Daniel Mark Loughnane) *midfield: angled lft to outer over 2f out: pushed along and hdwy to chse ldr over 1f out: rdn and kpt on same pce ins fnl f* **10/1**
-151 **4** *1 1/2* **Rockwood**[13] 2772 6-8-4 **77** (v) AndrewMullen 2 76
(Karen McLintock) *hld up: hdwy over 2f out: swtchd lft arnd wknd rival over 1f out: rdn and kpt on* **16/1**
0-51 **5** *1/2* **Prying Pandora (FR)**[13] 2789 4-8-8 **81** PaulHanagan 13 78
(Richard Fahey) *hld up: pushed along and hdwy to chse ldrs over 2f out: rdn over 1f out: no ex ins fnl f: lost 4th towards fin* **6/1**[2]
00-0 **6** *1/2* **Mywayistheonlyway (IRE)**[42] 1910 4-8-5 **78** PaddyAspell 11 74
(Grant Tuer) *dwlt: hld up: midfield 1/2-way: rdn over 2f out: one pce* **100/1**
3016 **7** *2 1/2* **Testa Rossa (IRE)**[13] 2773 7-8-6 **79** (b) SamJames 6 70
(Jim Goldie) *hld up in midfield: rdn over 2f out: nvr threatened* **20/1**
0-02 **8** *3/4* **Moonlightnavigator (USA)**[13] 2799 5-9-1 **88** JasonHart 7 77
(John Quinn) *led narrowly: rdn whn hdd over 2f out: wknd ins fnl f* **10/1**
0-00 **9** *2 1/4* **Instant Attraction (IRE)**[14] 2767 6-9-7 **94** JackGarritty 12 78
(Jedd O'Keeffe) *prom: rdn to ld over 2f out: hdd over 1f out: wknd ins fnl f* **7/1**
643 **10** *1 3/4* **Mulligatawny (IRE)**[12] 2838 4-9-0 **87** TonyHamilton 1 67
(Roger Fell) *hld up on outside: rdn over 2f out: sn btn* **10/1**
31-0 **11** *2 1/2* **Lavetta**[44] 1860 5-9-1 **88** JoeFanning 9 62
(Sally Haynes) *prom: racd keenly: rdn over 2f out: wknd over 1f out* **25/1**
035- **12** *1/2* **Illustrissime (USA)**[215] 7699 4-9-0 **87** BenCurtis 5 60
(Tony Coyle) *prom: rdn over 2f out: wknd over 2f out* **33/1**
000- **13** *18* **Jacob Black**[187] 8122 6-8-8 **81** PJMcDonald 4 12
(Kenny Johnson) *trckd ldrs: wknd qckly 3f out and eased* **100/1**
1m 40.04s (1.44) **Going Correction** +0.325s/f (Slow) **13** Ran SP% **120.1**
Speed ratings (Par 107): **105,102,101,100,99 99,96,95,93,91 89,88,70**
CSF £14.05 CT £111.68 TOTE £2.90: £1.40, £2.00, £3.90; EX 15.30 Trifecta £104.80.
**Owner** Al Shaqab Racing **Bred** Gestut Wittekindshof **Trained** Newmarket, Suffolk
**FOCUS**
This wasn't the strongest of handicaps and the early pace was moderate but the winner proved in a different league.

## 3256 DISSINGTON DASH H'CAP 6f (Tp)
**8:20** (8:23) (Class 6) (0-60,60) 4-Y-O+ **£3,234** (£962; £481; £240) **Stalls** Centre

Form RPR
3516 **1** **Dream Ally (IRE)**[76] 1246 7-8-11 **55** PhilDennis(5) 10 65
(John Weymes) *trckd ldrs: pushed along 2f out: rdn to chal appr fnl f: led narrowly 110yds out: kpt on* **20/1**
406- **2** *3/4* **Vecheka (IRE)**[75] 2778 6-8-11 **50** (p) TonyHamilton 9 58
(Chris Grant) *s.i.s: sn midfield racing keenly: pushed along and hdwy 2f out: rdn to ld appr fnl f: hdd narrowly 110yds out: hld towards fin* **33/1**
3342 **3** *3 3/4* **Hadley**[19] 2627 4-8-11 **50** BenCurtis 7 47
(Tracy Waggott) *prom: led 4f out: rdn over 2f out: hdd appr fnl f: no ex* **9/2**[1]
-300 **4** *hd* **Tango Sky (IRE)**[12] 2843 8-9-7 **60** PaulMulrennan 2 56
(Paul Midgley) *dwlt: hld up: hdwy into midfield 1/2-way: rdn 2f out: kpt on same pce* **10/1**
0253 **5** *2* **Sea Of Green**[8] 2950 5-8-12 **51** SamJames 5 41
(Jim Goldie) *stdd s: hld up: pushed along over 2f out: rdn and kpt on fr over 1f out: nvr threatened* **8/1**[3]
6533 **6** *3/4* **Cool Strutter (IRE)**[19] 2633 5-9-2 **55** PaulHanagan 1 43
(Karen Tutty) *hld up: bit short of room 2f out: kpt on ins fnl f: nvr threatened* **9/2**[1]
000 **7** *nk* **Captain Scooby**[20] 2589 11-9-0 **53** (b) ConnorBeasley 11 40
(Richard Guest) *slowly away: bhd tl sme late hdwy* **12/1**
0555 **8** *1 1/2* **Silver Bid (USA)**[19] 2627 5-9-1 **54** ShaneGray 6 36
(Karen Tutty) *chsd ldrs: rdn 1/2-way: wknd ins fnl f* **9/1**
-400 **9** *nk* **Gaelic Wizard (IRE)**[19] 2633 9-8-9 **53** (v) GemmaTutty(5) 3 34
(Karen Tutty) *hld up: nvr threatened* **12/1**
04- **10** *3 3/4* **Ypres**[245] 6910 8-8-12 **51** PJMcDonald 4 22
(Jason Ward) *chsd ldrs: rdn over 2f out: wknd fnl f* **14/1**
3005 **11** *1/2* **Sandstream**[28] 2346 4-8-13 **52** (t) JasonHart 13 24
(Tracy Waggott) *led narrowly: hdd 4f out: rdn over 2f out and wknd* **15/2**[2]
13 **12** *2 1/4* **Wimboldsley**[128] 386 6-8-11 **50** DavidAllan 8 12
(Scott Dixon) *prom: rdn 1/2-way: wknd over 1f out* **9/1**
0000 **13** *5* **Hab Reeh**[19] 2633 9-8-7 **46** oh1 (p) JamesSullivan 14
(Ruth Carr) *trckd ldrs: rdn over 2f out: wknd* **25/1**
1m 13.53s (1.03) **Going Correction** +0.325s/f (Slow) **13** Ran SP% **121.9**
Speed ratings (Par 101): **106,105,100,99,97 96,95,93,93,88 87,84,81**
CSF £559.98 CT £3476.22 TOTE £27.80: £7.00, £17.90, £1.50; EX 1447.40 TRIFECTA Not won..
**Owner** High Moor Racing 4 **Bred** Noel & Roger O'Callaghan **Trained** Middleham Moor, N Yorks
**FOCUS**
A 46-60 handicap run at a decent pace, but most of the runners were exposed and many tricky to win with. The first two were clear.

## 3257 SURGO CONSTRUCTION H'CAP 5f (Tp)
**8:50** (8:51) (Class 5) (0-75,75) 3-Y-O+ **£5,175** (£1,540; £769; £384) **Stalls** Centre

Form RPR
2215 **1** **Henley**[12] 2837 5-9-8 **73** BenCurtis 5 87
(Tracy Waggott) *mde all: rdn clr appr fnl f: edgd lft ins fnl f: reduced advantage towards fin but nvr in danger* **9/2**[2]
2-46 **2** *1/2* **Manshood (IRE)**[12] 2821 4-9-6 **71** (b) PaulMulrennan 6 83+
(Paul Midgley) *midfield: pushed along 1/2-way: briefly bit short of room over 1f out: rdn and r.o wl fnl f: wnt 2nd 110yds out: gaining at fin* **5/1**[3]
522 **3** *3 3/4* **Pushkin Museum (IRE)**[40] 1979 6-9-3 **68** (p) GrahamLee 7 67
(Patrick Morris) *trckd ldrs: rdn to chse ldr appr fnl f: lost 2nd 110yds out: wknd* **11/1**

3062 **4** 2 ½ **Poppy In The Wind**[19] 2631 5-9-3 **75**........................(v) BenRobinson(7) 9 65
(Alan Brown) *s.i.s: sn pushed along towards rr: kpt on fnl f: nvr threatened* **7/1**

0-30 **5** 1 ½ **Kachess**[23] 2503 3-9-3 **75**........................ JoeFanning 10 56
(Tom Dascombe) *dwlt: hld up: nvr threatened* **8/1**

1506 **6** 2 **Slingsby**[33] 2161 6-9-5 **73**........................(b) NathanEvans(3) 3 50
(Michael Easterby) *dwlt: a outpcd in rr: passed btn rivals fnl f* **4/1**[1]

0-46 **7** ½ **Flash City (ITY)**[21] 2551 9-9-4 **69**........................ JamesSullivan 1 44
(Ruth Carr) *midfield: rdn 2f out: sn wknd* **33/1**

140- **8** ½ **More Beau (USA)**[168] 8389 6-9-4 **69**........................(p) PaulHanagan 8 43
(Noel Wilson) *prom: rdn 2f out: wknd fnl f* **11/1**

-335 **9** 1 ¾ **Lawless Louis**[13] 2776 3-9-3 **75**........................ DanielTudhope 4 39
(David O'Meara) *prom: rdn 2f out: wknd appr fnl f* **4/1**[1]

59.73s (0.23) **Going Correction** +0.325s/f (Slow)
**WFA** 3 from 4yo+ 7lb **9** Ran SP% **118.1**
Speed ratings (Par 103): **111,110,104,100,97 94,93,93,90**
CSF £27.98 CT £235.93 TOTE £5.90: £2.30, £2.40, £2.40; EX 32.50 Trifecta £349.50.
**Owner** David Tate **Bred** Dandy's Farm **Trained** Spennymoor, Co Durham

**FOCUS**
This wasn't the strongest of 56-75 handicaps with most of the runners exposed, but the pace was decent, the winner came into it in good form and the first two were clear.
T/Jkpt: Not won. T/Plt: £1,116.60 to a £1 stake. Pool: £61,370.76 - 40.12 winning units. T/Qpdt: £100.90 to a £1 stake. Pool: £5,306.96 - 38.90 winning units. **Andrew Sheret**

## 3186 WOLVERHAMPTON (A.W) (L-H)

Thursday, June 1

**OFFICIAL GOING: Tapeta: standard**
Wind: Light behind turning fresher race after 2 Weather: Fine

### 3258 UNCLE FRED'S 80TH BIRTHDAY CELEBRATION CLAIMING STKS 5f 21y (Tp)
**1:50** (1:50) (Class 6) 3-Y-O+ **£2,264** (£673; £336; £168) **Stalls** Low

Form RPR

0-02 **1** **Point North (IRE)**[82] 1147 10-9-5 70........................(b) RobertWinston 5 76
(John Balding) *chsd ldr: rdn to ld ins fnl f: r.o* **9/2**[2]

0160 **2** 1 ½ **Dutch Golden Age (IRE)**[47] 1794 5-9-12 88........(v[1]) SilvestreDeSousa 1 78
(Gary Moore) *led: shkn up 1/2-way: rdn over 1f out: hdd ins fnl f: styd on same pce: eased whn hld nr fin* **1/7**[1]

0-6 **3** 1 ¼ **Digital Revolution**[16] 2699 3-8-5 0........................ CamHardie 4 56
(Antony Brittain) *chsd ldrs: pushed along over 3f out: outpcd 1/2-way: rdn over 1f out: styd on ins fnl f* **80/1**[3]

**4** 15 **Baby Say Yes** 3-8-9 0........................ RoystonFfrench 2 6
(John Norton) *s.i.s: outpcd* **100/1**

1m 2.23s (0.33) **Going Correction** +0.05s/f (Slow)
**WFA** 3 from 5yo+ 7lb **4** Ran SP% **107.9**
Speed ratings (Par 101): **99,96,94,70**
CSF £5.76 TOTE £5.60; EX 8.60 Trifecta £12.20.
**Owner** Billy Herring **Bred** Barronstown Stud **Trained** Scrooby, S Yorks

**FOCUS**
An uncompetitive claimer to open the card. The odds-on favourite was entitled to win at the weights, but that didn't prove the case. The race has been given a token rating through the winner.

### 3259 DOWNLOAD THE AT THE RACES APP MAIDEN STKS 6f 20y (Tp)
**2:20** (2:20) (Class 5) 3-Y-O **£3,234** (£962; £481; £240) **Stalls** Low

Form RPR

**1** **Always Amazing** 3-9-5 0........................ LukeMorris 4 83+
(Robert Cowell) *w ldrs: shkn up to ld over 1f out: pushed out* **11/8**[1]

02 **2** 1 ½ **World Power (IRE)**[32] 2180 3-9-0 0........................ PatCosgrave 6 72
(Paul Cole) *pushed along in rr early: hdwy over 3f out: rdn over 2f out: hung lft ins fnl f: styd on to go 2nd post* **3/1**[3]

3436 **3** *nk* **Arnarson**[36] 2087 3-9-5 78........................(p[1]) SilvestreDeSousa 1 76
(Ed Dunlop) *led 1f: led again 4f out: rdn and hdd over 1f out: styd on same pce wl ins fnl f* **11/4**[2]

**4** 5 **El Nefous (IRE)** 3-9-0 0........................ RobertWinston 5 55
(George Peckham) *w ldrs: led 5f out tl 4f out: hung rt over 3f out: sn pushed along: styd on same pce fr over 1f out* **16/1**

0 **5** *nse* **New Delhi (IRE)**[10] 2898 3-9-0 0........................ DaneO'Neill 2 55
(Mark Johnston) *prom: rdn over 1f out: sn edgd rt: no ex fnl f* **12/1**

00 **6** 2 **Tawfeer**[24] 2467 3-9-5 0........................(p[1]) RyanPowell 7 53?
(James Unett) *prom: lost pl over 3f out: rdn over 1f out: wknd fnl f* **250/1**

6-0 **7** 11 **Clip Art**[5] 3085 3-9-0 0........................ TimmyMurphy 8 13
(Jamie Osborne) *s.i.s: hung lft: outpcd* **100/1**

1m 14.81s (0.31) **Going Correction** +0.05s/f (Slow) **7** Ran SP% **108.7**
Speed ratings (Par 99): **99,97,96,89,89 87,72**
CSF £5.11 TOTE £1.90: £1.80, £2.20; EX 6.40 Trifecta £12.20.
**Owner** Abdulla Al Mansoori **Bred** Whitsbury Manor Stud **Trained** Six Mile Bottom, Cambs

**FOCUS**
A moderate maiden, but a nice first time out winner.

### 3260 HILLTOP EQUESTRIAN CENTRE - AVAILABLE TO RENT H'CAP 6f 20y (Tp)
**2:50** (2:51) (Class 6) (0-60,62) 3-Y-O **£2,587** (£770; £384; £192) **Stalls** Low

Form RPR

006 **1** **Frank's Legacy**[90] 1004 3-8-11 **50**........................(p[1]) SilvestreDeSousa 5 57
(Ivan Furtado) *pushed along in rr early: hdwy over 4f out: hung rt over 3f out: rdn over 1f out: r.o to ld wl ins fnl f: jst hld on* **4/1**[2]

-040 **2** *nk* **Kings Heart (IRE)**[9] 2927 3-9-4 **62**........................(h) RachealKneller(5) 4 68
(Mark Usher) *hld up: hdwy over 1f out: swtchd rt ins fnl f: r.o wl* **5/2**[1]

00-3 **3** 1 ¼ **My Girl Maisie (IRE)**[13] 2792 3-8-13 **52**........................ DougieCostello 13 54
(Richard Guest) *hld up: hdwy and swtchd rt ins fnl f: r.o to go 3rd post* **9/2**[3]

60-0 **4** *nse* **Miss Rosina (IRE)**[52] 1688 3-9-0 **60**........................ JaneElliott(7) 12 62
(George Margarson) *sn led: pushed clr 2f out: hdd and unable qck wl ins fnl f* **12/1**

6500 **5** 1 ½ **Mahna Mahna (IRE)**[23] 2507 3-9-1 **54**........................ WilliamCarson 8 51
(David W Drinkwater) *led early: plld hrd and remained handy: rdn over 2f out: no ex ins fnl f* **11/1**

**6** 2 ¼ **Flying Expectation (ITY)**[118] 560 3-9-1 **54**........................ LukeMorris 3 45
(Des Donovan, Ire) *s.i.s: hdwy 5f out: rdn and hung lft over 1f out: no ex fnl f* **15/2**

-640 **7** *hd* **Paquita Bailarina**[15] 2734 3-9-2 **55**........................ TomQueally 1 45
(James Given) *broke wl: n.m.r and lost pl over 5f out: rdn over 2f out: r.o ins fnl f* **9/1**

000- **8** 1 ¼ **Kath's Boy (IRE)**[240] 7047 3-9-0 **53**........................ RobertWinston 11 39
(Tony Carroll) *hung lft sn after s: mid-div: rdn over 1f out: hmpd ins fnl f: nvr trbld ldrs* **28/1**

6200 **9** ½ **Tink**[29] 2309 3-8-9 **48**........................(h[1]) CamHardie 10 35
(Mark Brisbourne) *s.i.s: hld up: effrt whn hmpd ins fnl f: nvr on terms* **25/1**

-005 **10** 1 **Henrietta's Dream**[16] 2699 3-8-7 **46** oh1........................(v) RoystonFfrench 6 30
(John Wainwright) *chsd ldrs: nt clr run wl over 3f out: rdn over 1f out: wknd fnl f* **200/1**

0004 **11** ½ **Red Shanghai (IRE)**[24] 2470 3-8-4 **46** oh1........................ NoelGarbutt(3) 2 26
(Charles Smith) *n.m.r sn after s: hld up: rdn over 2f out: n.d* **40/1**

00-4 **12** 6 **Tess Graham**[16] 2699 3-8-7 **46** oh1........................(p) RyanPowell 7 8
(Sarah Hollinshead) *hmpd sn after s: in rr: ct wd fr 1/2-way tl wknd 2f out* **50/1**

1m 15.43s (0.93) **Going Correction** +0.05s/f (Slow) **12** Ran SP% **116.7**
Speed ratings (Par 97): **95,94,92,92,90 87,87,85,85,83 83,75**
CSF £13.61 CT £47.15 TOTE £6.30: £2.60, £1.20, £1.80; EX 18.60 Trifecta £56.20.
**Owner** The Giggle Factor & Ubs Partners **Bred** Lady Fairhaven **Trained** Wiseton, Nottinghamshire

**FOCUS**
A low-grade sprint handicap featuring plenty of non-winners, but they went a good pace, suiting the closers. The third and fourth help set the early level.

### 3261 FOLLOW AT THE RACES ON TWITTER H'CAP 1m 4f 51y (Tp)
**3:20** (3:20) (Class 6) (0-65,71) 3-Y-O **£2,587** (£770; £384; £96; £96) **Stalls** Low

Form RPR

0-53 **1** **True Romance (IRE)**[16] 2702 3-9-7 **65**........................ TomEaves 2 70
(James Given) *mde virtually all: qcknd 3f out: rdn over 1f out: styd on gamely* **11/2**[3]

2411 **2** 2 ¼ **La Vie En Rose**[7] 2991 3-9-13 **71** 6ex........................ SilvestreDeSousa 6 72
(Mark Johnston) *prom: nt clr run and lost pl over 10f out: swtchd rt over 4f out: pushed along over 2f out: rdn and hung lft over 1f out: r.o to go 2nd nr fin: no ch w wnr* **5/4**[1]

-145 **3** *shd* **Padleyourowncanoe**[37] 2060 3-9-0 **58**........................(b) DaneO'Neill 3 59
(Daniel Mark Loughnane) *hld up: hdwy over 5f out: rdn over 2f out: styd on* **10/1**

65-3 **4** ½ **All About The Pace**[37] 2060 3-8-10 **54**........................ SteveDrowne 1 54
(Mark Usher) *chsd ldrs: rdn to chse wnr over 1f out: styd on same pce ins fnl f* **33/1**

014- **4** *dht* **Oxford Blu**[189] 8080 3-9-6 **64**........................(v) LukeMorris 8 64
(Sir Mark Prescott Bt) *prom: edgd lft after 1f: sn chsng ldr: rdn over 3f out: lost 2nd over 2f out: styd on same pce ins fnl f* **7/2**[2]

0004 **6** 3 ¼ **Tor**[30] 2273 3-9-7 **65**........................ AdamKirby 7 60
(Iain Jardine) *prom: hmpd and lost pl after 1f: hdwy 10f out: rdn over 2f out: no ex fnl f* **11/2**[3]

60-0 **7** 3 ¼ **Every Nice Girl (USA)**[52] 1685 3-8-11 **60**........................ GeorgeWood(5) 4 50
(Marco Botti) *s.i.s: hld up: rdn over 2f out: nvr on terms* **28/1**

60-6 **8** 24 **Just Heather (IRE)**[110] 681 3-8-2 **46** oh1........................ RoystonFfrench 5
(John Wainwright) *chsd ldrs: lost pl 8f out: rdn and wknd 3f out* **200/1**

2m 40.64s (-0.16) **Going Correction** +0.05s/f (Slow) **8** Ran SP% **113.4**
Speed ratings (Par 97): **102,100,100,100,100 97,95,79**
CSF £12.60 CT £65.69 TOTE £6.00: £1.70, £1.10, £2.70; EX 13.50 Trifecta £81.30.
**Owner** Suzanne & Nigel Williams **Bred** Tower Place Bloodstock **Trained** Willoughton, Lincs
■ Stewards' Enquiry : Luke Morris caution; careless riding

**FOCUS**
A fair handicap for the grade and they didn't go flat out. The winner made all. The winner has been rated to his previous best, with the runner-up to form.

### 3262 WATCH TODAY'S REPLAYS ON THE ATR APP H'CAP 1m 142y (Tp)
**3:50** (3:51) (Class 4) (0-85,85) 3-Y-O **£5,175** (£1,540; £769; £384) **Stalls** Low

Form RPR

2-51 **1** **Mukalal**[28] 2330 3-9-4 **82**........................ DaneO'Neill 9 89
(Marcus Tregoning) *chsd ldrs: led 7f out: rdn over 1f out: hung rt ins fnl f: jst hld on* **13/2**

1150 **2** *hd* **Vantage Point (IRE)**[17] 2690 3-9-1 **79**........................(p) SilvestreDeSousa 4 85
(Gary Moore) *chsd ldrs: rdn and ev ch ins fnl f: r.o* **20/1**

1-1 **3** 1 ½ **Pavillon**[22] 2517 3-9-6 **84**........................ AdamKirby 6 87+
(Clive Cox) *hld up: swtchd rt and hdwy over 1f out: rdn and edgd lft ins fnl f: r.o* **9/4**[1]

1-41 **4** ¾ **Me Too Nagasaki (IRE)**[12] 2818 3-9-6 **84**........................ LukeMorris 8 85+
(Jeremy Noseda) *hld up: hdwy u.p and hung lft fr over 1f out: r.o: nt rch ldrs* **6/1**[3]

22-3 **5** *shd* **El Cap (USA)**[43] 1889 3-8-13 **77**........................ WilliamCarson 13 78
(Sir Michael Stoute) *sn led: hdd 7f out: chsd ldrs: wnt 2nd 2f out: rdn and ev ch over 1f out: styd on same pce ins fnl f* **11/1**

10- **6** 1 ¾ **Dowayla (IRE)**[227] 7409 3-9-6 **84**........................(p[1]) PatCosgrave 11 81
(Saeed bin Suroor) *prom: chsd wnr over 6f out: tl rdn 2f out: no ex wl ins fnl f* **15/2**

-100 **7** 1 ½ **Jupiter Light**[20] 2567 3-9-3 **81**........................ RobertTart 7 75
(John Gosden) *hld up: hung lft and styd on fr over 1f out: nvr trbld ldrs* **11/1**

132- **8** 2 **Muirsheen Durkin**[227] 7416 3-9-2 **80**........................ DougieCostello 1 69
(Neville Bycroft) *hld up: pushed along and hdwy over 1f out: wknd ins fnl f* **33/1**

1-06 **9** 3 ½ **Annie Fior (IRE)**[56] 1582 3-9-1 **79**........................(h) TomQueally 10 60
(Denis Coakley) *hld up: a in rr* **66/1**

0-1 **10** ¾ **Weloof (FR)**[75] 1259 3-9-3 **81**........................ GavinLerena 2 60
(Ed Dunlop) *prom: rdn over 2f out: wknd fnl f* **5/1**[2]

01- **11** 4 **Quinteo (IRE)**[247] 6850 3-9-1 **79**........................ TomEaves 3 49
(Jo Hughes) *hld up: wknd over 2f out* **66/1**

1m 49.37s (-0.73) **Going Correction** +0.05s/f (Slow) **11** Ran SP% **114.2**
Speed ratings (Par 101): **105,104,103,102,102 101,99,98,94,94 90**
CSF £127.88 CT £378.38 TOTE £7.50: £2.10, £4.40, £1.50; EX 132.60 Trifecta £426.40.
**Owner** Hamdan Al Maktoum **Bred** Shadwell Estate Company Limited **Trained** Whitsbury, Hants
■ Stewards' Enquiry : William Carson three-day ban; careless riding

**FOCUS**
The feature race was a fair handicap, but they didn't go that fast and the winner made all.

### 3263 VISIT ATTHERACES.COM H'CAP (DIV I) 1m 142y (Tp)
**4:20** (4:20) (Class 6) (0-60,61) 4-Y-O+ **£2,264** (£673; £336; £168) **Stalls** Low

Form RPR

0-25 **1** **Muthraab Aldaar (IRE)**[64] 1427 4-9-6 **59**........................ JackMitchell 6 70
(Jim Boyle) *led 1f: chsd ldr tl led 2f out: shkn up over 1f out: styd on wl: eased nr fin* **3/1**[2]

0216 **2** 2 ¾ **The Dukkerer (IRE)**[17] 2688 6-9-6 **59**........................ TomEaves 7 63
(James Given) *chsd ldr tl led over 7f out: qcknd 3f out: hdd 2f out: sn rdn: no ex ins fnl f* **12/1**

1602 **3** *hd* **Grey Destiny**[9] 2918 7-9-5 **58**........................ CamHardie 3 62
(Antony Brittain) *s.s: hld up: edgd lft and r.o ins fnl f: nrst fin* **10/1**

-410 **4** ½ **Caribbean Spring (IRE)**[8] 2976 4-9-0 **60**........................ JaneElliott(7) 5 63
(George Margarson) *chsd ldrs: rdn over 1f out: styd on same pce fnl f* **8/1**

1221 **5** 2 1/4 **Lord Murphy (IRE)**[33] 2166 4-9-8 **61** AdamKirby 1 59
(Daniel Mark Loughnane) *hld up: rdn over 2f out: nt trble ldrs* **2/1**[1]
44 **6** 7 **Kafeel (USA)**[30] 2255 6-9-2 **55** (p) TomQueally 8 38
(Gary Moore) *s.i.s: rdn 3f out: a in rr* **7/2**[3]
00/0 **7** 3 1/2 **Crossley**[9] 2919 8-8-0 **46** oh1 (p) KieranSchofield(7) 4 22
(Neville Bycroft) *hld up: rdn over 3f out: wknd over 2f out* **200/1**
63-5 **8** 1 3/4 **Fitzwilliam**[9] 2914 5-8-9 **48** SilvestreDeSousa 2 20
(Mick Channon) *prom: rdn over 2f out: wknd wl over 1f out* **14/1**
1m 51.0s (0.90) **Going Correction** +0.05s/f (Slow) **8** Ran SP% **115.6**
Speed ratings (Par 101): **98,95,95,94,92 86,83,82**
CSF £38.60 CT £322.27 TOTE £4.50: £1.90, £2.40, £3.10; EX 45.20 Trifecta £157.00.
**Owner** Epsom Equine Spa Partnership **Bred** G Devlin **Trained** Epsom, Surrey

**FOCUS**
A moderate handicap run at just a steady tempo and 1.63s slower than the previous handicap. The winner was well placed before pulling clear. It's been rated around the second and third.

## 3264 VISIT ATTHERACES.COM H'CAP (DIV II) 1m 142y (Tp)
**4:50** (4:50) (Class 6) (0-60,60) 4-Y-0+ **£2,264** (£673; £336; £168) **Stalls** Low

Form RPR
-442 **1** **Makhfar (IRE)**[29] 2313 6-9-6 **59** (p) SteveDrowne 6 65
(Mark Usher) *chsd ldrs: rdn to ld ins fnl f: r.o* **11/4**[1]
0-43 **2** 1 1/4 **Sakhalin Star (IRE)**[17] 2688 6-9-3 **56** (p[1]) DougieCostello 3 59
(Richard Guest) *led: hdd 6f out: chsd ldr tl led again over 3f out: rdn and hdd over 1f out: styd on same pce: wnt 2nd again wl ins fnl f* **7/2**[2]
46-0 **3** 1 1/4 **Sooqaan**[44] 1868 6-9-6 **59** CamHardie 4 60
(Antony Brittain) *hld up: hdwy over 2f out: styd on to go 3rd post* **11/2**[3]
0-06 **4** nk **Life Of Luxury**[33] 2167 4-9-5 **58** WilliamCarson 2 58
(Mark Brisbourne) *chsd ldrs: wnt 2nd over 2f out: led over 1f out: rdn and hdd ins fnl f: wknd towards fin* **7/2**[2]
2200 **5** 1 1/4 **Cahar Fad (IRE)**[19] 2626 5-8-12 **51** (bt) LukeMorris 5 48
(Steph Hollinshead) *pushed along and prom: n.m.r and lost pl over 7f out: hdwy u.p over 1f out: hung rt ins fnl f: no ex towards fin* **6/1**
02/6 **6** 20 **Blue Valentino**[49] 1754 8-8-0 **46** (p[1]) JordanUys(7) 8 1
(Lisa Williamson) *s.s: a in rr: rdn and wknd over 3f out* **33/1**
3-00 **7** 9 **The Firm (IRE)**[24] 2464 8-9-7 **60** (v) AdamKirby 7
(J R Jenkins) *sn chsng ldr: led 6f out: edgd rt and hdd over 3f out: shkn up and wknd over 2f out* **11/1**
1m 50.91s (0.81) **Going Correction** +0.05s/f (Slow) **7** Ran SP% **112.1**
Speed ratings (Par 101): **98,96,95,95,94 76,68**
CSF £12.03 CT £47.11 TOTE £3.00: £1.10, £2.80; EX 10.20 Trifecta £60.40.
**Owner** Roemex Ltd **Bred** Centaur Bloodstock Agency **Trained** Upper Lambourn, Berks

**FOCUS**
The second division was run marginally faster than the first. They went a fair pace before slowing halfway up the back straight. The first five came well clear.

## 3265 WOLVERHAMPTON HOLIDAY INN H'CAP 7f 36y (Tp)
**5:20** (5:20) (Class 6) (0-65,65) 4-Y-0+ **£2,264** (£673; £336; £168) **Stalls** High

Form RPR
3542 **1** **Air Of York (IRE)**[8] 2961 5-9-2 **60** (p) LukeMorris 2 74+
(John Flint) *chsd ldrs: shkn up to ld over 1f out: rdn clr fnl f* **7/2**[1]
-413 **2** 4 1/2 **Caledonia Laird**[22] 2511 6-9-5 **63** IrineuGoncalves 1 64
(Jo Hughes) *s.i.s: hld up: hdwy over 1f out: r.o to go 2nd nr fin: no ch w wnr* **4/1**[2]
4042 **3** 1/2 **Misu Pete**[7] 3001 5-8-0 **51** oh3 JaneElliott(7) 7 51
(Mark Usher) *mid-div: hdwy over 1f out: r.o to go 3rd post* **6/1**[3]
450 **4** nk **Noble Act**[49] 1755 4-9-0 **65** DarraghKeenan(7) 3 64
(Phil McEntee) *led: rdn and hdd over 1f out: no ex ins fnl f* **25/1**
0055 **5** 1 **Dark Confidant (IRE)**[19] 2633 4-9-2 **60** TomEaves 11 56
(Richard Fahey) *mid-div: hdwy u.p over 1f out: nt trble ldrs* **10/1**
0-50 **6** 1/2 **Iceaxe**[31] 2224 4-9-4 **62** RoystonFfrench 6 57
(John Holt) *chsd ldrs: wnt 2nd over 2f out: rdn over 1f out: no ex ins fnl f: nt clr run towards fin* **40/1**
00-0 **7** 1/2 **Rock Of Monaco**[66] 1406 4-8-7 **51** oh3 (v[1]) CamHardie 12 45
(Antony Brittain) *hld up: rdn and r.o ins fnl f: nvr nrr* **22/1**
0-06 **8** shd **Black Truffle (FR)**[8] 2961 7-8-4 **55** NicolaCurrie(7) 4 49
(Mark Usher) *mid-div: hdwy 2f out: sn rdn: no ex fnl f* **16/1**
056 **9** 3 3/4 **Top Offer**[45] 1842 8-9-2 **60** (p) PatCosgrave 5 44
(Patrick Morris) *hld up: rdn over 1f out: nvr on terms* **15/2**
**10** 1 3/4 **See You In Malta (IRE)**[45] 1844 4-8-12 **56** (p) TomQueally 10 36
(Jennie Candlish) *rn wout declared tongue strap: s.i.s: hld up: hung rt over 3f out: wknd over 2f out* **25/1**
-263 **11** 2 3/4 **Ettie Hart (IRE)**[9] 2915 4-8-8 **52** SilvestreDeSousa 8 25
(Mick Channon) *chsd ldrs: rdn over 2f out: wknd fnl f: eased* **7/1**
5-05 **12** 15 **Firesnake (IRE)**[133] 303 4-8-8 **59** (p) JordanUys(7) 9
(Lisa Williamson) *chsd ldr tl rdn over 2f out: sn wknd: eased fnl f* **33/1**
1m 28.89s (0.09) **Going Correction** +0.05s/f (Slow) **12** Ran SP% **113.2**
Speed ratings (Par 101): **101,95,95,94,93 93,92,92,88,86 83,65**
CSF £15.05 CT £80.50 TOTE £4.40: £1.50, £1.80, £1.60; EX 15.60 Trifecta £80.00.
**Owner** Mrs Lynn Cullimore **Bred** Hugh Ryan **Trained** Kenfig Hill, Bridgend

**FOCUS**
A moderate handicap, but several in-form runners gave it substance. They went an even gallop. Straightforward form.
T/Plt: £91.80 to a £1 stake. Pool: £50,622.64 - 402.40 winning units. T/Qpdt: £10.50 to a £1 stake. Pool: £6,125.52 - 430.57 winning units. **Colin Roberts**

3266 - 3273a (Foreign Racing) - See Raceform Interactive

# 1459 FONTAINEBLEAU
Thursday, June 1
**OFFICIAL GOING: Turf: good to soft**

## 3274a PRIX DES ERABLES (CLAIMER) (4YO) (TURF) 1m 1f
**1:20** 4-Y-0 **£8,119** (£3,247; £2,435; £1,623; £811)

RPR
**1** **High Draw (FR)**[10] 2893 4-9-4 0 TonyPiccone 2 76
(K R Burke) *qckly into stride: led after 1f: pushed along over 2f out: briefly hdd over 1f out: rdn to regain ld ins fnl f: kpt on wl* **133/10**
**2** hd **Witchcraft (FR)**[58] 4-9-0 0 DelphineSantiago(4) 7 75
(J-M Beguigne, France) **3/1**[2]
**3** 1 1/4 **Heartbeat (IRE)**[62] 4-9-1 0 (b) StephanePasquier 4 70
(F Chappet, France) **161/10**
**4** 3/4 **Amiral**[54] 4-9-1 0 VincentCheminaud 8 68
(J-F Doucet, France) **23/1**
**5** 1/2 **Dani Blue (FR)**[21] 4-9-1 0 ChristopheSoumillon 10 67
(Mme P Butel, France) **61/10**[3]
**6** 1 3/4 **Talismana (IRE)**[28] 4-8-6 0 ClementLecoeuvre(5) 1 59
(E Lellouche, France) **112/10**
**7** 1 1/4 **Beau Temps (FR)**[10] 4-9-5 0 MickaelBarzalona 3 65
(S Smrczek, Germany) **9/5**[1]
**8** 8 **Effywind (FR)**[26] 4-8-13 0 EddyHardouin 6 42
(K Borgel, France) **33/1**
**9** dist **Blink (FR)**[17] 4-8-11 0 FabriceVeron 5
(N Caullery, France) **19/2**
**10** 1/2 **Texas Ranger (FR)**[77] 4-9-1 0 (b) Pierre-CharlesBoudot 9
(H-A Pantall, France) **172/10**

PARI-MUTUEL (all including 1 euro stake): WIN 14.30 PLACE 2.90, 1.80, 3.60 DF 26.30 SF 49.30.
**Owner** Tim Dykes & Mrs E Burke **Bred** Assoc Aleyrion Bloodstock Ltd **Trained** Middleham Moor, N Yorks

## 3275a PRIX DES VERNES (CLAIMER) (3YO FILLIES) (TURF) 1m 2f
**2:55** 3-Y-0 **£8,119** (£3,247; £2,435; £1,623; £811)

RPR
**1** **Wootalove (FR)**[17] 2697 3-9-4 0 MickaelBarzalona 1 67
(Mme Pia Brandt, France) **105/10**
**2** 1 1/4 **Ave Sothia (FR)**[39] 3-9-1 0 GeraldMosse 2 61
(T Castanheira, France) **101/10**
**3** snk **Selati (IRE)**[15] 3-8-4 0 (p) ThomasTrullier(7) 4 57
(N Clement, France) **92/10**
**4** nk **Eclipse De Sivola (FR)** 3-8-2 0 MlleAdelineMerou(9) 8 56
(K Borgel, France) **115/10**
**5** 4 **Zamira (FR)**[80] 3-9-1 0 TheoBachelot 11 52
(S Wattel, France) **10/1**
**6** 2 1/2 **Berlin Calling (IRE)**[169] 3-9-1 0 ClementLecoeuvre(3) 7 50
(Gerald Geisler, Germany) **71/10**[2]
**7** 2 1/2 **Artifix (IRE)** 3-8-11 0 (b[1]) MaximeGuyon 12 38
(F Head, France) **89/10**[3]
**8** hd **Trapped (FR)**[22] 2536 3-9-1 0 VincentCheminaud 9 42
(F Belmont, France) **74/1**
**9** 3 **My Soul**[29] 3-9-4 0 (p) ChristopheSoumillon 13 39
(Mme P Butel, France) **47/10**[1]
**10** 1 1/4 **Flawed Diamond (FR)**[50] 1726 3-9-1 0 (p) TonyPiccone 3 34
(K R Burke) *trckd ldrs early: tk clsr order 3f out: rdn over 2f out: little rspnse and eased fnl f* **236/10**
**11** 12 **Malefique (FR)**[59] 3-9-1 0 Pierre-CharlesBoudot 10 10
(H-A Pantall, France) **102/10**
**12** nk **Mydearlaura (FR)**[18] 3-9-1 0 (p) FabriceVeron 14 9
(L Gadbin, France) **176/10**
**13** 20 **Classica (FR)**[176] 3-8-11 0 GabrieleCongiu 6
(J-P Gauvin, France) **134/10**
**14** 12 **Tabarka (FR)** 3-8-10 0 MlleMarylineEon(5) 5
(J Boisnard, France) **15/1**
2m 3.4s **14** Ran SP% **117.5**
PARI-MUTUEL (all including 1 euro stake): WIN 11.50 PLACE 3.70, 3.60, 3.60 DF 46.10 SF 76.20.

**Owner** Meridian Racing Club **Bred** E Nagell-Erichsen **Trained** France

# 3021 BATH (L-H)
Friday, June 2
**OFFICIAL GOING: Good to firm (9.7)**
Wind: Light across Weather: Overcast

## 3276 SUNBETS.CO.UK H'CAP 1m 5f 11y
**5:45** (5:46) (Class 6) (0-65,66) 3-Y-0 **£2,264** (£673; £336; £168) **Stalls** High

Form RPR
00-0 **1** **Newt**[18] 2686 3-9-4 **62** LukeMorris 4 69
(Sir Mark Prescott Bt) *mde all: flashed tail over 4f out: drvn along over 2f out: styd on gamely* **7/2**[1]
000- **2** 1 3/4 **Imphal**[214] 7726 3-8-13 **57** MartinDwyer 6 61
(Marcus Tregoning) *racd keenly in 2nd pl: rdn over 4f out: styd on same pce ins fnl f* **7/2**[1]
-464 **3** 3/4 **Plato's Kode (IRE)**[17] 2711 3-9-2 **60** (tp) DaneO'Neill 1 63
(Seamus Durack) *trckd ldrs: racd keenly: rdn over 2f out: no ex wl ins fnl f* **7/2**[1]
4300 **4** 1 3/4 **Rock N Roll Global (IRE)**[27] 2394 3-9-7 **65** (b[1]) RobertWinston 5 65
(Richard Hughes) *hld up: rdn over 2f out: n.m.r 1f out: nt rch ldrs* **7/2**[1]
050 **5** nse **Air Ministry (IRE)**[21] 2584 3-8-13 **64** (b) TristanPrice(7) 3 64
(Michael Bell) *hld up: rdn over 2f out: kpt on: nt trble ldrs* **11/1**[3]
-053 **6** 1 1/4 **Kiruna Peak (IRE)**[18] 2686 3-9-1 **66** KeithQuinn(7) 2 64
(Mick Channon) *s.i.s: sn prom: rdn over 3f out: no ex fnl f* **5/1**[2]
2m 50.98s (-1.02) **Going Correction** -0.025s/f (Good) **6** Ran SP% **113.9**
Speed ratings (Par 97): **102,100,100,99,99 98**
CSF £16.24 TOTE £3.90: £1.90, £2.20; EX 11.20 Trifecta £62.80.
**Owner** B Haggas **Bred** J B Haggas **Trained** Newmarket, Suffolk

**FOCUS**
Some starts have been moved at this track following remeasuring, so some races will not have speed figures until there is sufficient data to calculate updated median times. A modest 3yo handicap. They went an, at best, respectable gallop on good to firm ground.

## 3277 SUNBETS.CO.UK LIVE CASINO / EBF NOVICE STKS 5f 10y
**6:20** (6:24) (Class 5) 2-Y-0 **£3,234** (£962; £481; £240) **Stalls** Centre

Form RPR
24 **1** **Dahik (IRE)**[22] 2556 2-9-2 0 DaneO'Neill 8 81+
(Roger Varian) *a.p: led over 1f out: edgd lft and rdn clr fnl f* **1/1**[1]
5 **2** 5 **Haveoneyerself (IRE)**[22] 2556 2-8-9 0 DarraghKeenan(7) 4 63
(John Butler) *disp ld tl wnt on wl over 1f out: sn hdd: styd on same pce fnl f* **12/1**
**3** 1 **Ursus Belle (IRE)** 2-8-11 0 KieranO'Neill 6 54
(Richard Hannon) *sn outpcd: swtchd rt and hdwy over 1f out: edgd lft ins fnl f: nrst fin* **9/1**[2]
**4** 1 3/4 **Go Bananas** 2-8-4 0 JordanUys(7) 5 48
(Brian Meehan) *dwlt: outpcd: swtchd rt over 1f out: nvr trbld ldrs* **14/1**
44 **5** hd **Data Protection**[17] 2706 2-9-2 0 MartinDwyer 1 52
(William Muir) *sn pushed along to dispute ld tl rdn and hdd wl over 1f out: no ex fnl f* **10/1**[3]

0 6 *26* **Rusty Blade (IRE)**[22] 2556 2-9-2 0 ................................ RobertWinston 7
(Daniel Mark Loughnane) *broke wl enough: sn hung lft and outpcd: eased wl over 1f out* **33/1**
1m 2.66s (0.16) **Going Correction** -0.025s/f (Good) **6** Ran SP% **86.4**
Speed ratings (Par 93): **97,89,87,84,84 42**
CSF £6.79 TOTE £1.30: £1.10, £4.30; EX 6.40 Trifecta £24.70.
**Owner** Hamdan Al Maktoum **Bred** Tally-Ho Stud **Trained** Newmarket, Suffolk
■ Fab was withdrawn. Price at time of withdrawal 9/4. Rule 4 applies to all bets - deduction 30p in the pound.
**FOCUS**
A fair juvenile novice contest. They went a decent gallop and the favourite outclassed these opponents from about 2f out. The second and fifth help guide with the level.

## 3278 SUN BETS DOWNLOAD THE APP H'CAP 5f 160y
**6:50** (6:51) (Class 4) (0-80,81) 3-Y-O+ **£4,568** (£1,367; £683; £342; £170) **Stalls** Centre

Form RPR
5-33 **1** **Trick Of The Light (IRE)**[21] 2579 3-8-11 **76** .................. DavidEgan(7) 8 83+
(Roger Varian) *trckd ldrs: rdn to go 2nd over 1f out: styd on to ld wl ins fnl f* **2/1**[1]
5263 **2** *1 ½* **Swendab (IRE)**[23] 2514 9-8-7 **64** ..................(b) BenRobinson(7) 9 68
(John O'Shea) *chsd ldr tl led 2f out: rdn and edgd lft over 1f out: hdd wl ins fnl f* **33/1**
3000 **3** *1* **Sumou (IRE)**[4] 3161 4-9-10 **74** .................. RobertWinston 2 75
(Milton Bradley) *led: rdn and hdd 2f out: styd on u.p* **25/1**
434 **4** *½* **Rosealee (IRE)**[3] 3176 4-9-5 **76** .................. FinleyMarsh(7) 6 75
(Jeremy Gask) *hld up in tch: racd keenly: rdn over 1f out: styd on same pce wl ins fnl f* **7/1**[3]
-031 **5** *3* **Babyfact**[16] 2725 6-9-7 **71** .................. DaneO'Neill 1 60
(Malcolm Saunders) *prom: nt clr run and lost pl over 2f out: rallied over 1f out: no ex wl ins fnl f* **9/1**
-320 **6** *1 ¼* **Geoff Potts (IRE)**[27] 2404 4-9-6 **70** ..................(h) LiamJones 4 55
(Jeremy Gask) *s.i.s: hdwy u.p and hung lft fr over 1f out: nt trble ldrs* **20/1**
61-1 **7** *2 ½* **Mr Pocket (IRE)**[42] 1940 3-9-9 **81** ..................(b) LukeMorris 10 56
(Paul Cole) *s.i.s: plld hrd and hdwy over 3f out: rdn over 2f out: wknd fnl f* **5/2**[2]
-116 **8** *1 ½* **Go Amber Go**[7] 3021 5-9-3 **67** ..................(b) WilliamCarson 7 39
(Rod Millman) *led: rdn and hdd 2f out: wknd over 1f out* **12/1**
2355 **9** *3 ¼* **Burning Thread (IRE)**[63] 1465 10-9-7 **78** ..................(b) AdamMcLean(7) 3 39
(David Elsworth) *prom: n.m.r and lost pl after 1f: n.d after* **20/1**
51-4 **10** *10* **Wild Dancer**[29] 2335 4-9-10 **74** .................. RobHornby 5 2
(Patrick Chamings) *s.i.s: outpcd* **7/1**[3]
1m 10.49s (-0.71) **Going Correction** -0.025s/f (Good)
**WFA** 3 from 4yo+ 8lb **10** Ran SP% **120.9**
Speed ratings (Par 105): **103,101,99,99,95 93,90,88,83,70**
CSF £83.78 CT £1368.41 TOTE £3.20: £1.30, £7.00, £6.20; EX 115.00 Trifecta £1310.70.
**Owner** Jon Collins & Chris Fahy **Bred** Forenaghts Stud Farm Ltd **Trained** Newmarket, Suffolk
**FOCUS**
A fair handicap. They went a proper gallop and a relatively unexposed 3yo came to the fore.

## 3279 BET & WATCH AT SUNBETS.CO.UK MAIDEN FILLIES' STKS 5f 160y
**7:20** (7:23) (Class 5) 3-Y-O+ **£2,911** (£866; £432; £216) **Stalls** Centre

Form RPR
540 **1** **Under The Covers**[4] 3139 4-9-8 66 .................. RyanPowell 8 82
(Ronald Harris) *sn led at quick pce: rdn ins fnl f: styd on wl* **9/2**[2]
34-2 **2** *3* **Dealer's Choice (IRE)**[20] 2619 3-8-7 80 ..................(h) DavidEgan(7) 2 70
(Roger Varian) *broke wl sn pushed along and lost pl: hdwy over 2f out: rdn to chse wnr over 1f out: hung lft ins fnl f: styd on same pce* **1/5**[1]
04 **3** *11* **Hell Of A Lady**[21] 2581 3-9-0 0 .................. RobHornby 4 34
(Michael Attwater) *chsd ldrs: hmpd after 1f: rdn over 2f out: wknd over 1f out* **16/1**[3]
**4** *1 ¼* **Bird For Life** 3-8-7 0 .................. NicolaCurrie(7) 1 30
(Mark Usher) *s.s: outpcd: r.o ins fnl f: nvr nrr* **16/1**[3]
0- **5** *1 ¼* **Wedgewood Wonder**[235] 7216 3-9-0 0 .................. WilliamCarson 3 26
(Tony Carroll) *racd keenly in 2nd pl: rdn 1/2-way: edgd rt and wknd over 1f out* **40/1**
**6** *6* **Picc And Go** 4-9-8 0 .................. KieranO'Neill 5
(Matthew Salaman) *s.s: pushed along in rr: hdwy 2f out: rdn and wknd over 1f out* **33/1**
00-0 **7** *10* **Sixties Symphony**[14] 2782 3-9-0 0 .................. LiamJones 6
(John Flint) *chsd ldrs: rdn 1/2-way: wknd over 1f out* **66/1**
1m 10.39s (-0.81) **Going Correction** -0.025s/f (Good)
**WFA** 3 from 4yo 8lb **7** Ran SP% **120.2**
Speed ratings (Par 100): **104,100,85,83,82 74,60**
CSF £6.16 TOTE £7.80: £2.20, £1.02; EX 9.00 Trifecta £30.40.
**Owner** Ridge House Stables Ltd **Bred** Llety Farms **Trained** Earlswood, Monmouths
**FOCUS**
A fair fillies' maiden. They went a proper gallop, and the right two horses came clear, but not in the expected order.

## 3280 SUN BETS LIKE US ON FACEBOOK H'CAP 5f 160y
**7:50** (7:52) (Class 6) (0-65,65) 4-Y-O+ **£2,264** (£673; £336; £168) **Stalls** Centre

Form RPR
2310 **1** **Compton Prince**[9] 2962 8-8-9 **53** ..................(b) LukeMorris 9 59
(Milton Bradley) *mid-div: hdwy over 2f out: rdn over 1f out: styd on to ld post* **9/1**[3]
05/0 **2** *nse* **Thewestwalian (USA)**[6] 3084 9-8-1 **52** .................. MollyKing(7) 11 58
(Peter Hiatt) *s.i.s: hld up: swtchd rt over 2f out: hdwy over 1f out: r.o wl* **25/1**
00-4 **3** *hd* **Jaganory (IRE)**[17] 2709 5-8-4 **55** ..................(p) DavidEgan(7) 13 60
(Christopher Mason) *w ldrs: led over 2f out: rdn and edgd lft fnl f: hdd post* **10/1**
-030 **4** *¾* **Spellmaker**[21] 2589 8-8-10 **54** .................. RobHornby 3 57
(Tony Newcombe) *chsd ldrs: rdn over 1f out: r.o* **10/1**
0045 **5** *¾* **Burauq**[16] 2724 5-7-10 **47** ..................(b) MillyNaseb(7) 6 47
(Milton Bradley) *hood removed late: dwlt: hld up: swtchd rt and hdwy over 1f out: r.o* **16/1**
-654 **6** *nk* **Catalinas Diamond (IRE)**[16] 2724 9-8-1 **48** ..................(t) AaronJones(3) 12 48
(Pat Murphy) *s.i.s: hld up: swtchd rt over 2f out: hdwy over 1f out: r.o* **16/1**
/0-2 **7** *½* **Harrison Stickle**[23] 2514 5-8-13 **64** .................. BenRobinson(7) 1 65
(John Gallagher) *w ldrs: rdn over 1f out: nt clr run ins fnl f: styd on same pce towards fin* **6/4**[1]
0314 **8** *nk* **Kingstreet Lady**[16] 2725 4-8-8 **52** .................. KieranO'Neill 14 49
(Richard Price) *hld up: nt clr run and rdn ins fnl f: nt trble ldrs* **6/1**[2]
00-0 **9** *3* **Sabato (IRE)**[16] 2724 4-7-11 **46** .................. RichardOliver(5) 7 33
(Fergal O'Brien) *prom: pushed along over 2f out: no ex fnl f* **33/1**
0044 **10** *1* **Molly Jones**[9] 2969 8-8-5 **54** .................. MitchGodwin(5) 8 37
(Matthew Salaman) *chsd ldrs: rdn over 1f out: no ex ins fnl f* **9/1**[3]
0F00 **11** *4 ½* **Mobley Chaos**[30] 2294 7-7-9 **46** oh1 ..................(p) DarraghKeenan(7) 2 15
(John Flint) *led 3f: wknd over 1f out* **25/1**
0001 **12** *3 ¼* **Zophilly (IRE)**[16] 2724 4-8-6 **50** ..................(t) LiamJones 17 8
(Jeremy Gask) *prom on outer: rdn over 3f out: wknd wl over 1f out* **20/1**
00-0 **13** *1 ¾* **Zorlu (IRE)**[133] 332 4-8-2 **49** ..................(b) EdwardGreatrex(3) 15 1
(John O'Shea) *s.s: outpcd* **50/1**
0 **14** *1 ½* **Jesse Tree (IRE)**[31] 2255 4-7-13 **46** oh1 ..................(t[1]) NathanAlison(3) 10
(John Flint) *plld hrd and prom: lost pl wl over 2f out: eased* **20/1**
1m 12.1s (0.90) **Going Correction** -0.025s/f (Good) **14** Ran SP% **126.4**
Speed ratings (Par 101): **93,92,92,91,90 90,89,89,85,83 77,73,71,69**
CSF £229.73 CT £2316.94 TOTE £10.70: £2.90, £9.00, £3.40; EX 271.90.
**Owner** E A Hayward **Bred** Whitsbury Manor Stud **Trained** Sedbury, Gloucs
**FOCUS**
A modest handicap. They went a decent gallop and it produced a thrilling three-way photo in a typically bunched finish to a sprint on this track. Straightforward form rated around the second and third to their best.

## 3281 SUN BETS FOLLOW US ON TWITTER H'CAP 5f 10y
**8:20** (8:20) (Class 5) (0-75,77) 4-Y-O+ **£2,911** (£866; £432; £216) **Stalls** Centre

Form RPR
1113 **1** **Major Valentine**[20] 2621 5-8-10 **70** .................. BenRobinson(7) 8 75
(John O'Shea) *w ldrs 2f: rdn to chse ldr over 2f out: styd on to ld nr fin* **5/2**[1]
4232 **2** *nk* **The Big Lad**[18] 2680 5-9-3 **77** ..................(b) NicolaCurrie(7) 7 81
(Richard Hughes) *sn pushed along in rr: hdwy over 1f out: r.o wl* **9/2**[2]
30-0 **3** *nse* **Edged Out**[28] 2360 7-8-13 **71** .................. MitchGodwin(5) 2 75
(Christopher Mason) *w ldrs tl led 3f out: rdn and edgd lft ins fnl f: hdd nr fin* **20/1**
154- **4** *shd* **Our Lord**[301] 5105 5-8-6 **59** .................. LukeMorris 5 62
(Michael Attwater) *hld up: hdwy over 1f out: sn rdn: r.o* **14/1**
-202 **5** *1 ½* **Silverrica (IRE)**[7] 3021 7-9-2 **74** .................. GeorgiaCox(5) 6 72
(Malcolm Saunders) *chsd ldrs: rdn over 1f out: styd on same pce wl ins fnl f* **5/2**[1]
0663 **6** *8* **Kyllukey**[7] 3021 4-9-9 **76** .................. RobertWinston 3 45
(Milton Bradley) *led 2f: sn rdn: wknd over 1f out* **11/2**[3]
1-50 **7** *1 ½* **Quantum Dot (IRE)**[9] 2967 6-8-8 **61** ..................(b) RobHornby 4 25
(Ed de Giles) *pushed along to chse ldrs: wknd over 1f out* **11/1**
-200 **8** *3 ¾* **Fly True**[9] 2967 4-9-1 **68** ..................(h) DaneO'Neill 1 18
(Jeremy Gask) *s.s: a bhd* **12/1**
1m 2.36s (-0.14) **Going Correction** -0.025s/f (Good) **8** Ran SP% **118.2**
Speed ratings (Par 103): **100,99,99,99,96 84,81,75**
CSF £14.60 CT £186.40 TOTE £3.60: £1.40, £1.80, £3.80; EX 14.60 Trifecta £114.60.
**Owner** Pete Smith **Bred** J R Salter **Trained** Elton, Gloucs
**FOCUS**
A fair handicap. They went a decent gallop and a likeable sprinter eked out another win.

## 3282 SUN BETS MUSIC NIGHTS H'CAP 1m
**8:50** (8:50) (Class 4) (0-80,80) 4-Y-O+ **£4,690** (£1,395; £697; £348) **Stalls** Low

Form RPR
5301 **1** **Mister Musicmaster**[23] 2511 8-8-10 **68** .................. SteveDrowne 6 74
(Ron Hodges) *prom early: plenty to do whn runners c bk into view over 3f out: hdwy over 2f out: r.o to ld wl ins fnl f: comf* **10/1**
-660 **2** *¾* **British Embassy (IRE)**[7] 3030 5-9-0 **79** ..................(p[1]) JoshuaBryan(7) 4 83
(Bill Turner) *sn led: clr whn runners c bk into view over 3f out: rdn and hdd wl ins fnl f* **16/1**
631 **3** *½* **King Oswald (USA)**[9] 2974 4-8-4 **62** 6ex ..................(p) RyanPowell 7 65
(James Unett) *hld up: stl wl in rr whn runners c bk into view over 3f out: stl last over 2f out: hung lft and r.o ins fnl f: nt rch ldrs* **2/1**[2]
1551 **4** *4* **Captain Courageous (IRE)**[7] 3036 4-9-3 **80** 6ex ........ JennyPowell(5) 2 73
(Ed Walker) *chsd ldr: wl off the pce whn runners c bk into view over 3f out: rdn over 2f out: no ex ins fnl f* **7/4**[1]
5-24 **5** *½* **Hot Mustard**[7] 3028 7-8-6 **64** .................. RobHornby 5 56
(William Muir) *chsd ldrs early: 3rd pl and wl off the pce whn pushed along over 3f out: no ex fnl f* **4/1**[3]
04-4 **6** *½* **Saint Helena (IRE)**[16] 2722 9-8-0 **65** ..................(b) JordanUys(7) 1 56
(Mark Gillard) *pushed along to chse ldrs early: rdn in 4th and wl off the pce whn field c bk into view over 3f out: 6th 1f out: no ex* **14/1**
42-0 **7** *1 ½* **Peak Storm**[4] 3144 8-9-4 **79** .................. EdwardGreatrex(3) 8 66
(John O'Shea) *s.i.s: in rr and rdn whn runners c into view over 3f out: n.d* **12/1**
1m 40.61s (-0.19) **7** Ran SP% **119.0**
CSF £150.63 CT £452.25 TOTE £7.00: £1.80, £5.00; EX 128.70 Trifecta £937.80.
**Owner** Mrs L Sharpe & Mrs S G Clapp **Bred** Mrs J Fuller And S Dutfield **Trained** Charlton Mackrell, Somerset
**FOCUS**
The feature contest was a fair handicap. The mirk had descended with rain and fog. Visibility was poor throughout. A previous dual C&D winner came through to win readily but the form should be treated with a degree of caution.
T/Plt: £102.70 to a £1 stake. Pool: £40,449.00 - 393.70 winning units. T/Qpdt: £25.70 to a £1 stake. Pool: £3,724.00 - 144.60 winning units. **Colin Roberts**

# 2987 CATTERICK (L-H)
Friday, June 2
**OFFICIAL GOING: Good to firm (good in places; watered; 8.9)**
Wind: Light half behind Weather: Overcast

## 3283 EBF NOVICE STKS 5f
**1:50** (1:51) (Class 5) 2-Y-O **£2,911** (£866; £432; £216) **Stalls** Low

Form RPR
2 **1** **Consequences (IRE)**[16] 2740 2-9-2 0 .................. DanielTudhope 5 86+
(David O'Meara) *trckd ldr: led jst ins fnl f: nudged clr: easily* **2/11**[1]
04 **2** *2 ½* **Pursuing The Dream (IRE)**[7] 3029 2-8-11 0 .................. DougieCostello 4 68
(Jamie Osborne) *led: rdn over 1f out: hdd jst ins fnl f: sn no ch wnr* **11/1**[3]
025 **3** *3* **Shay C**[11] 2882 2-9-2 0 .................. TomEaves 2 63
(Declan Carroll) *trckd ldr: racd keenly: rdn over 1f out: wknd ins fnl f* **20/1**
**4** *1 ½* **W G Grace (IRE)** 2-9-2 0 .................. PJMcDonald 6 57+
(Mark Johnston) *hld up in tch on outer: pushed along 1/2-way: nvr threatened* **9/1**[2]
50 **5** *¾* **I Am Dandy (IRE)**[14] 2786 2-9-2 0 .................. PaulMulrennan 1 54+
(James Ewart) *in tch: pushed along 2f out: grad wknd* **200/1**
**6** *3 ¼* **Haxby Juniors** 2-8-11 0 .................. CamHardie 3 37
(Antony Brittain) *dwlt: hld up: nvr threatened* **150/1**

7 2 1/2 **Cobbler Quinn (IRE)** 2-9-2 0 PhillipMakin 7 33
(Keith Dalgleish) *s.i.s: sn in tch: rdn along 1/2-way: wknd over 1f out* **22/1**

59.58s (-0.22) **Going Correction** -0.175s/f (Firm) **7** Ran SP% **113.2**
Speed ratings (Par 93): **94,90,85,82,81 76,72**
CSF £2.94 TOTE £1.20: £1.10, £2.60; EX 3.20 Trifecta £11.20.
**Owner** Nick Bradley Racing 15 **Bred** L Lynch & R Sherrard **Trained** Upper Helmsley, N Yorks

**FOCUS**
After the opening race, the jockeys were calling the ground "good". This maiden went to Lowther Stakes winner Queen Kindly a year ago and Consequences looks another nice prospect. The runner-up and fifth anchor the form.

## 3284 CATTERICKBRIDGE.CO.UK (S) STKS 1m 5f 192y
**2:25** (2:25) (Class 6) 4-Y-0+ **£2,264** (£673; £336; £168) **Stalls** Low

Form RPR
5134 **1** **Viewpoint (IRE)**[10] 2941 8-9-1 74 AlistairRawlinson(3) 4 67+
(Michael Appleby) *trckd ldr in 2nd: rdn to ld over 1f out: kpt on* **5/6**[1]
4031 **2** 1 3/4 **Retrieve (AUS)**[11] 2891 9-9-4 90 (t) DougieCostello 5 64+
(Jamie Osborne) *hld up in tch in 4th: pushed along to chse ldr appr fnl f: rdn and sn one pce ins fnl f* **5/4**[2]
0660 **3** 5 **Ibreeq (IRE)**[29] 2340 4-8-12 48 (p[1]) ConnorBeasley 3 50
(Roger Fell) *led: rdn over 2f out: hdd over 1f out: sn wknd* **33/1**
-005 **4** 3 1/2 **Moccasin (FR)**[22] 2546 8-8-12 42 (b) PJMcDonald 1 45
(Geoffrey Harker) *dwlt: sn in tch in 3rd: rdn over 2f out: wknd over 1f out* **16/1**[3]

3m 9.41s (5.81) **Going Correction** -0.20s/f (Firm) **4** Ran SP% **107.8**
Speed ratings (Par 101): **75,74,71,69**
CSF £2.12 TOTE £1.80; EX 2.30 Trifecta £5.70.There was no bid for the winner.
**Owner** Mick Appleby Racing **Bred** F Dunne **Trained** Oakham, Rutland

**FOCUS**
Race run over an extra 6yds. This seller was essentially a two-horse race. The third and fourth set the level for now.

## 3285 LIONWELD KENNEDY H'CAP 5f
**3:00** (3:00) (Class 5) (0-70,69) 3-Y-0 **£2,911** (£866; £432; £216) **Stalls** Low

Form RPR
5-02 **1** **Glyder**[11] 2897 3-8-10 58 RoystonFfrench 1 65
(John Holt) *trckd ldrs: rdn to ld over 1f out: strly pressed thrght fnl f: hld on wl* **11/4**[2]
21 **2** shd **Berryessa (IRE)**[111] 679 3-9-7 69 DavidAllan 5 76
(Rae Guest) *dwlt: hld up: hdwy to trck ldrs 1/2-way: pushed along over 1f out: rdn to join ldr 1f out: kpt on: jst failed* **5/2**[1]
6526 **3** 2 3/4 **Joysunny**[4] 3141 3-7-13 50 oh1 NathanEvans(3) 7 47
(Michael Easterby) *prom: rdn 2f out: wknd fnl 110yds* **5/1**
422 **4** shd **Lambrini Legacy**[18] 2674 3-8-12 60 (h) KevinStott 3 56
(Lisa Williamson) *outpcd in rr tl kpt on ins fnl f* **12/1**
-430 **5** 1 **Hamidans Girl (IRE)**[10] 2924 3-9-7 69 PhillipMakin 6 62
(Keith Dalgleish) *midfield: rdn and outpcd 1/2-way: no threat after* **9/2**[3]
3050 **6** 2 **Prazeres**[28] 2372 3-9-1 63 (p[1]) DougieCostello 2 49
(Les Eyre) *led: rdn whn hdd over 1f out: sn wknd* **15/2**
1-06 **7** 13 **Newgate Sioux**[11] 2897 3-8-11 59 DuranFentiman 4
(Tony Coyle) *a rr* **33/1**

59.26s (-0.54) **Going Correction** -0.175s/f (Firm) **7** Ran SP% **112.5**
Speed ratings (Par 99): **97,96,92,92,90 87,66**
CSF £9.72 TOTE £3.10: £1.70, £1.70; EX 9.30 Trifecta £23.40.
**Owner** Jobsworth Racing **Bred** Mrs J McMahon & Mickley Stud **Trained** Peckleton, Leics

**FOCUS**
Moderate handicap form.

## 3286 MACMILLAN CANCER SUPPORT MAIDEN STKS 1m 4f 13y
**3:35** (3:37) (Class 5) 3-Y-0+ **£3,234** (£962; £481; £240) **Stalls** Low

Form RPR
35-2 **1** **Beach Break**[16] 2721 3-8-13 77 (b) PhillipMakin 6 83
(Ralph Beckett) *mde all: rdn 2f out: kpt on to draw clr ins fnl f* **6/4**[1]
55 **2** 5 **Montanna**[12] 2857 3-8-13 0 JackGarritty 2 74
(Jedd O'Keeffe) *trckd ldr in 2nd: rdn over 3f out: sn outpcd and dropped to 3rd: styd on fnl f: regained 2nd nr fin* **9/2**[3]
3-42 **3** 1/2 **Lester Kris (IRE)**[14] 2807 3-8-13 74 DanielTudhope 3 73
(Richard Hannon) *in tch in 3rd: hdwy to go 2nd over 3f out: rdn over 2f out: wknd ins fnl f: lost 2nd nr fin* **13/8**[2]
**4** 10 **Flowers Will Bloom (IRE)** 3-8-8 0 SamJames 4 52
(David O'Meara) *midfield: rdn along over 4f out: sn btn* **10/1**
**5** 5 **Notnow Seamus**[23] 6-9-11 0 NathanEvans(3) 5 49
(Marjorie Fife) *s.i.s: hld up: rdn over 4f out: sn btn* **25/1**
**6** 76 **Karapiro Boy** 3-8-13 0 ConnorBeasley 1
(Roger Fell) *slowly away: a rr: t.o fnl 4f* **100/1**

2m 34.15s (-4.75) **Going Correction** -0.20s/f (Firm)
**WFA** 3 from 6yo 15lb **6** Ran SP% **110.2**
Speed ratings (Par 103): **107,103,103,96,93 42**
CSF £8.39 TOTE £2.10: £1.10, £3.20; EX 9.30 Trifecta £17.80.
**Owner** K Abdullah **Bred** Juddmonte Farms Ltd **Trained** Kimpton, Hants

**FOCUS**
Race run over an extra 6yds. The winner had things his own way in front in this ordinary maiden.

## 3287 FOLLOW @BRITISHEBF ON TWITTER FILLIES' H'CAP 7f 6y
**4:10** (4:10) (Class 4) (0-80,79) 3-Y-0+ **£6,469** (£1,925; £962; £481) **Stalls** Low

Form RPR
1404 **1** **Bint Arcano (FR)**[14] 2805 4-10-0 79 JoeDoyle 5 88
(Julie Camacho) *trckd ldr: pushed along to ld over 1f out: edgd lft: kpt on wl* **7/2**[3]
5400 **2** 2 3/4 **Maureb (IRE)**[6] 3063 5-9-2 67 (p) DuranFentiman 2 69
(Tony Coyle) *led: rdn whn hdd over 1f out: one pce and no ch wnr ins fnl f* **14/1**
12-0 **3** 4 1/2 **Totally Magic (IRE)**[18] 2685 5-8-13 64 CamHardie 4 53
(Richard Whitaker) *s.i.s: hld up: pushed along over 2f out: kpt on to go modest 3rd ins fnl f: no threat ldng pair* **17/2**
6052 **4** 1/2 **Be Royale**[9] 2974 7-8-10 64 (t) AlistairRawlinson(3) 3 52
(Michael Appleby) *midfield: rdn over 2f out: one pce and nvr threatened* **10/1**
-205 **5** 1 1/2 **Invermere**[34] 2138 4-9-7 79 ConnorMurtagh(7) 8 63
(Richard Fahey) *trckd ldr on outer: rdn over 2f out: wknd fnl f* **11/4**[1]
4-02 **6** hd **Little Miss Kodi (IRE)**[11] 2888 4-9-7 75 CharlieBennett(3) 7 58
(Daniel Mark Loughnane) *in tch: rdn over 2f out: edgd rt over 1f out: wknd fnl f* **3/1**[2]
0-06 **7** 3/4 **Quick N Quirky (IRE)**[11] 2884 4-9-10 75 (bt) DavidAllan 6 56
(Tim Easterby) *trckd ldr: rdn 3f out: wknd fnl f* **8/1**

8 2 1/2 **Duck Egg Blue (IRE)**[222] 7560 3-8-12 73 (p[1]) DougieCostello 1 44
(Patrick Holmes) *dwlt: a rr* **33/1**

1m 24.72s (-2.28) **Going Correction** -0.20s/f (Firm)
**WFA** 3 from 4yo+ 10lb **8** Ran SP% **114.2**
Speed ratings (Par 102): **105,101,96,96,94 94,93,90**
CSF £49.97 CT £385.31 TOTE £4.50: £1.30, £3.70, £4.10; EX 39.80 Trifecta £284.50.
**Owner** G B Turnbull Ltd **Bred** Rabbah Bloodstock Limited **Trained** Norton, N Yorks

**FOCUS**
Race run over an extra 6yds. Not many got into this fair fillies' handicap.

## 3288 RACINGUK.COM H'CAP 5f 212y
**4:55** (4:56) (Class 4) (0-85,87) 4-Y-0+ **£4,851** (£1,443; £721; £360) **Stalls** Low

Form RPR
4312 **1** **Lucky Beggar (IRE)**[13] 2837 7-9-7 83 DavidAllan 2 91
(David C Griffiths) *chsd ldrs: pushed along 2f out: rdn to ld ins fnl f: kpt on* **9/4**[1]
-004 **2** 1 1/4 **Stanghow**[7] 3052 5-9-7 83 CamHardie 9 87
(Antony Brittain) *pressed ldr: led over 2f out: sn rdn: hdd ins fnl f: one pce* **10/1**
40-0 **3** nk **Harwoods Volante (IRE)**[13] 2840 6-9-11 87 DanielTudhope 7 90
(David O'Meara) *dwlt: hld up: pushed along and hdwy on inner over 1f out: rdn and kpt on ins fnl f* **4/1**[2]
0465 **4** 3/4 **Seamster**[13] 2835 10-8-10 79 (t) CameronNoble(7) 4 80+
(David Loughnane) *dwlt: hld up in rr: pushed along and hdwy on outside over 1f out: rdn and kpt on fnl f* **6/1**[3]
4413 **5** 3/4 **Space War**[30] 2305 10-8-4 69 NathanEvans(3) 1 67
(Michael Easterby) *midfield: rdn 2f out: kpt on ins fnl f: nvr threatened* **8/1**
-030 **6** 1 1/2 **Racquet**[13] 2821 4-8-4 69 RachelRichardson(3) 3 62
(Ruth Carr) *led narrowly: hdd over 2f out: sn rdn: wknd ins fnl f* **8/1**
0000 **7** 1/2 **Cosmic Chatter**[13] 2840 7-9-3 79 (p) JackGarritty 5 71
(Ruth Carr) *hld up in midfield: rdn over 2f out: no imp* **7/1**
5100 **8** 1 1/2 **Florencio**[49] 1778 4-9-5 81 (p) ConnorBeasley 8 68
(Roger Fell) *midfield: rdn over 2f out: wknd fnl f* **16/1**

1m 11.58s (-2.02) **Going Correction** -0.20s/f (Firm) **8** Ran SP% **114.8**
Speed ratings (Par 105): **105,103,102,101,100 98,98,96**
CSF £26.12 CT £85.95 TOTE £2.50: £1.20, £2.40, £1.70; EX 13.30 Trifecta £54.30.
**Owner** David Kilpatrick **Bred** Mrs Cherry Faeste **Trained** Bawtry, S Yorks

**FOCUS**
Race run over an extra 6yds. Modest handicap form.

## 3289 NEVER MISS A RACE ON RACING UK H'CAP (DIV I) 5f 212y
**5:30** (5:30) (Class 6) (0-65,64) 3-Y-0+ **£2,264** (£673; £336; £168) **Stalls** Low

Form RPR
6132 **1** **Sir Geoffrey (IRE)**[8] 2994 11-8-7 48 (b) PaddyPilley(5) 7 56
(Scott Dixon) *mde all: rdn over 1f out: kpt on* **3/1**[2]
25-0 **2** 1 1/4 **Exotic Guest**[13] 2843 7-9-12 62 (p) JackGarritty 4 66
(Ruth Carr) *midfield: pushed along whn briefly short of room over 1f out: rdn and hdwy to go 2nd ins fnl f: kpt on* **9/2**[3]
4001 **3** 3 1/4 **Nuala Tagula (IRE)**[14] 2777 4-9-7 57 (t) DougieCostello 8 51+
(John Quinn) *midfield: smooth hdwy on outer 2f out: drvn appr fnl f: edgd lft and sn no further imp: no ex in 3rd fnl 75yds* **8/1**
4504 **4** 2 1/2 **Tafteesh (IRE)**[13] 2843 4-9-11 64 NathanEvans(3) 9 50
(Michael Easterby) *s.i.s: hld up: rdn and hung lft over 1f out: nvr threatened* **9/4**[1]
535 **5** 3/4 **Bismarck The Flyer (IRE)**[33] 2182 3-8-13 57 (p[1]) AndrewMullen 6 38
(Ollie Pears) *chsd ldr: rdn over 2f out: wknd fnl f* **6/1**
0-00 **6** 1 3/4 **Zaytoon (IRE)**[22] 2547 4-8-9 45 PJMcDonald 5 23
(Micky Hammond) *a outpcd in rr* **16/1**
015- **7** 3 **Roman Times (IRE)**[262] 6436 4-9-0 57 ConnorMurtagh(7) 1 25
(Colin Teague) *chsd ldr: rdn over 2f out: wknd over 1f out* **11/1**

1m 12.49s (-1.11) **Going Correction** -0.20s/f (Firm)
**WFA** 3 from 4yo+ 8lb **7** Ran SP% **113.6**
Speed ratings (Par 101): **99,97,93,89,88 86,82**
CSF £16.62 CT £95.67 TOTE £3.20: £1.90, £2.80; EX 20.20 Trifecta £69.20.
**Owner** General Sir Geoffrey Howlett **Bred** P Rabbitte **Trained** Babworth, Notts

**FOCUS**
Race run over an extra 6yds. Moderate sprint form, and the slower division by 0.33sec.

## 3290 NEVER MISS A RACE ON RACING UK H'CAP (DIV II) 5f 212y
**6:05** (6:06) (Class 6) (0-65,62) 3-Y-0+ **£2,264** (£673; £336; £168) **Stalls** Low

Form RPR
4010 **1** **Castlerea Tess**[30] 2306 4-9-8 58 (p) CallumRodriguez(5) 3 65
(Sarah Hollinshead) *chsd ldr: rdn over 2f out: kpt on to ld 75yds out* **8/1**[3]
3353 **2** 3/4 **Penny Dreadful**[20] 2631 5-9-12 57 (p) DavidAllan 6 62
(Scott Dixon) *led: rdn over 1f out: hdd 75yds out: no ex* **11/8**[1]
6501 **3** 3/4 **Searanger (USA)**[8] 2989 4-9-12 62 6ex CliffordLee(5) 7 65
(Rebecca Menzies) *midfield: rdn and hdwy over 1f out: kpt on* **15/8**[2]
00-6 **4** 1 1/2 **Deben**[8] 2989 4-9-4 56 DanielleMooney(7) 9 54
(John Weymes) *hld up: rdn and hdwy over 1f out: kpt on fnl f* **28/1**
0000 **5** 5 **Rat Catcher (IRE)**[20] 2628 7-9-0 45 (b) KevinStott 4 27
(Lisa Williamson) *midfield: rdn over 2f out: wknd over 1f out* **25/1**
5000 **6** 5 **Disclosure**[8] 3001 6-9-5 50 TomEaves 8 16
(Declan Carroll) *a rr* **11/1**
00-5 **7** 12 **Mr Enthusiastic**[25] 2455 3-8-8 45 JoeDoyle 5
(Noel Wilson) *s.i.s: sn chsd ldr: rdn over 2f out: wknd over 1f out* **14/1**

1m 12.16s (-1.44) **Going Correction** -0.20s/f (Firm)
**WFA** 3 from 4yo+ 8lb **7** Ran SP% **110.3**
Speed ratings (Par 101): **101,100,99,97,90 83,67**
CSF £18.12 CT £27.31 TOTE £10.10: £2.40, £1.90; EX 27.60 Trifecta £40.30.
**Owner** Graham Brothers Racing Partnership **Bred** Graham Brothers Racing Partnership **Trained** Upper Longdon, Staffs

**FOCUS**
Race run over an extra 6yds. Very moderate form, but the quicker division by 0.33sec. Not many got into it.

T/Plt: £29.20 to a £1 stake. Pool: £30,071.00 - 1,027.78 winning units. T/Qpdt: £13.90 to a £1 stake. Pool: £2,117.00 - 151.30 winning units. **Andrew Sheret**

# 2815 DONCASTER (L-H)

Friday, June 2

**OFFICIAL GOING: Good (7.7) changing to good to soft after race 2 (6.30) changing to soft after race 3 (7.00)**

Wind: Virtually nil Weather: Rain

## 3291 WELDRICKS PHARMACY IN SUPPORT OF WESTON PARK H'CAP 1m 3f 197y

**6:00** (6:00) (Class 5) (0-75,76) 3-Y-O **£4,528** (£1,347; £673; £336) **Stalls** Low

Form RPR

46-4 **1** **Solar Cross**[23] 2527 3-9-3 **74** KieranShoemark(3) 3 82
(Roger Charlton) *trckd ldrs: hdwy and cl up 3f out: rdn to ld 1 1/2f out: drvn ins fnl f: kpt on strly* **5/1[2]**

13-0 **2** 1 **Je Suis Charlie**[44] 1886 3-9-6 **74** LouisSteward 5 80
(Michael Bell) *sn led at stdy pce: hdd over 7 out and prom: effrt to chal 2f out: rdn and ev ch ent fnl f: sn drvn and kpt on same pce* **9/1**

-451 **3** 1¾ **Road To Dubai (IRE)**[27] 2394 3-9-2 **75** GeorgeWood(5) 7 78
(George Scott) *in tch: hdwy on outer over 3f out: cl up 2f out: rdn wl over 1f out: drvn and kpt on same pce fnl f* **5/1[2]**

-214 **4** nk **Blushing Red (FR)**[14] 2784 3-9-7 **75** AntonioFresu 4 78+
(Ed Dunlop) *t.k.h: hld up towards rr: hdwy 3f out: effrt on inner 2f out and sn chsng ldrs: rdn and ev ch over 1f out: drvn and kpt on same pce fnl f* **8/1[3]**

4-23 **5** 1¼ **Mistress Quickly (IRE)**[32] 2227 3-9-7 **75** PhillipMakin 10 76+
(Ralph Beckett) *t.k.h: hld up in rr: hdwy 3f out: in tch 2f out: sn rdn and kpt on fnl f: nrst fin* **4/1[1]**

31-0 **6** nk **Castellated**[35] 2118 3-9-5 **73** PatCosgrave 11 73
(Richard Hannon) *trckd ldr: hdwy to ld wl over 2f out: rdn and hdd 1 1/2f out: sn drvn and grad wknd fnl f* **20/1**

53-0 **7** 2¼ **Chocolate Box (IRE)**[21] 2588 3-9-4 **72** JamieSpencer 9 68
(Luca Cumani) *in tch: effrt 3f out: sn rdn along and n.d* **16/1**

505 **8** 6 **Akamanto (IRE)**[16] 2721 3-9-8 **76** TomMarquand 6 63
(Richard Hannon) *chsd ldrs: rdn along 3f out: sn wknd* **20/1**

-514 **9** 4½ **Teodoro (IRE)**[23] 2526 3-9-6 **74** RichardKingscote 8 54
(Tom Dascombe) *hmpd s and t.k.h: hld up in rr: hdwy on outer over 3f out: rdn along over 2f out: n.d* **4/1[1]**

044 **10** ¾ **Indian Red**[58] 1559 3-8-11 **65** JoeyHaynes 1 43
(Mark H Tompkins) *t.k.h: trckd ldrs on inner: pushed along wl over 3f out: rdn wl over 2f out: sn wknd* **66/1**

503- **11** hd **Ettihadi (IRE)**[212] 7768 3-9-7 **75** DanielMuscutt 12 53
(Tim Vaughan) *t.k.h: hld up: a in rr* **25/1**

20-2 **12** 12 **Akkadian Empire**[72] 1300 3-9-7 **75** GrahamLee 2 34
(Iain Jardine) *t.k.h: chsd ldrs tl led over 7f out: pushed along 4f out: rdn and hdd wl over 2f out: sn wknd* **25/1**

2m 37.67s (2.77) **Going Correction** +0.30s/f (Good) **12** Ran SP% **119.0**
Speed ratings (Par 99): **102,101,100,99,99 98,97,93,90,89 89,81**
CSF £45.79 CT £240.02 TOTE £6.20: £2.00, £3.50, £1.40; EX 62.50 Trifecta £344.20.
**Owner** De Zoete, Inglett, Mercer And Smartt **Bred** Usk Valley Stud **Trained** Beckhampton, Wilts

**FOCUS**
Race distance increased by 12yds. A 1m4f handicap for 3yos featuring several lightly raced likely improvers. However, it was a muddling contest with a moderate early pace and several spoilt their chance by refusing to settle.

## 3292 NAPOLEONS CASINO & RESTAURANT SHEFFIELD SUPPORTING WPCC FILLIES' H'CAP 1m 2f 43y

**6:30** (6:31) (Class 5) (0-70,70) 4-Y-O+ **£4,528** (£1,347; £673; £336) **Stalls** Low

Form RPR

4662 **1** **Livella Fella (IRE)**[7] 3053 4-9-6 **69** PhillipMakin 5 77
(Keith Dalgleish) *mde all: pushed along and qcknd 4f out: rdn wl over 1f out: drvn ins fnl f: kpt on wl towards fin* **10/3[3]**

6-06 **2** ¾ **Miss Ranger (IRE)**[21] 2587 5-9-3 **66** BenCurtis 2 72
(Brian Ellison) *trckd ldng pair: hdwy to trck wnr 1/2-way: effrt over 2f out: rdn wl over 1f out: drvn ins fnl f: kpt on* **11/4[2]**

4224 **3** 10 **Ms Gillard**[31] 2282 4-9-5 **68** JamieSpencer 7 54
(David Simcock) *hld up in rr: hdwy wl over 2f out: rdn wl over 1f out kpt on fnl f: n.d* **11/4[2]**

3-10 **4** 2¼ **Reckless Wave (IRE)**[14] 2781 4-9-2 **65** ThomasBrown 4 47
(Ed Walker) *in tch: hdwy 4f out: chsd ldng pair over 2f out and sn rdn: drvn wl over 1f out: sn one pce* **5/2[1]**

0-06 **5** 4½ **Astrosecret**[16] 2728 4-8-10 **59** JoeyHaynes 1 32
(Mark H Tompkins) *in tch on inner: pushed along 4f out: rdn 3f out: sn outpcd* **33/1**

006- **6** 6 **Serangoon**[260] 6520 4-8-7 **56** oh3 TomMarquand 6 17
(Michael Appleby) *chsd wnr to 1/2-way: prom: pushed along over 4f out: rdn wl over 3f out: sn outpcd* **33/1**

2m 11.47s (2.07) **Going Correction** +0.30s/f (Good) **6** Ran SP% **110.9**
Speed ratings (Par 100): **103,102,94,92,89 84**
CSF £12.55 TOTE £3.40: £2.20, £2.00; EX 14.60 Trifecta £37.80.
**Owner** Middleham Park Racing XXIII **Bred** Manister House Stud **Trained** Carluke, S Lanarks

**FOCUS**
Race distance increased by 12yds. An ordinary fillies' handicap run at a fair gallop. Few got involved and the first two finished a long way clear of the rest.

## 3293 BUCKINGHAM INSURANCE FIGHTING CANCER WITH WPCC MAIDEN STKS 1m (S)

**7:00** (7:02) (Class 5) 3-Y-O **£4,528** (£1,347; £673; £336) **Stalls** High

Form RPR

0-2 **1** **Commander**[41] 1961 3-9-5 0 HarryBentley 4 88+
(Roger Varian) *led 11/2f: prom: hdwy over 2f out: slt ld wl over 1f out: sn rdn: drvn and hdd ins fnl f: rallied gamely to ld again towards fin* **1/1[1]**

0 **2** hd **Cape To Cuba**[39] 2019 3-8-9 0 GeorgeWood(5) 2 82
(James Fanshawe) *trckd ldrs: hdwy over 2f out: rdn to chal jst over 1f out: slt ld ins fnl f: hdd and no ex towards fin* **33/1**

34- **3** 3¾ **The Statesman**[179] 8227 3-9-5 0 PhillipMakin 9 78
(Ian Williams) *hld up towards rr: hdwy 3f out: rdn to chse ldrs wl over 1f out: drvn and kpt on same pce fnl f* **7/1[3]**

0-4 **4** 1¼ **Azaly (IRE)**[52] 1692 3-9-5 0 PaulMulrennan 5 76
(Owen Burrows) *cl up: rdn along over 2f out: ev ch over 1f out: sn drvn and wknd fnl f* **20/1**

2- **5** 4½ **Mudallel (IRE)**[252] 6751 3-9-5 0 PatCosgrave 1 65
(Ed Dunlop) *plld hrd: chsd ldrs on outer: led after 11/2f: pushed along 3f out: rdn and hdd 2f out: sn wknd* **5/2[2]**

50 **6** 1 **Sir Gnet (IRE)**[14] 2783 3-9-5 0 (h) RichardKingscote 3 63
(Ed Dunlop) *t.k.h: trckd ldrs: pushed along over 2f out: sn rdn and wknd* **66/1**

6 **7** 1¼ **Quinquereme**[15] 2753 3-9-0 0 DanielTudhope 6 55
(Michael Bell) *hld up towards rr: hdwy 3f out: rdn along 2f out: sn wknd* **50/1**

4 **8** ¾ **Warsaw Road (IRE)**[14] 2798 3-9-5 0 JamieSpencer 8 58
(Luca Cumani) *dwlt and towards rr: hdwy 3f out: in tch and rdn over 2f out: sn edgd lft and wknd* **8/1**

**9** 20 **Seaside Dreamer** 3-9-5 0 LouisSteward 7 12
(Michael Bell) *in tch on outer: pushed along 1/2-way: sn rdn and outpcd fnl 3f* **25/1**

1m 43.82s (4.52) **Going Correction** +0.30s/f (Good) **9** Ran SP% **117.2**
Speed ratings (Par 99): **89,88,85,83,79 78,77,76,56**
CSF £49.77 TOTE £1.80: £1.10, £7.70, £2.00; EX 53.00 Trifecta £245.30.
**Owner** China Horse Club International Limited **Bred** Highclere Stud & Hmh Management **Trained** Newmarket, Suffolk

**FOCUS**
The ground looked definitely on the soft side for this maiden, which was run at no more than an ordinary gallop. The third horse looks the key to the form.

## 3294 BLUE LINE TAXIS BARNSLEY SUPPORTING WPCC H'CAP 7f 6y

**7:30** (7:32) (Class 3) (0-95,96) 4-Y-O+ **£12,291** (£3,657; £1,827; £913) **Stalls** High

Form RPR

-050 **1** **Burnt Sugar (IRE)**[27] 2381 5-8-12 **85** PJMcDonald 10 93
(Roger Fell) *hld up towards rr: hdwy whn bmpd wl over 1f out: chsd ldrs and swtchd rt jst over 1f out: rdn to chal ent fnl f: led last 100 yds* **8/1**

-400 **2** ¾ **Intense Style (IRE)**[13] 2840 5-8-5 **85** (p) JaneElliott(7) 9 91
(Les Eyre) *cl up: led wl over 2f out: rdn and edgd lft ent fnl f: sn drvn: hdd last 100 yds: kpt on same pce* **16/1**

-456 **3** ¾ **Ballymore Castle (IRE)**[13] 2833 5-8-7 **80** AndrewMullen 14 84
(Richard Fahey) *hld up towards rr: hdwy nr stands rail 2f out: chsd ldrs over 1f out: chal ent fnl f: ev ch tl drvn and kpt on same pce last 75 yds* **12/1**

0-02 **4** 3½ **Ice Lord (IRE)**[13] 2833 5-9-3 **90** HarryBentley 7 85
(Chris Wall) *trckd ldrs: hdwy over 2f out: chal over 1f out: sn rdn and ev ch: drvn and wknd ent fnl f:* **5/1[2]**

-060 **5** shd **Bertiewhittle**[20] 2606 9-8-12 **90** RowanScott(5) 3 85
(David Barron) *dwlt and towards rr: hdwy on outer 2f out: rdn over 1f out: kpt on fnl f: nrst fin* **25/1**

0-43 **6** 1¼ **Truth Or Dare**[14] 2799 6-9-0 **87** JamieSpencer 11 78
(James Bethell) *hld up in rr: hdwy 2f out: swtchd rt and rdn over 1f out: kpt on fnl f* **9/2[1]**

000- **7** 1½ **Final Frontier (IRE)**[216] 7706 4-9-9 **96** PaulMulrennan 8 83
(Clive Cox) *dwlt: towards rr tl sme late hdwy* **16/1**

S-52 **8** 1½ **Ghalib (IRE)**[20] 2617 5-9-2 **89** (p[1]) PatCosgrave 6 73
(Amy Murphy) *chsd ldrs: rdn along over 2f out: grad wknd* **9/1**

6-12 **9** nk **Gallipoli (IRE)**[27] 2384 4-9-1 **91** AdamMcNamara(3) 4 74
(Richard Fahey) *chsd ldrs: rdn along 3f out: drvn and wknd 2f out* **6/1[3]**

2202 **10** 2 **Lexington Times (IRE)**[14] 2795 5-8-4 **80** RachelRichardson(3) 1 58
(Ruth Carr) *chsd ldrs on outer: rdn along over 2f out: grad wknd* **16/1**

0640 **11** 3¾ **Calder Prince (IRE)**[21] 2568 4-9-0 **87** RichardKingscote 13 55
(Tom Dascombe) *led: rdn along and hdd wl over 2f out: sn wknd* **7/1**

1101 **12** 1¼ **Welliesinthewater (IRE)**[23] 2518 7-9-2 **89** (v) DanielTudhope 12 54
(Derek Shaw) *chsd ldrs: rdn along wl over 2f out: drvn and wkng whn edgd lft wl over 1f out* **10/1**

1m 27.46s (1.16) **Going Correction** +0.30s/f (Good) **12** Ran SP% **121.0**
Speed ratings (Par 107): **105,104,103,99,99 97,96,94,93,91 87,85**
CSF £131.67 CT £1561.53 TOTE £11.00: £3.40, £5.10, £4.60; EX 206.20 Trifecta £3300.80.
**Owner** Middleham Park Racing XL & Partner **Bred** Ballylinch Stud **Trained** Nawton, N Yorks

**FOCUS**
After heavy rain the going had changed to soft for this 7f handicap which was run at an ordinary gallop and the first three were clear.

## 3295 ALAN WOOD PLUMBING & HEATING SUPPORTING WPCC H'CAP 5f 3y

**8:00** (8:00) (Class 4) (0-85,90) 3-Y-O+ **£5,175** (£1,540; £769; £384) **Stalls** High

Form RPR

-631 **1** **Tumblewind**[7] 3052 7-10-0 **90** 6ex LewisEdmunds(5) 8 98
(Richard Whitaker) *trckd ldrs: hdwy 2f out: n.m.r and squeezed through to ld over 1f out: rdn and kpt on wl fnl f* **5/2[1]**

-000 **2** ¾ **My Name Is Rio (IRE)**[13] 2840 7-9-11 **82** ConnorBeasley 10 87
(Michael Dods) *towards rr: rdn along 1/2-way: hdwy wl over 1f out: rdn to chse wnr ins fnl f: sn drvn and no imp* **5/1[3]**

-526 **3** ¾ **Bashiba (IRE)**[11] 2899 6-9-11 **87** (t) RowanScott(5) 6 89
(Nigel Tinkler) *dwlt and rr: pushed along 1/2-way: hdwy on outer wl over 1f out: rdn and styd on wl fnl f* **8/1**

0325 **4** 2 **Tylery Wonder (IRE)**[9] 2951 7-9-9 **80** (v) PaulMulrennan 3 75
(Paul Midgley) *cl up: led over 2f out: sn rdn: drvn: edgd lft and hdd over 1f out: kpt on same pce* **11/2**

-661 **5** 1¾ **Coolfitch (IRE)**[14] 2806 3-9-5 **86** JoshDoyle(3) 7 72
(David O'Meara) *trckd ldrs: hdwy and cl up 2f out: rdn and edgd rt over 1f out: sn drvn and grad wknd* **3/1[2]**

2103 **6** 8 **You're Cool**[41] 1981 5-8-12 **69** JoeDoyle 2 29
(John Balding) *led: rdn along and hdd over 2f out: cl up and drvn whn n.m.r and squeezed out over 1f out: wknd* **16/1**

426- **7** 2 **Harome (IRE)**[209] 7820 3-8-10 **81** BenSanderson(7) 4 31
(Roger Fell) *chsd ldrs: rdn along over 2f out: sn drvn and wknd* **8/1**

1m 0.9s (0.40) **Going Correction** +0.30s/f (Good)
**WFA** 3 from 4yo+ 7lb **7** Ran SP% **113.7**
Speed ratings (Par 105): **108,106,105,102,99 86,83**
CSF £15.18 CT £85.20 TOTE £2.90: £2.10, £2.50; EX 15.30 Trifecta £72.40.
**Owner** R M Whitaker **Bred** Hellwood Stud Farm **Trained** Scarcroft, W Yorks

**FOCUS**
A strongly run sprint and quite an impressive success by the in-foal winner.

## 3296 PENTAGON SUPPORTING WESTON PARK CANCER CHARITY H'CAP 7f 6y

**8:30** (8:32) (Class 5) (0-70,72) 3-Y-O **£4,528** (£1,347; £673; £336) **Stalls** High

Form RPR

0-01 **1** **Pursuing Steed**[24] 2507 3-8-12 **64** CharlieBennett(3) 6 76
(Hughie Morrison) *hld up towards rr: pushed along 1/2-way: hdwy on wd outside over 2f out: rdn to chal jst over 1f out: drvn to ld ins fnl f: kpt on wl towards fin* **3/1[1]**

-322 **2** 1 **Coverham (IRE)**[24] 2507 3-8-12 **61** RyanTate 4 70
(James Eustace) *hld up towards rr: hdwy over 2f out: rdn to chse ldr over 1f out: chal ent fnl f: ev ch tl drvn and kpt on same pce last 75 yds* **7/2[2]**

6-42 **3** *1* **Bruny Island (IRE)**[14] 2794 3-8-8 **57**.............................. StevieDonohoe 5 63
(Charlie Fellowes) *t.k.h: in tch: hdwy on outer to ld 2f out: rdn and edgd rt over 1f out: jnd and drvn 1f out: hdd ins fnl f: kpt on same pce* **3/1**[1]

3-52 **4** *6* **Eponina (IRE)**[25] 2470 3-9-2 **65**........................................ GrahamLee 7 56
(Ben Haslam) *prom: hdwy and cl up over 2f out: rdn wl over 1f out: drvn and wknd appr fnl f* **25/1**

60-0 **5** *1* **Haworth**[13] 2820 3-9-7 **70**................................................. PJMcDonald 12 58
(James Bethell) *in tch: hdwy over 2f out: rdn along wl over 1f out: no imp* **16/1**

0-60 **6** *½* **Dusty Bin**[99] 875 3-8-12 **61**................................................... BenCurtis 2 48
(Roy Bowring) *hld up in rr: hdwy on outer 2f out: rdn over 1f out: kpt on fnl f* **18/1**

3563 **7** *3 ¼* **Alfonso Manana (IRE)**[20] 2630 3-9-5 **68**............(b) RichardKingscote 13 46
(James Given) *chsd ldr: cl up over 2f out: sn rdn and wknd* **14/1**

14-0 **8** *1 ¾* **Allux Boy (IRE)**[34] 2145 3-9-7 **70**................................. AndrewMullen 8 44
(Nigel Tinkler) *led: rdn along 3f out: drvn and hdd 2f out: sn wknd* **25/1**

34-5 **9** *1 ¾* **Ocean Princess (IRE)**[63] 1474 3-9-0 **63**...................... PaulMulrennan 11 32
(Michael Dods) *trckd ldrs: hdwy over 2f out: rdn along and n.m.r wl over 1f out: sn wknd* **16/1**

30-4 **10** *8* **Mont Royal (FR)**[30] 2304 3-9-8 **71**................................. DanielTudhope 9 20
(Ollie Pears) *hld up: a rr* **12/1**[3]

-6 **11** *1* **Showdance Kid**[39] 2036 3-9-4 **72**..............................(v[1]) CliffordLee(5) 10 18
(K R Burke) *prom: hdwy and cl up over 2f out: sn rdn and wknd wl over 1f out* **14/1**

340- **12** *1 ½* **Miss Anticipation (IRE)**[226] 7467 3-9-5 **71**.......... KieranShoemark(3) 14 13
(Roger Charlton) *t.k.h: chsd ldrs: rdn along over 2f out: sn wknd* **25/1**

1m 28.99s (2.69) **Going Correction** +0.30s/f (Good) **12** Ran SP% **121.8**
Speed ratings (Par 99): **96,94,93,86,85 85,81,79,77,68 67,65**
CSF £13.38 CT £32.96 TOTE £3.80: £2.10, £1.30, £1.40; EX 14.40 Trifecta £39.40.
**Owner** Caveat Emptor Partnership **Bred** A E Smith And Co **Trained** East Ilsley, Berks

**FOCUS**
A moderately run handicap run at an ordinary gallop in which the first three finished clear.
T/Plt: £236.70 to a £1 stake. Pool: £57,792.00 - 244.09 winning units. T/Qpdt: £46.70 to a £1 stake. Pool: £5,152.00 - 110.12 winning units. **Joe Rowntree**

## 2083 EPSOM (L-H)
Friday, June 2

**OFFICIAL GOING: Good (overall 7.5; home straight: far side 7.1, stand side 7.7)**
Wind: light, across Weather: light cloud, shower before and during race 5

### 3297 INVESTEC WOODCOTE STKS (CONDITIONS RACE) (PLUS 10 RACE) 6f 3y
**2:00** (2:00) (Class 2) 2-Y-O

**£24,900** (£7,456; £3,728; £1,864; £932; £468) **Stalls** High

Form RPR
14 **1** *2* **Cardsharp**[20] 2607 2-9-5 0........................................ SilvestreDeSousa 4 94
(Mark Johnston) *led: rdn 2f out: drvn and hdd 1f out: kpt on same pce ins fnl f: fin 2nd: later awrdd the r* **7/4**[2]

1 **2** *1 ¾* **Zap**[15] 2769 2-9-5 0.............................................................. PaulHanagan 5 89
(Richard Fahey) *junked rt sn after s: in tch in midfield: effrt ent fnl 2f: hdwy and rdn to chse ldng pair over 1f out: kpt on but no imp ins fnl f: fin 3rd: plcd 2nd* **4/1**[3]

041 **3** *3* **Campion**[7] 3022 2-9-0 0........................................................ SeanLevey 1 75
(Richard Hannon) *t.k.h: chsd ldng pair: rdn over 2f out: outpcd and lost 3rd over 1f out: wknd ins fnl f: fin 4th: plcd 3rd* **14/1**

514 **4** *1 ½* **Diamond Pursuit**[7] 3025 2-9-0 0.................................... FrannyNorton 3 70
(Jo Hughes) *a last trio: effrt over 1f out: no real imp tl kpt on steadily ins fnl f: nvr trbld ldrs: fin 5th: plcd 4th* **66/1**

31 **5** *nk* **Ventura Dragon (IRE)**[11] 2882 2-9-5 0......................... TonyHamilton 2 74
(Richard Fahey) *off the pce in 5th: drvn over 2f out: no imp tl modest late hdwy ins fnl f: nvr trbld ldrs: fin 6th: plcd 5th* **14/1**

51 **6** *6* **Holdenhurst**[10] 2910 2-9-5 0.................................................. FranBerry 6 56
(Sylvester Kirk) *hmpd sn after s: a in rr: pushed along 4f out: rdn over 2f out: no prog and bhd over 1f out: fin 7th: plcd 6th* **33/1**

51 **D** **De Bruyne Horse**[12] 2852 2-9-5 0.................................... RyanMoore 7 100
(Richard Hannon) *sn chsng ldr: rdn over 2f out: hdwy u.p to ld 1f out: styd on strly: rdn out: later disqualified - prohibited substance in sample* **13/8**[1]

1m 8.54s (-0.86) **Going Correction** -0.05s/f (Good) **7** Ran SP% **112.2**
Speed ratings (Par 99): **100,98,94,92,91 83,103**
CSF £4.55 TOTE £2.60: £1.40, £1.60; EX 5.00 Trifecta £12.70.
**Owner** Sheikh Hamdan bin Mohammed Al Maktoum **Bred** Godolphin **Trained** Middleham Moor, N Yorks

**FOCUS**
A muggy day, and the going was given as good (GoingStick: 7.5; Home straight: Far side 7.1; Stands' side 7.7). The rail was out up to 5yds from the Mile marker to the winning post, adding 10yds to 6f, 20yds to 7f and 26yds to all races of 1m+. Although no longer carrying Listed status, this race looked up to standard. The time suggested the ground was on the fast side of good. The runner-up is perhaps the key to the form.

### 3298 INVESTEC CLICK & INVEST MILE H'CAP 1m 113y
**2:35** (2:35) (Class 2) (0-105,105) 4-Y-O+

**£24,900** (£7,456; £3,728; £1,864; £932; £468) **Stalls** Low

Form RPR
0-21 **1** **G K Chesterton (IRE)**[14] 2799 4-8-10 **94**...................(p[1]) WilliamBuick 6 104+
(Charlie Appleby) *mde all: dictated stdy gallop tl qcknd over 3f out: rdn over 2f out: over 2 l clr over 1f out: styd on and a doing enough ins fnl f* **3/1**[1]

0000 **2** *1* **Mythical Madness**[16] 2735 6-8-11 **95**..................(v) SilvestreDeSousa 11 102
(David O'Meara) *t.k.h: hld up in tch in midfield: effrt in 6th 2f out: clsd u.p 2f out: chsd clr wnr 150yds out: styd on wl but nvr getting to wnr* **20/1**

3-00 **3** *½* **Home Cummins (IRE)**[15] 2767 5-8-8 **92**.....................(p) PaulHanagan 7 98
(Richard Fahey) *t.k.h: trckd ldng trio: effrt over 2f out: styd u.p 1f out to go 3rd 100yds out: kpt on wl but nvr getting to wnr* **14/1**[3]

6110 **4** *1 ½* **Forceful Appeal (USA)**[8] 3014 9-7-9 **86** oh4.................. DavidEgan(7) 1 88
(Simon Dow) *trckd ldng pair: swtchd rt 2f out and sn rdn to chse clr wnr: kpt on but no imp: lost 2nd and kpt on same pce fnl 150yds* **33/1**

1100 **5** *1* **Chevallier**[81] 1177 5-8-9 **93**.................................................. LukeMorris 8 93
(Archie Watson) *t.k.h: trckd wnr: rdn over 2f out: lost 2nd wl over 1f out: stl battling for placings but no imp on wnr: keeping on same pce whn sltly squeezed for room ins fnl f* **33/1**

3-53 **6** *½* **Spring Offensive (IRE)**[27] 2406 5-8-9 **93**...................... AndreaAtzeni 5 94+
(Richard Fahey) *t.k.h: trckd ldng quartet: effrt on inner over 2f out: kpt on but no imp on wnr over 1f out: hld whn nt clr run ins fnl f: eased towards fin* **7/1**[2]

241- **7** *½* **Sixties Groove (IRE)**[205] 7869 4-9-0 **98**...........................(p) AdamKirby 9 96+
(Jeremy Noseda) *t.k.h: hld up in tch in last quartet: outpcd whn wnr qcknd over 3f out: shkn up over 1f out: hdwy and styd on wl ins fnl f: gng on fin but nvr threatening ldrs* **7/1**[2]

0003 **8** *½* **Mutarakez (IRE)**[13] 2828 5-8-4 **88**...................................... KierenFox 10 84
(Brian Meehan) *t.k.h: hld up in tch in midfield: outpcd and rdn whn wnr qcknd over 3f out: no imp and wnt lft u.p over 1f out: swtchd rt and styd on ins fnl f: no threat to ldrs* **7/1**[2]

0-03 **9** *1* **Stipulate**[27] 2406 8-8-4 **93**........................................ MeganNicholls(5) 12 87
(Brian Ellison) *stdd s: hld up in last quartet: outpcd whn wnr qcknd over 3f out: rdn over 2f out: no threat to ldrs but kpt on ins fnl f* **20/1**

0-00 **10** *1 ½* **Cricklewood Green (USA)**[8] 3014 6-8-2 **86** oh4.... JosephineGordon 3 77
(Sylvester Kirk) *bustled along early: t.k.h after 1f and hld up in last quartet: outpcd whn wnr qcknd and rdn over 3f out: no imp and wl hld whn swtchd rt over 1f out* **25/1**

0-10 **11** *1 ¼* **Calvados Spirit**[13] 2828 4-8-2 **89**................................ HollieDoyle(3) 4 77
(William Muir) *stdd s: t.k.h: hld up in rr: outpcd whn wnr qcknd over 3f out: rdn and no hdwy over 2f out: n.d* **20/1**

02-0 **12** *2* **Remarkable**[20] 2606 4-9-7 **105**..................................(b) FrankieDettori 2 88
(John Gosden) *dwlt and rousted along early: rdn and outpcd whn wnr qcknd over 3f out: no imp whn carried lft and hmpd over 1f out: wknd and bhd ins fnl f* **3/1**[1]

1m 46.95s (0.85) **Going Correction** -0.05s/f (Good) **12** Ran SP% **118.2**
Speed ratings (Par 109): **94,93,92,91,90 90,89,89,88,86 85,84**
CSF £73.35 CT £740.63 TOTE £3.70: £1.40, £5.10, £3.80; EX 84.80 Trifecta £1001.50.
**Owner** Godolphin **Bred** Darley **Trained** Newmarket, Suffolk

**FOCUS**
It was another very competitive edition of this 1m handicap on paper. However, the hold-up horses stood zero chance due to a stop-start pace. Race distance increased by 26yds.

### 3299 INVESTEC CORONATION CUP (GROUP 1) 1m 4f 6y
**3:10** (3:14) (Class 1) 4-Y-O+

**£238,182** (£90,300; £45,192; £22,512; £11,298; £5,670) **Stalls** Centre

Form RPR
12-0 **1** **Highland Reel (IRE)**[69] 1379 5-9-0 123.............................. RyanMoore 3 123
(A P O'Brien, Ire) *led: jnd 3 out: sn rdn and hdd jst over 2f out: sustained battle w chalr and led again over 1f out and sn forged ahd: styd on wl: rdn out* **9/4**[1]

6-41 **2** *1 ¾* **Frontiersman**[26] 2431 4-9-0 109........................................ JamesDoyle 10 119+
(Charlie Appleby) *hld up in last pair: 9th st: rdn and hdwy on outer over 2f out: hung bdly lft fr 2f out but str run to chse wnr ins fnl f: rdr trying to switch rt but horse stl hanging and kpt on wout threatening wnr* **9/1**

3-51 **3** *3 ½* **Hawkbill (USA)**[13] 2822 4-9-0 117..................................(p) WilliamBuick 4 114
(Charlie Appleby) *chsd ldr over 10f out: 2nd st: sn rdn to chal and led over 2f out: sustained battle w wnr tl hdd and wnt rt over 1f out: no ex and lost 2nd ins fnl f: wknd fnl 100yds* **11/2**[3]

-142 **4** *1* **Elbereth**[26] 2432 6-8-11 107.................................................. OisinMurphy 6 109
(Andrew Balding) *dwlt: sn rcvrd and in midfield: 5th st: rdn over 2f out: no imp tl kpt on ins fnl f to snatch 4th last stride: nvr enough pce to threaten ldrs* **33/1**

111- **5** *shd* **Journey**[230] 7351 5-8-11 120.........................................(h) FrankieDettori 2 109
(John Gosden) *t.k.h: chsd wnr for over 1f: stdd bk and hld up in 4th tl wnt 3rd st: rdn over 2f out: no imp and carried lft whn lost 3rd over 1f out: wknd ins fnl f: lost 4th last stride* **7/2**[2]

1U5- **6** *1* **Idaho (IRE)**[229] 7405 4-9-0 119.................................... SeamieHeffernan 7 110
(A P O'Brien, Ire) *hld up in midfield: 6th st: sn rdn: outpcd and lost pl over 2f out: rallied 1f out and kpt on under hands and heels riding ins fnl f: no threat to ldrs* **11/1**

2-65 **7** *½* **Red Verdon (USA)**[8] 3012 4-9-0 113.............................(p[1]) PatSmullen 8 109
(Ed Dunlop) *hld up in midfield: 7th st: rdn over 2f out: no imp and sltly impeded over 1f out: kpt on same pce after and nvr threatened ldrs* **33/1**

40-1 **8** *1 ¼* **Air Pilot**[54] 1654 8-9-0 114........................................................ FranBerry 9 107
(Ralph Beckett) *stdd after s: hld up in rr: 10th st: effrt jst over 2f out: no imp u.p over 1f out: nvr trbld ldrs* **25/1**

2114 **9** *¾* **Prize Money**[69] 1379 4-9-0 115.......................................(h) OlivierPeslier 1 106
(Saeed bin Suroor) *chsd ldng pair tl 4th st: rdn over 2f out: sn struggling: lost pl over 1f out: wknd fnl f* **10/1**

0-32 **10** *2* **US Army Ranger (IRE)**[21] 2571 4-9-0 114.............. DonnachaO'Brien 5 103
(A P O'Brien, Ire) *stdd s: hld up in last trio: 8th st: rdn and no hdwy ent fnl 2f: bhd ins fnl f* **8/1**

2m 33.34s (-5.56) **Going Correction** -0.05s/f (Good) **10** Ran SP% **116.6**
Speed ratings (Par 117): **116,114,112,111,111 111,110,109,109,108**
CSF £23.14 CT £98.80 TOTE £2.90: £1.20, £3.30, £2.00; EX 27.30 Trifecta £215.40.
**Owner** Derrick Smith & Mrs John Magnier & Michael Tabor **Bred** Hveger Syndicate **Trained** Cashel, Co Tipperary

**FOCUS**
Race distance increased by 26yds. A bigger field than normal for this Group 1, and it looked quite a competitive race on paper. The O'Brien-trained horses had been late arriving at the track due to a flight delay (arrived at about 2pm), and they had to pass the vet before taking part, but it had no impact on the favourite, who was the best horse in the race on ratings, and proved it.

### 3300 INVESTEC WEALTH & INVESTMENT H'CAP 1m 2f 17y
**3:45** (3:48) (Class 2) 4-Y-O+

**£31,125** (£9,320; £4,660; £2,330; £1,165; £585) **Stalls** Low

Form RPR
30-0 **1** **Not So Sleepy**[16] 2735 5-9-8 **98**...........................................(t) AdamKirby 2 105
(Hughie Morrison) *taken down early: dwlt: in tch in midfield: hdwy to chse ldrs over 1f out: nt clr run and swtchd rt 1f out: barging match w rival and squeezed through to chse ldr ins fnl f: r.o wl to ld last strides* **10/1**[3]

-306 **2** *nk* **Innocent Touch (IRE)**[16] 2735 6-9-2 **92**.......................... TonyHamilton 5 98
(Richard Fahey) *chsd ldr: clsd to chal 2f out: rdn to ld over 1f out: kpt on wl u.p tl hdd last strides* **16/1**

41-0 **3** *nk* **What About Carlo (FR)**[8] 2999 6-9-10 **100**.................... TomQueally 8 105
(Eve Johnson Houghton) *hld up in midfield: effrt 2f out: nt clr run and trying to swtchd rt but hemmed in over 1f out tl hdwy ins fnl f: r.o strly fnl 100yds: nt quite rch ldrs* **14/1**

5-40 **4** *nk* **Examiner (IRE)**[62] 1492 6-9-2 **92**..........................................(t) FranBerry 1 97
(Stuart Williams) *chsd ldrs: effrt to chse ldng pair wl over 1f out: sn drvn: barging w wnr jst ins fnl f: kpt on u.p* **16/1**

-512 **5** ½ **Brorocco**[22] 2552 4-9-0 **90**......(h) OisinMurphy 9 94+
(Andrew Balding) *taken down early: stdd after s: t.k.h: hld up in tch in last trio: hdwy on inner over 2f out: 5th whn nt clr run 1f out: switching rt ins fnl f: styd on wout quite getting on terms* **11/4**[1]

4046 **6** *nk* **Great Hall**[27] 2396 7-9-10 **100**...... ShaneKelly 11 103
(Mick Quinn) *hld up in tch in midfield: swtchd rt and effrt 2f out: hdwy u.p ins fnl f: styd on wl towards fin: nvr quite getting to ldrs* **33/1**

4-30 **7** *nk* **Top Beak (IRE)**[13] 2828 4-8-13 **89**......(t) JamesDoyle 6 92
(Hughie Morrison) *hld up in tch in midfield on outer: effrt 2f out: kpt on wl fnl 100yds: nvr quite enough pce to rch ldrs* **16/1**

U250 **8** ½ **Final**[16] 2735 5-9-2 **92**...... FrannyNorton 10 97+
(Mark Johnston) *niggled along early: in tch in rr: hdwy towards inner jst over 1f out: styng on whn stuck bhd wkng rival ins fnl f: swtchd rt and kpt on towards fin* **10/1**[3]

1321 **9** *shd* **Storm King**[22] 2558 8-8-7 **83**...... SamHitchcott 3 84
(David C Griffiths) *led: jnd and rdn over 2f out: hdd over 1f out: no ex and wknd ins fnl f* **20/1**

45-1 **10** ¾ **Fidaawy**[34] 2136 4-9-8 **98**......(h) JimCrowley 12 98
(Sir Michael Stoute) *chsd ldrs on outer: rdn 2f out: unable qck and lost pl over 1f out: hld and kpt on same pce ins fnl f* **4/1**[2]

1-50 **11** ½ **Speed Company (IRE)**[16] 2735 4-9-8 **98**...... JasonHart 13 97
(John Quinn) *hld up in last pair: effrt ent fnl 2f: edging lft and no imp over 1f out: swtchd rt and kpt on ins fnl f: nvr trbld ldrs* **14/1**

0055 **12** ¾ **Imshivalla (IRE)**[13] 2817 6-8-4 **80**......(h) PaulHanagan 7 77
(Richard Fahey) *chsd ldrs: rdn and unable qck over 1f out: lost pl over 1f out: wl hld whn nt clr run ins fnl f* **12/1**

2-20 **13** ¾ **Grapevine (IRE)**[27] 2396 4-9-0 **90**...... AndreaAtzeni 4 86
(Charles Hills) *hld up in midfield: shkn up and effrt over 1f out: nt clr run and hmpd 1f out: swtchd rt and pushed along ins fnl f: sn n.m.r again and coasted home* **12/1**

0040 **14** *nk* **Abareeq**[8] 2999 4-8-11 **87**...... SilvestreDeSousa 14 82
(Mark Johnston) *hld up in tch towards rr: rdn and swtchd lft 2f out: swtchd lft again over 1f out: nt clr run and swtchd rt 1f out: stl nowhere to go and coasted home fnl 100yds* **16/1**

2m 6.96s (-2.74) **Going Correction** -0.05s/f (Good) **14 Ran SP% 124.8**
Speed ratings (Par 109): **108,107,107,107,106 106,106,106,105,105 104,104,103,103**
CSF £166.37 CT £2261.94 TOTE £11.80: £3.90, £5.80, £3.60; EX 217.90 Trifecta £2692.40.
**Owner** Lady Blyth **Bred** Lord Blyth **Trained** East Ilsley, Berks

**FOCUS**
Another decent handicap. There was a muddling early pace, though, and it proved a rough race inside the final furlong. Race distance increased by 26yds.

## 3301 INVESTEC OAKS (GROUP 1) (FILLIES) 1m 4f 6y
**4:30** (4:33) (Class 1) 3-Y-O

**£283,550** (£107,500; £53,800; £26,800; £13,450; £6,750) **Stalls** Centre

Form RPR

1-31 **1** **Enable**[23] 2523 3-9-0 107...... FrankieDettori 9 123
(John Gosden) *chsd ldng pair: 3rd st: rdn and clsd to ld over 2f out: sn wnt clr w runner up: forged ent fnl f: styd on strly and drew clr fnl f: readily* **6/1**[2]

31-2 **2** *5* **Rhododendron (IRE)**[26] 2434 3-9-0 116...... RyanMoore 5 115
(A P O'Brien, Ire) *hld up in 4th: 4th st: clsd to join ldrs over 2f out: sn wnt clr w wnr: rdn over 1f out: no ex and unable to go w wnr ent fnl f: outstyd by wnr but kpt on for clr 2nd* **8/11**[1]

2 **3** *6* **Alluringly (USA)**[23] 2523 3-9-0 106...... SeamieHeffernan 7 105
(A P O'Brien, Ire) *hld up in midfield: 6th st: rdn and hdwy to chse clr ldng pair 2f out: sn no imp and outpcd: wl hld in 3rd and plugged on same pce after* **16/1**

41-1 **4** 3¾ **Horseplay**[26] 2436 3-9-0 100...... OisinMurphy 3 99+
(Andrew Balding) *t.k.h: hld up in last trio: 7th st: rdn and carried rt over 2f out: hdwy to go modest 4th 1f out: kpt on but no ch w ldrs* **14/1**

11-3 **5** *1* **Coronet**[19] 2665 3-9-0 103...... AndreaAtzeni 6 98+
(John Gosden) *sn dropped to rr and niggled along: 8th st: swtchd rt and rdn over 2f out: no ch but kpt on to pass btn rivals 1f out: wnt modest 5th ins fnl f: n.d* **12/1**[3]

1-2 **6** 2¾ **Isabel De Urbina (IRE)**[26] 2436 3-9-0 98...... FranBerry 8 93
(Ralph Beckett) *hld up in last trio: 9th st: sn rdn: no prog and no ch after: plugged on to pass btn rivals fnl f* **33/1**

5-42 **7** 2¾ **Pocketfullofdreams (FR)**[20] 2613 3-9-0 99......(h) DonnachaO'Brien 1 89
(A P O'Brien, Ire) *sn led and set decent gallop: 5 l clr st: rdn and hdd over 2f out: sn btn and dropped out: wl bhd ins fnl f* **50/1**

15-1 **8** 1¾ **Sobetsu**[19] 2665 3-9-0 113...... WilliamBuick 10 86
(Charlie Appleby) *led for 1f: chsd ldr: 2nd st: sn rdn to cl: ev ch briefly over 2f out: 3rd and totally outpcd by ldng pair 2f out: wknd over 1f out* **6/1**[2]

21 **9** *7* **Natavia**[13] 2827 3-9-0 102...... PatSmullen 2 75
(Roger Charlton) *hld up in midfield: 5th st: rdn and outpcd whn edgd rt over 2f out: bhd over 1f out* **12/1**[3]

2m 34.13s (-4.77) **Going Correction** -0.05s/f (Good) **9 Ran SP% 119.3**
Speed ratings (Par 110): **113,109,105,103,102 100,98,97,93**
CSF £11.07 CT £71.45 TOTE £6.40: £2.00, £1.10, £3.90; EX 12.10 Trifecta £93.60.
**Owner** K Abdullah **Bred** Juddmonte Farms Ltd **Trained** Newmarket, Suffolk
■ Daddys Lil Darling was withdrawn. Price at time of withdrawal 33/1. Rule 4 does not apply.

**FOCUS**
Race distance increased by 26yds. While the favourite set a good standard, this looked an Oaks with depth to it. Some interest was lost when the American challenger Daddys Lil Darling bolted to post, unseated Olivier Peslier and was withdrawn. It was run in a thunderstorm, the pace was a good one (time was 0.79sec slower than the Coronation Cup), set by Pocketfullofdreams, and stamina came to the fore. The winner and third came from the Cheshire Oaks.

## 3302 INVESTEC SAVINGS SURREY STKS (LISTED RACE) 7f 3y
**5:15** (5:15) (Class 1) 3-Y-O

**£22,684** (£8,600; £4,304; £2,144; £1,076; £540) **Stalls** Low

Form RPR

0-04 **1** **Solomon's Bay (IRE)**[13] 2830 3-9-0 95...... SilvestreDeSousa 3 110+
(Roger Varian) *hld up in last pair: swtchd rt and effrt over 2f out: hdwy to chal ent fnl f: led ins fnl f: r.o wl: rdn out* **8/1**

-303 **2** ¾ **Seven Heavens**[13] 2830 3-9-0 103...... FrankieDettori 7 107
(John Gosden) *taken down early: dwlt: t.k.h and sn rcvrd to chse ldr: upsides and travelling strly 3f out: led and rdn over 2f out: hdd jst ins fnl f: kpt on but a hld after* **5/2**[2]

**3** 2¼ **True Valour (IRE)**[32] 2242 3-9-0 101...... RyanMoore 1 101
(J P Murtagh, Ire) *t.k.h: chsd ldrs on inner: nt clrest of runs 2f out: swtchd rt and rdn to chse ldng pair 1f out: kpt on same pce and no imp after* **3/1**[3]

4120 **4** 1¾ **Mr Scaramanga**[41] 1959 3-9-3 100...... PatSmullen 5 99
(Simon Dow) *hld up in last pair: effrt over 2f out: rdn and hdwy to chse ldng pair briefly over 1f out: sn outpcd: wl hld 4th and one pced ins fnl f* **22/1**

50-0 **5** ¾ **Koropick (IRE)**[13] 2823 3-9-0 105...... JamesDoyle 4 94
(Hugo Palmer) *chsd ldrs on outer: rdn over 2f out: struggling to qckn and n.m.r over 1f out: wl hld and kpt on same pce ins fnl f* **25/1**

134- **6** 2¼ **Kodiline (IRE)**[277] 5977 3-9-0 95...... AdamKirby 6 88
(Clive Cox) *sn led: rdn and hdd over 1f out: sn drvn: lost pl and btn 1f out: wknd ins fnl f: eased towards fin* **16/1**

2531 **7** 3¾ **Sutter County**[6] 3071 3-9-0 103...... AndreaAtzeni 2 78
(Mark Johnston) *t.k.h: chsd ldrs but unbalanced on early downhill run: rdn 3f out: dropped to rr and btn 2f out: wknd* **2/1**[1]

1m 21.97s (-1.33) **Going Correction** -0.05s/f (Good) **7 Ran SP% 112.1**
Speed ratings (Par 107): **105,104,101,99,98 96,91**
CSF £27.21 TOTE £9.20: £3.70, £1.70; EX 28.40 Trifecta £127.80.
**Owner** Prince A A Faisal **Bred** Nawara Stud Company Ltd S A **Trained** Newmarket, Suffolk

**FOCUS**
Just an average Listed event for 3yos. They went a sound pace, no more, and the runner-up sets the level. Race distance increased by 20yds.

## 3303 INVESTEC FOREIGN EXCHANGE H'CAP 7f 3y
**5:50** (5:51) (Class 2) (0-100,95) 3-Y-O

**£24,900** (£7,456; £3,728; £1,864; £932; £468) **Stalls** Low

Form RPR

2-53 **1** **Juanito Chico (IRE)**[21] 2567 3-8-6 **80**......(h) SilvestreDeSousa 4 91+
(William Jarvis) *t.k.h: hld up in tch in midfield: swtchd rt over 2f out: nt clr run and swtchd rt again over 1f out: str run ins fnl f to ld fnl 50yds: sn in command* **4/1**[1]

-452 **2** *1* **Wahash (IRE)**[13] 2818 3-9-4 **92**...... FrankieDettori 2 100
(Richard Hannon) *led: rdn and fnd ex over 1f out: kpt on wl tl hdd and nt match pce of wnr fnl 50yds* **7/1**

30-2 **3** 1¼ **Black Trilby (IRE)**[11] 2894 3-8-5 **79**......(h[1]) SamHitchcott 3 84
(Clive Cox) *chsd ldr: rdn over 2f out: clsd and drvn to press wnr 2f out: unable qck over 1f out: kpt on same pce ins fnl f* **5/1**[3]

2030 **4** *3* **Dr Julius No**[35] 2126 3-9-2 **90**...... ShaneKelly 8 87+
(Richard Hughes) *dwlt: t.k.h: hld up in last pair: effrt on outer ent fnl 2f: sltly impeded and wnt rt over 1f out: hdwy u.p ins fnl f: styd on wl to go 4th cl home* **20/1**

15-0 **5** ½ **Plant Pot Power (IRE)**[23] 2520 3-8-10 **84**...... SeanLevey 7 79
(Richard Hannon) *t.k.h: wl in tch in midfield: effrt over 2f out: chsd ldng pair but hanging lft over 1f out: no ex and wknd ins fnl f* **25/1**

10-2 **6** 1¼ **Musawaat**[13] 2820 3-8-13 **87**...... JimCrowley 6 79
(Charles Hills) *hld up towards rr: effrt on outer whn pushed rt over 1f out: hdwy ins fnl f: styd on but no threat to ldrs* **15/2**

2-31 **7** *nk* **Firefright (IRE)**[34] 2135 3-8-10 **84**...... AndreaAtzeni 11 75
(Jeremy Noseda) *hld up in midfield: rdn 3f out: no imp and edgd rt over 1f out: kpt on same pce after* **9/2**[2]

3312 **8** *shd* **Atteq**[28] 2374 3-8-7 **81**......(t) PaulHanagan 9 72
(Richard Fahey) *t.k.h: in tch in midfield: effrt 2f out: nt clrest of runs over 1f out: swtchd rt ins fnl f: kpt on but no threat to ldrs* **16/1**

3051 **9** *3* **Zamjar**[22] 2557 3-8-8 **82**......(b) JosephineGordon 1 65
(Ed Dunlop) *t.k.h: chsd ldrs: rdn over 1f out: unable qck and wknd ins fnl f* **20/1**

120- **10** 2½ **Eaton Square**[223] 7544 3-9-7 **95**......(p) RyanMoore 5 71
(John Gosden) *hld up in last quartet: pushed along ent fnl 2f: nt clrest of runs 2f out: no prog: n.d* **7/1**

-210 **11** *1* **Aardwolf (USA)**[6] 3071 3-9-5 **93**...... FrannyNorton 10 66
(Mark Johnston) *t.k.h: chsd ldrs: rdn 2f out: lost pl qckly over 1f out: wknd ins fnl f* **20/1**

4140 **12** *29* **Alkashaaf (USA)**[84] 1124 3-8-4 **81**...... HollieDoyle(3) 12
(Archie Watson) *wnt rt s: sn bhd and nvr travelling: lost tch over 2f out: t.o* **33/1**

1m 21.62s (-1.68) **Going Correction** -0.05s/f (Good) **12 Ran SP% 118.6**
Speed ratings (Par 105): **107,105,104,101,100 99,98,98,95,92 91,57**
CSF £29.14 CT £130.02 TOTE £4.80: £1.80, £2.40, £2.10; EX 27.50 Trifecta £166.20.
**Owner** Tony Verrier **Bred** Miss Catherine Monaghan **Trained** Newmarket, Suffolk

**FOCUS**
This good-quality 3yo handicap was run at a sound pace and the principals were clear at the finish. Race distance increased by 20yds.
T/Jkpt: Not won. T/Plt: £207.00 to a £1 stake. Pool: £185,181.00 - 894.3 winning units. T/Qpdt: £51.10 to a £1 stake. Pool: £13,383.00 - 261.55 winning units. **Steve Payne**

# 3069 GOODWOOD (R-H)
Friday, June 2

**OFFICIAL GOING: Good (7.3)**
Wind: light breeze across Weather: sunny

## 3304 THREE FRIDAY NIGHTS AMATEUR RIDERS' H'CAP 1m 1f 11y
**6:10** (6:11) (Class 5) (0-70,68) 4-Y-O+ **£3,743** (£1,161; £580; £290) **Stalls** Low

Form RPR

-260 **1** **Strictly Art (IRE)**[78] 1225 4-9-11 **56**...... MissJCooley(5) 8 63
(Alan Bailey) *mde all: kpt on strly fnl f: pushed out* **11/2**[2]

04-0 **2** *2* **Pink Ribbon (IRE)**[14] 2785 5-11-0 **68**......(p) MrAlexFerguson 3 71
(Sylvester Kirk) *trckd ldrs: rdn over 2f out: chsd wnr ent fnl f: kpt on but a being hld* **11/4**[1]

2301 **3** 3¾ **Gabrial The Thug (FR)**[31] 2276 7-10-11 **65**......(t) MrSWalker 5 61
(Ian Williams) *hld up in tch: hdwy over 2f out: sn rdn: kpt on fnl f but nt pce to get on terms* **11/4**[1]

0-40 **4** 1½ **Knight Of The Air**[33] 2178 5-10-2 **63**...... MrsCPownall(7) 7 56
(Joseph Tuite) *trckd ldrs: rdn to chse wnr over 2f out tl ent fnl f: no ex* **16/1**

6604 **5** 3½ **Solveig's Song**[9] 2956 5-10-8 **62**......(p) MrRBirkett 2 48
(Steve Woodman) *hld up in tch: rdn 2f out: nt pce to get on terms: fdd ins fnl f* **11/2**[2]

6026 **6** *3* **Fairy Mist (IRE)**[10] 2916 10-9-2 **49** oh1...... MissTannyaBagoban(7) 1 29
(John Bridger) *plld hrd: hdwy to press wnr after 2f: pushed along 4f out: wknd over 1f out* **8/1**[3]

5256 **7** *8* **Gaelic Silver (FR)**[28] 2365 11-10-4 **65**......(v[1]) MissBeckyButler(7) 4 29
(Gary Moore) *v.s.a: a towards rr* **16/1**

5-05 **8** *10* **Tarseekh**[30] 2297 4-10-6 **65**...... PoppyBridgwater(5) 6 9
(Chris Gordon) *trckd ldrs: rdn 3f out: wknd 2f out* **12/1**

1m 58.27s (1.97) **Going Correction** +0.225s/f (Good) **8 Ran SP% 114.7**
Speed ratings (Par 103): **100,98,94,93,90 87,80,71**
CSF £21.10 CT £50.11 TOTE £6.20: £2.00, £1.40, £1.40; EX 18.50 Trifecta £90.50.

**Owner** AB Racing Limited **Bred** Lismacue Mare Syndicate **Trained** Newmarket, Suffolk
**FOCUS**
Some starts have been moved at this track following remeasuring, so some races will not have speed figures until there is sufficient data to calculate updated median times. First 2f of the mile course dolled out 5yds and top bend dolled out 3yds. Warm, drying conditions, with the track missing the rain that hit other parts of the south east. This was a moderate race.

## 3305 GLORIOUS EBF NOVICE STKS 6f
**6:40** (6:46) (Class 5) 2-Y-O **£3,234** (£962; £481; £240) **Stalls** High

Form RPR
1 **Snazzy Jazzy (IRE)** 2-8-13 0 HectorCrouch(3) 4 73
(Clive Cox) *racd center: a.p: overall ldr jst over 2f out: drifted lft but kpt on wl fnl f* **7/1**[3]
2 1 1/4 **Alrahaal (IRE)** 2-9-2 0 FergusSweeney 8 69
(Marcus Tregoning) *racd stands' side: pressed ldr: rdn 2f out: kpt on ins fnl f: wnt 2nd fnl strides* **16/1**
0 3 shd **Merchant Marine (IRE)**[25] [2473] 2-9-2 0 (v[1]) FranBerry 2 69
(Ralph Beckett) *led center gp tl rdn jst over 2f out: sn rdn to chse wnr: kpt o n but a being hld fnl f: lost 2nd fnl strides* **9/2**[2]
4 hd **Collateral (IRE)** 2-9-2 0 MartinHarley 3 68
(James Tate) *racd center: trckd ldrs: effrt 2f out: kpt on same pce fnl f* **9/2**[2]
5 1 1/4 **Margub** 2-9-2 0 PatDobbs 6 65
(Marcus Tregoning) *racd stands' side: trckd ldrs: rdn 2f out: kpt on same pce fnl f* **12/1**
6 hd **Island Court (IRE)** 2-9-2 0 LiamKeniry 7 64
(J S Moore) *racd stands' side: sn pushed along in last pair but in tch: hdwy 2f out: kpt on same pce fnl f* **33/1**
7 nk **Frostbite** 2-9-2 0 JohnFahy 9 63
(Eve Johnson Houghton) *led stands' side gp: rdn to chse wnr 2f out: kpt on same pce fnl f* **10/1**
0 8 11 **Aiya (IRE)**[14] [2779] 2-9-2 0 DavidProbert 5 30+
(Andrew Balding) *racd center: stmbld leaving stalls: prom: rdn over 2f out: wknd jst over 1f out* **7/4**[1]
9 16 **Good Impression** 2-9-2 0 GavinLerena 1
(Amanda Perrett) *racd center: s.i.s: last pair but in tch: rdn over 2f out: wknd over 1f out* **14/1**

1m 13.25s (1.05) **Going Correction** 0.0s/f (Good) **9** Ran SP% **117.5**
Speed ratings (Par 93): **98,96,96,95,94 94,93,78,57**
CSF £112.05 TOTE £7.00: £2.30, £4.60, £1.70; EX 88.40 Trifecta £1379.30.
**Owner** Mrs Olive Shaw **Bred** Bluegate Stud **Trained** Lambourn, Berks
**FOCUS**
The favourite bombed out and there was just over 3l covering the first seven, so the bare form is probably just ordinary, but a likeable winner.

## 3306 COATES & SEELY FILLIES' NOVICE STKS (PLUS 10 RACE) 5f
**7:10** (7:10) (Class 5) 2-Y-O **£3,234** (£962; £481) **Stalls** High

Form RPR
1 **Short Call (IRE)** 2-9-0 0 CharlesBishop 1 80+
(Mick Channon) *trckd ldng pair: led over 1f out: sn drifted lft: r.o wl: readily* **11/4**[3]
2 2 3/4 **Looks A Million** 2-9-0 0 FranBerry 4 70
(Joseph Tuite) *racd keenly: hung rt: pressed ldr: rdn and ev ch over 1f out: hld ent fnl f: nt pce of wnr* **2/1**[2]
242 3 3 **Auntie Pam (IRE)**[22] [2556] 2-9-0 0 (p) MartinHarley 2 59
(Tom Dascombe) *led: rdn and hdd over 1f out: hld whn squeezed up ent fnl f* **1/1**[1]

1m 0.08s (-0.12) **3** Ran SP% **110.0**
CSF £7.85 TOTE £3.70; EX 7.60 Trifecta £8.70.
**Owner** Jaber Abdullah **Bred** M Wurtenberger & R Stockli **Trained** West Ilsley, Berks
**FOCUS**
Only the third-placed finisher had previous form and she looks an unreliable guide, but the first two are probably nice fillies. The opening level is fluid.

## 3307 EBF STALLIONS BREEDING WINNERS FILLIES STKS (H'CAP) 6f
**7:40** (7:44) (Class 3) (0-90,91) 3-Y-O+ **£9,703** (£2,887; £1,443; £721) **Stalls** High

Form RPR
-212 1 **Angel Of Darkness**[37] [2094] 3-8-5 **78** CallumShepherd(3) 1 85
(Charles Hills) *trckd ldrs: rdn 2f out: led jst ins fnl f: kpt on wl: rdn out* **5/1**[3]
-366 2 1 **Iseemist (IRE)**[20] [2623] 6-10-0 **90** FergusSweeney 2 96
(John Gallagher) *led: rdn over 1f out: hdd jst ins fnl f: kpt on but no ex* **11/4**[1]
0-40 3 shd **Belledesert**[20] [2623] 4-9-7 **83** AdamBeschizza 4 88
(Steph Hollinshead) *trckd ldrs: rdn over 2f out: kpt on ins fnl f: nrly snatched 2nd fnl stride* **5/1**[3]
-441 4 2 1/4 **Southern Belle (IRE)**[12] [2856] 4-10-1 **91** 6ex MartinHarley 5 89
(Robert Cowell) *rrd leaving stalls: bhd: swtchd rt and hdwy u.p over 1f out: kpt on into 4th ins fnl f but nvr any threat to ldrs* **3/1**[2]
000- 5 1 3/4 **Dainty Dandy (IRE)**[217] [7667] 3-9-6 **90** (t[1]) DavidProbert 3 81
(Paul Cole) *trckd ldrs: rdn over 1f out: nt pce to mount chal* **8/1**
/463 6 1/2 **Jersey Breeze (IRE)**[10] [2917] 4-8-9 **71** GeorgeDowning 6 62
(Mick Channon) *chsd ldrs: hung rt: rdn over 2f out: fdd ins fnl f* **14/1**
-012 7 4 1/2 **Black Bess**[10] [2912] 4-9-11 **87** JackMitchell 7 64
(Jim Boyle) *chsd ldrs tl outpcd 1/2-way: nvr bk on terms* **5/1**[3]

1m 11.16s (-1.04) **Going Correction** 0.0s/f (Good)
**WFA** 3 from 4yo+ 8lb **7** Ran SP% **119.4**
Speed ratings (Par 107): **106,104,104,101,99 98,92**
CSF £20.37 TOTE £5.10: £2.90, £2.00; EX 23.80 Trifecta £91.30.
**Owner** D James, J Gompertz, S Jenkins **Bred** Stratford Place Stud **Trained** Lambourn, Berks
■ Stewards' Enquiry : Martin Harley two-day ban: used whip down shoulder in forehand position (Jun 25-26)
**FOCUS**
A useful fillies' handicap.

## 3308 CAPITAL FM H'CAP 1m 3f 218y
**8:10** (8:13) (Class 5) (0-75,77) 4-Y-O+ **£4,528** (£1,347; £673; £336) **Stalls** High

Form RPR
6-60 1 **Thames Knight**[16] [2741] 5-8-12 **75** TylerSaunders(7) 8 82
(Marcus Tregoning) *mid-div: hdwy over 3f pout: shkn up to ld over 1f out: kpt on wl fnl f* **8/1**
4431 2 1 1/2 **Light Of Air (FR)**[18] [2678] 4-9-5 **75** TimmyMurphy 1 79
(Gary Moore) *prom: rdn and ev ch over 2f out: chsd wnr over 1f out: kpt on but a being hld fnl f* **5/1**[3]
4122 3 nk **Deep Challenger (IRE)**[10] [2913] 5-9-3 **73** FergusSweeney 6 77
(Jamie Osborne) *hld up towards rr: hdwy 2f out: sn rdn: styd on fnl f: wnt 3rd fnl 120yds* **5/1**[3]
41-1 4 1/2 **Balancing Time**[65] [1430] 4-9-5 **75** (p) JimCrowley 9 78
(Amanda Perrett) *trckd ldr: chal over 2f out: sn rdn: ev ch over 1f out: styd on same pce fnl f* **7/2**[2]
/045 5 1/2 **Bostonian**[38] [2059] 7-9-2 **75** CallumShepherd(3) 7 77
(Shaun Lycett) *led: rdn whn strly pressed wl over 2f out: sn edgd lft: hdd over 1f out: kpt on w ev ch tl no ex fnl 140yds* **20/1**
36-3 6 3/4 **East India**[23] [2512] 5-9-1 **74** (h) HectorCrouch(3) 11 75
(George Baker) *nvr really travelling towards rr: hdwy over 4f out: sn drvn: chsd ldrs 2f out: styd on same pce fnl f* **10/1**
-026 7 7 **Takbeer (IRE)**[9] [2965] 5-9-4 **74** (p) DavidProbert 5 64
(Nikki Evans) *slowly away: towards rr: hdwy 5f out: effrt 3f out: wknd over 1f out* **25/1**
1-60 8 1 **Elusive Cowboy (USA)**[17] [507] 4-9-2 **72** (b) PatDobbs 4 60
(Stuart Edmunds) *trckd ldrs: rdn over 2f out: sn wknd* **33/1**
0336 9 1 1/4 **River Dart (IRE)**[63] [1466] 5-9-7 **77** GeorgeDowning 10 63
(Tony Carroll) *mid-div: effrt over 2f out: wknd over 1f out* **18/1**
511/ 10 3/4 **Candyman Can (IRE)**[547] [8092] 7-9-2 **72** (h) LiamKeniry 3 57
(Henry Spiller) *a towards rr* **20/1**
4- 11 3/4 **Saint Contest (FR)**[153] [7512] 4-9-7 **77** FranBerry 2 61
(Alan King) *mid-div: rdn and hdwy over 2f out: nvr threatened ldrs: wknd over 1f out* **3/1**[1]

2m 40.04s (1.64) **Going Correction** +0.225s/f (Good) **11** Ran SP% **122.3**
Speed ratings (Par 103): **103,102,101,101,101 100,95,95,94,93 93**
CSF £47.30 CT £227.48 TOTE £11.00: £2.90, £2.20, £1.80; EX 64.50 Trifecta £325.30.
**Owner** R C C Villers **Bred** Mr & Mrs A E Pakenham **Trained** Whitsbury, Hants
**FOCUS**
Add 10yds. A fair handicap but the early pace seemed modest and the first six were covered by just 3.5l.

## 3309 TINIE & CHARLESY DJ SET MAIDEN FILLIES' STKS 1m
**8:40** (8:46) (Class 5) 3-Y-O+ **£3,234** (£962; £481; £240) **Stalls** Low

Form RPR
34-2 1 **Shaaqaaf (IRE)**[15] [2753] 3-9-0 **85** JimCrowley 2 75+
(John Gosden) *trckd ldrs: led over 2f out: shkn up to draw clr: r.o wl: comf* **1/4**[1]
5 2 2 3/4 **Characterized**[11] [2908] 3-9-0 0 TimmyMurphy 4 69
(Geoffrey Deacon) *trckd ldr: chal 3f out: rdn and ev ch briefly 2f out: kpt on but sn hld: jst hld on for 2nd* **6/1**[3]
3 hd **Caravela (IRE)** 3-9-0 0 CharlesBishop 8 68+
(Mick Channon) *s.i.s: bhd: hdwy whn swtchd lft over 2f out: kpt on nicely fnl f: nrly snatched 2nd at fin* **5/1**[2]
0 4 7 **Kalani Rose**[11] [2908] 3-9-0 0 JackMitchell 3 52
(Ben De Haan) *in tch: rdn over 2f out: styd on but nt pce to get involved* **25/1**
0 5 4 1/2 **Estrellada**[8] [3007] 3-9-0 0 GavinLerena 9 42
(Mick Channon) *s.i.s: a towards rr* **14/1**
6 1 3/4 **Percipio** 3-9-0 0 FergusSweeney 1 38
(Alan King) *towards rr: rdn over 2f out: little imp* **8/1**
6 7 1 1/4 **African Quest**[21] [2580] 3-8-11 0 HectorCrouch(3) 7 35
(Gary Moore) *racd keenly on outer: carried lft s: in tch: hdwy over 3f out: rdn over 2f out: wknd over 1f out* **25/1**
50 8 nse **La Goulue**[31] [2266] 3-9-0 0 (b[1]) DavidProbert 6 35
(John Gallagher) *unsettled stalls: wnt lft s: trckd ldrs: rdn over 2f out: wknd over 1f out* **40/1**
0-4 9 1 **Sniper Viper**[27] [2405] 3-9-0 0 (b) GeorgeDowning 5 32
(Daniel Kubler) *led tl rdn over 2f out: wknd over 1f out* **50/1**

1m 40.28s (0.38) **Going Correction** +0.225s/f (Good) **9** Ran SP% **140.8**
Speed ratings (Par 100): **107,104,104,97,92 90,89,89,88**
CSF £4.02 TOTE £1.20: £1.02, £2.00, £2.00; EX 4.60 Trifecta £11.90.
**Owner** Ms Hissa Hamdan Al Maktoum **Bred** George Kent **Trained** Newmarket, Suffolk
**FOCUS**
Add 12yds. An uncompetitive fillies' maiden.
T/Plt: £58.20 to a £1 stake. Pool: £41,035.00 - 704.79 winning units. T/Qpdt: £18.10 to a £1 stake. Pool: £2,840.00 - 156.38 winning units. **Tim Mitchell**

# 2944 SAINT-CLOUD (L-H)
Friday, June 2

**OFFICIAL GOING: Turf: good**

## 3310a PRIX DE PENTHIEVRE (CLAIMER) (3YO) (LADY RIDERS) (TURF) 1m
**1:10** 3-Y-O **£8,119** (£3,247; £2,435; £1,623; £811)

RPR
1 **Vatican Hill (IRE)**[10] 3-9-5 0 ow1 MlleMarylineEon 8 71
(P Monfort, France) **18/1**
2 1/2 **Munawer**[18] [2677] 3-9-0 0 ow1 MlleIsisMagnin(5) 5 70
(J Phelippon, France) **6/4**[1]
3 1/2 **Hard Drink (USA)**[40] 3-8-5 0 ow1 MlleOphelieThiebaut(7) 6 62
(C Laffon-Parias, France) **81/10**
4 snk **La Cumparsita (FR)**[63] 3-8-9 0 ow1 (p) DelphineSantiago 12 59
(C Lerner, France) **111/10**
5 snk **A Magic Man (IRE)**[18] [2697] 3-9-5 0 ow1 MllePaulineDominois 4 68
(Henk Grewe, Germany) **42/10**[2]
6 shd **Buttonwood**[14] 3-8-9 0 MlleZoePfeil(3) 10 61
(Antonio Marcialis, Italy) **56/1**
7 1 **Highly Bay (FR)**[33] 3-8-5 0 ow1 MlleLucieOger(7) 2 59
(H-A Pantall, France) **123/10**
8 1 **La Dame En Rouge (FR)**[66] [1415] 3-8-4 0 ow1 MlleLeaBails(5) 9 53
(J Phelippon, France) **125/10**
9 hd **Teddy Edward**[231] [7328] 3-8-7 0 ow1 MlleCoraliePacaut(5) 11 56
(J Bossert, France) **84/1**
10 3/4 **Iron Islands**[53] [1678] 3-9-0 0 ow1 (b[1]) MmeAlexiaCeccarello(5) 1 61
(K R Burke) *sn settled in midfield: shkn up and nt qckn 2 1/2f out: rdn but no imp fr 2f out: wl hld fnl f* **28/1**
11 1 3/4 **Idroscalo (GER)** 3-8-9 0 ow1 MlleLauraGrosso(3) 3 50
(Antonio Marcialis, Italy) **71/10**[3]
12 10 **Zing (FR)**[234] 3-8-13 0 ow2 (b) MlleAudeDuporte 7 28
(C Boutin, France) **82/1**

1m 44.61s (-2.89) **12** Ran SP% **118.6**
PARI-MUTUEL (all including 1 euro stake): WIN 19.00; PLACE 4.10, 1.60, 2.70; DF 21.70; SF 75.20.
**Owner** Ecurie Michel Doineau **Bred** Mrs Gillian McCalmont **Trained** France

# 3291 DONCASTER (L-H)

Saturday, June 3

**OFFICIAL GOING: Soft (good to soft in places; 6.4)**

Wind: Light against Weather: Fine & dry

## 3311 BETFRED CELEBRATING 50 YEARS OF SUCCESS H'CAP 1m 6f 115y

1:55 (1:56) (Class 5) (0-70,70) 4-Y-O+ £3,881 (£1,155; £577; £288) Stalls Low

Form RPR

53-5 1 **Incus**[10] 2966 4-7-9 **51** oh5 DavidEgan(7) 12 62
(Ed de Giles) *trckd ldrs: hdwy and cl up over 4f out: led over 3f out: rdn and edgd lft wl over 1f out: sn clr: kpt on strly* **12/1**

602- 2 5 **Lady Natasha (IRE)**[222] 7582 4-8-9 **61** JordanVaughan(3) 6 65
(K R Burke) *hld up: hdwy over 3f out: chsd wnr 2f out: sn rdn: drvn and no imp fnl f* **12/1**

6040 3 1 1/4 **Spiritoftomintoul**[28] 2388 8-9-0 **63** (t) GeorgeDowning 2 65
(Tony Carroll) *stdd s and hld up in rr: hdwy over 3f out: swtchd rt to outer and rdn 2f out: styd on wl appr fnl f* **10/1**

034/ 4 5 **Attention Seaker**[433] 6827 7-8-13 **62** DuranFentiman 13 57
(Tim Easterby) *hld up in rr: hdwy 4f out: rdn along over 3f out: chsd ldrs over 2f out: sn drvn and kpt on one pce* **20/1**

5-05 5 nk **Ivanhoe**[15] 2781 7-9-2 **65** (b) DaneO'Neill 3 60
(Michael Blanshard) *hld up towards rr: hdwy over 3f out: rdn along whn n.m.r 2f out: sn one pce* **8/1**

30/1 6 1 1/4 **Mishko (IRE)**[26] 2460 6-9-2 **68** KieranShoemark(3) 10 61
(Steve Gollings) *trckd ldrs: hdwy over 3f out: rdn along wl over 2f out: sn drvn and btn* **4/1**[2]

55-3 7 4 **Waiting For Richie**[28] 2386 4-9-5 **68** AndrewMullen 8 55
(Tom Tate) *cl up: led after 1f: jnd 1/2-way: pushed along 4f out: rdn and hdd over 3f out: drvn over 2f out: sn wknd* **10/3**[1]

-020 8 3 1/2 **Ice Galley (IRE)**[16] 2770 4-9-7 **70** TonyHamilton 4 53
(Philip Kirby) *in tch: pushed along over 4f out: rdn wl over 3f out: sn wknd* **9/1**

000 9 4 **Melanna (IRE)**[93] 992 6-8-12 **66** CallumRodriguez(5) 5 43
(Richard Ford) *led 1f: prom: rdn along 4f out: sn wknd* **9/2**[3]

-000 10 27 **Tarakkom (FR)**[18] 2712 5-7-9 **51** oh1 RPWalsh(7) 11
(Peter Hiatt) *prom: cl up 1/2-way: rdn along over 4f out: sn wknd and bhd* **25/1**

3m 14.37s (6.97) **Going Correction** +0.45s/f (Yiel) 10 Ran SP% **115.5**
Speed ratings (Par 103): **99,96,95,93,92 92,90,88,86,71**
CSF £145.19 CT £1493.71 TOTE £15.00: £3.50, £2.80, £3.30; EX 231.60 Trifecta £2300.70.
**Owner** Mange Tout II **Bred** Lilly Hall Farm **Trained** Ledbury, H'fords

**FOCUS**
Rail movements add 12 yards to the distances of Race 1, 5 and 6. A modest staying handicap. They went a respectable gallop on ground officially described as soft, good to soft in places. The winning time concurred with that assessment.

## 3312 BETFRED TV EBF FILLIES' NOVICE STKS (PLUS 10 RACE) 6f 111y

2:30 (2:32) (Class 4) 2-Y-O £4,528 (£1,347; £673; £336) Stalls Centre

Form RPR

1 **Natural (IRE)** 2-9-0 0 SeanLevey 9 78+
(Richard Hannon) *mde all: shkn up and qcknd over 1f out: rdn ins fnl f: kpt on strly* **11/10**[1]

2 1 3/4 **Time Change** 2-9-0 0 HarryBentley 14 73+
(Ralph Beckett) *trckd ldrs: hdwy on outer wl over 2f out: rdn to chse wnr over 1f out: kpt on fnl f* **12/1**

3 3/4 **Paramount Love** 2-9-0 0 TonyHamilton 15 71+
(Richard Fahey) *hld up towards rr: hdwy 1/2-way: chsd ldrs 2f out:. sn rdn: kpt on fnl f* **16/1**

4 hd **Falcon's Vision** 2-9-0 0 JamieSpencer 8 70+
(David Simcock) *in tch: hdwy to chse ldrs wl over 2f out: rdn wl over 1f out: kpt on same pce* **14/1**

4 5 1 1/2 **Silca Mistress**[7] 3070 2-9-0 0 CharlesBishop 3 66
(Mick Channon) *trckd ldrs: chsd wnr 1/2-way: rdn along 2f out: kpt on one pce* **8/1**[2]

6 2 1/4 **Deadly Reel (IRE)** 2-9-0 0 RichardKingscote 6 60
(Archie Watson) *midfield: hdwy over 2f out: sn rdn along and no imp* **20/1**

7 1 1/2 **Juliet Capulet (IRE)** 2-8-11 0 KieranShoemark(3) 1 56
(John Gosden) *dwlt and rr: sme hdwy over 2f out: sn rdn along and n.d* **8/1**[2]

8 1 **Daffrah** 2-9-0 0 MartinHarley 4 53
(James Tate) *in tch on outer: pushed along 3f out: rdn over 2f out: n.d* **20/1**

0 9 1 **Sensory (IRE)**[10] 2958 2-9-0 0 RobertTart 13 50
(John Gosden) *prom: rdn along over 2f out: sn wknd* **8/1**[2]

10 1/2 **Mountain Meadow** 2-8-11 0 AdamMcNamara(3) 5 49
(Richard Fahey) *dwlt: a towards rr* **18/1**

11 2 1/4 **Boss Koko** 2-9-0 0 DuranFentiman 12 43
(Tim Easterby) *a towards rr* **66/1**

12 3/4 **Thundercloud** 2-9-0 0 DavidProbert 7 41
(Scott Dixon) *t.k.h: a towards rr* **50/1**

5 13 4 1/2 **Dubai Classic (IRE)**[14] 2836 2-9-0 0 BenCurtis 2 38+
(K R Burke) *prom: pushed along 3f out: rdn and wknd over 2f out: rr and eased fnl f* **9/1**[3]

1m 22.74s (2.84) **Going Correction** +0.45s/f (Yiel) 13 Ran SP% **129.4**
Speed ratings (Par 92): **101,99,98,97,96 93,91,90,89,89 86,85,80**
CSF £17.34 TOTE £2.20: £1.60, £3.30, £4.60; EX 22.50 Trifecta £396.40.
**Owner** Qatar Racing Limited **Bred** D Noonan & Loughphilip Bloodstock **Trained** East Everleigh, Wilts

**FOCUS**
A fair juvenile fillies' novice contest. They went a respectable gallop on the testing ground and a well-backed debutante won in taking fashion.

## 3313 BETFRED TREBLE ODDS ON LUCKY 15'S MAIDEN STKS 5f 3y

3:05 (3:05) (Class 5) 3-Y-O+ £3,234 (£962; £481; £240) Stalls Centre

Form RPR

4 1 **Fortitude (IRE)**[21] 2619 3-9-0 0 HarryBentley 3 71+
(Hugo Palmer) *trckd ldrs: hdwy 2f out: chal over 1f out: rdn to ld ins fnl f: readily* **5/4**[1]

020- 2 2 **Jabbarockie**[270] 6218 4-9-12 64 NeilFarley 6 72
(Eric Alston) *qckly away and led: jnd over 2f out and sn rdn: drvn over 1f out: hdd ins fnl f: kpt on same pce* **8/1**

02-0 3 2 1/4 **Angel Palanas**[11] 2927 3-9-5 63 BenCurtis 7 61
(K R Burke) *chsd ldng pair: effrt 2f out and sn rdn: drvn and kpt on same pce fnl f* **5/1**[3]

-652 4 1 1/4 **Double Spin**[11] 2924 3-9-0 63 MartinHarley 1 51
(Robert Cowell) *chsd ldr: hdwy and cl up over 2f out: rdn wl over 1f out: sn drvn and wknd* **11/4**[2]

0-65 5 2 1/4 **Harwood**[8] 3054 3-8-12 64 PatrickVaughan(7) 2 48
(David O'Meara) *in tch: rdn along over 2f out: sn wknd* **10/1**

0 6 1 1/4 **Texas Wedge**[5] 3157 3-9-2 0 (b[1]) KieranShoemark(3) 4 44
(William Muir) *.dwlt: a rr* **25/1**

1m 1.55s (1.05) **Going Correction** +0.45s/f (Yiel)
**WFA** 3 from 4yo 7lb 6 Ran SP% **111.8**
Speed ratings (Par 103): **109,105,102,100,96 94**
CSF £12.03 TOTE £2.30: £1.40, £2.30; EX 9.80 Trifecta £35.40.
**Owner** Isa Salman **Bred** Epona Bloodstock Ltd **Trained** Newmarket, Suffolk

**FOCUS**
An ordinary sprint maiden. They went a proper gallop and the well-backed, unexposed favourite won well.

## 3314 BETFRED SUPPORTS JACK BERRY HOUSE FILLIES' H'CAP 7f 6y

3:40 (3:40) (Class 3) (0-95,88) 4-Y-O+ £8,821 (£2,640; £1,320; £660) Stalls Centre

Form RPR

-622 1 **Florenza**[15] 2805 4-9-0 **81** JamieSpencer 6 87
(Chris Fairhurst) *led: pushed along and hdd over 2f out: cl up and rdn wl over 1f out: drvn and rallied to ld again ins fnl f: kpt on wl towards fin* **11/10**[1]

531- 2 1/2 **Sante (IRE)**[290] 5544 4-9-2 **83** GavinLerena 5 88+
(Charles Hills) *t.k.h: trckd wnr: cl up 1/2-way: slt ld over 2f out: rdn and edgd lft wl over 1f out: drvn and hdd ins fnl f: kpt on same pce towards fin* **5/1**[3]

66-4 3 1 **Yeah Baby Yeah (IRE)**[32] 2268 4-8-12 **86** (p) DavidEgan(7) 1 88
(Gay Kelleway) *trckd ldng pair: hdwy and cl up 2f out: rdn over 1f out and ev ch whn n.m.r on inner ent fnl f: sn drvn and kpt on same pce* **7/1**

000- 4 1 3/4 **Fourth Way (IRE)**[227] 7472 4-9-7 **88** DavidProbert 4 86
(Ralph Beckett) *hld up in rr: effrt over 2f out: sn rdn along and no imp* **9/4**[2]

1m 29.83s (3.53) **Going Correction** +0.45s/f (Yiel) 4 Ran SP% **107.6**
Speed ratings (Par 104): **97,96,95,93**
CSF £6.65 TOTE £1.70; EX 4.20 Trifecta £6.70.
**Owner** 980 Racing **Bred** 980 Racing **Trained** Middleham, N Yorks

**FOCUS**
The feature contest was a decent little fillies' handicap. They went an, at best, respectable gallop on the testing ground.

## 3315 BETFRED WATCH SKY SPORTS IN OUR SHOPS H'CAP 1m 3f 197y

4:15 (4:15) (Class 4) (0-85,86) 4-Y-O+ £5,175 (£1,540; £769; £384) Stalls Low

Form RPR

5/30 1 **Sgt Reckless**[40] 2021 10-8-12 **81** DavidEgan(7) 9 90
(Mick Channon) *hld up towards rr: hdwy on outer 3f out: chal wl over 1f out: rdn to ld appr fnl f: kpt on wl* **8/1**

-241 2 2 **Hermann**[16] 2752 4-9-7 **83** (p[1]) SeanLevey 7 89
(Richard Hannon) *led: pushed along 3f out: rdn over 2f out: jnd wl over 1f out and sn drvn: hdd appr fnl f: kpt on same pce* **6/5**[1]

640- 3 nk **Azzir (IRE)**[208] 7847 5-8-9 **74** JordanVaughan(3) 3 79
(K R Burke) *trckd ldng pair on inner: hdwy to chse ldr 3f out: rdn along 2f out: drvn over 1f out: kpt on same pce* **12/1**

3052 4 1 1/4 **Chancery (USA)**[7] 3091 9-9-3 **86** (p) PatrickVaughan(7) 6 89
(David O'Meara) *hld up towards rr: hdwy over 3f out: rdn to chse ldrs wl over 1f out: kpt on same pce* **6/1**[3]

0-14 5 nse **Archippos**[22] 2574 4-9-7 **83** PaddyAspell 12 86
(Philip Kirby) *trckd ldrs: hdwy over 3f out: rdn wl over 2f out: sn drvn and kpt on one pce* **9/2**[2]

33-0 6 5 **Chebsey Beau**[21] 2622 7-8-6 **68** HarryBentley 8 63
(John Quinn) *.trckd ldr: pushed along 4f out: rdn over 3f out: sn drvn and wknd* **16/1**

153/ 7 2 3/4 **Parole (IRE)**[700] 3905 5-8-8 **70** DuranFentiman 4 61
(Tim Easterby) *hld up: a towards rr* **20/1**

-064 8 3/4 **Bertie Moon**[16] 2752 7-9-2 **78** (p) TrevorWhelan 11 67
(Lydia Pearce) *hld up in rr: effrt and sme hdwy on inner over 3f out: sn rdn along and wknd* **14/1**

0-00 9 2 1/4 **Wotabreeze (IRE)**[21] 2629 4-8-11 **73** KevinStott 5 59
(John Quinn) *chsd ldrs: rdn along over 3f out: sn wknd* **20/1**

2m 39.27s (4.37) **Going Correction** +0.45s/f (Yiel) 9 Ran SP% **118.8**
Speed ratings (Par 105): **103,101,101,100,100 97,95,94,93**
CSF £18.55 CT £117.05 TOTE £12.20: £3.20, £1.10, £3.50; EX 25.90 Trifecta £227.60.
**Owner** George Materna **Bred** Miss Bridget Coyle **Trained** West Ilsley, Berks

**FOCUS**
Race distance increased 12 yards. A decent middle-distance handicap. They went a sensible gallop on the testing ground.

## 3316 BETFRED MOBILE CLASSIFIED STKS (PLUS 10 RACE) 1m 2f 43y

5:10 (5:11) (Class 3) 3-Y-O £7,762 (£2,310; £1,154; £577) Stalls Low

Form RPR

1-00 1 **Good Omen**[100] 887 3-9-3 90 JamieSpencer 3 99+
(David Simcock) *hld up in rr: hdwy on outer wl over 2f out: cl up over 1f out: rdn to ld appr fnl f: pushed out* **9/2**[3]

61 2 1 3/4 **Daawy (IRE)**[35] 2159 3-9-3 87 RobertWinston 6 93
(William Haggas) *trckd ldr: hdwy 3f out: cl up and pushed along 2f out: rdn and ev ch whn n.m.r appr fnl f: drvn to chse wnr ins fnl f: no imp* **4/5**[1]

65-5 3 2 3/4 **Monticello (IRE)**[151] 31 3-9-3 90 RichardKingscote 1 88
(Mark Johnston) *led: pushed along and qcknd 3f out: rdn 2f out: drvn and hdd appr fnl f: kpt on same pce* **7/1**

1-6 4 3 1/4 **Youmkin (USA)**[38] 2084 3-9-3 88 DaneO'Neill 4 81
(Saeed bin Suroor) *trckd ldng pair: hdwy 3f out: cl up 2f out: sn rdn and ev ch: drvn and wknd appr fnl f* **10/3**[2]

2m 16.0s (6.60) **Going Correction** +0.45s/f (Yiel) 4 Ran SP% **109.3**
Speed ratings (Par 103): **91,89,87,84**
CSF £8.82 TOTE £5.80; EX 9.90 Trifecta £14.80.
**Owner** Mrs Q J Guo **Bred** Hascombe And Valiant Studs **Trained** Newmarket, Suffolk

**FOCUS**
Race distance increased 12 yards. A decent 3yo classified contest. They went a modest gallop on the testing ground.

## 3317 BETFRED FOLLOW US ON TWITTER H'CAP 1m (S)
**5:40** (5:41) (Class 4) (0-85,86) 3-Y-O **£5,175** (£1,540; £769; £384) **Stalls** Centre

| Form | | | | RPR |
|---|---|---|---|---|
| 41 | 1 | | **Afaak**[21] 2632 3-9-8 **86** DaneO'Neill 14 (Charles Hills) *hld up towards rr: hdwy on outer over 2f out: chsd ldrs over 1f out: rdn to chal ins fnl f: kpt on wl to ld last 50 yds* **12/1** | 97 |
| -221 | 2 | ¾ | **Mountain Angel (IRE)**[18] 2704 3-9-2 **80** HarryBentley 13 (Roger Varian) *trckd ldrs: hdwy 2f out: cl up and rdn over 1f out: drvn to ld ins fnl f: hdd and no ex last 50 yds* **6/1** | 89 |
| 31-3 | 3 | 1 ¾ | **Mojito (IRE)**[7] 3082 3-9-5 **83** RobertWinston 6 (William Haggas) *hld up towards rr: gd hdwy on inner over 2f out: trckd ldrs over 1f out: rdn to chal and ev ch ent fnl f: sn drvn and kpt on* **11/4**[1] | 88+ |
| -322 | 4 | nse | **Marzouq (USA)**[44] 1907 3-9-0 **85** DavidEgan(7) 4 (Jeremy Noseda) *prom: pushed along and cl up 2f out: rdn wl over 1f out: drvn and ev ch ent fnl f: kpt on* **11/1** | 90 |
| 2-14 | 5 | hd | **Multi Facets (IRE)**[22] 2567 3-9-6 **84** JamieSpencer 5 (David Simcock) *dwlt and hld up towards rr: hdwy over 2f out: swtchd lft and chsd ldrs over 1f out: rdn and ev ch ent fnl f: drvn and kpt on same pce last 50 yds* **10/3**[2] | 89 |
| 6-1 | 6 | ¾ | **Music Seeker (IRE)**[15] 2798 3-9-8 **86** RyanTate 12 (James Eustace) *rr: pushed along and bhd over 3f out: hdwy on outer 2f out: sn rdn and kpt on fnl f* **16/1** | 89 |
| 41 | 7 | 1 | **Rumpole**[26] 2475 3-9-3 **81** SeanLevey 8 (Hughie Morrison) *trckd ldrs: hdwy over 2f out: rdn to ld 11/2f out: drvn and hdd ins fnl f: wknd last 100 yds* **14/1** | 82 |
| 0-45 | 8 | 1 ½ | **George Reme (IRE)**[29] 2376 3-8-12 **76** KevinStott 2 (John Quinn) *towards rr: hdwy over 2f out: sn rdn and kpt on fnl f* **40/1** | 73 |
| 021- | 9 | hd | **Sound Bar**[225] 7503 3-9-4 **82** (h[1]) RichardKingscote 11 (Ralph Beckett) *hld up: hdwy over 2f out: rdn along to chse ldrs whn n.m.r over 1f out: sn wknd* **11/2**[3] | 79 |
| -366 | 10 | 1 ½ | **Whip Nae Nae (IRE)**[15] 2784 3-9-4 **82** GavinLerena 3 (Richard Hannon) *led: pushed along over 2f out: rdn and hdd 11/2f out: sn drvn and grad wknd* **16/1** | 75 |
| 5-20 | 11 | 3 | **Prancing Oscar (IRE)**[54] 1680 3-8-3 **67** DuranFentiman 15 (Ben Haslam) *chsd ldrs on outer: rdn along over 2f out: sn wknd* **50/1** | 53 |
| -310 | 12 | 1 ¾ | **Nick Vedder**[36] 2118 3-8-6 **73** JordanVaughan(3) 10 (K R Burke) *chsd ldr: rdn along over 2f out: wknd wl over 1f out* **50/1** | 55 |

1m 41.27s (1.97) **Going Correction** +0.45s/f (Yiel) 12 Ran SP% **120.2**
Speed ratings (Par 101): **108,107,105,105,105 104,103,102,101,100 97,95**
CSF £82.97 CT £263.47 TOTE £12.20: £3.40, £2.30, £1.50; EX 65.00 Trifecta £325.90.
**Owner** Hamdan Al Maktoum **Bred** Shadwell Estate Company Limited **Trained** Lambourn, Berks

**FOCUS**
A decent 3yo handicap and form that is worth noting off a respectable gallop.
T/Plt: £1,131.40 to a £1 stake. Pool: £77,081.14 - 49.73 winning units. T/Qpdt: £63.00 to a £1 stake. Pool: £4,314.62 - 50.60 winning units. **Joe Rowntree**

# 3297 EPSOM (L-H)
Saturday, June 3

**OFFICIAL GOING: Good (good to firm in places; 7.6; 5f course: 8.0)**
Wind: light, half against Weather: sunny

## 3318 INVESTEC PRIVATE BANKING H'CAP 1m 2f 17y
**2:00** (2:00) (Class 2) (0-105,101) 3-Y-O
**£31,125** (£9,320; £4,660; £2,330; £1,165; £585) **Stalls** Low

| Form | | | | RPR |
|---|---|---|---|---|
| 6-21 | 1 | | **Drochaid**[24] 2520 3-8-8 **88** OisinMurphy 3 (Andrew Balding) *taken down early: t.k.h: hld up in 4th: effrt over 2f out: hdwy u.p to chal 1f out: led 150yds out: styd on: pushed out towards fin* **11/2** | 95 |
| -151 | 2 | nk | **Emenem**[38] 2088 3-8-3 **83** FrannyNorton 7 (Simon Dow) *hld up in tch in last trio: effrt 3 out: hdwy to chse ldrs whn nt clr run over 1f out: swtchd sharply lft ent fnl f: hdwy to chse wnr wl ins fnl f: r.o wl: nvr quite getting to wnr* **9/2**[3] | 89 |
| 11-2 | 3 | 1 | **Desert Skyline (IRE)**[14] 2829 3-9-4 **98** FranBerry 6 (David Elsworth) *stdd after s: hld up in rr: effrt 3f out: hdwy u.p 1f out: styd on strly fnl 100yds to go 2nd towards fin: nvr getting to ldng pair* **4/1**[2] | 102+ |
| 1-43 | 4 | 1 ¼ | **Tartini (USA)**[21] 2614 3-9-1 **95** FrankieDettori 8 (John Gosden) *dwlt: sn rcvrd and in tch in midfield: effrt over 2f out: sn chsng ldrs: clsd and ev ch briefly 1f out: sn outpcd and wknd fnl 75yds* **7/2**[1] | 97 |
| 0253 | 5 | 2 ¼ | **Masham Star (IRE)**[7] 3077 3-9-7 **101** JamesDoyle 4 (Mark Johnston) *broke wl: sn stdd to trck ldr: rdn to ld 2f out: hrd pressed 1f out: sn hdd and btn: wknd fnl 100yds* **10/1** | 98 |
| 2-01 | 6 | 1 | **Mister Blue Sky (IRE)**[21] 2625 3-8-0 **80** oh2 RyanPowell 1 (Sylvester Kirk) *t.k.h: chsd ldrs: effrt over 2f out: sn outpcd: bhd whn nt clr run and hmpd 1f out: swtchd rt and kpt on same pce ins fnl f* **12/1** | 76+ |
| 2-31 | 7 | nk | **Hajaj (IRE)**[22] 2567 3-7-12 **80** ow1 AaronJones(3) 5 (Charlie Fellowes) *hld up in tch in last trio: effrt over 2f out: chsng ldrs but keeping on same pce whn pushed lft and hmpd 1f out: nt rcvr and no imp after* **8/1** | 77+ |
| 332 | 8 | 2 ¼ | **Bristol Missile (USA)**[24] 2527 3-8-2 **82** KieranO'Neill 2 (Richard Hannon) *sn led: rdn and hdd 2f out: no ex u.p over 1f out: wknd ins fnl f* **9/1** | 72 |

2m 5.96s (-3.74) **Going Correction** -0.10s/f (Good) 8 Ran SP% **113.7**
Speed ratings (Par 105): **110,109,108,107,106 105,105,103**
CSF £30.01 CT £108.89 TOTE £7.20: £2.20, £1.90, £1.70; EX 33.10 Trifecta £96.40.
**Owner** Mick and Janice Mariscotti **Bred** Meon Valley Stud **Trained** Kingsclere, Hants
■ Stewards' Enquiry : Franny Norton seven-day ban: careless riding (Jun 17-23)

**FOCUS**
All distances as advertised. Oisin Murphy, who won the opener said of the ground: "it's riding lovely, it's just good. I couldn't find any good to firm in it." while Frankie Dettori called it "beautiful good, good to firm ground." Traditionally a good handicap, they went a pretty steady gallop and the winner was well placed in comparison to the placed runners. The fourth has been rated to his Derby Trial form.

## 3319 PRINCESS ELIZABETH STKS (SPONSORED BY INVESTEC) (GROUP 3) (F&M) 1m 113y
**2:35** (2:35) (Class 1) 3-Y-O+
**£39,697** (£15,050; £7,532; £3,752; £1,883; £945) **Stalls** Low

| Form | | | | RPR |
|---|---|---|---|---|
| 1-51 | 1 | | **Laugh Aloud**[28] 2392 4-9-6 110 (t) JamesDoyle 5 (John Gosden) *led for 1f: restrained and t.k.h: chsd ldng pair after 2f: 3rd st: nudged along and clsd smoothly jst over 2f out: led over 1f out: sn rdn and readily qcknd clr: v easily* **4/5**[1] | 112 |
| 2312 | 2 | 5 | **Absolute Blast (IRE)**[50] 1775 5-9-6 105 PatSmullen 8 (Archie Watson) *chsd ldrs tl wnt 2nd 6f out: 2nd st: clsd to join ldr 3f out: rdn over 2f out: unable qck w wnr over 1f out: no ch w wnr but kpt on to win battle for 2nd ins fnl f* **8/1**[3] | 101 |
| 1101 | 3 | nk | **Tisbutadream (IRE)**[21] 2605 3-8-8 93 SilvestreDeSousa 10 (David Elsworth) *led after 1f: jnd and rdn 3f out: hdd over 1f out: sn outpcd by wnr and btn: kpt on but lost battle for 2nd ins fnl f* **12/1** | 98 |
| | 4 | ½ | **Silver Meadow (IRE)**[27] 2449 4-9-6 93 (t[1]) FrankieDettori 6 (F-H Graffard, France) *hld up in last pair: 9th st: rdn and hdwy jst over 2f out: wnt 4th and switching rt ins fnl f: kpt on towards fin: no ch w wnr* **25/1** | 99+ |
| 6-04 | 5 | 1 ½ | **Crowning Glory (FR)**[28] 2392 4-9-6 93 FranBerry 1 (Ralph Beckett) *chsd ldng trio: 4th st: rdn and outpcd over 2f out: no ch w wnr and kpt on same pce fnl 2f* **20/1** | 95 |
| -446 | 6 | nk | **Silver Step (FR)**[27] 2432 4-9-9 107 (h) WilliamBuick 2 (Mme Pia Brandt, France) *hld up in rr: 10th st: hdwy and drifting lft over 1f out: kpt on ins fnl f: nvr trbld ldrs* **16/1** | 98+ |
| 3-20 | 7 | 2 ¾ | **Urban Fox**[27] 2434 3-8-8 104 DavidAllan 4 (James Tate) *midfield: 7th st: rdn 3f out: sn outpcd: wl hld and plugged on same pce fnl 2f* **11/2**[2] | 86 |
| 0054 | 8 | nk | **Epsom Icon**[21] 2605 4-9-6 95 JimCrowley 11 (Mick Channon) *t.k.h: hld up in midfield: 6th st: rdn and outpcd over 2f out: wl hld and plugged on same pce after* **14/1** | 88 |
| 0-60 | 9 | nk | **Kilmah**[27] 2434 3-8-8 100 FrannyNorton 7 (Mark Johnston) *in tch in midfield: 5th st: rdn 3f out: sn outpcd: wknd over 1f out* **25/1** | 85 |
| 0-61 | 10 | 3 ¾ | **Czabo**[69] 1387 4-9-9 99 AndreaAtzeni 9 (Mick Channon) *dwlt and rousted along leaving stalls: hld up in last trio: 8th st: rdn and no hdwy over 2f out: bhd over 1f out: eased wl ins fnl f* **20/1** | 81 |

1m 41.54s (-4.56) **Going Correction** -0.10s/f (Good)
**WFA** 3 from 4yo+ 12lb 10 Ran SP% **119.5**
Speed ratings (Par 113): **116,111,111,110,109 109,106,106,106,102**
CSF £7.42 TOTE £1.70: £1.10, £2.50, £3.00; EX 9.40 Trifecta £61.70.
**Owner** Godolphin **Bred** Darley **Trained** Newmarket, Suffolk

**FOCUS**
They didn't go that quick early and the first three were in those positions throughout, but with that said the winner stamped her class. The runner-up has been rated close to her AW form.

## 3320 INVESTEC DIOMED STKS (GROUP 3) 1m 113y
**3:10** (3:11) (Class 1) 3-Y-O+
**£39,697** (£15,050; £7,532; £3,752; £1,883; £945) **Stalls** Low

| Form | | | | RPR |
|---|---|---|---|---|
| 1311 | 1 | | **Sovereign Debt (IRE)**[36] 2129 8-9-10 114 JamesSullivan 2 (Ruth Carr) *hld up in tch in midfield: 4th st: effrt and clsd 2f out: rdn to ld over 1f out: hld on wl towards fin: rdn out* **4/1**[3] | 117 |
| 0424 | 2 | nk | **Gabrial (IRE)**[23] 2553 8-9-5 113 FrankieDettori 6 (Richard Fahey) *hld up in last pair: 6th st: rdn and hdwy 2f out: edging lft and chsd wnr 1f out: kpt on wl to press wnr towards fin: hld cl home* **7/1** | 111 |
| 2121 | 3 | ½ | **Oh This Is Us (IRE)**[21] 2610 4-9-5 110 PatDobbs 4 (Richard Hannon) *hld up in tch in midfield: 5th st: clsd to chse ldrs and nt clr run 2f out: trying to switch rt but hemmed in and leaned on ent fnl f: 3rd and drifted lft jst ins fnl f: styd on wl* **7/2**[2] | 110+ |
| 2-10 | 4 | 1 | **Kool Kompany (IRE)**[36] 2129 5-9-5 114 JamesDoyle 3 (Richard Hannon) *hld up in tch in last pair: 7th st: effrt jst over 2f out: squeezed for room and hmpd over 1f out: swtchd rt 1f out: r.o wl ins fnl f: nvr getting to ldrs* **7/1** | 109+ |
| 1223 | 5 | 2 ½ | **Folkswood**[23] 2553 4-9-5 113 (p) WilliamBuick 5 (Charlie Appleby) *chsd ldr: 2nd st: rdn to ld 2f out: hdd and no ex u.p over 1f out: wknd ins fnl f* **10/3**[1] | 102 |
| 2-15 | 6 | ½ | **Ballet Concerto**[28] 2396 4-9-5 102 RyanMoore 1 (Sir Michael Stoute) *chsd ldrs: 3rd st: effrt on inner over 2f out: gap clsd and nt clr run ent fnl f: shuffled bk to rr and no threat to ldrs after* **11/2** | 101+ |
| -621 | 7 | 1 | **Custom Cut (IRE)**[27] 2440 8-9-8 108 (p) DanielTudhope 7 (David O'Meara) *led: rdn over 2f out: hdd 2f out: jst beginnning to struggled whn squeezed for room and hmpd ent fnl f: wknd ins fnl f* **16/1** | 102 |

1m 42.61s (-3.49) **Going Correction** -0.10s/f (Good) 7 Ran SP% **111.6**
Speed ratings (Par 113): **111,110,110,109,107 106,105**
CSF £29.84 TOTE £4.60: £2.30, £3.10; EX 29.70 Trifecta £108.30.
**Owner** Lady O'Reilly, J P Hames & T Dorman **Bred** Yeomanstown Stud **Trained** Huby, N Yorks

**FOCUS**
Run at a sound gallop early, it was a repeat result of the Bet365 Mile at Sandown, with Sovereign Debt just getting the better of Gabrial, this time under a penalty. The third didn't get the best of runs, but wasn't unlucky. The winner has been rated back to his old best.

## 3321 INVESTEC CORPORATE BANKING "DASH" H'CAP 5f
**3:45** (3:47) (Class 2) 3-Y-O+
**£61,590** (£18,540; £9,270; £4,620; £2,320; £1,170) **Stalls** High

| Form | | | | RPR |
|---|---|---|---|---|
| 3050 | 1 | | **Caspian Prince (IRE)**[7] 3092 8-9-8 **107** (t) TomEaves 1 (Tony Coyle) *pressed ldng pair tl led 2f out: drvn and forged ahd ins fnl f: jst hld on: all out* **25/1** | 114 |
| 1-43 | 2 | shd | **Dark Shot**[28] 2391 4-8-2 **87** MartinDwyer 10 (Andrew Balding) *s.i.s: bhd: last 2f out: nt clr run over 1f out: swtchd lft and rdn 1f out: hdwy and switching bk rt ins fnl f: r.o v strly fnl 100yds: snatched 2nd on post: jst failed* **10/1** | 94+ |

-641 **3** nse **Duke Of Firenze**[16] 2764 8-9-8 **107** 4ex................................ DavidAllan 12 113
(David C Griffiths) *racd in last pair: clsd 1/2-way: effrt and swtchd rt over 1f out: hdwy u.p and hung lft ins fnl f: r.o wl to go 2nd towards fin: nt quite rch wnr: lost 2nd on post* **9/1**[3]

0-12 **4** ¾ **A Momentofmadness**[28] 2391 4-8-6 **91**...............(h) SilvestreDeSousa 5 95
(Charles Hills) *taken down early: broke sltly early: led and crossed to r towards stands rail: hdd 2f out: stl ev ch and rdn over 1f out: no ex and kpt on same pce ins fnl f: lost 2 pls towards fin* **8/1**[2]

1214 **5** shd **Edward Lewis**[14] 2839 4-8-12 **100** 4ex............................ JoshDoyle(3) 11 103+
(David O'Meara) *hld up in midfield: effrt whn nt clr run and hmpd over 1f out: swtchd lft and hdwy u.p ins fnl f: r.o strly towards fin: nt rch ldrs* **14/1**

3640 **6** ½ **Boom The Groom (IRE)**[50] 1772 6-9-5 **104**.................. AdamKirby 18 106+
(Tony Carroll) *taken down early: hld up towards rr: nt clrest of runs over 1f out: effrt jst over 1f out: hdwy ins fnl f: kpt on strly fnl 100yds: nvr threatened ldrs* **8/1**[2]

00-1 **7** hd **Desert Law (IRE)**[49] 1800 9-8-9 **94**.................................. OisinMurphy 9 95
(Paul Midgley) *in tch in midfield: effrt and shifting lft over 1f out: hdwy u.p ins fnl f: kpt on wl fnl 75yds: nt rch ldrs* **8/1**[2]

0-11 **8** nk **El Astronaute (IRE)**[24] 2524 4-8-9 **94** 4ex..................... JasonHart 7 94
(John Quinn) *pressed ldr: rdn and hung lft over 1f out: unable qck and styd on same pce ins fnl f* **12/1**

0340 **9** ½ **Line Of Reason (IRE)**[7] 3092 7-8-12 **97**.................(p) PaulMulrennan 15 95
(Paul Midgley) *in tch in midfield: clsd to chse ldng trio jst over 1f out: rdn and styd on same pce ins fnl f* **12/1**

-110 **10** ½ **Kimberella**[28] 2397 7-9-3 **109**.................................... ConnorMurtagh(7) 20 105
(Richard Fahey) *in tch in midfield: rdn over 1f out: unable qck and carried lft ins fnl f: kpt on same pce* **6/1**[1]

0-20 **11** 1 **Exceed The Limit**[15] 2780 4-8-7 **92**................................. KieranO'Neill 17 85
(Robert Cowell) *hld up in tch in midfield: effrt over 1f out: sn hung lft and no imp ins fnl f* **25/1**

-403 **12** shd **Olivia Fallow (IRE)**[12] 2899 5-7-11 **85**......................... AaronJones(3) 19 77
(Paul Midgley) *hld up in tch in midfield: effrt whn nt clr run and hmpd on stands rail over 1f out: kpt on but no threat to ldrs ins fnl f* **16/1**

-311 **13** nse **Excessable**[12] 2899 4-8-2 **87** 4ex....................................(t) RobHornby 13 79
(Tim Easterby) *hld up in tch in midfield: rdn and lost pl 2f out: no threat to ldrs but kpt on ins fnl f* **8/1**[2]

-210 **14** 1 ¼ **Majestic Hero (IRE)**[24] 2524 5-8-7 **92**........................... TomMarquand 2 80
(Ronald Harris) *chsd ldrs: rdn and unable qck over 1f out: wknd ins fnl f* **33/1**

00-0 **15** ½ **Move In Time**[16] 2764 9-9-1 **100**....................................(v) DanielTudhope 8 86
(David O'Meara) *chsd ldrs: rdn over 1f out: losing pl whn squeezed for room and hmpd 1f out: no ch after* **33/1**

2522 **16** ½ **Bowson Fred**[43] 1946 5-9-1 **100**........................................ JamesSullivan 14 84
(Michael Easterby) *chsd ldrs: rdn over 2f out: lost pl and btn over 1f out: wknd ins fnl f* **14/1**

-650 **17** ¾ **Union Rose**[7] 3092 5-8-8 **93**....................................... FergusSweeney 16 74
(Ronald Harris) *hld up in rr: effrt over 1f out: sn rdn and no imp: nvr trbld ldrs* **33/1**

-000 **18** 2 ¾ **Blithe Spirit**[13] 2856 6-8-2 **90**.......................................... HollieDoyle(3) 4 61
(Eric Alston) *chsd ldrs: rdn and lost pl over 1f out: wknd fnl f* **50/1**

6105 **19** 2 ¼ **Sign Of The Kodiac (IRE)**[22] 2566 4-8-6 **91**............(b[1]) FrannyNorton 3 54
(James Given) *in tch in midfield: rdn and lost pl 2f out: bhd fnl f* **25/1**

54.92s (-0.78) **Going Correction** +0.075s/f (Good) **19** Ran SP% **134.7**
Speed ratings (Par 109): **109,108,108,107,107 106,106,105,105,104 102,102,102,100,99 98,97,93,89**
CSF £264.61 CT £2533.53 TOTE £30.60: £6.20, £3.00, £2.60, £2.50; EX 601.50 Trifecta £5089.80.
**Owner** Stephen Louch **Bred** Ballygallon Stud Limited **Trained** Norton, N Yorks
■ Stewards' Enquiry : Tom Eaves two-day ban (17-18 Jun): used whip above permitted level

**FOCUS**
The pace was with those drawn low, albeit they crossed over to race centre to stands' side. There was a bunched finish, with the three pace horses finishing first, fourth and eighth. The winner has been rated better than ever, with the third helping to set the standard.

## 3322 INVESTEC DERBY (GROUP 1) (ENTIRE COLTS & FILLIES) 1m 4f 6y
**4:30** (4:35) (Class 1) 3-Y-O

**£921,537** (£349,375; £174,850; £87,100; £43,712; £21,937) **Stalls** Centre

Form RPR

40-2 **1** **Wings Of Eagles (FR)**[23] 2555 3-9-0 109.............................. PBBeggy 14 121+
(A P O'Brien, Ire) *hmpd sn after s: hld up off the pce in rr: 16th st: clsng whn nt clr run ent fnl 2f: stl plenty to do whn nt clr run carried lft and swtchd rt over 1f out: 7th and hdwy 1f out: str run to ld nr fin* **40/1**

1 **2** ¾ **Cliffs Of Moher (IRE)**[22] 2569 3-9-0 107...............(t) RyanMoore 13 119+
(A P O'Brien, Ire) *hld up towards rr: 14th st: rdn and hdwy on outer over 2f out: str run to ld 1f out: kpt on u.p ins fnl f: hdd and no ex nr fin* **5/1**[2]

1-1 **3** nk **Cracksman**[38] 2084 3-9-0 109.......................................... FrankieDettori 7 118
(John Gosden) *broke wl and t.k.h early: stdd bk and handy in main gp after: 5th st: sn rdn and clsd to chse ldr over 2f out: drvn to ld over 1f out: hdd 1f out: kpt on but unable qck fnl 100yds* **7/2**[1]

1-16 **4** ¾ **Eminent (IRE)**[28] 2399 3-9-0 112........................................ JimCrowley 4 117
(Martyn Meade) *hld up towards rr: 12th st: rdn and effrt 3f out: hdwy over 2f out: chsd ldrs 1f out: kpt on u.p and ev ch 100yds out: keeping on same pce whn squeezed and n.m.r towards fin* **5/1**[2]

132 **5** 1 ¾ **Benbatl**[16] 2766 3-9-0 111.............................................(t[1]) OisinMurphy 16 114
(Saeed bin Suroor) *stdd s: hld up wl off the pce in rr: 18th st: effrt over 2f out: stl plenty to do but only 1 l bhd wnr 2f out: hdwy over 1f out: styd on wl ins fnl f: snatched 4th last strides* **20/1**

3-43 **6** nk **Capri (IRE)**[27] 2442 3-9-0 110............................... SeamieHeffernan 10 113+
(A P O'Brien, Ire) *midfield: 8th st: sn rdn and clsd to chse ldrs 2f out: unable qck and edgd rt 1f out: kpt on same pce ins fnl f* **16/1**

4-21 **7** 1 **Douglas Macarthur (IRE)**[27] 2442 3-9-0 111........ ColmO'Donoghue 19 111
(A P O'Brien, Ire) *sn led: clr w rival after 3f: rdn and kicked clr 3f out: drvn and hdd over 1f out: no ex u.p and wknd ins fnl f* **25/1**

-401 **8** 1 ¾ **Best Solution (IRE)**[21] 2614 3-9-0 113............................. PatCosgrave 8 109
(Saeed bin Suroor) *chsd ldr for 1f: prom in chsng gp: 4th st: rdn and clsd 3f out: chsd wnr briefly over 2f out: unable qck and btn 1f out: wknd ins fnl f* **12/1**

1-52 **9** 1 ¼ **Glencadam Glory**[21] 2614 3-9-0 100............................(h) JamesDoyle 18 107
(John Gosden) *hld up towards rr: 15th st: effrt on outer over 2f out: no real imp tl styd on to pass btn horses ins fnl f: nvr trbld ldrs* **33/1**

3211 **10** nk **Permian (IRE)**[16] 2766 3-9-0 113.......................................... WilliamBuick 3 106
(Mark Johnston) *sn prom in main gp: 6th st: rdn 3f out: unable qck and outpcd 2f out: wknd ins fnl f* **8/1**[3]

1 **11** nk **Dubai Thunder**[15] 2783 3-9-0 100........................................ AdamKirby 1 106
(Saeed bin Suroor) *hld up in midfield: 9th st: sn rdn: unable qck and no imp over 2f out: edgd lft and wknd over 1f out* **9/1**

1 **12** 2 ½ **Venice Beach (IRE)**[23] 2555 3-9-0 111.................(tp) DonnachaO'Brien 9 102
(A P O'Brien, Ire) *prom in main gp: 3rd st: lost pl u.p over 2f out: hung lft and wknd over 1f out* **12/1**

23-2 **13** ½ **Salouen (IRE)**[46] 1861 3-9-0 110............................................ FranBerry 11 101+
(Sylvester Kirk) *hld up towards rr: 13th st: effrt but stl plenty to do whn clipped heels and stmbld bdly over 2f out: no threat to ldrs but switching rt and trying to rally whn nt clr run again ins fnl f: nvr threatened* **33/1**

3131 **14** 2 ¼ **Khalidi**[8] 3032 3-9-0 111........................................................ PatSmullen 6 97
(John Gosden) *hld up in midfield: 10th st: rdn and no imp wl over 2f out: sn wl btn and wknd over 1f out* **20/1**

31-1 **15** 2 ¼ **Crowned Eagle**[19] 2690 3-9-0 97.................................(p[1]) AndreaAtzeni 12 94
(John Gosden) *hld up in midfield on outer: sltly hmpd sn after s: 6th st: sn rdn: edgd rt and unable qck: lost pl and btn 2f out: wknd* **33/1**

0-14 **16** 2 ¼ **Rekindling**[16] 2766 3-9-0 111.......................................... WayneLordan 15 90
(Joseph Patrick O'Brien, Ire) *hld up in midfield: 11th st: sn rdn and struggling whn sltly impeded 3f out: wknd and bhd over 1f out* **25/1**

30-3 **17** 5 **The Anvil (IRE)**[23] 2555 3-9-0 109.......................................... AnaO'Brien 2 82
(A P O'Brien, Ire) *rousted along early: chsd ldr after 1f and clr w him after 3f: 2nd st: sn rdn and lost 2nd over 2f out: dropped out qckly: bhd ins fnl f* **66/1**

-241 **18** 10 **Pealer (GER)**[26] 2468 3-9-0 85.................................(t) SilvestreDeSousa 5 66
(John Gosden) *stdd s: t.k.h: hld up and a towards rr: 17th st: lost tch and eased fnl f* **100/1**

2m 33.02s (-5.88) **Going Correction** -0.10s/f (Good) **18** Ran SP% **128.9**
Speed ratings (Par 113): **115,114,114,113,112 112,111,110,109,109 109,107,107,105,104 102,99,92**
CSF £223.80 CT £921.34 TOTE £56.60: £10.80, £2.60, £1.80; EX 585.10 Trifecta £4230.30.
**Owner** Derrick Smith & Mrs John Magnier & Michael Tabor **Bred** Mme Aliette Forien & Mr Gilles Forien **Trained** Cashel, Co Tipperary
■ Stewards' Enquiry : Seamie Heffernan four-day ban: used whip above permitted level (Jun 17-19, 25)
Frankie Dettori four-day ban: used whip above permitted level (Jun 17-19, 25)

**FOCUS**
18 runners and no hiding place, with two of the Ballydoyle outsiders ensuring the gallop was strong, and the race for the line began swinging off Tattenham Corner, the placed runners making their move early and being mown down late by a strong-staying type who overcame trouble in running to win with a bit in hand. Although the winner was a big price, there's every reason to believe it's strong form. The place figures fit the race standard.

## 3323 INVESTEC OUT OF THE ORDINARY H'CAP 1m 4f 6y
**5:15** (5:16) (Class 2) (0-100,100) 4-Y-O+

**£24,900** (£7,456; £3,728; £1,864; £932; £468) **Stalls** Centre

Form RPR

0-06 **1** **Soldier In Action (FR)**[15] 2804 4-9-6 **99**........................... JamesDoyle 9 107+
(Mark Johnston) *chsd ldr: rdn to ld 2f out: strly pressed and edgd rt 1f out: forged ahd ins fnl f: styd on strly and drew clr fnl 100yds* **12/1**

4060 **2** 2 **Eddystone Rock (IRE)**[38] 2086 5-9-4 **97**................(h) JimCrowley 12 101
(John Best) *hld up in tch in last quartet: swtchd rt and effrt 3f out: str run but hanging lft over 1f out: chal 1f out: no ex u.p and outpcd fnl 100yds* **15/2**[3]

56-0 **3** 1 ½ **Carntop**[21] 2604 4-9-7 **100**...............................................(h[1]) PatDobbs 4 102+
(Ralph Beckett) *stdd s: hld up in tch in rr: effrt on inner over 1f out: nt clr run ent fnl f: swtchd rt ins fnl f: r.o wl to snatch 3rd last strides: no threat to ldng pair* **25/1**

025- **4** hd **Shraaoh (IRE)**[287] 5653 4-9-0 **93**........................................ FrankieDettori 2 95
(Sir Michael Stoute) *chsd ldrs: effrt and shkn up ent fnl 2f: rdn and unable qck over 1f out: kpt on same pce ins fnl f: lost 3rd last strides* **5/4**[1]

3065 **5** hd **Sennockian Star**[23] 2552 7-8-12 **91**......................... SilvestreDeSousa 1 92
(Mark Johnston) *led: rdn and hdd 2f out: unable qck u.p over 1f out: styd on same pce ins fnl f* **16/1**

61-2 **6** hd **Whinging Willie (IRE)**[38] 2085 8-8-4 **81** ow2............(v) SamHitchcott 10 84
(Gary Moore) *stdd after s: hld up in last pair: hdwy on outer to chse ldrs over 3f out: rdn ent fnl 2f: stl chsng ldrs whn squeezed out and hmpd jst over 1f out: kpt on same pce ins fnl f* **10/1**

00-3 **7** hd **Barwick**[38] 2085 9-8-10 **89**................................................ FrannyNorton 3 90
(George Baker) *s.i.s and pushed along early: hdwy into midfield after 2f: effrt on inner but nt clr run 2f out: switching rt fr over 1f out: kpt on ins fnl f: no threat to ldrs* **12/1**

4-31 **8** 4 **Spinners Ball (IRE)**[26] 2478 4-8-2 **81** oh3........................ MartinDwyer 6 75
(Sylvester Kirk) *sn chsng ldrs: rdn jst over 2f out: wanting to hang lft and lost pl over 1f out: btn whn nt clr run 1f out: wknd ins fnl f* **16/1**

-243 **9** ¾ **Gawdawpalin (IRE)**[38] 2086 4-8-10 **89**........................... TomMarquand 5 82
(Sylvester Kirk) *in tch in midfield: effrt 3f out: squeezed for room and dropped to rr over 1f out: wknd ins fnl f* **9/2**[2]

0-44 **10** 3 **Green Light**[29] 2375 6-8-7 **86**...............................................(v) TomEaves 7 74
(Brian Ellison) *hld up in tch: effrt whn nt clr run 2f out: nvr able to cl bhd ins fnl f* **16/1**

2m 37.94s (-0.96) **Going Correction** -0.10s/f (Good) **10** Ran SP% **120.4**
Speed ratings (Par 109): **99,97,96,96,96 96,96,93,92,90**
CSF £102.04 CT £2230.22 TOTE £13.10: £3.10, £2.70, £6.00; EX 103.10 Trifecta £892.60.
**Owner** A D Spence **Bred** Randolf Peters **Trained** Middleham Moor, N Yorks

**FOCUS**
A good handicap. The early pace wasn't strong and the time was 4.92sec slower than the Derby. Muddling form. The winner has been rated back to the level of his Goodwood win.

## 3324 INVESTEC ASSET MANAGEMENT H'CAP 6f 3y
**5:50** (5:51) (Class 2) (0-100,98) 4-Y-O+

**£24,900** (£7,456; £3,728; £1,864; £932; £468) **Stalls** High

Form RPR

-500 **1** **Reputation (IRE)**[17] 2736 4-8-10 **87**..................................(v) JasonHart 15 98
(John Quinn) *chsd ldrs: 3rd and swtchd rt over 1f out: styd on wl u.p to ld towards fin: drvn out* **25/1**

1-41 **2** ½ **Naggers (IRE)**[14] 2840 6-9-4 **95**...................................... PaulMulrennan 3 104+
(Paul Midgley) *hld up in midfield: effrt 2f out: hdwy u.p and hung lft 1f out: styd on strly ins fnl f to go 2nd towards fin: nvr quite getting to wnr* **5/2**[1]

-006 **3** 1 ¼ **George Bowen (IRE)**[17] 2736 5-8-9 **86**................................ TomEaves 6 91
(Richard Fahey) *towards rr: rdn over 2f out: hdwy u.p to chse ldng trio over 1f out: pressing ldrs ins fnl f: kpt on same pce wl ins fnl f* **15/2**[3]

4543 **4** shd **Watchable**[7] 3092 7-9-4 **95**.......................................(v) DanielTudhope 16 100
(David O'Meara) *led for 1f: chsd ldr after tl rdn to ld over 1f out: drvn ins fnl f: hdd and lost 3 pls towards fin* **8/1**

0360 **5** 1 ¼ **Ninjago**[17] 2736 7-8-12 **89**.................................................(b) OisinMurphy 14 90
(Paul Midgley) *in tch in midfield: effrt 2f out: no imp and carried lft ent fnl f: kpt on same pce ins fnl f* **12/1**

3006 **6** 3/4 **Holiday Magic (IRE)**[21] 2606 6-9-3 **94** AdamKirby 5 93+
(Michael Easterby) *s.i.s: in rr: nt clr run and trying to switch rt over 1f out: stl plenty to do over 1f out: r.o strly to pass btn horses ins fnl f: nvr trbld ldrs* **14/1**

20-0 **7** 1/2 **Ashpan Sam**[15] 2780 8-8-12 **89** (p) WilliamCarson 17 86
(David W Drinkwater) *bustled along leaving stalls: led after 1f out: rdn and hdd over 1f out: no ex and wknd ins fnl f* **16/1**

3121 **8** 3/4 **Lucky Beggar (IRE)**[1] 3288 7-8-12 **89** 6ex DavidAllan 10 84
(David C Griffiths) *taken down early: chsd ldrs: shkn up 2f out: jostled wl over 1f out and sn unable qck: wknd ins fnl f* **10/1**

3600 **9** hd **Pearl Spectre (USA)**[37] 2115 6-8-7 **87** CallumShepherd(3) 13 81
(Phil McEntee) *midfield: rdn: outpcd and lost pl over 2f out: rallied and styd on u.p ins fnl f: no threat to ldrs* **40/1**

4-21 **10** 3/4 **Paddy Power (IRE)**[14] 2835 4-7-12 **81** ow1 ConnorMurtagh(7) 9 74
(Richard Fahey) *hld up in rr: effrt over 2f out: sme hdwy ins fnl f: nvr trbld ldrs* **9/1**

-005 **11** 1/2 **B Fifty Two (IRE)**[8] 3052 8-8-5 **82** (t) JamesSullivan 4 72
(Marjorie Fife) *hld up in tch in midfield: effrt on inner 2f out: sn rdn and no imp: wl hld and kpt on same pce ins fnl f* **25/1**

-106 **12** nk **In The Red (IRE)**[21] 2617 4-8-3 **83** NoelGarbutt(3) 2 72
(Martin Smith) *chsd ldrs: rdn and unable qck over 2f out: lost pl and btn over 1f out: wknd ins fnl f* **33/1**

5160 **13** 1/2 **Suzi's Connoisseur**[28] 2390 6-9-5 **96** (t) PatDobbs 1 83
(Stuart Williams) *chsd ldrs: rdn 2f out: unable qck and btn over 1f out: wknd ins fnl f* **20/1**

20-1 **14** 1/2 **Blaine**[15] 2780 7-9-0 **98** (b) JoshuaBryan(7) 8 84
(Brian Barr) *midfield: lost pl and rdn 2f out: sn btn and wknd ins fnl f* **11/2**[2]

-040 **15** 3 1/2 **Clear Spring (IRE)**[8] 3034 9-8-13 **90** LiamJones 7 65
(John Spearing) *s.i.s: a bhd* **20/1**

/-40 **16** 5 **Sir Ottoman (FR)**[46] 1863 4-9-1 **95** (t[1]) EdwardGreatrex(3) 11 54
(Mohamed Moubarak) *a towards rr: wd and dropped to last over 3f out: nvr on terms after* **33/1**

1m 7.99s (-1.41) **Going Correction** -0.10s/f (Good) **16** Ran SP% **131.7**
Speed ratings (Par 109): **105,104,102,102,100 99,99,98,97,96 96,95,95,94,89 83**
CSF £87.73 CT £586.47 TOTE £36.80: £5.50, £1.30, £2.20, £2.20; EX 169.40 Trifecta £1072.90.

**Owner** Fulbeck Horse Syndicate Ltd **Bred** Moyns Park Estate And Stud Ltd **Trained** Settrington, N Yorks

**FOCUS**
A low draw is often an advantage in this race, but the winner, fourth and seventh, who were all drawn wide, had the early speed to clear their rivals heading into the first turn. The winner has been rated to his best.
T/Jkpt: Not won. T/Plt: £503.60 to a £1 stake. Pool: £392,420.77 - 568.81 winning units. T/Qpdt: £315.10 to a £1 stake. Pool: £22,956.62 - 53.90 winning units. **Steve Payne**

## 3244 LINGFIELD (L-H)
### Saturday, June 3

**OFFICIAL GOING: Turf course - good to firm (good in places; 7.4); polytrack: standard**
Wind: mild breeze against Weather: cloudy

## 3325 TAKE THAT EXPERIENCE AT LINGFIELD PARK - JUNE 17 AMATEUR RIDERS' H'CAP 1m 2f (P)
**5:45** (5:45) (Class 5) (0-75,75) 4-Y-0+ **£2,807** (£870; £435; £217) **Stalls** Low

Form RPR
4050 **1** **The Gay Cavalier**[15] 2785 6-9-13 **67** (t) MissHVKnowles(7) 7 74
(John Ryan) *s.i.s: last pair: hdwy over 2f out: r.o strly fnl f: led fnl stride* **12/1**

10-0 **2** hd **Duke Of Yorkshire**[62] 1519 7-10-5 **69** (p) MissEEasterby(3) 9 75
(Tim Easterby) *sn led: rdn whn jnd 2f out: kpt on gamely ins fnl f: hdd fnl stride* **10/1**

0450 **3** 1 **Zephyros (GER)**[19] 1284 6-9-8 **62** PoppyBridgwater(7) 5 66
(David Bridgwater) *mid-div tl lost pl over 2f out: rdn and hdwy over 1f out: running on strly whn nt clr run fnl 75yds: kpt on to go 3rd cl home* **9/2**[3]

224- **4** 1/2 **Jersey Jewel (FR)**[214] 7732 5-10-2 **70** (p) MissCAGreenway(7) 6 73
(Tom Dascombe) *trckd ldrs: chal 2f out: rdn and ev ch ent fnl f: no ex fnl 75yds: lost 2 pls cl home* **11/2**

0641 **5** 4 **Black Dave (IRE)**[10] 2968 7-10-2 **68** MrJFlook(5) 1 63
(David Evans) *broke wl: prom: rdn over 2f out: hld turning in: fdd fnl f* **7/2**[2]

2100 **6** 8 **Ravenhoe (IRE)**[12] 2884 4-10-4 **72** MissEmmaBedford(7) 2 51
(Mark Johnston) *mid-div tl dropped rr 4f out: rdn whn squeezed up in rails turning in: wknd* **9/1**

0050 **7** 19 **Silver Alliance**[17] 2729 9-9-11 **58** (p) MrRBirkett 3
(Julia Feilden) *trckd ldrs: rdn over 2f out: sn wknd* **12/1**

5-20 **P** **Marcano (IRE)**[35] 2133 5-11-0 **75** (t) MrPMillman 8
(Rod Millman) *hld up last pair: hdwy over 4f out: rdn whn lost action wl over 1f out: sn p.u* **11/4**[1]

2m 6.98s (0.38) **Going Correction** -0.075s/f (Stan) **8** Ran SP% **116.9**
Speed ratings (Par 103): **95,94,94,93,90 84,68,**
CSF £125.46 CT £627.68 TOTE £9.10: £2.80, £3.20, £1.70; EX 107.10 Trifecta £388.60.
**Owner** The Gay Cavaliers Partnership **Bred** Philip Newton **Trained** Newmarket, Suffolk

**FOCUS**
All distances as advertised. Not a great race for the grade. They went a steady pace and the winner finished best.

## 3326 GAVIN HEPBURN MEMORIAL H'CAP 1m 4f (P)
**6:20** (6:20) (Class 6) (0-60,62) 3-Y-0 **£2,264** (£673; £336; £168) **Stalls** Low

Form RPR
0-04 **1** **Conkering Hero (IRE)**[65] 1445 3-9-8 **61** LiamKeniry 2 76+
(Joseph Tuite) *mde all: drew 6 l clr 2f out: kpt up to work but in n.d after: easily* **10/1**

40-6 **2** 3 1/4 **Let's Be Happy (IRE)**[32] 2259 3-9-8 **61** ShaneKelly 1 67
(Richard Hughes) *trckd ldrs: rdn to chse wnr over 2f out: kpt on but nvr threatened to get on terms* **15/2**[3]

00-5 **3** 1/2 **Lady Of York**[19] 2679 3-8-7 **46** JoeyHaynes 4 51
(Alan Bailey) *mid-div: hdwy 2f out: sn rdn to chal for hld 2nd: styd on same pce* **16/1**

0225 **4** 3 3/4 **Too Many Shots**[18] 2705 3-9-5 **58** KierenFox 10 59
(John Best) *trckd ldrs: rdn whn short of room and lost pl 2f out: styd on again ent fnl f: wnt 4th fnl 140yds* **9/4**[1]

600- **5** 1 **Kenyan (FR)**[157] 8556 3-8-1 **47** (t[1]) FinleyMarsh(7) 8 45
(Seamus Durack) *hld up: hdwy into midfield turning in: sn rdn: kpt on but nt pce to get on terms* **8/1**

5-56 **6** 1 1/2 **Charlie Rascal (FR)**[7] 3087 3-9-6 **59** TomMarquand 11 54
(Peter Chapple-Hyam) *chsd ldrs: rdn wl over 2f out: sn one pce* **10/1**

-560 **7** 3 **Netley Abbey**[19] 2679 3-8-13 **52** (p[1]) TimmyMurphy 3 42
(Karen George) *mid-div: rdn wl over 2f out: nvr any imp* **18/1**

50-0 **8** 5 **Cape Cruiser (USA)**[18] 2711 3-9-9 **62** (p[1]) FranBerry 6 44
(Ralph Beckett) *struggling over 4f out: a towards rr* **11/4**[2]

000 **9** 2 1/4 **Geordielad**[10] 2957 3-8-9 **48** FergusSweeney 12 27
(Jamie Osborne) *racd freely: slowly away: stdy prog on outer to dispute ld 5f out tl 3f out: wknd 2f out* **20/1**

000 **10** 3 **Mushareefa (IRE)**[22] 2585 3-8-11 **50** (p[1]) AntonioFresu 7 24
(Ed Dunlop) *mid-div: struggling 4f out: nvr threatened: wknd over 1f out* **16/1**

2m 32.36s (-0.64) **Going Correction** -0.075s/f (Stan) **10** Ran SP% **120.3**
Speed ratings (Par 97): **99,96,96,94,93 92,90,87,85,83**
CSF £85.46 CT £1207.74 TOTE £12.10: £3.40, £2.40, £3.60; EX 88.40 Trifecta £730.80.
**Owner** C R Lambourne, M Forbes, D Losse **Bred** J Hutchinson **Trained** Lambourn, Berks

**FOCUS**
Plenty of unexposed types in this open handicap which was run at a steady pace. A step forward from the winner, with the runner-up rated to her mark.

## 3327 #TAKETHEREINS17 H'CAP 1m 2f (P)
**6:50** (6:53) (Class 6) (0-60,62) 3-Y-0 **£2,264** (£673; £336; £168) **Stalls** Low

Form RPR
-000 **1** **Deleyll**[31] 2315 3-8-12 **50** (b) AdamBeschizza 9 57
(John Butler) *hld up bhd: gd hdwy over 2f out: rdn for str chal over 1f out: kpt on wl to ld ins fnl f: drvn out* **12/1**

4500 **2** 1/2 **Malt Teaser (FR)**[28] 2394 3-9-10 **62** KierenFox 2 68
(John Best) *led for 3f: trckd ldr: rdn to ld over 1f out: sn strly pressed: hdd ins fnl f: kpt on* **7/2**[2]

40-5 **3** 4 1/2 **Power Home (IRE)**[40] 2018 3-9-2 **59** PaddyPilley(5) 4 57
(Denis Coakley) *trckd ldrs: rdn over 2f out: styd on but nt pce to mount chal* **8/1**

0-04 **4** 3 1/4 **Let's Sway**[19] 2679 3-9-1 **53** (h) LemosdeSouza 14 44
(Amy Murphy) *plld hrd: hdwy to ld after 3f: rdn and hdd over 1f out: no ex ins fnl f* **20/1**

600 **5** 1/2 **Chunkyfunkymonkey**[39] 2066 3-9-7 **59** (p[1]) LouisSteward 5 49
(John Ryan) *mid-div: rdn and hdwy over 1f out: styd on fnl f but nt pce to get on terms* **12/1**

4-40 **6** 1 1/2 **Bizet (IRE)**[42] 1968 3-9-10 **62** (b[1]) JimCrowley 1 50
(John Ryan) *s.i.s: mid-div after 2f: rdn over 2f out: styd on fnl f but nt pce to get on terms* **5/1**[3]

060- **7** 3/4 **Take A Turn (IRE)**[171] 8353 3-9-10 **62** TomQueally 10 48
(David Lanigan) *s.i.s: towards rr: struggling 3f out: hdwy over 1f out: no further imp fnl f* **6/1**

0560 **8** 2 3/4 **Swallow Dancer**[35] 2137 3-9-1 **53** (t[1]) SamHitchcott 7 34
(Harry Dunlop) *a mid-div* **25/1**

000- **9** 3 1/4 **Broughtons Admiral**[205] 7882 3-9-5 **57** TimmyMurphy 12 32
(Henry Spiller) *s.i.s: towards rr: sme minor late prog: n.d* **25/1**

6542 **10** 5 **Madam Prancealot (IRE)**[16] 2758 3-8-6 **51** KatherineGlenister(7) 11 16
(David Evans) *mid-div: rdn over 2f out: nvr threatened: wknd over 1f out* **14/1**

0-00 **11** 15 **Royal Sentiment (IRE)**[7] 3087 3-8-13 **51** LiamKeniry 8
(Mark Usher) *mid-div: rdn over 2f out: sn wknd* **33/1**

0-03 **12** 2 1/2 **Mr Mac**[40] 2018 3-9-5 **57** (h) CharlesBishop 6
(Peter Hedger) *trckd ldrs: rdn over 2f out: sn hld: looked to lose action whn eased ent fnl f* **3/1**[1]

2m 6.49s (-0.11) **Going Correction** -0.075s/f (Stan) **12** Ran SP% **126.7**
Speed ratings (Par 97): **97,96,93,90,90 88,88,86,83,79 67,65**
CSF £55.25 CT £377.20 TOTE £16.70: £4.30, £1.80, £2.70; EX 98.40 Trifecta £524.40.
**Owner** Tramore Tree **Bred** Genesis Green Stud Ltd **Trained** Newmarket, Suffolk

**FOCUS**
A modest handicap run at an honest pace. The front two finished clear. The third and fourth help set the level.

## 3328 MCMILLAN WILLIAMS SOLICITORS MAIDEN AUCTION STKS 4f 217y
**7:20** (7:22) (Class 5) 2-Y-0 **£2,911** (£866; £432; £216) **Stalls** Centre

Form RPR
42 **1** **Magic Applause (IRE)**[9] 2988 2-9-0 0 SilvestreDeSousa 3 70+
(George Scott) *in tch: hdwy over 2f out: str chal fnl f: led fnl 100yds: r.o: rdn out* **5/2**[1]

**2** 1 **Connery (IRE)** 2-8-13 0 MitchGodwin(5) 8 70
(Sylvester Kirk) *trckd ldr: led 2f out: sn rdn: hdd fnl 100yds: kpt on but no ex* **12/1**

00 **3** 3 **Terri Rules (IRE)**[16] 2750 2-9-0 0 AdamBeschizza 6 55
(Julia Feilden) *trckd ldrs: rdn and ev ch over 1f out: kpt on same pce fnl f* **25/1**

**4** 1 **Royal Liberty** 2-9-3 0 OisinMurphy 2 55
(Mark Johnston) *s.i.s: last trio: hdwy over 1f out: kpt on to go 4th ins fnl f but nt pce to get on terms* **11/4**[2]

35 **5** nk **Princess Lyla (IRE)**[11] 2910 2-8-11 0 ShaneKelly 7 48
(Richard Hughes) *led tl rdn 2f out: sn one pce* **5/1**[3]

36 **6** 2 3/4 **Royal Crown (IRE)**[23] 2545 2-9-0 0 PatCosgrave 5 41
(David O'Meara) *sn pushed along in 4th: rdn over 2f out: wknd over 1f out:* **10/1**

6 **7** 3/4 **Alaskan Star (IRE)**[8] 3029 2-9-5 0 JimCrowley 4 43
(Amanda Perrett) *last trio: rdn over 2f out: nvr gng pce to get involved* **5/1**[3]

**8** 2 1/4 **Red For Danger** 2-8-13 0 CharlesBishop 1 29+
(Eve Johnson Houghton) *s.i.s: sn struggling: a towards rr* **8/1**

59.85s (1.65) **Going Correction** +0.175s/f (Good) **8** Ran SP% **120.3**
Speed ratings (Par 93): **93,91,86,85,84 80,78,75**
CSF £35.18 TOTE £3.30: £1.30, £4.30, £5.20; EX 39.00 Trifecta £753.50.
**Owner** Redman, Philipps & McClean **Bred** Ms A O'Callaghan **Trained** Newmarket, Suffolk

**FOCUS**
The first turf race of the evening. They went a sound pace for this fair maiden. The opening level is fluid.

## 3329 ORPHEUS CENTRE MAIDEN FILLIES' STKS 7f
**7:50** (7:52) (Class 5) 3-Y-0+ **£2,911** (£866; £432; £216) **Stalls** Centre

Form RPR
2-32 **1** **Isabel's On It**[26] 2463 3-9-0 75 PatCosgrave 6 82+
(William Haggas) *trckd ldrs: led over 1f out: qcknd clr: easily* **8/11**[1]

**2** 4 **Unified** 3-8-11 0 HectorCrouch(3) 5 66
(Clive Cox) *mid-div: pushed along and hdwy over 2f out: rdn over 1f out: kpt on to go 2nd ent fnl f but nvr any threat to easy wnr* **9/1**[3]

3 2 ½ **Scribbler** 3-9-0 0 AdamBeschizza 7 59
(Rae Guest) *s.i.s: sn trcking ldrs: rdn 2f out: kpt on same pce fnl f* **20/1**

4 nk **Gold Dust** 3-9-0 0 JohnFahy 4 59
(Clive Cox) *towards rr: stdy prog fr 2f out: kpt on fnl f but nvr gng pce to get involved* **12/1**

2 5 4 **Euqranian (USA)**[12] 2908 3-9-0 0 (h) SilvestreDeSousa 9 48
(Jeremy Noseda) *led: rdn and hdd over 1f out: wknd fnl f* **7/4[2]**

03 6 2 ¼ **Dr Goodhead (FR)**[16] 2753 3-8-11 0 CallumShepherd(3) 2 42
(Charles Hills) *mid-div: rdn over 2f out: nvr any imp: wknd fnl f* **14/1**

05 7 5 **Golden Cannon**[22] 2580 6-9-10 0 DannyBrock 8 32
(Sheena West) *racd keenly: pressed ldr: rdn 3f out: wknd over 1f out* **40/1**

8 6 **Violet's Lads (IRE)** 3-9-0 0 KieranO'Neill 3 12
(Brett Johnson) *s.i.s: a towards rr* **40/1**

60-0 9 18 **Denver Spirit (IRE)**[16] 2753 3-9-0 0 ShaneKelly 1
(Luca Cumani) *sn struggling: a towards rr* **25/1**

1m 24.05s (0.75) **Going Correction** +0.175s/f (Good)
**WFA** 3 from 6yo 10lb **9** Ran SP% **132.1**
Speed ratings (Par 100): **102,97,94,94,89 87,81,74,53**
CSF £10.79 TOTE £1.70: £1.02, £2.90, £7.20; EX 12.60 Trifecta £190.10.
**Owner** Lael Stable **Bred** R Jackson **Trained** Newmarket, Suffolk

**FOCUS**
An uncompetitive maiden. They went a sound pace and the winner did it well.

## 3330 RACING WELFARE H'CAP 6f
**8:20** (8:21) (Class 4) (0-85,85) 4-Y-0+ **£4,690** (£1,395; £697; £348) **Stalls** Centre

Form RPR

-145 1 **Diamond Lady**[7] 3074 6-8-12 **79** HollieDoyle(3) 4 88
(William Stone) *broke sharply: mde all: kpt on wl fnl f: rdn out* **7/1**

3-15 2 ¾ **Compas Scoobie**[31] 2320 4-9-2 **80** SilvestreDeSousa 1 87+
(Roger Varian) *stdd s: last: hdwy whn bmpd over 2f out: rdn over 1f out: chsd wnr ent fnl f: kpt on but a being hld* **2/1[1]**

20-2 3 1 ¾ **Tanasoq (IRE)**[35] 2147 4-9-0 **78** JimCrowley 7 79
(Owen Burrows) *travelled wl trcking ldr most of way tl rdn 2f out: sn edgd lft: kpt on same pce* **5/2[2]**

5-25 4 3 ½ **Goring (GER)**[19] 2692 5-9-6 **84** JohnFahy 6 74
(Eve Johnson Houghton) *in tch: rdn over 1f out: kpt on but nt pce to threaten* **4/1[3]**

3230 5 hd **Highly Sprung (IRE)**[8] 3052 4-9-4 **82** OisinMurphy 3 71
(Mark Johnston) *trckd ldr: rdn 2f out: kpt on same pce fnl f* **8/1**

1/6- 6 1 ¼ **Human Nature (IRE)**[280] 5881 4-9-0 **85** (t[1]) MillyNaseb(7) 5 70
(Stuart Williams) *mid-div: swtchd lft over 2f out: sn rdn: nvr any imp* **25/1**

050- 7 3 ½ **Zebstar (IRE)**[369] 2736 4-9-5 **83** MartinDwyer 8 57
(Gay Kelleway) *in tch: hdwy over 2f out: sn rdn: wknd ent fnl f* **20/1**

1-60 8 nk **Consulting**[14] 2835 4-8-12 **79** (t) AaronJones(3) 2 52
(Stuart Williams) *a towards rr* **33/1**

1m 10.15s (-1.05) **Going Correction** +0.175s/f (Good) **8** Ran SP% **117.1**
Speed ratings (Par 105): **114,113,110,106,105 104,99,99**
CSF £21.56 CT £45.84 TOTE £8.20: £1.90, £1.10, £1.40; EX 28.00 Trifecta £97.60.
**Owner** The Going Great Guns Partnership **Bred** Mickley Stud **Trained** West Wickham, Cambs

**FOCUS**
They went a sound pace for this fair handicap.

## 3331 INJURED JOCKEYS FUND FILLIES' H'CAP 4f 217y
**8:50** (8:50) (Class 5) (0-70,72) 3-Y-0+ **£2,911** (£866; £432; £216) **Stalls** Centre

Form RPR

0600 1 **Flowing Clarets**[10] 2969 4-9-2 **58** WilliamCarson 11 65
(John Bridger) *trckd ldrs: rdn 2f out: led ent fnl f: r.o wl* **14/1**

123 2 1 **Monteamiata (IRE)**[17] 2725 3-9-9 **72** ThomasBrown 8 72
(Ed Walker) *mid-div: rdn over 2f out: no imp tl hdwy jst over 1f out: r.o strly fnl f: snatched 2nd cl home* **13/8[1]**

0-54 3 nk **Staffa (IRE)**[29] 2367 4-8-10 **52** OisinMurphy 3 54+
(Denis Coakley) *s.i.s: last: shkn up and hdwy over 1f out: swtchd lft ins fnl f: chalng for 2nd fnl 120yds: kpt on* **8/1**

-000 4 hd **Bobby Vee**[26] 2474 3-8-10 **62** JackDuern(3) 5 60
(Dean Ivory) *prom: rdn to ld over 1f out: hdd ent fnl f: kpt on but no ex whn losing 2 pls cl home* **11/1**

-536 5 2 **Exquisite Ruby**[36] 2121 3-8-12 **64** CallumShepherd(3) 12 55
(Charles Hills) *sn trcking ldrs: rdn over 2f out: swtchd lft ins fnl f: kpt on same pce* **12/1**

5401 6 ½ **Annie Salts**[42] 1981 4-10-0 **70** (h) SilvestreDeSousa 9 62
(Chris Dwyer) *led: rdn 2f out: sn hdd: no ex fnl f* **4/1[2]**

34-6 7 2 **Katrine (IRE)**[49] 1786 3-9-7 **70** (h) JimCrowley 6 60
(David O'Meara) *mid-div: rdn 2f out: no imp whn hmpd jst ins fnl f: no threat after* **5/1[3]**

2243 8 1 ½ **Fabulous Flyer**[59] 1557 4-8-6 **51** oh1 HectorCrouch(3) 1 31
(Jeremy Gask) *towards rr: drvn along over 2f out: little imp: fdd fnl f* **14/1**

3-04 9 1 ½ **Cherry Kool**[19] 2680 4-9-7 **66** (t) AaronJones(3) 4 40
(Stuart Williams) *in tch: rdn over 2f out: wknd ent fnl f* **16/1**

58.73s (0.53) **Going Correction** +0.175s/f (Good)
**WFA** 3 from 4yo 7lb **9** Ran SP% **121.1**
Speed ratings (Par 100): **102,100,99,99,96 95,92,90,87**
CSF £39.06 CT £212.73 TOTE £18.70: £3.70, £1.70, £2.20; EX 50.30 Trifecta £634.10.
**Owner** Wood Marshall Bridger **Bred** R A Fahey **Trained** Liphook, Hants
■ Stewards' Enquiry : Callum Shepherd caution: careless riding

**FOCUS**
A strongly run handicap.
T/Plt: £378.20 to a £1 stake. Pool: £59,293.65 - 114.44 winning units. T/Qpdt: £12.30 to a £1 stake. Pool: £7,539.19 - 451.01 winning units. **Tim Mitchell**

# 3043 MUSSELBURGH (R-H)
Saturday, June 3

**OFFICIAL GOING: Good to firm (7.8)**
Wind: Light across Weather: Cloudy, showers after 3rd and 5th

## 3332 EDINBURGH GIN'S SEASIDE H'CAP 7f 33y
**1:40** (1:40) (Class 5) (0-70,71) 3-Y-0+ **£3,234** (£962; £481; £240) **Stalls** Low

Form RPR

50-2 1 **Wigan Warrior**[10] 2957 3-9-3 **71** JosephineGordon 5 73
(David Brown) *hld up: sn pushed along: rdn and hdwy on outer over 2f out: led 1f out: kpt on* **9/4[1]**

40-6 2 ¾ **Full Of Promise**[14] 2843 4-9-2 **60** PaulHanagan 1 64
(Richard Fahey) *trckd ldrs: pushed along 2f out: briefly short of room wl over 1f out: rdn to chal ins fnl f: kpt on* **4/1[2]**

0466 3 1 **Ralphy Boy (IRE)**[8] 3045 8-9-10 **68** PJMcDonald 2 69
(Alistair Whillans) *led: rdn over 2f out: hdd 1f out: no ex fnl 50yds* **5/1[3]**

0004 4 5 **Ellaal**[8] 3048 8-9-8 **66** JackGarritty 4 54
(Ruth Carr) *trckd ldrs: rdn 2f out: wknd fnl f* **9/4[1]**

0454 5 4 **Secret Missile**[2] 3239 7-9-12 **70** (p) ConnorBeasley 3 47
(David C Griffiths) *prom: rdn over 2f out: wknd fnl f* **15/2**

1m 28.21s (-0.79) **Going Correction** -0.025s/f (Good)
**WFA** 3 from 4yo+ 10lb **5** Ran SP% **110.0**
Speed ratings (Par 103): **103,102,101,95,90**
CSF £11.39 TOTE £2.80: £1.80, £2.80; EX 11.00 Trifecta £25.40.
**Owner** Peter Onslow & David H Brown **Bred** Peter Onslow **Trained** Averham Park, Notts

**FOCUS**
All distances as advertised. Good to firm prior to the opener, a moderate handicap in which the jockeys reported that the ground was riding on the quick side.

## 3333 EBFSTALLIONS.COM EDINBURGH CASTLE STKS (A CONDITIONS RACE) (PLUS 10 RACE) 5f 1y
**2:15** (2:17) (Class 2) 2-Y-0
**£12,450** (£3,728; £1,864; £932; £466; £234) **Stalls** High

Form RPR

4 1 **It Dont Come Easy (IRE)**[17] 2740 2-9-2 0 PaulHanagan 5 95
(Richard Fahey) *trckd ldr: rdn 2f out: chal ent fnl f: r.o wl: led towards fin* **7/2[2]**

1 2 hd **Rebel Assault (IRE)**[9] 2988 2-9-1 0 JoeFanning 6 93
(Mark Johnston) *led: pushed along 2f out: rdn and pressed ent fnl f: kpt on wl but hdd towards fin* **2/5[1]**

026 3 10 **Rocket Man Dan (IRE)**[17] 2740 2-9-2 0 DougieCostello 3 58
(Keith Dalgleish) *dwlt: hld up: rdn along 1/2-way: kpt on to go remote 3rd ins fnl f* **20/1**

01 4 6 **Brandy Station (IRE)**[31] 2299 2-9-6 0 BarryMcHugh 4 40
(Tony Coyle) *trckd ldrs: rdn 2f out: wknd ins fnl f* **28/1**

04 5 2 ¼ **Angel Force (IRE)**[9] 2988 2-8-11 0 JosephineGordon 2 23
(David C Griffiths) *pressed ldr: rdn 1/2-way: wknd fnl f* **50/1**

52 6 nk **Marnie James**[15] 2771 2-9-2 0 DavidNolan 1 27
(Iain Jardine) *trckd ldrs: rdn 1/2-way: wknd fnl f* **12/1[3]**

57.66s (-2.74) **Going Correction** -0.50s/f (Hard) 2y crse rec **6** Ran SP% **111.5**
Speed ratings (Par 99): **101,100,84,75,71 71**
CSF £5.23 TOTE £4.40: £1.90, £1.10; EX 6.20 Trifecta £25.60.
**Owner** A Rhodes Haulage And P Timmins **Bred** Limestone And Tara Studs **Trained** Musley Bank, N Yorks

**FOCUS**
The winner of this interesting juvenile sprint traditionally heads to Royal Ascot, where the 2011 winner triumphed (clocked 58.02s in this race), while two others were placed. They went very quick from the stalls, and the juvenile course record, which had stood since 1994, was broken. The first two came clear and this form can be rated as fairly decent. The runner-up's debut effort could be rated this high.

## 3334 EDINBURGH GIN'S FILLIES' STKS (REGISTERED AS THE MAGGIE DICKSON STAKES) (LISTED RACE) 7f 33y
**2:50** (2:51) (Class 1) 3-Y-0+
**£22,684** (£8,600; £4,304; £2,144; £1,076; £540) **Stalls** Low

Form RPR

3-26 1 **Unforgetable Filly**[27] 2434 3-8-4 105 JosephineGordon 5 106+
(Hugo Palmer) *midfield: pushed along 3f out: swtchd lft to outer 2f out: sn rdn and hdwy: led ins fnl f: edgd rt: kpt on wl* **5/2[2]**

52-3 2 1 ¾ **Pirouette**[21] 2616 4-9-0 105 CharlieBennett 9 105
(Hughie Morrison) *prom: rdn to ld over 1f out: hdd ins fnl f: kpt on but no ch w wnr* **9/4[1]**

2-00 3 nse **Glitter Girl**[21] 2623 3-8-4 98 LukeMorris 7 101
(William Haggas) *trckd ldrs: rdn over 2f out: kpt on ins fnl f* **11/2**

3511 4 hd **Hells Babe**[15] 2805 4-9-0 87 AlistairRawlinson 10 104
(Michael Appleby) *led: rdn over 2f out: hdd over 1f out: kpt on* **14/1**

0614 5 1 ½ **Realtra (IRE)**[21] 2616 5-9-3 105 (b) JackMitchell 2 103
(Roger Varian) *trckd ldr: keen early: rdn 2f out: no ex fnl 75yds* **3/1[3]**

0036 6 7 **Summer Icon**[21] 2616 4-9-0 95 GrahamLee 4 81
(Mick Channon) *s.i.s: hld up: nvr threatened* **25/1**

130- 7 2 ¾ **Excellent Sounds**[217] 7687 4-9-0 77 JoeFanning 3 74
(Hughie Morrison) *hld up: n.m.r on inner 3f out: rdn over 2f out: sn wknd* **66/1**

10- 8 2 **Conselice**[272] 4-9-0 105 PJMcDonald 6 69
(K R Burke) *hld up in midfield: rdn over 2f out: wknd over 1f out* **40/1**

1m 26.93s (-2.07) **Going Correction** -0.025s/f (Good)
**WFA** 3 from 4yo+ 10lb **8** Ran SP% **114.2**
Speed ratings (Par 108): **110,108,107,107,106 98,94,92**
CSF £8.44 TOTE £3.10: £1.20, £1.40, £1.80; EX 9.40 Trifecta £29.70.
**Owner** Dr Ali Ridha **Bred** Rabbah Bloodstock Limited **Trained** Newmarket, Suffolk

**FOCUS**
A decent Listed event for fillies, but a lack of an early gallop produced a bunched finish from the first five home, who finished clear of the rest.

## 3335 EDINBURGH GIN'S EDINBURGH CUP H'CAP 1m 5f 216y
**3:25** (3:26) (Class 2) 3-Y-0
**£49,800** (£14,912; £7,456; £3,728; £1,864; £936) **Stalls** Low

Form RPR

21-3 1 **Time To Study (FR)**[14] 2824 3-9-7 **89** JoeFanning 10 96+
(Mark Johnston) *trckd ldr: led 4f out: pushed along and strly pressed over 2f out: rdn ent fnl f: hld on gamely* **15/8[1]**

5411 2 hd **Alabaster**[32] 2264 3-8-13 **81** (p[1]) LukeMorris 6 87+
(Sir Mark Prescott Bt) *led for 4f: trckd ldr: rdn to chal strly over 2f out: edgd lft ent fnl f: styd on but a jst hld* **4/1[3]**

26-1 3 ¾ **Euro Nightmare (IRE)**[29] 2376 3-9-0 **82** GrahamLee 2 87
(Keith Dalgleish) *midfield: pushed along and hdwy to chse ldrs over 2f out: rdn over 1f out: styd on* **13/2**

1-20 4 hd **Mister Manduro (FR)**[27] 2437 3-9-6 **88** PJMcDonald 3 93
(Mark Johnston) *midfield on inner: rdn over 3f out: styd on fr over 1f out* **7/2[2]**

-312 5 2 ¼ **Look My Way**[32] 2264 3-8-5 **73** JimmyQuinn 5 75
(Andrew Balding) *in tch: rdn to chse ldrs over 2f out: no ex fnl f* **11/1**

3431 6 ½ **Cray (IRE)**[19] 2686 3-8-6 **74** (p[1]) JosephineGordon 8 75+
(James Bethell) *trckd ldr: led 10f out: hung lft on bnd over 4f out and sn hdd: rdn over 3f out: no ex fnl f* **18/1**

663 7 ¾ **Albert's Back**[26] 2467 3-8-2 **73** NathanEvans(3) 4 73
(Michael Easterby) *hld up in midfield: rdn over 2f out: one pce nvr threatened* **25/1**

-120 **8** *2 ¾* **The Blues Master (IRE)**[24] 2526 3-8-8 **76**.................. RoystonFfrench 9 72
(Mark Johnston) *hld up: rdn over 3f out: nvr threatened* **40/1**

5-10 **9** *2* **Taxmeifyoucan (IRE)**[15] 2807 3-8-6 **74**.......................(p) PaulHanagan 7 67
(Keith Dalgleish) *a rr: hung rt u.p over 2f out* **18/1**

3m 2.57s (-2.73) **Going Correction** -0.025s/f (Good) **9** Ran SP% **115.5**
Speed ratings (Par 105): **106,105,105,105,104 103,103,101,100**
CSF £9.40 CT £39.60 TOTE £2.60: £1.20, £1.60, £2.00; EX 9.40 Trifecta £25.40.
**Owner** Abdulla Al Mansoori **Bred** E A R L Haras Du Quesnay **Trained** Middleham Moor, N Yorks

**FOCUS**
A competitive renewal of the Edinburgh Cup, but not the strongest, with the top weight rated 89 for this 3yo handicap. They didn't go fast and there was a sprint from the home bend, producing a bunched finish. The right horses were involved at the line, however, and the form looks okay.

## 3336 IAN MACLEOD DISTILLERS H'CAP 1m 2y
**4:00** (4:00) (Class 3) (0-90,90) 3-Y-O **£12,938** (£3,850; £1,924; £962) **Stalls** Low

Form RPR

-315 **1** **Thomas Cranmer (USA)**[8] 3045 3-9-5 **88**......................... JoeFanning 1 93
(Mark Johnston) *mde all: rdn over 1f out: kpt on wl* **9/2**[3]

303 **2** *1 ½* **The Eagle's Nest (IRE)**[23] 2547 3-8-3 **72**........................ ShaneGray 2 74
(Richard Fahey) *trckd ldr: rdn 2f out: kpt on but a hld* **20/1**

16 **3** *¾* **Yamarhaba Malayeen (IRE)**[22] 2567 3-8-13 **82**.............. GrahamLee 4 82+
(Simon Crisford) *hld up in rr: racd keenly: stmbld sltly 7f out: pushed along and hdwy on outside over 2f out: rdn over 1f out: one pce ins fnl f* **6/4**[1]

-110 **4** *7* **Morning Suit (USA)**[11] 2922 3-9-7 **90**.............................. PJMcDonald 3 74
(Mark Johnston) *hld up: rdn over 2f out: wknd over 1f out* **10/1**

0-51 **5** *hd* **Desert Dream**[33] 2231 3-8-12 **81**..................................... LukeMorris 6 65
(Sir Michael Stoute) *hld up: rdn over 3f out: sn btn* **2/1**[2]

-420 **6** *3 ¾* **Lord Commander**[15] 2807 3-8-8 **77**................................. PaulHanagan 5 52
(Richard Fahey) *trckd ldr: rdn over 2f out: wknd over 1f out* **12/1**

1m 39.39s (-1.81) **Going Correction** -0.025s/f (Good) **6** Ran SP% **113.1**
Speed ratings (Par 103): **108,106,105,98,98 94**
CSF £74.81 TOTE £6.20: £2.20, £7.70; EX 83.90 Trifecta £315.80.
**Owner** Sheikh Hamdan bin Mohammed Al Maktoum **Bred** Darley **Trained** Middleham Moor, N Yorks

**FOCUS**
An average 3yo handicap in which they once again didn't go fast, allowing the winner to nick it. The first two in the market were well supported but may not have been suited by the run of the race. They finished in two groups of three, with the former coming clear.

## 3337 EDINBURGH GIN DISTILLERY H'CAP 5f 1y
**4:55** (4:55) (Class 4) (0-85,87) 4-Y-O+ **£6,469** (£1,925; £962; £481) **Stalls** High

Form RPR

0-11 **1** **Longroom**[26] 2453 5-8-3 **70**.................................................. PhilDennis(5) 7 84+
(Noel Wilson) *trckd ldrs: squeezed through gap appr fnl f: led ins fnl f: pushed clr: readily* **5/2**[1]

0-20 **2** *2 ½* **Midnight Malibu (IRE)**[12] 2899 4-9-4 **83**............ RachelRichardson(3) 4 88
(Tim Easterby) *prom: rdn 2f out: led appr fnl f: hdd ins fnl f: kpt on but no ch wnr* **11/1**

0111 **3** *1 ½* **Royal Brave (IRE)**[10] 2951 6-9-6 **82**.............................. DougieCostello 5 82
(Rebecca Bastiman) *dwlt: hld up: sme hdwy over 1f out: rdn and kpt on ins fnl f: wnt 3rd towards fin* **13/2**

-063 **4** *nk* **Landing Night (IRE)**[19] 2683 5-9-0 **76**.........................(tp) PJMcDonald 3 75
(Rebecca Menzies) *chsd ldrs: rdn 2f out: kpt on same pce: lost 3rd nr fin* **14/1**

-060 **5** *½* **Showdaisy**[113] 664 4-9-11 **87**........................................(p) PaulHanagan 9 84
(Keith Dalgleish) *dwlt: hld up: sme hdwy whn short of room ent fnl f: kpt on pushed out ins fnl f but too much to do* **8/1**

0-64 **6** *1 ¾* **Lexington Place**[12] 2899 7-9-6 **82**................................ JackGarritty 2 72
(Ruth Carr) *s.i.s: hld up in rr: pushed along over 1f out: keeping on whn hmpd ins fnl f: nt rcvr* **9/2**[2]

-440 **7** *1 ¾* **Desert Ace (IRE)**[4] 3183 6-8-10 **77**..............................(b) CliffordLee(5) 1 61
(Iain Jardine) *sn led: racd towards centre and wd of main field: rdn 1/2-way: hdd appr fnl f: wknd ins fnl f* **13/2**

0621 **8** *2 ¼* **Bosham**[23] 2551 7-9-0 **79**...........................................(bt) NathanEvans(3) 6 55
(Michael Easterby) *w ldr: rdn 1/2-way: lost pl whn bit short of room 1f out: eased* **5/1**[3]

57.54s (-2.86) **Going Correction** -0.50s/f (Hard) **8** Ran SP% **116.2**
Speed ratings (Par 105): **102,98,95,95,94 91,88,85**
CSF £32.19 CT £162.01 TOTE £3.00: £1.30, £3.30, £1.90; EX 32.20 Trifecta £208.20.
**Owner** Marwood Racing Limited **Bred** Juddmonte Farms Ltd **Trained** Marwood, Co Durham
■ Stewards' Enquiry : Dougie Costello caution: careless riding

**FOCUS**
A competitive sprint handicap featuring several last-time-out winners. The winner impressed and recorded a time only 0.44s outside the course record.

## 3338 EDINBURGH GIN'S RHUBARB AND GINGER APPRENTICE H'CAP 1m 5f 216y
**5:30** (5:30) (Class 5) (0-70,76) 4-Y-O+ **£3,234** (£962; £481; £240) **Stalls** Low

Form RPR

-313 **1** **Mr Globetrotter (USA)**[37] 1834 4-9-8 **69**....................... CliffordLee(3) 3 74
(Iain Jardine) *trckd ldr in 2nd: rdn over 2f out: led narrowly appr fnl f: hdd ins fnl f: rallied u.p to ld again towards fin* **7/4**[2]

005- **2** *nk* **Schmooze (IRE)**[360] 3018 8-8-1 **52**..................... LeanneFerguson(7) 2 56
(Linda Perratt) *hld up in tch: hdwy 2f out: led narrowly ins fnl f: kpt on pushed out: hdd towards fin* **20/1**

-213 **3** *½* **Jonny Delta**[3] 3193 10-8-5 **56**.......................................... SeanMooney(7) 1 59
(Jim Goldie) *led: rdn 2f out: hdd appr fnl f: kpt on same pce* **6/5**[1]

5051 **4** *6* **Lady Clitico (IRE)**[23] 2549 6-9-9 **67**.............................(p) NathanEvans 4 61
(Rebecca Menzies) *in tch in 3rd: pushed along over 3f out: rdn over 2f out: wknd over 1f out* **7/2**[3]

3m 4.02s (-1.28) **Going Correction** -0.025s/f (Good) **4** Ran SP% **108.8**
Speed ratings (Par 103): **102,101,101,98**
CSF £21.74 TOTE £2.90; EX 16.20 Trifecta £46.40.
**Owner** New Approach Racing Limited **Bred** Jane Schosberg **Trained** Carruthertown, D'fries & G'way
■ Stewards' Enquiry : Sean Mooney four-day ban (17-19 & 25 Jun): used whip above permitted level
Clifford Lee two-day ban (17-18 Jun): used whip above permitted level

**FOCUS**
A tight little handicap, but thee of them were in a line a furlong out. They didn't appear to go that fast, and the time was 1.45s slower than the Edinburgh Cup earlier on the card.
T/Plt: £34.50 to a £1 stake. Pool: £53,643.93 - 1133.52 winning units. T/Qpdt: £19.20 to a £1 stake. Pool: £3148.96 - 121.20 winning units. **Andrew Sheret**

# 3252 NEWCASTLE (A.W) (L-H)
Saturday, June 3

**OFFICIAL GOING: Tapeta: standard**
Wind: Fresh, half against Weather: Sunny, warm

## 3339 GRAHAM WYLIE FOUNDATION EBF NOVICE STKS 6f (Tp)
**6:10** (6:11) (Class 5) 2-Y-O **£2,937** (£2,937; £673; £336) **Stalls** Centre

Form RPR

34 **1** **Benadalid**[12] 2896 2-9-2 0.............................................. RoystonFfrench 7 71
(Chris Fairhurst) *trckd ldrs: rdn over 2f out: rallied over 1f out: kpt on wl fnl f to dead-heat on line* **7/1**[3]

1 **1** *dht* **Guzman (IRE)**[28] 2403 2-9-6 0..................................... TonyHamilton 1 75
(Richard Fahey) *trckd ldrs: effrt and rdn over 1f out: led ins fnl f: kpt on u.p: jnd on line* **3/1**[2]

2 **3** *1 ½* **Bustam (IRE)**[10] 2948 2-9-2 0...........................................(h) PhillipMakin 8 67
(John Quinn) *t.k.h early: led: rdn over 1f out: hdd ins fnl f: kpt on same pce* **8/15**[1]

00 **4** *1* **Sam James (IRE)**[10] 2948 2-9-2 0.................................... DavidNolan 6 64
(Iain Jardine) *in tch: drvn along and outpcd over 2f out: rallied over 1f out: sn no imp* **33/1**

5 **5** *1 ½* **Plundered (IRE)**[35] 2148 2-9-2 0........................................ BenCurtis 4 59
(David Brown) *disp ld to over 1f out: rdn and wknd fnl f* **14/1**

**6** *7* **Brough Lane Lass (IRE)** 2-8-11 0............................. ConnorBeasley 5 33
(John Weymes) *bhd and sn pushed along: struggling 1/2-way: sn wknd* **66/1**

**7** *1* **Hello My Sunshine** 2-9-2 0............................................ BarryMcHugh 3 35
(Karen McLintock) *s.i.s: rn green in rr: struggling 1/2-way: kpt on fnl f: nvr able to chal* **25/1**

**8** *18* **Cuillin Hills** 2-9-2 0........................................................ AndrewMullen 2
(Keith Dalgleish) *s.i.s: rn green in rr: no ch fr 1/2-way* **25/1**

1m 15.52s (3.02) **Going Correction** +0.275s/f (Slow) **8** Ran SP% **121.5**
Speed ratings (Par 93): **90,90,88,86,84 75,74,50**
WIN: B £5.10, G £2.20; PL: B £1.90, Bus £1.02, G £1.20; EX: B/G £12.60, G/B £19.00; CSF: B/G £12.15, G/B £14.60; TF: B/G/Bus £17.20, G/B/Bus £27.60;.
**Owner** Merchants and Missionaries **Bred** Casablanca Jewel Partnership **Trained** Musley Bank, N Yorks
**Owner** Mrs Shirley France **Bred** P Balding **Trained** Middleham, N Yorks

**FOCUS**
Stalls: Straight races - centre. Races 3, 4 & 5 - far side. Race 2 - inside. A thrilling opener which saw the main protagonists flash past the winning line as one. The form looks fair. Benadalid has been rated as repeating his debut form.

## 3340 NORTHSEALOGISTICS.CO.UK H'CAP 2m 56y (Tp)
**6:40** (6:42) (Class 6) (0-65,64) 4-Y-O+ **£3,234** (£962; £481; £240) **Stalls** Low

Form RPR

4046 **1** **Whitecliff Park (IRE)**[4] 3192 4-8-10 **58**..................(p) BenRobinson(7) 14 68+
(Brian Ellison) *s.i.s: sn pushed into midfield: hdwy on wd outside to ld over 2f out: rdn and clr whn veered both ways fr over 1f out: kpt on wl* **11/2**[3]

0/54 **2** *4 ½* **Nachi Falls**[35] 2164 4-9-9 **64**..............................................(t) LukeMorris 8 69
(Nigel Hawke) *hld up midfield: stdy hdwy over 4f out: effrt and ev ch briefly over 2f out: drvn and hung lft over 1f out: nt pce of wnr* **3/1**[1]

6-00 **3** *5* **Stanarley Pic**[32] 2270 6-9-6 **60**........................................... NeilFarley 10 59
(Sally Haynes) *hld up: hdwy on outside 3f out: rdn 2f out: outpcd by first two fr over 1f out* **22/1**

6435 **4** *3 ½* **Jan Smuts (IRE)**[12] 2889 9-8-13 **56**.........................(tp) SammyJoBell(3) 9 50
(Wilf Storey) *hld up: pushed along 3f out: hdwy over 1f out: kpt on: nvr able to chal* **9/1**

242- **5** *1 ½* **Cape Hideaway**[11] 7592 5-9-8 **62**....................................(p) DavidNolan 4 55
(Mark Walford) *trckd ldrs: effrt and ev ch briefly over 2f out: wknd over 1f out* **10/3**[2]

560 **6** *2* **Absolute Angel**[47] 1830 6-9-1 **55**........................................... BenCurtis 1 45
(Peter Niven) *in tch: effrt and rdn 3f out: wknd over 1f out* **14/1**

516- **7** *1 ¼* **Byronegetonefree**[37] 6920 6-8-12 **52**................................ GrahamLee 7 41
(Stuart Coltherd) *chsd ldng pair: wnt 2nd over 5f out: led over 3f out to over 2f out: rdn and wknd over 1f out* **12/1**

3523 **8** *¾* **Ted's Brother (IRE)**[51] 1754 9-8-9 **49** ow1..............(h) StevieDonohoe 13 37
(Laura Morgan) *hld up: rdn along 3f out: sn no imp: btn over 1f out* **11/1**

0450 **9** *16* **Psychology**[47] 1834 4-8-11 **52**........................................ AndrewMullen 12 21
(Kenny Johnson) *missed break: hld up: stdy hdwy 3f out: rdn and wknd 2f out* **16/1**

205- **10** *17* **Nashville (IRE)**[331] 4045 8-9-3 **57**................................... TonyHamilton 6 5
(Andrew Crook) *hld up on ins: drvn along over 3f out: wknd over 2f out* **40/1**

10-0 **11** *¾* **Kazoey**[35] 2162 4-7-13 **47**.................................................... PaulaMuir(7) 2
(Chris Fairhurst) *led to over 3f out: rdn and wknd qckly over 2f out* **40/1**

-520 **12** *5* **Madam Lilibet (IRE)**[18] 2712 8-9-4 **58**............................... PaddyAspell 3
(Sharon Watt) *hld up in tch: drvn and lost pl after 4f: rdn and struggling fr 4f out* **33/1**

05-0 **13** *78* **Omid**[12] 2889 9-8-8 **48**.......................................................(tp) BarryMcHugh 5
(Kenneth Slack) *chsd ldr to over 5f out: rdn and wknd qckly over 3f out: t.o* **20/1**

3m 38.5s (3.30) **Going Correction** +0.275s/f (Slow) **13** Ran SP% **119.0**
Speed ratings (Par 101): **102,99,97,95,94 93,93,92,84,76 75,73,34**
CSF £20.79 CT £338.75 TOTE £7.80: £2.80, £1.50, £7.50; EX 33.70 Trifecta £423.80.
**Owner** D Gilbert, M Lawrence, A Bruce **Bred** Rosetown Bloodstock Ltd **Trained** Norton, N Yorks

**FOCUS**
A fair staying handicap which saw two potentially well-handicapped horses fight out the finish. The winner has been rated back to his best.

## 3341 BRITISH MASTERS AT CLOSE HOUSE FILLIES' H'CAP 1m 4f 98y (Tp)
**7:10** (7:12) (Class 4) (0-85,82) 3-Y-O+ **£7,762** (£2,310; £1,154; £577) **Stalls** High

Form RPR

/6-2 **1** **Stoney Broke**[17] 2728 4-9-5 **73**........................................ DanielMuscutt 4 87
(James Fanshawe) *hld up in tch: smooth hdwy to press ldr over 2f out: rdn to ld appr fnl f: kpt on wl* **11/2**[2]

14-1 **2** *1 ½* **Kullu (IRE)**[22] 2575 4-9-13 **81**..............................(h) StevieDonohoe 9 93
(Charlie Fellowes) *t.k.h: prom on outside: smooth hdwy to ld over 2f out: rdn and hdd appr fnl f: kpt on same pce last 100yds* **1/1**[1]

205- **3** *10* **Wor Lass**[253] 6740 9-9-9 **82**...................................... GarryWhillans(5) 6 78
(Donald Whillans) *hld up on outside: hdwy on outside over 2f out: rdn and edgd lft over 1f out: tk modest 3rd wl ins fnl f: no imp* **50/1**

-316 **4** ½ **Vogueatti (USA)**14 2817 4-9-6 **79** GeorgeWood(5) 8 74
(Marco Botti) *hld up: hdwy over 3f out: effrt and chsd clr ldng pair over 2f out to wl ins fnl f: one pce* **9/1**

43-0 **5** 2½ **Island Flame (IRE)**17 2741 4-9-4 **75** AdamMcNamara(3) 5 66
(Richard Fahey) *dwlt: hld up: rdn along and effrt over 2f out: wknd over 1f out* **10/1**

1-5 **6** 4½ **Di Alta (IRE)**11 2929 3-8-8 **77** LukeMorris 2 61
(Ed Walker) *trckd ldrs: rdn and outpcd 2f out: sn wknd* **8/1**3

0-50 **7** ½ **Age Of Elegance (IRE)**10 2953 5-9-7 **75** (p) TonyHamilton 7 58
(Roger Fell) *pressed ldr to over 2f out: sn rdn and wknd* **16/1**

5234 **8** 8 **Star Of Lombardy (IRE)**8 3046 4-9-7 **75** JoeFanning 3 45
(Mark Johnston) *led: rdn and hdd over 2f out: sn wknd: eased whn no ch over 1f out* **16/1**

/ **9** 26 **Catchy Lass (IRE)**57 1616 8-9-3 **76** (t) ConorMcGovern(5) 1 5
(Anthony Mulholland, Ire) *dwlt: hld up on ins: drvn and outpcd 3f out: btn fnl 2f* **16/1**

2m 41.75s (0.65) **Going Correction** +0.275s/f (Slow)
**WFA** 3 from 4yo+ 15lb 9 Ran SP% **115.2**
Speed ratings (Par 102): **108,107,100,100,98 95,95,89,72**
CSF £11.30 CT £248.25 TOTE £6.40: £1.40, £1.30, £5.50; EX 17.80 Trifecta £1045.40.
**Owner** Merry Fox Stud Limited **Bred** Merry Fox Stud Limited **Trained** Newmarket, Suffolk

**FOCUS**
A decent handicap in which the front two pulled a long way clear, so the form looks reliable. It's been rated on the positive side.

## 3342 PARKDEAN RESORTS 73 AWARD-WINNING HOLIDAY PARKS MAIDEN STKS 1m 2f 42y (Tp)
**7:40** (7:41) (Class 5) 3-Y-0+ **£4,528** (£1,347; £673; £336) **Stalls** High

Form RPR

6-0 **1** **Lady Bergamot (FR)**19 2689 3-8-4 0 GeorgeWood(5) 8 78
(James Fanshawe) *trckd ldrs: led gng wl 3f out: rdn and edgd lft wl over 1f out: kpt on wl fnl f* **8/1**3

6 **2** 1½ **Abjar**32 2260 3-9-0 0 PhillipMakin 9 80
(Sir Michael Stoute) *in tch: drvn and outpcd over 2f out: rallied over 1f out: kpt on fnl f to take 2nd nr fin: nt pce of wnr* **8/13**1

0 **3** nk **Light Of Joy (USA)**31 2311 3-8-9 0 StevieDonohoe 11 74
(David Lanigan) *in tch: smooth hdwy to press wnr over 2f out: rdn and ev ch over 1f out: kpt on same pce ins fnl f: lost 2nd cl home* **9/2**2

6 **4** 3¾ **Vindicator (IRE)**35 2159 3-9-0 0 ConnorBeasley 4 72
(Michael Dods) *hld up midfield: stdy hdwy over 2f out: effrt and rdn wl over 1f out: one pce fnl f* **66/1**

0 **5** hd **Sparte Quercus (IRE)**19 2689 4-9-13 0 GrahamLee 10 73
(Ed Dunlop) *midfield: stdy hdwy over 2f out: drvn over 1f out: outpcd fnl f* **25/1**

**6** ¾ **Cape Coast** 3-9-0 0 JoeFanning 5 73+
(Mark Johnston) *colty in preliminaries: led 2f: cl up: effrt whn nt clr run over 2f out: sn outpcd: one pce fr over 1f out* **8/1**3

**7** 6 **Captor** 3-9-0 0 DougieCostello 2 58+
(David Simcock) *dwlt: hld up: stdy hdwy on outside over 2f out: sn rdn: wknd over 1f out* **14/1**

60 **8** 12 **Toronto Sound**9 2997 3-9-0 0 LukeMorris 12 34
(Sir Mark Prescott Bt) *s.i.s: hld up: rdn and outpcd over 4f out: struggling fr over 2f out* **33/1**

550- **9** 2¼ **Python**263 6452 5-9-13 28 NeilFarley 6 31
(Andrew Crook) *hld up on ins: drvn along over 3f out: wknd fnl 2f* **200/1**

4364 **10** nk **Lord Rob**11 2919 6-9-8 46 (b1) CallumRodriguez(5) 13 30
(David Thompson) *dwlt: hdwy on outside to ld after 2f: rdn and hdd 3f out: wknd 2f out* **40/1**

00- **11** 12 **Saint Cuthberts**232 7329 3-9-0 0 BenCurtis 3
(David Brown) *in tch on ins: drvn and outpcd over 4f out: sn wknd* **150/1**

0- **12** 10 **Canizay (IRE)**278 5952 3-9-0 0 TonyHamilton 1
(Roger Fell) *t.k.h: hld up: struggling over 3f out: sn wknd* **100/1**

2m 11.73s (1.33) **Going Correction** +0.275s/f (Slow)
**WFA** 3 from 4yo+ 13lb 12 Ran SP% **121.9**
Speed ratings (Par 103): **105,103,103,100,100 99,95,85,83,83 73,65**
CSF £13.50 TOTE £10.50: £2.90, £1.10, £2.10; EX 19.10 Trifecta £60.50.
**Owner** Andrew & Julia Turner **Bred** Sarl Elevage Du Haras De Bourgeauville **Trained** Newmarket, Suffolk

**FOCUS**
A fair maiden won by a nice prospect who can go on to better things.

## 3343 HERES TO THE WILD SPIRITS POETICLICENSEDISTILLERY.CO.UK H'CAP 1m 2f 42y (Tp)
**8:10** (8:14) (Class 6) (0-65,65) 4-Y-0+ **£3,234** (£962; £481; £240) **Stalls** High

Form RPR

0002 **1** **Archipeligo**2 3242 6-9-6 **59** (p) DavidNolan 13 74
(Iain Jardine) *hld up: smooth hdwy over 2f out: plld to outside and led on bit over 1f out: shkn up and sn qcknd clr: v readily* **2/1**1

00-0 **2** 7 **Diamond Runner (IRE)**19 2687 5-8-12 **51** (b) JoeFanning 10 53
(Lawrence Mullaney) *hld up: smooth hdwy on outside to ld over 2f out: hdd and rdn over 1f out: kpt on fnl f: no ch w ready wnr* **14/1**

0-43 **3** 1¼ **Hussar Ballad (USA)**45 1891 8-9-12 **65** CamHardie 4 65
(Antony Brittain) *hld up: stdy hdwy whn n.m.r over 2f out: rdn and kpt on fnl f: nvr able to chal* **5/1**2

-400 **4** 2½ **Sehail (USA)**32 2282 4-9-4 **57** (v1) LukeMorris 12 53
(George Peckham) *trckd ldrs: rdn over 3f out: kpt on same pce fr 2f out* **20/1**

2135 **5** ½ **Kerry Icon**19 2687 4-8-8 **52** (h) CliffordLee(5) 8 47
(Iain Jardine) *prom: drvn along over 2f out: wknd fr over 1f out* **9/1**

2240 **6** ½ **Swanswaу**26 2466 4-9-5 **65** HarrisonShaw(7) 14 59
(Michael Easterby) *hld up: pushed along 3f out: hdwy over 1f out: sn no imp* **6/1**3

13-0 **7** 1½ **Calliope**54 1679 4-9-9 **62** GrahamLee 7 53
(Kenneth Slack) *in tch: hdwy and ev ch briefly 3f out: drvn and wknd over 1f out* **18/1**

4000 **8** 5 **Dan's Hopeforglory**19 2688 5-8-11 **50** AndrewMullen 11 32
(Peter Niven) *bhd: pushed along over 3f out: sme late hdwy: nvr on terms* **66/1**

-336 **9** 3½ **Percy Verence**5 3155 4-9-2 **55** RoystonFfrench 1 31
(Tracy Waggott) *t.k.h: cl up: n.m.r briefly 2f out: sn rdn and wknd* **11/1**

-050 **10** 4½ **Druid's Diamond**10 2955 4-8-12 **51** DougieCostello 6 19
(Mark Walford) *led to over 2f out: outpcd whn hmpd over 1f out: sn btn* **16/1**

5215 **11** 2¼ **Mr Sundowner (USA)**8 3043 5-9-1 **57** (t) SammyJoBell(3) 9 31+
(Wilf Storey) *dwlt: hld up: stdy hdwy and in tch over 2f out: outpcd whn bdly hmpd over 1f out: wknd* **8/1**

4/00 **12** hd **Sandgate**2 3252 5-8-10 **54** PhilDennis(5) 2 19
(Kenny Johnson) *t.k.h: in tch: rdn over 2f out: sn wknd* **100/1**

2m 12.24s (1.84) **Going Correction** +0.275s/f (Slow) 12 Ran SP% **118.8**
Speed ratings (Par 101): **103,97,96,94,94 93,92,88,85,82 80,80**
CSF £33.44 CT £128.78 TOTE £3.20: £2.00, £3.80, £1.90; EX 40.40 Trifecta £193.30.
**Owner** Mckenzie & Moore **Bred** Dachel Stud **Trained** Carrutherstown, D'fries & G'way

**FOCUS**
A modest handicap which produced an easy winner which will not have gone unnoticed by the handicapper.

## 3344 TECHNOLOGY SERVICES GROUP H'CAP 7f 14y (Tp)
**8:40** (8:41) (Class 5) (0-70,70) 4-Y-0+ **£4,528** (£1,347; £673; £336) **Stalls** Centre

Form RPR

2020 **1** **Barwah (USA)**19 2685 6-9-5 **68** AndrewMullen 6 75
(Peter Niven) *hld up in tch: rdn over 2f out: hdwy to ld appr fnl f: edgd lft: hld on wl cl home* **7/1**

2-60 **2** hd **Kirkham**19 2684 4-9-0 **63** (p1) JoeDoyle 1 69
(Julie Camacho) *cl up: ev ch over 2f out to over 1f out: rdn and kpt on fnl f: hld nr fin* **6/1**3

2-50 **3** nk **Wealth Tax**15 2785 4-9-7 **70** LukeMorris 10 75
(Ed Dunlop) *prom: drvn over 2f out: kpt on fnl f: hld cl home* **7/2**2

-324 **4** 2 **Lucky Lodge**36 2119 7-9-1 **64** (p) CamHardie 3 64
(Antony Brittain) *in tch: rdn over 2f out: effrt over 1f out: kpt on same pce ins fnl f* **8/1**

0602 **5** nk **Faintly (USA)**11 2919 6-8-12 **61** (b) JackGarritty 8 60+
(Ruth Carr) *t.k.h: hld up: smooth hdwy whn nt clr run over 1f out: swtchd lft: one pce fnl f* **2/1**1

4000 **6** 2 **Hernando Torres**31 2301 9-8-8 **64** (t) HarrisonShaw(7) 7 57
(Michael Easterby) *cl up: led over 2f out: rdn and hdd appr fnl f: sn outpcd* **16/1**

0012 **7** ½ **Chelwood Gate (IRE)**10 2968 7-9-7 **70** (v) JoeFanning 9 62
(Conor Dore) *dwlt: hld up: effrt and pushed along over 2f out: one pce fr over 1f out* **14/1**

00-2 **8** 7 **Destination Aim**34 2179 10-8-11 **60** GrahamLee 2 33
(Fred Watson) *led at ordinary gallop: rdn and hdd over 2f out: wknd over 1f out* **14/1**

-000 **9** shd **Cookie Ring (IRE)**9 3001 6-7-12 **54** (p) PaulaMuir(7) 5 27
(Patrick Holmes) *dwltf: hld up: stdy hdwy 1/2-way: rdn and wknd over 2f out* **50/1**

1m 29.43s (3.23) **Going Correction** +0.275s/f (Slow) 9 Ran SP% **114.6**
Speed ratings (Par 103): **92,91,91,89,88 86,85,77,77**
CSF £48.13 CT £172.61 TOTE £8.10: £2.10, £2.70, £1.60; EX 56.30 Trifecta £356.00.
**Owner** Keep The Faith Partnership **Bred** Shadwell Farm LLC **Trained** Barton-le-Street, N Yorks

**FOCUS**
An ordinary handicap which produced an exciting finish. It's been rated around the first two to their previous C&D form.

## 3345 NORTH SEA LOGISTICS H'CAP 5f (Tp)
**9:10** (9:11) (Class 6) (0-65,67) 3-Y-0+ **£3,234** (£962; £481; £240) **Stalls** Centre

Form RPR

2344 **1** **Horsforth**11 2925 5-9-9 **63** (b) CliffordLee(5) 5 70
(Richard Guest) *chsd ldr: led 2f out: rdn and edgd lft ins fnl f: kpt on wl* **6/4**1

5-00 **2** 1¼ **Oriental Splendour (IRE)**18 2700 5-10-4 **67** JackGarritty 7 70
(Ruth Carr) *hld up in tch: effrt and chsd wnr over 1f out: kpt on same pce ins fnl f* **9/1**

2050 **3** 2½ **Windforpower (IRE)**9 2990 7-9-11 **60** (p) BenCurtis 6 54
(Tracy Waggott) *trckd ldrs: effrt and drvn along 2f out: kpt on same pce appr fnl f* **5/1**3

4-66 **4** ½ **Wilde Extravagance (IRE)**28 2404 4-9-13 **62** JoeDoyle 1 54
(Julie Camacho) *prom: rdn over 2f out: kpt on same pce fnl f* **7/2**2

4-60 **5** ¾ **Hot Hannah**21 2630 3-9-6 **67** (b1) CallumRodriguez(5) 3 53
(Michael Dods) *led at decent gallop: edgd lft and hdd 2f out: outpcd fnl f* **9/1**

2500 **6** nk **Novabridge**21 2628 9-9-3 **57** (b) GemmaTutty(5) 4 45
(Karen Tutty) *fly j. s: bhd and pushed along: hdwy over 1f out: no imp fnl f* **14/1**

40-0 **7** 3½ **Lady Joanna Vassa (IRE)**52 1722 4-9-6 **55** ConnorBeasley 2 30
(Richard Guest) *t.k.h: in tch: rdn over 1f out: sn wknd* **14/1**

600- **8** ½ **Sunrise Dance**295 5368 8-8-5 **45** (t) PhilDennis(5) 8 19
(Kenny Johnson) *walked to post: dwlt: bhd and outpcd: struggling fr 1/2-way* **66/1**

1m 1.41s (1.91) **Going Correction** +0.275s/f (Slow)
**WFA** 3 from 4yo+ 7lb 8 Ran SP% **113.7**
Speed ratings (Par 101): **95,93,89,88,87 86,80,80**
CSF £16.15 CT £54.47 TOTE £2.50: £1.70, £2.20, £1.70; EX 16.30 Trifecta £62.00.
**Owner** Morecool Racing **Bred** Laundry Cottage Stud Farm **Trained** Ingmanthorpe, W Yorks

**FOCUS**
A moderate sprint handicap which produced a decisive winner. The winner has been rated as repeating her latest C&D form.
T/Plt: £15.10 to a £1 stake. Pool: £64,296 - 3106.41 winning units. T/Qpdt: £5.50 to a £1 stake. Pool: £5,075.86 - 672.66 winning units. **Richard Young**

3346 - 3352a (Foreign Racing) - See Raceform Interactive

# 2977 MAISONS-LAFFITTE (R-H)
Saturday, June 3

**OFFICIAL GOING: Turf: soft**

## 3353a PRIX DE CHEFFREVILLE (MAIDEN) (3YO FILLIES) (TURF) 1m 2f 110y
**1:40** 3-Y-0
**£12,051** (£4,871; £3,589; £2,307; £1,410; £897)

RPR

**1** **Style Icon (FR)** 3-8-11 0 AlexisBadel 2 70
(H-F Devin, France) **179/10**

**2** ½ **Lady Valdean**234 7286 3-9-2 0 MickaelBarzalona 11 74
(Jose Santos) *broke wl and led: 1l ld and lened whn drvn wl over 1 1/2f out: hdd ins fnl f: no ex* **29/1**

**3** ¾ **Miss Melbourne (FR)** 3-9-2 0 (p) TheoBachelot 13 73
(A De Watrigant, France) **106/10**

**4** ¾ **Scarlett Lady (FR)**28 3-9-2 0 AurelienLemaitre 8 71
(M Delzangles, France) **18/5**2

**5** 2 **Etatinka (FR)**168 3-9-2 0 OlivierPeslier 7 67
(J-M Beguigne, France) **36/5**

6 2 1/2 **Pachinko (USA)**[44] 3-9-2 0 VincentCheminaud 6 62
(A Fabre, France) **23/5**[3]
7 4 1/2 **Belfast (FR)**[12] 3-9-2 0 Pierre-CharlesBoudot 3 54
(F-H Graffard, France) **23/10**[1]
8 2 1/2 **Eyes Designer**[31] 3-8-6 0 MlleJuliaZambudioPerez(10) 10 45
(M Delcher Sanchez, France) **93/1**
9 7 **April Angel (FR)**[166] 3-8-10 0 MathieuPelletan(6) 1 35
(P Demercastel, France) **104/1**
10 shd **Star Quality**[61] 3-9-2 0 ChristopheSoumillon 12 35
(P Bary, France) **131/10**
11 3 **Elpy Bere (FR)** 3-9-2 0 GeraldMosse 5 29
(J-P Dubois, France) **55/1**
12 2 **Dalakania (IRE)**[94] 3-9-2 0 MaximeGuyon 4 25
(C Laffon-Parias, France) **186/10**
13 6 **Circumcanes (IRE)** 3-9-2 0 GregoryBenoist 9 13
(M Nigge, France) **41/1**

2m 15.41s (135.41) **13** Ran SP% **117.7**
PARI-MUTUEL (all including 1 euro stake): WIN 18.90 PLACE 5.40, 7.40, 3.90 DF 219.00 SF 387.80.
**Owner** Mme Henri Devin **Bred** Mme H Devin **Trained** France

## 3354a PRIX DU PALAIS-ROYAL (GROUP 3) (3YO+) (STRAIGHT) (TURF) 7f
**3:20** 3-Y-0+ **£34,188** (£13,675; £10,256; £6,837; £3,418)

RPR
1 **Inns Of Court (IRE)**[20] 2666 3-8-8 0 MickaelBarzalona 7 113+
(A Fabre, France) *w.w in fnl pair: hdwy ins fnl 2f: sustained run on outer to ld ins fnl f: drvn out* **8/5**[1]
2 1 1/4 **Attendu (FR)**[33] 2248 4-9-4 0 MaximeGuyon 8 113
(C Laffon-Parias, France) *w.w towards rr on outer: drvn to dispute ld wl over 1 1/2f out: hdd ins fnl f: styd on at same pce* **9/2**[2]
3 hd **Karar**[33] 2248 5-9-4 0 GregoryBenoist 1 112
(F-H Graffard, France) *trckd ldr: led briefly 2f out: sn drvn: hdd and lost pl wl over 1 1/2f out: styd on again last 150yds: jst missed 2nd* **13/2**
4 3/4 **Spectre (FR)**[33] 2248 4-9-1 0 Pierre-CharlesBoudot 3 107
(M Munch, Germany) *hld up in fnl pair: hdwy u.p 1 1/2f out: styd on ins fnl f: nvr on terms* **48/10**[3]
5 snk **Djiguite (FR)**[33] 2248 5-9-4 0 GeraldMosse 6 110
(D Smaga, France) *chsd ldrs: drvn 2 1/2f out: drvn to dispute ld wl over 1 1/2f out: sn hdd: one pce fnl f* **67/10**
6 3 **Blessed Silence (FR)**[27] 2449 4-9-1 0 OlivierPeslier 5 99
(J-M Beguigne, France) *dwlt: sn rcvrd to chse ldng trio under restraint: drvn and nt qckn wl over 1f out: wl hld fnl f* **121/10**
7 2 1/2 **For Ever (FR)**[20] 6-9-4 0 (b) AntoineCoutier 4 95
(Carina Fey, France) *led: hdd 2f out: grad dropped away wl over 1f out* **18/1**
8 10 **Walec**[43] 5-9-4 0 CristianDemuro 2 68
(P Sogorb, France) *dwlt: towards rr on inner: drvn and lost pl wl over 1 1/2f out: wl btn fnl f* **185/10**

1m 25.43s (-2.57) **8** Ran SP% **118.2**
**WFA** 3 from 4yo+ 10lb
PARI-MUTUEL (all including 1 euro stake): WIN 2.60 PLACE 1.40, 1.60, 1.80 DF 5.70 SF 10.40.
**Owner** Godolphin SNC **Bred** Darley **Trained** Chantilly, France

**FOCUS**
The standard is set around the second, third, sixth and seventh.

## 3355a PRIX SOLEIL (CLAIMER) (3YO) (TURF) 6f
**3:50** 3-Y-0 **£9,829** (£3,931; £2,948; £1,965; £982)

RPR
1 **Dark American (FR)**[24] 3-9-1 0 ChristopheSoumillon 3 83
(J-C Rouget, France) **17/5**[2]
2 1 3/4 **Larno (FR)**[23] 3-9-1 0 MaximeGuyon 5 77
(C Escuder, France) **6/4**[1]
3 3/4 **Nuee Ardente (FR)**[24] 3-8-11 0 StephanePasquier 7 71
(K Borgel, France) **9/2**[3]
4 2 **If I Say So**[5] 3-8-11 0 (p) EddyHardouin 2 64
(M Boutin, France) **102/10**
5 snk **Lord Cooper**[22] 2579 3-9-13 0 (p) MickaelBarzalona 4 80
(Jose Santos) *chsd ldrs: cl 4th 1/2-way: rdn and nt qckn over 1 1/2f out: lost pl and dropped to last appr fnl f: kpt on again last 150yds* **104/10**
6 snk **Glicourt (FR)**[5] 3-8-11 0 GeraldMosse 10 63
(M Boutin, France) **247/10**
7 1/2 **Soho Universe (FR)**[23] 3-9-1 0 (b) Pierre-CharlesBoudot 9 66
(H-A Pantall, France) **83/10**
8 snk **Stormy (FR)**[24] 2536 3-9-4 0 (b) AurelienLemaitre 8 68
(S Cerulis, France) **214/10**

1m 12.94s (-0.46) **8** Ran SP% **117.7**
PARI-MUTUEL (all including 1 euro stake): WIN 4.40 PLACE 1.50, 1.20, 1.40 DF 5.50 SF 12.60.
**Owner** Ecurie Antonio Caro **Bred** Chevotel De La Hauquerie **Trained** Pau, France

3356 - 3365a (Foreign Racing) - See Raceform Interactive

# 3117 CHANTILLY (R-H)
Sunday, June 4

**OFFICIAL GOING: Turf: good to soft; polytrack: standard**

## 3366a PRIX DE ROYAUMONT (GROUP 3) (3YO FILLIES) (TURF) 1m 4f
**1:20** 3-Y-0 **£34,188** (£13,675; £10,256; £6,837; £3,418)

RPR
1 **Kitesurf**[28] 2447 3-9-0 0 MickaelBarzalona 3 103
(A Fabre, France) *settled bhd ldrs: rowed along and clsd 2f out: led over 1 1/2f out: drvn and styd on fnl f: a holding runner-up* **13/2**[3]
2 1 1/4 **Bebe D'Amour (FR)**[22] 3-9-0 0 ChristopheSoumillon 4 101
(J-Y Artu, France) *w.w in midfield: drvn to cl wl over 1 1/2f out: chsd ldr fnl f: nvr on terms* **20/1**
3 1 3/4 **Lady Paname (FR)**[28] 2447 3-9-0 0 TonyPiccone 8 98
(E Lellouche, France) *settled in fnl pair: drvn 2 1/2f out: hdwy appr 1 1/2f out: 4th and styng on ent fnl f: nt pce to trble front two* **11/1**
4 2 **Layali (FR)**[36] 2168 3-9-0 0 GregoryBenoist 1 96
(F Rohaut, France) *chsd ldng pair: cl 5th and drvn over 1 1/2f out: grad outpcd by ldrs: one pce fnl f* **12/1**
5 1 3/4 **Satine (FR)**[16] 3-9-0 0 StephanePasquier 9 92
(N Clement, France) *w.w in rr: clsd on outer over 1 1/2f out: kpt on at same pce fnl f: nvr in contention* **20/1**
6 3/4 **Glittering Jewel (USA)**[23] 2564 3-9-0 0 WilliamBuick 6 91
(Charlie Appleby) *racd a little freely: trckd ldr on outer: pushed along 2 1/2f out: sn rdn and no imp: dropped away fnl 1 1/2f* **6/1**[2]
7 1 1/4 **Musawaah (USA)**[28] 2447 3-9-0 0 AurelienLemaitre 5 89
(F Head, France) *led under a tight hold: scrubbed along 2f out: hdd over 1 1/2f out: wknd appr fnl f* **8/13**[1]
8 15 **Bluesacha Rosetgri (FR)**[16] 3-9-0 0 SylvainRuis 7 65
(R Le Gal, France) *settled in midfield: outpcd and rdn ins fnl 2f: wl btn appr fnl f: eased* **40/1**
9 10 **Szolnok (USA)**[28] 2447 3-9-0 0 CristianDemuro 2 49
(S Cerulis, France) *a little outpcd early: sn towards rr of midfield on inner: rdn and no imp over 1 1/2f out: wknd over 1f out: eased* **50/1**

2m 29.62s (-1.38) **9** Ran SP% **119.5**
PARI-MUTUEL (all including 1 euro stake): WIN 4.10; PLACE 2.80, 3.80, 4.30; DF 23.40; SF 43.60.
**Owner** Godolphin SNC **Bred** Peter Winkworth **Trained** Chantilly, France

**FOCUS**
The standard is set around the third, fourth, sixth and eighth.

## 3367a PRIX DE SANDRINGHAM (GROUP 2) (3YO FILLIES) (TURF) 1m
**1:55** 3-Y-0 **£63,333** (£24,444; £11,666; £7,777; £3,888)

RPR
1 **La Sardane (FR)**[49] 1825 3-8-11 0 (p) FranckBlondel 3 108+
(B De Montzey, France) *trckd ldr under a tight grip: drvn to chal fr 1 1/2f out: led ent fnl f: rdn clr: a in control* **20/1**
2 1 **Gold Luck (FR)**[21] 2665 3-8-11 0 MaximeGuyon 4 106+
(F Head, France) *settled in 3rd: angled out and rowed along w 2f to run: styd on fnl f: nt pce to chal wnr* **7/2**[3]
3 nk **Senga (USA)**[22] 2644 3-8-11 0 StephanePasquier 2 105+
(P Bary, France) *hld up in rr: reminders 2f out: rdn and styd on appr fnl f: nvr able to get on terms* **9/4**[2]
4 3/4 **Speed As (FR)**[28] 2446 3-8-11 0 IoritzMendizabal 1 103
(F Chappet, France) *led single-file field: pushed along 1 1/2f out: hdd ent fnl f: kpt on at same pce* **10/1**
5 nk **Heuristique (IRE)**[22] 2644 3-8-11 0 Pierre-CharlesBoudot 5 103
(F-H Graffard, France) *w.w one fr last: drvn fr 1 1/2f out: kpt on fnl f: nt pce to get in contention* **6/5**[1]

1m 39.79s (1.79) **5** Ran SP% **112.3**
PARI-MUTUEL (all including 1 euro stake): WIN 23.80; PLACE 5.50, 2.50; SF 61.30.
**Owner** Team Valor International **Bred** Scea Plessis & J Guillemin **Trained** France

**FOCUS**
This was steadily run. The winner, second and fourth help with setting the level.

## 3368a QIPCO PRIX DU JOCKEY CLUB (GROUP 1) (3YO COLTS & FILLIES) (TURF) 1m 2f 110y
**3:15** 3-Y-0 **£732,564** (£293,076; £146,538; £73,205; £36,666)

RPR
1 **Brametot (IRE)**[21] 2666 3-9-2 0 CristianDemuro 1 117+
(J-C Rouget, France) *dwlt: slow to stride: w.w in rr: hdwy on outer over 1 1/2f out: 8th and rdn ent fnl f: r.o to ld fnl strides* **13/8**[1]
2 shd **Waldgeist**[27] 2483 3-9-2 0 Pierre-CharlesBoudot 5 116
(A Fabre, France) *racd in midfield between horses: rdn and hdwy appr fnl f: sustained run to ld 50yds out: hdd fnl strides* **9/1**
3 1 **Recoletos (FR)**[27] 2483 3-9-2 0 OlivierPeslier 12 114
(C Laffon-Parias, France) *dwlt: sn rcvrd to chse ldrs: rowed along to chal 1 1/2f out: led ent fnl f: hdd 50yds out: no ex* **4/1**[2]
4 1/2 **The Taj Mahal (IRE)**[35] 2191 3-9-2 0 (b) DonnachaO'Brien 2 113
(A P O'Brien, Ire) *led on inner: rdn and hdd appr 2f out: rallied u.p to regain ld 1 1/2f out: hdd ent fnl f: styd on gamely* **66/1**
5 1 **War Decree (USA)**[45] 1904 3-9-2 0 RyanMoore 8 111+
(A P O'Brien, Ire) *stdd leaving stalls to switch ins: settled towards rr: 2nd last and niggled along 2 1/2f out: angled out and began to cl 2f out: nt clr run over 1 1/2f out: rdn and styd on fnl f: nt pce to get on terms* **12/1**
6 nk **Orderofthegarter (IRE)**[21] 2666 3-9-2 0 (p) SeamieHeffernan 9 113+
(A P O'Brien, Ire) *w.w towards rr: drvn to cl on inner fr 2 1/2f out: chsd ldrs over 1f out: keeping on but hld whn sltly impeded 75yds out* **22/1**
7 shd **Bay Of Poets (IRE)**[23] 2569 3-9-2 0 WilliamBuick 3 110
(Charlie Appleby) *racd in midfield on inner: chsd ldrs on run to fnl f: kpt on at same pce u.p* **10/1**
8 1 3/4 **Rivet (IRE)**[21] 2666 3-9-2 0 FrankieDettori 4 107+
(William Haggas) *racd keenly: restrained bhd ldng pair: drvn to ld appr 2f out: hdd 1 1/2f out: rallied u.p: wknd fnl 100yds* **11/2**[3]
9 3/4 **Be My Sheriff (GER)**[32] 3-9-2 0 TheoBachelot 6 105
(M Rulec, Germany) *trckd ldr on outer: hrd rdn and nt qckn over 1 1/2f out: grad lft bhd fnl f* **40/1**
10 snk **D'bai (IRE)**[12] 2944 3-9-2 0 (p) JamesDoyle 7 105
(Charlie Appleby) *w.w in fnl pair: last and drvn 2f out: sme modest late prog: nvr in contention* **66/1**
11 1 1/4 **Soleil Marin (IRE)**[49] 1826 3-9-2 0 MickaelBarzalona 11 103
(A Fabre, France) *hld up towards rr on outer: short-lived effrt u.p 1 1/2f out: nvr involved* **11/1**
12 3 1/2 **Plumatic**[28] 2448 3-9-2 0 MaximeGuyon 10 96+
(A Fabre, France) *racd keenly: hld up in midfield on outer: rdn and btn wl over 1f out* **20/1**

2m 6.51s (-2.29) **12** Ran SP% **123.1**
PARI-MUTUEL (all including 1 euro stake): WIN 2.70; PLACE 1.40, 2.10, 1.80; DF 11.90; SF 15.40.
**Owner** Al Shaqab Racing & Gerard Augustin-Normand **Bred** H Cardemil **Trained** Pau, France

**FOCUS**
This looked a bang up to scratch renewal of the Prix du Jockey Club, and should be strong form for the coming weeks and months. The time was said to be good without being outstanding. The fourth and ninth limit the form.

## 3369a GRAND PRIX DE CHANTILLY (GROUP 2) (4YO+) (TURF) 1m 4f
**4:00** 4-Y-0+ **£63,333** (£24,444; £11,666; £7,777; £3,888)

RPR
1 **Silverwave (FR)**[34] 2249 5-9-4 0 Pierre-CharlesBoudot 5 114+
(P Bary, France) *w.w in rr: angled out and hdwy appr 1 1/2f out: chal ent fnl f: rdn to ld 75yds out* **5/6**[1]
2 nk **Talismanic**[27] 2485 4-9-0 0 MickaelBarzalona 1 109
(A Fabre, France) *led: hdd after 3f and trckd ldr: led over 2f out: styd on u.p: hdd 75yds out: no ex* **10/3**[2]
3 3/4 **Apilobar (FR)**[24] 2559 4-9-0 0 CristianDemuro 2 108
(F Vermeulen, France) *racd keenly: hld up bhd ldr: led after 3f: hdd over 2f out: rallied u.p 1 1/2f out: styd on same pce fnl f* **20/1**

4 ½ **Left Hand**[12] 2946 4-9-3 0 ........ MaximeGuyon 4 110
(C Laffon-Parias, France) *hld up bhd ldrs on outer: 3rd and drvn along 1 1/2f out: one pce fnl f* **11/2**[3]

5 1 ¼ **Doha Dream (FR)**[246] 6971 4-9-4 0 ........ GregoryBenoist 3 109
(A Fabre, France) *w.w bhd ldrs on inner: drvn and n.m.r wl over 1f out: nvr really in clr fnl f: nt given a hrd time late on* **6/1**

2m 29.45s (-1.55) 5 Ran SP% **112.1**
PARI-MUTUEL (all including 1 euro stake): WIN 2.00; PLACE 1.20, 1.50; SF 4.50.
**Owner** Hspirit **Bred** Mlle M-L Collet, J Collet & Mme M Collet **Trained** Chantilly, France

**FOCUS**
The third limits the form.

## 3370a PRIX DU GROS-CHENE (GROUP 2) (3YO+) (TURF) 5f
**4:40** 3-Y-O+ **£63,333** (£24,444; £11,666; £7,777; £3,888)

RPR

1 **Muthmir (IRE)**[29] 2397 7-9-3 0 ........(p) JimCrowley 3 113
(William Haggas) *w.w in last: hdwy over 1 1/2f out: rdn to ld 75yds out: r.o* **4/1**[2]

2 1 **Finsbury Square (IRE)**[22] 2643 5-9-3 0 ........(b) ChristopheSoumillon 4 109
(F Chappet, France) *w.w towards rr: gd hdwy 1 1/2f out: led ent fnl f: rdn and styd on: hdd 75yds out: no ex* **9/2**[3]

3 1 ¼ **Plusquemavie (IRE)**[14] 2867 6-9-3 0 ........(b) CristianDemuro 10 105
(V Fazio, Italy) *racd in midfield: styd on over 1f out: got up for 3rd cl home: nvr on terms w front two* **33/1**

4 shd **Largent Du Bonheur (FR)**[22] 2643 4-9-3 0 ......(b[1]) VincentCheminaud 7 104
(M Delzangles, France) *chsd ldr: led after 1/2-way: hdd ent fnl f: one pce* **20/1**

5 ½ **Son Cesio (FR)**[22] 2643 6-9-3 0 ........ Pierre-CharlesBoudot 9 102
(H-A Pantall, France) *racd keenly: hld up bhd ldrs: drvn and nt qckn over 1 1/2f out: kpt on ins fnl f: nt pce to get on terms* **5/1**

6 3 ½ **Aladdine**[24] 2561 3-8-7 0 ........ AurelienLemaitre 6 84
(F Head, France) *chsd ldrs: rdn and no imp 2f out: dropped away fnl f* **6/4**[1]

7 ½ **Willytheconqueror (IRE)**[21] 2657 4-9-3 0 ........ MartinDwyer 1 88
(William Muir) *chsd ldrs: pushed along 1/2-way: lost pl wl over 1f out: one pce fnl f* **18/1**

8 snk **Hit The Bid**[53] 1742 3-8-10 0 ........ LeighRoche 8 84
(D J Bunyan, Ire) *chsd ldrs: 2nd and ev ch wl over 1f out: wknd ins fnl f* **40/1**

9 1 ¾ **Daring Match (GER)**[34] 6-9-3 0 ........ AlexanderPietsch 11 81
(J Hirschberger, Germany) *led: hdd after 1/2-way: wknd wl over 1f out* **33/1**

10 1 ¼ **Love Spirit**[22] 2643 7-9-3 0 ........ MaximeGuyon 2 77
(Louis Baudron, France) *settled in fnl pair: drvn and no imp 1 1/2f out: bhd and eased fnl f* **22/1**

58.01s (-0.29)
**WFA** 3 from 4yo+ 7lb 10 Ran SP% **117.5**
PARI-MUTUEL (all including 1 euro stake): WIN 8.00; PLACE 2.30, 1.80, 4.80; DF 15.10; SF 27.80.
**Owner** Hamdan Al Maktoum **Bred** Sunderland Holdings Ltd **Trained** Newmarket, Suffolk

**FOCUS**
It's been rated around the balance of the first four.

# 2667 HOPPEGARTEN (R-H)
Sunday, June 4

**OFFICIAL GOING: Turf: soft**

## 3371a SOLDIER HOLLOW - DIANA-TRIAL (GROUP 2) (3YO FILLIES) (TURF) 1m 2f
**5:00** 3-Y-O **£34,188** (£13,247; £6,837; £3,418; £2,136)

RPR

1 **Tusked Wings (IRE)**[21] 3-9-2 0 ........ FilipMinarik 4 104
(Jean-Pierre Carvalho, Germany) *racd keenly: hld up in rr: drvn and clsd fr 2f out: rdn to chal ldr wl over 1f out: sustained run to ld fnl strides: all out* **89/10**

2 shd **Well Spoken (GER)**[224] 7563 3-9-2 0 ........ AdriedeVries 5 103
(Markus Klug, Germany) *led: drvn wl over 1 1/2f out: styd on u.p whn chal wl over 1f out: hdd fnl strides* **33/10**[3]

3 4 **Litaara (GER)** 3-9-2 0 ........ AndraschStarke 2 95
(P Schiergen, Germany) *hld up in fnl trio: prog to press ldrs bef 1/2-way: readily outpcd by ldrs over 1f out: one pce fnl f* **16/5**[2]

4 1 ½ **Shy Angel** 3-9-2 0 ........ EduardoPedroza 3 92
(A Wohler, Germany) *hld up in midfield: cl 4th and rdn 1 1/2f out: one pce fnl f* **21/10**[1]

5 3 ½ **Margie's Music (FR)** 3-9-2 0 ........ DanielePorcu 6 85
(P Schiergen, Germany) *racd in midfield: outpcd and rdn appr 1 1/2f out: sn btn* **33/1**

6 nse **Gondora (GER)**[49] 3-9-2 0 ........ BauyrzhanMurzabayev 8 85
(R Dzubasz, Germany) *sn racing in midfield: hrd rdn to chse ldrs 1 1/2f out: sn btn* **84/10**

7 6 **Pemina (GER)**[224] 7563 3-9-2 0 ........ StephenHellyn 1 73
(J Hirschberger, Germany) *racd v keenly: hld up in fnl trio: rdn and btn 2f out* **53/10**

8 10 **Walatah (GER)** 3-9-2 0 ........ MartinSeidl 7 53
(Markus Klug, Germany) *racd keenly: pressed ldr: rdn and nt qckn over 2f out: sn wknd* **89/10**

2m 10.5s (3.80) 8 Ran SP% **129.0**
PARI-MUTUEL (all including 10 euro stake): WIN 99 PLACE: 22, 15, 19; SF: 495.
**Owner** Stall Ullmann **Bred** Gestut Schlenderhan **Trained** Germany

3372 - 3382a (Foreign Racing) - See Raceform Interactive

# 3193 AYR (L-H)
Monday, June 5

**OFFICIAL GOING: Good (good to firm in places; 8.1)**
Wind: light against, making no material difference Weather: Overcast

## 3383 BET WITH PADDOCK BOOKMAKERS ON COURSE MAIDEN STKS 1m
**5:55** (5:57) (Class 5) 3-Y-O+ **£3,234** (£962; £481; £240) **Stalls** Low

Form RPR

2 1 **Born To Be Alive (IRE)**[21] 2681 3-8-12 0 ........ CliffordLee[(5)] 6 92
(K R Burke) *trckd ldrs: rdn to ld 2f out: edgd rt but sn clr: pushed out fnl f: easily* **1/2**[1]

-324 2 8 **Lamloom (IRE)**[15] 2857 3-9-3 78 ........ DanielTudhope 5 74
(David O'Meara) *prom: pushed along to ld over 2f out: hdd 2f out: one pce and sn no ch wnr* **2/1**[2]

0 3 1 ¾ **Drumochter**[124] 503 3-8-9 0 ........ CallumShepherd[(3)] 3 65
(Charles Hills) *trckd ldrs: rdn over 2f out: one pce* **9/1**[3]

00 4 1 ¼ **Donnachies Girl (IRE)**[14] 2887 4-9-4 0 ........ RowanScott[(5)] 7 65
(Alistair Whillans) *midfield: pushed along over 2f out: kpt on same pce* **66/1**

5 11 **Red Star Dancer (IRE)** 3-9-3 0 ........ ShaneGray 1 41
(Linda Perratt) *slowly away: a towards rr* **66/1**

6 11 **High Anxiety** 3-8-12 0 ........ ConnorBeasley 8 11
(John Weymes) *racd keenly: sn led: rdn whn hdd over 2f out: wknd* **33/1**

00- 7 14 **Brendan (IRE)**[401] 1849 4-10-0 0 ........(h[1]) SamJames 4
(Jim Goldie) *a rr* **100/1**

1m 41.08s (-2.72) **Going Correction** -0.25s/f (Firm)
**WFA** 3 from 4yo 11lb 7 Ran SP% **116.9**
Speed ratings (Par 103): **103,95,93,92,81 70,56**
CSF £1.85 TOTE £1.50: £1.10, £1.30; EX 2.00 Trifecta £3.80.
**Owner** Tim Dykes & Mrs E Burke **Bred** Barbara Prendergast **Trained** Middleham Moor, N Yorks

**FOCUS**
Races 2, 3 & 4 distances as advertised, races 1, 5 & 6 increased by 6yds and race 7 increased by 12yds. The going was officially described as good, good to firm in places. A maiden with little depth and the favourite won in good style. The fourth is perhaps the key to the form.

## 3384 BET WITH TATTERSALLS BOOKMAKERS ON COURSE FILLIES' H'CAP 6f
**6:25** (6:25) (Class 5) (0-75,71) 3-Y-O+ **£3,234** (£962; £481; £240) **Stalls** Centre

Form RPR

6-32 1 **Love Oasis**[4] 3239 3-9-2 **67** ........ PJMcDonald 3 72
(Mark Johnston) *dwlt: sn in tch: pushed along and bit outpcd 3f out: hdwy 2f out: led over 1f out: rdn and kpt on* **6/4**[1]

2 nk **Duchess Of France (IRE)**[16] 2850 4-9-7 **71** ........(t) DannySheehy[(7)] 5 77+
(Adrian Paul Keatley, Ire) *hld up in tch: briefly short of room over 2f out: pushed along and edgd rt over 1f out: swtchd lft ins fnl f: r.o wl* **4/1**[2]

-030 3 1 ¼ **Mininggold**[15] 2858 4-9-6 **68** ........(p) CallumRodriguez[(5)] 6 70
(Michael Dods) *chsd ldr: rdn and ev ch over 1f out: one pce ins fnl f* **11/1**

54-0 4 ¾ **Lotara**[152] 45 5-9-2 **59** ........ SamJames 1 59
(Jim Goldie) *hld up: rdn and outpcd 1/2-way: kpt on wl fnl f: nrst fin* **12/1**

0-00 5 shd **Harbour Lightning**[10] 3047 3-8-9 **60** ........ ShaneGray 8 57
(Noel Wilson) *in tch: rdn over 2f out: kpt on* **28/1**

-466 6 2 ½ **Reckless Serenade (IRE)**[4] 3239 3-8-13 **69** ........ RowanScott[(5)] 4 58
(Keith Dalgleish) *prom: rdn over 2f out: wknd over 1f out* **11/2**[3]

2060 7 2 ¼ **Sarabi**[6] 3170 4-9-1 **63** ........(p) PaddyPilley[(5)] 7 47
(Scott Dixon) *sn led: rdn whn hdd over 1f out: wknd fnl f* **16/1**

3235 8 6 **Bloomin Lovely (IRE)**[80] 1243 3-9-2 **67** ........ JasonHart 2 30
(John Quinn) *chsd ldrs: rdn over 2f out: wknd over 1f out* **8/1**

1m 14.06s (1.66) **Going Correction** +0.275s/f (Good)
**WFA** 3 from 4yo+ 8lb 8 Ran SP% **111.9**
Speed ratings (Par 100): **99,98,96,95,95 92,89,81**
CSF £7.02 CT £44.49 TOTE £2.20: £1.10, £1.90, £2.90; EX 8.20 Trifecta £32.40.
**Owner** Crone Stud Farms Ltd **Bred** New England, Mount Coote & P Barrett **Trained** Middleham Moor, N Yorks

**FOCUS**
A fair handicap but not the strongest for the level. The third has been rated close to her recent form.

## 3385 BET WITH RAILS BOOKMAKERS ON COURSE H'CAP 6f
**6:55** (6:55) (Class 6) (0-60,62) 3-Y-O+ **£2,587** (£770; £384; £192) **Stalls** Centre

Form RPR

2535 1 **Sea Of Green**[4] 3256 5-9-3 **51** ........(p) PJMcDonald 7 59
(Jim Goldie) *s.i.s: sn midfield: rdn and hdwy over 1f out: led 75yds out: kpt on wl* **4/1**[2]

0640 2 ¾ **Misu Moneypenny**[33] 2294 4-9-0 **53** ........(p) PaddyPilley[(5)] 4 59
(Scott Dixon) *w ldr: led 1/2-way: rdn 2f out: hdd 75yds out: one pce* **10/1**

5-03 3 2 ¼ **Bunce (IRE)**[4] 3238 9-9-9 **62** ........ LewisEdmunds[(5)] 3 61
(Linda Perratt) *hld up: rdn and hdwy over 1f out: kpt on ins fnl f* **7/1**

036- 4 1 ¾ **Mo Henry**[17] 2809 5-9-6 **61** ........(v) DannySheehy[(7)] 10 55
(Adrian Paul Keatley, Ire) *midfield: rdn and hdwy to chse ldr over 1f out: no ex ins fnl f* **7/2**[1]

0-46 5 ¾ **Insurplus (IRE)**[17] 2776 4-9-12 **60** ........(b[1]) SamJames 9 52
(Jim Goldie) *led narrowly: hdwy 1/2-way: rdn and edgd rt over 2f out: sn outpcd and btn* **7/2**[1]

-401 6 ¾ **Goninodaethat**[12] 2949 9-9-6 **61** ........ SeanMooney[(7)] 5 50
(Jim Goldie) *chsd ldrs: rdn over 2f out: wknd ins fnl f* **10/1**

0015 7 4 **Frangarry (IRE)**[6] 3186 5-9-9 **60** ........ CallumShepherd[(3)] 1 37
(Alan Bailey) *s.i.s: hld up: rdn over 2f out: nvr threatened* **13/2**[3]

056- 8 2 ¾ **Red Shadow**[495] 341 8-8-7 **46** oh1 ........(p) RowanScott[(5)] 8 15
(Alistair Whillans) *chsd ldrs: rdn 1/2-way: wknd over 1f out* **50/1**

-000 9 19 **Warleggan (FR)**[5] 3196 3-8-4 **46** oh1 ........ ShaneGray 6
(Linda Perratt) *a rr* **50/1**

00-0 10 2 **Piccolino**[33] 2311 3-7-12 **47** oh1 ow1 ........(p[1]) ConnorMurtagh[(7)] 2
(John David Riches) *midfield: rdn 1/2-way: wknd and bhd* **80/1**

1m 14.6s (2.20) **Going Correction** +0.275s/f (Good)
**WFA** 3 from 4yo+ 8lb 10 Ran SP% **113.6**
Speed ratings (Par 101): **96,95,92,89,88 87,82,78,53,50**
CSF £41.97 CT £269.46 TOTE £5.00: £1.60, £2.90, £2.10; EX 49.70 Trifecta £338.10.
**Owner** James Callow **Bred** Frank Brady **Trained** Uplawmoor, E Renfrews


The Form Book Flat, Raceform Ltd, Newbury, RG14 5SJ

**FOCUS**
A modest, open looking handicap and they went a good pace. The third has been rated back to the level of last autumn's form here.

## 3386 BET WITH BOOKMAKERS INSIDE BAR H'CAP 6f
**7:25** (7:25) (Class 4) (0-85,85) 3-Y-0+ **£5,822** (£1,732; £865; £432) **Stalls** Centre

Form RPR
5-10 **1** **Muscika**[19] 2739 3-9-0 **79**........ DanielTudhope 5 87+
(David O'Meara) *hld up in tch: rdn and hdwy over 1f out: drvn and kpt on wl: led 50yds out* **5/2**[2]
0300 **2** ¾ **Tatlisu (IRE)**[30] 2381 7-9-7 **85**........ ConnorMurtagh(7) 6 92
(Richard Fahey) *hld up in tch: hdwy 2f out: rdn to ld 1f out: kpt on but hdd 50yds out* **8/1**
2102 **3** 3 ¼ **Aprovado (IRE)**[12] 2951 5-9-7 **83**........(p) CallumRodriguez(5) 3 80
(Michael Dods) *led narrowly: rdn over 2f out: hdd 1f out: no ex* **15/2**[3]
0-2 **4** 2 ¼ **The Mcgregornator (IRE)**[5] 3195 3-8-1 **73**........(tp) DannySheehy(7) 2 60
(Adrian Paul Keatley, Ire) *hld up: rdn and outpcd 1/2-way: plugged on to go modest 4th over 1f out: nvr threatened* **5/4**[1]
020- **5** 7 **Naples Bay**[212] 7820 3-8-12 **77**........ JasonHart 8 42
(John Quinn) *sn trckd ldrs racing keenly: rdn over 2f out: wknd over 1f out* **15/2**[3]
01-3 **6** 6 **Danish Duke (IRE)**[13] 2923 6-9-1 **72**........(p) TomEaves 4 20
(Ruth Carr) *pressed ldr: rdn over 2f out: wknd over 1f out* **12/1**
00-6 **7** 5 **Dawoodi**[5] 3195 3-8-10 **75**........ PJMcDonald 7 5
(Linda Perratt) *chsd ldrs: rdn 1/2-way: wknd and bhd* **66/1**

1m 13.3s (0.90) **Going Correction** +0.275s/f (Good)
**WFA** 3 from 5yo+ 8lb **7 Ran SP% 116.8**
Speed ratings (Par 105): **105,104,99,96,87 79,72**
CSF £23.41 CT £133.52 TOTE £3.90: £1.90, £3.40; EX 28.80 Trifecta £113.60.
**Owner** Gallop Racing & Dynast Racing **Bred** Dukes Stud & Overbury Stallions Ltd **Trained** Upper Helmsley, N Yorks

**FOCUS**
A useful sprint and the front two pulled nicely clear of the rest.

## 3387 BET WITH ON COURSE BOOKMAKERS H'CAP 7f 50y
**7:55** (7:56) (Class 6) (0-60,60) 3-Y-0+ **£2,587** (£770; £384; £192) **Stalls** High

Form RPR
-400 **1** **Rioja Day (IRE)**[5] 3196 7-8-13 **52**........(b) SeanMooney(7) 8 59
(Jim Goldie) *led for 1f: chsd ldrs: rdn 3f out: chal strly over 1f out: kpt on: led post* **12/1**
0350 **2** shd **Magic Journey (IRE)**[73] 1348 3-8-10 **52**........ JasonHart 11 55
(John Quinn) *s.i.s: sn midfield racing keenly: rdn and hdwy over 2f out: led narrowly over 1f out: kpt on but hdd post* **7/1**[3]
6025 **3** 3 ¼ **Hollywood Harry (IRE)**[10] 3047 3-9-3 **59**........(p) ConnorBeasley 9 54
(Keith Dalgleish) *chsd ldrs: rdn 3f out: one pce* **9/2**[2]
**4** ½ **Legend Status (IRE)**[43] 1996 3-8-6 **55**........(t) DannySheehy(7) 13 48+
(Adrian Paul Keatley, Ire) *slowly away: hld up in rr: stl lot to do over 2f out: rdn and hdwy on outside over 1f out: kpt on* **11/1**
523 **5** hd **Ss Vega**[5] 3198 4-9-2 **48**........ SamJames 1 45
(Jim Goldie) *midfield on inner: rdn over 2f out: kpt on same pce* **4/1**[1]
0052 **6** 1 **Highly Focussed (IRE)**[17] 2792 3-8-11 **53**........ ShaneGray 6 43
(Ann Duffield) *hld up in midfield: pushed along over 2f out: swtchd lft over 1f out: sn hdwy: one pce ins fnl f* **7/1**[3]
0050 **7** hd **New Decade**[5] 3196 8-9-0 **46** oh1........ PJMcDonald 14 40
(Jim Goldie) *hld up: rdn over 2f out: kpt on ins fnl f: nvr threatened* **12/1**
00-0 **8** ½ **Nellie's Dancer**[28] 2470 3-8-11 **58**........ PaddyPilley(5) 12 47
(Scott Dixon) *hld up: rdn and hdwy on outer 2f out: wknd ins fnl f* **22/1**
225 **9** 1 ¼ **Bonnie Gals**[32] 2338 3-8-13 **60**........ RowanScott(5) 5 46
(Keith Dalgleish) *hld up: nvr threatened* **12/1**
**10** ¾ **Kings Of Luxor**[17] 2809 4-9-0 **46** oh1........(b1) RobsonAguiar 4 34
(R P Burns, Ire) *hld up: nvr threatened* **14/1**
60-0 **11** 4 ½ **Diamond Avalanche (IRE)**[29] 2429 4-9-4 **50**........(p1) DanielTudhope 2 26
(Patrick Holmes) *trckd ldrs: rdn over 2f out: wknd over 1f out* **18/1**
00-0 **12** 3 **Riponian**[40] 2082 7-9-4 **55** ow1........(bt1) GarryWhillans(5) 3 24
(Susan Corbett) *stmbld s: plld hrd and sn prom: rn wd on bnd 4f out but led: rdn 3f out: hdd over 2f out: wknd* **33/1**
4-00 **13** 1 ¾ **Vintage Dream (IRE)**[13] 2927 3-9-3 **59**........ TomEaves 7 20
(Noel Wilson) *racd keenly: led after 1f: hdd 4f out: remained prom: rdn to ld again over 2f out: hdd over 1f out: wknd* **20/1**

1m 32.13s (-1.27) **Going Correction** -0.25s/f (Firm)
**WFA** 3 from 4yo+ 10lb **13 Ran SP% 118.6**
Speed ratings (Par 101): **97,96,93,92,92 91,91,90,89,88 83,79,77**
CSF £90.64 CT £443.01 TOTE £14.50: £4.10, £3.10, £2.30; EX 123.40 Trifecta £379.60.
**Owner** Ayrshire Racing & Partner **Bred** Mrs Eleanor Commins **Trained** Uplawmoor, E Renfrews

**FOCUS**
Race distance increased by 6yds. A modest handicap. It's been rated as ordinary form.

## 3388 BEST ODDS WITH ON COURSE BOOKMAKERS H'CAP 7f 50y
**8:25** (8:27) (Class 4) (0-85,84) 3-Y-0+ **£5,822** (£1,732; £865; £432) **Stalls** High

Form RPR
024 **1** **Safe Voyage (IRE)**[17] 2772 4-9-7 **84**........ JoshQuinn(7) 6 93
(John Quinn) *hld up: swtchd to wd outside 2f out: rdn and r.o wl: led 30yds out* **14/1**
1053 **2** 1 ½ **Chaplin Bay (IRE)**[10] 3045 5-8-13 **74**........(p) LewisEdmunds(5) 8 79
(Ruth Carr) *hld up: rdn and hdwy on outer over 2f out: led appr fnl f: kpt on but hdd 30yds out* **7/2**[2]
0-02 **3** 2 **Jay Kay**[5] 3199 8-8-13 **74**........(h) CliffordLee(5) 3 74
(K R Burke) *dwlt: hld up in midfield: rdn and outpcd over 2f out: kpt on ins fnl f* **10/3**[1]
5406 **4** 2 ¼ **Party Tiger**[16] 2820 3-8-2 **71**........(p) SammyJoBell(3) 5 61
(Richard Fahey) *racd keenly in midfield: rdn to chse ldrs 2f out: wknd ins fnl f* **14/1**
-604 **5** 2 ¼ **Fieldsman (USA)**[5] 3199 5-10-0 **84**........ DanielTudhope 4 72
(David O'Meara) *in tch: rdn over 2f out: wknd ins fnl f* **7/2**[2]
2624 **6** ½ **Tailor's Row (USA)**[32] 2348 3-9-1 **81**........ PJMcDonald 2 64
(Mark Johnston) *led: rdn over 2f out: hdd 2f out: wknd ins fnl f* **15/2**
00-0 **7** 9 **Majdool (IRE)**[13] 2922 4-9-13 **83**........ TomEaves 7 47
(Noel Wilson) *trckd ldr: rdn to ld 2f out: hdd appr fnl f: wknd* **66/1**
21-5 **8** 5 **Saint Equiano**[17] 2775 3-9-2 **82**........ ConnorBeasley 1 29
(Keith Dalgleish) *dwlt: tk str hold and sn trckd ldrs: rdr lost irons over 3f out: eased over 1f out* **9/2**[3]

1m 32.27s (-1.13) **Going Correction** -0.25s/f (Firm)
**WFA** 3 from 4yo+ 10lb **8 Ran SP% 112.3**
Speed ratings (Par 105): **96,94,92,89,86 86,76,70**
CSF £60.35 CT £205.83 TOTE £14.70: £3.40, £1.60, £1.60; EX 63.70 Trifecta £440.90.
**Owner** Ross Harmon **Bred** Schneider Adolf **Trained** Settrington, N Yorks

**FOCUS**
Race distance increased by 6yds. A useful handicap run at an even pace. A pb from the winner, with the runner-up rated a bit off.

## 3389 TOMMY MORTON 60 YEARS ON COURSE H'CAP 1m 7f
**8:55** (8:55) (Class 5) (0-70,71) 4-Y-0+ **£3,234** (£962; £481; £240) **Stalls** Low

Form RPR
4354 **1** **Vercingetorix (IRE)**[1] 2546 6-9-0 **68**........(p) JamieGormley(7) 5 78
(Iain Jardine) *pressed ldr: rdn 3f out: led over 1f out: styd on wl* **8/1**
0-55 **2** 3 **Braes Of Lochalsh**[23] 2609 6-9-7 **68**........(p) SamJames 6 74
(Jim Goldie) *trckd ldrs: wnt prom on outside over 7f out: led narrowly 3f out: sn rdn: hdd over 1f out: no ex fnl f* **4/1**[2]
5-12 **3** 1 ¼ **Stoneham**[45] 1344 6-9-5 **71**........(h) LewisEdmunds(5) 7 75
(Iain Jardine) *hld up: rdn over 3f out: styd on fnl 2f: nrst fin* **5/1**[3]
51-2 **4** 14 **Buzz Boy (ITY)**[5] 3193 4-7-13 **53**........(b) DannySheehy(7) 1 39
(Adrian Paul Keatley, Ire) *led narrowly: rdn whn hdd 3f out: wknd* **6/5**[1]
2-05 **5** 9 **Esspeegee**[12] 2972 4-7-13 **49** oh2........(p) NathanAlison(3) 3 23
(Alan Bailey) *dwlt: hld up in tch: rdn over 4f out: wknd* **14/1**
000/ **6** 1 **Aumit Hill**[557] 8006 4-8-3 **50** oh2 ow1........(b1) ShaneGray 2 23
(John Quinn) *trckd ldrs: lost pl over 7f out: rdn over 3f out: wknd* **17/2**
43/5 **7** 14 **Cadore (IRE)**[18] 2456 9-8-0 **50**........(p) SammyJoBell(3) 8 5
(Lucy Normile) *hld up in tch: rdn over 7f out: sn bhd* **40/1**

3m 21.51s (1.11) **Going Correction** -0.25s/f (Firm) **7 Ran SP% 112.9**
Speed ratings (Par 103): **87,85,84,77,72 71,64**
CSF £38.66 CT £176.22 TOTE £9.10: £3.80, £3.10; EX 36.50 Trifecta £146.30.
**Owner** Graeme Slesser **Bred** M Henochsberg & Madame D Ades-Hazan **Trained** Carrutherstown, D'fries & G'way

**FOCUS**
Race distance increased by 12yds. A fair handicap run at a good pace. The third has been rated close to her AW form.
T/Plt: £56.10 to a £1 stake. Pool: £69,884.04 - 908.99 winning units T/Qpdt: £35.60 to a £1 stake. Pool: £5,185.39 - 107.56 winning units **Andrew Sheret**

# 3164 LEICESTER (R-H)
Monday, June 5

**OFFICIAL GOING: Good to soft (str 7.1, rnd 6.7)**
Wind: Strong behind Weather: Overcast

## 3390 RAGDALE MAIDEN AUCTION STKS 6f
**2:20** (2:21) (Class 5) 2-Y-0 **£3,881** (£1,155; £577; £288) **Stalls** High

Form RPR
45 **1** **Shazzab (IRE)**[14] 2896 2-8-7 0........ JoeDoyle 5 68
(Richard Fahey) *chsd ldrs: shkn up over 2f out: rdn and r.o to ld wl ins fnl f* **10/1**
**2** ½ **Simpson (IRE)** 2-9-0 0........ LukeMorris 2 74+
(Ed Walker) *a.p: shkn up to ld over 1f out: edgd lft: hdd wl ins fnl f* **7/2**[2]
42 **3** 4 **Porchy Party (IRE)**[20] 2698 2-9-2 0........ RichardKingscote 18 64
(Tom Dascombe) *led: rdn and hdd over 1f out: no ex ins fnl f* **9/4**[1]
6 **4** hd **Major Peirson (IRE)**[20] 2706 2-8-12 0........ FrannyNorton 8 59
(Jo Hughes) *chsd ldr: rdn and ev ch wl over 1f out: no ex ins fnl f* **14/1**
**5** 1 ¾ **Blue Havana (IRE)** 2-8-9 0........ CamHardie 4 51
(John Quinn) *.hld up in tch: shkn up over 2f out: styd on same pce fnl f* **28/1**
**6** ½ **Followthesteps (IRE)** 2-9-2 0........ DavidNolan 16 56
(Ivan Furtado) *prom: rdn over 1f out: wknd wl ins fnl f* **25/1**
**7** ½ **Boreagh Lass (IRE)** 2-8-8 0 ow1........ FergusSweeney 14 47+
(Henry Candy) *pushed along: hung rt and rn green in rr: swtchd rt over 2f out: r.o ins fnl f: nvr nrr* **7/1**[3]
**8** shd **Roman Spinner** 2-8-7 0........(t1) AdamBeschizza 11 45+
(Rae Guest) *mid-div: pushed along and hdwy 2f out: no ex fnl f* **25/1**
**9** 1 ¾ **Cheeky Rascal (IRE)** 2-9-2 0........ TomMarquand 9 49
(Richard Hannon) *mid-div: pushed along 4f out: effrt over 2f out: nt trble ldrs* **16/1**
**10** 3 ¾ **Alifax** 2-9-2 0........ DougieCostello 13 38
(Jamie Osborne) *prom: rdn over 2f out: wknd fnl f* **33/1**
**11** 1 ½ **Vallesa (IRE)** 2-8-4 0........ AaronJones(3) 15 24
(David Brown) *s.i.s: nvr on terms* **66/1**
**12** 2 ½ **Crystal Casque** 2-8-7 0........ RyanTate 10 17
(Rod Millman) *sn pushed along towards rr: wknd over 2f out* **33/1**
**13** 2 **Dream Of Delphi (IRE)** 2-9-0 0........ PatCosgrave 1 18
(William Haggas) *s.s: outpcd* **7/1**[3]
**14** 6 **Four Fifty Three** 2-8-12 0........ HarryBentley 7
(Mark H Tompkins) *s.s: sn pushed along and a in rr* **100/1**
**15** hd **Billy Booth (IRE)** 2-9-2 0........ MartinDwyer 3 1
(Gay Kelleway) *hdwy into mid-div: over 4f out: rdn: hung lft and wknd over 2f out* **33/1**
**16** 1 ½ **Bullseye Bullet** 2-8-12 0........ SteveDrowne 6
(Mark Usher) *s.i.s: sn pushed along in rr: wknd over 2f out* **100/1**

1m 12.48s (-0.52) **Going Correction** -0.025s/f (Good) **16 Ran SP% 123.1**
Speed ratings (Par 93): **102,101,96,95,93 92,92,91,89,84 82,79,76,68,68 66**
CSF £41.95 TOTE £12.50: £2.90, £2.00, £2.10; EX 52.70 Trifecta £190.00.
**Owner** Darren Barton **Bred** Pat Todd **Trained** Musley Bank, N Yorks

**FOCUS**
Cam Hardie said of the ground: "It's good to soft but loose enough." Two came clear in this ordinary maiden, the winner's experience counting late on. It's been rated as ordinary form in line with the race average.

## 3391 HICKLING (S) STKS 6f
**2:50** (2:50) (Class 5) 3-5-Y-0 **£3,234** (£962; £481; £240) **Stalls** High

Form RPR
0-00 **1** **Kody Ridge (IRE)**[19] 2720 3-8-11 **67**........(h) DougieCostello 7 66
(David Dennis) *chsd ldrs: rdn to ld ins fnl f: r.o: comf* **14/1**
40-0 **2** 1 ½ **Jack Nevison**[19] 2727 4-9-5 **70**........(p1) TrevorWhelan 1 63
(John O'Shea) *a.p: rdn and ev ch 1f out: edgd lft: no ex wl ins fnl f* **8/1**
1000 **3** nk **Oakley Pride (IRE)**[7] 3151 3-9-1 **60**........(vt) LukeMorris 5 64
(Gay Kelleway) *prom: pushed along 1/2-way: rdn over 1f out: r.o* **25/1**
3- **4** ½ **Bourbonisto**[213] 7792 3-8-11 **64**........ CamHardie 4 59
(Ben Haslam) *prom: lost pl after 1f: pushed along 4f out: hdwy u.p over 1f out: r.o* **3/1**[2]
-322 **5** 1 **Black Bubba (IRE)**[6] 3166 3-8-4 **58**........ KatherineGlenister(7) 8 56
(David Evans) *sn led: rdn over 1f out: hdd ins fnl f: no ex towards fin* **2/1**[1]
3033 **6** 3 ¼ **Loumarin (IRE)**[11] 2994 5-8-7 **53**........(p) RayDawson(7) 10 43
(Michael Appleby) *w ldrs tl pushed along 4f out: rdn and hung lft over 2f out: styd on same pce fr over 1f out* **9/2**[3]

-300 **7** 1 ¾ **Spiritofedinburgh (IRE)**[7] 3163 3-8-8 70.........(v[1]) KieranShoemark(3) 9 41
(Brendan Powell) *w ldr tl rdn 1/2-way: hung rt over 2f out: wknd fnl f* **14/1**

-500 **8** 5 **Monsieur Paddy**[61] 1558 4-9-9 59.............................. GeorgeDowning 6 32
(Tony Carroll) *hld up: rdn over 2f out: wknd wl over 1f out* **33/1**

00-0 **9** 3 **Diminutive (IRE)**[24] 2589 5-9-4 51.........................(p) StevieDonohoe 3 18
(Grace Harris) *chsd ldrs: rdn over 2f out: wknd wl over 1f out* **25/1**

1m 12.5s (-0.50) **Going Correction** -0.025s/f (Good)
**WFA** 3 from 4yo+ 8lb **9** Ran SP% **111.6**
Speed ratings (Par 103): **102,100,99,98,97 93,90,84,80**
CSF £113.10 TOTE £16.70: £4.60, £2.80, £6.20; EX 129.90 Trifecta £821.90.The winner was claimed by Mr Roger Fell for 9,500 guineas. Jack Nevison was claimed by Mr Michael Appleby for £7,000.
**Owner** A Killoran **Bred** Tally-Ho Stud **Trained** Hanley Swan, Worcestershire

**FOCUS**
Two of the higher-rated runners came to the fore, with the winner challenging up the stands' rail. The runner-up has been rated around a stone below last year's best, and the third is perhpas the key.

## 3392 SWANNINGTON H'CAP 1m 2f
**3:20** (3:21) (Class 4) (0-80,80) 3-Y-O **£6,301** (£1,886; £943; £472; £235) **Stalls** Low

Form RPR

0-1 **1** **Meteor Light (IRE)**[34] 2266 3-9-7 **80**.....................(h) AdamBeschizza 14 91+
(Ed Vaughan) *hld up in tch: racd keenly: shkn up over 2f out: rdn to ld over 1f out: r.o* **15/2**

00-4 **2** ½ **Cotinga**[18] 2761 3-8-12 **71**.............................................. OisinMurphy 8 79
(Ralph Beckett) *hld up: pushed along over 3f out: hdwy u.p over 1f out: r.o wl* **12/1**

61-1 **3** 1 **Rake's Progress**[17] 2794 3-8-13 **72**................................. GavinLerena 2 78
(Heather Main) *chsd ldrs: rdn over 3f out: outpcd over 2f out: rallied over 1f out: r.o* **9/2**[1]

060- **4** 1 ¼ **Prosecution**[180] 8246 3-8-5 **64**....................................... FrannyNorton 15 68
(Hughie Morrison) *hld up: plld hrd: shkn up over 2f out: r.o ins fnl f: nt rch ldrs* **12/1**

15 **5** hd **Comrade Conrad (IRE)**[21] 2690 3-9-4 **80**............ KieranShoemark(3) 4 83
(Roger Charlton) *w ldr tl settled into 2nd pl 8f out: rdn and ev ch over 1f out: no ex wl ins fnl f* **6/1**[2]

0-16 **6** nk **Lightly Squeeze**[21] 2690 3-9-0 **73**..............................(p) HarryBentley 7 76
(Philip Hide) *hld up in tch: racd keenly: rdn over 2f out: sn outpcd: rallied over 1f out: styd on same pce wl ins fnl f* **20/1**

46-4 **7** 1 ¼ **Our Boy (IRE)**[47] 1875 3-8-8 **74**..................................... DavidEgan(7) 1 74
(David Evans) *led: qcknd over 3f out: rdn and hdd over 1f out: no ex ins fnl f* **25/1**

22-1 **8** 5 **Interweave**[60] 1581 3-9-5 **78**.......................................(v[1]) RyanMoore 12 68
(Sir Michael Stoute) *s.s: hld up: shkn up and swtchd lft over 2f out: rdn over 1f out: no imp: eased ins fnl f* **6/1**[2]

2-1 **9** ½ **Evening Hill**[20] 2707 3-9-3 **76**......................................... ShaneKelly 9 65
(Richard Hughes) *chsd ldrs: rdn over 2f out: wknd fnl f* **9/1**

-310 **10** 1 **Cloud Dragon (IRE)**[37] 2145 3-9-2 **75**............................ JamesDoyle 3 62
(Hugo Palmer) *chsd ldrs: rdn over 3f out: wknd wl over 1f out* **16/1**

4-00 **11** 5 **Go On Mayson**[10] 3040 3-8-9 **68**................................. StevieDonohoe 10 45
(David Evans) *hld up: rdn over 3f out: sn wknd* **50/1**

1-30 **12** 22 **Manangatang (IRE)**[21] 2690 3-9-2 **75**............................. AndreaAtzeni 13 8
(Luca Cumani) *hld up: pushed along 1/2-way: hdwy over 3f out: rdn over 2f out: sn wknd* **7/1**[3]

2m 8.87s (0.97) **Going Correction** -0.025s/f (Good) **12** Ran SP% **112.9**
Speed ratings (Par 101): **95,94,93,92,92 92,91,87,87,86 82,64**
CSF £87.28 CT £449.77 TOTE £8.70: £2.80, £3.20, £1.90; EX 103.60 Trifecta £696.70.
**Owner** Ballymore Sterling Syndicate **Bred** Nordkappe Partnership **Trained** Newmarket, Suffolk

**FOCUS**
A decent little handicap and a winner very much on the up. It's been rated at face value around the second, third, fifth and sixth.

## 3393 BREEDERS BACKING RACING EBF MAIDEN STKS (DIV I) 1m 53y
**3:50** (3:53) (Class 5) 3-Y-O **£4,528** (£1,347; £673; £336) **Stalls** Low

Form RPR

**1** **Contango (IRE)** 3-9-5 0................................................ OisinMurphy 8 77
(Andrew Balding) *a.p: shkn up to ld 2f out: rdn and edgd rt ins fnl f: styd on* **7/1**

00 **2** 1 **Unit Of Assessment (IRE)**[17] 2783 3-9-5 0.................. HarryBentley 2 74
(William Knight) *chsd ldrs: rdn and ev ch fr over 1f out: no ex towards fin* **16/1**

5- **3** 1 ½ **Ebtkaar (IRE)**[198] 8034 3-9-5 0...................................... AndreaAtzeni 7 71
(Roger Varian) *sn led: pushed along 1/2-way: hdd 2f out: rdn and ev ch 1f out: no ex wl ins fnl f* **5/2**[2]

**4** 1 ¼ **Verity** 3-9-0 0.................................................................. RyanMoore 6 63+
(Sir Michael Stoute) *prom: pushed along over 3f out: nt clr run over 2f out: rdn over 1f out: styd on same pce ins fnl f* **11/10**[1]

0-0 **5** 3 ¼ **Niseko**[28] 2476 3-9-5 0.............................................(b[1]) DougieCostello 5 61
(William Muir) *broke wl: sn lost pl: in rr and pushed along 4f out: rdn and hung rt fr over 1f out: styd on: nt trble ldrs* **66/1**

**6** 1 ½ **Ididitforyoooo (IRE)** 3-9-5 0...................................... TomMarquand 10 57
(Brian Meehan) *s.s: sn pushed along in rr: kpt on ins fnl f: nvr on terms* **16/1**

00 **7** nk **Ruled By The Moon**[30] 2383 3-9-5 0............................ DavidNolan 4 57
(Ivan Furtado) *broke wl: sn lost pl: shkn up over 1f out: nvr on terms* **66/1**

0 **8** 2 ¼ **Careyanne**[47] 1889 3-9-0 0.......................................... RobertTart 3 46
(Brian Baugh) *hld up: rdn over 3f out: n.d* **100/1**

**9** 60 **Soqrat** 3-9-5 0...................................................................... JimCrowley 9
(Ed Dunlop) *w ldr: ev ch over 2f out: sn wknd: eased fr over 1f out* **13/2**[3]

1m 47.07s (1.97) **Going Correction** -0.025s/f (Good) **9** Ran SP% **117.8**
Speed ratings (Par 99): **89,88,86,85,82 80,80,77,17**
CSF £109.60 TOTE £9.50: £2.00, £3.20, £1.10; EX 114.60 Trifecta £482.10.
**Owner** Kennet Valley Thoroughbreds XII **Bred** Thomas Hassett **Trained** Kingsclere, Hants

**FOCUS**
The quicker of the two divisions, but it perhaps didn't have the depth of the second leg. The third has been rated close to his AW debut effort for now.

## 3394 BREEDERS BACKING RACING EBF MAIDEN STKS (DIV II) 1m 53y
**4:20** (4:20) (Class 5) 3-Y-O **£4,528** (£1,347; £673; £336) **Stalls** Low

Form RPR

**1** **Monaadhil (IRE)** 3-9-5 0.................................................. JimCrowley 2 76+
(Marcus Tregoning) *s.i.s: sn prom: rdn over 1f out: r.o to ld wl ins fnl f* **10/1**

42 **2** ½ **Wonderfillo (IRE)**[75] 1299 3-9-5 0................................... LukeMorris 4 75
(Paul Cole) *chsd ldrs: shkn up to ld over 1f out: rdn and hdd wl ins fnl f* **3/1**[2]

6 **3** 3 ¼ **Powderhouse (IRE)**[21] 2681 3-9-5 0............................(p[1]) JamesDoyle 1 68
(Charlie Appleby) *chsd ldr: rdn and ev ch over 1f out: wknd towards fin* **11/2**

6- **4** 2 **Eternal Dream**[350] 3463 3-9-5 0....................................... OisinMurphy 9 63
(William Knight) *led: rdn and hdd over 1f out: sn hung rt: wknd ins fnl f* **8/1**

**5** shd **Mesbaar** 3-9-5 0.................................................................. AndreaAtzeni 6 63
(Roger Varian) *s.i.s: hld up: pushed along 1/2-way: styd on fr over 1f out: nvr trbld ldrs* **11/4**[1]

06 **6** 1 **Aladdin Sane (IRE)**[18] 2751 3-8-12 0............................. JordanUys(7) 3 60
(Brian Meehan) *hld up: racd keenly: rdn over 2f out: n.d* **50/1**

06 **7** shd **Upended**[17] 2798 3-9-5 0............................................... MartinHarley 8 60
(Chris Wall) *hld up: shkn up over 2f out: nvr nr to chal* **50/1**

00 **8** 1 ¾ **Tallulah's Quest (IRE)**[17] 2798 3-9-0 0.......................... AdamBeschizza 7 51
(Julia Feilden) *hld up: rdn over 3f out: n.d* **100/1**

0- **9** 10 **Meyrick**[297] 5356 3-9-5 0................................................... PatCosgrave 5 33
(William Haggas) *s.i.s: hld up: wknd 2f out* **7/2**[3]

1m 48.75s (3.65) **Going Correction** -0.025s/f (Good) **9** Ran SP% **114.4**
Speed ratings (Par 99): **80,79,76,74,74 73,73,71,61**
CSF £39.72 TOTE £10.20: £2.80, £1.40, £1.70; EX 37.80 Trifecta £212.30.
**Owner** Hamdan Al Maktoum **Bred** Oak Hill Stud **Trained** Whitsbury, Hants

**FOCUS**
The slower of the two legs, but more depth. The level is a bit fluid.

## 3395 SHARNFORD FILLIES' CONDITIONS STKS 7f
**4:55** (4:55) (Class 3) 3-Y-O+ **£7,561** (£2,263; £1,131; £566; £282) **Stalls** High

Form RPR

260- **1** **Bletchley**[261] 6555 3-8-8 103.........................................(h[1]) OisinMurphy 2 103
(Ralph Beckett) *chsd ldr: shkn up to ld ins fnl f: r.o wl* **9/4**[2]

40- **2** 1 ¾ **Same Jurisdiction (SAF)**[246] 6991 5-9-4 107.................. RyanMoore 3 102
(Ed Dunlop) *led main gp: led overall and qcknd over 2f out: rdn over 1f out: hdd ins fnl f: styd on same pce* **9/2**

01 **3** 2 **Present Tense**[33] 2316 3-8-8 0..................................... DavidProbert 1 93
(John Gosden) *trckd ldrs: rdn over 1f out: styd on same pce* **11/4**[3]

422- **4** nse **Aljuljalah (USA)**[221] 7650 4-9-4 96............................... AndreaAtzeni 4 97
(Roger Varian) *hld up in tch: racd keenly early: rdn over 1f out: styd on same pce* **2/1**[1]

3 **5** 7 **Voi**[124] 510 3-8-5 0.............................................................. NoelGarbutt(3) 6 74?
(Conrad Allen) *racd alone and overall ldr on stands' side: hung rt and hdd over 2f out: wknd over 1f out* **100/1**

1m 24.66s (-1.54) **Going Correction** -0.025s/f (Good)
**WFA** 3 from 4yo+ 10lb **5** Ran SP% **109.9**
Speed ratings (Par 104): **107,105,102,102,94**
CSF £12.32 TOTE £2.90: £1.40, £2.40; EX 11.80 Trifecta £26.50.
**Owner** Qatar Racing Limited **Bred** Qatar Bloodstock Ltd **Trained** Kimpton, Hants

**FOCUS**
A good little conditions race. The winner has been rated to form.

## 3396 OLD DALBY H'CAP 7f
**5:25** (5:26) (Class 5) (0-75,75) 4-Y-O+ **£3,881** (£1,155; £577; £288) **Stalls** High

Form RPR

0-23 **1** **Manton Grange**[34] 2267 4-9-7 **75**.................................... JamesDoyle 11 87
(George Baker) *hld up: hdwy 2f out: led 1f out: rdn out* **5/1**[2]

-003 **2** 1 ½ **Flyboy (IRE)**[14] 2888 4-9-4 **75**.............................(b) AdamMcNamara(3) 3 83
(Richard Fahey) *s.i.s: hld up: hdwy over 1f out: rdn and ev ch ins fnl f: no ex towards fin* **9/2**[1]

0342 **3** 2 **Flying Fantasy**[33] 2318 5-9-0 **68**.................................... BenCurtis 7 71
(Michael Appleby) *s.i.s: sn chsng ldrs: led over 1f out: sn rdn and hdd: styd on same pce ins fnl f* **5/1**[2]

640- **4** 1 ¼ **Bryght Boy**[223] 7601 4-8-9 **63**....................................... LukeMorris 5 62
(Ed Walker) *hld up: hdwy 1/2-way: rdn and ev ch over 1f out: wknd wl ins fnl f* **12/1**

0062 **5** ¾ **King Of Swing**[6] 3177 4-8-13 **67**.................................. ShaneKelly 13 64
(Richard Hughes) *prom: racd keenly: rdn over 1f out: edgd rt and styd on same pce fnl f* **12/1**

61-6 **6** 2 **Pacific Salt (IRE)**[34] 2267 4-8-13 **67**............................ RobHornby 8 59
(Pam Sly) *s.i.s: hld up: rdn over 1f out: nt trble ldrs* **14/1**

00-5 **7** ¾ **Big Chill (IRE)**[23] 2618 5-9-0 **71**............................ CharlieBennett(3) 2 61
(Patrick Chamings) *sn led: rdn over 2f out: hdd over 1f out: wknd fnl f* **14/1**

003 **8** 1 ½ **Glorious Poet**[12] 2960 4-9-7 **75**.................................... TomMarquand 10 61
(John Spearing) *w ldrs: rdn over 2f out: nt clr run over 1f out: sn wknd* **6/1**[3]

-035 **9** 1 ¼ **Taskeen (IRE)**[24] 2592 4-9-6 **74**.................................. DavidNolan 6 56
(Roger Fell) *w ldrs: rdn over 2f out: n.m.r over 1f out: wknd fnl f* **9/1**

05-4 **10** 1 ¾ **Another Boy**[17] 2795 4-9-5 **73**.................................(p) OisinMurphy 9 51
(Ralph Beckett) *prom: lost pl over 5f out: rdn and wknd wl over 1f out* **10/1**

0-30 **11** 2 ¼ **Sister Dude**[7] 3142 4-9-0 **68**........................................ MartinHarley 12 40
(Jonathan Portman) *sn pushed along in rr: wknd over 2f out* **25/1**

1m 23.74s (-2.46) **Going Correction** -0.025s/f (Good) **11** Ran SP% **117.5**
Speed ratings (Par 103): **113,111,109,107,106 104,103,101,100,98 95**
CSF £27.74 CT £121.52 TOTE £6.60: £2.70, £1.30, £2.00; EX 30.90 Trifecta £172.00.
**Owner** Goltz, Finegold & McGeever **Bred** Follow The Flag Partnership **Trained** Manton, Wilts

**FOCUS**
A modest handicap, the first two came from off the pace. The runner-up has been rated close to his late 2016 form.

## 3397 COPLOW H'CAP 7f
**6:00** (6:00) (Class 6) (0-60,60) 4-Y-O+ **£2,587** (£770; £384; £192) **Stalls** High

Form RPR

-000 **1** **Poor Duke (IRE)**[28] 2454 7-8-13 **52**...............................(p) RobertTart 12 61
(Michael Mullineaux) *w ldrs: led main gp over 5f out: overall ldr over 4f out: rdn over 1f out: styd on wl: eased nr fin* **16/1**

222 **2** 1 ¼ **Tidal's Baby**[33] 2294 8-9-6 **59**.................................(p) GeorgeDowning 6 63
(Tony Carroll) *hld up: hdwy over 2f out: rdn over 1f out: edgd lft ins fnl f: styd on same pce* **6/1**

1064 **3** hd **Magic Mirror**[13] 2916 4-8-12 **51**..................................(p) TomMarquand 8 54
(Mark Rimell) *chsd ldrs: rdn over 2f out: styd on u.p* **5/1**[2]

0 **4** 2 ¾ **See You In Malta (IRE)**[4] 3265 4-9-3 **56**...................... DavidNolan 2 53
(Jennie Candlish) *mid-div: hdwy over 2f out: rdn over 1f out: styd on same pce ins fnl f* **9/1**

-061 **5** 2 ½ **Intimately**[18] 2762 4-8-13 **59**................................ Pierre-LouisJamin(7) 10 49
(Jonathan Portman) *s.s: bhd: styd on fr over 1f out: nt trble ldrs* **11/2**[3]

0251 **5** dht **Magic Moments**[19] 2732 4-9-6 **59**................................. MartinHarley 5 49
(Alan King) *chsd ldrs: rdn and ev ch over 1f out: wknd ins fnl f* **11/4**[1]

0400 **7** 4 **Qortaaj**[13] 2916 4-9-4 **57**...(e[1]) ShaneKelly 13 37
(David Loughnane) *mid-div: shkn up over 2f out: nvr trbld ldrs* **16/1**

000- **8** 2 ½ **Doctor Bong**[185] 8190 5-9-0 **60**...(b) BenRobinson(7) 14 34
(Grace Harris) *s.i.s: sn pushed along in rr: nvr on terms* **16/1**

000- **9** 2 ¾ **My Time**[276] 6105 8-8-7 **46** oh1...(h) JimmyQuinn 7 13
(Michael Mullineaux) *in rr: rdn 1/2-way: n.d* **50/1**

05-0 **10** 4 **Clubland (IRE)**[154] 22 8-9-4 **60**... AlistairRawlinson(3) 18 17
(Roy Bowring) *racd alone stands' side: overall ldr tl over 4f out: sn hung rt: wknd 2f out* **16/1**

6005 **11** ½ **Doodle Dandy (IRE)**[12] 2961 4-9-4 **57**... DougieCostello 15 13
(David Bridgwater) *led main gp tl over 5f out: remained handy tl rdn and wknd over 2f out* **10/1**

/00- **12** 4 ½ **Purana**[431] 1162 6-8-7 **46** oh1...(t[1]) IrineuGoncalves 9
(Ms N M Hugo) *prom: jnd wnr 5f out tl rdn wl over 2f out: sn wknd* **66/1**

1m 25.0s (-1.20) **Going Correction** -0.025s/f (Good) **12** Ran SP% **119.1**
Speed ratings (Par 101): **105,103,103,100,97 97,92,89,86,82 81,76**
CSF £109.66 CT £570.05 TOTE £18.40: £4.20, £1.70, £2.10; EX 207.80 Trifecta £547.90.
**Owner** Michael Mullineaux **Bred** Corrin Stud **Trained** Alpraham, Cheshire

**FOCUS**
Moderate handicap form. The runner-up helps pin the level.
T/Plt: £67.20 to a £1 stake. Pool: £56,213.48 - 610.55 winning units T/Qpdt: £16.00 to a £1 stake. Pool: £3,998.20 - 184.28 winning units **Colin Roberts**

# 2836 THIRSK (L-H)

## Monday, June 5

**OFFICIAL GOING: Good changed to good to soft after race 1 (2.00)**
Wind: Moderate half behind Weather: Rain then sunny periods and showers

## 3398 WATCH RACING UK IN HD NOVICE AUCTION STKS (DIV I) 6f

**2:00** (2:01) (Class 5) 2-Y-O **£2,911** (£866; £432; £216) **Stalls** Centre

Form RPR

0 **1** **Another Day Of Sun (IRE)**[11] 3002 2-9-0 0... SilvestreDeSousa 3 71+
(Mick Channon) *cl up: led wl over 1f out: rdn and edgd rt appr fnl f: kpt on* **5/6**[1]

6 **2** 1 ¼ **Mr Wagyu (IRE)**[37] 2154 2-9-1 0... JasonHart 4 68
(John Quinn) *sn slt ld: pushed along over 2f out: rdn and hdd wl over 1f out: carried sltly rt approachring fnl f: kpt on* **16/1**

0 **3** ¾ **Emerald Rocket (IRE)**[14] 2896 2-8-13 0... BenCurtis 6 64
(K R Burke) *trckd ldng pair: hdwy and cl up over 2f out: rdn along wl over 1f : edgd lft ins fnl f: kpt on same pce* **16/1**

00 **4** ½ **Archie Perkins (IRE)**[20] 2698 2-8-13 0... JosephineGordon 11 63
(Nigel Tinkler) *chsd ldrs: rdn along wl over 1f out: kpt on same pce fnl f* **100/1**

600 **5** 2 ¼ **Mount Hellvelyn**[14] 2896 2-8-12 0... JamesSullivan 1 55
(Clive Mulhall) *towards rr: hdwy 2f out: sn rdn and kpt on fnl f* **18/1**

**6** ¾ **Byron's Choice** 2-9-2 0... PaulMulrennan 9 57+
(Michael Dods) *wnt lft s: towards rr tl styd on fnl 2f* **8/1**[3]

5 **7** 2 ¼ **Mabo**[16] 2816 2-9-1 0... PaulHanagan 10 50
(Richard Fahey) *trckd ldrs: pushed along over 2f out: rdn wl over 1f out: sn no imp* **3/1**[2]

000 **8** hd **Rock On Bertie (IRE)**[17] 2786 2-9-0 0... TomEaves 7 47
(Nigel Tinkler) *hld up: a towards rr* **66/1**

**9** 1 **Aliento** 2-8-8 0... AndrewMullen 5 38
(Ollie Pears) *a towards rr* **66/1**

6 **10** 1 ¾ **Harvest Day**[9] 3093 2-8-4 0...(t) NathanEvans(3) 2 32
(Michael Easterby) *t.k.h: chsd ldrs on outer: rdn along over 2f out: wknd over 1f out* **20/1**

**11** 6 **Hamba Moyo (IRE)** 2-8-10 0... DuranFentiman 8 17
(Tim Easterby) *hmpd s: green and a bhd* **33/1**

1m 13.96s (1.26) **Going Correction** +0.15s/f (Good) **11** Ran SP% **119.4**
Speed ratings (Par 93): **97,95,94,93,90 89,86,86,85,82 74**
CSF £17.59 TOTE £1.80: £1.10, £4.50, £3.70; EX 19.90 Trifecta £171.30.
**Owner** M Channon **Bred** Patrick J Gleeson **Trained** West Ilsley, Berks

**FOCUS**
Stands' side running rail was positioned three metres inside its regular position along the entire length of the straight course to facilitate turf recovery within the protected area. A rainy day and the going was changed to good to soft after this opening race. They raced middle to stands' side in what looked a pretty modest novice race. The fifth's pre-race form anchors the form for now.

## 3399 WATCH RACING UK IN HD NOVICE AUCTION STKS (DIV II) 6f

**2:30** (2:33) (Class 5) 2-Y-O **£2,911** (£866; £432; £216) **Stalls** Centre

Form RPR

642 **1** **Jedi Master (IRE)**[16] 2816 2-9-0 0... PaulHanagan 10 67
(Richard Fahey) *trckd ldrs: hdwy over 2f out: chal wl over 1f out and sn edgd lft: rdn to ld ent fnl f: sn drvn and hung lft: kpt on* **8/15**[1]

**2** 1 ½ **Kannapolis (IRE)** 2-8-5 0... HarrisonShaw(7) 5 61+
(Michael Easterby) *dwlt: green and outpcd in rr: rdn along 1/2-way: hdwy 2f out: swtchd rt over 1f out: styd on wl fnl f* **40/1**

06 **3** ¾ **Monkey Magic**[24] 2590 2-8-9 0... SilvestreDeSousa 6 55
(Nigel Tinkler) *led 1f: cl up: rdn to ld again jst over 2f out: hdd wl over 1f out: drvn and carried sltly lft ins fnl f: kpt on same pce* **8/1**[3]

0 **4** 1 ¾ **Acromatic (IRE)**[17] 2771 2-9-2 0... JackGarritty 9 57
(John Quinn) *trckd ldrs: pushed along over 2f out: rdn wl over 1f out: kpt on same pce* **16/1**

0 **5** 3 **Eyes Of Fire**[42] 2029 2-9-1 0... AndrewMullen 1 47
(Ollie Pears) *rapid hdwy to ld after 150 yds: pushed along 1/2-way: rdn and hdd over 2f out: sn drvn and grad wknd* **16/1**

**6** ¾ **Makofitwhatyouwill** 2-8-13 0... TomEaves 3 43
(Nigel Tinkler) *green and outpcd in rr: pushed along 1/2-way: styd on fnl 2f* **50/1**

**7** 1 **Jaffar** 2-8-13 0...(be[1]) JosephineGordon 8 40
(Scott Dixon) *sn rdn along: a towards rr* **18/1**

60 **8** 3 **Heavenly Pulse (IRE)**[14] 2882 2-9-1 0... TonyHamilton 4 33
(Ann Duffield) *midfield: rdn along wl over 2f out: n.d* **66/1**

**9** nk **Curzon (IRE)** 2-8-12 0... JoshDoyle(3) 2 32
(David O'Meara) *t.k.h: trckd ldrs: rdn along over 2f out: sn wknd* **9/2**[2]

**10** 8 **Rickyroadboy** 2-8-12 0... GrahamLee 11 5
(Mark Walford) *wnt rt s:. in tch: pushed along 1/2-way: rdn along over 2f out: sn wknd* **33/1**

1m 14.13s (1.43) **Going Correction** +0.15s/f (Good) **10** Ran SP% **120.4**
Speed ratings (Par 93): **96,94,93,90,86 85,84,80,79,69**
CSF £42.14 TOTE £1.40: £1.02, £11.50, £2.30; EX 49.60 Trifecta £220.10.
**Owner** Kevin Hart & Partner **Bred** Mrs Eithne McDonnell **Trained** Musley Bank, N Yorks

**FOCUS**
Another modest-looking novice contest. The suspicion is that the winner was below form.

## 3400 PAY FOR RACING UK VIA PHONE BILL H'CAP 1m 4f 8y

**3:00** (3:02) (Class 6) (0-65,64) 4-Y-O+ **£2,911** (£866; £432; £216) **Stalls** High

Form RPR

100- **1** **Tonto's Spirit**[51] 5227 5-8-5 **48**... AndrewMullen 1 55
(Kenneth Slack) *mde all: rdn over 2f out: drvn over 1f out: kpt on wl u.p towards fin* **5/2**[1]

0322 **2** 1 ½ **Stoneboat Bill**[12] 2955 5-8-13 **63**... GerO'Neill(7) 2 68
(Declan Carroll) *hld up towards rr: hdwy on outer over 3f out: sn chsng ldrs: rdn to chal on wd outside wl over 1f out: drvn and ev ch ent fnl f: no ex last 50 yds* **5/1**[3]

6-06 **3** 1 **Steccando (IRE)**[36] 2183 4-9-4 **61**... TonyHamilton 12 65
(Sally Haynes) *in tch: hdwy over 4f out: trckd ldrs 3f out: effrt and cl up wl over 1f out: sn rdn and ev ch ent fnl f: sn drvn and kpt on same pce* **20/1**

000- **4** 2 **Flying Power**[198] 8038 9-8-7 **50**... PaddyAspell 7 51
(John Norton) *trckd ldrs: hdwy and cl up 4f out: rdn along over 2f out: drvn over 1f out: grad wknd* **50/1**

005- **5** 2 ½ **Danzella**[276] 6097 5-8-2 **45**... DuranFentiman 11 42
(Chris Fairhurst) *trckd ldrs: pushed along over 4f out: rdn 3f out: drvn along 2f out: grad wknd* **33/1**

2115 **6** 2 ¾ **My Renaissance**[5] 853 7-8-13 **61**... JaneElliott(5) 10 54
(Sam England) *trckd wnr: pushed along over 3f out: rdn over 2f out: drvn wl over 1f out: sn wknd* **9/2**[2]

1442 **7** 6 **Surround Sound**[10] 3043 7-9-3 **63**...(t) RachelRichardson(3) 9 47
(Tim Easterby) *hld up in rr: effrt and sme hdwy on outer over 3f out: rdn along over 2f out: n.d* **6/1**

50-0 **8** 3 ¼ **Correggio**[39] 2108 7-9-7 **64**... PaulHanagan 6 43
(Micky Hammond) *trckd ldrs: pushed along over 4f out: rdn 3f out: sn btn* **10/1**

0222 **9** 7 **Hannington**[21] 2687 6-9-3 **60**...(t) SilvestreDeSousa 3 28
(Michael Appleby) *a towards rr* **5/1**[3]

00-0 **10** 1 ¾ **Dutch Barney**[37] 2140 7-7-9 **45**...(p[1]) RPWalsh(7) 4 11
(Barry Leavy) *a rr* **100/1**

2m 39.34s (3.14) **Going Correction** +0.15s/f (Good) **10** Ran SP% **114.1**
Speed ratings (Par 101): **95,94,93,92,90 88,84,82,77,76**
CSF £14.24 CT £199.41 TOTE £4.20: £1.60, £1.70, £3.90; EX 15.50 Trifecta £171.90.
**Owner** A Slack **Bred** Mrs J M Quy **Trained** Hilton, Cumbria

**FOCUS**
A moderate handicap in which the winner got an easy lead. The runner-up helps pin the level of the form.

## 3401 RACING UK HD ON SKY432 H'CAP 6f

**3:30** (3:32) (Class 5) (0-75,77) 4-Y-O+ **£3,234** (£962; £481; £240) **Stalls** Centre

Form RPR

2021 **1** **Meshardal (GER)**[11] 2990 7-8-13 **67**...(p) JamesSullivan 5 76
(Ruth Carr) *hld up: hdwy on outer to trck ldrs over 2f out: rdn over 1f out: styd on wl fnl f to ld nr fin* **7/2**[1]

510- **2** nk **Round The Island**[232] 7386 4-8-4 **61**... NathanEvans(3) 3 69
(Richard Whitaker) *racd centre: led 2f: cl up: rdn to ld again ent fnl f: sn drvn and edgd lft: hdd and no ex nr fin* **25/1**

00-0 **3** ½ **Pomme De Terre (IRE)**[36] 2184 5-9-9 **77**...(b) PaulMulrennan 1 83
(Michael Dods) *cl up towards far side: led after 2f: rdn along wl over 1f out: hdd ent fnl f: sn drvn and kpt on same pce towards fin* **7/1**[3]

5635 **4** 1 ¾ **Buccaneers Vault (IRE)**[9] 3095 5-9-5 **73**...(v[1]) GrahamLee 7 73
(Paul Midgley) *hld up: hdwy wl over 2f out: chsd ldrs over 1f out: sn rdn and no imp ins fnl f* **6/1**[2]

21-3 **5** 2 ¼ **Questo**[44] 1972 5-8-7 **61**... JoeFanning 9 54
(Tracy Waggott) *in tch centre: hdwy 1/2-way: sn chsng ldrs: rdn wl over 1f out: wknd appr fnl f* **7/2**[1]

55-6 **6** 3 ¼ **Vincenzo Coccotti (USA)**[18] 2763 5-8-11 **68**... HollieDoyle(3) 2 51
(Ken Cunningham-Brown) *chsd ldrs centre: rdn along wl over 2f out: sn one pce* **7/1**[3]

-050 **7** 1 ¼ **Bernie's Boy**[14] 2888 4-9-5 **73**...(p) TonyHamilton 4 52
(Roger Fell) *racd centre: a towards rr* **25/1**

-450 **8** ¾ **Dinneratmidnight**[16] 2837 6-9-4 **72**...(bt) KevinStott 8 48
(Richard Guest) *a towards rr* **14/1**

-360 **9** ¾ **Rose Marmara**[15] 2856 4-9-7 **75**...(t) BarryMcHugh 11 49
(Brian Rothwell) *a towards rr* **12/1**

0-00 **10** 4 ½ **Etienne Gerard**[16] 2821 5-9-1 **69**...(p) SilvestreDeSousa 12 29
(Nigel Tinkler) *racd nr stands rail: prom: rdn along over 2f out: sn drvn and wknd* **8/1**

1-00 **11** 32 **Oh James**[16] 2821 4-8-13 **67**...(h) AndrewMullen 6
(Tim Easterby) *wnt rt and bmpd s: a bhd: detached fr 1/2-way* **33/1**

1m 11.89s (-0.81) **Going Correction** +0.15s/f (Good) **11** Ran SP% **119.8**
Speed ratings (Par 103): **111,110,109,107,104 100,98,97,96,90 47**
CSF £104.17 CT £595.13 TOTE £4.50: £1.50, £4.90, £2.90; EX 82.20 Trifecta £637.00.
**Owner** The Hollinbridge Partnership & Ruth Carr **Bred** Gestut Hofgut Heymann **Trained** Huby, N Yorks

**FOCUS**
A fair sprint handicap. The winner has been rated 6lb off last year's peak, with the second running a small pb.

## 3402 PENELOPE DENNY OVER THE HILL H'CAP 7f 218y

**4:00** (4:05) (Class 5) (0-70,72) 4-Y-O+ **£3,557** (£1,058; £529; £264) **Stalls** Low

Form RPR

2133 **1** **Kenstone (FR)**[39] 2116 4-8-13 **65**...(p) HollieDoyle(3) 16 81
(Adrian Wintle) *.in tch: smooth hdwy 3f out: sn cl up: led wl over 1f out and sn rdn clr: readily* **15/2**[3]

6650 **2** 6 **Green Howard**[35] 2224 9-9-0 **63**...(b) DuranFentiman 17 66
(Rebecca Bastiman) *hld up: hdwy over 2f out: rdn wl over 1f out: chsd wnr ins fnl f: sn no imp* **14/1**

16-0 **3** 1 ¾ **Mango Chutney**[38] 2120 4-9-0 **63**...(p) PhillipMakin 3 62
(John Davies) *trckd ldrs: hdwy over 3f out: rdn along 2f out: drvn over 1f out: kpt on same pce* **12/1**

3401 **4** 1 ½ **Kiwi Bay**[12] 2955 12-9-5 **68**... PaulMulrennan 13 64
(Michael Dods) *t.k.h: hld up towards rr: hdwy 3f out: rdn along 2f out: kpt on u.p fnl f* **12/1**

3-04 **5** 1 ¾ **Bold Spirit**[11] 2990 6-8-5 **59**...(vt) PhilDennis(5) 15 51+
(Declan Carroll) *led: rdn along and jnd over 2f out: hdd wl over 1f out: sn drvn and wknd appr fnl f* **14/1**

-060 **6** ½ **Framley Garth (IRE)**[37] 2146 5-8-11 **67**... PaulaMuir(7) 7 58
(Patrick Holmes) *bhd: pushed along 3f out: hdwy on wd outside 2f out: sn rdn and kpt on fnl f: nvr nr ldrs* **20/1**

0506 **7** *1* **Willsy**[6] 3181 4-8-11 **65** (b[1]) GemmaTutty(5) 14 54
(Karen Tutty) *midfield: hdwy on outer over 3f out: rdn to chse ldrs over 2f out: sn drvn and no imp* **20/1**

-500 **8** *4 1/2* **Sunnua (IRE)**[14] 2900 4-8-13 **69** SebastianWoods(7) 11 48
(Richard Fahey) *midfield: in tch on inner over 3f out: effrt whn nt clr run wl over 1f out: sn swtchd rt and rdn: n.d* **13/2**[1]

0-3 **9** *hd* **Rayaa**[46] 1897 4-9-7 **70** (t) GrahamLee 1 48
(John Butler) *in tch on inner: n.m.r and swtchd rt over 2f out: sn rdn and n.d* **8/1**

1403 **10** *1 1/4* **Rebel State (IRE)**[28] 2458 4-8-11 **60** JackGarritty 2 35
(Jedd O'Keeffe) *chsd ldrs: rdn along wl over 2f out: sn wknd* **10/1**

-050 **11** *4 1/2* **Mr Cool Cash**[28] 2466 5-9-3 **66** JoeFanning 4 32
(Richard Guest) *chsd ldr: rdn along over 2f out: sn drvn and wknd* **7/1**[2]

-045 **12** *nk* **In Focus (IRE)**[27] 2501 6-8-8 **57** (t[1]) PaulHanagan 10 22
(Philip Kirby) *a towards rr* **16/1**

4-23 **13** *2* **Royal Holiday (IRE)**[82] 1210 10-9-5 **68** (p) BarryMcHugh 12 28
(Marjorie Fife) *chsd ldrs: rdn along 3f out: sn wknd* **16/1**

2220 **14** *nse* **Tadaawol**[21] 2685 4-9-9 **72** (p) TonyHamilton 8 32
(Roger Fell) *trckd ldrs: hdwy to chse ldr 1/2-way: rdn along wl over 2f out: sn wknd* **7/1**[2]

00-0 **15** *1/2* **The King's Steed**[13] 2918 4-8-2 **51** oh6 AndrewMullen 6 10
(Micky Hammond) *a towards rr* **40/1**

0060 **16** *nk* **Nelson's Bay**[13] 2918 8-8-1 **53** SammyJoBell(3) 5 12
(Wilf Storey) *a rr* **50/1**

50-0 **17** *99* **Favourite Treat (USA)**[38] 2119 7-9-7 **70** (e) JamesSullivan 9 +
(Ruth Carr) *awkward and stmbld s: rdr lost iron: a bhd: virtually p.u 2f out* **16/1**

1m 40.42s (0.32) **Going Correction** +0.15s/f (Good) **17** Ran SP% **130.6**
Speed ratings (Par 103): **104,98,96,94,93 92,91,87,86,85 81,80,78,78,78 77,**
CSF £111.13 CT £1327.63 TOTE £6.20: £1.70, £3.40, £3.30, £3.40; EX 131.30 Trifecta £1658.80.
**Owner** Glyn Byard **Bred** Guy Pariente Holding Sprl **Trained** Westbury-On-Severn, Gloucs

**FOCUS**
It was pouring with rain. The winner proved extremely well handicapped.

## 3403 RACINGUK.COM/DAYPASS H'CAP 6f
**4:35** (4:37) (Class 6) (0-65,65) 3-Y-O £2,911 (£866; £432; £216) **Stalls** Centre

Form RPR

06-0 **1** **Uncle Charlie (IRE)**[14] 2885 3-9-4 **62** KevinStott 1 67
(Ann Duffield) *in tch towards far rail: hdwy 2f out: swtchd lft and rdn over 1f out: clpse up and drvn ins fnl f: styd on to ld nr fin* **10/1**

2345 **2** *nk* **Sheepscar Lad (IRE)**[35] 2223 3-9-7 **65** SilvestreDeSousa 7 69
(Nigel Tinkler) *racd towards far side: prom: rdn wl over 1f out: led ins fnl f: sn drvn: hdd and no ex nr fin* **8/1**

3-50 **3** *1* **Kroy**[15] 2853 3-8-12 **56** (p[1]) AndrewMullen 17 57
(Ollie Pears) *racd nr stands rail: hdwy 1/2-way: cl up 2f out: rdn to ld 11/2f out and sn edgd lft: drvn and hung lft 1f out: hdd ins fnl f: kpt on* **18/1**

0044 **4** *1 3/4* **Cupid's Arrow (IRE)**[11] 2993 3-9-3 **61** JamesSullivan 5 60
(Ruth Carr) *racd towards far side: hld up: hdwy over 2f out: n.m.r and swtchd rt over 1f out: sn rdn and kpt on fnl f* **5/1**[2]

30-0 **5** *nk* **Foxy Boy**[14] 2897 3-9-2 **60** PaulMulrennan 6 55
(Michael Dods) *racd towards far side: prom: rdn along wl over 1f out: drvn and kpt on fnl f* **20/1**

20-3 **6** *3/4* **Gaval**[13] 2924 3-9-7 **65** PhillipMakin 3 58
(David Barron) *prom far side: rdn along over 2f out: sn drvn and wknd fnl f* **10/1**

0-00 **7** *1* **Decadent Times (IRE)**[11] 2993 3-8-13 **57** BarryMcHugh 8 47
(Marjorie Fife) *racd towards far side: in tch: swtchd rt and hdwy to chal centre 2f out: rdn and slt ld wl over 1rf out: sn hdd: drvn and grad wknd* **16/1**

6206 **8** *3/4* **Dapper Man (IRE)**[14] 2885 3-9-3 **61** (p) TonyHamilton 18 48
(Roger Fell) *racd towards stands side: prom: rdn along over 2f out: drvn wl over 1f out: grad wknd* **33/1**

-126 **9** *4 1/2* **Stubytuesday**[23] 2630 3-9-4 **65** NathanEvans(3) 13 39
(Michael Easterby) *racd towards stands side: chsd ldrs: rdn along over 2f out: sn no imp* **11/2**[3]

**10** *3/4* **Edgar Allan Poe (IRE)**[227] 7519 3-9-5 **63** DuranFentiman 10 35
(Rebecca Bastiman) *prom towards stands side: rdn along over 2f out: sn one pce* **50/1**

-241 **11** *2* **Arnold**[15] 2853 3-9-7 **65** JoeFanning 12 31
(Ann Duffield) *chsd ldrs stands side: rdn along 2f out: sn wknd* **7/2**[1]

336- **12** *shd* **Harvest Moon**[188] 8139 3-9-0 **65** SebastianWoods(7) 9 30
(Richard Fahey) *a towards rr far side* **18/1**

20-6 **13** *hd* **My Cherry Blossom**[23] 2631 3-8-11 **58** RachelRichardson(3) 4 23
(Tim Easterby) *overall ldr far side: rdn along over 2f out: hdd wl over 1f out: sn wknd* **16/1**

0260 **14** *2 3/4* **Stringybark Creek**[18] 2757 3-9-4 **62** GrahamLee 11 18
(Mick Channon) *racd towards stands side: chsd ldrs: rdn along 1/2-way: sn wknd* **20/1**

606 **F** **Noble Sword**[13] 2924 3-8-12 **56** JackGarritty 2
(Jedd O'Keeffe) *cl up far side: rdn along wl over 2f out: sn wknd and rr whn clipped heels and fell wl over 1f out* **25/1**

1m 12.5s (-0.20) **Going Correction** +0.15s/f (Good) **15** Ran SP% **124.1**
Speed ratings (Par 97): **107,106,105,102,102 101,100,99,93,92 89,89,89,85,**
CSF £84.21 CT £1475.52 TOTE £14.30: £4.00, £2.50, £5.70; EX 128.80 Trifecta £3388.00.
**Owner** David Barker & Partner **Bred** Knocklong House Stud **Trained** Constable Burton, N Yorks
■ Stewards' Enquiry : Kevin Stott seven-day ban (19-25 Jun): careless riding

**FOCUS**
The runners were spread across the track, with the main action unfolding far side. It's been rated as straightforward, limited form.

## 3404 FOLLOW @RACING_UK ON TWITTER MAIDEN FILLIES' STKS 7f 218y
**5:05** (5:12) (Class 5) 3-Y-O+ £3,557 (£1,058; £529; £264) **Stalls** Low

Form RPR

05 **1** **Lyric Harmony (IRE)**[14] 2898 3-9-0 0 KevinStott 8 76
(Giles Bravery) *in tch: hdwy 3f out: led 2f out: sn rdn and edgd lft : clr ent fnl f: rdn out* **7/4**[1]

**2** *3/4* **White Rosa (IRE)** 3-9-0 0 JosephineGordon 4 73
(Hugo Palmer) *in tch: hdwy 3f out: trckd ldrs whn n.m.r and swtchd rt 11/2f out: sn rdn to chse wnr: drvn ins fnl f: kpt on* **11/4**[2]

5 **3** *7* **Les Pecheurs (IRE)**[32] 2344 3-8-7 0 DanielleMooney(7) 6 57
(James Ewart) *prom: hdwy and cl up 3f out: rdn along 2f out: sn carried sltly lft: drvn over 1f out: kpt on one pce* **66/1**

0 **4** *4 1/2* **Best Of My Love (IRE)**[10] 3039 3-9-0 0 SilvestreDeSousa 1 47
(Mick Channon) *led: rdn along 3f out: hdd 2f out: sn drvn and wknd* **10/1**[3]

6-0 **5** *2 3/4* **Harbour Belle**[14] 2898 3-9-0 0 PaulMulrennan 11 40
(Michael Dods) *midfield: hdwy wl over 2f out: sn rdn and plugged on: nvr nr ldrs* **25/1**

6 **6** *1/2* **Super Ruby**[20] 2704 3-8-11 0 JordanVaughan(3) 2 39
(K R Burke) *chsd ldrs on inner: hdwy over 3f out: rdn along over 2f out: sn drvn and grad wknd* **25/1**

6 **7** *10* **Powercell (IRE)**[21] 2682 3-8-11 0 RachelRichardson(3) 5 16
(Tim Easterby) *sn outpcd: a bhd* **25/1**

000- **8** *10* **Ingleby Erin**[307] 4987 4-9-8 42 NathanEvans(3) 10
(Colin Teague) *prom: trckd ldr after 3f: rdn along over 3f out: sn wknd* **125/1**

**9** *5* **Love Candy (IRE)** 3-9-0 0 NeilFarley 9
(Sally Haynes) *a towards rr* **28/1**

00 **10** *20* **Catskill**[13] 2924 3-8-9 0 MeganNicholls(5) 7
(Wilf Storey) *sn outpcd and a bhd* **100/1**

1m 43.63s (3.53) **Going Correction** +0.15s/f (Good)
**WFA** 3 from 4yo 11lb **10** Ran SP% **90.4**
Speed ratings (Par 100): **88,87,80,75,73 72,62,52,47,27**
CSF £3.25 TOTE £2.20: £1.10, £1.10, £13.70; EX 4.80 Trifecta £253.00.
**Owner** Mrs C Cashman **Bred** Rathbarry Stud **Trained** Newmarket, Suffolk
■ Isabella was withdrawn. Price at time of withdrawal 9/4. Rule 4 applies to all bets - deduction 30p in the pound.

**FOCUS**
Not much depth to this maiden, with Isabella refusing to enter the stalls, but the first two pulled clear and are probably fair enough fillies. The winner has been rated in line with the better view of her latest effort.

## 3405 WATCH ROYAL ASCOT HERE TUESDAY 20TH JUNE FILLIES' H'CAP 1m 4f 8y
**5:35** (5:36) (Class 5) (0-70,66) 3-Y-O+ £3,557 (£1,058; £529; £264) **Stalls** High

Form RPR

-012 **1** **Dyna Might**[5] 3207 3-8-1 **54** (p) AndrewMullen 6 61
(Ollie Pears) *prom: cl up 1/2-way: rdn to dispute ld over 4f out: slt ld wl over 2f out: drvn clr appr fnl f: kpt on strly* **9/4**[1]

0-55 **2** *1* **Duke's Girl**[18] 2761 3-8-13 **66** PaulMulrennan 9 70
(Michael Bell) *hld up: hdwy to trck ldng pair over 5f out: effrt over 2f out and sn rdn: drvn to chse wnr ent fnl f: kpt on* **3/1**[2]

-013 **3** *1 3/4* **Mrs Biggs**[10] 3043 5-8-10 **53** PhilDennis(5) 3 54
(Declan Carroll) *led: pushed along and jnd over 4f out: rdn over 3f out: hdd wl over 2f out and sn drvn: kpt on same pce* **6/1**

-314 **4** *4* **Lady Turpin (IRE)**[74] 1330 4-9-0 **59** SebastianWoods(7) 4 54
(Richard Fahey) *t.k.h early: trckd ldrs: pushed along and lost pl 5f out: rdn along over 2f out: kpt on one pce* **10/1**

3350 **5** *nk* **Spirit Of Rome (IRE)**[20] 2705 3-8-2 **58** HollieDoyle(3) 7 52
(James Bethell) *prom: pushed along over 4f out: rdn over 3f out: drvn along over 2f out: one pce* **4/1**[3]

505- **6** *2* **Pennerley**[238] 7214 4-9-9 **61** PaulHanagan 8 52
(Micky Hammond) *t.k.h early: trckd ldrs: pushed along over 4f out: rdn along 3f out: sn outpcd* **11/1**

000- **7** *hd* **Cadmium**[216] 7754 6-8-8 **53** LaurenSteade(7) 5 44
(Micky Hammond) *hld up: hdwy over 4f out: rdn along and in tch on outer 3f out: drvn over 2f out: wknd* **50/1**

-240 **8** *2 1/4* **Fillydelphia (IRE)**[10] 3043 6-8-11 **56** PaulaMuir(7) 2 43
(Patrick Holmes) *chsd ldrs: rdn along 5f out: sn lost pl and bhd* **16/1**

2m 48.6s (12.40) **Going Correction** +0.15s/f (Good)
**WFA** 3 from 4yo+ 15lb **8** Ran SP% **115.3**
Speed ratings (Par 100): **64,63,62,59,59 57,57,56**
CSF £9.21 CT £34.45 TOTE £2.40: £1.30, £1.10, £1.70; EX 6.80 Trifecta £54.20.
**Owner** Ownaracehorse Ltd (ownaracehorse.co.uk) **Bred** Northmore Stud **Trained** Norton, N Yorks

**FOCUS**
A modest handicap. The winner has been rated to her latest Beverley effort.
T/Jkpt: Part Won. Pool: £10,000.00 - 0.5 winning unit. T/Plt: £105.20 to a £1 stake. Pool: £61,896.13 - 429.49 winning units T/Qpdt: £56.10 to a £1 stake. Pool: £5,204.08 - 68.56 winning units **Joe Rowntree**

# 3156 WINDSOR (R-H)
### Monday, June 5

**OFFICIAL GOING: Good to firm (good in places), changing to good after race 3 (6.40), changing to soft after race 5 (7.40)**
Wind: Moderate, across Weather: Overcast, raining from race 3

## 3406 SKY BET EBF STALLIONS NOVICE STKS (PLUS 10 RACE) 5f 21y
**5:40** (5:40) (Class 4) 2-Y-O £3,946 (£1,174; £586; £293) **Stalls** Low

Form RPR

1 **1** **Nine Below Zero**[9] 3083 2-9-8 0 FranBerry 1 90+
(Ralph Beckett) *pressed ldr: led 1/2-way: shkn up over 1f out: drew clr fnl f: readily* **6/4**[1]

4 **2** *3 3/4* **Midsummer Knight**[9] 3083 2-9-2 0 CharlesBishop 4 71
(Mick Channon) *chsd ldng pair: wnt 2nd wl over 1f out: drvn and cl enough sn after: outpcd fnl f* **10/1**

0 **3** *2 1/4* **Lethal Lunch**[56] 1681 2-9-2 0 SeanLevey 5 62
(Richard Hannon) *s.i.s: in rr tl effrt on outer 1/2-way: rdn to take 3rd over 1f out: stl looked green and no imp: stmbld last strides* **4/1**[3]

422 **4** *nk* **Choice Encounter**[21] 2691 2-9-2 0 JamieSpencer 2 65
(Michael Bell) *settled in last: pushed along 2f out: kpt on same pce and nvr able to threaten* **15/8**[2]

64 **5** *11* **The Golden Cue**[14] 2890 2-9-2 0 RoystonFfrench 3 22
(Steph Hollinshead) *led to 1/2-way: wknd qckly wl over 1f out* **20/1**

59.78s (-0.52) **Going Correction** +0.075s/f (Good) **5** Ran SP% **108.6**
Speed ratings (Par 95): **107,101,97,96,79**
CSF £15.46 TOTE £2.30: £1.30, £3.30; EX 11.20 Trifecta £27.80.
**Owner** P K Gardner **Bred** Springcombe Park Stud **Trained** Kimpton, Hants

**FOCUS**
A fair juvenile novice stakes and a decisive winner in a decent time. The second and third set the opening level.

## 3407 TRAILFINDERS CARIBBEAN HOLIDAYS MAIDEN STKS 6f 12y
**6:10** (6:10) (Class 5) 3-Y-O+ £2,911 (£866; £432; £216) **Stalls** Low

Form RPR

332- **1** **Madame Bounty (IRE)**[324] 4405 3-9-0 71 LiamKeniry 2 73
(Ed Walker) *mde all and racd against nr side rail: rdn and styd on wl fr over 1f out* **9/4**[2]

33 **2** *1 ¼* **Dirchill (IRE)**[16] 2819 3-9-5 0 FranBerry 6 74
(David Barron) *trckd ldng pair: rdn to chse wnr 2f out: styd on and drew clr of rest but nvr able to chal seriously* **8/11**[1]
60 **3** *9* **Fivos**[12] 2957 3-9-5 0 SeanLevey 5 45
(David Bridgwater) *chsd wnr to 2f out: wknd but hld on for 3rd* **50/1**
**4** *shd* **Astone Man (FR)** 3-9-5 0 RobertWinston 4 45
(Tony Carroll) *in tch in rr: rn green and racd wd fr 1/2-way: outpcd over 2f out: plugged on to press for 3rd nr fin* **14/1**
54- **5** *3* **Papa Delta**[366] 2902 3-9-5 0 WilliamCarson 1 35
(Tony Carroll) *stdd s: t.k.h and hld up: effrt 1/2-way: wknd 2f out* **20/1**
000- **6** *7* **Aegean Secret**[265] 6448 3-9-0 44 MitchGodwin(5) 7 13
(John Bridger) *chsd ldrs on outer: rdn 1/2-way: sn wknd* **66/1**
**7** *2 ½* **Make Sail** 3-9-0 0 FergusSweeney 3
(Tony Carroll) *hld up in tch: wknd qckly over 2f out* **8/1**[3]
1m 12.1s (-0.90) **Going Correction** +0.075s/f (Good) **7** Ran SP% **114.7**
Speed ratings (Par 103): **109,107,95,95,91 81,78**
CSF £4.23 TOTE £3.10: £1.60, £1.10; EX 4.00 Trifecta £39.90.
**Owner** Paola Hewins Olivia Hoare **Bred** Mount Coote Partnership **Trained** Upper Lambourn, Berks

**FOCUS**
A modest 3yo maiden in which the market leaders came well clear. The first two have been rated to their maiden form.

## 3408 TRAILFINDERS AWARD-WINNING TRAVEL MAIDEN AUCTION STKS 1m 2f
**6:40** (6:40) (Class 5) 3-Y-O **£2,911** (£866; £432; £216) **Stalls** Centre

Form RPR
2-32 **1** **Shadow Warrior**[34] 2273 3-9-1 70 JoeyHaynes 5 76
(Paul D'Arcy) *taken down early: t.k.h: trckd ldng pair: rdn to ld between them wl over 1f out: styd on and in command fnl f* **9/2**[3]
6 **2** *1 ¾* **Mancini**[12] 2963 3-9-4 0 RichardKingscote 9 75
(Jonathan Portman) *trckd ldr: shkn up to chal over 2f out: wnr wnt past wl over 1f out: chsng after: styd on but readily hld* **3/1**[2]
**3** *8* **Josh The Plod (IRE)** 3-8-6 0 JasonWatson(7) 2 54
(Andrew Balding) *dwlt: hld up in last pair: pushed along and sme prog 3f out: outpcd by ldrs but kpt on steadily to take 3rd ins fnl f* **16/1**
4-22 **4** *1* **Steaming (IRE)**[16] 2841 3-9-1 80 FranBerry 4 54
(Ralph Beckett) *led: rdn and hdd wl over 1f out: wknd tamely* **4/6**[1]
50- **5** *2* **Bermondsey Belle (IRE)**[160] 8537 3-8-10 0 RoystonFfrench 7 45
(Lucy Wadham) *chsd ldrs: rdn 3f out: wknd over 2f out* **20/1**
0 **6** *3 ¾* **Desert Song**[21] 2689 3-9-1 0 FergusSweeney 1 43
(Pat Phelan) *hld up in last pair: effrt to go 4th over 3f out: wknd over 2f out* **50/1**
**7** *28* **Stellekaya (IRE)** 3-8-13 0 TomQueally 6
(Mark H Tompkins) *dropped to last and struggling 1/2-way: t.o* **50/1**
2m 11.7s (3.00) **Going Correction** +0.075s/f (Good) **7** Ran SP% **117.7**
Speed ratings (Par 99): **91,89,83,82,80 77,55**
CSF £18.91 TOTE £6.20: £2.70, £2.30; EX 22.30 Trifecta £198.80.
**Owner** Mrs Jan Harris **Bred** Mrs L H Field **Trained** Newmarket, Suffolk

**FOCUS**
Rail movements added 14yds to the race distance. This modest maiden auction was run at a steady pace early, but the first two came clear and the winner disappointed. The runner-up has been rated as improving slightly on his debut run.

## 3409 GET THE SKY BET ADVANTAGE H'CAP 1m 3f 99y
**7:10** (7:11) (Class 4) (0-85,84) 4-Y-O+ **£4,690** (£1,395; £697; £348) **Stalls** Centre

Form RPR
16-4 **1** **West Drive (IRE)**[12] 2965 4-9-3 80 (p[1]) HarryBentley 6 89
(Roger Varian) *hld up in midfield: shoved along over 3f out: prog on outer over 2f out: drvn to ld last 75yds: hld on wl* **5/2**[1]
03-6 **2** *shd* **Opposition**[18] 2752 4-9-4 81 PatCosgrave 8 90
(Ed Dunlop) *hld up in midfield: prog 3f out: rdn to chal over 1f out: led jst ins fnl f: hdd last 75yds: nt qckn nr fin* **6/1**
6022 **3** *3 ½* **Essenaitch (IRE)**[14] 2909 4-8-8 71 StevieDonohoe 10 74
(David Evans) *t.k.h: hld up in last pair: prog 3f out: rdn and nt qckn over 1f out: r.o ins fnl f to take 3rd nr fin* **8/1**
0-20 **4** *1 ¾* **Croquembouche (IRE)**[24] 2574 8-9-0 84 RossaRyan(7) 2 84
(Ed de Giles) *led: hanging lft fr 4f out whn urged along: hrd pressed over 2f out: hdd & wknd jst ins fnl f* **5/1**[3]
420 **5** *1 ¼* **Priors Brook**[61] 1555 6-8-7 77 JoshuaBryan(7) 5 75
(Andrew Balding) *trckd ldng pair: rdn to chal 2f out to over 1f out: fdd sn after* **7/2**[2]
530- **6** *5* **Jazzy (IRE)**[21] 6300 4-8-12 75 (tp) TomQueally 4 64
(Martin Keighley) *trckd ldng pair: reminder 4f out: wknd jst over 2f out* **25/1**
00-4 **7** *2* **Ravenous**[23] 2617 6-9-4 81 KieranO'Neill 3 67
(Luke Dace) *restless stalls: trckd ldr: chal 3f out tl wknd qckly 2f out* **5/1**[3]
-050 **8** *5* **Ibazz**[84] 1178 4-9-5 82 RobertWinston 7 60
(Ian Williams) *hld up in last: shuffled along and no prog 3f out: nvr involved and eased over 1f out* **16/1**
2m 30.8s (1.30) **Going Correction** +0.075s/f (Good) **8** Ran SP% **119.3**
Speed ratings (Par 105): **98,97,95,94,93 89,88,84**
CSF £19.02 CT £107.38 TOTE £3.70: £1.40, £1.80, £2.00; EX 15.60 Trifecta £40.70.
**Owner** H R H Sultan Ahmad Shah **Bred** Airlie Stud **Trained** Newmarket, Suffolk

**FOCUS**
Rail movements added 14yds to the race distance. The going was changed to Good before this race. A competitive handicap in the rain-softened ground and a close finish. A pb from the winner, with the runner-up rated as improving and the third to his recent effort.

## 3410 SKY BET WINDSOR SPRINT SERIES H'CAP (QUALIFIER) 6f 12y
**7:40** (7:40) (Class 3) (0-95,95) 4-Y-O+ **£7,439** (£2,213; £1,106; £553) **Stalls** Low

Form RPR
-362 **1** **Stake Acclaim (IRE)**[16] 2835 5-9-1 89 RobertWinston 2 105
(Dean Ivory) *only one to r against nr side rail: mde all: clr 1/2-way: rdn over 1f out: nvr remotely threatened* **10/1**
11-0 **2** *4* **Upstaging**[10] 3034 5-9-3 94 KieranShoemark(3) 5 97
(Paul Cole) *chsd ldrs in centre: struggling 1/2-way: rallied 2f out: styd on to take 2nd last stride: no ch w wnr* **14/1**
-142 **3** *hd* **Ice Age (IRE)**[17] 2780 4-8-12 86 CharlesBishop 8 89
(Eve Johnson Houghton) *led gp in centre: nt on terms w wnr fr 1/2-way: no imp over 1f out: lost 2nd last stride* **7/2**[2]
1-14 **4** *1 ½* **Jordan Sport**[105] 842 4-9-5 93 (h) JamieSpencer 10 91
(David Simcock) *pressed ldr in centre tl 1f out: one pce* **7/1**
-305 **5** *¾* **Charles Molson**[23] 2606 6-9-4 92 PatCosgrave 12 87
(Patrick Chamings) *chsd ldrs in centre: rdn and effrt 2f out: kpt on but nvr pce to threaten* **5/1**[3]
300 **6** *hd* **Dougan**[52] 1769 5-9-6 94 FranBerry 9 89
(David Evans) *settled in last trio: effrt on outer over 2f out: shkn up and kpt on but nvr able to threaten* **16/1**
4-10 **7** *½* **Udontdodou**[19] 2736 4-9-0 88 SeanLevey 3 81
(Richard Guest) *chsd ldrs in centre: rdn 2f out: no imp over 1f out: fdd* **3/1**[1]
331- **8** *2 ¼* **Summer Chorus**[247] 6946 4-8-12 86 (h) DavidProbert 4 72
(Andrew Balding) *stdd s: hld up in last trio: shkn up over 2f out: no prog* **8/1**
3005 **9** *½* **Eljaddaaf (IRE)**[17] 2780 6-8-11 88 (h) JackDuern(3) 7 72
(Dean Ivory) *a in last trio: rdn and no prog 2f out* **20/1**
0-13 **10** *4 ½* **Little Palaver**[24] 2566 5-9-1 92 HectorCrouch(3) 6 62
(Clive Cox) *prom in centre 4f: wknd qckly* **9/1**
1m 12.37s (-0.63) **Going Correction** +0.075s/f (Good) **10** Ran SP% **123.9**
Speed ratings (Par 107): **107,101,101,99,98 98,97,94,93,87**
CSF £148.75 CT £609.26 TOTE £11.30: £2.90, £4.20, £1.50; EX 140.70 Trifecta £1094.90.
**Owner** M J Yarrow **Bred** G Devlin **Trained** Radlett, Herts

**FOCUS**
The feature race and a good class sprint handicap, but a runaway winner. The winner has been rated to the best view of his form.

## 3411 SKY BET BEST ODDS GUARANTEED H'CAP 5f 21y
**8:10** (8:11) (Class 4) (0-80,81) 3-Y-O **£4,690** (£1,395; £697; £348) **Stalls** Low

Form RPR
246 **1** **Blitz**[38] 2130 3-9-4 80 HectorCrouch(3) 7 85
(Clive Cox) *chsd ldr: styd towards nr side rail fr 1/2-way and led over 1f out: drvn and hdd fnl f: rallied to ld last stride* **11/8**[1]
1-00 **2** *nse* **Awesome Allan (IRE)**[25] 2557 3-9-5 78 (t) FranBerry 6 83
(David Evans) *chsd ldng pair: styd towards nr side fr 1/2-way and chsd ldr over 1f out: drvn to ld narrowly fnl f: hdd last stride* **3/1**[3]
004- **3** *5* **Secret Potion**[223] 7589 3-9-0 73 FergusSweeney 5 60
(Ronald Harris) *outpcd and pushed along early: styd in centre fr 1/2-way and sn no ch: hanging lft over 1f out: tk modest 3rd nr fin* **16/1**
113 **4** *½* **Fethiye Boy**[19] 2720 3-8-13 72 DavidProbert 4 57
(Ronald Harris) *led: 3 l clr whn styd in centre fr 1/2-way: hdd over 1f out: wknd* **11/4**[2]
1-50 **5** *hd* **Big Lachie**[35] 2215 3-9-3 79 CharlieBennett(3) 9 63
(Daniel Mark Loughnane) *hld up in last: styd in centre fr 1/2-way and sn no ch: pushed along and nvr nr ldrs after* **6/1**
1m 0.85s (0.55) **Going Correction** +0.075s/f (Good) **5** Ran SP% **113.9**
Speed ratings (Par 101): **98,97,89,89,88**
CSF £6.11 TOTE £2.60: £1.50, £1.60; EX 6.80 Trifecta £58.50.
**Owner** The Blitz Partnership **Bred** David Jamison & Gordon Roddick **Trained** Lambourn, Berks

**FOCUS**
A fair 3yo sprint handicap that was weakened by the withdrawal of half the field, mainly due to the ground. It produced a desperate finish.

## 3412 TRAILFINDERS UNFORGETTABLE HOLIDAY H'CAP 1m 31y
**8:40** (8:40) (Class 5) (0-75,77) 3-Y-O **£2,911** (£866; £432; £216) **Stalls** Low

Form RPR
2-62 **1** **Pillar Of Society (IRE)**[32] 2330 3-9-7 75 SeanLevey 13 84
(Richard Hannon) *mde all: styd against nr side rail in st: had rest in trble 2f out: shkn up over 1f out: styd on wl: unchal* **6/1**[3]
45-4 **2** *3 ½* **Hernandes (FR)**[16] 2820 3-9-5 73 LiamKeniry 9 74
(Ed Walker) *chsd wnr after 3f: rdn over 2f out: kpt on but no imp after* **8/1**
56-3 **3** *1 ¼* **Suspect Package (USA)**[23] 2625 3-9-6 74 (h) DanielMuscutt 2 72
(James Fanshawe) *chsd ldrs: rdn and prog over 2f out: chsd ldng pair wl over 1f out: kpt on same pce* **10/3**[1]
0-20 **4** *1* **See The Master (IRE)**[17] 2778 3-9-7 75 SamHitchcott 11 71
(Clive Cox) *in tch in midfield: rdn and prog fr 2f out: kpt on to take 4th fnl f: no ch* **16/1**
00-4 **5** *1 ¼* **Fair Power (IRE)**[40] 2088 3-9-0 73 MitchGodwin(5) 5 66
(Sylvester Kirk) *towards rr: effrt 3f out: shkn up and kpt on one pce fnl 2f: no ch* **11/1**
64-1 **6** *2* **Keepup Kevin**[17] 2793 3-9-5 73 JohnFahy 3 61
(Pam Sly) *t.k.h: chsd wnr 3f: styd prom tl wknd 2f out* **7/2**[2]
6-03 **7** *nk* **Famous Dynasty (IRE)**[10] 3024 3-8-8 62 DavidProbert 1 50
(Michael Blanshard) *hld up in last pair: effrt 3f out: prog into midfield 2f out: shkn up and no hdwy over 1f out* **20/1**
43-5 **8** *½* **Broughtons Knight**[17] 2793 3-9-2 70 StevieDonohoe 4 57
(Henry Spiller) *dwlt: hld up in rr: in it but kpt on fr over 2f out* **16/1**
41-2 **9** *8* **Raj Balaraaj (GER)**[35] 2220 3-9-1 69 PatCosgrave 8
(George Baker) *hld up towards rr: rdn 2f out: sn no ch in centre of trck* **14/1**
2530 **10** *3 ¼* **Dubai Waves**[34] 2284 3-9-2 70 JackMitchell 7 31
(Hugo Palmer) *nvr bttr than midfield: no prog over 2f out: bhd over 1f out* **16/1**
06-0 **11** *9* **Ede's E Rider**[124] 502 3-8-2 56 oh1 KieranO'Neill 6
(Pat Phelan) *t.k.h: prom: styd in centre in st: wknd 3f out: sn bhd* **50/1**
4461 **12** *5* **El Torito (IRE)**[33] 2293 3-9-6 77 (p) CharlieBennett(3) 10 5
(Jim Boyle) *a wl in rr: bhd fnl 2f* **16/1**
3432 **13** *16* **Arsenio Lupin**[23] 2625 3-9-9 77 (t) AntonioFresu 12 45
(Denis Quinn) *chsd ldrs on outside: struggling over 3f out; t.o* **8/1**
1m 45.33s (0.63) **Going Correction** +0.075s/f (Good) **13** Ran SP% **127.1**
Speed ratings (Par 99): **99,95,94,93,92 90,89,89,81,77 68,63,47**
CSF £57.18 CT £198.70 TOTE £7.30: £2.20, £2.80, £2.10; EX 72.00 Trifecta £336.30.
**Owner** Mrs J Wood **Bred** Jas Linnane, J Moore & B Gardiner **Trained** East Everleigh, Wilts

**FOCUS**
Rail movements added 14yds to the race distance. Another fair handicap but very few got into it and the winner made all and became the fifth winner of the evening to stick to the stands' rail in the straight. A clear pb from the winner, with the runner-up rated to form and the third close to his latest effort.

T/Plt: £45.00 to a £1 stake. Pool: £76,926.90 - 1,247.55 winning units T/Qpdt: £17.80 to a £1 stake. Pool: £7,855.63 - 325.84 winning units **Jonathan Neesom**

3413 - 3420a (Foreign Racing) - See Raceform Interactive

# [2706]CHEPSTOW (L-H)

Tuesday, June 6

**OFFICIAL GOING: Soft (6.2)**

Wind: strong breeze, behind them at times in the home straight Weather: showers and sunny spells

## 3421 CAPITOL SKODA FILLIES' NOVICE STKS (PLUS 10 RACE) 6f 16y

**2:00** (2:05) (Class 5) 2-Y-O **£3,234** (£962; £481; £240) **Stalls** Centre

Form RPR

3 **1** **So Hi Society (IRE)**[11] 3022 2-8-12 0 RichardKingscote 5 84
(Archie Watson) *trckd ldrs: led 2f out: sn drvn: jnd ins fnl f: on top cl home* **5/1**[3]

**2** *nk* **Oriental Song (IRE)** 2-8-12 0 DaneO'Neill 8 83
(Owen Burrows) *trckd ldrs: rdn to chse wnr over 1f out: ev ch ins fnl f tl hld cl home* **7/1**

4 **3** *2* **Reflect Alexander (IRE)**[15] 2905 2-8-12 0 FranBerry 12 77
(David Evans) *led narrowly: rdn over 2f out: sn hdd: kpt on same pce: hld by first two fnl f* **8/1**

5 **4** *2 ¼* **Angel Islington (IRE)**[15] 2905 2-8-12 0 DavidProbert 14 70
(Andrew Balding) *s.i.s: sn chsng ldrs: rdn and lsightly outpcd 2f out: styd on fnl f: tk 4th cl home* **11/2**

4 **5** *shd* **Miss Mo Brown Bear (IRE)**[13] 2958 2-8-12 0 TomMarquand 11 70
(Richard Hannon) *chsd ldrs: rdn over 2f out: kpt on same pce* **9/2**[2]

1 **6** *shd* **Holy Tiber (IRE)**[17] 2816 2-8-13 0 KieranShoemark(3) 4 74
(George Scott) *wnt lft leaving stalls: cl up: rdn and ev ch 2f out: wknd appr fnl f: lost 4th cl home* **9/4**[1]

0 **7** *1 ¾* **Isoletta**[35] 2265 2-8-12 0 LiamKeniry 6 65+
(Ed Walker) *hld up in midfield: nudged along over 2f out and outpcd by ldrs: rdn and grad fdd fnl f* **66/1**

4 **8** *6* **Inuk (IRE)**[7] 3174 2-8-12 0 ShaneKelly 7 47
(Richard Hughes) *w ldr 3f: sn rdn and grad wknd* **25/1**

**9** *nse* **Gone To Sea (IRE)** 2-8-12 0 CharlesBishop 13 46
(David Evans) *s.i.s: rdn 1/2-way: a towards rr* **66/1**

**10** *1 ¾* **Shoyd** 2-8-12 0 KieranO'Neill 1 41
(Richard Hannon) *s.i.s: a in rr* **20/1**

0 **11** *nk* **Runthatbymeagain (IRE)**[47] 1908 2-8-12 0 JohnFahy 10 40
(David Evans) *a towards rr* **80/1**

1m 11.94s (-0.06) **Going Correction** +0.05s/f (Good) **11** Ran SP% **117.4**
Speed ratings (Par 90): **102,101,98,95,95 95,93,85,85,82 82**
CSF £37.99 TOTE £6.40: £2.00, £2.50, £2.60; EX 46.50 Trifecta £313.80.
**Owner** K Sohi **Bred** Robert Ryan, Brendan Quinn & Joan Quinn **Trained** Upper Lambourn, W Berks

**FOCUS**
There had been loads of rain around and the ground was soft. This looked an ordinary fillies' novice race and they raced middle to stands' side. The level is a bit fluid, with the third rated to form for now.

## 3422 VANGUARDIA CONSULTING H'CAP 1m 14y

**2:30** (2:37) (Class 5) (0-70,72) 3-Y-O+ **£3,234** (£962; £481; £240) **Stalls** Centre

Form RPR

0145 **1** **Admirable Art (IRE)**[13] 2974 7-9-12 68 RobertWinston 10 79
(Tony Carroll) *broke wl: sn midfield: hdwy over 2f out: led appr fnl f: rdn out* **9/1**

30-5 **2** *1 ¾* **Spirit Of Belle**[62] 1559 3-8-9 69 KatherineGlenister(7) 3 73
(David Evans) *s.i.s: sn chsng ldrs: rdn to ld over 3f out: hdd appr fnl f: unable qck* **8/1**[3]

5002 **3** *2* **Tripartite (IRE)**[21] 2708 4-10-0 70 MartinLane 17 72
(Jeremy Gask) *cl up: chal 3f out: sn drvn and upsides tl over 1f out: no ex ins fnl f* **5/1**[1]

1160 **4** *2* **Daily Trader**[21] 2711 3-8-12 65 FranBerry 5 60
(David Evans) *hld up: hdwy over 3f out: rdn over 2f out: sn chsng ldrs: styd on same pce fnl f* **5/1**[1]

605- **5** *4 ½* **Pick A Little**[182] 8240 9-9-8 69 MitchGodwin(5) 2 56
(Michael Blake) *prom: rdn over 2f out: kpt on but outpcd by ldrs* **16/1**

14-3 **6** *¾* **Barista (IRE)**[21] 2708 9-9-6 62 CharlesBishop 14 48
(Brian Forsey) *in rr: rdn over 3f out: stl last 2f out: styd on u.p fnl f* **7/1**[2]

4-06 **7** *1 ¾* **Solent Meads (IRE)**[11] 3041 3-9-1 68 (b) GeorgeDowning 13 47
(Daniel Kubler) *t.k.h towards rr: drvn 3f out: modest late hdwy* **12/1**

344 **8** *hd* **Art's Desire (IRE)**[18] 2782 3-9-1 68 LiamKeniry 12 46
(Ed Walker) *s.i.s: hld up: pushed along and clsd over 3f out: no imp on ldrs fnl 2f* **8/1**[3]

66-0 **9** *½* **Zaria**[21] 2708 6-9-4 60 (p) TomMarquand 4 40
(Richard Price) *midfield: rdn over 3f out: wknd 2f out* **16/1**

0000 **10** *4 ½* **Imperial Link**[8] 3142 5-8-4 53 oh1 ow2 (p) BenRobinson(7) 9 23
(John O'Shea) *led tl rdn and hdd over 3f out: wknd 2f out* **8/1**[3]

0-00 **11** *½* **Wilspa's Magic (IRE)**[20] 2724 4-8-9 51 oh4 DavidProbert 8 20
(Ron Hodges) *cl up: rdn over 2f out: wknd and hung lft over 1f out* **50/1**

23-5 **12** *¾* **Edge (IRE)**[19] 2762 6-8-7 56 (b) KeelanBaker(7) 16 23
(Bernard Llewellyn) *s.s: in rr: rdn and sme hdwy 3f out: wknd 2f out* **16/1**

344- **13** *8* **Lady Bayside**[292] 5571 9-9-7 68 GeorgiaCox(5) 15 16
(Malcolm Saunders) *reluctant to enter stalls: sn chsd along in midfield: rdn 3f out: wknd 2f out* **20/1**

1m 35.96s (-0.24) **Going Correction** +0.05s/f (Good)
**WFA** 3 from 4yo+ 11lb **13** Ran SP% **121.2**
Speed ratings (Par 103): **103,101,99,97,92 92,90,90,89,85 84,83,75**
CSF £80.45 CT £421.80 TOTE £11.60: £3.50, £3.30, £2.80; EX 117.90 Trifecta £612.70.
**Owner** D Morgan **Bred** Longview Stud & Bloodstock Ltd **Trained** Cropthorne, Worcs

**FOCUS**
The action was up the middle of the track in this modest handicap.

## 3423 ALAN BUSHELL ON COURSE BOOKMAKER H'CAP 7f 16y

**3:00** (3:05) (Class 6) (0-65,65) 3-Y-O **£2,264** (£673; £336; £168) **Stalls** Centre

Form RPR

0344 **1** **Love And Be Loved**[7] 3191 3-8-0 51 WilliamCox(7) 16 60
(John Flint) *racd alone stands' side: led overall 3f: styd cl up: led over 1f out: edgd lft ins fnl f: pushed out* **7/1**[3]

5260 **2** *2* **Whatalove**[14] 2911 3-7-11 46 oh1 (h[1]) RichardOliver(5) 9 50
(Martin Keighley) *cl up: led 4f out: drvn and hdd over 1f out: kpt on gamely to hold 2nd* **7/1**[3]

-332 **3** *hd* **Topmeup**[69] 1428 3-8-9 53 JohnFahy 5 57
(David Evans) *hld up: rdn and hdwy on far side over 2f out: ch ent fnl f: edgd rt and unable qck* **10/1**

600- **4** *1 ¾* **Tis Wonderful (IRE)**[244] 7065 3-9-7 65 SamHitchcott 4 64
(Clive Cox) *s.i.s: towards rr tl hdwy on far side over 3f out: drvn and ch 1f out: one pce* **13/2**[2]

2503 **5** *2 ½* **Viola Park**[20] 2726 3-8-10 54 (p) FrannyNorton 15 47
(Ronald Harris) *cl up: rdn 2f out: kpt on same pce* **7/2**[1]

0205 **6** *1 ¾* **Met By Moonlight**[20] 2720 3-9-5 63 DavidProbert 3 52
(Ron Hodges) *t.k.h in midfield: rdn to chse ldrs over 2f out: wknd fnl f* **11/1**

0460 **7** *¾* **Neptune Star**[14] 2911 3-8-4 48 (h) LiamJones 6 35
(Jeremy Gask) *towards rr: rdn 3f out: styd on fnl 2f: nvr able to threaten ldrs* **16/1**

00-4 **8** *1 ¼* **Tally's Son**[15] 2895 3-8-4 55 BenRobinson(7) 8 39
(Grace Harris) *w ldrs: drvn 3f out: wknd wl over 1f out* **12/1**

000- **9** *3* **Felstead Queen**[223] 7615 3-8-7 51 ow1 TomMarquand 12 27
(Joseph Tuite) *drvn 4f out: a in rr* **33/1**

5-66 **10** *½* **Rebel Heart**[19] 2757 3-8-13 57 (v) CharlesBishop 13 32
(Bill Turner) *chsd ldrs: rdn 3f out: wknd 2f out* **8/1**

1013 **11** *8* **Chamasay**[51] 1817 3-9-6 64 FranBerry 14 19
(David Evans) *chsd ldrs: rdn 3f out: wknd 2f out: eased fnl f* **8/1**

1m 23.55s (0.35) **Going Correction** +0.05s/f (Good) **11** Ran SP% **116.7**
Speed ratings (Par 97): **100,97,97,95,92 90,89,88,84,84 75**
CSF £54.94 CT £500.55 TOTE £7.80: £2.70, £2.70, £2.50; EX 73.60 Trifecta £980.10.
**Owner** D A Poole **Bred** Sarah McNicholas **Trained** Kenfig Hill, Bridgend

**FOCUS**
A moderate handicap in which the winner raced alone on the stands' side, with the others middle to far side. The second and third have been rated close to their marks.

## 3424 MONMOUTHSHIRE BUSINESS AWARDS H'CAP 6f 16y

**3:30** (3:32) (Class 4) (0-85,87) 3-Y-O+ **£4,851** (£1,443; £721; £360) **Stalls** Centre

Form RPR

0504 **1** **Satchville Flyer**[21] 2708 6-9-1 72 FranBerry 10 79
(David Evans) *s.i.s: hld up: rdn over 2f out: chsd ldrs and hanging lft over 1f out: r.o to ld post* **13/2**

4000 **2** *shd* **Sir Billy Wright (IRE)**[8] 3161 6-9-5 83 KatherineGlenister(7) 4 89
(David Evans) *chsd ldrs: drvn to ld over 2f out: edgd rt over 1f out: rdr briefly dropped reins appr fnl f: hdd post* **6/1**[3]

-103 **3** *½* **Bonjour Steve**[14] 2932 6-8-4 66 oh4 (p) MitchGodwin(5) 2 70
(Richard Price) *hld up: hdwy over 2f out: rdn to chal over 1f out: kpt on u.p: jst hld* **12/1**

-005 **4** *2* **Munfallet (IRE)**[17] 2840 6-9-13 87 KieranShoemark(3) 7 85
(David Brown) *w ldrs: rdn over 2f out: unable qck ent fnl f* **4/1**[1]

1053 **5** *3 ¼* **Dandy Flame (IRE)**[19] 2757 3-8-12 77 ShaneKelly 1 63
(Richard Hughes) *chsd ldrs: rdn over 2f out: one pce fnl f* **8/1**

016- **6** *1 ½* **Ginzan**[248] 6946 9-9-5 81 GeorgiaCox(5) 9 64
(Malcolm Saunders) *chsd ldrs: sn pushed along: rdn and nt clr run over 2f out: nvr able to threaten* **20/1**

00-0 **7** *nk* **Cincuenta Pasos (IRE)**[40] 2113 6-10-0 85 DaneO'Neill 6 67
(Joseph Tuite) *s.i.s: towards rr: swtchd lft and hdwy 2f out: drvn and no imp fnl f* **7/1**

0014 **8** *½* **Englishman**[10] 3074 7-9-12 83 DavidProbert 8 63
(Milton Bradley) *led narrowly tl drvn and hdd over 2f out: wkng whn n.m.r appr fnl f* **9/2**[2]

6-50 **9** *½* **Vincentti (IRE)**[8] 3136 7-9-4 75 (p) FrannyNorton 3 54
(Ronald Harris) *hld up: rdn over 2f out: no hdwy* **14/1**

000 **10** *9* **Equally Fast**[24] 2608 5-9-2 73 (h) LiamKeniry 5 23
(Peter Hiatt) *cl up tl rdn and fnd nthing 2f out: wknd qckly: eased fnl f* **14/1**

1m 11.82s (-0.18) **Going Correction** +0.05s/f (Good)
**WFA** 3 from 5yo+ 8lb **10** Ran SP% **115.2**
Speed ratings (Par 105): **103,102,102,99,95 93,92,92,91,79**
CSF £44.69 CT £467.86 TOTE £7.90: £2.50, £2.30, £3.30; EX 48.90 Trifecta £676.20.
**Owner** A Cooke & P D Evans **Bred** Newsells Park Stud **Trained** Pandy, Monmouths

**FOCUS**
A fair sprint handicap in which they raced middle to stands' side.

## 3425 GD ENVIRONMENTAL - TAKING WASTE FURTHER FILLIES' H'CAP 1m 2f

**4:00** (4:01) (Class 5) (0-70,72) 3-Y-O+ **£3,234** (£962; £481; £240) **Stalls** Low

Form RPR

34-5 **1** **Twenty Times (IRE)**[37] 2172 3-8-13 67 ShaneKelly 6 80+
(Richard Hughes) *chsd along briefly leaving stalls: trckd ldrs: shkn up 2f out: drvn 1f out: hung rt and led 100yds out: readily* **6/1**

426 **2** *3 ¼* **Many Waters (USA)**[46] 1944 3-9-4 72 DavidProbert 1 79+
(Andrew Balding) *hld up: nt clr run on far side and swtchd rt briefly over 2f out: drvn in 5th over 1f out: styd on: wnt 2nd nr fin* **5/2**[1]

3-11 **3** *¾* **Miss Inga Sock (IRE)**[21] 2710 5-9-2 62 GeorgiaCox(5) 8 68
(Eve Johnson Houghton) *midfield: hdwy 3f out: led 2f out: rdn and hdd 100yds out: no ex: lost 2nd nr fin* **11/2**[3]

3-65 **4** *½* **Lassana Angel**[19] 2760 3-8-9 66 KieranShoemark(3) 3 70
(Roger Charlton) *midfield: rdn to cl on ldrs 3f out: hung lft u.p over 1f out: styd on* **9/2**[2]

06-4 **5** *8* **Star Of Doha**[19] 2759 3-9-3 71 FranBerry 9 59
(Ralph Beckett) *prom: trckd ldr after 2f: drvn to ld over 2f out: sn hdd: wknd fnl f* **8/1**

6-00 **6** *shd* **Moonlight Silver**[19] 2754 3-8-11 65 MartinDwyer 10 53
(William Muir) *hld up: drvn 3f out: no real imp: styd on fnl f* **22/1**

60-4 **7** *12* **Distant High**[32] 2358 6-9-2 57 (p) TomMarquand 5 22
(Richard Price) *in rr: rdn over 4f out: wknd over 2f out* **12/1**

-310 **8** *3* **Alnasl (IRE)**[10] 3088 3-9-1 69 RichardKingscote 4 27
(Archie Watson) *led tl hdd over 2f out: sn wknd* **15/2**

044 **9** *8* **Cecilator**[19] 2760 3-8-11 65 LiamKeniry 7 7
(Noel Williams) *trckd ldr 2f: styd prom: drvn 4f out: wknd over 2f out* **22/1**

2m 8.82s (-1.78) **Going Correction** +0.05s/f (Good)
**WFA** 3 from 5yo+ 13lb **9** Ran SP% **115.7**
Speed ratings (Par 100): **109,106,105,105,99 98,89,86,80**
CSF £21.42 CT £85.75 TOTE £6.00: £1.90, £1.30, £2.20; EX 23.20 Trifecta £50.80.
**Owner** True Reds **Bred** Kildaragh Stud **Trained** Upper Lambourn, Berks

**FOCUS**
A fair fillies' handicap.

## 3426 DRIBUILD MAIDEN STKS (DIV I) 1m 4f

**4:30** (4:30) (Class 5) 3-Y-O+ **£3,234** (£962; £481; £240) **Stalls** Low

Form RPR

4-2 **1** **Zenon (IRE)**[19] 2751 3-8-10 0 KieranShoemark(3) 10 87+
(John Gosden) *trckd ldr: rdn to ld wl over 1f out: styd on wl* **10/11**[1]

3 **2** *3* **Dark Pearl (IRE)**[18] 2783 3-8-13 0 LiamKeniry 3 82
(Ed Walker) *led tl rdn and hdd wl over 1f out: kpt on same pce* **7/2**[3]

3-2 **3** 4 1/2 **Hawridge Flyer**[18] 2783 3-8-13 0 .......... FranBerry 1 75
(Stuart Kittow) *chsd along early: trckd ldng pair: rdn over 2f out: sn outpcd by first two* **2/1**[2]

000- **4** 7 **Ocean Gale**[301] 5252 4-9-4 41 .......... MitchGodwin(5) 7 59?
(Richard Price) *a in 4th: rdn 3f out: qckly outpcd by ldrs but kpt on* **150/1**

55U **5** 11 **Belgravian (FR)**[17] 2842 3-8-13 0 .......... JackMitchell 8 46
(Archie Watson) *t.k.h in midfield: drvn in 5th 3f out: no imp on ldrs: grad wknd fnl 2f* **14/1**

6-0 **6** 8 **Royal Sunday (FR)**[18] 2783 3-8-13 0 .......... (h1) FergusSweeney 5 33
(Alan King) *t.k.h towards rr: clsd 4f out: drvn 3f out: wknd 2f out* **25/1**

6-00 **7** 15 **House Of Frauds (IRE)**[83] 1205 9-10-0 33 .......... MartinDwyer 4 9
(Tony Newcombe) *t.k.h early: hld up in last: drvn 4f out: t.o fnl 3f* **150/1**

**8** nk **River Roquette (IRE)** 3-8-8 0 .......... LiamJones 9 4
(J S Moore) *s.i.s: sn pushed along in rr: lost tch over 3f out: t.o* **66/1**

**9** 44 **Saintmont (FR)** 3-8-13 0 .......... ShaneKelly 6
(Christian Williams) *dwlt: sn in midfield: hung lft over 4f out: sn eased and bhd: t.o* **40/1**

2m 39.04s (0.04) **Going Correction** +0.05s/f (Good)
**WFA** 3 from 4yo+ 15lb **9** Ran SP% **123.7**
Speed ratings (Par 103): **101,99,96,91,84 78,68,68,39**
CSF £5.09 TOTE £2.00: £1.10, £1.50, £1.20; EX 6.00 Trifecta £9.00.
**Owner** Shirke Dhunjibhoy Desai Magnier & Tabor **Bred** V B Shirke, K N Dhunjibhoy & B M Desai **Trained** Newmarket, Suffolk

**FOCUS**
This only really concerned the first three but they'd each shown plenty of ability and the winner looks quite decent.

## 3427 DRIBUILD MAIDEN STKS (DIV II) 1m 4f
**5:00** (5:03) (Class 5) 3-Y-0+ **£3,234** (£962; £481; £240) **Stalls** Low

Form RPR

**1** **Great Sound (IRE)** 3-8-13 0 .......... FranBerry 7 88+
(John Gosden) *s.i.s: looked green in rr: rdn 4f out: hdwy 2f out: wnt 2nd 1f out: led 150yds out: comf* **3/1**[3]

04 **2** 1 3/4 **Kazawi**[13] 2963 3-8-10 0 .......... KieranShoemark(3) 3 81
(Roger Charlton) *led: rdn over 2f out: 2 l up ent fnl f: hdd 150yds out: qckly outpcd by wnr* **5/2**[1]

4-24 **3** 2 **Lexington Law (IRE)**[24] 2609 4-10-0 85 .......... TomMarquand 4 78
(Alan King) *trckd ldrs: wnt 2nd 3f out: rdn 2f out: lost 2nd 1f out: styd on same pce* **11/4**[2]

**4** 4 1/2 **Cold Shoulder** 3-8-13 0 .......... DavidProbert 6 73+
(Andrew Balding) *t.k.h early: midfield: rdn over 3f out: nt clr run briefly on rail over 1f out: styd on to go 4th ins fnl f* **8/1**

46 **5** 1 1/2 **Mudajaj (USA)**[20] 2721 3-8-13 0 .......... DaneO'Neill 9 68
(Charles Hills) *trckd ldrs: drvn 3f out: outpcd over 1f out: lost 4th ins fnl f* **7/1**

0-3 **6** 1 1/2 **Sheila's Fancy (IRE)**[74] 1342 3-8-13 0 .......... LiamKeniry 8 66
(J S Moore) *trckd ldr: drvn and lost 2nd 3f out: grad wknd fr over 1f out* **33/1**

2-43 **7** 11 **Henry Croft**[111] 737 4-10-0 80 .......... GeorgeDowning 5 48
(Tony Carroll) *t.k.h early: in rr: rdn over 3f out: sn wknd* **16/1**

5 **8** 17 **Striker (IRE)**[38] 2143 3-8-13 0 .......... RichardKingscote 1 21
(Tom Dascombe) *s.s: in midfield after 2f: drvn 4f out: wknd qckly: t.o* **33/1**

2m 40.29s (1.29) **Going Correction** +0.05s/f (Good)
**WFA** 3 from 4yo 15lb **8** Ran SP% **115.6**
Speed ratings (Par 103): **97,95,94,91,90 89,82,70**
CSF £11.10 TOTE £4.00: £1.80, £1.50, £1.40; EX 13.00 Trifecta £30.50.
**Owner** Bermuda Thoroughbred Racing Limited **Bred** Churchtown House Stud **Trained** Newmarket, Suffolk

**FOCUS**
A promising performance from the winner.

## 3428 LABYRINTH CHALLENGE CHEPSTOW 8TH & 9TH JULY H'CAP 1m 4f
**5:30** (5:30) (Class 5) (0-70,72) 3-Y-0+ **£3,234** (£962; £481; £240) **Stalls** Low

Form RPR

00-2 **1** **Knight Destroyer (IRE)**[21] 2711 3-8-12 **68** .......... FranBerry 10 80+
(Jonjo O'Neill) *trckd ldrs: wnt 2nd 1/2-way: shkn up to ld over 2f out: sn in command: styd on strly* **5/4**[1]

-456 **2** 4 1/2 **Rahmah (IRE)**[18] 2781 5-9-11 **66** .......... KieranO'Neill 15 70
(Geoffrey Deacon) *dwlt bdly: clsd into midfield after 2f: shkn up 5f out: drvn 3f out: wnt 2nd over 1f out: styd on but no ch w wnr* **7/1**[2]

-045 **3** 1 **Dizzey Heights (IRE)**[21] 2710 5-9-9 **64** .......... MartinLane 7 66
(Stuart Kittow) *chsd ldr after 2f to 1/2-way: remained prom: drvn fnl 4f: styd on same pce u.p* **14/1**

20/0 **4** 3/4 **Taroum (IRE)**[32] 2364 10-8-4 **52** .......... (bt) WilliamCox(7) 9 53
(John Flint) *chsd ldrs: drvn 3f out: sn outpcd: styd on again fnl f* **33/1**

00-0 **5** 1 1/2 **Tobougaloo**[31] 2388 6-9-4 **62** .......... KieranShoemark(3) 6 61
(Stuart Kittow) *hld up: hdwy over 3f out: rdn to go 3rd 2f out: no ex, hung sltly lft and lost 2 pls fnl f* **8/1**[3]

0422 **6** 4 1/2 **Innoko (FR)**[13] 2964 7-9-4 **59** .......... (h) GeorgeDowning 8 51
(Tony Carroll) *midfield: drvn 4f out: sn outpcd by ldrs: styd on fnl f* **7/1**[2]

-060 **7** 3 **Invictus (GER)**[14] 2913 5-9-7 **69** .......... CameronNoble(7) 14 56
(David Loughnane) *mounted on crse: led: rdn and hdd over 2f out: wknd over 1f out* **16/1**

/663 **8** 6 **Eben Dubai (IRE)**[20] 2722 5-8-13 **54** .......... CharlesBishop 5 31
(Tracey Barfoot-Saunt) *t.k.h towards rr: drvn on outer 3f out: no imp* **20/1**

45-0 **9** 3 1/4 **Mr Caffrey**[18] 2781 5-9-6 **61** .......... (b) MartinDwyer 11 33
(John Flint) *dwlt bdly: detached in last and rel to r early: nvr on terms* **10/1**

0-00 **10** 22 **Bohemian Rhapsody (IRE)**[38] 2153 8-9-9 **64** .......... (p) ShaneKelly 2
(Brendan Powell) *chsd ldrs tl drvn and lost pl over 5f out: t.o fnl 2f* **14/1**

2m 40.28s (1.28) **Going Correction** +0.05s/f (Good)
**WFA** 3 from 4yo+ 15lb **10** Ran SP% **116.6**
Speed ratings (Par 103): **97,94,93,92,91 88,86,82,80,66**
CSF £10.21 CT £85.43 TOTE £1.80: £1.02, £3.00, £4.40; EX 11.20 Trifecta £80.80.
**Owner** Ms Diane Carr **Bred** Colm McEvoy **Trained** Cheltenham, Gloucs

**FOCUS**
The only 3yo in the line-up, the winner was far too well handicapped for these, although the form doesn't look worth much in behind.
T/Jkpt: Not Won. T/Plt: £222.20 to a £1 stake. Pool: £82,962.32 - 272.51 winning units T/Qpdt: £17.00 to a £1 stake. Pool: £7,682.36 - 332.7 winning units **Richard Lowther**

# 2681 WETHERBY (L-H)
Tuesday, June 6

**OFFICIAL GOING: Soft (good to soft in places) changing to soft after race 4 (3:40) changing to soft (heavy in places) after race 7 (5.10)**
Wind: Strong behind Weather: Heavy rain

## 3429 BRITISH STALLION STUDS EBF NOVICE MEDIAN AUCTION STKS (DIV I) 5f 110y
**2:10** (2:11) (Class 5) 2-Y-0 **£3,881** (£1,155; £577; £288) **Stalls** High

Form RPR

06 **1** **Magnus (IRE)**[15] 2896 2-9-2 0 .......... BenCurtis 6 74
(Tom Dascombe) *prom: chal wl over 2f out: rdn to take slt ld and edgd lft over 1f out: drvn and hung lft ent fnl f: styd on* **8/1**[3]

**2** nk **Tough Remedy (IRE)** 2-9-2 0 .......... PJMcDonald 7 73+
(Keith Dalgleish) *trckd ldrs: hdwy 21/2f out: chal between rivals and ev ch whn n.m.r and squeezed out ent fnl f: swtchd rt and rdn: styd on wl towards fin: unlucky* **16/1**

54 **3** 2 1/2 **Dontgiveuponbob**[19] 2769 2-9-2 0 .......... TonyHamilton 1 65
(Richard Fahey) *led: pushed along 3f out: rdn over 2f out: hdd wl over 1f out: drvn and hld whn bmpd 110 yds out* **4/7**[1]

4 **4** 4 1/2 **Jo's Girl (IRE)**[11] 3022 2-8-11 0 .......... DougieCostello 4 45
(Jamie Osborne) *trckd ldrs: hdwy on outer and cl up 2f out: rdn over 1f out: grad wknd* **8/1**[3]

**5** 4 **Sulafaat (IRE)** 2-8-11 0 .......... JasonHart 3 32
(Mark Johnston) *cl up: pushed along over 3f out: rdn wl over 2f out: sn wknd* **5/1**[2]

0 **6** 2 1/4 **Bad Dog**[8] 3149 2-8-9 0 .......... HarrisonShaw(7) 9 30
(Michael Easterby) *dwlt: green and a rr* **50/1**

1m 8.7s (2.70) **Going Correction** +0.525s/f (Yiel) **6** Ran SP% **110.4**
Speed ratings (Par 93): **103,102,99,93,87 84**
CSF £104.65 TOTE £10.40: £3.20, £6.50; EX 51.50 Trifecta £215.70.
**Owner** Living Legend Racing Partnership IV **Bred** Stowell Park Stud **Trained** Malpas, Cheshire

**FOCUS**
After about 19mm of rain during the previous 24hrs the going was changed to good to soft, soft in places. An ordinary novice event in which the odds-on favourite underperformed. The opening level is fluid.

## 3430 BRITISH STALLION STUDS EBF NOVICE MEDIAN AUCTION STKS (DIV II) 5f 110y
**2:40** (2:40) (Class 5) 2-Y-0 **£3,881** (£1,155; £577; £288) **Stalls** High

Form RPR

6421 **1** **Jedi Master (IRE)**[1] 3399 2-9-6 0 .......... AdamMcNamara(3) 6 82
(Richard Fahey) *trckd ldng pair: effrt 2f out: rdn to ld ent fnl f: drvn out* **7/4**[1]

**2** 1 1/4 **Mearing** 2-9-2 0 .......... StevieDonohoe 7 71+
(Charlie Fellowes) *dwlt and rr: hdwy over 2f out: rdn over 1f out: styd on wl fnl f* **16/1**

4 **3** 1 1/4 **Twentytwowontdo (IRE)**[17] 2836 2-8-11 0 .......... DanielTudhope 3 62
(David O'Meara) *slt ld on inner: hdd over 3f out: cl up: rdn to dispute ld over 1f out: drvn ins fnl f: kpt on* **9/4**[2]

0 **4** nk **Admiral Rooke (IRE)**[18] 2786 2-9-2 0 .......... PaulMulrennan 5 66
(Michael Dods) *trckd ldrs: hdwy over 2f out: rdn over 1f out: kpt on fnl f* **11/1**

6 **5** nk **Rampant Lion (IRE)**[8] 3156 2-9-2 0 .......... JasonHart 2 65+
(Mark Johnston) *green and towards rr: pushed along over 2f out: rdn wl over 1f out: styd on strly fnl f: nrst fin* **5/1**[3]

66 **6** 2 1/2 **Funkadelic**[8] 3149 2-9-2 0 .......... PJMcDonald 4 57
(Ben Haslam) *cl up: slt ld over 3f out: pushed along 2f out: sn rdn: hdd ent fnl f: sn wknd* **10/1**

00 **7** 1 3/4 **Elixsoft (IRE)**[15] 2896 2-8-11 0 .......... TonyHamilton 1 46
(Roger Fell) *chsd ldrs: rdn along 1/2-way: sn wknd* **33/1**

**8** 3 **Money For Luck (IRE)** 2-9-2 0 .......... TomEaves 9 41
(Brian Ellison) *trckd ldrs: effrt on outer 1/2-way: rdn along over 2f out: sn wknd* **33/1**

1m 8.43s (2.43) **Going Correction** +0.525s/f (Yiel) **8** Ran SP% **113.0**
Speed ratings (Par 93): **104,102,100,100,99 96,94,90**
CSF £30.73 TOTE £2.80: £1.20, £3.70, £1.10; EX 26.90 Trifecta £164.20.
**Owner** Kevin Hart & Partner **Bred** Mrs Eithne McDonnell **Trained** Musley Bank, N Yorks

**FOCUS**
Th second division of a fair novice event was run in a slightly quicker time than the first leg. The third has been rated as running a similar race to her debut and helps set the level, along with the winner and the time.

## 3431 ROA/RACING POST OWNERS' JACKPOT H'CAP 1m
**3:10** (3:10) (Class 6) (0-60,60) 3-Y-0 **£3,234** (£962; £481; £240) **Stalls** Low

Form RPR

5403 **1** **Brother McGonagall**[16] 2853 3-9-7 **60** .......... CamHardie 1 69
(Tim Easterby) *hld up towards rr: stdy hdwy 3f out: chsd ldrs wl over 1f out: rdn ent fnl f: styd on strly to ld nr line* **9/1**

-043 **2** hd **Snookered (IRE)**[7] 3191 3-9-7 **60** .......... PaulHanagan 4 69
(Richard Fahey) *trckd ldng pair: hdwy over 3f out: led 2f out and sn rdn: drvn ins fnl f: hdd and no ex nr line* **5/2**[1]

40-5 **3** 3 1/4 **Ocean Temptress**[43] 2017 3-9-6 **59** .......... JosephineGordon 5 61
(John Ryan) *wnt rt s: trckd ldr: hdwy 3f out: rdn along 2f out: chal over 1f out and ev ch: drvn ent fnl f: kpt on same pce* **9/1**

00-3 **4** 8 **Treagus**[29] 2470 3-9-6 **59** .......... StevieDonohoe 11 43
(Charlie Fellowes) *in tch: hdwy over 3f out: rdn along over 2f out: sn drvn and one pce* **5/1**[2]

0-00 **5** 3/4 **Pindaric**[21] 2703 3-9-4 **57** .......... AndrewMullen 7 40
(Alan Lockwood) *dwlt and reminders s: nvr bttr than midfield* **13/2**

063- **6** 1/2 **Casaclare (IRE)**[274] 6189 3-9-7 **60** .......... GrahamLee 6 42
(Jonjo O'Neill) *hmpd s: a towards rr* **16/1**

0-30 **7** nse **He's A Toff (IRE)**[21] 2702 3-9-1 **54** .......... JasonHart 2 35
(Tim Easterby) *a towards rr* **12/1**

564 **8** 3/4 **England Expects**[28] 2495 3-9-2 **60** .......... (h1) CliffordLee(5) 3 40
(K R Burke) *a rr* **6/1**[3]

6005 **9** 1 **Naupaka**[22] 2686 3-9-2 **55** .......... (p1) BenCurtis 9 33
(Brian Ellison) *led: pushed along 3f out: rdn over 2f out: sn hdd: drvn wl over 1f out: sn wknd* **16/1**

0-00 **10** *19* **Pennington**[11] 3024 3-9-7 **60**......................(b[1]) PJMcDonald 10
(Mark Johnston) *midfield: pushed along over 3f out: sn rdn and wknd* **25/1**

1m 44.3s (3.30) **Going Correction** +0.525s/f (Yiel) **10** Ran SP% **116.2**
Speed ratings (Par 97): **104,103,100,92,91 91,91,90,89,70**
CSF £31.64 CT £213.50 TOTE £13.00: £2.50, £1.20, £2.50; EX 35.30 Trifecta £211.80.
**Owner** Reality Partnerships VI **Bred** J P Coggan **Trained** Great Habton, N Yorks
■ Stewards' Enquiry : Paul Hanagan two-day ban: used his whip above the permitted level (Jun 25-26)

**FOCUS**
A modest handicap run at an even pace. Sound form, with the second and third rated to their latest efforts.

## 3432 YORKSHIRE POST MAGAZINE H'CAP 1m 2f
**3:40** (3:42) (Class 5) (0-70,70) 4-Y-0+ **£3,234** (£962; £481; £240) **Stalls** Centre

Form RPR
0-00 **1** **Auxiliary**[6] 3205 4-9-3 **66**......................(p) DanielTudhope 10 75
(Patrick Holmes) *hld up: hdwy 4f out: trckd ldrs over 2f out: sn chsng clr ldr: rdn to chal ins fnl f: kpt on wl to ld last 100 yds* **12/1**
0530 **2** *¾* **Arithmetic (IRE)**[13] 2953 4-8-13 **62**...................... JackGarritty 3 69
(Ruth Carr) *led 1f: trckd ldng pair: hdwy to ld over 3f out: clr 2f out: rdn over 1f out: jnd and drvn ins fnl f: hdd last 100 yds: no ex* **11/2**[1]
0646 **3** *5* **False Id**[11] 3036 4-9-1 **64**...................... BarryMcHugh 14 61
(Marjorie Fife) *hld up in rr: hdwy on outer 3f out: rdn along 2f out: kpt on u.p fnl f* **10/1**
6-00 **4** *nk* **Suitor**[43] 2030 5-9-7 **70**......................(p[1]) TomEaves 4 66
(Brian Ellison) *trckd ldrs: hdwy over 3f out: rdn over 2f out: drvn wl over 1f out: kpt on same pce* **7/1**[3]
0 **5** *2 ¼* **Apalis (FR)**[5] 3252 5-9-2 **68**...................... NathanEvans(3) 2 59
(Michael Easterby) *trckd ldrs: pushed along over 3f out: rdn over 2f out: kpt on one pce* **8/1**
4-04 **6** *shd* **Lopito De Vega (IRE)**[17] 2815 5-9-1 **64**...................... StevieDonohoe 1 55
(David C Griffiths) *in tch: hdwy on inner 3f out: sn pushed along: rdn to chse ldrs 2f out: sn drvn and kpt on one pce* **11/2**[1]
664 **7** *hd* **Senatus (FR)**[15] 2887 5-9-4 **67**......................(h) GrahamLee 11 58
(Karen McLintock) *hld up in rr: hdwy 3f out: rdn along over 2f out: n.d* **6/1**[2]
0-50 **8** *18* **Beadlam (IRE)**[30] 2430 4-8-13 **62**...................... TonyHamilton 13 17
(Roger Fell) *rr: rdn along detached over 4f out: nvr a factor* **22/1**
056 **9** *3 ½* **Eez Eh (IRE)**[13] 2953 4-9-6 **69**......................(p) ConnorBeasley 6 17
(Keith Dalgleish) *cl up: led over 4f out: hdd over 3f out: sn rdn along and wknd* **7/1**[3]
45-0 **10** *3* **Frankster (FR)**[34] 2301 4-9-1 **64**......................(t) PJMcDonald 9 6
(Micky Hammond) *chsd ldrs: rdn along over 3f out: sn wknd* **25/1**
0110 **11** *19* **Dunquin (IRE)**[48] 1891 5-9-7 **70**...................... AndrewMullen 5
(John Mackie) *led after 1f: hdd over 4f out: rdn along over 3f out: sn wknd* **8/1**

2m 14.25s (5.25) **Going Correction** +0.525s/f (Yiel) **11** Ran SP% **117.3**
Speed ratings (Par 103): **100,99,95,95,93 93,93,78,75,73 58**
CSF £76.49 CT £695.52 TOTE £13.90: £3.80, £2.20, £3.50; EX 106.90 Trifecta £929.60.
**Owner** Mrs C M Clarke, Foulrice Park Racing Ltd **Bred** The Pocock Family **Trained** Middleham, N Yorks
■ Never Give In was withdrawn. Price at time of withdrawal 50/1. Rule 4 does not apply

**FOCUS**
A fair handicap and the first two pulled clear of the rest. The winner has been rated to last year's best, and the runner-up to his better 3yo figures over a mile.

## 3433 CONISTON HOTEL COUNTRY ESTATE AND SPA H'CAP 1m
**4:10** (4:13) (Class 4) (0-80,82) 4-Y-0+ **£5,175** (£1,540; £769; £384) **Stalls** Low

Form RPR
1563 **1** **Magic City (IRE)**[25] 2586 8-9-2 **77**...................... NathanEvans(3) 4 85
(Michael Easterby) *in tch: hdwy 3f out: chsd ldr 2f out: rdn over 1f out: chal ins fnl f: led last 100 yds: kpt on wl* **8/1**
0-30 **2** *1 ¼* **Dutch Artist (IRE)**[22] 2684 5-9-3 **75**......................(p) DanielTudhope 8 80
(David O'Meara) *sn led and racd wd: c wd home turn to stands side: clr 2f out: rdn jst over 1f out: drvn ins fnl f: hdd last 100 yds: kpt on same pce* **11/2**
100- **3** *1 ½* **Hitman**[287] 5743 4-9-5 **77**...................... DuranFentiman 7 79
(Rebecca Bastiman) *hld up towards rr.: hdwy 3f out: swtchd rt to stands rail and rdn wl over 1f out: kpt on wl fnl f* **50/1**
5-04 **4** *¾* **Stanley (GER)**[34] 2301 6-9-4 **76**...................... GrahamLee 13 76
(Jonjo O'Neill) *trckd ldrs: hdwy 3f out: rdn along 2f out: kpt on same pce fnl f* **4/1**[2]
-010 **5** *1 ¼* **Zlatan (IRE)**[17] 2828 4-9-4 **79**......................(p) CallumShepherd(3) 11 76+
(Ed de Giles) *broke wl and restrained to rr: hld up and last: racd centre and hdwy wl over 2f out: rdn wl over 1f out: styd on fnl f* **5/1**[3]
0-56 **6** *3 ¼* **Miss Van Gogh**[16] 2855 5-9-7 **82**...................... AdamMcNamara(3) 10 72+
(Richard Fahey) *in tch on inner styd towards far side and hdwy 3f out: rdn along over 2f out: sn drvn and btn* **5/2**[1]
43-5 **7** *1 ¼* **Ski Blast**[28] 2505 6-9-1 **73**...................... DavidNolan 6 60
(Ivan Furtado) *chsd ldrs: rdn along 3f out: grad wknd* **20/1**
5524 **8** *1 ½* **Red Touch (USA)**[49] 1867 5-9-0 **75**......................(p) AlistairRawlinson(3) 2 58
(Michael Appleby) *chsd ldng pair: c towards stands side: 3f out: sn rdn along and wknd* **20/1**
0002 **9** *27* **Like No Other**[22] 2684 4-8-10 **75**......................(b) PaulaMuir(7) 1
(Les Eyre) *prom on inner: styd towards far side over 3f out and rdn along: sn wknd: bhd and eased over 1f out* **7/1**

1m 44.22s (3.22) **Going Correction** +0.525s/f (Yiel) **9** Ran SP% **115.7**
Speed ratings (Par 105): **104,102,101,100,99 96,94,93,66**
CSF £50.20 CT £2060.80 TOTE £9.00: £2.40, £1.70, £7.40; EX 64.60 Trifecta £860.60.
**Owner** A Turton, J Blackburn & Mrs L Folwell **Bred** Miss Annmarie Burke **Trained** Sheriff Hutton, N Yorks

**FOCUS**
The going had eased again and was changed to soft before this race. A fair handicap run at a good pace and not many got into it. It's been rated around the runner-up, with the third close to his 3yo form.

## 3434 LAKES LUXURY LODGES AT FAR GRANGE H'CAP 7f
**4:40** (4:40) (Class 4) (0-80,82) 3-Y-0 **£5,175** (£1,540; £769; £384) **Stalls** Low

Form RPR
25-1 **1** **Dan Troop**[33] 2338 3-9-0 **73**...................... PaulHanagan 3 81+
(Richard Fahey) *t.k.h early: hld up in rr: wd to stands rail over 3f out: hdwy to trckd ldrs over 1f out: nt much swtchd lft ent fnl f: swtchd rt to stands rail and rdn ins fnl f: fin strly to ld on line* **9/2**[3]
4641 **2** *nse* **Right Action**[15] 2886 3-9-1 **74**...................... TonyHamilton 12 81
(Richard Fahey) *t.k.h early: trckd ldng pair: wd towards stands rail over 3f out: led wl over 2f out: rdn wl over 1f out: drvn ins fnl f: hdd on line* **10/1**
01-4 **3** *1* **Golden Apollo**[20] 2739 3-9-8 **81**...................... AndrewMullen 8 85
(Tim Easterby) *t.k.h early: trckd ldr: wd towards stands side over 3f out and sn led: rdn and hdd over 2f out: drvn and ev ch over 1f out tl no ex last 75 yds* **3/1**[1]
3-10 **4** *¾* **Hajjam**[33] 2334 3-9-0 **73**......................(h) PhillipMakin 10 75
(David O'Meara) *trckd ldrs: wd st towards stands side over 3f out: sn chsng ldrs: rdn and n.m.r over 1f out: swtchd lft and drvn ins fnl f: kpt on* **9/2**[3]
23-3 **5** *1 ¾* **Hydroxide**[50] 1837 3-9-9 **82**......................(t) JosephineGordon 5 80+
(Hugo Palmer) *hld up and bhd: hdwy towards centre over 2f out: sn rdn and kpt on fnl f* **4/1**[2]
30-1 **6** *1 ½* **Grinty (IRE)**[33] 2345 3-9-1 **74**...................... PaulMulrennan 1 68
(Michael Dods) *trckd ldrs: wd st to stands rail over 3f out: sn cl up: rdn along and ev ch 2f out: drvn over 1f out: wknd ent fnl f* **8/1**
1-04 **7** *4* **Sumner Beach**[8] 3146 3-9-6 **79**......................(t) TomEaves 2 62
(Brian Ellison) *trckd ldrs on inner: styd towards centre home st and sn rdn along: wknd 2f out* **8/1**
31-0 **8** *50* **Man Of Verve (IRE)**[24] 2630 3-9-3 **76**...................... JasonHart 9
(John Quinn) *t.k.h: led: styd towards centre and hdd over 3f out: sn wknd* **25/1**

1m 31.4s (4.40) **Going Correction** +0.525s/f (Yiel) **8** Ran SP% **116.5**
Speed ratings (Par 101): **95,94,93,92,90 89,84,27**
CSF £48.94 CT £157.99 TOTE £5.10: £1.50, £2.60, £2.00; EX 27.30 Trifecta £118.00.
**Owner** Mrs Janis Macpherson **Bred** Liam Sheridan **Trained** Musley Bank, N Yorks

**FOCUS**
A decent 3yo handicap and a 1-2 for Richard Fahey. The runner-up has been rated as running his best race since his second 2yo start. The third helps set the standard, with the the fourth to his AW form.

## 3435 LIFE & STYLE MEDIAN AUCTION MAIDEN STKS 1m
**5:10** (5:13) (Class 6) 3-4-Y-0 **£2,587** (£770; £384; £192) **Stalls** Low

Form RPR
04 **1** **Star Gypsy (FR)**[12] 2997 3-9-3 0...................... DanielTudhope 6 81+
(Luca Cumani) *mde all: wd st to stands rail: rdn wl over 1f out: kpt on strly fnl f* **5/2**[1]
5- **2** *3 ¼* **Thornton**[390] 2193 3-9-3 0...................... PaulMulrennan 7 74+
(Michael Dods) *trckd ldrs: wd st and hdwy over 3f out: trckd wnr over 2f out: rdn and cl up wl over 1f out: drvn appr fnl f and kpt on same pce* **7/1**[3]
**3** *3 ½* **Amazing Grazing (IRE)** 3-9-3 0...................... TomEaves 9 66
(Brian Ellison) *trckd ldrs: wd st to stands rail: chsd ldng pair: rdn wl over 2f out: drvn wl over 1f out: kpt on same pce* **20/1**
03 **4** *nk* **Tidal Watch (IRE)**[18] 2782 3-9-3 0...................... GrahamLee 5 65
(Jonjo O'Neill) *in tch: hdwy and wd st: chsd ldrs wl over 2f out: sn rdn and no imp* **7/2**[2]
22-3 **5** *4 ½* **War Of Succession**[52] 1804 3-9-3 84...................... OisinMurphy 4 56
(Andrew Balding) *chsd wnr: rdn along wl over 2f out: sn drvn and grad wknd* **5/2**[1]
**6** *½* **Global Roar** 4-9-9 0...................... PhilDennis(5) 1 57
(John Weymes) *t.k.h: trckd ldrs: racd towards centre home st: rdn along wl over 2f out: sn drvn and wknd* **100/1**
0 **7** *hd* **Bombero (IRE)**[14] 2930 3-9-3 0...................... DougieCostello 10 54
(Ed de Giles) *a towards rr* **50/1**
00 **8** *4* **Starboard Watch**[14] 2930 3-8-12 0...................... AndrewMullen 11 40
(James Given) *wnt rt s: a towards rr* **66/1**
0-0 **9** *6* **Arquus (IRE)**[36] 2231 4-9-11 0...................... CallumShepherd(3) 2 35
(Ed de Giles) *hld up: a towards rr* **50/1**
**10** *6* **Xylophone** 3-8-12 0...................... BenCurtis 3 14
(Archie Watson) *dwlt: a rr* **15/2**

1m 47.34s (6.34) **Going Correction** +0.525s/f (Yiel)
**WFA** 3 from 4yo 11lb **10** Ran SP% **114.8**
Speed ratings (Par 101): **89,85,82,81,77 76,76,72,66,60**
CSF £19.91 TOTE £3.70: £1.50, £1.80, £4.40; EX 22.20 Trifecta £243.20.
**Owner** Simon Capon **Bred** Stilvi Compania Financiera **Trained** Newmarket, Suffolk

**FOCUS**
A fair maiden and they finished well strung out. There's no real anchor to the form and the opening level is fluid.

## 3436 RACING UK PROFITS RETURNED TO RACING H'CAP 1m 6f
**5:40** (5:42) (Class 6) (0-60,59) 4-Y-0+ **£2,587** (£770; £384; £192) **Stalls** Low

Form RPR
5-00 **1** **Adherence**[8] 3155 4-9-3 **55**...................... BarryMcHugh 11 64
(Tony Coyle) *trckd ldrs: hdwy and wd st towards stands rail: chsd ldr 2f out: rdn to chal wl over 1f out: drvn to ld appr fnl f: kpt on* **7/1**
0423 **2** *2 ¼* **With Hindsight (IRE)**[13] 2972 9-9-4 **59**...................... AdamMcNamara(3) 1 64
(Steve Gollings) *led: wd st to stands rail: pushed along over 2f out: sn jnd and rdn: drvn and hdd appr fnl f: kpt on same pce* **11/4**[1]
050- **3** *8* **Aneedh**[172] 8400 7-9-2 **54**......................(p) GrahamLee 3 49
(Clive Mulhall) *hld up in tch: hdwy over 3f out: rdn to chse ldrs 2f out: sn drvn and kpt on one pce* **12/1**
0344 **4** *3 ¾* **Major Rowan**[8] 3155 6-9-7 **59**...................... PhillipMakin 2 49
(John Davies) *rrd and lost several l s: sn w field: hld up in rr: pushed along 4f out: wd to stands rail st: rdn 3f out: drvn along 2f out: plugged on* **4/1**[2]
0665 **5** *4 ½* **Yul Finegold (IRE)**[7] 3192 7-9-5 **57**...................... PaulMulrennan 8 41
(Conor Dore) *trckd ldng pair: hdwy to chse ldr over 3f out: rdn along over 2f out: sn drvn and grad wknd* **12/1**
/6-6 **6** *8* **Aristocracy**[21] 2712 6-9-0 **52**...................... TrevorWhelan 6 26
(Fergal O'Brien) *chsd ldrs: rdn along over 3f out: drvn and wknd over 2f out* **5/1**[3]
0432 **7** *3 ¾* **Dream Serenade**[13] 2972 4-8-10 **55**......................(h) RayDawson(7) 10 24
(Michael Appleby) *trckd ldrs: hdwy to trck ldr after 4f: rdn along 4f out: sn drvn and wknd wl over 2f out* **4/1**[2]
426/ **8** *6* **Stickleback**[555] 2763 8-9-2 **54**......................(p) PJMcDonald 7 15
(Micky Hammond) *dwlt: a bhd* **33/1**

3m 16.16s (11.16) **Going Correction** +0.525s/f (Yiel) **8** Ran SP% **114.2**
Speed ratings (Par 101): **89,87,83,81,78 73,71,68**
CSF £26.52 CT £227.97 TOTE £10.40: £3.10, £1.10, £4.20; EX 34.00 Trifecta £349.90.
**Owner** M A Scaife **Bred** Wrottesley Limited **Trained** Norton, N Yorks

**FOCUS**
Only a moderate handicap. It's been rated around the front two.
T/Plt: £1,563.90 to a £1 stake. Pool: £53,988.85 - 25.2 winning units T/Qpdt: £102.50 to a £1 stake. Pool: £5,240.89 - 37.8 winning units **Joe Rowntree**

## 2970 YARMOUTH (L-H)

Tuesday, June 6

**OFFICIAL GOING: Good changing to good to soft after race 2 (2:50) changing to soft after race 5 (4:20)**

Wind: strong, across Weather: rain and windy

### 3437 INJURED JOCKEYS FUND NOVICE STKS 6f 3y

**2:20** (2:23) (Class 5) 2-Y-O **£3,234** (£962; £481; £240) **Stalls** Centre

Form RPR

0 **1** **Enjazaat**[18] 2779 2-9-2 0 JimCrowley 9 85+
(Owen Burrows) *mde all: pushed along and readily wnt clr over 1f out: in n.d fnl f: unchal: v easily* **1/1**[1]

**2** *6* **Zaaki** 2-9-2 0 PatCosgrave 4 67+
(Mohamed Moubarak) *stdd s: t.k.h: hld up in tch in last pair: swtchd lft and effrt 2f out: hung lft but sme hdwy over 1f out: no ch w wnr but kpt on ins fnl f to snatch 2nd on post* **10/1**

**3** *nse* **Immortal Romance (IRE)** 2-9-2 0 JamieSpencer 6 67+
(Michael Bell) *chsd wnr: rdn ent fnl 2f: outpcd by wnr over 1f out: wl hld and kpt on same pce ins fnl f: lost 2nd on post* **9/4**[2]

**4** *4½* **Jan's Joy** 2-8-8 0 AaronJones(3) 2 48
(Stuart Williams) *chsd ldng pair: shkn up over 1f out: sn rdn and outpcd: wl hld 4th and wknd ins fnl f* **33/1**

00 **5** *1* **Tony Soprano (IRE)**[7] 3187 2-9-2 0 GavinLerena 5 50
(Martyn Meade) *stdd s: hld up in tch in midfield: rdn ent fnl 2f: sn rdn and outpcd over 1f out: wl hld 5th and wknd ins fnl f* **8/1**[3]

**6** *1* **Retained (FR)** 2-8-11 0 KierenFox 7 42
(John Best) *hld up in tch towards rr: effrt ent fnl 2f: edging lft and no hdwy over 1f out: wl hld and plugged on same pce ins fnl f* **16/1**

0 **7** *6* **Macho Guest (IRE)**[14] 2926 2-9-2 0 TomQueally 3 29
(George Margarson) *t.k.h: hld up in tch in midfield: effrt ent fnl 2f: sn struggling and btn over 1f out: fdd fnl f* **25/1**

**8** *3¾* **Koin** 2-8-11 0 JoeyHaynes 1 13
(Mark H Tompkins) *s.i.s: a rr: rdn ent fnl 2f: no rspnse and lost tch over 1f out* **66/1**

1m 14.99s (0.59) **Going Correction** +0.275s/f (Good) **8** Ran SP% **115.1**
Speed ratings (Par 93): **107,99,98,92,91 90,82,77**
CSF £12.56 TOTE £1.80: £1.02, £2.30, £1.90; EX 14.10 Trifecta £31.10.
**Owner** Hamdan Al Maktoum **Bred** C J Mills **Trained** Lambourn, Berks

**FOCUS**
Jockeys riding in the first felt the ground was on the slow side of good. All about the favourite, who ran out a quite impressive winner. The form will take time to settle.

### 3438 BBC RADIO NORFOLK MAIDEN STKS 1m 3y

**2:50** (2:56) (Class 5) 3-Y-O+ **£3,234** (£962; £481; £240) **Stalls** Centre

Form RPR

5 **1** **Rigoletto (SWI)**[18] 2778 3-9-3 0 JamieSpencer 13 78+
(Luca Cumani) *hld up in tch in midfield: swtchd lft and gd hdwy ent fnl 2f: drvn to chal ent fnl f: led 100yds out: styd on strly* **3/1**[2]

45 **2** *1* **Mabrook**[18] 2783 3-9-3 0 (h) MartinHarley 10 76
(Marco Botti) *led: rdn over 1f out: drvn and hdd 100yds out: styd on same pce after* **7/2**[3]

00 **3** *nk* **Wicker**[15] 2908 3-8-5 0 (t[1]) FinleyMarsh(7) 6 70
(Jane Chapple-Hyam) *chsd ldrs: wnt 2nd over 3f out: rdn wl over 1f out: cl 3rd and squeezed for room 1f out: swtchd lft and kpt on same pce ins fnl f* **66/1**

23 **4** *hd* **Musical Terms**[10] 3062 3-9-3 0 RyanMoore 1 75+
(William Haggas) *hld up in tch in midfield: nt clr run 2f out: effrt jst over 1f out: keeping on whn nt clrest of runs and swtchd lft wl ins fnl f: styd on towards fin: nt clr run and eased last strides* **5/4**[1]

0 **5** *3½* **Kyshoni (IRE)**[21] 2707 3-8-12 0 AntonioFresu 3 62
(Mike Murphy) *t.k.h: hld up in tch in midfield: effrt 2f out: 5th and no imp 1f out: wknd ins fnl f* **150/1**

**6** *3½* **Ginger Lady (IRE)** 3-8-5 0 GabrieleMalune(7) 4 54
(Mark H Tompkins) *hld up in tch in rr: effrt 2f out: hdwy into midfield over 1f out: 6th and no imp ins fnl f* **100/1**

**7** *7* **Khataaf (IRE)** 3-9-3 0 JimCrowley 9 43
(Roger Varian) *chsd ldrs tl over 3f out: rdn ent fnl 2f: sn struggling and lost pl over 1f out: wknd fnl f* **8/1**

00- **8** *¾* **Canadian Royal**[195] 8066 3-9-3 0 (t) AdamBeschizza 8 41
(Stuart Williams) *t.k.h: hld up in tch in midfield: rdn ent fnl 2f: lost pl and btn over 1f out: wknd fnl f* **100/1**

**9** *2½* **Just Surprise Me (IRE)** 4-9-7 0 (t[1]) DavidEgan(7) 15 38
(Mohamed Moubarak) *chsd ldrs tl rdn and unable qck ent fnl 2f: lost pl and wknd over 1f out* **20/1**

6 **10** *1¾* **Dixon**[34] 2314 3-9-3 0 JoeyHaynes 5 31
(Mark H Tompkins) *stdd s: hld up in tch in rr: rdn 2f out: sn struggling: wknd over 1f out* **50/1**

00 **11** *1½* **Tilsworth Lukey**[66] 1488 4-9-7 0 GinaMangan(7) 11 31
(J R Jenkins) *t.k.h: hld up in tch in rr: swtchd lft and hdwy into midfield 5f out: rdn over 2f out: sn struggling: wknd over 1f out* **200/1**

0 **12** *3½* **Reckless Woman (IRE)**[78] 1286 3-8-12 0 (h[1]) SilvestreDeSousa 14 15
(Jeremy Noseda) *a towards rr: pushed along 1/2-way: rdn over 2f out: wknd wl over 1f out* **28/1**

1m 42.74s (2.14) **Going Correction** +0.275s/f (Good)
**WFA** 3 from 4yo 11lb **12** Ran SP% **117.6**
Speed ratings (Par 103): **100,99,98,98,95 91,84,83,81,79 78,74**
CSF £13.36 TOTE £3.80: £1.70, £1.80, £12.80; EX 15.70 Trifecta £383.00.
**Owner** Simon Capon **Bred** Stall Schloss Berg **Trained** Newmarket, Suffolk
■ Abaad was withdrawn. Price at time of withdrawal 33/1. Rule 4 does not apply

**FOCUS**
The ground was changed to good to soft after this, a fair maiden.

### 3439 BURLINGTON PALM HOTEL OF GREAT YARMOUTH H'CAP 1m 3f 104y

**3:20** (3:22) (Class 6) (0-60,62) 4-Y-O+ **£2,264** (£673; £336; £168) **Stalls** Low

Form RPR

3040 **1** **Askari**[24] 2615 4-9-11 **62** PatCosgrave 3 71
(Tom Clover) *trckd ldng pair: shkn up 3f out: rdn to ld wl over 1f out: clr 1f out: styd on wl* **4/1**[2]

4151 **2** *3* **Albert Boy (IRE)**[8] 3148 4-9-0 **58** FinleyMarsh(7) 2 65+
(Scott Dixon) *rrd as stalls opened and slowly away: sn rcvrd and hld up in tch in rr: effrt on inner 2f out: swtchd rt jst ins fnl f: styd on to go 2nd towards fin: no ch w wnr* **11/10**[1]

0-00 **3** *¾* **Saga Sprint (IRE)**[21] 2710 4-9-3 **61** GinaMangan(7) 1 64
(J R Jenkins) *t.k.h: hld up in tch in last pair: effrt on inner over 2f out: 4th and rdn over 1f out: swtchd rt and chsd clr wnr ins fnl f: kpt on same pce and no imp: lost 2nd towards fin* **33/1**

2530 **4** *2* **Go On Gal (IRE)**[13] 2964 4-9-2 **56** ShelleyBirkett(3) 4 56
(Julia Feilden) *led: hrd pressed and rdn jst over 2f out: hdd and unable qck u.p over 1f out: wknd ins fnl f* **6/1**

20-0 **5** *5* **Shift On Sheila**[22] 2688 4-9-4 **55** RobHornby 5 47
(Pam Sly) *chsd ldr: rdn and ev ch jst over 2f out: unable qck and outpcd over 1f out: wknd ins fnl f* **5/1**[3]

0603 **6** *½* **Stun Gun**[20] 2729 7-9-0 **51** (p) KierenFox 6 42
(Derek Shaw) *wl in tch in midfield: effrt swtchd rt 2f out: sn no imp u.p: wknd fnl f* **8/1**

2m 37.28s (8.58) **Going Correction** +0.275s/f (Good) **6** Ran SP% **112.6**
Speed ratings (Par 101): **79,76,76,74,71 70**
CSF £8.92 TOTE £4.70: £2.60, £1.10; EX 9.10 Trifecta £84.10.
**Owner** C F E Hill **Bred** Saleh Al Homaizi & Imad Al Sagar **Trained** Newmarket, Suffolk

**FOCUS**
A moderate handicap but the form is reasonable for the level. There's no anchor to the level and the form may prove a bit better than rated.

### 3440 LOWESTOFT HYDRAULIC H'CAP 1m 2f 23y

**3:50** (3:51) (Class 6) (0-55,55) 4-Y-O+ **£2,264** (£673; £336; £168) **Stalls** Low

Form RPR

00-0 **1** **Theydon Girls**[27] 2515 4-8-9 **46** oh1 MarcMonaghan(3) 2 58+
(Peter Charalambous) *taken down early: mde all: travelling best over 2f out: pushed along and clr 2f out: kpt on and nvr seriously chal: eased towards fin* **16/1**

0030 **2** *4½* **Flying Author (IRE)**[56] 1698 6-8-12 **46** oh1 (p) SilvestreDeSousa 1 48
(Phil McEntee) *chsd ldrs: rdn 3f out: 3rd and no imp on wnr on wnr over 1f out: wnt 2nd 150yds out: plugged on but no threat to wnr* **5/1**[3]

0055 **3** *1½* **Sexy Secret**[20] 2729 6-9-1 **52** (p) SimonPearce(3) 5 51
(Lydia Pearce) *chsd ldr: rdn 3f out: kpt on same pce u.p fnl 2f: lost 2nd 150yds out: plugged on* **3/1**[2]

**4** *8* **Avocet (USA)**[260] 4-9-4 **55** ShelleyBirkett(3) 4 40
(Julia Feilden) *hld up in tch in rr of main gp: effrt over 2f out: no imp: 5th and wl btn over 1f out: wnt modest 4th nr fin* **12/1**

2011 **5** *1* **Street Art (IRE)**[20] 2729 5-9-4 **55** (bt) HollieDoyle(3) 8 38
(Mike Murphy) *t.k.h: hld up in tch in midfield: wnt 4th and travelling strly 3f out: rdn and pressed for 2nd over 1f out: no imp: 4th and btn over 1f out: fdd fnl f* **1/1**[1]

65-0 **6** *1¼* **Links Bar Marbella (IRE)**[25] 2581 4-8-12 **46** oh1 KierenFox 6 27
(Eric Wheeler) *hld up in tch in 6th: drvn 4f out: outpcd 3f out: no ch fnl 2f* **50/1**

0405 **7** *8* **Sarakova (IRE)**[24] 2626 4-8-12 **46** oh1 (p[1]) RyanPowell 9 12
(Kevin Frost) *sn detached in last: n.d* **8/1**

-000 **8** *30* **Overrider**[62] 1563 7-8-12 **46** oh1 (bt) JoeFanning 7
(Shaun Lycett) *t.k.h: chsd ldrs: shkn up 3f out: sn btn: bhd and eased fnl 2f* **33/1**

2m 11.86s (1.36) **Going Correction** +0.275s/f (Good) **8** Ran SP% **121.3**
Speed ratings (Par 101): **105,101,100,93,93 92,85,61**
CSF £99.00 CT £315.65 TOTE £17.40: £4.20, £1.30, £1.30; EX 110.00 Trifecta £516.90.
**Owner** E O'Riordan **Bred** Altitude Bloodstock **Trained** Newmarket, Suffolk

**FOCUS**
A lowly handicap and bit of a surprise result, the winner making all. The form is very moderate in behind the winner.

### 3441 JOHN KEMP 4 X 4 CENTRE OF NORWICH H'CAP 1m 3y

**4:20** (4:23) (Class 4) (0-80,82) 4-Y-O+ **£4,851** (£1,443; £721; £360) **Stalls** Centre

Form RPR

4252 **1** **Intrude**[20] 2730 5-9-7 **80** (t) MartinHarley 3 94
(Stuart Williams) *hld up in tch in last pair: clsd to ld on bit over 2f out: sn cruised clr: rdn out ins fnl f tl eased towards fin: v easily* **5/1**[3]

6013 **2** *16* **Berrahri (IRE)**[22] 2685 6-9-1 **74** KierenFox 5 51
(John Best) *chsd ldr for 1f: rdn 1/2-way and dropped to last 3f out: no ch w wnr over 1f out: plugged on to take modest 2nd ins fnl f* **3/1**[2]

342- **3** *nk* **Singapore Sling**[167] 8481 4-9-0 **73** (h[1]) TomQueally 4 50
(James Fanshawe) *hld up in tch in last pair: effrt over 2f out: wnt 2nd 2f out but immediately totally outpcd by wnr: lost modest 2nd ins fnl f* **5/2**[1]

0030 **4** *5* **Aqua Libre**[55] 1718 4-8-11 **73** (t) MarcMonaghan(3) 1 38
(Philip McBride) *dwlt: sn rcvrd and chsd ldr after 1f tl rdn and lost pl over 2f out: wl btn over 1f out* **8/1**

0561 **5** *12* **Thaqaffa (IRE)**[35] 2267 4-9-9 **82** SilvestreDeSousa 2 19
(Amy Murphy) *led tl rdn and hdd over 2f out: sn struggling and wl btn over 1f out: wl bhd and eased ins fnl f* **5/2**[1]

1m 41.15s (0.55) **Going Correction** +0.275s/f (Good) **5** Ran SP% **109.9**
Speed ratings (Par 105): **108,92,91,86,74**
CSF £19.84 TOTE £5.00: £2.80, £1.50; EX 17.50 Trifecta £48.70.
**Owner** Happy Valley Racing & Breeding Limited **Bred** Wallace Holmes & Partners **Trained** Newmarket, Suffolk

**FOCUS**
They appeared to go a good gallop and the early leaders fell away, with the winner storming clear for a rampant success.

### 3442 LADIES NIGHT AT GREAT YARMOUTH RACECOURSE H'CAP 1m 3y

**4:50** (4:52) (Class 6) (0-60,62) 3-Y-O+ **£2,264** (£673; £336; £168) **Stalls** Centre

Form RPR

0243 **1** **Swilly Sunset**[13] 2976 4-9-12 **59** SilvestreDeSousa 10 67
(Anthony Carson) *hld up in rr: hdwy to chse ldrs 3f out: sn rdn and chal 2f out: led 1f ou: edgd lft u.p but doing enough ins fnl f: eased cl hone* **6/4**[1]

40-3 **2** *½* **Break The Silence**[34] 2296 3-8-3 **54** ow1 FinleyMarsh(7) 12 58
(Scott Dixon) *chsd ldr tl led 3f out: ducked lft oer 2f out: sn rdn: hdd 1f out: edgd lft u.p: kpt on but a jst hld after* **16/1**

4230 **3** *½* **Harlequin Rock**[20] 2729 4-9-12 **59** PatCosgrave 1 65
(Mick Quinn) *t.k.h: hld up in tch in midfield: clsd 3f out: rdn to chse ldng pair 2f out: pressing ldng pair and drvn whn bmpd jst ins fnl f: edging lft and kpt on same pce after* **5/1**[2]

54-6 **4** *8* **Tommy's Secret**[20] 2731 7-9-13 **60** MartinHarley 9 45
(Jane Chapple-Hyam) *pressed ldr tl 3f out: sn rdn: outpcd and btn over 1f out: wknd fnl f* **7/1**

3000 **5** *3½* **Chandrayaan**[20] 2733 10-8-6 **46** oh1 (v) GinaMangan(7) 5 22
(John E Long) *hld up in tch towards rr: effrt 3f out: no imp u.p 2f out: wknd and wl btn 1f out* **50/1**

0000 **6** *2¼* **Seeing Things (IRE)**[7] 3191 3-8-11 **58** (t) MarcMonaghan(3) 8 26
(Philip McBride) *hld up in tch: effrt over 2f out: sn struggling: wl btn over 1f out* **16/1**

0656 7 1 **Moving Robe (IRE)**[20] 2729 4-8-10 **46** oh1 NoelGarbutt(3) 2 14
(Conrad Allen) *led tl 3f out: sn u.p and struggling: wknd wl over 1f out* **12/1**

04-6 8 1 3/4 **Banta Bay**[28] 2507 3-8-10 **54** (v1) KierenFox 3 15
(John Best) *chsd ldrs tl 1/2-way: sn lost pl and u.p: no ch fnl 2f* **6/1**[3]

-555 9 nk **Cloud Nine (FR)**[19] 2763 4-9-8 **55** JoeFanning 6 18
(Tony Carroll) *hld up in tch: rdn 3f out: sn btn and bhd fnl 2f* **6/1**[3]

1P0P 10 8 **Tilsworth Micky**[66] 1490 5-9-13 **60** TomQueally 11
(J R Jenkins) *hld up in tch in rr: hdwy nr stands' rail 3f out: hung lft and btn 2f out: wl bhd and eased ins fnl f* **33/1**

1m 43.34s (2.74) **Going Correction** +0.275s/f (Good)
**WFA** 3 from 4yo+ 11lb 10 Ran SP% **122.1**
Speed ratings (Par 101): **97,96,96,87,83 80,79,77,77,68**
CSF £32.10 CT £109.09 TOTE £2.30: £1.40, £4.80, £1.40; EX 39.00 Trifecta £217.90.
**Owner** Alderson Carson Francis Hart **Bred** Aston House Stud **Trained** Newmarket, Suffolk

**FOCUS**
Three came clear in this low-grade handicap, the favourite always just doing enough despite drifting left and taking the placed runners with him.

## 3443 WEDDINGS & PRIVATE PARTIES AT YARMOUTH RACECOURSE H'CAP 7f 3y
**5:20** (5:21) (Class 5) (0-75,77) 3-Y-O **£2,911** (£866; £432; £216) **Stalls** Centre

Form RPR

-240 1 **Always Thankful**[5] 3246 3-9-1 **69** SilvestreDeSousa 7 76
(Ismail Mohammed) *hld up in tch in rr: pushed along over 3f out: swtchd lft 2f out: rdn to chal over 1f out and sn clr w ldr: sustained effrt u.p to ld 50yds out: styd on* **15/8**[1]

26-6 2 1/2 **Casina Di Notte (IRE)**[38] 2145 3-9-6 **74** (b) DanielMuscutt 1 78
(Marco Botti) *trckd ldr: gng best over 2f out: shkn up to ld over 1f out: sn rdn and clr w wnr: hdd and one pced fnl 50yds* **4/1**[3]

220 3 3 **Golden Guest**[18] 2793 3-8-7 **66** JaneElliott(5) 11 62
(George Margarson) *stdd s: hld up in tch in rr: effrt over 2f out: sn hung lft and outpcd by ldng pair over 1f out: 3rd and kpt on same pce fnl f* **8/1**

-222 4 1 3/4 **Wonder Of Dubai (IRE)**[18] 2793 3-9-5 **73** MartinHarley 10 63
(Michael Bell) *stdd s: t.k.h and sn trcking ldng pair: rdn to ld 2f out: sn hdd and outpcd: wknd fnl f* **2/1**[2]

4-25 5 4 1/2 **Valley Of Rocks (IRE)**[8] 3150 3-9-7 **75** JoeFanning 6 52
(Mark Johnston) *t.k.h: led: rdn over 2f out: sn hdd and lost pl over 1f out: wknd fnl f* **5/1**

1m 28.98s (2.38) **Going Correction** +0.275s/f (Good) 5 Ran SP% **115.9**
Speed ratings (Par 99): **97,96,92,90,84**
CSF £10.29 TOTE £2.80: £1.60, £3.30; EX 12.20 Trifecta £49.60.
**Owner** Saeed H Al Tayer **Bred** T J Cooper **Trained** Newmarket, Suffolk

**FOCUS**
A race hit by non-runners, the front pair came clear late on, with the favourite just prevailing.
T/Plt: £49.60 to a £1 stake. Pool: £65,505.02 - 963.14 winning units T/Qpdt: £17.10 to a £1 stake. Pool: £4.824.32 - 207.58 winning units **Steve Payne**

# 3310 SAINT-CLOUD (L-H)
Tuesday, June 6

**OFFICIAL GOING: Turf: soft**

## 3444a PRIX DE VILLE-D'AVRAY (CLAIMER) (2YO) (TURF) 6f
**11:40** 2-Y-O **£11,538** (£4,615; £3,461; £2,307; £1,153)

RPR

1 **Like Lightning (IRE)**[18] 2779 2-9-1 0 IoritzMendizabal 7 80
(J S Moore) *qckly into stride: settled bhd ldrs in 4th: pushed along and sn u.p over 2f out: drvn to ld over 1f out: styd on wl fnl f* **61/10**[3]

2 2 **So Sora (FR)**[24] 2642 2-8-11 0 StephanePasquier 10 70
(P Adda, France) **5/2**[1]

3 snk **Jurisprudance (FR)**[8] 2-8-8 0 (p) MickaelBarzalona 5 67
(M Boutin, France) **44/5**

4 shd **Fancy Dresser (FR)**[8] 2-8-11 0 (b) AntoineHamelin 4 69
(Matthieu Palussiere, France) **15/2**

5 hd **Uchronique (FR)**[8] 2-8-8 0 AlexisBadel 11 66
(M Boutin, France) **37/1**

6 1/2 **Le Gitan (FR)**[42] 2073 2-9-1 0 MaximeGuyon 9 71
(M Pimbonnet, France) **67/10**

7 2 1/2 **Wooldix (FR)** 2-9-4 0 ChristopheSoumillon 3 67
(C Escuder, France) **7/2**[2]

8 2 **You Make Me Smile (FR)** 2-8-5 0 MlleLauraGrosso(10) 8 58
(N Clement, France) **39/1**

9 3 **Reboot (IRE)**[23] 2664 2-9-1 0 (b1) TonyPiccone 1 49
(Matthieu Palussiere, France) **141/10**

10 1/2 **Lovely Demon (FR)** 2-8-8 0 (p) AntoineWerle 6 40
(T Lemer, France) **41/1**

11 9 **Lastyouni (FR)**[61] 1594 2-8-8 0 (p) FabriceVeron 2 13
(Matthieu Palussiere, France) **22/1**

1m 19.71s (2.91) 11 Ran SP% **118.3**
PARI-MUTUEL (all including 1 euro stake): WIN 7.10 PLACE 2.00, 1.40, 1.80 DF 11.80 SF 24.40.
**Owner** Ciara Doyle & J S Moore **Bred** James Doyle **Trained** Upper Lambourn, Berks

## 3445a PRIX KEFALIN (MAIDEN) (2YO) (TURF) 6f
**12:10** 2-Y-O **£11,538** (£4,615; £3,461; £2,307; £1,153)

RPR

1 **Zone Regard (IRE)**[23] 2664 2-8-13 0 StephanePasquier 11 76
(M Delcher Sanchez, France) **47/10**[3]

2 hd **Victoria's Angel (IRE)** 2-8-13 0 AlexisBadel 2 75
(H-F Devin, France) **79/10**

3 1 **Day Of Rest (FR)** 2-8-11 0 MaximeGuyon 7 70
(George Baker) *settled midfield: dropped to rr over 4f out: brought wd into the st and rdn over 2f out: hdwy down the middle of the crse over 1f out: styd on wl fnl f to be nrest at the fin* **92/10**

4 3/4 **Amiral Chop (FR)** 2-8-10 0 (p) FlorentGavilan(6) 9 73
(A Chopard, France) **144/10**

5 nse **Marvellous Night (FR)**[23] 2664 2-8-13 0 TheoBachelot 4 70
(H De Nicolay, France) **246/10**

6 3/4 **We Ride The World (IRE)**[23] 2664 2-9-2 0 ChristopheSoumillon 5 71
(Louis Baudron, France) **13/5**[2]

7 1/2 **Digicode (FR)** 2-8-11 0 AntoineHamelin 3 64
(Matthieu Palussiere, France) **155/10**

8 3 **Le Professeur (FR)** 2-8-11 0 PierreBazire 10 55
(P Dhaese, France) **64/1**

9 3 1/2 **Kickass D'Aumone (FR)** 2-8-11 0 TonyPiccone 6 45
(S Jesus, France) **39/1**

10 1 1/2 **Cristot (FR)**[23] 2664 2-9-2 0 CristianDemuro 8 45
(J-C Rouget, France) **5/2**[1]

11 5 **Pif D'Avril (FR)**[18] 2881 2-8-13 0 AurelienLemaitre 1 27
(F-X De Chevigny, France) **50/1**

1m 19.25s (2.45) 11 Ran SP% **117.4**
PARI-MUTUEL (all including 1 euro stake): WIN 5.70 PLACE 2.10, 3.50, 3.10 DF 18.60 SF 51.60.
**Owner** A Mouknass & Ecurie Pandora Racing **Bred** Paul McCarthy **Trained** France

## 3446a PRIX DE LA ROCHE GUYON (CLAIMER) (3YO) (TURF) 1m
**2:55** 3-Y-O **£9,829** (£3,931; £2,948; £1,965; £982)

RPR

1 **Tap Tap Boom**[22] 2697 3-9-10 0 TheoBachelot 6 87
(George Baker) *qckly into stride: settled 3rd: pushed along over 3f out: stdy hdwy to take ld over 2f out: rdn and drew clr fnl f* **11/5**[1]

2 5 **Douceur D'Antan (FR)**[27] 2536 3-8-11 0 MaximeGuyon 10 62
(P Adda, France) **119/10**

3 1/2 **Berjou (FR)**[96] 3-9-1 0 CristianDemuro 2 65
(Mme Pia Brandt, France) **9/2**

4 1 3/4 **Magical Forest (IRE)**[77] 1293 3-9-1 0 ChristopheSoumillon 5 61
(G Botti, France) **43/10**[3]

5 1 **La Fibrossi (FR)**[22] 2697 3-9-2 0 Pierre-CharlesBoudot 3 60
(H-A Pantall, France) **42/10**[2]

6 3/4 **Desert Heights (IRE)**[42] 3-8-11 0 (b) AurelienLemaitre 8 53
(N Caullery, France) **232/10**

7 8 **Flying Ballerina (IRE)**[18] 3-8-8 0 RaphaelMarchelli 4 31
(F Alloncle, France) **44/1**

8 1 1/4 **Sublissimo (FR)**[22] 2697 3-9-1 0 RonanThomas 9 36
(J Phelippon, France) **143/10**

9 30 **Zanati (IRE)**[23] 3-9-1 0 AntoineHamelin 7
(Hedi Ghabri, France) **37/1**

10 19 **Grey Magic (FR)**[26] 3-9-1 0 MickaelBarzalona 1
(N Caullery, France) **116/10**

1m 46.73s (-0.77) 10 Ran SP% **118.7**
PARI-MUTUEL (all including 1 euro stake): WIN 3.20 PLACE 1.80, 2.70, 2.00 DF 19.80 SF 30.30.
**Owner** Steve & Jolene De'Lemos **Bred** London Thoroughbred Services Ltd **Trained** Manton, Wilts

# 3237 HAMILTON (R-H)
Wednesday, June 7

**OFFICIAL GOING: Soft (5.5)**
Wind: fresh against in home straight Weather: Sunny

## 3447 BB FOODSERVICE NOVICE AUCTION STKS (PLUS 10 RACE) (A £20,000 BB FOODSERVICE 2YO SERIES QUALIFIER) 6f 6y
**2:10** (2:10) (Class 4) 2-Y-O **£5,175** (£1,540; £769; £384) **Stalls** High

Form RPR

2 1 **Miss Bar Beach (IRE)**[41] 2105 2-8-7 0 ConnorBeasley 5 72+
(Keith Dalgleish) *trckd ldrs: pushed along to ld over 1f out: rdn and edgd lft ent fnl f: kpt on wl to draw clr* **11/8**[1]

03 2 4 1/2 **Time For Treacle**[16] 2890 2-8-7 0 BarryMcHugh 6 58
(Ben Haslam) *led narrowly: rdn whn hdd over 1f out: one pce and sn no ch wnr* **11/2**[3]

0 3 1 **If We Can Can**[20] 2750 2-8-12 0 JoeFanning 1 60
(Mark Johnston) *pressed ldr: rdn 2f out: sn one pce: no ex fnl 110yds* **6/1**

4 1/2 **Lina's Star (IRE)** 2-8-8 0 PaulHanagan 2 55
(Richard Fahey) *pressed ldr: rdn over 1f out: sn one pce: wknd fnl 110yds* **2/1**[2]

1m 15.27s (3.07) **Going Correction** +0.40s/f (Good) 4 Ran SP% **105.1**
Speed ratings (Par 95): **95,89,87,87**
CSF £8.17 TOTE £1.60; EX 6.00 Trifecta £12.00.
**Owner** Middleham Park Racing Cxv **Bred** Tyrone Molloy **Trained** Carluke, S Lanarks

**FOCUS**
Distance as advertised. The first of many races on the card hit with multiple non-runners. All about the favourite, who handled the conditions well and raced clear. The runner-up is perhaps the key to the level.

## 3448 NEILSLAND AND EARNOCK JULIAN WATSON MEMORIAL MAIDEN STKS 6f 6y
**2:40** (2:41) (Class 5) 3-Y-O+ **£4,528** (£1,347; £673; £336) **Stalls** Centre

Form RPR

40 1 **Souls In The Wind (IRE)**[45] 1997 3-9-0 0 TadhgO'Shea 3 67
(John Patrick Shanahan, Ire) *prom: led over 2f out: rdn and jnd over 1f out: flashed tail ins fnl f: kpt on and on top cl home* **6/4**[2]

43 2 1/2 **Don Valentino (IRE)**[9] 3150 3-9-5 0 DanielTudhope 2 70
(David O'Meara) *trckd ldrs on outer: racd quite keenly: pushed along to join ldr over 1f out: drvn ins fnl f: no ex towards fin* **11/8**[1]

006 3 1 1/2 **Tilly Tinker**[12] 3054 3-8-11 0 NathanEvans(3) 5 60
(Michael Easterby) *trckd ldrs: rdn over 2f out: edgd rt over 1f out: kpt on ins fnl f* **8/1**

-0 4 6 **Starfall**[27] 2547 4-9-13 0 ShaneGray 7 48
(Christopher Wilson) *sn led: rdn whn hdd over 2f out: wknd over 1f out* **200/1**

5 nk **Danny Mc D** 4-9-13 0 DavidNolan 1 47
(Iain Jardine) *s.i.s: hld up: rdn over 2f out: wknd over 1f out* **6/1**[3]

1m 15.16s (2.96) **Going Correction** +0.40s/f (Good)
**WFA** 3 from 4yo 8lb 5 Ran SP% **108.0**
Speed ratings (Par 103): **96,95,93,85,84**
CSF £3.74 TOTE £2.00: £1.10, £1.70; EX 3.60 Trifecta £8.30.
**Owner** Thistle Bloodstock Limited **Bred** Mrs C L Weld **Trained** Kells, Co Kilkenny

**FOCUS**
Modest maiden form. It's been rated around the runner-up to the better view of his Redcar latest.

## 3449 HAMILTON PARK SUPPORTING RACING TO SCHOOL H'CAP 1m 5f 16y
**3:10** (3:10) (Class 6) (0-65,60) 4-Y-O+ **£3,234** (£962; £481; £240) **Stalls** High

Form RPR

1 **Mistiness (IRE)**[6] 3271 6-8-9 **51** (b) RobbieDowney(3) 8 67
(Keith Henry Clarke, Ire) *dwlt: hld up: rdn and hdwy 3f out: led 1f out: styd on wl to draw clr* **15/8**[2]

5230 **2** 7 **Ted's Brother (IRE)**4 3340 9-8-4 **48** JaneElliott(5) 9 53
(Laura Morgan) *in tch: racd quite keenly: rdn to chse ldr over 2f out: led over 1f out: hdd 1f out: edgd rt and wknd* **12/1**

1 **3** 2 1/4 **High Expectations (FR)**7 3193 6-8-12 **51** 6ex JoeFanning 4 53+
(Gordon Elliott, Ire) *chsd ldr: led 3f out: sn rdn: hdd over 1f out: sn wknd* **11/10**1

/060 **4** 1/2 **Jebulani**12 3043 7-8-3 **45** (p1) NathanEvans(3) 2 46
(Barry Murtagh) *hld up in tch: rdn over 2f out: plugged on* **50/1**

40-0 **5** 17 **Operateur (IRE)**36 2272 9-8-7 **46** PaulHanagan 1 23
(Ben Haslam) *chsd ldr: rdn 3f out: sn wknd* **20/1**

6040 **6** 1 **Firestorm (GER)**42 2095 6-9-1 **54** GrahamLee 5 30+
(Richard Ford) *led: clr 11f out tl over 7f out: pushed along whn hdd 3f out: sn wknd* **8/1**3

2m 55.89s (1.99) **Going Correction** +0.40s/f (Good) 6 Ran SP% **107.9**
Speed ratings (Par 101): **109,104,103,103,92 91**
CSF £21.17 CT £28.87 TOTE £2.20: £1.10, £4.30; EX 18.80 Trifecta £26.00.
**Owner** Phoenix Platinum Syndicate **Bred** S F Bloodstock **Trained** Drumree, Co. Meath
■ Stewards' Enquiry : Robbie Downey four-day ban: excessive use of the whip (Jun 25-28)

**FOCUS**
Distance increased by 8yds. There was an easy winner of this lowly handicap, although not the favourite who could only manage third having made his move too soon. The winner has been rated as replicating his Irish win last time out.

## 3450 ALEX FERGUSSON MEMORIAL H'CAP 1m 68y
3:40 (3:42) (Class 6) (0-65,67) 4-Y-0+ £3,234 (£962; £481; £240) Stalls Low

Form RPR

-304 **1** **Dark Crystal**6 3241 6-9-4 **61** DavidNolan 7 67
(Linda Perratt) *in tch: trckd ldr over 2f out: pushed along to ld over 1f out: rdn clr ins fnl f: pushed out towards fin* **15/2**3

0606 **2** 2 1/4 **Framley Garth (IRE)**2 3402 5-9-3 **67** PaulaMuir(7) 1 68
(Patrick Holmes) *dwlt: hld up in rr: rdn and hdwy 2f out: stl only 4th jst ins fnl f: styd on wl: wnt 2nd towards fin* **7/2**2

00-0 **3** nk **Hellavashock**15 2918 4-8-6 **54** RowanScott(5) 2 54
(Alistair Whillans) *hld up in tch: rdn and hdwy over 2f out: styd on fnl f* **9/1**

5201 **4** 2 1/4 **Amy Blair**6 3242 4-9-7 **64** 6ex (h) ConnorBeasley 4 59+
(Keith Dalgleish) *led: rdn over 2f out: hdd over 1f out: wknd ins fnl f* **4/5**1

0-00 **5** 7 **Stardrifter**14 2953 5-9-7 **64** GrahamLee 3 44
(Linda Perratt) *chsd ldr: rdn over 2f out: wknd over 1f out* **20/1**

/6-0 **6** 21 **Lawman's Justice (IRE)**55 1758 4-9-1 **58** JasonHart 5
(John Quinn) *hld up in tch: rdn over 3f out: sn wknd* **16/1**

1m 50.31s (1.91) **Going Correction** +0.40s/f (Good) 6 Ran SP% **110.2**
Speed ratings (Par 101): **106,103,103,101,94 73**
CSF £32.21 CT £224.81 TOTE £5.60: £3.40, £2.60; EX 32.20 Trifecta £105.40.
**Owner** Nil Sine Labore Partnership **Bred** R Biggs **Trained** East Kilbride, S Lanarks

**FOCUS**
Distance increased by 8yds. A modest handicap. The third is the key to the level.

## 3451 WEATHERBYS HAMILTONIAN H'CAP 1m 1f 35y
4:10 (4:12) (Class 4) (0-80,82) 4-Y-0+ £7,762 (£2,310; £1,154; £577) Stalls Low

Form RPR

0-11 **1** **Gulf Of Poets**49 1892 5-9-4 **78** NathanEvans(3) 13 90+
(Michael Easterby) *trckd ldrs: led gng wl over 2f out: rdn over 1f out: edgd lft ent fnl f: kpt on wl: eased towards fin* **9/2**2

3-41 **2** 1 1/4 **Fivehundredmiles (IRE)**19 2773 4-9-3 **74** (b) TadhgO'Shea 6 82
(John Patrick Shanahan, Ire) *trckd ldrs: rdn over 2f out: kpt on but no threat wnr* **9/2**2

-004 **3** hd **Carnageo (FR)**18 2838 4-9-10 **81** PaulHanagan 1 88
(Richard Fahey) *prom: rdn and bit outpcd over 2f out: styd on fnl f* **11/4**1

1411 **4** 3/4 **Cosmic Ray**12 3048 5-9-1 **72** (h) JoeFanning 14 77
(Les Eyre) *led: racd keenly: rdn whn hdd over 2f out: no ex fnl 110yds* **5/1**3

34/- **5** 1 **Poetic Choice**28 2531 6-9-2 **76** RobbieDowney(3) 4 79
(Keith Henry Clarke, Ire) *dwlt: hld up: rdn and sme hdwy 2f out: one pce fnl f* **12/1**

-466 **6** 3 1/2 **Archie's Advice**6 3240 6-9-6 **77** JasonHart 8 73
(Keith Dalgleish) *hld up: rdn over 2f out: nvr threatened* **11/2**

34-4 **7** 1 **Tectonic (IRE)**7 3197 8-8-9 **66** (p) ConnorBeasley 12 59
(Keith Dalgleish) *racd keenly in midfield: rdn over 2f out: wknd ins fnl f* **16/1**

-002 **8** nk **Alexandrakollontai (IRE)**19 2789 7-9-6 **82** (b) RowanScott(5) 7 75
(Alistair Whillans) *a rr* **20/1**

2m 1.89s (2.19) **Going Correction** +0.40s/f (Good) 8 Ran SP% **113.4**
Speed ratings (Par 105): **106,104,104,104,103 100,99,98**
CSF £24.59 CT £64.70 TOTE £5.00: £1.80, £2.30, £1.10; EX 25.00 Trifecta £89.70.
**Owner** L Hall, A Chandler, J Blackburn **Bred** Juddmonte Farms Ltd **Trained** Sheriff Hutton, N Yorks

**FOCUS**
Distance increased by 8yds. A fair handicap, it paid to race handily. The winner has been rated as resuming his progress back from a break, with the runner-up rated to his latest win here.

## 3452 WEATHERBYS PRINTING SERVICES H'CAP 6f 6y
4:40 (4:40) (Class 4) (0-80,79) 4-Y-0+ £6,469 (£1,925; £962; £481) Stalls Centre

Form RPR

0-22 **1** **Inexes**14 2952 5-9-5 **77** (p) BarryMcHugh 7 84
(Marjorie Fife) *hld up: swtchd lft to chse ldr towards stands' side 1/2-way: rdn 2f out: led 110 yds out: kpt on* **3/1**2

-445 **2** 3/4 **Honeysuckle Lil (IRE)**17 2856 5-8-12 **73** (p) RachelRichardson(3) 8 78
(Tim Easterby) *racd towards stands' side: led: pushed along over 1f out: rdn and edgd rt ent fnl f: hdd 110yds out: no ex* **9/2**3

4-3 **3** 2 3/4 **Dandyleekie (IRE)**18 2821 5-9-7 **79** (p) DanielTudhope 3 75
(David O'Meara) *racd centre: hld up: pushed along 2f out: rdn to go 3rd ins fnl f: nvr threatened ldng pair towards stands' side* **7/4**1

**4** 3/4 **Dandy Dude (IRE)**12 3060 4-8-6 **67** RobbieDowney(3) 4 61
(Keith Henry Clarke, Ire) *racd centre: chsd ldr: rdn over 2f out: wknd ins fnl f* **17/2**

-004 **5** 3 **Royal Connoisseur (IRE)**23 2684 6-9-3 **78** AdamMcNamara(3) 2 62
(Richard Fahey) *racd centre: chsd ldr: rdn over 2f out: wknd fnl f* **5/1**

1m 13.71s (1.51) **Going Correction** +0.40s/f (Good) 5 Ran SP% **106.7**
Speed ratings (Par 105): **105,104,100,99,95**
CSF £15.13 TOTE £3.60: £1.60, £3.50; EX 17.90 Trifecta £40.00.
**Owner** 21st Century Racing **Bred** Meon Valley Stud **Trained** Stillington, N Yorks

**FOCUS**
Little got into this ordinary sprint, the front two coming clear towards the stands' side. The winner has been rated as finding a bit on his recent 1m form.

## 3453 WATCH RACING UK IN HD APPRENTICE H'CAP 5f 7y
5:15 (5:16) (Class 6) (0-65,67) 4-Y-0+ £3,234 (£962; £481; £240) Stalls Centre

Form RPR

66-0 **1** **Kinglami**37 2229 8-9-11 **66** (p) BenRobinson(5) 1 75
(John O'Shea) *chsd ldrs: rdn 2f out: led ins fnl f: kpt on* **4/1**3

000 **2** 1 1/2 **Tinsill**7 3201 6-8-9 **48** (p) RowanScott(3) 6 52
(Nigel Tinkler) *sn led: rdn 2f out: hdd ins fnl f: no ex* **5/1**

00-0 **3** 1 1/4 **Molans Mare (IRE)**4 3347 7-8-9 **45** RobbieDowney 2 44
(Keith Henry Clarke, Ire) *outpcd in rr tl kpt on fnl f: wnt 3rd 75yds out: nrst fin* **11/4**1

2214 **4** 3 **Roy's Legacy**17 2858 8-9-10 **67** TobyEley(7) 5 55
(Shaun Harris) *prom: rdn 2f out: wknd ins fnl f* **9/2**

0-50 **5** nk **Perfect Words (IRE)**25 2633 7-9-8 **58** (p) NathanEvans 3 45
(Marjorie Fife) *chsd ldrs: rdn 1/2-way: wknd fnl f* **3/1**2

40-0 **6** hd **Reflation**18 2843 5-9-5 **62** (p) PaulaMuir(7) 8 49
(Patrick Holmes) *dwlt: sn chsd ldrs: rdn 1/2-way: wknd fnl f* **14/1**

1m 2.63s (2.63) **Going Correction** +0.40s/f (Good) 6 Ran SP% **113.2**
Speed ratings (Par 101): **94,91,89,84,84 84**
CSF £24.05 CT £62.61 TOTE £5.20: £2.00, £3.00; EX 28.80 Trifecta £111.50.
**Owner** Pete Smith & Phil Hart Racing **Bred** Cheveley Park Stud Ltd **Trained** Elton, Gloucs

**FOCUS**
Little got into this moderate sprint. The second and third pin the level.
T/Plt: £88.00 to a £1 stake. Pool: £54,106.31 - 448.66 winning units T/Qpdt: £26.50 to a £1 stake. Pool: £2,999.46 - 83.70 winning units **Andrew Sheret**

# 3208 KEMPTON (A.W) (R-H)
Wednesday, June 7

**OFFICIAL GOING: Polytrack: standard to slow**
Wind: Light across (away from stands) Weather: Warm, breezy, dark cloud

## 3454 100% PROFITS BOOST AT 32REDSPORT.COM H'CAP 7f (P)
5:55 (5:56) (Class 5) (0-75,77) 4-Y-0+ £2,911 (£866; £432; £216) Stalls Low

Form RPR

0114 **1** **Believe It (IRE)**39 2163 5-9-2 **77** (b) StephenCummins(7) 6 87
(Richard Hughes) *sn led and mde rest: rdn ent 2f out: qcknd clr of rivals over 1f out: kpt on wl ins fnl f: rdn out* **8/1**

0-51 **2** 1 **Helfire**14 2961 4-8-10 **67** CharlieBennett(3) 13 74+
(Hughie Morrison) *hld up in rr on inner: shkn up and tk clsr order over 2f out: nt clrest run over 1f out: swtchd to inner and rdn ent fnl f: kpt on wl: n.d to wnr* **7/1**3

4011 **3** 1 1/2 **Papou Tony**56 1728 4-9-5 **73** LiamKeniry 7 76
(George Baker) *in rr: shkn up ent st and angled to outer: rdn over 2f out: picked up wl fr over 1f out: tk 3rd post: nvr nrr* **11/2**2

1335 **4** shd **Gulland Rock**21 2731 6-8-11 **70** MitchGodwin(5) 11 73
(Anthony Carson) *cl up bhd ldr: rdn over 2f out: kpt on wl and chsd wnr ent fnl f: wknd and lost 3rd post* **20/1**

3214 **5** 3/4 **Saleh (IRE)**68 1462 4-9-9 **77** AdamKirby 2 78
(Lee Carter) *broke wl: sn settled bhd ldrs on rail: rdn over 2f out: kpt on tl no ex ent fnl f* **9/2**1

-30 **6** shd **Rayaa**2 3402 4-9-2 **70** (t) TomQueally 10 71
(John Butler) *chsd ldrs on outer and t.k.h: rdn 2f out: kpt on one pce ent fnl f* **25/1**

0-00 **7** 1 1/4 **Good Luck Charm**12 3030 8-8-11 **68** HectorCrouch(3) 4 65
(Gary Moore) *hld up in rr-div: shkn up over 2f out: sn rdn: kpt on nicely fr over 1f out* **25/1**

3155 **8** 3/4 **Dream Farr (IRE)**18 2821 4-9-7 **75** (t) ThomasBrown 9 70
(Ed Walker) *hld up in rr: shkn up and prog gng wl on rail over 1f out: swtchd off rail and shkn up: nt clr run again and nudged out after* **9/1**

0004 **9** nk **Mezmaar**7 3214 8-9-3 **71** (h) SteveDrowne 8 65
(Mark Usher) *t.k.h: cl up bhd ldrs: rdn 2f out: kpt on one pce fr over 1f out* **8/1**

/642 **10** hd **Bumptious**14 2975 4-9-7 **75** StevieDonohoe 1 69
(Ismail Mohammed) *chsd ldrs on outer: rdn over 2f out: kpt on one pce tl wknd ent fnl f* **8/1**

1211 **11** 1 **Prince Of Time**36 2278 5-8-10 **69** CallumRodriguez(5) 12 60
(Richard Ford) *hld up in mid-div: rdn 2f out: kpt on one pce fr over 1f out* **16/1**

0200 **12** 1/2 **Fairway To Heaven (IRE)**25 2608 8-9-0 **73** JennyPowell(5) 5 63
(Lee Carter) *settled in mid-div on outer: rdn 2f out: no imp ent fnl f* **33/1**

33 **13** 3 1/2 **Corporal Maddox**14 2968 10-8-12 **66** (p) OisinMurphy 3 46
(Ronald Harris) *settled in mid-div: swtchd to inner and rdn 2f out: sn no ex: hmpd ent fnl f and eased* **20/1**

1m 25.42s (-0.58) **Going Correction** +0.125s/f (Slow) 13 Ran SP% **115.4**
Speed ratings (Par 103): **108,106,105,105,104 104,102,101,101,101 100,99,95**
CSF £55.76 CT £348.08 TOTE £9.20: £2.80, £2.80, £1.80; EX 64.10 Trifecta £437.00.
**Owner** Richard Hughes **Bred** The Kathryn Stud **Trained** Upper Lambourn, Berks

**FOCUS**
A fair handicap, dominated by the winner from the front. The second and third did well to get involved from well off the pace. Another pb from the winner, with the fourth helping to set the standard.

## 3455 32RED CASINO FILLIES' H'CAP (LONDON MILE SERIES QUALIFIER) 1m (P)
6:25 (6:26) (Class 4) (0-85,78) 4-Y-0+ £4,690 (£1,395; £697; £348) Stalls Low

Form RPR

-104 **1** **Tegara**6 3233 4-9-0 **74** HollieDoyle(3) 3 82
(David Simcock) *sn cl up in last and t.k.h: shkn up over 2f out and swtchd to outer: rdn over 1f out: ev ch and marginally led ent fnl f: hung rt and rdn out after* **5/2**2

1-24 **2** 1 3/4 **Karisma (IRE)**39 2138 4-9-7 **78** RyanMoore 4 82
(Roger Varian) *cl up bhd ldr in 3rd and t.k.h: shkn up 2f out: sn rdn and ev ch ent fnl f: kpt on one pce* **10/11**1

5504 **3** 3/4 **Here's Two**22 2710 4-8-11 **68** JimCrowley 1 70
(Ron Hodges) *sn led and set mod gallop: shkn up 2f out: kpt on tl hdd ent fnl f: kpt on one pce in duel for 3rd* **11/2**3

2264 **4** nse **First Experience**44 2028 6-9-4 **75** (p) AdamKirby 2 77
(Lee Carter) *sn cl up w ldr: shkn up 2f out: sn rdn: ev ch over 1f out: no ex wl ins fnl f in duel for 3rd* **9/1**

1m 40.67s (0.87) **Going Correction** +0.125s/f (Slow) 4 Ran SP% **106.3**
Speed ratings (Par 102): **100,98,97,97**
CSF £5.08 TOTE £3.80; EX 5.20 Trifecta £7.80.

**Owner** Tick Tock Partnership **Bred** Rabbah Bloodstock Limited **Trained** Newmarket, Suffolk
**FOCUS**
They didn't go a great gallop and it turned into a bit of a dash up the straight.

## 3456 32RED ON THE APP STORE MAIDEN STKS 7f (P)
**6:55** (6:59) (Class 4) 3-Y-0+ **£4,690** (£1,395; £697; £348) **Stalls** Low

Form RPR

1 **Don't Give Up** 3-9-4 0 OisinMurphy 4 82+
(Saeed bin Suroor) *sn cl up and led: shkn up over 2f out: rdn wl over 1f out and scooted clr of rivals: in command ent fnl f and rdn out: easily* **6/4**[1]

0 2 5 **Right About Now (IRE)**[19] 2778 3-9-4 0 StevieDonohoe 10 68
(Ismail Mohammed) *covered up in mid-div: shkn up over 2f out and swtchd to inner: kpt on wl passed btn horses fr over 1f out: tk 2nd wl ins fnl f* **20/1**

3 ¾ **Hyperloop** 3-9-4 0 PatCosgrave 14 66+
(William Haggas) *hmpd s: hld up in rr: shkn up over 2f out: sn rdn and gd prog fr rr: kpt on wl ent fnl f: likely improver* **7/1**[3]

3 4 ¾ **Khitaamy (IRE)**[36] 2266 3-9-4 0 JimCrowley 2 64
(Ed Dunlop) *chsd ldr on inner: rdn over 2f out: kpt on one pce after* **9/4**[2]

5 1 ¾ **St James's Park (IRE)** 4-10-0 0 AntonioFresu 5 63
(Luke McJannet) *reluctant to load: sn settled in mid-div on rail: travelling wl over 2f out: rdn over 1f out in centre: kpt on: can do bttr* **100/1**

6 4 **Beach Party** 3-8-13 0 RobertWinston 9 43
(Hughie Morrison) *in rr-div on outer: rdn 2f out: one pce after* **22/1**

6 7 ¾ **Pioneertown (IRE)**[6] 3234 3-9-1 0 RosieJessop(3) 7 46
(Sir Mark Prescott Bt) *mid-div on outer w little cover: shkn up on outer over 2f out: sn rdn: kpt on one pce after* **33/1**

64 8 ½ **My Illusionist**[14] 2957 3-9-4 0 AdamKirby 13 45
(Harry Dunlop) *wnt lft s and hmpd rival: gd spd and styd in centre tl pressed wnr first bnd: shkn up over 2f out: sn lft bhd: pushed out after* **14/1**

4/0 9 1 **Paradise Found**[9] 3157 6-9-6 0 HectorCrouch(3) 11 41
(Emma Owen) *sn cl up bhd ldrs: rdn over 2f out: wknd fr over 1f out* **100/1**

10 4 ½ **Good Bond** 5-10-0 0 SteveDrowne 8 34
(Linda Jewell) *covered up in mid-div: rdn over 2f out: sn no imp* **250/1**

11 ½ **Tyrolean**[410] 4-10-0 0 TomQueally 3 33
(Seamus Durack) *a in rr: sme prog fr over 1f under hands and heels* **75/1**

0 12 ½ **Wolfcatcherjack (IRE)**[8] 3188 3-9-4 0 RyanPowell 6 28
(Sir Mark Prescott Bt) *hld up in rr on inner: rdn over 2f out: sn hld* **100/1**

13 4 ½ **Henriqua** 3-8-8 0 PaddyPilley(5) 1 10
(Denis Coakley) *a in rr and rn green: shkn up to hold pl wl over 4f out: rdn ent st: sn hld* **50/1**

1m 26.41s (0.41) **Going Correction** +0.125s/f (Slow)
**WFA** 3 from 4yo+ 10lb 13 Ran SP% **119.8**
Speed ratings (Par 105): **102,96,95,94,92 88,87,86,85,80 79,79,74**
CSF £39.81 TOTE £2.40: £1.20, £4.20, £2.40; EX 33.60 Trifecta £153.70.
**Owner** Godolphin **Bred** Darley **Trained** Newmarket, Suffolk
■ Sand Shoe was withdrawn. Price at time of withdrawal 14/1. Rule 4 applies \n\x\x to bets struck prior to withdrawal - deduction 5p in the pound. New market formed
**FOCUS**
A good performance from the winner, who knew his job first time out. The race has been rated at face value, with the fourth a bit below his debut effort.

## 3457 32RED.COM H'CAP (LONDON MIDDLE DISTANCE SERIES QUALIFIER) 1m 2f 219y(P)
**7:25** (7:28) (Class 4) (0-80,78) 3-Y-0 **£4,690** (£1,395; £697; £348) **Stalls** Low

Form RPR

-115 1 **Arab Moon**[32] 2395 3-9-3 74 JimCrowley 10 83+
(William Knight) *hld up in rr-divsion on outer: shkn up over 2f out and smooth prog on outer: stl plenty to do whn rdn over 1f out: kpt on strly ins fnl f and led nr fin: snug* **11/2**[2]

02-0 2 1 **Footman (GER)**[30] 2475 3-9-4 75 PatCosgrave 3 80
(Richard Hughes) *broke wl and led: sn settled bhd ldrs on inner: gng wl wen nt clr run over 2f out: rdn over 1f out: kpt on wl and led 150yds out: hdd nr fin* **12/1**

13- 3 hd **Winston C (IRE)**[285] 5847 3-9-6 77 LouisSteward 12 81
(Michael Bell) *chsd ldrs on outer: ct on heels and tk false step ent first bnd where almost c down: sn rcvrd: rdn over 2f out: kpt on wl fr over 1f out: can do bttr* **12/1**

34-4 4 ½ **Second Page**[53] 1787 3-9-3 74 KieranO'Neill 13 77
(Richard Hannon) *pressed ldr: rdn over 2f out: no ex and wknd ins fnl f* **25/1**

250 5 nk **Ply**[19] 2783 3-9-1 75 KieranShoemark(3) 6 77+
(Roger Charlton) *hld up in rr: rdn 2f out: kpt on wl fr over 1f out: nvr nrr* **11/2**[2]

0-61 6 2 **Nathan Mayer**[26] 2588 3-9-2 73 RyanMoore 7 72
(Sir Michael Stoute) *in rr-div on inner: shkn up over 2f out: rdn 2f out: nt picked up tl ent fnl f* **10/3**[1]

5311 7 nk **Arctic Sea**[33] 2361 3-9-3 74 DavidProbert 9 73
(Paul Cole) *hld up in last trio: t.k.h at times: rdn over 2f out: kpt on encouragingly fr over 1f out past btn horses: can do bttr* **8/1**[3]

043- 8 1 ½ **Sussex Ranger (USA)**[182] 8246 3-8-13 73 HectorCrouch(3) 1 69
(Gary Moore) *hld up in mid-div on inner: nudged along on bnd ent st: rdn over 2f out: kpt on one pce* **9/1**

40-4 9 6 **Presence Process**[145] 209 3-8-6 63 JimmyQuinn 8 49
(Pat Phelan) *mid-div: rdn over 2f out: kpt on one pce* **40/1**

-210 10 2 ½ **Solajan (IRE)**[26] 2520 3-9-6 77 (h) AdamKirby 4 59
(Ed Dunlop) *t.k.h in mid-div: rdn over 2f out: sn hld and wknd* **20/1**

16 11 1 **Falcon Cliffs (IRE)**[13] 3006 3-9-5 76 OisinMurphy 11 56
(Joseph Tuite) *sn led: rdn over 2f out: wknd fr over 1f out* **20/1**

6-00 12 1 **Gravity Wave (IRE)**[40] 2132 3-8-10 72 MitchGodwin(5) 2 50
(Sylvester Kirk) *a in rr: t.k.h: rdn ent st: sn hld* **20/1**

310 13 7 **Investigation**[19] 2807 3-9-7 78 RobHornby 5 44
(Andrew Balding) *completely missed break and detached in rr: sn ct up on heels of rr gp: tk fierce hold at times: rdn ent st: no imp and pushed out* **14/1**

2m 20.68s (-1.22) **Going Correction** +0.125s/f (Slow) 13 Ran SP% **117.6**
Speed ratings (Par 101): **109,108,108,107,107 106,105,104,100,98 97,97,92**
CSF £62.43 CT £764.83 TOTE £4.80: £1.70, £4.30, £3.50; EX 79.20 Trifecta £783.00.
**Owner** Angmering Park Thoroughbreds Iv **Bred** Genesis Green Stud Ltd **Trained** Patching, W Sussex

**FOCUS**
A handicap that should throw up a few winners. It's been rated around the fourth to his one previous standout run.

## 3458 32RED H'CAP 1m 3f 219y(P)
**7:55** (7:56) (Class 3) (0-90,86) 4-Y-0+
**£7,158** (£2,143; £1,071; £535; £267; £134) **Stalls** Low

Form RPR

0315 1 **Langlauf (USA)**[32] 2387 4-8-9 79 (p) DavidEgan(5) 6 86
(Rod Millman) *hld up in last trio on outer: shkn up and gd prog on outer fr 2f out: kpt on wl and pressed runner-up deep ins fnl f: led nr fin* **10/1**

0-56 2 nk **Fleeting Visit**[25] 2603 4-9-2 81 JohnFahy 7 87
(Eve Johnson Houghton) *pushed along leaving stalls to sit handy: rdn over 2f out in centre and led: kpt on wl and strly pressed deep ins fnl f: jst lost out* **4/1**[3]

154/ 3 1 ¾ **Clowance One**[567] 7893 5-8-12 80 KieranShoemark(3) 1 83
(Roger Charlton) *chsd ldrs on inner: rdn over 2f out: kpt on wl fr over 1f out: ev ch ent fnl f: no ex fnl 100yds* **10/3**[2]

/3-0 4 1 ¾ **Fergall (IRE)**[25] 1502 10-9-5 84 SteveDrowne 3 84
(Seamus Mullins) *in last trio: rdn 2f out: kpt on one pce* **8/1**

1/0- 5 1 **Murgan**[382] 2484 5-9-6 85 OisinMurphy 5 84
(Stuart Kittow) *chsd ldrs: rdn ent 2f out: sn no imp and pushed out* **8/1**

-110 6 nk **Captain Peacock**[20] 2752 4-9-7 86 (v) JimCrowley 9 84
(William Knight) *hld up in last trio: swtchd to inner and rdn 2f out: kpt on tl no imp on ldrs ent fnl f* **11/4**[1]

52 7 4 ½ **Methag (FR)**[19] 2781 4-8-9 74 FergusSweeney 2 65
(Alex Hales) *in last trio: rdn over 2f out: sn no imp and pushed out fr over 1f out* **20/1**

060- 8 6 **Zambeasy**[247] 7015 6-8-12 80 HectorCrouch(3) 8 62
(Philip Hide) *led and tk v t.k.h: rdn and hdd 2f out: sn wknd* **14/1**

2m 32.85s (-1.65) **Going Correction** +0.125s/f (Slow) 8 Ran SP% **112.5**
Speed ratings (Par 107): **110,109,108,107,106 106,103,99**
CSF £48.08 CT £162.34 TOTE £9.90: £2.40, £2.10, £1.80; EX 55.40 Trifecta £264.80.
**Owner** Tony Bloom **Bred** Darley **Trained** Kentisbeare, Devon
**FOCUS**
They didn't go a great gallop here. A pb from the winner back on the AW, with the runner-up rated pretty much to form.

## 3459 FOLLOW @RACING_UK ON TWITTER H'CAP 1m 7f 218y(P)
**8:25** (8:26) (Class 4) (0-80,79) 4-Y-0+ **£4,690** (£1,395; £697; £348) **Stalls** Low

Form RPR

2413 1 **Denmead**[32] 2388 4-9-5 75 RobertWinston 2 82+
(John Butler) *mde all and dictated pce: rdn over 2f out: kpt on wl fr over 1f out: fnd plenty and rdn out cl home* **5/1**[3]

5050 2 1 ¾ **Lanceur (FR)**[20] 2752 8-9-7 79 HollieDoyle(3) 7 83+
(William Stone) *hld up in rr: gng wl over 2f out waiting for cutaway whn n.m.r: taken off heels and swtchd to outer over 1f out: kpt on wl ins fnl f: no imp on wnr* **14/1**

455- 3 ¾ **Pastoral Music**[182] 8254 4-9-0 73 CharlieBennett(3) 6 76
(Hughie Morrison) *mid-div on inner: rdn 3f out: kpt on fr over 1f out: one pce fnl f* **9/2**[2]

23-5 4 hd **Southern States**[57] 1697 4-8-6 62 (e[1]) KieranO'Neill 3 65
(Lydia Richards) *chsd ldr on outer: rdn 3f out: one pce ins fnl f* **8/1**

6-30 5 nse **Chelsea's Boy (IRE)**[15] 2928 4-9-5 75 RyanMoore 1 78
(Ralph Beckett) *sluggish s: chsd ldrs on inner: rdn 3f out: one pce fr over 1f out* **4/1**[1]

-424 6 1 ¾ **Plymouth Sound**[11] 3086 5-9-7 76 (v) CharlesBishop 5 77
(Eve Johnson Houghton) *covered up in mid-div and t.k.h: rdn over 2f out: kpt one pce fr over 1f out* **8/1**

1-33 7 3 **Hepplewhite**[14] 2966 4-9-2 72 MartinDwyer 9 69
(William Muir) *in rr-div: rdn wl over 2f out: rdn 3f out: no imp on ldr* **9/2**[2]

6636 8 13 **Treble Strike (USA)**[77] 1303 4-8-5 64 (p) JackDuern(3) 8 46
(Dean Ivory) *in rr: niggled along at 1/2-way: reminder and prog on outer wl over 3f out: rdn over 2f out: sn hld* **20/1**

5554 9 7 **See And Be Seen**[7] 3213 7-8-6 66 (p) MitchGodwin(5) 4 39
(Sylvester Kirk) *prom on outer: rdn wl over 3f out: sn btn and wknd* **16/1**

3m 31.83s (1.73) **Going Correction** +0.125s/f (Slow) 9 Ran SP% **112.6**
Speed ratings (Par 105): **100,99,98,98,98 97,96,89,86**
CSF £69.34 CT £333.90 TOTE £7.40: £2.90, £2.80, £1.70; EX 48.60 Trifecta £190.90.
**Owner** John O'Donnell & Noel Kelly **Bred** J O'Donnell & N Kelly **Trained** Newmarket, Suffolk
**FOCUS**
This was steadily run, the pace dictated by the winner. The fourth helps set the standard.
T/Plt: £204.70 to a £1 stake. Pool: £66,138.65 - 235.81 winning units T/Qpdt: £28.60 to a £1 stake. Pool: £7,094.50 - 183.24 winning units **Cathal Gahan**

# 2852 RIPON (R-H)
Wednesday, June 7

**OFFICIAL GOING: Good to soft (watered; 7.1)**
Wind: moderate 1/2 behind Weather: overcast

## 3460 BRITISH STALLION STUDS EBF NOVICE STKS 5f
**6:35** (6:40) (Class 5) 2-Y-0 **£3,234** (£962; £481; £240) **Stalls** High

Form RPR

1 **Another Batt (IRE)**[25] 2635 2-9-2 0 SilvestreDeSousa 2 92+
(George Scott) *swtchd lft after s: mde all: shkn up and wnt clr 1f out: v easily* **1/3**[1]

0 2 5 **Gangland**[19] 2786 2-9-2 0 (h) TonyHamilton 8 69
(Richard Fahey) *chsd ldrs: drvn over 2f out: 2nd 1f out: no ch w wnr* **5/1**[2]

3 1 ¼ **Nomorecalls (IRE)** 2-9-2 0 PhillipMakin 1 65
(Robert Cowell) *chsd ldrs: kpt on same pce appr fnl f* **6/1**[3]

4 1 ¼ **Call Dawn** 2-8-4 0 HarrisonShaw(7) 5 55
(Michael Easterby) *s.i.s: hdwy to chse ldrs over 2f out: keeping on same pce whn carried rt 150yds out* **33/1**

5 hd **Camacho Chief (IRE)** 2-9-2 0 PaulMulrennan 6 59
(Michael Dods) *chsd ldrs: drvn over 2f out: edgd rt 150yds out: kpt on same pce* **8/1**

00 6 1 ¼ **Furni Factors**[49] 1872 2-9-2 0 JackGarritty 3 55
(Ronald Thompson) *sn chsng ldrs: one pce over 1f out* **50/1**

0 7 4 **Your Just Desserts (IRE)**[18] 2836 2-8-11 0 PJMcDonald 7 35
(Micky Hammond) *mid-div: hdwy over 2f out: wknd appr fnl f* **50/1**

8 3 ¾ **Miss Mazzie** 2-8-11 0 JamesSullivan 4 22
(Michael Easterby) *s.s: bhd and drvn along: nvr on terms* **25/1**



The Form Book Flat, Raceform Ltd, Newbury, RG14 5SJ

9 1 **Westfield Wonder** 2-9-2 0 AndrewMullen 9 23
(Ronald Thompson) *dwlt: sn outpcd: sme hdwy over 2f out: lost pl over 1f out: sn bhd* **66/1**

1m 0.47s (0.47) **Going Correction** -0.075s/f (Good) **9** Ran SP% **129.3**
Speed ratings (Par 93): **93,85,83,81,80 78,72,66,64**
CSF £3.18 TOTE £1.20: £1.02, £1.80, £2.50; EX 3.60 Trifecta £10.20.
**Owner** Excel Racing **Bred** J W Nicholson **Trained** Newmarket, Suffolk

**FOCUS**
The going was given as good to soft. An uncompetitive novice event but hard not to be impressed by the facile winner. A small step forward from the winner, with the runner-up and sixth suggesting this is a sensible opening level.

## 3461 EURA AUDIT UK H'CAP 1m
**7:05** (7:09) (Class 5) (0-70,72) 3-Y-O **£3,234** (£962; £481; £240) **Stalls** Low

Form RPR
0-05 **1** **Heatongrad (IRE)**[25] [2625] 3-9-7 **69** TonyHamilton 1 74
(Richard Fahey) *mde all: drvn 3f out: hld on clsng stages* **11/2**[2]
4552 **2** ½ **Mama Africa (IRE)**[16] [2900] 3-9-2 **64** SilvestreDeSousa 9 68
(David Barron) *mid-div: t.k.h: effrt over 2f out: styd on to take 2nd last 100yds: clsng at fin* **6/1**[3]
0-41 **3** 1 ½ **Alfred Richardson**[44] [2035] 3-9-10 **72** PhillipMakin 10 73
(John Davies) *mid-div: effrt over 2f out: styd on fnl f: tk 3rd post* **8/1**
3-36 **4** *shd* **Fortuities (IRE)**[15] [2921] 3-9-6 **68** JackGarritty 2 68
(Jedd O'Keeffe) *chsd ldrs: kpt on same pce fnl f* **9/1**
1-0 **5** *shd* **Scots Piper**[19] [2793] 3-9-7 **69** PJMcDonald 12 69
(Mark Johnston) *sn chsng ldrs: effrt over 2f out: kpt on same pce fnl f* **16/1**
0-14 **6** *hd* **Four Wishes**[16] [2886] 3-9-1 **63** JamesSullivan 6 63+
(Tim Easterby) *hld up towards rr: nt clr run fr mover 3f out tl over 1f out: styd on* **15/2**
04-3 **7** 1 ¾ **Dance Teacher (IRE)**[19] [2793] 3-9-7 **69** FranBerry 7 65
(Ralph Beckett) *s.i.s: hdwy over 3f out: kpt on same pce appr fnl f* **7/4**[1]
0-56 **8** 1 ½ **Thomas Crown (IRE)**[34] [2345] 3-9-0 **62** AndrewMullen 5 54
(Roger Fell) *mid-div: drvn to chse ldrs over 3f out: one pce fnl 2f* **25/1**
-630 **9** *nk* **Baby Helmet**[103] [895] 3-8-8 **61** GemmaTutty(5) 3 52
(Karen Tutty) *w ldr: t.k.h: wknd over 1f out* **33/1**
020- **10** 20 **Mulwith (IRE)**[286] [5799] 3-8-13 **61** PaulMulrennan 8 6
(Scott Dixon) *t.k.h in rr: hdwy over 3f out: lost pl over 3f out: sn heavily eased: t.o* **50/1**

1m 42.37s (0.97) **Going Correction** +0.10s/f (Good) **10** Ran SP% **113.5**
Speed ratings (Par 99): **99,98,97,96,96 96,94,93,93,73**
CSF £36.70 CT £269.59 TOTE £6.60: £2.10, £2.50, £1.60; EX 34.70 Trifecta £197.50.
**Owner** Middleham Park Racing XXXV & Partner **Bred** M Morgan **Trained** Musley Bank, N Yorks

**FOCUS**
A fair handicap, in which the pace was ordinary, and they finished in a bit of a heap. A small pb from the winner., but modest form.

## 3462 RIPON FARM SERVICES H'CAP 6f
**7:35** (7:35) (Class 4) (0-85,85) 3-Y-O **£5,175** (£1,540; £769; £384) **Stalls** High

Form RPR
6 **1** **Impart**[27] [2557] 3-9-2 **83** JoshDoyle(3) 5 86
(David O'Meara) *w ldr: led appr fnl f: drvn rt out* **7/1**
0-13 **2** *nk* **Dandy Highwayman (IRE)**[19] [2775] 3-9-2 **80** AndrewMullen 8 82
(Ollie Pears) *trckd ldrs: drvn 3f out: sn sltly outpcd: hdwy on ins over 1f out: styd on to take 2nd post* **3/1**[1]
2440 **3** *shd* **Poet's Society**[13] [2992] 3-9-7 **85** PJMcDonald 2 87
(Mark Johnston) *led: hdd appr fnl f: kpt on same pce* **7/2**[2]
140- **4** *shd* **Night Law**[242] [7147] 3-8-11 **75** TonyHamilton 1 76+
(Richard Fahey) *dwlt: in rr: hdwy on outer over 2f out: chsng ldrs over 1f out: kpt on same pce* **10/1**
60-0 **5** 1 ½ **Angel Meadow**[19] [2806] 3-9-2 **80** (h[1]) SilvestreDeSousa 7 76
(Micky Hammond) *mid-div: effrt and n.m.r over 2f out: kpt on one pce over 1f out* **14/1**
-210 **6** 1 **Suitcase 'N' Taxi**[12] [3038] 3-8-10 **74** PaulMulrennan 3 66
(Tim Easterby) *chsd ldrs: drvn over 2f out: wknd last 150yds* **4/1**[3]
13-0 **7** *nk* **Glorious Rocket**[48] [1895] 3-8-13 **77** (h[1]) PhillipMakin 4 68
(David Barron) *s.i.s: in rr: kpt on fnl f: nvr a factor* **6/1**
60-0 **8** ½ **Groupie**[17] [2856] 3-9-4 **82** JamesSullivan 6 71
(Tom Tate) *mid-div: effrt over 2f out: one pce: nvr a threat* **25/1**

1m 13.1s (0.10) **Going Correction** -0.075s/f (Good) **8** Ran SP% **113.6**
Speed ratings (Par 101): **96,95,95,95,93 92,91,90**
CSF £27.94 CT £86.45 TOTE £10.90: £1.80, £1.10, £1.40; EX 38.80 Trifecta £124.00.
**Owner** Dr Marwan Koukash **Bred** Juddmonte Farms Ltd **Trained** Upper Helmsley, N Yorks

**FOCUS**
A useful 3yo handicap, in which it paid to race close to the pace. The third has been rated close to his turf best.

## 3463 DIRECTORS CUP H'CAP 6f
**8:05** (8:06) (Class 3) (0-95,95) 4-Y-O-**£7,561** (£2,263; £1,131; £566; £282) **Stalls** High

Form RPR
3030 **1** **Pipers Note**[11] [3092] 7-9-7 **95** JamesSullivan 1 105
(Ruth Carr) *chsd ldrs: led last 75yds: hld on towards fin* **15/2**
00-0 **2** *hd* **Snap Shots (IRE)**[20] [2764] 5-9-1 **89** (p) BarryMcHugh 8 98
(Tony Coyle) *led: hdd last 75yds: no ex cl home* **20/1**
312/ **3** 3 **Atletico (IRE)**[676] [4882] 5-9-0 **88** AndreaAtzeni 14 88+
(Roger Varian) *hld up towards rr: nt clr run over 2f out: styd on wl fnl f: tk 3rd post* **9/2**[2]
0-04 **4** *shd* **Eccleston**[18] [2840] 6-9-0 **88** (v) DanielTudhope 12 87+
(David O'Meara) *in rr: effrt and nt clr run over 2f out: hdwy over 1f out: styd on to take 4th post* **4/1**[1]
0-00 **5** *nk* **Another Wise Kid (IRE)**[44] [2031] 9-8-10 **84** GrahamLee 9 82
(Paul Midgley) *chsd ldrs: edgd rt over 1f out: kpt on same pce* **16/1**
-055 **6** 1 **Flying Pursuit**[21] [2736] 4-8-12 **86** (b) CamHardie 7 81
(Tim Easterby) *chsd ldrs: drvn over 2f out: edgd lft over 1f out: one pce* **7/1**
0232 **7** *nse* **Johnny Cavagin**[18] [2821] 8-8-8 **82** (t) AndrewMullen 11 80
(Ronald Thompson) *s.i.s: in rr: keeping on whn hmpd over 1f out: nt clr run ands eased 75yds out* **12/1**
-000 **8** 3 ½ **Scrutineer (IRE)**[19] [2780] 4-9-7 **95** SilvestreDeSousa 10 79
(Mick Channon) *chsd ldrs: wknd appr fnl f* **8/1**
0000 **9** ¾ **Kenny The Captain (IRE)**[18] [2840] 6-8-1 **78** RachelRichardson(3) 2 60
(Tim Easterby) *swtchd rt after 1f and racd alone far side: chsd ldrs: wknd over 1f out: eased clsng stages* **16/1**
60-0 **10** 3 ¼ **Shared Equity**[19] [2780] 6-9-7 **95** PJMcDonald 3 66
(Jedd O'Keeffe) *chsd ldrs: drvn 3f out: lost pl wl over 1f out* **13/2**[3]
1210 **11** 3 ½ **Zylan (IRE)**[18] [2840] 5-8-4 **85** BenSanderson(7) 6 45
(Roger Fell) *chsd ldrs: lost pl wl over 1f out* **16/1**

1m 11.39s (-1.61) **Going Correction** -0.075s/f (Good) **11** Ran SP% **117.0**
Speed ratings (Par 107): **107,106,102,102,102 100,100,96,95,90 86**
CSF £145.45 CT £767.53 TOTE £7.30: £2.50, £4.10, £2.50; EX 108.30 Trifecta £732.80.
**Owner** Cragg Wood Racing **Bred** Wadacre Stud **Trained** Huby, N Yorks

**FOCUS**
A strong, competitive sprint, and those ridden handily had the edge. The winner has been rated back to form, with the runner-up rated slightly higher than for his C&D win last August.

## 3464 RIPON RACES SUPPORTS RACING WELFARE H'CAP 2m
**8:35** (8:35) (Class 5) (0-75,77) 4-Y-O+ **£3,234** (£962; £481; £240) **Stalls** High

Form RPR
1-06 **1** **Wishing Well**[26] [2594] 5-9-6 **69** PJMcDonald 6 74
(Micky Hammond) *swtchd rt after s: hld up in mid-div: hdwy over 7f out: effrt over 3f out: styd on wl to ld last 75yds* **16/1**
0214 **2** 1 ½ **Akavit (IRE)**[13] [3004] 5-9-2 **68** CallumShepherd(3) 3 71
(Ed de Giles) *led: hdd and sltly hmpd over 1f out: kpt on same pce last 100yds* **4/1**[2]
40-3 **3** *shd* **Pumblechook**[12] [3050] 4-9-13 **77** SilvestreDeSousa 1 80
(Mark Johnston) *trckd ldrs: edgd rt and led over 1f out: hdd and no ex last 75yds* **6/5**[1]
0-00 **4** 1 **Stormin Tom (IRE)**[12] [3046] 5-9-5 **71** RachelRichardson(3) 2 74+
(Tim Easterby) *trckd ldrs: t.k.h: nt clr run on inner over 2f out: edgd rt and kpt on fnl f* **9/1**
30-0 **5** ¾ **Ingleby Hollow**[12] [3050] 5-9-10 **73** (p) DanielTudhope 7 74
(David O'Meara) *racd wd: sn trcking ldrs: drvn 3f out: hmpd over 1f out: one pce* **11/2**[3]
0-56 **6** *nk* **Medina Sidonia (IRE)**[16] [2889] 5-9-6 **69** (p) JasonHart 5 69
(Tim Easterby) *sn trcking ldrs: drvn 4f out: outpcd 3f out: kpt on wl fnl f* **16/1**
6314 **7** *nse* **Cavalieri (IRE)**[27] [2549] 7-8-13 **62** (tp) KevinStott 8 62
(Philip Kirby) *in rr: effrt and outpcd over 3f out: kpt on wl fnl f* **16/1**
0-65 **8** 11 **Sail With Sultana**[15] [2928] 6-8-5 **54** oh9 AndrewMullen 9 41
(Mark Rimell) *a last: reminders over 7f out: bhd fnl 3f* **25/1**

3m 33.67s (1.87) **Going Correction** +0.10s/f (Good) **8** Ran SP% **112.3**
Speed ratings (Par 103): **99,98,98,97,97 97,97,91**
CSF £76.09 CT £136.34 TOTE £18.20: £4.30, £1.10, £1.50; EX 78.90 Trifecta £206.70.
**Owner** The Pennies Dropped Partnership **Bred** D Hudson-Wood **Trained** Middleham, N Yorks

**FOCUS**
A fair staying handicap. The first two have been rated to form.

## 3465 SIS TRADING SERVICES MAIDEN STKS 1m 1f 170y
**9:05** (9:06) (Class 5) 3-Y-O+ **£3,234** (£962; £481; £240) **Stalls** Low

Form RPR
**1** **Strong Belief (IRE)** 3-9-1 0 PhillipMakin 9 93
(Charlie Appleby) *trckd ldrs: drvn to ld over 1f out: styd on strly: eased towards fin* **6/1**[3]
022 **2** 7 **Kilowatt**[18] [2842] 3-9-1 76 PaulMulrennan 5 79
(Tim Easterby) *trckd ldrs: 2nd over 5f out: drvn over 3f out: chsd wnr fnl f: no imp* **8/1**
**3** ¾ **Northwest Frontier (IRE)** 3-9-1 0 PaulHanagan 2 77
(Richard Fahey) *mid-div: sn drvn along: outpcd over 5f out: hdwy over 2f out: styd on wl fnl f: tk 3rd nr fin* **9/1**
2 **4** ¾ **Circulation**[20] [2760] 3-8-10 0 FranBerry 7 71
(Ralph Beckett) *trckd ldrs: effrt over 2f out: kpt on one pce over 1f out* **9/4**[2]
22 **5** *nk* **Maratha (IRE)**[15] [2930] 3-9-1 0 (v) SilvestreDeSousa 10 75
(Simon Crisford) *swtchd rt after s: led: t.k.h: wnt clr over 6f out: drvn over 2f out: hdd over 1f out: wknd clsng stages* **6/4**[1]
4-5 **6** 11 **Mount Rock**[38] [2185] 3-9-1 0 JamesSullivan 4 53
(Michael Easterby) *mid-div: drvn over 5f out: sn outpcd and bhd* **16/1**
5-0 **7** 9 **Sir Runs A Lot**[25] [2632] 5-10-0 0 AndrewMullen 3 35
(David Barron) *in rr: drvn over 3f out: sn bhd* **50/1**
**8** 42 **Formative**[59] 4-10-0 0 (t[1]) GrahamLee 8
(Noel Wilson) *dwlt: in rr: bhd fnl 6f* **66/1**
0/0 **P** **Rip N Roar (IRE)**[26] [2580] 5-10-0 0 JackMitchell 1
(Tom Clover) *s.i.s: in rr: sme hdwy over 2f out: poor 6th whn p.u appr fnl f* **66/1**

2m 4.61s (-0.79) **Going Correction** +0.10s/f (Good)
**WFA** 3 from 4yo+ 13lb **9** Ran SP% **117.0**
Speed ratings (Par 103): **107,101,100,100,99 91,83,50,**
CSF £53.11 TOTE £7.40: £1.90, £2.50, £2.20; EX 43.60 Trifecta £449.70.
**Owner** Godolphin **Bred** Jim Bradley **Trained** Newmarket, Suffolk

**FOCUS**
Not a bad maiden, taken in good style by a 3yo newcomer. It's been rated at face value for now, with the runner-up rated to his penultimate C&D effort.
T/Jkpt: Not Won. T/Plt: £76.60 to a £1 stake. Pool: £92,847.41 - 884.24 winning units T/Qpdt: £30.80 to a £1 stake. Pool: £7,468.51 - 179.30 winning units **Walter Glynn**

# 3258 WOLVERHAMPTON (A.W) (L-H)
Wednesday, June 7

**OFFICIAL GOING: Tapeta: standard**
Wind: blustery, behind Weather: dry, mild

## 3466 FCL GLOBAL FORWARDING H'CAP 5f 21y (Tp)
**1:50** (1:50) (Class 6) (0-65,67) 3-Y-O+ **£2,264** (£673; £336; £168) **Stalls** Low

Form RPR
05-0 **1** **Krystallite**[153] [71] 4-10-1 **67** JosephineGordon 8 73
(Scott Dixon) *chsd ldr: drvn and chal over 1f out: rdn and r.o wl ins fnl f: led nr line* **11/2**[3]
0102 **2** *nse* **Cruise Tothelimit (IRE)**[8] [3186] 9-9-4 **63** (bt) ConnorMurtagh(7) 4 69
(Patrick Morris) *led: rdn over 1f out: jnd ins fnl f: r.o wl: hdd nr line* **4/1**[2]
1536 **3** 1 ¼ **Dashing Poet**[21] [2720] 3-9-5 **64** (h) MartinLane 6 62
(Jeremy Gask) *mid-div: hdwy over 2f out: hrd rdn over 1f out: r.o one pce ins fnl f* **7/2**[1]
0066 **4** 1 ½ **Barnsdale**[13] [2995] 4-8-5 **50** oh5 MeganEllingworth(7) 1 46
(John Holt) *hld up in rr: hdwy on outer 2f out: hrd rdn 1f out: r.o wl: nvr nrr* **150/1**
0263 **5** 1 ¼ **Vale Of Flight (IRE)**[33] [2370] 4-9-8 **60** RichardKingscote 10 51
(Luke McJannet) *chsd ldrs: pushed along 2f out: rdn over 1f out: one pce* **7/2**[1]
/000 **6** *shd* **My Meteor**[21] [2724] 10-8-7 **50** oh5 PaddyPilley(5) 7 41
(Natalie Lloyd-Beavis) *mid-div: rdn wl over 1f out: onr pce ins fnl f* **80/1**

0006 **7** *shd* **Elusivity (IRE)**[15] 2932 9-10-1 **67**..................(p) DavidProbert 2 58
(Conor Dore) *mid-div: effrt over 2f out: hrd rdn 1f out: no imp* **10/1**

1424 **8** *nk* **Borough Boy (IRE)**[8] 3170 7-10-1 **67**..................(v) DougieCostello 5 57
(Derek Shaw) *hld up: pushed along over 1f out: rdn and one pce ins fnl f* **8/1**

00-0 **9** *1 1/2* **Your Gifted (IRE)**[8] 3186 10-9-10 **62**..................(v) KevinStott 3 46
(Lisa Williamson) *mid-div: drvn 2f out: hrd rdn and wknd ins fnl f* **40/1**

60-0 **10** *6* **Lucky Clover**[37] 2214 6-9-6 **58**.................. MartinHarley 9 21
(Malcolm Saunders) *a in rr: rdn and wknd fr 2f out* **12/1**

1m 1.19s (-0.71) **Going Correction** -0.075s/f (Stan)
**WFA** 3 from 4yo+ 7lb **10** Ran SP% **112.1**
Speed ratings (Par 101): **102,101,99,97,95 95,95,94,92,82**
CSF £26.54 CT £86.31 TOTE £6.70: £2.00, £1.70, £1.70; EX 27.30 Trifecta £107.00.
**Owner** Paul J Dixon And The Chrystal Maze Ptn **Bred** Paul Dixon & Crystal Maze Partnership **Trained** Babworth, Notts

**FOCUS**
Not a bad sprint handicap for the class and it was run at a brisk pace. The runner-up and fourth help set the level.

## 3467 FCL GLOBAL FORWARDING NOVICE STKS 6f 20y (Tp)

**2:20** (2:23) (Class 5) 2-Y-O £2,911 (£866; £432; £216) **Stalls** Low

Form RPR

**1** **Running Cloud (IRE)** 2-9-2 0.................. CharlesBishop 3 82+
(Eve Johnson Houghton) *trckd ldrs: pushed along in 3rd 2f out: wnt 2nd over 1f out: sn chal lde: led appr fnl f: briefly rdn and sn wl on top: comf* **9/1**[3]

3 **2** *4* **Makanah**[20] 2769 2-9-2 0.................. JimCrowley 8 69
(Simon Crisford) *disp ld tl wnt on wl over 2f out: pushed along over 1f out: hdd appr fnl f: briefly rdn: one pce* **1/4**[1]

5 **3** *3 1/2* **Wildnightinvegas (IRE)**[23] 2691 2-9-2 0.................. TomMarquand 11 59
(Richard Hannon) *chsd ldrs: drvn 2f out: rdn over 1f out: r.o to take 3rd ins fnl f* **8/1**[2]

**4** *2 1/2* **Arty But Poor** 2-9-2 0.................. KevinStott 1 51
(Oliver Greenall) *disp ld tl relegated to 2nd wl over 2f out: sn drvn: one pce fnl f* **66/1**

5 **5** *3/4* **Vegas Boy (IRE)**[35] 2292 2-9-2 0..................(t[1]) DougieCostello 9 49
(Jamie Osborne) *mid-div: rdn 2f out: rn wd and one pce fr wl over 1f out* **33/1**

0 **6** *3/4* **Roses In June (IRE)**[16] 2904 2-8-11 0.................. LiamJones 7 42
(J S Moore) *mid-div: rdn 2f out: swtchd wd over 1f out: one pce fnl f* **100/1**

45 **7** *1 1/4* **Shovel It On (IRE)**[54] 1767 2-9-2 0.................. AdamBeschizza 4 43
(David Evans) *mid-div: drvn 2f out: rdn over 1f out: one pce* **20/1**

65 **8** *1/2* **Bond Angel**[12] 3023 2-8-4 0.................. KatherineGlenister(7) 6 36
(David Evans) *in rr: drvn 2f out: rdn over 1f out: no imp* **80/1**

**9** *3/4* **Bumble Beeze (IRE)** 2-9-2 0.................. RichardKingscote 13 43+
(Tom Dascombe) *slowly away and sn pushed along: nvr a factor* **10/1**

0 **10** *hd* **Xaar Island**[36] 2277 2-8-11 0.................. RoystonFfrench 12 33
(David Evans) *hld up: pushed along and rn wd 2f out: one pce* **66/1**

**11** *14* **Anythingwithapulse (IRE)** 2-8-8 0.................. CharlieBennett(3) 5
(Daniel Mark Loughnane) *hld up: pushed along 3f out: sn rdn and wknd* **100/1**

**12** *37* **Admissible** 2-9-2 0.................. ShaneKelly 10
(Richard Hughes) *mid-div: veered rt over 2f out: dropped away qckly and eased* **80/1**

1m 13.63s (-0.87) **Going Correction** -0.075s/f (Stan) **12** Ran SP% **125.3**
Speed ratings (Par 93): **102,96,92,88,87 86,85,84,83,83 64,15**
CSF £12.21 TOTE £15.80: £2.70, £1.02, £2.30; EX 24.20 Trifecta £79.60.
**Owner** HP Racing Running Cloud **Bred** The Kathryn Stud **Trained** Blewbury, Oxon

**FOCUS**
A novice event lacking depth. There was a turn up, but the winner impressed. There's no real anchor to the form.

## 3468 FCL GLOBAL FORWARDING MAKING LOGISTICS PERSONAL H'CAP (DIV I) 6f 20y (Tp)

**2:50** (2:53) (Class 6) (0-60,62) 4-Y-O+ £2,264 (£673; £336; £168) **Stalls** Low

Form RPR

-263 **1** **Titus Secret**[11] 3084 5-9-7 **60**.................. JosephineGordon 5 71+
(Malcolm Saunders) *mde all: pushed along 2f out: rdn 1f out: hung lft and rt ins fnl f but r.o wl: comf* **11/8**[1]

3-05 **2** *1 1/4* **Forever Yours (IRE)**[14] 2962 4-9-6 **62**.................. JackDuern(3) 8 69
(Dean Ivory) *mid-div on outer: prog 2f out: drvn over 1f out: rdn and r.o wl ins fnl f: a hld by wnr* **11/2**[2]

4-00 **3** *3 1/4* **Goadby**[26] 2589 6-8-9 **48**..................(v[1]) RoystonFfrench 4 45
(John Holt) *racd in cl 2nd: pushed along 2f out: sn lost 2nd: rdn 1f out: styd on one pce* **18/1**

55-5 **4** *hd* **Joaldo**[64] 1544 5-8-7 **46** oh1..................(p[1]) CamHardie 9 43
(Antony Brittain) *mid-div: drvn and effrt over 1f out: r.o wl ins fnl f: nvr nrr* **8/1**[3]

2400 **5** *1/2* **Justice Rock**[42] 2091 4-8-2 **46** oh1.................. DavidEgan(5) 6 41
(Phil McEntee) *mid-div: rdn over 1f out: one pce* **12/1**

-606 **6** *nk* **Classic Flyer**[14] 2967 5-9-3 **56**..................(v) FrannyNorton 3 50
(Christine Dunnett) *chsd ldrs: effrt 2f out: sn rdn and no ex* **16/1**

0002 **7** *1 1/2* **Insolenceofoffice (IRE)**[35] 2306 9-8-3 **49**..........(v) ConnorMurtagh(7) 1 39
(Richard Ford) *mid-div: hrd rdn 2f out: wknd fnl f* **11/1**

-000 **8** *3 1/4* **The Perfect Show**[8] 3186 4-9-5 **58**..................(p[1]) RobertWinston 10 38
(Milton Bradley) *hld up: pushed along fr 2f out: no imp* **28/1**

000 **9** *nk* **Captain Scooby**[6] 3256 11-9-0 **53**..................(b) DougieCostello 7 32
(Richard Guest) *slowly away and sn pushed along: rdn 2f out: nvr a factor* **12/1**

0-00 **10** *2 1/4* **Secret Look**[44] 2043 7-9-8 **61**.................. TomMarquand 2 33
(Richard Phillips) *hld up: rdn and no hdwy fnl 2 fs* **12/1**

0-00 **11** *14* **Tamarin**[11] 3062 5-8-7 **46** oh1..................(v) LiamJones 11
(Lisa Williamson) *hld up: rdn and racd wd 2f out: wknd* **125/1**

1m 13.89s (-0.61) **Going Correction** -0.075s/f (Stan) **11** Ran SP% **115.4**
Speed ratings (Par 101): **101,99,95,94,94 93,91,87,86,83 65**
CSF £8.37 CT £93.46 TOTE £2.30: £1.50, £1.80, £5.00; EX 9.70 Trifecta £105.70.
**Owner** M S Saunders **Bred** M S Saunders **Trained** Green Ore, Somerset

**FOCUS**
A weak sprint handicap in which two came clear. The third and fourth offer some perspective on the level of the form.

## 3469 FCL GLOBAL FORWARDING MAKING LOGISTICS PERSONAL H'CAP (DIV II) 6f 20y (Tp)

**3:20** (3:22) (Class 6) (0-60,61) 4-Y-O+ £2,264 (£673; £336; £168) **Stalls** Low

Form RPR

-421 **1** **Deeds Not Words (IRE)**[14] 2962 6-9-8 **61**..................(p) DavidProbert 10 78+
(Michael Wigham) *slowly away: rcvrd qckly into midfield: hdwy 3f out: effrt and pushed along 2f out: cut down ldr appr fnl f: sn in front: c clr: readily* **9/4**[1]

423 **2** *3 1/4* **Strictly Carter**[35] 2306 4-9-4 **57**.................. RobertWinston 6 62
(Alan Bailey) *trckd ldrs: wnt 2nd over 2f out: pushed along over 1f out and passed by wnr: rdn fnl f: r.o to take 2nd last 100yds* **4/1**[3]

2442 **3** *2 1/2* **Mr Chuckles (IRE)**[23] 2675 4-8-8 **52**..................(be) DavidEgan(5) 3 50
(Daniel Mark Loughnane) *chsd ldrs: drvn 2f out: rdn appr fnl f: r.o to take 3rd last 50yds* **3/1**[2]

010- **4** *1 1/4* **O Dee**[279] 6046 5-9-8 **61**..................(t[1]) OscarPereira 9 55
(Jose Santos) *led at fast pce: 5 l clr 2f out: advantage sn whittled away: rdn and hdd appr fnl f: wknd* **12/1**

0202 **5** *1 3/4* **Doctor Parkes**[13] 2995 11-9-0 **60**.................. MillyNaseb(7) 8 49
(Natalie Lloyd-Beavis) *hld up: effrt on inner 2f out: rdn and r.o one pce fnl f* **33/1**

-024 **6** *1 3/4* **Generalyse**[14] 2962 8-9-2 **55**..................(b) JosephineGordon 7 38
(Anabel K Murphy) *mid-div early: lost pl 1/2-way and bustled along: rdn 2f out: no ex* **14/1**

0600 **7** *1/2* **Jeanie's Place**[14] 2969 4-8-9 **48**..................(bt[1]) AdamBeschizza 1 30
(Charlie Wallis) *slowly away: racd in rr: chsd along 2f out: sn rdn and no imp* **25/1**

500 **8** *5* **Spirit Of Gondree (IRE)**[14] 2961 9-8-7 **46** oh1..........(b) FrannyNorton 5 13
(Milton Bradley) *chsd ldr: pushed along 2f out: wknd qckly* **7/1**

1m 14.03s (-0.47) **Going Correction** -0.075s/f (Stan) **8** Ran SP% **109.4**
Speed ratings (Par 101): **100,95,92,90,88 86,85,78**
CSF £10.35 CT £23.53 TOTE £2.90: £1.30, £1.50, £1.30; EX 10.40 Trifecta £24.10.
**Owner** D Hassan **Bred** B Holland, S Hillen & J Cullinan **Trained** Newmarket, Suffolk
■ Stewards' Enquiry : Oscar Pereira caution: careless riding

**FOCUS**
The second division of the weak sprint handicap was run at a frantic pace. The runner-up helps pin the level.

## 3470 FCL GLOBAL FORWARDING MAKING LOGISTICS PERSONAL CLAIMING STKS 1m 4f 51y (Tp)

**3:50** (3:50) (Class 6) 4-Y-O+ £2,264 (£673; £336; £168) **Stalls** Low

Form RPR

/60- **1** **Azari**[40] 5-9-7 0.................. MeganNicholls(5) 7 87+
(Paul Nicholls) *mid-div: hdwy on outer gng wl 3f out: pushed along 2f out: chal ent fnl f: rdn and sn on top: comf* **8/1**

1341 **2** *1 3/4* **Viewpoint (IRE)**[5] 3284 8-9-4 **80**.................. AlistairRawlinson(3) 2 78
(Michael Appleby) *trckd ldrs: hdwy on outer to ld over 2f out: pushed along and 1 l clr wl over 1f out: jnd ent fnl f: sn passed by wnr: no ex* **6/5**[1]

0312 **3** *9* **Retrieve (AUS)**[5] 3284 9-9-10 **85**..................(t) DougieCostello 1 67
(Jamie Osborne) *led tl 1/2-way: regained ld 3f out: hdd over 2f out: rdn and weakened wl over 1f out* **9/4**[2]

5463 **4** *5* **Dakota City**[30] 2461 6-9-8 **68**..................(v) AdamBeschizza 3 57
(Julia Feilden) *hld up in last: impr on inner 4f out: hrd rdn 2f out: no further prog* **5/1**[3]

6050 **5** *3 3/4* **Just Fred (IRE)**[15] 2914 4-9-1 **45**..................(tp) DavidEgan(5) 4 49
(Neil Mulholland) *mid-div: drvn 3f out: rdn 2f out: no ex* **100/1**

0 **6** *3* **Columbian Cartel**[14] 2957 4-9-1 0.................. GeorgiaDobie(7) 6 46
(J S Moore) *hld up: struggling 4f out: rdn and wknd fr 3f out* **200/1**

100/ **7** *7* **Irish Hawke (IRE)**[15] 6183 5-9-2 **79**..................(bt) ConnorMurtagh(7) 5 36
(Donald McCain) *chsd ldr tl led 1/2-way: hdd 3f out: sn u.p: fdd fnl 2 fs* **33/1**

2m 37.74s (-3.06) **Going Correction** -0.075s/f (Stan) **7** Ran SP% **108.4**
Speed ratings (Par 101): **107,105,99,96,94 92,87**
CSF £16.35 TOTE £9.60: £2.90, £1.30; EX 19.30 Trifecta £41.10.The winner was claimed by Mr T. Dascombe for £18,000.
**Owner** M Adams & D Coles **Bred** Yeguada De Milagro Sa **Trained** Ditcheat, Somerset

**FOCUS**
The first pair came clear in this fair claimer. Straightforward form.

## 3471 CONTACT US AT FCLGF.COM H'CAP 7f 36y (Tp)

**4:20** (4:21) (Class 4) (0-85,84) 4-Y-O+ £4,690 (£1,395; £697; £348) **Stalls** High

Form RPR

2310 **1** **Wink Oliver**[7] 3203 5-9-0 **77** 6ex..................(p) DougieCostello 7 86+
(Jo Hughes) *hld up: smooth hdwy on outer wl over 1f out: pushed along fnl f: led last stride* **8/1**

6-00 **2** *nse* **Eqleem**[28] 2528 4-8-7 **77**.................. KatherineGlenister(7) 9 83
(David Evans) *mid-div: prog 2f out: rdn and chal 1f out: led ins fnl f: hdd last stride* **20/1**

6002 **3** *nk* **Kingsley Klarion (IRE)**[9] 3140 4-9-0 **77**.................. FrannyNorton 2 82
(Mark Johnston) *mid-div on inner: plld out to chal over 1f out: rdn and r.o wl fnl f* **6/1**[3]

-131 **4** *3/4* **Art Echo**[19] 2795 4-8-13 **76**..................(t) BenCurtis 1 79
(John Mackie) *trckd ldrs: hdwy and wnt 2nd 2f out: ev ch and rdn over 1f out: no ex ins fnl f* **11/2**[2]

1255 **5** *nk* **Tavener**[7] 3199 5-8-7 **77**..................(p) FinleyMarsh(7) 6 79
(David C Griffiths) *led: pushed along 2f out: rdn ent fnl f: sn hdd and no ex* **8/1**

3100 **6** *3 1/2* **Dutiful Son (IRE)**[14] 2960 7-8-13 **81**.................. DavidEgan(5) 8 74
(Simon Dow) *hld up: pushed along 2f out and racd wd: hrd rdn 1f out. no ex* **11/1**

43-0 **7** *3/4* **Pirate's Treasure**[26] 2586 4-9-3 **80**.................. MartinHarley 4 71
(Jennie Candlish) *hed up: effrt 2f out: r.o under hand riding ins fnl f* **16/1**

2403 **8** *1/2* **Joey's Destiny (IRE)**[56] 1718 7-9-7 **84**.................. CamHardie 5 73
(Antony Brittain) *mid-div: pushed along 2f out: rdn over 1f out: one pce* **15/2**

12 **9** *1/2* **Vroom (IRE)**[52] 1820 4-8-9 **79**..................(p) RhiainIngram(7) 11 67
(Gay Kelleway) *trckd ldrs: drvn 3f out: rdn over 1f out: no imp* **20/1**

3-00 **10** *1 1/4* **Mr Christopher (IRE)**[49] 1890 5-8-13 **76**..........(p) RichardKingscote 10 61
(Tom Dascombe) *trckd ldr: drvn and lost pl over 2f out: wknd* **12/1**

00 **11** *hd* **Golden Raven (IRE)**[14] 2960 5-9-5 **82**.................. RobHornby 3 66
(Jamie Osborne) *hld up: pushed along 2f out: no imp* **9/2**[1]

1m 27.82s (-0.98) **Going Correction** -0.075s/f (Stan) **11** Ran SP% **113.3**
Speed ratings (Par 105): **102,101,101,100,100 96,95,94,94,92 92**
CSF £149.73 CT £1037.66 TOTE £9.20: £2.50, £7.70, £2.00; EX 294.70 Trifecta £1839.70.



The Form Book Flat, Raceform Ltd, Newbury, RG14 5SJ

**Owner** P & L Partners **Bred** Norman Court Stud **Trained** Lambourn. Berks

**FOCUS**

A competitive handicap, run at a sound pace. The form makes sense rated around the second, third fourth and fifth.

## 3472 FCLGF.COM MAIDEN FILLIES' STKS 7f 36y (Tp)
**4:55** (4:58) (Class 5) 3-Y-O+ **£3,234** (£962; £481; £240) **Stalls** High

Form RPR

33 **1** **Inshiraah (FR)**[8] 3188 3-9-0 0 .......... HarryBentley 2 76+
(George Peckham) *mid-div: hdwy and 4th 2f out: qcknd to ld 1f out: rdn: r.o wl and in command ins fnl f* **11/8**[1]

4-35 **2** ¾ **Getna (USA)**[26] 2564 3-9-0 75 .......... TomMarquand 3 72
(Richard Hannon) *trckd ldrs: effrt and wnt 2nd wl over 1f out: rdn and led briefly appr fnl f: sn hdd: r.o wl: but a hld* **5/2**[2]

3-5 **3** 1 ¾ **Angel's Quest (FR)**[13] 3007 3-9-0 0 .......... ShaneKelly 9 69+
(Richard Hughes) *mid-div: effrt and n.m.r over 1f out: r.o wl fnl furling: nvr nrr* **5/2**[2]

55-5 **4** 3 **Summer Falls (IRE)**[140] 283 4-9-7 61 .......... AaronJones(3) 11 63
(Rae Guest) *hld up: hdwy 2f out: pushed along fnl f: r.o* **20/1**

0 **5** 1 ¼ **Bicolour (USA)**[23] 2681 3-9-0 0 .......... FrannyNorton 6 56
(Mark Johnston) *mid-div: niggled after 3 fs: pushed along 3f out: rdn 2f out: styd on ins fnl f* **14/1**[3]

**6** 1 **Delilah Park** 3-8-7 0 .......... RossaRyan(7) 8 53
(Philip McBride) *slowly away: sme hdwy fnl 2 fs: nvr a threat* **33/1**

0 **7** hd **Emilene**[8] 3188 3-9-0 0 .......... (h) KierenFox 4 53
(Mark Brisbourne) *led: pushed along over 2f out: hrd rdn and hdd over 1f out: no ex* **200/1**

00 **8** 1 ¾ **Tisa River (IRE)**[54] 1762 3-9-0 0 .......... GeorgeDowning 10 48
(Milton Bradley) *trckd ldrs: rdn and chal ldrs over 1f out: wknd qckly* **200/1**

4660 **9** ¾ **Tranquil Tracy**[44] 2016 3-9-0 42 .......... PaddyAspell 5 46
(John Norton) *chsd ldrs: drvn 2f out: no imp ent fnl f* **200/1**

0 **10** 4 ½ **Easy Wind**[138] 331 3-8-7 0 .......... ManuelFernandes(7) 7 34
(Sir Mark Prescott Bt) *mid-div: pushed along over 2f out: rdn 1f out: no ex* **80/1**

00 **11** 1 ¼ **Morning Sequel**[21] 2721 4-9-10 0 .......... DougieCostello 1 34
(Neil Mulholland) *hld up in last: effrt over 2f out: sn rdn: no imp* **200/1**

1m 29.14s (0.34) **Going Correction** -0.075s/f (Stan)
**WFA** 3 from 4yo 10lb **11** Ran SP% **116.8**
Speed ratings (Par 100): **95,94,92,88,87 86,85,83,83,77 76**
CSF £4.92 TOTE £2.50: £1.10, £1.10, £1.50; EX 6.30 Trifecta £10.40.
**Owner** Fawzi Abdulla Nass **Bred** Jean-Philippe Dubois **Trained** Newmarket, Suffolk

**FOCUS**

There was just an ordinary pace on here but it's still straightforward enough form. It's been rated around the second and the fourth.

## 3473 FCL GLOBAL FORWARDING MAKING LOGISTICS PERSONAL FILLIES' H'CAP 7f 36y (Tp)
**5:25** (5:28) (Class 6) (0-65,65) 3-Y-O+ **£2,587** (£770; £384; £192) **Stalls** High

Form RPR

2041 **1** **Dusky Maid (IRE)**[13] 2993 3-9-4 **65** .......... JoeDoyle 9 70
(James Given) *a.p: pushed along in 2nd over 1f out: led u.p ins fnl f: r.o wl* **10/3**[2]

6-00 **2** nk **Pyjamarama**[26] 2587 3-9-2 **63** .......... HarryBentley 3 68+
(Roger Varian) *trckd ldrs: drvn 2f out: hdwy over 1f out: hrd rdn and r.o strly ins fnl f: nt rch wnr* **3/1**[1]

-340 **3** nk **Do You Know (IRE)**[26] 2587 3-9-3 **64** .......... (bt[1]) TomMarquand 7 67
(Marco Botti) *mid-div: rdn wl over 1f out: r.o wl ins fnl f* **11/1**

**4** ¾ **Mags Well (IRE)**[22] 2716 3-8-6 **60** .......... RossaRyan(7) 5 61
(Edmond Daniel Linehan, Ire) *trck ldrs: gd hdwy to ld wl over 1f out: hrd rdn and hdd ins fnl f: no ex cl home* **16/1**

424 **5** nse **Zilza (IRE)**[67] 1489 3-9-4 **65** .......... (t) FrannyNorton 12 66
(Conrad Allen) *led: drvn and hdd wl over 1f out: pushed along and r.o again one pce fnl f* **9/1**[3]

2-24 **6** 1 ¼ **Tennessee Rose (IRE)**[9] 3162 3-9-2 **63** .......... MartinHarley 4 61
(Luke McJannet) *t.k.h early: trckd ldrs: 4th on inner 2f out: rdn over 1f out: one pce* **3/1**[1]

5205 **7** shd **Binky Blue (IRE)**[8] 3172 5-9-11 **62** .......... (h) ShaneKelly 10 64
(Daniel Mark Loughnane) *hld up: pushed along and hdwy 2f out: rdn fnl f: r.o: nvr nrr* **11/1**

000- **8** ¾ **Wishing Tree**[244] 7097 4-9-0 **51** oh1 .......... BenCurtis 1 51
(Brian Ellison) *hld up: rdn wl over 1f out: sme late hdwy* **25/1**

000- **9** 4 **Bradfield Magic (IRE)**[175] 8361 3-9-2 **63** .......... GavinLerena 2 48
(Charles Hills) *hld up: hrd drvn 2f out: no imp* **22/1**

3-00 **10** 1 **Sakhee's Jem**[14] 2969 4-9-5 **63** .......... CameronNoble(7) 8 49
(Gay Kelleway) *slowly away: a in rr* **25/1**

1m 29.11s (0.31) **Going Correction** -0.075s/f (Stan)
**WFA** 3 from 4yo+ 10lb **10** Ran SP% **117.7**
Speed ratings (Par 98): **95,94,94,93,93 91,91,91,86,85**
CSF £13.54 CT £97.58 TOTE £4.60: £1.60, £1.60, £3.60; EX 18.70 Trifecta £112.00.
**Owner** The Cool Silk Partnership **Bred** L O'Donovan **Trained** Willoughton, Lincs

**FOCUS**

There was a bunched finish in this moderate fillies' handicap. The runner-up has been rated back to form.

T/Plt: £12.10 to a £1 stake. Pool: £65,150.68 - 3,914.75 winning units T/Qpdt: £7.60 to a £1 stake. Pool: £4,778.36 - 459.77 winning units **Keith McHugh**

3474 - 3481a (Foreign Racing) - See Raceform Interactive

# 2882 CARLISLE (R-H)
Thursday, June 8

**OFFICIAL GOING: Soft (good to soft in places) changing to soft after race 3 (7.10)**

Wind: Moderate, against in home straight of nearly 3f Weather: Heavy showers developing

## 3482 CARLETON FILLIES' NOVICE STKS (PLUS 10 RACE) 5f
**6:10** (6:12) (Class 5) 2-Y-O **£3,396** (£1,010; £505; £252) **Stalls** Low

Form RPR

4 **1** **Ellthea (IRE)**[17] 2904 2-8-9 0 .......... CliffordLee(5) 1 77+
(K R Burke) *racd keenly: hld up in rr: hdwy to ld over 1f out: edgd rt ins fnl f: r.o: comf* **9/4**[2]

5 **2** 2 **Mable Lee (IRE)**[14] 2988 2-9-0 0 .......... TomEaves 6 70
(Iain Jardine) *hld up: pushed along over 2f out: edgd lft wl over 1f out: styd on ins fnl f: tk 2nd towards fin: no imp on wnr* **33/1**

6 **3** ½ **Silver Starlight**[14] 2987 2-8-11 0 .......... RachelRichardson(3) 2 68
(Tim Easterby) *racd keenly: hld up in tch: hdwy on inner 2f out: ch over 1f out: kpt on ins fnl f: nt pce of wnr* **16/1**

6210 **4** 1 **Faithful Promise**[20] 2801 2-9-7 0 .......... FrannyNorton 5 71
(Mark Johnston) *led: rdn and hdd over 1f out: no ex ins fnl f* **11/2**[3]

0 **5** 3 ¾ **Lil Gem (IRE)**[19] 2836 2-9-0 0 .......... PJMcDonald 3 51
(Keith Dalgleish) *w ldr tl rdn over 1f out: faltered whn wkng fnl 150yds* **10/1**

**6** 1 ½ **Wirral Girl (IRE)** 2-9-0 0 .......... TonyHamilton 8 46+
(Richard Fahey) *sed awkwardly: trckd ldrs: rdn and lost pl over 1f out: wknd ins fnl f* **1/1**[1]

1m 4.82s (4.02) **Going Correction** +0.80s/f (Soft) **6** Ran SP% **114.1**
Speed ratings (Par 90): **99,95,95,93,87 85**
CSF £57.42 TOTE £3.20: £1.60, £5.20; EX 50.70 Trifecta £561.10.
**Owner** Mrs M Gittins **Bred** George Kent **Trained** Middleham Moor, N Yorks

**FOCUS**

The going was changed to soft, good to soft in places. They went a sound gallop which suited the closers. The second and third probably dictate the level.

## 3483 RACING UK IN HD NOVICE AUCTION STKS 5f 193y
**6:40** (6:41) (Class 5) 2-Y-O **£3,396** (£1,010; £505; £252) **Stalls** Low

Form RPR

10 **1** **Izzy Bizu (IRE)**[20] 2801 2-9-4 0 .......... PJMcDonald 3 82
(Mark Johnston) *mde all: r.o to draw clr ins fnl f: rdn out* **4/1**[2]

2 **2** 5 **Ajwan**[19] 2836 2-8-11 0 .......... PaulHanagan 4 60
(Richard Fahey) *chsd ldrs: pushed along 3f out: wnt 2nd over 2f out: no imp on wnr fr ovor 1f out* **0/15**[1]

**3** 2 ¼ **Fabella Bere (FR)** 2-8-11 0 .......... BenCurtis 1 53+
(K R Burke) *in rr: pushed along 3f out: sn outpcd: styd on ins fnl f: nt pce to chal: can improve* **12/1**

**4** ¾ **Tanaya** 2-8-13 0 .......... AdamMcNamara(3) 2 56
(Richard Fahey) *chsd wnr: rdn and lost 2nd over 2f out: one pce fnl f* **11/2**[3]

0 **5** 3 ¾ **Foxxy Brown**[19] 2836 2-8-11 0 .......... TonyHamilton 6 40
(Richard Fahey) *racd keenly: hld up: effrt over 2f out: no imp: wknd fnl f* **28/1**

1m 18.82s (5.12) **Going Correction** +0.80s/f (Soft) **5** Ran SP% **111.8**
Speed ratings (Par 93): **97,90,87,86,81**
CSF £6.75 TOTE £4.70: £1.80, £1.10; EX 7.50 Trifecta £26.10.
**Owner** Lowther Racing & P D Savill **Bred** Mark Salmon **Trained** Middleham Moor, N Yorks

**FOCUS**

An interesting maiden run at a decent pace. The winner clearly improved but it's tricky form to pin down.

## 3484 WATCH RACING UK IN HD H'CAP 1m 1f
**7:10** (7:11) (Class 5) (0-70,72) 3-Y-O **£3,396** (£1,010; £505; £252) **Stalls** Low

Form RPR

0-01 **1** **Archi's Affaire**[7] 3243 3-9-7 **69** 6ex .......... PaulMulrennan 8 76
(Michael Dods) *midfield: pushed along over 3f out: hdwy over 2f out: r.o to ld fnl 110yds: edgd lft: in command towards fin* **2/1**[1]

4-34 **2** 2 **Golconda Prince (IRE)**[18] 2854 3-9-1 **63** .......... PaulHanagan 4 66
(Richard Fahey) *trckd ldrs: rdn to ld over 1f out: hdd fnl 110yds: no ex towards fin* **7/2**[2]

103 **3** ¾ **Musikel (IRE)**[16] 2931 3-9-6 **71** .......... (p) JordanVaughan(3) 6 72
(K R Burke) *hld up in rr: hdwy over 3f out: edgd lft over 1f out whn chsng ldrs: trying to chal ins fnl f whn edgd rt: styd on same pce fnl 110yds* **4/1**[3]

663 **4** 4 ½ **Elite Icon**[72] 1414 3-8-4 **52** .......... JamesSullivan 2 44
(Iain Jardine) *hld up: rdn and outpcd 3f out: plugged on fnl f: no imp* **16/1**

1-54 **5** 2 ¼ **Dream Team**[96] 1029 3-9-7 **69** .......... (p) ConnorBeasley 5 56
(Michael Dods) *hld up: rdn over 3f out: no imp and one pce fnl f* **20/1**

000- **6** 2 ¾ **Devil's Guard (IRE)**[219] 7741 3-8-3 **51** .......... AndrewMullen 1 32
(Keith Dalgleish) *racd keenly: prom: rdn over 2f out: wknd over 1f out* **16/1**

5045 **7** hd **Coral Princess (IRE)**[8] 3196 3-8-5 **53** .......... FrannyNorton 3 34
(Keith Dalgleish) *led: rdn 2f out: hdd over 1f out: sn wknd* **11/1**

5501 **8** 26 **Cartavio (IRE)**[12] 3088 3-9-10 **72** .......... LiamKeniry 7
(Andrew Balding) *chsd ldr tl rdn and wknd over 2f out* **5/1**

2m 4.04s (6.44) **Going Correction** +0.80s/f (Soft) **8** Ran SP% **117.1**
Speed ratings (Par 99): **103,101,100,96,94 92,91,68**
CSF £9.35 CT £25.59 TOTE £2.20: £1.20, £1.20, £1.40; EX 11.00 Trifecta £33.90.
**Owner** D Neale **Bred** Miss K Rausing **Trained** Denton, Co Durham

**FOCUS**

Due to rail movements add 16yds. A competitive contest for the grade run at a good pace. The form looks strong, the winner confirming his Hamilton running.

## 3485 CUMWHINTON MAIDEN STKS 1m 1f
**7:45** (7:46) (Class 5) 3-Y-O+ **£3,396** (£1,010; £505; £252) **Stalls** Low

Form RPR

53 **1** **Pilgrim's Treasure (USA)**[24] 2681 3-9-2 0 .......... (p[1]) PhillipMakin 5 85
(Charlie Appleby) *chsd ldr: rdn to ld over 2f out: styd on wl* **9/4**[2]

**2** 2 ½ **Torcello (IRE)** 3-9-2 0 .......... LiamKeniry 3 80
(Andrew Balding) *in rr and green: pushed along most of way: hdwy over 1f out: styd on to take 2nd ins fnl f: no imp on wnr* **11/1**

-322 **3** 6 **Jamacho**[23] 2703 3-9-2 76 .......... TomEaves 7 67
(Brian Ellison) *led: rdn and hdd over 2f out: wknd ins fnl f* **6/1**

33 **4** 4 ½ **Stararchitecture (IRE)**[16] 2930 3-9-2 0 .......... (t) BenCurtis 1 58
(William Haggas) *hld up: rdn over 2f out: no imp over 1f out: wl btn ins fnl f* **7/4**[1]

33 **5** 15 **Born To Boom (IRE)**[39] 2185 3-8-11 0 .......... CliffordLee(5) 4 41
(K R Burke) *prom: rdn over 2f out: wknd over 1f out* **3/1**[3]

2m 3.92s (6.32) **Going Correction** +0.80s/f (Soft)
**WFA** 3 from 4yo 12lb **5** Ran SP% **114.8**
Speed ratings (Par 103): **103,100,95,91,78**
CSF £24.44 TOTE £3.70: £1.80, £4.10; EX 15.50 Trifecta £90.80.
**Owner** Godolphin **Bred** Darley **Trained** Newmarket, Suffolk

**FOCUS**

The going was eased to soft prior to the fourth. Due to rail movements add 16yds. The pace was honest for this fair maiden. Improvement from the winner.

## 3486 RACING UK H'CAP 1m 3f 39y
**8:20** (8:21) (Class 4) (0-85,87) 4-Y-O+ **£5,498** (£1,636; £817; £408) **Stalls** High

Form RPR

0-60 **1** **Swaheen**[17] 2893 5-9-7 **79** .......... JoeDoyle 1 87
(Julie Camacho) *chsd ldrs: wnt chalng 2nd wl over 1f out: led narrowly fnl 110yds: kpt on* **3/1**[2]

-642 **2** *hd* **Rainbow Rebel (IRE)**[10] 3154 4-10-1 **87**........................ FrannyNorton 6 94
(Mark Johnston) *led for 2f: chsd ldr after tl regained ld over 2f out: pressed wl over 1f out: hdd narrowly fnl 110yds: kpt on: jst hld* **7/4**[1]

0566 **3** *6* **Top Of The Glas (IRE)**[16] 2920 6-9-2 **74**........................ TomEaves 2 71
(Brian Ellison) *in rr: hdwy to chse ldrs over 7f out: rdn and outpcd over 2f out: keeping on u.p whn edgd rt over 1f out: one pce and no imp ins fnl f* **15/2**

1236 **4** *2 1/4* **Lac Leman (GER)**[22] 2741 6-9-7 **79**........................(h) GrahamLee 7 72
(Pauline Robson) *hld up: rdn over 2f out: kpt on ins fnl f: nvr able to trble ldrs* **4/1**[3]

00-0 **5** *nk* **Another Go (IRE)**[67] 1517 4-9-2 **74**........................ NeilFarley 4 66
(Sally Haynes) *hld up: rdn 2f out: no imp over 1f out* **18/1**

40-0 **6** *6* **Brandon Castle**[57] 1716 5-8-10 **68**........................(h) PJMcDonald 8 50
(Simon West) *plld hrd: led after 2f: rdn and hdd over 2f out: wknd fnl f* **6/1**

2m 33.29s (10.19) **Going Correction** +0.80s/f (Soft) **6** Ran SP% **112.7**
Speed ratings (Par 105): **94,93,89,87,87 83**
CSF £8.76 CT £33.13 TOTE £3.90: £2.40, £1.80; EX 10.10 Trifecta £35.60.
**Owner** Judy & Richard Peck **Bred** Ashbrittle Stud **Trained** Norton, N Yorks

**FOCUS**
Due to rail movements add 16yds. A fair handicap run at a sound pace in the ground. The winner was close to his best, with the runner-up to form.

## 3487 RACING UK DAY PASS JUST £10 H'CAP 7f 173y
**8:50** (8:50) (Class 5) (0-70,71) 4-Y-0+ **£3,396** (£1,010; £505; £252) **Stalls** Low

Form RPR

0/36 **1** **Geordie George (IRE)**[16] 2919 5-8-11 **60**........................(t) GrahamLee 5 66
(Rebecca Menzies) *hld up: rdn and hdwy over 1f out: led ins fnl f: styd on: in command towards fin* **7/2**[2]

3-06 **2** *3/4* **Mustaqbal (IRE)**[31] 2458 5-9-3 **71**........................(p) CallumRodriguez(5) 1 75
(Michael Dods) *hld up: hdwy over 3f out: swtchd lft and effrt on inner over 2f out: chalng over 1f out: nt qckn ins fnl f: kpt on but hld after* **11/4**[1]

2-00 **3** *1 1/4* **Jordan James (IRE)**[9] 3181 4-9-7 **70**........................(p[1]) TomEaves 2 71
(Brian Ellison) *led: rdn over 2f out: hdd ins fnl f: styd on same pce fnl 100yds* **4/1**[3]

-400 **4** *6* **Someone Exciting**[26] 2633 4-8-5 **59**........................ LewisEdmunds(5) 4 46+
(David Thompson) *racd keenly: prom: lost pl 3f out: bdly hmpd and nrly fell over 2f out: n.d after* **7/2**[2]

0253 **5** *hd* **Chiswick Bey (IRE)**[13] 3049 9-9-5 **71**........................ AdamMcNamara(3) 3 58
(Richard Fahey) *prom: rdn 2f out: wknd over 1f out* **9/2**

1m 47.91s (7.91) **Going Correction** +0.80s/f (Soft) **5** Ran SP% **109.3**
Speed ratings (Par 103): **92,91,90,84,83**
CSF £13.15 TOTE £4.80: £2.50, £1.40; EX 14.30 Trifecta £50.70.
**Owner** Fletcher, Outhart, Moran & Maddison **Bred** Azienda Agricola Rosati Colarieti **Trained** Mordon, Durham
■ Stewards' Enquiry : Adam McNamara four-day ban: failed to ride out a horse that would have finished fourth (Jun 25-28)
Callum Rodriguez seven-day ban: careless riding (Jun 22-28)

**FOCUS**
Due to rail movements add 14yds. They went a fair pace for this open handicap. Not easy form to assess.

## 3488 WREAY H'CAP 6f 195y
**9:20** (9:21) (Class 5) (0-70,69) 4-Y-0+ **£3,396** (£1,010; £505; £252) **Stalls** Low

Form RPR

0-00 **1** **Reinforced**[19] 2843 4-9-0 **62**........................(t[1]) AndrewMullen 7 71
(Michael Dods) *mde all: rdn 2f out: pressed ins fnl f: gamely fnd ex towards fin* **9/1**

5336 **2** *1 1/2* **Cool Strutter (IRE)**[7] 3256 5-8-9 **57**........................ SamJames 2 62
(Karen Tutty) *midfield: rdn and hdwy over 1f out: chalng ins fnl f: no ex towards fin* **7/2**[2]

0-55 **3** *4 1/2* **Mitchum**[7] 3238 8-8-12 **65**........................ PhilDennis(5) 4 58
(Ron Barr) *racd keenly: prom: rdn 2f out: ev ch wl over 1f out: nt qckn: kpt on same pce ins fnl f* **14/1**

6250 **4** *1 1/4* **Crazy Tornado (IRE)**[15] 2952 4-9-7 **69**........................(h) ConnorBeasley 3 59
(Keith Dalgleish) *midfield: rdn over 2f out: outpcd over 1f out: edgd lft ent fnl f: sn swtchd rt: kpt on towards fin but n.d* **11/4**[1]

-003 **5** *1* **Fidelma Moon (IRE)**[10] 3151 5-9-0 **65**........................ JordanVaughan(3) 6 52
(K R Burke) *prom: rdn and ev ch 2f out: outpcd over 1f out: no imp after* **5/1**

6-05 **6** *1/2* **Popsies Joy (IRE)**[8] 3203 4-9-0 **65**........................(be[1]) RachelRichardson(3) 8 51
(Tim Easterby) *bolted on way to s: in tch: effrt 2f out: wknd ins fnl f* **4/1**[3]

6-05 **7** *1 1/4* **Lukoutoldmakezebak**[20] 2792 4-8-2 **50** oh5........................ JamesSullivan 1 33
(David Thompson) *stdd s: hld up: pushed along 3f out: rdn whn checked ent fnl f: n.d* **25/1**

6-00 **8** *1 3/4* **Off The Scale (IRE)**[38] 2224 5-9-2 **64**........................ GrahamLee 5 42
(Rebecca Menzies) *hld up: pushed along 3f out: nvr a threat* **12/1**

1m 32.3s (5.20) **Going Correction** +0.80s/f (Soft) **8** Ran SP% **113.8**
Speed ratings (Par 103): **102,100,95,93,92 92,90,88**
CSF £40.13 CT £442.50 TOTE £7.90: £2.80, £1.50, £3.10; EX 52.50 Trifecta £486.50.
**Owner** W G McHarg & M Pearson **Bred** Maze Rattan Limited **Trained** Denton, Co Durham
■ Stewards' Enquiry : Rachel Richardson stewards noted jockey was unable to get her feet in the irons before going out on to the track, resulting in filly running free to post; however having been examined by the vet at the start, filly was deemed fit to race

**FOCUS**
Due to rail movements add 14yds. A strongly run handicap. The winner built on last autumn's progress.
T/Plt: £57.40 to a £1 stake. Pool: £58,560.12 - 743.78 winning units. T/Qpdt: £12.50 to a £1 stake. Pool: £4,928.13 - 291.30 winning units. **Darren Owen**

# 3076 HAYDOCK (L-H)
Thursday, June 8

**OFFICIAL GOING: Soft (good to soft in places) changing to soft after race 1 (2.10)**
Wind: Fresh half against Weather: Cloudy with sunny periods and heavy showers

## 3489 188BET.CO.UK H'CAP 1m 3f 140y
**2:10** (2:10) (Class 5) (0-70,69) 3-Y-0 **£3,557** (£1,058; £529; £264) **Stalls** Centre

Form RPR

0-16 **1** **Brimham Rocks**[20] 2807 3-9-7 **69**........................ SilvestreDeSousa 1 83+
(Ralph Beckett) *led 1f: trckd ldrs on inner: hdwy to ld wl over 2f out: rdn clr wl over 1f out: kpt on strly* **13/8**[1]

01-5 **2** *7* **Nordic Combined (IRE)**[20] 2807 3-8-13 **68**........................ BenRobinson(7) 11 70
(Brian Ellison) *in tch: pushed along 1/2-way: rdn along and outpcd over 4f out: hdwy on wd outside 3f out: sn rdn: drvn over 1f out: kpt on nvr nr wnr* **5/1**[2]

-640 **3** *nk* **Legato (IRE)**[29] 2527 3-9-4 **66**........................ RichardKingscote 7 67
(Tom Dascombe) *hld up towards rr: hdwy 4f out: rdn along to chse ldrs over 2f out: drvn over 1f out: kpt on same pce* **12/1**

0-63 **4** *4* **Zamadance**[14] 2991 3-9-0 **62**........................ AntonioFresu 8 57
(Ed Dunlop) *hld up towards rr: hdwy over 4f out: rdn along to chse ldng pair wl over 2f out: sn drvn and no imp* **16/1**

3651 **5** *1 1/2* **American Craftsman (IRE)**[8] 3207 3-9-0 **62** 6ex....(p) ConnorBeasley 6 55
(Roger Fell) *cl up: led over 4f out: pushed along 3f out: sn hdd and rdn: drvn wl over 1f out: sn wknd* **13/2**[3]

2250 **6** *2 1/2* **Good Time Ahead (IRE)**[18] 2854 3-9-5 **67**........................ PaddyAspell 9 56
(Philip Kirby) *dwlt and rr tl sme late hdwy* **33/1**

0-64 **7** *1 1/4* **Kuraka**[14] 2991 3-9-4 **69**........................ JordanVaughan(3) 4 56
(K R Burke) *trckd ldrs: hdwy 4f out: rdn along 3f out sn drvn and wknd* **9/1**

0-00 **8** *1 1/4* **Nobleman (GER)**[33] 2395 3-8-8 **56**........................(h) LiamKeniry 10 41
(Hughie Morrison) *prom: rdn along over 4f out: sn wknd* **8/1**

0-60 **9** *6* **Silver Gleam (IRE)**[9] 3180 3-8-5 **53**........................ RoystonFfrench 3 28
(Chris Fairhurst) *cl up: slt ld after 1f: pushed along and hdd over 4f out: sn rdn along and wknd 3f out* **20/1**

1335 **10** *4 1/2* **Critical Thinking (IRE)**[13] 3041 3-8-10 **65**........................ FinleyMarsh(7) 2 33
(Kevin Frost) *in tch: rdn along over 4f out: sn drvn and wknd* **9/1**

650 **11** *36* **Company Trader (IRE)**[19] 2841 3-7-13 **50** oh2........................ HollieDoyle(3) 5
(Sharon Watt) *a rr: outpcd and bhd fnl 3f* **50/1**

2m 34.8s (1.80) **Going Correction** +0.375s/f (Good) **11** Ran SP% **122.4**
Speed ratings (Par 99): **109,104,104,101,100 98,97,97,93,90 66**
CSF £9.78 CT £77.95 TOTE £2.30: £1.10, £2.50, £3.80; EX 10.70 Trifecta £46.00.
**Owner** Mr and Mrs David Aykroyd **Bred** Mr & Mrs David Aykroyd **Trained** Kimpton, Hants
■ Stewards' Enquiry : Ben Robinson two-day ban: excessive use of the whip (Jun 25-26)

**FOCUS**
There was 7mm of rain overnight and the going was given as soft, good to soft in places (GoingStick: 6.8). All races were run on the Inner Home Straight. Race distance increased by 10yds. A modest handicap. The winner reversed York form with the runner-up.

## 3490 SCOTLAND V ENGLAND BETTING AT 188BET NOVICE STKS (PLUS 10 RACE) 5f
**2:40** (2:42) (Class 4) 2-Y-0 **£4,528** (£1,347; £673; £336) **Stalls** High

Form RPR

06 **1** **Darkanna (IRE)**[17] 2904 2-8-11 0........................ BarryMcHugh 7 80
(Richard Fahey) *hmpd on inner after 100 yds and sn bhd: swtchd lft to outer and hdwy 1/2-way: chsd ldrs on outer and rdn over 1f out: chal ent fnl f: styd on wl to ld last 100 yds* **14/1**

**2** *3/4* **Gift In Time (IRE)** 2-9-2 0........................ JoeDoyle 3 82+
(James Given) *chsd ldr and led after 150yds: pushed along over 1f out: jnd and rdn ent fnl f: hdd and no ex last 100 yds* **11/4**[3]

2 **3** *7* **Seyaady**[17] 2882 2-9-2 0........................ JoeFanning 2 57
(Mark Johnston) *t.k.h: led early: cl up: rdn along 2f out: drvn over 1f out: grad wknd* **9/4**[2]

20 **4** *2 3/4* **Big Time Maybe (IRE)**[29] 2522 2-9-2 0........................ RichardKingscote 5 47
(Tom Dascombe) *sltly hmpd after 100 yds: trckd ldrs: effrt over 2f out and sn rdn: drvn along wl over 1f out and sn wknd* **13/8**[1]

02 **5** *1/2* **Dragon's Teeth (IRE)**[54] 1792 2-9-2 0........................ DougieCostello 4 45
(Jo Hughes) *edgd rt after 100 yds: sn chsng ldng pair: rdn along 2f out: sn wknd* **12/1**

00 **6** *2 1/2* **Sir Walter (IRE)**[15] 2948 2-9-2 0........................ PatCosgrave 1 36
(Eric Alston) *wnt lft s: in tch: rdn along over 2f out: sn wknd* **66/1**

1m 2.9s (2.10) **Going Correction** +0.375s/f (Good) **6** Ran SP% **111.4**
Speed ratings (Par 95): **98,96,85,81,80 76**
CSF £51.33 TOTE £15.90: £4.40, £3.00; EX 67.30 Trifecta £319.90.
**Owner** The Cool Silk Partnership **Bred** Mountarmstrong Stud **Trained** Musley Bank, N Yorks

**FOCUS**
The first two came well clear in this novice event, some of them seeming unable to show their form on this soft ground.

## 3491 188BET EBF MAIDEN FILLIES' STKS (PLUS 10 RACE) 6f
**3:10** (3:14) (Class 5) 2-Y-0 **£3,557** (£1,058; £529; £264) **Stalls** High

Form RPR

2 **1** **Ertiyad**[27] 2563 2-9-0 0........................ PatCosgrave 8 79+
(William Haggas) *mde all: shkn up ins fnl f: rdn and kpt on wl towards fin* **4/9**[1]

**2** *1/2* **Maybride** 2-9-0 0........................ BarryMcHugh 3 78+
(Richard Fahey) *trckd ldrs: hdwy 2f out: rdn over 1f out: chal ins fnl f: sn ev ch: kpt on wl u.p* **11/4**[2]

0 **3** *2 1/2* **Kirbec (IRE)**[49] 1909 2-9-0 0........................ ConnorBeasley 12 70
(Keith Dalgleish) *trckd ldrs: pushed along 2f out: rdn over 1f out: kpt on same pce fnl f* **20/1**

**4** *nk* **Supersymmetry (IRE)** 2-9-0 0........................ RichardKingscote 10 69
(Tom Dascombe) *dwlt and towards rr: hdwy over 2f out: rdn along over 2f out: kpt on fnl f* **7/1**[3]

**5** *nk* **Peggy's Angel** 2-9-0 0........................ DougieCostello 6 68+
(Jo Hughes) *cl up: rdn 2f out: drvn over 1f out: wknd fnl f* **33/1**

**6** *2 1/4* **Fleeting Freedom** 2-9-0 0........................ RobertTart 5 61
(Alan Bailey) *green and sn rdn along in rr: swtchd wd and hdwy 2f out: sn in tch: grad wknd fr over 1f out* **25/1**

**7** *3 1/4* **Excellent Times** 2-9-0 0........................ JamesSullivan 11 52
(Tim Easterby) *wnt rt s: green and a towards rr* **16/1**

**8** *3/4* **Fenagh (IRE)** 2-9-0 0........................ LiamKeniry 7 49
(David Loughnane) *trckd ldrs: effrt over 2f out: sn rdn and wknd* **33/1**

**9** *1* **Harbour Rose** 2-9-0 0........................ PaddyAspell 4 46
(Philip Kirby) *sltly hmpd after 1f and towards rr: hdwy and in tch over 2f out: sn rdn and wknd* **50/1**

0 **10** *17* **Snoop**[13] 3037 2-9-0 0........................ SamJames 13
(David Loughnane) *t.k.h: cl up: rdn along 1/2-way: sn wknd* **100/1**

1m 17.27s (3.47) **Going Correction** +0.375s/f (Good) **10** Ran SP% **131.7**
Speed ratings (Par 90): **91,90,87,86,86 83,78,77,76,53**
CSF £2.25 TOTE £1.50: £1.02, £1.60, £4.30; EX 3.10 Trifecta £18.50.
**Owner** Sheikh Juma Dalmook Al Maktoum **Bred** Ms J Allison **Trained** Newmarket, Suffolk

**FOCUS**
They went quite steady early and the odds-on favourite was always best placed. The form can't be rated any higher.

## 3492 RUGBY UNION BETTING AT 188BET H'CAP 6f
**3:40** (3:41) (Class 4) (0-85,85) 4-Y-O+ **£5,822** (£1,732; £865; £432) **Stalls** High

| Form | | | | RPR |
|---|---|---|---|---|
| 666- | **1** | | **Adam's Ale**[259] 6718 8-8-12 **76**.....(p) BarryMcHugh 5 (Marjorie Fife) *trckd ldrs: hdwy on bit and cl up over 2f out: led 11/2f out and sn qcknd clr: rdr dropped rein wl ins fnl f: kpt on* **7/1** | 87 |
| 22-0 | **2** | 3 | **Rantan (IRE)**[49] 1910 4-9-4 **82**..... SilvestreDeSousa 1 (David Barron) *wnt lft s and rr: hdwy on outer 2f out: rdn over 1f out: chsd wnr ins fnl f: kpt on* **2/1**[1] | 83 |
| 0003 | **3** | nk | **Amood (IRE)**[16] 2922 6-8-8 **72**.....(p) JoeFanning 6 (Simon West) *hld up in rr: hdwy 2f out: rdn over 1f out: kpt on fnl f* **7/1** | 72 |
| 0-42 | **4** | 1 ¾ | **Signore Piccolo**[9] 3170 6-8-12 **76**.....(h) SamJames 2 (David Loughnane) *slt ld: rdn along and hdd over 2f out: sn drvn and grad wknd* **7/2**[2] | 71 |
| 1000 | **5** | hd | **Florencio**[6] 3288 4-9-3 **81**..... ConnorBeasley 3 (Roger Fell) *trckd ldrs: hdwy over 2f out: rdn wl over 1f out: sn drvn and kpt on same pce* **20/1** | 75 |
| 1164 | **6** | nk | **Art Collection (FR)**[33] 2381 4-9-7 **85**..... JamesSullivan 4 (Ruth Carr) *trckd ldrs: pushed along over 2f out: sn rdn and wknd* **9/2**[3] | 78 |
| 03 | **7** | 1 | **New Road Side**[7] 3253 4-8-9 **78**..... CliffordLee(5) 8 (Richard Guest) *cl up: led over 2f out: rdn and hdd 11/2f out: sn drvn and wknd* **8/1** | 68 |

1m 16.21s (2.41) **Going Correction** +0.375s/f (Good) **7 Ran SP% 114.6**
Speed ratings (Par 105): **98,94,93,91,91 90,89**
CSF £21.57 CT £102.62 TOTE £10.00: £3.70, £1.70; EX 29.60 Trifecta £149.10.

**Owner** Mrs M Hills **Bred** Mrs M J Hills **Trained** Stillington, N Yorks

**FOCUS**
Quite a competitive sprint on paper, but the winner did it easily. He's rated to last year's form.

## 3493 BEST ODDS GUARANTEED AT 188BET MAIDEN STKS (PLUS 10 RACE) 6f 212y
**4:10** (4:10) (Class 4) 3-Y-O **£5,822** (£1,732; £865; £432) **Stalls** Low

| Form | | | | RPR |
|---|---|---|---|---|
| 0 | **1** | | **Rubens Dream**[40] 2135 3-9-5 0..... SilvestreDeSousa 4 (Charles Hills) *dwlt and bhd: racd wd home st: hdwy 3f out: rdn wl over 1f out: drvn and styd on strly fnl f to ld nr line* **13/2** | 78+ |
| 23 | **2** | shd | **Peach Melba**[7] 3234 3-9-0 0..... JoeFanning 2 (Mark Johnston) *led: pushed along over 2f out: rdn over 1f out: drvn ins fnl f: hdd on line* **6/4**[1] | 72 |
| -232 | **3** | nk | **Benjamin Thomas (IRE)**[13] 3054 3-9-5 75.....(v[1]) DougieCostello 5 (John Quinn) *trckd ldrs: hdwy 4f out: chsd ldr over 2f out: rdn wl over 1f out: drvn and ev ch ins fnl f: kpt on* **11/4**[2] | 76 |
| 5 | **4** | 6 | **Mio Ragazzo**[20] 2791 3-9-5 0..... AntonioFresu 1 (Marco Botti) *trckd ldr: pushed along wl over 2f out: rdn wl over 1f out: grad wknd* **9/2**[3] | 60 |
| 6 | **5** | hd | **Mac O'Polo (IRE)**[12] 3062 3-9-5 0..... RichardKingscote 3 (Tom Dascombe) *trckd ldrs: pushed along over 3f out: rdn wl over 2f out: drvn and wknd wl over 1f out* **8/1** | 60 |
| 66 | **6** | 2 ¼ | **Super Ruby**[3] 3404 3-8-11 0..... JordanVaughan(3) 6 (K R Burke) *hld up towards rr: hdwy 3f out: rdn along 2f out: sn drvn and wknd* **25/1** | 49 |
| 0 | **7** | 9 | **D'Waterside**[26] 2620 3-9-5 0..... SamJames 7 (David Loughnane) *chsd ldrs: rdn along wl over 3f out: sn wknd* **40/1** | 31 |

1m 32.34s (1.64) **Going Correction** +0.375s/f (Good) **7 Ran SP% 115.6**
Speed ratings (Par 101): **105,104,104,97,97 94,84**
CSF £17.13 TOTE £6.90: £2.60, £1.40; EX 18.10 Trifecta £44.30.

**Owner** Tony Wechsler & Ann Plummer **Bred** Cheveley Park Stud Ltd **Trained** Lambourn, Berks

**FOCUS**
Just a fair maiden and there was little to choose between the first three at the line. The form is rated around the third.

## 3494 LIVE CASINO AT 188BET H'CAP (FOR LADY AMATEUR RIDERS) 1m 6f
**4:40** (4:40) (Class 5) (0-75,73) 4-Y-O+ **£3,431** (£1,064; £531; £266) **Stalls** Low

| Form | | | | RPR |
|---|---|---|---|---|
| 56-3 | **1** | | **Zenafire**[19] 2609 8-9-13 **65**.....(p) MlleBarbaraGuenet 3 (Sarah Hollinshead) *trckd ldr: hdwy to ld 3f out: rdn wl clr 2f out: kpt on strly: unchal* **6/5**[1] | 76 |
| 5-03 | **2** | 16 | **Barizan (IRE)**[16] 2928 11-9-9 **66**.....(vt) PoppyBridgwater(5) 6 (Brendan Powell) *prom: pushed along after 4f: sn rdn along and lost pl: rr tl hdwy u.p wl over 2f out: plugged on to take remote 2nd nr fin* **5/1**[3] | 55 |
| 0/16 | **3** | ¾ | **Mishko (IRE)**[5] 3311 6-9-9 **68**..... MissSATrotter(7) 1 (Steve Gollings) *trckd ldrs: hdwy 3f out: chsd wnr 2f out and sn rdn: drvn and no imp fnl f: lost remote 2nd nr fin* **5/1**[3] | 56 |
| 622- | **4** | 23 | **Kristjano (GER)**[98] 6090 5-10-4 **70**.....(p) BryonyFrost 2 (Jimmy Frost) *prom: pushed along and lost pl over 6f out: bhd fnl 3f* **10/1** | 25 |
| 030 | **5** | 1 ¾ | **Entihaa**[54] 1798 9-10-4 **73**.....(p[1]) MissJodieHughes(3) 5 (Dai Burchell) *led: rdn along 4f out: hdd 3f out: sn drvn and wknd* **9/1** | 26 |
| -525 | **6** | ½ | **Nafaath (IRE)**[8] 3193 11-9-5 **62**.....(p) MissAMcCain(5) 7 (Donald McCain) *dwlt and rr: hdwy on inner to trck ldrs whn n.m.r and hmpd 7f out: rdn along 4f out sn wknd* **9/2**[2] | 14 |

3m 18.36s **Going Correction** +0.375s/f (Good) **6 Ran SP% 116.1**
Speed ratings (Par 103): **68,58,58,45,44 44**
CSF £8.08 TOTE £2.40: £1.50, £2.30; EX 8.00 Trifecta £30.80.

**Owner** Robert Moseley **Bred** R J R Moseley & Mrs E Coquelin **Trained** Upper Longdon, Staffs

■ Stewards' Enquiry : Miss S A Trotter seven-day ban: failed to ride out a horse that could have finished second (tbn)

**FOCUS**
Race distance increased by 26yds. This was well run given the conditions and they finished strung out. A weak race in which the winner had plenty in his favour.

T/Plt: £44.00 to a £1 stake. Pool: £63,670.31 - 1054.36 winning units. T/Qpdt: £5.80 to a £1 stake. Pool: £4,519.94 - 579.96 winning units. **Joe Rowntree**

# 3460 RIPON (R-H)
Thursday, June 8

**OFFICIAL GOING: Good to soft (7.4)**
Wind: fresh half behind Weather: Cloudy, odd shower

## 3495 WESTGATE EBF NOVICE STKS 6f
**2:00** (2:03) (Class 5) 2-Y-O **£3,234** (£962; £481; £240) **Stalls** High

| Form | | | | RPR |
|---|---|---|---|---|
| 53 | **1** | | **Collingham Park (IRE)**[31] 2452 2-9-2 0..... GrahamLee 3 (Jedd O'Keeffe) *prom: pushed along to ld over 1f out: rdn and styd on to draw clr fnl f* **9/4**[1] | 75+ |
| 40 | **2** | 4 | **Go Now Go Now (IRE)**[23] 2698 2-9-2 0..... FrannyNorton 7 (Mark Johnston) *prom: rdn 1/2-way: outpcd and lost pl 2f out: plugged on fnl f: wnt 2nd post* **9/2**[3] | 63 |
| 0 | **3** | nk | **Shaheen (IRE)**[20] 2786 2-9-2 0..... JasonHart 6 (John Quinn) *led: rdn whn hdd over 1f out: wknd ins fnl f: lost 2nd post* **5/2**[2] | 62 |
| | **4** | ½ | **Kylie Rules** 2-8-11 0..... ShaneGray 5 (Ann Duffield) *dwlt: hld up: pushed along and sme hdwy over 1f out: plugged on fnl f* **33/1** | 56 |
| 0 | **5** | 5 | **Reinbeau Prince**[23] 2698 2-9-2 0..... TonyHamilton 1 (Richard Fahey) *hld up: pushed along and hung rt 1/2-way: a towards rr* **14/1** | 46 |
| 60 | **6** | 6 | **Harvest Day**[3] 3398 2-8-4 0.....(t) HarrisonShaw(7) 2 (Michael Easterby) *in tch: pushed along 1/2-way: edgd rt over 1f out: wknd* **40/1** | 23 |

1m 14.75s (1.75) **Going Correction** +0.20s/f (Good) **6 Ran SP% 89.6**
Speed ratings (Par 93): **96,90,90,89,82 74**
CSF £7.56 TOTE £2.10: £1.10, £1.80; EX 5.50 Trifecta £9.80.

**Owner** Ingham Racing Syndicate **Bred** John Dunleavy **Trained** Middleham Moor, N Yorks

**FOCUS**
No changes to race distances. After riding in the opener Franny Norton said: "I thought it was soft ground" and Graham Lee said: "It is betweeen soft and good to soft." A fair novice event. The well supported \bSandie Gem\p was withdrawn after she wouldn't go in the stalls.

## 3496 KIRKGATE H'CAP 6f
**2:30** (2:30) (Class 5) (0-70,73) 3-Y-O **£3,234** (£962; £481; £240) **Stalls** High

| Form | | | | RPR |
|---|---|---|---|---|
| -011 | **1** | | **Kaeso**[9] 3184 3-9-5 **68** 6ex..... TomEaves 7 (Nigel Tinkler) *trckd ldrs: pushed along whn short of room over 1f out tl jst ins fnl f: rdn and kpt on wl: led towards fin* **9/4**[1] | 73+ |
| 2042 | **2** | ½ | **Seaview**[16] 2927 3-9-2 **68**..... AaronJones(3) 4 (David Brown) *dwlt: sn midfield: rdn and hdwy on outer over 1f out: kpt on* **8/1** | 71 |
| -000 | **3** | hd | **Vintage Dream (IRE)**[3] 3387 3-8-10 **59**.....(p[1]) GrahamLee 3 (Noel Wilson) *led: rdn over 2f out: edgd rt ins fnl f: one pce and hdd towards fin* **40/1** | 61 |
| 0004 | **4** | 1 ¾ | **Spare Parts (IRE)**[34] 2362 3-8-3 **52**..... FrannyNorton 2 (Charles Hills) *prom: rdn over 2f out: no ex fnl 110yds* **11/1** | 49 |
| 45-4 | **5** | 3 ¾ | **Swag (IRE)**[14] 3000 3-9-4 **70**.....(t) NathanEvans(3) 5 (Michael Easterby) *midfield: rdn over 2f out: wknd over 1f out* **4/1**[2] | 55 |
| 12-1 | **6** | 1 ¼ | **Control Centre (IRE)**[7] 3239 3-9-10 **73** 6ex..... DanielTudhope 1 (Marjorie Fife) *chsd ldrs: rdn to chal 2f out: wknd fnl f* **5/1**[3] | 54 |
| 0600 | **7** | 1 ½ | **Trick Of The Lyte (IRE)**[26] 2630 3-8-11 **60**..... JasonHart 6 (John Quinn) *a towards rr* **28/1** | 36 |
| 3-22 | **8** | hd | **Springforth**[20] 2775 3-9-4 **67**..... PaulHanagan 8 (Richard Fahey) *rrd s and slowly away: hld up: pushed along 1/2-way: nvr threatened* **4/1**[2] | 42 |

1m 13.7s (0.70) **Going Correction** +0.20s/f (Good) **8 Ran SP% 112.8**
Speed ratings (Par 99): **103,102,102,99,94 93,91,90**
CSF £20.67 CT £551.65 TOTE £3.10: £1.10, £2.50, £9.80; EX 23.80 Trifecta £413.20.

**Owner** M Webb **Bred** Sir Eric Parker **Trained** Langton, N Yorks

■ Stewards' Enquiry : Aaron Jones two-day ban: used whip in incorrect place (Jun 25-26)

**FOCUS**
Modest sprint handicap form.

## 3497 RIPONBET OUR PROFITS STAY IN RACING H'CAP 1m 1f 170y
**3:00** (3:00) (Class 4) (0-85,83) 4-Y-O+ **£5,175** (£1,540; £769; £384) **Stalls** Low

| Form | | | | RPR |
|---|---|---|---|---|
| 4216 | **1** | | **Sands Chorus**[12] 3065 5-9-7 **83**..... PaulMulrennan 3 (James Given) *mde all: pushed along over 2f out: rdn fnl f: kpt on* **3/1**[1] | 92 |
| -600 | **2** | 1 ¼ | **Mukhayyam**[22] 2741 5-9-5 **81**.....(p) DuranFentiman 2 (Tim Easterby) *trckd ldrs on inner: pushed along and short of room over over 1f out: short of room again ins fnl f: kpt on to go 2nd post: nvr able to chal* **17/2** | 87+ |
| 0406 | **3** | hd | **Jacbequick**[8] 3204 6-9-3 **82**.....(p) JoshDoyle(3) 4 (David O'Meara) *prom: rdn over 2f out: one pce ins fnl f: lost 2nd post* **8/1**[3] | 87 |
| 56-5 | **4** | 1 ¼ | **Indy (IRE)**[17] 2893 6-8-12 **74**..... JasonHart 5 (John Quinn) *in tch: rdn over 2f out: kpt on* **10/3**[2] | 76 |
| -000 | **5** | 6 | **Maraakib (IRE)**[22] 2741 5-9-7 **83**..... DanielTudhope 7 (David O'Meara) *in tch on outer: rdn over 2f out: wknd fnl f* **3/1**[1] | 73 |
| 600- | **6** | 5 | **Salmon Sushi**[181] 8283 6-9-4 **80**..... AndrewMullen 6 (Tim Easterby) *hld up: rdn along 3f out: wknd over 1f out* **16/1** | 60 |
| 0-14 | **7** | 11 | **Toboggan's Fire**[20] 2789 4-9-6 **82**..... JoeyHaynes 1 (Ann Duffield) *dwlt: a towards rr* **9/1** | 39 |

2m 6.33s (0.93) **Going Correction** +0.20s/f (Good) **7 Ran SP% 110.6**
Speed ratings (Par 105): **104,103,102,101,97 93,84**
CSF £26.53 TOTE £3.70: £2.30, £3.60; EX 25.20 Trifecta £122.00.

**Owner** The Cool Silk Partnership **Bred** Worksop Manor Stud **Trained** Willoughton, Lincs

**FOCUS**
This wasn't truly run, the winner dictating, and only the first three became seriously involved. The third looks the best guide.

## 3498 WEATHERBYS GENERAL STUD BOOK ONLINE H'CAP 1m
**3:30** (3:34) (Class 3) (0-95,94) 4-Y-O+ **£7,762** (£2,310; £1,154; £577) **Stalls** Low

| Form | | | | RPR |
|---|---|---|---|---|
| 0524 | **1** | | **Boots And Spurs**[10] 3144 8-8-5 **78**.....(v) FrannyNorton 11 (Scott Dixon) *trckd ldr: rdn over 2f out: kpt on fnl f: led 30 yds out* **14/1** | 85 |
| 2613 | **2** | hd | **Roller**[47] 1969 4-8-10 **86**..... NathanEvans(3) 8 (Michael Easterby) *midfield: rdn and hdwy over 1f out: chal ins fnl f: kpt on* **9/2**[1] | 92+ |

-311 **3** ½ **Gurkha Friend**[18] 2855 5-9-6 **93** TomEaves 7 98
(Karen McLintock) *trckd ldr: rdn to chal 2f out: led narrowly over 1f out: hdd 30yds out* **6/1**[2]

0-30 **4** 2 **Candelisa (IRE)**[19] 2828 4-9-7 **94** (p) GrahamLee 6 94
(Jedd O'Keeffe) *hld up: rdn over 2f out: styd on fr over 1f out: nvr threatened ldrs* **16/1**

-665 **5** ¾ **Qeyaadah (IRE)**[22] 2730 4-8-12 **85** BenCurtis 5 84+
(Michael Appleby) *midfield on inner: swtchd lft and n.m.r 2f out: pushed along over 1f out: rdn and kpt on ins fnl f* **16/1**

13-0 **6** ¾ **Just Hiss**[40] 2136 4-9-1 **88** PaulMulrennan 2 85
(Tim Easterby) *in tch on inner: pushed along over 2f out: outpcd over 1f out: no threat after* **14/1**

1430 **7** 2 **Swift Emperor (IRE)**[10] 3154 5-9-5 **92** PhillipMakin 9 84
(David Barron) *sn led: rdn and jnd over 2f out: hdd over 1f out: wknd ins fnl f* **12/1**

0-00 **8** nk **Stamp Hill (IRE)**[26] 2606 4-9-5 **92** TonyHamilton 3 84
(Richard Fahey) *in tch: rdn over 2f out: wknd fnl f* **9/1**[3]

6220 **9** ½ **Two For Two (IRE)**[22] 2735 9-8-10 **90** BenSanderson(7) 4 80
(Roger Fell) *slowly away: hld up: rdn over 2f out: nvr threatened* **9/1**[3]

0-64 **10** 1½ **Bahama Moon (IRE)**[58] 1704 5-9-0 **87** AndrewMullen 10 74
(David Barron) *dwlt: a towards rr* **20/1**

1m 41.44s (0.04) **Going Correction** +0.20s/f (Good) **10** Ran SP% **90.0**
Speed ratings (Par 107): **107,106,106,104,103 102,100,100,100,98**
CSF £45.64 CT £186.14 TOTE £13.90: £3.70, £1.70, £1.30; EX 58.40 Trifecta £296.10.
**Owner** S Chappell **Bred** Miss G Abbey **Trained** Babworth, Notts
■ Kharbetation was withdrawn. Price at time of withdrawal 3-1. Rule 4 applies to all bets - deduction 25p in the pound.

**FOCUS**
A decent handicap, but one that was weakened when favourite \bKharbetation\p again refused to enter the stalls. It was another race that suited those who raced up with the generous gallop. The winner's best form since last autumn.

## 3499 FOLLOW @RIPONRACES ON TWITTER H'CAP 1m 1f 170y
**4:00** (4:00) (Class 5) (0-70,72) 3-Y-O **£3,234** (£962; £481; £240) **Stalls** Low

Form RPR

-363 **1** **Barwell (IRE)**[39] 2186 3-9-3 **65** PaulMulrennan 7 78
(Michael Dods) *midfield: keen early: pushed along and hdwy over 3f out: led 2f out: sn rdn: styd on wl to draw clr fnl f* **9/2**[2]

00-0 **2** 2¾ **Cornerstone Lad**[39] 2185 3-8-13 **61** JackGarritty 3 68
(Micky Hammond) *midfield on inner: bit short of room over 2f out and swtchd lft: rdn and hdwy over 1f out: wnt 2nd 110yds out: styd on but no threat wnr* **11/1**

0-43 **3** 1½ **Racemaker**[18] 2854 3-9-7 **69** NeilFarley 9 73
(Andrew Crook) *midfield on outer: rdn and hdwy 3f out: chal 2f out: no ex ins fnl f: lost 2nd 110yds out* **10/1**

3151 **4** 2 **Metronomic (IRE)**[27] 2591 3-9-0 **62** AndrewMullen 2 62
(Peter Niven) *trckd ldr: rdn over 2f out: grad wknd over 1f out* **7/1**

2-30 **5** 5 **Warm Love**[18] 2854 3-9-10 **72** DanielTudhope 1 62
(David O'Meara) *led: rdn whn hdd 2f out: wknd fnl f* **11/2**[3]

600 **6** 2 **Rock Island Line**[39] 2185 3-9-0 **65** NathanEvans(3) 5 51
(Mark Walford) *hld up: nvr threatened* **14/1**

405 **7** 8 **Oregon Point (USA)**[35] 2345 3-9-9 **71** DuranFentiman 6 40
(Tim Easterby) *hld up: rdn over 4f out: sn btn* **28/1**

26-5 **8** 18 **Powerful Love (IRE)**[18] 2854 3-9-10 **72** JasonHart 4
(Mark Johnston) *prom: rdn over 4f out: wknd over 2f out* **11/2**[3]

2-51 **9** 4 **Reinstorm**[23] 2703 3-9-1 **63** PaulHanagan 8
(Richard Fahey) *hld up in midfield: rdn over 3f out: sn wknd* **3/1**[1]

2m 8.27s (2.87) **Going Correction** +0.20s/f (Good) **9** Ran SP% **114.0**
Speed ratings (Par 99): **96,93,92,91,87 85,79,64,61**
CSF £51.92 CT £467.40 TOTE £5.10: £2.00, £3.60, £3.10; EX 62.60 Trifecta £774.10.
**Owner** Tullpark Limited **Bred** Tullpark Ltd **Trained** Denton, Co Durham

**FOCUS**
This modest handicap was run at a steady initial gallop. It was run on softening ground and the time was nearly 2sec slower than that for the earlier Class 4 handicap. Improvement from the winner.

## 3500 SIS STREAMING CONTENT GLOBALLY MAIDEN STKS 1m
**4:30** (4:30) (Class 5) 3-Y-O **£3,234** (£962; £481; £240) **Stalls** Low

Form RPR

5 **1** **Anif (IRE)**[47] 1962 3-9-5 0 DaneO'Neill 6 77
(Charles Hills) *mde all: pushed clr over 1f out: rdn out fnl f* **9/2**[3]

2 **2** 1¼ **Liquid Gold (IRE)**[23] 2704 3-9-0 0 PaulHanagan 5 69
(Richard Fahey) *hld up in tch: rdn along over 3f out: edgd rt and nt at ease on trck: styd on to go 2nd ins fnl f but no threat wnr* **11/8**[1]

**3** 2¼ **Kings Will Dream (IRE)** 3-9-5 0 PaulMulrennan 1 70
(Micky Hammond) *hld up in tch on inner: pushed along whn bit short of room 2f out: kpt on ins fnl f: wnt 3rd post* **33/1**

52 **4** hd **Bob Maxwell (IRE)**[20] 2791 3-9-5 0 PhillipMakin 2 68
(David Barron) *trckd ldr: rdn over 2f out: no ex fnl f: lost 3rd post* **10/3**[2]

0-20 **5** 5 **Highland Cradle**[24] 2689 3-9-5 79 (p[1]) DanielTudhope 4 57
(Sir Michael Stoute) *trckd ldr: rdn over 2f out: wknd over 1f out* **10/3**[2]

1m 43.43s (2.03) **Going Correction** +0.20s/f (Good) **5** Ran SP% **109.4**
Speed ratings (Par 99): **97,95,93,93,88**
CSF £11.07 TOTE £4.60: £1.90, £1.20; EX 11.10 Trifecta £75.30.
**Owner** Hamdan Al Maktoum **Bred** Shadwell Estate Company Limited **Trained** Lambourn, Berks

**FOCUS**
Another winner from the front in what looked an interesting little maiden. The form looks a bit fluid.

## 3501 LADIES DAY 22ND JUNE BOOK NOW H'CAP 1m 4f 10y
**5:00** (5:00) (Class 5) (0-70,69) 4-Y-O+ **£3,234** (£962; £481; £240) **Stalls** Low

Form RPR

/600 **1** **Marmion**[35] 2333 5-9-6 **68** (h[1]) DanielTudhope 7 77
(Les Eyre) *hld up: pushed along and hdwy over 3f out: rdn to chal strly 2f out: styd on: led 75yds out* **5/1**[3]

503 **2** 1 **Hurricane Hollow**[19] 2841 7-9-7 **69** PhillipMakin 5 76
(David Barron) *s.i.s: sn trckd ldr: led 10f out: pushed along 3f out: strly pressed 2f out: sn hrd drvn: hdd 75yds out: no ex* **6/4**[1]

0-20 **3** 7 **Young Tom**[22] 2729 4-8-12 **60** RoystonFfrench 3 56
(Michael Appleby) *in tch: rdn over 3f out: one pce in 3rd fnl 2f* **4/1**[2]

6-60 **4** 3 **Rockliffe**[8] 3205 4-8-12 **60** GrahamLee 4 51
(Micky Hammond) *midfield: rdn over 3f out: plugged on: nvr threatened* **17/2**

04-0 **5** 7 **Gold Merlion (IRE)**[112] 769 4-9-5 **67** JasonHart 1 47
(Mark Johnston) *led for 2f: trckd ldr: rdn over 4f out: wknd over 2f out* **12/1**

23-6 **6** 1½ **Hayward Field (IRE)**[31] 2456 4-9-1 **68** PhilDennis(5) 6 45
(Noel Wilson) *hld up: rdn over 3f out: sn wknd* **16/1**

/0-5 **7** 32 **Callaghan (GER)**[36] 2308 4-8-8 **61** (t) LewisEdmunds(5) 2
(Tom Gretton) *midfield: rdn over 4f out: wknd qckly and t.o* **7/1**

2m 46.68s (9.98) **Going Correction** +0.20s/f (Good) **7** Ran SP% **113.3**
Speed ratings (Par 103): **74,73,68,66,62 61,39**
CSF £12.70 TOTE £5.40: £2.20, £1.30; EX 14.70 Trifecta £29.00.
**Owner** RP Racing Ltd **Bred** Carwell Equities Ltd **Trained** Catwick, N Yorks

**FOCUS**
A moderate handicap lacking horses in form and run in the worst of the ground. The first two came clear.
T/Plt: £64.80 to a £1 stake. Pool: £75,612.57 - 851.23 winning units. T/Qpdt: £24.10 to a £1 stake. Pool: £4,909.11 - 150.68 winning units. **Andrew Sheret**

# 3009 SANDOWN (R-H)
## Thursday, June 8

**OFFICIAL GOING: Round course - good (good to soft in places; 6.6); sprint course - good to soft (good in places; 6.2)**
Wind: Moderate, against in home straight Weather: Overcast, frequent showers from race 3 onwards

## 3502 BRITISH STALLION STUDS EBF FILLIES' NOVICE STKS (PLUS 10 RACE) 5f 10y
**6:00** (6:00) (Class 5) 2-Y-O **£3,881** (£1,155; £577; £288) **Stalls** High

Form RPR

2 **1** **Looks A Million**[6] 3306 2-9-0 0 OisinMurphy 4 74
(Joseph Tuite) *chsd ldrs: wnt 2nd 1/2-way on outer: sn urged along to press ldr who was gng much bttr: kpt pestering and wore her down to ld last 100yds* **8/1**[3]

31 **2** ¾ **Validator**[19] 2836 2-9-7 0 RyanMoore 1 78
(William Haggas) *tall: led against rail: gng bttr than rest fr 1/2-way: shkn up whn pressed 1f out: rdn and hdd last 100yds: fnd nil* **1/2**[1]

**3** 1 **Glaceon (IRE)** 2-9-0 0 SeanLevey 3 67+
(Richard Hannon) *tall: lw: in tch: plld out wd and pushed along 1/2-way: tk 3rd over 1f out: rn green w tail swishing but kpt on fnl f: nrst fin* **5/1**[2]

**4** 4½ **Utterly Charming (IRE)** 2-9-0 0 SamHitchcott 2 51
(Clive Cox) *w'like: sn pushed along to stay in tch: nvr pce to threaten but won battle for modest 4th nr fin* **10/1**

00 **5** nk **Hope And Glory (IRE)**[14] 2987 2-8-9 0 PaddyPilley(5) 7 50
(Tom Dascombe) *w'like: str: chsd ldr to 1/2-way: sn rdn: wknd over 1f out* **66/1**

6 **6** 5 **Olive Mabel**[10] 3135 2-8-11 0 JackDuern(3) 5 32
(Dean Ivory) *w'like: s.i.s: a in last pair and stl looked green: nvr a factor* **50/1**

**7** 3¾ **Star Of Siena** 2-9-0 0 JosephineGordon 6 19
(John Ryan) *w'like: lengthy: s.s: a struggling in last pair* **25/1**

1m 2.5s (0.90) **Going Correction** +0.025s/f (Good) **7** Ran SP% **110.8**
Speed ratings (Par 90): **93,91,90,83,82 74,68**
CSF £11.82 TOTE £6.80: £3.00, £1.10; EX 14.90 Trifecta £37.60.
**Owner** Peter Gleeson **Bred** Hackcanter Ltd & Mr P Gleeson **Trained** Lambourn, Berks

**FOCUS**
All distances as advertised and Sprint track at full width. Three came clear in what was probably just an ordinary novice event and there was a slight turn-up. The second is rated to her maiden win.

## 3503 CLARENDELLE, INSPIRED BY HAUT-BRION H'CAP 1m 6f
**6:30** (6:30) (Class 4) (0-85,84) 3-Y-O **£5,822** (£1,732; £865; £432) **Stalls** Low

Form RPR

6-13 **1** **Jukebox Jive (FR)**[29] 2526 3-9-1 **83** DavidEgan(5) 3 90
(Anthony Honeyball) *trckd ldr: led over 2f out: drvn over 1f out: kpt on and hld on gamely* **10/3**[2]

50-5 **2** nk **Veiled Secret (IRE)**[14] 2991 3-8-5 **68** LukeMorris 8 74+
(Sir Mark Prescott Bt) *hld up in last: rdn 3f out: prog 2f out but racd awkwardly: tk 2nd jst over 1f out: clsd on wnr grad u.str.p but stl racd awkwardly: jst hld* **6/1**[3]

4-32 **3** ¾ **Splash Around**[20] 2784 3-9-2 **79** RyanMoore 7 84
(Sir Michael Stoute) *lw: trckd ldng trio: pushed along 3f out: sed to cl 2f out but tk a long time abt it: disp 2nd over 1f out: kpt on but nt pce to chal properly* **6/5**[1]

2123 **4** 3 **Wefait (IRE)**[12] 3081 3-9-1 **78** JamesDoyle 4 78
(Richard Hannon) *lw: disp 2nd pl to over 2f out: sn rdn: hld whn hung lft over 1f out: one pce after* **7/1**

2-14 **5** nk **Pete So High (GER)**[37] 2264 3-8-12 **75** (p) SeanLevey 10 74
(Richard Hannon) *dwlt but sn pushed up to ld and set gd pce: hdd over 2f out: styd cl up tl wknd jst over 1f out* **9/1**

54-3 **6** 10 **Avantgardist (GER)**[101] 959 3-8-7 **70** JosephineGordon 1 55
(Pat Phelan) *a in last pair: often had to be pushed along fr 11f out: last and struggling 4f out: sn no ch* **40/1**

3m 6.15s (1.65) **Going Correction** +0.025s/f (Good) **6** Ran SP% **107.8**
Speed ratings (Par 101): **96,95,95,93,93 87**
CSF £20.96 CT £30.51 TOTE £4.00: £2.10, £2.80; EX 20.20 Trifecta £50.10.
**Owner** R W Huggins **Bred** Ronald Wallace Huggins **Trained** Mosterton, Dorset

**FOCUS**
A fair staying handicap for 3yos that was run at a sound gallop. The form is rated around the fourth and fifth.

## 3504 RAINBOW TRUST CHILDREN'S CHARITY H'CAP 1m
**7:00** (7:03) (Class 4) (0-85,87) 3-Y-O **£5,822** (£1,732; £865; £432) **Stalls** Low

Form RPR

6-1 **1** **Surrey Hope (USA)**[92] 1083 3-9-6 **83** OisinMurphy 6 91
(Joseph Tuite) *str: lw: trckd ldr: led 2f out: rdn over 1f out: hrd pressed ins fnl f but kpt on wl* **8/1**[3]

-414 **2** ½ **Me Too Nagasaki (IRE)**[7] 3262 3-9-7 **84** JamesDoyle 12 90+
(Jeremy Noseda) *lw: hld up in 8th: shkn up and prog on outer fr 2f out: drvn to chse wnr last 75yds: styd on but nvr quite got there* **9/2**[2]

1-20 **3** ¾ **Glorious Forever**[19] 2824 3-9-7 **84** LukeMorris 10 89
(Ed Walker) *lw: wl in tch: rdn over 2f out: styd on u.p to dispute 2nd wl ins fnl f: nvr quite able to chal* **16/1**

0-1 **4** nk **Almoreb (IRE)**[20] 2778 3-9-5 **82** JimCrowley 5 86
(Richard Hannon) *led: shkn up and hdd 2f out: styd pressing wnr tl no ex and lost 2 pls last 75yds* **8/1**[3]

-16 **5** *1 ¼* **Dancing Breeze (IRE)**[20] 2802 3-9-10 **87** FrankieDettori 9 88+
(John Gosden) *lw: stdd s: hld up in 9th: prog and swtchd rt wl over 1f out: rdn and clsd on ldrs fnl f: no imp last 100yds* **8/1**[3]

-102 **6** *1 ¼* **Glory Of Paris (IRE)**[21] 2757 3-9-0 **77** WilliamCarson 1 75
(Rod Millman) *chsd ldrs: lost pl and drvn 2f out: struggling in rr over 1f out: styd on again last 100yds* **16/1**

-244 **7** *nse* **Berkshire Boy (IRE)**[27] 2565 3-9-6 **83** (b) RobHornby 2 81
(Andrew Balding) *dwlt: hld up in 10th: rdn over 2f out: no prog tl styd on fnl f: gng on at fin but no ch* **14/1**

6551 **8** *nk* **Chance To Dream (IRE)**[10] 3162 3-9-0 **77** 6ex KierenFox 11 74+
(John Best) *dwlt: hld up in last: rdn wl over 2f out: no prog tl kpt on wl fnl 150yds: no ch* **25/1**

31-0 **9** *nk* **Pivoine (IRE)**[48] 1945 3-9-4 **81** RyanMoore 3 78
(Sir Michael Stoute) *trckd ldrs: rdn over 2f out: disp 3rd jst over 1f out but no imp: wknd ins fnl f* **3/1**[1]

1502 **10** *1 ¼* **Vantage Point (IRE)**[7] 3262 3-9-2 **79** (p) FranBerry 7 73
(Gary Moore) *trckd ldng pair: rdn over 2f out: wknd jst over 1f out* **16/1**

05-1 **11** *30* **Envoy**[16] 2930 3-9-6 **83** RyanTate 8 8
(James Eustace) *hld up in 7th: pushed along and making no prog whn hmpd: hit rail and stmbld bdly over 1f out: nrly fell and eased after* **9/1**

1m 42.99s (-0.31) **Going Correction** +0.025s/f (Good) **11** Ran SP% **114.7**
Speed ratings (Par 101): **102,101,100,100,99 97,97,97,97,96 66**
CSF £42.73 CT £574.04 TOTE £8.60: £3.00, £1.50, £4.30; EX 45.30 Trifecta £494.60.
**Owner** Surrey Racing (sh) **Bred** Nancy Mazzoni **Trained** Lambourn, Berks
■ Stewards' Enquiry : Frankie Dettori four-day ban: careless riding (Jun 26-29)

**FOCUS**
A good handicap run at a fair gallop. The favourite was disappointing but it was won by a promising sort who built on his Kempton win.

## 3505 BOODLES DIAMOND H'CAP — 1m 1f 209y
**7:35** (7:37) (Class 3) (0-90,88) 3-Y-O
**£8,092** (£2,423; £1,211; £605; £302; £152) **Stalls** Low

Form RPR

1- **1** **Frontispiece**[278] 6108 3-9-0 **81** RyanMoore 7 88
(Sir Michael Stoute) *trckd ldrs: led 2f out: sn drvn: kpt on wl fnl f: a jst holding on nr fin* **5/2**[2]

0-21 **2** *nk* **On To Victory**[17] 2894 3-9-3 **84** (h) TomMarquand 1 90
(Eve Johnson Houghton) *t.k.h: hld up in last pair: prog on inner and waiting for room briefly 2f out: drvn and hdwy to chse wnr ins fnl f: clsd nr fin: jst too late* **7/2**[3]

2321 **3** *1 ¼* **Hold Sway (IRE)**[21] 2751 3-9-6 **87** (p) JamesDoyle 6 90
(Charlie Appleby) *lw: trckd ldr: led jst over 2f out: sn hdd and nt qckn: one pce and lost 2nd ins fnl f* **9/4**[1]

51-0 **4** *½* **Rosarno (IRE)**[24] 2690 3-9-0 **81** (bt[1]) JimCrowley 3 83
(Charles Hills) *hld up in last pair: prog on outer over 2f out: hanging and nt qckn over 1f out: kpt on same pce after* **25/1**

10-2 **5** *½* **Trading Punches (IRE)**[21] 2755 3-9-7 **88** SeanLevey 2 89
(David Brown) *wl in tch: nt clr run over 2f out to over 1f out: hanging and nt qckn after* **9/1**

2-04 **6** *7* **Ghayyar (IRE)**[29] 2520 3-9-3 **84** FrankieDettori 4 71
(Richard Hannon) *t.k.h: trckd ldrs: lost pl 2f out: wknd over 1f out* **7/1**

10-4 **7** *4 ½* **Viking Hoard (IRE)**[39] 2174 3-8-10 **77** DavidProbert 5 55
(Harry Dunlop) *led to jst over 2f out: wknd qckly over 1f out* **25/1**

2m 9.5s (-1.00) **Going Correction** +0.025s/f (Good) **7** Ran SP% **111.8**
Speed ratings (Par 103): **105,104,103,103,102 97,93**
CSF £11.14 TOTE £3.10: £2.00, £2.10; EX 12.80 Trifecta £27.80.
**Owner** The Queen **Bred** The Queen **Trained** Newmarket, Suffolk

**FOCUS**
A useful 3yo handicap, little got into it but the form looks good. The first three could prove better than the bare figures.

## 3506 BRITISH EBF MAIDEN STKS — 1m 1f 209y
**8:05** (8:08) (Class 5) 3-4-Y-O
**£3,881** (£1,155; £577; £288) **Stalls** Low

Form RPR

46-2 **1** **Jake's Hill**[24] 2689 3-9-1 79 CharlesBishop 6 89
(Eve Johnson Houghton) *trckd ldr: chal fr over 2f out and sn clr of rest: drvn ahd jst ins fnl f: kpt on wl* **4/1**[2]

04-2 **2** *¾* **Mafaaheem (IRE)**[49] 1906 3-9-1 88 JimCrowley 5 87
(Owen Burrows) *led: hrd pressed by wnr and clr of rest 2f out: hdd jst ins fnl f: kpt on wl* **9/4**[1]

**3** *shd* **Pouvoir Magique (FR)** 3-9-1 0 JamesDoyle 11 94+
(John Gosden) *athletic: lw: broke on terms but sn restrained into last: stl there wl over 2f out: rapid prog after: tk 3rd jst over 1f out but stl 5 l bhd ldng pair: clsd all the way to the fin: promising debut but should have won* **6/1**[3]

44 **4** *5* **Sonnetist**[7] 3248 3-9-1 0 SeanLevey 15 77
(Richard Hannon) *str: prom: chsd ldng pair over 2f out but sn outpcd by them: no imp after: lost 3rd jst over 1f out* **25/1**

**5** *shd* **Great White Shark (FR)** 3-8-10 0 DanielMuscutt 8 72
(James Fanshawe) *athletic: slowly away but sn rcvrd into midfield: shkn up over 2f out: outpcd sn after: swtchd lft and kpt on one fr over 1f out* **12/1**

60 **6** *½* **Magellan**[20] 2783 3-8-12 0 KieranShoemark(3) 2 76
(Roger Charlton) *wl in tch bhd ldrs: outpcd and shkn up 2f out: kpt on one pce after* **8/1**

0 **7** *1 ¾* **Precision**[45] 2039 3-9-1 0 RyanMoore 14 72+
(Sir Michael Stoute) *cmpt: hld up in rr: pushed along over 2f out: reminder over 1f out: kpt on steadily and shaped w sme promise* **8/1**

0-4 **8** *2 ½* **Two Dollars (IRE)**[16] 2921 3-9-1 0 TrevorWhelan 7 67
(William Jarvis) *a in midfield: rdn over 2f out and sn outpcd: no imp ldrs after* **66/1**

0 **9** *1 ¼* **Sputnik Planum (USA)**[27] 2584 3-9-1 0 TomQueally 10 65+
(David Lanigan) *str: bit bkwd: hld up in rr: shkn up over 2f out: plld out and kpt on fr over 1f out: nt disgracd* **66/1**

**10** *5* **Opera Queen** 3-8-10 0 DavidProbert 9 50
(Andrew Balding) *w'like: hld up in last quartet: no prog over 2f out: nvr a factor* **25/1**

0 **11** *nk* **High Wells**[34] 2359 3-9-1 0 OisinMurphy 13 54
(Seamus Durack) *w'like: broke on terms but sn restrained into last pair: shkn up and no prog over 2f out* **33/1**

**12** *nk* **Your Ladyship (IRE)** 3-8-10 0 FranBerry 1 48
(Ralph Beckett) *athletic: dwlt: but sn rcvrd to chse ldng pair: wknd over 2f out* **9/1**

0-5 **13** *16* **Montycristo**[124] 576 4-9-11 0 HectorCrouch(3) 3 22
(Philip Hide) *racd on outer: wl in tocuh tl hung lft and wknd over 2f out: t.o* **100/1**

2m 9.13s (-1.37) **Going Correction** +0.025s/f (Good)
**WFA** 3 from 4yo 13lb **13** Ran SP% **119.6**
Speed ratings (Par 103): **106,105,105,101,101 100,99,97,96,92 92,91,79**
CSF £12.74 TOTE £5.10: £2.20, £1.30, £2.00; EX 14.80 Trifecta £80.60.
**Owner** Mrs Virginia Neale **Bred** Cherry Park Stud **Trained** Blewbury, Oxon

**FOCUS**
A decent maiden, the front three came clear with the the first two up there from the word go, but the story of the race was the run of the third, who came from last place to be beaten under a length. The second looks the most soild guide.

## 3507 SPORTSPAGES FILLIES' H'CAP — 1m 1f
**8:40** (8:41) (Class 5) (0-75,76) 3-Y-O+
**£3,881** (£1,155; £577; £288) **Stalls** Low

Form RPR

34-1 **1** **Titi Makfi**[7] 3241 3-9-4 **76** 6ex JamesDoyle 2 86
(Mark Johnston) *led to over 7f out: trckd ldng pair after: led again 2f out and committed for home: in command fnl f: rdn out* **9/4**[1]

21- **2** *1 ¼* **Gallifrey**[170] 8464 3-9-4 **76** JimCrowley 8 83+
(Lucy Wadham) *str: hld up in last trio: prog on outer 2f out: drvn and styd on to take 2nd last 100yds: unable to threaten wnr* **11/4**[2]

0-40 **3** *1 ½* **Prize Diva**[16] 2929 3-8-0 **63** (p[1]) DavidEgan(5) 6 67
(David Elsworth) *t.k.h: trckd ldrs on outer: shoved along over 3f out: responded to chse wnr 2f out: no imp 1f out: lost 2nd last 100yds: one pce* **16/1**

5-42 **4** *1* **Carol (IRE)**[16] 2929 3-9-4 **76** RyanMoore 5 78
(Ed Dunlop) *lw: trckd ldrs: rdn and nt qckn 2f out: one pce fr over 1f out* **13/2**[3]

0-02 **5** *shd* **Peloton**[10] 3163 3-8-7 **65** KieranO'Neill 10 67+
(Pat Phelan) *hld up in last: gng bttr than many but stl there 2f out: prog over 1f out: reminders and styd on fnl f: nvr nrr* **8/1**

60-6 **6** *3 ½* **Junoesque**[16] 2931 3-8-5 **63** LukeMorris 9 57
(John Gallagher) *hld up in midfield: rdn on outer over 2f out: no imp over 1f out: wknd fnl f* **33/1**

0-35 **7** *2 ¼* **Vigee Le Brun (IRE)**[13] 3031 3-8-10 **68** TomMarquand 3 57
(Brian Meehan) *a towards rr: rdn and no prog over 2f out: wl btn after* **8/1**

-100 **8** *1 ¾* **Ejayteekay**[26] 2605 4-9-11 **74** CharlieBennett(3) 4 61
(Hughie Morrison) *t.k.h and plld way into ld over 7f out: hdd & wknd 2f out* **25/1**

056- **9** *shd* **Starlight Circus (IRE)**[170] 8464 3-8-10 **68** DanielMuscutt 1 53
(Marco Botti) *prom early but sn shuffled bk to rr on inner: rdn and no prog over 2f out: wl btn over 1f out* **16/1**

1442 **10** *¾* **Ixelles Diamond (IRE)**[43] 2095 6-8-11 **57** JosephineGordon 7 42
(Lee Carter) *t.k.h and trckd ldr over 7f out to jst over 2f out: wknd* **25/1**

1m 56.77s (1.07) **Going Correction** +0.025s/f (Good)
**WFA** 3 from 4yo+ 12lb **10** Ran SP% **115.4**
Speed ratings (Par 100): **96,94,93,92,92 89,87,85,85,85**
CSF £8.07 CT £77.94 TOTE £3.20: £1.60, £1.60, £4.70; EX 10.30 Trifecta £139.50.
**Owner** Paul & Clare Rooney **Bred** Floors Farming **Trained** Middleham Moor, N Yorks

**FOCUS**
Just an ordinary handicap, but a progressive winner. The winner backed up her Hamilton victory.
T/Jkpt: Not won. T/Plt: £53.90 to a £1 stake. Pool: £77,364.35 - 1047.23 winning units. T/Qpdt: £10.80 to a £1 stake. Pool: £7644.19 - 522.38 winning units. **Jonathan Neesom**

3508 - 3514a (Foreign Racing) - See Raceform Interactive

# DIEPPE (R-H)
Thursday, June 8

**OFFICIAL GOING: Turf: good to soft**

## 3515a PRIX CAMILLE SAINT-SAENS (CONDITIONS) (2YO) (TURF) — 5f 110y
**5:55** 2-Y-O
**£11,111** (£4,444; £3,333; £2,222; £1,111)

RPR

**1** **Cead Mile Failte (FR)** 2-8-13 0 AntoineHamelin 6 81
(Matthieu Palussiere, France) **37/10**[3]

**2** *1 ½* **Neeran**[33] 2-8-7 0 GregoryBenoist 3 70
(H-F Devin, France) **4/1**

**3** *nse* **Lamchope (FR)**[26] 2642 2-8-10 0 ChristopheSoumillon 1 73
(Y Barberot, France) **21/10**[1]

**4** *nk* **Morever (FR)**[33] 2-8-7 0 MaximeGuyon 4 69
(Mme P Butel, France) **121/10**

**5** *2 ½* **White Feather**[25] 2664 2-9-0 0 MickaelBarzalona 7 68
(Jo Hughes) *qckly away: led on stands rail: pushed along and hdd over 2f out: drvn and styd on one pce fnl f* **23/10**[2]

**6** *5 ½* **Norwegian Lord (FR)**[44] 2073 2-8-5 0 ow1(p) MlleLauraPoggionovo(10) 5 51
(F Sanchez, France) **228/10**

**7** *7 ½* **Zeebullet (IRE)**[11] 2-8-2 0 MathieuPelletan(5) 2 18
(M Delcher Sanchez, France) **35/1**

PARI-MUTUEL (all including 1 euro stake): WIN 4.70 PLACE 2.50, 3.30, SF 27.40.
**Owner** Mrs Theresa Marnane **Bred** Haras De Grandcamp Earl **Trained** France

# 2910 BRIGHTON (L-H)
Friday, June 9

**OFFICIAL GOING: Good to soft (good in places from 6f to 2f; 7.5)**
Wind: gusty 1/2 behind Weather: fine and sunny but very breezy

## 3516 NEXERE.COM NOVICE STKS — 5f 60y
**2:20** (2:20) (Class 5) 2-Y-O
**£2,911** (£866; £432; £216) **Stalls** Low

Form RPR

6 **1** **Billy Dylan (IRE)**[21] 2779 2-9-2 0 SeanLevey 2 80
(Richard Hannon) *s.i.s: sn mid-div: styd on to ld last 150yds: edgd lft: drvn out* **11/8**[1]

3 **2** *1 ½* **Bath And Tennis (IRE)**[11] 3135 2-8-11 0 RyanPowell 3 71
(Sir Mark Prescott Bt) *trckd ldrs on ins: nt clr run over 1f out: keeping on whn hmpd clsng stages* **6/1**[3]

60 **3** *hd* **City Guest (IRE)**[10] 3164 2-9-2 0 TomQueally 1 74
(George Margarson) *in rr: hdwy over 2f out: n.m.r: swtchd rt over 1f out: styd on wl last 100yds* **66/1**

4 ¾ **Gotti (USA)** 2-9-2 0....(b[1]) GeraldMosse 5 72
(Jeremy Noseda) *in rr: sn drvn along: hdwy over 1f out: kpt on fnl 75yds* **9/2[2]**

4 **5** ¾ **Catapult**[10] 3169 2-9-2 0.... PaoloSirigu 6 69
(Robert Eddery) *chsd ldrs: led briefly 1f out: kpt on same pce* **12/1**

433 **6** ½ **Kodiac Express (IRE)**[18] 2904 2-8-11 0.... ShaneKelly 7 62
(Mike Murphy) *trckd ldrs on outer: t.k.h: kpt on one pce fnl f* **8/1**

523 **7** 7 **Spoof**[24] 2698 2-9-2 0....(h) JimCrowley 4 42
(Charles Hills) *trckd ldrs: led briefly over 1f out: sn wknd* **9/2[2]**

50 **8** 4 **Butterfly Spirit**[14] 3029 2-8-11 0.... WilliamCarson 8 22
(Michael Attwater) *led: hdd over 1f out: wknd* **80/1**

**9** 5 **Lisbon Legend** 2-9-2 0.... GeorgeDowning 9 9
(Tony Carroll) *sn outpcd in rr: bhd fnl 2f* **100/1**

1m 4.53s (2.23) **Going Correction** +0.275s/f (Good) 9 Ran SP% **115.3**
Speed ratings (Par 93): **93,90,90,89,87 87,75,69,61**
CSF £10.24 TOTE £2.20: £1.10, £2.00, £11.40; EX 12.10 Trifecta £298.70.
**Owner** Sullivan Bloodstock Limited **Bred** River Downs Stud **Trained** East Everleigh, Wilts
■ Stewards' Enquiry : Sean Levey caution: careless riding

**FOCUS**
The ground had changed overnight to good to soft, good in places. A decent enough novice stakes for the course. It was pretty rough at times, but the first two are probably decent.

## 3517 KEW ELECTRICAL H'CAP — 5f 215y
**2:50** (2:51) (Class 5) (0-75,77) 3-Y-0 **£2,911** (£866; £432; £216) **Stalls** Low

Form RPR

2611 **1** **Goodwood Crusader (IRE)**[49] 1940 3-9-2 **77**.... FinleyMarsh(7) 6 88
(Richard Hughes) *hld up in last: hdwy over 2f out: str run to ld last 200yds: styd on wl* **6/1**

3114 **2** 1 ¼ **Tai Hang Dragon (IRE)**[31] 2503 3-9-7 **75**.... SeanLevey 3 82
(Richard Hannon) *chsd ldrs: drvn over 2f out: hung lft over 1f out: tk 2nd last 150yds* **4/1[2]**

16-6 **3** 6 **Compton Poppy**[34] 2407 3-9-7 **75**.... GeorgeDowning 7 63
(Tony Carroll) *in rr: hdwy over 2f out: hung lft and kpt on to take modest 3rd last 75yds* **20/1**

2-1 **4** 1 **Otomo**[38] 2252 3-9-5 **73**.... SilvestreDeSousa 5 58
(Philip Hide) *sn w ldrs: led over 3f out: hdd last 200yds: wknd* **10/11[1]**

53-3 **5** 3 ¼ **Island Cloud**[31] 2503 3-9-1 **69**....(p[1]) JimCrowley 2 43
(Heather Main) *led tl over 3f out: swtchd rt 2f out: lost pl over 1f out* **9/2[3]**

3130 **6** ½ **Peachey Carnehan**[49] 1940 3-9-6 **74**....(v) WilliamCarson 1 47
(Michael Attwater) *w ldrs: lost pl over 1f out* **33/1**

1m 11.76s (1.56) **Going Correction** +0.275s/f (Good) 6 Ran SP% **112.6**
Speed ratings (Par 99): **100,98,90,89,84 84**
CSF £29.80 TOTE £5.40: £1.80, £1.90; EX 22.60 Trifecta £115.10.
**Owner** Goodwood Racehorse Owners Group (23) Ltd **Bred** Tally-Ho Stud **Trained** Upper Lambourn, Berks

**FOCUS**
The leaders went off too quick in this 3yo sprint handicap and the first three home were the last three at halfway. The winner has been rated in line with his Bath maiden win.

## 3518 MOTORCLEAN LTD H'CAP — 5f 215y
**3:20** (3:20) (Class 4) (0-80,78) 4-Y-0+ **£4,690** (£1,395; £697; £348) **Stalls** Low

Form RPR

332 **1** **Black Caesar (IRE)**[17] 2917 6-8-13 **70**.... SilvestreDeSousa 2 77
(Philip Hide) *trckd ldr: led after 2f: hld on wl clsng stages* **11/4[2]**

6214 **2** ¾ **Nezar (IRE)**[27] 2608 6-9-7 **78**.... JimCrowley 3 83
(Dean Ivory) *trckd ldrs: chal over 1f out: no ex last 50yds* **6/4[1]**

3204 **3** 1 ¼ **Flexible Flyer**[28] 2582 8-9-7 **78**....(h) DavidProbert 4 79
(Chris Dwyer) *sn chsng ldrs on inner: effrt 3f out: swtchd rt and kpt on same pce last 150yds* **8/1**

-432 **4** shd **Morache Music**[13] 3074 9-9-7 **78**....(p) LiamKeniry 6 79
(Patrick Chamings) *trckd ldrs: t.k.h: drvn 3f out: hung lft over 1f out: kpt on clsng stages* **4/1[3]**

0-05 **5** 1 **Bahamian Heights**[10] 3170 6-9-4 **75**....(h) GeorgeDowning 5 72
(Robert Cowell) *awkward s and s.i.s: in rr: hdwy 3f out: chsng ldrs over 1f out: kpt on same pce* **20/1**

3643 **6** 3 ¼ **Childesplay**[63] 1599 6-9-3 **74**.... SeanLevey 1 61
(Heather Main) *led 2f: chsd ldrs: wknd fnl f* **17/2**

1m 12.22s (2.02) **Going Correction** +0.275s/f (Good) 6 Ran SP% **113.1**
Speed ratings (Par 105): **97,96,94,94,92 88**
CSF £7.42 TOTE £3.40: £1.80, £1.60; EX 7.70 Trifecta £28.40.
**Owner** The Long Furlong **Bred** Miss Hilary Mullen **Trained** Findon, W Sussex

**FOCUS**
A cracking duel between two willing horses under top-class jockeys and a fair result. A small pb from the winner, with the runner-up rated to his recent form.

## 3519 ROUTE MOBILE H'CAP — 1m 1f 207y
**3:50** (3:50) (Class 6) (0-65,65) 4-Y-0+ **£2,264** (£673; £336; £168) **Stalls** High

Form RPR

-113 **1** **Miss Inga Sock (IRE)**[3] 3425 5-8-13 **62**.... GeorgiaCox(5) 8 68
(Eve Johnson Houghton) *trckd ldrs: led 2f out: hld on clsng stages* **2/1[1]**

1-04 **2** nk **Mr Frankie**[81] 1284 6-8-12 **56**.... LiamKeniry 1 61
(John Spearing) *t.k.h: sn eased into mid-div: hdwy to chse ldrs over 2f out: chsd wnr last 100yds: no ex nr fin* **15/2**

2601 **3** 1 ½ **Strictly Art (IRE)**[7] 3304 4-8-11 **62** 6ex.... JoshuaBryan(7) 5 65
(Alan Bailey) *led after 1f: hdd 6f out: hdd 2f out: kpt on same pce fnl 150yds* **7/1**

43-6 **4** 1 ½ **Transmitting**[16] 2956 4-9-7 **65**....(h[1]) HarryBentley 9 65
(Ed Vaughan) *dwlt: in rr: effrt over 2f out: styd on wl to take 4th nr fin* **7/2[2]**

1054 **5** ½ **Siouxperhero (IRE)**[45] 2055 8-9-4 **62**....(b) TomMarquand 3 61
(William Muir) *trckd ldrs: effrt over 2f out: one pce fnl f* **33/1**

0-06 **6** 5 **Funny Oyster (IRE)**[17] 2914 4-8-7 **51** oh1.... SamHitchcott 2 40
(Chris Gordon) *led 1f: led 6f out: hdd 2f out: wknd and eased fnl f* **25/1**

4062 **7** nk **Betsalottie**[25] 2679 4-8-13 **57**.... WilliamCarson 4 46
(John Bridger) *mid-div: effrt over 3f out: lost pl 2f out* **4/1[3]**

-054 **8** ½ **Machiavelian Storm (IRE)**[17] 2915 5-8-7 **51** oh6.... KieranO'Neill 6 39
(Richard Mitchell) *s.i.s: sn mid-div: drvn over 3f out: hung lft and wknd over 1f out* **66/1**

6045 **9** 1 ½ **Solveig's Song**[7] 3304 5-9-2 **60**....(p) JimCrowley 7 45
(Steve Woodman) *hld up in rr: hdwy over 3f out: lost pl over 1f out* **12/1**

2m 6.45s (2.85) **Going Correction** +0.275s/f (Good) 9 Ran SP% **115.8**
Speed ratings (Par 101): **99,98,97,96,95 91,91,91,90**
CSF £17.78 CT £88.67 TOTE £3.10: £1.50, £2.50, £2.20; EX 19.40 Trifecta £103.50.
**Owner** The Ascot Colts & Fillies Club **Bred** R F Johnson Houghton **Trained** Blewbury, Oxon

**FOCUS**
A decent race for the level with the winner well-ridden to claim a 3rd win in her last 4 starts. The winner has been rated to her best from the last few years.

## 3520 ROUTEMOBILE.COM H'CAP — 1m 3f 198y
**4:20** (4:20) (Class 5) (0-75,75) 3-Y-O **£2,911** (£866; £432; £216) **Stalls** High

Form RPR

54-1 **1** **Quloob**[30] 2513 3-9-7 **75**.... JimCrowley 1 91+
(Owen Burrows) *trckd ldrs: led over 1f out: forged wl clr: eased clsng stages* **10/3[3]**

5-03 **2** 8 **Chaparrachik (IRE)**[34] 2394 3-9-5 **73**.... PatDobbs 4 73
(Amanda Perrett) *dwlt: sn chsng ldrs: drvn 3f out: kpt on to take modest 2nd last 100yds* **7/1**

3-02 **3** 3 **Je Suis Charlie**[7] 3291 3-9-6 **74**.... LouisSteward 6 69
(Michael Bell) *led: hdd over 1f out: one pce* **2/1[1]**

-432 **4** 1 ¼ **Koeman**[13] 3068 3-9-7 **75**.... SilvestreDeSousa 5 68
(Mick Channon) *mid-div: effrt over 3f out: hung lft and kpt on one pce fnl f* **11/4[2]**

0-40 **5** nk **Aware (IRE)**[15] 2997 3-9-0 **71**....(t[1]) CallumShepherd(3) 8 64
(Charles Hills) *hld up in rr: hdwy 3f out: drvn and one pce over 1f out* **20/1**

-065 **6** 3 ¼ **General Allenby**[10] 3180 3-8-7 **61** oh15....(be) RyanPowell 7 49
(Henry Tett) *s.i.s: in rr: bhd fnl 3f* **50/1**

334 **7** 3 ¼ **Tristram**[35] 2359 3-9-7 **75**.... ShaneKelly 2 58
(Richard Hughes) *hld up in mid-div: effrt over 2f out: lost pl over 1f out* **10/1**

1600 **8** 75 **Oberyn (IRE)**[13] 3087 3-8-5 **64**.... MitchGodwin(5) 3
(Sylvester Kirk) *hld up in rr: drvn over 4f out: lost pl over 3f out: heavily eased over 1f out: virtually p.u: t.o* **33/1**

2m 35.79s (3.09) **Going Correction** +0.275s/f (Good) 8 Ran SP% **114.3**
Speed ratings (Par 99): **100,94,92,91,91 89,87,37**
CSF £25.97 CT £57.17 TOTE £3.80: £1.30, £2.10, £1.10; EX 26.60 Trifecta £70.40.
**Owner** Hamdan Al Maktoum **Bred** Shadwell Estate Company Limited **Trained** Lambourn, Berks

**FOCUS**
An interesting and open-looking 3yo handicap for the grade, but the progressive winner took them apart. The winning jockey said the ground was now riding good. The runner-up has been rated in line with his maiden form.

## 3521 HACIENDA CLASSICAL 9 SEPT H'CAP — 7f 211y
**4:50** (4:50) (Class 5) (0-70,69) 4-Y-O+ **£2,911** (£866; £432; £216) **Stalls** Low

Form RPR

2-06 **1** **Galinthias**[17] 2913 5-9-5 **67**.... HarryBentley 3 70
(Simon Dow) *sn trcking ldrs: pushed along over 4f out: led last 100yds: edgd rt: jst hld on* **6/1**

50-1 **2** shd **Many Dreams (IRE)**[22] 2763 4-9-4 **69**.... HectorCrouch(3) 4 71+
(Gary Moore) *t.k.h: trckd ldrs: nt clr run and swtchd rt 2f out: hung lft and styd on strly last 75yds: jst failed* **2/1[2]**

0104 **3** ½ **Tulip Dress**[11] 3139 4-9-2 **64**.... JimCrowley 5 65
(Anthony Carson) *hld up in last but wl in tch: trcking ldrs over 3f out: led over 1f out: edgd lft and hdd last 100yds: no ex* **15/8[1]**

1313 **4** 1 **Shifting Star (IRE)**[25] 2677 12-9-3 **65**....(vt) WilliamCarson 6 65
(John Bridger) *led: hdd narrowly over 1f out: keeping on one pce whn hmpd and eased clsng stages* **3/1[3]**

1m 38.39s (2.39) **Going Correction** +0.275s/f (Good) 4 Ran SP% **107.4**
Speed ratings (Par 103): **99,98,98,97**
CSF £17.68 TOTE £8.70; EX 20.00 Trifecta £24.00.
**Owner** Meadows, Snell, Taylor, Dow **Bred** Barry Walters Farms **Trained** Ashtead, Surrey

**FOCUS**
A small field but an incredibly tight contest with little more than a length covering them at the line. The winner has been rated to his early AW maiden form.

## 3522 TRAILWALKER 100KM CHALLENGE 29-30 JULY H'CAP — 6f 210y
**5:20** (5:21) (Class 6) (0-60,62) 4-Y-O+ **£2,264** (£673; £336; £168) **Stalls** Low

Form RPR

0044 **1** **Live Dangerously**[17] 2914 7-9-0 **52**.... WilliamCarson 11 59
(John Bridger) *hld up in rr: effrt on outer over 2f out: led 1f out: edgd lft: kpt on* **11/2[1]**

6632 **2** 1 ¼ **With Approval (IRE)**[17] 2916 5-9-6 **58**....(p) GeorgeDowning 1 62
(Laura Mongan) *wnt rt s: chsd ldrs: upsides over 1f out: kpt on same pce to take 2nd last 50yds* **11/2[1]**

4066 **3** 1 **Aye Aye Skipper (IRE)**[37] 2294 7-8-7 **45**....(bt) KieranO'Neill 7 46
(Ken Cunningham-Brown) *in rr: hdwy on outer over 2f out: edgd lft and n.m.r over 1f out: kpt on to take 3rd nr fin* **16/1**

4304 **4** ½ **Caledonian Gold**[15] 3001 4-9-1 **53**.... JoeyHaynes 6 53
(Paul D'Arcy) *trckd ldrs: led brifely over 1f out: kpt on same pce* **7/1[3]**

2630 **5** 3 ¾ **Ettie Hart (IRE)**[8] 3265 4-9-0 **52**.... SilvestreDeSousa 9 41
(Mick Channon) *chsd ldrs: effrt over 2f out: one pce* **6/1[2]**

3356 **6** 1 **Rafaaf (IRE)**[22] 2762 9-9-4 **56**....(p) LiamKeniry 4 43
(Peter Hiatt) *dwlt and hmpd s: t.k.h in rr: hdwy 2f out: kpt on fnl f: nvr a factor* **14/1**

3142 **7** 2 ¼ **Andalusite**[15] 2996 4-9-7 **59**....(v) FergusSweeney 3 40+
(John Gallagher) *hmpd s: led after 2f: hdd over 1f out: sn wknd* **11/2[1]**

4226 **8** 2 ¼ **Noble Deed**[16] 2962 7-9-4 **59**....(p) CallumShepherd(3) 2 36
(Michael Attwater) *hmpd s: mid-div: hdwy on ins over 2f out: sn chsng ldrs: wknd and eased last 150yds* **20/1**

0045 **9** 1 ¾ **Locommotion**[16] 2968 5-9-2 **54**.... JohnFahy 10 24
(Matthew Salaman) *led 2f: wknd over 1f out* **10/1**

6330 **10** 1 ¼ **Bold Max**[17] 2916 6-8-7 **45**....(p) SamHitchcott 8 12
(Zoe Davison) *in rr: effrt on outer over 2f out: nvr a factot* **20/1**

4230 **11** 5 **Broughtons Fancy**[16] 2961 4-9-10 **62**.... ShaneKelly 5 15
(Gary Moore) *hmpd s: mid-div: drvn over 2f out: sn lost pl: eased clsng stages* **11/2[1]**

1m 24.39s (1.29) **Going Correction** +0.275s/f (Good) 11 Ran SP% **119.5**
Speed ratings (Par 101): **103,101,100,99,95 94,91,89,87,85 80**
CSF £35.88 CT £462.15 TOTE £7.30: £2.20, £2.30, £4.80; EX 33.40 Trifecta £846.70.
**Owner** W A Wood **Bred** Manor Farm Stud & Mrs A J Ralli **Trained** Liphook, Hants

**FOCUS**
A modest but competitive Class 6 won in typical Brighton fashion. The second, third and fourth offer perspective to the level.

T/Plt: £77.10 to a £1 stake. Pool: £55,737.00 - 722.69 winning units. T/Qpdt: £26.20 to a £1 stake. Pool: £3,809.00 - 145.38 winning units. **Walter Glynn**

# [3482]CARLISLE (R-H)
Friday, June 9

**OFFICIAL GOING: Soft (6.7)**
Wind: fairly strong half behind in straight Weather: Fine

## 3523 RACING UK IN HD NOVICE STKS 5f
**2:10** (2:11) (Class 5) 2-Y-O **£3,396** (£1,010; £505; £252) **Stalls** Low

Form RPR
0 1 **John Kirkup**[16] 2948 2-9-2 0 PaulMulrennan 4 77
(Michael Dods) *in tch: pushed along 3f out: hdwy appr fnl f: sn chsd ldr: rdn to ld 75yds out: kpt on* **12/1**
0 2 1 1/4 **Charnock Richard**[10] 3169 2-9-2 0 TomEaves 1 73
(David Brown) *prom: rdn to ld over 1f out: edgd lft ins fnl f: hdd 75yds out: one pce* **22/1**
3 3 hd **Move It Move It**[21] 2786 2-9-2 0 DougieCostello 2 72
(Keith Dalgleish) *trckd ldrs: rdn over 1f out: kpt on* **1/1**[1]
30 4 6 **Seen The Lyte (IRE)**[15] 2987 2-8-11 0 JasonHart 3 45
(John Quinn) *led narrowly: racd keenly: rdn whn hdd over 1f out: wknd ins fnl f* **10/1**[3]
5 hd **Burn Some Dust (IRE)** 2-9-2 0 BenCurtis 8 49
(Brian Ellison) *hld up: pushed along over 3f out: nvr threatened* **33/1**
6 nk **Stopwatch** 2-9-2 0 GrahamLee 6 48
(Karen McLintock) *s.i.s: hld up: sn pushed along: nvr threatened* **18/1**
332 7 1 1/2 **Rockin Fella (IRE)**[39] 2222 2-9-2 0 PJMcDonald 5 43
(K R Burke) *pressed ldr: racd keenly: rdn over 1f out: wknd fnl f* **2/1**[2]

1m 4.13s (3.33) **Going Correction** +0.45s/f (Yiel) **7 Ran SP% 112.7**
Speed ratings (Par 93): **91,89,88,79,78 78,75**
CSF £209.33 TOTE £15.00: £4.20, £7.60; EX 174.00 Trifecta £610.60.
**Owner** Mrs Suzanne Kirkup & Kevin Kirkup **Bred** W M Lidsey **Trained** Denton, Co Durham

**FOCUS**
Rail on inside line, distances as advertised. It was a bright day yet the going was still on the soft side after downpours the previous night. This wasn't a bad novice event and they went a respectable pace, coming up the centre of the home straight. The third has been rated to his Tapeta debut, but the form will take time to settle down.

## 3524 THURSBY H'CAP 5f
**2:40** (2:41) (Class 5) (0-70,72) 3-Y-0+ **£3,396** (£1,010; £505; £252) **Stalls** Low

Form RPR
5-02 1 **Exotic Guest**[7] 3289 7-9-5 62 (p) JamesSullivan 6 68
(Ruth Carr) *in tch: trckd ldr 2f out: pushed along to ld appr fnl f: rdn and strly pressed ins fnl f: hld on all out* **8/1**
-462 2 hd **Manshood (IRE)**[8] 3257 4-10-0 71 (b) PaulMulrennan 2 77
(Paul Midgley) *hld up: pushed along over 3f out: rdn and hdwy 2f out: chal strly ins fnl f: kpt on* **13/8**[1]
64-5 3 hd **Muatadel**[81] 1290 4-9-11 68 TonyHamilton 5 73
(Roger Fell) *trckd ldr: rdn over 1f out: chal strly ins fnl f: kpt on* **11/1**
-302 4 shd **Jack Luey**[8] 3238 10-9-12 69 (b) DanielTudhope 4 74
(Lawrence Mullaney) *led: rdn whn hdd appr fnl f: outpcd in 4th ins fnl f: rallied towards fin* **3/1**[2]
4654 5 3 **David's Beauty (IRE)**[9] 3201 4-9-2 59 (p) GrahamLee 3 53
(Brian Baugh) *chsd ldr on outside: rdn 2f out: one pce* **20/1**
-404 6 1 3/4 **Rose Eclair**[27] 2631 4-9-10 67 (b) JasonHart 7 55
(Tim Easterby) *dwlt and bmpd s: hld up: rdn over 2f out: nvr threatened* **8/1**
0-23 7 5 **Wild Acclaim (IRE)**[28] 2595 3-9-8 72 PaulHanagan 1 39
(Ann Duffield) *in tch on outer: rdn 2f out: wknd ins fnl f: eased* **13/2**[3]

1m 4.4s (3.60) **Going Correction** +0.45s/f (Yiel)
**WFA** 3 from 4yo+ 7lb **7 Ran SP% 111.7**
Speed ratings (Par 103): **89,88,88,88,83 80,72**
CSF £20.52 CT £141.86 TOTE £9.40: £3.10, £1.80; EX 21.40 Trifecta £325.20.
**Owner** Mrs Ruth A Carr **Bred** D Cantillon And E Cantillon **Trained** Huby, N Yorks

**FOCUS**
This modest sprint handicap threw up tight three-way finish on the stands' side. Ordinary form.

## 3525 LONGTOWN H'CAP 5f 193y
**3:10** (3:12) (Class 6) (0-60,60) 3-Y-O **£2,911** (£866; £432; £216) **Stalls** Low

Form RPR
0-33 1 **My Girl Maisie (IRE)**[8] 3260 3-8-13 52 ConnorBeasley 12 58+
(Richard Guest) *hld up on outer: gd hdwy over 2f out: pushed along to ld wl over 1f out: rdn and kpt on fnl f* **2/1**[1]
45-0 2 1 1/2 **Hamba Kashe (IRE)**[50] 1913 3-9-7 60 JasonHart 4 62
(Tim Easterby) *chsd ldr: rdn over 2f out: ev ch over 1f out: one pce ins fnl f* **13/2**
4-03 3 hd **Guiding Star**[16] 2949 3-8-9 48 (p) DougieCostello 2 49
(Patrick J McKenna, Ire) *chsd ldrs: angled lft over 1f out: rdn and kpt on wl fnl f* **11/1**
3000 4 1/2 **Albizu Campos**[36] 2349 3-8-7 46 oh1 FrannyNorton 6 45
(Lawrence Mullaney) *squeezed out sltly s: hld up: swtchd lft to wd outside 2f out: sn rdn and hdwy: kpt on same pce fnl f* **6/1**[3]
064 5 4 1/2 **Zone In**[24] 2704 3-9-7 60 TonyHamilton 1 46
(Roger Fell) *led for 1f: prom: rdn over 2f out: wknd fnl f* **11/2**[2]
064- 6 1 **Atrafan (IRE)**[245] 7109 3-9-7 60 BenCurtis 7 43
(Alan Brown) *midfield: rdn over 2f out: wknd ins fnl f* **9/1**
0-00 7 1 1/4 **Melaniemillie**[24] 2699 3-9-0 53 JamesSullivan 5 32
(Ruth Carr) *hld up: rdn over 2f out: nvr threatened* **11/1**
00-0 8 shd **Tael O' Gold**[21] 2790 3-8-11 50 (p[1]) TomEaves 11 29
(Iain Jardine) *midfield: rdn over 2f out: wknd fnl f* **40/1**
600- 9 3 **I Wouldn't Bother**[205] 7974 3-9-7 60 (bt[1]) GrahamLee 3 30
(Daniel Kubler) *racd keenly and led after 1f: rdn whn hdd wl over 1f out: wknd* **12/1**
0-50 10 10 **Nifty Niece (IRE)**[18] 2897 3-8-8 47 (p) PaulHanagan 8
(Ann Duffield) *midfield: rdn over 2f out: wknd over 1f out: eased* **33/1**

1m 15.57s (1.87) **Going Correction** +0.45s/f (Yiel) **10 Ran SP% 116.1**
Speed ratings (Par 97): **105,103,102,102,96 94,93,92,88,75**
CSF £14.97 CT £117.63 TOTE £3.90: £1.70, £2.30, £2.50; EX 21.70 Trifecta £139.30.
**Owner** Alfa Site Services Ltd **Bred** Patrick M Ryan **Trained** Ingmanthorpe, W Yorks

**FOCUS**
A moderate 3yo sprint handicap. They kept far side this time. A small step up from the winner back on turf.

## 3526 BRITISH STALLION STUDS EBF FILLIES' H'CAP 5f 193y
**3:40** (3:42) (Class 4) (0-85,87) 3-Y-O+ **£6,469** (£1,925; £962; £481) **Stalls** Low

Form RPR
4-00 1 **Savannah Slew**[19] 2856 3-8-11 76 (b[1]) PaulMulrennan 5 83
(James Given) *dwlt: hld up in tch: rdn over 1f out: hdwy to chal ins fnl f: kpt on: led towards fin* **5/1**[3]
-504 2 nk **Storm Cry**[14] 3045 3-9-0 79 FrannyNorton 8 85
(Mark Johnston) *chsd ldr: rdn to chal over 1f out: led 1f out: kpt on but hdd towards fin* **7/2**[2]
5-04 3 3 1/2 **Partitia**[28] 2570 3-9-6 85 StevieDonohoe 2 80
(Sir Michael Stoute) *trckd ldr: rdn to ld narrowly over 1f out: hdd 1f out: wknd fnl 110yds* **9/4**[1]
4002 4 3 1/4 **Maureb (IRE)**[7] 3287 5-8-9 66 oh3 (p) DuranFentiman 9 52
(Tony Coyle) *led: rdn over 2f out: hdd over 1f out: wknd fnl f* **9/1**
0-16 5 5 **Savannah's Dream**[21] 2806 3-9-2 81 DanielTudhope 7 49
(David O'Meara) *hld up: rdn over 2f out: wknd fnl f* **7/2**[2]
611- 6 1 1/4 **Spin Doctor**[211] 7893 3-9-5 84 PaulHanagan 6 48
(Richard Fahey) *trckd ldr: rdn over 2f out: wknd over 1f out* **7/1**

1m 15.36s (1.66) **Going Correction** +0.45s/f (Yiel)
**WFA** 3 from 4yo+ 8lb **6 Ran SP% 114.4**
Speed ratings (Par 102): **106,105,100,96,89 88**
CSF £23.19 CT £49.47 TOTE £5.90: £2.40, £2.00; EX 29.40 Trifecta £100.00.
**Owner** Dachel Stud **Bred** Dachel Stud **Trained** Willoughton, Lincs

**FOCUS**
Not a bad fillies' sprint handicap. Two came clear late on down the centre. The winner has been rated back to her 2yo form.

## 3527 RACING UK DAY PASS JUST £10 H'CAP 1m 6f 32y
**4:10** (4:10) (Class 4) (0-85,85) 4-Y-O+ **£5,498** (£1,636; £817; £408) **Stalls** Low

Form RPR
-122 1 **Kensington Star**[21] 2774 4-9-4 82 (p) JasonHart 3 91+
(Keith Dalgleish) *trckd ldrs: short of room over 3f out and lost pl: rdn and hung lft to stands' rail over 1f out: hdwy and sn ev ch: styd on: led towards fin* **11/4**[1]
0640 2 shd **Card High (IRE)**[14] 3046 7-8-5 72 (t) NathanEvans[(3)] 1 79
(Wilf Storey) *midfield: pushed along and hdwy 2f out: rdn to ld narrowly appr fnl f: styd on: hdd towards fin* **14/1**
4-04 3 1 1/2 **Arthur Mc Bride (IRE)**[13] 3076 8-9-5 83 (t) TomEaves 4 88
(Nigel Twiston-Davies) *led: rdn over 2f out: hdd appr fnl f: one pce* **10/1**
1-64 4 3 1/4 **Silva Eclipse**[22] 2770 4-9-2 80 (p[1]) PaulMulrennan 2 81
(Jedd O'Keeffe) *trckd ldrs: rdn to chal over 2f out: wknd ins fnl f* **7/2**[3]
0-01 5 2 **Injam (IRE)**[22] 2770 4-9-7 85 GrahamLee 7 83
(Jedd O'Keeffe) *trckd ldrs on outer: rdn 3f out: edgd rt over 1f out: wknd fnl f* **10/3**[2]
05-3 6 14 **Wor Lass**[6] 3341 9-8-13 82 CliffordLee[(5)] 8 62
(Donald Whillans) *slowly away: hld up in rr: wnt a little in snatches: rdn over 3f out: wknd over 2f out* **12/1**
6-00 7 10 **Saved By The Bell (IRE)**[22] 2770 7-9-4 82 (p) DanielTudhope 6 49
(David O'Meara) *prom: rdn over 3f out: wknd qckly and eased* **8/1**
342 8 1 3/4 **Codeshare**[34] 2386 5-9-6 84 PJMcDonald 5 49
(Sally Haynes) *hld up: rdn over 3f out: wknd over 2f out: eased* **12/1**

3m 10.46s (2.96) **Going Correction** +0.45s/f (Yiel) **8 Ran SP% 114.2**
Speed ratings (Par 105): **109,108,108,106,105 97,91,90**
CSF £41.81 CT £335.47 TOTE £4.80: £1.80, £4.20, £2.00; EX 40.40 Trifecta £442.20.
**Owner** J S Morrison **Bred** Cheveley Park Stud Ltd **Trained** Carluke, S Lanarks

**FOCUS**
A fair staying handicap that served up a proper test. The third sets the standard.

## 3528 RACING UK IN HD H'CAP 1m 3f 39y
**4:40** (4:41) (Class 4) (0-85,86) 3-Y-O **£5,498** (£1,636; £817; £408) **Stalls** High

Form RPR
0-15 1 **Shymkent**[14] 3032 3-9-9 86 DanielTudhope 3 94+
(David O'Meara) *trckd ldrs: pushed along to chal 2f out: rdn to ld narrowly appr fnl f: edgd rt ins fnl f: styd on: all out* **10/3**[2]
046 2 nse **Immortalised**[19] 2857 3-8-9 77 CliffordLee[(5)] 2 84
(K R Burke) *led: rdn 3f out: hdd appr fnl f: styd on: jst failed* **7/1**
51-1 3 2 **Melting Dew**[15] 2998 3-9-5 82 StevieDonohoe 4 86
(Sir Michael Stoute) *hld up: rdn over 3f out: no imp tl styd on ins fnl f: nrst fin* **13/8**[1]
5-13 4 3 3/4 **Addicted To You (IRE)**[38] 2264 3-8-11 74 JasonHart 1 71
(Mark Johnston) *trckd ldrs: rdn along 4f out: wknd ins fnl f* **5/1**[3]
13 5 4 1/2 **Voski (USA)**[13] 3068 3-9-6 83 FrannyNorton 6 73
(Mark Johnston) *prom on outer: rdn 3f out: edgd rt over 1f out and wknd* **5/1**[3]
02- 6 14 **Something Brewing (FR)**[279] 3-9-7 84 TomEaves 5 50
(Iain Jardine) *hld up: rdn over 3f out: sn wknd* **18/1**

2m 28.79s (5.69) **Going Correction** +0.45s/f (Yiel) **6 Ran SP% 112.3**
Speed ratings (Par 101): **97,96,95,92,89 79**
CSF £25.74 TOTE £5.50: £2.50, £2.70; EX 26.80 Trifecta £74.70.
**Owner** Nurlan Bizakov **Bred** Hesmonds Stud Ltd **Trained** Upper Helmsley, N Yorks

**FOCUS**
An interesting 3yo handicap. There was something of an uneven pace on and it saw another bobbing finish, this time down the middle again. The third has been rated in line with his AW win.

## 3529 RACING UK IN GLORIOUS HD H'CAP (DIV I) 1m 1f
**5:10** (5:10) (Class 6) (0-60,62) 4-Y-O+ **£2,911** (£866; £432; £216) **Stalls** Low

Form RPR
0-04 1 **Beverley Bullet**[17] 2918 4-9-1 54 (p[1]) DanielTudhope 9 62
(Lawrence Mullaney) *mde all: rdn clr 2f out: kpt on* **7/2**[1]
040- 2 2 1/4 **Old China**[299] 5438 4-9-9 62 SamJames 1 66
(John Davies) *trckd ldrs: rdn to chse ldr 2f out: wandered appr fnl f: kpt on* **9/2**[3]
/5-0 3 2 1/2 **Modern Tutor**[17] 2937 8-8-9 48 TomEaves 4 47
(Miss Nicole McKenna, Ire) *midfield: rdn over 2f out: kpt on fnl f* **16/1**
3060 4 nk **Leonard Thomas**[25] 2687 7-8-7 53 (p) JamieGormley[(7)] 2 51
(Philip Kirby) *slowly away: hld up in rr: bhd tl styd on fr over 1f out* **9/1**
0506 5 nk **Never Say (IRE)**[28] 2591 4-8-7 46 oh1 (p) FrannyNorton 7 43
(Jason Ward) *hld up: pushed along over 2f out: styd on fnl f* **25/1**
0226 6 3/4 **New Abbey Angel (IRE)**[9] 3196 4-9-7 60 (v) ConnorBeasley 3 56
(Keith Dalgleish) *hld up: hdwy 3f out: rdn and one pce in 4th over 1f out: wknd fnl 50yds* **7/2**[1]

-000 **7** 4½ **Scruffy McGuffy**[16] 2955 4-9-4 **57**....(p) ShaneGray 10 44
(Ann Duffield) *prom: rdn over 2f out: wknd fnl f* **12/1**
200- **8** 6 **Bertha Burnett (IRE)**[131] 7581 6-8-8 **47**.... JamesSullivan 8 22
(Brian Rothwell) *a towards rr* **33/1**
2-60 **9** ¾ **May Mist**[102] 954 5-9-5 **58**.... GrahamLee 5 31
(Trevor Wall) *trckd ldrs: rdn over 3f out: sn wknd* **25/1**
030- **10** 5 **Highfield Lass**[192] 8142 6-8-7 **46**....(p) AndrewMullen 6 9
(Michael Dods) *racd keenly in midfield: rdn over 2f out: wknd over 1f out* **4/1**[2]

2m 1.14s (3.54) **Going Correction** +0.45s/f (Yiel) **10** Ran SP% **116.8**
Speed ratings (Par 101): **102,100,97,97,97 96,92,87,86,82**
CSF £18.97 CT £227.75 TOTE £3.00: £1.50, £1.60, £4.60; EX 17.90 Trifecta £242.40.
**Owner** Mrs Jean Stapleton & Rob Wilson **Bred** Keith Trowbridge **Trained** Great Habton, N Yorks

**FOCUS**
They were strung out early in this weak handicap and the winner dictated. The runner-up has been rated as improving a bit.

## 3530 RACING UK IN GLORIOUS HD H'CAP (DIV II) 1m 1f
**5:40** (5:41) (Class 6) (0-60,60) 4-Y-O+ **£2,911** (£866; £432; £216) **Stalls** Low

Form RPR
05-0 **1** **Im Dapper Too**[10] 3181 6-9-7 **60**.... SamJames 2 66
(John Davies) *trckd ldrs: pushed along 3f out: rdn to ld appr fnl f: edgd lft ins fnl f: kpt on wl* **3/1**[2]
5 **2** 1¾ **Colour Contrast (IRE)**[16] 2955 4-9-6 **59**.... DavidNolan 5 62
(Iain Jardine) *midfield: rdn and hdwy over 2f out: chal over 1f out: hung rt ent fnl f: kpt on same pce* **5/2**[1]
5054 **3** 1 **Mount Cheiron (USA)**[8] 3242 6-8-5 **47**.... NathanEvans(3) 3 48
(Richard Ford) *midfield: rdn over 2f out: kpt on* **7/1**
0-34 **4** nk **Joyful Star**[9] 3196 7-9-0 **53**.... PaulMulrennan 8 53
(Fred Watson) *hld up: pushed along over 2f out: sme hdwy over 1f out: styd on ins fnl f* **7/1**
3360 **5** 1¼ **Percy Verence**[6] 3343 4-9-2 **55**....(t) BenCurtis 6 52
(Tracy Waggott) *prom: rdn to ld 2f out: hdd appr fnl f: wknd ins fnl f* **10/1**
4-03 **6** 1¼ **Remember Rocky**[16] 2955 8-8-12 **58**....(b) KieranSchofield(7) 7 53
(Lucy Normile) *chsd ldrs on outer: rdn and outpcd over 3f out: no threat after* **6/1**[3]
00-0 **7** 2¾ **Eeny Mac (IRE)**[35] 2378 10-8-7 **46**....(p) FrannyNorton 4 35
(John Wainwright) *hld up: rdn over 3f out: hdd 2f out: sn wknd* **25/1**
05 **8** 5 **Thatsthewaytodoit (IRE)**[11] 3137 4-8-9 **48**.... AndrewMullen 9 27
(Daniel Mark Loughnane) *hld up: rdn over 3f out: sn wknd* **14/1**

2m 1.26s (3.66) **Going Correction** +0.45s/f (Yiel) **8** Ran SP% **112.5**
Speed ratings (Par 101): **101,99,98,98,97 96,93,89**
CSF £10.54 CT £45.61 TOTE £3.60: £1.10, £1.90, £2.20; EX 15.30 Trifecta £75.20.
**Owner** Christopher Davies **Bred** Christopher T Dawson **Trained** Piercebridge, Durham

**FOCUS**
This second division of the weak 1m1f handicap was run at a modest pace. The winner has been rated to last year's best, with the runner-up to his Ayr form.
T/Plt: £3,525.90 to a £1 stake. Pool: £46,014.00 - 13.05 winning units. T/Qpdt: £54.20 to a £1 stake. Pool: £4,442.00 - 81.90 winning units. **Andrew Sheret**

# 3304 GOODWOOD (R-H)
Friday, June 9
**OFFICIAL GOING: Good to soft (7.0)**
Wind: light against Weather: sunny periods

## 3531 RACING UK APPRENTICE H'CAP 1m 1f 197y
**5:55** (5:57) (Class 5) (0-75,75) 3-Y-0 **£3,234** (£962; £481; £240) **Stalls** Low

Form RPR
4513 **1** **Road To Dubai (IRE)**[7] 3291 3-9-5 **75**.... FletcherYarham(7) 5 84
(George Scott) *little slowly away: sn chsng clr ldrs: rdn over 2f out: clsd on front pair over 1f out: str run ins fnl f: led cl home* **9/2**[2]
2233 **2** 1¼ **Alexander M (IRE)**[14] 3041 3-9-7 **70**.... RichardOliver 2 76
(Mark Johnston) *led at decent pce: sn clr w one other: rdn whn strly chal wl over 2f out: kpt on gamely: hdd cl home* **6/1**
4-03 **3** hd **Galactic Prince**[15] 2998 3-9-7 **75**.... WilliamCox(5) 7 81
(Andrew Balding) *trckd ldrs in chsng gp: rdn over 2f out: hdwy over 1f out: r.o wl fnl 120yds: wnt 3rd towards fin: nrly snatched 2nd* **7/2**[1]
6005 **4** ¾ **Chunkyfunkymonkey**[6] 3327 3-8-5 **59**....(p) JackOsborn(5) 3 63
(John Ryan) *chsd ldr: clr of remainder: chal 3f out: sn rdn: ev ch ent fnl f: no ex whn losing 2 pls fnl 100yds* **33/1**
1 **5** 4 **Mam'Selle (IRE)**[22] 2760 3-9-10 **73**.... GeorgiaCox 8 69
(William Haggas) *hld up: rdn and sme hdwy over 1f out: styd on but nt pce to get on terms* **9/2**[2]
566- **6** 5 **Leonidas (IRE)**[225] 7648 3-8-13 **67**.... TylerSaunders(5) 1 53
(Marcus Tregoning) *s.i.s: last: nvr gng pce to get involved* **11/2**[3]
-553 **7** hd **Fields Of Fortune**[13] 3088 3-9-4 **70**....(h) JoshuaBryan(3) 4 56
(Richard Hannon) *hld up in chsng gp: rdn wl over 2f out: nvr any imp: wknd over 1f out* **8/1**
2-35 **8** 5 **Harry Beau**[13] 3088 3-9-0 **68**.... RossaRyan(5) 6 44
(Richard Hannon) *chsd clr ldrs: rdn over 2f out edgd rt over 1f out: wknd ent fnl f* **10/1**

2m 10.7s (2.60) **Going Correction** +0.30s/f (Good) **8** Ran SP% **111.4**
Speed ratings (Par 99): **101,100,99,99,96 92,91,87**
CSF £29.77 CT £101.05 TOTE £5.00: £1.50, £2.00, £1.60; EX 29.80 Trifecta £90.70.
**Owner** Mohammed Al Nabouda **Bred** Rabbah Bloodstock Limited **Trained** Newmarket, Suffolk

**FOCUS**
There was 4mm of rain the previous evening but it had been dry since and the going was given as good to soft (GoingStick: 7.0). The first two furlongs of the Mile course was dolled out 5yds, and the top bend was dolled out 3yds. Race distance increased by 10yds. This was run at a good pace. It's been rated around the runner-up.

## 3532 GUNCAST SWIMMING POOLS H'CAP 6f
**6:30** (6:31) (Class 5) (0-70,74) 4-Y-O+ **£3,234** (£962; £481; £240) **Stalls** High

Form RPR
1504 **1** **Artscape**[17] 2932 5-9-7 **70**.... JamesDoyle 7 81
(Dean Ivory) *travelled wl trcking ldrs: disp ld wl over 1f out: sn rdn: kpt on wl fnl f: edgd ahd and drifted rt cl home* **5/1**[2]
4-61 **2** hd **Curious Fox**[10] 3177 4-9-4 **74** 6ex.... TylerSaunders(7) 6 84
(Anthony Carson) *s.i.s: towards rr: hdwy over 2f out: disp ld wl over 1f out: sn rdn: kpt on wl fnl f: hdd cl home* **9/2**[1]
-650 **3** 2¼ **Showmethewayavrilo**[24] 2709 4-9-3 **66**.... JosephineGordon 9 69+
(Malcolm Saunders) *dwlt: bhd: hdwy 2f out: chsd ldng pair fnl f: kpt on* **10/1**

0-00 **4** 2¾ **Hurricane Rock**[72] 1427 4-8-11 **60**.... HarryBentley 3 54
(Simon Dow) *mid-divison: hdwy 2f out: sn rdn: kpt on but nt pce to chal* **8/1**
0304 **5** 2 **Hamish McGonagain**[10] 3177 4-9-4 **67**....(p) RobertTart 12 55
(Jeremy Gask) *mid-div: effrt 2f out: nt pce to get on terms* **11/1**
5421 **6** ¾ **Air Of York (IRE)**[8] 3265 5-9-5 **68** 6ex....(p) DanielMuscutt 8 54
(John Flint) *trckd ldr tl rdn 2f out: sn wknd* **15/2**
0-42 **7** hd **Langley Vale**[13] 3084 8-8-13 **62**....(v) JackMitchell 1 47
(Roger Teal) *trckd ldr: led briefly 2f out whn rdn: wknd jst over 1f out* **9/2**[1]
10-1 **8** ½ **Mad Endeavour**[35] 2367 6-9-3 **66**....(b) TomQueally 10 49
(Stuart Kittow) *led at decent pce: rdn and hdd 2f out: sn wknd* **6/1**[3]
-002 **9** 1¼ **Flying Sakhee**[16] 2969 4-8-1 **55**.... RichardOliver(5) 11 34
(John Bridger) *towards rr: effrt whn nt clr run jst over 1f out: nvr threatened to get involved* **14/1**

1m 12.77s (0.57) **Going Correction** +0.30s/f (Good) **9** Ran SP% **114.3**
Speed ratings (Par 103): **108,107,104,101,98 97,97,96,94**
CSF £27.45 CT £215.35 TOTE £5.80: £2.00, £1.90, £3.20; EX 32.60 Trifecta £185.40.
**Owner** Harlequin Direct Ltd & D Bloy **Bred** Darley **Trained** Radlett, Herts

**FOCUS**
A competitive sprint run at a good gallop. The runner-up backed up her AW latest.

## 3533 FEVER TREE MAIDEN STKS 1m 1f 197y
**7:05** (7:08) (Class 5) 3-Y-0+ **£3,234** (£962; £481; £240) **Stalls** Low

Form RPR
0-4 **1** **Tuff Rock (USA)**[21] 2783 3-9-1 0.... JimCrowley 4 82
(Ed Walker) *s.i.s: last but in tch: hdwy into 3rd over 2f out: sn rdn: wnt 2nd jst over 1f out: styd on to take narrow advantage fnl 120yds: jst hld on: all out* **11/4**[2]
0-23 **2** nse **Meccabah (FR)**[30] 2527 3-8-10 75.... DavidProbert 2 77
(Andrew Balding) *led: rdn over 1f out: narrowly hdd fnl 120yds: rallied gamely cl home: jst failed* **4/1**[3]
52 **3** 7 **Grieg Hall**[30] 2521 3-9-1 0.... JamesDoyle 3 68
(John Gosden) *pressed ldr: rdn 2f out: drifted lft whn hld in 3rd ent fnl f: fdd* **6/4**[1]
0-5 **4** 4½ **Clemento (IRE)**[32] 2476 3-9-1 0.... AndreaAtzeni 5 59
(Roger Charlton) *chsd ldrs: shkn up 7f out: effrt wl over 2f out: nt pce to chal: fdd fnl f* **4/1**[3]
0 **5** 19 **Lord Kitten (USA)**[41] 2152 3-9-1 0....(b[1]) TomQueally 1 21
(David Lanigan) *trckd ldrs: rdn 3f out: wknd 2f out* **25/1**

2m 10.42s (2.32) **Going Correction** +0.30s/f (Good)
**WFA** 3 from 4yo+ 13lb **5** Ran SP% **110.5**
Speed ratings (Par 103): **102,101,96,92,77**
CSF £13.78 TOTE £3.60: £1.70, £2.00; EX 12.00 Trifecta £26.00.
**Owner** H H Sheikh Mohammed Bin Khalifa Al Thani **Bred** Orpendale/Chelston/Wynatt **Trained** Upper Lambourn, Berks
■ Spanish Queen was withdrawn. Price at time of withdrawal 100-1. Rule 4 does not apply

**FOCUS**
Race distance increased by 10yds. There was a tight finish to this fair maiden. It's been rated around the runner-up to her penultimate AW form.

## 3534 BESPOKE PROPERTIES H'CAP 1m 6f
**7:40** (7:41) (Class 3) (0-95,93) 4-Y-O+
**£9,337** (£2,796; £1,398; £699; £349; £175) **Stalls** Low

Form RPR
5242 **1** **Getback In Paris (IRE)**[11] 3160 4-9-3 **89**.... ShaneKelly 2 97
(Richard Hughes) *mid-div: gd hdwy over 3f out: rdn over 2f out: led over 1f out: styd on wl: rdn out* **6/1**[3]
5-23 **2** ½ **Rydan (IRE)**[104] 921 6-8-12 **84**.... TomQueally 5 91
(Gary Moore) *mid-div: hdwy over 2f out: sn rdn: chsd wnr jst over 1f out: hung rt: styd on wl towards fin but hld* **22/1**
6-23 **3** 4½ **Champagne Champ**[21] 2788 5-9-7 **93**.... JimCrowley 8 94
(Rod Millman) *trckd ldr: rdn wl over 2f out: nt pce to chal: styd on gamely ins fnl f: regained 2nd cl home* **6/1**[3]
26-5 **4** ½ **Parliamentarian (IRE)**[13] 3076 4-9-3 **89**....(p[1]) JamesDoyle 6 89
(Charlie Appleby) *led: rdn and hdd over 1f out: no ex fnl f: lost 3rd cl home* **10/3**[1]
4-24 **5** 1½ **Sam Missile (IRE)**[21] 2774 4-9-3 **89**.... DanielMuscutt 7 87
(James Fanshawe) *hld up: hdwy 3f out: sn rdn in 5th: styd on same pce fnl 2f* **6/1**[3]
1040 **6** 3¾ **Gavlar**[21] 2788 6-9-4 **93**....(v) CallumShepherd(3) 4 86
(William Knight) *racd keenly: trckd ldrs: rdn wl over 2f out: sn one pce* **16/1**
22-1 **7** 2¼ **Admiral's Sunset**[23] 2723 4-8-8 **83**.... CharlieBennett(3) 10 73
(Hughie Morrison) *trckd ldrs: rdn wl over 2f out: sn hld: wknd ent fnl f* **8/1**
**8** 4 **Age Of Wisdom (IRE)**[230] 4-8-7 **82**.... HectorCrouch(3) 1 66
(Gary Moore) *hld up: hdwy over 3f out: rdn over 2f out: nvr threatened: wknd over 1f out* **40/1**
5-60 **9** ¾ **Glaring**[13] 3073 6-9-1 **87**....(p) PatDobbs 9 70
(Amanda Perrett) *in tch: outpcd over 3f out: n.d after* **20/1**
1/15 **10** 3¾ **Mr Khalid**[16] 2959 4-9-3 **89**.... AndreaAtzeni 3 67
(Roger Charlton) *in tch: rdn 3f out: wknd 2f out* **7/2**[2]

3m 6.92s (3.32) **Going Correction** +0.30s/f (Good) **10** Ran SP% **116.7**
Speed ratings (Par 107): **102,101,99,98,98 95,94,92,91,89**
CSF £130.12 CT £828.23 TOTE £6.80: £2.10, £5.30, £2.00; EX 101.00 Trifecta £1811.80.
**Owner** G B & G H Firmager **Bred** Elusive Wave Syndicate **Trained** Upper Lambourn, Berks

**FOCUS**
Race distance increased by 10yds. An interesting handicap, and the first two both took a step up for trying this trip for the first time. The runner-up has been rated close to his winter AW form, while the third helps set the standard.

## 3535 DELIVEROO PRESENTS: MEALS FOR WINNERS FILLIES' H'CAP 1m 1f 197y
**8:15** (8:16) (Class 3) (0-90,84) 3-Y-O+ **£9,703** (£2,887; £1,443; £721) **Stalls** Low

Form RPR
21-1 **1** **White Chocolate (IRE)**[22] 2761 3-8-9 **78**.... JimCrowley 5 85
(David Simcock) *hld up 5th: swtchd lft and hdwy wl over 2f out: sn rdn: led over 1f out: drifted rt: styd on wl* **5/4**[1]
4-41 **2** 1¾ **Nathania**[23] 2721 3-8-10 **79**.... ShaneKelly 6 84
(Richard Hughes) *trckd ldrs: chal 2f out: sn rdn w ev ch: styd on but a being hld ins fnl f: snatched up whn short of room cl home* **5/1**
01-3 **3** 1¾ **Mittens**[37] 2302 3-8-11 **80**.... DavidProbert 4 80
(Sir Michael Stoute) *stmbld leaving stalls: trckd ldr: led over 2f out: sn rdn: hdd over 1f out: kpt on same pce fnl f* **7/2**[2]
255- **4** ½ **Iconic Belle**[304] 5266 3-8-6 **75**.... SilvestreDeSousa 2 74
(Mick Channon) *trckd ldrs: pushed along 4f out: rdn wl over 2f out: styd on but nt pce to threaten* **12/1**

14-3 **5** *6* **Berengaria (IRE)**[20] 2817 3-9-1 **84**.................................... JamesDoyle 1 71
(Mark Johnston) *led: rdn and hdd over 2f out: sn hld: wknd over 1f out* **4/1**[3]

2m 11.33s (3.23) **Going Correction** +0.30s/f (Good) 5 Ran SP% **111.0**
Speed ratings (Par 104): **99,97,96,95,91**
CSF £7.99 TOTE £2.10: £1.40, £2.10; EX 7.30 Trifecta £23.80.
**Owner** The Rumble Racing Club **Bred** Scuderia Waldeck Srl **Trained** Newmarket, Suffolk

**FOCUS**
Race distance increased by 10yds. A fair handicap won by an improving filly. Muddling form.

## 3536 PETE TONG FILLIES' H'CAP 6f
**8:50** (8:50) (Class 5) (0-70,70) 3-Y-O **£3,408** (£1,006; £503) **Stalls** High

Form RPR
22-0 **1** **Coral Sea**[153] 119 3-9-7 **70**.................................... JimCrowley 8 80
(Charles Hills) *hld up: rdn and hdwy fr 2f out: led jst over 1f out: r.o wl: readily* **8/1**

0-34 **2** *3 ¼* **Sweet Pursuit**[17] 2911 3-8-2 **51**.................................... KieranO'Neill 4 51
(Rod Millman) *prom: rdn to chal over 2f out: ev ch jst over 1f out: kpt on but nt pce of wnr* **5/1**[2]

2-00 **3** *hd* **Mad Rose (IRE)**[32] 2474 3-8-12 **66**.............................. MitchGodwin(5) 9 65
(Jonathan Portman) *towards rr: rdn 2f out: no imp tl r.o ins fnl f: fin strly: nrly snatched 2nd* **25/1**

-264 **4** *2 ¼* **Royal Peace (IRE)**[10] 3173 3-9-2 **65**.............................. TomMarquand 6 57
(Richard Hannon) *led: rdn and hdd jst over 1f out: no ex* **14/1**

6316 **5** *nk* **Everkyllachy (IRE)**[10] 3171 3-8-7 **56**..................(b) JosephineGordon 7 47
(J S Moore) *mid-div: rdn 2f out: kpt on ins fnl f but nt pce to get on terms* **8/1**

2420 **6** *½* **Global Alexander (IRE)**[31] 2503 3-9-4 **70**.............. HectorCrouch(3) 10 59
(Clive Cox) *trckd ldrs: chal over 2f out: rdn and ev ch over 1f out tl ent fnl f: fdd fnl 100yds* **15/2**[3]

503- **7** *nse* **Bombay Dream**[214] 7845 3-9-3 **66**..............................(p[1]) AndreaAtzeni 5 55
(William Haggas) *mid-div: pushed along 3f out: nvr gng pce to get on terms* **5/2**[1]

00-5 **8** *1* **Cool Breeze (IRE)**[32] 2463 3-8-3 **52**......................... SilvestreDeSousa 1 38
(David Simcock) *s.i.s: bhd: hdwy 3f out: rdn and ch over 1f out: fdd fnl 120yds* **8/1**

0-52 **9** *4 ½* **Incentive**[23] 2725 3-9-0 **63**.................................... TomQueally 3 34
(Stuart Kittow) *sn prom: rdn over 2f out: sn hld: wknd fnl f* **5/1**[2]

1m 13.62s (1.42) **Going Correction** +0.30s/f (Good) 9 Ran SP% **117.5**
Speed ratings (Par 96): **102,97,97,94,94 93,93,91,85**
CSF £48.57 CT £973.12 TOTE £7.50: £2.20, £2.10, £4.80; EX 54.40 Trifecta £1056.00.
**Owner** P Winkworth **Bred** Peter Winkworth **Trained** Lambourn, Berks

**FOCUS**
A modest sprint but the winner looks capable of taking higher rank. The runner-up has been rated close to her latest effort.
T/Jkpt: Not won. T/Plt: £156.00 to a £1 stake. Pool: £59,064.00 - 378.47 winning units. T/Qpdt: £49.80 to a £1 stake. Pool: £4,744.00 - 95.11 winning units. **Tim Mitchell**

# 3489 HAYDOCK (L-H)
Friday, June 9

**OFFICIAL GOING: Soft (7.2)**
Wind: Light, half against in home straight of over 4f Weather: Fine

## 3537 188BET HAYDOCK PARK TRAINING SERIES APPRENTICE H'CAP (PART OF THE RACING EXCELLENCE INITIATIVE) 1m 2f 42y
**6:15** (6:15) (Class 5) (0-70,75) 4-Y-O+ **£3,557** (£1,058; £529; £264) **Stalls** Centre

Form RPR
45-4 **1** **The Major**[15] 3009 4-9-5 **70**.................................... TristanPrice(7) 11 78
(Michael Bell) *trckd ldrs: led 3f out: rdn over 2f out: pushed out ins fnl f* **3/1**[1]

6621 **2** *2* **Livella Fella (IRE)**[7] 3292 4-10-3 **75** 6ex......................... RowanScott 10 79
(Keith Dalgleish) *w ldr: led 4f out: hdd 3f out: kpt on u.p ins fnl f: no real imp on wnr* **4/1**[2]

-534 **3** *1 ¾* **Maroc**[21] 2785 4-9-10 **68**..............................(p) CameronNoble 5 69
(Nikki Evans) *led: rdn and hdd 4f out: outpcd 3f out: edgd rt over 1f out: rallied ins fnl f: styd on towards fin* **13/2**[3]

650 **4** *1 ½* **Competition**[21] 2791 5-9-7 **65**..............................(t) PaddyPilley 3 63
(Brian Rothwell) *hld up: hdwy 3f out: rdn over 2f out: kpt on ins fnl f: nvr able to chal* **20/1**

000- **5** *7* **Merchant Of Medici**[204] 7992 10-8-0 **51** oh1............. LaurenSteade(7) 4 35
(Micky Hammond) *hld up: in midfield 5f out: effrt to chse ldrs over 2f out: one pce over 1f out: nvr able to chal* **20/1**

4412 **6** *1* **Melabi (IRE)**[25] 2678 4-9-10 **68**.............................. CallumRodriguez 6 50
(Richard Ford) *hld up: outpcd over 3f out: nvr able to trble ldrs* **3/1**[1]

0246 **7** *2 ¼* **Warfare**[21] 2787 8-9-11 **69**.................................... PhilDennis 7 46
(Tim Fitzgerald) *trckd ldrs: rdn and lost pl over 3f out: n.d after* **8/1**

0066 **8** *17* **Raashdy (IRE)**[24] 2708 4-8-11 **60**.............................. MollyKing(5) 2 3
(Peter Hiatt) *in tch: rdn and lost pl 5f out: lft bhd over 3f out* **12/1**

2m 16.96s (4.26) **Going Correction** +0.325s/f (Good) 8 Ran SP% **111.7**
Speed ratings (Par 103): **95,93,92,90,85 84,82,69**
CSF £14.31 CT £68.86 TOTE £4.70: £1.80, £1.50, £2.50; EX 16.00 Trifecta £74.00.
**Owner** M L W Bell Racing Ltd **Bred** B Buckley **Trained** Newmarket, Suffolk

**FOCUS**
All races run on Inner Home Straight. Race distance increased by 22yds. Not the strongest of handicaps and though the pace seemed a fair one, the first three were in the first three throughout and the form is nothing out of the ordinary. The runner-up has been rated to form.

## 3538 DAILY RACING SPECIALS AT 188BET EBF NOVICE STKS 6f
**6:50** (6:55) (Class 4) 2-Y-O **£4,528** (£1,347; £673; £336) **Stalls** High

Form RPR
2 **1** **Raydiance**[17] 2926 2-9-2 0.................................... PJMcDonald 4 82+
(K R Burke) *edgy in stalls: towards rr: hdwy ent fnl 2f: led over 1f out: edgd rt wl ins fnl f: r.o wl to draw away towards fin* **2/1**[2]

**2** *2 ½* **Poet's Prince** 2-9-2 0.................................... OisinMurphy 3 75
(Mark Johnston) *led: rdn and hdd over 1f out: u.p and cl 2nd but hld whn checked briefly wl ins fnl f: kpt on same pce towards fin* **12/1**

4 **3** *2* **The Right Choice (IRE)**[24] 2698 2-9-2 0......................... TonyHamilton 6 69
(Richard Fahey) *in tch: rdn and hung lft 2f out: nt qckn over 1f out: kpt on ins fnl f: nvr able to chal* **9/1**[3]

2 **4** *nk* **Red Force One**[22] 2769 2-9-2 0.............................. RichardKingscote 7 68
(Tom Dascombe) *trckd ldrs: rdn and ev ch 2f out: sn hung lft and outpcd: no real imp fnl f* **11/10**[1]

6 **5** *2 ¾* **Skyva**[24] 2698 2-9-2 0.................................... MartinLane 2 59
(Brian Ellison) *hld up: pushed along 3f out: effrt to chse ldrs 2f out: no imp over 1f out: no ex fnl f* **33/1**

0 **6** *3 ½* **Brockey Rise (IRE)**[14] 3037 2-9-2 0......................... RoystonFfrench 1 49
(David Evans) *chsd ldr tl over 2f out: sn rdn: wknd over 1f out* **100/1**

1m 15.42s (1.62) **Going Correction** +0.325s/f (Good) 6 Ran SP% **102.6**
Speed ratings (Par 95): **102,98,96,95,91 87**
CSF £19.51 TOTE £3.10: £1.40, £3.10; EX 23.80 Trifecta £48.50.
**Owner** Ontoawinner 14 & Mrs E Burke **Bred** Hungerford Park Stud **Trained** Middleham Moor, N Yorks
■ Green Power was withdrawn. Price at time of withdrawal 9-1. Rule 4 applies to all bets - deduction 10p in the pound.

**FOCUS**
Quite an interesting juvenile event though the favourite was disappointing and Green Power, who had beaten the winner on his previous start, was withdrawn after bursting through the front of the stalls. The winner at least matched his debut effort, but the fourth has been rated below his debut form.

## 3539 188BET.CO.UK ACHILLES STKS (LISTED RACE) 5f
**7:25** (7:27) (Class 1) 3-Y-O+
**£20,982** (£7,955; £3,981; £1,983; £995; £499) **Stalls** High

Form RPR
1504 **1** **Final Venture**[13] 3079 5-9-4 110..............................(h) OisinMurphy 2 111
(Paul Midgley) *mde all: rdn over 1f out: strly pressed wl ins fnl f: kpt on gamely* **9/4**[1]

2-12 **2** *nk* **Kyllang Rock (IRE)**[22] 2768 3-8-11 102......................... MartinHarley 9 107
(James Tate) *hld up: hdwy travelling strly and swtchd lft wl ovor 1f out: str chal wl ins fnl f: kpt on but jst hld* **5/2**[2]

11-0 **3** *3* **Rosie Briar**[37] 2289 3-8-9 96.................................... RobHornby 4 94
(Andrew Balding) *hld up in tch: hdwy over 1f out: sn rdn whn chsng ldrs: no ex fnl 75yds* **14/1**

2-50 **4** *1* **Monsieur Joe (IRE)**[26] 2657 10-9-4 105......................... MartinLane 3 96
(Paul Midgley) *in tch: pushed along 3f out: rdn over 1f out: kpt on ins fnl f: nt pce to chal* **14/1**

-405 **5** *1 ¾* **Soie D'Leau**[13] 3092 5-9-4 95.................................... TonyHamilton 8 89
(Kristin Stubbs) *prom: rdn and ev ch over 1f out: wknd ins fnl f* **9/1**

2-26 **6** *hd* **Ornate**[34] 2397 4-9-4 109.................................... LukeMorris 5 89
(Robert Cowell) *chsd ldrs: ev ch 2f out: sn rdn: wknd ins fnl f* **7/2**[3]

2-00 **7** *2 ¾* **Glenrowan Rose (IRE)**[49] 1936 4-8-13 94......................... PhillipMakin 1 74
(Keith Dalgleish) *towards rr: rdn over 2f out: u.p whn nt clr run 1f out: nvr on terms* **22/1**

60-3 **8** *1 ¼* **Canny Kool**[28] 2573 5-9-4 95.................................... DougieCostello 6 74
(Brian Ellison) *hld up: pushed along and outpcd over 1f out: nvr a threat* **33/1**

1m 1.76s (0.96) **Going Correction** +0.325s/f (Good)
**WFA** 3 from 4yo+ 7lb 8 Ran SP% **112.2**
Speed ratings (Par 111): **105,104,99,98,95 95,90,88**
CSF £7.74 TOTE £2.80: £1.10, £1.40, £3.70; EX 9.90 Trifecta £58.90.
**Owner** Taylor's Bloodstock Ltd **Bred** Newsells Park Stud **Trained** Westow, N Yorks

**FOCUS**
Not the strongest of Listed events as only four of the eight runners had a rating of 100 or more but the first two were clear and the runner-up is a progressive sort. The winner and third have been rated to form.

## 3540 US OPEN GOLF BETTING AT 188BET H'CAP 7f 212y
**8:00** (8:00) (Class 5) (0-75,74) 4-Y-O+ **£3,557** (£1,058; £529; £264) **Stalls** Low

Form RPR
00-1 **1** **La Celebs Ville (IRE)**[41] 2140 4-9-5 **72**..................(p) RichardKingscote 2 81
(Tom Dascombe) *a.p: rdn 2f out: led narrowly fnl 110yds: kpt on gamely* **15/8**[1]

060- **2** *hd* **Chosen Character (IRE)**[273] 6280 9-9-7 **74**..............(vt) MartinHarley 9 82
(Tom Dascombe) *led: rdn 2f out: sn pressed: hdd narrowly fnl 110yds: kpt on* **16/1**

064- **3** *2 ½* **Ya Jammeel**[342] 3886 4-8-9 **67**.................................... DavidEgan(5) 3 69
(Mick Channon) *in tch: hdwy over 3f out: rdn to chse ldrs over 2f out: kpt on same pce fnl 75yds* **6/1**[3]

6300 **4** *1 ¾* **Captain Revelation**[25] 2685 5-9-0 **72**......................... PaddyPilley(5) 5 70
(Tom Dascombe) *prom: rdn 4f out: lost pl over 3f out: kpt on fr over 1f out but no imp* **9/1**

-056 **5** *hd* **Short Work**[13] 3095 4-9-3 **73**..............................(p) JoshDoyle(3) 4 70
(David O'Meara) *racd keenly: hld up in tch: rdn 3f out: hdwy over 1f out: edgd lft u.p: no imp fnl f* **9/1**

0-05 **6** *3 ¼* **My Lucille (IRE)**[24] 2708 4-9-5 **72**.............................. AdamBeschizza 1 62
(Chris Wall) *racd keenly: hld up in tch: rdn over 2f out: nvr able to chal* **9/2**[2]

/0-0 **7** *2 ¾* **Hidden Oasis (IRE)**[18] 2893 6-9-7 **74**......................(p) DougieCostello 6 58
(Jonjo O'Neill) *hld up in rr: hdwy 4f out: rdn to chse ldrs over 2f out: wknd over 1f out* **7/1**

606- **8** *nk* **Ingleby Angel (IRE)**[234] 7436 8-9-6 **73**..................(p[1]) RoystonFfrench 8 56
(Colin Teague) *chsd ldrs tl rdn and lost pl 3f out: n.d after* **25/1**

0-56 **9** *4* **Still On Top**[37] 2303 4-9-2 **69**..............................(h) CamHardie 10 43
(Tim Easterby) *in rr: u.p over 4f out: nvr a threat* **18/1**

1m 43.35s (-0.35) **Going Correction** +0.325s/f (Good) 9 Ran SP% **114.7**
Speed ratings (Par 103): **114,113,111,109,109 106,103,103,99**
CSF £35.55 CT £154.79 TOTE £2.50: £1.20, £4.20, £2.10; EX 28.30 Trifecta £171.00.
**Owner** Newport Rangers **Bred** Bernard Cooke **Trained** Malpas, Cheshire

**FOCUS**
A typical Haydock older-horse mile handicap which was run at a fair clip, and trainer Tom Dascombe was responsible for three of the first four. The runner-up has been rated close to his 2016 form.

## 3541 FREE SPINS AT 188BET CASINO FILLIES' H'CAP 6f 212y
**8:35** (8:35) (Class 4) (0-85,88) 4-Y-O+ **£5,822** (£1,732; £865; £432) **Stalls** Low

Form RPR
-020 **1** **Courier**[18] 2884 5-9-7 **83**.................................... BarryMcHugh 5 89+
(Marjorie Fife) *mde all: rdn over 1f out: pushed out wl ins fnl f: won a shade comf* **7/2**[3]

5021 **2** *½* **Rebel Surge (IRE)**[11] 3147 4-9-12 **88** 6ex.................(p) StevieDonohoe 4 91
(Richard Spencer) *hld up: rdn over 2f out: hdwy to take 2nd over 1f out: styd towards fin: nvr able to chal wnr* **11/4**[2]

6024 **3** *2 ¾* **Willbeme**[29] 2550 9-8-4 **66**.................................... LukeMorris 3 62
(Simon West) *racd keenly: chsd wnr: rdn over 2f out: lost 2nd over 1f out: kpt on same pce ins fnl f* **9/2**

-340 **4** *2 ¾* **Appleberry (IRE)**[20] 2821 5-8-12 **77**..................(h) AlistairRawlinson(3) 2 65
(Michael Appleby) *in rr: u.p over 2f out: nvr a threat* **8/1**

044- 5 9 **Golden Glimmer (IRE)**[321] 4630 4-9-6 **82**.............. RichardKingscote 1 58
(Tom Dascombe) *racd keenly: chsd ldrs: effrt over 2f out: wknd over 1f out: eased whn btn ins fnl f* **2/1**[1]

1m 31.0s (0.30) **Going Correction** +0.325s/f (Good) **5** Ran SP% **111.5**
Speed ratings (Par 102): **111,110,107,104,93**
CSF £13.55 TOTE £4.60: £2.10, £1.80; EX 14.60 Trifecta £52.50.
**Owner** Daniel Gath Homes Ltd **Bred** Stratford Place Stud And Watership Down **Trained** Stillington, N Yorks

**FOCUS**
A small field fillies' and mares' handicap run at a fair pace. Probably just ordinary form. The winner has been rated to form, and the runner-up to the best of her form in Britain.

## 3542 WORLD CUP QUALIFIERS AT 188BET MAIDEN FILLIES' STKS 1m 3f 140y
**9:10** (9:12) (Class 5) 3-Y-0+ **£3,557** (£1,058; £529; £264) **Stalls** Centre

Form RPR
33-2 1 **God Given**[20] 2834 3-8-12 79.......................................... JamieSpencer 10 79+
(Luca Cumani) *chsd ldr: led over 4f out: rdn over 1f out: edgd lft ins fnl f: r.o wl to draw clr clr fnl 110yds* **2/7**[1]

0 2 4 **Mod**[25] 2681 3-8-7 0.......................................... GeorgeWood(5) 7 75+
(James Fanshawe) *in tch: effrt 3f out: rdn and chalng over 1f out: no ex fnl 110yds* **10/1**

-044 3 nk **Amelia Dream**[13] 3088 3-8-7 70.......................................... DavidEgan(5) 4 71
(Mick Channon) *chsd ldrs: effrt over 3f out: rdn over 2f out: nt qckn over 1f out: styd on towards fin: no ch w wnr* **6/1**[2]

3 4 1 ½ **Relevant (IRE)**[20] 2842 3-8-12 0.......................................... PJMcDonald 2 69
(K R Burke) *chsd ldrs: effrt over 3f out: rdn over 2f out: nt qckn over 1f out: hung lft ins fnl f: kpt on same pce* **8/1**[3]

5 1 **Fire Leopard** 3-8-9 0.......................................... ShelleyBirkett(3) 5 67+
(David O'Meara) *plld hrd in midfield: rdn over 1f out: kpt on ins fnl f: nvr able to chal* **12/1**

4 6 hd **Becuna (USA)**[90] 1143 3-8-12 0.......................................... DannyBrock 9 67
(Michael Bell) *midfield: rdn and hdwy 3f out: chsd ldrs over 2f out: one pce ins fnl f* **22/1**

00 7 9 **Breton Belle (IRE)**[20] 2834 3-8-12 0.......................................... MartinDwyer 1 52
(David Simcock) *dwlt: in rr: rdn over 3f out: nvr on terms* **50/1**

8 1 **Shine Baby Shine** 3-8-12 0.......................................... PaddyAspell 6 51
(Philip Kirby) *dwlt: hld up: rdn over 3f out: nvr on terms* **50/1**

-05 9 1 ¼ **Sambuca Nera**[20] 2841 3-8-12 0.......................................... JoeDoyle 8 49
(James Given) *led: hdd over 4f out: rdn and lost pl over 3f out: wknd over 2f out* **50/1**

5 10 6 **Lagopus**[79] 1300 4-9-13 0.......................................... MartinLane 3 39
(David Simcock) *hld up: struggling over 3f out: nvr on terms* **33/1**

2m 39.62s (6.62) **Going Correction** +0.325s/f (Good)
**WFA** 3 from 4yo 15lb **10** Ran SP% **133.1**
Speed ratings (Par 100): **90,87,87,86,85 85,79,78,77,73**
CSF £5.88 TOTE £1.20: £1.02, £3.00, £1.90; EX 7.70 Trifecta £22.70.
**Owner** St Albans Bloodstock Limited **Bred** St Albans Bloodstock Llp **Trained** Newmarket, Suffolk

**FOCUS**
Race distance increased by 10yds. This looked a one-sided maiden run at a moderate gallop. The long odds-on favourite looked to have a fight on her hands 2f out but won well in the end. It's been rated around the third.
T/Plt: £24.60 to a £1 stake. Pool: £51,209.00 - 2,079.72 winning units. T/Qpdt: £5.80 to a £1 stake. Pool: £4,249.00 - 724.66 winning units. **Darren Owen**

# 3466 WOLVERHAMPTON (A.W) (L-H)
Friday, June 9

**OFFICIAL GOING: Tapeta: standard**
Wind: light breeze, behind Weather: Cloudy, cool

## 3543 EBC GROUP: IT SERVICES & SOLUTIONS H'CAP 6f 20y (Tp)
**2:00** (2:00) (Class 6) (0-65,66) 3-Y-O **£2,587** (£770; £384; £192) **Stalls** Low

Form RPR
66-0 1 **Iron Lady (IRE)**[17] 2911 3-8-8 **47**.......................................... MartinDwyer 2 60+
(William Muir) *trckd ldr: led wl over 1f out: pushed along ent fnl f: reminders and r.o strly: readily* **10/1**

0402 2 1 ¾ **Kings Heart (IRE)**[8] 3260 3-9-2 **60**........................(h) RachealKneller(5) 3 68
(Mark Usher) *hld up: hdwy on outer over 1f out: r.o u.p fnl f: nvr nrr* **13/8**[1]

050 3 2 ¾ **New Tale**[25] 2682 3-8-11 **50**.......................................... RobHornby 6 49
(Olly Williams) *trckd ldrs: pushed along over 1f out: rdn and r.o one pce fnl f* **10/1**

35-1 4 ¾ **Blue Rocks**[45] 2065 3-9-7 **60**.......................................... KevinStott 7 57
(Lisa Williamson) *mid-div: 3rd 2f out: drvn over 1f out: rdn and no ex fnl f* **7/2**[2]

-4P0 5 1 **Three C's (IRE)**[32] 2474 3-9-8 **66**........................(tp) DavidEgan(5) 4 59
(David Dennis) *mid-div: pushed along 3f out: rdn 2f out: swtchd and no hdwy fr over 1f out* **9/1**

3-00 6 1 ¼ **Bearag**[15] 2993 3-9-7 **60**.......................................... PhillipMakin 5 49
(David O'Meara) *hld up: drvn over 2f out: nvr a factor* **13/2**[3]

-656 7 1 ½ **Cosmic Sky**[21] 2792 3-8-8 **50**........................(be[1]) RachelRichardson(3) 1 35
(Tim Easterby) *led: hrd rdn and hdd wl over 1f out: fdd* **10/1**

1m 14.53s (0.03) **Going Correction** +0.025s/f (Slow) **7** Ran SP% **110.9**
Speed ratings (Par 97): **100,97,94,93,91 90,88**
CSF £25.18 TOTE £12.40: £5.30, £1.10; EX 31.70 Trifecta £284.10.
**Owner** Perspicacious Punters Racing Club **Bred** Horizon Bloodstock Limited **Trained** Lambourn, Berks

**FOCUS**
A modest 3yo handicap, run 2.33sec outside standard on standard Tapeta. It's been rated at face value.

## 3544 EBC GROUP: TELEPHONY & CONNECTIVITY H'CAP (DIV I) 5f 21y (Tp)
**2:30** (2:31) (Class 6) (0-55,61) 3-Y-O+ **£2,264** (£673; £336; £168) **Stalls** Low

Form RPR
5161 1 **Dream Ally (IRE)**[8] 3256 7-9-13 **61** 6ex.......................................... PhilDennis(5) 2 67
(John Weymes) *mid-div: pushed along and hdwy over 1f out: rdn and led ent fnl f: pushed out hands and heels last 100yds: comf* **4/1**[1]

-322 2 ½ **Maggi May (IRE)**[45] 2065 3-9-2 **52**.......................................... PatCosgrave 7 52
(David Brown) *trckd ldrs: drvn over 1f out: rdn and ev ch fnl f: r.o but nt pce of wnr* **4/1**[1]

5304 3 nk **Storm Trooper (IRE)**[27] 2628 6-9-12 **55**........................(p) BarryMcHugh 10 57
(Marjorie Fife) *racd wd: mid-div: hdwy over 3f out: rdn wl over 1f out: fin wl on stands' side* **9/2**[2]

0-02 4 nk **Harpers Ruby**[114] 742 7-9-9 **52**.......................................... PaddyAspell 5 53
(Lynn Siddall) *led: rdn and hdd ent fnl f: no ex* **16/1**

2632 5 nk **Swendab (IRE)**[7] 3278 9-9-7 **57**........................(b) BenRobinson(7) 9 57
(John O'Shea) *chsd ldr: rdn wl over 1f out: one pce ins fnl f* **9/2**[2]

5006 6 1 ¾ **Celerity (IRE)**[35] 2362 3-8-3 **46** oh1........................(v) KeelanBaker(7) 4 37
(David Evans) *in rr early: drvn 2f out: rdn over 1f out: one pce* **25/1**

/55- 7 7 **Roryslittlesister (IRE)**[46] 2047 7-8-10 **46** oh1......(t) GearoidBrouder(7) 1 14
(S M Duffy, Ire) *mid-div: n.m.r and snatched up over 2f out: sn rdn and wknd* **11/1**[3]

0005 8 ½ **Rat Catcher (IRE)**[7] 3290 7-9-3 **46** oh1........................(b) RobHornby 6 13
(Lisa Williamson) *hld up: pushed along 2f out: rdn over 1f out: no imp* **33/1**

0500 9 22 **Give Us A Belle (IRE)**[16] 2967 8-9-3 **46**........................(b[1]) AdamBeschizza 8
(Christine Dunnett) *slowly away: sn pushed along: lost tch fr 1/2-way* **28/1**

1m 1.67s (-0.23) **Going Correction** +0.025s/f (Slow)
**WFA** 3 from 4yo+ 7lb **9** Ran SP% **100.8**
Speed ratings (Par 101): **102,101,100,100,99 96,85,84,49**
CSF £15.17 CT £49.53 TOTE £4.50: £1.30, £1.20, £2.10; EX 22.80 Trifecta £76.90.
**Owner** High Moor Racing 4 **Bred** Noel & Roger O'Callaghan **Trained** Middleham Moor, N Yorks
■ Camino was withdrawn. Price at time of withdrawal 8/1. Rule 4 applies to all bets - deduction 10p in the pound.
■ Stewards' Enquiry : Paddy Aspell caution: careless riding

**FOCUS**
Low-grade handicap form. The quicker division by 0.11sec. Ordinary form rated around the balance of the first five.

## 3545 EBC GROUP: TELEPHONY & CONNECTIVITY H'CAP (DIV II) 5f 21y (Tp)
**3:00** (3:00) (Class 6) (0-55,59) 3-Y-O+ **£2,264** (£673; £336; £168) **Stalls** Low

Form RPR
0523 1 **Dandilion (IRE)**[10] 3186 4-10-0 **56**........................(t) LukeMorris 5 62
(Alex Hales) *mid-div: pushed along 2f out: 5th and rdn over 1f out: hdwy ins fnl f: got up u.str.p last 50yds* **2/1**[1]

5501 2 nk **Seneca Chief**[11] 3141 3-9-10 **59** 6ex........................(h) PatCosgrave 9 61
(Daniel Kubler) *hld up: hdwy over 1f out: rdn fnl f: fin wl* **5/2**[2]

-064 3 ½ **Mostashreqah**[11] 3136 4-9-3 **45**........................(p) RichardKingscote 6 48
(Milton Bradley) *led: pushed along and 1 l clr over 1f out: maintained same advantage tl rdn ins fnl f and ct last 50yds* **17/2**

0664 4 nk **Barnsdale**[2] 3466 4-8-10 **45**.......................................... MeganEllingworth(7) 3 47
(John Holt) *trckd ldrs: drvn over 1f out: sn rdn: r.o fnl f* **33/1**

0005 5 ½ **Something Lucky (IRE)**[21] 2800 5-9-12 **57**........................(p) HollieDoyle(3) 10 57
(Daniel Steele) *slowly away: in rr: hdwy on inner over 1f out: hrd rdn: fin wl* **7/1**[3]

5440 6 ½ **Chandresh**[15] 2994 4-9-3 **45**........................(b) PhillipMakin 4 43
(Robert Cowell) *chsd ldr: niggled wl over 1f out: rdn and no ex fnl f* **9/1**

-450 7 ½ **Essaka (IRE)**[17] 2917 5-9-5 **54**.......................................... AledBeech(7) 2 51
(Tony Carroll) *in rr early: effrt on outer 2f out: racd wd and u.p over 1f out: one pce* **18/1**

0002 8 nse **Percy Toplis**[11] 3141 3-9-4 **53**........................(v) AdamBeschizza 1 46
(Christine Dunnett) *trckd ldrs: ch and drvn over 1f out: sn hrd rdn: wknd fnl f* **14/1**

-000 9 5 **Artsteelwork**[11] 3141 3-8-10 **45**.......................................... AntonioFresu 7 20
(John Butler) *hld up: pushed along early: drvn wl over 1f out: sn rdn: wknd* **100/1**

1m 1.78s (-0.12) **Going Correction** +0.025s/f (Slow)
**WFA** 3 from 4yo+ 7lb **9** Ran SP% **110.8**
Speed ratings (Par 101): **101,100,99,99,98 97,96,96,88**
CSF £6.52 CT £29.79 TOTE £3.20: £1.40, £1.40, £2.70; EX 8.20 Trifecta £37.90.
**Owner** The Golden Horse Racing Club **Bred** Ballyhane Stud **Trained** Edgcote, Northamptonshire

**FOCUS**
The slower division, but only by 0.11sec. The first eight finished in a heap. The third and fourth help set a modest level.

## 3546 EBC GROUP: DIGITAL & PRINT SOLUTIONS CLAIMING STKS 1m 1f 104y (Tp)
**3:30** (3:30) (Class 6) 4-Y-O+ **£2,264** (£673; £336; £168) **Stalls** Low

Form RPR
3123 1 **Retrieve (AUS)**[2] 3470 9-9-13 85........................(tp) TimmyMurphy 3 83
(Jamie Osborne) *mid-div: hdwy 3f out: pushed along 2f out: led wl over 1f out: hrd rdn fnl f: all out* **7/2**[3]

6000 2 hd **Strong Steps**[19] 2855 5-9-6 86........................(p) BenSanderson(7) 2 82
(Roger Fell) *trckd ldr: led over 2f out: hdd wl over 1f out: rdn and rallied fnl f: jst hld* **2/1**[2]

136 3 nse **Mr Red Clubs (IRE)**[8] 3235 8-8-6 78........................(h) RayDawson(7) 6 68
(Michael Appleby) *hld up: pushed along 3f out: hdwy 2f out: u.p over 1f out: r.o strly ins fnl f: fin wl* **13/8**[1]

6-03 4 6 **Sooqaan**[8] 3264 6-8-9 59.......................................... CamHardie 4 52
(Antony Brittain) *mid-div: hdwy into 3rd 2f out: sn pushed along: rdn and wknd wl over 1f out* **8/1**

0-00 5 12 **The Dancing Lord**[10] 3172 8-8-9 59........................(t[1]) RoystonFfrench 1 28
(Adam West) *led: hdd over 2f out: hrd rdn and no ex* **50/1**

0004 6 22 **Steady Major (IRE)**[38] 2272 5-8-6 49........................(p) HollieDoyle(3) 5
(Mark Brisbourne) *mid-div: pushed along over 3f out: sn lost tch: eased* **20/1**

1m 58.98s (-1.82) **Going Correction** +0.025s/f (Slow) **6** Ran SP% **111.5**
Speed ratings (Par 101): **109,108,108,103,92 73**
CSF £10.79 TOTE £4.60: £2.40, £1.10; EX 11.40 Trifecta £15.80.
**Owner** Melbourne 10 Racing **Bred** Darley **Trained** Upper Lambourn, Berks

**FOCUS**
A cracking three-way finish to this claimer. The runner-up has been rated to his best yet for his current trainer.

## 3547 EBC GROUP: YOUR WORKPLACE TECHNOLOGY PARTNER H'CAP 1m 4f 51y (Tp)
**4:00** (4:00) (Class 5) (0-70,69) 4-Y-O+ **£2,911** (£866; £432; £216) **Stalls** Low

Form RPR
0/1- 1 **Lugano**[245] 7105 4-9-7 **69**.......................................... LukeMorris 11 84+
(Sir Mark Prescott Bt) *c across fr wd draw to trck ldr: tk over after 5f: mde rest: pushed along and qcknd pce 3f out: drvn 2f out: rdn fnl f: r.o strly* **2/1**[1]

1252 2 3 ½ **Boychick (IRE)**[16] 2956 4-9-6 **68**.......................................... RichardKingscote 7 75
(Ed Walker) *led 5f: styd prom and chsd ldr in 2nd: tried to cl 2f out: rdn and styd on wl: but nvr a serious threat* **11/4**[2]

-433 3 ¾ **Hussar Ballad (USA)**[6] 3343 8-9-3 **65**.......................................... CamHardie 6 70
(Antony Brittain) *mid-div: hdwy on outer 2f out: rdn over 1f out: r.o ins fnl f* **8/1**

2310 4 2 ½ **Pour L'Amour (IRE)**[21] 2781 4-9-4 **66**.......................................... DaneO'Neill 8 67
(Daniel Mark Loughnane) *trckd ldrs: drvn in 4th 2f out: hrd rdn wl over 1f out: styd on one pce* **9/1**

3056 5 1 ¾ **Yasir (USA)**[32] 2460 9-8-6 **61**.......................................... KatherineGlenister(7) 1 59
(Conor Dore) *mid-div: rdn over 1f out: no prog fnl f* **40/1**

5000 **6** 3/4 **Fast Play (IRE)**[16] 2956 5-9-7 **69**....(b) MartinLane 9 66
(Conor Dore) *hld up: pushed along and hdwy over 2f out: rdn ent fnl f: no ex* **66/1**
5045 **7** 1/2 **Karam Albaari (IRE)**[16] 2971 9-9-5 **67**....(v) PaddyAspell 10 63
(J R Jenkins) *hld up: pushed along fnl 2 fs: no imp* **80/1**
2151 **8** *nk* **Victor's Bet (SPA)**[9] 3208 8-8-12 **65**.... MeganNicholls(5) 4 61
(Ralph J Smith) *in rr: effrt on outer 3f out: one pce fnl 2 fs* **9/2**[3]
444 **9** 1 1/2 **Star Glitter (FR)**[32] 2456 4-9-4 **66**....(p[1]) PhillipMakin 2 59
(David O'Meara) *trckd ldrs: 3rd 3f out: drvn 2f out: lost pl and briefly rdn over 1f out: wknd* **12/1**
6/0- **10** 3/4 **Sailors Warn (IRE)**[69] 8477 10-9-2 **69**.... GeorgeWood(5) 3 61
(Ian Williams) *hld up: rousted along over 3f out: sn hrd rdn: no rspnse* **66/1**

2m 41.81s (1.01) **Going Correction** +0.025s/f (Slow) **10** Ran SP% **113.6**
Speed ratings (Par 103): **97,94,94,92,91 90,90,90,89,88**
CSF £7.20 CT £33.77 TOTE £2.70: £1.20, £1.70, £2.40; EX 8.50 Trifecta £59.50.
**Owner** Exors Of The Late J L C Pearce **Bred** Lordship Stud **Trained** Newmarket, Suffolk

**FOCUS**
This wasn't strongly run and turned into a bit of a dash for home from the three pole. The hold-up horses couldn't get involved. A small pb from the runner-up, with the third rated to form.

## 3548 EBC GROUP FILLIES' H'CAP 7f 36y (Tp)
**4:30** (4:30) (Class 4) (0-85,80) 4-Y-0+ **£4,690** (£1,395; £697) **Stalls** High

Form RPR
1136 **1** **Simply Me**[76] 1368 4-9-7 **80**....(p) RichardKingscote 4 85
(Tom Dascombe) *hld up: pushed along 2f out: hdwy and rdn wl over 1f out: jnd ldr ins fnl f: led last 100yds: hld on wl* **7/4**[2]
6212 **2** *shd* **French**[9] 3216 4-8-8 **67**....(p) CamHardie 1 71
(Antony Brittain) *chsd ldr: pushed along 2f out: led over 1f out: sn rdn: hdd last 100 yds: rallied but jst hld* **11/8**[1]
033 **3** *2* **Stosur (IRE)**[16] 2973 6-9-2 **75**....(b) LukeMorris 3 74
(Gay Kelleway) *led: drvn and hdd wl over 1f out: hrd rdn and no ex* **11/4**[3]

1m 29.88s (1.08) **Going Correction** +0.025s/f (Slow) 3 Ran SP% **105.1**
Speed ratings (Par 102): **94,93,91**
CSF £4.31 TOTE £2.50; EX 4.40 Trifecta £3.50.
**Owner** Laurence Bellman **Bred** Highclere Stud **Trained** Malpas, Cheshire

**FOCUS**
Just the three runners for the day's richest race, but it was run at what looked a reasonable gallop. Muddling form. A small pb from the winner, with the runner-up a shade below her recent turf form.

## 3549 EBC GROUP: MANAGED PRINT SERVICES MEDIAN AUCTION MAIDEN STKS 1m 142y (Tp)
**5:00** (5:03) (Class 5) 3-5-Y-O **£2,911** (£866; £432; £216) **Stalls** Low

Form RPR
62 **1** **Pastime**[16] 2970 3-9-2 0.... AdamBeschizza 3 75
(Gay Kelleway) *slowly away: sn rcvrd and racd in midfield: rowed along over 2f out: hdwy on outer over 1f out: rdn and led 150yds out: r.o wl* **14/1**
**2** 1/2 **Yaarmen (USA)** 3-9-2 0.... PatCosgrave 6 74+
(William Haggas) *slowly away: rcvrd to trck ldr: pushed along over 2f out: chal over 1f out: tk 2nd wl ins fnl f and r.o wl: hld by wnr: nt unduly knocked abt* **7/4**[2]
0- **3** *1* **Luminous**[270] 6414 3-8-6 0....(h[1]) GeorgeWood(5) 2 66
(Simon Crisford) *trckd ldrs: pushed along on inner over 1f out: rdn ins fnl f: r.o: nt gng pce of first two* **8/1**[3]
632 **4** *1* **Tadween (IRE)**[21] 2798 3-9-2 80.... DaneO'Neill 4 69
(Richard Hannon) *led: pushed along wl over 1f out: sn rdn: hdd 150yds out: wknd* **5/6**[1]
00 **5** *11* **Shamonix (IRE)**[18] 2908 3-8-11 0.... SteveDrowne 1 39
(Mark Usher) *hld up: drvn 3f out: wknd fnl 2f* **200/1**
40 **6** *7* **Striking For Gold**[119] 662 3-8-13 0.... JackDuern(3) 5 28
(Sarah Hollinshead) *hld up in last: pushed along and struggling fr 3f out: sn lost tch* **200/1**

1m 50.62s (0.52) **Going Correction** +0.025s/f (Slow) 6 Ran SP% **109.7**
Speed ratings (Par 103): **98,97,96,95,86 79**
CSF £37.33 TOTE £12.20: £4.00, £1.90; EX 30.40 Trifecta £146.60.
**Owner** Countrywide Classics Limited **Bred** Countrywide Classics Ltd **Trained** Exning, Suffolk

**FOCUS**
Just a modest maiden, with not a great deal to separate the first four. The form is a bit fluid.

## 3550 EBC GROUP: CYBER SECURITY SPECIALISTS APPRENTICE H'CAP 1m 142y (Tp)
**5:35** (5:36) (Class 6) (0-55,55) 4-Y-0+ **£2,264** (£673; £336; £168) **Stalls** Low

Form RPR
1 **1** **Society Ranger (IRE)**[46] 2051 4-9-3 **54**....(p) GearoidBrouder(3) 10 65+
(S M Duffy, Ire) *hld up: hdwy on outer 2f out: led 1f out: briefly rdn and sn clr: easily* **5/2**[1]
2460 **2** *5* **Pensax Lady (IRE)**[9] 3221 4-9-4 **55**.... DavidEgan(3) 7 55
(Daniel Mark Loughnane) *mid-div: rdn and n.m.r over 1f out: prog in clr and r.o wl fnl f: no ch w wnr* **13/2**[2]
6560 **3** 1/2 **Moving Robe (IRE)**[3] 3442 4-8-5 **46** oh1....(t) DarraghKeenan(7) 8 45
(Conrad Allen) *trckd ldrs: 3rd over 1f out: rdn appr fnl f: r.o one pce* **10/1**
0563 **4** *1* **Outlaw Torn (IRE)**[25] 2687 8-9-1 **54**....(e) BenSanderson(5) 6 51
(Richard Guest) *trckd ldr: led over 1f out: sn hdd: rdn and no ex fnl f* **7/1**[3]
1050 **5** 2 1/4 **Pivotal Dream (IRE)**[11] 3137 4-9-0 **48**.... JordanVaughan 9 40
(Mark Brisbourne) *mid-div: effrt and rdn over 1f out: one pce fnl f* **11/1**
0-01 **6** 2 3/4 **Suzi Icon**[15] 3001 5-9-2 **50**....(p) AlistairRawlinson 1 36
(Michael Appleby) *t.k.h: led tl hdd over 1f out: wknd and eased* **7/1**[3]
0000 **7** *2* **Overrider**[3] 3440 7-8-7 **46** oh1....(bt) AledBeech(5) 2 28
(Shaun Lycett) *prom: 3rd and niggled over 2f out: rdn wl over 1f out: fdd* **50/1**
0000 **8** 1 3/4 **Hercullian Prince**[10] 3172 5-9-2 **55**....(b) KatherineGlenister(5) 4 33
(Conor Dore) *trckd ldrs on inner: drvn 2f out: rdn 1f out: wknd* **25/1**
-050 **9** 3/4 **Ershaad (IRE)**[149] 167 5-8-13 **47**.... GeorgeWood 11 24
(Shaun Harris) *hld up: pushed along 2f out: rdn wl over 1f out: no imp* **16/1**
3341 **10** *5* **Sheer Intensity (IRE)**[17] 2915 4-9-0 **55**.... KeelanBaker(7) 13 21
(David Evans) *hmpd leaving stalls and lost many l: a in rr: nvr a factor* **12/1**
400- **11** *4* **Dark Illustrator**[366] 3020 4-8-9 **50**.... RyanTimby(7) 12 8
(Lynn Siddall) *wnt rt and hmpd rival leaving stalls losing several l: latched on to pack after 2 fs: effrt 2f out: sn rdn: fdd* **66/1**
0423 **U** **Misu Pete**[8] 3265 5-8-10 **51**.... NicolaCurrie(7) 5
(Mark Usher) *stmbld leaving stalls and uns rdr* **13/2**[2]

1m 49.44s (-0.66) **Going Correction** +0.025s/f (Slow) 12 Ran SP% **118.5**
Speed ratings (Par 101): **103,98,98,97,95 92,91,89,88,84 80,**
CSF £17.97 CT £141.61 TOTE £3.80: £1.30, £2.10, £5.20; EX 21.00 Trifecta £217.50.
**Owner** The Superb Partnership **Bred** Mrs Natasha Drennan **Trained** Errill, Co. Laois

**FOCUS**
They went a good clip in this lowly apprentice handicap. The form could be rated 4lb higher but this was all about the winner.
T/Plt: £14.40 to a £1 stake. Pool: £47,250.00 - 3,265.10 winning units. T/Qpdt: £5.80 to a £1 stake. Pool: £2,494.00 - 425.02 winning units. **Keith McHugh**

3551 - 3552a (Foreign Racing) - See Raceform Interactive

# 2641 BELMONT PARK (L-H)
Friday, June 9

**OFFICIAL GOING: Dirt: fast; turf: firm**

## 3553a BELMONT GOLD CUP INVITATIONAL STKS (GRADE 3) (4YO+) (TURF) 2m
**10:46** 4-Y-0+
**£178,861** (£65,040; £39,024; £19,512; £9,756; £6,504)

RPR
**1** **Red Cardinal (IRE)**[26] 2667 5-8-9 0.... EduardoPedroza 9 115+
(A Wohler, Germany) *midfield: rdn and hdwy on outer into st: chal over 1f out and led ent fnl f: styd on: drvn out: jst lasted* **14/5**[1]
**2** *nk* **St Michel**[30] 2519 4-8-3 0....(b[1]) IradOrtizJr 12 110+
(Sir Mark Prescott Bt) *hld up: rdn over 1f out: styd on into 2nd fnl f: clsng on wnr towards fin: jst failed to get up* **53/10**[3]
**3** *2* **Now We Can**[40] 2202 8-8-3 0.... JulienRLeparoux 3 106
(N Clement, France) **89/10**
**4** *nse* **Wicklow Brave**[42] 7756 8-8-11 0....(b) JavierCastellano 11 114
(W P Mullins, Ire) *fractious in stalls: dwlt: hld up: clsd home turn: angled out and rdn into st: chal over 1f out: outpcd by front pair fnl f: lost 3rd post* **18/5**[2]
**5** *nk* **Hunter O'Riley (USA)**[43] 4-8-6 0 ow1....(b) MikeESmith 1 110
(James J Toner, U.S.A) **142/10**
**6** *1* **Bullards Alley (USA)**[20] 5-8-9 0....(b) MarcelinoPedroza 8 111
(Tim Glyshaw, U.S.A) **67/1**
**7** *1* **Farz (USA)**[33] 5-8-5 0.... JoseLezcano 6 105
(Kiaran McLaughlin, U.S.A) **56/1**
**8** 1 1/2 **Wall Of Fire (IRE)**[28] 2571 4-8-3 0....(b) FlorentGeroux 4 103
(Hugo Palmer) *trckd clr ldr: clsd 1/2-way: rdn to ld into st: hdd over 1f out: no ex: wknd* **11/1**
**9** *hd* **Taghleeb (USA)**[27] 2641 6-8-9 0....(b) JoseLOrtiz 10 107
(Michael J Maker, U.S.A) **66/10**
**10** 1/2 **Clondaw Warrior (IRE)**[43] 6284 10-8-3 0....(h) JohnRVelazquez 5 101
(W P Mullins, Ire) *dwlt and hld up in last: no imp st: nvr a factor* **156/10**
**11** 5 1/4 **Roman Approval (USA)**[37] 6-8-6 0 ow1....(b) JoelRosario 7 97
(David Cannizzo, U.S.A) **224/10**
**12** *2* **Renown**[34] 6-8-9 0....(b) AngelCruz 2 98
(Elizabeth Voss, U.S.A) **222/10**

3m 18.79s 12 Ran SP% **119.9**

**Owner** Australian Bloodstock Stable **Bred** Lynch Bages Ltd **Trained** Germany

**FOCUS**
The standard is set around the third, fourth, fifth and sixth.

# 1181 COMPIEGNE (L-H)
Friday, June 9

**OFFICIAL GOING: Turf: heavy**

## 3554a PRIX DE CARLEPONT (CLAIMER) (3YO) (YOUNG JOCKEYS & APPRENTICES) (TURF) 1m 2f
**1:10** 3-Y-O **£9,829** (£3,931; £2,948; £1,474; £1,474)

RPR
**1** **Pando (IRE)**[82] 1269 3-9-1 0.... KyllanBarbaud(7) 5
(N Caullery, France) **49/10**[3]
**2** *nse* **Gnily (IRE)**[30] 3-8-2 0.... MlleLauraGrosso(9) 1
(N Clement, France) **6/4**[1]
**3** 2 1/2 **Good King (GER)** 3-9-1 0.... ClementLecoeuvre(3) 3
(Carmen Bocskai, Germany) **109/10**
**4** *hd* **Gasalto (FR)**[17] 3-8-10 0.... ClementGuitraud(8) 6
(Y Barberot, France) **189/10**
**4** *dht* **Copper Baked (FR)**[24] 2703 3-8-11 0.... GabrielLeDevehat(4) 4
(K R Burke) *racd keenly: hld up in fnl trio: drvn to cl wl over 2f out: nt clr run 1 1/2f fr home and angled out: hrd rdn and styd on fnl f: got up to share 4th fnl stride: nvr nrr* **123/10**
**6** 3/4 **Ospector (USA)**[21] 3-8-13 0....(b) ErwannLebreton(5) 9
(F Alloncle, France) **30/1**
**7** *1* **Ninian Des Aigles (FR)**[16] 3-8-13 0.... JeremieMonteiro(7) 7
(Mme C Barande-Barbe, France) **154/10**
**8** 3/4 **Mr Maximum (USA)**[13] 3-8-9 0....(p) JeromeMoutard(6) 2
(F-H Graffard, France) **29/10**[2]
**9** *1* **Hilarant (FR)**[18] 3-8-9 0....(p) AntonioOrani(6) 8
(C Laffon-Parias, France) **175/10**

2m 11.29s 9 Ran SP% **118.3**
PARI-MUTUEL (all including 1 euro stake): WIN 5.90 PLACE 1.60, 1.30, 2.30 DF 5.20 SF 14.00.
**Owner** Claude Bodin **Bred** Tinnakill Bloodstock **Trained** France

# 3200 BEVERLEY (R-H)
Saturday, June 10

**OFFICIAL GOING: Soft (good to soft in places) changing to good to soft (soft in places) after race 1 (2.05)**
Wind: Strong across Weather: Heavy cloud and showers

## 3555 MICHAEL AND EILEEN BIRTHDAY MEDIAN AUCTION MAIDEN STKS 7f 96y
**2:05** (2:06) (Class 5) 3-Y-O **£3,780** (£1,131; £565; £283; £141) **Stalls** Low

Form RPR
-533 **1** **Navarone (IRE)**[22] 2791 3-9-5 74.... PaulHanagan 1 75
(Richard Fahey) *t.k.h early: trckd ldng pair on inner: hdwy 2f out: n.m.r over 1f out: sn chal: rdn to ld ins fnl f: kpt on strly* **11/8**[1]

3-02 **2** 4 ½ **Valentino Boy (IRE)**[37] 2338 3-9-5 73 ................................ TomEaves 5 63
(Brian Ellison) *led: pushed along over 2f out: rdn wl over 1f out: drvn ent fnl f: sn hdd: kpt on same pce* **7/2**[3]

66-0 **3** 1 ¼ **Orientelle**[26] 2682 3-8-9 40 ................................ PhilDennis(5) 2 55
(Richard Whitaker) *trckd ldrs: hdwy over 2f out: rdn along wl over 1f out: kpt on fnl f* **66/1**

4-33 **4** ½ **Undiscovered Angel (FR)**[15] 3044 3-8-11 73 ........ JordanVaughan(3) 7 54
(K R Burke) *trckd ldrs: hdwy on outer 3f out: rdn along wl over 1f out: drvn and kpt on one pce fnl f* **5/2**[2]

40- **5** 11 **Seebring (IRE)**[350] 3654 3-9-0 0 ................................ MeganNicholls(5) 3 30
(Brian Ellison) *towards rr: pushed along 3f out: rdn 2f out: plugged on: n.d* **16/1**

6-00 **6** ¾ **Pontecarlo Boy**[37] 2349 3-9-5 45 ................................ CamHardie 8 28
(Richard Whitaker) *cl up: rdn along over 2f out: drvn over 1f out: sn wknd* **33/1**

**7** 2 ¾ **Silken Moonlight** 3-9-0 0 ................................ LouisSteward 4 16
(Scott Dixon) *dwlt: a in rr* **10/1**

**8** 9 **Dragons Thunder (IRE)** 3-8-12 0 ......................... KieranSchofield(7) 6
(Brian Ellison) *dwlt: a in bhd* **20/1**

1m 35.06s (1.26) **Going Correction** +0.20s/f (Good) **8** Ran SP% **117.1**
Speed ratings (Par 99): **100,94,93,92,80 79,76,66**
CSF £6.61 TOTE £2.30: £1.30, £1.60, £11.90; EX 6.50 Trifecta £317.50.
**Owner** Merchants and Missionaries **Bred** Michael O'Mahony **Trained** Musley Bank, N Yorks

**FOCUS**
Rail movements increase distances as follows: Race 1 and Race 7 plus 11 yards; Race 4, 5 and 6 plus 7 yards. An ordinary 3yo maiden. They went a respectable gallop on ground changed back to good to soft, soft in places after this race. The winning time concurred with that assessment. Modest form, rated around the winner.

## 3556 BRIAN YEARDLEY CONTINENTAL TWO YEAR OLD TROPHY CONDITIONS STKS (PLUS 10 RACE) (C&G) 5f

**2:40** (2:41) (Class 2) 2-Y-O

**£15,562** (£4,660; £2,330; £1,165; £582; £292) **Stalls** Low

Form RPR

142 **1** **Cardsharp**[8] 3297 2-9-0 0 ................................ JoeFanning 3 97
(Mark Johnston) *mde all: rdn over 1f out: edgd lft ins fnl f: kpt on wl* **6/4**[1]

41 **2** 2 ¼ **Rufus King**[15] 3051 2-9-2 0 ................................ PaulHanagan 4 91
(Mark Johnston) *wnt lft s: trckd ldng pair: hdwy wl over 1f out: rdn appr fnl f: sn drvn and kpt on* **6/1**[3]

**3** nse **Cool Spirit** 2-8-9 0 ................................ JoeDoyle 5 84
(James Given) *sltly hmpd s: in tch: hdwy over 2f out: effrt and n.m.r over 1f out: sn swtchd rt to inner and rdn: kpt on wl fnl f* **11/1**

021 **4** 2 ½ **Chatburn (IRE)**[12] 3149 2-9-0 0 ................................ TomEaves 2 80
(David O'Meara) *chsd wnr: rdn along wl over 1f out: drvn and wknd fnl f* **8/1**

3 **5** 1 ¼ **Areen Faisal (IRE)**[53] 1858 2-8-12 0 ................................ PhillipMakin 7 73
(Richard Fahey) *in tch: hdwy on outer 2f out: sn rdn and no imp* **11/2**[2]

1 **6** 2 **Excellently Poised**[56] 1803 2-9-2 0 ................................ ConnorBeasley 6 70
(Bryan Smart) *in rr: pushed along 1/2-way: effrt on outer 2f out: sn rdn and n.d* **11/2**[2]

21 **7** 1 ¼ **Joe's Spirit (IRE)**[12] 3135 2-9-0 0 ................................ LouisSteward 1 64
(Michael Bell) *chsd ldng pair on inner: pushed along over 2f out: rdn wl over 1f out: sn wknd* **15/2**

1m 4.35s (0.85) **Going Correction** +0.20s/f (Good) **7** Ran SP% **116.3**
Speed ratings (Par 99): **101,97,97,93,91 88,86**
CSF £11.40 TOTE £2.20: £1.30, £3.30; EX 10.40 Trifecta £121.30.
**Owner** Sheikh Hamdan bin Mohammed Al Maktoum **Bred** Godolphin **Trained** Middleham Moor, N Yorks

**FOCUS**
A good quality juvenile conditions contest won in 2011 by the smart Gabrial. The favourite controlled this race from the front at an even tempo, and continues to progress.

## 3557 HILARY NEEDLER TROPHY FILLIES' CONDITIONS STKS (PLUS 10 RACE) 5f

**3:15** (3:15) (Class 2) 2-Y-O

**£15,562** (£4,660; £2,330; £1,165; £582; £292) **Stalls** Low

Form RPR

**1** **Chica La Habana (IRE)** 2-8-9 0 ................................ AdamBeschizza 3 81+
(Robert Cowell) *dwlt and towards rr: hdwy 1/2-way: chsd ldrs over 1f out: sn rdn and styd on strly to ld last 110yds* **6/1**[3]

14 **2** ¾ **Maggies Angel (IRE)**[22] 2801 2-8-12 0 ................................ PaulHanagan 7 81
(Richard Fahey) *trckd ldrs: hdwy wl over 1f out: sn rdn: n.m.r and swtchd rt 1f out: sn drvn and kpt on wl towards fin* **9/2**[2]

**3** 2 ¼ **Ce De Nullis (IRE)** 2-8-9 0 ................................ (h[1]) ConnorBeasley 6 70+
(Paul Midgley) *green and towards rr: hdwy on outer wl over 1f out: rdn and kpt on wl fnl f* **33/1**

12 **4** ¾ **Rebel Assault (IRE)**[7] 3333 2-8-12 0 ................................ JoeFanning 2 71+
(Mark Johnston) *qckly away and led: rdn and edgd lft ent fnl f: hdd & wknd last 110yds* **2/5**[1]

5 **5** 1 ¼ **Moonlit Sands (IRE)**[16] 2987 2-8-12 0 ................................ TomEaves 1 66+
(Brian Ellison) *chsd ldrs on inner: rdn along and outpcd 1/2-way: hdwy wl over 1f out: kpt on fnl f* **20/1**

20 **6** 2 **Mount Victoria (IRE)**[22] 2801 2-8-12 0 ................................ JoeDoyle 5 59+
(James Given) *t.k.h: cl up: rdn along wl over 1f out: wknd appr fnl f* **16/1**

5512 **7** 19 **Popsi**[10] 3200 2-8-12 0 ................................ (p) CamHardie 4
(Marjorie Fife) *cl up: rdn along 2f out: sn wknd: bhd and eased fnl f* **25/1**

1m 5.02s (1.52) **Going Correction** +0.20s/f (Good) **7** Ran SP% **121.3**
Speed ratings (Par 96): **95,93,90,89,87 83,53**
CSF £34.13 TOTE £9.70: £4.20, £1.30; EX 33.30 Trifecta £792.20.
**Owner** The Cool Silk Partnership **Bred** Herbertstown & Diomed **Trained** Six Mile Bottom, Cambs

**FOCUS**
A good quality juvenile fillies' conditions contest won in 2015 by the smart Easton Angel. This was probably a more ordinary renewal. The favourite attempted to dominate at an even tempo up the far rail but got tired on the softer surface.

## 3558 HAPPY BIRTHDAY GRAHAM HALLETT FILLIES' H'CAP 1m 1f 207y

**3:50** (3:50) (Class 3) (0-95,92) 4-Y-0-**£7,158** (£2,143; £1,071; £535; £267) **Stalls** Low

Form RPR

11-2 **1** **High Hopes**[21] 2817 4-9-4 89 ................................ JoeFanning 5 98+
(David Simcock) *dwlt and hld up in rr: hdwy over 2f out: nt clr run wl over 1f out: swtchd lft to outer and effrt ent fnl f: qcknd to ld last 75yds: kpt on* **5/6**[1]

-515 **2** 1 ¾ **Prying Pandora (FR)**[9] 3255 4-8-10 81 ................................ PaulHanagan 4 85
(Richard Fahey) *trckd ldrs: hdwy 2f out: rdn to chal jst over 1f out: led ent fnl f: sn drvn: hdd last 75yds: kpt on same pce* **3/1**[2]

3340 **3** 3 ½ **Footlight**[22] 2774 4-8-4 75 ................................ ShaneGray 1 72
(Richard Fahey) *led: rdn along 2f out: drvn over 1f out: hdd ent fnl f: kpt on one pce* **9/2**[3]

50-0 **4** 4 **Sagely (IRE)**[28] 2605 4-9-7 92 ................................ TomEaves 3 81
(Ed Dunlop) *trckd ldrs on inner: hdwy over 2f out: cl up over 1f out: sn rdn: n.m.r and ev ch: drvn and wknd fnl f* **10/1**

00/0 **5** 3 **Lahayeb**[21] 2817 5-9-1 89 ................................ AlistairRawlinson(3) 2 72
(Michael Appleby) *trckd ldr: hdwy and cl up over 2f out: rdn along wl over 1f out: sn drvn and wknd* **14/1**

2m 9.2s (2.20) **Going Correction** +0.20s/f (Good) **5** Ran SP% **113.5**
Speed ratings (Par 104): **99,97,94,91,89**
CSF £3.79 TOTE £2.00: £1.50, £1.10; EX 3.90 Trifecta £7.60.
**Owner** Major M G Wyatt **Bred** Charlie Wyatt **Trained** Newmarket, Suffolk

**FOCUS**
Race distance increased 7 yards. A good little fillies' handicap. They went a sensible gallop on the good to surface and the clear favourite won readily. She's on the upgrade.

## 3559 AMBER, ALANA AND SONNY H'CAP 1m 1f 207y

**4:25** (4:25) (Class 5) (0-75,75) 4-Y-0+ **£3,780** (£1,131; £565; £283; £141) **Stalls** Low

Form RPR

-041 **1** **Miningrocks (FR)**[10] 3221 5-8-9 68 ................................ PhilDennis(5) 6 75
(Declan Carroll) *mde all: rdn over 1f out: edgd lft ins fnl f: hld on wl towards fin* **11/4**[1]

-564 **2** ½ **Perceived**[52] 1892 5-8-13 67 ................................ CamHardie 5 73
(Antony Brittain) *trckd ldrs: hdwy over 2f out: rdn to chse ldng pair over 1f out: chal ins fnl f: sn drvn and ev ch: no ex towards fin* **14/1**

50-0 **3** 3 **Hernandoshideaway**[15] 3050 5-9-7 75 ........................ (t[1]) ConnorBeasley 2 75
(Michael Dods) *trckd ldng pair: hdwy to chse wnr wl over 1f out: drvn and ev ch appr fnl f: sn edgd lft and kpt on same pce* **4/1**[2]

44-5 **4** 1 ¾ **Jan De Heem**[12] 3155 7-8-6 60 ................................ JoeDoyle 1 57
(Tina Jackson) *hld up in rr: hdwy 2f out: chsd ldrs: rdn and n.m.r ent fnl f: sn drvn and no imp* **7/1**

0-56 **5** 1 ½ **King Of The Celts (IRE)**[10] 3205 9-8-7 64 .......... RachelRichardson(3) 7 58
(Tim Easterby) *trckd wnr: pushed along wl over 2f out: sn rdn and grad wknd* **8/1**

00-3 **6** nk **Altharoos (IRE)**[10] 3204 7-9-7 75 ................................ PaulHanagan 8 68
(Micky Hammond) *in tch: hdwy to chse ldrs 3f out: rdn along 2f out: sn drvn and btn* **11/4**[1]

05-3 **7** shd **Dream Free**[10] 3205 4-8-9 63 ................................ TomEaves 4 56
(Mark Walford) *in rr: effrt and sme hdwy over 2f out: sn rdn and n.d* **6/1**[3]

2m 7.74s (0.74) **Going Correction** +0.20s/f (Good) **7** Ran SP% **117.9**
Speed ratings (Par 103): **105,104,102,100,99 99,99**
CSF £43.63 CT £156.02 TOTE £3.70: £2.00, £7.60; EX 44.30 Trifecta £234.70.
**Owner** Mrs Sarah Bryan **Bred** M Daguzan-Garros & Rolling Hills Farm **Trained** Malton, N Yorks

**FOCUS**
Race distance increased 7 yards. A fair handicap. One of the joint-favourites gamely made all off a respectable tempo, and is rated close to last year's C&D form..

## 3560 BERYL AND JOE TURNER MEMORIAL H'CAP 1m 100y

**5:00** (5:00) (Class 5) (0-70,72) 4-Y-0+ **£3,780** (£1,131; £565; £283; £141) **Stalls** Low

Form RPR

0500 **1** **Mr Cool Cash**[5] 3402 5-9-6 66 ................................ ConnorBeasley 2 73
(Richard Guest) *trckd ldng pair: hdwy 2f out: sn chal: rdn to ld over 1f out: drvn clr ins fnl f: kpt on* **7/1**

4045 **2** ½ **Character Onesie (IRE)**[12] 3144 5-9-12 72 ................... PaulHanagan 5 78
(Richard Fahey) *trckd ldrs: hdwy wl over 2f out: effrt and n.m.r over 1f out and sn rdn: drvn to chse wnr ins fnl f: kpt on* **3/1**[1]

6502 **3** 2 **Green Howard**[5] 3402 9-9-3 63 ................................ (b) JoeFanning 8 65
(Rebecca Bastiman) *stdd s and swtchd rt to inner: hld up and bhd: hdwy on inner 2f out: n.m.r and swtchd lft over 1f out: sn rdn and styd on fnl f* **7/2**[2]

0-52 **4** 3 ¼ **Thornaby Nash**[11] 3181 6-8-12 63 ............................ (p) GemmaTutty(5) 9 57
(Karen Tutty) *trckd ldrs: hdwy wl over 2f out: rdn along wl over 1f out: kpt on same pce* **11/2**[3]

-001 **5** ½ **Midlight**[10] 3196 5-8-11 57 ................................ (t) TomEaves 4 50
(Ruth Carr) *led: pushed along over 2f out: rdn and hdd over 1f out: sn drvn and wknd fnl f* **15/2**

25-0 **6** 2 **La Havrese (FR)**[15] 3053 6-9-0 60 ................................ PaddyAspell 3 49
(Lynn Siddall) *in tch: hdwy over 3f out: rdn along over 2f out: sn one pce* **20/1**

-064 **7** 1 ½ **Rosamaria (IRE)**[19] 2900 4-9-1 61 ................................ PhillipMakin 6 47
(Julie Camacho) *chsd ldr: rdn along over 2f out: sn drvn and wknd over 1f out* **13/2**

0052 **8** ½ **All You (IRE)**[10] 3205 5-9-0 67 ................................ (v) PatrickVaughan(7) 1 52
(David O'Meara) *hld up: effrt and sme hdwy over 3f out: rdn along over 2f out: n.d* **7/1**

4060 **9** 1 ½ **Shearian**[16] 2996 7-9-0 67 ................................ GerO'Neill(7) 10 48
(Declan Carroll) *in tch: pushed along 3f out: rdn over 2f out: sn wknd* **16/1**

00-0 **10** ½ **Ivors Involvement (IRE)**[18] 2918 5-8-2 48 oh2 ................ CamHardie 7 28
(Tina Jackson) *t.k.h: hld up: a towards rr* **33/1**

1m 48.58s (0.98) **Going Correction** +0.20s/f (Good) **10** Ran SP% **126.3**
Speed ratings (Par 103): **103,102,100,97,96 94,93,92,91,90**
CSF £30.83 CT £93.41 TOTE £9.10: £2.60, £2.00, £1.60; EX 35.20 Trifecta £121.90.
**Owner** I Lawson **Bred** T G Holdcroft **Trained** Ingmanthorpe, W Yorks

**FOCUS**
Race distance increased 7 yards. An ordinary handicap. They went a decent gallop and last year's winner won again. He's rated to his best.

## 3561 FURNISS AND JONES H'CAP 7f 96y

**5:35** (5:35) (Class 5) (0-70,70) 3-Y-O **£3,780** (£1,131; £565; £283; £141) **Stalls** Low

Form RPR

0-21 **1** **Pass The Cristal (IRE)**[18] 2911 3-8-11 60 ........................ PhillipMakin 4 65
(William Muir) *blind removed late and wnt rt s: t.k.h chsng ldng pair: hdwy on inner and cl up over 1f out: rdn to take slt ld ent fnl f: sn drvn and edgd lft: hld on gamely towards fin* **9/4**[1]

-002 **2** shd **Greenview Paradise (IRE)**[16] 2993 3-8-13 62 ..................... JoeDoyle 5 66
(Richard Fahey) *led: jnd and pushed along 2f out: rdn over 1f out: hdd narrowly and drvn ent fnl f: rallied gamely: jst hld* **12/1**

0-24 **3** 1 ½ **The Stalking Moon (IRE)**[11] 3171 3-9-5 68 ..................... CamHardie 3 68
(John Quinn) *hmpd at s: sn trcking ldrs: hdwy on outer over 2f out: rdn over 1f out: drvn and kpt on same pce fnl f* **7/2**[3]

3135 **4** 1 ½ **Il Sicario (IRE)**[19] 2885 3-9-6 69 ................................ (v[1]) JoeFanning 6 65
(Mark Johnston) *trckd ldr: pushed along over 2f out: rdn wl over 1f out: drvn and no imp fnl f* **9/2**

-031 **5** ½ **Champion Harbour (IRE)**[22] 2790 3-9-0 **63** .................. PaulHanagan 7 58
(Richard Fahey) *in tch: hdwy over 2f out: rdn along wl over 1f out: sn drvn and no imp* **10/3**[2]

21-0 **6** ¾ **Kilbaha Lady (IRE)**[40] 2228 3-8-11 **65** ............................ PhilDennis(5) 8 58
(Nigel Tinkler) *hld up: a towards rr* **16/1**

3-66 **7** 4 **Mr Coco Bean (USA)**[36] 2374 3-9-7 **70** ............................ TomEaves 2 52
(Ann Duffield) *hmpd s: a towards rr* **8/1**

1m 35.8s (2.00) **Going Correction** +0.20s/f (Good) 7 Ran SP% **118.9**
Speed ratings (Par 99): **96,95,94,92,91 91,86**
CSF £32.15 CT £95.34 TOTE £4.30: £2.70, £6.60; EX 39.10 Trifecta £159.90.
**Owner** O'Mulloy, Schwartz **Bred** Grangecon Stud **Trained** Lambourn, Berks

**FOCUS**
Race distance increased 7 yards. A modest 3yo handicap. They went a sensible gallop on the easy surface. The first two both improved a bit further.
T/Plt: £56.10 to a £1 stake. Pool: £50,877.96 - 661.07 winning units. T/Qpdt: £44.50 to a £1 stake. Pool: £2,601.86 - 43.20 winning units. **Joe Rowntree**

# [3283]CATTERICK (L-H)
## Saturday, June 10

**OFFICIAL GOING: Soft (7.4)**
Wind: light behind Weather: Steady rain

## 3562 TOTESCOOP6 PLAY TODAY NOVICE MEDIAN AUCTION STKS 5f
**1:40** (1:43) (Class 5) 2-Y-O **£2,911** (£866; £432; £216) **Stalls** Low

Form RPR
43 **1** **Twentytwowontdo (IRE)**[4] 3430 2-8-11 0 .................... RonanWhelan 5 69
(David O'Meara) *chsd ldr: rdn 2f out: led ins fnl f: kpt on* **7/4**[2]

431 **2** ¾ **Villa Tora**[9] 3237 2-9-4 0 ............................................ JasonHart 4 73
(Mark Johnston) *led: pushed along 2f out: rdn and hdd ins fnl f: kpt on but a hld* **10/11**[1]

**3** 5 **Undercover Brother** 2-9-2 0 .................................. SamJames 1 53
(David O'Meara) *dwlt: hld up: pushed along 1/2-way: kpt on fnl f* **8/1**[3]

**4** 6 **Show Princess** 2-8-6 0 ........................................ LewisEdmunds(5) 2 26
(Michael Appleby) *a outpcd in rr* **16/1**

00 **5** 4½ **Kyleque (IRE)**[21] 2816 2-9-2 0 ................................. KevinStott 3 15
(Paul Midgley) *racd alone far side: prom: rdn 1/2-way: wknd over 1f out* **33/1**

1m 1.21s (1.41) **Going Correction** +0.40s/f (Good) 5 Ran SP% **108.7**
Speed ratings (Par 93): **104,102,94,85,78**
CSF £3.57 TOTE £2.60: £1.40, £1.10; EX 3.40 Trifecta £8.10.
**Owner** York Thoroughbred Racing **Bred** Thomas & Seamus Whelan & David Harrison **Trained** Upper Helmsley, N Yorks

**FOCUS**
All distances as advertised. A wet day and no surprise to see them come stands' side in this opener. The form is taken at face value around the runner-up.

## 3563 TOTEQUADPOT FOUR PLACES IN FOUR RACES H'CAP 5f
**2:15** (2:16) (Class 6) (0-60,61) 4-Y-O+ **£3,234** (£962; £481; £240) **Stalls** Low

Form RPR
03 **1** **Lackaday**[16] 2990 5-9-7 **58** ............................................(p) TonyHamilton 8 65
(Noel Wilson) *led narrowly: drvn whn hdd appr fnl f: kpt on: led again towards fin* **5/1**[3]

2403 **2** hd **Culloden**[28] 2628 5-9-5 **56** ..............................................(v) KevinStott 10 62
(Shaun Harris) *pressed ldr: pushed along to ld narrowly appr fnl f: rdn ins fnl f: kpt on: hdd towards fin* **5/1**[3]

0-00 **3** 1 **Lady Joanna Vassa (IRE)**[7] 3345 4-9-1 **52** .................... PaddyAspell 4 54
(Richard Guest) *chsd ldrs on outer: rdn over 2f out: ev ch ins fnl f: one pce fnl 50yds* **25/1**

0013 **4** 1¼ **Nuala Tagula (IRE)**[8] 3289 4-9-6 **57** .................................(t) JasonHart 6 55+
(John Quinn) *dwlt: sn chsd ldrs: rdn over 2f out: kpt on same pce* **8/1**

1321 **5** ¾ **Sir Geoffrey (IRE)**[8] 3289 11-8-10 **52** ....................(b) LewisEdmunds(5) 7 47
(Scott Dixon) *prom: rdn over 2f out: no ex fnl 110yds* **7/2**[1]

3621 **6** 1 **Kodimoor (IRE)**[16] 2994 4-9-2 **58** .........................(bt) RobJFitzpatrick(5) 3 50
(Christopher Kellett) *dwlt: hld up: hdwy into midfield 1/2-way: rdn over 2f out: kpt on same pce* **9/2**[2]

6540 **7** nse **Silhuette (IRE)**[33] 2454 4-9-6 **57** .....................................(v) JackGarritty 1 48
(Colin Teague) *midfield: rdn 1/2-way: kpt on same pce* **16/1**

1-00 **8** 5 **Robbian**[151] 153 6-8-10 **54** ................................................ RPWalsh(7) 11 27
(Charles Smith) *sn bdly outpcd in rr: minor late hdwy* **20/1**

0-00 **9** 3½ **Caymus**[16] 2994 4-8-5 **45** ..............................................(t) SammyJoBell(3) 2 6
(Tracy Waggott) *a towards rr* **50/1**

5053 **10** 3 **Ambitious Icarus**[21] 2843 8-9-10 **61** ...............................(b[1]) SamJames 9 11
(Richard Guest) *dwlt: a towards rr* **11/2**

1m 0.69s (0.89) **Going Correction** +0.40s/f (Good) 10 Ran SP% **116.7**
Speed ratings (Par 101): **108,107,106,104,102 101,101,93,87,82**
CSF £29.58 CT £586.60 TOTE £6.10: £1.60, £2.00, £4.50; EX 32.20 Trifecta £589.20.
**Owner** Hoyle & Marwood **Bred** Andrew Parrish **Trained** Marwood, Co Durham

**FOCUS**
A moderate sprint handicap in which it paid to be handy. The runner-up helps with the opening level.

## 3564 TOTEEXACTA PICK THE 1ST AND 2ND CLASSIFIED CLAIMING STKS 1m 4f 13y
**2:50** (2:50) (Class 6) 4-Y-O+ **£2,264** (£673; £336; £168) **Stalls** Low

Form RPR
511- **1** **Collodi (GER)**[182] 6662 8-9-7 75 .............................. TonyHamilton 5 77+
(Neil Mulholland) *mde all: pushed clr over 2f out: easily* **4/6**[1]

5065 **2** 8 **Never Say (IRE)**[1] 3529 4-8-1 42 ow1 .........................(p) NathanEvans(3) 4 43
(Jason Ward) *chsd ldr: rdn 3f out: sn readily outpcd by wnr and hld in 2nd* **10/1**[3]

040- **3** 4 **Gabrial The Duke (IRE)**[281] 6083 7-9-0 71 .......................(b) KevinStott 3 47
(Patrick Morris) *hld up in tch: hdwy to trck ldr 4f out: rdn 3f out: wknd over 2f out* **7/4**[2]

-306 **4** 24 **Monzino (USA)**[73] 1436 9-8-9 45 ................................ DuranFentiman 2 6
(Michael Chapman) *in tch: pushed along and dropped to rr 8f out: wknd and t.o fnl 4f* **66/1**

2m 47.27s (8.37) **Going Correction** +0.40s/f (Good) 4 Ran SP% **106.9**
Speed ratings (Par 101): **88,82,80,64**
CSF £7.49 TOTE £1.60; EX 4.40 Trifecta £7.60.Never Say was claimed by Mrs Samantha England for £3000.
**Owner** Neil Mulholland Racing Club **Bred** Stiftung Gestut Fahrhof **Trained** Limpley Stoke, Wilts

**FOCUS**
An uneventful claimer. The runner-up sets the level.

## 3565 TOTETRIFECTA PICK THE 1,2,3 H'CAP 7f 6y
**3:25** (3:25) (Class 3) (0-90,91) 4-Y-O+ **£12,938** (£3,850; £1,924; £962) **Stalls** Low

Form RPR
1330 **1** **Fingal's Cave (IRE)**[19] 2884 5-9-4 **87** ................................. KevinStott 6 96
(Philip Kirby) *trckd ldrs: rdn over 2f out: led ins fnl f: kpt on* **16/1**

0-30 **2** 1¾ **Shouranour (IRE)**[21] 2838 7-8-9 **83** ......................(b) LewisEdmunds(5) 9 87
(Alan Brown) *prom: rdn to ld 2f out: hdd ins fnl f: one pce* **5/1**[3]

0-03 **3** 3 **Harwoods Volante (IRE)**[8] 3288 6-9-4 **87** ........................ SamJames 3 83
(David O'Meara) *trckd ldrs: rdn and bit outpcd 2f out: plugged on fnl f* **16/1**

-436 **4** ½ **Truth Or Dare**[8] 3294 6-9-0 **86** ...................................... NathanEvans(3) 2 81
(James Bethell) *midfield: rdn over 2f out: kpt on same pce* **6/1**

5-03 **5** ½ **Baron Bolt**[21] 2833 4-9-7 **90** ..........................................(p) AntonioFresu 8 84+
(Paul Cole) *s.i.s: hld up: rdn and sme hdwy over 1f out: one pce fnl f* **11/4**[1]

0511 **6** 1½ **Luis Vaz De Torres (IRE)**[15] 3045 5-9-2 **85** ...............(h) TonyHamilton 5 75
(Richard Fahey) *midfield: rdn over 2f out: no imp* **8/1**

4002 **7** 2¼ **Intense Style (IRE)**[8] 3294 5-9-1 **87** ......................(p) SammyJoBell(3) 7 71
(Les Eyre) *hld up: nvr threatened* **4/1**[2]

-000 **8** 1¼ **Gabrial The Tiger (IRE)**[31] 2528 5-8-12 **81** ..................... JackGarritty 1 62
(Richard Fahey) *led: rdn and hung lft whn hdd 2f out: sn wknd* **12/1**

03-3 **9** 1¾ **Sakhee's Return**[37] 2348 5-9-1 **84** .............................(t) DuranFentiman 4 60
(Tim Easterby) *hld up: rdn over 2f out: sn wknd* **12/1**

1m 27.99s (0.99) **Going Correction** +0.40s/f (Good) 9 Ran SP% **115.9**
Speed ratings (Par 107): **110,108,104,104,103 101,99,97,95**
CSF £94.26 CT £1323.78 TOTE £22.30: £5.20, £2.50, £4.90; EX 151.20 Trifecta £1348.20.
**Owner** RedHotGardogs **Bred** Rathasker Stud **Trained** East Appleton, N Yorks

**FOCUS**
This fair handicap was another race where it paid to be handy and close to the stsands' rail. The form is rated around the first two.

## 3566 TOTEPOOLLIVEINFO.COM VISIT FOR RACING RESULTS H'CAP 1m 7f 189y
**4:00** (4:00) (Class 5) (0-70,70) 4-Y-O+ **£3,234** (£962; £481; £240) **Stalls** Low

Form RPR
3131 **1** **Mr Globetrotter (USA)**[7] 3338 4-9-4 **70** ............... CallumRodriguez(5) 9 81
(Iain Jardine) *trckd ldr: led over 3f out: pushed clr over 2f out: styd on wl: easily* **9/4**[2]

4-50 **2** 6 **Question Of Faith**[12] 3155 6-8-2 **51** .......................... SammyJoBell(3) 4 55
(Martin Todhunter) *hld up: hdwy 5f out: ct bhd wkng rival 3f out and sn lot to do in 4th: rdn and edgd lft over 1f out: styd on: wnt 2nd towards fin* **2/1**[1]

3140 **3** nse **Cavalieri (IRE)**[3] 3464 7-9-2 **62** ........................................(tp) KevinStott 8 66
(Philip Kirby) *midfield: hdwy to go 2nd 3f out: sn rdn: one pce and no ch w wnr: lost 2nd towards fin* **15/2**

0335 **4** 14 **London Glory**[9] 3252 4-8-11 **63** ..............................(b) LewisEdmunds(5) 3 50
(David Thompson) *hld up: rdn 3f out: sn wknd* **7/2**[3]

00-5 **5** 14 **Duke Of Sonning**[13] 1870 5-9-3 **63** ...............................(b) DuranFentiman 7 33
(Shaun Harris) *led: rdn whn hdd over 3f out: wknd over 2f out* **50/1**

05-0 **6** 35 **Nashville (IRE)**[7] 3340 8-8-9 **55** ............................................. JasonHart 2
(Andrew Crook) *trckd ldr: lost pl over 7f out: sn bhd: t.o fnl 4f* **20/1**

25-6 **7** 10 **Kisumu**[30] 2549 5-9-1 **61** ........................................................ JackGarritty 5
(Micky Hammond) *midfield: rdn 4f out: wknd 3f out: t.o* **12/1**

3m 40.14s (8.14) **Going Correction** +0.40s/f (Good) 7 Ran SP% **112.5**
Speed ratings (Par 103): **95,92,91,84,77 60,55**
CSF £6.92 CT £25.90 TOTE £3.00: £1.60, £1.50; EX 8.00 Trifecta £30.20.
**Owner** New Approach Racing Limited **Bred** Jane Schosberg **Trained** Carrutherstown, D'fries & G'way

**FOCUS**
A very ordinary staying handicap. The winner improved again.

## 3567 TOTEPOOL LIKE US ON FACEBOOK H'CAP 7f 6y
**4:35** (4:35) (Class 4) (0-80,81) 4-Y-O+ **£5,175** (£1,540; £769; £384) **Stalls** Low

Form RPR
0136 **1** **Showboating (IRE)**[12] 3144 9-8-11 **75** ...................... LewisEdmunds(5) 8 85
(John Balding) *hld up in tch: rdn and hdwy 2f out: chal appr fnl f: kpt on: led at post* **7/2**[2]

216- **2** hd **Gilmer (IRE)**[235] 7443 6-8-5 **70** ow1 ........................ DanielleMooney(7) 5 79
(James Ewart) *hld up: racd keenly: rdn and gd hdwy over 1f out: chal appr fnl f: led 75yds out: pushed out: hdd post* **10/1**

4005 **3** 1½ **Young John (IRE)**[18] 2922 4-9-8 **81** ............................... TonyHamilton 3 85
(Richard Fahey) *trckd ldrs: rdn over 2f out: led narrowly over 1f out: hdd 75yds out: no ex* **10/3**[1]

2500 **4** 4½ **Tellovoi (IRE)**[14] 3095 9-8-13 **72** ........................................ SamJames 9 64
(Richard Guest) *led: rdn over 2f out: hdd over 1f out: wknd fnl f* **9/1**

54-0 **5** 1¾ **The Hooded Claw (IRE)**[101] 971 6-8-12 **71** ...................(p) KevinStott 4 59
(Patrick Morris) *prom: rdn over 2f out: wknd fnl f* **15/2**

30-6 **6** 1 **Market Choice (IRE)**[41] 2184 4-9-0 **73** ......................... AntonioFresu 10 58
(Tracy Waggott) *chsd ldrs: rdn over 2f out: wknd fnl f* **12/1**

00-0 **7** ½ **Lil Sophella (IRE)**[22] 2805 8-8-12 **78** ............................. PaulaMuir(7) 7 62
(Patrick Holmes) *s.i.s: a in rr* **17/2**

0023 **8** nk **Kingsley Klarion (IRE)**[3] 3471 4-9-1 **74** ............................... JasonHart 2 57
(Mark Johnston) *dwlt: hld up: hdwy and in tch over 3f out: rdn over 2f out: wknd over 1f out* **4/1**[3]

1m 29.28s (2.28) **Going Correction** +0.40s/f (Good) 8 Ran SP% **114.4**
Speed ratings (Par 105): **102,101,100,94,92 91,91,90**
CSF £37.79 CT £126.14 TOTE £4.00: £1.20, £2.80, £1.70; EX 40.00 Trifecta £206.10.
**Owner** M & Mrs L Cooke & A McCabe **Bred** Crone Stud Farms Ltd **Trained** Scrooby, S Yorks

**FOCUS**
A modest handicap, run at a sound pace. The winner's best turf form since Septermber 2015.

## 3568 COLLECT TOTEPOOL WINNINGS AT BETFRED SHOPS MEDIAN AUCTION MAIDEN STKS 5f 212y
**5:10** (5:11) (Class 6) 3-4-Y-O **£2,587** (£770; £384; £192) **Stalls** Low

Form RPR
2323 **1** **Benjamin Thomas (IRE)**[2] 3493 3-9-5 75 .........................(v) JasonHart 3 76
(John Quinn) *mde all: pushed along over 1f out: rdn clr ins fnl f: easily* **30/100**[1]

50 **2** 8 **Granny Roz**[19] 2898 3-9-0 0 ............................................... JackGarritty 5 47
(David Barron) *chsd ldr: rdn 2f out: one pce and no ch w wnr fnl f* **7/2**[2]

0 **3** 3 **Jennies Gem**[19] 2887 4-9-13 0 ............................................. KevinStott 1 45
(Ollie Pears) *chsd ldr: rdn over 2f out: sn one pce in 3rd* **33/1**

35 4 4 1/2 **Yorkshire Rover**[18] 2924 3-8-12 0.................................. KevinLundie(7) 8 30
(David Brown) *hld up: pushed along 3f out: rdn over 1f out: nvr threatened* **25/1**
5 3 1/2 **Snoring** 3-9-5 0.................................. SamJames 6 19
(John Davies) *slowly away: sn outpcd in rr: minor late hdwy* **12/1**[3]
-606 6 shd **Ivy Matilda**[28] 2627 4-9-5 38.................................(t[1]) NathanEvans(3) 4 16
(Colin Teague) *midfield: sn pushed along: wknd fnl 2f* **125/1**
0 7 3 1/4 **Pipers Way**[12] 3150 3-9-2 0.................................. SammyJoBell(3) 10 9
(Richard Fahey) *dwlt: hld up: nvr threatened* **14/1**
8 nk **Dandys Denouement** 3-9-0 0.............................(h[1]) MeganNicholls(5) 9 8
(Brian Ellison) *slowly away: a in rr* **14/1**

1m 15.84s (2.24) **Going Correction** +0.40s/f (Good)
**WFA** 3 from 4yo 8lb **8 Ran SP% 127.8**
Speed ratings (Par 101): **101,90,86,80,75 75,71,70**
CSF £2.23 TOTE £1.30: £1.10, £1.30, £7.10; EX 2.60 Trifecta £31.00.
**Owner** Hart Inn I **Bred** Frank Dunne **Trained** Settrington, N Yorks

**FOCUS**
With World Power a non-runner this was weak maiden. Few got involved. The winner is rated to this year's mark.
T/Plt: £49.20 to a £1 stake. Pool: £43,177.29 - 640.20 winning units. T/Qpdt: £25.00 to a £1 stake. Pool: £2,135.16 - 63.06 winning units. **Andrew Sheret**

# 3421 CHEPSTOW (L-H)
## Saturday, June 10

**OFFICIAL GOING: Soft**
Wind: slight and variable Weather: overcast, rain from race 3

## 3569 SOUTH WALES ARGUS H'CAP 5f 16y
**5:40** (5:43) (Class 6) (0-55,63) 3-Y-0+ **£2,587** (£770; £384; £192) **Stalls** Centre

Form RPR
-005 1 **Foxford**[17] 2969 6-9-2 50.................................. RobHornby 14 58
(Patrick Chamings) *trckd ldr stands' side and in 2nd overall: rdn to ld 1f out: pushed out* **11/2**[3]
4423 2 1 **Mr Chuckles (IRE)**[3] 3469 4-9-1 52.....................(p) CharlieBennett(3) 13 56
(Daniel Mark Loughnane) *trckd ldrs stands' side: rdn over 2f out: chsd wnr ins fnl f: r.o* **7/2**[1]
-466 3 1 1/2 **Stopdworldnletmeof**[20] 2853 3-8-2 46 oh1.............(v[1]) HollieDoyle(3) 12 42
(David Flood) *led on stands' side and overall: rdn 2f out: hdd 1f out: no ex and lost 2nd ins fnl f* **8/1**
0002 4 1 **Diamond Vine (IRE)**[24] 2724 9-8-12 46.....................(p) SamHitchcott 11 41
(Ronald Harris) *s.i.s: towards rr on stands' side: drvn over 3f out: r.o fnl f: nrst fin* **20/1**
0-00 5 nk **Diminutive (IRE)**[5] 3391 5-9-3 51.............................(p) TrevorWhelan 16 45
(Grace Harris) *chsd ldrs stands' side: rdn over 2f out: kpt on but nvr able to chal* **20/1**
606 6 1 **Clever Lady (IRE)**[33] 2463 3-8-2 46 oh1........................ NoelGarbutt(3) 8 34+
(David Evans) *chsd ldrs far side: tacked over to stands' side 1/2-way: drvn 2f out: kpt on but nvr able to chal* **25/1**
0-43 7 1 **Jaganory (IRE)**[8] 3280 5-9-3 56.................................(p) MitchGodwin(5) 3 43+
(Christopher Mason) *trckd ldrs far side: rdn to ld gp 1f out: kpt on but hld by those on other side: 1st in gp* **5/1**[2]
500- 8 hd **Tally's Song**[224] 7694 4-8-12 46 oh1.................................(p) JohnFahy 15 32
(Grace Harris) *towards rr on stands' side: gng wl enough whn nt clr run over 1f out: shkn up and kpt on fnl f* **66/1**
0-00 9 nk **Bushwise (IRE)**[26] 2675 4-9-4 52.............................(p) CharlesBishop 4 37+
(Milton Bradley) *chsd ldrs on far side: rdn over 2f out: kpt on same pce: 2nd in gp* **20/1**
1536 10 1/2 **Teepee Time**[33] 2453 4-9-0 48.................................. RobertTart 6 32+
(Michael Mullineaux) *led far side gp but a few l off the pce overall: rdn and hung rt 2f out: hdd on side 1f out: no ex: 3rd in gp* **14/1**
4035 11 nk **Blistering Dancer (IRE)**[38] 2298 7-8-7 46........................ GeorgeWood(5) 1 28+
(Tony Carroll) *cl up on far side: rdn over 2f out: wknd fnl f: 4th in gp* **8/1**
330 12 hd **Louis Vee (IRE)**[24] 2732 9-8-5 46 oh1........................(v[1]) RossaRyan(7) 5 28+
(John O'Shea) *awkward s: a towards rr on far side: 5th in gp* **12/1**
-350 13 1/2 **Majestic Girl (IRE)**[12] 3137 4-8-6 47.................................. TobyEley(7) 10 27
(Steve Flook) *dwlt: racd alone in centre and sn drvn along: a in rr* **16/1**
0060 14 3 1/4 **Arizona Snow**[24] 2724 5-8-5 46 oh1.............................(p) FinleyMarsh(7) 7 14+
(Ronald Harris) *chsd ldrs far side: rdn 2f out: edgd rt and grad wknd: last in gp* **14/1**

1m 0.1s (0.80) **Going Correction** +0.425s/f (Yiel)
**WFA** 3 from 4yo+ 7lb **14 Ran SP% 123.0**
Speed ratings (Par 101): **110,108,106,104,103 102,100,100,99,99 98,98,97,92**
CSF £23.65 CT £142.16 TOTE £7.00: £3.00, £2.40, £3.20; EX 32.10 Trifecta £213.20.
**Owner** The Foxford House Partnership **Bred** Mrs A K H Ooi **Trained** Baughurst, Hants

**FOCUS**
A cloudy evening with and a temperature of 19C. No less than 28mm of rain had fallen on the track in the four preceding days, including 14mm in the previous 24 hours and a further 1mm overnight. A very modest sprint handicap to start. Seven raced stands' side and six of them filled the first six places. The winner is rated close to last year's best.

## 3570 HAPPY BIRTHDAY PAUL FREEMAN / EBF NOVICE STKS 5f 16y
**6:10** (6:12) (Class 5) 2-Y-0 **£3,234** (£962; £481; £240) **Stalls** Centre

Form RPR
54 1 **Straight Ash (IRE)**[26] 2691 2-8-13 0.................................. HollieDoyle(3) 5 71+
(Richard Hannon) *awkward s: chsd ldrs: hung lft and hdwy on outer 1/2-way: drvn to ld 1f out: edgd rt: comf on top fnl 100yds* **6/4**[1]
0 2 2 **Frostbite**[8] 3305 2-9-2 0.................................. JohnFahy 8 64
(Eve Johnson Houghton) *dwlt: racd keenly and sn trcking first two: shkn up 2f out: sn ev ch: rdn fnl f: no ex fnl 100yds* **13/8**[2]
04 3 hd **Zain Smarts (IRE)**[16] 2987 2-8-8 0.................................. HectorCrouch(3) 7 58
(David Evans) *led: hung lft fr 2f out: hdd 1f out: r.o* **6/1**[3]
06 4 2 3/4 **Owen The Law**[11] 3165 2-9-2 0.................................. SteveDrowne 1 53
(David Evans) *trckd ldrs: rdn and lost 2nd 2f out: wknd fnl f* **14/1**
0 5 2 3/4 **Raven's Girl**[18] 2910 2-8-6 0.................................. GeorgeWood(5) 4 38
(Michael Madgwick) *dwlt: rdn 1/2-way: a in last* **50/1**
U **Rivas Rob Roy** 2-9-2 0.................................. CharlesBishop 3
(John Gallagher) *hung lft sn after leaving stalls: bucked several times and uns rdr after 100yds* **7/1**

1m 1.94s (2.64) **Going Correction** +0.425s/f (Yiel) **6 Ran SP% 113.5**
Speed ratings (Par 93): **95,91,91,87,82**
CSF £4.34 TOTE £2.00: £1.10, £1.50; EX 4.50 Trifecta £10.40.
**Owner** Palmer-Brown, Ensor, Blunt, Sullivan Ltd **Bred** Moyglare Stud Farm Ltd **Trained** East Everleigh, Wilts

**FOCUS**
A modest novices' sprint but won in fair style by an improver. The third and fourth and the time help pin the level.

## 3571 PERTEMPS NETWORK GROUP MAIDEN AUCTION STKS 7f 16y
**6:45** (6:46) (Class 5) 3-Y-O **£3,234** (£962; £481; £240) **Stalls** Centre

Form RPR
0-5 1 **Madeleine Bond**[17] 2957 3-9-0 0.................................. FergusSweeney 2 78
(Henry Candy) *mde all: rdn 2f out: sn clr: hung lft fnl f: easily* **2/1**[2]
0- 2 5 **Amenta (IRE)**[213] 7867 3-8-9 0.................................. PaddyPilley(5) 1 65
(Roger Charlton) *t.k.h in 4th: clsd into 2nd 1/2-way: drvn 2f out: unable qck and sn lft bhd by wnr: hung lft ins fnl f* **5/1**
5 3 2 1/2 **Jinkie Pink (IRE)**[50] 1947 3-9-0 0.................................. ThomasBrown 3 59
(Ed Walker) *hld up in last: stmbld jst over 4f out: rdn over 3f out: wnt modest 3rd 2f out: kpt on same pce* **15/8**[1]
-205 4 15 **La Guapita**[88] 1192 3-9-0 70.................................(h[1]) RobHornby 5 20
(Andrew Balding) *trckd ldrs: shkn up over 2f out: wknd qckly: wnt poor 4th towards fin* **4/1**[3]
00-0 5 hd **Money In My Pocket (IRE)**[14] 3134 3-8-7 63.........(p) RhiainIngram(7) 4 19
(Harry Dunlop) *trckd wnr to 1/2-way: rdn over 2f out: sn wknd: lost poor 4th towards fin* **14/1**

1m 25.96s (2.76) **Going Correction** +0.425s/f (Yiel) **5 Ran SP% 111.4**
Speed ratings (Par 99): **101,95,92,75,75**
CSF £12.15 TOTE £2.80: £1.50, £2.10; EX 12.80 Trifecta £34.90.
**Owner** Candy, Pritchard & Thomas **Bred** Hellwood Stud Farm **Trained** Kingston Warren, Oxon

**FOCUS**
Overcast skies made way for rain ahead of this modest maiden. The winner made all and although she won by a wide margin, she will not have many easier opportunities. Hard form to rate.

## 3572 MICHAEL MAINE MEMORIAL H'CAP 7f 16y
**7:15** (7:15) (Class 4) (0-85,87) 4-Y-O+ **£5,175** (£1,540; £769; £384) **Stalls** Centre

Form RPR
-254 1 **Goring (GER)**[7] 3330 5-9-5 83.................................. JohnFahy 3 90
(Eve Johnson Houghton) *trckd ldrs: led 2f out: sn shkn up: drvn and edgd rt fnl f: jst hld on* **5/1**[2]
-030 2 hd **Fox Trotter (IRE)**[15] 3030 5-8-12 83.................................. JordanUys(7) 4 89
(Brian Meehan) *hld up: carried lft and hdwy over 1f out: r.o wl u.p fnl f: jst failed* **6/1**[3]
0020 3 2 **Evanescent (IRE)**[17] 2961 8-8-2 73.................................. AledBeech(7) 1 74
(Tony Carroll) *led tl rdn and hdd 2f out: one pce* **50/1**
-030 4 1/2 **Ower Fly**[16] 3003 4-9-6 87.................................. HollieDoyle(3) 6 87
(Richard Hannon) *mainly chsd ldr tl rdn and lost 2nd over 2f out: kpt on same pce after* **6/1**[3]
1 5 2 **Alaadel**[21] 2819 4-8-13 77.................................. DaneO'Neill 5 72
(William Haggas) *s.i.s: hld up and tk sltly t.k.h: rdn over 2f out: edgd lft and sme hdwy over 1f out: no imp fnl f* **1/1**[1]
2-00 6 nk **Peak Storm**[8] 3282 8-8-13 77.................................(p) FergusSweeney 9 71
(John O'Shea) *chsd ldrs: briefly in 2nd 1/2-way: drvn over 2f out: one pce whn edgd rt over 1f out* **20/1**
0-00 7 shd **Cincuenta Pasos (IRE)**[4] 3424 6-9-4 85.............. CallumShepherd(3) 8 79
(Joseph Tuite) *chsd ldrs: rdn 2f out: wknd ins fnl f* **12/1**
-060 8 10 **Winklemann (IRE)**[17] 2960 5-8-12 76.............................(b[1]) DanielMuscutt 2 44
(John Flint) *dwlt: bhd: c over to r alone on stands' side after 3f: drvn over 2f out: nvr on terms* **12/1**

1m 26.15s (2.95) **Going Correction** +0.425s/f (Yiel) **8 Ran SP% 117.3**
Speed ratings (Par 105): **100,99,97,96,94 94,94,82**
CSF £35.84 CT £1345.33 TOTE £6.00: £1.90, £1.60, £10.70; EX 33.70 Trifecta £1090.90.
**Owner** G C Stevens **Bred** Westminster Race Horses Gmbh **Trained** Blewbury, Oxon

**FOCUS**
A fair handicap run at a decent pace fir the conditions. The winner came up the centre, with the runner-up widest of all up the far rail. The form is open to question but the winner is rated to his best.

## 3573 PICKWICK BOOKMAKERS H'CAP 6f 16y
**7:45** (7:47) (Class 5) (0-75,78) 4-Y-O+ **£3,234** (£962; £481; £240) **Stalls** Centre

Form RPR
6-01 1 **Kinglami**[3] 3453 8-8-13 66.................................(p) FergusSweeney 7 74
(John O'Shea) *hld up: rdn and hdwy 2f out: chsd ldr ins fnl f: r.o to ld post* **5/1**[3]
-02 2 nse **Spirit Of Rosanna**[25] 2709 5-8-7 60.........................(tp) AdamBeschizza 6 67
(Steph Hollinshead) *led far side and overall: rdn 2f out: r.o wl u.p: hdd post* **4/1**[2]
35-0 3 3/4 **Champagne Bob**[14] 3084 5-8-1 57.................................. HollieDoyle(3) 13 62
(Richard Price) *trckd one other on stands' side and towards rr overall: rdn and hdwy 1/2-way: hung lft 2f out: r.o fnl f: tk 3rd nr fin* **10/1**
3010 4 1/2 **Picket Line**[28] 2608 5-9-7 74.................................. TimmyMurphy 14 77
(Geoffrey Deacon) *led one other on stands' side but towards rr overall: shkn up and hdwy 2f out: rdn and ch fnl f: unable qck and lost 3rd nr fin* **14/1**
5041 5 hd **Satchville Flyer**[4] 3424 6-9-4 78 6ex.................... KatherineGlenister(7) 5 80
(David Evans) *t.k.h in midfield: clsd to chse ldrs 1/2-way: rdn 2f out: unable qck fnl f* **7/2**[1]
0216 6 nk **Indian Affair**[14] 3084 7-8-12 65.................................(bt) CharlesBishop 2 66
(Milton Bradley) *chsd ldr: drvn 2f out: lost 2nd ins fnl f: no ex towards fin* **10/1**
-500 7 3/4 **Vincentti (IRE)**[4] 3424 7-9-5 72.................................(p) SamHitchcott 3 71
(Ronald Harris) *s.i.s: sn chsng ldrs: rdn over 2f out: kpt on same pce fnl f* **33/1**
-003 8 1 1/2 **Oeil De Tigre (FR)**[40] 2229 6-9-0 67.................................. GeorgeDowning 8 61
(Tony Carroll) *s.i.s: towards rr: rdn and sme hdwy over 2f out: grad wknd fnl f* **8/1**
60-0 9 1 1/2 **Fantasy Justifier (IRE)**[25] 2709 6-8-5 65.................... FinleyMarsh(7) 11 54
(Ronald Harris) *hld up: shkn up over 1f out: drvn and no hdwy fnl f* **14/1**
4216 10 2 1/2 **Air Of York (IRE)**[1] 3532 5-9-1 68.............................(p) DanielMuscutt 10 49
(John Flint) *prom: rdn over 2f out: edgd rt and wknd over 1f out* **12/1**
11 2 1/4 **Windsorlot (IRE)**[78] 1350 4-8-6 59.................................. RobHornby 9 33
(Tony Carroll) *hld up: last and rdn 1/2-way: no hdwy* **22/1**
40-0 12 7 **Posh Bounty**[10] 3214 6-9-4 71.................................(h) JimmyQuinn 1 23
(Paul Burgoyne) *reluctant to go to post: prom: rdn 1/2-way: wknd wl over 1f out* **16/1**

1m 14.85s (2.85) **Going Correction** +0.425s/f (Yiel) **12 Ran SP% 122.4**
Speed ratings (Par 103): **98,97,96,96,96 95,94,92,90,87 84,74**
CSF £26.20 CT £202.50 TOTE £6.50: £2.10, £1.90, £3.00; EX 27.40 Trifecta £233.10.
**Owner** Pete Smith & Phil Hart Racing **Bred** Cheveley Park Stud Ltd **Trained** Elton, Gloucs

**FOCUS**
A run-of-the-mill sprint handicap and truly-run for the conditions. The winner was close to his Hamilton form.

## 3574 GSM AUTOMOTIVE BRECON Q1 AWARD H'CAP 1m 4f
**8:15** (8:16) (Class 5) (0-75,75) 4-Y-0+ **£3,234** (£962; £481; £240) **Stalls** Low

Form RPR
-521 **1** **Multigifted**[22] 2781 4-8-5 **64**........................................(t) GeorgeWood(5) 3 76+
(Michael Madgwick) *trckd ldr who wnt clr after 4f: clsd 4f out: led 3f out: rdn clr 2f out: styd on strly: eased towards fin* **9/4**[1]
0/5 **2** *7* **Iniesta (IRE)**[19] 2909 6-9-3 **71**........................................ TimmyMurphy 6 70
(Fergal O'Brien) *chsd ldrs: rdn over 2f out: kpt on same pce to go 2nd ins fnl f: no ch w wnr* **5/2**[2]
4-42 **3** *2 ½* **Glens Wobbly**[31] 2512 9-8-12 **73**.................................... JordanUys(7) 5 68
(Jonathan Geake) *chsd along leaving stalls to ld: clr after 4f tl reduced ld 4f out: rdn and hdd 3f out: no ch w wnr fr 2f out: wknd and lost 2nd ins fnl f* **9/2**
0-06 **4** *1 ¼* **Nabhan**[14] 3067 5-9-7 **75**..............................................(p) AdamBeschizza 2 68
(Bernard Llewellyn) *hld up: hdwy 4f out: one pce and no threat fnl 2f* **4/1**[3]
2220 **5** *nk* **Mazaaher**[15] 3036 7-8-11 **72**................................ KatherineGlenister(7) 1 65
(David Evans) *hld up: rdn 4f out: plugged on same pce* **15/2**
332- **6** *49* **Kaisan**[324] 4566 4-9-2 **70**..............................................(t[1]) DanielMuscutt 4
(Bernard Llewellyn) *chsd ldrs: rdn 4f out: wknd qckly: eased and t.o* **16/1**

2m 45.68s (6.68) **Going Correction** +0.675s/f (Yiel) **6 Ran SP% 115.2**
Speed ratings (Par 103): **104,99,97,96,96 63**
CSF £8.53 TOTE £3.70: £2.30, £1.60; EX 11.10 Trifecta £33.30.
**Owner** Mrs L N Harmes **Bred** Mrs L N Harmes **Trained** Denmead, Hants

**FOCUS**
A fair handicap run at a solid pace for the conditions and a runaway winner who improved again.

## 3575 CARDIFF AIRPORT H'CAP 1m 4f
**8:45** (8:46) (Class 6) (0-55,55) 4-Y-0+ **£2,587** (£770; £384; £192) **Stalls** Low

Form RPR
00-0 **1** **Grams And Ounces**[43] 924 10-9-4 **52**......................(tp) TimmyMurphy 8 62
(Grace Harris) *towards rr: hdwy 1/2-way: c stands' side ent st over 4f out: led 3f out: rdn 2f out: styd on wl* **16/1**
06-0 **2** *2 ½* **Lady Lunchalot (USA)**[10] 3208 7-9-6 **54**...................... SamHitchcott 14 60
(Polly Gundry) *hld up: hdwy 4f out: sn c stands' side: drvn to chse wnr over 1f out: edgd lft and no imp fnl f* **8/1**
**3** *7* **Miskin**[188] 8-9-7 **55**........................................................ RobHornby 2 51
(Robert Stephens) *midfield: clsd 4f out: rdn and chsd wnr over 2f out: lost 2nd over 1f out: one pce* **25/1**
3-05 **4** *1 ¼* **Eugenic**[15] 3028 6-9-3 **51**................................................ RyanTate 13 45
(Rod Millman) *towards rr: nt clr run over 3f out: sn clsd u.p: styd on to go 4th ins fnl f* **10/1**[3]
6630 **5** *1* **Eben Dubai (IRE)**[4] 3428 5-9-6 **54**................................ CharlesBishop 16 46
(Tracey Barfoot-Saunt) *led tl rdn and hdd 3f out: lost 2nd over 1f out: grad wknd* **20/1**
0-03 **6** *3 ¼* **Hint Of Grey (IRE)**[9] 2281 4-9-2 **55**..........................(h) GeorgeWood(5) 7 43
(Don Cantillon) *midfield: drvn 4f out: one pce and no imp fnl 2f* **5/4**[1]
60/2 **7** *½* **Granny Anne (IRE)**[54] 1933 9-8-8 **47** oh1 ow1............ PaddyPilley(5) 10 34
(Natalie Lloyd-Beavis) *midfield: rdn 4f out: kpt on one pce and nvr able to chal* **50/1**
2/00 **8** *2 ½* **Jeremy's Jet (IRE)**[39] 2276 6-9-7 **55**.......................... GeorgeDowning 6 38
(Tony Carroll) *midfield: rdn to chse ldrs 3f out: wknd 2f out* **12/1**
0-60 **9** *½* **Ring Eye (IRE)**[15] 3026 9-9-6 **54**.............................. FergusSweeney 11 36
(John O'Shea) *s.s: in rr tl modest hdwy u.p fnl 2f* **12/1**
06/5 **10** *¾* **Mesti Boleh**[33] 2467 6-9-4 **55**................................ CallumShepherd(3) 4 36
(Michael Scudamore) *hld up: sme hdwy u.p 3f out: wknd over 1f out* **16/1**
000- **11** *2 ¾* **Outback Guy (IRE)**[285] 5971 4-8-9 **46** oh1............ CharlieBennett(3) 12 23
(Daniel Mark Loughnane) *trckd wnr: lost 2nd 4f out: wknd over 2f out* **25/1**
000 **12** *2 ½* **Tsundoku (IRE)**[66] 1556 6-9-1 **49**.......................................... JohnFahy 9 22
(Alexandra Dunn) *s.s: sn detached in last: passed a few btn rivals late* **12/1**
550 **13** *3 ¾* **Brooke's Point**[17] 2964 4-8-5 **46** oh1.........................(p) RossaRyan(7) 17 14
(Neil Mulholland) *chsd ldrs: rdn over 3f out: sn wknd* **8/1**[2]
4044 **14** *nse* **The Greedy Boy**[19] 2891 4-8-9 **46** oh1........................(bt) HollieDoyle(3) 1 14
(Steve Flook) *chsd ldrs: rdn 4f out: grad wknd* **25/1**
445 **15** *11* **The Juggler**[10] 3208 4-9-3 **51**............................................ JimmyQuinn 3 2
(William Knight) *midfield: rdn 5f out: sn wknd: eased over 2f out: t.o* **7/1**
0-00 **16** *14* **Golden Cape**[12] 3148 4-8-12 **46** oh1..............................(p[1]) RobertTart 5
(Michael Mullineaux) *chsd ldrs: rdn 4f out: sn wknd: t.o* **50/1**
40 **17** *38* **Hong Kong Joe**[60] 1698 7-9-0 **48**.................................(v) SteveDrowne 15
(Lydia Richards) *a towards rr: drvn and lost tch 4f out: t.o* **20/1**

2m 46.91s (7.91) **Going Correction** +0.675s/f (Yiel) **17 Ran SP% 136.0**
Speed ratings (Par 101): **100,98,93,92,92 90,89,88,87,87 85,83,81,81,73 64,39**
CSF £583.75 CT £14786.75 TOTE £26.80: £4.30, £5.90, £6.40, £2.60; EX 385.30 Trifecta £1090.10.
**Owner** Grace Harris Racing **Bred** Brook Stud Bloodstock Ltd **Trained** Shirenewton, Monmouthshire

**FOCUS**
The visibility wasn't great by this stage. A very modest handicap but the pace was generous for the conditions and they finished well strung out, with the front two drawing clear. Despite this, the form looks open to question.
T/Plt: £107.30 to a £1 stake. Pool: £64,206.88 - 436.74 winning units. T/Qpdt: £50.00 to a £1 stake. Pool: £5,361.30 - 79.19 winning units. **Richard Lowther**

# 3062 CHESTER (L-H)
### Saturday, June 10

**OFFICIAL GOING: Good to soft changing to soft after race 2 (2.35)**
Wind: breezy, behind straight Weather: Mild, overcast with showers

## 3576 HALEWOOD WINES & SPIRITS NOVICE MEDIAN AUCTION STKS (PLUS 10 RACE) 6f 17y
**2:00** (2:02) (Class 4) 2-Y-0 **£6,225** (£1,864; £932; £466; £233; £117) **Stalls** Low

Form RPR
4 **1** **Armum (IRE)**[12] 3135 2-8-11 0........................................ DougieCostello 3 79
(Jamie Osborne) *trckd ldrs: 2 l 3rd over 1f out: rdn and chal wd appr fnl f: sn led: r.o wl* **5/1**
6 **2** *½* **Carouse (IRE)**[28] 2607 2-9-2 0............................................ OisinMurphy 2 83
(Andrew Balding) *chsd ldr: led over 1f out: sn rdn and passed by wnr: rallied u.p last 100yds but hld* **3/1**[2]
0 **3** *5* **Quayside**[11] 3169 2-8-13 0.......................................... AdamMcNamara(3) 1 68
(Richard Fahey) *mid-div: drvn over 1f out: rdn and r.o into 3rd fnl f* **9/2**[3]
1 **4** *4 ½* **Awsaaf**[11] 3187 2-9-8 0.................................................... DaneO'Neill 6 60
(Simon Crisford) *led: pushed along 2f out: hdd over 1f out: rdn and wknd* **2/1**[1]
002 **5** *hd* **Amazing Alice**[11] 3174 2-8-8 0.............................(p[1]) KieranShoemark(3) 10 48
(Archie Watson) *slowly away: effrt on outer 1/2-way: rdn wl over 1f out: one pce fnl f* **12/1**
**6** *hd* **Footsteps Forever (IRE)** 2-8-11 0.................................. FrannyNorton 9 48+
(Mark Johnston) *slowly away and last early: sme late hdwy: nt knocked abt* **8/1**
**7** *hd* **Couldn't Could She** 2-8-11 0........................................ StevieDonohoe 8 47
(Adam West) *in rr early: drvn 2f out: rdn over 1f out: one pce* **50/1**
00 **8** *1 ½* **Saria**[10] 3215 2-8-11 0.......................................................... MartinLane 5 43
(Daniel Mark Loughnane) *in rr: pushed along 2f out: no imp* **100/1**
**9** *7* **Gabrial The Devil (IRE)** 2-9-2 0........................................ DavidNolan 7 27
(David O'Meara) *mid-div: effrt 2f out: drvn over 1f out: fdd* **16/1**
0 **10** *11* **Renton**[14] 3066 2-9-2 0............................................................ NeilFarley 4
(Tony Coyle) *trckd ldrs: drvn 2f out: lost grnd qckly over 1f out* **40/1**

1m 16.89s (3.09) **Going Correction** +0.525s/f (Yiel) **10 Ran SP% 123.3**
Speed ratings (Par 95): **100,99,92,86,86 86,85,83,74,59**
CSF £21.63 TOTE £4.50: £1.30, £1.50, £2.30; EX 30.50 Trifecta £102.00.
**Owner** J A Osborne **Bred** Tally-Ho Stud **Trained** Upper Lambourn, Berks

**FOCUS**
The going was good to soft (soft in places) following 12mm of rain since midnight. After riding in the opener David Nolan, Martin Lane, Dane O'Neill and Oisin Murphy all called the ground soft. An interesting novice in which the first two pulled clear, and they finished quite strung out.

## 3577 JJ WHITLEY FILLIES' H'CAP 7f 127y
**2:35** (2:36) (Class 4) (0-80,80) 4-Y-0+ **£6,225** (£1,864; £932; £466; £233; £117) **Stalls** Low

Form RPR
-634 **1** **Alpine Dream (IRE)**[14] 3095 4-8-10 **69**..............................(b) PJMcDonald 2 76
(Tim Easterby) *mid-div: hdwy gng wl over 1f out: led and rdn ent fnl f: immediately jnd by 2nd: forged clr u.p last 100yds* **5/2**[1]
4212 **2** *1* **Forever A Lady (IRE)**[9] 3241 4-9-1 **74**.......................... DougieCostello 6 79
(Keith Dalgleish) *racd wd: hld up: pushed along over 1f out: hdwy and jnd wnr jst ins fnl f: rdn and no ex last 100yds* **11/2**[2]
-404 **3** *1 ¼* **Bush Beauty (IRE)**[12] 3147 6-8-6 **65**.................................... NeilFarley 4 68+
(Eric Alston) *hld up in last: effrt whn n.m.r wl over 1f out: plld wd and r.o wl fnl f* **7/1**
4011 **4** *½* **Moi Aussie**[17] 2976 4-8-4 **63**............................................(p) DannyBrock 3 64
(Michael Appleby) *led: pushed along over 1f out: rdn and sn hdd: wknd ins fnl f* **6/1**[3]
-424 **5** *½* **Arcane Dancer (IRE)**[10] 3203 4-8-2 **61**..........................(p) KieranO'Neill 7 61
(Lawrence Mullaney) *trckd ldrs: drvn 2f out: rdn and one pce ins fnl f* **8/1**
530- **6** *2 ¾* **American Hustle (IRE)**[268] 6502 5-8-3 **62**..................(p) FrannyNorton 1 56
(Brian Ellison) *trckd ldrs: n.m.r and hmpd over 1f out: lost pl: no ch after: position accepted* **11/2**[2]
1410 **7** *2 ¼* **Bahamian Bird**[14] 3095 4-9-4 **80**................................ AdamMcNamara(3) 8 68
(Richard Fahey) *chsd ldr: drvn 2f out: rdn over 1f out: wknd* **11/2**[2]

1m 36.68s (2.88) **Going Correction** +0.525s/f (Yiel) **7 Ran SP% 112.6**
Speed ratings (Par 102): **106,105,103,103,102 100,97**
CSF £15.89 CT £82.80 TOTE £2.40: £1.20, £3.30; EX 11.40 Trifecta £85.70.
**Owner** David & Yvonne Blunt **Bred** West Lodge Stud **Trained** Great Habton, N Yorks
■ Stewards' Enquiry : Adam McNamara four-day ban: used whip with excessive force (29th June - 2nd July)

**FOCUS**
The going was changed to soft. Not a bad fillies' handicap in which they went a sound gallop. They were bunched at the furlong marker, causing some interference, but the first three home came from behind. The winner has been rated close to form, and the runner-up to her mark.

## 3578 LIVERPOOL GIN H'CAP 7f 127y
**3:10** (3:10) (Class 3) (0-90,87) 3-Y-0 **£12,450** (£3,728; £1,864; £932; £466; £234) **Stalls** Low

Form RPR
2-13 **1** **Starlight Romance (IRE)**[24] 2739 3-9-3 **83**.......... AdamMcNamara(3) 5 89
(Richard Fahey) *mid-div: effrt over 1f out: hdwy u.p ent fnl f: r.o wl: led last few strides* **10/3**[1]
53-4 **2** *shd* **Vona (IRE)**[53] 1859 3-9-3 **87**.......................................... ConnorMurtagh(7) 2 92
(Richard Fahey) *trckd ldrs: pushed along 2f out: rdn to ld ins fnl f: r.o wl u.p: hdd last few strides* **10/1**
-025 **3** *1 ½* **Devil's Bridge (IRE)**[28] 2612 3-9-9 **86**.............................. KieranO'Neill 1 88
(Richard Hannon) *led: pushed along 2f out: rdn over 1f out: hdd ins fnl f: one pce* **5/1**[3]
1 **4** *1* **Casimiro (IRE)**[45] 2090 3-9-7 **87**.............................. KieranShoemark(3) 7 87
(Roger Charlton) *mid-div: drvn and hdwy on outer 2f out: hrd rdn and one pce fnl f* **4/1**[2]
3-14 **5** *1* **Itsakindamagic**[44] 2117 3-9-9 **86**..............................(t[1]) ThomasBrown 10 83+
(Andrew Balding) *t.k.h: hld up: hdwy on outer 2f out: rdn over 1f out: styd on fnl f: nvr nrr* **5/1**[3]
216- **6** *shd* **Roar (IRE)**[285] 5967 3-8-13 **76**................................................ MartinLane 9 73
(Brian Ellison) *mid-div: drvn 2f out: rdn over 1f out: one pce* **25/1**
61-4 **7** *5* **Subatomic**[19] 2894 3-9-0 **77**................................................ OisinMurphy 3 63
(Ralph Beckett) *hld up: effrt and drvn 2f out: no ex ent fnl f* **5/1**[3]
0-00 **8** *1 ¾* **The Amber Fort (USA)**[15] 3038 3-8-8 **71**.......................... PJMcDonald 11 53
(David O'Meara) *hld up: pushed along 2f out: no imp* **33/1**
030- **9** *9* **Lonely The Brave (IRE)**[248] 7073 3-9-3 **80**...................... FrannyNorton 8 41
(Mark Johnston) *chsd ldr: pushed along 2f out: wknd wl over 1f out: sn lost tch: eased* **16/1**

1m 36.64s (2.84) **Going Correction** +0.525s/f (Yiel) **9 Ran SP% 114.8**
Speed ratings (Par 103): **106,105,104,103,102 102,97,95,86**
CSF £37.31 CT £164.42 TOTE £5.20: £1.60, £4.50, £2.30; EX 47.90 Trifecta £162.30.
**Owner** Mrs H Steel **Bred** J F Tuthill **Trained** Musley Bank, N Yorks

**FOCUS**
A fair handicap, though it was robbed of the withdrawn favourite, which took some shine off. It paid to race handily. The third has been rated close to form.

## 3579 WILLOW WATER H'CAP 5f 15y
**3:45** (3:46) (Class 3) (0-95,90) 3-Y-0 **£9,337** (£2,796; £1,398; £699; £349; £175) **Stalls** Low

Form RPR
-532 **1** **Megan Lily (IRE)**[22] 2806 3-9-1 **87**.......................... AdamMcNamara(3) 2 92
(Richard Fahey) *trckd ldrs: effrt and rdn over 1f out: hdwy to ld ins fnl f: r.o wl u.p* **7/2**[2]

4403 **2** ½ **Poet's Society**[3] 3462 3-9-2 **85** FrannyNorton 1 88
(Mark Johnston) *disp ld tl hdd briefly over 1f out: sn rdn: rallied and r.o wl fnl f* **2/1**[1]

-014 **3** *nk* **Twizzell**[22] 2806 3-8-10 **79** PJMcDonald 4 81
(K R Burke) *hld up: pushed along 2f out: plld out to chal over 1f out: rdn and r.o ins fnl f: nvr nrr* **11/2**[3]

60- **4** ½ **Mayleaf Shine (IRE)**[286] 5940 3-9-6 **89** DougieCostello 5 89
(Iain Jardine) *hld up: hdwy wl over 1f out: swtchd to inner: rdn and r.o strly fnl f* **25/1**

61 **5** ½ **Impart**[3] 3462 3-9-3 **89** 6ex JoshDoyle(3) 6 86
(David O'Meara) *disp ld: led over 1f out: hrd rdn and hdd ins fnl f: no ex* **10/1**

51-6 **6** *3* **Rosabelle**[29] 2570 3-9-7 **90** StevieDonohoe 7 77
(Alan Bailey) *trckd ldrs: drvn 2f out: rdn over 1f out: no imp* **10/1**

22-1 **7** *2* **Tallinski (IRE)**[49] 1970 3-8-10 **79** MartinLane 3 59
(Brian Ellison) *hld up: drvn 2f out: sn struggling: nvr a factor* **7/1**

10-5 **8** *8* **Leontes**[80] 1311 3-9-6 **89** OisinMurphy 9 40
(Andrew Balding) *mid-div: pushed along 1/2-way: drvn and lost tch wl over 1f out: eased* **7/1**

1m 2.65s (1.65) **Going Correction** +0.525s/f (Yiel) **8** Ran SP% **118.0**
Speed ratings (Par 103): **107,106,105,104,104 99,96,83**
CSF £11.34 CT £37.68 TOTE £4.70: £2.10, £1.10, £2.60; EX 12.30 Trifecta £68.90.
**Owner** Nick Bradley Racing 1 **Bred** Irish National Stud **Trained** Musley Bank, N Yorks
■ Stewards' Enquiry : Franny Norton two-day ban: used whip above permitted level (Jun 25-26)
**FOCUS**
A fair sprint handicap in which the first two came from the lowest stalls. They went hard from the start. The runner-up has been rated close to his turf best.

## 3580 CRABBIE'S H'CAP — 1m 4f 63y
**4:20** (4:21) (Class 4) (0-85,86) 4-Y-0+
**£7,781** (£2,330; £1,165; £582; £291; £146) **Stalls** Low

Form RPR

-062 **1** **Miss Ranger (IRE)**[8] 3292 5-8-5 **69** FrannyNorton 4 76
(Brian Ellison) *mid-div: hdwy and drvn over 1f out: rdn to chal ins fnl f: r.o wl to ld last 100yds* **5/1**[3]

4114 **2** *1* **Monaco Rose**[15] 3033 4-8-3 **74** ConnorMurtagh(7) 2 79
(Richard Fahey) *trckd ldrs: hdwy to ld over 1f out: rdn fnl f: r.o but hdd last 100yds* **9/2**[2]

-044 **3** *1 ¼* **Marsh Pride**[19] 2906 5-9-6 **84** PJMcDonald 10 87
(K R Burke) *hld up: plenty to do 2f out: rdn and hdwy 1f out: r.o wl fnl f: nvr nrr* **10/1**

0-01 **4** ½ **Gabrial's Star**[11] 3190 8-9-5 **86** (p) AdamMcNamara(3) 7 88
(Richard Fahey) *hld up: drvn and hdwy over 1f out: rdn and r.o wl ins fnl f* **12/1**

1216 **5** *1* **Royal Flag**[35] 2386 7-8-8 **72** MartinLane 3 72
(Brian Ellison) *mid-div: effrt 2f out: brought wd over 1f out: r.o u.p fnl f* **11/1**

1633 **6** *1 ¾* **Modernism**[29] 2574 8-9-2 **80** (p) StevieDonohoe 1 78
(Ian Williams) *disp ld tl tk def advantage 4f out: pushed along 2f out: hdd wl over 1f out: rdn and wknd* **7/1**

1142 **7** *3 ½* **Luv U Whatever**[53] 1865 7-8-7 **71** WilliamCarson 6 63
(Michael Attwater) *trckd ldrs: reminders wl over 1f out: sn rdn and wknd* **22/1**

24-1 **8** *8* **St Mary's**[29] 2574 4-9-5 **83** OisinMurphy 5 62
(Andrew Balding) *mid-div: niggled 2f out: wknd qckly fr wl over 1f out* **2/1**[1]

15 **9** *3 ½* **Sean O'Casey (IRE)**[14] 3091 4-9-4 **82** TomMarquand 8 56
(Michael Appleby) *sweating: disp ld tl 4f out: drvn 2f out: wknd and eased* **11/1**

2m 45.21s (6.71) **Going Correction** +0.525s/f (Yiel) **9** Ran SP% **118.5**
Speed ratings (Par 105): **98,97,96,96,95 94,92,86,84**
CSF £28.58 CT £220.01 TOTE £6.30: £2.20, £1.20, £3.50; EX 35.10 Trifecta £233.50.
**Owner** Jane Greetham & Victoria Greetham **Bred** J F Tuthill **Trained** Norton, N Yorks
**FOCUS**
A good little middle-distance handicap featuring some in-form types. They didn't go flat out, and the gallop only picked up on the bend, though that didn't stop the winner coming from behind. The third has been rated close to her non-claiming best.

## 3581 WHITLEY NEILL GIN H'CAP — 6f 17y
**4:55** (4:56) (Class 4) (0-85,87) 4-Y-0+
**£7,781** (£2,330; £1,165; £582; £291; £146) **Stalls** Low

Form RPR

0-00 **1** **Dragon King (IRE)**[10] 3199 5-9-3 **81** (h) DougieCostello 1 89
(Iain Jardine) *mid-div: hdwy over 1f out: weaved way through to chal ent fnl f: rdn and led last 100yds: sn chal by runner-up: jst hld on* **9/1**

0650 **2** *shd* **Russian Realm**[10] 3199 7-9-3 **81** OisinMurphy 7 88
(Paul Midgley) *hld up: hdwy over 1f out: rdn and r.o strly fnl f: jst failed* **8/1**

2555 **3** *1 ½* **Tavener**[3] 3471 5-8-13 **77** (p) RoystonFfrench 4 79
(David C Griffiths) *2nd to 1/2-way where wnt on: drvn over 1f out: rdn ent fnl f: hdd last 100yds: kpt on u.p* **10/1**

1210 **4** *nk* **Lucky Beggar (IRE)**[7] 3324 7-9-9 **87** FrannyNorton 6 88
(David C Griffiths) *trckd ldrs: effrt to chal over 1f out: rdn and ev ch ins fnl f: nt qckn* **9/2**[2]

6005 **5** *1 ¼* **Ballesteros**[9] 3231 8-9-4 **82** DavidNolan 3 79
(Richard Fahey) *trckd ldrs: wnt 2nd 2f out: chal ldr u.p over 1f out: rdn and one pce fnl f* **7/1**[3]

00-0 **6** *1 ½* **Powerallied (IRE)**[52] 1876 4-9-0 **85** ConnorMurtagh(7) 11 77
(Richard Fahey) *mid-div: pushed along over 1f out: rdn ins fnl f: one pce* **16/1**

-652 **7** ¾ **Red Tycoon (IRE)**[28] 2608 5-9-3 **84** KieranShoemark(3) 2 74
(Ken Cunningham-Brown) *hld up: drvn 2f out: rdn and one pce fnl f* **7/2**[1]

-001 **8** *1* **Khelman (IRE)**[21] 2821 7-9-2 **83** AdamMcNamara(3) 5 70
(Richard Fahey) *hld up: pushed along 2f out: sme hdwy on inner u.p 1f out: wknd ins fnl f* **7/2**[1]

026- **9** ¾ **Echo Of Lightning**[259] 6772 7-8-13 **77** MartinLane 12 61
(Brian Ellison) *broke wl fr wd draw to chse ldrs: prom tl rdn and lost pl fr over 1f out* **33/1**

0034 **10** *5* **Gramercy (IRE)**[61] 1674 10-8-13 **77** (p) StevieDonohoe 8 45
(Ian Williams) *hld up: drvn over 1f out: rdn fnl f: no imp* **25/1**

4100 **11** *3 ¾* **Monumental Man**[36] 2368 8-9-6 **84** (p) WilliamCarson 9 40
(Michael Attwater) *led to 1/2-way: pushed along over 2f out: wknd* **33/1**

1m 17.55s (3.75) **Going Correction** +0.525s/f (Yiel) **11** Ran SP% **120.9**
Speed ratings (Par 105): **96,95,93,93,91 89,88,87,86,79 74**
CSF £79.84 CT £757.15 TOTE £12.00: £3.00, £3.50, £3.70; EX 116.50 Trifecta £2562.40.
**Owner** New Approach Racing Limited **Bred** Mountarmstrong Stud **Trained** Carrutherstown, D'fries & G'way
**FOCUS**
A mainly out-of-form bunch, bar the first two in the market, for this average sprint handicap. Stall one came out best. The winner has been rated to his winter AW level.

## 3582 TOMMY & SHEILA CLISHAM ANNIVERSARY H'CAP — 1m 2f 70y
**5:30** (5:30) (Class 4) (0-85,84) 4-Y-0+
**£6,225** (£1,864; £932; £466; £233; £117) **Stalls** Low

Form RPR

20-4 **1** **Al Destoor**[22] 2787 7-9-5 **82** (t) DavidNolan 10 96
(Jennie Candlish) *mid-div: 5th wl over 1f out: gd hdwy to ld appr fnl f: sn clr: easily* **11/2**[3]

2-33 **2** *5* **Lorelina**[19] 2906 4-9-1 **78** OisinMurphy 4 82
(Andrew Balding) *trckd ldrs: hdwy 2f out: rdn ent fnl f: r.o but no ch w wnr* **5/2**[1]

-052 **3** *1* **Jabbaar**[12] 3153 4-8-11 **74** PJMcDonald 11 76
(David Barron) *trckd ldr: led over 3f out: rdn over 1f out: sn hdd and one pce* **8/1**

5131 **4** *1 ¾* **Energia Fox (BRZ)**[14] 3065 6-9-4 **84** AdamMcNamara(3) 2 83
(Richard Fahey) *trckd ldrs: hdwy into 2nd 2f out: rdn and wknd ent fnl f* **3/1**[2]

/062 **5** *1 ¼* **Tobacco Road (IRE)**[9] 3235 7-9-2 **79** (tp) TomMarquand 12 75
(David Pipe) *hld up: drvn 2f out: sn rdn and r.o one pce* **10/1**

0002 **6** *2 ½* **Lord Franklin**[11] 3168 8-9-0 **77** NeilFarley 1 69
(Eric Alston) *led: hdd and drvn over 3f out: styd prom tl rdn and wknd over 1f out* **11/1**

-004 **7** ¾ **Buonarroti (IRE)**[9] 3240 6-9-4 **81** StevieDonohoe 8 71
(Declan Carroll) *hld up: rowed along over 1f out: fdd ins fnl f* **7/1**

1006 **8** *17* **Zoravan (USA)**[10] 3199 4-9-5 **82** (v) DougieCostello 7 40
(Keith Dalgleish) *mid-div: drvn over 1f: wknd qckly* **14/1**

2m 16.2s (5.00) **Going Correction** +0.525s/f (Yiel) **8** Ran SP% **116.7**
Speed ratings (Par 105): **101,97,96,94,93 91,91,77**
CSF £20.12 CT £110.74 TOTE £7.80: £2.80, £1.02, £3.60; EX 21.00 Trifecta £117.90.
**Owner** Glen's Fools 2 **Bred** Richard Moses Bloodstock **Trained** Basford Green, Staffs
**FOCUS**
An average handicap, but a clear-cut winner. As was the theme on the card, those that set the pace failed to get home, with the closers doing best. The runner-up has been rated close to form.
T/Plt: £148.60 to a £1 stake. Pool: £85,044.96 - 417.59 winning units. T/Qpdt: £47.20 to a £1 stake. Pool: £5,647.32 - 88.46 winning units. **Keith McHugh**

# 3537 HAYDOCK (L-H)
Saturday, June 10

**OFFICIAL GOING: Soft (6.7)**
Wind: Moderate, across in straight of over 4f Weather: Overcast

## 3583 BETWAY MIDDLE DISTANCE H'CAP — 1m 2f 100y
**1:45** (1:47) (Class 4) (0-85,87) 3-Y-O **£6,469** (£1,925; £962; £481) **Stalls** Centre

Form RPR

0-64 **1** **Reachforthestars (IRE)**[28] 2612 3-9-12 **87** DanielTudhope 3 94
(David O'Meara) *led: hdd over 6f out: continued to chse ldr: rdn to regain ld over 1f out: sn strly pressed: edgd rt ins fnl 100yds: gamely fnd ex* **16/1**

3-54 **2** *1* **Pirate Look (IRE)**[16] 2998 3-9-2 **77** RyanMoore 5 82
(Marco Botti) *midfield: rdn and hdwy 2f out: chalng whn lugged lft over 1f out: upsides ins fnl f: pushed sltly rt ins fnl 100yds: hld nr fin* **8/1**

43-2 **3** *1 ¼* **Another Eclipse (IRE)**[20] 2857 3-9-6 **81** JamieSpencer 2 84
(David Simcock) *hld up in rr: pushed along 3f out: rdn over 2f out: hdwy for press over 1f out: styng on whn nt clr run towards fin: nvr able to chal front two* **4/1**[2]

-630 **4** *nk* **Society Red**[14] 3077 3-9-3 **78** BarryMcHugh 7 80
(Richard Fahey) *hld up: effrt 3f out: no imp tl styd on towards fin: nt pce to chal* **11/1**

12-6 **5** *shd* **Mister Belvedere**[35] 2385 3-9-12 **87** PaulMulrennan 4 89
(Michael Dods) *prom: rdn over 2f out: nt qckn: kpt on one pce ins fnl f* **12/1**

2-21 **6** ½ **Materialist**[20] 2857 3-9-6 **81** (h) AndreaAtzeni 8 82+
(Roger Varian) *plld hrd: sn prom: led over 6f out: rdn over 2f out: hdd over 1f out: stl there tl fdd ins fnl 100yds* **5/2**[1]

1- **7** *1 ½* **High Waves (IRE)**[212] 7883 3-9-6 **81** PatCosgrave 1 79
(Saeed bin Suroor) *trckd ldrs: rdn over 2f out: outpcd over 1f out: wknd ins fnl f* **5/1**[3]

-163 **8** *nk* **Doctor Bartolo (IRE)**[23] 2755 3-9-3 **78** DavidProbert 6 76
(Charles Hills) *racd keenly: hld up in rr: rdn wl over 2f out: nvr a threat* **7/1**

2m 19.65s (4.15) **Going Correction** +0.35s/f (Good) **8** Ran SP% **110.8**
Speed ratings (Par 101): **97,96,95,94,94 94,93,93**
CSF £127.35 CT £591.73 TOTE £11.10: £3.00, £2.50, £1.90; EX 113.70 Trifecta £385.60.
**Owner** Geoff & Sandra Turnbull **Bred** Roundhill Stud & T Stewart **Trained** Upper Helmsley, N Yorks
**FOCUS**
All races were run over the Stands' Side Home Straight. Allowing for rail position on bends, the actual race distance as 1m2f 121yds. Rain in the run up to racing would only have made the ground softer and after riding in the first, Danny Tudhope and Ryan Moore described the ground as soft, while Jamie Spencer felt it was: "Heavy - very wet." A race run at a good clip courtesy of the over-racing favourite, little got into it from of the pace. A length pb from the runner-up, with the third to his maiden form.

## 3584 BETWAY SPRINT H'CAP — 6f
**2:20** (2:20) (Class 4) (0-80,82) 3-Y-O **£6,469** (£1,925; £962; £481) **Stalls** High

Form RPR

1- **1** **Pennsylvania Dutch**[282] 6053 3-9-10 **81** BenCurtis 7 90+
(William Haggas) *sed awkwardly: plld hrd in rr: swtchd lft over 2f out: hdwy ent fnl f: r.o to ld fnl 75yds* **5/1**

-405 **2** ½ **Bellevarde (IRE)**[18] 2927 3-8-5 **62** JamesSullivan 3 66
(Richard Price) *a.p: rdn over 1f out: chalng ins fnl f: nt pce of wnr nr fin* **25/1**

2-31 **3** *nse* **Fantasy Keeper**[18] 2927 3-9-0 **71** RyanMoore 5 75+
(Michael Appleby) *hld up: rdn over 2f out: edgd rt over 1f out: prog ins fnl f: fin wl* **10/3**[1]

1552 **4** ½ **Full Intention**[15] 3038 3-9-11 **82** RichardKingscote 10 84
(Tom Dascombe) *prom: led 2f out: sn rdn: edgd lft ins fnl f: hdd fnl 75yds: no ex* **4/1**[2]

0-05 **5** *1 ¼* **Haworth**[8] 3296 3-8-10 **67** DavidProbert 4 65
(James Bethell) *hld up: rdn and hdwy 2f out: nt clr run whn chsng ldrs ent fnl f: kpt on u.p after but nt pce of front few* **9/1**

14-0 **6** *1 1/2* **Maakaasib**[37] 2334 3-9-10 **81** ............(e[1]) GrahamLee 9 74
(Simon Crisford) *led: hdd 2f out: sn rdn: stl ev ch ins fnl f: fdd fnl 75yds* **14/1**

-002 **7** *hd* **Awesome Allan (IRE)**[5] 3411 3-9-7 **78**............ DanielTudhope 1 71
(David Evans) *prom: rdn over 1f out: fdd wl ins fnl f* **9/2**[3]

41-0 **8** *1 1/4* **Desperados Destiny**[32] 2499 3-9-4 **75**............ PaulMulrennan 11 64
(Michael Dods) *midfield: rdn over 2f out: lost pl over 1f out: one pce fnl f* **20/1**

30-5 **9** *3/4* **Stoneyford Lane (IRE)**[22] 2806 3-9-4 **75**............ RoystonFfrench 6 61
(Steph Hollinshead) *chsd ldrs: rdn and lost pl over 2f out: n.d after* **10/1**

1m 14.65s (0.85) **Going Correction** +0.35s/f (Good) **9** Ran SP% **112.3**
Speed ratings (Par 101): **108,107,107,106,104 102,102,101,100**
CSF £112.51 CT £473.34 TOTE £4.50: £1.10, £7.00, £1.50; EX 115.90 Trifecta £1785.20.
**Owner** Lael Stable **Bred** Lael Stables **Trained** Newmarket, Suffolk

**FOCUS**
Distance as advertised. They raced centre-to-stands' side and the winner came from off the pace down the centre. It's been rated around the fourth to his C&D latest.

## 3585 BETWAY DASH H'CAP 6f
**2:55** (2:56) (Class 3) (0-95,95) 4-Y-O+ **£9,703** (£2,887; £1,443; £721) **Stalls** High

Form RPR

0502 **1** **Handsome Dude**[21] 2840 5-8-10 **84**............(b) DavidProbert 13 92
(David Barron) *a.p under stands' rail: rdn over 1f out: r.o to ld fnl strides* **8/1**

0001 **2** *hd* **Major Pusey**[12] 3161 5-8-8 **82**............ FergusSweeney 1 89
(John Gallagher) *led: rdn over 2f out: r.o u.p: hdd fnl strides* **12/1**

0-02 **3** *shd* **Snap Shots (IRE)**[3] 3463 5-9-1 **89**............(p) BarryMcHugh 4 96
(Tony Coyle) *a.p: rdn 2f out: chalng ins fnl f: r.o u.p: jst hld* **13/2**[2]

000 **4** *1 1/4* **Toofi (FR)**[15] 3034 6-9-1 **89**............ RobertWinston 10 92
(John Butler) *dwlt: in rr: rdn 2f out: prog ins fnl f: styd on towards fin: nt pce of ldrs* **14/1**

0066 **5** *shd* **Holiday Magic (IRE)**[7] 3324 6-9-6 **94**............ RyanMoore 8 97
(Michael Easterby) *in tch: rdn 2f out: effrt to chse ldrs ins fnl f: styd on same pce towards fin* **11/1**

4200 **6** *nk* **Taexali (IRE)**[14] 3092 4-9-2 **95**............ CliffordLee(5) 9 97
(John Patrick Shanahan, Ire) *in rr: pushed along over 3f out: hdwy 2f out: rdn whn chsng ldrs over 1f out: kpt on same pce fnl 75yds* **16/1**

-044 **7** *1/2* **Eccleston**[3] 3463 6-9-0 **88**............(v) DanielTudhope 7 88
(David O'Meara) *hld up: rdn 2f out: styd on ins fnl f: nt rch ldrs* **11/2**[1]

0000 **8** *3/4* **Cosmic Chatter**[8] 3288 7-8-2 **76** oh1............(p) JamesSullivan 2 74
(Ruth Carr) *in tch: rdn over 2f out: nt qckn over 1f out: one pce ins fnl f* **40/1**

50-6 **9** *1 1/4* **Reflektor (IRE)**[29] 2573 4-9-6 **94**............ RichardKingscote 12 88
(Tom Dascombe) *prom: rdn 2f out: wknd ins fnl f* **8/1**

-634 **10** *1/2* **Northgate Lad (IRE)**[24] 2736 5-9-1 **89**............ BenCurtis 11 81
(Brian Ellison) *towards rr: rdn 2f out: one pce ins fnl f* **8/1**

33 **11** *3/4* **Dandyleekie (IRE)**[3] 3452 5-8-2 **79**............(p) ShelleyBirkett(3) 5 69
(David O'Meara) *hld up: rdn 2f out: sme hdwy sn after: no imp fnl f* **7/1**[3]

0505 **12** *6* **Eltezam (IRE)**[21] 2833 4-9-5 **93**............(h) TomMarquand 6 64
(Richard Hannon) *chsd ldrs tl rdn and wknd 2f out* **16/1**

3-50 **13** *9* **Memories Galore (IRE)**[70] 1501 5-8-10 **84**............ PaulMulrennan 3 26
(Roger Fell) *stdd s: sn chsd ldrs: rdn over 1f out: wknd ent fnl f* **22/1**

1m 13.98s (0.18) **Going Correction** +0.35s/f (Good) **13** Ran SP% **115.8**
Speed ratings (Par 107): **112,111,111,109,109 109,108,107,106,105 104,96,84**
CSF £97.31 CT £684.80 TOTE £8.70: £3.00, £4.20, £2.60; EX 102.20 Trifecta £637.10.
**Owner** W D & Mrs D A Glover **Bred** Fifehead Farms M C Denning **Trained** Maunby, N Yorks

**FOCUS**
Distance as advertised. A decent little sprint, they raced centre-to-stands' side and there was little between the front three at the line. The winner has been rated close to his best, with the third to last year's C&D form.

## 3586 BETWAY PINNACLE STKS (GROUP 3) 1m 3f 175y
**3:30** (3:32) (Class 1) 4-Y-O+
**£35,727** (£13,545; £6,778; £3,376; £1,694; £850) **Stalls** High

Form RPR

50-2 **1** **Bateel (IRE)**[41] 2202 5-9-0 **103**............(h) RichardKingscote 8 110+
(F-H Graffard, France) *hld up: hdwy gng wl over 2f out: led over 1f out: pushed out ins fnl f: readily* **2/1**[1]

15-6 **2** *1 1/2* **Dubka**[35] 2389 4-9-0 **97**............ RyanMoore 6 106
(Sir Michael Stoute) *broke wl: led for over 1f: chsd ldr tl regained ld over 2f out: rdn and hdd over 1f out: kpt on u.p ins fnl f: sn no ch w wnr* **7/1**[3]

0-11 **3** *2 3/4* **Ajman Princess (IRE)**[35] 2389 4-9-0 **107**............ AndreaAtzeni 4 102
(Roger Varian) *chsd ldrs: rdn over 1f out: styd on same pce ins fnl f: nt pce to trble front two* **11/4**[2]

0065 **4** *7* **Lucy The Painter (IRE)**[10] 3219 5-9-0 **93**............ DanielTudhope 9 91
(Ed de Giles) *hld up: pushed along over 3f out: hdwy over 2f out: sn tried to chal: one pce fr over 1f out* **16/1**

/15- **5** *3 1/4* **Return Ace**[210] 7946 5-9-0 **96**............ DanielMuscutt 3 86
(James Fanshawe) *midfield: rdn over 2f out: one pce and no imp fr over 1f out* **8/1**

5243 **6** *1* **Maleficent Queen**[17] 2954 5-9-0 **105**............ RobertWinston 7 84
(Keith Dalgleish) *in tch: effrt to chal over 2f out: wknd over 1f out* **8/1**

05-2 **7** *3* **Island Remede**[56] 1808 6-9-0 **97**............(b) GrahamLee 2 79
(Henry De Bromhead, Ire) *led after over 1f: rdn and hdd over 2f out: wknd over 1f out* **16/1**

-121 **8** *1* **Zain Arion (IRE)**[24] 2741 4-9-0 **85**............ PaulMulrennan 10 78
(John Butler) *midfield: rdn over 2f out: wknd over 1f out* **20/1**

-0 **9** *29* **Chinoiseries**[35] 2389 4-9-0 **89**............(h[1]) FergusSweeney 1 31
(David Simcock) *s.s: t.k.h bhd: in tch but in rr 7f out: struggling over 3f out: sn lft bhd* **25/1**

2m 36.91s (3.11) **Going Correction** +0.35s/f (Good) **9** Ran SP% **115.1**
Speed ratings (Par 113): **103,102,100,95,93 92,90,90,70**
CSF £16.64 TOTE £2.90: £1.30, £1.50, £1.40; EX 16.70 Trifecta £35.40.
**Owner** Al Asayl Bloodstock Ltd **Bred** Sheikh Sultan Bin Khalifa Al Nayhan **Trained** France

**FOCUS**
Allowing for rail position on bends the actual race distance was 1m3f 208yds. Run at a good gallop, the right three drew clear and the form looks rock-solid.

## 3587 BETWAY JOHN OF GAUNT STKS (GROUP 3) 7f 37y
**4:05** (4:05) (Class 1) 4-Y-O+
**£35,727** (£13,545; £6,778; £3,376; £1,694; £850) **Stalls** Low

Form RPR

-042 **1** **Absolutely So (IRE)**[28] 2610 7-9-0 **109**............ DavidProbert 3 112
(Andrew Balding) *plld hrd in midfield: hdwy 3f out: rdn over 1f out: r.o ins fnl f: gamely led towards fin* **6/1**[3]

23-3 **2** *1/2* **Jallota**[43] 2129 6-9-3 **111**............ JamieSpencer 8 113
(Charles Hills) *chsd ldr: rdn over 1f out: led ins fnl f: hdd and hld towards fin* **6/1**[3]

0-53 **3** *nk* **So Beloved**[28] 2610 7-9-0 **108**............ DanielTudhope 7 109
(David O'Meara) *dwlt: hld up: hdwy over 1f out: rdn to chal ins fnl f: styd on same pce nr fin* **8/1**

5-50 **4** *nk* **Mitchum Swagger**[21] 2825 5-9-0 **108**............ RyanMoore 2 108
(David Lanigan) *hld up: rdn and hdwy over 1f out: styd on ins fnl f: edgd lft clsng stages: nt quite pce of front trio* **3/1**[2]

10-3 **5** *nk* **Breton Rock (IRE)**[21] 2825 7-9-5 **112**............ AndreaAtzeni 4 112
(David Simcock) *hld up in rr: effrt over 1f out: prog ins fnl f: styd on: nt quite pce of ldrs* **11/4**[1]

0-13 **6** *1 3/4* **That Is The Spirit**[31] 2518 6-9-0 **100**............ PaulMulrennan 1 103
(David O'Meara) *led: sn clr: racd alone on far side in st: reduced advantage 3f out: rdn over 1f out: hdd ins fnl f: no ex fnl 50yds* **16/1**

10-0 **7** *1 1/2* **Growl**[24] 2737 5-9-0 **114**............ GrahamLee 5 99
(Richard Fahey) *chsd ldrs: rdn over 1f out: one pce ins fnl f* **7/1**

-000 **8** *2 3/4* **Dream Walker (FR)**[35] 2406 8-9-0 **95**............(t) BenCurtis 6 92
(Brian Ellison) *hld up: rdn over 2f out: no imp over 1f out* **50/1**

1m 32.97s (0.27) **Going Correction** +0.35s/f (Good) **8** Ran SP% **111.7**
Speed ratings (Par 113): **112,111,111,110,110 108,106,103**
CSF £39.56 TOTE £7.90: £2.40, £1.20, £3.00; EX 32.10 Trifecta £205.80.
**Owner** The George Smith Family Partnership **Bred** L Mulryan **Trained** Kingsclere, Hants

**FOCUS**
Allowing for rail position on bends the actual race distance was 7f 58yds. No hanging around for this Group 3, with That Is The Spirit opening up a clear lead, and all bar that one headed down the centre in the straight. Plenty had their chance and there was little to separate the first five at the line. The winner has been rated to his best.

## 3588 BETWAY H'CAP 7f 37y
**4:40** (4:40) (Class 4) (0-85,87) 3-Y-O **£6,469** (£1,925; £962; £481) **Stalls** Low

Form RPR

1-01 **1** **Mjjack (IRE)**[21] 2820 3-9-1 **83**............ CliffordLee(5) 5 98
(K R Burke) *chsd ldr: led wl over 1f out: styd on strly to go clr ins fnl f: comf* **10/3**[2]

10 **2** *4 1/2* **Sir Reginald Brown**[24] 2739 3-8-12 **75**............ GrahamLee 2 78
(Richard Fahey) *racd keenly: a.p: rdn 3f out: nt qckn over 2f out: kpt on to take 2nd ins fnl f: no ch w wnr* **9/2**[3]

5304 **3** *2 3/4* **Arc Royal**[14] 3082 3-9-4 **81**............ RichardKingscote 4 77
(Tom Dascombe) *led: rdn over 2f out: hdd wl over 1f out: lost 2nd ins fnl f: no ex* **7/1**

05-5 **4** *3/4* **Lady In Question (IRE)**[21] 2820 3-8-13 **76**............ BarryMcHugh 1 70
(Richard Fahey) *dwlt: hld up: hdwy over 3f out: rdn over 2f out: kpt on ins fnl f: nvr able to chal* **8/1**

312- **5** *1/2* **Fareeq**[244] 7185 3-9-3 **80**............ PatCosgrave 8 73
(William Haggas) *hld up: rdn 2f out: swtchd lft over 1f out: kpt on ins fnl f: nvr a danger* **12/1**

1-04 **6** *8* **Warrior's Spirit (IRE)**[23] 2755 3-9-3 **80**............ RyanMoore 6 52
(Richard Hannon) *n.m.r and hmpd s: bhd: rdn 3f out: nvr on terms* **3/1**[1]

216- **7** *2 1/2* **Maldonado (FR)**[259] 6791 3-9-0 **84**............ RyanTimby(7) 3 50
(Michael Easterby) *chsd ldrs: rdn 3f out: wknd 2f out* **40/1**

0206 **8** *1 3/4* **Letmestopyouthere (IRE)**[30] 2554 3-9-10 **87**............ DanielTudhope 7 48
(David Evans) *hld up: rdn 2f out: no imp over 1f out: wl btn ins fnl f* **10/1**

2-05 **9** *6* **Jumping Around (IRE)**[35] 2407 3-9-0 **77**............ RobertWinston 9 22
(Ian Williams) *chsd ldrs: rdn 3f out: wknd 2f out* **16/1**

1m 33.69s (0.99) **Going Correction** +0.35s/f (Good) **9** Ran SP% **115.0**
Speed ratings (Par 101): **108,102,99,98,98 89,86,84,77**
CSF £18.70 CT £97.68 TOTE £5.10: £2.00, £1.70, £2.60; EX 19.70 Trifecta £126.20.
**Owner** Mrs M Gittins **Bred** Derrymore House Syndicate **Trained** Middleham Moor, N Yorks

**FOCUS**
Allowing for rail position on bends the actual race distance was 7f 58yds. A fair handicap but very much one-way traffic with an easy winner. The level is a bit fluid, but the runner-up has been rated to his maiden form.

## 3589 BETWAY MILE H'CAP 1m 37y
**5:15** (5:15) (Class 3) (0-90,92) 4-Y-O+ **£9,703** (£2,887; £1,443; £721) **Stalls** Low

Form RPR

15-0 **1** **Zwayyan**[35] 2390 4-9-3 **85**............ PatCosgrave 8 96+
(William Haggas) *midfield: racd far side ent st over 4f out: hdwy over 2f out: rdn and str chal fr over 1f out: edgd lft clsng stages: r.o to ld post* **4/1**[2]

-032 **2** *hd* **Ionization (IRE)**[22] 2772 4-9-1 **88**............ CliffordLee(5) 10 98
(John Patrick Shanahan, Ire) *midfield: c wd ent st over 4f out: hdwy 3f out: rdn to ld 2f out: carried hd high and strly pressed after: edgd lft clsng stages: hdd post* **7/1**

0505 **3** *2 1/2* **Abushamah (IRE)**[10] 3204 6-8-6 **74**............(p) JamesSullivan 12 78
(Ruth Carr) *hld up: c wd ent st over 4f out: rdn 2f out: hdwy over 1f out: styd on ins fnl f: edgd lft clsng stages: nt rch front pair* **14/1**

-111 **4** *2* **Commodity (IRE)**[17] 2960 4-9-1 **83**............ RyanMoore 3 82
(Sir Michael Stoute) *led: r far side ent st over 4f out: hdd over 3f out: rdn over 2f out: no ex ins fnl f* **5/2**[1]

0002 **5** *1/2* **Strong Steps**[1] 3546 5-9-4 **86**............(b) PaulMulrennan 11 84
(Roger Fell) *hld up: racd far side ent st over 4f out: rdn and hdwy over 1f out: kpt on ins fnl f: nt pce to chal* **22/1**

431- **6** *shd* **I Am Not Here (IRE)**[183] 8283 6-9-3 **85**............ BenCurtis 7 83+
(Brian Ellison) *chsd ldrs: c wd ent st over 4f out: rdn over 2f out: kpt on towards fin* **12/1**

-000 **7** *nk* **Gabrial's Kaka (IRE)**[14] 3064 7-9-6 **88**............ GrahamLee 4 85
(Richard Fahey) *midfield: c wd ent st over 4f out: rdn over 2f out: no imp over 1f out: kpt on same pce ins fnl f* **12/1**

025- **8** *2 1/2* **Little Lady Katie (IRE)**[221] 7744 5-9-1 **86**............ JordanVaughan(3) 9 78
(K R Burke) *prom: c wd ent st over 4f out: led over 3f out: rdn and hdd 2f out: wknd ins fnl f* **12/1**

3-51 **9** *3 3/4* **Red Tea**[47] 2030 4-9-7 **89**............ DavidProbert 1 72
(Peter Hiatt) *in tch: c wd ent st over 4f out: rdn over 2f out: wknd over 1f out* **11/2**[3]

0563 **10** *3/4* **Baltic Prince (IRE)**[88] 1189 7-7-10 **71**............ MillyNaseb(7) 2 52
(Tony Carroll) *prom: racd far side ent st over 4f out: rdn over 2f out: sn wknd* **50/1**

1140 **11** *2 3/4* **Hammer Gun (USA)**[31] 2518 4-9-1 **83**............(v) DanielTudhope 13 58
(Derek Shaw) *midfield: racd wd ent st over 4f out: hdwy over 3f out: rdn over 2f out: wknd over 1f out* **25/1**

0600 **12** *8* **Mansfield**[21] 2838 4-8-7 **75**............ KieranO'Neill 6 32
(Michael Wigham) *missed break: plld hrd: in rr: racd wd ent st over 4f out: rdn over 2f out: nvr a threat* **66/1**

00- **13** 8 **Accurate**[212] 7897 4-9-10 **92** ........ RobertWinston 5 30
(Ian Williams) *trckd ldrs: c wd ent st over 4f out: wknd over 2f out* **33/1**

1m 48.4s (3.70) **Going Correction** +0.35s/f (Good) **13** Ran SP% **120.8**
Speed ratings (Par 107): **95,94,92,90,89 89,89,86,83,82 79,71,63**
CSF £30.95 CT £365.40 TOTE £4.70: £1.70, £2.90, £4.70; EX 32.40 Trifecta £378.40.
**Owner** Al Shaqab Racing **Bred** Newsells Park Stud & Cheveley Park Stud **Trained** Newmarket, Suffolk

**FOCUS**
Allowing for rail position on bends the actual race distance was 1m 58yds. They went a steady gallop for the first half of this and split into two groups in the straight initially, although ended up spread across the track. The fifth has been rated close to his claimer figure the previous day.
T/Plt: £69.50 to a £1 stake. Pool: £156,089.08 - 1,638.39 winning units. T/Qpdt: £11.40 to a £1 stake. Pool: £11,134.54 - 720.48 winning units. **Darren Owen**

## 2829 NEWMARKET (R-H)
### Saturday, June 10

**OFFICIAL GOING: Good (7.4)**
Wind: medium to strong, across Weather: sunny

## 3590 MARGARET GIFFEN MEMORIAL EBF NOVICE STKS (PLUS 10 RACE) (DIV I) 6f
**1:25** (1:25) (Class 4) 2-Y-O **£4,528** (£1,347; £673; £336) **Stalls** High

Form RPR

**1** **Glorious Journey** 2-9-2 0 ........ WilliamBuick 3 82+
(Charlie Appleby) *t.k.h: trckd ldrs: effrt over 1f out: rdn to ld ins fnl f: r.o wl and a jst holding runner-up after* **1/1**[1]

4 **2** nk **Grand Koonta (IRE)**[22] 2779 2-9-2 0 ........ AdamKirby 6 81
(Clive Cox) *chsd ldr tl rdn to ld wl over 1f out: drvn and hdd ins fnl f: kpt on wl but a jst hld after* **3/1**[2]

**3** 1 ½ **Take Me With You (USA)** 2-8-11 0 ........ GeraldMosse 8 72+
(Jeremy Noseda) *hld up in tch in midfield: effrt over 1f out: hdwy to chse ldng pair ins fnl f: kpt on wl but nvr threatening ldrs* **8/1**[3]

**4** ¾ **Amourice (IRE)** 2-8-11 0 ........ MartinDwyer 10 69+
(Jane Chapple-Hyam) *mounted on crse: t.k.h: hld up in tch in midfield: swtchd rt and effrt over 1f out: kpt on wl ins fnl f wout threatening ldrs* **150/1**

**5** ½ **Maksab (IRE)** 2-9-2 0 ........ SilvestreDeSousa 5 73+
(Mick Channon) *hld up in tch in last trio: swtchd rt and effrt 2f out: hdwy 1f out: kpt on wl ins fnl f: nvr trbld ldrs* **25/1**

5 **6** nk **Al Fujairah**[15] 3037 2-9-2 0 ........ PatDobbs 9 72
(Richard Hannon) *led and set stdy gallop: rdn and hdd wl over 1f out: 3rd and unable qck 1f out: wknd wl ins fnl f* **9/1**

**7** ½ **Cosmopolitan Queen** 2-8-11 0 ........ ShaneKelly 7 65+
(David Elsworth) *hld up in tch in last pair: effrt over 1f out: kpt on steadily ins fnl f: nvr trbld ldrs* **33/1**

50 **8** 1 ½ **Starboy (IRE)**[12] 3135 2-9-2 0 ........ MartinHarley 4 66
(George Scott) *stdd s: t.k.h: hld up in tch in last pair: effrt over 1f out: kpt on same pce and no imp ins fnl f* **66/1**

**9** 1 ¼ **Qayes** 2-9-2 0 ........ FrankieDettori 1 62+
(John Gosden) *hld up in tch in midfield on outer: clsd to chse ldrs 1/2-way: rdn and lost pl over 1f out: wknd ins fnl f* **9/1**

1m 15.53s (3.03) **Going Correction** +0.025s/f (Good) **9** Ran SP% **115.1**
Speed ratings (Par 95): **80,79,77,76,75 75,74,72,71**
CSF £3.89 TOTE £1.70: £1.10, £1.30, £2.40; EX 4.50 Trifecta £19.00.
**Owner** Godolphin **Bred** Normandie Stud Ltd **Trained** Newmarket, Suffolk

**FOCUS**
Stands' Side of July course used with stalls on the far side except 1m2f, 1m4f & 1m6f: centre. The first fixture on the July course in 2017. There was 25.5mm of rain on Monday/Tuesday, 1mm of overnight rain on Wednesday and 1mm of rain Thursday evening, but it had been dry since. The early pace was slow - the time was 2.01sec off the second division - and the bare form might prove muddling. The level and anchors for the race will become clear in time.

## 3591 MARGARET GIFFEN MEMORIAL EBF NOVICE STKS (PLUS 10 RACE) (DIV II) 6f
**1:55** (1:56) (Class 4) 2-Y-O **£4,528** (£1,347; £673; £336) **Stalls** High

Form RPR

4 **1** **Folk Tale (IRE)**[16] 3002 2-9-2 0 ........ WilliamBuick 8 76
(Charlie Appleby) *t.k.h: hld up in tch in midfield: effrt over 1f out: rdn to ld and edgd lft ent fnl f: hld on wl ins fnl f: rdn out* **13/8**[1]

**2** nk **Faraasah (IRE)** 2-9-2 0 ........ JimCrowley 9 75+
(Brian Meehan) *trckd ldrs: effrt and rdn to press ldrs ent fnl f: ev ch ins fnl f: kpt on wl but a jst hld* **8/1**

0 **3** nk **Dichato (USA)**[15] 3037 2-9-2 0 ........ FrankieDettori 4 74
(John Gosden) *hld up in rr: effrt and swtchd rt over 1f out: sn rdn: hdwy ins fnl f: styd on strly to go 3rd towards fin: nt quite rch ldrs* **8/1**

52 **4** ½ **Tangled (IRE)**[12] 3135 2-9-2 0 ........ PatDobbs 2 75
(Richard Hannon) *hld up in tch towards rr: clsd and nt clr run over 1f out: sn swtchd lft: hdwy and swtchd rt jst ins fnl f: chsng ldrs and swtchd rt again ins fnl f: kpt on: n.m.r cl home* **6/1**[3]

**5** 2 ¼ **Global Wealth** 2-9-2 0 ........ SilvestreDeSousa 6 66
(Ed Dunlop) *dwlt: hld up in tch in midfield: rdn and outpcd wl over 1f out: hdwy ins fnl f: swtchd rt and kpt on wl fnl 75yds: no threat to ldrs* **25/1**

5 **6** ½ **Montague (IRE)**[16] 3002 2-9-2 0 ........ TimmyMurphy 7 64
(Jamie Osborne) *t.k.h: led tl 1/2-way: styd pressing ldr: rdn over 1f out: no ex u.p 1f out: wknd ins fnl f* **16/1**

0 **7** nk **Devil's Cowboy (IRE)**[53] 1858 2-8-13 0 ........ CallumShepherd(3) 5 64
(Charles Hills) *trckd ldrs: unable tp qckn u.p over 1f out: lost pl 1f out and wknd ins fnl f* **33/1**

**8** 3 ½ **Polar Light** 2-8-11 0 ........ ShaneKelly 3 48
(David Elsworth) *in tch in midfield: rdn over 2f out: dropped to rr and bhd 1f out: wknd ins fnl f* **50/1**

**9** nk **Encrypted** 2-9-2 0 ........ JamesDoyle 1 52+
(Hugo Palmer) *ducked sharply rt leaving stalls: sn rcvrd to chse ldr and t.k.h: led 1/2-way: rdn and hdd ent fnl f: sn struggling: wknd qckly ins fnl f* **11/4**[2]

1m 13.52s (1.02) **Going Correction** +0.025s/f (Good) **9** Ran SP% **115.9**
Speed ratings (Par 95): **94,93,93,92,89 88,88,83,83**
CSF £15.51 TOTE £2.30: £1.10, £3.00, £2.70; EX 15.60 Trifecta £74.20.
**Owner** Godolphin **Bred** Godolphin **Trained** Newmarket, Suffolk

**FOCUS**
A more truly run race than the first division. It's been rated around the winner, fourth, and a few down the field.

## 3592 ANIMAL HEALTH TRUST CELEBRATING 75 YEARS H'CAP 7f
**2:30** (2:31) (Class 2) (0-105,103) 3-Y-O
**£28,012** (£8,388; £4,194; £2,097; £1,048; £526) **Stalls** High

Form RPR

1-35 **1** **Parfait (IRE)**[12] 3146 3-8-3 **85** ........ (p[1]) MartinDwyer 14 104
(John Gosden) *mde all: clr 1/2-way: rdn over 1f out: styd on strly ins fnl f: unchal* **11/1**

201- **2** 7 **Six Strings**[193] 8140 3-8-5 **87** ........ AndrewMullen 12 88
(Richard Fahey) *t.k.h: hld up in midfield: effrt over 2f out: rdn to chse clr wnr 2f out: no imp but battled on gamely to hold 2nd ins fnl f* **14/1**

12-0 **3** shd **Town Charter (USA)**[14] 3071 3-8-0 **87** ........ RichardOliver(5) 11 88
(Mark Johnston) *hld up towards rr: hmpd over 2f out: effrt 2f out: hdwy over 1f out: styd on wl u.p ins fnl f and battling for 2nd cl home: no ch w wnr* **25/1**

-531 **4** nse **Juanito Chico (IRE)**[8] 3303 3-8-5 **87** ........ (h) SilvestreDeSousa 5 88+
(William Jarvis) *stdd s: t.k.h: hld up towards rr: effrt over 2f out: hdwy u.p over 1f out: battling for 2nd fnl f: kpt on but no imp on wnr* **11/4**[1]

6-00 **5** hd **Rebel De Lope**[30] 2554 3-8-3 **85** ........ JimmyQuinn 7 85
(Charles Hills) *stdd s: hld up in tch towards rr: effrt and shifting lft over 1f out: swtchd rt and drvn over 1f out: battling for placings and kpt on ins fnl f: no ch w wnr* **20/1**

1-41 **6** 1 **Omran**[18] 2922 3-9-2 **98** ........ FrankieDettori 1 95
(Marco Botti) *hld up in midfield on outer: hdwy 1/2-way: rdn and disputing 2nd 2f out: no imp on wnr: wknd ins fnl f* **4/1**[2]

1-04 **7** 1 **Ahlan Bil Zain (FR)**[21] 2818 3-7-12 **83** ........ AaronJones(3) 2 78
(David Simcock) *hld up towards rr: effrt jst over 2f out: sme hdwy whn nt clrest of runs briefly over 1f out: styd on steadily u.p ins fnl f: no ch w wnr* **25/1**

0-35 **8** ½ **Mutawakked (IRE)**[21] 2831 3-8-0 **82** ........ RyanPowell 9 76
(Brian Meehan) *taken down early: chsd ldr: rdn 3f out: lost 2nd and unable qck 2f out: wknd ins fnl f* **40/1**

23-0 **9** 1 ½ **Novoman (IRE)**[56] 1801 3-8-8 **90** ........ LiamJones 4 80
(William Haggas) *stdd and wnt rt s: hld up towards rr: swtchd rt and effrt 2f out: sme hdwy over 1f out: plugged on same pce ins fnl f: nvr threatened ldrs* **16/1**

1304 **10** 3 ¼ **Law And Order (IRE)**[16] 3013 3-9-7 **103** ........ (v[1]) AdamKirby 13 84
(James Tate) *prom in chsng gp: rdn 3f out: struggling 2f out and losing pl whn n.m.r over 1f out: wknd ins fnl f* **12/1**

3151 **11** 1 ¼ **Thomas Cranmer (USA)**[7] 3336 3-8-11 **93** ........ JimCrowley 10 71
(Mark Johnston) *chsd chsng gp ldrs: rdn 3f out: lost pl 2f out: bhd ins fnl f* **9/1**

0-61 **12** shd **Harmonise**[23] 2754 3-7-9 **82** oh7 ........ DavidEgan(5) 8 60
(Mick Channon) *prom in main gp: rdn 1/2-way: lost pl and bhd 2f out: wknd over 1f out* **20/1**

24-0 **13** 2 ½ **Mutahaady (IRE)**[29] 2565 3-8-6 **88** ........ JosephineGordon 6 59
(K R Burke) *midfield: rdn 3f out: sn struggling and dropped to rr 2f out: no ch after* **33/1**

-123 **14** 7 **Ejaaby**[12] 3146 3-8-5 **87** ........ HarryBentley 3 40
(Roger Varian) *midfield: rdn 3f out: sn struggling and dropped to rr 3f: wl bhd and eased ins fnl f* **15/2**[3]

1m 24.22s (-1.48) **Going Correction** +0.025s/f (Good) **14** Ran SP% **119.6**
Speed ratings (Par 105): **109,101,100,100 99,98,97,96,92 90,90,87,79**
CSF £139.36 CT £2229.36 TOTE £13.10: £3.80, £4.40, £7.60; EX 182.10 Trifecta £3849.60.
**Owner** Godolphin **Bred** Mogeely Stud **Trained** Newmarket, Suffolk

**FOCUS**
This looked a competitive handicap but the winner was allowed a completely free lead. The level is a bit fluid.

## 3593 PORSCHE CENTRE CAMBRIDGE H'CAP 6f
**3:05** (3:05) (Class 2) (0-105,99) 3-Y-O+ **£12,938** (£3,850; £1,924; £962) **Stalls** High

Form RPR

211/ **1** **Culturati**[610] 7087 4-9-9 **94** ........ WilliamBuick 6 107
(Charlie Appleby) *racd in centre tl gps merged 2f out: trckd ldrs: rdn to ld over 1f out: in command and r.o strly ins fnl f* **5/1**[1]

5-12 **2** 1 ½ **Scorching Heat**[12] 3146 3-8-3 **82** ........ JimmyQuinn 3 88
(Andrew Balding) *stmbld sltly leaving stalls: racd in centre tl gps merged 2f out: sn rcvrd to ld gp and chsd ldrs overall: rdn to press ldrs over 1f out: chsd wnr and kpt on same pce ins fnl f* **7/1**[3]

-031 **3** ¾ **Boy In The Bar**[15] 3034 6-9-6 **91** ........ (v) JosephineGordon 10 97
(Ian Williams) *racd on far side: trckd ldrs: effrt 2f out: hdwy u.p over 1f out: wnt 3rd ins fnl f: kpt on but no threat to wnr* **7/1**[3]

0-30 **4** 2 ¼ **Out Do**[14] 3092 8-10-0 **99** ........ (v) HarryBentley 2 98
(David O'Meara) *racd in centre tl gps merged 2f out: hld up towards rr: effrt 2f out: hdwy u.p 1f out: styd on ins fnl f: no threat to wnr* **16/1**

-325 **5** nk **Stellarta**[15] 3034 6-9-10 **95** ........ AdamKirby 9 93
(Michael Blanshard) *racd on far side: hld up in rr: effrt over 1f out: hdwy u.p over 1f out: styd on ins fnl f: nvr trbld ldrs* **33/1**

0033 **6** ¾ **Go Far**[15] 3034 7-9-6 **98** ........ (v) JoshuaBryan(7) 12 93
(Alan Bailey) *racd on far side: overall ldr tl over 2f out: edgd rt u.p and unable qck over 1f out: wknd wl ins fnl f* **16/1**

0320 **7** nk **Moonraker**[15] 3034 5-8-13 **89** ........ DavidEgan(5) 8 83
(Mick Channon) *racd on far side: t.k.h: chsd overall ldr tl rdn to ld over 2f out: hdd over 1f out: sn btn and wknd ins fnl f* **16/1**

/0-1 **8** ¾ **Al Qahwa (IRE)**[24] 2736 4-9-13 **98** ........ JamesDoyle 11 90
(David O'Meara) *racd on far side: in tch in midfield: effrt 2f out: no imp u.p over 1f out: wknd ins fnl f* **7/1**[3]

2250 **9** ½ **Outer Space**[31] 2518 6-9-5 **90** ........ TimmyMurphy 5 80
(Jamie Osborne) *racd in centre tl gps merged 2f out: effrt over 1f out: stl in rr whn nt clr run and hmpd 1f out: nvr trbld ldrs* **66/1**

1-34 **10** ½ **Spring Loaded (IRE)**[31] 2524 5-9-10 **95** ........ JoeyHaynes 7 84
(Paul D'Arcy) *swtchd lft sn after s and racd on far side: hld up in tch: effrt over 1f out: no imp u.p 1f out: nvr trbld ldrs* **14/1**

0106 **11** 1 **Gunmetal (IRE)**[22] 2780 4-9-9 **94** ........ SilvestreDeSousa 1 80
(Charles Hills) *racd in centre tl gps merged 2f out: hld up towards rr: effrt 2f out: sn drvn and no imp: nvr trbld ldrs* **5/1**[1]

-112 **12** 1 **Gin In The Inn (IRE)**[31] 2528 4-9-7 **92** ........ FrankieDettori 4 74
(Richard Fahey) *racd in centre tl gps merged 2f out: in tch in midfield: rdn 2f out: sn struggling and lost pl over 1f out: wknd ins fnl f* **6/1**[2]

010- 13 1 1/2 **New Bidder**[232] 7497 6-9-13 **98**.................................(b) AndrewMullen 13 76
(David Barron) *racd on far side: stdd s: hld up in rr: n.d* **50/1**
1m 11.54s (-0.96) **Going Correction** +0.025s/f (Good) **13** Ran SP% **115.8**
**WFA** 3 from 4yo+ 8lb
Speed ratings (Par 109): **107,105,104,101,100 99,99,98,97,96 95,94,92**
CSF £37.62 CT £253.93 TOTE £5.80: £2.50, £2.50, £2.40; EX 42.80 Trifecta £208.70.
**Owner** Godolphin **Bred** New England Stud & Mount Coote Stud **Trained** Newmarket, Suffolk

**FOCUS**
There were two groups early, with one bunch far side and the others just off them, more towards the middle, but there didn't look to be a bias. The third has been rated to last year's C&D form.

## 3594 JOHN SUNLEY MEMORIAL H'CAP 1m 6f
**3:40** (3:40) (Class 2) (0-105,103) 4-Y-0+
**£28,012** (£8,388; £4,194; £2,097; £1,048; £526) **Stalls** Centre

Form RPR
0-21 **1** **Jaameh (IRE)**[14] 3067 4-8-11 **93**..................................... JimCrowley 12 103+
(Mark Johnston) *trckd ldrs: effrt and rdn to chse ldr wl over 1f out: styd on to ld ins fnl f: jst hld on* **9/2**[1]

1240 **2** *hd* **Byron Flyer**[14] 3067 6-8-5 **87**............................................ HarryBentley 9 95+
(Ian Williams) *hld up in midfield: effrt over 2f out: 5th and drvn 1f out: styd on to chse wnr wl ins fnl f: clsng qckly towards fin: jst hld* **8/1**

13-4 **3** *1 1/4* **Cape Cova (IRE)**[22] 2797 4-9-5 **101**.................................(b) TomQueally 15 108
(John Gosden) *trckd ldrs: clsd to join ldrs and travelling wl 3f out: led ent fnl 2f: sn rdn and drifted rt over 1f out: hdd ins fnl f: styd on same pce after* **8/1**

2-02 **4** *3 1/4* **Nakeeta**[14] 3090 6-9-7 **103**..........................................(h) FrankieDettori 16 105
(Iain Jardine) *t.k.h: hld up in tch towards rr: stdy hdwy 5f out: rdn to chse ldrs 2f out: no ex jst ins fnl f: wknd fnl 100yds* **8/1**

3-20 **5** *1 3/4* **Batts Rock (IRE)**[14] 3073 4-8-2 **84**........................... JosephineGordon 4 84
(Michael Bell) *chsd ldrs: drvn to chse ldrs over 2f out: unable qck over 1f out: wknd ins fnl f* **7/1**[3]

5-04 **6** *7* **Southdown Lad (IRE)**[22] 2804 4-8-11 **93**.............. SilvestreDeSousa 10 83
(William Knight) *hld up in tch in last quartet: effrt 4f out: swtchd lft and rdn over 2f out: hdwy into midfield but no imp over 1f out: wknd fnl f* **13/2**[2]

1063 **7** *1 3/4* **Gabrial's King (IRE)**[14] 3067 8-8-7 **89**.......................... JoeyHaynes 14 76
(Richard Fahey) *hld up in tch in rr: rdn and effrt 3f out: hdwy into midfield but no imp over 1f out: wknd fnl f* **28/1**

0 **8** *nk* **Cosmelli (ITY)**[14] 3073 4-9-3 **99**...............................(b) MartinDwyer 3 86
(Gay Kelleway) *chsd ldr: rdn and ev ch 3f out: led over 1f out tl hdd and unable qck ent fnl 2f: wknd over 1f out* **100/1**

1-36 **9** *1/2* **Amazing Red (IRE)**[22] 2774 4-8-1 **88**........................... DavidEgan(5) 11 74
(Ed Dunlop) *t.k.h: in tch in midfield: hdwy to ld 3f out: sn rdn and hdd over 2f out: sn btn: wknd and hung lft over 1f out* **9/1**

5-13 **10** *6* **Hot Beat (IRE)**[116] 728 5-9-0 **96**....................................... MartinHarley 7 74
(David Simcock) *stdd s: hld up in rr: clsd 4f out: effrt and no rspnse over 1f out: sn btn and fdd ins fnl f* **12/1**

-406 **11** *9* **Angel Gabrial (IRE)**[14] 3073 8-8-8 **90**........................... AndrewMullen 8 55
(Richard Fahey) *in tch in midfield: rdn 3f out: sn struggling: wknd over 1f out* **10/1**

6400 **12** *24* **Intense Tango**[42] 2157 6-8-9 **91**............................................ ShaneKelly 5 23
(K R Burke) *led tl rdn and hdd 3f out: sn dropped out: wl bhd and virtually p.u ins fnl f: t.o* **40/1**

6-50 **13** *105* **Blue Rambler**[128] 540 7-9-2 **98**...................................... GeorgeDowning 6
(Ian Williams) *chsd ldrs: rdn over 5f out: dropped out and bhd whn eased 2f out: t.o* **25/1**

6024 **14** *1* **Tawdeea**[30] 2559 5-9-5 **101**...............................................(p) JamesDoyle 13
(David O'Meara) *hld up in rr: rdn over 3f out: sn btn: eased fnl 2f: t.o* **14/1**
2m 53.98s (-3.72) **14** Ran SP% **121.5**
CSF £39.11 CT £287.19 TOTE £4.50: £1.90, £3.20, £2.90; EX 46.30 Trifecta £419.90.
**Owner** Hamdan Al Maktoum **Bred** Peter & Hugh McCutcheon **Trained** Middleham Moor, N Yorks

**FOCUS**
A decent staying handicap. The form is set around the third and fourth.

## 3595 PRICE BAILEY MAIDEN FILLIES' STKS 7f
**4:15** (4:15) (Class 5) 3-Y-0+ **£3,881** (£1,155; £577; £288) **Stalls** High

Form RPR
56-3 **1** **Lady Freyja**[46] 2066 3-9-0 70.............................................. GeraldMosse 1 84
(John Ryan) *mde all: rdn and edging lft over 1f out: asserting and gng clr ent fnl f: r.o strly: eased towards fin: easily* **6/1**[3]

0-33 **2** *7* **Alouja (IRE)**[15] 3039 3-9-0 79........................................... JamesDoyle 2 66
(Hugo Palmer) *chsd ldrs: effrt 2f out: rdn and unable qck w wnr over 1f out: wl hld 2nd and kpt on same pce fnl 150yds* **9/4**[2]

0-4 **3** *1 1/4* **Miss Patience**[63] 1626 3-9-0 0...........................(h[1]) SilvestreDeSousa 10 63
(Peter Chapple-Hyam) *t.k.h: hld up in last quartet: pushed along and effrt 2f out: no ch w wnr but kpt on steadily fnl f to go 3rd wl ins fnl f* **16/1**

00- **4** *1* **Heart Of Gold**[301] 5400 3-8-9 0........................................ DavidEgan(5) 9 60
(William Muir) *chsd ldrs: rdn 2f out: unable qck and outpcd over 1f out: wl hld and plugged on same pce ins fnl f* **25/1**

3- **5** *1/2* **Luqyaa**[224] 7696 3-9-0 0..................................................... JimCrowley 8 59
(John Gosden) *hld up in tch in last trio: swtchd rt over 2f out: pushed and hdwy into midfield over 1f out: sn no imp and edgd lft ins fnl f: plugged on same pce after* **15/8**[1]

34 **6** *1 1/4* **Omneeya**[33] 2463 3-9-0 0.................................................. MartinHarley 7 56
(Marco Botti) *chsd wnr: rdn 2f out: drvn and unable qck w wnr over 1f out: wl btn and lost 2nd 150yds out: wknd fnl 100yds* **15/2**

60 **7** *1 1/4* **Quinquereme**[8] 3293 3-9-0 0.......................................... JosephineGordon 3 53
(Michael Bell) *restless in stalls: in tch in midfield: rdn over 2f out: outpcd and btn over 1f out: wl hld and plugged on same pce after* **66/1**

0- **8** *1 3/4* **Ghaseedah**[192] 8152 3-9-0 0...................................(h[1]) HarryBentley 4 48
(Simon Crisford) *restless in stalls: s.i.s: in tch in midfield: shkn up jst over 2f out: rdn and unable qck over 1f out: wknd ins fnl f* **14/1**

**9** *3 1/4* **Linda Doris (IRE)** 3-9-0 0................................................ MartinDwyer 6 40
(Gay Kelleway) *a in rr: rdn over 2f out: sn struggling and bhd over 1f out* **66/1**

5 **10** *1 3/4* **Deciding Vote**[24] 2727 3-9-0 0........................................... TomQueally 5 35
(Chris Wall) *stdd s: a in rr: n.d* **40/1**
1m 25.61s (-0.09) **Going Correction** +0.025s/f (Good) **10** Ran SP% **113.4**
Speed ratings (Par 100): **101,93,91,90,89 88,87,85,81,79**
CSF £18.94 TOTE £6.80: £2.20, £1.10, £4.00; EX 15.30 Trifecta £174.20.
**Owner** Jon A Thompson **Bred** P And Mrs A G Venner **Trained** Newmarket, Suffolk

**FOCUS**
An ordinary-looking fillies' maiden and the winner got the run of it in front, but she did this pretty well. The fourth has been rated similar to her previous efforts.

## 3596 ANIMAL HEALTH TRUST H'CAP 1m 4f
**4:50** (4:50) (Class 4) (0-80,78) 3-Y-0 **£5,175** (£1,540; £769; £384) **Stalls** Centre

Form RPR
4-31 **1** **Amlad (IRE)**[52] 1874 3-9-7 **78**................................... SilvestreDeSousa 2 87
(Ed Dunlop) *mde all: rdn 2f out: styd on strly and in command fnl f: rdn out* **4/1**[2]

6-15 **2** *2 3/4* **Maori Bob (IRE)**[101] 967 3-8-7 **64**............................ JosephineGordon 8 68
(Michael Bell) *chsd ldrs tl wnt 2nd over 2f out: rdn 2f out: drvn and styd on same pce fr over 1f out* **25/1**

6-44 **3** *2 1/4* **Cubswin (IRE)**[29] 2564 3-9-1 **72**........................................ HarryBentley 4 72
(Roger Charlton) *t.k.h: hld up in tch in last trio: clsd and nt clrest of runs over 2f out: hdwy u.p over 1f out: 3rd and kpt on same pce u.p ins fnl f* **10/1**

4-43 **4** *4* **Really Super**[21] 2834 3-9-6 **77**............................................... FranBerry 1 71
(Ralph Beckett) *t.k.h: chsd ldrs: 3rd and u.p 2f out: no imp over 1f out: wknd ins fnl f* **2/1**[1]

46-0 **5** *4* **Medalla De Oro**[37] 2347 3-8-11 **68**.................................... WilliamBuick 5 55
(Peter Chapple-Hyam) *stdd s: t.k.h: hld up in rr: swtchd lft 3f out: sn rdn: unable qck and edgd bk rt over 2f out: sn struggling and wl btn over 1f out* **20/1**

5-24 **6** *1* **Bedouin (IRE)**[22] 2807 3-9-4 **75**.......................................(b) AdamKirby 3 61
(Luca Cumani) *hld up in tch in midfield: clsd and nt clr run 3f out: rdn over 2f out: no imp and btn 5th whn hung rt over 1f out: wknd fnl f* **9/2**[3]

623 **7** *nk* **Marqoom**[42] 2159 3-9-2 **73**..................................................... JimCrowley 6 58
(Mark Johnston) *chsd wnr: rdn over 4f out: lost pl qckly over 2f out: wl btn over 1f out* **8/1**

-343 **8** *1/2* **Sufi**[24] 2721 3-9-6 **77**.......................................................... PatDobbs 7 61
(Richard Hannon) *hld up in tch in midfield: short-lived effrt u.p over 2f out: sn btn and wknd over 1f out: fin lame* **7/1**
2m 32.38s (-0.52) **Going Correction** +0.025s/f (Good) **8** Ran SP% **112.8**
Speed ratings (Par 101): **102,100,98,96,93 92,92,92**
CSF £88.79 CT £924.42 TOTE £4.30: £1.40, £5.60, £3.00; EX 81.70 Trifecta £769.60.
**Owner** Abdullah Saeed Al Naboodah **Bred** Barouche Stud Ireland Ltd **Trained** Newmarket, Suffolk

**FOCUS**
The winner was allowed a clear lead. The third has been rated to her maiden form.

## 3597 BET SOLUTIONS INTERNATIONAL PLC H'CAP 1m 2f
**5:25** (5:27) (Class 2) (0-100,100) 4-Y-0+ **£12,938** (£3,850; £1,924; £962) **Stalls** Centre

Form RPR
-222 **1** **Kapstadt (FR)**[14] 3065 7-8-10 **89**............................................ FranBerry 12 99
(Ian Williams) *hld up in tch in midfield: effrt and rdn to chse ldrs 2f out: styd on to ld 1f out: kpt on wl ins fnl f: forged ahd towards fin: rdn out* **9/1**[3]

300/ **2** *1* **First Flight (IRE)**[700] 4165 6-9-2 **95**................................ GeraldMosse 11 103
(Heather Main) *hld up in rr of main gp: swtchd lft and hdwy in centre over 2f out: str chal jst ins fnl f: kpt on but outpcd towards fin* **33/1**

-005 **3** *2 1/2* **Beardwood**[12] 3154 5-8-9 **88**...................................... SilvestreDeSousa 3 91
(Mark Johnston) *hld up in tch in midfield: nt clr run and swtchd lft over 2f out: swtchd bk rt and hdwy u.p 2f out: chsd ldrs and edgd lft ins fnl f: styd on to go 3rd towards fin* **8/1**[2]

0234 **4** *1/2* **Pactolus (IRE)**[39] 2261 6-8-6 **88**..................................(t) AaronJones(3) 6 90
(Stuart Williams) *hld up in tch in midfield: nt clr run over 2f out: swtchd lft and effrt over 1f out: chsd ldrs jst ins fnl f: kpt on same pce and lost 3rd towards fin* **40/1**

0-45 **5** *3 3/4* **Berkshire (IRE)**[14] 3069 6-9-7 **100**..................................(p[1]) AdamKirby 4 95
(Paul Cole) *sn led: rdn over 2f out: hdd 1f out: sn wknd* **12/1**

0-0 **6** *1 1/4* **Munaashid (USA)**[16] 3014 4-8-2 **81** oh1.................. JosephineGordon 15 73
(Ed Dunlop) *hld up in tch in midfield: hdwy to chse ldrs and rdn 2f out: unable qck over 1f out: wknd ins fnl f* **50/1**

/301 **7** *1/2* **Sgt Reckless**[7] 3315 10-8-2 **86**........................................ DavidEgan(5) 5 77
(Mick Channon) *hld up in tch in midfield: rdn 3f out: hdwy to chse ldrs 2f out tl unable qck over 1f out: wknd ins fnl f* **16/1**

3-66 **8** *nk* **Hibou**[12] 3154 4-8-10 **89**...............................................(b) MartinDwyer 14 79
(Iain Jardine) *stdd after s: hld up off the pce in last pair: clsd and in tch 4f out: effrt ent fnl 2f: no imp u.p over 1f out: wknd ins fnl f* **16/1**

5/1- **9** *hd* **Firnas**[394] 2175 4-9-2 **95**...................................................... WilliamBuick 1 85
(Charlie Appleby) *plld hrd early: t.k.h: swtchd lft and chsd ldr jst over 2f out: ev ch but unable qck u.p over 1f out: wknd ins fnl f* **6/4**[1]

62-4 **10** *nk* **Awake My Soul (IRE)**[24] 2735 8-9-0 **93**..................... AndrewMullen 13 82
(Tom Tate) *taken down early: t.k.h: chsd ldrs: rdn to chse ldr briefly over 2f out: losing pl whn short of room 2f out: sn lost pl and wknd fnl f* **9/1**[3]

0040 **11** *1 1/4* **Top Notch Tonto (IRE)**[23] 2767 7-8-13 **99**............(t) BenRobinson(7) 10 86
(Brian Ellison) *stdd s: hld up off the pce in last trio: clsd and in tch 4f out: rdn 3f out: no imp and wknd over 1f out* **25/1**

-040 **12** *shd* **Majeed**[119] 699 7-9-2 **100**.......................................... GeorgeBuckell(5) 9 87
(David Simcock) *stdd s: hld up wl off the pce in rr: clsd and in tch 4f out: swtchd lft and effrt 2f out: sn no imp: wknd fnl f* **10/1**

0466 **13** *19* **Great Hall**[8] 3300 7-9-6 **99**................................................. ShaneKelly 8 48
(Mick Quinn) *hld up in tch in rr of main gp: rdn over 2f out: drvn and wl btn 2f out: bhd and eased ins fnl f* **16/1**

21/0 **14** *6* **Mootaharer (IRE)**[38] 2290 4-8-11 **90**................................ JimCrowley 7 27
(Charles Hills) *chsd ldr tl over 2f out: sn dropped out and bhd fnl f* **20/1**
2m 2.21s (-3.29) **Going Correction** +0.025s/f (Good) **14** Ran SP% **121.5**
Speed ratings (Par 109): **114,113,111,110,107 106,106,106,106,105 104,104,89,84**
CSF £290.36 CT £2478.71 TOTE £11.40: £2.90, £10.60, £2.80; EX 365.10 Trifecta £4373.00.
**Owner** Anchor Men **Bred** Charles Barel **Trained** Portway, Worcs

**FOCUS**
A decent handicap. The winner has been rated close to his old French form.

T/Jkpt: Not won. T/Plt: £120.80 to a £1 stake. Pool: £85,741.00 - 709.60 winning units. T/Qpdt: £110.40 to a £1 stake. Pool: £5,911.00 - 53.50 winning units. **Steve Payne**

3598 - 3610a (Foreign Racing) - See Raceform Interactive

## 3353 MAISONS-LAFFITTE (R-H)

Saturday, June 10

**OFFICIAL GOING: Turf: good**

### 3611a PRIX LA FLECHE (LISTED RACE) (2YO) (TURF) 5f
4:30 2-Y-0

**£24,102** (£9,743; £7,179; £4,615; £2,820; £1,794)

RPR

1 **Ardenode (IRE)**35 2-9-2 0 FabriceVeron 3 100
(E J O'Neill, France) **67/10**
2 *hd* **Unfortunately (IRE)**22 [2771] 2-9-2 0 TonyPiccone 9 99
(K R Burke) *hld up in rr: rdn and gd hdwy on wd outside fr 2f out: styd on wl to press wnr strly last 100yds: jst hld* **66/10**
3 *1 1/2* **Mister Picnic (FR)**35 2-9-2 0 Francois-XavierBertras 2 94
(D Guillemin, France) **16/51**
4 *3* **Rioticism (FR)**24 2-8-13 0 AntoineHamelin 6 80
(Matthieu Palussiere, France) **51/103**
5 *hd* **Lady Anjorica (IRE)**16 [2987] 2-8-13 0 GregoryBenoist 4 79
(Keith Dalgleish) *towards rr of midfield: pushed along 2 1/2f out: rdn 1 1/2f out: sme hdwy clsng stages: n.d* **183/10**
6 *hd* **Listen Alexander (IRE)**19 [2904] 2-8-13 0 MaximeGuyon 5 79
(David Evans) *trckd ldrs: rdn 2 1/2f out: outpcd 1 1/2f out: no imp fnl f* **105/10**
7 *shd* **Pimpinehorse (FR)**63 2-9-2 0 ChristopheSoumillon 7 81
(R Chotard, France) **47/102**
8 *hd* **Get Even**22 [2801] 2-8-13 0 MickaelBarzalona 10 78
(Jo Hughes) *towards rr: rdn over 3f out: hdwy into midfield 2 1/2f out: wknd steadily fnl f* **165/10**
9 *2* **Mon Amie Chop (FR)** 2-8-13 0 StephanePasquier 1 70
(J-P Gauvin, France) **74/10**
10 *nk* **Gaelic Spirit (IRE)**10 [3215] 2-8-13 0 IoritzMendizabal 8 69
(Joseph Tuite) *midfield: pushed along and outpcd 2 1/2f out: wknd steadily fr over 1f out: eased clsng stages* **41/1**

58.69s **10** Ran SP% **117.8**
PARI-MUTUEL (all including 1 euro stake): WIN 7.70 PLACE 2.40, 2.60, 1.80 DF 26.70 SF 49.10.
**Owner** Mrs Susan Davis & Mrs Melissa O'Neill **Bred** R & M Bloodstock **Trained** France

### 3612a PRIX DES LILAS (LISTED RACE) (3YO FILLIES) (STRAIGHT) (TURF) 1m
5:30 3-Y-0 **£23,504** (£9,401; £7,051; £4,700; £2,350)

RPR

1 **Thais (FR)**28 [2644] 3-9-0 0 ChristopheSoumillon 6 107
(P Bary, France) **5/1**
2 *1* **Ambivalence (IRE)**26 3-9-0 0 MaximeGuyon 4 105
(H-A Pantall, France) **47/103**
3 *3* **Lady Frankel**27 [2665] 3-9-0 0 VincentCheminaud 2 98
(A Fabre, France) **19/101**
4 *1 3/4* **Charly Nova (FR)**42 [2170] 3-9-0 0 MickaelBarzalona 9 94
(F Rossi, France) **11/2**
5 *3/4* **Niedziela (IRE)**35 [2421] 3-9-0 0 CristianDemuro 5 92
(C Lerner, France) **25/1**
6 *nk* **La Poutanesca (IRE)**35 [2421] 3-9-0 0 GregoryBenoist 1 91
(D Smaga, France) **159/10**
7 *5* **Flower Fashion (FR)**35 [2421] 3-9-0 0 StephanePasquier 3 80
(N Clement, France) **7/22**
8 *1 3/4* **Erica Bing**31 [2523] 3-9-0 0 TheoBachelot 7 76
(Jo Hughes) *prom: rdn and lost pl qckly 2 1/2f out: sn struggling: eased ins fnl f* **50/1**

1m 35.48s (-6.82) **8** Ran SP% **118.0**
PARI-MUTUEL (all including 1 euro stake): WIN 6.00 PLACE 1.70, 1.80, 1.40 DF 17.70 SF 29.80.
**Owner** Ecurie J-L Bouchard & Mme G Sandor **Bred** G Sandor & Mme G Sandor **Trained** Chantilly, France

### 3613a PRIX MARCHAND D'OR (LISTED RACE) (3YO) (TURF) 6f 110y
6:00 3-Y-0 **£23,504** (£9,401; £7,051; £4,700; £2,350)

RPR

1 **Aiming For Rio (FR)**27 3-8-7 0 MickaelBarzalona 6 106+
(A Fabre, France) *led gp of five on far side (2nd overall): rdn 1 1/2f out: led 1f out: sn in command: rdn out* **31/5**
2 *2* **City Light (FR)**30 [2561] 3-8-10 0 ChristopheSoumillon 1 103
(S Wattel, France) **21/101**
3 *shd* **Incampo (FR)**34 [2446] 3-8-10 0 MaximeGuyon 7 103
(H-A Pantall, France) **59/10**
4 *1* **Battle In Seattle (FR)**86 [1236] 3-8-10 0 AntoineHamelin 5 100
(A De Royer-Dupre, France) **5/13**
5 *3 1/2* **Simmie (IRE)**21 [2823] 3-8-10 0 TonyPiccone 2 90
(K R Burke) *chsd other runner on nr side (midfield overall): rdn over 2f out: outpcd ent fnl f: sn no imp* **11/52**
6 *2 1/2* **L'Invincible (FR)**24 3-8-7 0 TheoBachelot 3 79
(J-P-J Dubois, France) **153/10**
7 *4 1/2* **Aufsteiger (FR)**12 3-8-10 0 IoritzMendizabal 4 69
(P Schiergen, Germany) **29/1**

1m 16.34s **7** Ran SP% **118.0**
PARI-MUTUEL (all including 1 euro stake): WIN 7.20 PLACE 3.50, 2.00 SF 26.50.
**Owner** Godolphin SNC **Bred** Earl Haras Du Logis & Julian Ince **Trained** Chantilly, France

### 3614a PRIX HAMPTON (LISTED RACE) (3YO+) (TURF) 5f
6:30 3-Y-0+ **£22,222** (£8,888; £6,666; £4,444; £2,222)

RPR

1 **Rosa Imperial (IRE)**23 4-8-13 0 MickaelBarzalona 8 104+
(A Fabre, France) *s.i.s: in rr: rdn and gd hdwy fr under 2f out: drvn and kpt on strly fr under 1f out: led 75yds out: readily* **6/51**
2 *1 1/2* **Val Nanda (IRE)**48 3-8-6 0 IvanRossi 5 96
(Cristiana Signorelli, Italy) **183/10**
3 *hd* **Spiritfix**19 4-8-13 0 MaximeGuyon 3 98+
(A Fabre, France) **32/5**
4 *nk* **Clem Fandango (FR)**30 [2561] 3-8-9 0 GregoryBenoist 9 97
(Keith Dalgleish) *racd in midfield: rdn under 2f out: hdwy to chse ldrs ins fnl f: no ex clsng stages* **48/103**
5 *3* **California Tee**282 [6068] 3-8-6 0 AntoineHamelin 6 83
(Matthieu Palussiere, France) **58/1**
6 *3/4* **Shot In The Dark (FR)**23 4-9-2 0 StephanePasquier 4 87
(F Chappet, France) **12/1**
7 *hd* **Sir Robert Cheval**27 [2657] 6-9-2 0 ChristopheSoumillon 1 86
(Robert Cowell) *towards rr: rdn and brief effrt 2f out: wknd ins fnl f* **9/22**
8 *4* **Becquamis (FR)**30 [2561] 3-8-13 0 (p) AntoineWerle 7 73
(T Lemer, France) **209/10**
9 *1 1/2* **Eskimo Point (IRE)**28 [2643] 5-9-5 0 (p) TonyPiccone 2 69
(Mario Hofer, Germany) **178/10**

57.08s
**WFA** 3 from 4yo+ 7lb **9** Ran SP% **118.8**
PARI-MUTUEL (all including 1 euro stake): WIN 2.20 PLACE 1.40, 3.00, 1.90 DF 20.90 SF 32.90.
**Owner** Godolphin SNC **Bred** Darley **Trained** Chantilly, France

## 3531 GOODWOOD (R-H)

Sunday, June 11

**OFFICIAL GOING: Straight course - good to soft; round course - good (7.2)**
Wind: light breeze against Weather: sunny with some cloud

### 3615 NSPCC SPEAK OUT STAY SAFE MAIDEN FILLIES' STKS 1m 1f 197y
2:00 (2:02) (Class 5) 3-Y-0+ **£4,528** (£1,347; £673; £336) **Stalls** Low

Form RPR

2 1 **Lightening Dance**24 [2759] 3-8-13 0 JimCrowley 2 77
(Amanda Perrett) *w'like: mid-div: hdwy over 2f out: rdn whn chalng over 1f out: led jst ins fnl f: styd on wl: rdn out* **2/11**
0 2 *nk* **Sileel (USA)**48 [2019] 3-8-13 0 (v1) JosephineGordon 8 76
(Ed Dunlop) *str: trckd ldrs: chal over 2f out: sn rdn: led over 1f out: hdd jst ins fnl f: styd on wl* **33/1**
3-3 3 *nk* **Italian Heiress**20 [2908] 3-8-10 0 HectorCrouch(3) 1 76+
(Clive Cox) *lengthy: lw: trckd ldrs: nt clrest of runs over 2f out: rdn over 1f out: swtchd rt ins fnl f: styd on strly towards fin* **8/13**
6 4 *2 1/4* **Paris Rooftops (IRE)**17 [3007] 3-8-13 0 JamieSpencer 7 71
(Luca Cumani) *trckd ldr: rdn and v ch over 2f out tl jst ins fnl f: no ex fnl 100yds* **4/12**
5 *3/4* **Tarte Tropezienne (IRE)** 3-8-13 0 PatCosgrave 11 69+
(William Haggas) *unf: dwlt: bhd hdwy but nt clrest of runs 3f out: styd on nicely fnl f wout threatening to get on terms: improve* **10/1**
0-63 6 *3 3/4* **Trilliant (IRE)**24 [2759] 3-8-13 78 OisinMurphy 3 62
(Ed Walker) *lw: led: rdn wl over 2f out whn strly pressed: hdd over 1f out: fdd ins fnl f* **4/12**
6 7 *3 3/4* **Shanandoa**24 [2759] 6-9-5 0 (h) JoshuaBryan(7) 10 55
(Brian Barr) *bit bkwd: s.i.s: towards rr: hdwy into midfield 3f out: sn rdn: one pce fnl 2f* **100/1**
0 8 *1/2* **Queen Beatrice**20 [2908] 3-8-13 0 MartinDwyer 6 53
(William Muir) *leggy: racd keenly in midfield: rdn over 2f out: no imp* **100/1**
9 *nse* **Artic Nel** 3-8-13 0 GeorgeDowning 9 53
(Ian Williams) *w'like: s.i.s: a towards rr* **66/1**
6 10 *nse* **Celtik Secret**20 [2908] 3-8-13 0 SilvestreDeSousa 5 53
(Hughie Morrison) *leggy: trckd ldrs: rdn 3f out: wknd over 1f out* **16/1**
11 *23* **Dukinta (IRE)** 3-8-13 0 JamesDoyle 4 7
(Hugo Palmer) *athletic: sn pushed along in midfield: rdn 3f out: wknd over 1f out* **10/1**

2m 10.42s (2.32) **Going Correction** +0.275s/f (Good)
**WFA** 3 from 6yo 13lb **11** Ran SP% **114.9**
Speed ratings (Par 100): **101,100,100,98,98 95,92,91,91,91 73**
CSF £78.31 TOTE £2.80: £1.30, £9.00, £2.20; EX 90.20 Trifecta £899.80.
**Owner** Mrs Alexandra J Chandris **Bred** Mrs J Chandris **Trained** Pulborough, W Sussex

**FOCUS**
First 2f of the Mile course dolled out 5yds. They went a fair enough pace in this modest fillies' maiden and there was something of a slow-motion finish.

### 3616 SUTTON WINSON BACKING THE NSPCC H'CAP 1m 3f 44y
2:30 (2:32) (Class 5) (0-75,80) 4-Y-0+ **£4,528** (£1,347; £673; £336) **Stalls** High

Form RPR

6-42 1 **Silver Ghost (IRE)**17 [3009] 4-9-7 **75** CharlesBishop 3 86+
(Eve Johnson Houghton) *mde all: styd on gamely to assert fnl f: rdn out* **11/41**
-601 2 *1 3/4* **Thames Knight**9 [3308] 5-9-5 **80** TylerSaunders(7) 11 87
(Marcus Tregoning) *lw: mid-div: hdwy wl over 2f out: rdn in cl 3rd jst over 1f out: wnt 2nd jst ins fnl f: styd on but a being hld by wnr* **15/2**
-365 3 *1 1/2* **Cordite (IRE)**17 [3009] 6-9-2 **70** (h) PatCosgrave 4 74
(Jim Boyle) *trckd ldr: rdn and ev ch over 1f out: styd on but no ex ins fnl f* **9/1**
5511 4 *2 1/2* **Fast And Hot (IRE)**20 [2909] 4-8-13 **74** (b) RossaRyan(7) 2 74
(Richard Hannon) *trckd ldrs: nt clr run briefly 3f out: sn rdn to dispute cl 3rd: nt quite pce to get on terms: no ex fnl 120yds* **6/12**
6300 5 *3/4* **Archangel Raphael (IRE)**13 [2369] 5-9-5 **73** (v1) PatDobbs 8 72
(Amanda Perrett) *s.i.s: towards rr: hdwy on rails fr 3f out: rdn to chse ldrs over 1f out: styd on but nt pce to get involved* **40/1**
0223 6 *shd* **Essenaitch (IRE)**6 [3409] 4-9-3 **71** JamesDoyle 12 70
(David Evans) *mid-div: hdwy over 3f out: rdn over 2f out: styd on same pce* **7/13**
132/ 7 *3* **Milky Way (IRE)**673 [5154] 5-9-1 **72** HectorCrouch(3) 9 66
(Gary Moore) *hld up towards rr: midfield whn rdn over 2f out: no further imp on ldrs* **14/1**
-560 8 *1 1/4* **Ban Shoof**19 [2913] 4-9-1 **69** TimmyMurphy 1 61
(Gary Moore) *hld up towards rr: nvr any imp on ldrs fr 3f out* **66/1**
0/ 9 *1/2* **Azzuri**9 [6510] 5-9-4 **77** (t) DavidEgan(5) 5 68
(Dan Skelton) *lw: in tch: rdn over 2f out: wknd over 1f out* **8/1**
1-43 10 *3 3/4* **Art Of Swing (IRE)**23 [2781] 5-9-2 **70** TomQueally 10 54
(Gary Moore) *lw: mid-div: pushed along 4f out: nvr threatened: wknd over 1f out* **16/1**
1-14 11 *5* **Balancing Time**9 [3308] 4-9-7 **75** (p) JimCrowley 7 51
(Amanda Perrett) *trckd ldrs: rdn over 2f out: wknd over 1f out* **8/1**
3605 12 *12* **Rightway (IRE)**18 [2956] 6-8-5 **64** GeorgiaCox(5) 6 19
(Tony Carroll) *s.i.s: towards rr of midfield: effrt 3f out: wknd 2f out* **33/1**

2m 27.29s (0.79) **Going Correction** +0.275s/f (Good) **12** Ran SP% **116.9**
Speed ratings (Par 103): **108,106,105,103,103 103,101,100,99,97 93,84**
CSF £22.56 CT £165.02 TOTE £3.40: £1.50, £2.90, £3.40; EX 25.40 Trifecta £257.20.
**Owner** Mrs Jennifer Simpson Racing **Bred** George Delahunt **Trained** Blewbury, Oxon

**FOCUS**
Race distance increased by 10yds. It paid to be handy in this modest handicap but the form looks solid.

## 3617 CSS SEISMIC SWEEPSTAKE H'CAP 5f
**3:05** (3:05) (Class 4) (0-85,87) 6-Y-O+ **£6,469** (£1,925; £962; £481) **Stalls** High

| Form | | | | RPR |
|---|---|---|---|---|
| 0214 | **1** | | **Zac Brown (IRE)**[29] 2621 6-8-6 **75**...(t) DavidEgan(5) 3 (Charlie Wallis) *awkwardly away and squeezed up s: trckd ldrs: rdn to ld over 1f out: r.o wl* **9/2**[2] | 88 |
| -503 | **2** | ½ | **Pettochside**[15] 3074 8-8-13 **77**... JosephineGordon 1 (John Bridger) *prom: rdn for str chal over 1f out: ev ch ins fnl f: hld towards fin* **7/2**[1] | 88 |
| 4654 | **3** | 3 ¾ | **Seamster**[9] 3288 10-8-7 **78**...(t) CameronNoble(7) 2 (David Loughnane) *prom: rdn and ev ch 2f out: hld in 3rd ent fnl f: kpt on same pce* **8/1** | 76 |
| 20-0 | **4** | 1 | **Intibaah**[150] 194 7-9-4 **82**...(b) PatCosgrave 5 (George Baker) *prom: rdn 2f out: kpt on same pce fnl f* **10/1** | 76 |
| 6104 | **5** | nk | **Dungannon**[37] 2368 10-9-2 **87**...(b) JoshuaBryan(7) 4 (Andrew Balding) *squeezed up s: trckd ldrs: rdn 2f out: kpt on but nt pce to get on terms* **10/1** | 80 |
| 0-26 | **6** | ½ | **Waseem Faris (IRE)**[36] 2391 8-9-6 **84**... PatDobbs 6 (Ken Cunningham-Brown) *lw: rrd leaving stalls: chsd ldrs: rdn 2f out: kpt on same pce* **10/1** | 75 |
| 00-2 | **7** | 1 ¼ | **Ladweb**[22] 2839 7-9-2 **85**... GeorgeBuckell(5) 8 (John Gallagher) *led: rdn and hdd over 1f out: fdd fnl 100yds* **11/2** | 72 |
| 1032 | **8** | 1 | **Fredricka**[10] 3253 6-9-1 **79**...(p) SilvestreDeSousa 7 (Chris Dwyer) *prom: rdn over 2f out: fdd ins fnl f* **5/1**[3] | 62 |

59.43s (-0.77) **Going Correction** 0.0s/f (Good) **8** Ran SP% **110.8**
Speed ratings: **106,105,99,97,97 96,94,92**
CSF £19.30 CT £106.28 TOTE £5.10: £1.80, £1.50, £2.90; EX 19.20 Trifecta £113.70.
**Owner** Dab Hand Racing **Bred** Tally-Ho Stud **Trained** Ardleigh, Essex

**FOCUS**
The first pair came clear down the middle in this fair sprint handicap.

## 3618 MAYWAL H'CAP 2m
**3:40** (3:40) (Class 3) (0-90,89) 4-Y-O+ **£9,703** (£2,887; £1,443; £721) **Stalls** Low

| Form | | | | RPR |
|---|---|---|---|---|
| 11-2 | **1** | | **London Prize**[29] 728 6-9-4 **84**... JamesDoyle 3 (Ian Williams) *in tch: hdwy over 2f out: rdn to ld over 1f out: styd on strly to draw clr fnl f: comf* **7/4**[1] | 99 |
| 2-42 | **2** | 8 | **Medburn Cutler**[17] 3004 7-8-10 **76**...(p) SilvestreDeSousa 9 (Paul Henderson) *lw: pressed ldr: rdn and ev ch fr over 2f out tl jst over 1f out: styd on but sn hld by comfortable wnr* **8/1** | 81 |
| 62/1 | **3** | 3 ¾ | **Sternrubin (GER)**[41] 2234 6-9-2 **82**...(h) TomQueally 4 (Philip Hobbs) *sn led: rdn and drifted lft fr over 2f out: hdd over 1f out: fdd fnl 120yds* **10/3**[2] | 84 |
| 4-56 | **4** | 1 ½ | **Mazalto (IRE)**[36] 2388 4-8-4 **71** oh1... KieranO'Neill 2 (Pat Phelan) *hld up: rdn wl over 2f out: styd on fnl 2f to go 4th wl ins fnl f but nvr gng pce to get involved* **33/1** | 70 |
| 0-33 | **5** | nk | **Paris Protocol**[15] 3076 4-9-8 **89**... JimCrowley 7 (Richard Hannon) *trckd ldrs: rdn over 2f out: styd on same pce fnl 2f* **6/1**[3] | 87 |
| 0-54 | **6** | 2 ¼ | **Fitzwilly**[18] 2966 7-8-0 **71** oh4... DavidEgan(5) 5 (Mick Channon) *hld up: struggling in last pair whn drifted to center over 3f out: sme minor late prog but nvr any threat to ldrs* **14/1** | 67 |
| 1-05 | **7** | ½ | **Michael's Mount**[30] 2574 4-8-11 **78**...(p) OisinMurphy 1 (Ed Dunlop) *trckd ldrs: rdn over 2f out: nt quite pce to mount chal: wknd ent fnl f* **12/1** | 73 |
| 0/ | **8** | 1 | **Milord (GER)**[29] 8-9-2 **82**...(p) TrevorWhelan 6 (Kim Bailey) *in tch: rdn over 3f out: sn one pce* **40/1** | 76 |
| -051 | **9** | 28 | **Chartbreaker (FR)**[17] 3004 6-9-0 **80**...(p) PatCosgrave 8 (Chris Gordon) *rn in snatches: rousted along leaving stalls: sn in tch: drifted to center u.p over 3f out: wknd over 1f out* **12/1** | 40 |

3m 30.66s (1.66) **Going Correction** +0.275s/f (Good) **9** Ran SP% **112.3**
Speed ratings (Par 107): **106,102,100,99,99 98,97,97,83**
CSF £15.95 CT £41.85 TOTE £2.70: £1.40, £1.70, £1.50; EX 13.20 Trifecta £53.40.
**Owner** Mrs Margaret Forsyth **Bred** P And Mrs A G Venner **Trained** Portway, Worcs

**FOCUS**
This was was run at a sound pace and the placed horses set a useful level.

## 3619 NSPCC LETTING THE FUTURE IN (S) STKS 5f
**4:15** (4:19) (Class 4) 2-Y-O **£6,469** (£1,925; £962; £481) **Stalls** High

| Form | | | | RPR |
|---|---|---|---|---|
| 2366 | **1** | | **Milton Road**[10] 3245 2-8-13 0... SilvestreDeSousa 4 (Mick Channon) *trckd ldrs: swtchd rt 2f out: rdn to ld ent fnl f: r.o* **7/4**[1] | 65 |
| 4364 | **2** | 1 ¼ | **Quick Skips Lad (IRE)**[29] 2642 2-8-8 0...(b[1]) DavidEgan(5) 2 (J S Moore) *disp ld: rdn 2f out: hdd ent fnl f: kpt on same pce* **11/4**[2] | 60 |
| 05 | **3** | hd | **Tie Em Up Tel (IRE)**[38] 2343 2-8-13 0... JamesDoyle 3 (David Evans) *disp ld: rdn 2f out: hdd ent fnl f: kpt on same pce* **9/2**[3] | 59 |
| 00 | **4** | 7 | **Dolly Dagger**[23] 2801 2-8-8 0... KieranO'Neill 7 (Mark Usher) *rousted along leaving stalls: chsd ldrs: rdn 3f out: drifted rt over 1f out: wknd ent fnl f* **9/1** | 29 |
| | **5** | 2 | **One Drunken Night** 2-8-6 0... CameronNoble(7) 1 (Gay Kelleway) *leggy: chsd ldrs: rdn 2f out: wknd ent fnl f* **8/1** | 26 |
| 40 | **6** | 5 | **Cranworth Phoenix**[24] 2756 2-8-8 0... RyanTate 6 (Brian Barr) *leggy: prom tl rdn 2f out: sn wknd* **16/1** | 3 |

1m 0.89s (0.69) **Going Correction** 0.0s/f (Good) **6** Ran SP% **108.2**
Speed ratings (Par 95): **94,92,91,80,77 69**
CSF £6.17 TOTE £2.00: £1.50, £1.50; EX 5.40 Trifecta £11.00.The winner was bought in for 9,500gns.
**Owner** M Channon **Bred** M P Bishop **Trained** West Ilsley, Berks
■ Rachael's Rocket was withdrawn. Price at time of withdrawal 25-1. Rule 4 does not apply.

**FOCUS**
A typically weak 2yo seller. The winner didn't have to match his pre-race best.

## 3620 BETFRED SUPPORTS THE NSPCC H'CAP 7f
**4:45** (4:46) (Class 3) (0-90,92) 3-Y-O+ **£9,703** (£2,887; £1,443; £721) **Stalls** Low

| Form | | | | RPR |
|---|---|---|---|---|
| 4-10 | **1** | | **Aventinus (IRE)**[31] 2554 3-8-12 **84**... JackMitchell 2 (Hugo Palmer) *a.p: led 2f out: kpt on wl fnl f: rdn out* **6/1** | 87 |
| 3654 | **2** | ¾ | **Medburn Dream**[16] 3030 4-9-6 **82**... SilvestreDeSousa 4 (Paul Henderson) *lw: trckd ldrs: nt clr run over 1f out: rdn whn swtchd lft ent fnl f: kpt on but nt pce to get to wnr* **3/1**[2] | 87 |
| 030 | **3** | hd | **Professor**[17] 3003 7-9-9 **85**... JosephineGordon 5 (Michael Attwater) *trckd ldrs: chal over 2f out: sn rdn: ev ch ent fnl f: kpt on but no ex fnl 120yds* **14/1** | 89 |
| 3030 | **4** | 1 | **Mister Music**[13] 3144 8-9-4 **80**... GeorgeDowning 8 (Tony Carroll) *hld up last: rdn and stdy prog fr 2f out: kpt on to go 4th ins fnl f but nt pce to threaten ldrs* **25/1** | 82 |
| 5302 | **5** | nk | **The Warrior (IRE)**[17] 3003 5-10-0 **90**...(v) JimCrowley 9 (Amanda Perrett) *hld up: cl up but nt clr run jst over 1f out: kpt on whn clr in side fnl f but nt pce to threaten* **5/1**[3] | 91 |
| 60-0 | **6** | ½ | **Scottish Glen**[22] 2833 11-9-13 **92**... HectorCrouch(3) 6 (Patrick Chamings) *in tch: rdn to chse ldrs over 2f out: kpt on same pce fnl f* **16/1** | 92 |
| 1301 | **7** | nk | **Athassel**[11] 3214 8-9-0 **83**... KatherineGlenister(7) 7 (David Evans) *hld up: racing keenly whn short of room on rails 4f out: rdn over 2f out: kpt on but nt pce to get on terms* **25/1** | 84+ |
| 1-25 | **8** | ¾ | **Tai Sing Yeh (IRE)**[15] 3082 3-8-10 **85**...(t) CallumShepherd(3) 3 (Charles Hills) *s.i.s: in tch: rdn 2f out: kpt on but nt pce to mount chal* **8/1** | 78 |
| 4-12 | **9** | 6 | **Time To Exceed (IRE)**[27] 2692 4-9-7 **83**... DaneO'Neill 1 (Henry Candy) *lw: sn led: rdn and hdd 2f out: disputing 3rd but hld whn looked to lose action and eased ins fnl f* **11/4**[1] | 64 |

1m 27.63s (0.63) **Going Correction** +0.275s/f (Good)
**WFA** 3 from 4yo+ 10lb **9** Ran SP% **114.0**
Speed ratings (Par 107): **107,106,105,104,104 103,103,102,95**
CSF £24.00 CT £237.71 TOTE £7.00: £2.60, £1.60, £3.10; EX 31.40 Trifecta £333.10.
**Owner** Seventh Lap Racing **Bred** Dr Philip J Brown **Trained** Newmarket, Suffolk

**FOCUS**
Race distance increased by 10yds. A fair handicap, run at an average pace.

## 3621 WILLEXCELL CONSULTING SUPPORTS THE NSPCC H'CAP 7f
**5:20** (5:20) (Class 5) (0-75,76) 3-Y-O **£4,528** (£1,347; £673; £336) **Stalls** Low

| Form | | | | RPR |
|---|---|---|---|---|
| 140 | **1** | | **Cyrus Dallin**[16] 3040 3-9-7 **75**...(h[1]) MartinDwyer 2 (William Muir) *trckd ldrs: rdn over 2f out: drifted rt whn ldng over 1f out: kpt on wl fnl f* **33/1** | 81 |
| -160 | **2** | 2 | **Alemaratalyoum (IRE)**[13] 3162 3-9-3 **71**... SilvestreDeSousa 9 (Ed Dunlop) *mid-div: rdn and hdwy over 2f out: wnt 3rd jst over 1f out: kpt on to go 2nd ins fnl f but a being hld by wnr* **11/1** | 72 |
| -130 | **3** | ¾ | **Gala Celebration (IRE)**[17] 3000 3-8-8 **67**...(h) GeorgeBuckell(5) 6 (John Gallagher) *lw: led: rdn and hdd over 1f out: no ex fnl f* **10/1** | 66 |
| 0-00 | **4** | 3 | **Diable D'Or (IRE)**[41] 2215 3-9-6 **74**... CharlesBishop 10 (Eve Johnson Houghton) *mid-div: hdwy 3f out: nt clr run over 2f out and again briefly whn rdn over 1f out: nt pce to get on terms* **16/1** | 65 |
| 2041 | **5** | nk | **Jet Setter (IRE)**[12] 3166 3-9-2 **70**... GeorgeDowning 7 (Tony Carroll) *hld up: rdn and stdy prog fr 2f out: kpt on wl ins fnl f but no threat to ldrs* **20/1** | 60 |
| 6466 | **6** | 2 | **Hisar (IRE)**[23] 2778 3-9-5 **73**... ShaneKelly 5 (Ronald Harris) *trckd ldrs: rdn over 2f out: sn one pce* **25/1** | 58 |
| 4-21 | **7** | 3 ½ | **Crafty Madam (IRE)**[15] 3085 3-9-4 **72**... AdamKirby 1 (Clive Cox) *trckd ldrs: rdn and ch 2f out: wknd fnl f* **7/4**[1] | 47 |
| 100 | **8** | 3 | **Mori Yoshinari (IRE)**[27] 2690 3-9-5 **73**...(b[1]) PatDobbs 8 (Richard Hannon) *s.i.s: towards rr: rdn over 2f out: little imp* **20/1** | 40 |
| 03-0 | **9** | hd | **Himself**[43] 2151 3-9-8 **76**... TomMarquand 4 (Richard Hannon) *trckd ldrs: rdn over 2f out: wknd jst over 1f out* **8/1**[3] | 43 |
| 4540 | **10** | 1 ¾ | **Gunmaker (IRE)**[15] 3088 3-9-0 **68**...(h[1]) JamieSpencer 3 (David Simcock) *lw: s.i.s: towards rr: swtchd lft over 3f out: effrt over 2f out: nvr threatened: wknd over 1f out* **9/1** | 30 |
| 2110 | **11** | hd | **Dark Destroyer (IRE)**[51] 1945 3-9-3 **76**... DavidEgan(5) 11 (Joseph Tuite) *racd keenly: hld up: effrt in center over 2f out: nvr threatened: wknd over 1f out* **7/2**[2] | 37 |

1m 28.78s (1.78) **Going Correction** +0.275s/f (Good) **11** Ran SP% **119.3**
Speed ratings (Par 99): **100,97,96,93,93 90,86,83,83,81 80**
CSF £348.46 CT £3940.14 TOTE £23.50: £4.60, £2.50, £3.90; EX 830.80 Trifecta £4671.30.
**Owner** C L A Edginton **Bred** J A And Mrs Duffy **Trained** Lambourn, Berks

**FOCUS**
Race distance increased by 10yds. This wasn't a bad 3yo handicap. The leaders went off hard early on.
T/Jkpt: £7,580.70 to a £1 stake. Pool: £15,162.00 - 2 winning units. T/Plt: £27.50 to a £1 stake. Pool: £87,811.00 - 3,182.24 winning units. T/Qpdt: £8.00 to a £1 stake. Pool: £6,686.00 - 825.46 winning units. **Tim Mitchell**

# 3215 NOTTINGHAM (L-H)
Sunday, June 11

**OFFICIAL GOING: Good to soft (soft in places; 6.8)**
Wind: stiff breeze, against in straight

## 3622 BETTINGGODS.COM FREE RACING TIPS EBF MAIDEN STKS 5f 8y
**1:50** (1:51) (Class 5) 2-Y-O **£3,881** (£1,155; £577; £288) **Stalls** Centre

| Form | | | | RPR |
|---|---|---|---|---|
| | **1** | | **Abel Handy (IRE)** 2-9-5 0... TomEaves 2 (Declan Carroll) *mde all: pushed along and 1 l clr over 1f out: briefly rdn and extended advantage fnl f: comf* **16/1** | 80+ |
| | **2** | 2 ½ | **Roman River** 2-9-5 0... RobertWinston 3 (Martin Smith) *trckd wnr: ev ch 2f out: shkn up and effrt over 1f out: no imp: but r.o steadily fnl f* **8/1** | 71 |
| 05 | **3** | 1 | **Bodybuilder**[15] 3083 2-9-2 0... HollieDoyle(3) 7 (Richard Hannon) *prom: effrt and rdn over 1f out: one pce fnl f* **11/4**[1] | 67 |
| 0 | **4** | 3 ¾ | **Peter Leonard**[15] 3093 2-9-5 0... TonyHamilton 1 (Richard Fahey) *mid-div: pushed along 2f out: rdn over 1f out: one pce* **6/1** | 54 |
| 4 | **5** | nk | **W G Grace (IRE)**[9] 3283 2-9-5 0... FrannyNorton 6 (Mark Johnston) *prom: drvn wl over 1f out: rdn briefly and no ex: eased fnl f* **3/1**[2] | 52 |
| 0 | **6** | 2 ½ | **Cent Flying**[24] 2750 2-9-5 0... DougieCostello 5 (William Muir) *slowly away: rcvrd to latch on to pack: drvn along 2f out: rdn appr fnl f: no ex* **9/2**[3] | 43 |
| 0 | **7** | 4 | **Bee Machine (IRE)**[71] 1496 2-9-5 0... StevieDonohoe 8 (Declan Carroll) *hld up: struggling in rr whn sltly hmpd by rival over 1f out: eased after* **8/1** | 29+ |
| 0 | **U** | | **Peas On Earth**[11] 3215 2-9-0 0... KierenFox 4 (Derek Shaw) *hld up: in rr whn appeared to clip heels and uns rdr wl over 1f out* **100/1** | |

1m 2.76s (1.26) **Going Correction** -0.025s/f (Good) **8** Ran SP% **113.2**
Speed ratings (Par 93): **88,84,82,76,75 71,65,**
CSF £132.89 TOTE £14.90: £3.70, £2.80, £1.10; EX 193.50 Trifecta £777.00.
**Owner** F Gillespie **Bred** Mr & Mrs G Middlebrook **Trained** Malton, N Yorks

**FOCUS**
Rails on outer track and all distances as advertised. After a dry morning the going was changed to good to soft. An ordinary maiden taken from the front by a newcomer. The third helps set the opening level.

## 3623 BETTINGGOODS.COM BETTING TIPSTERS H'CAP — 1m 6f
**2:20** (2:21) (Class 5) (0-70,69) 4-Y-0+ — **£3,234** (£962; £481; £240) **Stalls** Low

Form — RPR

3-51 **1** — **Incus**$^{8}$ [3311] 4-8-9 **57** .......... AndreaAtzeni 4 — 64+
(Ed de Giles) *racd in 3rd first m: pushed along briefly 3f out: hdwy to ld over 2f out: sn 2 l clr: rdn fnl f: drvn out last 100 yds: advantage dwindling at line* — **5/4**$^{1}$

0403 **2** *nk* **Spiritoftomintoul**$^{8}$ [3311] 8-8-11 **62** ow2 .......... (t) CliffordLee$^{(5)}$ 5 — 70
(Tony Carroll) *hld up in last: hdwy 3f out: rdn 2f out: wnt 2nd over 1f out: r.o wl u.p fnl f: clsng on wnr nr fin* — **7/4**$^{2}$

413 **3** *6* **Hallstatt (IRE)**$^{40}$ [2270] 11-9-1 **63** .......... (t) BenCurtis 6 — 61
(John Mackie) *chsd ldr: drvn along and ev ch 2f out where passed by wnr: hrd rdn over 1f out: fdd fnl f* — **7/1**$^{3}$

3330 **4** *3 ¾* **Marshall Aid (IRE)**$^{18}$ [2966] 4-9-1 **63** .......... (v$^{1}$) DougieCostello 2 — 55
(Mark Usher) *led: extended ld to 3 l 1/2-way: rdn and hdd over 2f out: wknd* — **11/1**

-645 **5** *16* **Aumerle**$^{45}$ [2111] 5-9-3 **65** .......... GrahamLee 1 — 35
(Shaun Lycett) *hld up in 4th: pushed along over 3f out: sn rdn and wknd: eased fnl 2 fs* — **14/1**

3m 5.98s (-1.02) **Going Correction** -0.025s/f (Good) — **5 Ran SP% 108.3**
Speed ratings (Par 103): **101,100,97,95,86**
CSF £3.53 TOTE £1.80: £1.10, £1.80; EX 3.90 Trifecta £9.60.
**Owner** Mange Tout II **Bred** Lilly Hall Farm **Trained** Ledbury, H'fords

**FOCUS**
A modest handicap for the grade, with the top-weight rated 5lb below the ceiling.

## 3624 BETTINGGOODS.COM HORSE RACING TIPS H'CAP — 5f 8y
**2:55** (2:57) (Class 6) (0-65,65) 3-Y-0 — **£2,587** (£770; £384; £192) **Stalls** Centre

Form — RPR

3-05 **1** — **Sitar**$^{25}$ [2725] 3-8-13 **62** .......... (h$^{1}$) GeorgeWood$^{(5)}$ 6 — 67+
(James Fanshawe) *slowly away: in rr tl hdwy 2f out: rdn appr fnl f and stl plenty to do: qcknd ins fnl f: str run to ld last 50yds* — **5/1**$^{1}$

3340 **2** *½* **Bithynia (IRE)**$^{15}$ [3063] 3-9-7 **65** .......... FrannyNorton 8 — 68
(Christopher Kellett) *led: drvn and 1 l clr appr fnl f: rdn and r.o but ct last 50yds* — **25/1**

0004 **3** *½* **Bobby Vee**$^{8}$ [3331] 3-9-3 **61** .......... (p$^{1}$) RobertWinston 4 — 62
(Dean Ivory) *mid-div: hdwy 2f out: chal 1f out: rdn and r.o ins fnl f* — **5/1**$^{1}$

20U2 **4** *2 ½* **Lightoller (IRE)**$^{16}$ [3035] 3-8-12 **63** .......... (b) KeithQuinn$^{(7)}$ 11 — 55
(Mick Channon) *prom: ev ch 2f out: rdn appr fnl f: one pce* — **13/2**$^{2}$

-606 **5** *2 ¾* **Dusty Bin**$^{9}$ [3296] 3-8-12 **59** .......... AlistairRawlinson$^{(3)}$ 10 — 42
(Roy Bowring) *mid-div: pushed along and effrt 2f out: sn rdn: r.o one pce fnl f* — **8/1**

0050 **6** *1* **Henrietta's Dream**$^{10}$ [3260] 3-8-7 **51** oh6 .......... (b$^{1}$) RoystonFfrench 5 — 30
(John Wainwright) *in rr: reminder 1/2-way: pushed along and hdwy fr 2f out: nvr nrr* — **125/1**

-000 **7** *1* **Miss Pepper (IRE)**$^{20}$ [2897] 3-8-4 **51** oh6 .......... (h) SammyJoBell$^{(3)}$ 9 — 26
(Paul Midgley) *mid-div: drvn 2f out: sme late hdwy* — **33/1**

00-0 **8** *hd* **Kath's Boy (IRE)**$^{10}$ [3260] 3-8-7 **51** oh1 .......... JoeyHaynes 2 — 26
(Tony Carroll) *chsd ldrs: reminders over 1f out: drvn and wknd fnl f* — **25/1**

-443 **9** *¾* **Jorvik Prince**$^{20}$ [2897] 3-8-13 **57** .......... (p$^{1}$) SamJames 12 — 29
(Karen Tutty) *prom: pushed along 1/2-way: rdn over 1f out: no ex* — **7/1**$^{3}$

0-35 **10** *1* **Flashing Light**$^{20}$ [2897] 3-8-12 **56** .......... DavidAllan 3 — 24
(Tim Easterby) *a in rr: no hdwy u.p* — **16/1**

163 **11** *1 ½* **Cryptonite (IRE)**$^{12}$ [3184] 3-9-2 **60** .......... (p) AndrewMullen 7 — 23
(Michael Appleby) *chsd ldrs: drvn 2f out: rdn and wknd* — **5/1**$^{1}$

-605 **12** *3* **Hot Hannah**$^{8}$ [3345] 3-9-6 **64** .......... (b) ConnorBeasley 1 — 16
(Michael Dods) *prom early: struggling fr 1/2-way: weakend qckly* — **8/1**

1m 2.34s (0.84) **Going Correction** -0.025s/f (Good) — **12 Ran SP% 115.4**
Speed ratings (Par 97): **92,91,90,86,82 80,78,78,77,75 73,68**
CSF £134.48 CT £656.70 TOTE £5.60: £2.10, £4.90, £2.00; EX 91.30 Trifecta £869.40.
**Owner** Manor Farm Stud & John Rose **Bred** Manor Farm Stud (rutland) **Trained** Newmarket, Suffolk

**FOCUS**
A modest 3yo handicap in which, apart from the winner, nothing got into it from off the pace. The winner has been rated back to last year's best.

## 3625 MERLIN INFLATABLES UK H'CAP — 5f 8y
**3:30** (3:32) (Class 3) (0-95,95) 4-Y-0+ — **£9,703** (£2,887; £1,443; £721) **Stalls** Centre

Form — RPR

233 **1** — **Escalating**$^{16}$ [3052] 5-8-2 **83** .......... (tp) RayDawson$^{(7)}$ 3 — 91
(Michael Appleby) *trckd ldrs: reminders wl over 1f out: hdwy ent fnl f: hrd rdn and r.o wl to ld last 10yds* — **6/1**$^{3}$

3621 **2** *nk* **Stake Acclaim (IRE)**$^{6}$ [3410] 5-9-7 **95** 6ex .......... RobertWinston 1 — 102
(Dean Ivory) *prom: 2nd after 2f: led over 1f out: 1 l clr ins fnl f: clsd down by wnr nr fin and ct last 10yds* — **11/4**$^{1}$

5-30 **3** *1 ¼* **Confessional**$^{15}$ [3092] 10-9-2 **90** .......... (e) DavidAllan 2 — 93
(Tim Easterby) *chsd ldrs: pushed along 2f out: rdn ent fnl f: r.o: lugged bhd wnr 100yds out* — **11/1**

-401 **4** *½* **Elysian Flyer (IRE)**$^{22}$ [2837] 5-8-9 **83** .......... GrahamLee 6 — 84
(Paul Midgley) *mid-div: effrt and rdn over 1f out: pushed along and r.o wl fnl f* — **8/1**

6311 **5** *¾* **Tumblewind**$^{9}$ [3295] 7-9-2 **95** .......... LewisEdmunds$^{(5)}$ 9 — 93
(Richard Whitaker) *prom: 3rd 2f out: rdn over 1f out: one pce fnl f* — **5/1**$^{2}$

300- **6** *½* **Huntsmans Close**$^{172}$ [8484] 7-9-2 **90** .......... PhillipMakin 7 — 86
(Robert Cowell) *led: reminder 2f out: drvn and hdd over 1f out: no ex* — **25/1**

-646 **7** *1 ¼* **Lexington Place**$^{8}$ [3337] 7-8-6 **80** .......... JamesSullivan 8 — 72
(Ruth Carr) *hld up: pushed along and effrt over 1f out: rdn and no rspnse fnl f* — **12/1**

2-35 **8** *1 ¾* **Oh So Sassy**$^{30}$ [2578] 7-9-2 **90** .......... AdamBeschizza 10 — 75
(Chris Wall) *racd alone stands' side: prom: u.p and jnd rest of field over 1f out: wknd* — **25/1**

2110 **9** *shd* **Treaty Of Rome (USA)**$^{34}$ [2462] 5-8-2 **76** oh1 .......... (v) FrannyNorton 5 — 61
(Derek Shaw) *hld up: niggled over 2f out: sn rdn and wknd* — **25/1**

1m 1.08s (-0.42) **Going Correction** -0.025s/f (Good) — **9 Ran SP% 96.3**
Speed ratings (Par 107): **102,101,99,98,97 96,94,91,91**
CSF £16.01 CT £95.82 TOTE £6.10: £1.70, £1.30, £2.80; EX 20.40 Trifecta £117.30.
**Owner** The Horse Watchers **Bred** Juddmonte Farms Ltd **Trained** Oakham, Rutland
■ Foolaad was withdrawn. Price at time of withdrawal 9-2. Rule 4 applies to all bets - deduction 15p in the pound.

**FOCUS**
A good-quality sprint.

## 3626 LEXUS NOTTINGHAM MAIDEN FILLIES' STKS (PLUS 10 RACE) — 1m 75y
**4:05** (4:14) (Class 5) 3-Y-0 — **£3,881** (£1,155; £577; £288) **Stalls** Centre

Form — RPR

04 **1** — **Best Of My Love (IRE)**$^{6}$ [3404] 3-9-0 0 .......... RobHornby 1 — 74
(Mick Channon) *led: pushed along 2f out: rdn ent fnl f: r.o wl: hld on by dwindling margin* — **50/1**

23- **2** *shd* **Kitty Boo**$^{221}$ [7761] 3-8-9 0 .......... (h$^{1}$) GeorgeWood$^{(5)}$ 9 — 73+
(Luca Cumani) *hld up: hdwy over 3f out: drvn appr 2f out: rdn ent fnl f: str run last 100yds: clsd on wnr: jst failed* — **3/1**$^{3}$

32 **3** *½* **Hindsight**$^{27}$ [2682] 3-8-11 0 .......... AlistairRawlinson$^{(3)}$ 10 — 72
(Michael Appleby) *prom early: t.k.h and settled into midfield: hdwy 3f out: 2nd 2f out: rdn fnl f: one pce* — **7/1**

**4** *2 ½* **Pequeninha** 3-9-0 0 .......... StevieDonohoe 2 — 66
(David Simcock) *reluctant to go in stalls: chsd ldrs: drvn 2f out: no ex fnl f* — **33/1**

6-22 **5** *nk* **Sasini**$^{16}$ [3039] 3-9-0 80 .......... DavidProbert 7 — 65
(Charles Hills) *mid-div early: wnt 2nd after 2f: remained prom tl rdn and wknd 2f out* — **5/2**$^{2}$

0 **6** *5* **Lupin (USA)**$^{24}$ [2759] 3-9-0 0 .......... (v$^{1}$) RichardKingscote 3 — 54
(Sir Michael Stoute) *looked difficult ride: t.k.h in mid-div: reminders 3f out: no imp on ldrs* — **9/1**

3 **7** *1 ¼* **UAE Queen**$^{20}$ [2898] 3-9-0 0 .......... AndreaAtzeni 5 — 51
(Roger Varian) *chsd ldrs: drvn 2f out: one pce: eased* — **2/1**$^{1}$

4 **8** *1 ¾* **Velvet Charm**$^{24}$ [2753] 3-9-0 0 .......... (h) MartinLane 6 — 47
(Rae Guest) *slowly away: mod hdwy over 3f out: nvr a threat* — **33/1**

**9** *8* **Naralsaif (IRE)** 3-9-0 0 .......... KierenFox 4 — 29
(Derek Shaw) *hld up: drvn 3f out: nvr a factor* — **100/1**

1m 48.91s (-0.09) **Going Correction** -0.025s/f (Good) — **9 Ran SP% 118.2**
Speed ratings (Par 96): **99,98,98,95,95 90,89,87,79**
CSF £198.61 TOTE £32.60: £9.50, £1.40, £2.20; EX 206.00 Trifecta £5127.50.
**Owner** Tadhg Geary **Bred** Patrick Jones **Trained** West Ilsley, Berks
■ Book Of Dust was withdrawn. Price at time of withdrawal 100-1. Rule 4 does not apply.

**FOCUS**
Not a bad 3yo maiden but it seemed hard work in the sticky ground.

## 3627 BETTINGGOODS.COM PROFESSIONAL TIPSTERS H'CAP — 1m 75y
**4:35** (4:38) (Class 5) (0-70,72) 3-Y-0 — **£3,234** (£962; £481; £240) **Stalls** Centre

Form — RPR

0-64 **1** — **Jumira Prince (IRE)**$^{42}$ [2171] 3-9-6 **69** .......... AndreaAtzeni 6 — 77+
(Roger Varian) *mid-div: gng wl: hdwy on inner 3f out: squeezed through over 1f out: sn rdn and led: r.o wl* — **5/2**$^{1}$

45-0 **2** *1* **Flood Defence (IRE)**$^{23}$ [2793] 3-8-12 **61** .......... AdamBeschizza 15 — 67+
(Chris Wall) *hld up: trckd wnr on inner fr 3f out: n.m.r over 1f out: rdn and r.o wl in clr* — **33/1**

-631 **3** *shd* **Dragons Voice**$^{19}$ [2931] 3-9-9 **72** .......... GrahamLee 13 — 78
(Philip Hide) *prom: hdwy on outer to ld over 2f out: hdd over 1f out: kpt on u.p* — **6/1**$^{3}$

-005 **4** *nk* **Time To Sea (IRE)**$^{19}$ [2931] 3-9-2 **65** .......... RobertWinston 5 — 70
(John Butler) *mid-div: hdwy 2f out: rdn over 1f out: r.o ins fnl f* — **8/1**

5522 **5** *½* **Mama Africa (IRE)**$^{4}$ [3461] 3-9-1 **64** .......... PhillipMakin 7 — 68
(David Barron) *hld up: hdwy 3f out: r.o u.p fnl f* — **4/1**$^{2}$

5424 **6** *1 ¾* **Fairy Lock (IRE)**$^{23}$ [2790] 3-8-3 **52** .......... JamesSullivan 9 — 52
(David Barron) *mid-div: rdn over 1f out: one pce fnl f* — **12/1**

4012 **7** *1 ½* **Badenscoth**$^{13}$ [3162] 3-9-5 **71** .......... (h) JackDuern$^{(3)}$ 10 — 67
(Dean Ivory) *hld up: drvn 2f out: rdn ent fnl f: mod late hdwy* — **7/1**

3155 **8** *hd* **Bazwind (IRE)**$^{53}$ [1888] 3-8-12 **66** .......... (v) CliffordLee$^{(5)}$ 1 — 62
(David Evans) *trckd ldrs: drvn 2f out and n.m.r: one pce fnl f* — **16/1**

320- **9** *2 ¾* **Salieri (FR)**$^{214}$ [7865] 3-9-3 **66** .......... FergusSweeney 3 — 56
(Alan King) *hld up: pushed along 3f out: no imp appr fnl f* — **20/1**

0-40 **10** *2 ¼* **Bridal March**$^{20}$ [2886] 3-8-11 **60** .......... (p$^{1}$) BenCurtis 4 — 44
(John Mackie) *led: pushed along 3f out: hdd over 2f out: fdd* — **33/1**

3544 **11** *2 ¼* **De Vegas Kid (IRE)**$^{39}$ [2315] 3-8-7 **56** .......... JimmyQuinn 11 — 35
(Tony Carroll) *trckd ldr: pushed along 2f out: wknd* — **12/1**

10-0 **12** *15* **Iftitah (IRE)**$^{17}$ [3000] 3-9-2 **65** .......... (t) StevieDonohoe 12 — 10
(George Peckham) *mid-div on outer: pushed along 2f out: wknd qckly* — **50/1**

0-60 **13** *¾* **Just Heather (IRE)**$^{10}$ [3261] 3-8-2 **51** oh6 ow1 .......... RoystonFfrench 2
(John Wainwright) *hld up: nvr a factor* — **100/1**

00-0 **14** *43* **Jupiter Ascending**$^{11}$ [3207] 3-8-2 **51** oh6 .......... (bt) AndrewMullen 14
(Michael Appleby) *mid-div: drvn 4f out: no rspnse: eased* — **66/1**

1m 46.58s (-2.42) **Going Correction** -0.025s/f (Good) — **14 Ran SP% 122.8**
Speed ratings (Par 99): **111,110,109,109,109 107,105,105,102,100 98,83,82,39**
CSF £107.47 CT £489.77 TOTE £3.80: £2.20, £7.70, £2.30; EX 112.60 Trifecta £733.50.
**Owner** Sheikh Mohammed Obaid Al Maktoum **Bred** Deer Forest Stud **Trained** Newmarket, Suffolk

**FOCUS**
A fair 3yo handicap and they finished in a bit of a heap, but the form looks solid for the level.

## 3628 BETTINGGOODS.COM FREE HORSE RACING TIPS H'CAP — 1m 2f 50y
**5:10** (5:11) (Class 6) (0-65,66) 4-Y-0+ — **£2,587** (£770; £384; £192) **Stalls** Low

Form — RPR

005 **1** — **Incredible Dream (IRE)**$^{32}$ [2521] 4-8-8 **55** .......... (p$^{1}$) JackDuern$^{(3)}$ 8 — 63
(Dean Ivory) *hld up: plld out fr inner 3f out: hdwy 2f out: sn rdn: jnd ldrs ins fnl f: r.o u.p to ld cl home* — **16/1**

2631 **2** *½* **Sir Jack**$^{13}$ [3143] 4-8-11 **60** .......... CliffordLee$^{(5)}$ 11 — 67
(Tony Carroll) *trckd ldrs: pushed along to chal 2f out: rdn and led ins fnl f: r.o but ct cl home* — **9/2**$^{2}$

3-00 **3** *1 ¾* **Spinart**$^{20}$ [2909] 4-9-7 **65** .......... RobHornby 9 — 69
(Pam Sly) *trckd ldrs: hdwy to ld 3f out: hrd rdn over 1f out: hdd ins fnl f: no ex* — **7/1**

-134 **4** *nse* **Angelical (IRE)**$^{13}$ [3148] 4-8-13 **60** .......... CharlieBennett$^{(3)}$ 1 — 64
(Daniel Mark Loughnane) *trckd ldrs on inner: effrt over 1f out: rdn and one pce fnl f* — **11/1**

3222 **5** *3* **Stoneboat Bill**$^{6}$ [3400] 5-8-12 **63** .......... GerO'Neill$^{(7)}$ 7 — 61
(Declan Carroll) *hld up in last: drvn and hdwy over 2f out: no ex ent fnl f* — **11/4**$^{1}$

4362 **6** *1 ¾* **Fantasy Gladiator**$^{11}$ [3221] 11-9-4 **62** .......... (p$^{1}$) AndrewMullen 4 — 57
(Michael Appleby) *mid-div: rdn and no imp fnl 2 fs* — **5/1**$^{3}$

3422 **7** *10* **Little Choosey**$^{29}$ [2626] 7-9-4 **62** .......... (bt) JimmyQuinn 3 — 39
(Roy Bowring) *trckd ldrs: effrt and pushed along over 2f out: sn rdn and wknd* — **12/1**

0503 **8** *1* **Einstein**$^{59}$ [1758] 4-8-12 **56** .......... (t) AdamBeschizza 12 — 31
(Mrs Ilka Gansera-Leveque) *chsd ldr: led briefly over 3f out: hdd and rdn 3f out: no ex* — **20/1**

6-06 **9** *3 ½* **Balmont Belle (IRE)**[50] 1985 7-8-1 48 ow2.............. GeorgeWood(5) 10 19
(Barry Leavy) *hld up: drvn 4f out: rdn over 3f out: one pce and no hdwy fnl 2 fs* **25/1**

0356 **10** *¾* **Playtothewhistle**[43] 2153 6-9-1 62.....................(v) AlistairRawlinson(3) 2 30
(Michael Appleby) *hld up on inner: u.p over 2f out: wknd* **20/1**

4022 **11** *6* **Adventureman**[16] 3048 5-9-4 62..............................(p) JamesSullivan 5 19
(Ruth Carr) *led: rdn and hdd over 3f out: fdd* **12/1**

2m 11.54s (-2.76) **Going Correction** -0.025s/f (Good) 11 Ran SP% **117.0**
Speed ratings (Par 101): **110,109,108,108,105 104,96,95,92,92 87**
CSF £83.86 CT £562.98 TOTE £36.30: £7.90, £2.00, £2.90; EX 190.00 Trifecta £2734.60.
**Owner** Black Star Racing **Bred** Rabbah Bloodstock Limited **Trained** Radlett, Herts

**FOCUS**
A modest handicap run at a good pace. The third and fourth suggest the form could be better than rated.
T/Plt: £90.10 to a £1 stake. Pool: £63,191.00 - 701.23 winning units. T/Qpdt: £24.50 to a £1 stake. Pool: £6,569.00 - 268.02 winning units. **Keith McHugh**

3629 - 3631a (Foreign Racing) - See Raceform Interactive

## 3598 CURRAGH (R-H)
Sunday, June 11

**OFFICIAL GOING: Soft changing to soft to heavy on straight course after race 2 (2.45)**

### 3632a TRM BALLYOGAN STKS (GROUP 3) (F&M) 6f
**3:55** (3:56) 3-Y-0+

**£31,769** (£10,230; £4,846; £2,153; £1,076; £538)

RPR

**1** **Penny Pepper (IRE)**[21] 2860 5-9-6 87.............................. ChrisHayes 7 98
(Kevin Prendergast, Ire) *bit slowly away: racd in 10th to 1/2-way: swtchd lft over 1f out and prog into 7th ent fnl f: styd on strly on outer clsng stages to ld on line* **16/1**

**2** *hd* **Only Mine (IRE)**[15] 3099 4-9-6 105.............................. GaryCarroll 8 97
(Joseph G Murphy, Ire) *sn trckd ldr in 2nd: rdn and no imp on ldr appr fnl f: kpt on strly clsng stages into 2nd cl home* **9/4**[1]

**3** *hd* **Alphabet**[15] 3078 3-8-12 95......................................(t) SeamieHeffernan 4 95
(A P O'Brien, Ire) *led: extended advantage over 1f out: clr ent fnl f: strly pressed clsng stages: hdd cl home and dropped to 3rd* **12/1**

**4** *1* **Florida Times (IRE)**[22] 2823 3-8-12 91.................. DanielTudhope 12 92
(David O'Meara) *chsd ldrs in 3rd: rdn and no imp ent fnl f: kpt on same pce: dropped to 4th fnl 50yds* **8/1**

**5** *nk* **Elusive Beauty (IRE)**[14] 3111 3-8-12 94.................. ShaneFoley 5 91
(K J Condon, Ire) *racd towards rr: pushed along in 11th at 1/2-way: 9th ent fnl f: kpt on wl into 5th clsng stages: nrst fin* **16/1**

**6** *2* **Peticoatgovernment (IRE)**[15] 3097 4-9-6 92........................ WJLee 11 86
(W McCreery, Ire) *chsd ldrs: 5th at 1/2-way: rdn and nt qckn over 1f out: no ex fnl 100yds* **5/1**[2]

**7** *¾* **Wowcha (IRE)**[260] 6770 4-9-6 78..........................................(v) PBBeggy 6 84
(John Quinn) *racd in mid-div: pushed along in 7th at 1/2-way: no imp appr fnl f: kpt on one pce* **33/1**

**8** *3* **Music Box (IRE)**[6] 3420 3-8-12 87.............................. WayneLordan 10 72
(A P O'Brien, Ire) *sn chsd ldrs: rdn in 3rd at 1/2-way: wknd ins fnl f* **6/1**[3]

**9** *6 ½* **Poet's Princess**[22] 2831 3-8-12 88................................ KevinManning 9 51
(Hughie Morrison) *racd in rr for most: modest late hdwy wout ever threatening* **12/1**

**10** *½* **Buying Trouble (USA)**[15] 3080 4-9-6 97................ DeclanMcDonogh 1 52
(David Evans) *chsd ldrs far side: pushed along in 6th at 1/2-way: nt qckn over 1f out: wknd* **9/1**

**11** *8 ½* **Evil Spell**[29] 2623 5-9-6 95..................................................... ColinKeane 3 25
(Robert Cowell) *racd in mid-div: 8th at 1/2-way: rdn and no imp 2f out: wknd: eased clsng stages* **25/1**

**12** *2* **Smoulder**[10] 3268 3-8-12 84........................................ MichaelHussey 2 16
(A P O'Brien, Ire) *hld up: rdn 1/2-way and dropped to rr under 2f out: no ex* **50/1**

1m 16.34s (0.84) **Going Correction** +0.10s/f (Good)
**WFA** 3 from 4yo+ 8lb 12 Ran SP% **118.7**
Speed ratings: **98,97,97,96,95 93,92,88,79,78 67,64**
CSF £51.41 TOTE £21.90: £5.90, £1.30, £3.50; DF 70.90 Trifecta £838.50.
**Owner** J F Tuthill **Bred** J F Tuthill **Trained** Friarstown, Co Kildare

**FOCUS**
A thrilling finish in which the winner, who is reportedly in-foal, picked up late on the near-side to edge out the favourite who was meeting Kevin Prendergast's mare on 18lb better than handicap terms. On balance, this has to be considered a sub-standard Group 3 race, only the runner-up holding a rating above 97. The winner ran a personal best.

3633 - 3635a (Foreign Racing) - See Raceform Interactive

## 2869 COLOGNE (R-H)
Sunday, June 11

**OFFICIAL GOING: Turf: good**

### 3636a 182ND OPPENHEIM-UNION-RENNEN (GROUP 2) (3YO) (TURF) 1m 3f
**2:55** 3-Y-0 **£34,188** (£13,247; £6,837; £3,418; £2,136)

RPR

**1** **Colomano**[49] 2002 3-9-2 0.......................................... AndreasHelfenbein 3 105+
(Markus Klug, Germany) *w.w in rr: shkn up and clsd over 2f out: sustained run to ld fnl 150yds: drvn out* **27/10**[2]

**2** *½* **Windstoss (GER)**[63] 3-9-2 0........................................... MaximPecheur 8 104
(Markus Klug, Germany) *led after 1f: 2l clr and nudged along 2f out: rdn and edgd lft fr 1 1/2f out: styd on fnl f: hdd fnl 150yds and rallied* **92/10**

**3** *2 ¼* **Northsea Star (GER)**[41] 2246 3-9-2 0........................ AndraschStarke 1 100+
(Markus Klug, Germany) *racd keenly: hld up under restraint: hdd after 1f: remained cl up bhd ldrs: 4l 3rd and drvn 2 1/2f out: styd on fr over 1f out: nt pce to trble front two* **36/5**

**4** *½* **Warring States (JPN)**[41] 2246 3-9-2 0........................ EduardoPedroza 4 99+
(A Wohler, Germany) *racd towards rr: hdwy over 1 1/2f out: styd on fnl f: nvr nrr* **21/10**[1]

**5** *3 ¼* **Shanjo (GER)** 3-9-2 0..................................................... MartinSeidl 5 93
(Markus Klug, Germany) *chsd ldrs: drvn in 2nd over 2f out: sn rdn: dropped away fnl f* **26/5**

**6** *1* **Monreal (IRE)**[34] 2483 3-9-2 0........................................ FilipMinarik 2 92
(Jean-Pierre Carvalho, Germany) *racd keenly: hld up bhd ldrs: drvn and lost pl 3 1/2f out: wl hld fnl 1 1/2f* **29/10**[3]

**7** *3 ½* **Oriental Khan (GER)** 3-9-2 0......................(b) BauyrzhanMurzabayev 6 85
(R Dzubasz, Germany) *chsd ldrs on outer: rdn and lost pl 2f out: sn bhd* **30/1**

**8** *6 ½* **Khan (GER)**[63] 3-9-2 0....................................................... AntoineHamelin 7 74
(Henk Grewe, Germany) *w.w in fnl trio: last and drvn 2 1/2f out: sn wknd u.p* **244/10**

2m 14.44s (-6.36) 8 Ran SP% **130.2**
PARI-MUTUEL (all including 10 euro stake): WIN 37; PLACE 16, 21, 18; SF 265.
**Owner** Stall Reckendorf **Bred** Gestut Fahrhof **Trained** Germany

## 3020 LYON PARILLY (R-H)
Sunday, June 11

**OFFICIAL GOING: Turf: good**

### 3637a GRAND PRIX DE LYON (LISTED RACE) (4YO+) (TURF) 1m 4f
**5:05** 4-Y-0+ **£25,641** (£10,256; £7,692; £5,128; £2,564)

RPR

**1** **Holdthasigreen (FR)**[42] 2202 5-9-10 0........................(p) TonyPiccone 2 111+
(C Le Lay, France) **89/10**

**2** *¾* **Smart Whip (FR)**[25] 6-9-1 0........................................ EddyHardouin 7 101
(C Lotoux, France) **5/1**[3]

**3** *1 ½* **Master's Spirit (IRE)**[43] 2169 6-9-1 0................ ChristopheSoumillon 3 99
(J Reynier, France) **17/10**[1]

**4** *nk* **Murafej (IRE)**[42] 2202 5-9-1 0........................ Francois-XavierBertras 6 98
(F Rohaut, France) **39/10**[2]

**5** *1 ¼* **Pump Pump Palace (FR)**[31] 2559 4-9-1 0........ Pierre-CharlesBoudot 4 96
(J-P Gauvin, France) **63/10**

**6** *8 ½* **Galapiat**[15] 3072 4-9-1 0.............................................. IoritzMendizabal 5 83
(Mark Johnston) **7/1**

**7** *1* **Beraymi (IRE)**[270] 6497 4-8-11 0.................................... TheoBachelot 8 68
(J Reynier, France) **164/10**

**D** *3 ½* **Delegation (FR)**[39] 7-8-11 0........................................... CyrilleStefan 1 74
(J Albrecht, Czech Republic) **61/1**

2m 28.55s (-4.96) 8 Ran SP% **117.8**
PARI-MUTUEL (all including 1 euro stake): WIN 9.90; PLACE 2.50, 2.00, 1.40; DF 23.70; SF 58.50.
**Owner** Claude Le Lay **Bred** J Gilbert & C Le Lay **Trained** France

3638 - 3647a (Foreign Racing) - See Raceform Interactive

## 3383 AYR (L-H)
Monday, June 12

**OFFICIAL GOING: Soft (6.8)**
Wind: strong against Weather: changeable, very breezy

### 3648 TOTEPLACEPOT RACING'S FAVOURITE BET EBF NOVICE STKS 6f
**2:00** (2:01) (Class 5) 2-Y-0 **£3,234** (£962; £481; £240) **Stalls** High

Form RPR

0 **1** **Jackontherocks**[19] 2948 2-8-11 0......................... CallumRodriguez(5) 7 72
(Michael Dods) *hmpd sn after s: chsd ldrs: swtchd lft 2f out: kpt on to ld last 100yds: hld on cl home* **18/1**

3 **2** *nk* **Weellan**[22] 2852 2-9-2 0................................................... JasonHart 1 71+
(John Quinn) *t.k.h: w ldrs: led over 4f out: hdd over 1f out: swtchd lft and styd on strly last 150yds: jst hld* **4/1**[2]

**3** *1* **Here In The Dark** 2-9-2 0.......................................... ConnorBeasley 5 68
(Keith Dalgleish) *dwlt: sn chsng ldrs: led over 1f out: hdd and no ex last 100yds* **40/1**

**4** *3 ½* **Safrani (IRE)** 2-9-2 0........................................................ PhillipMakin 6 58
(David O'Meara) *chsd ldrs: wknd last 150yds* **7/2**[1]

**5** *4 ½* **Tommy Shelby (FR)** 2-9-2 0............................................ BarryMcHugh 10 44
(Richard Fahey) *s.i.s: in rr: kpt on fnl f: nvr a factor* **14/1**[3]

6 **6** *shd* **Crown Of Cortez**[24] 2771 2-9-2 0.................................. PaulHanagan 8 44
(Richard Fahey) *chsd ldrs: drvn 3f out: lost pl over 1f out* **7/2**[1]

065 **7** *5* **Lord Of The Glen**[24] 2771 2-8-9 0.............................. SeanMooney(7) 4 29
(Jim Goldie) *sn chsng ldrs: wknd over 1f out* **22/1**

032 **8** *4 ½* **Poignant**[35] 2459 2-9-2 0................................................... BenCurtis 9 16
(Archie Watson) *hmpd sn after s: towards rr: n.m.r on inner over 3f out: sn drvn: lost pl over 2f out* **4/1**[2]

004 **9** *25* **Sam James (IRE)**[9] 3339 2-9-2 0.................................. DavidNolan 3
(Iain Jardine) *edgd rt sn after s: led tl over 4f out: lost pl over 2f out: sn bhd* **18/1**

1m 18.79s (6.39) **Going Correction** +0.80s/f (Soft) 9 Ran SP% **108.4**
Speed ratings (Par 93): **89,88,87,82,76 76,69,63,30**
CSF £80.01 TOTE £20.60: £4.70, £1.60, £7.20; EX 94.70 Trifecta £3383.10.
**Owner** M J K Dods **Bred** T Ellison, B Olkowicz And C Speller **Trained** Denton, Co Durham

**FOCUS**
Inner rail moved in 4yds. There had been 58mm of rain since the previous Monday, so soft ground. This looked an ordinary novice race and it proved quite attritional in the conditions.

### 3649 TOTEPOOLLIVEINFO.COM MEDIAN AUCTION MAIDEN FILLIES' STKS 1m 2f
**2:30** (2:30) (Class 5) 3-4-Y-0 **£3,234** (£962; £481; £240) **Stalls** Low

Form RPR

5-4 **1** **Paradise Cove**[21] 2908 3-9-0 0....................................... BenCurtis 3 74
(William Haggas) *led: pushed along over 2f out: wnt clr appr fnl f: v readily* **4/7**[1]

0 **2** *5* **Master Me (IRE)**[17] 3039 3-8-10 0 ow1......................... CliffordLee(5) 1 65
(K R Burke) *chsd ldng pair: effrt 3f out: kpt on to take 2nd 1f out: no ch w wnr* **7/1**[3]

5203 **3** *1* **Glorvina (IRE)**[13] 3175 3-9-0 67...................................... PhillipMakin 4 62
(David O'Meara) *trckd wnr: chal 3f out: sn drvn: one pce over 1f out* **3/1**[2]

**4** *14* **Alfa Queen (IRE)** 3-9-0 0.............................................. DavidNolan 2 34
(Iain Jardine) *dwlt: sn chsng ldrs: drvn over 3f out: lost pl 2f out: sn bhd* **16/1**

2m 15.65s (3.65) **Going Correction** +0.475s/f (Yiel) 4 Ran SP% **107.0**
Speed ratings (Par 100): **104,100,99,88**
CSF £4.91 TOTE £1.50; EX 4.00 Trifecta £5.60.
**Owner** Biddestone Racing Partnership XXI **Bred** Biddestone Stud Ltd **Trained** Newmarket, Suffolk

**FOCUS**
Add 12yds. The favourite dominated in this weak fillies' maiden. The winner progressed just nominally from her reappearance.

## 3650 TOTEPOOL RACECOURSE DEBIT CARD BETTING AVAILABLE H'CAP 1m 2f
**3:00** (3:01) (Class 6) (0-60,58) 4-Y-0+ **£2,587** (£770; £384; £192) **Stalls** Low

Form RPR
36-3 **1** **Rubis**17 3053 4-9-7 **58** PaulHanagan 1 63
(Richard Fahey) *trckd ldr tl over 6f out: 2nd over 2f out: led appr fnl f: pushed out* **3/1**2

**2** 1 1/4 **Reinas Queen (IRE)**11 3272 4-8-13 **53** (p) SammyJoBell(3) 4 56
(Sarah Dawson, Ire) *led: drvn over 3f out: hdd appr fnl f: kpt on same pce* **10/3**3

0-03 **3** 1 1/2 **Haymarket**11 3242 8-8-12 **49** PJMcDonald 6 49
(R Mike Smith) *trckd ldng pair: 2nd over 6f out: effrt over 3f out: kpt on same pce over 1f out* **2/1**1

646 **4** 3 1/2 **Tambour**11 3242 4-9-7 **58** DougieCostello 3 52
(Keith Dalgleish) *s.i.s: hdwy 8f out: drvn 3f out: one pce* **10/1**

6000 **5** 18 **Scannermandango**12 3196 4-8-1 **45** (t1) SeanMooney(7) 5 6
(Jim Goldie) *dwlt: in rr: lost pl over 4f out: sn bhd* **28/1**

-005 **6** 1/2 **Whitchurch**21 2891 5-8-10 **47** (b1) JamesSullivan 2 7
(Iain Jardine) *mid-div: drvn 3f out: sn lost pl and bhd* **5/1**

2m 16.6s (4.60) **Going Correction** +0.475s/f (Yiel) **6 Ran SP% 110.6**
Speed ratings (Par 101): **100,99,97,95,80 80**
CSF £12.93 TOTE £3.10: £1.10, £2.10; EX 11.80 Trifecta £28.00.
**Owner** Mr & Mrs P Ashton **Bred** Mr & Mrs P Ashton **Trained** Musley Bank, N Yorks

**FOCUS**
Add 12yds. A moderate handicap in which the winner is rated to her mark.

## 3651 @TOTEPOOLRACING WIN RACING TICKETS ON TWITTER H'CAP 1m 1f 20y
**3:30** (3:30) (Class 4) (0-85,86) 4-Y-0+ **£5,822** (£1,732; £865; £432) **Stalls** Low

Form RPR
0-23 **1** **Royal Regent**19 2953 5-8-9 **76** SammyJoBell(3) 9 86
(Lucy Normile) *hld up in rr: smooth hdwy on outside over 3f out: led over 1f out: hld on clsng stages* **9/2**2

-411 **2** 1/2 **Gworn**12 3197 7-9-0 **78** PJMcDonald 6 87
(R Mike Smith) *in rr: swtchd rt and hdwy on outside 2f out: chsd wnr fnl f: no ex towards fin* **9/2**2

-001 **3** 3 **Finn Class (IRE)**23 2838 6-9-8 **86** ConnorBeasley 7 89
(Michael Dods) *mid-div: hdwy over 4f out: chsng ldrs over 2f out: hung lft and one pce fnl f* **7/1**

-305 **4** 3 3/4 **Timeless Art (IRE)**18 3014 4-9-2 **85** CliffordLee(5) 4 80
(K R Burke) *chsd ldrs: outpcd over 1f out: kpt on one pce to take modest 4th clsng stages* **7/2**1

00-3 **5** 1 **Royal Shaheen (FR)**19 2952 4-9-3 **81** JamesSullivan 3 74
(Alistair Whillans) *chsd ldrs: nt clr run over 2f out: one pce over 1f out: n.m.r clsng stages* **9/1**

50-0 **6** nse **Le Chat D'Or**44 2155 9-9-7 **85** (bt) PhillipMakin 2 78
(Michael Dods) *s.i.s: sn mid-div: outpcd and lost pl over 2f out: sme late hdwy* **12/1**

31-6 **7** hd **Dark Devil (IRE)**12 3212 4-9-8 **86** PaulHanagan 8 78
(Richard Fahey) *trckd ldrs: chal over 2f out: fdd appr fnl f* **11/2**3

005 **8** 1 1/4 **Maraakib (IRE)**4 3497 5-9-2 **83** (p1) JoshDoyle(3) 10 73
(David O'Meara) *trckd ldrs: led over 2f out: hdd over 1f out: grad wknd* **18/1**

010 **9** 8 **Spes Nostra**19 2953 9-8-13 **77** (b) JoeFanning 5 50
(Iain Jardine) *led: hdd over 2f out: sn lost pl* **33/1**

2m 0.96s (3.46) **Going Correction** +0.475s/f (Yiel) **9 Ran SP% 112.4**
Speed ratings (Par 105): **103,102,99,96,95 95,95,94,87**
CSF £24.18 CT £137.14 TOTE £5.60: £1.90, £1.80, £2.90; EX 27.40 Trifecta £127.30.
**Owner** Steve Dick **Bred** Steve Dick **Trained** Duncrievie, Perth & Kinross

**FOCUS**
Add 12yds. The first two finishers came from the last two places and the third also raced out the back. The winner is rated back to last year's best.

## 3652 TOTEPOOL LIKE US ON FACEBOOK H'CAP 7f 50y
**4:00** (4:01) (Class 5) (0-75,83) 4-Y-0+ **£3,234** (£962; £481; £240) **Stalls** High

Form RPR
3041 **1** **Dark Crystal**5 3450 6-8-8 **67** 6ex ow1 LewisEdmunds(5) 6 76
(Linda Perratt) *charged gate and 1/2 rrd s: led early: trckd ldrs: led over 1f out: drvn out* **5/1**3

0403 **2** 1 1/4 **Magistral**35 2456 7-9-0 **68** (p) PJMcDonald 8 74
(R Mike Smith) *mid-div: hdwy over 2f out: chsd wnr fnl 100yds: kpt on same pce* **18/1**

3314 **3** 3 **Vallarta (IRE)**12 3195 7-9-6 **74** JamesSullivan 10 72
(Ruth Carr) *t.k.h: racd wd: sn led: hdd over 1f out: kpt on one pce* **10/1**

-221 **4** 3/4 **Inexes**5 3452 5-10-1 **83** 6ex (p) BarryMcHugh 9 79
(Marjorie Fife) *mid-div: hdwy over 3f out: sn chsng ldrs: kpt on one pce over 1f out* **10/3**1

00-6 **5** shd **Royal Duchess**34 2500 7-9-2 **70** DougieCostello 3 66
(Lucy Normile) *s.v.s: in rr: hdwy over 1f out: styng on wl at fin* **14/1**

-023 **6** 1 **Jay Kay**7 3388 8-9-1 **74** (h) CliffordLee(5) 2 67
(K R Burke) *s.i.s: sn trcking ldr: one pce over 1f out* **4/1**2

0-06 **7** 1/2 **Mywayistheonlyway (IRE)**11 3255 4-9-8 **76** PaddyAspell 11 68
(Grant Tuer) *chsd ldrs: one pce fnl 2f* **28/1**

0555 **8** 3 1/4 **Dark Confidant (IRE)**11 3265 4-8-5 **59** PaulHanagan 5 42
(Richard Fahey) *in rr: sn pushed along: nvr a factor* **18/1**

4001 **9** 1/2 **Rioja Day (IRE)**7 3387 7-7-12 **59** 6ex ow1 (b) ConnorMurtagh(7) 4 41
(Jim Goldie) *chsd ldrs: lost pl over 2f out* **22/1**

0000 **10** 2 3/4 **Slemy (IRE)**28 2684 6-9-4 **72** DavidNolan 12 47
(Ruth Carr) *s.i.s: swtchd lft after s: in rr: hung lft over 1f out: nvr on terms* **28/1**

-302 **11** 9 **Dutch Artist (IRE)**6 3433 5-9-4 **75** (p) JoshDoyle(3) 7 27
(David O'Meara) *rr-div: brief effrt over 2f out: sn wknd: bhd whn eased clsng stages* **5/1**3

1m 33.88s (0.48) **Going Correction** +0.475s/f (Yiel) **11 Ran SP% 113.9**
Speed ratings (Par 103): **116,114,111,110,110 109,108,104,104,101 90**
CSF £84.91 CT £855.42 TOTE £5.60: £1.70, £4.20, £4.50; EX 100.20 Trifecta £1193.00.
**Owner** Nil Sine Labore Partnership **Bred** R Biggs **Trained** East Kilbride, S Lanarks

**FOCUS**
Add 12yds. Not much got into this. The rider's claim helped the winner to a pb.

## 3653 TOTEPOOL BETTING ON ALL UK RACING H'CAP 5f
**4:30** (4:30) (Class 4) (0-80,82) 3-Y-0+ **£5,822** (£1,732; £865; £432) **Stalls** High

Form RPR
0002 **1** **My Name Is Rio (IRE)**10 3295 7-10-4 **82** ConnorBeasley 7 91
(Michael Dods) *hld up racing towards stands' side: effrt over 1f out: led last 150yds: edgd lft: drvn out* **15/8**1

000 **2** 1 1/2 **Dark Defender**33 2528 4-10-4 **82** (v) DougieCostello 3 86
(Keith Dalgleish) *wnt lft s: w ldrs: hung rt and kpt on same pce last 100yds* **17/2**

4016 **3** nk **Goninodaethat**7 3385 9-8-4 **61** SeanMooney(7) 2 64
(Jim Goldie) *sltly hmpd s: sn trcking ldrs: t.k.h: effrt over 1f out: kpt on same pce last 150yds* **20/1**

033 **4** 2 1/4 **Bunce (IRE)**7 3385 9-8-11 **61** JoeFanning 6 56
(Linda Perratt) *hld up wl in tch: effrt over 1f out: one pce* **10/1**

130 **5** nse **Suwaan (IRE)**14 3152 3-9-0 **71** JamesSullivan 4 63
(Ruth Carr) *swtchd rt s: overall ldr towards stands' side: hdd last 150yds: wknd towards fin* **11/2**3

0350 **6** 2 1/2 **One Boy (IRE)**29 2656 6-9-8 **72** PJMcDonald 5 58
(Paul Midgley) *chsd ldr towards stands' side: wknd fnl f* **9/2**2

-350 **7** 3 1/4 **Grandad's World (IRE)**17 3052 5-10-0 **78** PaulHanagan 1 52
(Richard Fahey) *chsd ldrs: drvn over 2f out: lost pl over 1f out* **9/2**2

1m 2.32s (2.92) **Going Correction** +0.80s/f (Soft)
**WFA** 3 from 4yo+ 7lb **7 Ran SP% 110.9**
Speed ratings (Par 105): **108,105,105,101,101 97,92**
CSF £17.57 TOTE £3.00: £1.70, £4.70; EX 21.50 Trifecta £209.70.
**Owner** K Kirkup & Mrs T Galletley **Bred** Anthony J Keane **Trained** Denton, Co Durham
■ Stewards' Enquiry : Sean Mooney two-day ban: used whip above permitted level (Jun 26-27)

**FOCUS**
A fair sprint handicap. The winner is still rated a length off last year's best.

## 3654 COLLECT TOTEPOOL WINNINGS AT BETFRED SHOPS H'CAP (FOR LADY AMATEUR RIDERS) 1m 5f 26y
**5:00** (5:00) (Class 6) (0-65,61) 4-Y-0+ **£2,495** (£774; £386; £193) **Stalls** Low

Form RPR
00-1 **1** **Tonto's Spirit**7 3400 5-10-0 **54** 6ex (h1) MissAWaugh 2 66+
(Kenneth Slack) *mde all: coasted home: v easily* **4/6**1

0430 **2** 2 1/4 **Thackeray**14 3155 10-9-5 **45** MissJoannaMason 4 50
(Chris Fairhurst) *hld up in last but wl in tch: hdwy over 4f out: 2nd 2f out: no ch w wnr* **12/1**

02-2 **3** 6 **Lady Natasha (IRE)**9 3311 4-10-7 **61** MrsCBartley 1 57
(K R Burke) *sn trcking ldrs: 3rd 2f out: wknd fnl f* **11/4**2

30-0 **4** 9 **Sherman McCoy**152 174 11-10-4 **58** (p) MissBeckySmith 5 41
(Marjorie Fife) *sn trcking ldrs: upsides over 7f out: drvn over 2f out: sn wknd: bhd whn eased clsng stages* **10/1**3

260- **5** 1/2 **Gunner Lindley (IRE)**9 5971 10-10-3 **57** MissETodd 3 40
(Stuart Coltherd) *chsd wnr: drvn over 6f out: outpcd over 5f out: lost pl over 3f out: sn bhd* **25/1**

3m 4.44s (10.44) **Going Correction** +0.475s/f (Yiel) **5 Ran SP% 107.3**
Speed ratings (Par 101): **86,84,80,75,75**
CSF £1.57 TOTE £1.50: £1.10, £4.60; EX 8.00 Trifecta £14.70.
**Owner** A Slack **Bred** Mrs J M Quy **Trained** Hilton, Cumbria

**FOCUS**
Add 24yds. A moderate race but a well-handicapped winner. The form is given a token rating around the third.
T/Jkpt: Part won. £10,000 to a £1 stake. 0.5 winning units. T/Plt: £210.90 to a £1 stake. Pool: £73,394.75 - 253.97 winning units T/Qpdt: £23.50 to a £1 stake. Pool: £7,484.90 - 234.90 winning units **Walter Glynn**

# 3516 BRIGHTON (L-H)
Monday, June 12

**OFFICIAL GOING: Good to firm (good in places; 8.5) changing to good to firm after race 1 (2.15)**
Wind: medium to strong, half against Weather: bright spells

## 3655 "NASHVILLE" NOVICE AUCTION STKS 5f 215y
**2:15** (2:16) (Class 5) 2-Y-0 **£2,911** (£866; £432; £216) **Stalls** Centre

Form RPR
4 **1** **Royal Liberty**9 3328 2-9-0 0 SilvestreDeSousa 3 72
(Mark Johnston) *chsd ldr tl rdn to ld over 1f out: drvn ins fnl f: a holding on: rdn out* **11/4**2

43 **2** nk **Alaska (IRE)**13 3169 2-8-10 0 MitchGodwin(5) 4 72
(Sylvester Kirk) *trckd ldrs: swtchd rt and rdn to chse wnr over 1f out: kpt on but no imp on wnr tl clsd towards fin: nvr quite getting to wnr* **2/1**1

0 **3** nk **Mrs Teasdale**12 3210 2-8-11 0 OisinMurphy 8 67
(Archie Watson) *s.i.s: off the pce in last pair: stl last 2f out: sme hdwy 1f out: str run to go 3rd wl ins fnl f: gng on strly at fin: nvr quite getting to ldrs* **25/1**

04 **4** 1 3/4 **Move To The Front (IRE)**20 2910 2-9-1 0 (b) AdamKirby 7 65
(Clive Cox) *last trio and niggled along: hdwy and rdn over 1f out: 4th and keeping on but nt threatening ldrs whn nt clrest of runs and eased towards fin* **9/2**3

003 **5** 4 **Terri Rules (IRE)**9 3328 2-8-11 0 AdamBeschizza 5 49
(Julia Feilden) *chsd ldrs: effrt 2f out: 3rd and no ex 1f out: hung lft and wknd ins fnl f* **25/1**

2 **6** 3/4 **Hateya (IRE)**20 2910 2-8-9 0 WilliamCarson 6 44
(Jim Boyle) *s.i.s: off the pce in last pair: rdn 3f out: nvr trbld ldrs* **9/2**3

20 **7** 6 **Super Florence (IRE)**27 2706 2-8-9 0 JohnFahy 1 25
(Eve Johnson Houghton) *led tl rdn and hdd over 1f out: sn btn and fdd ins fnl f* **12/1**

0 **8** 4 1/2 **The Kiddie Kid**11 3244 2-8-6 0 KeithQuinn(7) 9 15
(Mick Channon) *midfield: rdn over 2f out: lost pl and bhd over 1f out: wknd fnl f* **33/1**

1m 11.59s (1.39) **Going Correction** +0.20s/f (Good) **8 Ran SP% 114.7**
Speed ratings (Par 93): **98,97,97,94,89 88,80,74**
CSF £8.51 TOTE £4.20: £1.40, £1.10, £4.70; EX 10.10 Trifecta £121.40.
**Owner** Ali Saeed **Bred** Equine Breeding Limited **Trained** Middleham Moor, N Yorks

**FOCUS**
All distances increased by 3yds. The ground was changed to good to firm all round following this opener. An ordinary juvenile contest, rated around the runner-up.

## 3656 CALL STAR SPORTS ON 08000 521321 FILLIES' H'CAP — 7f 211y
2:45 (2:46) (Class 5) (0-70,72) 3-Y-O — £2,911 (£866; £432; £216) **Stalls** Centre

Form / RPR

1566 **1** **Nastenka**[25] 2761 3-9-8 **71**............................ ThomasBrown 3 78
(Ed Walker) *hld up in tch: swtchd rt and effrt over 1f out: hdwy u.p to chal ins fnl f: r.o wl to ld towards fin* **11/2**

-222 **2** *nk* **Al Nafoorah**[20] 2931 3-9-7 **70**............................ AntonioFresu 4 76
(Ed Dunlop) *t.k.h: hld up in tch: effrt over 1f out: styd on u.p to ld 100yds out: r.o but hdd and unable qck towards fin* **9/4**[1]

-003 **3** *1 ½* **Ashazuri**[14] 3163 3-8-6 **62**............................(h) Pierre-LouisJamin(7) 1 65
(Jonathan Portman) *w ldr tl led 4f out: rdn and hdd over 1f out: kpt on and stl ev ch tl no ex 100yds out: outpcd towards fin* **8/1**

-564 **4** *½* **Whiteley (IRE)**[14] 3142 3-8-8 **62**............................ DavidEgan(5) 5 64
(Mick Channon) *trckd ldrs: swtchd lft and effrt on inner over 2f out: rdn to ld over 1f out: hdd and no ex 100yds out: outpcd towards fin* **3/1**[2]

625 **5** *3 ¾* **Hamster Jam (IRE)**[17] 3039 3-9-9 **72**............................ AdamKirby 7 65
(Mark Johnston) *led tl 4f out: styd w ldr: shkn up 2f out: unable qck u.p over 1f out: wknd ins fnl f* **4/1**[3]

0-60 **6** *8* **Moonstone Rock**[11] 3246 3-8-11 **60**............................(p) WilliamCarson 2 35
(Jim Boyle) *t.k.h: trckd ldrs: rdn and lost pl over 1f out: sn hung lft and wknd* **12/1**

1m 36.89s (0.89) **Going Correction** +0.20s/f (Good) **6** Ran SP% **110.0**
Speed ratings (Par 96): **103,102,101,100,96 88**
CSF £17.52 TOTE £5.80: £2.60, £2.10; EX 19.80 Trifecta £98.60.
**Owner** Miss K Rausing **Bred** Miss K Rausing **Trained** Upper Lambourn, Berks

**FOCUS**
Race distance increased by 3yds. The pace slowed after a couple of furlongs and then only picked up again once they'd come down the hill. Modest fillies' form.

## 3657 STARSPORTSBET.CO.UK H'CAP — 1m 1f 207y
3:15 (3:16) (Class 6) (0-55,56) 3-Y-O — £2,264 (£673; £336; £168) **Stalls** High

Form / RPR

-000 **1** **About Glory**[11] 3250 3-9-4 **52**............................(b[1]) TomMarquand 3 59
(Richard Hannon) *hld up in tch in midfield: nt clrest of runs of runs ent fnl 2f: rdn and hdwy ent fnl f: led ins fnl f: styd on strly and drew clr towards fin* **16/1**

606 **2** *2 ½* **California Cliffs (IRE)**[40] 2316 3-9-7 **55**............................ DavidProbert 9 57
(Rae Guest) *hld up in tch in midfield: swtchd rt and rdn to chse ldrs over 1f out: drvn and led ins fnl f: sn hdd and outpcd by wnr fnl 100yds* **12/1**

00-0 **3** *1 ½* **Henry Did It (IRE)**[26] 2726 3-9-4 **52**............................ TomQueally 7 51
(Tony Carroll) *hld up towards rr: swtchd rt and hdwy over 1f out: styd on u.p ins fnl f to go 3rd nr fin: nvr trbld ldrs* **20/1**

6000 **4** *¾* **Greyjoy (IRE)**[13] 3191 3-8-8 **47**............................ MitchGodwin(5) 11 45
(Sylvester Kirk) *wl in tch in midfield: effrt 2f out: pressed ldrs and drvn over 1f out: drifted rt 1f out: unable qck and styd on same pce ins fnl f* **12/1**

0-00 **5** *1* **Peking Flyer (IRE)**[13] 3191 3-9-3 **51**............................(t) OisinMurphy 6 47
(Ed Walker) *dwlt: hld up in midfield: effrt 2f out: no imp tl hdwy ins fnl f: styd on fnl 100yds: nvr trbld ldrs* **17/2**

000 **6** *shd* **King Kevin**[18] 2997 3-9-5 **53**............................(v[1]) SilvestreDeSousa 8 49
(Ed Dunlop) *midfield tl hdwy to ld after 2f: rdn 2f out: drvn and hdd over 1f out: ev ch tl no ex ins fnl f: wknd qckly towards fin* **6/1**[1]

600 **7** *hd* **Tojosimbre**[58] 1787 3-9-2 **50**............................(h) ShaneKelly 15 45
(Richard Hughes) *stdd s: hld up in rr: pushed along 2f out: awkward hd carriage but styd on ins fnl f: nvr trbld ldrs* **20/1**

-050 **8** *2* **Diamante (IRE)**[27] 2705 3-9-2 **50**............................ GeorgeDowning 13 41
(Daniel Kubler) *chsd ldrs: wnt 2nd over 4f out: drvn to ld over 1f out: edgd lft 1f out: hdd & wknd ins fnl f* **12/1**

0-00 **9** *4 ½* **Pushjockeypush**[61] 1727 3-9-7 **55**............................(t) HarryBentley 10 38
(Stuart Williams) *midfield: rdn 4f out: wknd u.p over 1f out* **12/1**

50-0 **10** *3* **Think So (IRE)**[11] 3248 3-9-2 **50**............................ AdamKirby 5 27
(Mark Johnston) *midfield: pushed along 4f out: no hdwy u.p 2f out: sn wknd* **8/1**

0042 **11** *2 ½* **Sublime**[17] 3024 3-8-13 **47**............................(p) KieranO'Neill 14 19
(Rod Millman) *chsd ldrs: rdn 2f out: unable qck and btn over 1f out: fdd ins fnl f* **13/2**[2]

0-55 **12** *8* **Pitch High (IRE)**[26] 2733 3-9-4 **55**............................ ShelleyBirkett(3) 2 12
(Julia Feilden) *led tl 8f out: chsd ldrs: rdn 3f out: son struggling: wknd wl over 1f out* **10/1**

-050 **13** *9* **Holyroman Princess**[16] 3087 3-9-2 **50**............................(b) RyanTate 12
(Rod Millman) *midfield: effrt u.p and wd 3f out: sn btn and bhd over 1f out* **7/1**[3]

000- **14** *49* **Twaddle**[273] 6412 3-8-12 **46** oh1............................ MartinLane 4
(Rae Guest) *a rr: lost tch 5f out: t.o and virtually p.u fnl f* **20/1**

00-0 **15** *1 ¼* **Champagne Reign (IRE)**[26] 2726 3-9-2 **50**............................(b[1]) LiamJones 16
(J S Moore) *a towards rr: bhd 3f out: lost tch and hung lft 2f out: t.o and virtually p.u fnl f: burst blood vessel* **33/1**

2m 5.62s (2.02) **Going Correction** +0.20s/f (Good) **15** Ran SP% **124.7**
Speed ratings (Par 97): **99,97,95,95,94 94,94,92,88,86 84,78,70,31,30**
CSF £191.26 CT £3859.92 TOTE £17.60: £5.70, £4.60, £7.80; EX 278.00 Trifecta £5320.90.
**Owner** Ali Bahbahani **Bred** T Cummins **Trained** East Everleigh, Wilts

**FOCUS**
Race distance increased by 3yds. Lowly handicap form and a race that set up for the closers. The placed horses help with the level.

## 3658 FOLLOW US ON TWITTER @STARSPORTS_BET H'CAP — 1m 3f 198y
3:45 (3:46) (Class 4) (0-85,87) 4-Y-O+ — £4,690 (£1,395; £697; £348) **Stalls** High

Form / RPR

-321 **1** **Wapping (USA)**[17] 3027 4-9-7 **85**............................(b) TomQueally 2 93
(David Lanigan) *mde all and dictated stdy gallop: shkn up and qcknd 2f out: wandered rt and then lft u.p: hld on wl ins fnl f* **7/2**[2]

0061 **2** *nk* **Impressive Day (IRE)**[20] 2913 4-8-11 **75**............................(p) AdamBeschizza 5 82
(Gary Moore) *trckd ldrs: wnt 2nd and bmpd 3f out: rdn 2f out: lost 2nd but stl cl enough 1f out: chsd wnr again ins fnl f: styd on but a hld* **4/1**[3]

3-11 **3** *2* **Mornington**[42] 2218 4-9-2 **87**............................ TylerSaunders(7) 3 93+
(Marcus Tregoning) *trckd ldr tl swtchd rt and bmpd 3f out: effrt on inner 2f out: 2nd and pressing wnr 1f out: nt clrest of runs and lost 2nd ins fnl f: outpcd towards fin* **11/8**[1]

30-4 **4** *6* **Rubensian**[20] 2913 4-8-8 **77**............................ GeorgeBuckell(5) 1 71
(David Simcock) *t.k.h: hld up in tch: effrt 2f out: no imp u.p over 1f out: wknd ins fnl f* **5/1**

0-15 **5** *1* **Roy Rocket (FR)**[20] 2913 7-8-3 **72**............................ DavidEgan(5) 4 64
(John Berry) *hld up in rr: effrt 2f out: no imp and wknd ins fnl f* **9/1**

2m 40.16s (7.46) **Going Correction** +0.20s/f (Good) **5** Ran SP% **111.0**
Speed ratings (Par 105): **83,82,81,77,76**
CSF £17.36 TOTE £3.90: £1.90, £2.10; EX 19.20 Trifecta £39.00.
**Owner** Lord Lloyd-Webber **Bred** W S Farish & Watership Down Stud **Trained** Newmarket, Suffolk

**FOCUS**
Race distance increased by 3yds. A fair little handicap, although they went steady. The form is rated around the runner-up.

## 3659 CALL STAR SPREADS ON 0808 2349709 H'CAP — 5f 60y
4:15 (4:15) (Class 5) (0-75,71) 4-Y-O+ — £2,911 (£649; £649; £216) **Stalls** Centre

Form / RPR

4436 **1** **Come On Dave (IRE)**[13] 3176 8-9-6 **70**............................(v) DanielMuscutt 4 75
(John Butler) *taken down early: chsd ldr tl led 2f out: drvn 1f out: hld on cl home: all out* **11/4**[2]

341 **2** *nk* **Zipedeedodah (IRE)**[19] 2967 5-9-2 **71**............................(t) DavidEgan(5) 3 75
(Joseph Tuite) *dwlt: t.k.h: trckd ldrs: rdn to chse wnr jst over 1f out: styd on and ev ch whn rdr dropped reins 100yds out: kpt on wl but nvr quite getting to wnr* **7/4**[1]

4216 **2** *dht* **Hurricane Alert**[42] 2214 5-8-5 **55**............................ KieranO'Neill 2 59
(Mark Hoad) *taken down early: squeezed for room leaving stalls: hld up in tch: nt clr run 2f out: 4th and swtchd rt 1f out: styd on strly fnl 100yds: nt quite rch wnr* **16/1**

6001 **4** *2* **Flowing Clarets**[9] 3331 4-8-11 **61**............................ WilliamCarson 5 58
(John Bridger) *in tch: effrt 2f out: unable qck u.p over 1f out: kpt on fnl 100yds but nvr threatening ldrs* **7/2**[3]

5222 **5** *1 ¼* **Entertaining Ben**[22] 2858 4-8-11 **68**............................(p) FinleyMarsh(7) 1 61
(Amy Murphy) *led tl 2f out: unable qck u.p over 1f out: wknd ins fnl f* **4/1**

1m 3.31s (1.01) **Going Correction** +0.20s/f (Good) **5** Ran SP% **111.1**
Speed ratings (Par 103): **99,98,98,95,93**
WIN: £3.90; PL: HA £2.20, COD £1.70, £0.60; EX: £3.60, £17.90; CSF: COD\Z£4.05, COD\HA £18.04; TF: COD\Z\HA £26.20, COD\HA\Z £67.20;.
**Owner** Royale Racing Syndicate **Bred** Mrs Eithne Hamilton **Trained** Newmarket, Suffolk

**FOCUS**
Race distance increased by 3yds. A modest sprint, there was little between the front three as they hit the line and the outsider of the field looked a bit unlucky. The winner is rated in line with his recent AW level.

## 3660 STARSPREADS.COM H'CAP — 5f 215y
4:45 (4:45) (Class 6) (0-60,67) 3-Y-O+ — £2,264 (£673; £336; £168) **Stalls** Centre

Form / RPR

4211 **1** **Deeds Not Words (IRE)**[5] 3469 6-10-8 **67** 6ex............(p) DavidProbert 2 77+
(Michael Wigham) *hld up in midfield: clsd and nt clr run 2f out: gap opened and effrt over 1f out: styd on to ld ins fnl f: r.o wl and drew clr towards fin* **1/1**[1]

4331 **2** *1 ¼* **Frank Cool**[49] 2024 4-9-10 **55**............................ GeorgeDowning 7 58
(Tony Carroll) *trckd ldrs: effrt to chal and hung lft to far rail over 1f out: kpt on u.ps tl unable qck w wnr 100yds out: one pce after: burst blood vessel* **11/2**[3]

-060 **3** *hd* **Sixties Habana**[20] 2911 3-9-0 **53**............................ ShaneKelly 1 53
(Pat Phelan) *led: rdn over 1f out: hdd and styd on same pce ins fnl f* **11/1**

3054 **4** *¾* **Jack The Laird (IRE)**[19] 2968 4-9-9 **57**............................(b[1]) JackDuern(3) 8 57
(Dean Ivory) *hld up in midfield: effrt and shkn up over 1f out: no imp tl styd on wl ins fnl f: nvr enough pce to threaten ldrs* **8/1**

0035 **5** *1* **New Rich**[16] 3084 7-9-11 **56**............................(v) CharlesBishop 4 53
(Eve Johnson Houghton) *chsd ldr tl over 1f out: sn u.p and hung lft: kpt on same pce ins fnl f* **5/1**[2]

-404 **6** *11* **Knight Of The Air**[10] 3304 5-10-2 **61**............................ SamHitchcott 5 23
(Joseph Tuite) *s.i.s: a 6th and nvr on terms: effrt 2f out: no imp: wl hld and eased ins fnl f* **12/1**

300- **7** *nk* **Nip Down The Jug**[264] 6663 3-9-2 **55**............................ KierenFox 9 14
(Michael Attwater) *s.i.s: a detached in last* **33/1**

1m 11.45s (1.25) **Going Correction** +0.20s/f (Good)
**WFA** 3 from 4yo+ 8lb **7** Ran SP% **112.1**
Speed ratings (Par 101): **99,97,97,96,94 80,79**
CSF £6.58 CT £36.03 TOTE £1.90: £1.30, £2.60; EX 8.30 Trifecta £37.10.
**Owner** D Hassan **Bred** B Holland, S Hillen & J Cullinan **Trained** Newmarket, Suffolk

**FOCUS**
Race distance increased by 3yds. Not much of a race but the winner was strong in the finish to complete a hat-trick. The race is rated around the in-form runner-up.

## 3661 FOLLOW US ON TWITTER @STARSPREADS_BET APPRENTICE H'CAP — 6f 210y
5:15 (5:15) (Class 6) (0-55,57) 3-Y-O+ — £2,264 (£673; £336; £168) **Stalls** Centre

Form / RPR

1550 **1** **Tigerfish (IRE)**[11] 3246 3-8-4 **50**............................(p) KatherineGlenister(7) 9 53
(William Stone) *hld up in tch: shkn up over 1f out: hdwy and swtchd lft 1f out: styd on to chal ins fnl f: led and rdr dropped whip towards fin* **4/1**[2]

345 **2** *hd* **Welsh Inlet (IRE)**[65] 1618 9-9-11 **57**............................ MitchGodwin(3) 6 63
(John Bridger) *led: rdn 2f out: hrd pressed and battled on gamely fr over 1f out: hdd towards fin* **14/1**

4-53 **3** *nk* **Lawfilly**[26] 2733 3-8-7 **53**............................ NicolaCurrie(7) 13 55
(Richard Hughes) *t.k.h: hld up in tch in rr: hdwy on outer over 1f out: ev ch and pushed along 1f out: kpt on: no ex cl home* **5/1**[3]

50-3 **4** *hd* **Fanfair**[20] 2911 3-9-2 **55**............................ HollieDoyle 3 57
(Richard Hannon) *in tch in midfield: swtchd lft 2f out: effrt whn nt clr run and swtchd rt over 1f out: ev ch and drvn ins fnl f: unable qck cl home* **7/2**[1]

36-0 **5** *2 ¼* **Captain Marmalade (IRE)**[25] 2763 5-9-5 **55**............................ RossaRyan(7) 7 55
(Jimmy Fox) *s.i.s: hld up in tch: clsd 2f out: gap opened and hdwy 2f out: rdn and ev ch 1f out: no ex and jst getting outpcd whn n.m.r wl ins fnl f: wknd towards fin* **9/1**

0-05 **6** *1 ¼* **Aberdonian**[20] 2911 3-8-3 **49** ow3............................ FinleyMarsh(7) 8 41
(Jeremy Gask) *hld up in tch in midfield: effrt to chal and hung lft over 1f out: no ex ins fnl f: wknd fnl 100yds* **7/1**

0-00 **7** *shd* **Sabato (IRE)**[10] 3280 4-8-10 **46** oh1............................ GeorgiaDobie(7) 5 41
(Fergal O'Brien) *s.i.s: hld up in tch in rr: rdn and hdwy jst over 1f out: kpt on same pce ins fnl f* **50/1**

3-50 **8** *4 ½* **Fitzwilliam**[11] 3263 5-8-10 **46** oh1............................ KeithQuinn(7) 10 29
(Mick Channon) *chsd ldrs: rdn and ev ch 2f out tl unable qck over 1f out: wknd fnl f* **16/1**

6305 **9** *nk* **Ettie Hart (IRE)**[3] 3522 4-9-1 **51**............................ LenkaHelmecka(7) 11 33
(Mick Channon) *chsd ldr tl 2f out: lost pl over 1f out: wknd fnl f* **8/1**

-600 **10** *1 ½* **King Otto**[24] 2792 3-8-8 **52**..............................(t[1]) DavidEgan(5) 4 32
(Phil McEntee) *chsd ldrs: effrt u.p to press ldrs 2f out: jst getting outpcd whn short of room and bdly hmpd 1f out: wknd fnl f* **12/1**

0-00 **U** **Just Marion (IRE)**[124] 614 5-9-3 **46** oh1.......................... LouisSteward 1
(Clare Ellam) *uns rdr leaving stalls: fatally injured while loose* **50/1**

1m 24.74s (1.64) **Going Correction** +0.20s/f (Good)
**WFA** 3 from 4yo+ 10lb **11** Ran SP% **116.7**
Speed ratings (Par 101): **98,97,97,97,94 93,93,87,87,85**
CSF £58.48 CT £289.66 TOTE £4.90: £1.70, £2.70, £1.70; EX 78.20 Trifecta £366.90.
**Owner** Miss Caroline Scott **Bred** Swordlestown Little **Trained** West Wickham, Cambs
■ Stewards' Enquiry : Finley Marsh three-day ban: careless riding (Jun 26-28)

**FOCUS**
Race distance increased by 3yds. A wide-open finale but the market got it right, with the winner well backed. A compressed finish and very weak form.
T/Plt: £325.70 to a £1 stake. Pool: £79,481.59 - 178.12 winning units. T/Qpdt: £111.40 to a £1 stake. Pool: £6,272.84 - 41.64 winning units. **Steve Payne**

# 3049 PONTEFRACT (L-H)

Monday, June 12

**OFFICIAL GOING: Good (good to firm in places; 8.4)**
Wind: Moderate behind in straight Weather: Cloudy

## 3662 HUDDERSFIELD GIANTS FILLIES' NOVICE AUCTION STKS (PLUS 10 RACE) 6f

**6:40** (6:41) (Class 5) 2-Y-O **£3,881** (£1,155; £577; £288) **Stalls** Low

Form RPR

2 **1** **Miss Dd (IRE)**[13] 3179 2-8-12 0.............................. RichardKingscote 9 69
(Tom Dascombe) *mde all: pushed clr wl over 1f out: hung bdly rt to stands rail ins fnl f: rdn out* **2/1**[1]

**2** *1 ½* **Dance To Paris** 2-9-0 0.............................. GrahamLee 11 66
(Lucy Wadham) *midfield: hdwy on outer 2f out: rdn to chse ldrs over 1f out: kpt on fnl f* **14/1**

6 **3** *nk* **Peace Prevails**[59] 1776 2-9-0 0.............................. TonyHamilton 8 65+
(Richard Fahey) *towards rr and sn pushed along: hdwy 2f out: rdn along to chse ldrs and swtchd lft ent fnl f: kpt on wl towards fin* **6/1**[2]

30 **4** *½* **Flo's Melody**[23] 2816 2-8-11 0.............................. AdamMcNamara(3) 3 64
(Richard Fahey) *prom: hdwy to chse ldr 2f out: rdn wl over 1f out: drvn and kpt on fnl f* **6/1**[2]

5 **5** *1 ¾* **Paco Bleue**[13] 3179 2-8-10 0.............................. DavidAllan 5 57+
(Tim Easterby) *green and sn outpcd in rr: hdwy over 2f out: rdn along on outer over 1f out: kpt on wl fnl f* **6/1**[2]

**6** *½* **Fastalong (IRE)** 2-8-11 0.............................. RachelRichardson(3) 2 59+
(Tim Easterby) *towards rr: effrt and n.m.r on inner 1/2-way: nt clr run wl over 1f out: sn swtchd rt and rdn: styd on wl fnl f* **20/1**

0 **7** *1 ¼* **Miss Van Winkle**[13] 3179 2-8-12 0.............................. FrannyNorton 4 50
(Mark Johnston) *chsd ldrs: rdn along 2f out: drvn wl over 1f out: grad wknd* **10/1**[3]

**8** *1 ½* **Sandama (IRE)** 2-8-12 0.............................. JackGarritty 7 46
(Richard Fahey) *t.k.h: green and a towards rr* **6/1**[2]

003 **9** *6* **Dark Hedges**[18] 2988 2-8-10 0.............................. DuranFentiman 10 24
(Olly Williams) *chsd wnr: rdn along over 2f out: drvn wl over 1f out: sn wknd* **50/1**

0 **10** *1 ¼* **Boss Koko**[9] 3312 2-8-10 0.............................. CamHardie 6 20
(Tim Easterby) *chsd ldrs: rdn along over 2f out: sn drvn and wknd* **50/1**

0 **11** *3 ¾* **French Silk**[23] 2836 2-8-10 0.............................. RoystonFfrench 1 8
(Chris Fairhurst) *in tch on inner: pushed along 1/2-way: rdn over 2f out: sn wknd* **66/1**

1m 20.07s (3.17) **Going Correction** +0.275s/f (Good) **11** Ran SP% **116.4**
Speed ratings (Par 90): **89,87,86,85,83 82,81,79,71,69 64**
CSF £32.51 TOTE £3.00: £1.30, £4.70, £1.90; EX 31.40 Trifecta £170.10.
**Owner** First Capital Cashflow Ltd & Partners **Bred** Michael G Daly **Trained** Malpas, Cheshire

**FOCUS**
The rail was dolled out from 6f to the winning post adding approximately 8 yards to all the races. An ordinary juvenile fillies' novice contest. They went a respectable gallop on ground officially described as good, good to firm in places. The winning time was over six seconds slower than standard, though. Just fair form which has a fluid look to it.

## 3663 TONY BETHELL MEMORIAL H'CAP (ROUND 3 OF THE PONTEFRACT STAYERS CHAMPIONSHIP 2017) 2m 1f 27y

**7:10** (7:10) (Class 4) (0-80,80) 4-Y-O+ **£5,822** (£1,732; £865; £432) **Stalls** Low

Form RPR

34-1 **1** **Frederic**[21] 2889 6-9-10 **80**.............................. GrahamLee 2 95+
(Keith Dalgleish) *hld up in tch: smooth hdwy 3f out: cl up over 1f out: pushed along to ld ins fnl f: cleverly* **5/4**[1]

55-2 **2** *1 ½* **All For The Best (IRE)**[51] 1405 5-9-3 **73**..............(tp) DanielTudhope 6 79
(Robert Stephens) *trckd ldrs: hdwy and cl up over 6f out: led over 2f out: rdn along and jnd over 1f out: drvn and hdd ins fnl f: kpt on: no ch w wnr* **11/2**[3]

1-11 **3** *4 ½* **Aurora Gray**[146] 280 4-9-8 **79**.............................. RichardKingscote 13 81
(Hughie Morrison) *hld up in rr: hdwy over 4f out: rdn along on outer 2f out: drvn and styd on fnl f: nrst fin* **8/1**

0623 **4** *nk* **Teak (IRE)**[14] 3138 10-8-5 **61** oh1..............................(b) FrannyNorton 5 62
(Ian Williams) *chsd ldr: rdn along and outpcd 3f out: kpt on u.p appr fnl f* **5/1**[2]

-566 **5** *1* **Medina Sidonia (IRE)**[5] 3464 5-8-13 **69**..............(b[1]) JasonHart 10 69
(Tim Easterby) *plld hrd. sn led and clr: pushed along over 4f out: rdn and hdd over 2f out: sn drvn and kpt on one pce appr fnl f* **12/1**

0-00 **6** *2 ¾* **Rock On Bollinski**[20] 2928 7-9-0 **70**..............(p) BenCurtis 11 67
(Brian Ellison) *slowly away: rapid hdwy to chse ldrs after 3f: rdn along over 3f out: drvn 2f out: sn one pce* **50/1**

6-21 **7** *1* **Tuscan Gold**[49] 2032 10-8-9 **65**..............(p) TomEaves 7 61
(Micky Hammond) *hld up towards rr: hdwy 6f out: rdn to chse ldrs 3f out: sn drvn and no imp* **25/1**

4-22 **8** *4 ½* **Serenity Now (IRE)**[22] 2471 9-8-11 **72**..............(p) BenRobinson(5) 4 64
(Brian Ellison) *in tch: hdwy on inner 6f out: rdn along 3f out: drvn 2f out: sn wknd* **25/1**

0324 **9** *4* **Riptide**[21] 2889 11-8-6 **62**.............................. RoystonFfrench 9 50
(Michael Scudamore) *hld up in rr: hdwy 7f out: rdn along over 3f out: drvn and btn 2f out* **33/1**

616 **10** *18* **Uncle Bernie (IRE)**[24] 2788 7-9-4 **74**..............(p) AndrewMullen 8 44
(Sarah Hollinshead) *hld up in rr: hdwy on outer 5f out: chsd ldrs over 3f out: sn rdn along and wknd* **14/1**

01-0 **11** *7* **La Bacouetteuse (FR)**[21] 2889 12-8-10 **66**..............(b) DavidAllan 1 29
(Iain Jardine) *hld up: a rr: rdn along 4f out: sn outpcd* **33/1**

3m 53.54s (8.94) **Going Correction** +0.275s/f (Good) **11** Ran SP% **117.5**
Speed ratings (Par 105): **89,88,86,86,85 84,83,81,79,71 68**
CSF £7.57 CT £40.16 TOTE £2.20: £1.10, £1.80, £3.20; EX 9.40 Trifecta £33.50.
**Owner** Paul & Clare Rooney **Bred** Fittocks Stud **Trained** Carluke, S Lanarks

**FOCUS**
Race distance increased 8 yards. A fairly decent staying handicap. Plenty of these horses raced too freely after getting lit up in a scrum for the lead. The winning time once again suggested the ground was riding slower than the official description. The winner is a big improver.

## 3664 MR WOLF SPRINT H'CAP 6f

**7:40** (7:40) (Class 3) (0-90,87) 3-Y-O

**£9,337** (£2,796; £1,398; £699; £349; £175) **Stalls** Low

Form RPR

1-43 **1** **Golden Apollo**[6] 3434 3-9-1 **81**.............................. DavidAllan 5 98
(Tim Easterby) *hld up in tch: hdwy on outer wl over 1f out: rdn and qcknd wl to ld appr fnl f: sn clr: easily* **7/2**[1]

23-0 **2** *5* **Parnassian (IRE)**[26] 2739 3-9-6 **86**.............................. BenCurtis 3 85
(K R Burke) *trckd ldrs on inner: effrt and nt clr run 11/2f out: swtchd rt and rdn ent fnl f: styd on* **8/1**

3211 **3** *¾* **El Hombre**[17] 3038 3-9-2 **87**.............................. RowanScott(5) 6 84
(Keith Dalgleish) *cl up: chal 2f out: rdn wl over 1f out: slt ld briefly appr fnl f: sn hdd and drvn: kpt on same pce* **4/1**[2]

2-10 **4** *¾* **Esprit De Corps**[23] 2831 3-9-2 **82**.............................. RichardKingscote 8 76
(Roger Charlton) *swtchd lft s and rr: pushed along and outpcd 1/2-way: hdwy wl over 1f out: kpt on fnl f* **9/1**

1-34 **5** *4* **Holmeswood**[23] 2831 3-9-5 **85**..............................(b[1]) AndrewMullen 2 66
(Michael Dods) *sn led: rdn along over 2f out: hdd over 1f out: sn drvn and wknd* **7/2**[1]

-111 **6** *11* **Black Isle Boy (IRE)**[12] 3195 3-9-7 **87**.............................. DanielTudhope 7 33
(David O'Meara) *trckd ldrs: hdwy on outer 2f out: rdn over 1f out: wknd appr fnl f: eased whn btn* **5/1**[3]

44-3 **7** *3 ½* **The Nazca Lines (IRE)**[18] 2992 3-8-9 **75**.............................. JasonHart 4 10
(John Quinn) *led early: sn restrained to trck ldrs: pushed along 2f out: sn rdn and wknd* **12/1**

1m 17.37s (0.47) **Going Correction** +0.275s/f (Good) **7** Ran SP% **109.9**
Speed ratings (Par 103): **107,100,99,98,93 78,73**
CSF £28.81 CT £106.36 TOTE £4.60: £2.10, £3.50; EX 30.40 Trifecta £146.20.
**Owner** David Scott **Bred** Cheveley Park Stud Ltd **Trained** Great Habton, N Yorks

**FOCUS**
Race distance increased 8 yards. A decent 3yo sprint handicap. They went a strong gallop and it helped to come from off the pace, so the winner could be flattered. The winning time was more akin to good ground on this occasion.

## 3665 WAKEFIELD TRINITY H'CAP 1m 4f 5y

**8:10** (8:12) (Class 4) (0-80,82) 3-Y-O **£6,469** (£1,925; £962; £481) **Stalls** Low

Form RPR

2-22 **1** **Special Relation (IRE)**[149] 237 3-9-7 **76**.............................. RichardKingscote 2 84+
(Hughie Morrison) *trckd ldrs on inner: hdwy 5f out: swtchd rt to outer over 2f out: rdn to chal over 1f out: led jst ins fnl f: kpt on strly* **7/4**[1]

0046 **2** *2* **Tor**[11] 3261 3-8-13 **75**.............................. JamieGormley(7) 1 79
(Iain Jardine) *t.k.h: led: pushed along 3f out: rdn over 2f out: drvn over 1f out: hdd jst ins fnl f: kpt on* **14/1**

2210 **3** *6* **Specialist (IRE)**[36] 2437 3-9-7 **76**.............................. FrannyNorton 5 70
(Mark Johnston) *trckd ldng pair: pushed along 4f out: rdn along and sltly outpcd wl over 2f out: plugged on u.p fnl f* **13/2**

-531 **4** *½* **True Romance (IRE)**[11] 3261 3-9-0 **69**.............................. TomEaves 4 63
(James Given) *hld up in rr: hdwy on outer over 3f out: rdn to chse ldng pair wl over 2f out: drvn wl over 1f out: sn one pce* **3/1**[3]

201 **5** *2 ¾* **Globetrotter (IRE)**[37] 2408 3-9-13 **82**.............................. DavidAllan 3 71
(James Tate) *t.k.h early: trckd ldr: hdwy and cl up 3f out: rdn along 2f out: sn drvn and wknd over 1f out* **5/2**[2]

2m 42.59s (1.79) **Going Correction** +0.275s/f (Good) **5** Ran SP% **109.9**
Speed ratings (Par 101): **105,103,99,99,97**
CSF £23.48 TOTE £2.70: £1.80, £5.00; EX 16.10 Trifecta £98.90.
**Owner** Bruton Street Uk - Ill **Bred** Tony Ashley **Trained** East Ilsley, Berks

**FOCUS**
Race distance increased 8 yards. A decent middle-distance 3yo handicap. They went a respectable gallop and an anticipated improver upped in trip came through to win well. The form is rated around the second.

## 3666 CASTLEFORD TIGERS H'CAP 6f

**8:40** (8:41) (Class 5) (0-70,70) 3-Y-O+ **£3,881** (£1,155; £577; £288) **Stalls** Low

Form RPR

10-2 **1** **Round The Island**[7] 3401 4-8-12 **61**.............................. LewisEdmunds(5) 12 72
(Richard Whitaker) *in tch: gd hdwy on outer 2f out: led over 1f out: sn rdn clr and edgd lft: kpt on strly* **5/1**[1]

-044 **2** *2 ¼* **Mr Orange (IRE)**[21] 2883 4-9-7 **65**..............................(p) TonyHamilton 7 69
(Paul Midgley) *t.k.h: in tch: hdwy 2f out and sn n.m.r: rdn over 1f out: chsd wnr ins fnl f: kpt on* **11/2**[2]

2005 **3** *nk* **Fleckerl (IRE)**[13] 3177 7-9-10 **68**..............................(p) KevinStott 5 71
(Conor Dore) *towards rr: hdwy wl over 1f out: sn rdn and kpt on strly fnl f* **14/1**

-512 **4** *hd* **Siege Of Boston (IRE)**[119] 724 4-9-12 **70**..............(t) FrannyNorton 3 72+
(John Butler) *towards rr: hdwy wl over 1f out: rdn to chse ldrs and swtchd lft ins fnl f: kpt on wl towards fin* **7/1**[3]

2122 **5** *2 ½* **French**[3] 3548 4-9-12 **70**..............................(p) CamHardie 8 64+
(Antony Brittain) *chsd ldrs: hdwy and cl up over 2f out: rdn to chal and ev ch wl over 1f out: drvn and edgd lft jst ins fnl f: kpt on* **11/2**[2]

2560 **6** *hd* **Ticks The Boxes (IRE)**[20] 2923 5-9-12 **70**..............(p) TomEaves 14 63
(John Wainwright) *dwlt and rr: hdwy wl over 1f out: rdn and styd on wl fnl f* **40/1**

0101 **7** *nse* **Castlerea Tess**[10] 3290 4-8-11 **60**..............(p) CallumRodriguez(5) 10 53
(Sarah Hollinshead) *dwlt and rr: hdwy wl over 1f out: sn rdn and kpt on fnl f* **12/1**

1600 **8** *nk* **Cliff (IRE)**[16] 3095 7-8-12 **63**.............................. FayeMcManoman(7) 11 58+
(Nigel Tinkler) *dwlt and bhd: hdwy on inner whn nt clr run over 1f out: swtchd rt and rdn: kpt on fnl f* **14/1**

3030 **9** *½* **Compton Park**[46] 2104 10-9-8 **69**..............(t) NathanEvans(3) 2 60
(Les Eyre) *prom: hdwy and cl up 2f out: slt ld wl over 1f out: sn rdn and hdd: hld whn bmpd ins fnl f* **8/1**

-000 **10** *6* **Be Bold**[51] 1971 5-9-10 **68**.............................. DanielTudhope 1 39
(Rebecca Bastiman) *in tch on inner: hdwy 2f out: sn rdn and no imp appr fnl f* **16/1**

460- **11** *1* **Le Laitier (FR)**[369] 3013 6-9-2 **60** ........ DavidAllan 13 28
(Scott Dixon) *nvr bttr than midfield* **25/1**

0-00 **12** *nk* **Total Power**[13] 3186 4-9-4 **62** ........ BenCurtis 4 29
(Brian Ellison) *dwlt: t.k.h: a towards rr* **25/1**

5360 **13** *8* **Meandmyshadow**[12] 3216 9-9-7 **68** ........ (b) JoshDoyle(3) 6 10
(Alan Brown) *cl up: led wl over 2f out: rdn and hdd wl over 1f out: sn wknd* **20/1**

0306 **14** *32* **Racquet**[10] 3288 4-9-8 **66** ........ JackGarritty 9
(Ruth Carr) *prom: rdn along 2f out: sn drvn and wknd* **16/1**

66-0 **15** *40* **Niqnaaqpaadiwaaq**[45] 2120 5-9-2 **60** ........ NeilFarley 16
(Eric Alston) *qckly away and led: rdn along 1/2-way: hdd wl over 2f out: sn drvn sn wknd* **20/1**

1m 18.42s (1.52) **Going Correction** +0.275s/f (Good) **15** Ran SP% **123.5**
Speed ratings (Par 103): **100,97,96,96,93 92,92,92,91,83 82,81,71,28,**
CSF £29.73 CT £382.29 TOTE £5.70: £2.00, £2.30, £5.00; EX 33.20 Trifecta £475.60.
**Owner** Nice Day Out Partnership **Bred** R Dollar, T Adams & G F Pemberton **Trained** Scarcroft, W Yorks

**FOCUS**
Race distance increased 8 yards. A modest sprint handicap. They went a decent gallop and the favourite came through to win readily from a wide draw. He confirmed his improved latest form.

## 3667 FEATHERSTONE ROVERS H'CAP 5f 3y
**9:10** (9:12) (Class 5) (0-75,77) 4-Y-0+ **£3,881** (£1,155; £577; £288) **Stalls** Low

Form RPR

-002 **1** **Oriental Splendour (IRE)**[9] 3345 5-8-13 **67** ........ JackGarritty 12 78
(Ruth Carr) *in tch: wd st: hdwy wl over 1f out: rdn to ld jst ins fnl f: sn clr: kpt on strly* **10/1**

6251 **2** *3 1/2* **Jacob's Pillow**[12] 3201 6-8-9 **68** ........ (p) RowanScott(5) 14 66
(Rebecca Bastiman) *hld up in rr: wd st: hdwy over 1f out: sn rdn and kpt on strly fnl f* **14/1**

0040 **3** *nk* **Twentysvnthlancers**[12] 3202 4-8-11 **65** ........ (p[1]) GrahamLee 3 62
(Paul Midgley) *towards rr: gd hdwy on inner 2f out: chsd ldrs over 1f out: rdn and ev ch ent fnl f: sn drvn and kpt on same pce* **16/1**

5161 **4** *1 1/4* **Crosse Fire**[12] 3202 5-8-12 **66** ........ DavidAllan 8 59
(Scott Dixon) *trckd ldng pair: hdwy and wd st: rdn over 1f out: drvn and kpt on same pce fnl f* **4/1**[1]

43-0 **5** *1 1/2* **Astrophysics**[17] 3052 5-9-4 **72** ........ PaddyAspell 4 59
(Lynn Siddall) *trckd ldrs on inner: hdwy 2f out and sn cl up: rdn and ev ch 1f out: kpt on same pce* **14/1**

06-0 **6** *nse* **Star Citizen**[23] 2821 5-9-6 **74** ........ JasonHart 15 61
(Fred Watson) *stdd s and swtchd lft: bhd: hdwy and wd st: rdn wl over 1f out: fin strly* **66/1**

-562 **7** *1/2* **Pearl Acclaim (IRE)**[14] 3136 7-9-4 **72** ........ (p) DanielTudhope 7 57
(David O'Meara) *cl up: rdn along 2f out: drvn over 1f out: grad wknd fnl f* **9/2**[2]

6503 **8** *3/4* **Archimedes (IRE)**[12] 3201 4-8-11 **65** ........ (p) FrannyNorton 10 48
(David C Griffiths) *chsd ldrs on outer: wd st: rdn along wl over 1f out: kpt on one pce* **16/1**

-664 **9** *shd* **Wilde Extravagance (IRE)**[9] 3345 4-8-11 **65** ........ JoeDoyle 9 47
(Julie Camacho) *in tch: rdn along wl over 1f out: sn no imp* **13/2**

0000 **10** *1* **Coiste Bodhar (IRE)**[20] 2932 6-8-8 **67** ........ PaddyPilley(5) 6 46
(Scott Dixon) *qckly away and led: rdn wl over 1f out: drvn and hdd jst ins fnl f: sn wknd* **20/1**

30 **11** *1* **New Road Side**[4] 3492 4-9-4 **77** ........ (v) CliffordLee(5) 5 52
(Richard Guest) *chsd ldrs: rdn along 2f out: wknd over 1f out* **6/1**[3]

-050 **12** *nse* **Bond Bombshell**[27] 2700 4-8-7 **68** ........ PatrickVaughan(7) 13 43
(David O'Meara) *dwlt: a towards rr* **33/1**

-005 **13** *1/2* **Kestrel Call (IRE)**[12] 3202 4-8-9 **63** ........ (t[1]) BenCurtis 2 36
(Michael Appleby) *a towards rr* **16/1**

1m 4.12s (0.82) **Going Correction** +0.275s/f (Good) **13** Ran SP% **115.1**
Speed ratings (Par 103): **104,98,97,95,93 93,92,91,91,89 88,88,87**
CSF £134.57 CT £2295.12 TOTE £9.40: £3.00, £4.00, £5.30; EX 84.10 Trifecta £1609.80.
**Owner** M Baldam & Mrs R Carr **Bred** H R H Sultan Ahmad Shah **Trained** Huby, N Yorks

**FOCUS**
Race distance increased 8 yards. A fair sprint handicap. They went a strong pace and it paid to be ridden more patiently. The winner is worth more at face value.
T/Plt: £201.40 to a £1 stake. Pool: £84,899.42 - 307.70 winning units. T/Qpdt: £90.90 to a £1 stake. Pool: £4,805.42 - 39.10 winning units. **Joe Rowntree**

# 3406 WINDSOR (R-H)
Monday, June 12

**OFFICIAL GOING: Good to firm (good in places; 8.2)**
Wind: Fresh, behind in home straight Weather: Fine

## 3668 EBF STALLIONS NOVICE STKS (PLUS 10 RACE) 6f 12y
**6:00** (6:03) (Class 4) 2-Y-0 **£3,946** (£1,174; £586; £293) **Stalls** Low

Form RPR

**1** **Buridan (FR)** 2-9-2 0 ........ FrankieDettori 1 82+
(Richard Hannon) *broke wl: w ldr: led against rail over 2f out: rdn over 1f out: hld on nr fin* **8/11**[1]

0 **2** *nk* **Mr Top Hat**[24] 2779 2-9-2 0 ........ DaneO'Neill 10 81
(David Evans) *wl in tch on outer: rdn 2f out: styd on to take 2nd ins fnl f: clsd on wnr nr fin: jst hld* **40/1**

202 **3** *hd* **Angel Of The South (IRE)**[21] 2905 2-8-11 0 ........ RobertWinston 9 75
(Dean Ivory) *hld up: swtchd to nr side rail and rdn 2f out: r.o wl fnl f: tk 3rd last 75yds and clsd on ldng pair fin* **5/1**[3]

2 **4** *2 1/2* **Prince Ahwahnee**[13] 3165 2-9-2 0 ........ AdamKirby 7 72
(Clive Cox) *narrow ld to over 2f out: pressed wnr to over 1f out: wknd ins fnl f* **5/2**[2]

**5** *1 3/4* **Expecting** 2-9-2 0 ........ PaulMulrennan 8 67
(Charles Hills) *trckd ldrs: effrt 2f out: cl up over 1f out: hld whn short of room jst ins fnl f: fdd* **16/1**

0 **6** *2 3/4* **General Zoff**[13] 3165 2-9-2 0 ........ MartinDwyer 4 58
(William Muir) *outpcd and rn green in rr: sn pushed along: nvr a factor but kpt on fnl f* **80/1**

**7** *nk* **Coal Stock (IRE)** 2-9-2 0 ........ SeanLevey 2 57
(David Evans) *rn green and outpcd in last: nvr a factor but kpt on fnl 2f* **50/1**

**8** *6* **Ivy Leaguer** 2-8-9 0 ........ JordanUys(7) 5 37
(Brian Meehan) *rn green and outpcd in rr: bhd over 1f out* **50/1**

P **Rivendicato** 2-8-11 0 ........ OisinMurphy 6
(Joseph Tuite) *pressed ldrs tl wknd 2f out: lost action and eased fnl f: p.u and dismntd nr fin* **16/1**

1m 12.7s (-0.30) **Going Correction** -0.10s/f (Good) **9** Ran SP% **122.5**
Speed ratings (Par 95): **98,97,97,94,91 88,87,79,**
CSF £49.63 TOTE £1.70: £1.10, £9.30, £1.60; EX 45.80 Trifecta £194.80.
**Owner** Al Shaqab Racing **Bred** S C A La Perrigne **Trained** East Everleigh, Wilts

■ Stewards' Enquiry : Dane O'Neill caution: careless riding

**FOCUS**
Rail moved out 8yds over last three meetings' running lines on stands' rail from 6f to winning post. All distances as advertised. This wasn't a bad novice event and the third makes it look straightforward enough. The time was just fair.

## 3669 CONGRATULATIONS SPORTING LIFE PICK-7 WINNER SHANE ROCHE MAIDEN STKS 6f 12y
**6:30** (6:30) (Class 5) 3-Y-0+ **£2,911** (£866; £432; £216) **Stalls** Low

Form RPR

-033 **1** **Think Fashion (IRE)**[14] 3157 3-9-0 78 ........ (p[1]) WilliamBuick 1 74
(Brian Meehan) *mde all: kicked on 1/2-way: shkn up over 1f out and racd w hd at awkward angle after: hrd pressed ins fnl f: drvn and hld on* **10/3**[3]

2 **2** *nk* **Cobalty Isle (IRE)**[16] 3085 3-9-5 0 ........ DaneO'Neill 2 78
(Henry Candy) *pressed wnr: urged along and nt keep tabs 1/2-way: rallied over 1f out: chal ins fnl f: nt qckn nr fin* **11/8**[1]

54 **3** *3* **Pride Of Angels**[14] 3157 4-9-8 0 ........ TimmyMurphy 6 65
(Gary Moore) *pressed ldng pair: shkn up wl over 1f out: steadily fdd fnl f* **25/1**

2-5 **4** *shd* **Mudallel (IRE)**[10] 3293 3-9-5 0 ........ JamesDoyle 3 68
(Ed Dunlop) *chsd ldng trio: pushed along 1/2-way: no imp whn rdn over 1f out: kpt on* **9/4**[2]

**5** *nse* **Dark Magic** 3-9-5 0 ........ (h[1]) RobertWinston 4 68+
(Dean Ivory) *s.s: wl bhd in last pair: picked up wl and styd on fr 2f out: gng on at fin* **12/1**

4 **6** *13* **Bird For Life**[10] 3279 3-8-9 0 ........ LuluStanford(5) 7 21
(Mark Usher) *s.s: rn green and outpcd in last pair: bhd over 1f out* **66/1**

**7** *1* **Intoxikating** 3-9-5 0 ........ (t[1]) MartinDwyer 5 23
(Gay Kelleway) *s.i.s: outpcd and rn green in 5th: hanging and no prog 1/2-way: bhd over 1f out* **33/1**

1m 12.13s (-0.87) **Going Correction** -0.10s/f (Good)
**WFA** 3 from 4yo 8lb **7** Ran SP% **111.9**
Speed ratings (Par 103): **101,100,96,96,96 79,77**
CSF £7.96 TOTE £4.60: £1.90, £1.30; EX 8.50 Trifecta £74.40.
**Owner** Mrs Perle O'Rourke **Bred** Mrs P O'Rourke **Trained** Manton, Wilts

■ Stewards' Enquiry : Dane O'Neill two-day ban: careless riding (Jun 26-27)
William Buick caution: careless riding

**FOCUS**
A modest sprint maiden, rated around the third. The winner is still rated below her standout 2yo run.

## 3670 SKY BET EXTRA PLACE RACE EVERY DAY H'CAP 1m 2f
**7:00** (7:00) (Class 4) (0-85,84) 4-Y-0+ **£4,690** (£1,395; £697; £348) **Stalls** Centre

Form RPR

166- **1** **Hollywood Road (IRE)**[44] 6870 4-8-13 **81** ........ (b) GeorgeWood(5) 8 89
(Don Cantillon) *hld up in 6th: urged along fr 1/2-way and looked in trble: prog on outer fr 3f out: rdn to ld jst ins fnl f: hrd pressed after and hld on wl* **9/2**[3]

65-3 **2** *nk* **Biotic**[42] 2233 6-8-11 **74** ........ RyanTate 1 81
(Rod Millman) *stdd s: hld up in last: stdy prog on outer fr 3f out: cajoled along to chal fnl f: drvn last 150yds: nt qckn and hld nr fin* **5/2**[1]

0-04 **3** *2* **Harlequin Striker (IRE)**[19] 2960 5-9-4 **81** ........ DaneO'Neill 7 84
(Dean Ivory) *trckd ldr: rdn over 2f out: tried to chal over 1f out but pair on outer wnt past sn after* **14/1**

2412 **4** *shd* **Hermann**[9] 3315 4-9-7 **84** ........ (p) SeanLevey 4 87
(Richard Hannon) *taken down early: led: styd against nr side rail in st: rdn 2f out: hdd & wknd jst ins fnl f* **7/2**[2]

2010 **5** *5* **Pendo**[26] 2730 6-9-4 **81** ........ KierenFox 3 74
(John Best) *taken down early: trckd ldng pair: nt qckn over 2f out: lost pl and fdd over 1f out* **16/1**

33-5 **6** *23* **Blaze Of Hearts (IRE)**[19] 2965 4-9-0 **77** ........ RobertWinston 2 54
(Dean Ivory) *in tch: rdn 3f out: wknd 2f out: heavily eased over 1f out and t.o* **5/1**

0-04 **7** *3* **Oasis Spear**[20] 2920 5-9-5 **82** ........ WilliamBuick 5 23
(Chris Wall) *t.k.h: hld up in tch: wknd 3f out: t.o* **6/1**

2m 8.15s (-0.55) **Going Correction** -0.10s/f (Good) **7** Ran SP% **112.5**
Speed ratings (Par 105): **98,97,96,96,92 73,71**
CSF £15.63 CT £141.39 TOTE £5.60: £2.00, £2.00; EX 16.10 Trifecta £107.10.
**Owner** Mrs Catherine Reed **Bred** Tally-Ho Stud **Trained** Newmarket, Suffolk

**FOCUS**
Not a bad handicap. There was an uneven pace on and the first pair came clear down the middle. A length pb from the winner.

## 3671 SKY BET BEST ODDS GUARANTEED H'CAP 1m 3f 99y
**7:30** (7:30) (Class 3) (0-95,94) 4-Y-0+ **£7,439** (£2,213; £1,106; £553) **Stalls** Centre

Form RPR

56-4 **1** **Stockhill Diva**[42] 2234 7-8-12 **85** ........ PatDobbs 3 88
(Brendan Powell) *hld up in 3rd: trckd ldr on outer over 3f out: shkn up to ld over 1f out: hrd rdn fnl f: hld on* **12/1**

113 **2** *hd* **Jacob Cats**[19] 2959 8-9-6 **93** ........ (v) SilvestreDeSousa 1 95
(William Knight) *s.s: t.k.h: hld up in last: rdn to chse ldng pair 3f out: wnt 2nd over 1f out on outer: chal ins fnl f: jst hld* **2/1**[2]

2201 **3** *1 1/4* **Gaelic Tiger**[11] 3240 4-9-2 **89** ........ (v[1]) JamesDoyle 4 89
(David O'Meara) *trckd ldr: led over 3f out but styd away fr nr side rail: drvn and hdd over 1f out: wandered and fnd little in 3rd pl after* **13/8**[1]

-204 **4** *99* **Croquembouche (IRE)**[7] 3409 8-8-8 **84** ........ CallumShepherd(3) 2
(Ed de Giles) *led to over 3f out: wknd rapidly and sn t.o: virtually p.u* **9/4**[3]

2m 29.87s (0.37) **Going Correction** -0.10s/f (Good) **4** Ran SP% **109.9**
Speed ratings (Par 107): **94,93,92,20**
CSF £35.31 TOTE £8.20; EX 18.30 Trifecta £50.10.
**Owner** Mrs M Fairbairn & E Gadsden **Bred** Mrs M Fairbairn And E Gadsden **Trained** Upper Lambourn, Berks

**FOCUS**
A good-quality little handicap, if ordinary for the grade with a surprise return to form from the winner. There was a fair enough pace on.

## 3672 SKY BET WINDSOR SPRINT SERIES H'CAP (QUALIFIER) 5f 21y
**8:00** (8:00) (Class 4) (0-85,87) 3-Y-O **£5,013** (£1,491; £745; £372) **Stalls** Low

Form RPR

031 **1** **Mabs Cross**[20] 2924 3-8-10 **74** ........ PaulMulrennan 5 86+
(Michael Dods) *hld up: prog towards outer 2f out: pushed into ld jst over 1f out and swiftly 2 l clr: comf* **7/2**[2]

1-63 **2** 3/4 **Open Wide (USA)**[17] 3038 3-9-2 **80** ........(p[1]) GavinLerena 4 88
(Amanda Perrett) *dwlt: hld up in tch: prog towards nr side 2f out: rdn to chse wnr ins fnl f: r.o but nvr any ch to chal* **7/2**[2]

-044 **3** 2 3/4 **Tahoo (IRE)**[18] 2992 3-9-4 **82** ........ OisinMurphy 2 80
(K R Burke) *pressed ldr: chal 2f out: upsides jst over 1f out: sn outpcd: kpt on* **8/1**

1621 **4** 1 1/4 **Arzaak (IRE)**[18] 2992 3-9-8 **86** ........(b) SilvestreDeSousa 8 80
(Chris Dwyer) *taken down early: chsd ldrs: drvn on outer 2f out: outpcd and one pce fnl f* **3/1**[1]

0-30 **5** 1 **Nayyar**[45] 2130 3-9-7 **85** ........(t[1]) WilliamBuick 3 75
(Charles Hills) *taken down early: chsd ldrs: rdn and nt qckn wl over 1f out: sn outpcd and no ch* **11/2**[3]

31-0 **6** hd **Broadhaven Honey (IRE)**[30] 2631 3-8-11 **75** ........ MartinDwyer 7 64
(Tony Carroll) *taken down early: led: rdn and hdd jst over 1f out: wknd* **25/1**

31-0 **7** 1/2 **Dagonet (IRE)**[17] 3038 3-9-0 **81** ........(t) KieranShoemark(3) 6 68
(Roger Charlton) *outpcd in last: kpt on fnl f: nvr a factor* **16/1**

00-5 **8** 7 **Dainty Dandy (IRE)**[10] 3307 3-9-9 **87** ........(t) DavidProbert 1 49
(Paul Cole) *taken down early: chsd ldng pair: wknd qckly 2f out* **12/1**

58.74s (-1.56) **Going Correction** -0.10s/f (Good) **8** Ran SP% **113.4**
Speed ratings (Par 101): **108,106,102,100,98 98,97,86**
CSF £15.89 CT £89.05 TOTE £4.70: £1.60, £1.60, £2.50; EX 17.00 Trifecta £86.20.
**Owner** David W Armstrong **Bred** Highfield Farm Llp **Trained** Denton, Co Durham

**FOCUS**
A fair 3yo sprint handicap. Again the centre of the home straight was the place to be. The winner built on her taking maiden win.

## 3673 SKY BET HORSERACING CASH OUT CLASSIFIED STKS 6f 12y
**8:30** (8:31) (Class 5) 3-Y-O **£2,911** (£866; £432; £216) **Stalls** Low

Form RPR

0-06 **1** **Farleigh Mac**[18] 3000 3-9-0 73 ........ DavidProbert 8 83
(Andrew Balding) *taken down early: mde virtually all: tk field to centre fr 1/2-way: gng best 2f out: drvn and kpt on wl fnl f* **6/1**[2]

2326 **2** 1 1/4 **Cappananty Con**[20] 2927 3-9-0 73 ........(t) RobertWinston 9 79
(Dean Ivory) *stdd s: hld up in last pair: prog on outer over 2f out: rdn to chse wnr over 1f out: styd on but nvr able to chal* **11/1**

-120 **3** 1 1/4 **Comprise**[24] 2806 3-9-0 75 ........ JamieSpencer 2 75
(Michael Bell) *hld up: prog over 2f out: rdn to chse ldrs over 1f out: kpt on same pce fnl f* **7/1**[3]

2-55 **4** 3/4 **Nibras Again**[17] 3038 3-9-0 72 ........ SilvestreDeSousa 4 75
(Ismail Mohammed) *hld up in tch: rdn 2f out: nt clr run over 1f out: styd on same pce fnl f* **2/1**[1]

36-5 **5** 1/2 **Malcolm The Pug (IRE)**[11] 3234 3-9-0 75 ........ SeanLevey 5 71
(Richard Hannon) *t.k.h: trckd ldrs: chsd wnr briefly: wl over 1f out and shkn up briefly: pushed along and fdd fnl f* **8/1**

3-51 **6** shd **Zebulon (IRE)**[33] 2510 3-9-0 74 ........ PatDobbs 1 71
(Richard Hannon) *sltly awkward s: hld up in last pair: rdn 2f out: kpt on one pce and nvr able to threaten* **6/1**[2]

04-3 **7** 4 **Secret Potion**[7] 3411 3-9-0 73 ........ OisinMurphy 7 58
(Ronald Harris) *pressed ldng pair to 1/2-way: sn lost pl u.p* **33/1**

2241 **8** nse **Secret Strategy (IRE)**[28] 2674 3-9-0 74 ........ AdamBeschizza 3 58
(Julia Feilden) *in tch tl rdn and wknd 2f out* **14/1**

424- **9** 10 **Sheikspear**[231] 7578 3-8-11 75 ........ CallumShepherd(3) 6 26
(Ed de Giles) *chsd wnr to wl over 1f out: wknd qckly and eased* **6/1**[2]

1m 11.69s (-1.31) **Going Correction** -0.10s/f (Good) **9** Ran SP% **117.7**
Speed ratings (Par 99): **104,102,100,99,99 98,93,93,80**
CSF £70.74 TOTE £7.90: £2.20, £3.50, £2.10; EX 69.00 Trifecta £366.40.
**Owner** Farleigh Racing **Bred** Farleigh Court Racing Partnership **Trained** Kingsclere, Hants

**FOCUS**
This modest 3yo classified contest saw the winner dominate down the middle. The winner is rated back to a better view of his 2yo form.

## 3674 BOYZONE AT ROYAL WINDSOR RACECOURSE 26TH AUGUST H'CAP 1m 3f 99y
**9:00** (9:01) (Class 6) (0-60,61) 3-Y-O **£2,264** (£673; £336; £168) **Stalls** Centre

Form RPR

-006 **1** **The Secrets Out**[26] 2732 3-8-10 **49** ........(h) KieranO'Neill 4 56
(Luke Dace) *led after 2f: mde rest: rdn 3f out: wandered u.p but kpt on fnl 2f* **16/1**

0001 **2** 2 1/2 **Deleyll**[9] 3327 3-9-3 **56** ........(b) AdamBeschizza 11 59
(John Butler) *chsd ldng trio after 4f: rdn and clsd 3f out: racd against nr side rail and chsd wnr over 2f out: drvn and no imp after* **8/1**

2510 **3** nk **Av A Word**[11] 3250 3-9-6 **59** ........(p) GeorgeDowning 12 62
(Daniel Kubler) *hld up in last quartet: gd prog over 3f out: rdn and styd on fr over 1f out: nvr able to chal* **8/1**

-000 **4** 2 **Crystal Secret**[18] 3007 3-8-6 **50** ........ MitchGodwin(5) 14 49+
(John Bridger) *stdd into rr after s: last and urged along 5f out: stl in last pair and no ch over 2f out: styd on strly fnl f but all too late* **33/1**

000 **5** 1 1/2 **Our Kim (IRE)**[18] 2997 3-8-10 **54** ........ DavidEgan(5) 2 51
(Mohamed Moubarak) *hld up in 7th: rdn 3f out: no imp ldrs 2f out: hung bdly rt jst ins fnl f* **16/1**

-406 **6** 3 3/4 **Bizet (IRE)**[9] 3327 3-9-7 **60** ........(p) RobertWinston 1 52
(John Ryan) *hld up in 8th: rdn 3f out: one pce and wl hld whn hmpd ins fnl f* **12/1**

-044 **7** shd **Let's Sway**[9] 3327 3-8-12 **51** ........(h) LemosdeSouza 10 43
(Amy Murphy) *t.k.h: led 2f out: chsd wnr: chal over 3f out but wandered and nt qckn: lost 2nd and wknd over 2f out: hmpd ins fnl f* **14/1**

-003 **8** shd **Light Gunner (IRE)**[16] 3087 3-8-13 **52** ........ MartinDwyer 9 44
(Henry Tett) *chsd ldrs in 6th: rdn and no prog 3f out: wl btn whn hmpd ins fnl f* **7/1**[3]

005- **9** 2 3/4 **Beyond Beyond**[166] 8556 3-9-2 **55** ........ OisinMurphy 7 42
(Hughie Morrison) *chsd ldrs in 5th: rdn and wknd over 2f out: hmpd ins fnl f* **6/1**[2]

0-05 **10** 5 **Darcey Lou**[40] 2315 3-8-9 **48** ........ KierenFox 5 26
(John Best) *chsd ldng pair: rdn 3f out: wknd 2f out* **25/1**

3450 **11** 2 1/4 **Beauchamp Opal**[24] 2790 3-9-4 **57** ........ StevieDonohoe 6 32
(Charlie Fellowes) *hld up in last quartet and wl off the pce: rdn and no prog 3f out* **9/1**

000 **12** 27 **Red Master (IRE)**[18] 2997 3-9-2 **55** ........(b[1]) SilvestreDeSousa 3
(Ed Dunlop) *hld up in last quartet: rdn and no prog over 3f out: sn btn: eased fnl 2f* **11/4**[1]

2m 29.98s (0.48) **Going Correction** -0.10s/f (Good) **12** Ran SP% **118.6**
Speed ratings (Par 97): **94,92,91,90,89 86,86,86,84,80 79,59**
CSF £138.62 CT £1115.50 TOTE £18.10: £4.50, £2.40, £2.20; EX 46.30 Trifecta £2352.10.
**Owner** G Collacott **Bred** Copped Hall Farm & Stud **Trained** Pulborough, W Sussex

**FOCUS**
A moderate 3yo handicap, run at a solid pace. The winner is rated a bit closer to his better 2yo form.
T/Plt: £357.80 to a £1 stake. Pool: £96,264.44 - 196.36 winning units. T/Qpdt: £98.00 to a £1 stake. Pool: £7,298.58 - 55.10 winning units. **Jonathan Neesom**

3675 - 3681a (Foreign Racing) - See Raceform Interactive

# 3554 COMPIEGNE (L-H)
Monday, June 12

**OFFICIAL GOING: Turf: good to soft**

## 3679a PRIX DE LA HARPE (MAIDEN) (2YO) (TURF) 7f
**1:20** 2-Y-O **£11,538** (£4,615; £3,461; £2,307; £1,153)

RPR

**1** **Namibie** 2-8-13 0 ........ MaximeGuyon 9 74
(H-A Pantall, France) **11/5**[1]

**2** snk **Shyamala**[69] 2-8-13 0 ........ FabriceVeron 6 73
(E J O'Neill, France) **235/10**

**3** hd **Tosen Gift (IRE)** 2-8-9 0 ........ AurelienLemaitre 12 69
(S Kobayashi, France) **38/1**

**4** snk **Swiss Bank (IRE)** 2-9-2 0 ........(b) AntoineHamelin 13 76
(Matthieu Palussiere, France) **213/10**

**5** 2 1/2 **Land Of Mind**[37] 2-9-2 0 ........ StephanePasquier 4 69
(M Delcher Sanchez, France) **67/10**[3]

**6** 4 **Samphire (FR)** 2-8-9 0 ........ AlexisBadel 3 52
(H-F Devin, France) **128/10**

**7** 3/4 **Kyvon Des Aigles (FR)**[43] 2-9-2 0 ........ RonanThomas 2 57
(Mme C Barande-Barbe, France) **93/10**

**8** 1 3/4 **Assonance (FR)**[48] 2-8-13 0 ........ GregoryBenoist 5 49
(H-F Devin, France) **119/10**

**9** 1/2 **Cambiko (FR)** 2-8-13 0 ........ IoritzMendizabal 11 48
(M Le Forestier, France) **55/1**

**10** snk **Sens Des Affaires (FR)**[24] 2881 2-9-2 0 ........(p) TheoBachelot 10 50
(Y Barberot, France) **73/10**

**11** snk **Jasmine A La Plage (FR)**[14] 2-8-13 0 ........ EddyHardouin 7 47
(Matthieu Palussiere, France) **128/10**

**12** 1 1/2 **Mafeking**[24] 2779 2-9-2 0 ........ CristianDemuro 1 46
(Harry Dunlop) *dwlt: pushed along early: rdn over 3f out: drvn over 2f out: sn no imp: eased fnl f* **26/5**[2]

**13** 1 1/4 **Playcity (FR)**[53] 1929 2-8-10 0 ........ JeromeMoutard(6) 8 43
(J-P Lopez, France) **88/1**

1m 27.11s **13** Ran SP% **118.4**
PARI-MUTUEL (all including 1 euro stake): WIN 3.20; PLACE 1.80, 5.40, 8.20; DF 34.20; SF 45.60.
**Owner** Ecurie Skymarc Farm **Bred** E Puerari, Oceanic Bloodstock Inc & Mme A Graverea **Trained** France

## 3680a PRIX RIDGWAY (LISTED RACE) (3YO COLTS & GELDINGS) (TURF) 1m 2f
**2:55** 3-Y-O **£23,504** (£9,401; £7,051; £4,700; £2,350)

RPR

**1** **Afandem (FR)**[94] 1138 3-8-11 0 ........ GregoryBenoist 4 105+
(J-C Rouget, France) **33/10**[2]

**2** hd **Glen Shiel**[32] 3-8-11 0 ........ MickaelBarzalona 3 105
(A Fabre, France) *settled bhd ldr: hdwy to chal over 1f out: led ins fnl f: drvn and hdd fnl 75yds* **39/10**

**3** 1 1/2 **Finche**[29] 3-8-11 0 ........ VincentCheminaud 5 102
(A Fabre, France) **7/5**[1]

**4** snk **Cultivator (FR)** 3-8-11 0 ........ ChristopheSoumillon 2 101
(F Rossi, France) **37/10**[3]

**5** 1 **Temple Church (IRE)**[32] 2560 3-8-11 0 ........ IoritzMendizabal 6 99
(Hughie Morrison) *dwlt: tk a t.k.h: hdwy 2f out: u.p and styd on one pce fnl f* **108/10**

**6** snk **Real Value (FR)**[15] 3115 3-8-11 0 ........ TonyPiccone 1 99
(Mario Hofer, Germany) **244/10**

2m 11.61s **6** Ran SP% **119.0**
PARI-MUTUEL (all including 1 euro stake): WIN 4.30 PLACE 2.20, 2.10, SF 14.50.
**Owner** Al Shaqab Racing **Bred** E Robin & M Robin **Trained** Pau, France

3681a (Foreign Racing) - See Raceform Interactive

# 3325 LINGFIELD (L-H)
Tuesday, June 13

**OFFICIAL GOING: Turf course - good to firm (good in places; watered; 7.9); aw course - polytrack: standard to slow**
Wind: Nil Weather: Fine, warm

## 3682 TAKE THAT EXPERIENCE AT LINGFIELD PARK - JUNE 17 MAIDEN STKS 1m 1f
**5:50** (5:51) (Class 5) 3-Y-O+ **£2,911** (£866; £432; £216) **Stalls** Low

Form RPR

2-4 **1** **Sporting Times**[21] 2930 3-9-0 0 ........ JamesDoyle 2 79+
(Ed Dunlop) *chsd ldng pair: rdn over 2f out: clsd over 1f out: led jst ins fnl f: styd on wl* **15/8**[2]

444- **2** 1 1/4 **Asaas (USA)**[243] 7307 3-9-0 80 ........ SilvestreDeSousa 4 76
(Roger Varian) *t.k.h: led: rdn and narrowly hdd 2f out: upsides 1f out: kpt on same pce* **5/2**[3]

64 **3** 2 1/2 **Abaad (IRE)**[137] 437 3-9-0 0 ........ StevieDonohoe 1 71
(Mohamed Moubarak) *dwlt: racd in 5th: rdn 3f out: no real prog and stl 6 l bhd ldng trio over 1f out: styd on strly fnl f to take 3rd last strides* **25/1**

2- **4** *hd* **Creek Walk (USA)**[208] 7988 3-9-0 0................................ PatCosgrave 6 71
(Saeed bin Suroor) *trckd ldr: rdn to ld narrowly 2f out to jst ins fnl f: fnd little and fdd: eased and lost 3rd last strides* **6/4**[1]

0- **5** *6* **Everlasting Sea**[246] 7208 3-8-9 0................................ RobHornby 5 53
(Stuart Kittow) *chsd ldng trio: rdn over 2f out: no imp* **50/1**

0 **6** *10* **Tyrolean**[6] 3456 4-9-12 0................................ DavidProbert 7 39
(Seamus Durack) *stdd s: hld up in 6th: shkn up over 2f out: no prog and bhd over 1f out* **20/1**

0 **7** *3* **Sampaquita (FR)**[19] 3007 3-8-9 0................................ FergusSweeney 3 25
(Gary Moore) *awkward s: a in last pair: bhd fnl 3f* **66/1**

**8** *9* **Clearance** 3-8-7 0................................ GabrieleMalune(7) 8 12
(Mark H Tompkins) *dwlt: rn green and a detached in last* **50/1**

1m 55.3s (-1.30) **Going Correction** +0.05s/f (Good)
**WFA** 3 from 4yo 12lb **8** Ran SP% **117.4**
Speed ratings (Par 103): **107,105,103,103,98 89,86,78**
CSF £6.89 TOTE £2.80: £1.10, £1.20, £3.80; EX 7.50 Trifecta £59.60.
**Owner** Mrs I H Stewart-Brown & M J Meacock **Bred** Mrs I Stewart-Brown & M Meacock **Trained** Newmarket, Suffolk
■ Stewards' Enquiry : Pat Cosgrave five-day ban (reduced from 10 on appeal): failed to ride out on a horse that would have finished third (Jun 27-Jul 1)

**FOCUS**
The watered ground on the turf course was given as good to firm, good in places. Rail movements added 8yds to all turf races. A fair maiden rated around the second and fourth.

## 3683 HAPPY 25TH WEDDING ANNIVERSARY BARRY & ANN H'CAP 1m 2f
**6:20** (6:20) (Class 5) (0-70,71) 4-Y-O+ **£2,911** (£866; £432; £216) **Stalls Low**

Form RPR

006 **1** **C'Est No Mour (GER)**[29] 2689 4-9-7 **70**................................ TomMarquand 6 75
(Peter Hedger) *hld up in rr: shkn up over 2f out: clsd on ldrs over 1f out: rdn and r.o to ld last 100yds* **8/1**

-633 **2** *1* **Ghinia (IRE)**[19] 3009 6-9-8 **71**................................ RobHornby 7 74
(Pam Sly) *chsd clr ldrs: clsd on inner over 2f out: sn rdn to chal: led 1f out: hdd and one pce last 100yds* **9/4**[1]

3-54 **3** *½* **Pack It In (IRE)**[34] 2512 4-9-7 **70**................................(b) JamesDoyle 9 72
(Brian Meehan) *racd wd: in tch: rdn over 4f out to 2f out: clsd grad fr over 1f out: styd on to take 3rd last strides* **13/2**

-560 **4** *nk* **Daisy Boy (IRE)**[32] 2562 6-9-5 **71**................................(t) AaronJones(3) 3 72
(Stuart Williams) *trckd ldr and clr of rest after 3f: chal and upsides over 2f out: nt qckn over 1f out: outpcd fnl f* **5/1**[2]

0-60 **5** *nk* **Megalala (IRE)**[21] 2914 16-7-9 **51** oh4................................ MillyNaseb(7) 5 52
(John Bridger) *led at gd pce and clr w one rival after 3f: rdn and jnd over 2f out: battled on wl but hdd and one pce 1f out* **33/1**

5010 **6** *½* **Becca Campbell (IRE)**[21] 2913 4-9-1 **69**................................(p) GeorgiaCox(5) 4 69+
(Eve Johnson Houghton) *hld up in last: detached in rr 4f out: shkn up 3f out: kpt on steadily fnl 2f: nrst fin but nvr a threat* **5/1**[2]

1160 **7** *4* **Smiley Bagel (IRE)**[24] 2815 4-9-6 **69**................................ RichardKingscote 8 61
(Ed Walker) *chsd clr ldrs: rdn over 2f out: no prog over 1f out: sn wknd* **6/1**[3]

440- **8** *37* **Inn The Bull (GER)**[236] 7076 4-9-4 **67**................................ FergusSweeney 1
(Alan King) *in tch to 4f out: sn struggling: t.o* **10/1**

2m 7.6s (-2.90) **Going Correction** +0.05s/f (Good) **8** Ran SP% **114.9**
Speed ratings (Par 103): **113,112,111,111,111 110,107,78**
CSF £26.55 CT £125.86 TOTE £8.30: £3.20, £1.20, £2.70; EX 36.00 Trifecta £277.50.
**Owner** D Wilbrey **Bred** Graf U Grafin V Stauffenberg **Trained** Hook, Hampshire

**FOCUS**
Race distance increased by 8yds. A modest affair in which they finished in a bit of a heap. The form is rated around the second to recent figures.

## 3684 HAPPY 30TH BIRTHDAY SIOBHAN BARDEN FILLIES' H'CAP 1m 3f 133y
**6:50** (6:50) (Class 4) (0-80,81) 4-Y-O+ **£4,690** (£1,395; £697; £348) **Stalls High**

Form RPR

2-55 **1** **Pacharana**[18] 3033 4-9-6 **78**................................ LukeMorris 5 84
(Luca Cumani) *trckd ldr: rdn over 2f out: led wl over 1f out: drvn out and kpt on fnl f* **5/1**[2]

0-44 **2** *1* **Saumur**[25] 2781 5-9-0 **72**................................ JamesDoyle 4 76
(Denis Coakley) *trckd ldng pair: chal fr 3f out: led briefly 2f out: chsd wnr after: kpt on fnl f but a hld* **15/8**[1]

0-32 **3** *1* **Rosie Royale (IRE)**[27] 2723 5-8-9 **72**................................ GeorgeWood(5) 3 74
(Roger Teal) *led: steered field on wd crse fr 7f out: rdn and hdd 2f out: one pce after* **7/1**[3]

4-22 **4** *¾* **All My Love (IRE)**[20] 2965 5-9-7 **79**................................ RobHornby 6 80
(Pam Sly) *trckd ldng trio: shkn up over 2f out: nt clrest of runs but nt qckn wl over 1f out: one pce after* **15/8**[1]

5-45 **5** *2½* **Tuolumne Meadows**[34] 2515 4-9-0 **72**................................(b[1]) DavidProbert 2 69
(Paul Cole) *s.s: sn in tch in last: effrt on inner and cl up over 2f out: fdd over 1f out: eased last strides* **9/1**

2m 38.69s (7.19) **Going Correction** +0.05s/f (Good) **5** Ran SP% **108.7**
Speed ratings (Par 102): **78,77,76,76,74**
CSF £14.43 TOTE £5.30: £2.70, £1.30; EX 14.50 Trifecta £48.10.
**Owner** S Stuckey **Bred** Stuart Stuckey **Trained** Newmarket, Suffolk
■ Stewards' Enquiry : James Doyle two-day ban: used whip above permitted level (Jun 27-28)

**FOCUS**
Race distance increased by 8yds. This was steadily run and it paid to race handily. A length pb from the winner.

## 3685 INJURED JOCKEYS FUND H'CAP 2m 68y
**7:20** (7:20) (Class 5) (0-75,72) 4-Y-O+ **£2,911** (£866; £432; £216) **Stalls Low**

Form RPR

2142 **1** **Akavit (IRE)**[6] 3464 5-9-6 **68**................................ SilvestreDeSousa 8 75
(Ed de Giles) *mde all: sent for home over 3f out and maintained 3 l ld after: rdn over 1f out: kpt on wl* **7/4**[1]

5321 **2** *1¾* **Night Generation (GER)**[16] 2332 5-9-2 **64**................................(tp) DaneO'Neill 6 68+
(Chris Gordon) *trckd ldrs: lost pl 5f out: outpcd in last quartet downhill 4f out: prog over 2f out: styd on fr over 1f out to take 2nd last 75yds* **8/1**

10-1 **3** *1* **Danglydontask**[53] 1935 6-9-2 **64**................................(b) LukeMorris 7 66
(David Arbuthnot) *s.i.s: sn pushed up to chse wnr: rdn 3f out: hanging and no imp 2f out: lost 2nd last 75yds* **14/1**

0420 **4** *nk* **Bamako Du Chatelet (FR)**[40] 2336 6-9-9 **71**................................(p) JamesDoyle 5 73
(Ian Williams) *in tch: prog to chse ldrs 5f out: clr in ldng quartet 4f out: drvn over 2f out: kpt on one pce over 1f out* **13/2**[3]

3420 **5** *2* **Bridey's Lettuce (IRE)**[25] 2781 5-9-4 **66**................................(h) KierenFox 2 66
(John Best) *hld up in last: outpcd in last quartet 4f out: prog on inner wl over 2f out: one pce and no imp on ldrs over 1f out* **10/1**

1-02 **6** *4½* **McCools Gold**[21] 2928 4-9-4 **67**................................(p) MartinHarley 1 61
(Alan King) *trckd ldrs: rdn 3f out: nt qckn over 2f out: wknd over 1f out* **7/2**[2]

36-6 **7** *6* **Daghash**[31] 2622 8-9-9 **71**................................ RichardKingscote 4 58
(Stuart Kittow) *hld up in rr: outpcd in last quartet 4f out: rdn and no prog after* **7/1**

5-42 **8** *8* **Ruler Of The Nile**[34] 1561 5-9-10 **72**................................(p) LiamKeniry 3 49
(Robert Stephens) *hld up: outpcd in last quartet 4f out: wknd 3f out* **25/1**

3m 36.14s (1.34) **Going Correction** +0.05s/f (Good) **8** Ran SP% **115.1**
Speed ratings (Par 103): **98,97,96,96,95 93,90,86**
CSF £16.87 CT £149.19 TOTE £2.40: £1.20, £1.80, £3.00; EX 15.40 Trifecta £109.20.
**Owner** Simon Treacher & Partner **Bred** Tenuta Genzianella Di Manuela Martinelli **Trained** Ledbury, H'fords

**FOCUS**
Race distance increased by 8yds. The winner was soon out in front and dominated throughout. The runner-up is rated close to form.

## 3686 RACING WELFARE (S) STKS 6f 1y(P)
**7:50** (7:51) (Class 6) 3-Y-O+ **£2,264** (£673; £336; £168) **Stalls Low**

Form RPR

0025 **1** **Nag's Wag (IRE)**[40] 2335 4-9-5 72................................ LiamKeniry 4 69+
(George Baker) *trckd ldrs gng wl: wnt 2nd over 2f out: rdn to ld over 1f out: kpt on* **11/8**[1]

000- **2** *1¼* **Lucky Di**[188] 8252 7-8-11 60................................ CharlesBishop 3 57
(Peter Hedger) *hld up: prog 2f out: shkn up and styd on to take 2nd ins fnl f: nvr able to chal* **11/4**[2]

2343 **3** *2¼* **Bookmaker**[39] 2367 7-9-5 57................................(p) MitchGodwin(5) 6 62
(John Bridger) *rdn in last bef 1/2-way: no prog tl kpt on fr over 1f out to take 3rd nr fin* **4/1**[3]

/0-0 **4** *¾* **Little Cupcake**[36] 2454 6-8-4 43................................(v) JackOsborn(7) 7 47
(Denis Quinn) *sn pressed ldr on outer: led wl over 3f out: drvn and hdd over 1f out: wknd ins fnl f* **33/1**

000- **5** *8* **Shillbourne Lad (IRE)**[178] 8425 3-8-6 33 ow3..........(t[1]) PaddyPilley(5) 2 27
(Bill Turner) *led to wl over 3f out: wknd wl over 1f out* **66/1**

04/0 **6** *27* **Rain Wind And Fire (USA)**[55] 1890 5-9-2 70..............(b[1]) ShaneKelly 5
(Ronald Harris) *in tch: effrt on outer 1/2-way: wknd qckly over 2f out: virtually p.u over 1f out* **9/2**

1m 14.08s (2.18) **Going Correction** +0.40s/f (Slow)
**WFA** 3 from 4yo+ 8lb **6** Ran SP% **111.4**
Speed ratings (Par 101): **101,99,96,95,84 48**
CSF £5.32 TOTE £2.30: £1.20, £2.00; EX 5.80 Trifecta £10.50.
**Owner** Popbitch Racing Club **Bred** Mrs Ann Foley & Mr William Neville **Trained** Manton, Wilts

**FOCUS**
An ordinary seller, and the winner didn't need to run to her mark to win. Straightforward form.

## 3687 #TAKETHEREINS17 FILLIES' NOVICE STKS (PLUS 10 RACE) 6f 1y(P)
**8:20** (8:23) (Class 5) 2-Y-O **£2,911** (£866; £432; £216) **Stalls Low**

Form RPR

3 **1** **Elizabeth Bennet (IRE)**[17] 3070 2-9-0 0................................ JamesDoyle 4 88+
(Charles Hills) *trckd ldng pair: pushed along 2f out: led over 1f out and qckly drew clr: v comf* **13/8**[1]

6 **2** *5* **Sardenya (IRE)**[17] 3070 2-8-11 0................................ KieranShoemark(3) 7 70
(Roger Charlton) *trckd ldrs gng wl: pushed along and outpcd 2f out: styd on wl to take 2nd last 75yds: no ch w wnr* **10/1**

**3** *1¼* **Moggy (USA)** 2-9-0 0................................ ShaneKelly 8 66
(Richard Hughes) *chsd ldr to over 1f out: sn outpcd: kpt on* **40/1**

**4** *nse* **Golden Footsteps (IRE)** 2-9-0 0................................ LiamKeniry 6 66
(Ed Walker) *led: shkn up 2f out: hdd and outpcd over 1f out: fdd and lost 2 pls last 75yds* **11/4**[2]

0 **5** *3½* **Laura Knight (IRE)**[17] 3070 2-9-0 0................................ SilvestreDeSousa 2 55+
(Gary Moore) *settled in last quartet: outpcd 2f out: prog over 1f out: nvr any ch but kpt on steadily fnl f* **10/1**

**6** *1½* **Arizona Mist (IRE)** 2-9-0 0................................ DaneO'Neill 11 50
(Simon Crisford) *trckd ldrs: outpcd fr 2f out: sn no ch* **10/1**

6 **7** *2* **Patty Patch**[14] 3179 2-9-0 0................................(h) StevieDonohoe 12 43
(Richard Spencer) *wl in tch in midfield: outpcd over 2f out: fdd* **16/1**

**8** *hd* **Watch Tan** 2-9-0 0................................ PatCosgrave 9 43
(George Baker) *dwlt: sn in midfield and gng wl enough: outpcd over 2f out: shkn up and no prog over 1f out: wknd fnl f* **66/1**

5 **9** *½* **Silver Bullet (IRE)**[42] 2265 2-9-0 0................................ RichardKingscote 3 41+
(Tom Dascombe) *cl up whn no room on inner after 1f and lost several pls: struggling in rr sn after 1/2-way* **8/1**[3]

4 **10** *shd* **Go Bananas**[11] 3277 2-8-7 0................................ JordanUys(7) 1 41
(Brian Meehan) *s.s: a wl in rr* **25/1**

0 **11** *½* **Deauville Society (IRE)**[14] 3179 2-9-0 0................................ LukeMorris 10 39
(Sir Mark Prescott Bt) *dwlt: a wl in rr: no ch fnl 2f* **25/1**

**12** *9* **Phillimore** 2-9-0 0................................ TomMarquand 5 10
(Richard Hannon) *dwlt: a struggling: t.o* **14/1**

1m 12.9s (1.00) **Going Correction** +0.40s/f (Slow) **12** Ran SP% **127.3**
Speed ratings (Par 90): **109,102,100,100,95 93,91,91,90,90 89,77**
CSF £20.88 TOTE £2.60: £1.20, £3.70, £8.40; EX 24.50 Trifecta £853.10.
**Owner** Mr & Mrs T O'Donohoe **Bred** Awbeg Stud **Trained** Lambourn, Berks

**FOCUS**
A good performance from the winner, who drew right away in the closing stages. She'll rate a good bit higher.

## 3688 RYAN VEHICLES H'CAP 1m 1y(P)
**8:50** (8:51) (Class 6) (0-55,55) 4-Y-O+ **£2,264** (£673; £336; £168) **Stalls High**

Form RPR

-040 **1** **Spryt (IRE)**[68] 1587 5-8-8 **49**................................(t[1]) DarraghKeenan(7) 3 55
(John Butler) *mostly trckd ldr: shkn up to ld jst over 1f out: urged along and hld on wl* **9/1**

00-3 **2** *hd* **Cainhoe Star**[27] 2732 4-9-5 **53**................................ LukeMorris 2 60
(Anthony Carson) *mostly chsd ldng pair: effrt whn nt clr run on inner 1f out and swtchd: styd on to press wnr nr fin: a jst hld* **11/4**[1]

5-0 **3** *nk* **Patanjali (IRE)**[18] 3028 4-9-7 **55**................................ CharlesBishop 11 61
(Eve Johnson Houghton) *hld up in last pair: gd prog over 1f out: nt clr run ins fnl f and swtchd to inner: styd on but too late to rch ldng pair* **6/1**[3]

00-5 **4** *½* **Alketios (GR)**[21] 2915 6-9-7 **55**................................ DaneO'Neill 10 59
(Chris Gordon) *s.i.s: sn in midfield: prog to chse ldng trio over 1f out: styd on to chal fnl f: nt qckn last 100yds* **16/1**

0-13 **5** *½* **Buzz Lightyere**[21] 2916 4-9-6 **54**................................ LiamKeniry 7 56
(Philip Hide) *racd wd: towards rr: rdn over 2f out: prog fnl f: styd on to take 5th nr fin: n.d* **4/1**[2]

0000 **6** *¾* **Hercullian Prince**[4] 3550 5-9-1 **49**................................(b) MartinHarley 5 50
(Conor Dore) *hld up in last pair: gng wl 3f out: pushed along and kpt on same pce fr over 1f out: nvr in chalng position* **18/1**

2053 **7** ¾ **Free To Roam (IRE)**[15] 3137 4-8-13 **47**....................(p) StevieDonohoe 1 46
(Luke McJannet) *led: rdn and hdd jst over 1f out: wknd and lost several pls last 100yds* **10/1**

000- **8** *hd* **Arctic Flower (IRE)**[188] 8248 4-8-11 **50**.................... MitchGodwin(5) 12 48
(John Bridger) *slowly away: racd wd in rr: effrt over 2f out: one pce and no imp on ldrs* **33/1**

0500 **9** *hd* **Frap**[14] 3192 4-8-9 **48**....................(v[1]) GeorgeWood(5) 4 46
(Ian Williams) *nvr bttr than midfield: shkn up 3f out: one pce and no prog* **12/1**

112 **10** 1½ **Living Leader**[44] 2178 8-9-2 **55**.................... BenRobinson(5) 8 49
(Grace Harris) *chsd ldrs: reminder over 3f out: lost pl and btn over 2f out* **7/1**

0001 **11** *nk* **Just Fab (IRE)**[15] 3137 4-9-0 **51**....................(b) CharlieBennett(3) 6 45
(Lee Carter) *cl up bhd ldrs tl wknd wl over 1f out* **9/1**

1m 41.63s (3.43) **Going Correction** +0.40s/f (Slow) **11** Ran SP% **124.3**
Speed ratings (Par 101): **98,97,97,97,96 95,95,94,94,93 92**
CSF £35.96 CT £172.89 TOTE £12.10: £3.60, £1.40, £2.20; EX 51.80 Trifecta £314.70.
**Owner** J Butler **Bred** Moyglare Stud Farm Ltd **Trained** Newmarket, Suffolk

**FOCUS**
There was a tight finish to this low-grade handicap. Weak form.
T/Plt: £33.20 to a £1 stake. Pool: £71,699.15 - 1,573.34 winning units. T/Qpdt: £7.40 to a £1 stake. Pool: £5,421.11 - 537.96 winning units. **Jonathan Neesom**

## 3083 SALISBURY (R-H)
Tuesday, June 13

**OFFICIAL GOING: Good to firm (8.5)**
Wind: nil Weather: sunny, very warm

### 3689 BATHWICK TYRES NOVICE AUCTION STKS (PLUS 10 RACE) (DIV I) 6f
**2:00** (2:00) (Class 4) 2-Y-O **£4,528** (£1,347; £673; £336) **Stalls** Low

Form RPR

2 **1** **Initiative (IRE)**[26] 2750 2-9-0 0.................... DaneO'Neill 9 79
(Henry Spiller) *q str: trckd ldrs: shkn up whn green over 2f out: led jst ins fnl f: r.o wl: readily* **6/5**[1]

**2** *1* **Autumn Leaves** 2-8-9 0.................... SamHitchcott 8 71+
(Clive Cox) *q tall: athletic: s.i.s: sn mid-div: rdn 3f out: hdwy jst over 1f out: kpt on wl to go 2nd fnl 50yds: fin strly* **9/1**[3]

66 **3** 2¼ **Jungle Queen (IRE)**[35] 2502 2-8-9 0.................... CharlesBishop 4 64
(Eve Johnson Houghton) *q str: trckd ldrs: rdn 2f out: swtchd lft over 1f out: kpt on to go 3rd towards fin* **11/1**

23 **4** *nk* **Joegogo (IRE)**[17] 3083 2-9-0 0.................... FranBerry 1 68
(David Evans) *w'like: led: rdn 2f out: hdd jst ins fnl f: no ex and lost 2 pls towards fin* **11/4**[2]

0 **5** *nk* **Alifax**[8] 3390 2-9-0 0.................... TimmyMurphy 2 69+
(Jamie Osborne) *w'like: on toes: hld up: pushed along and hdwy fr 2f out: rdn whn nt clr run briefly ins fnl f: kpt on wl* **20/1**

00 **6** 1¼ **Hastenplace**[26] 2756 2-8-9 0.................... OisinMurphy 6 58
(Rod Millman) *leggy: on toes: w ldr: rdn over 2f out: ev ch ent fnl f: no ex fnl 120yds* **12/1**

**7** *8* **Spot Lite** 2-9-2 0.................... WilliamCarson 3 39
(Rod Millman) *w'like: sltly on toes: s.i.s: sn outpcd: a towards rr* **20/1**

**8** *4* **May Spirit** 2-8-7 0.................... KieranO'Neill 10 17
(Michael Blanshard) *cl-cpld: sn pushed along in mid-div: wknd 2f out* **66/1**

**9** 1½ **Grand Acclaim (IRE)** 2-8-12 0.................... LukeMorris 5 17
(Harry Dunlop) *cmpt: noisy & green in prelims: sn outpcd: a towards rr* **25/1**

1m 14.08s (-0.72) **Going Correction** -0.20s/f (Firm) **9** Ran SP% **113.0**
Speed ratings (Par 95): **96,94,91,91,90 89,78,73,71**
CSF £11.93 TOTE £1.80: £1.10, £3.30, £3.10; EX 11.20 Trifecta £71.20.
**Owner** Saville House Racing Club **Bred** J F Tuthill **Trained** Newmarket, Suffolk

**FOCUS**
Sam Hitchcott described the ground as "good to firm but consistent and safe." The first division of an ordinary novice. The winner did quite well to build on his debut form.

### 3690 BATHWICK TYRES NOVICE AUCTION STKS (PLUS 10 RACE) (DIV II) 6f
**2:30** (2:30) (Class 4) 2-Y-O **£4,528** (£1,347; £673; £336) **Stalls** Low

Form RPR

6 **1** **Simply Breathless**[26] 2750 2-8-7 0.................... SamHitchcott 2 71
(Clive Cox) *leggy: chsd ldr: rdn over 2f out: led fnl 140yds: kpt on wl: readily* **15/2**

4 **2** 1¼ **Groundnut**[15] 3156 2-8-12 0.................... RichardKingscote 3 72
(Jonathan Portman) *w'like: trckd ldr: rdn to chal 2f out: edgd lft in 3rd ent fnl f: kpt on to regain 2nd towards fin* **2/1**[1]

333 **3** ½ **Aquadabra (IRE)**[42] 2265 2-8-9 0.................... CharlesBishop 9 67
(Mick Channon) *leggy: lw: led: rdn over 1f out: hdd fnl 140yds: no ex: lost 2nd towards fin* **7/2**[2]

**4** *nk* **Kimifive (IRE)** 2-9-2 0.................... OisinMurphy 1 73+
(Joseph Tuite) *cmpt: mid-div: hdwy 2f out: sn swtchd lft: kpt on nicely fnl f* **12/1**

6 **5** *nk* **Safe Waters**[21] 2910 2-8-7 0.................... JosephineGordon 8 63+
(Eve Johnson Houghton) *w'like: outpcd in last trio: hdwy 2f out: kpt on ins fnl f but nt pce to get on terms* **7/1**

**6** *3* **Divine Intuition (IRE)** 2-9-0 0.................... SeanLevey 4 61+
(Richard Hannon) *cmpt: bit bkwd: s.i.s: sn mid-div: hdwy 2f out: sn rdn and hld: fdd fnl f* **4/1**[3]

**7** 1¼ **Ojala (IRE)** 2-9-0 0.................... TomMarquand 10 57
(Simon Dow) *q str: s.i.s: outpcd towards rr: nvr on terms* **18/1**

0 **8** 3¼ **Rio Santos**[22] 2890 2-8-7 0.................... AliceMills(5) 6 44
(Rod Millman) *leggy: cl up: rdn over 2f out: sn wknd* **50/1**

**9** *14* **Powerful Rose** 2-8-9 0.................... LukeMorris 5
(Michael Blanshard) *unf: bmpd leaving stalls: sn outpcd: a in rr* **50/1**

1m 14.15s (-0.65) **Going Correction** -0.20s/f (Firm) **9** Ran SP% **116.7**
Speed ratings (Par 95): **96,94,93,93,92 88,87,82,64**
CSF £23.14 TOTE £10.20: £2.70, £1.60, £1.20; EX 27.70 Trifecta £106.70.
**Owner** The Hold Your Breath Syndicate **Bred** Highgate Stud **Trained** Lambourn, Berks

**FOCUS**
The more competitive of the two divisions, although the time was fractionally slower. A few of these are likely to progress significantly from the bare form.

### 3691 BATHWICK TYRES MAIDEN STKS 6f 213y
**3:00** (3:02) (Class 4) 3-Y-O+ **£5,175** (£1,540; £769; £384) **Stalls** Low

Form RPR

5 **1** **La Rav (IRE)**[25] 2798 3-9-4 0.................... JamieSpencer 11 87+
(Luca Cumani) *tall: q lengthy: lw: wnt lft s: mid-div: hdwy over 2f out: sn rdn: led jst ins fnl f: edgd rt: r.o wl: readily* **11/4**[1]

0 **2** 4½ **Blazed (IRE)**[14] 3188 3-9-1 0.................... KieranShoemark(3) 3 70
(Roger Charlton) *athletic: racd keenly: trckd ldr: rdn over 2f out: kpt on ins fnl f but nt pce of ready wnr* **9/2**[2]

0 **3** ¾ **Mulsanne Chase**[25] 2778 3-9-4 0.................... SteveDrowne 1 68
(Brian Barr) *mid-div: rdn over 2f out: hdwy over 1f out: kpt on wl fnl f: wnt 3rd towards fin* **25/1**

04 **4** 1¼ **Saaheq**[12] 3234 3-9-4 0....................(b[1]) DaneO'Neill 10 65
(Brian Meehan) *q str: warm: prom: led 4f out: rdn 2f out: hdd jst ins fnl f: no ex fnl 100yds* **13/2**

4- **5** *nk* **Tuscany (IRE)**[296] 5676 3-9-4 0.................... LukeMorris 4 64
(Paul Cole) *q str: bit bkwd: trckd ldrs: rdn over 2f out: sn one pce* **8/1**

-5 **6** *hd* **Plutonian (IRE)**[14] 3188 3-9-4 0.................... GavinLerena 13 64
(Charles Hills) *q str: sltly on toes: cl up: rdn over 2f out: sn one pce* **6/1**[3]

0 **7** ½ **Allofmelovesallofu**[20] 2957 3-9-4 0.................... PatDobbs 7 62
(Ken Cunningham-Brown) *q tall: mid-div: rdn over 2f out: kpt on fnl f* **100/1**

5 **8** *hd* **Queen Moon (IRE)**[28] 2707 3-8-13 0.................... ThomasBrown 6 57+
(Andrew Balding) *q str: awkward leaving stalls and nrly uns rdr: towards rr: drvn in midfield over 2f out: styd on fnl f but nvr any threat* **33/1**

**9** ½ **Important Mission (USA)** 3-9-4 0.................... LiamJones 12 60+
(William Haggas) *q str: bmpd leaving stalls: sn mid-div: rdn wl over 2f out: nvr any imp* **6/1**[3]

60 **10** *nse* **Canford Tor (IRE)**[25] 2782 3-9-4 0.................... FergusSweeney 5 60+
(Henry Candy) *s.i.s: a towards rr* **28/1**

0- **11** *9* **Millie May**[181] 8354 3-8-10 0.................... HollieDoyle(3) 14 31
(Jimmy Fox) *a towards rr* **150/1**

66 **12** *nse* **Harbour Force (FR)**[21] 2930 3-9-4 0.................... MartinDwyer 9 36
(William Muir) *chsd ldrs tl 3f out: sn wknd* **16/1**

0 **13** *6* **Captive (FR)**[25] 2782 3-9-4 0.................... SeanLevey 8 20
(Richard Hannon) *led tl 4f out: wknd 2f out* **20/1**

1m 26.53s (-2.07) **Going Correction** -0.20s/f (Firm) **13** Ran SP% **120.4**
Speed ratings (Par 105): **103,97,97,95,95 95,94,94,93,93 83,83,76**
CSF £13.83 TOTE £3.80: £1.60, £1.90, £6.80; EX 18.10 Trifecta £251.80.
**Owner** Simon Capon **Bred** Mrs Alison Lewis **Trained** Newmarket, Suffolk

**FOCUS**
An ordinary maiden, but a taking performance from the favourite who is potentially smart. There's a bit of doubt over what the bare form's worth.

### 3692 SHARP'S DOOM BAR H'CAP 5f
**3:30** (3:31) (Class 5) (0-70,72) 3-Y-O **£3,396** (£1,010; £505; £252) **Stalls** Low

Form RPR

03-2 **1** *hd* **Secret Agent**[27] 2720 3-8-11 **65**.................... GeorgeWood(5) 9 69
(William Muir) *trckd ldrs: rdn for str chal 2f out: kpt on w ev ch whn carried sltly lft fnl f: jst hld: fin 2nd: plcd 1st after stewards' inquiry* **5/1**[2]

-215 **2** **Red Alert**[26] 2757 3-9-7 **70**.................... JosephineGordon 5 74
(Joseph Tuite) *led: rdn whn strly chal fr 2f out: drifted lft fnl f: hld on: all out: fin 1st disqualified: plcd 2nd* **4/1**[1]

50-5 **3** *shd* **Coronation Cottage**[57] 1837 3-8-10 **62**.................... CharlieBennett(3) 1 65
(Malcolm Saunders) *broke wl: trckd ldr: rdn for str chal fr 2f out: kpt on w ev ch thrght fnl f: jst hld* **33/1**

5413 **4** ¾ **Jashma (IRE)**[18] 3035 3-9-6 **69**.................... ShaneKelly 4 70
(Richard Hughes) *lw: hld up: hdwy over 2f out: rdn to chse ldrs over 1f out: kpt on but nt quite pce to chal* **4/1**[1]

0U24 **5** *1* **Lightoller (IRE)**[2] 3624 3-9-0 **63**....................(b) GavinLerena 7 60
(Mick Channon) *trckd ldrs: rdn 2f out: nt pce to chal but kpt on ins fnl f* **15/2**[3]

0046 **6** *nk* **Kings Academy**[14] 3166 3-8-13 **65**....................(t) KieranShoemark(3) 8 61
(Paul Cole) *unsettled stalls: in tch: rdn over 2f out: kpt on but nt pce to get on terms* **9/1**

21-0 **7** *hd* **Foxcatcher**[26] 2757 3-9-9 **72**....................(b) AdamKirby 2 69
(Clive Cox) *hmpd s: in tch: hdwy 2f out: sn rdn: nt clrest of runs but nt pce to chal whn clr over 1f out: no ex ins fnl f* **5/1**[2]

5363 **8** *2* **Dashing Poet**[6] 3466 3-9-1 **64**....................(h) MartinLane 6 53
(Jeremy Gask) *racd keenly: hld up: effrt 2f out: nt pce to get involved* **8/1**

-666 **9** *nk* **Compton Lane**[26] 2758 3-9-4 **67**.................... WilliamCarson 3 55
(Rod Millman) *hld up: rdn whn swtchd rt over 1f out: nt pce to get involved* **20/1**

1m 0.33s (-0.67) **Going Correction** -0.20s/f (Firm) **9** Ran SP% **113.9**
Speed ratings (Par 99): **96,97,96,95,93 93,92,89,89**
CSF £24.94 CT £593.75 TOTE £5.90: £1.90, £1.80, £6.40; EX 29.00 Trifecta £726.30.
**Owner** Mrs Michelle Morgan **Bred** Carmel Stud **Trained** Lambourn, Berks
■ Stewards' Enquiry : Josephine Gordon two-day ban: careless riding in that she failed to take sufficient measures to correct her mount from drifting left-handed (Jun 27-28)

**FOCUS**
A modest sprint. They raced down the centre and the race was decided in the stewards' room, Secret Agent being promoted. The third is the key to the form.

### 3693 BRITISH STALLION STUDS EBF MARGADALE FILLIES' H'CAP 1m 1f 201y
**4:00** (4:02) (Class 3) (0-90,82) 3-Y-O+
**£12,450** (£3,728; £1,864; £932; £466; £234) **Stalls** Low

Form RPR

0-52 **1** **Billesdon Bess**[26] 2761 3-8-9 **79**.................... HollieDoyle(3) 7 91
(Richard Hannon) *lw: mde all: drifted lft whn rdn over 1f out: strly chal ent fnl f: kpt on gamely to assert towards fin* **4/1**[2]

21-3 **2** ¾ **Dubara**[54] 1907 3-9-1 **82**.................... JamieSpencer 6 93+
(Luca Cumani) *s.i.s: last: hdwy over 3f out: rdn to chal and drifted lft jst over 1f out: ev ch ins fnl f: no ex towards fin* **2/1**[1]

4-01 **3** 2¼ **Harebell (IRE)**[21] 2929 3-8-10 **77**....................(h) FranBerry 1 83
(Ralph Beckett) *racd keenly trcking ldrs: rdn over 2f out: kpt on to chse ldng pair ent fnl f but nt pce to get on terms* **9/2**[3]

**4** 2¾ **Fengate**[200] 4-9-9 **80**.................... KieranShoemark(3) 4 82
(Roger Charlton) *q tall: trckd ldr: rdn over 2f out: lost 2nd over 1f out: no ex ent fnl f* **12/1**

15- **5** 4½ **Kind Of Beauty (IRE)**[264] 6713 3-8-11 **78**.................... JosephineGordon 3 70
(Hugo Palmer) *lw: trckd ldrs: rdn over 3f out: nt pce to get involved: wknd fnl f* **8/1**

-112 **6** *2 ¼* **Perfect Quest**[22] 2906 4-9-12 **80**........................................(t) AdamKirby 2 68
(Clive Cox) *hld up in tch: rdn over 2f out: nvr threatened: wknd fnl f* **7/1**

1 **7** *5* **Hidden Charms (IRE)**[82] 1333 3-8-7 **74**.......................... OisinMurphy 5 51
(David Simcock) *hld up in last pair: struggling and detached over 2f out: n.d after* **8/1**

2m 6.71s (-3.19) **Going Correction** -0.20s/f (Firm)
**WFA** 3 from 4yo 13lb 7 Ran SP% **113.9**
Speed ratings (Par 104): **104,103,101,99,95 94,90**
CSF £12.35 TOTE £4.40: £1.90, £1.60; EX 13.20 Trifecta £46.10.
**Owner** Pall Mall Partners & Partners **Bred** Stowell Hill Partners **Trained** East Everleigh, Wilts

**FOCUS**
A useful little fillies' handicap. The winner showed last season's Listed form didn't flatter her.

## 3694 BATHWICK TYRES H'CAP 1m 4f 5y

**4:30** (4:31) (Class 5) (0-70,70) 4-Y-0+ **£4,204** (£1,251; £625; £312) **Stalls** Low

Form RPR

1450 **1** **Cotton Club (IRE)**[19] 3004 6-9-7 **70**.............................. WilliamCarson 7 76
(Rod Millman) *lw: in tch: hdwy to ld over 2f out: sn rdn: jst ahd whn drifted rt over 1f out: styd on: rdn out* **4/1**[3]

4-00 **2** *1 ¼* **Onorina (IRE)**[38] 2388 5-9-4 **67**.......................................... OisinMurphy 5 70
(Jim Boyle) *trckd ldrs: led 3f out: sn rdn and hdd: ev ch 2f out: hld ent fnl f: styd on* **7/4**[1]

254/ **3** *shd* **Benbecula**[56] 5582 8-8-13 **67**..............................................(b) AliceMills(5) 2 69
(Richard Mitchell) *disp early: trckd ldr after 2f: chal 4f out tl rdn over 2f out: styd on to chal for 2nd fnl f but hld by wnr* **20/1**

25-6 **4** *1 ½* **Goldslinger (FR)**[47] 2111 5-9-5 **68**...................................... AdamKirby 9 67
(Dean Ivory) *lw: sn led: rdn and hdd 3f out: hld 2f out: styd on again fnl f* **7/2**[2]

0-04 **5** *7* **Loving Your Work**[22] 2909 6-8-10 **59**................................ PatDobbs 8 47
(Ken Cunningham-Brown) *hld up: hdwy over 3f out: rdn over 2f out: nvr threatened: wknd fnl f* **9/2**

6-10 **6** *1 ¼* **Staplehurst (IRE)**[136] 461 4-8-7 **56**................................(t) KieranO'Neill 1 42
(Geoffrey Deacon) *chsd ldrs: rdn 3f out: sn hld: wknd fnl f* **12/1**

020/ **7** *1 ¼* **Garcon De Soleil**[553] 8143 4-8-4 **53**.................................... LiamJones 6 37
(Michael Blanshard) *racd keenly: hld up: hdwy over 3f out: sn rdn: nvr threatened ldrs: wknd fnl f* **50/1**

2m 35.33s (-2.67) **Going Correction** -0.20s/f (Firm) 7 Ran SP% **111.2**
Speed ratings (Par 103): **100,99,99,98,93 92,91**
CSF £10.77 CT £114.19 TOTE £4.50: £2.20, £1.70; EX 11.90 Trifecta £101.00.
**Owner** David Little The Links Partnership **Bred** Patrick Gleeson **Trained** Kentisbeare, Devon

**FOCUS**
A modest handicap run at a fair gallop. The form is best rated around the runner-up.

## 3695 MOLSON COORS H'CAP 6f 213y

**5:00** (5:03) (Class 6) (0-60,60) 3-Y-0 **£3,234** (£962; £481; £240) **Stalls** Low

Form RPR

150 **1** **Beepeecee**[22] 2903 3-9-0 **60**........................................(p) FinleyMarsh(7) 14 68
(Richard Hughes) *hld up: hdwy over 2f out: led wl over 1f out: kpt on strly to assert ins fnl f: rdn out* **10/1**

0-00 **2** *¾* **Opening Time**[27] 2726 3-9-2 **55**..........................................(b) SeanLevey 8 61
(Richard Hannon) *little slowly away: sn trcking ldrs: rdn to chal whn edgd lft and bmpd ldr 2f out: ev ch ent fnl f: no ex fnl 120yds* **4/1**[2]

3323 **3** *½* **Topmeup**[7] 3423 3-9-0 **53**............................................................ FranBerry 9 58
(David Evans) *mid-div: hdwy 3f out: rdn to ld briefly whn bmpd 2f out: edgd rt: ev ch ent fnl f: no ex fnl 120yds* **7/4**[1]

00-0 **4** *4 ½* **Coachella (IRE)**[25] 2790 3-8-11 **53**.......................... CallumShepherd(3) 1 45
(Ed de Giles) *mid-div: rdn and hdwy 2f out: ev ch over 1f out: no ex ent fnl f* **11/1**

6640 **5** *½* **Hidden Stash**[21] 2911 3-8-12 **58**..................................(v) MichaelColes(7) 10 49+
(Andrew Balding) *awkward leaving stalls: last: rdn over 2f out: styd on fr over 1f out but nvr any threat* **9/1**

-460 **6** *2* **Primadonia**[14] 3191 3-9-5 **58**.................................................. ShaneKelly 6 44
(Richard Hughes) *lw: trckd ldrs: rdn and ev ch 2f out: fdd fnl f* **14/1**

00-0 **7** *3 ½* **Gaia Princess (IRE)**[15] 3162 3-9-5 **58**............................ TimmyMurphy 3 34
(Gary Moore) *hld up towards rr: rdn over 2f out: styd on past btn horses fnl f but nvr any imp on ldrs* **16/1**

60-4 **8** *2* **Royal Melody**[27] 2726 3-9-1 **57**..............................(p) KieranShoemark(3) 11 28
(Heather Main) *disp ld tl clr ldr over 2f out: rdn and hdd sn after: wknd ent fnl f* **15/2**[3]

60-0 **9** *3 ½* **Golden Harbour (FR)**[130] 545 3-8-5 **50** ow1.........(t) JoshuaBryan(7) 13 12
(Brian Barr) *hung lft over 1f out: a towards rr* **40/1**

0-60 **10** *15* **Harbour Town**[14] 3173 3-9-5 **58**............................................ AdamKirby 7
(Harry Dunlop) *disp ld tl over 2f out: sn wknd* **16/1**

1m 27.11s (-1.49) **Going Correction** -0.20s/f (Firm) 10 Ran SP% **116.4**
Speed ratings (Par 97): **100,99,98,93,92 90,86,84,80,63**
CSF £49.76 CT £108.10 TOTE £10.40: £2.90, £1.40, £1.20; EX 63.50 Trifecta £229.70.
**Owner** BPC Partnership **Bred** Equine Origin Ltd **Trained** Upper Lambourn, Berks

**FOCUS**
A moderate handicap, the front three came clear. The winner's previous form could easily be rated this high.

## 3696 SHADWELL STUD RACING EXCELLENCE APPRENTICE H'CAP (WHIPS SHALL BE CARRIED BUT NOT USED) 6f

**5:30** (5:33) (Class 5) (0-75,77) 4-Y-0+ **£4,528** (£1,347; £673; £336) **Stalls** Low

Form RPR

00-0 **1** **Gold Hunter (IRE)**[17] 3074 7-9-11 **74**..........................(p) JoshuaBryan 4 82
(Steve Flook) *trckd ldrs: swtchd lft over 1f out: r.o ins fnl f: led fnl stride* **14/1**

2002 **2** *shd* **Bahamian Dollar**[15] 3161 4-9-11 **77**.................... KatherineGlenister(3) 6 84
(David Evans) *lw: prom: led 2f out: sn rdn: kpt on: hdd fnl stride* **4/1**[1]

16-1 **3** *2* **Swanton Blue (IRE)**[17] 3084 4-9-4 **70**........................... RossaRyan(3) 10 71
(Ed de Giles) *led tl 2f out: sn rdn: kpt on but no ex ins fnl f* **9/2**[2]

1650 **4** *shd* **Born To Finish (IRE)**[31] 2608 4-9-5 **73**.......................... WilliamCox(5) 8 73+
(Jamie Osborne) *on toes: hld up: hdwy over 2f out: sn rdn: r.o fnl f: nrly snatched 3rd fnl stride* **7/1**[3]

0051 **5** *1 ½* **Passing Star**[15] 3136 6-9-10 **73**......................................(tp) RayDawson 1 68
(Daniel Kubler) *lw: mid-div: rdn 2f out: kpt on wl fnl f* **9/1**

0-14 **6** *nk* **One Big Surprise**[29] 2676 5-9-6 **74**..................(p) StephenCummins(5) 12 69
(Richard Hughes) *warm: on toes: mid-div: rdn over 1f out: kpt on ins fnl f* **7/1**[3]

-621 **7** *2* **Danecase**[19] 3008 4-9-6 **74**............................................ TheodoreLadd(5) 5 62
(David Dennis) *slowly away and sn swtchd rt after s: towards rr: sme minor late prog: nvr any threat* **7/1**[3]

4163 **8** *shd* **Anonymous John (IRE)**[13] 3214 5-9-7 **75**.................... NicolaCurrie(5) 7 63
(Dominic Ffrench Davis) *towards rr: sme late prog: nvr any threat* **11/1**

-001 **9** *½* **Perfect Pastime**[21] 2917 9-8-10 **64**..........................(p) IsobelFrancis(5) 3 50
(Jim Boyle) *mid-div: hdwy 2f out: sn rdn: wknd fnl f* **25/1**

0315 **9** *dht* **Babyfact**[11] 3278 6-9-8 **71**................................................ JordanUys 2 57
(Malcolm Saunders) *chsd ldrs: rdn over 2f out: drifted lft over 1f out: wknd ent fnl f* **16/1**

5/02 **11** *3 ¼* **Thewestwalian (USA)**[11] 3280 9-8-2 **56** oh3................. MollyKing(5) 11 32
(Peter Hiatt) *mid-div: effrt over 2f out: wknd over 1f out* **28/1**

125- **12** *7* **Beauden Barrett**[185] 8319 4-9-9 **75**..............................(t) FinleyMarsh(3) 9 28
(Jeremy Gask) *a towards rr* **14/1**

1m 13.23s (-1.57) **Going Correction** -0.20s/f (Firm) 12 Ran SP% **120.5**
Speed ratings (Par 103): **102,101,99,99,97 96,94,93,93,93 88,79**
CSF £70.43 CT £307.84 TOTE £18.50: £4.80, £1.70, £2.20; EX 111.50 Trifecta £661.90.
**Owner** Glyn Byard **Bred** Airlie Stud And Sir Thomas Pilkington **Trained** Leominster, Herefordshire

**FOCUS**
A competitive little handicap. The winner is rated to last year's best.
T/Jkpt: Not Won. T/Plt: £14.40 to a £1 stake. Pool: £74,939.91 - 3,783.17 winning units. T/Qpdt: £7.40 to a £1 stake. Pool: £5,446.56 - 543.33 winning units. **Tim Mitchell**

# 3437 YARMOUTH (L-H)

Tuesday, June 13

**OFFICIAL GOING: Good to firm (watered; 7.8)**
Wind: light, across Weather: light cloud, bright spells

## 3697 NORFOLK CHAMBER OF COMMERCE MAIDEN FILLIES' STKS (PLUS 10 RACE) 6f 3y

**2:15** (2:16) (Class 5) 2-Y-0 **£3,557** (£1,058; £529; £264) **Stalls** Centre

Form RPR

**1** **Hermosita** 2-9-0 0.............................................................. AndreaAtzeni 5 77
(Roger Varian) *fly j. as stalls opened: chsd ldrs: wnt 2nd and rdn jst over 2f out: steadily clsd and str chal jst ins fnl f: r.o wl to ld towards fin* **9/4**[1]

**2** *nk* **First Drive** 2-9-0 0................................................................ RyanMoore 2 76
(Michael Bell) *led: 2 l clr 2f: sn pushed along: jnd jst ins fnl f: hdd and unable qck towards fin* **13/2**

**3** *2* **Eirene** 2-9-0 0.................................................................. RobertWinston 7 70+
(Dean Ivory) *s.i.s: hld up in tch in last trio: pushed along and effrt ent fnl 2f: hdwy over 1f out: edging lft but kpt on wl to go 3rd towards fin* **18/1**

**4** *½* **Early Dawn** 2-9-0 0................................................................ HarryBentley 1 68
(Marco Botti) *in tch in midfield: rdn jst over 2f out: chsd clr ldng pair jst over 1f out: kpt on wout threatening ldrs: lost 3rd towards fin* **7/1**

**5** *1* **Royal Parks** 2-9-0 0.............................................................. MartinHarley 9 65
(James Tate) *in tch in midfield: effrt ent fnl 2f: wnt 4th 1f out: kpt on steadily but nvr enough pce to threaten ldrs* **11/2**[3]

**6** *1* **Lucifugous (IRE)** 2-9-0 0.................................................. DanielMuscutt 11 62
(Stuart Williams) *taken down early: s.i.s: hld up in tch in rr: hdwy into midfield 4f out: rdn and outpcd 2f out: rallied 1f out: edging lft and kpt on wl ins fnl f: no threat to ldrs* **33/1**

**7** *2 ¾* **Gold Eagle** 2-9-0 0.................................................................. DavidAllan 10 53
(Philip McBride) *chsd ldrs: rdn ent fnl 2f: 3rd and outpcd over 1f out: wknd ins fnl f* **25/1**

**8** *6* **Tell Me (IRE)** 2-9-0 0............................................................ JimCrowley 8 34
(Simon Crisford) *in tch towards rr: pushed along over 3f out: outpcd and btn 2f out: sn wknd* **4/1**[2]

**9** *½* **Honey Blossom** 2-9-0 0........................................................ JoeyHaynes 3 32
(Mark H Tompkins) *dwlt: a in rr: rdn and struggling ent fnl 2f: wknd over 1f out* **100/1**

**10** *3 ¼* **Alacritas** 2-9-0 0.................................................................. JoeFanning 12 22
(David Simcock) *chsd ldr tl jst over 2f out: sn u.p and lost pl: bhd fnl f* **9/1**

**11** *11* **Rock On Baileys** 2-9-0 0................................................ LemosdeSouza 4
(Chris Dwyer) *t.k.h: hld up in tch: effrt over 2f out: sn struggling: wknd wl over 1f out: wl bhd ins fnl f* **50/1**

1m 13.39s (-1.01) **Going Correction** -0.25s/f (Firm) 11 Ran SP% **117.0**
Speed ratings (Par 90): **96,95,92,92,90 89,85,77,77,72 58**
CSF £16.76 TOTE £3.10: £1.20, £2.10, £5.10; EX 17.30 Trifecta £182.50.
**Owner** Newsells Park Stud **Bred** Newsells Park Stud **Trained** Newmarket, Suffolk
■ Tivoli (6-4) was withdrawn. Rule 4 applies to all bets struck prior to withdrawal, but not to SP bets. Deduction - 40p in the pound. New market formed.

**FOCUS**
Race distances as advertised. This race for unraced fillies lost some of its interest when favourite Tivoli was withdrawn after injuring Frankie Dettori in the paddock, but it should still prove a fertile source of winners. Smart filly Urban Fox won a division last year, with Listed scorer On Her Toes third in the other division.

## 3698 WEDDINGS & PRIVATE PARTIES AT YARMOUTH RACECOURSE MAIDEN H'CAP 1m 3f 104y

**2:45** (2:45) (Class 5) (0-75,74) 4-Y-0+ **£2,911** (£866; £432; £216) **Stalls** Low

Form RPR

0/64 **1** **Hawkerland (IRE)**[50] 2039 4-9-4 **71**.................................... RyanMoore 5 77
(Marcus Tregoning) *chsd ldrs: pushed along to cl and upsides over 3f out: rdn over 2f out: sustained duel w ldr after: kpt on wl u.p but a jst hld tl forged ahd last strides* **5/6**[1]

0455 **2** *hd* **Bostonian**[11] 3308 7-9-7 **74**................................................ JimCrowley 3 79
(Shaun Lycett) *bmpd s: sn led: jnd over 3f out: rdn over 2f out: sustained duel w wnr after: battled on wl and looked to be jst holding chalr tl hdd and no ex last strides* **4/1**[3]

0-36 **3** *½* **Falak (IRE)**[19] 2997 4-9-3 **70**.............................................. AndreaAtzeni 1 74
(Roger Varian) *trckd ldng pair: effrt 3f out: hrd drvn over 1f out: kpt on steadily u.p and grad clsd on ldng pair ins fnl f: nvr quite getting to ldrs* **3/1**[2]

0002 **4** *7* **St Andrews (IRE)**[18] 3028 4-8-2 **55** oh3.......................(p[1]) RyanPowell 4 48
(Ian Williams) *hld up in tch in rr: effrt in 4th 3f out: no imp and outpcd 2f out: wl hld 4th over 1f out* **11/1**

0-06 **5** *11* **Rob's Legacy**[39] 2364 4-8-2 **55** oh10.......................(v[1]) RoystonFfrench 2 29
(Shaun Harris) *hld up in tch in last pair: rdn and dropped to last over 3f out: bhd fnl 2f* **100/1**

2m 27.1s (-1.60) **Going Correction** -0.20s/f (Firm) 5 Ran SP% **108.9**
Speed ratings (Par 103): **97,96,96,91,83**
CSF £4.45 TOTE £1.70: £1.10, £1.80; EX 3.60 Trifecta £7.50.
**Owner** Guy Brook **Bred** Mount Coote Partnership **Trained** Whitsbury, Hants

**FOCUS**
This modest event was run at a muddling pace. The first two improved a bit from their maiden form.

## 3699 WELL BALANCED LEDGER JOHN H SIMPSON ACCOUNTANTS FILLIES' H'CAP — 1m 2f 23y
**3:15** (3:15) (Class 5) (0-70,69) 4-Y-0+ **£2,911** (£866; £432) **Stalls** Low

Form | | | | RPR
2243 **1** **Ms Gillard**[11] 3292 4-9-5 **67**....(v[1]) JimCrowley 1 72
(David Simcock) *hld up in 3rd: effrt ent fnl 3f: rdn over 2f out: styd on u.p and chal 1f out: kpt on to ld fnl 50yds* **9/4**[2]

-411 **2** *nk* **Favorite Girl (GER)**[19] 789 9-9-4 **69**.... AlistairRawlinson(3) 3 73
(Michael Appleby) *rousted along leaving stalls: chsd ldr: rdn over 3f out: drvn and ev ch over 2f out: led wl over 1f out: kpt on wl tl hdd and unable qck fnl 50yds* **7/2**[3]

0-01 **3** *10* **Theydon Girls**[7] 3440 4-8-3 **51** 6ex.... JimmyQuinn 4 41
(Peter Charalambous) *taken down early: led: rdn ent 3f out: drvn and hrd pressed over 2f out: hdd wl over 1f out: no ex and btn 1f out: wknd ins fnl f* **10/11**[1]

2m 6.27s (-4.23) **Going Correction** -0.20s/f (Firm) **3** Ran SP% **105.4**
Speed ratings (Par 100): **108,107,99**
CSF £8.14 TOTE £3.30; EX 7.80 Trifecta £6.10.
**Owner** Miss K Rausing **Bred** Miss K Rausing **Trained** Newmarket, Suffolk

**FOCUS**
A disappointing turnout for this fillies' handicap, which went to the last to challenge. The pace was sound and the winner is rated to form.

## 3700 RACING WELFARE H'CAP — 1m 3y
**3:45** (3:45) (Class 4) (0-80,81) 3-Y-O **£4,851** (£1,443; £721; £360) **Stalls** Centre

Form | | | | RPR
14 **1** **Moolazim**[54] 1895 3-9-6 **79**.... RyanMoore 8 90+
(Marco Botti) *t.k.h: hld up wl in tch in midfield: pushed along and qcknd to ld over 1f out: clr and r.o strly ins fnl f: readily* **9/2**[3]

3-23 **2** *2 ½* **Glendun (USA)**[19] 3000 3-9-2 **75**.... RyanTate 4 78
(James Eustace) *chsd ldr for 1f: styd trcking ldrs: rdn ent fnl 2f: 4th and outpcd over 1f out: rallied u.p and styd on ins fnl f to go 2nd 50yds out: no threat to wnr* **9/1**

3-10 **3** *½* **Fujaira Bridge (IRE)**[32] 2569 3-9-8 **81**.... AndreaAtzeni 10 83+
(Roger Varian) *hld up in tch in last trio: effrt 2f out: hdwy ent fnl f: styd on u.p ins fnl f to go 2nd nr fin: no threat to wnr* **7/2**[2]

313 **4** *½* **Excel Again**[18] 3040 3-9-5 **78**.... MartinHarley 2 79
(James Tate) *dwlt: sn rcvrd and chsd ldr after 1f: ev ch u.p over 1f out: outpcd by wnr but wnt 2nd ins fnl f: kpt on same pce and lost 2 pls fnl 50yds* **5/1**

41-3 **5** *nk* **Hersigh**[22] 2894 3-9-7 **80**.... KevinStott 3 80
(Saeed bin Suroor) *led: rdn and hdd over 1f out: sn outpcd by wnr: kpt on same pce and lost 3 pls fnl 150yds* **10/1**

-140 **6** *¾* **Millie's Kiss**[34] 2517 3-8-5 **71**.... CameronNoble(7) 6 69
(Philip McBride) *t.k.h: hld up in tch in last trio: drifting rt 1/2-way: hdwy u.p over 1f out: kpt on ins fnl f: nvr trbld ldrs* **40/1**

1 **7** *½* **Hakeem**[49] 2066 3-9-4 **77**.... JimCrowley 9 74
(William Haggas) *in tch in midfield: rdn over 2f out: sn outpcd and wl hld over 1f out: kpt on again ins fnl f but no threat to ldrs* **11/4**[1]

51-4 **8** *1* **Kodiac Khan (IRE)**[47] 2106 3-9-7 **80**.... JoeFanning 11 75
(Mark Johnston) *hld up in tch in midfield: rdn wl over 1f out: swtchd lft ins fnl f: kpt on same pce after* **20/1**

0-45 **9** *5* **Salt Whistle Bay (IRE)**[118] 737 3-8-13 **72**.... TomQueally 5 55
(Rae Guest) *t.k.h: hld up in tch in midfield: lost 2f out: sn u.p and btn: wknd fnl f* **33/1**

5-00 **10** *2* **Justice Frederick (IRE)**[64] 1685 3-8-9 **68**....(t) JoeyHaynes 7 47
(Paul D'Arcy) *rrd as stalls opened: t.k.h: hld up in tch in last trio: shkn up 2f out: sn rdn and btn: wknd fnl f* **66/1**

1m 38.62s (-1.98) **Going Correction** -0.25s/f (Firm) **10** Ran SP% **114.5**
Speed ratings (Par 101): **99,96,96,95,95 94,93,92,87,85**
CSF £41.69 CT £159.59 TOTE £5.10: £1.90, £2.50, £1.40; EX 37.90 Trifecta £215.30.
**Owner** Sheikh Mohammed Bin Khalifa Al Maktoum **Bred** Essafinaat **Trained** Newmarket, Suffolk

**FOCUS**
A decent handicap ontested by some unexposed types, but they didn't go a great gallop. The winner built on his debut win.

## 3701 JME LTD OF LOWESTOFT CLASSIFIED STKS — 1m 3y
**4:15** (4:16) (Class 6) 3-Y-O **£2,264** (£673; £336; £168) **Stalls** Centre

Form | | | | RPR
0404 **1** **Patching**[13] 3217 3-9-0 60....(v[1]) KevinStott 2 70
(Giles Bravery) *hld up in tch in midfield: rdn and hdwy to ld over 1f out: hung rt but gng clr 1f out: r.o strly* **7/2**[3]

0-53 **2** *4 ½* **Ocean Temptress**[7] 3431 3-9-0 59.... JimCrowley 5 59
(John Ryan) *hld up in tch in midfield: rdn and chsd ldrs over 1f out: no ch w wnr ins fnl f but kpt on to go 2nd towards fin* **11/4**[1]

0-32 **3** *nk* **Break The Silence**[7] 3442 3-9-0 53.... DavidAllan 3 58
(Scott Dixon) *chsd ldr tl led jst over 2f out: hdd and unable qck over 1f out: kpt on same pce and lost 2nd towards fin* **3/1**[2]

6-00 **4** *2 ¾* **Ripper Street (IRE)**[12] 3250 3-9-0 55....(h) TomQueally 7 52
(Christine Dunnett) *stdd s: hld up in tch in last trio: effrt and hdwy u.p over 1f out: swtchd lft and no imp ins fnl f* **100/1**

-360 **5** *1 ½* **Camaradorie (IRE)**[27] 2734 3-8-11 58.... SimonPearce(3) 8 48
(Lydia Pearce) *trckd ldrs: rdn and ev ch 2f out tl unable qck over 1f out: wknd ins fnl f* **20/1**

0-40 **6** *7* **Mungo Madness**[112] 848 3-8-11 58.... ShelleyBirkett(3) 1 31
(Julia Feilden) *hld up in tch in last pair: effrt u.p and edging rt over 2f out: no imp whn bdly hmpd and swtchd lft over 1f out: wknd fnl f* **20/1**

5644 **7** *nk* **Cookie's Star**[14] 3166 3-8-7 60.... CameronNoble(7) 4 31
(Philip McBride) *hld up in tch in midfield: rdn over 2f out: sn struggling and outpcd: wknd fnl f* **16/1**

0-62 **8** *7* **Permanent**[12] 3250 3-9-0 60....(p) GeorgeDowning 6 14
(Daniel Kubler) *led tl jst over 2f out: sn u.p and lost pl: wknd over 1f out* **9/2**

600 **9** *10* **Nonnie And Norny**[44] 2180 3-9-0 41.... RoystonFfrench 9
(Shaun Harris) *in tch: rdn over 2f out: sn struggling and bhd over 1f out: wknd fnl f* **100/1**

1m 39.15s (-1.45) **Going Correction** -0.25s/f (Firm) **9** Ran SP% **109.5**
Speed ratings (Par 97): **97,92,92,89,87 80,80,73,63**
CSF £12.17 TOTE £4.10: £1.50, £1.10, £1.60; EX 12.70 Trifecta £33.80.
**Owner** D B Clark & Mrs M V Penfold **Bred** Bugley Stud (crinolette) Partnership **Trained** Newmarket, Suffolk

**FOCUS**
A very modest event but one with an easy with an easy winner. Straightforward form. The first five all came down the stands' side in the latter stages. It was slower by 0.53sec than the preceding Class 4 handicap.

## 3702 NORFOLK AND SUFFOLK ANIMAL TRUST H'CAP — 7f 3y
**4:45** (4:47) (Class 6) (0-65,66) 4-Y-O+ **£2,264** (£673; £336; £168) **Stalls** Centre

Form | | | | RPR
4600 **1** **Himalayan Queen**[20] 2969 4-9-4 **62**.... AndreaAtzeni 8 69
(William Jarvis) *hld up in tch in last trio: travelling strly but nt clr run wl over 1f out: swtchd rt and clr run 1f out: rdn and r.o wl to ld fnl 50yds* **6/1**[3]

05 **2** *¾* **The Happy Hammer (IRE)**[20] 2976 11-8-2 **46**.... JoeyHaynes 3 51
(Eugene Stanford) *hld up in tch in last trio: swtchd lft and effrt 2f out: hdwy to chal 1f out: drvn to ld ins fnl f: hdd and styd on same pce fnl 50yds* **16/1**

-000 **3** *1 ¼* **Steal The Scene (IRE)**[13] 3203 5-9-8 **66**.... TrevorWhelan 11 68
(Kevin Frost) *trckd ldrs: clsd to ld on bit 2f out: shkn up over 1f out: rdn 1f out: hdd and one pce ins fnl f* **9/2**[2]

00-0 **4** *hd* **Pennine Warrior**[13] 3203 6-8-11 **55**....(p) DavidAllan 7 56
(Scott Dixon) *trckd ldrs: rdn 3f out: ev ch 2f out tl no ex ins fnl f: styd on same pce fnl 100yds* **7/1**

6-60 **5** *1 ¼* **Kingfisher Girl**[31] 2633 4-7-13 **46** oh1....(t[1]) NoelGarbutt(3) 10 44
(Michael Appleby) *hld up in tch in rr: effrt 2f out: chsng ldrs whn nt clrest of runs jst over 1f out: kpt on same pce u.p ins fnl f* **50/1**

40- **6** *shd* **African Trader (USA)**[235] 7514 4-9-4 **62**.... RobertWinston 6 59
(Daniel Mark Loughnane) *hld up in tch in rr: swtchd rt ent fnl 2f: effrt over 1f out: kpt on ins fnl f: nvr trbld ldrs* **8/1**

6444 **7** *½* **Chetan**[17] 3084 5-9-6 **64**....(tp) LouisSteward 2 60
(Charlie Wallis) *taken down early: led: rdn over 2f out: hdd 2f out: unable qck u.p over 1f out: wknd ins fnl f* **9/2**[2]

0453 **8** *4 ½* **Tigserin (IRE)**[15] 3139 4-9-3 **61**....(p[1]) KevinStott 9 45
(Giles Bravery) *chsd ldr: rdn and ev ch ent fnl 2f: lost pl and short of room over 1f out: wknd ins fnl f* **4/1**[1]

-506 **9** *7* **Iceaxe**[12] 3265 4-9-7 **65**.... RoystonFfrench 1 30
(John Holt) *stdd s: t.k.h: in tch in midfield: rdn over 2f out: wknd over 1f out* **12/1**

-000 **10** *1* **Sakhee's Jem**[6] 3473 4-9-2 **60**....(v[1]) BenCurtis 5 22
(Gay Kelleway) *stdd after s and swtchd lft to r towards fin: sn chsng ldrs: rdn over 2f out: sn dropped out: bhd fnl f* **16/1**

1m 25.25s (-1.35) **Going Correction** -0.25s/f (Firm) **10** Ran SP% **115.7**
Speed ratings (Par 101): **97,96,94,94,93 92,92,87,79,78**
CSF £95.83 CT £483.63 TOTE £6.90: £2.50, £4.30, £1.80; EX 98.70 Trifecta £622.20.
**Owner** Miss Samantha Dare **Bred** Usk Valley Stud **Trained** Newmarket, Suffolk
■ Stewards' Enquiry : Joey Haynes two-day ban: used whip above the permitted level (Jun 27-28)

**FOCUS**
Moderate handicap form. The winner is rated to her mark.

## 3703 HAPPY 50TH BIRTHDAY GLENN TUBBY H'CAP — 6f 3y
**5:15** (5:16) (Class 6) (0-60,62) 3-Y-O **£2,264** (£673; £336; £168) **Stalls** Centre

Form | | | | RPR
0-43 **1** **Sadieroseclifford (IRE)**[15] 3141 3-8-11 **50**.... KevinStott 5 58
(Giles Bravery) *stdd after s: hld up in tch: hdwy to trck ldrs ent fnl 2f: rdn to ld over 1f out: kpt on wl ins fnl f: rdn out* **6/1**

653 **2** *1 ¼* **Agnethe (IRE)**[20] 2970 3-9-9 **62**.... JoeyHaynes 1 66
(Paul D'Arcy) *chsd ldrs: clsd to join ldrs 3f out: rdn and ev ch ent fnl 2f: chsd wnr and kpt on same pce u.p ins fnl f* **5/1**[3]

00-2 **3** *hd* **Wotadoll**[27] 2734 3-8-12 **54**.... JackDuern(3) 12 57
(Dean Ivory) *chsd ldrs: ev ch 1/2-way: rdn ent fnl 2f: kpt on same pce u.p ins fnl f* **9/4**[1]

-400 **4** *½* **African Girl**[35] 2507 3-8-7 **49**.... SimonPearce(3) 4 51
(Lydia Pearce) *chsd ldrs: rdn ent fnl 2f: kpt on pressing ldrs but unable qck and one pce ins fnl f* **12/1**

-500 **5** *4 ½* **Shouldertoshoulder**[21] 2911 3-8-11 **50**.... RoystonFfrench 6 37
(Stuart Williams) *hld up in tch towards rr: effrt ent fnl 2f: 6th and no imp 1f out: plugged on* **20/1**

5061 **6** *2 ¾* **Ebitda**[22] 2897 3-8-12 **51**.... DavidAllan 2 30
(Scott Dixon) *pressed ldrs: led jst over 2f out: sn rdn and hdd over 1f out: unable qck over 1f out: wknd ins fnl f* **5/2**[2]

00-0 **7** *¾* **Compton Brave**[27] 2734 3-8-7 **46** oh1.... JimmyQuinn 11 22
(J R Jenkins) *in rr: effrt u.p 2f out: no imp and wl btn fnl f* **66/1**

006 **8** *2 ½* **Tawfeer**[12] 3259 3-9-4 **57**....(p) RyanPowell 8 25
(James Unett) *in tch in midfield: pushed along 4f out: rdn and outpcd over 2f out: wl btn over 1f out* **40/1**

2000 **9** *6* **Sir Harry Collins (IRE)**[15] 3141 3-8-12 **51**....(p) RobertWinston 7
(Richard Spencer) *led: rdn and hdd over 2f out: sn btn: bhd fnl f* **25/1**

2436 **10** *9* **Billy's Boots**[42] 2252 3-9-4 **57**.... TomQueally 10
(J R Jenkins) *a towards rr: lost tch u.p over 1f out* **33/1**

1m 13.81s (-0.59) **Going Correction** -0.25s/f (Firm) **10** Ran SP% **113.5**
Speed ratings (Par 97): **93,91,91,90,84 80,79,76,68,56**
CSF £32.84 CT £88.36 TOTE £7.00: £2.10, £1.60, £1.60; EX 38.50 Trifecta £116.40.
**Owner** Eric Rayner **Bred** Rabbah Bloodstock Limited **Trained** Newmarket, Suffolk

**FOCUS**
The first four finished clear in this very ordinary handicap. The second to fourth help with the level.
T/Plt: £57.80 to a £1 stake. Pool: £79,150.63 - 999.14 winning units. T/Qpdt: £21.20 to a £1 stake. Pool: £5,114.81 - 177.80 winning units. **Steve Payne**

## [3447] HAMILTON (R-H)

Wednesday, June 14

**OFFICIAL GOING: Good (good to soft in places)**

Wind: Breezy, half behind Weather: Overcast Rails: +8yds to Races 3 & 5

### 3704 MARIAN GARDINER CELEBRATIONS AMATEUR RIDERS' H'CAP 6f 6y
5:55 (5:57) (Class 6) (0-60,60) 4-Y-0+ £3,119 (£967; £483; £242) Stalls Centre

Form RPR
-051 **1** **Concur (IRE)**[15] 3185 4-10-3 49....................(tp) MrPMillman 7 56
(Rod Millman) *midfield against stands' rail: hdwy over 1f out: pushed along and led wl ins fnl f: r.o* **5/1**[2]

0060 **2** 1 ¼ **Minty Jones**[14] 3201 8-9-9 46 oh1....................(v) MrLewisStones(5) 2 49
(Michael Mullineaux) *led and sn tacked over towards stands' side: rdn and edgd rt over 1f out: edgd lft and hdd wl ins fnl f: one pce* **33/1**

-005 **3** 1 ½ **Whipphound**[21] 2950 9-9-13 50....................(p) MissEmilyBullock(5) 3 49
(Ruth Carr) *prom: effrt and pressed wnr over 1f out to ins fnl f: kpt on: hld nr fin* **17/2**

52 **4** 1 **Kensington Palace (IRE)**[15] 3185 4-10-11 57........ MissBeckySmith 13 53
(Marjorie Fife) *s.i.s: bhd and outpcd: hdwy over 1f out: kpt on: nt pce to chal* **11/4**[1]

3004 **5** ¾ **Tango Sky (IRE)**[13] 3256 8-10-12 58.................... MrSWalker 1 52
(Paul Midgley) *hld up in tch on outside: effrt and hdwy over 1f out: edgd lft: one pce ins fnl f* **5/1**[2]

04-0 **6** ½ **Bahamian Sunshine**[21] 2950 4-9-12 49 ow1..............(p) MrMEnnis(5) 10 41
(Lee Smyth, Ire) *restless in stalls: in tch: drvn along over 3f out: rallied: kpt on same pce over 1f out* **25/1**

4000 **7** 1 ¼ **Gaelic Wizard (IRE)**[13] 3256 9-10-9 55....................(v) MissETodd 5 43
(Karen Tutty) *pressed ldr tl rdn and wknd over 1f out* **12/1**

0500 **8** ¾ **New Decade**[9] 3387 8-10-0 46 oh1.................... MrAlexFerguson 12 32
(Jim Goldie) *towards rr: drvn along 1/2-way: no imp fr over 1f out* **18/1**

5400 **9** shd **Silhuette (IRE)**[4] 3563 4-10-11 57....................(v) MissCWalton 8 43
(Colin Teague) *s.i.s: bhd: hdwy and in tch over 1f out: wknd over 1f out* **10/1**

-465 **10** ¾ **Insurplus (IRE)**[9] 3385 4-10-9 60....................(v) MissRHill(5) 6 43
(Jim Goldie) *midfield: drvn and outpcd over 2f out: btn over 1f out* **13/2**[3]

00-0 **11** 1 ¼ **Jacksonfire**[15] 3185 5-10-0 46 oh1....................(p) MissMMullineaux 9 26
(Michael Mullineaux) *towards rr: effrt 1/2-way: wknd wl over 1f out* **80/1**

00-0 **12** 9 **Sunrise Dance**[11] 3345 8-9-7 46 oh1....................(t) MrKYeoman(7) 11
(Kenny Johnson) *missed break: a outpcd and wl bhd* **100/1**

1m 13.82s (1.62) **Going Correction** +0.225s/f (Good) **12** Ran SP% **114.9**
Speed ratings (Par 101): **98,96,94,93,92 91,89,88,88,87 85,73**
CSF £162.83 CT £1366.26 TOTE £4.50: £1.90, £9.30, £2.40; EX 172.30 Trifecta £1704.00.
**Owner** Miss Gloria Abbey **Bred** Miss Annmarie Burke **Trained** Kentisbeare, Devon

**FOCUS**
A drying day and the going was upgraded to good, good to soft in places although clerk of the course Sulekha Varma confirmed it still on the slow side after walking the course mid-afternoon. Those drawn high were at an advantage in this weak sprint handicap for amateur riders.

### 3705 HAMILTON AUDI WHISTLEBERRY ROAD NOVICE AUCTION STKS 5f 7y
6:25 (6:26) (Class 5) 2-Y-0 £3,881 (£1,155; £577; £288) Stalls High

Form RPR
45 **1** **Danehill Desert (IRE)**[23] 2890 2-9-2 0.................... TonyHamilton 2 70
(Richard Fahey) *trckd ldr: rdn to ld 1f out: sn hrd pressed: hld on gamely cl home* **4/1**[2]

5 **2** shd **Camacho Chief (IRE)**[7] 3460 2-9-2 0.................... PaulMulrennan 1 70
(Michael Dods) *in tch: hdwy on outside over 1f out: drvn and disp ld ins fnl f: kpt on: jst hld* **11/2**[3]

2 **3** nk **Tough Remedy (IRE)**[8] 3429 2-9-2 0.................... PJMcDonald 4 73+
(Keith Dalgleish) *trckd ldrs: pushed along over 2f out: effrt whn nt clr run appr fnl f: angled rt and kpt on wl last 100yds: jst hld* **8/13**[1]

5 **4** 2 ¾ **Ty Rock Brandy (IRE)**[13] 3237 2-8-8 0.................... ShaneBKelly(3) 5 54
(Lee Smyth, Ire) *t.k.h: led: rdn edgd lft and hdd 1f out: kpt on same pce* **40/1**

6 **5** 3 ¼ **Stopwatch**[5] 3523 2-9-2 0.................... GrahamLee 3 47
(Karen McLintock) *dwlt: sn pushed along in rr: drvn and outpcd over 2f out: no imp fr over 1f out* **12/1**

1m 0.86s (0.86) **Going Correction** +0.225s/f (Good) **5** Ran SP% **107.4**
Speed ratings (Par 93): **102,101,101,96,91**
CSF £23.19 TOTE £4.60: £2.20, £2.60; EX 18.40 Trifecta £29.70.
**Owner** Percy/Green Racing **Bred** Newlands House Stud **Trained** Musley Bank, N Yorks
■ Stewards' Enquiry : P J McDonald 2 day ban - guilty of careless riding in that he allowed his mount to drift left when insufficiently clear (28/29 June)
Paul Mulrennan 2 day ban - used whip above the permitted level (28/29 June)

**FOCUS**
A modest novice event that threw up a tight three-way finish.

### 3706 WATCH RACING UK IN HD H'CAP 1m 3f 15y
6:55 (6:55) (Class 6) (0-65,67) 4-Y-0+ £3,234 (£962; £481; £240) Stalls High

Form RPR
-224 **1** **Highway Robber**[13] 3252 4-8-6 50.................... NathanEvans(3) 6 58
(Wilf Storey) *mde all: rdn and hrd pressed fr over 2f out: edgd lft ins fnl f: kpt on strly* **4/1**[2]

00-3 **2** 1 ¼ **Yensir**[13] 3252 4-9-12 67.................... PaddyAspell 8 73
(Grant Tuer) *pressed wnr: smooth hdwy to chal over 2f out: rdn over 1f out: one pce whn carried lft ins fnl f* **10/3**[1]

0- **3** 2 ¼ **Ruth Melody (IRE)**[173] 8514 5-9-4 62.................... ShaneBKelly(3) 2 64+
(Lee Smyth, Ire) *prom: drvn along over 3f out: sn outpcd: rallied over 1f out: chsd clr ldng pair ins fnl f: kpt on* **13/2**

5340 **4** 2 ¾ **Paddy's Rock (IRE)**[89] 1249 6-8-3 49.................... RowanScott(5) 9 47
(Lynn Siddall) *t.k.h in midfield: drvn and outpcd over 3f out: rallied over 1f out: no imp* **11/2**[3]

00-0 **5** 3 ½ **Cadmium**[9] 3405 6-8-12 53.................... PJMcDonald 3 45
(Micky Hammond) *blkd s: hld up on ins: effrt and chsd clr ldng pair over 2f out to ins fnl f: wknd* **9/1**

50-0 **6** 1 ¾ **Python**[11] 3342 5-8-4 45.................... CamHardie 5 35
(Andrew Crook) *hld up: drvn along over 3f out: sn outpcd: n.d after* **80/1**

05-2 **7** hd **Schmooze (IRE)**[11] 3338 8-8-11 52.................... GrahamLee 11 41
(Linda Perratt) *hld up: rdn along over 3f out: sn outpcd: btn fnl 2f* **7/1**

05/0 **8** 6 **Dizoard**[58] 1834 7-8-4 45....................(h) JamesSullivan 4 25
(Iain Jardine) *t.k.h: hld up: struggling over 3f out: sn wknd* **6/1**

0005 **9** 3 ¾ **Clayton Hall (IRE)**[16] 2591 4-8-12 53....................(t[1]) PaulMulrennan 1 27
(John Wainwright) *t.k.h: chsd ldrs: hdwy over 4f out: rdn: edgd rt and wknd over 2f out* **22/1**

2m 29.78s (4.18) **Going Correction** +0.225s/f (Good) **9** Ran SP% **114.2**
Speed ratings (Par 101): **93,92,90,88,85 84,84,80,77**
CSF £17.53 CT £83.44 TOTE £5.10: £1.60, £1.30, £2.20; EX 21.90 Trifecta £81.50.
**Owner** Gremlin Racing **Bred** Raymond Clive Tooth **Trained** Muggleswick, Co Durham

**FOCUS**
Race distance increased by 8yds. The two market leaders dominated this ordinary handicap.

### 3707 HAMILTON AUDI 2ND ANNIVERSARY CELEBRATION H'CAP 5f 7y
7:25 (7:25) (Class 4) (0-80,79) 3-Y-0+ £7,762 (£2,310; £1,154; £577) Stalls Centre

Form RPR
2151 **1** **Henley**[13] 3257 5-9-11 78.................... BenCurtis 1 87
(Tracy Waggott) *prom on far side of centre gp: hdwy to ld over 1f out: clr whn drifted lft ins fnl f: r.o* **9/2**[2]

4452 **2** 2 **Honeysuckle Lil (IRE)**[7] 3452 5-9-3 73..........(p) RachelRichardson(3) 6 75
(Tim Easterby) *in tch centre: effrt and hdwy over 1f out: chsd wnr ins fnl f: r.o* **7/2**[1]

6543 **3** ¾ **Seamster**[3] 3617 10-9-6 78....................(t) RowanScott(5) 7 77
(David Loughnane) *cl up in centre: rdn along and ev ch over 1f out: one pce ins fnl f* **13/2**

4515 **4** 1 **Casterbridge**[13] 3239 5-9-8 75.................... NeilFarley 2 71
(Eric Alston) *cl up in centre: effrt and ev ch briefly over 1f out: nt qckn ins fnl f* **11/1**

6553 **5** 1 ½ **Aguerooo (IRE)**[23] 2883 4-9-10 77....................(v[1]) AndrewMullen 5 67
(Ollie Pears) *hld up bhd ldng gp in centre: drvn and outpcd over 2f out: rallied over 1f out: hung lft: kpt on fnl f: nvr able to chal* **14/1**

0634 **6** 1 ¼ **Landing Night (IRE)**[11] 3337 5-9-8 75....................(tp) PJMcDonald 3 61
(Rebecca Menzies) *prom in centre: drvn along over 2f out: wknd over 1f out* **9/1**

4400 **7** 1 ¾ **Desert Ace (IRE)**[11] 3337 6-9-7 74....................(b) JasonHart 10 54
(Iain Jardine) *cl up stands' side tl rdn and wknd wl over 1f out* **10/1**

0-21 **8** hd **Bronze Beau**[13] 3238 10-9-2 69....................(tp) ShaneGray 4 48
(Kristin Stubbs) *led centre gp to over 1f out: sn rdn and wknd* **25/1**

6222 **9** ¾ **Silvanus (IRE)**[19] 3052 12-9-12 79.................... GrahamLee 9 55
(Paul Midgley) *hmpd s: in tch stands' side: struggling over 2f out: sn btn* **11/2**[3]

10-2 **10** nk **Economic Crisis (IRE)**[15] 3183 8-9-9 76.................... PaulMulrennan 8 51
(Colin Teague) *cl up stands' side tl rdn and wknd wl over 1f out* **12/1**

1m 0.49s (0.49) **Going Correction** +0.225s/f (Good) **10** Ran SP% **114.8**
Speed ratings (Par 105): **105,101,100,99,96 94,91,91,90,89**
CSF £20.26 CT £103.71 TOTE £5.50: £2.00, £1.80, £2.10; EX 26.90 Trifecta £179.20.
**Owner** David Tate **Bred** Dandy's Farm **Trained** Spennymoor, Co Durham

**FOCUS**
A competitive sprint handicap. The middle proved the place to be and it's solid form, with another pb from the winner.

### 3708 FOLLOW @HAMILTONPARKRC ON TWITTER H'CAP 1m 68y
7:55 (7:55) (Class 6) (0-60,66) 3-Y-0+ £3,234 (£962; £481; £240) Stalls Low

Form RPR
4031 **1** **Brother McGonagall**[8] 3431 3-9-9 66 6ex.................... CamHardie 11 72+
(Tim Easterby) *hld up: pushed along over 3f out: hdwy wl over 1f out: led ins fnl f: rdn out* **11/4**[1]

5-00 **2** ½ **Match My Fire (IRE)**[14] 3193 4-10-0 60....................(p) PaulMulrennan 5 68
(Michael Dods) *prom: effrt and chsd ldr over 2f out: rdn and edgd rt over 1f out: chal briefly ins fnl f: kpt on: hld towards fin* **8/1**

250 **3** 1 ½ **Bonnie Gals**[9] 3387 3-9-3 60.................... DougieCostello 13 62
(Keith Dalgleish) *s.i.s: hld up: stdy hdwy and swtchd lft over 2f out: effrt and chsd ldrs ins fnl f: r.o* **28/1**

2-40 **4** 3 **Penelope Pitstop**[13] 3242 5-8-12 47.................... ShaneBKelly(3) 6 45
(Lee Smyth, Ire) *hld up in tch: effrt on outside over 2f out: edgd rt over 1f out: outpcd fnl f* **8/1**

6042 **5** ¾ **Panther In Pink (IRE)**[14] 3196 3-8-2 48...............(h) SammyJoBell(3) 12 41
(Ann Duffield) *early ldr: pressed ldr: regained ld over 3f out: rdn and hdd ins fnl f: sn wknd* **10/1**

00-0 **6** 4 **Hazy Manor (IRE)**[23] 2903 3-8-10 53....................(t[1]) TomEaves 2 38
(Julia Brooke) *chsd ldrs: drvn and outpcd over 2f out: n.d after* **33/1**

1651 **7** ½ **Symbolic Star (IRE)**[22] 2918 5-9-4 57..................(p) ConnorMurtagh(7) 1 43
(Barry Murtagh) *missed break: hld up: smooth hdwy over 3f out: rdn and hung rt over 1f out: sn wknd* **5/1**[3]

-432 **8** 2 ¾ **Sakhalin Star (IRE)**[13] 3264 6-9-10 56....................(p) ConnorBeasley 7 36
(Richard Guest) *t.k.h: sn led: hdd over 3f out: rdn and wknd 2f out* **4/1**[2]

006 **9** ½ **What's Up Walter**[142] 378 3-8-4 47.................... PaddyAspell 9 23
(Philip Kirby) *hld up: drvn along and outpcd wl over 2f out: sn wknd* **50/1**

006- **10** 1 **Ten In The Hat (IRE)**[233] 7570 3-8-4 47.................... AndrewMullen 3 21
(Shaun Harris) *hld up midfield on ins: drvn and struggling 3f out: sn wknd* **14/1**

4603 **11** 7 **I'm Super Too (IRE)**[14] 3203 10-9-3 54..................(p) GemmaTutty(5) 14 16
(Karen Tutty) *t.k.h: in tch on outside: rdn over 3f out: wknd over 2f out* **16/1**

/000 **12** 6 **Sandgate**[11] 3343 5-9-2 48....................(t[1]) BenCurtis 4
(Kenny Johnson) *t.k.h: stdd into midfield: struggling over 3f out: wknd over 2f out* **80/1**

1m 50.34s (1.94) **Going Correction** +0.225s/f (Good)
**WFA** 3 from 4yo+ 11lb **12** Ran SP% **116.8**
Speed ratings (Par 101): **99,98,97,94,93 89,88,86,85,84 77,71**
CSF £24.30 CT £517.43 TOTE £3.50: £1.20, £2.20, £5.70; EX 27.80 Trifecta £515.60.
**Owner** Reality Partnerships VI **Bred** J P Coggan **Trained** Great Habton, N Yorks

**FOCUS**
Race distance increased by 8yds. This moderate handicap was run at a solid pace. The winner posted an effort in keeping with his Wetherby form.

### 3709 HAMILTON AUDI RS PERFORMANCE H'CAP 6f 6y
8:25 (8:26) (Class 4) (0-80,80) 3-Y-0 £7,762 (£2,310; £1,154; £577) Stalls Centre

Form RPR
-132 **1** **Dandy Highwayman (IRE)**[7] 3462 3-9-7 80.................... AndrewMullen 9 90
(Ollie Pears) *prom on nr side of gp: hdwy to ld over 1f out: sn rdn: drifted lft wl ins fnl f: kpt on* **11/4**[1]

26-2 **2** 1 ½ **Hee Haw (IRE)**[36] 2495 3-8-10 69.................... ConnorBeasley 8 76+
(Keith Dalgleish) *t.k.h: hld up on nr side of gp: hdwy to chse wnr fnl f: keeping on but hld whn n.m.r nr fin* **9/2**[2]

0-36 **3** 1 ¼ **Eltanin (IRE)**[15] 3184 3-8-8 67....................(p[1]) JasonHart 5 68
(John Quinn) *trckd ldrs: effrt and drvn along 2f out: kpt on same pce ins fnl f* **14/1**

4361 **4** *1 ½* **Intense Romance (IRE)**[22] 2925 3-8-11 **75**.......... CallumRodriguez(5) 2 71
(Michael Dods) *prom on far side of gp: effrt and ev ch over 1f out: rdn and outpcd ins fnl f* **9/2**[2]

0-46 **5** *2 ¾* **Ventura Secret (IRE)**[16] 3152 3-8-6 **65**........................ JamesSullivan 6 52
(Tim Easterby) *flyj. and blkd s: bhd: rdn and hdwy over 1f out: kpt on ins fnl f: nvr able to chal* **10/1**

46-6 **6** *1 ¼* **Greengairs**[141] 385 3-8-5 **64**..........................................(p) ShaneGray 7 47
(Keith Dalgleish) *hld up bhd ldng gp: drvn along and outpcd over 2f out: no imp over 1f out* **28/1**

2-03 **7** *nk* **Angel Palanas**[11] 3313 3-8-1 **63**.................................. NathanEvans(3) 3 45
(K R Burke) *led tl rdn and hdd over 1f out: wknd fnl f* **10/1**

0-05 **8** *2 ½* **Angel Meadow**[7] 3462 3-9-7 **80**......................................(h) PJMcDonald 1 54
(Micky Hammond) *dwlt: hld up: drvn and outpcd over 2f out: btn over 1f out* **12/1**

3-10 **9** *1 ½* **Dubai Art**[14] 3211 3-9-4 **77**............................................... TonyHamilton 4 47
(Richard Fahey) *prom tl rdn: hung rt and wknd 2f out* **7/1**[3]

1m 13.1s (0.90) **Going Correction** +0.225s/f (Good) **9** Ran SP% **111.5**
Speed ratings (Par 101): **103,101,99,97,93 92,91,88,86**
CSF £14.05 CT £139.56 TOTE £3.10: £1.10, £1.90, £3.90; EX 14.80 Trifecta £156.20.
**Owner** Ontoawinner & Ollie Pears **Bred** Michael M Byrne **Trained** Norton, N Yorks

**FOCUS**
Not a bad 3yo sprint handicap. They went a decent pace down the middle and the winner continues to progress.

## 3710 AUCHINRAITH H'CAP — 5f 7y
**8:55** (8:57) (Class 6) (0-55,57) 4-Y-O+ **£3,234** (£962; £481; £240) **Stalls** Centre

Form — RPR

-060 **1** **Dutch Dream**[21] 2950 4-9-0 **45**........................................ JamesSullivan 10 57+
(Linda Perratt) *hld up: gd hdwy on nr side of main centre gp over 1f out: led ins fnl f: rdn and kpt on strly* **28/1**

-232 **2** *1 ¾* **Cheeni**[21] 2950 5-9-1 **46**..................................................(p) PJMcDonald 12 51
(Jim Goldie) *hld up bhd ldng gp in centre: hdwy and ev ch ins fnl f: sn chsng wnr: kpt on* **6/1**[3]

5004 **3** *1 ½* **Very First Blade**[26] 2777 8-8-12 **48**................................(p) PhilDennis(5) 13 47
(Michael Mullineaux) *trckd ldrs in centre: drvn along wl over 1f out: kpt on ins fnl f* **18/1**

-024 **4** *hd* **Harpers Ruby**[5] 3544 7-9-0 **45**........................................... PaddyAspell 5 44
(Lynn Siddall) *racd far side: w ldrs thrght tl rdn and no ex ins fnl f* **16/1**

-003 **5** *¾* **Lady Joanna Vassa (IRE)**[4] 3563 4-9-7 **52**.................. ConnorBeasley 3 48
(Richard Guest) *upset in stalls: chsd far side ldr: rdn: edgd lft and ev ch briefly over 1f out: one pce ins fnl f* **5/1**[2]

2340 **6** *hd* **Our Place In Loule**[15] 3185 4-9-5 **50**................................. TomEaves 11 45
(Noel Wilson) *w ldrs in centre: led over 2f out to ins fnl f: kpt on same pce* **7/1**

0134 **7** *2 ¼* **Nuala Tagula (IRE)**[4] 3563 4-9-12 **57**..............................(t) JasonHart 14 44
(John Quinn) *dwlt: t.k.h and prom on nr side of centre gp: rdn over 2f out: outpcd over 1f out* **7/2**[1]

20- **8** *1* **Mighty Bond**[365] 3268 5-9-3 **48**............................................ BenCurtis 2 31
(Tracy Waggott) *dwlt: bhd far side: rdn and hung lft 1/2-way: no imp over 1f out* **33/1**

002 **9** *1 ¼* **Tinsill**[7] 3453 6-8-10 **46**..................................................(p) LewisEdmunds(5) 4 25
(Nigel Tinkler) *sn swtchd to far side of centre gp: rdn and effrt 1/2-way: wknd over 1f out* **6/1**[3]

2-34 **10** *2 ½* **Tribesman**[134] 495 4-9-6 **51**.........................................(bt) BarryMcHugh 8 21
(Marjorie Fife) *wnt lft s: hld up in centre: shortlived effrt 1/2-way: btn fnl f* **7/1**

00-0 **11** *3 ¾* **Knockamany Bends (IRE)**[14] 3202 7-9-4 **49**..........(tp) PaulMulrennan 7 5
(John Wainwright) *led centre gp to over 2f out: wknd over 1f out* **40/1**

0604 **12** *1 ½* **Under Approval**[20] 2994 6-8-9 **45**................................(p) GemmaTutty(5) 6
(Karen Tutty) *chsd ldrs in centre gp: drvn over 2f out: edgd rt and wknd wl over 1f out* **22/1**

1m 0.59s (0.59) **Going Correction** +0.225s/f (Good) **12** Ran SP% **116.8**
Speed ratings (Par 101): **104,101,98,98,97 96,93,91,89,85 79,77**
CSF £180.76 CT £3128.13 TOTE £27.40: £5.50, £1.80, £5.10; EX 233.70 Trifecta £4155.90.
**Owner** B Jordan **Bred** Lark Copse Ltd **Trained** East Kilbride, S Lanarks

**FOCUS**
The middle again proved the place to be in this moderate sprint handicap. It was a good winning time for the class.
T/Plt: £197.40 to a £1 stake. Pool: £67,454.59. 249.34 winning units. T/Qpdt: £8.80 to a £1 stake. Pool: £7,021.64. 585.39 winning units. **Richard Young**

# 3583 HAYDOCK (L-H)
Wednesday, June 14

**OFFICIAL GOING: Good to soft (good in places; 7.7)**
Wind: Light, half against in home straight of over 4f Weather: Fine

## 3711 CULTURE CLUB HERE 22ND JULY H'CAP — 1m 6f
**2:00** (2:00) (Class 4) (0-85,80) 3-Y-O **£5,822** (£1,732; £865; £432) **Stalls** Low

Form — RPR

1 **1** **Ottonian**[25] 2842 3-9-7 **80**.................................................. WilliamBuick 6 90+
(Charlie Appleby) *hld up: hdwy 3f out: led over 1f out: sn rdn: pushed out and r.o wl fnl f: comf* **7/4**[1]

-552 **2** *2 ¼* **Duke's Girl**[9] 3405 3-8-7 **66**............................................ PaulHanagan 7 70
(Michael Bell) *t.k.h: led: rdn over 2f out: hdd over 1f out: unable to go w wnr ins fnl f* **9/2**[3]

1200 **3** *½* **The Blues Master (IRE)**[11] 3335 3-9-2 **75**.................... FrannyNorton 5 78
(Mark Johnston) *chsd ldr to 3f out: sn rdn: kpt on u.p ins fnl f: no ch w wnr* **11/1**

0-61 **4** *2 ¼* **New Society (IRE)**[15] 3180 3-8-10 **69**............................ PJMcDonald 4 69
(James Bethell) *chsd ldrs: ev ch over 2f out: rdn and unable qck over 1f out: kpt on same pce ins fnl f* **11/2**

4-60 **5** *5* **Lethal Impact (JPN)**[21] 2963 3-9-5 **78**........................... JamieSpencer 2 71
(David Simcock) *hld up in rr: rdn over 2f out: no imp* **4/1**[2]

-641 **6** *1 ¼* **Perfect In Pink**[16] 3145 3-9-7 **80**.................................... GrahamLee 1 71
(Mick Channon) *plld hrd: hld up: rdn over 2f out: outpcd over 1f out: wl btn ins fnl f* **7/1**

3m 10.85s **Going Correction** -0.175s/f (Firm) **6** Ran SP% **110.8**
Speed ratings (Par 101): **67,65,65,64,61 60**
CSF £9.57 TOTE £2.10: £1.20, £2.30; EX 8.00 Trifecta £40.70.
**Owner** Godolphin **Bred** Darley **Trained** Newmarket, Suffolk

**FOCUS**
All races on Inner home straight. Distance increased by 50yds. A fair 3yo maiden run at a sound gallop and a taking effort from the favourite. The form makes sense.

## 3712 BRITISH STALLION STUDS EBF FILLIES' NOVICE STKS (PLUS 10 RACE) — 6f
**2:30** (2:32) (Class 5) 2-Y-O **£3,557** (£1,058; £529; £264) **Stalls** Centre

Form — RPR

1 **1** **Dance Diva**[15] 3179 2-9-4 0............................................... PaulHanagan 4 78
(Richard Fahey) *in tch: effrt and green 2f out: led wl over 1f out: r.o ins fnl f* **13/8**[1]

**2** *1* **Vodka Pigeon** 2-9-0 0........................................ RichardKingscote 6 71
(Tom Dascombe) *hld up: rdn and hdwy 2f out: chalng ins fnl f: styd on: nt quite pce of wnr nr fin* **15/2**[3]

426 **3** *¾* **Noble Manners (IRE)**[21] 2948 2-9-0 0............................ FrannyNorton 5 69
(Mark Johnston) *a.p: rdn and ev ch over 1f out: unable qck ins fnl f* **10/1**

0 **4** *¾* **Dathanna (IRE)**[23] 2905 2-9-0 0.................................(h1) WilliamBuick 7 67
(Charlie Appleby) *racd keenly: hld up: hdwy 2f out: rdn over 1f out: wl there ins fnl f: one pce nr fin* **5/2**[2]

4356 **5** *½* **Felisa**[18] 3066 2-9-0 0.................................................. ConnorBeasley 1 65
(David Evans) *in tch: rdn whn forced lft 2f out: unable qck: kpt on same pce ins fnl f* **16/1**

0 **6** *¾* **Song Of Summer**[21] 2958 2-9-0 0.................................. DanielTudhope 9 63
(Archie Watson) *chsd ldrs: rdn over 1f out: no ex fnl 100yds* **16/1**

56 **7** *5* **Atalanta Queen**[19] 3023 2-9-0 0...................................... JamieSpencer 2 48
(Brian Meehan) *disp ld: def advantage over 2f out: hdd wl over 1f out: wknd ins fnl f* **12/1**

430 **8** *1 ¾* **Floss The Hoss (IRE)**[18] 3066 2-9-0 0......................... TomMarquand 11 43
(David Evans) *little bit keen to post: disp ld tl rdn over 2f out: sn wknd* **40/1**

0 **9** *1* **Milan Reef (IRE)**[15] 3179 2-9-0 0...................................... SamJames 8 40
(David Loughnane) *hld up: rdn over 1f out: nvr a threat* **100/1**

**10** *13* **Lady Jayne (IRE)** 2-9-0 0.......................................... JosephineGordon 10 1
(Ian Williams) *missed break and wnt rt s: in rr: struggling 2f out: nvr on terms* **33/1**

1m 13.47s (-0.33) **Going Correction** -0.175s/f (Firm) **10** Ran SP% **113.3**
Speed ratings (Par 90): **95,93,92,91,91 90,83,81,79,62**
CSF £14.02 TOTE £2.40: £1.10, £3.00, £2.80; EX 14.90 Trifecta £56.20.
**Owner** Cheveley Park Stud **Bred** Cheveley Park Stud Ltd **Trained** Musley Bank, N Yorks

**FOCUS**
Distance as advertised. Just an ordinary novice but a useful winner on the up. The third and fifth offer perspective.

## 3713 WATCH RACING UK IN HD H'CAP — 7f 212y
**3:00** (3:01) (Class 3) (0-90,84) 3-Y-O **£9,056** (£2,695; £1,346; £673) **Stalls** Low

Form — RPR

-314 **1** **Fire Brigade**[18] 3077 3-9-3 **80**........................................... WilliamBuick 6 87+
(Michael Bell) *in rr: hdwy over 2f out: rdn to chal over 1f out: led ins fnl f: r.o gamely* **4/1**[1]

1-16 **2** *hd* **Original Choice (IRE)**[33] 2565 3-9-6 **83**......................... MartinHarley 8 89+
(William Haggas) *led for 1f: chsd ldr tl regained ld over 2f out: rdn whn edgd rt jst over 1f out: edgd lft and hdd ins fnl f: continued to run on for press but jst hld* **5/1**[2]

1 **3** *1 ¾* **Hugin (IRE)**[26] 2791 3-9-7 **84**......................................... JamieSpencer 9 86+
(David Simcock) *hld up: hdwy on outer 2f out: edgd lft whn chsng ldrs ins fnl f: r.o: nt get to front pair* **7/1**[3]

-346 **4** *hd* **In First Place**[19] 3040 3-9-1 **78**.......................................... PaulHanagan 2 80
(Richard Fahey) *chsd ldrs: rdn 2f out: unable qck over 1f out: styd on ins fnl f: nt pce of ldrs* **12/1**

1- **5** *nk* **Omeros**[237] 7483 3-9-6 **83**............................................ JosephineGordon 7 84
(Hugo Palmer) *racd keenly: chsd ldrs: rdn over 2f out: ch over 1f out: kpt on same pce fnl 100yds* **9/1**

44-1 **6** *1 ½* **Zefferino**[33] 2580 3-9-6 **83**............................................. AndreaAtzeni 5 83+
(Roger Charlton) *hld up: effrt on outer over 2f out: hdwy over 1f out: keeping on u.p but hld in 6th whn n.m.r and snatched up abt 110yds out: eased after* **8/1**

2-10 **7** *¾* **International Law**[33] 2567 3-9-2 **79**..........................(v1) TomMarquand 11 75
(Brian Meehan) *racd keenly: led after 1f: rdn and hdd over 2f out: kpt on u.p tl no ex fnl 100yds* **33/1**

31-0 **8** *¾* **Makkaar (IRE)**[14] 3199 3-9-7 **84**...................................... DaneO'Neill 1 78
(Mark Johnston) *s.i.s: midfield: rdn over 2f out: no imp* **18/1**

3211 **9** *½* **Sidewinder (IRE)**[19] 3040 3-9-4 **81**........................ RichardKingscote 10 74
(Tom Dascombe) *racd 3 wd in midfield: hdwy over 3f out: rdn over 2f out: fdd ins fnl f* **7/1**[3]

1-03 **10** *1 ¾* **Intimate Art (IRE)**[13] 3232 3-9-6 **83**................................... DavidProbert 4 72
(Andrew Balding) *hld up: rdn and carried hd awkwardly over 2f out: no imp: wknd over 1f out* **7/1**[3]

410- **11** *hd* **Rock N Rolla (IRE)**[271] 6536 3-9-7 **84**........................... ConnorBeasley 3 73
(Keith Dalgleish) *midfield: lost pl over 3f out: outpcd after* **28/1**

1m 40.74s (-2.96) **Going Correction** -0.175s/f (Firm) **11** Ran SP% **114.6**
Speed ratings (Par 103): **107,106,105,104,104 103,102,101,101,99 99**
CSF £22.70 CT £134.69 TOTE £4.60: £1.50, £2.10, £2.20; EX 29.30 Trifecta £179.30.
**Owner** The Fitzrovians **Bred** Stowell Hill Ltd **Trained** Newmarket, Suffolk

**FOCUS**
Distance increased by 11yds. A useful handicap, with the right two fighting it out, although there wasn't much of a gallop on. The winner continues to progress and the fourth helps with the standard.

## 3714 LOWTON MAIDEN STKS (PLUS 10 RACE) — 7f 212y
**3:30** (3:31) (Class 4) 3-Y-O **£4,690** (£1,395; £697; £348) **Stalls** Low

Form — RPR

4 **1** **Addeybb (IRE)**[26] 2778 3-9-5 0........................................ MartinHarley 3 93+
(William Haggas) *sn taken bk and in rr: rdn and hdwy 2f out: tried to chal over 1f out: r.o to ld cl home* **10/3**[2]

3-23 **2** *½* **Mutarabby (IRE)**[27] 2751 3-9-5 87.................................(p1) DaneO'Neill 6 92
(Saeed bin Suroor) *chsd ldrs: led over 2f out: rdn whn pressed after: hdd cl home* **2/1**[1]

**3** *nk* **Sharja Bridge** 3-9-5 0.................................................... AndreaAtzeni 2 91+
(Roger Varian) *chsd ldrs: effrt over 2f out: a little green: str chal after and upsides: r.o u.p fnl f: hld cl home* **7/1**[3]

30 **4** *7* **Mellor Brook (IRE)**[38] 2429 3-9-5 0................................ ConnorBeasley 1 75
(Bryan Smart) *led: rdn and hdd over 2f out: wknd over 1f out* **20/1**

**5** *½* **Naaeebb (USA)** 3-9-5 0................................................ JosephineGordon 4 74
(Saeed bin Suroor) *in rr: niggled along 5f out: hdwy over 3f out: rdn whn chsng ldrs over 2f out: wknd over 1f out* **2/1**[1]



The Form Book Flat, Raceform Ltd, Newbury, RG14 5SJ

5 6 6 **Long Socks**22 2930 3-9-5 0 FergusSweeney 5 60
(Alan King) *chsd leer tl rdn over 2f out: wknd over 1f out* **40/1**
1m 40.87s (-2.83) **Going Correction** -0.175s/f (Firm) 6 Ran SP% **109.4**
Speed ratings (Par 101): **107,106,106,99,98 92**
CSF £9.88 TOTE £3.70: £1.40, £1.70; EX 11.70 Trifecta £42.40.
**Owner** Sheikh Ahmed Al Maktoum **Bred** Rabbah Bloodstock Limited **Trained** Newmarket, Suffolk
■ Stewards' Enquiry : Dane O'Neill two-day ban: used whip above the permitted level (Jun 28-29)
**FOCUS**
Distance increased by 11yds. A useful maiden and a couple of these can go on to make good handicappers. The form is rated on the positive side.

## 3715 RACING UK HD H'CAP 6f 212y
**4:00** (4:01) (Class 4) (0-85,82) 3-Y-O **£5,822** (£1,732; £865; £432) **Stalls** Low

Form RPR
2-21 1 **Merlin**32 2620 3-9-4 **79** WilliamBuick 6 86
(Michael Bell) *broke wl: led early: w ldr: rdn 2f out whn chalng: edgd rt ent fnl f: sn led: kpt on gamely nr fin* **4/1**3
1-60 2 ½ **Brogan**15 3167 3-9-3 **78** RichardKingscote 2 83
(Tom Dascombe) *trckd ldrs: rdn over 2f out: styd on to take 2nd fnl 50yds: nt quite able to chal wnr* **9/1**
5042 3 ½ **Storm Cry**5 3526 3-9-4 **79** FrannyNorton 7 83
(Mark Johnston) *sn led: rdn 2f out: pressed whn intimidated and pushed sltly rt ent fnl f: sn hdd: lost 2nd fnl 50yds: no ex* **7/2**2
25-2 4 1½ **Vaulted**19 3047 3-8-7 **68** PaulHanagan 3 68
(Richard Fahey) *hld up in midfield: rdn over 2f out: effrt whn swtchd rt over 1f out: styd on towards fin: nt pce to chal* **10/1**
40-0 5 1 **Captain Hawk**22 2027 3-8-11 **72** JosephineGordon 1 69
(Ian Williams) *hld up: rdn and outpcd 3f out: prog whn swtchd rt fnl 150yds: styd on: nt quite rch ldrs* **20/1**
1-42 6 hd **Rely On Me (IRE)**15 3167 3-9-7 **82** DavidProbert 8 78
(Andrew Balding) *hld up in midfield: bmpd over 2f out: rdn whn chsng ldrs over 1f out: one pce fnl 100yds* **3/1**1
45-0 7 2¼ **Used To Be**50 2071 3-8-11 **72** MartinHarley 4 62
(K R Burke) *hld up in rr: rdn over 2f out: no imp* **25/1**
3-22 8 ½ **Falbon**20 3000 3-9-5 **80** (p1) AndreaAtzeni 5 69
(Marco Botti) *racd keenly: trckd ldrs: rdn whn edgd rt over 2f out: nt qckn over 1f out: fdd ins fnl f* **9/2**
1m 26.91s (-3.79) **Going Correction** -0.175s/f (Firm) 8 Ran SP% **113.1**
Speed ratings (Par 101): **114,113,112,111,110 109,107,106**
CSF £38.35 CT £137.09 TOTE £4.50: £1.50, £3.10, £1.50; EX 45.20 Trifecta £166.80.
**Owner** The Queen **Bred** The Queen **Trained** Newmarket, Suffolk
**FOCUS**
Distance increased by 11yds. They appeared to go a good gallop but still little got into it, with the winner putting up a game effort. The third is rated close to her latest form.

## 3716 TENSATIONAL SATURDAYS AT HAYDOCK PARK H'CAP 1m 3f 140y
**4:30** (4:32) (Class 3) (0-95,95) 4-Y-O+ **£9,056** (£2,695; £1,346; £673) **Stalls** Centre

Form RPR
-220 1 **Marmajuke Bay**28 2741 4-8-10 **84** (p) SteveDrowne 4 93
(Mark Usher) *racd keenly: mde all: rdn whn pressed over 2f out: fnd plenty ins fnl f: r.o wl* **16/1**
0-11 2 2½ **Mutadaffeq (IRE)**19 3050 4-9-0 **88** DanielTudhope 6 93+
(David O'Meara) *hld up: rdn and hdwy 2f out: styd on ins fnl f: tk 2nd towards fin: nt trble wnr* **9/4**2
221- 3 ¾ **First Voyage (IRE)**231 7627 4-8-9 **83** WilliamBuick 1 87+
(Charlie Appleby) *chsd wnr to 7f out: regained 2nd over 3f out: sn chalng: rdn over 1f out: unable qck and go w wnr ins fnl f: no ex and lost 2nd towards fin* **6/5**1
3-00 4 3¼ **Mustajeer**38 2431 4-9-7 **95** DaneO'Neill 5 93
(Owen Burrows) *sweating: in tch: rdn and outpcd over 2f out: edgd lft u.p over 1f out: kpt on ins fnl f but no ch* **9/1**
0-00 5 1 **Parish Boy**34 2552 5-9-0 **88** JosephineGordon 3 85
(David Loughnane) *chsd ldrs: wnt 2nd 7f out: rdn and lost 2nd over 3f out: btn 2f out* **40/1**
6-55 6 nk **Sindarban (IRE)**49 2085 6-9-1 **89** JamieSpencer 2 85
(Keith Dalgleish) *s.s: hld up: hdwy over 3f out: rdn and no imp over 2f out: wl btn over 1f out* **13/2**3
2m 30.74s (-2.26) **Going Correction** -0.175s/f (Firm) 6 Ran SP% **107.9**
Speed ratings (Par 107): **100,98,97,95,95 94**
CSF £48.17 TOTE £13.10: £4.20, £1.50; EX 37.20 Trifecta £60.00.
**Owner** The Ridgeway Alchemist's **Bred** The Welldiggers Partnership **Trained** Upper Lambourn, Berks
**FOCUS**
Distance increased by 26yds. Bit of a turn up in this decent handicap, with little getting into it and the winner making all. The form is taken at face value.

## 3717 TYLDESELEY MAIDEN STKS 1m 3f 140y
**5:00** (5:00) (Class 5) 3-Y-O+ **£3,557** (£1,058; £529; £264) **Stalls** Centre

Form RPR
0-52 1 **UAE King**33 2576 3-8-13 84 AndreaAtzeni 1 91+
(Roger Varian) *led: hdd after 2f: chsd ldr: regained ld over 3f out: rdn whn pressed over 1f out: sn edgd rt: kpt on wl* **6/5**1
2 1 **Festival Of Ages (USA)** 3-8-13 0 WilliamBuick 4 89+
(Charlie Appleby) *hld up in midfield: hdwy 3f out: rdn to chal over 1f out: unable qck ins fnl f: kpt on nr fin: can improve* **11/4**2
5-5 3 3¼ **Joshua Reynolds**74 1497 3-8-13 0 (p1) RobertTart 3 84
(John Gosden) *midfield: hdwy to trck ldrs after 4f: pushed along over 3f out: rdn over 2f out: one pce fnl f* **4/1**3
4 3¾ **Assiduous** 3-8-13 0 FrannyNorton 5 78
(Mark Johnston) *prom: lost pl 6f out: rallied 3f out: rdn to chal over 2f out: edgd lft u.p over 1f out: one pce* **33/1**
5 5 shd **Uber Cool (IRE)**30 2681 3-8-13 0 MartinHarley 8 78
(Jane Chapple-Hyam) *in tch: swtchd to outer and hdwy over 6f out: sn prom: rdn to chal over 2f out: one pce u.p fr over 1f out* **11/1**
4 6 10 **Flowers Will Bloom (IRE)**12 3286 3-8-8 0 PaulHanagan 2 57
(David O'Meara) *chsd ldrs: lost pl after 4f: pushed along 5f out: no imp after* **33/1**
0-4 7 3¾ **Inspector (IRE)**25 2842 3-8-13 0 (t) JosephineGordon 10 56
(Hugo Palmer) *hld up: pushed along over 3f out: no imp on ldrs* **25/1**
0- 8 3 **Moans Cross (USA)**224 7769 3-8-13 0 FergusSweeney 7 51
(Alan King) *racd keenly: hld up in rr: rdn over 2f out: nvr a threat* **50/1**
000 9 58 **Tamarin**7 3468 5-9-9 35 (p) SteveDrowne 9
(Lisa Williamson) *racd keenly: in tch: led after 2f: hdd over 3f out: sn wknd: eased whn wl btn 2f out: t.o* **200/1**
P **War Brigade (FR)** 3-8-13 0 (h1) JamieSpencer 6
(David Simcock) *s.i.s: plld hrd: hld up: stmbld after 2f: p.u after 4f: dismntd: sddle slipped* **20/1**
2m 32.05s (-0.95) **Going Correction** -0.175s/f (Firm)
**WFA** 3 from 5yo 15lb 10 Ran SP% **117.4**
Speed ratings (Par 103): **96,95,93,90,90 83,81,79,40,**
CSF £4.28 TOTE £2.10: £1.10, £1.80, £1.60; EX 5.90 Trifecta £12.90.
**Owner** Sheikh Mohammed Obaid Al Maktoum **Bred** Darley **Trained** Newmarket, Suffolk
**FOCUS**
Distance increased by 26yds. The right horses dominated this maiden and it's a race that should produce decent winners. The winner set a decent standard and is rated close to form.
T/Plt: £17.30 to a £1 stake. Pool: £75,882.38. 3,192.96 winning units. T/Qpdt: £10.10 to a £1 stake. Pool: £3,953.21. 286.99 winning units. **Darren Owen**

# 3454KEMPTON (A.W) (R-H)
Wednesday, June 14
**OFFICIAL GOING: Polytrack: standard to slow**
Wind: Behind last 3f, moderate becoming light Weather: Sunny, very warm

## 3718 FOLLOW @RACING_UK ON TWITTER APPRENTICE H'CAP (JOCKEY CLUB GRASSROOTS MIDDLE DISTANCE QUALIFIER) 1m (P)
**6:10** (6:10) (Class 5) (0-75,83) 4-Y-O+ **£3,234** (£962; £481; £240) **Stalls** Low

Form RPR
1141 1 **Believe It (IRE)**7 3454 5-10-1 **83** 6ex (b) StephenCummins(5) 3 95
(Richard Hughes) *mde all: rdn 2f out: kpt on and a holding rivals* **9/4**1
/1-1 2 1¼ **Phosphorescence (IRE)**50 2070 7-9-6 **74** (b) FinleyMarsh(5) 11 82
(George Scott) *chsd wnr: rdn and nt qckn 2f out: kpt on after but nvr able to chal seriously* **5/1**2
00-0 3 1¾ **Easy Code**20 3008 4-9-5 **68** GeorgiaCox 14 72
(William Haggas) *hld up in 8th: rdn and prog on inner to chse ldng pair 2f out: kpt on same pce after* **25/1**
-251 4 2 **Muthraab Aldaar (IRE)**13 3263 4-8-11 **65** IsobelFrancis(5) 6 64
(Jim Boyle) *t.k.h: trckd ldng pair 3f: pushed along in 4th and no imp fnl 2f* **15/2**
-020 5 1½ **Ataman (IRE)**20 3009 5-9-10 **73** GeorgeWood 2 69
(Chris Wall) *wl in tch: rdn over 2f out: one pce and no prog* **6/1**3
5060 6 2¾ **Runaiocht (IRE)**14 3208 7-8-9 **61** (b) JordanUys(3) 13 51
(Paul Burgoyne) *taken down early: s.i.s: mostly in last quartet: drvn over 2f out: plugged on fr over 1f out: no ch* **50/1**
0-50 7 1½ **Cat Silver**21 2960 4-9-6 **69** PaddyPilley 12 55
(Roger Charlton) *prog to chse ldng pair after 3f: rdn and wknd 2f out* **11/1**
055 8 ½ **Gracious George (IRE)**104 986 7-8-11 **65** RossaRyan(5) 10 50
(Jimmy Fox) *dwlt: a wl in rr: rdn and no prog over 2f out* **25/1**
0524 9 1¼ **Be Royale**12 3287 7-8-11 **63** (t) RayDawson(3) 5 45
(Michael Appleby) *s.s: last to 3f out: no significant hdwy after* **25/1**
3263 10 1¼ **Secret Glance**37 2466 5-8-8 **62** KieranSchofield(5) 4 41
(Adrian Wintle) *racd wd in midfield: lost pl 3f out: sn wknd* **25/1**
-016 11 4½ **Ebbisham (IRE)**23 2909 4-9-7 **70** (p) GeorgeBuckell 8 39
(Jim Boyle) *chsd ldrs tl wknd qckly wl over 2f out* **8/1**
1222 P **Spiritual Star (IRE)**53 1982 8-9-7 **73** BenRobinson(3) 7
(Lee Carter) *dwlt: a in rr: rdn and wknd qckly 3f out: p.u over 1f out* **16/1**
1m 39.53s (-0.27) **Going Correction** -0.05s/f (Stan) 12 Ran SP% **116.2**
Speed ratings (Par 103): **99,97,96,94,92 89,88,87,86,85 80,**
CSF £11.53 CT £223.17 TOTE £3.30: £1.80, £2.20, £5.80; EX 11.40 Trifecta £174.70.
**Owner** Mrs W Watson & Emily Scott **Bred** The Kathryn Stud **Trained** Upper Lambourn, Berks
**FOCUS**
Another well judged ride by Stephen Cummins on Believe It, who continues to rack up the wins at this track (now 5-7 here). The first pair were Iways 1-2, but a slightly positive view has been taken of the form.

## 3719 100% PROFIT BOOST AT 32REDSPORT.COM H'CAP 6f (P)
**6:40** (6:40) (Class 5) (0-75,77) 3-Y-O **£3,234** (£962; £481; £240) **Stalls** Low

Form RPR
16 1 **Sparkalot**30 2692 3-9-7 **75** JimCrowley 5 85+
(Simon Dow) *dwlt: hld up in 5th: prog on outer jst over 2f out: rdn to ld jst over 1f out: styd on wl and in command last 150yds* **11/8**1
-214 2 1¾ **Cajmere**124 657 3-9-4 **77** PaddyPilley(5) 7 80
(Tom Dascombe) *led: jnd 2f out: hdd and one pce jst over 1f out* **33/1**
443- 3 shd **Dimitre**233 7574 3-9-2 **73** HectorCrouch(3) 3 76
(Henry Candy) *nudged by rival s: trckd ldng trio: effrt to chal and upsides 2f out to jst over 1f out: kpt on one pce* **11/2**3
016 4 3¾ **Who Told Jo Jo (IRE)**44 2235 3-9-0 **68** FranBerry 2 59
(Joseph Tuite) *wnt lft s: t.k.h early but outpcd in last bef 1/2-way: nvr on terms after: plugged on over 1f out* **20/1**
406- 5 ¾ **Queens Royale**203 8065 3-8-1 **62** RayDawson(7) 4 50
(Michael Appleby) *dwlt: outpcd in last pair: nvr on terms: plugged on over 1f out* **25/1**
-301 6 ½ **Team Meeting (USA)**15 3173 3-9-8 **76** PatCosgrave 8 63
(Saeed bin Suroor) *trckd ldng pair: tried to chal 2f out: wknd over 1f out* **2/1**2
3006 7 7 **Beach Dancer (IRE)**21 2957 3-8-3 **57** ow1 (e1) MartinDwyer 1 21
(William Knight) *t.k.h: w ldr after 2f to jst over 2f out: wknd rapidly* **14/1**
1m 12.61s (-0.49) **Going Correction** -0.05s/f (Stan) 7 Ran SP% **109.0**
Speed ratings (Par 99): **101,98,98,93,92 91,82**
CSF £48.41 CT £174.41 TOTE £1.90: £1.10, £8.60; EX 23.90 Trifecta £101.70.
**Owner** R Moss, C Brennan, H Redknapp **Bred** Mrs James Wigan **Trained** Ashtead, Surrey
**FOCUS**
There was a disputed pace and that played into the hands of the winner, who built on his C&D maiden win.

## 3720 32RED/BRITISH STALLION STUDS EBF MAIDEN STKS 1m 3f 219y(P)
**7:10** (7:11) (Class 5) 3-Y-O **£3,234** (£962; £481; £240) **Stalls** Low

Form RPR
3 1 **Petitioner (IRE)**53 1984 3-9-2 0 KieranShoemark(3) 5 85+
(Roger Charlton) *hld up in midfield: prog over 2f out to ld over 1f out: drvn and edgd lft ins fnl f: jst hld on* **9/2**2
60 2 hd **Qaviy Cash**26 2783 3-9-5 0 (t) JackMitchell 7 84
(Hugo Palmer) *hld up in midfield: waiting for a gap over 2f out: prog to chse wnr jst over 1f out and sn chalng w hd sltly awkward: nudged 50yds out: clsng at fin: jst hld* **8/1**
54 3 1¼ **Marine One**27 2751 3-9-5 0 FranBerry 14 82
(David Simcock) *stdd s and hld up in last fr wdst draw: sme prog but only 10th 3f out: gd hdwy on outer 2f out to chal over 1f out: effrt flattened out but kpt on fnl f* **10/1**

6 **4** *1 ¼* **Cape Coast**[11] 3342 3-9-5 0 HarryBentley 13 80+
(Mark Johnston) *chsd ldrs: trapped out wd and urged along fr 4f out: responded to press ldrs over 1f out: one pce ins fnl f* **10/1**

0 **5** *5* **Forever Song**[53] 1967 3-9-5 0 JamesDoyle 10 72
(Charlie Appleby) *hld up but sn in midfield: rdn and nt clrest of runs on inner wl over 2f out: prog to chal wl over 1f out: sn wknd* **7/2**[1]

0-5 **6** *1* **Uptown Funk (IRE)**[33] 2584 3-9-5 0 (p[1]) MartinDwyer 2 70
(John Gosden) *trckd ldng pair: lost pl fr 2f out and squeezed for room over 1f out: one pce after* **8/1**

6 **7** *1 ¾* **Stylish Dancer**[33] 2564 3-9-0 0 ShaneKelly 3 63
(Luca Cumani) *chsd ldrs: urged along fr 4f out: effrt on inner and rt on terms 2f out: wknd over 1f out* **14/1**

4-44 **8** *½* **Master Archer (IRE)**[47] 2118 3-9-5 77 TomQueally 11 67
(James Fanshawe) *trckd ldrs: prog to go 2nd over 2f out gng strly: rdn to chal wl over 1f out: sn wknd tamely* **13/2**[3]

54 **9** *5* **Park Paddocks (IRE)**[28] 2721 3-9-5 0 PatCosgrave 1 59
(William Haggas) *pushed up to ld: rdn over 2f out: hdd & wknd qckly over 1f out* **8/1**

05 **10** *7* **Buldan**[27] 2751 3-9-5 0 JimCrowley 9 48
(Sir Michael Stoute) *trckd ldr to over 2f out: wknd rapidly* **10/1**

66 **11** *12* **Act Swiftly (IRE)**[13] 3248 3-9-5 0 LiamJones 4 28
(J S Moore) *sn pushed along and wl in rr: t.o 3f out* **200/1**

00 **12** *9* **Astroshadow**[16] 3145 3-9-0 0 TomMarquand 8 9
(Mark H Tompkins) *dwlt: a wl in rr: t.o 3f out* **200/1**

0 **13** *4* **Iley Boy**[21] 2963 3-9-0 0 GeorgeBuckell(5) 12 8
(John Gallagher) *dwlt: a wl in rr: t.o 3f out* **200/1**

**14** *87* **Flooded** 3-8-12 0 (h[1]) RayDawson(7) 6
(Daniel Kubler) *dwlt: last and losing tch 1/2-way: sn t.o* **100/1**

2m 32.89s (-1.61) **Going Correction** -0.05s/f (Stan) **14** Ran SP% **123.5**
Speed ratings (Par 99): **103,102,102,101,97 97,96,95,92,87 79,73,71,13**
CSF £42.20 TOTE £5.30: £2.30, £3.10, £3.40; EX 47.10 Trifecta £444.10.
**Owner** B E Nielsen **Bred** Bjorn Nielsen **Trained** Beckhampton, Wilts

**FOCUS**
The first four pulled clear of the rest in this maiden, which was sound run. Just fair form.

## 3721 32RED ON THE APP STORE H'CAP (LONDON MIDDLE DISTANCE SERIES QUALIFIER) 1m 2f 219y(P)

**7:40** (7:41) (Class 5) (0-70,72) 3-Y-O **£3,234** (£962; £481; £240) **Stalls** Low

Form RPR

-505 **1** **Cribbs Causeway (IRE)**[19] 3024 3-8-11 **62** KieranShoemark(3) 10 74
(Roger Charlton) *swift move fr wdst draw to ld after 1f: mde rest: kicked on 4f out: drvn clr wl over 1f out: kpt on wl* **11/1**

-360 **2** *3* **Quothquan (FR)**[20] 3005 3-9-5 **72** GeorgeWood(5) 6 78
(Michael Madgwick) *hld up in midfield: hrd rdn wl over 2f out: prog to take 3rd over 1f out: kpt on fnl f to take 2nd last strides* **9/2**[1]

2321 **3** *nk* **Bonnie Arlene (IRE)**[19] 3053 3-9-7 **69** JamesDoyle 1 74
(Mark Johnston) *led 1f: chsd wnr: rdn over 3f out: tried to chal over 2f out: no ex over 1f out: lost 2nd last strides* **5/1**[2]

3-52 **4** *3 ¼* **Orithia (USA)**[43] 2259 3-8-13 **61** (t) RobertWinston 5 60
(Seamus Durack) *hld up in last: pushed along and prog on inner over 2f out: shkn up briefly to take 4th over 1f out: nvr nr to chal* **12/1**

5002 **5** *1 ¼* **Malt Teaser (FR)**[11] 3327 3-9-4 **66** KierenFox 3 63
(John Best) *hld up in midfield: prog to chse clr ldng pair over 2f out to over 1f out: fdd* **15/2**

1-06 **6** *3* **Castellated**[12] 3291 3-9-9 **71** TomMarquand 9 63
(Richard Hannon) *hld up in last trio: rdn and no prog over 2f out* **9/1**

4-40 **7** *4* **Secret Soul**[43] 2269 3-9-4 **66** (h[1]) FranBerry 2 50
(Ralph Beckett) *trckd ldng pair: rdn 4f out: lost pl and wknd over 2f out* **7/1**

0-05 **8** *7* **Penny Red**[15] 3178 3-9-4 **66** JimCrowley 8 38
(William Knight) *hld up in last trio: brief effrt over 2f out: sn shkn up and dropped to rr again* **10/1**

0560 **9** *25* **Meteoric Riser (USA)**[19] 3024 3-9-0 **62** (p[1]) ShaneKelly 4
(Richard Hughes) *chsd ldrs: drvn 4f out: sn wknd: t.o and virtually p.u fnl f* **20/1**

061 **10** *1 ½* **I'm Running Late**[15] 3175 3-9-9 **71** PatCosgrave 7
(Dean Ivory) *chsd ldrs on outer: urged along 5f out: wknd rapidly over 2f out: t.o and virtually p.u fnl f* **6/1**[3]

2m 19.53s (-2.37) **Going Correction** -0.05s/f (Stan) **10** Ran SP% **113.3**
Speed ratings (Par 99): **106,103,103,101,100 98,95,90,71,70**
CSF £58.23 CT £280.72 TOTE £7.60: £2.80, £1.60, £1.70; EX 54.80 Trifecta £236.30.
**Owner** Nick Bradley Racing 13 **Bred** N Bradley **Trained** Beckhampton, Wilts

**FOCUS**
The pace generally held up here. The winner built on her maiden promise, with a small pb from the second.

## 3722 32RED.COM FILLIES' H'CAP 7f (P)

**8:10** (8:10) (Class 4) (0-85,85) 3-Y-O **£5,175** (£1,540; £769; £384) **Stalls** Low

Form RPR

1-4 **1** **Tribute Act**[27] 2754 3-8-11 **75** TomQueally 4 87+
(James Fanshawe) *dwlt: hld up in last pair: prog and threaded between rivals fr 2f out: burst through to ld 1f out: pushed clr: impressive* **9/4**[1]

1-53 **2** *1 ¾* **Ventura Blues (IRE)**[15] 3171 3-9-2 **80** PatDobbs 6 84
(Richard Hannon) *hld up in last pair: nt clr run wl over 2f out: swtchd to outer and prog over 1f out: drvn and styd on wl to take 2nd last strides: no ch w wnr* **14/1**

0-25 **3** *nk* **Raven's Lady**[32] 2605 3-9-2 **85** GeorgeWood(5) 3 88
(Marco Botti) *trckd ldrs: wnt 2nd over 1f out: chalng whn wnr shot past sn after: no ch after and lost 2nd last strides* **8/1**

021- **4** *shd* **Parlance (IRE)**[237] 7484 3-9-7 **85** JimCrowley 5 87
(Sir Michael Stoute) *hld up in last trio: rdn and prog on outer 2f out: tried to chal jst over 1f out but sn outpcd: kpt on wl* **8/1**

1 **5** *3* **Yaraki**[32] 2619 3-9-2 **80** PatCosgrave 10 74
(William Haggas) *dwlt: rcvrd fr wdst draw to ld after 1f: rdn 2f out: hdd and fdd 1f out* **9/2**[2]

21-3 **6** *1 ¼* **Shenanigans (IRE)**[25] 2820 3-9-3 **81** HarryBentley 8 72
(Roger Varian) *chsd ldng pair but trapped out wd: rdn 3f out: lost pl fr 2f out: one pce u.p after* **13/2**[3]

-332 **7** *2 ¼* **Illaunmore (USA)**[13] 3233 3-9-1 **82** KieranShoemark(3) 1 67
(John Gosden) *trckd ldrs: prog to take 2nd 2f out to over 1f out: sn wknd* **7/1**

41-0 **8** *2 ¾* **Odelouca (IRE)**[37] 2474 3-8-3 **67** ow1 MartinDwyer 7 45
(Brendan Powell) *led 1f: chsd ldr to 2f out: steadily wknd* **50/1**

1660 **9** *6* **Mitigate**[19] 3031 3-8-11 **75** (p[1]) ShaneKelly 2 36
(David Elsworth) *hld up in midfield: shkn up and no prog over 2f out: sn wknd* **25/1**

41-6 **10** *4* **Syndicate**[19] 3031 3-8-12 **76** FranBerry 9 27
(Ralph Beckett) *nvr gng wl: u.p and lost midfield pl over 2f out: sn bhd* **16/1**

1m 24.84s (-1.16) **Going Correction** -0.05s/f (Stan) **10** Ran SP% **115.4**
Speed ratings (Par 98): **104,102,101,101,98 96,94,90,84,79**
CSF £36.57 CT £217.17 TOTE £3.80: £1.30, £3.50, £2.40; EX 34.10 Trifecta £171.00.
**Owner** Elite Racing Club **Bred** Elite Racing Club **Trained** Newmarket, Suffolk

**FOCUS**
The closers came to the fore in this well run fillies' handicap and the winner was impressive. The winner has more to offer.

## 3723 32RED CASINO H'CAP 7f (P)

**8:40** (8:40) (Class 4) (0-80,82) 4-Y-O+ **£5,175** (£1,540; £769; £384) **Stalls** Low

Form RPR

0-56 **1** **North Creek**[21] 2960 4-9-5 **78** JamesDoyle 3 85
(Chris Wall) *prom in chsng gp: shkn up wl over 2f out: prog to chse ldr over 1f out: drvn to ld last 100yds and edgd rt: kpt on* **2/1**[1]

-105 **2** *nk* **Twin Point**[35] 2528 6-9-8 **81** (t) StevieDonohoe 4 87
(Charlie Fellowes) *prom in chsng gp: rdn and clsd to ld over 1f out: hdd last 100yds: hld whn nudged sn after* **7/2**[2]

-603 **3** *1 ¼* **Imperial State**[21] 2975 4-9-6 **79** (tp) TomMarquand 7 82
(George Scott) *hld up towards rr: shkn up over 2f out: prog to take 3rd fnl f: kpt on but unable to chal* **11/2**[3]

0-33 **4** *2* **Wings Of Esteem (IRE)**[21] 2974 4-9-2 **75** AntonioFresu 9 72
(Luke McJannet) *dwlt: hld up in last trio: rdn and styd on same pce fr 2f out to take 4th nr fin* **8/1**

2526 **5** *¾* **Until Midnight (IRE)**[21] 2975 7-9-0 **80** JoshuaBryan(7) 8 75
(Eugene Stanford) *in tch: rdn over 2f out: one pce and no real prog after* **14/1**

21/F **6** *1* **Porta Rosa (USA)**[14] 3214 4-9-9 **82** JimCrowley 2 75
(Mohamed Moubarak) *in tch in chsng gp: prog on inner and on terms over 1f out: wknd quite qckly fnl f* **20/1**

0300 **7** *¾* **Among Angels**[14] 3214 5-9-2 **75** (b) ShaneKelly 5 66
(Daniel Mark Loughnane) *drvn to try to ld but had to chse clr ldr: wknd wl over 1f out* **20/1**

10-0 **8** *nk* **Acrux**[53] 1969 4-9-7 **80** TomQueally 10 70
(David Lanigan) *dwlt: t.k.h and hld up in last: reminders and nt looking keen 2f out: no significant prog* **10/1**

5-00 **9** *3 ¾* **Molten Lava (IRE)**[21] 2961 5-8-4 **63** (p) MartinDwyer 1 43
(Christian Williams) *t.k.h: hld up in last pair: shkn up and over 2f out: sn no prog and wknd* **40/1**

04-0 **10** *9* **Multitask**[14] 3214 7-9-1 **74** TimmyMurphy 6 29
(Gary Moore) *sn led and blasted clr on wd route: 8 l ahd 1/2-way: wknd rapidly and hdd over 1f out* **20/1**

1m 25.58s (-0.42) **Going Correction** -0.05s/f (Stan) **10** Ran SP% **114.5**
Speed ratings (Par 105): **100,99,98,95,95 93,93,92,88,78**
CSF £7.96 CT £32.03 TOTE £3.00: £1.30, £1.60, £2.40; EX 9.80 Trifecta £44.50.
**Owner** Michael Bringloe **Bred** Alexis Chetioui **Trained** Newmarket, Suffolk

**FOCUS**
The runaway leader was ignored and the market leaders came to the fore. A fairly ordinary race for the grade.

## 3724 WATCH RACING UK ON SKY 432 H'CAP 1m 7f 218y(P)

**9:10** (9:10) (Class 6) (0-60,60) 4-Y-O+ **£2,587** (£770; £384; £192) **Stalls** Low

Form RPR

6003 **1** **Golly Miss Molly**[41] 2332 6-9-5 **58** (b) MartinLane 2 65
(Martin Bosley) *wl in tch in 6th: rdn and prog over 2f out to chse ldr over 1f out: led jst ins fnl f: drvn clr* **8/1**[3]

423- **2** *3 ½* **Intimidator (IRE)**[338] 4197 6-9-4 **57** StevieDonohoe 3 60
(Miss Joey Ellis) *hld up in midfield: rdn and prog over 2f out: tk 3rd over 1f out: kpt on u.p fnl f to take 2nd last stride* **10/1**

40/6 **3** *nse* **Wintour Leap**[21] 2966 6-9-5 **58** LiamKeniry 4 61
(Robert Stephens) *trckd ldng trio: quick prog to ld wl over 1f out: hdd and one pce jst ins fnl f: lost 2nd last stride* **12/1**

0-20 **4** *4* **Author's Dream**[41] 2332 4-9-4 **58** JimCrowley 1 56
(William Knight) *hld up in last pair: urged along 4f out: prog over 2f out: kpt on to take 4th fnl f but no threat* **7/4**[1]

133- **5** *6* **Mr Lando**[297] 5680 8-9-1 **57** NoelGarbutt(3) 8 48
(Johnny Farrelly) *t.k.h: led and clr: 12 l ahd 1/2-way: hdd & wknd wl over 1f out* **25/1**

0404 **6** *¾* **L'Ami De Rouge**[13] 3251 4-8-11 **51** RyanTate 7 41
(Ralph J Smith) *hld up in midfield: rdn and no imp ldrs wl over 2f out: no ch after* **14/1**

11-4 **7** *4* **Work (IRE)**[8] 2712 4-9-5 **59** (bt[1]) PatDobbs 6 44
(David Pipe) *hld up in last trio: shkn up 3f out: passed a few but nvr any ch* **20/1**

00-5 **8** *4* **Jackblack**[31] 738 5-9-0 **60** (h) RossaRyan(7) 10 40
(Brett Johnson) *hld up in last pair: drvn 3f out: no great prog* **14/1**

0000 **9** *1* **Tarakkom (FR)**[11] 3311 5-8-9 **48** (p[1]) RobHornby 5 27
(Peter Hiatt) *chsd clr ldr to over 2f out: wknd qckly* **20/1**

0-01 **10** *1* **Tractive Effort**[119] 738 4-8-9 **49** KierenFox 9 27
(Michael Attwater) *chsd ldrs in 5th: rdn 3f out: hung bdly lft fr over 2f out and wknd* **14/1**

56/ **11** *3 ½* **In The House (IRE)**[341] 4121 5-9-2 **55** FranBerry 12 29
(Lucinda Egerton) *nvr bttr than midfield: wknd u.p 3f out* **50/1**

1104 **12** *2 ¼* **Briac (FR)**[41] 2332 6-9-0 **53** DanielMuscutt 14 24
(Mark Pattinson) *t.k.h: disp 2nd pl bhd clr ldr to over 2f out: wknd qckly* **4/1**[2]

3m 30.58s (0.48) **Going Correction** -0.05s/f (Stan) **12** Ran SP% **119.6**
Speed ratings (Par 101): **96,94,94,92,89 88,86,84,84,83 82,80**
CSF £81.86 CT £965.92 TOTE £10.30: £2.80, £2.70, £3.50; EX 67.60 Trifecta £1844.30.
**Owner** John Carey **Bred** Brook Stud Bloodstock Ltd **Trained** Chalfont St Giles, Bucks

**FOCUS**
A moderate staying contest run at a decent tempo. The winner is entitled to rate this high.

T/Plt: £40.20 to a £1 stake. Pool: £69,991.41. 1,270.46 winning units. T/Qpdt: £10.70 to a £1 stake. Pool: £6,639.61. 457.58 winning units. **Jonathan Neesom**

## [3697]YARMOUTH (L-H)

Wednesday, June 14

**OFFICIAL GOING: Good to firm (8.0)**

Wind: Light, across Weather: sunny and warm

### 3725 BRITISH STALLION STUDS EBF NOVICE STKS (PLUS 10 RACE) 5f 42y

**2:10** (2:11) (Class 4) 2-Y-O **£4,528** (£1,347; £673; £336) **Stalls** Centre

Form RPR

**1** **Viscount Loftus (IRE)** 2-9-2 0 ... SilvestreDeSousa 5 80
(Mark Johnston) *racd keenly: mde all: rdn over 1f out: sustained duel w runner up fnl f: drvn and hld on wl towards fin* **7/1[2]**

1 **2** *nse* **One Minute (IRE)**[33] 2577 2-9-3 0 ... PatCosgrave 2 80
(William Haggas) *trckd wnr: pushed along and chal over 1f out: sustained duel w wnr fnl f: kpt on wl: jst hld* **1/3[1]**

5 **3** *1 1/2* **Onefootinparadise**[15] 3169 2-8-6 0 ... DavidEgan(5) 1 69
(Philip McBride) *in tch in 4th: effrt to chse ldng pair 2f out: kpt on ins fnl f: nvr quite enough pce to get on terms* **14/1[3]**

**4** *9* **May Girl** 2-8-11 0 ... LukeMorris 3 37
(Robert Cowell) *s.i.s: niggled along in rr: rdn and edgd lft 1/2-way: wknd over 1f out* **33/1**

**5** *6* **Sovereign State** 2-9-2 0 ... AdamKirby 4 20
(Robert Cowell) *chsd ldrs: shkn up 1/2-way: rdn and lost pl 2f out: sn wknd* **7/1[2]**

1m 1.78s (-0.92) **Going Correction** -0.375s/f (Firm) **5** Ran SP% **109.6**
Speed ratings (Par 95): **92,91,89,75,65**
CSF £9.95 TOTE £6.40: £2.80, £1.10; EX 10.70 Trifecta £43.00.
**Owner** Mrs Christine E Budden & Partners **Bred** Mrs C E Budden & Partners **Trained** Middleham Moor, N Yorks

**FOCUS**
The ground has been slightly watered overnight and the good to firm surface will surely dry out on a hot day. A solid novice stakes with the first three looking worth following.

### 3726 HAVEN SEASHORE HOLIDAY PARK H'CAP 1m 3f 104y

**2:40** (2:41) (Class 6) (0-55,57) 4-Y-O+ **£2,587** (£770; £384; £192) **Stalls** Low

Form RPR

3-44 **1** **Hope Is High**[21] 2964 4-9-4 **52** ... SilvestreDeSousa 1 62
(John Berry) *led for 1f: chsd ldr tl led again 5f out: rdn over 3f out: styd on wl u.p fr over 1f out: rdn out* **7/4[1]**

-011 **2** *2 1/2* **Zubaidah**[13] 3251 5-9-3 **56** ...(tp) DavidEgan(5) 2 62
(Jane Chapple-Hyam) *trckd ldrs: wnt 2nd and bmpd bnd over 4f out: rdn over 3f out: kpt on u.p but unable to get to wnr: styd on same pce ins fnl f* **9/4[2]**

2600 **3** *hd* **Dove Mountain (IRE)**[15] 3192 6-9-7 **55** ...(tp) LukeMorris 10 61
(Anabel K Murphy) *hld up in midfield: hdwy on inner 4f out: rdn over 2f out: drvn to chse ldng pair wl over 1f out: kpt on wl ins fnl f: nvr getting on terms w wnr* **25/1**

064- **4** *1 3/4* **Three Loves (IRE)**[315] 5012 4-9-4 **52** ... AdamBeschizza 3 55
(Stuart Williams) *hld up in tch in midfield: clsd to trck ldrs 4f out: rdn ent fnl 2f out: unable qck: kpt on same pce u.p fr over 1f out* **25/1**

0022 **5** *1 1/4* **Tyrsal (IRE)**[21] 2971 6-9-6 **57** ... HollieDoyle(3) 4 58
(Clifford Lines) *stdd s: hld up in rr: clsd into midfield 4f out: rdn to press for 3rd 2f out: no imp on ldng pair: 5th and plugged on same pce ins fnl f* **4/1[3]**

6200 **6** *10* **The Ginger Berry**[14] 3208 7-8-11 **52** ...(h) JoshuaBryan(7) 6 37
(Dr Jon Scargill) *hld up on midfield: clsd to trck ldrs 4f out: rdn 2f out: little rspnse and sn drvn and outpcd: wknd fnl f* **9/1**

0055 **7** *5* **Awesome Rock (IRE)**[19] 3026 8-8-5 **46** oh1 ... RhiainIngram(7) 11 23
(Roger Ingram) *stdd after s and dropped into midfield: effrt 3f out: sn struggling: wl btn 7th over 1f out* **40/1**

/0P- **8** *10* **Oracle Boy**[463] 865 6-9-4 **52** ... JoeyHaynes 8 13
(Michael Chapman) *a rr: lost tch 3f out* **100/1**

6000 **9** *1 1/4* **Thou Swell (IRE)**[25] 2815 5-9-2 **53** ...(v) CharlieBennett(3) 7 12
(Shaun Harris) *rousted along and hdwy to ld after 1f: hdd 5f out: hit rail and bmpd rival bnd over 4f out: sn dropped out u.p: wl bhd over 2f out* **33/1**

06-6 **10** *8* **Serangoon**[12] 3292 4-9-0 **51** ... AlistairRawlinson(3) 5
(Michael Appleby) *taken down early: awkward leaving stalls: chsd ldrs: rdn 6f out: lost pl 4f out: sn wl bhd: t.o* **40/1**

00-0 **11** *nk* **Daring Knight**[20] 2993 4-9-9 **57** ...(b) StevieDonohoe 9
(Clare Ellam) *nvr gng wl in rr: t.o fnl 3f* **100/1**

2m 23.6s (-5.10) **Going Correction** -0.375s/f (Firm) **11** Ran SP% **114.6**
Speed ratings (Par 101): **103,101,101,99,98 91,87,80,79,73 73**
CSF £5.25 CT £64.65 TOTE £2.70: £1.10, £1.50, £6.00; EX 7.00 Trifecta £74.20.
**Owner** Mrs Emma Berry **Bred** Miss K Rausing **Trained** Newmarket, Suffolk

**FOCUS**
A competitive Class 6 won by a jockey at the top of his game. The jockey considered the going easier on the round course.

### 3727 SEADELL SHOPS & HOLIDAY CHALETS HEMSBY H'CAP 1m 2f 23y

**3:10** (3:11) (Class 5) (0-75,77) 3-Y-O **£2,911** (£866; £432; £216) **Stalls** Low

Form RPR

63-2 **1** **Daira Prince (IRE)**[37] 2475 3-9-7 **77** ... SilvestreDeSousa 1 82+
(Roger Varian) *t.k.h: chsd ldr tl led over 3f out: rdn over 2f out: drvn and kpt on wl fr over 1f out: a jst holding on cl home* **2/1[1]**

014- **2** *hd* **Seafarer (IRE)**[292] 5829 3-8-10 **73** ... TylerSaunders(7) 5 77+
(Marcus Tregoning) *dwlt: hld up in tch in midfield: nt clr run over 2f out: swtchd rt ent fnl 2f out: rdn and hdwy on outer over 1f out: wnt 2nd fnl 50yds: clsd on wnr but nvr quite getting up* **16/1**

-414 **3** *1/2* **Paddy A (IRE)**[26] 2793 3-8-11 **72** ... DavidEgan(5) 6 75
(Philip McBride) *in tch in midfield: clsd to chse ldrs 3f out: 3rd and drvn over 1f out: kpt on u.p ins fnl f* **11/1**

14-4 **4** *1/2* **Tamayef (IRE)**[30] 2690 3-9-4 **77** ... MarcMonaghan(3) 9 79
(Hugo Palmer) *chsd ldng pair tl wnt 2nd 3f out: rdn ent fnl 2f: kpt on u.p and pressing wnr 1f out: kpt on same pce and a hld after: lost 2 pls fnl 50yds* **12/1**

05-2 **5** *3 1/2* **Beyond Recall**[46] 2144 3-9-3 **73** ... AdamKirby 3 68
(Luca Cumani) *trckd ldrs: effrt 2f out: unable qck u.p over 1f out: wknd ins fnl f* **9/1**

555- **6** *3/4* **Poseidon (IRE)**[229] 7658 3-9-3 **73** ... ThomasBrown 10 67
(Ed Walker) *stdd and dropped in after s: hld up in tch in last trio: rdn 3f out: no imp: swtchd rt 2f out: hdwy to pass btn rivals 1f out: kpt on: nvr trbld ldrs* **11/2[2]**

1-56 **7** *1 3/4* **X Rated (IRE)**[32] 2612 3-9-5 **75** ... HarryBentley 2 65
(Mark Johnston) *led tl 3f out: lost 2nd 3f out: rdn and unable qck over 2f out: wknd fnl f* **9/1**

4-04 **8** *nk* **See The City (IRE)**[33] 2588 3-9-4 **74** ... RyanTate 4 63
(James Eustace) *hld up in tch in midfield: rdn over 2f out: unable qck and outpcd over 1f out: wl hld fnl f* **7/1[3]**

610- **9** *1/2* **First Quest (USA)**[238] 7471 3-9-6 **76** ...(b[1]) JimmyQuinn 8 64
(Ed Dunlop) *s.i.s: hld up in tch in last trio: hdwy on inner 4f out: rdn over 2f out: sn struggling: wknd over 1f out* **33/1**

01-5 **10** *1 3/4* **Diamond Bear (USA)**[30] 2677 3-9-6 **76** ... LukeMorris 7 61
(Sir Mark Prescott Bt) *hld up in last trio: swtchd rt and effrt over 2f out: no imp: bhd fnl f* **12/1**

2m 5.95s (-4.55) **Going Correction** -0.375s/f (Firm) **10** Ran SP% **113.8**
Speed ratings (Par 99): **103,102,102,102,99 98,97,97,96,95**
CSF £36.85 CT £283.25 TOTE £2.70: £1.10, £5.20, £3.20; EX 43.70 Trifecta £462.00.
**Owner** Sheikh Mohammed Obaid Al Maktoum **Bred** Castlemartin Sky & Skymarc Farm **Trained** Newmarket, Suffolk

**FOCUS**
A decent 3yo handicap that saw Silvestre De Sousa complete a tremendous hat-trick. A bit of a muddling race, but the winner was unexposed.

### 3728 INJURED JOCKEYS FUND H'CAP 6f 3y

**3:40** (3:44) (Class 6) (0-55,57) 4-Y-O+ **£2,264** (£673; £336; £168) **Stalls** Centre

Form RPR

4005 **1** **Justice Rock**[7] 3468 4-8-7 **46** oh1 ...(t[1]) DavidEgan(5) 6 54
(Phil McEntee) *in rr of main gp: hdwy to chse ldrs over 2f out: pushed into ld over 1f out: kpt on to forge ahd wl ins fnl f: rdn out* **14/1**

5-53 **2** *3/4* **Robbie Roo Roo**[21] 2962 4-9-6 **54** ...(bt) AdamBeschizza 1 60
(Mrs Ilka Gansera-Leveque) *chsd ldrs tl led 4f out: rdn and hdd over 1f out: kpt on u.p and ev ch after tl jst outpcd wl ins fnl f* **4/1[1]**

-006 **3** *3/4* **Manipura**[22] 2925 4-9-3 **51** ...(p) MartinLane 12 54+
(Derek Shaw) *v.s.a and lost many l: grad rcvrd and clsd onto bk of field 1/2-way: rdn and hdwy over 1f out: chsd ldng pair and edgd lft u.p jst ins fnl f: kpt on same pce fnl 100yds* **16/1**

-003 **4** *2 3/4* **Goadby**[7] 3468 6-9-0 **48** ...(v) RoystonFfrench 9 42
(John Holt) *led for 2f: chsd ldr tl wl over 1f out: no ex u.p 1f out: wknd ins fnl f* **11/1**

3-00 **5** *1 1/4* **Jazz Legend (USA)**[33] 2589 4-9-7 **55** ...(h[1]) JimmyQuinn 10 45
(Anabel K Murphy) *t.k.h: hld up towards rr of main gp: hdwy 1/2-way: drvn and unable qck over 1f out: kpt on same pce ins fnl f* **28/1**

6402 **6** *nk* **Misu Moneypenny**[9] 3385 4-9-5 **53** ...(p) LukeMorris 5 42
(Scott Dixon) *in tch in midfield: shkn up over 2f out: rdn to chse ldrs but unable qck over 1f out: kpt on same pce ins fnl f* **11/2[3]**

0063 **7** *3/4* **Humour (IRE)**[20] 3001 6-8-12 **46** oh1 ...(v) StevieDonohoe 13 33
(Christine Dunnett) *in tch in midfield: rdn to chse ldrs 2f out: drvn and unable qck over 1f out: wknd ins fnl f* **16/1**

0006 **8** *nk* **Pleadings (USA)**[28] 2727 4-8-12 **46** ...(tp) LouisSteward 4 32
(Charlie Wallis) *in rr of main gp: reminder over 4f out: hdwy over 2f out: rdn and no imp over 1f out: plugged on same pce ins fnl f* **14/1**

0-40 **9** *2 1/2* **Refuse Colette (IRE)**[21] 2969 8-9-4 **57** ... LuluStanford(5) 14 35
(Mick Quinn) *in tch in midfield and racd towards stands' side thrght: rdn and unable qck whn nt clr run over 1f out: wknd ins fnl f* **7/1**

1050 **10** *1 1/2* **Autumn Tonic (IRE)**[20] 3001 5-8-12 **53** ...(b) JoshuaBryan(7) 11 26
(Charlie Wallis) *hld up in midfield: rdn 2f out: sn struggling and btn: wknd fnl f* **33/1**

6066 **11** *nk* **Classic Flyer**[7] 3468 5-9-8 **56** ...(v) AdamKirby 8 28
(Christine Dunnett) *chsd ldr for over 1f: styd prom tl lost pl u.p over 2f out: wknd fnl f* **16/1**

5050 **12** *2 1/4* **Multi Quest**[21] 2969 5-9-1 **49** ...(b) RyanPowell 2 14
(John E Long) *chsd ldrs: rdn and losing pl whn n.m.r jst over 2f out: bhd over 1f out* **9/1**

550- **13** *2* **Diamondsaretrumps (IRE)**[469] 789 4-9-0 **48**...(p[1]) SilvestreDeSousa 3 7
(Chris Dwyer) *in tch in midfield: effrt u.p over 2f out: no hdwy: wl btn and eased fnl f* **9/2[2]**

0400 **14** *18* **Silver Springs (IRE)**[35] 2509 4-8-5 **46** oh1 ... RhiainIngram(7) 7
(Roger Ingram) *chsd ldrs tl 1/2-way: sn dropped out and bhd: t.o* **66/1**

1m 12.82s (-1.58) **Going Correction** -0.375s/f (Firm) **14** Ran SP% **123.3**
Speed ratings (Par 101): **95,94,93,89,87 87,86,85,82,80 80,77,74,50**
CSF £70.05 CT £961.87 TOTE £15.70: £4.20, £1.80, £4.80; EX 101.00 Trifecta £1435.70.
**Owner** Steve Jakes **Bred** Ashbrittle Stud **Trained** Newmarket, Suffolk

**FOCUS**
A competitive low-grade sprint that seemed to show a bias to the near side.

### 3729 ROA/RACING POST OWNERS JACKPOT FILLIES' H'CAP 6f 3y

**4:10** (4:12) (Class 5) (0-75,77) 3-Y-O+ **£3,234** (£962; £481; £240) **Stalls** Centre

Form RPR

135 **1** **In The Spotlight (IRE)**[36] 2503 3-8-7 **69** ... CameronNoble(7) 7 76+
(Henry Spiller) *stdd s: hld up in last pair: smooth hdwy to join ldr 2f out: pushed into ld over 1f out: r.o wl to ins fnl f: pushed out* **9/1**

/000 **2** *1 1/2* **Flower Cup**[21] 2969 4-8-10 **57** ...(b[1]) SilvestreDeSousa 2 61
(Chris Dwyer) *led: rdn 2f out: drvn and hdd over 1f out: styd on same pce u.p ins fnl f* **8/1**

11-2 **3** *3/4* **Hackney Road**[55] 1899 4-10-0 **75** ... AdamKirby 5 77
(John Butler) *stdd s: hld up in last pair: effrt 2f out: rdn and hdwy to chse ldrs over 1f out: kpt on to go 3rd towards fin: nvr threatening wnr* **11/4[2]**

10-0 **4** *nk* **Reedanjas (IRE)**[63] 1732 3-9-3 **77** ... DavidEgan(5) 3 76
(Gay Kelleway) *t.k.h: wl in tch in midfield: rdn to chse ldng pair 2f out: drvn over 1f out: kpt on same pce ins fnl f: lost 3rd towards fin* **16/1**

0-56 **5** *7* **Giennah (IRE)**[36] 2506 3-9-3 **75** ... CharlieBennett(3) 8 52
(Daniel Mark Loughnane) *t.k.h: chsd ldrs: effrt 2f out: sn outpcd and wknd fnl f* **14/1**

1-05 **6** *nk* **Sayem**[15] 3167 3-9-6 **75** ... LukeMorris 6 51
(Ed Walker) *in tch in midfield: shkn up 2f out: sn outpcd and no hdwy whn rdn over 1f out: wknd fnl f* **2/1[1]**

3-64 **7** *3/4* **Racing Angel (IRE)**[25] 2835 5-9-1 **67** ... LuluStanford(5) 4 42
(Mick Quinn) *broke wl: sn stdd and chsd ldr: rdn over 2f out: lost pl 2f out and sn wknd* **11/2[3]**

450 **8** *12* **Langham**[20] 2993 4-8-12 **62** ...(p) AlistairRawlinson(3) 1
(Michael Appleby) *taken down early: chsd ldrs tl rdn and lost pl over 2f out: wl bhd fnl f* **28/1**

1m 11.84s (-2.56) **Going Correction** -0.375s/f (Firm)
**WFA** 3 from 4yo+ 8lb **8** Ran SP% **112.5**
Speed ratings (Par 100): **102,100,99,98,89 88,87,71**
CSF £75.14 CT £252.25 TOTE £9.00: £2.80, £2.40, £1.10; EX 44.40 Trifecta £222.10.
**Owner** Dethrone Racing **Bred** Ms Patricia Walsh **Trained** Newmarket, Suffolk

**FOCUS**
A low-key fillies handicap won decisively as the market leaders underperformed. The runner-up's first form since she was a 2yo.

## 3730 FOLLOW US ON FACEBOOK AT YARMOUTH RACECOURSE H'CAP 1m 3y
4:40 (4:40) (Class 4) (0-80,80) 4-Y-0+ £4,690 (£1,395; £697; £348) Stalls Centre

Form RPR
-135 1 **Selection (FR)**[26] 2796 4-9-5 78 SilvestreDeSousa 4 88+
(William Haggas) *dwlt: sn rcvrd to ld and dictated stdy gallop: rdn ent fnl 2f: styd on wl and asserted ins fnl f: eased towards fin* **5/2**[2]
2-P1 2 2 **Chiefofchiefs**[30] 2689 4-9-7 80 StevieDonohoe 2 83
(Charlie Fellowes) *t.k.h: trckd wnr: rdn over 2f out: stl pressing ldr whn wandered lft 1f out: styd on same pce after* **7/4**[1]
3644 3 hd **Suqoor**[21] 2975 4-9-6 79 (p) AdamBeschizza 5 82
(Chris Dwyer) *broke wl: sn restrained to trck ldrs: effrt ent fnl 2f: kpt on same pce u.p ins fnl f* **9/1**
-214 4 ½ **Anastazia**[21] 2974 5-8-9 68 JoeyHaynes 6 70
(Paul D'Arcy) *trckd ldrs: effrt ent fnl 2f out: kpt on same pce u.p ins fnl f* **11/1**
313 5 5 **King Oswald (USA)**[12] 3282 4-8-4 63 RyanPowell 3 53
(James Unett) *hld up in tch: clsd 1/2-way: rdn over 1f out: sn edging lft and outpcd: wknd ins fnl f* **5/1**[3]
0331 6 nse **Ross Raith Rover**[28] 2731 4-8-8 67 (p) PaoloSirigu 1 57
(Robert Eddery) *hld p in tch in last pair: effrt over 2f out: no imp and carried lft over 1f out: wknd ins fnl f* **9/1**

1m 38.4s (-2.20) **Going Correction** -0.375s/f (Firm) **6 Ran SP% 109.9**
Speed ratings (Par 105): **96,94,93,93,88 88**
CSF £6.96 TOTE £2.90: £2.00, £1.10; EX 7.80 Trifecta £25.90.
**Owner** Highclere Thoroughbred Racing - Siyouni **Bred** F Bozo, M Bozo, M Bozo & J Bozo **Trained** Newmarket, Suffolk

**FOCUS**
A moderate Class 4 but the winner undoubtedly has potential and brought up a four-timer for Silvestre De Sousa. The form is rated through the runner-up.

## 3731 LADIES NIGHT AT YARMOUTH RACECOURSE APPRENTICE H'CAP 1m 3y
5:10 (5:10) (Class 6) (0-65,63) 4-Y-0+ £2,264 (£673; £336; £168) Stalls Centre

Form RPR
2553 1 **Lunar Deity**[42] 2319 8-9-3 59 (t) MillyNaseb(5) 5 78
(Stuart Williams) *dwlt: hld up in tch: clsd 1/2-way: rdn to ld over 1f out: r.o strly: easily* **9/4**[2]
5042 2 10 **Rustique**[28] 2731 5-9-12 63 (h) JennyPowell 7 58
(Ed Walker) *hld up in 3rd: clsd 1/2-way: rdn and ev ch 2f out: outpcd by wnr and wl hld 1f out: plugged on to hold 2nd ins fnl f* **2/1**[1]
6315 3 ½ **Hold Firm**[20] 2996 5-9-6 62 GabrieleMalune(5) 2 56
(Mark H Tompkins) *chsd ldr tl led over 2f out: sn rdn and hdd over 1f out: wl btn but battling for 2nd ins fnl f: plugged on* **7/1**
4-64 4 1 **Tommy's Secret**[8] 3442 7-9-6 60 (p1) DavidEgan(3) 4 51
(Jane Chapple-Hyam) *racd in 4th: effrt over 2f out: outpcd over 1f out: wl btn 4th and plugged on fnl f* **11/4**[3]
5-20 5 13 **Jonnie Skull (IRE)**[36] 2255 11-8-8 45 (vt) CharlieBennett 3
(Phil McEntee) *led: rdn 3f out: hdd over 2f out: sn struggling: wknd wl over 1f out* **16/1**

1m 37.54s (-3.06) **Going Correction** -0.375s/f (Firm) **5 Ran SP% 109.2**
Speed ratings (Par 101): **100,90,89,88,75**
CSF £7.02 TOTE £3.20: £1.30, £1.50; EX 7.50 Trifecta £16.40.
**Owner** W E Enticknap & Partner **Bred** Hermes Services Ltd **Trained** Newmarket, Suffolk

**FOCUS**
A low-key finale won by a street.
T/Plt: £21.40 to a £1 stake. Pool: £63,088.60. 2,147.99 winning units. T/Qpdt: £13.10 to a £1 stake. Pool: £3,312.97. 186.90 winning units. **Steve Payne**

3732 - 3739a (Foreign Racing) - See Raceform Interactive

3711
# HAYDOCK (L-H)
Thursday, June 15

**OFFICIAL GOING: Good (8.4)**
Wind: Moderate, half against in straight of over 4f Weather: Showers

## 3740 RACINGUK.COM/FREETRIAL HAYDOCK PARK APPRENTICE TRAINING SERIES H'CAP 1m 3f 140y
6:05 (6:05) (Class 5) (0-70,75) 4-Y-0+ £3,557 (£1,058; £529; £264) Stalls Centre

Form RPR
/1-1 1 **Lugano**[6] 3547 4-9-12 75 6ex ManuelFernandes(5) 6 91+
(Sir Mark Prescott Bt) *chsd ldrs: wnt 2nd 4f out: led 3f out: rdn over 1f out: edgd lft and styd on wl to draw clr ins fnl f* **1/1**[1]
-004 2 4½ **Suitor**[5] 3432 5-9-9 70 (p) BenRobinson(3) 2 75
(Brian Ellison) *chsd clr ldr tl 4f out: regained 2nd over 2f out: edgd lft u.p over 1f out: no imp on wnr ins fnl f* **9/1**[3]
6-31 3 1½ **Zenafire**[7] 3494 8-9-13 71 6ex (p) MeganNicholls 7 74
(Sarah Hollinshead) *hld up in midfield: stdy hdwy over 3f out: styd on ins fnl f: nvr able to chal* **9/2**[2]
-000 4 6 **King Of Paradise (IRE)**[14] 3242 8-8-5 52 JoshQuinn(3) 1 45
(Eric Alston) *led: sn clr: reduced advantage 4f out: hdd 3f out: one pce and wl hld fnl 2f* **50/1**
1512 5 ½ **Albert Boy (IRE)**[9] 3439 4-9-6 64 PaddyPilley 10 56
(Scott Dixon) *in tch: rdn whn swtchd lft over 2f out: no imp over 1f out* **14/1**
000- 6 ½ **Inspector Norse**[237] 7500 6-8-7 56 HannahWorrall(5) 3 47
(Tim Easterby) *midfield: rdn and outpcd over 2f out: plugged on fnl f* **33/1**
4-11 7 1¼ **Up Ten Down Two (IRE)**[76] 1469 8-9-7 70 (t) RyanTimby(5) 8 59
(Michael Easterby) *midfield: rdn over 2f out: no imp* **20/1**
-046 8 2½ **Lopito De Vega (IRE)**[9] 3432 5-9-6 64 RowanScott 9 49
(David C Griffiths) *hld up: rdn over 4f out: nvr able to get on terms* **11/1**
05-5 9 4½ **Danzella**[10] 3400 5-8-7 51 oh6 RobJFitzpatrick 4 29
(Chris Fairhurst) *hld up: struggling over 2f out: nvr a threat* **25/1**
4126 10 ¾ **Melabi (IRE)**[6] 3537 4-9-10 68 (p1) CallumRodriguez 5 45
(Richard Ford) *s.i.s: in rr: stdy hdwy over 2f out: no imp on ldrs: wknd fnl f* **14/1**

2m 30.37s (-2.63) **Going Correction** -0.125s/f (Firm) course record **10 Ran SP% 113.4**
Speed ratings (Par 103): **103,100,99,95,94 94,93,91,88,88**
CSF £9.70 CT £28.94 TOTE £2.00: £1.10, £3.00, £1.80; EX 13.20 Trifecta £47.90.
**Owner** Exors Of The Late J L C Pearce **Bred** Lordship Stud **Trained** Newmarket, Suffolk

**FOCUS**
All races on Inner home straight. Race distance increased by 26yds. The going was officially good though there was a heavy shower prior to this race which was quite a competitive handicap for apprentices with three of the ten winners last time out. The pace was decent and the winner is a progressive sort. The second is rated to his old turf best.

## 3741 SILK MILL BAR RIPPONDEN WELCOMES YOU H'CAP 5f
6:35 (6:40) (Class 4) (0-85,86) 3-Y-0+ £5,822 (£1,732; £865; £432) Stalls Centre

Form RPR
-424 1 **Signore Piccolo**[7] 3492 6-9-8 78 (h) PaulMulrennan 3 88
(David Loughnane) *midfield: hdwy over 1f out: sn rdn: led ins fnl f: r.o* **11/1**
6615 2 1½ **Coolfitch (IRE)**[13] 3295 3-9-6 86 JoshDoyle(3) 1 88
(David O'Meara) *missed break: hld up in rr: hdwy gng wl over 1f out: chalng wl ins fnl f: styd on to take 2nd fnl 75yds: nt pce of wnr towards fin* **14/1**
5263 3 hd **Bashiba (IRE)**[13] 3295 6-9-11 86 (t) RowanScott(5) 7 90
(Nigel Tinkler) *hld up in rr: nt clr run over 1f out: rdn and hdwy ent fnl f: r.o towards fin: nt trble wnr* **9/1**[3]
1503 4 ½ **Foxtrot Knight**[16] 3183 5-9-9 79 JackGarritty 8 81
(Ruth Carr) *chsd ldr: led 2f out: rdn over 1f out: hdd ins fnl f: no ex towards fin* **11/1**
2013 5 1½ **Invincible Ridge (IRE)**[22] 2951 9-9-10 80 LukeMorris 10 77
(Eric Alston) *hld up in midfield: rdn over 2f out: kpt on u.p ins fnl f: nvr able to chal* **25/1**
-104 6 1¼ **Black Grass**[16] 3183 4-9-4 81 HarrisonShaw(7) 4 74
(Michael Easterby) *dwlt: sn chsd ldrs: effrt whn swtchd lft wl over 1f out: styd on same pce ins fnl f* **18/1**
6500 7 1¼ **Union Rose**[12] 3321 5-10-2 86 (p) MartinHarley 2 74
(Ronald Harris) *in tch: rdn and forced lft by rival wl over 1f out: one pce fnl f* **9/1**[3]
66-1 8 ¾ **Adam's Ale**[7] 3492 8-9-12 82 6ex (p) BarryMcHugh 9 67
(Marjorie Fife) *chsd ldrs tl rdn and wknd over 1f out* **3/1**[1]
0165 9 2 **Sandra's Secret (IRE)**[19] 3063 4-9-11 81 FrannyNorton 5 59
(Les Eyre) *led: hdd 2f out: sn rdn: wknd fnl 150yds* **7/1**[2]
0143 10 2¼ **Twizzell**[5] 3579 3-9-2 79 PJMcDonald 11 46
(K R Burke) *hld up: effrt 2f out: no imp on ldrs: wknd 1f out* **3/1**[1]

59.92s (-0.88) **Going Correction** -0.125s/f (Firm)
**WFA** 3 from 4yo+ 7lb **10 Ran SP% 114.9**
Speed ratings (Par 105): **102,99,99,98,96 94,92,90,87,84**
CSF £151.49 CT £1475.10 TOTE £11.80: £3.00, £4.30, £2.80; EX 164.60 Trifecta £3468.40.
**Owner** Lancashire Lads Partnership **Bred** Capt J H Wilson **Trained** Market Drayton, Shropshire
■ Stewards' Enquiry : Harrison Shaw two-day ban: careless riding (Jun 29-30)

**FOCUS**
A strongly-run sprint in which the first three all came from off the pace, in fact after 2f the first three were the last three which suggests they went off too hard. The winner's best form since 2015.

## 3742 NORMAN AND HIS SWIFTS NOVICE STKS (PLUS 10 RACE) 6f 212y
7:05 (7:07) (Class 4) 2-Y-0 £4,528 (£1,347; £673; £336) Stalls Low

Form RPR
34 1 **Leeshaan (IRE)**[16] 3165 2-9-2 0 MartinHarley 9 76
(James Tate) *midfield: hdwy over 2f out: rdn to ld wl over 1f out: kpt on ins fnl f: hld on wl fnl strides* **9/2**[3]
2 nk **Stage Magic (IRE)** 2-9-2 0 WilliamBuick 3 75+
(Charlie Appleby) *midfield: effrt over 2f out: rn green whn chsng ldrs and rdr eased off over 1f out: abt 3 l down ins fnl f: picked up fnl 75yds: fin strly: one to nte* **6/4**[1]
3 ¾ **Coastal Drive** 2-9-2 0 KieranO'Neill 4 73
(Richard Hannon) *chsd ldrs: wnt 2nd over 3f out: led jst over 2f out: hdd wl over 1f out: edgd lft appr fnl f: styd on same pce fnl 75yds* **20/1**
4 1¼ **Knight In Armour (IRE)** 2-9-2 0 FrannyNorton 10 70
(Mark Johnston) *hld up: rdn 2f out: hdwy over 1f out: cl up trying to chal ins fnl f: one pce fnl 75yds* **6/1**
0 5 1¼ **Jaffar**[10] 3399 2-9-2 0 (be) PJMcDonald 2 66
(Scott Dixon) *led: rdn and hdd jst over 2f out: kpt on same pce ins fnl f* **66/1**
6 6 3 **Ferik (IRE)**[20] 3037 2-9-2 0 AndrewMullen 6 58
(David Evans) *chsd ldrs: rdn and outpcd over 2f out: n.d after* **8/1**
7 ¾ **Kraka (IRE)** 2-9-2 0 RichardKingscote 5 56
(Tom Dascombe) *dwlt: hld up: green and rdn over 2f out: sme hdwy over 1f out: no imp fnl f* **4/1**[2]
0 8 2½ **Lever Du Soleil (FR)**[25] 2852 2-9-2 0 DavidAllan 8 50
(Tim Easterby) *chsd ldr tl over 3f out: rdn and wknd 2f out* **66/1**
9 14 **Partry Flyer (IRE)** 2-9-2 0 KevinStott 7 12
(Oliver Greenall) *completely missed break: in rr: rdn over 2f out: lft bhd over 1f out* **50/1**

1m 29.78s (-0.92) **Going Correction** -0.125s/f (Firm) **9 Ran SP% 113.3**
Speed ratings (Par 95): **100,99,98,97,95 92,91,88,72**
CSF £11.19 TOTE £5.80: £1.60, £1.10, £4.20; EX 14.30 Trifecta £97.50.
**Owner** Saeed Manana **Bred** Karis Bloodstock Ltd & Rathbarry Stud **Trained** Newmarket, Suffolk

**FOCUS**
Race distance increased by 11yds. One of the first 7f juvenile events of the season, and often a race that throws up a few winners. It went to the most exposed horse in the line-up and the first five were clear. Not easy form to assess.

## 3743 LET R & M CONNECT YOU H'CAP 7f 212y
7:40 (7:40) (Class 3) (0-95,96) 4-Y-0+ £9,056 (£2,695; £1,346; £673) Stalls Low

Form RPR
0002 1 **Mythical Madness**[13] 3298 6-9-11 96 (v) PhillipMakin 5 105
(David O'Meara) *racd keenly: hld up in midfield: n.m.r on bnd 6f out: hdwy 2f out: r.o ins fnl f: led fnl 150yds: in command towards fin* **11/1**
6400 2 1¾ **Calder Prince (IRE)**[13] 3294 4-9-0 85 RichardKingscote 8 90
(Tom Dascombe) *led: rdn over 2f out: hdd fnl 150yds: styd on same pce towards fin* **9/1**
5053 3 nk **Abushamah (IRE)**[5] 3589 6-8-3 74 (p) JamesSullivan 4 78
(Ruth Carr) *racd keenly: hld up in midfield: hdwy 2f out: chsd ldrs 1f out: styd on towards fin: nt pce to mount serious chal* **8/1**[3]
-043 4 ½ **Fuwairt (IRE)**[19] 3064 5-9-5 90 PJMcDonald 9 93
(Roger Fell) *hld up in rr: hdwy on outer 1f out: styd on ins fnl f: nt quite pce to chal* **12/1**
-030 5 ¾ **Ice Slice (IRE)**[19] 3064 6-9-7 92 RyanTate 3 93
(James Eustace) *a.p: rdn 2f out: unable qck over 1f out: styd on same pce ins fnl f* **8/1**[3]

6132 **6** *nk* **Roller**[7] 3498 4-8-12 **86**...................................... NathanEvans(3) 7 87
(Michael Easterby) *racd keenly in midfield: effrt over 1f out whn nt clr run and clipped heels: styd on ins fnl f: nt quite get to ldrs* **3/1**[1]

2-00 **7** *hd* **Mountain Rescue (IRE)**[21] 3014 5-9-1 **86**.................... WilliamBuick 12 86
(Chris Wall) *racd wd on bk st: prom: rdn over 2f out: fdd wl ins fnl f* **10/1**

0-00 **8** *1 ½* **Zealous (IRE)**[66] 1677 4-8-5 **76**........................................ LukeMorris 10 73
(Sally Haynes) *hld up: rdn over 2f out: nvr a threat* **50/1**

-004 **9** *hd* **London Protocol (FR)**[26] 2833 4-9-1 **91**...................... CliffordLee(5) 11 87
(K R Burke) *prom: n.m.r and hmpd on bnd 6f out: rdn over 2f out: wknd 1f out* **10/1**

4316 **10** *2* **Eternal**[17] 3160 5-9-1 **86**.......................................................... KevinStott 6 78
(Declan Carroll) *racd keenly in tch: n.m.r on bnd 6f out: rdn over 2f out: losing pl whn edgd rt: slipped and bmpd over 1f out: wknd ins fnl f* **16/1**

2521 **11** *7* **Intrude**[9] 3441 5-9-1 **86** 6ex..............................................(t) MartinHarley 1 62
(Stuart Williams) *hld up in rr: rdn over 2f out: nvr a threat* **11/2**[2]

1m 39.32s (-4.38) **Going Correction** -0.125s/f (Firm) **11** Ran SP% **114.7**
Speed ratings (Par 107): **116,114,113,113,112 112,112,110,110,108 101**
CSF £103.54 CT £838.36 TOTE £11.00: £2.60, £3.30, £2.70; EX 87.20 Trifecta £584.90.
**Owner** J C G Chua **Bred** Highbank Stud Llp **Trained** Upper Helmsley, N Yorks

**FOCUS**
Race distance increased by 11yds. Probably not form to rely on, for the early pace was slow and several runners spoilt their chance by pulling hard. Then several met trouble, and finally they then went for home a fair way out. The winner and third came from off the pace, whereas the second had the run of the race. The winner is rated to his AW form.

## 3744 COVERS 33 RIPPONDEN SUPPORTS THE SILK MILL H'CAP 1m 2f 42y
**8:10** (8:10) (Class 4) (0-80,84) 4-Y-0+ **£5,822** (£1,732; £865; £432) **Stalls** Centre

Form RPR

-111 **1** **Gulf Of Poets**[8] 3451 5-9-8 **84** 6ex................................ NathanEvans(3) 6 97+
(Michael Easterby) *hld up in midfield: hdwy gng wl over 2f out: produced to ld ins fnl f: r.o wl and in command after* **7/2**[1]

1341 **2** *1 ¼* **Boycie**[21] 3009 4-8-13 **79**.................................................. TinaSmith(7) 12 84
(Richard Hannon) *midfield on outer: hdwy over 1f out: styd on ins fnl f: tk 2nd post: nt pce to trble wnr* **13/2**[3]

40-3 **3** *nse* **Azzir (IRE)**[12] 3315 5-8-12 **74**.................................... JordanVaughan(3) 2 79
(K R Burke) *prom: rdn over 2f out: led over 1f out: hdd ins fnl f: unable to go w wnr: styd on same pce u.p towards fin* **10/1**

4063 **4** *nse* **Jacbequick**[7] 3497 6-9-4 **80**..............................................(p) JoshDoyle(3) 7 85
(David O'Meara) *midfield: lost pl and outpcd over 3f out: rallied ins fnl f: r.o towards fin* **10/1**

0063 **5** *nk* **Save The Bees**[17] 3153 9-9-0 **78**....................................... PhilDennis(5) 1 82
(Declan Carroll) *led: rdn over 2f out: hdd over 1f out: styd on same pce fnl 100yds* **16/1**

3-16 **6** *1 ¾* **Lopes Dancer (IRE)**[62] 1781 5-9-4 **77**.................................. NeilFarley 4 78
(Sally Haynes) *trckd ldrs: rdn over 2f out: unable qck over 1f out: keeping on u.p whn nt clr run fnl 75yds: sn eased* **40/1**

2-16 **7** *¾* **Caponova (IRE)**[35] 2558 4-9-9 **82**........................... RichardKingscote 10 81
(Tom Dascombe) *racd keenly: hld up: rdn over 2f out: kpt on ins fnl f: nvr able to trble ldrs* **9/2**[2]

3063 **8** *1 ¼* **Berlusca (IRE)**[101] 1065 8-9-3 **76**........................................ DavidNolan 8 73
(David O'Meara) *hld up: hdwy over 2f out: no bttr than midfield: one pce fnl f* **40/1**

5302 **9** *1 ¼* **Arithmetic (IRE)**[9] 3432 4-8-3 **62**................................. JamesSullivan 3 56
(Ruth Carr) *prom: ev ch over 2f out: rdn over 1f out: wknd ins fnl f: eased whn btn fnl 150yds* **7/1**

0-06 **10** *nse* **Brandon Castle**[7] 3486 5-8-9 **68**....................................(e[1]) LukeMorris 11 62
(Simon West) *hld up in rr: rdn over 2f out: no imp* **28/1**

142- **11** *13* **So Celebre (GER)**[68] 7229 4-9-3 **76**............................ StevieDonohoe 5 44
(Ian Williams) *in tch: rdn and lost pl over 2f out: bhd fnl 2f* **9/2**[2]

2m 11.25s (-1.45) **Going Correction** -0.125s/f (Firm) **11** Ran SP% **116.8**
Speed ratings (Par 105): **100,99,98,98,98 97,96,95,94,94 84**
CSF £25.77 CT £205.98 TOTE £4.30: £1.40, £2.70, £2.80; EX 22.40 Trifecta £263.90.
**Owner** L Hall, A Chandler, J Blackburn **Bred** Juddmonte Farms Ltd **Trained** Sheriff Hutton, N Yorks

**FOCUS**
Race distance increased by 33yds. A fair gallop to this handicap and a cosy success by the progressive winner, who was value for extra.

## 3745 SILK MILL SUPPORTING WHITWORTH WATERSKI ACADEMY H'CAP 1m 2f 42y
**8:40** (8:42) (Class 5) (0-70,71) 3-Y-0 **£3,557** (£1,058; £529; £264) **Stalls** Centre

Form RPR

3631 **1** **Barwell (IRE)**[7] 3499 3-9-8 **71** 6ex.............................. PaulMulrennan 13 81
(Michael Dods) *in tch: dropped in and racd in midfield over 6f out: hdwy 3f out: led jst over 2f out: r.o wl and in command fnl 100yds* **7/4**[1]

600- **2** *1 ¼* **Breanski**[208] 8034 3-9-2 **65**................................................ PhillipMakin 11 72
(David O'Meara) *hld up: hdwy 2f out: wnt 2nd over 1f out: ch and styd on ins fnl f: no imp on wnr fnl 100yds* **33/1**

056- **3** *4* **Siyahamba (IRE)**[213] 7954 3-8-8 **57**........................... ConnorBeasley 12 56
(Bryan Smart) *hld up: hdwy on outer 2f out: styd on ins fnl f: nt rch front two* **66/1**

640 **4** *nk* **Melodine**[84] 1333 3-9-2 **65**..............................................(p[1]) LukeMorris 9 63
(Sir Mark Prescott Bt) *midfield: rdn over 2f out: hdwy over 1f out: kpt on u.p ins fnl f: nvr able to chal* **14/1**

0-02 **5** *1 ½* **Size Matters**[30] 2702 3-8-7 **56**............................................... JasonHart 7 51
(Mark Walford) *led: rdn over 2f out: sn hdd: outpcd over 1f out: no ex fnl 100yds* **8/1**[3]

04-6 **6** *¾* **Fleetfoot Jack (IRE)**[49] 2107 3-9-3 **66**............................. DavidNolan 10 60
(David O'Meara) *midfield: rdn over 2f out: one pce fnl f* **20/1**

0022 **7** *½* **Tread Lightly**[14] 3243 3-9-5 **68**........................................... DavidAllan 8 61
(Tim Easterby) *trckd ldrs: rdn and ev ch over 2f out: fdd ins fnl f* **9/2**[2]

05-5 **8** *1 ¾* **Ingleby Mackenzie**[17] 3163 3-9-2 **65**............................ CharlesBishop 6 54
(Mick Channon) *trckd ldrs: rdn over 2f out: one pce ins fnl f* **20/1**

0-52 **9** *4* **Spirit Of Belle**[9] 3422 3-9-6 **69**.................................. AndrewMullen 2 50
(David Evans) *midfield: niggled along 6f out: rdn and lost pl over 3f out: n.d after* **8/1**[3]

-60 **10** *¾* **Showdance Kid**[13] 3296 3-9-2 **70**..................................... CliffordLee(5) 4 50
(K R Burke) *towards rr: pushed along over 3f out: nvr a threat* **33/1**

-004 **11** *4 ½* **Nigh Or Never (IRE)**[24] 2903 3-8-10 **59**..............(p[1]) RichardKingscote 3 30
(Tom Dascombe) *prom: rdn wl over 2f out: wknd over 1f out* **9/1**

2m 12.23s (-0.47) **Going Correction** -0.125s/f (Firm) **11** Ran SP% **110.3**
Speed ratings (Par 99): **96,95,91,91,90 89,89,87,84,84 80**
CSF £73.37 CT £2367.87 TOTE £2.30: £1.30, £7.30, £6.60; EX 68.60 Trifecta £1060.00.
**Owner** Tullpark Limited **Bred** Tullpark Ltd **Trained** Denton, Co Durham
■ Shambra was withdrawn. Price at time of withdrawal 12-1. Rule 4 applies to all bets - deduction 5p in the pound.

**FOCUS**
Race distance increased by 33yds. This was run at a strong gallop and the first two finished clear. The winner is progressive and the runner-up unexposed.
T/Plt: £159.30 to a £1 stake.Pool: £77,690.65 - 355.83 winning units. T/Qpdt: £21.20 to a £1 stake. Pool: £7,521.38 - 261.98 winning units. **Darren Owen**

# 2822 NEWBURY (L-H)
Thursday, June 15

**OFFICIAL GOING: Good (good to firm in places; 6.3)**
Wind: strong against Weather: cloudy periods

## 3746 BE WISER INSURANCE NOVICE STKS (PLUS 10 RACE) (DIV I) 6f 110y
**1:30** (1:34) (Class 4) 2-Y-0 **£4,043** (£1,203; £601; £300) **Stalls** Centre

Form RPR

**1** **Bullington Bandit (IRE)** 2-9-2 0............................(p[1]) StevieDonohoe 6 84
(Jane Chapple-Hyam) *hmpd leaving stalls: sn mid-div: bmpd 2f out: sn shkn up and hdwy: r.o strly fnl f: led towards fin* **80/1**

**2** *nk* **Being There (FR)** 2-9-2 0.............................................. WilliamBuick 8 83+
(Charlie Appleby) *hld up: hanging lft but hdwy fr 2f out: rdn whn swtchd lft ent fnl f: r.o wl: wnt 2nd cl home* **3/1**[3]

**3** *¾* **Curiosity (IRE)** 2-9-2 0...................................................... JamesDoyle 2 81+
(Hugo Palmer) *hld up: hdwy fr 3f out: led 2f out: sn drifted rt: kpt on but no ex whn hdd cl home* **5/2**[2]

4 **4** *1* **Rogue**[26] 2826 2-9-2 0.......................................................... RyanMoore 9 78+
(Richard Hannon) *led tl 2f out: sn rdn: drifted rt jst over 1f out: kpt on same pce fnl f* **7/4**[1]

**5** *½* **Lifeboat (IRE)** 2-9-2 0.............................................. SilvestreDeSousa 7 77+
(Charles Hills) *hld up: hdwy 2f out: sn rdn: chal for 2nd briefly jst ins fnl f: sn no ex* **20/1**

**6** *2 ¼* **Anna Nerium** 2-8-11 0........................................................ SeanLevey 3 66
(Richard Hannon) *mid-div: hdwy over 2f out: sn rdn in cl 3rd: wknd ins fnl f* **25/1**

**7** *3 ½* **El Borracho (IRE)** 2-9-2 0............................................ HarryBentley 10 61
(Simon Dow) *mid-div: rdn 2f out: sn drifted lft: nt pce to get on terms: fdd fnl f* **100/1**

**8** *6* **Motabassim (IRE)** 2-9-2 0..................................................... PatDobbs 1 45+
(Brian Meehan) *prom tl rdn 2f out: sn wknd* **33/1**

**9** *1* **Mutafarrid (IRE)** 2-9-2 0................................................... JimCrowley 4 42+
(Owen Burrows) *prom tl rdn 2f out: sn wknd* **8/1**

**10** *3* **Lucky's Dream** 2-9-2 0........................................................ FranBerry 5 34
(David Evans) *wnt rt s: mid-div: rdn over 2f out: sn wknd* **40/1**

1m 23.1s (3.80) **Going Correction** +0.20s/f (Good) **10** Ran SP% **117.3**
Speed ratings (Par 95): **86,85,84,83,83 80,76,69,68,65**
CSF £300.87 TOTE £71.10: £19.00, £1.50, £1.30; EX 193.30 Trifecta £5120.00.
**Owner** Bryan Hirst **Bred** Asterra Holdings Ltd **Trained** Dalham, Suffolk

**FOCUS**
William Buick assessed the ground as "Good to firm", while Harry Bentley said: "Lovely, very nice." Stevie Donohoe's verdict was: "It's a bit lively." They raced into a headwind for much of the afternoon and the time for the opener was slow. Just one runner had previous racecourse experience in this novice event. Several could prove better than the bare form.

## 3747 BE WISER INSURANCE NOVICE STKS (PLUS 10 RACE) (DIV II) 6f 110y
**2:00** (2:04) (Class 4) 2-Y-0 **£4,043** (£1,203; £601; £300) **Stalls** Centre

Form RPR

**1** **Expert Eye** 2-9-2 0.............................................................. RyanMoore 8 89+
(Sir Michael Stoute) *t.k.h early: trckd ldrs: shkn up to chal jst over 1f out: r.o wl to ld fnl 140yds: readily* **6/1**[2]

2 **2** *1 ½* **Mutakatif (IRE)**[20] 3037 2-9-2 0........................................ JimCrowley 7 84
(Charles Hills) *trckd ldr: led narrowly jst over 1f out: sn drvn: hdd fnl 140yds: kpt on but nt pce of wnr* **4/7**[1]

**3** *2 ¼* **Barraquero (IRE)** 2-9-2 0............................................... WilliamBuick 4 78
(Brian Meehan) *in tch: hdwy over 2f out: led over 1f out: rdn and narrowly hdd jst outside fnl f: no ex fnl 100yds* **14/1**

**4** *3 ½* **Petrus (IRE)** 2-9-2 0...................................................... JamieSpencer 10 68
(Brian Meehan) *hld up: hdwy 2f out: kpt on but nt pce to get on terms* **20/1**

**5** *2 ¼* **Diva Star** 2-8-5 0 ow1.............................................. TylerSaunders(7) 2 58
(Marcus Tregoning) *hld up: rdn over 2f out: kpt on fr over 1f out but nvr gng pce to get involved* **33/1**

**6** *2* **Magnificent** 2-9-2 0.............................................................. PatDobbs 5 57
(Richard Hannon) *s.i.s: sn mid-div: rdn over 2f out: sn one pce* **20/1**

**7** *1 ½* **Corazon Espinado (IRE)** 2-9-2 0................................ HarryBentley 1 52+
(Simon Dow) *led: rdn and hdd over 1f out: wknd fnl f* **33/1**

**8** *2 ½* **Cuban Heel** 2-9-2 0.............................................................. AdamKirby 9 46
(Clive Cox) *s.i.s: a last pair* **13/2**[3]

**9** *1 ¼* **Glacier (IRE)** 2-9-2 0.......................................................... SeanLevey 6 42
(Richard Hannon) *s.i.s: sn mid-div: rdn over 2f out: wknd over 1f out* **16/1**

1m 21.29s (1.99) **Going Correction** +0.20s/f (Good) **9** Ran SP% **119.2**
Speed ratings (Par 95): **96,94,91,87,85 82,81,78,76**
CSF £9.74 TOTE £6.80: £2.00, £1.02, £3.90; EX 14.10 Trifecta £61.40.
**Owner** K Abdullah **Bred** Juddmonte Farms Ltd **Trained** Newmarket, Suffolk

**FOCUS**
The quicker division by 1.81sec. Again the wind was a factor. The field was well strung out and the winner looks a likely improver.

## 3748 CROSSLAND EBF STALLIONS MAIDEN FILLIES' STKS (PLUS 10 RACE) 1m (S)
**2:30** (2:36) (Class 4) 3-Y-0 **£5,336** (£1,588; £793; £396) **Stalls** Centre

Form RPR

**1** **Standing Rock (IRE)** 3-9-0 0.......................................... WilliamBuick 5 83+
(John Gosden) *mid-div: pushed along over 2f out: hdwy over 1f out: led fnl 120yds: r.o wl: pushed out* **10/1**

-252 **2** *1 ¼* **Spinnaka (IRE)**[24] 2898 3-9-0 76...................................... JamieSpencer 1 79
(Luca Cumani) *mid-div: hdwy to ld over 2f out: edgd rt: sn rdn: hdd fnl 120yds: no ex* **11/4**[1]

**3** *nk* **What A Home (IRE)** 3-9-0 0.............................................. JamesDoyle 3 78+
(William Haggas) *hld up last: hdwy fr 2f out: rdn ent fnl f: kpt on wl to go 3rd fnl 120yds: clsng on 2nd at fin* **7/1**

2 **4** *2 ½* **Unified**[12] 3329 3-9-0 0........................................................ AdamKirby 6 73
(Clive Cox) *led: rdn and hdd 2f out: kpt on same pce fnl f* **7/1**

**5** *½* **Shimmering Light** 3-9-0 0................................................ RyanMoore 8 71
(Michael Bell) *mi-div: rdn jst over 2f out: styd on but nt pce to get on terms fnl f* **6/1**[3]

3 **6** *nk* **Deleyla**[19] 3075 3-9-0 0 SilvestreDeSousa 7 71
(Roger Varian) *trckd ldrs: rdn to chse ldr 2f out: nt quite pce to chal: fdd fnl 100yds* **5/1**[2]

60 **7** *1* **Know The Truth**[24] 2908 3-9-0 0 DavidProbert 11 68
(Andrew Balding) *s.i.s: towards rr: hdwy over 2f out: drifted lft u.p over 1f out: no further imp fnl f* **40/1**

42 **8** *6* **Highway One (USA)**[27] 2778 3-9-0 0 PatCosgrave 10 61
(George Baker) *hld up: hdwy over 3f out: rdn over 2f out: fdd fnl f* **6/1**[3]

55 **9** *15* **Vixen (IRE)**[27] 2782 3-9-0 0 HarryBentley 9 20
(Geoffrey Deacon) *prom: rdn over 2f out: sn hung rt: wknd* **66/1**

4-0 **10** *5* **Dancing Dragon (IRE)**[34] 2585 3-9-0 0 LiamKeniry 12 9
(George Baker) *in tch: rdn over 2f out: sn wknd* **66/1**

**11** *1 1/4* **Brave Tart** 3-8-7 0 MillyNaseb(7) 4 6
(Martin Smith) *trckd ldrs: rdn over 2f out: sn wknd* **100/1**

**12** *11* **Qelmim (IRE)** 3-9-0 0 SeanLevey 2
(Richard Hannon) *trckd ldrs: rdn over 2f out: wknd qckly* **16/1**

1m 40.93s (1.23) **Going Correction** +0.20s/f (Good) **12** Ran SP% **118.3**
Speed ratings (Par 98): **101,99,99,96,96 96,95,89,74,69 67,56**
CSF £37.39 TOTE £11.50: £3.60, £1.60, £2.80; EX 46.30 Trifecta £389.60.

**Owner** Rachel Hood & Mrs P Shanahan **Bred** P A Byrne **Trained** Newmarket, Suffolk

**FOCUS**
The principals came from towards the rear in what looked a fair fillies' maiden. The runner-up sets a fair standard.

## 3749 LORD WEINSTOCK MEMORIAL EBF STALLIONS STKS (REGD AS BALLYMACOLL STUD) (LISTED RACE) (FILLIES) 1m 2f

**3:05** (3:06) (Class 1) 3-Y-O
**£28,355** (£10,750; £5,380; £2,680; £1,345; £675) **Stalls** Centre

Form RPR

1-24 **1** **Elas Ruby**[21] 3006 3-9-0 84 JamesDoyle 8 96
(John Gosden) *trckd ldrs: rdn wl over 2f out: led ent fnl f: kpt on strly* **9/1**

1-51 **2** *3 3/4* **Ebbesbourne (IRE)**[19] 3094 3-9-0 85 (h) RyanMoore 6 88+
(Sir Michael Stoute) *hld up: pushed along over 3f out: rdn and stdy prog fr jst over 2f out: 6th whn nt clr run ent fnl f: r.o fnl 140yds: wnt 2nd cl home* **6/1**[2]

0-1 **3** *shd* **Smart Together (USA)**[20] 3039 3-9-0 82 WilliamBuick 7 87
(John Gosden) *mid-div: pushed along over 3f out: rdn and hdwy fr 2f out: chalng for 3rd whn hung lft ent fnl f: kpt on fnl 140yds* **16/1**

1-33 **4** *1/2* **Indian Blessing**[21] 3006 3-9-0 86 DavidProbert 4 86
(Ed Walker) *trckd ldr: led 2f out: sn rdn: hdd ent fnl f: kpt on same pce* **8/1**[3]

31 **5** *1 1/2* **Pleasant Surprise (IRE)**[43] 2307 3-9-0 80 JamieSpencer 5 83
(Luca Cumani) *led: rdn and hdd 2f out: kpt on but hld tl no ex fnl 100yds* **12/1**

-232 **6** *3/4* **Pattie**[16] 3182 3-9-0 73 SilvestreDeSousa 2 82
(Mick Channon) *hld up last pair: rdn 2f out: sn hung lft: nt pce to get involved* **33/1**

1-4 **7** *nse* **Talaayeb**[39] 2434 3-9-0 109 JimCrowley 1 82
(Owen Burrows) *dwlt: last pair: hdwy over 2f out: rdn in 3rd over 1f out: fdd ins fnl f* **4/7**[1]

0-1 **8** *6* **Fleur Forsyte**[28] 2759 3-9-0 81 DanielMuscutt 3 70
(James Fanshawe) *plld hrd: trckd ldrs: rdn over 2f out: wknd over 1f out* **14/1**

2m 7.52s (-1.28) **Going Correction** +0.20s/f (Good) **8** Ran SP% **122.2**
Speed ratings (Par 104): **113,110,109,109,108 107,107,102**
CSF £65.86 TOTE £11.80: £3.10, £1.90, £3.80; EX 64.30 Trifecta £474.10.

**Owner** Newsells Park Stud **Bred** Newsells Park Stud **Trained** Newmarket, Suffolk

**FOCUS**
Race run over an additional 28yds. Probably just an ordinary edition of this Listed event,rated a little below the race standard, but it was run at a good gallop. Two of the last five winners, Great Heavens and Speedy Boarding, have gone on to win in Group 1 company.

## 3750 COMAX H'CAP 1m (S)

**3:40** (3:40) (Class 4) (0-85,87) 4-Y-O+ **£6,469** (£1,925; £962; £481) **Stalls** Centre

Form RPR

6410 **1** **Kestrel Dot Com**[15] 3212 5-9-6 83 (b) SilvestreDeSousa 7 91
(Chris Dwyer) *mid-div: hdwy 2f out: rdn to ld ins fnl f: r.o wl* **15/2**[3]

2226 **2** *1/2* **Golden Wedding (IRE)**[15] 3214 5-9-5 82 CharlesBishop 8 88
(Eve Johnson Houghton) *a.p: rdn to ld over 1f out: hdd ins fnl f: kpt on wl but sn hld by wnr* **11/1**

0-00 **3** *1 1/4* **Wind In My Sails**[22] 2960 5-9-7 84 (h) JamieSpencer 6 89+
(Ed de Giles) *hld up last: hdwy whn nt clr run briefly jst over 1f out: r.o strly ins fnl f: snatched 3rd fnl stride* **9/1**

-341 **4** *nse* **Exceeding Power**[119] 769 6-8-12 75 FranBerry 3 78
(Martin Bosley) *s.i.s: mid-div: rdn and hdwy over 1f out: kpt on ins fnl f: wnt 3rd fnl 120yds: lost 3rd fnl stride* **12/1**

50-3 **5** *1/2* **Buckland Beau**[65] 1706 6-8-11 74 StevieDonohoe 1 76
(Charlie Fellowes) *mid-div: hdwy 2f out: sn rdn: kpt on same pce ins fnl f* **12/1**

-000 **6** *1 1/2* **Cricklewood Green (USA)**[13] 3298 6-9-2 79 PatDobbs 9 77
(Sylvester Kirk) *hld up: hdwy over 1f out: sn rdn: kpt on but nt pce to get involved* **16/1**

4041 **7** *1 1/4* **Ripoll (IRE)**[15] 3212 4-8-10 78 (t) MitchGodwin(5) 11 74+
(Sylvester Kirk) *led: rdn and hdd over 1f out: no ex ins fnl f* **8/1**

4050 **8** *hd* **Kingston Kurrajong**[15] 3212 4-9-3 80 JimCrowley 14 75
(Michael Attwater) *mid-div: rdn over 1f out: nt pce to get on terms* **20/1**

0-40 **9** *3/4* **Mullionheir**[149] 275 5-9-7 84 KierenFox 10 77
(John Best) *in tch: rdn over 2f out: fdd ins fnl f* **25/1**

0-22 **10** *1/2* **Directorship**[17] 3144 11-9-5 82 AdamKirby 2 74
(Patrick Chamings) *hld up: rdn 2f out: little imp* **14/1**

2-60 **11** *2 3/4* **Dubai's Secret**[22] 2960 4-9-7 84 SeanLevey 5 70
(David Brown) *in tch: rdn 2f out: sn wknd* **10/1**

53-2 **12** *5* **Capton**[66] 1683 4-8-12 75 FergusSweeney 12 49+
(Henry Candy) *trckd ldr: hung lft whn rdn 2f out: sn wknd* **5/1**[1]

-025 **13** *16* **Tomahawk Kid**[17] 3160 4-9-5 82 JamesDoyle 13 20
(Ian Williams) *in tch: rdn over 2f out: wknd over 1f out: eased fnl f* **11/2**[2]

1m 41.13s (1.43) **Going Correction** +0.20s/f (Good) **13** Ran SP% **118.9**
Speed ratings (Par 105): **100,99,98,98,97 96,94,94,94,93 90,85,69**
CSF £87.08 CT £761.13 TOTE £7.10: £2.50, £3.10, £3.20; EX 74.30 Trifecta £279.10.

**Owner** Mrs Nicola Thorne **Bred** Shadwell Estate Company Limited **Trained** Newmarket, Suffolk

**FOCUS**
The main action unfolded centre to far side in this fair, competitive handicap. The winner backed up his Yarmouth win.

## 3751 BE WISER INSURANCE "CONFINED" H'CAP 7f (S)

**4:15** (4:15) (Class 5) (0-75,70) 3-Y-O **£3,234** (£962; £481; £240) **Stalls** Centre

Form RPR

0-02 **1** **Limelite (IRE)**[14] 3246 3-9-7 70 RyanMoore 8 75
(Richard Hannon) *in tch: hdwy over 1f out: led ent fnl f: drifted lft: kpt on wl: rdn out* **3/1**[1]

-002 **2** *3/4* **Pyjamarama**[8] 3473 3-9-0 63 SilvestreDeSousa 4 66
(Roger Varian) *trckd ldr: rdn for str chal over 1f out: kpt on w ev ch fnl f: hld towards fin* **10/3**[2]

5-62 **3** *shd* **Fair Selene**[23] 2911 3-8-11 60 (v) GavinLerena 7 63
(Heather Main) *unsettled stalls and slowly away: bhd: hdwy whn bmpd 2f out: sn rdn: r.o strly fnl f* **10/1**

4450 **4** *1 3/4* **Major Cornwallis (IRE)**[21] 2993 3-8-10 62 AdamMcNamara(3) 6 60
(Richard Fahey) *led: rdn whn strly chal wl over 1f out: hdd ent fnl f: no ex* **16/1**

-533 **5** *3/4* **Lawfilly**[3] 3661 3-8-4 53 JimmyQuinn 5 49
(Richard Hughes) *trckd ldrs: swtchd rt 2f out: sn rdn: nt pce to chal: 4th and hld whn hmpd ent fnl f: kpt on same pce* **11/2**

40-0 **6** *2 1/2* **Feel The Vibes**[47] 2151 3-9-2 65 DavidProbert 3 54
(Michael Blanshard) *hld up: rdn 2f out: nvr threatened: fdd fnl f* **25/1**

20-0 **7** *hd* **Herm (IRE)**[38] 2474 3-9-3 66 AdamKirby 2 55
(David Evans) *trckd ldrs: rdn over 2f out: wknd ent fnl f* **4/1**[3]

2203 **8** *2* **Golden Guest**[9] 3443 3-9-3 66 TomQueally 1 49
(George Margarson) *hld up: effrt 2f out: nvr threatened: wknd fnl f* **8/1**

1m 28.37s (2.67) **Going Correction** +0.20s/f (Good) **8** Ran SP% **113.4**
Speed ratings (Par 99): **92,91,91,89,88 85,85,82**
CSF £12.94 CT £86.42 TOTE £3.90: £1.50, £1.60, £3.00; EX 10.70 Trifecta £61.20.

**Owner** Mrs E Roberts **Bred** J K Thoroughbreds **Trained** East Everleigh, Wilts

**FOCUS**
Runners couldn't have won since May last year, but must have contested at least three Flat handicaps and been placed at least once. All the field were maidens. Modest form, rated around the third.

## 3752 INSURE WISER H'CAP 1m 4f

**4:50** (4:50) (Class 5) (0-70,75) 3-Y-O **£3,234** (£962; £481; £240) **Stalls** Centre

Form RPR

01-2 **1** **King's Coinage (IRE)**[54] 1968 3-9-4 67 (h) LiamKeniry 2 75+
(Ed Walker) *hld up: hdwy but nt clrest of runs 2f out and again over 1f out but gamely squeezed through: led jst ins fnl f: r.o wl* **10/1**

3-00 **2** *3/4* **Chocolate Box (IRE)**[13] 3291 3-9-7 70 (p[1]) JamieSpencer 10 76+
(Luca Cumani) *hld up: tried to go for same gap as wnr 2f out but squeezed out: sn swtchd rt and rdn: edgd lft but r.o strly fnl f: nvr threatening to rch wnr* **8/1**

6-05 **3** *1 1/2* **Medalla De Oro**[5] 3596 3-9-5 68 (h[1]) JackMitchell 8 71
(Peter Chapple-Hyam) *led: rdn over 1f out: hdd ins fnl f: kpt on but no ex* **9/1**

-161 **4** *1* **Brimham Rocks**[7] 3489 3-9-12 75 6ex FranBerry 1 76
(Ralph Beckett) *trckd ldrs: rdn to chse ldr over 1f out tl ent fnl f: kpt on same pce* **11/8**[1]

-601 **5** *4 1/2* **Bayston Hill**[20] 3024 3-9-7 70 DanielMuscutt 6 64
(Mark Usher) *in tch: hdwy over 2f pout: sn rdn: fdd fnl 120yds* **10/1**

1512 **6** *3/4* **Bartholomew J (IRE)**[20] 3041 3-9-0 66 SimonPearce(3) 5 59
(Lydia Pearce) *hld up: rdn over 2f out: nvr threatened: hung lft and fdd fnl f* **13/2**[3]

3023 **7** *3* **Star Maker**[16] 3178 3-9-1 69 (b[1]) MitchGodwin(5) 7 57
(Sylvester Kirk) *sn trcking ldrs: rdn over 2f out: wknd fnl f* **6/1**[2]

00-4 **8** *8* **Born To Please**[20] 3024 3-8-2 51 JimmyQuinn 4 26
(Mark Usher) *plld hrd trcking ldrs: rdn 2f out: sn wknd* **33/1**

2m 36.1s (0.60) **Going Correction** +0.20s/f (Good) **8** Ran SP% **112.0**
Speed ratings (Par 99): **106,105,104,103,100 100,98,93**
CSF £82.44 CT £742.39 TOTE £9.40: £2.60, £2.50, £3.50; EX 59.90 Trifecta £1091.40.

**Owner** Brook Stud Partnership **Bred** Calumet Farm Llc **Trained** Upper Lambourn, Berks

**FOCUS**
This was run over an additional 28yds. Modest handicap form, the first two held up into a headwind.

## 3753 WISER ACADEMY AMATEUR RIDERS' H'CAP 1m 2f

**5:20** (5:21) (Class 5) (0-70,71) 4-Y-O+ **£3,119** (£967; £483; £242) **Stalls** Centre

Form RPR

5-41 **1** **The Major**[6] 3537 4-10-9 70 MrBJames(5) 8 79
(Michael Bell) *racd keenly: trckd ldrs: led wl over 1f out: styd on: rdn out* **13/8**[1]

4503 **2** *1/2* **Zephyros (GER)**[12] 3325 6-10-1 62 PoppyBridgwater(5) 1 69
(David Bridgwater) *mid-div: pushed along and stdy prog fr 3f out: wnt 3rd over 1f out: styd on to go 2nd fnl 120yds: clsng on wnr at fin* **8/1**[2]

0-02 **3** *2* **Duke Of Yorkshire**[12] 3325 7-10-11 70 (p) MissEEasterby(3) 5 73
(Tim Easterby) *prom: led after 4f: rdn and hdd wl over 1f out: sn hld: no ex fnl 120yds* **14/1**

3123 **4** *1/2* **Attain**[20] 3028 8-11-0 70 MrSWalker 7 72
(Archie Watson) *in tch: rdn over 2f out: styd on same pce* **8/1**[2]

4331 **5** *2 1/2* **Party Royal**[22] 2964 7-10-7 63 (p) MrDHDunsdon 15 60
(Nick Gifford) *hld up towards rr: swtchd to center over 3f out: rdn and stdy prog fr over 2f out: styd on but nvr gng pce to get on terms fnl f* **20/1**

420- **6** *2* **Wordismybond**[268] 6656 8-10-10 71 ow1 MrJamiePerrett(5) 14 64
(Brendan Powell) *mid-div: rdn and hdwy over 2f out: drifted lft over 1f out: styd on same pce fnl f* **33/1**

-604 **7** *3/4* **Pretty Jewel**[16] 3192 4-9-10 59 ow3 (h) DrMVoikhansky(7) 2 51
(Kevin Frost) *hld up towards rr: stdy prog whn nt clrest of runs over 2f out: styd on but nvr gng pce to get involved* **33/1**

4-02 **8** *1 1/2* **Pink Ribbon (IRE)**[13] 3304 5-11-0 70 (p) MrAlexFerguson 13 59
(Sylvester Kirk) *towards rr of mid-div: drvn 3f out: sme late prog: n.d* **20/1**

0-35 **9** *1/2* **McDelta**[71] 1556 7-10-4 60 (p) MissPFuller 9 48
(Geoffrey Deacon) *mid-div: rdn over 2f out: little imp* **14/1**

-004 **10** *nse* **Best Example (USA)**[22] 2971 5-10-13 69 (p) MrRBirkett 3 56
(Julia Feilden) *trckd ldrs: rdn over 2f out: wknd ent fnl f* **9/1**[3]

6011 **11** *1 3/4* **Master Of Heaven**[23] 2914 4-9-7 56 (p) MissSStevens(7) 4 40
(Jim Boyle) *led for 4f: chsd ldr tl rdn wl over 2f out: wknd jst over 1f out* **12/1**

000- **12** *nk* **Silver Dixie (USA)**[370] 3109 7-10-11 70 MissHayleyMoore(3) 6 53
(Peter Hedger) *hld up last: sme prog in center over 2f out but nvr threatened to get on terms: wknd fnl f* **16/1**

40-0 **13** *4½* **Classic Mission**[15] 3208 6-10-3 **62**............................(p) MrJHarding(3) 12 36
(Jonathan Portman) *hld up towards rr: hdwy over 3f out: wknd over 1f out* **33/1**

0-61 **14** *8* **Berkeley Vale**[29] 2722 6-10-11 **67**........................(b) MissAnnaHesketh 10 25
(Roger Teal) *mid-div: hdwy 5f out: effrt 4f out: wknd over 2f out* **16/1**

/23- **15** *6* **Red Dragon (IRE)**[498] 435 7-9-9 **56**.......................... MrHFNugent(5) 16 2
(Michael Blanshard) *trckd ldrs: rdn 3f out: sn wknd* **25/1**

2560 **16** *1¼* **Gaelic Silver (FR)**[13] 3304 11-10-0 **63**..............(p) MissBeckyButler(7) 11 7
(Gary Moore) *hmpd leaving stalls: a towards rr* **50/1**

2m 10.0s (1.20) **Going Correction** +0.20s/f (Good) **16** Ran SP% **127.3**
Speed ratings (Par 103): **103,102,101,100,98 97,96,95,94,94 93,93,89,83,78 77**
CSF £13.43 CT £152.21 TOTE £2.60: £1.10, £2.70, £3.50, £1.80; EX 18.10 Trifecta £157.90.
**Owner** M L W Bell Racing Ltd **Bred** B Buckley **Trained** Newmarket, Suffolk

**FOCUS**
This was run over an extra 28yds. A couple went out clear in this modest handicap for amateurs, including the third. The winner may be capable of a bit better.
T/Plt: £285.40 to a £1 stake. Pool: £69,937.86 - 178.84 winning units. T/Qpdt: £128.20 to a £1 stake. Pool: £5,487.11 - 31.66 winning units. **Tim Mitchell**

## 3622 NOTTINGHAM (L-H)
Thursday, June 15

**OFFICIAL GOING: Good to firm (good in places)**
Wind: Moderate against Weather: Cloudy with sunny periods

### 3754 MYRACING.COM EBF NOVICE STKS 6f 18y
**1:40** (1:43) (Class 5) 2-Y-O **£3,234** (£962; £481; £240) **Stalls** High

Form RPR

**1** **Great Prospector (IRE)** 2-9-2 0.................................. PaulHanagan 12 88+
(Richard Fahey) *hld up in rr: stdy hdwy on outer 1/2-way: chsd ldrs 2f out: rdn over 1f out: led jst ins fnl f: kpt on wl* **11/1**

**2** *2* **Tale Of Tails (IRE)** 2-9-2 0................................................ BenCurtis 10 82
(Brian Ellison) *towards rr: swtchd lft and hdwy on inner over 2f out: rdn wl over 1f out: styd on wl fnl f* **100/1**

25 **3** *¾* **Kit Marlowe**[26] 2826 2-9-2 0............................................ FrannyNorton 3 79
(Mark Johnston) *cl up: led 1/2-way: rdn along wl over 1f out: drvn and hdd jst ins fnl f: kpt on same pce* **15/8**[1]

43 **4** *¾* **Central City (IRE)**[36] 2522 2-9-2 0........................... JosephineGordon 5 77
(Hugo Palmer) *slt ld: hdd 1/2-way: cl up: rdn and ev ch over 1f out: drvn and kpt on same pce fnl f* **11/4**[2]

**5** *½* **Cosa Nostra (IRE)** 2-9-2 0.............................................. DavidNolan 4 76
(Richard Fahey) *trckd ldrs: pushed along over 2f out: rdn wl over 1f out: sn drvn and kpt on same pce* **28/1**

**6** *shd* **Manthoor (IRE)** 2-9-2 0.................................................... DaneO'Neill 1 75
(Owen Burrows) *trckd ldrs: hdwy 2f out: rdn over 1f out: wknd fnl f* **14/1**

**7** *1* **Etefaaq (IRE)** 2-9-2 0.................................................... TomMarquand 11 72
(Richard Hannon) *chsd ldrs on outer: rdn along 2f out: grad wknd* **20/1**

**8** *10* **Bib And Tucker** 2-9-2 0................................................ RobertWinston 2 42
(David Brown) *a towards rr* **66/1**

**9** *¾* **Flavius Titus** 2-9-2 0........................................................ AndreaAtzeni 6 40
(Roger Varian) *chsd ldrs: rdn along over 2f out: sn wknd* **3/1**[3]

0 **10** *6* **Westfield Wonder**[8] 3460 2-9-2 0........................................ TomEaves 8 22
(Ronald Thompson) *cl up: rdn along over 2f out: sn wknd* **200/1**

**11** *6* **Final Rock** 2-9-2 0.............................................................. LukeMorris 9 4
(Sir Mark Prescott Bt) *dwlt: a bhd* **40/1**

1m 15.36s (0.66) **Going Correction** -0.05s/f (Good) **11** Ran SP% **115.1**
Speed ratings (Par 93): **93,90,89,88,87 87,86,72,71,63 55**
CSF £792.74 TOTE £12.70: £3.10, £11.10, £1.10; EX 415.60.
**Owner** Mr And Mrs J D Cotton **Bred** Patrick Gleeson **Trained** Musley Bank, N Yorks

**FOCUS**
Outer track used. Distances as advertised. A breezy day, and the watered ground (5mm applied to the bends on Wednesday evening) was given as good to firm, good in places (GoingStick: 8.3). An interesting novice race in which the first two came from well off the pace. The form has been given a chance as rated.

### 3755 CARLING CUSTOMER MAIDEN STKS 1m 75y
**2:10** (2:14) (Class 5) 3-Y-O+ **£3,234** (£962; £481; £240) **Stalls** Centre

Form RPR

0-24 **1** **Alwahsh (IRE)**[31] 2681 3-9-2 76...................................(p[1]) MartinHarley 1 89+
(William Haggas) *mde all: rdn clr wl over 1f out: kpt on strly* **5/4**[1]

52 **2** *7* **Alqalsar (IRE)**[27] 2782 3-9-2 0........................................... DaneO'Neill 2 73
(Brian Meehan) *trckd wnr: hdwy 3f out: rdn along wl over 1f out: sn drvn and no imp* **3/1**[2]

60 **3** *shd* **Pioneertown (IRE)**[8] 3456 3-9-2 0................................... LukeMorris 15 73+
(Sir Mark Prescott Bt) *hld up in midfield: hdwy 3f out: n.m.r and swtchd lft over 1f out: sn rdn and kpt on fnl f* **50/1**

**4** *1* **Arabic Culture (USA)** 3-9-2 0................................. JosephineGordon 3 70+
(Saeed bin Suroor) *s.i.s and lost several l s: green and bhd: hdwy and n.m.r 2f out: sn swtchd rt to outer and rdn over 1f out: styd on wl fnl f* **7/2**[3]

**5** *3½* **Sukoot (IRE)** 3-9-2 0........................................................... TomEaves 5 62
(Ed Dunlop) *chsd ldng pair: pushed along 3f out: rdn 2f out: sn drvn and grad wknd* **25/1**

**6** *½* **Swaffham Bulbeck (IRE)** 3-9-2 0.................................. GrahamLee 13 61+
(Ed Vaughan) *hld up: hdwy over 2f out: rdn wl over 1f out: kpt on fnl f* **50/1**

0 **7** *1¾* **Khataaf (IRE)**[9] 3438 3-9-2 0........................................(t[1]) AndreaAtzeni 6 57
(Roger Varian) *chsd ldrs: rdn along over 2f out: grad wknd* **10/1**

00 **8** *1¼* **Bombero (IRE)**[9] 3435 3-8-13 0........................... CallumShepherd(3) 11 54+
(Ed de Giles) *towards rr: hdwy 3f out: n.m.r wl over 1f out: sn one pce* **200/1**

**9** *½* **Decision Maker (IRE)** 3-8-13 0........................... AlistairRawlinson(3) 7 53
(Roy Bowring) *a towards rr* **150/1**

**10** *shd* **Sanguine** 3-8-11 0...............................................(h[1]) AndrewMullen 9 48
(George Peckham) *in tch: hdwy to chse ldrs 3f out: rdn along over 2f out: sn drvn and wknd* **50/1**

00 **11** *nk* **Wolfcatcherjack (IRE)**[8] 3456 3-9-2 0................................. RyanPowell 8 52
(Sir Mark Prescott Bt) *hld up: pushed along and hdwy on inner over 3f out: n.m.r and hmpd over 2f out: n.d* **200/1**

5-0 **12** *2* **Wootyhoot (FR)**[38] 2475 3-8-11 0.......................(h[1]) GeorgeWood(5) 10 48
(James Fanshawe) *midfield: hdwy and in tch over 3f out: sn rdn along and wknd over 2f out* **28/1**

0-4 **13** *nse* **Mirimar (IRE)**[147] 310 3-9-2 0.................................. AdamBeschizza 16 48
(Ed Vaughan) *a towards rr* **25/1**

0- **14** *2¼* **Red Bordeaux (FR)**[247] 7239 3-9-2 0........................... GeorgeDowning 4 42
(Tony Carroll) *in tch: hdwy over 3f out: rdn along wl over 2f out: sn drvn and wknd* **200/1**

1m 44.33s (-4.67) **Going Correction** -0.275s/f (Firm)
**WFA** 3 from 4yo 11lb **14** Ran SP% **119.9**
Speed ratings (Par 103): **112,105,104,103,100 99,98,96,96,96 96,94,93,91**
CSF £4.68 TOTE £2.30: £1.20, £1.40, £8.80; EX 6.50 Trifecta £94.30.
**Owner** Hamdan Al Maktoum **Bred** Shadwell Estate Company Limited **Trained** Newmarket, Suffolk
■ Stewards' Enquiry : Alistair Rawlinson three-day ban: careless riding (Jun 29-30, Jul 1)

**FOCUS**
The favourite dominated from the off and had the rest in trouble some way out. The form seems sound with the field well stretched.

### 3756 MYRACING.COM TIPS FOR EVERY RACE H'CAP 1m 6f
**2:45** (2:45) (Class 6) (0-60,61) 4-Y-O+ **£2,587** (£770; £384; £192) **Stalls** Low

Form RPR

00-3 **1** **Wassail**[20] 3026 4-8-6 **47**........................................ CallumShepherd(3) 16 52
(Ed de Giles) *prom: trckd ldr after 3f: hdwy to ld wl over 3f out: rdn wl over 1f out: kpt on wl towards fin* **11/2**[2]

4602 **2** *nk* **Crakehall Lad (IRE)**[35] 2549 6-8-2 **45**..........................(b) PhilDennis(5) 5 50
(Andrew Crook) *trckd ldrs: hdwy 3f out: rdn wl over 1f out: drvn ins fnl f: kpt on wl towards fin* **11/1**

60-5 **3** *nk* **Sigurd (GER)**[25] 2364 5-8-10 **48**........................................ GrahamLee 10 53
(Jonjo O'Neill) *in tch: hdwy to trck ldrs 1/2-way: effrt 3f out: rdn along to chse ldng pair wl over 1f out: drvn and kpt on wl fnl f* **6/1**[3]

0-00 **4** *¾* **Honourable Knight (IRE)**[22] 2966 9-8-7 **45**.................. PaulHanagan 2 49
(Mark Usher) *led 2f: prom: cl up over 3f out: rdn to chse wnr over 2f out: drvn over 1f out: kpt on u.p fnl f* **40/1**

0-02 **5** *1¾* **My Mo (FR)**[30] 2712 5-8-12 **55**....................................(p) DavidEgan(5) 14 56
(David Dennis) *trckd ldrs: pushed along 3f out: rdn along and outpcd 2f out: kpt on u.p fnl f* **9/2**[1]

034- **6** *¾* **Angel In The Snow**[139] 7992 4-8-11 **49**............................... BenCurtis 11 50+
(Brian Ellison) *hld up and bhd: hdwy 3f out: rdn along wl over 1f out: styd on fnl f: nrst fin* **8/1**

-003 **7** *1* **Stanarley Pic**[12] 3340 6-9-7 **59**.......................................... NeilFarley 13 58
(Sally Haynes) *hld up in rr: hdwy on outer 3f out: rdn along wl over 1f out: sn drvn and no imp* **9/1**

000- **8** *1* **Desktop**[286] 6102 5-9-4 **56**................................................ CamHardie 7 54
(Antony Brittain) *t.k.h: trckd ldrs: hdwy over 3f out: rdn along to chse ldng pair over 2f out: drvn over 1f out: sn one pce* **11/1**

-603 **9** *nk* **Mr Standfast**[24] 2891 4-8-9 **47**......................................... FrannyNorton 8 44
(Alan Phillips) *cl up: led after 2f: pushed along over 4f out: hdd wl over 3f out: sn rdn along and wknd wl over 2f out* **25/1**

0-04 **10** *3½* **Little Orchid**[22] 2972 4-8-6 **47**............................... ShelleyBirkett(3) 9 40
(Julia Feilden) *a rr* **11/1**

5000 **11** *nk* **Lineman**[68] 1629 7-9-1 **53**...............................................(p) JamesSullivan 1 45
(Sarah Hollinshead) *a towards rr* **12/1**

0400 **12** *4½* **Le Tissier**[42] 2332 4-9-0 **52**.............................................(b[1]) LukeMorris 15 39
(Michael Attwater) *midfield: hdwy over 4f out: rdn along over 3f out: sn wknd* **10/1**

3m 6.82s (-0.18) **Going Correction** -0.275s/f (Firm) **12** Ran SP% **117.0**
Speed ratings (Par 101): **89,88,88,88,87 86,86,85,85,83 83,80**
CSF £63.95 CT £377.55 TOTE £5.40: £1.70, £3.10, £3.40; EX 78.90 Trifecta £639.30.
**Owner** Simon Treacher & Partner **Bred** Usk Valley Stud **Trained** Ledbury, H'fords

**FOCUS**
It paid to race handily in this weak staying handicap. Improved form from the winner.

### 3757 MYRACING.COM FREE HORSE RACING TIPS! H'CAP 6f 18y
**3:20** (3:21) (Class 3) (0-90,90) 4-Y-O+
**£9,337** (£2,796; £1,398; £699; £349; £175) **Stalls** High

Form RPR

0063 **1** **George Bowen (IRE)**[12] 3324 5-9-3 **86**............................ PaulHanagan 3 97
(Richard Fahey) *trckd ldrs: hdwy 2f out: led ent fnl f: sn rdn and qcknd clr: readily* **2/1**[1]

-041 **2** *4½* **Love Island**[14] 3253 8-8-12 **84**....................................(h) NathanEvans(3) 2 81
(Richard Whitaker) *in tch: hdwy 2f out: rdn to chse ldrs over 1f out: drvn and kpt on wl fnl f* **14/1**

-500 **3** *hd* **Seeking Magic**[20] 3034 9-9-7 **90**..........................................(t) RyanTate 4 86
(Clive Cox) *led: pushed along 2f out: jnd and rdn over 1f out: hdd ent fnl f: sn drvn and kpt on same pce* **12/1**

0140 **4** *2* **Englishman**[9] 3424 7-9-0 **83**.......................................... RobertWinston 8 73
(Milton Bradley) *trckd ldrs: hdwy 2f out: rdn over 1f out: sn no imp* **25/1**

2320 **5** *nk* **Johnny Cavagin**[8] 3463 8-8-13 **82**..................................(t) TomEaves 10 71
(Ronald Thompson) *towards rr: hdwy wl over 1f out: sn rdn and kpt on fnl f* **16/1**

2-12 **6** *shd* **Magical Effect (IRE)**[40] 2404 5-8-11 **80**........................ JamesSullivan 7 68
(Ruth Carr) *t.k.h: trckd ldr: pushed along 2f out: sn rdn and wknd over 1f out* **3/1**[2]

11-0 **7** *½* **Syrian Pearl**[40] 2381 6-9-4 **87**...................................... AdamBeschizza 5 74
(Chris Wall) *hld up: hdwy on outer over 2f out: rdn to chse ldrs wl over 1f out: sn drvn and wknd* **8/1**[3]

0-30 **8** *½* **War Whisper (IRE)**[20] 3030 4-9-0 **83**............................. TomMarquand 6 68
(Richard Hannon) *a towards rr* **8/1**[3]

2-02 **9** *1½* **Rantan (IRE)**[7] 3492 4-8-13 **82**........................................ AndrewMullen 9 62
(David Barron) *chsd ldrs: rdn along 2f out: sn drvn and wknd* **14/1**

1m 12.68s (-2.02) **Going Correction** -0.05s/f (Good) **9** Ran SP% **111.3**
Speed ratings (Par 107): **111,105,104,102,101 101,100,100,98**
CSF £30.18 CT £229.62 TOTE £3.00: £1.40, £3.60, £3.30; EX 31.30 Trifecta £185.50.
**Owner** M A Scaife **Bred** Kevin Blake **Trained** Musley Bank, N Yorks

**FOCUS**
A good performance from the winner, who ended a long losing streak in style. This form is worth more at face value.

### 3758 DOOM BAR SUMMER H'CAP 6f 18y
**3:55** (3:57) (Class 6) (0-65,67) 3-Y-O+ **£2,587** (£770; £384; £192) **Stalls** High

Form RPR

5004 **1** **Soaring Spirits (IRE)**[23] 2917 7-10-1 **66** ow1...........(p) RobertWinston 6 73
(Dean Ivory) *prom: chal wl over 1f out: rdn ins fnl f: led last 100 yds* **10/1**

4060 **2** *¾* **Athollblair Boy (IRE)**[29] 2731 4-9-12 **63**.............................. TomEaves 10 68
(Nigel Tinkler) *trckd ldrs: smooth hdwy 2f out: led jst over 1f out: sn rdn: hdd and no ex last 100 yds* **14/1**

3244 **3** *hd* **Lucky Lodge**[12] 3344 7-9-12 **63**.........................................(v) CamHardie 1 67
(Antony Brittain) *in tch: hdwy wl over 1f out: rdn and kpt on wl fnl f* **12/1**

5400 **4** *1¾* **Gung Ho Jack**[33] 2608 8-10-0 **65**................................ JosephineGordon 3 64
(John Best) *towards rr: rdn along and hdwy wl over 1f out: kpt on wl u.p fnl f* **8/1**[3]

6610 **5** *nse* **Fortinbrass (IRE)**[38] 2469 7-9-11 **62**.................................... JoeDoyle 4 61
(John Balding) *prom: rdn along 2f out: sn drvn and kpt on same pce* **28/1**

0530 **6** *½* **Ambitious Icarus**[5] 3563 8-9-10 **61**..........................(e) ConnorBeasley 13 58
(Richard Guest) *dwlt and rr: rdn along and hdwy 2f out: styd on fnl f* **16/1**

5030 **7** *hd* **Archimedes (IRE)**[3] 3667 4-10-0 **65**........................(tp) PaulHanagan 14 62
(David C Griffiths) *led: pushed along 2f out: sn rdn and hdd jst over 1f out: wknd ins fnl f* **12/1**

1444 **8** *1 ¾* **Bogsnog (IRE)**[34] 2589 7-9-5 **56**.................................... JamesSullivan 9 47
(Ruth Carr) *trckd ldrs: effrt 2f out: sn rdn and no imp* **7/1**[2]

0-00 **9** *½* **Pyroclastic (IRE)**[54] 1978 5-8-6 **46** oh1....................(t) ShelleyBirkett(3) 2 36
(Nick Kent) *a towards rr* **50/1**

-000 **10** *6* **Bushwise (IRE)**[5] 3569 4-8-10 **52**.................................(p) DavidEgan(5) 8 24
(Milton Bradley) *chsd ldrs: rdn along over 2f out: sn wknd* **33/1**

53-6 **11** *6* **Loveatfirstsight**[17] 3139 4-9-9 **60**.......................................... LiamJones 7 14
(Michael Attwater) *a towards rr* **33/1**

1004 **12** *2* **First Excel**[15] 3202 5-8-13 **57**.......................................(b) KevinLundie(7) 11 5
(Roy Bowring) *dwlt: sn in tch towards stands side: hdwy and prom wl over 2f out: rdn along wl over 1f out: sn wknd* **8/1**[3]

0-00 **13** *5* **Sixties Symphony**[13] 3279 3-8-1 **46** oh1..................... RoystonFfrench 5
(John Flint) *a towards rr* **100/1**

42-2 **14** *1 ½* **Arctic Angel (IRE)**[22] 2962 4-9-11 **67**....................(h) GeorgeWood(5) 12
(James Fanshawe) *in tch towards stands side: chsd ldrs 1/2-way and sn pushed along: rdn 2f out: sn wknd* **6/4**[1]

1m 14.72s (0.02) **Going Correction** -0.05s/f (Good)
**WFA** 3 from 4yo+ 8lb **14** Ran SP% **124.0**
Speed ratings (Par 101): **97,96,95,93,93 92,92,90,89,81 73,70,64,62**
CSF £141.34 CT £1759.86 TOTE £12.00: £3.30, £4.90, £3.20; EX 157.90 Trifecta £1395.50.
**Owner** Mrs Doreen Carter **Bred** Kevin & Meta Cullen **Trained** Radlett, Herts

**FOCUS**
A modest sprint thrown open by the poor performance of the hot favourite. Straightforward form.

## 3759 @MYRACINGTIPS FOLLOW NOW ON TWITTER FILLIES' H'CAP (JC GRASSROOTS MIDDLE DISTANCE SERIES) 1m 2f 50y

**4:30** (4:30) (Class 5) (0-75,77) 3-Y-O **£3,234** (£962; £481; £240) **Stalls** Low

Form RPR

-403 **1** **Prize Diva**[7] 3507 3-8-4 **63**.......................................(p) DavidEgan(5) 5 71
(David Elsworth) *trckd ldr: cl up 4f out: led 3f out: pushed along 2f out: rdn over 1f out: jnd ins fnl f: sn drvn and kpt on wl* **5/1**[3]

522- **2** *2 ¾* **Jive Talking (IRE)**[204] 8074 3-9-3 **71**............................. LouisSteward 8 74
(Michael Bell) *hld up: stdy hdwy on outer 3f out: rdn to chse wnr ent fnl f: sn ev ch: drvn and no ex last 100 yds* **5/1**[3]

0412 **3** *1 ¾* **Mirzam (IRE)**[19] 3087 3-9-4 **75**....................................... NathanEvans(3) 3 74
(Mick Channon) *trckd ldrs on inner: hdwy over 3f out: effrt over 2f out and sn n.m.r: swtchd rt to outer over 1f out and sn drvn: kpt on* **7/2**[2]

12 **4** *¾* **Ocean Drive (IRE)**[139] 439 3-9-9 **77**.............................. AndreaAtzeni 7 75
(William Haggas) *led 1f: trckd ldrs: hdwy 3f out: chsd wnr 2f out: sn rdn: drvn and one pce appr fnl f* **9/4**[1]

3-36 **5** *2* **Nurse Nightingale**[28] 2760 3-9-4 **72**......................... JosephineGordon 2 66
(Hugo Palmer) *trckd ldrs: pushed along on inner: over 3f out: rdn wl over 2f out: sn btn* **8/1**

-515 **6** *8* **Waves (IRE)**[17] 3142 3-9-1 **69**...................................... RobertWinston 6 52
(Eve Johnson Houghton) *t.k.h: hld up in rr: hdwy on outer over 3f out: rdn along over 2f out: sn drvn and btn* **8/1**

50-0 **7** *1 ¾* **Darwasl**[34] 2564 3-8-12 **66**..........................................(b[1]) DaneO'Neill 4 41
(Brian Meehan) *cl up: led after 1f: pushed along and hdd 3f out: sn rdn and wknd* **16/1**

2m 9.33s (-4.97) **Going Correction** -0.275s/f (Firm) **7** Ran SP% **114.4**
Speed ratings (Par 96): **108,105,104,103,102 95,94**
CSF £29.88 CT £98.06 TOTE £6.30: £2.90, £2.40; EX 30.20 Trifecta £116.30.
**Owner** J C Smith **Bred** Littleton Stud **Trained** Newmarket, Suffolk

**FOCUS**
A fair fillies' handicap, and there's more to come from the winner. A small pb from the runner-up.

## 3760 @MYRACINGTIPS JOIN 230,000 TWITTER FOLLOWERS H'CAP (DIV I) 1m 2f 50y

**5:00** (5:00) (Class 6) (0-60,62) 4-Y-O+ **£2,587** (£770; £384; £192) **Stalls** Low

Form RPR

/05- **1** **St Dunstan (IRE)**[323] 4764 4-9-0 **53**...................................(v) JasonHart 2 59
(John Quinn) *t.k.h early: trckd ldrs on inner: hdwy over 2f out: rdn to chse ldng pair ent fnl f: sn chal and n.m.r: squeezed through and drvn to ld nr fin* **10/1**

2642 **2** *hd* **Bling King**[31] 2688 8-9-7 **60**.........................................(p) LouisSteward 8 66
(Geoffrey Harker) *trckd ldrs: hdwy and cl up 3f out: chal 2f out: rdn to take slt ld over 1f: sn drvn: hdd and no ex nr fin* **15/8**[1]

-063 **3** *nk* **Cool Music (IRE)**[16] 3192 7-9-0 **53**.................................(p) CamHardie 6 58
(Antony Brittain) *sn led: pushed along 3f out: rdn 2f out: drvn and hdd over 1f out: kpt on gamely u.p fnl f* **5/1**[3]

/003 **4** *3* **Frontline Phantom (IRE)**[113] 865 10-8-4 **50**........... RussellHarris(7) 5 49
(K R Burke) *hld up: hdwy on outer 3f out: rdn along to chse ldrs wl over 1f out: kpt on same pce fnl f* **14/1**

6036 **5** *1 ¼* **Stun Gun**[9] 3439 7-8-12 **51**...........................................(p) MartinLane 7 48
(Derek Shaw) *stdd s and hld up in rr: hdwy on outer over 2f out: rdn wl over 1f out: kpt on fnl f* **16/1**

3516 **6** *1 ½* **The Lock Master (IRE)**[17] 3148 10-9-4 **60**......(p) AlistairRawlinson(3) 11 54
(Michael Appleby) *chsd ldrs: pushed along 4f out: rdn 3f out: drvn on outer 2f out: grad wknd* **10/1**

0-66 **7** *shd* **Patent**[38] 2471 4-9-1 **54**...............................................(p[1]) GrahamLee 3 49
(Peter Niven) *hld up: effrt and sme hdwy 3f out: rdn along over 2f out: n.d* **9/2**[2]

030- **8** *nse* **Cosmic Dust**[187] 8306 4-8-4 **48**.......................................(h) PhilDennis(5) 1 42
(Richard Whitaker) *in tch: effrt on inner whn nt clr run over 2f out: n.d after* **25/1**

50-0 **9** *1* **Its A Sheila Thing**[23] 2914 4-8-2 **46**............................ GeorgeWood(5) 10 38
(Tony Carroll) *trckd ldr: cl up over 4f out: chal over 2f out and sn rdn: drvn wl over 1f out: sn wknd* **9/1**

2m 13.69s (-0.61) **Going Correction** -0.275s/f (Firm) **9** Ran SP% **114.2**
Speed ratings (Par 101): **91,90,90,88,87 86,85,85,85**
CSF £28.80 CT £107.52 TOTE £9.40: £3.10, £1.10, £2.20; EX 33.10 Trifecta £113.40.
**Owner** S A T Quinn **Bred** Michael O'Mahony **Trained** Settrington, N Yorks

**FOCUS**
This was steadily run and developed into a bit of a dash. Straightforward, low-grade form.

## 3761 @MYRACINGTIPS JOIN 230,000 TWITTER FOLLOWERS H'CAP (DIV II) 1m 2f 50y

**5:30** (5:30) (Class 6) (0-60,62) 4-Y-O+ **£2,587** (£770; £384; £192) **Stalls** Low

Form RPR

0-02 **1** **Diamond Runner (IRE)**[12] 3343 5-8-12 **51**...............(b) RobertWinston 4 60+
(Lawrence Mullaney) *trckd ldrs: hdwy over 2f out: nt clr run and swtchd rt to outer over 1f out: sn rdn to chal: led last 100yds: kpt on strly* **10/3**[1]

2162 **2** *1 ¾* **The Dukkerer (IRE)**[14] 3263 6-9-6 **59**............................... TomEaves 2 63
(James Given) *trckd ldng pair: hdwy over 2f out: n.m.r over 1f out: rdn to take slt ld appr fnl f: sn drvn: hdd last 100yds: kpt on same pce* **4/1**[2]

5634 **3** *1* **Outlaw Torn (IRE)**[6] 3550 8-9-1 **54**..........................(e) ConnorBeasley 11 56
(Richard Guest) *trckd ldr: hdwy and cl up over 4f out: led over 3f out: jnd and rdn 2f out: drvn and hdd appr fnl f: kpt on u.p* **9/2**[3]

0-5 **4** *½* **Touch The Clouds**[125] 665 6-8-4 **46** oh1..................... HollieDoyle(3) 7 47
(William Stone) *hld up and bhd: hdwy 3f out: effrt on outer 2f out: sn rdn along and kpt on wl fnl f* **20/1**

2406 **5** *3* **Inflexiball**[20] 3053 5-9-3 **56**............................................ RoystonFfrench 9 51
(John Mackie) *t.k.h: trckd ldrs: pushed along wl over 2f out: sn rdn and n.d* **5/1**

-003 **6** *1 ¾* **Scent Of Power**[17] 3143 5-8-4 **48**..................................(t) JaneElliott(5) 12 40
(Barry Leavy) *in tch: hdwy over 4f out: chsd ldrs 3f out: sn rdn and one pce* **6/1**

0404 **7** *2 ¼* **Nouvelle Ere**[15] 3208 6-9-4 **57**.................................(t) GeorgeDowning 3 45
(Tony Carroll) *led: pushed along 4f out: sn hdd: rdn and wknd over 2f out* **15/2**

0660 **8** *hd* **Raashdy (IRE)**[6] 3537 4-9-7 **60**...............................(b[1]) TrevorWhelan 10 47
(Peter Hiatt) *chsd ldrs: rdn along 3f out: sn drvn and wknd* **16/1**

2m 11.26s (-3.04) **Going Correction** -0.275s/f (Firm) **8** Ran SP% **114.6**
Speed ratings (Par 101): **101,99,98,98,96 94,92,92**
CSF £16.82 CT £59.40 TOTE £4.10: £1.50, £1.60, £1.60; EX 14.80 Trifecta £57.70.
**Owner** Bawtry Racing Club **Bred** Edmond Kent **Trained** Great Habton, N Yorks

**FOCUS**
The pace was better in this division and the time was 2.43sec quicker. The second and third help pin a modest level.
T/Jkpt: Not won. T/Plt: £463.50 to a £1 stake. Pool: £61,645.84 - 97.08 winning units. T/Qpdt: £100.00 to a £1 stake. Pool: £3,936.18 - 29.10 winning units. **Joe Rowntree**

3762 - 3764a (Foreign Racing) - See Raceform Interactive

# 3508 LEOPARDSTOWN (L-H)

Thursday, June 15

**OFFICIAL GOING: Good (good to firm in places)**

## 3765a OLIVER BRADY MEMORIAL SHABRA CHARITY BALLYCORUS STKS (GROUP 3) 7f

**7:20** (7:19) 3-Y-O+

**£31,769** (£10,230; £4,846; £2,153; £1,076; £538)

RPR

**1** **Flight Risk (IRE)**[229] 7706 6-9-9 108.............................. KevinManning 1 112+
(J S Bolger, Ire) *racd in rr: travelled wl to cl on inner over 1f out: led 1f out and sn qcknd clr: styd on strly* **12/1**

**2** *2 ½* **Don't Touch**[243] 7350 5-9-9 0......................................... TonyHamilton 5 105
(Richard Fahey) *chsd ldrs in 3rd: rdn over 2f out: almost on terms appr fnl f: sn nt qckn w wnr: kpt on same pce in 2nd* **5/2**[2]

**3** *2 ¾* **Psychedelic Funk**[25] 2863 3-8-13 104.............................. ColinKeane 2 94
(G M Lyons, Ire) *hld up in 6th: rdn over 2f out: wnt 4th appr fnl f: sn rdn and swtchd rt: kpt on same pce into 3rd cl home* **4/1**[3]

**4** *½* **Gordon Lord Byron (IRE)**[19] 3099 9-10-0 112................ ChrisHayes 3 101
(T Hogan, Ire) *bit slowly away: gd hdwy to dispute after 2f: hdd narrowly 3f out: nt qckn in 3rd ins fnl f: dropped to 4th cl home* **12/1**

**5** *1 ¾* **Firmament**[19] 3089 5-9-9 0............................................ DanielTudhope 6 92
(David O'Meara) *settled off ldrs in 5th: rdn and no imp over 1f out: kpt on one pce* **7/4**[1]

**6** *½* **Marshall Jennings (IRE)**[7] 3510 5-9-9 102............ ColmO'Donoghue 4 90
(Mrs John Harrington, Ire) *led and jnd after 2f: led again narrowly 3f out tl hdd 1f out: sn no ex* **12/1**

**7** *5 ½* **Sevenleft (IRE)**[7] 3510 4-9-9 97....................................(t) RonanWhelan 7 76
(Ms Sheila Lavery, Ire) *sn chsd ldrs in 4th: rdn 1/2-way: nt qckn under 2f out: sn dropped to rr and no ex* **20/1**

1m 28.31s (-0.39) **Going Correction** +0.275s/f (Good)
**WFA** 3 from 4yo+ 10lb **7** Ran SP% **112.8**
Speed ratings: **113,110,107,106,104 103,97**
CSF £41.05 TOTE £13.00: £4.30, £1.90; DF 45.60 Trifecta £225.50.
**Owner** Mrs J S Bolger **Bred** James F Hanly **Trained** Coolcullen, Co Carlow

**FOCUS**
A race that worked out perfectly for the winner, a horse that deserved to pick up one of these. He has been rated back to his best.

3766 - 3768a (Foreign Racing) - See Raceform Interactive

# 3569 CHEPSTOW (L-H)

Friday, June 16

**OFFICIAL GOING: Good to firm (8.5)**

Wind: light breeze, across them in the home straight Weather: fine

## 3769 EBF NOVICE STKS (PLUS 10 RACE) 6f 16y

**5:55** (5:55) (Class 4) 2-Y-O **£4,851** (£1,443; £721; £360) **Stalls** Centre

Form RPR

3 **1** **Klosters (IRE)**[23] 2958 2-8-8 0................................ KieranShoemark(3) 2 73+
(Roger Charlton) *trckd ldrs: clsd 1/2-way: led narrowly 2f out: asserted early ins fnl f: pushed out* **11/10**[1]

30 **2** *2* **Airshow**[63] 1767 2-9-2 0......................................(h) ThomasBrown 5 71
(Rod Millman) *mainly trckd ldr: chal and bmpd over 2f out: ev ch after tl no ex early ins fnl f* **12/1**

03 **3** *1 ¼* **Merchant Marine (IRE)**[14] 3305 2-9-2 0..........................(v) PatDobbs 8 67
(Ralph Beckett) *led tl hdd 2f out: rdn and kpt on same pce* **7/2**[2]

0 **4** *3 ½* **Bin Daahir**[21] 3025 2-9-2 0............................................ DaneO'Neill 7 57
(Charles Hills) *chsd ldrs: rdn 1/2-way and sn sltly outpcd: styd on appr fnl f but no threat* **12/1**

| Form | Pos | Dist | Horse | RPR |
|---|---|---|---|---|
| | 5 | 1 ¼ | **That's My Girl (IRE)** 2-8-11 0 KieranO'Neill 6 (Richard Hannon) *chsd ldrs early: rdn and lost pl after 2f: sn swtchd lft: one pce and no real imp fnl 2f* **16/1** | 48 |
| 24 | 6 | nk | **Zain Flash**[24] 2926 2-9-2 0 JFEgan 9 (David Evans) *chsd ldrs: rdn 1/2-way: wknd over 1f out* **9/1**[3] | 52 |
| 00 | 7 | nk | **Mysaan (IRE)**[29] 2750 2-9-2 0 (b[1]) JosephineGordon 4 (Brian Meehan) *stmbld sltly sn after leaving stalls: towards rr: rdn 1/2-way: wknd over 1f out* **9/1**[3] | 51 |
| | 8 | 1 ¼ | **Stockings Lane (IRE)** 2-9-2 0 AdamBeschizza 1 (Steph Hollinshead) *s.i.s: in rr: rdn and hung lft 1/2-way: sme hdwy on outer 2f out: fdd fnl f* **40/1** | 47 |

1m 11.04s (-0.96) **Going Correction** -0.175s/f (Firm) 8 Ran SP% **113.5**
Speed ratings (Par 95): **99,96,94,90,88 87,87,85**
CSF £16.04 TOTE £1.90: £1.10, £3.20, £1.50; EX 14.80 Trifecta £57.50.
**Owner** Nick Bradley Racing 46 & Partner **Bred** Mrs Eleanor Commins **Trained** Beckhampton, Wilts

**FOCUS**
A glorious summer evening and the meeting started with an official description of 'good to firm' with Kieran Shoemark after the first stating it was "very quick". No more than a fair novice, and it has been rated around the 3rd.

## 3770 BET FREE BETS AT BETFREEBETS.UK MAIDEN FILLIES' STKS 1m 4f
**6:25** (6:26) (Class 5) 3-Y-O+ **£3,234** (£962; £481; £240) **Stalls** Low

| Form | Pos | Dist | Horse | RPR |
|---|---|---|---|---|
| 4 | 1 | | **Sure To Explore (IRE)**[18] 3145 3-9-0 0 DaneO'Neill 10 (William Muir) *trckd ldrs: rdn over 2f out: led appr fnl f: drvn out* **10/1**[3] | 70 |
| 3-33 | 2 | ½ | **So Sleek**[18] 3145 3-9-0 80 JosephineGordon 6 (Luca Cumani) *hld up: niggled along 5f out: drvn and hdwy on outer over 2f out: styd on wl to go 2nd ins fnl fnl f: clsng on wnr towards fin* **6/5**[1] | 69 |
| 4-32 | 3 | 3 | **Inconceivable (IRE)**[37] 2515 3-9-0 76 PatDobbs 2 (Ralph Beckett) *led: jnd 4f out: rdn 3f out: hdd appr fnl f: one pce* **11/8**[2] | 64 |
| 43-5 | 4 | 1 ¼ | **What A Scorcher**[42] 2357 6-10-0 68 RobHornby 1 (Nikki Evans) *s.i.s: sn rcvrd to trck ldr: chal 4f out: rdn 3f out: ev ch tl n.m.r in cl 3rd ent fnl f: no ex* **12/1** | 62 |
| | 5 | 1 ¾ | **Infanta Isabella** 3-9-0 0 LiamKeniry 4 (George Baker) *trckd ldrs: shkn up in 3rd over 2f out: grad fdd fnl f* **16/1** | 59 |
| 5450 | 6 | shd | **Tenby Two**[17] 3180 3-9-0 62 CharlesBishop 5 (Mick Channon) *hld up: rdn 3f out: one pce* **20/1** | 59 |
| 0-0 | 7 | 2 ¼ | **Franny Nisbet**[18] 3145 3-8-11 0 KieranShoemark(3) 7 (William Muir) *hld up: drvn over 3f out: sn outpcd: styd on fnl 2f but nvr a threat* **50/1** | 55 |
| 0 | 8 | 32 | **Maitresse (IRE)**[42] 2359 3-9-0 0 KieranO'Neill 9 (Seamus Durack) *chsd ldrs: rdn 4f out: wknd 3f out: t.o* **50/1** | 4 |
| 0 | 9 | 26 | **Ruby Taylor**[23] 2963 5-9-7 0 (h) JordanUys(7) 8 (Nick Lampard) *s.s: a last: drvn over 5f out: t.o fnl 4f* **200/1** | |

2m 34.93s (-4.07) **Going Correction** -0.40s/f (Firm)
**WFA** 3 from 5yo+ 14lb 9 Ran SP% **119.4**
Speed ratings (Par 100): **97,96,94,93,92 92,91,69,52**
CSF £23.11 TOTE £14.70: £3.20, £1.10, £1.10; EX 34.50 Trifecta £79.30.
**Owner** Newsells Park Stud **Bred** Newsells Park Stud **Trained** Lambourn, Berks

**FOCUS**
A maiden won by Sir Michael Stoute's useful filly Dubka in 2016. The betting suggested this was a two horse race, but they had to be content with place positions.

## 3771 HICKS LOGISTICS H'CAP 1m 2f
**7:00** (7:00) (Class 5) (0-75,75) 4-Y-O+ **£2,911** (£866; £432; £216) **Stalls** Low

| Form | Pos | Dist | Horse | RPR |
|---|---|---|---|---|
| -604 | 1 | | **Jufn**[25] 2893 4-9-7 75 (h) TrevorWhelan 1 (John Butler) *led at stdy gallop: increased pce 3f out: drvn over 1f out: styd on wl* **11/4**[1] | 82 |
| /10- | 2 | 1 | **Squiggley**[232] 7653 4-9-4 72 DaneO'Neill 2 (Henry Candy) *in 2nd thrght: drvn over 2f out: kpt on wl but hld by wnr fnl f* **7/2**[2] | 77 |
| /040 | 3 | 2 ¼ | **Matravers**[44] 2291 6-8-12 69 AaronJones(3) 6 (Mary Hambro) *hld up: rdn and nt clr run in last over 2f out: hdwy over 1f out: styd on to go 3rd ins fnl f: too much to do* **8/1** | 71 |
| 4266 | 4 | 1 | **Jack Of Diamonds (IRE)**[22] 3009 8-9-1 72 (b) KieranShoemark(3) 4 (Roger Teal) *trckd ldrs: drvn 2f out: one pce and lost 3rd ins fnl f* **5/1**[3] | 71 |
| 5-33 | 5 | 1 ½ | **Frantical**[16] 3221 5-7-10 57 AledBeech(7) 8 (Tony Carroll) *t.k.h towards rr: rdn 2f out: one pce and unable to threaten ldrs* **5/1**[3] | 53 |
| 00-6 | 6 | 2 ¼ | **Golden Isles (IRE)**[24] 2915 4-8-2 56 oh1 JimmyQuinn 3 (Heather Main) *hld up in 5th: rdn over 2f out: unable qck: fdd fnl f* **12/1** | 47 |
| 0-40 | 7 | 1 | **Distant High**[10] 3425 6-8-3 57 (p) JosephineGordon 5 (Richard Price) *s.i.s: sn chsng ldrs: rdn 3f out: wknd over 1f out* **7/1** | 46 |

2m 9.02s (-1.58) **Going Correction** -0.40s/f (Firm) 7 Ran SP% **113.5**
Speed ratings (Par 103): **90,89,87,86,85 83,82**
CSF £12.33 CT £66.15 TOTE £3.60: £1.80, £2.40; EX 8.10 Trifecta £81.70.
**Owner** C Benham/D Whitford/P Bennison/K Quinn **Bred** Shadwell Estate Company Limited **Trained** Newmarket, Suffolk

**FOCUS**
The market gave everything a chance in this modest handicap, but the favourite won nicely.

## 3772 BEST BETTING SITES AT BETTINGSITES.LTD.UK FILLIES H'CAP 1m 14y
**7:30** (7:31) (Class 5) (0-70,68) 4-Y-O+ **£2,911** (£866; £432; £216) **Stalls** Centre

| Form | Pos | Dist | Horse | RPR |
|---|---|---|---|---|
| 0-35 | 1 | | **Fantasy Queen**[45] 2285 4-9-1 62 CharlesBishop 6 (Eve Johnson Houghton) *trckd ldng pair: rdn over 2f out: led over 1f out: edgd sltly lft fnl f: drvn out* **6/4**[1] | 68 |
| 5043 | 2 | 1 ½ | **Here's Two**[9] 3455 4-9-7 68 DaneO'Neill 5 (Ron Hodges) *cl 2nd: rdn and ev ch 2f out tl unable qck ins fnl f* **9/4**[2] | 71 |
| 6650 | 3 | 2 ¼ | **Smart Mover (IRE)**[31] 2708 4-8-9 56 RobHornby 2 (Nikki Evans) *led: rdn 2f out: hdd over 1f out: sn hung lft ins fnl f* **8/1** | 54 |
| 3410 | 4 | 2 ¼ | **Sheer Intensity (IRE)**[7] 3550 4-8-1 55 KatherineGlenister(7) 3 (David Evans) *dwlt bdly: in tch after 2f: rdn over 2f out: sn outpcd by ldrs: kpt on fnl f* **10/3**[3] | 48 |
| 56-0 | 5 | 8 | **Whitstable Pearl (IRE)**[21] 3028 4-8-4 51 RoystonFfrench 1 (Sophie Leech) *dwlt bdly: in tch after 2f: rdn 3f out: sn outpcd: wknd over 1f out* **16/1** | 25 |

1m 34.03s (-2.17) **Going Correction** -0.40s/f (Firm) 5 Ran SP% **110.8**
Speed ratings (Par 103): **94,92,90,88,80**
CSF £5.20 TOTE £2.40: £1.10, £1.60; EX 4.70 Trifecta £16.10.
**Owner** Mrs Zara Campbell-Harris **Bred** Mrs Z C Campbell-Harris **Trained** Blewbury, Oxon

**FOCUS**
Modest form.

## 3773 CHEPSTOW PLANT INTERNATIONAL H'CAP 7f 16y
**8:05** (8:05) (Class 5) (0-75,78) 4-Y-O+ **£2,911** (£866; £432; £216) **Stalls** Centre

| Form | Pos | Dist | Horse | RPR |
|---|---|---|---|---|
| 23-3 | 1 | | **Carpe Diem Lady (IRE)**[51] 2087 4-9-7 75 (v[1]) PatDobbs 3 (Ralph Beckett) *mde all: racd towards far side tl tacked over fr 3f out: stands' side by 1f out where shkn up: drvn fnl 150yds: hld on gamely* **2/1**[1] | 80 |
| 025 | 2 | ½ | **Bounty Pursuit**[85] 1334 5-8-8 67 MitchGodwin(5) 10 (Michael Blake) *s.i.s: hld up on nr side: hdwy over 2f out: drvn to chse wnr over 1f out: r.o wl: jst hld* **8/1** | 70 |
| 0415 | 3 | hd | **Satchville Flyer**[6] 3573 6-9-3 78 6ex KatherineGlenister(7) 5 (David Evans) *wnt to post early: t.k.h and hld up nr side: drvn over 2f out: swtchd lft 2f out and sn hung to far rail: r.o u.p fnl f* **9/2**[2] | 81 |
| 0-53 | 4 | 1 | **Bella's Venture**[29] 2763 4-8-7 61 JosephineGordon 1 (John Gallagher) *chsd wnr towards far side and prom overall: rdn over 2f out: kpt on same pce fnl f* **7/1** | 61 |
| 0003 | 5 | hd | **Sumou (IRE)**[14] 3278 4-9-4 72 RobertWinston 6 (Milton Bradley) *led gp of five on nr side and prom overall: drvn over 1f out: one pce: wnt wrong after fin* **5/1**[3] | 71 |
| 00-0 | 6 | 1 | **Doctor Bong**[11] 3397 5-8-6 60 (b) JimmyQuinn 9 (Grace Harris) *chsd ldrs on nr side: drvn 3f out: styd on one pce* **20/1** | 57 |
| 330 | 7 | 3 ¼ | **Corporal Maddox**[9] 3454 10-8-12 66 (p) LiamKeniry 8 (Ronald Harris) *chsd ldrs nr side: drvn 2f out: wknd fnl f* **16/1** | 54 |
| 06-0 | 8 | ¾ | **Bergholt (IRE)**[53] 2022 4-8-7 61 KieranO'Neill 2 (Tim Vaughan) *racd towards far side: outpcd and qckly detached in last: chsd along 1/2-way: no real imp* **15/2** | 47 |

1m 22.13s (-1.07) **Going Correction** -0.175s/f (Firm) 8 Ran SP% **114.2**
Speed ratings (Par 103): **99,98,98,97,96 95,91,91**
CSF £18.86 CT £64.78 TOTE £2.70: £1.10, £2.80, £2.00; EX 19.00 Trifecta £82.30.
**Owner** Mrs Angie Dawes **Bred** Stonethorn Stud Farms Ltd **Trained** Kimpton, Hants
■ Stewards' Enquiry : Jimmy Quinn two-day ban: used whip with his arm above shoulder height (Jun 30-Jul 1)
Pat Dobbs two-day ban: used whip above the permitted level (Jun 30-Jul 1)

**FOCUS**
Ordinary form. The field was in two groups early before merging, but they went a good gallop.

## 3774 GRAHAM PLUMBERS MERCHANT CHALLENGE H'CAP 6f 16y
**8:35** (8:36) (Class 5) (0-70,72) 3-Y-O+ **£2,911** (£866; £432; £216) **Stalls** Centre

| Form | Pos | Dist | Horse | RPR |
|---|---|---|---|---|
| 6503 | 1 | | **Showmethewayavrilo**[7] 3532 4-9-12 66 JosephineGordon 6 (Malcolm Saunders) *chsd ldrs: rdn to ld over 1f out: drvn and hld on wl* **11/2**[3] | 74 |
| 1322 | 2 | ¾ | **Delfie Lane**[39] 2474 3-9-3 71 (p) FinleyMarsh(7) 10 (Richard Hughes) *midfield: hdwy over 2f out: sltly hmpd appr fnl f: r.o* **9/4**[1] | 74 |
| 2166 | 3 | shd | **Indian Affair**[6] 3573 7-9-11 65 (bt) RobertWinston 7 (Milton Bradley) *towards rr: hdwy 1/2-way: drvn 2f out: r.o u.p* **11/2**[3] | 69 |
| 3140 | 4 | ½ | **Kingstreet Lady**[14] 3280 4-8-12 52 RobHornby 13 (Richard Price) *chsd ldrs: rdn 2f out: disp 2nd 1f out tl wl ins fnl f* **14/1** | 54 |
| -032 | 5 | 1 ¼ | **Arthurthedelegator**[25] 2886 3-9-7 68 KevinStott 1 (Oliver Greenall) *towards rr: hdwy 2f out: styd on u.p fnl f* **9/2**[2] | 64 |
| 6066 | 6 | ¾ | **Clever Lady (IRE)**[6] 3569 3-7-13 49 oh4 NoelGarbutt(3) 8 (David Evans) *chsd ldrs: rdn 2f out: nt clr run and lost grnd over 1f out: r.o ins fnl f* **28/1** | 46+ |
| 5000 | 7 | ¾ | **Vincentti (IRE)**[6] 3573 7-9-11 72 (p) WilliamCox(7) 9 (Ronald Harris) *midfield: drvn 2f out: kpt on same pce fnl f* **14/1** | 66 |
| 0024 | 8 | 1 ¼ | **Diamond Vine (IRE)**[6] 3569 9-8-9 49 oh3 (p) RoystonFfrench 5 (Ronald Harris) *in rr: rdn and outpcd over 3f out: r.o fnl f: nvr any ch* **33/1** | 39 |
| 0050 | 9 | ¾ | **Divine Call**[20] 3084 10-8-11 51 (b) ThomasBrown 3 (Milton Bradley) *in rr: rdn over 2f out: sme hdwy fnl f* **25/1** | 38 |
| 0000 | 10 | nk | **Royal Normandy**[20] 3084 5-8-9 49 oh4 (b) JimmyQuinn 12 (Grace Harris) *led: rdn and hdd over 1f out: sn jinked lft: wknd fnl f* **50/1** | 35 |
| -505 | 11 | 1 ¼ | **Monarch Maid**[16] 3216 6-9-11 65 LiamKeniry 14 (Peter Hiatt) *s.i.s: sn chsng ldrs: rdn over 2f out: wknd appr fnl f* **14/1** | 47 |
| -403 | 12 | 8 | **Kaaber (USA)**[31] 2709 6-8-8 53 (b) JaneElliott(5) 4 (Roy Brotherton) *towards rr: sme hdwy u.p 1/2-way: wknd over 1f out* **9/1** | 10 |

1m 10.5s (-1.50) **Going Correction** -0.175s/f (Firm)
**WFA** 3 from 4yo+ 7lb 12 Ran SP% **121.9**
Speed ratings (Par 103): **103,102,101,101,99 98,97,95,94,94 92,82**
CSF £18.16 CT £74.55 TOTE £7.40: £2.70, £1.20, £2.30; EX 22.90 Trifecta £137.30.
**Owner** Pat Hancock & Eric Jones **Bred** Eric Jones, Pat Hancock **Trained** Green Ore, Somerset

**FOCUS**
A run-of-the-mill sprint handicap. They went a good pace, but it's just modest form.

## 3775 SELECTSECURITYUK.COM H'CAP 2m
**9:05** (9:05) (Class 6) (0-65,67) 4-Y-O+ **£2,264** (£673; £336; £168) **Stalls** Low

| Form | Pos | Dist | Horse | RPR |
|---|---|---|---|---|
| 0061 | 1 | | **Dovils Date**[23] 2966 8-9-7 65 KieranO'Neill 6 (Tim Vaughan) *mde virtually all: rdn over 2f out: styd on wl u.p* **3/1**[2] | 72 |
| /542 | 2 | ¾ | **Nachi Falls**[13] 3340 4-9-1 66 (t) JoshuaBryan(7) 8 (Nigel Hawke) *trckd ldrs: rdn to chse wnr 2f out: styd on wl fnl f: unable qck towards fin* **15/8**[1] | 72 |
| 5540 | 3 | 5 | **See And Be Seen**[9] 3459 7-9-2 65 (p) MitchGodwin(5) 5 (Sylvester Kirk) *hld up: rdn 3f out: hdwy 2f out: wnt 3rd ins fnl f: no threat to first two* **5/1** | 65 |
| 46-1 | 4 | 4 ½ | **Kashgar**[42] 2364 8-9-9 67 TimmyMurphy 1 (Bernard Llewellyn) *hld up: hdwy 5f out: rdn to chse wnr 3f out: lost 2nd 2f out: one pce: wknd towards fin* **7/2**[3] | 62 |
| 5-50 | 5 | 5 | **Skylark Lady (IRE)**[21] 3026 4-8-13 57 (p) CharlesBishop 9 (Nikki Evans) *chsd ldrs: drvn over 3f out: wknd over 1f out* **25/1** | 46 |
| 0-55 | 6 | 2 ¾ | **Urban Space**[42] 2363 11-8-9 60 (t) WilliamCox(7) 3 (John Flint) *s.i.s: hld up: drvn 3f out: one pce and no imp* **12/1** | 45 |
| 000- | 7 | 36 | **Kirkman (IRE)**[247] 7270 6-8-2 46 JimmyQuinn 7 (Peter Hiatt) *pressed wnr: rdn over 3f out: sn lost 2nd: wknd over 1f out: eased fnl f: t.o* **25/1** | |

3m 31.9s (-7.00) **Going Correction** -0.40s/f (Firm) 7 Ran SP% **114.1**
Speed ratings (Par 101): **101,100,98,95,93 92,74**
CSF £9.01 CT £24.99 TOTE £4.10: £1.90, £1.50; EX 10.00 Trifecta £29.50.
**Owner** Itsfuninit **Bred** Cranford Stud **Trained** Aberthin, Vale of Glamorgan

**FOCUS**
A moderate staying race.
T/Plt: £3.40 to a £1 stake.Pool: £50,993.00 - 14,577.13 winning units. T/Qpdt: £2.70 to a £1 stake.Pool: £3,027.00 - 1,120.10 winning units. **Richard Lowther**

## 3615 GOODWOOD (R-H)

Friday, June 16

**OFFICIAL GOING: Straight course - good; round course - good to firm (watered; 7.8)**

Wind: virtually nil Weather: mainly sunny

### 3776 FEDERATION OF BLOODSTOCK AGENTS NOVICE AUCTION STKS (PLUS 10 RACE) 6f

**6:05** (6:05) (Class 4) 2-Y-O **£6,469** (£1,925; £962; £481) **Stalls** High

Form RPR

2 **1** **Royal Household**[20] 3093 2-8-13 0 HollieDoyle(3) 3 77+
(Richard Hannon) *unf: racd keenly: sn led: rdn over 1f out: styd on strly and drew clr ins fnl f: readily* **5/6**[1]

521 **2** 3 ¼ **May Remain**[21] 3029 2-9-8 0 JamieSpencer 6 73
(Paul Cole) *trckd wnr: effrt to chal wl over 1f out: no ex u.p and btn ins fnl f: wknd fnl 75yds* **7/2**[2]

**3** 1 **Rainbow Jazz (IRE)** 2-9-2 0 SteveDrowne 1 64
(Mark Usher) *w'like: q tall: v noisy in prelims: sn trcking ldrs: rdn 2f out: unable qck w ldrs over 1f out: styd on same pce ins fnl f* **20/1**

**4** nk **Spanish Star (IRE)** 2-8-13 0 CharlieBennett(3) 7 63
(Patrick Chamings) *cl-cpld: dwlt: rcvrd to trck ldrs after 2f: effrt 2f out: unable qck w ldrs over 1f out: kpt on same pce ins fnl f* **25/1**

**5** 2 ½ **Expediate** 2-9-2 0 DougieCostello 4 56
(Robert Cowell) *cmpt: dwlt: niggled along in rr: rdn and hdwy into 5th over 1f out: kpt on same pce and no imp ins fnl f* **8/1**

**6** 2 **Champs Inblue** 2-9-2 0 ShaneKelly 2 50
(Pat Phelan) *w'like: q tall: rn green: hld up in last pair: rdn over 2f out: no imp: wl hld and kpt on same pce fr over 1f out* **25/1**

0 **7** ¾ **Dream Of Delphi (IRE)**[11] 3390 2-8-11 0 JimCrowley 5 42
(William Haggas) *cmpt: chsd ldrs early: grad lost pl: rdn over 2f out: bhd and wl hld over 1f out* **6/1**[3]

1m 13.8s (1.60) **Going Correction** +0.15s/f (Good) 7 Ran SP% **114.6**
Speed ratings (Par 95): **95,90,89,88,85 82,81**
CSF £3.88 TOTE £1.70: £1.10, £1.60; EX 3.60 Trifecta £29.10.
**Owner** HP Racing Royal Household **Bred** Dusting Partnership **Trained** East Everleigh, Wilts

**FOCUS**
Races 2, 5 & 6 increased by 10yds. The going was good on the Straight course and good to firm on the Round course. The winner proved hard to catch under the stands' rail. This has been rated around the 2nd.

### 3777 LAYLA'S 40TH BIRTHDAY APPRENTICE H'CAP 7f

**6:35** (6:35) (Class 4) (0-85,87) 4-Y-O+ **£6,469** (£1,925; £962; £481) **Stalls** Low

Form RPR

1060 **1** **In The Red (IRE)**[13] 3324 4-8-13 **80** MillyNaseb(5) 4 86
(Martin Smith) *hld up in last trio: pushed along over 2f out: hdwy u.p 1f out: r.o strly to ld towards fin* **10/1**

0005 **2** nk **Majestic Moon (IRE)**[21] 3030 7-9-8 **84** ShelleyBirkett 1 89
(Julia Feilden) *led: rdn wl over 1f out: kpt on wl u.p tl hdd and no ex towards fin* **8/1**

-501 **3** ¾ **Noble Peace**[21] 3030 4-9-6 **85** DavidEgan(3) 7 88+
(Henry Candy) *lw: bustled along in midfield early: nt clr run over 2f out: trying to force a way through whn squeezed for room over 1f out: hdwy and swtchd lft ins fnl f: r.o strly: nvr getting to ldng pair* **3/1**[1]

44-1 **4** ¾ **Joe Packet**[20] 3074 10-8-10 **79** Pierre-LouisJamin(7) 8 80
(Jonathan Portman) *hld up in last pair: hdwy on outer wl over 1f out: chsd ldr 1f out: styd on and ev ch 100yds out: no ex and jst outpcd towards fin* **14/1**

340 **5** 2 **Fiftyshadesofgrey (IRE)**[41] 2390 6-9-9 **85** (p) HectorCrouch 3 81
(George Baker) *dwlt: sn rcvrd and in tch in midfield: clsd and nt clrest of runs over 2f out: effrt to chse ldr 2f out: sn rdn: unable qck and lost 2nd 1f out: wknd fnl 100yds* **4/1**[3]

6-22 **6** 1 **Pastoral Player**[21] 3030 10-9-11 **87** CharlieBennett 5 80
(Hughie Morrison) *taken down early: squeezed for room leaving stalls: hld up in tch in last trio: swtchd lft and effrt jst over 2f out: hdwy to chse ldrs and edgd rt over 1f out: no imp 1f out and kpt on same pce ins fnl f* **7/2**[2]

00-6 **7** 1 ¾ **Field Of Vision (IRE)**[18] 3161 4-8-9 **78** SophieScardifield(7) 2 66
(Joseph Tuite) *restless in stalls: t.k.h: chsd ldng pair: swtchd lft over 2f out: rdn and unable qck over 1f out: lost pl and wknd ins fnl f* **25/1**

60-0 **8** 2 ½ **Monteverdi (FR)**[18] 3161 4-9-8 **84** (b[1]) LucyKBarry 6 66
(Jamie Osborne) *wnt rt s: chsd ldng trio: effrt 2f out: keeping on same pce whn pushed rt and hmpd over 1f out: dropped to rr and wl hld fnl f* **8/1**

6000 **9** ¾ **Pearl Spectre (USA)**[13] 3324 6-9-9 **85** HollieDoyle 9 65
(Phil McEntee) *chsd ldr tl 2f out: unable qck u.p whn bdly hmpd over 1f out: dropped to rr and n.d after* **12/1**

1m 26.79s (-0.21) **Going Correction** -0.25s/f (Firm) 9 Ran SP% **116.7**
Speed ratings (Par 105): **91,90,89,88,86 85,83,80,79**
CSF £87.83 CT £303.51 TOTE £11.00: £2.70, £2.90, £1.60; EX 91.60 Trifecta £451.70.
**Owner** Sunville Rail Limited **Bred** Airlie Stud **Trained** Newmarket, Suffolk
■ Stewards' Enquiry : David Egan eight-day ban: careless riding (Jun 30-Jul 7)

**FOCUS**
Race distance increased by 10yds. An average handicap and they went a sound gallop.

### 3778 SIR ERIC PARKER MEMORIAL H'CAP 1m 1f 197y

**7:10** (7:11) (Class 3) (0-90,89) 3-Y-O **£9,703** (£2,887; £1,443; £721) **Stalls** Low

Form RPR

41 **1** **Mudaarab (USA)**[44] 2300 3-9-3 **85** JimCrowley 1 91
(Sir Michael Stoute) *q str: lw: w ldr for 2f: trckd ldr after: pushed along 2f out: clsd u.p and ev ch ent fnl f: led ins fnl f: r.o wl: rdn out* **3/1**[2]

00-6 **2** 1 **Bear Valley (IRE)**[49] 2132 3-9-6 **88** DavidProbert 3 92
(Mark Johnston) *led and set stdy gallop: rdn wl over 1f out: edgd lft u.p ent fnl f: hdd and styd on same pce ins fnl f* **10/1**

40-1 **3** hd **Eynhallow**[22] 3005 3-8-13 **81** JamieSpencer 4 85+
(Roger Charlton) *stdd s: t.k.h: hld up in last pair: pushed along to cl over 2f out: swtchd lft 2f out: rdn ent fnl f: wnt 4th and hung rt ins fnl f: r.o wl towards fin* **5/4**[1]

41-0 **4** nk **Anythingtoday (IRE)**[49] 2132 3-9-0 **82** JamesDoyle 5 85
(Hugo Palmer) *lw: t.k.h: hld up in midfield: clsd and swtchd rt 2f out: switching lft and drvn to press ldrs ent fnl f: kpt on same pce fnl 150yds* **6/1**[3]

6-40 **5** 2 ¾ **Zymyran**[27] 2824 3-8-13 **81** HarryBentley 6 79
(David Simcock) *hld up in tch in last pair: clsd over 2f out: rdn wl over 1f out: unable qck u.p ent fnl f: wknd ins fnl f* **9/1**

43-4 **6** 1 ¼ **Jackhammer (IRE)**[65] 1725 3-9-7 **89** SilvestreDeSousa 2 84
(William Knight) *t.k.h: chsd ldng pair: rdn over 2f out: unable qck over 1f out: wknd ins fnl f* **8/1**

2m 9.46s (1.36) **Going Correction** -0.25s/f (Firm) 6 Ran SP% **113.9**
Speed ratings (Par 103): **84,83,83,82,80 79**
CSF £31.41 TOTE £3.40: £2.00, £3.50; EX 20.90 Trifecta £91.30.
**Owner** Hamdan Al Maktoum **Bred** Grousemont Farm **Trained** Newmarket, Suffolk

**FOCUS**
A fair handicap featuring a couple of last-time-out winners, though it was run at a slow tempo, favouring those ridden prominently.

### 3779 SUSSEX ROOF GARDEN H'CAP 1m 3f 218y

**7:40** (7:43) (Class 4) (0-85,83) 3-Y-O **£6,469** (£1,925; £962; £481) **Stalls** High

Form RPR

-033 **1** **Galactic Prince**[7] 3531 3-8-13 **75** DavidProbert 5 82
(Andrew Balding) *hld up in tch in midfield: clsd to trck ldrs 4f out: pressed wnr and stl travelling strly 2f out: sn rdn: led ins fnl f: kpt on wl: rdn out* **4/1**[2]

5131 **2** nk **Road To Dubai (IRE)**[7] 3531 3-8-13 **75** SilvestreDeSousa 7 81
(George Scott) *led and set stdy gallop: qcknd over 3f out: rdn and wnt clr w wnr 2f out: hdd and wnt sharply lft u.p ins fnl f: kpt on but hld towards fin* **13/8**[1]

4324 **3** 2 ½ **Koeman**[7] 3520 3-8-8 **75** DavidEgan(5) 2 77
(Mick Channon) *hld up in tch: rdn over 3f out: hdwy to dispute 3rd but outpcd by ldng pair 2f: hung lft over 1f out: kpt on to go 3rd ins fnl f: nvr enough pce to threaten ldrs* **16/1**

0015 **4** ½ **Duke Of Bronte**[27] 2824 3-9-7 **83** JimCrowley 6 84
(Rod Millman) *lw: chsd ldr tl 5f out: pushed along and outpcd 2f out: rallied ins fnl f: styd on to go 4th towards fin: no threat to ldng pair* **5/1**[3]

4-51 **5** hd **Twenty Times (IRE)**[10] 3425 3-8-11 **73** 6ex ShaneKelly 3 73
(Richard Hughes) *hld up wl in tch in midfield: lost pl and rdn 2f out: sme hdwy on inner ent fnl f: styd on ins fnl f: wout threatening ldng pair* **13/2**

5530 **6** ¾ **Fields Of Fortune**[7] 3531 3-8-8 **70** HarryBentley 4 69
(Richard Hannon) *chsd ldrs tl wnt 2nd 5f out: rdn over 2f out: sn dropped to 3rd and unable qck 2f out: kpt on same pce after: lost 3 pls ins fnl f* **25/1**

055- **7** ½ **City Limits**[268] 6663 3-9-0 **76** (t) LukeMorris 1 74
(Luca Cumani) *lw: hld up in tch in last pair: effrt over 2f out: no imp u.p over 1f out: kpt on same pce ins fnl f* **9/1**

0-22 **8** 6 **War At Sea (IRE)**[116] 840 3-9-5 **81** JamieSpencer 8 70
(David Simcock) *stdd s and dropped in bhd: hdwy on outer to press for 3rd 2f out: outpcd and btn whn swtchd rt over 1f out: wknd ins fnl f* **14/1**

2m 43.49s (5.09) **Going Correction** -0.25s/f (Firm) 8 Ran SP% **114.5**
Speed ratings (Par 101): **73,72,71,70,70 70,69,65**
CSF £10.92 CT £90.69 TOTE £4.40: £1.90, £1.10, £5.10; EX 12.30 Trifecta £86.30.
**Owner** J C Smith **Bred** Littleton Stud **Trained** Kingsclere, Hants

**FOCUS**
An interesting handicap in which it again paid to race prominently off an ordinary gallop.

### 3780 LADY'S NEWSPAPER H'CAP 1m

**8:15** (8:19) (Class 4) (0-85,85) 3-Y-O **£6,469** (£1,925; £962; £481) **Stalls** Low

Form RPR

4120 **1** **I'vegotthepower (IRE)**[27] 2824 3-8-13 **77** (v) SilvestreDeSousa 8 91
(Brian Meehan) *wnt lft s: sn led: rdn 2f out: drvn and hdd 1f out: battled bk u.p to ld again ins fnl f: edging lft and hld on wl towards fin* **8/1**

3224 **2** hd **Marzouq (USA)**[13] 3317 3-9-2 **85** DavidEgan(5) 4 98
(Jeremy Noseda) *in tch in midfield and niggled along at times: hdwy to chse wnr and edgd lft u.p over 2f out: led 1f out: drvn and hdd ins fnl f: kpt on but a jst hld after* **15/8**[1]

2155 **3** 7 **Tafaakhor (IRE)**[16] 3211 3-9-5 **83** JimCrowley 7 80
(Richard Hannon) *hld up in tch in rr of main gp: nt clrest of runs over 2f out: rdn to chse ldng pair and edgd rt over 1f out: no imp and wknd ins fnl f* **9/2**[2]

1- **4** 1 ¼ **Mr Minerals**[182] 8404 3-9-2 **80** ShaneKelly 2 74+
(Richard Hughes) *str: lw: stdd s: t.k.h: hld up in tch: clsd to chse ldrs whn bdly hmpd jst over 2f out: no ch w ldrs after: kpt on to go modest 4th ins fnl f* **6/1**

6-10 **5** 2 ¾ **Masterofdiscovery**[51] 2088 3-8-11 **75** (b) JohnFahy 6 63
(Clive Cox) *chsd ldrs: rdn whn pushed rt and bmpd over 2f out: sn struggling: 4th and wknd over 1f out* **14/1**

300 **6** 4 ½ **Poetic Force (IRE)**[35] 2567 3-9-0 **78** GeorgeDowning 5 55
(Tony Carroll) *taken down early: chsd ldrs: wnt 2nd 1/2-way tl pushed rt and bmpd over 2f out: no ch after: wknd over 1f out* **16/1**

3-00 **7** 2 **Haulani (USA)**[22] 2998 3-8-12 **76** (t) JamieSpencer 3 49
(Philip Hide) *stdd s: sn detached in last and nvr gng wl: n.d* **9/1**

651 **8** 1 **Gloriosus (USA)**[16] 3206 3-9-3 **81** JamesDoyle 1 51
(Mark Johnston) *chsd wnr tl 1/2-way: losing pl whedm n.m.r ent fnl 2f: sn dropped and wknd fnl f* **5/1**[3]

1m 37.51s (-2.39) **Going Correction** -0.25s/f (Firm) 8 Ran SP% **117.6**
Speed ratings (Par 101): **101,100,93,92,89 85,83,82**
CSF £24.17 CT £79.28 TOTE £6.60: £2.00, £1.20, £1.70; EX 28.30 Trifecta £111.60.
**Owner** S E Sangster & Partner **Bred** D Farrington, P Gately, T Killarney **Trained** Manton, Wilts
■ Stewards' Enquiry : David Egan 2 day ban - guilty of careless riding (9/10 July)

**FOCUS**
Race distance increased by 10yds. An average handicap in which they went a fair gallop. They finished strung out, and the first two went clear. The winner was given a good ride from the front by Silvestre De Sousa, who was riding his sixth winner of the day.

### 3781 SIGMA MAIDEN STKS 1m

**8:45** (8:48) (Class 5) 3-Y-O+ **£3,234** (£962; £481; £240) **Stalls** Low

Form RPR

42- **1** **Harbour Rock**[255] 7034 3-9-0 0 JamieSpencer 3 79+
(David Simcock) *stdd s: hld up in rr: effrt 2f out: clsd to chal u.p jst over 1f out: drvn to ld jst ins fnl f: styd on to assert towards fin: eased cl home* **3/1**[2]

3-24 **2** ½ **Envisaging (IRE)**[135] 504 3-9-0 76 SilvestreDeSousa 4 78
(James Fanshawe) *t.k.h: hld up in 3rd: clsd to ld 2f out: sn edgd rt u.p: drvn and hdd jst ins fnl f: kpt on but nt quite match pce of wnr fnl 100yds* **9/2**[3]

2-22 **3** 3 ¼ **Cool Team (IRE)**[22] 2997 3-9-0 79 (t[1]) JamesDoyle 1 71
(Hugo Palmer) *lw: chsd ldr: effrt to press ldrs over 2f out: struggling to qckn whn sltly impeded wl over 1f out: 3rd and no imp fnl f* **8/11**[1]

63-0 **4** *1* **Brise De Mer (FR)**[39] 2484 3-9-0 77.................................... JimCrowley 2 68
(George Baker) *sltly on toes: led tl 2f out: outpcd and nt that much room sn after: pushed along in 4th and kpt on same pce fnl f* **9/1**
1m 39.85s (-0.05) **Going Correction** -0.25s/f (Firm) **4** Ran SP% **111.1**
Speed ratings (Par 103): **90,89,86,85**
CSF £15.25 TOTE £3.40; EX 12.00 Trifecta £15.90.
**Owner** Qatar Racing Limited **Bred** Christopher Humber **Trained** Newmarket, Suffolk
**FOCUS**
Race distance increased by 10yds. Not a strong maiden, but they went a fair gallop and there was a tight finish involving the first two, who came clear of the third.
T/Plt: £72.00 to a £1 stake. Pool: £46,042.00 - 638.67 winning units. T/Qpdt: £21.90 to a £1 stake. Pool: £3,042.00 - 138.28 winning units. **Steve Payne**

## 3502 SANDOWN (R-H)

Friday, June 16

**OFFICIAL GOING: Good (good to firm in places) changing to good to firm (good in places) after race 2 (2.35)**
Wind: Moderate, against in home straight Weather: Fine

### 3782 BRITISH STALLION STUDS EBF NOVICE STKS 5f 10y
**2:00** (2:01) (Class 5) 2-Y-O **£3,881** (£1,155; £577; £288) **Stalls** Low

Form RPR
65 **1** **Branscombe**[15] 3254 2-9-2 0.................................... SilvestreDeSousa 1 77+
(Mark Johnston) *hung lft after s but qckly away: mde all: shkn up over 1f out: kpt on and a in command: jinked lft nr fin* **8/1**
**2** *1* **Global Passion (FR)** 2-9-2 0.................................... WilliamBuick 3 73+
(Charles Hills) *trckd ldng trio: swtchd lft 2f out: rdn and prog over 1f out: styd on fnl f to take 2nd last strides* **9/2**[2]
3 **3** *hd* **Glaceon (IRE)**[8] 3502 2-8-11 0.................................... RyanMoore 7 68
(Richard Hannon) *chsd wnr 2f: sn pushed along: rdn to chse wnr again fnl f: kpt on but nvr pce to chal: lost 2nd last strides* **5/4**[1]
0 **4** *1 ½* **New Empire**[29] 2769 2-9-2 0.................................... JimCrowley 5 67+
(Peter Chapple-Hyam) *dwlt: in tch in rr: pushed along over 1f out: kpt on steadily fnl f* **11/2**[3]
0 **5** *1 ¾* **Wiff Waff**[18] 3135 2-9-2 0....................................(t[1]) SeanLevey 9 61
(Stuart Williams) *prom: chsd wnr after 2f: rdn 2f out: no imp and wknd fnl f* **40/1**
**6** *nse* **Dream Prospect** 2-9-2 0.................................... HarryBentley 10 61
(Roger Charlton) *dwlt: racd on outer: in tch: rdn over 1f out: one pce and no imp ldrs* **15/2**
0 **7** *1 ½* **Mossketeer**[15] 3245 2-9-2 0.................................... KierenFox 2 55
(John Best) *hld up in 5th: shkn up over 1f out: no prog* **25/1**
6 **8** *8* **Haven's View**[39] 2473 2-9-2 0.................................... ShaneKelly 4 27
(Richard Hughes) *dwlt: in tch in rr tl wknd over 1f out* **16/1**
**9** *10* **Swift Fox** 2-9-2 0.................................... TimmyMurphy 8
(Gary Moore) *dwlt: outpcd and a wl bhd* **66/1**
1m 1.97s (0.37) **Going Correction** -0.10s/f (Good) **9** Ran SP% **114.5**
Speed ratings (Par 93): **93,91,91,88,85 85,83,70,54**
CSF £42.90 TOTE £9.90: £2.90, £1.20, £1.10; EX 50.50 Trifecta £120.40.
**Owner** Sheikh Hamdan bin Mohammed Al Maktoum **Bred** Godolphin **Trained** Middleham Moor, N Yorks
**FOCUS**
Round course railed out from 1m1f, around home bend and out 6yds in home straight, adding 19yds to all round course distances. A warm, sunny day. This looked an ordinary novice race.

### 3783 EBFSTALLIONS.COM JUDY MAYNARD "HELLO DARLING" MAIDEN STKS 7f
**2:35** (2:37) (Class 5) 2-Y-O **£3,881** (£1,155; £577; £288) **Stalls** Low

Form RPR
**1** **Falmouth Light (FR)** 2-9-5 0.................................... SilvestreDeSousa 2 78
(Mark Johnston) *pressed ldr: led 2f out: sn shkn up: rdn fnl f: hung lft nr fin but hld on* **5/1**[3]
**2** *hd* **Master Of Wine (GER)** 2-9-5 0.................................... DavidProbert 6 77
(Andrew Balding) *trckd ldrs: shkn up 2f out: prog to take 2nd fnl f: styd on nr fin: jst hld* **8/1**
**3** *1* **George Villiers (IRE)** 2-9-5 0.................................... RobertTart 7 75+
(John Gosden) *hld up in 6th: rn green whn shkn up jst over 2f out: prog over 1f out: tk 3rd ins fnl f: styd on and nrst fin* **9/4**[1]
**4** *3* **Connect** 2-9-5 0.................................... SamHitchcott 10 67
(Clive Cox) *t.k.h early: cl up on outer: shkn up and nt qckn 2f out: one pce after* **8/1**
5 **5** *hd* **Musbaq (USA)**[26] 2852 2-9-5 0.................................... JimCrowley 1 66
(Mark Johnston) *led to 2f out: wknd fnl f* **7/1**
**6** *1 ¼* **Sallab (IRE)** 2-9-5 0.................................... RyanMoore 9 63
(Richard Hannon) *trckd ldrs: pushed along and lost pl over 2f out: no ch over 1f out* **10/3**[2]
**7** *1* **Font Vert (FR)** 2-9-5 0.................................... FranBerry 3 60+
(Ralph Beckett) *a in rr: pushed along and no prog 2f out* **18/1**
**8** *3 ½* **Giovanni Medici** 2-9-5 0.................................... TomQueally 8 51
(Seamus Durack) *slowly away: rn green in detached last: threatening to make prog whn n.m.r 2f out: wknd fnl f* **66/1**
0 **9** *14* **Vice Marshal (IRE)**[17] 3164 2-9-5 0.................................... StevieDonohoe 4 13
(Charlie Fellowes) *a in rr: wknd over 2f out: t.o* **50/1**
1m 30.09s (0.59) **Going Correction** -0.275s/f (Firm) **9** Ran SP% **114.0**
Speed ratings (Par 93): **85,84,83,80,79 78,77,73,57**
CSF £43.83 TOTE £6.20: £2.30, £2.50, £1.40; EX 49.20 Trifecta £182.30.
**Owner** Abdulla Al Mansoori **Bred** Rashit Shaykhutdinov **Trained** Middleham Moor, N Yorks
**FOCUS**
Add 19yds. The ground was changed to good to firm, good in places after this race. Not much got involved and the bare form is probably just fair to useful, but a few of these ought to progress, not least the winner.

### 3784 RACING UK FREE FOR A MONTH H'CAP 7f
**3:10** (3:10) (Class 5) (0-75,77) 3-Y-O **£3,881** (£1,155; £577; £288) **Stalls** Low

Form RPR
564- **1** **Call Me Grumpy (IRE)**[231] 7664 3-9-1 69.................... SilvestreDeSousa 6 83+
(Roger Varian) *hld up in midfield: smooth prog fr 2f out: led jst over 1f out: pushed clr: comf* **7/4**[1]
0-20 **2** *2 ¼* **Endless Gold**[35] 2567 3-9-7 75....................(p[1]) WilliamBuick 5 78
(Charlie Appleby) *trckd ldr after 2f to over 1f out: shkn up and styd on fnl f to take 2nd again nr fin* **3/1**[2]
6-3 **3** *½* **Halawain (USA)**[44] 2304 3-9-6 74.................................... JamesDoyle 12 75
(John Quinn) *led: rdn over 1f out: sn hdd and outpcd: lost 2nd nr fin* **20/1**

4136 **4** *nse* **Revel**[25] 2894 3-9-6 74....................................(t) HarryBentley 14 75+
(Stuart Williams) *t.k.h: hld up in 11th and off the pce: shkn up on outer over 2f out: prog over 1f out: styd on to take 4th last strides* **20/1**
1-60 **5** *shd* **Thaaqib**[21] 3040 3-9-9 77....................................(b[1]) JimCrowley 10 78
(Charles Hills) *hld up towards rr: pushed along fr 2f out: styd on steadily: nvr nrr* **12/1**
5-66 **6** *½* **Teqany (IRE)**[44] 2293 3-9-4 72.................................... DavidProbert 11 72
(Owen Burrows) *hld up towards rr: shkn up 2f out: kpt on fr over 1f out: nvr pce to threaten* **12/1**
650 **7** *½* **Jumping Jack (IRE)**[34] 2625 3-9-4 72....................(h[1]) ShaneKelly 4 70
(Richard Hughes) *trckd ldrs on inner: pushed along 2f out: nt qckn over 1f out: kpt on same pce fnl f* **20/1**
0-13 **8** *½* **Derek Duval (USA)**[85] 1332 3-9-3 74....................(t) AaronJones[(3)] 8 71+
(Stuart Williams) *hld up in midfield on inner: nvr clrest of runs whn trying to make prog fr 2f out: kpt on same pce fnl f* **10/1**[3]
20-3 **9** *nse* **Bequia (IRE)**[45] 2280 3-9-0 75.................................... JoshuaBryan[(7)] 9 72
(Martyn Meade) *t.k.h: trckd ldrs: rdn over 2f out: lost pl fnl f* **33/1**
0-45 **10** *nk* **Milburn Jack**[51] 2090 3-9-5 73.................................... SamHitchcott 3 69
(Clive Cox) *t.k.h: trckd ldr 2f: styd prom tl wknd fnl f* **14/1**
1-60 **11** *nk* **Native Soldier (IRE)**[29] 2755 3-9-9 77....................(h[1]) TomQueally 2 72
(William Haggas) *awkward s and slowly away: detached in last pair: hanging whn shkn up over 2f out: nvr on terms but kpt on fnl f* **25/1**
060- **12** *6* **Innstigator**[167] 8591 3-8-9 63.................................... LukeMorris 7 42
(Ralph J Smith) *chsd ldrs tl 2f out: wknd over 1f out* **50/1**
060- **13** *16* **Singula**[241] 7424 3-8-12 66.................................... FergusSweeney 1 2
(Alan King) *awkward s and slowly away: a detached in last: t.o* **33/1**
1m 28.68s (-0.82) **Going Correction** -0.275s/f (Firm) **13** Ran SP% **118.5**
Speed ratings (Par 99): **93,90,89,89,89 89,88,87,87,87 87,80,62**
CSF £5.65 CT £80.09 TOTE £2.80: £1.40, £1.30, £5.20; EX 9.30 Trifecta £118.80.
**Owner** Willie Leung **Bred** Peter Kelly **Trained** Newmarket, Suffolk
**FOCUS**
Add 19yds. Plenty for the notebook in behind the winner, who proved really well handicapped.

### 3785 GEORGE LINDON-TRAVERS MEMORIAL H'CAP 1m 1f 209y
**3:45** (3:46) (Class 3) (0-90,89) 4-Y-O+
**£9,337** (£2,796; £1,398; £699; £349; £175) **Stalls** Low

Form RPR
-411 **1** **Shargiah (IRE)**[24] 2920 4-9-7 89.................................... SilvestreDeSousa 2 104+
(Roger Varian) *trckd ldrs: shkn up and clsd to ld 2f out: drvn into clr ld over 1f out: kpt on wl* **11/8**[1]
14-3 **2** *2 ½* **Artful Rogue (IRE)**[163] 38 6-8-12 80.................................... GavinLerena 4 87
(Amanda Perrett) *hld up in 7th: nt clr run and squeezed between rivals wl 1f out: shkn up and prog to take 2nd last 150yds: styd on wl but no ch to threaten* **33/1**
-232 **3** *3 ½* **Prendergast Hill (IRE)**[21] 3027 5-8-12 80................(p) DougieCostello 1 80
(Ed de Giles) *hld up in midfield: rdn and prog whn nudged by rival wl over 1f out: styd on to take 2nd briefly jst ins fnl f: one pce after* **10/1**
-245 **4** *1 ½* **Cape Banjo (USA)**[23] 2960 4-8-11 79.................................... FranBerry 6 76
(Ralph Beckett) *led at gd pce: jnd after 2f: rdn and hdd 2f out: steadily fdd* **14/1**
344- **5** *hd* **Richie McCaw**[251] 7159 4-8-9 77.................................... DavidProbert 8 74+
(Ian Williams) *hld up in last: gd prog on wd outside over 2f out: chsd wnr over 1f out to to jst ins fnl f: wknd* **7/2**[2]
65-1 **6** *1 ½* **Solo Hunter**[46] 2233 6-9-0 89....................................(b) JoshuaBryan[(7)] 7 83
(Martyn Meade) *prog to join ldr at gd pce after 2f to 2f out: steadily wknd* **8/1**
0660 **7** *1 ½* **Zamperini (IRE)**[29] 2752 5-8-11 79.................................... MartinDwyer 3 70
(Mike Murphy) *hld up in last trio: rdn and struggling over 3f out: no prog after* **16/1**
115- **8** *10* **Proctor**[266] 6735 4-9-0 82.................................... MartinLane 5 53
(Stuart Kittow) *trckd ldrs: rdn and wknd 3f out: eased over 1f out* **14/1**
-300 **9** *2 ¼* **Top Beak (IRE)**[14] 3300 4-9-5 87....................................(t) SeanLevey 9 53
(Hughie Morrison) *trckd ldr 2f: styd prom to 3f out: hrd rdn and btn whn nudged by rival wl over 1f out: wknd qckly* **7/1**[3]
2m 5.8s (-4.70) **Going Correction** -0.275s/f (Firm) **9** Ran SP% **119.2**
Speed ratings (Par 107): **107,105,102,101,100 99,98,90,88**
CSF £59.22 CT £356.93 TOTE £2.30: £1.10, £6.10, £3.30; EX 43.00 Trifecta £268.90.
**Owner** Saif Ali **Bred** Rabbah Bloodstock Limited **Trained** Newmarket, Suffolk
**FOCUS**
Add 19yds. A decent handicap.

### 3786 SUPPORTING BRITISH STALLIONS EBF FILLIES' H'CAP 1m
**4:20** (4:21) (Class 4) (0-85,82) 3-Y-O **£6,469** (£1,925; £962; £481) **Stalls** Low

Form RPR
1 **1** **Time Chaser**[53] 2019 3-9-6 81.................................... JamesDoyle 9 88+
(Roger Charlton) *trckd ldr: led 2f out: rdn and hdd over 1f out: led again ins fnl f: drvn out* **6/4**[1]
31 **2** *nk* **Tirania**[25] 2908 3-9-7 82.................................... SilvestreDeSousa 4 88+
(William Haggas) *trckd ldng trio: clsd 2f out: rdn to ld over 1f out: hung lft and hdd ins fnl f: drvn and kpt on wl nr fin* **6/4**[1]
104- **3** *nk* **Stellar Surprise**[256] 7016 3-9-1 76.................................... HarryBentley 1 81
(Stuart Williams) *trckd ldng pair to 2f out: eased off rail and rdn to take 3rd again over 1f out: drvn and r.o fnl f: gaining at fin* **16/1**
061- **4** *4* **Medicean Ballet (IRE)**[240] 7466 3-9-1 76.................................... FergusSweeney 2 72
(Henry Candy) *dwlt: hld up in 7th: pushed along over 2f out: kpt on to take 4th fnl f: no ch but nt disgracd* **20/1**
213- **5** *1 ¾* **Golden Nectar**[184] 8360 3-9-2 77.................................... GeorgeDowning 6 69
(Laura Mongan) *hld up in last: hung lft and stl there 2f out: no ch but kpt on ins fnl f* **50/1**
0-21 **6** *½* **Highland Pass**[20] 3062 3-9-3 78....................................(h) DavidProbert 3 69
(Andrew Balding) *trckd ldrs in 5th: nt clr run over 2f out: shkn up and wknd wl over 1f out* **5/1**[2]
42-0 **7** *nk* **Midnight Vixen**[45] 2269 3-8-11 72.................................... RyanMoore 8 62
(Sir Michael Stoute) *led: rdn and hdd 2f out: sn wknd* **20/1**
200- **8** *2* **High On Love (IRE)**[251] 7147 3-9-6 81.................................... StevieDonohoe 7 66
(Charlie Fellowes) *t.k.h: hld up in 8th: pushed along and no ch whn nt clr run over 1f out: sn wknd* **33/1**
4325 **9** *1 ¾* **Plead**[27] 2827 3-9-6 81....................................(b) JackMitchell 5 62
(Archie Watson) *in tch in 6th tl wknd u.p 2f out* **12/1**[3]
1m 43.5s (0.20) **Going Correction** -0.275s/f (Firm) **9** Ran SP% **124.7**
Speed ratings (Par 98): **88,87,87,83,81 81,80,78,77**
CSF £3.87 CT £26.01 TOTE £2.50: £1.20, £1.10, £4.10; EX 5.50 Trifecta £53.00.
**Owner** K Abdullah **Bred** Juddmonte Farms Ltd **Trained** Beckhampton, Wilts

**FOCUS**
Add 19yds. A useful fillies' handicap.

## 3787 BECK H'CAP — 1m 1f 209y
4:50 (4:50) (Class 4) (0-80,80) 3-Y-O — £5,822 (£1,732; £865; £432) Stalls Low

Form | | | | RPR
1000 1 **Jupiter Light**[15] 3262 3-9-6 79 ....(b[1]) RobertTart 2 89
(John Gosden) *hld up tl trckd ldrs 1/2-way: waiting for room on inner over 2f out: gap appeared and chsd ldr over 1f out: drvn and styd on strly to ld last stride* **7/1**
41 2 *shd* **Archetype (FR)**[22] 2997 3-9-7 80 .... MartinLane 8 89
(Simon Crisford) *led: rdn over 1f out: styd on wl fnl f but hdd last stride* **3/1**[1]
00-1 3 *4* **Dream Machine (IRE)**[21] 3041 3-8-13 72 .... LouisSteward 4 73
(Michael Bell) *t.k.h: trckd ldr after 2f to over 1f out: sn btn but clung on for 3rd* **3/1**[1]
4-25 4 *nk* **Romanor**[32] 2689 3-9-7 80 ....(h) LukeMorris 7 80
(Ed Walker) *t.k.h: hld up: hrd rdn and nt qckn 2f out: kpt on fnl f to press for 3rd nr fin* **8/1**
2315 5 *nse* **Mullarkey**[28] 2784 3-9-1 74 .... KierenFox 1 74
(John Best) *chsd ldr 2f: rdn 3f out: steadily wknd fr 2f out* **11/2**[2]
6-53 6 *3* **Zamalight**[51] 2092 3-9-7 80 .... GavinLerena 5 74
(Amanda Perrett) *t.k.h: hld up in rr: rdn and no prog over 2f out: sn btn* **14/1**
-042 7 *hd* **Lunar Jet**[35] 2588 3-8-13 72 .... TomQueally 3 66
(John Mackie) *trckd ldrs: gng wl enough 3f out: shkn up and no rspnse 2f out: sn wknd* **6/1**[3]
-322 8 *20* **Testbourne (IRE)**[52] 2067 3-8-11 73 .... JordanVaughan(3) 6 27
(K R Burke) *hld up in rr: rdn over 2f out: hanging and fnd nil: wknd rapidly: t.o* **25/1**

2m 9.43s (-1.07) **Going Correction** -0.275s/f (Firm) **8 Ran SP% 113.8**
Speed ratings (Par 101): **93,92,89,89,89 87,86,70**
CSF £28.03 CT £76.38 TOTE £8.70: £2.40, £1.50, £1.50; EX 37.70 Trifecta £202.80.
**Owner** George Strawbridge **Bred** George Strawbridge **Trained** Newmarket, Suffolk

**FOCUS**
Add 19yds. A fair 3yo handicap.

## 3788 DR LUCY FREE H'CAP — 1m 6f
5:25 (5:25) (Class 5) (0-75,75) 3-Y-O — £3,881 (£1,155; £577; £288) Stalls Low

Form | | | | RPR
-601 1 **Dominating (GER)**[16] 3220 3-9-2 70 .... SilvestreDeSousa 2 80+
(Mark Johnston) *led 4f: sn in 3rd: reminder 1/2-way: effrt on inner to go 2nd 3f out and rdn to ld 2f out: carried hd awkwardly but kpt on u.p fnl f* **7/4**[1]
3125 2 *1* **Look My Way**[13] 3335 3-8-12 73 .... JoshuaBryan(7) 3 81
(Andrew Balding) *pressed ldr: led after 4f: rdn 3f out: hdd 2f out: kpt on after and clr of rest but a hld* **5/1**[3]
14-4 3 *8* **Oxford Blu**[15] 3261 3-8-10 64 ....(b[1]) LukeMorris 1 61
(Sir Mark Prescott Bt) *slowly away: racd in last: rdn 4f out: no prog u.p over 2f out: kpt on to take modest 3rd ins fnl f* **6/1**
-032 4 *2 ¾* **Chaparrachik (IRE)**[7] 3520 3-9-5 73 .... GavinLerena 5 66
(Amanda Perrett) *t.k.h: trckd ldrs: shkn up and nt qckn 3f out: sn wknd* **13/2**
2144 5 *hd* **Blushing Red (FR)**[14] 3291 3-9-7 75 .... WilliamBuick 4 68
(Ed Dunlop) *t.k.h: trckd ldrs: rdn to take 3rd over 2f out: lft bhd by ldng pair after: wknd fnl f* **10/3**[2]
220 6 *½* **Ulysses (GER)**[53] 2039 3-9-6 74 ....(b[1]) FranBerry 7 66
(Ralph Beckett) *drvn to go prom: chsd ldr after 4f to 3f out: sn wknd u.p* **16/1**

3m 3.19s (-1.31) **Going Correction** -0.275s/f (Firm) **6 Ran SP% 109.6**
Speed ratings (Par 99): **92,91,86,85,85 84**
CSF £10.26 TOTE £2.40: £1.40, £3.60; EX 10.70 Trifecta £45.60.
**Owner** A D Spence **Bred** Gestut Etzean **Trained** Middleham Moor, N Yorks

**FOCUS**
Add 19yds. A fair staying handicap.
T/Plt: £4.90 to a £1 stake.Pool: £60,274.00 - 12,122.99 winning units. T/Qpdt: £2.90 to a £1 stake.Pool: £4,076.00 - 1,380.67 winning units. **Jonathan Neesom**

# 3089 YORK (L-H)
Friday, June 16

**OFFICIAL GOING: Good to firm (good in places; 7.3)**
Wind: Strong half against Weather: Cloudy

## 3789 COOPERS MARQUEES BRITISH EBF NOVICE STKS (PLUS 10 RACE) — 5f
1:50 (1:52) (Class 3) 2-Y-O — £7,762 (£2,310; £1,154; £577) Stalls High

Form | | | | RPR
3 1 **Tulip Fever**[16] 3215 2-8-11 0 .... PatCosgrave 4 72+
(William Haggas) *dwlt: t.k.h towards rr: hdwy 2f out: chsd ldrs over 1f out: rdn and qcknd to ld narrowly ins fnl f: sn drvn: edgd lft and hld on wl towards fin* **5/2**[1]
2 2 *shd* **Sosian**[15] 3254 2-8-11 0 .... PaulHanagan 2 72+
(Richard Fahey) *pushed along and outpcd in rr: hdwy on outer wl over 1f out: rdn to chal ent fnl f: sn drvn: green and edgd rt: kpt on wl: jst hld* **4/1**[3]
3 3 *2* **Magic Mark**[25] 2882 2-8-11 0 .... CliffordLee(5) 1 70
(K R Burke) *trckd ldrs: cl up on outer 1/2-way: rdn and ev ch over 1f out: n.m.r jst ins fnl f: kpt on* **7/2**[2]
4 *hd* **Rumshak (IRE)** 2-9-2 0 .... PaulMulrennan 7 69+
(Michael Dods) *cl up: led wl over 1f out: green and wandered appr fnl f: sn hdd and kpt on same pce* **6/1**
0 5 *1 ½* **Laith Alareen**[31] 2698 2-9-2 0 ....(t[1]) PhillipMakin 9 64
(David O'Meara) *cl up: rdn wl over 1f out: slt ld jst over 1f out: hdd and drvn ins fnl f: wknd towards fin* **33/1**
06 6 *2* **Bad Dog**[10] 3429 2-8-13 0 .... NathanEvans(3) 5 56
(Michael Easterby) *towards rr: pushed along 2f out: sn rdn and n.d* **66/1**
4 7 *hd* **Hard Graft**[21] 3037 2-9-2 0 .... AndreaAtzeni 6 56
(David Brown) *led: pushed along over 2f out: rdn and hdd wl over 1f out: sn wknd* **4/1**[3]
526 8 *3 ¾* **Marnie James**[13] 3333 2-9-2 0 .... TomEaves 8 42
(Iain Jardine) *a towards rr* **22/1**

1m 0.35s (1.05) **Going Correction** +0.125s/f (Good) **8 Ran SP% 113.9**
Speed ratings (Par 97): **96,95,92,92,89 86,86,80**
CSF £12.51 TOTE £3.20: £1.20, £1.50, £1.50; EX 11.20 Trifecta £35.80.
**Owner** Mrs Deborah June James **Bred** Mrs D J James **Trained** Newmarket, Suffolk

**FOCUS**
Rail moved out 10yds on south bend from 9f to entrance to home straight. Riders after the fast confirmed the official going description. This wasn't a bad novice event. They went a decent pace down the centre and the two promising market leaders fought it out.

## 3790 PETER "SOOTY" SUTTON MEMORIAL H'CAP — 1m 2f 56y
2:20 (2:22) (Class 3) (0-95,102) 4-Y-O+
£12,450 (£3,728; £1,864; £932; £466; £234) Stalls Low

Form | | | | RPR
114 1 **Big Country (IRE)**[40] 2431 4-9-7 94 .... AndreaAtzeni 7 104+
(Michael Appleby) *trckd ldrs: hdwy over 2f out: chal over 1f out: rdn to take narrow advantage ent fnl f: sn drvn and edgd lft: hld on wl towards fin* **9/4**[1]
2-12 2 *nk* **Burguillos**[28] 2804 4-9-5 92 .... MartinHarley 8 101
(Alan King) *hld up: hdwy over 3f out: trckd ldrs 2f out: effrt: nt clr run and swtchd lft over 1f out: sn rdn to chal ent fnl f: sn drvn and ev ch: kpt on* **4/1**[2]
-024 3 *nk* **Dance King**[20] 3091 7-8-9 82 ....(tp) DavidAllan 10 90
(Tim Easterby) *hld up in midfield: hdwy over 2f out: rdn over 1f out: styd on strly fnl f* **12/1**
3062 4 *1* **Innocent Touch (IRE)**[14] 3300 6-9-5 92 .... TonyHamilton 9 98
(Richard Fahey) *trckd ldr: hdwy and cl up 2f out: rdn to dispute ld over 1f out: ev ch tl drvn and hld whn n.m.r ins fnl f* **12/1**
6422 5 *1* **Rainbow Rebel (IRE)**[8] 3486 4-9-0 87 .... FrannyNorton 2 91
(Mark Johnston) *plld hrd: trckd ldng pair on inner: hdwy and cl up 3f out: rdn along over 2f out: drvn over 1f out: kpt on same pce* **15/2**[3]
6430 6 *1* **Mulligatawny (IRE)**[15] 3255 4-9-0 87 .... ConnorBeasley 11 89
(Roger Fell) *midfield: hdwy over 2f out: rdn along wl over 1f out: kpt on fnl f* **25/1**
23 7 *hd* **Madroos**[20] 3095 4-8-4 80 ....(t[1]) NathanEvans(3) 1 82
(Michael Easterby) *plld hrd early: trckd ldrs on inner: hdwy 3f out: rdn along wl over 1f out: drvn and kpt on same pce fnl f* **10/1**
3-06 8 *hd* **Just Hiss**[8] 3498 4-8-12 88 .... RachelRichardson(3) 13 89
(Tim Easterby) *chsd ldrs on outer: rdn along over 2f out: grad wknd* **22/1**
210 9 *hd* **Storm King**[14] 3300 8-8-10 83 .... DanielMuscutt 4 84
(David C Griffiths) *led: rdn along 2f out: hdd ent fnl f: wknd* **25/1**
0013 10 *1* **Euchen Glen**[18] 3154 4-9-1 88 .... PJMcDonald 5 87
(Jim Goldie) *in tch on inner: pushed along and hdwy to chse ldrs over 2f out: rdn wl over 1f out: sn drvn and wknd* **14/1**
-030 11 *1 ½* **Stipulate**[14] 3298 8-8-13 91 .... MeganNicholls(5) 3 87
(Brian Ellison) *s.i.s and bhd: sme hdwy on outer over 3f out: rdn along over 2f out: n.d* **20/1**
440- 12 *4 ½* **Power Game**[226] 7765 5-9-4 91 .... DanielTudhope 14 78
(David O'Meara) *hld up: a towards rr* **25/1**
-330 13 *18* **Mica Mika (IRE)**[106] 991 9-8-9 82 .... PaulHanagan 12 33
(Richard Fahey) *dwlt: a rr* **40/1**

2m 11.0s (-1.50) **Going Correction** +0.025s/f (Good) **13 Ran SP% 116.8**
Speed ratings (Par 107): **107,106,106,105,104 104,103,103,103,102 101,98,83**
CSF £8.86 CT £87.91 TOTE £3.00: £1.60, £1.80, £3.40; EX 11.70 Trifecta £100.60.
**Owner** The Horse Watchers **Bred** Mrs Jacqueline O'Brien **Trained** Oakham, Rutland
■ Stewards' Enquiry : Andrea Atzeni 4 day ban - used his whip in the incorrect place (30 June - 3 July)

**FOCUS**
There was a muddling pace on in this decent handicap. The right horses came to the fore, though, and it's strong form. Race distance increased 32yds.

## 3791 SKF ROUS (S) STKS — 6f
2:55 (2:57) (Class 3) 2-Y-O — £9,703 (£2,887; £1,443; £721) Stalls High

Form | | | | RPR
40 1 **Seaella (IRE)**[17] 3179 2-8-9 0 .... JasonHart 7 69
(John Quinn) *racd centre: mde most. rdn over 1f out: drvn ins fnl f: kpt on wl towards fin* **13/2**[3]
2436 2 *1 ½* **The Love Doctor (IRE)**[27] 2826 2-9-0 0 .... DanielTudhope 18 69
(David Evans) *racd towards stands side: prom: hdwy over 2f out: rdn to chal over 1f out: drvn and ev ch ent fnl f: kpt on same pce towards fin* **3/1**[1]
21 3 *1 ¼* **Our Little Pony**[16] 3200 2-8-9 0 .... RichardKingscote 14 60
(Lawrence Mullaney) *racd towards stands side: prom: hdwy 2f out: rdn and ev ch ent fnl f: sn drvn and kpt on same pce* **9/2**[2]
0 4 *1* **Christmas Night**[16] 3200 2-9-0 0 .... JamesSullivan 15 62
(Ollie Pears) *racd towards stands side: towards rr: hdwy 2f out: sn rdn and kpt on wl fnl f* **66/1**
3661 5 *1* **Milton Road**[5] 3619 2-9-0 0 .... GrahamLee 8 59
(Mick Channon) *chsd ldrs centre: rdn along wl over 1f out: sn drvn and grad wknd* **13/2**[3]
6 *¾* **Where's Jeff** 2-8-7 0 .... HarrisonShaw(7) 16 57+
(Michael Easterby) *dwlt and bhd towards stands side: hdwy 2f out: rdn and kpt on wl fnl f: nrst fin* **33/1**
0 7 *4* **Laydee Victoria (IRE)**[25] 2896 2-8-9 0 .... JoeDoyle 2 40
(Ollie Pears) *racd towards centre: midfield: hdwy 2f out: sn rdn and no imp* **9/1**
03 8 *nse* **Placebo Effect (IRE)**[43] 2343 2-9-0 0 .... TomEaves 9 45
(Ollie Pears) *t.k.h: hld up towards rr: hdwy 2f out: sn rdn and kpt on fnl f* **20/1**
046 9 *1 ¾* **Faradays Spark (IRE)**[15] 3237 2-8-11 0 .... AdamMcNamara(3) 10 40
(Richard Fahey) *nvr bttr than midfield* **14/1**
05 10 *1 ¼* **Eyes Of Fire**[11] 3399 2-9-0 0 .... AndrewMullen 4 36
(Ollie Pears) *t.k.h: chsd ldrs centre: rdn along 2f out: sn wknd* **25/1**
06 11 *shd* **Roses In June (IRE)**[9] 3467 2-8-6 0 ....(p[1]) CallumShepherd(3) 13 31
(J S Moore) *racd towards stands side: a towards rr* **28/1**
05 12 *1* **Foxxy Brown**[8] 3483 2-8-9 0 .... TonyHamilton 17 28
(Richard Fahey) *a towards rr* **33/1**
0 13 *hd* **Mr Carbonator**[17] 3187 2-9-0 0 .... PaulHanagan 5 32
(Richard Fahey) *dwlt: a towards rr* **10/1**
50 14 *1* **Budgie**[17] 3165 2-9-0 0 .... JoeyHaynes 1 29
(Mark H Tompkins) *dwlt: a towards rr* **50/1**
0 15 *1 ½* **Miss Mazzie**[9] 3460 2-8-6 0 .... NathanEvans(3) 11 19
(Michael Easterby) *dwlt: a rr* **66/1**
55 16 *3* **Holmfirst**[16] 3200 2-9-0 0 .... PaulMulrennan 6 15
(Paul Midgley) *cl up centre: rdn along over 2f out: sn edgd lft and wknd* **33/1**
17 *17* **Lady Ensign** 2-8-9 0 .... CamHardie 3
(Mark Brisbourne) *cl up on outer: rdn along and hung bdly lft to far rail wl over 2f out: sn bhd* **66/1**

1m 13.18s (1.28) **Going Correction** +0.125s/f (Good) **17 Ran SP% 122.9**
Speed ratings (Par 97): **96,94,92,91,89 88,83,83,80,79 79,77,77,76,74 70,47**
CSF £23.86 TOTE £7.50: £2.50, £1.80, £1.50; EX 37.30 Trifecta £222.50.

**Owner** Bill Hobson **Bred** Miss Siobhan Ryan **Trained** Settrington, N Yorks

**FOCUS**

The principals dominated this valuable 2yo seller.

## 3792 JIGSAW SPORTS BRANDING H'CAP 7f

3:30 (3:33) (Class 3) (0-90,91) 4-Y-O+ £7,762 (£2,310; £1,154; £577) Stalls Low

Form RPR

025 **1** **Be Kool (IRE)**[21] 3049 4-8-4 **73**........................(v) CamHardie 13 85
(Brian Ellison) *cl up: rdn to ld over 1f out: drvn clr ins fnl f: styd on wl* **33/1**

/21- **2** 1 3/4 **Sun Lover**[260] 6905 4-9-2 **85**........................ AndreaAtzeni 14 92+
(Roger Varian) *hld up: hdwy 2f out: n.m.r and rdn over 1f out: chsd wnr ins fnl f: sn drvn and no imp towards fin* **11/2[1]**

1-56 **3** 1 1/4 **Classic Seniority**[27] 2840 5-9-6 **89**........................(p) DanielTudhope 1 93
(Marjorie Fife) *trckd ldrs on inner: hdwy over 2f out: rdn and ev ch over 1f out: drvn and kpt on same pce fnl f* **13/2[3]**

4126 **4** shd **War Department (IRE)**[87] 1295 4-9-7 **90**........................(v) GrahamLee 17 94
(Keith Dalgleish) *midfield: hdwy on outer over 2f out: effrt and nt clr run jst over 1f out: sn swtchd rt and rdn: styd on wl fnl f* **40/1**

0605 **5** nk **Bertiewhittle**[14] 3294 9-9-1 **89**........................ RowanScott(5) 9 92
(David Barron) *hld up in rr: hdwy 2f out: swtchd rt to outer ent fnl f: sn rdn and fin wl* **20/1**

-302 **6** nk **Shouranour (IRE)**[6] 3565 7-8-11 **83**........................(b) JoshDoyle(3) 19 85
(Alan Brown) *led: jnd and rdn 2f out: drvn and hdd over 1f out: grad wknd fnl f* **20/1**

2020 **7** nk **Lexington Times (IRE)**[14] 3294 5-8-11 **80**........................ JackGarritty 5 81
(Ruth Carr) *midfield: hdwy 2f out: rdn to chse ldrs over 1f out: drvn and kpt on same pce fnl f* **28/1**

0532 **8** 1/2 **Chaplin Bay (IRE)**[11] 3388 5-8-5 **74**........................(p) JamesSullivan 6 74
(Ruth Carr) *hld up and bhd: hdwy 2f out: effrt and n.m.r over 1f out: sn rdn and kpt on fnl f* **12/1**

3101 **9** 1/2 **Wink Oliver**[9] 3471 5-8-11 **80** 6ex........................(p) IrineuGoncalves 11 79
(Jo Hughes) *hld up in tch: hdwy on outer 3f out: chsd ldrs 2f out: sn rdn and edgd lft: grad wknd* **33/1**

3-30 **10** hd **Sakhee's Return**[6] 3565 5-8-12 **84**........................(t) RachelRichardson(3) 10 82
(Tim Easterby) *trckd ldrs: pushed along over 2f out: rdn wl over 1f out: drvn and wknd appr fnl f* **9/1**

4563 **11** hd **Ballymore Castle (IRE)**[14] 3294 5-8-11 **80**........................ PaulHanagan 18 78
(Richard Fahey) *dwlt and rr tl sme late hdwy* **10/1**

-000 **12** 3/4 **Roll On Rory**[27] 2840 4-8-13 **87**........................ CliffordLee(5) 4 82
(Jason Ward) *a towards rr* **25/1**

0560 **13** hd **God Willing**[27] 2840 6-9-3 **86**........................ TomEaves 12 81
(Declan Carroll) *chsd ldrs: rdn along 2f out: sn drvn and wknd* **14/1**

-020 **14** 1 **Moonlightnavigator (USA)**[15] 3255 5-9-5 **88**........................ JasonHart 15 80
(John Quinn) *cl up: rdn along over 2f out: sn wknd* **33/1**

1-05 **15** nk **Gothic Empire (IRE)**[45] 2283 5-9-5 **88**........................ DanielMuscutt 8 79
(James Fanshawe) *in tch: rdn along over 2f out: sn drvn and wknd* **6/1[2]**

-002 **16** 3/4 **Penwortham (IRE)**[20] 3064 4-9-4 **90**........................(h) AdamMcNamara(3) 16 79
(Richard Fahey) *hld up towards rr: hdwy on outer over 3f out: chsd ldrs over 2f out: sn rdn and wknd* **16/1**

6353 **17** shd **Firmdecisions (IRE)**[45] 2283 7-9-8 **91**........................ PatCosgrave 7 80
(Dean Ivory) *midfield: rdn along over 2f out: sn wknd* **12/1**

10/0 **18** 1 1/2 **Roaring Forties (IRE)**[27] 2840 4-9-2 **85**........................ DuranFentiman 3 70
(Rebecca Bastiman) *in tch on inner: rdn along wl over 2f out: sn wknd* **80/1**

-500 **19** hd **Related**[30] 2736 7-9-1 **84**........................ PaulMulrennan 2 69
(Paul Midgley) *a rr* **20/1**

1m 25.27s (-0.03) **Going Correction** +0.025s/f (Good) **19** Ran SP% **124.1**

Speed ratings (Par 107): **101,99,97,97,97 96,96,95,95,95 94,93,93,92,92 91,91,89,89**

CSF £187.51 CT £1402.36 TOTE £48.00: £8.50, £1.50, £2.20, £9.40; EX 489.90 Trifecta £5798.80 Part won..

**Owner** Miss Jessica J Bell **Bred** E Lonergan **Trained** Norton, N Yorks

**FOCUS**

This developed into a dash for home and those held up were at a distinct disadvantage.

## 3793 EBF BREEDERS SERIES FILLIES' H'CAP 6f

4:05 (4:05) (Class 2) (0-100,92) 3-Y-O+

£18,675 (£5,592; £2,796; £1,398; £699; £351) Stalls Centre

Form RPR

31-0 **1** **Eartha Kitt**[34] 2616 3-8-13 **84**........................(p1) RichardKingscote 8 92+
(Tom Dascombe) *.dwlt and rr: hdwy over 1f out: swtchd rt and rdn jst ins fnl f: styd on strly to ld nr line* **15/2**

4414 **2** 1/2 **Southern Belle (IRE)**[14] 3307 4-9-11 **89**........................ PhillipMakin 12 97
(Robert Cowell) *wnt rt s: in tch: hdwy on outer wl over 1f out: rdn to chal ins fnl f: drvn to ld last 50 yds: hdd and no ex nr line* **7/1[3]**

6-42 **3** 1 1/2 **The Feathered Nest (IRE)**[26] 2856 3-8-12 **83**........................ PaulHanagan 4 84
(Richard Fahey) *hld up in tch: hdwy on inner over 2f out: rdn to chse ldr ent fnl f: sn drvn and ev ch: kpt on same pce* **11/4[1]**

0-01 **4** nk **Turanga Leela**[20] 3063 3-8-10 **84**........................(b1) GeorgeWood(3) 2 84
(Ian Williams) *led: rdn clr over 1f out: drvn and wandered ins fnl f: hdd & wknd last 50 yds* **14/1**

1244 **5** 1 3/4 **Queen In Waiting (IRE)**[21] 3034 3-9-3 **88**........................ FrannyNorton 11 82
(Mark Johnston) *trckd ldng pair: hdwy to chse ldr wl over 1f out: sn rdn and wknd ent fnl f* **7/2[2]**

14-3 **6** 1 **Fruit Salad**[41] 2409 4-8-7 **74**........................ NathanEvans(3) 7 67
(James Bethell) *chsd ldrs: rdn along wl over 1f out: grad wknd* **8/1**

100- **7** 3/4 **Shamsaya (IRE)**[218] 7893 3-9-3 **88**........................ AndreaAtzeni 10 77
(Simon Crisford) *hld up: a towards rr* **14/1**

6150 **8** 4 1/2 **Shypen**[28] 2805 4-9-2 **83**........................ AdamMcNamara(3) 1 59
(Richard Fahey) *chsd ldrs: rdn along over 2f out: sn wknd* **20/1**

210- **9** 5 **Hope Solo (IRE)**[335] 4394 3-9-4 **89**........................ DavidAllan 5 47
(Tim Easterby) *chsd ldng pair: rdn along over 2f out: sn drvn and wknd* **25/1**

40-0 **10** 1 1/2 **Tallulah Rose**[58] 1883 3-9-2 **92**........................ CliffordLee(5) 6 46
(K R Burke) *chsd ldr: rdn along 2f out: sn wknd* **12/1**

1m 11.18s (-0.72) **Going Correction** +0.125s/f (Good)

**WFA** 3 from 4yo 7lb **10** Ran SP% **113.9**

Speed ratings (Par 96): **109,108,106,105,103 102,101,95,88,86**

CSF £57.67 CT £183.78 TOTE £8.40: £2.10, £2.30, £1.40; EX 65.60 Trifecta £206.00.

**Owner** Chasemore Farm **Bred** Chasemore Farm **Trained** Malpas, Cheshire

**FOCUS**

This was a weak fillies' handicap for the class with the top weight 11lb lower than the race ceiling.

## 3794 IRISH THOROUGHBRED MARKETING H'CAP 1m 5f 188y

4:40 (4:41) (Class 3) (0-90,88) 4-Y-O+ £7,762 (£2,310; £1,154; £577) Stalls Low

Form RPR

-441 **1** **Theydon Grey**[20] 3091 4-9-0 **86**........................ GeorgiaCox(5) 6 93
(William Haggas) *led 3f: trckd ldr: cl up 3f out: led 2f out: sn pushed along and carried hd high : rdn ins fnl f: hld on wl towards fin* **10/3[1]**

5-30 **2** nk **Waiting For Richie**[13] 3311 4-8-2 **69** oh1........................ JamesSullivan 8 75
(Tom Tate) *trckd ldrs: pushed along 3f out: sn rdn and outpcd over 2f out: hdwy over 1f out: styd on strly fnl f* **16/1**

1131 **3** 3/4 **Monjeni**[34] 2609 4-8-12 **79**........................(v) AndreaAtzeni 9 84
(Ian Williams) *hld up in rr: hdwy over 2f out: rdn to chse ldrs on inner and hung lft over 1f out: drvn ins fnl f: styd on wl towards fin* **7/2[2]**

1215 **4** hd **On Fire**[29] 2770 4-8-7 **74**........................(p) PaulHanagan 2 79
(James Bethell) *t.k.h: trckd ldrs: hdwy and cl up 4f out: chal 2f out and sn rdn: drvn and ev ch ent fnl f: no ex last 50 yds* **6/1[3]**

-041 **5** 1/2 **Mark Hopkins**[20] 3086 5-9-7 **88**........................ GrahamLee 4 92
(David Elsworth) *trckd ldr: led after 3f: stdd pce 1/2-way: pushed along and jnd 3f out: sn rdn and hdd 2f out: cl up: drvn ent fnl f: kpt on same pce* **10/3[1]**

3-31 **6** 6 **Belabour**[139] 457 4-9-1 **82**........................ PaulMulrennan 3 77
(Mark Brisbourne) *hld up: hdwy 4f out: chsd ldrs over 2f out: sn rdn and no imp* **25/1**

10-0 **7** 1/2 **Transpennine Star**[34] 2629 4-8-9 **76**........................ ConnorBeasley 7 70
(Michael Dods) *in tch: hdwy over 3f out: rdn along wl over 2f out: sn btn* **16/1**

-545 **8** 10 **Western Prince**[21] 3050 4-8-10 **77**........................(h) BenCurtis 5 56
(Michael Appleby) *dwlt: t.k.h and hld up in rr: hdwy on inner over 3f out and sn chsng ldrs: rdn along 2f out: sn btn* **14/1**

120- **9** nk **Multellie**[238] 7498 5-9-4 **85**........................ DavidAllan 1 64
(Tim Easterby) *t.k.h: in tch: hdwy over 4f out: rdn along over 3f out: wknd over 2f out* **12/1**

3m 4.78s (4.58) **Going Correction** +0.025s/f (Good) **9** Ran SP% **112.6**

Speed ratings (Par 107): **87,86,86,86,86 82,82,76,76**

CSF £54.53 CT £195.69 TOTE £4.00: £1.60, £4.30, £1.50; EX 53.90 Trifecta £382.10.

**Owner** The Going Grey Partnership **Bred** Pinnacle Bloodstock Ltd **Trained** Newmarket, Suffolk

**FOCUS**

This decent staying handicap suited those racing handily. Race distance increased 32yds.

## 3795 EVENTMASTERS.CO.UK APPRENTICE H'CAP 1m 3f 188y

5:15 (5:19) (Class 4) (0-80,81) 4-Y-O-£7,762 (£2,310; £1,154; £288; £288) Stalls Centre

Form RPR

3-62 **1** **Opposition**[11] 3409 4-9-13 **81**........................ AdamMcNamara 7 89
(Ed Dunlop) *trckd ldrs: hdwy 3f out: cl up 2f out: rdn to chal over 1f out: drvn to ld ins fnl f: kpt on gamely towards fin* **5/2[1]**

-531 **2** 3/4 **Panko (IRE)**[23] 2965 4-9-12 **80**........................ CallumShepherd 10 86
(Ed de Giles) *trckd ldr: hdwy 3f out: led over 2f out: jnd and rdn over 1f out: drvn and hdd ins fnl f: kpt on* **4/1[2]**

-345 **3** 1 1/4 **Peterhouse (USA)**[18] 3153 5-9-5 **76**........................(p) CliffordLee(3) 6 80
(Jason Ward) *trckd ldrs: hdwy over 4f out: pushed along 3f out: rdn and n.m.r 2f out: swtchd rt to outer and drvn over 1f out: styd on to chse ldng pair ins fnl f: no imp towards fin* **4/1[2]**

-002 **4** 2 **Itlaaq**[21] 3050 11-9-9 **77**........................(t) NathanEvans 5 78
(Michael Easterby) *trckd ldrs: hdwy 3f out: chsd ldrs and rdn 2f out: drvn over 1f out: kpt on same pce fnl f* **8/1**

4-54 **4** dht **Jan De Heem**[6] 3559 7-8-0 **61** oh1........................ ConnorMurtagh(7) 11 62
(Tina Jackson) *hld up in tch: gd hdwy on outer 3f out: chsd ldrs 2f out: rdn and ev ch over 1f out: kpt on same pce fnl f* **20/1**

4440 **6** 4 1/2 **Mysterial**[21] 3050 7-8-13 **70**........................ PhilDennis(3) 4 64
(Declan Carroll) *led: pushed along over 3f out: rdn and hdd over 2f out: sn drvn and grad wknd* **15/2[3]**

0-03 **7** 1 1/2 **Saxo Jack (FR)**[21] 3036 7-9-4 **77**........................(t) BenRobinson(5) 2 68
(Sophie Leech) *hld up: hdwy over 3f out: chsd ldrs 2f out: sn rdn and btn* **10/1**

-045 **8** 1/2 **Satish**[21] 3036 4-9-2 **70**........................(v) JoshDoyle 8 60
(David O'Meara) *hld up: a towards rr* **20/1**

0 **9** 6 **Song Of Love (IRE)**[28] 2804 5-9-2 **77**........................(p) AidenBlakemore(3) 9 58
(Shaun Harris) *prom: rdn along over 3f out: sn wknd* **33/1**

110- **10** 3 3/4 **Alphabetical Order**[400] 2194 9-9-5 **80**........................ ZakWheatley(7) 12 55
(David O'Meara) *a towards rr* **25/1**

2m 34.43s (1.23) **Going Correction** +0.025s/f (Good) **10** Ran SP% **116.8**

Speed ratings (Par 105): **96,95,94,93,93 90,89,89,85,82**

CSF £11.63 CT £38.62 TOTE £3.20: £1.40, £1.60, £1.50; EX 14.20 Trifecta £43.60.

**Owner** Highclere Thoroughbred Racing(Melbourne) **Bred** Cheveley Park Stud Ltd **Trained** Newmarket, Suffolk

**FOCUS**

This modest apprentice handicap was another race where it paid to be handy. Race distance increased 32yds.

T/Jkpt: Not won. T/Plt: £11.90 to a £1 stake.Pool: £98,169.00 - 8,226.79 winning units. T/Qpdt: £9.50 to a £1 stake.Pool: £5,701.00 - 597.87 winning units. **Joe Rowntree**

3796 - 3804a (Foreign Racing) - See Raceform Interactive

# 3276 BATH (L-H)

Saturday, June 17

**OFFICIAL GOING: Firm (good to firm in places; 9.4)**

Wind: Light breeze Weather: Very warm and sunny

## 3805 TOTEPLACEPOT SIX PLACES IN SIX RACES H'CAP 1m 3f 137y

1:55 (1:56) (Class 6) (0-60,58) 4-Y-O+ £2,264 (£673; £336; £168) Stalls Low

Form RPR

0-01 **1** **Grams And Ounces**[7] 3575 10-9-6 **57**........................(tp) TimmyMurphy 10 63
(Grace Harris) *trckd ldr: led over 3f out: chal and rdn over 1f out: r.o wl fnl f* **3/1[2]**

-301 **2** 3/4 **Filament Of Gold (USA)**[46] 2272 6-9-1 **55**........................(p) KieranShoemark(3) 6 60
(Roy Brotherton) *mid-div: effrt and pushed along over 2f out: rdn and chal over 1f out: r.o ins fnl f: hld* **6/1**

66/0 **3** shd **Vexillum (IRE)**[22] 3026 8-8-5 **45**........................(p) CallumShepherd(3) 8 50
(Neil Mulholland) *in rr: hdwy 3f out: hrd rdn over 1f out: styd on wl ins fnl f: nrst fin* **22/1**

4322 **4** 1/2 **Powered (IRE)**[16] 3251 4-8-13 **57**........................ KatherineGlenister(7) 1 61
(David Evans) *hld up: hdwy gng wl over 3f out: 3rd and rdn ent fnl f: kpt on u.p* **11/4[1]**

6024 **5** 5 **Golden Muscade (USA)**[22] 3026 4-9-3 **54** LukeMorris 7 50
(Brian Barr) *settled in 4th: hdwy into 2nd on outer over 3f out: hrd rdn 2f out: wknd ent fnl f* **10/3**[3]

10 **6** 12 **Petrify**[22] 3026 7-9-7 **58** (tp) LiamKeniry 4 34
(Bernard Llewellyn) *slowly away and in rr: prog into mid-div after 4f: rdn and wknd over 3f out* **11/1**

0/04 **7** 7 **Taroum (IRE)**[11] 3428 10-8-13 **50** (bt) DanielMuscutt 2 14
(John Flint) *trckd ldrs: drvn along over 3f out: sn rdn and fdd* **10/1**

0505 **8** 11 **Just Fred (IRE)**[10] 3470 4-8-8 **45** (t[1]) JimmyQuinn 9
(Neil Mulholland) *led: hdd over 3f out: drvn and no ex* **20/1**

2m 28.79s (-1.81) **Going Correction** -0.15s/f (Firm) **8** Ran SP% **115.6**
Speed ratings (Par 101): **100,99,99,99,95 87,83,75**
CSF £21.65 CT £332.72 TOTE £4.60: £1.90, £2.20, £5.70; EX 22.20 Trifecta £216.20.
**Owner** Grace Harris Racing **Bred** Brook Stud Bloodstock Ltd **Trained** Shirenewton, Monmouthshire

**FOCUS**
A dry, warm afternoon with a temperature of 22C. The ground had tightened up and the official going had changed to Firm, Good to Firm in places. The stalls were positioned on the inside for this very modest handicap and the first four finished close up.

## 3806 TOTEPOOLLIVEINFO.COM VISIT FOR RACING RESULTS/BRITISH EBF MAIDEN STKS 5f 10y

**2:25** (2:25) (Class 5) 3-Y-0+ **£3,881** (£1,155; £577; £288) **Stalls** Centre

Form RPR

3-4 **1** **Bella Alissa**[44] 2344 3-9-0 0 (p[1]) RobertWinston 7 70
(Robert Cowell) *disp ld tl led 2f out: sn pushed along: rdn appr fnl f: r.o wl: readily* **5/4**[1]

22-0 **2** 1 1/4 **Subjective**[21] 3085 3-9-5 74 (b[1]) LukeMorris 4 70
(David Simcock) *racd in 3rd: plld out and shkn up to mount chal 2f out: sn rdn: r.o one pce ins fnl f* **7/4**[2]

5365 **3** 1 1/2 **Exquisite Ruby**[14] 3331 3-9-0 61 SteveDrowne 6 60
(Charles Hills) *disp ld tl 2f out: drvn along appr fnl f: sn rdn and no ex* **4/1**[3]

6 **4** 2 1/4 **Picc And Go**[15] 3279 4-9-6 0 JohnFahy 3 54
(Matthew Salaman) *hld up in last: drvn along 2f out: tk 4th over 1f out: rdn ins fnl f: no imp* **33/1**

06 **5** 8 **Texas Wedge**[14] 3313 3-9-2 0 (b) KieranShoemark(3) 5 28
(William Muir) *settled in 4th: tk false step after 1f: chsd along over 2f out: reminder and wknd over 1f out* **10/1**

1m 2.15s (-0.35) **Going Correction** -0.275s/f (Firm)
**WFA** 3 from 4yo 6lb **5** Ran SP% **112.8**
Speed ratings (Par 103): **91,89,86,83,70**
CSF £3.86 TOTE £2.40: £1.20, £1.30; EX 4.20 Trifecta £9.20.
**Owner** Saleh Al Homaizi & Imad Al Sagar **Bred** Saleh Al Homaizi & Imad Al Sagar **Trained** Six Mile Bottom, Cambs

**FOCUS**
The stalls were placed in the centre for this modest sprint maiden in which the market spoke correctly.

## 3807 TOTEPOOL BETTING ON ALL UK RACING/EBFSTALLIONS.COM FILLIES' NOVICE STKS (PLUS 10 RACE) 5f 10y

**3:00** (3:00) (Class 4) 2-Y-0 **£4,592** (£1,366; £683; £341) **Stalls** Centre

Form RPR

3 **1** **Lynn's Memory**[22] 3023 2-9-0 0 JimmyQuinn 6 71
(Joseph Patrick O'Brien, Ire) *trckd ldrs early: wnt 2nd after 2f: hdwy to ld 2f out: shkn up over 1f out: sn rdn: r.o wl u.p fnl f* **6/1**[3]

**2** 1/2 **Tonkolili (IRE)** 2-8-11 0 KieranShoemark(3) 9 69+
(William Muir) *in rr: hdwy on outer 2f out: shkn up over 1f out: reminder ent fnl f: r.o strly: clsng nr fin* **20/1**

1 **3** 2 1/4 **Short Call (IRE)**[15] 3306 2-9-6 0 CharlesBishop 4 67
(Mick Channon) *trckd ldrs: pushed along and hdwy over 2f out: rdn appr fnl f: r.o to take 3rd nr fin* **6/4**[2]

02 **4** nk **Awesome**[22] 3022 2-9-0 0 LukeMorris 5 60
(Clive Cox) *led: hdd 2f out: sn drvn along: one pce and lost 3rd wl ins fnl f* **6/5**[1]

0 **5** 1 3/4 **Cove Beach**[39] 2502 2-9-0 0 RobertWinston 8 53
(Paul Cole) *mid-div: pushed along 2f out: swtchd to inner over 1f out: no hdwy and eased ins fnl f* **20/1**

**6** nk **Diamond Express (IRE)** 2-8-9 0 MitchGodwin(5) 7 52
(Roger Teal) *slowly away: in rr: effrt 3f out: briefly n.m.r: pushed along and no imp last 2f* **33/1**

0 **7** 7 **Red For Danger**[14] 3328 2-9-0 0 JohnFahy 1 26
(Eve Johnson Houghton) *racd in 2nd tl lost grnd qckly over 2f out: wknd* **20/1**

1m 1.65s (-0.85) **Going Correction** -0.275s/f (Firm) **7** Ran SP% **117.0**
Speed ratings (Par 92): **95,94,90,90,87 86,75**
CSF £100.34 TOTE £7.60: £2.00, £8.40; EX 110.70 Trifecta £360.90.
**Owner** Nick Bradley Racing Club **Bred** The Roxelana Partnership **Trained** Owning Hill, Co Kilkenny

**FOCUS**
The stalls were placed in the centre for this fair fillies' novices' sprint. The form should hold firm.

## 3808 TOTEQUADPOT INSURE YOUR PLACEPOT LAST FOUR H'CAP 1m

**3:35** (3:36) (Class 3) (0-90,88) 4-Y-0+ **£7,439** (£2,213; £1,106; £553) **Stalls** Low

Form RPR

0641 **1** **Realize**[24] 2975 7-9-4 **85** (t) LiamKeniry 4 96+
(David Simcock) *t.k.h: trckd ldrs: trapped in pocket on inner 2f out: swtchd and waited for gap over 1f out: qcknd between horses whn in clr: sn led: pushed out ins fnl f: comf* **11/4**[1]

3-00 **2** 2 1/2 **Palawan**[17] 3212 4-9-3 **84** TimmyMurphy 5 87
(Jamie Osborne) *mid-div on outer: prog into 3rd 2f out: led ins fnl f: sn hdd: rdn and r.o but no ch w wnr* **16/1**

0-44 **3** 1/2 **Midhmaar**[23] 3014 4-9-7 **88** (p[1]) DanielMuscutt 6 90
(Owen Burrows) *led at stdy gallop: qcknd pce 3f out: pushed along 2f out: rdn and hdd ins fnl f: r.o one pce* **3/1**[2]

100 **4** nk **Calvados Spirit**[15] 3298 4-9-2 **86** (h[1]) KieranShoemark(3) 9 87
(William Muir) *trckd ldr: pushed along 2f out: rdn wl over 1f out: nt qckn fnl f* **6/1**

-104 **5** 1 3/4 **Reaver (IRE)**[17] 3212 4-9-3 **84** CharlesBishop 3 81
(Eve Johnson Houghton) *hld up: hdwy and chsd along 2f out: rdn ent fnl f: no ex* **4/1**[3]

1010 **6** 1 1/4 **Wink Oliver**[1] 3792 5-9-1 **82** (p) IrineuGoncalves 1 76
(Jo Hughes) *hld up: pushed along on outer 2f out: reminders and no imp fnl 2f* **12/1**

3011 **7** shd **Mister Musicmaster**[15] 3282 8-8-4 **71** LukeMorris 2 65
(Ron Hodges) *mid-div: drvn and effrt 2f out: sn rdn: one pce* **7/1**

3010 **8** 3 1/4 **Athassel**[6] 3620 8-8-9 **83** KatherineGlenister(7) 7 70
(David Evans) *slowly away: in rr tl effrt 3f out: rdn 2f out: wknd* **14/1**

1m 40.55s (-0.25) **Going Correction** -0.15s/f (Firm) **8** Ran SP% **118.7**
Speed ratings (Par 107): **95,92,92,91,89 88,88,85**
CSF £48.50 CT £143.43 TOTE £3.30: £1.40, £5.00, £1.20; EX 62.80 Trifecta £260.20.
**Owner** Twenty Stars Partnership **Bred** M J Watson **Trained** Newmarket, Suffolk

**FOCUS**
Stall placement on the inside for this decent handicap run at a pedestrian early pace. The winner is well ahead of the handicapper and the form looks viable.

## 3809 @TOTEPOOLRACING WIN RACING TICKETS ON TWITTER H'CAP 1m

**4:10** (4:14) (Class 6) (0-60,61) 4-Y-0+ **£2,264** (£673; £336; £168) **Stalls** Low

Form RPR

0663 **1** **Aye Aye Skipper (IRE)**[8] 3522 7-8-7 **45** (b) SteveDrowne 11 57
(Ken Cunningham-Brown) *mid-div: hdwy 2f out: pushed along over 1f out: led ins fnl f: rdn and r.o wl: rn wout declared tongue tie* **8/1**

2232 **2** 3 1/4 **Mowhoob**[18] 3172 7-9-2 **54** LukeMorris 1 58
(Brian Barr) *trckd ldrs: 3rd and niggled 3f out: pushed along 2f out: rdn and ev ch ent fnl f: r.o to take 2nd last 50yds* **4/1**[2]

5501 **3** hd **Mamnoon (IRE)**[22] 3028 4-9-4 **59** (b) KieranShoemark(3) 6 63
(Roy Brotherton) *trckd ldrs: drvn over 1f out: rdn and led briefly ins fnl f: sn hdd and one pce: lost 2nd last 50yds* **9/4**[1]

-400 **4** 2 **Overhaugh Street**[16] 3252 4-9-6 **61** (b[1]) CallumShepherd(3) 5 60
(Ed de Giles) *led: hdd and drvn ent fnl f: no ex last 150yds* **12/1**

5550 **5** 2 1/2 **Cloud Nine (FR)**[11] 3442 4-9-1 **53** JimmyQuinn 13 46
(Tony Carroll) *hld up: hdwy 2f out: sn rdn: r.o ins fnl f* **17/2**

4004 **6** 3 1/4 **Rising Sunshine (IRE)**[19] 3137 4-8-7 **45** (bt) ThomasBrown 7 30
(Milton Bradley) *trckd ldr: niggled 3f out: rdn over 2f out: one pce ent fnl f* **12/1**

0654 **7** nse **Rocket Ronnie (IRE)**[98] 1145 7-8-13 **51** (b) RobertWinston 3 36
(Brian Barr) *hld up: hdwy on outer 2f out: drvn and no imp fr wl over 1f out* **5/1**[3]

-500 **8** 2 **Fitzwilliam**[5] 3661 5-8-7 **45** RobHornby 4 25
(Mick Channon) *mid-div: effrt 3f out: rdn 2f out: one pce* **10/1**

000- **9** nse **Paca Punch**[320] 4939 4-8-7 **45** DannyBrock 9 25
(John Flint) *mid-div: chsd along 3f out: wknd fnl 2f* **50/1**

5306 **10** 3 1/4 **Gavarnie Encore**[58] 1894 5-8-8 **46** KieranO'Neill 12 18
(Michael Blanshard) *mid-div: pushed along on inner over 2f out: rdn over 1f out: one pce fnl f* **16/1**

4-00 **11** 9 **Saxony**[131] 601 6-8-4 **45** NoelGarbutt(3) 10
(Matthew Salaman) *in rr: drvn 3f out: no imp* **66/1**

/6-0 **12** 26 **Max Beddow (IRE)**[25] 2915 4-8-13 **51** (t[1]) LiamKeniry 8
(Geoffrey Deacon) *a in rr* **50/1**

1m 39.31s (-1.49) **Going Correction** -0.15s/f (Firm) **12** Ran SP% **124.8**
Speed ratings (Par 101): **101,97,97,95,93 89,89,87,87,84 75,49**
CSF £42.08 CT £101.30 TOTE £10.90: £2.60, £1.90, £1.10; EX 53.30 Trifecta £156.50.
**Owner** John Pearl **Bred** Ballyhane Stud **Trained** Danebury, Hants
■ Stewards' Enquiry : Steve Drowne Three-day ban; jockey weighed in 2lb over (1st-3rd July)

**FOCUS**
The stalls were positioned on the inside for this low-grade handicap, which was truly-run.

## 3810 TOTEPOOL RACECOURSE DEBIT CARD BETTING AVAILABLE H'CAP 5f 160y

**4:45** (4:48) (Class 6) (0-65,67) 3-Y-0 **£2,835** (£848; £424; £212; £105) **Stalls** Centre

Form RPR

0-04 **1** **Pastfact**[31] 2720 3-9-3 **58** LiamKeniry 9 63+
(Malcolm Saunders) *mid-div on outer: hdwy gng wl 2f out: led over 1f out: shkn up: briefly faltered but sn rcvrd: appeared to hamper 3rd wl ins fnl f: rdn to assert last 100yds* **9/4**[1]

05-0 **2** nk **Harlequin Rose (IRE)**[43] 2362 3-8-8 **49** (v) JimmyQuinn 4 53
(Patrick Chamings) *in rr: trckd wnr through over 2f out: shkn up to chal appr fnl f: sn rdn: hld last 100yds* **7/1**

4P05 **3** 3 **Three C's (IRE)**[8] 3543 3-9-7 **62** (tp) TimmyMurphy 2 59
(David Dennis) *prom: ev ch 2f out: pushed along over 1f out: rdn fnl f: btn whn n.m.r and appeared hmpd by wnr wl ins fnl f* **9/1**

3240 **4** nk **Tooty Fruitti**[31] 2720 3-9-4 **59** IrineuGoncalves 3 52
(Jo Hughes) *hld up: hdwy to cl on ldrs gng wl 2f out: briefly n.m.r: swtchd and sn in clr: rdn 1f out: no ex* **7/1**

00-0 **5** 7 **Swan Serenade**[71] 1596 3-8-6 **52** LuluStanford(5) 7 22
(Jonathan Portman) *prom: drvn over 2f out: sn lost pl: one pce fnl f* **12/1**

5005 **6** 3/4 **Mahna Mahna (IRE)**[16] 3260 3-8-11 **52** ThomasBrown 6 20
(David W Drinkwater) *prom: pushed along and lost pl 2f out: one pce fnl f* **5/1**[3]

3225 **7** 7 **Black Bubba (IRE)**[12] 3391 3-9-2 **57** SteveDrowne 8 1
(David Evans) *led narrowly tl hdd over 1f out: sn rdn and wknd* **11/4**[2]

1m 11.45s (0.25) **Going Correction** -0.275s/f (Firm) **7** Ran SP% **116.8**
Speed ratings (Par 97): **87,86,82,82,72 71,62**
CSF £19.30 CT £120.51 TOTE £3.10: £1.60, £3.10; EX 21.30 Trifecta £112.60.
**Owner** Premier Conservatory Roofs **Bred** M S Saunders & D Collier **Trained** Green Ore, Somerset
■ Stewards' Enquiry : Liam Keniry caution; careless riding

**FOCUS**
The stalls were positioned in the centre. A modest 3yo sprint handicap and the pace was solid.

## 3811 COLLECT TOTEPOOL WINNINGS AT BETFRED SHOPS H'CAP 5f 160y

**5:20** (5:22) (Class 6) (0-65,67) 3-Y-0+ **£2,522** (£750; £375; £187) **Stalls** Centre

Form RPR

-430 **1** **Jaganory (IRE)**[7] 3569 5-9-3 **56** (p) LuluStanford(5) 14 62
(Christopher Mason) *disp ld tl led on own over 2f out: rdn appr fnl f: hld on grimly u.p last 150yds* **6/1**[3]

-523 **2** nse **Captain Ryan**[23] 3008 6-9-13 **61** KieranO'Neill 2 67
(Geoffrey Deacon) *trckd ldrs: hdwy 2f out: rdn and r.o wl ins fnl f: jst failed* **2/1**[1]

P643 **3** shd **Wedgewood Estates**[24] 2969 6-9-6 **54** JimmyQuinn 1 60
(Tony Carroll) *mid-div: pushed along over 1f out: rdn and r.o wl fnl f* **12/1**

0300 **4** 2 **Miracle Garden**[25] 2932 5-10-2 **67** (v[1]) KieranShoemark(3) 13 66
(Ian Williams) *mid-div: effrt and rdn over 1f out: r.o ins fnl f* **13/2**

0-00 **5** nk **Lucky Clover**[10] 3466 6-9-7 **55** (p) LiamKeniry 11 53
(Malcolm Saunders) *disp tl lost share of ld over 2f out: rdn and one pce fnl 2f* **25/1**

6546 **5** dht **Catalinas Diamond (IRE)**[15] 3280 9-8-13 **47** (t) SteveDrowne 7 45
(Pat Murphy) *mid-div: effrt over 2f out: rdn and r.o ins fnl f* **16/1**

/020 **7** 1/2 **Thewestwalian (USA)**[4] 3696 9-8-12 **53** MollyKing(7) 8 49
(Peter Hiatt) *slowly away: hdwy on outer 2f out: rdn and no ex ent fnl f* **12/1**

240- **8** 1 **Time Medicean**[247] 7301 11-9-5 **60** AledBeech(7) 12 53
(Tony Carroll) *mid-div: one pce fnl 2f* **20/1**

0455 **9** *hd* **Burauq**[15] 3280 5-8-12 **46**....................(b) ThomasBrown 16 38
(Milton Bradley) *chsd ldrs: no ex fnl 2f* **12/1**

00-0 **10** *2 ¼* **Tally's Song**[7] 3569 4-8-6 **45**....................(p) JennyPowell(5) 4 30
(Grace Harris) *mid-div: no ex fr 2f out* **40/1**

0440 **11** *2 ½* **Molly Jones**[15] 3280 8-9-0 **51**.................... NoelGarbutt(3) 10 40
(Matthew Salaman) *mid-div: pushed along: n.m.r and no ex fnl 2f* **16/1**

3101 **12** *2 ¾* **Compton Prince**[15] 3280 8-9-7 **55**....................(b) RobertWinston 15 23
(Milton Bradley) *mid-div: drvn 2f out: wknd* **5/1**[2]

510/ **13** *¾* **Satellite Express (IRE)**[897] 11 6-9-4 **52**....................(bt[1]) TimmyMurphy 6 17
(Tim Pinfield) *mid-div: rdn over 2f out: wknd* **20/1**

1m 10.7s (-0.50) **Going Correction** -0.275s/f (Firm) **13** Ran SP% **128.3**
Speed ratings (Par 101): **92,91,91,89,88 88,88,86,86,83 80,76,75**
CSF £18.84 CT £156.44 TOTE £7.60: £2.10, £1.40, £3.90; EX 31.20 Trifecta £232.40.
**Owner** Brian Hicks **Bred** Canice Farrell Jnr **Trained** Caewent, Monmouthshire

**FOCUS**
Stall placement was in the centre of the track for this low-key sprint handicap. The front three finished in a heap.
T/Plt: £200.40 to a £1 stake. Pool: £60,217.73 - 219.29 winning units T/Qpdt: £58.70 to a £1 stake. Pool: £3,915.38 - 49.30 winning units **Keith McHugh**

## 3390 LEICESTER (R-H)
### Saturday, June 17

**OFFICIAL GOING: Good to firm (good in places; watered; 7.9)**
Wind: Almost nil Weather: Sunny

### 3812 SIX HILLS H'CAP 5f
**6:10** (6:10) (Class 5) (0-70,68) 3-Y-0+ **£3,881** (£1,155; £577; £288) **Stalls** High

Form RPR

3-15 **1** **Ocelot**[35] 2631 3-9-5 **65**.................... TomMarquand 2 75+
(Robert Cowell) *prom: pushed along 3f out: shkn up to ld over 1f out: rdn clr ins fnl f: edgd rt towards fin* **6/1**[3]

5623 **2** *2 ¼* **Burtonwood**[18] 3170 5-9-7 **66**....................(p) LewisEdmunds(5) 5 70
(Julie Camacho) *sn pushed along in rr: hdwy over 1f out: sn rdn: styd on to go 2nd wl ins fnl f: edgd rt towards fin* **15/8**[1]

5131 **3** *¾* **Mighty Zip (USA)**[23] 2995 5-9-1 **62**....................(p) JordanUys(7) 6 63
(Lisa Williamson) *chsd ldrs: rdn and ev ch over 1f out: styd on same pce ins fnl f* **10/1**

2225 **4** *hd* **Entertaining Ben**[5] 3659 4-9-7 **68**....................(p) FinleyMarsh(7) 1 69
(Amy Murphy) *chsd ldrs: rdn and ev ch over 1f out: edgd lft and styd on same pce ins fnl f* **6/1**[3]

5440 **5** *1 ¼* **Emjayem**[35] 2621 7-9-7 **68**.................... MeganEllingworth(7) 4 64
(John Holt) *sn pushed along in rr: hdwy on outer over 1f out: no ex wl ins fnl f* **16/1**

-021 **6** *hd* **Glyder**[15] 3285 3-9-3 **63**.................... RoystonFfrench 8 56
(John Holt) *racd keenly: w ldr: rdn and ev ch over 1f out: no ex wl ins fnl f* **5/1**[2]

-040 **7** *½* **Cherry Kool**[14] 3331 4-9-9 **63**....................(h[1]) PatDobbs 3 57
(Stuart Williams) *sn outpcd: styd on fnl f: nvr trbld ldrs* **18/1**

4210 **8** *1* **Pearl Noir**[17] 3201 7-9-3 **64**....................(b) RPWalsh(7) 7 54
(Scott Dixon) *sn pushed along to ld: rdn and hdd over 1f out: wknd ins fnl f* **11/1**

30 **9** *7* **Wimboldsley**[16] 3256 6-8-10 **50**.................... JoeDoyle 9 15
(Scott Dixon) *w ldrs 2f: nt clr run sn after: wknd 2f out* **25/1**

59.64s (-0.36) **Going Correction** -0.25s/f (Firm)
**WFA** 3 from 4yo+ 6lb **9** Ran SP% **112.4**
Speed ratings (Par 103): **92,88,87,86,84 84,83,82,70**
CSF £17.04 CT £109.73 TOTE £6.50: £2.10, £1.40, £2.90; EX 20.40 Trifecta £152.30.
**Owner** Manor Farm Stud (rutland) **Bred** Manor Farm Stud & Mrs A J Ralli **Trained** Six Mile Bottom, Cambs

**FOCUS**
A modest but competitive sprint handicap, although the winner scored in good style. The time was pretty good for the grade.

### 3813 HUNGARTON CLAIMING STKS 1m 2f
**6:40** (6:42) (Class 6) 3-4-Y-0 **£3,234** (£962; £481; £240) **Stalls** Low

Form RPR

1354 **1** **Il Sicario (IRE)**[7] 3561 3-9-2 67.................... PJMcDonald 5 77
(Mark Johnston) *hld up: pushed along and hdwy over 2f out: rdn to chse ldr over 1f out: led ins fnl f: styd on wl* **5/2**[2]

6312 **2** *3 ¼* **Sir Jack**[6] 3628 4-9-9 60.................... JimCrowley 7 66
(Tony Carroll) *prom: led over 2f out: rdn and edgd rt over 1f out: hdd and no ex ins fnl f* **2/1**[1]

6-00 **3** *3 ½* **Maestro Mac (IRE)**[42] 2388 4-9-8 70.................... CharlieBennett(3) 2 61
(Hughie Morrison) *hld up in tch: pushed along over 2f out: nt clr run and lost pl wl over 1f out: swtchd lft sn after: styd on to go 3rd wl ins fnl f* **4/1**[3]

6104 **4** *2* **Log Off (IRE)**[19] 3143 3-8-2 60 ow1.................... RoystonFfrench 3 46
(David Evans) *hld up: hdwy over 2f out: rdn over 1f out: wknd fnl f* **14/1**

5-00 **5** *2 ½* **Miss Monro (IRE)**[19] 3142 3-8-1 53....................(b[1]) JoeDoyle 1 41
(Brian Ellison) *chsd ldrs: rdn over 2f out: wknd over 1f out* **25/1**

60-0 **6** *3 ½* **Iberica Road (USA)**[149] 306 4-9-6 75.................... PaddyAspell 4 41
(Grant Tuer) *led: rdn and hdd over 2f out: wknd over 1f out* **14/1**

4440 **7** *20* **Star Glitter (FR)**[8] 3547 4-9-11 64....................(v[1]) DanielTudhope 8 8
(David O'Meara) *racd keenly: wnt 2nd after 1f tl rdn and hung rt over 2f out: sn wknd and eased* **7/1**

06 **8** *6* **Columbian Cartel**[10] 3470 4-8-12 0.................... GeorgiaDobie(7) 6
(J S Moore) *s.i.s and a in rr: lost tch fnl 4f* **66/1**

2m 6.51s (-1.39) **Going Correction** -0.075s/f (Good)
**WFA** 3 from 4yo 12lb **8** Ran SP% **113.1**
Speed ratings (Par 101): **102,99,96,95,93 90,74,69**
CSF £7.71 TOTE £3.20: £1.50, £1.10, £1.70; EX 7.80 Trifecta £24.30.Il Sicario was claimed by Mr Bill Turner for £15000.
**Owner** P D Savill **Bred** Lynn Lodge Stud **Trained** Middleham Moor, N Yorks

**FOCUS**
Mixed levels of ability in this claimer but two came clear and the winner was suited by the longer trip. He posted a pb.

### 3814 H.A.C. PIPELINE SUPPLIES H'CAP 6f
**7:10** (7:11) (Class 4) (0-80,81) 3-Y-0 **£6,469** (£1,925; £962; £481) **Stalls** High

Form RPR

6111 **1** **Goodwood Crusader (IRE)**[8] 3517 3-9-1 **81**.................... FinleyMarsh(7) 2 89+
(Richard Hughes) *broke wl: settled to trck ldrs after 1f: lost pl over 3f out: hdwy over 1f out: rdn to ld and edgd lft ins fnl f: r.o wl* **11/4**[1]

44-0 **2** *1 ½* **Parys Mountain (IRE)**[53] 2072 3-9-0 **73**....................(h) JimCrowley 5 76
(David Brown) *trckd ldrs: racd keenly: rdn over 1f out: edgd lft ins fnl f: styd on to go 2nd towards fin* **11/2**[3]

31- **3** *nk* **Fivetwoeight**[185] 8352 3-9-5 **78**.................... LukeMorris 3 80
(Peter Chapple-Hyam) *hld up: racd keenly: hdwy over 3f out: rdn to ld over 1f out: hdd and hmpd ins fnl f: styd on same pce towards fin* **4/1**[2]

-130 **4** *1* **Sword Exceed (GER)**[33] 2692 3-9-6 **79**.................... TomMarquand 6 78
(Ivan Furtado) *led: rdn and hdd over 1f out: styd on same pce ins fnl f* **9/1**

3-00 **5** *½* **Glorious Rocket**[10] 3462 3-9-2 **75**....................(h) PatDobbs 4 72
(David Barron) *stdd at s: hld up: racd keenly: shkn up over 1f out: running on whn short of room ins fnl f: nvr able to chal* **14/1**

31 **6** *shd* **Moonwise (IRE)**[26] 2887 3-9-6 **79**.................... FranBerry 7 76+
(Ralph Beckett) *s.i.s: hld up: shkn up over 2f out: r.o u.p ins fnl f: nt rch ldrs* **11/4**[1]

110 **7** *nse* **Man About Town (IRE)**[35] 2630 3-8-9 **68**.................... PJMcDonald 1 65
(K R Burke) *w ldr: rdn and ev ch over 1f out: no ex wl ins fnl f* **20/1**

6-20 **8** *3 ¾* **Red Gunner**[45] 2304 3-9-4 **77**.................... DanielTudhope 8 70
(David O'Meara) *trckd ldrs: rdn over 1f out: styng on same pce whn nt clr run ins fnl f: eased* **20/1**

1m 11.63s (-1.37) **Going Correction** -0.25s/f (Firm) **8** Ran SP% **114.9**
Speed ratings (Par 101): **99,97,96,95,94 94,94,89**
CSF £18.46 CT £57.98 TOTE £3.10: £1.30, £1.20, £2.00; EX 16.20 Trifecta £58.80.
**Owner** Goodwood Racehorse Owners Group (23) Ltd **Bred** Tally-Ho Stud **Trained** Upper Lambourn, Berks

**FOCUS**
The feature race and a competitive 3yo sprint handicap but, despite the early pace being nothing special, the winner completed a four-timer in good style.

### 3815 BRITISH STALLION STUDS EBF FILLIES' NOVICE STKS (PLUS 10 RACE) 6f
**7:40** (7:43) (Class 4) 2-Y-0 **£4,528** (£1,347; £505; £505) **Stalls** High

Form RPR

101 **1** **Izzy Bizu (IRE)**[9] 3483 2-9-6 0.................... PJMcDonald 8 83
(Mark Johnston) *mde all: rdn over 1f out: styd on wl* **6/4**[1]

042 **2** *1 ½* **Mraseel (IRE)**[24] 2958 2-9-0 0....................(p) LukeMorris 10 73
(James Tate) *w wnr 1f: remained handy: swtchd rt over 4f out: rdn and ev ch fr over 1f out tl styd on same pce wl ins fnl f* **4/1**[2]

**3** *1 ¾* **Point Hope (IRE)** 2-9-0 0.................... PatDobbs 3 67
(Richard Hannon) *hld up: hdwy over 1f out: styd on: nt trble ldrs* **8/1**

0 **3** *dht* **Little Miss Lilly**[26] 2905 2-8-11 0.................... HectorCrouch(3) 9 67
(Clive Cox) *plld hrd: jnd wnr 5f out tl pushed along 4f out: rdn and edgd rt over 1f out: kpt on* **16/1**

**5** *4* **Blazing Beryl (IRE)** 2-9-0 0.................... KierenFox 1 55
(Brian Meehan) *in rr: pushed along over 3f out: rdn over 2f out: styd on ins fnl f: nvr nrr* **33/1**

**6** *1 ½* **Be Mindful (IRE)** 2-8-11 0.................... CallumShepherd(3) 2 51
(Charles Hills) *s.i.s: in rr: shkn up over 1f out: styd on ins fnl f: nrst fin* **25/1**

00 **7** *1* **Sensory (IRE)**[14] 3312 2-9-0 0....................(b[1]) TomMarquand 11 48
(John Gosden) *hld up: plld hrd and hdwy over 4f out: rdn and hung rt over 1f out: wknd fnl f* **10/1**

**8** *1 ½* **Choral Music** 2-9-0 0.................... PaddyAspell 6 43
(Jonathan Portman) *s.i.s: hld up: pushed along and sme hdwy 2f out: wknd fnl f* **50/1**

5 **9** *3 ¾* **Gigi (IRE)**[18] 3174 2-9-0 0.................... FranBerry 7 32
(Charles Hills) *hld up: hdwy over 3f out: rdn over 2f out: wknd over 1f out* **6/1**[3]

**10** *2 ¼* **Royal Wave** 2-9-0 0.................... JimCrowley 13 25
(William Knight) *hld up: hdwy over 3f out: shkn up and wknd over 2f out* **16/1**

**11** *9* **Elegant Joan** 2-9-0 0.................... GeorgeDowning 4
(Kevin Frost) *in rr: swtchd lft over 2f out: sn hung rt: n.d* **66/1**

**12** *16* **Bucks Frizz (IRE)** 2-9-0 0.................... DanielTudhope 12
(David Evans) *chsd ldr: lost pl over 3f out: wkng whn hmpd over 2f out* **22/1**

1m 12.01s (-0.99) **Going Correction** -0.25s/f (Firm) **12** Ran SP% **120.8**
Speed ratings (Par 92): **96,94,91,91,86 84,83,81,76,73 61,39**
WIN: IB 2.40; PL: IB 1.20, LML 2.40 , M 1.60, PH 1.30 ; EX: 8.60; CSF: 6.84; TF: IB/M/LML 38.00, IB/M/PH 17.60;.
**Owner** Lowther Racing & P D Savill **Bred** Mark Salmon **Trained** Middleham Moor, N Yorks

**FOCUS**
This juvenile fillies' novice stakes featured a number of runners from major yards and was run 0.38 secs slower than the preceding 3yo handicap. It has been rated around the race averages and the winner's latest winning Carlisle form.

### 3816 HUTTON'S WHOLESALE DRINKS 10TH ANNIVERSARY H'CAP 7f
**8:10** (8:12) (Class 4) (0-80,82) 3-Y-0+ **£6,301** (£1,886; £943; £472; £235) **Stalls** High

Form RPR

00-4 **1** **Mamillius**[71] 1606 4-10-1 **81**.................... FranBerry 3 88
(George Baker) *w ldrs tl led over 5f out: rdn over 1f out: styd on u.p* **11/8**[1]

160- **2** *nk* **Peak Princess (IRE)**[231] 7698 3-9-7 **82**.................... TomMarquand 10 85
(Richard Hannon) *hld up in tch: pushed along and hung rt over 4f out: outpcd over 2f out: rallied and hung rt fr over 1f out: kpt on u.p nr fin* **3/1**[2]

0-00 **3** *¾* **Favourite Treat (USA)**[12] 3402 7-9-4 **70**....................(e) JamesSullivan 6 74
(Ruth Carr) *hld up: hdwy over 1f out: ev ch ins fnl f: sn rdn: nt run on* **11/1**

-255 **4** *6* **Valley Of Rocks (IRE)**[11] 3443 3-8-9 **70**.................... PJMcDonald 5 55
(Mark Johnston) *racd keenly: w wnr over 5f out tl rdn over 2f out: no ex fnl f* **6/1**[3]

060- **5** *hd* **Case Key**[247] 7308 4-9-1 **74**.................... RayDawson(7) 8 61
(Michael Appleby) *chsd ldrs: rdn 1/2-way: no ex fnl f* **7/1**

3500 **6** *3 ¾* **Rockley Point**[29] 2800 4-9-7 **73**.................... JoeyHaynes 7 50
(Paul D'Arcy) *s.i.s: hld up: rdn over 2f out: n.d* **16/1**

-600 **7** *1* **Consulting**[14] 3330 4-9-6 **75**....................(vt[1]) AaronJones(3) 9 49
(Stuart Williams) *plld hrd: led tl over 5f out: remained handy: rdn over 2f out: wknd over 1f out* **33/1**

1m 23.45s (-2.75) **Going Correction** -0.25s/f (Firm)
**WFA** 3 from 4yo+ 9lb **7** Ran SP% **111.0**
Speed ratings (Par 105): **105,104,103,96,96 92,91**
CSF £5.19 CT £27.30 TOTE £2.20: £1.50, £1.90; EX 6.50 Trifecta £36.00.
**Owner** The Mamillius Partnership **Bred** East Bloodstock & Mr S Graham **Trained** Manton, Wilts

**FOCUS**
Another competitive handicap but a strange race, with the favourite proving the most straightforward.

## 3817 HARBY H'CAP — 1m 3f 179y
**8:40** (8:41) (Class 5) (0-75,77) 4-Y-0+ — **£3,234** (£962; £481; £240) **Stalls** Low

Form — RPR

0-33 **1** **Pumblechook**[10] 3464 4-9-11 **77** ........ RichardKingscote 1 — 85
(Mark Johnston) *chsd ldr 2f: remained handy: rdn to chse ldr over 1f out: led ins fnl f: jst hld on* **11/4**[2]

5604 **2** *shd* **Daisy Boy (IRE)**[4] 3683 6-9-5 **71** ........(vt[1]) JimCrowley 3 — 78
(Stuart Williams) *led: qcknd over 3f out: rdn over 1f out: hdd ins fnl f: styd on* **5/2**[1]

-210 **3** *2 1/4* **Desert Cross**[29] 2781 4-9-0 **66** ........ FranBerry 5 — 69
(Jonjo O'Neill) *hld up: pushed along over 3f out: hdwy over 1f out: nt rch ldrs* **7/1**

3363 **4** *2 1/4* **Bridge Of Sighs**[25] 2913 5-9-7 **73** ........ TomMarquand 6 — 73
(Martin Smith) *hld up: rdn over 2f out: hdwy over 1f out: hung rt and no ex ins fnl f* **11/1**

1223 **5** *3* **Deep Challenger (IRE)**[15] 3308 5-9-7 **73** ........ FergusSweeney 2 — 68
(Jamie Osborne) *chsd ldrs: wnt 2nd 10f out: rdn over 2f out: lost 2nd over 1f out: wknd fnl f* **3/1**[3]

02-2 **6** *28* **San Quentin (IRE)**[37] 2546 6-9-7 **73** ........(b) LukeMorris 4 — 23
(Dr Richard Newland) *s.s and rel to r: a bhd* **10/1**

2m 31.96s (-1.94) **Going Correction** -0.075s/f (Good) — **6** Ran SP% **110.2**
Speed ratings (Par 103): **103,102,101,99,97 79**
CSF £9.64 TOTE £3.40: £1.70, £2.10; EX 10.10 Trifecta £35.60.
**Owner** Christopher W T Johnston **Bred** Castlemartin Sky & Skymarc Farm **Trained** Middleham Moor, N Yorks

**FOCUS**
A small but closely matched field in this middle-distance handicap and it produced a good finish between the market leaders.

## 3818 ASFORDBY H'CAP — 5f
**9:10** (9:11) (Class 6) (0-60,59) 3-Y-0 — **£3,234** (£962; £481; £240) **Stalls** High

Form — RPR

3-50 **1** **The Big Short**[45] 2306 3-9-6 **58** ........ JimCrowley 3 — 65
(Charles Hills) *mde all: rdn over 1f out: edgd lft ins fnl f: styd on* **5/2**[1]

0-55 **2** *1 1/4* **Defining Moment**[31] 2734 3-9-3 **55** ........ LukeMorris 6 — 58
(Rae Guest) *hld up: pushed along 1/2-way: hdwy over 1f out: r.o* **7/2**[2]

3222 **3** *1* **Maggi May (IRE)**[8] 3544 3-9-1 **53** ........(p[1]) PJMcDonald 7 — 52
(David Brown) *chsd ldrs: rdn 1/2-way: hung lft ins fnl f: styd on* **9/2**[3]

-005 **4** *3/4* **Cherry Leyf**[84] 1363 3-9-3 **55** ........(t[1]) PatDobbs 4 — 51
(Stuart Williams) *chsd ldrs: rdn over 1f out: styd on same pce ins fnl f* **20/1**

0-40 **5** *1/2* **Tess Graham**[16] 3260 3-8-7 **45** ........(p) JamesSullivan 5 — 39
(Sarah Hollinshead) *hld up: hdwy over 1f out: no ex wl ins fnl f* **28/1**

-660 **6** *3* **Rebel Heart**[11] 3423 3-9-1 **58** ow3 ........(v) RyanWhile(5) 1 — 42
(Bill Turner) *chsd ldrs: rdn 1/2-way: wknd ins fnl f* **13/2**

54-5 **7** *nk* **Papa Delta**[12] 3407 3-8-11 **49** ........ GeorgeDowning 2 — 32
(Tony Carroll) *prom: pushed along 1/2-way: rdn: hung lft and wknd ins fnl f* **12/1**

00-0 **8** *3/4* **I Wouldn't Bother**[8] 3525 3-9-5 **57** ........(t) TomMarquand 8 — 37
(Daniel Kubler) *hld up: rdn 1/2-way: wknd over 1f out* **20/1**

4224 **9** *6* **Lambrini Legacy**[15] 3285 3-9-0 **59** ........(h) JordanUys(7) 9 — 17
(Lisa Williamson) *hld up: plld hrd: rdn and wknd over 1f out* **10/1**

-065 **10** *9* **Sweet Amazement**[19] 3141 3-8-9 **47** ow1 ........ FergusSweeney 11
(Mark Usher) *hld up: sme hdwy 1/2-way: rdn and wknd over 1f out* **25/1**

59.76s (-0.24) **Going Correction** -0.25s/f (Firm) — **10** Ran SP% **115.9**
Speed ratings (Par 97): **91,89,87,86,85 80,80,78,69,54**
CSF £10.33 CT £36.67 TOTE £3.50: £1.50, £1.10, £1.90; EX 10.20 Trifecta £49.80.
**Owner** Kennet Valley Thoroughbreds XI **Bred** Habton Farms **Trained** Lambourn, Berks

**FOCUS**
This low-grade but competitive handicap was run 0.12 secs slower than the opening contest. The favourite made all and posted a minor pb.
T/Plt: £6.10 to a £1 stake. Pool: £59,870.07 - 7,073.13 winning units. T/Qpdt: £3.20 to a £1 stake. Pool: £4,259.65 - 959.22 winning units. **Colin Roberts**

# 3682 LINGFIELD (L-H)
## Saturday, June 17

**OFFICIAL GOING: Good to firm (good in places; watered; 7.6)**
Wind: light breeze Weather: warm and humid

## 3819 INJURED JOCKEYS FUND H'CAP — 1m 2f
**5:50** (5:51) (Class 6) (0-60,62) 3-Y-0 — **£2,264** (£673; £336; £168) **Stalls** Low

Form — RPR

-524 **1** **Orithia (USA)**[3] 3721 3-9-8 **61** ........(t) ShaneKelly 9 — 66
(Seamus Durack) *trckd ldrs: hdwy 3f out: led appr 2f out: sn rdn: r.o wl fnl f* **11/4**[1]

00-0 **2** *nk* **Broughtons Admiral**[14] 3327 3-9-2 **55** ........ PatCosgrave 3 — 59
(Henry Spiller) *hld up: effrt 2f out on far rail: sn ev ch: rdn and r.o ins fnl f* **20/1**

5300 **3** *2 1/4* **Hold Me Tight (IRE)**[19] 3162 3-9-0 **53** ........ LiamJones 6 — 53
(J S Moore) *hld up: prog and drvn over 2f out: rdn and r.o wl appr fnl f: nvr nrr* **16/1**

60-0 **4** *3 1/2* **Take A Turn (IRE)**[14] 3327 3-9-7 **60** ........ TomQueally 1 — 54
(David Lanigan) *trckd ldrs: effrt on inner 3f out: sn ev ch: rdn wl over 1f out: grad wknd* **10/1**

0006 **5** *1 1/2* **King Kevin**[5] 3657 3-9-0 **53** ........(v) MartinHarley 7 — 44
(Ed Dunlop) *mid-div: rdn over 2f out: sme late hdwy but nvr a threat* **4/1**[2]

5-00 **6** *1 1/4* **Kitsey (IRE)**[22] 3024 3-9-0 **60** ........ RossaRyan(7) 2 — 48
(Richard Hannon) *hld up: drvn 2f out: rdn and one pce appr fnl f* **14/1**

4460 **7** *1 1/2* **Born To Reason (IRE)**[56] 1968 3-9-6 **59** ........ RyanPowell 4 — 44
(Kevin Frost) *led: hdd appr 2f out: sn rdn and wknd* **7/1**

6-40 **8** *3 1/2* **Russian Regard (IRE)**[21] 3087 3-9-7 **60** ........ RenatoSouza 8 — 39
(Jonathan Portman) *a in rr: rdn and no hdwy fr 3f out* **11/1**

0-35 **9** *1/2* **Midnight Man (FR)**[26] 2902 3-9-6 **62** ........ JordanVaughan(3) 5 — 40
(K R Burke) *prom: drvn 3f out: sn rdn: fdd* **8/1**

-650 **10** *15* **Pentito Rap (USA)**[22] 3024 3-8-7 **46** ........ SamHitchcott 12
(Rod Millman) *prom: rdn and lost pl over 3f out: wknd qckly* **6/1**[3]

6000 **11** *2 1/2* **Joy**[25] 2911 3-8-4 **46** oh1 ........ GeorgeWood(3) 11
(Laura Mongan) *mid-div: pushed along 5f out: rdn and lost tch 3f out* **33/1**

4300 **12** *2 1/2* **Toolatetodelegate**[31] 2726 3-8-8 **52** ........ RachealKneller(5) 10
(Brian Barr) *mid-div: rn wd over 3f out: sn lost tch* **33/1**

2m 10.25s (-0.25) **Going Correction** -0.075s/f (Good) — **12** Ran SP% **125.2**
Speed ratings (Par 97): **98,97,95,93,91 90,89,86,86,74 72,70**
CSF £67.90 CT £775.03 TOTE £3.50: £1.40, £5.90, £4.90; EX 54.70 Trifecta £595.80.
**Owner** Stephen Tucker & Ownaracehorse **Bred** A Guida, J Guida & T Keenan **Trained** Upper Lambourn, Berkshire

**FOCUS**
Add 16yds to race distance. This was a maiden handicap, in effect, given the lack of winning form in the book, and was an extremely weak affair.

## 3820 HAPPY 21ST BIRTHDAY AMY H'CAP — 1m 2f
**6:20** (6:21) (Class 5) (0-70,71) 4-Y-0+ — **£2,911** (£866; £432; £216) **Stalls** Low

Form — RPR

0023 **1** **Tripartite (IRE)**[11] 3422 4-9-6 **69** ........ AdamBeschizza 5 — 78
(Jeremy Gask) *mid-div: hdwy 3f out: drvn 2f out: sn rdn and fnd stride ent fnl f: led u.p last 150yds: r.o wl* **7/2**[3]

2-34 **2** *1 1/2* **Monsieur Glory**[17] 3205 4-9-7 **70** ........(v) PatCosgrave 9 — 76
(Tom Clover) *prom: led 3f out: rdn 2f out: r.o u.p ent fnl f: hdd and no ex last 150yds* **5/2**[1]

23-6 **3** *2 1/4* **Iballisticvin**[17] 3208 4-9-2 **65** ........ TomQueally 10 — 68
(Gary Moore) *mid-div: hdwy over 2f out and sn ev ch: hrd rdn over 1f out: one pce fnl f* **10/1**

64-3 **4** *3 3/4* **Ya Jammeel**[8] 3540 4-9-4 **67** ........ CharlesBishop 2 — 61
(Mick Channon) *prom: ev ch 3f out: sn rdn: wknd fnl 2f* **11/4**[2]

000 **5** *4 1/2* **Arrowzone**[49] 2163 6-9-7 **70** ........ RyanPowell 6 — 55
(Kevin Frost) *hld up: effrt and plenty to do 3f out: rdn wl over 1f out: r.o ins fnl f* **12/1**

2-00 **6** *1 3/4* **Onehelluvatouch**[53] 2055 4-8-10 **59** ........(e[1]) SamHitchcott 7 — 41
(Philip Hide) *hld up: drvn 3f out: rdn 2f out: wknd appr fnl f* **20/1**

6650 **7** *8* **Al Khafji**[35] 2622 4-9-1 **64** ........(b) JackMitchell 8 — 30
(Jeremy Gask) *a in rr: rdn and no hdwy fnl 2f* **7/1**

6-0 **8** *36* **Mr Andros**[106] 1007 4-9-6 **69** ........ MartinDwyer 3
(Brendan Powell) *led: hdd 3f out: wknd qckly* **25/1**

2m 8.92s (-1.58) **Going Correction** -0.075s/f (Good) — **8** Ran SP% **115.4**
Speed ratings (Par 103): **103,101,100,97,93 92,85,56**
CSF £12.83 CT £78.27 TOTE £4.70: £1.50, £1.50, £3.00; EX 13.40 Trifecta £72.80.
**Owner** The Salt House Syndicate **Bred** Tally-Ho Stud **Trained** Stockbridge, Hants

**FOCUS**
Add 16yds to race distance. The first three home all came here in good form and the gallop looked an even one, so this looks reliable form for the grade.

## 3821 KEW ELECTRICAL FILLIES' NOVICE MEDIAN AUCTION STKS (PLUS 10 RACE) — 4f 217y
**6:50** (6:52) (Class 5) 2-Y-0 — **£2,264** (£673; £336; £168) **Stalls** Centre

Form — RPR

4 **1** **Utterly Charming (IRE)**[9] 3502 2-9-0 **0** ........ SamHitchcott 9 — 74+
(Clive Cox) *trckd ldrs: drvn 2f out: rdn and swtchd to rail ent fnl f: briefly n.m.r: 1 l down 150yds out: r.o strly u.p to ld last 2 strides* **8/1**

223 **2** *nk* **Three Little Birds**[16] 3230 2-8-9 **0** ........ MitchGodwin(5) 11 — 73
(Sylvester Kirk) *led: pushed along 2f out: 1 l clr ent fnl f: rdn and r.o wl: ct last 2 strides* **11/2**[3]

043 **3** *3/4* **Firenze Rosa (IRE)**[22] 3029 2-9-0 **0** ........ AdamBeschizza 6 — 70
(John Bridger) *a.p: ev ch 2f out: rdn appr fnl f: one pce* **16/1**

226 **4** *2 1/2* **Take Shelter**[28] 2832 2-9-0 **0** ........ MartinHarley 2 — 61
(James Tate) *chsd ldrs: 4th and rdn over 1f out: no imp* **7/4**[1]

0 **5** *1 1/2* **Hunni**[24] 2958 2-9-0 **0** ........ PatCosgrave 14 — 56
(Tom Clover) *hld up: pushed along 2f out: r.o ins fnl f* **20/1**

**6** *3/4* **Lady Marigold (IRE)** 2-9-0 **0** ........ CharlesBishop 10 — 53
(Eve Johnson Houghton) *mid-div: effrt 2f out: styd on one pce fnl f* **20/1**

5 **7** *2* **Dreamboat Annie**[19] 3156 2-9-0 **0** ........ StevieDonohoe 3 — 46
(Mark Usher) *mid-div: rdn over 1f out: one pce fnl f* **25/1**

**8** *2 1/4* **Dusty** 2-9-0 **0** ........ RyanTate 5 — 37
(Mick Channon) *mid-div: no hdwy fnl 2f* **25/1**

4 **9** *1 1/4* **Prezzie**[16] 3244 2-9-0 **0** ........ MartinDwyer 7 — 33
(William Muir) *mid-div: drvn 2f out: no imp* **12/1**

0 **10** *3/4* **Disapproval (IRE)**[25] 2910 2-9-0 **0** ........ TomQueally 12 — 30
(Daniel Kubler) *hld up: pushed along over 1f out: nvr a factor* **25/1**

**11** *2 3/4* **Arden Pearl (IRE)** 2-9-0 **0** ........(h[1]) JackMitchell 8 — 20
(Archie Watson) *a in rr: no hdwy whn drvn 2f out* **18/1**

43 **12** *1 1/2* **Jonnysimpson (IRE)**[17] 3210 2-9-0 **0** ........ ShaneKelly 13 — 15
(Brendan Powell) *prom tl drvn and wknd qckly 2f out* **9/2**[2]

57.97s (-0.23) **Going Correction** -0.175s/f (Firm) — **12** Ran SP% **120.9**
Speed ratings (Par 90): **94,93,92,88,85 84,81,77,75,74 70,67**
CSF £48.39 TOTE £10.50: £2.70, £1.80, £4.80; EX 52.70 Trifecta £1101.30.
**Owner** Mrs Patricia J Burns **Bred** Mrs Louise Lyons **Trained** Lambourn, Berks

**FOCUS**
Not a particularly strong fillies' maiden but the winner is at least unexposed and going the right way.

## 3822 COMMODORE KITCHENS FILLIES' H'CAP — 6f
**7:20** (7:22) (Class 4) (0-80,82) 3-Y-0 — **£4,690** (£1,395; £697; £348) **Stalls** Centre

Form — RPR

3-32 **1** **Beck And Call**[19] 3157 3-8-12 **75** ........ GeorgiaCox(5) 5 — 82
(Henry Candy) *trckd ldrs: pushed along 2f out: led over 1f out: hrd rdn and hld on wl fnl f* **6/1**[3]

2135 **2** *nk* **Pepita (IRE)**[38] 2517 3-9-7 **79** ........ PatCosgrave 6 — 85
(Richard Hannon) *chsd ldr: pushed along to ld 2f out: rdn and hdd over 1f out: rallied and r.o wl u.p ins fnl f* **8/1**

2-1 **3** *shd* **Cartographer**[24] 2970 3-9-10 **82** ........ JamieSpencer 7 — 87+
(Martyn Meade) *hld up: hdwy between horses over 1f out: rdn and ev ch ent fnl f: r.o but hld last 50yds* **6/4**[1]

216- **4** **Ariena (IRE)**[296] 5794 3-9-7 **79** ........ JohnFahy 2 — 83
(Clive Cox) *trckd ldrs: drvn and swtchd over 1f out: hrd rdn ent fnl f: r.o* **18/1**

-200 **5** *1/2* **Jule In The Crown**[18] 3167 3-9-10 **82** ........ CharlesBishop 3 — 84
(Mick Channon) *mid-div: drvn over 2f out: sn hrd rdn: r.o fnl f* **14/1**

61 **6** *1 3/4* **Edged In Blue**[53] 2072 3-8-5 **64** ow2 ........ JordanVaughan(3) 1 — 62
(K R Burke) *mid-div: drvn to chal over 2f out: rdn and no ex ent fnl f* **20/1**

535- **7** *1* **Sparkle**[192] 8244 3-9-0 **72** ........ MartinHarley 4 — 65
(Ed Dunlop) *in rr: rdn wl over 1f out: no imp* **16/1**

21-3 **8** *4* **Cashla Bay**[18] 3167 3-9-9 **81** ........ RobertTart 8 — 61
(John Gosden) *led: pushed along and hdd 2f out: drvn and no ex* **5/2**[2]

1m 9.87s (-1.33) **Going Correction** -0.175s/f (Firm) — **8** Ran SP% **116.5**
Speed ratings (Par 98): **101,100,100,99,99 96,95,90**
CSF £53.57 CT £108.05 TOTE £7.00: £1.90, £1.60, £1.10; EX 49.10 Trifecta £110.30.
**Owner** Major M G Wyatt **Bred** Dunchurch Lodge Stud Company **Trained** Kingston Warren, Oxon



The Form Book Flat, Raceform Ltd, Newbury, RG14 5SJ

**FOCUS**
A competitive 0-80 fillies' handicap given the five of the eight runners were rated 79 or higher, but they finished in a heap so mixed messages from this form.

## 3823 DENISE CALVER BIRTHDAY H'CAP 7f
7:50 (7:52) (Class 6) (0-55,53) 3-Y-O+ £2,264 (£673; £336; £168) Stalls Centre

Form RPR
6062 1 **Emily Goldfinch**19 3137 4-9-7 50 DannyBrock 10 62
(Phil McEntee) *mde all: pushed along 2f out: 1 l clr whn rdn over 1f out: r.o wl fnl f* 8/1[3]
0-04 2 1 3/4 **Lesanti**29 2792 3-8-5 50 RossaRyan(7) 2 54
(Ed de Giles) *trckd ldrs: pushed along 2f out: rdn over 1f out: r.o wl to take 2nd last 150yds* 9/2[2]
00-0 3 2 **Arctic Flower (IRE)**4 3688 4-9-7 50 MartinHarley 12 52
(John Bridger) *prom: rdn and ev ch in 2nd 2f out: kpt on one pce ent fnl f: lost 2nd last 150yds* 8/1[3]
0651 4 1 1/2 **Gypsy Rider**45 2294 8-9-6 49 PatCosgrave 13 47
(Henry Tett) *trckd ldrs: rdn 2f out: one pce fnl f* 8/1[3]
0020 5 3 1/2 **Flying Sakhee**8 3532 4-9-5 53 MitchGodwin(5) 9 41
(John Bridger) *mid-div: effrt 2f out: no ex u.p ins fnl f* 12/1
210 6 1 1/4 **Sir Jamie**46 2255 4-9-1 47 GeorgeWood(3) 6 32
(Tony Carroll) *mid-div: rdn over 1f out: one pce* 9/1
0-00 7 shd **Seventii**58 1906 3-8-12 50 JFEgan 1 32
(Robert Eddery) *in rr early: effrt u.p 2f out: one pce* 25/1
-005 8 2 **The Dancing Lord**8 3546 8-9-10 53 (tp) JohnFahy 3 32
(Adam West) *mid-div: rdn 2f out: no imp* 33/1
0640 9 4 **Quintus Cerialis (IRE)**30 2763 5-9-8 51 (vt1) AdamBeschizza 11 20
(Karen George) *mid-div: drvn along 2f out: fdd* 20/1
0000 10 1/2 **Bassino (USA)**25 2916 4-8-13 47 (v1) RachealKneller(5) 7 14
(James Bennett) *hld up: rdn over 2f out: no imp* 20/1
0-60 11 2 1/2 **Ashford Island**19 3137 4-9-2 45 (b) ShaneKelly 5 5
(Adam West) *prom tl rdn and lost pl 2f out* 33/1
0044 12 nk **Spare Parts (IRE)**9 3496 3-8-13 51 JamieSpencer 8 8
(Charles Hills) *in rr: drvn 3f out: hrd rdn 2f out: little rspnse* 3/1[1]
00-6 13 3/4 **Aegean Secret**12 3407 3-8-7 45 (v1) RyanTate 16
(John Bridger) *trckd ldrs: rdn 2f out: wknd* 25/1
00-3 14 3 1/4 **Royal Caper**24 2961 7-9-9 52 StevieDonohoe 4
(Miss Joey Ellis) *mid-div: n.m.r 3f out: rdn and struggling fr 2f out* 10/1
4403 U **Captain Sedgwick (IRE)**45 2309 3-8-4 47 JaneElliott(5) 15
(John Spearing) *uns rdr after 2f* 14/1
1m 22.98s (-0.32) **Going Correction** -0.175s/f (Firm)
**WFA** 3 from 4yo+ 9lb 15 Ran SP% **133.1**
Speed ratings (Par 101): **94,92,89,88,84 82,82,80,75,75 72,71,70,67,**
CSF £44.26 CT £322.17 TOTE £10.70: £3.70, £1.60, £3.20; EX 67.00 Trifecta £478.20.
**Owner** McHugh & Paxton **Bred** J M Paxton & Mrs S J Wrigley **Trained** Newmarket, Suffolk
**FOCUS**
Quantity over quality here. The speed held up and very few could make an impact from off the pace.

## 3824 SHARON SIMMONS MEMORIAL MEDIAN AUCTION MAIDEN STKS 7f
8:20 (8:26) (Class 6) 3-4-Y-O £2,264 (£673; £336; £168) Stalls Centre

Form RPR
40 1 **Warsaw Road (IRE)**15 3293 3-9-3 0 PatCosgrave 5 77
(Luca Cumani) *hld up: plenty to do 2f out: hdwy 1f out: sn chal ldr: pushed out to ld ins fnl f: reminder 50yds out: comf* 4/1[3]
42-2 2 1 **Nuncio**26 2901 3-9-3 73 TomQueally 7 74
(Daniel Kubler) *chsd ldr: led over 2f out: 1 l clr and rdn appr fnl f: r.o but ct ins fnl f* 3/1[2]
3-33 3 3 **Margherita**24 2957 3-8-12 75 SilvestreDeSousa 8 61
(Roger Varian) *trckd ldrs: drvn 2f out: sn hrd rdn: one pce fnl f* 10/11[1]
40-0 4 2 1/2 **Tesko Fella (IRE)**21 3085 3-9-3 66 (p1) AntonioFresu 6 59
(Luke McJannet) *chsd ldrs: drvn wl over 1f out: rdn appr fnl f: no ex* 16/1
00 5 1/2 **Easy Wind**10 3472 3-8-12 0 RyanPowell 9 53
(Sir Mark Prescott Bt) *in rr: struggling 1/2-way: pushed along fr 2f out: r.o ins fnl f: nvr nrr* 40/1
5- 6 1 **Solitary Sister (IRE)**339 4261 3-8-12 0 (t1) StevieDonohoe 2 52
(Richard Spencer) *slowly away and flashed tail: in rr: pushed along 1/2-way: rdn over 1f out: sme late hdwy* 8/1
00- 7 nk **Clandon**269 6674 4-9-5 0 RossaRyan(7) 1 57
(Brett Johnson) *mid-div on outer: rdn appr 2f out: fdd fnl f* 66/1
0 8 7 **Hanningfield**16 3234 3-9-3 0 DannyBrock 4 35
(Michael Bell) *led: hdd over 2f out: sn hrd rdn: wknd qckly* 25/1
1m 23.82s (0.52) **Going Correction** -0.175s/f (Firm)
**WFA** 3 from 4yo 9lb 8 Ran SP% **122.2**
Speed ratings (Par 101): **90,88,85,82,82 80,80,72**
CSF £17.54 TOTE £5.10: £1.60, £1.30, £1.10; EX 17.50 Trifecta £28.00.
**Owner** Mrs A Silver & Partner **Bred** Tally-Ho Stud **Trained** Newmarket, Suffolk
**FOCUS**
The front two came clear of the disappointing odds-on favourite and this looks a maiden of little depth.

## 3825 #TAKETHEREINS MAIDEN STKS 6f
8:50 (8:52) (Class 5) 3-Y-O+ £2,911 (£866; £432; £216) Stalls Centre

Form RPR
42- 1 **Tundra**248 7279 3-8-10 0 SilvestreDeSousa 1 78
(Roger Varian) *trckd ldrs: jnd runner-up 2f out: rdn wl over 1f out: r.o resolutely u.p to ld wl ins fnl f* 2/1[2]
-422 2 nk **Buxted Dream (USA)**16 3234 3-9-1 82 JamieSpencer 3 82
(Luca Cumani) *led: chal by wnr 2f out: rdn wl over 1f out: responded and r.o: hdd wl ins fnl f* 8/15[1]
0 3 14 **Good Bond**10 3456 5-9-8 0 RobertTart 2 39
(Linda Jewell) *t.k.h: chsd ldr: drvn over 2f out: losing tch w ldrs whn rdn over 1f out: jst hld on for 3rd fnl f* 50/1
0-0 4 shd **Dawn Goddess**154 237 3-8-10 0 ShaneKelly 4 32
(Gary Moore) *t.k.h: chsd ldrs: drvn and dropped to last over 2f out: rdn over 1f out: styd on fnl f* 28/1
0-0 5 1/2 **Meyrick**12 3394 3-9-1 0 PatCosgrave 5 35
(William Haggas) *hld up in last: hdwy over 2f out: sn pushed along: wknd ins fnl f* 10/1[3]
1m 11.14s (-0.06) **Going Correction** -0.175s/f (Firm)
**WFA** 3 from 5yo 7lb 5 Ran SP% **113.1**
Speed ratings (Par 103): **93,92,73,73,73**
CSF £3.52 TOTE £2.90: £1.40, £1.10; EX 3.40 Trifecta £28.30.
**Owner** Prince A A Faisal **Bred** Nawara Stud Co Ltd **Trained** Newmarket, Suffolk
■ Stewards' Enquiry : Jamie Spencer two-day ban; used his whip down the shoulder in the forehand (Jul 1-2)

**FOCUS**
This turned into a match between the two with the best form and they pulled well clear of three modest-looking rivals.
T/Plt: £116.60 to a £1 stake. Pool: £62,608.35 - 391.81 winning units. T/Qpdt: £18.30 to a £1 stake. Pool: £5,567.49 - 224.55 winning units. **Keith McHugh**

# 3332 MUSSELBURGH (R-H)
Saturday, June 17

**OFFICIAL GOING: Good to firm (7.9)**
Wind: Breezy, half against in sprints and in over 3f of home straight in races on the round course Weather: Cloudy, bright

## 3826 EBF STALLIONS MAIDEN STKS 5f 1y
1:35 (1:36) (Class 5) 2-Y-O £3,234 (£962; £481; £240) Stalls High

Form RPR
1 **Roland Rocks (IRE)** 2-9-5 0 CamHardie 2 82
(John Ryan) *s.i.s: hld up: stdy hdwy whn n.m.r wl over 1f out: rdn to ld ins fnl f: kpt on wl* 20/1
00 2 1 **Jive Lady (IRE)**18 3169 2-9-0 0 JoeFanning 8 73
(Mark Johnston) *led: rdn over 1f out: edgd rt and hdd ins fnl f: kpt on: hld towards fin* 17/2
63 3 1 1/2 **Palmer (IRE)**31 2740 2-9-5 0 ConnorBeasley 3 73
(Bryan Smart) *in tch on outside: hdwy over 1f out: rdn and edgd lft ins fnl f: kpt on: nt pce to chal* 5/2[1]
3 4 nk **Ce De Nullis (IRE)**7 3557 2-9-0 0 (h) MartinLane 6 67
(Paul Midgley) *s.i.s: sn prom: rdn along 2f out: kpt on same pce ins fnl f* 5/1[3]
32 5 1/2 **Donny Belle**17 3215 2-9-0 0 TomEaves 4 65
(David Brown) *w ldr to over 1f out: drvn and outpcd fnl f* 5/1[3]
62 6 1/2 **Shobrom (IRE)**43 2373 2-9-5 0 TonyHamilton 1 68
(Richard Fahey) *in tch: hdwy and rdn 2f out: wknd ins fnl f* 10/3[2]
0 7 3 3/4 **Free Spirited**18 3165 2-9-5 0 DavidNolan 7 55
(Richard Fahey) *noisy and green in paddock: in tch: rdn and outpcd 1/2-way: btn over 1f out* 20/1
0263 8 3/4 **Rocket Man Dan (IRE)**14 3333 2-9-5 0 DougieCostello 5 52
(Keith Dalgleish) *in tch: rdn and outpcd 1/2-way: wknd wl over 1f out* 9/1
1m 0.29s (-0.11) **Going Correction** -0.225s/f (Firm) 8 Ran SP% **115.0**
Speed ratings (Par 93): **91,89,87,86,85 84,78,77**
CSF £177.26 TOTE £26.20: £6.50, £2.80, £1.30; EX 219.20 Trifecta £778.60.
**Owner** Gerry McGladery **Bred** E Heary **Trained** Newmarket, Suffolk
**FOCUS**
All races run over the advertised distances. After the first winning jockey Cam Hardie said the ground was "good to firm", while second-placed Joe Fanning said it was "quick". A decent maiden with a surprise outcome.

## 3827 WILLIAM HILL TARTAN TROPHY CONSOLATION RACE H'CAP 5f 1y
2:05 (2:07) (Class 3) 4-Y-O+ £25,876 (£7,700; £3,848; £1,924) Stalls High

Form RPR
6245 1 **Orient Class**28 2839 6-8-11 84 ConnorMurtagh(7) 9 93
(Paul Midgley) *trckd ldrs: led over 1f out: drvn out fnl f* 16/1
2141 2 1 1/4 **Zac Brown (IRE)**6 3617 6-8-10 81 6ex (t) DavidEgan(5) 14 86+
(Charlie Wallis) *s.i.s: hld up towards rr: hdwy over 1f out: wnt 2nd ins fnl f: kpt on fin* 13/2[2]
0605 3 shd **Showdaisy**14 3337 4-9-2 87 (p) RowanScott(5) 7 91
(Keith Dalgleish) *s.i.s: bhd: hdwy and prom 1/2-way: effrt and disp 2nd pl ins fnl f: kpt on: hld nr fin* 11/1
0042 4 3/4 **Stanghow**15 3288 5-9-3 83 CamHardie 2 84
(Antony Brittain) *cl up: effrt and rdn over 1f out: kpt on same pce ins fnl f* 22/1
0022 5 3/4 **Rasheeq (IRE)**21 3092 4-9-7 90 RachelRichardson(3) 10 89+
(Tim Easterby) *t.k.h: hld up: hdwy whn nt clr run 1/2-way: effrt and rdn over 1f out: kpt on ins fnl f* 4/1[1]
-226 6 1/2 **Straightothepoint**24 2951 5-9-4 84 (p) ConnorBeasley 8 81
(Bryan Smart) *trckd ldrs: effrt and drvn along 2f out: kpt on same pce ins fnl f* 8/1
3333 7 1/2 **Fast Track**46 2262 6-9-9 89 DougieCostello 13 84
(David Barron) *hld up in tch: effrt and rdn 2f out: kpt on same pce fnl f* 14/1
4030 8 shd **Olivia Fallow (IRE)**14 3321 5-9-5 85 GrahamLee 1 80
(Paul Midgley) *bhd on outside: rdn and hdwy over 1f out: kpt on fnl f: nvr able to chal* 14/1
2305 9 nse **Highly Sprung (IRE)**14 3330 4-9-3 83 JoeFanning 12 78+
(Mark Johnston) *sn pushed along towards rr: hdwy over 1f out: kpt on fnl f: nvr able to chal* 22/1
-414 10 nk **Tommy G**24 2951 4-8-6 77 PhilDennis(5) 11 71
(Jim Goldie) *s.i.s: bhd: hdwy over 1f out: no imp whn n.m.r briefly ins fnl f* 14/1
3254 11 nk **Tylery Wonder (IRE)**15 3295 7-9-0 80 (b) MartinLane 5 72
(Paul Midgley) *led: rdn and hdd over 1f out: wknd and eased ins fnl f* 28/1
3110 12 1 1/2 **Excessable**14 3321 4-9-9 89 6ex (t) DavidAllan 15 76
(Tim Easterby) *hld up on ins: rdn over 2f out: wknd wl over 1f out* 13/2[2]
4-04 13 1/2 **Lotara**12 3384 5-7-7 66 oh7 MillyNaseb(7) 6 51
(Jim Goldie) *bhd and outpcd: nvr on terms* 66/1
2050 14 3 1/4 **Meadway**59 1876 6-9-7 87 (p) TomEaves 3 61
(Bryan Smart) *in tch on outside: rdn over 2f out: wknd over 1f out* 18/1
-210 U **Paddy Power (IRE)**14 3324 4-8-12 81 SammyJoBell(3) 4
(Richard Fahey) *rrd and uns rdr leaving stalls* 7/1[3]
58.91s (-1.49) **Going Correction** -0.225s/f (Firm) 15 Ran SP% **123.4**
Speed ratings (Par 107): **102,100,99,98,97 96,95,95,95,95 94,92,91,86,**
CSF £114.41 CT £1249.20 TOTE £21.90: £5.60, £2.60, £3.30; EX 151.60 Trifecta £1561.10.
**Owner** F Brady,A Williams,P Lindley,S Wibberley **Bred** Frank Brady **Trained** Westow, N Yorks
**FOCUS**
A very competitive consolation race for the Scottish Sprint Cup, effectively a 0-90. The first two both had the stands' rail in the latter stages.

## 3828 WILLIAM HILL MARES AND FILLIES' H'CAP 1m 2y
2:35 (2:37) (Class 3) (0-90,88) 3-Y-O+ £12,938 (£3,850; £1,924; £962) Stalls Low

Form RPR
-243 1 **Lincoln Rocks**29 2789 4-10-0 88 DavidNolan 6 97
(David O'Meara) *mde all: hrd pressed and rdn over 1f out: edgd lft: hld on gamely fnl f* 10/1
1-1 2 1/2 **Khamaary (IRE)**26 2900 3-9-3 87 JoeFanning 4 93
(Mark Johnston) *t.k.h early: pressed ldr: rdn and disp ld over 1f out to ins fnl f: kpt on same pce nr fin* 1/1[1]

4304 **3** 2½ **Hidden Rebel**[26] 2884 5-9-10 **84** ConnorBeasley 9 86
(Alistair Whillans) *hld up: rdn over 2f out: kpt on fnl f: nvr able to chal* **12/1**

0020 **4** shd **Alexandrakollontai (IRE)**[10] 3451 7-9-4 **78** (b) DougieCostello 1 80
(Alistair Whillans) *prom: drvn and outpcd 2f out: kpt on ins fnl f: no imp* **28/1**

213 **5** ½ **Acadian Angel (IRE)**[26] 2885 3-7-12 **73** DavidEgan(5) 10 72
(John Quinn) *t.k.h: hld up in tch: effrt and rdn 2f out: edgd lft: kpt on same pce fnl f* **13/2**[3]

3-13 **6** 2½ **Normandie Lady**[16] 3233 4-9-2 **83** ConnorMurtagh(7) 2 78
(Richard Fahey) *t.k.h: prom: drvn and outpcd 2f out: btn fnl f* **5/1**[2]

2122 **7** ¾ **Forever A Lady (IRE)**[7] 3577 4-9-2 **76** GrahamLee 8 69
(Keith Dalgleish) *trckd ldrs: drvn and edgd rt wl over 1f out: wknd fnl f* **14/1**

0-00 **8** ¾ **Lil Sophella (IRE)**[7] 3567 8-9-2 **76** NeilFarley 3 68
(Patrick Holmes) *s.i.s: hld up: rdn over 2f out: no imp fr over 1f out* **33/1**

6223 **9** 10 **Amber Mystique**[19] 3147 4-9-1 **75** TonyHamilton 5 44
(Kristin Stubbs) *hld up bhd ldng gp: rdn and outpcd over 2f out: btn over 1f out* **33/1**

3520 **10** 6 **Fiendish (USA)**[26] 2894 3-8-0 **75** RichardOliver(5) 7 28
(Mark Johnston) *hld up on outside: hdwy and cl up over 3f out: rdn and wknd over 2f out* **33/1**

1m 38.72s (-2.48) **Going Correction** -0.125s/f (Firm)
**WFA** 3 from 4yo+ 10lb **10** Ran SP% **115.7**
Speed ratings (Par 104): **107,106,104,103,103 100,100,99,89,83**
CSF £19.71 CT £126.74 TOTE £14.40: £3.80, £1.02, £3.90; EX 32.20 Trifecta £187.70.
**Owner** Peter Smith P C Coaches Limited **Bred** James Ortega Bloodstock **Trained** Upper Helmsley, N Yorks

**FOCUS**
The principals were always prominent in this decent handicap for fillies.

## 3829 WILLIAM HILL SCOTTISH SPRINT CUP H'CAP 5f 1y
**3:10** (3:14) (Class 2) 4-Y-O+
**£62,250** (£18,640; £9,320; £4,660; £2,330; £1,170) **Stalls** High

Form RPR

3400 **1** **Line Of Reason (IRE)**[14] 3321 7-8-12 **97** JoeFanning 8 106
(Paul Midgley) *hld up: hdwy on outside over 1f out: kpt on wl fnl f to ld nr fin* **11/1**

2004 **2** nk **Harry Hurricane**[21] 3092 5-8-13 **98** (b) TrevorWhelan 7 106
(George Baker) *trckd ldrs gng wl: shkn up to ld ent fnl f: edgd rt and kpt on u.p: hdd nr fin* **9/1**

1100 **3** ¾ **Kimberella**[14] 3321 7-9-3 **109** ConnorMurtagh(7) 14 114
(Richard Fahey) *bhd: hdwy on outside over 1f out: rdn and kpt on fnl f: nrst fin* **9/1**

0501 **4** ¾ **Caspian Prince (IRE)**[14] 3321 8-9-12 **111** 6ex (t) TomEaves 4 113
(Tony Coyle) *w ldr: led 1/2-way tl hdd ent fnl f: kpt on same pce* **16/1**

310- **5** ½ **Mirza**[238] 7537 10-9-3 **107** (p) DavidEgan(5) 2 108
(Rae Guest) *hld up in tch: effrt and edgd lft over 1f out: kpt on same pce ins fnl f* **33/1**

1320 **6** ¾ **Robot Boy (IRE)**[30] 2764 7-9-0 **99** DougieCostello 11 97
(David Barron) *in tch: drvn along over 2f out: rallied: kpt on same pce ins fnl f* **14/1**

-110 **7** nse **El Astronaute (IRE)**[14] 3321 4-8-9 **94** JasonHart 5 92
(John Quinn) *led to 1/2-way: cl up tl drvn and no ex ins fnl f* **14/1**

-240 **8** nse **East Street Revue**[21] 3092 4-8-9 **94** (b) DuranFentiman 1 91
(Tim Easterby) *hld up on outside: hdwy 2f out: rdn and no imp fnl f* **16/1**

1041 **9** ¾ **Stepper Point**[16] 3231 8-8-9 **94** 6ex (v) GrahamLee 6 89
(William Muir) *in tch: rdn over 2f out: kpt on same pce fr over 1f out* **25/1**

-303 **10** shd **Confessional**[6] 3625 10-8-7 **92** (e) CamHardie 17 86
(Tim Easterby) *bhd: angled rt and hdwy over 1f out: kpt on fnl f: nvr able to chal* **22/1**

0-64 **11** nse **Orion's Bow**[35] 2611 6-9-2 **104** RachelRichardson(3) 13 98+
(Tim Easterby) *midfield: no room fr 1/2-way: eased whn no ch last 100yds* **11/2**[1]

0-06 **12** ½ **Jack Dexter**[28] 2839 8-8-2 **92** PhilDennis(5) 12 84+
(Jim Goldie) *bhd and pushed along: nt clr run over 1f out to ins fnl f: n.d* **25/1**

-346 **13** nk **Gamesome (FR)**[21] 3092 6-8-7 **92** ShaneGray 15 83+
(Paul Midgley) *bhd: rdn whn nt clr run over 1f out: no imp fnl f* **8/1**[3]

0-10 **14** nse **Desert Law (IRE)**[14] 3321 9-8-9 **94** MartinLane 3 85
(Paul Midgley) *chsd ldrs: drvn along 1/2-way: wknd fnl f* **7/1**[2]

6413 **15** nk **Duke Of Firenze**[14] 3321 8-9-8 **107** DavidAllan 16 97
(David C Griffiths) *dwlt: bhd: hdwy over 1f out: no imp whn bmpd bdly ent fnl f: sn btn* **7/1**[2]

5220 **16** ½ **Bowson Fred**[14] 3321 5-8-8 **100** HarrisonShaw(7) 9 88
(Michael Easterby) *towards rr: drvn along 1/2-way: sn no imp: btn fnl f* **20/1**

0-00 **17** 1 **Move In Time**[14] 3321 9-9-0 **99** ow2 DavidNolan 10 84
(David O'Meara) *bhd: rdn whn nt clr run over 1f out: sn n.d* **28/1**

58.1s (-2.30) **Going Correction** -0.225s/f (Firm) **17** Ran SP% **128.1**
Speed ratings (Par 109): **109,108,107,106,105 104,104,103,102,102 102,101,101,101,100 99,98**
CSF £101.20 CT £985.98 TOTE £13.10: £3.40, £2.40, £2.80, £3.70; EX 137.40 Trifecta £1159.40.
**Owner** Taylor's Bloodstock Ltd **Bred** Corduff Stud Ltd, J Corcoran & J Judd **Trained** Westow, N Yorks

**FOCUS**
A high-class sprint handicap run at a blistering pace, and run just a tenth of a second outside the standard time. There was a blnaket finish and several just didn't get the chance to show what they were capable of.

## 3830 STOBO CASTLE LADIES DAY GOLD CUP H'CAP 1m 7f 217y
**3:45** (3:48) (Class 3) (0-85,87) 4-Y-O+ **£12,938** (£3,850; £1,924; £962) **Stalls** High

Form RPR

4-61 **1** **Great Fighter**[22] 3046 7-8-13 **79** (v) PhilDennis(5) 1 87+
(Jim Goldie) *s.i.s: hld up: stdy hdwy over 2f out: rdn to ld appr fnl f: kpt on wl* **11/4**[2]

1221 **2** 1½ **Kensington Star**[8] 3527 4-9-10 **85** (p) JasonHart 8 91
(Keith Dalgleish) *prom: effrt and wnt 2nd over 2f out to over 1f out: kpt on fnl f to regain 2nd nr fin: nt pce of wnr* **9/4**[1]

111 **3** nk **Sebastian's Wish (IRE)**[22] 3043 4-9-1 **76** JoeFanning 14 82
(Keith Dalgleish) *led to 1/2-way: regained ld over 3f out: rdn: edgd lft and hdd appr fnl f: kpt on: no ex and lost 2nd nr fin* **9/2**[3]

-123 **4** 1½ **Stoneham**[12] 3389 6-8-3 **71** (h) JamieGormley(7) 9 75
(Iain Jardine) *s.i.s: hld up: hdwy on outside 2f out: edgd rt: kpt on fnl f: nvr able to chal* **18/1**

0-06 **5** ½ **Buyer Beware (IRE)**[22] 3046 5-8-9 **70** ConnorBeasley 10 73
(Patrick Holmes) *in tch: drvn and outpcd over 2f out: rallied over 1f out: kpt on fnl f: nvr able to chal* **50/1**

1032 **6** nse **Cosmic Tigress**[22] 3046 6-7-9 **61** DavidEgan(5) 12 64
(John Quinn) *prom: rdn over 2f out: hdwy and ch briefly over 1f out: kpt on same pce ins fnl f* **14/1**

5-36 **7** 2¼ **Wor Lass**[8] 3527 9-8-13 **79** GarryWhillans(5) 7 79
(Donald Whillans) *hld up: pushed along over 2f out: hdwy whn nt clr run over 1f out: sn n.d* **25/1**

1311 **8** nk **Mr Globetrotter (USA)**[7] 3566 4-8-10 **76** CallumRodriguez(5) 3 76
(Iain Jardine) *hld up: rdn along 3f out: no imp fr over 1f out* **7/1**

05 **9** 2½ **Apalis (FR)**[11] 3432 5-8-4 **65** CamHardie 5 62
(Michael Easterby) *hld up: rdn along over 2f out: sn outpcd: n.d after* **33/1**

3-66 **10** 7 **An Fear Ciuin (IRE)**[13] 666 6-9-3 **78** (p) DougieCostello 13 67
(R Mike Smith) *chsd ldrs tl rdn and wknd fr 2f out* **28/1**

-004 **11** nk **Stormin Tom (IRE)**[10] 3464 5-8-7 **71** (p1) RachelRichardson(3) 11 59
(Tim Easterby) *cl up: led 1/2-way to over 3f out: rdn and wknd 2f out* **18/1**

5330 **12** 2¾ **Falcon's Fire (IRE)**[16] 3240 4-8-12 **73** GrahamLee 2 58
(Keith Dalgleish) *hld up: drvn along over 3f out: wknd fnl 2f* **20/1**

3m 28.38s (-5.12) **Going Correction** -0.125s/f (Firm) **12** Ran SP% **122.3**
Speed ratings (Par 107): **107,106,106,105,105 105,103,103,102,99 98,97**
CSF £9.05 CT £27.79 TOTE £3.80: £1.20, £1.50, £1.90; EX 11.10 Trifecta £45.10.
**Owner** J Fyffe **Bred** Darley **Trained** Uplawmoor, E Renfrews

**FOCUS**
A decent staying handicap, run at a solid gallop.

## 3831 MADELEINE CUP H'CAP (DIV I) 7f 33y
**4:20** (4:22) (Class 6) (0-55,55) 3-Y-O+ **£3,234** (£962; £481; £240) **Stalls** Low

Form RPR

061- **1** **Great Colaci**[169] 8589 4-9-8 **53** DavidNolan 8 59
(Gillian Boanas) *prom: drvn over 2f out: rallied over 1f out: kpt on wl fnl f to ld nr fin* **4/1**[2]

-506 **2** nk **Kelpie Spirit (IRE)**[40] 2455 3-8-7 **52** DavidEgan(5) 5 54
(John Weymes) *hld up: rdn and hdwy 2f out: kpt on wl fnl f: hld cl home* **12/1**

6063 **3** hd **Harbour Patrol (IRE)**[44] 2342 5-9-2 **47** (b) DuranFentiman 12 52
(Rebecca Bastiman) *pressed ldr: led 3f out: 3 l clr whn rdn and hung rt over 1f out: kpt on fnl f: hdd nr fin* **10/1**

00-6 **4** 2 **Devil's Guard (IRE)**[9] 3484 3-8-9 **49** (v1) GrahamLee 11 45
(Keith Dalgleish) *t.k.h: hld up: pushed along and hdwy over 1f out: kpt on fnl f: no imp* **10/1**

6464 **5** ½ **Jessie Allan (IRE)**[18] 3185 6-8-10 **46** oh1 PhilDennis(5) 2 44
(Jim Goldie) *midfield: effrt and drvn over 2f out: kpt on same pce fr over 1f out* **14/1**

5030 **6** hd **Let Right Be Done**[17] 3196 5-9-2 **47** (p) ShaneGray 3 44
(Linda Perratt) *chsd ldrs: hdwy and ev ch over 3f out: outpcd 2f out: n.d after* **7/1**[3]

3502 **7** 2 **Magic Journey (IRE)**[12] 3387 3-9-1 **55** (p1) JasonHart 9 44
(John Quinn) *t.k.h in midfield: drvn and outpcd over 2f out: n.d after* **5/2**[1]

0665 **8** 1¾ **Ryedale Rio (IRE)**[18] 3185 4-9-6 **51** (b) DavidAllan 6 38
(Tim Easterby) *s.i.s: hld up: outpcd whn hung rt over 2f out: sn no imp* **10/1**

0-00 **9** ½ **Tael O' Gold**[8] 3525 3-8-7 **47** (p) JoeFanning 10 30
(Iain Jardine) *s.i.s: hld up: rdn and shortlived effrt on outside 2f out: sn n.d* **25/1**

0-00 **10** 3 **Equity**[26] 2897 3-9-1 **55** (b1) TomEaves 1 30
(David Brown) *t.k.h: led: blkd bnd ent st: rdn and wknd 2f out* **14/1**

40-0 **11** 1½ **Myllachy**[48] 2181 3-8-5 **48** (b1) RachelRichardson(3) 4 19
(Tim Easterby) *t.k.h: in tch: struggling over 2f out: btn whn blkd over 1f out* **14/1**

1m 29.0s **Going Correction** -0.125s/f (Firm)
**WFA** 3 from 4yo+ 9lb **11** Ran SP% **119.9**
Speed ratings (Par 101): **95,94,94,92,91 91,89,87,86,83 81**
CSF £52.65 CT £465.39 TOTE £4.30: £1.70, £3.90, £3.30; EX 59.70 Trifecta £741.40.
**Owner** Rug, Grub & Pub Partnership **Bred** Reveley Farms **Trained** Lingdale, Redcar & Cleveland

**FOCUS**
Low-grade handicap form. It was the slightly quicker division.

## 3832 MADELEINE CUP H'CAP (DIV II) 7f 33y
**4:55** (4:56) (Class 6) (0-55,56) 3-Y-O+ **£3,234** (£962; £481; £240) **Stalls** Low

Form RPR

0-00 **1** **Clear As A Bell (IRE)**[27] 2853 3-8-11 **51** DavidAllan 7 55
(Tim Easterby) *mde virtually all: hrd pressed fr 1/2-way: hld on gamely fnl f* **14/1**

5044 **2** ¾ **Secret City (IRE)**[24] 2950 11-9-1 **46** oh1 (b) DuranFentiman 5 51
(Rebecca Bastiman) *s.i.s: hld up: hdwy 2f out: kpt on fnl f to take 2nd nr fin* **12/1**

0406 **3** nk **Cyflymder (IRE)**[22] 3048 11-8-12 **46** oh1 RachelRichardson(3) 12 50
(David C Griffiths) *trckd ldrs: effrt and rdn 2f out: edgd lft ins fnl f: kpt on* **11/1**

-352 **4** nse **Rosie Crowe (IRE)**[24] 2976 5-9-6 **51** (v) TrevorWhelan 1 55
(Shaun Harris) *chsd ldrs: drvn and outpcd 3f out: rallied over 1f out: kpt on ins fnl f* **11/4**[1]

60-5 **5** ¾ **Verdi (IRE)**[71] 1600 3-8-12 **52** CamHardie 2 51
(John Ryan) *midfield: rdn along over 2f out: hdwy over 1f out: kpt on same pce ins fnl f* **5/1**[2]

1-06 **6** hd **Peny Arcade**[29] 2790 3-8-10 **55** RowanScott(5) 8 53
(Alistair Whillans) *bhd and sn pushed along: hdwy on outside 2f out: kpt on fnl f: nrst fin* **13/2**[3]

0-00 **7** ¾ **Diamond Avalanche (IRE)**[12] 3387 4-9-3 **48** (p) DougieCostello 4 47
(Patrick Holmes) *hld up: drvn over 2f out: kpt on fnl f: no imp* **22/1**

0450 **8** shd **Coral Princess (IRE)**[9] 3484 3-8-11 **51** GrahamLee 11 50
(Keith Dalgleish) *hld up: pushed along over 2f out: hdwy and in tch whn nt clr run over 1f out: sn n.d* **8/1**

2405 **9** shd **A Bit Of Ginger**[18] 3191 3-9-1 **55** ShaneGray 9 51
(Ann Duffield) *t.k.h: cl up: disp ld fr 1/2-way to over 1f out: outpcd ins fnl f* **7/1**

0-64 **10** 3½ **Deben**[15] 3290 4-9-1 **53** DanielleMooney(7) 6 42
(John Weymes) *s.i.s: hld up: drvn and outpcd over 2f out: sn btn* **8/1**

00-0 **11** nk **Whisper A Word (IRE)**[48] 2180 3-8-6 **46** oh1 JasonHart 3 32
(Tim Easterby) *hld up in tch: rdn and outpcd over 2f out: sn btn* **22/1**

1m 29.24s (0.24) **Going Correction** -0.125s/f (Firm)
**WFA** 3 from 4yo+ 9lb **11** Ran SP% **122.8**
Speed ratings (Par 101): **93,92,91,91,90 90,89,89,89,85 85**
CSF £178.27 CT £1950.63 TOTE £16.70: £5.00, £3.80, £4.60; EX 202.20 Trifecta £2886.70.
**Owner** Habton Farms **Bred** Drumlin Bloodstock **Trained** Great Habton, N Yorks

**FOCUS**
This was slightly the slower division. Poor handicap form, with a pair of 11yos filling the placings.

## 3833 GAYNOR WINYARD H'CAP 7f 33y
**5:30** (5:32) (Class 5) (0-75,77) 4-Y-0+ **£3,234** (£962; £481; £240) **Stalls** Low

Form RPR
001- **1** **Big Storm Coming**[193] 8241 7-9-7 **74** TomEaves 8 82
(David Brown) *trckd ldrs: smooth hdwy to ld 2f out: drvn and edgd rt ins fnl f: r.o* **12/1**
5351 **2** *1 1/4* **Sea Of Green**[12] 3385 5-7-11 **55** (p) DavidEgan(5) 1 60
(Jim Goldie) *prom: rdn over 2f out: hdwy to chse wnr ins fnl f: r.o* **10/1**
4/24 **3** *nk* **Dark Profit (IRE)**[88] 1296 5-9-2 **69** (p) GrahamLee 3 73
(Keith Dalgleish) *in tch on outside: effrt and rdn wl over 1f out: kpt on same pce ins fnl f* **9/2**[2]
P-45 **4** *1 1/4* **Flinty Fell (IRE)**[16] 3241 4-9-1 **68** (h) JoeFanning 10 69
(Keith Dalgleish) *t.k.h: hld up: pushed along over 2f out: effrt over 1f out: no imp ins fnl f* **7/1**
5553 **5** *2 1/4* **Tavener**[7] 3581 5-9-10 **77** (p) DavidAllan 7 72
(David C Griffiths) *pressed ldr: ev ch over 2f out to wl over 1f out: outpcd fnl f* **7/2**[1]
-056 **6** *1 1/4* **Popsies Joy (IRE)**[9] 3488 4-8-9 **62** (p[1]) DuranFentiman 5 53
(Tim Easterby) *flyj. s: bhd: rdn and effrt over 2f out: no imp fr over 1f out* **10/1**
2504 **7** *1 1/2* **Crazy Tornado (IRE)**[9] 3488 4-9-0 **67** (h) ConnorBeasley 4 54
(Keith Dalgleish) *midfield: drvn and outpcd over 2f out: n.d after* **9/2**[2]
0263 **8** *2 1/2* **Top Of The Bank**[18] 3177 4-9-5 **72** (p) TonyHamilton 2 53
(Kristin Stubbs) *led tl rdn and hdd 2f out: sn wknd* **16/1**
0235 **9** *1 1/4* **Miss Goldsmith (IRE)**[22] 3048 4-8-4 **60** (h) SammyJoBell(3) 9 37
(Richard Fahey) *s.i.s: bhd: rdn over 2f out: btn whn hung rt over 1f out* **6/1**[3]
350 **10** *2* **Order Of Service**[21] 3095 7-9-6 **73** (v) TrevorWhelan 6 45
(Shaun Harris) *s.v.s: bhd: shortlived effrt over 2f out: hung rt and btn over 1f out* **20/1**

1m 27.8s (-1.20) **Going Correction** -0.125s/f (Firm) **10** Ran SP% **121.9**
Speed ratings (Par 103): **101,99,99,97,95 93,92,89,87,85**
CSF £131.32 CT £644.77 TOTE £11.60: £3.80, £2.90, £1.80; EX 98.60 Trifecta £638.90.
**Owner** Fishlake Commercial Motors Ltd **Bred** Bearstone Stud Ltd **Trained** Averham Park, Notts
■ Stewards' Enquiry : David Egan two-day ban; used whip above the permitted level (Jul 11-12)

**FOCUS**
An ordinary handicap, but the quickest of the three 7f races.
T/Plt: £156.20 to a £1 stake. Pool: £91,426.44 - 427.21 winning units T/Qpdt: £14.90 to a £1 stake. Pool: £5,827.96 - 288.0 winning units **Richard Young**

# 3782 SANDOWN (R-H)
Saturday, June 17

**OFFICIAL GOING: Good to firm (firm in places; sprint 7.7, round 7.8)**
Wind: Almost nil Weather: Fine, hot

## 3834 RANDOX.COM H'CAP (JOCKEY CLUB GRASSROOTS FLAT SPRINT SERIES QUALIFIER) 5f 10y
**2:10** (2:11) (Class 4) (0-80,82) 4-Y-0+ **£5,822** (£1,732; £865; £432) **Stalls** Low

Form RPR
0603 **1** **Rio Ronaldo (IRE)**[19] 3161 5-9-3 **76** AntonioFresu 6 84+
(Mike Murphy) *dwlt: hld up and last to 1/2-way: stdy prog on outer fr 2f out: shkn up and r.o fnl f to ld last strides: cleverly* **5/2**[1]
13-0 **2** *nk* **Royal Mezyan (IRE)**[28] 2835 6-9-5 **78** StevieDonohoe 12 85
(Henry Spiller) *chsd ldrs: rdn wl over 1f out: clsd u.p to ld 100yds out: kpt on wl but hdd last strides* **20/1**
1000 **3** *1/2* **Foxy Forever (IRE)**[28] 2835 7-9-7 **80** (t) AdamKirby 10 85
(Michael Wigham) *s.i.s: hld up in last trio: prog towards inner wl over 1f out: squeezed through to chal ins fnl f: outpcd nr fin* **16/1**
1130 **4** *1 3/4* **Oriental Relation (IRE)**[22] 3052 6-9-6 **79** (b) JoeDoyle 8 78
(James Given) *pressed ldr: led at 1/2-way: drvn over 1f out: hdd & wknd last 100yds* **6/1**[2]
6612 **5** *1* **Taajub (IRE)**[24] 2967 10-8-13 **72** FergusSweeney 5 67
(Peter Crate) *walked to post early: hld up: detached in last whn swtchd to wd outside over 1f out: r.o last 100yds: nrst fin* **17/2**
2322 **6** *nk* **The Big Lad**[15] 3281 5-9-5 **78** (b) ShaneKelly 11 75
(Richard Hughes) *chsd ldrs: rdn wl over 1f out: keeping on but nt gng to win whn hmpd jst ins fnl f* **8/1**[3]
3606 **7** *1 1/4* **Just Us Two (IRE)**[18] 3183 5-9-5 **78** (v[1]) MartinHarley 9 68
(Robert Cowell) *cl up: jnd ldr 2f out gng wl: rdn and fnd nil jst over 1f out: wknd tamely* **8/1**[3]
0030 **8** *nk* **Very Honest (IRE)**[35] 2608 4-8-13 **79** RossaRyan(7) 7 68
(Brett Johnson) *chsd ldrs: rdn 2f out: no prog and wknd fnl f* **16/1**
6504 **9** *1 3/4* **Secret Asset (IRE)**[22] 3021 12-7-10 **62** (v) RPWalsh(7) 4 44
(Lisa Williamson) *led against rail to 1/2-way: wknd over 1f out* **14/1**
000- **10** *1/2* **Musical Comedy**[224] 7825 6-9-9 **82** PatCosgrave 3 63
(Mike Murphy) *trckd ldng pair against rail: rdn 2f out: wknd over 1f out* **8/1**[3]
50-0 **P** **Zebstar (IRE)**[14] 3330 4-9-6 **79** MartinDwyer 1
(Gay Kelleway) *in tch tl broke down and p.u after 2f* **12/1**

1m 0.11s (-1.49) **Going Correction** -0.25s/f (Firm) **11** Ran SP% **117.6**
Speed ratings (Par 105): **101,100,99,96,95 94,92,92,89,88**
CSF £60.06 CT £690.31 TOTE £2.90: £1.50, £6.30, £5.00; EX 67.40 Trifecta £3096.80.
**Owner** The Castaways **Bred** Knocktoran Stud & Kildaragh Stud **Trained** Westoning, Beds

**FOCUS**
A scorcher of a day and ground on the quick side, with both the sprint and round course being described as good to firm, firm in places (firm places in the home straight on round course) going into the seven-race card. A competitive sprint handicap run at what appeared a strong gallop, setting it up for the closers.

## 3835 RANDOX HEALTH SCURRY STKS (LISTED RACE) 5f 10y
**2:40** (2:41) (Class 1) 3-Y-0
**£20,982** (£7,955; £3,981; £1,983; £995; £499) **Stalls** Low

Form RPR
333- **1** **Battaash (IRE)**[253] 7113 3-9-0 **100** DaneO'Neill 9 115
(Charles Hills) *s.i.s: t.k.h: hld up in rr: prog on outer 1/2-way: led over 1f out and sn clr: edgd rt fnl f but nvr threatened* **11/1**
0-05 **2** *1 1/4* **Koropick (IRE)**[15] 3302 3-9-0 **100** JackMitchell 6 110
(Hugo Palmer) *hld up towards rr: rdn and prog over 1f out: r.o wl to take 2nd last 75yds: no ch to threaten wnr* **25/1**
-211 **3** *1 3/4* **Copper Knight (IRE)**[21] 3092 3-9-0 **101** PatCosgrave 8 104
(Tim Easterby) *pressed ldng pair on outer: rdn to ld briefly wl over 1f out: outpcd by wnr sn after: lost 2nd last 75yds* **7/2**[1]
122- **4** *3/4* **Gheedaa (USA)**[196] 8209 3-8-9 **86** HarryBentley 3 96
(William Haggas) *s.i.s: hld up in last: taken to outer over 1f out: drvn and r.o fnl f: nvr nrr* **15/2**
10-4 **5** *1* **Ardad (IRE)**[30] 2768 3-9-5 **106** WilliamBuick 1 102
(John Gosden) *trckd ldrs against rail: pushed along over 1f out: outpcd sn after but kpt on fnl f: nt disgracd* **4/1**[2]
15-1 **6** *1 1/2* **Fashion Queen**[30] 2768 3-8-12 **101** RyanMoore 4 90
(David O'Meara) *led against rail to over 2f out: wknd over 1f out* **9/2**[3]
6-41 **7** *3/4* **Equimou**[41] 2425 3-8-9 **103** MartinHarley 5 84
(Robert Eddery) *hld up in tch gng wl: shkn up over 1f out: nt clr run sn after and then no prog* **6/1**
0113 **8** *1 1/4* **Quench Dolly**[28] 2831 3-8-9 **93** FergusSweeney 7 80
(John Gallagher) *pressed ldr: narrow ld over 2f out to wl over 1f out: wknd sn after* **10/1**
5321 **9** *6* **Megan Lily (IRE)**[7] 3579 3-8-9 **90** AdamMcNamara 2 58
(Richard Fahey) *chsd ldrs: rdn 2f out: sn wknd* **16/1**

59.36s (-2.24) **Going Correction** -0.25s/f (Firm) **9** Ran SP% **113.6**
Speed ratings (Par 107): **107,105,102,101,99 97,95,93,84**
CSF £238.73 TOTE £14.70: £3.40, £6.50, £1.50; EX 344.30 Trifecta £1760.80.
**Owner** Hamdan Al Maktoum **Bred** Ballyphilip Stud **Trained** Lambourn, Berks

**FOCUS**
A wide open renewal of this Listed sprint, on paper at least, but it produced a very impressive winner who dipped under the standard time.

## 3836 RANDOX H'CAP 7f
**3:15** (3:19) (Class 3) (0-95,92) 3-Y-0
**£8,715** (£2,609; £1,304; £652; £326; £163) **Stalls** Low

Form RPR
-610 **1** **Burrishoole Abbey (IRE)**[22] 3038 3-8-10 **81** MartinHarley 5 86
(K R Burke) *trckd ldng trio gng wl: shkn up and prog to go 2nd over 1f out: rdn to ld ins fnl f: jst hld on* **20/1**
0-23 **2** *hd* **Black Trilby (IRE)**[15] 3303 3-8-11 **82** (h) SamHitchcott 4 86
(Clive Cox) *chsd ldng pair: rdn 3f out: responded to press to cl on inner over 1f out: tk 2nd last 75yds: jst failed* **10/3**[2]
-541 **3** *3/4* **Battered**[31] 2739 3-9-7 **92** (p[1]) RyanMoore 2 94
(William Haggas) *hld up in 5th: shkn up over 2f out: clsd on outer over 1f out: edgd lft and nt qckn jst ins fnl f: styd on nr fin* **5/4**[1]
14-4 **4** *hd* **Akhlaaq**[58] 1901 3-9-3 **88** DaneO'Neill 1 90
(Owen Burrows) *stdd s: t.k.h: hld up in last pair: shkn up on outer over 2f out: grad clsd over 1f out: kpt on but nvr quite able to chal* **15/2**
11- **5** *hd* **Love Dreams (IRE)**[355] 3712 3-9-6 **91** WilliamBuick 3 92
(Mark Johnston) *problematic to post: reluctant to enter stalls and fractious in them: mde most: rdn 2f out: hdd ins fnl f: wilted and lost pls nr fin* **11/2**[3]
-226 **6** *1* **Sea Shack**[17] 3211 3-8-9 **80** HarryBentley 7 79
(William Knight) *trckd ldr: rdn over 2f out: lost 2nd over 1f out: one pce after and lost pls ins fnl f* **7/1**
5220 **7** *4* **Spirit Of Sarwan (IRE)**[35] 2625 3-8-6 **77** (p) AdamBeschizza 6 65
(Julia Feilden) *dwlt: hld up in last pair: rdn 3f out: no prog 2f out: fdd* **25/1**

1m 27.64s (-1.86) **Going Correction** -0.175s/f (Firm) **7** Ran SP% **115.8**
Speed ratings (Par 103): **103,102,101,101,101 100,95**
CSF £87.35 TOTE £24.90: £7.30, £1.80; EX 122.60 Trifecta £468.70.
**Owner** Mrs M Gittins **Bred** Grange Stud **Trained** Middleham Moor, N Yorks

**FOCUS**
Add 19yds to race distance. One or two progressive 3yo's in here but they finished in a bit of a heap and the key horse (Battered) probably wasn't at his best, so there are reasons to doubt this strength of this form.

## 3837 RANDOX HEALTH H'CAP 1m
**3:50** (3:52) (Class 2) (0-100,97) 3-Y-0+
**£18,675** (£5,592; £2,796; £1,398; £699; £351) **Stalls** Low

Form RPR
41-2 **1** **Greenside**[23] 3014 6-9-11 **94** RyanMoore 2 105+
(Henry Candy) *trckd ldng pair: waiting for a gap fr 2f out to over 1f out: prog between rivals to ld ins fnl f: urged along and qckly asserted* **13/8**[1]
11-1 **2** *1 1/4* **Laidback Romeo (IRE)**[23] 3014 5-10-0 **97** AdamKirby 10 104
(Clive Cox) *hld up in midfield: prog 2f out: rdn to chal jst over 1f out: nt pce of wnr but kpt on to take 2nd last stride* **4/1**[2]
0-00 **3** *shd* **Glory Awaits (IRE)**[30] 2767 7-9-7 **90** (b) StevieDonohoe 4 96
(David Simcock) *led: rdn over 2f out: sn hdd: kpt on wl and upsides 1f out: outpcd by wnr sn after: lost 2nd last stride* **33/1**
-005 **4** *1* **General Macarthur (USA)**[45] 2310 4-9-5 **93** (t) GeorgeBuckell(5) 11 97+
(David Simcock) *stdd s fr wdst draw and hld up in last: prog on outer over 2f out: urged along and kpt on fr over 1f out: nvr nr enough to chal* **33/1**
0-33 **5** *nk* **Alnashama**[17] 3212 5-9-6 **89** DaneO'Neill 3 92
(Charles Hills) *trckd ldr: led 2f out: rdn and hdd ins fnl f: wknd* **14/1**
-003 **6** *nk* **Home Cummins (IRE)**[15] 3298 5-9-6 **92** (p) AdamMcNamara(3) 8 95
(Richard Fahey) *hld up in last pair: rdn over 2f out: prog on inner fnl f: kpt on but nvr able to threaten* **12/1**
0016 **7** *nse* **Alejandro (IRE)**[23] 3014 8-9-7 **90** (e[1]) ShaneKelly 6 93
(David Loughnane) *wl in tch: looked poised to chal 2f out: nt qckn over 1f out then tightened for room: one pce after* **33/1**
0221 **8** *1/2* **Palmerston**[17] 3204 4-8-10 **82** AlistairRawlinson(3) 9 83
(Michael Appleby) *trckd ldng pair: rdn to chal over 1f out: upsides jst ins fnl f: sn wknd* **10/1**
5-10 **9** *1* **Taurean Star (IRE)**[35] 2606 4-9-8 **91** JamieSpencer 5 90
(Michael Bell) *awkward s: hld up in rr: pushed along over 1f out: one pce and nvr really in it* **8/1**[3]
3025 **10** *shd* **The Warrior (IRE)**[6] 3620 5-9-7 **90** (v) GavinLerena 7 89
(Amanda Perrett) *hld up in last trio: pushed along 2f out: one pce and making little imp whn short of room jst ins fnl f* **20/1**
-003 **11** *hd* **Sir Roderic (IRE)**[23] 3014 4-9-12 **95** WilliamBuick 1 95
(Rod Millman) *wl in tch in midfield: lost pl fr 2f out: pushed along in rr 1f out: no prog after: eased last strides: nvr in it* **8/1**[3]

1m 42.69s (-0.61) **Going Correction** -0.175s/f (Firm) **11** Ran SP% **117.4**
Speed ratings (Par 109): **96,94,94,93,93 93,93,92,91,91 91**
CSF £7.24 CT £143.69 TOTE £2.50: £1.30, £1.60, £10.20; EX 7.40 Trifecta £289.30.
**Owner** Clayton, Frost, Kebell & Turner **Bred** Lordship Stud **Trained** Kingston Warren, Oxon

**FOCUS**
Add 19yds to race distance. Not too many of these have a particularly progressive profile but the right horses came to the fore, with the first two home the same pair that dominated a C&D handicap (albeit in a different order) last month.

## 3838 RANDOXHEALTH.COM H'CAP 1m 1f
4:25 (4:25) (Class 3) (0-90,89) 3-Y-O

£8,715 (£2,609; £1,304; £652; £326; £163) Stalls Low

Form RPR
34-3 1 **The Statesman**[15] 3293 3-8-8 76 MartinDwyer 6 83
(Ian Williams) *t.k.h: trckd ldng trio: clsd over 2f out: rdn to ld over 1f out: drvn out and kpt on* 15/2
-310 2 1 1/4 **Hajaj (IRE)**[14] 3318 3-8-12 80 StevieDonohoe 7 84
(Charlie Fellowes) *hld up in 6th: rdn and prog 2f out: chal jst over 1f out: chsd wnr after: kpt on but no imp last 100yds* 13/2
0304 3 1/2 **Dr Julius No**[15] 3303 3-9-7 89 ShaneKelly 2 92
(Richard Hughes) *led 1f: sn in 3rd: effrt again 2f out: rdn over 1f out: kpt on fnl f to take 3rd last strides* 7/1
41- 4 hd **Intrepidly (USA)**[255] 7064 3-9-3 85 RyanMoore 1 88
(Jeremy Noseda) *trckd ldr after 3f: rdn to ld over 2f out: hdd and one pce over 1f out* 5/2[1]
163- 5 1/2 **Blushing Rose**[266] 6787 3-8-10 78 WilliamBuick 8 79
(Sir Michael Stoute) *hld up in last pair: promising hdwy on outer over 2f out and looked a threat over 1f out: fdd fnl f* 5/1[3]
1240 6 1/2 **Shamrokh (IRE)**[58] 1907 3-9-0 85 AlistairRawlinson(3) 3 85
(Michael Appleby) *hld up in 5th: shkn up over 2f out: nt qckn and no imp on ldrs: kpt on nr fin* 25/1
1-23 7 1 1/4 **War Chief**[23] 3005 3-9-0 82 (h) FergusSweeney 5 80
(Alan King) *stdd s: t.k.h: hld up in last pair: shkn up over 2f out: no prog* 4/1[2]
0-00 8 4 1/2 **Comedy School (USA)**[22] 3033 3-9-4 86 AdamKirby 4 74
(Mark Johnston) *led after 1f to over 2f out: sn wknd* 20/1
1m 57.38s (1.68) **Going Correction** -0.175s/f (Firm) 8 Ran SP% 111.4
Speed ratings (Par 103): **85,83,83,83,82 82,81,77**
CSF £52.18 CT £350.24 TOTE £8.30: £2.30, £2.00, £2.10; EX 51.70 Trifecta £302.60.
**Owner** Randolph & Mortimer Racing **Bred** Barry Walters **Trained** Portway, Worcs
**FOCUS**
Add 19yds to race distance. A decent little 3yo handicap run at what appeared an even gallop and a few of these could easily rate higher in the future.

## 3839 RANDOX HEALTH BRITISH EBF MAIDEN STKS 1m 1f 209y
5:00 (5:00) (Class 5) 3-Y-O £3,881 (£1,155; £577; £288) Stalls Low

Form RPR
3320 1 **Bristol Missile (USA)**[14] 3318 3-9-5 80 RyanMoore 1 78
(Richard Hannon) *trckd ldng pair: prog to ld 2f out: rdn over 1f out: kpt on and a holding rivals* 1/1[1]
2 3/4 **Musaahim (USA)** 3-9-5 0 JackMitchell 10 77+
(Roger Varian) *racd wd: trckd ldrs: shkn up over 2f out: prog to take 2nd jst over 1f out: rn green but kpt on fnl f and steadily clsng at fin* 8/1
54 3 1 3/4 **Touwari (IRE)**[45] 2314 3-9-5 0 (b) RobertTart 3 73
(John Gosden) *led: rdn: hdd and nt qckn 2f out: one pce after and lost 2nd jst over 1f out* 11/2[3]
4 2 **Munthany (USA)** 3-9-5 0 DaneO'Neill 5 69
(Charles Hills) *trckd ldr to over 2f out: shkn up and one pce after* 9/2[2]
6 5 6 **Ididitforyoooo (IRE)**[12] 3393 3-9-5 0 WilliamBuick 7 57
(Brian Meehan) *stdd s: hld up in last pair: shkn up 3f out: prog 2f out: pushed along in 5th fnl f and nvr on terms* 12/1
6 3/4 **My Name Is Jeff** 3-9-5 0 AdamBeschizza 8 56
(Julia Feilden) *hld up in last pair: prog into midfield 2f out but no on terms w ldrs: no imp after* 40/1
00 7 1 3/4 **High Wells**[9] 3506 3-9-5 0 FergusSweeney 4 52
(Seamus Durack) *hld up in rr: pushed along 1/2-way: nvr a factor but plugged on over 1f out* 50/1
00 8 shd **Kings City (IRE)**[17] 3209 3-8-12 0 GabrieleMalune(7) 6 52
(Luca Cumani) *chsd ldrs: shkn up and lost pl 2f out: no ch after* 20/1
50 9 3/4 **Corredordel Viento (USA)**[29] 2783 3-9-5 0 HarryBentley 2 50
(Simon Dow) *in tch: rdn and lft bhd over 2f out* 25/1
10 27 **The Iron Factor (USA)** 3-9-5 0 (t[1]) StevieDonohoe 9
(David Lanigan) *in tch 6f: sn wknd: t.o* 25/1
2m 8.32s (-2.18) **Going Correction** -0.175s/f (Firm) 10 Ran SP% 119.2
Speed ratings (Par 99): **101,100,99,97,92 92,90,89,89,68**
CSF £9.41 TOTE £1.80: £1.10, £3.10, £2.10; EX 9.30 Trifecta £34.60.
**Owner** Michael Cohen & Michael Daffey **Bred** Kenneth L Ramsey & Sarah K Ramsey **Trained** East Everleigh, Wilts
**FOCUS**
Add 19yds to race distance. This was won by the standard-setting favourite but there was notable promise from a couple of the newcomers, particularly the runner-up.

## 3840 RANDOX FOOD H'CAP 1m 6f
5:35 (5:36) (Class 4) (0-85,87) 4-Y-O+ £6,469 (£1,925; £962; £481) Stalls Low

Form RPR
131- 1 **Machine Learner**[245] 7359 4-9-5 82 (b[1]) RyanMoore 4 89
(Joseph Tuite) *hld up in tch: cl up bhd ldrs fr 2f out and waiting: brought through rivals 1f out and sn jnd ldr: urged along and won on the nod* 9/2[3]
-502 2 nse **Taper Tantrum (IRE)**[19] 3138 5-9-1 78 (p[1]) LouisSteward 1 84
(Michael Bell) *led: rdn and pressed over 2f out: kpt on wl after: jnd fnl f: btn on the nod* 7/1
-421 3 1/2 **Fire Jet (IRE)**[35] 2622 4-9-7 84 BenCurtis 8 89
(John Mackie) *hld up in rr: rdn and wandered over 2f out but prog sn after to chal over 1f out: upsides jst ins fnl f: nt qckn last 100yds* 11/4[2]
31-1 4 1/2 **Vuela**[42] 2387 4-9-6 83 JamieSpencer 9 87
(Luca Cumani) *trckd ldr after 3f: chal over 2f out: stl nrly upsides 1f out: one pce last 150yds* 15/8[1]
1425 5 4 1/2 **Ayr Of Elegance**[23] 3004 5-8-11 74 HarryBentley 3 72
(Philip Hide) *awkward s: hld up in last pair: rdn and no prog over 2f out: n.d after: plugged on* 13/2
23/6 6 3 1/4 **Cool Sky**[21] 3076 8-9-6 83 (p[1]) StevieDonohoe 6 76
(Ian Williams) *trckd ldr 3f: styd prom tl wknd over 2f out* 7/1
140/ 7 1 **Authorized Too**[82] 7305 6-9-0 77 (p) FergusSweeney 7 69
(Noel Williams) *hld up in last: swift move to chse ldng pair 5f out: rdn and wknd over 2f out* 25/1
3m 8.14s (3.64) **Going Correction** -0.175s/f (Firm) 7 Ran SP% 121.8
Speed ratings (Par 105): **82,81,81,81,78 76,76**
CSF £38.12 CT £104.98 TOTE £5.90: £2.30, £3.60; EX 47.10 Trifecta £169.00.
**Owner** Michael Geoghegan **Bred** Bearstone Stud Ltd **Trained** Lambourn, Berks
■ Pleasure Dome (10-1) was withdrawn not under orders. Rule 4 \n\x\x applies to all bets struck prior to withdrawal, but not to SP bets. Deduct 5p in the pound. New market formed
■ Stewards' Enquiry : Louis Steward two-day ban: used whip above the permitted level (Jul 1-2); caution: careless riding
**FOCUS**
Add 19yds to race distance. A decent little handicap fought out by some in-form horses but this was run at a leisurely tempo, resulting in a relatively slow time given the conditions.
T/Plt: £378.20 to a £1 stake. Pool: £105,957.84 - 204.47 winning units. T/Qpdt: £47.00 to a £1 stake. Pool: £6,072.09 - 95.46 winning units. **Jonathan Neesom**

# 3789 YORK (L-H)
Saturday, June 17

**OFFICIAL GOING: Good to firm (7.4)**
Wind: Fresh half against Weather: Fine, dry & blustery

## 3841 QUEEN MOTHER'S CUP H'CAP (FOR LADY AMATEUR RIDERS) 1m 3f 188y
1:50 (1:51) (Class 3) (0-95,92) 3-Y-O+

£11,992 (£3,746; £1,872; £936; £468; £236) Stalls Centre

Form RPR
0-36 1 **Tapis Libre**[19] 3153 9-9-12 76 MissJoannaMason 7 87
(Jacqueline Coward) *trckd ldrs: hdwy over 3f out: led 2f out: sn rdn: kpt on wl fnl f* 8/1
6002 2 1 1/4 **Mukhayyam**[9] 3497 5-10-3 81 (p) MissEEasterby 2 90
(Tim Easterby) *hld up in rr: hdwy on inner wl over 2f out: chsd ldrs over 1f out: rdn and styd on wl fnl f* 4/1[1]
60-1 3 3/4 **Azari**[10] 3470 5-10-12 90 MissAnnaHesketh 4 98
(Tom Dascombe) *hld up: hdwy on outer over 4f out: chsd ldrs over 2f out: rdn wl over 1f out: styd on fnl f* 10/1
2452 4 nse **Masterpaver**[92] 1240 6-9-11 81 MissFMcSharry(6) 6 89
(Richard Fahey) *trckd ldrs: hdwy 4f out: chsd wnr wl over 1f out: rdn and edgd lft ins fnl f: kpt on same pce* 11/2[2]
-412 5 10 **Charismatic Man (IRE)**[17] 3213 4-10-11 89 MsLO'Neill 5 81
(Ralph Beckett) *trckd ldrs on inner: pushed along over 3f out: rdn over 2f out: sn drvn and one pce* 6/1[3]
0524 6 1 **Chancery (USA)**[14] 3315 9-10-2 86 (p) MissCarlyScott(6) 9 76
(David O'Meara) *hld up: hdwy 3f out: rdn along wl over 1f out: n.d* 8/1
0550 7 4 **Imshivalla (IRE)**[15] 3300 6-10-0 78 (h) MissEmmaSayer 8 62
(Richard Fahey) *t.k.h: prom: trckd ldr after 3f: led over 5f out: pushed clr over 3f out: rdn along over 2f out: sn hdd & wknd* 12/1
-110 8 9 **Samtu (IRE)**[31] 2741 6-10-3 81 MissBeckySmith 1 50
(Marjorie Fife) *hld up: a towards rr* 14/1
0-20 9 2 1/2 **Purple Rock (IRE)**[22] 3046 5-10-7 85 (t) MissCWalton 3 50
(Michael Easterby) *in tch: hdwy to chse ldrs over 4f out: rdn along over 3f out: sn wknd* 8/1
-115 10 3 1/2 **Corton Lad**[29] 2774 7-11-0 92 (tp) MrsCBartley 10 52
(Keith Dalgleish) *sn led: pushed along and hdd over 5f out: rdn over 4f out: sn wknd* 14/1
1100 11 3 1/2 **Be Perfect (USA)**[21] 3091 8-10-4 85 (p) MissEmilyBullock(3) 11 39
(Ruth Carr) *trckd ldrs: rdn along wl over 3f out: sn wknd* 25/1
2m 34.13s (0.93) **Going Correction** +0.075s/f (Good) 11 Ran SP% 117.0
Speed ratings (Par 107): **99,98,97,97,90 90,87,81,79,77 75**
CSF £39.78 CT £328.41 TOTE £8.80: £2.80, £1.80, £3.60; EX 36.60 Trifecta £318.70.
**Owner** Mrs Susan E Mason **Bred** Sedgecroft Stud **Trained** Dalby, North Yorks
**FOCUS**
Race 1 increased by 32yds, race 3 by 28yds and race 5 by 31yds. The going was good to firm ahead of the opener, traditionally a competitive lady riders' event. They went a good pace and the first four came clear.

## 3842 JCB H'CAP 7f
2:20 (2:23) (Class 2) (0-105,104) 3-Y-O+

£24,900 (£7,456; £3,728; £1,864; £932; £468) Stalls Low

Form RPR
6446 1 **Viscount Barfield**[21] 3064 4-9-0 90 (h) DavidProbert 9 99
(Andrew Balding) *hld up in rr: hdwy 3f out: swtchd rt wl over 1f out: nt clr run and swtchd lft over 1f out: sn rdn and chal ins fnl f: drvn to ld last 100yds: kpt on* 11/1
4066 2 3/4 **Mutawathea**[23] 3003 6-9-4 99 (p) LewisEdmunds(5) 12 106
(Simon Crisford) *hld up: hdwy on wd outside wl over 1f out: rdn to chse ldng pair ent fnl f: sn drvn and ev ch: kpt on* 20/1
0134 3 hd **Salateen**[58] 1902 5-10-0 104 PhillipMakin 15 110
(David O'Meara) *sn led: pushed along 2f out: rdn over 1f out: drvn and hdd ent fnl f: sn edgd lft: kpt on u.p* 12/1
-404 4 1/2 **Above The Rest (IRE)**[21] 3064 6-9-11 101 (h) SilvestreDeSousa 18 106
(David Barron) *trckd ldr: hdwy 2f out: rdn to take slt ld ent fnl f: sn drvn: hdd last 100yds: kpt on same pce* 10/1[3]
-456 5 1 **Mazyoun**[31] 2739 3-8-3 88 (b) JosephineGordon 10 91+
(Hugo Palmer) *hld up in rr: hdwy 2f out: effrt and nt clr run towards outer over 1f out: swtchd lft and rdn ent fnl f: styd on: nrst fin* 10/1[3]
1506 6 1/2 **Twin Appeal (IRE)**[25] 2922 6-9-2 92 (b) AndrewMullen 3 93
(David Barron) *trckd ldrs towards inner: hdwy over 2f out: rdn wl over 1f out: drvn and kpt on same pce fnl f* 33/1
3301 7 1/2 **Fingal's Cave (IRE)**[7] 3565 5-9-3 93 KevinStott 6 93
(Philip Kirby) *hld up: hdwy towards outer over 2f out: rdn along wl over 1f out: kpt on fnl f* 25/1
3113 8 3 1/4 **Gurkha Friend**[9] 3498 5-9-4 94 DanielTudhope 1 85
(Karen McLintock) *prom: rdn along wl over 1f out: drvn and wknd appr fnl f* 10/1[3]
-653 9 nse **Get Knotted (IRE)**[21] 3089 5-9-8 98 (p) PaulMulrennan 8 89
(Michael Dods) *chsd ldrs: rdn along 2f out: sn drvn and no imp* 7/1[1]
-050 10 hd **Baraweez (IRE)**[64] 1769 7-9-1 96 BenRobinson(5) 13 86
(Brian Ellison) *towards rr tl sme late hdwy* 25/1
0011 11 2 1/4 **Theodorico (IRE)**[21] 3095 4-9-1 91 PJMcDonald 11 75
(David Loughnane) *prom: hdwy to chse ldr over 4f out: rdn along wl over 2f out: sn wknd* 8/1[2]
000- 12 1 1/2 **Farlow (IRE)**[294] 5871 9-9-3 93 BarryMcHugh 4 73
(Richard Fahey) *a towards rr* 40/1
060- 13 1/2 **Tanzeel (IRE)**[315] 5174 6-9-4 94 (t) JimCrowley 5 73
(Charles Hills) *a towards rr* 20/1
5001 14 3/4 **Reputation (IRE)**[14] 3324 4-9-1 91 (v) FranBerry 7 68
(John Quinn) *a towards rr* 16/1
-120 15 4 1/2 **Gallipoli (IRE)**[15] 3294 4-9-0 90 PaulHanagan 17 55
(Richard Fahey) *hld up towards rr: hdwy on wd outside over 2f out: sn rdn along and wknd* 16/1


The Form Book Flat, Raceform Ltd, Newbury, RG14 5SJ

0501 **16** *1 1/2* **Burnt Sugar (IRE)**[15] 3294 5-8-13 **89** ...................... RichardKingscote 14 50
(Roger Fell) *hld up: hdwy on wd outside over 2f out: rdn along wl over 1f out: sn wknd* **14/1**

-044 **17** *2* **Shady McCoy (USA)**[23] 3003 7-8-13 **89** ........................ JamesDoyle 16 44
(Ian Williams) *hld up towards rr: hdwy on wd outside over 2f out: rdn along wl over 1f out: sn drvn and wknd* **8/1**[2]

-000 **18** *10* **Heaven's Guest (IRE)**[35] 2606 7-9-4 **94** ............................ JackGarritty 2 22
(Richard Fahey) *in tch on inner: rdn along wl over 2f out: sn wknd* **12/1**

1m 24.11s (-1.19) **Going Correction** +0.075s/f (Good)
**WFA** 3 from 4yo+ 9lb **18** Ran SP% **126.7**
Speed ratings (Par 109): **109,108,107,107,106 105,105,101,101,101 98,96,96,95,90 88,86,74**
CSF £227.74 CT £2705.04 TOTE £13.00: £3.50, £4.10, £3.30, £3.00; EX 263.90 Trifecta £3680.30.
**Owner** David Brownlow **Bred** Rockwell Bloodstock **Trained** Kingsclere, Hants

**FOCUS**
A quality handicap featuring a number of recent winners. They went a sound gallop and came down the middle of the home straight.

## 3843 BEST WESTERN HOTELS GANTON STKS (LISTED RACE) 7f 192y

**2:55** (2:55) (Class 1) 3-Y-O+

**£28,355** (£10,750; £5,380; £2,680; £1,345; £675) **Stalls** Low

Form RPR

4-11 **1** **Arabian Hope (USA)**[51] 2117 3-8-6 94 .................(h) JosephineGordon 1 107
(Saeed bin Suroor) *trckd ldrs: hdwy 3f out: chsd ldr 2f out: sn rdn to chal whn wandered and hit on chin by ldrs whip: drvn ins fnl f: kpt on gamely to ld nr line* **6/1**[3]

56-1 **2** *hd* **Golden Stunner (IRE)**[21] 3089 4-9-2 102 ............................ FranBerry 2 109
(Ralph Beckett) *led 1 1/2f: trckd ldr: led again 1/2-way: rdn along 2f out: drvn ent fnl f: kpt on wl: hdd nr line* **9/2**[2]

15-0 **3** *3/4* **Thikriyaat (IRE)**[30] 2767 4-9-7 109 ..................................... JimCrowley 10 112
(Sir Michael Stoute) *hld up towards rr: hdwy on outer over 2f out: rdn over 1f out: drvn to chal ins fnl f: ev ch tl no ex towards fin* **9/2**[2]

4242 **4** *1/2* **Gabrial (IRE)**[14] 3320 8-9-7 113 ........................................ PaulHanagan 4 111
(Richard Fahey) *hld up: hdwy over 3f out: chsd ldrs 2f out: drvn and ev ch ent fnl f: kpt on same pce* **6/1**[3]

1-32 **5** *2 1/4* **Spark Plug (IRE)**[21] 3069 6-9-7 112 ..............................(p) JamesDoyle 8 106
(Brian Meehan) *in tch: hdwy 3f out: rdn to chal over 1f out: ev ch ent fnl f: sn drvn and wknd last 100yds* **3/1**[1]

-064 **6** *nk* **Mondialiste (IRE)**[23] 3012 7-9-7 110 ............................ DanielTudhope 6 105
(David O'Meara) *hld up in rr: hdwy wl over 2f out: rdn to chse ldrs 1 1/2f out: sn drvn and no imp* **8/1**

0540 **7** *1 3/4* **Epsom Icon**[14] 3319 4-9-2 95 ........................................ PaulMulrennan 9 96
(Mick Channon) *hld up towards rr: hdwy over 3f out: rdn along and in tch 2f out: sn drvn and no imp* **40/1**

6210 **8** *2 1/4* **Custom Cut (IRE)**[14] 3320 8-9-12 107 .............................. PhillipMakin 5 101
(David O'Meara) *prom: rdn along 3f out: sn wknd* **25/1**

-151 **9** *1 3/4* **Khafoo Shememi (IRE)**[23] 3013 3-9-0 107 ....................... SeanLevey 7 93
(Richard Hannon) *t.k.h: cl up: led after 1 1/2f: hdd 1/2-way and sn pushed along: rdn 3f out: sn wknd* **10/1**

1m 37.29s (-1.71) **Going Correction** +0.075s/f (Good)
**WFA** 3 from 4yo+ 10lb **9** Ran SP% **116.4**
Speed ratings (Par 111): **111,110,110,109,107 107,105,103,101**
CSF £33.44 TOTE £6.90: £2.50, £2.00, £1.70; EX 35.30 Trifecta £221.50.
**Owner** Godolphin **Bred** Hill 'N' Dale Equine Holdings Inc Et Al **Trained** Newmarket, Suffolk

**FOCUS**
Race distance increased by 28yds. A really good Listed event that has grown in stature with three of the last five victors taking a Group 2/3 during their next two outings, including Ascot's Summer Mile. This year's renewal was well represented with several improving youngsters, who fought out the finish. They once again came down the middle.

## 3844 CATHERINE KINLOCH PAVER MEMORIAL MACMILLAN CHARITY H'CAP 6f

**3:30** (3:32) (Class 2) (0-105,104) 3-Y-O

**£62,250** (£18,640; £9,320; £4,660; £2,330; £1,170) **Stalls** Centre

Form RPR

-431 **1** **Golden Apollo**[5] 3664 3-8-3 **86** 6ex ................................. JamesSullivan 1 97
(Tim Easterby) *towards rr: hdwy on inner over 2f out: chsd ldrs over 1f out: sn rdn: drvn to chal ins fnl f: kpt on strly to ld nr fin* **5/1**[2]

3-60 **2** *nk* **The Wagon Wheel (IRE)**[21] 3071 3-8-2 **85** oh1 ow2..(b[1]) JoeyHaynes 2 95
(Richard Fahey) *hld up towards rr: hdwy over 2f out: rdn to chse ldrs over 1f out: sn cl up: drvn to take slt ld last 75yds: hdd and no ex nr fin* **20/1**

-103 **3** *1* **Justanotherbottle (IRE)**[19] 3159 3-8-3 **86** ................. RoystonFfrench 7 93
(Declan Carroll) *prom: effrt to ld over 1f out and sn rdn: jnd and drvn appr fnl f: hdd and no ex last 75yds* **20/1**

4032 **4** *nk* **Poet's Society**[7] 3579 3-8-3 **86** .................................... AndrewMullen 15 92
(Mark Johnston) *prom: rdn along and sltly outpcd over 1f out: swtchd lft and drvn ent fnl f: styd on wl towards fin* **33/1**

1-21 **5** *1 1/2* **Ekhtiyaar**[28] 2831 3-8-11 **94** ............................................ JimCrowley 11 95
(Roger Varian) *towards rr: smooth hdwy 1/2-way: trckd ldrs 2f out: rdn and n.m.r over 1f out: drvn and kpt on fnl f* **5/2**[1]

615 **6** *hd* **Impart**[7] 3579 3-8-1 **87** ............................................ ShelleyBirkett[(3)] 18 88
(David O'Meara) *trckd ldrs: hdwy over 2f out: rdn to dispute ld over 1f out: ev ch tl drvn and wknd ins fnl f* **40/1**

-512 **7** *1* **Turin Redstar**[37] 2557 3-8-6 **89** ...............................(p) PJMcDonald 13 86+
(Ralph Beckett) *hmpd s and bhd: hdwy towards outer over 2f out: rdn wl over 1f out: styd on fnl f* **11/1**

3355 **8** *1 1/4* **Tomily (IRE)**[19] 3159 3-9-0 **97** ............................................ JamesDoyle 14 90
(Richard Hannon) *in tch: rdn along 2f out: kpt on fnl f* **33/1**

34-5 **9** *hd* **Perfect Angel (IRE)**[28] 2823 3-9-1 **98** ........................... DavidProbert 16 91
(Andrew Balding) *towards rr: hdwy over 2f out: rdn wl over 1f out: no imp* **14/1**

1-40 **10** *nse* **Private Matter**[28] 2823 3-9-7 **104** ..................................... PaulHanagan 10 99+
(Richard Fahey) *chsd ldrs: rdn along 2f out: wknd over 1f out* **33/1**

60-0 **11** *1/2* **Medici Banchiere**[58] 1901 3-8-12 **95** ........................ RichardKingscote 17 86
(K R Burke) *chsd ldrs on outer: rdn along over 2f out: sn drvn and wknd* **33/1**

20-1 **12** *1 1/2* **Danielsflyer (IRE)**[42] 2400 3-9-4 **101** ...................... SilvestreDeSousa 8 87
(David Barron) *hld up and bhd: swtchd lft and sme hdwy on inner wl over 2f out: rdn along wl over 1f out: n.d* **8/1**[3]

34-6 **13** *3/4* **Kodiline (IRE)**[15] 3302 3-8-10 **93** .................................(h[1]) PaulMulrennan 4 77
(Clive Cox) *chsd ldrs: rdn along over 2f out: grad wknd* **25/1**

4330 **14** *hd* **Sayesse**[19] 3146 3-8-3 **86** ............................................ JosephineGordon 6 69
(Mick Channon) *a towards rr* **33/1**

1-11 **15** *hd* **Carlton Frankie**[46] 2271 3-8-4 **90** ................................. NathanEvans[(3)] 12 73
(Michael Easterby) *sn led: rdn along 2f out: hdd over 1f out: sn wknd* **9/1**

4522 **16** *1/2* **Wahash (IRE)**[15] 3303 3-9-1 **98** ............................................ SeanLevey 5 79
(Richard Hannon) *in tch: rdn along over 2f out: sn wknd* **16/1**

1-04 **17** *1 3/4* **Gulliver**[33] 2692 3-8-7 **90** ............................................(bt) AndreaAtzeni 3 65
(Hugo Palmer) *dwlt and wnt lft s: a in rr* **10/1**

5501 **18** *nk* **Smokey Lane (IRE)**[19] 3146 3-9-2 **99** ................................... FranBerry 9 73
(David Evans) *midfield: rdn along wl over 2f out: sn wknd* **20/1**

1m 11.41s (-0.49) **Going Correction** +0.05s/f (Good) **18** Ran SP% **131.6**
Speed ratings (Par 105): **105,104,103,102,100 100,99,97,97,97 96,94,93,93,93 92,90,89**
CSF £110.04 CT £1915.08 TOTE £5.50: £1.80, £4.80, £4.40, £6.60; EX 126.10 Trifecta £3959.60.
**Owner** David Scott **Bred** Cheveley Park Stud Ltd **Trained** Great Habton, N Yorks
■ Stewards' Enquiry : Andrew Mullen caution: careless riding

**FOCUS**
A typically competitive renewal of this valuable 3yo sprint handicap. There didn't appear to be any draw bias.

## 3845 ICE & EASY FROZEN ALCOHOLIC SLUSHIES H'CAP 1m 177y

**4:05** (4:08) (Class 4) (0-80,80) 4-Y-O+ **£7,762** (£2,310; £1,154; £577) **Stalls** Low

Form RPR

3-14 **1** **Visitant**[19] 3153 4-9-3 **76** .................................................. JamesDoyle 4 88+
(David Thompson) *hld up in tch on inner: hdwy 3f out: led 1 1/2f out: sn rdn: drvn and styd on wl fnl f* **3/1**[1]

40-2 **2** *1 3/4* **Throckley**[35] 2629 6-9-7 **80** ................................................(t) SamJames 5 87
(John Davies) *trckd ldng pair: effrt over 2f out: rdn along over 1f out: drvn and kpt on wl fnl f* **9/1**

3-54 **3** *nk* **Dark Intention (IRE)**[21] 3065 4-9-0 **73** .................(h) JosephineGordon 3 79
(Lawrence Mullaney) *hld up in tch towards inner: hdwy over 3f out: cl up 2f out: rdn to ld briefly wl over 1f out: sn hdd and drvn: kpt on same pce* **13/2**[3]

43-2 **4** *3 1/2* **Destroyer**[21] 3095 4-9-6 **79** ............................................ JamesSullivan 18 77
(Tom Tate) *hld up: hdwy on wd outside over 2f out: rdn over 1f out: drvn: edgd lft and kpt on wl fnl f* **14/1**

1514 **5** *1/2* **Rockwood**[16] 3255 6-9-4 **77** ..........................................(v) DavidProbert 20 74
(Karen McLintock) *dwlt and hld up in rr: hdwy on wd outside over 2f out: rdn wl over 1f out: kpt on fnl f* **12/1**

-042 **6** *3/4* **Hanseatic**[22] 3049 8-9-2 **75** ..........................................(p) PaulMulrennan 8 70
(Michael Easterby) *midfield: hdwy wl over 2f out: rdn to chse ldrs wl over 1f out: no imp appr fnl f* **10/1**

64-6 **7** *1* **Madrinho (IRE)**[28] 2838 4-9-6 **79** ...................................... BarryMcHugh 2 72
(Tony Coyle) *prom: chsd ldng pair over 3f out: rdn along over 2f out: grad wknd* **16/1**

06-0 **8** *nse* **Ingleby Angel (IRE)**[8] 3540 8-8-10 **69** ................................. KevinStott 17 62
(Colin Teague) *towards rr: hdwy over 2f out and sn rdn: drvn over 1f out: styd on fnl f* **33/1**

-061 **9** *1/2* **Talent Scout (IRE)**[17] 3203 11-8-5 **69** ....................(p) GemmaTutty[(5)] 14 61
(Karen Tutty) *led: rdn along over 2f out: hdd wl over 1f out: sn wknd* **50/1**

1000 **10** *1* **Pivotman**[17] 3204 9-8-6 **68** ..........................................(t) NathanEvans[(3)] 16 57
(Michael Easterby) *bhd: hdwy over 2f out: sn rdn and styd on fnl f* **66/1**

5001 **11** *3 1/2* **Mr Cool Cash**[7] 3560 5-8-3 **69** ........................................ WilliamCox[(7)] 13 50
(Richard Guest) *chsd ldrs: rdn along wl over 2f out: sn drvn and wknd* **25/1**

00-3 **12** *hd* **Hitman**[11] 3433 4-9-4 **77** ............................................... PJMcDonald 1 58
(Rebecca Bastiman) *chsd ldrs: rdn along wl over 2f out: sn drvn and wknd* **16/1**

3044 **13** *nk* **Zodiakos (IRE)**[17] 3204 4-9-4 **77** ............................(p[1]) SilvestreDeSousa 9 57
(Roger Fell) *midfield: sme hdwy on inner 3f out: rdn along over 2f out: sn wknd* **6/1**[2]

400- **14** *hd* **Woody Bay**[225] 7796 7-9-4 **77** ............................................ PaulHanagan 10 57
(Mark Walford) *cl up: disp ld 3f out: rdn over 2f out: sn drvn and wknd* **16/1**

0500 **15** *1/2* **Shamaheart (IRE)**[44] 2348 7-9-6 **79** ...........................(p) PhillipMakin 15 57
(Geoffrey Harker) *dwlt: a towards rr* **33/1**

0201 **16** *1/2* **Barwah (USA)**[14] 3344 6-8-12 **71** ..................................... AndrewMullen 7 48
(Peter Niven) *a towards rr* **40/1**

-060 **17** *1 1/2* **Quick N Quirky (IRE)**[15] 3287 4-8-13 **72** ......................(p) JackGarritty 6 46
(Tim Easterby) *a towards rr* **25/1**

-150 **18** *nk* **Sunglider (IRE)**[19] 3153 4-9-5 **78** ..........................(vt) DanielTudhope 11 51
(David O'Meara) *in tch: hdwy to chse ldrs 3f out: rdn along over 2f out: sn drvn and wknd* **16/1**

0565 **19** *8* **Short Work**[8] 3540 4-8-9 **71** ...................................(p) ShelleyBirkett[(3)] 12 26
(David O'Meara) *a towards rr* **28/1**

1m 50.92s (-1.08) **Going Correction** +0.075s/f (Good) **19** Ran SP% **132.5**
Speed ratings (Par 105): **107,105,105,102,101 100,100,100,99,98 95,95,95,94,94 94,92,92,85**
CSF £29.02 CT £156.85 TOTE £4.20: £1.50, £2.20, £2.20, £3.60; EX 33.10 Trifecta £177.60.
**Owner** N Park **Bred** Cheveley Park Stud Ltd **Trained** Bolam, Co Durham

**FOCUS**
Add 31yds. A wide-open handicap, but a tidy winner who came up the far side. They went an even gallop.

## 3846 REG GRIFFIN APPRECIATION EBFSTALLIONS.COM MAIDEN STKS (PLUS 10 RACE) 6f

**4:40** (4:40) (Class 3) 2-Y-O **£7,762** (£2,310; £1,154; £577) **Stalls** High

Form RPR

**1** **International Man** 2-9-5 0 ................................................... JackGarritty 5 80+
(Richard Fahey) *trckd ldrs: hdwy over 2f out: sn cl up: rdn to chal over 1f out: led ins fnl f: edgd lft and kpt on wl towards fin* **13/2**

**2** *1 1/2* **Arbalet (IRE)** 2-9-5 0 ............................................................ JamesDoyle 8 75+
(Hugo Palmer) *dwlt and hld up in rr: swtchd lft and hdwy on inner over 2f out: chsd ldrs over 1f out and sn rdn: drvn ins fnl f: kpt on* **9/4**[1]

3 **3** *hd* **Astraea**[18] 3179 2-8-11 0 ............................................... NathanEvans[(3)] 9 70
(Michael Easterby) *in tch on outer: pushed along over 2f out: hdwy wl over 1f out: sn rdn and kpt on fnl f* **10/1**

02 **4** *nk* **Knockout Blow**[21] 3066 2-9-5 0 ................................ SilvestreDeSousa 3 74
(Mark Johnston) *trckd ldr: cl up 1/2-way: led 2f out: jnd and rdn over 1f out: drvn and hdd ins fnl f: kpt on* **11/4**[2]

**5** *3 1/2* **Knowing Glance (IRE)** 2-9-5 0 ............................................. PaulHanagan 7 62
(Richard Fahey) *t.k.h: in tch: green and pushed along 1/2-way: rdn wl over 1f out: sn no imp* **6/1**[3]

**6** *3/4* **Don Pepe (IRE)** 2-9-5 0 ........................................................ SeanLevey 4 60
(Richard Hannon) *trckd ldrs: hdwy 1/2-way: cl up on outer over 2f out: sn rdn and wknd wl over 1f out* **6/1**[3]

**7** *4 1/2* **Dark Freedom (IRE)** 2-9-5 0 ............................................ DavidProbert 6 46
(Charles Hills) *green: a towards rr* **14/1**

0 8 21 **Cathie's Dream (USA)**[23] 2988 2-9-0 0 ........................ PaulMulrennan 1
(Noel Wilson) *sn led: rdn along and hdd 2f out: sn wknd* **33/1**
1m 13.82s (1.92) **Going Correction** +0.05s/f (Good) 8 Ran SP% **118.0**
Speed ratings (Par 97): **89,87,86,86,81 80,74,46**
CSF £22.32 TOTE £7.80: £2.40, £1.30, £2.70; EX 23.90 Trifecta £192.60.
**Owner** P D Smith Holdings Ltd **Bred** Bearstone Stud Ltd **Trained** Musley Bank, N Yorks
**FOCUS**
An average maiden in which Richard Fahey was having his fourth winner since 2010. It may not be strong form as the principals finished close-up.

## 3847 RIEVAULX SPORTING SUPPORTING MACMILLAN H'CAP 6f
**5:15** (5:15) (Class 4) (0-80,80) 3-Y-O+ **£7,762** (£2,310; £1,154; £577) **Stalls** Centre

Form RPR
0211 **1** **Meshardal (GER)**[12] 3401 7-9-3 **69** ........................ (p) JamesSullivan 12 79+
(Ruth Carr) *hld up: hdwy and nt clr run wl over 1f out: sn swtchd lft and rdn: styd on strly fnl f to ld last 75yds* **7/1**[3]
-010 **2** ½ **Tricky Dicky**[23] 2990 4-9-6 **72** ........................ SamJames 19 80
(Olly Williams) *hld up in tch nr stands' rail: hdwy wl over 1f out: sn rdn: styd on strly fnl f* **16/1**
32-5 **3** *nk* **My Dad Syd (USA)**[42] 2404 5-9-8 **74** ........................ (v) JamesDoyle 4 81+
(Ian Williams) *trckd ldrs towards centre: hdwy 2f out: rdn and ev ch over 1f out: drvn and edgd rt ins fnl f: kpt on* **11/2**[2]
34-5 **4** ¾ **Hilary J**[26] 2899 4-10-0 **80** ........................ JoeyHaynes 10 85
(Ann Duffield) *sn led: rdn over 1f out: drvn ins fnl f: hdd and no ex last 75yds* **10/1**
0033 **5** *1* **Amood (IRE)**[9] 3492 6-9-6 **72** ........................ (p) DavidProbert 20 73
(Simon West) *towards rr nr stands' rail: hdwy wl over 1f out: rdn and styd on wl fnl f* **25/1**
0000 **6** *shd* **Kenny The Captain (IRE)**[10] 3463 6-9-2 **75** ........ RobertDodsworth(7) 5 76
(Tim Easterby) *chsd ldrs centre: cl up 2f out: rdn and ev ch ent fnl f: hld whn n.m.r last 100yds* **25/1**
04-5 **7** 1¾ **Storm Melody**[35] 2608 4-9-8 **74** ........................ KevinStott 9 70
(Jonjo O'Neill) *chsd ldrs towards centre: rdn along wl over 1f out: drvn and one pce fnl f* **9/1**
1211 **8** 2½ **Kinloch Pride**[35] 2628 5-9-2 **68** ........................ (p) PaulHanagan 17 56
(Noel Wilson) *racd nr stands' rail: cl up: rdn along wl over 1f out: drvn and wknd fnl f* **10/1**
0050 **9** 1¼ **B Fifty Two (IRE)**[14] 3324 8-9-13 **79** ........................ (t) BarryMcHugh 13 63
(Marjorie Fife) *chsd ldrs centre: rdn along 2f out: sn wknd* **20/1**
3-12 **10** *nk* **Ancient Astronaut**[29] 2800 4-9-11 **77** ........................ (h) JackGarritty 16 60
(John Quinn) *in tch towards stands' side: rdn along over 2f out: sn drvn and grad wknd* **10/1**
53-0 **11** *1* **Point Of Woods**[32] 2700 4-8-11 **68** ........................ MeganNicholls(5) 11 47
(Tina Jackson) *chsd ldrs centre: rdn along 2f out: grad wknd* **50/1**
0005 **12** *5* **Florencio**[9] 3492 4-9-6 **79** ........................ (h) BenSanderson(7) 2 42
(Roger Fell) *stmbld bdly at s: racd towards far side: a towards rr* **33/1**
0-00 **13** 4½ **See The Sun**[28] 2840 6-10-0 **80** ........................ AndrewMullen 6 29
(Tim Easterby) *prom centre: rdn along wl over 1f out: sn drvn and wknd* **16/1**
-640 **14** 1¼ **Money Team (IRE)**[28] 2821 6-9-10 **76** ........................ SilvestreDeSousa 8 21
(David Barron) *dwlt: a towards rr* **9/1**
0624 **15** ¾ **Poppy In The Wind**[16] 3257 5-9-8 **74** ........................ (v) JosephineGordon 3 17
(Alan Brown) *a towards rr* **20/1**
34-0 **16** 3¾ **Duke Cosimo**[48] 2184 7-9-12 **78** ........................ PaulMulrennan 15 9
(Michael Herrington) *dwlt: a bhd* **16/1**
2-10 **P** **Harbour Grey (IRE)**[31] 2739 3-9-4 **77** ........................ SeanLevey 7
(Richard Hannon) *chsd ldrs centre: lost pl 1/2-way: lost action over 2f out and p.u* **9/2**[1]
1m 12.48s (0.58) **Going Correction** +0.05s/f (Good)
**WFA** 3 from 4yo+ 7lb 17 Ran SP% **133.1**
Speed ratings (Par 105): **98,97,96,95,94 94,92,88,87,86 85,78,72,71,70 65,**
CSF £113.72 CT £709.75 TOTE £8.40: £2.40, £3.80, £1.90, £2.40; EX 194.80 Trifecta £1128.70.

**Owner** The Hollinbridge Partnership & Ruth Carr **Bred** Gestut Hofgut Heymann **Trained** Huby, N Yorks
**FOCUS**
A competitive sprint handicap and a strong pace, which helped the winner come from behind.
T/Jkpt: Not Won. T/Plt: £599.80 to a £1 stake. Pool: £229,673.67 - 279.52 winning units. T/Qpdt: £55.50 to a £1 stake. Pool: £12,559.98 - 167.22 winning units. **Joe Rowntree**

3848 - 3854a (Foreign Racing) - See Raceform Interactive

# 3366 CHANTILLY (R-H)
Saturday, June 17
**OFFICIAL GOING: Polytrack: standard; turf: good**

## 3855a PRIX PAUL DE MOUSSAC LONGINES (GROUP 3) (3YO) (TURF) 1m
**1:50** 3-Y-O **£34,188** (£13,675; £10,256; £6,837; £3,418)

RPR
**1** **Trais Fluors**[25] 2944 3-8-13 0 ow2 ........................ VincentCheminaud 1 112+
(A Fabre, France) *settled in fnl pair: crept clsr over 2 1/2f out: styng on whn nt clr run 1f out: r.o to ld fnl 50yds: readily* **9/10**[1]
**2** *1* **Stunning Spirit**[41] 2448 3-8-13 0 ow2 ........................ AurelienLemaitre 5 108+
(F Head, France) *racd keenly early: hld up bhd ldr: rdn to go 2nd 1f out: styd on wl to ld 100yds out: hdd fnl 50yds: no ex* **39/10**[2]
**3** 1½ **Roc Angel (FR)**[40] 2484 3-8-13 0 ow2 ........................ TonyPiccone 2 104
(F Chappet, France) *chsd ldr: drvn but no imp 1 1/2f out: styd on but nt pce of front two ins fnl f: tk 3rd cl home* **164/10**
**4** *hd* **Yuman (FR)**[49] 2170 3-8-13 0 ow2 ........................ Pierre-CharlesBoudot 3 104
(H-A Pantall, France) *led: drvn 1 1/2f out: hdd fnl 100yds: no ex: lost 3rd cl home* **76/10**
**5** ¾ **Ratiocination (IRE)**[25] 2944 3-8-13 0 ow2 ........................ StephanePasquier 4 102
(P Bary, France) *racd keenly: hld up towards rr: drvn to cl 1 1/2f out: styd on ins fnl f: nt pce to get on terms* **73/10**
**6** 2½ **Markazi (FR)**[62] 1824 3-8-13 0 ow2 ........................ (p) ChristopheSoumillon 6 96
(J-C Rouget, France) *w.w in rr: rdn and short-lived effrt wl over 1f out: one pce fnl f* **11/2**[3]
1m 37.65s (-0.35) 6 Ran SP% **117.8**
PARI-MUTUEL (all including 1 euro stake): WIN: 1.90; PLACE: 1.20, 1.70; SF: 4.10.
**Owner** Scea Haras De Saint Pair **Bred** Scea Haras De Saint Pair **Trained** Chantilly, France

## 3856a LA COUPE LONGINES (GROUP 3) (4YO+) (TURF) 1m 2f
**3:00** 4-Y-O+ **£34,188** (£13,675; £10,256; £6,837; £3,418)

RPR
**1** **Robin Of Navan (FR)**[20] 3118 4-9-1 0 ow1 ........................ CristianDemuro 3 115+
(Harry Dunlop) *racd freely: hld up bhd ldr: shkn up to ld 1 1/2f out: styd on 2 l clr ins fnl f: pushed out: won easing down* **9/10**[1]
**2** ½ **Garlingari (FR)**[188] 8329 6-9-1 0 ow1 ........................ (p) RonanThomas 1 114+
(Mme C Barande-Barbe, France) *chsd ldng pair on inner: 2 l 3rd and drvn 1 1/2f out: styd on fnl f: nvr able to chal wnr* **17/2**
**3** *2* **First Sitting**[21] 3069 6-9-1 0 ow1 ........................ GeraldMosse 2 110
(Chris Wall) *hld up in fnl pair: drvn but n.m.r 1 1/2f out: sn angled out and rdn: styd on same pce fnl f* **5/1**[3]
**4** 1½ **Shutterbug (FR)**[24] 2977 5-9-1 0 ow1 ........................ (b) AntoineHamelin 6 107
(M Figge, Germany) *led: drvn 2f out: hdd 1 1/2f out: grad dropped away fnl f* **10/1**
**5** ½ **That Which Is Not (USA)**[25] 2946 4-8-11 0 ow1 .... StephanePasquier 5 102
(F-H Graffard, France) *racd keenly: hld up in rr: drvn and no real imp 1 1/2f out: one pce fnl f* **16/5**[2]
**6** *10* **Cafe Royal (GER)**[40] 2485 6-9-1 0 ow1 ........................ MaximeGuyon 4 86
(A Schutz, France) *chsd ldng pair on outer: rdn and lost pl 1 1/2f out: last and wl hld whn eased ins fnl f* **131/10**
1m 59.45s (-5.35) 6 Ran SP% **119.8**
PARI-MUTUEL (all including 1 euro stake): WIN: 1.90; PLACE: 1.60, 2.90; SF: 11.30.
**Owner** Cross, Deal, Foden, Sieff **Bred** Mme Monique Lepeudry **Trained** Lambourn, Berks

# 3311 DONCASTER (L-H)
Sunday, June 18
**OFFICIAL GOING: Good to firm (watered; 7.8)**
Wind: Light against Weather: Sunny Rails: Moved out on round course from 1m2f to straight. Races 3, 4 & 7 increased by 12y

## 3857 YORKSHIRE WILDLIFE PARK FOUNDATION H'CAP 7f 213y(R)
**2:00** (2:01) (Class 4) (0-85,85) 4-Y-O+ **£5,175** (£1,540; £769; £384) **Stalls** Low

Form RPR
0-05 **1** ½ **Sovereign Bounty**[33] 2701 5-9-0 **78** ........................ PJMcDonald 2 83
(Jedd O'Keeffe) *a.p: chsd wnr over 1f out: sn rdn and ev ch: styd on: fin 2nd: awrdd the r* **7/2**[2]
36-5 **2** ¾ **Blind Faith (IRE)**[25] 2973 4-9-1 **79** ........................ JamieSpencer 7 82+
(Luca Cumani) *awkward s: hld up: hdwy over 1f out: rdn and r.o to go 3rd wl ins fnl f: nt rch ldrs: fin 3rd: plcd 2nd* **7/1**
5441 **3** 1¾ **Mon Beau Visage (IRE)**[23] 3049 4-9-1 **79** ........................ (p) DanielTudhope 6 78
(David O'Meara) *hld up: hdwy over 1f out: sn rdn: styd on same pce ins fnl f: fin 4th: plcd 3rd* **2/1**[1]
66/4 **4** 1¼ **Groor**[101] 1119 5-9-7 **85** ........................ SeanLevey 3 81
(Mohamed Moubarak) *s.i.s: hld up: hdwy over 2f out: rdn over 1f out: no ex ins fnl f: fin 5th: plcd 4th* **20/1**
0-03 **5** ¾ **Midnight Macchiato (IRE)**[30] 2795 4-9-0 **78** ........................ PhillipMakin 8 73
(David Brown) *led: rdn and hdd 2f out: no ex ins fnl f: fin 6th: plcd 5th* **5/1**
1040 **6** ¾ **Dutch Art Dealer**[77] 1512 6-9-7 **85** ........................ (p[1]) DavidNolan 5 78
(Ivan Furtado) *hld up: hdwy over 1f out: no ex fnl f: fin 7th: plcd 6th* **20/1**
00-0 **7** *31* **Jacob Black**[17] 3255 6-8-11 **75** ........................ DougieCostello 4
(Kenny Johnson) *prom: racd alone centre fr 4f out tl wknd wl over 2f out: fin 8th: plcd 7th* **66/1**
4636 **D** **Intensical (IRE)**[20] 3140 6-8-11 **75** ........................ (p) SilvestreDeSousa 1 81
(Ivan Furtado) *chsd ldr tl wnt upsides over 3f out: led 2f out: sn rdn: edgd rt ins fnl f: styd on u.p: later disqualified: prohibited substance fnd in sample* **9/2**[3]
1m 37.96s (-1.74) **Going Correction** -0.20s/f (Firm) 8 Ran SP% **113.9**
Speed ratings (Par 105): **99,98,97,95,95 94,63,100**
CSF £20.04 CT £107.69 TOTE £5.50: £1.50, £1.80, £2.50; EX 20.00 Trifecta £123.60.
**Owner** Caron & Paul Chapman **Bred** West Dereham Abbey Stud **Trained** Middleham Moor, N Yorks
**FOCUS**
The going was good to firm ahead of the opener, an average handicap in which only one of the last nine winners of the race followed-up. They didn't go flat out, before sprinting halfway up the straight.

## 3858 PROJECT POLAR EBF FILLIES' NOVICE STKS (PLUS 10 RACE) 7f 6y
**2:30** (2:35) (Class 5) 2-Y-O **£3,881** (£1,155; £577; £288) **Stalls** Centre

Form RPR
**1** **Quivery (USA)** 2-9-0 0 ........................ JamieSpencer 8 83+
(Jeremy Noseda) *s.i.s: hld up: hdwy over 1f out: shkn up and edgd lft ins fnl f: r.o to ld nr fin: readily* **9/4**[2]
**2** ¾ **Arabian Gift (IRE)** 2-9-0 0 ........................ WilliamBuick 10 81+
(Charlie Appleby) *wnt rt s: hld up: hdwy over 2f out: led over 1f out: rdn and hung lft ins fnl f: hdd nr fin* **2/1**[1]
3 **3** 3¼ **Paramount Love**[15] 3312 2-9-0 0 ........................ PaulHanagan 2 73
(Richard Fahey) *hld up: hdwy over 2f out: ev ch over 1f out: rdn and hung lft ins fnl f: styd on same pce* **4/1**[3]
**4** 2¼ **One Second** 2-9-0 0 ........................ SilvestreDeSousa 5 67
(Mark Johnston) *dwlt: rn green in rr: hdwy over 2f out: led wl over 1f out: sn rdn: hung rt and hdd: hung lft and wknd wl ins fnl f* **6/1**
**5** 2¾ **Tig Tog (IRE)** 2-9-0 0 ........................ SeanLevey 1 60
(Richard Hannon) *prom: led over 2f out: rdn and hdd wl over 1f out: hmpd sn after: wknd ins fnl f* **14/1**
0 **6** ½ **Thundercloud**[15] 3312 2-9-0 0 ........................ PJMcDonald 7 58
(Scott Dixon) *chsd ldr: ev ch over 2f out: sn rdn: wknd over 1f out* **100/1**
0 **7** 1½ **Daffrah**[15] 3312 2-9-0 0 ........................ DanielTudhope 3 54
(James Tate) *hld up in tch: racd keenly: rdn over 2f out: wknd over 1f out* **16/1**
0 **8** 2½ **Mountain Meadow**[15] 3312 2-9-0 0 ........................ JackGarritty 6 48
(Richard Fahey) *hld up in tch: pushed along 1/2-way: wknd wl over 1f out* **33/1**
**9** 1¾ **Headwear (IRE)** 2-9-0 0 ........................ PhillipMakin 9 43
(David Brown) *chsd ldrs: rdn over 2f out: wknd over 1f out* **50/1**
0 **10** *9* **Foxy's Spirit**[52] 2105 2-9-0 0 ........................ DavidAllan 4 20
(Tim Easterby) *led: rdn and hdd over 2f out: wknd wl over 1f out* **100/1**
1m 26.52s (0.22) **Going Correction** -0.20s/f (Firm) 10 Ran SP% **117.8**
Speed ratings (Par 90): **90,89,85,82,79 79,77,74,72,62**
CSF £7.19 TOTE £3.70: £1.30, £1.30, £1.50; EX 8.80 Trifecta £26.20.
**Owner** Marc Keller **Bred** Elm Tree Farm Llc **Trained** Newmarket, Suffolk

**FOCUS**
A fair maiden in which they went a good clip, setting it up for the closers. The first two went clear and look decent types.

## 3859 INTO AFRICA CLASSIFIED STKS 1m 2f 43y
**3:00** (3:00) (Class 5) 3-Y-O **£3,881** (£1,155; £577; £288) **Stalls** Low

Form RPR
2332 1 **Alexander M (IRE)**[9] 3531 3-9-0 70 SilvestreDeSousa 4 74
(Mark Johnston) *chsd ldrs: led over 7f out: clr over 4f out: rdn over 1f out: styd on u.p* **11/10**[1]
41- 2 *nk* **Crushed (IRE)**[233] 7659 3-9-0 69 BenCurtis 1 73
(William Haggas) *s.i.s: hld up: hdwy to chse wnr over 2f out: rdn over 1f out: edgd lft ins fnl f: styd on* **7/4**[2]
4-44 3 3 ½ **Second Page**[11] 3457 3-8-8 71 RossaRyan(7) 2 67
(Richard Hannon) *led 1f: racd keenly: remained handy: wnt 2nd over 6f out tl rdn over 2f out: sn outpcd: styd on to go 3rd nr fin* **3/1**[3]
1-04 4 *nk* **Three Duchesses**[26] 2929 3-8-9 70 LuluStanford(5) 3 66
(Michael Bell) *plld hrd: led after 1f tl over 7f out: pushed along over 4f out: styd on same pce fr over 1f out* **10/1**

2m 10.41s (1.01) **Going Correction** -0.20s/f (Firm) **4** Ran SP% **118.1**
Speed ratings (Par 99): **87,86,83,83**
CSF £3.80 TOTE £2.00; EX 4.00 Trifecta £6.80.
**Owner** Mrs Christine E Budden **Bred** Christine E Budden & Partners **Trained** Middleham Moor, N Yorks
■ Doctor Cross (11-1) was withdrawn not under orders. Rule 4 \n\x\x applies to all bets struck prior to withdrawal. Deduct 5p in the pound. New\n\x\x market formed

**FOCUS**
A modest little 3yo event in which the favourite made all.

## 3860 SAFARI VILLAGE MAIDEN STKS 1m 3f 197y
**3:30** (3:30) (Class 5) 3-Y-O+ **£3,234** (£962; £481; £240) **Stalls** Low

Form RPR
22 1 **Humble Hero (IRE)**[25] 2963 3-9-0 0 BenCurtis 4 82+
(William Haggas) *s.i.s: sn prom: led 10f out: rdn over 1f out: styd on wl* **4/5**[1]
-62 2 3 ¾ **Chief Craftsman**[37] 2584 3-9-0 0 JamieSpencer 5 76
(Luca Cumani) *prom: chsd wnr 4f out: rdn over 1f out: swtchd lft and no ex wl ins fnl f* **6/1**[3]
3 2 **Helf (IRE)** 3-9-0 0 SeanLevey 2 73
(Richard Hannon) *s.i.s: hld up: hdwy over 3f out: rdn over 1f out: styd on same pce fnl f* **20/1**
35 4 *shd* **Sea Sovereign (IRE)**[25] 2963 4-10-0 0 TimmyMurphy 6 73
(Mark Pitman) *led 2f: chsd ldr tl over 4f out: rdn over 2f out: no ex ins fnl f* **20/1**
5-32 5 *hd* **Fibonacci**[46] 2314 3-9-0 85 WilliamBuick 1 72
(Hugo Palmer) *prom: pushed along and hung lft fr over 4f out: styd on same pce fr over 1f out* **9/4**[2]
4500 6 43 **Psychology**[15] 3340 4-10-0 49 (t) DougieCostello 7 4
(Kenny Johnson) *s.i.s: hld up: wknd over 3f out* **200/1**

2m 34.28s (-0.62) **Going Correction** -0.20s/f (Firm)
**WFA** 3 from 4yo+ 14lb **6** Ran SP% **110.6**
Speed ratings (Par 103): **94,91,90,90,89 61**
CSF £6.00 TOTE £1.70: £1.30, £2.10; EX 5.30 Trifecta £46.70.
**Owner** Mrs S Magnier/M Tabor/M Jooste & D Smith **Bred** Lynch Bages & Camas Park Stud **Trained** Newmarket, Suffolk

**FOCUS**
A fair maiden in which four of the last five winners of the race won during their next two outings, including a Listed race. The favourite made all.

## 3861 YORKSHIRE WILDLIFE PARK H'CAP 6f 2y
**4:00** (4:00) (Class 3) (0-95,98) 3-Y-O+ **£7,762** (£2,310; £1,154; £577) **Stalls** Centre

Form RPR
0301 1 **Pipers Note**[11] 3463 7-10-3 98 JamesSullivan 5 106
(Ruth Carr) *hld up in tch: rdn to ld 1f out: all out* **6/1**[3]
006 2 *hd* **Dougan**[13] 3410 5-9-6 92 DavidEgan(5) 8 99
(David Evans) *mid-div: hdwy over 1f out: rdn and edgd rt ins fnl f: r.o wl* **7/1**
4-00 3 ½ **Red Pike (IRE)**[50] 2156 6-9-9 90 ConnorBeasley 6 96
(Bryan Smart) *trckd ldr tl led wl over 1f out: sn rdn: hdd 1f out: styd on u.p* **9/1**
0110 4 ½ **Wentworth Falls**[32] 2736 5-10-1 96 PhillipMakin 3 100
(Geoffrey Harker) *s.i.s: hld up: hdwy over 1f out: sn rdn: no ex towards fin* **9/2**[2]
2221 5 2 ¾ **Evergate**[20] 3159 3-9-3 91 SilvestreDeSousa 2 84+
(Robert Cowell) *hld up: swtchd rt over 2f out: hdwy over 1f out: rdn and hung lft ins fnl f: no ex* **5/2**[1]
-410 6 1 ½ **Scofflaw**[20] 3146 3-8-7 81 PaulHanagan 4 70
(Richard Fahey) *hld up: rdn over 2f out: nt trble ldrs* **10/1**
000- 7 *hd* **Son Of Africa**[271] 6642 5-10-0 95 (h[1]) HarryBentley 9 85
(Henry Candy) *s.i.s: hld up: shkn up over 2f out: nt trble ldrs* **16/1**
0-05 8 1 **Bossipop**[39] 2524 4-9-3 84 (b) DavidAllan 10 71
(Tim Easterby) *chsd ldrs: rdn over 2f out: wknd ins fnl f* **25/1**
0-00 9 4 **Ashpan Sam**[15] 3324 8-9-6 87 (p) WilliamCarson 7 61
(David W Drinkwater) *led: rdn over 2f out: hdd wl over 1f out: wknd fnl f* **25/1**
3662 10 3 ¾ **Iseemist (IRE)**[16] 3307 6-9-9 90 FergusSweeney 11 52
(John Gallagher) *chsd ldrs: rdn over 2f out: wknd over 1f out* **16/1**
00-1 11 1 ¾ **Zanetto**[49] 2184 7-9-8 89 JasonHart 1 45
(John Quinn) *s.i.s: a in rr: rdn and wknd over 1f out* **20/1**

1m 11.21s (-2.39) **Going Correction** -0.20s/f (Firm)
**WFA** 3 from 4yo+ 7lb **11** Ran SP% **116.8**
Speed ratings (Par 107): **107,106,106,105,101 99,99,98,92,87 85**
CSF £45.98 CT £372.72 TOTE £5.80: £2.40, £2.40, £2.60; EX 43.30 Trifecta £384.90.
**Owner** Cragg Wood Racing **Bred** Wadacre Stud **Trained** Huby, N Yorks

**FOCUS**
A competitive sprint handicap featuring several last time out winners, and the form looks solid as the right horses came to the fore.

## 3862 BREN SLINGSBY H'CAP 7f 213y(R)
**4:30** (4:30) (Class 4) (0-80,81) 3-Y-O **£5,175** (£1,540; £769; £384) **Stalls** Low

Form RPR
0-51 1 **Helovaplan (IRE)**[49] 2186 3-9-1 74 ConnorBeasley 2 86+
(Bryan Smart) *s.i.s: hld up: hdwy over 2f out: led over 1f out: rdn out* **8/1**
421 2 1 ¾ **Komodo (IRE)**[34] 2682 3-9-4 77 DanielTudhope 11 85
(Jedd O'Keeffe) *chsd ldrs: rdn over 1f out: edgd lft and chsd wnr ins fnl f: styd on* **13/2**[3]
5-04 3 1 ½ **Ascot Week (USA)**[22] 3062 3-9-5 78 DaneO'Neill 6 83
(Owen Burrows) *hld up: hdwy over 2f out: rdn over 1f out: styd on same pce ins fnl f* **25/1**
-302 4 3 ½ **Inner Circle (IRE)**[23] 3040 3-9-7 80 SeanLevey 10 77
(Richard Hannon) *chsd ldr tl led over 2f out: rdn and hdd over 1f out: wknd ins fnl f* **8/1**
3-53 5 ¾ **Fayez (IRE)**[18] 3199 3-9-8 81 PhillipMakin 4 76
(David O'Meara) *s.i.s: hld up: hdwy over 2f out: rdn over 1f out: wknd fnl f* **20/1**
-003 6 1 ¼ **Aelius**[23] 3047 3-8-3 65 NathanEvans(3) 8 57
(Michael Easterby) *s.i.s: in rr: pushed along over 4f out: nvr nrr* **10/1**
2-00 7 *nse* **Natajack**[19] 3188 3-8-13 75 AdamMcNamara(3) 12 67
(Richard Fahey) *s.i.s: ct wd 2f: rdn and hung lft fr over 2f out: nvr on terms* **33/1**
41-3 8 *shd* **Dellaguista (IRE)**[23] 3031 3-9-2 75 (p[1]) WilliamBuick 7 67
(William Haggas) *mid-div: hdwy over 2f out: wknd ins fnl f* **4/1**[1]
5-05 9 1 ¾ **Procurator (IRE)**[37] 2567 3-9-5 78 KieranO'Neill 3 66
(Richard Hannon) *pushed along early in rr: hdwy over 6f out: rdn and wknd over 1f out* **8/1**
-135 10 ½ **Proud Archi (IRE)**[23] 3040 3-9-7 80 PaulMulrennan 1 66
(Michael Dods) *led over 5f: wknd fnl f* **10/1**
3032 11 6 **The Eagle's Nest (IRE)**[15] 3336 3-9-0 73 PaulHanagan 9 46
(Richard Fahey) *hld up: rdn over 2f out: wkng whn hmpd over 1f out* **6/1**[2]
0-10 12 3 ¾ **Weloof (FR)**[17] 3262 3-9-7 80 SilvestreDeSousa 5 44
(Ed Dunlop) *prom: rdn over 3f out: wknd wl over 1f out* **10/1**

1m 37.71s (-1.99) **Going Correction** -0.20s/f (Firm) **12** Ran SP% **119.8**
Speed ratings (Par 101): **101,99,97,94,93 92,92,92,90,89 83,80**
CSF £58.49 CT £1277.34 TOTE £10.90: £3.10, £2.60, £6.50; EX 85.30 Trifecta £3915.40.
**Owner** The Smart Set **Bred** Ross Moorhead **Trained** Hambleton, N Yorks

**FOCUS**
An open 3yo handicap with several unexposed runners, and two of them fought out the finish. There was a good pace and the first three came clear, suggesting the form is solid.

## 3863 WILDLIFE ADVENTURE APPRENTICE H'CAP 1m 6f 115y
**5:00** (5:00) (Class 5) (0-70,68) 4-Y-O+ **£3,234** (£962; £481) **Stalls** Low

Form RPR
2421 1 **Graceful Lady**[25] 2972 4-8-11 62 DavidEgan(5) 3 66
(Robert Eddery) *plld hrd: let at stdy pce tl qcknd over 3f out: rdn over 2f out: styd on gamely* **10/11**[1]
3354 2 *nk* **Wordiness**[36] 2622 9-8-11 64 KatherineGlenister(7) 1 67
(David Evans) *s.i.s: sn racd keenly in 2nd pl: rdn and ev ch fr over 1f out: edgd rt ins fnl f: nt qckn nr fin* **5/2**[3]
0651 3 8 **Gambol (FR)**[23] 3026 7-8-10 63 (v) LukeCatton(7) 4 56
(Ian Williams) *hld up in tch: plld hrd: rdn over 2f out: sn outpcd* **9/4**[2]

3m 14.64s (7.24) **Going Correction** -0.20s/f (Firm) **3** Ran SP% **111.7**
Speed ratings (Par 103): **72,71,67**
CSF £3.56 TOTE £1.80; EX 3.40 Trifecta £3.60.
**Owner** Graham & Lynn Knight **Bred** J C Sillett **Trained** Newmarket, Suffolk

**FOCUS**
Just the three runners for this moderate staying handicap, though two of them won last time out, and there was an exciting finish. The pace was slow.
T/Plt: £65.30 to a £1 stake. Pool: £106,996.55 - 1,194.99 winning units. T/Qpdt: £28.50 to a £1 stake. Pool: £6,148.17 - 159.50 winning units. **Colin Roberts**

# 3689 SALISBURY (R-H)
Sunday, June 18

**OFFICIAL GOING: Good to firm (watered; 8.6)**
Wind: nil Weather: very warm (30)

## 3864 DEREK BURRIDGE GOLF & RACING TROPHIES H'CAP 1m 4f 5y
**2:15** (2:15) (Class 6) (0-65,67) 3-Y-O **£3,234** (£962; £481; £240) **Stalls** Low

Form RPR
00-1 1 **Pow Wow**[22] 3087 3-9-7 67 KieranShoemark(3) 3 78+
(Roger Charlton) *mde all: rdn 3f out: styd on wl* **4/6**[1]
000 2 ½ **Theglasgowwarrior**[34] 2689 3-9-6 63 LouisSteward 2 70+
(Michael Bell) *trckd wnr: rdn over 2f out: styd on ins fnl f but a being hld* **14/1**
0-30 3 2 **Black Prince (FR)**[33] 2711 3-8-10 53 (t[1]) JFEgan 6 57
(Anthony Honeyball) *s.i.s: pushed along early in last: rdn over 2f out: stdy prog fr over 1f out: styd on to go 3rd towards fin but nt pce to get on terms* **16/1**
-030 4 ¾ **Famous Dynasty (IRE)**[13] 3412 3-9-3 60 DanielMuscutt 8 63
(Michael Blanshard) *hld up in tch: hdwy over 2f out: sn rdn: disp 2nd over 1f out tl no ex fnl 120yds* **16/1**
045- 5 ¾ **Zoffanist (IRE)**[242] 7458 3-9-7 64 JimCrowley 4 66
(Amanda Perrett) *in tch: rdn over 2f out: sn one pce* **7/1**[3]
4-35 6 ½ **Eolian**[27] 2892 3-9-10 67 (p[1]) DavidProbert 5 68
(Andrew Balding) *trckd wnr: rdn over 2f out: styd on tl no ex fnl 120yds* **9/2**[2]
0-50 7 9 **See The Sea (IRE)**[31] 2754 3-9-10 67 TomMarquand 7 53
(Richard Hannon) *trckd wnr: rdn 3f out: wknd over 1f out* **14/1**
0440 8 12 **Cecilator**[12] 3425 3-9-5 62 (p[1]) LiamKeniry 1 29
(Noel Williams) *hld up in tch: rdn over 3f out: wknd over 2f out* **50/1**

2m 35.11s (-2.89) **Going Correction** -0.30s/f (Firm) **8** Ran SP% **117.7**
Speed ratings (Par 97): **97,96,95,94,94 94,88,80**
CSF £13.01 CT £90.39 TOTE £1.60: £1.10, £2.80, £2.30; EX 12.20 Trifecta £92.40.
**Owner** Philip Newton **Bred** Philip Newton **Trained** Beckhampton, Wilts

**FOCUS**
Clerk of the course Jeremy Martin reported that 16mm of water had been applied in the days leading up to racing. The stalls were on the stands' side for this moderate opener, won with some ease by a well-backed favourite plainly better than the grade.

## 3865 THINK CARS SSANGYONG PADDOCK AREA DISPLAY H'CAP 5f
**2:45** (2:45) (Class 4) (0-85,84) 3-Y-O+ **£5,175** (£1,540; £769; £384) **Stalls** Low

Form RPR
0-03 1 **Edged Out**[16] 3281 7-8-10 71 MitchGodwin(5) 4 79
(Christopher Mason) *trckd ldr: rdn 2f out: r.o wl ins fnl f: led fnl 120yds: rdn out* **12/1**
1-10 2 ¾ **Mr Pocket (IRE)**[16] 3278 3-9-5 81 (t[1]) DavidProbert 5 84
(Paul Cole) *cl up: nt best of runs fr 2f out: rdn and r.o whn clr jst ins fnl f: wnt 2nd towards fin* **4/1**[3]
040- 3 ¾ **Shackled N Drawn (USA)**[192] 8280 5-9-5 75 TomMarquand 2 78
(Peter Hedger) *led: rdn ent fnl f: hdd fnl 120yds: no ex* **25/1**

6-50 **4** *shd* **Super Julius**[51] 2130 3-9-1 77 RobertWinston 8 77
(Eve Johnson Houghton) *cl up: rdn over 2f out: kpt on same pce fnl f* **9/4**[1]

54-3 **5** *¾* **Justice Lady (IRE)**[29] 2835 4-9-9 79 ShaneKelly 1 79
(David Elsworth) *t.k.h early: cl up: nt clrest of runs fr 2f out: snatched up jst over 1f out: kpt on whn clr but no threat to ldrs* **3/1**[2]

-266 **6** *½* **Waseem Faris (IRE)**[7] 3617 8-10-0 84 PatDobbs 7 82
(Ken Cunningham-Brown) *hld up: rdn over 2f out: swtchd lft ent fnl f: kpt on but nt pce to get on terms* **8/1**

2025 **7** *½* **Silverrica (IRE)**[16] 3281 7-9-6 76 JosephineGordon 3 72
(Malcolm Saunders) *chsd ldr: rdn 2f out: nt pce to chal: fdd ins fnl f* **9/1**

6-63 **8** *¾* **Compton Poppy**[9] 3517 3-8-10 72 GeorgeDowning 6 63
(Tony Carroll) *awkwardly away: in last pair: effrt 2f out: nvr threatened: fdd ins fnl f* **16/1**

59.18s (-1.82) **Going Correction** -0.225s/f (Firm) course record
**WFA** 3 from 4yo+ 6lb **8** Ran SP% **114.3**
Speed ratings (Par 105): **105,103,102,102,101 100,99,98**
CSF £59.38 CT £1188.50 TOTE £14.60: £3.10, £1.60, £5.60; EX 56.20 Trifecta £1229.10.
**Owner** Christopher And Annabelle Mason Racing **Bred** Christopher & Annabelle Mason **Trained** Caewent, Monmouthshire

**FOCUS**
Stalls on far side. Just a reasonable sprint for the grade, and the fact the winner lowered the twelve year-old course record by 0.62 seconds underlined the quickness of the prevailing conditions.

## 3866 WATERAID MILDREN CONSTRUCTION MAIDEN FILLIES' STKS (PLUS 10 RACE) 1m 1f 201y
**3:15** (3:15) (Class 4) 3-Y-O **£5,175** (£1,540; £769; £384) **Stalls** Low

Form RPR

24-0 **1** **Neshmeya**[51] 2131 3-9-0 81 JimCrowley 5 81
(Charles Hills) *mid-div: hdwy 2f out: rdn over 1f out: led fnl 100yds: kpt on wl* **7/2**[3]

0 **2** *nk* **Superioritycomplex (IRE)**[58] 1947 3-9-0 0 PatDobbs 8 80
(Sir Michael Stoute) *a.p: rdn 2f out: tk narrow advantage ent fnl f: hdd fnl 100yds: kpt on but no ex cl home* **12/1**

**3** *1* **Mahabba (IRE)** 3-8-11 0 KieranShoemark(3) 3 78
(Luca Cumani) *trckd ldrs: rdn whn swtchd lft ent fnl f: kpt on* **12/1**

42 **4** *¾* **Extra Mile**[48] 2227 3-9-0 0 (v) FranBerry 1 77
(Saeed bin Suroor) *led: rdn 2f out: hdd ent fnl f: no ex fnl 120yds* **2/1**[1]

4 **5** *1 ½* **Nathalie**[48] 2227 3-9-0 0 DanielMuscutt 9 74
(James Fanshawe) *trckd ldrs: chal 2f out: rdr dropped whip whn ev ch over 1f out: kpt on same pce* **9/4**[2]

2-0 **6** *1 ½* **The Jean Genie**[58] 1944 3-9-0 0 SamHitchcott 10 71+
(Clive Cox) *last pair: rdn over 2f out: styd on fnl f but nt pce to get involved* **9/1**

**7** *1* **Line Of Beauty** 3-9-0 0 MartinLane 7 69+
(Simon Crisford) *hld up: hdwy 4f out: rdn over 2f out: sn one pce* **25/1**

0-6 **8** *7* **Lagertha (IRE)**[29] 2834 3-9-0 0 JosephineGordon 4 55
(Hugo Palmer) *prom for 4f: trckd ldrs: rdn 3f out: wknd jst over 1f out* **33/1**

0 **9** *6* **Opera Queen**[10] 3506 3-9-0 0 DavidProbert 6 43
(Andrew Balding) *a towards rr* **25/1**

6 **10** *shd* **Percipio**[16] 3309 3-9-0 0 TomMarquand 2 43
(Alan King) *a towards rr* **66/1**

2m 8.0s (-1.90) **Going Correction** -0.30s/f (Firm) **10** Ran SP% **123.8**
Speed ratings (Par 98): **95,94,93,93,92 90,90,84,79,79**
CSF £45.66 TOTE £5.60: £1.50, £3.20, £2.70; EX 65.50 Trifecta £519.60.
**Owner** Hamdan Al Maktoum **Bred** J Wigan & G Strawbridge **Trained** Lambourn, Berks

**FOCUS**
Stalls on inner. A race which went last year to recent Spring Lodge Stakes scorer Playful Sound, but this year's edition went to what appeared beforehand to be the most exposed runner in the field. The pace was respectable.

## 3867 BRITISH STALLION STUDS EBF CATHEDRAL STKS (LISTED RACE) 6f
**3:45** (3:46) (Class 1) 3-Y-O+
**£27,220** (£10,320; £5,164; £2,572; £1,291; £648) **Stalls** Low

Form RPR

-320 **1** **Eqtiraan (IRE)**[29] 2831 3-8-12 105 JimCrowley 1 103
(Richard Hannon) *trckd ldrs: rdn over 1f out: led fnl 100yds: r.o wl* **4/1**[2]

6251 **2** *nk* **Mythmaker**[36] 2611 5-9-5 104 PatDobbs 3 104
(Bryan Smart) *disp ld: rdn over 2f out: hdd fnl 100yds: kpt on* **9/2**[3]

-544 **3** *1 ¼* **Pixeleen**[36] 2623 5-9-0 86 JosephineGordon 5 95
(Malcolm Saunders) *disp ld: rdn over 2f out: hdd fnl 120yds: no ex* **16/1**

010/ **4** *¾* **Glass Office**[729] 3380 7-9-5 108 ShaneKelly 2 98
(David Simcock) *hld up: hdwy 2f out: rdn over 1f out: nt pce to chal but kpt on fnl f* **20/1**

-432 **5** *nk* **Dark Shot**[15] 3321 4-9-5 89 DavidProbert 4 97
(Andrew Balding) *trckd ldrs: rdn 2f out: nt quite pce to chal: no ex fnl 70yds* **9/1**

3-04 **6** *1 ¼* **Spring Fling**[22] 3080 6-9-0 94 KieranShoemark 8 88
(Henry Candy) *racd keenly in mid-div: effrt in centre 2f out: nt pce to threaten* **10/1**

5000 **7** *½* **Dark Emerald (IRE)**[78] 1493 7-9-5 102 (vt) FranBerry 7 91
(Brendan Powell) *s.i.s: last: rdn over 2f out: kpt on ins fnl f but nt pce to get involved* **25/1**

-213 **8** *nk* **Mr Lupton (IRE)**[27] 2907 4-9-5 113 TonyHamilton 10 90
(Richard Fahey) *trckd ldrs: rdn over 2f out: fdd ins fnl f* **11/4**[1]

3255 **9** *hd* **Stellarta**[8] 3593 6-9-0 92 TomMarquand 6 84
(Michael Blanshard) *mid-div: rdn 2f out: nvr any imp* **33/1**

25/6 **10** *19* **Tropics (USA)**[27] 2907 9-9-5 109 RobertWinston 9 29
(Dean Ivory) *bmpd leaving stalls: in mid-div: effrt over 2f out: wknd over 1f out: eased fnl f* **6/1**

1m 11.76s (-3.04) **Going Correction** -0.225s/f (Firm)
**WFA** 3 from 4yo+ 7lb **10** Ran SP% **115.7**
Speed ratings (Par 111): **111,110,108,107,107 105,105,104,104,79**
CSF £21.60 TOTE £4.50: £1.40, £1.90, £5.40; EX 21.90 Trifecta £188.40.
**Owner** Hamdan Al Maktoum **Bred** Victor Stud Bloodstock & Brendan Cummins **Trained** East Everleigh, Wilts

**FOCUS**
Stalls on far side. A perfectly decent renewal of one of Salisbury's highlights and a time 0.54 quicker than standard, but very few actually got into it.

## 3868 TOBY BALDING MEMORIAL NOVICE STKS (PLUS 10 RACE) 6f
**4:15** (4:19) (Class 3) 2-Y-O **£10,350** (£3,080; £1,539; £769) **Stalls** Low

Form RPR

**1** **Nyaleti (IRE)** 2-8-11 0 JFEgan 1 88
(Mark Johnston) *led: rdn whn narrowly hdd 2f out: rallied to ld jst over 1f out: kpt on strly: rdn out* **16/1**

32 **2** *¾* **Billesdon Brook**[22] 3070 2-8-11 0 TomMarquand 2 86
(Richard Hannon) *pressed wnr: led 2f out: rdn and edgd lft over 1f out: hdd jst bef fnl f: kpt on but hld fnl 100yds* **10/11**[1]

**3** *5* **Shabaaby** 2-9-2 0 JimCrowley 4 76
(Owen Burrows) *trckd ldrs: nt clr run briefly over 2f out: sn rdn: nt pce to get on terms: kpt on fnl f* **6/1**[3]

**4** *nk* **Watheer** 2-9-2 0 PatDobbs 5 75
(Marcus Tregoning) *in tch: rdn over 2f out: sn one pce* **16/1**

**5** *hd* **Ragstone View (IRE)** 2-9-2 0 ShaneKelly 6 75
(Richard Hughes) *hld up in last pair: swtchd lft over 1f out: kpt on ins fnl f but nt pce to get involved* **25/1**

**6** *½* **Alba Power (IRE)** 2-9-2 0 JosephineGordon 7 73
(Hugo Palmer) *in tch: rdn 3f out: one pce fnl 2f* **10/1**

3 **7** *2 ¾* **Luna Eclipse (IRE)**[31] 2756 2-9-2 0 DavidProbert 8 65
(Andrew Balding) *trckd ldrs: rdn over 2f out: nt pce to get on terms: fdd ins fnl f* **7/2**[2]

**8** *37* **London's Burning** 2-9-2 0 FranBerry 3
(Ralph Beckett) *dwlt: rn green: sn outpcd: a detached in last* **33/1**

1m 12.76s (-2.04) **Going Correction** -0.225s/f (Firm) **8** Ran SP% **116.5**
Speed ratings (Par 97): **104,103,96,95,95 95,91,42**
CSF £31.87 TOTE £15.20: £3.50, £1.10, £1.80; EX 38.20 Trifecta £174.10.
**Owner** 3 Batterhams and A Reay **Bred** SF Bloodstock LLC **Trained** Middleham Moor, N Yorks

**FOCUS**
Stalls on far side. Salouen finished a nose second in this contest last year prior to placing in two Group 1s and running in the Derby. The first two home in this year's renewal pulled miles clear of the remainder at the end of a well-run event, and the winner in particular looks well above average.

## 3869 CARA GLASS FILLIES' H'CAP 6f 213y
**4:45** (4:47) (Class 5) (0-75,77) 3-Y-O+ **£3,881** (£1,155; £577; £288) **Stalls** Centre

Form RPR

30-0 **1** **Excellent Sounds**[15] 3334 4-9-13 77 CharlieBennett(3) 9 86
(Hughie Morrison) *mid-div: hdwy over 2f out: led over 1f out: kpt on: pushed out* **16/1**

55-2 **2** *nk* **Bassmah**[19] 3171 3-9-6 76 TomMarquand 8 83+
(Ismail Mohammed) *s.i.s: bhd: shkn up 2f out: hdwy ent fnl f: r.o wl: wnt 2nd fnl 70yds: nt quite rch wnr* **4/1**[3]

1-40 **3** *1 ¾* **Sarangoo**[33] 2708 9-9-9 75 GeorgiaCox(5) 1 78
(Malcolm Saunders) *disp ld tl clr ldr after 2f: rdn edgd lft and hdd over 1f out: drifted rt fnl 150yds: no ex cl home* **16/1**

1142 **4** *½* **Tai Hang Dragon (IRE)**[9] 3517 3-9-5 75 PatDobbs 10 76+
(Richard Hannon) *hld up in last pair: hdwy but nt clr run over 2f out: running on in cl 3rd whn snatched up on rails fnl 150yds: swtchd lft: kpt on again towards fin but no ch after* **7/2**[2]

51-0 **5** *¾* **Phalaborwa**[19] 3167 3-9-7 77 AdamBeschizza 2 74
(Ed Vaughan) *led for 2f: trckd ldr: rdn and ev ch over 1f out: sn edgd rt: kpt on same pce fnl f* **7/1**

5-30 **6** *1* **Miss Icon**[24] 3000 3-9-1 71 DavidProbert 6 65
(Patrick Chamings) *trckd ldrs: rdn w ch 2f out: fdd fnl 120yds* **14/1**

15-5 **7** *2 ½* **Chica De La Noche**[144] 392 3-9-2 72 JimCrowley 7 62+
(Simon Dow) *hld up: hdwy whn nt clr run briefly 2f out: sn rdn: nt qckn: snatched up whn hld and short of room ins fnl f* **11/4**[1]

43-0 **8** *2* **Heavenly Angel**[59] 1913 3-9-3 73 FranBerry 5 55
(Richard Hannon) *mid-div: rdn over 2f out: wknd ent fnl f* **20/1**

3-21 **9** *1 ¼* **Aimez La Vie (IRE)**[23] 3044 3-9-6 76 TonyHamilton 3 54
(Richard Fahey) *mid-div: hdwy 3f out: sn rdn: wknd over 1f out* **15/2**

2-40 **10** *10* **Dynamic Girl (IRE)**[48] 2229 4-9-7 68 (p) MartinDwyer 4 22
(Brendan Powell) *trckd ldrs: rdn over 2f out: wknd over 1f out* **20/1**

1m 26.12s (-2.48) **Going Correction** -0.225s/f (Firm)
**WFA** 3 from 4yo+ 9lb **10** Ran SP% **121.1**
Speed ratings (Par 100): **105,104,102,102,101 100,97,94,93,82**
CSF £82.18 CT £1081.05 TOTE £18.20: £4.20, £2.30, £5.00; EX 93.30 Trifecta £2282.30.
**Owner** Helena Springfield Ltd **Bred** Meon Valley Stud **Trained** East Ilsley, Berks

**FOCUS**
Stalls in centre. A well-stocked fillies' handicap for the grade, and a decent pace from the outset, but not hard to imagine the second might have won with better luck.

## 3870 SHADWELL STUD RACING EXCELLENCE APPRENTICE H'CAP (WHIPS CAN BE CARRIED BUT NOT USED) 1m
**5:15** (5:16) (Class 6) (0-65,64) 3-Y-O **£3,234** (£962; £481; £240) **Stalls** Low

Form RPR

0033 **1** **Ashazuri**[6] 3656 3-9-4 62 (h) Pierre-LouisJamin(5) 6 70
(Jonathan Portman) *trckd ldr: led over 1f out: kpt on wl whn strly chal thrght fnl f: hld on* **5/1**[3]

02-6 **2** *shd* **Halinka (IRE)**[24] 2993 3-9-8 64 FinleyMarsh(3) 3 72
(Roger Varian) *trckd ldr: swtchd lft 2f out: str chal sn after: ev ch thrght fnl f: jst hld* **5/1**[3]

3441 **3** *3 ½* **Love And Be Loved**[12] 3423 3-9-2 55 JordanUys 4 55
(John Flint) *led: hdd over 1f out: kpt on but no ex fnl f* **6/1**

00-4 **4** *1 ¾* **Tis Wonderful (IRE)**[12] 3423 3-9-6 64 WilliamCox(5) 7 60
(Clive Cox) *trckd ldrs: effrt 2f out: kpt on same pce fnl f* **3/1**[1]

3314 **5** *3 ¾* **Scala Regia (FR)**[86] 1348 3-9-5 63 ManuelFernandes(5) 1 50
(Sir Mark Prescott Bt) *short of room and snatched up after 1f: in tch: swtchd lft over 3f out: nvr threatened: one pce fnl 2f* **9/2**[2]

60-0 **6** *½* **Socrates**[20] 3163 3-9-5 63 TylerSaunders(5) 8 49
(Daniel Kubler) *v awkwardly away: bhd: nvr gng pce to get involved* **25/1**

5-40 **7** *6* **Bay Watch (IRE)**[122] 763 3-9-5 63 (p) JasonWatson(5) 2 35
(Andrew Balding) *trckd ldrs: ch 2f out: wknd ent fnl f* **6/1**

0146 **8** *3 ¼* **Brother In Arms (IRE)**[41] 2474 3-9-8 64 AledBeech(3) 5 29
(Tony Carroll) *a towards rr* **9/1**

1m 41.76s (-1.74) **Going Correction** -0.225s/f (Firm) **8** Ran SP% **118.9**
Speed ratings (Par 97): **99,98,95,93,89 89,83,80**
CSF £31.44 CT £155.87 TOTE £5.40: £1.70, £2.00, £1.90; EX 28.40 Trifecta £202.00.
**Owner** RWH Partnership **Bred** G Wickens And J Homan **Trained** Upper Lambourn, Berks

**FOCUS**
Stalls on far side. A moderate finale with some early scrimmaging, but the stewards were satisfied that Halinka's lurch across Scala Regia after a furlong didn't improve the former's placing. The initial pace was moderate.

T/Jkpt: Not Won. T/Plt: £518.90 to a £1 stake. Pool: £95,007.47 - 133.64 winning units. T/Qpdt: £118.40 to a £1 stake. Pool: £6,916.17 - 43.20 winning units. **Tim Mitchell**

3871 - 3872a (Foreign Racing) - See Raceform Interactive

## 2808 CORK (R-H)

Sunday, June 18

**OFFICIAL GOING: Good to firm (good in places on round course)**

### 3873a MIDSUMMER SPRINT STKS (LISTED RACE) 5f

2:50 (2:51) 3-Y-0+

£22,692 (£7,307; £2,500; £2,500; £769; £384)

RPR

1 **Hit The Bid**[14] 3370 3-9-6 97 LeighRoche 1 105+
(D J Bunyan, Ire) *chsd ldrs: impr to chal gng wl fr 2f out: rdn to ld 1f out and sn edgd lft: kpt on wl u.p wl ins fnl f* **20/1**

2 ¾ **Go Kart (IRE)**[29] 2846 4-9-4 86 (v) ColinKeane 4 96
(P J Prendergast, Ire) *towards rr far side: impr after 1/2-way to chse ldrs 1 1/2f out where rdn: wnt 2nd ins fnl f and kpt on wl clsng stages: nt match wnr* **7/1**

3 1 ¾ **Abstraction (IRE)**[287] 6167 7-9-9 94 RonanWhelan 5 95
(Miss Natalia Lupini, Ire) *cl up: cl 2nd bef 1/2-way: impr to ld narrowly briefly over 1f out: sn hdd and no imp on wnr u.p in 3rd ins fnl f: jnd for 3rd on line* **16/1**

3 dht **Alphabet**[7] 3632 3-8-12 95 (t) WayneLordan 10 88
(A P O'Brien, Ire) *w.w in rr early: tk clsr order fr 1/2-way: rdn bhd ldrs over 1f out and u.p in 4th ins fnl f: kpt on clsng stages to dead-heat for 3rd* **7/2**[1]

5 ½ **Monsieur Joe (IRE)**[9] 3539 10-9-9 102 GaryCarroll 9 93
(Paul Midgley) *prom tl sn settled bhd ldrs nr side: pushed along fr 1/2-way: rdn under 2f out and no imp on wnr u.p in 5th wl ins fnl f: kpt on same pce* **6/1**[3]

6 ¾ **Ostatnia (IRE)**[29] 2846 5-9-4 94 (v) WJLee 3 86
(W McCreery, Ire) *chsd ldrs: disp cl 3rd after 1/2-way: rdn 1 1/2f out and sn no ex: one pce ins fnl f* **9/2**[2]

7 shd **Gorane (IRE)**[28] 2863 3-8-12 99 DeclanMcDonogh 8 83+
(Henry De Bromhead, Ire) *chsd ldrs early: short of room briefly at 1/2-way: nt clr run bhd horses 1 1/2f out: swtchd rt ins fnl f and kpt on clsng stages: nvr trbld ldrs* **9/2**[2]

8 ½ **Yulong Baobei (IRE)**[55] 2046 3-9-1 102 ShaneFoley 6 84
(M Halford, Ire) *broke wl to ld: narrow advantage bef 1/2-way: rdn 2f out and hdd u.p over 1f out: wknd fnl f* **10/1**

9 ½ **Pious Alexander (IRE)**[62] 1844 3-8-12 0 (t[1]) PatSmullen 11 80
(Edward Lynam, Ire) *towards rr thrght: stl gng wl 2f out: short of room between horses 1f out where checked and no imp after: eased clsng stages* **12/1**

10 ½ **Misty Birnam (SAF)**[322] 3-9-9 107 ChrisHayes 7 85
(J A Stack, Ire) *towards rr thrght: pushed along fr 2f out and no imp under hands and heels ins fnl f: eased clsng stages* **20/1**

57.4s (-1.80)
**WFA** 3 from 4yo+ 6lb **10 Ran SP% 117.6**
PL: 1.02 Alphabet, 3.10 Abstraction. TF: HTB&GK&AB: 1948.30, HTB&GK&ALP: 662.60 CSF £154.68 TOTE £22.50: £5.80, £2.10; DF 167.10.
**Owner** Straight To Victory Syndicate **Bred** W And R Barnett Ltd **Trained** The Curragh, Co Kildare

**FOCUS**
A competitive sprint won in good style by a fast horse who brought off one of the biggest shocks of the 2016 season. He was a big price here again, a little surprising seeing he had run in a Group 2 event in France on his previous start and was taking a significant drop in class.

### 3874a MUNSTER OAKS STKS (GROUP 3) (F&M) 1m 4f

3:20 (3:22) 3-Y-0+

£35,299 (£11,367; £5,384; £2,393; £1,196; £598)

RPR

1 **Santa Monica**[35] 2658 4-9-9 95 WJLee 9 99+
(Charles O'Brien, Ire) *mid-div: 7th 1/2-way: gng wl into st: rdn in 5th 2f out and clsd u.p over 1f out: short of room briefly and swtchd rt in 3rd ins fnl f: r.o wl between horses to ld cl home* **20/1**

2 nk **Butterflies (IRE)**[36] 2637 3-8-9 96 WayneLordan 10 99
(A P O'Brien, Ire) *hld up bhd ldrs in 5th: effrt on outer 2f out: rdn to ld over 1f out: strly pressed wl ins fnl f and hdd cl home* **9/1**

3 1 ¼ **Glamorous Approach (IRE)**[7] 3633 4-9-9 103 KevinManning 6 97
(J S Bolger, Ire) *settled bhd ldr in 2nd: impr to ld over 2f out where rdn: hdd u.p over 1f out: no ex in 3rd wl ins fnl f: kpt on same pce* **9/4**[1]

4 1 **Flying Fairies (IRE)**[36] 2637 4-9-9 96 GaryCarroll 4 95
(John M Oxx, Ire) *mid-div: 6th 1/2-way: rdn over 2f out and clsd u.p ins fnl f where n.m.r and checked sltly in 4th: kpt on same pce clsng stages* **14/1**

5 hd **Bengala (FR)**[56] 1998 3-8-9 0 DeclanMcDonogh 1 95
(John M Oxx, Ire) *hld up towards rr: 8th 1/2-way: rdn 2f out and sme hdwy u.p in 7th 1f out: kpt on same pce in 5th clsng stages: nvr nrr* **4/1**[2]

6 ½ **Sea Swift (IRE)**[49] 2190 4-9-9 99 (h) PatSmullen 8 94
(D K Weld, Ire) *chsd ldrs: 4th 1/2-way: rdn in 4th 2f out and no ex u.p over 1f out: no imp on ldrs whn n.m.r between horses ins fnl f: one pce clsng stages* **4/1**[2]

7 5 ½ **Key To My Heart (IRE)**[36] 2637 3-8-9 100 (b) ColmO'Donoghue 7 85
(A P O'Brien, Ire) *sn led: rdn and hdd over 2f out: no ex in 3rd over 1f out: wknd and eased ins fnl f* **11/2**[3]

8 2 ¾ **Pavlenko (JPN)**[42] 2439 3-8-9 0 (p[1]) MichaelHussey 2 81
(A P O'Brien, Ire) *towards rr thrght: 9th 1/2-way: pushed along under 5f out and no imp into st: one pce fnl 2f* **20/1**

9 17 **Red Stars (IRE)**[56] 1999 4-9-9 99 (h) NGMcCullagh 5 53
(John M Oxx, Ire) *settled bhd ldrs: 3rd 1/2-way: rdn under 3f out and sn no ex: wknd and eased fnl 2f* **16/1**

10 3 **Like A Star (IRE)**[242] 7479 4-9-9 77 (b) DonnachaO'Brien 3 49
(A P O'Brien, Ire) *a bhd: pushed along in rr under 3f out and no imp: wknd and eased fnl 2f* **50/1**

2m 33.83s (-14.07)
**WFA** 3 from 4yo 14lb **10 Ran SP% 120.2**
CSF £190.34 TOTE £15.40: £7.30, £3.20, £1.20; DF 208.50 Trifecta £1132.90.
**Owner** Mrs John Magnier & Exors of the Late Mrs Jacquelin **Bred** D J Erwin Bloodstock **Trained** Straffan, Co Kildare

**FOCUS**
A second long-priced winner of the afternoon in one of the feature-races. A career-best by winner and second in getting the better of the in-form favourite.

3875 - 3878a (Foreign Racing) - See Raceform Interactive

## 3855 CHANTILLY (R-H)

Sunday, June 18

**OFFICIAL GOING: Turf: good**

### 3879a PRIX HOCQUART LONGINES (GROUP 2) (3YO COLTS & FILLIES) (TURF) 1m 4f

1:50 3-Y-0

£63,333 (£24,444; £11,666; £7,777; £3,888)

RPR

1 **Ice Breeze**[26] 2947 3-9-3 0 ow1 VincentCheminaud 5 111+
(P Bary, France) *settled in midfield: relegated to last 3f out: gd hdwy on outer 2f out: rdn to chse ldr 1f out: led last 100yds: drvn out* **19/10**[1]

2 hd **Shakeel (FR)**[26] 2947 3-9-3 0 ow1 ChristopheSoumillon 1 110+
(A De Royer-Dupre, France) *w.w next to last: moved up qckly to trck ldr on outer sn after 1/2-way: led under 3f out: drvn 1 1/2f out: hdd last 100yds: no ex* **33/10**

3 ¾ **Falcon Wings**[26] 2947 3-9-3 0 ow1 OlivierPeslier 2 109
(N Clement, France) *sn led single-file field at mod pce: hdd under 3f out: sn rdn and rallied: styd on at same pce fnl f* **99/10**

4 ¾ **Mask Of Time (IRE)**[22] 3103 3-9-3 0 ow1 Pierre-CharlesBoudot 3 108
(A Fabre, France) *dwlt: racd in rr: drvn to chse ldng pair over 2f out: kpt on same pce fnl f* **27/10**[2]

5 2 ½ **Galipad**[24] 3020 3-9-3 0 ow1 MaximeGuyon 4 104
(A Fabre, France) *racd keenly: restrained bhd ldr: 3rd sn after 1/2-way: outpcd and drvn 2f out: no imp fnl f* **16/5**[3]

2m 33.09s (2.09) **5 Ran SP% 117.7**
PARI-MUTUEL (all including 1 euro stake): WIN 2.90; PLACE 1.40, 1.60, SF 6.40.
**Owner** K Abdullah **Bred** Juddmonte Farms **Trained** Chantilly, France

### 3880a PRIX BERTRAND DU BREUIL LONGINES (GROUP 3) (4YO+) (TURF) 1m

2:25 4-Y-0+

£34,188 (£13,675; £10,256; £6,837; £3,418)

RPR

1 **Taareef (USA)**[260] 6975 4-9-5 0 ow1 IoritzMendizabal 1 119
(J-C Rouget, France) *led: hdd after 1 1/2f: chsd new ldr: drvn to cl over 2f out: sustained run to ld 130yds out: styd on fnl f* **51/10**[3]

2 1 ¾ **Zelzal (FR)**[280] 6394 4-9-1 0 ow1 GregoryBenoist 4 111+
(J-C Rouget, France) *settled in fnl pair: plenty to do 3f out: 6th and shkn up 1 1/2f fr home: hdwy wl over 1f out: r.o fnl f: too much to do* **1/1**[1]

3 ½ **Siyoushake (IRE)**[48] 2248 5-9-0 0 ow1 StephanePasquier 3 109
(F Head, France) *chsd ldrs on outer: 5 l 3rd and rdn appr 1 1/2f out: styd on u.p fnl f* **114/10**

4 3 **Black Max (FR)**[25] 2977 4-9-1 0 ow1 Pierre-CharlesBoudot 7 103
(H-A Pantall, France) *racd keenly: plld way to front after 1 1/2f: sn clr: rdn over 2f out: hdd fnl 130yds: wknd* **69/10**

5 shd **Zalamea (IRE)**[48] 2248 4-9-1 0 ow1 EddyHardouin 5 103
(Carina Fey, France) *chsd ldrs on inner: outpcd and drvn more than 1 1/2f out: styd on at same pce fnl f* **235/10**

6 snk **Nordic Dream (IRE)**[25] 2977 4-9-1 0 ow1 VincentCheminaud 6 102
(A Fabre, France) *w.w in rr: rdn along and little imp wl over 1 1/2f out: kpt on u.p fnl f: nvr in contention* **129/10**

7 ¾ **Kourkan (FR)**[48] 2248 4-9-1 0 ow1 ChristopheSoumillon 2 101
(J-M Beguigne, France) *settled in fnl trio: short-lived effrt over 1 1/2f out: sn btn* **42/10**[2]

1m 34.57s (-3.43) **7 Ran SP% 117.6**
PARI-MUTUEL (all including 1 euro stake): WIN 6.10; PLACE 2.30, 1.60, SF 11.60.
**Owner** Hamdan Al Maktoum **Bred** Dixiana Farms Llc **Trained** Pau, France

### 3881a PRIX DE DIANE LONGINES (GROUP 1) (3YO FILLIES) (TURF) 1m 2f 110y

3:05 3-Y-0

£488,376 (£195,384; £97,692; £48,803; £24,444)

RPR

1 **Senga (USA)**[14] 3367 3-9-1 0 ow1 StephanePasquier 8 112
(P Bary, France) *reluctant to enter stalls: w.w towards rr of midfield on outer: 10th 3f out: drvn and began to cl more than 2f out: str run to ld 1 1/2f out: sn rdn and edgd rt: styd on fnl f* **218/10**

2 1 **Sistercharlie (IRE)**[56] 2003 3-9-1 0 ow1 Pierre-CharlesBoudot 6 110+
(H-A Pantall, France) *w.w towards rr: clsd into midfield wl bef 1/2-way: n.m.r 2 1/2f out: sltly impeded 1 1/2f out: 5th and plenty to do ent fnl f: r.o wl: wnt 2nd post* **121/10**

3 nse **Terrakova (IRE)**[26] 2945 3-9-1 0 ow1 MaximeGuyon 4 110+
(F Head, France) *w.w towards rr: impeded by wkng Rhododendron 3 1/2f out and forced wd: hdwy more than 2f out: rdn to chse two clr ldrs 1 1/2f out: r.o u.p fnl f: wnt 2nd but nvr on terms w wnr: lost 2nd post* **53/10**[3]

4 ½ **Shutter Speed**[32] 2738 3-9-1 0 ow1 FrankieDettori 14 109
(John Gosden) *settled in midfield on outer: 8th and clsng more than 2 1/2f out: rdn to chse ldr 1 1/2f out: no ex ins fnl f: dropped two pls late on and jst hld 4th* **23/10**[1]

5 nse **Turf Laurel (IRE)**[21] 3117 3-9-1 0 ow1 CristianDemuro 13 109
(S Kobayashi, France) *racd keenly: hld up in fnl trio: began to cl more than 1 1/2f out: styd on u.p fnl f: nrest at fin* **69/1**

6 4 **Mademoiselle Marie (FR)**[26] 2945 3-9-1 0 ow1 TonyPiccone 9 101
(K Borgel, France) *w.w towards rr: styd on u.p fr 1 1/2f out: nrest at fin* **56/1**

7 hd **Panthelia (FR)**[26] 2945 3-9-1 0 ow1 Jean-BernardEyquem 7 101
(P Sogorb, France) *settled in fnl trio: beginning to cl whn sltly impeded 1 1/2f out: angled out sn after: styd on u.p fnl f: nvr nrr* **39/1**

8 4 ½ **Yellow Storm (FR)**[14] 3-9-1 0 ow1 MlleMarylineEon 5 92
(Alain Couetil, France) *slowly away: sn rcvrd to r in fnl trio: late prog u.p: nvr in contention* **51/1**

9 hd **Monroe Bay (IRE)**[21] 3117 3-9-1 0 ow1 (b) GeraldMosse 3 92
(P Bary, France) *chsd ldrs towards inner: cl up and n.m.r 2f out: sn rdn and no imp: wl hld fnl f* **25/1**

10 snk **Kitesurf**[14] 3366 3-9-1 0 ow1 MickaelBarzalona 12 91
(A Fabre, France) *settled promly on outer: 5th and rdn wl over 2f out: no imp: wknd appr fnl f* **126/10**

11 4 **Vue Fantastique (FR)**[35] 2665 3-9-1 0 ow1 OlivierPeslier 15 83
(F Chappet, France) *w.w in tch: 5th and gng wl over 2f out: sltly hmpd 1 1/2f out: nt qckn wl over 1f out: wknd fnl f* **183/10**

12 2 ½ **Haya Of Fortune (FR)**[39] 3-9-1 0 ow1 TheoBachelot 16 79
(N Leenders, France) *led: hdd after 2f: chsd ldr: led again over 2 1/2f out: drvn along 2f out: hdd 1 1/2f out: sn wknd* **74/1**

13 1 1/4 **Festive (FR)**[36] 2644 3-9-1 0 ow1 JulienAuge 1 76
(Eric Saint-Martin, France) *w.w in midfield on inner: rdn but nt qckn over 1 1/2f out: sn dropped away* **83/1**

14 9 **Normandie (GER)**[21] 3117 3-9-1 0 ow1 GregoryBenoist 2 59
(Mme Pia Brandt, France) *cl up: led after 2f: hdd over 2 1/2f out: styd cl up tl rdn 1 1/2f out: wknd sn after* **71/1**

F **Onthemoonagain (FR)**[50] 2168 3-9-1 0 ow1 ChristopheSoumillon 10
(J-C Rouget, France) *settled in midfield: 7th and looking to cl whn n.m.r and fell 1 1/2f out* **104/10**

P **Rhododendron (IRE)**[16] 3301 3-9-1 0 ow1 RyanMoore 11
(A P O'Brien, Ire) *w.w bhd ldng gp: rdr looked down 4f out and eased her bk through field: p.u sn after* **17/5**[2]

2m 5.97s (-2.83) **16** Ran SP% **117.6**
PARI-MUTUEL (all including 1 euro stake): WIN 22.80; PLACE 5.20, 4.10, 2.80; DF 107.60; SF 258.30.
**Owner** Flaxman Stables Ireland Ltd **Bred** Flaxman Holdings Limited **Trained** Chantilly, France

**FOCUS**
This was a pretty rough renewal of the Prix De Diane, with a leading candidate coming down in the home straight. Only the runner-up got herself out of trouble in the latter stages, with the others involved in the finish racing wide. The 4th, 6th and 7th help set the level, with the winner, 2nd and 3rd posting pbs.

## 1661 DUSSELDORF (R-H)
Sunday, June 18

**OFFICIAL GOING: Turf: good**

### 3882a WEMPE 97TH GERMAN 1000 GUINEAS (GROUP 2) (3YO FILLIES) (TURF) 1m
4:15 3-Y-O **£59,829** (£23,931; £12,820; £6,837; £3,418)

RPR

1 **Unforgetable Filly**[15] 3334 3-9-2 0 JamesDoyle 5 104+
(Hugo Palmer) *settled in midfield: 5th and drvn over 2f out: str run to ld 100yds out: sn clr* **11/5**[2]

2 1 3/4 **Peace In Motion (USA)**[35] 2665 3-9-2 0 (b) MarcLerner 11 100
(Waldemar Hickst, Germany) *w.w cl up: 4th and drvn 2 1/2f out: styd on u.p fr 1 1/2f out: tk 2nd cl home: no ch w wnr* **7/1**

3 nk **Arazza (GER)**[62] 1846 3-9-2 0 AlexanderPietsch 9 99
(J Hirschberger, Germany) *trckd ldr on outer: sltly outpcd whn ldr kicked over 2f out: drvn to chal ldr wl over 1f out: led ent fnl f: hdd 100yds out: lost 2nd cl home* **89/10**

4 nk **Delectation**[36] 2644 3-9-2 0 EduardoPedroza 7 99+
(A Wohler, Germany) *w.w towards rr on outer: 8th and plenty to do whn rdn over 1 1/2f out: r.o wl fnl f: nvr nrr* **21/10**[1]

5 4 **Cristal Fizz (IRE)**[36] 2644 3-9-2 0 PatCosgrave 3 89+
(William Haggas) *stdd s: racd keenly: hld up in midfield on inner: lost pl and pushed along over 3f out: rdn and styd on fr 1 1/2f out: nt pce to get involved* **4/1**[3]

6 1 1/4 **Alwina (GER)**[49] 3-9-2 0 ClementLecoeuvre 6 87
(Henk Grewe, Germany) *led: wnt nrly 3 l clr over 2f out: hdd ent fnl f: wknd* **31/1**

7 nk **Celebrity (GER)**[13] 3-9-2 0 OliverWilson 8 86
(D Moser, Germany) *racd in rr: wl adrift appr 1/2-way: last and hrd rdn over 2f out: styd on late: nvr in contention* **142/10**

8 1/2 **Hargeisa (USA)**[62] 1846 3-9-2 0 MartinHarley 10 85
(Mario Hofer, Germany) *settled in fnl pair: hrd rdn and clsd a little over 1 1/2f out: no further imp fnl f* **122/10**

9 1/2 **Viva La Flora (GER)**[43] 2421 3-9-2 0 AndraschStarke 1 84
(P Schiergen, Germany) *chsd ldng pair: rdn and lost pl wl over 2f out: sn wknd* **194/10**

10 2 1/2 **Diaphora (GER)**[29] 3-9-2 0 MartinSeidl 4 78
(Markus Klug, Germany) *hld up towards rr of midfield: outpcd and drvn ins fnl 2f: wl hld more than 1f out* **242/10**

1m 35.49s (-5.67) **10** Ran SP% **132.3**
PARI-MUTUEL (all including 10 euro stake): WIN 32 PLACE: 13, 22, 24; SF: 255.
**Owner** Dr Ali Ridha **Bred** Rabbah Bloodstock Limited **Trained** Newmarket, Suffolk

## LE LION-D'ANGERS (R-H)
Sunday, June 18

**OFFICIAL GOING: Turf: good**

### 3883a PRIX URBAN SEA - FONDS EUROPEEN DE L'ELEVAGE (LISTED RACE) (4YO+ FILLIES & MARES) (TURF) 1m 2f
4:00 (4:00) 4-Y-O+ **£20,512** (£8,205; £6,153; £4,102; £2,051)

RPR

1 **Game Theory (IRE)**[42] 2449 5-9-3 0 ow1 SebastienMaillot 8 103
(N Clement, France) **26/5**[3]

2 1 **Capricious Cantor (IRE)**[24] 2999 4-8-13 0 ow2 RonanThomas 2 97
(Ed Dunlop) *dwlt: sn rcvrd to ld after 1f: pushed along over 2f out: hdd and rdn over 1f out: rallied ins fnl f and styd on wl cl home* **109/10**

3 hd **Madiva (FR)**[46] 5-8-13 0 ow2 ValentinSeguy 5 97
(C Lotoux, France) **162/10**

4 hd **Mint Julep (FR)**[51] 4-8-13 0 ow2 AlexisBadel 6 96
(J E Hammond, France) **113/10**

5 1 **Astral Merit (FR)**[163] 7-8-13 0 ow2 (b) FabriceVeron 1 94
(F Monnier, France) **9/2**[2]

6 nse **Via Firenze (IRE)**[25] 2977 4-8-13 0 ow2 HugoJourniac 4 94
(Mme Pia Brandt, France) **9/10**[1]

7 2 **Girl's Hope (IRE)**[12] 4-8-13 0 ow2 StephaneBreux 3 90
(F-H Graffard, France) **141/10**

8 1 **Sisene (IRE)**[77] 1530 4-8-13 0 ow2 AlexandreRoussel 7 88
(P Monfort, France) **38/1**

PARI-MUTUEL (all including 1 euro stake): WIN 6.20; PLACE 2.20, 3.20, 3.70; DF 16.30; SF 29.20.
**Owner** Mme James Norton **Bred** M Henochsberg, P Klein & J-L Burgat **Trained** Chantilly, France

## 3120 SAN SIRO (R-H)
Sunday, June 18

**OFFICIAL GOING: Turf: good**

### 3884a GRAN PREMIO DI MILANO (GROUP 2) (3YO+) (TURF) 1m 4f
4:30 3-Y-O+ **£78,632** (£34,598; £18,871; £9,435)

RPR

1 **Full Drago (ITY)**[28] 2866 4-9-5 0 DarioVargiu 4 106
(Stefano Botti, Italy) *mde all: set stdy pce: grad raised tempo fr 1/2-way: rdn whn chal over 1f out: styd on wl u.p* **76/100**[1]

2 1 1/4 **Way To Paris**[41] 2485 4-9-5 0 PierantonioConvertino 8 104
(Antonio Marcialis, Italy) *w.w wl in tch on outer: trckd ldr fr 3f out: drvn to chal over 1f out: styd on u.str.p: no ex last 75yds* **66/10**

3 1 1/4 **Quelindo (GER)**[28] 2866 5-9-5 0 AlbertoSanna 6 102+
(Gabor Maronka, Hungary) *w.w in rr: last tl rdn and styd on fr 1 1/2f out: tk 3rd cl to home: nvr able to chal* **33/1**

4 nk **Time To Choose**[35] 2663 4-9-5 0 FabioBranca 3 102
(Stefano Botti, Italy) *settled one fr last: hdwy over 2f out: chsd ldrs into fnl f: one pce u.p: lost 3rd cl home* **6/1**

5 4 **Wild Hacked (USA)**[36] 2604 4-9-5 0 AndreaAtzeni 1 95
(Marco Botti) *cl up on inner: outpcd and drvn 4f out: 5 l 3rd and keeping on u.p 2f out: wandered u.p over 1f out: wl hld in fnl f* **19/5**[2]

6 2 1/2 **Moonshiner (GER)**[41] 2485 4-9-5 0 MichaelCadeddu 5 91
(Jean-Pierre Carvalho, Germany) *trckd ldr under a tight hold: outpcd and lost pl 4f out: hld whn impeded over 1f out* **89/20**[3]

7 9 **Time Chant**[28] 2866 5-9-5 0 MarioEsposito 7 77
(Stefano Botti, Italy) *settled towards rr: rdn and short-lived effrt 2 1/2f out: sn btn: eased fnl f* **26/1**

P **Refuse To Bobbin (IRE)**[28] 2866 7-9-5 0 LucaManiezzi 2
(M Narduzzi, Italy) *settled towards rr: stl wl in tch whn tk a false step and p.u 3f out* **269/10**

2m 29.1s (-2.40) **8** Ran SP% **133.7**
PARI-MUTUEL (all including 1 euro stake): WIN 1.76 PLACE 1.22, 2.03, 4.79 DF 5.73.
**Owner** Dioscuri Srl **Bred** Massimo Dragoni **Trained** Italy

3885 - 3894a (Foreign Racing) - See Raceform Interactive

## 3523 CARLISLE (R-H)
Monday, June 19

**OFFICIAL GOING: Good (good to firm in places; watered; 7.6)**
Wind: Breezy, half against in over 2f of home straight Weather: Sunny, warm
Rails: 6yds added to all races over 7f+

### 3895 CHAMPAGNE CHARLIES CLUB NOVICE AUCTION STKS 5f 193y
2:00 (2:02) (Class 5) 2-Y-O **£3,396** (£1,010; £505; £252) Stalls Low

Form RPR

1 1 **Ghost Serge (IRE)**[18] 3244 2-9-9 0 BenCurtis 3 87
(Archie Watson) *trckd ldr: led 2f out: rdn and edgd rt ins fnl f: kpt on strly* **5/6**[1]

0 2 1 1/4 **Arcavallo (IRE)**[28] 2896 2-9-2 0 PaulMulrennan 6 76
(Michael Dods) *in tch: hdwy and ev ch 2f out: kpt on ins fnl f: nt pce of wnr* **8/1**[3]

3 shd **Han Solo Berger (IRE)** 2-9-2 0 DougieCostello 12 75+
(Keith Dalgleish) *dwlt: hld up on outside: pushed along over 2f out: effrt and angled rt over 1f out: kpt on ins fnl f: nrst fin* **25/1**

462 4 3/4 **Our Man In Havana**[20] 3187 2-9-2 0 RoystonFfrench 11 73
(Tom Dascombe) *trckd ldrs: drvn and edgd lft over 1f out: kpt on same pce ins fnl f* **7/1**[2]

5 5 **Alfa McGuire (IRE)** 2-9-2 0 ConnorBeasley 10 58+
(Bryan Smart) *t.k.h in rr: pushed along and hdwy over 1f out: kpt on fnl f: bttr for r* **9/1**

64 6 2 3/4 **Ventura Crest (IRE)**[29] 2852 2-9-2 0 JamesSullivan 8 49
(Tim Easterby) *in tch: drvn along over 2f out: wknd over 1f out* **40/1**

7 1 1/4 **Cameo Star (IRE)** 2-9-2 0 PaulHanagan 5 45
(Richard Fahey) *dwlt: hld up bhd ldng gp: effrt over 2f out: wknd over 1f out* **9/1**

5 8 shd **Blue Havana (IRE)**[14] 3390 2-8-11 0 JasonHart 7 40
(John Quinn) *s.i.s: bhd and outpcd: sme late hdwy: nvr on terms* **10/1**

9 1 3/4 **Grimeford Lane (IRE)** 2-9-2 0 AndrewMullen 1 39
(Michael Dods) *noisy and green in paddock: hld up on ins: pushed along and edgd rt wl over 1f out: sn btn* **40/1**

0 10 10 **Rickyroadboy**[14] 3399 2-8-13 0 NathanEvans(3) 2 8
(Mark Walford) *led tl rdn and hdd 2f out: sn wknd* **150/1**

11 13 **Ray Purchase** 2-9-2 0 JoeFanning 4
(Keith Dalgleish) *t.k.h early: trckd ldrs on outside tl rdn and wknd fr 2f out* **50/1**

1m 14.49s (0.79) **Going Correction** -0.10s/f (Good) **11** Ran SP% **118.6**
Speed ratings (Par 93): **90,88,88,87,80 76,75,75,72,59 42**
CSF £7.93 TOTE £1.70: £1.10, £2.70, £5.60; EX 9.60 Trifecta £143.10.
**Owner** Champagne Charlies Club & Partners **Bred** Tally-Ho Stud **Trained** Upper Lambourn, W Berks
■ Stewards' Enquiry : Ben Curtis caution: careless riding

**FOCUS**
A warm day in Cumbria with conditions drying out all the time. Not much depth to this maiden and the first four finished some way clear. Ordinarily, Ghost Serge would have had a difficult task under a 7lb penalty but he has a terrific attitude and is probably a level or two above these rivals. The winning time was quite slow (3.49 seconds above standard). A step forward from the runner-up.

### 3896 BRITISH STALLION STUDS EBF MAIDEN FILLIES' STKS (PLUS 10 RACE) 5f 193y
2:30 (2:34) (Class 5) 3-Y-O **£4,690** (£1,395; £697; £348) Stalls Low

Form RPR

1 **Clon Coulis (IRE)** 3-9-0 0 BenCurtis 5 86
(David Barron) *.trckd ldrs on outside: led wl over 1f out: pushed clr fnl f* **10/1**

022 2 4 **World Power (IRE)**[18] 3259 3-9-0 73 (p[1]) JoeFanning 3 73
(Paul Cole) *t.k.h early: pressed ldr: ev ch over 2f out to over 1f out: kpt on same pce fnl f* **10/11**[1]

3 6 **Evies Wish (IRE)**[241] 7519 3-9-0 73 PaulHanagan 1 54
(John C McConnell, Ire) *led to wl over 1f out: sn rdn and wknd* **15/8**[2]

4 2¾ **Butterworth Brow** 3-9-0 0 ........ ConnorBeasley 2 45
(Bryan Smart) *unruly in paddock: trckd ldrs tl rdn and wknd over 1f out*
**11/2**[3]

4 5 14 **Palace Ball**[24] 3044 3-9-0 0 ........ TomEaves 4
(Stuart Coltherd) *hld up: struggling 1/2-way: lost tch fnl 2f* **80/1**

1m 13.11s (-0.59) **Going Correction** -0.10s/f (Good) **5** Ran SP% **112.9**
Speed ratings (Par 96): **99,93,85,82,63**
CSF £20.53 TOTE £9.10: £5.20, £1.10; EX 21.50 Trifecta £37.20.
**Owner** Ms Colette Twomey **Bred** Collette Twomey **Trained** Maunby, N Yorks

**FOCUS**
The big two in the market didn't set a particularly daunting standard and they were emphatically put in their place by a newcomer. The winning time was over a second quicker than the opener, but this winner was carrying 9lb less.

## 3897 MOLSON COORS H'CAP 5f 193y
**3:00** (3:04) (Class 5) (0-70,71) 3-Y-0+ **£3,396** (£1,010; £505; £252) **Stalls** Low

Form RPR

6-22 1 **Hee Haw (IRE)**[5] 3709 3-9-6 **69** ........ PaulMulrennan 6 81+
(Keith Dalgleish) *trckd ldrs gng wl: shkn up to ld wl over 1f out: pushed clr ins fnl f: readily* **11/4**[1]

4-53 2 2¼ **Roys Dream**[18] 3239 3-9-5 **68** ........ JoeFanning 2 73
(Paul Collins) *hld up midfield: stdy hdwy gng wl over 1f out: carried lft 1f out: chsd wnr wl ins fnl f: r.o* **12/1**

-021 3 ¾ **Exotic Guest**[10] 3524 7-9-9 **65** ........(p) JamesSullivan 3 70
(Ruth Carr) *trckd ldrs: effrt and chsng wnr whn drifted lft 1f out: lost 2nd and one pce wl ins fnl f* **10/1**

0243 4 nk **Willbeme**[10] 3541 9-9-9 **65** ........(t[1]) JasonHart 14 69
(Simon West) *dwlt: hld up midfield on outside: rdn and outpcd wl over 1f out: styng on whn checked ins fnl f: r.o fin* **14/1**

1-35 5 1½ **Questo**[14] 3401 5-9-3 **59** ........ BenCurtis 1 58
(Tracy Waggott) *hld up on ins: rdn along over 2f out: hdwy over 1f out: kpt on fnl f: nvr able to chal* **5/1**[2]

60-4 6 1½ **Silk Mill Blue**[38] 2595 3-8-4 **58** ........ PhilDennis(5) 10 50
(Richard Whitaker) *hld up in tch: rdn and outpcd 2f out: no imp fnl f* **20/1**

2060 7 ½ **Salvatore Fury (IRE)**[37] 2608 7-9-13 **69** ........(p) AndrewMullen 8 61
(Keith Dalgleish) *hld up midfield: stdy hdwy whn nt clr run wl over 1f out: sn rdn and outpcd: n.d after* **25/1**

1-36 8 ¾ **Danish Duke (IRE)**[14] 3386 6-9-12 **71** ........(p) NathanEvans(3) 12 61
(Ruth Carr) *hld up: rdn along over 2f out: hdwy over 1f out: sn no imp* **20/1**

14-0 9 3½ **Gun Case**[27] 2923 5-10-0 **70** ........ DougieCostello 13 49
(Alistair Whillans) *dwlt: bhd and outpcd: effrt over 2f out: sn no imp: btn over 1f out* **25/1**

-022 10 nk **Portland Street (IRE)**[31] 2776 4-9-13 **69** ........(b) ConnorBeasley 11 47
(Bryan Smart) *cl up: rdn over 2f out: edgd lft and wknd over 1f out* **5/1**[2]

6-01 11 nse **Uncle Charlie (IRE)**[14] 3403 3-9-3 **66** ........ PaulHanagan 7 42
(Ann Duffield) *in tch: drvn over 2f out: wknd over 1f out* **7/1**[3]

4135 12 nse **Space War**[17] 3288 10-9-5 **68** ........ RyanTimby(7) 5 46
(Michael Easterby) *dwlt: bhd and outpcd: drvn along 1/2-way: n.d* **40/1**

0066 13 1½ **Newstead Abbey**[42] 2464 7-9-13 **69** ........ TomEaves 9 42
(Michael Herrington) *hld up on ins: struggling over 2f out: sn btn* **22/1**

04-0 14 4 **Mercers Row**[37] 2633 10-8-6 **55** ........(p) ConnorMurtagh(7) 15 15
(Michael Herrington) *led tl rdn and hdd wl over 1f out: sn wknd* **80/1**

1m 13.95s (0.25) **Going Correction** -0.10s/f (Good)
**WFA** 3 from 4yo+ 7lb **14** Ran SP% **121.2**
Speed ratings (Par 103): **94,91,90,89,87 85,84,83,79,78 78,78,76,71**
CSF £34.56 CT £250.77 TOTE £4.40: £2.30, £3.40, £3.00; EX 36.70 Trifecta £424.80.
**Owner** Mrs Janis Macpherson **Bred** Ballinvana House Stud **Trained** Carluke, S Lanarks

**FOCUS**
A competitive enough race for the grade and they appeared to go a decent gallop. The winner, who has been knocking on the door, was one of the four 3yo's in the line-up and he looks capable of holding his own in better races. The runner-up has been rated to form, with the third to his latest 5f win here.

## 3898 THURSBY H'CAP (JOCKEY CLUB GRASSROOTS FLAT MIDDLE DISTANCE SERIES QUALIFIER) 1m 1f
**3:30** (3:32) (Class 5) (0-70,70) 4-Y-0+ **£3,396** (£1,010; £505; £252) **Stalls** Low

Form RPR

126 1 **Lucent Dream (IRE)**[26] 2955 6-9-0 **63** ........(t) BenCurtis 7 75+
(John C McConnell, Ire) *stdd s: hld up: hdwy on outside over 2f out: led and rdn over 1f out: edgd rt: kpt on wl fnl f* **3/1**[1]

05-3 2 2½ **Maulesden May (IRE)**[19] 3197 4-9-1 **69** ........ RowanScott(5) 10 73
(Keith Dalgleish) *in tch: rdn along over 2f out: rallied to chse (clr) wnr ins fnl f: kpt on: no imp* **6/1**[3]

560 3 1¼ **Eez Eh (IRE)**[13] 3432 4-9-4 **67** ........(v[1]) ConnorBeasley 6 68
(Keith Dalgleish) *pressed ldr: led over 2f out: sn rdn: hdd over 1f out: kpt on same pce and lost 2nd ins fnl f* **9/2**[2]

45-6 4 1 **Omotesando**[18] 3252 7-9-1 **64** ........ JoeFanning 9 63
(Oliver Greenall) *prom: effrt and rdn over 2f out: edgd lft over 1f out: kpt on same pce ins fnl f* **9/2**[2]

4153 5 nk **Celtic Artisan (IRE)**[21] 2301 6-9-0 **70** ........(bt) PaulaMuir(7) 8 68
(Rebecca Menzies) *led: rdn and hdd over 2f out: outpcd fr over 1f out* **17/2**

6504 6 2¾ **Competition**[10] 3537 5-9-0 **63** ........(t) JamesSullivan 3 55
(Brian Rothwell) *prom: rdn and edgd rt over 2f out: wknd over 1f out* **11/1**

5-00 7 3¼ **Sir Runs A Lot**[12] 3465 5-9-2 **65** ........ AndrewMullen 11 50
(David Barron) *hld up: rdn along 1/2-way: struggling fnl 2f* **25/1**

0340 8 3¼ **Restive (IRE)**[26] 2953 4-9-4 **67** ........(h) TomEaves 12 45
(Iain Jardine) *stdd and swtchd rt s: hld up: rdn along over 2f out: sn n.d: btn over 1f out* **6/1**[3]

1m 57.65s (0.05) **Going Correction** +0.025s/f (Good) **8** Ran SP% **112.6**
Speed ratings (Par 103): **100,97,96,95,95 93,90,87**
CSF £20.58 CT £78.62 TOTE £4.20: £1.30, £1.80, £1.80; EX 22.20 Trifecta £103.10.
**Owner** Ms Caroline Ahearn **Bred** Roland H Alder **Trained** Stamullen, Co Meath

**FOCUS**
Add 6yds to race distance. This looked an open little handicap on paper but they went a decent gallop and it was won in emphatic fashion by a horse who looks ahead of the game all of sudden. The runner-up has been rated to form, with the third close to his best since his C&D win here in September.

## 3899 RACING UK H'CAP 7f 173y
**4:00** (4:00) (Class 5) (0-70,72) 4-Y-0+ **£3,396** (£1,010; £505; £252) **Stalls** Low

Form RPR

0-62 1 **Full Of Promise**[16] 3332 4-8-13 **61** ........ PaulHanagan 4 71
(Richard Fahey) *hld up: hdwy and angled lft over 2f out: led over 1f out: clr whn edgd rt ins fnl f: kpt on wl* **11/2**[3]

3035 2 2½ **So It's War (FR)**[19] 3198 6-9-3 **65** ........(p) AndrewMullen 1 69
(Keith Dalgleish) *hld up: hdwy on outside over 1f out: drvn and chsd (clr) wnr ins fnl f: kpt on: nt pce to chal* **9/1**

4004 3 2½ **Someone Exciting**[11] 3487 4-8-6 **59** ........ PhilDennis(5) 7 57
(David Thompson) *dwlt: hld up: hdwy over 2f out: effrt and chsd wnr over 1f out to ins fnl f one pce* **20/1**

-062 4 4 **Mustaqbal (IRE)**[11] 3487 5-9-5 **72** ........(p) CallumRodriguez(5) 8 61
(Michael Dods) *hld up: pushed along and hdwy over 2f out: rdn and no imp fr over 1f out* **4/1**[1]

0505 5 ½ **Curzon Line**[20] 3181 8-9-4 **69** ........ NathanEvans(3) 3 57
(Michael Easterby) *led: rdn over 2f out: drifted lft and hdd over 1f out: sn wknd* **9/2**[2]

1006 6 3 **Ravenhoe (IRE)**[16] 3325 4-9-9 **71** ........ JoeFanning 5 52
(Mark Johnston) *hld up: rdn and outpcd over 2f out: rallied over 1f out: no imp fnl f* **10/1**

0415 7 ½ **African Blessing**[28] 2888 4-9-10 **72** ........ BenCurtis 10 52
(David Barron) *prom: drvn along over 2f out: wknd over 1f out* **4/1**[1]

0044 8 shd **Ellaal**[16] 3332 8-9-3 **65** ........ JamesSullivan 2 45
(Ruth Carr) *in tch: rdn and lost pl over 2f out: n.d after* **16/1**

4663 9 3½ **Ralphy Boy (IRE)**[16] 3332 8-9-5 **67** ........ PaulMulrennan 6 39
(Alistair Whillans) *hld up midfield: smooth hdwy and cl up over 2f out: rdn whn checked over 1f out: sn wknd* **12/1**

00-4 10 1¾ **Know Your Name**[58] 1983 6-9-0 **62** ........ TomEaves 11 30
(Donald McCain) *trckd ldrs: rdn over 2f out: wknd wl over 1f out* **40/1**

0450 11 2¾ **In Focus (IRE)**[14] 3402 6-8-1 **54** ........ RichardOliver(5) 9 15
(Philip Kirby) *pressed ldr: drvn along over 2f out: wknd wl over 1f out* **22/1**

1m 39.6s (-0.40) **Going Correction** +0.025s/f (Good) **11** Ran SP% **117.8**
Speed ratings (Par 103): **103,100,98,94,93 90,90,89,86,84 81**
CSF £52.93 CT £940.87 TOTE £4.20: £2.20, £3.00, £6.40; EX 54.60 Trifecta £1233.80.

**Owner** Richard Fahey Ebor Racing Club Ltd **Bred** Mrs Sheila Oakes **Trained** Musley Bank, N Yorks

■ Stewards' Enquiry : Nathan Evans caution: careless riding

**FOCUS**
Add 6yds to race distance. They looked to go a strong gallop here and some of these finished very tired, notably the pacemaker. They came over to the stands side in the straight. The winner produced the best time performance on the card so far. The runner-up has been rated close to his recent form.

## 3900 BRITISH STALLION STUDS EBF FILLIES' H'CAP 6f 195y
**4:30** (4:30) (Class 4) (0-80,78) 3-Y-0 **£6,469** (£1,925; £962; £481) **Stalls** Low

Form RPR

-116 1 **Miss Sheridan (IRE)**[23] 3094 3-9-0 **74** ........ NathanEvans(3) 1 78
(Michael Easterby) *mde all: rdn and hrd pressed over 2f out: edgd lft over 1f out: hld on wl fnl f* **11/4**[2]

25-1 2 ¾ **Contentment**[23] 3075 3-9-7 **78** ........ BenCurtis 3 80
(William Haggas) *dwlt: hld up in tch: hdwy to press wnr over 1f out: sn rdn: kpt on fnl f: hld nr fin* **13/8**[1]

0022 3 ½ **Greenview Paradise (IRE)**[9] 3561 3-8-8 **65** ........ PaulHanagan 5 66
(Richard Fahey) *pressed wnr: drvn and outpcd 2f out: kpt on ins fnl f: nt pce to chal* **10/1**

6465 4 1¼ **Whatsthemessage (IRE)**[101] 1124 3-8-10 **67** ........ JoeFanning 2 65
(Keith Dalgleish) *prom: drvn and outpcd wl over 1f out: kpt on same pce fnl f* **15/2**

-442 5 shd **Seduce Me**[19] 3217 3-9-6 **77** ........(p) PaulMulrennan 4 74
(K R Burke) *trckd ldrs: chal over 2f out to over 1f out: sn drvn along: outpcd appr fnl f* **10/3**[3]

1m 28.94s (1.84) **Going Correction** +0.025s/f (Good) **5** Ran SP% **108.7**
Speed ratings (Par 98): **90,89,88,87,87**
CSF £7.44 TOTE £3.60: £1.90, £1.50; EX 8.70 Trifecta £37.90.

**Owner** J Blackburn & A Turton & Partner **Bred** Drumlin Bloodstock **Trained** Sheriff Hutton, N Yorks

■ Stewards' Enquiry : Nathan Evans caution: careless riding

**FOCUS**
A reasonably competitive little handicap in which they came over to the stands side in the straight. Experience may have told on the closing stages as the winner toughed this out. The runner-up has been been rated to her maiden form, and third to her latest effort.

## 3901 WATCH RACING UK ON 3 DEVICES H'CAP 1m 3f 39y
**5:00** (5:01) (Class 5) (0-70,70) 3-Y-0 **£3,396** (£1,010; £505; £252) **Stalls** High

Form RPR

60-2 1 **Solo Mission**[47] 2315 3-9-6 **69** ........(p[1]) TomQueally 5 74+
(William Haggas) *hld up in last pl: stdy hdwy over 3f out: rdn to ld wl over 1f out: edgd rt ins fnl f: styd on wl* **1/1**[1]

6-50 2 2¾ **Powerful Love (IRE)**[11] 3499 3-9-7 **70** ........(b[1]) JoeFanning 1 71
(Mark Johnston) *sn pushed along and led after 1f: rdn and hdd wl over 1f out: rallied: kpt on same pce fnl f* **5/1**[2]

6620 3 2¼ **Knightsbridge Liam (IRE)**[88] 1331 3-8-8 **57** ........ JamesSullivan 4 54
(Michael Easterby) *trckd ldrs: effrt over 2f out: one pce whn checked over 1f out: sn no ex* **16/1**

6634 4 1¼ **Elite Icon**[11] 3484 3-7-13 **51** oh1 ........ NathanEvans(3) 3 46
(Iain Jardine) *hld up in tch: pushed along and outpcd 2f out: no imp fnl f* **11/2**[3]

00-3 5 5 **Royal Cosmic**[18] 3243 3-8-5 **54** ........ PaulHanagan 6 41
(Richard Fahey) *prom: effrt and rdn whn checked wl over 1f out: sn wknd* **8/1**

00-2 6 29 **Moonlight Blue (IRE)**[27] 2921 3-9-6 **69** ........ PaulMulrennan 2 10
(Michael Dods) *t.k.h early: led 1f: pressed ldr: rdn and lost pl over 2f out: sn wknd: eased whn no ch over 1f out* **6/1**

2m 24.91s (1.81) **Going Correction** +0.025s/f (Good) **6** Ran SP% **113.3**
Speed ratings (Par 99): **94,92,90,89,85 64**
CSF £6.55 TOTE £1.80: £1.10, £2.50; EX 6.70 Trifecta £49.80.

**Owner** Mohamed Obaida **Bred** Rabbah Bloodstock Limited **Trained** Newmarket, Suffolk

**FOCUS**
Add 6yds to race distance. An weak little 3yo handicap which was effectively a maiden given non of the six runners had won a race. The fourth has been rated near his mark.

T/Plt: £25.20 to a £1 stake. Pool: £64,249.45 - 1857.55 winning units T/Qpdt: £11.40 to a £1 stake. Pool: £4,129.43 - 268.04 winning units **Richard Young**

3754 **NOTTINGHAM** (L-H)
Monday, June 19
**OFFICIAL GOING: Good to firm (good in places; watered; 8.1)**
Wind: Nil Weather: Overcast

## 3902 ROYAL ASCOT BETTING AT 188BET FILLIES' NOVICE AUCTION STKS (PLUS 10 RACE) 6f 18y
**6:00** (6:01) (Class 5) 2-Y-O **£3,234** (£962; £481; £240) **Stalls** High

Form RPR
623 1 **Lexington Grace (IRE)**25 2987 2-9-0 0 SeanLevey 11 69
(Richard Hannon) *chsd ldrs: rdn over 1f out: led ins fnl f: r.o* **5/1**2
62 2 ¾ **Hello Girl**19 3210 2-9-0 0 RobertWinston 6 67
(Dean Ivory) *led: racd keenly: shkn up over 1f out: hdd ins fnl f: kpt on* **11/8**1
3 nk **Raven's Raft (IRE)** 2-8-11 0 AlistairRawlinson(3) 14 66
(Michael Appleby) *a.p: pushed along 1/2-way: rdn over 1f out: r.o* **20/1**
4 7 **Just For Fun** 2-8-11 0 AdamMcNamara(3) 9 45
(Richard Fahey) *dwlt: outpcd: r.o ins fnl f: nvr nrr* **8/1**3
00 5 1 ¼ **Deauville Society (IRE)**6 3687 2-9-0 0 LukeMorris 1 41
(Sir Mark Prescott Bt) *s.i.s: sn rcvrd into mid-div: pushed along over 3f out: sn outpcd: nvr on terms after* **33/1**
6 nk **Tranquil Soul** 2-9-0 0 MartinLane 2 40+
(David Lanigan) *green to post: s.i.s and hmpd s: outpcd: styd on ins fnl f* **25/1**
0 7 ¾ **Vallesa (IRE)**14 3390 2-9-0 0 SilvestreDeSousa 3 38
(David Brown) *s.i.s and hmpd s: sn outpcd: rdn over 2f out: nvr on terms* **16/1**
8 ¾ **Eesha Beauty (IRE)** 2-9-0 0 DanielMuscutt 5 36
(Marco Botti) *edgd lft s: chsd ldrs: rdn over 2f out: wknd fnl f* **16/1**
6 9 1 ½ **Headline Act**19 3210 2-9-0 0 JackMitchell 13 31
(Archie Watson) *mid-div: rdn over 2f out: sn wknd* **11/1**
55 10 ¾ **Paco Bleue**7 3662 2-8-11 0 RachelRichardson(3) 8 29
(Tim Easterby) *chsd ldrs over 3f* **8/1**3
11 2 **Oneroa (IRE)** 2-9-0 0 DavidProbert 10 23
(Daniel Mark Loughnane) *s.i.s: sn pushed along in rr: rdn and hung lft fr over 3f out: wknd over 1f out* **33/1**
0 12 8 **Harbour Rose**11 3491 2-9-2 0 ow2 DavidNolan 7 1
(Philip Kirby) *sn outpcd* **66/1**

1m 12.53s (-2.17) **Going Correction** -0.70s/f (Hard) 12 Ran SP% **117.1**
Speed ratings (Par 90): **86,85,84,75,73 73,72,71,69,68 65,54**
CSF £11.33 TOTE £5.60: £2.10, £1.10, £6.70; EX 11.30 Trifecta £211.80.
**Owner** Middleham Park Racing XII & A E Denham **Bred** Tally-Ho Stud **Trained** East Everleigh, Wilts

**FOCUS**
Watered good to firm ground and a hot, sunny evening for a fixture on the outside course. Rail movements added 6yds to races 4, 5 and 6. The stalls were on the outer for this opening big-field fillies' novice event, in which very few got involved off a decent pace. It's been rated around the runner-up.

## 3903 DAILY RACING SPECIALS AT 188BET H'CAP 5f 8y
**6:30** (6:31) (Class 5) (0-75,76) 4-Y-O+ **£3,150** (£943; £471; £236; £117) **Stalls** High

Form RPR
3532 1 **Penny Dreadful**17 3290 5-7-11 57 (p) RPWalsh(7) 1 73
(Scott Dixon) *mde all: grad crossed over to stands' side rail fr wd draw: rdn clr fr over 1f out* **6/1**2
540- 2 5 **Sir Dudley (IRE)**261 6962 4-9-3 73 (b) AdamMcNamara(3) 7 71
(James Given) *chsd ldrs: rdn to chse wnr over 1f out: edgd rt: no imp fnl f* **6/1**2
2030 3 2 ¾ **Normal Equilibrium**40 2516 7-9-7 74 DavidNolan 6 62
(Ivan Furtado) *s.i.s: hld up: hdwy over 1f out: styd on to go 3rd ins fnl f: nt rch ldrs* **8/1**
2-50 4 shd **Kiringa**26 2967 4-8-6 59 LukeMorris 8 47
(Robert Cowell) *chsd ldrs: hmpd sn after s: rdn and outpcd 1/2-way: n.d after* **12/1**
6636 5 1 ¾ **Kyllukey**17 3281 4-9-6 73 RobertWinston 2 54
(Milton Bradley) *hld up: hdwy over 1f out: wknd ins fnl f* **16/1**
3506 6 1 ½ **One Boy (IRE)**7 3653 6-9-5 72 MartinLane 5 48
(Paul Midgley) *sn outpcd: nvr nrr* **15/2**3
522- 7 ½ **Dyllan (IRE)**293 5992 4-9-9 76 SilvestreDeSousa 4 50
(Ruth Carr) *s.i.s: in rr: sme hdwy u.p over 1f out: wknd ins fnl f* **2/1**1
8 2 ½ **Candelaria**387 2704 4-9-1 68 DavidProbert 3 33
(Jonjo O'Neill) *chsd wnr tl rdn over 1f out: wknd fnl f* **15/2**3

57.58s (-3.92) **Going Correction** -0.70s/f (Hard) course record 8 Ran SP% **110.1**
Speed ratings (Par 103): **103,95,90,90,87 85,84,80**
CSF £38.41 CT £273.07 TOTE £7.60: £1.90, £2.00, £3.00; EX 50.80 Trifecta £352.70.
**Owner** Sexy Six Partnership **Bred** B A McGarrigle **Trained** Babworth, Notts
■ Stewards' Enquiry : David Probert caution: allowed his mount to drift right-handed shortly after the start

**FOCUS**
Stalls on outer. A reasonable contest for the grade, but the winner took it apart in a course record time and once again very few featured. The runner-up has been rated a length off last year's turf form.

## 3904 188BET FILLIES' H'CAP 5f 8y
**7:00** (7:00) (Class 4) (0-85,83) 3-Y-O+ **£5,175** (£1,540; £769; £384) **Stalls** High

Form RPR
-613 1 **Rose Berry**23 3063 3-9-7 82 (h) SilvestreDeSousa 3 88
(Chris Dwyer) *chsd ldrs: pushed along and outpcd 3f out: hdwy over 1f out: rdn to ld and edgd rt ins fnl f: r.o* **15/8**1
1321 2 ½ **Socialites Red**19 3216 4-8-8 70 (p) RPWalsh(7) 7 76
(Scott Dixon) *chsd ldrs: outpcd 1/2-way: rdn and nt clr run over 1f out: r.o wl towards fin* **6/1**
2415 3 1 ½ **Yorkshiredebut (IRE)**21 3152 3-9-0 75 MartinLane 8 74
(Paul Midgley) *edgd rt s: sn w ldrs: led 1/2-way: rdn: edgd lft and hdd ins fnl f: styd on same pce* **8/1**
212 4 hd **Berryessa (IRE)**17 3285 3-8-12 73 DavidProbert 6 71
(Rae Guest) *hld up: hdwy and nt clr run over 1f out: swtchd lft ins fnl f: nvr able to chal* **11/2**3
101 5 hd **Lydia's Place**20 3183 4-9-7 81 CliffordLee(5) 1 81
(Richard Guest) *disp ld to 1/2-way: rdn over 1f out: styd on same pce ins fnl f* **6/1**
-202 6 2 ¾ **Midnight Malibu (IRE)**16 3337 4-9-11 83 RachelRichardson(3) 4 73
(Tim Easterby) *racd keenly: disp ld to 1/2-way: rdn over 1f out: wknd ins fnl f* **9/2**2

58.12s (-3.38) **Going Correction** -0.70s/f (Hard)
**WFA** 3 from 4yo 6lb 6 Ran SP% **108.0**
Speed ratings (Par 102): **99,98,95,95,95 90**
CSF £12.30 CT £60.14 TOTE £2.50: £1.40, £3.60; EX 11.90 Trifecta £66.20.
**Owner** Strawberry Fields Stud **Bred** Aljw Bloodstock **Trained** Newmarket, Suffolk

**FOCUS**
Stalls on outer. A good little contest despite the absentees, with most of these lining up in decent form.

## 3905 188BET.CO.UK H'CAP 1m 2f 50y
**7:30** (7:30) (Class 4) (0-85,85) 4-Y-O+ **£5,175** (£1,540; £769; £384) **Stalls** Low

Form RPR
530- 1 **Nayel (IRE)**290 6081 5-9-6 85 (p1) SeanLevey 4 93
(Richard Hannon) *mde all: qcknd 3f out: rdn clr fr over 1f out: comf* **4/1**3
2-41 2 2 ½ **Rotherwick (IRE)**18 3249 5-9-6 85 (t) LukeMorris 5 88
(Paul Cole) *chsd wnr: rdn over 2f out: hung lft ins fnl f: styd on same pce* **2/1**1
0-03 3 1 ¼ **Red Rannagh (IRE)**18 3249 4-9-3 82 (h1) FergusSweeney 3 83
(David Simcock) *s.s: hld up: racd keenly: pushed along and outpcd over 3f out: hdwy u.p over 1f out: hung lft and styd on ins fnl f: nt rch ldrs* **6/1**
5003 4 2 ¼ **Worlds His Oyster**23 3065 4-9-3 82 JasonHart 2 78
(John Quinn) *hld up in tch: pushed along over 3f out: styd on same pce fr over 1f out* **3/1**2
0/05 5 7 **Lahayeb**9 3558 5-9-3 85 AlistairRawlinson(3) 1 68
(Michael Appleby) *trckd ldrs: racd keenly: rdn over 2f out: wknd over 1f out* **25/1**
6-06 6 1 ½ **High Baroque (USA)**93 1258 5-9-2 81 DavidNolan 7 61
(Richard Fahey) *hld up in tch: rdn over 2f out: wknd wl over 1f out* **11/2**

2m 9.62s (-4.68) **Going Correction** -0.70s/f (Hard) 6 Ran SP% **111.8**
Speed ratings (Par 105): **90,88,87,85,79 78**
CSF £12.36 TOTE £4.80: £2.70, £1.50; EX 7.40 Trifecta £61.60.
**Owner** R Hannon **Bred** John Cullinan **Trained** East Everleigh, Wilts

**FOCUS**
Actual race distance 1m2f56yds. Stalls on inner. A tight contest on paper, and the winning rider's tactical nous proved decisive. The winner has been rated to the balance of his form over the past year.

## 3906 READ SILVESTRE DE SOUSA AT 188BET H'CAP 1m 75y
**8:00** (8:02) (Class 6) (0-65,65) 4-Y-O+ **£2,587** (£770; £384; £192) **Stalls** Centre

Form RPR
0-24 1 **Whitkirk**24 3049 4-9-6 64 JackGarritty 4 74+
(Jedd O'Keeffe) *led 1f: remained handy: nt clr run over 6f out: led again over 2f out: rdn over 1f out: r.o wl* **7/4**1
-003 2 2 ½ **Tom's Anna (IRE)**37 2626 7-7-11 46 oh1 DavidEgan(5) 6 50
(Sean Regan) *prom: rdn to chse wnr over 1f out: styd on same pce fnl f* **10/1**
2050 3 3 **Binky Blue (IRE)**12 3473 5-8-13 60 CharlieBennett(3) 2 57
(Daniel Mark Loughnane) *s.i.s: plld hrd and sn prom: rdn over 2f out: styd on same pce fnl f* **20/1**
0643 4 ¾ **Magic Mirror**14 3397 4-8-7 51 (p) FergusSweeney 9 47
(Mark Rimell) *s.i.s: hld up: r.o ins f: nt rch ldrs* **7/1**
31-0 5 nk **Carcharias (IRE)**68 1729 4-9-3 64 CallumShepherd(3) 10 59
(Ed de Giles) *plld hrd: hdwy to ld over 6f out: hdd over 2f out: no ex fnl f* **16/1**
0-00 6 ½ **The King's Steed**14 3402 4-8-2 46 oh1 JimmyQuinn 5 40
(Micky Hammond) *hld up: rdn over 3f out: nvr trbld ldrs* **50/1**
-000 7 hd **Pyroclastic (IRE)**4 3758 5-7-13 46 oh1 (t) ShelleyBirkett(3) 3 40
(Nick Kent) *hld up: hdwy over 3f out: wknd over 1f out* **40/1**
10-6 8 4 **Kafoo**51 2163 4-9-7 65 SilvestreDeSousa 1 50
(Ed Dunlop) *s.i.s: hdwy to ld 7f out: sn hdd: remained handy: rdn over 3f out: wknd ins fnl f* **7/2**2
5212 9 1 **Indigo Princess**21 3147 4-9-0 65 RayDawson(7) 8 48
(Michael Appleby) *chsd ldrs: lost pl over 5f out: wknd over 1f out* **9/2**3
-006 10 25 **Zaytoon (IRE)**17 3289 4-8-2 46 oh1 LukeMorris 7
(Micky Hammond) *plld hrd and prom: rdn over 3f out: wknd over 2f out* **66/1**

1m 43.14s (-5.86) **Going Correction** -0.70s/f (Hard) 10 Ran SP% **114.9**
Speed ratings (Par 101): **101,98,95,94,94 93,93,89,88,63**
CSF £19.94 CT £262.20 TOTE £2.70: £1.10, £3.10, £5.20; EX 17.40 Trifecta £195.40.
**Owner** T S Ingham **Bred** Whatton Manor Stud **Trained** Middleham Moor, N Yorks

**FOCUS**
Actual race distance 1m81yds. Stalls in centre. Moderate fare, and a lot of getting in each other's way initially, but indisputably the right result on the night.

## 3907 BEST ODDS GUARANTEED AT 188BET H'CAP 1m 6f
**8:30** (8:31) (Class 5) (0-75,77) 4-Y-O+ **£3,234** (£962; £481; £240) **Stalls** Low

Form RPR
1-11 1 **Lugano**4 3740 4-9-10 77 LukeMorris 1 92+
(Sir Mark Prescott Bt) *trckd ldrs: shkn up over 4f out: led 2f out: sn edgd lft: styd on strly* **4/11**1
133 2 4 ½ **Hallstatt (IRE)**8 3623 11-8-10 63 (t) DavidProbert 4 67
(John Mackie) *hld up: hdwy over 2f out: rdn over 1f out: styd on to go 2nd nr fin: no ch w wnr* **14/1**
22-3 3 nk **Tyrell (IRE)**19 3213 4-9-5 72 (v) FergusSweeney 2 76
(Alan King) *led 2f: chsd ldr tl led again 3f out: rdn and hdd 2f out: no ex fnl f* **6/1**2
66-6 4 4 ½ **Art Scholar (IRE)**41 2504 10-8-2 62 RayDawson(7) 7 59
(Michael Appleby) *hld up: hdwy over 2f out: sn rdn: wknd fnl f* **33/1**
6-5 5 9 **Maoi Chinn Tire (IRE)**24 3046 10-9-7 74 (p) DavidNolan 5 59
(Jennie Candlish) *prom: rdn over 2f out: wknd over 1f out* **25/1**
0-05 6 10 **Ingleby Hollow**12 3464 5-9-4 71 (p) DanielTudhope 3 42
(David O'Meara) *led after 2f: rdn and hdd 3f out: wknd over 1f out* **10/1**3

3m 0.75s (-6.25) **Going Correction** -0.70s/f (Hard) 6 Ran SP% **110.1**
Speed ratings (Par 103): **89,86,86,83,78 72**
CSF £6.60 TOTE £1.20: £1.10, £4.70; EX 6.40 Trifecta £21.30.
**Owner** Exors Of The Late J L C Pearce **Bred** Lordship Stud **Trained** Newmarket, Suffolk

**FOCUS**
Actual race distance 1m6f6yds. Stalls on inner. This was all about the four-timer seeking favourite, and he did not disappoint.
T/Plt: £24.20 to a £1 stake. Pool: £64,218.43 - 1936.35 winning units T/Qpdt: £6.60 to a £1 stake. Pool: £5,148.72 - 572.9 winning units **Colin Roberts**

# 3429 WETHERBY (L-H)

Monday, June 19

**OFFICIAL GOING: Good to firm (watered; 8.9)**

Wind: Light behind Weather: Fine, dry & hot

## 3908 WATCH RACING UK WITH FREE TRIAL NOW NOVICE MEDIAN AUCTION STKS 7f

**2:15** (2:17) (Class 5) 2-Y-O £3,881 (£1,155; £577; £288) **Stalls** Low

Form RPR

2 **1** **Indomeneo**[31] 2786 2-9-2 0 .......... TonyHamilton 5 77
(Richard Fahey) *mde all: rdn and qcknd wl over 1f out: drvn ins fnl f: hld on gamely* **2/1**[1]

4 **2** *hd* **Power And Peace (IRE)**[18] 3245 2-8-11 0 .......... HarryBentley 8 71
(David Simcock) *trckd ldng pair: hdwy 2f out: rdn to chal over 1f out: drvn to dispute ld and ev ch ins fnl f: no ex nr liner* **9/4**[2]

6 **3** *hd* **Deadly Reel (IRE)**[16] 3312 2-8-11 0 .......... JackMitchell 3 71
(Archie Watson) *t.k.h: trckd wnr: hdwy over 2f out: sn cl up: rdn wl over 1f out: drvn and ev ch ins fnl f: no ex nr fin* **5/1**[3]

**4** *½* **Barford (IRE)** 2-9-2 0 .......... RobHornby 2 75
(Pam Sly) *dwlt: green and towards rr: hdwy on outer 1/2-way: chsd ldrs over 2f out: rdn and cl up over 1f out: drvn and ev ch ins fnl f: no ex towards fin* **8/1**

**5** *7* **Kingfast (IRE)** 2-9-2 0 .......... GrahamLee 7 56
(David Dennis) *dwlt: green towards rr: pushed along 1/2-way: rdn along over 2f out: n.d* **16/1**

**6** *½* **Ideal Candy (IRE)** 2-8-4 0 .......... RussellHarris(7) 4 49
(Andrew Crook) *t.k.h: chsd ldrs: rdn along and green wl over 2f out: sn outpcd* **50/1**

**7** *7* **Toohottotouch** 2-9-2 0 .......... PhillipMakin 1 35
(Michael Dods) *green and a rr* **12/1**

1m 28.77s (1.77) **Going Correction** -0.35s/f (Firm) **7** Ran SP% **107.4**

Speed ratings (Par 93): **75,74,74,73,65 65,57**

CSF £5.82 TOTE £2.50: £1.70, £1.10; EX 5.20 Trifecta £10.50.

**Owner** Middleham Park Racing LX **Bred** Hungerford Park Stud **Trained** Musley Bank, N Yorks

■ Urban Soul was withdrawn. Price at time of withdrawal 20/1. Rule 4 does not apply.

**FOCUS**

A race that played out as the market anticipated, there was little between the first four at the line. Ordinary form.

## 3909 ANDREWS BOWEN SAFETRACK H'CAP 1m 6f

**2:45** (2:47) (Class 5) (0-75,76) 3-Y-O £3,881 (£1,155; £577; £288) **Stalls** Low

Form RPR

55-4 **1** **Davy's Dilemma**[45] 2376 3-9-7 **75** .......... PhillipMakin 4 81
(Michael Dods) *hld up: hdwy over 3f out: chsd ldrs over 2f out: rdn over 1f out: styd on to ld ins fnl f* **8/1**

-430 **2** *hd* **Laureate**[28] 2892 3-8-12 **66** .......... PJMcDonald 8 71
(Mark Johnston) *hld up in tch: hdwy 5f out: chsd ldr over 3f out: led wl over 1f out: drvn and hdd ins fnl f: kpt on* **16/1**

0462 **3** *¾* **Tor**[7] 3665 3-9-0 **75** .......... JamieGormley(7) 7 79
(Iain Jardine) *hld up in rr: hdwy on inner over 3f out: trckd ldrs 2f out: rdn wl over 1f out: kpt on strly fnl f* **7/1**

-434 **4** *½* **Really Super**[9] 3596 3-9-8 **76** ..........(p[1]) MartinHarley 9 79
(Ralph Beckett) *hld up in rr: stdy hdwy on outer over 3f out: trckd wnr 2f out: rdn and edgd lft over 1f out: sn drvn and kpt on same pce u.p fnl f* **10/3**[1]

0536 **5** *4 ½* **Kiruna Peak (IRE)**[17] 3276 3-8-10 **64** ..........(v[1]) GrahamLee 2 61
(Mick Channon) *hld up towards rr: hdwy on outer 3f out: rdn along to chse ldrs 2f out: sn drvn and no imp* **14/1**

0-22 **6** *7* **Plage Depampelonne**[19] 3220 3-8-12 **66** .......... HarryBentley 6 53
(James Bethell) *in tch: pushed along and hdwy over 3f out: rdn along to chse ldrs 2f out: sn drvn and wknd* **4/1**[2]

0-40 **7** *½* **Two Dollars (IRE)**[11] 3506 3-9-1 **69** .......... TrevorWhelan 1 55
(William Jarvis) *in tch: hdwy 4f out: rdn along 3f out: drvn and btn 2f out* **33/1**

5522 **8** *6* **Breakwater Bay (IRE)**[25] 2991 3-8-9 **63** .......... DavidAllan 5 41
(Tim Easterby) *set str pce: pushed along 3f out: rdn over 2f out: hdd wl over 1f out and sn wknd* **6/1**

2-33 **9** *51* **Migyaas (USA)**[51] 2164 3-9-2 **73** ..........(v[1]) AlistairRawlinson(3) 3
(Saeed bin Suroor) *reminders s and sn cl up: disp ld 6f out: rdn along 4f out: sn lost pl and bhd* **5/1**[3]

3m 0.41s (-4.59) **Going Correction** -0.35s/f (Firm) **9** Ran SP% **113.1**

Speed ratings (Par 99): **99,98,98,98,95 91,91,87,58**

CSF £122.55 CT £934.32 TOTE £8.30: £2.40, £4.10, £2.80; EX 108.70 Trifecta £1448.60.

**Owner** D Neale **Bred** Wansdyke Farms Limited **Trained** Denton, Co Durham

**FOCUS**

Run at a good gallop, with a pair of tearaway leaders, the first four pulled clear and the form looks reasonable for the level. A small pb from the winner, with the fourth rated to her maiden form.

## 3910 D M KEITH H'CAP 1m 2f

**3:15** (3:15) (Class 5) (0-75,73) 4-Y-O+ £3,881 (£1,155; £577; £288) **Stalls** Centre

Form RPR

-500 **1** **Age Of Elegance (IRE)**[16] 3341 5-9-7 **73** ..........(p) TonyHamilton 5 78
(Roger Fell) *set stdy pce: pushed along and qcknd over 2f out: rdn wl over 1f out: drvn ent fnl f and sn hdd: rallied gamely to ld again last 75 yds* **3/1**[3]

52-0 **2** *¾* **Scottish Summit (IRE)**[24] 3050 4-9-4 **70** .......... SamJames 8 74
(Geoffrey Harker) *trckd wnr: hdwy over 2f out: cl up 11/2f out: sn rdn: led ins fnl f: sn drvn and edgd lft: hdd and no ex last 75 yds* **16/1**

03-0 **3** *1 ½* **Quoteline Direct**[20] 3181 4-8-10 **62** ..........(h) PJMcDonald 1 63
(Micky Hammond) *trckd ldng pair on inner: pushed along over 2f out: rdn and n.m.r over 1f out: drvn and kpt on fnl f* **12/1**

-355 **4** *½* **Bollihope**[27] 2920 5-9-6 **72** .......... RobHornby 7 72
(Richard Guest) *dwlt: hld up in rr: hdwy ion outer wl over 2f out: chsd ldrs wl over 1f out: rdn and edgd lft appr fnl f: sn drvn and kpt on same pce* **11/4**[2]

0525 **5** *hd* **Trinity Star (IRE)**[19] 3197 6-9-2 **68** ..........(b) PhillipMakin 6 68
(Michael Dods) *t.k.h: trckd ldrs: hdwy over 2f out: rdn along wl over 1f out: n.m.r and edgd lft appr fnl f: sn drvn and kpt on same pce* **7/4**[1]

-000 **6** *9* **Glance My Way (IRE)**[23] 3065 4-9-2 **68** ..........(b) DavidAllan 2 50
(Tim Easterby) *trckd ldrs: pushed along 3f out: rdn over 2f out: sn drvn and wknd* **18/1**

/00- **7** *5* **Never Give In**[251] 7246 4-9-1 **67** .......... MartinHarley 4 39
(John Weymes) *dwlt: t.k.h in rr: rdn along 3f out: drvn over 2f out: sn outpcd and bhd* **33/1**

2m 10.55s (1.55) **Going Correction** -0.35s/f (Firm) **7** Ran SP% **109.8**

Speed ratings (Par 103): **79,78,77,76,76 69,65**

CSF £42.97 CT £461.72 TOTE £3.80: £1.70, £5.10; EX 47.60 Trifecta £327.70.

**Owner** R G Fell & K Hamilton **Bred** Ladyswood Stud **Trained** Nawton, N Yorks

**FOCUS**

A modest handicap, it paid to race handy with them going a steady pace and first three home up there throughout. It's been rated cautiously, with the runner-up to form.

## 3911 START YOUR RACING UK FREE TRIAL NOW FILLIES' H'CAP 1m

**3:45** (3:45) (Class 5) (0-75,75) 3-Y-O+ £3,881 (£1,155; £577; £288) **Stalls** Low

Form RPR

2222 **1** **Al Nafoorah**[7] 3656 3-8-13 **70** .......... GrahamLee 1 78
(Ed Dunlop) *mde all: pushed along and qcknd 2f out: rdn and kpt on strly fnl f* **9/4**[1]

2-03 **2** *2 ½* **Totally Magic (IRE)**[17] 3287 5-8-9 **61** .......... LewisEdmunds(5) 6 65
(Richard Whitaker) *t.k.h: trckd wnr: pushed along over 2f out: rdn wl over 1f out: drvn and kpt on fnl f* **3/1**[2]

4-32 **3** *1 ¼* **Cheerfilly (IRE)**[24] 3044 3-9-4 **75** .......... MartinHarley 8 74
(Tom Dascombe) *t.k.h: trckd ldrs on outer: hdwy over 2f out: rdn and edgd lft over 1f out: drvn and kpt on fnl f* **7/2**[3]

210 **4** *½* **Rinaria (IRE)**[32] 2754 3-8-11 **71** ..........(h[1]) JordanVaughan(3) 5 69+
(K R Burke) *dwlt and hld up in rr: hdwy on outer over 2f out: rdn wl over 1f out: kpt on u.p fnl f* **12/1**

-054 **5** *¾* **Beatbybeatbybeat**[20] 3189 4-9-7 **68** ..........(v) CamHardie 7 66
(Antony Brittain) *trckd ldrs: hdwy 3f out: rdn along 2f out: sn drvn and no imp* **14/1**

455- **6** *1 ¾* **Sepal (USA)**[262] 6922 4-9-10 **71** ..........(h[1]) DavidNolan 2 65
(Iain Jardine) *trckd ldng pair on inner: hdwy 3f out: rdn along 2f out: sn drvn and grad wknd* **9/1**

4554 **7** *hd* **Lozah**[20] 3181 4-8-13 **60** .......... TonyHamilton 4 54
(Roger Fell) *dwlt: hld up in rr: hdwy 3f out: rdn along and n.m.r on inner 2f out: sn drvn and btn* **12/1**

1m 38.82s (-2.18) **Going Correction** -0.35s/f (Firm) course record

**WFA** 3 from 4yo+ 10lb **7** Ran SP% **110.0**

Speed ratings (Par 100): **96,93,92,91,91 89,89**

CSF £8.39 CT £19.71 TOTE £3.20: £1.70, £1.70; EX 9.20 Trifecta £29.90.

**Owner** Mohammed Jaber **Bred** Aston Mullins Stud **Trained** Newmarket, Suffolk

**FOCUS**

Another all-the-way winner, the favourite ending a frustrating run of second. The third has been rated to her maiden form.

## 3912 UNBOX RACING UK FOR FREE NOW H'CAP 7f

**4:15** (4:17) (Class 6) (0-65,66) 4-Y-O+ £3,234 (£962; £481; £240) **Stalls** Low

Form RPR

6-03 **1** **Mango Chutney**[14] 3402 4-9-4 **62** ..........(p) PhillipMakin 15 71
(John Davies) *trckd ldrs: hdwy over 2f out: sn cl up: rdn to ld ent fnl f: kpt on strly* **9/2**[1]

263- **2** *1 ½* **Rosy Ryan (IRE)**[185] 8401 7-8-9 **53** .......... JoeDoyle 11 58
(Tina Jackson) *hld up in midfield: hdwy 3f out: chsd ldrs wl over 1f out: sn rdn and kpt on fnl f* **16/1**

5-50 **3** *¾* **Picks Pinta**[18] 3239 6-9-0 **63** .......... LewisEdmunds(5) 4 66
(John David Riches) *in tch: hdwy on inner over 2f out: led wl over 1f out: sn rdn and hung rt: hdd and drvn ent fnl f: kpt on same pce* **16/1**

524 **4** *nk* **Kensington Palace (IRE)**[5] 3704 4-8-13 **57** .......... BarryMcHugh 10 59
(Marjorie Fife) *in tch: hdwy 3f out: sn chsng ldrs: rdn and hung lft over 1f out: sn drvn and kpt on same pce* **5/1**[2]

2233 **5** *nk* **Cabal**[20] 3181 10-9-4 **62** ..........(b) DavidAllan 3 63
(Geoffrey Harker) *hld up towards rr: gd hdwy on inner wl over 1f out: sn rdn and kpt on wl fnl f* **6/1**[3]

6023 **6** *¾* **Grey Destiny**[18] 3263 7-9-2 **60** .......... CamHardie 14 59
(Antony Brittain) *swtchd lft s and t.k.h: hld up in rr: hdwy over 2f out: rdn over 1f out: kpt on fnl f* **20/1**

-056 **7** *1* **Danot (IRE)**[19] 3203 5-9-1 **59** ..........(p) JackGarritty 8 56
(Jedd O'Keeffe) *hld up towards rr: hdwy wl over 2f out: rdn along wl over 1f out: kpt on fnl f* **11/1**

0102 **8** *½* **The Name's Paver**[19] 3198 4-9-7 **65** .......... GrahamLee 12 61
(Noel Wilson) *trckd ldr: cl up 1/2-way: rdn along wl over 2f out: wkng whn hmpd over 1f out* **9/1**

0003 **9** *nk* **Steal The Scene (IRE)**[6] 3702 5-9-8 **66** ..........(b[1]) TrevorWhelan 7 63
(Kevin Frost) *trckd ldrs: hdwy over 2f out: rdn along whn hmpd over 1f out: nt rcvr* **9/1**

4132 **10** *hd* **Caledonia Laird**[18] 3265 6-9-5 **63** .......... IrineuGoncalves 2 57
(Jo Hughes) *midfield: effrt on outer wl over 2f out: sn rdn along: n.d* **10/1**

-050 **11** *3* **Lukoutoldmakezebak**[11] 3488 4-8-4 **48** ow2 .......... RoystonFfrench 9 34
(David Thompson) *a towards rr* **100/1**

/0-0 **12** *½* **Dylan's Storm (IRE)**[20] 3181 5-8-13 **57** ..........(p) PJMcDonald 1 41
(Peter Niven) *towards rr: sme hdwy on inner over 2f out: sn rdn and n.d* **33/1**

30-6 **13** *¾* **American Hustle (IRE)**[9] 3577 5-8-11 **60** ..........(p) BenRobinson(5) 6 42
(Brian Ellison) *led: pushed along wl over 2f out: sn rdn: hdd wl over 1f out: grad wknd* **12/1**

0-54 **14** *½* **Check 'Em Tuesday (IRE)**[129] 655 4-9-1 **62** .......... CharlieBennett(3) 13 43
(Daniel Mark Loughnane) *hld up and swtchd lft s: a towards rr* **20/1**

30-0 **15** *9* **Mr Conundrum**[149] 362 4-8-5 **49** .......... PaddyAspell 5 6
(Lynn Siddall) *chsd ldrs: rdn along 3f out: drvn over 2f out: sn wknd* **100/1**

1m 25.89s (-1.11) **Going Correction** -0.35s/f (Firm) **15** Ran SP% **120.5**

Speed ratings (Par 101): **92,90,89,89,88 87,86,86,85,85 82,81,80,80,69**

CSF £72.92 CT £1093.95 TOTE £4.90: £2.30, £5.90, £5.50; EX 90.40 Trifecta £1883.80.

**Owner** The Sexy Fish Partnership **Bred** P Taylor **Trained** Piercebridge, Durham

**FOCUS**

Moderate form, although the winner was well backed. A minor pb from the winner, with the form straightforward in behind.

## 3913 RACINGUK.COM/FREETRIAL H'CAP 1m

**4:45** (4:47) (Class 6) (0-60,59) 3-Y-O £3,234 (£962; £481; £240) **Stalls** Low

Form RPR

2 **1** **Secret Memories (IRE)**[33] 2726 3-9-5 **57** ..........(t) PJMcDonald 15 63
(Miss Katy Brown, Ire) *trckd ldrs: hdwy over 2f out: rdn to ld over 1f out: drvn out* **7/1**[3]

5640 **2** *½* **England Expects**[13] 3431 3-9-5 **57** ..........(h) MartinHarley 16 62
(K R Burke) *hld up in rr: hdwy over 2f out: rdn over 1f out: chsd wnr ins fnl f: sn drvn and kpt on* **10/1**

-300 3 nk **He's A Toff (IRE)**[13] 3431 3-9-0 52..............................(b) GrahamLee 3 56
(Tim Easterby) *trckd ldrs on inner: hdwy 3f out: rdn and cl up 2f out: drvn over 1f out: kpt on u.p fnl f* **16/1**

4155 4 nk **Jack Blane**[56] 2016 3-9-3 55.............................. RobHornby 12 59
(Daniel Kubler) *prom: cl up over 3f out: led 2f out: sn rdn and hdd over 1f out: drvn and kpt on fnl f* **11/1**

4246 5 1 3/4 **Fairy Lock (IRE)**[8] 3627 3-9-0 52.............................. JackGarritty 13 52
(David Barron) *towards rr: hdwy on outer wl over 2f out: rdn along wl over 1f out: kpt on fnl f* **3/1**[1]

0 6 1 **Edgar Allan Poe (IRE)**[14] 3403 3-9-7 59.............................. DuranFentiman 9 59
(Rebecca Bastiman) *midfield: effrt over 2f out: rdn wl over 1f out: kpt on fnl f* **25/1**

466 7 3/4 **Lakeski**[49] 2227 3-9-3 55.............................. BarryMcHugh 10 51
(Scott Dixon) *prom on outer: hdwy and cl up 3f out: rdn along 2f out: sn drvn and grad wknd* **66/1**

5062 8 1/2 **Kelpie Spirit (IRE)**[2] 3831 3-8-11 52.............................. CharlieBennett(3) 1 46
(John Weymes) *hld up: hdwy on inner 2f out: sn rdn and kpt on: nt rch ldrs* **8/1**

6-03 9 2 1/2 **Orientelle**[9] 3555 3-8-12 55..............................(p[1]) LewisEdmunds(5) 6 46
(Richard Whitaker) *t.k.h: chsd ldr: cl up 1/2-way: rdn along 3f out: sn wknd* **13/2**[2]

0253 10 2 3/4 **Hollywood Harry (IRE)**[14] 3387 3-9-6 58..............................(p) PhillipMakin 5 40
(Keith Dalgleish) *led: pushed along 3f out: rdn over 2f out: sn hdd & wknd* **7/1**[3]

6300 11 nk **Baby Helmet**[12] 3461 3-9-1 58.............................. GemmaTutty(5) 4 40
(Karen Tutty) *midfield: rdn along 3f out: n.d* **33/1**

-560 12 1 3/4 **Thomas Crown (IRE)**[12] 3461 3-9-7 59..............................(p[1]) TonyHamilton 7 37
(Roger Fell) *nvr bttr than midfield* **33/1**

6400 13 1 1/4 **Paquita Bailarina**[18] 3260 3-9-1 53.............................. HarryBentley 14 28
(James Given) *a rr* **10/1**

1m 39.36s (-1.64) **Going Correction** -0.35s/f (Firm) **13 Ran SP% 118.1**
Speed ratings (Par 97): **94,93,93,92,91 90,89,88,86,83 83,81,80**
CSF £71.95 CT £1116.44 TOTE £7.80: £2.40, £3.70, £5.20; EX 82.60 Trifecta £1176.50.
**Owner** S & M O'Brien Partnership **Bred** Windflower Overseas Holdings Inc **Trained** Enniscorthy, Co Wexford

**FOCUS**
A pretty lowly handicap. Modest form.

## 3914 RACING UK FREE FOR A MONTH H'CAP (DIV I) 5f 110y
**5:15** (5:17) (Class 6) (0-60,60) 3-Y-O+ **£3,234** (£962; £481; £240) **Stalls** High

Form RPR

2060 1 **Dapper Man (IRE)**[14] 3403 3-9-1 58..............................(b) TonyHamilton 3 68
(Roger Fell) *cl up: rdn to ld over 1f out: sn clr: kpt on strly* **6/1**[3]

5306 2 3 3/4 **Ambitious Icarus**[4] 3758 8-9-10 60..............................(b) RobHornby 10 58
(Richard Guest) *trckd ldrs on outer: hdwy over 2f out: rdn over 1f out: drvn and kpt on fnl f: no ch w wnr* **7/2**[1]

4032 3 3/4 **Culloden**[9] 3563 5-9-5 58..............................(v) CharlieBennett(3) 9 53
(Shaun Harris) *hld up in rr: hdwy on wd outside 2f out: rdn over 1f out: kpt on fnl f* **4/1**[2]

0616 4 1/2 **Ebitda**[6] 3703 3-8-8 51.............................. PJMcDonald 2 43
(Scott Dixon) *led: rdn over 2f out: drvn and hdd over 1f out: wknd fnl f* **4/1**[2]

0-00 5 2 3/4 **Pavers Pride**[28] 2897 3-9-1 58.............................. MartinHarley 4 40
(Noel Wilson) *trckd ldrs: hdwy over 2f out: rdn along wl over 1f out: sn drvn: edgd lft and one pce* **17/2**

6660 6 nse **Lady Molly (IRE)**[24] 3047 3-8-11 54.............................. JoeDoyle 1 36
(Keith Dalgleish) *cl up on inner: rdn along and disp ld 2f out: sn drvn and wknd over 1f out* **7/1**

-604 7 3 1/4 **Spike (IRE)**[25] 2989 4-9-5 55..............................(b) GrahamLee 5 29
(Donald McCain) *chsd ldrs on inner: rdn over 2f out: sn drvn and wknd* **11/1**

6040 8 5 **Under Approval**[5] 3710 6-8-10 46 oh1..............................(p) ShaneGray 8 3
(Karen Tutty) *dwlt: sn rdn along: a bhd* **33/1**

1m 4.25s (-1.75) **Going Correction** -0.35s/f (Firm) course record
**WFA** 3 from 4yo+ 6lb **8 Ran SP% 110.8**
Speed ratings (Par 101): **105,100,99,98,94 94,90,83**
CSF £25.54 CT £89.60 TOTE £6.10: £2.30, £1.50, £1.60; EX 32.40 Trifecta £104.60.
**Owner** R G Fell **Bred** William Joseph Martin **Trained** Nawton, N Yorks

**FOCUS**
The first leg of a lowly sprint, it produced an emphatic winner. The winner has been rated back to last year's form.

## 3915 RACING UK FREE FOR A MONTH H'CAP (DIV II) 5f 110y
**5:50** (5:51) (Class 6) (0-60,60) 3-Y-O+ **£3,234** (£962; £481; £240) **Stalls** High

Form RPR

-050 1 **Thatcherite (IRE)**[19] 3201 9-9-10 60..............................(t) BarryMcHugh 3 68
(Tony Coyle) *dwlt and towards rr: hdwy on wd outside wl over 1f out: str run ent fnl f: led last 75 yds* **9/2**[2]

0-06 2 1 1/4 **Spoken Words**[26] 2949 8-8-10 46 oh1.............................. PaddyAspell 6 49
(John David Riches) *trckd ldr: hdwy and cl up over 2f out: rdn over 1f out: led ent fnl f: sn drvn: hdd and no ex last 75 yds* **33/1**

04-0 3 nse **Ypres**[18] 3256 8-9-6 56..............................(p) CamHardie 5 59
(Jason Ward) *trckd ldrs: hdwy 2f out: rdn over 1f out: drvn and ev ch ins fnl f: kpt on same pce* **9/1**

3024 4 2 1/4 **Lizzy's Dream**[26] 2949 9-8-10 46.............................. DuranFentiman 1 41
(Rebecca Bastiman) *trckd ldng pair on inner: hdwy and cl up 3f out: led 2f out and sn rdn: drvn and hdd ent fnl f: grad wknd* **9/1**

0-50 5 1 1/4 **Nefetari**[115] 899 4-8-5 46 oh1..............................(b) LewisEdmunds(5) 8 37
(Alan Brown) *chsd ldrs: hdwy and cl up over 2f out: rdn and ev ch over 1f out: drvn and wknd ent fnl f* **16/1**

-005 6 nk **Harbour Lightning**[14] 3384 3-9-1 58.............................. PJMcDonald 10 46
(Noel Wilson) *in tch on outer: rdn along 2f out: sn wknd* **6/1**[3]

0035 7 1/2 **Lady Joanna Vassa (IRE)**[5] 3710 4-9-2 52.............................. RobHornby 2 41
(Richard Guest) *dwlt and bhd: hdwy 3f out: chsd ldrs 2f out: sn rdn and wknd over 1f out* **5/2**[1]

6066 8 1/2 **Chip Or Pellet**[19] 3202 4-8-11 47..............................(b) GrahamLee 9 34
(Nigel Tinkler) *a towards rr* **6/1**[3]

0-50 9 1 1/2 **Mr Enthusiastic**[17] 3290 3-8-3 46 oh1..............................(h[1]) RoystonFfrench 4 26
(Noel Wilson) *led: rdn along 3f out: hdd over 2f out and sn wknd* **33/1**

000 10 4 1/2 **Captain Scooby**[12] 3468 11-9-0 50..............................(b) TonyHamilton 7 17
(Richard Guest) *s.i.s and a bhd* **16/1**

1m 5.06s (-0.94) **Going Correction** -0.35s/f (Firm)
**WFA** 3 from 4yo+ 6lb **10 Ran SP% 113.0**
Speed ratings (Par 101): **92,90,90,87,85 85,84,83,81,75**
CSF £132.36 CT £1264.50 TOTE £4.80: £1.70, £7.60, £2.90; EX 94.40 Trifecta £3056.10.
**Owner** Brian Kerr **Bred** Taroka Equine Investments **Trained** Norton, N Yorks

**FOCUS**
The slower of the two divisions. The runner-up helps pin the modest level of the form.
T/Jkpt: £19,097.30 to a £1 stake. Pool: £28,646.05 - 1.5 winning units T/Plt: £540.70 to a £1 stake. Pool: £71,339.22 - 96.31 winning units T/Qpdt: £104.50 to a £1 stake. Pool: £4,477.38 - 31.7 winning units **Joe Rowntree**

# 3668 WINDSOR (R-H)
## Monday, June 19

**OFFICIAL GOING: Good to firm (7.8)**
Wind: Almost nil Weather: Fine, 32 degrees

## 3916 ROYAL WINDSOR RACECOURSE APPRENTICE H'CAP 1m 3f 99y
**5:45** (5:45) (Class 6) (0-65,65) 4-Y-O+ **£2,264** (£673; £336; £168) **Stalls** Centre

Form RPR

3224 1 **Powered (IRE)**[2] 3805 4-8-11 57.............................. KeelanBaker(7) 2 64
(David Evans) *hld up in last: prog on wd outside fr 3f out: led over 1f out: styd on wl: readily* **5/1**[3]

-441 2 2 1/4 **Hope Is High**[5] 3726 4-9-0 58 6ex.............................. DarraghKeenan(5) 3 61
(John Berry) *cl up: dropped to last pair and pushed along 4f out: effrt 3f out: kpt on to take 2nd ins fnl f: no ch w wnr* **5/6**[1]

0006 3 1 **Moojaned (IRE)**[70] 1684 6-9-9 65.............................. RossaRyan(3) 5 67
(John Flint) *led: styd against rail in st: hrd rdn and hdd over 1f out: one pce* **8/1**

3304 4 hd **Marshall Aid (IRE)**[8] 3623 4-9-5 63.............................. NicolaCurrie(5) 4 64
(Mark Usher) *chsd ldrs: disp 2nd over 2f out to over 1f out: nt qckn and one pce after* **9/2**[2]

3022 5 3 1/2 **Flying Author (IRE)**[8] 3958 6-8-4 46 oh1..............................(p) FinleyMarsh(3) 1 42
(Phil McEntee) *chsd ldr 4f: styd prom: rdn 3f out: fdd 2f out* **14/1**

-024 6 27 **Shirataki (IRE)**[19] 3221 9-8-8 52.............................. MollyKing(5) 6 5
(Peter Hiatt) *s.i.s: rcvrd to chse ldr after 4f: chal 4f out: wknd 3f out: sn t.o* **20/1**

2m 28.72s (-0.78) **Going Correction** +0.025s/f (Good) **6 Ran SP% 111.9**
Speed ratings (Par 101): **103,101,100,100,97 78**
CSF £9.60 TOTE £4.80: £2.50, £1.10; EX 10.70 Trifecta £41.30.
**Owner** Mrs E Evans **Bred** Colman Carroll **Trained** Pandy, Monmouths
■ Stewards' Enquiry : Darragh Keenan four-day ban: used whip above permitted level (July 3-6)

**FOCUS**
Race distances as advertiseed. Rail moved out 8yds from the stands' side inner position from 6f to winning post. They went a solid pace in this ordinary handicap, confined to apprentice riders. It's been rated as straightforward form.

## 3917 EBF STALLIONS NOVICE STKS 5f 21y
**6:15** (6:15) (Class 5) 2-Y-O **£2,911** (£866; £432; £216) **Stalls** Low

Form RPR

4 1 **Gotti (USA)**[10] 3516 2-9-2 0.............................. GeraldMosse 9 75
(Jeremy Noseda) *sn in last trio: prog on wd outside 1/2-way: drvn to chal ins fnl f: led last strides* **3/1**[2]

43 2 hd **Indian Warrior**[35] 2691 2-9-2 0.............................. JamesDoyle 7 74
(Ed Dunlop) *trckd ldrs: chal four wd 2f out: hrd rdn to ld jst over 1f out: kpt on but hdd last strides* **2/1**[1]

0 3 3/4 **Zalshah**[66] 1767 2-9-2 0.............................. TomMarquand 2 71
(Richard Hannon) *trckd ldrs: effrt 2f out: styd on to take 3rd nr fin: jst unable to chal* **9/1**

5 4 1/2 **Expecting**[7] 3668 2-9-2 0.............................. GavinLerena 10 70
(Charles Hills) *w ldng pair: led briefly over 1f out: pressed ldr after tl nt qckn ins fnl f* **15/2**

032 5 1 1/2 **Demons Rock (IRE)**[20] 3169 2-9-2 0.............................. RichardKingscote 5 64
(Tom Dascombe) *trckd ldrs: rdn 2f out: no imp over 1f out: one pce after* **4/1**[3]

6 1 **Time For Wine (IRE)** 2-8-11 0.............................. FranBerry 6 56
(David Evans) *s.i.s: last and off the pce: nvr a factor but kpt on fr over 1f out on wd outside* **33/1**

043 7 shd **Zain Smarts (IRE)**[9] 3570 2-8-11 0.............................. JFEgan 3 55
(David Evans) *broke smartly: led against nr side rail: hdd and fdd over 1f out* **25/1**

8 3/4 **Iconic Knight (IRE)** 2-9-2 0.............................. LiamKeniry 1 57
(Ed Walker) *s.i.s: a wl in rr: kpt on ins fnl f* **25/1**

06 9 1 1/4 **Cent Flying**[8] 3622 2-9-2 0..............................(t[1]) MartinDwyer 8 53
(William Muir) *w ldr: stl upsides 2f out: fdd over 1f out* **33/1**

0 10 hd **Lastoneforthecraic (IRE)**[21] 3156 2-8-11 0.............................. AdamBeschizza 4 47
(David Evans) *towards rr: pushed along by 1/2-way: nvr on terms* **80/1**

1m 0.77s (0.47) **Going Correction** -0.05s/f (Good) **10 Ran SP% 114.9**
Speed ratings (Par 93): **94,93,92,91,89 87,87,86,84,84**
CSF £8.75 TOTE £3.60: £1.30, £1.10, £2.90; EX 10.00 Trifecta £64.90.
**Owner** Phoenix Thoroughbred Limited **Bred** Jack Mandato & Hidden Brook Farm **Trained** Newmarket, Suffolk
■ Stewards' Enquiry : Gavin Lerena two-day ban: used whip above permitted level (July 3-4)

**FOCUS**
Not a bad novice event. The first pair fought it out down the middle. The runner-up helps set the standard.

## 3918 BURNING BRIGHT PRODUCTIONS (S) STKS 6f 12y
**6:45** (6:47) (Class 5) 2-Y-O **£2,911** (£866; £432; £216) **Stalls** Low

Form RPR

053 1 **Tie Em Up Tel (IRE)**[8] 3619 2-8-11 0.............................. JFEgan 5 64
(David Evans) *chsd ldrs: rdn and clsd on outer fr 2f out: led over 1f out: styd on and sn clr* **15/8**[1]

060 2 4 **Roses In June (IRE)**[3] 3791 2-8-6 0.............................. LiamJones 8 47
(J S Moore) *jnd ldng pair after 2f: chal fr 1/2-way: upsides over 1f out: wandered and one pce after* **14/1**

05 3 1 **Give Em A Clump (IRE)**[59] 1934 2-8-11 0.............................. AdamBeschizza 7 49
(David Evans) *wl in rr: long way off the pce in last pair 1/2-way: shkn up 2f out: styd on wl on outer fr over 1f out: tk 3rd nr fin* **12/1**

3642 4 hd **Quick Skips Lad (IRE)**[8] 3619 2-8-11 0..............................(b) LiamKeniry 3 48
(J S Moore) *led to 1/2-way: styd pressing ldrs: one pce over 1f out* **7/2**[3]

00 5 2 **Runthatbymeagain (IRE)**[13] 3421 2-8-7 0 ow1.............................. TomMarquand 4 38
(David Evans) *wl in rr: long way off the pce in last pair 1/2-way: kpt on fr over 1f out: nrst fin* **25/1**

060 6 2 1/4 **Mirek (IRE)**[27] 2910 2-8-6 0..............................(h) MitchGodwin(5) 6 36
(Jonathan Portman) *chsd ldrs: no imp in 5th 2f out: fdd over 1f out* **33/1**

0 7 3/4 **Bumble Beeze (IRE)**[12] 3467 2-8-11 0.............................. RichardKingscote 10 33+
(Tom Dascombe) *swvd bdly lft s: rcvrd to join ldng pair: led 1/2-way: hdd over 1f out: hanging and wknd rapidly* **2/1**[2]

00 8 *shd* **The Kiddie Kid**[7] 3655 2-8-12 0 ow1 GavinLerena 9 34
(Mick Channon) *pressed ldr 2f: sn lost pl: wl in rr fnl 2f* **33/1**
1m 14.35s (1.35) **Going Correction** -0.05s/f (Good) **8** Ran SP% **114.4**
Speed ratings (Par 93): **89,83,82,82,79 76,75,75**
CSF £27.73 TOTE £2.80: £1.10, £3.40, £3.40; EX 24.70 Trifecta £143.00.The winner was bought in for £7,500
**Owner** Power Geneva Ltd & Partner **Bred** Albert Ennis **Trained** Pandy, Monmouths
**FOCUS**
This is usually and okay race for the grade. The winner has been rated slightly better than par for the grade.

## 3919 SKY BET ADVANTAGE FOR ROYAL ASCOT H'CAP 6f 12y
**7:15** (7:16) (Class 4) (0-85,85) 4-Y-O+ **£4,690** (£1,395; £697; £348) **Stalls** Low

Form RPR
0022 1 **Bahamian Dollar**[6] 3696 4-8-6 **77** KatherineGlenister[(7)] 6 85
(David Evans) *racd on outer: sn cl up bhd ldrs: chal over 1f out: shkn up to ld jst ins fnl f: kpt on wl* **2/1**[1]
-14 2 *½* **King Of Spin**[21] 3161 4-9-3 **81** ShaneKelly 8 87
(Richard Hughes) *pushed up to ld but crossed to nr side rail: rdn 2f out: hdd jst ins fnl f: edgd lft and kpt on* **3/1**[2]
-445 3 *2½* **Cool Bahamian (IRE)**[21] 3161 6-9-5 **83** (b) CharlesBishop 1 81
(Eve Johnson Houghton) *pressed ldrs: cl up 2f out: drvn and kpt on one pce after* **7/1**
16-6 4 *2* **Ginzan**[13] 3424 9-8-8 **79** FinleyMarsh[(7)] 9 71
(Malcolm Saunders) *t.k.h: mostly chsd ldr to over 1f out: wknd last 150yds* **16/1**
1110 5 *¾* **Whitecrest**[20] 3177 9-8-10 **74** TomMarquand 7 64
(John Spearing) *racd on outer: chsd ldrs: rdn and no imp over 2f out: no hdwy after* **33/1**
-623 6 *hd* **Handytalk (IRE)**[24] 3030 4-9-0 **78** PatDobbs 5 67
(Rod Millman) *tk fierce hold: hld up: tried to make prog over 2f out: swtchd to nr side rail and no imp over 1f out* **5/1**[3]
5356 7 *4½* **Pretty Bubbles**[23] 3063 8-9-5 **83** (v) JamesDoyle 2 58
(J R Jenkins) *hld up: off the pce in rr 1/2-way: rdn 2f out: no great prog* **10/1**
/0-0 8 *nk* **Lawmaking**[35] 2692 4-9-7 **85** LiamKeniry 4 59
(Henry Spiller) *hld up in last: long way off the pce whn shkn up 2f out: nvr in it* **50/1**
0104 9 *1* **Picket Line**[9] 3573 5-8-9 **73** KieranO'Neill 3 43
(Geoffrey Deacon) *hld up: outpcd 1/2-way: shkn up and nvr on terms after: wknd fnl f* **12/1**
1m 11.89s (-1.11) **Going Correction** -0.05s/f (Good) **9** Ran SP% **115.1**
Speed ratings (Par 105): **105,104,101,98,97 97,91,90,89**
CSF £7.91 CT £33.88 TOTE £3.10: £1.40, £1.40, £2.40; EX 9.80 Trifecta £39.60.
**Owner** Shropshire Wolves **Bred** Burns Farm Stud **Trained** Pandy, Monmouths
**FOCUS**
A fair sprint handicap which saw another winner come down the middle. The runner-up has been rated to his penultimate C&D win.

## 3920 SKY BET SPECIALS AT ROYAL ASCOT H'CAP 1m 31y
**7:45** (7:46) (Class 4) (0-80,80) 4-Y-O+ **£4,690** (£1,395; £697; £348) **Stalls** Low

Form RPR
3134 1 **Shifting Star (IRE)**[10] 3521 12-8-6 **65** (vt) WilliamCarson 6 74
(John Bridger) *led: styd against nr side rail in st: drvn and hdd jst over 1f out: rallied gamely fnl f to ld last strides* **8/1**
-231 2 *hd* **Manton Grange**[14] 3396 4-9-7 **80** JamesDoyle 7 88
(George Baker) *hld up towards rr: stdy prog on outer 3f out: led jst over 1f out: kpt on wl fnl f but hdd last strides* **10/11**[1]
00-0 3 *2¾* **Fit For The Job (IRE)**[34] 2708 5-8-13 **72** FranBerry 8 73
(Jonjo O'Neill) *s.i.s: t.k.h: hld up in last pair: shkn up over 3f out: prog on outer 2f out: kpt on fnl f: nvr able to chal* **15/2**[3]
505/ 4 *4* **Ogbourne Downs**[581] 7874 7-9-0 **76** KieranShoemark[(3)] 3 68
(Ben Pauling) *s.s: t.k.h: hld up in last pair: gd prog 3f out to chse ldrs: rdn over 2f out: fdd fnl f* **8/1**
21-5 5 *1¾* **Venutius**[31] 2795 10-9-2 **75** GavinLerena 2 63
(Charles Hills) *prom: chsd wnr over 3f out to over 2f out: wknd over 1f out* **16/1**
622- 6 *1¼* **The Salmon Man**[194] 8255 5-8-13 **72** PatDobbs 1 57
(Brendan Powell) *s.i.s: hld up in midfield: rdn over 2f out: wknd wl over 1f out* **9/2**[2]
-050 7 *½* **Tarseekh**[17] 3304 4-8-2 **61** KieranO'Neill 5 45
(Chris Gordon) *nvr btr than midfield: pushed along 3f out: lost pl then n.m.r over 2f out: wknd* **40/1**
20- 8 *1¾* **Udogo**[59] 1616 6-9-2 **80** JennyPowell[(5)] 9 60
(Brendan Powell) *chsd ldr: rdn 1/2-way: sn lost 2nd and wknd over 2f out* **25/1**
-606 9 *6* **Ready (IRE)**[88] 1329 7-9-2 **80** (p) PaddyPilley[(5)] 4 46
(Clare Ellam) *hld up: struggling in last sn after 1/2-way: bhd over 1f out* **40/1**
1m 43.84s (-0.86) **Going Correction** +0.025s/f (Good) **9** Ran SP% **119.2**
Speed ratings (Par 105): **105,104,102,98,96 95,94,92,86**
CSF £16.05 CT £60.25 TOTE £10.50: £2.30, £1.10, £2.90; EX 21.70 Trifecta £135.60.
**Owner** Night Shadow Syndicate **Bred** Hardys Of Kilkeel Ltd **Trained** Liphook, Hants
**FOCUS**
A modest handicap, run at a sound pace. It's been rated cautiously.

## 3921 ETON CROWN & CUSHION MAIDEN STKS 1m 2f
**8:15** (8:18) (Class 5) 3-Y-O+ **£2,911** (£866; £432; £216) **Stalls** Centre

Form RPR
44 1 **Marie Josephe**[30] 2834 3-8-11 0 ShaneKelly 5 74
(Richard Hughes) *mde virtually all: jnd over 3f out: steered away fr nr side rail in st: shkn up to assert jst over 1f out: pushed out fnl f* **15/2**
0 2 *2* **Love Conquers (JPN)**[52] 2131 3-8-11 0 FranBerry 6 70
(Ralph Beckett) *trckd wnr: chal and upsides over 3f out to over 1f out: one pce u.p after* **7/2**[3]
2-52 3 *¾* **Prerogative (IRE)**[45] 2359 3-9-2 **79** (p) PatDobbs 7 73
(Richard Hannon) *trckd ldng pair 3f: rdn to go 3rd again over 2f out: kpt on fnl f but nvr able to chal* **7/4**[1]
5- 4 *nk* **Percy B Shelley**[189] 8340 3-9-2 0 (t[1]) JamesDoyle 8 72+
(John Gosden) *hld up in midfield: shkn up and nt qckn wl over 2f out: kpt on fr over 1f out to press for 3rd nr fin* **2/1**[2]
05 5 *1½* **Sparte Quercus (IRE)**[16] 3342 4-10-0 0 AntonioFresu 1 69+
(Ed Dunlop) *t.k.h: hld up bhd ldrs: shkn up wl over 2f out: racd awkwardly and steadily outpcd* **25/1**
0 6 *2¾* **Bringit (IRE)**[38] 2580 3-9-2 0 TomMarquand 2 64
(Jamie Osborne) *t.k.h: trckd ldng pair after 3f out to over 2f out: wknd over 1f out* **66/1**
7 *nse* **Amazing Steps (IRE)** 3-9-2 0 StevieDonohoe 9 64
(Charlie Fellowes) *hld up in last pair: lost tch over 4f out: wl bhd 3f out: styd on in encouraging style fnl f* **16/1**
8 *½* **Pretty Obvious (FR)**[38] 4-10-0 0 TimmyMurphy 4 63
(Jonjo O'Neill) *hld up in tch: shkn up 3f out: steadily wknd* **50/1**
9 *19* **The Last Melon**[303] 5-9-9 0 (h) RachealKneller[(5)] 3 25
(James Bennett) *sn in rr: lost tch over 4f out: t.o* **200/1**
0-6 10 *4* **So Much Water (FR)**[65] 1787 5-9-9 0 JFEgan 10 12
(John Berry) *sn dropped to rr: wknd over 4f out: t.o* **100/1**
2m 10.94s (2.24) **Going Correction** +0.025s/f (Good)
**WFA** 3 from 4yo+ 12lb **10** Ran SP% **118.4**
Speed ratings (Par 103): **92,90,89,89,88 86,86,85,70,67**
CSF £34.06 TOTE £10.20: £2.10, £2.00, £1.10; EX 50.70 Trifecta £96.90.
**Owner** Normandie Stud Ltd **Bred** Normandie Stud Ltd **Trained** Upper Lambourn, Berks
**FOCUS**
Few managed to land a blow in this modest maiden. Muddling form.

## 3922 BEST OF BRITISH FESTIVAL 1-3 JULY H'CAP 1m 2f
**8:45** (8:52) (Class 5) (0-70,69) 3-Y-O **£2,911** (£866; £432; £216) **Stalls** Centre

Form RPR
1 **African**[71] 1656 3-9-6 **68** StevieDonohoe 2 77+
(Charlie Fellowes) *v reluctant to go nr or enter the stalls: hld up in rr: 8th and pushed along 3f out: rapid prog between rivals 2f out: rdn to ld ins fnl f: hung lft but enough in hand* **7/1**[2]
60-4 2 *¾* **Prosecution**[14] 3392 3-9-2 **64** RichardKingscote 8 71+
(Hughie Morrison) *pressed ldr: chal over 2f out: shkn up to ld wl over 1f out: kpt on but hdd ins fnl f* **11/8**[1]
66-5 3 *2* **Hawridge Glory (IRE)**[21] 3162 3-8-10 **58** PatDobbs 12 61
(Rod Millman) *led: styd against nr side rail in st: rdn and hdd over 1f out: outpcd fnl f* **7/1**[2]
-434 4 *1* **It's How We Roll (IRE)**[21] 3163 3-9-5 **67** (b) TomMarquand 11 68
(John Spearing) *wl in tch: rdn wl over 2f out and no prog: kpt on same pce over 1f out* **8/1**[3]
100 5 *1* **Broad Appeal**[27] 2931 3-8-12 **65** MitchGodwin[(5)] 9 64
(Jonathan Portman) *wl in tch: rdn 3f out and no prog: kpt on fr over 1f out: n.d* **16/1**
-000 6 *1½* **Gravity Wave (IRE)**[12] 3457 3-9-0 **69** FinleyMarsh[(7)] 7 65
(Sylvester Kirk) *hld up in rr: rdn 3f out and sn struggling: tried to rally over 1f out: no great prog* **7/1**[2]
455 7 *4½* **Olympic Legend (IRE)**[119] 846 3-9-2 **67** GeorgeWood[(3)] 10 54
(Martin Bosley) *chsd ldng pair: rdn over 3f out: wknd 2f out* **25/1**
0-56 8 *8* **Red Emperor (IRE)**[31] 2782 3-9-3 **65** GavinLerena 6 36
(Amanda Perrett) *hld up in last pair: lost tch completely 4f out: reminder and briefly clsd 3f out: sn wknd and bhd* **16/1**
-535 9 *2¼* **Sandy Shores**[115] 895 3-9-2 **64** JamesDoyle 1 31
(Brian Meehan) *chsd ldrs: pushed along 4f out: wknd over 2f out: sn bhd* **10/1**
2m 10.82s (2.12) **Going Correction** +0.025s/f (Good) **9** Ran SP% **115.4**
Speed ratings (Par 99): **92,91,89,89,88 87,83,77,75**
CSF £16.99 CT £71.40 TOTE £9.70: £2.60, £1.10, £2.40; EX 23.50 Trifecta £104.00.
**Owner** Mohammed Bin Hamad Khalifa Al Attiya **Bred** Mrs F H Hay **Trained** Newmarket, Suffolk
**FOCUS**
A modest 3yo handicap, run at a routine pace. The third and fourth help set the standard.
T/Plt: £9.60 to a £1 stake. Pool: £92,934.44 - 7060.8 winning units T/Qpdt: £4.60 to a £1 stake. Pool: £8,411.23 - 1341.56 winning units **Jonathan Neesom**

3923 - (Foreign Racing) - See Raceform Interactive

# 2603 ASCOT (R-H)
Tuesday, June 20

**OFFICIAL GOING: Good to firm (good in places; stand side 8.6, centre 8.3, far side 8.5, round 7.7) changed to good to firm after race 1 (2.30)**
Wind: Nil Weather: Hot & Sunny

## 3924 QUEEN ANNE STKS (GROUP 1) (BRITISH CHAMPIONS SERIES) 1m (S)
**2:30** (2:33) (Class 1) 4-Y-O+
**£388,463** (£147,275; £73,706; £36,716; £18,426; £9,247) **Stalls** Centre

Form RPR
2-31 1 **Ribchester (IRE)**[31] 2825 4-9-0 125 WilliamBuick 1 125
(Richard Fahey) *lw: prom in chsng gp: wnt 2nd 3f out: clsd and upsides ldr whn carried lft over 1f out: sn led and hung lft u.p ent fnl f: edging lft u.p but r.o wl ins fnl f: rdn out* **11/10**[1]
33-5 2 *1¼* **Mutakayyef**[87] 1378 6-9-0 120 JimCrowley 9 122
(William Haggas) *hld up in midfield: hdwy and trcking wnr through fr 3f out: effrt to chse wnr and edgd lft jst over 1f out: styd on u.p but no imp on wnr ins fnl f* **5/1**[2]
0213 3 *nk* **Deauville (IRE)**[23] 3108 4-9-0 114 (p) RyanMoore 6 121
(A P O'Brien, Ire) *prom in main gp: clsd on clr ldr over 2f out: chsd ldrs and rdn 2f out: clsd u.p to press ldng pair whn carried lft jst over 1f out: styd on but no imp on wnr ins fnl f* **12/1**
0-04 4 *1* **Spectre (FR)**[17] 3354 4-8-11 109 StephanePasquier 13 116
(M Munch, Germany) *leggy: hld up towards rr of main gp: hdwy over 2f out: rdn to chse ldng trio over 1f out: kpt on same pce ins fnl f* **50/1**
0-52 5 *3¼* **Kaspersky (IRE)**[20] 3218 6-9-0 110 MichellePayne 3 112
(Jane Chapple-Hyam) *lw: stdd s: hld up in last pair: effrt ent fnl 2f: rdn and hdwy on far side over 1f out: kpt on but no imp ins fnl f: nvr trbld ldrs* **66/1**
560- 6 *nk* **Dutch Connection**[227] 7837 5-9-0 116 JamesDoyle 2 111
(Charles Hills) *hld up in midfield: effrt jst over 2f out: hdwy u.p towards far side over 1f out: kpt on but no imp ins fnl f: nvr trbld ldrs* **25/1**
2063 7 *nk* **Cougar Mountain (IRE)**[44] 2440 6-9-0 112 (tp) DonnachaO'Brien 7 110
(A P O'Brien, Ire) *swtg: hld up in rr: rdn and hdwy jst over 2f out: swtchd lft and hdwy over 1f out: kpt on u.p ins fnl f: nvr threatened ldrs* **33/1**
1213 8 *1½* **Oh This Is Us (IRE)**[17] 3320 4-9-0 110 PatDobbs 15 107
(Richard Hannon) *hld up in last trio: swtchd rt and hdwy jst over 2f out: kpt on same pce u.p fnl f: nvr trbld ldrs* **33/1**
13-2 9 *hd* **Lightning Spear**[31] 2825 6-9-0 120 JamieSpencer 14 106
(David Simcock) *hld up towards rr: swtchd lft ent fnl 2f: sme hdwy u.p over 1f out: nvr getting on terms w ldrs and no imp ins fnl f* **11/2**[3]
3-32 10 *5* **Jallota**[10] 3587 6-9-0 112 SilvestreDeSousa 12 95
(Charles Hills) *hld up towards rr: rdn over 2f out: no imp u.p over 1f out: wknd ins fnl f* **40/1**

3- **11** 1 **American Patriot (USA)**$^{67}$ 1783 4-9-0 115..........(b) JohnRVelazquez 16 92
(Todd Pletcher, U.S.A) *str: lw: hld up in midfield: lost pl over 2f out: sn bhd and wl hld over 1f out* **20/1**

-104 **12** shd **Kool Kompany (IRE)**$^{17}$ 3320 5-9-0 114.............................. PatSmullen 8 92
(Richard Hannon) *hld up in midfield: effrt 3f out: struggling u.p and btn 2f out: wknd over 1f out* **50/1**

515- **13** ¾ **Miss Temple City (USA)**$^{198}$ 8216 5-8-11 114.............(t) EdgarSPrado 4 87
(H Graham Motion, U.S.A) *athletic: led main gp and chsd clr ldng pair tl over 2f out: sn rdn and lost pl: wl btn and eased fnl f* **20/1**

-450 **14** 1 **Toscanini (IRE)**$^{31}$ 2825 5-9-0 110.................................. PaulHanagan 10 88
(Richard Fahey) *swtg: led and set str gallop: rdn and edgd lft over 1f out: sn hdd and btn: fdd ins fnl f* **150/1**

1-42 **15** nk **Ennaadd**$^{48}$ 2290 4-9-0 113.......................................... AndreaAtzeni 11 88
(Roger Varian) *lw: prom in main gp: rdn and lost pl over 2f out: wknd over 1f out* **16/1**

1256 **16** 36 **Dutch Uncle**$^{55}$ 2086 5-9-0 88..........................................(p) MartinHarley 5 5
(Robert Cowell) *chsd ldr and clr of field: rdn 1/2-way: lost pl 3f out: bhd and eased fr wl over 1f out: t.o* **200/1**

1m 36.6s (-4.20) **Going Correction** -0.25s/f (Firm) **16** Ran SP% **121.5**
Speed ratings (Par 117): **111,109,109,108,105 104,104,103,102,97 96,96,96,95,94 58**
CSF £5.43 CT £48.63 TOTE £2.40: £1.60, £1.60, £3.00; EX 8.50 Trifecta £74.60.

**Owner** Godolphin **Bred** A Thompson & M O'Brien **Trained** Musley Bank, N Yorks

■ Stewards' Enquiry : Jim Crowley caution; careless riding

**FOCUS**
The running rail on the round course was 3yds out from its innermost position from approx 9f out to the home straight. The round course was watered on Sunday night, and the straight was watered on Monday, with watering finishing at 1pm Monday. It was a baking hot day and, following this opening race, the official going was changed from good to firm, good in places to just good to firm. The pace was strong, thanks to Toscanini and Dutch Uncle racing in a clear lead for much of the way, and the winner lowered the course record. The action unfolded middle to far side. The winner has been rated to his improved Lockinge figure, with the runner-up and fifth to form.

## 3925 COVENTRY STKS (GROUP 2) 6f
**3:05** (3:10) (Class 1) 2-Y-O

**£85,065** (£32,250; £16,140; £8,040; £4,035; £2,025) **Stalls** Centre

Form RPR

1 **1** **Rajasinghe (IRE)**$^{32}$ 2786 2-9-1 0.................................. StevieDonohoe 9 108
(Richard Spencer) *leggy: athletic: walked to post early: s.i.s and bmpd s: pushed along into midfield early: in tch w ldrs 1/2-way: effrt 2f out: led 1f out: r.o gamely* **11/1**

21 **2** hd **Headway**$^{24}$ 3066 2-9-1 0.................................................. PatCosgrave 13 107
(William Haggas) *str: lw: hld up: rdn and hdwy over 1f out: r.o and str chal wl ins fnl f: jst hld* **33/1**

**3** nk **Murillo (USA)**$^{26}$ 3015 2-9-1 0.............................................(t) RyanMoore 4 106
(A P O'Brien, Ire) *str: hld up: rdn and hdwy 2f out: r.o to press ldrs ins fnl f: jst hld* **8/1**$^{3}$

1 **4** nk **Brother Bear (IRE)**$^{24}$ 3098 2-9-1 0......................... ColmO'Donoghue 8 106
(Mrs John Harrington, Ire) *str: wnt lft leaving stalls: a.p: led 2f out: rdn and drifted lft over 1f out: sn hdd: rallied on nr side rail wl ins fnl f: r.o towards fin but hld* **4/1**$^{1}$

14 **5** ¾ **Aqabah (USA)**$^{24}$ 3098 2-9-1 0....................................(h$^{1}$) WilliamBuick 10 103
(Charlie Appleby) *tall: midfield: impr to go prom after 2f: rdn over 2f out: chalng 1f out: no ex fnl 50yds* **16/1**

1 **6** ½ **Prince Of The Dark**$^{25}$ 3025 2-9-1 0...........................(p$^{1}$) AdamKirby 18 102
(Clive Cox) *athletic: hld up: rdn 2f out: hdwy over 1f out: styd on ins fnl f: nt quite rch ldrs* **12/1**

**7** nk **Romanised (IRE)**$^{57}$ 2044 2-9-1 0...............................(t$^{1}$) ShaneFoley 17 101
(K J Condon, Ire) *w'like: s.i.s: in rr: rdn over 2f out: nt clr run over 1f out and swtchd rt: edgd lft ent fnl f: styd on: nt quite pce to chal* **12/1**

511 **8** ½ **De Bruyne Horse**$^{18}$ 3297 2-9-1 0.................................... SeanLevey 11 99
(Richard Hannon) *midfield: effrt and hdwy 2f out: chalng over 1f out: one pce fnl 75yds* **5/1**$^{2}$

1 **9** 1¼ **Nebo (IRE)**$^{32}$ 2779 2-9-1 0.............................................. JimCrowley 1 95
(Charles Hills) *cmpt: chsd ldrs: rdn 2f out: kpt on same pce fr over 1f out* **10/1**

1 **10** 1 **Chookie Dunedin**$^{27}$ 2948 2-9-1 0............................ DougieCostello 16 92+
(Keith Dalgleish) *cmpt: midfield: nt clr run over 2f out: sn swtchd rt: kpt on ins fnl f: nt pce to trble ldrs* **66/1**

11 **11** 1 **Denaar (IRE)**$^{31}$ 2826 2-9-1 0........................................... PatSmullen 12 89
(Richard Hannon) *led: rdn and hdd 2f out: wknd 1f out* **11/1**

**12** ½ **Arawak (USA)**$^{25}$ 2-9-1 0.....................................(bt) JohnRVelazquez 14 88
(Wesley A Ward, U.S.A) *tall: lengthy: prom: rdn 1/2-way: wknd over 1f out* **8/1**$^{3}$

1 **13** hd **Zaman**$^{24}$ 3093 2-9-1 0.................................................... JamesDoyle 7 87
(Charlie Appleby) *athletic: lw: midfield: rdn over 2f out: sn wknd* **20/1**

3 **14** 1 **U S Navy Flag (USA)**$^{24}$ 3098 2-9-1 0...............(t) SeamieHeffernan 5 84
(A P O'Brien, Ire) *lengthy: lw: hld up: rdn and swtchd rt whn hdwy over 2f out: chsd ldrs over 1f out: fdd ins fnl f* **33/1**

2 **15** hd **Connery (IRE)**$^{17}$ 3328 2-9-1 0........................................ MartinDwyer 15 83
(Sylvester Kirk) *w'like: chsd ldrs: rdn over 2f out: wknd over 1f out* **150/1**

41 **16** nk **Red Roman**$^{33}$ 2750 2-9-1 0................................ ChristopheSoumillon 3 82
(Charles Hills) *hld up: u.p 2f out: nvr able to trble ldrs* **33/1**

233 **17** 1 **Haddaf (IRE)**$^{26}$ 3010 2-9-1 0........................................ AndreaAtzeni 2 79
(James Tate) *prom: rdn 2f out: wknd over 1f out* **28/1**

0 **18** 14 **Ivy Leaguer**$^{8}$ 3668 2-9-1 0........................................ SilvestreDeSousa 6 36
(Brian Meehan) *unf: broke wl: racd keenly: handy tl wknd 2f out: lft bhd fnl f* **100/1**

1m 12.39s (-2.11) **Going Correction** -0.25s/f (Firm) 2y crse rec **18** Ran SP% **126.1**
Speed ratings (Par 105): **104,103,103,102,101 101,100,100,98,97 95,95,94,93,93 92,91,72**
CSF £352.57 CT £3166.99 TOTE £14.60: £4.30, £10.40, £2.90; EX 461.60 Trifecta £5760.30.

**Owner** Rebel Racing **Bred** James & Geoff Mulcahy **Trained** Newmarket, Suffolk

■ Stewards' Enquiry : William BuickM four-day ban; used his whip above the permitted level (4th-7th July)

**FOCUS**
Distance as advertised. Not the strongest edition of the race, with there being no stand-out performer, and there was a bit of a surprise result. Both the third and fourth had claims to being unfortunate. Predictably they raced centre-to-stands' side, with the winner coming down the middle, and with the ground so fast it was no surprise to see 2yo course record fall. It's been rated an ordinary renewal.

## 3926 KING'S STAND STKS (GROUP 1) (BRITISH CHAMPIONS SERIES AND GLOBAL SPRINT CHALLENGE) 5f
**3:40** (3:44) (Class 1) 3-Y-0+

**£226,840** (£86,000; £43,040; £21,440; £10,760; £5,400) **Stalls** Centre

Form RPR

13-1 **1** **Lady Aurelia (USA)**$^{66}$ 1813 3-8-9 121...................... JohnRVelazquez 18 124
(Wesley A Ward, U.S.A) *lw: ponied to s: trckd ldrs: wnt 2nd and moving rt 1/2-way: led wl over 1f out: sn rdn: qcknd and r.o strly fnl f: impressive* **7/2**$^{2}$

60-2 **2** 3 **Profitable (IRE)**$^{38}$ 2643 5-9-4 116.................................... JamesDoyle 1 118
(Clive Cox) *taken down early: hld up wl in tch in midfield: effrt and edgd lft over 1f out: chsd wnr 1f out: kpt on but nvr matching pce of wnr ins fnl f* **14/1**

21-1 **3** hd **Marsha (IRE)**$^{45}$ 2397 4-9-1 116............................................ LukeMorris 9 114
(Sir Mark Prescott Bt) *lw: hld up in tch in midfield: effrt 2f out: hdwy u.p to chse ldrs 1f out: kpt on wl ins fnl f but nvr threatening wnr* **11/4**$^{1}$

-101 **4** ½ **Muthmir (IRE)**$^{16}$ 3370 7-9-4 109.......................................(p) JimCrowley 2 116
(William Haggas) *swtg: hld up in tch in midfield: clsd 2f out: effrt ent fnl f: swtchd lft ins fnl f: kpt on wl fnl 100yds but no threat to wnr* **16/1**

60-0 **5** 1¼ **Take Cover**$^{24}$ 3079 10-9-4 111............................................ DavidAllan 11 111
(David C Griffiths) *taken down early and led to post: led tl hdd wl over 1f out: hung rt u.p over 1f out: lost 2nd 1f out: no ex and wknd ins fnl f* **66/1**

2-03 **6** shd **Alpha Delphini**$^{24}$ 3079 6-9-4 110...........................(v$^{1}$) ConnorBeasley 14 111
(Bryan Smart) *hld up in tch in midfield: effrt whn bmpd over 2f out: kpt on same pce u.p fnl f* **20/1**

0-00 **7** nk **Cotai Glory**$^{24}$ 3079 5-9-4 110.................................. SilvestreDeSousa 16 110
(Charles Hills) *taken down early: wl in tch in midfield: rdn and bmpd over 2f out: unable qck u.p over 1f out: kpt on same pce ins fnl f* **28/1**

45-1 **8** nk **Signs Of Blessing (IRE)**$^{38}$ 2643 6-9-4 118.......... StephanePasquier 13 109
(F Rohaut, France) *hld up in tch in midfield: swtchd lft and effrt wl over 1f out: sme hdwy u.p 1f out: no imp and one pce ins fnl f* **5/1**$^{3}$

5041 **9** 1½ **Final Venture**$^{11}$ 3539 5-9-4 110.......................................(h) PatDobbs 3 103
(Paul Midgley) *taken down early: chsd ldrs: rdn 2f out: no ex and jst getting outpcd whn squeezed for room and hmpd over 1f out: wknd ins fnl f* **40/1**

6-32 **10** 1¼ **Goldream**$^{24}$ 3079 8-9-4 111.........................................(p) MartinHarley 12 99
(Robert Cowell) *wl in tch in midfield: effrt 2f out: unable qck u.p over 1f out: wknd ins fnl f* **12/1**

10-2 **11** nk **Ardhoomey (IRE)**$^{37}$ 2657 5-9-4 111.................................(t) ColinKeane 5 98
(G M Lyons, Ire) *hld up in last quartet: effrt u.p over 1f out: swtchd rt and sme hdwy ent fnl f: nt clrest of runs and no imp ins fnl f: nvr trbld ldrs* **20/1**

-151 **12** nse **Priceless**$^{24}$ 3079 4-9-1 110.............................................. AdamKirby 7 95
(Clive Cox) *taken down early: chsd ldrs: unable qck u.p over 1f out: btn whn carried lft ins fnl f: wknd fnl 100yds* **11/1**

-330 **13** nse **Willytheconqueror (IRE)**$^{16}$ 3370 4-9-4 104................. MartinDwyer 4 97
(William Muir) *hld up in last quartet: effrt over 1f out: no imp fnl f: nvr trbld ldrs* **125/1**

4420 **14** 1¼ **Gracious John (IRE)**$^{45}$ 2397 4-9-4 107................................. JFEgan 10 93
(David Evans) *swtg: wl in tch in midfield: pushed along over 2f out: unable qck over 1f: wknd ins fnl f* **80/1**

-026 **15** 2¾ **Washington DC (IRE)**$^{24}$ 3079 4-9-4 111.....................(t) RyanMoore 17 83
(A P O'Brien, Ire) *lw: a towards rr: effrt over 1f out: no prog: n.d* **8/1**

1200 **16** ½ **Medicean Man**$^{87}$ 1376 11-9-4 109..............................(tp) AndreaAtzeni 15 81
(Jeremy Gask) *a in rr: n.d* **66/1**

0-00 **17** 25 **Just Glamorous (IRE)**$^{37}$ 2657 4-9-4 108................................. ShaneKelly 8
(Ronald Harris) *chsd ldr tl 1/2-way: sn lost pl: bhd and eased fnl f* **100/1**

57.45s (-3.05) **Going Correction** -0.25s/f (Firm)
**WFA** 3 from 4yo+ 6lb **17** Ran SP% **126.7**
Speed ratings (Par 117): **114,109,108,108,106 105,105,104,102,100 100,100,99,97,93 92,52**
CSF £49.96 CT £166.14 TOTE £3.00: £1.70, £4.50, £1.50; EX 51.30 Trifecta £229.80.

**Owner** Stonestreet Stables/G Bolton/P Leidel **Bred** Stonestreet Thoroughbred Holdings LLC **Trained** North America

■ Stewards' Enquiry : David Allan caution; careless riding
James Doyle caution; careless riding

**FOCUS**
A brilliant winner of the King's Stand. The runner-up has been rated to last year's winning figure in this race, with the fourth close to his best.

## 3927 ST JAMES'S PALACE STKS (GROUP 1) (BRITISH CHAMPIONS SERIES) (ENTIRE COLTS) 7f 213y(R)
**4:20** (4:23) (Class 1) 3-Y-O

**£226,840** (£86,000; £43,040; £21,440; £10,760; £5,400) **Stalls** Low

Form RPR

1-12 **1** **Barney Roy**$^{45}$ 2399 3-9-0 118........................................ JamesDoyle 4 122
(Richard Hannon) *lw: racd keenly: in tch: effrt over 2f out: edgd lft sn after: r.o to ld ent fnl f: in control nr fin* **5/2**$^{2}$

-445 **2** 1 **Lancaster Bomber (USA)**$^{24}$ 3100 3-9-0 117.......... DonnachaO'Brien 1 119
(A P O'Brien, Ire) *warm: led for nrly 2f: trckd ldr after: regained ld jst over 2f out: rdn and edgd rt over 1f out: hdd ent fnl f: r.o u.p: hld nr fin* **12/1**

11P2 **3** hd **Thunder Snow (IRE)**$^{24}$ 3100 3-9-0 118.........(p$^{1}$) ChristopheSoumillon 2 118
(Saeed bin Suroor) *trckd ldrs: swtchd lft 2f out: chalng fr over 1f out: nt pce of wnr wl ins fnl f: no ex fnl strides* **6/1**$^{3}$

1-11 **4** 3¼ **Churchill (IRE)**$^{24}$ 3100 3-9-0 123........................................ RyanMoore 5 111
(A P O'Brien, Ire) *swtg: hld up: pushed along over 2f out: sn wnt sltly lft: rdn to chse ldrs over 1f out but unable to chal: eased whn no imp and wl hld fnl 75yds* **1/2**$^{1}$

3-16 **5** 3½ **Forest Ranger (IRE)**$^{33}$ 2766 3-9-0 106.............................. TonyHamilton 6 103
(Richard Fahey) *hld up in rr: rdn over 1f out: kpt on u.p ins fnl f: no imp on ldrs* **33/1**

-230 **6** nk **Rivet (IRE)**$^{16}$ 3368 3-9-0 115........................................ AndreaAtzeni 7 102
(William Haggas) *chsd ldr: led after nrly 2f: rdn and hdd jst over 2f out: u.p and outpcd over 1f out: wknd ins fnl f* **16/1**

1204 **7** 2¼ **Mr Scaramanga**$^{18}$ 3302 3-9-0 100.................................. HarryBentley 3 97
(Simon Dow) *missed break: hld up towards rr: rdn over 2f out: hung rt over 1f out: one pce after* **66/1**

30-0 **8** *43* **Peace Envoy (FR)**[37] 2666 3-9-0 109....................(b[1]) SeamieHeffernan 8
(A P O'Brien, Ire) *lw: ref to settle whn towards rr on outer: rdn over 2f out: eased whn wl btn over 1f out* **33/1**

1m 37.22s (-3.48) **Going Correction** -0.125s/f (Firm) course record **8** Ran SP% **130.5**
Speed ratings (Par 113): **112,111,110,107,104 103,101,58**
CSF £36.19 CT £179.49 TOTE £3.90: £1.40, £2.90, £2.30; EX 41.00 Trifecta £150.50.
**Owner** Godolphin **Bred** Eliza Park International Pty Ltd **Trained** East Everleigh, Wilts
■ Stewards' Enquiry : James Doyle two-day ban; used whip above permitted level (Jul 4-5)

**FOCUS**
Distance increased by 5yds. They went a nice gallop, nothing mad, and yet still smashed the old course record by over a second. The story of the race was the underwhelming effort from red-hot favourite Churchill, who had beaten the first three home previously and clearly failed to give his running. The runner-up has been rated up a length on his Guineas form, and the third close to form.

## 3928 ASCOT STKS (A H'CAP) 2m 3f 210y
**5:00** (5:00) (Class 2) (0-100,100) 4-Y-O+
**£49,800** (£14,912; £7,456; £3,728; £1,864; £936) **Stalls** Low

Form RPR

211/ **1** **Thomas Hobson**[52] 7526 7-9-10 **100**.............................. RyanMoore 11 115+
(W P Mullins, Ire) *hld up in detached last trio: clsd onto bk of field 12f out: wl in tch but stl rr of ldng gp 3f out: swtchd lft: rdn and qcknd jst over 2f out: led over 1f out: r.o strly and stormed clr fnl f: v readily* **4/1**[1]

-132 **2** *6* **Endless Acres (IRE)**[32] 2788 4-9-4 **96**....................(v) StevieDonohoe 17 105
(Charlie Fellowes) *lw: prom: chsd ldr 3f out: ev ch u.p over 2f out: carried lft and unable qck over 1f out: chsd clr wnr and kpt on same pce fnl f* **10/1**

35-4 **3** *1 ¾* **Who Dares Wins (IRE)**[41] 2525 5-9-3 **93**................(p) TomMarquand 10 100
(Alan King) *racd keenly: chsd ldrs tl wnt 2nd 12f out: swtchd lft to ld and jostling w rival 4f out: hrd pressed and drvn over 2f out: hung lft over 1f out: sn hdd and outpcd by wnr: 3rd and kpt on same pce fnl f* **5/1**[2]

2-31 **4** *2 ½* **Rainbow Dreamer**[60] 1942 4-9-1 **93**.............................(v) AndreaAtzeni 7 98+
(Alan King) *lw: t.k.h: hld up towards rr of main gp: hdwy 7f out: nt clrest of run over 3f out: effrt to chse ldrs and swtchd rt 3f out: hung lft u.p and kpt on same pce fr over 1f out* **12/1**

-002 **5** *½* **Suegioo (FR)**[24] 3076 8-9-10 **100**................................(p) TonyHamilton 8 104
(Richard Fahey) *lw: hld up in detached last trio: clsd into bk of field 12f out: effrt on inner over 2f out: styd on ins fnl f: no ch w wnr* **25/1**

01-6 **6** *½* **Star Rider**[60] 1942 5-9-5 **95**...............................................(p) AdamKirby 2 99
(Hughie Morrison) *in tch in midfield: clsd 6f out: nt clr run and switching lft bnd over 2f out: styd on same pce fnl 2f* **20/1**

3-55 **7** *1 ¼* **Magic Circle (IRE)**[41] 2525 5-9-8 **98**..................... SilvestreDeSousa 20 101+
(Ralph Beckett) *in tch in midfield: hdwy to chse ldrs over 3f out: 3rd and pressing ldng pair u.p 2f out: sn no ex and btn over 1f out: wknd ins fnl f* **6/1**[3]

3231 **8** *5* **Yorkidding**[24] 3076 5-9-9 **99**...................................... RichardKingscote 6 97
(Mark Johnston) *lw: niggled along early: midfield: hdwy on inner 6th: 7th and wl in tch whn rdn 3f out: struggling and outpcd 2f out: wknd over 1f out* **14/1**

05/2 **9** *3 ½* **High Secret (IRE)**[24] 3073 6-9-0 **95**........................ MeganNicholls(5) 18 89
(Paul Nicholls) *warm: stdd and dropped in bhd after s: hld up in detached last trio: clsd onto bk of field 12f out: effrt over 2f out: sn rdn and no imp: wl hld whn swtchd rt over 1f out* **25/1**

0552 **10** *1* **Oceane (FR)**[39] 2562 5-9-4 **94**..................................(p) FergusSweeney 4 87
(Alan King) *hld up towards rr of main gp: effrt and swtchd lft over 3f out: no imp and outpcd over 2f out: wknd over 1f out* **20/1**

40- **11** *5* **Wolfcatcher (IRE)**[17] 3246 5-9-1 **91**...............................(tp) WilliamBuick 14 79
(Ian Williams) *hld up in midfield: hdwy 6f out: rdn to chse ldrs 3f out: bmpd over 2f out and sn struggling: edgd lft and wknd over 1f out* **33/1**

13-5 **12** *29* **Cleonte (IRE)**[45] 2398 4-9-8 **100**......................................... JimCrowley 5 59
(Andrew Balding) *warm: hld up towards rr of main gp: effrt 3f out: sn struggling and wknd jst over 2f out: eased fnl f: t.o* **33/1**

1-15 **13** *8* **Cartwright**[32] 2797 4-9-3 **95**...............................................(v[1]) LukeMorris 16 46
(Sir Mark Prescott Bt) *swtg: t.k.h: chsd ldrs: ev ch and jostling w rival 4f out: lost pl qckly over 2f out: eased over 1f out: t.o* **33/1**

30-0 **14** *13* **Shrewd**[66] 1802 7-9-5 **100**.............................................. CliffordLee(5) 12 38
(Iain Jardine) *swtg: hld up in midfield: hdwy 6f out: rdn and lost pl 3f out: wl bhd and eased over 1f out: t.o* **33/1**

46-5 **15** *9* **Moorside**[45] 2389 4-9-3 **95**................................................ PatSmullen 19 24
(Charles Hills) *t.k.h: chsd ldrs: rdn 4f out: sn lost pl: wl bhd and eased over 1f out: t.o* **50/1**

334/ **16** *20* **Beyond Conceit (IRE)**[74] 4873 8-9-2 **92**....................(h) JamieSpencer 3
(Nicky Henderson) *hld up in midfield: dropped to rr of ldng gp 4f out: sn wl btn and eased: t.o* **5/1**[2]

400/ **17** *117* **Iniciar (GER)**[287] 7-9-10 **100**......................................(b) DougieCostello 1
(David Pipe) *swtg: led: 6 l clr 6f out: hdd 4f out: sn dropped out and t.o whn virtually p.u fnl f* **66/1**

055- **18** *130* **Galizzi (USA)**[333] 4581 6-9-3 **93**...................................(t) DanielMuscutt 9
(Tim Vaughan) *chsd ldr for 8f: sn rdn and lost pl: t.o and virtually p.u fnl 5f* **50/1**

4m 17.62s (-7.18) **Going Correction** -0.125s/f (Firm)
**WFA** 4 from 5yo+ 1lb **18** Ran SP% **125.5**
Speed ratings (Par 109): **109,106,105,104,104 104,104,102,100,100 98,86,83,78,74 66, ,**
CSF £39.00 CT £212.90 TOTE £4.50: £1.60, £3.90, £1.60, £2.80; EX 56.90 Trifecta £351.70.
**Owner** Mrs S Ricci **Bred** Mount Coote Stud And M H Dixon **Trained** Muine Beag, Co Carlow

**FOCUS**
Add 11yds. The pace looked on from the start and nothing could live with the winner in the straight.

## 3929 WINDSOR CASTLE STKS (LISTED RACE) 5f
**5:35** (5:40) (Class 1) 2-Y-O
**£45,368** (£17,200; £8,608; £4,288; £2,152; £1,080) **Stalls** Centre

Form RPR

14 **1** **Sound And Silence**[26] 3010 2-9-3 0........................(p[1]) WilliamBuick 12 101
(Charlie Appleby) *midfield: hdwy 2f out: nosed ahd ins fnl f: sn edgd rt: r.o gamely and kpt finding nr fin* **16/1**

1 **2** *nk* **Roussel (IRE)**[21] 3169 2-9-3 0........................................... JamesDoyle 5 100
(Charlie Appleby) *prom: rdn to ld over 1f out:: hdd narrowly ins fnl f: rallied gamely: jst hld nr fin* **12/1**

3 **3** *1 ¼* **James Garfield (IRE)**[21] 3165 2-9-3 0............................. HarryBentley 4 95+
(George Scott) *str: s.i.s: midfield: rdn and hung rt fr 2f out: hdwy over 1f out: r.o ins fnl f: nt pce to chal front pair* **25/1**

2 **4** *¾* **Mokaatil**[24] 3083 2-9-3 0...................................................... JimCrowley 13 93
(Owen Burrows) *athletic: lw: s.i.s: hld up: swtchd rt and hdwy over 2f out: r.o u.p ins fnl f: no further prog towards fin* **25/1**

2U2 **5** *1* **Last Page**[25] 3025 2-9-3 0.......................................................(p[1]) JFEgan 18 89
(David Evans) *a.p: rdn to chal over 1f out: stl wl there ins fnl f: styd on same pce fnl 100yds* **66/1**

**6** *½* **Elizabeth Darcy (IRE)**[27] 2-8-12 0.................................(b) EdgarSPrado 2 82
(Wesley A Ward, U.S.A) *str: led: rdn and hdd over 1f out: stl ev ch ins fnl f: no ex fnl 100yds* **9/1**[3]

31 **7** *1 ¼* **Dragons Tail (IRE)**[40] 2556 2-9-3 0.......................... RichardKingscote 6 83
(Tom Dascombe) *chsd ldrs: n.m.r and lost pl over 2f out: outpcd over 1f out: rallied ins fnl f: r.o and gng on towards fin* **14/1**

1 **8** *nk* **Another Batt (IRE)**[13] 3460 2-9-3 0......................... SilvestreDeSousa 23 82
(George Scott) *w'like: midfield: rdn and hdwy over 2f out: styd on ins fnl f: nt rch ldrs* **9/1**[3]

112 **9** *½* **Corinthia Knight (IRE)**[48] 2286 2-9-3 0.............................. LukeMorris 20 80
(Archie Watson) *midfield: rdn and hdwy over 2f out: no imp over 1f out: styd on same pce ins fnl f* **33/1**

16 **10** *1 ¼* **Excellently Poised**[10] 3556 2-9-3 0............................. ConnorBeasley 1 75
(Bryan Smart) *w'like: chsd ldrs: rdn 2f out: fdd fnl 150yds* **66/1**

1 **11** *shd* **Marchingontogether**[42] 2502 2-8-12 0.......................... MartinHarley 10 70
(Ivan Furtado) *towards rr: rdn and outpcd 3f out: edgd rt and prog over 1f out: styd on ins fnl f: nrst fin* **33/1**

13 **12** *½* **Simmy's Copshop**[30] 2861 2-9-3 0............................. PaulHanagan 17 73
(Richard Fahey) *cmpt: in tch: rdn 2f out: unable qck wl over 1f out: styd on same pce ins fnl f* **25/1**

431 **13** *1* **Declarationoflove (IRE)**[43] 2473 2-9-3 0........................ PatCosgrave 21 70
(Tom Clover) *w'like: hld up: towards rr: sme hdwy u.p over 1f out: one pce fnl f: nvr able to trble ldrs* **66/1**

4 **14** *½* **T For Tango (IRE)**[30] 2861 2-9-3 0................................. PatSmullen 16 68
(J A Nash, Ire) *hld up: pushed along over 2f out: kpt on ins fnl f: nvr able to trble ldrs* **40/1**

35 **15** *¾* **Areen Faisal (IRE)**[10] 3556 2-9-3 0............................. TonyHamilton 24 65
(Richard Fahey) *lw: prom: outpcd 2f out: wknd fnl f* **66/1**

5323 **16** *nk* **Autumn Lodge**[22] 3156 2-9-3 0............................................. JohnFahy 22 64
(J S Moore) *s.i.s: in rr: u.p 2f out: nvr a threat* **200/1**

**17** *2 ½* **Nootka Sound (USA)**[54] 2-8-12 0.......................(b) JohnRVelazquez 11 50+
(Wesley A Ward, U.S.A) *str: restless in stalls: prom: rdn whn n.m.r and lost pl over 2f out: allowed to coast home whn wl btn ins fnl f* **9/2**[2]

061 **18** *nse* **Magnus (IRE)**[14] 3429 2-9-3 0........................................... AndreaAtzeni 19 55
(Tom Dascombe) *cmpt: towards rr: outpcd over 2f out: nvr a threat* **66/1**

603 **19** *1 ¼* **City Guest (IRE)**[11] 3516 2-9-3 0........................................ TomQueally 9 50
(George Margarson) *leggy: towards rr: rdn and outpcd over 2f out: nvr a threat* **100/1**

241 **20** *hd* **Dahik (IRE)**[18] 3277 2-9-3 0................................................ DaneO'Neill 15 50+
(Roger Varian) *hld up: rdn over 2f out: sn n.m.r and lost pl: n.d after* **40/1**

01 **21** *nk* **June Dog**[21] 3165 2-9-3 0...................................................... SeanLevey 8 49+
(Richard Hannon) *chsd ldrs: lost pl and n.m.r 3f out: nt clr run and swtchd rt whn bhd ins fnl f: sn eased* **66/1**

**22** *2 ¾* **Declarationofpeace (USA)**[41] 2529 2-9-3 0................(t) RyanMoore 14 39+
(A P O'Brien, Ire) *str: lw: hld up: sme hdwy ent fnl 2f: no imp on ldrs: eased whn n.d ins fnl f* **13/8**[1]

59.2s (-1.30) **Going Correction** -0.25s/f (Firm) **22** Ran SP% **129.3**
Speed ratings (Par 101): **100,99,97,96,94 93,91,91,90,88 88,87,86,85,84 83,79,79,77,77 76,72**
CSF £183.29 CT £4852.93 TOTE £19.50: £4.90, £3.20, £8.50; EX 208.10 Trifecta £6151.90.
**Owner** Godolphin **Bred** Godolphin **Trained** Newmarket, Suffolk

**FOCUS**
Strong Listed form, with a one-two for Godolphin, although the big gamble of the race dropped out to finish last of the 22 runners. It's been rated in line with the Coventry, with the fifth the key to the level.
T/Jkpt: Not Won. T/Plt: £585.60 to a £1 stake. Pool: £684,170.44 - 852.76 winning units T/Qpdt: £75.70 to a £1 stake. Pool: £34,775.57 - 339.94 winning units **Steve Payne & Darren Owen**

# 3555 BEVERLEY (R-H)
## Tuesday, June 20

**OFFICIAL GOING: Good to firm (watered; 8.0)**
Wind: Moderate behind Weather: Cloudy

## 3930 HORSE COMES FIRST NOVICE MEDIAN AUCTION STKS 7f 96y
**6:00** (6:02) (Class 5) 2-Y-O **£3,780** (£1,131; £565; £283; £141) **Stalls** Low

Form RPR

343 **1** **Ventura Knight (IRE)**[19] 3245 2-9-2 0.................................. JoeFanning 6 77+
(Mark Johnston) *sn led: pushed along and qcknd over 2f out: rdn clr over 1f out: kpt on strly* **15/8**[2]

**2** *4 ½* **Equidae** 2-9-2 0........................................................................ PhillipMakin 5 66
(James Tate) *trckd ldng pair: hdwy to chse wnr over 2f out: rdn along wl over 1f out: kpt on wl u.p fnl f* **8/1**

5 **3** *½* **Global Wealth**[10] 3591 2-9-2 0....................................... PaulMulrennan 4 65
(Ed Dunlop) *t.k.h early: hld up in tch: effrt on outer over 2f out and sn pushed along: rdn wl over 1f out: drvn and kpt on same pce fnl f* **7/4**[1]

05 **4** *1 ½* **Reinbeau Prince**[12] 3495 2-9-2 0....................................... JackGarritty 1 61
(Richard Fahey) *hld up in tch on inner: swtchd lft and pushed along 2f out: sn rdn and no imp fnl f* **33/1**

0 **5** *6* **Far Dawn**[32] 2786 2-9-2 0.................................................... GrahamLee 3 47
(Simon Crisford) *trckd wnr: pushed along 3f out: rdn over 2f out: sn drvn and wknd* **11/4**[3]

550 **6** *1 ½* **Highland Bobby**[22] 3149 2-8-13 0...................................... JoshDoyle(3) 2 43
(David O'Meara) *hld up: a rr* **16/1**

1m 33.87s (0.07) **Going Correction** -0.125s/f (Firm) **6** Ran SP% **117.7**
Speed ratings (Par 93): **94,88,88,86,79 78**
CSF £17.96 TOTE £2.80: £1.60, £2.70; EX 18.20 Trifecta £36.20.
**Owner** Middleham Park Racing XXXVII **Bred** L K I Bloodstock Ltd **Trained** Middleham Moor, N Yorks

**FOCUS**
Race distance increased by 7yds in races 1, 2, 4, 5 and 6. The going was good to firm prior to the opener, a moderate juvenile event in which the winner made all. The winner has been rated as improving slightly.

## 3931 HAPPY BIRTHDAY ROBERT MAXSTED MAIDEN FILLIES' STKS 7f 96y
**6:30** (6:30) (Class 5) 3-Y-O+ **£3,780** (£1,131; £565; £283) **Stalls** Low

Form RPR

0U-3 **1** **Harba (IRE)**[48] 2316 3-8-8 0.............................................. GeorgiaCox(5) 3 76
(William Haggas) *led: pushed along over 2f out: jnd and rdn over 1f out: drvn and hdd narrowly ins fnl f: rallied wl to ld again last 75 yds: hld on gamely* **7/4**[1]

0 **2** *nk* **Flourishing**[60] 1948 3-8-13 0 GrahamLee 4 75
(Sir Michael Stoute) *trckd wnr: hdwy over 2f out: chal over 1f out: sn rdn: tk narrow advantage ins fnl f: green and hdd last 75 yds: kpt on towards fin* **9/4**[2]

05 **3** *5* **New Delhi (IRE)**[19] 3259 3-8-13 0 JoeFanning 1 61
(Mark Johnston) *trckd ldng pair: pushed along and hdwy over 2f out: rdn along wl over 1f out: sn one pce* **13/2**[3]

**4** *1* **Waiting A Lot (IRE)** 3-8-13 0 PhillipMakin 2 58
(David O'Meara) *dwlt and green in rr: pushed along and sme hdwy over 2f out: sn rdn and n.d* **9/4**[2]

1m 32.51s (-1.29) **Going Correction** -0.125s/f (Firm) **4** Ran SP% **111.2**
Speed ratings (Par 100): **102,101,95,94**
CSF £6.15 TOTE £2.50; EX 5.10 Trifecta £14.70.
**Owner** Al Shaqab Racing **Bred** Summerville Bloodstock Investments **Trained** Newmarket, Suffolk

**FOCUS**
Race distance increased by 7yds. Not the most competitive maiden and they didn't go fast, allowing the winner to make all. The first fought it out and came clear. The level is fluid.

## 3932 BRITISH STALLION STUDS WEATHERBYS HAMILTON EBF CONDITIONS STKS 5f
**7:00** (7:02) (Class 3) 3-Y-O+ **£8,715** (£2,609; £1,304) **Stalls** Low

Form RPR
6511 **1** **Judicial (IRE)**[39] 2573 5-9-3 107 (e) JoeDoyle 2 110+
(Julie Camacho) *trckd ldng pair: effrt and nt clr run over 1f out: stdd and swtchd lft: rdn and qcknd wl to ld last 100 yds: sn clr* **1/2**[1]

4055 **2** *3 ¼* **Soie D'Leau**[11] 3539 5-9-0 94 (p[1]) JoeFanning 4 95
(Kristin Stubbs) *trckd ldr: hdwy and cl up 2f out: rdn to ld appr fnl f: hdd and no ex last 100 yds* **11/2**[3]

2-00 **3** *5* **Thesme**[24] 3079 5-8-9 103 TomEaves 5 72
(Nigel Tinkler) *led: jnd and rdn 2f out: hdd appr fnl f: sn wknd* **5/2**[2]

59.77s (-3.73) **Going Correction** -0.55s/f (Hard) course record **3** Ran SP% **110.6**
Speed ratings (Par 107): **107,101,93**
CSF £3.63 TOTE £1.30; EX 3.50 Trifecta £3.00.
**Owner** Elite Racing Club **Bred** Elite Racing Club **Trained** Norton, N Yorks

**FOCUS**
Just the three runners for this conditions sprint, but an impressive winner who broke the course record, set in this race 12 months ago. The winner has been rated to form.

## 3933 MORCO PRODUCTS 225TH ANNIVERSARY FILLIES' H'CAP 1m 4f 23y
**7:30** (7:30) (Class 4) (0-80,80) 3-Y-O+ **£5,040** (£1,508; £754) **Stalls** Low

Form RPR
41-4 **1** **Camerone (IRE)**[38] 2613 3-9-0 80 PhillipMakin 2 85
(Ralph Beckett) *trckd ldr: led briefly after 2f: sn hdd and cl up: chal over 2f out and sn rdn: drvn over 1f out: styd on ins fnl f to ld on line* **11/10**[2]

-225 **2** *shd* **High On Light**[123] 781 4-9-7 73 AndrewMullen 1 78
(David Barron) *led: hung lft at path and hdd briefly after 2f: sn led again: pushed along wl over 2f out: sn rdn: drvn appr fnl f: hdd nr line* **8/1**[3]

4112 **3** *11* **La Vie En Rose**[19] 3261 3-8-8 74 JoeFanning 3 68
(Mark Johnston) *trckd ldng pair: hdwy over 3f out: pushed along wl over 2f out: rdn wl over 1f out: sn btn* **1/1**[1]

2m 36.68s (-3.12) **Going Correction** -0.125s/f (Firm)
**WFA** 3 from 4yo 14lb **3** Ran SP% **108.7**
Speed ratings (Par 102): **105,104,97**
CSF £6.98 TOTE £2.50; EX 8.30 Trifecta £10.50.
**Owner** H H Sheikh Mohammed Bin Khalifa Al Thani **Bred** Al Shahania Stud **Trained** Kimpton, Hants
■ Stewards' Enquiry : Andrew Mullen four-day ban; used whip above permitted level (4th-7th July)

**FOCUS**
Race distance increased by 7yds. Just three runners for this fillies' handicap, but it provided a thrilling finish from the front two, who set a sound gallop. The runner-up has been rated back to form.

## 3934 KATHY GILLETT MEMORIAL H'CAP 1m 100y
**8:00** (8:01) (Class 5) (0-75,74) 3-Y-O+ **£3,780** (£1,131; £565; £283; £141) **Stalls** Low

Form RPR
-413 **1** **Alfred Richardson**[13] 3461 3-9-2 72 PhillipMakin 7 77+
(John Davies) *hld up in rr: hdwy wl over 2f out and sn pushed along: rdn to chse ldrs over 1f out: drvn and styd on strly fnl f to ld nr fin* **15/8**[1]

-040 **2** *½* **Yorkee Mo Sabee (IRE)**[29] 2888 4-9-13 73 JoeFanning 1 79
(Mark Johnston) *trckd ldng pair: hdwy to ld 2f out: rdn over 1f out: drvn ins fnl f: hdd and no ex towards fin* **7/2**[2]

-450 **3** *1 ¼* **George Reme (IRE)**[17] 3317 3-9-4 74 (v[1]) JasonHart 8 75
(John Quinn) *t.k.h: hld up: hdwy on inner to chse ldrs 2f out: nt clr run and swtchd lft over 1f out: sn rdn and kpt ion fnl f* **4/1**[3]

5004 **4** *hd* **Tellovoi (IRE)**[10] 3567 9-9-3 70 (h) WilliamCox[(7)] 4 73
(Richard Guest) *trckd ldrs: hdwy to chse ldng pair over 2f out: rdn wl over 1f out: drvn appr fnl f: kpt on same pce* **12/1**

1302 **5** *1 ¾* **Make On Madam (IRE)**[20] 3203 5-9-5 70 RowanScott[(5)] 5 69
(Les Eyre) *t.k.h: trckd ldrs on outer: rdn along 2f out: sn drvn and kpt on one pce* **5/1**

0-03 **6** *3* **Marbooh (IRE)**[22] 3140 4-10-0 74 (t) DavidNolan 6 66
(David O'Meara) *led: pushed along 3f out: rdn and hdd 2f out: sn drvn and grad wknd* **14/1**

-500 **7** *6* **Beadlam (IRE)**[14] 3432 4-8-12 58 (b[1]) PJMcDonald 2 36
(Roger Fell) *t.k.h: prom: rdn along over 2f out: drvn over 1f out: grad wknd* **9/1**

0-00 **8** *1 ¾* **Dylan's Storm (IRE)**[1] 3912 5-8-11 57 (p) AndrewMullen 3 31
(Peter Niven) *towards rr: rdn along 3f out: sn drvn and outpcd* **50/1**

1m 46.19s (-1.41) **Going Correction** -0.125s/f (Firm)
**WFA** 3 from 4yo+ 10lb **8** Ran SP% **120.0**
Speed ratings (Par 103): **102,101,100,100,98 95,89,87**
CSF £9.12 CT £24.25 TOTE £2.60: £1.30, £1.70, £1.50; EX 12.10 Trifecta £43.90.
**Owner** K Kirkup & J Davies **Bred** J J Davies & K Kirkup **Trained** Piercebridge, Durham

**FOCUS**
Race distance increased by 7yds. A modest handicap and they didn't go fast, though it didn't prevent the favourite coming from last place. The runner-up helps set the standard.

## 3935 RACING UK H'CAP 1m 1f 207y
**8:30** (8:32) (Class 6) (0-65,66) 4-Y-O+ **£2,587** (£770; £384; £192) **Stalls** Low

Form RPR
-215 **1** **Bit Of A Quirke**[27] 2953 4-9-7 63 JasonHart 10 70
(Mark Walford) *trckd ldr: hdwy and cl up over 2f out: rdn to ld wl over 1f out: drvn ins fnl f: kpt on wl* **11/4**[1]

2-01 **2** *1* **Bromance**[20] 3205 4-9-4 60 (p) JoeFanning 12 65
(Peter Niven) *hld up in rr: stdy hdwy on outer over 4f out: chsd ldrs 2f out: rdn over 1f out: drvn and ev ch ins fnl f: kpt on* **10/3**[2]

0520 **3** *shd* **All You (IRE)**[10] 3560 5-9-10 66 (v) PhillipMakin 13 71
(David O'Meara) *in tch: hdwy over 2f out: chsd ldrs and n.m.r jst over 1f out: swtchd rt and rdn ins fnl f: kpt on wl towards fin* **14/1**

-305 **4** *1 ¼* **Lean On Pete (IRE)**[20] 3205 8-9-2 58 AndrewMullen 11 61
(Ollie Pears) *prom on outer: swtchd rt to inner and effrt 2f out: sn rdn along: drvn and ev ch ent fnl f: no ex last 50 yds styd on and ev ch ins fnl f: drvn and no ex last 50 yds* **12/1**

-021 **5** *¾* **Diamond Runner (IRE)**[5] 3761 5-9-1 57 6ex (b) PaulMulrennan 1 59
(Lawrence Mullaney) *hld up in rr: hdwy over 2f out: rdn and n.m.r over 1f out: drvn and styd on fnl f* **4/1**[3]

42-0 **6** *nse* **Judicious**[51] 2183 10-9-0 56 SamJames 8 57
(Geoffrey Harker) *trckd ldrs: hdwy over 3f out: rdn 2f out: drvn over 1f out: sn n.m.r and kpt on same pce* **12/1**

-030 **7** *hd* **Bahamian C**[25] 3036 6-9-2 61 (t) AdamMcNamara[(3)] 4 62
(Richard Fahey) *dwlt: t.k.h in rr: hdwy over 2f out: rdn to chse ldrs over 1f out: drvn and kpt on fnl f* **12/1**

-565 **8** *nse* **King Of The Celts (IRE)**[10] 3559 9-9-4 63 (p[1]) RachelRichardson[(3)] 2 65
(Tim Easterby) *in tch on inner: hdwy over 2f out: rdn along and nt clr run over 1f out: no imp* **12/1**

6030 **9** *1 ½* **I'm Super Too (IRE)**[6] 3708 10-8-7 54 (p) GemmaTutty[(5)] 3 52
(Karen Tutty) *t.k.h: hld up towards rr: hdwy 2f out: n.m.r over 1f out: sn rdn and n.d* **20/1**

0-60 **10** *¾* **Great Return**[24] 3062 4-9-0 63 JordanUys[(7)] 7 59
(Lisa Williamson) *trckd ldrs: pushed along over 2f out: sn rdn and wknd* **33/1**

6/40 **11** *¾* **Tin Pan Alley**[20] 3205 9-9-6 62 DavidNolan 5 57
(David C Griffiths) *sn led: rdn along and jnd over 2f out: drvn and hdd wl over 1f out: sn wknd* **18/1**

-604 **12** *1 ½* **Rockliffe**[12] 3501 4-9-0 56 PJMcDonald 14 48
(Micky Hammond) *in tch: hdwy to chse ldrs 3f out: rdn along over 2f out: drvn wl over 1f out: sn wknd* **50/1**

0000 **13** *1 ¼* **Cookie Ring (IRE)**[17] 3344 6-8-7 49 (b) JoeDoyle 9 39
(Patrick Holmes) *stmbld and dwlt s: a bhd* **50/1**

2m 6.26s (-0.74) **Going Correction** -0.125s/f (Firm) **13** Ran SP% **124.1**
Speed ratings (Par 101): **97,96,96,95,94 94,94,94,93,92 91,90,89**
CSF £11.74 CT £112.86 TOTE £4.00: £1.70, £1.60, £4.40; EX 14.90 Trifecta £157.30.
**Owner** A Quirke **Bred** Dr A Gillespie **Trained** Sherriff Hutton, N Yorks

**FOCUS**
Race distance increased by 7yds. An open handicap featuring a couple of recent winners, but they didn't go fast and finished in a heap.
T/Plt: £46.80 to a £1 stake. Pool: £40,069.05 - 624.75 winning units T/Qpdt: £11.60 to a £1 stake. Pool: £3,732.64 - 238.03 winning units **Joe Rowntree**

# 3655 BRIGHTON (L-H)
### Tuesday, June 20

**OFFICIAL GOING: Good to firm (good in places; watered; 8.4)**
Wind: light 1/2 against Weather: fine and sunny, very warm

## 3936 IRISH STALLION FARMS EBF MAIDEN STKS 5f 215y
**5:40** (5:43) (Class 5) 2-Y-O **£3,881** (£1,155; £577; £288) **Stalls** Centre

Form RPR
432 **1** **Alaska (IRE)**[8] 3655 2-9-0 0 MitchGodwin[(5)] 5 72
(Sylvester Kirk) *trckd ldrs: effrt 2f out: led 1f out: hung lft: drvn out* **1/1**[1]

U **2** *¾* **Rivas Rob Roy**[10] 3570 2-9-2 0 HectorCrouch[(3)] 2 70
(John Gallagher) *outpcd and drvn 4f out: hdwy over 2f out: swtchd rt 1f out: styd on wl to take 2nd last 50yds* **9/1**

0320 **3** *1 ¾* **Poignant**[8] 3648 2-9-5 0 RobertWinston 3 65
(Archie Watson) *led: drvn over 2f out: hdd 1f out: keeppuing on same pce whn n.m.r on inner 100yds out* **9/2**[3]

3 **4** *½* **Ursus Belle (IRE)**[18] 3277 2-9-0 0 KieranO'Neill 4 57
(Richard Hannon) *chsd ldrs: effrt over 2f out: styd on fnl 100yds* **4/1**[2]

025 **5** *1* **Dragon's Teeth (IRE)**[12] 3490 2-8-12 0 FinleyMarsh[(7)] 6 59
(Jo Hughes) *chsd ldrs: one pce fnl f* **16/1**

**6** *2 ¼* **Prime Chief (IRE)** 2-9-5 0 LiamKeniry 7 52
(George Baker) *dwlt: hdwy to chse ldrs 4f out: wknd 1f out* **8/1**

1m 10.28s (0.08) **Going Correction** -0.175s/f (Firm) **6** Ran SP% **115.2**
Speed ratings (Par 93): **92,91,88,88,86 83**
CSF £11.63 TOTE £1.70: £1.10, £5.20; EX 15.40 Trifecta £52.40.
**Owner** John Wardley & Neil Simpson **Bred** Tally-Ho Stud **Trained** Upper Lambourn, Berks

**FOCUS**
Rail movements increased the race distance by 6yds. Two stood out on RPR ratings in this ordinary juvenile maiden and they dominated the race until late on, when the runner-up split them. The winner has been rated to his slightly revised pre-race level.

## 3937 LABYRINTH CHALLENGE 18 AUG H'CAP 6f 210y
**6:10** (6:10) (Class 6) (0-65,66) 3-Y-O **£2,264** (£673; £336; £168) **Stalls** Centre

Form RPR
-606 **1** **Moonstone Rock**[8] 3656 3-8-13 60 (b[1]) CharlieBennett[(3)] 6 63
(Jim Boyle) *s.i.s: sn wl in tch: hdwy on outer over 2f out: styd on fnl 150yds: led post* **20/1**

-236 **2** *hd* **Still Waiting**[32] 2794 3-9-5 63 CharlesBishop 4 65
(William Jarvis) *s.i.s: sn chsng ldrs: led narrowly last 75yds: hdd post* **13/2**

501 **3** *shd* **Beepeecee**[7] 3695 3-9-1 66 6ex (p) FinleyMarsh[(7)] 2 68
(Richard Hughes) *trckd ldrs: t.k.h: drvn over 2f out: styd on wl last 150yds: jst denied* **11/4**[2]

-300 **4** *1 ¼* **Al Mansor (IRE)**[32] 2794 3-9-8 66 TimmyMurphy 5 65
(Richard Hannon) *w ldr: led after 1f: hdd 1f out: wknd clsng stages* **4/1**[3]

5644 **5** *1 ½* **Whiteley (IRE)**[8] 3656 3-9-4 62 GavinLerena 3 58
(Mick Channon) *led 1f: chsd ldrs: hdwy on inner to ld 1f out: hdd & wknd last 75yds* **6/1**

-211 **6** *2 ½* **Pass The Cristal (IRE)**[10] 3561 3-9-7 65 DavidProbert 1 53
(William Muir) *hld up wl in tch: hdwy to chse ldrs over 2f out: wknd 1f out: eased clsng stages* **2/1**[1]

1m 23.1s **Going Correction** -0.175s/f (Firm) **6** Ran SP% **112.4**
Speed ratings (Par 97): **93,92,92,91,89 86**
CSF £136.06 TOTE £25.90: £7.70, £3.00; EX 126.20 Trifecta £569.90.
**Owner** Inside Track Racing Club **Bred** Sean Gollogly **Trained** Epsom, Surrey



The Form Book Flat, Raceform Ltd, Newbury, RG14 5SJ

**FOCUS**
Rail movements increased the race distance by 6yds. A modest but competitive looking 3yo handicap that produced a terrific three-way finish. The winner has been rated back to his 2yo form.

## 3938 CELEBRATING 21 YEARS OF GEO-ENVIRONMENTAL H'CAP 6f 210y
**6:40** (6:40) (Class 4) (0-80,78) 4-Y-O+ **£4,690** (£1,395; £697; £348) **Stalls** Centre

Form RPR
352 **1** **Honiara**$^{116}$ 896 4-9-7 **78**....................(b) DavidProbert 2 83
(Paul Cole) *led: edgd rt over 1f out: edgd lft last 75yds: all out* **13/8**$^{2}$
-465 **2** *nk* **Fast Dancer (IRE)**$^{24}$ 3065 5-9-6 **77**....................(v$^{1}$) RobertWinston 1 83+
(Joseph Tuite) *detached in last: outpcd 4f out: hdwy over 2f out: hug lft over 1f out: chsng ldrs whn rdr dropped whip 100yds out: swtchd lft and squeezed through: jst hld* **6/4**$^{1}$
321 **3** *½* **Black Caesar (IRE)**$^{11}$ 3518 6-9-1 **72**.................... LiamKeniry 3 75
(Philip Hide) *trckd ldrs: drvn over 2f out: no ex fnl 50yds* **9/2**$^{3}$
-000 **4** *2* **Good Luck Charm**$^{13}$ 3454 8-8-10 **70**....................(b) HectorCrouch$^{(3)}$ 4 72
(Gary Moore) *sn chsng ldrs: swtchd ins appr fnl f: almost upsides and keeping on whn bdly hmpd and eased nr fin* **6/1**

1m 20.78s (-2.32) **Going Correction** -0.175s/f (Firm) **4** Ran SP% **110.6**
Speed ratings (Par 105): **106,105,105,102**
CSF £4.56 TOTE £1.90; EX 4.70 Trifecta £5.30.
**Owner** Meyrick Wright Asprey PJL Racing Wilcock **Bred** Scea Haras De Saint Pair **Trained** Whatcombe, Oxon

**FOCUS**
Rail movements increased the race distance by 6yds. The feature race and a tightly knit contest despite the small field. The time was 2.22 secs faster than the preceding contest and produced a desperate finish.

## 3939 GESL.NET H'CAP 1m 1f 207y
**7:10** (7:11) (Class 6) (0-60,61) 3-Y-O **£2,264** (£673; £336; £168) **Stalls** High

Form RPR
0-62 **1** **Let's Be Happy (IRE)**$^{17}$ 3326 3-9-8 **61**....................(p$^{1}$) ShaneKelly 8 67
(Richard Hughes) *sn chsng ldrs: chal over 3f out: styd on wl fnl f: led nr fin* **3/1**$^{2}$
0-05 **2** *½* **Niseko**$^{15}$ 3393 3-9-8 **61**....................(b) RobHornby 1 66
(William Muir) *led: hung lft over 1f out: wknd and hdd nr fin* **14/1**
-634 **3** *½* **Zamadance**$^{12}$ 3489 3-9-7 **60**.................... DavidProbert 3 64
(Ed Dunlop) *trckd ldrs: t.k.h: kpt on fnl 100yds* **4/1**$^{3}$
0 **4** *4 ½* **Performance Art (IRE)**$^{33}$ 2759 3-8-11 **50**.................... SteveDrowne 7 46
(Seamus Mullins) *mid-div: drvn 5f out: outpcd over 2f out: kpt on fnl f* **33/1**
00-0 **5** *½* **Dragonite (IRE)**$^{162}$ 149 3-8-7 **49**.................... CharlieBennett$^{(3)}$ 5 44
(Daniel Mark Loughnane) *dwlt: hld up towards rr: t.k.h: effrt 3f out: kpt on fnl f* **16/1**
0054 **6** *3 ¾* **Chunkyfunkymonkey**$^{11}$ 3531 3-9-4 **57**.................... RobertWinston 6 44
(John Ryan) *hld up in rr: hdwy over 3f out: hmpd over 2f out: drvn and no imp over 1f out: eased clsng stages* **9/4**$^{1}$
-304 **7** *nk* **Mystical Nelly**$^{19}$ 3250 3-9-0 **56**.................... GeorgeWood$^{(3)}$ 2 43
(Jonathan Portman) *trckd ldrs: drvn over 2f out: wknd over 1f out* **8/1**
0004 **8** *15* **Greyjoy (IRE)**$^{8}$ 3657 3-8-3 **47**.................... MitchGodwin$^{(5)}$ 4 5
(Sylvester Kirk) *mid-div: hdwy over 5f out: lost pl over 1f out: heavily eased last 100yds* **6/1**

2m 2.11s (-1.49) **Going Correction** -0.175s/f (Firm) **8** Ran SP% **116.7**
Speed ratings (Par 97): **98,97,97,93,93 90,89,77**
CSF £44.40 CT £171.63 TOTE £3.70: £1.40, £3.80, £1.60; EX 43.70 Trifecta £128.90.
**Owner** Catch The Pigeon Syndicate **Bred** Cbs Bloodstock & John O' Connor **Trained** Upper Lambourn, Berks

**FOCUS**
Rail movements increased the race distance by 6yds. This moderate 3yo handicap is often won by an improver and that might be the case again. The early pace was modest and very few got into the race.

## 3940 LOVE FAIRS ANTIQUES 27 AUG H'CAP 7f 211y
**7:40** (7:40) (Class 6) (0-60,60) 4-Y-O+ **£2,264** (£673; £336; £168) **Stalls** Centre

Form RPR
5531 **1** **Lunar Deity**$^{6}$ 3731 8-8-13 **59**....................(t) MillyNaseb$^{(7)}$ 3 69+
(Stuart Williams) *trckd ldrs: 2nd over 1f out: rdn to ld last 100yds: styd on wl* **4/9**$^{1}$
**2** *2 ½* **Take A Drop (IRE)**$^{137}$ 562 4-8-7 **46** oh1....................(h$^{1}$) KieranO'Neill 7 50
(Seamus Mullins) *wnt lft s: led after 1f: hdd and no ex last 100yds* **25/1**
5000 **3** *7* **Frap**$^{7}$ 3688 4-8-9 **48**....................(b$^{1}$) ShaneKelly 1 36
(Ian Williams) *reminders after s: led 1f: chsd ldrs: edgd rt and one pce fnl 2f* **14/1**
5-00 **4** *2 ½* **Waggle (IRE)**$^{22}$ 3137 4-8-7 **46** oh1....................(b$^{1}$) AdamBeschizza 5 28
(Michael Wigham) *hld up towards rr: effrt over 3f out: one pce fnl 2f* **12/1**$^{3}$
0441 **5** *6* **Live Dangerously**$^{11}$ 3522 7-9-2 **55**.................... WilliamCarson 6 23
(John Bridger) *hld up towards rr: t.k.h: effrt on outer over 3f out: lost pl over 1f out: eased clsng stages* **4/1**$^{2}$
0000 **6** *3* **Tamarin**$^{6}$ 3717 5-8-3 **46** oh1 ow3....................(p) FinleyMarsh$^{(7)}$ 4 10
(Lisa Williamson) *hmpd s: sn trcking ldrs: t.k.h: drvn over 3f out: lost pl over 1f out* **50/1**

1m 33.83s (-2.17) **Going Correction** -0.175s/f (Firm) **6** Ran SP% **109.4**
Speed ratings (Par 101): **103,100,93,91,85 82**
CSF £13.70 CT £63.98 TOTE £1.40: £1.10, £8.80; EX 10.60 Trifecta £59.10.
**Owner** W E Enticknap & Partner **Bred** Hermes Services Ltd **Trained** Newmarket, Suffolk

**FOCUS**
Rail movements increased the race distance by 6yds. A low-grade mile handicap that was a match according to the betting, but the favourite won decisively. It's been rated tentatively around the runner-up's better Irish figures.

## 3941 THE HUMAN LEAGUE 8 SEPT H'CAP 5f 215y
**8:10** (8:10) (Class 5) (0-70,77) 3-Y-O+ **£2,911** (£866; £432; £216) **Stalls** Centre

Form RPR
4636 **1** **Jersey Breeze (IRE)**$^{18}$ 3307 4-10-0 **70**....................(v$^{1}$) GavinLerena 2 78
(Mick Channon) *sn led: hdd narrowly 100yds out: kpt on to regain ld clsng stages* **4/1**$^{3}$
223 **2** *¾* **Pushkin Museum (IRE)**$^{19}$ 3257 6-9-11 **67**.................... ShaneKelly 5 72
(Patrick Morris) *led early: trckd ldrs: hung lft and led narrowly 100yds out: hdd and no ex clsng stages* **8/1**
2260 **3** *1 ¾* **Noble Deed**$^{11}$ 3522 7-9-0 **56**....................(p) KierenFox 6 56
(Michael Attwater) *chsd ldrs: drvn over 2f out: kpt on fnl f* **10/1**
0331 **4** *¾* **Swiss Cross**$^{9}$ 3957 10-10-0 **77** 6ex....................(tp) FinleyMarsh$^{(7)}$ 4 74
(Phil McEntee) *in rr: effrt over 2f out: sn outpcd kpt on fnl 100yds* **4/1**$^{3}$
4036 **5** *¾* **Baby Gal**$^{19}$ 3246 3-8-10 **62**.................... CharlieBennett$^{(3)}$ 1 55
(Jim Boyle) *trckd ldrs: upsides over 1f out: fdd last 100yds* **3/1**$^{2}$
3246 **6** *1 ½* **Gold Club**$^{24}$ 3074 6-10-2 **72**....................(p) MartinLane 3 62
(Tom Clover) *hld up in rr: drvn over 2f out: chsng ldrs over 1f out: wknd last 150yds* **11/4**$^{1}$

1m 8.88s (-1.32) **Going Correction** -0.175s/f (Firm)
**WFA** 3 from 4yo+ 7lb **6** Ran SP% **111.9**
Speed ratings (Par 103): **101,100,97,96,95 93**
CSF £33.59 TOTE £5.30: £3.30, £2.60; EX 38.40 Trifecta £158.00.
**Owner** Mrs Susan Bunney **Bred** Guy O'Callaghan **Trained** West Ilsley, Berks

**FOCUS**
Rail movements increased the race distance by 6yds. This ordinary sprint handicap was run 1.40 secs faster than the earlier juvenile contest. The runner-up has been rated to this year's AW form.

## 3942 HACIENDA CLASSICAL 9 SEPT H'CAP 5f 60y
**8:40** (8:40) (Class 6) (0-60,56) 3-Y-O+ **£2,264** (£673; £336; £168) **Stalls** Centre

Form RPR
0203 **1** **Camino**$^{46}$ 2370 4-8-13 **45**.................... MartinLane 6 50
(Andi Brown) *dwlt: in rr: hdwy over 2f out: upsides last 100yds: kpt on to ld nr fin* **4/1**$^{3}$
5040 **2** *nk* **Archie Stevens**$^{21}$ 3186 7-9-5 **56**.................... PaddyPilley$^{(5)}$ 2 60
(Clare Ellam) *led: drvn over 2f out: jnd last 100yds: hdd nr fin* **8/1**
0050 **3** *1 ¼* **Rat Catcher (IRE)**$^{11}$ 3544 7-8-13 **45**....................(b) RobHornby 3 44
(Lisa Williamson) *chsd ldrs: drvn over 2f out: kpt on same pce fnl f* **20/1**
0050 **4** *½* **Ask The Guru**$^{88}$ 1340 7-9-4 **50**....................(p) KierenFox 1 48
(Michael Attwater) *mid-div: drvn over 2f out: one pce over 1f out* **7/2**$^{2}$
0-05 **5** *hd* **Ginger Truffle**$^{146}$ 397 3-8-13 **51**.................... KieranO'Neill 4 46
(Brett Johnson) *t.k.h in rr: hdwy 2f out: kpt on same pce fnl f* **5/1**
0032 **6** *½* **Deer Song**$^{26}$ 3008 4-9-10 **56**.................... WilliamCarson 5 51
(John Bridger) *sn chsng ldr: drvn over 2f out: wknd last 100yds* **7/4**$^{1}$

1m 1.63s (-0.67) **Going Correction** -0.175s/f (Firm)
**WFA** 3 from 4yo+ 6lb **6** Ran SP% **111.1**
Speed ratings (Par 101): **98,97,95,94,94 93**
CSF £33.14 TOTE £5.70: £2.50, £3.10; EX 35.40 Trifecta £198.30.
**Owner** In For A Penny In For A Pound **Bred** D R Tucker **Trained** Newmarket, Suffolk

**FOCUS**
Rail movements increased the race distance by 6yds. Another moderate sprint handicap but another close finish and the field finished in a bunch.
T/Plt: £540.30 to a £1 stake. Pool: £44,371.32 - 59.95 winning units T/Qpdt: £29.90 to a £1 stake. Pool: £4,106.60 - 101.38 winning units **Walter Glynn**

# 3398 THIRSK (L-H)
Tuesday, June 20

**OFFICIAL GOING: Good to firm (watered; 8.5)**
Wind: Breezy, half against in home straight in sprints and in 3f of home straight on round course Weather: Overcast

## 3943 BRITISH STALLION STUDS EBF FILLIES' NOVICE STKS (PLUS 10 RACE) 6f
**2:10** (2:11) (Class 5) 2-Y-O **£3,557** (£1,058; £529; £264) **Stalls** Centre

Form RPR
45 **1** **Silca Mistress**$^{17}$ 3312 2-9-0 0.................... GrahamLee 1 70+
(Mick Channon) *w ldrs: led over 1f out: pushed along and edgd lft over 1f out: kpt on strly fnl f* **11/4**$^{1}$
**2** *1 ¾* **Elysee Star** 2-8-9 0.................... RobJFitzpatrick$^{(5)}$ 5 64
(Ben Haslam) *prom: hdwy and ev ch over 1f out: kpt on fnl f: nt rch wnr* **66/1**
**3** *¾* **Porrima (IRE)** 2-9-0 0.................... CamHardie 7 62+
(Ben Haslam) *missed break: hld up: shkn up and hdwy over 1f out: kpt on fnl f: nrst fin* **33/1**
**4** *nse* **Poppy Walton (IRE)** 2-9-0 0.................... AndrewMullen 2 62
(Ollie Pears) *green in preliminaries: led: rdn and hdd over 2f out: rallied: kpt on same pce ins fnl f* **40/1**
**5** *shd* **Javelin** 2-9-0 0.................... DavidNolan 10 62+
(Richard Fahey) *hld up bhd ldng gp: effrt and pushed along over 1f out: kpt on same pce ins fnl f* **11/4**$^{1}$
**6** *nk* **Mecca's Spirit (IRE)** 2-9-0 0.................... PaulMulrennan 6 61+
(Michael Dods) *trckd ldrs: effrt and pushed along over 1f out: kpt on same pce ins fnl f* **7/2**$^{2}$
**7** *nk* **Bibbidibobbidiboo (IRE)** 2-9-0 0.................... JoeyHaynes 8 60+
(Ann Duffield) *hld up: shkn up and hdwy over 1f ou: kpt on fnl f: nvr able to chal* **16/1**
6 **8** *4* **Brough Lane Lass (IRE)**$^{17}$ 3339 2-8-9 0.................... PhilDennis$^{(5)}$ 3 47
(John Weymes) *in tch: pushed along over 2f out: wknd over 1f out* **100/1**
**9** *2 ¼* **Hermana Santa (IRE)** 2-9-0 0.................... TomEaves 11 40
(David Barron) *hld up in tch: effrt over 2f out: wknd wl over 1f out* **9/1**
**10** *4* **Sovereign Katie (IRE)** 2-9-0 0.................... JoeDoyle 9 27
(Ollie Pears) *t.k.h early: w ldrs to over 2f out: sn lost pl and struggling* **33/1**
**11** *2 ¼* **Lady Grand** 2-9-0 0.................... JackGarritty 4 20
(Richard Fahey) *wnt bdly lft s: bhd and green: struggling over 2f out: sn btn* **6/1**$^{3}$

1m 14.32s (1.62) **Going Correction** +0.25s/f (Good) **11** Ran SP% **116.5**
Speed ratings (Par 90): **99,96,95,95,95 95,94,89,86,81 78**
CSF £209.46 TOTE £3.70: £1.60, £16.40, £7.00; EX 177.00 Trifecta £4392.60 Part won..
**Owner** Aldridge Racing Partnership **Bred** Aldridge Racing Partnership **Trained** West Ilsley, Berks

**FOCUS**
The rails had been moved altering race distances as follows: Races 3, 6 and 7 add 10 yards; Race 5 add 30 yards. An ordinary juvenile fillies' novice contest. They went an, at best, respectable gallop on seemingly heavily watered ground, officially described as good to firm, good in places. Ordinary form.

## 3944 BOOK TICKETS ONLINE THIRSKRACECOURSE.NET FOR DISCOUNT H'CAP 5f
**2:45** (2:46) (Class 6) (0-65,66) 3-Y-O+ **£3,408** (£1,006; £503) **Stalls** Centre

Form RPR
25-5 **1** **Eternalist**$^{64}$ 1828 4-9-0 **56**....................(h) SeanMooney$^{(7)}$ 10 64
(Jim Goldie) *t.k.h: mde all: rdn and edgd lft over 1f out: hld on wl fnl f* **17/2**
-460 **2** *½* **Flash City (ITY)**$^{19}$ 3257 9-10-3 **66**.................... JamesSullivan 4 73
(Ruth Carr) *hld up: hdwy nr side of gp over 1f out: rdn and chsd wnr ins fnl f: kpt on fin* **14/1**
0503 **3** *1 ½* **Windforpower (IRE)**$^{17}$ 3345 7-9-10 **59**....................(p) BenCurtis 2 60
(Tracy Waggott) *cl up on far side of gp: drvn along 1/2-way: rallied: kpt on ins fnl f* **14/1**

-350 **4** *nse* **Thornaby Princess**[26] 2994 6-8-12 **47**....................(p) RoystonFfrench 1 48
(Colin Teague) *hld up in tch on far side of gp: rdn and effrt over 1f out: kpt on ins fnl f: nt pce to chal* **20/1**

0333 **5** *hd* **Roaring Rory**[20] 3202 4-9-8 **62**....................(p) LewisEdmunds(5) 6 62
(Ollie Pears) *prom: rdn and outpcd 1/2-way: rallied fnl f: kpt on* **4/1**[1]

6400 **6** *1/2* **Groundworker (IRE)**[38] 2628 6-9-6 **58**....................(t) SammyJoBell(3) 5 56
(Paul Midgley) *hld up bhd ldng gp: hdwy 1/2-way: rdn and one pce over 1f out* **15/2**

-660 **7** *nk* **Young Tiger**[20] 3202 4-9-4 **53**.................................... AndrewMullen 9 50
(Tom Tate) *cl up on nr side of gp tl rdn and outpcd over 1f out: n.d after* **4/1**[1]

3441 **8** *1* **Horsforth**[17] 3345 5-9-10 **66**....................................(b) WilliamCox(7) 7 60
(Richard Guest) *wnt rt s: trckd ldrs tl rdn and wknd over 1f out* **6/1**[3]

40- **9** *1/2* **Camanche Grey (IRE)**[270] 6745 6-9-3 **52**.................... GrahamLee 3 44
(Ben Haslam) *hld up on far side of gp: rdn along and effrt over 1f out: sn no imp* **50/1**

5-01 **10** *10* **Krystallite**[13] 3466 4-10-0 **63**.................... JosephineGordon 8 19
(Scott Dixon) *blkd s: t.k.h: cl up tl wknd and eased fr 2f out* **9/2**[2]

59.98s (0.38) **Going Correction** +0.25s/f (Good) **10** Ran SP% **114.8**
Speed ratings (Par 101): **106,105,102,102,102 101,101,99,98,82**
CSF £118.25 CT £1681.05 TOTE £11.00: £3.30, £4.70, £3.60; EX 143.90 Trifecta £1109.80.
**Owner** Zen Racing & J S Goldie **Bred** Johnnie Delta Racing **Trained** Uplawmoor, E Renfrews

**FOCUS**
A modest sprint handicap. They went a respectable gallop on the heavily watered ground and the relatively unexposed winner made the most of a drop in grade. The first two help pin the opening level.

## 3945 EBF STALLIONS BREEDING WINNERS MAIDEN STKS 7f 218y
**3:20** (3:23) (Class 5) 3-Y-0+ **£3,881** (£1,155; £577; £288) **Stalls** Low

Form RPR

0222 **1** **Time's Arrow (IRE)**[20] 3206 3-9-4 81.................... JoeFanning 4 59+
(Sir Michael Stoute) *trckd ldr: led over 2f out: rdn clr over 1f out* **2/11**[1]

40-0 **2** *3 1/4* **Newspeak (IRE)**[42] 2496 5-10-0 51....................(v[1]) GrahamLee 3 53
(Fred Watson) *t.k.h: prom: pushed along and chsd (clr) wnr over 1f out: kpt on fnl f: nt pce to chal* **66/1**

53 **3** *3/4* **Les Pecheurs (IRE)**[15] 3404 3-8-6 0.................... DanielleMooney(7) 1 44
(James Ewart) *hld up on ins: shkn up and hdwy 2f out: edgd lft: kpt on fnl f: nvr nrr* **14/1**[3]

60 **4** *1 1/4* **Powercell (IRE)**[15] 3404 3-8-10 0.................... RachelRichardson(3) 7 41+
(Tim Easterby) *s.i.s: t.k.h and sn prom: effrt and chsd wnr over 2f out to over 1f out: sn outpcd* **33/1**

36/ **5** *2 1/4* **Media World (IRE)**[637] 6612 4-10-0 0.................... JoeDoyle 2 43
(Julie Camacho) *t.k.h: hld up: rdn and outpcd over 2f out: n.d after* **20/1**

05 **6** *nk* **Bicolour (USA)**[13] 3472 3-8-13 0.................... PJMcDonald 5 35
(Mark Johnston) *led to over 2f out: rdn and wknd over 1f out* **6/1**[2]

1m 43.48s (3.38) **Going Correction** +0.25s/f (Good)
**WFA** 3 from 4yo+ 10lb **6** Ran SP% **114.8**
Speed ratings (Par 103): **93,89,89,87,85 85**
CSF £29.76 TOTE £1.10: £1.02, £19.70; EX 21.50 Trifecta £127.10.
**Owner** Flaxman Stables Ireland Ltd **Bred** Flaxman Stables Ireland Ltd **Trained** Newmarket, Suffolk
■ Global Roar was withdrawn. Price at time of withdrawal 50/1. Rule 4 does not apply.

**FOCUS**
Race distance increased 10 yards. A fair, if uncompetitive, maiden. They went a respectable gallop, and the long odds-on favourite won easily, but the modest winning time confirms that the heavily watered ground isn't riding on the quick side of good. It's been rated negatively.

## 3946 LADIES' DAY @THIRSKRACES SATURDAY 9TH SEPTEMBER H'CAP 6f
**3:55** (3:56) (Class 4) (0-85,84) 3-Y-0+ **£4,851** (£1,443; £721; £360) **Stalls** Centre

Form RPR

2112 **1** **The Armed Man**[20] 3201 4-8-7 **70**.................... PaulaMuir(7) 1 79
(Chris Fairhurst) *mde all: pushed along and hrd pressed fr 1/2-way: hld on gamely towards fin* **9/2**[2]

-060 **2** *nk* **Highland Acclaim (IRE)**[137] 547 6-9-13 **83**....................(h) DavidNolan 2 91
(David O'Meara) *in tch: hdwy and ev ch over 1f out: sn rdn: kpt on fnl f: hld nr fin* **14/1**

0-21 **3** *1 1/2* **Round The Island**[8] 3666 4-8-8 **69** 6ex.................... LewisEdmunds(5) 6 72
(Richard Whitaker) *prom: effrt and rdn over 1f out: kpt on same pce wl ins fnl f* **2/1**[1]

0401 **4** *2 1/2* **Merdon Castle (IRE)**[29] 2883 5-9-8 **78**....................(e) JamesSullivan 5 73
(Ruth Carr) *hld up: pushed along 1/2-way: hdwy over 1f out: kpt on fnl f: nvr rchd ldrs* **15/2**[3]

2100 **5** *3/4* **Zylan (IRE)**[13] 3463 5-9-7 **84**.................... BenSanderson(7) 4 77
(Roger Fell) *cl up: rdn over 2f out: outpcd fr over 1f out* **10/1**

0-00 **6** *nk* **Groupie**[13] 3462 3-9-2 **79**.................... PaulMulrennan 8 69
(Tom Tate) *hld up: pushed along 1/2-way: no imp whn edgd lft over 1f out* **28/1**

5433 **7** *3/4* **Seamster**[6] 3707 10-9-1 **78**....................(t) CameronNoble(7) 7 67
(David Loughnane) *dwlt: bhd and pushed along: shortlived effrt on nr side of gp over 2f out: sn n.d* **10/1**

1614 **8** *3/4* **Crosse Fire**[8] 3667 5-8-10 **66**.................... JosephineGordon 12 53
(Scott Dixon) *hld up in tch away fr main gp: hung lft thrght: hdwy over 2f out: rdn and wknd wl over 1f out* **8/1**

0-00 **9** *8* **Majdool (IRE)**[15] 3388 4-9-9 **79**....................(p[1]) GrahamLee 10 40
(Noel Wilson) *cl up: rdn over 2f out: wknd wl over 1f out* **66/1**

410- **10** *3/4* **Robben Rainbow**[277] 6536 3-9-4 **81**.................... AndrewMullen 11 38
(David Barron) *missed break: bhd and outpcd: nvr on terms* **10/1**

1m 12.66s (-0.04) **Going Correction** +0.25s/f (Good)
**WFA** 3 from 4yo+ 7lb **10** Ran SP% **113.3**
Speed ratings (Par 105): **110,109,107,104,103 102,101,100,90,89**
CSF £63.46 CT £162.12 TOTE £5.30: £1.60, £3.80, £1.40; EX 71.10 Trifecta £231.90.
**Owner** Mrs C A Arnold **Bred** C W Fairhurst **Trained** Middleham, N Yorks
■ Stewards' Enquiry : David Nolan two-day ban: used whip above the permitted level (Jul 4-5)

**FOCUS**
A decent sprint handicap. They went a respectable gallop and an in-form sprinter proved thoroughly game in the finish. The third has been rated to his Pontefract win.

## 3947 THEAKSTON BEST BITTER H'CAP 1m 4f 8y
**4:35** (4:35) (Class 4) (0-80,81) 4-Y-0+ **£4,851** (£1,443; £721; £360) **Stalls** High

Form RPR

4524 **1** **Masterpaver**[3] 3841 6-9-5 **81**.................... AdamMcNamara(3) 3 90
(Richard Fahey) *chsd ldrs: rdn and outpcd 5f out: rallied and edgd lft 2f out: led 1f out: drvn out* **5/4**[1]

34-5 **2** *2* **New World Power (JPN)**[45] 2386 4-9-8 **81**.................... TomEaves 6 87
(David Simcock) *hld up: hdwy to chse ldr over 4f out: led over 2f out to 1f out: rdn and one pce* **15/8**[2]

13-4 **3** *2 1/4* **Desert Way (IRE)**[48] 2302 4-9-7 **80**.................... PJMcDonald 2 82
(Rebecca Menzies) *pressed ldr: led over 5f out to over 2f out: rallied: drvn and outpcd over 1f out* **10/1**

40-0 **4** *1 1/2* **Carthage (IRE)**[34] 2741 6-8-7 **71**.................... BenRobinson(5) 1 71
(Brian Ellison) *led to over 5f out: rallied: drvn and outpcd fr 2f out* **16/1**

2-60 **5** *4 1/2* **Under Attack (IRE)**[27] 2965 4-9-6 **79**....................(h) JamesSullivan 4 72
(Ruth Carr) *t.k.h early: hld up in tch: outpcd over 3f out: btn fnl 2f* **9/2**[3]

2m 42.62s (6.42) **Going Correction** +0.25s/f (Good) **5** Ran SP% **112.4**
Speed ratings (Par 105): **88,86,85,84,81**
CSF £3.98 TOTE £2.00: £1.10, £1.50; EX 4.00 Trifecta £10.40.
**Owner** Exors of the Late Mrs A M Riney **Bred** Mrs A M Riney **Trained** Musley Bank, N Yorks

**FOCUS**
Race distance increased 30 yards. A fair little middle-distance handicap. They went a modest gallop but the well-backed favourite obliged in decisive fashion. A small pb from the runner-up.

## 3948 EBF STALLIONS MAIDEN STKS 7f
**5:10** (5:14) (Class 5) 3-Y-0 **£3,881** (£1,155; £577; £288) **Stalls** Low

Form RPR

3 **1** **Raselasad (IRE)**[29] 2887 3-9-5 0.................... RoystonFfrench 3 75
(Tracy Waggott) *mde all at stdy pce: hrd pressed and rdn over 2f out: hld on gamely fnl f* **12/1**[3]

0 **2** *1/2* **Dandys Denouement**[10] 3568 3-9-5 0.................... TomEaves 4 74
(Brian Ellison) *trckd wnr: chal and rdn over 2f out: kpt on fnl f: hld nr fin* **100/1**

3-35 **3** *1 1/4* **Hydroxide**[14] 3434 3-9-5 81....................(t) JosephineGordon 2 70
(Hugo Palmer) *t.k.h: trckd ldrs: effrt and rdn 2f out: kpt on same pce ins fnl f* **5/4**[2]

5 **4** *1 1/2* **Akdaar**[52] 2135 3-9-5 0.................... JackMitchell 1 66
(Roger Varian) *prom: effrt and pushed along 2f out: kpt on same pce fnl f* **4/5**[1]

03 **5** *6* **Oriental Lilly**[20] 3194 3-9-0 0.................... PJMcDonald 6 45
(Jim Goldie) *dwlt: hld up: pushed along over 2f out: sn no imp* **25/1**

0- **6** *5* **Ninedarter**[227] 7818 3-9-5 0.................... CamHardie 7 37
(Antony Brittain) *hld up in tch: drvn and struggling over 2f out: sn wknd* **100/1**

1m 29.7s (2.50) **Going Correction** +0.25s/f (Good) **6** Ran SP% **113.5**
Speed ratings (Par 99): **95,94,93,91,84 78**
CSF £519.08 TOTE £14.30: £4.80, £13.10; EX 161.80 Trifecta £742.30.
**Owner** David Tate **Bred** Shadwell Estate Company Limited **Trained** Spennymoor, Co Durham

**FOCUS**
Race distance increased 10 yards. A fair 3yo maiden. They went a modest gallop and it proved difficult to make up any ground on the heavily watered surface.

## 3949 NEXT MEETING @THIRSKRACES WEDNESDAY 5TH JULY H'CAP 7f
**5:45** (5:47) (Class 5) (0-70,70) 3-Y-0+ **£3,557** (£1,058; £529; £264) **Stalls** Low

Form RPR

-154 **1** **Tanawar (IRE)**[20] 3198 7-9-6 **62**....................(b) JamesSullivan 11 69
(Ruth Carr) *hld up: stdy hdwy on ins over 2f out: effrt and pushed along over 1f out: kpt on wl fnl f to ld nr fin* **10/1**

-602 **2** *nk* **Kirkham**[17] 3344 4-9-6 **65**....................(p) AdamMcNamara(3) 1 71
(Julie Camacho) *trckd ldrs: hdwy to ld over 1f out: sn rdn: kpt on fnl f: hdd nr fin* **6/1**[3]

5124 **3** *1/2* **Siege Of Boston (IRE)**[8] 3666 4-10-0 **70**....................(t) TrevorWhelan 5 75
(John Butler) *prom: rdn along over 2f out: edgd both ways ins fnl f: kpt on fin* **3/1**[1]

0-40 **4** *nk* **Mont Royal (FR)**[18] 3296 3-9-3 **68**.................... AndrewMullen 2 69+
(Ollie Pears) *s.i.s: hld up: effrt on ins 2f out: rdn and kpt on ins fnl f* **12/1**

0300 **5** *1 3/4* **Compton Park**[8] 3666 10-9-8 **69**....................(t) LewisEdmunds(5) 3 69
(Les Eyre) *s.i.s: hld up on ins: pushed along and effrt whn nt clr run wl over 1f out: kpt on fnl f: no imp* **13/2**

-000 **6** *2 3/4* **Etienne Gerard**[15] 3401 5-9-7 **66**....................(p) RachelRichardson(3) 9 58
(Nigel Tinkler) *t.k.h: hld up on outside: pushed along over 2f out: no imp fr over 1f out* **25/1**

0350 **7** *1* **Taskeen (IRE)**[15] 3396 4-10-0 **70**.................... DavidNolan 8 59
(Roger Fell) *hld up bhd ldng gp: rdn over 2f out: no imp over 1f out* **4/1**[2]

60-0 **8** *hd* **Le Laitier (FR)**[8] 3666 6-9-4 **60**.................... JosephineGordon 10 49
(Scott Dixon) *trckd ldrs: rdn over 2f out: blkd wl over 1f out: sn wknd* **25/1**

6114 **9** *1/2* **Endeavour (IRE)**[21] 3184 3-9-1 **66**.................... BarryMcHugh 4 50
(Marjorie Fife) *led at ordinary gallop: rdn and hdd over 1f out: sn wknd* **8/1**

60-0 **10** *1 1/4* **Redvers (IRE)**[36] 2684 9-9-7 **68**....................(p) PhilDennis(5) 7 52
(Noel Wilson) *s.i.s: hld up: rdn over 2f out: sn btn* **20/1**

20-0 **11** *6* **Mulwith (IRE)**[13] 3461 3-8-7 **58**.................... PJMcDonald 6 23
(Scott Dixon) *cl up tl rdn and wknd over 2f out* **50/1**

1m 27.86s (0.66) **Going Correction** +0.25s/f (Good)
**WFA** 3 from 4yo+ 9lb **11** Ran SP% **114.9**
Speed ratings (Par 103): **106,105,105,104,102 99,98,98,97,96 89**
CSF £64.21 CT £229.80 TOTE £12.70: £2.90, £2.10, £1.40; EX 52.70 Trifecta £237.00.
**Owner** G Scruton, D Williamson & R Carr **Bred** J Hanly, Castlemartin Sky & Skymarc Far **Trained** Huby, N Yorks
■ Stewards' Enquiry : Andrew Mullen two-day ban; careless riding (4th-5th July)

**FOCUS**
Race distance increased 10 yards. A modest handicap. They went a respectable gallop. One of the paddock picks beforehand narrowly landed a thrilling finale. The winner has been rated back to the level of last year's form.
T/Plt: £1,586.20 to a £1 stake. Pool: £47,696.08 - 21.95 winning units T/Qpdt: £111.40 to a £1 stake. Pool: £3,387.29 - 22.50 winning units **Richard Young**

3950 - 3958a (Foreign Racing) - See Raceform Interactive

# 3924 ASCOT (R-H)
Wednesday, June 21

**OFFICIAL GOING: Good to firm (watered; stand side 8.7, centre 8.4, far side 8.5, round 7.9)**
Wind: virtually nil Weather: hot and sunny

## 3959 JERSEY STKS (GROUP 3) 7f
**2:30** (2:36) (Class 1) 3-Y-O
**£51,039** (£19,350; £9,684; £4,824; £2,421; £1,215) **Stalls** Centre

Form RPR

1-2 **1** **Le Brivido (FR)**[38] 2666 3-9-1 121.................... Pierre-CharlesBoudot 10 116+
(A Fabre, France) *cmpt: racd in centre gp: a.p: rdn to ld gp over 2f out: r.o ins fnl f: got up to ld overall towards fin: 1st of 14 in gp* **2/1**[1]

-006 **2** *nk* **Spirit Of Valor (USA)**25 3100 3-9-1 106............(bt) DonnachaO'Brien 20 115
(A P O'Brien, Ire) *str: racd in stands' side gp: chsd ldr tl over 4f out: swtchd rt over 2f out: led overall over 1f out: edgd rt ent fnl f: r.o for press: hdd and hld towards fin: 1st of 6 in gp* **66/1**

0-33 **3** *2 1/4* **Mubtasim (IRE)**25 3078 3-9-1 107................................. PatCosgrave 15 109
(William Haggas) *lw: racd in stands' side gp: hld up in rr: hdwy 2f out: effrt and swtchd lft over 1f out: racd on rail ins fnl f: r.o towards fin: nt quite pce to trble front two: 2nd of 6 in gp* **20/1**

-351 **4** *hd* **Parfait (IRE)**11 3592 3-9-1 100...................................(p) WilliamBuick 18 109
(John Gosden) *cmpt: racd in stands' side gp: led overall: rdn 3f out: hdd over 1f out: edgd rt ent fnl f: styd on same pce fnl 100yds: 3rd of 6 in gp* **25/1**

125 **5** *nk* **Dream Castle**46 2399 3-9-1 113.............................. JosephineGordon 19 108
(Saeed bin Suroor) *racd in stands' side gp: a.p and t.k.h: rdn over 2f out: unable qck over 1f out: styd on same pce fnl 100yds: 4th of 6 in gp* **9/2**2

1-13 **6** *2* **Daban (IRE)**45 2434 3-9-1 111....................................... AndreaAtzeni 13 102
(John Gosden) *lw: racd in centre gp: trckd ldrs: effrt over 2f out: unable qck over 1f out: styd on same pce ins fnl f: 2nd of 14 in gp* **7/1**3

1-22 **7** *2 1/4* **Chessman (IRE)**25 3082 3-9-1 93...................................... AdamKirby 1 96+
(John Gosden) *str: lw: racd in centre gp: hld up: rdn and hdwy over 2f out: chsd ldrs over 1f out: kpt on ins fnl f: nvr able to chal: 3rd of 14 in gp* **20/1**

3 **8** *nk* **True Valour (IRE)**19 3302 3-9-1 101.................................. ShaneFoley 8 95
(J P Murtagh, Ire) *w'like: racd in centre gp: midfield: rdn over 2f out: hdwy over 1f out: styd on fnl 100yds: gng on at fin: 4th of 14 in gp* **80/1**

0-13 **9** *2 3/4* **Bacchus**40 2565 3-9-1 99.............................................(p) KevinManning 3 88
(Brian Meehan) *warm: racd in centre gp: midfield: rdn over 2f out: chsd ldrs over 1f out: styd on same pce fnl 100yds: 5th of 14 in gp* **66/1**

1 **10** *nk* **Beat The Bank**61 1859 3-9-1 106.................................... OisinMurphy 17 87
(Andrew Balding) *racd in stands' side gp: in tch: effrt 3f out: rdn and carried rt over 2f out: one pce and no imp fnl f: 5th of 6 in gp* **18/1**

1431 **11** *hd* **Winning Ways (IRE)**40 2565 3-9-1 101.......................(t) GeraldMosse 2 87
(Jeremy Noseda) *warm: racd in centre gp: hld up: rdn and hdwy 2f out: kpt on but no imp fnl f: 6th of 14 in gp* **14/1**

6-56 **12** *1/2* **Sir Dancealot (IRE)**49 2289 3-9-1 106............................... ShaneKelly 9 85
(David Elsworth) *lw: s.i.s: racd in centre gp: in rr: swtchd lft and hdwy 2f out: kpt on ins fnl f: nt trble ldrs: 7th of 14 in gp* **66/1**

10-2 **13** *1 1/4* **Escobar (IRE)**27 3013 3-9-1 106....................................... PatSmullen 16 82
(Hugo Palmer) *swtg: s.s and n.m.r early strides: racd in stands' side gp: towards rr: swtchd rt and effrt 3f out: sn hung lft: kpt on but no imp fnl f: 6th of 6 in gp* **25/1**

5-41 **14** *1 1/4* **Taamol (IRE)**32 2830 3-9-1 103.....................................(p1) JimCrowley 5 79
(Sir Michael Stoute) *swtg: racd in centre gp: midfield: rdn whn n.m.r and swtchd rt jst over 2f out: sn lost pl: n.d after: 8th of 14 in gp* **20/1**

23-1 **15** *nse* **Whitecliffsofdover (USA)**31 2860 3-9-1 110............(bt1) RyanMoore 12 78
(A P O'Brien, Ire) *racd in centre gp: led overall tl rdn over 2f out: wknd over 1f out: eased whn btn ins fnl f: 9th of 14 in gp* **12/1**

-041 **16** *2* **Solomon's Bay (IRE)**19 3302 3-9-1 108.............. SilvestreDeSousa 7 73
(Roger Varian) *racd in centre gp: hld up: rdn and edgd lft 2f out: no imp on ldrs fnl f: 10th of 14 in gp* **33/1**

5310 **17** *1 1/4* **Sutter County**19 3302 3-9-1 108..................................... JamesDoyle 4 70
(Mark Johnston) *racd in centre gp: prom: rdn over 2f out: wknd over 1f out: 11th of 14 in gp* **66/1**

16-6 **18** *3 1/4* **Barrington (IRE)**32 2823 3-9-1 97.............................(t) GavinLerena 14 61
(Charles Hills) *racd in centre gp: hld up and t.k.h: rdn and outpcd over 2f out: nvr a threat: 12th of 14 in gp* **100/1**

1006 **19** *1 1/4* **Top Score**25 3071 3-9-1 109........................................... OlivierPeslier 6 58
(Saeed bin Suroor) *racd in centre gp: s.s: in rr: wnt into midfield after 1f: sn prom: rdn and wknd 2f out: 13th of 14 in gp* **33/1**

54 **20** *nk* **Glastonbury Song (IRE)**25 3100 3-9-1 105.................... ColinKeane 11 57
(G M Lyons, Ire) *leggy: racd in centre gp: hld up in midfield: niggled along 4f out: wknd 2f out: 14th of 14 in gp* **22/1**

1m 25.05s (-2.55) **Going Correction** -0.075s/f (Good) **20** Ran SP% **124.0**
Speed ratings (Par 109): **111,110,108,107,107 105,102,102,99,98 98,98,96,95,95 92,91,87,86,85**
CSF £195.59 CT £2245.69 TOTE £2.90: £1.50, £14.70, £6.30; EX 150.50 Trifecta £2861.90.
**Owner** HRH Prince Faisal Bin Khaled **Bred** J Bugada & Mme B Bugada **Trained** Chantilly, France

**FOCUS**
Day two was another scorcher. Clerk of the course Chris Stickels put 5mm of water on the whole course to maintain safe, quick ground and there was another brisk time in the opener. The running rail on the round course was 3yds out from its innermost position from approx 9f out to the home straight. This was a decent edition of the Jersey Stakes. They split into two groups and five of the first four home raced towards the stands' rail. The level is a bit fluid.

## 3960 QUEEN MARY STKS (GROUP 2) (FILLIES) 5f
**3:05** (3:11) (Class 1) 2-Y-O

**£62,381** (£23,650; £11,836; £5,896; £2,959; £1,485) **Stalls** Centre

Form RPR

1 **1** **Heartache**26 3023 2-9-0 0........................................................ AdamKirby 20 107+
(Clive Cox) *unf: scope: racd nr side to centre: trckd overall ldr tl led wl over 1f out: sn rdn: styd on strly and drew clr ins fnl f: rdn out: 1st of 17 in gp* **5/1**2

**2** *2 1/2* **Happy Like A Fool (USA)**73 2-9-0 0..........................(b) RyanMoore 18 98
(Wesley A Ward, U.S.A) *str: lw: ponied to s: led nr side to centre gp and overall ldr: hdd and rdn wl over 1f out: kpt on u.p tl no ex and outpcd by wnr ins fnl f: hld on to 2nd cl home: 2nd of 17 in gp* **10/11**1

31 **3** *1/2* **Out Of The Flames**30 2904 2-9-0 0.............................. OisinMurphy 17 96
(Richard Hannon) *racd nr side to centre: chsd ldrs: rdn 2f out: sltly outpcd over 1f out: rallied and kpt on u.p ins fnl f: pressing for 2nd cl home but no threat to wnr: 3rd of 17 in gp* **14/1**

**4** *hd* **Now You're Talking (IRE)**25 3096 2-9-0 0............ DonnachaO'Brien 13 95
(Joseph Patrick O'Brien, Ire) *athletic: racd nr side to centre: stdd s: hld up towards rr: hdwy 1/2-way: rdn to chse ldrs over 1f out: 3rd and kpt on same pce u.p ins fnl f: lost 3rd last strides: 4th of 17 in gp* **66/1**

512 **5** *1* **Neola**33 2801 2-9-0 0........................................................... GrahamLee 14 92
(Mick Channon) *racd nr side to centre: wl in tch in midfield: rdn 2f out: unable qck u.p over 1f out: kpt on same pce ins fnl f: 5th of 17 in gp* **16/1**

042 **6** *nk* **Pursuing The Dream (IRE)**19 3283 2-9-0 0............ DougieCostello 23 91+
(Jamie Osborne) *racd nr side to centre: stdd and short of room leaving stalls: hld up in rr: clsd over 1f out: shkn up ent fnl f: rdn and r.o wl ins fnl f: nvr gng to rch ldrs: 6th of 17 in gp* **150/1**

061 **7** *hd* **Darkanna (IRE)**13 3490 2-9-0 0.................................. BarryMcHugh 10 90
(Richard Fahey) *w'like: racd nr side to centre: hld up in midfield: effrt over 2f out: swtchd rt and hdwy 2f out: kpt on u.p ins fnl f: no threat to wnr: 7th of 17 in gp* **100/1**

**8** *1/2* **Treasuring**18 3346 2-9-0 0............................................ ColinKeane 12 88
(G M Lyons, Ire) *str: lw: racd nr side to centre: chsd ldrs: rdn 2f out: unable qck u.p over 1f out: wknd ins fnl f: 8th of 17 in gp* **25/1**

5 **9** *shd* **Missy Mischief (USA)**25 3070 2-9-0 0........................ GeraldMosse 11 88
(Jeremy Noseda) *str: racd nr side to centre: hld up in tch in midfield: effrt 2f out: chsd ldrs and hung rt over 1f out and sn no ex: wknd ins fnl f: 9th of 17 in gp* **50/1**

2 **10** *hd* **Maybride**13 3491 2-9-0 0.................................................. PaulHanagan 16 87
(Richard Fahey) *str: racd nr side to centre: hld up in tch in midfield: lost pl and dropped towards rr wl over 1f out: rallied and sme hdwy whn nt clr run and swtchd rt ins fnl f: kpt on but no threat to ldrs: 10th of 17 in gp* **50/1**

1 **11** *1/2* **Mrs Gallagher**40 2563 2-9-0 0................................. SilvestreDeSousa 1 85+
(William Jarvis) *lw: racd far side: t.k.h: hld up and midfield overall: hdwy 2f out: pressing overall ldrs whn hung lft over 1f out: no ex 1f out and wknd ins fnl f: 1st of 6 in gp* **10/1**3

525 **12** *shd* **Lady Anjorica (IRE)**11 3611 2-9-0 0.....................(p1) ConnorBeasley 19 85
(Keith Dalgleish) *w'like: racd nr side to centre: in tch in midfield: rdn and lost pl ent fnl 2f: rallied u.p and kpt on again ins fnl f: no threat to ldrs: 11th of 17 in gp* **150/1**

5 **13** *nk* **Mamba Noire (FR)**31 2861 2-9-0 0...................................... ShaneFoley 8 84
(K J Condon, Ire) *unf: racd nr side to centre: stdd and swtchd lft after s: hld up in rr: rdn and hdwy into midfield over 1f out: kpt on same pce and no imp ins fnl f: 12th of 17 in gp* **33/1**

6 **14** *shd* **Sirici (IRE)**31 2861 2-9-0 0.............................................. ChrisHayes 9 83
(J A Stack, Ire) *str: racd nr side to centre: hld up in tch in midfield: rdn 2f out: unable qck u.p over 1f out: wknd ins fnl f: 13th of 17 in gp* **100/1**

22 **15** *3/4* **Mother Of Dragons (IRE)**26 3029 2-9-0 0................ JamieSpencer 24 81
(Joseph Tuite) *racd nr side to centre: stdd s: hld up in rr: effrt over 1f out: sme hdwy and swtchd rt ent fnl f: no imp after: nvr trbld ldrs: 14th of 17 in gp* **100/1**

1 **16** *nk* **Formidable Kitt**63 1884 2-9-0 0............................... RichardKingscote 5 80
(Tom Dascombe) *racd far side: t.k.h: chsd gp ldr and prom overall: rdn to ld gp and pressing ldrs over 1f out: sn outpcd and wknd ins fnl f: 2nd of 6 in gp* **16/1**

32 **17** *1/2* **Bath And Tennis (IRE)**12 3516 2-9-0 0.......................... LukeMorris 15 78
(Sir Mark Prescott Bt) *str: racd nr side to centre: chsd ldrs: rdn ent fnl 2f: sn struggling and lost pl over 1f out: wknd ins fnl f: 15th of 17 in gp* **66/1**

64 **18** *nk* **Rioticism (FR)**11 3611 2-9-0 0.................................... AntoineHamelin 4 77+
(Matthieu Palussiere, France) *leggy: racd far side: hld up in tch: swtchd lft and rdn 2f out: no imp u.p over 1f out: wknd ins fnl f: 3rd of 6 in gp* **100/1**

1 **19** *1 1/2* **Debutante's Ball (IRE)**36 2706 2-9-0 0........................... LiamJones 6 71+
(J S Moore) *unf: racd far side: hld up in tch: effrt over 2f out: sme hdwy u.p 2f out: no imp and btn over 1f out: wknd fnl f: 4th of 6 in gp* **100/1**

61 **20** *2 3/4* **Wings Of The Rock (IRE)**21 3215 2-9-0 0....................... DavidAllan 2 61+
(Scott Dixon) *w'like: racd far side: led gp and chsd ldrs overall: rdn and pressing ldrs 2f out: hung lft: lost gp ld and btn over 1f out: wknd ins fnl f: 5th of 6 in gp* **100/1**

1 **21** *2 3/4* **Chica La Habana (IRE)**11 3557 2-9-0 0.......................... JimCrowley 22 52
(Robert Cowell) *str: racd nr side to centre: in tch in midfield: rdn over 2f out: sn struggling and lost pl: bhd fnl f: 16th of 17 in gp* **25/1**

40 **22** *hd* **Go Bananas**8 3687 2-9-0 0.................................................. KierenFox 3 51+
(Brian Meehan) *racd far side: chsd gp ldrs and wl in tch overall: rdn 2f out: sn lost pl: bhd fnl f: 6th of 6 in gp* **200/1**

2141 **23** *7* **Emilia James**20 3230 2-9-0 0........................................... JamesDoyle 7 26
(Mark Johnston) *w'like: racd far side tl swtchd lft to join nr side to centre gp after 1f: chsd ldrs: rdn 2f out: sn lost pl: bhd ins fnl f: 17th of 17 in gp* **33/1**

59.63s (-0.87) **Going Correction** -0.075s/f (Good) **23** Ran SP% **124.8**
Speed ratings (Par 102): **103,99,98,97,96 95,95,94,94,94 93,93,92,92,91 90,90,89,87,82 78,78,66**
CSF £8.89 CT £66.51 TOTE £6.10: £1.90, £1.20, £3.40; EX 14.00 Trifecta £110.10.
**Owner** The Hot To Trot Syndicate - Heartache **Bred** Whitsbury Manor Stud **Trained** Lambourn, Berks

**FOCUS**
Distance as advertised. They split into two groups, with the bigger gathering more stands' side coming out on top. The big two in the market came to the fore, although the red-hot favourite had to make do with second. It's been rated an ordinary renewal, with less than 3.5l covering the first ten home.

## 3961 DUKE OF CAMBRIDGE STKS (GROUP 2) (F&M) 1m (S)
**3:40** (3:44) (Class 1) 4-Y-O+

**£114,270** (£43,322; £21,681; £10,800; £5,420; £2,720) **Stalls** Centre

Form RPR

13-2 **1** **Qemah (IRE)**39 2616 4-9-0 114.................................. GregoryBenoist 10 116+
(J-C Rouget, France) *warm: stdd s: racd in stands' side gp: hld up: hdwy over 3f out: rdn to ld jst over 1f out: r.o ins fnl f: drvn out: 1st of 11 in gp* **5/2**1

0-15 **2** *3/4* **Aljazzi**45 2432 4-9-0 101..................................................(h) AdamKirby 14 114
(Marco Botti) *racd in stands' side gp: hld up in rr: rdn over 2f out: hdwy over 1f out: chalng wl ins fnl f: r.o u.p: hld towards fin: 2nd of 11 in gp* **40/1**

6-33 **3** *nk* **Usherette (IRE)**24 3118 5-9-0 110.......................... MickaelBarzalona 13 115+
(A Fabre, France) *racd in stands' side gp: taken bk early: hld up: nt clr run wl over 1f out: sn swtchd rt: hdwy ent fnl f: sn swtchd lft: r.o and clsd towards fin: 3rd of 11 in gp* **11/4**2

-3 **4** *3/4* **Smart Call (SAF)**34 2765 5-9-0 119................................ RyanMoore 11 112
(Sir Michael Stoute) *lw: racd stands' side: led overall: rdn and hdd jst over 1f out: stl there ins fnl f: no ex towards fin: 4th of 11 in gp* **9/2**3

0-03 **5** *2* **Aim To Please (FR)**45 2432 4-9-0 102......................... PJMcDonald 15 107
(F Doumen, France) *stdd s: racd in stands' side gp: hld up in rr: hdwy over 2f out: rdn to chse ldrs over 1f out: kpt on u.p ins fnl f but no imp: 5th of 11 in gp* **40/1**

5-13 **6** *1/2* **Turret Rocks (IRE)**25 3101 4-9-0 109.......................... KevinManning 7 106
(J S Bolger, Ire) *racd in stands' side gp: prom: effrt 3f out: outpcd over 1f out: kpt on same pce ins fnl f: 6th of 11 in gp* **16/1**

1-30 **7** *hd* **Dawn Of Hope (IRE)**54 2129 4-9-0 110......................... AndreaAtzeni 16 106
(Roger Varian) *racd in stands' side gp: in tch: effrt over 2f out: cl up over 1f out: no ex fnl 150yds: 7th of 11 in gp* **33/1**

2-32 **8** *2 1/4* **Pirouette**18 3334 4-9-0 105.............................................. JimCrowley 9 100
(Hughie Morrison) *racd in stands' side gp: midfield: lost pl and red-hot outpcd over 2f out: plugged on ins fnl f: 8th of 11 in gp* **14/1**

**9** *nk* **Greta G (ARG)**326 3-8-13 110........................................ OlivierPeslier 8 100
(John Gosden) *str: racd in stands' side gp: trckd ldrs: lost pl 3f out: nt clr run and swtchd rt 2f out and outpcd: plugged on ins fnl f: 9th of 11 in gp* **14/1**

-130 **10** *nk* **Furia Cruzada (CHI)**[88] 1380 5-9-3 108...................... AurelienLemaitre 3 102
(S Kobayashi, France) *racd in centre gp: chsd gp ldr tl over 2f out: sn rdn: swtchd lft whn outpcd over 1f out: intimidated by rival after: led gp ins fnl f: one pce and no imp on ldrs: 1st of 3 in gp* **66/1**

40-2 **11** *5* **Same Jurisdiction (SAF)**[16] 3395 5-9-0 103.................. GavinLerena 4 87
(Ed Dunlop) *stdd s: swtchd lft early to r in stands' side gp: in tch: chalng over 2f out: wknd over 1f out: 10th of 11 in gp* **125/1**

0-11 **12** *1* **Mix And Mingle (IRE)**[39] 2616 4-9-0 113.................. WilliamBuick 1 85
(Chris Wall) *lw: racd in centre gp: hld up in rr: wnt 2nd over 2f out: led gp over 1f out: no imp on ldrs: hung lft over 1f out: hdd in gp ins fnl f: sn wknd: 2nd of 3 in gp* **8/1**

1042 **13** *3 ½* **Opal Tiara (IRE)**[25] 3101 4-9-3 109............................ OisinMurphy 12 80
(Mick Channon) *racd in stands' side gp: prom: rdn and struggling to hold pl whn n.m.r wl over 1f out: sn eased: 11th of 11 in gp* **33/1**

0366 **14** *1 ½* **Summer Icon**[18] 3334 4-9-0 95.......................................... GrahamLee 2 74
(Mick Channon) *led centre gp: rdn over 2f out: hdd in gp over 1f out: sn wknd: 3rd of 3 in gp* **150/1**

1m 38.34s (-2.46) **Going Correction** -0.075s/f (Good)
**WFA** 3 from 4yo+ 10lb **14** Ran SP% **117.5**
Speed ratings (Par 115): **109,108,107,107,105 104,104,102,101,101 96,95,92,90**
CSF £116.28 CT £299.44 TOTE £3.10: £1.40, £11.00, £1.50; EX 97.40 Trifecta £456.90.
**Owner** Al Shaqab Racing **Bred** Ecurie Cadran Bissons Sas lei **Trained** Pau, France

**FOCUS**
A rock-solid Group 2 for fillies and mares. They went a sound pace near the stands' side and the form makes some sense. The runner-up is the key to the form, apparently running a big pb, but otherwise the form makes sense with the third to seventh all running within a length of their marks.

## 3962 PRINCE OF WALES'S STKS (GROUP 1) (BRITISH CHAMPIONS SERIES) 1m 1f 212y

**4:20** (4:23) (Class 1) 4-Y-0+

**£425,325** (£161,250; £80,700; £40,200; £20,175; £10,125) **Stalls** Low

Form RPR

2-01 **1** **Highland Reel (IRE)**[19] 3299 5-9-0 123.......................... RyanMoore 6 123
(A P O'Brien, Ire) *swtg: pressed ldr: rdn to chal 2f out: battled on wl to ld ins fnl f: styd on strly and gng away at fin* **9/4**[2]

1161 **2** *1 ¼* **Decorated Knight**[24] 3108 5-9-0 118............................ AndreaAtzeni 4 120
(Roger Charlton) *swtg: trckd ldrs: effrt ent fnl 2f: drvn and str chal over 1f out tl unable to match pce of wnr 100yds out: wnt 2nd and kpt on same pce fnl 50yds* **10/1**

24-1 **3** *shd* **Ulysses (IRE)**[54] 2127 4-9-0 116.......................................... JimCrowley 7 120
(Sir Michael Stoute) *dwlt: t.k.h and hld up in midfield: effrt over 2f out: hdwy and str chal over 1f out: led 1f out tl hdd ins fnl 1f: outpcd by wnr 100yds out: kpt on same pce and lost 2nd 50yds out* **9/2**[3]

31-4 **4** *¾* **Queen's Trust**[34] 2765 4-8-11 118.................................. OlivierPeslier 1 115
(Sir Michael Stoute) *hmpd and dropped to rr after 1f: effrt 2f out: hdwy u.p 1f out: styd on wl ins fnl f: nvr getting on terms w wnr* **16/1**

212- **5** *1* **Scottish (IRE)**[249] 7378 5-9-0 115...................................... JamesDoyle 5 116
(Charlie Appleby) *led: rdn and hrd pressed 2f out: drvn and hdd 1f out: no ex and wknd ins fnl f* **20/1**

2-21 **6** *nk* **Mekhtaal**[24] 3118 4-9-0 115.......................................... GregoryBenoist 2 115
(J-C Rouget, France) *str: lw: t.k.h early: hld up in tch in last trio: effrt ent fnl 2f out: kpt on same pce and no imp fnl f* **17/2**

3-45 **7** *1 ½* **Johannes Vermeer (IRE)**[24] 3108 4-9-0 109.........(t) DonnachaO'Brien 3 112
(A P O'Brien, Ire) *swtg: in tch in midfield: effrt ent fnl 2f: unable qck and lost pl over 1f out: hld and kpt on same pce ins fnl f* **50/1**

P3-1 **8** *½* **Jack Hobbs**[88] 1379 5-9-0 123........................................(b) WilliamBuick 8 111
(John Gosden) *lw: stdd s: t.k.h: hld up in last pair: clsd on outer 3f out: effrt over 2f out: no imp and edgd rt u.p over 1f out: wknd ins fnl f* **2/1**[1]

2m 5.04s (-2.36) **Going Correction** +0.20s/f (Good) **8** Ran SP% **114.5**
Speed ratings (Par 117): **117,116,115,115,114 114,113,112**
CSF £25.04 CT £93.71 TOTE £3.00: £1.20, £2.50, £1.60; EX 22.90 Trifecta £79.80.
**Owner** Derrick Smith & Mrs John Magnier & Michael Tabor **Bred** Hveger Syndicate **Trained** Cashel, Co Tipperary

■ Stewards' Enquiry : Donnacha O'Brien three-day ban: careless riding (July 5-7)

**FOCUS**
Distance increased by 11yds. They didn't go overly fast and the winner received a good ride, always being well placed. The winner has been rated pretty much to form.

## 3963 ROYAL HUNT CUP (HERITAGE H'CAP) 1m (S)

**5:00** (5:04) (Class 2) 3-Y-0+

**£108,937** (£32,620; £16,310; £8,155; £4,077; £2,047) **Stalls** Centre

Form RPR

4003 **1** **Zhui Feng (IRE)**[39] 2606 4-9-0 100............................(p) MartinDwyer 26 110
(Amanda Perrett) *lw: racd in stands' side gp: mde all: rdn over 1f out: edgd rt ins fnl f: r.o: kpt finding more towards fin: 1st of 26 in gp* **25/1**

212- **2** *½* **Blair House (IRE)**[242] 7546 4-8-11 97.................(b) MickaelBarzalona 22 106
(Charlie Appleby) *racd in stands' side gp: midfield: hdwy 3f out: edgd rt and str chal ins fnl f: r.o u.p: hld nr fin: 2nd of 26 in gp* **16/1**

6/-0 **3** *nk* **Tashweeq (IRE)**[54] 2129 4-9-6 106.................................. DaneO'Neill 18 114
(John Gosden) *racd in stands' side gp: midfield: hdwy 2f out: rdn to chal over 1f out: edgd rt ins fnl f: no ex fnl strides: 3rd of 26 in gp* **66/1**

-156 **4** *1 ¾* **Ballet Concerto**[18] 3320 4-9-2 102................................... RyanMoore 11 106
(Sir Michael Stoute) *racd in stands' side gp: midfield: hdwy 2f out: rdn to chse ldrs over 1f out: cl up ins fnl f: checked 150yds out: edgd lft and styd on towards fin: 4th of 26 in gp* **20/1**

1-21 **5** *1 ¼* **Tabarrak (IRE)**[49] 2290 4-9-11 111..................................... JimCrowley 30 112
(Richard Hannon) *racd in stands' side gp: trckd ldrs: rdn over 2f out: sn outpcd: hung rt ins fnl f: styd on: nt pce to chal: 5th of 26 in gp* **10/1**

2-00 **6** *shd* **Remarkable**[19] 3298 4-9-2 105...........................(b) KieranShoemark[(3)] 15 106
(John Gosden) *racd in stands' side gp: midfield: rdn 2f out: hdwy over 1f out: r.o ins fnl f: gng on at fin: 6th of 26 in gp* **25/1**

00-0 **7** *nk* **Gm Hopkins**[39] 2606 6-9-5 105......................................... JamesDoyle 29 105+
(John Gosden) *lw: racd in stands' side gp: hld up: rdn over 1f out: no imp tl hung rt and prog ins fnl f: fin wl: 7th of 26 in gp* **20/1**

-045 **8** *nk* **Master The World (IRE)**[125] 776 6-9-5 105..................(p) PatDobbs 8 105+
(David Elsworth) *racd in stands' side gp: hld up in rr: hdwy over 1f out: styd on ins fnl f: one pce nr fin: nt rch ldrs: 8th of 26 in gp* **50/1**

-311 **9** *hd* **Fastnet Tempest (IRE)**[25] 3064 4-8-13 99...............(p) PatCosgrave 14 101+
(William Haggas) *lw: racd in stands' side: hld up: nt clr run and hdwy wl over 1f out: swtchd lft ent fnl f: r.o: fin strly: 9th of 26 in gp* **15/2**[2]

0036 **10** *¾* **Elleval (IRE)**[45] 2440 7-8-9 100........................................ OisinOrr[(5)] 3 97
(David Marnane, Ire) *racd in stands' side gp: hld up: rdn over 2f out: hdwy over 1f out: styd on towards fin: nt pce to trble ldrs: 10th of 26 in gp* **66/1**

0241 **11** *shd* **Another Touch**[21] 3218 4-8-10 103 5ex.................. ConnorMurtagh[(7)] 25 100
(Richard Fahey) *lw: racd in stands' side gp: prom: rdn and hung rt wl over 1f out: styd on same pce fnl 150yds: 11th of 26 in gp* **20/1**

-001 **12** *½* **Withernsea (IRE)**[32] 2828 6-8-11 97.............................. PaulHanagan 32 93
(Richard Fahey) *racd in stands' side gp: prom and t.k.h: rdn over 2f out: unable qck over 1f out: no ex fnl 100yds: 12th of 26 in gp* **66/1**

2320 **13** *hd* **Hors De Combat**[39] 2606 6-9-3 103................................... OisinMurphy 23 101
(Denis Coakley) *racd in stands' side gp: midfield: rdn 2f out: nt clr run and swtchd lft over 1f out: nt clr run and prog ins fnl f whn swtchd rt: styd on wl towards fin: 13th of 26 in gp* **16/1**

0-50 **14** *hd* **Bossy Guest (IRE)**[39] 2606 5-9-3 103.................... SilvestreDeSousa 13 98
(Mick Channon) *racd in stands' side gp: hld up: rdn 2f out: prog whn swtchd rt ins fnl f: fin ok: 14th of 26 in gp* **16/1**

052- **15** *nse* **Abe Lincoln (USA)**[370] 3299 4-8-13 99........................(t[1]) GeraldMosse 31 94
(Jeremy Noseda) *racd in stands' side gp: prom: rdn 2f out: unable qck over 1f out: no ex and fdd fnl 100yds: 15th of 26 in gp* **13/2**[1]

50-0 **16** *shd* **Boomshackerlacker (IRE)**[60] 1960 7-9-0 100................ LiamKeniry 28 95
(George Baker) *racd in stands' side gp: in tch and racd keenly: rdn and swtchd rt ent fnl 2f: hung rt sn after: one pce fnl f: 16th of 26 in gp* **100/1**

-100 **17** *½* **Bravery (IRE)**[34] 2767 4-9-4 104.................................. DanielTudhope 20 98
(David O'Meara) *racd in stands' side gp: midfield: rdn 2f out: no imp over 1f out: styd on same pce fnl 150yds: 17th of 26 in gp* **40/1**

0516 **18** *shd* **Cote D'Azur**[34] 2767 4-8-11 97............................ RichardKingscote 16 90
(Les Eyre) *racd in stands' side gp: midfield: effrt 2f out: one pce ins fnl f: 18th of 26 in gp* **40/1**

-211 **19** *nk* **G K Chesterton (IRE)**[19] 3298 4-8-13 99 5ex...........(p) WilliamBuick 19 92
(Charlie Appleby) *racd in stands' side gp: trckd ldrs: effrt and carried rt ent fnl 2f: stl wl there over 1f out: no ex fnl 150yds: 19th of 26 in gp* **11/1**

-301 **20** *shd* **El Vip (IRE)**[20] 3255 4-8-13 99 5ex................................ JamieSpencer 12 92
(Luca Cumani) *lw: racd in stands' side gp: hld up: swtchd lft under 2f out: kpt on ins fnl f: nvr able to trble ldrs: 20th of 26 in gp* **9/1**[3]

-334 **21** *nk* **Belgian Bill**[130] 698 9-9-0 100.......................................... TrevorWhelan 2 92+
(George Baker) *racd on far side: chsd gp ldr and t.k.h: rdn to ld gp 2f out: no imp on other side: no ex nr fin but 1st of 3 in gp* **66/1**

-142 **22** *nse* **George William**[39] 2606 4-8-12 98.................................... SeanLevey 1 90+
(Richard Hannon) *wnt lft s: racd on far side: hld up: rdn over 2f out: outpcd after: kpt on towards fin: no ch w other side: 2nd of 3 in gp* **12/1**

1-30 **23** *1* **Yuften**[81] 1494 6-9-5 105............................................... AndreaAtzeni 4 94+
(Roger Charlton) *warm: racd far side: led gp: hdd over 2f out: kpt on same pce ins fnl f: no ch w other side: 3rd of 3 in gp* **20/1**

-005 **24** *¾* **Big Baz (IRE)**[21] 3218 7-9-2 102...................................... DougieCostello 17 90
(William Muir) *racd stands' side: in tch: effrt over 2f out: one pce fnl f: 21st of 26 in gp* **100/1**

33-5 **25** *1 ½* **Von Blucher (IRE)**[39] 2610 4-8-13 99................................(t) PJMcDonald 27 83
(Rebecca Menzies) *racd stands' side: trckd ldrs: effrt over 2f out: one pce over 1f out: fdd fnl f: 22nd of 26 in gp* **33/1**

20-1 **26** *2 ¼* **Banksea**[60] 1960 4-9-4 104................................................... LukeMorris 7 83
(Luca Cumani) *racd in stands' side gp: hld up: rdn over 2f out: kpt on ins fnl f: nvr a threat: 23rd of 26 in gp* **10/1**

-035 **27** *2 ¼* **Castle Harbour**[27] 3003 4-9-2 102.................................(b[1]) PatSmullen 9 76
(John Gosden) *lw: racd in stands' side gp: hld up in midfield and t.k.h: rdn 2f out: no imp: bhd and outpcd ins fnl f: 24th of 26 in gp* **40/1**

20-2 **28** *4 ½* **Early Morning (IRE)**[53] 2141 6-9-2 102.............................. AdamKirby 21 66
(Harry Dunlop) *racd in stands' side gp: trckd ldrs: rdn to chal 2f out and carried rt: wknd fnl f: 25th of 26 in gp* **33/1**

1600 **29** *1 ¼* **My Target (IRE)**[25] 3064 6-8-11 97.................................. OlivierPeslier 10 58
(Michael Wigham) *racd in stands' side gp: hld up in midfield: wknd over 1f out: 26th of 26 in gp* **100/1**

1m 37.82s (-2.98) **Going Correction** -0.075s/f (Good) **29** Ran SP% **137.8**
Speed ratings (Par 109): **111,110,110,108,107 107,106,106,106,105 105,104,104,104,104 104,103,103,103,103 103,103,102,10**
CSF £354.02 TOTE £29.20: £7.90, £5.00, £19.10, £4.10; EX 559.90 Trifecta £28890.50 Part won..
**Owner** John Connolly & Odile Griffith **Bred** Es Que Syndicate & Irish National Stud **Trained** Pulborough, W Sussex

■ Stewards' Enquiry : Dane O'Neill four-day ban: used whip above permitted level (July 5-9)

**FOCUS**
One of the most competitive handicaps of the Flat campaign. Not surprisingly the stands' side proved the place to be and the placed horses help to give the form a sound look, although the pace wasn't frantic. The fourth and fifth have been rated close to form.

## 3964 SANDRINGHAM H'CAP (LISTED RACE) (FILLIES) 1m (S)

**5:35** (5:44) (Class 1) (0-110,104) 3-Y-0

**£45,368** (£17,200; £8,608; £4,288; £2,152; £1,080) **Stalls** Centre

Form RPR

- **1** **Con Te Partiro (USA)**[32] 3-9-5 102............................(t[1]) JamieSpencer 11 110
(Wesley A Ward, U.S.A) *tall: athletic: ponied to s: stdd s: hld up in rr: clsd 2f out: swtchd lft to trck runner up and n.m.r briefly over 1f out: sn making hdwy u.p: styd on strly ins fnl f to ld 50yds out: gng away at fin* **20/1**

045 **2** *1 ¼* **Rain Goddess (IRE)**[39] 2644 3-9-7 104.............................. RyanMoore 18 109
(A P O'Brien, Ire) *w'like: hld up in rr: clsd over 2f out: rdn and hdwy wl over 1f out: carried rt and chal 1f out: drvn to ld 100yds out: hdd and no ex 50yds out* **7/1**[2]

14-4 **3** *1* **Paco's Angel**[74] 1621 3-9-0 97.......................................... ShaneKelly 23 100
(Richard Hughes) *hld up in tch in midfield: hmpd 1/2-way: clsd to trck ldrs 2f out: swtchd rt but then hung rt and rdn to ld over 1f out: hdd 100yds out: styd on same pce after* **33/1**

2-11 **4** *1* **Queen Of Time**[26] 3031 3-8-7 90 oh3............................ HarryBentley 13 91+
(Henry Candy) *hld up in tch in midfield: hdwy ent fnl 2f: drvn and chsd ldrs 1f out: kpt on same pce ins fnl f* **8/1**[3]

5-14 **5** *nk* **Classical Times**[33] 2802 3-8-13 96................................... JamesDoyle 20 96
(Peter Chapple-Hyam) *hld up towards rr: smooth hdwy against stands' rail jst over 2f out: drvn and ev ch 1f out tl no ex 100yds out: wknd towards fin* **50/1**

200 **6** *2* **Asking (IRE)**[24] 3110 3-8-13 96.....................................(t) AnaO'Brien 14 91+
(A P O'Brien, Ire) *swtg: wl in tch in midfield: impeded 1/2-way: rdn to chse ldrs 2f out: drvn and ev ch over 1f out tl no ex jst ins fnl f: wknd fnl 100yds* **33/1**

-165 **7** *shd* **Dancing Breeze (IRE)**[13] 3504 3-8-7 90 oh3.................. MartinDwyer 6 85+
(John Gosden) *lw: s.i.s: effrt jst over 2f out: hdwy u.p over 1f out: styd on same pce and no imp ins fnl f* **25/1**

13-2 **8** *1 ¾* **On Her Toes (IRE)**[33] 2802 3-9-1 98................................. PatCosgrave 8 89
(William Haggas) *lw: in tch in midfield: swtchd lft 2f out: hdwy whn swtchd bk rt jst over 1f out: kpt on ins fnl f: no threat to ldrs* **10/1**

1013 **9** *1¼* **Tisbutadream (IRE)**[18] 3319 3-9-0 **97**..................... SilvestreDeSousa 2 85+
(David Elsworth) *taken down early: hld up in tch in midfield: effrt u.p over 2f out: chsd ldrs 2f out tl no ex 1f out: wknd ins fnl f* **14/1**

121 **10** *nk* **Cheval Blanche (USA)**[52] 2177 3-8-7 **90** oh4........... TomMarquand 24 78
(Michael Bell) *lw: sn led: rdn: hung lft and hdd over 1f out: stl ev ch but no ex 1f out: wknd ins fnl f* **25/1**

-600 **11** *½* **Kilmah**[18] 3319 3-8-13 **96**............................................ RichardKingscote 7 82
(Mark Johnston) *chsd ldr: wnt lft 1/2-way: rdn over 2f out: lost 2nd over 1f out: sn btn and wknd ins fnl f* **33/1**

516 **12** *½* **Bean Feasa**[24] 3110 3-9-5 **102**........................................ KevinManning 1 87
(J S Bolger, Ire) *str: bustled along leaving stalls: in tch in midfield: effrt to chse ldrs 2f out: unable qck u.p over 1f out: wknd ins fnl f* **14/1**

350- **13** *¾* **Marie Of Lyon**[286] 6260 3-8-7 **90** oh2.............................. PaulHanagan 10 74
(Richard Fahey) *hld up towards rr: effrt and sme hdwy whn hung rt over 1f out: sn no imp and wknd ins fnl f* **66/1**

-216 **14** *4* **Prosper**[32] 2827 3-8-7 **90** oh2.......................................(h[1]) AndreaAtzeni 19 64
(Roger Varian) *midfield: hmpd and lost pl 1/2-way: rdn 3f out: no imp u.p over 1f out: wknd ins fnl f* **20/1**

2-12 **15** *3½* **Gymnaste (IRE)**[21] 3211 3-8-7 **90** oh1...................... JosephineGordon 4 56+
(John Gosden) *tall: lw: t.k.h: chsd ldrs: rdn to chal 2f out tl no ex over 1f out: sn wknd* **6/1**[1]

6-31 **16** *2¼* **Lady Freyja**[11] 3595 3-8-7 **90** oh5........................................ LukeMorris 5 51
(John Ryan) *trckd ldrs: rdn to press ldrs jst over 2f out tl no ex and btn over 1f out: sn wknd* **40/1**

0-06 **17** *½* **Baileys Showgirl (FR)**[27] 3013 3-8-12 **95**.................... FranBerry 3 55
(Mark Johnston) *dwlt: in rr: effrt over 2f out: no imp 2f out: wknd over 1f out* **100/1**

1-13 **18** *1½* **Sibilance**[33] 2802 3-8-10 **93**.................................................. PatDobbs 16 50
(Ralph Beckett) *in tch in midfield: effrt ent fnl 2f: no imp and sn struggling: wknd and bhd 1f out* **7/1**[2]

54-0 **19** *½* **Drumfad Bay (IRE)**[31] 2860 3-9-0 **97**..................... ColmO'Donoghue 9 52
(Mrs John Harrington, Ire) *midfield: lost pl 1/2-way: u.p and struggling whn swtchd rt over 2f out: wknd over 1f out* **20/1**

013 **20** *2¼* **Present Tense**[16] 3395 3-8-12 **95**.............................. PatSmullen 15 45
(John Gosden) *wl in tch in midfield: hmpd 4f out: rdn over 2f out: little rspnse and btn whn wandered over 1f out: sn wknd: bhd whn eased ins fnl f* **25/1**

20-3 **21** *10* **Grecian Light (IRE)**[94] 1270 3-9-5 **102**........................ WilliamBuick 17 29
(Charlie Appleby) *in tch in midfield: impeded 1/2-way: towards rr and no hdwy u.p over 2f out: t.o and eased fnl f* **20/1**

-045 **22** *37* **Miss Infinity (IRE)**[35] 2738 3-9-0 **97**............................ AdamKirby 22
(Mark Johnston) *wl in tch in midfield: rdn 1/2-way: sn struggling and dropped to rr 2f out: eased and t.o ins fnl f* **50/1**

-153 **23** *5* **Really Special**[118] 887 3-9-4 **101**.................................. OisinMurphy 21
(Saeed bin Suroor) *chsd ldrs tl lost pl 4f out: bhd and eased 2f out: t.o* **8/1**[3]

10-2 **24** *4½* **Salamah (IRE)**[42] 2517 3-8-7 **90** oh10.............................. ShaneFoley 12
(Michael Bell) *chsd ldrs: rdn over 3f out: sn struggling: bhd and eased 2f out: t.o* **66/1**

1m 38.84s (-1.96) **Going Correction** -0.075s/f (Good) **24** Ran SP% **133.7**
Speed ratings (Par 104): **106,104,103,102,102 100,100,98,97,97 96,96,95,91,87 85,85,83,83,80 70,33,28,24**
CSF £139.42 CT £4721.06 TOTE £20.80: £4.70, £2.20, £8.70, £2.50; EX 99.20 Trifecta £4262.30.
**Owner** Hat Creek Racing **Bred** K C Garrett Farm Llc **Trained** North America
■ Stewards' Enquiry : Ana O'Brien two-day ban: used whip above permitted level (July 5-6)

**FOCUS**
Those racing more towards the stands' side again came out on top and, with the pace collapsing, the race very much set up for the closers. A pb from the third, with the winner rated as fitting the race standard.
T/Jkpt: Not won. T/Plt: £156.90 to a £1 stake. Pool: £595,813.10 - 2771.36 winning units T/Qpdt: £61.80 to a £1 stake. Pool: £35,909.39 - 429.89 winning units **Steve Payne & Darren Owen**

# 3230 CHELMSFORD (A.W) (L-H)

Wednesday, June 21

**OFFICIAL GOING: Polytrack: standard**
Weather: Fine

## 3965 PLACEPOT QUADPOT TWO BETS ONE SLIP NOVICE AUCTION STKS 7f (P)

**6:10** (6:11) (Class 5) 2-Y-O **£4,528** (£1,347; £673; £336) **Stalls** Low

Form RPR

**1** **Capla Temptress (IRE)** 2-8-10 0.................................. AntonioFresu 4 68
(Marco Botti) *hld up: hdwy over 1f out: r.o wl ins fnl f to ld post* **20/1**

05 **2** *nse* **Alifax**[8] 3689 2-9-1 0........................................................ TimmyMurphy 2 73
(Jamie Osborne) *a.p: chsd ldr over 1f out: rdn to ld ins fnl f: hdd post* **3/1**[2]

64 **3** *hd* **Uther Pendragon (IRE)**[61] 1934 2-9-0 0..........................(p[1]) JohnFahy 8 71
(J S Moore) *a.p: rdn over 1f out: r.o* **16/1**

532 **4** *¾* **Zabaletaswansong (GER)**[23] 3156 2-9-2 0....................... KieranO'Neill 10 71
(Richard Hannon) *sn led: rdn and hdd ins fnl f: unable qck towards fin* **2/1**[1]

0 **5** *nk* **Barbarianatthegate**[23] 3156 2-9-2 0...........................(b[1]) TomQueally 9 71
(Brian Meehan) *chsd ldr: pushed along over 3f out: rdn and lost 2nd over 1f out: styd on* **16/1**

**6** *½* **Danzan (IRE)** 2-9-0 0...................................................... DavidProbert 1 67
(Andrew Balding) *mid-div: hdwy over 1f out: r.o* **9/1**

**7** *2* **Neverbeen To Paris (IRE)** 2-9-1 0.............................. LouisSteward 3 63+
(Michael Bell) *hld up: racd keenly: hdwy over 2f out: rdn over 1f out: edgd lft: styd on* **4/1**[3]

**8** *3* **Galloping Hogan (IRE)** 2-8-10 0.............................. MitchGodwin(5) 7 55
(Sylvester Kirk) *hld up: pushed along 4f out: sme hdwy press over 2f out: styd on same pce fr over 1f out* **25/1**

**9** *1* **Gemologist (IRE)** 2-8-10 0.......................................................... JFEgan 5 47
(Mark Johnston) *pushed along early in rr: rdn over 1f out: n.d* **8/1**

0 **10** *2½* **Four Fifty Three**[16] 3390 2-8-13 0.................................... JoeyHaynes 6 43
(Mark H Tompkins) *hld up: rdn over 1f out: nvr on terms* **50/1**

1m 29.92s (2.72) **Going Correction** +0.225s/f (Slow) **10** Ran SP% **121.8**
Speed ratings (Par 93): **93,92,92,91,91 90,88,85,84,81**
CSF £81.72 TOTE £23.20: £6.70, £1.70, £5.30; EX 133.20 Trifecta £2126.20.
**Owner** Les Boyer Partnership **Bred** Pier House Stud **Trained** Newmarket, Suffolk

**FOCUS**
Standard going ahead of the opener, a moderate novice event in which they didn't go fast and finished in a heap.

## 3966 TOTEPOOL BETTING ON ALL UK RACING H'CAP 1m 2f (P)

**6:40** (6:43) (Class 4) (0-80,80) 4-Y-O+ **£8,086** (£2,406; £1,202; £601) **Stalls** Low

Form RPR

316- **1** **Angrywhitepyjamas (IRE)**[322] 5026 4-9-1 **77**........... GeorgeWood(3) 5 89
(William Muir) *sn led: hdd after 1f: remained handy: chsd ldr over 4f out: rdn to ld and edgd lft over 1f out: r.o wl* **10/3**[1]

000- **2** *4½* **Classic Villager**[247] 7412 5-9-7 **80**.............................(h[1]) RobertWinston 8 83
(Dean Ivory) *led at stdy pce after 1f: qcknd over 2f out: rdn and hdd over 1f out: edgd lft and no ex ins fnl f* **9/2**[2]

1553 **3** *2* **Foie Gras**[27] 2996 7-8-10 **69**........................................ AdamBeschizza 11 68
(Chris Dwyer) *prom: rdn over 2f out: edgd lft over 1f out: styd on same pce fnl f* **14/1**

501 **4** *hd* **The Gay Cavalier**[18] 3325 6-8-10 **69**..............................(t) JackMitchell 9 68+
(John Ryan) *hld up: rdn over 1f out: r.o ins fnl f: nvr nrr* **11/2**[3]

624- **5** *1¼* **Warrior Prince**[350] 4027 4-9-4 **77**................................ AntonioFresu 6 73
(Ed Dunlop) *prom: racd keenly: shkn up over 2f out: edgd lft and wknd fnl f* **6/1**

3-00 **6** *shd* **Pirate's Treasure**[14] 3471 4-9-4 **77**.............................. TomQueally 10 73
(Jennie Candlish) *s.i.s: hld up: hdwy over 3f out: rdn over 2f out: styd on same pce fr over 1f out* **16/1**

0120 **7** *½* **Chelwood Gate (IRE)**[18] 3344 7-8-9 **68**..........................(v) MartinLane 4 63
(Conor Dore) *hld up: rdn over 1f out: nvr nrr* **20/1**

0-65 **8** *½* **Vizier**[22] 3168 4-8-7 **73**.............................................(p) PatrickVaughan(7) 2 67
(David O'Meara) *hld up in tch: rdn over 1f out: wknd fnl f* **20/1**

553 **9** *½* **Craftsmanship (FR)**[22] 3168 6-9-3 **76**............................(p) PaoloSirigu 3 69
(Robert Eddery) *hld up: rdn over 1f out: n.d* **9/2**[2]

0605 **10** *3¾* **Mezzotint (IRE)**[23] 3140 8-9-1 **74**.................................... DavidProbert 1 59
(Lee Carter) *chsd ldr tl over 4f out: rdn over 2f out: wknd over 1f out* **10/1**

2m 13.17s (4.57) **Going Correction** +0.225s/f (Slow) **10** Ran SP% **120.3**
Speed ratings (Par 105): **90,86,84,84,83 83,83,82,82,79**
CSF £18.79 CT £183.78 TOTE £3.10: £2.10, £3.00, £5.30; EX 21.80 Trifecta £153.00.
**Owner** O'Mulloy, Collenette, Clark **Bred** J & J Waldron **Trained** Lambourn, Berks

**FOCUS**
An average handicap in which they didn't go fast, and the first two were up with the pace throughout, making it hard for those coming from behind. The level is a bit fluid.

## 3967 TOTEPOOL LIVE INFO DOWNLOAD THE APP H'CAP 5f (P)

**7:10** (7:13) (Class 2) (0-105,102) 3-Y-O+ **£16,172** (£4,812; £2,405; £1,202) **Stalls** Low

Form RPR

130 **1** **Encore D'Or**[25] 3079 5-10-0 **102**........................................... LukeMorris 1 110
(Robert Cowell) *chsd ldr 1f: remained handy: rdn to ld ins fnl f: r.o* **11/4**[2]

3100 **2** *nk* **Royal Birth**[46] 2397 6-9-11 **102**......................................(t) AaronJones(3) 3 109
(Stuart Williams) *half-rrd s: hld up: racd keenly: swtchd lft 4f out: nt clr run 1/2-way: hdwy over 1f out: rdn to chse wnr ins fnl f: r.o* **6/1**

-124 **3** *1* **A Momentofmadness**[18] 3321 4-9-3 **91**..............(h) SilvestreDeSousa 7 94+
(Charles Hills) *s.i.s: hld up: hung rt 1/2-way: rdn over 1f out: r.o to go 3rd wl ins fnl f: nt rch ldrs* **15/8**[1]

144 **4** *1¼* **Jordan Sport**[16] 3410 4-9-4 **92**..........................................(h) JackMitchell 5 91
(David Simcock) *jnd ldr after 1f: rdn and ev ch over 1f out: styd on same pce ins fnl f* **9/2**[3]

0015 **5** *1* **Brother Tiger**[22] 3176 8-8-9 **83** oh2............................................ JFEgan 4 78
(David C Griffiths) *led: rdn over 1f out: hdd and no ex ins fnl f* **33/1**

5414 **6** *½* **Dynamo Walt (IRE)**[20] 3231 6-8-11 **85**............................(v) KierenFox 9 78
(Derek Shaw) *s.i.s: in rr: rdn over 1f out: r.o towards fin: nvr nrr* **20/1**

-200 **7** *nk* **Exceed The Limit**[18] 3321 4-9-2 **90**.............................. RobertWinston 6 82
(Robert Cowell) *in rr: hdwy u.p over 1f out: edgd lft ins fnl f: nt trble ldrs* **11/1**

00-6 **8** *¾* **Huntsmans Close**[10] 3625 7-9-2 **90**.......................... GeorgeDowning 2 83
(Robert Cowell) *prom: rdn over 1f out: styng on same pce whn nt clr run wl ins fnl f* **25/1**

6210 **9** *½* **Bosham**[18] 3337 7-8-11 **88**...........................................(bt) NathanEvans(3) 8 76
(Michael Easterby) *chsd ldrs: rdn over 1f out: no ex fnl f* **25/1**

1m 0.23s (0.03) **Going Correction** +0.225s/f (Slow) **9** Ran SP% **117.6**
Speed ratings (Par 109): **108,107,105,103,102 101,101,99,99**
CSF £18.89 CT £38.21 TOTE £3.60: £1.40, £1.60, £1.30; EX 17.70 Trifecta £38.90.
**Owner** Mrs Morley,G Johnson,Newsells Park Stud **Bred** Newsells Park Stud **Trained** Six Mile Bottom, Cambs

**FOCUS**
A fair sprint for the track. They went a sound gallop and the form looks solid. Small personal bests from the first two.

## 3968 TOTEPOOL LIKE US ON FACEBOOK FILLIES' H'CAP 1m 6f (P)

**7:40** (7:41) (Class 2) (0-105,98) 4-Y-O+ **£16,172** (£4,812; £2,405; £1,202) **Stalls** Low

Form RPR

3151 **1** **Langlauf (USA)**[14] 3458 4-8-0 **82**...................................(p) DavidEgan(5) 6 89
(Rod Millman) *chsd ldr tl led 3f out: rdn over 1f out: styd on* **5/1**[3]

4-42 **2** *nk* **Jelly Monger (IRE)**[26] 3033 5-8-9 **86**...................... SilvestreDeSousa 3 92
(Dominic Ffrench Davis) *a.p: racd keenly: chsd wnr over 2f out: rdn over 1f out: carried hd high: styd on u.p* **5/1**[3]

1-3 **3** *1¼* **Notice (IRE)**[26] 3033 4-8-1 **81**......................................... AaronJones(3) 7 85
(David Simcock) *hld up: hdwy u.p and hung lft fr over 1f out: styd on to go 3rd towards fin: nt rch ldrs* **10/1**

3-12 **4** *¾* **Graceland (FR)**[34] 2770 5-8-5 **87**.............................. LuluStanford(5) 4 90
(Michael Bell) *s.s: hld up: plld hrd: swtchd rt and hdwy over 1f out: rdn and edgd lft ins fnl f: styd on same pce* **9/4**[1]

00-2 **5** *7* **Elysian Fields (GR)**[46] 2389 6-9-7 **98**............................ JackMitchell 1 91
(Amanda Perrett) *chsd ldrs: rdn over 2f out: wknd ins fnl f* **5/1**[3]

515- **6** *1¾* **Cliff Face (IRE)**[210] 8068 4-9-4 **95**................................... LukeMorris 2 86
(Sir Mark Prescott Bt) *hld up: rdn whn hmpd over 1f out: hung lft and wknd fnl f* **7/2**[2]

-001 **7** *¾* **Perfect Summer (IRE)**[23] 3158 7-7-13 **79** oh3........(b) GeorgeWood(3) 5 69
(Ian Williams) *led at stdy pce tl qcknd 4f out: hdd 3f out: sn rdn: wknd over 1f out* **25/1**

3m 7.02s (3.82) **Going Correction** +0.225s/f (Slow) **7** Ran SP% **115.9**
Speed ratings (Par 96): **98,97,97,96,92 91,91**
CSF £30.69 TOTE £6.00: £2.90, £3.30; EX 22.90 Trifecta £168.60.
**Owner** Tony Bloom **Bred** Darley **Trained** Kentisbeare, Devon

**FOCUS**
A tight fillies' staying handicap in which they didn't go much of a gallop. The first four came clear.

## 3969 @TOTEPOOLRACING WIN RACING TICKETS ON TWITTER H'CAP 6f (P)
**8:10** (8:10) (Class 3) (0-95,97) 4-Y-0+ **£9,703** (£2,887; £1,443; £721) **Stalls** Centre

Form RPR
-100 **1** **Udontdodou**[16] 3410 4-8-13 **87** RobertWinston 4 102
(Richard Guest) *sn pushed along and prom: led over 1f out: rdn out* **13/8**[1]
1-60 **2** *1 ¾* **Mazzini**[26] 3034 4-8-12 **89** GeorgeWood(3) 2 98
(James Fanshawe) *hld up: hdwy over 1f out: chsd wnr ins fnl f: styd on same pce* **5/2**[2]
5121 **3** *2* **Dark Side Dream**[23] 3140 5-7-10 **77** MillyNaseb(7) 7 80
(Chris Dwyer) *awkward s: sn rcvrd into mid-div: hdwy 1/2-way: rdn over 1f out: styd on to go 3rd wl ins fnl f* **8/1**
2112 **4** *¾* **Menelik (IRE)**[22] 3176 8-8-6 **80** (bt) DavidProbert 9 80
(Des Donovan, Ire) *chsd ldrs: rdn over 1f out: no ex ins fnl f* **16/1**
1065 **5** *1* **Top Boy**[42] 2516 7-8-9 **83** (v) MartinLane 3 80
(Derek Shaw) *stdd s: hld up: plld hrd: hdwy over 1f out: sn rdn and hung lft: nt trble ldrs* **25/1**
5434 **6** *1 ¼* **Watchable**[18] 3324 7-9-7 **95** (v) DanielTudhope 6 88
(David O'Meara) *led: hdd over 4f out: chsd ldr: rdn and ev ch over 1f out: wknd ins fnl f* **7/1**[3]
2500 **7** *hd* **Outer Space**[11] 3593 6-9-2 **90** TimmyMurphy 8 82
(Jamie Osborne) *sn outpcd: r.o towards fin* **25/1**
0230 **8** *½* **Kingsley Klarion (IRE)**[11] 3567 4-8-4 **78** SilvestreDeSousa 10 69
(Mark Johnston) *sn pushed along in rr: n.d* **12/1**
1-5 **9** *4* **Song Of Shadows**[28] 2975 4-8-6 **80** (t) AdamBeschizza 11 58
(Michael Wigham) *s.i.s: hld up: hdwy u.p over 1f out: wknd fnl f* **20/1**
1/F6 **10** *hd* **Porta Rosa (USA)**[7] 3723 4-8-8 **82** JFEgan 5 59
(Mohamed Moubarak) *w ldr tl led over 4f out: rdn and hdd over 1f out: wknd and eased ins fnl f* **25/1**

1m 12.26s (-1.44) **Going Correction** +0.225s/f (Slow) **10** Ran SP% **120.2**
Speed ratings (Par 107): **118,115,113,112,110 109,108,108,102,102**
CSF £5.50 CT £22.79 TOTE £3.20: £1.30, £1.20, £2.20; EX 7.10 Trifecta £48.80.
**Owner** Mrs Alison Guest **Bred** Times Of Wigan Ltd **Trained** Ingmanthorpe, W Yorks

**FOCUS**
An average sprint handicap in which they went a good clip, and the right horses came from behind to occupy the first two places. It's been rated on the positive side, with the third rated close to his recent form.

## 3970 TOTEPOOLLIVEINFO.COM MAIDEN STKS 6f (P)
**8:40** (8:42) (Class 5) 3-Y-0 **£5,175** (£1,540; £769; £384) **Stalls** Centre

Form RPR
4 **1** **Summerghand (IRE)**[46] 2383 3-9-5 0 DanielTudhope 7 78
(David O'Meara) *hld up: hdwy over 2f out: rdn and hung lft fr over 1f out: styd on to ld wl ins fnl f: jst hld on* **7/2**[3]
063- **2** *shd* **Zumran**[306] 5598 3-8-9 **63** DavidEgan(5) 6 73
(Philip McBride) *chsd ldrs: rdn and ev ch whn n.m.r wl ins fnl f: r.o: rdr dropped whip nr fin* **25/1**
0 **3** *nk* **Noble Masterpiece**[40] 2580 3-9-5 0 StevieDonohoe 2 77
(Sir Michael Stoute) *s.i.s: hld up: plld hrd: hdwy over 1f out: r.o wl* **5/1**
62-0 **4** *nk* **Star Catch**[58] 2033 3-9-0 76 DavidProbert 4 71
(Charles Hills) *led: plld hrd: rdn over 1f out: hdd wl ins fnl f: no ex nr fin* **8/1**
34 **5** *3 ¼* **Khitaamy (IRE)**[14] 3456 3-9-5 0 AntonioFresu 3 66
(Ed Dunlop) *trckd ldrs: racd keenly: rdn over 1f out: hung lft and no ex ins fnl f* **5/2**[1]
2-6 **6** *2* **Lovely Acclamation (IRE)**[30] 2898 3-9-0 0 SilvestreDeSousa 8 54
(Ismail Mohammed) *s.i.s: sn rcvrd to chse ldr: rdn and lost 2nd over 1f out: wknd ins fnl f* **3/1**[2]
**7** *3* **Emilysbutterscotch** 3-9-0 0 AdamBeschizza 5 45
(Rae Guest) *hld up: pushed along over 3f out: n.d* **25/1**
00- **8** *4* **Magicinthemaking (USA)**[294] 6034 3-9-0 0 (h[1]) RobertWinston 1 32
(Mike Murphy) *broke wl: sn stdd and lost pl: swtchd rt over 4f out: bhd fr 1/2-way* **25/1**

1m 14.03s (0.33) **Going Correction** +0.225s/f (Slow) **8** Ran SP% **115.1**
Speed ratings (Par 99): **106,105,105,105,100 98,94,88**
CSF £84.69 TOTE £4.60: £1.10, £5.70, £2.80; EX 83.50 Trifecta £944.50.
**Owner** Hamad Rashed Bin Ghedayer **Bred** Airlie Stud **Trained** Upper Helmsley, N Yorks

**FOCUS**
An open maiden and they may have gone too fast, with the two market fancies disappointing having raced up with the pace. The winner came from behind. The runner-up is the key to the form.

## 3971 SHIRES IN CONCERT HERE 7TH JULY H'CAP 7f (P)
**9:10** (9:15) (Class 6) (0-65,67) 3-Y-0+ **£3,234** (£962; £481; £240) **Stalls** Low

Form RPR
423U **1** **Misu Pete**[12] 3550 5-9-0 **51** SilvestreDeSousa 2 58
(Mark Usher) *w ldr early: lost pl over 3f out: pushed along over 2f out: hdwy over 1f out: sn edgd lft: rdn to ld wl ins fnl f: r.o* **10/3**[1]
5660 **2** *¾* **Out Of The Ashes**[22] 3170 4-10-2 **67** (t) StevieDonohoe 14 72
(Mohamed Moubarak) *chsd ldrs: led 5f out tl over 4f out: chsd ldr: rdn to ld ins fnl f: sn hdd: styd on* **12/1**
0454 **3** *¾* **Zabdi**[28] 2961 4-9-10 **61** (t[1]) DavidProbert 1 64
(Lee Carter) *hld up: hdwy over 1f out: nt clr run ins fnl f: r.o* **8/1**
0-10 **4** *½* **See You Mush**[52] 2181 3-8-12 **58** (b) AdamBeschizza 8 57
(Mrs Ilka Gansera-Leveque) *plld hrd and prom: led over 4f out: rdn and hdd ins fnl f: styd on same pce* **9/1**
4022 **5** *nk* **Kings Heart (IRE)**[12] 3543 3-8-13 **64** (h) RachealKneller(5) 11 63
(Mark Usher) *prom: rdn over 1f out: styng on whn hmpd ins fnl f* **10/1**
0-54 **6** *1 ¼* **Mythical Spirit (IRE)**[70] 1727 3-9-1 **61** LukeMorris 6 55
(James Tate) *sn led: hdd 5f out: remained handy: rdn over 1f out: no ex ins fnl f* **4/1**[2]
-052 **7** *hd* **Forever Yours (IRE)**[14] 3468 4-9-12 **63** RobertWinston 10 61+
(Dean Ivory) *s.i.s and hmpd sn after s: hld up: nt clr run: swtchd lft and hdwy over 1f out: nt clr run again wl ins fnl f: nt trble ldrs* **5/1**[3]
3403 **8** *nk* **Do You Know (IRE)**[14] 3473 3-9-2 **65** (bt) GeorgeWood(3) 12 58
(Marco Botti) *hld up: rdn over 1f out: r.o ins fnl f: nvr nrr* **10/1**
4504 **9** *13* **Noble Act**[20] 3265 4-9-6 **64** DarraghKeenan(7) 9 25
(Phil McEntee) *hld up: hdwy over 3f out: sn hung rt and wknd* **16/1**
-000 **10** *3* **The Firm (IRE)**[20] 3264 8-9-9 **60** (b) JimmyQuinn 4 13
(J R Jenkins) *free to post: hld up: plld hrd: wknd over 2f out* **33/1**
6000 **11** *9* **Mime Dance**[75] 1603 6-9-11 **62** (p) TimmyMurphy 7
(John Butler) *hld up in tch: wknd wl over 2f out* **25/1**

1m 27.83s (0.63) **Going Correction** +0.225s/f (Slow)
**WFA** 3 from 4yo+ 9lb **11** Ran SP% **119.4**
Speed ratings (Par 101): **105,104,103,102,102 100,100,100,85,82 71**
CSF £45.47 CT £307.49 TOTE £3.90: £1.60, £3.90, £3.30; EX 47.60 Trifecta £351.40.
**Owner** The Mark Usher Racing Club **Bred** A C M Spalding **Trained** Upper Lambourn, Berks

**FOCUS**
A moderate handicap in which they set a sound pace, but they finished quite bunched up, suggesting the form isn't look strong. The winner ending a 19-race losing run. Straightforward form rated around the first three.
T/Plt: £119.10 to a £1 stake. Pool: £64,483.32 - 395.11 winning units T/Qpdt: £15.50 to a £1 stake. Pool: £6,684.96 - 319.12 winning units **Colin Roberts**

# 3704 HAMILTON (R-H)
### Wednesday, June 21

**OFFICIAL GOING: Good to firm (firm in places; 7.8)**
Wind: Almost nil Weather: Overcast

## 3972 RACINGUK.COM NOVICE AUCTION STKS (PLUS 10 RACE) 5f 7y
**2:10** (2:12) (Class 4) 2-Y-0 **£5,175** (£1,540; £769; £384) **Stalls** High

Form RPR
3 **1** **Undercover Brother**[11] 3562 2-9-2 0 SamJames 3 71
(David O'Meara) *mde all cl to stands' rail: rdn and hrd pressed fr over 1f out: hld on gamely fnl f* **11/1**
52 **2** *hd* **Haveoneyerself (IRE)**[19] 3277 2-9-2 0 TonyHamilton 2 70
(John Butler) *pressed wnr: rdn and ev ch fr over 1f out: kpt on fnl f: hld cl home* **9/1**[3]
2 **3** *2* **Verhoyen**[11] 3599 2-9-2 0 (h) WJLee 1 63
(M C Grassick, Ire) *trckd ldrs on outside: outpcd and edgd rt over 1f out: kpt on ins fnl f: nt rch first two* **11/10**[1]
0 **4** *6* **Curzon (IRE)**[16] 3399 2-8-13 0 JoshDoyle(3) 8 41
(David O'Meara) *t.k.h: trckd ldrs tl rdn and wknd wl over 1f out* **25/1**
4312 **5** *2 ¼* **Villa Tora**[11] 3562 2-9-3 0 JoeFanning 6 34
(Mark Johnston) *dwlt and wnt rt s: t.k.h and sn prom: rdn over 1f out: sn wknd* **13/8**[2]
0 **6** *nse* **Money For Luck (IRE)**[15] 3430 2-8-11 0 BenRobinson(5) 4 33
(Brian Ellison) *blkd s: sn outpcd and bhd: hdwy on outside over 2f out: rdn and edgd rt over 1f out: sn wknd* **40/1**

1m 0.06s (0.06) **Going Correction** -0.125s/f (Firm) **6** Ran SP% **110.3**
Speed ratings (Par 95): **94,93,90,80,77 77**
CSF £93.74 TOTE £10.10: £5.50, £4.70; EX 50.20 Trifecta £140.20.
**Owner** P Sutherland **Bred** Mechanical Facilities Services Ltd **Trained** Upper Helmsley, N Yorks
■ Stewards' Enquiry : Sam James caution: careless riding

**FOCUS**
The going was good to firm, firm in places. A fair contest run at a sound gallop. The first two home were always prominent. It's been rated as ordinary form.

## 3973 BRITISH STALLION STUDS EBF MAIDEN STKS (PLUS 10 RACE) (A £20,000 BB FOODSERVICE 2YO SERIES QUAL) 6f 6y
**2:45** (2:45) (Class 4) 2-Y-0 **£5,175** (£1,540; £769; £384) **Stalls** High

Form RPR
43 **1** **Armed Response**[33] 2771 2-9-5 0 JackGarritty 7 79
(Jedd O'Keeffe) *mde all against stands' rail: rdn over 1f out: drew clr fnl f* **7/1**
2 **2** *3 ¼* **Poet's Prince**[12] 3538 2-9-5 0 JoeFanning 3 69
(Mark Johnston) *pressed wnr thrght: rdn and edgd rt over 1f out: outpcd ins fnl f* **1/1**[1]
**3** *2 ¾* **Phoenix Lightning (IRE)** 2-9-2 0 TonyHamilton 1 57
(Richard Fahey) *trckd ldrs: effrt and rdn wl over 1f out: wknd ins fnl f* **4/1**[2]
55 **4** *3 ¾* **Plundered (IRE)**[18] 3339 2-9-5 0 BenCurtis 8 48+
(David Brown) *prom: drvn and outpcd 2f out: btn fnl f* **22/1**
5 **5** *nk* **Northern Law (IRE)**[25] 3093 2-9-5 0 JasonHart 4 47+
(John Quinn) *s.i.s: sn pushed along in rr: drvn and outpcd over 3f out: n.d after* **9/2**[3]
**6** *11 ½* **Drover** 2-8-11 0 RowanScott(5) 2 7+
(Keith Dalgleish) *dwlt: t.k.h: hld up in tch on outside: drvn and struggling over 2f out: sn wknd* **14/1**
**7** *6* **Barney George** 2-9-2 0 TomEaves 5
(Iain Jardine) *missed break: bhd and outpcd: nvr on terms* **33/1**

1m 12.59s (0.39) **Going Correction** -0.125s/f (Firm) **7** Ran SP% **114.6**
Speed ratings (Par 95): **92,87,84,79,78 63,55**
CSF £14.58 TOTE £9.50: £4.20, £1.10; EX 16.80 Trifecta £60.50.
**Owner** Caron & Paul Chapman **Bred** Alvediston Stud **Trained** Middleham Moor, N Yorks

**FOCUS**
A truly run maiden which favoured those prominent. Again the winner came up the stands rail.

## 3974 SAM COLLINGWOOD-CAMERON H'CAP 6f 6y
**3:20** (3:20) (Class 5) (0-75,73) 3-Y-0+ **£3,881** (£1,155; £577; £288) **Stalls** High

Form RPR
4-02 **1** **Parys Mountain (IRE)**[4] 3814 3-9-7 **73** (h) BenCurtis 7 83
(David Brown) *mde all against stands' rail: rdn over 1f out: drew clr ins fnl f* **9/4**[1]
0000 **2** *2 ½* **Cosmic Chatter**[11] 3585 7-10-0 **73** (p) JamesSullivan 8 77
(Ruth Carr) *t.k.h: prom: effrt and rdn over 1f out: chsd (clr) wnr ins fnl f: kpt on: nt pce to chal* **9/2**[3]
0206 **3** *1 ¼* **Steelriver (IRE)**[39] 2621 7-9-9 **68** PaulMulrennan 3 68
(David Barron) *missed break: hld up: rdn along over 1f out: kpt on ins fnl f* **7/1**
6-60 **4** *nk* **Manatee Bay**[25] 3095 7-9-9 **73** (p) PhilDennis(5) 4 74+
(Noel Wilson) *t.k.h: hld up bhd ldng gp: no room fr over 2f out tl last 100yds: styng on whn nt clr run towards fin* **25/1**
-321 **5** *hd* **Love Oasis**[16] 3384 3-9-5 **71** JoeFanning 6 67
(Mark Johnston) *pressed wnr: drvn along over 2f out: outpcd ins fnl f* **10/3**[2]
0600 **6** *½* **Salvatore Fury (IRE)**[2] 3897 7-9-10 **69** (p) AndrewMullen 5 66
(Keith Dalgleish) *t.k.h: trckd ldrs: effrt and rdn over 1f out: outpcd ins fnl f* **14/1**
0325 **7** *1 ¼* **Extrasolar**[22] 3183 7-9-13 **72** (p) PhillipMakin 1 65
(Geoffrey Harker) *in tch on outside: rdn and effrt 2f out: wknd ins fnl f* **9/1**
2410 **8** *¾* **Arnold**[16] 3403 3-8-13 **65** ShaneGray 2 53
(Ann Duffield) *hld up: rdn along on outside over 2f out: wknd over 1f out* **12/1**

1m 10.78s (-1.42) **Going Correction** -0.125s/f (Firm)
**WFA** 3 from 7yo 7lb **8** Ran SP% **112.7**
Speed ratings (Par 103): **104,100,99,98,98 97,96,95**
CSF £12.16 CT £59.19 TOTE £3.20: £1.10, £1.70, £2.40; EX 13.00 Trifecta £63.40.
**Owner** J C Fretwell **Bred** Yeomanstown Stud **Trained** Averham Park, Notts

**FOCUS**
A competitive contest for the grade. It was run at a sound tempo with the winner again making all up the stands rails.

## 3975 FOLLOW @HAMILTONPARKRC ON TWITTER H'CAP 1m 68y
**3:55** (3:56) (Class 5) (0-70,72) 3-Y-O **£3,881** (£1,155; £577; £288) **Stalls** Low

Form RPR
-225 **1** **Cliff Bay (IRE)**[20] 3243 3-9-1 **63**................................ PaulMulrennan 14 70+
(Keith Dalgleish) *hld up: stdy hdwy to trck ldrs whn nt clr run over 2f out: effrt and swtchd lft over 1f out: led ins fnl f: kpt on strly* **5/1**[3]
00-2 **2** ½ **Breanski**[6] 3745 3-9-0 **65**................................ JoshDoyle(3) 1 71
(David O'Meara) *s.i.s: hld up: stdy hdwy to press ldrs over 2f out: rdn and led briefly ins fnl f: edgd lft and kpt on: hld cl home* **2/1**[1]
-146 **3** 1 **Four Wishes**[14] 3461 3-9-1 **63**................................ DavidNolan 10 67
(Tim Easterby) *trckd ldrs: effrt whn blkd over 2f out: rdn and ev ch over 1f out: kpt on same pce ins fnl f* **4/1**[2]
0-06 **4** 1 ½ **Kiribati**[26] 3047 3-9-3 **65**................................ JoeFanning 6 66
(Mark Johnston) *led: rdn over 2f out: hdd ins fnl f: sn outpcd* **9/1**
-051 **5** ½ **Heatongrad (IRE)**[14] 3461 3-9-7 **72**................................ AdamMcNamara(3) 12 71
(Richard Fahey) *pressed ldr: ev ch over 2f out to over 1f out: no ex ins fnl f* **4/1**[2]
0-20 **6** 17 **Akkadian Empire**[19] 3291 3-9-10 **72**................................(h[1]) TomEaves 4 32
(Iain Jardine) *hld up: rdn and outpcd 4f out: sn n.d: btn fnl 2f* **20/1**
000 **7** 3 ½ **Foxy Rebel**[37] 2681 3-8-4 **52**................................ JamesSullivan 3 4
(Ruth Carr) *hld up midfield: outpcd and edgd lft over 3f out: btn fnl 2f* **20/1**
000- **8** 2 ¼ **She's Zoff (IRE)**[248] 7380 3-8-2 **50**................................ CamHardie 11 26
(John Quinn) *trckd ldrs: effrt whn blkd over 2f out: wknd wl over 1f out* **33/1**

1m 46.27s (-2.13) **Going Correction** -0.125s/f (Firm) **8** Ran SP% **112.5**
Speed ratings (Par 99): **105,104,103,102,101 84,81,78**
CSF £14.76 CT £42.92 TOTE £5.90: £2.10, £1.10, £1.90; EX 18.90 Trifecta £66.00.
**Owner** David McKenzie **Bred** John Hutchinson **Trained** Carluke, S Lanarks
■ Stewards' Enquiry : David Nolan seven-day ban: improper riding (July 6-12). four-day ban: acted in a violent manor towards other jockey (July 13-19)
Paul Mulrennan two-day ban: careless riding (July 5-6)

**FOCUS**
Race run over an extra 13yds. A strongly run handicap with the first five home finishing a long way clear. It's been rated around the third.

## 3976 BOTHWELL CASTLE H'CAP 1m 68y
**4:35** (4:35) (Class 4) (0-80,82) 3-Y-O+ **£7,762** (£2,310; £1,154; £577) **Stalls** Low

Form RPR
4-11 **1** **Titi Makfi**[13] 3507 3-9-6 **82**................................ JoeFanning 2 90+
(Mark Johnston) *led 1f: pressed ldr: regained ld gng wl over 2f out: rdn and edgd rt over 1f out: hld on wl fnl f* **4/6**[1]
02-0 **2** 1 ¼ **Imperial Focus (IRE)**[65] 1832 4-9-10 **76**................................ JoeDoyle 4 80
(Simon Waugh) *cl up: led after 1f to over 2f out: rallied: kpt on u.p fnl f: nt pce of wnr* **16/1**
0411 **3** nse **Dark Crystal**[9] 3652 6-9-1 **72** 6ex................................ LewisEdmunds(5) 1 76
(Linda Perratt) *trckd ldrs: effrt and rdn 2f out: disp 2nd pl fnl f: hld nr fin* **7/1**[3]
442 **4** 1 ½ **Haraz (IRE)**[21] 3204 4-9-10 **76**................................(v) DavidNolan 6 77
(David O'Meara) *in tch: stdy hdwy over 2f out: effrt and rdn over 2f out: no ex ins fnl f* **5/1**[2]
4666 **5** 1 ¼ **Archie's Advice**[14] 3451 6-9-4 **75**................................(p) RowanScott(5) 8 73
(Keith Dalgleish) *s.i.s: hld up: pushed along and effrt over 2f out: sn outpcd: kpt on ins fnl f: no imp* **20/1**
0523 **6** 3 ¾ **Jabbaar**[11] 3582 4-9-8 **74**................................ TomEaves 3 63
(David Barron) *prom: effrt and rdn over 2f out: wknd over 1f out* **8/1**

1m 46.06s (-2.34) **Going Correction** -0.125s/f (Firm)
**WFA** 3 from 4yo+ 10lb **6** Ran SP% **110.9**
Speed ratings (Par 105): **106,104,104,103,101 98**
CSF £12.80 CT £41.04 TOTE £1.40: £1.10, £6.40; EX 12.20 Trifecta £43.40.
**Owner** Paul & Clare Rooney **Bred** Floors Farming **Trained** Middleham Moor, N Yorks

**FOCUS**
Race run over an extra 13yds. The pace was steady for this fair handicap with the field racing up the far side. A pb from the second, with the third to her latest career best.

## 3977 SAINTS & SINNERS RACENIGHT NEXT WEEK H'CAP 1m 1f 35y
**5:10** (5:10) (Class 6) (0-60,62) 3-Y-O+ **£3,234** (£962; £481; £240) **Stalls** Low

Form RPR
0-03 **1** **Regal Mirage (IRE)**[30] 2903 3-8-4 **47**................................ JamesSullivan 2 52
(Tim Easterby) *trckd ldrs: rdn and outpcd over 2f out: rallied over 1f out: led ins fnl f: kpt on strly* **14/1**
6422 **2** ¾ **Bling King**[6] 3760 8-9-9 **60**................................(p) CliffordLee(5) 1 65
(Geoffrey Harker) *prom: hdwy to ld over 1f out: hdd ins fnl f: kpt on: hld nr fin* **3/1**[1]
02-1 **3** ¾ **Clenymistra (IRE)**[30] 2903 3-9-2 **62**................................ JoshDoyle(3) 11 64
(David O'Meara) *t.k.h early: led: rdn and hdd over 1f out: rallied: kpt on same pce ins fnl f* **10/1**
2266 **4** ½ **New Abbey Angel (IRE)**[12] 3529 4-9-7 **58**................................(v) RowanScott(5) 7 60
(Keith Dalgleish) *hld up midfield: pushed along and carried hd high 2f out: kpt on ins fnl f* **18/1**
050- **5** nse **Frozon**[201] 8194 4-9-3 **54**................................ BenRobinson(5) 3 56
(Brian Ellison) *s.i.s: sn midfield: rdn and outpcd over 2f out: rallied fnl f: nt pce to chal* **8/1**[3]
52 **6** hd **Colour Contrast (IRE)**[12] 3530 4-9-13 **59**................................(p[1]) DavidNolan 6 61
(Iain Jardine) *s.i.s: hld up: rdn and hdwy 2f out: kpt on same pce ins fnl f* **5/1**[2]
5023 **7** 1 ¾ **Green Howard**[11] 3560 9-10-2 **62**................................(b) DuranFentiman 9 60
(Rebecca Bastiman) *s.i.s: hld up: pushed along and effrt over 2f out: rdn and no imp over 1f out* **12/1**
2503 **8** nk **Bonnie Gals**[7] 3708 3-9-0 **57**................................(p[1]) JoeFanning 4 53
(Keith Dalgleish) *hld up: hdwy on outside 2f out: drvn and outpcd fnl f* **3/1**[1]
5-26 **9** 3 **Single Estate**[21] 3207 3-8-7 **50**................................ JoeDoyle 5 40
(Simon Waugh) *prom tl rdn and wknd fr 2f out* **16/1**
-005 **10** nk **Stardrifter**[14] 3450 5-9-10 **61**................................ LewisEdmunds(5) 10 52
(Linda Perratt) *pressed ldr to over 2f out: sn rdn and wknd* **16/1**
0-06 **11** 13 **Trulove**[28] 2950 4-9-0 **46** oh1................................ TomEaves 8 11
(John David Riches) *hld up: rdn and hung rt over 2f out: sn wknd: t.o* **100/1**

1m 58.97s (-0.73) **Going Correction** -0.125s/f (Firm)
**WFA** 3 from 4yo+ 11lb **11** Ran SP% **119.2**
Speed ratings (Par 101): **98,97,96,96,96 96,94,94,91,91 79**
CSF £56.64 CT £456.81 TOTE £16.80: £3.90, £1.60, £2.70; EX 80.50 Trifecta £708.00.
**Owner** Ryedale Partners No 7 **Bred** Norelands, Lofts Hall & A Gold **Trained** Great Habton, N Yorks

**FOCUS**
Race run over an extra 13yds. An open handicap. Straightforward form, with third rated to her Redcar form.

## 3978 HAMILTON-PARK.CO.UK APPRENTICE H'CAP 1m 4f 15y
**5:45** (5:47) (Class 6) (0-60,60) 4-Y-O+ **£3,234** (£962; £481; £240) **Stalls** High

Form RPR
004 **1** **Donnachies Girl (IRE)**[16] 3383 4-9-4 **60**................................ RowanScott(3) 6 69
(Alistair Whillans) *hld up: rdn along over 2f out: hdwy over 1f out: led ins fnl f: styd on wl* **8/1**[3]
4404 **2** 1 ¼ **Thorntoun Care**[21] 3193 6-9-0 **60**................................(p[1]) JamieGormley(7) 5 67
(Iain Jardine) *hld up: stdy hdwy 3f out: rdn to ld over 1f out: hdd ins fnl f: kpt on same pce* **4/1**[2]
0-11 **3** 1 ½ **Tonto's Spirit**[9] 3654 5-9-6 **59** 6ex................................(h) AdamMcNamara 3 64
(Kenneth Slack) *led: rdn over 2f out: hung lft and hdd over 1f out: sn no ex* **10/11**[1]
360/ **4** 2 **Uriah Heep (FR)**[41] 6520 8-9-4 **60**................................ LewisEdmunds(3) 2 61
(R Mike Smith) *s.i.s: hld up: pushed along and effrt over 2f out: kpt on fnl f: no imp* **14/1**
3-02 **5** 1 **Moon Over Rio (IRE)**[30] 2891 6-9-1 **57**................................ MeganNicholls(3) 4 57
(Ben Haslam) *prom: effrt and ch over 2f out: wknd fnl f* **14/1**
5-20 **6** 1 ¾ **Schmooze (IRE)**[7] 3706 8-8-6 **52**................................ LeanneFerguson(7) 8 49
(Linda Perratt) *hld up: drvn and outpcd 3f out: rallied over 1f out: no imp ins fnl f* **14/1**
6-50 **7** 5 **Celtic Power**[26] 3043 5-8-6 **52**................................ SeanMooney(7) 7 41
(Jim Goldie) *hld up: drvn and outpcd over 3f out: n.d after* **14/1**
0-60 **8** nk **Indian Giver**[20] 3242 9-8-8 **50**................................ PhilDennis(3) 1 39
(John David Riches) *pressed ldr to over 2f out: sn rdn and wknd* **25/1**
0000 **9** 13 **Dan's Hopeforglory**[18] 3343 5-8-5 **47**................................ GemmaTutty(3) 9 15
(Peter Niven) *chsd ldrs tl rdn and wknd fr 3f out* **66/1**

2m 37.09s (-1.51) **Going Correction** -0.125s/f (Firm) **9** Ran SP% **115.5**
Speed ratings (Par 101): **100,99,98,96,96 95,91,91,82**
CSF £40.04 CT £56.72 TOTE £10.80: £3.00, £1.60, £1.02; EX 45.90 Trifecta £118.70.
**Owner** Mrs Karen Spark **Bred** Darley **Trained** Newmill-On-Slitrig, Borders

**FOCUS**
Race run over an extra 13yds. A modest handicap. The runner-up helps pin the level.
T/Plt: £215.90 to a £1 stake. Pool: £50,711.26 - 171.45 winning units T/Qpdt: £9.30 to a £1 stake. Pool: £4,493.24 - 357 winning units **Richard Young**

# 3495 RIPON (R-H)
Wednesday, June 21

**OFFICIAL GOING: Good (good to firm in places home straight; watered; 8.2)**
Wind: Light behind Weather: Cloudy

## 3979 RAYE WILKINSON APPRENTICE H'CAP 6f
**6:50** (6:51) (Class 6) (0-65,63) 3-Y-O+ **£3,234** (£962; £481; £240) **Stalls** High

Form RPR
6000 **1** **Cliff (IRE)**[9] 3666 7-10-0 **63**................................ FayeMcManoman 5 70
(Nigel Tinkler) *midfield: hdwy on outer over 3f out: sn chsd ldr: pushed along to ld over 1f out: strly pressed fnl 75yds: jst hld on* **6/1**
3362 **2** hd **Cool Strutter (IRE)**[13] 3488 5-9-7 **56**................................ SophieScardifield 10 62
(Karen Tutty) *chsd ldrs: rdn along 2f out: chal strly fnl 75yds: kpt on* **5/1**[3]
0-03 **3** hd **Carlovian**[27] 2989 4-8-10 **45**................................ MichaelColes 3 51
(Mark Walford) *prom: pushed along and sltly outpcd 3f out: edgd rt towards centre 2f out: rdn and kpt on wl fnl f: edgd lft towards fin* **5/2**[1]
5013 **4** 1 ¾ **Searanger (USA)**[19] 3290 4-9-11 **60**................................ SharnaArmstrong 1 61
(Rebecca Menzies) *prom: led over 3f out: hdd over 1f out: no ex fnl 110yds* **11/2**
0000 **5** nk **Gaelic Wizard (IRE)**[7] 3704 9-9-6 **55**................................ GeorgiaDobie 2 55
(Karen Tutty) *s.i.s: hld up on outside: pushed along 2f out: kpt on fnl f: nrst fin* **14/1**
0-00 **6** 1 ¼ **Ivors Involvement (IRE)**[11] 3560 5-8-10 **45**................................ ZakWheatley 9 41
(Tina Jackson) *s.i.s: outpcd in rr tl kpt on ins fnl f* **33/1**
00-5 **7** 4 **Hit The Lights (IRE)**[27] 2994 7-9-3 **52**................................(p) MeganEllingworth 8 36
(Marjorie Fife) *led: hdd over 3f out: remained cl up tl wknd fnl f* **16/1**
63-0 **8** 7 **Peach Pavlova (IRE)**[30] 2886 3-9-7 **63**................................ TommyO'Connor 4 24
(Ann Duffield) *chsd ldrs: pushed along over 2f out: edgd rt and wknd over 1f out* **16/1**
0012 **9** 3 ¼ **Kyllach Me (IRE)**[39] 2633 5-9-10 **59**................................(v) HarryRussell 7 12
(Bryan Smart) *hld up: rdn over 3f out: sn outpcd and btn* **4/1**[2]
5-30 **10** hd **Port Master**[140] 511 3-9-1 **57**................................ LukeCatton 6 8
(Ann Duffield) *dwlt: a rr* **66/1**

1m 11.7s (-1.30) **Going Correction** -0.20s/f (Firm)
**WFA** 3 from 4yo+ 7lb **10** Ran SP% **117.8**
Speed ratings (Par 101): **100,99,99,97,96 95,89,80,76,75**
CSF £36.50 CT £97.06 TOTE £7.20: £2.60, £2.00, £1.50; EX 42.80 Trifecta £222.80.
**Owner** W F Burton **Bred** John O'Connor **Trained** Langton, N Yorks

**FOCUS**
A low-grade sprint to open proceedings and in a race confined to riders who hadn't ridden a winner prior to Sunday 18th June, it was Faye McManoman who was celebrating her breakthrough success. Straightforward form rated around the second and third.

## 3980 BONDGATE FILLIES' NOVICE STKS (PLUS 10 RACE) 5f
**7:20** (7:21) (Class 5) 2-Y-O **£3,234** (£962; £481; £240) **Stalls** High

Form RPR
63 **1** **Silver Starlight**[13] 3482 2-9-0 0................................ AndrewMullen 5 67
(Tim Easterby) *pressed ldr: rdn to ld narrowly appr fnl f: hld on all out* **9/1**[3]
304 **2** shd **Seen The Lyte (IRE)**[12] 3523 2-9-0 0................................ JasonHart 3 67
(John Quinn) *racd keenly: led narrowly: rdn 2f out: hdd narrowly appr fnl f: kpt on: jst failed* **16/1**
**3** 2 ¼ **Kalagia (IRE)** 2-9-0 0................................ PaulMulrennan 4 59
(Mark Johnston) *chsd ldng pair: pushed along 2f out: rdn to chal appr fnl f: rn green and one pce fnl 75yds* **5/6**[1]
**4** 3 ¼ **Corton Lass** 2-9-0 0................................ RoystonFfrench 2 47+
(Keith Dalgleish) *s.i.s: hld up: sn pushed along and rn green: kpt on ins fnl f* **25/1**
**5** 2 ½ **La Belle Mayson** 2-9-0 0................................ TonyHamilton 7 38
(Richard Fahey) *in tch: pushed along 1/2-way: wknd appr fnl f* **7/2**[2]
**6** 2 ¼ **Rema Al Kuwait (IRE)** 2-9-0 0................................ PhillipMakin 1 30
(David O'Meara) *chsd ldrs on outer: rdn 1/2-way: wknd over 1f out* **10/1**

7 ¾ **Daffy Jane** 2-8-11 0 RachelRichardson(3) 6 27
(Nigel Tinkler) *dwlt: a towards rr* **12/1**
59.0s (-1.00) **Going Correction** -0.20s/f (Firm) 7 Ran SP% **113.3**
Speed ratings (Par 90): **100,99,96,91,87 83,82**
CSF £127.87 TOTE £6.10: £2.40, £5.70; EX 66.70 Trifecta £287.60.
**Owner** Reality Partnerships I **Bred** Mrs Fiona Denniff **Trained** Great Habton, N Yorks

**FOCUS**
The two with previous experience were always to the fore and fought out a head-bobbing finish.

## 3981 ALISON MEMORIAL FOR YORKSHIRE KIDNEY RESEARCH FILLIES' H'CAP 1m 1f 170y
**7:50** (7:50) (Class 4) (0-85,86) 3-Y-O+ **£5,175** (£1,540; £769; £384) **Stalls** Low

Form RPR
6-13 **1** **Euro Nightmare (IRE)**[18] 3335 3-9-2 **84** JasonHart 6 91+
(Keith Dalgleish) *prom: rdn and bit outpcd over 2f out: styd on wl fnl f: led post* **6/4**[1]
10-6 **2** *nse* **Dowayla (IRE)**[20] 3262 3-9-1 **83** RoystonFfrench 3 89
(Saeed bin Suroor) *led: set stdy pce: pushed along and qcknd over 2f out: drvn ins fnl f: kpt on but hdd post* **5/2**[2]
-660 **3** *3* **Katebird (IRE)**[22] 3178 3-8-0 **68** oh2 AndrewMullen 4 68
(Mark Johnston) *trckd ldrs: rdn over 2f out: briefly chse ldr appr fnl f: one pce ins fnl f* **12/1**
-120 **4** *¾* **Pernickety**[27] 3009 4-9-0 **70** PaulMulrennan 5 68
(Lucy Wadham) *dwlt: hld up: racd keenly: pushed along over 2f out: kpt on ins fnl f: nvr able to chal* **5/1**[3]
340 **5** *½* **Coillte Cailin (IRE)**[95] 1258 7-9-13 **86** ShelleyBirkett(3) 1 83
(David O'Meara) *hld up: pushed along whn bit short of room on rail over 2f out: angled lft off rail over 1f out: nvr threatened* **18/1**
5152 **6** *nk* **Prying Pandora (FR)**[11] 3558 4-9-11 **81** TonyHamilton 2 78
(Richard Fahey) *trckd ldrs: rdn over 2f out: wknd ins fnl f* **7/1**
2m 4.1s (-1.30) **Going Correction** -0.025s/f (Good)
**WFA** 3 from 4yo+ 12lb 6 Ran SP% **110.7**
Speed ratings (Par 102): **104,103,101,100,100 100**
CSF £5.25 TOTE £2.50: £1.90, £1.60; EX 6.50 Trifecta £27.70.
**Owner** J S Morrison **Bred** Miss Annmarie Burke **Trained** Carluke, S Lanarks

**FOCUS**
Race run over an extra 4yds. A steady pace for this fillies' handicap but it produced another thrilling finish.

## 3982 WELLS MEMORIAL CHALLENGE TROPHY H'CAP 5f
**8:20** (8:28) (Class 3) (0-95,88) 3-Y-O **£7,561** (£2,263; £1,131; £566) **Stalls** High

Form RPR
26-0 **1** **Harome (IRE)**[19] 3295 3-8-12 **79** PaulMulrennan 3 81
(Roger Fell) *chsd ldng pair: pushed along over 1f out: rdn to chal ins fnl f: kpt on: led post* **10/1**
0310 **2** *nse* **Jack Flash (FR)**[33] 2806 3-9-1 **82** (h) JasonHart 6 84
(Les Eyre) *led narrowly: drvn over 1f out: kpt on: hdd post* **10/11**[1]
-060 **3** *½* **Monks Stand (USA)**[35] 2739 3-8-11 **78** (p) DavidAllan 4 78
(Tim Easterby) *sn pushed along and outpcd in 4th tl kpt on ins fnl f* **13/2**[3]
40-4 **4** *nse* **Night Law**[14] 3462 3-8-8 **75** TonyHamilton 7 75
(Richard Fahey) *pressed ldr: rdn over 1f out: no ex fnl 50yds* **7/2**[2]
58.64s (-1.36) **Going Correction** -0.20s/f (Firm) 4 Ran SP% **97.0**
Speed ratings (Par 103): **102,101,101,101**
CSF £15.89 TOTE £7.70; EX 16.30 Trifecta £35.90.
**Owner** R G Fell **Bred** Limestone & Tara Studs **Trained** Nawton, N Yorks
■ Dakota Gold was withdrawn (6-5) Rule 4 applies to bets struck at board prices prior to withdrawal but not SP bets - deduction 50p in the pound. New market formed. Rozy Boys was withdrawn (11-2) Rule 4 applies to all bets - deduction 15p in the pound

**FOCUS**
Drama before the race with 6-5 favourite Dakota Gold getting worked up in the stalls and having to be withdrawn. As the field loaded a second time, Rozy Boys reared up and went over backwards before being withdrawn. In the race itself the pace was strong and the runner-up emerges with plenty of credit. The winner has been rated back to his 2yo best, with the runner-up to his penultimate C&D win.

## 3983 IT'S LADIES DAY TOMORROW H'CAP 1m 4f 10y
**8:50** (8:52) (Class 5) (0-75,74) 4-Y-O+ **£3,234** (£962; £481; £240) **Stalls** Centre

Form RPR
-502 **1** **Theos Lolly (IRE)**[33] 2787 4-9-6 **73** TonyHamilton 1 83+
(Richard Fahey) *in tch: hdwy on outer over 2f out: led over 2f out: pushed clr: eased towards fin* **7/4**[1]
344- **2** *2* **Chant (IRE)**[272] 6719 7-9-3 **70** ShaneGray 3 74
(Ann Duffield) *led: rdn 3f out: hdd over 1f out: one pce and sn no ch w wnr* **14/1**
2340 **3** *1* **Star Of Lombardy (IRE)**[18] 3341 4-9-6 **73** PaulMulrennan 5 75
(Mark Johnston) *trckd ldr: rdn 3f out: styd on same pce* **7/2**[3]
05 **4** *5* **Fisherman's Blues (IRE)**[47] 2375 4-8-10 **63** JamesSullivan 2 57
(Peter Niven) *stdd s: hld up in rr: pushed along over 2f out: nvr threatened* **28/1**
6001 **5** *nk* **Marmion**[13] 3501 5-9-7 **74** (h) PhillipMakin 6 68
(Les Eyre) *hld up: rdn over 3f out: nvr threatened* **2/1**[2]
05-6 **6** *16* **Pennerley**[16] 3405 4-8-6 **59** AndrewMullen 4 27
(Micky Hammond) *midfield: rdn over 3f out: sn wknd: eased* **11/1**
2m 35.19s (-1.51) **Going Correction** -0.025s/f (Good) 6 Ran SP% **110.4**
Speed ratings (Par 103): **104,102,102,98,98 87**
CSF £24.54 TOTE £2.20: £1.20, £5.20; EX 25.30 Trifecta £81.90.
**Owner** M J Macleod **Bred** Mrs Claire Doyle **Trained** Musley Bank, N Yorks

**FOCUS**
Race run over an extra 4yds. Not a strong race for the grade but the winner did it comfortably. Although the field were strung out early, the pace didn't appear especially quick. The winner has been rated back to the level of his C&D win last year.

## 3984 SIS MAIDEN STKS 6f
**9:20** (9:20) (Class 5) 3-Y-O **£3,234** (£962; £481; £240) **Stalls** High

Form RPR
432 **1** **Don Valentino (IRE)**[14] 3448 3-9-5 70 PhillipMakin 7 76
(David O'Meara) *mde all: rdn over 2f out: strly pressed fnl 75yds: kpt on* **11/4**[2]
06-4 **2** *hd* **Equiano Springs**[26] 3054 3-9-5 74 JamesSullivan 8 75
(Tom Tate) *trckd ldr: racd keenly: pushed along over 1f out: rdn ins fnl f: chal strly fnl 75yds: kpt on: jst hld* **9/4**[1]
452 **3** *10* **Yorkshire Pudding**[23] 3150 3-8-11 65 RachelRichardson(3) 6 38
(Tim Easterby) *trckd ldr towards outer: rdn over 2f out: wknd fnl f* **11/2**
**4** *2* **Mohsen** 3-9-5 0 RoystonFfrench 2 37
(Marcus Tregoning) *dwlt: sn in tch towards outer: rdn over 2f out: edgd lft and sn no hdwy: wknd ins fnl f* **7/2**[3]
4 **5** *1½* **Melrose Girl**[23] 3150 3-9-0 0 ConnorBeasley 5 27
(Bryan Smart) *dwlt: hld up in midfield: swtchd rt to outer 3f out: sn pushed along: wknd fnl f* **8/1**
**6** *8* **Oscar Ranger (IRE)** 3-9-5 0 TonyHamilton 3 7
(Richard Fahey) *dwlt: a towards rr* **14/1**
6-0 **7** *1¼* **Ginger Love**[72] 1680 3-9-5 0 PaulMulrennan 1 3
(Bryan Smart) *hld up: nvr threatened* **20/1**
4 **8** *14* **Baby Say Yes**[20] 3258 3-9-0 0 PaddyAspell 9
(John Norton) *plld hrd and sn trckd ldr: lost pl 3f out: sn wknd and bhd* **100/1**
1m 11.05s (-1.95) **Going Correction** -0.20s/f (Firm) 8 Ran SP% **118.6**
Speed ratings (Par 99): **105,104,91,88,86 76,74,55**
CSF £9.81 TOTE £4.00: £1.80, £2.00, £2.00; EX 11.10 Trifecta £44.30.
**Owner** Clipper Logistics **Bred** Ann & Joe Hallinan **Trained** Upper Helmsley, N Yorks

**FOCUS**
A wide-range of abilities on show in the closing maiden and the two market principals pulled clear of the rest.
T/Plt: £2,278.50 to a £1 stake. Pool: £55,871.66 - 17.9 winning units T/Qpdt: £673.00 to a £1 stake. Pool: £4,456.86 - 4.9 winning units **Andrew Sheret**

3985 - 3992a (Foreign Racing) - See Raceform Interactive

# 3959 ASCOT (R-H)
### Thursday, June 22

**OFFICIAL GOING: Good to firm (going stick: stand side 9.1, centre 8.3, far side 9.0, round 7.9)**
Wind: Light, Against Weather: Cloudy

## 3993 NORFOLK STKS (GROUP 2) 5f
**2:30** (2:33) (Class 1) 2-Y-O
**£56,710** (£21,500; £10,760; £5,360; £2,690; £1,350) **Stalls** Centre

Form RPR
6 **1** **Sioux Nation (USA)**[26] 3098 2-9-1 0 RyanMoore 2 108
(A P O'Brien, Ire) *str: warm: racd far side: hld up in midfield overall: rdn and hdwy over 1f out: edgd lft u.p but overall ldr jst ins fnl f: styd on: rdn out: 1st of 4 in gp* **14/1**
11 **2** *½* **Santry (IRE)**[36] 2740 2-9-1 0 JimCrowley 16 106+
(Declan Carroll) *racd stands side: trckd ldrs: nt clr run and swtchd rt 2f out: hdwy u.p between rivals ent fnl f: chsd wnr 100yds out: kpt on wl but a hld: 1st of 13 in gp* **13/2**[1]
1421 **3** *1½* **Cardsharp**[12] 3556 2-9-1 0 JamesDoyle 15 101
(Mark Johnston) *lw: racd stands side: chsd ldr: rdn 2f out: edgd rt u.p and impeded over 1f out: kpt on same pce ins fnl f: 2nd of 13 in gp* **8/1**[3]
012 **4** *¾* **Frozen Angel (IRE)**[28] 3010 2-9-1 0 RichardKingscote 3 98
(Tom Dascombe) *racd far side: led gp and chsd ldrs overall: ev ch whn rdn and edgd lft over 1f out: no ex and styd on same pce ins fnl f: 2nd of 4 in gp* **9/1**
41 **5** *1* **It Dont Come Easy (IRE)**[19] 3333 2-9-1 0 PaulHanagan 5 94
(Richard Fahey) *racd far side: chsd gp ldrs and in tch in midfield overall: hdwy and carried lft over 1f out: kpt on same pce ins fnl f: 3rd of 4 in gp* **8/1**[3]
1 **6** *nse* **True Blue Moon (IRE)**[32] 2861 2-9-1 0 DonnachaO'Brien 17 94+
(Joseph Patrick O'Brien, Ire) *leggy: racd stands side: s.i.s: in rr: rdn 1/2-way: hdwy jst over 1f out: swtchd rt ins fnl f: styd on strly: nvr trbld ldrs: 3rd of 13 in gp* **16/1**
**7** *nk* **McErin (USA)**[49] 2-9-1 0 (b) DavidRomeroFlores 10 93
(Wesley A Ward, U.S.A) *tall: str: racd stands side: led: rdn and edgd lft over 1f out: hdd jst ins fnl f: no ex and wknd wl ins fnl f: 4th of 13 in gp* **13/2**[1]
13 **8** *1¼* **Koditime (IRE)**[33] 2826 2-9-1 0 AdamKirby 18 89
(Clive Cox) *cmpt: racd stands side: hld up in tch in midfield: swtchd rt and effrt wl over 1f out: sn hung rt and no imp: kpt on same pce ins fnl f: 5th of 13 in gp* **9/1**
21 **9** *nk* **Consequences (IRE)**[20] 3283 2-9-1 0 DanielTudhope 6 88
(David O'Meara) *racd stands side: trckd ldrs: swtchd rt and effrt to chal 2f out: no ex u.p 1f out: wknd ins fnl f: 6th of 13 in gp* **16/1**
211 **10** *1½* **Havana Grey**[28] 3010 2-9-1 0 PJMcDonald 14 82
(K R Burke) *str: lw: racd stands side: travelled strly and wl in tch in midfield: effrt to press ldrs 2f out: unable qck u.p and jst getting outpcd whn nudged ent fnl f: wknd ins fnl f: 7th of 13 in gp* **7/1**[2]
61 **11** *nse* **Billy Dylan (IRE)**[13] 3516 2-9-1 0 SeanLevey 7 82
(Richard Hannon) *racd stands side: hld up in tch in midfield: effrt 2f out: carried rt and no imp oer 1f out: wknd ins fnl f: 8th of 13 in gp* **50/1**
11 **12** *2* **Nine Below Zero**[17] 3406 2-9-1 0 PatSmullen 4 75
(Ralph Beckett) *str: racd far side: pressed gp ldr and chsd ldrs overall: rdn and effrt over 1f out: carried lft and unable qck sn after: wknd ins fnl f: 4th of 4 in gp* **9/1**
1 **13** *1¾* **Pilkington**[21] 3254 2-9-1 0 PaulMulrennan 12 68
(David O'Meara) *str: racd stands side: stdd s: a towards rr of gp: rdn 2f out: no prog: wknd fnl f: 9th of 13 in gp* **50/1**
1 **14** *1¼* **Viscount Loftus (IRE)**[8] 3725 2-9-1 0 SilvestreDeSousa 13 64
(Mark Johnston) *str: lw: racd stands side: chsd ldrs: rdn 2f out: unable qck and losing pl whn sltly short of room jst over 1f out: wknd fnl f: 10th of 13 in gp* **20/1**
2 **15** *3* **Gift In Time (IRE)**[14] 3490 2-9-1 0 JoeDoyle 11 53
(James Given) *racd stands side: s.i.s: sn rcvrd and in tch in midfield: effrt 2f out: sn u.p and no hdwy: wknd over 1f out: 11th of 13 in gp* **40/1**
04 **16** *5* **New Empire**[6] 3782 2-9-1 0 MartinHarley 9 35
(Peter Chapple-Hyam) *racd stands side: awkward leaving stalls and s.i.s: a towards rr: rdn over 2f out: lost tch over 1f out: 12th of 13 in gp* **100/1**
**17** *23* **Poorauldjosephine** 2-8-12 0 (b[1]) LiamJones 8
(David Flood) *leggy: racd stands side: awkward leaving stalls: sn outpcd: t.o 1/2-way: 13th of 13 in gp* **200/1**
1m 0.88s (0.38) **Going Correction** +0.15s/f (Good) 17 Ran SP% **122.4**
Speed ratings (Par 105): **102,101,98,97,96 95,95,93,92,90 90,87,84,82,77 69,32**
CSF £98.87 CT £820.99 TOTE £17.50: £4.80, £2.70, £3.30; EX 147.50 Trifecta £1875.90.
**Owner** Michael Tabor & Derrick Smith & Mrs John Magnier **Bred** Fethard Bloodstock **Trained** Cashel, Co Tipperary

**FOCUS**

Day three saw a lot more cloud cover and much cooler conditions, meaning the 5mm applied to the whole course once more overnight would've taken longer to evaporate. After riding in the opener James Doyle said: 'The ground is better than yesterday, it is not as quick, while Pat Smullen said: 'It is lively but there is no jar, they have put enough water on.'\n\x\x The running rail on the round course was again 3yds out from its innermost position from approx 9f out to the home straight. This looked a wide-open Norfolk Stakes. A brisk pace collapsed from the furlong marker and the first two home were wide apart on the track. The third sets the standard. It's been rated as a par renewal, with the fourth to his C&D conditions form.

## 3994 HAMPTON COURT STKS (GROUP 3) (FORMERLY THE TERCENTENARY STAKES) 1m 1f 212y

**3:05** (3:09) (Class 1) 3-Y-O

**£51,039** (£19,350; £9,684; £4,824; £2,421; £1,215) **Stalls** Low

Form RPR

1325 **1** **Benbatl**[19] 3322 3-9-0 113........(t) OisinMurphy 6 115
(Saeed bin Suroor) *trckd ldrs: effrt over 2f out: sn tk 2nd: r.o to ld wl over 1f out: sn edgd rt: kpt on wl towards fin and a doing enough* **9/2**[2]

1156 **2** *½* **Orderofthegarter (IRE)**[18] 3368 3-9-0 110........(t[1]) RyanMoore 14 114+
(A P O'Brien, Ire) *w'like: hld up in midfield: plld to outer and hdwy over 2f out: str run and edgd rt over 1f out: sn tk 2nd: r.o wl and clsd nr fin* **10/3**[1]

1-4 **3** *¾* **Mirage Dancer**[41] 2569 3-9-0 100........ AndreaAtzeni 3 113
(Sir Michael Stoute) *athletic: midfield: rdn and hdwy over 2f out: unable qck over 1f out: edgd rt fnl 110yds: styd on wl towards fin: lacked pce of front two* **7/1**

5-24 **4** *¾* **The Taj Mahal (IRE)**[18] 3368 3-9-0 113........(b) SeamieHeffernan 10 111
(A P O'Brien, Ire) *str: led: rdn over 2f out: hdd wl over 1f out: kpt on u.p: styd on same pce fnl 100yds* **8/1**

3 **5** *5* **Exultant (IRE)**[26] 3100 3-9-0 110........ ShaneFoley 4 101+
(M Halford, Ire) *leggy: hld up in midfield: rdn over 2f out: hdwy whn nt clr run over 1f out: styd on to take 4th ins fnl f: no imp on front quartet* **6/1**[3]

1212 **6** *½* **Speedo Boy (FR)**[47] 2401 3-9-0 100........ SilvestreDeSousa 16 100
(Ian Williams) *lw: midfield on outer: effrt 3f out: rdn and outpcd over 2f out: styd on ins fnl f: nt pce to chal* **20/1**

1-22 **7** *1* **Fearless Fire (IRE)**[33] 2824 3-9-0 91........ AdamKirby 12 98
(Andrew Balding) *lw: prom racing 3 wd: rdn and lost pl over 2f out: one pce fr over 1f out* **16/1**

3-14 **8** *1* **Tamleek (USA)**[42] 2555 3-9-0 107........ JimCrowley 1 96
(Saeed bin Suroor) *lw: trckd ldrs: rdn over 2f out: unable qck wl over 1f out: kpt on same pce ins fnl f* **9/1**

2-40 **9** *nk* **Kings Gift (IRE)**[39] 2666 3-9-0 101........ PaulMulrennan 7 96
(Michael Dods) *hld up: rdn over 2f out: denied a run fr wl over 1f out: swtchd lft then rt: kpt on ins fnl f: nvr able to trble ldrs* **66/1**

4241 **10** *2½* **Grey Britain**[33] 2829 3-9-0 99........ GeraldMosse 11 90
(John Ryan) *chsd ldr: pushed along over 3f out: rdn over 2f out: sn lost 2nd: wknd 1f out* **33/1**

0-25 **11** *nk* **Rodaini (USA)**[28] 3013 3-9-0 102........(b[1]) JamieSpencer 15 90
(Simon Crisford) *stdd s: hld up: rdn and swtchd lft 2f out: no imp over 1f out: outpcd and btn whn edgd rt ins fnl f: nvr able to get on terms w ldrs* **66/1**

-320 **12** *1* **Bay Of Poets (IRE)**[18] 3368 3-9-0 110........ WilliamBuick 9 88
(Charlie Appleby) *lw: midfield: rdn and nt clr run over 2f out: sn swtchd rt: sme hdwy over 1f out: no imp on ldrs: wknd fnl 150yds* **10/1**

-635 **13** *1¼* **Savile Row (FR)**[32] 2869 3-9-0 104........(p) PaulHanagan 13 85
(Frau Erika Mader, Germany) *bhd: outpcd 3f out: nvr a threat* **50/1**

2m 5.4s (-2.00) **Going Correction** +0.15s/f (Good) **13** Ran SP% **116.8**
Speed ratings (Par 109): **114,113,113,112,108 108,107,106,106,104 103,103,102**
CSF £18.55 CT £103.09 TOTE £5.50: £2.00, £1.70, £2.10; EX 21.30 Trifecta £94.40.
**Owner** Godolphin **Bred** Darley **Trained** Newmarket, Suffolk

**FOCUS**
Distance increased by 11yds. Strong Group 3 form, with the right horses coming to the fore, and the first four clear. Sound form with the winner rated to form.

## 3995 RIBBLESDALE STKS (GROUP 2) (FILLIES) 1m 3f 211y

**3:40** (3:44) (Class 1) 3-Y-O

**£121,926** (£46,225; £23,134; £11,524; £5,783; £2,902) **Stalls** Low

Form RPR

1-35 **1** **Coronet**[20] 3301 3-9-0 103........ OlivierPeslier 1 107+
(John Gosden) *w'like: hld up off the pce in midfield: effrt over 2f out: hdwy to chse ldrs whn nt clr run and swtchd lft over 1f out: chsd ldng pair 150yds out: r.o strly u.p to ld cl home* **9/1**

511 **2** *nk* **Mori**[28] 3006 3-9-0 91........ PatSmullen 10 105
(Sir Michael Stoute) *lw: hld up off the pce in midfield: effrt and clsd over 2f out: hdwy to chse wnr and 2 l down ent fnl f: styd on and grad clsd to ld 50yds out: hdd and no ex cl home* **2/1**[1]

-321 **3** *1* **Hertford Dancer**[40] 2613 3-9-0 99........ JimCrowley 8 103
(John Gosden) *str: racd off the pce in 3rd: effrt to chse ldr and clsng 2f out: led wl over 1f out: drvn and 2 l clr 1f out: kpt on tl hdd 50yds out: no ex and outpcd towards fin* **16/1**

40-4 **4** *1½* **Rich Legacy (IRE)**[43] 2523 3-9-0 103........ OisinMurphy 12 101
(Ralph Beckett) *hld up off the pce in last trio: effrt and nt that much room wl over 1f out: hdwy u.p 1f out: wnt 4th 100yds out: styd on wl but nvr threatening ldrs* **40/1**

21 **5** *1¼* **Apphia (IRE)**[28] 3007 3-9-0 81........ JamesDoyle 9 99
(Hugo Palmer) *hld up off the pce in midfield: swtchd rt and effrt over 2f out: keeping on whn swtchd lft over 1f out: hdwy 1f out and kpt on wl ins fnl f: no threat to ldrs* **66/1**

23 **6** *2¼* **Alluringly (USA)**[20] 3301 3-9-0 105........ RyanMoore 4 95
(A P O'Brien, Ire) *lengthy: lw: racd off the pce in 4th: swtchd lft and effrt to cl on ldr over 2f out: wnt 2nd briefly 1f out: no ex u.p 1f out: wknd ins fnl f* **5/2**[2]

5-12 **7** *½* **Coconut Creme**[28] 3006 3-9-0 86........ PatCosgrave 3 94
(William Haggas) *taken down early: stdd after s: t.k.h: hld up off the pce in last trio: effrt over 2f out: sme hdwy and switching lft over 1f out: no imp and kpt on same pce ins fnl f* **20/1**

134 **8** *nse* **The Sky Is Blazing (IRE)**[26] 3094 3-9-0 86........(p[1]) SilvestreDeSousa 5 94+
(William Haggas) *led: wnt clr after 2f: stl clr and rdn over 2f out: c bk to field and hdd over 1f out: wknd fnl f* **20/1**

3-13 **9** *1¼* **Serenada**[36] 2738 3-9-0 100........ AndreaAtzeni 11 92
(Roger Varian) *chsd clr ldr: rdn and effrt over 2f out: lost 2nd but clsng on ldr 2f out: unable qck over 1f out: btn whn n.m.r jst ins fnl f: wknd fnl 100yds* **16/1**

0-14 **10** *hd* **Gracious Diana**[33] 2827 3-9-0 98........(t[1]) AdamKirby 6 93
(John Gosden) *lw: hld up off the pce in rr: reminder 5f out: effrt over 2f out: keeping on but nt threatening ldrs whn squeezed for room over 1f out: wl hld fnl f* **20/1**

12 **9** **Naughty Or Nice (IRE)**[33] 2847 3-9-0 0........(b[1]) DeclanMcDonogh 7 70+
(John M Oxx, Ire) *w'like: t.k.h: hld up off the pce in midfield: effrt whn sddle slipped and rdr kicked feet out of the irons 3f out: lost any ch and dropped to rr 2f out: sn swtchd rt and wl btn* **7/1**[3]

2m 32.06s (-0.44) **Going Correction** +0.15s/f (Good) **12** Ran SP% **120.3**
Speed ratings (Par 108): **107,106,106,105,104 102,102,102,101,101 98,92**
CSF £26.00 CT £298.80 TOTE £10.40: £2.80, £1.40, £4.60; EX 34.90 Trifecta £453.90.
**Owner** Denford Stud **Bred** Denford Stud Ltd **Trained** Newmarket, Suffolk

**FOCUS**
Race run over an extra 11yds. This year's Ribblesdale was a searching test thanks to tearaway leader The Sky Is Blazing. It's been rated at the bottom end of the race standard. The fourth has been rated as getting close to her May Hill form.

## 3996 GOLD CUP (GROUP 1) (BRITISH CHAMPIONS SERIES) 2m 3f 210y

**4:20** (4:22) (Class 1) 4-Y-O+

**£226,840** (£86,000; £43,040; £21,440; £10,760; £5,400) **Stalls** Low

Form RPR

0-41 **1** **Big Orange**[28] 3011 6-9-2 117........(p) JamesDoyle 7 119
(Michael Bell) *lw: led for 2f: chsd ldr: regained ld after 6f: mde rest: rdn over 2f out: over 2 l clr over 1f out: edgd lft ins fnl f: edgd rt sn after and jnd fnl 100yds: hld on gamely* **5/1**[2]

4-21 **2** *shd* **Order Of St George (IRE)**[27] 3057 5-9-2 120........ RyanMoore 13 118
(A P O'Brien, Ire) *hld up: hdwy on outer w work to do over 2f out: wnt 2nd over 1f out where over 2 l down and edgd rt: str chal fnl 100yds: r.o u.p: jst hld* **5/6**[1]

41-0 **3** *6* **Harbour Law**[50] 2288 4-9-0 114........ JimCrowley 5 113
(Laura Mongan) *a.p: wnt 2nd over 3f out: rdn to chal over 2f out: lost 2nd over 1f out: unable to go w front two fnl 150yds: kpt on u.p whn no ch after* **33/1**

01-3 **4** *½* **She Is No Lady**[28] 3011 5-8-13 101........ FranBerry 8 109
(Ralph Beckett) *lw: sn in midfield: hdwy 3f out: rdn to chse ldrs over 2f out: outpcd whn edgd rt over 1f out: kpt on u.p whn no ch ins fnl f* **50/1**

50-1 **5** *2¾* **Torcedor (IRE)**[60] 1999 5-9-2 111........ ColmO'Donoghue 1 110
(Mrs John Harrington, Ire) *in tch: rdn 3f out: outpcd over 2f out: edgd lft and bmpd ins fnl f: styd on fnl 100yds: nt pce of ldrs* **20/1**

1-33 **6** *½* **Sheikhzayedroad**[89] 1374 8-9-2 117........(h) MartinHarley 3 109
(David Simcock) *racd keenly in midfield: pushed along 4f out: rdn and swtchd lft over 2f out: hdwy sn after: hung rt and bmpd ins fnl f: kpt on u.p: no imp on ldrs* **10/1**

51-1 **7** *1¼* **Sweet Selection**[50] 2288 5-8-13 105........ SilvestreDeSousa 10 105
(Hughie Morrison) *in tch: rdn and lost pl 3f out: outpcd whn edgd lft over 2f out: one pce ins fnl f* **14/1**

-352 **8** *hd* **Prince Of Arran**[50] 2288 4-9-0 107........ TomQueally 14 108
(Charlie Fellowes) *hld up: hdwy over 3f out: rdn to chse ldrs over 2f out: kpt on same pce ins fnl f tl no ex towards fin* **66/1**

5-32 **9** *4* **Nearly Caught (IRE)**[39] 2667 7-9-2 113........ AdamKirby 12 104
(Hughie Morrison) *lw: trckd ldrs: pushed along briefly 1 m out: pushed along 5f out: rdn 3f out: hung rt u.p over 2f out: wknd fnl f* **66/1**

22-4 **10** *2¾* **Endless Time (IRE)**[34] 2803 5-8-13 112........ WilliamBuick 6 99
(Charlie Appleby) *in rr: rdn 3f out: sme hdwy over 2f out: nvr able to trble ldrs: wl btn 1f out* **20/1**

6-14 **11** *10* **Harrison**[26] 3090 4-9-0 109........ GrahamLee 11 93
(Mick Channon) *in rr: rdn over 2f out: no imp: wl bhd over 1f out* **66/1**

2-00 **12** *40* **Quest For More (IRE)**[28] 3011 7-9-2 116........(b) JamieSpencer 9 57
(Roger Charlton) *sed awkwardly: prom on outer tl led after 2f: hdd after 6f: chsd ldr tl over 3f out: wknd qckly: eased whn wl btn over 1f out* **25/1**

3-04 **13** *13* **Trip To Paris (IRE)**[71] 1733 6-9-2 107........ AndreaAtzeni 2 45
(Ed Dunlop) *midfield: rdn and lost pl over 3f out: eased whn bhd over 1f out* **50/1**

13-2 **14** *23* **Simple Verse (IRE)**[34] 2803 5-8-13 113........ OisinMurphy 4 21
(Ralph Beckett) *hld up: rdn 3f out: sme hdwy over 2f out: no imp: eased whn wl btn over 1f out: virtually p.u wl ins fnl f* **15/2**[3]

4m 22.4s (-2.40) **Going Correction** +0.15s/f (Good)
**WFA** 4 from 5yo+ 1lb **14** Ran SP% **123.5**
Speed ratings (Par 117): **110,109,107,107,106 106,105,105,103,102 98,82,77,68**
CSF £8.93 CT £131.71 TOTE £5.90: £2.00, £1.10, £7.60; EX 11.60 Trifecta £274.90.
**Owner** W J and T C O Gredley **Bred** Stetchworth & Middle Park Studs **Trained** Newmarket, Suffolk
■ Stewards' Enquiry : James Doyle two-day ban: used whip above the permitted level (Jul 6-7)

**FOCUS**
Distance increased by 11yds. A thrilling Gold Cup, with the big two pulling 6l clear, and the extremely game winner denying the favourite, who came from a long way off the pace, back-to-back wins in the race. The winner slowed the pace to get in a breather before the straight and that proved crucial. The winner has been rated to his best, with the third close to his St Leger form.

## 3997 BRITANNIA STKS (C&G) (HERITAGE H'CAP) 1m (S)

**5:00** (5:05) (Class 2) (0-105,105) 3-Y-O

**£74,700** (£22,368; £11,184; £5,592; £2,796; £1,404) **Stalls** Centre

Form RPR

2135 **1** **Bless Him (IRE)**[26] 3071 3-8-9 **90**........(h) JamieSpencer 3 102
(David Simcock) *racd far side: stdd s: hld up in rr: clsd and squeezed through gap wl over 1f out: rdn to ld overall 1f out: styd on and a doing enough towards fin: 1st of 8 in gp* **25/1**

10-1 **2** *½* **Ronald R (IRE)**[47] 2402 3-9-0 **95**........ DanielTudhope 1 107+
(Michael Bell) *racd far side: hld up in rr: clsd and gng for same gap as wnr whn squeezed out wl over 1f out: sn swtchd lft and hdwy in 3rd 1f out: chsd wnr 100yds out: styd on strly to press wnr nr fin: 2nd of 8 in gp* **16/1**

1112 **3** *1½* **Tricorn (IRE)**[21] 3232 3-9-4 **99**........ JamesDoyle 7 107
(John Gosden) *racd far side: in tch in midfield: effrt to chal 2f out: led gp and overall ldr over 1f out tl hdd 1f out: no ex u.p: lost 2nd and outpcd fnl 100yds: 3rd of 8 in gp* **14/1**[3]

2112 **4** *4* **Indian Dandy (IRE)**[26] 3077 3-8-11 **92**........(h) TomQueally 27 90+
(Marco Botti) *racd stands' side: hld up in rr: clsd and nt clr run 2f out: swtchd lft and hdwy u.p over 1f out: styd on strly ins fnl f: nvr getting on terms w far side ldrs: 1st of 21 in gp* **25/1**

-014 **5** *hd* **Leshlaa (USA)**[33] 2829 3-9-8 **103**........ SilvestreDeSousa 19 101
(Saeed bin Suroor) *racd stands' side: hld up towards rr: swtchd rt and hdwy jst over 2f out: led gp and 4th overall 1f out: no ex and outpcd by far side ldrs ins fnl f: lost 4th last strides: 2nd of 21 in gp* **25/1**

10-5 **6** *¾* **Simply Brilliant**[36] 2739 3-8-10 **91**........ PaulHanagan 6 87
(Richard Fahey) *racd far side: pressed gp ldr and prom overall: rdn to ld gp and overall ldr 2f out: hdd over 1f out: wknd ins fnl f: 3rd of 8 in gp* **33/1**



The Form Book Flat, Raceform Ltd, Newbury, RG14 5SJ

411 **7** *nse* **Afaak**[19] 3317 3-8-11 **92**........................................ JimCrowley 10 88+
(Charles Hills) *racd stands' side: t.k.h: hld up in tch in midfield: clsd to trck ldrs and wnt lft 2f out: drvn over 1f out: 5th overall 1f out: outpcd ins fnl f: 3rd of 21 in gp* **8/1**[2]

6-11 **7** *dht* **Leader's Legacy (USA)**[40] 2612 3-8-13 **94**.................(t) GeraldMosse 2 90
(Saeed bin Suroor) *racd far side: in tch in midfield overall: effrt to press ldrs 2f out: unable qck u.p over 1f out: wknd ins fnl f: 4th of 8 in gp* **14/1**[3]

15-0 **9** *1 ½* **Medieval (IRE)**[47] 2402 3-9-3 **98**.............................(b) FranBerry 21 91
(Paul Cole) *racd stands' side: hld up in tch: swtchd rt and effrt 2f out: hrd drvn and sme hdwy over 1f out: no imp ins fnl f: 4th of 21 in gp* **100/1**

0-11 **10** *1* **City Of Joy**[21] 3232 3-8-13 **94**........................................ RyanMoore 17 84+
(Sir Michael Stoute) *racd stands' side: hld up in tch towards rr: clsd and nt clr run 2f out: sme room and effrt 1f out: nt clr run again and swtchd lft ins fnl f: styd on towards fin: nvr able to threaten: 5th of 21 in gp* **8/1**[2]

1-12 **11** *nk* **Son Of The Stars**[47] 2402 3-9-0 **95**................................ OisinMurphy 20 85+
(Richard Hannon) *racd stands' side: hld up wl in tch in midfield: clsd to trck ldrs 2f out: effrt 2f out: disputing gp ld and chsng overall ldrs over 1f out: no ex 1f out: wknd ins fnl f: 6th of 21 in gp* **11/2**[1]

1-50 **12** *½* **Via Serendipity**[47] 2402 3-8-9 **90**.................(t) JosephineGordon 28 79
(Hugo Palmer) *racd stands' side: t.k.h: hld up in tch in midfield: effrt wl over 1f out: no imp u.p 1f out: edgd rt and kpt on same pce ins fnl f: 7th of 21 in gp* **40/1**

-121 **13** *¾* **Sabador (FR)**[22] 3199 3-8-12 **93**.................................... PJMcDonald 30 80+
(Ed Walker) *racd stands' side: hld up towards rr: nt clr run 2f out: weaving through and hdwy 1f out: swtchd lft ins fnl f: kpt on but nvr any hope of threatening ldrs: 8th of 21 in gp* **16/1**

-202 **14** *1* **Medahim (IRE)**[26] 3071 3-9-0 **95**.............................. GregoryBenoist 22 80
(Richard Hannon) *racd stands' side: trckd ldrs: clsd to press gp ldr over 3f out: rdn to ld gp and ev ch 2f out tl outpcd over 1f out: wknd ins fnl f: 9th of 21 in gp* **33/1**

0-24 **15** *nk* **Executive Force**[42] 2560 3-9-3 **98**................................ PatCosgrave 23 82
(William Haggas) *racd stands' side: hld up in midfield: clsd and nt clrest of runs 2f out: effrt and hdwy u.p over 1f out: chsd gp ldrs but no imp 1f out: wknd ins fnl f: 10th of 21 in gp* **20/1**

41-4 **16** *hd* **Colibri (IRE)**[55] 2126 3-8-12 **93**.................................... PatSmullen 32 76
(Hugo Palmer) *racd stands' side: hld up in tch in midfield: effrt 2f out: rdn to chse gp ldrs over 1f out: sn no imp and outpcd: wknd ins fnl furlon: 11th of 21 in gp* **16/1**

-416 **17** *2* **Omran**[12] 3592 3-9-3 **98**.............................................. DanielMuscutt 33 77
(Marco Botti) *racd stands' side: hld up in tch in midfield: nt clr run over 2f out: swtchd rt 2f out: no hdwy u.p over 1f out: wknd ins fnl f: 12th of 21 in gp* **50/1**

1-33 **18** *¾* **Capezzano (USA)**[110] 1040 3-9-1 **96**............................... WilliamBuick 5 73
(Charlie Appleby) *racd far side: in tch in midfield overall: effrt to chal u.p 2f out: no ex and btn over 1f out: wknd ins fnl f: 6th of 8 in gp* **33/1**

0221 **19** *2 ¾* **Rusumaat (IRE)**[26] 3077 3-9-10 **105**................................. DaneO'Neill 25 76
(Mark Johnston) *racd stands' side: chsd ldrs: rdn 2f out: sn lost pl: wknd fnl f: 13th of 21 in gp* **20/1**

0-32 **20** *2* **The Grape Escape (IRE)**[40] 2612 3-8-11 **92**.................... PatDobbs 12 58
(Richard Hannon) *racd stands' side: t.k.h: chsd ldrs: rdn 2f out: unable qck and lost pl over 1f out: wknd fnl f: 14th of 21 in gp* **25/1**

63-0 **21** *1 ¼* **Sultan Baybars**[21] 3232 3-8-12 **93**................................(h) HarryBentley 8 56
(Roger Varian) *racd far side: led gp and pressed overall ld: rdn ev ch 2f out: no ex over 1f out: wknd fnl f: 7th of 8 in gp* **66/1**

3- **22** *hd* **Moritzburg**[18] 3362 3-8-11 **92**.........................................(p) ShaneFoley 18 55
(M Halford, Ire) *racd stands' side: overall ldr tl 2f out: lost gp ld and btn over 1f out: sn wknd: 15th of 21 in gp* **50/1**

**23** *2 ½* **Lightening Fast**[59] 2050 3-8-10 **91**................................. ColinKeane 9 48
(G M Lyons, Ire) *racd far side: chsd gp ldrs: rdn over 2f out: lost pl u.p and btn over 1f out: wknd ins fnl f: 8th of 8 in gp* **25/1**

-114 **24** *8* **Horroob**[26] 3071 3-8-9 **90**.............................................. AndreaAtzeni 29 29
(Roger Varian) *racd stands' side: t.k.h: hld up in midfield: effrt whn hmpd and lost pl 2f out: nt rcvr: wknd over 1f out: 16th of 21 in gp* **16/1**

1510 **25** *6* **Thomas Cranmer (USA)**[12] 3592 3-8-12 **93**......... RichardKingscote 14 18
(Mark Johnston) *racd stands' side: chsd ldrs: rdn 1/2-way: lost pl and bhd 2f out: wknd: 17th of 21 in gp* **66/1**

0-11 **26** *1 ¼* **Keyser Soze (IRE)**[22] 3211 3-8-12 **93**........................ StevieDonohoe 31 15
(Richard Spencer) *racd stands' side: t.k.h: chsd ldrs: rdn and lost pl ent fnl 2f: btn and hmpd over 1f out: bhd ins fnl f: 18th of 21 in gp* **8/1**[2]

2535 **27** *4* **Masham Star (IRE)**[19] 3318 3-9-4 **99**............................... AdamKirby 15 12
(Mark Johnston) *racd stands' side: hld up in tch in midfield: effrt to chse ldrs and drvn whn impeded 2f out: sn outpcd and lost pl over 1f out: eased ins fnl f: t.o: 19th of 21 in gp* **66/1**

61-3 **28** *1 ½* **Hyde Park**[26] 3071 3-9-1 **96**........................................... GrahamLee 26 5
(John Gosden) *racd stands' side: t.k.h: chsd ldrs: rdn over 2f out: struggling and losing pl whn hmpd over 1f out: bhd and eased ins fnl f: 20th of 21 in gp* **25/1**

13-5 **29** *29* **Maths Prize**[62] 1943 3-8-6 **90**.............................. KieranShoemark(3) 13
(Roger Charlton) *restless in stalls: racd stands' side: rdn 1/2-way: sn struggling bhd 2f out: virtually p.u ins fnl f: t.o: 21st of 21 in gp* **14/1**[3]

1m 40.59s (-0.21) **Going Correction** +0.15s/f (Good) **29 Ran SP% 145.5**
Speed ratings (Par 105): **107,106,105,101,100 100,100,100,98,97 97,96,95,94,94 94,92,91,88,86 85,85,83,75,69 67,63,62,3**
CSF £365.89 TOTE £30.80: £6.00, £5.10, £3.20, £8.60; EX 682.50 Trifecta £3486.00.
**Owner** Qatar Racing Limited **Bred** Knocklong House Stud **Trained** Newmarket, Suffolk

**FOCUS**
Predictably the huge field split into two groups, with eight sticking to the far side and the first three came from that pack. A typical Royal Ascot handicap in many respects with numerous eyecatchers. It's been rated in line with the race averages.

## 3998 KING GEORGE V STKS (H'CAP) 1m 3f 211y
**5:35** (5:40) (Class 2) (0-105,104) 3-Y-O

**£56,025** (£16,776; £8,388; £4,194; £2,097; £1,053) **Stalls** Low

Form RPR

1-12 **1** **Atty Persse (IRE)**[27] 3042 3-8-7 **93**..................(p[1]) KieranShoemark(3) 22 104+
(Roger Charlton) *lw: prom: rdn to ld over 2f out: edgd rt over 1f out: qcknd clr ins fnl f: r.o wl and in command fnl 100yds* **7/1**[2]

-202 **2** *3* **First Nation**[55] 2132 3-8-10 **93**...................................... WilliamBuick 18 98
(Charlie Appleby) *trckd ldrs: rdn and swtchd lft over 2f out: edgd rt over 1f out: sn wnt 2nd: unable to go w wnr ins fnl f: no imp: all out to hold on for 2nd fin* **8/1**[3]

0-62 **3** *hd* **Bear Valley (IRE)**[6] 3778 3-8-5 **88**................................ PJMcDonald 10 93
(Mark Johnston) *broke wl: in tch: rdn over 2f out: swtchd lft whn chsng ldrs over 1f out: styd on ins fnl f: fin wl: no ch w wnr* **20/1**

-211 **4** *nk* **Drochaid**[19] 3318 3-8-10 **93**.......................................... OisinMurphy 7 97+
(Andrew Balding) *racd keenly in midfield: rdn and hdwy whn nt clr run and hmpd over 1f out: r.o ins fnl f: gng on at fin* **14/1**

1 **5** *1 ¼* **Homesman (USA)**[25] 3109 3-9-7 **104**...........................(b) RyanMoore 16 106+
(A P O'Brien, Ire) *str: hld up: swtchd lft and rdn over 2f out: hdwy over 1f out: sn hung rt: styd on ins fnl f: nt rch ldrs* **8/1**[3]

0-6 **6** *nk* **Utah (IRE)**[25] 3109 3-8-13 **96**................................ SeamieHeffernan 13 98
(A P O'Brien, Ire) *cmpt: swtg: squeezed out s: midfield: rdn whn plld out and hdwy over 2f out: intimidated by rival over 1f out: styd on ins fnl f: one pce nr fin* **10/1**

-251 **7** *hd* **Never Surrender (IRE)**[43] 2527 3-8-5 **88**.......................... PaulHanagan 12 89
(Charles Hills) *wnt lft s: racd keenly: led after 1f: rdn and hdd over 2f out: outpcd by wnr over 1f out: sn lost 2nd: no ex fnl 100yds* **25/1**

-134 **8** *hd* **Bin Battuta**[46] 2437 3-8-10 **93**.................................(v[1]) PatCosgrave 5 94+
(Saeed bin Suroor) *s.i.s: towards rr: hmpd over 4f out: last and rdn over 2f out: swtchd rt and hdwy over 1f out: r.o ins fnl f: fin wl* **20/1**

216 **9** *½* **Janszoon**[26] 3081 3-8-7 **90**...................................(b) MickaelBarzalona 21 90
(Charlie Appleby) *lengthy: midfield: effrt over 2f out: bmpd over 1f out: styd on same pce ins fnl f* **16/1**

-151 **10** *1 ¼* **Shymkent**[13] 3528 3-8-8 **91**.......................................... HarryBentley 2 89
(David O'Meara) *hld up in midfield: lost pl over 4f out: pushed along to go pce 3f out: rdn over 2f out: styd on fnl f: nt pce to rch ldrs* **33/1**

4-31 **11** *nse* **Master Singer (USA)**[30] 2921 3-8-13 **96**...................(p[1]) AndreaAtzeni 15 94
(John Gosden) *str: lw: trckd ldrs: rdn over 2f out: hung lft u.p over 1f out: fdd ins fnl f* **4/1**[1]

-001 **12** *1 ¾* **Good Omen**[19] 3316 3-8-10 **93**....................................... JamieSpencer 19 88
(David Simcock) *swtg: stdd s: hld up: rdn over 2f out: kpt on fnl f: nvr able to trble ldrs* **14/1**

216 **13** *½* **Oasis Charm**[46] 2437 3-8-7 **90**................................. ColmO'Donoghue 9 85
(Charlie Appleby) *dwlt: midfield: rdn over 2f out: n.m.r and hmpd over 1f out: no imp after* **25/1**

4101 **14** *1 ¾* **Sofia's Rock (FR)**[26] 3081 3-9-3 **100**.............................. JimCrowley 20 92
(Mark Johnston) *lw: chsd ldrs: rdn over 2f out: struggling to hold pl whn n.m.r and hmpd over 1f out: sn dropped away* **7/1**[2]

4 **15** *2 ¼* **Twin Star (IRE)**[25] 3109 3-9-2 **99**................................... RonanWhelan 1 87
(Ms Sheila Lavery, Ire) *cmpt: bmpd early: in rr: checked over 4f out: rdn over 2f out: nvr able to get on terms* **25/1**

-434 **16** *nk* **Tartini (USA)**[19] 3318 3-8-12 **95**...................................... GrahamLee 6 83
(John Gosden) *hld up in midfield: rdn and outpcd over 2f out: n.d after* **14/1**

4-54 **17** *2* **Majoris (IRE)**[47] 2401 3-8-12 **95**.................................(bt[1]) PatSmullen 4 80
(Hugo Palmer) *hld up: rdn over 2f out: nvr on terms* **50/1**

-641 **18** *1 ¼* **Reachforthestars (IRE)**[12] 3583 3-8-8 **91**........................ ShaneFoley 11 74
(David O'Meara) *led for 1f: remained prom: rdn over 2f out: wknd over 1f out* **33/1**

2m 31.68s (-0.82) **Going Correction** +0.15s/f (Good) **18 Ran SP% 131.1**
Speed ratings (Par 105): **108,106,105,105,104 104,104,104,104,103 103,102,101,100,99 98,97,96**
CSF £59.08 CT £1115.07 TOTE £7.50: £2.30, £2.70, £4.80, £3.30; EX 77.40 Trifecta £2789.60.
**Owner** Godolphin **Bred** Bjorn Nielsen **Trained** Beckhampton, Wilts

**FOCUS**
Race run over an extra 11yds. Run at a good gallop, this didn't prove as competitive as expected, with there being a clear-cut winner. The runner-up down to the seventh have all been rated close to their marks.
T/Jkpt: Not won. T/Plt: £447.30 to a £1 stake. Pool: £652,822.00. 1,065.18 winning units.
T/Qpdt: £59.80 to a £1 stake. Pool: £39,793.96. 492.22 winning units.
**Steve Payne & Darren Owen**

# 3965 CHELMSFORD (A.W) (L-H)
## Thursday, June 22

**OFFICIAL GOING: Polytrack: standard**
Wind: Fresh, behind Weather: Cloudy with sunny spells

## 3999 CHELMSFORD CITY #THEPLACETOBE THIS SUMMER NOVICE AUCTION STKS 6f (P)
**1:50** (1:50) (Class 5) 2-Y-O **£5,175** (£1,540; £769; £384) **Stalls** Centre

Form RPR

0025 **1** **Amazing Alice**[12] 3576 2-8-11 0.................................(p) JackMitchell 1 82
(Archie Watson) *mde all: pushed clr over 1f out: easily* **8/1**[3]

6 **2** *7* **Goldenground (IRE)**[21] 3244 2-8-13 0.................... GeorgeWood(3) 8 66
(Henry Spiller) *hld up: pushed along 1/2-way: hdwy over 1f out: r.o to go 2nd towards fin: no ch w wnr* **12/1**

2 **3** *nk* **Simpson (IRE)**[17] 3390 2-9-2 0........................................ LukeMorris 3 65
(Ed Walker) *dwlt: hdwy over 3f out: rdn and hung lft fr over 1f out: styng on same pce whn chsd wnr ins fnl f tl towards fin* **10/11**[1]

434 **4** *2 ½* **Central City (IRE)**[7] 3754 2-9-2 0.......................(b[1]) JosephineGordon 5 60
(Hugo Palmer) *prom: chsd wnr over 2f out: sn rdn: lost 2nd and wkng whn hmpd ins fnl f* **7/4**[2]

60 **5** *8* **Misty Breese (IRE)**[21] 3244 2-8-11 0................................ JoeyHaynes 2 29
(Paul D'Arcy) *prom: rdn over 2f out: wknd over 1f out* **50/1**

**6** *1* **Mr Little (IRE)** 2-9-2 0.................................................. TimmyMurphy 7 31
(Jamie Osborne) *chsd ldrs: lost pl over 4f out: wknd wl over 2f out* **20/1**

**7** *10* **Korak Boy (IRE)** 2-9-2 0.................................................. LiamKeniry 4
(Joseph Tuite) *racd keenly in 2nd pl tl rdn over 2f out: wknd over 1f out* **25/1**

1m 13.9s (0.20) **Going Correction** +0.175s/f (Slow) **7 Ran SP% 118.1**
Speed ratings (Par 93): **105,95,95,91,81 79,66**
CSF £90.43 TOTE £11.10: £4.10, £7.90; EX 102.70 Trifecta £206.10.
**Owner** C R Hirst **Bred** Home Farm **Trained** Upper Lambourn, W Berks

**FOCUS**
A fair event on paper but a race that didn't take anywhere near as much winning as had seemed likely given both market leaders disappointed. The winner raced close to the inside rail throughout.

## 4000 HEART ESSEX H'CAP 2m (P)
**2:20** (2:21) (Class 5) (0-70,72) 4-Y-O+ **£5,175** (£1,540; £769; £384) **Stalls** Low

Form RPR

4211 **1** **Graceful Lady**[4] 3863 4-8-12 **62**.................................... DavidEgan(5) 2 69
(Robert Eddery) *s.i.s: hld up: hdwy over 3f out: led over 2f out: rdn over 1f out: edgd lft ins fnl f: styd on* **3/1**[2]

5403 **2** *½* **See And Be Seen**[6] 3775 7-8-13 **63**.....................(p) MitchGodwin(5) 5 69
(Sylvester Kirk) *prom: lost pl over 12f out: hdwy and nt clr run over 2f out: chsd wnr over 1f out: sn rdn: styd on* **8/1**

3212 **3** *11* **Night Generation (GER)**[9] 3685 5-9-5 **64**.....................(tp) LukeMorris 4 57
(Chris Gordon) *hld up in tch: rdn over 2f out: wknd fnl f* **5/2**[1]



The Form Book Flat, Raceform Ltd, Newbury, RG14 5SJ

3-54 **4** 5 **Southern States**$^{15}$ 3459 4-9-2 **61**......(e) SteveDrowne 7 48
(Lydia Richards) *disp ld tl wnt on over 3f out: rdn and hdd over 2f out: wknd over 1f out* **9/2**

30-6 **5** 12 **Jazzy (IRE)**$^{17}$ 3409 4-9-10 **72**......(tp) GeorgeWood$^{(3)}$ 1 44
(Martin Keighley) *disp ld tl rdn over 3f out: wknd over 1f out* **4/1**$^{3}$

11-3 **6** 21 **Master Dancer**$^{48}$ 2363 6-9-7 **66**......(p) DavidProbert 6 13
(Tim Vaughan) *chsd ldrs: rdn over 3f out: wknd wl over 2f out* **6/1**

3m 34.38s (4.38) **Going Correction** +0.175s/f (Slow) **6** Ran SP% **117.2**
Speed ratings (Par 103): **96,95,90,87,81 71**
CSF £27.28 TOTE £4.30: £1.80, £4.60; EX 32.40 Trifecta £66.40.
**Owner** Graham & Lynn Knight **Bred** J C Sillett **Trained** Newmarket, Suffolk

**FOCUS**
A modest handicap in which the gallop increased after 5f. The first two pulled clear in the straight and the winner came down the centre. The runner-up has been rated to his recent best.

## 4001 OLIVER'S PLANTS LTD H'CAP 1m (P)
**2:55** (2:56) (Class 3) (0-90,92) 4-Y-0+ **£12,938** (£3,850; £1,924; £962) **Stalls** Low

Form RPR

-503 **1** **Wealth Tax**$^{19}$ 3344 4-8-3 **71**...... JoeyHaynes 1 78
(Ed Dunlop) *trckd ldrs: nt clr run and lost pl over 2f out: hdwy and n.m.r over 1f out: rdn and r.o to ld towards fin* **10/1**

-215 **2** nk **Ballard Down (IRE)**$^{22}$ 3212 4-9-7 **92**......(v) CallumShepherd$^{(3)}$ 8 98
(William Knight) *s.i.s: hld up: hdwy on outer over 2f out: rdn to ld ins fnl f: edgd lft: hdd towards fin* **6/1**$^{3}$

0030 **3** ½ **Mutarakez (IRE)**$^{20}$ 3298 5-9-6 **88**...... DougieCostello 10 93
(Brian Meehan) *hld up: rdn: hung lft and hmpd over 1f out: continued to hang lft and r.o ins fnl f: nt rch ldrs* **7/1**

1400 **4** 1 ¾ **Hammer Gun (USA)**$^{12}$ 3589 4-9-1 **83**......(v) MartinLane 3 86+
(Derek Shaw) *hmpd sn after s: hld up: hdwy and nt clr run over 1f out: running on whn carried lft and nowhere to go wl ins fnl f: nvr able to chal* **12/1**

4630 **5** 1 **Bold Prediction (IRE)**$^{33}$ 2828 7-9-2 **84**...... LukeMorris 6 83
(Ed Walker) *led 1f: chsd ldr tl rdn to ld over 1f out: hdd: carried lft and no ex ins fnl f* **5/1**$^{2}$

0-12 **6** 2 **Lastmanlastround (IRE)**$^{22}$ 3212 4-8-8 **81**...... DavidEgan$^{(5)}$ 7 75+
(Rae Guest) *prom: nt clr run over 1f out: sn swtchd lft: no ex ins fnl f: b.b.v* **3/1**$^{1}$

3661 **7** hd **Bint Dandy (IRE)**$^{29}$ 2973 6-9-0 **87**......(b) LewisEdmunds$^{(5)}$ 9 81
(Chris Dwyer) *hld up in tch: rdn and ev ch fr over 1f out: styng on same pce whn nt clr run wl ins fnl f* **6/1**$^{3}$

-520 **8** 5 **Michele Strogoff**$^{22}$ 3199 4-9-7 **89**...... TomEaves 4 71
(Tony Coyle) *chsd ldrs: rdn over 1f out: wknd fnl f* **10/1**

00-0 **9** 1 **Accurate**$^{12}$ 3589 4-9-7 **89**...... GeorgeDowning 2 69
(Ian Williams) *s.i.s: hld up: pushed along over 3f out: nvr on terms* **25/1**

0-35 **10** 4 ½ **Dream Of Summer (IRE)**$^{40}$ 2617 4-8-12 **80**......(b$^{1}$) DavidProbert 5 49
(Andrew Balding) *racd keenly: led after 1f: rdn and hdd over 1f out: wknd fnl f* **7/1**

1m 40.31s (0.41) **Going Correction** +0.175s/f (Slow) **10** Ran SP% **125.0**
Speed ratings (Par 107): **104,103,103,101,100 98,98,93,92,87**
CSF £73.91 CT £473.41 TOTE £10.60: £3.30, £1.40, £3.30; EX 71.60 Trifecta £427.50.
**Owner** Mhs Partners & E Dunlop **Bred** Barry Walters **Trained** Newmarket, Suffolk
■ Stewards' Enquiry : Dougie Costello 2 day ban - guilty of careless riding (6/7 July)

**FOCUS**
A competitive handicap in which the gallop was reasonable. The winner raced centre-to-far side in the straight. The third has been rated to his recent best.

## 4002 LEXUS IPSWICH H'CAP 1m 2f (P)
**3:30** (3:32) (Class 3) (0-95,93) 4-Y-0+ **£12,938** (£3,850; £1,924; £481) **Stalls** Low

Form RPR

1120 **1** **Ickymasho**$^{24}$ 3160 5-9-6 **92**...... LukeMorris 5 102
(Jonathan Portman) *chsd ldrs: led over 1f out: rdn clr and edgd lft ins fnl f: jst hld on* **14/1**

1264 **2** nk **Banditry (IRE)**$^{24}$ 3154 5-9-4 **90**...... DavidProbert 6 99+
(Ian Williams) *hld up: hdwy u.p over 1f out: edgd lft and r.o to go 2nd wl ins fnl f: nt quite rch wnr* **13/8**$^{1}$

0-04 **3** 4 **Sagely (IRE)**$^{12}$ 3558 4-9-3 **89**...... TomEaves 3 90
(Ed Dunlop) *hld up: hdwy over 2f out: rdn over 1f out: styd on same pce fnl f* **25/1**

0053 **4** ½ **Beardwood**$^{12}$ 3597 5-9-2 **88**......(p) MartinLane 2 88
(Mark Johnston) *pushed along to chse ldr after 1f: rdn and ev ch over 1f out: no ex ins fnl f* **4/1**$^{2}$

4-51 **4** dht **Zzoro (IRE)**$^{34}$ 2796 4-9-2 **88**...... GavinLerena 1 88
(Amanda Perrett) *led: rdn and hdd over 1f out: edgd lft and no ex ins fnl f* **5/1**$^{3}$

1231 **6** 1 ½ **Retrieve (AUS)**$^{13}$ 3546 9-8-12 **84**......(tp) DougieCostello 4 81
(Jamie Osborne) *hld up: effrt over 1f out: no ex ins fnl f* **25/1**

-121 **7** 3 ½ **Celebration Day (IRE)**$^{21}$ 3235 4-8-11 **86**...... GeorgeWood$^{(3)}$ 7 76
(Simon Crisford) *chsd ldrs: rdn over 3f out: wknd wl over 1f out* **4/1**$^{2}$

4/63 **8** nk **Farquhar (IRE)**$^{34}$ 2797 6-9-4 **93**......(h) AlistairRawlinson$^{(3)}$ 8 82
(Michael Appleby) *half rrd s: hld up: pushed along over 2f out: nvr on terms* **10/1**

-550 **9** 58 **Calvinist**$^{92}$ 1309 4-9-3 **89**...... RobertWinston 9
(Ian Williams) *hld up: hung lft 4f out: wknd over 2f out: eased* **16/1**

2m 7.2s (-1.40) **Going Correction** +0.175s/f (Slow) **9** Ran SP% **124.1**
Speed ratings (Par 107): **112,111,108,108,108 106,104,103,57**
CSF £40.05 CT £605.72 TOTE £13.70: £3.50, £1.20, £7.30; EX 58.50 Trifecta £709.30.
**Owner** C R Lambourne, M Forbes, D Losse **Bred** Allseasons Bloodstock **Trained** Upper Lambourn, Berks

**FOCUS**
A decent handicap in which the gallop was only fair. The first two deserve credit for pulling clear in the closing stages. A clear pb from the winner.

## 4003 LOVE THAT HAT MEDIAN AUCTION MAIDEN FILLIES' STKS 1m 2f (P)
**4:05** (4:13) (Class 4) 3-4-Y-0 **£8,086** (£2,406; £1,202; £601) **Stalls** Low

Form RPR

5 **1** **Distant (USA)**$^{22}$ 3209 3-9-0 0...... DavidProbert 1 73+
(Roger Charlton) *trckd ldrs: shkn up to ld over 1f out: drvn out* **4/6**$^{1}$

**2** nk **Lewinsky (IRE)** 3-9-0 0...... JackMitchell 2 72+
(Hugo Palmer) *s.i.s: sn rcvrd and hld up in tch: rdn over 1f out: ev ch ins fnl f: styd on* **10/1**

3-63 **3** 3 ½ **Canterbury Quad (FR)**$^{30}$ 2929 3-9-0 78...... LouisSteward 6 66
(Henry Spiller) *a.p: rdn and ev ch over 1f out: no ex ins fnl f: edgd lft towards fin* **7/2**$^{2}$

00 **4** 2 ½ **Kimene**$^{33}$ 2834 3-9-0 0...... AdamBeschizza 4 60
(William Stone) *chsd ldr tl rdn over 2f out: no ex ins fnl f* **50/1**

33- **5** ½ **Miss Fay (IRE)**$^{266}$ 6888 3-9-0 0......(v$^{1}$) LukeMorris 5 59
(Michael Bell) *s.i.s: hld up: pushed along and hdwy over 2f out: rdn and hung lft over 1f out: nt clr run and swtchd rt ins fnl f: styd on same pce* **7/1**$^{3}$

0 **6** 1 **Xylophone**$^{16}$ 3435 3-9-0 0...... RobertWinston 3 57
(Archie Watson) *led: qcknd over 2f out: rdn and hdd over 1f out: sn hung lft: wknd ins fnl f* **20/1**

35 **7** nk **Voi**$^{17}$ 3395 3-8-11 0......(t$^{1}$) NoelGarbutt$^{(3)}$ 12 56
(Conrad Allen) *hld up: styd on ins fnl f: nvr nrr* **20/1**

**8** ½ **Lady Macha** 3-8-11 0...... GeorgeWood$^{(3)}$ 10 55+
(Marco Botti) *s.s: hld up: rdn over 1f out: nvr nrr* **10/1**

0-4 **9** ½ **Autumn Glow**$^{23}$ 3175 3-8-7 0...... JackOsborn$^{(7)}$ 13 54?
(Miss Joey Ellis) *mid-div: rdn over 3f out: wknd over 2f out: hung lft over 1f out* **50/1**

50 **10** 18 **Lagopus**$^{13}$ 3542 4-9-12 0...... MartinLane 7 18
(David Simcock) *hld up: rdn over 2f out: nvr on terms* **50/1**

0 **11** ½ **Naralsaif (IRE)**$^{11}$ 3626 3-8-11 0...... AaronJones$^{(3)}$ 9 17
(Derek Shaw) *hld up in tch: plld hrd early: stdd and lost pl 8f out: wknd over 2f out* **50/1**

2m 12.15s (3.55) **Going Correction** +0.175s/f (Slow)
**WFA** 3 from 4yo 12lb **11** Ran SP% **130.3**
Speed ratings (Par 102): **92,91,88,86,86 85,85,85,84,70 69**
CSF £9.94 TOTE £1.70: £1.02, £3.00, £1.40; EX 10.50 Trifecta £26.90.
**Owner** K Abdullah **Bred** Juddmonte Farms Inc **Trained** Beckhampton, Wilts
■ Stellekaya was withdrawn. Price at time of withdrawal 66-1. Rule 4 does not apply.

**FOCUS**
Not much strength in depth but decent-enough form from the principals. The gallop was fair. The opening level is fluid.

## 4004 ESSEX LIFE H'CAP 1m 6f (P)
**4:45** (4:45) (Class 4) (0-85,84) 3-Y-0 **£8,086** (£2,406; £1,202; £601) **Stalls** Low

Form RPR

4112 **1** **Alabaster**$^{19}$ 3335 3-9-7 **84**......(b$^{1}$) LukeMorris 3 92+
(Sir Mark Prescott Bt) *mde virtually all: racd keenly: qcknd over 2f out: rdn over 1f out: hung lft ins fnl f: styd on u.p* **4/5**$^{1}$

4316 **2** 1 ¼ **Cray (IRE)**$^{19}$ 3335 3-8-11 **74**...... JackMitchell 2 79
(James Bethell) *hld up: hdwy on outer over 2f out: rdn to chse wnr over 1f out: styd on same pce ins fnl f* **7/1**

2003 **3** 3 **The Blues Master (IRE)**$^{8}$ 3711 3-8-12 **75**......(b$^{1}$) MartinLane 1 76
(Mark Johnston) *disp 2nd after 1f: rdn over 2f out: styd on same pce fr over 1f out* **6/1**$^{3}$

-323 **4** ½ **Splash Around**$^{14}$ 3503 3-9-3 **80**...... GavinLerena 4 80
(Sir Michael Stoute) *led early: disp 2nd pl tl rdn over 1f out: no ex fnl f* **11/4**$^{2}$

3m 3.26s (0.06) **Going Correction** +0.175s/f (Slow) **4** Ran SP% **109.0**
Speed ratings (Par 101): **106,105,103,103**
CSF £6.71 TOTE £1.60; EX 7.90 Trifecta £15.40.
**Owner** Charles C Walker - Osborne House **Bred** Miss K Rausing **Trained** Newmarket, Suffolk

**FOCUS**
Only four runners and a muddling gallop but a useful effort from thie winner, whose form continues on an upward curve.

## 4005 GREENE KING IPA H'CAP 5f (P)
**5:20** (5:21) (Class 5) (0-70,72) 3-Y-0+ **£5,175** (£1,540; £769; £384) **Stalls** Low

Form RPR

6443 **1** **Saved My Bacon (IRE)**$^{21}$ 3231 6-9-13 **72**......(h) LewisEdmunds$^{(5)}$ 10 81
(Chris Dwyer) *s.i.s: hld up: hung rt over 3f out: rdn over 1f out: str run to ld wl ins fnl f* **9/2**$^{3}$

2635 **2** 1 ¼ **Vale Of Flight (IRE)**$^{15}$ 3466 4-9-4 **58**......(p$^{1}$) AntonioFresu 5 62
(Luke McJannet) *s.i.s: sn rdn over 1f out: r.o wl to go 2nd nr fin* **14/1**

4-31 **3** ½ **Absolutely Awesome**$^{23}$ 3186 3-9-8 **68**...... RobertWinston 3 68+
(John Butler) *sn w ldr: led over 1f out: rdn and hdd wl ins fnl f* **5/2**$^{1}$

0-02 **4** nk **Show Palace**$^{33}$ 2843 4-9-10 **64**...... DavidNolan 4 65
(Jennie Candlish) *dwlt: hdwy over 3f out: rdn and carried rt over 1f out: styd on* **4/1**$^{2}$

5620 **5** 1 ¼ **Pearl Acclaim (IRE)**$^{10}$ 3667 7-10-1 **72**......(p) ShelleyBirkett$^{(3)}$ 6 69
(David O'Meara) *led: rdn: hung rt and hdd over 1f out: no ex ins fnl f* **10/1**

4240 **6** 1 **Borough Boy (IRE)**$^{15}$ 3466 7-9-11 **65**......(v) MartinLane 8 58
(Derek Shaw) *prom: rdn 1/2-way: styd on same pce fnl f* **16/1**

6012 **7** ¾ **Classic Pursuit**$^{40}$ 2621 6-9-13 **67**......(p) LukeMorris 2 57
(Michael Appleby) *prom: rdn over 1f out: no ex ins fnl f* **9/2**$^{3}$

-635 **8** 3 ¼ **Corridor Kid (IRE)**$^{30}$ 2932 4-9-13 **67**......(v) TomEaves 1 46
(Derek Shaw) *s.i.s: hld up: hung rt 2f out: hdwy over 1f out: wknd ins fnl f* **10/1**

2144 **9** ½ **Roy's Legacy**$^{15}$ 3453 8-9-5 **66**...... AidenBlakemore$^{(7)}$ 9 43
(Shaun Harris) *w ldrs tl over 3f out: rdn over 1f out: wknd fnl f* **20/1**

0020 **10** nse **Percy Toplis**$^{13}$ 3545 3-8-1 **50**......(v) AaronJones$^{(3)}$ 7 25
(Christine Dunnett) *s.i.s: rdn over 1f out: a in rr* **33/1**

1m 0.73s (0.53) **Going Correction** +0.175s/f (Slow)
**WFA** 3 from 4yo+ 6lb **10** Ran SP% **123.4**
Speed ratings (Par 103): **102,100,99,98,96 95,93,88,87,87**
CSF £69.65 CT £200.10 TOTE £4.90: £1.60, £4.90, £1.60; EX 76.40 Trifecta £500.80.
**Owner** Mrs J Hughes & Mrs C Kemp **Bred** Kenneth Heelan **Trained** Newmarket, Suffolk

**FOCUS**
A strongly run race and one that teed things up for the finishers. The winner raced in the centre in the straight. The winner has been rated close to her best.
T/Plt: £549.30 to a £1 stake. Pool: £46,449.88. 61.73 winning units. T/Qpdt: £17.10 to a £1 stake. Pool: £4,579.78. 197.86 winning units. **Colin Roberts**

# 3819 LINGFIELD (L-H)
Thursday, June 22

**OFFICIAL GOING: Polytrack: standard**
Wind: breezy Weather: cloudy and mild

## 4006 RACING WELFARE H'CAP 1m 1y(P)
**5:50** (5:51) (Class 6) (0-60,60) 3-Y-0 **£2,264** (£673; £252) **Stalls** High

Form RPR

-402 **1** **Varun's Bride (IRE)**$^{23}$ 3191 3-9-4 **57**...... TomMarquand 11 62
(Richard Hannon) *mde all: pushed along 2f out: 1 l clr whn rdn appr fnl f: ld diminishing and r.o u.p fnl f: hld on wl* **8/1**

-326 **2** nk **Epsom Secret**$^{21}$ 3250 3-9-0 **53**...... KieranO'Neill 9 57+
(Pat Phelan) *mid-div: plenty to do and drvn 2f out: rdn appr fnl f: r.o strly and clsng on wnr last 50yds* **8/1**

3233 **3** *nk* **Topmeup**[9] 3695 3-8-7 **53**..................(v[1]) KatherineGlenister(7) 6 57
(David Evans) *hld up: hdwy u.p on inner over 1f out: r.o wl fnl f: nvr nrr* **7/2**[1]

6-06 **3** *dht* **Casado (IRE)**[50] 2315 3-9-7 **60**.................. KierenFox 10 64+
(John Best) *hld up: hdwy 3f out: rdn over 1f out: r.o wl ins fnl f: nrst fin* **8/1**

0-02 **5** *¾* **How's Lucy**[36] 2733 3-9-0 **53**.................. DannyBrock 8 55
(Jane Chapple-Hyam) *racd in cl 2nd: drvn 2f out: rdn 1f out: no ex* **11/2**[3]

000- **6** *2* **Joshlee (IRE)**[241] 7571 3-9-3 **56**.................. ShaneKelly 1 53
(Richard Hughes) *trckd ldrs: rdn over 2f out: grad fdd* **8/1**

00 **7** *nse* **Beast**[23] 3173 3-9-1 **57**.................. CharlieBennett(3) 4 54
(Lee Carter) *trckd ldrs: pushed along in 4th 2f out: rdn over 1f out: wknd* **50/1**

4-60 **8** *2* **Banta Bay**[16] 3442 3-8-9 **51**.................. HectorCrouch(3) 5 44
(John Best) *hld up: drvn 2f out: rdn over 1f out: one pce fnl f* **10/1**

4-00 **9** *1* **Ronni Layne**[21] 3250 3-8-11 **55**.................. DavidEgan(5) 12 45
(Conrad Allen) *hld up: pushed along on outer 2f out: rdn over 1f out: no hdwy* **33/1**

0000 **10** *½* **Hippocampus (IRE)**[27] 3024 3-8-12 **58**.................. RossaRyan(7) 3 47
(Richard Hannon) *mid-div: drvn 2f out: rdn over 1f out: fdd* **12/1**

-645 **11** *2¾* **Nicky Baby (IRE)**[119] 875 3-9-2 **60**..................(p[1]) LuluStanford(5) 2 43
(Dean Ivory) *trckd ldrs on outer: niggled 1/2-way: rdn and wknd wl over 2f out* **9/2**[2]

1m 40.64s (2.44) **Going Correction** +0.20s/f (Slow) **11 Ran SP% 121.9**
Speed ratings (Par 97): **95,94,94,94,93 91,91,89,88,88 85**
WIN: 7.00; PL: VB 2.90, ES 3.50, C 1.10 T 1.00; EX: 44.40; CSF: 73.28; TC: VB-ES-C 203.95, VB-ES-T 135.31; TF: VB-ES-C 506.30, VB-ES-T 97.30.
**Owner** Middleham Park Racing CIII **Bred** Philip And Mrs Jane Myerscough **Trained** East Everleigh, Wilts

**FOCUS**
A tight finish to this competitive handicap.

## 4007 INJURED JOCKEYS FUND NOVICE STKS 6f 1y(P)
**6:20** (6:21) (Class 5) 2-Y-O **£3,234** (£962; £481; £240) **Stalls** Low

Form RPR

**1** **Tunes Of Glory** 2-9-2 0.................. RyanPowell 4 71
(Sir Mark Prescott Bt) *mde all: narrow ld whn pushed along over 1f out: hld on wl ins fnl f* **12/1**

**2** *hd* **Carricklane** 2-8-11 0.................. ShaneKelly 8 65
(Richard Hughes) *prom: effrt and almost alongside wnr over 1f out: pushed along and r.o wl fnl f: jst hld* **28/1**

6 **3** *nk* **Retained (FR)**[16] 3437 2-8-11 0.................. KierenFox 6 64
(John Best) *trckd ldrs: rdn in 4th over 1f out: styd on wl u.p fnl f: nvr nrr* **20/1**

00 **4** *hd* **Isoletta**[16] 3421 2-8-6 0.................. JennyPowell(5) 2 64
(Ed Walker) *trckd ldrs: hdwy on inner over 1f out: ev ch ins fnl f: r.o but hld last 100yds* **14/1**

**5** *¾* **Rude Awakening** 2-8-9 0.................. ManuelFernandes(7) 1 66+
(Sir Mark Prescott Bt) *hld up: pushed along and hdwy on inner over 1f out: r.o steadily under hands and heels ins fnl f* **20/1**

**6** *shd* **Chess Move (IRE)** 2-9-2 0.................. LiamKeniry 5 66
(George Baker) *mid-div: pushed along over 1f: r.o fnl f* **7/1**[2]

4 **7** *½* **Move Over**[26] 3093 2-9-2 0.................. TomMarquand 7 64
(Richard Hannon) *mid-div on outer: rdn along 2f out: one pce u.p appr fnl f: no ex* **8/11**[1]

6 **8** *¾* **Star Of Vendome (FR)**[23] 3174 2-8-11 0..................(t[1]) DavidProbert 3 57
(Harry Dunlop) *hld up: drvn over 1f out: one pce fnl f* **10/1**

**9** *nk* **Sun And Shadow** 2-9-2 0.................. ThomasBrown 9 61
(Ed Walker) *hld up: pushed along on outer wl over 1f out: rdn ins fnl f: nvr a factor* **8/1**[3]

1m 14.12s (2.22) **Going Correction** +0.20s/f (Slow) **9 Ran SP% 117.9**
Speed ratings (Par 93): **93,92,92,92,91 90,90,89,88**
CSF £301.47 TOTE £14.60: £3.30, £3.80, £5.80; EX 271.80 Trifecta £7764.80.
**Owner** Denford Stud **Bred** Denford Stud Ltd **Trained** Newmarket, Suffolk

**FOCUS**
The pace held up and it was tough to make up ground. They finished in a heap.

## 4008 LINE MANAGEMENT GROUP (S) STKS 5f 6y(P)
**6:50** (6:50) (Class 6) 3-Y-O+ **£2,587** (£770; £384; £192) **Stalls** High

Form RPR

0251 **1** **Nag's Wag (IRE)**[9] 3686 4-9-8 72.................. LiamKeniry 4 74
(George Baker) *trckd ldr: hdwy to ld over 1f out: sn clr: rdn and r.o wl fnl f: comf* **8/11**[1]

0253 **2** *2* **Picansort**[59] 2025 10-9-8 64..................(b) ShaneKelly 2 67
(Peter Crate) *racd in 3rd: drvn over 1f out: wnt 2nd ins fnl f: sn rdn and no imp* **9/4**[2]

4360 **3** *1½* **Billy's Boots**[9] 3703 3-8-11 57.................. KierenFox 1 55
(J R Jenkins) *t.k.h: led: pushed along over 1f out: rdn and hdd appr fnl f: no ex* **10/1**

0-04 **4** *1¼* **Little Cupcake**[9] 3686 6-8-0 43..................(v) JackOsborn(7) 3 42
(Denis Quinn) *a in last: pushed along 1/2-way: drvn wl over 1f out: sn rdn: no imp* **9/1**[3]

1m 0.8s (2.00) **Going Correction** +0.20s/f (Slow)
**WFA** 3 from 4yo+ 6lb **4 Ran SP% 107.8**
Speed ratings (Par 101): **92,88,86,84**
CSF £2.57 TOTE £1.60; EX 2.30 Trifecta £4.30.There was no bid for the winner.
**Owner** Popbitch Racing Club **Bred** Mrs Ann Foley & Mr William Neville **Trained** Manton, Wilts

**FOCUS**
A pretty uncompetitive seller.

## 4009 ENDLESS POOLS H'CAP 5f 6y(P)
**7:20** (7:20) (Class 6) (0-65,64) 4-Y-O+ **£2,264** (£673; £336; £168) **Stalls** High

Form RPR

-543 **1** **Staffa (IRE)**[19] 3331 4-8-9 **52**.................. LukeMorris 4 57
(Denis Coakley) *hld up: hdwy 2f out: drvn over 1f out: clsd on ldrs and rdn ent fnl f: r.o wl u.p to ld last 25yds* **7/2**[2]

2430 **2** *nk* **Fabulous Flyer**[19] 3331 4-8-6 **49**.................. AdamBeschizza 2 53
(Jeremy Gask) *mid-div: hdwy over 1f out: sn rdn and clsd on ldr: led ins fnl f: r.o but hdd last 25yds* **4/1**[3]

0060 **3** *2* **Elusivity (IRE)**[15] 3466 9-9-0 **64**..................(p) KatherineGlenister(7) 5 61
(Conor Dore) *chsd ldrs: pushed along over 1f out: rdn and one pce fnl f* **7/1**

2305 **4** *¾* **Powerful Wind (IRE)**[29] 2967 8-9-4 **61**..................(t) JFEgan 3 55
(Charlie Wallis) *led: 5 l clr 2f out: stl 4 l clr 1f out: rdn ins fnl f: wknd qckly and hdd ins fnl f: no ex* **3/1**[1]

230- **5** *hd* **Regal Miss**[211] 8078 5-8-13 **59**.................. CharlieBennett(3) 1 52
(Patrick Chamings) *chsd clr ldr: lost 2nd appr fnl f: sn rdn and no ex* **9/2**

5254 **6** *3* **Pharoh Jake**[29] 2967 9-8-12 **55**.................. WilliamCarson 6 38
(John Bridger) *a in rr: drvn over 1f out: no imp fnl f* **13/2**

59.89s (1.09) **Going Correction** +0.20s/f (Slow) **6 Ran SP% 111.2**
Speed ratings (Par 101): **99,98,95,94,93 89**
CSF £17.32 TOTE £4.10: £2.50, £2.20; EX 15.50 Trifecta £86.30.
**Owner** The Good Mixers **Bred** Kildaragh Stud **Trained** West Ilsley, Berks

**FOCUS**
With Powerful Wind setting a strong pace up front this was set up for the closers.

## 4010 ROA/RACING POST OWNERS JACKPOT FILLIES' H'CAP 1m 1y(P)
**7:50** (7:51) (Class 5) (0-75,77) 4-Y-O+ **£3,234** (£962; £481; £240) **Stalls** High

Form RPR

-512 **1** **Helfire**[15] 3454 4-9-0 **70**.................. CharlieBennett(3) 3 79+
(Hughie Morrison) *mid-div: hdwy on inner over 1f out: sn angled out: led ins fnl f: asserted under hands and heels: comf* **11/8**[1]

333 **2** *1½* **Stosur (IRE)**[13] 3548 6-9-1 **73**..................(b) DavidEgan(5) 5 77
(Gay Kelleway) *led: qcknd and pushed along 2f out: 1 l ld jst over 1f out: hdd by wnr ins fnl f: rdn and no ex* **10/1**

2644 **3** *½* **First Experience**[15] 3455 6-9-0 **74**..................(p) JoshuaBryan(7) 4 78+
(Lee Carter) *trckd ldrs: hdwy gng wl over 1f out: rdn ent fnl f: one pce* **16/1**

5125 **4** *1¾* **Auntie Barber (IRE)**[51] 2254 4-9-7 **77**.................. AaronJones(3) 2 76
(Stuart Williams) *hld up: rdn and effrt on inner over 1f out: one pce fnl f* **4/1**[3]

0-03 **5** *½* **Ede's The Mover**[23] 3172 4-8-2 **55**.................. KieranO'Neill 1 53
(Pat Phelan) *trckd ldrs: drvn and hdwy into 2nd over 1f out: sltly hmpd by wnr over 1f out: briefly lost momentum: no ex fnl f* **20/1**

306 **6** *5* **Rayaa**[15] 3454 4-9-1 **68**..................(t) JFEgan 7 54
(John Butler) *hld up: drvn 2f out: rdn wl over 1f out: no imp* **3/1**[2]

4420 **7** *¾* **Ixelles Diamond (IRE)**[14] 3507 6-8-3 **56**.................. LukeMorris 8 41
(Lee Carter) *prom: pushed along 2f out: rdn and weakend over 1f out* **20/1**

4104 **8** *¾* **Sheer Intensity (IRE)**[6] 3772 4-8-2 **55**.................. JimmyQuinn 6 38
(David Evans) *slowly away: in rr: u.p 2f out: nvr a factor* **20/1**

1m 38.64s (0.44) **Going Correction** +0.20s/f (Slow) **8 Ran SP% 116.4**
Speed ratings (Par 100): **105,103,103,101,100 95,95,94**
CSF £16.42 CT £150.41 TOTE £2.30: £1.30, £3.00, £4.40; EX 18.40 Trifecta £122.20.
**Owner** Deborah Collett & M J Watson **Bred** M J Watson **Trained** East Ilsley, Berks
■ Stewards' Enquiry : Charlie Bennett four-day ban: careless riding (Jul 6-7, 9-10)

**FOCUS**
A good performance from the winner, even if she did have to use her elbows. The third has been rated close to her recent best.

## 4011 KOMFORT PARTITIONING LIMITED AND AMF CEILINGS H'CAP 6f 1y(P)
**8:20** (8:23) (Class 6) (0-65,66) 3-Y-O+ **£2,587** (£770; £384; £192) **Stalls** Low

Form RPR

022- **1** **Debonaire David**[184] 8467 3-9-6 **64**..................(t) ShaneKelly 5 71+
(Richard Hughes) *trckd ldrs: hdwy 2f out: pushed along to ld over 1f out: chal by runner-up ins fnl f: rdn and asserted last 100yds* **11/10**[1]

1-53 **2** *1* **Nuzha**[154] 313 3-9-8 **66**..................(p[1]) AdamBeschizza 1 70+
(Karen George) *trckd ldrs: hdwy over 1f out out: sn rdn: chal wnr inide fnl f: r.o wl but hld last 100yds* **12/1**

00 **3** *4½* **Jesse Tree (IRE)**[20] 3280 4-8-4 **46** oh1..................(t) MitchGodwin(5) 4 39
(John Flint) *prom: led 2f out: sn pushed along: hdd over 1f out: rdn and one pce ins fnl f* **50/1**

0060 **4** *1½* **Pleadings (USA)**[8] 3728 4-8-9 **46**..................(b[1]) LukeMorris 2 34
(Charlie Wallis) *mid-div: drvn over 1f out: rdn and styd on one pce fnl f* **8/1**[3]

3-00 **5** *½* **Silver Penny**[36] 2725 3-9-0 **65**..................(p[1]) IsobelFrancis(7) 8 50
(Jim Boyle) *led: hdd 2f out: racd wd wl over 1f out: wknd fnl f* **25/1**

2000 **6** *¾* **Fly True**[20] 3281 4-10-1 **66**.................. MartinLane 9 50
(Jeremy Gask) *hld up: drvn 2f out: rdn over 1f out: no imp* **8/1**[3]

20-0 **7** *4½* **Keep It Dark**[28] 3008 8-9-7 **58**.................. DavidProbert 7 29
(William Knight) *trckd ldrs: drvn 2f out: wknd fnl f* **8/1**[3]

F000 **8** *11* **Mobley Chaos**[20] 3280 7-8-9 **46** oh1..................(b) JohnFahy 6
(John Flint) *hld up on outer: wknd 2f out* **33/1**

0146 **9** *11* **Fleeting Glimpse**[29] 2969 4-9-5 **59**.................. CharlieBennett(3) 3
(Patrick Chamings) *slowly away: immediately veered rt and lost 30 l: a bhd* **9/2**[2]

1m 13.13s (1.23) **Going Correction** +0.20s/f (Slow)
**WFA** 3 from 4yo+ 7lb **9 Ran SP% 115.6**
Speed ratings (Par 101): **99,97,91,89,89 88,82,67,52**
CSF £15.98 CT £429.62 TOTE £1.90: £1.10, £3.00, £10.70; EX 12.90 Trifecta £382.20.
**Owner** Sir David Seale **Bred** D R Tucker **Trained** Upper Lambourn, Berks

**FOCUS**
An ordinary race. Two of the three 3yos in the line-up came through to fight it out.

## 4012 GLENYS CURTIS MEMORIAL FILLIES' H'CAP 1m 4f (P)
**8:50** (8:50) (Class 5) (0-70,71) 3-Y-O **£3,234** (£962; £481; £240) **Stalls** Low

Form RPR

5051 **1** **Cribbs Causeway (IRE)**[8] 3721 3-9-2 **68** 6ex.................. KieranShoemark(3) 4 82+
(Roger Charlton) *mde all: qcknd 3f out and shot clr: 8 l ahd 2f out: extended advantage over 1f out: heavily eased ins fnl f: v easily* **1/1**[1]

-434 **2** *3¾* **Glenys The Menace (FR)**[23] 3178 3-9-4 **67**..................(h) KierenFox 7 70+
(John Best) *hld up: effrt 2f out: rdn and gd hdwy over 1f out: r.o wl to take 2nd ins fnl f but no ch w wnr* **8/1**[3]

3213 **3** *2¾* **Bonnie Arlene (IRE)**[8] 3721 3-9-6 **69**.................. DavidProbert 6 68
(Mark Johnston) *hld up: hdwy on outer 3f out: sn drvn into distant 2nd: rdn 1f out: one pce and lost 2nd pl ins fnl f* **4/1**[2]

5-34 **4** *1* **All About The Pace**[21] 3261 3-8-4 **53**.................. KieranO'Neill 1 50
(Mark Usher) *mid-div: drvn over 1f out: one pce fnl f* **16/1**

0443 **5** *2¾* **Amelia Dream**[13] 3542 3-9-2 **70**.................. DavidEgan(5) 3 63
(Mick Channon) *mid-div: drvn 3f out: hdwy into 3rd wl over 1f out: rdn and lost pl ent fnl f* **16/1**

0-53 **6** *4* **Power Home (IRE)**[19] 3327 3-8-4 **58** ow1.................. PaddyPilley(5) 8 44
(Denis Coakley) *chsd ldr: drvn whn wnr qcknd 3f out: sn lost tch w ldrs: rdn and wknd ent fnl f* **16/1**

060 **7** *1½* **Charming Loza**[35] 2760 3-9-8 **71**.................. StevieDonohoe 9 55
(Charlie Fellowes) *in rr: drvn 4f out: rdn wl over 1f out: one pce* **20/1**

6-30 **8** *10* **Doreen**[24] 3145 3-9-2 **65**.................. PatDobbs 10 33
(Sir Michael Stoute) *hld up: pushed along 4f out: drvn 2f out: no imp* **14/1**

33-3 **9** *12* **Settle Petal**[155] 284 3-9-2 **65**.................. JFEgan 2 14
(Pat Phelan) *trckd ldrs: drvn in 3rd 3f out: lost pl and eased 2f out* **33/1**



The Form Book Flat, Raceform Ltd, Newbury, RG14 5SJ

-530 **10** *65* **Star Of Bristol (USA)**31 2900 3-9-7 **70**..........................(b1) ShaneKelly 5
(Richard Hughes) *trckd ldrs: rdn and lost pl 4f out: sn struggling: heavily eased* **25/1**
2m 32.49s (-0.51) **Going Correction** +0.20s/f (Slow) **10** Ran SP% **117.0**
Speed ratings (Par 96): **109,106,104,104,102 99,98,91,83,40**
CSF £9.42 CT £24.61 TOTE £1.70: £1.10, £2.60, £1.70; EX 12.30 Trifecta £40.60.
**Owner** Nick Bradley Racing 13 **Bred** N Bradley **Trained** Beckhampton, Wilts
**FOCUS**
This proved uncompetitive, with the winner following up her Kempton win in great style.
T/Plt: £201.10 to a £1 stake. Pool: £45,282.86. 164.35 winning units. T/Qpdt: £8.10 to a £1 stake. Pool: £5,949.07. 542.68 winning units. **Keith McHugh**

# 3979 RIPON (R-H)
Thursday, June 22
**OFFICIAL GOING: Good (good to firm in places)**
Wind: Fresh, across Weather: Cloudy

## 4013 SIS CLAIMING STKS 6f
**2:10** (2:12) (Class 5) 3-Y-O+ **£3,234** (£962; £481; £240) **Stalls** High

Form RPR
3002 **1** **Tatlisu (IRE)**17 3386 7-9-3 87.................................... ConnorMurtagh(7) 5 84+
(Richard Fahey) *hld up: smooth hdwy over 2f out: led gng wl over 1f out: rdn out ins fnl f* **8/11**1
0000 **2** *1 3/4* **Mishaal (IRE)**33 2840 7-9-2 80...................................... BarryMcHugh 4 70
(Michael Herrington) *chsd ldr: rdn over 2f out: kpt on* **3/1**2
0500 **3** *1 1/4* **Bernie's Boy**17 3401 4-8-9 70.................................... BenSanderson(7) 2 66
(Roger Fell) *led for 1f: chsd ldr: rdn over 2f out: one pce* **10/1**3
4-03 **4** *1* **Ypres**3 3915 8-9-0 56...........................................................(p) CamHardie 3 61
(Jason Ward) *hld up in tch: rdn and hdwy on outer 2f out: ev ch appr fnl f: wknd ins fnl f* **28/1**
1214 **5** *1 3/4* **Noah Amor (IRE)**21 3238 4-8-13 71......................... PatrickVaughan(7) 1 61
(David O'Meara) *led after 1f: rdn 2f out: hdd over 1f out: wknd ins fnl f* **10/1**3
40-0 **6** *20* **More Beau (USA)**21 3257 6-8-9 67..............................(p) PhilDennis(5) 6
(Noel Wilson) *hld up: racd keenly: rdn 2f out and wknd* **16/1**
1m 11.94s (-1.06) **Going Correction** -0.25s/f (Firm) **6** Ran SP% **110.4**
Speed ratings (Par 103): **97,94,93,91,89 62**
CSF £2.95 TOTE £1.50: £1.10, £2.20; EX 3.60 Trifecta £11.70.
**Owner** Middleham Park Racing LIV **Bred** J C And Rocal Bloodstock **Trained** Musley Bank, N Yorks
**FOCUS**
The rail on bend from back straight to home straight dolled out by 2 yards adding approximately 4 yards to races on the round course during the afternoon. A decent claimer using official figures as a guide. The balance of the third and fourth helps set the level.

## 4014 SNOOTY FROX EBF NOVICE STKS 6f
**2:45** (2:46) (Class 5) 2-Y-O **£3,234** (£962; £481; £240) **Stalls** High

Form RPR
62 **1** **Mr Wagyu (IRE)**17 3398 2-9-2 0.......................................... JasonHart 1 72+
(John Quinn) *pressed ldr: rdn to ld narrowly over 1f out: pressed ins fnl f: kpt on wl* **7/1**
531 **2** *3/4* **Collingham Park (IRE)**14 3495 2-9-9 0.......................... JackGarritty 9 77
(Jedd O'Keeffe) *in tch: angled rt to outer 2f out: sn rdn: hdwy to chal appr fnl f: kpt on but a hld* **11/10**1
0 **3** *2 1/4* **Sorority**23 3174 2-8-11 0.............................................. AndrewMullen 10 57
(Mark Johnston) *prom: rdn over 2f out: one pce fnl f* **20/1**
04 **4** *1/2* **Dyson's Girl**23 3179 2-8-11 0...................................... ConnorBeasley 2 56
(Bryan Smart) *led narrowly: rdn over 2f out: hdd over 1f out: one pce* **5/1**3
0000 **5** *3 3/4* **Rock On Bertie (IRE)**17 3398 2-8-13 0.........(p1) RachelRichardson(3) 7 49
(Nigel Tinkler) *midfield: rdn over 2f out: one pce and nvr threatened* **50/1**
600 **6** *5* **Heavenly Pulse (IRE)**17 3399 2-9-2 0............................ ShaneGray 4 39+
(Ann Duffield) *hld up: nudged along and sme hdwy over 1f out: nvr threatened* **100/1**
**7** *3* **Bigdabog** 2-9-2 0.......................................................... NeilFarley 5 23
(Eric Alston) *hld up: nvr threatened* **50/1**
0 **8** *1 1/4* **Moakkad**23 3164 2-9-2 0.............................................. JoeFanning 6 19
(Mark Johnston) *dwlt: sn trckd ldrs: rdn over 2f out: sn wknd* **5/2**2
**9** *2 1/2* **Shades Of Mist** 2-9-2 0................................................ BenCurtis 3 11
(Ann Duffield) *s.i.s: sn trckd ldrs on outside racing keenly: rdn over 2f out: sn wknd* **28/1**
**10** *8* **David Fallow** 2-9-2 0................................................... CamHardie 8
(Paul Midgley) *a towards rr* **66/1**
1m 12.8s (-0.20) **Going Correction** -0.25s/f (Firm) **10** Ran SP% **120.0**
Speed ratings (Par 93): **91,90,87,86,81 74,70,69,65,55**
CSF £15.23 TOTE £8.20: £2.30, £1.10, £5.00; EX 20.70 Trifecta £109.30.
**Owner** The New Century Partnership **Bred** Danny O'Sullivan **Trained** Settrington, N Yorks
**FOCUS**
Two runners were backed more or less to the exclusion of the remainder, but neither proved good enough. The runner-up helps set the early standard.

## 4015 NORTH ORMESBY WMC TONY BENNETT MEMORIAL H'CAP 5f
**3:20** (3:21) (Class 5) (0-75,76) 3-Y-O+ **£3,234** (£962; £481; £240) **Stalls** High

Form RPR
6600 **1** **Tarboosh**56 2104 4-9-10 72........................................... CamHardie 3 82+
(Paul Midgley) *hld up in midfield: smooth hdwy 2f out: short of room appr fnl f and again jst ins fnl f: in clr fnl 110yds: qcknd wl to ld 25yds out* **12/1**
3350 **2** *1/2* **Lawless Louis**21 3257 3-9-2 73.................................(v1) JoshDoyle(3) 9 77
(David O'Meara) *chsd ldr: rdn to chal insidfe fnl f: kpt on* **15/2**
2100 **3** *3/4* **Pearl Noir**5 3812 7-9-2 64............................................(b) DavidAllan 1 67
(Scott Dixon) *led: rdn over 2f out: hdd 25yds out: no ex* **8/1**
-000 **4** *3/4* **Pea Shooter**47 2409 8-10-0 76........................................ BenCurtis 2 76+
(Brian Ellison) *slowly away: hld up: rdn and hdwy appr fnl f: kpt on: short of room on rail 50yds out and swtchd rt* **9/1**
0500 **5** *2 1/2* **Bond Bombshell**10 3667 4-8-13 68......................... PatrickVaughan(7) 5 59
(David O'Meara) *chsd ldr: rdn over 2f out: wknd ins fnl f* **33/1**
0021 **6** *nk* **Oriental Splendour (IRE)**10 3667 5-9-11 73 6ex........ JamesSullivan 4 63
(Ruth Carr) *midfield on outside: rdn over 2f out: wknd ins fnl f* **5/2**1
1230 **7** *2 1/2* **Spirit Of Zebedee (IRE)**61 1980 4-8-11 66................. JoshQuinn(7) 6 47
(John Quinn) *midfield: rdn over 2f out: losing pl whn short of room appr fnl f: wknd ins fnl f* **7/1**3
131 **8** *1 1/4* **Dusty Blue**59 2025 5-9-3 68........................................ NathanEvans(3) 8 45
(Michael Easterby) *hld up: rdn over 2f out: nvr threatened* **4/1**2
0403 **9** *4 1/2* **Twentysvnthlancers**10 3667 4-9-3 65............................ JackGarritty 10 26
(Paul Midgley) *midfield: rdn over 2f out: wknd ins fnl f and eased* **9/1**
58.84s (-1.16) **Going Correction** -0.25s/f (Firm)
**WFA** 3 from 4yo+ 6lb **9** Ran SP% **114.6**
Speed ratings (Par 103): **99,98,97,95,91 91,87,85,78**
CSF £97.56 CT £772.85 TOTE £14.70: £3.20, £2.10, £3.10; EX 116.30 Trifecta £684.30.
**Owner** The Guys & Dolls & Sandfield Racing **Bred** Landmark Racing Limited **Trained** Westow, N Yorks
■ Stewards' Enquiry : Patrick Vaughan two-day ban: careless riding (Jul 6-7)
**FOCUS**
A fair handicap that contained one 3yo taking on his elders again. It's been rated around the third.

## 4016 SLINGSBY GIN H'CAP 1m 4f 10y
**3:55** (3:57) (Class 4) (0-80,81) 3-Y-O **£5,175** (£1,540; £769; £384) **Stalls** Centre

Form RPR
0222 **1** **Kilowatt**15 3465 3-9-7 76.............................................. DavidAllan 5 87
(Tim Easterby) *dwlt: sn trckd ldr: led wl over 2f out: sn rdn: strly pressed thrght fnl 2f: hld on gamely* **6/5**1
131- **2** *hd* **Londinium**321 5109 3-9-12 81........................................ JoeFanning 1 91
(Mark Johnston) *trckd ldr: rdn to chal strly 2f out: styd on but a jst hld* **11/8**2
2-02 **3** *10* **Phoenix Dawn**26 3088 3-9-1 70.......................................(p) BenCurtis 4 64
(Brendan Powell) *led: rdn over 2f out: hdd wl over 2f out: wknd over 1f out* **11/2**3
2506 **4** *3 3/4* **Good Time Ahead (IRE)**14 3489 3-8-10 65..................... PaddyAspell 3 53
(Philip Kirby) *hld up: rdn over 2f out: sn wknd* **14/1**
2m 35.23s (-1.47) **Going Correction** -0.10s/f (Good) **4** Ran SP% **109.6**
Speed ratings (Par 101): **100,99,93,90**
CSF £3.22 TOTE £2.00; EX 3.90 Trifecta £6.70.
**Owner** Geoff & Sandra Turnbull **Bred** Geoff & Sandra Turnbull **Trained** Great Habton, N Yorks
**FOCUS**
Race distance increased by 4yds. Hard to know what to make of this form, as there were concerns for most of these to overcome. The winner has been rated as improving in line with his better maiden form.

## 4017 LADIES DAY H'CAP 1m 1f
**4:35** (4:35) (Class 3) (0-90,90) 4-Y-O+**£7,561** (£2,263; £1,131; £566; £282) **Stalls** Low

Form RPR
5631 **1** **Magic City (IRE)**16 3433 8-8-6 82.............................. HarrisonShaw(7) 6 89+
(Michael Easterby) *midfield: pushed along and hdwy over 2f out: rdn to ld over 1f out: kpt on: edgd rt nr fin* **9/1**
4306 **2** *3/4* **Mulligatawny (IRE)**6 3790 4-9-4 87............................ ConnorBeasley 8 92
(Roger Fell) *trckd ldrs: rdn to chal 2f out: kpt on* **7/2**2
0634 **3** *shd* **Jacbequick**7 3744 6-8-10 82.........................................(p) JoshDoyle(3) 1 87
(David O'Meara) *midfield: rdn and hdwy 2f out: kpt on fnl f* **11/2**3
2161 **4** *3/4* **Sands Chorus**14 3497 5-9-3 86........................................ JoeFanning 9 89
(James Given) *prom: rdn to ld over 2f out: hdd over 1f out: kpt on same pce: bit short of room nr fin* **5/2**1
06 **5** *4 1/2* **Beach Bar (IRE)**29 2968 6-9-2 85...................................(h) BenCurtis 7 79
(Brendan Powell) *led: rdn over 3f out: hdd over 2f out: grad wknd over 1f out* **18/1**
0160 **6** *1 1/2* **Alejandro (IRE)**5 3837 8-9-0 90.............................(e) CameronNoble(7) 2 81
(David Loughnane) *midfield: pushed along over 2f out: hung rt over 1f out and no imp* **6/1**
5241 **7** *3/4* **Boots And Spurs**14 3498 8-8-13 82..................................(v) DavidAllan 3 71
(Scott Dixon) *trckd ldrs: rdn over 2f out: wknd over 1f out* **6/1**
6000 **8** *hd* **Mansfield**12 3589 4-8-3 72............................................ RoystonFfrench 4 61
(Michael Wigham) *hld up: racd keenly: pushed along 2f out: nvr threatened* **50/1**
00-6 **9** *nk* **Salmon Sushi**14 3497 6-8-8 77.........................................(h) JasonHart 10 65
(Tim Easterby) *dwlt: hld up: threatening to make sme hdwy whn short of room over 1f out: no ch after* **25/1**
1m 51.78s (-2.92) **Going Correction** -0.10s/f (Good) **9** Ran SP% **115.8**
Speed ratings (Par 107): **108,107,107,106,102 101,100,100,100**
CSF £40.71 CT £193.33 TOTE £7.10: £2.90, £2.50, £2.10; EX 52.50 Trifecta £349.90.
**Owner** A Turton, J Blackburn & Mrs L Folwell **Bred** Miss Annmarie Burke **Trained** Sheriff Hutton, N Yorks
**FOCUS**
Race distance increased by 4yds. A strong looking race run at a good tempo. The runner-up helps set the standard, with the third to his recent best.

## 4018 OLD MUTUAL WEALTH PCA LADIES' DERBY H'CAP (FOR LADY AMATEUR RIDERS) 1m 4f 10y
**5:10** (5:12) (Class 6) (0-65,64) 4-Y-O+ **£3,119** (£967; £483; £242) **Stalls** Centre

Form RPR
31-6 **1** **Our Kylie (IRE)**33 2815 5-10-0 60............................... MissLWilson(3) 14 66
(Brian Ellison) *hld up: gd hdwy on outside over 3f out: led over 3f out: pushed along and wandered appr fnl f: idled ins fnl f: plld out more towards fin: shade cosily* **6/1**3
6013 **2** *3/4* **Strictly Art (IRE)**13 3519 4-10-0 62.............................. MissJCooley(5) 8 67
(Alan Bailey) *led: rdn whn hdd over 2f out: bit outpcd over 1f out: styd on ins fnl f* **6/1**3
2406 **3** *nse* **Swansway**19 3343 4-10-7 64............................ MissJoannaMason 11 69
(Michael Easterby) *midfield: rdn and hdwy to chse ldr appr fnl f: kpt on* **12/1**
16-0 **4** *nk* **Byronegetonefree**19 3340 6-9-8 51.................................. MissETodd 3 55
(Stuart Coltherd) *midfield: rdn 2f out: kpt on fnl f* **16/1**
00-5 **5** *1/2* **Merchant Of Medici**13 3537 10-9-5 48.................. MissBeckySmith 5 52+
(Micky Hammond) *hld up in midfield: bit tight for room over 2f out: hdwy over 1f out: styd on fnl f* **28/1**
6-31 **6** *1 3/4* **Rubis**10 3650 4-10-7 64 6ex...................................... MissEmmaSayer 10 65
(Richard Fahey) *trckd ldr: racd keenly: rdn and ev ch over 2f out: wknd ins fnl f* **11/2**2
0-00 **7** *2 1/2* **Graceful Act**31 2900 9-8-12 46................................. PoppyBridgwater(5) 7 43
(Ron Barr) *trckd ldrs: rdn over 2f out: wknd fnl f* **25/1**
2400 **8** *nk* **Fillydelphia (IRE)**17 3405 6-9-6 54............................ MissAMcCain(5) 2 50
(Patrick Holmes) *midfield on inner: pushed along over 2f out: nvr threatened* **18/1**
2150 **9** *nk* **Mr Sundowner (USA)**19 3343 5-10-0 57..........................(t) MissCWalton 4 53
(Wilf Storey) *trckd ldrs: rdn over 2f out: wknd fnl f* **8/1**
**10** *25* **Presenting Julio (IRE)**18 831 9-10-4 61..................(b) MsLO'Neill 12 17
(Gordon Elliott, Ire) *virtually ref to r and wl bhd thrght* **7/4**1
0P-0 **11** *4 1/2* **Oracle Boy**8 3726 6-9-9 52........................................... MissAWaugh 6
(Michael Chapman) *hld up: wknd 4f out and bhd* **100/1**

560- **12** *15* **Fledermaus (IRE)**[258] [7105] 7-9-2 **45**..............................(t) MissADeniel 9
(Tina Jackson) *midfield on outer: wknd qckly over 3f out and t.o.* **80/1**
2m 38.32s (1.62) **Going Correction** -0.10s/f (Good) **12** Ran SP% **119.8**
Speed ratings (Par 101): **90,89,89,89,88 87,86,85,85,69 66,56**
CSF £41.46 CT £426.46 TOTE £6.10: £1.80, £1.80, £2.30; EX 44.90 Trifecta £350.30.
**Owner** Morecool & Cool Racing **Bred** Lynn Lodge Stud **Trained** Norton, N Yorks
**FOCUS**
Race distance increased by 4yds. A fairly competitive event at a moderate level. The fourth is among those that helps pin the level.

## 4019 STRAY FM CELEBRATING LADIES DAY H'CAP 1m
**5:45** (5:45) (Class 5) (0-75,73) 4-Y-0+ **£3,234** (£962; £481; £240) **Stalls** Low

Form RPR
4114 **1** **Cosmic Ray**[15] [3451] 5-9-6 **72**..............................(h) JoeFanning 1 82
(Les Eyre) *t.k.h early: trckd ldrs: smooth hdwy to ld over 1f out: rdn clr ins fnl f* **13/8**[1]
6035 **2** *3 ¾* **Billy Bond**[21] [3242] 5-8-2 **57**..............................(b[1]) SammyJoBell(3) 4 58
(Richard Fahey) *hld up: stdy hdwy on outside 3f out: rdn and edgd rt over 1f out: rallied and chsd wnr wl ins fnl f: r.o* **11/2**
42-3 **3** *shd* **Singapore Sling**[16] [3441] 4-9-7 **73**..............................(h) ConnorBeasley 2 74
(James Fanshawe) *t.k.h: in tch: rdn and outpcd over 3f out: rallied over 1f out: kpt on fnl f: no imp* **9/4**[2]
0015 **4** *nse* **Midlight**[12] [3560] 5-8-4 **56**..............................(t) JamesSullivan 7 57
(Ruth Carr) *led to over 1f out: chsd wnr tl edgd lft: no ex and lost two pls wl ins fnl f* **4/1**[3]
0-40 **5** *6* **Almunther (IRE)**[26] [3095] 4-8-13 **65**.............................. JackGarritty 3 52
(Micky Hammond) *dwlt: sn trcking ldr: drvn and outpcd over 2f out: wknd wl over 1f out* **14/1**
1m 39.89s (-1.51) **Going Correction** -0.10s/f (Good) **5** Ran SP% **110.9**
Speed ratings (Par 103): **103,99,99,99,93**
CSF £10.90 TOTE £2.40: £1.10, £2.90; EX 8.10 Trifecta £26.20.
**Owner** Over The Moon Racing III **Bred** Winterbeck Manor Stud **Trained** Catwick, N Yorks
**FOCUS**
Race distance increased by 4yds. Probably ordinary form for the class. The winner has been rated back to his old best.
T/Plt: £93.10 to a £1 stake. Pool: £51,856.62. 406.47 winning units. T/Qpdt: £72.00 to a £1 stake. Pool: £2,919.48. 30.00 winning units. **Andrew Sheret**

# 3762 LEOPARDSTOWN (L-H)
Thursday, June 22
**OFFICIAL GOING: Good to firm**

## 4020a FORAN EQUINE IRISH EBF AUCTION RACE (PLUS 10 RACE) 7f
**6:00** (6:01) 2-Y-O **£15,769** (£4,871; £2,307; £1,025; £384)

RPR
**1** **Red Persian (IRE)**[21] [3267] 2-8-11 0.............................. KevinManning 3 78
(P J Prendergast, Ire) *t.k.h early to chse ldrs in 3rd: rdn and no imp in 4th under 2f out: 5th ent fnl f: styd on strly clsng stages to ld fnl strides* **5/2**[2]
**2** *nk* **Hyperlapse (IRE)** 2-8-13 0.............................. GaryCarroll 8 79
(G M Lyons, Ire) *hld up in 6th: rdn and swtchd rt 2f out: chsd ldrs in 4th ent fnl f: styd on strly into 2nd cl home* **10/1**
**3** *nk* **Bella Figura (IRE)**[21] [3267] 2-8-10 0.............................. NGMcCullagh 7 75+
(Mrs John Harrington, Ire) *led and jnd after 2f: hdd briefly over 1f out: regained ld ins fnl f tl strly pressed and hdd cl home where dropped to 3rd* **9/2**[3]
**4** *1 ½* **Rufus King**[12] [3556] 2-9-10 0.............................. WJLee 6 85+
(Mark Johnston) *sn pressed ldr in 2nd: on terms after 2f: rdn to ld briefly over 1f out: sn hdd and no ex clsng stages where dropped to 4th* **5/4**[1]
**5** *1 ¾* **Island Affair (IRE)** 2-8-6 0..............................(h[1]) RoryCleary 1 63
(Adrian McGuinness, Ire) *racd in mid-div: 5th at 1/2-way: rdn to chse ldrs in 3rd under 2f out: no imp ent fnl f: wknd* **50/1**
**6** *2 ¾* **Adnap (IRE)** 2-9-1 0.............................. WayneLordan 5 64
(Gavin Cromwell, Ire) *chsd ldrs in 4th tl nt qckn 2f out: sn one pce* **9/1**
**7** *shd* **Stormy Tale (IRE)**[10] [3675] 2-8-1 0.............................. KillianLeonard(5) 2 55
(Michael Mulvany, Ire) *hld up towards rr: pushed along 3f out: kpt on one pce fr over 1f out: nvr on terms* **66/1**
**8** *5 ½* **Only William (IRE)**[12] [3598] 2-9-0 0.............................. GaryHalpin(3) 4 51
(Gordon Elliott, Ire) *racd in rr thrght: no imp under 2f out* **33/1**
1m 33.39s (4.69) **Going Correction** +0.60s/f (Yiel) **8** Ran SP% **116.7**
Speed ratings: **97,96,96,94,92 89,89,83**
CSF £27.47 TOTE £2.90: £1.20, £2.90, £1.50; DF 32.20 Trifecta £99.10.
**Owner** Persian Red Partnership **Bred** Longrove Stud **Trained** Melitta Lodge, Co Kildare
**FOCUS**
A stewards enquiry took place after this opener, but sensibly, the result stood. The complexion of the race changed dramatically inside the final 100 yards or so. Rufus King and Bella Figura looked set to battle it out for top honours but ended up running out of petrol just a few strides from the line. That gave the newcomer Hyperlapse and Red Persian an invitation to go and win the race, and it was the latter who galloped on strongest for a trainer who is enjoying a fine season. The real story of the race is the success of the EBF Auction series. The winner cost just 5,000 euros but paid for himself a few times over with this win as he bagged connections a cheque in excess of 18,000 euros.

4021 - 4026a (Foreign Racing) - See Raceform Interactive

# LA TESTE DE BUCH (R-H)
Thursday, June 22
**OFFICIAL GOING: Turf: good**

## 4027a PRIX LA SORELLINA - TATTERSALLS (LISTED RACE) (3YO FILLIES) (TURF) 1m
**1:20** 3-Y-O **£23,504** (£9,401; £7,051; £4,700; £2,350)

RPR
**1** **Dallas Affair**[21] 3-9-3 0 ow1.............................. AurelienLemaitre 5 104+
(F Head, France) **6/4**[1]
**2** *2 ½* **Garance (FR)** 3-9-3 0 ow1.............................. IoritzMendizabal 4 97
(J-C Rouget, France) **12/5**[2]
**3** *1 ½* **Westit**[47] [2421] 3-9-3 0 ow1.............................. MaximeGuyon 9 93
(C Laffon-Parias, France) **18/1**
**4** *1 ½* **Maytime (FR)**[47] [2421] 3-9-3 0 ow1.............................. EnzoCorallo 10 90
(C Ferland, France) **25/1**
**5** *2 ½* **Niedziela (IRE)**[12] [3612] 3-9-3 0 ow1.............................. ChristopheSoumillon 1 84
(C Lerner, France) **78/10**[3]
**6** *3 ½* **Denitza (FR)**[38] 3-9-3 0 ow1.............................. JulienAuge 8 76
(C Ferland, France) **162/10**
**7** *2* **Golden State (USA)**[31] [2898] 3-9-3 0 ow1.............................. AlexisBadel 6 72
(Archie Watson) *wl into stride: settled bhd ldrs: pushed along over 3f out: sn rdn: u.p over 1f out but little rspnse: eased ins fnl f* **227/10**
**8** *2 ½* **Fuenteesteis (FR)**[29] [2978] 3-9-3 0 ow1(b[1]) Roberto-CarlosMontenegro 11 66
(R Avial Lopez, Spain) **40/1**
**9** *4* **Elegante Bere (FR)**[233] [7757] 3-9-3 0 ow1.............................. AlexandreGavilan 3 57
(D Guillemin, France) **19/2**
**10** *1 ½* **Honeymoon Trip (FR)** 3-9-3 0 ow1.............................. Pierre-CharlesBoudot 7 53
(L A Urbano-Grajales, France) **127/10**

PARI-MUTUEL (all including 1 euro stake): WIN 2.50; PLACE 1.40, 1.50, 2.90; DF 3.50; SF 5.00.
**Owner** George Strawbridge **Bred** Gestut Haus Ittlingen **Trained** France

# 3993 ASCOT (R-H)
Friday, June 23
**OFFICIAL GOING: Good to firm (stand side 9.0, centre 8.3, far side 8.6, round 7.4)**
Wind: light, against Weather: light cloud, bright spells

## 4028 ALBANY STKS (GROUP 3) (FILLIES) 6f
**2:30** (2:31) (Class 1) 2-Y-O
**£45,368** (£17,200; £8,608; £4,288; £2,152; £1,080) **Stalls** Centre

Form RPR
**1** **Different League (FR)**[31] 2-9-0 0.............................. AntoineHamelin 13 107+
(Matthieu Palussiere, France) *str: elected to r far side: t.k.h and prom: led overall under 5f out: rdn wl over 1f out: sn edgd lft: running on and looking in command: kpt on wl and a doing enough whn pressed nr fin: 1st of 12 in gp* **20/1**
1 **2** *nk* **Alpha Centauri (IRE)**[33] [2862] 2-9-0 0.............................. ColmO'Donoghue 1 106+
(Mrs John Harrington, Ire) *lengthy: racd far side: trckd ldrs: wnt 2nd in gp over 2f out: r.o ins fnl f: pressed wnr nr fin but a hld: 2nd of 12 in gp* **2/1**[1]
3 **3** *3* **Take Me With You (USA)**[13] [3590] 2-9-0 0.............................. GeraldMosse 20 96+
(Jeremy Noseda) *leggy: athletic: racd stands' side: a.p: rdn and big effrt over 2f out: led gp jst over 1f out: r.o ins fnl f: nt get to overall front two: 1st of 8 in gp* **20/1**
53 **4** *½* **Mistress Of Venice**[35] [2801] 2-9-0 0.............................. JimCrowley 18 95
(James Given) *racd stands' side: hld up in midfield: effrt over 2f out: hung rt after: hdwy u.p over 1f out: tk 2nd in gp fnl 75yds: r.o for press towards fin: 2nd of 8 in gp* **66/1**
51 **5** *½* **Madeline (IRE)**[27] [3070] 2-9-0 0.............................. AndreaAtzeni 21 93
(Roger Varian) *racd stands' side: a.p: rdn over 2f out: sn led gp: hdd jst over 1f out: styd on same pce fnl 100yds: 3rd of 8 in gp* **14/1**
2 **6** *nk* **Actress (IRE)**[33] [2862] 2-9-0 0.............................. WayneLordan 16 92
(A P O'Brien, Ire) *str: lw: racd stands' side: hld up in rr: hdwy over 2f out: cl up for press over 1f out: kpt on same pce fnl 100yds: 4th of 8 in gp* **25/1**
**7** *hd* **Clemmie (IRE)**[27] [3096] 2-9-0 0.............................. RyanMoore 2 92
(A P O'Brien, Ire) *athletic: lw: racd far side: towards rr: rdn and hdwy over 2f out: chsd ldrs over 1f out: styd on ins fnl f: no imp on front two in gp: 3rd of 12 in gp* **7/1**[2]
**8** *½* **Snowflakes (IRE)**[27] [3096] 2-9-0 0.............................. SeamieHeffernan 5 90+
(A P O'Brien, Ire) *str: racd far side: hld up in midfield: effrt and hdwy over 2f out: chsd ldrs over 1f out: styd on ins fnl f: nt pce of ldrs: 4th of 12 in gp* **12/1**
21 **9** *1 ¾* **Miss Bar Beach (IRE)**[16] [3447] 2-9-0 0.............................. GrahamLee 12 84
(Keith Dalgleish) *leggy: swtchd lft to r in stands' side gp early on: racd keenly and hld up: rdn over 2f out: edgd lft u.p over 1f out: kpt on: nvr able to trble ldrs: 5th of 8 in gp* **100/1**
**10** *1 ¼* **Princess Peggy (USA)**[29] 2-9-0 0..............................(b) DavidRomeroFlores 3 80
(Wesley A Ward, U.S.A) *athletic: racd far side: hld up: rdn over 2f out: nt clr run and swtchd lft over 1f out: styd on ins fnl f: nt pce to trble ldrs: 5th of 12 in gp* **25/1**
**11** *1* **Black Sails**[41] [2635] 2-9-0 0.............................. ColinKeane 4 77
(G M Lyons, Ire) *unf: racd far side: midfield: rdn and hdwy over 2f out: unable qck over 1f out: one pce ins fnl f: 6th of 12 in gp* **8/1**[3]
**12** *1* **Fairyland (USA)**[77] 2-9-0 0.............................. DonnachaO'Brien 14 74
(Wesley A Ward, U.S.A) *str: lw: ponied to s: racd stands' side: led gp: rdn over 2f out: sn hdd: wknd ins fnl f: 6th of 8 in gp* **8/1**[3]
3112 **13** *½* **Starlight Mystery (IRE)**[34] [2826] 2-9-0 0.............................. SilvestreDeSousa 11 75
(Mark Johnston) *dwlt: racd far side: hld up in rr: rdn and nt clr run over 1f out: kpt on ins fnl f: nvr able to rch ldrs: 7th of 12 in gp* **50/1**
1 **14** *shd* **Natural (IRE)**[20] [3312] 2-9-0 0.............................. OisinMurphy 10 72
(Richard Hannon) *str: racd far side: trckd ldrs: rdn and outpcd over 2f out: no imp after: 8th of 12 in gp* **12/1**
44 **15** *nk* **Jo's Girl (IRE)**[17] [3429] 2-9-0 0.............................. TimmyMurphy 19 71
(Jamie Osborne) *racd stands' side: in rr: rdn over 2f out: outpcd wl over 1f out: nvr a threat: 7th of 8 in gp* **125/1**
21 **16** *¾* **Ertiyad**[15] [3491] 2-9-0 0.............................. PatCosgrave 15 69+
(William Haggas) *swtchd rt early on to r far side: sn checked: hld up: rdn over 2f out: nvr able to get on terms: 9th of 12 in gp* **14/1**
**17** *½* **Whitefountainfairy (IRE)**[22] [3267] 2-9-0 0.............................. ShaneFoley 9 67
(Mrs John Harrington, Ire) *cmpt: racd far side: overall ldr tl under 5f out: remained handy: rdn and swtchd lft over 2f out: chsd ldrs over 1f out: wknd fnl 150yds: 10th of 12 in gp* **40/1**
1 **18** *1* **Electric Landlady (IRE)**[23] [3210] 2-9-0 0.............................. TomQueally 6 64
(Denis Coakley) *racd far side: keen and in tch: pushed along and outpcd over 2f out: u.p whn n.m.r and hmpd over 1f out: n.d after: 11th of 12 in gp* **66/1**
**19** *½* **Summer Shamal (FR)**[37] 2-9-0 0.............................. OlivierPeslier 8 62
(F-H Graffard, France) *racd far side: t.k.h: w ldr tl over 2f out: wknd over 1f out: 12th of 12 in gp* **66/1**
41 **20** *21* **Armum (IRE)**[13] [3576] 2-9-0 0.............................. DougieCostello 17
(Ed Dunlop) *str: racd stands' side: in tch: rdn and wknd 2f out: bhd over 1f out: 8th of 8 in gp* **50/1**
1m 14.6s (0.10) **Going Correction** +0.125s/f (Good) **20** Ran SP% **126.6**
Speed ratings (Par 100): **104,103,99,98,98 97,97,96,94,92 91,90,89,89,89 88,87,86,85,57**
CSF £56.70 CT £902.39 TOTE £28.80: £7.00, £1.40, £7.80; EX 103.10 Trifecta £1964.80.
**Owner** Mrs Theresa Marnane **Bred** Lotfi Kohli **Trained** France

**FOCUS**
There was 4mm of water dumped on the track following the previous day's racing, to maintain good to firm ground. The rail that had been in place on the round course for the first three days was removed, providing fresh ground from about 9f out to the home straight. Therefore the rail was at its innermost position, and race distances were as advertised. There were two groups and the winner and second pulled clear on the far side, but the next four finishers raced stands' side, so it's hard to be dogmatic about any bias. The runner-up has been rated to her pre-race form.

## 4029 KING EDWARD VII STKS (GROUP 2) (C&G) 1m 3f 211y
3:05 (3:05) (Class 1) 3-Y-O

£127,597 (£48,375; £24,210; £12,060; £6,052; £3,037) Stalls Low

Form RPR

2110 **1** **Permian (IRE)**[20] 3322 3-9-0 113 WilliamBuick 11 114
(Mark Johnston) *chsd ldr tl rdn to ld over 2f out: styd on wl u.p fr over 1f out: rdn out: gamely* 6/1[2]

1310 **2** ½ **Khalidi**[20] 3322 3-9-0 111 OlivierPeslier 5 113
(John Gosden) *lw: t.k.h early: trckd ldrs tl sttld bk into midfield 7f out: rdn and outpcd over 2f out: rallied to chse ldrs 1f out: chsd wnr wl ins fnl f: r.o wl but nvr quite getting to wnr* 10/1

2-13 **3** 1¼ **Crystal Ocean**[36] 2766 3-9-0 110 AndreaAtzeni 7 111
(Sir Michael Stoute) *lw: hld up in tch in midfield swtchd lft and effrt to press ldrs and rdn 3f out: chsd wnr and edgd rt 2f out: kpt on u.p but nvr able to cl: lost 2nd wl ins fnl f* 9/4[1]

4-23 **4** 1 **Raheen House (IRE)**[28] 3032 3-9-0 109 JamieSpencer 3 110+
(Brian Meehan) *hld up in last trio: clsd whn nt clr run and swtchd lft ent fnl 2f: hdwy 1f out: edging rt but kpt on wl ins fnl f: snatched 4th last strides: nvr trbld ldrs* 25/1

-520 **5** nk **Glencadam Glory**[20] 3322 3-9-0 106 (h) RobertTart 2 109
(John Gosden) *led to post: sn led: rdn and hdd over 2f out: 4th and no ex u.p 1f out: styd on same pce ins fnl f* 25/1

13 **6** shd **Call To Mind**[34] 2829 3-9-0 95 JimCrowley 6 109
(William Haggas) *dwlt: sn swtchd rt and hdwy to r in midfield: effrt over 2f out: sme hdwy but forced to switch lft fr over 1f out: swtchd lft again and kpt on wl ins fnl f: nvr threatened ldrs* 14/1

3-20 **7** 1¼ **Salouen (IRE)**[20] 3322 3-9-0 110 FranBerry 9 108
(Sylvester Kirk) *hld up in last trio: effrt over 2f out: swtchd lft and drvn over 1f out: hdwy and carried rt 1f out: keeping on but no threat to ldrs whn squeezed for room 150yds out: no imp after* 9/1

0-34 **8** ½ **Frankuus (IRE)**[41] 2614 3-9-0 102 SilvestreDeSousa 1 106
(Mark Johnston) *chsd ldrs: rdn over 2f out: 3rd and no ex u.p 1f out: wknd ins fnl f* 22/1

6 **9** 1 **Sir John Lavery (IRE)**[41] 2614 3-9-0 99 RyanMoore 13 105
(A P O'Brien, Ire) *hld up in tch towards rr: effrt over 2f out: switching rt and u.p over 1f out: kpt on steadily ins fnl f: nvr trbld ldrs* 8/1

4010 **10** 1½ **Best Solution (IRE)**[20] 3322 3-9-0 112 PatCosgrave 12 102
(Saeed bin Suroor) *chsd ldrs: rdn over 2f out: sltly impeded and swtchd lft 2f out: unable qck over 1f out: wknd ins fnl f* 13/2[3]

3-2 **11** nk **Intern (IRE)**[56] 2128 3-9-0 103 PatSmullen 4 102
(Ralph Beckett) *t.k.h: hld up in tch in last trio: nt clrest of runs 2f out: sn rdn: no imp and kpt on same pce fr over 1f out* 25/1

121- **12** 1¼ **Best Of Days**[272] 6783 3-9-0 110 (t[1]) JamesDoyle 8 100
(Hugo Palmer) *warm: in tch in midfield: rdn 3f out: lost pl u.p and edgd rt over 1f out: wknd ins fnl f* 10/1

2m 30.1s (-2.40) **Going Correction** +0.15s/f (Good) 12 Ran SP% 120.2
Speed ratings (Par 111): **114,113,112,112,111 111,111,110,110,109 108,108**
CSF £62.15 CT £173.01 TOTE £6.50: £2.30, £3.10, £1.40; EX 68.00 Trifecta £264.80.
**Owner** Sheikh Hamdan bin Mohammed Al Maktoum **Bred** Darley **Trained** Middleham Moor, N Yorks

**FOCUS**
The Derby form was well represented, with five of the field coming here from Epsom, including the first two home. It was an advantage to race handily. The first three have been rated to form, with the fourth close to his 2yo form.

## 4030 COMMONWEALTH CUP (GROUP 1) (BRITISH CHAMPIONS SERIES) 6f
3:40 (3:41) (Class 1) 3-Y-O

£226,840 (£86,000; £43,040; £21,440; £10,760; £5,400) Stalls Centre

Form RPR

11-1 **1** **Caravaggio (USA)**[33] 2863 3-9-3 119 RyanMoore 5 124
(A P O'Brien, Ire) *swtg: midfield: hdwy over 1f out: sn edgd rt: gd run to ld fnl 110yds: r.o strly* 5/6[1]

1-21 **2** ¾ **Harry Angel (IRE)**[27] 3078 3-9-3 118 AdamKirby 7 121
(Clive Cox) *displayed plenty of pce and led: rdn whn pressed over 1f out: hdd fnl 110yds: unable to go w wnr towards fin* 11/4[2]

23-1 **3** ½ **Blue Point (IRE)**[51] 2289 3-9-3 116 WilliamBuick 10 119
(Charlie Appleby) *lw: in tch: effrt to chal fr over 1f out: styd on u.p: kpt on same pce fnl 75yds* 9/2[3]

**4** 3 **Bound For Nowhere (USA)**[64] 3-9-3 0 DavidRomeroFlores 3 109
(Wesley A Ward, U.S.A) *str: lw: ponied to s: in tch: effrt over 2f out: nt clr run over 1f out: sn swtchd lft: styd on ins fnl f: nt pce to trble front three* 10/1

3 **5** 2 **Mr Scarlet**[33] 2863 3-9-3 100 PatSmullen 9 103
(Ms Sheila Lavery, Ire) *stdd s and checked early: hld up in rr: rdn and hdwy over 1f out: kpt on u.p ins fnl f: nvr able to chal* 80/1

50-4 **6** ½ **Tis Marvellous**[51] 2289 3-9-3 110 (t) GeraldMosse 4 101
(Clive Cox) *trckd ldrs after 1f: rdn and unable qck over 1f out: kpt on same pce fnl 110yds* 33/1

43 **7** ¾ **Straight Right (FR)**[43] 2561 3-9-3 106 OlivierPeslier 8 99
(C Ferland, France) *hld up: rdn over 2f out: kpt on u.p over 1f out: one pce ins fnl f: no imp* 66/1

3121 **8** 1¾ **Visionary (IRE)**[34] 2823 3-9-3 101 JamieSpencer 2 93
(Robert Cowell) *towards rr: sn niggled along: nvr able to get on terms u.p* 50/1

40-4 **9** ¾ **Intelligence Cross (USA)**[61] 1997 3-9-3 107 (bt[1]) SeamieHeffernan 1 91
(A P O'Brien, Ire) *lw: w ldr tl rdn over 2f out: outpcd over 1f out: wknd fnl f* 25/1

26-0 **10** 5 **Legendary Lunch (IRE)**[51] 2289 3-9-3 103 TomMarquand 12 75
(Richard Hannon) *sed awkwardly: hld up in midfield: effrt and no imp over 2f out: wkng whn hung rt over 1f out* 50/1

1-10 **11** 4½ **Victory Angel (IRE)**[48] 2400 3-9-3 92 SilvestreDeSousa 11 61
(Roger Varian) *towards rr: rdn and swtchd lft over 2f out: no imp on ldrs: wknd over 1f out: eased whn wl btn ins fnl f* 66/1

06-5 **12** 6 **Yalta (IRE)**[51] 2289 3-9-3 105 JamesDoyle 6 41
(Mark Johnston) *trckd ldrs: rdn over 2f out: wknd over 1f out: eased whn wl btn over 1f out* 50/1

1m 13.49s (-1.01) **Going Correction** +0.125s/f (Good) 12 Ran SP% 125.4
Speed ratings (Par 113): **111,110,109,105,102 102,101,98,97,91 85,77**
CSF £3.34 CT £7.68 TOTE £1.80: £1.10, £1.40, £1.70; EX 3.80 Trifecta £9.10.
**Owner** Mrs John Magnier & Michael Tabor & Derrick Smith **Bred** Windmill Manor Farms Inc Et Al **Trained** Cashel, Co Tipperary

**FOCUS**
Surely top-class sprinting form and this race, in only its third year, really was a fantastic idea. They raced towards the far side. Another step forward from the winner, with the third improving in line with the better view of his form.

## 4031 CORONATION STKS (GROUP 1) (BRITISH CHAMPIONS SERIES) (FILLIES) 7f 213y(R)
4:20 (4:21) (Class 1) 3-Y-O

£243,853 (£92,450; £46,268; £23,048; £11,567; £5,805) Stalls Low

Form RPR

211 **1** **Winter (IRE)**[26] 3110 3-9-0 118 RyanMoore 7 119+
(A P O'Brien, Ire) *hld up in tch in midfield: wnt 3rd and clsd on ldrs over 2f out: rdn to ld over 1f out: gng clr and edgd rt jst ins fnl f: r.o wl* 4/9[1]

-062 **2** 2¼ **Roly Poly (USA)**[26] 3110 3-9-0 107 (p) SeamieHeffernan 2 113
(A P O'Brien, Ire) *w ldr: shkn up and outpcd by wnr over 1f out: hung rt u.p and lost 2nd jst ins fnl f: rallied to chse wnr again 75yds out: kpt on but no threat to wnr* 12/1

-103 **3** nk **Hydrangea (IRE)**[26] 3110 3-9-0 107 (p) PBBeggy 5 112
(A P O'Brien, Ire) *chsd ldng pair tl over 2f out: shkn up 2f out: rdn jst over 1f out: rallied and styd on to go 3rd wl ins fnl f: no threat to wnr* 16/1

13-1 **4** 1 **Dabyah (IRE)**[62] 1958 3-9-0 112 JimCrowley 3 110
(John Gosden) *hld up in rr: clsd and nt clr run 2f out: swtchd lft and effrt over 1f out: hdwy to chse wnr briefly ins fnl f: no imp: lost 2nd and wknd fnl 75yds* 13/2[2]

6- **5** 1¾ **La Coronel (USA)**[49] 3-9-0 113 FlorentGeroux 6 106
(Mark Casse, Canada) *leggy: in tch in midfield on outer: rdn over 2f out: kpt on same pce fr over 1f out* 25/1

4-11 **6** ¾ **Tomyris**[35] 2802 3-9-0 100 AndreaAtzeni 4 104
(Roger Varian) *stdd after s: hld up in last pair: clsd and nt clr run wl over 1f out: gap opened and effrt jst over 1f out: no imp* 33/1

2-21 **7** nk **Precieuse (IRE)**[41] 2644 3-9-0 114 OlivierPeslier 1 107+
(F Chappet, France) *athletic: led: rdn and hdd over 1f out: immediately outpcd by wnr: bdly hmpd and snatched up jst ins fnl f: no ch after* 8/1[3]

1m 39.39s (-1.31) **Going Correction** +0.15s/f (Good) 7 Ran SP% 114.1
Speed ratings (Par 110): **112,109,109,108,106 105,105**
CSF £7.26 TOTE £1.40: £1.10, £4.60; EX 7.80 Trifecta £27.10.
**Owner** Mrs John Magnier & Michael Tabor & Derrick Smith **Bred** Laddies Poker Two Syndicate **Trained** Cashel, Co Tipperary
■ Stewards' Enquiry : Seamie Heffernan five-day ban: careless riding (July 7-11)
P B Beggy two-day ban: used whip above permitted level (Jul 7, 9)

**FOCUS**
The Irish Guineas form was confirmed, with the first three, all trained by Aidan O'Brien, repeating their finishing positions from the Curragh, albeit with the winning distance being reduced on this quicker ground. The second and third have been rated back to their 2yo bests.

## 4032 QUEEN'S VASE (GROUP 2) 1m 5f 211y
5:00 (5:00) (Class 1) 3-Y-O

£91,444 (£34,668; £17,350; £8,643; £4,337; £2,176) Stalls Low

Form RPR

1-12 **1** **Stradivarius (IRE)**[44] 2526 3-9-0 94 AndreaAtzeni 9 103+
(John Gosden) *midfield: hdwy whn nt clr run over 2f out: swtchd lft over 1f out: rn to ld fnl 120yds: rdn out* 11/2[2]

3-15 **2** nk **Count Octave**[43] 2555 3-9-0 103 OisinMurphy 3 102
(Andrew Balding) *hld up in tch: impr to trck ldrs 10f out: led 2f out: hdd fnl 120yds: styd on u.p: hld nr fin* 8/1

122 **3** 2 **Secret Advisor (FR)**[29] 3005 3-9-0 87 WilliamBuick 11 99
(Charlie Appleby) *hld up: hdwy on outer over 2f out: r.o ins fnl f: edgd rt: gng on at fin: nt rch front two* 10/1

**4** hd **Belgravia (IRE)**[34] 2847 3-9-0 97 (bt[1]) RyanMoore 7 99
(A P O'Brien, Ire) *str: hld up in midfield: rdn over 2f out: nt clr run and swtchd lft over 1f out: styd on u.p ins fnl f: one pce fnl 50yds* 5/1[1]

1-31 **5** 1 **Time To Study (FR)**[20] 3335 3-9-0 93 SilvestreDeSousa 2 98
(Mark Johnston) *led: hdd on bnd after 1f: regained ld after 2f: jnd over 5f out: hdd narrowly over 4f out: rdn and stl ev ch fr 2f out: edgd lft over 1f out: stl wl there ins fnl f: jinked lft fnl 75yds: no ex* 7/1[3]

1-23 **6** nk **Desert Skyline (IRE)**[20] 3318 3-9-0 100 FranBerry 5 98+
(David Elsworth) *squeezed out s: in rr: effrt whn swtchd lft over 2f out: rdn and hdwy over 1f out: styd on u.p ins fnl f: n.m.r and checked fnl 75yds: kpt on but no imp after* 8/1

-204 **7** ¾ **Mister Manduro (FR)**[20] 3335 3-9-0 90 JimCrowley 12 96
(Mark Johnston) *prom: rdn to chal 2f out: stl there 1f out: styd on same pce fnl 150yds* 25/1

-214 **8** ½ **Face The Facts (IRE)**[27] 3081 3-9-0 85 AdamKirby 1 97+
(John Gosden) *w'like: str: hld up: pushed along over 3f out: rdn and nt clr run 2f out: edgd lft ent fnl f: styng on whn nt clr run and snatched up fnl 75yds: sn swtchd rt: nvr able to rch ldrs* 33/1

32-1 **9** 2¼ **Alqamar**[35] 2807 3-9-0 87 (p) JamesDoyle 8 92
(Charlie Appleby) *racd keenly: trckd ldrs: lost pl 1 m out: rdn and outpcd over 2f out: kpt on u.p over 1f out: one pce ins fnl f* 14/1

**10** hd **Night Of Glory**[15] 3511 3-9-0 99 (p[1]) ShaneFoley 13 92
(M D O'Callaghan, Ire) *tall: prom: pushed along and outpcd over 3f out: u.p in tch over 2f out: wknd ent fnl f* 16/1

**11** 3½ **Haripour (IRE)**[20] 3348 3-9-0 94 (b) PatSmullen 10 87
(D K Weld, Ire) *lengthy: n.m.r and hmpd after 1f on bnd: dropped to midfield: hdwy over 2f out: no imp: wkng whn n.m.r over 1f out* 11/1

**12** 18 **Wisconsin (JPN)**[29] 3017 3-9-0 0 (p[1]) SeamieHeffernan 4 62
(A P O'Brien, Ire) *str: lw: hld up: pushed along early: led on bnd after 1f: sn hung bdly lft and racd v wd: hdd after 2f: racd keenly: c over 1 m out: disp ld over 5f out: led narrowly over 4f out tl 2f out: wknd over 1f out: sn eased* 8/1

1-52 **13** 5 **Fierce Impact (JPN)**[28] 3032 3-9-0 98 JamieSpencer 6 55
(David Simcock) *hld up: rdn over 2f out: nvr a threat* 14/1

3m 1.47s (0.47) **Going Correction** +0.15s/f (Good) 13 Ran SP% 121.3
Speed ratings (Par 111): **104,103,102,102,102 101,101,101,99,99 97,87,84**
CSF £50.02 CT £438.34 TOTE £6.20: £2.10, £3.40, £3.40; EX 65.00 Trifecta £794.20.
**Owner** B E Nielsen **Bred** Bjorn Nielsen **Trained** Newmarket, Suffolk

**FOCUS**

The Queen's Vase was newly upgraded from Listed status and the distance reduced from 2m, although the latter change made for a short run to the first bend and things got a little tight. John Gosden suggested afterwards they could move the start back a furlong and make it a 1m7f race in future. The runner-up helps set the standard based on his Classic trial form. The fifth and seventh have been rated close to their Musselburgh handicap form.

## 4033 DUKE OF EDINBURGH STKS (H'CAP) 1m 3f 211y

5:35 (5:39) (Class 2) (0-105,105) 3-Y-O+

**£49,800** (£14,912; £7,456; £3,728; £1,864; £936) Stalls Low

Form RPR

1/0- **1** **Rare Rhythm**[371] 3340 5-9-2 **97**........................................ WilliamBuick 19 108
(Charlie Appleby) *wl in tch in midfield: clsd to join ldr 9f out tl led over 2f out: sn rdn: edgd lft u.p ent fnl f: shifting bk rt u.p but styd on strly ins fnl f: rdn out* **20/1**

03-1 **2** 2 ¼ **Appeared**[41] 2603 5-9-6 **101**........................................(p[1]) AndreaAtzeni 18 108
(Roger Varian) *t.k.h: trckd ldrs: effrt to chse wnr: edging rt u.p jst ins fnl f: no ex and outpcd fnl 100yds* **13/2**

04-2 **3** 1 **Star Storm (IRE)**[41] 2604 5-9-5 **103**........................ GeorgeWood(3) 5 108
(James Fanshawe) *hld up in tch in midfield: clsd whn nt clrest of runs and swtchd rt 2f out: hdwy u.p to chse ldng pair 1f out: kpt on wl: no threat to ldr* **14/1**

0-21 **4** nk **Top Tug (IRE)**[27] 3073 6-9-10 **105**............................ PatSmullen 17 110
(Alan King) *lw: hld up in midfield on outer: effrt ent fnl 2f: hdwy u.p over 1f out: styd on wl ins fnl f: nvr threatening wnr* **8/1**

41-0 **5** ½ **Sixties Groove (IRE)**[21] 3298 4-9-3 **98**........................(p) AdamKirby 15 102+
(Jeremy Noseda) *lw: hld up towards rr: effrt and shifting lft ent fnl 2f: stl plenty to do and swtchd lft over 1f out: hdwy u.p 1f out: styd on strly ins fnl f: nvr threatened ldrs* **9/2[2]**

22-3 **6** hd **Mainstream**[47] 2431 4-9-3 **98**........................................(h) RyanMoore 11 101+
(Sir Michael Stoute) *s.i.s and wnt rt s: hld up in last quartet: hdwy and switching lft over 1f out: kpt on wl ins fnl f: nvr trbld ldrs* **5/1[3]**

-540 **7** hd **Lustrous Light (IRE)**[37] 2735 4-9-3 **98**........................ OisinMurphy 1 101
(Ralph Beckett) *in tch in midfield: effrt whn nt clrest of runs and bmpd 2f out: hdwy u.p ent fnl f: kpt on but no threat to wnr* **50/1**

/130 **8** ¾ **Red Galileo**[120] 890 6-9-7 **102**........................................ PatCosgrave 10 104
(Saeed bin Suroor) *chsd ldrs: rdn jst over 2f out: unable qck u.p over 1f out: wknd ins fnl f* **33/1**

6423 **9** shd **Mistiroc**[43] 2552 6-9-4 **99**........................................(v) JasonHart 14 101
(John Quinn) *trckd ldrs: effrt and cl 4th 2f out: no ex u.p jst over 1f out: wknd ins fnl f* **33/1**

0602 **10** ½ **Eddystone Rock (IRE)**[20] 3323 5-9-4 **99**........................(h) KierenFox 4 100
(John Best) *hld up in tch in midfield: nt clr run on inner 2f out: swtchd lft and rdn over 1f out: styd on ins fnl f: nvr threatening ldrs* **50/1**

56-0 **11** ½ **Shabeeb (USA)**[37] 2735 4-9-3 **98**................................(p[1]) JimCrowley 21 98
(Roger Varian) *lw: dwlt: hld up in last quartet: effrt and swtchd lft over 2f out: sn rdn and no imp: no threat to ldrs but sme hdwy and kpt on steadily ins fnl f* **25/1**

-061 **12** ½ **Soldier In Action (FR)**[20] 3323 4-9-10 **105**............. RichardKingscote 2 104
(Mark Johnston) *pressed ldr for 2f: styd chsng ldrs: rdn over 2f out: stuck bhd wkng rival and lost pl bef switching lft over 1f out: kpt on same pce and no threat to ldrs after* **20/1**

10-0 **13** 1 ¼ **Baydar**[29] 3012 4-9-5 **105**........................................ DavidEgan(5) 22 102
(Hugo Palmer) *hld up in tch in midfield: effrt u.p over 2f out: drvn and no hdwy over 1f out: wknd ins fnl f* **33/1**

0-20 **14** 1 ½ **Manjaam (IRE)**[27] 3073 4-9-2 **97**................................(b[1]) GeraldMosse 6 92
(Ed Dunlop) *t.k.h early: in tch in midfield on inner: shuffled bk towards rr over 2f out: swtchd lft and tried to rally over 1f out: no real imp* **25/1**

-001 **15** 5 **Master Carpenter (IRE)**[37] 2735 6-9-10 **105**..................... FranBerry 20 92
(Rod Millman) *in tch in midfield: hdwy to trck ldrs 4f out: rdn and unable qck over 1f out: lost pl and btn over 1f out: wl btn ins fnl f: eased towards fin* **25/1**

11-1 **16** ½ **Wadigor**[30] 2959 4-9-9 **104**........................................ SilvestreDeSousa 12 90
(Roger Varian) *lengthy: lw: wnt rt s: hld up in midfield: shuffled bk to rr 3f out: nt clr run and squeezed for room 2f out: effrt but stl plenty to do whn hmpd over 1f out: no ch after* **4/1[1]**

3-43 **17** ½ **Cape Cova (IRE)**[13] 3594 4-9-7 **102**............................(v[1]) TomQueally 16 87
(John Gosden) *s.i.s and bustled along early: hld up in last quartet: effrt and pushed wd over 2f out: no hdwy and bhd whn hung rt wl over 1f out* **12/1**

-053 **18** 1 ¼ **Oasis Fantasy (IRE)**[37] 2735 6-9-2 **97**........................ JamieSpencer 7 80
(David Simcock) *led: hdd over 2f out: sn u.p and unable qck: wknd over 1f out: bhd and eased ins fnl f* **20/1**

1210 **19** 5 **Petite Jack**[70] 1770 4-9-3 **98**........................................ JackMitchell 13 73
(Archie Watson) *hld up in last quartet: effrt whn squeezed for room and hmpd 2f out: n.d after: eased ins fnl f* **33/1**

2m 31.15s (-1.35) **Going Correction** +0.15s/f (Good) **19** Ran SP% **135.2**

Speed ratings (Par 109): **110,108,107,107,107 107,107,106,106,106 105,105,104,103,100 99,99,98,95**

CSF £139.43 CT £1947.78 TOTE £27.10: £5.00, £2.20, £3.90, £1.90; EX 202.70 Trifecta £3501.20.

**Owner** Godolphin **Bred** Highclere Stud And Floors Farming **Trained** Newmarket, Suffolk

■ Stewards' Enquiry : Adam Kirby five-day ban: careless riding (Jul 7-11)

**FOCUS**

A tactical race, Jamie Spencer setting a controlled pace up front, and it didn't pay to be too far off the gallop. For the 11th time in the last 12 years something drawn in double figures won. The third has been rated close to form.

T/Jkpt: Not won. T/Plt: £49.40 to a £1 stake. Pool: £475,571.00 - 9,615.59 winning units. T/Qpdt: £14.10 to a £1 stake. Pool: £28,151.00 - 1,985.47 winning units. **Steve Payne & Darren Owen**

# 3648 AYR (L-H)

## Friday, June 23

**OFFICIAL GOING: Good (good to firm in places; 7.9)**

Wind: Breezy, half against Weather: Overcast

## 4034 TENNENT'S BLACK T AMATEUR RIDERS' H'CAP 1m 2f

6:30 (6:31) (Class 6) (0-65,60) 4-Y-O+ **£3,119** (£967; £483; £242) Stalls Low

Form RPR

-033 **1** **Haymarket**[11] 3650 8-10-3 **49**........................................ MrsCBartley 7 56
(R Mike Smith) *mde all at decent gallop: rdn along over 2f out: styd on gamely fnl f* **11/2[2]**

2302 **2** ½ **Ted's Brother (IRE)**[16] 3449 9-9-10 **47**........................ MissAPeck(5) 11 53
(Laura Morgan) *prom: effrt and plld out over 1f out: chsd wnr ins fnl f: kpt on fin* **12/1**

526 **3** 2 ¾ **Colour Contrast (IRE)**[2] 3977 4-10-8 **59**........................(p) MrBLynn(5) 4 60
(Iain Jardine) *t.k.h early: prom: stdy hdwy over 2f out: rdn over 1f out: kpt on same pce ins fnl f* **11/8[1]**

00-6 **4** shd **Inspector Norse**[8] 3740 6-10-7 **56**........................(p) MissEEasterby(3) 5 57
(Tim Easterby) *pressed ldr: rdn over 2f out: no ex and lost two pls ins fnl f* **10/1[3]**

30-6 **5** 2 **Diamonds A Dancing**[23] 3198 7-10-9 **60**................(h) MissAMcCain(5) 1 57+
(Donald McCain) *hld up in midfield: stdy hdwy and edgd lft fr over 2f out: kpt on fnl f: nvr able to chal* **33/1**

0406 **6** 2 **Firestorm (GER)**[16] 3449 6-10-6 **52**........................ MissBeckySmith 13 45+
(Richard Ford) *s.i.s: bhd: hdwy 2f out: kpt on fnl f: no imp* **14/1**

0543 **7** hd **Mount Cheiron (USA)**[14] 3530 6-10-0 **46**........................(p) MissCWalton 2 39
(Richard Ford) *hld up: stdy hdwy 3f out: rdn and wknd over 1f out* **25/1**

0056 **8** 6 **Whitchurch**[11] 3650 5-10-1 **47**........................................(p) MrAlexFerguson 8 28
(Iain Jardine) *hld up: pushed along over 2f out: sn no imp* **28/1**

602- **9** 6 **Ronaldinho (IRE)**[25] 5801 7-10-2 **48**........................(tp) MissEmmaSayer 9 18
(Dianne Sayer) *midfield: rdn along over 3f out: wknd fnl 2f* **28/1**

0034 **10** nk **Frontline Phantom (IRE)**[8] 3760 10-9-13 **50**...... MissCAGreenway(5) 3 19
(K R Burke) *hld up: hdwy on outside over 2f out: rdn and wknd wl over 1f out* **22/1**

4030 **11** 1 ¾ **Rebel State (IRE)**[18] 3402 4-10-5 **58**........................ MissACawley(7) 6 24
(Jedd O'Keeffe) *bhd: pushed along over 3f out: nvr on terms* **10/1[3]**

0010 **12** 5 **Rioja Day (IRE)**[11] 3652 7-10-5 **56**........................(b) MissRHill(5) 14 12
(Jim Goldie) *a bhd: struggling over 3f out: sn btn* **22/1**

0-03 **13** 13 **Hellavashock**[16] 3450 4-10-3 **52**........................(p[1]) MrRyanNichol(3) 12
(Alistair Whillans) *trckd ldrs tl rdn and wknd 3f out* **16/1**

1/0- **14** 10 **Wolf Heart (IRE)**[351] 4038 9-10-1 **47**........................ MissAnnaHesketh 10
(Lucy Normile) *trckd ldrs: hmpd and lost pl over 3f out: sn wknd* **33/1**

2m 12.34s (0.34) **Going Correction** +0.10s/f (Good) **14** Ran SP% **121.2**

Speed ratings (Par 101): **102,101,99,99,97 96,95,91,86,86 84,80,70,62**

CSF £63.57 CT £140.48 TOTE £6.30: £2.10, £3.60, £1.20; EX 49.50 Trifecta £153.80.

**Owner** Ewan Ross **Bred** J Breslin **Trained** Galston, E Ayrshire

■ Stewards' Enquiry : Miss A Peck caution: careless riding. two-day ban: careless riding (tbc)

**FOCUS**

Distances as advertised. A low-grade handicap for amateur riders featuring a well-supported favourite. The pace was decent but few got involved and the finish concerned those who raced prominently. The form wouldn't be strong. The winner has been rated in line with his form from mid-2016 here.

## 4035 CALEDONIA BEST H'CAP 1m 2f

7:05 (7:09) (Class 4) (0-85,90) 3-Y-O+ **£6,469** (£1,925; £962; £481) Stalls Low

Form RPR

4112 **1** **Gworn**[11] 3651 7-9-7 **78**........................................ PJMcDonald 3 86
(R Mike Smith) *prom: effrt and rdn over 1f out: kpt on wl fnl f to ld nr fin* **5/1[3]**

3-21 **2** hd **Kasperenko**[44] 2521 3-9-2 **85**........................................ PaulMulrennan 2 92
(David Lanigan) *dwlt: sn pressing ldr: led over 2f out: rdn and hung lft over 1f out: kpt on wl fnl f: hdd nr fin* **7/4[2]**

-231 **3** 1 ¼ **Royal Regent**[11] 3651 5-9-8 **82** 6ex........................ SammyJoBell(3) 1 86
(Lucy Normile) *trckd ldrs: effrt and swtchd rt 1f out: kpt on same pce ins fnl f* **7/1**

-203 **4** 3 ½ **Glorious Forever**[15] 3504 3-9-1 **84**........................ LukeMorris 6 81
(Ed Walker) *led at ordinary gallop: rdn and hdd over 1f out: carried lft over 1f out: one pce whn hmpd ins fnl f* **6/4[1]**

0-00 **5** ¾ **Intiwin (IRE)**[23] 3197 5-8-9 **66**........................................ TomEaves 5 62
(Linda Perratt) *hld up in tch: rdn and outpcd over 2f out: rallied fnl f: no imp* **40/1**

0160 **6** 5 **Testa Rossa (IRE)**[22] 3255 7-9-1 **79**........................(b) SeanMooney(7) 7 65
(Jim Goldie) *hld up: rdn and outpcd 3f out: sn struggling* **22/1**

2m 12.32s (0.32) **Going Correction** +0.10s/f (Good)

**WFA** 3 from 5yo+ 12lb **6** Ran SP% **112.3**

Speed ratings (Par 105): **102,101,100,98,97 93**

CSF £14.26 TOTE £5.60: £1.90, £1.60; EX 14.70 Trifecta £37.10.

**Owner** R Gibson **Bred** Azienda Agricola F Lli Nencini **Trained** Galston, E Ayrshire

■ Stewards' Enquiry : Paul Mulrennan caution: careless riding

**FOCUS**

Although the official ground was good, good to firm in places, it didn't look any worse than good on the round course. This was run at a modest gallop though the time was similar to the other race over the same trip. This wouldn't be form to take literally with the third and fourth both meeting trouble.

## 4036 HEVERLEE MAIDEN STKS 1m 1f 20y

7:40 (7:43) (Class 5) 3-Y-O+ **£3,881** (£1,155; £577; £288) Stalls Low

Form RPR

3242 **1** **Lamloom (IRE)**[18] 3383 3-9-3 **78**........................................ DanielTudhope 7 79+
(David O'Meara) *mde all: rdn clr over 1f out: unchal* **2/1[2]**

22 **2** 3 ¼ **Liquid Gold (IRE)**[15] 3500 3-8-12 **0**........................ TonyHamilton 3 67
(Richard Fahey) *trckd ldrs: effrt and chsd wnr over 2f out: kpt on same pce fnl f* **11/8[1]**

3-3 **3** ½ **Bolder Bob (IRE)**[24] 3182 3-9-3 **0**........................................ BenCurtis 8 71+
(David Barron) *hld up in tch: effrt over 2f out: no imp over 1f out* **10/1**

4 1 **Starplex**[57] 7-9-9 **0**........................................ RowanScott(5) 4 70
(Keith Dalgleish) *hld up: rdn and effrt over 2f out: no imp appr fnl f* **25/1**

0- **5** 3 ¼ **Chinese Spirit (IRE)**[270] 6833 3-9-3 **0**........................ PJMcDonald 1 62
(R Mike Smith) *hld up in tch: rdn over 2f out: edgd lft and no imp over 1f out* **40/1**

64 **6** 3 ¼ **Vindicator (IRE)**[20] 3342 3-9-3 **0**........................ PaulMulrennan 6 55
(Michael Dods) *reluctant to enter stalls: hld up: rdn and outpcd over 2f out: sn n.d* **22/1**

335 **7** 2 ½ **Born To Boom (IRE)**[15] 3485 3-8-12 **73**........................ CliffordLee(5) 9 50
(K R Burke) *pressed wnr to over 2f out: rdn and wknd wl over 1f out* **13/2[3]**

4- **8** 4 **Traditional Dancer (IRE)**[41] 5581 5-10-0 **0**..................(p[1]) DavidNolan 2 43
(Iain Jardine) *slowly away: bhd and outpcd: nvr on terms* **18/1**

1m 57.18s (-0.32) **Going Correction** +0.10s/f (Good)

**WFA** 3 from 5yo+ 11lb **8** Ran SP% **113.8**

Speed ratings (Par 103): **105,102,101,100,97 95,92,89**

CSF £4.94 TOTE £3.10: £1.40, £1.10, £2.50; EX 5.20 Trifecta £22.60.

**Owner** Salem Rashid **Bred** M Duffy **Trained** Upper Helmsley, N Yorks

**FOCUS**
A fair maiden race in which the 78-rated winner made all setting a reasonable though not overly-strong gallop. The winner has been rated to his mark.

## 4037 TENNENT'S H'CAP 6f
**8:10** (8:12) (Class 3) (0-95,93) 3-Y-O+ **£9,056** (£2,695; £1,346; £673) **Stalls** Centre

Form RPR
0556 **1** **Flying Pursuit**[16] 3463 4-9-2 **84**........................(p[1]) RachelRichardson[(3)] 6 95
(Tim Easterby) *mde all: rdn over 1f out: kpt on strly fnl f* **7/1**[3]
5610 **2** 1 ¼ **Explain**[27] 3095 5-9-1 **80**..............................................(p) JamesSullivan 7 87
(Ruth Carr) *trckd ldrs: effrt and chsd wnr over 1f out: kpt on ins fnl f: nt pce to chal* **16/1**
-122 **3** 3 **Scorching Heat**[13] 3593 3-8-12 **84**................................ PaulMulrennan 4 79
(Andrew Balding) *t.k.h: pressed wnr to over 1f out: no ex fnl f* **5/4**[1]
-000 **4** 2 ¼ **Giant Spark**[37] 2736 5-9-4 **90**.................................... ConnorMurtagh[(7)] 1 80
(Paul Midgley) *in tch on outside: drvn along over 2f out: no imp over 1f out* **20/1**
0-22 **5** ½ **Glengarry**[28] 3045 4-9-8 **87**................................................ DavidNolan 8 76
(Keith Dalgleish) *hld up: rdn and outpcd over 2f out: kpt on fnl f: nvr able to chal* **4/1**[2]
4140 **6** 1 ¼ **Tommy G**[6] 3827 4-8-7 **77**................................................ PhilDennis[(5)] 11 62
(Jim Goldie) *hld up: rdn and outpcd over 2f out: n.d after* **11/1**
-033 **7** 3 ½ **Harwoods Volante (IRE)**[13] 3565 6-9-7 **86**................ DanielTudhope 10 59
(David O'Meara) *hld up: stdy hdwy over 2f out: rdn and wknd over 1f out* **12/1**
3605 **8** 1 **Ninjago**[20] 3324 7-9-9 **88**..................................................(b) LukeMorris 5 58
(Paul Midgley) *prom: rdn over 2f out: wknd over 1f out* **8/1**

1m 13.31s (0.91) **Going Correction** +0.10s/f (Good)
**WFA** 3 from 4yo+ 7lb **8** Ran SP% **114.7**
Speed ratings (Par 107): **97,95,91,88,87 86,81,80**
CSF £107.81 CT £228.84 TOTE £8.20: £2.10, £4.20, £1.10; EX 101.30 Trifecta £367.80.
**Owner** Ontoawinner, M Hulin & Partner **Bred** Crossfields Bloodstock Ltd **Trained** Great Habton, N Yorks

**FOCUS**
Not form to take literally as the pace was pretty ordinary and the first three were in the first three throughout. The runner-up has been rated to last year's best.

## 4038 MAGNERS H'CAP 1m 5f 26y
**8:45** (8:45) (Class 3) (0-90,90) 4-Y-O+ **£9,056** (£2,695; £1,346; £673) **Stalls** Low

Form RPR
0130 **1** **Euchen Glen**[7] 3790 4-9-5 **88**........................................ PaulMulrennan 3 95+
(Jim Goldie) *hld up in last pl: hdwy and edgd lft wl over 1f out: rdn to ld ins fnl f: comf* **8/1**[3]
-552 **2** ¾ **Braes Of Lochalsh**[18] 3389 6-8-2 **71** oh3.................(v[1]) JamesSullivan 4 76
(Jim Goldie) *led: rdn over 2f out: hdd ins fnl f: kpt on same pce* **18/1**
-111 **3** 4 ½ **Lugano**[4] 3907 4-9-0 **83** 6ex.................................................. LukeMorris 1 81
(Sir Mark Prescott Bt) *prom: hdwy on outside to chse ldr 3f out: sn rdn and hung lft: drvn and veered rt over 1f out: outpcd ins fnl f* **4/7**[1]
0655 **4** 9 **Sennockian Star**[20] 3323 7-9-7 **90**................................... PJMcDonald 5 75
(Mark Johnston) *trckd ldrs tl rdn and wknd fr 2f out* **16/1**
-112 **5** 9 **Mutadaffeq (IRE)**[9] 3716 4-9-5 **88**................................ DanielTudhope 6 59
(David O'Meara) *trckd ldr to 2f out: rdn and wknd 2f out* **3/1**[2]

2m 53.16s (-0.84) **Going Correction** +0.10s/f (Good) **5** Ran SP% **110.9**
Speed ratings (Par 107): **106,105,102,97,91**
CSF £100.38 TOTE £8.30: £3.30, £4.80; EX 64.60 Trifecta £217.50.
**Owner** W M Johnstone **Bred** W M Johnstone **Trained** Uplawmoor, E Renfrews

**FOCUS**
A bit of a stop-start gallop, though the winner came from last to first and the second made the running. The form is hard to evaluate as the two market leaders ran below their best. The runner-up has been rated close to last year's best.

## 4039 MENABREA H'CAP 7f 50y
**9:15** (9:16) (Class 5) (0-70,70) 3-Y-O+ **£3,881** (£1,155; £577; £288) **Stalls** High

Form RPR
/243 **1** **Dark Profit (IRE)**[6] 3833 5-9-13 **69**..........................(p) PaulMulrennan 13 81
(Keith Dalgleish) *prom: nt clr run over 2f out: effrt and led 1f out: edgd lft and qcknd clr fnl f: comf* **7/2**[2]
4032 **2** 2 ½ **Magistral**[11] 3652 7-9-12 **68**..........................................(p) PJMcDonald 10 73
(R Mike Smith) *hld up in midfield: effrt over 2f out: chsd wnr appr fnl f: kpt on: nt pce to chal* **3/1**[1]
-003 **3** nk **Favourite Treat (USA)**[6] 3816 7-10-0 **70**...................(e) JamesSullivan 3 74
(Ruth Carr) *hld up: effrt and plld out over 1f out: kpt on ins fnl f: nvr able to chal* **6/1**[3]
0-65 **4** 1 ¾ **Royal Duchess**[11] 3652 7-10-0 **70**....................................... JoeDoyle 12 70
(Lucy Normile) *trckd ldrs: led over 2f out to over 1f out: rdn and one pce fnl f* **17/2**
0306 **5** ¾ **Let Right Be Done**[6] 3831 5-8-6 **51** oh4.................(b) SammyJoBell[(3)] 6 49
(Linda Perratt) *hld up in midfield: stdy hdwy on outside over 2f out: rdn over 1f out: no imp fnl f* **25/1**
3512 **6** nse **Sea Of Green**[6] 3833 5-8-8 **55**.......................................(p) PhilDennis[(5)] 1 53
(Jim Goldie) *awkward s: hld up: effrt whn n.m.r over 2f out: rdn over 1f out: kpt on fnl f: nvr able to chal* **15/2**
-001 **7** nk **Reinforced**[15] 3488 4-9-9 **65**..........................................(tp) TomEaves 11 62
(Michael Dods) *led to over 2f out: rallied: outpcd fnl f* **8/1**
0050 **8** nk **Stardrifter**[2] 3977 5-8-12 **61**.................................. ConnorMurtagh[(7)] 14 57
(Linda Perratt) *hld up: rdn over 2f out: no imp over 1f out* **25/1**
20-0 **9** ¾ **Declamation (IRE)**[130] 724 7-8-13 **55**................................ BenCurtis 7 49
(Alistair Whillans) *cl up: ev ch over 2f out: rdn: edgd lft and wknd over 1f out* **20/1**
010- **10** 1 **Circuitous**[241] 7604 9-8-13 **60**....................................(v) RowanScott[(5)] 2 51
(Keith Dalgleish) *prom: rdn over 2f out: wknd over 1f out* **33/1**
3130 **11** ¾ **Newmarket Warrior (IRE)**[24] 3181 6-9-7 **70**.........(p) JamieGormley[(7)] 8 60
(Iain Jardine) *missed break: bhd: struggling over 3f out: nvr on terms* **11/1**
0-60 **12** 7 **Dawoodi**[18] 3386 3-9-5 **70**................................................ DavidNolan 9 38
(Linda Perratt) *t.k.h: hld up: rdn over 2f out: wknd wl over 1f out* **66/1**

1m 30.74s (-2.66) **Going Correction** +0.10s/f (Good)
**WFA** 3 from 4yo+ 9lb **12** Ran SP% **120.1**
Speed ratings (Par 103): **119,116,115,113,112 112,112,112,111,110 109,101**
CSF £13.69 CT £63.14 TOTE £4.50: £1.60, £1.60, £2.40; EX 15.70 Trifecta £80.70.
**Owner** Weldspec Glasgow Limited **Bred** Mrs S M Rogers & Sir Thomas Pilkington **Trained** Carluke, S Lanarks

**FOCUS**
Not a strong 51-70 handicap as not many came into it in particularly good form. The pace was decent and the well-backed winner scored in good style. The winner has been rated back to the better view of his early 2yo form, with the runner-up and third close to their latest efforts.

T/Plt: £89.70 to a £1 stake. Pool: £59,478.37 - 484.03 winning units. T/Qpdt: £72.70 to a £1 stake. Pool: £4,483.17 - 45.58 winning units. **Richard Young**

# [3805]BATH (L-H)
## Friday, June 23

**OFFICIAL GOING: Firm (10.9)**
Wind: light against Weather: overcast

## 4040 MARSTONS BREWERY H'CAP (BATH SUMMER STAYERS' SERIES QUALIFIER) 1m 3f 137y
**5:40** (5:40) (Class 6) (0-60,58) 4-Y-O+ **£2,264** (£673; £336; £168) **Stalls** Low

Form RPR
0-23 **1** **Hallingham**[53] 2219 7-9-4 **58**........................................ HectorCrouch[(3)] 3 67
(Ken Cunningham-Brown) *chsd clr ldr: rdn to cl on ldr over 3f out: chal jst ins fnl f: led fnl 100yds: styd on wl* **3/1**[2]
6305 **2** 1 **Eben Dubai (IRE)**[13] 3575 5-9-1 **52**................................ CharlesBishop 1 59
(Tracey Barfoot-Saunt) *racd keenly: led: sn 12 l clr: rdn over 1f out: hdd fnl 100yds: no ex* **7/1**[3]
-143 **3** 17 **Avocadeau (IRE)**[22] 3251 6-9-4 **55**...............................(p) MartinDwyer 5 35
(Stuart Kittow) *chsd clr ldr: rdn to cl on ldr over 3f out: drifted lft over 1f out: wknd ent fnl f* **2/1**[1]
6/03 **4** 2 **Vexillum (IRE)**[6] 3805 8-8-8 **45**.......................................(p) LiamKeniry 2 22
(Neil Mulholland) *hld up in last pair but in tch: rdn over 3f out: sn btn* **3/1**[2]
0540 **5** 7 **Machiavelian Storm (IRE)**[14] 3519 5-8-3 **45** ow2....... FinleyMarsh[(7)] 7 12
(Richard Mitchell) *s.i.s: in last pair in chsng gp: rdn over 3f out: sn btn* **12/1**
6045 **6** 13 **Kilim**[97] 1256 4-9-1 **52**..................................................(t) RoystonFfrench 6
(John Berry) *trckd ldrs in chsng gp: rdn over 3f out: sn btn* **8/1**

2m 29.76s (-0.84) **Going Correction** -0.075s/f (Good) **6** Ran SP% **114.6**
Speed ratings (Par 101): **99,98,87,85,81 72**
CSF £24.04 TOTE £3.60: £1.80, £3.40; EX 27.90 Trifecta £44.50.
**Owner** David Henery **Bred** John W Ford And Peter J Skinner **Trained** Danebury, Hants

**FOCUS**
A moderate middle-distance handicap. They went a respectable gallop on firm ground. The first two have been rated up on this year's form, with the runner-up close to his best.

## 4041 ANDERSONS WASTE MANAGEMENT H'CAP 1m 2f 37y
**6:10** (6:10) (Class 5) (0-75,77) 4-Y-O+ **£4,269** (£1,270; £634; £317) **Stalls** Low

Form RPR
-423 **1** **Glens Wobbly**[13] 3574 9-8-11 **72**...................................... JordanUys[(7)] 6 78
(Jonathan Geake) *led after 2f: hdd jst over 3f out: continued to press ldr u.p: rallied gamely to regain ld ins fnl f: styd on* **6/1**[3]
11-4 **2** 1 ¼ **Sharjah (IRE)**[20] 2352 7-9-9 **77**...................................(b) WilliamCarson 1 80
(Andrew Slattery, Ire) *led for 2f: trckd ldr: led jst over 3f out: rdn over 2f out: hdd ins fnl f: styd on but no ex* **9/4**[1]
2625 **3** hd **Russian Reward (IRE)**[50] 2333 5-9-4 **75**............(p) KieranShoemark[(3)] 2 77
(Amanda Perrett) *prom: trckd ldr after 2f: rdn to chse ldng pair wl over 2f out: edgd lft over 1f out: styd on towards fin* **5/2**[2]
1234 **4** hd **Attain**[8] 3753 8-8-8 **69**........................................................ FinleyMarsh[(7)] 3 71
(Archie Watson) *last pair but in tch: tk clsr order 3f out: sn rdn: nt clr run whn swtchd rt ins fnl f: styd on towards fin* **9/4**[1]
0-05 **5** 4 **Henryhudsonbridge (USA)**[37] 2722 5-8-3 **57**.......(tp) RoystonFfrench 5 51
(John Flint) *slowly away: last: rdn 3f out: styd on but nvr gng pce to get involved* **25/1**
4-46 **6** 15 **Saint Helena (IRE)**[21] 3282 9-8-10 **64**................................(b) JohnFahy 4 28
(Mark Gillard) *chsd ldrs: effrt 3f out: wknd over 1f out* **14/1**

2m 8.01s (-2.99) **Going Correction** -0.075s/f (Good) **6** Ran SP% **114.9**
Speed ratings (Par 103): **108,107,106,106,103 91**
CSF £20.56 TOTE £7.70: £2.40, £1.70; EX 26.90 Trifecta £52.30.
**Owner** Glen Symes **Bred** H J Manners **Trained** East Kennett, Wilts

**FOCUS**
A fair handicap. They went a contested gallop and a course specialist prevailed after an engaging battle with one of the joint-favourites. The winner has been rated close to his best.

## 4042 CHARLES SAUNDERS FOOD SERVICES MAIDEN FILLIES' STKS 1m 2f 37y
**6:45** (6:46) (Class 5) 3-Y-O+ **£5,040** (£1,508; £754; £377; £188) **Stalls** Low

Form RPR
03 **1** **Light Of Joy (USA)**[20] 3342 3-9-0 0.............................. RobertWinston 5 80+
(David Lanigan) *hld up: pushed along and hdwy over 2f out: led over 1f out: drifted lft: kpt on wl: pushed out* **9/4**[2]
35 **2** 1 ¼ **Feint**[42] 2585 3-9-0 0........................................................... LiamJones 6 75
(William Haggas) *trckd ldr: rdn to ld 2f out: hdd over 1f out: hld whn swtchd rt ins fnl f: kpt on* **9/2**[3]
55-4 **3** 3 ¾ **Iconic Belle**[14] 3535 3-9-0 73............................................... GrahamLee 1 67
(Mick Channon) *led: rdn and hdd 2f out: sn one pce* **7/1**
6-54 **4** 2 ¼ **Polly Glide (IRE)**[28] 3039 3-8-7 77........................... GabrieleMalune[(7)] 7 63+
(Luca Cumani) *trckd ldrs: sddle slipped after 1f and nvr rcvrd: effrt over 2f out: kpt on but unable to chal* **6/5**[1]
05 **5** 2 **Estrellada**[21] 3309 3-9-0 0.................................................. CharlesBishop 2 59
(Mick Channon) *hld up: effrt wl over 2f out: nt pce to get on terms* **33/1**
**6** 3 ½ **Nagamaat (IRE)** 3-9-0 0..................................................... TomMarquand 3 52
(Brian Meehan) *chsd ldrs: effrt wl over 2f out: nvr threatened: wknd jst over 1f out* **12/1**

2m 10.78s (-0.22) **Going Correction** -0.075s/f (Good) **6** Ran SP% **117.5**
Speed ratings (Par 100): **97,96,93,91,89 86**
CSF £13.55 TOTE £3.40: £1.80, £2.20; EX 15.60 Trifecta £50.90.
**Owner** Flaxman Stables Ireland Ltd **Bred** Flaxman Holdings Limited **Trained** Newmarket, Suffolk

**FOCUS**
A fair fillies' maiden. They went a modest gallop on the firm ground. The second favourite relished the surface to win well. The winner has been rated as building on her previous form.

## 4043 CHARLES SAUNDERS SEAFOOD FILLIES' H'CAP 5f 160y
**7:15** (7:16) (Class 5) (0-75,77) 3-Y-O+ **£3,557** (£1,058; £529; £264) **Stalls** Centre

Form RPR
6361 **1** **Jersey Breeze (IRE)**[3] 3941 4-9-9 **76** 6ex....................(v) KeithQuinn[(7)] 7 85
(Mick Channon) *a.p: led jst over 2f out: strly pressed over 1f out: r.o wl to assert ins fnl f* **7/4**[1]
U161 **2** 2 ¼ **Powerful Dream (IRE)**[28] 3021 4-10-0 **74**.......................(p) GrahamLee 6 75
(Ronald Harris) *trckd ldrs: str chal wl over 1f out: ev ch ent fnl f: sn no ex* **4/1**[3]
0-04 **3** shd **Reedanjas (IRE)**[9] 3729 3-9-3 **77**................................... FinleyMarsh[(7)] 2 76
(Gay Kelleway) *trckd ldrs: rdn in cl 3rd over 1f out: swtchd lft ent fnl f: kpt on same pce* **3/1**[2]

1404 **4** *4* **Kingstreet Lady**[7] 3774 4-8-4 **55** oh3......................(v[1]) MitchGodwin(5) 3 43
(Richard Price) *sn trcking ldrs: rdn over 2f out: nt pce to get on terms* **5/1**

56-3 **5** *2* **Welsh Rose**[50] 2335 4-9-10 **70**..........................................(h) LiamKeniry 5 51
(Ed de Giles) *led: hdd jst over 2f out: sn rdn and hld: wknd fnl f* **5/1**

4400 **6** *nk* **Molly Jones**[6] 3811 8-8-9 **55** oh4.......................................... JohnFahy 1 35
(Matthew Salaman) *trckd ldrs: rdn over 2f out: nt pce to threaten: fdd ins fnl f* **25/1**

1m 11.39s (0.19) **Going Correction** -0.075s/f (Good)
**WFA** 3 from 4yo+ 7lb **6** Ran SP% **118.5**
Speed ratings (Par 100): **95,92,91,86,83 83**
CSF £9.92 TOTE £3.00: £2.00, £1.90; EX 9.90 Trifecta £38.90.

**Owner** Mrs Susan Bunney **Bred** Guy O'Callaghan **Trained** West Ilsley, Berks

**FOCUS**
A fair fillies' sprint handicap. They went a respectable gallop and the right horses came to the fore. The runner-up has been rated to the balance of her form, with the third to her latest effort.

## 4044 GOOD MORNING DISPOSABLE MAIDEN AUCTION STKS 5f 10y
**7:50** (7:50) (Class 6) 2-Y-O £2,458 (£731; £365; £182) **Stalls** Centre

Form RPR

50 **1** **Dreamboat Annie**[6] 3821 2-9-0 0........................................ SteveDrowne 3 65
(Mark Usher) *trckd ldr: led narrowly ent fnl f: kpt on wl to assert fnl 120yds* **8/1**[3]

3230 **2** *1 ¼* **Autumn Lodge**[3] 3929 2-9-5 0.............................................. JohnFahy 2 65
(J S Moore) *led: hdd narrowly ent fnl f: sn rdn: kpt on but no ex fnl 120yds* **4/6**[1]

**3** *2* **Avenging Red (IRE)** 2-9-5 0.......................................... RoystonFfrench 4 57
(Adam West) *slowly away: last but wl in tch: hdwy over 2f out: sn rdn: kpt on but nt pce of front pair* **16/1**

**4** *3 ¾* **Arrogant (IRE)** 2-9-5 0................................................ OscarPereira 5 42
(Jose Santos) *trckd ldrs: snatched up after 1f: rdn over 2f out: hung lft jst over 1f out: sn wknd* **8/1**[3]

**5** *9* **Hugs And Pats** 2-9-5 0................................................ RobertWinston 1 6
(Dean Ivory) *trckd ldrs: outpcd over 2f out: wknd over 1f out* **11/4**[2]

1m 2.86s (0.36) **Going Correction** -0.075s/f (Good) **5** Ran SP% **114.8**
Speed ratings (Par 91): **94,92,88,82,68**
CSF £14.78 TOTE £9.00: £3.80, £1.10; EX 13.90 Trifecta £68.20.

**Owner** Ushers Court **Bred** Itchen Valley Stud **Trained** Upper Lambourn, Berks

**FOCUS**
A modest juvenile maiden. They went a respectable gallop but the favourite didn't really go through with his effort on the firm surface. The runner-up has been rated to his recent form.

## 4045 PLATINUM MOTOR GROUP H'CAP 1m 5f 11y
**8:25** (8:25) (Class 6) (0-65,67) 3-Y-O £2,458 (£731; £365; £182) **Stalls** High

Form RPR

00-2 **1** **Imphal**[21] 3276 3-8-10 **58**.........................................(p[1]) TylerSaunders(7) 7 69+
(Marcus Tregoning) *trckd ldrs early: wnt 2nd 10f out: rdn to ld over 2f out: jnd ent fnl f: styd on wl to assert: readily* **5/2**[2]

4643 **2** *1 ¾* **Plato's Kode (IRE)**[21] 3276 3-9-5 **60**.......................(tp) RobertWinston 1 68
(Seamus Durack) *hld up: hdwy 3f out: trckd wnr over 1f out: str chal ent fnl f: sn rdn: styd on but no ex fnl 120yds* **4/1**[3]

0-01 **3** *5* **Newt**[21] 3276 3-9-12 **67**................................................ LiamJones 3 68
(Sir Mark Prescott Bt) *racd keenly: led: rdn and hdd over 2f out: sn hld by wnr: lost 2nd over 1f out: no ex fnl f* **6/4**[1]

4506 **4** *5* **Tenby Two**[7] 3770 3-9-7 **62**............................................ GrahamLee 5 55
(Mick Channon) *hld up: rdn over 3f out: nt pce to get on terms* **14/1**

0505 **5** *1* **Air Ministry (IRE)**[21] 3276 3-9-6 **61**.............................(b) LouisSteward 4 53
(Michael Bell) *slowly away and rousted along: sn chsng ldrs: rdn in 4th 3f out: nvr threatened to get on terms* **8/1**

**6** *46* **Downtown Rebel (USA)**[34] 2849 3-8-13 **54**.......................... LiamKeniry 2
(Andrew Slattery, Ire) *trckd ldr: rdn over 3f out: sn wknd: eased whn btn* **14/1**

2m 50.04s (-1.96) **Going Correction** -0.075s/f (Good) **6** Ran SP% **113.0**
Speed ratings (Par 97): **103,101,98,95,95 66**
CSF £13.03 TOTE £3.50: £1.70, £2.20; EX 13.00 Trifecta £36.60.

**Owner** Mrs M E Slade **Bred** G S Bishop **Trained** Whitsbury, Hants

**FOCUS**
A modest 3yo staying handicap. The favourite was too keen and had to be restrained on the lead. She had nothing left to give once headed about 2f out.

## 4046 WAINWRIGHT BREWERY H'CAP (BATH SUMMER SPRINT SERIES QUALIFIER) 5f 160y
**8:55** (8:55) (Class 6) (0-65,67) 3-Y-O £2,458 (£731; £365; £182) **Stalls** Centre

Form RPR

U245 **1** **Lightoller (IRE)**[10] 3692 3-9-7 **63**..................................(b) GrahamLee 3 69
(Mick Channon) *trckd ldr: rdn for str chal over 1f out: kpt on to ld cl home* **6/1**[3]

6-01 **2** *hd* **Iron Lady (IRE)**[14] 3543 3-8-12 **54**.................................... MartinDwyer 2 59
(William Muir) *led: rdn whn strly chal over 1f out: kpt on ins fnl f: hdd cl home* **9/4**[2]

40-1 **3** *¾* **Zambezi Queen (IRE)**[49] 2362 3-9-4 **67**......................... RossaRyan(7) 4 70+
(Paul Cole) *awkwardly away: trckd ldng trio: nt best of runs whn swtchd rt then lft 2f out: clr run ins fnl f but nt pce to get on terms: kpt on to go 3rd towards fin* **8/11**[1]

2404 **4** *¾* **Tooty Fruitti**[6] 3810 3-9-3 **59**........................................ SteveDrowne 1 59
(Jo Hughes) *trckd ldrs: rdn to chal over 1f out: ev ch ent fnl f: no ex towards fin* **10/1**

1m 11.36s (0.16) **Going Correction** -0.075s/f (Good) **4** Ran SP% **112.0**
Speed ratings (Par 97): **95,94,93,92**
CSF £19.61 TOTE £7.00; EX 18.00 Trifecta £20.80.

**Owner** M Channon **Bred** Pat Heffernan **Trained** West Ilsley, Berks

**FOCUS**
A modest 3yo sprint handicap. They went a decent gallop and finished in a bit of heap.

T/Plt: £65.70 to a £1 stake. Pool: £44,985.02 - 499.79 winning units. T/Qpdt: £9.90 to a £1 stake. Pool: £4,182.49 - 309.68 winning units. **Tim Mitchell**

# 3590 NEWMARKET (R-H)
Friday, June 23

**OFFICIAL GOING: Good to firm (7.5)**
Wind: Light across Weather: Cloudy

## 4047 FLY LONDON SOUTHEND AIRPORT TO PERPIGNAN APPRENTICE H'CAP 1m
**5:50** (5:50) (Class 5) (0-70,69) 4-Y-O+ £3,881 (£1,155; £577; £288) **Stalls** High

Form RPR

260- **1** **Trulee Scrumptious**[268] 6876 8-9-3 **63**.............................(v) JoshQuinn(3) 8 74
(Peter Charalambous) *mde all: sn clr: rdn over 1f out: styd on wl: unchal* **7/2**[1]

1-66 **2** *7* **Pacific Salt (IRE)**[18] 3396 4-9-5 **67**.................................. WilliamCox(5) 2 62
(Pam Sly) *hld up: hdwy to chse wnr and hung lft fr over 1f out: sn rdn: no imp fnl f* **9/2**[2]

014 **3** *¾* **The Gay Cavalier**[2] 3966 6-9-7 **69**...............................(t) JackOsborn(5) 1 62
(John Ryan) *s.s: in rr: pushed along over 3f out: r.o wl ins fnl f: nt rch ldrs* **6/1**

0 **4** *1 ½* **Windsorlot (IRE)**[13] 3573 4-8-8 **56**.................................... AledBeech(5) 9 46
(Tony Carroll) *hld up: pushed along over 3f out: swtchd rt over 1f out: styd on fnl f: nt trble ldrs* **16/1**

0615 **5** *1* **Intimately**[18] 3397 4-8-11 **59**.................................... Pierre-LouisJamin(5) 7 46
(Jonathan Portman) *s.s: hdwy over 4f out: rdn over 1f out: no ex fnl f* **8/1**

1043 **6** *3 ¼* **Tulip Dress**[14] 3521 4-9-4 **64**.............................................. MillyNaseb(3) 3 44
(Anthony Carson) *chsd ldrs: lost pl over 4f out: hdwy over 1f out: rdn whn hmpd sn after: wknd ins fnl f* **11/2**[3]

0000 **7** *¾* **The Firm (IRE)**[2] 3971 8-8-12 **60**.................................(b) GinaMangan(5) 4 38
(J R Jenkins) *plld hrd and prom: wnt 2nd over 5f out tl rdn over 1f out: wknd ins fnl f* **50/1**

1450 **8** *¾* **Schottische**[109] 1067 7-8-11 **57**................................(b) JoshuaBryan(3) 5 34
(Alan Bailey) *mid-div: racd keenly: rdn over 2f out: wknd over 1f out* **14/1**

2303 **9** *3* **Harlequin Rock**[17] 3442 4-9-2 **59**.................................... LuluStanford 6 29
(Mick Quinn) *chsd wnr over 3f: remained handy in chsng gp tl rdn and wknd over 1f out: eased ins fnl f* **9/2**[2]

3064 **10** *2 ½* **Monzino (USA)**[13] 3564 9-8-2 **50** oh5.......................... TristanPrice(5) 10 14
(Michael Chapman) *s.s: a in rr: wknd over 3f out* **100/1**

1m 39.02s (-0.98) **Going Correction** +0.05s/f (Good) **10** Ran SP% **114.9**
Speed ratings (Par 103): **106,99,98,96,95 92,91,91,88,85**
CSF £18.78 CT £92.70 TOTE £3.90: £2.80, £1.50, £2.10; EX 17.90 Trifecta £117.70.

**Owner** pcracing.co.uk **Bred** Dxb Bloodstock Ltd **Trained** Newmarket, Suffolk

■ Stewards' Enquiry : Josh Quinn two-day ban: used whip when clearly winning (July 7-9)

**FOCUS**
Far side of July Course used. Stalls far side, except 1m2f: centre. Race distance increased by 19yds in race 2 and 6. The going was good to firm ahead of the opener, a modest apprentices' handicap. There was a well-backed runaway winner, who was given too much rope up front. The winner has been rated to her best.

## 4048 FLY LONDON SOUTHEND AIRPORT TO MILAN H'CAP 1m 2f
**6:20** (6:20) (Class 4) (0-85,87) 3-Y-O £5,175 (£1,540; £769; £384) **Stalls** Centre

Form RPR

4-13 **1** **Weekender**[28] 3042 3-10-0 **87**............................................ HarryBentley 6 93+
(John Gosden) *chsd ldr after 1f: rdn to ld ins fnl f: styd on u.p* **5/4**[1]

5-53 **2** *nk* **Monticello (IRE)**[20] 3316 3-10-0 **87**................................... DaneO'Neill 2 92
(Mark Johnston) *led: pushed along and qcknd over 2f out: rdn and hdd ins fnl f: styd on* **15/2**

13-3 **3** *1 ½* **Winston C (IRE)**[16] 3457 3-9-6 **79**.................................... GavinLerena 4 81
(Michael Bell) *chsd ldrs: rdn over 1f out: styd on same pce wl ins fnl f* **8/1**

-313 **4** *½* **Carigrad (IRE)**[41] 2612 3-9-6 **79**................................. JosephineGordon 3 80
(Hugo Palmer) *hld up: nt clr run over 2f out: hdwy over 1f out: sn rdn: edgd lft and styd on same pce wl ins fnl f* **9/2**[2]

41 **5** *4 ½* **Near Kettering**[24] 3182 3-9-7 **80**....................................... MartinHarley 7 72
(Luca Cumani) *hld up: hdwy over 4f out: rdn over 2f out: wknd ins fnl f* **13/2**[3]

4143 **6** *nk* **Paddy A (IRE)**[9] 3727 3-8-13 **72**...................................... StevieDonohoe 5 63
(Philip McBride) *broke wl: lost pl over 8f out: effrt over 1f out: wknd ins fnl f* **12/1**

-053 **7** *7* **Medalla De Oro**[8] 3752 3-8-7 **66**....................................(h) JimmyQuinn 1 43
(Peter Chapple-Hyam) *s.i.s: hdwy over 8f out: rdn over 2f out: wknd over 1f out* **16/1**

2m 5.59s (0.09) **Going Correction** +0.05s/f (Good) **7** Ran SP% **112.4**
Speed ratings (Par 101): **101,100,99,99,95 95,89**
CSF £10.93 TOTE £2.20: £1.50, £2.90; EX 11.00 Trifecta £60.00.

**Owner** K Abdullah **Bred** Juddmonte Farms Ltd **Trained** Newmarket, Suffolk

**FOCUS**
Race distance increased by 19yds. A competitive little handicap won by the progressive Baydar 12 months ago, and this year's winner also looks a nice handicapper. They didn't go fast and were bunched up the near side rail. The runner-up has been rated to his best since his 2yo Listed run last July.

## 4049 FLY LONDON SOUTHEND AIRPORT TO LYON NOVICE STKS (PLUS 10 RACE) 6f
**6:55** (6:58) (Class 4) 2-Y-O £4,528 (£1,347; £673; £336) **Stalls** High

Form RPR

2 **1** **Invincible Army (IRE)**[29] 3002 2-9-2 0................................ MartinHarley 5 94+
(James Tate) *a.p: led over 1f out: pushed clr fnl f* **8/13**[1]

**2** *5* **Tribal Quest (USA)** 2-9-2 0............................................ JamesDoyle 6 80+
(Charlie Appleby) *hld up: swtchd rt over 2f out: edgd lft over 1f out: edgd rt and r.o to go 2nd wl ins fnl f: no ch w wnr* **3/1**[2]

0 **3** *1 ½* **Tathmeen (IRE)**[29] 3002 2-9-2 0........................................ DaneO'Neill 1 73
(Richard Hannon) *trckd ldrs: racd keenly: rdn over 1f out: edgd lft ins fnl f: styd on same pce* **7/1**[3]

**4** *nk* **Rockies Spirit** 2-9-2 0.......................................................... JFEgan 7 72
(Denis Quinn) *led: rdn and hdd over 1f out: edgd rt and no ex ins fnl f* **66/1**

**5** *2 ½* **Robinson Crusoe (IRE)** 2-9-2 0....................................... SeanLevey 2 64
(Richard Hannon) *s.s: rn green early: hld up: effrt over 1f out: wknd ins fnl f* **16/1**

00 **6** *1 ¼* **Devil's Cowboy (IRE)**[13] 3591 2-8-13 0................. CallumShepherd(3) 4 64
(Charles Hills) *racd keenly in 2nd tl shkn up wl over 1f out: hmpd and wknd ins fnl f* **33/1**



The Form Book Flat, Raceform Ltd, Newbury, RG14 5SJ

7 *19* **Thunder North (IRE)** 2-9-2 0 ..... StevieDonohoe 3
(David Lanigan) *hld up: pushed along over 2f out: sn wknd* **33/1**

1m 11.8s (-0.70) **Going Correction** +0.05s/f (Good) **7** Ran SP% **112.7**
Speed ratings (Par 95): **106,99,97,96,93 91,66**
CSF £2.55 TOTE £1.60: £1.10, £2.00; EX 3.20 Trifecta £6.00.
**Owner** Saeed Manana **Bred** Rabbah Bloodstock Limited **Trained** Newmarket, Suffolk

**FOCUS**
A good pace for this novice in which the experienced form horse won comfortably.

## 4050 FLY LONDON SOUTHEND AIRPORT TO PRAGUE H'CAP 1m
**7:30** (7:33) (Class 5) (0-75,76) 3-Y-O **£3,881** (£1,155; £577; £288) **Stalls** High

Form RPR

002 **1** **Luna Bear**[42] 2580 3-9-4 **72** ..... TimmyMurphy 10 78+
(Gary Moore) *led: hdd over 6f out: chsd ldrs: nt clr run over 1f out: rdn and r.o to ld nr fin* **28/1**

0-03 **2** *1/2* **Turning Gold**[35] 2790 3-8-5 **59** ..... (b) RyanPowell 1 64
(Sir Mark Prescott Bt) *dwlt: hdwy and crossed over to ld over 6f out: rdn and hdd over 1f out: rallied to ld wl ins fnl f: hdd nr fin* **20/1**

3222 **3** *nk* **Coverham (IRE)**[21] 3296 3-8-10 **64** ..... RyanTate 8 68+
(James Eustace) *edgd rt s: hld up: pushed along over 2f out: hdwy over 1f out: rdn and r.o to go 3rd wl ins fnl f: nt rch ldrs* **10/3**[1]

400- **4** *1 1/2* **So Hoity Toity**[327] 4924 3-9-4 **75** ..... CharlieBennett(3) 9 76
(Hughie Morrison) *chsd ldrs: rdn over 2f out: styd on u.p* **20/1**

4-16 **5** *nse* **Keepup Kevin**[18] 3412 3-9-4 **72** ..... RobHornby 4 73
(Pam Sly) *hmpd s: sn prom: chsd ldr over 6f out: wnt upsides 1/2-way: rdn to ld over 1f out: hdd and unable qck wl ins fnl f* **7/2**[2]

-021 **6** *5* **Carducci**[23] 3217 3-9-8 **76** ..... SeanLevey 7 68+
(Richard Hannon) *hld up: hdwy over 2f out: sn rdn: wknd fnl f* **11/2**[3]

5530 **7** *4 1/2* **Trade Route (IRE)**[41] 2625 3-9-5 **73** ..... (p) JFEgan 3 52
(David Elsworth) *sn pushed along in rr: rdn and hung lft over 2f out: nvr nrr* **25/1**

0400 **8** *2 3/4* **Zoffany Bay (IRE)**[25] 3162 3-8-11 **68** ..... (b[1]) MarcMonaghan(3) 2 41
(George Peckham) *s.i.s: hld up: rdn over 2f out: wknd over 1f out* **25/1**

-064 **9** *1/2* **Claire's Secret**[35] 2794 3-8-11 **65** ..... DavidProbert 5 37
(Philip McBride) *s.i.s and hmpd s: hld up: rdn over 2f out: wknd over 1f out* **16/1**

6-62 **10** *9* **Casina Di Notte (IRE)**[17] 3443 3-9-7 **75** ..... (b) DanielMuscutt 11 26
(Marco Botti) *s.i.s: sn chsng ldrs: rdn and wknd over 1f out* **7/1**

1m 39.47s (-0.53) **Going Correction** +0.05s/f (Good) **10** Ran SP% **99.7**
Speed ratings (Par 99): **104,103,103,101,101 96,92,89,88,79**
CSF £315.44 CT £1309.29 TOTE £14.50: £3.20, £3.70, £1.50; EX 135.40 Trifecta £1209.10.
**Owner** Scuderia Vita Bella **Bred** Linda Sadler **Trained** Lower Beeding, W Sussex
■ Revel was withdrawn. Price at time of withdrawal was 4-1. Rule 4 applies to \n\x\x all bets - deduction 20p in the pound
■ Stewards' Enquiry : Rob Hornby four-day ban: failed to ride out for best possible finishing position (July 7-11)

**FOCUS**
A competitive 3yo handicap, though none of the last nine winners of the race managed to follow-up. They didn't go fast on the far rail and it paid to race prominently. The first five came clear. The third has been rated close to his penultimate run on good to firm.

## 4051 FLY LONDON SOUTHEND AIRPORT TO BUDAPEST FILLIES' H'CAP 7f
**8:00** (8:02) (Class 3) (0-95,90) 3-Y-O+ **£7,762** (£2,310; £1,154; £577) **Stalls** High

Form RPR

11-3 **1** **Roman Holiday (IRE)**[23] 3216 4-9-0 **76** ..... (p) HarryBentley 5 84
(Ed Vaughan) *s.i.s: racd keenly and sn prom: lost pl over 4f out: nt clr run over 2f out: hdwy and hung lft over 1f out: sn rdn: r.o to ld nr fin* **8/1**

2121 **2** *nk* **Angel Of Darkness**[21] 3307 3-8-8 **82** ..... CallumShepherd(3) 4 86+
(Charles Hills) *s.i.s: hld up: plld hrd: hdwy over 4f out: rdn to ld over 1f out: hdd nr fin* **9/2**[2]

1106 **3** *1* **Carolinae**[35] 2805 5-9-9 **85** ..... StevieDonohoe 1 89
(Charlie Fellowes) *stdd s: hld up: racd keenly: rdn over 1f out: r.o ins fnl f: edgd lft and unable qck towards fin* **6/1**[3]

6436 **4** *shd* **Childesplay**[14] 3518 6-8-11 **73** ..... GavinLerena 7 77
(Heather Main) *led at stdy pce: qcknd: hdd over 2f out: rdn and ev ch over 1f out: styd on same pce towards fin* **25/1**

21-2 **5** *2 1/4* **Panova**[28] 3031 3-8-13 **84** ..... WilliamBuick 8 79
(Sir Michael Stoute) *chsd ldrs: rdn over 2f out: ev ch over 1f out: no ex wl ins fnl f* **11/10**[1]

6-43 **6** *1 1/2* **Yeah Baby Yeah (IRE)**[20] 3314 4-9-6 **85** ..... (p) CharlieBennett(3) 3 79
(Gay Kelleway) *hld up: plld hrd: hdwy 4f out: rdn over 1f out: no ex fnl f* **14/1**

-000 **7** *3 3/4* **Island Vision (IRE)**[120] 887 3-9-5 **90** ..... JosephineGordon 2 70
(David Simcock) *hld up: plld hrd: rdn over 2f out: sn outpcd* **9/1**

620- **8** *1* **Clear Water (IRE)**[244] 7550 4-10-0 **90** ..... DavidProbert 6 71
(Michael Wigham) *prom: chsd ldr over 5f out tl led over 2f out: rdn and hdd over 1f out: wknd ins fnl f* **16/1**

1m 26.35s (0.65) **Going Correction** +0.05s/f (Good)
**WFA** 3 from 4yo+ 9lb **8** Ran SP% **117.6**
Speed ratings (Par 104): **98,97,96,96,93 92,87,86**
CSF £45.06 CT £237.00 TOTE £9.80: £2.70, £1.90, £2.10; EX 48.20 Trifecta £172.70.
**Owner** Bloomsbury Stud **Bred** Bloomsbury Stud **Trained** Newmarket, Suffolk

**FOCUS**
A good handicap featuring a couple of improving 3yo's, though they didn't go fast, and plenty were in with chance a furlong out. The form, however, looks solid enough, despite the favourite disappointing. The third has been rated to her AW form.

## 4052 FLY LONDON SOUTHEND AIRPORT TO DUBROVNIK EBFSTALLIONS.COM MAIDEN STKS (PLUS 10 RACE) 1m 2f
**8:35** (8:38) (Class 4) 3-Y-O **£5,175** (£1,540; £769) **Stalls** Centre

Form RPR

2 **1** **Yaarmen (USA)**[14] 3549 3-9-5 0 ..... DaneO'Neill 2 79
(William Haggas) *mde all: set stdy pce tl qcknd over 2f out: rdn over 1f out: edgd lft ins fnl f: styd on wl* **9/2**[2]

3 **2** *nk* **Playwriter (IRE)**[67] 1830 3-9-5 0 ..... WilliamBuick 3 78
(Charlie Appleby) *chsd wnr: ev ch fr over 2f out: rdn over 1f out: edgd lft ins fnl f: styd on* **2/1**[1]

**3** *3 1/2* **Perfect Spy** 3-8-11 0 ..... GeorgeWood(3) 5 66
(Luca Cumani) *hld up in tch: racd keenly: swtchd lft over 2f out: rdn and hung lft over 1f out: no ex ins fnl f* **8/1**[3]

2m 10.89s (5.39) **Going Correction** +0.05s/f (Good) **3** Ran SP% **62.6**
Speed ratings (Par 101): **80,79,76**
CSF £4.41 TOTE £2.20; EX 2.70 Trifecta £2.90.
**Owner** Hamdan Al Maktoum **Bred** Shadwell Farm LLC **Trained** Newmarket, Suffolk
■ Mountain Hunter was withdrawn. Price at time of withdrawal was Evs. Rule 4 applies to all bets - deduction 45p in the pound.

**FOCUS**
Race distance increased by 19yds for the maiden that was weakened by the late withdrawal of the favourite, Mountain Hunter. The level is fluid.

## 4053 FLY LONDON SOUTHEND AIRPORT TO VENICE FILLIES' H'CAP 5f
**9:05** (9:08) (Class 5) (0-70,70) 3-Y-O+ **£3,881** (£1,155; £577; £288) **Stalls** High

Form RPR

200- **1** **Sweet Zain (IRE)**[262] 7050 3-9-1 **63** ..... JFEgan 2 70
(John Butler) *sn pushed along in rr: rdn over 1f out: r.o wl ins fnl f: to ld nr fin* **20/1**

0-50 **2** *nk* **Cool Breeze (IRE)**[14] 3536 3-8-3 **51** oh2 ..... KieranO'Neill 11 57
(David Simcock) *s.i.s: hld up: hdwy over 1f out: rdn to ld wl ins fnl f: hdd nr fin* **14/1**

5231 **3** *shd* **Dandilion (IRE)**[14] 3545 4-9-3 **59** ..... (t) DavidProbert 1 67
(Alex Hales) *pushed along in rr early: swtchd rt 1/2-way: hdwy to ld over 1f out: rdn and hdd wl ins fnl f: r.o* **9/2**[2]

5321 **4** *3* **Penny Dreadful**[4] 3903 5-9-0 **63** 6ex ..... (p) RPWalsh(7) 5 60
(Scott Dixon) *led: rdn and hdd over 1f out: edgd rt and no ex ins fnl f* **11/10**[1]

-640 **5** *nk* **Racing Angel (IRE)**[9] 3729 5-9-11 **67** ..... TomQueally 9 63
(Mick Quinn) *prom: rdn over 1f out: no ex ins fnl f* **8/1**

0063 **6** *3 1/2* **Manipura**[9] 3728 4-8-9 **51** ..... (p) MartinLane 4 35
(Derek Shaw) *s.s: outpcd* **11/2**[3]

40-6 **7** *1 1/2* **Zig Zag Girl**[170] 41 3-8-11 **64** ..... DavidEgan(5) 7 40
(John Butler) *chsd ldrs: rdn over 1f out: wknd ins fnl f* **16/1**

0400 **8** *3/4* **Cherry Kool**[6] 3812 4-9-0 **63** ..... MillyNaseb(7) 10 38
(Stuart Williams) *w ldrs 2f: pushed along 2f out: wknd ins fnl f* **10/1**

3000 **9** *8* **Willow Spring**[93] 1304 5-8-2 **51** oh6 ..... JackOsborn(7) 3
(Denis Quinn) *w ldr: rdn 1/2-way: wknd over 1f out* **33/1**

59.01s (-0.09) **Going Correction** +0.05s/f (Good)
**WFA** 3 from 4yo+ 6lb **9** Ran SP% **121.6**
Speed ratings (Par 100): **102,101,101,96,96 90,88,86,74**
CSF £279.41 CT £1511.51 TOTE £21.90: £4.90, £3.20, £1.70; EX 383.30 Trifecta £2114.80.
**Owner** Asaad Al Banwan **Bred** Swettenham Stud, Carradale Ltd & T Stack **Trained** Newmarket, Suffolk

**FOCUS**
An average sprint handicap in which they went hard, suiting the closers. The first two have been rated as improving quite a bit.
T/Plt: £59.50 to a £1 stake. Pool: £56,604.72 - 694.07 winning units. T/Qpdt: £10.60 to a £1 stake. Pool: £4,668.29 - 325.21 winning units. **Colin Roberts**

# 3179 REDCAR (L-H)
### Friday, June 23

**OFFICIAL GOING: Good (good to firm in places; 8.5)**
Wind: Fresh & blustery across Weather: Cloudy

## 4054 RACINGUK.COM/FREETRIAL (S) STKS 7f
**1:50** (1:51) (Class 6) 2-Y-O **£2,897** (£855; £427) **Stalls** Centre

Form RPR

0460 **1** **Faradays Spark (IRE)**[7] 3791 2-8-11 0 ..... TonyHamilton 7 60
(Richard Fahey) *trckd ldng pair: hdwy 2f out: chal over 1f out: rdn ins fnl f: kpt on to ld nr fin* **4/1**[3]

053 **2** *1/2* **Give Em A Clump (IRE)**[4] 3918 2-8-11 0 ..... BenCurtis 4 59
(David Evans) *trckd ldng pair: hdwy and cl up over 2f out: rdn to take slt ld ent fnl f: sn drvn: hdd and no ex nr fin* **5/2**[1]

32 **3** *5* **Time For Treacle**[16] 3447 2-8-6 0 ..... CamHardie 2 40
(Ben Haslam) *wnt lft s: sn led: hdd 1/2-way: cl up: led again 2f out: rdn over 1f out: drvn and hdd ent fnl f: kpt on one pce* **11/4**[2]

050 **4** *3* **Foxxy Brown**[7] 3791 2-8-3 0 ..... SammyJoBell(3) 3 32
(Richard Fahey) *rr: pushed along 3f out: rdn 2f out: plugged on: n.d* **13/2**

0 **5** *1 1/4* **Tweeting**[24] 3179 2-8-3 0 ..... NathanEvans(3) 6 29
(John Quinn) *dwlt: t.k.h in rr: pushed along 1/2-way: rdn over 2f out: n.d* **12/1**

0 **6** *6* **Gone To Sea (IRE)**[17] 3421 2-8-6 0 ..... ConnorBeasley 5 12
(David Evans) *t.k.h: cl up: led 1/2-way: rdn along over 2f out: sn hdd & wknd* **6/1**

1m 25.2s (0.70) **Going Correction** +0.025s/f (Good) **6** Ran SP% **110.5**
Speed ratings (Par 91): **97,96,90,87,85 79**
CSF £13.94 TOTE £4.50: £1.70, £1.70; EX 17.30 Trifecta £37.00.
**Owner** Nick Bradley Racing 35 & Partner **Bred** Roundhill Stud **Trained** Musley Bank, N Yorks
■ Stewards' Enquiry : Ben Curtis two-day ban: used whip above permitted level (July 7-9)

**FOCUS**
Race distances as advertised. Naturally this is very modest form, but the time was only 3.2sec outside standard, suggesting the ground was riding quick.

## 4055 WATCH RACINGUK WITH FREE TRIAL NOW MAIDEN STKS 1m 2f 1y
**2:20** (2:24) (Class 5) 3-Y-O+ **£3,234** (£962; £481; £240) **Stalls** Low

Form RPR

3 **1** **Northwest Frontier (IRE)**[16] 3465 3-9-2 0 ..... TonyHamilton 1 74+
(Richard Fahey) *trckd ldrs: hdwy over 2f out: rdn to ld wl over 1f out: drvn and edgd rt ins fnl f: kpt on* **4/6**[1]

**2** *1 1/2* **Heron (USA)** 3-9-2 0 ..... PhillipMakin 8 71
(Hugo Palmer) *trckd ldrs: green and pushed along over 3f out: cl up and rdn 2f out: ev ch: kpt on same pce ins fnl f* **5/2**[2]

5 **3** *3/4* **Fire Leopard**[14] 3542 3-8-8 0 ..... ShelleyBirkett(3) 4 64
(David O'Meara) *trckd ldrs: hdwy 3f out: chal 2f out: sn rdn and ev ch tl drvn ins fnl f and kpt on same pce* **10/1**[3]

**4** *3/4* **Chartbuster (IRE)** 3-9-2 0 ..... JoeDoyle 10 68+
(Julie Camacho) *towards rr: hdwy on outer 3f out: rdn along 2f out: styd on wl fnl f* **16/1**

**5** *1/2* **Roddy (IRE)** 3-9-2 0 ..... AndrewMullen 3 67+
(Tom Tate) *dwlt and rr: hdwy over 4f out: chsd ldrs wl over 2f out:. sn rdn along: drvn and one pce fr over 1f out* **25/1**

**6** *2* **Broadway Dreams** 3-9-2 0 ..... BarryMcHugh 2 63
(Marjorie Fife) *dwlt and rr: hdwy into midfield 1/2-way: pushed along 3f out: rdn over 2f out: kpt on fnl f* **33/1**

0-5 **7** *5* **Zacchetto (USA)**[100] 1198 3-9-2 0 ..... JoeFanning 6 53
(Mark Johnston) *led 1f: trckd ldr: hdwy and cl up 3f out: rdn along 2f out: sn drvn and grad wknd* **14/1**

**8** *1 1/2* **Simmo's Partytrick (IRE)** 4-10-0 0 ..... SamJames 11 50
(Geoffrey Harker) *prom: led after 1f: pushed along 3f out: rdn over 2f out: hdd wl over 1f out: sn wknd* **33/1**

9 9 **Rambling Queen (IRE)**26 4-9-6 0 ..........................(t) NathanEvans(3) 5 27
(Brian Rothwell) *in tch on inner: pushed along over 3f out: sn rdn and wknd wl over 2f out* **100/1**

00-0 **10** 7 **Breton Blues**54 2183 7-10-0 42 ..........................(p) JackGarritty 7 18
(Fred Watson) *midfield: rdn along over 3f out: sn wknd* **100/1**

0-00 **11** 5 **Sai Kung Star**32 2903 3-8-6 35 .......................... LewisEdmunds(5) 9 3
(Nigel Tinkler) *in tch on outer: pushed along wl over 3f out: sn rdn and wknd* **100/1**

2m 6.82s (-0.28) **Going Correction** +0.025s/f (Good)
**WFA** 3 from 4yo+ 12lb **11 Ran SP% 122.9**
Speed ratings (Par 103): **102,100,100,99,99 97,93,92,85,79 75**
CSF £2.48 TOTE £1.70: £1.10, £1.20, £2.30; EX 3.40 Trifecta £11.50.
**Owner** Sir Robert Ogden **Bred** Sir Robert Ogden **Trained** Musley Bank, N Yorks

**FOCUS**
Not a strong maiden. The level is fluid.

## 4056 RACING UK FREE FOR A MONTH FILLIES' H'CAP 1m 2f 1y
**2:55** (2:56) (Class 4) (0-80,77) 3-Y-O+ **£5,175** (£1,540; £769; £384) **Stalls** Low

Form RPR

5-32 **1** **Maulesden May (IRE)**4 3898 4-9-6 69 .......................... PhillipMakin 1 75
(Keith Dalgleish) *trckd ldr: hdwy and cl up over 2f out: sn chal and rdn: led 11/2f out: drvn out* **5/2**3

-230 **2** 1 ¾ **Celestation**31 2929 3-9-2 77 .......................... JoeFanning 2 81
(Mark Johnston) *led: pushed along and qcknd over 3f out: jnd and rdn over 2f out: hdd and drvn 11/2f out: kpt on u.p fnl f* **7/4**1

3-05 **3** 2 ¾ **Island Flame (IRE)**20 3341 4-9-7 73 .......................... AdamMcNamara(3) 3 70
(Richard Fahey) *trckd ldng pair: hdwy over 3f out: rdn along over 2f out: drvn over 1f out: kpt on same pce* **6/1**

622 **4** 4 **Lucy's Law (IRE)**33 2854 3-8-8 69 .......................... AndrewMullen 4 59
(Tom Tate) *trckd ldng pair: hdwy over 3f out: rdn along over 2f out: sn drvn and wknd over 1f out* **9/4**2

2m 7.77s (0.67) **Going Correction** +0.025s/f (Good)
**WFA** 3 from 4yo 12lb **4 Ran SP% 110.0**
Speed ratings (Par 102): **98,96,94,91**
CSF £7.34 TOTE £3.10; EX 6.10 Trifecta £15.30.
**Owner** The County Set (Two) **Bred** Yeomanstown Stud **Trained** Carluke, S Lanarks

**FOCUS**
This wasn't truly run and it developed into a sprint over the last three furlongs or so. It was nearly a second slower than the maiden. The first two have been rated to form.

## 4057 RACING UK STRAIGHT MILE SERIES H'CAP (QUALIFIER) 7f 219y
**3:30** (3:30) (Class 3) (0-90,89) 3-Y-O+ **£7,762** (£2,310; £1,154; £577) **Stalls** Centre

Form RPR

4-00 **1** **Mutahaady (IRE)**13 3592 3-8-12 86 .......................... JordanVaughan(3) 5 90
(K R Burke) *trckd ldr: swtchd rt and hdwy over 1f out: rdn to chal jst ins fnl f: drvn and kpt on wl to ld towards fin* **8/1**3

100- **2** ½ **Ginger Jack**252 7316 10-9-9 89 .......................... LewisEdmunds(5) 6 94
(Jo Hughes) *set stdy pce: qcknd wl over 2f out: rdn and qcknd over 1f out: drvn ins fnl f: hdd towards fin* **11/1**

0533 **3** 2 ½ **Abushamah (IRE)**8 3743 6-8-13 74 ..........................(p) JackGarritty 3 73
(Ruth Carr) *t.k.h: hld up in rr: hdwy over 1f out: rdn ent fnl f: kpt on same pce* **7/4**2

2-03 **4** 1 **Town Charter (USA)**13 3592 3-9-2 87 .......................... JoeFanning 2 82
(Mark Johnston) *t.k.h early: trckd ldrs: hdwy over 2f out: rdn along wl over 1f out: drvn and kpt on same pce fnl f* **5/4**1

16-0 **5** shd **Maldonado (FR)**13 3588 3-8-6 80 .......................... NathanEvans(3) 1 75
(Michael Easterby) *t.k.h: chsd ldr: pushed along over 2f out: rdn wl over 1f out: drvn and kpt on same pce fnl f* **9/1**

1m 37.05s (0.45) **Going Correction** +0.025s/f (Good)
**WFA** 3 from 4yo+ 10lb **5 Ran SP% 110.3**
Speed ratings (Par 107): **98,97,95,94,93**
CSF £74.65 TOTE £8.10: £3.20, £3.50; EX 34.40 Trifecta £174.70.
**Owner** Tim Dykes, Mrs G Buchanan & E Burke **Bred** Kevin Blake **Trained** Middleham Moor, N Yorks

**FOCUS**
Not a strong handicap for the class. It wasn't truly run and the first two raced nearer to the stands' side than the others. The winner has been rated back to his 2yo best.

## 4058 WIN A VIP DAY @ REDCARRACING.CO.UK H'CAP 7f
**4:05** (4:05) (Class 5) (0-70,75) 3-Y-O **£3,234** (£962; £481; £240) **Stalls** Centre

Form RPR

-104 **1** **Hajjam**17 3434 3-9-10 72 ..........................(h) PhillipMakin 8 77
(David O'Meara) *hld up in rr: hdwy 2f out: chsd ldrs ent fnl f: sn rdn and styd on wl to ld last 50 yds* **3/1**2

64-1 **2** ½ **Call Me Grumpy (IRE)**7 3784 3-9-6 75 6ex .......................... CameronNoble(7) 5 79
(Roger Varian) *trckd ldrs: hdwy to ld wl over 1f out: rdn and edgd lft ins fnl f: hdd and no ex last 50 yds* **4/7**1

1-06 **3** 1 **Kilbaha Lady (IRE)**13 3561 3-8-10 63 .......................... LewisEdmunds(5) 10 64
(Nigel Tinkler) *hld up in rr: hdwy on outer 2f out: rdn to chse ldrs and hung lft over 1f out: sn drvn and kpt on* **16/1**

-000 **4** 1 ½ **Melaniemillie**14 3525 3-8-2 50 .......................... JoeDoyle 4 47
(Ruth Carr) *prom: pushed along 2f out: rdn over 1f out: drvn and kpt on same pce fnl f* **25/1**

36-0 **5** 1 **Harvest Moon**18 3403 3-9-0 62 .......................... JackGarritty 1 56
(Richard Fahey) *led: rdn along over 2f out: hdd wl over 1f out: sn drvn and wknd* **20/1**

0-00 **6** 3 **Nyx**32 2897 3-8-2 50 oh5 ..........................(v1) CamHardie 6 36
(Richard Guest) *t.k.h: in tch: hdwy 1/2-way: rdn along over 2f out: sn one pce* **100/1**

4-00 **7** hd **Allux Boy (IRE)**21 3296 3-9-5 67 .......................... AndrewMullen 7 53
(Nigel Tinkler) *trckd ldr: hdwy and cl up 3f out: rdn along over 2f out: drvn wl over 1f out: sn wknd* **10/1**3

40-0 **8** 7 **Flash Of White**51 2304 3-9-7 69 .......................... ConnorBeasley 3 36
(Bryan Smart) *prom on outer: pushed along over 2f out: sn rdn and wknd* **11/1**

1m 23.8s (-0.70) **Going Correction** +0.025s/f (Good) **8 Ran SP% 121.6**
Speed ratings (Par 99): **105,104,103,101,100 97,96,88**
CSF £5.32 CT £23.29 TOTE £4.50: £1.30, £1.02, £3.80; EX 6.40 Trifecta £32.90.
**Owner** Sheikh Abdullah Almalek Alsabah **Bred** Mrs Janis Macpherson **Trained** Upper Helmsley, N Yorks

**FOCUS**
The first two dominated the market and fought out the finish, ending up on the far side. The third has been rated to form.

## 4059 START YOUR RACINGUK FREE TRIAL NOW H'CAP 7f 219y
**4:45** (4:46) (Class 5) (0-70,71) 4-Y-O+ **£3,234** (£962; £481; £240) **Stalls** Centre

Form RPR

5230 **1** **Kicking The Can (IRE)**93 1312 6-8-4 57 ow2 .......................... LewisEdmunds(5) 6 63
(David Thompson) *trckd ldrs: hdwy on outer over 2f out: rdn to ld 11/2f out: drvn and edgd lft ins fnl f: jst hld on* **10/3**2

000- **2** nse **Connemera Queen**281 6502 4-9-3 65 .......................... BarryMcHugh 1 70
(Chris Grant) *trckd ldrs: hdwy and cl up 3f out: led over 2f out: rdn and hdd 11/2f out: drvn and rallied ins fnl f: sn ev ch: jst hld* **20/1**

2335 **3** 1 ¾ **Cabal**4 3912 10-9-0 62 ..........................(v) SamJames 4 63
(Geoffrey Harker) *hld up in rr: hdwy over 2f out: swtchd lft and chsd ldng pair wl over 1f out: drvn and no imp fnl f* **2/1**1

00 **4** 4 **Nonno Giulio (IRE)**28 3049 6-9-6 71 .......................... JoshDoyle(3) 5 63
(Tony Coyle) *sn led: hdd over 5f out: cl up: rdn along to dispute ld over 2f out: drvn over 1f out: grad wknd* **5/1**

400 **5** 5 **Drago (IRE)**27 3065 5-9-0 69 ..........................(h) PatrickVaughan(7) 2 49
(David O'Meara) *trckd ldrs: hdwy wl over 2f out: rdn wl over 1f out: sn wknd* **9/2**3

0024 **6** 3 ¾ **Maureb (IRE)**14 3526 5-9-3 65 ..........................(p) DuranFentiman 3 37
(Tony Coyle) *t.k.h: trckd ldrs: effrt and hdwy wl over 2f out: sn rdn and btn* **5/1**

0/0- **7** 15 **Excellent Addition (IRE)**472 867 7-8-2 50 oh1 ..........(t) AndrewMullen 7
(Lee James) *prom: led over 5f out: rdn along 3f out: hdd over 2f out: sn wknd* **100/1**

1m 36.43s (-0.17) **Going Correction** +0.025s/f (Good) **7 Ran SP% 113.7**
Speed ratings (Par 103): **101,100,99,95,90 86,71**
CSF £60.58 TOTE £4.60: £2.40, £7.90; EX 76.30 Trifecta £212.20.
**Owner** D Mawer **Bred** William J M Morrissey **Trained** Bolam, Co Durham

**FOCUS**
This was 0.62sec quicker than the earlier Class 3 handicap. The first two raced towards the stands' side before the winner edged left late on. The runner-up has been rated to the better view of her surprise maiden win here last year.

## 4060 UNBOX RACING UK FOR FREE NOW MAIDEN H'CAP 5f
**5:20** (5:20) (Class 5) (0-70,70) 3-Y-O+ **£3,234** (£962; £481; £240) **Stalls** Centre

Form RPR

0223 **1** **Flawlessly (FR)**25 3152 3-8-12 63 .......................... NathanEvans(3) 1 66
(James Bethell) *qckly away: mde all: rdn and hung lft to far rail over 1f out: kpt on wl towards fin* **11/8**1

4-53 **2** ½ **Muatadel**14 3524 4-10-0 70 .......................... ConnorBeasley 2 73
(Roger Fell) *chsd ldrs: rdn wl over 1f out: drvn and styd on strly fnl f* **5/2**2

300- **3** nk **Liberatum**230 7820 3-9-3 65 .......................... JackGarritty 3 65
(Ruth Carr) *t.k.h: trckd wnr: hdwy to chal over 1f out: sn rdn and edgd lft: drvn ins fnl f: no ex towards fin* **16/1**

0003 **4** 2 ½ **Vaux (IRE)**38 2699 3-8-4 52 .......................... AndrewMullen 7 43
(Ben Haslam) *hld up: hdwy 2f out and sn rdn: drvn over 1f out and no imp* **20/1**

3032 **5** 3 ¼ **Dundunah (USA)**23 3202 3-9-6 68 ..........................(t) PhillipMakin 5 47
(David O'Meara) *wnt lft s: trckd ldng pair: effrt 2f out and sn rdn: drvn over 1f out: sn wknd* **3/1**3

0-00 **6** 4 **By The Law**24 3181 4-9-5 61 ..........................(b1) CamHardie 4 28
(Tim Easterby) *sltly hmpd s: a rr* **12/1**

57.83s (-0.77) **Going Correction** +0.025s/f (Good)
**WFA** 3 from 4yo 6lb **6 Ran SP% 114.0**
Speed ratings (Par 103): **107,106,105,101,96 90**
CSF £5.21 TOTE £2.50: £1.20, £1.60; EX 4.50 Trifecta £25.60.
**Owner** John Dance **Bred** Eric Parker **Trained** Middleham Moor, N Yorks

**FOCUS**
Moderate handicap form. This time the principals ended up near the far fence. The winner has been rated back to her early 2yo best, and the third to his 2yo maiden form.
T/Plt: £473.00 to a £1 stake. Pool: £28,674.00 - 60.61 winning units. T/Qpdt: £276.50 to a £1 stake. Pool: £1,576.00 - 5.70 winning units. **Joe Rowntree**

4061 - 4067a (Foreign Racing) - See Raceform Interactive

# 4028 ASCOT (R-H)
### Saturday, June 24

**OFFICIAL GOING: Good to firm (firm in places on straight course; stand side 9.8, centre 9.0, far side 9.6, round 8.5)**
Wind: Almost nil Weather: Cloudy

## 4068 CHESHAM STKS (LISTED RACE) 7f
**2:30** (2:32) (Class 1) 2-Y-O
**£45,368** (£17,200; £8,608; £4,288; £2,152; £1,080) **Stalls** Centre

Form RPR

**1** **September (IRE)**16 3508 2-8-12 0 .......................... RyanMoore 6 101+
(A P O'Brien, Ire) *athletic: dwlt and bmpd leaving stalls: hld up towards rr: hdwy into midfield 1/2-way: effrt to go 3rd 2f out: sn chsng clr ldr and edging rt: qcknd to ld ins fnl f: styd on strly and sn clr: quite impressive* **11/8**1

1 **2** 2 ¼ **Nyaleti (IRE)**6 3868 2-8-12 0 .......................... JFEgan 2 95
(Mark Johnston) *str: lw: led: set str gallop and sn clr: edgd lft u.p over 1f out: hdd ins fnl f: no ex and sn outpcd by wnr: wknd towards fin but hld on to 2nd* **10/1**3

1 **3** shd **Masar (IRE)**30 3002 2-9-3 0 .......................... WilliamBuick 4 100
(Charlie Appleby) *lw: chsd clr ldr: effrt fnl 2f: 3rd and no imp over 1f out: carried rt 1f out and kpt on same pce ins fnl f: pressing for 2nd towards fin* **3/1**2

3 **4** 3 ½ **Bartholomeu Dias**30 3002 2-9-3 0 .......................... JimCrowley 1 91
(Charles Hills) *niggled along towards rr: sme hdwy over 1f out: 7th 1f out: styd on to pass btn horses ins fnl f and gng on at fin: nvr trbld ldrs* **40/1**

41 **5** 1 ¼ **Elysium Dream**33 2905 2-8-12 0 .......................... SeanLevey 5 83
(Richard Hannon) *str: lw: wnt lft s: chsd ldrs: rdn ent fnl 2f: 4th and outpcd over 1f out: wknd ins fnl f* **50/1**

23 **6** ½ **Bustam (IRE)**21 3339 2-9-3 0 ..........................(h) GregoryBenoist 3 86
(John Quinn) *lengthy: stdd s: t.k.h: hld up in tch in midfield: effrt over 2f out: sn outpcd u.p: wl hld but kpt on ins fnl f* **100/1**

155 **7** ¾ **Gold Town**28 3098 2-9-3 0 ..........................(p) JamesDoyle 7 84
(Charlie Appleby) *cmpt: chsd ldrs: rdn and unable qck whn edgd rt and impeded jst over 2f out: outpcd and wl hld over 1f out: kpt on same pce fnl f* **16/1**

3 **8** *2 ¾* **We Are The World**[33] 2896 2-9-3 0 ................................ OisinMurphy 8 77
(Archie Watson) *cmpt: chsd ldrs: rdn 3f out: sn lost pl and btn 2f out: wknd over 1f out* **50/1**

2 **9** *1* **Hey Gaman**[25] 3164 2-9-3 0 ........................................ AndreaAtzeni 15 75+
(James Tate) *str: t.k.h: hld up towards rr: swtchd rt over 2f out: no hdwy u.p wl over 1f out: wknd* **14/1**

3 **10** *3 ¾* **Match Maker (IRE)**[25] 3164 2-9-3 0 ..................(t[1]) SeamieHeffernan 14 65+
(Simon Crisford) *str: lw: hld up in tch in midfield: short of room: lost pl and dropped to rr 1/2-way: bhd and hung rt 2f out: no ch but plugged on to pass wl btn rivals fnl f* **12/1**

21 **11** *2 ¼* **Westerland**[25] 3164 2-9-3 0 ........................................ PatSmullen 13 59+
(John Gosden) *str: wl in tch in midfield: rdn 3f out: sn struggling and lost pl: wknd and bhd over 1f out* **10/1**[3]

2 **12** *2 ½* **Highlight Reel (IRE)**[23] 3245 2-9-3 0 .......................... JamieSpencer 10 52+
(Michael Bell) *unf: stdd s and swtchd rt after s: hld up in detached last: clsd and swtchd rt over 2f out: sn rdn and no prog: wl btn over 1f out: wknd fnl f* **25/1**

1 **13** *1 ½* **Optimum Time (IRE)**[26] 3156 2-9-3 0 ....................... CharlesBishop 12 49+
(Eve Johnson Houghton) *unf: scope: lw: stdd and swtchd rt after s: hld up in midfield: rdn and lost pl over 2f out: wknd u.p wl over 1f out* **25/1**

51 **14** *5* **Di Fede (IRE)**[31] 2958 2-8-12 0 .............................. RichardKingscote 9 31
(Ralph Beckett) *w'like: lengthy: chsd ldrs: rdn and lost pl over 2f out: wknd and bhd over 1f out* **100/1**

**15** *nk* **Abandon Ship (IRE)** 2-9-3 0 .......................................... AdamKirby 16 35
(Paul Cole) *tall: a towards rr: rdn 1/2-way: sn struggling: bhd 2f out* **33/1**

1m 26.7s (-0.90) **Going Correction** 0.0s/f (Good) **15** Ran SP% **124.5**
Speed ratings (Par 101): **105,102,102,98,96 96,95,92,91,86 84,81,79,74,73**
CSF £16.19 CT £40.32 TOTE £2.20: £1.20, £3.20, £1.50; EX 19.80 Trifecta £65.50.
**Owner** Mrs John Magnier & Michael Tabor & Derrick Smith **Bred** Orpendale And Chelston **Trained** Cashel, Co Tipperary

**FOCUS**
The rail that had been in place on the round course for the previous three days was removed, providing fresh ground from about 9f out to the Home straight. Therefore the rail was at its innermost position and race distances were as advertised. Strong Listed form, with the first three clear and a top-class prospect getting on top of what is clearly a very smart filly late on. They went a fast pace, ensuring no hiding place.

## 4069 WOLFERTON H'CAP (LISTED RACE) 1m 1f 212y

**3:05** (3:08) (Class 1) (0-110,109) 4-Y-O+

**£45,368** (£17,200; £8,608; £4,288; £2,152; £1,080) **Stalls** Low

Form RPR

-150 **1** **Snoano**[34] 2855 5-9-0 **102** .................................................. DavidAllan 5 110
(Tim Easterby) *hld up in midfield: nt clr run and hdwy over 2f out: sn swtchd lft: gd run to ld 1f out: hld on gamely nr fin* **25/1**

0400 **2** *nk* **Majeed**[14] 3597 7-8-12 **100** ........................................... JamieSpencer 7 107
(David Simcock) *slowly away: towards rr: hdwy over 1f out: sn trcking ldng bunch and briefly waited for run: r.o to take 2nd fnl 75yds: fin strly* **25/1**

6-42 **3** *1* **Kidmenever (IRE)**[121] 888 4-9-2 **104** ............................ WilliamBuick 10 109
(Charlie Appleby) *lw: in tch: tk clsr order over 3f out: chalng 4 wd over 2f out: stl ev ch 1f out: nt pce of wnr fnl 75yds: no ex nr fin* **6/1**[2]

200- **4** *½* **Maverick Wave (USA)**[224] 7934 6-9-0 **102** ...................... JamesDoyle 2 106
(John Gosden) *lw: led: rdn over 2f out: hdd 1f out: stl there ins fnl f: styd on same pce fnl 75yds* **20/1**

546- **5** *nk* **Ayrad (IRE)**[238] 7700 6-9-7 **109** ..................................... RyanMoore 14 112
(Roger Charlton) *midfield: effrt on outer over 2f out: prog ins fnl f: styd on towards fin: nt quite rch ldrs* **16/1**

210- **6** *nk* **Scarlet Dragon**[177] 8573 4-9-7 **109** ..........................(h) TomMarquand 11 111
(Eve Johnson Houghton) *hld up: hdwy on outer 2f out: prog ins fnl f: styd on over 1f out: one pce nr fin* **12/1**

0035 **7** *hd* **Restorer**[28] 3072 5-9-0 **102** ............................................ MartinDwyer 4 104
(William Muir) *racd keenly: in tch: nt clr run jst over 2f out: rdn over 1f out and plld to the lft: styd on u.p ins fnl f: nt pce to mount serious chal* **20/1**

0-50 **8** *nk* **Muntazah**[42] 2604 4-9-3 **105** ......................................(p[1]) DavidProbert 6 106
(Owen Burrows) *midfield: hdwy 3f out: nt clr run and swtchd lft over 2f out: chsd ldrs over 1f out: styd on same pce fnl 100yds* **16/1**

6503 **9** *nk* **Dragon Mall (USA)**[24] 3218 4-8-13 **101** ................(h) JosephineGordon 1 102
(David Simcock) *completely missed break: rdn along and looking reluctant: bhd: detached for 3f: rdn over 2f out: nt clr run over 1f out: r.o fnl 100yds: nt rch ldrs* **20/1**

2/60 **10** *1 ¼* **Tumbaga (USA)**[133] 698 6-8-12 **100** ....................... SilvestreDeSousa 12 98
(Saeed bin Suroor) *swtg: chsd ldr: rdn and chalng over 2f out: stl ev ch 1f out: fdd and no ex fnl 50yds* **16/1**

13-3 **11** *nk* **Central Square (IRE)**[49] 2396 5-9-5 **107** ...................(b) AndreaAtzeni 13 105
(Roger Varian) *in rr: rdn along early: rdn over 2f out: styd on u.p ins fnl f: prog whn n.m.r fnl 75yds: coasted home after: unable to trble ldrs* **7/1**[3]

1424 **12** *hd* **Elbereth**[22] 3299 6-9-5 **107** .......................................... OisinMurphy 16 104
(Andrew Balding) *racd keenly: trckd ldrs: chalng over 2f out: rdn over 1f out: keeping on same pce u.p whn n.m.r and hmpd fnl 75yds: no ex after* **8/1**

11-1 **13** *¾* **Khairaat (IRE)**[44] 2552 4-9-2 **104** ..................................... JimCrowley 3 100
(Sir Michael Stoute) *lw: racd keenly: trckd ldrs: nt clr run and swtchd lft jst over 2f out: unable qck over 1f out: one pce ins fnl f: nt pce to chal* **3/1**[1]

/0-3 **14** *hd* **Allez Henri (IRE)**[32] 6-9-0 **102** ..........................(p) AurelienLemaitre 8 97
(D & P Prod'Homme, France) *midfield: rdn over 2f out: keeping on whn n.m.r and snatched up ins fnl 75yds: nt trble ldrs* **50/1**

0021 **15** *6* **Mythical Madness**[9] 3743 6-8-13 **101** ......................(v) DanielTudhope 15 84
(David O'Meara) *hld up: rdn over 2f out: sme hdwy over 1f out: no imp and wl btn fnl f* **14/1**

20-0 **16** *2 ½* **Pacify**[63] 1960 5-8-12 **100** ........................................... PatSmullen 9 78
(Ralph Beckett) *lw: midfield: n.m.r and checked after 2f: hdwy 3f out: rdn to chse ldrs over 2f out: wknd 1f out* **8/1**

2m 4.94s (-2.46) **Going Correction** +0.10s/f (Good) **16** Ran SP% **130.0**
Speed ratings (Par 111): **113,112,111,111,111 111,110,110,110,109 109,109,108,108,103 101**
CSF £546.75 CT £4221.67 TOTE £38.00: £6.40, £5.70, £1.90, £4.60; EX 1214.40 Trifecta £27064.70 Part won..
**Owner** M J Macleod **Bred** Minster Stud **Trained** Great Habton, N Yorks

**FOCUS**
Another open-looking edition of this classy handicap. They were strung out early due to a decent pace and it proved a real test of the distance. The form makes sense with the runner-up rated close to his best.

## 4070 HARDWICKE STKS (GROUP 2) 1m 3f 211y

**3:40** (3:42) (Class 1) 4-Y-O+

**£127,597** (£48,375; £24,210; £12,060; £6,052; £3,037) **Stalls** Low

Form RPR

U5-6 **1** **Idaho (IRE)**[22] 3299 4-9-1 117 .................................. SeamieHeffernan 7 119
(A P O'Brien, Ire) *swtg: trckd ldng quartet: effrt to chse ldrs 2f out: rdn to press ldrs 1f out: led ins fnl f: r.o wl* **9/2**[2]

12-3 **2** *½* **Barsanti (IRE)**[28] 3072 5-9-1 108 ............................... AndreaAtzeni 14 118
(Roger Varian) *lw: hld up in last quartet: effrt whn pushed lft over 2f out: hdwy u.p to go 6th 1f out: r.o wl to chse wnr wl ins fnl f: clsng towards fin: nvr quite getting on terms* **20/1**

-126 **3** *1 ¼* **Chemical Charge (IRE)**[35] 2822 5-9-1 111 .................. OisinMurphy 12 116
(Ralph Beckett) *stdd after s: hld up in last quartet: swtchd rt and effrt on inner over 2f out: hdwy to chse ldrs but nt clr run ent fnl f: swtchd lft jst ins fnl f: r.o wl to go 3rd wl ins fnl f* **25/1**

22-1 **4** *1 ½* **Dartmouth**[36] 2803 5-9-1 118 ........................................... RyanMoore 4 114
(Sir Michael Stoute) *t.k.h early: chsd ldrs tl wnt 2nd after 2f: upsides over 2f out: drvn to ld over 1f out: hdd ins fnl f: no ex: outpcd and lost 2 pls wl ins fnl f* **9/4**[1]

420- **5** *nk* **Wings of Desire**[311] 5558 4-9-1 118 .......................... WilliamBuick 2 113
(John Gosden) *chsd ldr for 2f: styd trcking ldrs: effrt and cl 4th 2f out: stl chsng ldrs whn nt clr run ent fnl f: swtchd lft jst ins fnl f: kpt on but nvr getting on terms w ldrs after* **11/2**[3]

1-61 **6** *½* **Dal Harraild**[28] 3090 4-9-1 111 ........................................ PatCosgrave 6 113
(William Haggas) *led: jnd over 2f out: drvn and hdd over 1f out: no ex u.p jst ins fnl f: outpcd fnl 100yds* **13/2**

51-1 **7** *4* **Western Hymn**[43] 2571 6-9-1 111 ................................(p) JamesDoyle 3 106
(John Gosden) *hld up in tch in midfield: nt clrest of runs and swtchd lft over 2f out: no imp and edgd rt over 1f out: wl hld and kpt on same pce ins fnl f: eased towards fin* **12/1**

13-5 **8** *1 ¼* **Across The Stars (IRE)**[35] 2822 4-9-1 113 ................... OlivierPeslier 9 104
(Sir Michael Stoute) *stdd s: t.k.h: hld up in last quartet: effrt whn bmpd and pushed lft over 2f out: no imp over 1f out: wl hld and edgd rt ins fnl f* **16/1**

-310 **9** *1 ½* **Muntahaa (IRE)**[36] 2803 4-9-1 113 ................................... JimCrowley 1 102
(John Gosden) *hld up in tch in midfield: effrt ent fnl 2f: no imp u.p and btn over 1f out: wknd ins fnl f* **14/1**

50-4 **10** *1 ¾* **Stellar Mass (IRE)**[76] 1654 4-9-1 112 ........................... KevinManning 8 99
(J S Bolger, Ire) *w'like: t.k.h: chsd ldrs: 3rd and rdn 3f out: lost pl u.p jst over 2f out: wknd fnl f* **40/1**

1140 **11** *1 ½* **Prize Money**[22] 3299 4-9-1 115 ........................................ PatSmullen 11 97
(Saeed bin Suroor) *t.k.h: hld up in midfield: effrt 2f out: hrd drvn and no imp over 1f out: wknd ins fnl f* **10/1**

10-6 **12** *hd* **Arthenus**[57] 2127 5-9-1 108 .......................................(p) TomQueally 5 96
(James Fanshawe) *niggled along at times: a in rr: effrt over 2f out: no imp and wl btn whn edgd rt over 1f out* **66/1**

2m 28.94s (-3.56) **Going Correction** +0.10s/f (Good) **12** Ran SP% **119.5**
Speed ratings (Par 115): **115,114,113,112,112 112,109,108,107,106 105,105**
CSF £96.69 CT £2038.10 TOTE £5.70: £1.70, £5.80, £6.80; EX 116.20 Trifecta £1600.40.
**Owner** Michael Tabor & Derrick Smith & Mrs John Magnier **Bred** Hveger Syndicate **Trained** Cashel, Co Tipperary

**FOCUS**
This looked a good, competitive race beforehand and it was the horse with the most potential who came out on top, receiving an excellent ride from Seamie Heffernan. They didn't go overly fast early, with the market leaders all prominent, yet two of the outsiders managed to come from off the pace to fill the places. The winner has been rated back to something like his best, with the third in line with the better view of his Newbury form.

## 4071 DIAMOND JUBILEE STKS (GROUP 1) (BRITISH CHAMPIONS SERIES) 6f

**4:20** (4:21) (Class 1) 4-Y-O+

**£340,260** (£129,000; £64,560; £32,160; £16,140; £8,100) **Stalls** Centre

Form RPR

21-5 **1** **The Tin Man**[38] 2737 5-9-3 117 ...................................... TomQueally 3 120
(James Fanshawe) *n.m.r at s: hld up in midfield: nt clr run and hdwy 2f out: swtchd rt over 1f out: str run to ld fnl 150yds: hung lft: r.o wl* **9/2**[2]

0-21 **2** *nk* **Tasleet**[38] 2737 4-9-3 116 ...........................................(p) JimCrowley 12 119
(William Haggas) *hld up: rdn and hdwy over 1f out: edgd rt and str chal wl ins fnl f: running on and upsides whn bmpd towards fin: jst hld* **7/1**[3]

16-0 **3** *¾* **Limato (IRE)**[91] 1376 5-9-3 122 ...................................... RyanMoore 15 117
(Henry Candy) *in midfield: hdwy over 2f out: r.o and str chal ins fnl f: stl ev ch but possibly jst hld whn n.m.r and hmpd towards fin* **2/1**[1]

416- **4** *1 ¼* **Librisa Breeze**[252] 7350 5-9-3 113 ............................. RobertWinston 10 113
(Dean Ivory) *stdd s: hld up in midfield: nt clr run over 2f out and over 1f out whn bmpd: sn swtchd lft: r.o ins fnl f: fin wl* **11/1**

-032 **5** *¾* **Finsbury Square (IRE)**[20] 3370 5-9-3 106 ..................(b) OlivierPeslier 7 110
(F Chappet, France) *racd keenly: trckd ldrs: effrt 2f out: edgd rt over 1f out and ins fnl f: kpt on: nt pce to chal* **40/1**

0416 **6** *½* **Tupi (IRE)**[38] 2737 5-9-3 108 ............................................ SeanLevey 1 109
(Richard Hannon) *midfield: effrt whn n.m.r and bmpd over 1f out: r.o ins fnl f: gng on at fin* **66/1**

3-03 **7** *nse* **Suedois (FR)**[28] 3099 6-9-3 114 ...............................(v[1]) DanielTudhope 9 109
(David O'Meara) *prom travelling wl: rdn over 1f out: ev ch ins fnl f: styd on same pce fnl 100yds* **25/1**

11-6 **8** *½* **Aclaim (IRE)**[35] 2825 4-9-3 114 ...................................... JamieSpencer 11 107
(Martyn Meade) *hld up in midfield: nt clr run over 2f out: nt clr run and swtchd lft over 1f out: styd on ins fnl f: edgd lft clsng stages: nt rch ldrs* **25/1**

5/1- **9** *1* **Al Jazi (IRE)**[60] 2075 4-9-0 108 ................................... GregoryBenoist 16 101
(F Rohaut, France) *hld up in rr: rdn over 2f out: swtchd lft over 1f out w plenty to do: styd on ins fnl f: unable to trble ldrs* **33/1**

0-45 **10** *nk* **Kachy**[28] 3079 4-9-3 109 ...................................(t[1]) RichardKingscote 8 103
(Tom Dascombe) *led: jinked lft under 4f out: rdn over 1f out: hdd fnl 150yds: no ex* **33/1**

1-31 **11** *shd* **The Right Man**[91] 1376 5-9-3 116 ................... Francois-XavierBertras 2 103
(D Guillemin, France) *in tch: rdn and outpcd whn n.m.r and hmpd over 1f out: keeping on whn swtchd rt fnl 100yds: no imp after* **14/1**

2 **12** *6* **Long On Value (USA)**[91] 1376 6-9-3 115 .......................(t) JoelRosario 14 83
(William Mott, U.S.A) *ponied to s: hld up: rdn 2f out: no imp: outpcd over 1f out* **14/1**

1423 **13** *hd* **Comicas (USA)**[38] 2737 4-9-3 113..............................(b) WilliamBuick 6 83
(Charlie Appleby) *chsd ldr tl over 3f out: hung rt over 2f out: wknd over 1f out* **33/1**

0-02 **14** *shd* **Dancing Star**[33] 2907 4-9-0 108.............................. DavidProbert 5 79
(Andrew Balding) *trckd ldrs: rdn whn n.m.r and hmpd jst over 2f out: lost pl bef tk false step shortly afterwards: wknd over 1f out* **25/1**

31-3 **15** *4 ½* **Windfast (IRE)**[65] 1903 6-9-3 109.............................. SilvestreDeSousa 4 68
(Brian Meehan) *prom: rdn and outpcd over 2f out: wl btn fnl f* **66/1**

-045 **16** *12* **Mobsta (IRE)**[28] 3099 5-9-3 106..............................(v[1]) PatSmullen 19 30
(Mick Channon) *in rr: pushed along and outpcd over 2f out: nvr a threat* **100/1**

11-4 **17** *1 ½* **Kassia (IRE)**[65] 1903 4-9-0 100.............................. GrahamLee 13 22
(Mick Channon) *hld up: rdn over 2f out: wknd over 1f out* **100/1**

00-2 **18** *4 ½* **Magical Memory (IRE)**[38] 2737 5-9-3 114.............................. JamesDoyle 18 10
(Charles Hills) *hld up: rdn and hdwy over 2f out: no imp on ldrs: wknd over 1f out* **8/1**

0-00 **U** **Growl**[14] 3587 5-9-3 109..............................(p) PaulHanagan 17
(Richard Fahey) *rrd s and uns rdr in sing stalls* **40/1**

1m 12.02s (-2.48) **Going Correction** 0.0s/f (Good) **19** Ran SP% **127.0**
Speed ratings (Par 117): **116,115,114,112,111 111,111,110,109,108 108,100,100,100,94 78,76,70,**
CSF £32.96 CT £87.20 TOTE £5.20: £1.90, £2.80, £1.50; EX 42.20 Trifecta £176.30.

**Owner** Fred Archer Racing - Ormonde **Bred** Mrs Elizabeth Grundy **Trained** Newmarket, Suffolk

**FOCUS**

There was a searching pace on towards the far side in this year's Diamond Jubilee. The right horse came to the fore in a tight finish and it's top sprinting form. A small pb from the winner, with the fourth close to form. The sixth helps set the standard.

## 4072 WOKINGHAM STKS (HERITAGE H'CAP) 6f

**5:00** (5:04) (Class 2) (0-110,110) 3-Y-0+

**£108,937** (£32,620; £16,310; £8,155; £4,077; £2,047) **Stalls** Centre

Form RPR

304 **1** **Out Do**[14] 3593 8-8-13 **99**..............................(v) DanielTudhope 1 109
(David O'Meara) *racd far side: hld up in tch in midfield: clsd to press ldrs and travelling wl 2f out: rdn and qcknd to ld 1f out: kpt on u.p: rdn out: 1st of 14 in gp* **25/1**

2444 **2** *½* **Steady Pace**[121] 892 4-9-4 **104**.............................. JosephineGordon 6 112
(Saeed bin Suroor) *racd far side: hld up towards rr: hdwy jst over 2f out: chsng ldrs and forced to switch lft jst over 1f out: hdwy u.p ins fnl f: r.o to go 2nd nr fin: nvr quite getting to wnr: 2nd of 14 in gp* **16/1**

53-6 **3** *nk* **Projection**[48] 2433 4-9-0 **103**.............................. KieranShoemark(3) 28 110+
(Roger Charlton) *lw: taken down early: racd stands side: t.k.h: hld up in tch in midfield: clsd to join ldrs and travelling wl 2f out: rdn to ld gp and ev ch over 1f out: kpt on wl u.p ins fnl f: 1st of 13 in gp* **15/2**[2]

-403 **4** *nk* **Polybius**[133] 696 6-9-1 **101**.............................. OisinMurphy 31 107+
(David Simcock) *racd stands side: stdd s: hld up towards rr: clsd 2f out: rdn and hdwy over 1f out: chalng gp ldrs and pressing overall ldrs 1f out: kpt on u.p ins fnl f: 2nd of 13 in gp* **33/1**

22-6 **5** *½* **Danzeno**[28] 3089 6-9-1 **104**.............................. AlistairRawlinson(3) 16 108
(Michael Appleby) *lw: racd far side: wl in tch in midfield: effrt to chal 2f out: drvn and led overall over 1f out: hdd 1f out: styd on same pce ins fnl f: 3rd of 14 in gp* **16/1**

2145 **6** *¾* **Edward Lewis**[21] 3321 4-8-12 **101**.............................. JoshDoyle(3) 7 103
(David O'Meara) *racd far side: hld up in rr: clsd 2f out: nt clr run and swtchd lft over 1f out: hdwy u.p ins fnl f: kpt on fnl 100yds: nvr threatening ldrs: 4th of 14 in gp* **14/1**

0032 **7** *hd* **Eastern Impact (IRE)**[48] 2433 6-9-4 **104**.............................. StevieDonohoe 8 105
(Richard Fahey) *racd far side: wl in tch in midfield: clsd to chse ldrs but nt clr run 2f out: effrt and swtchd lft jst over 1f out: kpt on ins fnl f wout threatening ldrs: 5th of 14 in gp* **14/1**

3-14 **8** *1* **Raucous**[33] 2907 4-9-5 **105**..............................(b[1]) RyanMoore 21 103+
(William Haggas) *lw: racd stands side: stdd and swtchd lft s: hld up in rr: clsd 2f out: switching lft: hdwy and bumping w rival jst over 1f out: chsd gp ldrs and kpt on ins fnl f: nvr quite getting on terms: 3rd of 13 in gp* **11/2**[1]

0-21 **9** *shd* **Normandy Barriere (IRE)**[43] 2566 5-9-0 **100**.............................. WilliamBuick 26 98
(Nigel Tinkler) *racd stands side: wl in tch in midfield: effrt 2f out: chsng ldrs overall and drvn over 1f out: edgd rt and kpt on same pce ins fnl f: 4th of 13 in gp* **9/1**[3]

1124 **10** *¾* **Lancelot Du Lac (ITY)**[71] 1772 7-9-6 **106**.............................. RobertWinston 10 102
(Dean Ivory) *racd far side: t.k.h: overall ldr: rdn 2f out: hdd over 1f out: no ex u.p 1f out: wknd fnl 100yds: 6th of 14 in gp* **33/1**

0403 **11** *¾* **Amazour (IRE)**[42] 2611 5-8-13 **99**.............................. TomMarquand 2 92
(Ismail Mohammed) *racd far side: hld up towards rr: clsd and nt clr run 2f out: swtchd rt over 1f out: hdwy ins fnl f: kpt on but no threat to ldrs: 7th of 14 in gp* **14/1**

50-0 **12** *½* **Outback Traveller (IRE)**[42] 2606 6-9-4 **104**.............................. MartinHarley 23 96
(Robert Cowell) *racd stands side: hld up in tch in midfield: hdwy u.p and bumping w rival jst over 1f out: no imp ins fnl f: 5th of 13 in gp* **9/1**[3]

0030 **13** *¾* **Poyle Vinnie**[28] 3092 7-9-1 **101**..............................(p) SilvestreDeSousa 19 90
(Michael Appleby) *racd stands side: wl in tch in midfield: effrt to chal and drvn 2f out: no ex u.p ent fnl f: wknd fnl 150yds: 6th of 13 in gp* **50/1**

0042 **14** *1 ¾* **Harry Hurricane**[7] 3829 5-8-12 **98**..............................(b) TrevorWhelan 30 82
(George Baker) *racd stands side: restless in stalls: w gp ldr and prom overall: led gp and pressing overall ldrs 2f out: rdn and lost gp ld over 1f out: wknd ins fnl f: 7th of 13 in gp* **25/1**

43-0 **15** *hd* **Squats (IRE)**[42] 2606 5-8-13 **104**..............................(p) GeorgiaCox(5) 27 87
(William Haggas) *racd stands side: hld up in rr: effrt: swtchd rt and nt clr run wl over 1f out: sme hdwy fnl f: kpt on: nvr trbld ldrs: 8th of 13 in gp* **20/1**

4130 **16** *nk* **Duke Of Firenze**[7] 3829 8-9-7 **107**.............................. DavidAllan 11 89
(David C Griffiths) *racd far side: hld up in tch in midfield: swtchd lft and effrt u.p over 1f out: sn no imp: wknd ins fnl f: 8th of 14 in gp* **33/1**

55-5 **17** *½* **George Dryden (IRE)**[42] 2611 5-9-0 **100**.............................. GrahamLee 9 80
(Ann Duffield) *racd far side: taken down early: wl in tch in midfield: nt clr run 2f out and shuffled bk: gap opened and pushed along jst over 1f out: no ch of rcvring and kpt on same pce ins fnl f: 9th of 14 in gp* **66/1**

-550 **18** *nk* **First Selection (SPA)**[121] 888 4-9-0 **100**.............................. PatSmullen 24 79
(Simon Crisford) *racd stands side: taken down early: led gp and w ldrs overall tl 2f out: sn lost pl: wknd fnl f: 9th of 13 in gp* **50/1**

6-06 **19** *hd* **Birchwood (IRE)**[42] 2610 4-9-5 **105**..............................(b[1]) JamesDoyle 13 84
(Richard Fahey) *racd far side: chsd ldrs: drvn and ev ch 2f out tl lost pl qckly over 1f out: wknd ins fnl f: 10th of 14 in gp* **25/1**

044- **20** *1* **G Force (IRE)**[28] 3097 6-8-7 **100**.............................. DannySheehy(7) 29 76
(Adrian Paul Keatley, Ire) *racd stands side: squeezed for room sn after leaving stalls: sn in tch in midfield: effrt u.p jst over 2f out: no imp u.p and lost pl over 1f out: wknd fnl f: 10th of 13 in gp* **25/1**

6406 **21** *1 ¼* **Boom The Groom (IRE)**[21] 3321 6-9-4 **104**.............................. AdamKirby 15 76
(Tony Carroll) *racd far side: taken down early: hld up in midfield: effrt over 1f out: sn drvn and no imp: wknd fnl f: 11th of 14 in gp* **33/1**

-200 **22** *1* **Captain Colby (USA)**[36] 2780 5-8-12 **98**..............................(b) ThomasBrown 22 66
(Ed Walker) *swtg: racd stands side: dwlt and swtchd lft after s: hld up in rr: effrt over 2f out: sn drvn and no imp: wknd fnl f: 11th of 13 in gp* **50/1**

-155 **23** *nk* **Intisaab**[33] 2907 6-9-5 **108**..............................(p) ShelleyBirkett(3) 20 75
(David O'Meara) *racd stands side: in tch in midfield: rdn wl over 1f out: sn struggling and lost pl: wknd fnl f: 12th of 13 in gp* **25/1**

24-4 **24** *2 ½* **Certificate**[42] 2610 6-9-5 **110**.............................. DavidEgan(5) 18 69
(Roger Varian) *lw: racd stands side: swtchd rt after s: in tch in midfield: effrt 2f out: sn struggling and lost pl: bhd fnl f: 13th of 13 in gp* **16/1**

145- **25** *½* **Buckstay (IRE)**[266] 6942 7-9-8 **108**..............................(p) JamieSpencer 12 66
(Peter Chapple-Hyam) *racd far side: hld up in rr: clsd 2f out: stl plenty to do whn squeezed for room over 1f out: nt rcvr and no ch after: 12th of 14 in gp* **20/1**

-222 **26** *¾* **Muntadab (IRE)**[38] 2736 5-9-0 **100**..............................(v[1]) JimCrowley 17 55
(Roger Fell) *racd far side: swtchd rt s: pressed overall ldr: rdn 2f out: lost pl qckly over 1f out: bhd and eased ins fnl f: 13th of 14 in gp* **14/1**

041- **27** *3 ¾* **Shanghai Glory (IRE)**[258] 7191 4-9-1 **104**.............................. CallumShepherd(3) 14 47
(Charles Hills) *racd far side: chsd ldrs: losing pl u.p and towards rr whn squeezed for room and hmpd over 1f out: bhd and eased ins fnl f: 14th of 14 in gp* **50/1**

1m 13.02s (-1.48) **Going Correction** 0.0s/f (Good) **27** Ran SP% **141.3**
Speed ratings (Par 109): **109,108,107,107,106 105,105,104,104,103 102,101,100,98,97 97,96,96,96,94 93,91,91,88,87 86,81**
CSF £364.20 CT £3358.06 TOTE £48.70: £8.90, £5.00, £2.70, £9.30; EX 592.10 Trifecta £19990.80.

**Owner** Evan M Sutherland **Bred** Equibreed S R L **Trained** Upper Helmsley, N Yorks

■ Stewards' Enquiry : Kieran Shoemark two-day ban; used whip above the permitted level (Jul 9-10)

**FOCUS**

As competitive as ever, there was a pretty even split into two groups and it was those far side who held the advantage, with the winner coming from stall one. The runner-up has been rated back to his 2yo form.

## 4073 QUEEN ALEXANDRA STKS (CONDITIONS RACE) 2m 5f 143y

**5:35** (5:38) (Class 2) 4-Y-0+

**£49,800** (£14,912; £7,456; £3,728; £1,864; £936) **Stalls** Low

Form RPR

5-25 **1** **Oriental Fox (GER)**[28] 3073 9-9-5 102.............................. JoeFanning 3 100
(Mark Johnston) *trckd ldrs: rdn over 2f out: wnt chalng 2nd over 1f out: edgd rt ins fnl f: led fnl 150yds: styd on gamely* **10/1**

11/1 **2** *1 ¼* **Thomas Hobson**[4] 3928 7-9-2 100.............................. MartinHarley 13 96
(W P Mullins, Ire) *midfield: hdwy over 2f out: styd on to ld over 1f out: hdd fnl 150yds: hld and no ex nr fin* **2/1**[1]

-320 **3** *1 ¾* **US Army Ranger (IRE)**[22] 3299 4-9-0 112.............................. RyanMoore 7 94
(A P O'Brien, Ire) *midfield: hdwy over 2f out: rdn over 1f out to chse ldrs: styd on ins fnl f: tk 3rd towards fin: nt rch front two* **7/2**[3]

141- **4** *nk* **Qewy (IRE)**[224] 7947 7-9-2 110.............................. WilliamBuick 15 94
(Charlie Appleby) *lw: prom: led over 2f out: rdn and hdd over 1f out: styd on same pce u.p ins fnl f* **3/1**[2]

03-3 **5** *5* **Fun Mac (GER)**[45] 2525 6-9-5 103..............................(t) JimCrowley 20 93
(Hughie Morrison) *hld up: rdn over 2f out: hdwy over 1f out: styd on ins fnl f: nt trble ldrs* **14/1**

6-54 **6** *¾* **Guard of Honour (IRE)**[64] 1942 6-9-2 89..............................(b) PatCosgrave 11 89
(George Baker) *t.k.h: hld up: rdn over 2f out: hdwy over 1f out: nt trble ldrs and no imp fnl 100yds* **80/1**

3100 **7** *1 ¾* **First Mohican**[45] 2525 9-9-5 98..............................(h) JosephineGordon 4 90
(Alan King) *lw: midfield: rdn and hung rt over 2f out: one pce u.p fnl f: nvr able to trble ldrs* **40/1**

3-13 **8** *½* **October Storm**[30] 3004 4-9-0 77.............................. GrahamLee 8 87
(Mick Channon) *swtg: hld up: rdn over 2f out: swtchd lft u.p over 1f out: kpt on ins fnl f: no real imp* **33/1**

-043 **9** *3* **Arthur Mc Bride (IRE)**[15] 3527 8-9-2 83..............................(t) ThomasBrown 10 84
(Nigel Twiston-Davies) *led: rdn and hdd over 2f out: stl chsd ldrs u.p tl wknd 1f out* **66/1**

-422 **10** *1 ½* **Medburn Cutler**[13] 3618 7-9-2 76..............................(p) JFEgan 1 83
(Paul Henderson) *lw: in tch: rdn over 3f out: outpcd over 2f out: one pce over 1f out* **100/1**

3 **11** *1* **Motherland (IRE)**[29] 3057 4-9-0 103.............................. DonnachaO'Brien 6 82
(Joseph Patrick O'Brien, Ire) *w'like: swtg: prom: rdn over 2f out: one pce over 1f out: no ex fnl 100yds* **16/1**

**12** *7* **His Dream (IRE)**[54] 4-9-0 0.............................. JamieSpencer 14 76
(Jonjo O'Neill) *slowly away: in rr: struggling over 2f out: edgd lft and plugged on over 1f out: nvr a threat* **66/1**

-215 **13** *1 ¾* **Winning Story**[43] 2571 4-9-6 108..............................(p) SilvestreDeSousa 5 87
(Saeed bin Suroor) *trckd ldrs: rdn over 2f out: wknd over 1f out: eased whn btn ins fnl f* **10/1**

-335 **14** *13* **Paris Protocol**[13] 3618 4-9-0 88..............................(p[1]) PatSmullen 19 62
(Richard Hannon) *racd keenly in midfield: rdn and wknd over 2f out: eased whn btn over 1f out* **66/1**

/0-4 **15** *3* **Excellent Result (IRE)**[36] 2788 7-9-2 92..............................(p) StevieDonohoe 18 60
(Richard Spencer) *midfield tl rdn and wknd over 3f out* **66/1**

4 **16** *10* **Soiesauvage (FR)**[85] 1464 6-8-11 70..............................(t[1]) TrevorWhelan 12 46
(Sophie Leech) *lw: slowly away: racd keenly: hld up: lft bhd fnl 3f* **125/1**

4m 49.09s (-0.31) **Going Correction** +0.10s/f (Good)
**WFA** 4 from 6yo+ 1lb **16** Ran SP% **125.7**
Speed ratings (Par 109): **104,103,102,102,100 100,100,99,98,98 97,95,94,89,88 85**
CSF £30.69 CT £91.22 TOTE £11.60: £2.80, £1.50, £1.70; EX 48.60 Trifecta £222.70.

**Owner** Markus Graff **Bred** Gestut Auenquelle **Trained** Middleham Moor, N Yorks

**FOCUS**

This long-established marathon affair was run at a sound enough pace and it's decent staying form. The sixth, ninth and tenth have been rated close to their marks.

T/Jkpt: Not Won. T/Plt: £163.30 to a £1 stake. Pool: £645,439.50 - 2,884.02 winning units
T/Qpdt: £47.00 to a £1 stake. Pool: £37,791.70 - 594.84 winning units

**Steve Payne & Darren Owen**

4034 **AYR** (L-H)

Saturday, June 24

**OFFICIAL GOING: Good (good to firm in places; 8.1)**

Wind: Fresh, half against Weather: Overcast

## 4074 ARNOLD CLARK BRITISH STALLION STUDS EBF NOVICE AUCTION STKS (PLUS 10 RACE) 6f

**1:50** (1:53) (Class 4) 2-Y-O **£4,528** (£1,347; £673; £336) **Stalls** Centre

Form RPR

1 **French Flyer (IRE)** 2-8-13 0 PaulMulrennan 5 70+
(Michael Dods) *dwlt and wnt lft s: sn trcking ldrs: shkn up over 1f out: led and qcknd ins fnl f: promising* **7/1**3

2 2 1/4 **Up Sticks And Go** 2-9-1 0 AndrewMullen 1 65
(Keith Dalgleish) *w ldr: led wl over 1f out: rdn and hdd ins fnl f: nt pce of wnr* **4/1**2

3 1 **Onesarnieshort (FR)** 2-9-2 0 PhillipMakin 3 63
(David O'Meara) *t.k.h: hld up: stdy hdwy over 2f out: rdn and edgd lft over 1f out: kpt on same pce ins fnl f* **4/1**2

41 4 2 **Royal Liberty**12 3655 2-9-6 0 FrannyNorton 7 61
(Mark Johnston) *led: rdn over 2f out: hdd wl over 1f out: kpt on same pce fnl f* **1/1**1

0 5 nk **Billy Booth (IRE)**19 3390 2-9-2 0 (p1) AdamBeschizza 6 56
(Gay Kelleway) *trckd ldrs: effrt and rdn 2f out: outpcd fnl f* **20/1**

6 8 **Squirrelheed** 2-9-1 0 ConnorBeasley 4 31
(Richard Guest) *dwlt: hld up: rdn over 2f out: wknd wl over 1f out* **16/1**

1m 16.02s (3.62) **Going Correction** +0.525s/f (Yiel) 6 Ran SP% **113.1**

Speed ratings (Par 95): **96,93,91,89,88 77**

CSF £34.93 TOTE £6.90: £4.20, £2.90; EX 32.40 Trifecta £115.90.

**Owner** D Neale **Bred** Azienda Agricola La Rovere **Trained** Denton, Co Durham

**FOCUS**

All distances as advertised. Probably a fair juvenile novice though the previous winner perhaps didn't run to his best so the form is not easy to evaluate. The opening level is fluid.

## 4075 SUNSPORT H'CAP 7f 50y

**2:20** (2:22) (Class 3) (0-90,92) 3-Y-O

**£9,337** (£2,796; £1,398; £699; £349; £175) **Stalls** High

Form RPR

114- 1 **Lomu (IRE)**242 7600 3-9-7 **84** PaulMulrennan 2 89
(Keith Dalgleish) *t.k.h: hld up in tch: hdwy and swtchd rt over 1f out: rdn to ld ins fnl f: kpt on strly* **6/1**

5331 2 1/2 **Navarone (IRE)**14 3555 3-9-0 **77** TonyHamilton 6 80
(Richard Fahey) *t.k.h: trckd ldrs: hdwy to ld briefly over 1f out: kpt on: hld nr fin* **4/1**3

3120 3 1/2 **Atteq**22 3303 3-9-3 **80** (t) ConnorBeasley 1 84+
(Richard Fahey) *t.k.h: trckd ldrs: effrt whn nt clr run over 1f out: swtchd rt and kpt on ins fnl f: hld nr fin* **9/4**1

5521 4 1 3/4 **Our Charlie Brown**29 3047 3-8-10 **73** JamesSullivan 3 70
(Tim Easterby) *t.k.h: trckd ldr: led briefly over 1f out: rdn and one pce fnl f* **11/4**2

02-6 5 2 1/4 **Something Brewing (FR)**15 3528 3-9-3 **80** (b) TomEaves 5 71
(Iain Jardine) *dwlt: hld up: stdy hdwy on outside over 2f out: pushed along whn blkd over 1f out: sn btn* **20/1**

2100 6 1 **Aardwolf (USA)**22 3303 3-10-1 **92** FrannyNorton 4 80
(Mark Johnston) *led at ordinary gallop: rdn and hdd over 1f out: sn wknd* **9/2**

1m 32.11s (-1.29) **Going Correction** +0.10s/f (Good) 6 Ran SP% **114.7**

Speed ratings (Par 103): **111,110,109,107,105 104**

CSF £30.51 TOTE £6.40: £2.20, £2.20; EX 28.00 Trifecta £88.20.

**Owner** Steve Macdonald **Bred** Michael G Daly **Trained** Carluke, S Lanarks

**FOCUS**

A tight handicap for three-year-olds but not a reliable guide for the future as the pace was moderate several pulled hard and the third didn't get a run until too late. The runner-up has been rated to the better view of his form.

## 4076 NEWS SCOTLAND H'CAP 1m 2f

**2:55** (2:56) (Class 3) (0-95,96) 4-Y-O+ **£9,703** (£2,887; £1,443; £721) **Stalls** Low

Form RPR

-500 1 **Speed Company (IRE)**22 3300 4-9-8 **96** (h) PhillipMakin 4 103
(John Quinn) *dwlt: sn trcking ldrs: rdn to ld appr fnl f: hld on wl u.p cl home* **5/2**1

1606 2 nse **Testa Rossa (IRE)**1 4035 7-7-13 **80** ow1 (b) SeanMooney(7) 5 86
(Jim Goldie) *hld up: hdwy on outside over 1f out: edgd lft and kpt on wl fnl f: jst hld* **12/1**

-660 3 2 1/4 **Hibou**14 3597 4-8-13 **87** (p) TomEaves 7 89
(Iain Jardine) *s.i.s: hld up: rdn over 1f out: kpt on fnl f: nt rch first two* **7/1**3

0243 4 1/2 **Dance King**8 3790 7-8-10 **84** (tp) JamesSullivan 2 85+
(Tim Easterby) *trckd ldrs: nt clr run fr over 2f out to ent fnl f: kpt on same pce* **11/4**2

4225 5 shd **Rainbow Rebel (IRE)**8 3790 4-9-1 **89** FrannyNorton 1 89
(Mark Johnston) *led: rdn and hrd pressed over 2f out: hdd appr fnl f: sn one pce* **5/2**1

04-4 6 2 1/2 **Cape Of Glory (IRE)**127 779 4-8-12 **86** (p) AndrewMullen 3 81
(Keith Dalgleish) *pressed ldr: ev ch whn edgd both ways u.p over 1f out: wknd ins fnl f* **12/1**

2304 7 1 1/2 **Vettori Rules**56 2158 4-9-7 **95** AdamBeschizza 6 87
(Gay Kelleway) *hld up in tch: rdn over 2f out: wknd fnl f* **33/1**

2m 12.76s (0.76) **Going Correction** +0.10s/f (Good) 7 Ran SP% **114.6**

Speed ratings (Par 107): **100,99,98,97,97 95,94**

CSF £32.54 TOTE £3.30: £1.70, £4.00; EX 29.70 Trifecta £151.90.

**Owner** Mrs May Moo **Bred** Rathasker Stud **Trained** Settrington, N Yorks

**FOCUS**

A fair gallop to this 1m2f handicap but things got a bit tight late on and the form as a whole wouldn't be totally reliable. The runner-up has been rated to his best.

## 4077 SCOTTISH SUN ON SUNDAY CHAMPION H'CAP (FOR THE JOHNSTONE ROSE BOWL) 1m

**3:30** (3:30) (Class 2) (0-105,93) 4-Y-O+

**£18,675** (£5,592; £2,796; £1,398; £699; £351) **Stalls** Low

Form RPR

1231 1 **Nicholas T**31 2952 5-9-1 **87** JamesSullivan 6 94+
(Jim Goldie) *t.k.h: hld up: stdy hdwy over 2f out: effrt and rdn over 1f out: angled rt ins fnl f: kpt on wl to ld cl home* **10/3**1

4-12 2 1/2 **Sophie P**31 2954 4-9-4 **93** NathanEvans(3) 4 99
(R Mike Smith) *trckd ldrs: led over 2f out: rdn over 1f out: kpt on fnl f: hdd nr fin* **4/1**2

1264 3 nk **War Department (IRE)**8 3792 4-9-0 **91** (v) RowanScott(5) 5 96
(Keith Dalgleish) *dwlt: hld up: rdn and hdwy 2f out: kpt on fnl f: nrst fin* **12/1**

-536 4 3/4 **Spring Offensive (IRE)**22 3298 5-9-5 **91** TonyHamilton 9 95
(Richard Fahey) *pressed ldr: ev ch and rdn over 2f out: kpt on same pce ins fnl f* **11/2**

0-50 5 1 **Kentuckyconnection (USA)**38 2735 4-9-6 **92** ConnorBeasley 8 93
(Bryan Smart) *led at ordinary gallop: rdn and hdd over 2f out: rallied: one pce ins fnl f* **14/1**

0013 6 nk **Finn Class (IRE)**12 3651 6-9-0 **86** AndrewMullen 7 87
(Michael Dods) *hld up in tch on outside: stdy hdwy over 2f out: rdn and edgd lft over 1f out: one pce fnl f* **8/1**

-304 7 1/2 **Candelisa (IRE)**16 3498 4-9-6 **92** TomEaves 2 91
(Jedd O'Keeffe) *trckd ldrs: rdn and outpcd wl over 1f out: n.d after* **9/2**3

2005 8 1 1/4 **Lat Hawill (IRE)**28 3064 6-9-6 **92** (b1) JoeDoyle 1 89
(Keith Dalgleish) *hld up: pushed along whn hmpd and outpcd over 2f out: n.d after* **11/2**

1m 42.68s (-1.12) **Going Correction** +0.10s/f (Good) 8 Ran SP% **117.5**

Speed ratings (Par 109): **109,108,108,107,106 106,105,104**

CSF £17.32 CT £143.30 TOTE £4.40: £1.80, £2.00, £3.40; EX 10.60 Trifecta £132.90.

**Owner** W M Johnstone **Bred** W M Johnstone **Trained** Uplawmoor, E Renfrews

**FOCUS**

Not the strongest of races for this decent prize with the top weight 12lb below the ceiling of 105. The pace was ordinary though the winner came from last to first. The runner-up was confirming her recent improvement, and the third has been rated to his AW best.

## 4078 SCOTTISH SUN/BRITISH STALLION STUDS EBF LAND O'BURNS FILLIES' STKS (LISTED RACE) 5f

**4:10** (4:12) (Class 1) 3-Y-O+

**£28,355** (£10,750; £5,380; £2,680; £1,345; £675) **Stalls** Centre

Form RPR

-046 1 **Spring Fling**6 3867 6-9-4 94 JamesSullivan 11 101
(Henry Candy) *hld up: gd hdwy over 1f out: led ins fnl f: rdn and r.o strly* **6/1**3

0-0 2 1 1/4 **Rural Celebration**42 2623 6-9-4 84 (p) TomEaves 8 96
(Kevin Ryan) *prom: effrt and led briefly ent fnl f: kpt on: nt pce of wnr* **33/1**

4-50 3 nk **Queen Kindly**48 2434 3-8-12 107 TonyHamilton 9 93
(Richard Fahey) *hld up: pushed along over 2f out: hdwy over 1f out: kpt on fnl f: nrst fin* **7/4**1

-223 4 1 1/4 **Futoon (IRE)**28 3080 4-9-4 94 JoeDoyle 5 91
(Kevin Ryan) *prom: effrt and rdn over 1f out: kpt on same pce ins fnl f* **7/2**2

23-1 5 1/2 **Cosmopolitan Girl (IRE)**53 2253 4-9-4 86 AdamBeschizza 10 89
(Robert Cowell) *missed break: hld up: pushed along and hdwy over 1f out: kpt on same pce ins fnl f* **12/1**

0300 6 2 **Olivia Fallow (IRE)**7 3827 5-9-4 83 BenCurtis 3 82
(Paul Midgley) *bmpd s: hld up: rdn over 2f out: one pce fr over 1f out* **20/1**

0-50 7 1/2 **Mayfair Lady**28 3080 4-9-4 97 PhillipMakin 6 80
(Richard Fahey) *chsd clr ldr to over 1f out: sn rdn and no ex* **7/1**

2452 8 1/2 **Merry Banter**30 2992 3-8-12 85 ConnorBeasley 1 76
(Paul Midgley) *racd centre and jst away fr main gp: led and clr: rdn and hdd ent fnl f: sn wknd* **14/1**

-000 9 3/4 **Glenrowan Rose (IRE)**15 3539 4-9-4 93 AndrewMullen 7 75
(Keith Dalgleish) *in tch: drvn over 2f out: wknd over 1f out* **25/1**

60-4 10 1 1/4 **Mayleaf Shine (IRE)**14 3579 3-8-12 89 NathanEvans 4 69
(Iain Jardine) *hld up: rdn over 2f out: sn no imp: btn over 1f out* **20/1**

41 11 nse **Fortitude (IRE)**21 3313 3-8-12 72 JackMitchell 2 69
(Hugo Palmer) *bmpd s: sn cl up: rdn and edgd lft over 2f out: wknd over 1f out* **22/1**

50-0 12 nk **Shrill**64 1936 4-9-4 87 (p1) FrannyNorton 12 70
(Robert Cowell) *cl up: wnt 2nd briefly over 1f out: drvn and sn wknd* **40/1**

1m 1.08s (1.68) **Going Correction** +0.525s/f (Yiel)

**WFA** 3 from 4yo+ 6lb 12 Ran SP% **122.8**

Speed ratings (Par 108): **107,105,104,102,101 98,97,96,95,93 93,93**

CSF £200.78 TOTE £7.80: £2.30, £9.10, £1.20; EX 213.30 Trifecta £7071.30 Part won..

**Owner** Six Too Many & T A Frost **Bred** Mrs C R D Wilson **Trained** Kingston Warren, Oxon

**FOCUS**

Not a classy Listed sprint for fillies, but it was competitive contest, run at a strong gallop with the action taking place towards the stand side. The runner-up is the key to the form. The level is a bit fluid, but the first two suggest this is high enough.

## 4079 CLYDE 1'S BOWIE@BREAKFAST H'CAP 5f

**4:50** (4:53) (Class 3) (0-95,97) 3-Y-O+ **£9,703** (£2,887; £1,443; £721) **Stalls** Centre

Form RPR

6152 1 **Coolfitch (IRE)**9 3741 3-8-11 **86** PhillipMakin 2 94
(David O'Meara) *hld up: smooth hdwy over 1f out: squeezed between horses and led ins fnl f: shkn up and kpt on wl: readily* **15/2**

2113 2 1 1/4 **El Hombre**12 3664 3-8-7 **87** RowanScott(5) 6 90
(Keith Dalgleish) *w ldr: rdn over 2f out: chsd wnr ins fnl f: kpt on fin* **11/4**1

00-2 3 nk **Orvar (IRE)**43 2578 4-9-9 **92** JackMitchell 8 96
(Robert Cowell) *led: rdn over 1f out: edgd rt and hdd ins fnl f: kpt on same pce* **5/1**3

1406 4 hd **Tommy G**1 4037 4-8-5 **77** NathanEvans(3) 5 80
(Jim Goldie) *hld up in tch: rdn along over 1f out: r.o ins fnl f: no imp* **10/1**

00-0 5 nk **Son Of Africa**6 3861 5-9-12 **95** BenCurtis 1 97
(Henry Candy) *t.k.h: hld up in tch: hdwy over 1f out: kpt on same pce ins fnl f* **4/1**2

0021 6 hd **My Name Is Rio (IRE)**12 3653 7-9-4 **87** ConnorBeasley 3 88
(Michael Dods) *trckd ldrs: effrt and drvn along over 1f out: kpt on same pce ins fnl f* **5/1**3

6460 7 2 1/2 **Lexington Place**13 3625 7-8-9 **78** (p) JamesSullivan 7 70
(Ruth Carr) *walked to post: trckd ldrs tl rdn and wknd over 1f out* **9/1**

1m 1.28s (1.88) **Going Correction** +0.525s/f (Yiel)

**WFA** 3 from 4yo+ 6lb 7 Ran SP% **110.9**

Speed ratings (Par 107): **105,103,102,102,101 101,97**

CSF £26.66 CT £108.27 TOTE £7.40: £3.40, £2.00; EX 35.40 Trifecta £161.20.

**Owner** W Hoffman Racing **Bred** P Kelly **Trained** Upper Helmsley, N Yorks

■ Lightscameraction was withdrawn. Price at time of withdrawal 16/1. Rule 4 does not apply.

**FOCUS**
They didn't go flat out here and the two pacesetters were second and third but the winner came from last to first. The third has been rated to form, and the fourth pretty much to form despite being down in trip.

## 4080 LEITH H'CAP 6f
**5:25** (5:27) (Class 4) (0-80,85) 3-Y-0+ **£5,175** (£1,540; £769; £384) **Stalls** Centre

Form RPR

16-2 **1** **Gilmer (IRE)**[14] 3567 6-9-11 **75** TomEaves 5 83
(James Ewart) *stdd in last pl: hdwy over 1f out: rdn to ld ins fnl f: kpt on wl* **6/1**

1-00 **2** 1 1/4 **Chipping (IRE)**[35] 2820 3-9-1 **72** ConnorBeasley 1 74
(Michael Dods) *in tch: effrt and rdn over 1f out: kpt on fnl f to take 2nd nr fin* **9/2**[3]

002 **3** hd **Dark Defender**[12] 3653 4-9-13 **82** (v) RowanScott(5) 4 85
(Keith Dalgleish) *trckd ldrs: led over 2f out to over 1f out: kpt on same pce ins fnl f* **13/2**

2543 **4** 1/2 **September Issue**[102] 1185 4-10-0 **78** (p) AdamBeschizza 7 80
(Gay Kelleway) *t.k.h early: in tch: hdwy to ld over 1f out: sn rdn: hdd and no ex ins fnl f* **8/1**

3143 **5** 3 1/4 **Vallarta (IRE)**[12] 3652 7-9-10 **74** JamesSullivan 8 65
(Ruth Carr) *t.k.h: hld up: rdn over 2f out: no imp fr over 1f out* **7/2**[2]

1321 **6** 3/4 **Dandy Highwayman (IRE)**[10] 3709 3-10-0 **85** AndrewMullen 2 72
(Ollie Pears) *early ldr: cl up: rdn over 2f out: wknd fnl f* **9/4**[1]

0163 **7** 7 **Goninodaethat**[12] 3653 9-8-7 **60** NathanEvans(3) 6 27
(Jim Goldie) *dwlt: sn led: hdd over 2f out: wknd over 1f out* **16/1**

1m 13.95s (1.55) **Going Correction** +0.525s/f (Yiel)
**WFA** 3 from 4yo+ 7lb **7 Ran SP% 115.8**
Speed ratings (Par 105): **110,108,108,107,103 102,92**
CSF £33.67 CT £182.03 TOTE £6.80: £3.30, £2.90; EX 41.80 Trifecta £221.90.
**Owner** Mrs Stef Keniry **Bred** Darley **Trained** Langholm, Dumfries & G'way

**FOCUS**
Mainly exposed sorts in this all-aged sprint in which the first four finished clear and the main action was towards the stand side. The runner-up has been rated to his 2yo form and the third to his latest effort.
T/Plt: £488.50 to a £1 stake. Pool: £62,013.52 - 92.67 winning units T/Qpdt: £31.70 to a £1 stake. Pool: £4,517.18 - 105.16 winning units **Richard Young**

# 3740 HAYDOCK (L-H)
Saturday, June 24

**OFFICIAL GOING: Good to firm (watered; 9.5)**
Wind: breezy, against in straight Weather: Sunny intervals, warm Rails: all races on inner home straight

## 4081 BETFRED "DOUBLE DELIGHT" EBF FILLIES' H'CAP (JOCKEY CLUB GRASSROOTS FLAT SPRINT QUALIFIER) 5f
**6:30** (6:30) (Class 4) (0-85,87) 3-Y-0+ **£6,469** (£1,925; £962; £481) **Stalls** Centre

Form RPR

0311 **1** **Mabs Cross**[12] 3672 3-9-3 **82** PaulMulrennan 1 93+
(Michael Dods) *in rr early: sn trcking ldrs: smooth hdwy to ld over 1f out: pushed out and qcknd clr ins fnl f: readily* **10/11**[1]

2026 **2** 2 1/4 **Midnight Malibu (IRE)**[5] 3904 4-9-7 **83** RachelRichardson(3) 2 88
(Tim Easterby) *led tl hdd after 1f: remained prom: regained ld wl over 1f out: sn hdd by wnr: rdn ent fnl f: kpt on* **13/2**[3]

0-50 **3** 2 1/4 **Dainty Dandy (IRE)**[12] 3672 3-9-5 **84** (b[1]) DanielMuscutt 6 79
(Paul Cole) *prom: tacked over to stands' rail after 1f: pushed along 2f out: rdn over 1f out: one pce fnl f* **16/1**

4016 **4** 3 **Annie Salts**[21] 3331 4-8-3 **69** (h) MillyNaseb(7) 4 55
(Chris Dwyer) *mid-div: effrt and rdn over 2f out: no ex ent fnl f* **25/1**

-305 **5** 1 1/4 **Kachess**[23] 3257 3-8-8 **73** (v[1]) RobHornby 7 53
(Tom Dascombe) *hld up: pushed along bef 2f out: no imp fnl f* **9/1**

6053 **6** 1 1/2 **Showdaisy**[7] 3827 4-10-0 **87** (p) DavidNolan 5 63
(Keith Dalgleish) *slowly away: rcvrd to ld after 1f: pushed along 2f out: hdd wl over 1f out: rdn and wknd ent fnl f: eased* **11/4**[2]

1m 0.25s (-0.55) **Going Correction** +0.025s/f (Good)
**WFA** 3 from 4yo 6lb **6 Ran SP% 112.1**
Speed ratings (Par 102): **105,101,97,93,91 88**
CSF £7.57 TOTE £1.80: £1.20, £2.70; EX 7.80 Trifecta £54.70.
**Owner** David W Armstrong **Bred** Highfield Farm Llp **Trained** Denton, Co Durham

**FOCUS**
Just 1mm of rain overnight, and the watered ground (10mm on Tuesday and again on Wednesday) was given as good to firm (GoingStick: 9.5) to begin with, but changed to good to firm, firm in places after the opening race. All races were run on the Inner home straight. Just a small field but they split into two groups, the first two coming up the centre of the track and the third racing next to the stands' rail. The race has been rated at face value, with the runner-up to form.

## 4082 BETFRED "WIN GRAND FINAL TICKETS" H'CAP 1m 2f 42y
**7:00** (7:01) (Class 5) (0-75,73) 3-Y-0+ **£3,557** (£1,058; £529; £264) **Stalls** Centre

Form RPR

5140 **1** **Teodoro (IRE)**[22] 3291 3-9-2 **73** (h[1]) RichardKingscote 4 85
(Tom Dascombe) *slowly away: sn rcvrd to ld: mde rest: pushed along in narrow ld 3f out: 2 l ahd 2f out: rdn over 1f out: forged clr: comf* **9/4**[2]

15-1 **2** 6 **Thello**[130] 727 5-9-6 **70** CliffordLee(5) 5 70
(Jo Hughes) *led early: sn reined bk and hdd by wnr: mid-div taking t.k.h: wnt 3rd 5f out: drvn and wnt 2nd 2f out: rdn over 1f out: lft bhd by wnr ent fnl f* **10/1**

6-33 **3** 2 **Suspect Package (USA)**[19] 3412 3-9-2 **73** (h) DanielMuscutt 2 69
(James Fanshawe) *racd in last: hdwy 3f out: pushed along 2f out: rdn over 1f out and no immediate rspnse: r.o one pce to take 3rd ins fnl f* **11/8**[1]

5-64 **4** 1/2 **Omotesando**[5] 3898 7-9-0 **64** MeganNicholls(5) 1 59
(Oliver Greenall) *trckd wnr: pushed along 3f out: rdn and wknd ent fnl f* **9/1**

5010 **5** 4 1/2 **Cartavio (IRE)**[16] 3484 3-9-1 **72** RobHornby 6 58
(Andrew Balding) *mid-div: pushed along and reminder over 3f out: rdn over 2f out: losing tch and eased ins fnl f* **15/2**[3]

0630 **6** 11 **Berlusca (IRE)**[9] 3744 8-10-0 **73** DavidNolan 7 37
(David O'Meara) *racd in 5th: drvn 3f out: sn wknd: eased fnl 2f* **10/1**

2m 9.21s (-3.49) **Going Correction** -0.375s/f (Firm)
**WFA** 3 from 4yo+ 12lb **6 Ran SP% 112.8**
Speed ratings (Par 103): **98,93,91,91,87 78**
CSF £23.86 TOTE £3.40: £1.70, £3.80; EX 25.50 Trifecta £48.60.
**Owner** Laurence Bellman & Caroline Ingram **Bred** John Connaughton **Trained** Malpas, Cheshire

**FOCUS**
Race distance increased by 25yds. This was dominated by the winner, who took well to the fitting of a hood for the first time.

## 4083 BETFRED "WATCH SKY SPORTS IN OUR SHOPS" NOVICE STKS (PLUS 10 RACE) 6f 212y
**7:35** (7:35) (Class 4) 2-Y-0 **£4,528** (£1,347; £673; £336) **Stalls** Low

Form RPR

**1** **Albishr (IRE)** 2-9-2 0 TomMarquand 6 75
(Richard Hannon) *trckd ldr: 1 l down 3f out: pushed along to mount chal 2f out: rdn ent fnl f: r.o wl to ld last few strides* **8/1**

5 **2** hd **Iconic Sunset**[37] 2750 2-9-2 0 DavidAllan 3 74
(James Tate) *led: 1 l clr 3f out: pushed along to maintain advantage 2f out: chal and hrd rdn ins fnl f: r.o but ct last few strides* **3/1**[2]

5 **3** 1 1/2 **Chai Chai (IRE)**[28] 3066 2-9-2 0 RobHornby 2 73+
(Andrew Balding) *chsd ldrs: pushed along 2f out: tried to chal on inner of runner-up ent fnl f but n.m.r and lost impetus: one pce after* **3/1**[2]

**4** 1/2 **Dark Acclaim (IRE)** 2-9-2 0 DanielMuscutt 4 69+
(Marco Botti) *hld up: effrt and drvn 3f out: hrd rdn over 1f out: r.o fnl f* **14/1**

**5** 3/4 **King's Proctor (IRE)** 2-9-2 0 AndreaAtzeni 5 67
(Mark Johnston) *chsd ldrs on outer: drvn and ev ch over 2f out: rdn wl over 1f out: eased whn btn ins fnl f* **11/4**[1]

**6** 3 1/4 **Zoffalee (FR)** 2-9-2 0 RichardKingscote 1 58+
(Tom Dascombe) *mid-div: pushed along on outer over 2f out: no imp ent fnl f* **4/1**[3]

1m 29.05s (-1.65) **Going Correction** -0.375s/f (Firm) **6 Ran SP% 114.4**
Speed ratings (Par 95): **94,93,92,91,90 86**
CSF £32.83 TOTE £7.00: £4.70, £1.80; EX 32.90 Trifecta £138.10.
**Owner** Mohamed Saeed Al Shahi **Bred** Miss Ciara Doyle **Trained** East Everleigh, Wilts

**FOCUS**
Race distance increased by 3yds. The pace wasn't that strong, it paid to be prominent, and it got a bit messy late on with room hard to come by. The opening level is fluid.

## 4084 BETFRED "HAT TRICK HEAVEN" H'CAP 7f 212y
**8:05** (8:06) (Class 4) (0-80,80) 3-Y-0 **£5,822** (£1,732; £865; £432) **Stalls** Low

Form RPR

1464 **1** **Ray's The Money (IRE)**[29] 3040 3-8-12 **78** (v) TristanPrice(7) 4 85
(Michael Bell) *hld up on inner: effrt and plld out to mount chal over 2f out: rdn and hdwy over 1f out: str run ins fnl f: led last 75yds* **5/1**[3]

-350 **2** 3/4 **Mutawakked (IRE)**[14] 3592 3-9-6 **79** TomMarquand 1 84
(Brian Meehan) *trckd ldrs: drvn and hdwy on inner to ld 1f f out: sn hrd rdn: r.o ins fnl f: ct last 75yds* **15/2**

51 **3** 3 1/2 **Anif (IRE)**[16] 3500 3-9-5 **78** DanielMuscutt 5 75
(Charles Hills) *led: pushed along 2f out: rdn over 1f out: hdd 1f out: one pce* **5/1**[3]

2110 **4** 1/2 **Sidewinder (IRE)**[10] 3713 3-9-7 **80** RichardKingscote 2 75
(Tom Dascombe) *mid-div: hdwy 3f out: rdn and ev ch wl over 1f out: no ex* **9/2**[2]

-641 **5** 3/4 **Jumira Prince (IRE)**[13] 3627 3-9-1 **74** AndreaAtzeni 6 68
(Roger Varian) *hld up: hdwy over 3f out: sn drvn: rdn wl over 1f out: no imp* **13/8**[1]

0-21 **6** 12 **Wigan Warrior**[21] 3332 3-9-1 **74** PaulMulrennan 7 39
(David Brown) *racd in last: effrt on outer over 2f out: no further hdwy: one pce and eased ent fnl f* **17/2**

-050 **7** 4 1/2 **Jumping Around (IRE)**[14] 3588 3-9-2 **75** GeorgeDowning 3 29
(Ian Williams) *chsd ldr: pushed along and lost pl 2f out: wknd* **33/1**

1m 39.53s (-4.17) **Going Correction** -0.375s/f (Firm) **7 Ran SP% 114.8**
Speed ratings (Par 101): **105,104,100,100,99 87,83**
CSF £41.44 TOTE £5.90: £2.80, £3.90; EX 40.50 Trifecta £167.50.
**Owner** Mr & Mrs Ray Jenner **Bred** Ballybrennan Stud Ltd **Trained** Newmarket, Suffolk

**FOCUS**
Race distance increased by 3yds. The first two finished nicely clear, the winner showing a good turn of foot to take it. It's been rated around the runner-up to his 2yo form.

## 4085 BETFRED "PROUD SPONSOR OF SUPER LEAGUE" H'CAP 7f 212y
**8:35** (8:35) (Class 4) (0-85,84) 4-Y-0+ **£5,822** (£1,732; £865; £432) **Stalls** Low

Form RPR

5514 **1** **Captain Courageous (IRE)**[22] 3282 4-9-7 **84** RichardKingscote 7 93
(Ed Walker) *hld up: hdwy 3f out: pushed along to join ldr over 1f out: rdn and led ins fnl f: r.o wl: comf* **4/1**[3]

31-2 **2** 1 3/4 **Sante (IRE)**[21] 3314 4-9-7 **84** AndreaAtzeni 5 89+
(Charles Hills) *hld up: gd hdwy on inner 3f out: led 2f out: pushed along whn jnd over 1f out: rdn and hdd ins fnl f: r.o* **7/2**[2]

4414 **3** 1 3/4 **Mon Beau Visage (IRE)**[6] 3857 4-9-2 **79** (p) DavidNolan 2 80
(David O'Meara) *mid-div: n.m.r 3f out: swtchd wd and hdwy over 1f out: rdn and r.o fnl f* **5/1**

60-2 **4** 1 1/2 **Chosen Character (IRE)**[15] 3540 9-8-8 **78** (vt) ElishaWhittington(7) 3 75
(Tom Dascombe) *led: hdd 2f out: rdn appr fnl f: one pce* **10/1**

-052 **5** 1 1/2 **Sovereign Bounty**[6] 3857 5-9-1 **78** JackGarritty 1 72
(Jedd O'Keeffe) *t.k.h: trckd ldrs on inner: n.m.r over 2f out: rdn wl over 1f out: no ex* **11/4**[1]

0-35 **6** 1 **Royal Shaheen (FR)**[12] 3651 4-9-3 **80** PaulMulrennan 4 71
(Alistair Whillans) *mid-div: hdwy and ev ch 3f out: pushed along 2f out: drvn over 1f out: sn btn* **5/1**

0500 **7** 2 1/4 **Ibazz**[19] 3409 4-9-1 **78** GeorgeDowning 6 64
(Ian Williams) *chsd ldr: ev ch 3f out: pushed along 2f out: sn lost pl: rdn and wknd wl over 1f out* **33/1**

1m 39.53s (-4.17) **Going Correction** -0.375s/f (Firm) **7 Ran SP% 114.3**
Speed ratings (Par 105): **105,103,101,100,98 97,95**
CSF £18.34 TOTE £4.90: £2.30, £2.00; EX 16.40 Trifecta £50.90.
**Owner** Laurence Bellman **Bred** Edgeridge & Glenvale **Trained** Upper Lambourn, Berks
■ Stewards' Enquiry : Elisha Whittington two-day ban: used whip without giving her mount time to respond (Jul 9-10)

**FOCUS**
Race distance increased by 3yds. It paid to be held up here, the three at the back early in the straight coming through to finish in the first three.

## 4086 BETFRED "PASSIONATE ABOUT SUPER LEAGUE" MAIDEN STKS 7f 212y
**9:05** (9:05) (Class 5) 3-Y-0+ **£3,557** (£1,058; £529; £264) **Stalls** Low

Form RPR

03 **1** **Najashee (IRE)**[30] 2997 3-9-2 0 RichardKingscote 2 78+
(Owen Burrows) *2nd keeping cl tabs on ldr: jnd issue gng wl over 1f out: pushed along to ld ent fnl f: rdn and asserted last 100yds* **8/11**[1]

5- **2** *1 1/2* **Big Tour (IRE)**[227] 7867 3-9-2 0 ........ TomMarquand 1 73
(Saeed bin Suroor) *led: qcknd pce 2f out: rdn and jnd by wnr over 1f out: hdd and kpt on wl jst ins fnl f: wl hld last 100yds* **7/4**[2]

05 **3** *3* **Lord Kitten (USA)**[15] 3533 3-9-2 0 ........ (b) FrannyNorton 5 66
(David Lanigan) *chsd ldrs: pushed along 2f out: rdn over 1f out: no imp* **20/1**

50 **4** *10* **Queen Moon (IRE)**[11] 3691 3-8-11 0 ........ RobHornby 6 37
(Andrew Balding) *a in last: pushed along 3f out: wknd* **9/1**[3]

1m 41.81s (-1.89) **Going Correction** -0.375s/f (Firm) **4 Ran SP% 109.0**
Speed ratings (Par 103): **94,92,89,79**
CSF £2.27 TOTE £1.30; EX 2.50 Trifecta £6.30.
**Owner** Hamdan Al Maktoum **Bred** Skymarc Farm Inc And Ecurie Des Monceaux **Trained** Lambourn, Berks

**FOCUS**
Race distance increased by 3yds. This was a duel between the big two in the market from some way out. The runner-up has been rated in line with his 2yo debut run.
T/Plt: £251.50 to a £1 stake. Pool: £57,893.16 - 168.03 winning units T/Qpdt: £128.30 to a £1 stake. Pool: £4,736.52 - 27.30 winning units **Keith McHugh**

# 4006 LINGFIELD (L-H)

## Saturday, June 24

**OFFICIAL GOING: Good to firm (good in places; watered; 7.8)**
Wind: Strong behind Weather: Cloudy

## 4087 VISTAVIS LTD H'CAP 1m 3f 133y

**5:45** (5:46) (Class 6) (0-52,53) 3-Y-O+ **£2,264** (£673; £336; £168) **Stalls** High

Form RPR

0-53 **1** **Lady Of York**[21] 3326 3-8-6 **46** ........ JoeyHaynes 7 52
(Alan Bailey) *t.k.h in mid-div on outer: rdn over 2f out: on ldrs quarters over 1f out: kpt on wl and led jst ins fnl f: strly pressed and hrd rdn nr fin: hld on* **5/1**[3]

0061 **2** *nk* **The Secrets Out**[12] 3674 3-8-13 **53** ........ (h) KieranO'Neill 5 59
(Luke Dace) *pressed ldr on outer: rdn and led wl over 3f out: kpt on wl fr over 1f out: narrowly hdd jst ins fnl f: kpt on again at fin: jst lost out* **9/4**[1]

0063 **3** *2* **Lord E (IRE)**[23] 3247 3-8-9 **52** ........ HectorCrouch(3) 11 55
(Gary Moore) *in rr-div: rdn over 3f out: kpt on wl fr mid-div wl over 1f out: tk 3rd ins fnl f: no imp on ldng pair* **16/1**

00-4 **4** *2 1/2* **Flying Power**[19] 3400 9-9-9 **49** ........ RoystonFfrench 6 48
(John Norton) *trckd ldrs on outer: rdn over 3f out: kpt on wl tl wknd ent fnl f: no ex and lost 3rd ins fnl f* **20/1**

0004 **5** *2 3/4* **Crystal Secret**[12] 3674 3-8-4 **49** ........ MitchGodwin(5) 8 43
(John Bridger) *t.k.h in rr: pushed along at 1/2-way to hold pl: rdn wl over 2f out: kpt on one pce fr over 1f out* **8/1**

0440 **6** *3 1/2* **Let's Sway**[12] 3674 3-8-9 **49** ........ (h) LemosdeSouza 10 38
(Amy Murphy) *settled in last: rdn over 3f out: styd on fr over 1f out* **10/1**

5001 **7** *5* **Affair**[23] 3247 3-8-4 **51** ........ TheodoreLadd(7) 9 32
(Hughie Morrison) *led early: sn taken bk and sn trckd ldrs on outer w no cover: rdn over 4f out: no imp fr over 1f out* **14/1**

-006 **8** *3* **Coup De Vent**[50] 2358 6-9-6 **46** oh1 ........ TimmyMurphy 1 22
(John O'Shea) *settled bhd ldr on rail: rdn over 3f out: no imp* **50/1**

6000 **9** *10* **Tojosimbre**[12] 3657 3-8-8 **48** ........ ShaneKelly 3 8
(Richard Hughes) *settled in mid-div on rail: rdn over 3f out: sn hld* **7/2**[2]

-605 **10** *6* **Megalala (IRE)**[11] 3683 16-9-0 **47** ........ KatherineGlenister(7) 4
(John Bridger) *pushed along leaving stalls and sn led: wkng and hdd wl over 3f out: sn wknd* **14/1**

6-00 **11** *3* **Cranwell**[40] 2679 5-9-11 **51** ........ (h) LiamKeniry 12
(George Baker) *a in rr: rdn over 3f out: sn hld* **25/1**

2m 34.04s (2.54) **Going Correction** +0.50s/f (Yiel)
**WFA** 3 from 5yo+ 14lb **11 Ran SP% 119.6**
Speed ratings (Par 101): **111,110,109,107,105 103,100,98,91,87 85**
CSF £16.57 CT £172.10 TOTE £6.50: £2.10, £1.40, £4.10; EX 22.90 Trifecta £266.30.
**Owner** Miss Christine Calton **Bred** P D Smith Holdings Ltd **Trained** Newmarket, Suffolk

**FOCUS**
Race distance increased by 16yds in race 1, 2 and 3. The ground had been watered and the going was good to firm (good in places), though the slow times on the card suggest it may not have been that firm. The opener was a modest handicap in which they went a fair gallop. Very ordinary form.

## 4088 ROYAL BRITISH LEGION SURREY H'CAP 1m 2f

**6:15** (6:15) (Class 6) (0-65,65) 4-Y-O+ **£2,264** (£673; £336; £168) **Stalls** Low

Form RPR

0-66 **1** **Golden Isles (IRE)**[8] 3771 4-8-6 **53** ........ GeorgeWood(3) 5 59
(Heather Main) *settled bhd ldr: shkn up and led over 3f out: kpt on wl fr over 2f out: pressed on either side over 1f out: battled on ins fnl f: hld on post* **6/1**

0620 **2** *1/2* **Betsalottie**[15] 3519 4-8-12 **56** ........ WilliamCarson 2 61
(John Bridger) *settled bhd ldr: rdn over 2f out: kpt on wl and almost upside wnr over 1f out: no ex nr fin* **9/4**[2]

1344 **3** *3/4* **Angelical (IRE)**[13] 3628 4-8-13 **60** ........ CharlieBennett(3) 3 64
(Daniel Mark Loughnane) *settled bhd ldr: rdn over 2f out: kpt on wl and pressing wnr over 1f out: no ex nr fin* **15/8**[1]

3013 **4** *31* **Gabrial The Thug (FR)**[22] 3304 7-9-7 **65** ........ (t[1]) ShaneKelly 1 10
(Ian Williams) *settled bhd ldr on rail: shkn up and dropped to last wl over 3f out: rdn and no imp after: kpt on one pce fr 2f out for remote 4th: t.o* **5/1**[3]

-600 **5** *91* **Great Return**[4] 3935 4-9-5 **63** ........ CharlesBishop 4
(Lisa Williamson) *sn led: shkn up and hdd over 3f out: sn wknd: virtually p.u fr 2f out: allowed to come home in own time: t.o* **7/1**

2m 12.55s (2.05) **Going Correction** +0.50s/f (Yiel) **5 Ran SP% 109.0**
Speed ratings (Par 101): **111,110,110,85,12**
CSF £19.35 TOTE £7.70: £3.00, £1.40; EX 20.20 Trifecta £45.80.
**Owner** Donald M Kerr **Bred** J & J Waldron **Trained** Kingston Lisle, Oxon

**FOCUS**
Race distance increased by 16yds. A modest little handicap and the first three came clear having tracked a fair pace. The winner has been rated back to near last year's form.

## 4089 NEW MEMBERS WELCOME AT DARTFORD GOLF CLUB H'CAP 1m 3f 133y

**6:45** (6:45) (Class 5) (0-75,75) 4-Y-O+ **£2,911** (£866; £432; £216) **Stalls** High

Form RPR

4246 **1** **Plymouth Sound**[17] 3459 5-9-6 **74** ........ (v) CharlesBishop 3 83
(Eve Johnson Houghton) *hld up in 6th: shkn up and prog wl over 3f out: rdn over 2f out: kpt on wl and led ent fnl f: sn clr* **5/2**[2]

-330 **2** *5* **Hepplewhite**[17] 3459 4-9-3 **71** ........ (p) MartinDwyer 4 72
(William Muir) *chsd ldr: rdn and led wl over 2f out: kpt on tl hdd ent fnl f where lft bhd by wnr: pushed out after* **2/1**[1]

200- **3** *13* **Hurricane Volta (IRE)**[223] 7274 6-8-9 **66** ........ (p) GeorgeWood(3) 5 45
(Peter Hedger) *in rr: nt gng wl and pushed along at 1/2-way to hold tch: rdn 4f out: c wd in st: kpt on tl wknd fr 2f out* **12/1**

312 **4** *3 1/2* **Rum Swizzle**[44] 2358 5-9-6 **74** ........ ShaneKelly 6 48
(Harry Dunlop) *settled in 4th: gng wl over 3f out: sn rdn and no imp fr 2f out* **8/1**

455 **5** *9* **Tuolumne Meadows**[11] 3684 4-9-1 **69** ........ (b) DavidProbert 1 28
(Paul Cole) *sn led: rdn wl over 3f out: hdd over 2f out: wknd after* **12/1**

0612 **6** *9* **Impressive Day (IRE)**[12] 3658 4-9-7 **75** ........ (p) TimmyMurphy 2 31
(Gary Moore) *settled bhd ldr: began to struggle 5f out where pushed along: no imp 3f out: eased sn after* **3/1**[3]

2m 33.47s (1.97) **Going Correction** +0.50s/f (Yiel) **6 Ran SP% 113.4**
Speed ratings (Par 103): **113,109,101,98,92 86**
CSF £8.10 TOTE £3.30: £1.70, £1.60; EX 8.20 Trifecta £41.50.
**Owner** M Page, D Smith & R Whichelow **Bred** Mrs James Wigan **Trained** Blewbury, Oxon

**FOCUS**
Race distance increased by 16yds. A small handicap in which they seemed to go a fair gallop, and the winner came from last place and they finished well strung out. The winner has been rated to his 2016 form, with the runner-up a bit below his recent best.

## 4090 RON PEARCE MAIDEN AUCTION STKS 7f

**7:20** (7:22) (Class 6) 2-Y-O **£2,264** (£673; £336; £168) **Stalls** Centre

Form RPR

**1** **Bambino Lola** 2-8-9 0 ........ RoystonFfrench 2 75+
(Adam West) *hld up bhd ldrs: hld together over 3f out: shkn up over 2f out: rdn over 1f out: qcknd up and led ent fnl f: sn clr* **25/1**

03 **2** *3 1/2* **Mrs Teasdale**[12] 3655 2-8-13 0 ........ OisinMurphy 9 70
(Archie Watson) *prom: rdn and led wl over 1f out: kpt on tl hdd ent fnl f: no ch w wnr* **11/4**[2]

**3** *4 1/2* **Midnight Wilde** 2-9-1 0 ........ DannyBrock 5 60
(John Ryan) *settled off ldrs: rdn wl over 1f out: hdwy tl no ex ins fnl f* **5/1**

3 **4** *2 1/2* **Day Of Rest (FR)**[18] 3445 2-9-4 0 ........ LiamKeniry 10 56
(George Baker) *settled bhd ldrs: shkn up over 2f out: shuffled along after: no ex ins fnl f* **9/4**[1]

5 **5** *1 1/4* **Lyford (IRE)**[23] 3244 2-8-11 0 ........ MitchGodwin(5) 7 51
(Sylvester Kirk) *hld up in off ldrs: rdn over 2f out: no ex fr over 1f out* **14/1**

65 **6** *3 3/4* **Safe Waters**[11] 3690 2-8-9 0 ........ MartinDwyer 11 34
(Eve Johnson Houghton) *sn led on rail: j. path: rdn over 3f out: no ex fr over 1f out and wknd* **3/1**[3]

05 **7** *8* **Raven's Girl**[14] 3570 2-8-8 0 ........ GeorgeWood(3) 4 14
(Michael Madgwick) *a in rr: rdn on outer over 3f out: no ex fr over 1f out* **40/1**

**8** *1 3/4* **Lady Maldiva (IRE)** 2-8-8 0 ........ OscarPereira 6 6
(Jose Santos) *a in rr: rdn over 3f out and rn green: pushed out after* **33/1**

1m 25.93s (2.63) **Going Correction** +0.20s/f (Good) **8 Ran SP% 115.0**
Speed ratings (Par 91): **92,88,82,80,78 74,65,63**
CSF £92.57 TOTE £17.10: £4.60, £1.20, £1.50; EX 107.40 Trifecta £707.50.
**Owner** Maharaj Freeze **Bred** M E Broughton **Trained** Epsom, Surrey

**FOCUS**
A moderate juvenile event in which they went a fair pace along the stands' side rail.

## 4091 RACING WELFARE H'CAP 7f 135y

**7:50** (7:51) (Class 4) (0-85,85) 4-Y-O+ **£4,690** (£1,395; £697; £348) **Stalls** Centre

Form RPR

6542 **1** **Medburn Dream**[13] 3620 4-9-5 **83** ........ SilvestreDeSousa 4 94
(Paul Henderson) *pressed ldr: rdn over 2f out and led gng wl: rdn over 1f out and sprinted clr: heavily eased nr fin* **11/8**[1]

0052 **2** *9* **Majestic Moon (IRE)**[8] 3777 7-9-4 **85** ........ ShelleyBirkett(3) 1 74
(Julia Feilden) *broke wl and sn led: rdn and hdd over 2f out: wknd: kpt on again nr fin* **7/1**

6443 **3** *1/2* **Suqoor**[10] 3730 4-9-1 **79** ........ (p) DavidProbert 6 66
(Chris Dwyer) *hld up in mid-div: rdn over 2f out: kpt on tl lft bhd by wnr fr over 1f out* **4/1**[2]

0340 **4** *1 3/4* **Gramercy (IRE)**[14] 3581 10-8-11 **75** ........ (v[1]) ShaneKelly 2 58
(Ian Williams) *in rr: rdn over 2f out: kpt on one pce* **33/1**

0-06 **5** *3 1/2* **Munaashid (USA)**[14] 3597 4-9-1 **79** ........ JimCrowley 5 53
(Ed Dunlop) *hld up on rail: rdn over 2f out: no imp* **5/1**[3]

6610 **6** *1* **Plucky Dip**[31] 2975 6-9-2 **80** ........ DannyBrock 3 52
(John Ryan) *cl up: pushed along over 3f out: sn rdn and no ex* **14/1**

-002 **7** *2 1/4* **Palawan**[7] 3808 4-9-6 **84** ........ TimmyMurphy 7 50
(Jamie Osborne) *racd in mid-div: shkn up fr 3f out: no imp fr over 2f out and wknd* **13/2**

1m 31.62s (-0.68) **Going Correction** +0.20s/f (Good) **7 Ran SP% 114.2**
Speed ratings (Par 105): **111,102,101,99,96 95,93**
CSF £11.83 TOTE £2.20: £1.40, £3.10; EX 10.50 Trifecta £27.80.
**Owner** Eddie Evans **Bred** Eddie Evans **Trained** Whitsbury, Hants

**FOCUS**
An average handicap, but the well-backed favourite turned it into a procession. A clear pb from the winner, but the level is fluid.

## 4092 MOVE REVOLUTION MAIDEN STKS 6f

**8:20** (8:24) (Class 5) 3-Y-O+ **£2,911** (£866; £432; £216) **Stalls** Centre

Form RPR

4-22 **1** **Dealer's Choice (IRE)**[22] 3279 3-9-0 78 ........ (p[1]) SilvestreDeSousa 6 80
(Roger Varian) *early spd and pressed ldr: led 4f out: rdn over 2f out: wnt clr wl over 1f out: eased nr fin* **4/6**[1]

6-55 **2** *8* **Malcolm The Pug (IRE)**[12] 3673 3-9-5 72 ........ KieranO'Neill 3 59
(Richard Hannon) *settled bhd ldrs: rdn over 2f out: kpt on and ch 2f out: sn one pce and lft bhd: pushed out fnl f* **9/4**[2]

**3** *10* **Hydeandseek (FR)** 3-9-0 0 ........ KierenFox 5 22
(John Best) *reluctant to load: settled off the pce bhd ldrs: rdn over 3f out: no imp on ldrs fr over 1f out: jst hld remote 3rd* **25/1**

0- **4** *nse* **Spring Eternal**[295] 6078 3-9-0 0 ........ DavidProbert 1 22
(Charles Hills) *early pce and t.k.h: hung rt: hdd 4f out: grad wknd after and hld for remote 3rd* **8/1**[3]

53 **5** *9* **Napping**[61] 2024 4-9-7 0 ........ LiamKeniry 2
(Anabel K Murphy) *s.s: settled bhd ldrs: rdn over 2f out: no imp after* **25/1**

46- **6** *9* **Must Be Amazing**[231] 7818 3-9-0 0 ........ MartinLane 4
(Jeremy Gask) *s.s: outpcd in rr on outer: rdn over 2f out: sn hld* **25/1**

1m 12.11s (0.91) **Going Correction** +0.20s/f (Good)
**WFA** 3 from 4yo 7lb **6 Ran SP% 113.4**
Speed ratings (Par 103): **101,90,77,76,64 52**
CSF £2.34 TOTE £1.60: £1.10, £1.90; EX 2.50 Trifecta £22.10.
**Owner** J Shack **Bred** Jc Bloodstock & Goodwill Bloodstock **Trained** Newmarket, Suffolk

**FOCUS**
A small maiden and another clear-cut winner on the card. They went a good clip and finished well strung out for a sprint.

## 4093 ABBA REVIVIAL AT LINGFIELD PARK - 1ST JULY H'CAP 4f 217y
**8:50** (8:53) (Class 5) (0-75,76) 3-Y-O+ **£2,911** (£866; £432; £216) **Stalls** Centre

Form RPR
6325 **1** **Swendab (IRE)**[15] 3544 9-8-11 **64**....(b) BenRobinson[(5)] 1 70
(John O'Shea) *gd spd and sn pressed ldr in centre: shkn up over 2f out and led: rdn 2f out: kpt on strly ins fnl f* **10/1**
344 **2** *1* **Rosealee (IRE)**[22] 3278 4-9-12 **74**....(p[1]) MartinLane 4 76
(Jeremy Gask) *chsd ldrs: rdn 2f out: kpt on wl ins fnl f: jst hld 2nd* **5/1**
-001 **3** *nse* **Tailwind**[25] 3176 4-9-7 **76**....(b) RossaRyan[(7)] 7 78
(Richard Hannon) *settled bhd ldr on rail: rdn 2f out: styd on wl ins fnl f: jst failed for 2nd* **10/3**[2]
2162 **4** *nk* **Hurricane Alert**[12] 3659 5-8-2 **55**.... DavidEgan[(5)] 3 56
(Mark Hoad) *restless in stalls: hld up bhd ldrs: rdn 2f out: prog and kpt on wl fr over 1f out: no ex nr fin* **7/1**
-146 **5** *¾* **One Big Surprise**[11] 3696 5-9-11 **73**....(p) ShaneKelly 2 71+
(Richard Hughes) *in rr: rdn over 2f out: kpt on one pce: nvr involved* **4/1**[3]
-14 **6** *4 ½* **Otomo**[15] 3517 3-9-5 **73**.... LiamKeniry 6 53
(Philip Hide) *tk fierce hold bhd ldrs: shkn up over 2f out: sn rdn: no ex fr over 1f out* **11/4**[1]
1340 **7** *2 ¼* **Mossgo (IRE)**[50] 2368 7-9-3 **65**....(t) KierenFox 5 39
(John Best) *gd spd and sn led: rdn over 2f out: sn hdd: no ex and wknd fnl f* **16/1**

59.86s (1.66) **Going Correction** +0.20s/f (Good)
**WFA** 3 from 4yo+ 6lb **7 Ran SP% 113.9**
Speed ratings (Par 103): **94,92,92,91,90 83,79**
CSF £57.94 CT £203.51 TOTE £11.20: £6.80, £2.80; EX 62.90 Trifecta £260.10.
**Owner** E&G Racing: Swendab **Bred** P Brady **Trained** Elton, Gloucs

**FOCUS**
A small 5f handicap in which they went a good clip, though the winner came home alone down the centre. The second, third and fourth have been rated close to their recent marks.
T/Plt: £36.70 to a £1 stake. Pool: £56,612.37 - 1,124.94 winning units T/Qpdt: £7.20 to a £1 stake. Pool: £6,130.71 - 627.78 winning units **Cathal Gahan**

# [4047]NEWMARKET (R-H)
Saturday, June 24

**OFFICIAL GOING: Good to firm (watered; 7.6)**
Wind: Light across Weather: Cloudy with sunny spells

## 4094 ROYAL ASCOT BETTING AT 188BET EBF STALLIONS NOVICE STKS (PLUS 10 RACE) 7f
**2:10** (2:11) (Class 4) 2-Y-O **£4,528** (£1,347; £673; £336) **Stalls** Low

Form RPR
**1** **Cape Bunting (IRE)** 2-8-11 0.... HarryBentley 1 77+
(Mark Johnston) *chsd ldrs: shkn up to ld over 1f out: edgd lft ins fnl f: r.o: comf* **6/1**
4 **2** *1 ½* **Yafta**[28] 3066 2-9-2 0.... DaneO'Neill 6 78
(Richard Hannon) *chsd ldr: rdn and ev ch over 1f out: styd on same pce wl ins fnl f* **7/4**[1]
**3** *1 ¾* **Global Giant** 2-9-2 0.... FranBerry 7 73
(Ed Dunlop) *dwlt: hdwy over 4f out: shkn up and ev ch over 1f out: no ex wl ins fnl f* **5/1**[3]
05 **4** *2 ¾* **Contribute**[53] 2279 2-9-2 0.... PatDobbs 4 66
(Martyn Meade) *led: rdn and hdd over 1f out: wknd ins fnl f* **16/1**
**5** *3 ¼* **Main Street** 2-9-2 0.... RobertTart 2 57+
(John Gosden) *s.s: sn pushed along in rr: effrt on outer over 2f out: wknd fnl f* **3/1**[2]
**6** *3 ¾* **Extraction (USA)** 2-9-2 0.... GavinLerena 5 47
(Martyn Meade) *prom: lost pl over 4f out: pushed along over 2f out: wknd over 1f out* **14/1**
**7** *2 ¼* **Real Estate (IRE)** 2-9-2 0.... LukeMorris 3 41
(James Tate) *prom: pushed along 1/2-way: wknd wl over 1f out* **11/1**

1m 26.05s (0.35) **Going Correction** -0.075s/f (Good) **7 Ran SP% 113.2**
Speed ratings (Par 95): **95,93,91,88,84 80,77**
CSF £16.62 TOTE £6.90: £2.80, £1.30; EX 17.60 Trifecta £42.50.
**Owner** Sheikh Hamdan bin Mohammed Al Maktoum **Bred** Godolphin **Trained** Middleham Moor, N Yorks

**FOCUS**
Far side of July Course used. Stalls on the stands' side, except 1m5f: centre. The re-positioning of the bend into the home straight increased the distance of the 1m5f race by 19 yards. A fair juvenile novice contest. They went an, at best, respectable gallop on good to firm ground. A well-bred debutante won cosily. The opening level is fluid.

## 4095 EXTRA PLACE RACES AT 188BET H'CAP 1m 5f
**2:45** (2:47) (Class 5) (0-75,80) 4-Y-O+ **£3,881** (£1,155; £577; £288) **Stalls** Centre

Form RPR
-331 **1** **Pumblechook**[7] 3817 4-9-12 **80**.... HarryBentley 4 94
(Mark Johnston) *a.p: chsd ldr over 10f out: led on bit over 2f out: pushed clr fr over 1f out: easily* **1/1**[1]
1216 **2** *10* **Amanto (GER)**[30] 3004 7-9-0 **75**....(t) FinleyMarsh[(7)] 2 74
(Ali Stronge) *s.i.s: hld up: pushed along over 3f out: hdwy to chse wnr over 1f out: sn rdn: hung rt and no ex fnl f* **5/1**[3]
6655 **3** *4* **Excellent Puck (IRE)**[37] 2752 7-9-2 **70**.... LukeMorris 1 63
(Shaun Lycett) *chsd ldr over 2f: remained handy: rdn over 3f out: wknd over 1f out* **7/1**
6042 **4** *2* **Daisy Boy (IRE)**[7] 3817 6-9-5 **73**....(vt) FranBerry 3 63
(Stuart Williams) *led: rdn and hdd over 2f out: wknd over 1f out* **9/4**[2]

2m 44.06s (0.06) **Going Correction** -0.075s/f (Good) **4 Ran SP% 109.9**
Speed ratings (Par 103): **96,89,87,86**
CSF £6.35 TOTE £1.70; EX 5.00 Trifecta £16.90.
**Owner** Christopher W T Johnston **Bred** Castlemartin Sky & Skymarc Farm **Trained** Middleham Moor, N Yorks

**FOCUS**
Race distance increased 19 yards. A fairly decent little staying handicap. They went a respectable gallop and the favourite cleared right away from more exposed opposition. A clear step forward from the winner, but there are some doubts over the second and third.

## 4096 188BET EBF STALLIONS FILLIES' H'CAP 1m
**3:20** (3:23) (Class 4) (0-85,84) 3-Y-O+ **£6,469** (£1,925; £962; £481) **Stalls** Low

Form RPR
3-12 **1** **Ghadaayer (IRE)**[25] 3189 3-9-0 **80**.... DaneO'Neill 1 87
(Sir Michael Stoute) *a.p: rdn to chse ldr over 1f out: carried lft and r.o to ld towards fin* **11/4**[1]
3-53 **2** *nk* **Angel's Quest (FR)**[17] 3472 3-8-7 **73**.... ShaneKelly 2 79
(Richard Hughes) *led: qcknd over 2f out: rdn over 1f out: hung lft and hdd towards fin* **7/2**[3]
1-40 **3** *3 ½* **Fleeting Motion**[37] 2755 3-9-4 **84**.... PatDobbs 4 82
(Richard Hannon) *chsd ldr tl rdn and edgd lft over 1f out: no ex ins fnl f* **6/1**
1254 **4** *hd* **Auntie Barber (IRE)**[2] 4010 4-9-1 **74**.... AaronJones[(3)] 3 74
(Stuart Williams) *hld up: swtchd lft and hdwy over 1f out: rdn: hung rt and styd on same pce wl ins fnl f* **12/1**
10 **5** *2 ¼* **Ice Dancing (IRE)**[28] 3094 3-8-11 **77**.... LouisSteward 5 69
(Michael Bell) *hld up: hdwy 1/2-way: rdn over 1f out: hung rt and wknd ins fnl f* **33/1**
-610 **6** *2 ¼* **Harmonise**[14] 3592 3-8-9 **75**.... LukeMorris 6 62
(Mick Channon) *chsd ldrs: rdn and edgd lft over 1f out: wknd fnl f* **11/2**
051 **7** *2 ¼* **Lyric Harmony (IRE)**[19] 3404 3-8-10 **76** ow1.... FranBerry 7 58
(Giles Bravery) *hld up: pushed along over 3f out: rdn and wknd over 1f out* **3/1**[2]

1m 37.52s (-2.48) **Going Correction** -0.075s/f (Good)
**WFA** 3 from 4yo 10lb **7 Ran SP% 114.2**
Speed ratings (Par 102): **109,108,105,105,102 100,98**
CSF £12.68 TOTE £3.20: £1.60, £2.20; EX 9.70 Trifecta £47.10.
**Owner** Hamdan Al Maktoum **Bred** Shadwell Estate Company Limited **Trained** Newmarket, Suffolk

**FOCUS**
A decent fillies' handicap. They went a respectable gallop and the favourite was good enough to cut down the long-time leader in the closing stages. The third has been rated close to form, with the fourth to her turf form.

## 4097 188BET.CO.UK EBF STALLIONS MAIDEN STKS (PLUS 10 RACE) 1m
**4:00** (4:00) (Class 4) 3-Y-O **£5,175** (£1,540; £769; £384) **Stalls** Low

Form RPR
2- **1** **Game Starter (IRE)**[235] 7740 3-9-5 0.... MartinLane 7 94
(Saeed bin Suroor) *wnt lft s: sn prom: chsd ldr over 6f out: pushed along 1/2-way: rdn over 1f out: styd on to ld wl ins fnl f* **11/8**[2]
4-22 **2** *½* **Mafaaheem (IRE)**[16] 3506 3-9-5 88.... DaneO'Neill 6 92
(Owen Burrows) *led 7f out: rdn over 1f out: hung lft and hdd wl ins fnl f* **6/5**[1]
**3** *5* **Kryptos**[259] 7161 3-9-5 0.... FranBerry 5 80
(John Berry) *racd keenly: led 1f: settled to trck ldrs: shkn up over 1f out: edgd lft and wknd ins fnl f* **50/1**
**4** *7* **Wannabe Like You** 3-9-5 0.... PatDobbs 4 64
(William Haggas) *prom: pushed along over 3f out: wknd over 1f out* **7/1**[3]
0 **5** *2* **Miss Pacific**[23] 3234 3-8-7 0.... AarronMiller[(7)] 3 54
(William Jarvis) *dwlt: hld up: pushed along over 2f out: wknd over 1f out* **66/1**
40 **6** *4 ½* **Mystery Of War (IRE)**[25] 3188 3-9-5 0.... LouisSteward 1 48
(George Scott) *hld up: pushed along over 3f out: wknd over 1f out* **50/1**
03 **7** *7* **Mulsanne Chase**[11] 3691 3-9-5 0.... SteveDrowne 2 31
(Brian Barr) *hld up: pushed along over 3f out: wknd wl over 1f out* **20/1**

1m 39.52s (-0.48) **Going Correction** -0.075s/f (Good) **7 Ran SP% 110.2**
Speed ratings (Par 101): **99,98,93,86,84 80,73**
CSF £3.04 TOTE £2.10: £1.10, £1.30; EX 2.90 Trifecta £29.30.
**Owner** Godolphin **Bred** Darley **Trained** Newmarket, Suffolk

**FOCUS**
A decent 3yo maiden. They went a muddling gallop and the winning time was two seconds slower than the previous 1m fillies' handicap. The right two horses still came to the fore, though. The runner-up has been rated to form.

## 4098 READ SILVESTRE DE SOUSA AT 188BET H'CAP 5f
**4:40** (4:40) (Class 2) (0-105,103) 3-Y-O **£12,938** (£3,850; £1,924; £962) **Stalls** Low

Form RPR
2445 **1** **Queen In Waiting (IRE)**[8] 3793 3-8-0 **87**.... RichardOliver[(5)] 3 96
(Mark Johnston) *mde all: pushed along 1/2-way: rdn and hung lft fnl f: r.o gamely* **2/1**[2]
-113 **2** *nk* **Jumira Bridge**[37] 2768 3-8-11 **93**.... HarryBentley 4 101
(Roger Varian) *trckd ldrs: rdn: hung lft and ev ch ins fnl f: r.o* **6/4**[1]
1 **3** *2 ¼* **Always Amazing**[23] 3259 3-8-2 **84** oh1.... LukeMorris 1 84
(Robert Cowell) *chsd ldrs: rdn and ev ch over 1f out: edgd lft and styd on same pce ins fnl f* **11/2**[3]
-116 **4** *1 ½* **Ascot Day (IRE)**[26] 3159 3-8-4 **86**.... SamHitchcott 5 81
(David Simcock) *hld up: rdn over 1f out: no imp fnl f* **14/1**
-410 **5** *6* **Equimou**[7] 3835 3-9-7 **103**.... DaneO'Neill 6 89
(Robert Eddery) *w wnr tl shkn up wl over 1f out: wknd and eased fnl f* **13/2**

58.0s (-1.10) **Going Correction** -0.075s/f (Good) **5 Ran SP% 108.7**
Speed ratings (Par 105): **105,104,100,98,88**
CSF £5.25 TOTE £2.70: £1.40, £1.30; EX 5.70 Trifecta £12.90.
**Owner** Sheikh Hamdan bin Mohammed Al Maktoum **Bred** Darley **Trained** Middleham Moor, N Yorks

**FOCUS**
The feature contest was a good 3yo sprint handicap.They went a decent gallop and the right two horses came to the fore in the quickest winning time on the card so far. The third has been rated close to his AW maiden win.

## 4099 BEST ODDS GUARANTEED AT 188BET H'CAP 6f
**5:20** (5:22) (Class 4) (0-85,87) 3-Y-O+ **£5,175** (£1,540; £769; £384) **Stalls** Low

Form RPR
1111 **1** **Goodwood Crusader (IRE)**[7] 3814 3-9-2 **87**.... FinleyMarsh[(7)] 2 97
(Richard Hughes) *hld up: hdwy and n.m.r over 1f out: rdn to ld ins fnl f: r.o wl* **5/1**[3]
31-0 **2** *2* **Cold Snap (IRE)**[61] 2040 4-9-9 **80**.... DaneO'Neill 5 86
(William Jarvis) *trckd ldrs: led over 1f out: rdn and hdd ins fnl f: styd on same pce* **9/1**
2111 **3** *nk* **Meshardal (GER)**[7] 3847 7-8-12 **74**....(p) LewisEdmunds[(5)] 7 79
(Ruth Carr) *mid-div: hdwy over 1f out: rdn and ev ch ins fnl f: no ex towards fin* **11/4**[1]

416- **4** *2* **Spanish City**[219] 7990 4-9-13 **84**........ HarryBentley 9 83
(Roger Varian) *mid-div: pushed along over 2f out: hdwy over 1f out: sn rdn: no ex wl ins fnl f* **9/2**[2]
/6-6 **5** *1 3/4* **Human Nature (IRE)**[21] 3330 4-9-11 **82**........(t) SteveDrowne 10 75
(Stuart Williams) *sn prom: rdn and ev ch over 1f out: wknd ins fnl f* **50/1**
0-01 **6** *nk* **Gold Hunter (IRE)**[11] 3696 7-8-13 **77**........(p) JoshuaBryan(7) 12 69
(Steve Flook) *chsd ldrs: rdn and ev ch over 1f out: wknd ins fnl f* **14/1**
1451 **7** *nk* **Diamond Lady**[21] 3330 6-9-12 **83**........ MartinLane 6 74
(William Stone) *chsd ldr: wnt upsides 4f out: rdn and ev ch over 1f out: wknd ins fnl f* **14/1**
633- **8** *3 1/4* **Fang**[217] 8032 4-9-9 **80**........ FranBerry 4 61
(William Jarvis) *led: rdn and hdd over 1f out: wknd ins fnl f* **16/1**
0510 **9** *1* **Zamjar**[22] 3303 3-9-4 **82**........(v[1]) PatDobbs 8 58
(Ed Dunlop) *hld up in tch: rdn and wknd over 1f out* **10/1**
6000 **10** *1* **Consulting**[7] 3816 4-8-11 **71**........(vt) AaronJones(3) 1 45
(Stuart Williams) *hld up: rdn over 2f out: hung rt over 1f out: nvr on terms* **66/1**
31-0 **11** *1 1/4* **Summer Chorus**[19] 3410 4-10-1 **86**........(h) JimmyQuinn 3 56
(Andrew Balding) *s.i.s: sn pushed along and a bhd* **13/2**

1m 11.11s (-1.39) **Going Correction** -0.075s/f (Good)
**WFA** 3 from 4yo+ 7lb **11** Ran SP% **116.6**
Speed ratings (Par 105): **106,103,102,100,97 97,97,92,91,90 88**
CSF £49.13 CT £151.66 TOTE £5.00: £1.70, £2.90, £1.60; EX 55.60 Trifecta £221.10.
**Owner** Goodwood Racehorse Owners Group (23) Ltd **Bred** Tally-Ho Stud **Trained** Upper Lambourn, Berks

**FOCUS**
A decent sprint handicap. They went a proper gallop and a thriving 3yo won his fifth consecutive race in a good time. The third has been rated to last year's best for now.

## 4100 LIVE CASINO AT 188BET H'CAP 7f
**5:55** (5:55) (Class 4) (0-85,87) 3-Y-O **£5,175** (£1,540; £769; £384) **Stalls** Low

Form RPR
-130 **1** **Derek Duval (USA)**[8] 3784 3-8-7 **72**........(t) AaronJones(3) 7 81
(Stuart Williams) *hld up: hdwy over 2f out: rdn to ld and edgd rt wl ins fnl f: r.o* **12/1**
-211 **2** *1 1/2* **Merlin**[10] 3715 3-9-7 **83**........ FranBerry 6 88
(Michael Bell) *racd keenly: led: hdd over 5f out: remained handy: led again over 1f out: sn rdn: hdd and unable qck wl ins fnl f* **15/8**[1]
5533 **3** *1 1/2* **High Acclaim (USA)**[35] 2818 3-9-4 **87**........(p) FinleyMarsh(7) 3 88
(Roger Teal) *chsd ldrs: led over 4f out: hdd wl over 1f out: sn rdn: styd on same pce ins fnl f* **9/2**[3]
3-20 **4** *1 1/4* **King Of Paris**[37] 2751 3-9-2 **78**........ HarryBentley 1 76
(Roger Varian) *w ldrs: led over 5f out tl over 4f out: led again wl over 1f out: sn rdn and hdd: no ex ins fnl f* **4/1**[2]
01-0 **5** *1* **Textured (IRE)**[45] 2517 3-9-5 **81**........ PatDobbs 5 76
(Sir Michael Stoute) *hld up: rdn over 1f out: nt trble ldrs* **16/1**
-221 **6** *nk* **Farook (IRE)**[38] 2727 3-9-3 **79**........ DaneO'Neill 2 73
(Charles Hills) *chsd ldrs: rdn and hung rt over 1f out: no ex fnl f* **6/1**
163- **7** *5* **Anfaass (IRE)**[231] 7820 3-9-4 **80**........ LukeMorris 4 61
(George Margarson) *hld up: pushed along 1/2-way: effrt whn hmpd over 1f out: sn wknd* **9/1**

1m 24.73s (-0.97) **Going Correction** -0.075s/f (Good) **7** Ran SP% **110.8**
Speed ratings (Par 101): **102,100,98,97,96 95,89**
CSF £32.85 TOTE £15.40: £5.10, £1.70; EX 43.20 Trifecta £188.20.
**Owner** G & J Racing **Bred** SF Bloodstock LLC **Trained** Newmarket, Suffolk

**FOCUS**
A decent 3yo handicap. They went a respectable gallop and it is sound form. It's been rated around the third.
T/Plt: £8.60 to a £1 stake. Pool: £59,898.49 - 5,033.59 winning units T/Qpdt: £3.50 to a £1 stake. Pool: £2,998.44 - 631.24 winning units **Colin Roberts**

# 4054 REDCAR (L-H)
Saturday, June 24

**OFFICIAL GOING: Good to firm (good in places; watered; 8.5)**
Wind: Blustery, largely behind in straight Weather: Fine

## 4101 RACINGUK.COM/FREETRIAL BRITISH EBF NOVICE STKS 5f 217y
**1:35** (1:40) (Class 5) 2-Y-O **£3,234** (£962; £481; £240) **Stalls** Centre

Form RPR
03 **1** **Shaheen (IRE)**[16] 3495 2-9-2 0........(t[1]) JasonHart 7 75
(John Quinn) *mde all: pushed along 2f out: rdn appr fnl f: edgd lft ins fnl f: kpt on* **15/2**
02 **2** *1 1/2* **Gangland**[17] 3460 2-9-2 0........(h) JackGarritty 2 70
(Richard Fahey) *chsd ldrs: rdn 2f out: kpt on* **4/1**[2]
**3** *3/4* **Pacific Fleet (USA)** 2-9-2 0........ DanielMuscutt 5 68
(Archie Watson) *ponied to s: trckd ldr: rdn over 1f out: one pce ins fnl f* **13/2**
402 **4** *1 1/2* **Go Now Go Now (IRE)**[16] 3495 2-9-2 0........ PJMcDonald 1 63
(Mark Johnston) *prom: rdn over 2f out: no ex ins fnl f* **6/1**[3]
0 **5** *nse* **Gabrial The Devil (IRE)**[14] 3576 2-9-2 0........ DavidNolan 8 63
(David O'Meara) *eld up: pushed along 2f out: sltly hmpd 1f out: kpt on ins fnl f: nvr threatened ldrs* **16/1**
4 **6** *1 3/4* **Collateral (IRE)**[22] 3305 2-9-2 0........ DougieCostello 4 57
(James Tate) *dwlt and early reminder: hld up: pushed along to r in tch over 3f out: rdn over 2f out: sn no imp* **11/10**[1]
**7** *29* **The Gingerbreadman** 2-9-2 0........ DuranFentiman 3
(Chris Fairhurst) *slowly away: sn outpcd in rr: t.o 1/2-way* **80/1**

1m 10.65s (-1.15) **Going Correction** -0.225s/f (Firm) **7** Ran SP% **114.1**
Speed ratings (Par 93): **98,96,95,93,92 90,51**
CSF £37.13 TOTE £7.70: £3.20, £2.20; EX 35.20 Trifecta £195.80.
**Owner** Al Shaqab Racing **Bred** Tally-Ho Stud **Trained** Settrington, N Yorks

**FOCUS**
All distances as advertised. The ground was good to firm, good in places. After riding in the opener Dougie Costello described the ground as 'on the quick side of good'. They went a fair pace for this maiden with the field racing up the centre. The race has been rated at face value around the second and fourth.

## 4102 BETTY LEIGH BOUTIQUE FASHION SHOW H'CAP 1m 5f 218y
**2:05** (2:05) (Class 6) (0-65,62) 4-Y-O+ **£2,911** (£866; £432; £216) **Stalls** Low

Form RPR
0653 **1** **Adrakhan (FR)**[26] 3155 6-8-1 **45**........ SammyJoBell(3) 4 51
(Wilf Storey) *hld up in midfield: rdn and hdwy over 2f out: led over 1f out: styd on* **13/2**
3605 **2** *1 1/4* **Percy Verence**[15] 3530 4-8-12 **53**........ JasonHart 2 57
(Tracy Waggott) *trckd ldrs: briefly ct bhd wkng rival 2f out and swtchd lft: sn rdn: ev ch jst ins fnl f: kpt on* **8/1**
3354 **3** *1 1/2* **London Glory**[14] 3566 4-9-6 **61**........(b) JackGarritty 11 63
(David Thompson) *racd keenly in tch: bit short of room and shuffled bk over 2f out: sn swtchd rt to outer: rdn and hdwy over 1f out: styd on* **7/1**
4420 **4** *3/4* **Surround Sound**[19] 3400 7-9-4 **62**........(t) RachelRichardson(3) 3 63+
(Tim Easterby) *slowly away: hld up in rr: rapid hdwy on outer over 3f out: led over 2f out: sn rdn: hdd over 1f out: no ex fnl f* **9/2**[2]
-002 **5** *7* **Midnight Warrior**[26] 3155 7-8-8 **54**........(t) PhilDennis(5) 1 45
(Ron Barr) *prom: rdn over 3f out: wknd over 1f out* **5/1**[3]
0-60 **6** *3/4* **Chauvelin**[26] 3155 6-8-4 **52**........(b) FayeMcManoman(7) 8 42
(Nigel Tinkler) *hld up: pushed along 3f out: nvr threatened* **25/1**
3444 **7** *3 1/4* **Major Rowan**[18] 3436 6-9-2 **57**........ SamJames 9 42
(John Davies) *trckd ldr: led 10f out: rdn over 3f out: hdd over 2f out: sn wknd* **8/1**
4232 **8** *nk* **With Hindsight (IRE)**[18] 3436 9-9-1 **59**........ AdamMcNamara(3) 5 43
(Steve Gollings) *led: hdd 10f out: trckd ldr: rdn 3f out: wknd over 1f out* **4/1**[1]
6022 **9** *27* **Crakehall Lad (IRE)**[9] 3756 6-8-6 **47** ow1........(b) NeilFarley 12
(Andrew Crook) *midfield: rdn over 4f out: sn lost pl and bhd: eased* **10/1**

3m 1.12s (-3.58) **Going Correction** -0.225s/f (Firm) **9** Ran SP% **115.8**
Speed ratings (Par 101): **101,100,99,99,95 94,92,92,77**
CSF £57.45 CT £376.45 TOTE £10.50: £2.80, £3.00, £2.30; EX 70.10 Trifecta £383.60.
**Owner** W Storey **Bred** E A R L Haras Du Camp Benard **Trained** Muggleswick, Co Durham

**FOCUS**
The pace was honest for this open handicap. Straightforward form.

## 4103 H JARVIS 139TH ANNIVERSARY H'CAP 7f
**2:40** (2:40) (Class 3) (0-90,91) 4-Y-O+ **£7,762** (£2,310; £1,154; £577) **Stalls** Centre

Form RPR
6655 **1** **Qeyaadah (IRE)**[16] 3498 4-9-0 **84**........ RayDawson(7) 2 92
(Michael Appleby) *pressed ldr: led over 4f out: rdn 2f out: strly pressed ins fnl f: hld on wl* **11/2**
3023 **2** *1/2* **Horsted Keynes (FR)**[30] 3003 7-10-0 **91**........ DanielMuscutt 3 97
(David Simcock) *in tch: rdn over 2f out: hdwy to chal strly ins fnl f: kpt on but a hld* **5/1**[3]
4364 **3** *1/2* **Truth Or Dare**[14] 3565 6-9-3 **83**........ AdamMcNamara(3) 6 88
(James Bethell) *sltly awkward s: hld up: pushed along over 2f out: rdn and hdwy over 1f out: kpt on* **13/2**
0110 **4** *2 1/4* **Theodorico (IRE)**[7] 3842 4-10-0 **91**........ PJMcDonald 9 90
(David Loughnane) *in tch: rdn over 2f out: one pce* **5/1**[3]
-300 **5** *shd* **Sakhee's Return**[8] 3792 5-9-5 **82**........(t) DuranFentiman 1 80
(Tim Easterby) *trckd ldrs: rdn 2f out: no ex ins fnl f* **10/1**
0032 **6** *shd* **Flyboy (IRE)**[19] 3396 4-8-10 **76**........(b) SammyJoBell(3) 7 74
(Richard Fahey) *racd keenly: trckd ldrs: rdn to chal 2f out: wknd ins fnl f* **4/1**[1]
5320 **7** *1 3/4* **Chaplin Bay (IRE)**[8] 3792 5-8-8 **74**........(p) RachelRichardson(3) 4 67
(Ruth Carr) *hld up in rr: pushed along 2f out: rdn over 1f out: nvr threatened* **9/2**[2]
5000 **8** *1 3/4* **Related**[8] 3792 7-9-4 **81**........ CamHardie 5 70
(Paul Midgley) *hld up: rdn over 2f out: sn wknd* **20/1**
0-00 **9** *13* **Jacob Black**[6] 3857 6-8-12 **75**........ JasonHart 8 28
(Kenny Johnson) *led narrowly: hdd over 4f out: remained prom tl wknd over 1f out: eased* **66/1**

1m 23.0s (-1.50) **Going Correction** -0.225s/f (Firm) **9** Ran SP% **115.6**
Speed ratings (Par 107): **99,98,97,95,95 95,93,91,76**
CSF £33.16 CT £184.14 TOTE £7.90: £2.20, £1.80, £2.10; EX 43.30 Trifecta £293.20.
**Owner** C L Bacon **Bred** Norelands Bloodstock **Trained** Oakham, Rutland

**FOCUS**
Not a great race for the grade. The runner-up helps set the standard.

## 4104 MARKET CROSS JEWELLERS H'CAP 5f
**3:15** (3:19) (Class 4) (0-85,82) 3-Y-O **£6,469** (£1,925; £962; £481) **Stalls** Centre

Form RPR
154 **1** **Batten The Hatches**[29] 3038 3-9-3 **78**........(b[1]) PJMcDonald 2 89
(David Barron) *mde all: rdn and hung lft appr fnl f: kpt on wl* **5/4**[1]
4-30 **2** *2 3/4* **The Nazca Lines (IRE)**[12] 3664 3-8-11 **72**........(v) JasonHart 4 73
(John Quinn) *chsd ldr: rdn over 2f out: one pce* **8/1**
2604 **3** *hd* **Kamra (USA)**[26] 3152 3-9-0 **75**........(p) ShaneGray 3 75
(Michael Herrington) *chsd ldr: rdn over 2f out: one pce* **12/1**
220- **4** *nse* **Maazel (IRE)**[260] 7120 3-9-1 **76**........ DanielMuscutt 7 76
(Roger Varian) *dwlt: hld up in rr: rdn over 1f out: kpt on ins fnl f: nrst fin* **5/1**[3]
124 **5** *2 3/4* **Rock Of America (USA)**[68] 1838 3-9-7 **82**........ DavidNolan 6 72
(David O'Meara) *dwlt: sn chsd ldr: rdn 2f out: wknd ins fnl f* **7/2**[2]
1-41 **6** *hd* **Desert Sport (USA)**[45] 2508 3-9-3 **78**........ DougieCostello 1 67
(Robert Cowell) *half rrd s: hld up: sn pushed along: nvr threatened* **5/1**[3]

57.63s (-0.97) **Going Correction** -0.225s/f (Firm) **6** Ran SP% **118.8**
Speed ratings (Par 101): **98,93,93,93,88 88**
CSF £13.37 TOTE £2.30: £1.40, £3.90; EX 12.70 Trifecta £86.20.
**Owner** Harrowgate Bloodstock Ltd & Partner **Bred** Whitsbury Manor Stud **Trained** Maunby, N Yorks
■ Suwaan was withdrawn. Price at time of withdrawal 7/1. Rule 4 applies to bets struck at board prices prior to withdrawal but not to SP bets - deduction 10p in the pound. New market formed

**FOCUS**
A fair handicap run at a sound pace. The third has been rated to this year's form.

## 4105 WATCH RACINGUK WITH FREE TRIAL NOW CLAIMING STKS 7f
**3:50** (3:50) (Class 5) 3-Y-O+ **£3,234** (£962; £481; £240) **Stalls** Centre

Form RPR
04 **1** **Nonno Giulio (IRE)**[1] 4059 6-8-12 71........(p[1]) PatrickVaughan(7) 4 68
(Tony Coyle) *prom: led over 4f out: rdn over 2f out: strly pressed appr fnl f: kpt on wl* **6/1**
2350 **2** *1/2* **Miss Goldsmith (IRE)**[7] 3833 4-8-4 58........ ConnorMurtagh(7) 13 59
(Richard Fahey) *trckd ldrs: pushed along and hdwy to chal appr fnl f: rdn and kpt on fnl f* **9/1**
2200 **3** *shd* **Tadaawol**[19] 3402 4-9-4 71........(p) BenSanderson(7) 6 73
(Roger Fell) *dwlt: hld up: rdn and hdwy over 1f out: kpt on wl fnl 110yds* **4/1**[2]
0-06 **4** *nk* **Iberica Road (USA)**[7] 3813 4-9-5 72........ PaddyAspell 12 66
(Grant Tuer) *chsd ldrs: briefly short of room and swtchd lft appr fnl f: kpt on wl* **28/1**
2300 **5** *1* **Sophisticated Heir (IRE)**[40] 2683 7-9-6 77........(v) AdamMcNamara(3) 5 67
(Michael Herrington) *trckd ldrs: rdn over 2f out: no ex fnl 50yds* **7/1**

2601 **6** *1 ¾* **Pobbles**[26] 3151 3-8-5 67 (v) PJMcDonald 7 50
(George Scott) *slowly away: hld up: rdn and sme hdwy over 1f out: one pce ins fnl f* **11/4**[1]
000 **7** *½* **Golden Raven (IRE)**[17] 3471 5-9-11 79 DougieCostello 3 63
(Jamie Osborne) *hld up: rdn 2f out: nvr threatened* **11/2**[3]
4342 **8** *1 ½* **Monsieur Jimmy**[26] 3151 5-8-12 58 GerO'Neill(7) 2 53
(Declan Carroll) *hld up: rdn 2f out: nvr threatened* **8/1**
00-0 **9** *1 ¾* **Never Give In**[5] 3910 4-9-2 67 (t[1]) PhilDennis(5) 9 50
(John Weymes) *led: hdd over 4f out: rdn over 2f out: wknd over 1f out* **33/1**
00-0 **10** *6* **Bertha Burnett (IRE)**[15] 3529 6-8-12 45 BarryMcHugh 1 25
(Brian Rothwell) *a rr* **66/1**
0/06 **11** *4 ½* **Conjuror's Bluff**[51] 2342 9-9-3 32 (v[1]) JasonHart 11 18
(Fred Watson) *midfield: rdn over 2f out: sn wknd* **100/1**
00-0 **12** *9* **Jon H The Lawman (IRE)**[52] 2312 4-9-4 34 (b) GeorgeDowning 10
(Ronald Thompson) *chsd ldrs: rdn and lost pl over 2f out: wknd and bhd* **66/1**
000 **13** *11* **Catskill**[19] 3404 3-8-0 23 (t[1]) SammyJoBell(3) 8
(Wilf Storey) *hld up: rdn over 3f out: wknd and t.o* **80/1**

1m 23.44s (-1.06) **Going Correction** -0.225s/f (Firm)
**WFA** 3 from 4yo+ 9lb 13 Ran SP% **121.5**
Speed ratings (Par 103): **97,96,96,95,94 92,92,90,88,81 76,66,53**
CSF £58.16 TOTE £6.70: £2.30, £2.70, £1.70; EX 64.00 Trifecta £403.60.Miss Goldsmith was claimed by Miss L Egerton for £3,000. Nonno Giulio was claimed by Mr Conor Dore for £6,000
**Owner** Stephen Louch **Bred** Ballygallon Stud Limited **Trained** Norton, N Yorks
■ Stewards' Enquiry : Patrick Vaughan two-day ban; used whip above permitted level (9th-10th July)

**FOCUS**
An ordinary claimer. The winner has been rated close to his form since his handicap win here last September, and the runner-up to her penultimate turf run.

## 4106 RACING UK FREE FOR A MONTH MEDIAN AUCTION MAIDEN STKS 5f 217y
**4:30** (4:31) (Class 5) 3-5-Y-0 **£3,234** (£962; £481; £240) **Stalls** Centre

Form RPR
30-2 **1** **Peace Dreamer (IRE)**[38] 2727 3-9-0 63 DougieCostello 5 77
(Robert Cowell) *chsd ldr: rdn to ld appr fnl f: kpt on wl to draw clr* **2/1**[1]
502 **2** *7* **Granny Roz**[14] 3568 3-9-0 70 PJMcDonald 4 55
(David Barron) *led: rdn and hung lft over 1f out: hdd appr fnl f: one pce and no ch wnr* **9/4**[2]
2-02 **3** *2 ½* **Subjective**[7] 3806 3-9-0 72 (b) GeorgeBuckell(5) 8 52
(David Simcock) *chsd ldrs: rdn 2f out: sn one pce* **2/1**[1]
03 **4** *4 ½* **Jennies Gem**[14] 3568 4-9-12 0 JackGarritty 2 39
(Ollie Pears) *midfield: rdn over 2f out: sn outpcd* **14/1**
0506 **5** *¾* **Henrietta's Dream**[13] 3624 3-9-0 34 (v) CamHardie 6 30
(John Wainwright) *midfield: rdn over 2f out: sn outpcd* **100/1**
5 **6** *2* **Snoring**[14] 3568 3-9-5 0 SamJames 7 28
(John Davies) *slowly away: hld up: pushed along over 2f out: nvr threatened* **10/1**[3]
-04 **7** *5* **Starfall**[17] 3448 4-9-12 0 ShaneGray 1 14
(Christopher Wilson) *a rr* **50/1**
**8** *2* **Tap On The Bar** 3-9-5 0 (h[1]) BarryMcHugh 3 6
(John Wainwright) *slowly away: a rr* **50/1**

1m 9.53s (-2.27) **Going Correction** -0.225s/f (Firm)
**WFA** 3 from 4yo 7lb 8 Ran SP% **118.1**
Speed ratings (Par 103): **106,96,93,87,86 83,77,74**
CSF £7.12 TOTE £2.80: £1.20, £1.20, £1.10; EX 7.70 Trifecta £17.00.
**Owner** Mrs Jenny Hadida **Bred** Tally-Ho Stud **Trained** Six Mile Bottom, Cambs

**FOCUS**
The pace was sound for the uncompetitive maiden. The runner-up has been rated close to her debut sprint maiden form.

## 4107 UNBOX RACING UK FOR FREE NOW H'CAP 5f
**5:10** (5:13) (Class 6) (0-65,67) 3-Y-0 **£3,234** (£962; £481; £240) **Stalls** Centre

Form RPR
0-05 **1** **Foxy Boy**[19] 3403 3-9-0 **58** ShaneGray 1 67
(Michael Dods) *midfield: pushed along and hdwy over 1f out: rdn and kpt on wl fnl f: hdd 50yds out* **7/1**[2]
6110 **2** *1 ½* **Mr Strutter (IRE)**[30] 2989 3-9-3 **61** (h) JasonHart 5 65
(John Quinn) *chsd ldrs: rdn 2f out: kpt on* **8/1**[3]
0601 **3** *1 ¼* **Dapper Man (IRE)**[5] 3914 3-8-13 **64** 6ex (b) BenSanderson(7) 15 63
(Roger Fell) *pressed ldr: pushed along to ld over 2f out: rdn over 1f out: hdd 50yds out: no ex* **15/8**[1]
0-50 **4** *¾* **Bay Station**[25] 3184 3-9-7 **65** SamJames 10 61
(Jason Ward) *hld up: rdn and hdwy 2f out: kpt on fnl f* **33/1**
4305 **5** *½* **Hamidans Girl (IRE)**[22] 3285 3-9-9 **67** DougieCostello 13 62
(Keith Dalgleish) *dwlt: hld up: pushed along and hdwy over 1f out: kpt on fnl f* **16/1**
3402 **6** *½* **Bithynia (IRE)**[13] 3624 3-9-9 **67** (h[1]) NeilFarley 11 60
(Christopher Kellett) *chsd ldrs: rdn over 2f out: no ex fnl f* **16/1**
6164 **7** *1* **Ebitda**[5] 3914 3-8-7 **51** PJMcDonald 7 40
(Scott Dixon) *chsd ldrs: rdn over 2f out: wknd fnl f* **7/1**[2]
1020 **8** *hd* **Little Kingdom (IRE)**[32] 2925 3-8-8 **57** PhilDennis(5) 8 45
(Tracy Waggott) *chsd ldrs: rdn over 2f out: wknd fnl f* **16/1**
5263 **9** *nk* **Joysunny**[22] 3285 3-8-5 **49** CamHardie 2 36
(Michael Easterby) *chsd ldrs: rdn over 2f out: wknd fnl f* **14/1**
4430 **10** *nse* **Jorvik Prince**[13] 3624 3-8-8 **57** (b[1]) GemmaTutty(5) 14 44
(Karen Tutty) *led narrowly: rdn whn hdd over 2f out: wknd over 1f out* **20/1**
3440 **11** *1 ½* **Tranquil Daze (IRE)**[32] 2927 3-9-4 **65** (v[1]) AdamMcNamara(3) 9 47
(David Brown) *dwlt: hld up: rdn over 3f out: sn struggling* **20/1**
-000 **12** *¾* **Decadent Times (IRE)**[19] 3403 3-8-11 **55** BarryMcHugh 4 34
(Marjorie Fife) *hld up: sn rdn along: a towards rr* **8/1**[3]
606F **13** *1 ¾* **Noble Sword**[19] 3403 3-8-10 **54** (b[1]) JackGarritty 6 27
(Jedd O'Keeffe) *a towards rr* **33/1**
-060 **14** *1 ¾* **Newgate Sioux**[22] 3285 3-8-11 **55** DuranFentiman 12 22
(Tony Coyle) *chsd ldrs: rdn and lost pl 1/2-way: sn btn* **66/1**
600- **15** *3 ¾* **King Of Castilla**[197] 8285 3-8-7 **54** SammyJoBell(3) 3 7
(Colin Teague) *s.i.s: a rr* **66/1**

57.37s (-1.23) **Going Correction** -0.225s/f (Firm) 15 Ran SP% **124.7**
Speed ratings (Par 97): **100,97,95,94,93 92,91,90,90,90 87,86,83,81,75**
CSF £59.64 CT £153.01 TOTE £7.20: £2.40, £2.90, £1.40; EX 69.20 Trifecta £200.90.
**Owner** Sekura Group **Bred** Giles W Pritchard-Gordon (farming) Ltd **Trained** Denton, Co Durham

**FOCUS**
An open handicap run at a strong pace. A minor pb from the winner, with the runner-up rated to this year's selling win. A minor pb from the winner, with the runner-up rated to this year's selling win.

T/Plt: £160.50 to a £1 stake. Pool: £60,775.25 - 276.35 winning units T/Qpdt: £11.60 to a £1 stake. Pool: £3,783.46 - 239.60 winning units **Andrew Sheret**

4108 - 4115a (Foreign Racing) - See Raceform Interactive

# 3662 PONTEFRACT (L-H)
Sunday, June 25

**OFFICIAL GOING: Good to firm (watered; 8.9)**
Wind: Fresh half behind Weather: Cloudy with sunny periods

## 4116 BET TOTEPLACEPOT EBF FILLIES' NOVICE STKS (PLUS 10 RACE) 6f
**2:00** (2:02) (Class 5) 2-Y-0 **£4,528** (£1,347; £673; £336) **Stalls** Low

Form RPR
6 **1** **Footsteps Forever (IRE)**[15] 3576 2-9-0 0 SilvestreDeSousa 11 77
(Mark Johnston) *set stdy pce: pushed along and qcknd 2f out: jnd and rdn over 1f out: drvn ins fnl f: kpt on strly towards fin* **3/1**[2]
**2** *1 ½* **Procedure** 2-9-0 0 RyanMoore 5 72+
(Sir Michael Stoute) *prom: trckd wnr to 1/2-way: hdwy to chal wl over 1f out: rdn and ev ch ent fnl f: kpt on same pce last 100yds* **2/1**[1]
**3** *1 ¼* **Clubbable** 2-9-0 0 TonyHamilton 10 68+
(Richard Fahey) *trckd ldrs: hdwy on outer over 2f out: rdn along over 1f out: drvn and kpt on same pce fnl f* **13/2**[3]
**4** *¾* **Collateral Beauty** 2-9-0 0 JackGarritty 2 66
(Richard Fahey) *chsd wnr: pushed along wl over 2f out: rdn wl over 1f out: kpt on same pce* **17/2**
**5** *3 ¾* **Hogar Seguro (IRE)** 2-9-0 0 SamJames 7 54+
(David Loughnane) *dwlt and in rr: swtchd rt to outer and hdwy wl over 1f out: rdn and styd on wl fnl f* **50/1**
**6** *¾* **What Do You Think (IRE)** 2-9-0 0 AndrewMullen 12 51
(Michael Dods) *t.k.h: trckd ldrs: pushed along over 2f out: rdn wl over 1f out: grad wknd* **16/1**
0 **7** *shd* **Excellent Times**[17] 3491 2-9-0 0 DavidAllan 1 51
(Tim Easterby) *plld hrd: trckd ldrs: pushed along over 2f out: sn rdn and wknd over 1f out* **8/1**
**8** *3 ½* **Miss Perception** 2-9-0 0 RichardKingscote 9 40+
(Tom Dascombe) *dwlt: t.k.h towards rr: pushed along wl over 2f out: n.d* **14/1**
**9** *2 ¼* **Travel Lightly** 2-9-0 0 JamesSullivan 8 33
(Tim Easterby) *trckd ldrs whn hmpd and stmbld after 150yds: t.k.h and towards rr after* **33/1**
**10** *3 ½* **Madame Jo Jo** 2-8-9 0 CliffordLee(5) 4 21
(Sarah Hollinshead) *t.k.h in midfield: a towards rr* **40/1**
00 **11** *2 ¼* **Dream Of Delphi (IRE)**[9] 3776 2-9-0 0 PatCosgrave 6 14+
(William Haggas) *midfield whn hmpd after 150yds: towards rr after* **20/1**

1m 19.31s (2.41) **Going Correction** +0.10s/f (Good) 11 Ran SP% **118.0**
Speed ratings (Par 90): **87,85,83,82,77 76,76,71,68,63 60**
CSF £9.06 TOTE £3.90: £1.50, £1.10, £2.50; EX 12.30 Trifecta £29.30.
**Owner** J Keaney **Bred** J J Keaney **Trained** Middleham Moor, N Yorks

**FOCUS**
Race distance increased by 8yds in all races. The going was good to firm, and jockeys were in agreement that the ground was quick after the opener, a fair maiden in which the first four came clear. The form will take time to settle.

## 4117 BET TOTEEXACTA MAIDEN AUCTION STKS 1m 4f 5y
**2:30** (2:30) (Class 5) 3-Y-0 **£5,175** (£1,540; £769; £384) **Stalls** Low

Form RPR
64 **1** **Cape Coast**[11] 3720 3-9-0 0 SilvestreDeSousa 4 87+
(Mark Johnston) *set stdy pce: qcknd 3f out: pushed clr wl over 1f out: easily* **1/3**[1]
4 **2** *6* **Count Simon (IRE)**[26] 3182 3-9-1 0 LiamKeniry 2 73
(Andrew Balding) *trckd wnr: hdwy and cl up 3f out: sn pushed along: rdn 2f out: swtchd wd wl over 1f out: sn drvn and plugged on: no ch w wnr* **5/2**[2]
0 **3** *8* **Love Candy (IRE)**[20] 3404 3-8-10 0 NeilFarley 1 55
(Sally Haynes) *trckd ldng pair on inner: pushed along 3f out: rdn over 2f out: sn one pce* **25/1**[3]
0-45 **4** *1 ¼* **Our Cilla**[70] 1822 3-8-5 40 (p[1]) ShelleyBirkett(3) 3 51
(Julia Feilden) *in tch: pushed along 3f out: rdn over 2f out: sn drvn and one pce* **40/1**

2m 43.19s (2.39) **Going Correction** +0.10s/f (Good) 4 Ran SP% **109.9**
Speed ratings (Par 99): **96,92,86,85**
CSF £1.49 TOTE £1.20; EX 1.40 Trifecta £2.50.
**Owner** Ali Saeed **Bred** Mr & Mrs A E Pakenham **Trained** Middleham Moor, N Yorks

**FOCUS**
Race distance increased by 8yds. An uncompetitive maiden in which only the front two in the market could be considered, and the well backed favourite came clear having made all. The runner-up has been rated to form.

## 4118 BET TOTEQUADPOT H'CAP 1m 2f 5y
**3:00** (3:00) (Class 3) (0-90,89) 3-Y-0+
**£12,450** (£3,728; £1,864; £932; £466; £234) **Stalls** Low

Form RPR
4-00 **1** **Swiftsure (IRE)**[37] 2807 3-8-3 **76** JoeFanning 3 93+
(Sir Michael Stoute) *mde all: rdn clr wl over 1f out: easily* **7/2**[3]
21-0 **2** *6* **Sound Bar**[22] 3317 3-8-9 **82** RichardKingscote 4 82
(Ralph Beckett) *hld up in rr: effrt over 2f out: sn pushed along on outer: rdn and edgd lft over 1f out: kpt on fnl f* **11/4**[2]
3625 **3** *½* **Kingthistle**[24] 3240 4-8-13 **74** (t[1]) GrahamLee 1 73
(Rebecca Menzies) *trckd ldng pair: pushed along 3f out: rdn over 2f out: drvn wl over 1f out: kpt on same pce* **10/1**
0534 **4** *2 ¼* **Beardwood**[3] 4002 5-9-13 **88** (p) SilvestreDeSousa 6 89+
(Mark Johnston) *hld up in tch: hdwy on inner whn hmpd over 1f out: no ch after and short of room again ins fnl f* **5/2**[1]
143- **5** *2* **Niblawi (IRE)**[253] 7365 5-10-0 **89** RobertWinston 2 80
(Neil Mulholland) *trckd ldrs: pushed along 3f out: rdn over 2f out: sn drvn and wknd* **9/2**
1-33 **6** *6* **Apres Midi (IRE)**[27] 3158 4-9-5 **80** PJMcDonald 5 59
(K R Burke) *trckd wnr: pushed along 3f out: rdn over 2f out: sn drvn and wknd* **12/1**

2m 12.38s (-1.32) **Going Correction** +0.10s/f (Good)
**WFA** 3 from 4yo+ 12lb 6 Ran SP% **112.4**
Speed ratings (Par 107): **109,104,103,102,100 95**
CSF £13.56 TOTE £4.90: £2.40, £1.70; EX 15.50 Trifecta £90.20.
**Owner** The Queen **Bred** Darley **Trained** Newmarket, Suffolk

**FOCUS**
Race distance increased by 8yds. Not the strongest turnout for the prize, and none of the last 10 winners of the race managed to follow-up. They went an ordinary gallop and the winner made all. The form has been taken at face value, with the third close to form.

## 4119 TOTEPOOL PONTEFRACT CASTLE FILLIES' STKS (LISTED RACE) 1m 4f 5y
**3:30** (3:30) (Class 1) 4-Y-0+

**£25,519** (£9,675; £4,842; £2,412; £1,210; £607) **Stalls** Low

Form RPR

215- **1** **Abingdon (USA)**[290] 6259 4-9-0 107 ........ RyanMoore 1 111
(Sir Michael Stoute) *trckd ldrs on inner: hdwy over 2f out: sn swtchd rt to chal: led 1 1/2f out: sn rdn clr: styd on strly* **1/1**[1]

0654 **2** *10* **Lucy The Painter (IRE)**[15] 3586 5-9-0 93 ........ DanielTudhope 3 95
(Ed de Giles) *hld up in rr: hdwy on outer over 2f out: rdn wl over 1f out: styd on fnl f: no ch w wnr* **9/1**

**3** *3/4* **Shearling**[80] 4-9-0 0 ........ BenCurtis 4 94?
(Brian Ellison) *trckd ldrs: hdwy over 2f out: and sn rdn: drvn wl over 1f out: kpt on u.p fnl f* **40/1**

03-4 **4** *2 1/4* **Pure Art**[32] 2954 4-9-0 99 ........ RichardKingscote 5 90
(Ralph Beckett) *led: pushed along over 2f out: rdn and hdd 1 1/2f out: sn drvn and wknd* **7/1**

2310 **5** *9* **Yorkidding**[5] 3928 5-9-0 99 ........ SilvestreDeSousa 8 76
(Mark Johnston) *trckd ldrs on outer: rdn along wl over 2f out: sn wknd* **5/1**[2]

200- **6** *2* **Tioga Pass**[256] 7271 6-9-0 99 ........(p) LukeMorris 6 73
(Paul Cole) *in tch: pushed along on outer 4f out: rdn 3f out: sn wknd* **25/1**

111 **7** *hd* **Signe (IRE)**[64] 1964 4-9-0 85 ........ PatCosgrave 2 72
(William Haggas) *in tch: hdwy on inner: 4f out: rdn along wl over 2f out: sn btn* **6/1**[3]

00-4 **8** *33* **Colonial Classic (FR)**[50] 2389 4-9-0 97 ........ DanielMuscutt 7 19
(James Fanshawe) *chsd ldr: rdn along 3f out: sn wknd* **12/1**

2m 37.54s (-3.26) **Going Correction** +0.10s/f (Good) **8** Ran SP% **117.4**
Speed ratings (Par 108): **114,107,106,105,99 98,97,75**
CSF £11.73 TOTE £2.00: £1.10, £2.50, £8.40; EX 11.10 Trifecta £323.90.
**Owner** Ballymacoll Stud **Bred** Ballymacoll Stud **Trained** Newmarket, Suffolk

**FOCUS**
Race distance increased by 8yds. The feature race was a Listed event, though only the favourite had a mark in excess of 100, and she ran out an easy winner. They didn't go flat out. The winner has been rated to form for now.

## 4120 TOTETRIFECTA PONTEFRACT CUP H'CAP (ROUND 4 OF THE PONTEFRACT STAYERS CHAMPIONSHIP 2017) 2m 2f 2y
**4:00** (4:03) (Class 4) (0-85,89) 4-Y-0+ **£6,469** (£1,925; £962; £481) **Stalls** Low

Form RPR

1421 **1** **Akavit (IRE)**[12] 3685 5-8-11 72 ........ SilvestreDeSousa 6 79
(Ed de Giles) *mde all: rdn over 2f out: drvn and styd on strly fnl f* **3/1**[2]

-613 **2** *2 1/4* **La Fritillaire**[34] 2889 5-8-5 66 oh3 ........ AndrewMullen 10 69
(James Given) *hld up in midfield: hdwy 6f out: chsd ldrs 3f out: rdn and edgd lft wl over 1f out: sn drvn and kpt on fnl f* **16/1**

-113 **3** *nk* **Aurora Gray**[13] 3663 4-9-0 79 ........ CharlieBennett(3) 2 82
(Hughie Morrison) *trckd ldng pair: chsd wnr over 5f out: rdn along over 2f out: drvn wl over 1f out: kpt on* **5/1**[3]

4-11 **4** *1* **Frederic**[13] 3663 6-10-0 89 ........ GrahamLee 3 91
(Keith Dalgleish) *hld up in midfield: smooth hdwy over 4f out: trckd ldrs 3f out: effrt whn n.m.r and sltly hmpd wl over 1f out: sn rdn and kpt on same pce* **11/8**[1]

-210 **5** *1* **Tuscan Gold**[13] 3663 10-8-6 67 oh3 ow1 ........(p) PJMcDonald 5 68
(Micky Hammond) *hld up in rr: hdwy over 4f out: rdn to chse ldrs 2f out: drvn wl over 1f out: no imp* **33/1**

160 **6** *1/2* **Uncle Bernie (IRE)**[13] 3663 7-8-12 73 ........(p) JamesSullivan 4 74
(Sarah Hollinshead) *hld up in rr: hdwy on outer 5f out: chsd ldrs over 2f out and sn rdn: drvn wl over 1f out: no imp* **25/1**

-000 **7** *1 1/4* **Saved By The Bell (IRE)**[16] 3527 7-9-4 79 ........(v[1]) DanielTudhope 8 78
(David O'Meara) *t.k.h: trckd ldrs: pushed along 3f out: rdn over 2f out: sn drvn and btn* **12/1**

6234 **8** *16* **Teak (IRE)**[13] 3663 10-8-5 66 oh6 ........(v) LukeMorris 7 49
(Ian Williams) *trckd wnr: cl up 7f out: rdn along 5f out: wknd over 3f out* **16/1**

1100 **9** *2 1/2* **Samtu (IRE)**[8] 3841 6-9-3 78 ........ BarryMcHugh 1 59
(Marjorie Fife) *hld up towards rr: sme hdwy on inner over 5f out: rdn along 4f out: sn outpcd* **16/1**

410/ **10** *69* **Almagest**[308] 7409 9-9-1 76 ........(tp) LiamKeniry 11
(Robert Stephens) *a towards rr: outpcd and bhd fr over 3f out* **66/1**

-006 **11** *32* **Rock On Bollinski**[13] 3663 7-8-7 68 ........(p) BenCurtis 9
(Brian Ellison) *dwlt and reminders s: sn chsng ldrs: rdn along over 5f out: sn lost pl and bhd* **40/1**

3m 58.33s (2.13) **Going Correction** +0.10s/f (Good) **11** Ran SP% **119.8**
Speed ratings (Par 105): **99,98,97,97,96 96,96,89,87,57 43**
CSF £49.27 CT £239.46 TOTE £3.70: £1.30, £4.00, £1.70; EX 50.90 Trifecta £226.30.
**Owner** Simon Treacher & Partner **Bred** Tenuta Genzianella Di Manuela Martinelli **Trained** Ledbury, H'fords

**FOCUS**
Race distance increased by 8yds. A good staying handicap in which the right horses came to the fore. The winner made all at a sensible pace. The likes of the fifth from 4lb out of the handicap suggest the bare form is ordinary.

## 4121 BET TOTEWIN FILLIES' H'CAP 1m 6y
**4:30** (4:32) (Class 4) (0-85,81) 3-Y-0+ **£6,469** (£1,925; £962; £481) **Stalls** Low

Form RPR

2326 **1** **Pattie**[10] 3749 3-8-10 73 ........ SilvestreDeSousa 4 79
(Mick Channon) *t.k.h in rr: hdwy over 2f out: chsd ldng pair over 1f out: rdn to chse ldr ins fnl f: styd on strly to ld towards fin* **7/4**[2]

2104 **2** *3/4* **Rinaria (IRE)**[6] 3911 3-8-6 69 ........(h) JoeyHaynes 2 73
(K R Burke) *led: rdn clr over 1f out: drvn ins fnl f: hdd and no ex towards fin* **7/1**

2-26 **3** *7* **Aristocratic**[43] 2605 4-10-0 81 ........(v[1]) RyanMoore 1 71
(Sir Michael Stoute) *trckd ldr: hdwy and cl up over 2f out: rdn wl over 1f out: drvn appr fnl f: kpt on same pce* **11/8**[1]

5200 **4** *3 1/4* **Fiendish (USA)**[8] 3828 3-8-10 73 ........ JoeFanning 3 54
(Mark Johnston) *trckd ldng pair on inner: hdwy 3f out: rdn along 2f out: sn drvn and one pce* **16/1**

6341 **5** *7* **Alpine Dream (IRE)**[15] 3577 4-9-6 73 ........(b) DavidAllan 5 40
(Tim Easterby) *t.k.h: trckd ldrs: rdn along jst over 2f out: sn wknd* **13/2**[3]

1m 45.17s (-0.73) **Going Correction** +0.10s/f (Good)
**WFA** 3 from 4yo 10lb **5** Ran SP% **110.2**
Speed ratings (Par 102): **107,106,99,96,89**
CSF £13.58 TOTE £2.40: £1.60, £3.40; EX 13.60 Trifecta £28.10.
**Owner** M Channon **Bred** Mike Channon Bloodstock Ltd **Trained** West Ilsley, Berks

**FOCUS**
Race distance increased by 8yds. Not a strong race for the money and they didn't go fast, but that didn't stop the winner coming from behind. Silvester de Sousa was rode a four-timer. The runner-up has been rated to the better view of her maiden form.

## 4122 BET TOTEPLACE H'CAP 6f
**5:00** (5:03) (Class 5) (0-75,74) 3-Y-0 **£4,528** (£1,347; £673; £336) **Stalls** Low

Form RPR

350- **1** **Alfie's Angel (IRE)**[302] 5884 3-9-2 69 ........ ConnorBeasley 7 74
(Bryan Smart) *trckd ldrs: hdwy on outer wl over 1f out: sn rdn: drvn ent fnl f: styd on strly to ld on line* **10/1**

3452 **2** *shd* **Sheepscar Lad (IRE)**[20] 3403 3-9-1 68 ........ SilvestreDeSousa 6 72
(Nigel Tinkler) *t.k.h early: cl up: led 2f out: rdn over 1f out: drvn ins fnl f: hdd on line* **9/2**[3]

0506 **3** *3/4* **Prazeres**[23] 3285 3-8-7 60 ........ PJMcDonald 3 62
(Les Eyre) *hld up in rr: hdwy wl over 1f out: chsd ldrs and n.m.r 1f out: sn swtchd lft to inner and rdn: drvn and kpt on wl towards fin* **12/1**

6-33 **4** *3/4* **Halawain (USA)**[9] 3784 3-9-7 74 ........ PhillipMakin 2 73
(John Quinn) *trckd ldrs: hdwy to chse ldr over 1f out: sn rdn: drvn ins fnl f: kpt on same pce* **4/1**[2]

0-50 **5** *1 3/4* **Little Miss Lola**[26] 3171 3-8-5 58 ........ JoeFanning 8 52
(Sally Haynes) *cl up on outer: disp ld 1/2-way: rdn 2f out: drvn over 1f out: wknd ins fnl f* **25/1**

0332 **6** *1 1/4* **Logi (IRE)**[26] 3184 3-9-5 72 ........ TomEaves 5 62
(David Barron) *led: rdn along and hdd 2f out: sn drvn and wknd over 1f out* **5/1**

-465 **7** *1 1/2* **Ventura Secret (IRE)**[11] 3709 3-8-9 62 ........ JamesSullivan 4 47
(Tim Easterby) *in tch: hdwy over 2f out: swtchd rt to outer and rdn to chse ldrs over 1f out: sn drvn and btn* **12/1**

2106 **8** *10* **Suitcase 'N' Taxi**[18] 3462 3-9-6 73 ........ DavidAllan 1 37
(Tim Easterby) *dwlt: a towards rr: bhd and eased fnl f* **9/4**[1]

1m 16.83s (-0.07) **Going Correction** +0.10s/f (Good) **8** Ran SP% **113.9**
Speed ratings (Par 99): **104,103,102,101,99 97,95,82**
CSF £54.01 CT £552.91 TOTE £12.40: £2.60, £1.80, £3.90; EX 52.20 Trifecta £677.30.
**Owner** Ms Dawn Aldridge **Bred** Penolva Partnership **Trained** Hambleton, N Yorks

**FOCUS**
Race distance increased by 8yds. An average 3yo sprint handicap in which they went fast and set things up for the closers. A small pb from the winner, with the runner-up rated to his best.
T/Plt: £31.60 to a £1 stake. Pool: £77,782.16 - 1,792.77 winning units. T/Qpdt: £22.20 to a £1 stake. Pool: £4,998.42 - 166.38 winning units. **Joe Rowntree**

4123 - 4129a (Foreign Racing) - See Raceform Interactive

# 1196 DORTMUND (R-H)
Sunday, June 25

**OFFICIAL GOING: Turf: good**

## 4130a 30TH GROSSER PREIS DER WIRTSCHAFT - ALFRED ZIMMERMANN-MEMORIAL (GROUP 3) (3YO+) (TURF) 1m 165y
**4:10** 3-Y-0+ **£27,350** (£10,256; £5,128; £2,564; £1,709)

RPR

**1** **Wild Chief (GER)**[49] 6-9-3 0 ........ AlexanderPietsch 4 107
(J Hirschberger, Germany) *settled in midfield on inner: cl 3rd and travelling strly over 1 1/2f out: drvn to chse ldr ent fnl f: styd on u.p to ld fnl 125yds: rdn out* **15/2**

**2** *1 1/4* **Cashman (FR)**[32] 2977 4-9-1 0 ........ JozefBojko 3 102
(A Wohler, Germany) *sn led: kicked 2l clr 2f out: sn rdn and rallied: hdd fnl 125yds: no ex* **40/1**

**3** *1 1/2* **Noor Al Hawa (FR)**[120] 934 4-9-5 0 ........ EduardoPedroza 2 103
(A Wohler, Germany) *w.w towards rr: tk clsr order 2 1/2f out: 5th and drvn 2f out: styd on fnl f: nt pce to get on terms w front two* **6/5**[1]

**4** *1* **Dragon Lips (GER)**[35] 2869 3-8-8 0 ........ AndraschStarke 5 100
(Andreas Suborics, Germany) *a cl up on outer: chsd ldr wl over 1 1/2f out: outpcd by front two over 1f out: kpt on at one pce* **7/2**[2]

**5** *3/4* **El Loco (GER)**[31] 3019 4-9-1 0 ........ MartinSeidl 9 95
(Markus Klug, Germany) *w.w in rr: rowed along to cl ins fnl 2f: styd on fr 1f out: nvr nrr* **13/1**

**6** *1 1/4* **Wonnemond (GER)**[31] 3019 4-9-5 0 ........ BayarsaikhanGanbat 1 96
(S Smrczek, Germany) *cl up on inner: dropped to last over 3f out: last and drvn over 2f out: styd on u.p fr 1 1/2f out: nt trble ldrs* **41/10**[3]

**7** *1/2* **Palace Prince (GER)**[31] 3019 5-9-7 0 ........(p) FilipMinarik 8 97
(Jean-Pierre Carvalho, Germany) *settled in fnl trio: began to cl 1 1/2f out: kpt on at same pce fnl f: nvr in contention* **77/10**

**8** *11* **Boscaccio (GER)**[16] 4-9-1 0 ........ DennisSchiergen 10 67
(Christian Sprengel, Germany) *racd keenly: hld up in midfield on outer: outpcd and hrd rdn 1 1/2f out: dropped away fnl f* **102/10**

**9** *1/2* **Bonusdargent (FR)**[58] 5-9-3 0 ........ CyrilleStefan 7 68
(Mme Pia Brandt, France) *settled in midfield: rdn and no imp ins fnl 2f: sn wknd* **42/1**

1m 48.78s
**WFA** 3 from 4yo+ 11lb **9** Ran SP% **131.4**
PARI-MUTUEL (all including 10 euro stake): WIN 85 PLACE: 20, 53, 15; SF: 1558.
**Owner** Stall Furstenhof **Bred** Walter Hacker **Trained** Germany

# 3884 SAN SIRO (R-H)
Sunday, June 25

**OFFICIAL GOING: Turf: heavy**

## 4131a PREMIO PRIMI PASSI (GROUP 3) (2YO) (TURF) 6f
**4:55** 2-Y-0 **£29,914** (£13,162; £7,179; £3,589)

RPR

**1** **Ipompieridiviggiu (ITY)**[36] 2-8-11 0 ........ DarioVargiu 2 98
(Il Cavallo In Testa, Italy) *fly j. leaving stalls: sn rcvrd to ld: mde rest: drvn clr ins fnl f: comf* **4/1**[2]

2 3 1/2 **Sestilio Jet (FR)**[56] 2-8-11 0............................ PierantonioConvertino 6 88
(Antonio Marcialis, Italy) *hld up on ldr's quarters on outer: rdn to chse ldr over 1f out: styd on fnl f: nt pce of wnr* **107/20**
3 1/2 **Bonita Fransisca (FR)**[21] 2-8-8 0.................................. FabioBranca 3 83
(Antonio Marcialis, Italy) *w.w in rr: rdn to cl 1 1/2f out: kpt on ins fnl f: nvr on terms* **48/10**[3]
4 2 1/2 **Iframe (IRE)** 2-8-11 0.......................................... CristianDemuro 1 79
(Luigi Riccardi, Italy) *trckd ldr on inner: rdn and nt qckn 1 1/2f out: one pce fnl f* **87/100**[1]
5 3/4 **Captain Cirdan (IRE)** 2-8-11 0.................................... LucaManiezzi 8 76
(Marco Gasparini, Italy) *racd in fnl pair: rdn and nt qckn over 1 1/2f out: one pce u.p fnl f* **218/10**
6 4 1/2 **Gold And Rock (IRE)** 2-8-11 0..................................... SilvanoMulas 5 63
(Stefano Botti, Italy) *chsd ldrs towards outer: rdn and lost pl wl over 1f out: wknd fnl f* **41/5**
7 1 3/4 **Cracking Art** 2-8-11 0.............................................. NicolaPinna 7 58
(Il Cavallo In Testa, Italy) *dwlt: sn rcvrd to chse ldrs on outer: cl 3rd and drvn 1 1/2f out: sn no further imp: wknd fnl f* **127/10**
8 18 **Frisson Du Large (FR)** 2-8-11 0...................................... CarloFiocchi 4
(M Narduzzi, Italy) *w.w wl in tch three fr last: outpcd and driver 2f out: sn dropped last: lost tch and eased fnl f* **224/10**

1m 11.7s (-0.10) **8** Ran SP% **133.3**
PARI-MUTUEL (all including 1 euro stake): WIN 4.99 PLACE 2.01, 2.32, 2.27 DF 12.76.
**Owner** Il Cavallo In Testa **Bred** Azienda Agricola Rosati Colarieti **Trained** Italy

4132 - 4141a (Foreign Racing) - See Raceform Interactive

## 3957 LES LANDES
Friday, June 23

**OFFICIAL GOING: Turf: firm**

### 4142a GREEN VALLEY H'CAP (TURF) 5f 110y
**7:05** (7:05) 3-Y-0+ **£1,780** (£640; £380)

RPR
1 **Spanish Bounty**[40] 2669 12-9-5 ...................................... MissMHooper 3 47
(Mrs A Malzard, Jersey) **8/1**
2 2 **Monsieur Paddy**[18] 3391 4-10-2 ..................................... PaddyAspell 2 51
(Tony Carroll) **9/4**[2]
3 1 **Ron's Ballad**[12] 3957 4-8-12 ......................................... PhilipPrince 4 30
(K Kukk, Jersey) **5/1**[3]
4 2 **Country Blue (FR)**[40] 2669 8-10-12 ......................(p) MattieBatchelor 1 51
(Mrs A Malzard, Jersey) **1/2**[1]

**Owner** Malzard Racing **Bred** Farleigh Court Racing Partnership **Trained** St Ouen, Jersey

### 4143a GLORIOUS LES LANDES RACES H'CAP (TURF) 1m 100y
**8:15** (8:15) 3-Y-0+ **£1,780** (£640; £380)

RPR
1 **Captain James (FR)**[12] 3958 7-10-3 ................................. AliceMills 3 49
(Mrs C Gilbert, Jersey) **6/4**[2]
2 1 1/2 **Grey Panel (FR)**[12] 9-10-3 ........................................ JemmaMarshall 5 46
(T Le Brocq, Jersey) **3/1**[3]
3 5 **Brown Velvet**[40] 2672 5-9-12 ........................................ PaddyAspell 6 30
(Mrs C Gilbert, Jersey) **12/1**
4 5 **First Cat**[12] 3957 10-10-3 ............................................ PhilipPrince 4 24
(K Kukk, Jersey) **5/1**
5 5 **Sir Jamie**[6] 3823 4-10-12 ........................................... MattieBatchelor 1 22
(Tony Carroll) **1/1**[1]
6 8 **Toretto (IRE)**[371] 2080 9-10-9 ..................................... ThomasMarett 2 18
(Jan Coomer, Guernsey) **18/1**

**Owner** Crystal Racing **Bred** R Marot **Trained** Jersey

## 3769 CHEPSTOW (L-H)
Monday, June 26

**OFFICIAL GOING: Good to firm (watered; 9.1)**
Weather: sunny spells

### 4144 GOOD LUCK CAROLINE WILLIAMS MUM-TO-BE CLASSIFIED STKS 1m 14y
**2:00** (2:03) (Class 6) 3-Y-0 **£2,587** (£770; £384; £192) **Stalls** Centre

Form RPR
440 1 **Pinnata (IRE)**[58] 2152 3-9-0 65.............................(t) AdamBeschizza 8 72
(Stuart Williams) *wnt to post steadily: taken rt fr stalls to r against stands' rail: led: pressed 2f out: drvn fnl f: edgd lft towards fin and a holding runner-up* **12/1**
4041 2 1/2 **Patching**[13] 3701 3-9-0 65............................(v) JosephineGordon 4 71
(Giles Bravery) *t.k.h: trckd ldrs: rdn over 1f out: chsd wnr ins fnl f: r.o: a jst hld* **3/1**[2]
3350 3 2 1/2 **Critical Thinking (IRE)**[18] 3489 3-9-0 64.................... DougieCostello 6 65
(Kevin Frost) *a.p: rdn and ev ch 2f out tl unable qck ins fnl f* **10/1**[3]
2-62 4 nse **Halinka (IRE)**[8] 3870 3-9-0 64..................................... JackMitchell 1 65+
(Roger Varian) *hld up: rdn and hdwy on outer 2f out: unable qck and hung lft ins fnl f: lost 3rd cl home* **11/4**[1]
-000 5 8 **Go On Mayson**[21] 3392 3-9-0 63......................................... JFEgan 2 48
(David Evans) *chsd ldrs: rdn 1/2-way: wknd appr fnl f* **10/1**[3]
3062 6 3/4 **Auric Goldfinger (IRE)**[72] 1790 3-8-7 65....................(b) TinaSmith(7) 7 44
(Richard Hannon) *upset in stalls: s.i.s: sn chsng ldrs: rdn over 2f out: wknd over 1f out* **12/1**
-064 7 8 **Kiribati**[5] 3975 3-9-0 65.............................................. JoeFanning 5 25
(Mark Johnston) *hld up: shkn up 3f out: short-lived effrt and no imp 2f out: eased 1f out* **11/4**[1]
5600 8 8 **Meteoric Riser (USA)**[12] 3721 3-9-0 59................................(b[1]) RyanTate 3 5
(Richard Hughes) *in rr: struggling fr 1/2-way: lost tch over 2f out* **33/1**

1m 32.79s (-3.41) **Going Correction** -0.40s/f (Firm) **8** Ran SP% **114.8**
Speed ratings (Par 97): **101,100,98,97,89 89,81,73**
CSF £48.30 TOTE £16.80: £3.40, £1.40, £2.70; EX 68.00 Trifecta £1230.40.
**Owner** David N Reynolds & C D Watkins **Bred** Ammerland Verwaltung Gmbh & Co Kg **Trained** Newmarket, Suffolk

**FOCUS**
A couple of the key runners failed to live up to expectations and the form is just modest, but this was a pb from the winner. They raced stands' side and the winner was nearest the rail throughout.

### 4145 FEEDER - THE HOMECOMING MAIDEN FILLIES' STKS 1m 14y
**2:30** (2:32) (Class 5) 3-Y-0+ **£3,234** (£962; £481; £240) **Stalls** Centre

Form RPR
-424 1 **Carol (IRE)**[18] 3507 3-9-0 76........................................... JoeFanning 5 75+
(Ed Dunlop) *broke wl: t.k.h bhd ldrs: clsd to go 2nd 1/2-way: shkn up to ld over 1f out: asserted ins fnl f: comf* **11/8**[1]
-352 2 2 1/2 **Getna (USA)**[19] 3472 3-9-0 75..................................... TomMarquand 2 69
(Richard Hannon) *hld up last but wl in tch: impr a pl 1/2-way: rdn to chal on outer 2f out: sn unable qck: hld by wnr fnl f: kpt on to go 2nd last strides* **9/4**[2]
52 3 nk **Characterized**[24] 3309 3-9-0 0........................................ TimmyMurphy 4 68
(Geoffrey Deacon) *sn led: drvn and hdd over 1f out: kpt on same pce: lost 2nd fnl strides* **4/1**[3]
53 4 4 **Jinkie Pink (IRE)**[16] 3571 3-9-0 0................................. ThomasBrown 6 59
(Ed Walker) *racd keenly: trckd ldr tl dropped to last 1/2-way: rdn 3f out: outpcd and no threat fnl 2f* **11/2**

1m 33.55s (-2.65) **Going Correction** -0.40s/f (Firm)
**WFA** 3 from 4yo 10lb **4** Ran SP% **108.3**
Speed ratings (Par 100): **97,94,94,90**
CSF £4.71 TOTE £2.00; EX 3.10 Trifecta £5.30.
**Owner** Windflower Overseas Holdings Inc **Bred** Windflower Overseas Holdings Inc **Trained** Newmarket, Suffolk

**FOCUS**
A modest maiden that didn't take much winning.

### 4146 WESTERN POWER MEDIAN AUCTION MAIDEN STKS 1m 4f
**3:00** (3:00) (Class 5) 3-5-Y-0 **£3,234** (£962; £481; £240) **Stalls** Low

Form RPR
32 1 **Dark Pearl (IRE)**[20] 3426 3-8-13 0................................. LiamKeniry 4 79+
(Ed Walker) *mde all: pressed 2f out: shkn up and qckly drew clr: comf* **1/2**[1]
4 2 5 **Assiduous**[12] 3717 3-8-13 0........................................... JoeFanning 3 71+
(Mark Johnston) *in 2nd thrght: clsd over 2f out: sn hung lft u.p: outpcd by wnr and hld over 1f out* **11/4**[2]
0-5 3 4 1/2 **Everlasting Sea**[13] 3682 3-8-8 0.................................... RobHornby 1 57
(Stuart Kittow) *in 3rd thrght: rdn 3f out: outpcd by ldng pair over 1f out* **50/1**
4 6 **Normandie Attack (FR)** 3-8-13 0.................................... RobertTart 2 52
(Charlie Fellowes) *dwlt: a last: in tch tl outpcd 5f out: pushed along and nvr any imp after* **7/1**[3]

2m 37.21s (-1.79) **Going Correction** 0.0s/f (Good) **4** Ran SP% **107.8**
Speed ratings (Par 103): **105,101,98,94**
CSF £2.13 TOTE £1.50; EX 1.90 Trifecta £7.80.
**Owner** Chi Un Fred Ma **Bred** Northern Bloodstock Agency Ltd **Trained** Upper Lambourn, Berks

**FOCUS**
This looked a match but the short-price favourite was much the best.

### 4147 LYNNE'S LOVELY LADIES H'CAP 1m 2f
**3:30** (3:31) (Class 5) (0-75,75) 4-Y-0+ **£3,234** (£962; £481; £240) **Stalls** Low

Form RPR
205 1 **Priors Brook**[21] 3409 6-9-0 75................................ JoshuaBryan(7) 5 80
(Andrew Balding) *trckd ldr: led over 1f out: drvn out* **11/8**[1]
5114 2 1/2 **Fast And Hot (IRE)**[15] 3616 4-8-13 74........................(b) RossaRyan(7) 3 78
(Richard Hannon) *led and set modest gallop: shkn up 2f out: sn hdd: drvn and kpt on* **7/4**[2]
0-60 3 1 1/4 **Sark (IRE)**[38] 2781 4-8-13 67................................................ JFEgan 4 68
(David Evans) *hld up: rdn to chse ldng pair 2f out: kpt on fnl f but nvr able to chal* **7/2**[3]
-006 4 5 **Peak Storm**[16] 3572 8-9-7 75..................................(p) TrevorWhelan 1 66
(John O'Shea) *dwlt: sn in 3rd: rdn and dropped to last 2f out: outpcd and no ch after* **10/1**

2m 10.46s (-0.14) **Going Correction** 0.0s/f (Good) **4** Ran SP% **109.8**
Speed ratings (Par 103): **100,99,98,94**
CSF £4.16 TOTE £2.50; EX 4.60 Trifecta £7.80.
**Owner** Mrs L Alexander **Bred** Mrs L M Alexander **Trained** Kingsclere, Hants

**FOCUS**
A modest handicap run at a slow pace and the winner has been rated close to this year's form.

### 4148 CPL HOMEFIRE H'CAP 5f 16y
**4:00** (4:00) (Class 6) (0-60,61) 3-Y-0+ **£2,587** (£770; £384; £192) **Stalls** Centre

Form RPR
-500 1 **Quantum Dot (IRE)**[24] 3281 6-9-7 59...................(b) CallumShepherd(3) 4 67
(Ed de Giles) *mde all: rdn 1/2-way: drvn and hld on wl fnl f* **5/1**[2]
54-4 2 1 **Our Lord**[24] 3281 5-9-10 59.............................................. RobHornby 5 63
(Michael Attwater) *prom: chsd wnr 1/2-way: drvn over 1f out: unable qck towards fin* **9/4**[1]
0643 3 1 3/4 **Mostashreqah**[17] 3545 4-8-3 45..............................(p) MillyNaseb(7) 2 43
(Milton Bradley) *s.i.s: sn chsng ldrs: clsd 2f out: rdn and unable qck fnl f* **10/1**
0006 4 nk **My Meteor**[19] 3466 10-8-7 47.................................... PaddyPilley(5) 11 44
(Natalie Lloyd-Beavis) *midfield on stands' rail: rdn 2f out: sn disp 2nd: unable qck ins fnl f* **33/1**
6545 5 1 **David's Beauty (IRE)**[17] 3524 4-9-6 55.....................(p) TomMarquand 3 48
(Brian Baugh) *chsd wnr to 1/2-way: kpt on u.p tl fdd fnl f* **5/1**[2]
5465 6 hd **Catalinas Diamond (IRE)**[9] 3811 9-8-10 45........................(t) JFEgan 7 38
(Pat Murphy) *in rr: pushed along and sme hdwy 1/2-way: r.o fnl f* **5/1**[2]
0000 7 1 **Royal Normandy**[10] 3774 5-8-10 45................................(b) JimmyQuinn 1 34
(Grace Harris) *s.i.s: towards rr: rdn 1/2-way: kpt on fnl f but nvr able to threaten* **12/1**
0043 8 2 1/4 **Very First Blade**[12] 3710 8-8-12 47..........................(p) RobertTart 10 28
(Michael Mullineaux) *rdn after 2f: a towards rr* **7/1**[3]
066 9 1 **Celerity (IRE)**[17] 3544 3-7-11 45...............................(b) KeelanBaker(7) 8 20
(David Evans) *midfield: rdn 2f out: wknd appr fnl f* **16/1**
/000 10 12 **A Definite Diamond**[30] 3084 4-8-10 45.......................... MartinDwyer 6
(Grace Harris) *midfield: rdn after 2f: sn in rr: lost tch wl over 1f out* **66/1**

57.75s (-1.55) **Going Correction** -0.40s/f (Firm)
**WFA** 3 from 4yo+ 6lb **10** Ran SP% **120.4**
Speed ratings (Par 101): **96,94,91,91,89 89,87,84,82,63**
CSF £17.22 CT £111.93 TOTE £5.90: £2.00, £1.40, £3.20; EX 19.80 Trifecta £169.40.
**Owner** Mrs Yvonne Fleet **Bred** R N Auld **Trained** Ledbury, H'fords

**FOCUS**
Moderate sprinting form.

## 4149 HAPPY BIRTHDAY STUART ASH H'CAP — 6f 16y
**4:30** (4:30) (Class 6) (0-65,66) 3-Y-O+ **£2,587** (£770; £384; £192) **Stalls** Centre

Form RPR

1010 **1** **Castlerea Tess**[14] 3666 4-9-10 **60**....(p) SeanLevey 10 66
(Sarah Hollinshead) *hld up: hdwy over 3f out: rdn over 1f out: led 150yds out: kpt on wl* **4/1**[3]

1160 **2** 1 1/4 **Go Amber Go**[24] 3278 5-9-11 **66**.... LuluStanford(5) 14 68
(Rod Millman) *chsd ldrs: rdn to ld over 1f out: hdd 150yds out: no ex towards fin* **7/2**[2]

2025 **3** 1 1/4 **Doctor Parkes**[19] 3469 11-9-5 **60**.... PaddyPilley(5) 4 58
(Natalie Lloyd-Beavis) *chsd ldrs: pushed along after 2f: kpt on same pce fnl f* **16/1**

0-00 **4** 1 **Tally's Song**[9] 3811 4-8-9 **45**....(p) JimmyQuinn 15 40
(Grace Harris) *awkward s: sn prom: rdn over 2f out: unable qck fnl f* **50/1**

0-00 **5** 1 3/4 **Jacksonfire**[12] 3704 5-8-11 **47** ow2....(p) RobertTart 1 37
(Michael Mullineaux) *s.i.s: in rr: rdn after 2f: hdwy over 1f out: r.o fnl f: nrst fin* **14/1**

3-34 **6** nk **Quite A Story**[32] 3008 5-10-0 **64**.... JosephineGordon 8 53
(Patrick Chamings) *midfield: sltly outpcd over 2f out: drvn over 1f out: kpt on but nvr able to chal* **11/4**[1]

00-0 **7** nk **She's Rosanna**[27] 3166 3-8-2 **45**.... KieranO'Neill 3 31
(Steph Hollinshead) *led: rdn over 2f out: hdd over 1f out: wknd ins fnl f* **40/1**

300 **8** 1 1/4 **Louis Vee (IRE)**[16] 3569 9-8-4 **45**....(p) MitchGodwin(5) 12 29
(John O'Shea) *chsd ldrs: rdn 3f out: wknd over 1f out* **18/1**

0304 **9** hd **Spellmaker**[24] 3280 8-9-4 **54**.... MartinDwyer 11 41+
(Tony Newcombe) *nodded leaving stalls: a towards rr: rdn and outpcd 1/2-way: kpt on fnl f* **8/1**

0000 **10** 7 **The Perfect Show**[19] 3468 4-8-11 **54**....(b) MillyNaseb(7) 7 17
(Milton Bradley) *midfield: rdn over 2f out: wknd over 1f out* **20/1**

0-00 **11** 1 **Bold Grove**[88] 1456 5-8-9 **45**....(h) RobHornby 6 5
(Edward Bevan) *chsd ldrs: rdn and wkng whn n.m.r 2f out* **12/1**

4030 **12** 4 1/2 **Kaaber (USA)**[10] 3774 6-9-1 **51**....(b) TomMarquand 2
(Roy Brotherton) *s.i.s: a in rr* **14/1**

P0P0 **P** **Tilsworth Micky**[20] 3442 5-9-9 **59**.... KierenFox 5
(J R Jenkins) *a towards rr: rdn and no hdwy over 2f out: eased over 1f out: sn p.u and dismntd: bled fr the nose* **33/1**

1m 10.14s (-1.86) **Going Correction** -0.40s/f (Firm)
**WFA** 3 from 4yo+ 7lb **13** Ran SP% **124.3**
Speed ratings (Par 101): **96,94,92,91,89 88,88,86,86,76 75,69,**
CSF £18.58 CT £218.88 TOTE £5.20: £2.10, £2.10, £4.30; EX 23.30 Trifecta £237.20.
**Owner** Graham Brothers Racing Partnership **Bred** Graham Brothers Racing Partnership **Trained** Upper Longdon, Staffs

**FOCUS**
A pretty modest sprint, two of those towards the head of the market came to the fore. The runner-up and 4th help set the level, with the winner posting a minor pb.

## 4150 HUDSON HARRIS H'CAP — 7f 16y
**5:00** (5:01) (Class 6) (0-65,66) 3-Y-O **£2,587** (£770; £384; £192) **Stalls** Centre

Form RPR

0645 **1** **Chicago Star**[25] 3246 3-9-9 **66**.... JFEgan 10 73
(Mick Channon) *trckd ldrs: led over 2f out: drvn over 1f out: r.o wl* **7/2**[1]

2602 **2** 1/2 **Whatalove**[20] 3423 3-7-12 **46**....(h) RichardOliver(5) 11 52
(Martin Keighley) *chsd ldrs: drvn over 2f out: chsd wnr 100yds out: r.o* **8/1**

2644 **3** 1 **Royal Peace (IRE)**[17] 3536 3-9-5 **62**.... KieranO'Neill 1 65
(Richard Hannon) *led 1f: styd cl up: drvn 2f out: lost 2nd and no ex fnl 100yds* **12/1**

2333 **4** nk **Topmeup**[4] 4006 3-8-3 **53**....(v) KatherineGlenister(7) 4 55
(David Evans) *s.i.s: towards rr: swtchd lft and hdwy u.p over 3f out: chsng ldrs whn edgd rt over 1f out: kpt on same pce fnl f* **4/1**[2]

403U **5** 1/2 **Captain Sedgwick (IRE)**[9] 3823 3-8-4 **47**.... JimmyQuinn 2 48
(John Spearing) *s.i.s: in rr: rdn and hdwy over 2f out: nt clr run over 1f out: styd on fnl f* **25/1**

4413 **6** 1 3/4 **Love And Be Loved**[8] 3870 3-8-5 **55**.... WilliamCox(7) 9 51
(John Flint) *cl up tl led after 1f: rdn and hdd over 2f out: kpt on same pce* **5/1**[3]

400 **7** 4 **Accomplice**[33] 2957 3-9-5 **62**.... RobHornby 5 48
(Michael Blanshard) *midfield: rdn and outpcd 1/2-way: sme hdwy over 1f out: wknd ins fnl f* **33/1**

-002 **8** 7 **Opening Time**[13] 3695 3-8-13 **56**....(b) SeanLevey 3 23
(Richard Hannon) *chsd ldrs: stmbld sltly over 4f out: rdn 3f out: wknd over 1f out* **7/2**[1]

06-0 **9** 11 **Garth Rockett**[31] 3024 3-8-9 **52**.... MartinDwyer 6
(Brendan Powell) *prom: rdn 3f out: wknd 2f out: eased fnl f* **40/1**

55U5 **10** 24 **Belgravian (FR)**[20] 3426 3-9-5 **62**....(t[1]) RobertWinston 8
(Archie Watson) *restless in stalls: racd keenly in rr: nvr looked happy on trck: nt clr run on rail 4f out: sn pushed along and no hdwy: eased 2f out: virtually p.u* **6/1**

1m 21.15s (-2.05) **Going Correction** -0.40s/f (Firm) **10** Ran SP% **123.4**
Speed ratings (Par 97): **95,94,93,92,92 90,85,77,65,37**
CSF £33.84 CT £319.16 TOTE £4.70: £1.70, £2.50, £3.40; EX 33.80 Trifecta £404.80.
**Owner** Jon and Julia Aisbitt **Bred** Stuart Stuckey **Trained** West Ilsley, Berks

**FOCUS**
A moderate handicap and straightforward form.
T/Plt: £114.20 to a £1 stake. Pool: £67,623.89 - 432.16 winning units T/Qpdt: £16.80 to a £1 stake. Pool: £5,323.60 - 234.10 winning units **Richard Lowther**

# 3916 WINDSOR (R-H)
Monday, June 26

**OFFICIAL GOING: Good to firm (good in places; watered; 7.7)**
Wind: Almost nil Weather: Fine, warm

## 4151 BEST OF BRITISH FESTIVAL 1-3 JULY MAIDEN STKS — 6f 12y
**5:50** (5:56) (Class 5) 2-Y-O **£2,911** (£866; £432; £216) **Stalls** Low

Form RPR

**1** **Boomerang Betty (IRE)** 2-9-0 0.... DougieCostello 4 69
(Jamie Osborne) *in tch in midfield: pushed along 1/2-way: prog 2f out: rdn to chse ldr fnl f: drvn ahd last 100yds* **22/1**

**2** 1/2 **Exceedingly Diva** 2-8-7 0.... TylerSaunders(7) 7 68
(Marcus Tregoning) *s.i.s and pushed along early: then t.k.h in midfield: prog over 2f out: shkn up to ld over 1f out: hdd and nt qckn last 100yds* **16/1**

**3** nk **Downtown Mombasa (IRE)** 2-8-11 0.... EdwardGreatrex(3) 12 67
(Eve Johnson Houghton) *sn wl in rr: pushed along 1/2-way: sme prog and rdn 2f out: swtchd lft and weaved through rivals fnl f: fin wl* **20/1**

**4** 3/4 **Serjeant Painter** 2-9-2 0.... KieranShoemark(3) 15 69
(Marcus Tregoning) *racd on wd outside: wl in rr: prog jst over 2f out: shkn up over 1f out: styd on wl fnl f: nrst fin* **33/1**

**5** 1/2 **Yorbelucky** 2-9-5 0.... AdamKirby 6 68
(David Evans) *chsd clr ldng pair: shkn up 2f out: no imp over 1f out: one pce* **10/1**

**6** 1 **Swissal (IRE)** 2-9-5 0.... JimCrowley 2 65
(David Dennis) *wl in tch in midfield: pushed along 2f out: kpt on same pce fr over 1f out: nt disgracd* **25/1**

**7** 1 1/4 **Pheidippides** 2-9-5 0.... PatCosgrave 1 61
(Tom Clover) *slowly away: wl in rr: prog against nr side rail jst over 2f out: rdn and kpt on same pce fr over 1f out* **8/1**[3]

**8** 1 **Paco's Prince** 2-9-5 0.... MartinHarley 8 58
(Martin Smith) *in tch: outpcd 1/2-way: nvr on terms after but kpt on fnl f* **25/1**

**9** 3 3/4 **Mountain Peak** 2-9-5 0.... LiamKeniry 13 47
(Ed Walker) *wl in tch: no prog 2f out: fdd over 1f out* **16/1**

**10** shd **Two Seas** 2-9-5 0.... HarryBentley 10 47
(George Peckham) *w ldr: led 1/2-way: sn clr: rdn and hdd jst over 1f out: wknd rapidly* **10/1**

**11** 1/2 **Strategic (IRE)** 2-9-5 0.... RyanMoore 9 51+
(Richard Hannon) *slowly away: rn green and nvr gng wl: a wl in rr* **7/2**[2]

**12** 6 **Lady Of Authority** 2-9-0 0.... ShaneKelly 11 22
(Murty McGrath) *in tch to 1/2-way: sn wknd* **100/1**

**13** 1/2 **Tiepolo (IRE)** 2-9-5 0.... FranBerry 3 26
(Gary Moore) *led to 1/2-way: wknd rapidly over 2f out* **50/1**

**14** 23 **Keynote (IRE)** 2-9-5 0.... AndreaAtzeni 5
(Roger Varian) *chsd ldrs to 1/2-way: wknd v rapidly: t.o* **11/4**[1]

1m 13.8s (0.80) **Going Correction** -0.025s/f (Good) **14** Ran SP% **112.6**
Speed ratings (Par 93): **93,92,91,90,90 88,87,85,80,80 80,72,71,40**
CSF £266.71 TOTE £30.10: £5.50, £5.40, £5.00; EX 467.00 Trifecta £3564.10.
**Owner** Melbourne 10 Racing Partnership **Bred** Awbeg Stud **Trained** Upper Lambourn, Berks

■ City Gent was withdrawn. Price at time of withdrawal 8/1. Rule 4 applies to all bets - deduction 10p in the pound.

**FOCUS**
Rail moved out 8yds from the stands' side inner position from 6f to winning post. No previous form to go on in this 2yo maiden.

## 4152 YOUNG LIVES VS CANCER MAIDEN STKS — 1m 31y
**6:20** (6:25) (Class 5) 3-Y-O+ **£2,911** (£866; £432; £216) **Stalls** Low

Form RPR

-56 **1** **Plutonian (IRE)**[13] 3691 3-9-4 0.... JimCrowley 8 89
(Charles Hills) *mde all: clr 3f out: shkn up over 1f out: drew further away after* **3/1**[2]

0 **2** 10 **Violet's Lads (IRE)**[23] 3329 3-8-13 0.... JackMitchell 1 61
(Brett Johnson) *reluctant to enter the stalls: hld up in rr: prog over 3f out: chsd clr wnr wl over 1f out: hanging and racd awkwardly but beat others wl enough* **66/1**

5-3 **3** 3 1/4 **Ebtkaar (IRE)**[21] 3393 3-9-4 0.... AndreaAtzeni 3 58
(Roger Varian) *trckd ldng pair: rdn to chse wnr over 2f out to wl over 1f out: one pce* **10/11**[1]

0-04 **4** 4 **Tesko Fella (IRE)**[9] 3824 3-9-4 64....(h[1]) AntonioFresu 4 49
(Luke McJannet) *chsd wnr to over 2f out: wknd* **12/1**

- **5** nk **Keeper's Choice (IRE)** 3-8-13 0.... OisinMurphy 5 43
(Denis Coakley) *s.s: a in rr: lft bhd fr 3f out* **11/2**[3]

60 **6** 4 1/2 **African Quest**[24] 3309 3-8-10 0.... HectorCrouch(3) 2 33
(Gary Moore) *t.k.h: hld up in rr: outpcd fr 3f out: no prog after* **33/1**

00 **7** 4 **Lifeboat Lad (USA)**[38] 2782 3-9-4 0....(h) PatCosgrave 6 29
(Dean Ivory) *in tch to 3f out: wknd and bhd fnl 2f* **22/1**

05 **R** **Kyshoni (IRE)**[20] 3438 3-8-13 0.... ShaneKelly 9
(Mike Murphy) *swvd lft ldng stalls and rn off the trck* **8/1**

1m 43.0s (-1.70) **Going Correction** -0.025s/f (Good)
**WFA** 3 from 4yo 10lb **8** Ran SP% **120.4**
Speed ratings (Par 103): **107,97,93,89,89 84,80,**
CSF £183.57 TOTE £4.20: £1.50, £8.50, £1.10; EX 191.60 Trifecta £1086.40.
**Owner** Mrs Fitri Hay **Bred** Pier House Stud **Trained** Lambourn, Berks

**FOCUS**
This modest maiden proved a messy affair and the winner dominated. It's a hard race to rate.

## 4153 SKY BET TOP PRICE PROMISE H'CAP — 1m 31y
**6:50** (6:50) (Class 4) (0-85,80) 3-Y-O **£4,690** (£1,395; £697; £348) **Stalls** Low

Form RPR

1161 **1** **Sir Plato (IRE)**[28] 3163 3-9-3 **76**.... OisinMurphy 5 82
(Rod Millman) *tried to ld but forced to chse ldr: chal over 3f out: narrow ld 2f out: hdd jst ins fnl f: drvn ahd last 100yds: hld on* **7/2**[3]

410 **2** hd **Rumpole**[23] 3317 3-9-7 **80**.... AdamKirby 1 85
(Hughie Morrison) *won battle for ld: rdn and narrowly hdd 2f out: kpt on u.p to ld again jst ins fnl f: hdd last 100yds: jst hld* **6/4**[1]

5036 **3** nk **Fastnet Spin (IRE)**[27] 3167 3-8-8 **72**....(v) DavidEgan(5) 3 76
(David Evans) *hld up in last: prog to chse ldng pair over 1f out: drvn to chal fnl f: fnd little and hld nr fin* **16/1**

6-51 **4** 2 **Meshaykh (IRE)**[28] 3142 3-9-5 **78**.... RyanMoore 4 77
(Sir Michael Stoute) *trckd ldng pair: rdn over 2f out: nt qckn and lost 3rd over 1f out: one pce after* **11/4**[2]

01 **5** 1/2 **Rubens Dream**[18] 3493 3-9-7 **80**.... JimCrowley 2 78
(Charles Hills) *trckd ldrs: rdn and nt qckn over 2f out: one pce over 1f out* **5/1**

1m 44.53s (-0.17) **Going Correction** -0.025s/f (Good) **5** Ran SP% **111.4**
Speed ratings (Par 101): **99,98,98,96,96**
CSF £9.36 TOTE £4.70: £2.40, £2.20; EX 10.00 Trifecta £60.30.
**Owner** The Sir Plato Partnership **Bred** Noel Finegan **Trained** Kentisbeare, Devon

**FOCUS**
They went hard up front in this fair 3yo handicap and it saw a cracking finish.

## 4154 SKY BET ROYAL WINDSOR SPRINT SERIES H'CAP (QUALIFIER) 6f 12y
**7:20** (7:20) (Class 3) (0-95,95) 3-Y-O **£7,439** (£2,213; £1,106; £553) **Stalls** Low

Form RPR
3-02 **1** **Parnassian (IRE)**[14] 3664 3-8-12 **86** BenCurtis 1 92
(K R Burke) *hld up in last pair: prog 2f out: rdn over 1f out: clsd to ld last 100yds: sn in command* **10/3**[3]

-632 **2** ¾ **Open Wide (USA)**[14] 3672 3-8-9 **83** (p) AndreaAtzeni 3 86
(Amanda Perrett) *trckd ldrs: pushed along 1/2-way: rdn to chal jst over 1f out: upsides ins fnl f but limited rspnse and outpcd nr fin* **13/8**[1]

2060 **3** hd **Letmestopyouthere (IRE)**[16] 3588 3-8-11 **85** JFEgan 5 87
(David Evans) *trckd ldrs: pushed along 1/2-way: clsd on outer 2f out: rdn to ld ins fnl f: hdd and outpcd last 100yds* **20/1**

-360 **4** 1 ¾ **Volatile**[30] 3071 3-9-7 **95** MartinHarley 6 91
(James Tate) *led: rdn over 1f out: hdd & wknd jst ins fnl f* **17/2**

221 **5** 2 **Fair Cop**[28] 3157 3-8-8 **82** DavidProbert 2 72
(Andrew Balding) *racd against rail: pressed ldr to over 1f out: fdd* **11/4**[2]

3300 **6** 1 ¼ **Sayesse**[9] 3844 3-8-5 **84** (v[1]) DavidEgan(5) 4 70
(Mick Channon) *a in last pair: rdn and struggling 1/2-way: no prog after* **10/1**

1m 12.27s (-0.73) **Going Correction** -0.025s/f (Good) **6 Ran SP% 112.2**
Speed ratings (Par 103): **103,102,101,99,96 95**
CSF £9.19 TOTE £4.40: £1.70, £1.50; EX 8.90 Trifecta £81.30.
**Owner** Ontoawinner 14 & Mrs E Burke **Bred** Ballyhane Stud Ltd **Trained** Middleham Moor, N Yorks

**FOCUS**
The feature handicap was run at a solid pace and the principals came down the middle.

## 4155 APTUS INVESTMENT FUND FILLIES' H'CAP 1m 2f
**7:50** (7:50) (Class 4) (0-85,83) 3-Y-O **£4,690** (£1,395; £697; £348) **Stalls** Centre

Form RPR
2-60 **1** **Flying North**[31] 3031 3-9-3 **79** TimmyMurphy 1 86
(Richard Hannon) *mde all: kicked for home over 3f out and 3 l clr: rdn 2f out: styd on wl* **12/1**

21 **2** 1 ¾ **Lightening Dance**[15] 3615 3-9-2 **78** JimCrowley 3 82
(Amanda Perrett) *sn trckd ldng pair: rdn to chse wnr over 2f out: kpt on but no imp and nvr able to chal* **11/4**[3]

2-61 **3** 1 ¼ **Mouille Point**[55] 2269 3-9-2 **78** RyanMoore 4 79
(Richard Hannon) *trckd wnr: taken towards far side 3f out: sn lost 2nd: rdn and one pce fnl 2f* **15/8**[1]

3250 **4** shd **Plead**[10] 3786 3-9-3 **79** JackMitchell 2 80
(Archie Watson) *hld up in last: effrt 3f out: rdn and limited rspnse 2f out: no threat* **8/1**

1 **5** 1 ¼ **Maid To Remember**[45] 2585 3-9-7 **83** PatDobbs 5 81
(Ralph Beckett) *in tch: rdn over 2f out: one pce and nvr able to threaten* **9/4**[2]

2m 9.38s (0.68) **Going Correction** -0.025s/f (Good) **5 Ran SP% 111.0**
Speed ratings (Par 98): **96,94,93,93,92**
CSF £44.39 TOTE £11.50: £3.00, £1.40; EX 31.40 Trifecta £95.00.
**Owner** P T Tellwright **Bred** P T Tellwright **Trained** East Everleigh, Wilts
■ Stewards' Enquiry : Timmy Murphy regarding the apparent improvement in form, the trainer's representative said the filly had benefited from a flatter track

**FOCUS**
This fair fillies' handicap was run at an uneven pace. The winner has been rated to a better view of her nursery form, with the runner-up posting a length pb on maiden form.

## 4156 ROBJAN WEDDING H'CAP 1m 3f 99y
**8:20** (8:20) (Class 5) (0-75,77) 3-Y-O **£2,911** (£866; £432; £216) **Stalls** Centre

Form RPR
1234 **1** **Wefait (IRE)**[18] 3503 3-9-10 **77** SeanLevey 7 82
(Richard Hannon) *chsd clr ldr: clsd 4f out: chal 3f out: rdn to ld over 1f out: drvn out* **5/1**

0612 **2** 1 **The Secrets Out**[2] 4087 3-8-2 **55** oh2 (h) KieranO'Neill 1 58
(Luke Dace) *led at str pce: clr after 3f: breather 4f out: tried to kick on again 3f out but hanging u.p: hdd over 1f out: kpt on but hld* **3/1**[2]

43-0 **3** nk **Sussex Ranger (USA)**[19] 3457 3-9-2 **72** HectorCrouch(3) 5 75
(Gary Moore) *dwlt and pushed along early: urged along in last pair 4f out: rdn and clsd 3f out: drvn and nt qckn 2f out: styd on fnl f and nrly snatched 2nd* **8/1**

-616 **4** 1 ¾ **Nathan Mayer**[19] 3457 3-9-6 **73** RyanMoore 3 73
(Sir Michael Stoute) *dropped to last after 3f and detached sn after: stl detached 3f out: kpt on u.p fr 2f out: no threat* **9/4**[1]

2-02 **5** nk **Footman (GER)**[19] 3457 3-9-10 **77** ShaneKelly 2 76
(Richard Hughes) *hld up in 4th: gng wl 4f out: effrt 3f out: rdn over 2f out: racd awkwardly and fnd nil w tail swishing: no imp after* **9/2**[3]

0-40 **6** 1 **Arcadian Sea (IRE)**[32] 2997 3-8-4 **57** RoystonFfrench 9 54
(William Jarvis) *settled off the pce: urged along over 4f out: nvr on terms but plugged on fnl 2f* **20/1**

5-50 **7** nk **Ingleby Mackenzie**[11] 3745 3-8-4 **62** DavidEgan(5) 4 59
(Mick Channon) *chsd clr ldr: clsd 4f out: rdn over 3f out and sn lost pl: fdd over 1f out* **14/1**

2m 27.04s (-2.46) **Going Correction** -0.025s/f (Good) **7 Ran SP% 113.2**
Speed ratings (Par 99): **107,106,106,104,104 103,103**
CSF £19.92 CT £116.32 TOTE £8.00: £2.90, £2.30; EX 20.20 Trifecta £126.00.
**Owner** Mohamed Saeed Al Shahi **Bred** Conor Murphy & Rathmore Stud **Trained** East Everleigh, Wilts

**FOCUS**
There was a strong early pace on in this modest 3yo handicap. A small pb from the winner.

## 4157 SKY BET HORSERACING CASH OUT H'CAP 5f 21y
**8:50** (8:51) (Class 6) (0-65,67) 3-Y-O **£2,264** (£673; £336; £168) **Stalls** Low

Form RPR
-553 **1** **Zavikon**[40] 2734 3-9-3 **61** ShaneKelly 7 66
(Richard Hughes) *in tch in last pair: rdn and prog fr 2f out on outer: led ins fnl f: drvn out* **5/2**[1]

2451 **2** ½ **Lightoller (IRE)**[3] 4046 3-9-2 **67** 6ex (b) KeithQuinn(7) 1 70
(Mick Channon) *chsd ldrs: clsd against rail 1/2-way: drvn to ld over 1f out: hanging and racd awkwardly after: hdd and nt qckn ins fnl f* **11/2**[3]

3-35 **3** ¾ **Island Cloud**[17] 3517 3-9-5 **66** GeorgeWood(3) 4 66
(Heather Main) *in tch in last pair: rdn 2f out: prog fnl f: styd on to take 3rd last strides* **8/1**

5012 **4** nk **Seneca Chief**[17] 3545 3-9-4 **62** (h) GeorgeDowning 6 61
(Daniel Kubler) *trckd ldrs: rdn 2f out: chal over 1f out: one pce ins fnl f* **14/1**

2134 **5** ¾ **Mercers**[31] 3035 3-9-5 **63** JimCrowley 9 60
(Peter Crate) *racd on wd outside: wl in tch: rdn 2f out: nt qckn over 1f out: one pce after* **9/2**[2]

2400 **6** 2 **Popsilca**[40] 2734 3-8-8 **52** DavidProbert 5 41
(Mick Quinn) *led to over 1f out: wknd* **25/1**

03-0 **7** nk **Bombay Dream**[17] 3536 3-9-7 **65** (b[1]) PatCosgrave 8 53
(William Haggas) *trckd ldrs: rdn and nt qckn 2f out: no imp fnl f* **9/2**[2]

0-55 **8** 4 **Verdi (IRE)**[9] 3832 3-8-7 **51** DannyBrock 3 25
(John Ryan) *in tch in rr tl wknd wl over 1f out* **14/1**

0-04 **9** 10 **Miss Rosina (IRE)**[25] 3260 3-9-1 **59** JFEgan 2
(George Margarson) *wl away: chsd ldr to 2f out: sn wknd qckly* **10/1**

1m 0.88s (0.58) **Going Correction** -0.025s/f (Good) **9 Ran SP% 117.7**
Speed ratings (Par 97): **94,93,92,91,90 87,86,80,64**
CSF £16.78 CT £97.49 TOTE £3.50: £1.50, £2.10, £2.50; EX 17.90 Trifecta £116.40.
**Owner** Embleton, Galloway, Hanley & Lawrence **Bred** Crossfields Bloodstock Ltd **Trained** Upper Lambourn, Berks

**FOCUS**
This ordinary 3yo sprint handicap was run at a frantic early pace. Straightforward form.
T/Plt: £701.90 to a £1 stake. Pool: £80,126.82 - 83.33 winning units T/Qpdt: £21.80 to a £1 stake. Pool: £8,030.08 - 271.50 winning units **Jonathan Neesom**

# 3543 WOLVERHAMPTON (A.W) (L-H)
Monday, June 26

**OFFICIAL GOING: Tapeta: standard**
Wind: Light against Weather: Overcast

## 4158 INVEST CITY OF WOLVERHAMPTON AMATEUR RIDERS' (S) STKS 1m 4f 51y (Tp)
**2:15** (2:15) (Class 6) 4-Y-O+ **£2,183** (£677; £338; £169) **Stalls** Low

Form RPR
3412 **1** **Viewpoint (IRE)**[19] 3470 8-11-4 80 MissSBrotherton 5 82
(Michael Appleby) *hld up: hdwy over 5f out: chsd ldr over 3f out: shkn up to ld ins fnl f: styd on* **6/4**[1]

1420 **2** 1 ¼ **Luv U Whatever**[16] 3580 7-11-4 80 MrSWalker 4 80
(Michael Attwater) *a.p: led 4f out: rdn over 1f out: hdd ins fnl f: styd on same pce* **2/1**[2]

305 **3** 8 **Entihaa**[18] 3494 9-10-9 79 (p) MissJodieHughes(3) 1 61
(Dai Burchell) *hld up: nt clr run wl over 2f out: hdwy to go 3rd over 1f out: nvr on terms* **7/1**

6520 **4** 1 ¾ **Noguchi (IRE)**[60] 2111 12-10-5 63 (b) MissEBushe(7) 8 58
(Chris Dwyer) *hld up: pushed along over 3f out: styd on fr over 1f out: nvr on terms* **14/1**

534- **5** 7 **Medieval Bishop (IRE)**[354] 4045 8-10-7 52 MrMEnnis(5) 6 47
(Tony Forbes) *hld up: reminders over 4f out: hdwy over 3f out: wnt 3rd over 2f out: sn wknd* **50/1**

4050 **6** 8 **Sarakova (IRE)**[20] 3440 4-10-5 42 (b) DrMVoikhansky(7) 11 34
(Kevin Frost) *hld up: pushed along over 6f out: n.d* **100/1**

003 **7** 8 **Uphold**[55] 2272 10-10-12 52 (v) MrRBirkett 10 22
(Gay Kelleway) *prom: rdn over 3f out: sn wknd* **25/1**

000- **8** 4 ½ **Oyster Pearl (IRE)**[288] 6367 4-10-2 43 ow2 (t) MrJakeBament(7) 9 11
(Carroll Gray) *chsd ldr 8f: sn rdn: wknd wl over 2f out* **100/1**

0440 **9** 4 **The Greedy Boy**[16] 3575 4-10-7 43 (t[1]) MrJFlook(5) 3 8
(Steve Flook) *prom tl rdn and wknd wl over 2f out* **100/1**

0046 **10** 5 **Steady Major (IRE)**[17] 3546 5-10-9 48 (p) MissBeckyBrisbourne(3) 7
(Mark Brisbourne) *led 8f: sn rdn: wknd over 2f out* **100/1**

2316 **R** **Retrieve (AUS)**[4] 4002 9-10-11 84 (t) EmmaTaff(7) 2
(Jamie Osborne) *ref to r* **4/1**[3]

2m 39.88s (-0.92) **Going Correction** -0.05s/f (Stan) **11 Ran SP% 122.3**
Speed ratings (Par 101): **101,100,94,93,89 83,78,75,72,69**
CSF £4.86 TOTE £2.20: £1.10, £1.50, £2.30; EX 5.50 Trifecta £23.20.The winner was bought-in by Harriett Bethell for 7,000 guineas. Luv U Whatever was claimed by Mrs Marjorie Fife for £6,000. Retrieve was claimed by Mr T. Heal for £6,000.
**Owner** Mick Appleby Racing **Bred** F Dunne **Trained** Oakham, Rutland

**FOCUS**
An uncompetitive seller with the market leaders in control from a long way out.

## 4159 ROA/RACING POST OWNERS JACKPOT H'CAP 5f 21y (Tp)
**2:45** (2:45) (Class 5) (0-75,77) 3-Y-O **£3,557** (£1,058; £529; £264) **Stalls** Low

Form RPR
-504 **1** **Super Julius**[8] 3865 3-9-9 **77** (p[1]) CharlesBishop 2 86
(Eve Johnson Houghton) *led 1f: trckd ldrs: shkn up to ld over 1f out: rdn out* **3/1**[2]

3502 **2** 2 ½ **Lawless Louis**[4] 4015 3-9-2 **73** (v) JoshDoyle(3) 1 73
(David O'Meara) *hld up: hdwy over 1f out: rdn and r.o to go 2nd wl ins fnl f* **6/1**

-114 **3** 1 **Wild Approach (IRE)**[121] 926 3-9-2 **70** (p[1]) LukeMorris 6 66
(Robert Cowell) *prom: chsd ldr over 3f out tl rdn and hung lft fr over 1f out: styd on same pce ins fnl f* **4/1**[3]

235- **4** ½ **The Daley Express (IRE)**[186] 8494 3-9-7 **75** BenCurtis 8 70
(Ronald Harris) *hdwy over 3f out: rdn over 1f out: styd on same pce ins fnl f* **22/1**

-024 **5** 1 ¾ **Mr Skinnylegs**[35] 2897 3-8-4 **58** SilvestreDeSousa 5 46
(Brian Ellison) *pushed along to ld 4f out: rdn and hdd over 1f out: wknd ins fnl f* **11/4**[1]

51 **6** nk **Red Alert**[13] 3692 3-9-5 **73** OisinMurphy 7 60
(Joseph Tuite) *sn pushed along in rr: rdn and edgd lft over 1f out: n.d* **9/2**

5-14 **7** 1 **Blue Rocks**[17] 3543 3-8-1 **60** DavidEgan(5) 4 44
(Lisa Williamson) *sn pushed along and prom: lost pl after 1f: rdn and edgd lft over 1f out: wknd fnl f* **12/1**

1m 1.31s (-0.59) **Going Correction** -0.05s/f (Stan) **7 Ran SP% 116.2**
Speed ratings (Par 99): **102,98,96,95,92 92,90**
CSF £21.85 CT £72.70 TOTE £4.70: £1.60, £4.10; EX 23.40 Trifecta £129.30.
**Owner** B Miller **Bred** T R G Vestey **Trained** Blewbury, Oxon

**FOCUS**
Not a great race for the grade but it was run at a sound pace and the winner did it well. He has been rated back to his 2yo form.

## 4160 INVEST CITY OF WOLVERHAMPTON NOVICE STKS (PLUS 10 RACE) 5f 21y (Tp)
**3:15** (3:19) (Class 4) 2-Y-O **£3,946** (£1,174; £586; £293) **Stalls** Low

Form RPR
6 **1** **Followthesteps (IRE)**[21] 3390 2-9-2 0 TonyHamilton 8 75
(Ivan Furtado) *wnt lft s: sn chsng ldr: rdn to ld and hung lft wl ins fnl f: r.o* **7/1**

651 **2** ¾ **Branscombe**[10] 3782 2-9-8 0 SilvestreDeSousa 9 78
(Mark Johnston) *sn led: rdn over 1f out: hdd and unable qck wl ins fnl f* **3/1**[2]

34 **3** 5 **Story Minister (IRE)**[38] 2771 2-9-2 0 PJMcDonald 6 54
(Tom Dascombe) *hmpd s: sn prom: rdn over 1f out: styd on same pce fnl f* **7/2**[3]

**4** 2 ¾ **Spirited Boss** 2-9-2 0 SteveDrowne 1 44
(David Evans) *chsd ldrs: rdn over 1f out: wknd ins fnl f* **20/1**

0U **5** ¾ **Peas On Earth**[15] 3622 2-8-6 0 DavidEgan(5) 3 36+
(Derek Shaw) *hmpd s: sn outpcd: styd on fr over 1f out: nvr nrr* **100/1**

4 **6** shd **Arty But Poor**[19] 3467 2-9-2 0 KevinStott 10 41
(Oliver Greenall) *outpcd: styd on fnl f: nvr on terms* **16/1**

2 **7** 2 ½ **Fab (IRE)**[31] 3023 2-8-11 0 FergusSweeney 5 27+
(Jamie Osborne) *hmpd s: hdwy over 3f out: rdn over 1f out: sn wknd* **7/4**[1]

6 **8** 1 ¾ **Glamorous Rocket (IRE)**[31] 3022 2-8-11 0 BenCurtis 2 21
(Ronald Harris) *prom: lost pl over 3f out: rdn 1/2-way: wknd over 1f out* **66/1**

0 **9** 2 ¾ **Rue Cambon (IRE)**[35] 2904 2-8-11 0 AndrewMullen 4 18+
(George Peckham) *hmpd s: outpcd* **20/1**

**10** 1 **Midnight Blue** 2-8-11 0 LukeMorris 7 7
(Sir Mark Prescott Bt) *wnt lft and hmpd s: sn outpcd* **10/1**

1m 2.01s (0.11) **Going Correction** -0.05s/f (Stan) **10** Ran SP% **123.1**
Speed ratings (Par 95): **97,95,87,83,82 82,78,75,70,69**
CSF £29.17 TOTE £8.50: £2.60, £1.70, £1.70; EX 34.70 Trifecta £112.90.
**Owner** John L Marriott & Albert L Marriott **Bred** Dr D Harron **Trained** Wiseton, Nottinghamshire

**FOCUS**
An interesting contest run at a solid pace. The front two finished clear.

## 4161 JOIN THE BLACK COUNTRY CHAMBER OF COMMERCE CLAIMING STKS 6f 20y (Tp)
**3:45** (3:46) (Class 5) 3-Y-O **£3,105** (£924; £461; £230) **Stalls** Low

Form RPR

5630 **1** **Alfonso Manana (IRE)**[24] 3296 3-8-13 67 (b) RichardKingscote 3 71
(James Given) *a.p: rdn to ld wl ins fnl f: styd on* **11/4**[2]

1306 **2** 1 ¼ **Peachey Carnehan**[17] 3517 3-8-9 74 (v) WilliamCarson 4 63
(Michael Attwater) *led early: chsd ldr tl rdn to ld again over 1f out: hdd and unable qck wl ins fnl f* **5/2**[1]

-000 **3** 3 ½ **Equity**[9] 3831 3-8-9 52 ow1 (b) TomEaves 7 52
(David Brown) *sn led: rdn and hdd over 1f out: wknd wl ins fnl f* **25/1**

2-36 **4** shd **Five Star Frank**[28] 3157 3-9-4 72 CharlesBishop 6 60
(Eve Johnson Houghton) *hld up: pushed along 1/2-way: r.o ins fnl f: nt rch ldrs* **5/2**[1]

2250 **5** 1 **Black Bubba (IRE)**[9] 3810 3-8-7 54 (v[1]) BenCurtis 8 46
(David Evans) *hld up in tch: plld hrd: rdn over 2f out: styd on same pce fr over 1f out* **6/1**[3]

2000 **6** 1 **Tink**[25] 3260 3-8-1 45 (h) CamHardie 2 37
(Mark Brisbourne) *s.i.s: hld up: sme hdwy over 1f out: no ex ins fnl f* **80/1**

633 **7** ½ **Prancelina (IRE)**[47] 2508 3-7-12 60 DavidEgan(5) 1 37
(Phil McEntee) *chsd ldrs: rdn over 2f out: wknd ins fnl f* **12/1**

355 **8** 1 ¼ **Bismarck The Flyer (IRE)**[24] 3289 3-8-9 54 AndrewMullen 5 40
(Ollie Pears) *sn outpcd: rdn and swtchd lft over 1f out: nvr on terms* **14/1**

1m 14.27s (-0.23) **Going Correction** -0.05s/f (Stan) **8** Ran SP% **117.5**
Speed ratings (Par 99): **99,97,92,92,91 89,89,87**
CSF £10.43 TOTE £3.60: £1.30, £1.10, £7.90; EX 11.10 Trifecta £215.10.Peachey Carnehan was claimed by Mr Michael Mullineaux for £6,000.
**Owner** Stephanie Oliver **Bred** Chance For Romance Partnership **Trained** Willoughton, Lincs

**FOCUS**
An ordinary claimer run at a sound pace.

## 4162 INVEST CITY OF WOLVERHAMPTON H'CAP (DIV I) 7f 36y (Tp)
**4:15** (4:16) (Class 6) (0-60,60) 3-Y-O+ **£2,264** (£673; £336; £168) **Stalls** High

Form RPR

5035 **1** **Viola Park**[20] 3423 3-8-11 **54** (p) LukeMorris 4 62
(Ronald Harris) *chsd ldr: rdn to ld and hung lft fr over 1f out: styd on u.p* **7/2**[1]

4440 **2** 2 **Bogsnog (IRE)**[11] 3758 7-9-7 **55** JamesSullivan 5 61
(Ruth Carr) *led: rdn and hdd over 1f out: styd on same pce wl ins fnl f* **9/2**[2]

3-60 **3** nk **Loveatfirstsight**[11] 3758 4-9-10 **58** LiamJones 6 63
(Michael Attwater) *a.p: racd keenly: rdn over 2f out: r.o* **16/1**

5-54 **4** 1 ½ **Joaldo**[19] 3468 5-8-12 **46** oh1 (p) CamHardie 1 47
(Antony Brittain) *chsd ldrs: rdn over 2f out: styd on same pce ins fnl f* **8/1**

0-40 **5** ¾ **Royal Melody**[13] 3695 3-8-11 **54** (h[1]) PJMcDonald 3 50
(Heather Main) *plld hrd and prom: rdn 1/2-way: outpcd over 2f out: styd on ins fnl f* **7/1**

3500 **6** hd **Majestic Girl (IRE)**[16] 3569 4-8-12 **46** (b[1]) SilvestreDeSousa 10 45
(Steve Flook) *s.i.s: hld up: hdwy over 2f out: swtchd rt over 1f out: sn rdn and edgd lft: styd on* **15/2**

6065 **7** 2 ¾ **Dusty Bin**[15] 3624 3-8-6 **56** KevinLundie(7) 7 45
(Roy Bowring) *hld up: rdn 1/2-way: sme hdwy over 1f out: no ex ins fnl f* **5/1**[3]

00-2 **8** 2 ¼ **Lucky Di**[13] 3686 7-9-10 **58** CharlesBishop 11 44
(Peter Hedger) *s.i.s: hld up: rdn over 2f out: n.d* **13/2**

3015 **9** ½ **Fossa**[91] 1407 7-9-0 **51** (h) CharlieBennett(3) 9 35
(Mark Brisbourne) *hld up: shkn up over 2f out: rdn: hung lft and wknd over 1f out* **14/1**

0206 **10** 8 **Encapsulated**[52] 2367 7-9-1 **56** RhiainIngram(7) 2 20
(Roger Ingram) *hld up: pushed along 1/2-way: wknd over 2f out* **40/1**

1m 29.06s (0.26) **Going Correction** -0.05s/f (Stan)
**WFA** 3 from 4yo+ 9lb **10** Ran SP% **120.8**
Speed ratings (Par 101): **96,93,93,91,90 90,87,84,84,75**
CSF £19.84 CT £228.27 TOTE £4.30: £1.70, £1.60, £5.50; EX 22.00 Trifecta £307.40.
**Owner** John & Margaret Hatherell & RHS Ltd **Bred** Limestone Stud **Trained** Earlswood, Monmouths

**FOCUS**
The pace was honest for this modest handicap. It paid to race handy.

## 4163 INVEST CITY OF WOLVERHAMPTON H'CAP (DIV II) 7f 36y (Tp)
**4:45** (4:46) (Class 6) (0-60,59) 3-Y-O+ **£2,264** (£673; £336; £168) **Stalls** High

Form RPR

5003 **1** **Zebelini (IRE)**[55] 2278 5-8-5 **45** KevinLundie(7) 4 51
(Roy Bowring) *hmpd s: sn chsng ldr: led over 2f out: rdn out* **8/1**[3]

-060 **2** 1 ¼ **Black Truffle (FR)**[25] 3265 7-8-12 **52** NicolaCurrie(7) 8 55
(Mark Usher) *mid-div: hdwy over 2f out: chsd wnr over 1f out: rdn and edgd lft ins fnl f: styd on* **14/1**

5000 **3** 1 ¾ **Princess Way (IRE)**[108] 1123 3-8-13 **55** (v[1]) AndrewMullen 2 50
(David Evans) *sn prom: rdn over 2f out: edgd lft ins fnl f: styd on* **50/1**

5550 **4** ½ **Dark Confidant (IRE)**[14] 3652 4-9-12 **59** TonyHamilton 6 56
(Richard Fahey) *mid-div: hdwy over 1f out: sn rdn: r.o: nt rch ldrs* **5/1**[2]

-064 **5** 5 **Life Of Luxury**[25] 3264 4-9-10 **57** WilliamCarson 10 41
(Mark Brisbourne) *sn pushed along in rr: styd on fr over 1f out: nvr on terms* **5/1**[2]

0040 **6** 2 **Sparkling Cossack**[38] 2792 3-8-4 **46** (p) RoystonFfrench 9 22
(Jeremy Gask) *s.i.s: in rr: effrt and nt clr run over 1f out: nvr on terms* **25/1**

050 **7** nk **Thatsthewaytodoit (IRE)**[17] 3530 4-8-9 **45** (b[1]) CharlieBennett(3) 3 23
(Daniel Mark Loughnane) *edgd rt s: sn led: rdn and hdd over 2f out: wknd over 1f out* **8/1**[3]

-400 **8** 2 ¼ **Bridal March**[15] 3627 3-9-2 **58** (p) MartinLane 5 27
(John Mackie) *hmpd s: sn pushed along and a in rr* **9/1**

5060 **9** ½ **Win Lose Draw (IRE)**[33] 2976 5-9-8 **58** AlistairRawlinson(3) 7 29
(Michael Appleby) *prom: rdn over 2f out: sn wknd* **5/1**[2]

5-03 **10** 24 **Patanjali (IRE)**[13] 3688 4-9-9 **56** (p[1]) CharlesBishop 1
(Eve Johnson Houghton) *chsd ldrs: rdn over 2f out: wknd and eased over 1f out* **9/4**[1]

1m 28.75s (-0.05) **Going Correction** -0.05s/f (Stan)
**WFA** 3 from 4yo+ 9lb **10** Ran SP% **125.5**
Speed ratings (Par 101): **98,96,94,94,88 86,85,83,82,55**
CSF £121.91 CT £5345.16 TOTE £10.30: £3.00, £3.20, £8.90; EX 154.90 Trifecta £3100.00.
**Owner** K Nicholls **Bred** John McEnery **Trained** Edwinstowe, Notts
■ Stewards' Enquiry : Kevin Lundie two-day ban: used whip above permitted level (10-11 Jul)

**FOCUS**
A modest handicap run at a strong pace. The winner helps set the opening level.

## 4164 VOICE OF RACING DAY THIS FRIDAY MEDIAN AUCTION MAIDEN STKS 7f 36y (Tp)
**5:15** (5:17) (Class 5) 3-Y-O **£3,234** (£962; £481; £240) **Stalls** High

Form RPR

06- **1** **Sir Titan**[282] 6577 3-9-5 0 SteveDrowne 12 77
(Marcus Tregoning) *chsd ldr tl led wl over 1f out: sn shkn up: c readily clr fnl f: easily* **5/1**[2]

640 **2** 3 ½ **My Illusionist**[19] 3456 3-9-5 70 LukeMorris 2 68
(Harry Dunlop) *chsd ldrs: rdn to chse wnr over 1f out: edgd lft and no ex fnl f* **7/1**[3]

3-0 **3** 2 **Joys Delight**[164] 221 3-8-11 0 CharlieBennett(3) 6 58
(Daniel Mark Loughnane) *hld up in tch: rdn over 2f out: styd on same pce fr over 1f out* **28/1**

02 **4** 1 ¼ **Right About Now (IRE)**[19] 3456 3-9-5 0 SilvestreDeSousa 8 59
(Ismail Mohammed) *prom: rdn over 2f out: edgd lft and styd on same pce fr over 1f out* **4/7**[1]

65 **5** 2 **Mac O'Polo (IRE)**[18] 3493 3-9-5 0 RichardKingscote 9 54
(Tom Dascombe) *hld up in tch: shkn up over 2f out: sn outpcd* **5/1**[2]

46 **6** ½ **Bird For Life**[14] 3669 3-8-7 0 NicolaCurrie(7) 10 47
(Mark Usher) *hld up: sme hdwy over 1f out: nvr on terms* **66/1**

**7** ¾ **Monsieur Mel** 3-9-5 0 JamesSullivan 1 50
(Antony Brittain) *s.i.s and wnt lft s: nt clr run over 1f out: nvr on terms* **25/1**

00 **8** nk **Three's A Crowd (IRE)**[34] 2930 3-9-5 0 SamHitchcott 11 50
(Ed de Giles) *s.i.s: sn pushed along in rr: n.d* **40/1**

500 **9** 2 ¼ **La Goulue**[24] 3309 3-8-9 38 (p[1]) GeorgeBuckell(5) 7 39
(John Gallagher) *hld up in tch: pushed along over 2f out: wknd over 1f out* **66/1**

00 **10** 4 **Emilene**[19] 3472 3-9-0 0 WilliamCarson 4 28
(Mark Brisbourne) *led: plld hrd: hdd wl over 1f out: sn wknd* **40/1**

0-6 **P** **Ninedarter**[6] 3948 3-9-5 0 CamHardie 5
(Antony Brittain) *mid-div whn hmpd 6f out: sn lost pl: p.u over 3f out* **40/1**

1m 29.46s (0.66) **Going Correction** -0.05s/f (Stan) **11** Ran SP% **127.1**
Speed ratings (Par 99): **94,90,87,86,84 83,82,82,79,75**
CSF £40.67 TOTE £7.10: £1.90, £1.80, £5.80; EX 51.70 Trifecta £636.80.
**Owner** Wedgewood Estates **Bred** Mrs Liza Judd **Trained** Whitsbury, Hants

**FOCUS**
The pace was sound for this modest maiden.

## 4165 INVEST WOLVERHAMPTON - CITY OF OPPORTUNITY H'CAP 1m 142y (Tp)
**5:45** (5:47) (Class 6) (0-65,65) 4-Y-O+ **£2,264** (£673; £336; £168) **Stalls** Low

Form RPR

5030 **1** **Einstein**[15] 3628 4-8-11 **55** (vt[1]) AdamBeschizza 1 65
(Mrs Ilka Gansera-Leveque) *mde all: rdn clr over 1f out: hung rt ins fnl f: eased towards fin* **10/1**

4421 **2** 4 ½ **Makhfar (IRE)**[25] 3264 6-9-4 **62** (p) SteveDrowne 6 63
(Mark Usher) *hld up: hdwy over 2f out: rdn to chse wnr fnl f: edgd lft and no imp* **6/1**[3]

0006 **3** 1 ¼ **Hernando Torres**[23] 3344 9-9-2 **63** (tp) NathanEvans(3) 5 61
(Michael Easterby) *hld up in tch: rdn over 1f out: styd on same pce fnl f* **4/1**[2]

0236 **4** hd **Grey Destiny**[7] 3912 7-9-2 **60** CamHardie 9 58
(Antony Brittain) *s.s: hld up: hdwy over 1f out: r.o: nt rch ldrs* **8/1**

4043 **5** 2 **Bush Beauty (IRE)**[16] 3577 6-8-12 **56** NeilFarley 13 49
(Eric Alston) *hld up: hdwy over 1f out: nt trble ldrs* **16/1**

0565 **6** 3 ¾ **Yasir (USA)**[17] 3547 9-9-1 **59** LouisSteward 2 44
(Conor Dore) *hld up: nvr nrr* **25/1**

2215 **7** 1 ¾ **Lord Murphy (IRE)**[25] 3263 4-9-0 **61** CharlieBennett(3) 11 43
(Daniel Mark Loughnane) *chsd ldrs: rdn over 2f out: hung lft and wknd over 1f out* **7/1**

3144 **8** nk **Rattle On**[27] 3172 4-9-5 **63** (p) SilvestreDeSousa 4 44
(Jim Boyle) *chsd ldrs: wnt 2nd over 3f out: rdn over 2f out: wknd fnl f* **5/2**[1]

1-40 **9** 2 ¾ **Russian Ranger (IRE)**[32] 2996 4-9-4 **62** (p) LukeMorris 10 37
(Jonathan Portman) *prom: rdn over 3f out: hung lft and wknd over 1f out* **12/1**

0000 **10** 12 **Genuine Approval (IRE)**[35] 2909 4-8-12 **63** DarraghKeenan(7) 8 13
(John Butler) *hld up: a in rr* **50/1**

0000 **11** 1 ½ **Torch**[34] 2919 4-9-0 **58** (p) DanielMuscutt 3 5
(John Butler) *hld up: rdn 1/2-way: a in rr* **40/1**

06-0 **12** nse **Sailor Malan**[27] 3192 5-8-9 **53** (h) LiamJones 7
(Suzy Smith) *chsd wnr 5f: sn rdn: wknd over 2f out* **100/1**

1m 48.46s (-1.64) **Going Correction** -0.05s/f (Stan) **12** Ran SP% **118.4**
Speed ratings (Par 101): **105,101,99,99,97 94,93,92,90,79 78,78**
CSF £67.48 CT £288.71 TOTE £10.90: £3.60, £2.10, £2.10; EX 83.10 Trifecta £418.60.
**Owner** Brookside Breeders Club **Bred** Brookside Breeders Club **Trained** Newmarket, Suffolk

**FOCUS**
A strongly run handicap. This could be rated a bit higher.
T/Jkpt: £33,025.60 to a £1 stake. Pool: £627,487.32 - 19.0 winning units T/Plt: £176.80 to a £1 stake. Pool: £58,347.88 - 240.78 winning units T/Qpdt: £44.40 to a £1 stake. Pool: £6,498.36 - 108.28 winning units **Colin Roberts**

## 3444 SAINT-CLOUD (L-H)
Monday, June 26

**OFFICIAL GOING: Turf: good**

### 4166a PRIX D'ORGEVAL (CLAIMER) (2YO) (TURF) 7f
**2:20** 2-Y-O **£11,538** (£4,615; £3,461; £2,307; £1,153)

RPR
1 **Like Lightning (IRE)**[20] 3444 2-9-2 0 IoritzMendizabal 6 82
(J S Moore) *dwlt: sn pushed through to ld after 1f: pushed along to maintain advantage over 2f out: drvn over 1f out: styd on strly fnl f* **2/1**[2]
2 ¾ **All This Time (GER)** 2-8-11 0 CristianDemuro 3 75
(D Guillemin, France) **6/4**[1]
3 3 ½ **Palya (FR)**[11] 2-8-8 0 (p) AntoineHamelin 1 63
(Matthieu Palussiere, France) **5/1**[3]
4 1 ¾ **Fancy Dresser (FR)**[11] 2-8-11 0 (b) EddyHardouin 4 61
(Matthieu Palussiere, France) **11/1**
5 2 **Ardeatina** 2-8-5 0 ClementLecoeuvre(3) 8 52
(A Giorgi, Italy) **101/10**
6 2 **Jugeotte (FR)**[62] 2-8-11 0 AlexisBadel 7 50
(F Doumen, France) **28/1**
7 ¾ **Sens Des Affaires (FR)**[14] 3679 2-9-4 0 MaximeGuyon 5 55
(Y Barberot, France) **104/10**

1m 29.47s (-2.73) 7 Ran SP% **119.6**
PARI-MUTUEL (all including 1 euro stake): WIN 3.00; PLACE 1.20, 1.10, 1.20; DF 3.10; SF 8.20.
**Owner** Ciara Doyle & J S Moore **Bred** James Doyle **Trained** Upper Lambourn, Berks

## 3930 BEVERLEY (R-H)
Tuesday, June 27

**OFFICIAL GOING: Good to firm changing to good after race 3 (3.00)**
Wind: Moderate behind Weather: Heavy cloud and rain

### 4167 RACING UK IN GLORIOUS HD NOVICE AUCTION STKS 7f 96y
**2:00** (2:00) (Class 5) 2-Y-O **£3,780** (£1,131; £565; £283; £141) **Stalls** Low

Form RPR
500 1 **Poet's Dawn**[36] 2896 2-8-11 0 DavidAllan 3 72
(Tim Easterby) *trckd ldrs: hdwy on inner 3f out: swtchd lft 2f out and sn chal: rdn over 1f out: led jst ins fnl f: kpt on wl* **4/1**[3]
U23 2 1 ½ **Arabian Jazz (IRE)**[35] 2910 2-8-8 0 DannyBrock 7 64
(Michael Bell) *cl up: slt ld after 2f: pushed along wl over 2f out: jnd and rdn over 1f out: drvn and hdd jst ins fnl f: kpt on same pce* **11/10**[1]
3 9 **Duke Of Freedom** 2-9-1 0 DougieCostello 6 49
(Ann Duffield) *hld up in rr: hdwy wl over 2f out: rdn over 1f out: kpt on fnl f* **20/1**
05 4 ½ **Jaffar**[12] 3742 2-8-13 0 (be) PJMcDonald 2 46
(Scott Dixon) *dwlt: sn chsng ldrs: pushed along 4f out: rdn wl over 2f out: sn one pce* **13/2**
03 5 hd **If We Can Can**[20] 3447 2-8-13 0 JasonHart 4 46
(Mark Johnston) *slt ld 2f: cl up: rdn along wl over 2f out: drvn wl over 1f out: sn wknd* **7/2**[2]
00 6 4 ½ **Boss Koko**[15] 3662 2-8-6 0 DuranFentiman 5 28
(Tim Easterby) *a towards rr* **50/1**
0 7 shd **Hamba Moyo (IRE)**[22] 3398 2-8-11 0 (b[1]) RachelRichardson(3) 8 36
(Tim Easterby) *in tch: hdwy on outer 1/2-way: rdn along wl over 2f out: sn wknd* **40/1**

1m 33.64s (-0.16) **Going Correction** -0.15s/f (Firm) 7 Ran SP% **112.3**
Speed ratings (Par 93): **94,92,82,81,81 76,75**
CSF £8.50 TOTE £4.70: £2.00, £1.20; EX 9.90 Trifecta £117.60.
**Owner** Timothy O'Gram & Partner **Bred** Mrs J K Powell & Catridge Farm Stud **Trained** Great Habton, N Yorks

**FOCUS**
Rail movements meant all races except the last were run over seven yards further than the advertised distance. The riders said the ground was still good to firm despite rain in the morning and some drizzle during racing, but was a little loose on top. A modest novice event in which the first two came right away from the others.

### 4168 WATCH LIVE RACING AND BET WITH RACING UK H'CAP 7f 96y
**2:30** (2:30) (Class 5) (0-75,77) 3-Y-O+ **£3,780** (£1,131; £565; £283; £141) **Stalls** Low

Form RPR
0610 1 **Talent Scout (IRE)**[10] 3845 11-9-5 69 (p) GemmaTutty(5) 6 76
(Karen Tutty) *led 2f: chsd ldr: rdn and hdwy over 1f out: drvn to chal ins fnl f: styd on wl to ld fin* **18/1**
3025 2 nk **Make On Madam (IRE)**[7] 3934 5-9-11 70 (p) PJMcDonald 5 76
(Les Eyre) *trckd ldrs on inner: hdwy 2f out: rdn over 1f out: drvn ins fnl f and ev ch: kpt on* **8/1**[3]
0402 3 1 ¼ **Yorkee Mo Sabee (IRE)**[7] 3934 4-10-0 73 (h) JoeFanning 9 76
(Mark Johnston) *t.k.h: cl up: led after 2f out and sn clr: pushed along 2f out: rdn over 1f out: drvn ins fnl f: edgd lft last 100 yds: hdd and no ex towards fin* **4/1**[1]
4-60 4 1 **Madrinho (IRE)**[10] 3845 4-10-4 77 BarryMcHugh 2 77
(Tony Coyle) *in tch: hdwy on inner wl over 2f out: rdn to chse ldrs over 1f out: nt clr run ins fnl f: swtchd lft and kpt on towards fin* **5/1**[2]
0545 5 1 ¾ **Beatbybeatbybeat**[8] 3911 4-9-9 68 (v) CamHardie 3 64
(Antony Brittain) *trckd ldrs: hdwy over 2f out: rdn over 1f out: drvn and kpt on same pce fnl f* **25/1**
0566 6 1 **Popsies Joy (IRE)**[10] 3833 4-9-1 60 (p) DavidAllan 4 53
(Tim Easterby) *hld up towards rr: hdwy wl over 2f out: rdn to chse ldrs over 1f out: no imp fnl f* **9/1**
5000 7 1 ½ **Shamaheart (IRE)**[10] 3845 7-9-12 76 (v) CliffordLee(5) 11 65
(Geoffrey Harker) *dwlt and hld up towards rr: hdwy wl over 2f out: effrt and nt clr run over 1f out: sn swtchd lft and rdn: kpt on fnl f* **12/1**
-404 8 shd **Deansgate (IRE)**[39] 2791 4-9-11 70 (e) JoeDoyle 12 59
(Julie Camacho) *hld up in rr: swtchd lft to outer and hdwy over 2f out: sn rdn and n.d* **14/1**
0214 9 shd **Fine Example**[36] 2888 4-9-5 69 (b) LewisEdmunds(5) 7 58
(Kevin Ryan) *t.k.h early: trckd ldng pair: pushed along over 2f out: rdn wl over 1f out: sn drvn and wknd* **4/1**[1]
0000 10 1 ½ **Slemy (IRE)**[15] 3652 6-9-11 70 JamesSullivan 1 55
(Ruth Carr) *dwlt: a towards rr* **20/1**
3500 11 2 **Taskeen (IRE)**[7] 3949 4-9-11 70 TonyHamilton 8 49
(Roger Fell) *nvr bttr than midfield* **20/1**
3020 12 3 **Dutch Artist (IRE)**[15] 3652 5-10-4 77 (p) DanielTudhope 13 49
(David O'Meara) *chsd ldrs on outer: rdn along over 2f out: sn wknd* **8/1**[3]

1m 32.47s (-1.33) **Going Correction** -0.15s/f (Firm) **12** Ran SP% **121.9**
Speed ratings (Par 103): **101,100,99,98,96 94,93,93,93,91 89,85**
CSF £155.24 CT £706.04 TOTE £21.40: £4.70, £3.00, £1.40; EX 179.30 Trifecta £1757.70.
**Owner** Thoroughbred Homes Ltd **Bred** Johnston King **Trained** Osmotherley, N Yorks

**FOCUS**
Race run over an extra seven yards. This looks like solid form. The first pair were 1-2 over C&D last month and they repeated the trick. The winner has been rated as running his best race since 2015, and a pb from the runner-up.

### 4169 RACING UK ANDROID APP RACINGUK.COM/MOBILE H'CAP 1m 4f 23y
**3:00** (3:00) (Class 5) (0-70,68) 4-Y-O+ **£3,780** (£1,131; £565; £283; £141) **Stalls** Low

Form RPR
3054 1 **Lean On Pete (IRE)**[7] 3935 8-8-11 58 AndrewMullen 7 64
(Ollie Pears) *trckd ldr: hdwy 3f out: rdn to ld wl 2f out and sn edgd rt: drvn ent fnl f: hld on gamely towards fin* **7/1**
4434 2 hd **Tred Softly (IRE)**[32] 3043 4-8-10 57 (b) JasonHart 5 62
(John Quinn) *trckd ldng pair: hdwy over 2f out: rdn over 1f out: drvn to chal ins fnl f: ev ch: no ex nr fin* **11/2**[3]
3104 3 ¾ **Pour L'Amour (IRE)**[18] 3547 4-9-1 65 CharlieBennett(3) 8 68
(Daniel Mark Loughnane) *hld up in rr: hdwy on wd outside 2f out: rdn over 1f out: drvn and kpt on wl fnl f* **8/1**
0500 4 nk **Druid's Diamond**[24] 3343 4-7-13 49 NathanEvans(3) 1 52
(Mark Walford) *chsd ldrs: pushed along over 3f out: rdn along 2f out: drvn over 1f out: kpt on fnl f* **9/2**[2]
4406 5 hd **Mysterial**[11] 3795 7-9-0 68 GerO'Neill(7) 2 71
(Declan Carroll) *led: pushed along 3f out: rdn and hdd 2f out: n.m.r and swtchd lft over 1f out: sn drvn and ev ch: wknd ins fnl f* **9/4**[1]
0633 6 2 ¼ **Cool Music (IRE)**[12] 3760 7-8-6 53 (p) CamHardie 6 52
(Antony Brittain) *in tch: hdwy 3f out: rdn along 2f out: drvn over 1f out: kpt on same pce* **6/1**
0-00 6 dht **Correggio**[22] 3400 7-9-0 61 PJMcDonald 4 60
(Micky Hammond) *in tch: pushed along over 3f out: rdn 2f out: drvn to chse ldrs over 1f out: kpt on same pce fnl f* **12/1**
0365 8 19 **Stun Gun**[12] 3760 7-8-3 50 (p) JoeFanning 3 19
(Derek Shaw) *hld up in rr: pushed along wl over 2f out: sn rdn and bhd whn eased fnl f* **20/1**

2m 37.0s (-2.80) **Going Correction** -0.15s/f (Firm) **8** Ran SP% **114.7**
Speed ratings (Par 103): **103,102,102,102,102 100,100,87**
CSF £45.14 CT £315.23 TOTE £8.20: £2.10, £1.80, £2.70; EX 39.00 Trifecta £255.50.
**Owner** K C West **Bred** Mrs T Mahon **Trained** Norton, N Yorks

**FOCUS**
Race run over an extra seven yards. They finished in a heap in this modest handicap, which wasn't strongly run. The winner as been rated to his recent best.

### 4170 SKIDBY H'CAP 1m 1f 207y
**3:30** (3:33) (Class 4) (0-80,80) 4-Y-O+ **£6,301** (£1,886; £943; £472; £235) **Stalls** Low

Form RPR
1500 1 **Sunglider (IRE)**[10] 3845 4-9-4 77 (vt) DanielTudhope 6 85
(David O'Meara) *trckd ldrs: hdwy over 2f out: rdn to chal jst over 1f out: led ins fnl f: drvn out* **4/1**[2]
0635 2 1 ¼ **Save The Bees**[12] 3744 9-9-0 78 PhilDennis(5) 5 83
(Declan Carroll) *led: pushed along over 2f out: rdn wl over 1f out: drvn and hdd ins fnl f: no ex* **11/4**[1]
0-04 3 hd **Torremar (FR)**[32] 3050 4-9-0 73 (p) TomEaves 2 77
(Kevin Ryan) *chsd ldr: hdwy to chal 2f out: rdn over 1f out: drvn and ev ch ent fnl f: kpt on* **7/1**
2-34 4 3 ¼ **Toga Tiger (IRE)**[124] 885 10-9-7 80 DougieCostello 4 78
(Daniel Mark Loughnane) *dwlt and rr: hdwy over 2f out: rdn wl over 1f out: sn drvn and no imp* **10/1**
5-00 5 5 **Frankster (FR)**[21] 3432 4-8-2 61 oh1 (t) AndrewMullen 3 49
(Micky Hammond) *in tch: pushed along 3f out: rdn over 2f out: sn wknd* **50/1**
3-43 6 2 **Desert Way (IRE)**[7] 3947 4-9-7 80 PJMcDonald 7 64
(Rebecca Menzies) *trckd ldng pair: pushed along over 3f out: rdn wl over 2f out: sn wknd* **11/2**[3]
-012 7 2 ½ **Bromance**[7] 3935 4-8-2 61 oh1 (p) JamesSullivan 1 40
(Peter Niven) *hld up and bhd: effrt and sme hdwy on outer over 2f out: sn rdn and btn* **11/4**[1]

2m 5.02s (-1.98) **Going Correction** -0.15s/f (Firm) 7 Ran SP% **112.3**
Speed ratings (Par 105): **101,100,99,97,93 91,89**
CSF £14.83 TOTE £4.70: £2.50, £1.70; EX 18.40 Trifecta £76.40.
**Owner** G Brogan **Bred** Moyglare Stud Farm Ltd **Trained** Upper Helmsley, N Yorks

**FOCUS**
Following rain, the official going description was amended to good before this race, a fair handicap. It was run over an additional seven yards. The winner has been rated back to his previous C&D win.

### 4171 RACING UK ON SKY 432 H'CAP (DIV I) 1m 1f 207y
**4:00** (4:01) (Class 6) (0-65,66) 3-Y-O **£2,587** (£770; £384; £192) **Stalls** Low

Form RPR
6603 1 **Katebird (IRE)**[6] 3981 3-9-10 66 JoeFanning 4 74
(Mark Johnston) *trckd ldr: cl up 1/2-way: led wl over 2f out: rdn clr wl over 1f out: kpt on strly* **2/1**[1]
0-04 2 3 ½ **Bollin Ted**[27] 3207 3-8-3 45 DuranFentiman 8 46
(Tim Easterby) *trckd ldrs: hdwy to chse ldng pair over 2f out: rdn wl over 1f out: kpt on fnl f* **12/1**
4406 3 1 ¾ **Tewafeedj**[42] 2703 3-9-5 61 KevinStott 9 59
(Kevin Ryan) *in tch: hdwy on outer over 3f out: chsd ldrs over 2f out: rdn along and edgd rt over 1f out: kpt on same pce* **9/2**[3]
4-00 4 hd **Starlite Sienna (IRE)**[42] 2702 3-9-7 63 (p[1]) TonyHamilton 2 61
(Richard Fahey) *trckd ldrs: hdwy wl over 2f out: rdn along wl over 1f out: sn no imp* **10/1**
000- 5 1 ¼ **Spanish Beauty**[270] 6923 3-8-8 50 AndrewMullen 7 45
(Ollie Pears) *rr: pushed along 1/2-way: hdwy over 2f out: rdn and styng on whn n.m.r ent fnl f: one pce after* **50/1**
0044 6 1 **Clean Cut**[41] 2732 3-8-6 48 (p) RoystonFfrench 3 41
(Ivan Furtado) *led: rdn along and hdd wl over 2f out:. sn drvn and wknd wl over 1f out* **12/1**
0-05 7 3 ¼ **Trautmann (IRE)**[144] 545 3-9-0 59 CharlieBennett(3) 1 46
(Daniel Mark Loughnane) *chsd ldng pair: rdn along over 2f out: sn wknd* **22/1**

004- **8** ½ **Doctor Dynamite (IRE)**[363] 3772 3-9-4 **60**........................ DavidAllan 6 46
(Tim Easterby) *a towards rr* **7/1**

2-46 **9** 42 **Petit Filous**[39] 2793 3-9-7 **63**........................................ PaulMulrennan 10
(Giles Bravery) *a towards rr: rdn along 4f out: sn outpcd and bhd* **10/3**[2]

2m 5.75s (-1.25) **Going Correction** -0.15s/f (Firm) **9** Ran SP% **117.9**
Speed ratings (Par 97): **99,96,94,94,93 92,90,89,56**
CSF £29.02 CT £100.27 TOTE £3.00: £1.30, £3.50, £1.70; EX 33.90 Trifecta £226.00.
**Owner** J David Abell **Bred** Peter Grimes & The Late Jackie Grimes **Trained** Middleham Moor, N Yorks

**FOCUS**
Race run over an extra seven yards. A moderate handicap which was run at a good clip, and it was 1.10sec quicker than division two.

## 4172 RACING UK ON SKY 432 H'CAP (DIV II) 1m 1f 207y
**4:30** (4:30) (Class 6) (0-65,64) 3-Y-O **£2,587** (£770; £384; £192) **Stalls** Low

Form RPR

1514 **1** **Metronomic (IRE)**[19] 3499 3-9-4 **61**................................ AndrewMullen 5 66
(Peter Niven) *led:: rdn along 2f out: hdd jst over 1f out: drvn and rallied gamely ins fnl f to ld nr fin* **7/2**[2]

3004 **2** shd **Rosemay (FR)**[26] 3243 3-9-7 **64**............................................. JoeFanning 1 69
(Iain Jardine) *trckd ldng pair: swtchd lft and hdwy 2f out: sn chal: rdn to ld jst over 1f out: drvn ins fnl f: hdd and no ex nr fin* **7/2**[2]

00-0 **3** 2¾ **Mr C (IRE)**[37] 2857 3-8-6 **49**................................................. JoeDoyle 3 49
(Ollie Pears) *hld up: hdwy on inner over 2f out: chsd ldrs and n.m.r over 1f out: swtchd lft and rdn ent fnl f: kpt on* **10/1**

0-34 **4** 3 **Treagus**[21] 3431 3-9-1 **58**................................................. StevieDonohoe 8 52
(Charlie Fellowes) *trckd ldrs: hdwy over 2f out: rdn along wl over 1f out: sn drvn and kpt on same pce* **4/1**[3]

5600 **5** nse **Thomas Crown (IRE)**[8] 3913 3-9-2 **59**.......................(p) TonyHamilton 2 53
(Roger Fell) *dwlt and rr: hdwy over 2f out: rdn wl over 1f out: styd on fnl f: nrst fin* **18/1**

-052 **6** nk **Niseko**[7] 3939 3-9-4 **61**................................................(p[1]) DougieCostello 9 55
(William Muir) *trckd ldrs on outer: hdwy over 2f out: rdn over 1f out: drvn and kpt on same pce fnl f* **5/2**[1]

0-00 **7** ½ **Whisper A Word (IRE)**[10] 3832 3-8-0 **46** ow1.... RachelRichardson(3) 7 39
(Tim Easterby) *a towards rr* **40/1**

50-0 **8** 22 **Rainbow Chimes (IRE)**[167] 175 3-9-0 **57**........................ ShaneGray 6 8
(Ann Duffield) *cl up: pushed along 3f out: sn rdn and wknd 2f out* **25/1**

2m 6.85s (-0.15) **Going Correction** -0.15s/f (Firm) **8** Ran SP% **113.7**
Speed ratings (Par 97): **94,93,91,89,89 89,88,71**
CSF £15.98 CT £109.09 TOTE £3.80: £1.60, £1.40, £2.80; EX 18.20 Trifecta £136.50.
**Owner** Keep The Faith Partnership **Bred** Pier House Stud **Trained** Barton-le-Street, N Yorks

**FOCUS**
Race run over an extra seven yards. The slower division by 1.10sec. Like division one, it was won by the only previous winner, and the form is pretty moderate.

## 4173 RACING UK PROFITS ALL RETURNED TO RACING MEDIAN AUCTION MAIDEN STKS 1m 100y
**5:00** (5:00) (Class 5) 3-Y-O **£3,780** (£1,131; £565; £283; £141) **Stalls** Low

Form RPR

2-35 **1** **War Of Succession**[21] 3435 3-9-5 82.........................(b[1]) OisinMurphy 4 77
(Andrew Balding) *reminders s and sn led: rdn along wl over 1f out: drvn ins fnl f: kpt on* **11/8**[1]

0-3 **2** 2 **Luminous**[18] 3549 3-9-0 0...............................................(h) GrahamLee 5 67
(Simon Crisford) *sn chsng wnr: hdwy over 2f out: rdn over 1f out: drvn and kpt on same pce fnl f* **2/1**[2]

05-4 **3** 2¾ **William Booth (IRE)**[46] 2584 3-9-5 71.......................... PaulHanagan 1 66
(Daniel Mark Loughnane) *trckd ldng pair: hdwy 2f out: rdn over 1f out: sn drvn and no imp* **9/4**[3]

06 **4** 4 **Book Of Dust**[62] 2092 3-9-0 0.........................................(b[1]) KevinStott 2 51
(Giles Bravery) *a towards rr* **25/1**

00- **5** 5 **You Look Different**[231] 7855 3-9-0 0.............................. CamHardie 3 40
(Antony Brittain) *a towards rr* **66/1**

1m 47.07s (-0.53) **Going Correction** -0.15s/f (Firm) **5** Ran SP% **111.5**
Speed ratings (Par 99): **96,94,91,87,82**
CSF £4.55 TOTE £2.60: £1.40, £1.30; EX 4.30 Trifecta £6.40.
**Owner** Qatar Racing Limited **Bred** Hillwood Bloodstock **Trained** Kingsclere, Hants

**FOCUS**
Race run over an additional seven yards. There wasn't much depth to this maiden, and it has been rated around the runner-up and third.

## 4174 GO RACING IN YORKSHIRE FUTURE STARS APPRENTICE H'CAP 5f
**5:30** (5:30) (Class 6) (0-60,66) 3-Y-O+ **£2,587** (£770; £384; £192) **Stalls** Low

Form RPR

-051 **1** **Foxy Boy**[3] 4107 3-9-11 **64** 6ex........................................ CliffordLee 3 80+
(Michael Dods) *trckd ldrs: hdwy 2f out: led jst over 1f out: rdn clr fnl f: kpt on strly* **5/4**[1]

6013 **2** 5 **Dapper Man (IRE)**[3] 4107 3-9-6 **64** 6ex...............(b) BenSanderson(5) 13 62
(Roger Fell) *trckd ldrs: hdwy on outer 2f out: rdn and edgd rt ent fnl f: kpt on* **5/1**[2]

3335 **3** nk **Roaring Rory**[7] 3944 4-9-8 **62**...................................(p) SeamusCronin(7) 8 61
(Ollie Pears) *chsd ldrs: rdn along and hdwy over 1f out: nt clr run and swtchd lft ins fnl f: kpt on wl towards fin* **9/1**[3]

0402 **4** nk **Archie Stevens**[7] 3942 7-9-2 **56**.................................... WilliamCox(7) 9 54
(Clare Ellam) *slt ld: rdn along 2f out: drvn and hdd jst over 1f out: kpt on u.p fnl f* **16/1**

0501 **5** nk **Thatcherite (IRE)**[8] 3915 9-10-2 **66** 6ex....................(t) BenRobinson(3) 5 63
(Tony Coyle) *dwlt and bhd: rdn along 1/2-way: swtchd lft over 1f out: fin wl* **9/1**[3]

2540 **6** ¾ **See Vermont**[45] 2628 9-9-11 **58**.....................................(p) RowanScott 6 52
(Rebecca Bastiman) *stmbld s and towards rr: hdwy 2f out: edgd rt over 1f out: chsd ldrs and nt clr run ent fnl f: sn swtchd lft and rdn: kpt on towards fin* **12/1**

-505 **7** ½ **Nefetari**[8] 3915 4-8-13 **46** oh1.....................................(b) LewisEdmunds 10 38
(Alan Brown) *cl up: rdn to dispute ld wl over 1f out: edgd rt ent fnl f: sn wknd* **25/1**

4-00 **8** ¾ **Mercers Row**[8] 3897 10-9-3 **55**...............................(p) ConnorMurtagh(5) 2 45
(Michael Herrington) *prom on inner: rdn along wl over 1f out: grad wknd* **20/1**

0020 **9** ¾ **Tinsill**[13] 3710 6-8-7 **47**...............................................(p) FayeMcManoman(7) 11 34
(Nigel Tinkler) *bhd tl styd on appr fnl f* **33/1**

000- **10** ¾ **Miss Island Ruler**[269] 6950 3-8-2 **46**................................ AledBeech(5) 1 28
(Shaun Harris) *towards rr: effrt and nt clr run wl over 1f out: n.d* **50/1**

-405 **11** 1 **Tess Graham**[10] 3818 3-8-2 **46** oh1.....................(p) ManuelFernandes(5) 12 25
(Sarah Hollinshead) *chsd ldrs on wd outside: rdn along 2f out: hld whn n.m.r and swtchd lft over 1f out* **33/1**

3043 **12** 2 **Storm Trooper (IRE)**[18] 3544 6-9-7 **61**..................... HarrisonShaw(7) 14 34
(Marjorie Fife) *stmbld s: chsd ldrs towards outer: rdn along and edgd rt 2f out: sn wknd* **16/1**

0660 **13** shd **Chip Or Pellet**[8] 3915 4-8-11 **47**............................ PatrickVaughan(3) 15 20
(Nigel Tinkler) *a in rr* **25/1**

15-0 **14** 17 **Roman Times (IRE)**[25] 3289 4-9-8 **55**............................ MeganNicholls 4
(Colin Teague) *cl up: pushed along 1/2-way and sn lost pl: hld whn hmpd and hit inner rail over 1f out: sn eased* **40/1**

1m 2.03s (-1.47) **Going Correction** -0.15s/f (Firm)
**WFA** 3 from 4yo+ 6lb **14** Ran SP% **123.3**
Speed ratings (Par 101): **105,97,96,96,95 94,93,92,91,89 88,85,85,57**
CSF £6.49 CT £44.55 TOTE £2.20: £1.10, £1.80, £3.30; EX 9.30 Trifecta £49.90.
**Owner** Sekura Group **Bred** Giles W Pritchard-Gordon (farming) Ltd **Trained** Denton, Co Durham

**FOCUS**
A modest sprint handicap that was taken apart by the favourite.
T/Plt: £95.80 to a £1 stake. Pool: £76,403.07 - 582.02 winning units T/Qpdt: £27.20 to a £1 stake. Pool: £6,206.88 - 168/7 winning units **Joe Rowntree**

# 3936 BRIGHTON (L-H)
### Tuesday, June 27

**OFFICIAL GOING: Good to firm changing to good to firm (good in places) after race 5 (4:15)**
Wind: light, across Weather: cloudy, rain from race 3

## 4175 TRAILWALKER 100KM CHALLENGE 29-30 JULY NOVICE AUCTION STKS 5f 215y
**2:15** (2:15) (Class 5) 2-Y-O **£2,911** (£866; £432; £216) **Stalls** Centre

Form RPR

**1** **Pranceaboottheton (IRE)** 2-9-2 0.......................... DanielMuscutt 4 72+
(John Ryan) *bmpd leaving stalls: hld up wl in tch: effrt and swtchd rt over 1f out: rdn and hdwy to ld ins fnl f: r.o wl and drew clr fnl 100yds: readily* **11/1**

510 **2** 2½ **Holdenhurst**[25] 3297 2-9-4 0.......................................... MitchGodwin(5) 7 71
(Sylvester Kirk) *t.k.h: pressed ldr tl led wl over 2f out: drvn over 1f out: hdd ins fnl f: no ex and outpcd fnl 100yds* **11/8**[1]

0 **3** 1 **Iconic Knight (IRE)**[8] 3917 2-9-2 0.................................... LiamKeniry 6 61
(Ed Walker) *stdd s: t.k.h: trckd ldrs on outer: wnt 2nd and rdn 2f out: unable qck and one pce in 3rd fnl f* **7/4**[2]

00 **4** 2¼ **Red For Danger**[10] 3807 2-8-11 0.................................... CharlesBishop 2 49
(Eve Johnson Houghton) *stdd and bmpd s: effrt 2f out: no imp 1f out: edgd lft and wknd ins fnl f* **20/1**

50 **5** 10 **Cruel Clever Cat**[64] 2037 2-8-8 0.............................. HectorCrouch(3) 1 17
(John Gallagher) *t.k.h: led tl wl over 2f out: sn rdn: lost pl over 1f out: fdd fnl f* **4/1**[3]

1m 10.76s (0.56) **Going Correction** 0.0s/f (Good) **5** Ran SP% **111.6**
Speed ratings (Par 93): **96,92,91,88,75**
CSF £27.26 TOTE £14.90: £6.10, £1.10; EX 26.40 Trifecta £59.60.
**Owner** Peter Harper **Bred** Tally-Ho Stud **Trained** Newmarket, Suffolk

**FOCUS**
Distance increased by 6yds. Bit of a turn-up in this average novice. This has been rated through the 2nd/3rd/4th.

## 4176 TOTEPLACEPOT AT TOTESPORT.COM H'CAP 6f 210y
**2:45** (2:46) (Class 5) (0-70,71) 3-Y-O+ **£2,911** (£866; £432; £216) **Stalls** Centre

Form RPR

500 **1** **Jumping Jack (IRE)**[11] 3784 3-9-6 **71**................................ ShaneKelly 5 77
(Richard Hughes) *w ldr tl led over 1f out: rdn and kpt on wl ins fnl f: rdn out* **5/2**[1]

0004 **2** 1 **Good Luck Charm**[7] 3938 8-9-11 **70**........................(b) HectorCrouch(3) 3 76
(Gary Moore) *hld up in tch: clsd to trck ldrs 2f out: effrt to chse wnr ins fnl f: styd on but a hld fnl 100yds* **9/2**[2]

0041 **3** ¾ **Soaring Spirits (IRE)**[12] 3758 7-9-13 **69**..................(p) RobertWinston 7 73
(Dean Ivory) *led tl rdn and hdd over 1f out: kpt on same pce u.p ins fnl f* **9/2**[2]

3314 **4** nk **Swiss Cross**[7] 3941 10-9-12 **71**..........................(tp) CallumShepherd(3) 6 74
(Phil McEntee) *trckd ldrs: effrt 2f out: kpt on same pce u.p ins fnl f* **17/2**

05-5 **5** 2 **Pick A Little**[21] 3422 9-9-6 **67**.......................................... MitchGodwin(5) 1 65
(Michael Blake) *trckd ldrs: swtchd lft and effrt over 2f out: unable qck over 1f out: kpt on same pce fnl f* **6/1**[3]

452 **6** nk **Welsh Inlet (IRE)**[15] 3661 9-9-2 **58**.................................. WilliamCarson 8 55
(John Bridger) *dwlt: hld up in tch: c towards centre 3f out: sn rdn: outpcd u.p over 1f out: kpt on same pce after* **12/1**

6322 **7** 1½ **With Approval (IRE)**[18] 3522 5-9-2 **58**....................(p) GeorgeDowning 4 51
(Laura Mongan) *dwlt: hld up in tch: rdn ent fnl 2f: no imp and wl hld fnl f* **9/2**[2]

1m 23.42s (0.32) **Going Correction** 0.0s/f (Good)
**WFA** 3 from 5yo+ 9lb **7** Ran SP% **115.6**
Speed ratings (Par 103): **98,96,96,95,93 93,91**
CSF £14.29 CT £47.47 TOTE £3.10: £2.30, £1.30; EX 15.30 Trifecta £48.50.
**Owner** Danny Waters **Bred** R & R Bloodstock **Trained** Upper Lambourn, Berks

**FOCUS**
Add 6yds. A modest sprint but the winner has been rated to his best AW form.

## 4177 LABYRINTH CHALLENGE 18 AUG H'CAP 1m 1f 207y
**3:15** (3:16) (Class 6) (0-60,59) 3-Y-O+ **£2,264** (£673; £336; £168) **Stalls** High

Form RPR

5103 **1** **Av A Word**[15] 3674 3-9-2 **59**............................................(p) LukeMorris 5 64
(Daniel Kubler) *chsd ldrs: clsd to join ldrs wl over 2f out: rdn 2f out: drvn to ld 1f out: styd on fnl f* **2/1**[1]

0546 **2** ½ **Chunkyfunkymonkey**[7] 3939 3-9-0 **57**......................(p) DanielMuscutt 1 61
(John Ryan) *chsd ldrs tl led over 2f out: rdn 2f out: hdd 1f out: kpt on but a jst hld ins fnl f* **4/1**[2]

1044 **3** 1¼ **Log Off (IRE)**[10] 3813 3-8-12 **55**........................................ FranBerry 9 57
(David Evans) *t.k.h: hld up in tch in midfield: nt clrest of runs 3f out: swtchd rt and effrt over 2f out: chsd ldng pair jst ins fnl f: styd on: nvr gng to rch ldrs* **7/1**

0-50 **4** 4½ **Montycristo**[19] 3506 4-9-7 **55**.................................(b[1]) HectorCrouch(3) 7 48
(Philip Hide) *led tl 7f out: chsd ldr tl led again 4f out: hdd over 2f out: 3rd and outpcd u.p over 1f out: wknd ins fnl f* **33/1**

0006 **5** 3¾ **Herculian Prince**[14] 3688 5-9-2 **47**..................................(b) LiamKeniry 4 33
(Conor Dore) *hld up in last trio: effrt over 2f out: wl hld 5th and kpt on same pce fr over 1f out* **25/1**

0006 **6** *12* **Seeing Things (IRE)**[21] 3442 3-8-6 **54**..........................(t) DavidEgan(5) 6 17
(Philip McBride) *t.k.h: hld up in tch in midfield: effrt over 2f out: sn struggling and wknd over 1f out* **16/1**

503- **7** *3 1/2* **Solid Justice (IRE)**[208] 8180 6-8-11 **45**....................(v) NathanAlison(3) 3 2
(Mark Pattinson) *t.k.h: hld up in last trio: lost tch w ldrs over 2f out: no ch fnl 2f* **4/1**[2]

0000 **8** *18* **Silver Lining (IRE)**[92] 1402 5-9-0 **45**........................ AdamBeschizza 11
(Mark Hoad) *a in last trio: lost tch 2f out: t.o* **66/1**

0-00 **9** *6* **Fenner Hill Neasa (IRE)**[35] 2914 4-9-0 **45**........................ JFEgan 10
(Pat Phelan) *restless in stalls: s.i.s and flashed tail leaving stalls: t.k.h and hdwy to join ldr after 2f: led 7f out tl 4f out: lost pl and bhd 2f out: wknd: t.o* **16/1**

-005 **10** *2 1/4* **Peking Flyer (IRE)**[15] 3657 3-8-6 **49**.............................(t) LiamJones 8
(Ed Walker) *in tch in midfield: effrt on outer over 3f out: sn btn: bhd over 1f out: t.o* **11/2**[3]

2m 3.52s (-0.08) **Going Correction** 0.0s/f (Good)
**WFA** 3 from 4yo+ 12lb **10** Ran SP% **121.3**
Speed ratings (Par 101): **100,99,98,95,92 82,79,65,60,58**
CSF £10.31 CT £48.74 TOTE £2.80: £1.40, £1.60, £1.80; EX 9.60 Trifecta £44.10.
**Owner** Peter Onslow & Kevin Nash **Bred** Peter Onslow **Trained** Lambourn, Berks

**FOCUS**
Add 6yds. A moderate handicap that was predictably dominated by the 3yos, the first trio finishing clear and all posting minor pbs. Straightforward form.

## 4178 LOVE FAIRS ANTIQUES 27 AUG H'CAP 5f 60y
**3:45** (3:46) (Class 4) (0-80,81) 3-Y-O+ **£4,690** (£1,395; £697; £348) **Stalls** Centre

Form RPR

6-64 **1** **Ginzan**[8] 3919 9-9-12 **79**...................................... RobertWinston 4 85
(Malcolm Saunders) *racd off the pce in 3rd: clsd on ldr and rdn over 1f out: styd on to ld ins fnl f: eased cl home* **7/2**[2]

-102 **2** *nk* **Mr Pocket (IRE)**[9] 3865 3-9-8 **81**.................................(t) LukeMorris 1 84
(Paul Cole) *racd off the pce in 4th: swtchd rt over 2f out: unable qck and n.m.r over 1f out: swtchd rt ins fnl f: chsd wnr wl ins fnl f: r.o strly: nvr quite getting to wnr* **2/1**[1]

1000 **3** *1 1/4* **Monumental Man**[17] 3581 8-9-12 **79**.........................(p) WilliamCarson 6 80
(Michael Attwater) *sn led and wnt clr after 1f: rdn over 1f out: hdd ins fnl f: no ex and outpcd wl ins fnl f* **16/1**

623 **4** *hd* **Sandfrankskipsgo**[28] 3176 8-9-9 **76**........................ ShaneKelly 2 76
(Peter Crate) *chsd clr ldr: clsd over 1f out: rdn to chal briefly ins fnl f: unable qck and one pced wl ins fnl f* **5/1**

2410 **5** *2* **Secret Strategy (IRE)**[15] 3673 3-8-13 **72**.................. AdamBeschizza 3 63
(Julia Feilden) *sn niggled and off the pce in 5th: sme hdwy u.p over 1f out: no imp ins fnl f* **5/1**

146 **6** *6* **Otomo**[3] 4093 3-9-0 **73**.......................................(h[1]) LiamKeniry 5 43
(Philip Hide) *s.i.s: niggled along and off the pce in last: sme hdwy and edging lft u.p over 1f out: wknd ins fnl f* **9/2**[3]

1m 1.62s (-0.68) **Going Correction** 0.0s/f (Good)
**WFA** 3 from 8yo+ 6lb **6** Ran SP% **113.0**
Speed ratings (Par 105): **105,104,102,102,99 89**
CSF £11.10 TOTE £4.50: £2.30, £1.30; EX 13.40 Trifecta £132.40.
**Owner** Paul Nicholas & Partner **Bred** Hedsor Stud **Trained** Green Ore, Somerset

**FOCUS**
Add 6yds. A fair sprint in which the winner has been rated back to her best.

## 4179 MARC ALMOND AND THE SOUTH 8 SEPT H'CAP 5f 215y
**4:15** (4:15) (Class 6) (0-60,61) 3-Y-O+ **£2,264** (£673; £336; £168) **Stalls** Centre

Form RPR

4232 **1** **Strictly Carter**[20] 3469 4-9-5 **57**........................ JoshuaBryan(7) 9 64
(Alan Bailey) *t.k.h: hld up in tch in midfield: effrt to chse ldrs over 1f out: rdn to chal ins fnl f: kpt on u.p to ld wl ins fnl f: rdn out* **7/2**[2]

00-6 **2** *nk* **Wild Flower (IRE)**[89] 1451 5-9-3 **48**........................ KieranO'Neill 8 54
(Jimmy Fox) *w ldr: rdn 2f out: kpt on u.p to ld ins fnl f: sn hdd: kpt on wl u.p but a jst hld towards fin* **8/1**

5-33 **3** *3 1/4* **Seprani**[131] 763 3-9-6 **61**.................................(h) GeorgeWood(3) 6 55
(Marco Botti) *hld up in tch in midfield: rdn 3f out: hdwy to chse ldrs over 1f out: outpcd by ldng pair ins fnl f: kpt on to go 3rd towards fin* **7/2**[2]

-055 **4** *nk* **Ginger Truffle**[7] 3942 3-8-13 **51**........................ SamHitchcott 4 44
(Brett Johnson) *sn led: rdn over 1f out: hdd ins fnl f: sn outpcd and wknd wl ins fnl f* **16/1**

0544 **5** *2 1/4* **Jack The Laird (IRE)**[15] 3660 4-9-11 **56**..................(h[1]) RobertWinston 1 43
(Dean Ivory) *racd in last pair: rdn over 2f out: kpt on ins fnl f: nvr threatened ldrs* **9/4**[1]

-005 **6** *nk* **Jazz Legend (USA)**[13] 3728 4-9-8 **53**.................(h) JimmyQuinn 3 40
(Anabel K Murphy) *s.i.s: hld up in rr: effrt over 1f out: kpt on ins fnl f: nvr trbld ldrs* **10/1**

2603 **7** *1 1/2* **Noble Deed**[7] 3941 7-9-11 **56**.................................(p) KierenFox 2 38
(Michael Attwater) *taken down early: chsd ldr: rdn 2f out: unable qck and lost pl over 1f out: wknd fnl f* **6/1**[3]

0500 **8** *3 3/4* **Autumn Tonic (IRE)**[13] 3728 5-9-2 **52**.....................(b) DavidEgan(5) 7 22
(Charlie Wallis) *in tch in midfield: effrt over 2f out: unable qck and lost pl over 1f out: bhd 1f out: wknd* **33/1**

1m 9.23s (-0.97) **Going Correction** 0.0s/f (Good)
**WFA** 3 from 4yo+ 7lb **8** Ran SP% **118.5**
Speed ratings (Par 101): **106,105,101,100,97 97,95,90**
CSF £32.68 CT £106.40 TOTE £3.90: £1.40, £2.20, £1.70; EX 31.40 Trifecta £153.60.
**Owner** Barber Hood Bloodstock & Alan Bailey **Bred** Mickley Stud & Mr D Mossop **Trained** Newmarket, Suffolk

**FOCUS**
Add 6yds. Moderate sprinting form.

## 4180 THE HUMAN LEAGUE 8 SEPT H'CAP 7f 211y
**4:45** (4:46) (Class 6) (0-55,55) 3-Y-O+ **£2,264** (£673; £336; £168) **Stalls** Centre

Form RPR

-444 **1** **Luxford**[49] 2507 3-8-5 **46**...................................... MartinDwyer 13 59+
(John Best) *led for 1f: chsd ldr after: effrt over 1f out: led 1f out: styd on strly: readily* **5/1**[2]

5335 **2** *2 1/2* **Lawfilly**[12] 3751 3-8-12 **53**...................................... ShaneKelly 14 57
(Richard Hughes) *t.k.h: hld up towards rr: shifted rt and hdwy over 2f out: clsd and swtchd lft jst over 1f out: kpt on ins fnl f to chse wnr fnl 100yds: nvr a threat* **4/1**[1]

6-05 **3** *1/2* **Captain Marmalade (IRE)**[15] 3661 5-9-1 **53**.............. RossaRyan(7) 11 58
(Jimmy Fox) *stdd s: hld up towards rr: clsd and bmpd over 2f out: hdwy over 1f out: rdn and kpt on ins fnl f: wnt 3rd wl ins fnl f: nvr threatening wnr* **8/1**

0-54 **4** *1 3/4* **Alketios (GR)**[14] 3688 6-9-5 **55**........................ DavidEgan(5) 15 56
(Chris Gordon) *wl in tch in midfield: effrt 2f out: chsd ldrs 1f out: hung lft and kpt on same pce ins fnl f* **6/1**[3]

0-30 **5** *3* **Provoking (USA)**[35] 2914 4-9-5 **50**........................ JFEgan 16 44+
(David Evans) *t.k.h: led after 1f: rdn and hung lft over 1f out: hdd 1f out: wknd ins fnl f* **5/1**[2]

0505 **6** *1/2* **Pivotal Dream (IRE)**[18] 3550 4-9-1 **46**.................. KieranO'Neill 10 39
(Mark Brisbourne) *wl in tch in midfield: effrt over 2f out: unable qck u.p and no imp over 1f out: wl hld and one pce fnl f* **12/1**

0300 **7** *hd* **Lutine Charlie (IRE)**[35] 2916 10-9-1 **46** oh1..............(p) DanielMuscutt 7 39
(Emma Owen) *chsd ldrs: rdn 2f out: unable qck and btn over 1f out: wl hld and kpt on same pce ins fnl f* **20/1**

0266 **8** *4* **Fairy Mist (IRE)**[25] 3304 10-9-2 **47**..........................(v) WilliamCarson 3 30
(John Bridger) *chsd ldrs: drvn and no rspnse over 1f out: wl hld and eased ins fnl f* **7/1**

50-0 **9** *2* **Diamondsaretrumps (IRE)**[13] 3728 4-8-13 **47**.(t[1]) CallumShepherd(3) 2 26
(Phil McEntee) *in tch in midfield: rdn 2f out: sn outpcd and btn: wknd fnl f* **33/1**

6000 **10** *1 3/4* **King Otto**[15] 3661 3-8-8 **49**..........................................(bt[1]) LukeMorris 12 22
(Phil McEntee) *t.k.h: hld up in midfield: effrt 2f out: hung lft and btn over 1f out: wknd fnl f* **25/1**

-000 **11** *nk* **Caspian Gold (IRE)**[26] 3250 3-8-13 **54**........................ RyanTate 6 26
(Richard Hughes) *restless in stalls: hld up in rr: outpcd and rdn 2f out: sn wl btn* **16/1**

00-0 **12** *3/4* **Clandon**[10] 3824 4-9-10 **55**........................................ SamHitchcott 9 27
(Brett Johnson) *t.k.h: hld up in rr: u.p and no rspnse over 2f out: wl btn over 1f out* **50/1**

00-0 **13** *nk* **Nip Down The Jug**[15] 3660 3-8-11 **52**........................ KierenFox 1 22
(Michael Attwater) *taken down early: t.k.h: hld up in tch in midfield: hmpd and lost pl bnd 4f out: n.d after* **50/1**

-004 **14** *2* **Ripper Street (IRE)**[14] 3701 3-8-13 **54**.....................(h) AdamBeschizza 4 19
(Christine Dunnett) *hld up in tch in midfield: rdn and bmpd over 2f out: sn struggling: bhd over 1f out* **25/1**

-000 **15** *3 1/2* **Sabato (IRE)**[15] 3661 4-9-1 **46** oh1..........................(v[1]) TimmyMurphy 8
(Fergal O'Brien) *s.i.s: hdwy into midfield on outer after 2f: effrt on outer 3f out: lost pl and bhd over 1f out* **16/1**

1m 35.28s (-0.72) **Going Correction** 0.0s/f (Good)
**WFA** 3 from 4yo+ 10lb **15** Ran SP% **130.0**
Speed ratings (Par 101): **103,100,100,98,95 94,94,90,88,86 86,85,85,83,79**
CSF £25.39 CT £167.49 TOTE £6.70: £2.60, £1.50, £3.50; EX 26.40 Trifecta £98.20.
**Owner** Stuart Mair, Wendy Bush & Steve Summers **Bred** Best Breeding **Trained** Oad Street, Kent
■ Stewards' Enquiry : Rossa Ryan two-day ban: careless riding in that he allowed his horse to drift right-handed when looking for a run (Jul 11-12)
Adam Beschizza four-day ban: guilty of violent conduct in riders' changing room (Jul 11-13, 17)
Sam Hitchcott five-day ban: used whip when out of contention (Jul 11-15)
Kieren Fox seven-day ban: guilty of violent conduct in riders' changing room (Jul 11-15, 17-18)

**FOCUS**
Add 6yds. Lowly form, although two of the market leaders - both 3yos - came to the fore.

## 4181 HACIENDA CLASSICAL 9 SEPT AMATEUR RIDERS' H'CAP 1m 3f 198y
**5:15** (5:18) (Class 6) (0-65,65) 4-Y-O+ **£2,183** (£677; £338; £169) **Stalls** High

Form RPR

3403 **1** **Tempuran**[43] 2678 8-10-2 **58**..........................(v) PoppyBridgwater(5) 2 71
(David Bridgwater) *mde all: sn clr: pushed along over 1f out: styd on: unchal* **6/1**[2]

0132 **2** *9* **Strictly Art (IRE)**[5] 4018 4-10-11 **62**........................ MrRBirkett 4 61
(Alan Bailey) *chsd ldrs tl dropped to rr and bustled along 7f out: effrt in 3rd 2f out: kpt on to go 2nd wl ins fnl f: no ch w wnr* **7/4**[1]

3233 **3** *2 1/2* **Halling's Wish**[12] 3208 7-10-7 **65**..........................(b) MissBeckyButler(7) 1 60
(Gary Moore) *chsd clr wnr: rdn 2f out: no imp and lost wl btn 2nd wl ins fnl f* **7/1**[3]

640- **4** *3 3/4* **Royal Etiquette (IRE)**[106] 4950 10-9-6 **50**..............(t) MissIMarshall(7) 6 39
(Lawney Hill) *midfield: rdn 4f out: nvr on terms w wnr: plugged on* **25/1**

2241 **5** *7* **Powered (IRE)**[8] 3916 4-10-0 **56**........................ MissEMacKenzie(5) 7 33
(David Evans) *midfield: nvr on terms w wnr: rdn 2f out: no prog and wl btn whn hung lft and hit rail 1f out* **7/4**[1]

-040 **6** *7* **Little Orchid**[12] 3756 4-9-4 **46**........................ MrWillPettis(5) 3 12
(Julia Feilden) *hld up off the pce in last pair: hdwy to go 3rd but nt on terms w wnr 4f out: lost pl u.p over 2f out: wl btn after* **14/1**

000- **7** *4 1/2* **Beaumont's Party (IRE)**[23] 8586 10-9-13 **55**............... MissAPeck(5) 5 14
(Laura Morgan) *awkward leaving stalls: sn in midfield but nvr on terms w wnr: lost pl and bhd 4f out: no ch after* **12/1**

2m 35.97s (3.27) **Going Correction** 0.0s/f (Good) **7** Ran SP% **117.7**
Speed ratings (Par 101): **89,83,81,78,74 69,66**
CSF £17.76 TOTE £6.60: £3.00, £1.40; EX 18.00 Trifecta £94.30.
**Owner** David J Smith **Bred** Stiftung Gestut Fahrhof **Trained** Icomb, Gloucs

**FOCUS**
Add 6yds. Not form to put much faith in, the two market leaders disappointing as the winner slipped his field.
T/Jkpt: Not Won. T/Plt: £31.80 to a £1 stake. Pool: £90,302.01 - 2071.55 winning units T/Qpdt: £4.80 to a £1 stake. Pool: £7,023.39 - 1066.16 winning units **Steve Payne**

# 3812 LEICESTER (R-H)
Tuesday, June 27

**OFFICIAL GOING: Good to firm (good in places) changing to good after race 2 (6:40)**
Wind: Light behind Weather: Raining

## 4182 LANGHAM LADIES' H'CAP (FOR LADY AMATEUR RIDERS) 5f
**6:10** (6:10) (Class 5) (0-75,71) 3-Y-O+ **£3,743** (£1,161; £580; £290) **Stalls** High

Form RPR

3402 **1** **Vimy Ridge**[42] 2700 5-10-0 **71**..........................(t) MissJCooley(7) 7 79
(Alan Bailey) *s.i.s: sn outpcd: swtchd rt and hdwy over 1f out: led ins fnl f: pushed out* **3/1**[2]

4440 **2** *1 1/4* **Dodgy Bob**[27] 3203 4-9-12 **62**..........................(b) MissMMullineaux 8 66
(Michael Mullineaux) *prom: sn pushed along: chsd ldr 2f out: rdn and ev ch fr over 1f out tl edgd rt and styd on same pce wl ins fnl f* **16/1**

0120 **3** *3* **Classic Pursuit**[5] 4005 6-10-3 **67**..........................(b) MissSBrotherton 4 60
(Michael Appleby) *broke wl: sn stdd and lost pl: swtchd rt 1/2-way: hdwy over 1f out: sn rdn: styd on same pce ins fnl f* **5/2**[1]

3251 **4** *1 3/4* **Swendab (IRE)**[3] 4093 9-10-7 **71** 7ex..............(b) MissBrodieHampson 2 57
(John O'Shea) *chsd ldr tl rdn 2f out: no ex fnl f* **9/2**[3]



The Form Book Flat, Raceform Ltd, Newbury, RG14 5SJ

-210 **5** *nk* **Bronze Beau**[13] 3707 10-9-13 **68**........................(tp) MissKMargarson(5) 1 53
(Kristin Stubbs) *led: shkn up over 1f out: hdd ins fnl f: wknd towards fin* **12/1**

0246 **6** *6* **Generalyse**[20] 3469 8-9-10 **60**..............................(b) MissJoannaMason 3 24
(Anabel K Murphy) *s.i.s: outpcd* **12/1**

412 **7** *1* **Zipedeedodah (IRE)**[15] 3659 5-10-0 **71**....................(t) MrsCPownall(7) 5 31
(Joseph Tuite) *chsd ldrs: sn pushed along: wknd over 1f out* **9/2**[3]

1m 0.48s (0.48) **Going Correction** +0.125s/f (Good) **7** Ran SP% **111.2**
Speed ratings (Par 103): **101,99,94,91,90 81,79**
CSF £44.11 CT £130.39 TOTE £4.30: £1.90, £5.90; EX 49.00 Trifecta £211.90.
**Owner** Dr S P Hargreaves **Bred** Mrs Sheila Oakes **Trained** Newmarket, Suffolk

**FOCUS**
Despite a prolonged period of rain before racing the going remained good to firm, good in places. A fair handicap, in which the pace was good, and the closers came to the fore. Not strong form for the level.

## 4183 BRITISH STALLION STUDS EBF NOVICE STKS (PLUS 10 RACE) 7f
**6:40** (6:40) (Class 4) 2-Y-O **£5,175** (£1,540; £769; £384) **Stalls** High

Form RPR

5 **1** **Maksab (IRE)**[17] 3590 2-9-2 0.................................. SilvestreDeSousa 3 80
(Mick Channon) *chsd ldr 2f: remained handy: pushed along 1/2-way: led over 2f out: rdn and jnd over 1f out tl over 1f out tl lft clr wl ins fnl f* **2/1**[2]

6 **2** *2* **Rhosneigr (IRE)**[28] 3164 2-9-2 0.................................. DavidProbert 1 77
(Charles Hills) *prom: jnd ldr 5f out: ev ch fr over 1f out tl rdn and swvd rt wl ins fnl f: nt rcvr* **6/1**

**3** *1 ½* **Jazirat (IRE)** 2-9-2 0........................................(h[1]) MartinLane 2 71
(Charlie Appleby) *dwlt: rn green in rr: pushed along 1/2-way: rdn and edgd rt over 1f out: kpt on: nt trble ldrs* **4/1**[3]

1 **4** *5* **Falmouth Light (FR)**[11] 3783 2-9-8 0.............................. PJMcDonald 4 63
(Mark Johnston) *led: rdn and hdd over 2f out: wknd fnl f* **6/4**[1]

1m 25.32s (-0.88) **Going Correction** +0.125s/f (Good) **4** Ran SP% **107.6**
Speed ratings (Par 95): **110,107,106,100**
CSF £12.31 TOTE £3.20; EX 11.80 Trifecta £56.10.
**Owner** M Al-Qatami & K M Al-Mudhaf **Bred** D J And Mrs Deer **Trained** West Ilsley, Berks

**FOCUS**
An interesting little novice event and there was late drama.

## 4184 DEBORAH WHITEHORN'S BIRTHDAY CELEBRATION FILLIES' H'CAP 1m 53y
**7:10** (7:10) (Class 5) (0-70,71) 3-Y-O+ **£3,881** (£1,155; £577; £288) **Stalls** Low

Form RPR

001- **1** **Hope Against Hope (IRE)**[260] 7228 3-8-12 **61**............... PJMcDonald 1 69
(Mark Johnston) *sn pushed along to chse ldr: rdn and lost 2nd over 4f out: outpcd over 2f out: rallied over 1f out: led and flashed tail ins fnl f: styd on wl* **7/1**[3]

-001 **2** *3* **Clear As A Bell (IRE)**[10] 3832 3-8-5 **54**......................... JamesSullivan 2 55
(Tim Easterby) *led: rdn over 1f out: hdd ins fnl f: edgd lft and styd on same pce* **7/1**[3]

1622 **3** *¾* **The Dukkerer (IRE)**[12] 3761 6-9-6 **59**................................. TomEaves 6 60
(James Given) *chsd ldrs: rdn over 1f out: styd on same pce ins fnl f* **7/1**[3]

0036 **4** *1 ¼* **Scent Of Power**[12] 3761 5-8-4 **48** oh1............................(t) JaneElliott(5) 9 46
(Barry Leavy) *hld up in tch: chsd ldr over 3f out: rdn and ev ch over 1f out: no ex ins fnl f* **14/1**

6-00 **5** *1 ¼* **Zaria**[21] 3422 6-8-11 **57**............................................. KatherineGlenister(7) 5 53
(Richard Price) *hld up: hdwy over 3f out: rdn over 2f out: hung rt and no ex ins fnl f* **7/1**[3]

00-0 **6** *1 ½* **Delirium (IRE)**[29] 3142 3-8-8 **57**.................................(p[1]) RobHornby 11 47
(Ed de Giles) *s.i.s: sn rcvrd to chse ldrs: wnt 2nd over 4f out tl over 3f out: rdn over 2f out: wknd ins fnl f* **33/1**

6003 **7** *1 ¾* **Venetian Proposal (IRE)**[26] 3246 3-8-0 **49**..................(p) RyanPowell 7 35
(Zoe Davison) *hld up: stmbld over 4f out: hdwy over 2f out: sn rdn: wknd over 1f out* **16/1**

1440 **8** *2 ½* **Elusive Olivia (USA)**[46] 2587 3-9-4 **67**..........................(t) TomQueally 10 47
(Joseph Tuite) *hld up: rn wd bnd 5f out: sn outpcd: styd on ins fnl f* **14/1**

5240 **9** *½* **Be Royale**[13] 3718 7-9-1 **61**............................................... RayDawson(7) 8 42
(Michael Appleby) *hld up: hdwy over 3f out: rdn and wknd over 1f out* **11/1**

-446 **10** *4 ½* **Singing Sands (IRE)**[29] 3142 3-9-8 **71**.....................(t) FergusSweeney 3 40
(Seamus Durack) *hld up: racd keenly: effrt and nt clr run over 2f out: wknd fnl f* **9/2**[1]

3100 **11** *½* **Alnasl (IRE)**[21] 3425 3-9-1 **67**...............................(h) KieranShoemark(3) 4 35
(Archie Watson) *s.i.s: hld up: plld hrd: nt clr run 5f out: sme hdwy whn stmbld over 2f out: rdn and wknd over 1f out* **11/2**[2]

1m 46.29s (1.19) **Going Correction** +0.125s/f (Good)
**WFA** 3 from 5yo+ 10lb **11** Ran SP% **114.1**
Speed ratings (Par 100): **99,96,95,94,92 91,89,87,86,82 81**
CSF £53.60 CT £361.81 TOTE £5.40: £2.20, £1.70, £2.50; EX 43.90 Trifecta £168.40.
**Owner** Thurloe XXXI and Stuart & Ross Counsell **Bred** E Browne **Trained** Middleham Moor, N Yorks

**FOCUS**
The rain continued to fall and the going was changed to good before this race. A modest handicap but an improving winner.

## 4185 VIS-A-VIS SYMPOSIUMS H'CAP 1m 2f
**7:40** (7:40) (Class 5) (0-70,67) 4-Y-O+ **£3,881** (£1,155; £577; £288) **Stalls** Low

Form RPR

0600 **1** **Invictus (GER)**[21] 3428 5-9-5 **65**...............................(p[1]) PaulMulrennan 3 72
(David Loughnane) *mde all: led at stdy pce tl qckn d over 3f out: rdn over 2f out: styd on u.p: hung lft towards fin* **10/1**

3020 **2** *1 ¼* **Arithmetic (IRE)**[12] 3744 4-9-5 **65**................................. JamesSullivan 4 69
(Ruth Carr) *chsd wnr: rdn over 1f out: edgd rt u.p ins fnl f: styd on same pce towards fin* **4/1**[3]

1131 **3** *2 ¼* **Miss Inga Sock (IRE)**[18] 3519 5-9-1 **66**......................... GeorgiaCox(5) 6 66
(Eve Johnson Houghton) *chsd ldrs: pushed along over 3f out: rdn and nt clr run over 1f out: no ex ins fnl f* **3/1**[2]

0225 **4** *1 ¼* **Tyrsal (IRE)**[13] 3726 6-8-6 **57**............................................ PaddyPilley(5) 1 54
(Clifford Lines) *dwlt: hld up: hdwy 3f out: rdn over 2f out: sn outpcd: styd on ins fnl f* **5/1**

3423 **5** *3* **Flying Fantasy**[22] 3396 5-9-7 **67**.................................. SilvestreDeSousa 2 60
(Michael Appleby) *s.i.s: hld up: racd keenly: hdwy 3f out: rdn and hung rt over 1f out: wknd ins fnl f* **13/8**[1]

2m 10.44s (2.54) **Going Correction** +0.125s/f (Good) **5** Ran SP% **108.9**
Speed ratings (Par 103): **94,93,91,90,87**
CSF £46.11 TOTE £8.20: £3.60, £2.20; EX 56.20 Trifecta £317.40.
**Owner** Mike And Eileen Newbould **Bred** Westminster Race Horses Gmbh **Trained** Market Drayton, Shropshire

**FOCUS**
A modest handicap. The runner-up has been rated to his best.

## 4186 SKEFFINGTON H'CAP 1m 53y
**8:10** (8:10) (Class 5) (0-70,70) 3-Y-O **£3,881** (£1,155; £577; £288) **Stalls** Low

Form RPR

53-6 **1** **Alshibaa (IRE)**[37] 2854 3-9-7 **70**........................................... JimCrowley 4 77
(William Haggas) *chsd ldr: rdn over 2f out: styd on u.p to ld towards fin* **13/8**[1]

6-05 **2** *nk* **Duchess Of Fife**[28] 3189 3-9-0 **63**.........................(v[1]) SilvestreDeSousa 3 69
(William Knight) *led: rdn over 2f out: hdd towards fin* **9/1**

2554 **3** *2 ¾* **Valley Of Rocks (IRE)**[10] 3816 3-9-4 **67**......................... PJMcDonald 2 67
(Mark Johnston) *chsd ldrs: rdn over 2f out: swtchd rt wl ins fnl f: styd on same pce* **4/1**[2]

56-0 **4** *2 ¼* **Pioneering (IRE)**[58] 2185 3-9-4 **67**.................................... PhillipMakin 7 62
(David O'Meara) *hld up: hdwy and nt clr run over 1f out: no ex ins fnl f* **7/1**

-156 **5** *3* **Daring Guest (IRE)**[28] 3173 3-8-12 **66**.............................. JaneElliott(5) 5 54
(George Margarson) *hld up: plld hrd early: hdwy over 2f out: rdn over 1f out: hung rt and wknd fnl f* **5/1**[3]

0-00 **6** *nse* **Northdown**[39] 2794 3-9-4 **67**..........................................(p[1]) TomQueally 1 54
(David Lanigan) *s.i.s and pushed along early in rr: effrt over 2f out: rdn and hung rt over 1f out: nt run on* **11/1**

050- **7** *10* **Prince Of Clappers**[286] 6473 3-8-11 **60**......................... JamesSullivan 9 24
(Tim Easterby) *prom: shkn up over 2f out: sn wknd* **20/1**

1m 46.68s (1.58) **Going Correction** +0.125s/f (Good) **7** Ran SP% **110.4**
Speed ratings (Par 99): **97,96,93,91,88 88,78**
CSF £15.98 CT £46.38 TOTE £2.20: £1.60, £3.60; EX 18.00 Trifecta £55.10.
**Owner** Hamdan Al Maktoum **Bred** Shadwell Estate Company Limited **Trained** Newmarket, Suffolk

**FOCUS**
A modest handicap run at an ordinary pace. The winner built on his maiden form, and also a pb from the 2nd.

## 4187 BRUNTINGTHORPE H'CAP 1m 3f 179y
**8:45** (8:46) (Class 6) (0-60,60) 4-Y-O+ **£3,234** (£962; £481; £240) **Stalls** Low

Form RPR

1650 **1** **Shining Romeo**[43] 2022 5-9-7 **60**............................... SilvestreDeSousa 8 72
(Denis Quinn) *led 2f: chsd ldr tl led again 3f out: pushed clr fr over 1f out: eased towards fin* **9/4**[1]

6655 **2** *7* **Yul Finegold (IRE)**[21] 3436 7-9-1 **54**........................... PaulMulrennan 14 54
(Conor Dore) *racd wd early: sn w ldr: led 10f out tl 3f out: sn rdn: styd on same pce fr over 1f out* **20/1**

00-4 **3** *nk* **Ocean Gale**[21] 3426 4-8-11 **50**........................................ JamesSullivan 11 49
(Richard Price) *chsd ldrs: rdn over 4f out: outpcd over 2f out: styd on fnl f* **12/1**

0136 **4** *2 ¾* **Star Ascending (IRE)**[32] 3043 5-9-4 **57**......................(p) TomQueally 12 52
(Jennie Candlish) *s.i.s: hdwy over 9f out: rdn over 2f out: wknd fnl f* **8/1**[3]

665- **5** *1 ¼* **Rowlestonerendezvu**[255] 7369 4-8-11 **50**................ GeorgeDowning 2 43
(Tony Carroll) *hld up: hdwy over 2f out: rdn over 1f out: wkng whn hung lft ins fnl f* **10/1**

-106 **6** *1* **Staplehurst (IRE)**[14] 3694 4-8-10 **54**.........................(t) PaddyPilley(5) 9 45
(Geoffrey Deacon) *hld up: rdn over 3f out: nvr on terms* **25/1**

-041 **7** *1 ¾* **Infiniti (IRE)**[28] 3192 4-9-0 **58**............................................ JaneElliott(5) 7 47
(Barry Leavy) *hld up: pushed along over 5f out: hdwy over 3f out: rdn over 2f out: wknd wl over 1f out* **4/1**[2]

5166 **8** *11* **The Lock Master (IRE)**[12] 3760 10-9-1 **57**......(p) AlistairRawlinson(3) 10 28
(Michael Appleby) *prom: lost pl over 10f out: hdwy over 3f out: rdn and wknd over 2f out* **20/1**

4 **9** *3 ½* **Avocet (USA)**[21] 3440 4-9-0 **53**......................................... TonyHamilton 5 18
(Julia Feilden) *chsd ldrs tl rdn and wknd over 2f out* **33/1**

566- **10** *½* **Howardian Hills (IRE)**[395] 2700 4-9-1 **57**............... KieranShoemark(3) 3 22
(Victor Dartnall) *mid-div: rdn over 3f out: sn wknd* **8/1**[3]

400- **11** *19* **Rock Palm (IRE)**[295] 6194 4-9-2 **55**..................................... JimCrowley 1
(Laura Morgan) *mid-div: rdn and wknd over 3f out* **8/1**[3]

2m 34.99s (1.09) **Going Correction** +0.125s/f (Good) **11** Ran SP% **117.2**
Speed ratings (Par 101): **101,96,96,94,93 92,91,84,81,81 68**
CSF £55.71 CT £455.17 TOTE £2.90: £1.40, £5.70, £2.00; EX 43.80 Trifecta £902.50.
**Owner** John Mangan **Bred** Newsells Park Stud **Trained** Newmarket, Suffolk

**FOCUS**
A modest handicap and the well-backed favourite won as he liked.

## 4188 LEICESTER INTERACTIVE H'CAP 6f
**9:15** (9:15) (Class 5) (0-70,71) 3-Y-O **£2,911** (£866; £432; £216) **Stalls** High

Form RPR

3215 **1** **Love Oasis**[6] 3974 3-9-8 **71**............................................... PJMcDonald 3 80
(Mark Johnston) *w ldr tl led over 2f out: rdn over 1f out: edgd lft fnl f: r.o wl* **3/1**[3]

604- **2** *3 ½* **Screaming Gemini (IRE)**[195] 8354 3-9-7 **70**............(b[1]) AndreaAtzeni 2 68
(Roger Varian) *s.i.s: hdwy to chse ldr 5f out: rdn 1/2-way: styd on same pce fnl f* **11/4**[2]

-220 **3** *nk* **Springforth**[19] 3496 3-9-4 **67**........................................... TonyHamilton 4 64
(Richard Fahey) *sn led: hdd over 2f out: rdn over 1f out: no ex fnl f* **5/1**

-000 **4** *6* **Dravid**[40] 2758 3-8-4 **53**......................................................(h[1]) RyanPowell 5 31
(Rod Millman) *dwlt: outpcd: rdn over 1f out: nvr on terms* **25/1**

4052 **5** *¾* **Bellevarde (IRE)**[17] 3584 3-9-0 **63**................................. JamesSullivan 1 38
(Richard Price) *hld up in tch: rdn over 2f out: wknd ins fnl f* **5/2**[1]

4-10 **6** *¾* **Moonshine Dancer**[31] 3063 3-8-13 **69**................(h[1]) PatrickVaughan(7) 6 42
(Christian Williams) *prom: rdn over 2f out: wknd over 1f out* **25/1**

4-60 **7** *17* **Katrine (IRE)**[24] 3331 3-9-4 **67**...........................................(h) PhillipMakin 7
(David O'Meara) *plld hrd and prom: wknd over 1f out* **16/1**

1m 12.94s (-0.06) **Going Correction** +0.125s/f (Good) **7** Ran SP% **110.5**
Speed ratings (Par 99): **105,100,99,91,90 89,67**
CSF £10.85 TOTE £3.70: £1.90, £2.70; EX 12.40 Trifecta £50.20.
**Owner** Crone Stud Farms Ltd **Bred** New England, Mount Coote & P Barrett **Trained** Middleham Moor, N Yorks

**FOCUS**
A fair handicap run at a good pace.
T/Plt: £443.20 to a £1 stake. Pool: £63,692.50 - 104.89 winning units T/Qpdt: £71.70 to a £1 stake. Pool: £5,607.43 - 57.84 winning units **Colin Roberts**

4189 - 4195a (Foreign Racing) - See Raceform Interactive

# LE CROISE-LAROCHE

Tuesday, June 27

**OFFICIAL GOING: Turf: good**

## 4196a PRIX DE MONS (CLAIMER) (2YO) (TURF) 5f 110y
11:25 2-Y-O £6,410 (£2,564; £1,923; £1,282; £641)

RPR

1 **Quick Skips Lad (IRE)**[8] 3918 2-8-11 0...............(p) TonyPiccone 5 62
(J S Moore) *wl into stride: settled bhd ldrs: pushed along over 2f out: rdn and hdwy over 1f out: str run ins fnl f to assert cl home* **16/5**[2]

2 ¾ **Dragon's Teeth (IRE)**[7] 3936 2-9-1 0.............................. MaximeGuyon 8 63
(Jo Hughes) *disp ld early: settled 2nd: urged along over 2f out: rdn over 1f out: styd on wl fnl f* **76/10**

3 ¾ **Good To Talk**[14] 2-9-8 0...............................................(p) AntoineHamelin 1 68
(Matthieu Palussiere, France) **8/5**[1]

4 1 ½ **See You In Paris (IRE)** 2-8-8 0.................................. EddyHardouin 10 49
(Gianluca Bietolini, Italy) **30/1**

5 nk **Vida Loca (FR)**[14] 2-8-11 0...............................................(p) GregoryBenoist 9 51
(M Boutin, France) **152/10**

6 2 **Jurisprudance (FR)**[14] 2-9-1 0...............................(p) AurelienLemaitre 3 48
(M Boutin, France) **17/5**[3]

7 3 ½ **Norwegian Lord (FR)**[19] 3515 2-8-11 0.............(p) ClementGuitraud(8) 7 41
(Y Barberot, France) **208/10**

8 ¾ **Miss Milliner** 2-8-4 0.............................. GuillaumeTrolleyDePrevaux(4) 4 27
(Jo Hughes) *settled midfield: rdn over 1f out: limited rspnse and styd on one pce fnl f* **84/1**

9 ½ **Pif D'Avril (FR)**[21] 3445 2-8-8 0.................................. StephaneBreux 6 26
(F-X De Chevigny, France) **63/1**

10 ¾ **Sorina (GER)**[45] 2642 2-8-5 0.............................. ClementLecoeuvre(3) 11 23
(Henk Grewe, Germany) **157/10**

1m 6.2s **10** Ran SP% **119.3**

PARI-MUTUEL (all including 1 euro stake): WIN: 4.20; PLACE: 1.60, 2.00, 1.20; DF: 10.90; SF: 18.00.

**Owner** J S Moore **Bred** Tom McDonald **Trained** Upper Lambourn, Berks

# 4040 BATH (L-H)

Wednesday, June 28

**OFFICIAL GOING: Firm**

Wind: Light, across Weather: Overcast

## 4197 DRIBUILD GROUP H'CAP (BATH SUMMER STAYERS' SERIES QUALIFIER) 1m 5f 11y
6:00 (6:01) (Class 5) (0-75,73) 3-Y-O £2,911 (£866; £432; £216) Stalls High

Form RPR

0-11 1 **Pow Wow**[10] 3864 3-9-2 73 6ex.................................. PaddyPilley(5) 7 84
(Roger Charlton) *rrd over and uns rdr bhd stalls: sn w ldr: led after 2f: hdd over 8f out: led again over 6f out: rdn clr fr over 2f out: easily* **5/6**[1]

-145 2 9 **Pete So High (GER)**[20] 3503 3-9-7 73.........................(p) SteveDrowne 6 71
(Richard Hannon) *led 2f: racd keenly in 2nd pl tl led again over 8f out: hdd over 6f out: remained chsng wnr: edgd rt bnd over 4f out: rdn over 2f out: sn outpcd* **10/3**[2]

45-5 3 1 ½ **Zoffanist (IRE)**[10] 3864 3-8-12 64.................................. MartinDwyer 4 59
(Amanda Perrett) *racd keenly in 3rd pl tl dropped to last over 6f out: pushed along over 3f out: hdwy over 2f out: rdn and hung lft over 1f out: no ex* **4/1**[3]

3340 4 2 ½ **Tristram**[19] 3520 3-9-7 73.................................. TimmyMurphy 5 64
(Richard Hughes) *hld up: hdwy over 6f out: rdn over 2f out: wknd over 1f out* **7/1**

2m 51.7s (-0.30) **Going Correction** -0.05s/f (Good) **4** Ran SP% **110.1**

Speed ratings (Par 99): **98,92,91,90**

CSF £3.99 TOTE £1.90; EX 3.50 Trifecta £4.30.

**Owner** Philip Newton **Bred** Philip Newton **Trained** Beckhampton, Wilts

**FOCUS**

The complexion of the opener was somewhat changed during the day as three of the field came out, but it's hard to believe any of those would have troubled the progressive winner.

## 4198 HAPPY 60TH BIRTHDAY GRAHAM JAUNS H'CAP 5f 160y
6:30 (6:30) (Class 5) (0-75,75) 3-Y-O £4,568 (£1,367; £683; £342; £170) Stalls Centre

Form RPR

-041 1 **Pastfact**[11] 3810 3-8-8 62.................................. MartinDwyer 4 68
(Malcolm Saunders) *trckd ldrs: racd keenly: pushed along over 2f out: rdn to ld and hung lft ins fnl f: r.o: eased nr fin* **7/2**[2]

3-22 2 1 ¼ **Secret Agent**[15] 3692 3-8-11 68.................................. HectorCrouch(3) 5 70
(William Muir) *chsd ldr: rdn to ld 2f out: hdd ins fnl f: styd on same pce* **9/2**[3]

-306 3 ¾ **Miss Icon**[10] 3869 3-9-1 69.................................. TrevorWhelan 1 69
(Patrick Chamings) *chsd ldrs: shkn up over 1f out: nt clr run ins fnl f: styd on* **8/1**

223 4 1 **Del Parco**[37] 2895 3-9-7 75...............................................(p[1]) AdamKirby 3 71
(Clive Cox) *sn led: rdn and hdd 2f out: no ex wl ins fnl f* **13/8**[1]

351 5 5 **In The Spotlight (IRE)**[14] 3729 3-9-0 75.................................. CameronNoble(7) 2 55
(Henry Spiller) *s.s: sme hdwy over 2f out: hung lft and wknd over 1f out* **7/2**[2]

1m 10.33s (-0.87) **Going Correction** -0.05s/f (Good) **5** Ran SP% **111.8**

Speed ratings (Par 99): **103,101,100,99,92**

CSF £18.99 TOTE £4.70: £1.90, £3.00; EX 18.70 Trifecta £77.50.

**Owner** Premier Conservatory Roofs **Bred** M S Saunders & D Collier **Trained** Green Ore, Somerset

**FOCUS**

This race contained three last-time-out winners but none of them went off favourite. The winner progressed again, with the 2nd/3rd rated close to their best.

## 4199 LONGINES IRISH CHAMPIONS WEEKEND EBF FILLIES' NOVICE STKS (PLUS 10 RACE) 5f 160y
7:00 (7:01) (Class 4) 2-Y-O £4,690 (£1,395; £697; £348) Stalls Centre

Form RPR

0422 1 **Mraseel (IRE)**[11] 3815 2-9-0 0...............................(p) MartinHarley 5 76+
(James Tate) *mde all: rdn clr fnl f: comf* **9/4**[2]

4336 2 ¾ **Kodiac Express (IRE)**[19] 3516 2-9-0 0.................................. AntonioFresu 8 68
(Mike Murphy) *hld up: hdwy over 2f out: rdn over 1f out: r.o to go 2nd nr fin: no ch w wnr* **7/1**

31 3 ¾ **Tulip Fever**[12] 3789 2-9-6 0.................................. HarryBentley 6 71
(William Haggas) *prom: rdn to chse wnr over 1f out: styd on same pce ins fnl f: lost 2nd nr fin* **1/1**[1]

55 4 3 ¾ **Llamrei**[33] 3022 2-9-0 0.................................. SteveDrowne 1 53
(Jo Hughes) *chsd wnr tl rdn over 1f out: no ex fnl f* **33/1**

5 3 ¼ **Ladycammyofclare (IRE)** 2-9-0 0.................................. AdamKirby 4 42
(Mark Johnston) *hld up: hdwy over 3f out: rdn over 2f out: wknd over 1f out* **5/1**[3]

0 6 16 **Sunset Flyer**[37] 2904 2-9-0 0.................................. LemosdeSouza 7
(Amy Murphy) *hld up in tch: rdn over 2f out: wkng whn hung lft over 1f out* **50/1**

1m 11.66s (0.46) **Going Correction** -0.05s/f (Good) **6** Ran SP% **114.8**

Speed ratings (Par 92): **94,93,92,87,82 61**

CSF £18.49 TOTE £4.00: £2.00, £3.60; EX 17.90 Trifecta £29.50.

**Owner** Sheikh Hamed Dalmook Al Maktoum **Bred** Tally-Ho Stud **Trained** Newmarket, Suffolk

**FOCUS**

Only two of these seemed to be seriously fancied in the market, and one of those proved up to the task.

## 4200 CHAMPAGNE POMMERY H'CAP 5f 10y
7:30 (7:30) (Class 4) (0-85,84) 3-Y-O £6,469 (£1,925; £962; £481) Stalls Centre

Form RPR

134 1 **Fethiye Boy**[23] 3411 3-8-8 71.................................. RyanPowell 5 79
(Ronald Harris) *mde all: rdn and hung lft fnl f: styd on wl* **4/1**[2]

4134 2 1 ¼ **Jashma (IRE)**[15] 3692 3-8-1 69.................................. DavidEgan(5) 2 73
(Richard Hughes) *s.i.s: hdwy 4f out: rdn to chse wnr over 1f out: edgd lft ins fnl f: styd on same pce* **8/11**[1]

0-53 3 ¾ **Coronation Cottage**[15] 3692 3-8-2 65 oh1.................................. KieranO'Neill 1 66
(Malcolm Saunders) *chsd wnr tl rdn over 1f out: styng on same pce whn n.m.r wl ins fnl f* **5/1**[3]

1-06 4 9 **Broadhaven Honey (IRE)**[16] 3672 3-8-10 73...........(p[1]) MartinDwyer 4 42
(Tony Carroll) *broke wl: lost pl after 1f: sn bhd* **11/2**

1m 1.66s (-0.84) **Going Correction** -0.05s/f (Good) **4** Ran SP% **110.0**

Speed ratings (Par 101): **104,102,100,86**

CSF £7.64 TOTE £3.30; EX 6.80 Trifecta £9.70.

**Owner** Mrs Ruth M Serrell **Bred** Longdon Stud Ltd **Trained** Earlswood, Monmouths

**FOCUS**

The likely short-priced favourite Storm Over was taken out earlier in the day, so the race probably became much more competitive as a result.

## 4201 BIBBY FINANCIAL SERVICES H'CAP (BATH SUMMER SPRINT SERIES QUALIFIER) 5f 160y
8:00 (8:00) (Class 4) (0-85,86) 4-Y-O+ £4,568 (£1,367; £683; £342; £170) Stalls Centre

Form RPR

5443 1 **Pixeleen**[10] 3867 5-9-10 86.................................. AdamKirby 4 95
(Malcolm Saunders) *w ldrs: led 2 out: sn rdn: styd on gamely u.p* **6/5**[1]

5401 2 nk **Under The Covers**[26] 3279 4-8-13 75.................................. RyanPowell 2 83
(Ronald Harris) *dwlt: hdwy over 3f out: rdn over 1f out: r.o* **10/1**

403 3 1 **Belledesert**[26] 3307 4-9-7 83.................................. RoystonFfrench 6 88
(Steph Hollinshead) *prom: pushed along over 3f out: rdn over 1f out: r.o* **7/2**[2]

60-5 4 ½ **Case Key**[11] 3816 4-8-3 72...............................................(p[1]) RayDawson(7) 1 75
(Michael Appleby) *led: rdn and hdd 2f out: styd on same pce wl ins fnl f* **20/1**

3050 5 6 **Highly Sprung (IRE)**[11] 3827 4-9-3 79.................................. RichardKingscote 3 62
(Mark Johnston) *w ldrs tl rdn 1/2-way: wknd fnl f* **4/1**[3]

3004 6 ¾ **Miracle Garden**[11] 3811 5-7-12 65...............................................(v) DavidEgan(5) 5 46
(Ian Williams) *in tch but sn pushed along: sme hdwy over 2f out: rdn and wknd over 1f out* **8/1**

1m 9.85s (-1.35) **Going Correction** -0.05s/f (Good) **6** Ran SP% **112.6**

Speed ratings (Par 105): **107,106,105,104,96 95**

CSF £14.56 TOTE £1.90: £1.40, £3.20; EX 18.10 Trifecta £32.00.

**Owner** M S Saunders **Bred** Glebe Farm Stud **Trained** Green Ore, Somerset

**FOCUS**

The winner was well in after finishing third in a Listed race last time and wasn't far off that level.

## 4202 PARKER TRANSPORT SW LTD MAIDEN STKS 1m 3f 137y
8:30 (8:30) (Class 5) 3-Y-O+ £2,911 (£866; £432; £216) Stalls Low

Form RPR

1 **Rolling Maul (IRE)**[40] 9-9-7 0.................................. JoshuaBryan(7) 3 76
(Peter Bowen) *s.i.s: hld up: hdwy over 3f out: led over 1f out: sn rdn and edgd lft: styd on wl* **10/3**[3]

540 2 1 **Park Paddocks (IRE)**[14] 3720 3-9-0 73...........................(p[1]) MartinHarley 1 74
(William Haggas) *hld up: hdwy over 8f out: lost pl 7f out: nt clr run over 1f out: sn swtchd rt: rdn to chse wnr and edgd lft ins fnl f: styd on u.p* **2/1**[2]

66 3 3 ¼ **Dreamtide**[30] 3145 3-8-9 0...............................................(v[1]) MartinDwyer 5 64
(Amanda Perrett) *w ldr 3f: remained handy: wnt 2nd over 5f out: rdn and ev ch over 2f out: styd on same pce fnl f* **12/1**

543 4 ½ **Touwari (IRE)**[11] 3839 3-9-0 73...............................................(b) AdamKirby 4 68
(John Gosden) *trckd ldrs tl led 7f out: shkn up 4f out: rdn over 2f out: hdd over 1f out: nt run on* **11/8**[1]

2325 5 1 **Ceyhan**[73] 1818 5-10-0 73.................................. DougieCostello 2 66
(Jamie Osborne) *led over 4f: chsd ldr tl over 5f out: remained handy: ev ch over 2f out: rdn over 1f out: wknd wl ins fnl f* **12/1**

2m 31.5s (0.90) **Going Correction** -0.05s/f (Good)

**WFA** 3 from 5yo+ 14lb **5** Ran SP% **113.9**

Speed ratings (Par 103): **95,94,92,91,91**

CSF £10.83 TOTE £4.60: £1.70, £1.80; EX 11.60 Trifecta £54.50.

**Owner** Roddy Owen & Paul Fullagar **Bred** Rathmore Stud **Trained** Little Newcastle, Pembrokes

**FOCUS**

It's hard to say how strong this form actually is considering it contained some already exposed performers and a decent 9yo jumps horse making his Flat debut, but it has been rated around the 2nd.

## 4203 LEXUS BRISTOL H'CAP 1m
9:00 (9:00) (Class 5) (0-70,67) 4-Y-O+ £2,911 (£866; £432; £216) Stalls Low

Form RPR

3001 1 **Suitsus**[36] 2916 6-9-1 61...............................................(t) TimmyMurphy 5 66
(Geoffrey Deacon) *s.i.s: hld up: hdwy over 1f out: rdn and r.o to ld nr fin* **6/1**

6631 2 shd **Aye Aye Skipper (IRE)**[11] 3809 7-8-4 55...........................(b) GeorgiaCox(5) 2 60
(Ken Cunningham-Brown) *s.i.s: hld up: hdwy over 3f out: rdn to ld over 1f out: hdd nr fin* **11/4**[1]

0114 **3** ½ **Moi Aussie**[18] 3577 4-8-10 **63** RayDawson(7) 3 67
(Michael Appleby) *chsd ldr: rdn over 2f out: ev ch over 1f out: styd on* **5/1**
12 **4** 3¾ **Stormbound (IRE)**[56] 2297 8-9-7 **67** (b) AdamKirby 4 62
(Paul Cole) *chsd ldrs: rdn over 2f out: styd on same pce fnl f* **7/2**[2]
1120 **5** 1¼ **Living Leader**[15] 3688 8-8-3 **54** DavidEgan(5) 7 46
(Grace Harris) *prom: rdn and lost pl over 3f out: styd on same pce fr over 1f out* **14/1**
-245 **6** ½ **Hot Mustard**[26] 3282 7-9-3 **63** (p¹) MartinDwyer 1 53
(William Muir) *led: racd keenly: rdn over 2f out: hdd wl over 1f out: wknd ins fnl f* **4/1**[3]
3-50 **7** 1 **Edge (IRE)**[22] 3422 6-8-1 **54** (b) KeelanBaker(7) 6 42
(Bernard Llewellyn) *s.i.s: hld up: rdn over 2f out: nt trble ldrs* **14/1**

1m 40.71s (-0.09) **Going Correction** -0.05s/f (Good) **7** Ran SP% **113.2**
Speed ratings (Par 103): **98,97,97,93,92 91,90**
CSF £22.37 TOTE £7.50: £2.80, £2.00; EX 17.90 Trifecta £160.60.
**Owner** Suitsus Partnership **Bred** Mrs Susan Cole & Miss Lesley McGrath **Trained** Compton, Berks
■ Stewards' Enquiry : Timmy Murphy 2 day ban - used whip without giving the horse time to respond (12/13 Jul)

**FOCUS**
A competitive event run at a strong pace. The first two home were in the last three on the final bend.
T/Plt: £200.60 to a £1 stake. Pool: £64,400.71. 234.29 winning units. T/Qpdt: £38.90 to a £1 stake. Pool: £5,356.25. 101.86 winning units. **Colin Roberts**

# 3895 CARLISLE (R-H)
## Wednesday, June 28

**OFFICIAL GOING: Good to soft changing to good to soft (soft in places) after race 3 (3.00)**
Wind: Breezy, half against Weather: Overcast

## 4204 EDMUNDSON CABLETECH CARLISLE NOVICE AUCTION STKS 5f
**2:00** (2:02) (Class 5) 2-Y-O **£3,396** (£1,010; £505; £252) **Stalls** Low

Form RPR
01 **1** **John Kirkup**[19] 3523 2-9-9 0 PaulMulrennan 7 84
(Michael Dods) *hld up: hdwy on outside over 1f out: rdn: edgd rt and kpt on wl to ld nr fin* **4/1**[2]
**2** shd **Weeton (IRE)** 2-9-2 0 ConnorBeasley 4 77
(Bryan Smart) *taken early to post: hld up: hdwy and edgd rt over 1f out: edgd lft ins fnl f: carried rt: blkd and kpt on cl home: fin 3rd: promoted to 2nd* **15/2**
**3** shd **Falabelle (IRE)** 2-8-11 0 KevinStott 5 71
(Kevin Ryan) *trckd ldr: rdn to ld 1f out: drifted rt and hdd nr fin: fin 2nd: demoted to 3rd* **16/1**
3333 **4** 1½ **Aquadabra (IRE)**[15] 3690 2-8-11 0 GrahamLee 8 66
(Mick Channon) *t.k.h early: hld up on outside: rdn and edgd rt over 1f out: kpt on same pce ins fnl f* **7/1**[3]
23 **5** nse **Tough Remedy (IRE)**[14] 3705 2-9-2 0 PJMcDonald 6 71
(Keith Dalgleish) *sn in midfield: drvn and outpcd over 2f out: rallied fnl f: kpt on fin* **11/4**[1]
2 **6** 2 **Tember**[79] 1673 2-9-2 0 AndrewMullen 1 64
(David Barron) *trckd ldrs: drvn and edgd lft over 1f out: outpcd ins fnl f* **4/1**[2]
04 **7** 1 **Admiral Rooke (IRE)**[22] 3430 2-9-2 0 TomEaves 10 60
(Michael Dods) *hld up: pushed along and edgd rt over 1f out: no imp fnl f* **16/1**
**8** nk **Magic Pulse (IRE)** 2-8-11 0 (t¹) ShaneGray 2 54
(Ann Duffield) *led: rdn 2f out: hdd 1f out: sn btn* **80/1**
0354 **9** 2½ **Just For The Craic (IRE)**[28] 3200 2-9-2 0 JamesSullivan 9 50
(Ruth Carr) *trckd ldrs: rdn over 2f out: edgd rt and wknd fnl f* **25/1**
**10** 2 **Elements Quest (IRE)** 2-8-11 0 BenCurtis 3 42
(K R Burke) *.towards rr: drvn and outpcd over 2f out: wkng whn hmpd over 1f out* **10/1**

1m 4.38s (3.58) **Going Correction** +0.575s/f (Yiel) **10** Ran SP% **116.9**
Speed ratings (Par 93): **94,93,93,91,91 88,86,85,81,78**
CSF £34.26 TOTE £4.00: £1.40, £2.90, £4.20; EX 41.20 Trifecta £407.00.
**Owner** Mrs Suzanne Kirkup & Kevin Kirkup **Bred** W M Lidsey **Trained** Denton, Co Durham
■ Stewards' Enquiry : Kevin Stott 2 day ban - guilty of careless riding (12/13 Jul)

**FOCUS**
The course had endured 26mm of rain since the start of the week and the ground was downgraded to good to soft prior to the first. They kept far side in this modest novice event, which proved a bit of a messy race, and the winner came down the centre.

## 4205 TOTEPOOLLIVEINFO.COM EBF NOVICE STKS 5f 193y
**2:30** (2:31) (Class 5) 2-Y-O **£3,396** (£1,010; £505; £252) **Stalls** Low

Form RPR
6 **1** **Byron's Choice**[23] 3398 2-9-2 0 PaulMulrennan 2 77
(Michael Dods) *trckd ldrs: pushed along over 2f out: drifted lft and led ins fnl f: kpt on strly* **4/1**[2]
35 **2** 1½ **Star Of Zaam (IRE)**[30] 3149 2-9-2 0 BenCurtis 8 73
(K R Burke) *prom on outside: effrt: hung rt and led over 1f out: veered bdly lft and hdd ins fnl f: sn no ex* **3/1**[1]
**3** 1½ **Ingenuity** 2-9-2 0 JackGarritty 7 68+
(Jedd O'Keeffe) *dwlt: hld up: hdwy and edgd lft over 1f out: chsd clr ldng pair ins fnl f: r.o: bttr for r* **16/1**
**4** 3¾ **Birdette (IRE)** 2-8-11 0 PJMcDonald 6 51
(Mark Johnston) *trckd ldrs: effrt and ev ch briefly wl over 1f out: outpcd ins fnl f* **11/2**[3]
**5** 2 **Tebay (IRE)** 2-9-2 0 ConnorBeasley 3 50
(Michael Dods) *hld up on ins: pushed along and hdwy 2f out: no further imp and btn ins fnl f* **7/1**
1 **6** 7 **Our Kid (IRE)**[57] 2277 2-9-6 0 PaulHanagan 9 33
(Richard Fahey) *hld up: drvn and outpcd over 2f out: btn over 1f out* **3/1**[1]
04 **7** ½ **Acromatic (IRE)**[23] 3399 2-9-2 0 JasonHart 4 28
(John Quinn) *dwlt and wnt sltly lft leaving stalls: hdwy over 3f out: rdn and wknd fr 2f out* **12/1**
**8** 6 **Roundhay Park** 2-9-2 0 TomEaves 5 10
(Nigel Tinkler) *led: rdn and hdd over 1f out: sn wknd* **40/1**

1m 17.0s (3.30) **Going Correction** +0.575s/f (Yiel) **8** Ran SP% **113.9**
Speed ratings (Par 93): **101,99,97,92,89 80,79,71**
CSF £16.29 TOTE £4.70: £1.50, £1.30, £5.00; EX 19.90 Trifecta £214.40.
**Owner** A Wynn Williams & D Graham **Bred** Mr & Mrs C Booth & Mrs S Cammidge **Trained** Denton, Co Durham

**FOCUS**
This time the main action developed towards the stands' side. Ordinary form.

## 4206 TOTEPOOL CUMBERLAND PLATE H'CAP 1m 3f 39y
**3:00** (3:01) (Class 4) (0-85,85) 3-Y-O+
**£18,675** (£5,592; £2,796; £1,398; £699; £351) **Stalls** High

Form RPR
2434 **1** **Dance King**[4] 4076 7-9-6 **84** (tp) PaulMulrennan 4 91
(Tim Easterby) *hld up in tch: stdy hdwy over 2f out: effrt and rdn over 1f out: edgd lft and led ins fnl f: hld on wl* **8/1**
-562 **2** ½ **Fleeting Visit**[21] 3458 4-9-4 **82** (p) JohnFahy 16 88
(Eve Johnson Houghton) *led: rdn 2f out: edgd lft and hdd ins fnl f: rallied: hld nr fin* **12/1**
5246 **3** nk **Chancery (USA)**[11] 3841 9-9-6 **84** (p) DanielTudhope 13 89
(David O'Meara) *hld up on outside: effrt and pushed along 2f out: edgd rt and styd on fnl f: nrst fin* **16/1**
2-10 **4** nk **Admiral's Sunset**[19] 3534 4-8-13 **80** CharlieBennett(3) 14 85
(Hughie Morrison) *trckd ldrs: drvn and outpcd 2f out: rallied fnl f: kpt on fin* **11/1**
6-41 **5** ¾ **West Drive (IRE)**[23] 3409 4-9-6 **84** (b) AndreaAtzeni 15 88
(Roger Varian) *hld up midfield: stdy hdwy 3f out: drvn and outpcd 2f out: kpt on fnl f: nt pce to chal* **13/2**[3]
5312 **6** ¾ **Panko (IRE)**[12] 3795 4-9-1 **82** CallumShepherd(3) 11 84
(Ed de Giles) *trckd ldr: drvn over 2f out: kpt on same pce fr over 1f out* **8/1**
31 6 **7** ¾ **I Am Not Here (IRE)**[18] 3589 6-9-2 **85** BenRobinson(5) 1 86
(Brian Ellison) *hld up: drvn and outpcd over 2f out: kpt on fnl f: nvr able to chal* **6/1**[2]
-200 **8** 1 **Purple Rock (IRE)**[11] 3841 5-8-12 **83** (t) HarrisonShaw(7) 8 82
(Michael Easterby) *hld up on ins: rdn and outpcd over 2f out: rallied fnl f: no imp* **50/1**
20-0 **9** ½ **Multellie**[12] 3794 5-9-6 **84** CamHardie 9 83
(Tim Easterby) *t.k.h: hld up: drvn over 2f out: no imp fr over 1f out* **40/1**
00 **10** 1¼ **Tamayuz Magic (IRE)**[33] 3050 6-9-0 **81** (b) NathanEvans(3) 5 77
(Michael Easterby) *hld up: drvn along 3f out: no imp fr 2f out* **14/1**
0040 **11** hd **Buonarroti (IRE)**[18] 3582 6-9-2 **80** TomEaves 10 76
(Declan Carroll) *hld up: rdn on outside over 2f out: edgd rt and wknd over 1f out* **25/1**
-601 **12** nse **Swaheen**[20] 3486 5-9-4 **82** JoeDoyle 3 78
(Julie Camacho) *hld up: drvn along 3f out: sn n.d: btn fnl 2f* **7/1**
0022 **13** 1½ **Mukhayyam**[11] 3841 5-9-5 **83** (p) DavidAllan 7 77
(Tim Easterby) *t.k.h: trckd ldrs tl rdn and wknd wl over 1f out* **11/2**[1]
2110 **14** ½ **General Hazard (IRE)**[88] 1502 4-9-6 **84** BenCurtis 2 77
(Archie Watson) *hld up: rdn along and drifted lft fr over 2f out: sn btn* **22/1**

2m 29.98s (6.88) **Going Correction** +0.575s/f (Yiel) **14** Ran SP% **118.9**
Speed ratings (Par 105): **97,96,96,96,95 95,94,93,93,92 92,92,91,90**
CSF £95.53 CT £1507.18 TOTE £7.40: £2.90, £4.50, £4.40; EX 116.10 Trifecta £2510.90.
**Owner** Ambrose Turnbull **Bred** Meon Valley Stud **Trained** Great Habton, N Yorks

**FOCUS**
Add 27yds. This long-established handicap was typically competitive. They went a sound pace and the principals came down the middle late on.

## 4207 BOOKIES.COM CARLISLE BELL H'CAP 7f 173y
**3:30** (3:31) (Class 4) (0-85,85) 3-Y-O+
**£18,675** (£5,592; £2,796; £1,398; £699; £351) **Stalls** Low

Form RPR
0043 **1** **Carnageo (FR)**[21] 3451 4-9-2 **81** (b¹) PaulHanagan 8 91
(Richard Fahey) *hld up: rdn along over 2f out: hdwy on wd outside over 1f out: led ins fnl f: kpt on strly* **13/2**[1]
0-55 **2** ½ **King's Pavilion (IRE)**[51] 2457 4-9-6 **85** BenCurtis 17 93
(David Barron) *hld up on outside: effrt over 2f out: checked over 1f out: chsd wnr ins fnl f: kpt on: hld towards fin* **8/1**[2]
0643 **3** ½ **Georgian Bay (IRE)**[37] 2884 7-9-0 **84** (v) CliffordLee(5) 15 91
(K R Burke) *hld up: gd hdwy on outside to ld over 1f out: sn rdn and drifted rt: hdd and no ex ins fnl f* **10/1**[3]
5000 **4** 2½ **Silvery Moon (IRE)**[38] 2855 10-9-5 **84** DavidAllan 5 85
(Tim Easterby) *in tch: drvn and outpcd 2f out: kpt on ins fnl f: nt pce to chal* **13/2**[1]
-000 **5** 1 **Briyouni (FR)**[39] 2838 4-9-4 **83** (p¹) KevinStott 13 82
(Kevin Ryan) *hld up: effrt and hdwy 2f out: kpt on fnl f: nrst fin* **28/1**
44-1 **6** ¾ **Pensax Boy**[37] 2884 5-9-4 **83** (p¹) AndrewMullen 11 80
(Daniel Mark Loughnane) *s.i.s: hld up: rdn over 2f out: kpt on fnl f: no imp* **12/1**
0034 **7** shd **Worlds His Oyster**[9] 3905 4-9-3 **82** (v¹) JasonHart 3 79
(John Quinn) *trckd ldrs: effrt and rdn over 2f out: no ex fr over 1f out* **11/1**
2410 **8** ½ **Boots And Spurs**[6] 4017 8-9-3 **82** (v) PJMcDonald 9 78
(Scott Dixon) *prom: effrt and rdn 2f out: btn fnl f* **16/1**
-450 **9** hd **Rousayan (IRE)**[43] 2701 6-9-6 **85** (h) DanielTudhope 4 80
(David O'Meara) *s.i.s: hld up on ins: effrt and pushed along 2f out: no imp appr fnl f* **10/1**[3]
0025 **10** 2½ **Strong Steps**[18] 3589 5-9-5 **84** (b) TonyHamilton 6 73
(Roger Fell) *t.k.h early: led to over 1f out: hung rt and sn wknd* **20/1**
1-60 **11** 1 **Dark Devil (IRE)**[16] 3651 4-9-6 **85** DavidNolan 14 72
(Richard Fahey) *hld up in midfield on outside: hdwy and prom over 2f out: wknd over 1f out* **12/1**
0436 **12** 2¾ **Lagenda**[35] 2952 4-9-4 **83** (p) ShaneGray 16 64
(Kevin Ryan) *clsd up: rdn over 2f out: wknd appr fnl f* **33/1**
2541 **13** ½ **Goring (GER)**[18] 3572 5-9-6 **85** JohnFahy 2 65
(Eve Johnson Houghton) *prom: lost pl 2f out: sn btn* **8/1**[2]
3026 **14** ½ **Shouranour (IRE)**[12] 3792 7-9-3 **85** (b) JoshDoyle(3) 10 64
(Alan Brown) *hld up: drvn and outpcd over 2f out: btn over 1f out* **16/1**
6361 **15** 1¾ **Intensical (IRE)**[10] 3857 6-9-2 **81** 6ex (p) TomEaves 7 56
(Ivan Furtado) *hld up towards rr: drvn and outpcd over 2f out: sn btn* **33/1**
060 **16** 2 **Zoravan (USA)**[18] 3582 4-9-2 **81** (v) GrahamLee 1 51
(Keith Dalgleish) *t.k.h: hld up on ins: struggling over 2f out: sn btn* **33/1**

1m 43.09s (3.09) **Going Correction** +0.575s/f (Yiel) **16** Ran SP% **119.6**
Speed ratings (Par 105): **107,106,106,103,102 101,101,101,100,98 97,94,94,93,91 89**
CSF £51.42 CT £533.40 TOTE £5.50: £2.10, £2.50, £2.90, £2.00; EX 82.50 Trifecta £462.00.
**Owner** The Up For Anything Syndicate **Bred** Viktor Timoshenko **Trained** Musley Bank, N Yorks

**FOCUS**
Add 12yds. The year's Bell was run at a searching pace and it suited the closers, with the principals finishing clear down the middle. A small pb from the winner.

## 4208 EBFSTALLIONS.COM "ETERNAL" STKS (LISTED RACE) (FILLIES) 6f 195y
**4:00** (4:00) (Class 1) 3-Y-O

**£22,684** (£8,600; £4,304; £2,144; £1,076; £540) **Stalls** Low

Form RPR

0-65 **1** **Elusive Beauty (IRE)**[17] 3632 3-9-0 94 DanielTudhope 4 95
(K J Condon, Ire) *hld up: hdwy over 1f out: rdn to ld towards fin: comf* **11/2[3]**

60-1 **2** ½ **Bletchley**[23] 3395 3-9-0 103 (h) OisinMurphy 7 93
(Ralph Beckett) *hld up in midfield: hdwy and rdn over 1f out: led ins fnl f: hdd and no ex towards fin* **7/4[1]**

**3** *nk* **Aurora Butterfly (IRE)**[55] 2351 3-9-0 94 TonyHamilton 5 92
(W McCreery, Ire) *trckd ldrs: effrt and drvn along 2f out: kpt on ins fnl f* **16/1**

-321 **4** *shd* **Isabel's On It**[25] 3329 3-9-0 79 BenCurtis 11 92
(William Haggas) *t.k.h early: led: rdn over 1f out: hdd ins fnl f: kpt on same pce* **9/2[2]**

-001 **5** 1¾ **Savannah Slew**[19] 3526 3-9-0 80 (b) PaulMulrennan 3 87
(James Given) *stdd s: t.k.h: hld up: rdn 2f out: kpt on ins fnl f: nvr able to chal* **12/1**

3-00 **6** ½ **Pichola Dance (IRE)**[46] 2623 3-9-0 91 AndreaAtzeni 1 85
(Roger Varian) *hld up: drvn along after 3f: rallied 2f out: no further imp fnl f* **20/1**

30-0 **7** *nk* **Asidious Alexander (IRE)**[46] 2644 3-9-0 101 (v[1]) PaulHanagan 9 85
(Simon Crisford) *hld up in tch: hdwy over 2f out: rdn and edgd rt over 1f out: outpcd fnl f* **8/1**

63-1 **8** 7 **Bahamadam**[29] 3167 3-9-0 89 RobertWinston 10 66
(Eve Johnson Houghton) *hld up: drvn along and outpcd over 2f out: n.d after* **8/1**

0450 **9** 1½ **Miss Infinity (IRE)**[7] 3964 3-9-0 97 JoeFanning 2 62
(Mark Johnston) *trckd ldr: rdn along over 2f outs: wknd over 1f out* **20/1**

041 **10** ¾ **Best Of My Love (IRE)**[17] 3626 3-9-0 76 GrahamLee 8 60
(Mick Channon) *t.k.h early: trckd ldrs: lost pl over 2f out: btn over 1f out* **80/1**

1m 29.79s (2.69) **Going Correction** +0.575s/f (Yiel) **10** Ran SP% **116.5**
Speed ratings (Par 104): **107,106,106,105,103 103,103,95,93,92**
CSF £15.14 TOTE £6.50: £2.30, £1.20, £4.00; EX 18.50 Trifecta £163.20.
**Owner** David K Kelly **Bred** Peter McCutcheon **Trained** Rathbride, Co Kildare

**FOCUS**
Add 12yds. An ordinary fillies' race for the class and it threw up a bunched finish towards the near side. It's been rated around the winner and 3rd.

## 4209 EBF STALLIONS BREEDING WINNERS FILLIES' H'CAP 6f 195y
**4:30** (4:31) (Class 4) (0-80,78) 3-Y-O+ **£6,469** (£1,925; £962; £481) **Stalls** Low

Form RPR

4654 **1** **Whatsthemessage (IRE)**[9] 3900 3-8-8 67 AndrewMullen 5 72
(Keith Dalgleish) *t.k.h: mde all: rdn along and hrd pressed over 1f out: hld on gamely ins fnl f* **8/1**

0600 **2** ½ **Quick N Quirky (IRE)**[11] 3845 4-9-5 69 (p) DavidAllan 2 76
(Tim Easterby) *trckd ldrs: effrt and rdn 2f out: ev ch ins fnl f: kpt on: hld nr fin* **8/1**

0435 **3** ½ **Bush Beauty (IRE)**[2] 4165 6-9-1 65 NeilFarley 1 70
(Eric Alston) *hld up in tch: effrt and rdn 2f out: edgd rt and kpt on ins fnl f: nrst fin* **9/1**

-243 **4** 2¼ **The Stalking Moon (IRE)**[18] 3561 3-8-5 67 NathanEvans(3) 8 63
(John Quinn) *hld up in tch: hdwy and ev ch over 1f out: rdn and wknd ins fnl f* **5/2[1]**

4456 **5** ¾ **Enjoy Life (IRE)**[44] 2684 4-9-3 74 (p) SeamusCronin(7) 10 71
(Kevin Ryan) *pressed wnr: ev ch over 2f out to over 1f out: wknd ins fnl f* **6/1[3]**

0043 **6** 1¼ **Someone Exciting**[9] 3899 4-8-4 59 PhilDennis(5) 6 53
(David Thompson) *taken early to post: hld up hdwy nr side of gp over 2f out: rdn and wknd over 1f out* **8/1**

-241 **7** 10 **Favourite Royal (IRE)**[29] 3189 3-9-5 78 RobertWinston 9 42
(Eve Johnson Houghton) *hld up on outside: hdwy over 2f out: sn rdn: wknd over 1f out* **3/1[2]**

0063 **8** *hd* **Tilly Tinker**[21] 3448 3-8-2 61 CamHardie 7 24
(Michael Easterby) *trckd ldrs: lost pl 2f out: sn struggling* **25/1**

1m 31.45s (4.35) **Going Correction** +0.575s/f (Yiel)
**WFA** 3 from 4yo+ 9lb **8** Ran SP% **115.0**
Speed ratings (Par 102): **98,97,96,94,93 92,80,80**
CSF £69.73 CT £448.27 TOTE £9.40: £2.70, £2.70, £3.00; EX 84.70 Trifecta £1086.40.
**Owner** Ronnie Docherty **Bred** Lynn Lodge Stud **Trained** Carluke, S Lanarks

**FOCUS**
Add 12yds. A modest fillies' handicap, run at an average pace. The winner has been rated to her best since her early 2yo days.

## 4210 CARLISLE BELL CONSOLATION RACE H'CAP 7f 173y
**5:00** (5:01) (Class 4) (0-85,80) 3-Y-O+ **£6,469** (£1,925; £962; £481) **Stalls** Low

Form RPR

1361 **1** **Showboating (IRE)**[18] 3567 9-9-8 78 DanielTudhope 17 89
(John Balding) *hld up: hdwy on wd outside and led over 1f out: rdn and r.o wl fnl f* **9/1**

32-0 **2** 1¾ **Muirsheen Durkin**[27] 3262 3-9-0 80 (p) PaulHanagan 1 85
(Neville Bycroft) *in tch: smooth hdwy to chal over 1f out: sn rdn: kpt on same pce ins fnl f* **13/2[2]**

230 **3** 4 **Madroos**[12] 3790 4-9-6 79 NathanEvans(3) 8 77
(Michael Easterby) *hld up midfield: drvn and outpcd over 2f out: rallied appr fnl f: kpt on: nt rch first two* **7/2[1]**

0105 **4** ½ **Zlatan (IRE)**[22] 3433 4-9-6 79 (p) CallumShepherd(3) 5 76
(Ed de Giles) *hld up: smooth hdwy whn n.m.r briefly over 2f out: rdn over 1f out: no ex fnl f* **15/2**

0-32 **5** 2¼ **Yensir**[14] 3706 4-8-12 68 PaddyAspell 3 59
(Grant Tuer) *hld up midfield: effrt and prom over 1f out: wknd ins fnl f* **9/1**

011- **6** *shd* **Big Time Dancer (IRE)**[314] 5576 4-8-6 67 BenRobinson(5) 12 58
(Brian Ellison) *hld up: drvn and outpcd over 2f out: styd on steadily fnl f: nvr able to chal* **11/1**

1320 **7** *hd* **Dark Forest**[32] 3095 4-8-13 69 (p) BarryMcHugh 11 60
(Marjorie Fife) *mde most tl rdn and hdd over 1f out: wknd fnl f* **16/1**

1-01 **8** 3½ **Zeshov (IRE)**[55] 2339 6-9-6 78 DuranFentiman 15 61
(Rebecca Bastiman) *prom: rdn over 2f out: wknd over 1f out* **28/1**

302- **9** *shd* **Planetaria (IRE)**[236] 7796 4-9-10 80 AndrewMullen 4 62
(John Weymes) *pressed ldr: drvn over 2f out: wknd over 1f out* **50/1**

6-00 **10** *shd* **Ingleby Angel (IRE)**[11] 3845 8-8-11 67 KevinStott 13 49
(Colin Teague) *hld up: drvn and outpcd over 2f out: sn n.d: btn over 1f out* **22/1**

0-00 **11** ½ **Argaki (IRE)**[128] 841 7-8-12 68 GrahamLee 16 49
(Keith Dalgleish) *hld up: rdn and struggling over 2f out: sn btn* **20/1**

0426 **12** 1½ **Hanseatic**[11] 3845 8-8-12 75 (t) HarrisonShaw(7) 7 53
(Michael Easterby) *prom: rdn along over 2f out: wknd over 1f out* **15/2**

P-51 **13** *nk* **Frank Bridge**[30] 3144 4-9-7 77 RobertWinston 10 54
(Eve Johnson Houghton) *hld up midfield: drvn and struggling over 2f out: sn btn* **7/1[3]**

4-40 **14** 1 **Tectonic (IRE)**[21] 3451 8-8-9 65 (v) JasonHart 9 40
(Keith Dalgleish) *hld up: rdn over 2f out: sn wknd* **22/1**

1m 42.98s (2.98) **Going Correction** +0.575s/f (Yiel)
**WFA** 3 from 4yo+ 10lb **14** Ran SP% **124.7**
Speed ratings (Par 105): **108,106,102,101,99 99,99,95,95,95 95,93,93,92**
CSF £64.36 CT £258.83 TOTE £11.10: £3.50, £2.90, £2.00; EX 97.50 Trifecta £335.20.
**Owner** M & Mrs L Cooke & A McCabe **Bred** Crone Stud Farms Ltd **Trained** Scrooby, S Yorks

**FOCUS**
Add 12yds. This competitive consolation prize for the Bell was run at a decent pace. The winner has been ratec close to his winter AW form.
T/Jkpt: Not won. T/Plt: £497.20 to a £1 stake. Pool: £86,140.37. 126.46 winning units. T/Qpdt: £64.90 to a £1 stake. Pool: £7,319.56. 83.38 winning units. **Richard Young**

# 3718 KEMPTON (A.W) (R-H)
## Wednesday, June 28

**OFFICIAL GOING: Polytrack: standard to slow**
Wind: Moderate, half against in home straight Weather: Overcast

## 4211 RACING UK PROFITS RETURNED TO RACING APPRENTICE H'CAP 7f (P)
**5:40** (5:42) (Class 6) (0-60,60) 3-Y-O **£2,587** (£770; £384; £192) **Stalls** Low

Form RPR

0006 **1** **Dragon Dream (IRE)**[91] 1421 3-8-13 55 RhiainIngram(3) 6 65
(Roger Ingram) *led 2f out: trckd ldr: led again over 2f out and sent for home: ld dwindled ins fnl f but nvr seriously under threat* **12/1**

400 **2** ¾ **Happy Escape**[55] 2330 3-9-4 60 (t) PatrickVaughan(3) 8 68
(Joseph Tuite) *hld up in midfield and off the pce: prog over 2f out: chsd wnr jst ins fnl f: styd on to cl nr fin but nvr able to chal* **10/1**

4441 **3** 2½ **Luxford**[1] 4180 3-8-8 52 6ex LeviWilliams(5) 13 53
(John Best) *spd fr wd draw and w ldrs: chsd wnr over 1f out to jst ins fnl f: one pce* **4/1[1]**

0-00 **4** 1 **Kath's Boy (IRE)**[17] 3624 3-8-5 47 AledBeech(5) 7 46
(Tony Carroll) *hld up off the pce in midfield: no prog over 2f out: styd on fr over 1f out to take 4th last 75yds* **50/1**

0-23 **5** ¾ **Wotadoll**[15] 3703 3-9-1 54 LuluStanford 12 51
(Dean Ivory) *t.k.h and plld way into the ld after 2f: hdd over 2f out: steadily fdd* **7/1**

005 **6** 1 **Shamonix (IRE)**[19] 3549 3-8-2 46 oh1 TheodoreLadd(5) 9 40
(Mark Usher) *w ldrs to over 2f out: steadily wknd* **50/1**

0603 **7** ½ **Sixties Habana**[16] 3660 3-8-9 53 SophieRalston(5) 5 45
(Pat Phelan) *plld v hrd early: hld up in midfield: wl off the pce over 2f out and no ch: kpt on fr over 1f out* **6/1[3]**

4606 **8** 2¾ **Primadonia**[15] 3695 3-8-11 55 (b[1]) NicolaCurrie(5) 2 40
(Richard Hughes) *wnt lft s: wl in rr: prog on inner over 2f out: no hdwy over 1f out: wknd fnl f* **10/1**

5-00 **9** *hd* **Wootyhoot (FR)**[13] 3755 3-9-1 59 WilliamCox(5) 3 43+
(James Fanshawe) *dwlt then squeezed out s: mostly in last pair: nvr a factor but sme late prog* **5/1[2]**

0-04 **10** *shd* **Coachella (IRE)**[15] 3695 3-8-9 51 StephenCummins(3) 1 35
(Ed de Giles) *dwlt: t.k.h early in last pair: last and detached after 3f: nvr a factor but sme late hdwy* **8/1**

006 **11** *nse* **Golden Eye**[36] 2911 3-9-4 57 MitchGodwin 10 41
(Sylvester Kirk) *chsd clr ldrs tl wknd 2f out* **6/1[3]**

-600 **12** 2 **Parisian Chic (IRE)**[117] 1000 3-9-2 58 (p[1]) RossaRyan(3) 11 37
(Lee Carter) *chsd ldrs: hmpd after 1f: wknd over 2f out* **20/1**

-000 **13** 1 **Secret Willow**[65] 2016 3-8-2 46 oh1 GinaMangan(5) 4 22
(John E Long) *t.k.h: a towards rr: no ch over 2f out* **50/1**

6-00 **14** 17 **Clip Art**[27] 3259 3-8-10 49 GeorgiaCox 14
(Jamie Osborne) *fractious to post: slowly away: in midfield whn hung bdly lft bnd over 4f out and virtually unsteerable: t.o over 1f out* **33/1**

1m 26.29s (0.29) **Going Correction** 0.0s/f (Stan) **14** Ran SP% **128.3**
Speed ratings (Par 97): **98,97,94,93,92 91,90,87,87,87 87,84,83,64**
CSF £130.06 CT £590.72 TOTE £15.20: £3.80, £4.30, £2.60; EX 282.30 Trifecta £3228.10.
**Owner** Drag On Funds **Bred** Pier House Stud **Trained** Epsom, Surrey

**FOCUS**
An ordinary handicap.

## 4212 32RED.COM/BRITISH STALLION STUDS EBF FILLIES' NOVICE STKS (PLUS 10 RACE) 7f (P)
**6:10** (6:10) (Class 4) 2-Y-O **£4,592** (£1,366; £683; £341) **Stalls** Low

Form RPR

**1** **Codicil** 2-9-0 0 LukeMorris 1 71+
(Sir Mark Prescott Bt) *rn green early and shoved along: in tch disputing 5th: prog 2f out: rdn to chal fnl f: led last 50yds: hld on* **10/1**

**2** *hd* **Camomile Lawn (IRE)** 2-9-0 0 PatDobbs 8 70+
(Ralph Beckett) *dwlt: hld up in last pair: shkn up 2f out: prog on outer 1f out: styd on wl to take 2nd last stride: jst hld* **7/1[3]**

45 **3** *shd* **Miss Mo Brown Bear (IRE)**[22] 3421 2-8-7 0 RossaRyan(7) 6 70
(Richard Hannon) *pressed ldr: rdn to ld over 1f out: kpt on but hdd last 50yds: lost 2nd fnl stride* **7/1[3]**

0 **4** *hd* **Zoraya (FR)**[29] 3174 2-9-0 0 DavidProbert 4 69
(Paul Cole) *in tch disputing 5th: shkn up 2f out: prog fnl f: styd on to press ldrs nr fin* **50/1**

33 **5** 1 **Glaceon (IRE)**[12] 3782 2-9-0 0 SeanLevey 7 67
(Richard Hannon) *trckd ldng pair: rdn and nt qckn 2f out: kpt on same pce after* **9/2[2]**

0 **6** 1¾ **Polar Light**[18] 3591 2-9-0 0 FranBerry 3 62
(David Elsworth) *dwlt: mostly in last pair: rdn on inner 2f out: no real prog* **16/1**

2 **7** ½ **First Drive**[15] 3697 2-9-0 0 RyanMoore 5 61
(Michael Bell) *led: rdn 2f out: hdd over 1f out: wknd fnl f: eased last 75yds* **4/5[1]**

05 **8** *hd* **Laura Knight (IRE)**[15] 3687 2-9-0 0 ...................................... LiamKeniry 2 60
(Gary Moore) *t.k.h: trckd ldng pair: lost grnd qckly over 1f out* **20/1**

1m 27.44s (1.44) **Going Correction** 0.0s/f (Stan) 8 Ran SP% **120.4**
Speed ratings (Par 92): **91,90,90,90,89 87,86,86**
CSF £81.27 TOTE £11.80: £2.80, £2.90, £2.10; EX 66.90 Trifecta £551.00.
**Owner** Cheveley Park Stud **Bred** Cheveley Park Stud Ltd **Trained** Newmarket, Suffolk

**FOCUS**
A bit of a bunched finish to this novice race.

## 4213 32RED CASINO/EBFSTALLIONS.COM NOVICE STKS (PLUS 10 RACE) 6f (P)

**6:40** (6:41) (Class 4) 2-Y-0 **£4,592** (£1,366; £683; £341) **Stalls** Low

Form RPR

0 **1** **Encrypted**[18] 3591 2-9-2 0 ...................................... JosephineGordon 8 86+
(Hugo Palmer) *trckd ldng trio: pushed along over 2f out: clsd to ld jst over 1f out: sn clr: pushed out* **11/2**

0 **2** *2 ¼* **Cosmopolitan Queen**[18] 3590 2-8-11 0 ...................................... FranBerry 5 72
(David Elsworth) *chsd ldrs: shkn up over 2f out: prog over 1f out: styd on to take 2nd last 100yds: no ch w wnr* **9/2[3]**

46 **3** *¾* **Shania Says (IRE)**[29] 3187 2-8-8 0 ...................................... KieranShoemark(3) 4 70
(Tony Carroll) *led at gd pce: rdn and hdd jst over 1f out: one pce after* **25/1**

**4** *hd* **Rebel Streak** 2-9-2 0 ...................................... DavidProbert 3 74
(Andrew Balding) *dwlt: sn in 8th: pushed along over 2f out: prog over 1f out: styd on wl last 150yds and clsd qckly on plcd horses nr fin* **9/1**

32 **5** *½* **Makanah**[21] 3467 2-9-2 0 ...................................... JimCrowley 9 73
(Simon Crisford) *chsd ldr: rdn to chal over 1f out: wnr sn wnt past: one pce after* **15/8[1]**

2 **6** *1 ½* **Mearing**[22] 3430 2-9-2 0 ...................................... StevieDonohoe 2 68
(Charlie Fellowes) *chsd ldng pair to over 2f out: one pce fr over 1f out* **10/3[2]**

0 **7** *1 ½* **El Borracho (IRE)**[13] 3746 2-9-2 0 ...................................... LouisSteward 11 64
(Simon Dow) *stdd s: hld up and sn in 9th: pushed along over 2f out: nvr a threat but kpt on encouragingly fnl f* **33/1**

**8** *1 ½* **Yaafour** 2-9-2 0 ...................................... SeanLevey 7 59
(Richard Hannon) *chsd ldrs but trapped out wd: rdn over 2f out: wknd wl over 1f out* **12/1**

0 **9** *9* **Final Rock**[13] 3754 2-9-2 0 ...................................... LukeMorris 10 32
(Sir Mark Prescott Bt) *dropped to last after 2f and sn t.o* **50/1**

0 **10** *3 ¾* **Hornby**[34] 3002 2-9-2 0 ...................................... AdamBeschizza 6 21
(Michael Attwater) *stdd s: t.k.h early: chsd ldrs to over 2f out: wknd rapidly: t.o* **66/1**

1m 12.86s (-0.24) **Going Correction** 0.0s/f (Stan) 10 Ran SP% **119.4**
Speed ratings (Par 95): **101,98,97,96,96 94,92,90,78,73**
CSF £30.49 TOTE £8.00: £2.40, £2.00, £4.80; EX 36.00 Trifecta £588.80.
**Owner** K Abdullah **Bred** Juddmonte Farms Ltd **Trained** Newmarket, Suffolk

**FOCUS**
A good performance from the winner in this novice race.

## 4214 100% PROFIT AT 32REDSPORT.COM FILLIES' H'CAP 7f (P)

**7:10** (7:12) (Class 5) (0-70,70) 3-Y-0+ **£3,234** (£962; £481; £240) **Stalls** Low

Form RPR

-532 **1** **Robbie Roo Roo**[14] 3728 4-9-2 58 ......................................(vt) AdamBeschizza 6 65
(Mrs Ilka Gansera-Leveque) *trckd ldrs: gng strly whn waiting for a gap over 2f out: rdn and prog over 1f out: led last 150yds: drvn out* **10/1**

0411 **2** *½* **Dusky Maid (IRE)**[21] 3473 3-8-12 68 ...................................... LewisEdmunds(5) 3 71
(James Given) *trckd ldrs: pushed along over 2f out: prog to ld over 1f out: drvn and hdd last 150yds: kpt on wl* **3/1[1]**

3440 **3** *nse* **Art's Desire (IRE)**[22] 3422 3-9-0 65 ...................................... LiamKeniry 9 68+
(Ed Walker) *hld up in 11th: shkn up wl over 2f out: racd awkwardly but r.o fr over 1f out: fin wl and nrly snatched 2nd* **10/1**

600 **4** *hd* **Know The Truth**[13] 3748 3-9-2 67 ...................................... DavidProbert 2 69
(Andrew Balding) *hld up in 9th on outer: prog 2f out: clsd on ldrs and looked a threat 1f out: nt qckn last 100yds* **8/1[3]**

45 **5** *½* **Zilza (IRE)**[21] 3473 3-8-13 64 ......................................(t) JimCrowley 5 65
(Conrad Allen) *hld up in midfield: effrt over 1f out but squeezed out sn after: shkn up and styd on wl fnl f but no ch to chal* **10/1**

40-3 **6** *1 ½* **Doria Road (USA)**[78] 1705 3-8-13 64 ...................................... FranBerry 1 61
(Kevin Ryan) *wl in tch: prog on inner 2f out: chsd ldrs jst over 1f out: no hdwy after* **8/1[3]**

6434 **7** *1* **Magic Mirror**[9] 3906 4-8-12 54 ......................................(v) FergusSweeney 7 51
(Mark Rimell) *hld up in last trio: pushed along on inner over 2f out: prog over 1f out: urged along and styd on but nvr in time to threaten* **6/1[2]**

-665 **8** *¾* **Ocean Promise (USA)**[58] 2220 3-9-2 67 ......................................(p) ShaneKelly 4 59
(Richard Hughes) *led to over 1f out: wknd* **14/1**

5-00 **9** *hd* **Bois D'Ebene (IRE)**[27] 3246 3-9-0 68 ...................................... KieranShoemark(3) 12 59+
(Roger Charlton) *hld up in 10th: nt clr run wl over 1f out: styd on ins fnl f but no ch to be involved* **14/1**

-003 **10** *1* **Mad Rose (IRE)**[19] 3536 3-9-1 66 ...................................... LukeMorris 11 55
(Jonathan Portman) *pressed ldrs on outer: rdn over 2f out: stl upsides wl over 1f out: edgd lft and wknd* **20/1**

036 **11** *½* **Dr Goodhead (FR)**[25] 3329 3-8-11 62 ...................................... TomMarquand 13 49
(Charles Hills) *hld up in last pair: shkn up 3f out: nvr in it but styd on fnl f* **25/1**

1504 **12** *½* **Porto Ferro (IRE)**[27] 3246 3-9-0 65 ......................................(b) MartinLane 14 51
(Dr Jon Scargill) *chsd ldrs: rdn and no imp whn impeded over 1f out: wknd* **16/1**

35-0 **13** *2 ½* **Sparkle**[11] 3822 3-9-5 70 ...................................... WilliamBuick 10 49
(Ed Dunlop) *dwlt: a wl in rr* **8/1[3]**

0-00 **14** *2 ¾* **Posh Bounty**[18] 3573 6-9-5 68 ......................................(h) JordanUys(7) 8 43
(Paul Burgoyne) *t.k.h: w ldr to 2f out: wknd rapidly* **50/1**

1m 26.5s (0.50) **Going Correction** 0.0s/f (Stan) 14 Ran SP% **129.7**
**WFA** 3 from 4yo+ 9lb
Speed ratings (Par 100): **97,96,96,96,95 93,92,91,91,90 89,89,86,83**
CSF £42.33 CT £339.00 TOTE £9.60: £3.00, £2.30, £3.90; EX 39.70 Trifecta £776.00.
**Owner** Mrs I Gansera-Leveque **Bred** John James **Trained** Newmarket, Suffolk

**FOCUS**
A modest but competitive fillies' handicap, and a small pb from the winner.

## 4215 32RED H'CAP (LONDON MILE SERIES QUALIFIER) 1m (P)

**7:40** (7:41) (Class 4) (0-85,86) 3-Y-0+ **£5,175** (£1,540; £769; £384) **Stalls** Low

Form RPR

-P12 **1** **Chiefofchiefs**[14] 3730 4-9-11 81 ...................................... StevieDonohoe 2 90
(Charlie Fellowes) *trckd ldrs: effrt on inner over 2f out: rdn to ld over 1f out: edgd lft ins fnl f but styd on* **3/1[1]**

-103 **2** *½* **Abatement**[28] 3211 3-9-1 84 ...................................... KieranShoemark(3) 10 90
(Roger Charlton) *pressed ldrs on outer: chal over 1f out: chsd wnr after: styd on but a readily hld* **5/1[3]**

-234 **3** *2* **Election Day**[27] 3232 3-9-1 81 ...................................... WilliamBuick 6 82
(Mark Johnston) *led at mod pce: kicked on over 2f out: hdd over 1f out: one pce after but hld on for 3rd* **5/1[3]**

0304 **4** *nk* **Mister Music**[17] 3620 8-9-8 78 ...................................... GeorgeDowning 3 81
(Tony Carroll) *hld up in last trio: nt clr run wl over 1f out tl fnl f: styd on wl last 150yds: gaining at fin* **16/1**

1026 **5** *nk* **Glory Of Paris (IRE)**[20] 3504 3-8-13 79 ...................................... WilliamCarson 7 79
(Rod Millman) *hld up in midfield: rdn and nt qckn on outer 2f out: styd on again ins fnl f but nvr able to threaten* **9/2[2]**

2062 **6** *hd* **Mutamid**[28] 3214 5-10-0 84 ...................................... JimCrowley 5 85
(Ismail Mohammed) *hld up in last trio: shkn up 2f out: nt clr run briefly over 1f out: one pce fnl f* **8/1**

0253 **7** *1 ¾* **Devil's Bridge (IRE)**[18] 3578 3-9-6 86 ...................................... PatDobbs 8 81
(Richard Hannon) *hld up for 100yds but swift move to press ldrs and t.k.h: lost pl wl over 1f out: fdd* **9/1**

-045 **8** *¾* **Brilliant Vanguard (IRE)**[40] 2772 4-9-3 78 ...................................... LewisEdmunds(5) 9 73
(Kevin Ryan) *a in last pair: rdn and no prog over 2f out* **10/1**

5020 **9** *nk* **Vantage Point (IRE)**[20] 3504 3-9-4 84 ......................................(p) DavidProbert 4 76
(Gary Moore) *w ldr to over 2f out: steadily wknd over 1f out* **14/1**

1m 38.9s (-0.90) **Going Correction** 0.0s/f (Stan)
**WFA** 3 from 4yo+ 10lb 9 Ran SP% **119.3**
Speed ratings (Par 105): **104,103,101,101,100 100,98,98,97**
CSF £18.69 CT £74.50 TOTE £4.10: £1.80, £1.70, £1.90; EX 24.50 Trifecta £149.30.
**Owner** Mervyn Ayers **Bred** Executive Bloodlines **Trained** Newmarket, Suffolk

**FOCUS**
The pace wasn't that strong but the first two finished clear and both are on the up, with the 3rd helping to set the level.

## 4216 32RED ON THE APP STORE H'CAP (LONDON MIDDLE DISTANCE SERIES QUALIFIER) 1m 2f 219y(P)

**8:10** (8:10) (Class 4) (0-85,87) 4-Y-0+ **£5,175** (£1,540; £769; £384) **Stalls** Low

Form RPR

-310 **1** **Spinners Ball (IRE)**[25] 3323 4-8-11 78 ...................................... MitchGodwin(5) 11 85
(Sylvester Kirk) *trckd ldr: led 3f out and sn committed for home: hrd rdn 2f out: pressed on all sides ins fnl f: jst clung on* **8/1**

-013 **2** *hd* **Tom's Rock (IRE)**[36] 2920 4-9-5 81 ...................................... DanielMuscutt 10 88
(John Butler) *stdd s: hld up in last pair: prog 2f out: rdn over 1f out: clsd between rival nr fin: jst failed* **9/2[3]**

54/3 **3** *hd* **Clowance One**[21] 3458 5-9-1 80 ......................................(p[1]) KieranShoemark(3) 3 86
(Roger Charlton) *cl up: chsd wnr over 2f out: drvn to cl fr over 1f out: chal ins fnl f: jst hld and lost 2nd last strides* **11/4[2]**

645/ **4** *shd* **Castlelyons (IRE)**[656] 6286 5-9-11 87 ...................................... LiamKeniry 7 93
(Robert Stephens) *stdd s: hld up in last: gd prog on outer 2f out: clsd on wnr w others fnl f: nt qckn last 50yds* **33/1**

0-20 **5** *3* **The Otmoor Poet**[32] 3067 4-9-1 77 ......................................(p) LukeMorris 2 78
(Alex Hales) *hld up towards rr: prog 2f out: rdn and no imp on ldrs fnl f* **20/1**

4-32 **6** *1* **Artful Rogue (IRE)**[12] 3785 6-9-6 82 ...................................... JimCrowley 5 81
(Amanda Perrett) *hld up in last trio: prog 2f out: rdn and no hdwy or imp jst over 1f out* **5/2[1]**

5-03 **7** *1 ¼* **Silca Star**[42] 2728 4-8-13 75 ...................................... FergusSweeney 4 72
(Alan King) *t.k.h: trckd ldrs: effrt 2f out: no imp over 1f out: fdd ins fnl f* **16/1**

-224 **8** *2* **All My Love (IRE)**[15] 3684 5-9-2 78 ...................................... RobHornby 1 71
(Pam Sly) *hld up in midfield: prog on inner over 2f out: no hdwy over 1f out: wknd fnl f* **20/1**

150 **9** *4* **Sean O'Casey (IRE)**[18] 3580 4-9-1 80 ...................................... AlistairRawlinson(3) 8 66
(Michael Appleby) *chsd ldrs on outer: rdn over 2f out: wknd wl over 1f out* **20/1**

0625 **10** *11* **Tobacco Road (IRE)**[18] 3582 7-9-2 78 ......................................(tp) TomMarquand 9 44
(David Pipe) *led to 3f out: wknd rapidly over 2f out: hung lft fr over 1f out: t.o* **20/1**

0-10 **11** *11* **Instant Karma (IRE)**[51] 1719 6-9-7 83 ...................................... LouisSteward 6 29
(Michael Bell) *in tch: rdn and wknd wl over 1f out: virtually p.u ins fnl f: t.o* **14/1**

2m 19.3s (-2.60) **Going Correction** 0.0s/f (Stan) 11 Ran SP% **119.1**
Speed ratings (Par 105): **109,108,108,108,106 105,104,103,100,92 84**
CSF £40.59 CT £126.85 TOTE £11.20: £3.50, £2.10, £1.30; EX 63.20 Trifecta £261.80.
**Owner** E McCay **Bred** Lynch-Bages Ltd **Trained** Upper Lambourn, Berks
■ Stewards' Enquiry : Mitch Godwin four-day ban: used whip above the permitted level (Jul 12-13, 17-18)

**FOCUS**
The first four pulled clear of the rest and there was little to choose between them at the line.

## 4217 "HAPPY 70TH BIRTHDAY AUSTIN ALLISON" H'CAP 1m 7f 218y(P)

**8:40** (8:42) (Class 6) (0-65,65) 4-Y-0+ **£2,587** (£770; £384; £192) **Stalls** Low

Form RPR

0031 **1** **Golly Miss Molly**[14] 3724 6-9-4 62 ......................................(b) MartinLane 13 72
(Martin Bosley) *hld up in last trio 3f out: stl in last pair and drvn jst over 2f out: gd prog over 1f out: stormed into the ld 120yds out and qckly drew clr* **7/1**

4032 **2** *3 ¾* **See And Be Seen**[6] 4000 7-9-0 63 ......................................(p) MitchGodwin(5) 2 69
(Sylvester Kirk) *hld up in midfield: prog over 2f out: clsd to chal 1f out: led briefly ins fnl f: sn outpcd by wnr* **9/2[2]**

-005 **3** *1* **Woofie (IRE)**[30] 3143 5-9-2 60 ...................................... GeorgeDowning 14 64
(Laura Mongan) *led 5f: trckd ldr: led 3f out: drvn over 1f out: hdd and no ex ins fnl f* **25/1**

-544 **4** *hd* **Southern States**[6] 4000 4-9-3 61 ......................................(e) CharlesBishop 10 65
(Lydia Richards) *trckd ldrs: rdn to go 2nd briefly 2f out: kpt on same pce after* **13/2**

23-2 **5** *2 ¼* **Intimidator (IRE)**[14] 3724 6-9-0 58 ...................................... JimCrowley 11 59
(Miss Joey Ellis) *hld up in midfield: rdn and prog over 2f out: clsd on ldrs over 1f out: effrt fdd out tamely fnl f* **7/2[1]**

3102 **6** *2 ¼* **Ascendant**[14] 2332 11-9-1 59 ...................................... StevieDonohoe 9 58
(Johnny Farrelly) *rdn most of way: struggling in rr fr 1/2-way: kpt on u.p fnl 2f* **5/1[3]**

4446 **7** *1 ¼* **Money Talks**[35] 2964 7-8-11 55 ......................................(p) DanielMuscutt 7 52
(Michael Madgwick) *hld up in midfield: rdn wl over 2f out: no prog over 1f out* **10/1**

051/ **8** *nk* **Storming Harry**[685] 5307 5-8-9 53 ...................................... RobHornby 5 50
(Robin Dickin) *hld up in last to 1/2-way: rdn and sme prog over 2f out: no hdwy and btn over 1f out* **20/1**

4004 **9** 2¾ **Sehail (USA)**[25] 3343 4-8-11 **55**........................(b[1]) LukeMorris 8 49
(George Peckham) *t.k.h: prom tl wknd over 2f out* **14/1**
1040 **10** 6 **Briac (FR)**[14] 3724 6-8-8 **52**........................ WilliamCarson 6 38
(Mark Pattinson) *hld up in rr: pushed along on inner over 2f out: no prog and sn wknd* **14/1**
0450 **11** 1¼ **Karam Albaari (IRE)**[19] 3547 9-9-7 **65**........................(v) DavidProbert 12 50
(J R Jenkins) *hld up: last 1/2-way: rapid prog to chse ldrs 6f out: wknd over 2f out* **25/1**
60 **12** 2 **Mr Magill (FR)**[84] 1556 5-8-8 **52**........................(h[1]) AdamBeschizza 3 34
(Karen George) *tk fierce hold: hld up but plld way through to ld after 5f: hdd & wknd 3f out* **33/1**
5/0- **13** 11 **Toptempo**[509] 461 8-8-12 **56**........................ FergusSweeney 1 25
(Ralph J Smith) *chsd ldrs: urged along 4f out: wknd 3f out: t.o* **33/1**
3134 **14** 7 **Iona Island**[42] 2723 4-9-6 **64**........................ LiamKeniry 4 25
(Peter Hiatt) *prom: wknd rapidly wl over 2f out: t.o* **16/1**

3m 30.44s (0.34) **Going Correction** 0.0s/f (Stan) **14** Ran SP% **129.5**
Speed ratings (Par 101): **99,97,96,96,95 94,93,93,92,89 88,87,82,78**
CSF £39.09 CT £778.39 TOTE £6.90: £2.40, £2.00, £9.30; EX 44.10 Trifecta £696.40.
**Owner** John Carey **Bred** Brook Stud Bloodstock Ltd **Trained** Chalfont St Giles, Bucks

**FOCUS**
A modest stayers' event, but the winner is progressive.
T/Plt: £499.70 to a £1 stake. Pool: £75,049.64. 109.63 winning units. T/Qpdt: £13.90 to a £1 stake. Pool: £8,210.44. 434.68 winning units. **Jonathan Neesom**

## 3864 SALISBURY (R-H)

Wednesday, June 28

**OFFICIAL GOING: Good to soft (good in places) changing to good to soft after race 1 (2.10)**
Wind: mild breeze, against Weather: rain

### 4218 WHITSBURY MANOR STUD EBFSTALLIONS.COM BLAGRAVE MAIDEN STKS (PLUS 10 RACE) 6f 213y
**2:10** (2:10) (Class 4) 2-Y-O **£4,690** (£1,395; £697; £348) **Stalls** Centre

Form RPR
**1** **Christopher Wood (IRE)** 2-9-5 0........................ PatDobbs 11 78+
(Ralph Beckett) *trckd ldrs: swtchd rt over 1f out: kpt on wl to ld fnl 100yds: pushed out* **5/1**[3]
5 **2** ¾ **Lifeboat (IRE)**[13] 3746 2-9-5 0........................ JimCrowley 7 76
(Charles Hills) *led: rdn over 1f out: hdd fnl 100yds: kpt on but no ex* **11/4**[1]
**3** 2¾ **Al Jellaby** 2-9-5 0........................ AdamKirby 10 69+
(Clive Cox) *mid-div: hdwy over 1f out: kpt on nicely fnl f: wnt 3rd ins fnl 100yds* **10/3**[2]
**4** 1¼ **Preacher Man (IRE)** 2-9-5 0........................ DougieCostello 3 66
(Jamie Osborne) *in tch: rdn 2f out: ev ch whn edgd lft ent fnl f: no ex fnl 120yds* **11/1**
0 **5** 2¾ **Colorado Dream**[60] 2148 2-9-5 0........................(p[1]) TrevorWhelan 8 59
(George Baker) *prom tl rdn over 3f out: j. path sn after: one pce fnl 2f* **66/1**
5 **6** hd **Master Grey (IRE)**[36] 2926 2-9-5 0........................ FranBerry 2 61
(Rod Millman) *in tch: trckd ldr 5f out: rdn over 2f out: ev ch whn squeezed out ent fnl f: no ex fnl 120yds* **9/1**
**7** nk **Macaque** 2-9-5 0........................ DavidProbert 13 58
(Andrew Balding) *s.i.s: towards rr: rdn over 2f out: kpt on fnl f but nvr gng pce to get involved* **12/1**
**8** shd **Berkshire Royal** 2-9-5 0........................ RobHornby 4 58
(Andrew Balding) *s.i.s: hdwy to trck ldrs after 2f: effrt over 2f out: wknd ent fnl f* **16/1**
**9** 2 **Landue** 2-8-12 0........................ TylerSaunders(7) 5 53
(Marcus Tregoning) *towards rr: sme minor late prog: nvr trbld ldrs* **33/1**
**10** ¾ **Istanbul Pasha (IRE)** 2-9-5 0........................ JFEgan 6 51
(David Evans) *s.i.s: sn trcking ldrs: rdn 2f out: wknd ins fnl f* **25/1**
**11** nk **Champs De Reves** 2-9-5 0........................ RoystonFfrench 1 50
(Marcus Tregoning) *rn green: a towards rr* **16/1**
**12** 7 **Livingstones Quest (IRE)** 2-9-5 0........................ WilliamCarson 12 33
(Rod Millman) *wnt lft s: sn mid-div: lost pl whn short of room and snatched up over 4f out: wknd over 1f out* **40/1**
**13** 2¾ **Beringer** 2-9-5 0........................ FergusSweeney 9 26
(Alan King) *mid-div tl wknd 2f out* **18/1**

1m 30.02s (1.42) **Going Correction** +0.15s/f (Good) **13** Ran SP% **120.2**
Speed ratings (Par 95): **97,96,93,91,88 88,87,87,85,84 84,76,73**
CSF £18.65 TOTE £6.40: £2.20, £1.50, £1.60; EX 21.50 Trifecta £68.80.
**Owner** R A Green **Bred** Airlie Stud **Trained** Kimpton, Hants

**FOCUS**
Persistent rain in the 24 hours preceding the first resulted in the going changing from an overnight good to firm, firm in places to ground that was described as just good to soft after the first. Jim Crowley and Pat Dobbs were both inclined to agree with the official description. \n\x\x The three with experience didn't look to set a high standard, but all things considered this had the look of a fair maiden. They all came stands' side.

### 4219 INSPIRE FOUNDATION VETERANS' H'CAP 5f
**2:40** (2:41) (Class 4) (0-80,82) 6-Y-0+ **£5,175** (£1,540; £769; £384) **Stalls** Low

Form RPR
5032 **1** **Pettochside**[17] 3617 8-9-7 **80**........................ JosephineGordon 1 88+
(John Bridger) *trckd ldr: led over 1f out: sn in command: eased towards fin* **2/1**[1]
0-04 **2** ¾ **Intibaah**[17] 3617 7-9-6 **79**........................(b) JimCrowley 7 81
(George Baker) *s.i.s: last pair: swtchd to r alone on stands' side rails over 3f out: rdn and hdwy over 1f out: drifted rt but kpt on ins fnl f: wnt 2nd fnl 100yds: a being comf hld by wnr* **7/2**[2]
1003 **3** 1¾ **Pearl Noir**[6] 4015 7-8-4 **63**........................(b) KieranO'Neill 6 59
(Scott Dixon) *led: rdn and hdd over 1f out: kpt on same pce fnl f* **7/1**
2666 **4** 1 **Waseem Faris (IRE)**[10] 3865 8-9-9 **82**........................(h[1]) PatDobbs 3 74
(Ken Cunningham-Brown) *trckd ldrs: rdn over 2f out: kpt on same pce* **11/2**
4153 **5** 2½ **Satchville Flyer**[12] 3773 6-9-4 **77**........................ FranBerry 2 60
(David Evans) *trckd ldrs: rdn over 2f out: fdd ins fnl f* **4/1**[3]
3550 **6** 11 **Burning Thread (IRE)**[26] 3278 10-9-0 **73**........................(b) ShaneKelly 5 17
(David Elsworth) *hld up: rdn over 2f out: nvr any imp: wknd fnl f* **14/1**

1m 1.52s (0.52) **Going Correction** +0.15s/f (Good) **6** Ran SP% **110.1**
Speed ratings: **101,99,97,95,91 73**
CSF £8.78 TOTE £2.60: £1.30, £2.10; EX 9.20 Trifecta £32.50.
**Owner** P Cook **Bred** New Hall Stud **Trained** Liphook, Hants

**FOCUS**
A modest sprint restricted to those over the age of six.

### 4220 NEW FOREST FARM MACHINERY/JOHN DEERE AUCTION STKS (PLUS 10 RACE) 6f
**3:10** (3:10) (Class 3) 2-Y-O **£7,115** (£2,117; £1,058; £529) **Stalls** Low

Form RPR
**1** **Veejay (IRE)** 2-8-7 0........................ RobHornby 7 78+
(Mick Channon) *little slowly away: last pair: rdn over 2f out: no imp tl r.o strly ins fnl f: led fnl 50yds* **25/1**
53 **2** ¾ **Onefootinparadise**[14] 3725 2-7-11 0........................ DavidEgan(5) 4 71
(Philip McBride) *racd keenly: trckd ldrs: rdn 2f out: abt to mount chal whn short of room over 1f out: r.o to hold ev ch fnl 120yds: outpcd by wnr fnl 50yds* **4/1**[3]
2232 **3** 1 **Three Little Birds**[11] 3821 2-8-4 0........................ MartinDwyer 2 70
(Sylvester Kirk) *led: rdn whn strly chal 2f out: edgd lft ent fnl f: hdd fnl 50yds: no ex* **8/1**
4 **4** 1½ **Kimifive (IRE)**[15] 3690 2-8-13 0........................ FranBerry 6 75
(Joseph Tuite) *trckd ldr: chal over 3f out: rdn over 2f out: ev ch ent fnl f: no ex fnl 140yds* **12/1**
1 **5** 2 **Running Cloud (IRE)**[21] 3467 2-9-3 0........................ TomMarquand 5 73
(Eve Johnson Houghton) *last: struggling 1/2-way: nvr threatened: fdd ins fnl f* **6/4**[1]
01 **6** nk **Another Day Of Sun (IRE)**[23] 3398 2-9-1 0........................ JimCrowley 3 70
(Mick Channon) *trckd ldrs: rdn over 2f out: fdd ins fnl f* **11/4**[2]

1m 16.12s (1.32) **Going Correction** +0.15s/f (Good) **6** Ran SP% **109.3**
Speed ratings (Par 97): **97,96,94,92,90 89**
CSF £113.29 TOTE £22.20: £10.00, £2.50; EX 99.90 Trifecta £588.10.
**Owner** John & Zoe Webster **Bred** Messrs Billy McEnery & Paul McEnery **Trained** West Ilsley, Berks

**FOCUS**
A conditions race which which hasn't produced anything of note recently, but had in the past been taken by Milk It Mick and Sir Percy. The jury is out on the strength of this form with the sole newcomer, and outsider, staying on best to land the spoils.

### 4221 WHITSBURY MANOR STUD BIBURY CUP H'CAP 1m 4f 5y
**3:40** (3:40) (Class 3) (0-95,87) 3-Y-O
**£13,695** (£4,100; £2,050; £1,025; £512; £257) **Stalls** High

Form RPR
-212 **1** **On To Victory**[20] 3505 3-9-7 **87**........................(h) TomMarquand 1 101
(Eve Johnson Houghton) *trckd ldrs: led over 2f out: styd on strly to draw clr fnl f: rdn out* **10/3**[3]
2-12 **2** 8 **Stone The Crows**[32] 3081 3-9-3 **86**........................ KieranShoemark(3) 4 87
(Roger Charlton) *hld up bhd ldrs: rdn and hdwy over 2f out: chsd wnr wl over 1f out: no ex ins fnl f* **3/1**[2]
1 **3** ½ **Great Sound (IRE)**[22] 3427 3-9-7 **87**........................ FranBerry 7 87
(John Gosden) *slowly away: sn pushed along: trckd ldr: rdn over 3f out: hld over 2f out: styd on same pce* **15/8**[1]
442 **4** 1½ **Turnpike Trip**[28] 3209 3-9-0 **80**........................ FergusSweeney 3 78
(Henry Candy) *led for 3f: trckd ldr: rdn and ev ch 3f out tl over 2f out: sn hld: styd on same pce* **8/1**
3243 **5** 2¼ **Koeman**[12] 3779 3-8-2 **73**........................ DavidEgan(5) 2 67
(Mick Channon) *trckd ldrs: rdn over 2f out: sn one pce* **12/1**
30-1 **6** 6 **Redicean**[79] 1675 3-9-5 **85**........................ JosephineGordon 8 70
(Peter Chapple-Hyam) *trckd ldr: led after 3f: rdn and hdd over 2f out: wknd over 1f out* **8/1**

2m 37.44s (-0.56) **Going Correction** +0.15s/f (Good) **6** Ran SP% **112.8**
Speed ratings (Par 103): **107,101,101,100,98 94**
CSF £13.84 CT £22.74 TOTE £3.50: £1.40, £2.50; EX 13.90 Trifecta £34.50.
**Owner** HP Racing On To Victory **Bred** The Aston House Stud **Trained** Blewbury, Oxon

**FOCUS**
This is a traditionally a good handicap (Simple Verse won it in 2015 before going on to win the St Leger) and, with decent prize money on offer, it was a bit disappointing that the top rated horse was 8lb under the ceiling rating. That horse took the race apart though and he's one to follow wherever he turns up next, with this a clear pb.

### 4222 H S LESTER MEMORIAL H'CAP 1m 6f 44y
**4:10** (4:10) (Class 4) (0-85,87) 4-Y-O+ **£5,175** (£1,540; £769; £384) **Stalls** Far side

Form RPR
3330 **1** **Swashbuckle**[32] 3076 4-9-0 **85**........................ JoshuaBryan(7) 10 96
(Andrew Balding) *led: rdn and edgd ;lft fr 3f out: hdd 2f out: rallied to regain narrow ld ent fnl f: styd on gamely* **5/1**[2]
2/13 **2** ½ **Sternrubin (GER)**[17] 3618 6-9-3 **81**........................ TomQueally 3 91
(Philip Hobbs) *trckd ldrs: smooth hdwy to ld 2f out: sn rdn: hdd ent fnl f: no ex fnl 120yds* **3/1**[1]
4501 **3** 9 **Cotton Club (IRE)**[15] 3694 6-8-9 **73**........................ WilliamCarson 12 70
(Rod Millman) *hld up: rdn and hdwy over 2f out: wnt 3rd ent fnl f: styd on but nt pce to get on terms* **14/1**
13 **4** 2 **Rosa Damascena (FR)**[35] 2965 4-8-11 **75**........................ MartinHarley 5 70
(Alan King) *mid-div: rdn and hdwy over 2f out: chsd ldng pair over 1f out: styd on same pce fnl f* **8/1**
55-3 **5** 2¼ **Pastoral Music**[21] 3459 4-8-9 **73**........................ SeanLevey 12 64
(Hughie Morrison) *mid-div: rdn over 2f out: sn one pce* **8/1**
002- **6** nk **Buckle Street**[95] 7739 4-7-11 **66** oh2........................(tp) RichardOliver(5) 4 57
(Martin Keighley) *in tch: rdn to chse wnr over 3f out tl over 2f out: styd on same pce* **13/2**[3]
114- **7** 6 **Pleasure Dome**[44] 7215 4-9-9 **87**........................ ShaneKelly 7 70
(Jonjo O'Neill) *trckd ldrs: rdn over 3f out: wknd over 1f out* **20/1**
-600 **8** 3¼ **Glaring**[19] 3534 6-9-5 **83**........................(p) JimCrowley 1 61
(Amanda Perrett) *hld up: effrt 3f out: nvr threatened: wknd over 1f out* **12/1**
0-65 **9** 3 **Hatsaway (IRE)**[28] 3213 6-8-11 **75**........................ JFEgan 11 49
(Pat Phelan) *a towards rr* **7/1**
520 **10** 2¾ **Methag (FR)**[21] 3458 4-8-10 **74**........................ FergusSweeney 8 44
(Alex Hales) *a towards rr* **25/1**
3233 **11** 18 **Ardamir (FR)**[61] 2125 5-9-1 **82**........................ KieranShoemark(3) 9 27
(Laura Mongan) *prom tl 4f out: sn rdn: wknd over 2f out* **16/1**

3m 6.64s (-0.76) **Going Correction** +0.15s/f (Good) **11** Ran SP% **118.6**
Speed ratings (Par 105): **108,107,102,101,100 99,96,94,92,91 81**
CSF £20.52 CT £200.53 TOTE £5.90: £2.00, £1.50, £4.50; EX 24.60 Trifecta £279.40.
**Owner** Kingsclere Racing Club **Bred** Kingsclere Stud **Trained** Kingsclere, Hants

**FOCUS**
Flag start. A few fair sorts in this staying race and they looked to go a decent pace.

## 4223 MOLSON COORS H'CAP 1m
**4:40** (4:43) (Class 2) (0-100,95) 3-Y-0+
**£12,450** (£3,728; £1,864; £932; £466; £234) **Stalls** Low

Form RPR
-404 1 **Examiner (IRE)**[26] 3300 6-9-11 **92**..........................(t) RichardKingscote 8 100
(Stuart Williams) *trckd ldrs: rdn to ld ent fnl f: kpt on wl to assert fnl 120yds* **10/3**[2]
1104 2 1 3/4 **Morning Suit (USA)**[25] 3336 3-8-11 **88**.................................... JFEgan 5 90
(Mark Johnston) *led for over 1f: prom: rdn 2f out: ev ch ent fnl f: no ex fnl 100yds* **13/2**
0500 3 1/2 **Kingston Kurrajong**[13] 3750 4-8-11 **78**...................... AdamBeschizza 4 81
(Michael Attwater) *hld up: rdn 2f out: sn swtchd to stands' side: hdwy ent fnl f: kpt on to go 3rd fnl 120yds* **6/1**
0-06 4 3 1/4 **Storm Rock**[35] 2959 5-9-9 **90**........................................(p[1]) HarryBentley 9 85
(Harry Dunlop) *pressed ldr: led after 1f: rdn 2f out: hdd ent fnl f: no ex fnl 120yds* **4/1**[3]
0030 5 hd **Sir Roderic (IRE)**[11] 3837 4-9-9 **95**................................ DavidEgan(5) 3 90
(Rod Millman) *trckd ldrs: rdn over 2f out: nt pce to mount chal: no ex fnl 120yds* **2/1**[1]
65-4 6 8 **White Tower (IRE)**[69] 1912 3-8-1 **83**........................... RichardOliver(5) 2 57
(Mark Johnston) *trckd ldrs: rdn 3f out: edgd lft: wknd 2f out* **12/1**

1m 43.46s (-0.04) **Going Correction** +0.15s/f (Good)
**WFA** 3 from 4yo+ 10lb 6 Ran SP% **111.7**
Speed ratings (Par 109): **106,104,103,100,100 92**
CSF £24.07 CT £120.73 TOTE £3.70: £2.00, £2.20; EX 13.20 Trifecta £75.10.
**Owner** Hunscote Stud **Bred** River Downs Stud **Trained** Newmarket, Suffolk

**FOCUS**
Normally a good handicap, won in 2015 by Lightning Spear, but this renewal looked well below par - not helped by three non-runners. The winner has been rated to his best.

## 4224 BRITISH EBF VENTURE SECURITY MAIDEN STKS 1m 1f 201y
**5:10** (5:10) (Class 5) 3-Y-0+ **£4,204** (£1,251; £625; £312) **Stalls** Low

Form RPR
44-3 1 **See Of Rome**[44] 2689 3-9-2 77............................................ ShaneKelly 6 85
(Richard Hughes) *led: rdn and hdd 3f out: rallied to regain ld over 1f out: drifted lft: styd on strly to draw clr fnl f* **6/4**[1]
-523 2 5 **Prerogative (IRE)**[9] 3921 3-9-2 79.............................(p) TomMarquand 7 75
(Richard Hannon) *trckd ldr tl chal 3f out: sn rdn in cl 3rd: styd on again to regain 2nd fnl 90yds but no ch w wnr* **9/2**[3]
5- 3 1 **Working Class**[259] 7283 3-9-2 0.......................................... MartinHarley 8 73
(Peter Chapple-Hyam) *trckd ldrs: led 3f out: rdn and hdd over 1f out: no ex ins fnl f: lost 2nd fnl 90yds* **8/1**
62 4 1 1/4 **Mancini**[23] 3408 3-9-2 0............................................... RichardKingscote 4 71
(Jonathan Portman) *mid-div: hdwy 4f out: rdn w ev ch 3f out: sn outpcd: styd on ins fnl f to snatch 4th fnl strides* **11/4**[2]
00 5 nk **Sputnik Planum (USA)**[20] 3506 3-9-2 0........................... TomQueally 5 70
(David Lanigan) *hld up last trio: hdwy 3f out: sn rdn: wnt 4th 2f out: nt pce to get on terms: lost 4th fnl stride* **33/1**
444 6 6 **Sonnetist**[20] 3506 3-9-2 77.................................................. KieranO'Neill 3 58
(Richard Hannon) *mid-div: hdwy 4f out: rdn w ch 3f out: sn hld: wknd over 1f out* **8/1**
60 7 3/4 **Celtik Secret**[17] 3615 3-8-11 0............................................ RobHornby 9 51
(Hughie Morrison) *hld up last pair: hdwy over 3f out: sn rdn: nt pce to chal: wknd over 1f out* **33/1**
06 8 19 **Desert Song**[23] 3408 3-9-2 0..................................................... JFEgan 2 18
(Pat Phelan) *trckd ldrs: rdn 3f out: wknd and eased over 1f out* **66/1**
6 9 55 **Dartmoor Girl (IRE)**[59] 2175 3-8-11 0................................. DannyBrock 1
(Mark Gillard) *s.i.s: sn struggling in last: eased 3f out* **100/1**

2m 12.71s (2.81) **Going Correction** +0.15s/f (Good) 9 Ran SP% **115.4**
Speed ratings (Par 103): **94,90,89,88,87 83,82,67,23**
CSF £8.52 TOTE £2.10: £1.10, £1.80, £2.40; EX 8.40 Trifecta £41.90.
**Owner** John And Jordan Lund **Bred** Aston House Stud **Trained** Upper Lambourn, Berks

**FOCUS**
No more than a fair maiden, but the winner took it well, posting a pb, and there were a few in behind to be interested in for the future too.
T/Plt: £80.90 to a £1 stake. Pool: £59,169.88. 533.85 winning units. T/Qpdt: £29.70 to a £1 stake. Pool: £3,437.88. 85.54 winning units. **Tim Mitchell**

4225 - 4231a (Foreign Racing) - See Raceform Interactive

# ARGENTAN (R-H)
Wednesday, June 28

**OFFICIAL GOING: Turf: soft**

## 4232a PRIX CLAIRFEUILLE (MAIDEN) (3YO FILLIES) (TURF) 1m 2f 110y
**4:55** 3-Y-0 **£6,837** (£2,735; £2,051; £1,367; £683)

RPR
1 **Alacovia (FR)**[66] 3-9-2 0........................................ Pierre-CharlesBoudot 4 77
(P Bary, France) **56/10**[2]
2 2 1/2 **Nosongsosweet (IRE)**[264] 3-8-8 0............................ JeremyMoisan(8) 2 72
(M Delzangles, France) **79/1**
3 snk **Lady Valdean**[25] 3353 3-9-2 0................................................ JulienAuge 8 72
(Jose Santos) **23/10**[1]
4 1/2 **Belleire (FR)**[35] 2978 3-9-2 0............................................. JeromeCabre 3 71
(M Nigge, France) **13/2**
5 2 **Etatinka (FR)**[25] 3353 3-9-2 0............................................ MickaelForest 7 67
(J-M Beguigne, France) **6/1**[3]
6 1/2 **Love Money (FR)**[22] 3-8-8 0................................... QuentinGervais(8) 13 66
(Y Barberot, France) **21/1**
7 snk **Maklau (FR)**[32] 3134 3-9-2 0................................. ChristopherGrosbois 9 66
(J Boisnard, France) **78/10**
8 shd **Youmsovain (FR)**[15] 3-9-2 0.......................................... SebastienMaillot 5 66
(N Clement, France) **31/1**
9 1 **Cavalseulles (FR)**[37] 3-9-2 0.............................................. FabriceVeron 11 64
(L Gadbin, France) **9/1**
10 shd **Pretoria (FR)** 3-9-2 0.................................................... IoritzMendizabal 1 64
(E Libaud, France) **19/1**
11 2 **Anse De Bel'Amande (FR)**[32] 3134 3-9-2 0........... MathieuAndrouin 6 60
(F Lemercier, France) **106/1**
12 1 1/2 **Sunshada (FR)**[24] 3-9-2 0............................................. WilliamsSaraiva 14 57
(P Fleurie, France) **130/1**
13 7 **Sapotille (FR)**[32] 3134 3-8-11 0............................ MlleMarylineEon(5) 12 43
(E Libaud, France) **31/1**
14 4 **Simply Sweet (FR)**[64] 3-9-2 0.................................. ThibaultSpeicher 10 35
(Louis Baudron, France) **16/1**

2m 13.3s 14 Ran SP% **119.1**
**Owner** Ecurie Jean-Louis Bouchard **Bred** Haras Du Quesnay **Trained** Chantilly, France

## 4233a PRIX DE COMPIEGNE (CLAIMER) (4YO+) (TURF) 6f
**5:55** 4-Y-0+ **£6,410** (£2,564; £1,923; £1,282; £641)

RPR
1 **O Dee**[21] 3469 5-9-1 0.................................................................. JulienAuge 4 74
(Jose Santos) **48/10**[3]
2 2 1/2 **Zia Melody (FR)**[297] 4-8-8 0................................ ChristopherGrosbois 3 59
(J Boisnard, France) **37/1**
3 2 **Never Compromise (FR)**[342] 4-9-1 0............... ClementLecoeuvre(3) 8 63
(Henk Grewe, Germany) **3/1**[1]
4 3/4 **Image Seconde (FR)**[38] 5-9-1 0.......................................... DavidBreux 7 58
(J-F Lelievre, France) **17/1**
5 1/2 **Bonita Chica (FR)**[44] 5-9-2 0............................................. JeromeCabre 2 57
(F Monnier, France) **19/5**[2]
6 2 1/2 **Cracker'star (FR)**[40] 4-9-1 0...................................... MathieuAndrouin 12 48
(C Plisson, France) **60/1**
7 snk **Chef Oui Chef (FR)**[31] 7-9-1 0.................................(p) MrHugoBoutin 13 48
(M Boutin, France) **14/1**
8 shd **La Perle Doloise (FR)**[11] 4-9-1 0...............................(b) FabriceVeron 10 47
(A Bonin, France) **18/1**
9 1/2 **Night Call (FR)**[48] 4-7-12 0.........................(b) MmeAlexiaCeccarello(10) 1 39
(A Spanu, France) **45/1**
10 2 **Forza Libranno (FR)**[242] 4-9-4 0..........................(b) IoritzMendizabal 11 42
(F Chappet, France) **7/1**
11 2 **Amadeus Wolfe Tone (IRE)**[71] 8-8-11 0.......(p) AnthonyCaramanolis 9 29
(Leo Braem, Belgium) **9/1**
12 nk **Cruzador (IRE)**[38] 9-8-11 0........................................(p) RichardJuteau 14 28
(S Gouyette, France) **113/1**
13 2 **Flicka's Boy**[52] 2424 5-9-4 0...................................(p) AlexandreRoussel 5 28
(P Monfort, France) **11/1**

1m 15.2s 13 Ran SP% **118.7**
**Owner** Jose Santos Racing Ltd **Bred** Lofts Hall Stud & B Sangster **Trained** Upper Lambourn, Berks

3611
# MAISONS-LAFFITTE (R-H)
Wednesday, June 28

**OFFICIAL GOING: Turf: good**

## 4234a PRIX DE RIS-ORANGIS (GROUP 3) (3YO+) (TURF) 6f
**1:20** 3-Y-0+ **£34,188** (£13,675; £10,256; £6,837; £3,418)

RPR
1 **Rosa Imperial (IRE)**[18] 3614 4-8-11 0...................... MickaelBarzalona 7 110+
(A Fabre, France) *midfield in tch: rdn to chal 2f out: led fnl f: kpt on* **6/5**[1]
2 1 **Son Cesio (FR)**[24] 3370 6-9-1 0.......................... Pierre-CharlesBoudot 4 111
(H-A Pantall, France) *trckd ldr: travelled strly: rdn to ld 2f out: hdd fnl f: kpt on wout matching wnr after* **6/1**
3 3/4 **Attendu (FR)**[25] 3354 4-9-1 0.............................................. MaximeGuyon 1 108
(C Laffon-Parias, France) *niggled in midfield: kpt on for 3rd fnl f but nt pce to chal* **7/2**[2]
4 1 1/4 **Via Ravenna (IRE)**[46] 2644 3-8-9 0.......................... VincentCheminaud 2 103+
(A Fabre, France) *hmpd s: hld up: kpt on same pce u.p fnl 2f and nvr able to chal* **4/1**[3]
5 3/4 **Cersei**[37] 4-8-11 0.......................................................... StephanePasquier 5 98
(F Rohaut, France) *midfield: outpcd fnl 2f* **11/1**
6 1 1/4 **Love Spirit**[24] 3370 7-9-1 0........................................ Jean-BernardEyquem 6 98
(Louis Baudron, France) *led: rdn and hdd 2f out: no ex: wknd* **24/1**
7 3 **Rangali**[46] 2643 6-9-1 0....................................(b) Francois-XavierBertras 3 88
(D Guillemin, France) *wnt lft s: a in rr: brief effrt to improve on outer over 2f out: sn no ex: wl btn fnl f* **19/1**

1m 9.72s (-3.68)
**WFA** 3 from 4yo+ 7lb 7 Ran SP% **119.3**
PARI-MUTUEL (all including 1 euro stake): WIN 2.20; PLACE 1.50, 2.50; SF 10.30.
**Owner** Godolphin SNC **Bred** Darley **Trained** Chantilly, France

## 4235a PRIX DAPHNIS (GROUP 3) (3YO COLTS & GELDINGS) (ROUND) (TURF) 1m 1f
**2:55** 3-Y-0 **£34,188** (£13,675; £10,256; £6,837)

RPR
1 **Last Kingdom (USA)**[30] 3-8-11 0.......................... SilvestreDeSousa 2 110+
(A Fabre, France) *trckd ldr: gng best 2f out: rdn to chal and led ent fnl f: styd on: jst prevailed* **11/5**[3]
2 nk **Spotify (FR)**[45] 2666 3-8-11 0............................................ MaximeGuyon 4 109
(C Ferland, France) *hld up in tch: rdn to chal on rail 2f out: styd on and ev ch fnl f: jst hld* **13/10**[1]
3 2 **Neguev (IRE)**[89] 3-8-11 0..................................... Jean-BernardEyquem 1 105
(J-C Rouget, France) *led: rdn and strly pressed 2f out: hdd ent fnl f: hld in 3rd sn after* **2/1**[2]
4 snk **Roc Angel (FR)**[11] 3855 3-8-11 0......................................... TonyPiccone 5 105
(F Chappet, France) *hld up in tch: rdn and effrt on outer 2f out: sn outpcd: hld fnl f* **9/1**

1m 58.62s (3.92) 4 Ran SP% **118.1**
PARI-MUTUEL (all including 1 euro stake): WIN 3.20; PLACE 1.70, 1.50; SF 6.10.
**Owner** Prince A A Faisal **Bred** Michael Baum And Reiko Baum **Trained** Chantilly, France

4236 - 4243a (Foreign Racing) - See Raceform Interactive

# 3972 HAMILTON (R-H)

Thursday, June 29

**OFFICIAL GOING: Good to soft (good in places) changing to soft after race 2 (6.30)**

Wind: Breezy, half against Weather: Overcast, showers

## 4244 EXSEL GROUP SAINTS & SINNERS AMATEUR RIDERS' H'CAP (FOR THE SAINTS & SINNERS CHALLENGE CUP) 1m 5f 16y

**6:00** (6:02) (Class 5) (0-70,70) 4-Y-0+ **£3,743** (£1,161; £580; £290) **Stalls** High

| Form | | | | RPR |
|---|---|---|---|---|
| 0041 | 1 | | **Donnachies Girl (IRE)**[8] 3978 4-10-1 **60** MrRyanNichol(3) 11 (Alistair Whillans) *chsd ldrs: smooth hdwy to ld over 2f out: rdn and wandered fr over 1f out: kpt on strly* 5/2[1] | 69+ |
| -333 | 2 | 1 1/4 | **Canny Style**[40] 2815 4-10-12 **68** MissJoannaMason 10 (Kevin Ryan) *hld up: pushed along 3f out: hdwy to chse wnr over 1f out: kpt on ins fnl f: nt pce to chal* 4/1[3] | 74 |
| 4000 | 3 | 3 | **Fillydelphia (IRE)**[7] 4018 6-9-7 **54** (h) MissAMcCain(5) 6 (Patrick Holmes) *midfield: stdy hdwy over 3f out: rdn over 2f out: kpt on fnl f: nrst fin* 12/1 | 56 |
| -500 | 4 | 2 1/2 | **Celtic Power**[8] 3978 5-9-5 **52** (v) MissRHill(5) 1 (Jim Goldie) *led 3f: pressed ldr: regained ld 4f out: rdn and hdd over 2f out: one pce fr over 1f out* 16/1 | 50 |
| -023 | 5 | 1 | **Duke Of Yorkshire**[14] 3753 7-10-11 **70** (p) MissEEasterby(3) 9 (Tim Easterby) *trckd ldrs: drvn along over 2f out: wknd over 1f out* 11/2 | 66 |
| -206 | 6 | 8 | **Schmooze (IRE)**[8] 3978 8-9-10 **52** MrsCBartley 8 (Linda Perratt) *hld up: pushed along and hung rt wl over 1f out: sn outpcd: n.d after* 16/1 | 36 |
| 4032 | 7 | 3/4 | **Spiritoftomintoul**[18] 3623 8-10-1 **64** (t) MrGGilbertson(7) 7 (Tony Carroll) *missed break: bhd: shortlived effrt over 4f out: sn btn* 3/1[2] | 47 |
| 0-00 | 8 | nk | **Riponian**[24] 3387 7-9-10 **52** (t) MissCWalton 5 (Susan Corbett) *t.k.h early: pressed ldr: led after 3f to 4f out: rdn and wknd fr 2f out* 40/1 | 35 |

2m 59.36s (5.46) **Going Correction** +0.40s/f (Good) **8 Ran SP% 110.9**

Speed ratings (Par 103): **99,98,96,94,94 89,88,88**

CSF £11.90 CT £91.96 TOTE £3.00: £1.20, £1.80, £3.00; EX 12.00 Trifecta £90.70.

**Owner** Mrs Karen Spark **Bred** Darley **Trained** Newmill-On-Slitrig, Borders

**FOCUS**

Periods of rain throughout the day saw approximately 6mm fall on top of 12mm in the two days preceding this card. Rail alignment added 13 yards to the official distance of this very modest handicap for amateur riders. The pace was modest, run 13 seconds slower than standard, and the official going turned to soft afterwards. A race notable as the last for retiring jockey Ryan Nichol before pursuing another career. The unpenalised winner has been rated similar to latest.

## 4245 BB FOODSERVICE MAIDEN STKS (PLUS 10 RACE) (A £20,000 BB FOODSERVICE 2YO SERIES QUALIFIER) 6f 6y

**6:30** (6:30) (Class 4) 2-Y-0 **£5,175** (£1,540; £769; £384) **Stalls** High

| Form | | | | RPR |
|---|---|---|---|---|
| 03 | 1 | | **Quayside**[19] 3576 2-9-5 0 JackGarritty 5 (Richard Fahey) *mde all against stands' rail: shkn up over 1f out: kpt on strly fnl f* 9/4[2] | 75 |
| 03 | 2 | 3/4 | **Kirbec (IRE)**[21] 3491 2-9-0 0 AndrewMullen 2 (Keith Dalgleish) *prom: effrt and chsd wnr appr fnl f: kpt on ins fnl f: hld nr fin* 13/2 | 68 |
| | 3 | 3 1/2 | **Arch Gold (USA)** 2-9-5 0 JoeFanning 4 (Mark Johnston) *chsd wnr to over 1f out: rdn and wknd ins fnl f* 7/4[1] | 62+ |
| 3 | 4 | 1 1/4 | **Here In The Dark**[17] 3648 2-9-5 0 GrahamLee 1 (Keith Dalgleish) *in tch on outside: rdn over 2f out: no imp over 1f out: sn btn* 5/2[3] | 59+ |

1m 14.9s (2.70) **Going Correction** +0.375s/f (Good) **4 Ran SP% 109.0**

Speed ratings (Par 95): **97,96,91,89**

CSF £14.50 TOTE £3.60; EX 11.80 Trifecta £24.60.

**Owner** Bearstone Stud Limited **Bred** Bearstone Stud Ltd **Trained** Musley Bank, N Yorks

**FOCUS**

Few runners and they went no more than a steady pace early, but probably a decent juvenile maiden. The first two home had the benefit of a couple of runs under their belts and the winner is improving.

## 4246 EXSEL GROUP (S) H'CAP 5f 7y

**7:00** (7:00) (Class 6) (0-60,61) 3-Y-0+ **£3,234** (£962; £481; £240) **Stalls** Centre

| Form | | | | RPR |
|---|---|---|---|---|
| | 1 | | **Wee Jock (IRE)**[40] 2844 3-8-4 **45** RoystonFfrench 15 (John Patrick Shanahan, Ire) *mde all against stands' rail: pushed clr fr over 1f out: unchal* 5/2[1] | 58+ |
| -505 | 2 | 2 3/4 | **Perfect Words (IRE)**[22] 3453 7-9-7 **56** (p) BarryMcHugh 4 (Marjorie Fife) *prom: drvn along over 2f out: wnt 2nd over 1f out: kpt on fnl f: no imp* 5/1[3] | 61 |
| 0000 | 3 | 2 | **Miss Pepper (IRE)**[18] 3624 3-8-1 **45** (h) SammyJoBell(3) 11 (Paul Midgley) *t.k.h in midfield: hung rt and bmpd over 3f out: sn drvn along: hdwy over 1f out: kpt on fnl f: no imp* 9/1 | 41 |
| 0334 | 4 | hd | **Bunce (IRE)**[17] 3653 9-9-10 **59** GrahamLee 13 (Linda Perratt) *hld up: rdn and hdwy over 1f out: kpt on fnl f: nrst fin* 5/1[3] | 56 |
| 4026 | 5 | hd | **Misu Moneypenny**[15] 3728 4-9-5 **54** (p) BenCurtis 8 (Scott Dixon) *in tch: bmpd and outpcd over 3f out: rdn and hdwy over 1f out: no imp fnl f* 11/4[2] | 50 |
| 56-0 | 6 | 3 | **Red Shadow**[24] 3385 8-8-5 **45** (v) RowanScott(5) 7 (Alistair Whillans) *bhd and outpcd: drvn along 1/2-way: kpt on fnl f: nvr able to chal* 14/1 | 31 |
| 00-0 | 7 | 3/4 | **King Of Castilla**[5] 4107 3-8-13 **54** (p) KevinStott 9 (Colin Teague) *chsd ldrs: rdn over 2f out: wknd over 1f out* 50/1 | 35 |
| 0000 | 8 | shd | **Warleggan (FR)**[24] 3385 3-8-2 **46** ow1 (b) RachelRichardson(3) 14 (Linda Perratt) *hld up: drvn and outpcd over 2f out: btn over 1f out* 33/1 | 27 |
| 00-0 | 9 | 3/4 | **Kylla**[30] 3185 4-8-10 **45** (b[1]) TomEaves 3 (Shaun Harris) *wnt rt s: swtchd lft and sn cl up: rdn over 2f out: drifted rt and wknd appr fnl f* 66/1 | 25+ |
| 0-00 | 10 | 12 | **Sunrise Dance**[15] 3704 8-8-10 **45** (t) JackGarritty 5 (Kenny Johnson) *missed break: t.o thrght* 40/1 | |

1m 2.16s (2.16) **Going Correction** +0.375s/f (Good)

**WFA** 3 from 4yo+ 6lb **10 Ran SP% 114.1**

Speed ratings (Par 101): **97,92,89,89,88 83,82,82,81,62**

CSF £14.70 CT £97.34 TOTE £3.80: £1.90, £1.90, £1.80; EX 16.80 Trifecta £95.00.The winner was bought in for 7,200

**Owner** Thistle Bloodstock Limited **Bred** Thistle Bloodstock Limited **Trained** Kells, Co Kilkenny

**FOCUS**

A bargain-basement selling sprint and a winner who again came up the stands' rail.

## 4247 THISTLE BLOODSTOCK MAIDEN STKS 1m 1f 35y

**7:35** (7:37) (Class 5) 3-4-Y-0 **£3,881** (£1,155; £577; £288) **Stalls** Low

| Form | | | | RPR |
|---|---|---|---|---|
| -540 | 1 | | **Set In Stone (IRE)**[33] 3094 3-8-12 **73** TadhgO'Shea 7 (John Patrick Shanahan, Ire) *in tch: smooth hdwy to chse ldr over 1f out: shkn up to ld ent fnl f: kpt on wl towards fin* 2/1[1] | 67 |
| 2-03 | 2 | 1/2 | **Somnambulist**[53] 2429 3-9-3 **74** (h) GrahamLee 4 (Keith Dalgleish) *led: rdn 2f out: hdd ent fnl f: rallied: hld nr fin* 5/1 | 71 |
| 0220 | 3 | 3 3/4 | **Tread Lightly**[14] 3745 3-9-3 **70** DavidAllan 2 (Tim Easterby) *trckd ldrs: rdn and outpcd 2f out: rallied fnl f: kpt on: nt rch first two* 10/3[2] | 63 |
| 04- | 4 | nk | **Clarabel**[283] 6617 4-9-9 0 AndrewMullen 6 (John Weymes) *pressed ldr to over 2f out: sn drvn along: kpt on fnl f: no imp* 100/1 | 58 |
| 35 | 5 | 1 3/4 | **Unite The Clans (IRE)**[50] 2527 3-9-3 0 RoystonFfrench 5 (John Patrick Shanahan, Ire) *hld up: rdn and effrt over 2f out: no imp fr over 1f out* 9/2[3] | 59 |
| 5-00 | 6 | 1 | **Used To Be**[15] 3715 3-9-3 **69** BenCurtis 10 (K R Burke) *hld up on outside: smooth hdwy over 3f out: chsd ldr over 2f out to over 1f out: wknd ins fnl f* 16/1 | 57 |
| | 7 | nse | **Grey Diamond** 3-9-3 0 JoeFanning 8 (Mark Johnston) *hld up on outside: rdn along and effrt 3f out: sn no imp: btn over 1f out* 10/1 | 57 |
| 5 | 8 | 1 | **Red Star Dancer (IRE)**[24] 3383 3-9-3 0 KevinStott 9 (Linda Perratt) *hld up: rdn over 3f out: shortlived effrt 2f out: sn btn* 80/1 | 55 |
| | 9 | 3/4 | **Wee Bogus**[44] 4-9-9 0 RowanScott(5) 11 (Alistair Whillans) *hld up: drvn along over 3f out: btn fnl 2f* 50/1 | 54 |
| | 10 | 1 | **Precious Rock (IRE)** 3-9-3 0 JackGarritty 1 (Jedd O'Keeffe) *s.i.s: sn midfield: drvn and green over 3f out: btn fnl 2f* 12/1 | 51 |
| 45 | 11 | 21 | **Palace Ball**[10] 3896 3-8-12 0 TomEaves 3 (Stuart Coltherd) *towards rr: drvn and struggling 3f out: sn lost tch: t.o* 100/1 | 2 |

2m 4.04s (4.34) **Going Correction** +0.40s/f (Good)

**WFA** 3 from 4yo 11lb **11 Ran SP% 119.1**

Speed ratings (Par 103): **96,95,92,91,90 89,89,88,87,87 68**

CSF £12.56 TOTE £2.90: £1.20, £1.70, £1.50; EX 13.70 Trifecta £36.40.

**Owner** Thistle Bloodstock Limited **Bred** Thistle Bloodstock Limited **Trained** Kells, Co Kilkenny

**FOCUS**

Rail alignment added 13 yards to the official distance and they went a sensible clip for the conditions. Probably a modest maiden and it has been rated around the runner-up to his latest.

## 4248 BRITISH STALLION STUDS CAPTAIN J C STEWART EBF FILLIES' H'CAP 1m 68y

**8:10** (8:11) (Class 4) (0-80,80) 3-Y-0+ **£7,470** (£2,236; £1,118; £559; £279; £140) **Stalls** Low

| Form | | | | RPR |
|---|---|---|---|---|
| 0-33 | 1 | | **Company Asset (IRE)**[41] 2805 4-9-11 **77** KevinStott 10 (Kevin Ryan) *hld up in tch: shkn up over 2f out: hdwy to ld over 1f out: qcknd clr fnl f: readily* 7/2[2] | 90+ |
| 0 | 2 | 3 1/2 | **Duck Egg Blue (IRE)**[27] 3287 3-8-2 **71** (p) PaulaMuir(7) 4 (Patrick Holmes) *hld up midfield: drvn and outpcd over 2f out: rallied over 1f out: chsd (clr) wnr wl ins fnl f: kpt on* 25/1 | 73 |
| 4113 | 3 | 1 1/2 | **Dark Crystal**[6] 3976 6-9-1 **72** LewisEdmunds(5) 6 (Linda Perratt) *trckd ldrs: smooth hdwy to ld over 2f out: rdn and hdd over 1f out: one pce whn lost 2nd wl ins fnl f* 9/2[3] | 73 |
| 232 | 4 | nk | **Peach Melba**[21] 3493 3-8-13 **75** JoeFanning 3 (Mark Johnston) *t.k.h early: pressed ldr: led after 2f: hdd over 2f out: rallied and ev ch over 1f out: outpcd ins fnl f* 5/2[1] | 73 |
| 1220 | 5 | 2 3/4 | **Forever A Lady (IRE)**[12] 3828 4-9-10 **76** GrahamLee 1 (Keith Dalgleish) *led 2f: chsd ldr to over 3f out: rdn over 2f out: wknd fnl f* 7/1 | 70 |
| 55-6 | 6 | 1/2 | **Sepal (USA)**[10] 3911 4-8-12 **71** (h) JamieGormley(7) 8 (Iain Jardine) *s.i.s: hld up: pushed along and outpcd 3f out: n.d after* 20/1 | 63 |
| -566 | 7 | 5 | **Miss Van Gogh**[23] 3433 5-10-0 **80** JackGarritty 7 (Richard Fahey) *hld up: drvn along 3f out: sn no imp: btn fnl 2f* 5/1 | 61 |
| 401 | 8 | 14 | **Souls In The Wind (IRE)**[22] 3448 3-9-4 **80** TadhgO'Shea 9 (John Patrick Shanahan, Ire) *s.i.s: hld up: pushed along and outpcd wl over 2f out: sn btn* 16/1 | 27 |

1m 50.44s (2.04) **Going Correction** +0.40s/f (Good)

**WFA** 3 from 4yo+ 10lb **8 Ran SP% 112.6**

Speed ratings (Par 102): **105,101,100,99,96 96,91,77**

CSF £78.27 CT £400.05 TOTE £4.50: £1.50, £5.20, £1.70; EX 108.90 Trifecta £367.30.

**Owner** Hambleton Racing Ltd XVI **Bred** Newlands House Stud **Trained** Hambleton, N Yorks

**FOCUS**

Rail alignment added 13 yards to the official distance. A fair fillies' handicap for the grade and the winner took this well.

## 4249 PATERSONS OF GREENOAKHILL H'CAP 5f 7y

**8:40** (8:42) (Class 4) (0-80,80) 3-Y-0+ **£7,470** (£2,236; £1,118; £559; £279; £140) **Stalls** Centre

| Form | | | | RPR |
|---|---|---|---|---|
| 4000 | 1 | | **Desert Ace (IRE)**[15] 3707 6-9-3 **71** (p) TomEaves 3 (Iain Jardine) *mde all: sn crossed fr wd draw to r against stands' rail: rdn over 1f out: kpt on strly: unchal* 16/1 | 80 |
| 1046 | 2 | 1 1/4 | **Black Grass**[14] 3741 4-9-9 **80** NathanEvans(3) 4 (Michael Easterby) *chsd wnr on outside: rdn and edgd rt over 1f out: kpt on fnl f: nt pce of wnr* 7/1 | 85+ |
| 6-06 | 3 | 2 3/4 | **Star Citizen**[17] 3667 5-9-5 **73** KevinStott 11 (Fred Watson) *in tch: rdn over 2f out: hdwy over 1f out: kpt on fnl f: nvr rchd ldrs* 8/1 | 68 |
| 4522 | 4 | 1 1/4 | **Honeysuckle Lil (IRE)**[15] 3707 5-9-2 **73** (p) RachelRichardson(3) 1 (Tim Easterby) *prom on outside: drvn along over 2f out: outpcd fnl f* 5/2[1] | 63+ |
| 0-20 | 5 | 2 1/4 | **Economic Crisis (IRE)**[15] 3707 8-8-7 **75** AndrewMullen 6 (Colin Teague) *dwlt: hld up: rdn and hdwy over 1f out: no imp fnl f* 25/1 | 57 |
| 6006 | 6 | 3 1/2 | **Salvatore Fury (IRE)**[8] 3974 7-9-1 **69** (v) GrahamLee 8 (Keith Dalgleish) *hld up: rdn and outpcd over 2f out: no imp over 1f out* 14/1 | 38 |
| 5034 | 7 | 3/4 | **Foxtrot Knight**[14] 3741 5-9-10 **78** JackGarritty 7 (Ruth Carr) *hld up bhd ldng gp: effrt and rdn over 2f out: wknd over 1f out* 9/2[3] | 45 |

5154 **8** 2 **Casterbridge**[15] 3707 5-9-5 **73** NeilFarley 9 33
(Eric Alston) *chsd ldrs tl rdn and wknd wl over 1f out* **3/1**[2]

1m 1.21s (1.21) **Going Correction** +0.375s/f (Good) **8** Ran SP% **111.8**
Speed ratings (Par 105): **105,103,98,96,93 87,86,83**
CSF £116.48 CT £965.06 TOTE £18.20: £4.00, £2.30, £2.50; EX 93.00 Trifecta £845.80.
**Owner** Excelsior Racing Ltd **Bred** Kildaragh Stud **Trained** Carrutherstown, D'fries & G'way

**FOCUS**
A modest sprint handicap for the grade and the winner made most of the running up the stands' rail, which was the place to be all evening in these rain-softened conditions.

## 4250 RACINGUK.COM H'CAP — 6f 6y
**9:10** (9:11) (Class 5) (0-75,77) 3-Y-0+ **£3,881** (£1,155; £577; £288) **Stalls** Centre

Form RPR

-221 **1** **Hee Haw (IRE)**[10] 3897 3-9-9 **77** 6ex GrahamLee 10 86+
(Keith Dalgleish) *prom cl to stands' rail: effrt and rdn over 1f out: led ins fnl f: hld on wl cl home* **15/8**[1]

4622 **2** ½ **Manshood (IRE)**[20] 3524 4-9-13 **74** (b) BenCurtis 7 83
(Paul Midgley) *trckd ldrs: effrt and rdn 2f out: ev ch ins fnl f: kpt on: hld nr fin* **7/2**[2]

2-16 **3** ½ **Control Centre (IRE)**[21] 3496 3-9-5 **73** (p[1]) BarryMcHugh 8 78
(Marjorie Fife) *cl up against stands' rail: led 2f out: rdn and hdd ins fnl f: kpt on same pce* **14/1**

0006 **4** 1¾ **Kenny The Captain (IRE)**[12] 3847 6-9-9 **73** RachelRichardson[(3)] 1 75+
(Tim Easterby) *prom on outside: effrt and edgd lft over 1f out: ch ins fnl f: no ex nr fin* **11/2**[3]

31 **5** 4 **Lackaday**[19] 3563 5-9-0 **61** (p) PatrickMathers 5 50
(Noel Wilson) *led to 2f out: rdn and outpcd whn hmpd ent fnl f: sn btn* **16/1**

330 **6** ¾ **Dandyleekie (IRE)**[19] 3585 5-9-9 **77** (p) PatrickVaughan[(7)] 6 64
(David O'Meara) *hld up: rdn over 2f out: no imp fr over 1f out* **9/1**

0-04 **7** 5 **Pennine Warrior**[16] 3702 6-8-9 **56** oh2 (p) DavidAllan 3 27
(Scott Dixon) *hmpd s: bhd and pushed along: struggling 1/2-way: nvr on terms* **14/1**

20-5 **8** 1½ **Naples Bay**[24] 3386 3-9-7 **75** JasonHart 2 39
(John Quinn) *in tch: drvn along over 2f out: wknd wl over 1f out* **18/1**

5523 **9** 7 **The Magic Pencil (IRE)**[68] 1979 4-9-3 **64** (v) TomEaves 4 7
(Kevin Ryan) *chsd ldrs: drvn along over 2f out: wknd over 1f out* **14/1**

1m 14.16s (1.96) **Going Correction** +0.375s/f (Good)
**WFA** 3 from 4yo+ 7lb **9** Ran SP% **113.5**
Speed ratings (Par 103): **101,100,99,97,92 91,84,82,73**
CSF £8.02 CT £67.01 TOTE £2.70: £1.10, £1.30, £4.70; EX 7.40 Trifecta £77.30.
**Owner** Mrs Janis Macpherson **Bred** Ballinvana House Stud **Trained** Carluke, S Lanarks

**FOCUS**
A fairly competitive handicap for the grade and it was taken by an improving animal, and the race has been rated positively.
T/Plt: £197.70 to a £1 stake. Pool: £65,892.37 - 243.24 winning units. T/Qpdt: £37.10 to a £1 stake. Pool: £7,177.71 - 143 winning units. **Richard Young**

# 3746 NEWBURY (L-H)
### Thursday, June 29

**OFFICIAL GOING: Good to firm (good in places; watered; 6.3)**
Wind: virtually nil Weather: overcast

## 4251 PUMP TECHNOLOGY H'CAP — 7f (S)
**5:50** (5:52) (Class 5) (0-75,75) 3-Y-0+ **£3,234** (£962; £481; £240) **Stalls** High

Form RPR

-011 **1** **Pursuing Steed**[27] 3296 3-8-11 **70** CharlieBennett[(3)] 15 78+
(Hughie Morrison) *hld up bhd: rdn and hdwy over 1f out: led fnl 100yds: r.o strly* **3/1**[1]

3222 **2** 1¾ **Delfie Lane**[13] 3774 3-8-9 **72** (p) FinleyMarsh[(7)] 10 75
(Richard Hughes) *mid-div: hdwy over 2f out: rdn over 1f out: kpt on wl ins fnl f: wnt 2nd towards fin: nt pce of wnr* **6/1**[2]

1-40 **3** nk **Coastal Cyclone**[29] 3211 3-9-4 **74** DavidProbert 9 76
(Harry Dunlop) *led: rdn over 1f out: kpt on but no ex whn hdd fnl 100yds* **8/1**

-004 **4** nk **Diable D'Or (IRE)**[18] 3621 3-8-13 **72** EdwardGreatrex[(3)] 12 74+
(Eve Johnson Houghton) *hld up towards rr: nt best of runs but hdwy over 1f out: rdn and r.o wl fnl f but nt quite pce to threaten* **10/1**

6210 **5** hd **Danecase**[16] 3696 4-9-6 **74** RossaRyan[(7)] 8 78
(David Dennis) *s.i.s: sn trcking ldrs: rdn to chse ldr over 1f out: kpt on same pce fnl 120yds* **10/1**

6415 **6** 3½ **Black Dave (IRE)**[26] 3325 7-9-4 **65** DaneO'Neill 11 60
(David Evans) *chsd ldrs: rdn over 2f out: sn one pce* **25/1**

5-50 **7** ¾ **Chica De La Noche**[11] 3869 3-9-2 **72** JFEgan 3 62
(Simon Dow) *mid-div: hdwy over 2f out: rdn in cl 3rd wl over 1f out: wknd ent fnl f* **11/1**

1630 **8** shd **Anonymous John (IRE)**[16] 3696 5-9-6 **74** KatherineGlenister[(7)] 4 66
(Dominic Ffrench Davis) *nvr bttr than mid-div* **16/1**

-403 **9** 1¼ **Sarangoo**[11] 3869 9-9-9 **75** GeorgiaCox[(5)] 1 64
(Malcolm Saunders) *prom: rdn over 2f out: grad fdd* **13/2**[3]

44-0 **10** 1¾ **Sir Compton**[83] 1603 4-9-0 **61** MartinDwyer 13 45
(Stuart Kittow) *racd keenly: sn trcking ldrs: effrt over 2f out: wkng whn short of room over 1f out* **33/1**

0-00 **11** 1¾ **Topology**[35] 3009 4-9-12 **73** JackMitchell 2 53
(Joseph Tuite) *chsd ldrs: rdn over 3f out: sn btn* **12/1**

2000 **12** 1¼ **Fairway To Heaven (IRE)**[22] 3454 8-9-5 **71** JennyPowell[(5)] 14 47
(Lee Carter) *s.i.s: rdn 3f out: a towards rr* **66/1**

4610 **13** 2 **El Torito (IRE)**[24] 3412 3-9-5 **75** (p) SamHitchcott 16 43
(Jim Boyle) *mid-div: rdn over 2f out: wknd over 1f out* **20/1**

300 **14** 1 **Corporal Maddox**[13] 3773 10-8-9 **63** (p) WilliamCox[(7)] 7 31
(Ronald Harris) *chsd ldrs: rdn 3f out: wknd over 1f out* **50/1**

1m 26.01s (0.31) **Going Correction** +0.05s/f (Good)
**WFA** 3 from 4yo+ 9lb **14** Ran SP% **118.8**
Speed ratings (Par 103): **100,98,97,97,97 93,92,92,90,88 86,85,82,81**
CSF £18.29 CT £136.68 TOTE £3.60: £1.60, £2.10, £3.30; EX 10.90 Trifecta £101.10.
**Owner** Caveat Emptor Partnership **Bred** A E Smith And Co **Trained** East Ilsley, Berks

**FOCUS**
A fair handicap and the progressive winner did it well.

## 4252 WIN RACES WITH JONATHAN PORTMAN FILLIES' NOVICE AUCTION STKS (PLUS 10 RACE) — 6f
**6:20** (6:22) (Class 4) 2-Y-O **£3,946** (£1,174; £586; £293) **Stalls** High

Form RPR

5312 **1** **Queen Of Kalahari**[28] 3230 2-9-1 **70** CallumShepherd[(3)] 8 72
(Charles Hills) *mde all: rdn whn drifted lft ent fnl f: kpt on wl* **6/1**

0544 **2** nk **Controversial Lady (IRE)**[42] 2750 2-8-8 **57** LiamJones 11 61
(J S Moore) *trckd ldrs: hmpd whn swtchd rt ent fnl f: r.o fnl 100yds: swtchd lft to go 2nd cl home* **20/1**

6 **3** ¾ **Sienna Says**[30] 3169 2-8-12 **0** RobertWinston 1 63
(Tony Carroll) *prom: rdn to chse wnr 2f out: kpt on tl no ex cl home* **13/2**

0 **4** ¾ **One For June (IRE)**[29] 3215 2-9-0 **0** JamesDoyle 10 67+
(William Haggas) *in tch: pushed along 2f out: nt clr run ins fnl f: wnt 4th towards fin* **9/2**[2]

6231 **5** 1¼ **Lexington Grace (IRE)**[10] 3902 2-8-13 **66** RossaRyan[(7)] 5 68
(Richard Hannon) *cl up: hmpd over 1f out: sn rdn: kpt on ins fnl f but nt pce to get on terms* **4/1**[1]

**6** nk **Isabella Mayson** 2-8-8 **0** MartinDwyer 4 52
(Stuart Kittow) *s.i.s: last pair: kpt on ins fnl f but no threat to ldrs* **25/1**

0 **7** nse **Show Of Force**[29] 3210 2-8-12 **0** RichardKingscote 2 56
(Jonathan Portman) *in tch: squeezed up briefly 2f out: sn rdn: nt pce to get involved* **11/2**[3]

0 **8** 2 **Shoyd**[23] 3421 2-8-12 **0** KieranO'Neill 7 50
(Richard Hannon) *prom: edgd lft whn rdn 2f out: wknd fnl 120yds* **16/1**

05 **9** 4½ **Cove Beach**[12] 3807 2-9-0 **0** DavidProbert 9 38
(Paul Cole) *trckd ldrs: carried lft 2f out: sn rdn: wknd ins fnl f* **25/1**

421 **10** 1 **Magic Applause (IRE)**[26] 3328 2-8-11 **70** FletcherYarham[(7)] 3 39
(George Scott) *prom: effrt 2f out: wknd ent fnl f* **6/1**

**11** 9 **Changing (IRE)** 2-8-8 **0** WilliamCarson 6 2
(Daniel Kubler) *s.i.s: a bhd* **50/1**

1m 14.36s (1.36) **Going Correction** +0.05s/f (Good) **11** Ran SP% **115.8**
Speed ratings (Par 92): **92,91,90,89,87 87,87,84,78,77 65**
CSF £121.50 TOTE £6.90: £2.00, £4.20, £2.50; EX 108.60 Trifecta £673.10.
**Owner** Mrs J K Powell **Bred** Minster Stud **Trained** Lambourn, Berks

**FOCUS**
Ordinary form for the grade. They went a sound pace with the first two home racing against the stands rail.

## 4253 PUMPMATIC PUMP STATIONS BY PUMP TECHNOLOGY FILLIES' NOVICE STKS (PLUS 10 RACE) — 7f (S)
**6:50** (6:54) (Class 4) 2-Y-O **£3,946** (£1,174; £586; £293) **Stalls** High

Form RPR

2 **1** **Time Change**[26] 3312 2-9-0 **0** PatDobbs 12 75+
(Ralph Beckett) *trckd ldrs: nt clr run over 1f out: swtchd lft to push way through over 1f out: led sn after: hld on: rdn out* **11/4**[1]

5 **2** hd **Tig Tog (IRE)**[11] 3858 2-9-0 **0** TomMarquand 10 74+
(Richard Hannon) *hld up towards rr: hdwy over 1f out: rdn ent fnl f: r.o strly: pressed wnr fnl 75yds: jst hld* **20/1**

**3** 2 **Dance Me (USA)** 2-8-9 **0** MitchGodwin[(5)] 4 69
(Sylvester Kirk) *s.i.s: towards rr: hdwy over 2f out: rdn and drifted to far side over 1f out: kpt on ins fnl f* **20/1**

0 **4** 1 **Juliet Capulet (IRE)**[26] 3312 2-9-0 **0** (p[1]) RobertTart 3 66
(John Gosden) *trckd ldrs: rdn to chse wnr jst ins fnl f: kpt on same pce fnl 120yds* **10/1**

**5** ¾ **Sukhovey (USA)** 2-9-0 **0** KierenFox 8 64
(Michael Attwater) *trckd ldrs: sltly outpcd 2f out: kpt on ins fnl f* **100/1**

25 **6** nk **She Believes (IRE)**[28] 3245 2-9-0 **0** LiamKeniry 11 64
(Sylvester Kirk) *led: rdn and hdd jst over 1f out: sn no ex* **12/1**

**7** nk **So Crafty** 2-9-0 **0** CharlesBishop 6 63
(Eve Johnson Houghton) *mid-div: hdwy over 2f out: sn rdn to chse ldrs: kpt on same pce fnl f* **25/1**

**8** 1¼ **Richenza (FR)** 2-8-9 **0** PatrickO'Donnell[(5)] 5 59
(Ralph Beckett) *chsd ldrs: rdn 2f out: one pce fnl f* **25/1**

**9** ¾ **Mahaarat** 2-9-0 **0** DaneO'Neill 2 59+
(Sir Michael Stoute) *mid-div: pushed along 1/2-way: nvr gng pce to get involved* **9/1**

**10** 1¾ **Sunday Best** 2-9-0 **0** RichardKingscote 14 53
(Jonathan Portman) *slowly away and hmpd s: towards rr of mid-div: sme minor late prog: n.d* **50/1**

2023 **11** 1¾ **Angel Of The South (IRE)**[17] 3668 2-9-0 **75** RobertWinston 13 53
(Dean Ivory) *wnt rt s: mid-divison: effrt 2f out: nt pce to get on terms: hld whn nt clr run ins fnl f: eased* **9/2**[2]

**12** ¾ **Dark Blue (IRE)** 2-9-0 **0** JFEgan 15 46
(Mick Channon) *a towards rr* **25/1**

**13** 2½ **The Mums** 2-9-0 **0** JamesDoyle 16 39
(John Gosden) *mid-div: pushed along 1/2-way: wknd ent fnl f* **6/1**[3]

3 **14** 2¾ **Moggy (USA)**[16] 3687 2-9-0 **0** ShaneKelly 1 32
(Richard Hughes) *prom: rdn 2f out: bmpd jst over 1f out: sn wknd* **12/1**

**15** 7 **Filly Mignon** 2-9-0 **0** MartinDwyer 7 13
(Brendan Powell) *towards rr of mid-div: rdn wl over 2f out: wknd over 1f out* **100/1**

**16** 1 **Arachina (IRE)** 2-9-0 **0** DavidProbert 9 10
(Harry Dunlop) *prom tl rdn over 2f out: wknd over 1f out* **100/1**

1m 26.73s (1.03) **Going Correction** +0.05s/f (Good) **16** Ran SP% **119.6**
Speed ratings (Par 92): **96,95,93,92,91 91,90,89,88,86 84,83,80,77,69 68**
CSF £65.72 TOTE £3.60: £1.50, £6.20, £5.90; EX 59.90 Trifecta £883.10.
**Owner** R Barnett **Bred** W & R Barnett Ltd **Trained** Kimpton, Hants

**FOCUS**
The pace was honest for this interesting novice contest.

## 4254 PEGASUS PUMPS LTD H'CAP — 1m 2f
**7:25** (7:25) (Class 4) (0-85,84) 3-Y-0+ **£4,690** (£1,395; £697; £348) **Stalls** Centre

Form RPR

1630 **1** **Doctor Bartolo (IRE)**[19] 3583 3-8-8 **76** WilliamCarson 12 85
(Charles Hills) *trckd ldrs: rdn to take narrow advantage wl over 1f out: strly pressed fnl f: styd on wl to assert towards fin* **12/1**

531 **2** ¾ **Pilgrim's Treasure (USA)**[21] 3485 3-9-0 **82** (p) JamesDoyle 10 90
(Charlie Appleby) *prom: rdn to ld briefly jst over 2f out: kpt on w ev ch fnl f: no ex nring fin* **11/4**[1]

66-1 **3** 2 **Hollywood Road (IRE)**[17] 3670 4-9-11 **84** (b) GeorgeWood[(3)] 2 87
(Don Cantillon) *mid-div: rdn over 3f out: styd on fnl f: wnt 3rd fnl 110yds: nt pce of front pair* **8/1**

-054 **4** *1* **Primogeniture (IRE)**[51] 3504 6-9-11 **81**................ RichardKingscote 7 82
(Mary Hambro) *in tch: rdn 2f out: kpt on same pce fnl f: wnt 4th fnl strides* **33/1**

340- **5** *nk* **Ladurelli (IRE)**[274] 6870 5-9-8 **78**.............................. DavidProbert 8 78
(Paul Cole) *led: rdn and hdd over 2f out: kpt on same pce fnl f* **16/1**

2-41 **6** *¾* **Sporting Times**[16] 3682 3-9-1 **83**.............................. DaneO'Neill 5 82+
(Ed Dunlop) *mid-divsion on outer: effrt 2f out: nt pce to get on terms* **7/2**[2]

3412 **7** *nk* **Boycie**[14] 3744 4-9-2 **79**.............................. TinaSmith(7) 3 77
(Richard Hannon) *mid-div: rdn over 2f out: kpt on same pce fnl f* **10/1**

1-26 **8** *¾* **Makaarim**[110] 1142 3-9-1 **83**.............................. DanielMuscutt 9 80
(Marco Botti) *hld up: rdn 2f out: kpt on fnl f but nt pce to get on terms* **11/1**

0006 **9** *¾* **Cricklewood Green (USA)**[14] 3750 6-9-2 **77**.......... MitchGodwin(5) 11 72
(Sylvester Kirk) *hld up: rdn over 2f out: kpt on fnl f but nt pce to get involved* **22/1**

5-24 **10** *¾* **Wannabe Friends**[47] 2624 4-9-9 **79**.............................. ShaneKelly 6 73
(Richard Hughes) *hld up: effrt 3f out: nt pce to get involved* **6/1**[3]

110- **11** *½* **Unison (IRE)**[75] 7189 7-9-9 **79**.............................. DougieCostello 4 72
(Jeremy Scott) *trckd ldrs: rdn 3f out: sn one pce: no ex fnl 120yds* **25/1**

2m 8.43s (-0.37) **Going Correction** +0.10s/f (Good)
**WFA** 3 from 4yo+ 12lb 11 Ran SP% **116.4**
Speed ratings (Par 105): **105,104,102,102,101 101,100,100,99,99 98**
CSF £43.66 CT £288.53 TOTE £14.00: £3.80, £1.30, £1.90; EX 59.90 Trifecta £349.70.
**Owner** W Carson, C Corbett, M Gibbens, C Wright **Bred** Tally-Ho Stud **Trained** Lambourn, Berks

**FOCUS**
Add 10.5yds. They went an even tempo for this competitive handicap. It paid to race handy.

## 4255 JUNG PUMPEN & PUMP TECHNOLOGY H'CAP 1m
**8:00** (8:00) (Class 5) (0-70,70) 3-Y-O £3,881 (£1,155; £577; £288) **Stalls** High

Form RPR

0616 **1** **Kyllachys Tale (IRE)**[33] 3088 3-9-5 **68**.............................. JackMitchell 3 73
(Roger Teal) *led: narrowly hdd over 2f out: ld ent fnl f: shkn up towards fin: a holding on* **16/1**

506 **2** *nk* **Sir Gnet (IRE)**[27] 3293 3-9-2 **65**..............................(h) DavidProbert 1 69+
(Ed Dunlop) *mid-div: rdn and hdwy whn swtchd lft over 1f out: str run ins fnl f: nvr quite rching wnr* **16/1**

0306 **3** *¾* **Challow (IRE)**[31] 3162 3-9-3 **66**.............................. LiamKeniry 9 68
(Sylvester Kirk) *.prom: rdn into narrow ld over 2f out: hdd ent fnl f: no ex fnl 120yds* **11/1**

00-4 **4** *½* **Heart Of Gold**[19] 3595 3-8-11 **65**.............................. DavidEgan(5) 5 66
(William Muir) *racd keenly: trckd ldrs: rdn over 2f out: kpt on ins fnl f* **10/1**

-300 **5** *nk* **Sakurajima (IRE)**[31] 3162 3-8-12 **64**..................(t) CallumShepherd(3) 2 64
(Charles Hills) *s.i.s: towards rr: hdwy over 2f out: sn rdn: styd on fnl f but nt pce to get on terms* **11/1**

4-30 **6** *2½* **Dance Teacher (IRE)**[22] 3461 3-9-5 **68**.............................. PatDobbs 4 63
(Ralph Beckett) *mid-div: rdn over 2f out: nt pce to get involved* **3/1**[1]

0120 **7** *2½* **Badenscoth**[18] 3627 3-9-7 **70**..............................(h) RobertWinston 10 59
(Dean Ivory) *mid-divsion: hdwy 3f out: ev ch 2f out: sn rdn: fdd ins fnl f* **7/2**[2]

1-20 **8** *½* **Raj Balaraaj (GER)**[24] 3412 3-9-6 **69**.............................. FranBerry 7 57
(George Baker) *trckd ldrs: rdn over 2f out: wknd jst over 1f out* **8/1**[3]

0-00 **9** *2¾* **Herm (IRE)**[14] 3751 3-9-1 **64**..............................(t[1]) JFEgan 6 45
(David Evans) *mid-div: hdwy over 3f out: rdn to chse ldrs over 2f out: sn hld: wknd over 1f out* **16/1**

600 **10** *1¼* **Canford Tor (IRE)**[16] 3691 3-9-4 **67**.............................. DaneO'Neill 11 45
(Henry Candy) *s.i.s and ducked lft sn after s: bhd: latched on to main gp 5f out: rdn over 2f out: sn hung lft: nvr threatened* **9/1**

20-0 **11** *2½* **Salieri (FR)**[18] 3627 3-9-1 **64**.............................. TomMarquand 12 37
(Alan King) *s.i.s: a towards rr* **16/1**

1m 39.68s (0.98) **Going Correction** +0.10s/f (Good) 11 Ran SP% **117.6**
Speed ratings (Par 99): **99,98,97,97,97 94,92,91,88,87 85**
CSF £247.44 CT £2969.18 TOTE £20.60: £4.60, £3.20, £3.20; EX 312.40 Trifecta £1857.60.
**Owner** Barry Kitcherside **Bred** Old Carhue Stud **Trained** Great Shefford, Berks

**FOCUS**
Add 3.5yds. An open handicap.

## 4256 LEE SAN MARINE SANITATION H'CAP 6f
**8:30** (8:31) (Class 5) (0-70,72) 3-Y-O+ £3,881 (£1,155; £577; £288) **Stalls** High

Form RPR

0033 **1** **Delagate This Lord**[33] 3085 3-8-13 **67**..............................(p) DavidEgan(5) 11 73
(Michael Attwater) *racd stands' side: trckd ldrs: rdn 2f out: overall ldr over 1f out: kpt on: drvn out* **9/1**

6-13 **2** *nk* **Swanton Blue (IRE)**[16] 3696 4-9-11 **70**.............. CallumShepherd(3) 4 77
(Ed de Giles) *overall ldr in center: rdn and drifted rt whn hdd over 1f out: kpt on: hld nring fin* **15/2**[3]

5-66 **3** *1¼* **Vincenzo Coccotti (USA)**[24] 3401 5-9-7 **66**............ HectorCrouch(3) 5 69
(Ken Cunningham-Brown) *chsd ldr in center: rdn over 2f out: kpt on ins fnl f but nt pce to chal* **12/1**

1663 **4** *1¼* **Indian Affair**[13] 3774 7-9-2 **65**..............................(bt) FinleyMarsh(7) 3 64
(Milton Bradley) *mid-div in center gp: rdn over 2f out: hdwy over 1f out: kpt on same pce fnl f* **16/1**

2111 **5** *hd* **Deeds Not Words (IRE)**[17] 3660 6-10-1 **71**.............(p) DavidProbert 13 69
(Michael Wigham) *racd stands' side: mid-div: hdwy over 2f out: sn rdn: kpt on fnl f but nt pce to get on terms* **5/1**[1]

-222 **6** *1* **Excellent Sunset (IRE)**[29] 3194 3-9-9 **72**.............................. JamesDoyle 16 65+
(David Lanigan) *racd stands' side: hld up: hdwy fr 2f out: kpt on fnl f but nvr any threat* **8/1**

6504 **7** *½* **Born To Finish (IRE)**[16] 3696 4-10-2 **72**.............................. DougieCostello 8 66+
(Jamie Osborne) *s.i.s: racd stands' side: towards rr: kpt on fr over 1f out: n.d* **7/1**[2]

4440 **8** *2½* **Chetan**[16] 3702 5-9-6 **62**..............................(tp) AdamBeschizza 1 48
(Charlie Wallis) *a mid-div in center gp* **12/1**

5031 **9** *nk* **Showmethewayavrilo**[13] 3774 4-9-10 **69**.............. CharlieBennett(3) 6 54
(Malcolm Saunders) *rrd leaving stalls: sn chsng ldrs on stands' side: one pce fnl 2f* **7/1**[2]

0500 **10** *2½* **Divine Call**[13] 3774 10-8-9 **51** oh3..............................(b) MartinDwyer 2 28
(Milton Bradley) *hld up in center gp: rdn into midfield over 1f out: no further imp fnl f* **66/1**

0014 **11** *nk* **Flowing Clarets**[17] 3659 4-9-5 **61**.............................. WilliamCarson 12 37
(John Bridger) *racd stands' side: chsd ldrs: rdn over 2f out: wknd jst over 1f out* **25/1**

4301 **12** *5* **Jaganory (IRE)**[12] 3811 5-8-11 **58**..............................(p) LuluStanford(5) 14 18
(Christopher Mason) *racd stands' side: in tch tl wknd over 1f out* **20/1**

5006 **13** *1½* **Rockley Point**[12] 3816 4-10-1 **71**..............................(p) JoeyHaynes 15 26
(Paul D'Arcy) *racd stands' side: mid-div tl wknd over 1f out* **20/1**

0-00 **14** *1¼* **Hidden Oasis (IRE)**[20] 3540 6-10-1 **71**..............................(p) FranBerry 9 22
(Jonjo O'Neill) *s.i.s: a towards rr on stands' side* **16/1**

0-20 **15** *1¼* **Harrison Stickle**[27] 3280 5-9-8 **64**.............................. FergusSweeney 10 11
(John Gallagher) *led stands' side gp tl over 2f out: sn wknd* **25/1**

1m 12.74s (-0.26)
**WFA** 3 from 4yo+ 7lb 15 Ran SP% **120.4**
CSF £69.25 CT £844.82 TOTE £11.90: £4.20, £3.10, £3.50; EX 92.70 Trifecta £1008.60.
**Owner** Mrs M S Teversham **Bred** Mrs Monica Teversham **Trained** Epsom, Surrey

**FOCUS**
A competitive race for the grade.

## 4257 PUMP TECHNOLOGY APPRENTICE H'CAP 1m 3f
**9:00** (9:01) (Class 5) (0-70,72) 4-Y-O+ £3,234 (£962; £481; £240) **Stalls** Centre

Form RPR

-104 **1** **Reckless Wave (IRE)**[27] 3292 4-9-6 **64**.............................. JennyPowell 14 73
(Ed Walker) *mde all: kpt on wl fnl f: drvn out* **11/2**

40-0 **2** *1¼* **Inn The Bull (GER)**[16] 3683 4-9-9 **67**..............................(t[1]) PaddyPilley 3 74
(Alan King) *mid-div: hdwy 2f out: sn rdn: chsd wnr ent fnl f: kpt on: hld nring fin* **14/1**

-045 **3** *2½* **Loving Your Work**[16] 3694 6-8-11 **58**.............................. JoshuaBryan(3) 13 61
(Ken Cunningham-Brown) *hld up: hdwy 3f out: rdn over 2f out: chal for 2nd over 1f out: kpt on same pce ins fnl f* **5/1**[3]

2664 **4** *2½* **Jack Of Diamonds (IRE)**[13] 3771 8-9-7 **70**..............(b) RossaRyan(5) 2 69
(Roger Teal) *s.i.s: sn mid-div: hdwy over 3f out: rdn and hung lft over 1f out: styd on same pce* **9/2**[2]

-600 **5** *1¼* **Elusive Cowboy (USA)**[27] 3308 4-9-7 **70**.............................. WilliamCox(5) 10 67
(Chris Gordon) *trckd ldrs: outpcd over 2f out: styd on ins fnl f but n.d* **20/1**

-003 **6** *nse* **Maestro Mac (IRE)**[12] 3813 4-9-5 **68**.............................. TheodoreLadd(5) 12 65
(Hughie Morrison) *racd keenly: trckd ldrs: rdn wl over 2f out: nt pce to chal: no ex ins fnl f* **9/2**[2]

400 **7** *3½* **Hong Kong Joe**[19] 3575 7-8-2 **51** oh5.............................. AledBeech(5) 9 42
(Lydia Richards) *s.i.s: towards rr: styd on fnl f: nvr threatened ldrs* **25/1**

033 **8** *hd* **Camakasi (IRE)**[36] 2971 6-10-0 **72**.............................. CliffordLee 7 62
(Ali Stronge) *mid-div: hdwy over 3f out: sn rdn to chse ldrs: hld whn bmpd over 1f out: wknd* **4/1**[1]

0-00 **9** *3½* **Classic Mission**[14] 3753 6-8-9 **58**..................(b) Pierre-LouisJamin(5) 4 42
(Jonathan Portman) *s.i.s: a towards rr* **20/1**

-155 **10** *3* **Roy Rocket (FR)**[17] 3658 7-9-8 **71**.............................. NicolaCurrie(5) 1 50
(John Berry) *stdd s: bhd: hdwy over 3f out: short-lived effrt over 2f out* **14/1**

424/ **11** *4½* **Kingston Mimosa**[30] 6239 5-8-4 **51** oh2....................(p) JordanUys(3) 11 23
(Mark Gillard) *mid-div: effrt over 3f out: sn hung lft and wknd* **50/1**

2m 23.85s (2.65) **Going Correction** +0.10s/f (Good) 11 Ran SP% **117.1**
Speed ratings (Par 103): **94,93,91,89,88 88,85,85,83,81 77**
CSF £74.24 CT £411.76 TOTE £8.20: £2.70, £3.50, £1.80; EX 60.80 Trifecta £840.30.
**Owner** Mrs T Walker **Bred** John Connaughton **Trained** Upper Lambourn, Berks

**FOCUS**
Add 10.5yds. The pace was steady for this open contest.
T/Jkpt: Not won. T/Plt: £2,782.90 to a £1 stake. Pool: £75,291.28 - 19.75 winning units. T/Qpdt: £496.80 to a £1 stake. Pool: £6,881.54 - 10.25 winning units. **Tim Mitchell**

# 3339 NEWCASTLE (A.W) (L-H)
Thursday, June 29

**OFFICIAL GOING: Tapeta: standard**
Wind: Light Across Weather: Wet

## 4258 BETFRED "CELEBRATING 50 YEARS OF SUCCESS" NOVICE MEDIAN AUCTION STKS 7f 14y (Tp)
**2:00** (2:04) (Class 5) 2-Y-O £4,528 (£1,347; £673; £336) **Stalls** Centre

Form RPR

253 **1** **Kit Marlowe**[14] 3754 2-9-2 **87**.............................. PJMcDonald 1 74
(Mark Johnston) *wnt sltly lft s: w ldr: led over 2f out: rdn over 1f out: pressed thrght fnl f: kpt on wl* **11/4**[2]

32 **2** *nk* **Weellan**[17] 3648 2-9-2 **0**.............................. PhillipMakin 5 73
(John Quinn) *trckd ldrs: pushed along over 2f out: rdn over 1f out: edgd lft ins fnl f: kpt on* **5/2**[1]

341 **3** *hd* **Benadalid**[26] 3339 2-9-9 **73**.............................. RoystonFfrench 8 80
(Chris Fairhurst) *trckd ldrs: rdn to chal appr fnl f: kpt on* **8/1**

0 **4** *2¾* **Hello My Sunshine**[26] 3339 2-9-2 **0**.............................. GrahamLee 6 66
(Karen McLintock) *led narrowly: hdd over 2f out: rdn over 1f out: no ex fnl f* **50/1**

2 **5** *½* **Tale Of Tails (IRE)**[14] 3754 2-9-2 **0**.............................. BenCurtis 3 65
(Brian Ellison) *hld up: rdn and sme hdwy over 1f out: no ex fnl f* **3/1**[3]

0 **6** *¾* **Hemingford (IRE)**[31] 3156 2-9-2 **0**.............................. MartinLane 9 63
(Charlie Fellowes) *in tch: pushed along 2f out: briefly short of room appr fnl f: swtchd lft ins fnl f: one pce and nvr threatened* **14/1**

**7** *1* **Molly Mayhem (IRE)** 2-8-11 **0**.............................. PaulHanagan 2 55
(Richard Fahey) *trckd ldrs: pushed along 3f out: outpcd and lost pl over 1f out* **7/1**

**8** *1½* **Working Together** 2-8-11 **0**.............................. CamHardie 7 52
(Antony Brittain) *slowly away: hld up: nvr threatened* **100/1**

**9** *19* **Gift Of Loulins** 2-8-11 **0**.............................. BarryMcHugh 4
(Tony Coyle) *hld up: pushed along over 3f out: wknd over 2f out and bhd* **40/1**

1m 29.51s (3.31) **Going Correction** +0.25s/f (Slow) 9 Ran SP% **115.9**
Speed ratings (Par 93): **91,90,90,87,86 85,84,83,61**
CSF £10.07 TOTE £3.60: £1.30, £1.30, £2.30; EX 10.90 Trifecta £39.80.
**Owner** Sheikh Hamdan bin Mohammed Al Maktoum **Bred** Godolphin **Trained** Middleham Moor, N Yorks

**FOCUS**
A decent juvenile novice contest. They went an, at best, respectable gallop on standard Tapeta and the front three, including the two horses at the head of the betting, came clear of the fourth. The winner was entitled to win on these terms and has been rated below his best form.

## 4259 BETFRED TV NOVICE STKS (PLUS 10 RACE) 6f (Tp)
**2:30** (2:32) (Class 4) 2-Y-O £5,822 (£1,732; £865; £432) **Stalls** Centre

Form RPR

3 **1** **Curiosity (IRE)**[14] 3746 2-9-2 **0**.............................. JosephineGordon 8 80+
(Hugo Palmer) *in tch: hdwy to trck ldrs gng wl over 1f out: pushed along ins fnl f: kpt on to ld towards fin: shade cosily* **5/6**[1]

33 **2** *nk* **Move It Move It**[20] 3523 2-9-2 **0**.............................. GrahamLee 3 76
(Keith Dalgleish) *trckd ldrs: pushed along over 1f out: rdn to chal ins fnl f: led narrowly 50yds out: kpt on but hdd towards fin* **5/2**[2]



The Form Book Flat, Raceform Ltd, Newbury, RG14 5SJ

4 **3** ¾ **Big Les (IRE)**[28] 3254 2-9-2 0 TomEaves 2 74
(Karen McLintock) *led: pushed along over 1f out: rdn ins fnl f: hdd 50yds out: no ex* 15/2[3]
**4** ½ **Ulshaw Bridge (IRE)** 2-9-2 0 PaulHanagan 4 72
(James Bethell) *trckd ldrs: pushed along and bit outpcd appr fnl f: kpt on ins fnl f* 14/1
**5** ¾ **Spray The Sea (IRE)** 2-9-2 0 ConnorBeasley 7 70
(Bryan Smart) *s.i.s: hld up: hdwy and in tch over 1f out: rdn fnl f: one pce fnl 110yds* 11/1
**6** 9 **Odds On Oli** 2-9-2 0 TonyHamilton 6 43
(Richard Fahey) *stdd s: hld up: racd keenly: pushed along 2f out: sn outpcd and bhd* 20/1
5 **7** ½ **Burn Some Dust (IRE)**[20] 3523 2-9-2 0 BenCurtis 1 42
(Brian Ellison) *prom: rdn and lost pl 2f out: sn bhd* 33/1
60 **8** 4 ½ **Brough Lane Lass (IRE)**[9] 3943 2-8-11 0 LukeMorris 5 23
(John Weymes) *in tch: rdn over 2f out: wknd over 1f out* 100/1

1m 13.95s (1.45) **Going Correction** +0.25s/f (Slow) **8 Ran SP% 118.6**
Speed ratings (Par 95): **100,99,98,97,96 84,84,78**
CSF £3.15 TOTE £1.70: £1.10, £1.10, £2.50; EX 3.60 Trifecta £10.80.
**Owner** H Moorhead, C Fahy & J Collins **Bred** M Phelan **Trained** Newmarket, Suffolk

**FOCUS**
A fairly decent juvenile novice contest. They went a respectable gallop and it is sound form.

## 4260 BETFRED "SUPER LEAGUE" H'CAP 1m 2f 42y (Tp)
**3:05** (3:05) (Class 5) (0-75,76) 4-Y-0+ **£4,528** (£1,347; £673; £336) **Stalls** High

Form RPR
-222 **1** **Therthaar**[34] 3036 4-9-7 74 KevinStott 8 81
(Ismail Mohammed) *prom: led over 1f out: sn rdn: pressed ins fnl f: kpt on wl* 9/2[3]
-342 **2** hd **Henpecked**[28] 3252 7-9-3 70 (p) PaulHanagan 7 76
(Alistair Whillans) *trckd ldrs towards outer: smooth hdwy to chal over 1f out: rdn ins fnl f: one pce and a hld* 10/1
4200 **3** 1 ¾ **Strummer (IRE)**[36] 2953 4-8-10 63 (p) JoeDoyle 13 66
(Kevin Ryan) *hld up in midfield: pushed along and hdwy over 1f out: rdn to chse ldng pair ins fnl f: no ex fnl 50yds* 16/1
-166 **4** nk **Lopes Dancer (IRE)**[14] 3744 5-9-9 76 NeilFarley 9 78
(Sally Haynes) *midfield: rdn and hdwy to chse ldrs over 1f out: one pce fnl f* 14/1
0450 **5** shd **Satish**[13] 3795 4-9-0 67 (b) DanielTudhope 2 69+
(David O'Meara) *s.i.s: hld up: pushed along over 1f out: kpt on ins fnl f: nrst fin* 16/1
0-03 **6** ½ **Hernandoshideaway**[19] 3559 5-9-7 74 (bt[1]) ConnorBeasley 3 75+
(Michael Dods) *slowly away: hld up in rr: stl last over 1f out: swtchd rt to outside and kpt on wl fnl f: nrst fin* 11/1
0604 **7** shd **Leonard Thomas**[20] 3529 7-8-7 60 (p) PaddyAspell 11 61
(Philip Kirby) *hld up: sme hdwy over 1f out: rdn and kpt on fnl f: nvr threatened* 40/1
61 **8** hd **Auspicion**[28] 3252 5-9-4 71 AndrewMullen 12 71
(Tom Tate) *hld up in midfield on inner: bit short of room 2f out: rdn ent fnl f: kpt on: nvr able to chal* 10/3[1]
0021 **9** ½ **Archipeligo**[26] 3343 6-8-10 70 (p) JamieGormley[(7)] 4 69
(Iain Jardine) *trckd ldrs: rdn 2f out: one pce fnl f* 4/1[2]
-000 **10** ½ **Sikandar (IRE)**[23] 2629 5-8-10 68 (t) BenRobinson[(5)] 14 66
(Brian Ellison) *hld up: rdn and sme hdwy on outer over 2f out: one pce fnl f* 33/1
5642 **11** ½ **Perceived**[19] 3559 5-9-2 69 CamHardie 5 66
(Antony Brittain) *midfield: rdn and lost pl over 1f out: no threat after* 20/1
3 **12** 1 ¼ **Bishop Of Bling (IRE)**[52] 2468 4-9-1 68 LukeMorris 1 63
(Chris Wall) *midfield: rdn over 2f out: wknd over 1f out* 25/1
00 **13** 3 ¼ **Polar Forest**[152] 460 7-9-3 70 (e) PJMcDonald 10 58
(Richard Guest) *trckd ldrs: rdn 2f out: wknd fnl f* 16/1
2020 **14** 6 **Muqarred (USA)**[37] 2920 5-9-6 73 (p) TonyHamilton 6 49
(Roger Fell) *led: rdn whn hdd over 1f out: sn wknd* 66/1

2m 12.54s (2.14) **Going Correction** +0.25s/f (Slow) **14 Ran SP% 118.5**
Speed ratings (Par 103): **101,100,99,99,99 98,98,98,98,97 97,96,93,88**
CSF £45.44 CT £668.33 TOTE £5.00: £1.50, £2.80, £5.60; EX 42.20 Trifecta £1520.90.
**Owner** Sultan Ali **Bred** Cheveley Park Stud Ltd **Trained** Newmarket, Suffolk

**FOCUS**
A fair handicap. They went, at best, a respectable gallop and one of the market leaders gamely made the most of his prominent pitch throughout.

## 4261 BETFRED SEATON DELAVAL H'CAP 1m 5y (Tp)
**3:40** (3:40) (Class 2) (0-105,100) 4-Y-0+
**£21,787** (£6,524; £3,262; £1,631; £815; £409) **Stalls** Centre

Form RPR
2-22 **1** **Constantino (IRE)**[124] 918 4-8-11 90 (b) TonyHamilton 8 98
(Richard Fahey) *in tch: smooth hdwy 2f out: pushed along to ld appr fnl f: rdn and kpt on* 10/1
-505 **2** 1 ½ **Kentuckyconnection (USA)**[5] 4077 4-8-13 92 ConnorBeasley 13 97
(Bryan Smart) *chsd ldrs: rdn to ld over 2f out: hdd appr fnl f: one pce* 16/1
1363 **3** hd **Qaffaal (USA)**[35] 2999 6-8-9 91 NathanEvans[(3)] 3 96
(Michael Easterby) *hld up: rdn and hdwy over 1f out: kpt on* 15/2
66-0 **4** nse **One Word More (IRE)**[29] 3218 7-9-0 93 (h) DavidAllan 9 97
(Tim Easterby) *s.i.s: hld up: pushed along and hdwy 2f out: kpt on fnl f* 20/1
200- **5** hd **Claim The Roses (USA)**[220] 8049 6-8-12 91 PhillipMakin 2 95
(Ed Vaughan) *hld up in midfield: rdn and hdwy over 1f out: one pce ins fnl f* 22/1
-000 **6** 2 ¼ **Mountain Rescue (IRE)**[14] 3743 5-8-10 89 LukeMorris 1 88
(Chris Wall) *chsd ldrs: rdn over 2f out: wknd fnl f 110yds* 20/1
0400 **7** 5 **Top Notch Tonto (IRE)**[19] 3597 7-9-3 96 BenCurtis 14 83
(Brian Ellison) *prom: rdn over 2f out: wknd over 1f out* 11/1
3-36 **8** nse **Replenish (FR)**[41] 2799 4-9-1 94 TomQueally 10 81
(James Fanshawe) *midfield: rdn over 2f out: wknd over 1f out* 5/1[2]
-403 **9** 1 ¼ **Chestnut Fire**[28] 3255 5-8-6 90 LewisEdmunds[(5)] 11 74
(Daniel Mark Loughnane) *dwlt: hld up: rdn over 2f out: sn wknd* 7/1[3]
4300 **10** 4 ½ **Swift Emperor (IRE)**[21] 3498 5-8-11 90 PJMcDonald 7 64
(David Barron) *chsd ldrs: rdn over 2f out: sn wknd* 11/1
4004 **11** 2 ¼ **Hammer Gun (USA)**[7] 4001 4-8-4 83 (v) FrannyNorton 12 52
(Derek Shaw) *hld up: rdn 3f out: sn btn* 12/1
6121 **12** 29 **Briardale (IRE)**[31] 3154 5-9-7 100 PaulHanagan 6 2
(James Bethell) *led: rdn whn hdd over 2f out: wknd and eased* 7/2[1]

1m 38.43s (-0.17) **Going Correction** +0.25s/f (Slow) **12 Ran SP% 116.4**
Speed ratings (Par 109): **110,108,108,108,108 105,100,100,99,95 92,63**
CSF £151.06 CT £1287.07 TOTE £6.90: £2.30, £5.20, £2.30; EX 172.80 Trifecta £2213.90.
**Owner** Sir Robert Ogden **Bred** Sir Robert Ogden **Trained** Musley Bank, N Yorks

**FOCUS**
The feature contest was a good handicap. They went a decent gallop and there is no reason to doubt the form.

## 4262 BETFRED "WATCH SKY SPORTS IN OUR SHOPS" H'CAP (DIV I) 1m 5y (Tp)
**4:15** (4:18) (Class 6) (0-60,59) 3-Y-0+ **£3,234** (£962; £481; £240) **Stalls** Centre

Form RPR
6510 **1** **Symbolic Star (IRE)**[15] 3708 5-9-7 57 (p) CallumRodriguez[(5)] 8 68
(Barry Murtagh) *slowly away: hld up: pushed along and gd hdwy over 1f out: led ins fnl f: kpt on* 11/2[2]
-041 **2** 3 ½ **Beverley Bullet**[20] 3529 4-10-0 59 (p) DanielTudhope 9 62
(Lawrence Mullaney) *prom: led over 3f out: rdn along over 2f out: hdd ins fnl f: one pce and no ch w wnr* 7/2[1]
4600 **3** nk **Born To Reason (IRE)**[12] 3819 3-9-1 56 (h[1]) RyanPowell 5 57
(Kevin Frost) *midfield: rdn over 2f out: kpt on fnl f* 22/1
0000 **4** ½ **Swiftee (IRE)**[34] 3049 4-9-9 54 (b) DavidNolan 11 56
(Ivan Furtado) *led narrowly: rdn whn hdd over 3f out: remained prom: plugged on fnl f* 16/1
-034 **5** ¾ **Sooqaan**[20] 3546 6-9-13 58 CamHardie 7 58
(Antony Brittain) *midfield: rdn to chse ldrs over 2f out: no ex ins fnl f* 16/1
6600 **6** hd **Tranquil Tracy**[22] 3472 3-8-8 49 PaddyAspell 4 46
(John Norton) *s.i.s: hld up: rdn over 2f out: kpt on fnl f: nvr threatened* 100/1
0600 **7** 1 ¾ **Nelson's Bay**[24] 3402 8-9-4 52 NathanEvans[(3)] 6 48
(Wilf Storey) *hld up: rdn over 2f out: kpt on ins fnl f: nvr threatened* 16/1
0012 **8** 1 ¼ **Clear As A Bell (IRE)**[2] 4184 3-8-13 54 DavidAllan 2 47
(Tim Easterby) *prom: rdn over 2f out: wknd ins fnl f* 6/1[3]
00-6 **9** 1 ¼ **Kuiper Belt (USA)**[48] 2581 3-9-4 59 TomQueally 12 47
(David Lanigan) *racd keenly in midfield: pushed along over 2f out: rdn over 1f out: nvr threatened* 11/2[2]
550- **10** ¾ **Little Pippin**[196] 8386 4-9-5 50 PJMcDonald 1 38
(Tony Coyle) *hld up: rdn over 2f out: sme hdwy over 1f out: wknd ins fnl f* 50/1
4602 **11** 1 **Pensax Lady (IRE)**[20] 3550 4-9-9 54 LukeMorris 3 40
(Daniel Mark Loughnane) *midfield: rdn along over 3f out: sn wknd* 10/1
00-0 **12** hd **Wishing Tree**[22] 3473 4-8-12 48 BenRobinson[(5)] 13 34
(Brian Ellison) *a towards rr* 16/1
4050 **13** 2 **A Bit Of Ginger**[12] 3832 3-8-12 53 ShaneGray 10 32
(Ann Duffield) *racd keenly in tch: rdn over 2f out: wknd over 1f out* 20/1
000- **14** 3 ¼ **Bigbadboy (IRE)**[237] 7795 4-8-9 45 LewisEdmunds[(5)] 14 19
(Clive Mulhall) *trckd ldrs: rdn over 2f out: wknd* 33/1

1m 40.68s (2.08) **Going Correction** +0.25s/f (Slow)
**WFA** 3 from 4yo+ 10lb **14 Ran SP% 114.9**
Speed ratings (Par 101): **99,95,95,94,93 93,92,90,89,88 87,87,85,82**
CSF £22.39 CT £391.40 TOTE £6.30: £2.30, £1.80, £6.00; EX 28.10 Trifecta £474.90.
**Owner** Murtagh, O'Rourke & Trinders **Bred** Darley **Trained** Low Braithwaite, Cumbria

**FOCUS**
The first division of a modest handicap. They went a respectable gallop, and the winner has been rated near last summer's form.

## 4263 BETFRED "WATCH SKY SPORTS IN OUR SHOPS" H'CAP (DIV II) 1m 5y (Tp)
**4:50** (4:51) (Class 6) (0-60,59) 3-Y-0+ **£3,234** (£962; £481; £240) **Stalls** Centre

Form RPR
00-0 **1** **Belisa (IRE)**[78] 1730 3-9-3 58 DavidNolan 5 65
(Ivan Furtado) *hld up: hdwy over 2f out: rdn to ld over 1f out: kpt on* 8/1
-500 **2** 1 ¼ **Steel Helmet (IRE)**[35] 2991 3-8-13 59 BenRobinson[(5)] 3 63
(Brian Ellison) *trckd ldrs: rdn over 2f out: ev ch appr fnl f: kpt on same pce* 12/1
4645 **3** ½ **Jessie Allan (IRE)**[12] 3831 6-9-0 45 PJMcDonald 14 50
(Jim Goldie) *hld up: rdn and hdwy over 1f out: styd on wl fnl f: nrst fin* 20/1
3622 **4** nk **Cool Strutter (IRE)**[8] 3979 5-9-4 54 GemmaTutty[(5)] 1 58
(Karen Tutty) *hld up: pushed along and stl plenty to do 2f out: rdn and r.o ins fnl f: nrst fin* 7/1[3]
0004 **5** ¾ **State Residence (IRE)**[31] 3151 3-8-13 54 (vt[1]) DanielTudhope 13 55
(David O'Meara) *midfield: gd hdwy 2f out: drvn appr fnl f: sn one pce* 11/2[2]
2-00 **6** 1 **Eium Mac**[52] 2466 8-9-3 53 CallumRodriguez[(5)] 11 53
(Neville Bycroft) *led: rdn over 2f out: hdd over 1f out: wknd ins fnl f* 14/1
4500 **7** nk **Coral Princess (IRE)**[12] 3832 3-8-9 50 JasonHart 7 50
(Keith Dalgleish) *midfield: rdn over 1f out: kpt on fnl 110yds: nvr threatened* 14/1
0/60 **8** ¾ **Cline**[53] 2430 4-9-13 58 JoeDoyle 10 56
(Kevin Ryan) *chsd ldrs: rdn over 2f out: no ex fnl f* 20/1
0-00 **9** 1 **Rock Of Monaco**[28] 3265 4-9-3 48 (b[1]) CamHardie 8 44
(Antony Brittain) *trckd ldrs: rdn over 2f out: wknd fnl f* 25/1
0-23 **10** nse **Broctune Papa Gio**[37] 2919 10-9-8 58 LewisEdmunds[(5)] 6 54
(Gillian Boanas) *midfield: rdn over 2f out: no imp* 9/2[1]
-050 **11** ½ **Circuit**[51] 2507 3-8-3 47 (t[1]) NathanEvans[(3)] 9 40
(Wilf Storey) *s.i.s: hld up: nvr threatened* 50/1
00-0 **12** 7 **Saxon Gold (IRE)**[60] 2179 4-9-5 50 SamJames 4 29
(John Davies) *chsd ldrs: rdn over 3f out: wknd over 1f out* 50/1
320 **13** nk **Sakhalin Star (IRE)**[15] 3708 6-9-10 55 MartinLane 2 34
(Richard Guest) *prom: rdn over 3f out: wknd over 2f out* 8/1
-066 **14** 9 **Peny Arcade**[12] 3832 3-8-13 54 PaulHanagan 12 11
(Alistair Whillans) *chsd ldrs: rdn over 2f out: sn wknd* 15/2

1m 40.69s (2.09) **Going Correction** +0.25s/f (Slow)
**WFA** 3 from 4yo+ 10lb **14 Ran SP% 118.4**
Speed ratings (Par 101): **99,97,97,96,96 95,94,94,93,93 92,85,85,76**
CSF £92.14 CT £1893.71 TOTE £8.90: £3.00, £4.60, £5.20; EX 117.80 Trifecta £1612.90.
**Owner** John L Marriott & Albert L Marriott **Bred** Zalim Bifov **Trained** Wiseton, Nottinghamshire

**FOCUS**
The second division of a modest handicap. They went a respectable gallop and the race was won in an almost identical time. Improved form from the winner, with the 2nd/3rd helping to pin the level.

## 4264 BETFRED "SUPPORTS JACK BERRY HOUSE" H'CAP 7f 14y (Tp)
**5:20** (5:21) (Class 2) (0-105,101) 3-Y-0+
**£12,450** (£3,728; £1,864; £932; £466; £234) **Stalls** Centre

Form RPR
2643 **1** **War Department (IRE)**[5] 4077 4-9-4 91 (v) ConnorBeasley 1 99
(Keith Dalgleish) *trckd ldrs: rdn to ld appr fnl f: kpt on* 3/1[1]
0050 **2** 1 ½ **Florencio**[12] 3847 4-8-9 82 oh1 (p) PJMcDonald 3 86
(Roger Fell) *hld up in midfield: pushed along and hdwy over 1f out: rdn to go 2nd 110yds out: kpt on but nvr getting to wnr* 50/1

1010 3 ½ **Welliesinthewater (IRE)**[27] 3294 7-9-2 **89**..................(v) FrannyNorton 4 92
(Derek Shaw) *racd keenly in tch: rdn 2f out: kpt on same pce* **14/1**
241 4 *nk* **Safe Voyage (IRE)**[24] 3388 4-8-8 **88**................................ JoshQuinn(7) 2 90
(John Quinn) *hld up: rdn 2f out: kpt on fnl f: nvr threatened* **5/1**
-136 5 ¾ **That Is The Spirit**[19] 3587 6-10-0 **101**........................... DanielTudhope 7 101
(David O'Meara) *led: pushed along and edgd lft over 1f out: hdd appr fnl f: wknd fnl 110yds* **7/2[2]**
3-55 6 *nk* **Right Touch**[33] 3089 7-9-11 **98**........................................ PaulHanagan 5 97
(Richard Fahey) *hld up in midfield: racd quite keenly: rdn 2f out: nvr threatened* **9/2[3]**
3-50 7 1½ **Accession (IRE)**[35] 3003 8-9-9 **96**................................ MartinLane 8 91
(Charlie Fellowes) *trckd ldr: rdn over 2f out: wknd fnl f* **8/1**
0020 8 *hd* **Penwortham (IRE)**[13] 3792 4-9-3 **90**..........................(h) TonyHamilton 6 84
(Richard Fahey) *s.i.s: hld up: nvr threatened* **8/1**

1m 26.61s (0.41) **Going Correction** +0.25s/f (Slow) **8** Ran SP% **112.9**
Speed ratings (Par 109): **107,105,104,104,103 103,101,101**
CSF £127.19 CT £1800.73 TOTE £3.50: £1.40, £7.10, £3.10; EX 90.10 Trifecta £637.50.
**Owner** Weldspec Glasgow Limited **Bred** Tom McDonald **Trained** Carluke, S Lanarks

**FOCUS**
A good handicap. They went a respectable gallop and the winner registered his third C&D victory in a straightforward manner.

## 4265 BETFRED "FOLLOW US ON TWITTER" H'CAP 7f 14y (Tp)
**5:55** (5:55) (Class 5) (0-75,74) 3-Y-O **£4,528** (£1,347; £673; £336) **Stalls** Centre

Form RPR
621 1 **Pastime**[20] 3549 3-9-7 **74**......................................... JosephineGordon 10 86
(Gay Kelleway) *dwlt: hld up: smooth hdwy over 1f out: qcknd to ld ins fnl f: rdn clr: comf* **4/1[1]**
2-50 2 2¾ **Savannah Moon (IRE)**[31] 3142 3-8-10 **63**........................ JoeDoyle 7 67
(Kevin Ryan) *racd keenly: trckd ldrs: rdn over 2f out: ev ch ent fnl f: kpt on but no ch wnr fnl 110yds* **20/1**
0315 3 1¼ **Champion Harbour (IRE)**[19] 3561 3-8-10 **63**.................. PaulHanagan 5 64
(Richard Fahey) *hld up: pushed along and hdwy over 1f out: rdn and kpt on fnl f* **6/1[3]**
0444 4 *shd* **Cupid's Arrow (IRE)**[24] 3403 3-8-7 **60**........................ LukeMorris 6 61
(Ruth Carr) *led narrowly: rdn 2f out: hdd ins fnl f: no ex* **11/2[2]**
-363 5 2 **Eltanin (IRE)**[15] 3709 3-9-0 **67**..........................................(p) JasonHart 4 62
(John Quinn) *pressed ldr: rdn and edgd lft over 1f out: no ex fnl f* **7/1**
441 6 *shd* **Rey Loopy (IRE)**[41] 2792 3-8-9 **62**.................................. CamHardie 3 57
(Ben Haslam) *hld up: pushed along and hdwy 2f out: hmpd appr fnl f and again ins fnl f: no ch after but kpt on* **6/1[3]**
40-5 7 ½ **Seebring (IRE)**[19] 3555 3-8-3 **61** ow3......................(p[1]) BenRobinson(5) 9 55
(Brian Ellison) *chsd ldrs: rdn over 2f out: wknd ins fnl f* **16/1**
250 8 1½ **Hitchcock**[48] 2595 3-9-2 **69**................................................ ShaneGray 2 59
(Kevin Ryan) *trckd ldrs: rdn over 2f out: wknd ins fnl f* **25/1**
2530 9 1½ **Hollywood Harry (IRE)**[10] 3913 3-8-6 **59** ow1.........(p) ConnorBeasley 1 45
(Keith Dalgleish) *a towards rr* **12/1**
6-21 10 3 **Black Salt**[31] 3150 3-9-7 **74**............................................. PJMcDonald 8 52
(David Barron) *hld up: racd keenly and plld way to r promly 4f out: pushed along over 1f out: wknd fnl f* **6/1[3]**

1m 27.21s (1.01) **Going Correction** +0.25s/f (Slow) **10** Ran SP% **112.9**
Speed ratings (Par 99): **104,100,99,99,97 96,96,94,92,89**
CSF £84.30 CT £483.59 TOTE £4.40: £1.90, £5.30, £2.10; EX 58.90 Trifecta £669.80.
**Owner** Countrywide Classics Limited **Bred** Countrywide Classics Ltd **Trained** Exning, Suffolk

**FOCUS**
A fair 3yo handicap. They went a respectable gallop and the favourite ran out a commanding winner up the near rail.
T/Plt: £574.20 to a £1 stake. Pool: £85,468.35 - 108.64 winning units. T/Qpdt: £337.30 to a £1 stake. Pool: £5,334.19 - 11.70 winning units. **Andrew Sheret**

# 4094 NEWMARKET (R-H)
Thursday, June 29

**OFFICIAL GOING: Good to soft (soft in places; 6.6)**
Wind: virtually nil Weather: overcast

## 4266 BRITISH & IRISH LIONS BETTING AT 188BET NOVICE STKS (PLUS 10 RACE) 6f
**2:10** (2:13) (Class 4) 2-Y-O **£4,528** (£1,347; £673; £336) **Stalls** High

Form RPR
0 1 **Etefaaq (IRE)**[14] 3754 2-9-2 0................................................ SeanLevey 3 82
(Richard Hannon) *mde virtually all and set stdy gallop: rdn and qcknd over 1f out: r.o and a doing enough ins fnl f* **15/2**
03 2 ½ **Dichato (USA)**[19] 3591 2-9-2 0........................................... RyanMoore 4 80
(John Gosden) *stdd after s: hld up wl in tch in last pair: rdn over 2f out: swtchd rt and hdwy 1f out: styd on to chse wnr wl ins fnl f: clsng towards fin but nvr quite getting on terms* **7/4[1]**
1 3 ¾ **Roland Rocks (IRE)**[12] 3826 2-9-8 0.................................... AdamKirby 1 84
(John Ryan) *chsd ldrs on outer: reminder and rdn over 2f out: chsd wnr over 1f out: kpt on but a hld ins fnl f: lost 2nd wl ins fnl f* **8/1**
5 4 1 **Ragstone View (IRE)**[11] 3868 2-9-2 0................................. ShaneKelly 6 75
(Richard Hughes) *stdd after s and t.k.h early: trckd ldrs: effrt and rn green over 1f out: kpt on same pce ins fnl f* **7/2[3]**
60 5 3¾ **Patty Patch**[16] 3687 2-8-11 0..........................................(h) StevieDonohoe 2 59
(Richard Spencer) *t.k.h: w wnr: rdn 2f out: losing pl and impeded 1f out: wknd ins fnl f* **25/1**
6 1¾ **Nicklaus** 2-9-2 0..................................................................... JimCrowley 5 58
(William Haggas) *t.k.h: hld up wl in tch in last pair: effrt wl over 1f out: no imp and outpcd 1f out: wknd ins fnl f* **10/3[2]**

1m 15.65s (3.15) **Going Correction** +0.225s/f (Good) **6** Ran SP% **108.4**
Speed ratings (Par 95): **88,87,86,85,80 77**
CSF £19.68 TOTE £8.20: £3.70, £1.40; EX 22.00 Trifecta £117.30.
**Owner** Al Shaqab Racing **Bred** Grennanstown Stud & Cloneymore Farm **Trained** East Everleigh, Wilts

**FOCUS**
A fair novice, they raced on far rail and the winner had the run of things.

## 4267 WIMBLEDON TENNIS BETTING AT 188BET H'CAP 1m 4f
**2:40** (2:42) (Class 5) (0-75,77) 3-Y-O+ **£3,881** (£1,155; £577; £288) **Stalls** Centre

Form RPR
-235 1 **Mistress Quickly (IRE)**[27] 3291 3-9-0 **75**........................... PatDobbs 3 87+
(Ralph Beckett) *led for 2f: chsd ldr tl led again 4f out: rdn and kicked clr over 1f out: in command and styd on ins fnl f: comf* **10/3[1]**
0002 2 2½ **Theglasgowwarrior**[11] 3864 3-7-11 **63**.............................. DavidEgan(5) 6 70
(Michael Bell) *hld up in tch in midfield: effrt over 2f out: hdwy to chse clr wnr over 1f out: styd on for clr 2nd but no imp on wnr fnl f* **9/2[3]**
250 3 2 **Zorba The Greek**[80] 1683 5-9-9 **70**................................(h[1]) HarryBentley 11 74
(Ed Vaughan) *stdd s: hld up in last trio: clsd 4f out: clsd to chse ldrs whn swtchd rt and barging match w rival over 1f out: 3rd and styd on same pce fnl f* **11/1**
3453 4 2¼ **Peterhouse (USA)**[13] 3795 5-9-12 **76**..........................(v[1]) AaronJones(3) 5 78
(Jason Ward) *hld up in last trio: clsd 4f out: effrt whn swtchd lft and barging match w rival over 1f out: c off worse and hmpd sn after: wl hld 4th and kpt on same pce fnl f* **12/1**
55-6 5 6 **Poseidon (IRE)**[15] 3727 3-8-11 **72**.................................... JimCrowley 1 63
(Ed Walker) *t.k.h: hld up in midfield: clsd 4f out: effrt over 2f out: outpcd u.p over 1f out: wknd fnl f* **4/1[2]**
53-0 6 2 **Nucky Thompson**[35] 3009 4-9-13 **74**.......................(t[1]) StevieDonohoe 8 62
(Richard Spencer) *stdd after s: hld up in last trio: clsd and wl in tch 4f out: effrt 2f out: no imp and btn whn edgd lft 1f out: wknd fnl f* **33/1**
3430 7 10 **Sufi**[19] 3596 3-9-2 **77**............................................................... SeanLevey 9 49
(Richard Hannon) *chsd ldr for 2f: styd prom and chsd wnr again wl over 3f out tl over 1f out: sn lost pl: wknd fnl f* **7/1**
1436 8 11 **Paddy A (IRE)**[6] 4048 3-8-12 **73**.................................... WilliamBuick 10 27
(Philip McBride) *stdd after s: hld up in midfield: clsd to chse ldrs 4f out: rdn over 2f out: sn struggling and lost pl: bhd and eased ins fnl f* **11/2**
23-0 9 107 **The New Master**[61] 2152 4-9-11 **72**............................ SilvestreDeSousa 7
(David Elsworth) *t.k.h: hld up in midfield: ref to settle and hdwy to ld after 2f: hdd 4f out: sn dropped out and bhd: t.o and eased fnl 2f* **25/1**

2m 33.85s (0.95) **Going Correction** +0.175s/f (Good)
**WFA** 3 from 4yo+ 14lb **9** Ran SP% **112.0**
Speed ratings (Par 103): **103,101,100,98,94 93,86,79,**
CSF £17.54 CT £143.14 TOTE £4.00: £1.60, £1.80, £2.90; EX 18.70 Trifecta £113.20.
**Owner** Mrs M E Slade **Bred** Rockhart Trading Ltd **Trained** Kimpton, Hants

**FOCUS**
Distance increased by 19yds. A modest handicap but the right two came to the fore.

## 4268 188BET H'CAP 6f
**3:15** (3:15) (Class 4) (0-80,80) 3-Y-O **£5,175** (£1,540; £769; £384) **Stalls** High

Form RPR
2-45 1 **Stanhope**[47] 2620 3-9-1 **74**...................................................(v[1]) FranBerry 5 86
(Mick Quinn) *travelled strly thrght: pressed ldr tl led 2f out: rdn and qcknd clr over 1f out: in command and r.o wl fnl f: comf* **10/1**
3431 2 3 **Hart Stopper**[52] 2474 3-9-3 **76**........................................ LouisSteward 4 78+
(Michael Bell) *stdd s: in rr: effrt over 2f out: hdwy to chse clr wnr over 1f out: styd on same pce and no imp ins fnl f* **11/4[2]**
5-54 3 1¼ **Lady In Question (IRE)**[19] 3588 3-8-7 **73**............ ConnorMurtagh(7) 1 71
(Richard Fahey) *hld up in tch: clsd to chse ldrs over 3f out: rdn over 1f out: 3rd and styd on same pce ins fnl f* **7/2[3]**
353- 4 4½ **Bengal Lancer**[349] 4371 3-9-0 **73**................................... StevieDonohoe 2 57
(Ian Williams) *chsd ldrs tl over 3f out: dropped to rr and rdn 2f out: sn outpcd and wl hld* **10/1**
3262 5 *nk* **Cappananty Con**[17] 3673 3-9-3 **76**.................................... JimCrowley 3 59
(Dean Ivory) *in tch: clsd to chse ldrs 3f out: rdn and unable qck over 1f out: 4th and btn 1f out: wknd ins fnl f* **6/1**
2-10 6 8 **Mutoondresdashorse**[29] 3211 3-9-3 **76**............................ AdamKirby 7 33
(Paul Cole) *led tl 2f out: sn rdn and struggling: bhd 1f out: fdd ins fnl f* **9/4[1]**

1m 14.13s (1.63) **Going Correction** +0.225s/f (Good) **6** Ran SP% **112.1**
Speed ratings (Par 101): **98,94,92,86,85 75**
CSF £37.38 CT £116.14 TOTE £11.10: £4.00, £1.90; EX 41.70 Trifecta £150.80.
**Owner** Raymond Tooth **Bred** Raymond Clive Tooth **Trained** Newmarket, Suffolk

**FOCUS**
An ordinary handicap, they raced on the far rail, not going much of a gallop, and the winner was always well placed.

## 4269 188BET.CO.UK MAIDEN STKS 7f
**3:50** (3:50) (Class 5) 3-Y-O+ **£3,881** (£1,155; £577; £288) **Stalls** High

Form RPR
322- 1 **Saluti (IRE)**[204] 8243 3-9-5 79.......................................... RyanMoore 1 84
(Amanda Perrett) *trckd ldrs tl clsd to join ldrs 1/2-way: led over 2f out: rdn and kicked clr wl over 1f out: in command and styd on wl fnl f: comf* **9/4[2]**
2 3½ **Raawy** 3-9-5 0..................................................................... SilvestreDeSousa 8 75
(Simon Crisford) *t.k.h: hld up in tch: effrt over 2f out: hdwy to chse clr wnr over 1f out: clr 2nd and kpt on ins fnl f: no imp on wnr* **4/1[3]**
3 5 **Glenn Coco** 3-9-2 0.................................................................. AaronJones(3) 4 62
(Stuart Williams) *s.i.s: sn rcvrd and in tch in rr: shkn up wl over 1f out: n.m.r wl over 1f out: no ch w wnr but kpt on ins fnl f to snatch 3rd last stride* **66/1**
00 4 *shd* **Dream Start**[53] 2434 3-9-0 0........................................(t) StevieDonohoe 3 57
(John Ryan) *in tch: clsd to chse ldrs 5f out: rdn jst over 2f out: 3rd and outpcd over 1f out: wl hld and plugged on same pce ins fnl f: lost 3rd last stride* **33/1**
0- 5 *shd* **Mishari**[279] 6731 3-9-5 0........................................................ WilliamBuick 6 61
(David Lanigan) *t.k.h: w ldr tl rdn to ld 3f out: sn hdd: outpcd and btn over 1f out: wl hld and plugged on same pce fnl f* **8/1**
6 2¼ **Slow To Hand** 3-9-5 0............................................................ DannyBrock 7 56
(William Jarvis) *w ldrs tl 3f out: sn rdn and outpcd 2f out: lost pl and wl btn over 1f out: wknd* **50/1**
334- 7 1½ **Muhajjal**[278] 6777 3-9-5 81.................................................... JimCrowley 5 52
(Owen Burrows) *led tl 3f out: sn rdn and unable qck: lost pl and bhd 1f out: wknd* **5/4[1]**

1m 28.72s (3.02) **Going Correction** +0.225s/f (Good) **7** Ran SP% **112.7**
Speed ratings (Par 103): **91,87,81,81,81 78,76**
CSF £11.25 TOTE £3.10: £1.70, £2.60; EX 13.80 Trifecta £209.60.
**Owner** J E Bodie & Partners **Bred** J Hanly **Trained** Pulborough, W Sussex

**FOCUS**
No great depth to this maiden, with the favourite disappointing. The winner has been rated to a better view of his 2yo AW form.

## 4270 READ SILVESTRE DE SOUSA AT 188BET H'CAP 7f
**4:25** (4:25) (Class 2) (0-100,97) 3-Y-O+ **£12,938** (£3,850; £1,924; £962) **Stalls** High

Form RPR
2-20 1 **Makzeem**[35] 3014 4-9-5 **88**.................................................. RyanMoore 1 95+
(Roger Charlton) *trckd ldrs: clsd to press ldrs over 2f out: rdn to chal over 1f out: led ins fnl f: styd on wl: rdn out* **4/1[2]**
6100 2 1 **Supersta**[37] 2942 6-9-5 **88**.............................................(p) OisinMurphy 4 92
(Michael Appleby) *chsd ldr: rdn and ev ch over 1f out: unable qck u.p ins fnl f: wnt 2nd and kpt on same pce wl ins fnl f* **25/1**



The Form Book Flat, Raceform Ltd, Newbury, RG14 5SJ

5066 3 nk **Twin Appeal (IRE)**[12] 3842 6-9-8 **91**......................(b) SilvestreDeSousa 7 94
(David Barron) *t.k.h: hld up in tch in midfield: effrt 2f out: kpt on wl u.p ins fnl f: nvr getting on terms w wnr* **6/1**[3]

0440 4 nse **Shady McCoy (USA)**[12] 3842 7-9-5 **88**....................(h[1]) WilliamBuick 10 91
(Ian Williams) *hld up in tch in midfield: effrt wl over 1f out: drvn and hdwy 1f out: kpt on wl ins fnl f: nvr getting on terms w wnr* **8/1**

1-12 5 ¾ **Khamaary (IRE)**[12] 3828 3-8-13 **91**.................................... JimCrowley 3 89
(Mark Johnston) *led: rdn and hrd pressed over 1f out: drvn and hdd ins fnl f: no ex and wknd towards fin* **2/1**[1]

303 6 2 **Professor**[18] 3620 7-9-2 **85**................................................. SeanLevey 8 80
(Michael Attwater) *chsd ldrs tl over 2f out: midfield and unable qck u.p over 1f out: kpt on same pce ins fnl f* **16/1**

-024 7 2 ¼ **Ice Lord (IRE)**[27] 3294 5-9-7 **90**............................................ FranBerry 2 79
(Chris Wall) *stdd s: t.k.h: hld up in tch in last pair: effrt over 1f out: no imp: wl hld and kpt on same pce ins fnl f* **9/1**

5630 8 hd **Ballymore Castle (IRE)**[13] 3792 5-8-3 **79**...........(p) ConnorMurtagh(7) 9 68
(Richard Fahey) *s.i.s: hld up in last pair: effrt 2f out: sn rdn and no imp: wl hld and one pced ins fnl f* **7/1**

1m 27.6s (1.90) **Going Correction** +0.225s/f (Good)
**WFA** 3 from 4yo+ 9lb **8** Ran SP% **111.0**
Speed ratings (Par 109): **98,96,96,96,95 93,90,90**
CSF £85.90 CT £572.01 TOTE £4.30: £1.50, £5.00, £2.20; EX 84.80 Trifecta £306.50.
**Owner** D J Deer **Bred** D J And Mrs Deer **Trained** Beckhampton, Wilts

**FOCUS**
Useful handicap form.

## 4271 DAILY RACING SPECIALS AT 188BET H'CAP 1m
**5:00** (5:00) (Class 4) (0-85,87) 3-Y-O **£5,175** (£1,540; £769; £384) **Stalls** High

Form RPR
51 1 **Rigoletto (SWI)**[23] 3438 3-9-1 **79**......................................... AdamKirby 4 89
(Luca Cumani) *racd in centre: s.i.s and wnt rt leaving stalls: hld up in tch in rr: clsd to trck ldrs 3f out: effrt to chal wl over 1f out: led 1f out: styd on: rdn out* **3/1**[2]

-202 2 ½ **Endless Gold**[13] 3784 3-8-12 **76**....................................(p) WilliamBuick 3 85
(Charlie Appleby) *racd in centre: chsd ldr tl led over 3f out: rdn 2f out: hung lft over 1f out: hdd 1f out: kpt on but a hld ins fnl f* **4/1**

6-11 3 2 ¾ **Surrey Hope (USA)**[21] 3504 3-9-9 **87**............................... OisinMurphy 2 90
(Joseph Tuite) *racd in centre: stdd s: trckd ldrs: effrt to press ldr 2f out: 3rd and unable qck over 1f out: wknd fnl 100yds* **9/4**[1]

60-2 4 8 **Peak Princess (IRE)**[12] 3816 3-9-7 **85**.........................(p[1]) RyanMoore 6 69
(Richard Hannon) *racd far side: led tl over 3f out: sn rdn and outpcd: wknd over 1f out* **8/1**

-005 5 ¾ **Rebel De Lope**[19] 3592 3-9-7 **85**............................... SilvestreDeSousa 5 68
(Charles Hills) *racd far side: stdd and awkward leaving stalls: t.k.h: hld up in last pair: rdn over 2f out: no prog: wl btn over 1f out* **7/2**[3]

1m 41.49s (1.49) **Going Correction** +0.225s/f (Good) **5** Ran SP% **109.1**
Speed ratings (Par 101): **101,100,97,89,89**
CSF £14.59 TOTE £4.40: £1.90, £2.20; EX 16.50 Trifecta £44.60.
**Owner** Simon Capon **Bred** Stall Schloss Berg **Trained** Newmarket, Suffolk

**FOCUS**
A good 3yo handicap and a winner on the up. They split into two small groups, with those down the centre proving much the best.

## 4272 FREE SPINS AT 188BET CASINO H'CAP 5f
**5:35** (5:36) (Class 4) (0-85,86) 3-Y-O+ **£5,175** (£1,540; £769; £384) **Stalls** High

Form RPR
0324 1 **Poet's Society**[12] 3844 3-9-9 **86**...................................... WilliamBuick 4 92
(Mark Johnston) *led: pushed along 2f out: rdn and hrd pressed over 1f out: hdd ins fnl f: battled bk u.p to ld again towards fin: gamely* **15/8**[1]

152 2 nk **Compas Scoobie**[26] 3330 4-9-11 **82**..........................(b[1]) HarryBentley 3 89
(Roger Varian) *trckd ldrs: clsd and upsides over 1f out: drvn 1f out: kpt on but unable qck and nvr looked like gng past: wnt 2nd last strides* **7/2**[2]

4-35 3 hd **Justice Lady (IRE)**[11] 3865 4-9-8 **79**................................. SeanLevey 8 85
(David Elsworth) *t.k.h: hld up in tch in midfield: effrt and hdwy to chal over 1f out: drvn to ld ins fnl f: hdd and no ex towards fin* **9/2**

6031 4 2 **Rio Ronaldo (IRE)**[12] 3834 5-9-11 **82**........................ AntonioFresu 9 81
(Mike Murphy) *stdd s: t.k.h: hld up in tch in rr: effrt over 1f out: rdn 1f out: styd on same pce and no imp ins fnl f: eased cl home* **4/1**[3]

00-0 5 2 ¾ **Musical Comedy**[12] 3834 6-9-8 **79**.................................... AdamKirby 5 68
(Mike Murphy) *chsd wnr: rdn 1/2-way: lost pl u.p and btn over 1f out: wknd ins fnl f* **10/1**

0220 6 1 ¾ **Upavon**[105] 1222 7-9-6 **80**...............................................(t) AaronJones(3) 7 63
(Stuart Williams) *broke wl: sn restrained and hld up in tch in last pair: effrt 2f out: no imp and hung lft 1f out: wknd ins fnl f* **16/1**

1m 0.52s (1.42) **Going Correction** +0.225s/f (Good)
**WFA** 3 from 4yo+ 6lb **6** Ran SP% **110.2**
Speed ratings (Par 105): **97,96,96,93,88 85**
CSF £8.27 CT £22.35 TOTE £2.20: £1.30, £2.10; EX 7.20 Trifecta £19.20.
**Owner** Sheikh Hamdan bin Mohammed Al Maktoum **Bred** Darley **Trained** Middleham Moor, N Yorks

**FOCUS**
A useful sprint and a small pb from the winner.
T/Plt: £128.30 to a £1 stake. Pool: £66,617.21 - 378.99 winning units. T/Qpdt: £60.10 to a £1 stake. Pool: £3,928.51 - 48.30 winning units. **Steve Payne**

# 3902 NOTTINGHAM (L-H)
Thursday, June 29

**OFFICIAL GOING: Soft (good to soft in places; 7.0)**
Wind: Virtually nil Weather: Heavy cloud and light rain showers

## 4273 32RED CASINO NOVICE AUCTION STKS 6f 18y
**2:20** (2:21) (Class 5) 2-Y-O **£3,234** (£962; £481; £240) **Stalls** High

Form RPR
16 1 **Holy Tiber (IRE)**[23] 3421 2-9-4 0.................................... JamesDoyle 2 77
(George Scott) *wnt lft s: sn cl up: led 1/2-way: pushed along 2f out: rdn over 1f out: kpt on wl fnl f* **10/11**[1]

6 2 ½ **Sweet Vixen**[58] 2258 2-8-11 0..................................... JackMitchell 6 69
(Tom Clover) *trckd ldrs: swtchd lft and hdwy to chal wl over 1f out: rdn and ev ch whn edgd lft ins fnl f: kpt on* **14/1**

3 3 3 ½ **Silvington**[28] 3244 2-8-13 0................................... CharlieBennett(3) 7 63
(Daniel Mark Loughnane) *slt ld: hdd 1/2-way: rdn along 2f out: kpt on same pce fnl f* **4/1**[2]

004 4 3 ¼ **Archie Perkins (IRE)**[24] 3398 2-8-11 66............................ PhilDennis(5) 5 53
(Nigel Tinkler) *trckd ldng pair: pushed along 2f out: rdn wl over 1f out: sn one pce* **10/1**

5 4 ½ **Princess Jessica (FR)** 2-8-11 0................................ PatrickMathers 4 35
(Richard Fahey) *green: sn rdn along: outpcd fr 1/2-way* **7/1**[3]

6 13 **Viking Way (IRE)** 2-9-2 0................................................ RobHornby 8
(Olly Williams) *dwlt: green and a bhd* **16/1**

1m 16.92s (2.22) **Going Correction** +0.20s/f (Good) **6** Ran SP% **106.5**
Speed ratings (Par 93): **93,92,87,83,77 60**
CSF £13.16 TOTE £1.40: £1.10, £5.90; EX 12.70 Trifecta £46.50.
**Owner** Matt Bartram **Bred** Quiet Waters Syndicate **Trained** Newmarket, Suffolk

**FOCUS**
Races took place on the outer track. Rail set out 4 yards, adding 12 yards to races 2, 3, 4 and 7. There was little depth to this and the pace was steady.

## 4274 32RED.COM MAIDEN STKS 1m 2f 50y
**2:50** (2:58) (Class 5) 3-Y-O+ **£3,234** (£962; £481; £240) **Stalls** Low

Form RPR
6 1 **Intellect (IRE)**[82] 1624 3-9-0 0........................................ AndreaAtzeni 7 83
(Sir Michael Stoute) *trckd ldrs: hdwy 3f out: rdn over 1f out: styd on to ld last 75 yds* **7/4**[1]

0 2 ¾ **Stormy Blues**[65] 2066 3-9-0 0....................................(t[1]) MartinHarley 3 81
(Charlie Appleby) *trckd ldr: hdwy to ld wl over 2f out: rdn over 1f out: edgd lft ins fnl f: hdd and no ex last 75 yds* **3/1**[2]

3 1 ¼ **Airway** 3-8-11 0.................................................. GeorgeWood(3) 5 78
(James Fanshawe) *in tch: hdwy on outer 3f out: rdn to chse ldng pair over 1f out: chal and ev ch ent fnl f: sn drvn and kpt on same pce* **9/2**[3]

0 4 8 **Titan**[72] 1857 3-8-11 0........................................ KieranShoemark(3) 12 63
(Ed Dunlop) *led: pushed along over 3f out: hdd wl over 2f out and sn rdn: grad wknd fnl 2f* **5/1**

5 2 ¾ **Outofthequestion** 3-9-0 0............................................ FergusSweeney 9 58
(Alan King) *midfield: hdwy over 3f out: rdn along over 2f out: no imp* **16/1**

0 6 3 ¼ **Artic Nel**[18] 3615 3-8-9 0............................................... TomMarquand 10 47
(Ian Williams) *rr: hdwy wl over 2f out: sn rdn and plugged on: n.d* **20/1**

0 7 1 **Clearance**[16] 3682 3-9-0 0.................................................. JoeyHaynes 2 50
(Mark H Tompkins) *in tch on inner: pushed along over 3f out: rdn wl over 2f out: sn wknd* **66/1**

8 1 ¾ **Desi Daru (IRE)**[46] 5-9-12 0...................................................... RobertTart 4 46
(Conrad Allen) *a towards rr* **14/1**

00- 9 ¾ **French Silver (FR)**[275] 6850 3-8-9 0............................ GeorgeDowning 8 40
(Tony Carroll) *trckd ldr: pushed along 4f out: rdn over 3f out: sn wknd* **100/1**

40 10 8 **Benissimo (IRE)**[61] 2164 7-9-5 0.......................................... TobyEley(7) 1 30
(Tony Forbes) *dwlt: a rr* **33/1**

0 11 21 **Volturnus**[48] 2584 3-9-0 0................................................. DougieCostello 6
(Jamie Osborne) *towards rr: rdn along over 4f out: sn outpcd and bhd* **33/1**

2m 17.73s (3.43) **Going Correction** +0.175s/f (Good)
**WFA** 3 from 5yo+ 12lb **11** Ran SP% **121.9**
Speed ratings (Par 103): **93,92,91,85,82 80,79,78,77,71 54**
CSF £6.99 TOTE £2.90: £1.10, £1.50, £1.80; EX 8.50 Trifecta £15.70.
**Owner** Highclere T'Bred Racing - Thomas Hardy **Bred** Duncan A McGregor **Trained** Newmarket, Suffolk

■ Pouvoir Magique was withdrawn. Price at the time of withdrawal 2-5. Rule 4 applies to bets struck prior to the withdrawal but not to SP bets. Deduction 70p in the pound. New market formed.

**FOCUS**
The rail was set out 4 yards, adding 12 yards to this race. Betting suggested that this was a one-horse contest but there was drama before the off when that heavy odds-on favourite Pouvoir Magique unshipped his rider on the way to the start and was withdrawn.

## 4275 £10 FREE AT 32RED.COM MAIDEN STKS 1m 75y
**3:25** (3:25) (Class 5) 3-Y-O+ **£3,234** (£962; £481; £240) **Stalls** Centre

Form RPR
2- 1 **Zabeel Prince (IRE)**[248] 7583 4-9-12 0............................ AndreaAtzeni 5 82+
(Roger Varian) *t.k.h early: trckd ldrs: hdwy over 2f out: rdn over 1f out: led ins fnl f: sn clr* **11/8**[2]

02 2 3 **Cape To Cuba**[27] 3293 3-8-8 0....................................... GeorgeWood(3) 6 68
(James Fanshawe) *t.k.h early: trckd ldng pair: hdwy 3f out: led 2f out and sn rdn: drvn ent fnl f: sn hdd and kpt on same pce* **5/4**[1]

0 3 2 ¾ **Decision Maker (IRE)**[14] 3755 3-9-2 0........................... SteveDrowne 7 67
(Roy Bowring) *hld up towards rr: hdwy on outer 3f out: cl up 2f out: rdn and ev ch ent fnl f: sn drvn and kpt on same pce* **66/1**

-245 4 1 ¼ **Muqaatil (USA)**[61] 2145 3-9-2 73..............................(p[1]) TomMarquand 9 64
(Richard Hannon) *led: pushed along 3f out: rdn and hdd 2f out: sn wknd* **6/1**[3]

6 5 hd **Princess Ophelia**[48] 2572 3-8-4 0.................................... RayDawson(7) 3 59
(Michael Appleby) *trckd ldr on inner: cl up over 2f out: rdn wl over 1f out: sn wknd* **25/1**

0 6 5 **Pretty Obvious (FR)**[10] 3921 4-9-12 0.......................... TimmyMurphy 2 54
(Jonjo O'Neill) *dwlt: a rr* **50/1**

0-0 7 5 **Red Bordeaux (FR)**[14] 3755 3-9-2 0......................... GeorgeDowning 10 41
(Tony Carroll) *in tch: hdwy to chse ldrs 4f out: rdn along 3f out: sn wknd* **100/1**

1m 51.68s (2.68) **Going Correction** +0.175s/f (Good)
**WFA** 3 from 4yo 10lb **7** Ran SP% **109.1**
Speed ratings (Par 103): **93,90,87,86,85 80,75**
CSF £3.04 TOTE £2.30: £1.70, £1.10; EX 3.50 Trifecta £60.10.
**Owner** Sheikh Mohammed Obaid Al Maktoum **Bred** Roundhill Stud **Trained** Newmarket, Suffolk

**FOCUS**
The rail was set out 4 yards, adding 12 yards to this distance. Not much depth to this but the winner could be smart.

## 4276 PLAY JURASSIC WORLD AT 32RED H'CAP 1m 75y
**4:00** (4:00) (Class 5) (0-75,77) 3-Y-O **£3,234** (£962; £481; £240) **Stalls** Centre

Form RPR
623 1 **Finale**[128] 849 3-8-10 **67**............................................... GeorgeWood(3) 1 75+
(Hughie Morrison) *.trckd ldrs: hdwy 3f out: led over 2f out: rdn over 1f out: styd on wl* **17/2**

5225 2 2 **Mama Africa (IRE)**[18] 3627 3-8-12 **66**........................... JamesSullivan 7 69
(David Barron) *hld up towards rr: hdwy wl over 2f out: chsd wnr over 1f out: sn rdn and no imp ins fnl f* **4/1**[3]

-342 3 1 ½ **Golconda Prince (IRE)**[21] 3484 3-8-10 **64**................. PatrickMathers 4 64
(Richard Fahey) *in tch: hdwy 3f out: chsd ldrs 2f out: rdn over 1f out: drvn and kpt on same pce fnl f* **2/1**[1]

60-2 **4** 1¼ **Hellomoto**[64] 2077 3-8-6 **60**....................(p) JoeyHaynes 6 57
(Kevin Ryan) *sn led: pushed along 3f out: hdd over 2f out and sn rdn: drvn over 1f out: grad wknd* **14/1**

-666 **5** 1½ **Teqany (IRE)**[13] 3784 3-9-3 **71**.................... AndreaAtzeni 3 65
(Owen Burrows) *hld up: hdwy on inner 3f out: chsd ldrs over 2f out: sn rdn and wknd over 1f out* **11/4**[2]

6-00 **6** 3¾ **Iron Islands**[27] 3310 3-8-10 **69**....................(v[1]) CliffordLee[(5)] 8 54
(K R Burke) *dwlt: sn trcking ldrs: hdwy and cl up 1/2-way: rdn along 3f out: drvn over 2f out and sn wknd* **7/1**

0-00 **7** 20 **Jupiter Ascending**[18] 3627 3-7-9 **56** oh11....................(t) RPWalsh[(7)] 9
(Michael Appleby) *s.i.s and bhd: rapid hdwy to chse ldng pair over 5f out: cl up on outer 4f out: rdn along over 3f out: sn lost pl and bhd* **80/1**

1m 50.48s (1.48) **Going Correction** +0.175s/f (Good) **7** Ran SP% **110.9**
Speed ratings (Par 99): **99,97,95,94,92 89,69**
CSF £39.60 CT £90.80 TOTE £9.10: £3.10, £2.30; EX 37.20 Trifecta £75.30.
**Owner** T D Rootes & O F Waller **Bred** Shutford Stud **Trained** East Ilsley, Berks

**FOCUS**
The rail was set out 4 yards, adding 12 yards to this distance. Three non-runners, including two likely to be well fancied, made this less competitive than it looked originally. It featured no previous winners in the line-up. The winner showed improved form.

## 4277 32RED H'CAP 6f 18y
**4:35** (4:38) (Class 4) (0-80,80) 3-Y-0+ **£5,175** (£1,540; £769; £384) **Stalls** High

Form RPR

0-00 **1** **Zapper Cass (FR)**[29] 3195 4-9-7 **78**.................... JoshDoyle[(3)] 11 86
(Tony Coyle) *trckd ldrs: hdwy 2f out: cl up over 1f out: rdn ent fnl f: sn drvn and kpt on wl to ld nr line* **11/1**

0200 **2** hd **Lexington Times (IRE)**[13] 3792 5-9-11 **79**.................... JamesSullivan 2 86
(Ruth Carr) *hld up towards rr: hdwy wl over 2f out: trckd ldrs wl over 1f out: sn chal: rdn to ld ins fnl f: drvn and hdd nr line* **9/2**[1]

3212 **3** 1 **Socialites Red**[10] 3904 4-8-9 **70**....................(p) RPWalsh[(7)] 4 74
(Scott Dixon) *wnt rt s: cl up: led 1/2-way: rdn over 1f out: drvn and hdd ins fnl f: kpt on same pce* **5/1**[2]

1105 **4** 3 **Whitecrest**[10] 3919 9-9-6 **74**.................... MartinHarley 3 68
(John Spearing) *midfield: hdwy on outer over 2f out: rdn along to chse ldrs over 1f out: no imp fnl f* **16/1**

-020 **5** 4 **Rantan (IRE)**[14] 3757 4-9-12 **80**.................... RobHornby 10 61
(David Barron) *sn towards rr and pushed along 1/2-way: hdwy 2f out: sn rdn and kpt on fnl f* **5/1**[2]

5041 **6** 4 **Artscape**[20] 3532 5-9-8 **76**.................... SteveDrowne 7 45
(Dean Ivory) *chsd ldrs: rdn along over 2f out: sn drvn and wknd* **9/2**[1]

4553 **7** ½ **Yeeoow (IRE)**[29] 3195 8-9-3 **76**....................(p) CliffordLee[(5)] 8 43
(K R Burke) *chsd ldrs: rdn wl over 2f out: sn drvn and grad wknd* **7/1**[3]

531- **8** 1½ **Ace Master**[330] 5034 9-8-12 **73**....................(b) KevinLundie[(7)] 13 35
(Roy Bowring) *led: hdd 1/2-way: sn rdn along and wknd 2f out* **16/1**

050- **9** 1 **Cadeaux Boxer**[244] 7671 4-9-7 **75**.................... JohnFahy 9 34
(Martin Smith) *chsd ldrs: rdn along 1/2-way: sn wknd* **20/1**

400- **10** 8 **Kommander Kirkup**[254] 7433 6-9-5 **73**.................... FergusSweeney 5 6
(Michael Herrington) *dwlt and hmpd s: a rr* **12/1**

1m 15.99s (1.29) **Going Correction** +0.20s/f (Good)
**WFA** 3 from 4yo+ 7lb **10** Ran SP% **114.7**
Speed ratings (Par 105): **99,98,97,93,88 82,82,80,78,68**
CSF £59.01 CT £289.33 TOTE £14.50: £4.10, £1.90, £1.70; EX 69.60 Trifecta £502.90.
**Owner** Stephen Louch **Bred** Arunas Cicenas **Trained** Norton, N Yorks

**FOCUS**
A competitive contest for the level.

## 4278 32RED.COM H'CAP 5f 8y
**5:10** (5:11) (Class 5) (0-75,75) 4-Y-0+ **£3,234** (£962; £481; £240) **Stalls** High

Form RPR

50-1 **1** **Rainbow Orse**[37] 2932 5-9-4 **72**....................(p) AndreaAtzeni 1 83
(Robert Cowell) *trckd ldr: cl up 1/2-way: rdn to ld wl over 1f out: edgd rt ent fnl f: sn drvn and kpt on wl towards fin* **2/1**[1]

4602 **2** 1 **Flash City (ITY)**[9] 3944 9-8-12 **66**.................... JamesSullivan 4 73
(Ruth Carr) *t.k.h: trckd ldrs: hdwy over 2f out: chal wl over 1f out: sn rdn and ev ch: drvn ins fnl f: kpt on same pce* **9/2**[3]

06-0 **3** 2¼ **Wiley Post**[31] 3161 4-9-5 **73**....................(b) SteveDrowne 2 72
(Tony Carroll) *t.k.h: trckd ldrs: hdwy 2f out: rdn over 1f out: kpt on one pce* **12/1**

6140 **4** nk **Crosse Fire**[9] 3946 5-8-7 **66**.................... PaddyPilley[(5)] 8 64
(Scott Dixon) *led: rdn along 2f out: sn hdd and drvn: wknd appr fnl f* **3/1**[2]

033 **5** 2½ **Bonjour Steve**[23] 3424 6-8-11 **65**....................(p) RobHornby 5 54
(Richard Price) *trckd ldrs: hdwy 1/2-way: rdn along wl over 1f out: sn drvn and btn* **3/1**[2]

1m 2.06s (0.56) **Going Correction** +0.20s/f (Good) **5** Ran SP% **109.2**
Speed ratings (Par 103): **103,101,97,97,93**
CSF £10.98 TOTE £2.20: £1.50, £2.00; EX 4.50 Trifecta £17.70.
**Owner** G Johnson **Bred** D R Botterill **Trained** Six Mile Bottom, Cambs

**FOCUS**
Just a modest handicap but another pb from the winner, with the runner-up rated to his latest.

## 4279 32RED "HANDS AND HEELS" SERIES APPRENTICE H'CAP (PART OF THE RACING EXCELLENCE INITIATIVE) 1m 2f 50y
**5:45** (5:46) (Class 5) (0-70,71) 4-Y-0+ **£3,234** (£962; £481; £240) **Stalls** Low

Form RPR

0411 **1** **Miningrocks (FR)**[19] 3559 5-9-11 **71**.................... GerO'Neill 4 78
(Declan Carroll) *mde all: pushed along over 2f out: rdn over 1f out: kpt on* **4/6**[1]

500 **2** 1¼ **Deinonychus**[31] 3153 6-9-7 **67**....................(h) JordanUys 5 70
(Michael Appleby) *hld up: hdwy 3f out: rdn to chse wnr wl over 1f out: drvn and kpt on fnl f* **8/1**

-003 **3** 6 **Saga Sprint (IRE)**[23] 3439 4-8-11 **60**.................... GinaMangan[(3)] 3 51
(J R Jenkins) *trckd wnr on inner: pushed along 3f out: rdn over 2f out: drvn wl over 1f out: kpt on one pce* **7/1**[3]

405- **4** 4 **Eastern Lady (IND)**[371] 3570 4-9-8 **71**....................(t[1]) TobyEley[(3)] 8 55
(Richard Price) *trckd wnr: pushed along 3f out: rdn over 2f out: sn drvn and wknd* **20/1**

0115 **5** 28 **Street Art (IRE)**[23] 3440 5-8-9 **55**....................(bt) MillyNaseb 6
(Mike Murphy) *s.i.s and lost 10 l s: jnd field after 3f: effrt on outer 4f out: rdn along 3f out: sn wknd* **4/1**[2]

2m 17.77s (3.47) **Going Correction** +0.175s/f (Good) **5** Ran SP% **108.4**
Speed ratings (Par 103): **93,92,87,84,61**
CSF £6.39 TOTE £1.50: £1.10, £4.30; EX 8.00 Trifecta £18.20.
**Owner** Mrs Sarah Bryan **Bred** M Daguzan-Garros & Rolling Hills Farm **Trained** Malton, N Yorks

**FOCUS**
The rail was set out 4 yards, adding 12 yards to this distance. This took little winning, and doesn't appeal as strong form.

T/Plt: £22.00 to a £1 stake. Pool: £52,463.33 - 1734.30 winning units. T/Qpdt: £11.80 to a £1 stake. Pool: £3,592.44 - 224.04 winning units. **Joe Rowntree**

4280 - 4287a (Foreign Racing) - See Raceform Interactive

# 2664 DEAUVILLE (R-H)
### Thursday, June 29

**OFFICIAL GOING: Turf: soft; polytrack: standard**

## 4288a PRIX D'AURIGNY (MAIDEN) (3YO FILLIES) (POLYTRACK) 6f 110y
**4:10** 3-Y-0 **£10,683** (£4,273; £3,205; £2,136; £1,068)

RPR

**1** **Followmeifucan (IRE)**[90] 3-9-2 0.................... CristianDemuro 10 78
(C Lerner, France) **43/5**

**2** snk **Red Chois (IRE)**[75] 3-9-2 0.................... FabriceVeron 5 78
(E J O'Neill, France) **43/10**[2]

**3** snk **Iken Water (FR)** 3-8-13 0 ow2.................... Pierre-CharlesBoudot 1 74
(H-A Pantall, France) **106/10**

**4** hd **Moon Eclipse (FR)** 3-8-11 0.................... JeromeCabre 2 72
(M Nigge, France) **34/1**

**5** 2 **Mangaia (FR)**[43] 3-9-2 0.................... TheoBachelot 6 71
(S Wattel, France) **63/10**[3]

**6** 3 **Maariyah (FR)**[38] 3-9-2 0....................(b[1]) GregoryBenoist 9 62
(A Fabre, France) **5/2**[1]

**7** 3 **Babylove (FR)**[91] 1459 3-9-2 0.................... SoufianeSaadi 4 53
(H-A Pantall, France) **39/1**

**8** 4 **Dancing Break (FR)**[12] 3-9-2 0.................... StephanePasquier 8 42
(A Schutz, France) **52/1**

**9** 3 **Undiscovered Angel (FR)**[19] 3555 3-9-2 0....................(p) AntoineHamelin 12 33
(K R Burke) *wnt lft s: sn rcvrd and tacked across to inner: led after 1 1/2f: hdd after 2f and chsd clr ldr: drvn and nt qckn over 1 1/2f out: rdn and wknd appr fnl f* **15/2**

**10** 1¾ **Fanta Dielo (USA)**[86] 3-9-2 0.................... MickaelBarzalona 11 28
(Mme Pia Brandt, France) **17/1**

**P** **Aothea (GER)**[232] 7879 3-8-13 0.................... ClementLecoeuvre[(3)] 3
(Carmen Bocskai, Germany) **13/2**

PARI-MUTUEL (all including 1 euro stake): WIN 9.60; PLACE 3.10, 1.80, 3.60; DF 23.00; SF 53.70.
**Owner** Ecurie Patrick Klein & Ecurie Haras Du Cadran **Bred** Ecurie Patrick Klein, Ecurie Haras Du Cadran & J-L **Trained** France

## 4289a PRIX DE CORMEILLES (CLAIMER) (3YO) (YOUNG JOCKEYS & APPRENTICES) (POLYTRACK) 7f 110y
**6:10** 3-Y-0 **£9,829** (£3,931; £2,948; £1,965; £982)

RPR

**1** **Take Me Home (FR)**[23] 3-8-6 0.................... TristanBaron[(5)] 12 77
(H-A Pantall, France) **235/10**

**2** ¾ **Angel Baby (FR)**[20] 3-8-6 0.................... MathieuPelletan[(5)] 3 75
(J-C Rouget, France) **7/5**[1]

**3** 1½ **Sivinsk (FR)**[87] 3-8-9 0.................... MlleElauraCieslik[(10)] 6 75
(Simone Brogi, France) **42/10**[2]

**4** 1 **Ucel (IRE)**[25] 3-9-2 0....................(b) FlorentMalbran[(8)] 8 82
(F Chappet, France) **7/1**[3]

**5** 2 **Rajeline (FR)**[13] 3-8-8 0.................... AdrienMoreau[(3)] 2 64
(M Boutin, France) **26/1**

**6** shd **Power Of The Cross**[90] 3-8-9 0....................(p) MlleLauraGrosso[(8)] 5 65
(Charley Rossi, France) **9/1**

**7** 1¼ **Evasion Absolue (FR)**[22] 3-8-5 0.................... ClementLecoeuvre[(3)] 11 57
(E Lellouche, France) **231/10**

**8** hd **Flawed Diamond (FR)**[28] 3275 3-7-12 0(b) MmeAlexiaCeccarello[(10)] 10 53
(K R Burke) *sn led: pressed bef 1/2-way: rdn and hdd over 1 1/2f out: grad dropped away* **107/1**

**9** hd **Fils De L'Air (FR)**[28] 3-8-9 0....................(p) KyllanBarbaud[(6)] 4 63
(P Sogorb, France) **74/10**

**10** 3½ **Arpani (FR)**[25] 3-8-3 0....................(p) MlleCoraliePacaut[(10)] 13 48
(T Castanheira, France) **192/10**

**11** 1¼ **Sirma Traou Land (FR)**[19] 3-8-6 0....................(p) JackyNicoleau[(5)] 1 47
(B Legros, France) **47/1**

**12** snk **Admiralty Arch**[114] 3-8-10 0....................(p) TomLefranc[(8)] 9 54
(C Boutin, France) **32/1**

PARI-MUTUEL (all including 1 euro stake): WIN 24.50; PLACE 4.40, 1.30, 1.70; DF 29.50; SF 79.70.
**Owner** Cocheese Bloodstock Anstalt **Bred** Mme A Tamagni & Cocheese Bloodstock Anstalt **Trained** France

# 3576 CHESTER (L-H)
### Friday, June 30

**OFFICIAL GOING: Good to soft (6.8)**
Wind: Faint breeze Weather: Cloudy and cool, occasional drizzle

## 4290 EDMUNDSON ELECTRICAL APPRENTICE H'CAP 7f 127y
**6:10** (6:12) (Class 4) (0-80,80) 3-Y-0
**£6,225** (£1,864; £932; £466; £233; £117) **Stalls** Low

Form RPR

-022 **1** **Valentino Boy (IRE)**[20] 3555 3-8-10 **69**.................... BenRobinson[(5)] 11 76
(Brian Ellison) *mde all: pushed along over 1f out: jnd and rdn ent fnl f: fnd ex to regain advantage: r.o wl* **11/1**

6412 **2** ½ **Right Action**[24] 3434 3-9-0 **75**.................... ConnorMurtagh[(7)] 10 81
(Richard Fahey) *chsd ldr: drvn to chal ent fnl f: sn rdn: r.o but hld* **5/1**[3]

6221 **3** 1¼ **Heir Of Excitement (IRE)**[39] 2885 3-9-4 **75**.................... LewisEdmunds[(3)] 8 78
(Kevin Ryan) *trckd ldrs: drvn over 1f out: rdn fnl f: no imp on front two* **4/1**[2]

006 **4** shd **Poetic Force (IRE)**[14] 3780 3-8-13 **74**.................... AledBeech[(7)] 5 77+
(Tony Carroll) *mid-div: hdwy on outer wl over 1f out: sn rdn: r.o to take 4th ins fnl f* **9/1**

1104 **5** 1½ **Sidewinder (IRE)**[6] 4084 3-9-12 **80**....................(p) HectorCrouch 4 79
(Tom Dascombe) *worked up befhand and uns rdr: trckd ldrs in 4th: rdn wl over 1f out: no ex fnl f* **6/1**

-140 **6** ¾ **Blue Rocks**[4] 4159 3-8-0 **61** oh1 DarraghKeenan(7) 7 59
(Lisa Williamson) *hld up: effrt over 1f out: sn rdn: r.o one pce fnl f* **66/1**

30-0 **7** 1 ¾ **Lonely The Brave (IRE)**[20] 3578 3-9-10 **78** JoshDoyle 1 72
(Mark Johnston) *mid-div: pushed along 2f out: drvn and lost pl fr over 1f out* **16/1**

3043 **8** *nse* **Arc Royal**[20] 3588 3-9-9 **80** PaddyPilley(3) 3 74
(Tom Dascombe) *prom early: sn settled in mid-div: pushed along wl over 1f out: sn rdn and lost pl* **7/2**[1]

1303 **9** ¾ **Gala Celebration (IRE)**[19] 3621 3-8-9 **66** (h) GeorgeBuckell(3) 6 58
(John Gallagher) *racd in last: pushed along 3f out: nvr a factor* **6/1**

0415 **10** *hd* **Jet Setter (IRE)**[19] 3621 3-8-12 **69** MitchGodwin(3) 12 60
(Tony Carroll) *hld up: drvn wl over 1f out: rdn and no imp* **25/1**

1m 36.19s (2.39) **Going Correction** +0.40s/f (Good) **10** Ran SP% **117.0**
Speed ratings (Par 101): **104,103,102,102,100 99,98,98,97,97**
CSF £65.46 CT £227.22 TOTE £10.70: £2.20, £1.60, £2.00; EX 31.80 Trifecta £192.00.
**Owner** Mrs J A Martin **Bred** Diomed Bloodstock Ltd **Trained** Norton, N Yorks

**FOCUS**
Quite a competitive handicap for apprentices. It was run at a medium gallop and it paid to race prominently with the first three being in the first three throughout. The winner's best run since he was a 2yo, and the runner-up fits.

## 4291 CALL THE MBNA TEAM MAIDEN AUCTION STKS (PLUS 10 RACE) 7f 1y
**6:40** (6:46) (Class 4) 2-Y-O

**£6,225** (£1,864; £932; £466; £233; £117) **Stalls** Low

Form RPR

052 **1** **Alifax**[9] 3965 2-9-2 0 DougieCostello 2 70
(Jamie Osborne) *trckd ldrs: 3rd on inner 2f out: plld out to chal over 1f out: rdn appr fnl f: hdwy and r.o wl u.p to ld last few strides* **2/1**[2]

4 **2** ½ **Knight In Armour (IRE)**[15] 3742 2-9-2 0 FrannyNorton 5 69
(Mark Johnston) *led: pushed along over 1f out: 1 l clr ent fnl furong: sn rdn: r.o: hdd last few strides* **5/4**[1]

6 **3** ½ **Lucifugous (IRE)**[17] 3697 2-8-11 0 ShaneGray 10 62+
(Stuart Williams) *hld up: hdwy over 1f out: drvn ins fnl f: r.o wl* **12/1**

6 **4** 1 ½ **Fastalong (IRE)**[18] 3662 2-8-4 0 ConnorMurtagh(7) 11 59
(Tim Easterby) *mid-div: effrt 2f out: wnt 4th over 1f out: rdn and r.o ins fnl f* **16/1**

0 **5** 1 **Sausage Fingers**[29] 3245 2-8-11 0 PaddyPilley(5) 6 61
(Tom Dascombe) *pressed ldr: drvn over 1f out: rdn and lost pl fnl f* **20/1**

**6** ¾ **Aussie Wind** 2-9-2 0 LiamKeniry 12 59+
(Hugo Palmer) *hld up: t.k.h early: sme hdwy fnl 2 fs* **8/1**[3]

**7** 1 **Jaycols Star** 2-8-13 0 JordanVaughan(3) 3 56
(Philip Kirby) *mid-div: drvn 2f out: rdn over 1f out: no ex fnl f* **66/1**

**8** *hd* **Snooker Jim** 2-9-2 0 RoystonFfrench 4 56
(Steph Hollinshead) *slowly away: racd in rr: mod hdwy fnl 2 fs* **25/1**

0 **9** 2 **Bib And Tucker**[15] 3754 2-8-13 0 HectorCrouch(3) 9 51
(David Brown) *prom: rdn 2f out: lost pl over 1f out* **40/1**

00 **10** 2 ½ **Bumble Beeze (IRE)**[11] 3918 2-8-13 0 SammyJoBell(3) 1 44
(Tom Dascombe) *hld up: pushed along 2f out: no impresion* **14/1**

**11** ½ **Gas Monkey** 2-8-13 0 ShelleyBirkett(3) 7 43
(Julia Feilden) *mid-div: rdn and effrt on outer 2f out: wknd fnl f* **28/1**

00 **12** ½ **Foxy's Spirit**[12] 3858 2-8-11 0 PaulQuinn 8 37
(Tim Easterby) *a in rr: drvn over 1f out: no imp* **100/1**

1m 30.2s (3.70) **Going Correction** +0.40s/f (Good) **12** Ran SP% **126.1**
Speed ratings (Par 95): **94,93,92,91,90 89,88,87,85,82 82,81**
CSF £4.89 TOTE £2.80: £1.40, £1.10, £4.00; EX 6.50 Trifecta £30.30.
**Owner** A Signy, I Barratt, S Short & B Spiers **Bred** Mrs E A Bass **Trained** Upper Lambourn, Berks

**FOCUS**
The market suggested this was a two-horse affair and it worked out that way. They went a decent gallop but with the pack closing in the straight it may not be a particularly strong event. It's rated as just modest form.

## 4292 GROSVENOR SHOPPING CENTRE/EBF BREEDERS' SERIES FILLIES' H'CAP 1m 2f 70y
**7:10** (7:10) (Class 3) (0-90,90) 3-Y-O+ **£12,450** (£3,728; £1,864; £932) **Stalls** High

Form RPR

-111 **1** **Titi Makfi**[9] 3976 3-9-0 **88** 6ex FrannyNorton 3 96+
(Mark Johnston) *racd in 3rd: pushed along briefly 2f out: trcking ldrs wl over 1f out: rdn ent fnl f: qckned and led last 100yds: comf* **7/4**[2]

1-11 **2** 1 ¾ **White Chocolate (IRE)**[21] 3535 3-8-11 **85** LiamKeniry 2 90+
(David Simcock) *hld up in last: pushed along 2f out: stl last and drvn over 1f out: hdwy and rdn: r.o ins fnl f to take 2nd nr fin* **1/1**[1]

31-5 **3** *nk* **Empress Ali (IRE)**[40] 2855 6-10-0 **90** AndrewMullen 4 94
(Tom Tate) *trckd ldr: drvn 2f out: hdwy to ld ent fnl f: hrd rdn and hdd last 100yds: no ex: lost 2nd nr fin* **5/1**[3]

6212 **4** 2 ½ **Livella Fella (IRE)**[21] 3537 4-9-1 **77** SeanLevey 5 76
(Keith Dalgleish) *led: pushed along 2f out rdn wl over 1f out: hdd ent fnl f: wknd* **12/1**

2m 15.18s (3.98) **Going Correction** +0.40s/f (Good)
**WFA** 3 from 4yo+ 12lb **4** Ran SP% **110.7**
Speed ratings (Par 104): **100,98,98,96**
CSF £4.01 TOTE £2.40; EX 3.40 Trifecta £6.70.
**Owner** Paul & Clare Rooney **Bred** Floors Farming **Trained** Middleham Moor, N Yorks

**FOCUS**
Just four runners in this fillies' handicap but it featured two who had won their last three races. They came out on top but it was rather a muddling affair as they set off quite fast, then steadied but went for home quite a way out. The form is rated around the third.

## 4293 EUROGOLD CLAIMING STKS 7f 127y
**7:45** (7:47) (Class 4) 4-Y-O+

**£6,225** (£1,864; £932; £466; £233; £117) **Stalls** Low

Form RPR

5200 **1** **Michele Strogoff**[8] 4001 4-8-13 89 (b) JoshDoyle(3) 10 92
(Tony Coyle) *mde all: t.k.h early: kicked 2 l clr 2f out: 3 l clr 1f out: sn rdn: hld on wl ins fnl f* **9/1**

0250 **2** 2 **Strong Steps**[2] 4207 5-8-13 84 (b) ConnorBeasley 3 84
(Roger Fell) *trckd ldrs: pushed along and hdwy into 2nd over 1f out: rdn and r.o fnl f: no imp on wnr* **5/2**[1]

-600 **3** 2 ¼ **Dubai's Secret**[15] 3750 4-9-5 82 SeanLevey 7 85
(David Brown) *chsd ldrs: pushed along in 4th 2f out: rdn over 1f out: r.o to take 3rd ins fnl f* **12/1**

0000 **4** 2 ¼ **Dream Walker (FR)**[20] 3587 8-8-10 95 (t) BenRobinson(5) 5 75+
(Brian Ellison) *hld up: effrt over 2f out: drvn over 1f out: rdn and r.o to take 4th nr fin* **11/4**[2]

0000 **5** *shd* **Gabrial's Kaka (IRE)**[20] 3589 7-9-3 86 FrannyNorton 11 77+
(Richard Fahey) *hld up: effrt and pushed along 2f out: racd wd over 1f out: drvn and r.o fnl f* **6/1**[3]

0033 **6** *shd* **Favourite Treat (USA)**[7] 4039 7-8-10 71 (e) AndrewMullen 9 70
(Ruth Carr) *trckd ldr: 2 l bhd 2f out: rdn over 1f out: wknd* **20/1**

5000 **7** 1 ½ **Outer Space**[9] 3969 6-9-4 88 DougieCostello 2 74
(Jamie Osborne) *hld up: drvn 2f out: no imp* **13/2**

3650 **8** 4 **Al Khan (IRE)**[77] 1769 8-8-10 90 LewisEdmunds(5) 8 62
(Kevin Ryan) *mid-div: drvn 2f out: rdn 1f out: wknd* **8/1**

1231 **9** 10 **Alpha Tauri (USA)**[53] 2466 11-8-3 38 AledBeech(7) 12 33
(Charles Smith) *mid-div on outer: drvn along 2f out: sn lost pl* **33/1**

0006 **10** 8 **Tamarin**[10] 3940 5-7-11 35 (p) DarraghKeenan(7) 1 8
(Lisa Williamson) *hld up: drvn 2f out: rdn over 1f out: wknd qckly* **125/1**

-100 **11** 47 **Harry Holland**[135] 734 5-8-11 64 ShaneGray 6
(Oliver Greenall) *bmpd sn after s and shuffled bk to last: pushed along 3f out: sn lost tch and heavily eased* **66/1**

1m 36.1s (2.30) **Going Correction** +0.40s/f (Good) **11** Ran SP% **121.6**
Speed ratings (Par 105): **104,102,99,97,97 97,95,91,81,73 26**
CSF £32.31 TOTE £10.90: £2.30, £1.50, £3.70; EX 44.10 Trifecta £335.90.Strong Steps was claimed by Mr J. S. Goldie for £14,000.
**Owner** Stephen Louch **Bred** Razza Del Sole Societa Agricola Srl **Trained** Norton, N Yorks

**FOCUS**
A competitive claimer with eight of the eleven runners rated 80 or above though most of them had been struggling to run to their marks in recent outings. The pace was strong, there was trouble at the start and few got involved so probably not form to rely on.

## 4294 CLOSE BROTHERS ASSET FINANCE H'CAP 7f 1y
**8:15** (8:18) (Class 4) (0-85,85) 3-Y-O+

**£6,225** (£1,864; £932; £466; £233; £117) **Stalls** Low

Form RPR

6102 **1** **Explain**[7] 4037 5-9-1 **80** (p) LewisEdmunds(5) 4 94
(Ruth Carr) *trckd ldrs on inner: hdwy gng wl 2f out: pushed along to ld over 1f out: reminders ent fnl f: sn drew clr: readily* **5/2**[1]

-200 **2** 5 **Heir To A Throne (FR)**[39] 2884 4-9-11 **85** ShaneGray 7 86
(Kevin Ryan) *trckd ldr: drvn 2f out: 3rd over 1f out: rdn appr fnl f: r.o to take 2nd last 50yds* **9/1**

0000 **3** ½ **Gabrial The Tiger (IRE)**[20] 3565 5-9-4 **78** BarryMcHugh 3 78
(Richard Fahey) *led: rdn along and hdd over 1f out: one pce fnl f: lost 2nd last 50yds* **4/1**[3]

-002 **4** 1 ¼ **Eqleem**[23] 3471 4-9-5 **79** AndrewMullen 10 75
(David Evans) *trckd ldrs: pushed along 2f out: rdn wl over 1f out: r.o one pce fnl f* **25/1**

1141 **5** 1 ½ **Cosmic Ray**[8] 4019 5-9-4 **78** 6ex (h) FrannyNorton 1 74+
(Les Eyre) *mid-div: pushed along 2f out: rdn over 1f out: one pce and eased fnl f* **11/4**[2]

6602 **6** 2 **British Embassy (IRE)**[28] 3282 5-9-2 **79** (p) HectorCrouch(3) 11 66
(Bill Turner) *trckd ldrs: drvn 2f out: rdn over 1f out: wknd* **33/1**

0010 **7** *nk* **Khelman (IRE)**[20] 3581 7-9-5 **82** SammyJoBell(3) 9 69
(Richard Fahey) *hld up: effrt on inner 2f out: rdn entering fnl f: one pce* **16/1**

0-00 **8** 8 **Monteverdi (FR)**[14] 3777 4-9-10 **84** (b) DougieCostello 8 50
(Jamie Osborne) *hld up: pushed along 2f out: rdn over 1f out: no imp* **20/1**

-006 **9** 7 **Grand Inquisitor**[41] 2828 5-9-10 **84** DavidProbert 6 32
(Ian Williams) *slowly away: a in rr: rdn 2f out: no imp* **7/1**

0522 **10** 3 **Majestic Moon (IRE)**[6] 4091 7-9-8 **85** ShelleyBirkett(3) 12 25
(Julia Feilden) *chsd ldrs: pushed along 2f out: wknd qckly* **20/1**

1m 28.37s (1.87) **Going Correction** +0.40s/f (Good) **10** Ran SP% **119.9**
Speed ratings (Par 105): **105,99,98,97,95 93,92,83,75,72**
CSF £25.08 CT £90.41 TOTE £3.30: £1.50, £2.80, £1.50; EX 27.60 Trifecta £107.10.
**Owner** The Beer Stalkers & Ruth Carr **Bred** Tibthorpe Stud **Trained** Huby, N Yorks

**FOCUS**
Despite this being a strongly-run affair it paid to race in the first half dozen and nothing got into it from behind. With the winning rider's claim, the form makes sense.

## 4295 CALDWELL CONSTRUCTION H'CAP 1m 2f 70y
**8:50** (8:50) (Class 4) (0-80,82) 3-Y-O

**£6,225** (£1,864; £932; £466; £233; £117) **Stalls** High

Form RPR

1 **1** **Contango (IRE)**[25] 3393 3-9-6 **76** DavidProbert 4 84+
(Andrew Balding) *trckd ldrs: hdwy on outer to press ldr 2f out: shkn up over 1f out: led and reminders ent fnl f: r.o wl* **7/2**[2]

-023 **2** 1 ¼ **Je Suis Charlie**[21] 3520 3-9-7 **77** LouisSteward 7 82
(Michael Bell) *hld up: prog to go 2nd 1/2-way where bmpd 5th home: qcknd into ld 2f out: rdn over 1f out and rdr lost whip: hdd ent fnl f: no ex* **13/2**

31-2 **3** 1 ¾ **Londinium**[8] 4016 3-9-11 **81** FrannyNorton 1 83+
(Mark Johnston) *slowly away: racd in rr: hdwy on outer 2f out: drvn along over 1f out: rdn and r.o to take 3rd ins fnl f* **11/8**[1]

3503 **4** 3 **Critical Thinking (IRE)**[4] 4144 3-8-3 **64** JaneElliott(5) 2 60
(Kevin Frost) *mid-div: lost pl 1/2-way: last and drvn 2f out: rdn and swtchd wd over 1f out: sme late hdwy* **12/1**

5-42 **5** *shd* **Hernandes (FR)**[25] 3412 3-8-12 **73** JennyPowell(5) 3 69
(Ed Walker) *led tl hdd after 1f: remained prom: received bump fr runner-up 1/2-way: drvn and lost pl 2f out: one pce u.p fnl f* **9/2**[3]

1033 **6** *hd* **Musikel (IRE)**[22] 3484 3-8-12 **71** (p) JordanVaughan(3) 6 67
(K R Burke) *trckd ldrs early: in mid-div 1/2-way: lost pl and drvn 2f out: rdn and one pce ins fnl f* **14/1**

10-0 **7** 3 **Rock N Rolla (IRE)**[16] 3713 3-9-7 **82** (p[1]) RowanScott(5) 8 72
(Keith Dalgleish) *trckd early: ldr: led after 1f: remained in ld tl drvn and hdd 2f out: sn rdn and wknd* **25/1**

2m 17.21s (6.01) **Going Correction** +0.40s/f (Good) **7** Ran SP% **114.0**
Speed ratings (Par 101): **91,90,88,86,86 85,83**
CSF £25.95 CT £44.41 TOTE £4.00: £2.10, £2.50; EX 31.30 Trifecta £52.10.
**Owner** Kennet Valley Thoroughbreds XII **Bred** Thomas Hassett **Trained** Kingsclere, Hants

**FOCUS**
Quite an interesting handicap for 3-y-os with several open to improvement. However, it was a muddling affair with a stop-start gallop and a sprint up the straight to finish. The runner-up is rated to a better view of his form.

T/Plt: £118.70 to a £1 stake. Pool: £52,571.00 - 442.57 winning units. T/Qpdt: £36.30 to a £1 stake. Pool: £3,300.00 - 90.71 winning units. **Keith McHugh**

# [3857]DONCASTER (L-H)

Friday, June 30

**OFFICIAL GOING: Soft (6.0)**

Wind: Light half against Weather: Cloudy with sunny periods

## 4296 188BET SUPPORTS VOICE OF RACING DAY EBF FILLIES' NOVICE STKS (PLUS 10 RACE) 6f 2y

**2:00** (2:01) (Class 5) 2-Y-0 **£2,975** (£885; £442; £221) **Stalls High**

Form RPR

3 **1** **Eirene**[17] 3697 2-9-0 0 RobertWinston 4 77+
(Dean Ivory) *hld up in tch: hdwy on outer 2f out: rdn to ld appr fnl f: kpt on wl* **5/2**[1]

**2** 1 **Fabulous Red** 2-9-0 0 JimmyQuinn 6 76+
(Ed Dunlop) *trckd ldrs: hdwy over 2f out: chal over 1f out: n.m.r and swtchd lft jst ins fnl f: sn rdn and styd on wl towards fin* **25/1**

62 **3** nk **Sardenya (IRE)**[17] 3687 2-8-11 0 KieranShoemark(3) 5 73
(Roger Charlton) *trckd ldrs: hdwy and cl up 2f out: rdn and ev ch whn edgd rt ent fnl f: kpt on same pce* **7/2**[2]

**4** 2 1/2 **Jane Rose (IRE)** 2-9-0 0 RyanMoore 10 69+
(Richard Hannon) *trckd ldrs: effrt whn nt clr run and hmpd jst over 1f out: sn swtchd lft and kpt on wl towards fin* **9/2**[3]

63 **5** shd **Peace Prevails**[18] 3662 2-9-0 0 TonyHamilton 1 65
(Richard Fahey) *led: pushed along and hdd 2f out: rdn and hung rt over 1f out: sn drvn and grad wknd* **7/1**

06 **6** nk **Song Of Summer**[16] 3712 2-9-0 0 DanielTudhope 12 64
(Archie Watson) *cl up: led 2f out: sn rdn: drvn and hdd appr fnl f: grad wknd* **7/1**

**7** 3 **Optimickstickhill** 2-9-0 0 BarryMcHugh 8 55
(Scott Dixon) *wnt rt jst after s: chsd ldrs: rdn along over 2f out: sn wknd* **50/1**

**8** 3/4 **Lady Sandy (IRE)** 2-9-0 0 PJMcDonald 7 53
(David Barron) *dwlt: a towards rr* **12/1**

**9** 6 **Puds** 2-9-0 0 PaulHanagan 3 35
(Charles Hills) *green and sn pushed along in rr: outpcd and bhd fr 1/2-way* **14/1**

0 **10** 9 **Beau Times (IRE)**[71] 1908 2-9-0 0 DavidAllan 9 8
(Tim Easterby) *dwlt and hmpd shortly after s: green and a bhd* **50/1**

1m 15.29s (1.69) **Going Correction** +0.10s/f (Good) **10** Ran SP% **116.1**

Speed ratings (Par 90): **92,90,90,86,86 86,82,81,73,61**

CSF £70.31 TOTE £2.90: £1.10, £7.40, £2.20; EX 61.60 Trifecta £489.20.

**Owner** M J Yarrow **Bred** Scuderia Archi Romani **Trained** Radlett, Herts

**FOCUS**

The round course was railed out from 1m2f until the straight. There was 56mm of rain on Wednesday and 5mm on Thursday. This looks fairly ordinary form but the winner, second and fourth look likely improvers.

## 4297 EXTRA PLACE RACES AT 188BET NOVICE STKS (PLUS 10 RACE) 7f 6y

**2:30** (2:31) (Class 4) 2-Y-0 **£4,204** (£1,251; £625; £312) **Stalls High**

Form RPR

3 **1** **Learn By Heart**[35] 3037 2-9-2 0 RyanMoore 6 86+
(William Haggas) *green and pushed along towards rr: hdwy on outer 3f out: led wl over 1f out: sn pushed clr: styd on strly* **4/7**[1]

4 **2** 3 1/2 **One Second**[12] 3858 2-8-11 0 HarryBentley 7 70
(Mark Johnston) *trckd ldng pair: cl up 1/2-way: led over 2f out: rdn and hdd wl over 1f out: sn drvn and kpt on: no ch w wnr* **9/1**[3]

**3** 2 1/2 **Porth Swtan (IRE)** 2-9-2 0 PaulHanagan 4 68
(Charles Hills) *in tch: hdwy over 2f out: rdn over 1f out: kpt on fnl f* **11/1**

**4** 3/4 **El Chapo** 2-9-2 0 TonyHamilton 2 66
(Richard Fahey) *towards rr: hdwy 2f out: rdn and kpt on fnl f* **10/1**

3 **5** 3 1/4 **Coastal Drive**[15] 3742 2-9-2 0 SeanLevey 1 58
(Richard Hannon) *led: hdd 1/2-way: cl up on outer: rdn along 2f out: sn wknd* **9/2**[2]

**6** 1/2 **The Fettler (IRE)** 2-9-2 0 DavidNolan 5 57
(Kevin Frost) *dwlt: green and a rr* **33/1**

0005 **7** 1/2 **Rock On Bertie (IRE)**[8] 4014 2-8-13 54 (p) RachelRichardson(3) 3 55
(Nigel Tinkler) *cl up: led 1/2-way: rdn along over 2f out: sn drvn and wknd wl over 1f out* **100/1**

1m 29.13s (2.83) **Going Correction** +0.10s/f (Good) **7** Ran SP% **113.2**

Speed ratings (Par 95): **87,83,80,79,75 75,74**

CSF £6.67 TOTE £1.70: £1.10, £3.60; EX 5.70 Trifecta £26.80.

**Owner** The Queen **Bred** The Queen **Trained** Newmarket, Suffolk

**FOCUS**

A decent winner but the time and the seventh suggest the bare form is not much better.

## 4298 188BET H'CAP 7f 213y(R)

**3:00** (3:02) (Class 5) (0-70,72) 3-Y-O+ **£2,975** (£885; £442; £221) **Stalls Low**

Form RPR

5-02 **1** **Flood Defence (IRE)**[19] 3627 3-8-11 63 WilliamBuick 10 68+
(Chris Wall) *hld up towards rr: hdwy 3f out: swtchd rt to outer and gd hdwy 2f out: chsd ldrs over 1f out: rdn to chal ins fnl f: kpt on wl to ld nr line* **5/1**[1]

63-2 **2** nk **Rosy Ryan (IRE)**[11] 3912 7-8-11 53 JoeDoyle 1 59
(Tina Jackson) *in tch: hdwy 3f out to trck ldrs 3f out: sltly hmpd 11/2f out: sn rdn to chal: drvn to ld last 75 yds: hdd and no ex nr line* **14/1**

-025 **3** 3/4 **Size Matters**[15] 3745 3-8-4 56 AndrewMullen 15 58
(Mark Walford) *trckd ldrs: hdwy and cl up wl over 2f out: chal over 1f out: rdn to take slt ld ins fnl f: drvn and hdd last 75 yds: kpt on same pce* **8/1**

0220 **4** nk **Adventureman**[19] 3628 5-9-6 62 (p) JamesSullivan 16 66
(Ruth Carr) *led: pushed along wl over 2f out: rdn and edgd lft 11/2f out: sn hdd and drvn: ev ch ent fnl f: kpt on same pce* **20/1**

0010 **5** nk **Mr Cool Cash**[13] 3845 5-9-13 69 ConnorBeasley 5 72
(Richard Guest) *trckd ldrs: hdwy on outer 3f out: cl up 2f out: rdn to ld over 1f out: drvn and hdd ins fnl f: kpt on same pce* **11/1**

3-50 **6** 4 **Ski Blast**[24] 3433 6-10-0 70 DavidNolan 11 64+
(Ivan Furtado) *dwlt and rr: hdwy wl over 2f out: rdn wl over 1f out: kpt on fnl f* **20/1**

40-4 **7** 1 **Bryght Boy**[25] 3396 4-9-5 61 ThomasBrown 17 52
(Ed Walker) *dwlt and t.k.h in rr: hdwy on outer over 3f out: chsd ldrs 2f out: sn rdn and no imp appr fnl f* **15/2**[3]

0-02 **8** 1/2 **Jack Nevison**[25] 3391 4-9-11 67 PaulHanagan 3 57
(Michael Appleby) *t.k.h: hld up towards rr: hdwy on inner 3f out: rdn along over 2f out: n.d* **10/1**

-323 **9** 1 3/4 **Break The Silence**[17] 3701 3-8-3 55 PatrickMathers 2 39
(Scott Dixon) *cl up: rdn along over 3f out: sn wknd* **12/1**

6463 **9** dht **False Id**[24] 3432 4-9-7 63 BarryMcHugh 8 49
(Marjorie Fife) *hld up: hdwy on outer 3f out: pushed along to chse ldrs over 2f out: sn rdn and btn* **13/2**[2]

-166 **11** 1 **Ashwaq**[35] 3038 3-9-6 72 RyanMoore 12 54
(Richard Hannon) *in tch: pushed along over 3f out: sn rdn and btn* **13/2**[2]

0163 **12** 1/2 **Luath**[38] 2918 4-9-2 61 NathanEvans(3) 4 44
(Suzzanne France) *midfield: rdn along on inner over 3f out: sn wknd* **11/1**

000 **13** 7 **Our Boy Jack (IRE)**[31] 3172 8-10-2 72 (p) DavidProbert 7 39
(Conor Dore) *t.k.h: hld up: a rr* **50/1**

4660 **14** hd **Lakeski**[11] 3913 3-8-0 55 AaronJones(3) 6 19
(Scott Dixon) *chsd ldrs: rdn along over 3f out: sn wknd* **50/1**

1m 43.64s (3.94) **Going Correction** +0.10s/f (Good)

**WFA** 3 from 4yo+ 10lb **14** Ran SP% **119.8**

Speed ratings (Par 103): **84,83,82,82,82 78,77,76,75,75 74,73,66,66**

CSF £72.89 CT £570.53 TOTE £5.40: £2.00, £4.50, £3.20; EX 83.40 Trifecta £833.00.

**Owner** Horsetrader One **Bred** Mcr Bloodstock Ltd **Trained** Newmarket, Suffolk

**FOCUS**

A tight finish to this competitive handicap. They raced up the middle in the straight.

## 4299 188BET.CO.UK H'CAP 7f 213y(R)

**3:30** (3:32) (Class 3) (0-95,94) 3-Y-O **£7,762** (£2,310; £1,154; £577) **Stalls Low**

Form RPR

1-34 **1** **Century Dream (IRE)**[41] 2824 3-9-0 87 (t[1]) WilliamBuick 2 96
(Simon Crisford) *trckd ldng pair: smooth hdwy 3f out: rdn to ld 11/2f out: styd on wl: comf* **2/1**[1]

-125 **2** 2 1/4 **Mustarrid (IRE)**[34] 3077 3-9-7 94 JimCrowley 7 98
(Richard Hannon) *led: pushed along 3f out: rdn over 2f out: hdd 11/.2f out: sn drvn and kpt on same pce* **11/2**

-216 **3** 7 **Materialist**[20] 3583 3-8-8 81 (h) HarryBentley 1 69
(Roger Varian) *t.k.h: trckd ldr: pushed along wl over 2f out: sn rdn and kpt on one pce fr over 1f out* **4/1**[3]

-511 **4** 1 3/4 **Helovaplan (IRE)**[12] 3862 3-8-7 80 6ex ConnorBeasley 6 64
(Bryan Smart) *hld up in rr: hdwy over 3f out: rdn along wl over 2f out: sn no imp* **5/1**

141 **5** 22 **Moolazim**[17] 3700 3-8-13 86 RyanMoore 3 19
(Marco Botti) *trckd ldrs: hdwy on inner over 3f out: sn pushed along: rdn over 2f: sn btn and eased* **7/2**[2]

1m 43.42s (3.72) **Going Correction** +0.10s/f (Good) **5** Ran SP% **107.6**

Speed ratings (Par 103): **85,82,75,74,52**

CSF £12.37 TOTE £2.70: £1.30, £2.80; EX 12.10 Trifecta £47.10.

**Owner** Abdullah Saeed **Bred** Rabbah Bloodstock Limited **Trained** Newmarket, Suffolk

**FOCUS**

For one reason or another, only the winner looked to run his best race. They raced up the middle in the straight.

## 4300 READ SILVESTRE DE SOUSA AT 188BET MAIDEN FILLIES' STKS 1m 2f 43y

**4:00** (4:01) (Class 5) 3-Y-O+ **£2,975** (£885; £442; £221) **Stalls Low**

Form RPR

5 **1** **Great White Shark (FR)**[22] 3506 3-9-0 0 DanielMuscutt 11 86+
(James Fanshawe) *trckd ldrs: hdwy 3f out: chsd ldr over 1f out: sn rdn to chal: led ins fnl f: kpt on wl* **8/1**

02 **2** 1 1/2 **Superioritycomplex (IRE)**[12] 3866 3-9-0 0 RyanMoore 13 82
(Sir Michael Stoute) *trckd ldr on outer: cl up 3f out: led 2f out: rdn over 1f out: drvn and hdd ins fnl f: kpt on* **9/2**[3]

3 **3** hd **What A Home (IRE)**[15] 3748 3-9-0 0 BenCurtis 3 81
(William Haggas) *hld up towards rr: hdwy 3f out: rdn wl over 1f out. sn chsng ldrs: styd on wl fnl f* **11/4**[1]

23-2 **4** 5 **Kitty Boo**[19] 3626 3-9-0 75 (h) DanielTudhope 10 72
(Luca Cumani) *trckd ldrs: hdwy 3f out: rdn along wl over 1f out: drvn and kpt on one pce fnl f* **4/1**[2]

0 **5** nk **Saniyaat**[72] 1885 3-9-0 0 (v[1]) HarryBentley 4 71
(George Peckham) *midfield: hdwy on outer 3f out: rdn along to chse ldrs 2f out: kpt on u.p fnl f* **25/1**

0 **6** 1 1/4 **Dukinta (IRE)**[19] 3615 3-9-0 0 (b[1]) JackMitchell 12 69
(Hugo Palmer) *led: rdn along over 3f out: hdd 2f out: sn drvn and grad wknd* **50/1**

3 **7** 14 **Sugardrop**[36] 3007 3-9-0 0 SteveDrowne 9 42
(Amanda Perrett) *trckd ldng pair: pushed along 3f out: rdn 2f out: sn drvn and wknd* **8/1**

**8** 5 **Quite Sharp** 3-9-0 0 ShaneKelly 6 33
(Charlie Fellowes) *a towards rr* **33/1**

5 **9** 3/4 **Shimmering Light**[15] 3748 3-9-0 0 JimCrowley 5 31
(Michael Bell) *in tch on inner: rdn along over 3f out: sn wknd* **6/1**

**10** 1 1/4 **Chocolate Account (USA)** 3-9-0 0 JoeyHaynes 1 29
(Ed Dunlop) *chsd ldrs: rdn along wl over 3f out: sn wknd* **100/1**

0 **11** 5 **Dutch Melody**[38] 2930 3-9-0 0 TomMarquand 8 20
(Chris Wall) *a rr* **150/1**

**12** 24 **Incredible Red** 3-9-0 0 TonyHamilton 7
(Ed Dunlop) *a towards* **33/1**

2m 15.75s (6.35) **Going Correction** +0.625s/f (Yiel) **12** Ran SP% **114.7**

Speed ratings (Par 100): **99,97,97,93,93 92,81,77,76,75 71,52**

CSF £40.73 TOTE £9.80: £2.30, £1.90, £1.20; EX 49.40 Trifecta £322.70.

**Owner** Malcolm C Denmark **Bred** Mme Anne-Marie D'Estainville Gedik **Trained** Newmarket, Suffolk

■ Stewards' Enquiry : Ben Curtis seven-day ban: failed to take all reasonable and permissible measures to obtain the best possible placing (Jul 14-21)

**FOCUS**

Add 12yds. A useful enough fillies' maiden. They raced middle to stands' side in the straight.

## 4301 BEST ODDS GUARANTEED AT 188BET H'CAP 1m 6f 115y

**4:30** (4:31) (Class 4) (0-85,85) 4-Y-O+ **£4,851** (£1,443; £721; £360) **Stalls Low**

Form RPR

-015 **1** **Injam (IRE)**[21] 3527 4-9-7 85 JoeyHaynes 7 94
(Jedd O'Keeffe) *trckd ldr: hdwy to ld 3f out: rdn wl over 1f out: drvn and kpt on wl fnl f* **4/1**[2]

5522 **2** 2 **Braes Of Lochalsh**[7] 4038 6-7-11 68 (v) SeanMooney(7) 8 74
(Jim Goldie) *trckd ldng pair: chsd wnr 3f out: rdn wl over 1f out: ch ent fnl f: sn drvn and kpt on same pce* **5/2**[1]

10-0 **3** 10 **Alphabetical Order**[14] 3795 9-9-1 79 DanielTudhope 1 72
(David O'Meara) *hld up in rr: hdwy over 3f out: chsd ldrs 2f out: sn rdn: styd on one pce fnl f* **25/1**

4213 **4** 2 1/4 **Fire Jet (IRE)**[13] 3840 4-9-6 84 BenCurtis 6 74
(John Mackie) *hld up in tch: hdwy 4f out: chsd ldrs 3f out: rdn along over 2f out: drvn wl over 1f out: sn one pce* **9/2**[3]

-644 **5** 1/2 **Silva Eclipse**[21] 3527 4-9-1 79 ShaneKelly 9 69
(Jedd O'Keeffe) *in tch: hdwy over 4f out: rdn along over 3f out: sn wknd* **9/2**[3]

0024 **6** *7* **Itlaaq**[14] 3795 11-8-7 **76**............(t) MeganNicholls(5) 4 57
(Michael Easterby) *hld up in rr: hdwy over 5f out: chsd ldrs 3f out: sn rdn: drvn wl over 1f out: wknd* **12/1**
-511 **7** *13* **Incus**[19] 3623 4-7-11 **66** oh7............ JaneElliott(5) 3 30
(Ed de Giles) *led: rdn along and hdd 3f out: sn wknd and bhd* **11/2**
3m 14.58s (7.18) **Going Correction** +0.625s/f (Yiel) **7** Ran SP% **111.9**
Speed ratings (Par 105): **105,103,98,97,97 93,86**
CSF £13.77 CT £210.47 TOTE £5.20: £2.50, £2.00; EX 20.30 Trifecta £269.70.
**Owner** Miss S Long **Bred** John M Weld **Trained** Middleham Moor, N Yorks
■ Western Prince was withdrawn. Price at time of withdrawal 33-1. Rule 4 does not apply.

**FOCUS**
Add 12yds. Three of these including the first two finishers soon established a big break on the others and, although the field bunched up turning in, it seems clear the one-two had more efficient trips than the closers, as they pulled right away again in the closing stages. The action was up the middle.

## 4302 BRITISH & IRISH LIONS BETTING AT 188BET H'CAP (DIV I) 6f 2y
**5:00** (5:02) (Class 6) (0-65,67) 3-Y-O **£2,587** (£770; £384; £192) **Stalls** High

Form RPR
63-2 **1** **Zumran**[9] 3970 3-9-5 **63**............ WilliamBuick 5 73
(Philip McBride) *towards rr: hdwy and in tch 1/2-way: hdwy on inner to ld 2f out: sn rdn: drvn clr ins fnl f: kpt on strly* **5/1**[2]
063- **2** *2¼* **Yes You (IRE)**[359] 4002 3-8-1 **52**............ JamieGormley(7) 3 55
(Iain Jardine) *trckd ldrs: pushed along and sltly outpcd 2f out: sn swtchd lft to outer and rdn: styd on wl fnl f* **20/1**
3-4 **3** *1* **Bourbonisto**[25] 3391 3-8-13 **62**............ RobJFitzpatrick(5) 8 62
(Ben Haslam) *in tch: hdwy over 2f out: rdn to chse ldrs over 1f out: drvn and kpt on same pce fnl f* **8/1**[3]
64-6 **4** *2¼* **Atrafan (IRE)**[21] 3525 3-9-0 **58**............ SteveDrowne 18 52
(Alan Brown) *racd towards stands side: towards rr: hdwy wl over 2f out: rdn to chse ldrs over 1f out: swtchd lft and drvn ins fnl f: kpt on* **16/1**
331 **5** *nk* **My Girl Maisie (IRE)**[21] 3525 3-8-12 **56**............ BenCurtis 15 49
(Richard Guest) *racd towards stand side: hdwy to chse ldrs 2f out: rdn over 1f out and ev ch: drvn and edgd rt ins fnl f: one pce* **7/4**[1]
0-00 **6** *¾* **Morello (IRE)**[32] 3162 3-9-2 **60**............ TomMarquand 1 50
(Henry Candy) *dwlt: sn chsng ldrs on inner: hdwy and cl up 2f out: sn rdn: drvn and wknd appr fnl f* **12/1**
000- **7** *3* **Tilly Devine**[234] 7855 3-8-0 **47**............ AaronJones(3) 4 28
(Scott Dixon) *cl up: led 1/2-way: rdn along and hdd 2f out: sn drvn and grad wknd* **50/1**
-603 **8** *6* **Tagur (IRE)**[39] 2886 3-9-7 **65**............(p) JoeDoyle 7 28
(Kevin Ryan) *led: hdd 1/2-way and sn pushed along: rdn 2f out and sn wknd* **5/1**[2]
P053 **9** *nse* **Three C's (IRE)**[13] 3810 3-9-3 **61**............(tp) TimmyMurphy 14 24
(David Dennis) *prom: rdn along over 2f out: sn drvn and wknd* **14/1**
-431 **10** *1¾* **Sadieroseclifford (IRE)**[17] 3703 3-8-10 **54**............ RobHornby 17 12
(Giles Bravery) *nvr bttr than midfield* **12/1**
-006 **11** *shd* **Pontecarlo Boy**[20] 3555 3-8-2 **46** oh1............ CamHardie 10 4
(Richard Whitaker) *a towards rr* **25/1**
0645 **12** *2½* **Zone In**[21] 3525 3-8-9 **60**............ BenSanderson(7) 6 10
(Roger Fell) *chsd ldrs: rdn along over 2f out: sn drvn and wknd* **16/1**
00-0 **13** *3½* **Zarkavon**[45] 2704 3-8-2 **46** oh1............ PaddyAspell 13
(John Wainwright) *a towards rr: bhd fr 1/2-way* **100/1**
1m 14.53s (0.93) **Going Correction** +0.10s/f (Good) **13** Ran SP% **122.3**
Speed ratings (Par 97): **97,94,92,89,89 88,84,76,76,73 73,70,65**
CSF £109.30 CT £805.02 TOTE £4.00: £1.70, £5.40, £2.70; EX 66.50 Trifecta £1194.30.
**Owner** Martin Percival & Mrs C E Percival **Bred** Boyce Bloodstock & Mrs C E Percival **Trained** Newmarket, Suffolk

**FOCUS**
A moderate handicap won in good style. They raced middle to stands' side. The third's helpful for pinning the level.

## 4303 BRITISH & IRISH LIONS BETTING AT 188BET H'CAP (DIV II) 6f 2y
**5:30** (5:33) (Class 6) (0-65,66) 3-Y-O **£2,587** (£770; £384; £192) **Stalls** High

Form RPR
05-4 **1** **Metisian**[38] 2924 3-9-4 **62**............ DavidNolan 15 73+
(Jedd O'Keeffe) *towards rr: gd hdwy on outer over 2f out: chsd ldrs over 1f out: sn rdn: chal ent fnl f: led last 100 yds: kpt on strly* **17/2**
-002 **2** *2¼* **Majestic Stone (IRE)**[61] 2182 3-8-11 **55**............(v) BenCurtis 17 60
(Julie Camacho) *swtchd lft s and rr: hdwy over 2f out: rdn over 1f out: styd on strly fnl f: tk 2nd on line* **13/2**[1]
5065 **3** *hd* **Henrietta's Dream**[6] 4106 3-7-9 **46** oh1............(b) SophieRalston(7) 8 50
(John Wainwright) *prom: cl up over 2f out: rdn to ld wl over 1f out: jnd and drvn ent fnl f: hdd and no ex last 100 yds* **80/1**
04-0 **4** *nse* **One Too Many (IRE)**[39] 2900 3-9-6 **64**............ SeanLevey 16 68
(David Brown) *in tch: smooth hdwy on outer over 2f out: cl up over 1f out: chal ent fnl f: sn rdn and ev ch: no ex towards fin* **10/1**
3360 **5** *nk* **Darvie**[39] 2897 3-8-13 **57**............ SamJames 6 60
(David Barron) *dwlt and rr: hdwy 2f out: rdn over 1f out: kpt on wl fnl f* **16/1**
-524 **6** *1¾* **Eponina (IRE)**[28] 3296 3-9-2 **65**............ MeganNicholls(5) 5 63
(Ben Haslam) *towards rr: hdwy over 2f out: rdn to chse ldrs on inner over 1f out: drvn and edgd rt ent fnl f: kpt on same pce* **8/1**[3]
-010 **7** *nk* **Uncle Charlie (IRE)**[11] 3897 3-9-8 **66**............ JoeyHaynes 3 63
(Ann Duffield) *dwlt: sn in tch on inner: hdwy and cl up over 2f out: rdn wl over 1f out: grad wknd* **8/1**[3]
03-0 **8** *¾* **Twilight Spirit**[31] 3171 3-9-3 **61**............ ShaneKelly 10 56
(Tony Carroll) *chsd ldrs: rdn along over 2f out: grad wknd* **10/1**
0-00 **9** *½* **Nellie's Dancer**[25] 3387 3-8-8 **55**............(p[1]) AaronJones(3) 4 48
(Scott Dixon) *midfield: effrt over 2f out: sn rdn and kpt on fnl f* **20/1**
0-00 **10** *nse* **Myllachy**[13] 3831 3-8-2 **46** oh1............(b) CamHardie 14 39
(Tim Easterby) *in tch: rdn along* **25/1**
3000 **11** *1¾* **Backinanger**[37] 2949 3-8-8 **52**............(p) JoeDoyle 7 40
(Kevin Ryan) *keen: chsd ldrs: rdn along 2f out: grad wknd* **25/1**
003 **12** *hd* **Vintage Dream (IRE)**[22] 3496 3-9-2 **60**............(p) PaddyAspell 1 47
(Noel Wilson) *cl up: led 2f out: sn rdn: hdd over 1f out and sn wknd* **14/1**
60-0 **13** *1* **Innstigator**[14] 3784 3-9-2 **60**............ RobHornby 12 44
(Ralph J Smith) *chsd ldrs: rdn along over 2f out: sn drvn and wknd* **16/1**
-000 **14** *½* **Flying Onsite (FR)**[42] 2792 3-7-13 **50**............ FayeMcManoman(7) 18 33
(Nigel Tinkler) *dwlt: a rr* **16/1**
1140 **15** *1¾* **Endeavour (IRE)**[10] 3949 3-9-8 **66**............ TomMarquand 11 43
(Marjorie Fife) *led: rdn along and hdd 2f out: sn wknd* **12/1**
0043 **16** *12* **Bobby Vee**[19] 3624 3-9-4 **62**............ SteveDrowne 9
(Dean Ivory) *chsd ldrs: rdn along over 2f out:. sn wknd* **15/2**[2]
0-00 **17** *1½* **Mulwith (IRE)**[10] 3949 3-8-7 **58**............(b) RPWalsh(7) 13
(Scott Dixon) *.cl up: rdn along 1/2-way: sn lost pl and bhd* **50/1**
1m 14.82s (1.22) **Going Correction** +0.10s/f (Good) **17** Ran SP% **123.7**
Speed ratings (Par 97): **95,92,91,91,91 88,88,87,86,86 84,84,82,82,79 63,61**
CSF £59.88 CT £4307.10 TOTE £10.20: £2.60, £1.90, £7.60, £2.60; EX 75.40.
**Owner** Mrs Sarah Pearson **Bred** Mrs S M Pearson **Trained** Middleham Moor, N Yorks

**FOCUS**
A moderate handicap in which they raced middle to stands' side. The winner has more to offer.
T/Jkpt: £10,000.00 to a £1 stake. Pool: £10,000.00 - 1 winning unit. T/Plt: £21.50 to a £1 stake. Pool: £73,149.00 - 3,399.76 winning units. T/Qpdt: £13.50 to a £1 stake. Pool: £5,104.00 - 378.02 winning units. **Joe Rowntree**

# 4258 NEWCASTLE (A.W) (L-H)
Friday, June 30

**OFFICIAL GOING: Tapeta: standard**
Wind: Light, half behind on straight course and in over 3f of home straight on round course Weather: Overcast, showers

## 4304 BETFRED "TREBLE ODDS ON LUCKY15'S" H'CAP 1m 5y (Tp)
**6:00** (6:03) (Class 4) (0-85,82) 3-Y-0+ **£5,822** (£1,732; £865; £432) **Stalls** Centre

Form RPR
3134 **1** **Excel Again**[17] 3700 3-8-13 **77**............ DavidAllan 4 85+
(James Tate) *trckd ldrs: rdn 2f out: rallied and led 2f out: kpt on strly fnl f* **11/8**[1]
0335 **2** *½* **Amood (IRE)**[13] 3847 6-9-10 **78**............(p) JasonHart 5 86
(Simon West) *dwlt: hld up: smooth hdwy over 2f out: effrt and chsd wnr appr fnl f: kpt on: hld nr fin* **10/1**
3100 **3** *3* **Nick Vedder**[27] 3317 3-8-9 **73**............(p[1]) OisinMurphy 6 72
(K R Burke) *trckd ldrs: effrt and wnt 2nd briefly over 1f out: kpt on same pce fnl f* **11/1**
3153 **4** *2* **Champion Harbour (IRE)**[1] 4265 3-8-0 **64** oh1............ PatrickMathers 7 58
(Richard Fahey) *hld up on nr side of gp: hdwy and disp 2nd pl over 1f out: rdn and outpcd fnl f* **11/1**
1244 **5** *2* **Inaam (IRE)**[38] 2922 4-10-0 **82**............ JackGarritty 3 74
(Richard Fahey) *hld up: pushed along and effrt over 2f out: edgd lft and no ex fnl f* **5/1**[2]
1-40 **6** *2½* **Kodiac Khan (IRE)**[17] 3700 3-9-0 **78**............ PaulMulrennan 9 62
(Mark Johnston) *led or disp ld to 2f out: drvn and sn wknd* **7/1**[3]
000 **7** *nk* **Zealous (IRE)**[15] 3743 4-9-5 **73**............ JosephineGordon 2 58
(Sally Haynes) *t.k.h: cl up: rdn and outpcd over 2f out: edgd lft and sn wknd* **25/1**
3113 **8** *1* **Roman De Brut (IRE)**[32] 3144 5-9-6 **77**............ CharlieBennett(3) 8 60
(Daniel Mark Loughnane) *trckd ldrs: drvn along over 2f out: wknd over 1f out* **12/1**
-003 **9** *1* **Jordan James (IRE)**[22] 3487 4-9-1 **69**............(p) TomEaves 1 50
(Brian Ellison) *led or disp ld to 2f out: sn rdn and wknd* **25/1**
1m 38.73s (0.13) **Going Correction** +0.075s/f (Slow)
**WFA** 3 from 4yo+ 10lb **9** Ran SP% **112.4**
Speed ratings (Par 105): **102,101,98,96,94 92,91,90,89**
CSF £15.62 CT £106.18 TOTE £2.00: £1.10, £2.90, £2.80; EX 16.90 Trifecta £122.80.
**Owner** Sheikh Rashid Dalmook Al Maktoum **Bred** Darley **Trained** Newmarket, Suffolk

**FOCUS**
Just an ordinary handicap to kick off day two of Newcastle's three-day Northumberland Plate meeting and it was won by a lightly raced 3yo on the up.

## 4305 BETFRED "HOME OF GOALS GALORE" FILLIES' H'CAP 5f (Tp)
**6:30** (6:31) (Class 5) (0-75,75) 3-Y-0+ **£4,528** (£1,347; £673; £336) **Stalls** Centre

Form RPR
3614 **1** **Intense Romance (IRE)**[16] 3709 3-9-1 **75**............ CallumRodriguez(5) 9 81
(Michael Dods) *hld up: hdwy on nr side of gp over 1f out: chal ent fnl f: led last 50yds: kpt on wl* **5/2**[1]
4-36 **2** *nk* **Fruit Salad**[14] 3793 4-9-9 **72**............(p) FranBerry 7 79
(James Bethell) *hld up: hdwy on nr side of gp over 1f out: led ent fnl f: hdd and no ex last 30yds* **10/3**[2]
2110 **3** *1¾* **Kinloch Pride**[13] 3847 5-9-0 **68**............(p) PhilDennis(5) 2 69
(Noel Wilson) *cl up: rdn to ld over 1f out: hdd ent fnl f: sn one pce* **7/1**
2410 **4** *½* **Lady Cristal (IRE)**[32] 3152 3-8-11 **71**............(p) CliffordLee(5) 3 68
(K R Burke) *cl up: effrt and ch over 1f out: kpt on same pce fnl f* **8/1**
4046 **5** *½* **Rose Eclair**[21] 3524 4-9-1 **64**............ JasonHart 5 61
(Tim Easterby) *trckd ldr: effrt and drvn over 1f out: one pce fnl f* **12/1**
-043 **6** *nk* **Reedanjas (IRE)**[7] 4043 3-9-3 **75**............ NathanEvans(3) 6 69
(Gay Kelleway) *hld up bhd ldng gp: drvn and outpcd over 2f out: rallied fnl f: no imp* **10/1**
6-65 **7** *1¼* **Savannah Beau**[149] 514 5-9-6 **69**............(p) TomEaves 8 60
(Derek Shaw) *stdd s: hld up: effrt and hdwy over 1f out: no imp fnl f* **50/1**
554- **8** *1* **Paradwys (IRE)**[255] 7439 3-9-5 **74**............ OisinMurphy 1 60
(Archie Watson) *prom on far side of gp: drvn and outpcd over 2f out: btn over 1f out* **13/2**[3]
-010 **9** *2½* **Krystallite**[10] 3944 4-9-7 **70**............ JosephineGordon 4 49
(Scott Dixon) *t.k.h: led to over 1f out: rdn and wknd fnl f* **25/1**
59.55s (0.05) **Going Correction** +0.075s/f (Slow)
**WFA** 3 from 4yo+ 6lb **9** Ran SP% **111.2**
Speed ratings (Par 100): **102,101,98,97,97 96,94,93,89**
CSF £10.05 CT £47.41 TOTE £3.50: £1.30, £1.40, £1.80; EX 11.20 Trifecta £26.40.
**Owner** Hugh Malcolm Linsley **Bred** John O'Connor **Trained** Denton, Co Durham

**FOCUS**
A competitive little contest for the grade and the front two, who ended up coming away, both raced towards the stands side of the main group. The runner-up is rated to form.

## 4306 BETFRED GOSFORTH PARK CUP H'CAP 5f (Tp)
**7:00** (7:06) (Class 2) (0-105,104) 3-Y-0+
**£28,012** (£8,388; £4,194; £2,097; £1,048; £526) **Stalls** Centre

Form RPR
4001 **1** **Line Of Reason (IRE)**[13] 3829 7-9-8 **100**............ OisinMurphy 10 108
(Paul Midgley) *hld up: shkn up and gd hdwy over 1f out: led wl ins fnl f: keeping on whn j. winning line* **9/1**[3]
02-2 **2** *½* **Lexington Abbey**[76] 1800 6-9-4 **96**............(b) KevinStott 14 102
(Kevin Ryan) *hld up in tch on nr side of gp: hdwy to ld over 1f out: sn rdn and edgd lft: hdd and no ex wl ins fnl f* **12/1**
-640 **3** *¾* **Orion's Bow**[13] 3829 6-9-12 **104**............ DavidAllan 9 111+
(Tim Easterby) *hld up: nt clr run over 2f out tl swtchd rt appr over 1f out: gd hdwy fnl f: nrst fin* **2/1**[1]

-060 **4** ½ **Jack Dexter**[13] 3829 8-8-11 **89**............................ PaulMulrennan 4 91+
(Jim Goldie) *hld up midfield: effrt on far side of gp over 1f out: edgd lft: kpt on fnl f: no imp* **16/1**

3206 **5** 1¾ **Robot Boy (IRE)**[13] 3829 7-9-10 **102**............................ FranBerry 1 97
(David Barron) *led tl rdn and hdd over 1f out: outpcd ins fnl f* **12/1**

0552 **6** 2 **Soie D'Leau**[10] 3932 5-9-2 **94**............................(p) TonyHamilton 8 82
(Kristin Stubbs) *t.k.h: hld up midfield: effrt and drvn along 2f out: wknd ins fnl f* **11/1**

331 **7** ½ **Escalating**[19] 3625 5-8-2 **87**............................(tp) RayDawson(7) 5 73
(Michael Appleby) *hld up: rdn along over 2f out: edgd lft: no imp fr over 1f out* **14/1**

3030 **8** nse **Confessional**[13] 3829 10-8-11 **89**............................(e) JackGarritty 7 75
(Tim Easterby) *prom: effrt and drvn whn checked over 1f out: sn lost pl: n.d after* **40/1**

0225 **9** 3¾ **Rasheeq (IRE)**[13] 3827 4-8-10 **91**............................ RachelRichardson(3) 11 64
(Tim Easterby) *hld up: rdn on nr side of gp 2f out: sn no imp* **5/1**[2]

2100 **10** ½ **Doc Sportello (IRE)**[77] 1772 5-9-4 **101**............................(p) CliffordLee(5) 3 72
(Michael Herrington) *prom on far side of gp: rdn over 2f out: edgd lft and wknd over 1f out* **12/1**

5203 **11** 3½ **Distant Past**[49] 2578 6-8-13 **91**............................(p) TomEaves 6 49
(Kevin Ryan) *cl up: effrt and drvn along 2f out: wknd ins fnl f* **25/1**

44-0 **12** 1 **Afandem (IRE)**[50] 2561 3-9-5 **103**............................(b1) JosephineGordon 13 56
(Hugo Palmer) *hld up on nr side of gp: drvn along over 2f out: sn n.d: btn over 1f out* **11/1**

58.58s (-0.92) **Going Correction** +0.075s/f (Slow)
**WFA** 3 from 4yo+ 6lb **12** Ran SP% **118.6**
Speed ratings (Par 109): **110,109,108,107,104 101,100,100,94,93 87,86**
CSF £112.36 CT £303.52 TOTE £9.50: £2.60, £3.50, £1.40; EX 86.80 Trifecta £240.10.

**Owner** Taylor's Bloodstock Ltd **Bred** Corduff Stud Ltd, J Corcoran & J Judd **Trained** Westow, N Yorks

■ Hoofalong was withdrawn. Price at time of withdrawal 16-1. Rule 4 does not apply.

**FOCUS**
An ultra competitive sprint handicap and strong form. The winner's rated close to his 2016 peak.

## 4307 BETFRED "SUPPORTS JACK BERRY HOUSE" CLASSIFIED STKS 1m 4f 98y (Tp)
7:35 (7:35) (Class 5) 3-Y-O **£4,528** (£1,347; £673; £336) **Stalls** High

Form RPR

552 **1** **Montanna**[28] 3286 3-9-0 74............................ JackGarritty 8 79
(Jedd O'Keeffe) *prom: effrt and chsd ldr over 2f out: led ins fnl f: hld on wl* **16/1**

543 **2** ½ **Marine One**[16] 3720 3-9-0 73............................ OisinMurphy 7 78+
(David Simcock) *t.k.h early: hld up in last pl: stdy hdwy on outside over 2f out: rdn over 1f out: kpt on to take 2nd nr fin* **1/1**[1]

-443 **3** ½ **Second Page**[12] 3859 3-8-7 75............................(p1) RossaRyan(7) 5 77
(Richard Hannon) *t.k.h: cl up: led over 2f out: rdn and hdd ins fnl f: no ex and lost 2nd nr fin* **9/1**[3]

041 **4** 1¾ **Conkering Hero (IRE)**[27] 3326 3-9-0 72............................ FranBerry 4 74
(Joseph Tuite) *hld up: stdy hdwy over 2f out: sn rdn: kpt on same pce ins fnl f* **10/1**

100 **5** 4 **Taxmeifyoucan (IRE)**[27] 3335 3-9-0 72............................(p) JasonHart 1 68
(Keith Dalgleish) *hld up on ins: drvn and outpcd over 2f out: sme late hdwy: nvr rchd ldrs* **12/1**

4123 **6** 2½ **Mirzam (IRE)**[15] 3759 3-9-0 75............................ GrahamLee 2 64
(Mick Channon) *led 2f: prom tl rdn and wknd wl over 1f out* **9/1**[3]

0033 **7** 4 **The Blues Master (IRE)**[8] 4004 3-9-0 75............................(b) PaulMulrennan 6 57
(Mark Johnston) *dwlt: hdwy on outside to ld after 2f: set ordinary gallop: hdd over 2f out: wknd over 1f out* **9/1**[3]

3-22 **8** 14 **Bowban**[7] 777 3-9-0 74............................ TomEaves 3 35
(Brian Ellison) *t.k.h: cl up: drvn and outpcd over 2f out: sn wknd* **13/2**[2]

2m 41.98s (0.88) **Going Correction** +0.075s/f (Slow) **8** Ran SP% **116.0**
Speed ratings (Par 99): **100,99,99,98,95 93,91,81**
CSF £33.20 TOTE £14.60: £4.20, £1.10, £2.60; EX 52.90 Trifecta £315.40.

**Owner** Highbeck Racing **Bred** West Stow Stud Ltd **Trained** Middleham Moor, N Yorks

**FOCUS**
An interesting little classified stakes featuring several likely capable of better at some stage. However, they went very steady early on, resulting in quite a few racing freely, so it might not pay to place too much faith in the form.

## 4308 BETFRED MOBILE/EBF HOPPINGS STKS (LISTED RACE) (F&M) 1m 2f 42y (Tp)
8:05 (8:07) (Class 1) 3-Y-O+
**£28,355** (£10,750; £5,380; £2,680; £1,345; £675) **Stalls** High

Form RPR

260- **1** **More Mischief**[298] 6200 5-9-5 99............................ GrahamLee 4 105
(Jedd O'Keeffe) *chsd ldr: clr of rest 1/2-way: rdn to ld over 1f out: hld on gamely towards fin* **10/1**

11-6 **2** nk **Chain Of Daisies**[36] 3012 5-9-5 110............................ FergusSweeney 6 104
(Henry Candy) *led at ordinary gallop: clr w wnr 1/2-way: rdn and hdd over 1f out: rallied: kpt on fnl f: hld nr fin* **5/4**[1]

0-46 **3** nk **Very Dashing**[30] 3219 4-9-5 96............................ PhillipMakin 7 103
(Ralph Beckett) *t.k.h: hld up in rr: effrt whn n.m.r briefly over 2f out: sn chsng clr ldng pair: clsd fr over 1f out: swtchd lft ins fnl f: one pce whn n.m.r cl home* **15/2**

16-3 **4** 10 **Entsar (IRE)**[30] 3219 4-9-5 95............................ PaulHanagan 3 92
(William Haggas) *hld up in tch: rdn along over 2f out: wknd over 1f out* **3/1**[2]

1041 **5** 12 **Tegara**[23] 3455 4-9-5 78............................ OisinMurphy 5 64
(David Simcock) *hld up: drvn along 3f out: sn n.d: btn fnl 2f* **33/1**

5-20 **6** 3¼ **Materialistic**[55] 2392 4-9-5 96............................ DanielTudhope 2 58
(Luca Cumani) *chsd ldrs: drvn along 3f out: wknd over 1f out* **11/2**[3]

5400 **7** 31 **Epsom Icon**[13] 3843 4-9-5 95............................ PaulMulrennan 1
(Mick Channon) *prom: drvn and outpcd over 2f out: sn btn and lost tch* **25/1**

2m 7.98s (-2.42) **Going Correction** +0.075s/f (Slow) **7** Ran SP% **112.5**
Speed ratings (Par 111): **112,111,111,103,93 91,66**
CSF £22.33 TOTE £9.40: £3.60, £1.20; EX 26.90 Trifecta £125.90.

**Owner** Caron & Paul Chapman **Bred** Cliveden Stud **Trained** Middleham Moor, N Yorks

■ Stewards' Enquiry : Fergus Sweeney two-day ban: used whip above permitted level (Jul 17-18)

**FOCUS**
A decent fillies' Listed race in which there was a standout contender on the ratings but she was once again below par despite being allowed an easy lead. The front three finished a mile clear.

## 4309 BETFRED TV MAIDEN STKS 7f 14y (Tp)
**8:40** (8:41) (Class 5) 3-Y-O+ **£4,528** (£1,347; £673; £336) **Stalls** Centre

Form RPR

0 **1** **Important Mission (USA)**[17] 3691 3-9-3 0............................ PaulHanagan 12 83+
(William Haggas) *hld up midfield: stdy hdwy over 2f out: rdn to ld ent fnl f: edgd lft: pushed out* **5/1**[3]

4 **2** 1¼ **Tamih (IRE)**[31] 3188 3-9-3 0............................ JackMitchell 13 80+
(Roger Varian) *in tch on nr side of gp: smooth hdwy to ld 2f out: sn rdn: hung lft and hdd ent fnl f: kpt on same pce* **15/8**[1]

**3** 1½ **Kynren (IRE)** 3-9-3 0............................ FranBerry 4 76
(David Barron) *hld up: stdy hdwy over 2f out: effrt and prom over 1f out: kpt on same pce fnl f* **66/1**

22 **4** 2 **Cobalty Isle (IRE)**[18] 3669 3-9-3 0............................ FergusSweeney 11 71
(Henry Candy) *trckd ldrs: effrt and ev ch 2f out: outpcd fnl f* **9/4**[2]

03 **5** shd **Jessinamillion**[35] 3054 3-9-3 0............................ DanielTudhope 1 70
(James Bethell) *trckd ldrs: effrt and ev ch 2f out: drvn and sn no ex* **16/1**

0 **6** 1¾ **Soldier Blue (FR)**[66] 2066 3-9-3 0............................ BenCurtis 6 66
(Brian Ellison) *hld up in tch on outside: edgd lft and outpcd wl over 1f out: sn btn* **25/1**

5-2 **7** 1 **Thornton**[24] 3435 3-9-3 0............................ PaulMulrennan 10 63+
(Michael Dods) *in tch: effrt and pushed along 2f out: wknd fnl f* **8/1**

5 **8** ½ **Sukoot (IRE)**[15] 3755 3-9-3 0............................ OisinMurphy 2 62
(Ed Dunlop) *pressed ldr: rdn over 2f out: wknd over 1f out* **25/1**

**9** nk **Fikhaar** 3-8-12 0............................ KevinStott 8 56
(Kevin Ryan) *t.k.h: hld up midfield: rdn and outpcd over 2f out: n.d after* **50/1**

**10** 2 **Aclimatise** 3-9-3 0............................ JasonHart 3 55
(Mark Johnston) *led tl rdn and hdd 2f out: sn wknd* **50/1**

**11** 1¼ **Dream Ballad (IRE)** 3-9-3 0............................(t1) JosephineGordon 7 52
(Hugo Palmer) *slowly away: rn green in rr: struggling fr over 2f out: sn btn* **12/1**

00 **12** 2 **Maid In Brittain**[49] 2585 3-8-12 0............................ CamHardie 14 42
(Antony Brittain) *hld up: rdn over 3f out: struggling fnl 2f* **125/1**

**13** 1¾ **Good Man (IRE)**[26] 4-9-12 0............................ GrahamLee 9 45
(Karen McLintock) *dwlt: hld up: rdn along over 2f out: sn wknd* **50/1**

1m 26.49s (0.29) **Going Correction** +0.075s/f (Slow)
**WFA** 3 from 4yo 9lb **13** Ran SP% **122.8**
Speed ratings (Par 103): **101,99,97,95,95 93,92,91,91,89 87,85,83**
CSF £14.63 TOTE £6.70: £2.00, £1.30, £14.00; EX 25.00 Trifecta £1139.60.

**Owner** Sheikh Juma Dalmook Al Maktoum **Bred** Brian Kahn & More Than Ready Syndicate **Trained** Newmarket, Suffolk

**FOCUS**
Probably not a bad maiden and winners should come out of this.

## 4310 BETFRED "LIKE US ON FACEBOOK" H'CAP 6f (Tp)
**9:10** (9:11) (Class 5) (0-70,70) 3-Y-O+ **£4,528** (£1,347; £673; £336) **Stalls** Centre

Form RPR

0-50 **1** **Yarmouk (FR)**[39] 2885 3-9-1 **64**............................ PhillipMakin 12 73+
(Richard Fahey) *in tch: hdwy to ld 1f out: rdn out* **7/1**[3]

45-0 **2** 1½ **Interlink (USA)**[35] 3049 4-9-13 **69**............................ JosephineGordon 10 75
(Michael Appleby) *cl up: led over 2f out to 1f out: kpt on fnl f: nt pce of wnr* **6/1**[2]

-150 **3** ¾ **Epeius (IRE)**[38] 2923 4-9-8 **64**............................(p1) PaulMulrennan 8 68
(Ben Haslam) *hld up towards rr: drvn along 1/2-way: hdwy over 1f out: kpt on fnl f: nvr able to chal* **14/1**

0602 **4** ½ **Athollblair Boy (IRE)**[15] 3758 4-9-8 **64**............................ TomEaves 2 66
(Nigel Tinkler) *hld up on outside: rdn and hdwy over 1f out: kpt on fnl f: no imp* **9/1**

5126 **5** hd **Sea Of Green**[7] 4039 5-8-10 **57**............................(p) CallumRodriguez(5) 3 59
(Jim Goldie) *hld up in midfield: effrt and rdn over 1f out: kpt on ins fnl f: nvr able to chal* **16/1**

3060 **6** 1 **Racquet**[18] 3666 4-9-6 **62**............................ JamesSullivan 7 61
(Ruth Carr) *hld up: rdn over 2f out: kpt on fnl f: nvr able to chal* **33/1**

4064 **7** ½ **Party Tiger**[25] 3388 3-9-6 **69**............................(p) PaulHanagan 9 64
(Richard Fahey) *hld up in midfield: drvn along and hdwy whn n.m.r briefly appr fnl f: no imp* **9/1**

1611 **8** 1 **Dream Ally (IRE)**[21] 3544 7-9-4 **65**............................ PhilDennis(5) 1 59
(John Weymes) *prom: rdn along 2f out: outpcd appr fnl f* **12/1**

501- **9** 2 **Traveltalk (IRE)**[269] 7041 3-9-4 **67**............................(p) BenCurtis 5 52
(Brian Ellison) *hld up: rdn along after 2f: sme late hdwy: nvr rchd ldrs* **20/1**

4306 **10** 3¼ **Big Amigo (IRE)**[53] 2469 4-9-8 **69**............................ CliffordLee(5) 6 46
(Daniel Mark Loughnane) *hld up: rdn along 1/2-way: sn n.d* **25/1**

1225 **11** nse **French**[18] 3666 4-9-11 **67**............................(p) CamHardie 14 44
(Antony Brittain) *cl up: rdn over 2f out: wknd over 1f out* **12/1**

0 **12** 2¾ **Avenue Of Stars**[42] 2776 4-10-0 **70**............................(p) GrahamLee 4 38
(Karen McLintock) *hld up on outside: rdn over 2f out: wknd wl over 1f out* **22/1**

42 **13** 1¼ **Quiet Warrior (IRE)**[66] 2053 6-9-2 **61**............................ NathanEvans(3) 11 25
(Michael Easterby) *led to over 2f out: rdn and wknd over 1f out* **4/1**[1]

100 **14** 1¼ **Man About Town (IRE)**[13] 3814 3-9-4 **67**............................ DanielTudhope 13 42
(K R Burke) *w ldrs tl rdn and wknd over 1f out* **8/1**

1m 12.27s (-0.23) **Going Correction** +0.075s/f (Slow)
**WFA** 3 from 4yo+ 7lb **14** Ran SP% **121.7**
Speed ratings (Par 103): **104,102,101,100,100 98,98,96,94,89 89,86,84,82**
CSF £46.75 CT £586.36 TOTE £7.50: £2.60, £2.80, £2.70; EX 56.80 Trifecta £963.00.

**Owner** Sheikh Abdullah Almalek Alsabah **Bred** E A R L Ecurie Haras D'Elbe **Trained** Musley Bank, N Yorks

**FOCUS**
A wide open handicap.

T/Plt: £11.60 to a £1 stake. Pool: £60,132.00 - 5,180.25 winning units. T/Qpdt: £7.00 to a £1 stake. Pool: £4,985.00 - 709.34 winning units. **Richard Young**

# 4266 NEWMARKET (R-H)

Friday, June 30

**OFFICIAL GOING: Good to soft (6.9)**

Wind: light breeze Weather: overcast; 20 degrees; light rain after race two, heavy after race five

## 4311 FLY LONDON SOUTHEND AIRPORT TO PERPIGNAN H'CAP 1m

**5:50** (5:50) (Class 5) (0-75,74) 3-Y-O+ **£3,881** (£1,155; £577; £288) **Stalls** High

Form RPR

25-5 **1** **Redgrave (IRE)**[90] 1485 3-9-4 **74**....................................(h) JamesDoyle 3 80
(Charles Hills) *sltly impeded s: bhd: prog 3f out: wnt 2nd 2f out: led 1f out: hrd drvn and edgd lft wl ins fnl f: all out* **5/1**[3]

60-1 **2** *hd* **Trulee Scrumptious**[7] 4047 8-9-3 **63**............................(v) JimmyQuinn 8 71
(Peter Charalambous) *led: rdn and tried to qckn clr 2f out: hdd 1f out: edgd rt ins fnl f: rallied gamely fnl 75yds: carried lft and jst hld* **2/1**[1]

-334 **3** *3 3/4* **Wings Of Esteem (IRE)**[16] 3723 4-9-8 **68**...................... AntonioFresu 4 67
(Luke McJannet) *taken down early: j. awkwardly fr stalls: rdr unbalanced and lost iron: sn rcvrd to chse ldrs: 3rd and rdn 2f out: no imp and wl hld fnl f* **9/1**

0-03 **4** *nk* **Easy Code**[16] 3718 4-9-1 **66**............................................ GeorgiaCox(5) 7 64
(William Haggas) *prom: chsd ldr over 3f out tl rdn 2f out: onepced and btn 1f out* **6/1**

-056 **5** *nse* **My Lucille (IRE)**[21] 3540 4-9-9 **69**....................................... JimCrowley 6 67
(Chris Wall) *t.k.h: pressed ldrs: rdn 2f out: no ch w ldng pair fnl f* **8/1**

4066 **6** *6* **Bizet (IRE)**[18] 3674 3-8-4 **60** ow2.......................................... DannyBrock 5 42
(John Ryan) *drvn along and nvr travelling in rr: no ch fr 1/2-way* **25/1**

6-05 **7** *10* **Balgair**[39] 2894 3-8-13 **72**......................................... KieranShoemark(3) 1 31
(Jonathan Portman) *chsd ldrs: rdn over 3f out: sn racing awkwardly: struggling 2f out: eased and t.o* **7/2**[2]

01P- **8** *14* **Ice Alert (IRE)**[269] 7048 4-9-8 **68**.............................(t) RichardKingscote 2
(John Ryan) *pressed ldr tl rdn over 3f out: fdd 2f out: eased and t.o* **33/1**

1m 39.45s (-0.55) **Going Correction** -0.05s/f (Good)
**WFA** 3 from 4yo+ 10lb **8** Ran SP% **114.4**
Speed ratings (Par 103): **100,99,96,95,95 89,79,65**
CSF £15.45 CT £86.91 TOTE £6.10: £1.70, £1.20, £2.40; EX 18.30 Trifecta £81.20.
**Owner** Highclere Thoroughbred Racing - WB Yeats **Bred** Mrs T Mahon **Trained** Lambourn, Berks
■ Stewards' Enquiry : James Doyle two-day ban: careless riding (Jul 17-18)

**FOCUS**
The ground was officially described as good to soft, and there are showers during the evening. This modest handicap was run at a decent gallop, in a time 3.25sec outside the standard. The first two came close together, finishing clear, and the winner kept the race following an enquiry. There's a case for thinking him better than the bare form.

## 4312 FLY LONDON SOUTHEND AIRPORT TO MILAN EBF FILLIES' NOVICE STKS (PLUS 10 RACE) 6f

**6:20** (6:20) (Class 4) 2-Y-O **£4,528** (£1,347; £673; £336) **Stalls** High

Form RPR

2 **1** **Oriental Song (IRE)**[24] 3421 2-9-0 0................................ JimCrowley 3 88+
(Owen Burrows) *mde all: pushed along to go clr 1f out: easily* **13/8**[1]

**2** *6* **Kareva** 2-9-0 0.................................................................. JamesDoyle 2 70
(Charles Hills) *t.k.h: chsd ldrs: effrt 2f out: wnt 2nd 1f out: hung lft and no ch w easy wnr* **11/2**

2 **3** *2* **Vodka Pigeon**[16] 3712 2-9-0 0.................................. RichardKingscote 1 64
(Tom Dascombe) *taken down early: prominnt: pushed along over 2f out: sn racing awkwardly: btn over 1f out: impeded ins fnl f* **11/4**[2]

**4** *1/2* **Perfect Thought** 2-9-0 0............................................... RobertWinston 6 63
(William Haggas) *plld hrd: chsd ldrs: rdn and no ex over 1f out: impeded ins fnl f* **9/2**[3]

**5** *nk* **Graffitista (IRE)** 2-9-0 0........................................... SilvestreDeSousa 4 62
(George Scott) *stdd s: a bhd: btn wl over 1f out: sltly impeded ins fnl f* **8/1**

6 **6** *3 1/4* **Red Snapper**[58] 2292 2-8-7 0.......................................... MillyNaseb(7) 5 52
(William Stone) *pressed wnr tl rdn over 2f out: wl btn over 1f out* **50/1**

1m 13.04s (0.54) **Going Correction** -0.05s/f (Good) **6** Ran SP% **111.4**
Speed ratings (Par 92): **94,86,83,82,82 77**
CSF £10.91 TOTE £2.30: £1.60, £2.40; EX 11.50 Trifecta £28.30.
**Owner** Hadi Al-Tajir **Bred** Hadi Al-Tajir **Trained** Lambourn, Berks

**FOCUS**
The winner proved different class in this ordinary novice race and produced a big step up on her debut.

## 4313 FLY LONDON SOUTHEND AIRPORT TO LYON H'CAP 7f

**6:50** (6:51) (Class 4) (0-80,80) 3-Y-O **£5,175** (£1,540; £769; £384) **Stalls** High

Form RPR

0-60 **1** **Angel Down**[30] 3211 3-9-1 **77**.................................. KieranShoemark(3) 3 87
(Henry Candy) *bhd: hdwy 2f out: chsd ldr over 1f out: drvn and sustained effrt to get up cl home* **13/2**[3]

521 **2** *1/2* **Patchwork**[39] 2901 3-9-5 **78**................................................ RyanMoore 1 86
(Richard Hughes) *cl up: led over 2f out: rdn ins fnl f: ct cl home* **7/2**[2]

331 **3** *hd* **Inshiraah (FR)**[23] 3472 3-9-4 **77**........................................ JamesDoyle 9 84
(George Peckham) *pressed ldrs: rdn to chal 2f out: ev ch but hanging rt ins fnl f: no ex fnl 50yds* **10/1**

1401 **4** *3 1/4* **Cyrus Dallin**[19] 3621 3-9-7 **80**..........................................(h) MartinDwyer 4 79
(William Muir) *stdd s: bhd: drvn and prog 2f out: 4th ins fnl f: n.g.t w effrt* **9/1**

-532 **5** *3* **Ocean Temptress**[17] 3701 3-8-2 **61** oh3.............................. KieranO'Neill 2 52
(John Ryan) *led: rdn and hdd over 2f out: btn 1f out* **16/1**

2266 **6** *nk* **Sea Shack**[13] 3836 3-9-5 **78**.......................................... SilvestreDeSousa 7 68
(William Knight) *taken down early: prom tl rdn and lost pl wl over 1f out* **9/4**[1]

6324 **7** *3 1/2* **Tadween (IRE)**[21] 3549 3-9-5 **78**........................................ DaneO'Neill 6 59
(Richard Hannon) *towards rr: rdn over 2f out: nvr making any imp* **16/1**

441- **8** *1/2* **Mississippi Miss**[249] 7576 3-9-2 **75**........................... RichardKingscote 5 55
(Dr Jon Scargill) *plld hrd: sn prom: rdn and wknd over 2f out* **25/1**

12-5 **9** *2 1/4* **Fareeq**[20] 3588 3-9-6 **79**..............................................(t) JimCrowley 8 53
(William Haggas) *towards rr: drvn over 2f out: sn btn* **15/2**

1530 **10** *19* **Fear The Fury (USA)**[35] 3040 3-9-3 **76**.......................... MartinHarley 10
(K R Burke) *chsd ldrs: rdn 1/2-way: sn lost pl: t.o and eased 1f out* **25/1**

1m 25.1s (-0.60) **Going Correction** -0.05s/f (Good) **10** Ran SP% **116.6**
Speed ratings (Par 101): **101,100,100,96,93 92,88,88,85,63**
CSF £29.52 CT £228.01 TOTE £7.80: £2.40, £1.60, £3.10; EX 43.10 Trifecta £537.00.
**Owner** Thurloe Thoroughbreds XX **Bred** Kirtlington Stud & Mr C Budgett **Trained** Kingston Warren, Oxon

**FOCUS**
A fair race for the grade. The first two and the fourth raced on the stands' side, while the third home edged over there in the latter stages. The race is rated around the race average.

## 4314 FLY LONDON SOUTHEND AIRPORT TO PRAGUE H'CAP 1m 5f

**7:25** (7:26) (Class 4) (0-80,81) 3-Y-O **£5,175** (£1,540; £769; £384) **Stalls** Centre

Form RPR

5-53 **1** **Joshua Reynolds**[16] 3717 3-9-4 **77**..............................(b[1]) JimCrowley 5 93+
(John Gosden) *racd enthusiastically: sn pressing ldr: led gng best 3f out: rdn clr 1f out: styd on wl but kpt up to work tl eased cl home* **9/2**[2]

-152 **2** *4 1/2* **Maori Bob (IRE)**[20] 3596 3-8-1 **65**.................................. LuluStanford(5) 6 73
(Michael Bell) *plld hrd: cl up: rdn 2f out: difficult to steer after: chsd wnr vainly fnl f* **7/1**

1151 **3** *3 1/4* **Arab Moon**[23] 3457 3-9-7 **80**....................................... SilvestreDeSousa 1 83
(William Knight) *hld up in last pl: effrt 5f out: rdn and chsd wnr 2f out: one pce after: lost 2nd 1f out* **11/2**[3]

6-41 **4** *4 1/2* **Solar Cross**[28] 3291 3-9-7 **80**............................................. JamesDoyle 3 76
(Roger Charlton) *settled in 3rd or 4th: rdn over 2f out: struggling wl over 1f out* **11/8**[1]

55-0 **5** *6* **City Limits**[14] 3779 3-9-1 **74**..........................................(t) RyanMoore 2 61
(Luca Cumani) *settled towards rr: tk clsr order 5f out: chal 3f out: sn hrd drvn: wknd over 2f out* **9/1**

0462 **6** *11* **Immortalised**[21] 3528 3-9-8 **81**........................................ PJMcDonald 4 52
(K R Burke) *taken down early: led: set mod pce: rdn and hdd 3f out: dropped out tamely: t.o* **8/1**

2m 48.83s (4.83) **Going Correction** +0.40s/f (Good) **6** Ran SP% **109.3**
Speed ratings (Par 101): **101,98,96,93,89 83**
CSF £32.34 TOTE £5.40: £2.20, £2.50; EX 33.70 Trifecta £133.80.
**Owner** Castle Down Racing & Rachel Hood **Bred** Meon Valley Stud **Trained** Newmarket, Suffolk

**FOCUS**
Race run over an extra 19 yards. A fair handicap. None of these had run over this far and it proved quite a test in the conditions. It's a race with a good average and the winner was much improved.

## 4315 FLY LONDON SOUTHEND AIRPORT TO BUDAPEST EBFSTALLIONS.COM FILLIES' CONDITIONS STKS (PLUS 10 RACE) 6f

**7:55** (7:56) (Class 3) 3-Y-O **£9,056** (£2,695; £1,346; £673) **Stalls** High

Form RPR

253 **1** **Raven's Lady**[16] 3722 3-9-5 **85**............................................ RyanMoore 4 94
(Marco Botti) *cl up: led wl over 1f out: rdn to assert 1f out: comf* **6/4**[1]

1352 **2** *2 3/4* **Pepita (IRE)**[13] 3822 3-9-5 **80**............................................. JamesDoyle 3 85
(Richard Hannon) *led: rdn and hdd wl over 1f out: no match for wnr ins fnl f: hung rt fnl 100yds* **9/4**[2]

6-54 **3** *1 1/4* **Perfect Madge (IRE)**[40] 2856 3-9-5 **87**..................... SilvestreDeSousa 5 81
(Kevin Ryan) *cl up: drvn 2f out: onepced ins fnl f* **11/4**[3]

1-66 **4** *1/2* **Rosabelle**[20] 3579 3-9-1 **88**............................................ JoshuaBryan(7) 2 83
(Alan Bailey) *v ungainly leaving stalls and lost abt 6 l: rdn 1/2-way: on heels of plcd horses ent fnl f: racd rather awkwardly and no further imp* **6/1**

1m 12.26s (-0.24) **Going Correction** -0.05s/f (Good) **4** Ran SP% **111.7**
Speed ratings (Par 100): **99,95,93,93**
CSF £5.36 TOTE £2.10; EX 4.70 Trifecta £7.90.
**Owner** Heart of the South Racing & Partner **Bred** Rabbah Bloodstock Limited **Trained** Newmarket, Suffolk

**FOCUS**
Decent fillies' form, if not particularly strong for the grade. The winner built on her AW form.

## 4316 FLY LONDON SOUTHEND AIRPORT TO DUBROVNIK H'CAP 1m 2f

**8:30** (8:31) (Class 2) (0-100,100) 3-Y-O+ **£12,938** (£3,850; £1,924; £962) **Stalls** Centre

Form RPR

2642 **1** **Banditry (IRE)**[8] 4002 5-9-4 **90**.........................................(h) JamesDoyle 4 97
(Ian Williams) *settled towards rr: hrd drvn to improve 3f out: led 2f out: holding rivals ins fnl f* **4/1**[3]

-532 **2** *1 1/2* **Monticello (IRE)**[7] 4048 3-8-3 **87**........................................ JoeFanning 2 91
(Mark Johnston) *plld hrd: chsd ldrs: rdn over 2f out: sn outpcd: cajoled along and rallied and styd on ins fnl f: passed three rivals fnl 100yds and wnt 2nd cl home but nt rch wnr* **10/3**[2]

-612 **3** *1/2* **Noble Gift**[36] 2999 7-9-13 **99**............................................... JimCrowley 6 102
(William Knight) *taken down early: pressed ldr: rdn over 2f out: onepced ins fnl f: lost 2nd cl home* **14/1**

/1-0 **4** *nk* **Firnas**[20] 3597 4-9-9 **95**.................................................... WilliamBuick 3 97
(Charlie Appleby) *chsd ldrs: rdn over 2f out: ev ch of 2nd but hld by wnr ins fnl f* **9/2**

514 **5** *2 1/2* **Zzoro (IRE)**[8] 4002 4-9-2 **88**..........................................(p[1]) MartinDwyer 8 85
(Amanda Perrett) *led: rdn and hdd over 2f out: btn whn edgd lft appr fnl f: wkng cl home* **10/1**

14-2 **6** *14* **Al Neksh**[44] 2735 4-9-6 **92**................................................... RyanMoore 9 61
(William Haggas) *a last: rdn over 2f out: no rspnse and sn btn: eased ins fnl f: b.b.v* **15/8**[1]

2m 9.67s (4.17) **Going Correction** +0.40s/f (Good)
**WFA** 3 from 4yo+ 12lb **6** Ran SP% **111.8**
Speed ratings (Par 109): **99,97,97,97,95 83**
CSF £17.43 CT £163.07 TOTE £5.00: £2.10, £2.10; EX 19.70 Trifecta £172.70.
**Owner** Buxted Partnership **Bred** Darley **Trained** Portway, Worcs

**FOCUS**
Race run over an additional 19yds. A decent handicap, but one weakened by non-runners. Conditions were pretty testing by this stage. The winner backed up his AW latest.

## 4317 FLY LONDON SOUTHEND AIRPORT TO VENICE FILLIES' H'CAP 6f

**9:00** (9:00) (Class 4) (0-85,85) 3-Y-O+ **£5,175** (£1,540; £769; £384) **Stalls** High

Form RPR

2-13 **1** **Cartographer**[13] 3822 3-9-5 **83**.................................. SilvestreDeSousa 7 97
(Martyn Meade) *mde all: gng wl 2f out: rdn clr 1f out: kpt on wl: comf* **2/1**[1]

0423 **2** *3 1/2* **Storm Cry**[16] 3715 3-9-4 **82**............................................... JoeFanning 4 83
(Mark Johnston) *cl up: chsd wnr over 1f out: rdn and no imp* **4/1**[2]

21-4 **3** *3/4* **Parlance (IRE)**[16] 3722 3-9-7 **85**........................................ RyanMoore 2 84
(Sir Michael Stoute) *towards rr: pushed along 1/2-way: rdn and effrt 2f out: kpt on same pce after: wnt 3rd cl home* **5/1**[3]

1-01 **4** *1/2* **Magical Dreamer (IRE)**[31] 3171 3-9-3 **81**.................(h) DanielMuscutt 6 78
(James Fanshawe) *chsd ldrs: rdn and effrt 2f out: 3rd and hld 1f out: flashing tail ins fnl f: lost 3rd nr fin* **4/1**[2]

2031 **5** *3 1/4* **East Coast Lady (IRE)**[32] 3139 5-9-1 **72**............................ MartinLane 1 61
(William Stone) *racd freely and prom: rdn 2f out: wknd ins fnl f* **14/1**

2-01 **6** *1 ½* **Coral Sea**[21] 3536 3-9-0 **78** .................... JimCrowley 3 60
(Charles Hills) *taken down early: stdd s: a last: rdn and btn over 1f out* **6/1**

1m 12.79s (0.29) **Going Correction** -0.05s/f (Good)
**WFA** 3 from 4yo+ 7lb **6** Ran SP% **111.0**
Speed ratings (Par 102): **96,91,90,89,85 83**
CSF £9.93 TOTE £2.70: £1.80, £2.30; EX 9.10 Trifecta £35.50.
**Owner** The Snailwell Stud **Bred** Bearstone Stud Ltd **Trained** Newmarket, Suffolk

**FOCUS**
The winner set a fair pace in this fair handicap for fillies, which was run on the worst of the ground. The form is taken at face value, the winner backing up her maiden win.
T/Plt: £235.80 to a £1 stake. Pool: £47,987.00 - 203.47 winning units. T/Qpdt: £62.10 to a £1 stake. Pool: £3,697.00 - 59.51 winning units. **Iain Mackenzie**

# 3725 YARMOUTH (L-H)
## Friday, June 30

**OFFICIAL GOING: Good (7.1)**
Wind: virtually nil Weather: light cloud

## 4318 RIVERSIDE RENTALS OF NORFOLK NOVICE STKS (PLUS 10 RACE) 6f 3y
**2:10** (2:12) (Class 4) 2-Y-O £4,528 (£1,347; £673; £336) **Stalls** Centre

Form RPR
6 **1** **Alba Power (IRE)**[12] 3868 2-9-2 0 .................... JamesDoyle 5 89
(Hugo Palmer) *pressed ldr: effrt over 1f out: drvn to chal 1f out: led wl ins fnl f: r.o wl* **5/1**[3]

32 **2** *½* **Jellmood**[48] 2607 2-9-2 0 .................... AdamKirby 2 87
(Marco Botti) *led: shkn up over 1f out: rdn and hrd pressed 1f out: hdd and styd on same pce wl ins fnl f* **4/6**[1]

**3** *4* **Mosalim (IRE)** 2-9-2 0 .................... MartinHarley 1 75
(William Haggas) *trckd ldrs: shkn up 2f out: rdn and unable qckn over 1f out: wl hld and kpt on same pce fnl f* **7/2**[2]

**4** *6* **Poets Dream (IRE)** 2-9-2 0 .................... (t[1]) StevieDonohoe 4 57
(Mohamed Moubarak) *s.i.s: rn green in rr: rdn over 2f out: sn outpcd and wl btn over 1f out* **9/1**

1m 12.38s (-2.02) **Going Correction** -0.60s/f (Hard) **4** Ran SP% **108.9**
Speed ratings (Par 95): **89,88,83,75**
CSF £9.09 TOTE £4.40; EX 10.20 Trifecta £14.30.
**Owner** Fiona and Ian Carmichael-Jennings **Bred** Shehila Partnership **Trained** Newmarket, Suffolk

**FOCUS**
Just the four runners but this novice event was a lively betting heat. The first pair dominated. The race is rated through the runner-up to his Ascot form.

## 4319 VOICE OF RACING DAY FILLIES' H'CAP 1m 3f 104y
**2:40** (2:40) (Class 5) (0-70,75) 3-Y-O+ £2,911 (£866; £432; £216) **Stalls** Low

Form RPR
0511 **1** **Cribbs Causeway (IRE)**[8] 4012 3-9-6 **75** 6ex .................... JamesDoyle 1 83+
(Roger Charlton) *trckd ldrs: clsd to join ldrs and travelling best 2f out: shkn up to ld over 1f out: r.o wl to draw clr ins fnl f: easily* **1/1**[1]

-142 **2** *2 ¾* **Ominotago**[87] 1548 5-9-12 **68** .................... LukeMorris 2 70
(Michael Appleby) *led: drvn and hdd over 1f out: no ch wih wnr and kpt on same pce ins fnl f* **10/1**[3]

56-0 **3** *½* **Starlight Circus (IRE)**[22] 3507 3-8-7 **65** .................... GeorgeWood(3) 3 66
(Marco Botti) *in tch in last pair: rdn over 3f out: hdwy u.p over 1f out: 3rd and kpt on same pce ins fnl f* **20/1**

4031 **4** *5* **Prize Diva**[15] 3759 3-9-0 **69** .................... (p) SilvestreDeSousa 5 62
(David Elsworth) *chsd ldr: rdn over 3f out: lost pl and btn over 1f out: wknd ins fnl f* **7/4**[2]

1204 **5** *¾* **Pernickety**[9] 3981 4-10-0 **70** .................... (h) TrevorWhelan 4 62
(Lucy Wadham) *trckd ldrs: rdn over 2f out: lost pl and btn over 1f out: wknd ins fnl f* **11/1**

2m 23.87s (-4.83) **Going Correction** -0.35s/f (Firm)
**WFA** 3 from 4yo+ 13lb **5** Ran SP% **108.5**
Speed ratings (Par 100): **103,101,100,97,96**
CSF £11.12 TOTE £1.40: £1.10, £3.80; EX 7.20 Trifecta £41.40.
**Owner** Nick Bradley Racing 13 **Bred** N Bradley **Trained** Beckhampton, Wilts

**FOCUS**
Not a bad fillies' handicap.

## 4320 RACING WELFARE H'CAP 1m 2f 23y
**3:10** (3:14) (Class 6) (0-65,66) 3-Y-O+ £2,264 (£673; £336; £168) **Stalls** Low

Form RPR
5462 **1** **Chunkyfunkymonkey**[3] 4177 3-8-1 **57** .................... JackOsborn(7) 10 64
(John Ryan) *hld up in tch in last trio: hdwy 3f out: rdn to chal 2f out: led over 1f out: kpt on wl ins fnl f: rdn out* **9/2**[3]

5126 **2** *1* **Bartholomew J (IRE)**[15] 3752 3-9-0 **66** .................... SimonPearce(3) 11 71
(Lydia Pearce) *wl in tch in midfield on outer: effrt to chal 2f out: chsd wnr over 1f out: kpt on but a hld ins fnl f* **7/1**

600 **3** *1 ¼* **Toronto Sound**[27] 3342 3-8-6 **55** .................... LukeMorris 8 58
(Sir Mark Prescott Bt) *chsd ldr tl rdn to ld over 2f out: hdd and unable qck over 1f out: 3rd and kpt on same pce ins fnl f* **8/1**

56-3 **4** *½* **Castle Talbot (IRE)**[44] 2731 5-10-0 **65** .................... AdamKirby 1 67
(Tom Clover) *in tch in midfield: effrt 2f out: chsd ldrs 1f out: kpt on ins fnl f: nvr enough pce to threaten ldrs* **8/1**

0054 **5** *½* **Time To Sea (IRE)**[19] 3627 3-9-3 **66** .................... TrevorWhelan 3 67
(John Butler) *trckd ldrs: nt clr run and swtchd lft 2f out: sn rdn: kpt on same pce ins fnl f* **10/3**[2]

15-0 **6** *2* **Ode To Glory**[45] 2702 3-9-2 **65** .................... MartinDwyer 2 62
(Rae Guest) *dwlt: hld up in tch in last pair: hdwy on far rail 3f out: nt clr run 2f out: swtchd lft over 1f out: no threat to ldrs but kpt on ins fnl f* **16/1**

0051 **7** *3 ½* **Incredible Dream (IRE)**[19] 3628 4-9-8 **59** .................... (p) DaneO'Neill 9 50+
(Dean Ivory) *s.i.s and rousted along: clsd and in tch in last pair after 2f: rdn over 2f out: no hdwy and btn over 1f out: wknd* **3/1**[1]

0-0 **8** *nk* **Lady Kaviar (IRE)**[42] 2794 3-9-0 **63** .................... RyanPowell 4 54
(George Margarson) *t.k.h: trckd ldrs: nt clr run and shuffled bk 3f out: no threat to ldrs after* **33/1**

0005 **9** *¾* **Our Kim (IRE)**[18] 3674 3-8-5 **54** ow2 .................... JFEgan 6 43
(Mohamed Moubarak) *led: reminder 4f out: rdn and hdd over 2f out: sn struggling and losing pl whn hmpd over 1f out: sn wknd* **14/1**

2m 9.02s (-1.48) **Going Correction** -0.35s/f (Firm)
**WFA** 3 from 4yo+ 12lb **9** Ran SP% **116.5**
Speed ratings (Par 101): **91,90,89,88,88 86,84,83,83**
CSF £36.29 CT £245.92 TOTE £5.10: £1.60, £2.40, £2.60; EX 35.00 Trifecta £143.20.
**Owner** Jon A Thompson **Bred** Mrs Fiona Shaw **Trained** Newmarket, Suffolk

**FOCUS**
A moderate handicap in which it paid to be handy due to an ordinary pace. It was dominated by 3yos and the form looks solid enough.

## 4321 PLEASUREWOOD HILLS THEME PARK OF LOWESTOFT H'CAP 7f 3y
**3:40** (3:42) (Class 3) (0-95,97) 4-Y-O **£7,246** (£2,168; £1,084; £542; £270) **Stalls** Centre

Form RPR
0232 **1** **Horsted Keynes (FR)**[6] 4103 7-9-5 **91** .................... MartinHarley 6 98
(David Simcock) *hld up in tch: clsd to trck ldr 2f out: shkn up to ld over 1f out: rdn ins fnl f: a doing enough towards fin rdn out* **5/2**[2]

4-52 **2** *nk* **Brigliadoro (IRE)**[41] 2828 6-9-7 **93** .................... SilvestreDeSousa 1 98
(Philip McBride) *stdd and dropped in bhd after s: hld up in tch in rr: hdwy ent fnl 2f: rdn to chse ldrs over 1f out: chsd wnr ins fnl f: styd on wl and pressing wnr towards fin: a hld* **13/8**[1]

-035 **3** *2 ¼* **Baron Bolt**[20] 3565 4-9-3 **89** .................... (p) LukeMorris 5 88+
(Paul Cole) *trckd ldrs: nt clrest of runs 2f out: effrt over 1f out: kpt on u.p fnl 100yds: wnt 3rd last strides: no threat to ldng pair* **9/2**[3]

0-66 **4** *nk* **Basil Berry**[26] 2518 6-9-11 **97** .................... TrevorWhelan 3 95
(Chris Dwyer) *led: rdn and hdd over 1f out: no ex jst ins fnl f: wknd fnl 100yds and lost 3rd last strides* **20/1**

0-03 **5** *4 ½* **Archie (IRE)**[44] 2730 5-8-11 **83** .................... StevieDonohoe 2 69
(Tom Clover) *wl in tch in midfield: effrt 2f out: unable qck u.p and btn 1f out: wknd ins fnl f* **7/1**

1/00 **6** *4* **Mootaharer (IRE)**[20] 3597 4-9-0 **86** .................... DaneO'Neill 4 61
(Charles Hills) *chsd ldr tl lost pl u.p 2f out: bhd 1f out* **9/1**

1m 22.31s (-4.29) **Going Correction** -0.60s/f (Hard) **6** Ran SP% **112.1**
Speed ratings (Par 107): **100,99,97,96,91 87**
CSF £6.96 TOTE £3.20: £1.60, £1.10; EX 8.10 Trifecta £28.80.
**Owner** Mrs J M Simcock **Bred** Oceanic Bloodstock & Mme A Gravereaux **Trained** Newmarket, Suffolk

**FOCUS**
This good-quality little handicap was run at a fair pace. Strong form with the two market leaders coming clear.

## 4322 GROSVENOR CASINO OF GREAT YARMOUTH H'CAP 1m 3y
**4:10** (4:10) (Class 2) (0-105,102) 3-Y-O **£11,971** (£3,583; £1,791; £896; £446) **Stalls** Centre

Form RPR
-145 **1** **Multi Facets (IRE)**[27] 3317 3-8-3 **84** .................... KieranO'Neill 4 93
(David Simcock) *t.k.h: chsd ldng pair: clsd to chse ldr 2f out: rdn to chal over 1f out: led ins fnl f: r.o wl* **5/1**[3]

5-21 **2** *1 ½* **To Dibba**[39] 2895 3-8-2 **83** oh1 .................... SilvestreDeSousa 5 88
(Roger Varian) *chsd ldr: began to hang lft and shkn up over 2f out: cl 3rd and stl hanging and nt clrest of runs over 1f out: in the clr and rdn ins fnl f: styd on to snatch 2nd on post* **1/1**[1]

31-4 **3** *nse* **Naseem (IRE)**[63] 2132 3-8-9 **90** .................... (p[1]) DaneO'Neill 7 95
(John Gosden) *led: rdn over 1f out: hdd ins fnl f: no ex and styd on same pce fnl 100yds: lost 2nd on post* **4/1**[2]

3040 **4** *2* **Law And Order (IRE)**[20] 3592 3-9-7 **102** .................... MartinHarley 1 102
(James Tate) *stdd s: hld up in midfield: effrt 2f out: unable qck over 1f out: kpt on ins fnl f but nvr enough pce to threaten ldrs* **16/1**

3141 **5** *nk* **Fire Brigade**[16] 3713 3-8-3 **84** .................... LukeMorris 3 84
(Michael Bell) *hld up in midfield: clsd over 2f out: cl enough in 4th and drvn over 1f out: no ex jst ins fnl f: wknd wl ins fnl f* **6/1**

3-00 **6** *hd* **Novoman (IRE)**[20] 3592 3-8-7 **88** .................... LiamJones 6 87
(William Haggas) *stdd s: t.k.h: hld up in last pair: effrt 2f out: kpt on ins fnl f: nvr trbld ldrs* **22/1**

3-46 **7** *7* **Jackhammer (IRE)**[14] 3778 3-8-6 **87** .................... MartinDwyer 2 69
(William Knight) *t.k.h: hld up in last pair: effrt and rdn over 2f out: hung lft and no imp over 1f out: sn wknd* **25/1**

1m 34.77s (-5.83) **Going Correction** -0.60s/f (Hard) **7** Ran SP% **115.0**
Speed ratings (Par 105): **105,103,103,101,101 100,93**
CSF £10.57 TOTE £5.80: £2.60, £1.30; EX 13.40 Trifecta £39.50.
**Owner** Jos & Mrs Jane Rodosthenous **Bred** Malih L Al Basti **Trained** Newmarket, Suffolk

**FOCUS**
This decent 3yo handicap was another race in which it suited those racing handily. Straightforward form.

## 4323 HAVEN SEASHORE HOLIDAY PARK H'CAP 1m 3y
**4:40** (4:45) (Class 6) (0-55,55) 4-Y-O+ £2,264 (£673; £336; £168) **Stalls** Centre

Form RPR
0-32 **1** **Cainhoe Star**[17] 3688 4-9-6 **54** .................... LukeMorris 7 70+
(Anthony Carson) *in tch in midfield: clsd 1/2-way: rdn to ld over 1f out: styd on wl and drew clr fnl f: eased towards fin: easily* **11/8**[1]

-030 **2** *5* **Hymn For The Dudes**[111] 1145 4-9-2 **50** .................... AdamKirby 11 54
(Lee Smyth, Ire) *hld up in rr: stdy hdwy on bridle 3f out: rdn to chal over 1f out: no ex 1f out: outpcd by wnr but kpt on for 2nd ins fnl f* **5/1**[2]

-605 **3** *1 ¾* **Kingfisher Girl**[17] 3702 4-8-9 **46** oh1 .................... (tp) NoelGarbutt(3) 1 46
(Michael Appleby) *in tch in midfield: hdwy to chse ldrs and rdn 2f out: unable qck over 1f out: 3rd and no ch w wnr ins fnl f: plugged on* **25/1**

000- **4** *1* **Glittering**[258] 7369 4-9-4 **52** .................... RyanTate 6 50
(James Eustace) *in tch in midfield: hdwy and rdn to chse ldrs 2f out: unable qck over 1f out: plugged on same pce ins fnl f* **33/1**

5603 **5** *7* **Moving Robe (IRE)**[21] 3550 4-8-12 **46** oh1 .................... (t) JFEgan 2 28
(Conrad Allen) *nvr travelling towards rr: plugged on to pass btn rivals over 1f out: nvr trbld ldrs* **14/1**

0500 **6** *½* **Ershaad (IRE)**[21] 3550 5-8-12 **46** oh1 .................... (b) StevieDonohoe 14 26
(Shaun Harris) *pressed ldrs tl led over 2f out: sn rdn: hdd over 1f out: sn wknd* **33/1**

4055 **7** *2 ¾* **John Caesar (IRE)**[95] 1403 6-9-7 **55** .................... (p) MartinLane 8 29
(Rebecca Bastiman) *dwlt: hld up in rr: effrt and hdwy over 2f out: no imp and btn over 1f out: wknd fnl f* **7/1**[3]

1-04 **8** *1 ½* **Clever Divya**[135] 735 4-9-4 **52** .................... KierenFox 9 23
(J R Jenkins) *led for 1f: styd prom tl unable qck u.p ent fnl 2f: wknd over 1f out* **33/1**

6000 **9** *1 ¾* **Great Expectations**[26] 2800 9-9-0 **48** .................... (t) LiamJones 13 15
(J R Jenkins) *towards rr: no hdwy u.p over 2f out: wknd over 1f out* **50/1**

54-0 **10** *2 ¼* **Annoushka**[39] 2908 4-9-7 **55** .................... (h[1]) AdamBeschizza 3 16
(Mrs Ilka Gansera-Leveque) *in tch in midfield: effrt u.p over 2f out: sn struggling: wknd over 1f out* **12/1**

-404 **11** *2 ¼* **Penelope Pitstop**[16] 3708 5-8-13 **47** .................... MartinHarley 5 3
(Lee Smyth, Ire) *chsd ldrs: rdn 4f out: lost pl over 2f out: bhd over 1f out* **7/1**[3]

0633 **12** *5* **Harbour Patrol (IRE)**[13] 3831 5-9-0 **48** .................... (b) DuranFentiman 12
(Rebecca Bastiman) *dwlt: c to r against stands rail and led after 1f out: hdd over 2f out: sn dropped out* **8/1**

04/0 **13** *125* **Hustle (IRE)**[90] 1484 12-9-0 **55**.................................... GinaMangan(7) 10
(Clare Hobson) *dropped to last and rdn 1/2-way: sn hung rt and wl btn: t.o and virtually p.u fnl 2f* **66/1**

1m 35.98s (-4.62) **Going Correction** -0.60s/f (Hard) **13** Ran SP% **125.4**
Speed ratings (Par 101): **99,94,92,91,84 83,81,79,77,75 73,68,**
CSF £8.02 CT £135.73 TOTE £2.30: £1.20, £2.10, £7.10; EX 12.60 Trifecta £259.10.
**Owner** Hugh & Mindi Byrne & W H Carson **Bred** Cheveley Park Stud Ltd **Trained** Newmarket, Suffolk

**FOCUS**
A weak handicap that was all about the winner. The first four finished clear.

## 4324 NORFOLK AND SUFFOLK ANIMAL TRUST H'CAP 5f 42y
**5:10** (5:11) (Class 5) (0-75,75) 3-Y-O **£2,911** (£866; £432; £216) **Stalls** Centre

Form RPR
01-5 **1** **Wadood (IRE)**[62] 2160 3-9-7 **75**......................................(h[1]) LukeMorris 1 80
(Robert Cowell) *mde all: rdn wl over 1f out: drvn over 1f out: styd on and hld on wl ins fnl f* **4/1**

-040 **2** *½* **Miss Rosina (IRE)**[4] 4157 3-8-5 **59**.................................... RyanPowell 3 62
(George Margarson) *pressed wnr thrght: rdn and chalng jst over 1f out: edgd lft ins fnl f: kpt on but a jst hld* **14/1**

-051 **3** *nk* **Sitar**[19] 3624 3-8-10 **67**..................................................(h) GeorgeWood(3) 5 69+
(James Fanshawe) *stdd to rr after s: niggled along and outpcd 1/2-way: rdn over 1f out: hdwy ins fnl f: r.o wl towards fin: wnt 3rd cl home but nvr quite getting to ldrs* **2/1[1]**

2135 **4** *nk* **Midnightly**[35] 3035 3-9-3 **71**........................................(t[1]) AdamBeschizza 6 72
(Rae Guest) *trckd ldrs: effrt over 1f out: kpt on same pce ins fnl f* **3/1[3]**

03-0 **5** *5* **Franca Florio (IRE)**[69] 1975 3-9-5 **73**.................................. AdamKirby 4 56
(Kevin Ryan) *restless in stalls: in tch in 4th: effrt over 1f out: unable qck and btn 1f out: wknd ins fnl f* **11/4[2]**

1m 0.56s (-2.14) **Going Correction** -0.60s/f (Hard) **5** Ran SP% **111.7**
Speed ratings (Par 99): **93,92,91,91,83**
CSF £46.32 TOTE £4.90: £2.30, £6.30; EX 38.40 Trifecta £136.20.
**Owner** Abdulla Al Mansoori **Bred** Mrs Teresa Thornton **Trained** Six Mile Bottom, Cambs
■ Stewards' Enquiry : Ryan Powell two day ban: used whip above permitted level (Jul 17-18)

**FOCUS**
They went a solid pace in this modest sprint handicap.
T/Plt: £140.20 to a £1 stake. Pool: £48,426.00 - 345.36 winning units. T/Qpdt: £9.60 to a £1 stake. Pool: £4,461.00 - 460.82 winning units. **Steve Payne**

4325 - 4326a (Foreign Racing) - See Raceform Interactive

# 3629 CURRAGH (R-H)
Friday, June 30

**OFFICIAL GOING: Straight course - yielding (good to yielding in places); round course - good (good to yielding in places)**

## 4327a JOE.IE H'CAP 6f
**6:45** (6:45) (60-95,91) 3-Y-O+ **£10,529** (£3,264; £1,555; £700; £273)

RPR
**1** **Enter The Red (IRE)**[19] 3631 8-8-6 **69**..........................(b) ChrisHayes 10 77+
(Aidan Anthony Howard, Ire) *sn trckd ldr in 2nd: rdn 2f out and kpt on strly u.p to ld 200yds out: styd on wl* **9/1**

**2** *¾* **Sahreej (IRE)**[19] 3631 4-8-4 **74**.................................... DannySheehy(7) 4 80
(Adrian Paul Keatley, Ire) *chsd ldrs on outer: cl 8th 1/2-way: pushed along over 2f out and prog to go 5th over 1f out: kpt on wl cl home to go 2nd* **12/1**

**3** *shd* **Ma Fee Heela (FR)**[7] 4062 3-9-4 **88**.................................... PatSmullen 5 92
(M D O'Callaghan, Ire) *chsd ldrs: 6th 1/2-way: pushed along over 2f out and kpt on wl u.p to go 3rd cl home* **6/1[1]**

**4** *½* **Ducky Mallon (IRE)**[34] 3097 6-8-9 **72**..........................(t) NGMcCullagh 14 76+
(Donal Kinsella, Ire) *sn mid-div on rail: 7th 1/2-way: pushed along over 2f out and kpt on wl u.p to go 4th cl home: nrst fin* **14/1**

**5** *¾* **Golden Pearl**[26] 3359 4-9-2 **79**..........................................(t[1]) ShaneFoley 3 81
(M Halford, Ire) *mid-div: rdn over 2f out and sme prog u.p on outer: kpt on wl ins fnl f but nt pce to chal* **8/1[3]**

**6** *nse* **Have A Nice Day**[13] 3852 7-9-9 **91**.........................(p) DMSimmonson(5) 9 93
(John James Feane, Ire) *mid-div: rdn bhd ldrs fr 1/2-way: short of room under 2f out and taken to outer: kpt on wl u.p ins fnl f* **8/1[3]**

**7** *nk* **Tookiedoo (IRE)**[20] 3600 3-7-11 **74** oh3..........................(t) SeanDavis(7) 2 73
(J C Hayden, Ire) *cl-up: 5th 1/2-way: sn rdn and wnt 3rd u.p over 1f out: no ex wl ins fnl f and dropped to 7th* **16/1**

**8** *1* **St Brelades Bay (IRE)**[34] 3097 5-9-2 **79**............(v[1]) ColmO'Donoghue 6 76
(Mrs John Harrington, Ire) *rdn and reminders to ld early: crossed to stands rail: 3 l clr 1/2-way: sn pushed along: reduced advantage ent fnl f and sn hdd: wknd* **8/1[3]**

**9** *nk* **Red Sabor**[8] 4025 3-8-11 **81**.......................................... DeclanMcDonogh 7 75
(Andrew Slattery, Ire) *cl-up: 3rd 1/2-way: sn pushed along and lost pl u.p under 2f out: wknd* **16/1**

**10** *nk* **Russian Realm**[20] 3581 7-9-7 **84**................................................ WJLee 1 79
(Paul Midgley) *bit slowly away: towards rr: pushed along 2f out and short of room bhd horses: taken to nr side rail and sme modest prog u.p ins fnl f* **7/1[2]**

**11** *2 ½* **Fit For Function**[33] 3114 4-9-8 **85**...................................... GaryCarroll 8 72
(Joseph G Murphy, Ire) *chsd ldrs: 4th 1/2-way: rdn over 2f out but sn no ex u.p and wknd* **10/1**

**12** *6 ½* **Escondida (IRE)**[34] 3097 4-9-3 **80**.................................. KevinManning 11 47
(J S Bolger, Ire) *a towards rr: pushed along after 2f: nvr gng wl: bhd ent fnl f* **16/1**

**13** *1 ¼* **Ice Cold In Alex (IRE)**[42] 2811 3-8-6 **76**..................(t) WayneLordan 12 37
(K J Condon, Ire) *mid-div: rdn 1/2-way and sn no ex: one pce u.p: bhd ins fnl f and eased* **8/1[3]**

1m 12.33s (-3.17) **Going Correction** -0.35s/f (Firm)
**WFA** 3 from 4yo+ 7lb **13** Ran SP% **122.3**
Speed ratings: **107,106,105,105,104 104,103,102,102,101 98,89,87**
CSF £115.31 CT £734.18 TOTE £9.40: £3.10, £4.20, £2.00; DF 120.50 Trifecta £376.50.
**Owner** Mrs Nuala Howard **Bred** Pat Todd **Trained** Curragh, Co Kildare

**FOCUS**
The first handicap of Derby weekend and a competitive little heat.

4328 - 4331a (Foreign Racing) - See Raceform Interactive

# 4290 CHESTER (L-H)
Saturday, July 1

**OFFICIAL GOING: Good to soft (7.1)**
Wind: faint breeze Weather: warm and sunny, light cloud

## 4332 LAURENT PERRIER MAIDEN STKS 7f 127y
**1:45** (1:46) (Class 4) 3-Y-O+
**£6,225** (£1,864; £932; £466; £233; £117) **Stalls** Low

Form RPR
02 **1** **Flourishing**[11] 3931 3-8-13 0.................................................. SeanLevey 6 79+
(Sir Michael Stoute) *mde all: qcknd 2f out: 4 l clr and pushed along over 1f out: kpt up to work ins fnl f: easily* **7/2[2]**

0223 **2** *4 ½* **Greenview Paradise (IRE)**[12] 3900 3-8-13 64............ PatrickMathers 5 65
(Richard Fahey) *trckd ldrs: effrt and wnt 3rd 2f out: rdn over 1f out: r.o to take 2nd ent fnl f* **9/1**

5 **3** *nk* **Infamous Lawman (IRE)**[40] 2887 3-9-4 0...................... FrannyNorton 4 69
(Brian Ellison) *hld up: prog 2f out: pushed along over 1f out: rdn and r.o to take 3rd wl ins fnl f* **5/1**

2-54 **4** *½* **Mudallel (IRE)**[19] 3669 3-9-4 77............................................ KevinStott 7 68
(Ed Dunlop) *hld up: pushed along and hdwy over 2f out: 3rd and rdn over 1f out: no ex: lost 3rd fnl f* **9/2[3]**

424 **5** *9* **Haraz (IRE)**[10] 3976 4-9-10 75........................................(b[1]) JoshDoyle(3) 3 48
(David O'Meara) *trckd ldr: drvn 2f out: hrd rdn and wknd over 1f out* **10/3[1]**

**6** *2* **Ancient Foe** 3-9-4 0.................................................................. LiamKeniry 2 42
(Andrew Balding) *mid-div: drvn and lost pl wl over 2f out: nvr a threat* **7/2[2]**

00 **7** *5* **Careyanne**[26] 3393 3-8-13 0.................................................. NeilFarley 1 25
(Brian Baugh) *trckd ldrs: drvn 2f out: sn lost pl: wknd ent fnl f* **50/1**

0040 **8** *11* **Red Shanghai (IRE)**[30] 3260 3-8-10 42.......................... NoelGarbutt(3) 8
(Charles Smith) *a in rr: drvn and lost tch fr 1/2-way* **100/1**

1m 35.81s (2.01) **Going Correction** +0.30s/f (Good)
**WFA** 3 from 4yo 9lb **8** Ran SP% **115.3**
Speed ratings (Par 105): **101,96,96,95,86 84,79,68**
CSF £34.94 TOTE £2.40: £1.40, £2.30, £2.20; EX 24.00 Trifecta £156.80.
**Owner** Qatar Racing Limited **Bred** Aston House Stud **Trained** Newmarket, Suffolk

**FOCUS**
Add 13yds. Not a strong maiden. They went a fair pace and the winner did it well. The runner-up rather limits the form.

## 4333 BEEFEATER H'CAP 5f 15y
**2:20** (2:22) (Class 3) (0-95,97) 3-Y-O+
**£9,337** (£2,796; £1,398; £699; £349; £175) **Stalls** Low

Form RPR
0-60 **1** **Reflektor (IRE)**[21] 3585 4-9-5 **90**.................................... PaddyPilley(5) 4 97
(Tom Dascombe) *trckd ldrs: 3rd and pushed along 2f out: rdn and hdwy ent fnl f: r.o wl to ld last 50yds* **11/2[3]**

2104 **2** *shd* **Lucky Beggar (IRE)**[21] 3581 7-9-3 **86**.......................... NathanEvans(3) 2 92+
(David C Griffiths) *mid-div: n.m.r 2f out: hdwy and drvn over 1f out: sn rdn: r.o strly fnl f: tk 2nd nr fin* **4/1[2]**

0424 **3** *nk* **Stanghow**[14] 3827 5-9-2 **82**...................................................... SeanLevey 7 87
(Antony Brittain) *trckd ldrs: hdwy to go 2nd 2f out: pushed along over 1f out: rdn and led ent fnl f: r.o but hdd last 50yds: lost 2nd nr fin* **14/1**

2451 **4** *1 ½* **Orient Class**[14] 3827 6-9-1 **88**.................................. ConnorMurtagh(7) 11 88+
(Paul Midgley) *hld up: effrt and n.m.r 2f out: hdwy on inner over 1f out: r.o steadily ins fnl f* **20/1**

4451 **5** *¾* **Queen In Waiting (IRE)**[7] 4098 3-9-7 **92**.......................... FrannyNorton 1 87+
(Mark Johnston) *slowly away: settled in rr: last 1/2-way: pushed along 2f out: hdwy and rdn 1f out: r.o wl ins fnl f: nvr nrr* **7/4[1]**

0055 **6** *½* **Ballesteros**[21] 3581 8-9-0 **80**........................................... PatrickMathers 8 75
(Richard Fahey) *mid-div: rdn and brought wd over 1f out: r.o one pce fnl f* **25/1**

0000 **7** *hd* **Blithe Spirit**[28] 3321 6-9-4 **84**................................................ NeilFarley 6 78
(Eric Alston) *broke wl: trckd across to ld: rdn and hdd ent fnl f: no ex* **16/1**

156 **8** *shd* **Impart**[14] 3844 3-8-13 **87**...................................................... JoshDoyle(3) 5 79
(David O'Meara) *mid-div: pushed along 2f out: rdn over 1f out: one pce* **7/1**

3210 **9** *1* **Megan Lily (IRE)**[14] 3835 3-9-2 **90**............................... SammyJoBell(3) 9 78
(Richard Fahey) *mid-div: pushed along on outer 2f out: rdn and no ex fr over 1f out* **14/1**

0020 **10** *¾* **Awesome Allan (IRE)**[21] 3584 3-8-10 **81**............................(t) JohnFahy 3 67
(David Evans) *mid-div: rdn over 1f out: fdd* **10/1**

6-00 **11** *1* **Lightscameraction (IRE)**[158] 388 5-10-3 **97**................(b) KevinStott 10 81
(Gay Kelleway) *slowly away: hdwy 1/2-way: rdn over 1f out: no imp* **40/1**

6606 **12** *1 ¼* **Red Stripes (USA)**[116] 1071 5-8-0 **73** oh8.............. DarraghKeenan(7) 12 53
(Lisa Williamson) *a in rr: pushed along on outer 2f out: sn rdn: no imp* **66/1**

1m 2.16s (1.16) **Going Correction** +0.30s/f (Good)
**WFA** 3 from 4yo+ 5lb **12** Ran SP% **125.1**
Speed ratings (Par 107): **102,101,101,98,97 96,96,96,94,93 92,90**
CSF £28.49 CT £309.81 TOTE £7.30: £2.00, £1.80, £3.60; EX 33.10 Trifecta £258.80.
**Owner** David Lowe & Miss Amber Lowe **Bred** Hyde Park Stud & Paddy Conney **Trained** Malpas, Cheshire

**FOCUS**
Add 11yds. A competitive sprint handicap run at a sound pace. The winner is rated close to his best.

## 4334 WOODFORD RESERVE H'CAP 7f 1y
**2:55** (2:56) (Class 2) (0-100,100) 3-Y-O
**£12,450** (£3,728; £1,864; £932; £466; £234) **Stalls** Low

Form RPR
-132 **1** **Lualiwa**[45] 2739 3-8-3 **82**............................................................ JoeDoyle 2 92
(Kevin Ryan) *trckd ldr: pushed along to ld over 1f out: rdn and 1 l clr ent fnl f: responded to press: hld on wl* **3/1[1]**

-131 **2** *¾* **Starlight Romance (IRE)**[21] 3578 3-8-5 **87**.............. SammyJoBell(3) 3 95
(Richard Fahey) *trckd ldrs: n.m.r 2f out: sn in clr: hdwy to chse ldr ins fnl f: rdn and r.o: but hld* **3/1[1]**

3-42 **3** *2 ¾* **Vona (IRE)**[21] 3578 3-8-4 **90**................................... ConnorMurtagh(7) 4 91
(Richard Fahey) *chsd ldrs: 4th 2f out: effrt over 1f out: rdn and styd on to take 3rd ins fnl f* **7/1[2]**

-034 **4** *2* **Town Charter (USA)**[8] 4057 3-8-8 **87**............................ FrannyNorton 9 83
(Mark Johnston) *hld up: pushed along on inner over 1f out: sn rdn: r.o to take 4th ins fnl f* **14/1[3]**

6-00 **5** *nk* **Erica Bing**[21] 3612 3-8-4 **86**.............................. NathanEvans(3) 8 81
(Jo Hughes) *broke wl fr wd draw: led: pushed along and hdd over 1f out: rdn: grad wknd* **50/1**

1203 **6** *shd* **Atteq**[7] 4075 3-8-2 **81**.............................. (t) PatrickMathers 1 76
(Richard Fahey) *mid-div: pushed along 2f out: rdn and one pce ent fnl f* **3/1**[1]

5010 **7** *shd* **Smokey Lane (IRE)**[14] 3844 3-9-6 **99**.............................. JohnFahy 6 93
(David Evans) *hld up: drvn 2f out: rdn over 1f out: one pce* **20/1**

5220 **8** *1 1/2* **Wahash (IRE)**[14] 3844 3-9-5 **98**.............................. SeanLevey 5 88
(Richard Hannon) *hld up: drvn and no imp fr 2f out* **7/1**[2]

2040 **9** *3/4* **Mr Scaramanga**[11] 3927 3-9-7 **100**.............................. LiamKeniry 7 88
(Simon Dow) *mid-div: pushed along 2f out: rdn over 1f out: wknd* **14/1**[3]

1m 27.47s (0.97) **Going Correction** +0.30s/f (Good) 9 Ran SP% **120.1**
Speed ratings (Par 106): **106,105,102,99,99 99,99,97,96**
CSF £12.01 CT £59.13 TOTE £3.90: £1.30, £1.40, £2.50; EX 14.70 Trifecta £65.20.
**Owner** Mrs Rosie Richer **Bred** M E Broughton **Trained** Hambleton, N Yorks

**FOCUS**
Add 13yds. The pace was sound for this decent handicap. The winner was well in with the second on York form.

## 4335 MATTHEW CLARK NOVICE STKS (PLUS 10 RACE) 5f 15y
**3:25** (3:29) (Class 4) 2-Y-O **£6,469** (£1,925; £962; £481) **Stalls** Low

Form RPR

610 **1** **Billy Dylan (IRE)**[9] 3993 2-9-8 85.............................. SeanLevey 8 83
(Richard Hannon) *trckd over fr wd draw to r in mid-div: gng wl bhd ldrs 2f out: hdwy over 1f out: pushed along to ld ent fnl f: sn clr: reminders to maintain advantage: comf* **11/4**[2]

0325 **2** *1 3/4* **Demons Rock (IRE)**[12] 3917 2-8-11 75.............................. PaddyPilley(5) 6 71
(Tom Dascombe) *trckd ldrs: effrt on outer 2f out: hdwy and rdn over 1f out: r.o to take 2nd ins fnl f* **9/2**[3]

300 **3** *3/4* **Floss The Hoss (IRE)**[17] 3712 2-8-11 59.............................. JohnFahy 3 63
(David Evans) *disp ld tl led on own wl over 1f out: sn rdn and hdd: one pce and lost 2nd ins fnl f* **14/1**

06 **4** *3 1/2* **Brockey Rise (IRE)**[22] 3538 2-9-2 0.............................. PatrickMathers 2 55
(David Evans) *in rr: pushed along fr 3f out: styd on fnl 2 fs: nvr nrr* **33/1**

03 **5** *3/4* **Levante Player (IRE)**[35] 3066 2-9-2 0.............................. LiamKeniry 1 53
(Tom Dascombe) *disp ld tl wl over 1f out: sn pushed along: no ex* **11/4**[2]

024 **6** *4 1/2* **Knockout Blow**[14] 3846 2-9-2 77.............................. FrannyNorton 5 37
(Mark Johnston) *prom: drvn 2f out: hrd rdn over 1f out: wknd* **2/1**[1]

00 **7** *2* **Renton**[21] 3576 2-9-2 0.............................. NeilFarley 4 29
(Tony Coyle) *mid-div: lost pl and drvn 1/2-way: rdn over 1f out: no imp* **50/1**

0 **8** *1/2* **Kathy**[35] 3066 2-8-4 0.............................. RPWalsh(7) 7 23
(Scott Dixon) *slowly away losing several l: a in rr* **50/1**

1m 3.53s (2.53) **Going Correction** +0.30s/f (Good) 8 Ran SP% **118.4**
Speed ratings (Par 96): **91,88,87,81,80 73,69,69**
CSF £16.07 TOTE £3.30: £1.30, £1.70, £3.50; EX 15.30 Trifecta £109.00.
**Owner** Sullivan Bloodstock Limited **Bred** River Downs Stud **Trained** East Everleigh, Wilts

**FOCUS**
Add 11yds. An interesting maiden run at a strong gallop.

## 4336 HOP HOUSE 13 H'CAP 1m 4f 63y
**4:00** (4:02) (Class 4) (0-80,82) 3-Y-O+

**£6,225** (£1,864; £932; £466; £233; £117) **Stalls** Low

Form RPR

4-42 **1** **Hochfeld (IRE)**[131] 846 3-9-0 **77**.............................. FrannyNorton 1 90+
(Mark Johnston) *mid-div: hdwy 2f out: 3rd and stl plenty to do over 1f out: rdn and str run ent fnl f: clsd qckly on runner-up: led last 75yds: comf* **3/1**[2]

3-10 **2** *1 1/2* **Kajaki (IRE)**[44] 2770 4-9-11 **76**.............................. (p) KevinStott 5 83
(Kevin Ryan) *a handy: trckd ldr gng wl 2f out: sn led: rdn 3 l clr 1f out: clsd down by fast-fining wnr ins fnl f: hdd last 75yds* **6/1**[3]

1142 **3** *4* **Monaco Rose**[21] 3580 4-9-10 **75**.............................. PatrickMathers 2 76
(Richard Fahey) *mid-div: wd and drvn wl over 1f out: r.o wl to take 3rd wl ins fnl f* **3/1**[2]

0026 **4** *1/2* **Lord Franklin**[21] 3582 8-9-11 **76**.............................. NeilFarley 3 76
(Eric Alston) *led 2f: hdd but remained prom: drvn in 4th 2f out: kpt on u.p fnl f* **20/1**

-050 **5** *1 1/2* **Michael's Mount**[20] 3618 4-9-8 **76**.............................. (b[1]) NathanEvans(3) 8 73
(Ed Dunlop) *mid-div: hdwy to go 2nd 2f out: rdn over 1f out: no ex* **7/1**

0-42 **6** *2 1/2* **Cotinga**[26] 3392 3-8-6 **74**.............................. GeorgiaCox(5) 9 68
(Ralph Beckett) *in rr: effrt over 2f out: sme late hdwy* **11/4**[1]

0-00 **7** *2 3/4* **Foresee (GER)**[31] 3213 4-9-4 **74**.............................. PaddyPilley(5) 7 63
(Tony Carroll) *mid-div: pushed along 2f out: rdn and no ex fr over 1f out* **50/1**

060 **8** *11* **Brandon Castle**[16] 3744 5-9-0 **65**.............................. (e) JohnFahy 6 36
(Simon West) *t.k.h early: circled field to go prom after 4 fs: led 4f out: drvn and hdd 2f out: wknd* **20/1**

-005 **9** *2 3/4* **Parish Boy**[17] 3716 5-10-3 **82**.............................. (p[1]) SamJames 10 49
(David Loughnane) *prom: led after 2f: hdd 4f out: sn rdn and wknd* **33/1**

4333 **10** *2* **Hussar Ballad (USA)**[22] 3547 8-8-6 **64**.............................. ConnorMurtagh(7) 4 28
(Antony Brittain) *.hld up: rdn 2f out: fdd* **16/1**

2m 42.15s (3.65) **Going Correction** +0.30s/f (Good)
**WFA** 3 from 4yo+ 12lb 10 Ran SP% **123.8**
Speed ratings (Par 105): **99,98,95,95,94 92,90,83,81,80**
CSF £21.94 CT £60.99 TOTE £4.80: £1.70, £2.20, £1.50; EX 28.30 Trifecta £104.10.
**Owner** Sheikh Hamdan bin Mohammed Al Maktoum **Bred** Kenilworth House Stud **Trained** Middleham Moor, N Yorks

**FOCUS**
Add 20yds. The pace was honest for this fair handicap. There could be more to come from the winner.

## 4337 STELLA ARTOIS H'CAP 5f 15y
**4:35** (4:36) (Class 4) (0-85,83) 4-Y-O+

**£6,225** (£1,864; £932; £466; £233; £117) **Stalls** Low

Form RPR

0303 **1** **Normal Equilibrium**[12] 3903 7-8-10 **72**.............................. FrannyNorton 5 81
(Ivan Furtado) *led 2f: hdd but remained prom: regained ld 2f out: drvn over 1f out: rdn and forged clr ent fnl f: r.o wl* **8/1**

0-06 **2** *1 3/4* **Powerallied (IRE)**[21] 3581 4-9-7 **83**.............................. PatrickMathers 2 86+
(Richard Fahey) *trckd ldrs: effrt whn hmpd by 3rd wl over 1f out: rcvrd and rdn 1f out: r.o strly ins fnl f: tk 2nd nr fin* **5/2**[1]

2232 **3** *nk* **Pushkin Museum (IRE)**[11] 3941 6-8-3 **68**.............................. NathanEvans(3) 8 70
(Patrick Morris) *trckd ldrs: 4th 2f out: sn pushed along: hmpd runner-up wl over 1f out: hdwy and rdn to chse wnr ins fnl f: r.o but lost 2nd nr fin* **20/1**

0135 **4** *1/2* **Invincible Ridge (IRE)**[16] 3741 9-9-3 **79**.............................. NeilFarley 10 79
(Eric Alston) *mid-div: pushed along 2f out: rdn and r.o wl fnl f: nvr nrr* **33/1**

00-0 **5** *1/2* **Lexi's Hero (IRE)**[42] 2837 9-8-8 **75**.............................. (v) PaddyPilley(5) 7 73
(Patrick Morris) *prom: led after 2 fs: drvn and hdd 2f out: wknd ins fnl f* **25/1**

4241 **6** *1/2* **Signore Piccolo**[16] 3741 6-9-7 **83**.............................. (h) SamJames 1 82+
(David Loughnane) *mid-div: effrt and n.m.r on inner wl over 1f out: denied clr run ent fnl f: nt rcvr* **11/4**[2]

2220 **7** *1 1/2* **Silvanus (IRE)**[17] 3707 12-8-10 **79**.............................. ConnorMurtagh(7) 9 70
(Paul Midgley) *prom: pushed along and ev ch 2f out: wknd ent fnl f* **20/1**

442 **8** *1 1/4* **Rosealee (IRE)**[7] 4093 4-8-12 **74**.............................. (p) RyanTate 3 60
(Jeremy Gask) *mid-div: drvn 2f out: no ex fnl f* **5/1**[3]

1313 **9** *2* **Mighty Zip (USA)**[14] 3812 5-8-2 **64** oh2.............................. (p) PaulQuinn 12 43
(Lisa Williamson) *mid-div: chsd along on outer 2f out: wknd ent fnl f* **66/1**

1023 **10** *2* **Aprovado (IRE)**[26] 3386 5-9-2 **83**.............................. (p) CallumRodriguez(5) 4 55
(Michael Dods) *hld up: pushed along 2f out: drvn 1f out: sn rdn and wknd* **11/2**

0-00 **11** *2 1/2* **Kibaar**[56] 2409 5-9-7 **83**.............................. KevinStott 11 46
(Kevin Ryan) *a in rr* **20/1**

1m 2.31s (1.31) **Going Correction** +0.30s/f (Good) 11 Ran SP% **121.0**
Speed ratings (Par 105): **101,98,97,96,96 95,92,90,87,84 80**
CSF £26.71 CT £409.26 TOTE £9.70: £2.60, £1.40, £4.80; EX 39.70 Trifecta £892.10.
**Owner** John L Marriott & Albert L Marriott **Bred** D R Tucker **Trained** Wiseton, Nottinghamshire
■ Stewards' Enquiry : Nathan Evans three-day ban: careless riding (Jul 17-19)

**FOCUS**
Add 11yds. A competitive handicap run at a strong pace. It paid to race handy. The winner is rated to his better form for this yard.

## 4338 COCA COLA ZERO SUGAR H'CAP 1m 7f 196y
**5:10** (5:10) (Class 4) (0-85,87) 4-Y-O+

**£6,225** (£1,864; £932; £466; £233; £117) **Stalls** Low

Form RPR

-313 **1** **Zenafire**[16] 3740 8-8-7 **71**.............................. (p) SammyJoBell(3) 5 78
(Sarah Hollinshead) *racd in 4th: wnt 3rd over 2f out: pushed along to go 2nd over 1f out: rdn and ldr ent fnl f: r.o wl to assert last 50yds* **7/2**[2]

2-42 **2** *1/2* **Corpus Chorister (FR)**[49] 2622 4-9-7 **82**.............................. KevinStott 7 88
(David Menuisier) *led: kicked on 2f out: 1 l clr over 1f out: sn rdn: jnd ent fnl f: matched strides w wnr tl hdd 50 yds out: no ex* **4/1**[3]

2165 **3** *3 1/2* **Royal Flag**[21] 3580 7-8-9 **70**.............................. FrannyNorton 4 72
(Brian Ellison) *trckd ldrs: relegated to 4th and pushed along over 2f out: rdn over 1f out: r.o to take 3rd ins fnl f* **5/2**[1]

-014 **4** *1/2* **Gabrial's Star**[21] 3580 8-9-4 **86**.............................. (p) ConnorMurtagh(7) 2 87
(Richard Fahey) *racd in 5th: pushed along 3f out: rdn 2f out: styd on one pce into 4th ins fnl f* **7/2**[2]

4060 **5** *hd* **Angel Gabrial (IRE)**[21] 3594 8-9-12 **87**.............................. PatrickMathers 6 88
(Richard Fahey) *trckd ldr: drvn whn ldr kicked on 2f out: rdn wl over 1f out: no ex* **9/2**

40-3 **6** *16* **Gabrial The Duke (IRE)**[21] 3564 7-8-4 **68**.............................. (b) NathanEvans(3) 3 50
(Patrick Morris) *in rr: drvn over 3f out: lost tch fr 2f out* **20/1**

3m 34.06s (6.06) **Going Correction** +0.30s/f (Good) 6 Ran SP% **116.0**
Speed ratings (Par 105): **96,95,94,93,93 85**
CSF £18.45 TOTE £5.60: £1.70, £1.80; EX 22.50 Trifecta £69.60.
**Owner** Robert Moseley **Bred** R J R Moseley & Mrs E Coquelin **Trained** Upper Longdon, Staffs

**FOCUS**
Add 26yds. A tight handicap run at a steady pace. The winner was close to his best.
T/Plt: £104.40 to a £1 stake. Pool: £76,426.12 - 534.26 winning units. T/Qpdt: £11.20 to a £1 stake. Pool: £5,669.03 - 371.70 winning units. **Keith McHugh**

# 4296 DONCASTER (L-H)
Saturday, July 1

**OFFICIAL GOING: Good to soft**
Wind: Light against Weather: Cloudy

## 4339 SUNBETS.CO.UK H'CAP 7f 6y
**5:55** (5:59) (Class 4) (0-85,87) 4-Y-O+ **£5,175** (£1,540; £769; £384) **Stalls** Centre

Form RPR

1314 **1** **Art Echo**[24] 3471 4-8-12 **76**.............................. (t) ConnorBeasley 1 84
(John Mackie) *hld up: hdwy 3f out and sn in tch: chsd ldrs 2f out: rdn to chal ent fnl f: drvn to ld last 100 yds* **9/2**[1]

3205 **2** *1/2* **Johnny Cavagin**[16] 3757 8-9-2 **80**.............................. (t) StevieDonohoe 8 86
(Ronald Thompson) *rrd s and dwlt: sn in tch: trckd ldrs 1/2-way: hdwy to chal over 1f out: sn rdn: drvn and slt advantage ins fnl f: hdd and no ex last 100 yds* **11/2**[3]

1-00 **3** *shd* **King Of Naples**[42] 2833 4-9-2 **83**.............................. GeorgeWood(3) 10 89
(James Fanshawe) *trckd ldrs: hdwy to ld wl over 1f out: rdn and wandered jst over 1f out: drvn and hdd narrowly ins fnl f: kpt on* **13/2**

1535 **4** *1 1/4* **Satchville Flyer**[3] 4219 6-8-13 **77**.............................. TomQueally 5 79
(David Evans) *towards rr: pushed along and hdwy over 2f out: rdn wl over 1f out: styd on fnl f: nrst fin* **20/1**

4260 **5** *shd* **Hanseatic**[3] 4210 8-8-11 **75**.............................. (t[1]) CamHardie 12 77
(Michael Easterby) *cl up: rdn along 2f out: ev ch 1f out: drvn appr fnl f and kpt on same pce* **14/1**

4014 **6** *1/2* **Merdon Castle (IRE)**[11] 3946 5-9-0 **78**.............................. (e) JamesSullivan 3 79
(Ruth Carr) *towards rr: hdwy 2f out: rdn to chse ldrs over 1f out: no imp fnl f* **20/1**

65-0 **7** *1 1/2* **Tukhoom (IRE)**[35] 3095 4-8-13 **77**.............................. JoeDoyle 4 74
(Michael Herrington) *hld up towards rr: hdwy over 2f out: sn rdn along and n.d* **17/2**

26-0 **8** *1 3/4* **Echo Of Lightning**[21] 3581 7-8-6 **75**.............................. MeganNicholls(5) 9 67
(Brian Ellison) *led: rdn along 2f out: sn hdd and drvn: grad wknd* **33/1**

0400 **9** *shd* **Dutch Art Dealer**[13] 3857 6-9-5 **83**.............................. (p) DavidNolan 6 75
(Ivan Furtado) *dwlt: a towards rr* **20/1**

0020 **10** *1 1/2* **Intense Style (IRE)**[21] 3565 5-9-9 **87**.............................. (p) JasonHart 11 75
(Les Eyre) *chsd ldrs: rdn along 2f out: sn wknd* **5/1**[2]

0000 **11** *3 1/4* **Roll On Rory**[15] 3792 4-9-8 **86**.............................. (v) JFEgan 7 65
(Jason Ward) *chsd ldrs: rdn along 2f out: sn wknd* **8/1**



The Form Book Flat, Raceform Ltd, Newbury, RG14 5SJ

0304 **12** *4* **Ower Fly**[21] 3572 4-9-7 **85** SeanLevey 2 53
(Richard Hannon) *chsd ldrs: rdn along 3f out: sn wknd* **13/2**

1m 27.45s (1.15) **Going Correction** +0.225s/f (Good) **12** Ran SP% **122.4**
Speed ratings (Par 105): **102,101,101,99,99 99,97,95,95,93 89,85**
CSF £28.30 CT £167.65 TOTE £4.80: £2.10, £2.10, £2.80; EX 35.30 Trifecta £156.40.
**Owner** Annwell Inn Syndicate **Bred** Follow The Flag Partnership **Trained** Church Broughton , Derbys

■ Stewards' Enquiry : Stevie Donohoe two-day ban: used whip above permitted level (Jul 17-18)

**FOCUS**
Race distance increased by 12yds in races 6 & 7. The ground had dried out to good to soft ahead of the opener, a modest handicap lacking many in-form runners. They went a good gallop and came down the centre. The form is rated around the second and third.

## 4340 PANELCRAFT SUPERIOR ACCESS PANELS BRITISH STALLION STUDS EBF FILLIES' NOVICE STKS (PLUS 10 RACE) 7f 6y
**6:25** (6:27) (Class 5) 2-Y-O **£3,234** (£962; £481; £240) **Stalls** Centre

Form RPR
**1** **Model (FR)** 2-9-0 0 SeanLevey 4 74
(Richard Hannon) *t.k.h: trckd ldng pair: hdwy over 2f out: rdn to chal over 1f out: drvn to ld and hung rt ins fnl f: jst hld on* **11/8**[1]

4 **2** *hd* **Sultanaa**[42] 2832 2-9-0 0 StevieDonohoe 8 73
(Ismail Mohammed) *t.k.h: cl up: rdn to ld 11/2f out: drvn and hdd ins fnl f: ev ch whn bmpd and carried rt ins last 100 yds: rallied wl towards fin: jst failed* **2/1**[2]

0 **3** *1 3/4* **Gemologist (IRE)**[10] 3965 2-9-0 0 HarryBentley 1 69
(Mark Johnston) *led: rdn along and hdd 11/2f out: cl 3rd whn hmpd jst ins fnl f: kpt on same pce after* **10/1**

**4** *3/4* **Ruysch (IRE)** 2-9-0 0 LukeMorris 2 67
(Ed Dunlop) *in tch: hdwy to chse ldrs over 2f out: rdn along wl over 1f out: kpt on fnl f* **20/1**

**5** *3 1/4* **Zoffinia (IRE)** 2-9-0 0 TonyHamilton 3 59+
(Richard Fahey) *dwlt and rr tl styd on fnl 2f* **4/1**[3]

**6** *1* **Pearl's Calling (IRE)** 2-9-0 0 JamesSullivan 5 56
(David Barron) *green and rr: sme late hdwy* **16/1**

00 **7** *2* **Harbour Rose**[12] 3902 2-9-0 0 PaddyAspell 6 51
(Philip Kirby) *t.k.h: chsd ldrs: rdn 3f out: sn wknd* **50/1**

00 **8** *nk* **Mops Tango**[37] 2987 2-8-7 0 RayDawson(7) 7 50
(Michael Appleby) *chsd ldrs: rdn along 3f out: sn wknd* **40/1**

1m 31.44s (5.14) **Going Correction** +0.225s/f (Good) **8** Ran SP% **119.6**
Speed ratings (Par 91): **79,78,76,75,72 71,68,68**
CSF £4.51 TOTE £2.10: £1.10, £1.20, £3.20; EX 4.90 Trifecta £24.80.
**Owner** Hussain Alabbas Lootah **Bred** Rosemont Stud Pty Ltd **Trained** East Everleigh, Wilts

**FOCUS**
A modest juvenile event in which the first two pulled away from the third and fourth, who came clear of the rest. The winner leaned into the runner-up late on but it didn't alter the outcome. The first two look decent.

## 4341 REG GILKS MEMORIAL MAIDEN STKS 6f 2y
**6:55** (6:58) (Class 5) 3-Y-O+ **£3,234** (£962; £481; £240) **Stalls** Centre

Form RPR
**1** **Samarmadi** 3-9-6 0 HarryBentley 7 78+
(Hugo Palmer) *in tch: hdwy over 2f out: rdn along over 1f out: chal ent fnl f: kpt on wl to ld last 50 yds* **12/1**

332 **2** *1/2* **Dirchill (IRE)**[26] 3407 3-9-6 73 JamesSullivan 3 76
(David Barron) *trckd ldrs: hdwy 1/2-way: cl up 2f out: chal over 1f out: sn rdn: led ins fnl f: sn drvn: hdd and no ex last 50 yds* **3/1**[2]

2 **3** *1 3/4* **Ptarmigan Ridge**[42] 2819 3-9-6 0 DanielMuscutt 13 70
(James Fanshawe) *cl up: chal 2f out: rdn to take slt ld jst over 1f out: drvn and hdd ins fnl f: kpt on same pce* **1/1**[1]

**4** *1 1/4* **Mischief Managed (IRE)** 3-9-6 0 (e[1]) DavidAllan 10 66+
(Tim Easterby) *dwlt and rr: hdwy 2f out: styd on fnl f* **40/1**

**5** *1* **Wardy (IRE)** 3-9-6 0 DanielTudhope 9 63+
(Peter Chapple-Hyam) *towards rr: hdwy 2f out: rdn over 1f out: kpt on fnl f* **10/1**

50 **6** *1* **Deciding Vote**[21] 3595 3-9-1 0 FranBerry 5 55
(Chris Wall) *led: rdn along 2f out: drvn and hdd jst over 1f out: grad wknd* **66/1**

44 **7** *1 1/4* **Chatoyer (FR)**[78] 1762 3-9-6 0 SeanLevey 11 56+
(Richard Hannon) *t.k.h: hld up towards rr: sme hdwy wl over 1f out: n.d* **12/1**

0-30 **8** *1/2* **Gloriux**[35] 3085 3-9-6 72 LukeMorris 4 54
(Charles Hills) *t.k.h: trckd ldrs: hdwy 3f out and sn cl up: rdn along wl over 1f out: grad wknd* **7/1**[3]

-6 **9** *nk* **Fille The Force**[42] 2819 3-9-1 0 BarryMcHugh 8 48
(Scott Dixon) *prom: rdn along 1/2-way: sn wknd* **66/1**

00 **10** *2* **Naralsaif (IRE)**[9] 4003 3-9-1 0 JFEgan 1 42
(Derek Shaw) *dwlt: a towards rr* **150/1**

24 **11** *2 1/2* **Calypso Jo**[75] 1837 3-9-6 0 JoeDoyle 6 39
(Kevin Ryan) *a towards rr* **20/1**

6 **12** *1/2* **Oscar Ranger (IRE)**[10] 3984 3-9-6 0 TonyHamilton 12 37
(Richard Fahey) *awkward s and dwlt: green and a rr* **33/1**

1m 14.68s (1.08) **Going Correction** +0.225s/f (Good) **12** Ran SP% **125.8**
Speed ratings (Par 103): **101,100,98,96,95 93,92,91,90,88 84,84**
CSF £49.57 TOTE £14.90: £4.10, £1.50, £1.10; EX 60.30 Trifecta £122.00.
**Owner** Abdullah Menahi **Bred** Rabbah Bloodstock Limited **Trained** Newmarket, Suffolk

**FOCUS**
A fairly good maiden won by The Tin Man in 2015 and Medicean Man in 2009. They came down the middle and a debutant triumphed. The form is rated around the runner-up and the fourth.

## 4342 JORDAN ROAD SURFACING H'CAP 5f 143y
**7:25** (7:27) (Class 4) (0-85,87) 3-Y-O **£5,175** (£1,540; £769; £384) **Stalls** Centre

Form RPR
1033 **1** **Justanotherbottle (IRE)**[14] 3844 3-10-0 **87** DanielTudhope 3 96
(Declan Carroll) *qckly away: mde all: clr wl over 1f out: readily* **6/4**[1]

2-12 **2** *2* **Marseille (IRE)**[39] 2925 3-9-0 **73** JoeDoyle 6 74+
(Julie Camacho) *hmpd s: t.k.h towards rr: hdwy 1/2-way: rdn to chse wnr over 1f out: kpt on fnl f* **4/1**[3]

0603 **3** *1 3/4* **Monks Stand (USA)**[10] 3982 3-9-4 **77** (p) DavidAllan 2 72
(Tim Easterby) *chsd ldng pair: rdn along 2f out: drvn and kpt on same pce appr fnl f* **14/1**

-310 **4** *3* **Kodicat (IRE)**[49] 2630 3-8-12 **71** ShaneGray 1 56
(Kevin Ryan) *towards rr: hdwy over 2f out: sn rdn and kpt on same pce* **9/1**

643- **5** *3/4* **Somewhere Secret**[238] 7819 3-9-3 **76** RobertTart 5 59
(Michael Mullineaux) *hmpd s: a towards rr* **7/1**

210- **6** *3* **Loving**[246] 7667 3-9-7 **80** LukeMorris 4 53
(William Haggas) *swvd rt s: t.k.h: chsd wnr: rdn along: carried hd high and hung rt wl over 1f out: sn wknd* **3/1**[2]

1m 9.97s (1.17) **Going Correction** +0.225s/f (Good) **6** Ran SP% **114.2**
Speed ratings (Par 102): **101,98,96,92,91 87**
CSF £8.09 TOTE £2.20: £1.30, £1.80; EX 7.60 Trifecta £34.40.
**Owner** Steve Ryan & M J Tedham **Bred** John O'Connor **Trained** Malton, N Yorks

**FOCUS**
A tight handicap, though each of the last seven winners of the race failed to follow-up. They came up the middle and the well backed favourite made all. He showed improved form.

## 4343 M&G SERVICES ASBESTOS ABATEMENT & SURVEYING H'CAP 6f 2y
**7:55** (7:57) (Class 4) (0-85,86) 4-Y-O+ **£5,175** (£1,540; £769; £384) **Stalls** Centre

Form RPR
3215 **1** **Art Obsession (IRE)**[31] 3195 6-9-1 **79** LukeMorris 4 87
(Paul Midgley) *towards rr: hdwy 3f out: chsd ldrs and rdn along wl over 1f out: styd on u.p ent fnl f: led last 50 yds* **11/1**

0440 **2** *3/4* **Eccleston**[21] 3585 6-9-8 **86** (v) DanielTudhope 9 92
(David O'Meara) *prom: effrt wl over 1f out: sn rdn to chse ldr: drvn ins fnl f: kpt on wl towards fin* **7/2**[1]

0-03 **3** *nse* **Pomme De Terre (IRE)**[26] 3401 5-9-1 **79** (b) PaulMulrennan 12 84
(Michael Dods) *led: rdn along over 1f out: drvn and jnd ins fnl f: hdd and no ex last 50 yds* **7/1**[3]

023 **4** *1/2* **Dark Defender**[7] 4080 4-8-13 **82** (b) RowanScott(5) 5 86
(Keith Dalgleish) *prom: hdwy to chse ldr 2f out: rdn over 1f out: drvn ins fnl f: kpt on* **7/1**[3]

4 00 **5** *1/2* **Duke Cosimo**[14] 3847 7-8-11 **75** JoeDoyle 14 77+
(Michael Herrington) *hld up and bhd: hdwy wl over 1f out: rdn and nt clr run wl ins fnl f: sn swtchd rt and kpt on wl towards fin* **22/1**

0655 **6** *3/4* **Top Boy**[10] 3969 7-9-4 **82** (v) PhillipMakin 6 82
(Derek Shaw) *hld up towards rr: hdwy wl over 1f out: rdn and kpt on wl fnl f* **25/1**

-360 **7** *1 1/4* **Danish Duke (IRE)**[12] 3897 6-8-5 **69** (p) JamesSullivan 3 65
(Ruth Carr) *in tch: hdwy to trck ldrs over 2f out: effrt wl over 1f out: sn rdn and hld whn n.m.r ins fnl f* **16/1**

0221 **8** *nk* **Bahamian Dollar**[12] 3919 4-8-9 **80** KatherineGlenister(7) 1 75
(David Evans) *trckd ldrs: hdwy on inner over 2f out: sn cl up and ev ch: rdn over 1f out: sn drvn and wknd* **4/1**[2]

001 **9** *2 1/4* **Dragon King (IRE)**[21] 3581 5-9-7 **85** (h) DougieCostello 11 73
(Iain Jardine) *stdd s: keen hld and hld up towards rr: sme hdwy wl over 1rf out: n.d* **16/1**

1100 **10** *2* **Treaty Of Rome (USA)**[20] 3625 5-8-8 **72** (v) JFEgan 2 53
(Derek Shaw) *a towards rr* **50/1**

0102 **11** *4 1/2* **Tricky Dicky**[14] 3847 4-8-10 **74** DuranFentiman 15 41
(Olly Williams) *racd wd: chsd ldrs on outer: rdn along wl over 2f out: sn wknd* **4/1**[2]

0045 **12** *3/4* **Royal Connoisseur (IRE)**[24] 3452 6-8-13 **77** TonyHamilton 13 41
(Richard Fahey) *chsd ldrs: rdn along 1/2-way: sn wknd* **20/1**

6520 **13** *7* **Red Tycoon (IRE)**[21] 3581 5-9-6 **84** FranBerry 10 26
(Ken Cunningham-Brown) *prom: rdn along 1/2-way: sn wknd* **20/1**

1m 14.19s (0.59) **Going Correction** +0.225s/f (Good) **13** Ran SP% **127.0**
Speed ratings (Par 105): **105,104,103,103,102 101,99,99,96,93 87,86,77**
CSF £49.12 CT £315.48 TOTE £12.50: £3.80, £1.80, £2.50; EX 63.90 Trifecta £441.70.
**Owner** Pee Dee Tee Syndicate & T W Midgley **Bred** Lynch Bages Ltd & Camas Park Stud **Trained** Westow, N Yorks

■ Stewards' Enquiry : Luke Morris caution: careless riding

**FOCUS**
A competitive sprint handicap and a very tight finish with not much splitting the first four. The winner was back to his old best.

## 4344 LIKE SUN BETS ON FACEBOOK FILLIES' H'CAP 1m 2f 43y
**8:25** (8:26) (Class 5) (0-70,72) 4-Y-O+ **£3,234** (£962; £481; £240) **Stalls** Low

Form RPR
4065 **1** **Inflexiball**[16] 3761 5-8-5 **54** LukeMorris 3 62
(John Mackie) *in tch: hdwy 3f out: rdn to chse ldr over 1f out: drvn to chal ins fnl f: led last 100 yds* **7/2**[3]

05 **2** *nk* **Della Valle (GER)**[43] 2785 4-9-0 **63** DanielMuscutt 4 70
(Mike Murphy) *trckd ldr: hdwy to ld over 2f out: rdn clr over 1f out: drvn and edgd rt ins fnl f: sn hdd: rallied wl u.p: kpt on* **8/1**

2230 **3** *7* **Amber Mystique**[14] 3828 4-9-4 **72** JaneElliott(5) 1 65
(Kristin Stubbs) *hld up in rr: hdwy 3f out: rdn along 2f out: drvn and no imp appr fnl f* **8/1**

4112 **4** *1* **Favorite Girl (GER)**[18] 3699 9-8-13 **69** RayDawson(7) 7 60
(Michael Appleby) *sn led: rdn along over 3f out: hdd over 2f out: sn drvn and plugged on one pce* **5/2**[2]

0-00 **5** *2 3/4* **Bertha Burnett (IRE)**[7] 4105 6-8-2 **51** oh6 JamesSullivan 5 37
(Brian Rothwell) *hld up in rr: sme hdwy on inner 3f out: rdn along over 2f out: n.d* **33/1**

-321 **6** *1/2* **Maulesden May (IRE)**[8] 4056 4-9-8 **71** PhillipMakin 6 56
(Keith Dalgleish) *trckd ldng pair: pushed along 3f out: rdn over 2f out: sn btn* **6/4**[1]

2m 13.97s (4.57) **Going Correction** +0.35s/f (Good) **6** Ran SP% **116.0**
Speed ratings (Par 100): **95,94,89,88,86 85**
CSF £31.11 CT £209.79 TOTE £4.50: £2.00, £4.00; EX 31.70 Trifecta £182.70.
**Owner** Derbyshire Racing II **Bred** Derbyshire Racing **Trained** Church Broughton , Derbys

**FOCUS**
Race distance increased by 12yds. Not the most competitive of handicaps, and the first two came well clear. The winner is rated to this year's form.

## 4345 FOLLOW SUN BETS ON TWITTER H'CAP 1m 3f 197y
**8:55** (8:55) (Class 5) (0-70,71) 4-Y-O+ **£3,234** (£962; £481; £240) **Stalls** Low

Form RPR
404 **1** **Paddy's Rock (IRE)**[17] 3706 6-8-1 **53** oh4 ow2 (p) NathanEvans(3) 2 61
(Lynn Siddall) *hld up towards rr: stdy hdwy over 3f out: trckd ldrs 2f out: chsd clr ldr over 1f out: rdn ins fnl f: styd on wl to ld on line* **8/1**

0-60 **2** *nse* **The New Pharaoh (IRE)**[49] 2622 6-9-8 **71** FranBerry 3 79
(Chris Wall) *trckd ldrs: smooth hdwy 3f out: trckd ldr 2f out: led 11/2f out: sn rdn clr: drvn ins fnl f: hdd on line* **3/1**[1]

5-30 **3** *7* **Dream Free**[21] 3559 4-8-13 **62** (p[1]) JasonHart 7 59
(Mark Walford) *trckd ldr: hdwy to ld 3f out: rdn along and hdd 11/2f out: sn drvn and kpt on one pce* **8/1**

342/ **4** *nk* **Tropical Bachelor (IRE)**[698] 4942 11-8-3 **52** JamesSullivan 4 48
(Ruth Carr) *hld up in rr: hdwy on outer wl over 2f out: rdn along wl over 1f out: kpt on fnl f* **7/1**

0-05 **5** 1¼ **Art History (IRE)**[101] 1303 9-8-6 **55** PaddyAspell 11 49
(Philip Kirby) *trckd ldrs: pushed along over 4f out: rdn and outpcd 3f out: plugged on u.p appr fnl f* **14/1**

40-2 **6** 2 **Old China**[22] 3529 4-9-0 **63** SamJames 10 54
(John Davies) *in tch: hdwy 4f out: chsd ldrs 3f out: rdn along 2f out: sn drvn and wknd* **4/1**[2]

05-0 **7** 4½ **Petrucci (IRE)**[33] 164 5-9-0 **63** JFEgan 8 47
(Derek Shaw) *dwlt: a rr* **20/1**

0401 **8** 2¼ **Askari**[25] 3439 4-9-5 **68** StevieDonohoe 9 48
(Tom Clover) *chsd ldng pair: pushed along 4f out: rdn 3f out: sn wknd* **5/1**[3]

5125 **9** 17 **Albert Boy (IRE)**[16] 3740 4-9-0 **63** LukeMorris 5 16
(Scott Dixon) *led: rdn along 4f out: hdd 3f out: sn wknd* **6/1**

2m 37.95s (3.05) **Going Correction** +0.35s/f (Good) **9** Ran SP% **122.1**
Speed ratings (Par 103): **103,102,98,98,97 95,92,91,80**
CSF £34.24 CT £207.25 TOTE £9.60: £2.70, £1.50, £2.70; EX 39.10 Trifecta £310.10.
**Owner** Jimmy Kay **Bred** John O'Connor **Trained** Colton, N Yorks

**FOCUS**
Race distance increased by 12yds. They went a fair gallop. The first two came from behind and went clear. The runner-up looks the best guide.
T/Plt: £31.50 to a £1 stake. Pool: £65,848 - 2087.73 winning units. T/Qpdt: £21.00 to a £1 stake. Pool: £5,017 - 238.04 winning units. **Joe Rowntree**

# 4087 LINGFIELD (L-H)

Saturday, July 1

**OFFICIAL GOING: Good (good to soft in places on the straight course; 7.5)**
Wind: light, across Weather: sunny spells

## 4346 SIMON BOWDEN 50TH BIRTHDAY (S) STKS 1m 3f 133y
5:40 (5:40) (Class 6) 3-Y-0+ £2,264 (£673; £336; £168) **Stalls High**

Form RPR

0-00 **1** **Ablaze**[163] 305 3-8-2 47 EdwardGreatrex(3) 4 62
(Laura Mongan) *led for 1f: chsd ldrs after tl lft 2nd and impeded over 5f out: led over 2f out: sustained duel w chalr fnl 2f: kpt on wl to forge ahd wl ins fnl f* **20/1**

555 **2** 1¾ **Tuolumne Meadows**[7] 4089 4-9-3 65 (t[1]) SamHitchcott 3 58
(Paul Cole) *hld up in midfield: clsd to chse ldrs and impeded over 5f out: clsd to chal and wnt clr w wnr over 2f out: sustained battle w wnr after: drvn over 1f out: no ex and btn wl ins fnl f* **11/2**[3]

1-13 **3** 19 **King Olav (UAE)**[92] 1464 12-10-2 67 GeorgeDowning 5 41
(Tony Carroll) *chsd ldrs: 4th and rdn 7f out: lft 3rd over 5f out: drvn and outpcd over 2f out: wknd over 1f out* **8/1**

2010 **4** ½ **Grand Facile**[133] 820 5-9-5 58 (b) JasonWatson(7) 6 36
(Gary Moore) *bhd and sn niggled along: lost tch w ldng quartet 4f out: no ch after: plugged on to go modest 4th ins fnl f* **14/1**

0-00 **5** 1 **Barbary Prince**[136] 747 5-9-5 15 CharlieBennett(3) 1 30
(Shaun Harris) *a last trio: rdn 6f out: lost tch w ldng quartet 4f out: no ch after: plugged on* **100/1**

-305 **6** 2¾ **Chelsea's Boy (IRE)**[24] 3459 4-9-8 74 (b[1]) ShaneKelly 7 26
(Ralph Beckett) *rousted along leaving stalls: hdwy to chse ldr after 2f and t.k.h: reminder 6f out: lft in ld over 5f out: 4 l clr home turn over 3f out: drvn and hdd over 2f out: sn dropped out and wl btn 2f out* **4/6**[1]

400 **7** 64 **Yemnaak (FR)**[81] 1692 3-8-10 48 (v[1]) AntonioFresu 2
(George Peckham) *s.i.s and rousted along early: a towards rr: lost tch w ldng quartet 4f out: t.o over 2f out* **33/1**

06-6 **8** dist **Cottesloe (IRE)**[169] 220 8-9-8 65 (b) RobHornby 8
(Neil Mulholland) *led after 1f tl hdd over 5f out: immediately dropped out: t.o and virtually p.u fnl 4f* **9/2**[2]

2m 33.2s (1.70) **Going Correction** -0.225s/f (Firm)
**WFA** 3 from 4yo+ 12lb **8** Ran SP% **120.0**
Speed ratings (Par 101): **85,83,71,70,70 68,25,**
CSF £129.60 TOTE £28.50: £3.90, £1.70, £2.30; EX 218.30 Trifecta £1187.80.
**Owner** Mrs P J Sheen **Bred** Howard Barton Stud **Trained** Epsom, Surrey

**FOCUS**
It had been a dry day ahead of this evening meeting with a few sunny spells, with temperatures around 20C. Rail movement added 12 yards to the official distance. A weak middle-distance seller to start and run at a modest pace. The first two drew well clear and it provided a bit of a turn-up. The form is suspect.

## 4347 AMY BOWDITCH QUARTER CENTURY OLD-TIMER MAIDEN AUCTION STKS 1m 2f
6:10 (6:10) (Class 6) 3-Y-0 £2,587 (£770; £384; £192) **Stalls Low**

Form RPR

3642 **1** **Pondering**[30] 3247 3-8-4 62 (v[1]) EdwardGreatrex(3) 8 69
(Eve Johnson Houghton) *hld up in midfield: rdn 3f out: hdwy to ld wl over 1f out: styd on wl and clr ins fnl f: eased nr fin* **7/1**

50-5 **2** 4 **Bermondsey Belle (IRE)**[26] 3408 3-9-0 65 RobHornby 3 67
(Lucy Wadham) *chsd ldng trio: pushed along bnd over 3f out: drvn to chse ldrs and bumping w rival over 1f out: kpt on to go 2nd wl ins fnl f: no threat to wnr* **16/1**

-025 **3** 1¾ **Peloton**[23] 3507 3-8-7 69 KieranO'Neill 1 57
(Pat Phelan) *chsd ldng pair: effrt on inner 3f out: ev ch 2f out tl outpcd over 1f out: wknd ins fnl f and lost 2nd fnl 75yds* **6/4**[1]

-060 **4** 5 **Solent Meads (IRE)**[25] 3422 3-9-5 64 (b) GeorgeDowning 2 60
(Daniel Kubler) *led: rdn over 2f out: hdd wl over 1f out: sn struggling and btn 4th 1f out: wknd ins fnl f* **25/1**

**5** ½ **Fools And Kings** 3-9-0 0 JackMitchell 6 54+
(Robyn Brisland) *wnt lft s: hld up in rr of main gp: hdwy ent fnl 2f: shifting lft 2f out but clsd to chse ldrs over 1f out: sn u.p and no imp: wknd ins fnl f* **6/1**

3 **6** ¾ **Josh The Plod (IRE)**[26] 3408 3-8-9 0 JasonWatson(7) 5 54
(Andrew Balding) *dwlt and pushed lft leaving stalls: sn rcvrd and hld up in midfield: effrt and carried lft 2f out: drifting bk rt and no hdwy over 1f out: wknd fnl f* **9/2**[2]

000- **7** 3½ **Leapt**[248] 7621 3-9-2 67 ShaneKelly 9 48
(Richard Hughes) *v keen to post: stdd and dropped into rr of main gp after s: plld hrd: lost tch w ldrs 3f out: n.d after* **5/1**[3]

6-4 **8** 5 **Eternal Dream**[26] 3394 3-9-5 0 KierenFox 4 41
(William Knight) *chsd ldr: hung rt and wd bnd over 3f out: losing pl whn bmpd over 1f out: sn wknd* **16/1**

0 **9** 33 **Flooded**[17] 3720 3-8-5 0 (h) JordanUys(7) 7
(Daniel Kubler) *taken down early: v awkward leaving stalls: a detached in last and nvr travelling wl: lost tch 4f out: t.o* **50/1**

2m 8.58s (-1.92) **Going Correction** -0.225s/f (Firm) **9** Ran SP% **119.2**
Speed ratings (Par 98): **98,94,93,89,89 88,85,81,55**
CSF £113.65 TOTE £6.70: £1.80, £3.90, £1.10; EX 64.80 Trifecta £448.70.
**Owner** Eden Racing Club **Bred** Aston House Stud **Trained** Blewbury, Oxon

**FOCUS**
Rail movement added 12 yards to the official distance. A modest 3yo maiden run at no more than adequate pace and the front two came from off the pace.

## 4348 HARRY BOWDITCH FAREWELL TO NOTRE DAME USA H'CAP 1m 3f 133y
6:40 (6:41) (Class 5) (0-70,68) 3-Y-0 £2,911 (£866; £432; £216) **Stalls High**

Form RPR

0230 **1** **Star Maker**[16] 3752 3-9-7 68 OisinMurphy 4 78
(Sylvester Kirk) *hld up in tch in midfield: smooth hdwy to ld 2f out: sn rdn clr and in command 1f out: comf* **7/2**[2]

660- **2** 2 **Astute Boy (IRE)**[205] 8277 3-9-6 67 TomMarquand 9 73
(Ed Vaughan) *hld up in tch in last trio: effrt 3f out: hdwy and switching lft over 1f out: styd on to chse clr wnr 100yds: kpt on wl but nvr a threat to wnr* **14/1**

2254 **3** 1½ **Too Many Shots**[28] 3326 3-8-10 57 KierenFox 5 61
(John Best) *chsd ldrs: effrt 3f out: rdn 3f out: ev ch 2f out: sn outpcd by wnr and hung lft over 1f out: one pce after and lost 2nd 100yds out* **7/1**[3]

0304 **4** hd **Famous Dynasty (IRE)**[13] 3864 3-8-11 58 DavidProbert 8 62
(Michael Blanshard) *hld up in rr: clsd over 2f out: rdn and hdwy over 1f out: kpt on same pce ins fnl f* **17/2**

-003 **5** 3¼ **Mr Scaff (IRE)**[40] 2892 3-8-10 57 ow1 JackMitchell 6 55
(Paul Henderson) *chsd ldrs tl wnt 2nd 6f out: rdn and pressed ldrs over 2f out: carried lft and outpcd over 1f out: wknd ins fnl f* **7/1**[3]

1 **6** 3½ **Enola (IRE)**[30] 3248 3-9-6 67 AntonioFresu 1 60
(Ed Dunlop) *dwlt: hld up in tch in midfield: effrt 3f out: no imp u.p 2f out: wknd over 1f out* **10/1**

4-01 **7** 3½ **King Of Scotland (FR)**[40] 2892 3-9-2 66 CharlieBennett(3) 2 53
(Hughie Morrison) *dwlt: rousted along and sn rcvrd to trck ldrs: rdn over 2f out: fnd little and sn btn: wknd over 1f out* **3/1**[1]

-355 **8** 3¾ **Red Caravel (IRE)**[31] 3220 3-9-4 65 (b) ShaneKelly 7 46
(Richard Hughes) *hld up in last trio: effrt 3f out: sn btn and bhd* **20/1**

0045 **9** hd **Crystal Secret**[7] 4087 3-7-11 49 oh2 RichardOliver(5) 3 29
(John Bridger) *led for 2f out: chsd ldr tl 1/2-way: lost pl on downhill run 4f out: lost pl u.p 3f out: bhd over 1f out* **22/1**

000 **10** 1¼ **Nobleman (GER)**[23] 3489 3-8-6 53 (b[1]) KieranO'Neill 10 31
(Hughie Morrison) *s.i.s and rousted along: hdwy to ld after 2f: rdn and hdd 2f out: sn dropped out: bhd fnl f* **17/2**

2m 32.49s (0.99) **Going Correction** -0.225s/f (Firm) **10** Ran SP% **118.1**
Speed ratings (Par 100): **87,85,84,84,82 80,77,75,75,74**
CSF £52.45 CT £330.80 TOTE £4.00: £1.60, £4.20, £2.50; EX 59.90 Trifecta £434.40.
**Owner** J C Smith **Bred** Littleton Stud **Trained** Upper Lambourn, Berks

**FOCUS**
Rail movement added 12 yards to the official distance. A modest handicap and the pace was ordinary. The official going changed to good all over before this race.

## 4349 EUROPEAN BREEDERS FUND (EBF) NOVICE STKS 4f 217y
7:10 (7:11) (Class 5) 2-Y-0 £2,911 (£866; £432; £216) **Stalls Centre**

Form RPR

**1** **Special Purpose (IRE)** 2-8-11 0 OisinMurphy 2 79+
(William Haggas) *hld up wl in tch in midfield: effrt over 1f out: hdwy to chse ldr jst ins fnl f: sn swtchd lft and qcknd under hands and heels riding to ld wl ins fnl f: gng away at fin: easily* **7/2**[3]

03 **2** 1½ **Zalshah**[12] 3917 2-9-2 0 TomMarquand 4 76
(Richard Hannon) *chsd ldr tl led over 1f out: sn rdn: hdd and out pced by wnr wl ins fnl f* **10/3**[2]

432 **3** 3½ **Indian Warrior**[12] 3917 2-9-2 75 JamesDoyle 6 63
(Ed Dunlop) *led: rdn and hdd over 1f out: unable qck u.p: lost 2nd jst ins fnl f: wknd fnl 100yds* **10/11**[1]

0 **4** 3¼ **Rock On Baileys**[18] 3697 2-8-11 0 DavidProbert 1 47
(Chris Dwyer) *nt that wl away but sn rcvrd to press ldrs: rdn over 1f out: no ex and btn jst ins fnl f: fdd* **25/1**

40 **5** nse **Inuk (IRE)**[25] 3421 2-8-11 0 ShaneKelly 3 47
(Richard Hughes) *stdd after s: t.k.h: hld up in tch in last pair: effrt 2f out: sn rdn and outpcd: wl btn 1f out* **20/1**

0 **6** 3¼ **Corazon Espinado (IRE)**[16] 3747 2-9-2 0 JackMitchell 5 40
(Simon Dow) *in tch in rr: shkn up 1/2-way: rdn 2f out: sn outpcd and wknd over 1f out* **14/1**

58.89s (0.69) **Going Correction** +0.025s/f (Good) **6** Ran SP% **113.0**
Speed ratings (Par 94): **95,92,87,81,81 76**
CSF £15.68 TOTE £4.20: £2.00, £1.90; EX 16.80 Trifecta £25.70.
**Owner** Qatar Racing Limited **Bred** Epona Bloodstock Ltd **Trained** Newmarket, Suffolk

**FOCUS**
A decent little novice event and the winner could be quite smart.

## 4350 JOHN AND JOAN GOODALL MEMORIAL H'CAP 7f
7:40 (7:45) (Class 6) (0-65,66) 3-Y-0+ £2,587 (£770; £384; £192) **Stalls Centre**

Form RPR

4063 **1** **Cyflymder (IRE)**[14] 3832 11-8-6 46 EdwardGreatrex(3) 10 54
(David C Griffiths) *in tch in midfield: effrt u.p over 1f out: styd on to ld ins fnl f: sn in command: rdn out* **20/1**

-246 **2** 1¾ **Tennessee Rose (IRE)**[24] 3473 3-9-3 62 (t) AntonioFresu 12 62
(Luke McJannet) *hld up wl in tch in midfield: clsd to chse ldrs whn nt clr run and swtchd lft over 1f out: clr in ldng quartet ins fnl f: chsd wnr fnl 75yds: no imp* **9/2**[2]

-110 **3** ¾ **A Sure Welcome**[32] 3173 3-9-4 63 (p) TomMarquand 5 61
(John Spearing) *trckd ldng trio: effrt over 1f out: chsd wnr 100yds: sn lost 2nd and styd on same pce towards fin* **8/1**

0-03 **4** 2½ **Arctic Flower (IRE)**[14] 3823 4-8-6 48 MitchGodwin(5) 3 43
(John Bridger) *chsd ldr tl led jst over 2f out: rdn over 1f out: hdd ins fnl f: wknd fnl 100yds* **12/1**

0-00 **5** 3¼ **Iftitah (IRE)**[20] 3627 3-9-0 59 (t) SamHitchcott 9 42
(George Peckham) *stdd s: hld up in midfield: effrt over 1f out: sme hdwy ent fnl f: kpt on same pce ins fnl f: nvr trbld ldrs* **33/1**

4-66 **6** 1¼ **Mutineer**[40] 2886 3-9-7 66 RobHornby 11 45
(Daniel Kubler) *hld up in tch in midfield: effrt 2f out: no imp u.p over 1f out: wl hld and kpt on same pce fnl f* **20/1**

3433 **7** ¾ **Bookmaker**[18] 3686 7-9-6 57 (p) KieranO'Neill 14 37
(John Bridger) *hld up in tch: rdn: swtchd lft and effrt over 2f out: sme hdwy u.p over 1f out: wl hld and kpt on same pce ins fnl f* **12/1**

-004 **8** ½ **Hurricane Rock**[22] 3532 4-9-7 **58** JackMitchell 2 37
(Simon Dow) *chsd ldrs: effrt 2f out: drvn and unable qck over 1f out: sn btn and wknd ins fnl f* **14/1**

344 **9** ¾ **Freddy With A Y (IRE)**[54] 2465 7-9-10 **61** KierenFox 7 38
(J R Jenkins) *stdd s: hld up in rr: rdn 3f out: swtchd lft over 1f out: modest hdwy to pass btn horses ins fnl f: nvr trbld ldrs* **9/1**

066- **10** 4 **Sandacres**[311] 5769 4-9-11 **62** GeorgeDowning 13 28
(Laura Mongan) *chsd ldrs: rdn to chse ldr briefly ent fnl 2f: lost pl and btn over 1f out: wknd fnl f* **50/1**

013 **11** ½ **Beepeecee**[11] 3937 3-9-6 **65** (p) ShaneKelly 6 27
(Richard Hughes) *niggled along in midfield: rdn 2f out: sn u.p and no rspnse: wknd over 1f out* **15/2**

3354 **12** hd **Gulland Rock**[24] 3454 6-10-1 **66** SilvestreDeSousa 1 30
(Anthony Carson) *led tl rdn and hdd jst over 1f out: lost pl and btn over 1f out: no ch and eased ins fnl f* **4/1**[1]

3000 **13** 1 **Spiritofedinburgh (IRE)**[26] 3391 3-8-12 **62** JennyPowell(5) 4 21
(Brendan Powell) *hld up in last trio: rdn 2f out: no rspnse and sn wknd* **50/1**

60-0 **14** 2¾ **Sandwood Bay**[33] 3142 3-9-6 **65** (e) JoeyHaynes 16 16
(Mark H Tompkins) *hld up in midfield: nt clr run over 2f out: swtchd lft 2f out: sn rdn and btn: wknd over 1f out* **33/1**

1-00 **15** ½ **Odelouca (IRE)**[17] 3722 3-9-3 **62** (t[1]) DavidProbert 15 12
(Brendan Powell) *in tch in midfield: rdn over 2f out: sn struggling: wknd over 1f out* **16/1**

000 **16** 49 **Never You Mind (IRE)**[74] 1862 3-8-13 **58** OisinMurphy 18
(Charles Hills) *nvr travelling wl: sn bhd and u.p: lost tch and eased over 2f out: t.o* **6/1**[3]

1m 23.36s (0.06) **Going Correction** +0.025s/f (Good)
**WFA** 3 from 4yo+ 8lb **16** Ran SP% **132.6**
Speed ratings (Par 101): **100,98,97,94,90 89,88,87,86,82 81,81,80,77,76 20**
CSF £110.94 CT £822.43 TOTE £22.30: £3.50, £1.80, £2.30, £3.30; EX 209.60 Trifecta £3111.00.
**Owner** D Griffiths **Bred** Miss Laura G F Ferguson **Trained** Bawtry, S Yorks

**FOCUS**
A very modest handicap but competitive enough for the grade. The pace was not strong early and the front four drew a little way clear.

## 4351 BETFAIR RACING STAFF WEEK FILLIES' H'CAP 7f
**8:10** (8:12) (Class 5) (0-75,78) 3-Y-O+ **£3,234** (£962; £481; £240) **Stalls** Centre

Form RPR

1424 **1** **Tai Hang Dragon (IRE)**[13] 3869 3-9-6 **75** TomMarquand 3 88
(Richard Hannon) *hld up in tch: effrt to chse ldrs ent fnl 2f: drvn over 1f out: swtchd lft and clsd to press ldrs 1f out: led 100yds: sn clr: styd on* **6/1**[3]

5-22 **2** 4½ **Bassmah**[13] 3869 3-9-9 **78** SilvestreDeSousa 7 79
(Ismail Mohammed) *chsd ldrs tl wnt 2nd 1/2-way: rdn to ld over 1f out: drvn and hdd 100yds out: sn btn* **7/4**[2]

5-06 **3** 4 **Tremendous (IRE)**[49] 2619 3-8-6 **61** KieranO'Neill 5 52
(Richard Hannon) *broke wl: sn restrained and hld up in tch: shkn up over 2f out: edgd lft u.p wl over 1f out: sn edging bk rt and outpcd: wl hld and plugged on same pce fnl f: lft 3rd cl home* **25/1**

2-42 **4** ½ **Music Lesson**[35] 3075 3-9-1 **73** CharlieBennett(3) 6 62
(Hughie Morrison) *chsd ldr tl 1/2-way: rdn 3f out: outpcd and struggling over 2f out: wl btn 5th and plugged on same pce fnl f: lft 4th cl home* **8/1**

1 **5** nk **Express Lady (IRE)**[50] 2581 3-9-4 **73** JamesDoyle 4 69
(Hugo Palmer) *racd freely: led and eventually crossed to r against stands rail: rdn and hdd over 1f out: 3rd and btn whn sltly impeded jst ins fnl f: sn btn: stmbld: heavily eased and lost 2 pls cl home: dismntd* **11/8**[1]

0-30 **6** 23 **Bee Case**[154] 458 3-8-12 **67** (h[1]) JackMitchell 1
(Simon Dow) *a in rr: rdn 1/2-way: lost tch over 1f out: eased ins fnl f: t.o* **33/1**

1m 24.45s (1.15) **Going Correction** +0.025s/f (Good) **6** Ran SP% **110.7**
Speed ratings (Par 100): **94,88,84,83,83 57**
CSF £16.51 TOTE £5.70: £1.90, £1.60; EX 15.50 Trifecta £152.70.
**Owner** Rockcliffe Stud **Bred** Lynn Lodge Stud **Trained** East Everleigh, Wilts

**FOCUS**
A competitive fillies' handicap on paper but it was a muddling affair and while the winner did it nicely, the merit of the form is open to question.

## 4352 BETFAIR SUPPORTING RACING H'CAP 4f 217y
**8:40** (8:40) (Class 5) (0-70,71) 3-Y-O+ **£2,911** (£866; £432; £216) **Stalls** Centre

Form RPR

4361 **1** **Come On Dave (IRE)**[19] 3659 8-9-13 **71** (v) LiamKeniry 9 80
(John Butler) *taken down early: sn led and mde rest: clr and rdn over 1f out: styd on: nvr seriously chal* **6/1**

4-30 **2** 2 **Glacier Point**[39] 2927 3-9-4 **70** HectorCrouch(3) 7 70
(Clive Cox) *chsd ldrs: rdn 1/2-way: chsd clr wnr over 1f out: kpt on but nvr getting on terms* **11/2**

0140 **3** shd **Flowing Clarets**[2] 4256 4-9-3 **61** KieranO'Neill 8 62
(John Bridger) *sn outpcd in 7th and pushed along: hdwy between horses over 1f out: battling for 2nd 1f out: edgd lft and no imp in wnr ins fnl f* **4/1**[3]

2254 **4** 7 **Entertaining Ben**[14] 3812 4-9-8 **66** (v[1]) LemosdeSouza 6 42
(Amy Murphy) *chsd wnr tl wl over 1f out: sn rdn and unable qck: 4th and wknd fnl f* **20/1**

-501 **5** ½ **The Big Short**[14] 3818 3-9-0 **63** DavidProbert 4 35
(Charles Hills) *wl in tch in midfield: shkn up 2f out: sn rdn and unable qck: 5th and wknd fnl f* **7/2**[2]

4302 **6** 2 **Fabulous Flyer**[9] 4009 4-8-8 **52** ow1 RobHornby 5 19
(Jeremy Gask) *wl in tch in midfield: effrt 2f out: sn u.p and btn over 1f out: wknd fnl f* **20/1**

6352 **7** 3 **Vale Of Flight (IRE)**[9] 4005 4-8-11 **55** (p) SilvestreDeSousa 3 11
(Luke McJannet) *dwlt: sn rcvrd to chse ldrs: rdn 2f out: sn drvn and btn: wknd over 1f out* **3/1**[1]

2-06 **8** 2¼ **John Joiner**[32] 3170 5-8-11 **60** MitchGodwin(5) 2 8
(Peter Hedger) *a outpcd in rr* **8/1**

57.88s (-0.32) **Going Correction** +0.025s/f (Good)
**WFA** 3 from 4yo+ 5lb **8** Ran SP% **117.5**
Speed ratings (Par 103): **103,99,99,88,87 84,79,76**
CSF £39.90 CT £133.34 TOTE £5.60: £2.00, £2.10, £1.70; EX 60.80 Trifecta £231.70.
**Owner** Royale Racing Syndicate **Bred** Mrs Eithne Hamilton **Trained** Newmarket, Suffolk

**FOCUS**
A weak sprint handicap for the class.
T/Plt: £717.70 to a £1 stake. Pool: £41,570 - 57.92 winning units. T/Qpdt: £240.20 to a £1 stake. Pool: £3,045 - 12.67 winning units. **Steve Payne**

# 4304 NEWCASTLE (A.W) (L-H)
Saturday, July 1

**OFFICIAL GOING: Tapeta: standard**
Wind: Breezy, across Weather: Cloudy, bright

## 4353 BETFRED "CELEBRATING 50 YEARS OF SUCCESS" H'CAP 6f (Tp)
**1:50** (1:50) (Class 2) (0-100,99) 3-Y-O+
**£12,450** (£3,728; £1,864; £932; £466; £234) **Stalls** Centre

Form RPR

35-1 **1** **Unabated (IRE)**[101] 1311 3-9-8 **99** (t) DanielMuscutt 14 109+
(Marco Botti) *hld up in tch on nr side of gp: smooth hdwy over 2f out: shkn up to ld ent fnl f: kpt on strly* **13/2**[3]

6340 **2** nk **Northgate Lad (IRE)**[21] 3585 5-8-11 **87** BenRobinson(5) 12 97
(Brian Ellison) *dwlt: sn w ldrs: led over 1f out to ent fnl f: rallied: hld nr fin* **8/1**

3200 **3** 1½ **Moonraker**[21] 3593 5-9-6 **91** GrahamLee 1 96
(Mick Channon) *hld up on far side of gp: stdy hdwy and prom over 1f out: rdn and kpt on ins fnl f* **10/1**

6530 **4** nk **Get Knotted (IRE)**[14] 3842 5-9-12 **97** (p) PaulMulrennan 7 101
(Michael Dods) *hld up midfield: pushed along over 2f out: hdwy over 1f out: kpt on steadily ins fnl f* **9/1**

-221 **5** shd **Robero**[49] 2608 5-9-6 **91** FranBerry 13 95
(Michael Easterby) *disp ld on nr side of gp: led over 2f out to over 1f out: rdn and nt qckn fnl f* **11/2**[2]

-602 **6** 1 **Mazzini**[10] 3969 4-9-5 **90** TomQueally 3 91+
(James Fanshawe) *mounted on crse and taken early to post: hld up: pushed along over 2f out: hdwy over 1f out: rdn and no imp fnl f* **11/2**[2]

4030 **7** 1 **Amazour (IRE)**[7] 4072 5-9-13 **98** DaneO'Neill 4 96
(Ismail Mohammed) *hld up: pushed along over 2f out: hdwy on far side of gp over 1f out: nvr able to chal* **9/2**[1]

6050 **8** ½ **Ninjago**[8] 4037 7-9-0 **85** LukeMorris 10 81
(Paul Midgley) *hld up: rdn and hdwy over 1f out: no imp fnl f* **28/1**

0-10 **9** 6 **Al Qahwa (IRE)**[21] 3593 4-9-13 **98** DanielTudhope 8 75
(David O'Meara) *in tch: drvn along over 2f out: wknd over 1f out* **12/1**

00-0 **10** 1½ **Farlow (IRE)**[14] 3842 9-9-5 **90** PaulHanagan 2 62
(Richard Fahey) *sn bhd on far side of gp: rdn along and outpcd over 2f out: n.d after* **33/1**

20-1 **11** 3¼ **The Commendatore**[56] 2381 4-9-2 **87** BenCurtis 6 49
(David Barron) *cl up tl lost pl over 2f out: sn struggling* **16/1**

0-30 **12** 7 **Canny Kool**[22] 3539 5-9-7 **92** DougieCostello 9 31
(Brian Ellison) *s.v.s: nvr on terms* **50/1**

000- **13** hd **Teruntum Star (FR)**[266] 7156 5-9-11 **96** TomEaves 11 34
(Kevin Ryan) *led to over 2f out: sn rdn and wknd* **28/1**

1m 12.84s (0.34) **Going Correction** +0.325s/f (Slow)
**WFA** 3 from 4yo+ 6lb **13** Ran SP% **117.9**
Speed ratings (Par 109): **110,109,107,107,107 105,104,103,95,93 89,80,79**
CSF £54.99 CT £536.36 TOTE £7.60: £2.30, £3.00, £2.80; EX 71.40 Trifecta £489.00.
**Owner** Mubarak Al Naemi **Bred** Mubarak Al Naemi **Trained** Newmarket, Suffolk
■ Stewards' Enquiry : Tom Queally two-day ban: used whip above shoulder height (Jul 17-18)

**FOCUS**
A good sprint handicap run at a respectable gallop. The race developed stands' side and the first two horses home were drawn near that rail. The form is rated around the runner-up.

## 4354 BETFRED TV CHIPCHASE STKS (GROUP 3) 6f (Tp)
**2:25** (2:25) (Class 1) 3-Y-O+
**£39,697** (£15,050; £7,532; £3,752; £1,883; £945) **Stalls** Centre

Form RPR

-052 **1** **Koropick (IRE)**[14] 3835 3-8-11 104 JosephineGordon 8 113
(Hugo Palmer) *prom: effrt whn n.m.r briefly over 1f out: rdn and kpt on wl fnl f to ld cl home* **8/1**

1550 **2** hd **Intisaab**[7] 4072 6-9-3 107 (p) DanielTudhope 2 113
(David O'Meara) *dwlt: hld up: hdwy on far side to ld over 1f out: rdn and kpt on fnl f: hdd nr fin* **10/1**

1003 **3** nk **Kimberella**[14] 3829 7-9-3 109 PaulHanagan 11 112
(Richard Fahey) *prom on nr side of gp: nt clr run fr over 2f out: checked over 1f out: squeezed through and r.o wl fnl f: hld cl home* **7/2**[2]

6-62 **4** 2¼ **Aeolus**[49] 2611 6-9-3 103 GrahamLee 3 107+
(Ed Walker) *in tch: effrt whn no room fr over 2f out to appr fnl f: kpt on: nt rch first three* **12/1**

0410 **5** 2¼ **Final Venture**[11] 3926 5-9-3 109 (h) LukeMorris 10 98
(Paul Midgley) *t.k.h: led: rdn and hdd over 1f out: wknd ins fnl f* **15/2**[3]

0215 **6** 1½ **Solar Flair**[65] 2114 5-9-3 104 TomQueally 5 93
(William Knight) *in tch on far side of gp: lost pl over 3f out: kpt on fnl f: nvr able to chal* **22/1**

20-1 **7** 1 **Perfect Pasture**[40] 2907 7-9-3 110 (v) PaulMulrennan 4 90
(Michael Easterby) *dwlt: hld up on nr side of gp: rdn over 2f out: no imp fnl f* **15/2**[3]

45-2 **8** ½ **Don't Touch**[16] 3765 5-9-3 113 (v) TonyHamilton 1 88
(Richard Fahey) *in tch on far side of gp: effrt and rdn 2f out: wknd ent fnl f* **5/2**[1]

6-50 **9** 3 **Nameitwhatyoulike**[45] 2737 8-9-3 103 ConnorBeasley 6 78
(Bryan Smart) *chsd ldrs: wnt 2nd over 2f out to over 1f out: sn wknd* **33/1**

-266 **10** 8 **Ornate**[22] 3539 4-9-3 109 JoeFanning 9 53
(Robert Cowell) *pressed ldr to over 2f out: rdn and wknd wl over 1f out* **14/1**

1m 12.76s (0.26) **Going Correction** +0.325s/f (Slow)
**WFA** 3 from 4yo+ 6lb **10** Ran SP% **116.2**
Speed ratings (Par 113): **111,110,110,107,104 102,101,100,96,85**
CSF £84.72 TOTE £11.40: £2.60, £3.30, £1.40; EX 96.50 Trifecta £507.80.
**Owner** V I Araci **Bred** C M Farrell **Trained** Newmarket, Suffolk
■ Stewards' Enquiry : Luke Morris two-day ban: careless riding (Jul 17-18)

**FOCUS**
A good quality renewal of this Group 3 sprint. They went a respectable gallop and the second favourite was a particularly unlucky loser up the stands' rail. Straightforward form, the winner improving.

## 4355 BETFRED NORTHUMBERLAND VASE H'CAP (CONSOLATION RACE FOR THE NORTHUMBERLAND PLATE) 2m 56y (Tp)

**3:00** (3:00) (Class 2) 3-Y-0+

**£46,687** (£13,980; £6,990; £3,495; £1,747; £877) **Stalls** Low

Form / RPR

1-21 **1** **London Prize**[20] 3618 6-9-9 **89** 5ex........................................ FranBerry 11 97
(Ian Williams) *trckd ldrs: hdwy to ld 2f out: rdn and hrd pressed fnl f: hld on gamely* **7/4**[1]

-124 **2** *nk* **Graceland (FR)**[10] 3968 5-9-7 **87**.................................... LouisSteward 3 94
(Michael Bell) *dwlt: hld up midfield: effrt and rdn over 2f out: pressed wnr thrght fnl f: kpt on: hld nr fin* **9/1**

12-6 **3** *2 ½* **High Command (IRE)**[35] 3086 4-9-3 **83**.................... PaulMulrennan 12 87
(Roger Varian) *in tch: shkn up over 2f out: effrt over 1f out: kpt on same pce ins fnl f* **9/1**

2212 **4** *hd* **Kensington Star**[14] 3830 4-9-7 **87** 5ex..............................(v) JasonHart 1 91
(Keith Dalgleish) *chsd ldr: led 3f out to over 2f out: pressed wnr tl rdn and one pce fnl f* **7/1**[3]

0630 **5** *1 ¾* **Gabrial's King (IRE)**[21] 3594 8-9-9 **89**.......................... PaulHanagan 10 91
(Richard Fahey) *hld up: rdn over 2f out: hdwy over 1f out: kpt on: nvr able to chal* **22/1**

3036 **6** *½* **Tetradrachm**[31] 3213 4-8-13 **79**......................................(p[1]) JoeFanning 4 80
(David Simcock) *prom: effrt and rdn over 2f out: hung lft over 1f out: outpcd fnl f* **33/1**

-130 **7** *1 ½* **October Storm**[7] 4073 4-8-11 **77**....................................... GrahamLee 9 76
(Mick Channon) *midfield: drvn and outpcd over 2f out: kpt on fnl f: no imp* **6/1**[2]

1-60 **8** *¾* **I Am Not Here (IRE)**[3] 4206 6-9-0 **85**................. BenRobinson(5) 7 83
(Brian Ellison) *hld up: rdn and outpcd over 2f out: no imp fr over 1f out* **7/1**[3]

3100 **9** *2 ¼* **Royal Marskell**[50] 2562 8-9-8 **88**......................................(h) LukeMorris 6 84
(Gay Kelleway) *missed break: hld up: rdn along over 3f out: no imp fr over 2f out* **40/1**

-420 **10** *3* **Velvet Revolution**[35] 3076 4-9-3 **83**................................ MartinHarley 8 75
(Marco Botti) *hld up: stdy hdwy 3f out: sn rdn: struggling fr wl over 1f out* **11/1**

-440 **11** *2* **Green Light**[28] 3323 6-9-4 **84**...............................................(v) TomEaves 5 74
(Brian Ellison) *dwlt: t.k.h: hld up: struggling over 3f out: btn fnl 2f* **66/1**

400- **12** *4* **Flight Officer**[265] 7188 6-9-3 **90**................................... HarrisonShaw(7) 2 75
(Michael Easterby) *t.k.h: led at modest gallp: hdd 3f out: rallied: wknd wl over 1f out* **66/1**

3m 41.44s (6.24) **Going Correction** +0.325s/f (Slow) **12** Ran SP% **116.7**
Speed ratings (Par 109): **97,96,95,95,94 94,93,93,92,90 89,87**
CSF £17.17 CT £112.42 TOTE £2.20: £1.20, £2.10, £3.50; EX 16.40 Trifecta £80.30.
**Owner** Mrs Margaret Forsyth **Bred** P And Mrs A G Venner **Trained** Portway, Worcs

**FOCUS**
A decent staying handicap. They went a modest gallop into a headwind in the straight. The favourite delighted the crowd with a tough victory. The time was poor.

## 4356 STOBART RAIL NORTHUMBERLAND PLATE H'CAP (HERITAGE HANDICAP) 2m 56y (Tp)

**3:30** (3:32) (Class 2) 3-Y-0+

**£92,385** (£27,810; £13,905; £6,930; £3,480; £1,312) **Stalls** Low

Form / RPR

1-22 **1** **Higher Power**[37] 3011 5-9-9 **107**.......................................... TomQueally 13 114
(James Fanshawe) *prom: smooth hdwy to ld over 1f out: sn rdn and hrd pressed: hld on gamely fnl f* **11/2**[2]

-116 **2** *½* **Natural Scenery**[78] 1770 4-9-5 **103**......................... JosephineGordon 10 109
(Saeed bin Suroor) *prom: effrt and disp ld over 1f out to ins fnl f: kpt on: hld nr fin* **7/1**

61-1 **3** *nk* **Flymetothestars**[43] 2788 4-9-2 **100**.................................... LukeMorris 8 106
(Sir Mark Prescott Bt) *t.k.h in midfield: hdwy to press ldrs over 2f out: rdn and outpcd over 1f out: r.o ins fnl f* **11/4**[1]

0-33 **4** *¾* **Lord George (IRE)**[49] 2603 4-8-9 **96**....................... GeorgeWood(3) 17 101
(James Fanshawe) *hld up: hdwy on outside over 2f out: rdn over 1f out: kpt on fnl f: nvr able to chal* **17/2**

0-01 **5** *nk* **My Reward**[63] 2157 5-8-9 **93**................................................ DavidAllan 18 98
(Tim Easterby) *led at modest gallop for 4f: chsd ldr: regained ld 3f out: rdn and hdd over 1f out: one pce ins fnl f* **28/1**

6201 **6** *¾* **Sir Chauvelin**[43] 2774 5-9-0 **98**.......................................... PaulMulrennan 6 102
(Jim Goldie) *hld up: hdwy over 2f out: rdn over 1f out: kpt on same pce fnl f* **25/1**

-245 **6** *dht* **Sam Missile (IRE)**[22] 3534 4-8-8 **92**..........................(p) DanielMuscutt 19 96
(James Fanshawe) *hld up: stdy hdwy on outside over 2f out: rdn over 1f out: no imp fnl f* **25/1**

00 **8** *nk* **Cosmelli (ITY)**[21] 3594 4-9-1 **99**.......................................(b) TomEaves 15 102
(Gay Kelleway) *hld up: rdn over 3f out: hdwy on outside over 1f out: kpt on fnl f: nrst fin* **100/1**

0-60 **9** *1* **Clever Cookie**[35] 3090 9-9-10 **108**..............................(p) DanielTudhope 20 110
(Peter Niven) *hld up: pushed along over 3f out: hdwy over 1f out: styng on whn nt clr run briefly ins fnl f: sn no imp* **33/1**

0406 **10** *½* **Gavlar**[22] 3534 6-8-6 **93**..........................................(v) CallumShepherd(3) 12 95
(William Knight) *hld up midfield: effrt and rdn over 2f out: outpcd over 1f out: btn fnl f* **40/1**

-206 **11** *nk* **Good Run (FR)**[63] 2157 4-9-0 **98**........................................(p[1]) FranBerry 4 99
(Saeed bin Suroor) *t.k.h in midfield: rdn and effrt over 2f out: no imp fr over 1f out* **20/1**

22-3 **12** *nk* **Seamour (IRE)**[35] 3090 6-9-5 **103**.........................................(p) BenCurtis 11 104
(Brian Ellison) *hld up midfield: pushed along and shortlived effrt over 2f out: wknd over 1f out* **6/1**[3]

3105 **13** *nk* **Yorkidding**[6] 4119 5-9-1 **99**........................................................ JoeFanning 9 100
(Mark Johnston) *hld up: rdn over 2f out: no imp fr wl over 1f out: btn fnl f* **33/1**

-233 **14** *1* **Champagne Champ**[22] 3534 5-8-9 **93**..........................(p[1]) PaulHanagan 2 92
(Rod Millman) *pressed ldr: led and increased gallop after 4f: hdd 3f out: rdn and wknd wl over 1f out* **25/1**

0025 **15** *2 ¼* **Suegioo (FR)**[11] 3928 8-9-2 **100**....................................(p) TonyHamilton 7 97
(Richard Fahey) *hld up: drvn along and outpcd 3f out: nvr on terms after* **25/1**

1250 **16** *2 ½* **Winterlude (IRE)**[78] 1770 7-9-6 **104**.................................... DavidNolan 16 98
(Jennie Candlish) *hld up: stdy hdwy wl over 2f out: rdn and wknd over 1f out* **66/1**

-211 **17** *2* **Jaameh (IRE)**[21] 3594 4-9-0 **98** 5ex...................................... DaneO'Neill 5 89
(Mark Johnston) *in tch: rdn over 3f out: wknd over 2f out* **12/1**

-130 **18** *9* **Hot Beat (IRE)**[21] 3594 5-8-12 **96**.................................... MartinHarley 14 76
(David Simcock) *hld up: drvn and outpcd 3f out: btn fnl 2f* **25/1**

1150 **19** *1* **Corton Lad**[14] 3841 7-8-3 **92**..........................................(tp) RowanScott(5) 1 71
(Keith Dalgleish) *t.k.h: midfield: struggling 3f out: btn fnl 2f* **100/1**

2436 **P** **Maleficent Queen**[21] 3586 5-9-7 **105**..................................... GrahamLee 3
(Keith Dalgleish) *s.s and p.u immediately* **50/1**

3m 35.37s (0.17) **Going Correction** +0.325s/f (Slow) **20** Ran SP% **128.3**
Speed ratings (Par 109): **112,111,111,111,111 110,110,110,110,109 109,109,109,108,107 106,105,100,100,**
CSF £38.03 CT £133.80 TOTE £7.30: £2.10, £2.40, £1.30, £2.60; EX 54.50 Trifecta £282.70.
**Owner** Mrs Martin Armstrong **Bred** Mrs Martin Armstrong **Trained** Newmarket, Suffolk

**FOCUS**
A strong renewal of the feature heritage handicap. They went a muddling initial gallop but it picked up well after 4f. The form is sound in a race which developed into a thrilling battle between two fancied horses. Higher Power improved in line with his Sandown run.

## 4357 BETFRED "HOME OF GOALS GALORE" H'CAP 1m 4f 98y (Tp)

**4:05** (4:05) (Class 4) (0-80,81) 4-Y-0+ **£6,469** (£1,925; £962; £481) **Stalls** High

Form / RPR

-020 **1** **Airton**[49] 2629 4-9-2 **75**................................................. JosephineGordon 12 83
(James Bethell) *hld up on outside: hdwy over 2f out: rdn to ld ent fnl f: sn hrd pressed: hld on wl* **5/1**[2]

-313 **2** *½* **Cape Peninsular**[30] 3235 4-9-7 **80**...................................... MartinHarley 4 88+
(James Tate) *trckd ldrs: nt clr run over 2f out to over 1f out: effrt and ev ch fnl f: kpt on: hld towards fin* **7/2**[1]

0042 **3** *¾* **Suitor**[16] 3740 5-9-0 **78**.......................................(p) BenRobinson(5) 3 84
(Brian Ellison) *prom: effrt and disp ld over 1f: led appr fnl f to ent fnl f: kpt on same pce* **13/2**

2364 **4** *2 ¾* **Lac Leman (GER)**[23] 3486 6-9-4 **77**...........................(h) PaulMulrennan 2 79
(Pauline Robson) *in tch: effrt whn nt clr run over 2f out to over 1f out: rdn and one pce fnl f* **11/2**[3]

0-04 **5** *1 ¼* **Carthage (IRE)**[11] 3947 6-8-10 **69**............................................ BenCurtis 9 69
(Brian Ellison) *dwlt: hld up: pushed along over 2f out: hdwy over 1f out: kpt on fnl f: nvr able to chal* **33/1**

3543 **6** *nse* **London Glory**[7] 4102 4-8-2 **61**......................................(b) AndrewMullen 11 61
(David Thompson) *hld up midfield: hdwy to ld over 2f out: hdd appr fnl f: sn one pce* **9/1**

530 **7** *nk* **Dolphin Village (IRE)**[35] 3091 7-9-3 **81**..................(h) LewisEdmunds(5) 5 80
(Shaun Harris) *hld up: pushed along over 2f out: hdwy over 1f out: sn no imp* **22/1**

31/0 **8** *hd* **Bank Bonus**[121] 991 8-9-0 **73**...............................................(h) TomEaves 7 72
(Brian Ellison) *missed break: hld up: drvn over 3f out: kpt on fnl f: n.d* **66/1**

4232 **9** *1 ¼* **Go George Go (IRE)**[57] 2375 4-9-1 **74**................................ JoeFanning 10 71
(Sally Haynes) *trckd ldr: ev ch over 2f out: rdn and edgd lft over 1f out: wknd fnl f* **7/1**

3300 **10** *10* **Falcon's Fire (IRE)**[14] 3830 4-8-12 **71**.................................. GrahamLee 1 52
(Keith Dalgleish) *hld up midfield: drvn along over 2f out: sn outpcd: n.d after* **25/1**

-360 **11** *4 ½* **Wor Lass**[14] 3830 9-9-1 **79**............................................. GarryWhillans(5) 6 53
(Donald Whillans) *checked s: hld up: rdn and outpcd over 2f out: sn btn* **20/1**

5021 **12** *4* **Theos Lolly (IRE)**[10] 3983 4-9-6 **79**.................................. PaulHanagan 8 46
(Richard Fahey) *stmbld and wnt lft s: led at modest gallop: rdn and hdd over 2f out: wknd wl over 1f out* **8/1**

2m 42.69s (1.59) **Going Correction** +0.325s/f (Slow) **12** Ran SP% **118.6**
Speed ratings (Par 105): **107,106,105,104,103 103,103,103,102,95 92,89**
CSF £21.35 CT £116.93 TOTE £6.30: £2.00, £2.00, £2.40; EX 26.10 Trifecta £181.50.
**Owner** Clarendon Thoroughbred Racing **Bred** Clive Dennett **Trained** Middleham Moor, N Yorks
■ Stewards' Enquiry : Paul Mulrennan two-day ban: used whip without giving his mount time to respond (Jul 17-18)

**FOCUS**
A fairly decent middle-distance handicap. They went, at best, a respectable gallop and the favourite who finished second didn't get a run in a timely manner. The winner is progressive overall and the form is sound.

## 4358 BETFRED "SUPPORTS JACK BERRY HOUSE" H'CAP 1m 2f 42y (Tp)

**4:45** (4:45) (Class 4) (0-85,82) 4-Y-0+ **£6,469** (£1,925; £962; £481) **Stalls** High

Form / RPR

610 **1** **Auspicion**[2] 4260 5-8-10 **71**............................................... AndrewMullen 3 79
(Tom Tate) *hld up: pushed along and effrt over 2f out: hdwy over 1f out: led wl ins fnl f: kpt on* **7/2**[1]

-463 **2** *hd* **Gerry The Glover (IRE)**[46] 2701 5-9-0 **75**...........................(p) BenCurtis 1 82
(Brian Ellison) *t.k.h early: hld up: hdwy over 2f out: led over 1f out: rdn and hdd wl ins fnl f: r.o* **5/1**[3]

6062 **3** *1 ¼* **Testa Rossa (IRE)**[7] 4076 7-9-0 **82**..........................(b) SeanMooney(7) 4 86
(Jim Goldie) *hld in tch: stdy hdwy over 2f out: effrt and rdn over 1f out: kpt on ins fnl f* **6/1**

5145 **4** *3* **Rockwood**[14] 3845 6-9-2 **77**...................................................(v) GrahamLee 6 75
(Karen McLintock) *trckd ldrs gng wl: ev ch over 1f out: sn rdn: wknd last 75yds* **4/1**[2]

0-60 **5** *1 ½* **Salmon Sushi**[9] 4017 6-8-12 **73**...................................(h) PaulMulrennan 8 68
(Tim Easterby) *hld up: stdy hdwy whn nt clr run over 2f out: rdn and effrt over 1f out: no imp fnl f* **16/1**

0210 **6** *2 ½* **Archipeligo**[2] 4260 6-8-2 **70**..................................(p) JamieGormley(7) 9 60
(Iain Jardine) *hld up: stdy hdwy and gng wl whn nt clr run over 2f out to over 1f out: sn drvn and no imp* **7/2**[1]

0-00 **7** *5* **Street Poet (IRE)**[42] 2815 4-8-8 **69**.............................................. TomEaves 7 49
(Michael Herrington) *led: rdn over 2f out: hdd over 1f out: sn wknd* **66/1**

-066 **8** *8* **High Baroque (USA)**[12] 3905 5-9-4 **79**................................ PaulHanagan 2 43
(Richard Fahey) *in tch: drvn and outpcd over 2f out: wknd wl over 1f out* **9/1**

00-4 **9** *1 ¼* **Arabian Oasis**[51] 1561 5-8-7 **68**.......................................(p) JoeFanning 5 30
(Philip Kirby) *pressed ldr: rdn over 2f out: wknd wl over 1f out* **40/1**

2m 11.75s (1.35) **Going Correction** +0.325s/f (Slow) **9** Ran SP% **115.2**
Speed ratings (Par 105): **107,106,105,103,102 100,96,89,88**
CSF £21.22 CT £101.02 TOTE £4.60: £1.40, £1.80, £1.80; EX 25.20 Trifecta £90.70.
**Owner** David Storey **Bred** Lael Stables **Trained** Tadcaster, N Yorks

**FOCUS**
A fairly decent handicap and sound form. They may have gone off a tad too quickly into a headwind into the straight as it was hard work in the finish.

## 4359 BETFRED "WATCH SKY SPORTS IN OUR SHOPS" EBF NOVICE STKS (PLUS 10 RACE) 5f (Tp)
**5:15** (5:18) (Class 3) 2-Y-O **£7,561** (£2,263; £1,131; £566; £282) **Stalls** Centre

Form RPR
2330 **1** **Haddaf (IRE)**[11] 3925 2-9-2 99 ............ MartinHarley 6 89+
(James Tate) *mde virtually all: pushed along and drew clr over 1f out: easily* **2/5**[1]
0 **2** 4 **Lyrical Pursuit**[35] 3093 2-8-4 0 ............ HarrisonShaw(7) 8 70
(Michael Easterby) *fly-jmpd s: bhd: hdwy and shkn up over 1f out: chsd (clr) wnr wl ins fnl f: kpt on* **50/1**
**3** *shd* **Begging Bowl** 2-8-6 0 ............ LewisEdmunds(5) 5 70
(Michael Easterby) *dwlt: bhd and outpcd: hdwy over 1f out: chsd (clr) wnr briefly ins fnl f: one pce* **25/1**
5 **4** 4 **Knowing Glance (IRE)**[14] 3846 2-9-2 0 ............ PaulHanagan 7 60
(Richard Fahey) *disp ld to wl over 1f out: sn outpcd: wknd and lost two pls ins fnl f* **4/1**[2]
40 **5** 1 1/2 **Hard Graft**[15] 3789 2-9-2 0 ............ AndrewMullen 3 55
(David Brown) *prom: outpcd and hung lft wl over 1f out: sn wknd* **11/2**[3]
6 **6** 1 **Where's Jeff**[15] 3791 2-8-9 0 ............ RyanTimby(7) 1 51
(Michael Easterby) *chsd ldrs: drvn over 2f out: sn wknd* **20/1**
1m 1.73s (2.23) **Going Correction** +0.325s/f (Slow) **6** Ran SP% **117.4**
Speed ratings (Par 98): **95,88,88,82,79 78**
CSF £36.86 TOTE £1.30: £1.10, £9.40; EX 32.50 Trifecta £176.20.
**Owner** Saif Ali **Bred** Rabbah Bloodstock Limited **Trained** Newmarket, Suffolk
■ Skyva was withdrawn. Price at time of withdrawal 25-1. Rule 4 does not apply.
**FOCUS**
A good juvenile novice contest. They went a modest gallop but the clear form horse still won as he liked.
T/Jkpt: Not won. T/Plt: £79.10 to a £1 stake. Pool: £197.969.28 - 1825.44 winning units. T/Qpdt: £7.70 to a £1 stake. Pool: £15,981.44 - 1516.74 winning units. **Richard Young**

# 4311 NEWMARKET (R-H)
### Saturday, July 1
**OFFICIAL GOING: Good to soft changing to good after race 3 (3.15)**
Wind: Light across Weather: Cloudy with sunny spells

## 4360 BETWAY FRED ARCHER STKS (LISTED RACE) 1m 4f
**2:05** (2:05) (Class 1) 4-Y-O+
**£20,982** (£7,955; £3,981; £1,983; £995; £499) **Stalls** Centre

Form RPR
20-1 **1** **Lord Yeats**[43] 2804 4-9-0 99 ............ PJMcDonald 3 110
(Jedd O'Keeffe) *led: rdn and edgd lft over 2f out: hdd over 1f out: hung lft ins fnl f: r.o to ld nr fin* **9/1**
4-31 **2** *nk* **Second Step (IRE)**[35] 3072 6-9-3 110 ............ JamieSpencer 6 112
(Roger Charlton) *hld up: hdwy over 2f out: rdn to ld and edgd rt over 1f out: hdd nr fin* **4/1**[2]
13-3 **3** 3/4 **Mount Logan (IRE)**[35] 3069 6-9-0 109 ............ SilvestreDeSousa 1 108
(Roger Varian) *s.i.s: hld up: hdwy over 5f out: rdn over 2f out: sn outpcd: r.o ins fnl f* **4/1**[2]
-650 **4** 3 1/2 **Red Verdon (USA)**[29] 3299 4-9-0 110 ............ (b[1]) JamesDoyle 4 102
(Ed Dunlop) *chsd ldrs: rdn and ev ch whn hung rt over 2f out: hmpd and no ex ins fnl f* **5/1**[3]
013- **5** *shd* **Platitude**[274] 6917 4-9-0 108 ............ JimCrowley 7 102
(Sir Michael Stoute) *hld up: shkn up over 2f out: nvr nr to chal* **8/1**
0-53 **6** 2 **Midterm**[42] 2822 4-9-0 114 ............ WilliamBuick 2 101
(Sir Michael Stoute) *chsd ldr: rdn and ev ch whn hmpd over 2f out: eased whn btn ins fnl f* **2/1**[1]
2m 31.65s (-1.25) **Going Correction** +0.175s/f (Good) **6** Ran SP% **111.1**
Speed ratings (Par 111): **111,110,110,107,107 106**
CSF £43.05 TOTE £10.60: £3.50, £2.10; EX 48.50 Trifecta £185.30.
**Owner** Geoff & Sandra Turnbull **Bred** Geoff & Sandra Turnbull **Trained** Middleham Moor, N Yorks
■ Stewards' Enquiry : P J McDonald caution: careless riding
**FOCUS**
The re-positioning of the bend into the home straight increased the distance of the 1m2f & 1m4f races by 19yds. There was 2.5mm of rain during racing the previous evening, but this was a dry day. A couple of disappointing sorts in this but not the winner, who is improving and showed a tremendous attitude, and the form looks solid for the level. It's rated around the runner-up.

## 4361 BETWAY EMPRESS FILLIES' STKS (LISTED RACE) 6f
**2:40** (2:45) (Class 1) 2-Y-O
**£14,744** (£5,590; £2,797; £1,393; £699; £351) **Stalls** Low

Form RPR
11 **1** **Dance Diva**[17] 3712 2-9-0 83 ............ WilliamBuick 2 97+
(Richard Fahey) *a.p: shkn up to ld 2f out: rdn and edgd lft ins fnl f: r.o* **3/1**[1]
142 **2** 1 1/4 **Maggies Angel (IRE)**[21] 3557 2-9-0 86 ............ GeraldMosse 5 93
(Richard Fahey) *s.i.s: sn pushed along in rr: swtchd lft over 2f out: hdwy over 1f out: rdn and hung rt ins fnl f: r.o* **8/1**
31 **3** 1 **So Hi Society (IRE)**[25] 3421 2-9-0 0 ............ RobertWinston 11 90
(Archie Watson) *trckd ldrs: shkn up to chse wnr and edgd rt over 1f out: styd on same pce ins fnl f* **10/1**
43 **4** 3 3/4 **Reflect Alexander (IRE)**[25] 3421 2-9-0 0 ............ RobertTart 13 79
(David Evans) *chsd ldrs: rdn over 1f out: no ex ins fnl f* **50/1**
31 **5** *nse* **Elizabeth Bennet (IRE)**[18] 3687 2-9-0 0 ............ JamesDoyle 7 79+
(Charles Hills) *hld up: hdwy and nt clr run over 2f out: rdn and hung lft over 1f out: nvr trbld ldrs* **7/2**[2]
1 **6** *hd* **Tajaanus (IRE)**[42] 2832 2-9-0 0 ............ JimCrowley 4 84+
(Richard Hannon) *s.i.s: hld up: hdwy and nt clr run fr over 2f out tl swtchd lft over 1f out: nvr trbld ldrs* **13/2**[3]
0414 **7** 1 1/4 **Campion**[29] 3297 2-9-0 76 ............ TimmyMurphy 1 76
(Richard Hannon) *plld hrd and prom: stdd and lost pl over 4f out: nt clr run fr over 2f out tl fnl f: nvr trbld ldrs* **33/1**
21 **8** 1 1/2 **Miss Dd (IRE)**[19] 3662 2-9-0 0 ............ (p[1]) RichardKingscote 12 70
(Tom Dascombe) *led: hdd over 3f out: rdn over 1f out: wknd fnl f* **14/1**
4 **9** 2 1/2 **Amourice (IRE)**[21] 3590 2-9-0 0 ............ LiamJones 3 63+
(Jane Chapple-Hyam) *s.i.s: sn pushed along in rr: effrt and nt clr run over 2f out: wknd over 1f out* **25/1**
3415 **10** 3/4 **Daddies Girl (IRE)**[43] 2801 2-9-0 80 ............ (p[1]) OisinMurphy 14 60
(Rod Millman) *in tch and sn pushed along: rdn over 2f out: wkng whn hung rt over 1f out* **16/1**
5145 **11** 1/2 **Diamond Pursuit**[29] 3297 2-9-0 71 ............ PJMcDonald 10 59
(Jo Hughes) *w ldr tl led over 3f out: hdd over 2f out: rdn and wknd over 1f out* **100/1**
451 **12** 3/4 **Silca Mistress**[11] 3943 2-9-0 72 ............ SilvestreDeSousa 9 57
(Mick Channon) *w ldrs: led over 2f out: sn rdn and hdd: wknd over 1f out* **16/1**
1m 11.73s (-0.77) **Going Correction** -0.025s/f (Good) **12** Ran SP% **108.9**
Speed ratings (Par 99): **104,102,101,96,95 95,94,92,88,87 87,86**
CSF £23.00 TOTE £3.30: £1.30, £2.60, £3.30; EX 20.50 Trifecta £129.90.
**Owner** Cheveley Park Stud **Bred** Cheveley Park Stud Ltd **Trained** Musley Bank, N Yorks
■ Ellthea was withdrawn. Price at time of withdrawal 10-1. Rule 4 applies to all bets - deduction 5p in the pound.
**FOCUS**
Not of these offered a particularly high level of form beforehand, but the winner is an improver. Ellthea tried to get under the front of her stall and had to be withdrawn.

## 4362 BETWAY CRITERION STKS (GROUP 3) 7f
**3:15** (3:15) (Class 1) 3-Y-O+
**£34,026** (£12,900; £6,456; £3,216; £1,614; £810) **Stalls** Low

Form RPR
20-1 **1** **Home Of The Brave (IRE)**[63] 2150 5-9-3 114 ............ (t) JamesDoyle 1 117
(Hugo Palmer) *a.p: led 2f out: sn rdn: r.o gamely* **13/8**[1]
2140 **2** 3/4 **Jungle Cat (IRE)**[45] 2737 5-9-3 112 ............ (p) WilliamBuick 2 115
(Charlie Appleby) *chsd ldrs: rdn to chse wnr over 1f out: r.o* **8/1**
0-35 **3** 2 3/4 **Breton Rock (IRE)**[21] 3587 7-9-3 112 ............ OisinMurphy 5 108
(David Simcock) *hld up: hdwy and nt clr run over 1f out: sn rdn: styd on same pce ins fnl f* **6/1**[3]
140- **4** 2 **Ibn Malik (IRE)**[350] 4393 4-9-3 108 ............ SilvestreDeSousa 8 102
(Charles Hills) *led 6f out: hdd 2f out: sn rdn and hung rt: no ex ins fnl f* **8/1**
4310 **5** 1 **Winning Ways (IRE)**[10] 3959 3-8-9 101 ............ (t) GeraldMosse 7 96
(Jeremy Noseda) *hld up: hdwy over 1f out: sn rdn and edgd rt: no ex ins fnl f* **10/1**
33-1 **6** 3 1/2 **Ifwecan**[42] 2833 6-9-3 95 ............ RobertWinston 6 90
(Martin Smith) *led 1f: chsd ldr: rdn over 2f out: edgd rt over 1f out: wknd ins fnl f* **40/1**
5-03 **7** 6 **Thikriyaat (IRE)**[14] 3843 4-9-3 111 ............ JimCrowley 3 74
(Sir Michael Stoute) *sn prom: rdn over 2f out: wknd over 1f out* **5/1**[2]
156- **8** 4 1/2 **Richard Pankhurst**[267] 7115 5-9-3 114 ............ RobertTart 4 62
(John Gosden) *hld up in tch: lost pl over 2f out: sn wknd* **8/1**
1m 23.13s (-2.57) **Going Correction** -0.025s/f (Good)
**WFA** 3 from 4yo+ 8lb **8** Ran SP% **113.9**
Speed ratings (Par 113): **113,112,109,106,105 101,94,89**
CSF £15.37 TOTE £2.10: £1.30, £2.00, £1.90; EX 12.00 Trifecta £45.40.
**Owner** Godolphin **Bred** Earl Ecurie Du Grand Chene **Trained** Newmarket, Suffolk
**FOCUS**
The ground was changed to good all over following this race. This looked a rock-solid Group 3 beforehand but only three of these committed to racing near side from the off and they filled the first three places. The others raced more towards the middle for much of the way. Home Of The Brave is rated to form.

## 4363 BETWAY NOVICE STKS (PLUS 10 RACE) 7f
**3:50** (3:50) (Class 4) 2-Y-O **£4,528** (£1,347; £673; £336) **Stalls** Low

Form RPR
0 **1** **Tadleel**[43] 2779 2-9-2 0 ............ JimCrowley 4 77
(Ed Dunlop) *w ldr tl shkn up to ld over 1f out: drvn out* **5/2**[2]
**2** 1/2 **Dukhan** 2-9-2 0 ............ JamesDoyle 3 76
(Hugo Palmer) *hld up in tch: racd keenly: nt clr run over 1f out: rdn and r.o ins fnl f* **9/4**[1]
**3** 1 **Jack Regan** 2-9-2 0 ............ (t[1]) SilvestreDeSousa 2 73
(Charles Hills) *s.i.s: hld up: shkn up over 2f out: hdwy over 1f out: sn rdn: styd on same pce wl ins fnl f* **11/4**[3]
**4** 2 **Metatrons Cube (IRE)** 2-9-2 0 ............ RobertWinston 6 68
(Charles Hills) *w ldrs: shkn up and ev ch over 1f out: no ex wl ins fnl f* **14/1**
**5** 2 3/4 **Queen Adelaide** 2-8-11 0 ............ GeraldMosse 5 55
(John Ryan) *s.s: hld up: nvr on terms* **14/1**
**6** 1/2 **Letsbe Avenue (IRE)** 2-9-2 0 ............ TimmyMurphy 7 59
(Richard Hannon) *wnt lft s: sn prom: rdn and hung lft over 1f out: wknd ins fnl f* **17/2**
**7** 7 **Ruby's Gem** 2-8-11 0 ............ OisinMurphy 1 35
(Philip McBride) *led: rdn and hdd over 1f out: wknd ins fnl f* **25/1**
1m 27.35s (1.65) **Going Correction** -0.025s/f (Good) **7** Ran SP% **113.7**
Speed ratings (Par 96): **89,88,87,85,81 81,73**
CSF £8.47 TOTE £3.30: £1.60, £1.70; EX 9.00 Trifecta £16.70.
**Owner** Hamdan Al Maktoum **Bred** Anthony Byrne **Trained** Newmarket, Suffolk
**FOCUS**
The winner was the only one with experience and the bare form probably isn't that strong.

## 4364 BETWAY FILLIES' H'CAP 1m 4f
**4:20** (4:22) (Class 3) (0-95,95) 3-Y-O+ **£7,762** (£2,310; £1,154; £577) **Stalls** Centre

Form RPR
2-11 **1** **Melodic Motion (IRE)**[36] 3033 3-8-11 **90** ............ OisinMurphy 2 105+
(Ralph Beckett) *chsd ldr tl shkn up to ld over 1f out: rdn clr ins fnl f: eased towards fin* **5/2**[2]
21-2 **2** 3 3/4 **Gallifrey**[23] 3507 3-8-2 **81** ............ PaoloSirigu 3 88
(Lucy Wadham) *hld up: hdwy over 4f out: rdn over 2f out: chsd wnr ins fnl f: no imp* **3/1**[3]
-412 **3** 2 1/4 **Nathania**[22] 3535 3-8-4 **83** ............ SilvestreDeSousa 5 86
(Richard Hughes) *plld hrd: led: qcknd over 2f out: rdn and hdd over 1f out: wknd wl ins fnl f* **2/1**[1]
-551 **4** 2 1/4 **Pacharana**[18] 3684 4-8-13 **80** ............ JamesDoyle 6 79
(Luca Cumani) *sn prom: rdn over 2f out: wknd ins fnl f* **12/1**
15-6 **5** 3/4 **Cliff Face (IRE)**[10] 3968 4-10-0 **95** ............ WilliamBuick 1 93
(Sir Mark Prescott Bt) *s.s: hld up and bhd: hdwy u.p over 1f out: wknd ins fnl f* **20/1**
0443 **6** 3/4 **Marsh Pride**[21] 3580 5-9-3 **84** ............ PJMcDonald 4 80
(K R Burke) *hld up: effrt over 2f out: sn edgd rt: wknd over 1f out* **8/1**
2m 36.11s (3.21) **Going Correction** +0.175s/f (Good)
**WFA** 3 from 4yo+ 12lb **6** Ran SP% **110.5**
Speed ratings (Par 104): **96,93,92,90,90 89**
CSF £10.05 TOTE £2.90: £1.70, £1.80; EX 10.30 Trifecta £21.20.
**Owner** Qatar Racing Limited **Bred** Old Carhue & Graeng Bloodstock **Trained** Kimpton, Hants

**FOCUS**
Add 19yds. Strong form, the winner continuing to progress.

## 4365 BETWAY H'CAP (JOCKEY CLUB GRASSROOTS MIDDLE DISTANCE SERIES QUALIFIER) 1m 2f
**4:55** (4:56) (Class 4) (0-80,82) 3-Y-0+ **£5,175** (£1,540; £769; £384) **Stalls** Centre

Form RPR
16-6 **1** **Roar (IRE)**[21] 3578 3-8-12 **74** PJMcDonald 11 81
(Brian Ellison) *sn led: hdd over 8f out: chsd ldr: rdn over 2f out: led ins fnl f: drvn out* **13/2**

141- **2** *½* **Stamford Raffles**[197] 8399 4-10-0 **80** LiamJones 7 85+
(Jane Chapple-Hyam) *hld up: swtchd lft and hdwy over 2f out: rdn over 1f out: ev ch ins fnl f: styd on* **33/1**

-001 **3** *1* **Swiftsure (IRE)**[6] 4118 3-9-6 **82** 6ex WilliamBuick 3 86
(Sir Michael Stoute) *w ldr tl led over 8f out: shkn up 3f out: rdn over 1f out: edgd lft and hdd ins fnl f: styd on same pce* **13/8**[1]

1312 **4** *nk* **Road To Dubai (IRE)**[15] 3779 3-9-2 **78** SilvestreDeSousa 8 81
(George Scott) *hld up: hdwy over 2f out: rdn over 1f out: sn hung lft: ev ch and hung rt ins fnl f: no ex towards fin* **9/4**[2]

3-33 **5** *nk* **Italian Heiress**[20] 3615 3-9-1 **77** GeraldMosse 10 80
(Clive Cox) *trckd ldrs: rdn and ev ch over 1f out: styd on same pce ins fnl f* **11/2**[3]

3-50 **6** *1 ¾* **Broughtons Knight**[26] 3412 3-8-6 **68** DannyBrock 4 67
(Henry Spiller) *prom: racd keenly: shkn up over 1f out: styd on same pce fnl f* **12/1**

143 **7** *1 ¼* **The Gay Cavalier**[8] 4047 6-9-3 **69** (t) RichardKingscote 6 65
(John Ryan) *s.i.s: hld up: shkn up over 1f out: nt trble ldrs* **20/1**

-633 **8** *9* **Canterbury Quad (FR)**[9] 4003 3-9-1 **77** (p[1]) JimCrowley 9 56
(Henry Spiller) *hld up: rdn over 1f out: wknd fnl f* **22/1**

2m 8.05s (2.55) **Going Correction** +0.175s/f (Good)
**WFA** 3 from 4yo+ 10lb **8** Ran SP% **117.3**
Speed ratings (Par 105): **96,95,94,94,94 92,91,84**
CSF £192.59 CT £510.19 TOTE £8.30: £2.20, £3.70, £1.20; EX 339.40 Trifecta £1464.30.
**Owner** K Strangeway & J M Basquill **Bred** Wollemie Park Stud **Trained** Norton, N Yorks

**FOCUS**
Add 19yds. A fair handicap but the field finished compressed and the form looks a bit fluid.

## 4366 BETWAY EBF STALLIONS FILLIES' H'CAP 1m
**5:30** (5:31) (Class 3) (0-95,86) 3-Y-0+ **£9,056** (£2,695; £1,346; £673) **Stalls** Low

Form RPR
1-33 **1** **Mittens**[22] 3535 3-8-12 **79** RichardKingscote 3 93
(Sir Michael Stoute) *trckd ldrs: shkn up to ld and edgd rt over 1f out: pushed clr ins fnl f: comf* **2/1**[2]

4-21 **2** *3 ¾* **Shaaqaaf (IRE)**[29] 3309 3-9-4 **85** JimCrowley 6 90
(John Gosden) *chsd ldr tl led over 2f out: rdn: edgd rt and hdd over 1f out: no ex ins fnl f* **15/8**[1]

04-3 **3** *3 ¾* **Stellar Surprise**[15] 3786 3-8-13 **80** PJMcDonald 1 76
(Stuart Williams) *hld up: racd keenly: hdwy over 1f out: sn rdn: hung lft and wknd ins fnl f* **5/2**[3]

25-0 **4** *¾* **Little Lady Katie (IRE)**[21] 3589 5-9-9 **84** JordanVaughan[(3)] 5 80
(K R Burke) *led: pushed along and qcknd 3f out: rdn and hdd over 2f out: wknd fnl f* **11/2**

1m 39.51s (-0.49) **Going Correction** -0.025s/f (Good)
**WFA** 3 from 5yo 9lb **4** Ran SP% **112.1**
Speed ratings (Par 104): **101,97,93,92**
CSF £6.35 TOTE £2.90; EX 6.60 Trifecta £7.60.
**Owner** K Abdullah **Bred** Juddmonte Farms Ltd **Trained** Newmarket, Suffolk

**FOCUS**
A decent enough race despite the small field, and the winner was quite impressive.
T/Plt: £38.70 to a £1 stake. Pool: £114,718.14 - 2163.29 winning units. T/Qpdt: £4.00 to a £1 stake. Pool: £6,671.84 - 1205.41 winning units. **Colin Roberts**

# 4151 WINDSOR (R-H)
Saturday, July 1

**OFFICIAL GOING: Good to soft (good in places; 6.7)**
Wind: Moderate, behind Weather: Fine but cloudy, warm

## 4367 LIKE SUN BETS ON FACEBOOK NOVICE STKS 6f 12y
**2:10** (2:10) (Class 5) 2-Y-O **£2,911** (£866; £432; £216) **Stalls** Low

Form RPR
42 **1** **Grand Koonta (IRE)**[21] 3590 2-9-2 0 AdamKirby 5 80+
(Clive Cox) *led after 1f towards outer: shkn up 2f out: sn drew clr: comf* **1/2**[1]

**2** *3 ¾* **Popsicle (IRE)** 2-8-11 0 TomMarquand 3 62+
(Richard Hannon) *chsd ldrs: pushed along 1/2-way: styd on fr over 1f out to take 2nd last 75yds* **14/1**

4321 **3** *1* **Alaska (IRE)**[11] 3936 2-9-4 74 MitchGodwin[(5)] 10 71
(Sylvester Kirk) *prom on wd outside: rdn to chal 2f out: sn btn off: fdd fnl f and lost 2nd last 75yds* **7/1**[3]

**4** *1 ¼* **Jupiter** 2-9-2 0 FergusSweeney 4 60+
(Henry Candy) *led 1f: chsd wnr to over 2f out: one pce after* **25/1**

**5** *½* **Perfect Hustler (USA)** 2-9-2 0 AntonioFresu 8 59
(Jeremy Noseda) *slowly away: wl in rr: pushed along 1/2-way: kpt on fr over 1f out: n.d* **16/1**

**6** *¾* **Garden Oasis** 2-8-13 0 KieranShoemark[(3)] 7 56
(Sir Michael Stoute) *wl in rr: pushed along 1/2-way: nvr on terms but kpt on fnl f on outer* **8/1**

**7** *¾* **Golden Salute (IRE)** 2-8-11 0 DavidProbert 9 49
(Andrew Balding) *prom: chsd wnr briefly over 2f out: wknd wl over 1f out* **6/1**[2]

60 **8** *1 ½* **Haven's View**[15] 3782 2-9-2 0 ShaneKelly 1 50
(Richard Hughes) *a in rr: pushed along 1/2-way: no prog* **80/1**

55 **9** *¾* **Vegas Boy (IRE)**[24] 3467 2-8-9 0 NicolaCurrie[(7)] 6 47
(Jamie Osborne) *hld up in tch: lost grnd 1/2-way: wl in rr over 1f out* **33/1**

**10** *2* **Jazz Affair (IRE)** 2-9-2 0 RobHornby 2 41
(Jamie Osborne) *a in rr: wknd over 1f out* **33/1**

1m 13.95s (0.95) **Going Correction** +0.175s/f (Good) **10** Ran SP% **128.1**
Speed ratings (Par 94): **100,95,93,92,91 90,89,87,86,83**
CSF £11.43 TOTE £1.30: £1.02, £3.30, £2.00; EX 11.80 Trifecta £37.50.
**Owner** China Horse Club International Limited **Bred** Skymarc Farm **Trained** Lambourn, Berks

**FOCUS**
The rail was moved out 12 yards from the stands' side inner position from 6f to the winning post. A decent-looking opener, in which the market leader proved strong enough in the final stages to win comfortably.

## 4368 MPM FLOORING LTD MAIDEN STKS 5f 21y
**2:45** (2:47) (Class 5) 3-Y-O+ **£2,911** (£866; £432; £216) **Stalls** Low

Form RPR
4- **1** **African Friend (IRE)**[442] 1451 4-9-12 0 FergusSweeney 6 83+
(Henry Candy) *mde virtually all: drvn over 1f out: hrd pressed fnl f: hld on nr fin* **5/2**[1]

**2** *hd* **Indian Raj** 3-9-7 0 AdamKirby 3 80
(Stuart Williams) *slowly away: hld up in last pair: prog 1/2-way: chsd wnr wl over 1f out: str chal fnl f against far rail: nt qckn last strides* **4/1**[2]

0466 **3** *4* **Kings Academy**[18] 3692 3-9-7 63 (t) DavidProbert 2 66
(Paul Cole) *hld up in last pair: shuffled along 2f out: tk 3rd fnl f: nvr nr to chal* **9/2**[3]

543 **4** *hd* **Pride Of Angels**[19] 3669 4-9-7 67 ShaneKelly 5 62
(Gary Moore) *chsd ldrs: on terms 2f out: sn rdn: fdd jst over 1f out* **11/2**

26 **5** *shd* **Hollander**[35] 3085 3-9-4 0 KieranShoemark[(3)] 1 65
(William Muir) *w wnr to 1/2-way: fdd u.p over 1f out* **5/2**[1]

0 **6** *10* **Make Sail**[26] 3407 3-9-2 0 TomMarquand 4 24
(Tony Carroll) *chsd ldrs to 1/2-way: sn wknd: t.o* **50/1**

1m 0.83s (0.53) **Going Correction** +0.175s/f (Good)
**WFA** 3 from 4yo 5lb **6** Ran SP% **112.7**
Speed ratings (Par 103): **102,101,95,94,94 78**
CSF £12.95 TOTE £3.00: £2.10, £1.90; EX 9.90 Trifecta £64.70.
**Owner** Henry Candy **Bred** Tom Radley **Trained** Kingston Warren, Oxon

**FOCUS**
Hard to think this was anything more than a modest race of its type at this stage of the season. It's possible that the first two were on the best ground late on.

## 4369 LONGINES IRISH CHAMPIONS WEEKEND EBF FILLIES' CONDITIONS STKS (PLUS 10 RACE) 5f 21y
**3:20** (3:20) (Class 2) 2-Y-O **£10,893** (£3,262) **Stalls** Low

Form RPR
124 **1** **Rebel Assault (IRE)**[21] 3557 2-8-12 93 DavidProbert 2 92+
(Mark Johnston) *bttr away than rival: mde all: pushed along and drew away over 1f out* **1/3**[1]

2 **2** *7* **Tonkolili (IRE)**[14] 3807 2-8-12 0 KieranShoemark 5 67+
(William Muir) *unsettled in stall and much more slowly away than rival: rdn to try to chal 2f out: sn lft bhd* **9/4**[2]

1m 1.7s (1.40) **Going Correction** +0.175s/f (Good) **2** Ran SP% **105.8**
Speed ratings (Par 97): **95,83**
TOTE £1.10.
**Owner** Mrs Christine E Budden & Partners **Bred** Christine E Budden & Partners **Trained** Middleham Moor, N Yorks

**FOCUS**
Sadly, from five entries, including the Queen Mary third, only two lined up, creating a match. Straightforward form to understand.

## 4370 FOLLOW SUN BETS ON TWITTER H'CAP 1m 3f 99y
**3:55** (3:56) (Class 2) (0-100,100) 4-Y-0+ **£12,291** (£3,657; £1,827; £913) **Stalls** Centre

Form RPR
0-00 **1** **King Bolete (IRE)**[33] 3154 5-9-6 **99** (p[1]) JackMitchell 7 107
(Roger Varian) *mde all: kicked on over 3f out: 3 l clr over 1f out: rdn and ld dwindled ins fnl f but a holding on* **7/2**[2]

1-03 **2** *nk* **What About Carlo (FR)**[29] 3300 6-9-7 **100** CharlesBishop 5 107
(Eve Johnson Houghton) *trckd ldrs: shkn up and prog over 2f out: chsd wnr over 1f out: styd on and clsd ins fnl f: a hld* **11/4**[1]

4660 **3** *3 ¼* **Great Hall**[21] 3597 7-9-4 **97** AdamKirby 1 98
(Mick Quinn) *in tch in midfield: sltly outpcd 3f out: rdn over 2f out: styd on fr over 1f out to take 3rd last stride* **6/1**

00 **4** *shd* **Desert God (IND)**[156] 428 5-9-4 **97** ShaneKelly 9 98
(Richard Hughes) *prom: chsd wnr 1/2-way: rdn over 2f out: hanging and racd awkwardly after: lost 2nd over 1f out and lost 3rd last stride* **8/1**

1-2P **5** *2 ¼* **Plutocracy (IRE)**[117] 1068 7-8-11 **90** (p) KieranO'Neill 6 87
(Gary Moore) *hld up in midfield: shkn up over 2f out: effrt over 1f out but sn no prog* **20/1**

6-41 **6** *1 ¾* **Stockhill Diva**[19] 3671 7-8-8 **87** FergusSweeney 3 81
(Brendan Powell) *hld up in rr: stdy prog 4f out to chse ldrs 2f out: sn rdn: wknd over 1f out* **12/1**

132 **7** *1 ½* **Jacob Cats**[19] 3671 8-9-1 **94** (v) TomMarquand 4 86
(William Knight) *stdd s: hld up in last: rdn and no real prog 3f out* **9/1**

4600 **8** *3* **Warrior Of Light (IRE)**[55] 2431 6-8-8 **90** KieranShoemark[(3)] 8 77
(Brendan Powell) *chsd wnr to 1/2-way: urged along over 4f out: wknd over 2f out* **33/1**

1106 **9** *5* **Captain Peacock**[24] 3458 4-8-6 **85** (v) DavidProbert 2 63
(William Knight) *slowly away: hld up in rr: hld together 3f out: effrt over 2f out: hanging and fnd nil: wknd over 1f out* **9/2**[3]

2m 30.94s (1.44) **Going Correction** +0.175s/f (Good) **9** Ran SP% **117.9**
Speed ratings (Par 109): **101,100,98,98,96 95,94,92,88**
CSF £13.90 CT £56.09 TOTE £4.70: £1.80, £1.40, £2.00; EX 16.60 Trifecta £92.10.
**Owner** Sheikh Mohammed Obaid Al Maktoum **Bred** Ship Commodities International **Trained** Newmarket, Suffolk
■ Stewards' Enquiry : Shane Kelly caution: careless riding

**FOCUS**
A really competitive contest, but the winning jockey confirmed afterwards that he was allowed an easy lead and set fractions to suit. The winner ran to his best, with a small pb from the second.

## 4371 SUNBETS.CO.UK MIDSUMMER STKS (LISTED RACE) 1m 31y
**4:25** (4:25) (Class 1) 3-Y-O+ **£20,982** (£7,955; £3,981; £1,983; £995) **Stalls** Low

Form RPR
110- **1** **Morando (FR)**[259] 7354 4-9-4 104 JackMitchell 2 116
(Roger Varian) *hld up in 4th: prog in centre 2f out: drvn to ld 1f out but hrd pressed after: r.o wl and jst hld on* **11/4**[2]

6-25 **2** *shd* **Stormy Antarctic**[55] 2492 4-9-4 114 (b) JamieSpencer 5 115
(Ed Walker) *stdd s: hld up in last: swtchd rt 2f out: prog to chal 1f out: hrd rdn and r.o but nt qckn last strides* **6/4**[1]

04-1 **3** *2 ½* **Here Comes When (IRE)**[44] 2767 7-9-7 110 (h) DavidProbert 4 112
(Andrew Balding) *t.k.h: hld up in 3rd tl chsd ldr 3f out: rdn to chal against far rail 2f out: stl there 1f out: outpcd after* **3/1**[3]

-533 **4** *1 ¾* **So Beloved**[21] 3587 7-9-4 108 AdamKirby 1 105
(David O'Meara) *racd freely: led: rdn over 2f out: hdd & wknd 1f out* **12/1**

0-13 **5** 2 **Calderon (IRE)**[37] 3012 4-9-9 113 TomMarquand 3 106
(Richard Hannon) *chsd ldr to 3f out: wknd 2f out* **7/1**
1m 43.92s (-0.78) **Going Correction** +0.20s/f (Good) **5** Ran SP% **111.9**
Speed ratings (Par 111): **111,110,108,106,104**
CSF £7.46 TOTE £3.70: £1.80, £1.30; EX 7.80 Trifecta £17.40.
**Owner** H H Sheikh Mohammed Bin Khalifa Al Thani **Bred** Guy Pariente Holding Sprl **Trained** Newmarket, Suffolk

**FOCUS**
The feature race was run at a sound gallop, although the leader was left alone to dominate early. The winner improved on last year's form.

## 4372 GEOFF CRAMMAN MEMORIAL FILLIES' H'CAP 1m 31y
5:00 (5:01) (Class 5) (0-75,75) 3-Y-O+ £2,911 (£866; £432; £216) Stalls Low

Form RPR
-056 **1** **Sayem**[17] 3729 3-9-2 **72** JamieSpencer 9 79
(Ed Walker) *trckd clr ldng pair: clsd over 2f out: drvn to ld jst over 1f out: hrd pressed fnl f but readily hld on* **6/1**
-410 **2** ½ **Snow Squaw**[44] 2754 3-8-8 **71** JoshuaBryan(7) 8 77
(David Elsworth) *hld up in last off str pce: prog over 2f out: rdn to chal 1f out: styd on but no imp wnr nr fin* **16/1**
03-6 **3** 2 **Funky Footsteps (IRE)**[44] 2754 3-9-2 **72** CharlesBishop 6 73
(Eve Johnson Houghton) *hld up off the pce: rdn wl over 2f out: clsd and ch jst over 1f out: styd on same pce* **7/1**
2221 **4** 2 **Al Nafoorah**[12] 3911 3-9-5 **75** TomMarquand 7 72
(Ed Dunlop) *led at str pce and clr w one rival: rdn over 2f out: hdd & wknd jst over 1f out* **5/2**[1]
3-15 **5** 3 ¼ **Passcode**[43] 2794 3-8-13 **69** DavidProbert 2 58
(Andrew Balding) *hld up in 4th: rdn 3f out: no prog and btn 2f out: fdd* **5/1**[3]
0-12 **6** 1 ½ **Many Dreams (IRE)**[22] 3521 4-9-6 **70** HectorCrouch(3) 5 58
(Gary Moore) *pressed ldr and sn clr of rest: rdn 3f out: lost 2nd and wknd wl over 1f out* **7/2**[2]
1000 **P** **Ejayteekay**[23] 3507 4-9-11 **72** AdamKirby 4
(Hughie Morrison) *p.u sn after s: tack problems* **7/1**
1m 45.23s (0.53) **Going Correction** +0.175s/f (Good)
**WFA** 3 from 4yo 9lb **7** Ran SP% **112.6**
Speed ratings (Par 100): **104,103,101,99,96 94,**
CSF £86.32 CT £680.54 TOTE £6.60: £3.30, £6.90; EX 94.40 Trifecta £638.30.
**Owner** B Greenwood, I Dodds-Smith & R Hatter **Bred** Saleh Al Homaizi & Imad Al Sagar **Trained** Upper Lambourn, Berks

**FOCUS**
A fair handicap in which the gallop was overly strong from the outset.

## 4373 BARRIE HORSTED RETIREMENT APPRENTICE H'CAP 6f 12y
5:35 (5:35) (Class 5) (0-70,72) 4-Y-O+ £2,911 (£866; £432; £216) Stalls Low

Form RPR
2321 **1** **Captain Bob (IRE)**[43] 2800 6-9-5 **69** (p) JonathanFisher(7) 7 76
(Robert Cowell) *mde all: pushed along 2f out: shkn up and kpt on fnl f: nvr seriously under threat* **2/1**[1]
3213 **2** ¾ **Black Caesar (IRE)**[11] 3938 6-9-8 **72** SebastianWoods(7) 5 76
(Philip Hide) *chsd wnr to 1/2-way: shkn up 2f out: wnt 2nd again jst over 1f out: styd on but nvr able to chal* **5/2**[2]
-03 **3** ¾ **Champagne Bob**[21] 3573 5-8-9 **57** RossaRyan(5) 6 58
(Richard Price) *chsd ldrs: rdn 2f out: disp 2nd over 1f out: kpt on same pce fnl f* **3/1**[3]
0030 **4** 1 ¼ **Oeil De Tigre (FR)**[21] 3573 6-9-4 **66** AledBeech(5) 2 63
(Tony Carroll) *v awkward s and lost 3 l: sn rcvrd: chsd wnr 1/2-way to jst over 1f out: fdd* **5/1**
0010 **5** 8 **Perfect Pastime**[18] 3696 9-9-0 **64** (p) IsobelFrancis(7) 1 36
(Jim Boyle) *sn in last: lost tch bef 1/2-way: shkn up and no prog 2f out* **12/1**
1m 13.47s (0.47) **Going Correction** +0.175s/f (Good) **5** Ran SP% **111.3**
Speed ratings (Par 103): **103,102,101,99,88**
CSF £7.39 TOTE £2.50: £1.60, £1.70; EX 6.70 Trifecta £9.40.
**Owner** The Cool Silk Partnership **Bred** Martyn J McEnery **Trained** Six Mile Bottom, Cambs

**FOCUS**
This remained an open contest even after three came out.
T/Plt: £74.30 to a £1 stake. Pool: £56,780.80 - 557.27 winning units. T/Qpdt: £37.40 to a £1 stake. Pool: £3,016.72 - 59.67 winning units. **Jonathan Neesom**

# 3841 YORK (L-H)
Saturday, July 1

**OFFICIAL GOING: Good (good to soft in places; 6.7)**
Wind: fresh across Weather: Sunny

## 4374 SUN BETS DOWNLOAD THE APP NOVICE STKS (PLUS 10 RACE) 6f
1:55 (1:56) (Class 3) 2-Y-O £7,762 (£2,310; £1,154; £577) Stalls Low

Form RPR
**1** **Moseeb (IRE)** 2-9-2 0 MartinLane 4 76+
(Saeed bin Suroor) *racd keenly: mde all: pushed along 2f out: strly pressed jst ins fnl f: rdn and kpt on wl* **10/11**[1]
543 **2** ½ **Dontgiveuponbob**[25] 3429 2-9-2 79 BarryMcHugh 5 72
(Richard Fahey) *prom: rdn over 2f out: pressed ldr ins fnl f: kpt on but a hld* **5/1**[3]
02 **3** 2 **Queen Penn**[42] 2832 2-8-11 0 JackGarritty 1 61
(Richard Fahey) *trckd ldrs: pushed along over 2f out: rdn and one pce fnl f* **11/4**[2]
**4** 3 ¾ **Foxrush Take Time (FR)** 2-9-2 0 JFEgan 2 55
(Richard Guest) *dwlt: sn trckd ldrs: rdn over 2f out: wknd over 1f out* **14/1**
**5** ½ **Mr Greenlight** 2-9-2 0 JamesSullivan 3 53
(Tim Easterby) *dwlt: sn trckd ldrs racing keenly: rdn over 1f out: wknd ins fnl f* **8/1**
1m 13.83s (1.93) **Going Correction** +0.225s/f (Good) **5** Ran SP% **113.5**
Speed ratings (Par 98): **96,95,92,87,87**
CSF £6.26 TOTE £1.80: £1.10, £1.80; EX 5.50 Trifecta £10.60.
**Owner** Godolphin **Bred** Mrs Louise Quinn & Irish National Stud **Trained** Newmarket, Suffolk

**FOCUS**
Jockeys seemed to think the ground was more or less as described. "It's nice, good ground," said Barry McHugh. A reasonable little novice and, as the market suggested, the favourite made a winning debut.

## 4375 BET & WATCH AT SUNBETS.CO.UK FILLIES' H'CAP 7f
2:30 (2:30) (Class 3) (0-95,95) 4-Y-O+
£12,450 (£3,728; £1,864; £932; £466; £234) Stalls Low

Form RPR
21- **1** **Sainted**[372] 3614 4-8-9 **83** HarryBentley 4 96+
(William Haggas) *dwlt: hld up in midfield: smooth hdwy over 2f out: pushed along to ld over 1f out: rdn and edgd rt ent fnl f: kpt on wl to draw clr: comf* **11/10**[1]
3415 **2** 3 **Alpine Dream (IRE)**[6] 4121 4-8-2 **76** oh3 (b) JamesSullivan 1 78
(Tim Easterby) *hld up: pushed along and hdwy over 1f out: rdn and kpt on wl fnl f: wnt 2nd towards fin* **12/1**
-436 **3** ½ **Yeah Baby Yeah (IRE)**[8] 4051 4-8-10 **84** (p) MartinDwyer 2 85
(Gay Kelleway) *hld up: pushed along and hdwy 2f out: kpt on fnl f* **14/1**
0212 **4** nk **Rebel Surge (IRE)**[22] 3541 4-9-2 **90** (p) StevieDonohoe 8 90
(Richard Spencer) *midfield: rdn and hdwy to chse ldrs over 1f out: edgd rt and one pce ins fnl f* **8/1**[3]
3660 **5** ¾ **Summer Icon**[10] 3961 4-9-7 **95** JFEgan 3 93
(Mick Channon) *hld up: rdn and hdwy 2f out: ev ch over 1f out: no ex ins fnl f* **12/1**
6221 **6** 3 **Florenza**[28] 3314 4-8-10 **84** RoystonFfrench 5 74
(Chris Fairhurst) *trckd ldrs: rdn and outpcd over 3f out: no threat after* **5/1**[2]
2055 **7** ½ **Invermere**[29] 3287 4-8-4 **78** CamHardie 6 67
(Richard Fahey) *trckd ldrs: rdn over 2f out: wknd fnl f* **14/1**
0201 **8** 2 ½ **Courier**[22] 3541 5-9-0 **88** BarryMcHugh 7 70
(Marjorie Fife) *led for 1f: remained prom: rdn over 2f out: wknd over 1f out* **12/1**
00-4 **9** hd **Fourth Way (IRE)**[28] 3314 4-8-12 **86** PhillipMakin 10 67
(Ralph Beckett) *trckd ldrs: racd quite keenly: rdn over 2f out: wknd over 1f out* **12/1**
-400 **10** 2 ¾ **Maggie Pink**[133] 810 8-7-12 **77** JaneElliott(5) 9 51
(Michael Appleby) *dwlt: led after 1f: rdn over 2f out: hdd over 1f out: wknd* **20/1**
1m 24.64s (-0.66) **Going Correction** -0.25s/f (Firm) **10** Ran SP% **124.3**
Speed ratings (Par 104): **93,89,89,88,87 84,83,80,80,77**
CSF £17.95 CT £140.09 TOTE £1.90: £1.10, £3.10, £3.20; EX 18.40 Trifecta £352.20.
**Owner** Cheveley Park Stud **Bred** Cheveley Park Stud Ltd **Trained** Newmarket, Suffolk

**FOCUS**
A useful handicap, with it setting up for the closers, and a winner very much on the up. The likes of the fourth help with the standard.

## 4376 SUNBETS.CO.UK H'CAP 1m 2f 56y
3:05 (3:06) (Class 2) (0-105,98) 3-Y-O
£31,125 (£9,320; £4,660; £2,330; £1,165; £585) Stalls Low

Form RPR
20-1 **1** **Defoe (IRE)**[42] 2824 3-9-7 **98** HarryBentley 6 106+
(Roger Varian) *hld up: gd hdwy over 2f out: pushed along to ld narrowly ent fnl f: sn rdn: styd on wl pushed out fnl 75yds* **5/2**[1]
6304 **2** ½ **Society Red**[21] 3583 3-8-0 **77** JamesSullivan 3 84
(Richard Fahey) *trckd ldrs: pushed along over 2f out: rdn to chal appr fnl f: styd on wl but a jst hld* **16/1**
1512 **3** 1 ¼ **Emenem**[28] 3318 3-8-10 **87** JFEgan 4 92
(Simon Dow) *midfield: rdn and hdwy over 2f out: led narrowly over 1f out: hdd ent fnl f: remained cl up tl no ex fnl 75yds* **7/1**[3]
-435 **4** 1 ¼ **Temple Church (IRE)**[19] 3680 3-9-7 **98** StevieDonohoe 11 100
(Hughie Morrison) *prom: pressed ldr over 3f out: rdn over 2f out: one pce fnl f* **16/1**
-100 **5** hd **Cullingworth (IRE)**[35] 3077 3-8-6 **83** BarryMcHugh 7 85
(Richard Fahey) *hld up: pushed along over 2f out: rdn and styd on fnl f* **25/1**
10-2 **6** ¾ **Appointed**[35] 3094 3-8-8 **88** RachelRichardson(3) 12 88
(Tim Easterby) *midfield: rdn over 2f out: one pce and nvr threatened* **10/1**
4-31 **7** ½ **The Statesman**[14] 3838 3-8-3 **80** MartinDwyer 10 79
(Ian Williams) *midfield: rdn over 2f out: one pce and nvr threatened* **7/1**[3]
35-5 **8** 2 **Teofonic (IRE)**[55] 2436 3-8-13 **90** RoystonFfrench 2 86
(Mark Johnston) *trckd ldrs: rdn and outpcd over 3f out: no threat after* **25/1**
0-11 **9** ¾ **Meteor Light (IRE)**[26] 3392 3-8-9 **86** (h) AdamBeschizza 5 80
(Ed Vaughan) *hld up: rdn over 2f out: nvr threatened* **11/2**[2]
5-64 **10** ¾ **Star Of Rory (IRE)**[36] 3042 3-9-2 **93** PhillipMakin 9 86
(Tom Dascombe) *hld up: pushed along over 2f out: nvr threatened* **20/1**
4-21 **11** 3 **Everything For You (IRE)**[75] 1830 3-8-4 **81** ShaneGray 1 68
(Kevin Ryan) *prom: rdn 3f out: wknd over 1f out* **11/1**
-623 **12** ½ **Bear Valley (IRE)**[9] 3998 3-9-0 **91** JackGarritty 8 77
(Mark Johnston) *led: rdn over 2f out: hdd over 1f out: wknd* **8/1**
2m 9.45s (-3.05) **Going Correction** -0.25s/f (Firm) **12** Ran SP% **121.7**
Speed ratings (Par 106): **102,101,100,99,99 98,98,96,96,95 93,92**
CSF £47.56 CT £254.97 TOTE £3.30: £1.60, £4.60, £2.10; EX 50.10 Trifecta £419.60.
**Owner** Sheikh Mohammed Obaid Al Maktoum **Bred** Darley **Trained** Newmarket, Suffolk

**FOCUS**
A good 3yo handicap and the form looks sound. The winner can do better and the second and third improved.

## 4377 LIKE SUN BETS ON FACEBOOK H'CAP 7f 192y
3:35 (3:38) (Class 3) (0-95,95) 3-Y-O+
£12,450 (£3,728; £1,864; £932; £466; £234) Stalls Low

Form RPR
-060 **1** **Just Hiss**[15] 3790 4-9-2 **86** (p[1]) RachelRichardson(3) 6 97
(Tim Easterby) *mde most: pushed clr over 2f out: rdn ent fnl f: edgd rt ins fnl f: reduced advantage towards fin but nvr in danger* **8/1**[2]
3643 **2** 1 **Truth Or Dare**[7] 4103 6-9-2 **83** JamesSullivan 7 92
(James Bethell) *s.i.s: hld up: pushed along and stl plenty to do over 2f out: rdn and hdwy over 1f out: wnt 2nd ins fnl f: styd on wl but nvr getting to wnr* **8/1**[2]
4100 **3** 2 **Boots And Spurs**[3] 4207 8-8-10 **82** (v) GeorgeBuckell(5) 8 86
(Scott Dixon) *chsd ldrs: rdn 3f out: styd on* **16/1**
251 **4** shd **Be Kool (IRE)**[15] 3792 4-9-0 **81** (v) CamHardie 12 85
(Brian Ellison) *pressed ldr: rdn and outpcd over 2f out: styd on fnl f* **10/1**[3]

-000 **5** *1 ¾* **Comedy School (USA)**[14] 3838 3-8-6 **82**.................(b[1]) HarryBentley 13 80
(Mark Johnston) *dwlt: hld up: rdn over 3f out: styd on fr over 1f out: nrst fin* **20/1**

0004 **6** *nk* **Silvery Moon (IRE)**[3] 4207 10-9-3 **84**.......................... DuranFentiman 4 83
(Tim Easterby) *midfield: rdn over 2f out: kpt on same pce* **14/1**

0036 **7** *1 ¼* **Home Cummins (IRE)**[14] 3837 5-9-11 **92**.................(p) BarryMcHugh 5 89
(Richard Fahey) *midfield: rdn over 2f out: no imp* **5/1**[1]

40-0 **8** *¾* **Power Game**[15] 3790 5-9-8 **89**......................................... PhillipMakin 10 84
(David O'Meara) *hld up in midfield: rdn over 2f out: no imp* **18/1**

-652 **9** *1 ½* **Mohab**[46] 2701 4-9-1 **82**.........................................(p[1]) ShaneGray 11 73
(Kevin Ryan) *hld up: rdn over 2f out: nvr threatened* **10/1**[3]

-000 **10** *hd* **Instant Attraction (IRE)**[30] 3255 6-9-11 **92**...................... JackGarritty 1 83
(Jedd O'Keeffe) *chsd ldrs: rdn over 2f out: wknd fnl f* **5/1**[1]

0500 **11** *½* **Baraweez (IRE)**[14] 3842 7-10-0 **95**................................. StevieDonohoe 2 85
(Brian Ellison) *a towards rr* **8/1**[2]

0200 **12** *1 ¾* **Moonlightnavigator (USA)**[15] 3792 5-9-5 **86**......................... JFEgan 3 72
(John Quinn) *midfield: rdn over 3f out: wknd over 1f out* **8/1**[2]

3010 **13** *1 ¾* **Fingal's Cave (IRE)**[14] 3842 5-9-12 **93**......................... MartinLane 14 75
(Philip Kirby) *prom on outer: rdn over 3f out: wknd 2f out* **16/1**

2-65 **14** *2 ¼* **Something Brewing (FR)**[7] 4075 3-8-1 **77**.............(b) RoystonFfrench 9 52
(Iain Jardine) *midfield: rdn over 2f out: wknd* **33/1**

1m 35.58s (-3.42) **Going Correction** -0.25s/f (Firm)
**WFA** 3 from 4yo+ 9lb **14 Ran SP% 127.4**
Speed ratings (Par 107): **107,106,104,103,102 101,100,99,98,98 97,95,94,91**
CSF £74.96 CT £1032.24 TOTE £10.00: £3.00, £2.40, £5.30; EX 64.90 Trifecta £2022.20.
**Owner** The Sandmoor Partnership **Bred** Jeremy Gompertz **Trained** Great Habton, N Yorks

**FOCUS**
A useful handicap, the winner was always well placed. He's rated back to his best.

## 4378 SUNBETS.CO.UK YOUBETCHA BRITISH EBF MAIDEN FILLIES' STKS (PLUS 10 RACE) 7f 192y

**4:15** (4:16) (Class 4) 3-Y-O **£7,762** (£2,310; £1,154; £577) **Stalls** Low

Form RPR

**1** **Finishing Touch** 3-9-0 0................................................... MartinLane 1 83+
(Saeed bin Suroor) *dwlt: hld up: smooth hdwy 3f out: pushed along to ld over 1f out: rdn out fnl 75yds* **3/1**[2]

2522 **2** *¾* **Spinnaka (IRE)**[16] 3748 3-9-0 76.................................. StevieDonohoe 4 78
(Luca Cumani) *hld up in tch: rdn over 2f out: wnt 2nd ins fnl f: kpt on wl but nvr getting to wnr* **2/1**[1]

2 **3** *3 ¼* **White Rosa (IRE)**[26] 3404 3-9-0 0.................................. HarryBentley 2 71
(Hugo Palmer) *hld up in tch: rdn over 2f out: kpt on same pce: wnt modest 3rd towards fin* **2/1**[1]

4 **4** *¾* **Caridade (USA)**[40] 2898 3-9-0 0........................................ ShaneGray 6 69
(Kevin Ryan) *prom: led over 2f out: rdn whn hdd over 1f out: edgd lft and wknd ins fnl f:* **16/1**

03 **5** *2 ½* **Drumochter**[26] 3383 3-9-0 0.................................................. JFEgan 3 63
(Charles Hills) *trckd ldrs: rdn over 2f out: wknd fnl f* **14/1**

323 **6** *1 ¾* **Hindsight**[20] 3626 3-9-0 74........................................... CamHardie 5 59
(Michael Appleby) *led: hdd over 2f out: sn rdn: wknd over 1f out* **8/1**[3]

1m 38.07s (-0.93) **Going Correction** -0.25s/f (Firm) **6 Ran SP% 115.3**
Speed ratings (Par 99): **94,93,90,89,86 85**
CSF £9.83 TOTE £3.90: £1.80, £1.60; EX 10.10 Trifecta £18.50.
**Owner** Godolphin **Bred** Darley **Trained** Newmarket, Suffolk

**FOCUS**
A fair fillies' maiden and the front two came clear. The runner-up set the standard.

## 4379 FOLLOW SUN BETS ON TWITTER "JUMP JOCKEYS' NUNTHORPE" H'CAP (RIDDEN BY PROFESSIONAL JUMP JOCKEYS) 5f

**4:50** (4:51) (Class 3) (0-90,87) 4-Y-0+
**£12,450** (£3,728; £1,864; £932; £466; £234) **Stalls** Centre

Form RPR

2540 **1** **Tylery Wonder (IRE)**[14] 3827 7-10-13 **76**................(v) TomScudamore 2 88
(Paul Midgley) *mde all: racd centre: pushed clr over 1f out: kpt on wl: easily* **14/1**

030- **2** *4* **Fumbo Jumbo (IRE)**[259] 7358 4-11-7 **84**......................... SeanBowen 5 82
(Michael Dods) *awkward s: sn chse ldr: rdn over 2f out: wnt 2nd ins fnl f: kpt on but no ch wnr* **15/2**[3]

2633 **3** *½* **Bashiba (IRE)**[16] 3741 6-11-9 **86**..............................(t) AndrewTinkler 7 82
(Nigel Tinkler) *dwlt: hld up: rdn and hdwy over 1f out: kpt on fnl f* **11/1**

0600 **4** *½* **First Bombardment**[32] 3183 4-11-1 **78**........................ AidanColeman 15 72
(David O'Meara) *prom: rdn over 1f out: no ex ins fnl f* **33/1**

0500 **5** *hd* **B Fifty Two (IRE)**[14] 3847 8-10-13 **76**...............(bt) JeremiahMcGrath 13 69+
(Marjorie Fife) *hld up towards nr side: pushed along and hdwy over 1f out: kpt on fnl f* **25/1**

0462 **6** *1 ¼* **Black Grass**[2] 4249 4-11-3 **80**...................................... GavinSheehan 14 69+
(Michael Easterby) *midfield: rdn and outpcd over 2f out: bit short of room over 1f out: kpt on ins fnl f* **10/1**

4-54 **7** *¾* **Hilary J**[14] 3847 4-11-3 **80**............................................ JoshuaMoore 18 66
(Ann Duffield) *prom towards nr side: rdn over 1f out: wknd fnl 75yds* **13/2**[2]

-000 **8** *1 ¼* **See The Sun**[14] 3847 6-10-12 **75**.................................(p) JoeColliver 11 57
(Tim Easterby) *midfield: sn pushed along: one pce and nvr threatened* **25/1**

0001 **9** *nk* **Desert Ace (IRE)**[2] 4249 6-11-0 **77** 6ex.......................(p) CraigNichol 10 58
(Iain Jardine) *dwlt: hld up: rdn 2f out: kpt on ins fnl f: nvr threatened* **10/1**

1511 **10** *1* **Henley**[17] 3707 5-11-7 **84**............................................... PaddyBrennan 16 61
(Tracy Waggott) *chsd ldrs: rdn over 2f out: wknd fnl f* **5/1**[1]

4330 **11** *½* **Seamster**[11] 3946 10-10-13 **76**......................................(t) AlainCawley 6 51
(David Loughnane) *chsd ldrs: rdn over 2f out: wknd over 1f out* **33/1**

-040 **12** *½* **Mont Kiara (FR)**[44] 2764 4-11-10 **87**............................. BrianHughes 4 60
(Kevin Ryan) *hld up: rdn 2f out: nvr threatened* **9/1**

1650 **13** *nk* **Sandra's Secret (IRE)**[16] 3741 4-11-2 **79**..............(p[1]) NicodeBoinville 3 51
(Les Eyre) *prom: rdn 2f out: wknd fnl f* **14/1**

262- **14** *¾* **Apricot Sky**[249] 7591 7-11-5 **82**...................................... HenryBrooke 9 52
(Brian Ellison) *chsd ldrs: rdn over 2f out: wknd fnl f* **14/1**

3206 **15** *1 ¾* **Geoff Potts (IRE)**[29] 3278 4-10-5 **68** oh1........................ JamesBest 12 31
(Jeremy Gask) *a towards rr* **33/1**

0262 **16** *½* **Midnight Malibu (IRE)**[7] 4081 4-11-5 **82**........................ JamieMoore 8 43
(Tim Easterby) *chsd ldrs: rdn over 2f out: wknd fnl f* **10/1**

210U **17** *1* **Paddy Power (IRE)**[14] 3827 4-11-4 **81**.......................... WillKennedy 17 39
(Richard Fahey) *dwlt: hld up towards nr side: nvr threatened* **16/1**

-500 **18** *19* **Memories Galore (IRE)**[21] 3585 5-11-5 **82**........ SamTwiston-Davies 1
(Roger Fell) *v.s.a: a bhd: eased fnl f* **20/1**

59.54s (0.24) **Going Correction** +0.225s/f (Good) **18 Ran SP% 134.5**
Speed ratings (Par 107): **107,100,99,99,98 96,95,93,93,91 90,89,89,88,85 84,82,52**
CSF £116.39 CT £1235.05 TOTE £17.10: £3.30, £2.40, £3.40, £10.70; EX 190.20 Trifecta £2489.70.
**Owner** Taylor's Bloodstock Ltd **Bred** Michael Kavanagh **Trained** Westow, N Yorks

**FOCUS**
A sprint for jump jockeys and probably not form to take a great deal of notice of, although there was a clear-cut winner who's rated to last year's best. Those drawn low fared best.

## 4380 DREAM TEAM NEW SEASON FREE TO PLAY LADY RIDERS' H'CAP (PRO-AM LADY RIDERS' RACE) 1m 3f 188y

**5:25** (5:25) (Class 3) (0-90,91) 3-Y-0+ **£10,350** (£3,080; £1,539; £769) **Stalls** Low

Form RPR

6343 **1** **Jacbequick**[9] 4017 6-10-5 **82**......................................(p) ShelleyBirkett 7 90
(David O'Meara) *hld up: rdn and hdwy over 2f out: chal appr fnl f: led narrowly ins fnl f: edgd lft: kpt on* **7/1**

0-13 **2** *nk* **Azari**[14] 3841 5-11-0 **91**................................................... MissADeniel 5 98
(Tom Dascombe) *hld up: gd hdwy 3f out: led over 1f out: hdd narrowly ins fnl f: carrried lft: kpt on: hld nr fin* **9/2**[3]

0-23 **3** *6* **Sellingallthetime (IRE)**[61] 2218 6-9-10 **73**...........(p) MissSBrotherton 3 70
(Michael Appleby) *awkward s: sn midfield: rdn and hdwy to ld over 2f out: hdd over 1f out: grad wknd* **6/1**

0-00 **4** *5* **Multellie**[3] 4206 5-10-7 **84**........................................ RachelRichardson 4 73
(Tim Easterby) *led: rdn over 3f out: hdd over 2f out: wknd over 1f out* **7/1**

44-5 **5** *6* **Richie McCaw**[15] 3785 4-10-0 **77**........................................ MsLO'Neill 2 57
(Ian Williams) *hld up: hdwy to trck ldrs over 2f out: rdn and wknd over 1f out* **3/1**[2]

24-2 **6** *5* **Arrowtown**[42] 2815 5-9-8 **71**....................................(h) MissJoannaMason 8 43
(Michael Easterby) *hld up: rdn over 3f out: sn btn* **5/2**[1]

0/0- **7** *20* **Cousin Khee**[46] 3657 10-10-5 **82**.......................................... MissPFuller 6 22
(Hughie Morrison) *prom: rdn over 3f out: wknd* **16/1**

00S/ **8** *24* **White Nile (IRE)**[1068] 4759 8-10-3 **80**................................(t) LucyKBarry 1
(Laura Young) *trckd ldrs: lost pl over 5f out: sn wknd and bhd* **22/1**

2m 32.07s (-1.13) **Going Correction** -0.25s/f (Firm) **8 Ran SP% 121.3**
Speed ratings (Par 107): **93,92,88,85,81 78,64,48**
CSF £40.88 CT £206.20 TOTE £6.60: £1.80, £1.60, £1.80; EX 44.30 Trifecta £174.80.
**Owner** Walker Graham **Bred** Russ Wake **Trained** Upper Helmsley, N Yorks

**FOCUS**
No great gallop, but the closers came to the fore and the front pair finished clear. The winner's best form this year.
T/Plt: £128.70 to a £1 stake. Pool: £97,327.47 - 551.65 winning units. T/Qpdt: £46.70 to a £1 stake. Pool: £6267.92 - 99.22 winning units. **Andrew Sheret**

4381 - 4382a (Foreign Racing) - See Raceform Interactive

# 4325 CURRAGH (R-H)
Saturday, July 1

**OFFICIAL GOING: Straight course - good to yielding; round course - good**

## 4383a DUBAI DUTY FREE MILLENNIUM MILLIONAIRE CELEBRATION STKS (LISTED RACE) 1m

**3:10** (3:11) 3-Y-0+
**£25,213** (£8,119; £3,846; £1,709; £854; £427)

RPR

**1** **True Valour (IRE)**[10] 3959 3-9-0 100.................................... ShaneFoley 5 110
(J P Murtagh, Ire) *hld up towards rr: 7th 1/2-way: gng wl bhd ldrs over 2f out: prog on far rail ent fnl f to ld 200yds out: sn rdn and kpt on wl cl home where drifted lft* **6/1**[3]

**2** *½* **Sea Wolf (IRE)**[34] 3114 5-9-9 108......................................... ColinKeane 4 111+
(G M Lyons, Ire) *hld up towards rr: 8th 1/2-way: gng wl on outer in st: pushed along to chal under 2f out: prog to go 3rd ent fnl f: kpt on wl u.p to go 2nd cl home: nrst fin* **2/1**[1]

**3** *nk* **Alexios Komnenos (IRE)**[345] 4574 3-9-0 106......................... ChrisHayes 7 108+
(J A Stack, Ire) *mid-div: 6th 1/2-way: pushed along to chal 2f out and kpt on wl to ld ent fnl f: hdd 200yds out and sn no ex u.p: sltly hmpd and dropped to 3rd cl home* **4/1**[2]

**4** *1 ½* **Flight Risk (IRE)**[16] 3765 6-10-0 113............................... KevinManning 1 112+
(J S Bolger, Ire) *s.i.s: hld up in rr sltly detached: t.k.h briefly after 3f: pushed along over 2f out and prog into 5th ent fnl f: n.m.r between horses wl ins fnl f: r.o into 4th cl home* **4/1**[2]

**5** *2 ¼* **Texas Rock (IRE)**[41] 2860 6-9-12 102.................................(p) WJLee 2 106
(M C Grassick, Ire) *sn led narrowly: rdn who pressed for ld 2f out: hdd over 1f out and sn no ex u.p: dropped to 5th cl home* **12/1**

**6** *½* **Foxtrot Charlie (USA)**[20] 3633 4-9-9 100.........................(t) PatSmullen 6 101
(D K Weld, Ire) *chsd ldrs in 4th: pushed along to chal over 2f out and prog to go 3rd: no ex u.p fr 1 1/2f out and dropped to 6th ins fnl f* **33/1**

**7** *1* **Mjjack (IRE)**[21] 3588 3-9-0 94................................... ColmO'Donoghue 9 96
(K R Burke) *mid-div: 5th 1/2-way: rdn over 2f out but sn no imp u.p and one pce* **10/1**

**8** *6* **Dragon Fei (IRE)**[7] 4112 7-9-4 94.................................... LeighRoche 3 79
(Dermot Anthony McLoughlin, Ire) *cl-up: sn trckd ldr in cl 2nd: pushed along to chal over 2f out but sn no imp and wknd* **14/1**

**9** *¾* **Misty Birnam (SAF)**[13] 3873 3-9-9 104.............................. WayneLordan 8 83
(J A Stack, Ire) *cl-up on outer: t.k.h early: settled in 3rd 1/2-way: pushed along over 2f out and sn no imp: wknd ent fnl f* **33/1**

1m 38.21s (-7.79) **Going Correction** -0.725s/f (Hard)
**WFA** 3 from 4yo+ 9lb **9 Ran SP% 117.0**
Speed ratings: **109,108,108,106,104 103,102,96,96**
CSF £18.65 TOTE £7.00: £2.10, £1.10, £1.70; DF 27.00 Trifecta £66.90.
**Owner** Qatar Racing Limited **Bred** P O'Rourke **Trained** Coolaghknock Glebe,Co Kildare

**FOCUS**
A good, tough performance from the winner so soon after running at Ascot and he really seems to be thriving on racing.

## 4385a DUBAI DUTY FREE TENNIS CHAMPIONSHIP SUMMER FILLIES H'CAP (PREMIER HANDICAP) 7f
**4:10** (4:11) 3-Y-0+

**£25,213** (£8,119; £3,846; £1,709; £854; £427)

RPR

1 **Asking (IRE)**10 3964 3-9-7 **95**.......(t) AnaO'Brien(3) 1 100+
(A P O'Brien, Ire) *chsd ldrs: tk clsr order in 4th 3f out: pushed along to chal 2f out and prog between horses to dispute ld jst ins fnl f: led 150yds out: kpt on wl* **8/1**

2 ½ **Honor Oak (IRE)**20 3630 5-8-11 **74**....... ChrisHayes 6 81
(T Hogan, Ire) *chsd ldrs: 5th 3f out: rdn to chal under 2f out and disp ld fr 1f out: hdd 150yds out and no ex cl home* **12/1**

3 1 **Duchess Of France (IRE)**20 3630 4-9-6 **83**.......(t) PatSmullen 11 87
(Adrian Paul Keatley, Ire) *sn led: rdn whn pressed for ld under 2f out: kpt on wl u.p but hdd 1f out: no ex cl home* **5/1**3

4 shd **Groundfrost (IRE)**23 3509 3-8-8 **84**.......(h1) DMSimmonson(5) 5 85+
(John James Feane, Ire) *bit slowly away: hld up in rr: pushed along over 2f out and sn n.m.r between horses: rdn ent fnl f and gd prog u.p to go 4th cl home: nrst fin* **12/1**

5 nk **Tobacco Bay (IRE)**20 3630 3-9-0 **85**....... SeamieHeffernan 2 85+
(J P Murtagh, Ire) *hld up towards rr: pushed along and prog to chse ldrs over 2f out: n.m.r bhd horses fr over 1f out: fnd room and r.o again ins fnl f* **9/2**2

6 ½ **Waitaki (IRE)**15 3801 4-8-7 **70**.......(b) LeighRoche 13 72
(D K Weld, Ire) *hld up towards rr: pushed along and prog to chse ldrs over 2f out: n.m.r bhd horses fr over 1f out: r.o ins fnl f* **16/1**

7 ½ **Betty Loch**6 4124 3-8-7 **78**....... ShaneFoley 12 75
(M Halford, Ire) *mid-div: 8th 3f out: sn rdn but no ex u.p fr over 1f out and sn one pce* **16/1**

8 nk **Music Box (IRE)**8 4062 3-9-1 **86**.......(h) RyanMoore 4 82
(A P O'Brien, Ire) *hld up towards rr: stl gng wl under 2f out but n.m.r bhd horses thrght fnl 2f: pushed along ins fnl f but short of room again and eased cl home* **7/2**1

9 ¾ **Ventura Blues (IRE)**17 3722 3-8-10 **81**....... KevinManning 10 75
(Richard Hannon) *hld up in rr: rdn 2f out and sme prog u.p but no ex ins fnl f and wknd* **8/1**

10 1 ¼ **Valentana (IRE)**23 3510 5-9-7 **91**....... NathanCrosse(7) 3 85
(W McCreery, Ire) *mid-div: pushed along over 2f out and sn no imp: wknd ent fnl f* **14/1**

11 9 ½ **Art Nouvelle (IRE)**13 3872 3-9-2 **87**.......(p) DonnachaO'Brien 9 52
(Joseph Patrick O'Brien, Ire) *chsd ldrs: 3rd 3f out: sn pushed along to chal: no ex u.p under 2f out and wknd* **40/1**

12 2 ½ **Truffles (IRE)**62 2188 4-9-8 **85**....... RonanWhelan 7 47
(Ms Sheila Lavery, Ire) *cl-up: 4th whn stmbld on far rail after 2f: sn lost pl and pushed along: dropped to rr 3f out and no imp* **16/1**

13 hd **Tinder (IRE)**21 3601 3-9-9 **94**....... ColmO'Donoghue 8 52
(Mrs John Harrington, Ire) *sn trckd ldr in 2nd: t.k.h early: pushed along over 2f out: hit by rivals whip 2f out: sn lost pl and short of room: eased ent fnl f* **25/1**

1m 23.95s (-6.85) **Going Correction** -0.725s/f (Hard)
**WFA** 3 from 4yo+ 8lb **13** Ran SP% **125.3**
Speed ratings: **110,109,108,108,107 107,106,106,105,104 93,90,90**
CSF £105.54 CT £557.08 TOTE £9.00: £2.30, £3.90, £2.10; DF 137.70 Trifecta £860.30.
**Owner** Mrs Magnier & M Tabor & D Smith & Mrs A M O'Brien **Bred** Whisperview Trading Ltd **Trained** Cashel, Co Tipperary

**FOCUS**
They went quite a good clip in this contest, anything that stays a mile had the edge and the winner could well be one to step back up into stakes company.

## 4386a GAIN RAILWAY STKS (GROUP 2) 6f
**4:40** (4:41) 2-Y-0

**£57,991** (£18,675; £8,846; £3,931; £1,965; £982) **Stalls** Centre

RPR

1 **Beckford**49 2634 2-9-3 0....... DeclanMcDonogh 9 113
(Gordon Elliott, Ire) *chsd ldrs: 3rd 1/2-way: gng wl 2f out and sn pushed along to ld narrowly 1f out: kpt on wl u.p ins fnl f and hld on wl cl home* **11/2**3

2 1 **Verbal Dexterity (IRE)**21 3598 2-9-3 0....... KevinManning 2 110
(J S Bolger, Ire) *disp ld: dropped to cl 2nd 1/2-way: led 2f out and sn rdn: kpt on strly u.p but hdd 1f out: no ex wl ins fnl f* **10/3**2

3 1 ¼ **Murillo (USA)**11 3925 2-9-3 0.......(t) RyanMoore 4 106
(A P O'Brien, Ire) *chsd ldrs: 4th 1/2-way: rdn over 2f out and kpt on wl u.p to go 3rd 1f out: no ex u.p cl home and hld* **6/4**1

4 2 ¼ **De Bruyne Horse**11 3925 2-9-3 0....... PatSmullen 5 99
(Richard Hannon) *disp ld: led narrowly 1/2-way: pushed along over 2f out and sn hdd: kpt on wl u.p but no ex in 4th fr 1f out* **7/1**

5 hd **Folk Tale (IRE)**21 3591 2-9-3 0.......(h1) ColmO'Donoghue 1 99
(Charlie Appleby) *hld up towards rr: 6th 1/2-way: rdn over 2f out and prog u.p to go 5th ent fnl f but sn no ex and one pce* **20/1**

6 hd **True Blue Moon (IRE)**9 3993 2-9-3 0....... DonnachaO'Brien 8 98
(Joseph Patrick O'Brien, Ire) *chsd ldrs: 5th 1/2-way: rdn over 2f out and hung rt u.p ent fnl f: sn no ex and one pce* **9/1**

7 shd **Commander Grigio (IRE)**34 3107 2-9-3 0....... ChrisHayes 3 98
(J A Stack, Ire) *towards rr: pushed along over 2f out and taken to outer ent fnl f: kpt on same pce u.p but nvr nr to chal* **7/1**

8 9 ½ **Devastating Power (IRE)**19 3675 2-9-3 0....... RonanWhelan 6 69
(Brendan W Duke, Ire) *in rr: rdn over 2f out and no imp: nvr in contention* **200/1**

1m 11.71s (-3.79) **Going Correction** -0.475s/f (Firm) **8** Ran SP% **118.7**
Speed ratings: **106,104,103,100,99 99,99,86**
CSF £25.21 TOTE £6.90: £1.90, £1.30, £1.10; DF 27.10 Trifecta £85.80.
**Owner** Newtown Anner Stud Farm Ltd **Bred** Joyce Wallsgrove **Trained** Longwood, Co Meath

**FOCUS**
The deepest renewal of this contest for a number of years, the winner could be capable of something very significant. The third and fourth backed up their Coventry form.

## 4387a DUBAI DUTY FREE IRISH DERBY (GROUP 1) (ENTIRE COLTS & FILLIES) 1m 4f
**5:20** (5:20) 3-Y-0

**£730,769** (£243,589; £115,384; £51,282; £25,641; £12,820)

RPR

1 **Capri (IRE)**28 3322 3-9-0 113....... SeamieHeffernan 1 120
(A P O'Brien, Ire) *cl-up: sn trckd clr ldr in 2nd: pushed along over 2f out and sn led: kpt on strly u.p whn chal ent fnl f: reduced advantage wl ins fnl f but hld on wl* **6/1**3

2 nk **Cracksman**28 3322 3-9-0 117....... PatSmullen 7 120+
(John Gosden) *hld up in mid-div: 6th 1/2-way: pushed along over 2f out and taken to outer in st: rdn and kpt on wl u.p: edgd rt ins fnl f: wnt 2nd cl home* **3/1**2

3 shd **Wings Of Eagles (FR)**28 3322 3-9-0 120....... RyanMoore 3 119
(A P O'Brien, Ire) *hld up in mid-div: 5th 1/2-way: pushed along 3f out and prog to chse wnr ent fnl f: kpt on wl u.p but no ex cl home and hld* **2/1**1

4 1 ½ **Waldgeist**27 3368 3-9-0 117....... Pierre-CharlesBoudot 8 117
(A Fabre, France) *hld up in rr: 8th 1/2-way: gng wl bhd ldrs over 2f out: pushed along between horses under 2f out and prog to go 4th ent fnl f: short of room sltly ins fnl f but sn no ex and hld in 4th* **3/1**2

5 2 ¼ **Douglas Macarthur (IRE)**28 3322 3-9-0 111....... DonnachaO'Brien 6 113
(A P O'Brien, Ire) *chsd ldrs in 3rd: pushed along 3f out and tk clsr order in 2nd 2f out: no ex u.p ent fnl f and dropped to 5th* **12/1**

6 3 **The Taj Mahal (IRE)**9 3994 3-9-0 113.......(b) WayneLordan 5 109
(A P O'Brien, Ire) *chsd ldrs in 4th: rdn over 2f out but sn no ex u.p and one pce fr over 1f out* **20/1**

7 3 ½ **Dubai Sand (IRE)**55 2442 3-9-0 104.......(p1) KevinManning 9 103
(J S Bolger, Ire) *hld up in rr: 9th 1/2-way: rdn 3f out and sn no imp: wnt modest 6th ins fnl f but nvr in contention* **100/1**

8 1 **The Anvil (IRE)**28 3322 3-9-0 108....... AnaO'Brien 2 101
(A P O'Brien, Ire) *sn led and wnt clr: 3 l clr 1/2-way: pushed along 3f out: hdd 2f out and no ex u.p: wknd* **66/1**

9 1 ½ **Grandee (IRE)**23 3511 3-9-0 102....... ColmO'Donoghue 4 99
(Mrs John Harrington, Ire) *cl-up: sn settled off str pce in 6th: rdn over 2f out and no imp u.p: wknd* **33/1**

2m 35.45s (-3.05) **Going Correction** +0.10s/f (Good) **9** Ran SP% **115.5**
Speed ratings: **114,113,113,112,111 109,106,106,105**
CSF £23.81 CT £48.57 TOTE £6.60: £1.70, £1.20, £1.10; DF 23.70 Trifecta £69.60.
**Owner** Derrick Smith & Mrs John Magnier & Michael Tabor **Bred** Lynch Bages Ltd & Camas Park Stud **Trained** Cashel, Co Tipperary

**FOCUS**
A tenacious performance from the winner, who appeared to appreciate the demands of the Curragh more than the undulations of Epsom. Although any Classic winner deserves respect and can only beat the best of his generation, perhaps it's too early to say that this current crop of 3yos are at an outstanding standard. The form ties into Epsom and Chantilly, with the level set around the 2nd/4th/5th/7th.

4384 - 4388a (Foreign Racing) - See Raceform Interactive

# 4288 DEAUVILLE (R-H)
Saturday, July 1

**OFFICIAL GOING: Turf: soft; polytrack: standard**

## 4389a PRIX DE CROISSANVILLE (CLAIMER) (2YO) (TURF) 6f
**11:20** 2-Y-0 **£9,829** (£3,931; £2,948; £1,965; £982)

RPR

1 **Uchronique (FR)**16 2-9-1 0....... AlexisBadel 8 71
(M Boutin, France) **119/10**

2 ¾ **Attilia (IRE)**18 2-8-8 0....... CristianDemuro 6 62
(A Giorgi, Italy) **17/2**

3 2 ½ **Le Gitan (FR)**25 3444 2-9-1 0....... ChristopheSoumillon 7 61
(C Boutin, France) **19/5**3

4 snk **Shesgotthelot**32 3174 2-9-1 0....... TonyPiccone 2 61
(J S Moore) *sn chsng ldrs: rdn whn outpcd by ldng pair under 2f out: kpt on u.p fnl f* **5/2**1

5 1 ¼ **Palya (FR)**5 4166 2-9-5 0.......(p) AntoineHamelin 5 61
(Matthieu Palussiere, France) **17/5**2

6 shd **Fancy Dresser (FR)**5 4166 2-9-5 0.......(b) ClementLecoeuvre(3) 4 64
(Matthieu Palussiere, France) **26/5**

7 ¾ **Freddo Du Desert (FR)**16 2-9-1 0.......(p) ThibaultSpeicher 3 55
(Louis Baudron, France) **178/10**

8 2 ½ **Reboot (IRE)**25 3444 2-8-11 0....... EddyHardouin 1 43
(Matthieu Palussiere, France) **154/10**

1m 13.51s (2.51) **8** Ran SP% **118.0**
PARI-MUTUEL (all including 1 euro stake): WIN 12.90; PLACE 2.80, 3.00, 2.10; DF 34.50; SF 85.00.
**Owner** Ecurie Rogier **Bred** M Boutin & Mme C Sineux **Trained** France

## 4390a PRIX DE LA PORTE MAILLOT (GROUP 3) (3YO+) (STRAIGHT) (TURF) 7f
**12:50** 3-Y-0+ **£34,188** (£13,675; £10,256; £6,837; £3,418)

RPR

1 **Inns Of Court (IRE)**28 3354 3-8-11 0....... MickaelBarzalona 2 117+
(A Fabre, France) *slt fly jump leaving stalls: sn trckd ldr: drvn and qcknd to ld over 1f out: sn rdn: r.o fnl f: won a shade cosily* **1/2**1

2 ¾ **African Ride**48 2666 3-8-8 0....... MaximeGuyon 1 112
(C Laffon-Parias, France) *hld up in fnl pair: drvn to cl on outer over 1 1/2f out: rdn to chal 1f out: styd on u.p fnl f: a hld by wnr* **41/10**2

3 2 **Aladdine**27 3370 3-8-8 0....... AurelienLemaitre 5 107
(F Head, France) *led: hdd after 1f: remained cl up: 4th and rdn appr fnl f: kpt on but nt pce to trble front two* **42/10**3

4 2 **Johnny Barnes (IRE)**40 2907 5-9-2 0....... ChristopheSoumillon 3 104
(John Gosden) *chsd ldr: led after 1f: kicked for home ins fnl 1 1/2f: rdn and hdd over 1f out: grad lft bhd fnl f* **96/10**

5 8 **Princess Asta (FR)**90 4-9-2 0.......(b) OlivierPeslier 4 83
(Mario Hofer, Germany) *w.w in rr: clsd on outer to chse ldng pair 2 1/2f out: sn drvn and nt qckn: dropped away fnl 1 1/2f* **168/10**

1m 24.26s (-4.04)
**WFA** 3 from 4yo+ 8lb **5** Ran SP% **120.6**
PARI-MUTUEL (all including 1 euro stake): WIN 1.50; PLACE 1.10, 1.10; SF 3.10.

**Owner** Godolphin SNC **Bred** Darley **Trained** Chantilly, France

## 4391a PRIX DU BOIS (GROUP 3) (2YO) (TURF) 5f
1:50 2-Y-O £34,188 (£13,675; £10,256; £6,837; £3,418)

RPR

1 **Zonza (FR)**[45] 2-8-10 0 CristianDemuro 2 102
(D Guillemin, France) *settled bhd front rnk between horses: angled out and hdwy 2f out: pushed along and led appr 1f out: rdn ins fnl f: r.o: readily* **53/10**

2 3/4 **Elizabeth Darcy (IRE)**[11] 3929 2-8-11 0 ow1 (b) OlivierPeslier 6 101
(Wesley A Ward, U.S.A) *cl up on outer: drvn to chal wl over 1f out: r.o fnl f: a hld by wnr* **29/10**[2]

3 1 **Ardenode (IRE)**[21] 3611 2-9-0 0 FabriceVeron 7 100
(E J O'Neill, France) *w.w bhd front rnk on outer: drvn in pursuit of ldrs over 1f out: styd on fnl f: nt pce to trble first two* **17/5**[3]

4 1 1/2 **Hergame**[34] 2-8-10 0 MaximeGuyon 3 91
(F Head, France) *wnt lft s: chsd ldr: drvn 2f out but nt qckn: n.m.r over 1f out: nt gaining whn impeded ins fnl f: kpt on at same pce* **6/4**[1]

5 shd **Debutante's Ball (IRE)**[10] 3960 2-8-10 0 TonyPiccone 5 90
(J S Moore) *racd in rr: outpcd and niggled along over 2f out: adrift and rdn over 1 1/2f out: styd on ins fnl f: nvr trbld ldrs* **29/1**

6 1 1/4 **Vik The Billy**[41] 2-8-10 0 FedericoBossa 4 86
(Sergio Dettori, Italy) *broke wl and led: qckly swtchd ins to rail: hdd appr 1f out: grad lft bhd* **142/10**

7 nk **Yori (IRE)**[34] 2-8-10 0 IoritzMendizabal 1 85
(P Vovcenko, Germany) *chsd ldr on inner: outpcd and rdn wl over 1 1/2f out: dropped away ins fnl f* **189/10**

58.56s (1.06) 7 Ran SP% 119.2
PARI-MUTUEL (all including 1 euro stake): WIN 6.30; PLACE 2.80, 2.30; SF 31.70.
**Owner** Alain Jathiere **Bred** H Rousseau & J-P Dubois **Trained** France

**FOCUS**
The form is rated in line with the race average.

# HAMBURG (R-H)
Saturday, July 1

**OFFICIAL GOING: Turf: heavy**

## 4392a PFERDEWETTEN.DE - GROSSER HANSA-PREIS (GROUP 2) (3YO+) (TURF) 1m 4f
3:25 3-Y-O+ £34,188 (£13,247; £6,837; £3,418; £2,136)

RPR

1 **Dschingis Secret (GER)**[34] 3116 4-9-6 0 MartinSeidl 3 118
(Markus Klug, Germany) *trckd ldr on outer: led gng strly over 2f out: drifted lft into centre of crse 1 1/2f out: rdn appr fnl f and edgd rt: drvn clr* **16/5**[3]

2 3 3/4 **Iquitos (GER)**[34] 3116 5-9-6 0 AndraschStarke 5 112
(H-J Groschel, Germany) *settled in last: began to cl on outer 2 1/2f out: chsd ldr 1 1/2f out: kpt on fnl f: no ch w wnr* **11/10**[1]

3 2 1/2 **Nepal (GER)**[55] 2450 4-9-3 0 MichaelCadeddu 2 105
(Dr A Bolte, Germany) *w.w bhd ldrs: rdn and styd on along rail over 1 1/2f out: one pce u.p fnl f* **32/5**

4 2 1/4 **Guignol (GER)**[34] 3116 5-9-6 0 FilipMinarik 6 104
(Jean-Pierre Carvalho, Germany) *sn led and swtchd ins to rail: drvn and hdd appr 2f out: kpt on at one pce* **2/1**[2]

5 44 **Space Cowboy (GER)**[41] 5-9-6 0 DanielePorcu 1 34
(Markus Klug, Germany) *racd keenly: restrained bhd ldrs: rdn and no imp over 3f out: lost tch 2f out: eased fnl f* **78/10**

2m 38.38s (3.83)
**WFA** 3 from 4yo+ 12lb 5 Ran SP% 129.6
PARI-MUTUEL (all including 10 euro stake): WIN 42 PLACE: 17, 14; SF: 89.
**Owner** Horst Pudwill **Bred** Gestut Park Wiedingen **Trained** Germany

## 4393a PREIS DER MITGLIEDER DES HAMBURGER RENN-CLUBS (GROUP 3) (3YO FILLIES) (TURF) 1m 3f
4:35 3-Y-O £27,350 (£10,256; £5,128; £2,564; £1,709)

RPR

1 **Lacazar (GER)**[26] 3-9-2 0 AndraschStarke 7 104
(P Schiergen, Germany) *settled cl up on outer: rdn and chsd ldr towards stands' side ins last 2f: str run fr over 1f out: led fnl 100yds: styd on wl* **47/10**[2]

2 1 1/2 **Diana Storm (GER)**[42] 3-9-2 0 JozefBojko 1 101
(Waldemar Hickst, Germany) *w.w cl up on inner: drvn to chal wl over 1f out: led ins fnl f: hdd 100yds out: no ex* **17/2**

3 2 1/4 **Navaro Girl (IRE)**[76] 3-9-2 0 DanielePorcu 11 97
(P Schiergen, Germany) *w.w in rr: hdwy over 1 1/2f out: styd on fnl f: nvr nrr* **188/10**

4 3 1/4 **Alicante (GER)**[42] 3-9-2 0 MartinSeidl 9 91
(Markus Klug, Germany) *towards rr and ct out wd first bnd: sn chsng ldr on outer: cl 4th and drvn wl over 1f out: one pce fnl f* **9/1**

5 3/4 **Well Spoken (GER)**[27] 3371 3-9-2 0 AndreasHelfenbein 8 90
(Markus Klug, Germany) *sn led and cut ins to rail: 4l clr bef 1/2-way: 2l ld and rdn ins fnl 2f: hdd ins fnl f: wknd* **6/5**[1]

6 3 **Gondora (GER)**[27] 3371 3-9-2 0 BauyrzhanMurzabayev 4 84
(R Dzubasz, Germany) *hmpd s: towards rr on inner: drvn to hold pl over 3f out: hrd rdn and no imp wl over 1 1/2f out: nvr in contention* **223/10**

7 9 1/2 **Gaea (GER)** 3-9-2 0 FilipMinarik 6 67
(Jean-Pierre Carvalho, Germany) *hld up towards rr: no imp whn rdn 2 1/2f out: wl bhd fr under 2f out* **76/10**

8 hd **Megera (FR)**[42] 3-9-2 0 EduardoPedroza 3 67
(A Wohler, Germany) *wnt sltly rt s and collided w rival: racd in midfield: rdn and btn ins fnl 2f* **59/10**[3]

9 9 1/2 **Gen Chi (GER)** 3-9-2 0 MichaelCadeddu 10 50
(P Vovcenko, Germany) *hld up in fnl pair: rdn and no imp fr 3f out: lost tch fnl 2f* **22/1**

10 9 1/2 **Rosamunde (FR)**[35] 3-9-2 0 AlexanderPietsch 2 33
(Andreas Suborics, Germany) *wnt lft s and collided w rival: sn rcvrd to chse ldr: wknd ins fnl 2f* **133/10**

2m 29.73s (5.03) 10 Ran SP% 130.3
PARI-MUTUEL (all including 10 euro stake): WIN 57 PLACE: 25, 29, 45; SF: 427.
**Owner** Gestut Haus Zoppenbroich **Bred** Frau Ina Emma Zimmermann **Trained** Germany

4394 - 4406a (Foreign Racing) - See Raceform Interactive

# 4367 WINDSOR (R-H)
Sunday, July 2

**OFFICIAL GOING: Good**
Wind: Fresh, half behind Weather: Fine, warm

## 4407 BERKS, BUCKS & OXON MASONIC 300YR CELEBRATION H'CAP 6f 12y
2:10 (2:11) (Class 3) (0-95,97) 3-Y-O £7,439 (£2,213; £1,106; £553) Stalls Low

Form RPR

1 1 **Lahore (USA)**[64] 2139 3-8-11 83 SilvestreDeSousa 3 91+
(Roger Varian) *t.k.h: hld up bhd ldrs: clsd against rail to take 2nd wl over 1f out: drvn to chal fnl f: led last 100yds* **13/8**[1]

1130 2 1/2 **Quench Dolly**[15] 3835 3-9-2 93 GeorgeBuckell(5) 1 98
(John Gallagher) *led: drifted off rail over 2f out: hrd pressed over 1f out: kpt on wl but hdd and hld last 100yds* **11/2**

312- 3 1/2 **Nobly Born**[352] 4352 3-9-8 97 KieranShoemark(3) 4 101+
(John Gosden) *settled in last: effrt whn nt clr run jst over 2f out and swtchd rt: styd on to take 3rd fnl f: fin wl but too late to chal* **5/1**

5333 4 2 1/4 **High Acclaim (USA)**[8] 4100 3-9-1 87 (p) JamesDoyle 2 84
(Roger Teal) *pressed ldr: rdn over 2f out: lost 2nd and fdd wl over 1f out* **4/1**[2]

21- 5 1 3/4 **Dark Power (IRE)**[270] 7072 3-8-6 78 SamHitchcott 5 69
(Clive Cox) *chsd ldng pair on outer: rdn over 2f out: fdd over 1f out* **9/2**[3]

1m 11.94s (-1.06) **Going Correction** -0.075s/f (Good) 5 Ran SP% 108.3
Speed ratings (Par 104): **104,103,102,99,97**
CSF £10.38 TOTE £1.90: £1.20, £3.10; EX 11.00 Trifecta £40.40.
**Owner** Prince A A Faisal **Bred** Nawara Stud Company Ltd **Trained** Newmarket, Suffolk

**FOCUS**
The rail was moved out 12yds from the stands' side inner position from 6f to Winning Post. A glorious sunny day and conditions were drying all the time. Three of the five runners in this opener are lightly-raced and open to improvement, not least the winner who ultimately made it 2-2 a shade cosily.

## 4408 MASONIC CHARITABLE FOUNDATION H'CAP 1m 2f
2:40 (2:42) (Class 3) (0-90,90) 3-Y-O £7,762 (£2,310; £1,154; £577) Stalls Centre

Form RPR

-016 1 **Mister Blue Sky (IRE)**[29] 3318 3-8-3 77 MitchGodwin(5) 5 82
(Sylvester Kirk) *sn hld up and in 5th bef 1/2-way: prog against rail over 2f out: edgd lft then impeded over 1f out and swtchd: drvn and r.o to ld nr fin* **9/2**[3]

0-1 2 hd **Valcartier (IRE)**[81] 1730 3-9-7 90 JamesDoyle 4 94
(John Gosden) *pressed ldr: led 3f out: rdn 2f out: edgd rt wl over 1f out: kpt on u.p but hdd nr fin* **6/5**[1]

1-56 3 1/2 **Count Calabash (IRE)**[43] 2824 3-9-5 88 CharlesBishop 2 91
(Eve Johnson Houghton) *chsd ldng pair to 1/2-way: rdn 3f out: cl enough over 1f out: drvn and styd on but a hld* **10/3**[2]

-220 4 1/2 **War At Sea (IRE)**[16] 3779 3-8-9 78 (h[1]) FranBerry 6 80
(David Simcock) *stdd s: hld up in last: shkn up and prog on outer over 2f out: cl enough over 1f out: nt qckn ins fnl f* **20/1**

3102 5 3/4 **Hajaj (IRE)**[15] 3838 3-8-12 81 StevieDonohoe 3 82
(Charlie Fellowes) *dwlt: sn rcvrd: chsd ldng pair 1/2-way: shkn up wl over 2f out: styd pressing ldrs tl lost pl 1f out: one pce after* **6/1**

1-5 6 18 **Kitten's Johnstown (USA)**[73] 1912 3-9-1 84 KevinStott 1 49
(Kevin Ryan) *led to 3f out: wknd 2f out: t.o* **20/1**

2m 9.76s (1.06) **Going Correction** -0.025s/f (Good) 6 Ran SP% 110.5
Speed ratings (Par 104): **94,93,93,93,92 78**
CSF £10.04 TOTE £5.50: £2.40, £1.40; EX 13.70 Trifecta £42.00.
**Owner** Deauville Daze Partnership 1 **Bred** Shadwell Estate Company Limited **Trained** Upper Lambourn, Berks

■ Stewards' Enquiry : Mitch Godwin two-day ban; used whip above the permitted level (19th-20th July) caution; careless riding

**FOCUS**
A competitive little handicap in which only two lengths separated the first five home at the line. The pace looked sound and the form looks solid enough.

## 4409 BERKS, BUCKS & OXON ROYAL ARCH FREEMASONS' MAIDEN STKS 1m 31y
3:10 (3:13) (Class 4) 3-5-Y-O £6,145 (£1,828; £913; £456) Stalls Low

Form RPR

3- 1 **Whispering Bell (IRE)**[277] 6874 3-8-11 0 (h[1]) KieranShoemark(3) 2 90
(John Gosden) *free to post: t.k.h: mde all: skipped clr 3f out: drvn over 1f out: kpt on wl fnl f* **7/4**[1]

25 2 4 1/2 **Euqranian (USA)**[29] 3329 3-9-0 0 (h) JamesDoyle 7 79
(Jeremy Noseda) *trckd ldrs: shkn up to go 2nd 2f out: drew clr of rest but no imp on wnr fnl f* **11/4**[2]

3 7 **Graphite (IRE)** 3-9-5 0 FranBerry 12 68
(David Simcock) *in tch: pushed along over 3f out: sn outpcd: kpt on to take 3rd over 1f out: no ch* **12/1**

0 4 5 **Good Business (IRE)**[44] 2798 3-9-0 0 LukeMorris 4 51
(Jeremy Noseda) *chsd ldrs: outpcd and rdn 3f out: one pce fnl 2f and tk modest 4th* **50/1**

4 5 2 1/2 **Gold Dust**[29] 3329 3-8-11 0 HectorCrouch(3) 6 45
(Clive Cox) *wl in tch: shkn up and outpcd 3f out: no ch fnl 2f* **5/1**[3]

6 6 4 **Mark Of Excellence (IRE)**[41] 2895 3-9-5 0 (p[1]) SilvestreDeSousa 5 41
(Saeed bin Suroor) *trckd wnr: outpcd 3f out and shkn up: lost 2nd and wknd 2f out* **5/1**[3]

00 7 6 **Queen Beatrice**[21] 3615 3-9-0 0 MartinDwyer 8 22
(William Muir) *wl in rr: lft bhd fr 4f out and pushed along: no ch after* **66/1**

0-0 8 7 **Millie May**[19] 3691 3-9-0 0 KieranO'Neill 1
(Jimmy Fox) *a towards rr: urged along 4f out: sn bhd* **125/1**

9 7 **Acker Bilk (IRE)** 3-9-5 0 TomQueally 9
(David Lanigan) *s.i.s: a wl bhd* **25/1**

0- 10 30 **Here I Go Again (IRE)**[265] 7225 3-8-12 0 (h[1]) JacobMitchell(7) 10
(Christine Dunnett) *uns rdr bef gng in stall: s.i.s: racd wd in rr: wknd 4f out: t.o* **125/1**

1m 43.73s (-0.97) **Going Correction** -0.025s/f (Good)
**WFA** 3 from 4yo 9lb 10 Ran SP% 112.9
Speed ratings (Par 105): **103,98,91,86,84 80,74,67,60,30**
CSF £6.24 TOTE £2.70: £1.20, £1.30, £2.80; EX 7.40 Trifecta £38.60.
**Owner** George Strawbridge **Bred** Epona Bloodstock Ltd **Trained** Newmarket, Suffolk
■ Discovered was withdrawn. Price at time of withdrawal 16-1. Rule 4 does not apply.

**FOCUS**
Probably not much depth to this maiden and they finished well strung out. Out of interest, the first three home were all sired by Galileo.

## 4410 GRAND MASTER'S GOLDEN JUBILEE H'CAP 1m 31y
**3:40** (3:40) (Class 2) (0-105,100) 3-Y-O+ **£12,938** (£3,850; £1,924; £962) **Stalls** Low

Form RPR
10-0 **1** **Murad Khan (FR)**[45] 2767 4-9-12 **98**........................(h[1]) JamesDoyle 2 107+
(Hugo Palmer) *trckd ldng pair: rdn over 2f out: clsd over 1f out: led ins fnl f: drvn out* **8/1**
222- **2** 1 ½ **Easy Tiger**[373] 3622 5-8-10 **82**........................ MartinDwyer 4 87
(Malcolm Saunders) *trckd ldr: shkn up to ld wl over 1f out: edgd lft and hdd ins fnl f: no ex* **25/1**
1-P2 **3** ¾ **Chelsea Lad (IRE)**[45] 2767 4-9-12 **98**........................(h[1]) SeanLevey 5 101
(Martyn Meade) *trckd ldrs: rdn over 2f out: kpt on to take 3rd fnl f: nvr pce to chal* **9/4**[1]
0054 **4** ½ **General Macarthur (USA)**[15] 3837 4-9-7 **93**..............(t) LukeMorris 8 95+
(David Simcock) *hld up in last trio: rdn over 2f out: prog over 1f out: styd on u.p to press for 3rd nr fin* **20/1**
4-04 **5** ½ **Storm Ahead (IRE)**[44] 2799 4-8-11 **90**.................. TylerSaunders[(7)] 10 91
(Marcus Tregoning) *in tch in midfield: effrt on outer over 2f out: drvn and ch of a pl 1f out: one pce* **5/1**[2]
5421 **6** ½ **Medburn Dream**[8] 4091 4-9-7 **93**........................ SilvestreDeSousa 1 92
(Paul Henderson) *led: rdn over 2f out: hdd wl over 1f out: wknd fnl f* **5/1**[2]
6433 **7** *hd* **Georgian Bay (IRE)**[4] 4207 7-8-9 **84**..................(v) JordanVaughan[(3)] 7 83
(K R Burke) *hld up in last trio: effrt on wd outside over 2f out: rdn and no rspnse wl over 1f out: one pce after* **10/1**
-300 **8** 3 **Doncha (IRE)**[45] 2767 6-9-13 **99**........................ PatCosgrave 3 91
(Robert Eddery) *s.i.s: sn in midfield: rdn and no prog over 2f out: n.d after* **11/2**[3]
012- **9** 2 **Lady Perignon**[291] 6483 4-8-9 **81** oh1........................ DavidProbert 9 68
(Andrew Balding) *t.k.h: trckd ldng trio: rdn over 2f out: wknd over 1f out* **25/1**
0000 **10** 17 **Dark Emerald (IRE)**[14] 3867 7-10-0 **100**........................(t) FranBerry 6 48
(Brendan Powell) *snatched up sn after s: a in last trio: shkn up and no prog over 2f out: wknd and eased over 1f out: t.o* **33/1**

1m 44.01s (-0.69) **Going Correction** -0.025s/f (Good) **10** Ran SP% **115.1**
Speed ratings (Par 109): **102,100,99,99,98 98,98,95,93,76**
CSF £189.42 CT £596.54 TOTE £10.80: £3.40, £3.90, £1.40; EX 131.00 Trifecta £775.00.
**Owner** V I Araci **Bred** S C E A Haras De Manneville **Trained** Newmarket, Suffolk

**FOCUS**
Competitive enough despite the fact that the topweight was rated 5lb below the ceiling mark for the grade. The gallop looked fairly even and no reason why this form shouldn't hold up.

## 4411 UNITED GRAND LODGE OF ENGLAND TERCENTENARY SPRINT H'CAP 6f 12y
**4:15** (4:16) (Class 2) (0-105,98) 3-Y-O+
**£11,827** (£3,541; £1,770; £885; £442; £222) **Stalls** Low

Form RPR
1-02 **1** **Upstaging**[27] 3410 5-9-10 **94**........................(p) LukeMorris 3 102
(Paul Cole) *chsd ldrs: drvn 2f out: clsd and c between rivals fnl f: edgd lft but led last 75yds* **14/1**
1404 **2** ½ **Englishman**[17] 3757 7-8-12 **82**........................ MartinDwyer 8 88
(Milton Bradley) *chsd ldrs: rdn 2f out: clsd on outer 1f out: styd on to take 2nd last strides* **25/1**
2550 **3** *hd* **Stellarta**[14] 3867 6-9-7 **91**........................ TomMarquand 9 97
(Michael Blanshard) *in tch: rdn sn after 1/2-way: prog on outer 2f out: drvn and styd on ins fnl f to take 3rd last stride* **20/1**
1423 **4** *shd* **Ice Age (IRE)**[27] 3410 4-9-2 **86**........................ SilvestreDeSousa 6 91
(Eve Johnson Houghton) *mde most: rdn 2f out: kpt on u.p but hdd last lost pls last 75yds* **5/2**[1]
4325 **5** *shd* **Dark Shot**[14] 3867 4-9-6 **90**........................ DavidProbert 2 95
(Andrew Balding) *w ldr and racd against rail: shkn up over 1f out and nt qckn: lost pls last 75yds* **5/1**[2]
6212 **6** *nk* **Stake Acclaim (IRE)**[21] 3625 5-10-0 **98**........................ RobertWinston 14 102
(Dean Ivory) *pressed ldrs: rdn 2f out: stl chalng ins fnl f: jst hld whn carried lft last 75yds* **6/1**
0-03 **7** ½ **Lincoln (IRE)**[46] 2736 6-9-9 **93**........................ GrahamLee 10 96+
(Mick Channon) *stdd s: hld up in last trio: stdy prog nr side over 1f out: trying to cl on ldrs whn nt clr run ins fnl f: nt rcvr* **9/1**
130/ **8** 1 ¼ **Secondo (FR)**[328] 7-9-3 **87**........................ FranBerry 13 89+
(Joseph Tuite) *stdd s: hld up in last: prog over 1f out: drvn and styng on w ch of a pl whn hmpd 50yds out: nt rcvr* **66/1**
0062 **9** 1 ¼ **Dougan**[14] 3861 5-9-5 **94**........................ CliffordLee[(5)] 11 89
(David Evans) *sn in rr: shkn up on outer 2f out: nvr pce to threaten* **11/2**[3]
0-10 **10** 1 ¾ **Blaine**[29] 3324 7-10-0 **98**........................(b) JamesDoyle 12 87
(Brian Barr) *in tch on outer: rdn 2f out: wknd jst over 1f out* **20/1**
5206 **11** *nk* **Kadrizzi (FR)**[37] 3034 4-9-11 **95**........................(p) PatCosgrave 4 83
(Dean Ivory) *in tch in midfield: u.p sn after 1/2-way: wknd over 1f out* **12/1**
6620 **12** *hd* **Iseemist (IRE)**[14] 3861 6-9-6 **90**........................ FergusSweeney 7 77
(John Gallagher) *w ldrs to 2f out: wknd sn after* **33/1**
10-0 **13** 6 **New Bidder**[22] 3593 6-9-12 **96**........................(b) JosephineGordon 5 64
(David Barron) *moved poorly to post: nvr beyond midfield: wknd 2f out* **40/1**

1m 11.94s (-1.06) **Going Correction** -0.075s/f (Good) **13** Ran SP% **119.5**
Speed ratings (Par 109): **104,103,103,102,102 102,101,100,98,96 95,95,87**
CSF £330.32 CT £6986.83 TOTE £15.00: £4.10, £9.40, £5.30; EX 545.70 Trifecta £9482.90.
**Owner** H R H Sultan Ahmad Shah **Bred** Glebe Stud **Trained** Whatcombe, Oxon

**FOCUS**
An ultra-competitive sprint handicap despite nothing being within 7lb of the ceiling rating for the grade. There was only around a length covering the first six home.

## 4412 ROYAL ARCH FREEMASONS' CELEBRATION H'CAP 5f 21y
**4:45** (4:45) (Class 3) (0-95,95) 3-Y-O **£7,762** (£2,310; £1,154; £577) **Stalls** Low

Form RPR
43 **1** **Tahoo (IRE)**[20] 3672 3-8-6 **80**........................ SilvestreDeSousa 2 87
(K R Burke) *fast away: mde all: against rail: drvn jst over 1f out: kpt on wl fnl f* **3/1**[2]
2123 **2** ½ **Major Jumbo**[44] 2806 3-8-10 **89**........................ LewisEdmunds[(5)] 3 94
(Kevin Ryan) *pressed wnr: rdn over 1f out: stl chalng ins fnl f: no ex last 100yds* **9/4**[1]
1404 **3** 4 ½ **Just An Idea (IRE)**[43] 2823 3-8-13 **87**........................ JosephineGordon 1 76
(Harry Dunlop) *chsd ldng pair: rdn and no imp over 1f out: fdd fnl f* **8/1**
3550 **4** 2 ¼ **Tomily (IRE)**[15] 3844 3-9-7 **95**........................ SeanLevey 5 76
(Richard Hannon) *chsd ldng pair: rdn 1/2-way: no imp over 1f out: wknd fnl f* **7/2**[3]
1521 **5** ½ **Coolfitch (IRE)**[8] 4079 3-9-0 **91**........................ JoshDoyle[(3)] 4 70+
(David O'Meara) *rel to r and lft 10 l: t.k.h and in tch after 2f: no prog 2f out: fdd* **7/2**[3]

59.4s (-0.90) **Going Correction** -0.075s/f (Good) **5** Ran SP% **111.3**
Speed ratings (Par 104): **104,103,96,92,91**
CSF £10.27 TOTE £4.00: £2.00, £1.40; EX 11.00 Trifecta £42.70.
**Owner** Nick Bradley Racing 19 **Bred** Tally-Ho Stud **Trained** Middleham Moor, N Yorks

**FOCUS**
This looked a good quality sprint on paper but it became significantly weaker when Coolfitch, one of the key form contenders, blew the start and a couple of the others didn't run to anything like their best, so likely this isn't strong form for the grade.

## 4413 MARK MASONS CELEBRATION H'CAP 1m 3f 99y
**5:20** (5:23) (Class 4) (0-80,82) 4-Y-O+ **£6,145** (£1,828; £913; £456) **Stalls** Centre

Form RPR
0061 **1** **C'Est No Mour (GER)**[19] 3683 4-9-1 **73**........................ TomMarquand 1 83+
(Peter Hedger) *hld up off the pce in rr: prog over 3f out: rdn to cl 2f out: drvn to ld 1f out: styd on* **5/1**[2]
60-0 **2** 1 ½ **Zambeasy**[25] 3458 6-9-6 **78**........................ GrahamLee 8 85
(Philip Hide) *trckd ldrs: clsd over 3f out: rdn to chal over 2f out: nt go by ldr u.p: chsd wnr fnl f but wandered and sn hld* **13/2**[3]
0-40 **3** 2 ½ **Ravenous**[27] 3409 6-9-6 **78**........................ KieranO'Neill 9 81
(Luke Dace) *trckd ldrs: prog to go 2nd over 3f out: rdn to ld over 2f out: hdd and one pce 1f out* **12/1**
033 **4** *nk* **Red Rannagh (IRE)**[13] 3005 4-9-10 **82**........................ FergusSweeney 10 84
(David Simcock) *s.s: wl bhd in last early: effrt 4f out: rdn over 2f out: kpt on to take 4th fnl f: nrst fin* **8/1**
3653 **5** 6 **Cordite (IRE)**[21] 3616 6-8-12 **70**........................ PatCosgrave 5 62
(Jim Boyle) *t.k.h: led after 2f: hdd over 2f out: sn wknd* **4/1**[1]
0262 **6** *nk* **Clovelly Bay (IRE)**[86] 1602 6-8-11 **76**........................ TylerSaunders[(7)] 2 68
(Marcus Tregoning) *hld up off the pce: prog 3f out: rdn to chse ldrs 2f out and cl enough over 1f out: sn wknd* **7/1**
4-0 **7** 1 ¾ **Saint Contest (FR)**[30] 3308 4-9-3 **75**........................(h[1]) FranBerry 4 64
(Alan King) *hld up off the pce in rr: rdn over 3f out and in tch: wknd jst over 2f out* **20/1**
4030 **8** 24 **Navajo War Dance**[31] 3240 4-9-1 **78**........................ CliffordLee[(5)] 7 26
(K R Burke) *led at gd pce but hdd after 2f: rdn 1/2-way: wknd over 3f out: t.o and eased* **12/1**
2454 **9** 2 ½ **Cape Banjo (USA)**[16] 3785 4-9-7 **79**........................ SilvestreDeSousa 6 23
(Ralph Beckett) *had to be dismntd and led to s: prom: chsd ldr 7f out to over 3f out: wknd qckly and eased: t.o* **4/1**[1]

2m 27.68s (-1.82) **Going Correction** -0.025s/f (Good) **9** Ran SP% **113.8**
Speed ratings (Par 105): **105,103,102,101,97 97,96,78,76**
CSF £36.79 CT £367.11 TOTE £5.10: £1.80, £2.60, £2.70; EX 42.40 Trifecta £467.00.
**Owner** D Wilbrey **Bred** Graf U Grafin V Stauffenberg **Trained** Hook, Hampshire

**FOCUS**
Run of the mill handicap form for the grade but the pace looked sound and that enabled the hold-up horses to play their hands in the straight.
T/Plt: £151.30 to a £1 stake. Pool: £78,155.00 - 516.40 winning units. T/Qpdt: £70.40 to a £1 stake. Pool: £5,729.00 - 81.37 winning units. **Jonathan Neesom**

4414 - 4415a (Foreign Racing) - See Raceform Interactive

# 4381 CURRAGH (R-H)
Sunday, July 2

**OFFICIAL GOING: Good (good to yielding in places on straight course)**

## 4416a TOTE ROCKINGHAM H'CAP (PREMIER HANDICAP) 5f
**2:45** (2:50) 3-Y-O+
**£50,427** (£16,239; £7,692; £3,418; £1,709; £854) **Stalls** Centre

RPR
**1** **Tithonus (IRE)**[69] 2045 6-8-8 **86**........................(bt[1]) RoryCleary 2 93
(Denis Gerard Hogan, Ire) *sn led on far side: strly pressed ins fnl f: jst hld on cl home* **14/1**
**2** *nk* **Hit The Bid**[14] 3873 3-9-8 **105**........................ LeighRoche 18 109+
(D J Bunyan, Ire) *hld up on stands' side: gd prog appr fnl f: styd on strly fnl 100yds into 2nd cl home: jst hld* **12/1**
**3** *nk* **Patrick (IRE)**[76] 1845 5-8-10 **88**........................ DeclanMcDonogh 9 93
(Richard John O'Brien, Ire) *chsd ldrs towards far side: 2nd after 1/2-way: kpt on wl ins fnl f: dropped to 3rd cl home* **50/1**
**4** *nk* **Spirit Quartz (IRE)**[36] 3097 9-9-5 **104**........................ DylanHogan[(7)] 5 108
(Barry John Murphy, Ire) *chsd ldrs in centre of trck: wnt 3rd after 1/2-way: kpt on wl tl no imp in 4th fnl 50yds* **25/1**
**5** *nse* **Patuano (IRE)**[22] 3601 3-7-11 **87** oh4........................ NathanCrosse[(7)] 14 89
(W McCreery, Ire) *racd in mid-div in centre of trck: prog to chse ldrs appr fnl f: kpt on wl clsng stages into 5th: nvr nrr* **14/1**
**6** *shd* **Celebration**[43] 2846 4-9-0 **92**........................ ColinKeane 20 95+
(G M Lyons, Ire) *racd in rr on stands' side tl prog appr fnl f: kpt on strly clsng stages into 6th: nvr nrr* **6/1**[2]
**7** ¾ **Go Kart (IRE)**[14] 3873 4-8-9 **94**........................(v) SeanDavis[(7)] 1 95
(P J Prendergast, Ire) *racd in mid-div on far side: clsr to chse ldrs at 1/2-way: wnt 4th ins fnl f: no ex fnl 50yds* **16/1**
**8** *nk* **Desert Law (IRE)**[15] 3829 9-9-1 **93**........................ GaryCarroll 10 93
(Paul Midgley) *hld up in centre of trck: prog to chse ldrs ent fnl f: kpt on wl: nvr nrr* **12/1**
**9** ¾ **Maarek**[36] 3097 10-9-8 **100**........................ SeamieHeffernan 3 97
(Miss Evanna McCutcheon, Ire) *racd towards rr on far side: prog over 1f out: kpt on wl: nvr on terms* **20/1**
**10** *hd* **Naggers (IRE)**[29] 3324 6-9-6 **98**........................ PatSmullen 16 94
(Paul Midgley) *chsd ldrs on stands' side: rdn and no imp ent fnl f: kpt on one pce* **11/4**[1]
**11** *nse* **Ostatnia (IRE)**[14] 3873 5-9-1 **93**........................(b) WJLee 19 89
(W McCreery, Ire) *racd in mid-div on stands' side: no imp towards rr ent fnl f: kpt on again clsng stages* **14/1**
**12** *shd* **Accalia (IRE)**[14] 3872 4-8-4 **82** oh7........................(vt) NGMcCullagh 6 78
(J C Hayden, Ire) *trckd ldr in 2nd towards far side: 4th at 1/2-way: rdn and wknd ins fnl f* **25/1**
**13** 1 **Elysian Flyer (IRE)**[21] 3625 5-8-5 **83**........................ ChrisHayes 4 75
(Paul Midgley) *chsd ldrs on far side: rdn and no imp ent fnl f: kpt on one pce* **16/1**

14 *nse* **Rattling Jewel**[21] 3631 5-8-12 **90**.................................(p) WayneLordan 7 82
(Miss Nicole McKenna, Ire) *racd in mid-div in centre of trck: short of room over 1f out: sn no imp* **10/1**[3]

15 *½* **Cenotaph (USA)**[36] 3097 5-9-1 **93**...............................(b[1]) RyanMoore 15 83
(A P O'Brien, Ire) *racd towards rr towards stands' side: kpt on one pce fnl f: nvr on terms* **12/1**

16 *¾* **Sors (IRE)**[21] 3631 5-8-11 **94**.......................... KillianLeonard(5) 11 81
(Andrew Slattery, Ire) *fractious in stalls: racd in mid-div in centre of trck: rdn and no imp whn swtchd rt 1f out: nvr on terms* **16/1**

17 *¾* **Idyllic Acrylic**[22] 3601 3-7-11 **87** oh8.......................... DannySheehy(7) 13 70
(W M Roper, Ire) *prom in centre of trck tl 1/2-way: wknd towards rr appr fnl f* **33/1**

18 *¾* **Majestic Hero (IRE)**[29] 3321 5-8-13 **91**.......................... KevinManning 8 73
(Ronald Harris) *chsd ldrs in centre of trck to 1/2-way: rdn and nt qckn appr fnl f: wknd* **25/1**

19 *¾* **Yulong Baobei (IRE)**[14] 3873 3-9-0 **97**.......................(h[1]) ShaneFoley 17 74
(M Halford, Ire) *prom on stands' side: rdn 1/2-way and sn dropped towards rr: no ex* **25/1**

58.4s (-4.50) **Going Correction** -0.625s/f (Hard)
**WFA** 3 from 4yo+ 5lb **19** Ran SP% **135.8**
Speed ratings: **111,110,110,109,109 109,108,107,106,106 106,105,104,104,103 102,101,99,98**
CSF £174.50 CT £8211.26 TOTE £23.00: £4.60, £3.00, £8.50, £4.10; DF 425.90.

**Owner** T & M Racing Partnership **Bred** K N Dhunjibhoy & B M Desai **Trained** Cloughjordan, Co Tipperary

**FOCUS**
As competitive as ever in this historic handicap sprint handicap. The pace was towards the centre of the track and the fair side, and the runner-up was possibly a little unlucky not to have some company for his late challenge up the stands' rail. The Turf Club's handicappers should be well pleased by the blanket-finish and the winner was closer to the pick of last season's form.

## 4417a FINLAY VOLVO INTERNATIONAL STKS (GROUP 3) 1m 2f
**3:15** (3:20) 3-Y-0+

**£32,777** (£10,555; £5,000; £2,222; £1,111; £555)

RPR

1 **Johannes Vermeer (IRE)**[11] 3962 4-9-8 111..................(t) RyanMoore 4 113+
(A P O'Brien, Ire) *chsd ldrs in 3rd: clsr to press ldr in 2nd ent fnl f: styd on wl for press to ld cl home* **5/2**[1]

2 *½* **Success Days (IRE)**[35] 3108 5-9-11 113........................(t[1]) ShaneFoley 1 115
(K J Condon, Ire) *sn led: strly pressed ent fnl f: kpt on wl: hdd cl home* **6/1**

3 *2 ¼* **Moonlight Magic**[35] 3108 4-9-8 114..........................(t[1]) KevinManning 6 108
(J S Bolger, Ire) *trckd ldr in 2nd: rdn in 3rd under 2f out: no imp on principals ent fnl f in 3rd: kpt on same pce* **11/2**

4 *1 ½* **The Grey Gatsby (IRE)**[260] 7353 6-9-8 117....................... PatSmullen 5 105
(D K Weld, Ire) *hld up in 4th: clsr in 2nd over 2f out: nt qckn ins fnl f and dropped to 4th ins fnl f: nt hrd-rdn* **11/4**[2]

5 *hd* **Air Pilot**[30] 3299 8-9-11 114.................................................. ColinKeane 3 107
(Ralph Beckett) *racd in rr: rdn along in 5th under 2f out: kpt on same pce ins fnl f: nvr on terms* **7/2**[3]

6 *15* **Shamreen (IRE)**[294] 6383 4-9-10 108........................................ LeighRoche 2 76
(D K Weld, Ire) *racd in rr: rdn and detached over 1f out: sn eased* **20/1**

2m 10.3s (1.00) **Going Correction** +0.05s/f (Good) **6** Ran SP% **111.9**
Speed ratings: **98,97,95,94,94 82**
CSF £17.50 TOTE £3.10: £1.40, £3.30; DF 18.70 Trifecta £67.90.

**Owner** Tabor/Smith/Magnier/China Horse Club **Bred** Desert Star Phoenix Jvc **Trained** Cashel, Co Tipperary

**FOCUS**
An interesting contest for this level in that the six-runner field included two former Group 1 winners attempting to re-establish themselves. The runner-up helps with the standard but the time doesn't back the level of form.

## 4418a GRANGECON STUD STKS (GROUP 3) (FILLIES) 6f
**3:45** (3:50) 2-Y-0

**£32,777** (£10,555; £5,000; £2,222; £1,111; £555) **Stalls** Centre

RPR

1 **Clemmie (IRE)**[9] 4028 2-9-0 0...........................................(t) RyanMoore 8 106+
(A P O'Brien, Ire) *chsd ldrs in 4th: clsr to trck ldr in 2nd after 1/2-way: led appr fnl f: rdn clr ins fnl 100yds* **6/4**[1]

2 *2 ¾* **Butterscotch (IRE)**[4] 4225 2-9-0 0..........................(t) SeamieHeffernan 6 98
(A P O'Brien, Ire) *led: pressed under 2f out and hdd appr fnl f: no match for wnr fnl 100yds: kpt on same pce* **3/1**[2]

3 *¾* **Mamba Noire (FR)**[11] 3960 2-9-0 0.......................................... ShaneFoley 5 96
(K J Condon, Ire) *racd in mid-div: pushed along 1/2-way: prog to chse ldng pair in 3rd appr fnl f: kpt on wl clsng stages: nvr nrr* **25/1**

4 *1* **Too Familiar (IRE)**[22] 3599 2-9-0 0.................................. NGMcCullagh 3 93
(J P Murtagh, Ire) *racd in rr: clsr after 1/2-way: wnt 4th 1f out: kpt on wl clsng stages: nvr nrr* **4/1**[3]

5 *2 ¾* **Sometimesadiamond (IRE)**[16] 3797 2-9-0 0..............(p[1]) RonanWhelan 4 84
(J S Bolger, Ire) *trckd ldr in 2nd to 1/2-way: sn rdn and nt qckn in 5th: no imp ent fnl f* **8/1**

6 *hd* **Fille Du Septembre (IRE)**[93] 1476 2-9-0 0....................... PatSmullen 2 84
(D K Weld, Ire) *racd towards rr: pushed along 2f out: kpt on one pce ins fnl f: nvr nrr* **20/1**

7 *2 ¼* **Drombeg Dream (IRE)**[28] 3358 2-9-0 0.......................................... WJLee 1 77
(Augustine Leahy, Ire) *chsd ldrs in 3rd: sn pushed along and dropped to rr at 1/2-way: kpt on one pce fnl f* **66/1**

8 *2 ½* **Gasta (IRE)**[22] 3599 2-9-0 0........................................... KevinManning 7 75
(J S Bolger, Ire) *hld up: clsr to chse ldrs in 3rd on outer after 1/2-way: rdn and nt qckn appr fnl f: sn no ex: eased* **11/1**

1m 11.87s (-3.63) **Going Correction** -0.625s/f (Hard) **8** Ran SP% **114.5**
Speed ratings: **99,95,94,93,89 89,86,82**
CSF £5.96 TOTE £2.30: £1.02, £1.50, £4.60; DF 6.30 Trifecta £69.30.

**Owner** Michael Tabor & Derrick Smith & Mrs John Magnier **Bred** Liberty Bloodstock **Trained** Cashel, Co Tipperary

**FOCUS**
A one-two for Aidan O'Brien. The winner, a sister to stablemate Churchill, showed the form of Royal Ascot's Albany Stakes in a good light.

## 4419a PRETTY POLLY STKS (GROUP 1) (F&M) 1m 2f
**4:20** (4:20) 3-Y-0+

**£113,461** (£36,538; £17,307; £7,692; £3,846; £1,923)

RPR

1 **Nezwaah**[39] 2954 4-9-8 108................................................ AndreaAtzeni 5 115+
(Roger Varian) *hld up: pushed along in 7th 3f out: gd prog under 2f out: led 1f out and sn qcknd clr: styd on strly* **13/2**

2 *3 ¼* **Rain Goddess (IRE)**[11] 3964 3-8-12 108.....................(t[1]) RyanMoore 11 110+
(A P O'Brien, Ire) *racd in rr: 9th 3f out: prog on inner appr fnl f in 4th: kpt on wl into 2nd fnl 100yds: nt rch wnr* **6/1**[3]

3 *1 ½* **Turret Rocks (IRE)**[11] 3961 4-9-8 109.......................... RonanWhelan 8 106
(J S Bolger, Ire) *chsd ldrs in 4th: rdn in 4th ent fnl f: kpt on again cl home into 3rd on line* **25/1**

4 *hd* **Zhukova (IRE)**[50] 2641 5-9-8 115....................................... PatSmullen 2 105
(D K Weld, Ire) *chsd clr ldr in 2nd: clsr 3f out: led under 2f out tl hdd 1f out: no imp in 3rd fnl 100yds: kpt on same pce and dropped to 4th on line* **7/2**[2]

5 *1 ½* **Laganore (IRE)**[21] 3633 5-9-8 108....................................... ColinKeane 4 102
(A J Martin, Ire) *racd in mid-div: 6th 3f out: clsr on outer over 1f out: kpt on same pce fnl f: nvr on terms* **20/1**

6 *½* **Intricately (IRE)**[35] 3110 3-8-12 108.......................... DonnachaO'Brien 1 102
(Joseph Patrick O'Brien, Ire) *racd in mid-div: 5th at 1/2-way: rdn 4f out: nt qckn over 1f out: kpt on same pce* **14/1**

7 *1 ¾* **Smart Call (SAF)**[11] 3961 5-9-8 111....................................... JimCrowley 3 98
(Sir Michael Stoute) *chsd ldrs in 3rd: clsr to press ldr in 2nd under 2f out: nt qckn ent fnl f: sn no ex* **13/2**

8 *nk* **Santa Monica**[14] 3874 4-9-8 99................................................... WJLee 10 97
(Charles O'Brien, Ire) *hld up: 10th 3f out: rdn 2f out: kpt on ins fnl f: nvr nrr* **66/1**

9 *2* **Pocketfullofdreams (FR)**[4] 4231 3-8-12 97.........(h) SeamieHeffernan 9 94
(A P O'Brien, Ire) *racd towards rr: last 3f out: kpt on under hands and heels fnl f: nvr on terms* **33/1**

10 *2 ¾* **Journey**[30] 3299 5-9-8 119..........................................(h) KevinManning 6 88
(John Gosden) *hld up: rdn 3f out in 8th: rdr dropped whip under 2f out: no imp over 1f out: nt hrd-rdn clsng stages* **15/8**[1]

11 *1 ¼* **Creggs Pipes (IRE)**[36] 3101 5-9-8 109...................... DeclanMcDonogh 7 85
(Andrew Slattery, Ire) *led and sn clr: advantage reduced under 3f out and hdd under 2f out: wknd qckly* **25/1**

2m 6.19s (-3.11) **Going Correction** +0.05s/f (Good)
**WFA** 3 from 4yo+ 10lb **11** Ran SP% **121.5**
Speed ratings: **114,111,110,110,108 108,107,106,105,103 102**
CSF £43.92 CT £935.05 TOTE £7.90: £2.80, £2.70, £7.10; DF 56.80 Trifecta £1245.40.
**Owner** Sheikh Ahmed Al Maktoum **Bred** Darley **Trained** Newmarket, Suffolk

**FOCUS**
A couple of the established older mares disappointed, and the three-year-olds did not boast strong credentials, but it was hard not to be impressed by the authority shown by the winner who is clearly reaching her peak as a four-year-old. The second and third help with the standard.

## 4420a COMER GROUP INTERNATIONAL CURRAGH CUP (GROUP 2) 1m 6f
**4:50** (4:51) 3-Y-0+

**£60,512** (£19,487; £9,230; £4,102; £2,051; £1,025)

RPR

1 **Rekindling**[29] 3322 3-8-11 109.......................................... WayneLordan 5 113+
(Joseph Patrick O'Brien, Ire) *hld up in 5th: rdn along in rr 2f out: swtchd rt and gd hdwy appr fnl f in 5th: styd on strly into 2nd fnl 100yds: led cl home* **4/1**[3]

2 *½* **Wicklow Brave**[23] 3553 8-9-11 115........................... DeclanMcDonogh 3 111
(W P Mullins, Ire) *trckd ldr in 2nd: rdn to ld under 2f out and clr ent fnl f: strly pressed and hdd cl home* **11/8**[1]

3 *1* **Elidor**[38] 3011 7-9-11 108................................................. RonanWhelan 6 110
(Mick Channon) *hld up in 6th: prog to chse ldng pair in 3rd over 1f out: dropped to 4th ins fnl f: kpt on same pce into 3rd fnl 100yds* **25/1**

4 *½* **Stellar Mass (IRE)**[8] 4070 4-9-11 110............................ KevinManning 7 109
(J S Bolger, Ire) *racd in rr: prog on outer over 1f out in 4th: kpt on wl wout getting on terms* **20/1**

5 *2 ¾* **Wisconsin (JPN)**[9] 4032 3-8-11 94........................... SeamieHeffernan 2 106
(A P O'Brien, Ire) *led: rdn 3f out: hdd under 2f out: wknd ins fnl f* **7/1**

6 *16* **Belgravia (IRE)**[9] 4032 3-8-11 99...................................(bt) RyanMoore 1 84
(A P O'Brien, Ire) *chsd ldrs in 3rd: rdn and nt qckn under 2f out: wknd qckly appr fnl f* **3/1**[2]

7 *42* **Forgotten Rules (IRE)**[88] 1571 7-9-11 107.....................(h) PatSmullen 4 24
(D K Weld, Ire) *settled off ldrs in 4th: rdn and no imp whn qckly eased under 2f out: lost action* **10/1**

3m 3.33s (-6.07) **Going Correction** +0.05s/f (Good)
**WFA** 3 from 4yo+ 14lb **7** Ran SP% **117.3**
Speed ratings: **119,118,118,117,116 107,83**
CSF £10.37 TOTE £5.30: £2.60, £1.70; DF 12.70 Trifecta £138.10.
**Owner** Lloyd J Williams **Bred** The Pocock Family **Trained** Owning Hill, Co Kilkenny

**FOCUS**
A performance of real substance from a potentially high-class stayer \bRekindling\p. His success continued the strong run for three-year-olds in this race as they have now won the past three renewals. The winner is rated back to his best.

4421 - (Foreign Racing) - See Raceform Interactive

# 4392 HAMBURG (R-H)
Sunday, July 2

**OFFICIAL GOING: Turf: soft**

## 4422a IDEE 148TH DEUTSCHES DERBY (GROUP 1) (3YO COLTS & FILLIES) (TURF) 1m 4f
**2:40** 3-Y-0 **£333,333** (£111,111; £66,666; £33,333; £11,111)

RPR

1 **Windstoss (GER)**[21] 3636 3-9-2 0.............................. MaximPecheur 11 113
(Markus Klug, Germany) *hld up towards rr: rdn 3f out: wd into st: styd on fr 2 1/2f out: led cl home* **13/2**

2 *1* **Enjoy Vijay (GER)**[35] 3115 3-9-2 0.............................. AndraschStarke 12 111
(P Schiergen, Germany) *hld up in rr: gd hdwy fr 5f out: in tch 4f out: rdn to ld over 2f out: hung rt 1f out: hdd and no ex cl home* **57/10**[3]

3 3/4 **Rosenpurpur (GER)**[27] 3-9-2 0........................................ DanielePorcu 3 110
(P Schiergen, Germany) *midfield: dropped towards rr 5f out: rdn 3f out: wd into st and crossed towards stands' side rail: styd on wl fr 2f out: nrst fin* **227/10**

4 1 **Shanjo (GER)**[21] 3636 3-9-2 0.................................... IoritzMendizabal 19 108
(Markus Klug, Germany) *midfield: rdn 3f out: kpt on wl fr 2f out: flashed tail under 2f out: nrst fin* **228/10**

5 2 1/4 **Promise Of Peace (JPN)**[79] 3-9-2 0............................(p) JozefBojko 15 105
(A Wohler, Germany) *trckd ldrs: led after 4f: sn clr: rdn over 2f out: hdd 2f out: wknd steadily fnl f* **31/1**

6 3 **Monreal (IRE)**[21] 3636 3-9-2 0........................................ FabriceVeron 14 100
(Jean-Pierre Carvalho, Germany) *led: hdd after 2 1/2f: trckd ldrs after: rdn over 3f out: nt clr run over 2f out: wknd steadily fr over 1f out* **162/10**

7 nk **Parviz (IRE)**[27] 3-9-2 0........................................................ MarcLerner 18 100
(Waldemar Hickst, Germany) *towards rr of midfield: rdn 3f out: crossed towards stands' side in st: kpt on steadily fr 2f out: n.d* **92/10**

8 nse **Kastano (GER)**[35] 3115 3-9-2 0.......................................... MartinSeidl 6 99
(Markus Klug, Germany) *hld up towards rr: stdy hdwy fr 5f out: rdn under 2f out: chsd ldrs briefly 2f out: wknd fnl f* **135/10**

9 nk **Amun (GER)** 3-9-2 0.................................................... StephenHellyn 10 99
(C Von Der Recke, Germany) *hld up towards rr: rdn under 3f out: wd into st and crossed towards stands' side: kpt on fr over 1f out: n.d* **53/1**

10 1 **Ming Jung (FR)**[35] 3115 3-9-2 0........................................ RenePiechulek 2 97
(Markus Klug, Germany) *midfield on inner: dropped towards rr and rdn under 3f out: drvn and kpt on steadily fr 2f out* **58/1**

11 3 3/4 **Gepard (GER)**[27] 3-9-2 0............................................ MichaelCadeddu 9 91
(C Zschache, Germany) *midfield: dropped towards rr 4f out: rdn 3f out: sme late hdwy: n.d* **73/1**

12 hd **Khan (GER)**[21] 3636 3-9-2 0.................................... ClementLecoeuvre 13 91
(Henk Grewe, Germany) *in tch in midfield: rdn along after 4f: dropped towards rr 5f out: rdn and kpt on steadily fr under 3f out: n.d* **49/1**

13 1 1/4 **Colomano**[21] 3636 3-9-2 0...................................... AndreasHelfenbein 17 89
(Markus Klug, Germany) *hld up towards rr: stdy hdwy fr 7f out: in tch whn rdn 2 1/2f out: wknd appr fnl f* **7/2**[1]

14 2 **Sternkranz (GER)** 3-9-2 0................................................ SibylleVogt 5 86
(Markus Klug, Germany) *trckd ldrs: pushed along and dropped to midfield 4f out: rdn 2 1/2f out: wknd 2f out* **75/1**

15 2 1/4 **Oriental Khan (GER)**[21] 3636 3-9-2 0...........(b) BauyrzhanMurzabayev 8 82
(R Dzubasz, Germany) *a towards rr* **56/1**

16 9 1/2 **Sargas (IRE)**[27] 3-9-2 0.......................................................... FilipMinarik 1 67
(Jean-Pierre Carvalho, Germany) *prom: led after 2 1/2f: hdd after 4f: rdn 2 1/2f out: wknd qckly 2f out: eased over 1f out* **96/10**

17 16 **Northsea Star (GER)**[21] 3636 3-9-2 0........................ AlexanderPietsch 16 41
(Markus Klug, Germany) *in tch: rdn and outpcd 2 1/2f out: wknd qckly over 2f out* **107/10**

18 10 **Warring States (JPN)**[21] 3636 3-9-2 0........................ EduardoPedroza 4 25
(A Wohler, Germany) *in tch: rdn and lost pl 4f out: sn wl btn: eased 2f out* **26/5**[2]

2m 41.52s (6.97) **18** Ran SP% **128.6**
PARI-MUTUEL (all including 10 euro stake): WIN 75 PLACE: 28, 25, 55; SF: 476.
**Owner** Gestut Rottgen **Bred** Gestut Rottgen **Trained** Germany

**FOCUS**
They were spread across the track in the straight.

## 4166 SAINT-CLOUD (L-H)
### Sunday, July 2

**OFFICIAL GOING: Turf: good to soft**

**4423a** **GRAND PRIX DE SAINT-CLOUD (GROUP 1) (4YO+) (TURF)** **1m 4f**
**2:55** 4-Y-0+ **£195,350** (£78,153; £39,076; £19,521; £9,777)

RPR

1 **Zarak (FR)**[35] 3118 4-9-2 0.................................... ChristopheSoumillon 4 119+
(A De Royer-Dupre, France) *hld up towards rr: gd hdwy on outer fr 2 1/2f out: rdn under 2f out: led 1f out: kpt on wl* **5/1**[3]

2 3/4 **Silverwave (FR)**[28] 3369 5-9-2 0.......................................... GeraldMosse 1 118
(P Bary, France) *in tch: pushed along and hdwy 2 1/2f out: rdn to ld 2f out: drvn 1 1/2f out: hdd 1f out: kpt on* **11/4**[1]

3 1 1/4 **Armande (IRE)**[40] 2946 4-8-13 0.................................. Pierre-CharlesBoudot 7 113
(A Fabre, France) *hld up in midfield: rdn and hdwy fr over 2f out: kpt on wl: nvr quite able to chal* **16/1**

4 snk **My Dream Boat (IRE)**[43] 2822 5-9-2 0..............................(p) AdamKirby 10 116
(Clive Cox) *hld up towards rr: drvn and gd hdwy fr 2 1/2f out: ev ch appr fnl f: no ex last 100yds* **17/2**

5 2 1/2 **Left Hand**[28] 3369 4-8-13 0...............................................(p) MaximeGuyon 3 109
(C Laffon-Parias, France) *in tch: rdn 2 1/2f out: kpt on same pce tl no ex last 100yds* **22/1**

6 10 **Hawkbill (USA)**[30] 3299 4-9-2 0.........................................(p) WilliamBuick 9 102+
(Charlie Appleby) *racd freely: trckd ldrs: chsd ldr after 3f: led 3 1/2f out: rdn 2 1/2f out: hdd 2f out: sn wknd* **9/2**[2]

7 18 **Tiberian (FR)**[55] 2485 5-9-2 0............................................... OlivierPeslier 2 67+
(Alain Couetil, France) *chsd ldr: led after 2 1/2f: hdd 3 1/2f out: pushed along briefly 2 1/2f out: short of room over 2f out: wknd qckly* **12/1**

8 18 **Robin Of Navan (FR)**[15] 3856 4-9-2 0.............................. CristianDemuro 8 38+
(Harry Dunlop) *led: hdd after 2 1/2f: trckd ldrs after: rdn 2 1/2f out: wknd qckly 2f out: eased 1 1/2f out* **16/1**

9 6 **Erupt (IRE)**[62] 2249 5-9-2 0........................................... StephanePasquier 6 29+
(F-H Graffard, France) *racd in midfield: rdn 3 1/2f out: wknd over 2f out: eased under 2f out* **11/2**

U **Doha Dream (FR)**[28] 3369 4-9-2 0...................................... GregoryBenoist 5
(A Fabre, France) *hld up in rr: rdn 2 1/2f out: making hdwy whn hmpd and uns rdr under 2f out* **25/1**

2m 27.76s (-12.64) **10** Ran SP% **115.1**
PARI-MUTUEL (all including 1 euro stake): WIN: 5.90; PLACE: 2.10, 1.60, 2.50; DF: 9.10; SF: 22.90.
**Owner** H H Aga Khan **Bred** Sa Aga Khan **Trained** Chantilly, France

**FOCUS**
While there is no doubt this was a classy contest, and it was run at a good gallop (the winning time was much quicker that the 3yo Group 2 fillies race that followed it over the same distance), the final stages were a little unsatisfactory with a few of the field tailing off down the home straight for one reason or another.

**4424a** **PRIX DE MALLERET (GROUP 2) (3YO FILLIES) (TURF)** **1m 4f**
**3:35** 3-Y-O **£63,333** (£24,444; £11,666; £7,777; £3,888)

RPR

1 **Strathspey**[38] 3-8-11 0............................................ MickaelBarzalona 5 103+
(A Fabre, France) *hld up towards rr: rdn 2 1/2f out: hdwy fr 2f out: styd on strly fnl f: led last stride* **14/1**

2 shd **Listen In (IRE)**[70] 2003 3-8-11 0.................................... AurelienLemaitre 11 103
(F Head, France) *led: rdn under 3f out: clr ent fnl f: wknd clsng stages: hdd last stride* **13/2**

3 1 1/4 **Elas Ruby**[17] 3749 3-8-11 0................................................ OlivierPeslier 4 101
(John Gosden) *midfield: rdn and outpcd fr 2 1/2f out: styd on fr 1 1/2f out: nrst fin* **10/1**

4 1 **Horseplay**[30] 3301 3-8-11 0................................................ OisinMurphy 2 99
(Andrew Balding) *trckd ldrs: rdn and kpt on same pce fr 2 1/2f out* **7/2**[3]

5 3 **Baiyouna (FR)**[41] 3-8-11 0.................................... ChristopheSoumillon 8 95
(A De Royer-Dupre, France) *hld up towards rr: rdn and kpt on fr 2 1/2f out: nvr gng pce to chal* **10/3**[2]

6 3/4 **Satine (FR)**[28] 3366 3-8-11 0.......................................... StephanePasquier 3 93
(N Clement, France) *in tch: rdn 2 1/2f out: wknd steadily fnl f* **28/1**

7 1 1/4 **Estelle Ma Belle (FR)**[26] 3-8-11 0..................................... MaximeGuyon 7 91
(T Castanheira, France) *hld up in midfield: rdn under 3f out: wknd over 1f out* **33/1**

8 snk **Normandel (FR)**[20] 3681 3-8-11 0.................................... CristianDemuro 6 91
(Mme Pia Brandt, France) *in tch in midfield: hdwy to chse ldr 6f out: rdn 2 1/2f out: wknd 1 1/2f out* **12/1**

9 1/2 **Rythmique (IRE)**[40] 2945 3-8-11 0.......................... Jean-BernardEyquem 10 90
(J-C Rouget, France) *hld up in rr: rdn and kpt on steadily on wd outside fr 2 1/2f out: n.d* **17/2**

10 2 1/2 **Gipoia (FR)**[39] 2978 3-8-11 0......................................... VincentCheminaud 1 86
(M Delzangles, France) *in tch: rdn 2 1/2f out: wknd appr fnl f* **40/1**

11 15 **Vintage Folly**[46] 2738 3-8-11 0............................................. WilliamBuick 9 62
(Hugo Palmer) *midfield: rdn over 3f out: lost pl appr 2f out: sn btn: eased fnl f* **3/1**[1]

2m 31.95s (-8.45) **11** Ran SP% **126.4**
PARI-MUTUEL (all including 1 euro stake): WIN: 18.50; PLACE: 4.60, 2.30, 3.30; DF: 45.00; SF: 116.80.
**Owner** Godolphin SNC **Bred** Darley **Trained** Chantilly, France

4425a (Foreign Racing) - See Raceform Interactive

## 4244 HAMILTON (R-H)
### Monday, July 3

**OFFICIAL GOING: Good (good to soft in places)**
Wind: Breezy, across Weather: Cloudy, bright

**4426** **FOLLOW US ON TWITTER @HAMILTONPARKRC H'CAP (FOR GENTLEMAN AMATEUR RIDERS)** **6f 6y**
**6:15** (6:16) (Class 5) (0-70,71) 3-Y-O+ **£3,743** (£1,161; £580; £290) **Stalls Centre**

Form RPR

0213 1 **Exotic Guest**[14] 3897 7-11-1 **65**..........................................(p) MrBLynn(5) 6 72
(Ruth Carr) *t.k.h early: prom: carried lft after 1f: effrt and edgd rt over 1f out: led ins fnl f: hld on towards fin* **4/1**[2]

2364 2 hd **El Principe**[41] 2923 4-11-0 **66**..........................................(h) MrJMAndrews(7) 3 72
(Les Eyre) *led: rdn over 1f out: hdd ins fnl f: rallied: hld cl home* **4/1**[2]

-011 3 1 3/4 **Kinglami**[23] 3573 8-11-12 **71**..............................................(p) MrSWalker 7 71
(John O'Shea) *in tch: effrt and edgd rt over 1f out: kpt on same pce ins fnl f* **3/1**[1]

0511 4 1 1/4 **Concur (IRE)**[19] 3704 4-10-9 **54**.......................................(tp) MrPMillman 4 50
(Rod Millman) *cl up against stands' rail: rdn 2f out: outpcd ins fnl f* **3/1**[1]

2434 5 2 1/2 **Willbeme**[14] 3897 9-11-3 **65**...............................................(t) MrJoeWright(3) 2 53
(Simon West) *cl up: rdn and ev ch over 1f out: wknd ins fnl f* **7/1**[3]

6 5 **Molecule (IRE)**[13] 3956 3-10-5 **56**........................................ MrJamesKing 1 27
(John Patrick Shanahan, Ire) *prom on outside: rdn over 2f out: wknd over 1f out* **9/1**

0-06 7 6 **Reflation**[26] 3453 5-10-7 **59**............................................(p) MrJCummins(7) 5 12
(Patrick Holmes) *s.s: hung rt thrght and a struggling in last pl* **66/1**

1m 13.92s (1.72) **Going Correction** +0.175s/f (Good)
**WFA** 3 from 4yo+ 6lb **7** Ran SP% **114.0**
Speed ratings (Par 103): **95,94,92,90,87 80,72**
CSF £20.16 TOTE £5.50: £2.30, £2.80; EX 19.60 Trifecta £69.70.
**Owner** Ruth Carr Racing 1 **Bred** D Cantillon And E Cantillon **Trained** Huby, N Yorks
■ Stewards' Enquiry : Mr P Millman two-day ban: careless riding (Jul 19, 22)
Mr J M Andrews two-day ban: used whip above permitted level (Jul 19, 22)

**FOCUS**
Races 4, 5 , 6 and 7 increased by 2yds. Quite a competitive sprint handicap for amateur riders which featured two horses going for their third win on the trot. The pace was sound. The runner-up has been rated to form.

**4427** **RACINGUK.COM NOVICE STKS (PLUS 10 RACE)** **5f 7y**
**6:45** (6:45) (Class 4) 2-Y-O **£5,175** (£1,540; £769; £384) **Stalls High**

Form RPR

3 1 **Kalagia (IRE)**[12] 3980 2-8-11 0.............................................. JoeFanning 2 72
(Mark Johnston) *mde all: shkn up over 1f out: kpt on wl fnl f* **2/1**[2]

633 2 2 1/4 **Palmer (IRE)**[16] 3826 2-9-2 76........................................ ConnorBeasley 5 69
(Bryan Smart) *t.k.h: trckd ldrs: effrt and chsd wnr over 1f out: kpt on same pce fnl f* **13/8**[1]

4 3 3/4 **Corton Lass**[12] 3980 2-8-11 0............................................... GrahamLee 1 61
(Keith Dalgleish) *t.k.h: trckd ldrs on outside: rdn over 1f out: kpt on same pce ins fnl f* **11/1**

3320 4 1 1/2 **Rockin Fella (IRE)**[24] 3523 2-9-2 72.................................(p1) BenCurtis 6 61
(K R Burke) *pressed wnr tl rdn and no ex fr over 1f out* **5/1**[3]

66 5 1/2 **Ventura Gold (IRE)**[63] 2222 2-9-2 0..................................... DavidNolan 4 59
(Richard Fahey) *hld up in last pl: pushed along over 2f out: no imp fr over 1f out* **7/1**

1m 0.87s (0.87) **Going Correction** +0.175s/f (Good) **5** Ran SP% **108.9**
Speed ratings (Par 96): **100,96,95,92,92**
CSF £5.52 TOTE £2.70: £1.40, £1.60; EX 5.90 Trifecta £17.80.
**Owner** Mrs Jane Newett **Bred** Philip & Orla Hore **Trained** Middleham Moor, N Yorks
■ Le Gros Serpant was withdrawn. Price at time of withdrawal 33/1. Rule 4 does not apply

**FOCUS**
This didn't look the strongest of juvenile novice events, the early pace was fairly moderate and several pulled hard as a result.

## 4428 HAMILTON-PARK.CO.UK H'CAP — 5f 7y
7:15 (7:15) (Class 5) (0-70,71) 3-Y-O+ — £3,881 (£1,155; £577; £288) Stalls High

Form — RPR

2105 **1** **Bronze Beau**[6] 4182 10-9-12 **68**........................(tp) ShaneGray 7 77
(Kristin Stubbs) *mde all against stands' rail: rdn clr fnl f* **14/1**

0030 **2** 2 **Vintage Dream (IRE)**[3] 4303 3-8-13 **60**..................(b[1]) PatrickMathers 6 60
(Noel Wilson) *pressed wnr thrght: rdn along 2f out: kpt on ins fnl f: nt pce to chal* **7/2**[1]

3055 **3** nk **Hamidans Girl (IRE)**[9] 4107 3-9-5 **66**........................ GrahamLee 10 65
(Keith Dalgleish) *hld up in tch: rdn and hdwy over 1f out: kpt on fnl f: nrst fin* **9/2**[2]

-030 **4** 1 1/2 **Angel Palanas**[19] 3709 3-9-0 **61**........................(p[1]) BenCurtis 1 54
(K R Burke) *prom: rdn along over 2f out: kpt on same pce appr fnl f* **7/1**

6664 **5** 3/4 **Compton River**[53] 2551 5-9-11 **67**........................ ConnorBeasley 3 60
(Bryan Smart) *prom: rdn along 2f out: kpt on same pce ins fnl f* **9/2**[2]

0066 **6** 1 1/2 **Salvatore Fury (IRE)**[4] 4249 7-9-6 **67**........................(v) RowanScott(5) 4 54
(Keith Dalgleish) *hld up: pushed along 2f out: no imp appr fnl f* **9/1**

3-05 **7** 1/2 **Astrophysics**[21] 3667 5-10-1 **71**........................ PaddyAspell 5 56
(Lynn Siddall) *hld up: hdwy and hung rt 2f out: wknd fnl f* **5/1**[3]

60-0 **8** hd **Imperial Legend (IRE)**[180] 45 8-9-12 **68**........................(p) PhillipMakin 2 53
(Alan Brown) *dwlt: hld up: stdy hdwy on outside after 2f: rdn and wknd over 1f out* **9/1**

1m 0.46s (0.46) **Going Correction** +0.175s/f (Good)
**WFA** 3 from 4yo+ 5lb — **8** Ran SP% **114.4**
Speed ratings (Par 103): **103,99,99,96,95 93,92,92**
CSF £62.65 CT £232.08 TOTE £11.10: £3.80, £2.00, £2.00; EX 73.80 Trifecta £180.90.
**Owner** G J Daly & Kristin Stubbs **Bred** Meon Valley Stud **Trained** Norton, N Yorks

**FOCUS**
Not the strongest of sprints as most of the runners, the winner being a notable exception, have been struggling to win a race. The winner has been rated to his 2015 non-claiming form for now.

## 4429 CHATELHERAULT H'CAP — 1m 4f 15y
7:45 (7:45) (Class 3) (0-90,91) 3-Y-O+
£9,337 (£2,796; £1,398; £699; £349; £175) Stalls Low

Form — RPR

1000 **1** **Be Perfect (USA)**[16] 3841 8-9-9 **84**........................(p) JackGarritty 3 88
(Ruth Carr) *trckd ldr: led over 2f out: sn rdn: hld on wl fnl f* **40/1**

0-41 **2** 3/4 **Al Destoor**[23] 3582 7-10-2 **91**........................(t) DavidNolan 2 93
(Jennie Candlish) *hld up: hdwy on outside over 2f out: kpt on fnl f to take 2nd towards fin* **4/1**[3]

6554 **3** nk **Sennockian Star**[10] 4038 7-9-13 **88**........................ JoeFanning 7 90
(Mark Johnston) *chsd ldrs: rdn over 2f out: wnt 2nd over 1f out: kpt on fnl f: lost 2nd towards fin* **14/1**

2-65 **4** nk **Mister Belvedere**[23] 3583 3-8-13 **86**........................ PaulMulrennan 5 89
(Michael Dods) *in tch: drvn and outpcd 3f out: rallied and edgd rt wl over 1f out: one pce fnl f* **9/4**[1]

-323 **5** 1/2 **Warp Factor (IRE)**[31] 3091 4-9-5 **80**........................ TadhgO'Shea 4 81
(John Patrick Shanahan, Ire) *hld up in tch: stdy hdwy to chse ldrs over 2f out: rdn and outpcd fnl f* **3/1**[2]

60-2 **6** 3/4 **My Brother (IRE)**[32] 3240 4-9-9 **84**........................(p) PhillipMakin 6 84
(Lee Smyth, Ire) *cl up: : rdn and outpcd over 2f out: rallied over 1f out: no imp fnl f* **13/2**

4-46 **7** 1 **Cape Of Glory (IRE)**[9] 4076 4-9-10 **85**........................(b) GrahamLee 1 83
(Keith Dalgleish) *dwlt: bhd: rdn and outpcd over 2f out: n.d after* **25/1**

2013 **8** 1 1/2 **Gaelic Tiger**[21] 3671 4-10-0 **89**........................(v) DanielTudhope 8 85
(David O'Meara) *led to over 2f out: rdn and wknd fnl f* **7/1**

2m 35.36s (-3.24) **Going Correction** -0.225s/f (Firm)
**WFA** 3 from 4yo+ 12lb — **8** Ran SP% **114.6**
Speed ratings (Par 107): **101,100,100,100,99 99,98,97**
CSF £193.77 CT £2395.25 TOTE £12.80: £4.90, £1.50, £2.80; EX 178.70 Trifecta £608.90.
**Owner** The Beer Stalkers & Ruth Carr **Bred** Joseph Allen **Trained** Huby, N Yorks

**FOCUS**
Race distance increased by 2yds. A moderately run affair in which it paid to race handy and with the first five in a bit of a heap it isn't likely to be strong form. It's been rated around the winner and third for now.

## 4430 RACING UK PROFITS RETURNED TO RACING H'CAP — 1m 3f 15y
8:15 (8:15) (Class 5) (0-75,75) 3-Y-O+ — £3,881 (£1,155; £577; £288) Stalls Low

Form — RPR

602 **1** **Qaviy Cash**[19] 3720 3-9-3 **75**........................(t[1]) JosephineGordon 8 92+
(Hugo Palmer) *trckd ldr: led over 2f out: rdn and hld on wl fnl f* **15/8**[1]

011 **2** nk **Archi's Affaire**[25] 3484 3-9-3 **75**........................ PaulMulrennan 1 90
(Michael Dods) *prom: pushed along 3f out: rallied: edgd rt and chsd wnr over 1f out: ev ch ins fnl f: kpt on: hld cl home* **2/1**[2]

1 **3** 7 **What Wonders Weave (IRE)**[16] 3854 3-9-3 **75**........................ TadhgO'Shea 5 78
(John Patrick Shanahan, Ire) *hld up in tch: smooth hdwy to chse ldrs over 2f out: rdn and lost 2nd over 1f out: sn outpcd* **13/2**[3]

-510 **4** 2 3/4 **Reinstorm**[25] 3499 3-8-1 **62**........................ SammyJoBell(3) 9 60
(Richard Fahey) *chsd ldrs: effrt and rdn over 2f out: wknd over 1f out* **16/1**

-502 **5** nk **Powerful Love (IRE)**[14] 3901 3-8-12 **70**........................(b) JoeFanning 7 68
(Mark Johnston) *t.k.h: led to over 2f out: rdn and wknd over 1f out* **15/2**

650 **6** 4 1/2 **Vizier**[12] 3966 4-9-9 **70**........................(v[1]) DanielTudhope 4 64
(David O'Meara) *hed up in tch: effrt and chsd wnr over 2f out to over 1f out: sn wknd* **20/1**

-001 **7** 3/4 **Auxiliary**[27] 3432 4-9-11 **72**........................(p) JackGarritty 2 60
(Patrick Holmes) *hld up in tch: rdn and outpcd over 2f out: btn over 1f out* **25/1**

100 **8** 1 1/4 **Spes Nostra**[21] 3651 9-9-12 **73**........................(b) DougieCostello 3 59
(Iain Jardine) *hld up: drvn and outpcd over 3f out: btn fnl 2f* **33/1**

211- **9** 5 **Galilee Chapel (IRE)**[185] 8586 8-9-2 **70**........................(b) RhonaPindar(7) 6 47
(Alistair Whillans) *hld up: drvn and struggling 3f out: sn wknd* **40/1**

2m 22.26s (-3.34) **Going Correction** -0.225s/f (Firm)
**WFA** 3 from 4yo+ 11lb — **9** Ran SP% **113.1**
Speed ratings (Par 103): **103,102,97,95,95 92,91,90,87**
CSF £5.39 CT £17.81 TOTE £2.80: £1.20, £1.10, £2.10; EX 6.70 Trifecta £27.80.
**Owner** V I Araci **Bred** Newsells Park Stud **Trained** Newmarket, Suffolk

**FOCUS**
Race distance increased by 2yds. A race in which the market was dominated by two horses and the pair pulled a long way clear of the rest. The pace was fair. It's hard to pin down the level.

## 4431 BOOK NOW FOR MUSIC FESTIVAL RACENIGHT FILLIES' H'CAP — 1m 1f 35y
8:45 (8:46) (Class 4) (0-85,87) 3-Y-O+ — £7,762 (£2,310; £1,154; £577) Stalls Low

Form — RPR

-331 **1** **Company Asset (IRE)**[4] 4248 4-9-13 **83** 6ex........................ KevinStott 6 95+
(Kevin Ryan) *hld up: hdwy over 2f out: effrt and hung rt over 1f out: sn swtchd lft and bmpd 1f out: sn led and qcknd: comf* **9/4**[1]

2302 **2** 2 1/4 **Celestation**[10] 4056 3-8-11 **77**........................ JoeFanning 3 80
(Mark Johnston) *t.k.h early: led tl hung lft bnd over 5f out: pressed ldr: regained ld and rdn over 2f out: hdd ins fnl f: nt pce of wnr* **7/1**[3]

-131 **3** 1/2 **Euro Nightmare (IRE)**[12] 3981 3-9-7 **87**........................ GrahamLee 4 89
(Keith Dalgleish) *trckd ldr: carried wd bnd over 5f out: effrt over 2f out: hung rt and bmpd 1f out: sn one pce* **9/4**[1]

3043 **4** 1/2 **Hidden Rebel**[16] 3828 5-10-0 **84**........................ PaulMulrennan 7 86
(Alistair Whillans) *hld up: pushed along over 4f out: hdwy over 1f out: kpt on fnl f: nvr able to chal* **12/1**

5000 **5** 1 3/4 **Sunnua (IRE)**[28] 3402 4-8-11 **67**........................ JackGarritty 2 65
(Richard Fahey) *trckd ldrs: effrt and rdn over 2f out: outpcd whn checked over 1f out: sn n.d* **12/1**

5401 **6** 1/2 **Set In Stone (IRE)**[4] 4247 3-8-13 **79** 6ex........................ TadhgO'Shea 1 75
(John Patrick Shanahan, Ire) *dwlt: t.k.h and sn trckd ldrs: led bnd over 5f out: hdd over 2f out: rallied: wknd fnl f* **7/2**[2]

1m 57.57s (-2.13) **Going Correction** -0.225s/f (Firm)
**WFA** 3 from 4yo+ 10lb — **6** Ran SP% **111.6**
Speed ratings (Par 102): **100,98,97,97,95 95**
CSF £18.23 TOTE £3.20: £1.90, £2.30; EX 17.00 Trifecta £59.00.
**Owner** Hambleton Racing Ltd XVI **Bred** Newlands House Stud **Trained** Hambleton, N Yorks

**FOCUS**
Race distance increased by 2yds. Just six runners for this fillies' handicap but three were last-time out winners so it was quite a competitive affair. There was a fair bit of trouble but the winner looked the best filly in the race. The pace was fair. The third and fourth have been rated close to their marks.

## 4432 RACING UK HD H'CAP — 1m 68y
9:15 (9:16) (Class 5) (0-70,69) 3-Y-O+ — £3,881 (£1,155; £577; £288) Stalls Low

Form — RPR

2014 **1** **Amy Blair**[26] 3450 4-9-10 **65**........................(h) ConnorBeasley 3 71
(Keith Dalgleish) *t.k.h early: mde all: rdn and hrd pressed fr over 1f out: hld on gamely fnl f* **4/1**[3]

-400 **2** 3/4 **Catastrophe**[38] 3048 4-9-0 **55**........................ PhillipMakin 7 59
(John Quinn) *hld up in tch: rdn over 2f out: kpt on wl fnl f to take 2nd nr fin* **12/1**

0432 **3** nse **Snookered (IRE)**[27] 3431 3-8-7 **64**........................ ConnorMurtagh(7) 10 66
(Richard Fahey) *pressed ldr: drvn and ev ch over 1f out: kpt on fnl f: no ex and lost 2nd nr fin* **11/4**[1]

-206 **4** shd **Akkadian Empire**[12] 3975 3-9-5 **69**........................(h) DavidNolan 6 71
(Iain Jardine) *hld up: rdn and effrt over 2f out: kpt on fnl f nrst fin* **25/1**

06-4 **5** 3/4 **Princess Nearco (IRE)**[33] 3206 3-9-0 **64**........................ DougieCostello 1 64
(Patrick Holmes) *missed break: hld up in tch: rdn over 2f out: kpt on fnl f: nvr able to chal* **20/1**

-364 **6** 3/4 **Fortuities (IRE)**[26] 3461 3-9-3 **67**........................ JackGarritty 4 65
(Jedd O'Keeffe) *prom: rdn along over 2f out: no ex fnl f* **7/2**[2]

4-36 **7** 1/2 **Royal Icon**[34] 3189 3-9-1 **65**........................ KevinStott 11 62
(Kevin Ryan) *trckd ldrs: rdn over 2f out: drifted lft and outpcd fnl f* **12/1**

1m 47.37s (-1.03) **Going Correction** -0.225s/f (Firm)
**WFA** 3 from 4yo+ 9lb — **7** Ran SP% **92.9**
Speed ratings (Par 103): **96,95,95,95,94 93,93**
CSF £30.77 CT £76.01 TOTE £4.40: £2.50, £4.70; EX 24.40 Trifecta £79.30.
**Owner** J Fyffe **Bred** Summertree Stud **Trained** Carluke, S Lanarks
■ Fleetfoot Jack was withdrawn. Price at time of withdrawal 7/2. Rule 4 applies to all bets - deduction 20p in the pound

**FOCUS**
Race distance increased by 2yds. Just a fair gallop to this handicap in which 3l covered the seven runners. It's been rated as ordinary form for now.
T/Plt: £70.70 to a £1 stake. Pool: £84,705.13 - 874.26 winning units T/Qpdt: £26.30 to a £1 stake. Pool: £7,842.98 - 220.64 winning units **Richard Young**

# 4116 PONTEFRACT (L-H)
Monday, July 3

**OFFICIAL GOING: Good (good to firm in places; 8.2)**
Wind: Fresh behind Weather: Cloudy with sunny periods

## 4433 ROY FOWLER - A LIFETIME IN RACING H'CAP — 5f 3y
2:00 (2:00) (Class 5) (0-75,75) 3-Y-O+ — £3,881 (£1,155; £577; £288) Stalls Low

Form — RPR

0303 **1** **Miningold**[28] 3384 4-9-2 **68**........................(p) CallumRodriguez(5) 6 81
(Michael Dods) *trckd ldrs: smooth hdwy wl over 1f out: rdn to ld ins fnl f: kpt on wl towards fin* **16/1**

-402 **2** nk **Boundsy (IRE)**[35] 3152 3-9-7 **73**........................ PaulHanagan 3 83
(Richard Fahey) *trckd ldrs: hdwy on inner 2f out: rdn to chal ins fnl f: sn drvn and ev ch: kpt on* **9/4**[1]

31-0 **3** 2 1/2 **Perfect Symphony (IRE)**[67] 2104 3-9-8 **74**........................(p) KevinStott 12 75
(Kevin Ryan) *midfield: hdwy over 2f out: rdn to chse ldrs and edgd lft over 1f out: drvn and kpt on fnl f* **25/1**

0216 **4** 1/2 **Oriental Splendour (IRE)**[11] 4015 5-9-12 **73**........................ JamesSullivan 5 74+
(Ruth Carr) *hld up towards rr: hdwy 2f out: swtchd rt to outer wl over 1f out: sn rdn and styd on fnl f* **11/2**[3]

121 **5** 1 3/4 **Spirit Of Wedza (IRE)**[57] 2424 5-9-9 **70**........................ JoeDoyle 4 65
(Julie Camacho) *prom: rdn along 2f out: sn drvn and grad wknd* **13/2**

2512 **6** hd **Jacob's Pillow**[21] 3667 6-9-7 **68**........................(p) DanielTudhope 1 62
(Rebecca Bastiman) *trckd ldr: pushed along 2f out: rdn over 1f out: drvn and wknd fnl f* **4/1**[2]

300 **7** nk **New Road Side**[21] 3667 4-9-9 **75**........................(v) CliffordLee(5) 11 68
(Richard Guest) *qckly away: led and swtchd lft to wards inner: pushed along 2f out: rdn over 1f out: hdd ins fnl f: wknd* **33/1**

2030 **8** nk **Indian Pursuit (IRE)**[72] 1979 4-9-4 **65**........................ JasonHart 2 57
(John Quinn) *clsd up: rdn along 2f out: drvn and wknd over 1f out* **12/1**

0-66 **9** 1 **Market Choice (IRE)**[23] 3567 4-9-11 **72**........................ PJMcDonald 7 60
(Tracy Waggott) *hld up towards rr: sme hdwy over 1f out: keeping on whn n.m.r ins fnl f: n.d* **16/1**

1310 **10** 1 ½ **Dusty Blue**[11] 4015 5-9-4 **68**........................................ NathanEvans(3) 13 51
(Michael Easterby) *hld up: a rr* **25/1**

4500 **11** nse **Dinneratmidnight**[28] 3401 6-9-8 **69**............................ FrannyNorton 9 52
(Richard Guest) *a towards rr* **14/1**

1350 **12** 1 ¼ **Space War**[14] 3897 10-8-13 **67**....................................(t) RyanTimby(7) 10 45
(Michael Easterby) *dwlt: a rr* **50/1**

1m 2.35s (-0.95) **Going Correction** -0.10s/f (Good)
**WFA** 3 from 4yo+ 5lb **12** Ran SP% **118.2**
Speed ratings (Par 103): **103,102,98,97,94 94,94,93,92,89 89,87**
CSF £50.32 CT £950.46 TOTE £15.30: £3.90, £1.40, £7.00; EX 75.30 Trifecta £1035.20.
**Owner** Mrs C E Dods **Bred** Mrs G S Rees **Trained** Denton, Co Durham

**FOCUS**
The rail was dolled out from 6f to the winning post adding approximately 8 yards to all races. An ordinary 5f handicap. They went a strong gallop on drying ground officially described as good, good to firm in places. The winning time concurred with that assessment. A length pb from the winner.

## 4434 BRITISH STALLION STUDS EBF SPINDRIFTER CONDITIONS STKS (PLUS 10 RACE) 6f
**2:30** (2:30) (Class 2) 2-Y-O **£12,450** (£3,728; £1,864; £932) **Stalls** Low

Form RPR

10 **1** **Zaman**[13] 3925 2-8-12 0........................................ WilliamBuick 2 101
(Charlie Appleby) *trckd ldr: pushed along 2 1/2f out and sn outpcd: rdn wl over 1f out: styd on strly fnl f to ld nr line* **15/8**[1]

512 **2** nk **Unfortunately (IRE)**[23] 3611 2-8-12 0.......................... CliffordLee 4 100
(K R Burke) *stdd and hld up in rr: gd hdwy on outer jst over 2f out: sn chsng ldr: rdn to take slt advantage ins fnl f: drvn and edgd lft 75 yds out: faltered and edgd rt nr fin: hdd nr line* **9/4**[2]

1011 **3** ½ **Izzy Bizu (IRE)**[16] 3815 2-8-7 84.............................. PJMcDonald 3 94
(Mark Johnston) *led: rdn along 2f out: jnd over 1f out: hdd narrowly and drvn ins fnl f: cl up whn n.m.r on inner 75 yds out: kpt on same pce* **9/2**

13 **4** 7 **Zap**[31] 3297 2-9-2 0............................................... PaulHanagan 1 82
(Richard Fahey) *trckd ldng pair on inner: pushed along 2f out: rdn wl over 1f out: sn btn* **3/1**[3]

1m 16.56s (-0.34) **Going Correction** -0.10s/f (Good) **4** Ran SP% **108.7**
Speed ratings (Par 100): **98,97,96,87**
CSF £6.36 TOTE £2.70; EX 6.00 Trifecta £18.00.
**Owner** Godolphin **Bred** Laundry Cottage Stud Farm **Trained** Newmarket, Suffolk

**FOCUS**
Race distance increased 8 yards. The feature contest was a good quality, little juvenile conditions contest. They went a respectable gallop and the favourite needed every yard of this stiff 6f to get his head in front in a race of changing fortunes.

## 4435 EBFSTALLIONS.COM FILLIES' H'CAP 6f
**3:00** (3:01) (Class 3) (0-90,90) 3-Y-O+
**£9,337** (£2,796; £1,398; £699; £349; £175) **Stalls** Low

Form RPR

000- **1** **Avon Breeze**[259] 7413 8-9-1 **82**.............................. LewisEdmunds(5) 3 90
(Richard Whitaker) *in tch: hdwy 2f out: nt clr run and swtchd rt jst over 1f out: sn rdn and squeezed through to ld last 100 yds: kpt on wl* **7/1**

-043 **2** ½ **Partitia**[24] 3526 3-9-2 **84**........................................ WilliamBuick 1 89
(Sir Michael Stoute) *trckd ldng pair on inner: nt clr run and swtchd rt 1 1/2f out: sn rdn to chal: ev ch ins fnal f: sn drvn and kpt on* **15/8**[1]

-423 **3** shd **The Feathered Nest (IRE)**[17] 3793 3-9-1 **83**.................. PaulHanagan 7 88
(Richard Fahey) *dwlt and rr: hdwy on outer wl over 1f out: sn rdn: styd on to chal ins fnl f: kpt on* **3/1**[2]

10-0 **4** 2 ¼ **Hope Solo (IRE)**[17] 3793 3-9-5 **87**.............................. DavidAllan 8 86+
(Tim Easterby) *rr: pushed along and outpcd 1/2-way: hdwy wl over 1f out: rdn and kpt on fnl f* **33/1**

0- **5** 1 **Tilly Trotter (IRE)**[71] 1997 3-9-5 **87**............................ DanielTudhope 6 82
(Declan Carroll) *in tch: pushed along over 2f out: hdwy and cl up on outer over 1f out: sn rdn and edgd lft: drvn and kpt on same pce fnl f* **20/1**

11-6 **6** 1 **Spin Doctor**[24] 3526 3-9-2 **84**.................................. TonyHamilton 5 75
(Richard Fahey) *trckd ldr: hdwy 2f out and sn chal: rdn to take slt ld ent fnl f: sn drvn: hdd & wknd* **25/1**

0000 **7** 2 ¼ **Glenrowan Rose (IRE)**[9] 4078 4-10-0 **90**...............(h[1]) AndrewMullen 4 75
(Keith Dalgleish) *trckd ldrs: pushed along 2f out: sn rdn and hld whn hmpd and squeezed out 1 1/2f out* **20/1**

2151 **8** 1 **Love Oasis**[6] 4188 3-8-9 **77** 6ex................................ PJMcDonald 2 58
(Mark Johnston) *led: rdn along 2f out: drvn and hdd ent fnl f: sn wknd* **7/2**[3]

1m 16.29s (-0.61) **Going Correction** -0.10s/f (Good)
**WFA** 3 from 4yo+ 6lb **8** Ran SP% **110.8**
Speed ratings (Par 104): **100,99,99,96,94 93,90,89**
CSF £18.95 CT £45.59 TOTE £7.00: £1.90, £1.20, £1.30; EX 21.60 Trifecta £75.80.
**Owner** Grange Park Racing II & Partner **Bred** Hellwood Stud Farm **Trained** Scarcroft, W Yorks

**FOCUS**
Race distance increased 8 yards. A fairly good fillies' handicap. They went a respectable gallop and it is sound form. The second has been rated close to her 2yo best.

## 4436 WAYNE CONWAY MEMORIAL H'CAP 1m 4f 5y
**3:30** (3:32) (Class 5) (0-70,71) 3-Y-O **£3,881** (£1,155; £577; £288) **Stalls** Low

Form RPR

5220 **1** **Breakwater Bay (IRE)**[14] 3909 3-9-0 **63**.......................... DavidAllan 2 73
(Tim Easterby) *t.k.h early: hld up in tch: hdwy on inner 4f out: rdn to chse ldrs 2f out: led 1 1/2f out: kpt on wl fnl f* **9/2**[2]

-614 **2** 2 ½ **New Society (IRE)**[19] 3711 3-9-6 **69**.......................... PJMcDonald 10 74
(James Bethell) *prom: chsd ldr over 3f out: rdn along 2f out: ev ch over 1f out: sn drvn and kpt on same pce* **7/1**

0-02 **3** hd **Cornerstone Lad**[25] 3499 3-9-0 **63**.............................. WilliamBuick 9 68
(Micky Hammond) *hld up in rr: hdwy on outer over 3f out: chsd ldrs 2f out: sn rdn: drvn and kpt on wl fnl f* **11/4**[1]

0121 **4** 4 **Dyna Might**[28] 3405 3-8-12 **61**..................................(p) AndrewMullen 6 59
(Ollie Pears) *trckd ldrs: hdwy over 3f out: chsd ldng pair 2f out and sn rdn: swtchd lft and drvn ins fnl f: sn one pce* **13/2**[3]

6203 **5** 3 ¾ **Knightsbridge Liam (IRE)**[14] 3901 3-8-7 **56**.................. JamesSullivan 8 48
(Michael Easterby) *t.k.h: led and sn clr at str pce: rn wd bnd 7f out: pushed along 3f out: rdn 2f out: hdd 1 1/2f out and sn wknd* **12/1**

0-35 **6** nk **Royal Cosmic**[14] 3901 3-8-3 **52**................................ PatrickMathers 4 44
(Richard Fahey) *hld up towards rr: hdwy over 2f out: sn rdn and plugged on appr fnl f* **22/1**

6230 **7** 4 **Marqoom**[23] 3596 3-9-8 **71**........................................ DaneO'Neill 12 56
(Mark Johnston) *chsd ldrs: pushed along over 5f out: rdn over 3f out: sn outpcd* **9/1**

0-00 **8** 9 **Mystic Maeve (IRE)**[34] 3180 3-7-13 **51** oh6............(b[1]) NathanEvans(3) 5 22
(Roger Fell) *chsd clr ldr: rdn along over 4f out: sn wknd* **100/1**

4050 **9** 16 **Oregon Point (USA)**[25] 3499 3-9-7 **70**.....................(b[1]) TonyHamilton 3 15
(Tim Easterby) *t.k.h early: a rr* **25/1**

0000 **10** 13 **Red Master (IRE)**[21] 3674 3-8-5 **54**...........................(p[1]) PaulHanagan 7
(Ed Dunlop) *a towards rr* **20/1**

2m 40.38s (-0.42) **Going Correction** -0.10s/f (Good) **10** Ran SP% **102.3**
Speed ratings (Par 100): **97,95,95,92,90 89,87,81,70,61**
CSF £26.65 CT £73.34 TOTE £4.40: £1.60, £1.70, £1.40; EX 30.60 Trifecta £141.90.
**Owner** Reality Partnerships III **Bred** George Delahunt **Trained** Great Habton, N Yorks
■ Gee Sixty Six was withdrawn. Price at time of withdrawal 6/1. Rule 4 applies to all bets - deduction 10p in the pound.

**FOCUS**
Race distance increased 8 yards. A modest middle-distance 3yo handicap. They went a muddling initial gallop but that tempo increased. The third helps set the standard.

## 4437 15TH WILFRED UNDERWOOD MEMORIAL CLASSIFIED STKS 6f
**4:00** (4:00) (Class 5) 3-Y-O **£3,881** (£1,155; £577; £288) **Stalls** Low

Form RPR

4321 **1** **Don Valentino (IRE)**[12] 3984 3-9-0 75.......................... DanielTudhope 3 86+
(David O'Meara) *mde all: rdn and qcknd clr over 1f out: readily* **5/2**[2]

2135 **2** 2 ¼ **Acadian Angel (IRE)**[16] 3828 3-9-0 73.......................... JasonHart 5 77
(John Quinn) *hld up: hdwy on outer wl over 1f out: rdn to chse wnr ins fnl f: no imp towards fin* **3/1**[3]

0-16 **3** 5 **Grinty (IRE)**[27] 3434 3-9-0 74.................................. AndrewMullen 4 61
(Michael Dods) *trckd ldng pair: hdwy to chse wnr 2f out: sn rdn and edgd lft over 1f out: sn drvn and kpt on same pce fnl f* **17/2**

1-30 **4** ¾ **Dellaguista (IRE)**[15] 3862 3-9-0 74..............................(p) PaulHanagan 1 59
(William Haggas) *in tch on inner: pushed along over 2f out: rdn wl over 1f out: sn btn* **9/4**[1]

0-44 **5** nk **Night Law**[12] 3982 3-9-0 75.................................. TonyHamilton 2 58
(Richard Fahey) *t.k.h: trckd wnr: pushed along over 2f out: rdn wl over 1f out: sn drvn and wknd* **11/2**

1m 16.24s (-0.66) **Going Correction** -0.10s/f (Good) **5** Ran SP% **110.3**
Speed ratings (Par 100): **100,97,90,89,88**
CSF £10.31 TOTE £2.50: £1.40, £1.70; EX 8.60 Trifecta £44.80.
**Owner** Clipper Logistics **Bred** Ann & Joe Hallinan **Trained** Upper Helmsley, N Yorks

**FOCUS**
Race distance increased 8 yards. An ordinary little 3yo Classified Stakes. The second favourite's jockey Daniel Tudhope got the front-running fractions spot on. The runner-up has been rated to form.

## 4438 PONTEFRACT RACECOURSE SUPPORTING RACING STAFF WEEK H'CAP 1m 6y
**4:30** (4:31) (Class 4) (0-80,81) 3-Y-O+ **£5,822** (£1,732; £865; £432) **Stalls** Low

Form RPR

3-24 **1** **Destroyer**[16] 3845 4-9-13 **79**.................................. JamesSullivan 7 83
(Tom Tate) *trckd ldr: cl up 2f out: slt ld jst over 1f out: jnd and rdn ins fnl f: hld on wl towards fin* **11/4**[2]

-621 **2** shd **Full Of Promise**[14] 3899 4-9-1 **67**.............................. PaulHanagan 8 71
(Richard Fahey) *trckd ldrs: hdwy over 2f out: chal ent fnl f: sn rdn and ev ch: drvn and no ex nr fin* **7/1**

5255 **3** 2 **Trinity Star (IRE)**[14] 3910 6-8-10 **67**..................(b) CallumRodriguez(5) 1 66
(Michael Dods) *hld up in tch: hdwy wl over 1f out: rdn to chse ldng pair ins fnl f: kpt on same pce* **5/2**[1]

4023 **4** 2 **Yorkee Mo Sabee (IRE)**[6] 4168 4-9-9 **75**...................(h) FrannyNorton 4 70
(Mark Johnston) *led: pushed along over 2f out: sn rdn: hdd over 1f out: grad wknd* **3/1**[3]

0-30 **5** 2 ¼ **Hitman**[16] 3845 4-9-10 **76**...................................... DuranFentiman 6 66
(Rebecca Bastiman) *hld up in tch: hdwy over 2f out: rdn to chse ldrs over 1f out: drvn and one pce ins fnl f* **25/1**

6510 **6** 2 ¾ **Gloriosus (USA)**[17] 3780 3-9-6 **81**.............................. WilliamBuick 2 62
(Mark Johnston) *trckd ldng pair: pushed along over 2f out: rdn wl over 1f out: sn drvn and wknd* **6/1**

1m 45.03s (-0.87) **Going Correction** -0.10s/f (Good)
**WFA** 3 from 4yo+ 9lb **6** Ran SP% **110.9**
Speed ratings (Par 105): **100,99,97,95,93 90**
CSF £20.93 CT £50.02 TOTE £3.60: £1.70, £2.50; EX 20.70 Trifecta £58.40.
**Owner** T T Racing **Bred** Whitsbury Manor Stud **Trained** Tadcaster, N Yorks

**FOCUS**
Race distance increased 8 yards. A fair handicap. They went a respectable gallop and once again it is sound form. The winner has been rated back to his best.

## 4439 JP MEMORIAL LADIES' H'CAP (FOR LADY AMATEUR RIDERS) 1m 2f 5y
**5:00** (5:00) (Class 5) (0-70,72) 3-Y-O+ **£3,743** (£1,161; £580; £290) **Stalls** Low

Form RPR

00-1 **1** **Exclusive Waters (IRE)**[146] 607 7-9-10 **57**.................. MissPFuller 7 71
(Tina Jackson) *midfield: hdwy 4f out: chsd ldrs 3f out: led over 2f out and sn rdn clr: kpt on wl fnl f* **33/1**

4014 **2** 6 **Kiwi Bay**[28] 3402 12-10-0 **68**................................ MissSEDods(7) 5 70
(Michael Dods) *midfield: hdwy and in tch over 4f out: trckd ldrs 3f out: rdn to chse wnr over 1f out: kpt on same pce* **12/1**

2133 **3** ½ **Bonnie Arlene (IRE)**[11] 4012 3-9-7 **69**................ MissEmmaBedford(5) 11 71
(Mark Johnston) *hld up towards rr: hdwy over 3f out: rdn along over 2f out: styd on to chse ldrs over 1f out: kpt on same pce* **6/1**[2]

2151 **4** 7 **Bit Of A Quirke**[13] 3935 4-10-5 **66**.............................. MissETodd 1 53
(Mark Walford) *led: pushed along 3f out: hdd over 2f out and sn rdn: drvn over 1f out: grad wknd* **2/1**[1]

50-5 **5** 1 **Frozon**[12] 3977 4-9-1 **53**..............................(p[1]) PoppyBridgwater(5) 2 38
(Brian Ellison) *.trckd ldrs: hdwy over 4f out: rdn along over 3f out: drvn over 2f out: plugged on one pce* **6/1**[2]

0-64 **6** nse **Inspector Norse**[10] 4034 6-9-4 **54**......................(p) MissEEasterby(3) 12 39
(Tim Easterby) *hld up in rr: hdwy on wd outside 3f out: rdn along 2f out: sn drvn and plugged on one pce* **7/1**[3]

0624 **7** 5 **Mustaqbal (IRE)**[14] 3899 5-10-4 **72**.......................... MissCADods(7) 3 47
(Michael Dods) *trckd ldrs: rdn along over 3f out: sn outpcd* **11/1**

0-05 **8** 10 **Cadmium**[19] 3706 6-9-4 **51**..................................(p) MissCWalton 6 6
(Micky Hammond) *a towards rr* **20/1**

66-1 **9** 4 **City Ground (USA)**[77] 1932 10-10-6 **67**...................... MissSBrotherton 10 14
(Michael Appleby) *hld up: a towards rr* **7/1**[3]

6603 **10** 11 **Ibreeq (IRE)**[31] 3284 4-8-11 **49** oh1.....................(b[1]) MissEmilyBullock(5) 8
(Roger Fell) *prom: chsd ldng pair 6f out: rdn along 4f out: sn lost pl and bhd* **33/1**

3-03 **11** nse **Quoteline Direct**[14] 3910 4-10-0 **61**.......................(h) MissBeckySmith 9
(Micky Hammond) *a towards rr* **20/1**

6400 **12** *10* **Stag Party (IRE)**[48] 2705 3-8-6 **49** oh4..........................(tp) MissAWaugh 4
(Julia Brooke) *prom: rdn along over 4f out: sn wknd* **33/1**
2m 14.28s (0.58) **Going Correction** -0.10s/f (Good)
**WFA** 3 from 4yo+ 10lb **12** Ran SP% **121.3**
Speed ratings (Par 103): **93,88,87,82,81 81,77,69,66,57 57,49**
CSF £373.22 CT £2703.82 TOTE £23.20: £7.20, £4.30, £2.10; EX 284.90 Trifecta £1409.80.
**Owner** Ms Sara Hattersley **Bred** M M Sammon **Trained** Liverton, Cleveland
**FOCUS**
Race distance increased 8 yards. A modest handicap for lady amateur riders. The strong early pace fell apart and an outsider came through to pick up the pieces. The winner has been rated back to his old turf best.
T/Jkpt: Not Won. T/Plt: £54.20 to a £1 stake. Pool: £89,295.73 - 54.20 winning units T/Qpdt: £6.50 to a £1 stake. Pool: £8,319.00 - 945.22 winning units **Joe Rowntree**

## 4407 WINDSOR (R-H)
Monday, July 3
**OFFICIAL GOING: Good (good to firm in places; 7.9)**
Wind: Moderate, behind Weather: Fine, warm

## 4440 EBF STALLIONS FILLIES' NOVICE MEDIAN AUCTION STKS (PLUS 10 RACE) 5f 21y
**6:00** (6:01) (Class 5) 2-Y-O **£3,881** (£1,155; £577; £288) **Stalls** Low

Form RPR
**1** **Flying Sparkle (IRE)** 2-9-0 0.......................................... HayleyTurner 2 78+
(Michael Bell) *trckd ldrs: led 2f out: rdn over 1f out and sn clr: pushed out last 150yds: comf* **11/2**[3]
05 **2** *2 1/4* **Hunni**[16] 3821 2-9-0 0.......................................... PatCosgrave 7 70
(Tom Clover) *chsd ldrs: rdn over 1f out: sn chsd wnr: styd on but no imp* **9/1**
0 **3** *1 1/4* **Dusty**[16] 3821 2-9-0 0.......................................... RyanTate 16 65+
(Mick Channon) *dwlt: sn in midfield on outer: rdn and prog 2f out: kpt on to take 3rd ins fnl f* **12/1**
**4** *1/2* **Polly's Gold (IRE)** 2-9-0 0.......................................... ShaneKelly 11 64+
(Richard Hughes) *jst in tch in midfield: prog 2f out: rdn and kpt on fnl f: nrst fin* **25/1**
20 **5** *hd* **Fab (IRE)**[7] 4160 2-9-0 0.......................................... TimmyMurphy 9 63
(Jamie Osborne) *walked to post early then dismntd at s: last to enter stalls: dwlt: wl in rr: rdn and prog on outer 1/2-way: racd awkwardly over 1f out: kpt on* **7/2**[1]
50 **6** *2 3/4* **Silver Bullet (IRE)**[20] 3687 2-9-0 0..........................(p[1]) LiamKeniry 1 53
(Tom Dascombe) *in tch in midfield: urged along 1/2-way: no threat to ldrs over 1f out: kpt on* **16/1**
**7** *2* **Misty Spirit** 2-9-0 0.......................................... FranBerry 8 46
(David Elsworth) *chsd ldrs: shkn up and wknd over 1f out* **10/1**
**8** *1* **Tea Rattle** 2-8-7 0.......................................... RPWalsh(7) 6 42
(Scott Dixon) *v.s.i.s: wl in rr on outer and rn green: nvr a factor but kpt on wl fnl f* **100/1**
0 **9** *nk* **Bucks Frizz (IRE)**[16] 3815 2-9-0 0.......................................... TomMarquand 3 41
(David Evans) *led against rail to 2f out: wknd over 1f out* **50/1**
4 **10** *1/2* **Jan's Joy**[27] 3437 2-8-11 0.......................................... AaronJones(3) 4 39
(Stuart Williams) *taken down early: chsd ldr to 1/2-way: wknd over 1f out* **14/1**
5 **11** *1 1/2* **That's My Girl (IRE)**[17] 3769 2-9-0 0.......................................... SeanLevey 12 34
(Richard Hannon) *jst in tch at rr of midfield: no prog 2f out: wknd* **5/1**[2]
**12** *3* **Smooth Sailing** 2-9-0 0.......................................... JamesDoyle 14 23
(Charles Hills) *dwlt: a detached in last quartet* **5/1**[2]
0 **13** *2 3/4* **Watch Tan**[20] 3687 2-9-0 0.......................................... TrevorWhelan 13 13
(George Baker) *pressed ldrs to wl over 1f out: wknd rapidly* **80/1**
00 **14** *nse* **Lastoneforthecraic (IRE)**[14] 3917 2-9-0 0.......................................... JohnFahy 15 13
(David Evans) *dwlt: a detached in last quartet* **100/1**
**15** *4* **Spix's Macaw** 2-8-9 0.......................................... MitchGodwin(5) 5
(Bill Turner) *sn pushed along and detached in last quartet: a bhd* **66/1**
**16** *3/4* **Raise A Little Joy** 2-9-0 0.......................................... TomQueally 10
(J R Jenkins) *v.s.a: a detached in last quartet* **80/1**
1m 0.35s (0.05) **Going Correction** 0.0s/f (Good) **16** Ran SP% **122.0**
Speed ratings (Par 91): **99,95,93,92,92 87,84,83,82,81 79,74,70,70,63 62**
CSF £53.35 TOTE £6.90: £2.40, £2.90, £3.50; EX 57.40 Trifecta £624.20.
**Owner** Karmaa Racing Limited **Bred** Newlands House Stud **Trained** Newmarket, Suffolk
**FOCUS**
Rail was out 12yds from the stands' side inner position from 6f to the winning post. Distances as advertised. There was "light selective watering" after racing the previous day, and during this card various connections said they considered the ground to be loose. This doesn't look strong form, but a likeable winner.

## 4441 ROYAL WINDSOR RACECOURSE (S) STKS 6f 12y
**6:30** (6:30) (Class 6) 3-Y-0+ **£2,264** (£673; £336; £168) **Stalls** Low

Form RPR
4324 **1** **Morache Music**[24] 3518 9-9-3 77..........................(p) DavidProbert 5 69+
(Patrick Chamings) *trckd ldng pair: chal over 1f out: urged along to ld jst ins fnl f: kpt on* **4/9**[1]
0000 **2** *3/4* **Vincentti (IRE)**[17] 3774 7-9-3 69..........................(p) SamHitchcott 3 66
(Ronald Harris) *led: rdn and hdd over 1f out: sn in 3rd: kpt on wl last 100yds to snatch 2nd fnl stride* **13/2**[3]
2511 **3** *shd* **Nag's Wag (IRE)**[11] 4008 4-9-8 71.......................................... LiamKeniry 4 71
(George Baker) *trckd ldr: shkn up to ld over 1f out: drvn and hdd jst ins fnl f: one pce and lost 2nd last stride* **10/3**[2]
6400 **4** *6* **Quintus Cerialis (IRE)**[16] 3823 5-8-10 49..........................(t[1]) RhiainIngram(7) 2 48
(Karen George) *s.s: detached in last: rdn and brief effrt over 2f out: sn no imp* **40/1**
1m 12.3s (-0.70) **Going Correction** 0.0s/f (Good) **4** Ran SP% **108.1**
Speed ratings (Par 101): **104,103,102,94**
CSF £3.86 TOTE £1.40; EX 4.30 Trifecta £5.60.Nag's Wag was claimed by Mr Conor Dore for £6,000
**Owner** The Berks & Hants Racing Partnership **Bred** Michael E Broughton **Trained** Baughurst, Hants
**FOCUS**
A fair seller despite the small field.

## 4442 JAMES DENLEY 60TH BIRTHDAY FILLIES' H'CAP 1m 3f 99y
**7:00** (7:00) (Class 5) (0-70,72) 3-Y-0+ **£2,911** (£866; £432; £216) **Stalls** Centre

Form RPR
-066 **1** **Castellated**[19] 3721 3-9-3 69.......................................... SeanLevey 2 78
(Richard Hannon) *trckd ldrs: rdn to ld over 2f out: in command over 1f out: drvn out* **11/4**[1]
0106 **2** *1 1/4* **Becca Campbell (IRE)**[20] 3683 4-9-11 69..........(p) EdwardGreatrex(3) 3 75
(Eve Johnson Houghton) *hld up in last: rdn and prog over 2f out: chsd wnr over 1f out: styd on and steadily clsd but nvr able to chal* **13/2**
-400 **3** *5* **Secret Soul**[19] 3721 3-8-12 64..........................(v[1]) DavidProbert 6 62
(Ralph Beckett) *led 2f: trckd ldr to 5f out: styd prom: drvn to ld briefly wl over 2f out: chsd wnr to over 1f out: one pce* **9/2**[3]
-633 **4** *2 3/4* **Mayflair**[140] 718 3-8-9 66..........................(b[1]) MitchGodwin(5) 7 60
(Jonathan Portman) *hld up in 5th: rdn wl over 2f out: kpt on one pce and no threat* **16/1**
-442 **5** *4* **Saumur**[20] 3684 5-10-3 72.......................................... TomQueally 4 58
(Denis Coakley) *hld up in rr: rdn on outer wl over 2f out: no imp ldrs over 1f out: wknd fnl f* **6/1**
5241 **6** *4* **Orithia (USA)**[16] 3819 3-8-13 65..........................(t) FergusSweeney 1 45
(Seamus Durack) *hld up in rr: rdn and effrt over 2f out: no imp ldrs over 1f out: wknd* **4/1**[2]
-006 **7** *17* **Onehelluvatouch**[16] 3820 4-9-1 56..........................(b) FranBerry 9 6
(Philip Hide) *trckd ldrs: pushed up to chal 5f out: drvn to ld over 3f out to over 2f out: wknd qckly: t.o and eased last 100yds* **33/1**
-306 **8** *1 3/4* **Angel Of Rome (IRE)**[34] 3178 3-9-1 67.......................................... ShaneKelly 8 15
(Richard Hughes) *led after 2f to over 3f out: wknd u.p over 2f out: eased over 1f out: t.o* **9/1**
2m 28.58s (-0.92) **Going Correction** 0.0s/f (Good)
**WFA** 3 from 4yo+ 11lb **8** Ran SP% **111.3**
Speed ratings (Par 100): **103,102,98,96,93 90,78,77**
CSF £19.84 CT £73.91 TOTE £3.70: £1.30, £2.20, £1.70; EX 22.80 Trifecta £96.20.
**Owner** Cheveley Park Stud **Bred** Cheveley Park Stud Ltd **Trained** East Everleigh, Wilts
**FOCUS**
The jockeys initially shunned the stands' rail on entering the straight, but that's where the first two ended up. Just a modest fillies' handicap. The winner has been rated back to her 2yo form.

## 4443 STRATEGIC PROPOSALS 30TH ANNIVERSARY H'CAP 1m 2f
**7:30** (7:31) (Class 4) (0-85,85) 3-Y-0+ **£4,690** (£1,395; £697; £348) **Stalls** Centre

Form RPR
41-4 **1** **Intrepidly (USA)**[16] 3838 3-9-4 85.......................................... JamieSpencer 4 98
(Jeremy Noseda) *hld up in 6th: prog 3f out: sustained chal fr wl over 1f out: hrd rdn to ld last 100yds* **5/2**[2]
1-04 **2** *nk* **Anythingtoday (IRE)**[17] 3778 3-9-1 82.......................................... JamesDoyle 7 94
(Hugo Palmer) *trckd ldrs: wnt 2nd 3f out: rdn to ld wl over 1f out: kpt on wl u.p but hdd last 100yds* **9/4**[1]
004 **3** *3* **Calvados Spirit**[16] 3808 4-9-11 85..........................(h) KieranShoemark(3) 2 90
(William Muir) *led at gd pce but pressed: drvn over 2f out: hdd wl over 1f out: kpt on same pce* **16/1**
5-32 **4** *7* **Biotic**[21] 3670 6-9-5 76.......................................... RyanTate 8 67
(Rod Millman) *stdd s: hld up in last pair: effrt 3f out: shkn up and no imp ldrs 2f out: wknd fnl f* **9/2**[3]
530 **5** *1* **Craftsmanship (FR)**[12] 3966 6-9-3 74.......................................... PaoloSirigu 3 63
(Robert Eddery) *s.s: hld up in last pair: rdn and effrt over 2f out: no imp ldrs over 1f out: wknd fnl f* **20/1**
20-0 **6** *17* **Udogo**[14] 3920 6-9-1 77.......................................... JennyPowell(5) 1 32
(Brendan Powell) *chsd ldrs: urged along 1/2-way: stl prom 3f out: sn wknd qckly: t.o* **66/1**
/64- **7** *1/2* **Matorico (IRE)**[226] 2472 6-9-11 82.......................................... FranBerry 6 36
(Jonjo O'Neill) *pressed ldr at gd pce: lost 2nd and wknd qckly 3f out: t.o* **14/1**
4113 **8** *22* **Rita's Man (IRE)**[35] 3162 3-8-7 74.......................................... TomMarquand 5
(Richard Hannon) *struggling and lost pl after 3f: last over 4f out: sn t.o* **5/1**
2m 8.27s (-0.43) **Going Correction** 0.0s/f (Good)
**WFA** 3 from 4yo+ 10lb **8** Ran SP% **113.0**
Speed ratings (Par 105): **101,100,98,92,91 78,77,60**
CSF £8.32 CT £68.59 TOTE £2.70: £1.10, £1.30, £3.60; EX 9.40 Trifecta £91.40.
**Owner** The Honorable Earle Mack & T Hind Racing **Bred** WinStar Farm LLC **Trained** Newmarket, Suffolk
**FOCUS**
A useful enough handicap. The principals gradually drifted towards the far side in the closing stages. The level is a bit fluid, but has been rated on the positive side around the third to his turf form.

## 4444 WINDSOR RACECOURSE SUPPORTING RACING STAFF WEEK MAIDEN STKS 1m 31y
**8:00** (8:03) (Class 5) 3-Y-O **£2,911** (£866; £432; £216) **Stalls** Low

Form RPR
44-2 **1** **Asaas (USA)**[20] 3682 3-9-5 80.......................................... SilvestreDeSousa 10 83
(Roger Varian) *reluctant to enter stalls: t.k.h: hld up in midfield: prog 3f out: rdn to chal wl over 1f out: drvn ahd last 75yds: hld on* **5/4**[1]
0 **2** *hd* **Jus Pires (USA)**[45] 2798 3-9-5 0..........................(t[1]) JamesDoyle 8 82
(Jeremy Noseda) *trckd ldrs: rdn over 2f out: led over 1f out but sn hrd pressed: hdd last 75yds: kpt on wl fnl strides* **4/1**[3]
00 **3** *7* **Street Marie (USA)**[39] 3007 3-8-11 0.......................................... KieranShoemark(3) 1 60
(John Gosden) *led: sent for home 3f out: hanging lft and hdd over 1f out: fdd* **20/1**
24 **4** *8* **Unified**[18] 3748 3-8-11 0.......................................... HectorCrouch(3) 6 42+
(Clive Cox) *s.i.s: wl in rr: off the pce 1/2-way: effrt 3f out: rchd v modest 4th over 1f out: no prog after* **9/4**[2]
4666 **5** *3/4* **Hisar (IRE)**[22] 3621 3-9-5 70..........................(p[1]) DavidProbert 2 45
(Ronald Harris) *chsd ldr to over 2f out: wknd qckly* **33/1**
**6** *2* **Big Bad Lol (IRE)** 3-9-5 0.......................................... RichardKingscote 3 41
(Ed Walker) *dwlt: rn green in last pair: lost tch 1/2-way: shkn up and plugged on fnl 2f* **20/1**
04 **7** *2* **Kalani Rose**[31] 3309 3-9-0 0.......................................... JackMitchell 7 31
(Ben De Haan) *chsd ldrs tl wknd over 2f out* **50/1**
050 **8** *15* **Kyshoni (IRE)**[7] 4152 3-9-0 0.......................................... ShaneKelly 4
(Mike Murphy) *reluctant to enter stalls: in tch to 1/2-way: sn wknd: t.o* **50/1**
**9** *3 1/2* **Light Humor (USA)** 3-9-0 0.......................................... JamieSpencer 9
(Jeremy Noseda) *sn in last pair and rn green: lost tch 1/2-way: t.o* **10/1**
1m 44.39s (-0.31) **Going Correction** 0.0s/f (Good) **9** Ran SP% **120.7**
Speed ratings (Par 100): **101,100,93,85,85 83,81,66,62**
CSF £6.67 TOTE £2.20: £1.02, £1.90, £5.40; EX 8.80 Trifecta £69.70.
**Owner** Prince A A Faisal **Bred** Nawara Stud Co Ltd **Trained** Newmarket, Suffolk
■ Stewards' Enquiry : Silvestre De Sousa two-day ban: used whip above permitted level (Jul 17-18)
James Doyle two-day ban: used whip above permitted level (Jul 17, 19)

**FOCUS**
The pace looked solid and the first two (who ended up far side) pulled clear of the third, who was in turn well ahead of the remainder. Fair form at least from the front two. The winner has been rated to the better view of his form.

## 4445 BOYZONE LIVE ON 26TH AUGUST MAIDEN FILLIES' STKS 6f 12y
**8:30** (8:36) (Class 5) 3-4-Y-0 **£2,911** (£866; £432; £216) **Stalls** Low

Form RPR
1 **Starsovertheriver (IRE)** 3-9-1 0 SeanLevey 9 68
(Ismail Mohammed) *chsd ldrs: outpcd and rdn 1/2-way: rallied on outer over 1f out: drvn ahd last 50yds* **4/1**[2]

2 *nk* **Charleston Belle** 3-9-1 0 PatCosgrave 12 67
(Giles Bravery) *hld up: gd prog 1/2-way: rdn to chse ldr over 1f out and sn chalng: jst hld and dropped to 3rd ins fnl f: kpt on wl to take 2nd again nr fin* **9/1**

346 3 *hd* **Omneeya**[23] 3595 3-9-1 71 TomMarquand 4 67
(Marco Botti) *cl up: trckd ldr 1/2-way: rdn to ld 2f out: hung lft fnl f: hdd last 50yds* **5/2**[1]

6650 4 *1 ¾* **Ocean Promise (USA)**[5] 4214 3-9-1 67 (b[1]) ShaneKelly 1 61
(Richard Hughes) *drvn to ld: hdd 2f out and nt qckn: styd on again nr fin* **9/2**[3]

5 *2 ¼* **Cherished (IRE)** 3-9-1 0 TimmyMurphy 2 54
(Geoffrey Deacon) *sn in last pair: pushed along over 2f out: kpt on steadily fr over 1f out: nt disgracd* **16/1**

6 *2 ¾* **Boogey Wonderland** 3-9-1 0 KieranO'Neill 13 45
(Scott Dixon) *slowly away: wl in rr: shkn up over 2f out: kpt on fr over 1f out* **25/1**

7 *2 ½* **Look Surprised**[105] 4-9-2 0 MitchGodwin(5) 8 38
(Roger Teal) *in tch: rdn and stl chsng ldrs 2f out: wknd over 1f out* **66/1**

64 8 *2* **Picc And Go**[16] 3806 4-9-7 0 JohnFahy 3 32
(Matthew Salaman) *chsd ldrs: rdn over 2f out: wknd over 1f out* **66/1**

9 *4 ½* **Here's The Deal** 3-8-12 0 CharlieBennett(3) 7 16
(Lisa Williamson) *slowly away: a in rr: in tch to over 2f out: wknd* **100/1**

00 10 *hd* **Willow Tiger Lily**[51] 2619 3-8-8 0 GinaMangan(7) 6 16
(J R Jenkins) *in tch to 1/2-way: wknd 2f out* **100/1**

00- 11 *11* **Sea My Diamond (IRE)**[287] 6622 3-8-12 0 HectorCrouch(3) 16
(Mark Hoad) *chsd ldr to 1/2-way: wknd qckly: t.o* **100/1**

1m 13.13s (0.13) **Going Correction** 0.0s/f (Good)
**WFA** 3 from 4yo 6lb **11** Ran SP% **92.4**
Speed ratings (Par 100): **99,98,98,96,93 89,86,83,77,77 62**
CSF £18.29 TOTE £4.10: £1.40, £2.40, £1.20; EX 33.80 Trifecta £75.50.
**Owner** Saeed Manana **Bred** Pat O'Rourke **Trained** Newmarket, Suffolk
■ Killay (8/1) was withdrawn. Rule 4 applies to bets struck prior to withdrawal but not to SP prices. Deduction 10p in the pound. New market formed. All Good (9/1) & Razzmatazz (2/1F) were withdrawn. Rule 4 applies to all bets - deduction 40p in the p35

## 4446 RONNIE SCOTT'S JAZZ CLUB H'CAP 1m 31y
**9:00** (9:03) (Class 5) (0-70,77) 3-Y-0+ **£2,911** (£866; £432; £216) **Stalls** Low

Form RPR
0-03 1 **Fit For The Job (IRE)**[14] 3920 5-10-2 72 (p) FranBerry 5 83
(Jonjo O'Neill) *hld up in 7th: prog towards outer over 2f out: rdn to ld jst over 1f out: styd on wl* **7/1**[3]

001 2 *1 ¼* **Jumping Jack (IRE)**[6] 4176 3-9-5 77 6ex FinleyMarsh(7) 2 82
(Richard Hughes) *in tch: pushed along over 2f out: prog wl over 1f out: drvn and styd on to take 2nd last 75yds* **7/2**[1]

3316 3 *nk* **Ross Raith Rover**[19] 3730 4-9-4 67 (p) JordanUys(7) 9 73
(Robert Eddery) *hld up in 8th: rdn on wd outside over 2f out: prog to chal over 1f out: chsd wnr after: no imp and lost 2nd last 75yds* **16/1**

1341 4 *3* **Shifting Star (IRE)**[14] 3920 12-9-13 69 (vt) WilliamCarson 12 68
(John Bridger) *pressed ldr: rdn over 2f out: stl ch over 1f out: fdd* **12/1**

3554 5 *1 ½* **Bollihope**[14] 3910 5-10-1 71 SeanLevey 11 67
(Richard Guest) *chsd ldng pair: rdn to ld briefly over 1f out: wknd fnl f* **14/1**

0-50 6 *¾* **Big Chill (IRE)**[28] 3396 5-9-11 70 CharlieBennett(3) 1 64
(Patrick Chamings) *led at gd pce: rdn over 2f out: hdd & wknd over 1f out* **12/1**

-354 7 *½* **Armagnac (IRE)**[41] 2931 3-9-4 69 JamieSpencer 7 60
(Michael Bell) *stdd after s: hld up wl in rr: rdn over 2f out: sme prog over 1f out: nvr a threat* **5/1**[2]

0605 8 *hd* **Candesta (USA)**[61] 2318 7-8-10 59 JackOsborn(7) 4 51
(Julia Feilden) *hld up in rr: rdn over 2f out against nr side: no great prog* **40/1**

4344 9 *1* **It's How We Roll (IRE)**[14] 3922 3-9-1 66 (b) TomMarquand 13 54
(John Spearing) *dwlt: mostly in last: kpt on fr over 1f out but nvr a factor* **10/1**

0-30 10 *1* **Inlawed**[38] 3038 3-9-3 68 RichardKingscote 14 54
(Ed Walker) *hld up towards rr: pushed along over 2f out: no imp ldrs over 1f out: wknd* **10/1**

6050 11 *3 ½* **Mezzotint (IRE)**[12] 3966 8-9-10 66 DavidProbert 10 46
(Lee Carter) *hld up wl in rr: rdn wl over 2f out: no significant prog* **33/1**

0-05 12 *1* **Lyrica's Lion (IRE)**[101] 1342 3-8-0 58 RhiainIngram(7) 8 33
(Michael Attwater) *chsd ldrs: lost pl and n.m.r over 2f out: wknd over 1f out* **66/1**

0500 13 *2* **Tarseekh**[14] 3920 4-9-0 56 PatCosgrave 6 29
(Chris Gordon) *a in rr: no prog over 2f out* **66/1**

121 14 *11* **Whispered Kiss**[34] 3172 4-9-9 65 ShaneKelly 3 12
(Mike Murphy) *plld hrd: prom: awkward bnd over 5f out: wknd qckly over 2f out: t.o* **8/1**

1m 45.33s (0.63) **Going Correction** 0.0s/f (Good)
**WFA** 3 from 4yo+ 9lb **14** Ran SP% **117.0**
Speed ratings (Par 103): **96,94,94,91,89 89,88,88,87,86 83,82,80,69**
CSF £30.10 CT £390.34 TOTE £7.80: £2.90, £1.50, £5.30; EX 34.00 Trifecta £587.00.
**Owner** John P McManus **Bred** Ballylinch Stud **Trained** Cheltenham, Gloucs

**FOCUS**
A modest handicap, and the main action was up the middle in the closing stages. A pb from the runner-up.
T/Plt: £26.50 to a £1 stake. Pool: £107,428.92 - 2954.6 winning units T/Qpdt: £4.60 to a £1 stake. Pool: £11,142.25 - 1761.57 winning units **Jonathan Neesom**

# 4158 WOLVERHAMPTON (A.W) (L-H)
Monday, July 3

**OFFICIAL GOING: Tapeta: standard**
Wind: Fresh half behind Weather: Cloudy with sunny spells

## 4447 FCL GLOBAL FORWARDING - MAKING LOGISTICS PERSONAL H'CAP 6f 20y (Tp)
**2:15** (2:15) (Class 6) (0-65,67) 3-Y-0 **£2,425** (£721; £360; £180) **Stalls** Low

Form RPR
22-1 1 **Debonaire David**[11] 4011 3-9-11 67 (t) ShaneKelly 3 75
(Richard Hughes) *s.i.s: hld up: racd keenly: hdwy over 1f out: rdn to ld ins fnl f: r.o* **9/4**[2]

-000 2 *½* **The Amber Fort (USA)**[23] 3578 3-9-8 67 JoshDoyle(3) 10 74
(David O'Meara) *prom: lost pl 4f out: hdwy on outer over 1f out: rdn and hung lft ins fnl f: r.o* **7/1**

-423 3 *nk* **Bruny Island (IRE)**[31] 3296 3-9-2 58 StevieDonohoe 4 64
(Charlie Fellowes) *hld up: plld hrd: hdwy over 1f out: swtchd lft ins fnl f: sn rdn: r.o* **13/8**[1]

354 4 *1* **Yorkshire Rover**[23] 3568 3-8-11 53 TomEaves 7 56
(David Brown) *chsd ldr tl led over 1f out: rdn and hdd ins fnl f: styd on same pce* **33/1**

-104 5 *2* **See You Mush**[12] 3971 3-9-2 58 (b) AntonioFresu 8 55
(Mrs Ilka Gansera-Leveque) *hld up: plld hrd: hmpd over 4f out: hdwy and nt clr run over 1f out: r.o: nt rch ldrs* **13/2**[3]

6445 6 *1 ¾* **Whiteley (IRE)**[13] 3937 3-9-3 59 JFEgan 11 50
(Mick Channon) *broke wl: sn lost pl: rdn over 1f out: r.o towards fin* **20/1**

0-63 7 *¾* **Digital Revolution**[32] 3258 3-8-12 54 CamHardie 2 43
(Antony Brittain) *plld hrd and prom: rdn over 1f out: wknd wl ins fnl f* **66/1**

000 8 *1 ¾* **Tisa River (IRE)**[26] 3472 3-8-8 50 LukeMorris 12 34
(Milton Bradley) *chsd ldrs: rdn over 1f out: wknd ins fnl f* **80/1**

065 9 *2* **Texas Wedge**[16] 3806 3-8-12 54 (p[1]) MartinDwyer 1 32
(William Muir) *prom: pushed along 1/2-way: rdn over 1f out: wknd fnl f* **33/1**

-000 10 *3 ¾* **Justice Frederick (IRE)**[20] 3700 3-9-7 63 (tp[1]) JoeyHaynes 9 30
(Paul D'Arcy) *s.i.s: last and drvn along 1/2-way: n.d* **40/1**

440- 11 *3 ¾* **Chevalier Du Lac (IRE)**[233] 7938 3-9-0 63 KatherineGlenister(7) 5 18
(Conor Dore) *led: rdn and hdd over 1f out: wknd fnl f* **50/1**

0503 12 *11* **New Tale**[24] 3543 3-8-8 50 RobHornby 6
(Olly Williams) *hld up: rdn and wknd over 2f out* **16/1**

1m 14.8s (0.30) **Going Correction** -0.05s/f (Stan) **12** Ran SP% **118.4**
Speed ratings (Par 98): **96,95,94,93,90 88,87,85,82,77 72,57**
CSF £17.34 CT £32.43 TOTE £2.70: £1.10, £2.60, £1.70; EX 19.90 Trifecta £45.80.
**Owner** Sir David Seale **Bred** D R Tucker **Trained** Upper Lambourn, Berks

**FOCUS**
Sound form for the class.

## 4448 RACING WELFARE'S RACING STAFF WEEK (S) STKS 5f 21y (Tp)
**2:45** (2:45) (Class 6) 3-Y-0+ **£2,264** (£673; £336; £168) **Stalls** Low

Form RPR
4044 1 **Tooty Fruitti**[10] 4046 3-8-7 57 ow1 JFEgan 5 67
(Jo Hughes) *hld up: hdwy over 1f out: rdn to ld and edgd lft wl ins fnl f: styd on* **11/4**[2]

6205 2 *½* **Pearl Acclaim (IRE)**[11] 4005 7-8-9 69 (h[1]) PatrickVaughan(7) 4 71
(David O'Meara) *chsd ldrs: wnt 2nd over 3f out tl led over 1f out: rdn and hdd wl ins fnl f: styd on same pce* **4/6**[1]

5360 3 *5* **Teepee Time**[23] 3569 4-8-12 47 (b[1]) PhilDennis(5) 1 54
(Michael Mullineaux) *led early: chsd ldr tl over 3f out: pushed along 1/2-way: styd on same pce fr over 1f out* **16/1**

0003 4 *5* **Equity**[7] 4161 3-8-11 52 (b) TomEaves 3 33
(David Brown) *sn led: rdn and hdd over 1f out: wknd fnl f* **6/1**[3]

5 *3 ¼* **Quick Monet (IRE)** 4-8-13 0 CharlieBennett(3) 2 24
(Shaun Harris) *dwlt: sn pushed along in rr: wknd over 1f out* **100/1**

1m 1.09s (-0.81) **Going Correction** -0.05s/f (Stan)
**WFA** 3 from 4yo+ 5lb **5** Ran SP% **107.8**
Speed ratings (Par 101): **104,103,95,87,82**
CSF £4.76 TOTE £2.20: £1.50, £1.10; EX 5.00 Trifecta £16.80.Pearl Acclaim was claimed by Mr D Griffiths for £6,000
**Owner** P & L Partners **Bred** Richard Kent **Trained** Lambourn, Berks

**FOCUS**
Not a seller to dwell on.

## 4449 WOLVERHAMPTON - CITY OF GEMS MEDIAN AUCTION MAIDEN STKS 1m 4f 51y (Tp)
**3:15** (3:15) (Class 6) 3-4-Y-0 **£2,264** (£673; £336; £168) **Stalls** Low

Form RPR
032 1 **Zack Mayo**[32] 3248 3-9-2 75 DavidProbert 1 75
(Philip McBride) *hld up: hdwy over 3f out: rdn and edgd rt over 1f out: led ins fnl f: styd on wl* **11/4**[2]

352- 2 *1* **Silver Link (IRE)**[259] 7406 3-8-11 79 JimCrowley 2 68
(Marcus Tregoning) *chsd ldr who wnt clr 9f out: rook clsr order over 5f out: rdn to ld and edgd rt 1f out: hdd ins fnl f: styd on same pce* **4/6**[1]

-500 3 *3* **Ingleby Mackenzie**[7] 4156 3-9-2 62 SilvestreDeSousa 3 69
(Mick Channon) *sn led: clr 9f out tl c bk to the field over 5f out: rdn over 2f out: hdd 1f out: no ex* **10/1**[3]

5 4 *17* **Cthulhu (USA)**[32] 3248 3-8-11 0 MartinDwyer 6 36
(William Muir) *s.i.s: hld up: hdwy over 4f out: rdn and wknd over 2f out* **14/1**

54 5 *3 ¾* **Toast Of London**[44] 2841 4-9-9 0 CamHardie 7 29
(Antony Brittain) *s.i.s: hld up: pushed along over 6f out: wknd over 5f out* **150/1**

6 *8* **Beauchamp Rose** 3-8-11 0 StevieDonohoe 5 18
(Charlie Fellowes) *sn pushed along in rr: wknd over 5f out* **22/1**

02 7 *8* **Master Me (IRE)**[21] 3649 3-8-8 0 JordanVaughan(3) 4 5
(K R Burke) *chsd ldrs: rdn over 4f out: wknd wl over 2f out* **25/1**

2m 37.96s (-2.84) **Going Correction** -0.05s/f (Stan)
**WFA** 3 from 4yo 12lb **7** Ran SP% **111.3**
Speed ratings (Par 101): **107,106,104,93,90 85,79**
CSF £4.62 TOTE £2.40: £1.90, £1.02; EX 5.10 Trifecta £16.40.
**Owner** Mrs Sarah Hamilton & Chris Budgett 1 **Bred** Mrs S Hamilton & Kirtlington Stud Ltd **Trained** Newmarket, Suffolk

**FOCUS**
An ordinary maiden, run at a sound pace. The winner is probably the best guide to the level.

## 4450 NEAL WOOD 8TH ANNIVERSARY MEMORIAL H'CAP 1m 4f 51y (Tp)
3:45 (3:45) (Class 4) (0-80,80) 3-Y-O £4,851 (£1,443; £721; £360) Stalls Low

Form RPR
3-33 1 **Winston C (IRE)**[10] 4048 3-9-6 79 LouisSteward 1 88+
(Michael Bell) *pushed along to ld after 1f: hdd over 5f out: led again over 3f out: rdn clr fnl f: eased nr fin* 5/2[1]
4-33 2 3 ½ **African Beat (IRE)**[144] 647 3-8-9 75 StephenCummins(7) 6 77
(Richard Hughes) *chsd ldrs: rdn to chse wnr fnl f: styd on same pce* 12/1
01-0 3 ¾ **Quinteo (IRE)**[32] 3262 3-9-4 77 (b[1]) JFEgan 7 78
(Jo Hughes) *hld up: rdn over 2f out: edgd lft and r.o to go 3rd wl ins fnl f: nt trble ldrs* 50/1
66-2 4 1 **Sable Island (IRE)**[75] 1874 3-9-7 80 JimCrowley 3 79
(Sir Michael Stoute) *led 1f: remained w ldr tl led again over 5f out: hdd over 3f out: rdn over 2f out: no ex fnl f* 11/4[2]
-443 5 hd **Cubswin (IRE)**[23] 3596 3-8-10 72 (h) KieranShoemark(3) 4 71
(Roger Charlton) *son chsng ldrs: rdn over 2f out: no ex fnl f* 4/1[3]
135 6 ½ **Voski (USA)**[24] 3528 3-9-7 80 SilvestreDeSousa 5 78
(Mark Johnston) *s.i.s: hld up: rdn over 2f out: edgd lft over 1f out: n.d* 11/4[2]

2m 39.27s (-1.53) **Going Correction** -0.05s/f (Stan) 6 Ran SP% 111.6
Speed ratings (Par 102): **103,100,100,99,99 99**
CSF £30.44 TOTE £2.90: £1.30, £4.20; EX 16.90 Trifecta £215.50.
**Owner** W J and T C O Gredley **Bred** Patrick F Kelly **Trained** Newmarket, Suffolk

**FOCUS**
A good-quality 3yo handicap, run at an uneven pace. The runner-up has been rated to form.

## 4451 WOLVERHAMPTON - CITY OF GEMS APPRENTICE CLAIMING STKS 7f 36y (Tp)
4:15 (4:15) (Class 6) 4-Y-0+ £2,264 (£673; £336; £168) Stalls High

Form RPR
4030 1 **Joey's Destiny (IRE)**[26] 3471 7-9-3 81 WilliamCox(7) 6 79
(Antony Brittain) *hld up: hdwy over 2f out: sn chsng ldr: rdn and r.o to ld towards fin* 11/4[2]
3005 2 1 ½ **Sophisticated Heir (IRE)**[9] 4105 7-9-5 77 (b) KieranShoemark 2 70
(Michael Herrington) *led 1f: chsd ldr tl led again over 4f out: rdn clr over 2f out: wknd and hdd towards fin* 15/8[1]
5504 3 ½ **Dark Confidant (IRE)**[7] 4163 4-9-0 59 AdamMcNamara 1 64
(Richard Fahey) *hld up: hdwy u.p over 1f out: r.o: nt rch ldrs* 11/2
/25- 4 8 **Rouge Nuage (IRE)**[395] 2862 7-9-9 83 RossaRyan(5) 5 58
(Conrad Allen) *hld up in tch: rdn over 2f out: hung lft and wknd fnl f* 4/1[3]
0035 5 4 ½ **Fidelma Moon (IRE)**[25] 3488 5-8-9 62 JordanVaughan 4 28
(K R Burke) *prom: chsd ldr 1/2-way tl rdn over 2f out: sn wknd* 7/1
000 6 25 **Spirit Of Gondree (IRE)**[26] 3469 9-8-12 42 (b) CallumShepherd 3
(Milton Bradley) *chsd ldr: led 6f out tl hdd over 4f out: wknd and eased over 2f out* 100/1

1m 28.8s **Going Correction** -0.05s/f (Stan) 6 Ran SP% 110.3
Speed ratings (Par 101): **98,96,95,86,81 52**
CSF £8.02 TOTE £3.40: £1.80, £1.20; EX 8.50 Trifecta £27.30.Dark Confidant was claimed by Mr D McCain Jnr for £5,000. Sophisticated Heir was claimed by Mr Kevin Frost for £7,500
**Owner** Antony Brittain **Bred** Brian Wallace **Trained** Warthill, N Yorks

**FOCUS**
They went hard up front early in this claimer. It's been given a token rating, with the third the key to the form.

## 4452 BRITISH STALLION STUDS EBF NOVICE STKS 7f 36y (Tp)
4:45 (4:45) (Class 5) 2-Y-O £2,911 (£866; £432; £216) Stalls High

Form RPR
3 1 **Global Humor (USA)**[32] 3254 2-9-2 0 SilvestreDeSousa 2 76
(Ed Dunlop) *chsd ldr tl shkn up to ld 1f out: styd on wl* 5/4[1]
21 2 1 **Indomeneo**[14] 3908 2-9-3 0 AdamMcNamara(3) 1 78
(Richard Fahey) *led: rdn and hdd 1f out: styd on same pce wl ins fnl f* 9/4[2]
0 3 1 **Kraka (IRE)**[18] 3742 2-9-2 0 RichardKingscote 3 72
(Tom Dascombe) *s.i.s: sn prom: rdn over 1f out: edgd lft ins fnl f: styd on* 5/1
4 1 ¾ **The Throstles** 2-9-2 0 TomEaves 8 67
(Kevin Frost) *hld up: hdwy over 1f out: nt clr run ins fnl f: r.o: nt rch ldrs* 66/1
5 hd **Finsbury Park** 2-8-13 0 GeorgeWood(3) 9 67
(Robyn Brisland) *hld up in tch: rdn 1/2-way: sn outpcd: r.o ins fnl f* 33/1
1 6 ½ **Tunes Of Glory**[11] 4007 2-9-9 0 LukeMorris 6 73
(Sir Mark Prescott Bt) *trckd ldrs: racd keenly: shkn up over 2f out: no ex fnl f* 4/1[3]
7 9 **Duggary** 2-9-2 0 CamHardie 7 43
(Kevin Frost) *s.i.s: a in rr: rdn and wknd over 2f out* 80/1
8 5 **Bansuri** 2-8-11 0 JFEgan 5 26
(Jo Hughes) *s.i.s: hld up: pushed along 1/2-way: wknd over 2f out* 80/1

1m 29.38s (0.58) **Going Correction** -0.05s/f (Stan) 8 Ran SP% 118.8
Speed ratings (Par 94): **94,92,91,89,89 88,78,72**
CSF £4.53 TOTE £1.90: £1.10, £1.10, £2.10; EX 4.80 Trifecta £17.80.
**Owner** Dr Johnny Hon **Bred** Russell L Reineman Stable, Inc **Trained** Newmarket, Suffolk

**FOCUS**
Not a bad novice contest. The first pair dominated. There's no real anchor to the form, but the time was slow.

## 4453 BETFAIR NOVICE FLAT AMATEUR RIDERS' H'CAP 1m 142y (Tp)
5:15 (5:16) (Class 6) (0-60,60) 3-Y-0+ £2,339 (£725; £362; £181) Stalls Low

Form RPR
0-40 1 **Know Your Name**[14] 3899 6-11-0 60 MissAMcCain 3 72+
(Donald McCain) *a.p: chsd ldr over 2f out: led wl over 1f out: rdn out* 9/1
50-0 2 3 ½ **Star Links (USA)**[35] 3137 11-9-11 46 oh1 (b) MrMSJohnson(3) 13 51
(John Butler) *sn chsng ldr: led over 4f out: rdn and hdd wl over 1f out: styd on same pce ins fnl f* 28/1
60 3 1 ½ **Top Offer**[32] 3265 8-10-12 58 (v[1]) MrTGillard 5 60
(Patrick Morris) *hld up: nt clr run over 2f out: hdwy u.p over 1f out: r.o: nt rch ldrs* 16/1
4500 4 2 ¼ **Schottische**[10] 4047 7-10-10 56 (b) MissJCooley 8 53
(Alan Bailey) *hmpd s: hld up: hdwy on outer over 2f out: styd on same pce fr over 1f out* 10/1
6540 5 nk **Rocket Ronnie (IRE)**[16] 3809 7-9-13 48 (p) MrSSayers(3) 2 44
(Brian Barr) *s.i.s: hld up: racd wd fr 3f out tl edgd lft and r.o ins fnl f: nvr nrr* 20/1
200 6 3 ¼ **Sakhalin Star (IRE)**[4] 4263 6-10-9 55 (e) MrTGreenwood 6 44
(Richard Guest) *sn led: hdd over 4f out: rdn over 2f out: wknd over 1f out* 6/1[2]
04-3 7 3 **Munaawib**[142] 684 9-10-11 60 (bt) MissSPeacock(3) 10 43
(Ray Peacock) *hmpd s: hld up: effrt and nt clr run over 2f out: sn wknd* 28/1
3000 8 ½ **Lutine Charlie (IRE)**[6] 4180 10-10-0 46 oh1 (p) MissEMacKenzie 1 28
(Emma Owen) *prom: racd keenly: lost pl 7f out: pushed along and nt clr run over 2f out: wknd over 2f out* 33/1
3060 9 ½ **Baker Street**[38] 3041 3-10-4 60 (p) MissCAGreenway 4 40
(Tom Dascombe) *hld up: racd wd fr 3f out: nvr on terms* 8/1
6650 10 9 **Ryedale Rio (IRE)**[16] 3831 4-10-5 54 (b) MissJGillam(3) 12 16
(Tim Easterby) *hood removed late and rdr lost iron briefly leaving stalls: sn prom: chsd ldr over 3f out tl over 2f out: wknd wl over 1f out* 20/1
-544 11 2 ¼ **Joaldo**[7] 4162 5-10-0 46 oh1 (p) MrMEnnis 7 3
(Antony Brittain) *hld up: plld hrd: hdwy over 5f out: rdn and wknd over 2f out* 7/1[3]
2036 12 1 **Muzaahim (IRE)**[41] 2918 6-10-11 57 (h) MissAPeck 9 12
(Laura Morgan) *hmpd s: a in rr* 6/1[2]
4021 13 3 ¾ **Varun's Bride (IRE)**[11] 4006 3-10-3 59 MrBJames 11 5
(Richard Hannon) *edgd lft s: chsd ldrs: pushed along over 4f out: nt clr run and lost pl over 3f out: sn wknd* 9/4[1]

1m 51.4s (1.30) **Going Correction** -0.05s/f (Stan)
**WFA** 3 from 4yo+ 10lb 13 Ran SP% 127.3
Speed ratings (Par 101): **92,88,87,85,85 82,79,79,78,70 68,67,64**
CSF £254.14 CT £4102.42 TOTE £10.10: £3.50, £6.70, £5.30; EX 343.60 Trifecta £8460.30.
**Owner** Livvys Racing Group **Bred** Mill Farm Stud **Trained** Cholmondeley, Cheshire

**FOCUS**
A moderate handicap and the amateur riders had, prior to April 1, 2017, not ridden more than three winners under any rules of racing. The level of the form is hard to pin.
T/Plt: £4.60 to a £1 stake. Pool: £78,111.29 - 12148.5 winning units T/Qpdt: £3.10 to a £1 stake. Pool: £5,152.13 - 1213.57 winning units **Colin Roberts**

# 4234 MAISONS-LAFFITTE (R-H)
Monday, July 3

**OFFICIAL GOING: Turf: soft**

## 4454a PRIX LE PAILLON (CONDITIONS) (4YO+) (STRAIGHT) (TURF) 1m
1:20 4-Y-0+ £11,965 (£4,786; £3,589; £2,393; £1,196)

RPR
1 **Dhevanafushi**[70] 4-9-0 0 MickaelBarzalona 8 95+
(H-A Pantall, France) 37/10[2]
2 hd **Al Erayg (IRE)**[433] 4-9-0 0 CristianDemuro 9 95
(F-H Graffard, France) 7/1
3 ¾ **Le Juge (IRE)**[18] 4-8-9 0 MllePaulineDominois(5) 5 93
(A Fabre, France) 17/10[1]
4 snk **Virginie (FR)**[53] 4-8-7 0 ClementLecoeuvre(3) 7 89
(T Clout, France) 143/10
5 hd **London Protocol (FR)**[18] 3743 4-9-0 0 (p) IoritzMendizabal 2 92
(K R Burke) *qckly into stride: settled bhd ldrs: pushed along over 2f out to keep in tch: drvn over 1f out: styd on one pce fnl f* 29/1
6 2 ½ **Diwan Senora (FR)**[42] 4-9-0 0 (p) JeromeCabre 1 87
(Y Barberot, France) 104/10
7 shd **King Platin (FR)**[18] 5-9-3 0 RonanThomas 4 89
(Mme C Barande-Barbe, France) 162/10
8 1 ¼ **Livinginafantasy (FR)**[228] 7998 4-8-10 0 TheoBachelot 6 80
(S Wattel, France) 34/1
9 2 ½ **Boxeur (IRE)**[50] 4-9-0 0 ChristopheSoumillon 3 78
(F Rossi, France) 39/10[3]

1m 38.53s (-3.77) 9 Ran SP% 118.5
PARI-MUTUEL (all including 1 euro stake): WIN 4.70; PLACE 1.40, 1.90, 1.20; DF 16.20; SF 29.40.
**Owner** Henri-Alex Pantall **Bred** H-A Pantall & Mme Y Chabot **Trained** France

## 4455a PRIX DE MARLY-LE-ROI (CLAIMER) (3YO FILLIES) (ROUND) (TURF) 1m 1f
2:20 3-Y-0 £9,829 (£3,931; £2,948; £1,965; £982)

RPR
1 **Bubble Bath**[62] 3-8-11 0 FranckBlondel 11 67
(M Pimbonnet, France) 7/2[2]
2 hd **Copper Baked (FR)**[24] 3554 3-9-1 0 TonyPiccone 3 71
(K R Burke) *wl into stride: settled in 3rd: hdwy to join ldr over 2f out: drvn and hdd over 1f out: rallied wl u.p ins fnl f to press ldr cl home: jst hld* 84/10
3 1 ½ **Magical Forest (IRE)**[27] 3446 3-9-4 0 ChristopheSoumillon 9 71
(G Botti, France) 14/5[1]
4 nk **Wootalove (FR)**[32] 3275 3-9-1 0 MickaelBarzalona 4 67
(Mme Pia Brandt, France) 19/5[3]
5 ¾ **Meteorite (FR)**[88] 3-8-11 0 AntoineHamelin 10 62
(S Smrczek, Germany) 222/10
6 snk **Parin** 3-8-11 0 AlexisBadel 13 62
(W Mongil, Germany) 177/10
7 ¾ **Douceur D'Antan (FR)**[7] 3-9-1 0 MaximeGuyon 2 64
(P Adda, France) 79/10
8 snk **Sabawa (FR)**[242] 3-8-11 0 (b[1]) MickaelBerto 5 60
(R Rohne, Germany) 69/1
9 ¾ **Armenian Girl (FR)**[27] 3-9-4 0 IoritzMendizabal 12 65
(A Lyon, France) 50/1
10 1 ¼ **April Angel (FR)**[17] 3-8-13 0 (p) MathieuPelletan(5) 1 63
(P Demercastel, France) 85/1
11 3 **Flying Ballerina (IRE)**[27] 3446 3-8-6 0 ErwannLebreton(5) 7 50
(F Alloncle, France) 118/1
12 ½ **Micolys (FR)**[9] 3-8-9 0 JeromeMoutard(6) 6 53
(J-M Lefebvre, France) 84/10
13 nk **Evalya Senora (FR)**[61] 3-8-7 0 ClementGuitraud(8) 8 52
(Y Barberot, France) 66/1

1m 55.19s (0.49) 13 Ran SP% 118.4
PARI-MUTUEL (all including 1 euro stake): WIN 4.50; PLACE 1.50, 2.00, 1.60; DF 17.30; SF 31.10.
**Owner** Fabrice Petit **Bred** Selwood B/S, Hoskins & Jonason **Trained** France


The Form Book Flat, Raceform Ltd, Newbury, RG14 5SJ

4456a (Foreign Racing) - See Raceform Interactive

## 4457a PRIX DU VESINET (CLAIMER) (4YO+) (TURF) 1m 4f 110y
3:55 4-Y-O+ £8,119 (£3,247; £2,435; £1,623; £811)

RPR

1 **Against Rules (FR)**[47] 5-9-1 0....................................(b) MaximeGuyon 1 85
(S Wattel, France) **2/1**[1]

2 3 ½ **Pachadargent (FR)**[41] 6-9-3 0............................ MlleElauraCieslik(10) 8 92
(J-P Gauvin, France) **22/5**[2]

3 shd **Santo Spirito**[17] 6-9-4 0............................................ MickaelBarzalona 4 83
(D & P Prod'Homme, France) **22/5**[2]

4 1 ¾ **Barwick**[30] 3323 9-9-4 0.................................................. TheoBachelot 11 80
(George Baker) *settled midfield: impr to take clsr order over 6f out: hdwy to chal ldrs over 2f out: rdn over 1f out: u.p and kpt on same pce fnl f* **23/5**[3]

5 nk **Parkori (FR)**[17] 9-9-8 0............................................ MrGuilainBertrand 10 84
(G Bertrand, France) **221/10**

6 1 ¼ **Corbellina (FR)** 6-8-4 0.......................................... JeromeMoutard(4) 6 68
(F Cheyer, France) **244/10**

7 ¾ **Ronchois**[18] 4-8-9 0......................................(b) ClementLecoeuvre(6) 2 74
(E Lellouche, France) **111/10**

8 2 **Track Star (FR)**[31] 5-9-1 0........................................... AntoineHamelin 3 71
(Gerard Martin, Austria) **269/10**

9 8 **Green Byron (FR)**[17] 7-8-10 0................................... MlleAudeDuporte(5) 5 59
(Mlle S Sine, France) **101/1**

10 ½ **Montaigne (FR)**[17] 4-9-1 0...................................... NicolasBarzalona(3) 9 61
(F-X Belvisi, France) **57/1**

11 1 ¼ **Parzival (IRE)**[271] 5-9-1 0.......................................... CristianDemuro 7 56
(G Botti, France) **136/10**

12 15 **La Fougasse (FR)**[989] 9-8-4 0....................................... MlleZoePfeil(7) 13 29
(R Kleparski, France) **93/1**

2m 40.6s (160.60) **12** Ran SP% **119.0**
PARI-MUTUEL (all including 1 euro stake): WIN 3.00; PLACE 1.30, 1.50, 1.50; DF 6.50; SF 11.90.
**Owner** L Haegel **Bred** J Hayoz **Trained** France

# 4175 BRIGHTON (L-H)

Tuesday, July 4

**OFFICIAL GOING: Good to firm (watered; 8.4)**
Wind: light, against Weather: sunny

## 4458 BRIGHTON RACECOURSE SUPPORTING RACING STAFF WEEK H'CAP 5f 215y
**2:15** (2:17) (Class 6) (0-55,56) 3-Y-O+ £2,587 (£770; £384; £192) **Stalls** Low

Form RPR

3540 1 **Cee Jay**[48] 2724 4-9-4 **54**.............................................. CharlieBennett(3) 6 60
(Patrick Chamings) *hld up in tch in midfield: hdwy over 1f out: chsd ldr and swtchd rt ins fnl f: clsd to ld fnl 75yds: r.o and a jst holding chalr after* **17/2**

5-02 2 shd **Harlequin Rose (IRE)**[17] 3810 3-8-13 **52**...................(v) DanielMuscutt 8 57
(Patrick Chamings) *hld up in rr of main gp: effrt 2f out: switching rt and hdwy over 1f out: clsd and str chal u.p fnl 100yds: r.o but a jst hld* **5/1**[2]

0-00 3 2 **Gaia Princess (IRE)**[21] 3695 3-8-12 **54**...................... HectorCrouch(3) 4 52
(Gary Moore) *wl in tch in midfield: clsd to trck ldrs on inner 2f out: rdn to ld over 1f out: drvn 1f out: hdd 75yds out: no ex and wknd towards fin* **12/1**

0440 4 1 ¾ **Spare Parts (IRE)**[17] 3823 3-8-11 **50**............................ LukeMorris 12 43
(Charles Hills) *chsd ldrs: rdn 2f out: hrd drvn and unable qck over 1f out: kpt on same pce ins fnl f* **8/1**

4310 5 ¾ **Sadierosecliffford (IRE)**[4] 4302 3-8-8 **54**..................... RayDawson(7) 7 44
(Giles Bravery) *t.k.h: hld up in tch in midfield: effrt 2f out: kpt on ins fnl f but nvr threatened ldrs* **7/1**[3]

-044 6 hd **Little Cupcake**[12] 4008 6-8-12 **45**....................................(v) DannyBrock 3 37
(Denis Quinn) *taken down early: squeezed for room sn after s and dropped to rr: hdwy into midfield 3f out: hdwy on inner over 1f out: kpt on ins fnl f: no threat to ldrs* **25/1**

0554 7 nk **Ginger Truffle**[7] 4179 3-8-7 **49**.................................. CallumShepherd(3) 1 38
(Brett Johnson) *led: rdn and hdd over 1f out: no ex u.p 1f out: wknd ins fnl f* **11/1**

-305 8 ½ **Provoking (USA)**[7] 4180 4-9-3 **50**............................ SilvestreDeSousa 11 38
(David Evans) *midfield: effrt 2f out: sme hdwy 1f out: nt clr run and no imp ins fnl f* **4/1**[1]

0503 9 ½ **Rat Catcher (IRE)**[14] 3942 7-8-12 **45**...........................(b) RobHornby 5 31
(Lisa Williamson) *taken down early: chsd ldrs: rdn 2f out: unable qck over 1f out: wknd ins fnl f* **16/1**

4024 10 4 **Archie Stevens**[7] 4174 7-9-2 **56**......................................... WilliamCox(7) 2 30
(Clare Ellam) *pressed ldr: rdn 2f out: sn outpcd and lost pl over 1f out: wknd ins fnl f* **9/1**

0203 11 2 **National Service (USA)**[51] 2669 6-8-12 **45**.................(tp) RyanPowell 15 12
(Clare Ellam) *awkward and wnt rt leaving stalls: hld up in rr: n.d* **16/1**

-040 12 shd **General Gerrard**[36] 3157 3-8-12 **54**...........................(t) GeorgeWood(3) 14 20
(Michael Madgwick) *in tch in midfield: rdn ent fnl 2f: sn struggling and lost pl over 1f out: wknd fnl f* **20/1**

-016 13 1 **Suzi Icon**[25] 3550 5-9-3 **50**................................................(p) LiamJones 9 14
(Michael Appleby) *nvr travelling wl and sn niggled along: lost pl and bhd over 1f out: wknd fnl f* **12/1**

-600 14 2 ¼ **Ashford Island**[17] 3823 4-8-9 **45**..............................(v[1]) NoelGarbutt(3) 16 2
(Adam West) *wnt lft and bdly hmpd leaving stall: nvr rcvrd and a bhd* **50/1**

603 15 1 **Fivos**[29] 3407 3-9-3 **56**.............................................(p[1]) TrevorWhelan 13 8
(David Bridgwater) *in tch in midfield: rdn 2f out: sn lost pl and wl btn: bhd ins fnl f* **16/1**

1m 10.1s (-0.10) **Going Correction** -0.125s/f (Firm)
**WFA** 3 from 4yo+ 6lb **15** Ran SP% **132.7**
Speed ratings (Par 101): **95,94,92,89,88 88,88,87,86,81 78,78,77,74,73**
CSF £54.55 CT £541.04 TOTE £10.50: £3.40, £1.60, £5.30; EX 58.90 Trifecta £1232.20.
**Owner** Mrs Betty Powell **Bred** Miss K J Keir **Trained** Baughurst, Hants

**FOCUS**
All distances as advertised. There had been 38mm of rainfall in the last seven days but warm enough, drying conditions for this meeting and the ground was given as good to firm. A moderate but competitive handicap.

## 4459 TOTEPLACEPOT AT TOTESPORT.COM H'CAP 7f 211y
**2:45** (2:46) (Class 6) (0-65,63) 4-Y-O+ £2,587 (£770; £384; £192) **Stalls** Low

Form RPR

2431 1 **Swilly Sunset**[28] 3442 4-9-6 **62**.................................. SilvestreDeSousa 7 74+
(Anthony Carson) *chsd ldrs: effrt to chal 2f out: rdn to ld ent fnl f: edgd lft and drew clr ins fnl f: eased towards fin: easily* **6/5**[1]

1-05 2 4 ½ **Carcharias (IRE)**[15] 3906 4-9-3 **62**.......................... CallumShepherd(3) 5 63
(Ed de Giles) *t.k.h: led: hrd pressed 2f out: drvn and hdd ent fnl f: sn brushed aside by wnr but kpt on to hold 2nd ins fnl f* **11/2**[3]

6155 3 ½ **Intimately**[11] 4047 4-9-0 **59**........................................... GeorgeWood(3) 6 59
(Jonathan Portman) *dwlt: hld up in last pair: effrt 2f out: 4th 1f out: kpt on to snatch 3rd last strides: no ch w wnr* **8/1**

0422 4 nk **Rustique**[20] 3731 5-9-7 **63**................................................ LukeMorris 3 62
(Ed Walker) *chsd ldr: ev ch 2f out tl unable to match pce of wnr ent fnl f: plugged on same pce and lost 3rd last strides* **4/1**[2]

0503 5 3 ¾ **Binky Blue (IRE)**[15] 3906 5-9-0 **59**..........................(h) CharlieBennett(3) 1 49
(Daniel Mark Loughnane) *hld up in tch in last pair: effrt on inner over 2f out: unable qck and btn over 1f out: wknd ins fnl f* **12/1**

526 6 2 **Welsh Inlet (IRE)**[7] 4176 9-9-2 **58**................................ WilliamCarson 4 44
(John Bridger) *in tch in midfield: shkn up 3f out: lost pl u.p and wl btn over 1f out: wknd fnl f* **14/1**

0-60 7 14 **Kafoo**[15] 3906 4-9-6 **62**.....................................................(p[1]) JoeyHaynes 2 15
(Ed Dunlop) *in tch in midfield: rdn 2f out: sn btn and dropped to rr: wl bhd ins fnl f* **20/1**

1m 34.74s (-1.26) **Going Correction** -0.125s/f (Firm) **7** Ran SP% **111.1**
Speed ratings (Par 101): **101,96,96,95,91 89,75**
CSF £7.63 TOTE £1.80: £1.20, £2.60; EX 8.80 Trifecta £41.10.
**Owner** Alderson Carson Francis Hart **Bred** Aston House Stud **Trained** Newmarket, Suffolk

**FOCUS**
A moderate handicap.

## 4460 TRAILWALKER 100KM CHALLENGE 29-30 JULY MAIDEN STKS 1m 1f 207y
**3:15** (3:16) (Class 5) 3-Y-O £2,911 (£866; £432; £216) **Stalls** High

Form RPR

3-23 1 **Another Eclipse (IRE)**[24] 3583 3-9-5 81........................ JamieSpencer 2 91+
(David Simcock) *trckd ldrs tl wnt 2nd 5f out: led over 2f out: pushed along and qcknd clr 2f out: in n.d 1f out: heavily eased towards fin* **2/5**[1]

4 2 5 **Frosting**[62] 2316 3-9-0 0................................................... PatCosgrave 3 74
(William Haggas) *chsd ldr tl 5f out: effrt and swtchd rt over 2f out: chsd clr wnr 2f out: clr 2nd but no ch w 1f out: kpt on same pce* **9/2**[2]

-536 3 6 **Zamalight**[18] 3787 3-9-5 79...................................(h[1]) SilvestreDeSousa 4 67
(Amanda Perrett) *sn led: jnd and rdn 3f out: hdd over 2f out: 3rd and wknd over 1f out* **11/2**[3]

4 1 ¼ **Seinfeld** 3-9-5 0................................................................ DanielMuscutt 5 65
(David Simcock) *hld up in rr: rdn wl over 2f out: outpcd and btn 2f out: wl hld whn nt clr run and swtchd lft ins fnl f* **25/1**

2m 3.05s (-0.55) **Going Correction** -0.125s/f (Firm) **4** Ran SP% **108.8**
Speed ratings (Par 100): **97,93,88,87**
CSF £2.61 TOTE £1.40; EX 2.70 Trifecta £4.00.
**Owner** Sheikh Juma Dalmook Al Maktoum **Bred** S F Bloodstock LLC **Trained** Newmarket, Suffolk

**FOCUS**
An uncompetitive maiden. The runner-up has been rated close to her debut form.

## 4461 LICENSED TRADE AUDITORS LICENSED-TRADE.CO.UK H'CAP 1m 1f 207y
**3:45** (3:48) (Class 6) (0-55,56) 4-Y-O+ £2,587 (£770; £384; £192) **Stalls** High

Form RPR

6003 1 **Dove Mountain (IRE)**[20] 3726 6-9-7 **55**..........................(bt[1]) LukeMorris 4 65
(Olly Murphy) *dwlt: hld up in tch in last trio: swtchd rt and hdwy between horses over 2f out: rdn to ld over 1f out: clr and styd on wl ins fnl f: rdn out* **3/1**[2]

-135 2 1 ¾ **Buzz Lightyere**[21] 3688 4-9-6 **54**............................. SilvestreDeSousa 2 62
(Philip Hide) *stmbld bdly leaving stalls: hld up in midfield: effrt over 2f out: chsd wnr over 1f out: kpt on but no imp ins fnl f: eased towards fin* **2/1**[1]

6202 3 1 ¾ **Betsalottie**[10] 4088 4-9-8 **56**........................................ WilliamCarson 10 59
(John Bridger) *led: rdn ent fnl 2f: hdd over 1f out: no ex and styd on same pce ins fnl f* **4/1**[3]

0500 4 ¾ **Silver Alliance**[31] 3325 9-9-4 **55**..............................(b) ShelleyBirkett(3) 6 56
(Julia Feilden) *hld up in tch in midfield: clsd to trck ldrs but nt clr run ent fnl 2f: fnlly able to switch rt and hdwy ins fnl f: styd on fnl 100yds: nvr any ch of threatening ldrs* **33/1**

460- 5 3 ½ **Storm Runner (IRE)**[377] 3522 9-8-7 **46** oh1.................... JaneElliott(5) 7 40
(George Margarson) *t.k.h: hld up in rr: swtchd rt and effrt wl over 2f out: nvr threatening to get on terms w ldrs: plugged on same pce fnl f* **66/1**

0110 6 hd **Master Of Heaven**[19] 3753 4-9-8 **56**..........................(p) PatCosgrave 5 50
(Jim Boyle) *chsd ldrs: nt clr run over 2f out: gap opened and tried to get through whn gap narrowed again and hmpd over 1f out: nvr able to cl and wknd ins fnl f* **8/1**

4-02 7 4 ½ **Rianna Star**[145] 646 4-9-4 **55**...................................... HectorCrouch(3) 3 40
(Gary Moore) *chsd ldr: rdn and ev ch ent fnl 2f: edging lft and outpcd ent fnl f: sn wknd* **12/1**

03-0 8 38 **Solid Justice (IRE)**[7] 4177 6-8-12 **46** oh1..................(v) DanielMuscutt 8
(Mark Pattinson) *hld up in tch in midfield: effrt and hanging lft ent fnl 2f: stl hanging and btn over 1f out: sn eased and virtually p.u ins fnl f: t.o* **14/1**

520- 9 12 **Lazizah**[360] 4159 4-9-4 **52**................................................ SteveDrowne 1
(Marcus Tregoning) *hld up in tch in midfield: dropped to rr and rdn over 2f out: lost tch over 1f out: virtually p.u ins fnl f: t.o* **14/1**

300- 10 3 ½ **Opera Buffa (IRE)**[264] 5625 4-8-7 **46**.......................(p) PaddyPilley(5) 9
(Steve Flook) *in tch in midfield: rdn over 2f out: sn lost pl and bhd over 1f out: virtually p.u ins fnl f: t.o* **80/1**

2m 3.3s (-0.30) **Going Correction** -0.125s/f (Firm) **10** Ran SP% **116.1**
Speed ratings (Par 101): **96,94,93,92,89 89,86,55,46,43**
CSF £9.29 CT £23.43 TOTE £4.20: £1.50, £1.40, £1.50; EX 12.00 Trifecta £47.40.
**Owner** Mrs Anabel K Murphy **Bred** Barnett Enterprises **Trained** Wilmcote, Warks

**FOCUS**
A moderate handicap.

## 4462 JANES SOLICITORS SILVER JUBILEE H'CAP — 1m 1f 207y
4:15 (4:18) (Class 5) (0-70,72) 3-Y-O — £2,911 (£866; £432; £216) Stalls High

Form — RPR

0-45 **1** **Fair Power (IRE)**[29] 3412 3-9-10 **72** .......... MitchGodwin(5) 3 — 83
(Sylvester Kirk) *hld up in rr: rdn over 4f out: hdwy to chse ldr and swtchd lft 2f out: led over 1f out: styd on strly and drew rt away ins fnl f: readily* **3/1**[2]

-621 **2** *7* **Let's Be Happy (IRE)**[14] 3939 3-9-7 **64** .......... (p) ShaneKelly 8 — 61
(Richard Hughes) *chsd ldr: effrt ent fnl 2f: rdn and fnd little over 1f out: chsd clr wnr and kpt on same pce ins fnl f* **9/4**[1]

0443 **3** *2 1/4* **Log Off (IRE)**[7] 4177 3-8-9 **55** .......... HectorCrouch(3) 5 — 48
(David Evans) *racd in 4th: rdn over 3f out: outpcd 2f out: no ch but plugged on ins fnl f to snatch 3rd last strides* **6/1**

-034 **4** *hd* **Born Legend (IRE)**[109] 1239 3-9-12 **72** .......... (b) CallumShepherd(3) 6 — 64+
(Charles Hills) *t.k.h: led: clr 7f out: rdn jst over 2f out: hdd over 1f out: sn btn and wknd ins fnl f* **33/1**

6404 **5** *1/2* **Melodine**[19] 3745 3-9-7 **64** .......... (p) LukeMorris 2 — 55
(Sir Mark Prescott Bt) *chsd ldng pair: rdn over 3f out: outpcd and btn 2f out: no ch whn swtchd rt ins fnl f* **4/1**[3]

5-01 **6** *9* **Rakematiz**[33] 3250 3-8-13 **63** .......... RossaRyan(7) 1 — 36
(Brett Johnson) *hld up in last pair: rdn 3f out: bhd and lost tch 3f out* **9/2**

2m 2.88s (-0.72) **Going Correction** -0.125s/f (Firm) — **6** Ran SP% **111.2**
Speed ratings (Par 100): **97,91,89,89,89 81**
CSF £9.97 CT £34.38 TOTE £3.90: £1.80, £1.60; EX 10.20 Trifecta £40.30.

**Owner** Fairway Racing **Bred** Pitrizzia Partnership **Trained** Upper Lambourn, Berks

**FOCUS**
This race looked to fall apart, with Born Legend doing way too much in front, the chasing pack getting after him too soon and some of these just not firing at all, and the winner came from last to win by a wide margin. The winner has been rated to the better view of her 2yo form.

## 4463 THE HUMAN LEAGUE 8 SEPT H'CAP — 6f 210y
4:45 (4:45) (Class 5) (0-70,72) 3-Y-O — £2,911 (£866; £432; £216) Stalls Low

Form — RPR

2030 **1** **Golden Guest**[19] 3751 3-8-9 **63** .......... JaneElliott(5) 7 — 68
(George Margarson) *hld up wl in tch in midfield: effrt to press ldr ent fnl f: rdn to ld ins fnl f: r.o wl and a jst doing enough towards fin* **12/1**

30-6 **2** *nk* **Lord Clenaghcastle (IRE)**[146] 625 3-9-4 **70** .......... HectorCrouch(3) 3 — 74
(Gary Moore) *led: rdn and fnd ex wl over 1f out: hrd pressed 1f out: hdd ins fnl f: kpt on wl but a jst hld after* **10/1**

436 **3** *1 1/2* **Miss Mirabeau**[94] 1488 3-8-12 **61** .......... (b[1]) LukeMorris 9 — 63+
(Sir Mark Prescott Bt) *stdd and dropped in bhd after s: hld up in last pair: nt clr run over 2f out: swtchd rt and effrt ent fnl 2f: hung bdly lft fr over 1f out: chsd ldrs ins fnl f: no imp fnl 100yds* **9/2**[3]

3334 **4** *nse* **Topmeup**[8] 4150 3-8-4 **53** .......... SilvestreDeSousa 2 — 53+
(David Evans) *dwlt: in tch in last pair: effrt 2f out: hdwy and nt clr run over 1f out: swtchd rt 1f out: hdwy ins fnl f: styd on wl fnl 100yds: nvr gng to rch ldrs* **9/4**[1]

6405 **5** *1/2* **Hidden Stash**[21] 3695 3-8-6 **55** .......... (v) RobHornby 8 — 54
(Andrew Balding) *chsd ldr: effrt over 2f out: unable qck udner press over 1f out: outpcd fnl 100yds* **7/1**

0-30 **6** *1* **Bequia (IRE)**[18] 3784 3-9-6 **72** .......... GeorgeWood(3) 5 — 68
(Martyn Meade) *t.k.h: trckd ldrs: rdn over 2f out: sltly outpcd whn n.m.r over 1f out: kpt on same pce ins fnl f* **6/1**

2362 **7** *1/2* **Still Waiting**[14] 3937 3-8-13 **62** .......... (p[1]) CharlesBishop 1 — 57
(William Jarvis) *wl in tch in midfield: effrt on inner to chse ldrs over 1f out: unable qck ent fnl f: wknd fnl 100yds* **7/2**[2]

1m 23.13s (0.03) **Going Correction** -0.125s/f (Firm) — **7** Ran SP% **114.7**
Speed ratings (Par 100): **94,93,91,91,91 90,89**
CSF £120.07 CT £624.88 TOTE £17.10: £6.60, £4.00; EX 128.30 Trifecta £928.80.

**Owner** John Guest Racing **Bred** P A & M J Reditt & Catridge Stud **Trained** Newmarket, Suffolk

■ Stewards' Enquiry : Hector Crouch two-day ban: used whip above permitted level (Jul 18-19)

**FOCUS**
Under 4l covered the seven runners, the favourite found trouble, the third-placed finisher looked a hard ride and the winner hardly had an appealing profile, so probably not strong form. The winner is the best guide to the level.

## 4464 HACIENDA CLASSICAL 9 SEPT H'CAP — 5f 60y
5:15 (5:15) (Class 5) (0-75,82) 3-Y-O+ — £2,911 (£866; £432; £216) Stalls Low

Form — RPR

5041 **1** **Super Julius**[8] 4159 3-10-4 **82** 6ex .......... (p) CharlesBishop 4 — 85
(Eve Johnson Houghton) *trckd ldr: shkn up: edgd lft and stmbld ent fnl 2f: drvn over 1f out: looked hld tl styd on wl ins fnl f to ld cl home* **5/4**[2]

3611 **2** *1/2* **Come On Dave (IRE)**[3] 4352 8-10-4 **77** 6ex .......... (v) DanielMuscutt 2 — 81
(John Butler) *taken down early: racd keenly: sn led: rdn over 1f out: drvn ins fnl f: hdd and no ex cl home* **11/10**[1]

0300 **3** *3/4* **Very Honest (IRE)**[17] 3834 4-9-10 **76** .......... RossaRyan(7) 1 — 77
(Brett Johnson) *trckd ldrs: effrt on inner over 1f out: swtchd rt 1f out: kpt on wl towards fin: nvr quite getting to ldrs* **9/1**[3]

0050 **4** *2 3/4* **Kestrel Call (IRE)**[22] 3667 4-8-8 **60** .......... (t) RayDawson(7) 3 — 51
(Michael Appleby) *hld up in tch in 4th: effrt ent fnl 2f: edging lft and no imp 1f out: wknd ins fnl f* **12/1**

1m 1.9s (-0.40) **Going Correction** -0.125s/f (Firm)
**WFA** 3 from 4yo+ 5lb — **4** Ran SP% **109.8**
Speed ratings (Par 103): **98,97,96,91**
CSF £3.03 TOTE £2.10; EX 2.90 Trifecta £4.00.

**Owner** B Miller **Bred** T R G Vestey **Trained** Blewbury, Oxon

**FOCUS**
A fair race despite the small field. The winner has been rated close to his latest AW win.

T/Plt: £270.90 to a £1 stake. Pool: £52,025.84 - 140.17 winning units T/Qpdt: £66.10 to a £1 stake. Pool: £5,913.21 - 66.18 winning units **Steve Payne**

# 4144 CHEPSTOW (L-H)
Tuesday, July 4

**OFFICIAL GOING: Good (good to firm in places; 8.0)**
Wind: almost nil Weather: fine

## 4465 WIMBLEDON BETTING AT 188BET NOVICE MEDIAN AUCTION STKS — 7f 16y
6:10 (6:12) (Class 6) 2-Y-O — £2,587 (£770; £384; £192) Stalls Centre

Form — RPR

**1** **Fortune's Pearl (IRE)** 2-9-2 0 .......... OisinMurphy 12 — 73
(Andrew Balding) *a.p: rdn over 2f out: led appr fnl f: sn hung lft: drvn fnl 100yds: jst hld on* **11/2**

66 **2** *shd* **Ferik (IRE)**[19] 3742 2-9-2 0 .......... JFEgan 5 — 73
(David Evans) *cl up: led after 2f: on stands' rail by 1/2-way: drvn over 2f out: hdd appr fnl f: r.o: jst hld* **16/1**

0 **3** *3/4* **Champs De Reves**[6] 4218 2-8-13 0 .......... KieranShoemark(3) 11 — 71+
(Marcus Tregoning) *in rr: rdn 3f out: nt clr run 2f out: r.o fnl f: tk 3rd last strides* **16/1**

63 **4** *shd* **Deadly Reel (IRE)**[15] 3908 2-8-11 0 .......... RichardKingscote 3 — 66
(Archie Watson) *prom: rdn and ev ch over 2f out: unable qck fnl 100yds: lost 3rd last strides* **9/2**[3]

0 **5** *3* **Giovanni Medici**[18] 3783 2-9-2 0 .......... TomQueally 2 — 63
(Seamus Durack) *prom: rdn 2f out: fdd fnl f* **33/1**

341 **6** *2* **Leeshaan (IRE)**[19] 3742 2-9-9 81 .......... MartinHarley 10 — 64
(James Tate) *hld up and t.k.h: impr to chse ldrs 1/2-way: rdn over 2f out: one pce over 1f out* **3/1**[2]

**7** *nse* **Mr Large (IRE)** 2-9-2 0 .......... DougieCostello 13 — 57
(Jamie Osborne) *chsd ldrs tl outpcd 1/2-way: styd on fnl f* **16/1**

**8** *nk* **Breath Caught** 2-9-2 0 .......... PatDobbs 1 — 56
(Ralph Beckett) *s.i.s: in tch on outer: rdn over 2f out: sn outpcd by ldrs: no hdwy fnl f* **11/4**[1]

0 **9** *3/4* **Landue**[6] 4218 2-8-9 0 .......... TylerSaunders(7) 7 — 54
(Marcus Tregoning) *s.i.s: sn midfield: rdn over 2f out: no imp* **20/1**

0 **10** *1/2* **Coal Stock (IRE)**[22] 3668 2-9-2 0 .......... FranBerry 6 — 53
(David Evans) *s.s: sn in tch: rdn after 3f: no imp whn hung lft over 1f out* **33/1**

55 **11** *3/4* **Lyford (IRE)**[10] 4090 2-9-2 0 .......... TomMarquand 4 — 51
(Sylvester Kirk) *led 2f: chsd ldrs: rdn 3f out: wknd over 1f out* **66/1**

**12** *12* **Travellers Joy** 2-8-11 0 .......... RyanTate 8 — 13
(Richard Hughes) *s.i.s: in rr: rdn 1/2-way: hung lft and lost tch over 2f out* **33/1**

1m 22.9s (-0.30) **Going Correction** -0.45s/f (Firm) — **12** Ran SP% **118.0**
Speed ratings (Par 92): **83,82,82,81,78 76,76,75,74,74 73,59**
CSF £82.98 TOTE £6.20: £2.00, £4.60, £5.30; EX 89.30 Trifecta £1418.50.
**Owner** Qatar Racing Limited **Bred** Miss Joann Lyons **Trained** Kingsclere, Hants

**FOCUS**
The official going of good, good to firm in places led to a raft of non-runners on the card. Not an obviously strong novice event to open proceedings but the winner is bred to be useful and could do no more than win on debut.

## 4466 DAILY RACING SPECIALS AT 188BET/EBF STALLIONS NOVICE STKS (PLUS 10 RACE) — 6f 16y
6:40 (6:43) (Class 4) 2-Y-O — £5,175 (£1,540; £769; £384) Stalls Centre

Form — RPR

3 **1** **Barraquero (IRE)**[19] 3747 2-9-2 0 .......... TomMarquand 4 — 92+
(Brian Meehan) *trckd ldrs: led 1f out: shkn up and qcknd clr: eased cl home: impressive: jinked and uns rdr after fin* **7/4**[1]

302 **2** *6* **Airshow**[18] 3769 2-9-2 73 .......... (h) OisinMurphy 7 — 71
(Rod Millman) *led 100yds: cl up: led again 3f out: rdn over 1f out: hdd 1f out: kpt on but no ch w easy wnr* **5/1**[3]

5 **3** *2 1/2* **Liva (IRE)**[46] 2779 2-9-2 0 .......... JFEgan 5 — 63
(David Evans) *sn towards rr: hdwy 1/2-way: nt clr run over 2f out: 5th whn swtchd lft 1f out: drvn and styd on wl to go 3rd nr fin* **3/1**[2]

6 **4** *1 1/4* **Dream Prospect**[18] 3782 2-8-13 0 .......... KieranShoemark(3) 9 — 59
(Roger Charlton) *t.k.h: chsd ldrs: pushed along 2f out: hld whn edgd rt ins fnl f: lost 3rd nr fin* **3/1**[2]

**5** *1/2* **Sarstedt** 2-9-2 0 .......... DaneO'Neill 10 — 57
(Henry Candy) *trckd ldrs: nt clr run over 2f out: sn rdn: one pce and lost 2 pls fnl f* **20/1**

**6** *2 1/2* **Pastamakesufaster** 2-8-11 0 .......... FranBerry 8 — 45+
(David Evans) *hld up in rr: swtchd lft and rdn over 1f out: modest late prog* **40/1**

06 **7** *3 1/4* **Cabanon Bay**[38] 3083 2-9-2 0 .......... JohnFahy 2 — 40
(Malcolm Saunders) *t.k.h in rr: lost tch and no ch fr 1/2-way* **33/1**

0 **8** *4 1/2* **Elegant Joan**[17] 3815 2-8-11 0 .......... StevieDonohoe 11 — 22
(Kevin Frost) *led after 100yds tl hdd 3f out: sn rdn: wknd fnl f* **66/1**

6 **P** **Mr Little (IRE)**[12] 3999 2-9-2 0 .......... DougieCostello 1
(Jamie Osborne) *midfield: rdn and outpcd fr 1/2-way: no ch whn p.u qckly jst ins fnl f: fatally injured* **50/1**

1m 9.88s (-2.12) **Going Correction** -0.45s/f (Firm) — **9** Ran SP% **116.6**
Speed ratings (Par 96): **96,88,84,83,82 79,74,68,**
CSF £10.73 TOTE £2.40: £1.10, £1.80, £1.50; EX 9.70 Trifecta £25.50.
**Owner** Manton Thoroughbreds II **Bred** Helen Smith & Sally Mullen **Trained** Manton, Wilts

**FOCUS**
Not a bad 2yo race for the track and the winner looked a good prospect in sauntering home clear of his rivals. The standard is set by the runner-up to his recent course form, and the third and fourth.

## 4467 188BET H'CAP — 6f 16y
7:10 (7:12) (Class 6) (0-65,66) 3-Y-O+ — £2,587 (£770; £384; £96; £96) Stalls Centre

Form — RPR

033 **1** **Champagne Bob**[3] 4373 5-8-13 **57** .......... KatherineGlenister(7) 2 — 68
(Richard Price) *prom: drvn 2f out: r.o to ld post* **4/1**[2]

2631 **2** *nse* **Titus Secret**[27] 3468 5-10-0 **65** .......... RobertWinston 14 — 76
(Malcolm Saunders) *cl up: led narrowly 1/2-way: shkn up and hung lft over 1f out: continued to hang u.p fnl f: hdd post* **13/8**[1]

-342 **3** *2 1/2* **Sweet Pursuit**[25] 3536 3-8-8 **51** .......... KieranO'Neill 11 — 53
(Rod Millman) *prom: rdn and ev ch 2f out: unable qck fnl f* **9/2**[3]

000- **4** *1 1/4* **Mallymkun**[213] 8206 5-9-9 **60** .......... FrannyNorton 15 — 60
(David Loughnane) *led to post: midfield: pushed along 1/2-way: drvn and r.o fnl f: clsng at fin* **14/1**

4550 **4** *dht* **Burauq**[17] 3811 5-8-2 **46** oh1 .......... (v) MillyNaseb(7) 3 — 46
(Milton Bradley) *chsd ldrs: drvn and ev ch 2f out tl one pce fnl f* **25/1**



The Form Book Flat, Raceform Ltd, Newbury, RG14 5SJ

1010 **6** 1 ½ **Compton Prince**[17] 3811 8-9-4 **55**....................(b) OisinMurphy 1 50
(Milton Bradley) *midfield: rdn 3f out: kpt on one pce fnl f* **25/1**

0240 **7** 1 ¾ **Diamond Vine (IRE)**[18] 3774 9-8-9 **46**....................(p) RyanPowell 7 36
(Ronald Harris) *outpcd and qckly rdn along in rr: edgd lft and sme prog fnl f* **40/1**

04 **8** ¾ **See You In Malta (IRE)**[29] 3397 4-9-0 **51**.................... TomQueally 9 39
(Jennie Candlish) *stmbld sn after s: in rr: drvn 2f out: no imp* **11/1**

0-00 **9** *nk* **Fantasy Justifier (IRE)**[24] 3573 6-9-12 **63**.................... MartinHarley 16 50
(Ronald Harris) *s.i.s: hld up: hdwy 1/2-way: rdn 2f out: sn outpcd by ldrs: wknd fnl f* **14/1**

-005 **10** 1 ¾ **Diminutive (IRE)**[24] 3569 5-8-12 **49**....................(p) TrevorWhelan 6 30
(Grace Harris) *midfield: rdn over 2f out: wknd over 1f out* **25/1**

0 **11** *11* **Candelaria**[15] 3903 4-10-1 **66**.................... FranBerry 13 14
(Jonjo O'Neill) *led to 1/2-way: sn rdn and wknd: eased fnl f* **20/1**

1m 10.33s (-1.67) **Going Correction** -0.45s/f (Firm)
**WFA** 3 from 4yo+ 6lb **11** Ran SP% **116.7**
Speed ratings (Par 101): **93,92,89,87,87 85,83,82,82,79 65**
CSF £9.95 CT £30.53 TOTE £5.30: £1.90, £1.20, £1.60; EX 13.10 Trifecta £55.30.
**Owner** M F Oseman **Bred** London Thoroughbred Services Ltd **Trained** Ullingswick, H'fords

**FOCUS**
Five non-runners but the bulk of the fancied horses stood their ground and this could prove solid form for the grade. Nothing got into the race from off the pace. Straightforward form.

## 4468 188BET.CO.UK H'CAP 1m 14y
**7:40** (7:47) (Class 5) (0-75,77) 3-Y-O+ **£3,234** (£962; £481; £240) **Stalls** Centre

Form RPR

-204 **1** **See The Master (IRE)**[29] 3412 3-9-4 **74**.................... AdamKirby 5 82
(Clive Cox) *mde all: drvn 2f out: r.o wl* **6/4**[1]

-050 **2** 1 ½ **Procurator (IRE)**[16] 3862 3-9-7 **77**.................... SeanLevey 9 81
(Richard Hannon) *t.k.h early: hld up in tch: shkn up wl over 1f out: chsd wnr ent fnl f: r.o but a hld* **11/4**[2]

-351 **3** 1 ¼ **Fantasy Queen**[18] 3772 4-9-1 **65**.................... EdwardGreatrex(3) 6 68
(Eve Johnson Houghton) *trckd ldng pair: rdn over 1f out and briefly in 2nd: unable qck fnl f* **4/1**[3]

0-04 **4** 1 ½ **Outback Blue**[54] 2558 4-9-12 **73**....................(t) StevieDonohoe 3 73
(David Evans) *hld up in last: rdn 2f out: r.o fnl f but nvr able to chal* **16/1**

0-40 **5** 1 ¼ **Viking Hoard (IRE)**[26] 3505 3-9-5 **75**.................... TomQueally 1 70
(Harry Dunlop) *t.k.h: trckd wnr: drvn wl over 1f out: nt qckn: wknd and hung lft ins fnl f* **10/1**

-000 **6** *nse* **Bois D'Ebene (IRE)**[6] 4214 3-8-9 **68**.................... KieranShoemark(3) 4 63
(Roger Charlton) *uns rdr and rn loose bef s: hld up in tch: drvn on outer over 2f out: nt pce to chal: hld whn carried lft ins fnl f* **7/1**

1m 34.09s (-2.11) **Going Correction** -0.45s/f (Firm)
**WFA** 3 from 4yo 9lb **6** Ran SP% **114.1**
Speed ratings (Par 103): **92,90,89,87,86 86**
CSF £6.02 CT £12.66 TOTE £2.30: £1.20, £1.80; EX 6.30 Trifecta £17.70.
**Owner** Mr And Mrs P Hargreaves **Bred** Amanda Brudenell & Anthea Gibson Fleming **Trained** Lambourn, Berks

**FOCUS**
One of the more interesting races on the card and the winner, although looking workmanlike, left the impression he was well ahead of his mark.

## 4469 RUGBY BETTING AT 188BET H'CAP 1m 4f
**8:10** (8:12) (Class 6) (0-55,55) 4-Y-O+ **£2,587** (£770; £384; £192) **Stalls** Low

Form RPR

0250 **1** **The Detainee**[46] 2781 4-9-7 **55**....................(p) AdamKirby 10 63+
(Neil Mulholland) *trckd ldrs tl lost pl 1/2-way: drvn and hdwy 3f out: led 1f out: styd on wl* **4/1**[2]

3 **2** 1 ½ **Miskin**[24] 3575 8-9-7 **55**.................... DaneO'Neill 15 61
(Robert Stephens) *cl up: trckd ldr after 2f: led over 3f out: rdn 2f out: drvn and hdd 1f out: hld fnl 100yds* **8/1**

-551 **3** *nk* **Miss Tree**[36] 3155 6-9-7 **55**.................... JasonHart 7 60
(John Quinn) *chsd ldrs: rdn 3f out: kpt on same pce u.p fnl f* **5/2**[1]

503- **4** 3 ¼ **Yourholidayisover (IRE)**[28] 1343 10-9-0 **48**....................(bt) FranBerry 8 48
(Tom Gretton) *hld up: hdwy 3f out: sn drvn: styd on fnl f* **20/1**

-600 **5** ¾ **Ring Eye (IRE)**[24] 3575 9-9-1 **52**.................... EdwardGreatrex(3) 9 51
(John O'Shea) *s.s: hld up in last: drvn on outer over 3f out: styd on fnl 2f* **14/1**

64-4 **6** *nk* **Three Loves (IRE)**[20] 3726 4-9-3 **51**.................... AdamBeschizza 16 49
(Stuart Williams) *led: drvn and hdd over 3f out: kpt on tl fdd fnl f* **5/1**[3]

600- **7** 5 **Arthur's Queen (FR)**[55] 2634 6-8-10 **51**.................... FinleyMarsh(7) 2 41
(Carroll Gray) *midfield: rdn over 3f out: wknd over 1f out* **25/1**

1066 **8** *nk* **Staplehurst (IRE)**[7] 4187 4-9-6 **54**....................(t[1]) TimmyMurphy 17 44
(Geoffrey Deacon) *s.i.s: sn chsng ldrs: drvn 2f out: no rspnse: wknd fnl f* **20/1**

-600 **9** 5 **May Mist**[25] 3529 5-9-2 **55**.................... JoshuaBryan(5) 6 37
(Trevor Wall) *t.k.h: trckd ldr 2f: styd prom: drvn 4f out: wknd over 2f out* **33/1**

-400 **10** ¾ **Moon Over Mobay**[34] 3208 4-8-10 **49**.................... MitchGodwin(5) 14 30
(Michael Blanshard) *towards rr: rdn 4f out: wknd over 2f out* **25/1**

00-0 **11** *shd* **Oyster Pearl (IRE)**[8] 4158 4-8-5 **46** oh1....................(t) WilliamCox(7) 4 26
(Carroll Gray) *midfield: clsd 1/2-way: rdn over 3f out: wknd over 2f out* **100/1**

/00- **12** *dist* **Don Padeja**[319] 257 7-8-13 **50**....................(t) KieranShoemark(3) 11
(Fergal O'Brien) *hld up towards rr: rdn 4f out: wknd rapidly: eased wl over 2f out: t.o* **5/1**[3]

2m 35.2s (-3.80) **Going Correction** -0.65s/f (Hard) **12** Ran SP% **120.8**
Speed ratings (Par 101): **86,85,84,82,82 81,78,78,75,74 74,**
CSF £33.16 CT £97.56 TOTE £6.00: £1.80, £2.30, £1.60; EX 41.40 Trifecta £124.50.
**Owner** Crowd Racing Partnership **Bred** Overbury Stallions Ltd & Dukes Stud **Trained** Limpley Stoke, Wilts

**FOCUS**
A low-grade handicap with five non-runners.

## 4470 PLAY ROULETTE AT 188BET H'CAP 1m 2f
**8:40** (8:43) (Class 6) (0-65,67) 4-Y-O+ **£1,678** (£1,678; £384; £192) **Stalls** Low

Form RPR

4-34 **1** **Ya Jammeel**[17] 3820 4-9-8 **66**.................... FrannyNorton 10 74
(Mick Channon) *cl up: led 3f out: drvn 2f out: jnd jst ins fnl f: r.o u.p* **15/8**[1]

4562 **1** *dht* **Rahmah (IRE)**[28] 3428 5-9-8 **66**.................... TimmyMurphy 7 74
(Geoffrey Deacon) *midfield: clsd 4f out: chsd ldr 2f out: chal and upsides jst ins fnl f: r.o u.p* **3/1**[2]

400 **3** 3 **Distant High**[18] 3771 6-8-9 **53**....................(v[1]) TomMarquand 8 55
(Richard Price) *wnt to post early: dwlt: in rr: hdwy 3f out: sn drvn: styd on fnl f: wnt 3rd cl home* **10/1**

-055 **4** *nk* **Henryhudsonbridge (USA)**[11] 4041 5-8-4 **55**....................(bt) JordanUys(7) 3 57
(John Flint) *t.k.h early: midfield: drvn 3f out: swtchd rt to chse ldrs 2f out: styd on same pce: lost 3rd cl home* **11/1**

-300 **5** 6 **Sister Dude**[29] 3396 4-9-2 **65**.................... MitchGodwin(5) 1 55
(Jonathan Portman) *trckd ldrs: rdn over 2f out: wknd appr fnl f* **14/1**

054/ **6** *16* **Dalgig**[738] 3642 7-9-2 **60**.................... TomQueally 5 20
(Jennie Candlish) *racd keenly: led: rdn and hdd 3f out: wknd over 1f out* **16/1**

05-1 **7** *1* **St Dunstan (IRE)**[19] 3760 4-8-11 **55**....................(v) JasonHart 6 13
(John Quinn) *chsd ldrs tl rdn and lost pl over 4f out: wknd 2f out: lost action and eased nr fin* **9/2**[3]

50 **8** *11* **Castanea**[118] 1082 5-8-2 **46** oh1.................... RyanPowell 11
(Ronald Harris) *chsd ldrs tl dropped to rr after 3f: rdn over 3f out: wl bhd fnl 2f* **25/1**

30-0 **9** *47* **Donttouchthechips (IRE)**[49] 2709 4-9-1 **59**....................(h[1]) RobHornby 9
(Nikki Evans) *s.i.s: t.k.h towards rr: hdwy to chse ldrs after 3f: drvn 4f out: sn lost pl: eased over 2f out: t.o* **33/1**

2m 6.13s (-4.47) **Going Correction** -0.65s/f (Hard) **9** Ran SP% **114.7**
Speed ratings (Par 101): **91,91,88,88,83 70,69,61,23**
WIN: 1.40 Ya Jammeel, 1.60 Rahmah; PL: 1.40 Ya Jammeel, 1.20 Rahmah, 2.70 Distant High; EX: 4.60, 4.80; CSF: 3.67, 4.47; TC: 21.11, 23.69; TF: 24.30, 30.30;.
**Owner** Business Moves Group & Partners **Bred** Ms Natalie Cleary **Trained** Compton, Berks
**Owner** M Channon **Bred** Rabbah Bloodstock Limited **Trained** West Ilsley, Berks

**FOCUS**
A steady early pace saw a few race with the choke out but the market principals came to the fore and the judge couldn't split them at the finish.

## 4471 READ SILVESTRE DE SOUSA AT 188BET H'CAP 2m
**9:10** (9:11) (Class 5) (0-75,75) 4-Y-O+ **£3,234** (£962; £481; £240) **Stalls** Low

Form RPR

/641 **1** **Hawkerland (IRE)**[21] 3698 4-8-12 **73**.................... TylerSaunders(7) 2 83+
(Marcus Tregoning) *trckd ldrs: wnt 2nd 3f out: drvn to ld 2f out: styd on wl: pushed along and in command fnl f: eased nr fin* **5/2**[1]

542 **2** *1* **Wordiness**[16] 3863 9-8-10 **64**.................... JFEgan 3 71
(David Evans) *s.i.s: hld up: hdwy 5f out: rdn 2f out: chsd wnr over 1f out: kpt on but a hld* **12/1**

-546 **3** 1 ¾ **Fitzwilly**[23] 3618 7-8-13 **67**.................... FrannyNorton 5 72
(Mick Channon) *led 100yds: chsd ldrs tl lost pl 1/2-way: clsd again 5f out: drvn 3f out: styd on same pce: wnt 3rd nr fin* **13/2**[3]

2-33 **4** *nk* **Tyrell (IRE)**[15] 3907 4-9-4 **72**....................(v) FergusSweeney 7 77
(Alan King) *trckd ldr tl led 4f out: sn drvn: hdd 2f out: one pce: wknd ins fnl f and lost 3rd nr fin* **5/1**[2]

**5** *17* **Moabit (GER)**[11] 5-9-2 **75**....................(t) MeganNicholls(5) 1 59
(Paul Nicholls) *led after 100yds: hdd 4f out: wknd 3f out* **5/2**[1]

0063 **6** *76* **Moojaned (IRE)**[15] 3916 6-8-2 **63**.................... JordanUys(7) 13
(John Flint) *t.k.h towards rr: hdwy 1/2-way: drvn over 4f out: wknd 3f out: sn eased: t.o* **28/1**

3240 **7** *10* **Riptide**[22] 3663 11-8-3 **60**.................... EdwardGreatrex(3) 4
(Michael Scudamore) *s.i.s: rdn after 4f: a in rr: bhd fnl 5f: t.o* **25/1**

0-13 **8** *59* **Danglydontask**[21] 3685 6-8-7 **64**....................(b) KieranShoemark(3) 10
(David Arbuthnot) *chsd ldrs tl dropped to rr 7f out: t.o fnl 5f* **8/1**

3m 27.28s (-11.62) **Going Correction** -0.65s/f (Hard) **8** Ran SP% **113.2**
Speed ratings (Par 103): **103,102,101,101,92 54,49,20**
CSF £34.47 CT £173.35 TOTE £3.30: £2.40, £2.30, £1.30; EX 24.60 Trifecta £177.50.
**Owner** Guy Brook **Bred** Mount Coote Partnership **Trained** Whitsbury, Hants

**FOCUS**
A solid gallop in the staying handicap and the winner looks a stayer on the upgrade. The third has been rated to form for now with the fourth close to form.
T/Jkpt: £10,573.00 to a £1 stake. Pool: £10,573.00 - 1.0 winning unit T/Plt: £39.20 to a £1 stake. Pool: £99,731.10 - 1,852.95 winning units T/Qpdt: £2.90 to a £1 stake. Pool: £10,361.32 - 2,617.57 winning units **Richard Lowther**

# 4426 HAMILTON (R-H)
Tuesday, July 4

**OFFICIAL GOING: Soft (good to soft in places; 7.1)**
Wind: Almost nil Weather: Overcast

## 4472 BB FOODSERVICE NOVICE AUCTION STKS (PLUS 10 RACE) (A £20,000 BB FOODSERVICE 2YO SERIES QUALIFIER) 6f 6y
**2:00** (2:01) (Class 4) 2-Y-O **£5,175** (£1,540; £769; £384) **Stalls** High

Form RPR

**1** **Poetic Steps (FR)** 2-8-11 0.................... PJMcDonald 5 73
(Mark Johnston) *prom: effrt and drvn along 2f out: hdwy to ld ins fnl f: edgd lft: pushed clr towards fin* **20/1**

0 **2** 2 **Austin Powers (IRE)**[35] 3165 2-9-2 0.................... JoeFanning 6 72
(Mark Johnston) *trckd ldr: effrt and rdn over 1f out: led briefly ins fnl f: kpt on: nt pce of wnr* **9/1**

431 **3** 1 ½ **Armed Response**[13] 3973 2-9-8 81.................... JackGarritty 9 73
(Jedd O'Keeffe) *led against stands' rail: rdn over 1f out: hdd ins fnl f: sn one pce* **13/8**[1]

2 **4** *shd* **Up Sticks And Go**[10] 4074 2-9-2 0.................... GrahamLee 7 67
(Keith Dalgleish) *trckd ldrs: nt clr run over 2f out: effrt and pushed along over 1f out: one pce fnl f* **10/3**[2]

**5** 5 **Wensley** 2-9-2 0.................... JosephineGordon 4 52+
(James Bethell) *s.i.s: t.k.h: hld up bhd ldng gp: hmpd and stmbld bdly over 3f out: sn pushed along: outpcd fr 2f out* **17/2**

0 **6** 2 **Sandama (IRE)**[22] 3662 2-8-11 0.................... TonyHamilton 3 41
(Richard Fahey) *hld up: rdn along over 2f out: no imp fr wl over 1f out* **8/1**[3]

0 **7** 3 **Ray Purchase**[15] 3895 2-9-2 0.................... PaulMulrennan 1 37
(Keith Dalgleish) *hld up: shkn up over 2f out: sn no imp: btn over 1f out* **50/1**

4 **8** 4 **Tanaya**[26] 3483 2-9-2 0.................... PhillipMakin 2 25
(Richard Fahey) *t.k.h: hld up in tch: blkd over 3f out: sn veered rt and outpcd: struggling fnl 2f* **12/1**

**9** *10* **Moremoneymoreparty (IRE)** 2-8-11 0.................... ConnorBeasley 8
(Richard Guest) *t.k.h: trckd ldrs: rdn over 2f out: wknd wl over 1f out* **9/1**

1m 15.04s (2.84) **Going Correction** +0.40s/f (Good) **9** Ran SP% **117.2**
Speed ratings (Par 96): **97,94,92,92,85 82,78,73,60**
CSF £189.55 TOTE £24.80: £4.90, £2.70, £1.30; EX 82.90 Trifecta £931.50.
**Owner** Kingsley Park 6 **Bred** Mark Johnston Racing Ltd **Trained** Middleham Moor, N Yorks

**FOCUS**
Races 2, 3, 4 and 5 all increased by 2yds. Bit of a turn up here, but reason to believe it could be okay form. There was a one-two for trainer Mark Johnston.

## 4473 FERNIEGAIR H'CAP — 1m 68y
**2:30** (2:31) (Class 6) (0-60,62) 3-Y-O — **£3,234** (£962; £481; £240) **Stalls** Low

Form — RPR

06 **1** **Edgar Allan Poe (IRE)**[15] 3913 3-9-6 **58** .................... DanielTudhope 8 70
(Rebecca Bastiman) *hld up midfield: pushed along and outpcd over 3f out: rallied and bk on bridle over 2f out: led over 1f out: pushed out last 75yds: comf* **15/2**[3]

0-64 **2** 1¼ **Devil's Guard (IRE)**[17] 3831 3-8-10 **48** ....................(v) GrahamLee 2 57
(Keith Dalgleish) *chsd ldng pair: clr of rest 1/2-way: led gng wl over 2f out: rdn and hdd over 1f out: rallied: one pce ins fnl f* **12/1**

**3** 6 **Ahundrednotout**[33] 3270 3-8-12 **50** .................... JamesSullivan 12 46+
(John James Feane, Ire) *midfield: outpcd 4f out: rallied and ev ch over 1f out: rdn and wknd ins fnl f* **2/1**[1]

-200 **4** 1¾ **Prancing Oscar (IRE)**[31] 3317 3-9-5 **62** ...........(p[1]) RobJFitzpatrick(5) 10 54
(Ben Haslam) *hld up: pushed along and hdwy over 2f out: no imp fr over 1f out* **8/1**

6402 **5** 4½ **England Expects**[15] 3913 3-9-4 **59** ....................(h) JordanVaughan(3) 11 41
(K R Burke) *s.i.s: hld up: drvn and outpcd over 3f out: rallied over 1f out: sn no imp* **5/1**[2]

053 **6** 7 **New Delhi (IRE)**[14] 3931 3-9-6 **58** .................... JoeFanning 5 25
(Mark Johnston) *prom: pushed along and edgd rt over 2f out: sn wknd* **8/1**

6-00 **7** ½ **Born To Boogie**[31] 2470 3-8-8 **46** ow1 .................... ConnorBeasley 7 12
(Chris Grant) *led to over 2f out: sn rdn and wknd* **66/1**

06-0 **8** 10 **Ten In The Hat (IRE)**[20] 3708 3-8-7 **45** .................... JosephineGordon 3
(Shaun Harris) *prom: drvn and outpcd 4f out: btn fnl 2f* **25/1**

5030 **9** 2¼ **Bonnie Gals**[13] 3977 3-9-7 **59** .................... PaulMulrennan 6
(Keith Dalgleish) *hld up: pushed along over 2f out: sn outpcd and btn* **8/1**

0425 **10** hd **Panther In Pink (IRE)**[20] 3708 3-8-9 **47** ....................(h) ShaneGray 13
(Ann Duffield) *pressed ldr: chal over 4f out: rdn and wknd qckly over 2f out* **16/1**

44-0 **11** 13 **Smiley Riley (IRE)**[57] 2470 3-9-1 **53** .................... BarryMcHugh 1
(Tony Coyle) *hld up: rdn and struggling 4f out: sn wknd* **20/1**

1m 50.96s (2.56) **Going Correction** +0.25s/f (Good) **11** Ran SP% **118.8**
Speed ratings (Par 98): **97,95,89,88,83 76,76,66,63,63 50**
CSF £92.60 CT £253.35 TOTE £8.00: £2.40, £3.30, £1.60; EX 104.20 Trifecta £438.90.
**Owner** I B Barker / P Bastiman **Bred** Paul, Ben & Charlie Cartan **Trained** Cowthorpe, N Yorks
■ Stewards' Enquiry : James Sullivan seven-day ban: careless riding (18-24 Jul)

**FOCUS**
Race distance increased by 2yds. Soon strung out, the race somewhat fell apart and the front two finished clear.

## 4474 RACINGUK.COM MAIDEN STKS — 1m 1f 35y
**3:00** (3:00) (Class 5) 3-Y-O+ — **£4,204** (£1,251; £625; £312) **Stalls** Low

Form — RPR

4 **1** **Starplex**[11] 4036 7-9-9 0 .................... RowanScott(5) 3 80+
(Keith Dalgleish) *hld up midfield: effrt over 2f out: rdn and led over 1f out: styd on wl fnl f* **7/1**[3]

6 **2** 1¼ **Broadway Dreams**[11] 4055 3-9-4 0 .................... JosephineGordon 10 75
(Marjorie Fife) *hld up: rdn and outpcd over 4f out: gd hdwy over 1f out: kpt on strly fnl f: nt rch wnr* **33/1**

2 **3** 1½ **Torcello (IRE)**[26] 3485 3-9-4 0 .................... LiamKeniry 9 72
(Andrew Balding) *hld up midfield on outside: effrt and rdn over 2f out: hung rt and hdwy to led briefly over 1f out: continued to edgd rt and one pce fnl f* **5/6**[1]

0-5 **4** 2 **Chinese Spirit (IRE)**[11] 4036 3-9-4 0 .................... PJMcDonald 7 68
(R Mike Smith) *hld up: rdn over 3f out: hdwy to chse ldrs over 1f out: outpcd fnl f* **40/1**

-032 **5** 8 **Somnambulist**[5] 4247 3-9-4 74 ....................(h) GrahamLee 11 51
(Keith Dalgleish) *cl up: rdn and edgd rt over 2f out: wknd over 1f out* **7/2**[2]

3502 **6** 1¼ **Miss Goldsmith (IRE)**[10] 4105 4-9-9 58 .................... NeilFarley 2 45
(Lucinda Egerton) *t.k.h: hld up in tch: stdy hdwy and cl up 4f out: rdn and wknd over 1f out* **50/1**

0 **7** 6 **Shine Baby Shine**[25] 3542 3-8-13 0 .................... PaddyAspell 6 31
(Philip Kirby) *s.i.s: hld up: rdn along over 3f out: sn outpcd: n.d after* **100/1**

3220 **8** 2¼ **Testbourne (IRE)**[18] 3787 3-9-1 70 ....................(t[1]) JordanVaughan(3) 8 31
(K R Burke) *led: rdn over 2f out: hdd over 1f out: sn wknd* **25/1**

355 **9** 4 **Unite The Clans (IRE)**[5] 4247 3-9-4 0 .................... TadhgO'Shea 4 23
(John Patrick Shanahan, Ire) *t.k.h: trckd ldrs: outpcd whn checked over 2f out: rdn and sn wknd* **15/2**

4 **10** 10 **Waiting A Lot (IRE)**[14] 3931 3-8-13 0 .................... DanielTudhope 1
(David O'Meara) *s.i.s: hld up: struggling 3f out: sn wknd* **16/1**

2m 1.1s (1.40) **Going Correction** +0.25s/f (Good)
**WFA** 3 from 4yo+ 10lb **10** Ran SP% **119.1**
Speed ratings (Par 103): **103,101,100,98,91 90,85,83,79,70**
CSF £209.32 TOTE £8.30: £2.30, £7.60, £1.10; EX 197.70 Trifecta £794.10.
**Owner** G & J Park **Bred** Jill Park **Trained** Carluke, S Lanarks

**FOCUS**
Race distance increased by 2yds. An average maiden, the favourite disappointed and the 7yo upstaged his younger rivals. It paid to race from off the pace. The form is a bit fluid, with the fourth perhaps the key.

## 4475 ALMADA MILE H'CAP — 1m 68y
**3:30** (3:31) (Class 2) (0-100,97) 3-Y-O+
**£18,675** (£5,592; £2,796; £1,398; £699; £351) **Stalls** Low

Form — RPR

6603 **1** **Hibou**[10] 4076 4-9-4 **87** ....................(b) DavidNolan 12 98
(Iain Jardine) *hld up: pushed along 3f out: hdwy over 1f out: led last 50yds: kpt on strly* **16/1**[3]

5350 **2** 1¼ **Masham Star (IRE)**[12] 3997 3-9-5 **97** .................... PJMcDonald 2 103
(Mark Johnston) *led: rdn over 2f out: hdd and no ex last 50yds* **5/1**[2]

0322 **3** 2¼ **Ionization (IRE)**[24] 3589 4-9-5 **93** .................... CliffordLee(5) 4 96
(John Patrick Shanahan, Ire) *in tch: effrt and rdn over 2f out: n.m.r over 1f out: sn edgd rt: kpt on ins fnl f* **5/1**[2]

1111 **4** 2½ **Gulf Of Poets**[19] 3744 5-9-4 **90** .................... NathanEvans(3) 1 87
(Michael Easterby) *trckd ldrs: rdn and wnt 2nd over 1f out: wknd ins fnl f* **4/1**[1]

1006 **5** 1½ **Aardwolf (USA)**[10] 4075 3-8-13 **91** .................... JoeFanning 6 83
(Mark Johnston) *prom: effrt and rdn over 2f out: edgd rt and wknd over 1f out* **16/1**[3]

-044 **6** nse **Highland Colori (IRE)**[64] 2232 9-9-13 **96** ....................(b) LiamKeniry 8 90
(Andrew Balding) *pressed ldr: drvn over 2f out: wknd over 1f out* **22/1**

2311 **7** nk **Nicholas T**[10] 4077 5-9-7 **90** .................... PaulMulrennan 3 83
(Jim Goldie) *hld up bhd ldng gp: pushed along 3f out: wknd wl over 1f out* **5/1**[2]

04 **8** 3¼ **Alexandrakollontai (IRE)**[17] 3828 7-8-9 **78** ...........(b) JamesSullivan 11 63
(Alistair Whillans) *hld up: drvn and outpcd wl over 3f out: btn fnl 2f* **20/1**

0050 **9** 1½ **Lat Hawill (IRE)**[10] 4077 6-9-7 **90** ....................(b) GrahamLee 13 72
(Keith Dalgleish) *hld up: struggling over 4f out: nvr on terms* **28/1**

600 **10** 1¼ **Zoravan (USA)**[6] 4207 4-8-7 **81** ....................(v) RowanScott(5) 9 60
(Keith Dalgleish) *t.k.h: cl up on outside tl rdn and wknd qckly fr over 2f out* **66/1**

31-3 **P** **Weekend Offender (FR)**[83] 1734 4-9-6 **89** .................... TomEaves 5
(Kevin Ryan) *leg ct in stalls and s.v.s: sn p.u* **4/1**[1]

1m 50.04s (1.64) **Going Correction** +0.25s/f (Good)
**WFA** 3 from 4yo+ 9lb **11** Ran SP% **115.8**
Speed ratings (Par 109): **101,99,97,95,93 93,93,89,88,87**
CSF £89.04 CT £475.04 TOTE £18.90: £3.90, £2.00, £1.80; EX 135.00 Trifecta £741.80.
**Owner** Tapas Partnership **Bred** Darley **Trained** Carrutherstown, D'fries & G'way

**FOCUS**
Race distance increased by 2yds. A decent handicap. The runner-up has been rated to his best, with the third close to her latest.

## 4476 HAMILTON PARK SUPPORTING RACING STAFF WEEK H'CAP — 1m 5f 16y
**4:00** (4:01) (Class 5) (0-75,77) 3-Y-O+ — **£4,528** (£1,347; £673; £336) **Stalls** Low

Form — RPR

5-41 **1** **Davy's Dilemma**[15] 3909 3-9-3 **77** .................... PaulMulrennan 7 88
(Michael Dods) *hld up in tch: smooth hdwy to ld over 2f out: shkn up and edgd rt over 1f out: kpt on wl fnl f* **9/5**[1]

-134 **2** 1¼ **Addicted To You (IRE)**[25] 3528 3-9-0 **74** .................... JoeFanning 5 83
(Mark Johnston) *cl up: led over 3f out: hdd over 2f out: rallied: kpt on same pce fnl f* **5/1**[3]

05-5 **3** 10 **Picture Painter (IRE)**[30] 2498 4-8-10 **57** .................... JamesSullivan 6 50
(Jim Goldie) *hld up: rdn and effrt over 2f out: chsd (clr) ldng pair over 1f out: kpt on fnl f: no imp* **7/1**

6323 **4** 8 **Archibelle**[56] 2496 3-8-6 **69** .................... NathanEvans(3) 8 51
(R Mike Smith) *hld up: rdn over 4f out: plugged on fr over 1f out: nvr on terms* **12/1**

2-23 **5** nse **Lady Natasha (IRE)**[22] 3654 4-8-11 **61** .................... JordanVaughan(3) 2 42
(K R Burke) *t.k.h and sddle sn slipped forward: hdd over 3f out: rdn and wknd over 2f out* **12/1**

4 **6** nk **Leven (IRE)**[23] 3635 3-8-0 **60** oh1 ....................(b[1]) RoystonFfrench 3 41
(John Patrick Shanahan, Ire) *trckd ldrs: effrt and rdn over 2f out: wknd wl over 1f out* **20/1**

0015 **7** 14 **Marmion**[13] 3983 5-9-12 **73** ....................(h) DanielTudhope 4 32
(Les Eyre) *hld up: effrt on outside over 3f out: drvn and wknd fnl 2f* **14/1**

26-5 **8** 6 **Wordsearch (USA)**[69] 2092 3-9-0 **74** .................... JosephineGordon 9 25
(Hugo Palmer) *t.k.h: trckd ldrs: drvn and outpcd over 3f out: sn wknd* **7/2**[2]

2m 58.15s (4.25) **Going Correction** +0.25s/f (Good)
**WFA** 3 from 4yo+ 13lb **8** Ran SP% **113.9**
Speed ratings (Par 103): **96,95,89,84,84 83,75,71**
CSF £10.94 CT £49.83 TOTE £2.40: £1.20, £1.70, £2.20; EX 11.70 Trifecta £56.00.
**Owner** D Neale **Bred** Wansdyke Farms Limited **Trained** Denton, Co Durham

**FOCUS**
Race distance increased by 2yds. Reasonable 3yo form, the front two finished clear and both look progressive types.

## 4477 RACINGUK.COM H'CAP — 6f 6y
**4:30** (4:32) (Class 4) (0-85,87) 3-Y-O+ — **£8,021** (£2,387; £1,192; £596) **Stalls** Centre

Form — RPR

2154 **1** **Sharp Defence (USA)**[46] 2775 3-9-8 **87** .................... TadhgO'Shea 9 99
(John Patrick Shanahan, Ire) *sn pushed along in tch: hdwy to ld over 1f out: drew clr fnl f* **7/2**[1]

0330 **2** 3¼ **Harwoods Volante (IRE)**[11] 4037 6-9-11 **84** .................... SamJames 4 87
(David O'Meara) *trckd ldrs: effrt and ev ch over 1f out: kpt on fnl f: nt pce of wnr* **14/1**

-005 **3** 1¼ **Another Wise Kid (IRE)**[27] 3463 9-9-9 **82** .................... GrahamLee 8 81
(Paul Midgley) *in tch: rdn over 2f out: hdwy over 1f out: kpt on fnl f: nvr able to chal* **7/1**[3]

-604 **4** 1 **Manatee Bay**[13] 3974 7-8-9 **73** ....................(p) PhilDennis(5) 10 69
(Noel Wilson) *s.i.s: hld up: rdn and effrt 2f out: no imp fnl f* **10/1**

2002 **5** nk **Lexington Times (IRE)**[5] 4277 5-9-6 **79** .................... JamesSullivan 2 74
(Ruth Carr) *hld up: rdn along over 2f out: hdwy over 1f out: sn no imp* **7/2**[1]

0054 **6** 6 **Munfallet (IRE)**[28] 3424 6-9-12 **85** .................... PhillipMakin 6 61
(David Brown) *pressed ldr: rdn over 2f out: wknd over 1f out* **7/2**[1]

-001 **7** 5 **Zapper Cass (FR)**[5] 4277 4-9-8 **84** 6ex .................... JoshDoyle(3) 1 44
(Tony Coyle) *s.i.s: hld up: shortlived effrt on outside over 2f out: wknd wl over 1f out* **6/1**[2]

3-00 **8** 5 **Bapak Asmara (IRE)**[43] 2899 5-9-6 **79** .................... TomEaves 7 23
(Kevin Ryan) *led against stands' rail: rdn over 2f out: wknd over 1f out* **25/1**

400- **9** 11 **Funding Deficit (IRE)**[201] 8389 7-8-10 **76** ...............(h) SeanMooney(7) 3
(Jim Goldie) *hld up: drvn and outpcd over 2f out: sn wknd* **40/1**

1m 13.71s (1.51) **Going Correction** +0.40s/f (Good)
**WFA** 3 from 4yo+ 6lb **9** Ran SP% **115.5**
Speed ratings (Par 105): **105,100,99,97,97 89,82,75,61**
CSF £56.34 CT £328.27 TOTE £4.00: £1.50, £3.20, £2.30; EX 52.00 Trifecta £371.00.
**Owner** Thistle Bloodstock Limited **Bred** Donato Lanni **Trained** Kells, Co Kilkenny

**FOCUS**
A fair sprint and no surprise to see it go to the 3yo. A clear pb from the winner, with the runner-up close to this year's form.

## 4478 RACING UK ON SKY 432 H'CAP (DIV I) — 5f 7y
**5:00** (5:02) (Class 6) (0-55,57) 3-Y-O+ — **£3,234** (£962; £481; £240) **Stalls** Centre

Form — RPR

0-0 **1** **Camanche Grey (IRE)**[14] 3944 6-8-13 **50** ............... RobJFitzpatrick(5) 7 60
(Ben Haslam) *hld up midfield: stdy hdwy over 2f out: led over 1f out: rdn and r.o wl fnl f* **12/1**

0601 **2** 1¾ **Dutch Dream**[20] 3710 4-9-4 **50** .................... JamesSullivan 10 54
(Linda Perratt) *hld up: pushed along and hdwy 2f out: kpt on fnl f: nt rch wnr* **4/1**[2]

2322 **3** ½ **Cheeni**[20] 3710 5-9-0 **46** ....................(p) PJMcDonald 3 48
(Jim Goldie) *hld up on far side of gp: rdn and effrt 2f out: kpt on ins fnl f* **5/1**[3]

2630 **4** 2 ½ **Joysunny**[10] 4107 3-8-7 **47** NathanEvans(3) 11 38
(Michael Easterby) *chsd clr ldr: rdn and hung rt over 1f out: outpcd fnl f* **11/2**

000 **5** *nk* **Captain Scooby**[15] 3915 11-9-1 **47** (b) TonyHamilton 4 39
(Richard Guest) *dwlt: bhd and pushed along: hdwy over 1f out: kpt on fnl f: nt pce to chal* **14/1**

005 **6** 2 ¼ **Six Of The Best**[102] 1349 5-8-13 **45** ConnorBeasley 6 29
(Bryan Smart) *in tch: drvn along over 2f out: outpcd over 1f out: btn fnl f* **33/1**

0430 **7** ½ **Very First Blade**[8] 4148 8-8-10 **47** (be) PhilDennis(5) 2 29
(Michael Mullineaux) *prom: effrt and rdn over 2f out: wknd appr fnl f* **16/1**

0323 **8** ½ **Culloden**[15] 3914 5-9-11 **57** (b) JosephineGordon 5 37
(Shaun Harris) *led at str gallop: hdd over 1f out: wknd qckly* **7/2**[1]

6606 **9** ¾ **Lady Molly (IRE)**[15] 3914 3-9-0 **51** GrahamLee 1 27
(Keith Dalgleish) *bhd on far side of gp: struggling over 2f out: sn wknd* **16/1**

223 **10** ¾ **Maggi May (IRE)**[17] 3818 3-9-2 **53** TomEaves 12 26
(David Brown) *bhd on nr side of gp: drvn along 1/2-way: sn btn* **15/2**

1m 2.45s (2.45) **Going Correction** +0.40s/f (Good)
**WFA** 3 from 4yo+ 5lb **10** Ran SP% **115.1**
Speed ratings (Par 101): **96,93,92,88,87 84,83,82,81,80**
CSF £58.83 CT £282.64 TOTE £15.40: £3.80, £1.80, £1.90; EX 81.00 Trifecta £627.30.
**Owner** Mrs C Barclay & Partners **Bred** Peter & Elizabeth Jones **Trained** Middleham Moor, N Yorks

**FOCUS**
Lowly sprint form, although they went pretty hard up front.

## 4479 RACING UK ON SKY 432 H'CAP (DIV II) 5f 7y
**5:30** (5:32) (Class 6) (0-55,55) 3-Y-O+ **£3,234** (£962; £481; £240) **Stalls** Centre

Form RPR

1 **1** **Wee Jock (IRE)**[5] 4246 3-8-12 **51** 6ex RoystonFfrench 11 60+
(John Patrick Shanahan, Ire) *mde all against stands' rail: shkn up ins fnl f: kpt on wl* **11/10**[1]

0602 **2** 1 ¼ **Minty Jones**[20] 3704 8-8-7 **46** (v) PhilDennis(5) 2 51
(Michael Mullineaux) *cl up in centre: rdn over 2f out: edgd lft over 1f out: kpt on ins fnl f* **8/1**

50-6 **3** 2 ¼ **Cool Run Girl (IRE)**[174] 179 3-8-6 **50** LewisEdmunds(5) 5 44
(Iain Jardine) *bhd on outside: rdn along 1/2-way: hdwy over 1f out: r.o fnl f: no imp* **16/1**

0200 **4** 1 ¾ **Tinsill**[7] 4174 6-8-8 **47** (p) RowanScott(5) 8 37
(Nigel Tinkler) *bhd and outpcd: hdwy over 1f out: kpt on fnl f: nvr able to chal* **6/1**[2]

0000 **5** 2 ¼ **Warleggan (FR)**[5] 4246 3-8-7 **46** oh1 (b) JamesSullivan 6 26
(Linda Perratt) *midfield: drvn over 2f out: hdwy and flashed tail fr over 1f out: no imp fnl f* **50/1**

5-00 **6** 2 ¾ **Roman Times (IRE)**[7] 4174 4-9-4 **55** (p) NathanEvans(3) 1 27
(Colin Teague) *in tch on far side of gp: drvn along over 2f out: wknd over 1f out* **33/1**

0450 **7** *nk* **La Haule Lady**[43] 2897 3-8-12 **51** (p) PaulMulrennan 9 20
(Paul Midgley) *in tch: rdn over 2f out: wknd over 1f out* **8/1**

-300 **8** 1 ¾ **Port Master**[13] 3979 3-9-2 **55** ShaneGray 4 18
(Ann Duffield) *dwlt: bhd and outpcd: nvr on terms* **66/1**

0244 **9** 4 **Harpers Ruby**[20] 3710 7-8-12 **46** oh1 PaddyAspell 7
(Lynn Siddall) *in tch: rdn over 2f out: wknd over 1f out* **15/2**[3]

1m 3.15s (3.15) **Going Correction** +0.40s/f (Good)
**WFA** 3 from 4yo+ 5lb **9** Ran SP% **108.2**
Speed ratings (Par 101): **90,88,84,81,78 73,73,70,63**
CSF £8.87 CT £66.95 TOTE £1.90: £1.10, £1.80, £4.00; EX 8.50 Trifecta £84.80.
**Owner** Thistle Bloodstock Limited **Bred** Thistle Bloodstock Limited **Trained** Kells, Co Kilkenny

**FOCUS**
Less open than division one.
T/Plt: £99.10 to a £1 stake. Pool: £46,075.84 - 339.33 winning units T/Qpdt: £24.70 to a £1 stake. Pool: £7,044.32 - 210.30 winning units **Richard Young**

4480 - 4486a (Foreign Racing) - See Raceform Interactive

# 4518 HAMBURG (R-H)
Tuesday, July 4

**OFFICIAL GOING: Turf: soft**

## 4487a SPARKASSE HOLSTEIN CUP (GROUP 3) (3YO+) (TURF) 1m 2f
**6:30** 3-Y-O+ **£27,350** (£10,256; £5,128; £2,564; £1,709)

RPR

**1** **Matchwinner (GER)**[57] 2485 6-9-0 0 StephenHellyn 2 106+
(A Kleinkorres, Germany) *hld up in 4th: dropped to rr after 4f: rdn and styd on fr 2f out: led 50yds out: drvn out* **12/5**[2]

**2** ¾ **Wai Key Star (GER)**[37] 3116 4-9-0 0 EduardoPedroza 5 104
(A Wohler, Germany) *led: hdd after 4f: rdn 2f out: led over 1f out: hdd 50yds out: no ex cl home* **7/5**[1]

**3** *hd* **El Loco (GER)**[9] 4130 4-9-0 0 AndreasHelfenbein 3 104
(Markus Klug, Germany) *t.k.h in 3rd: led after 4f: wnt clr 3f out: rdn 2f out: hdd over 1f out: kpt on same pce tl short of room clsng stages* **33/10**[3]

**4** 1 ½ **Devastar (GER)**[37] 3116 5-9-4 0 MartinSeidl 4 105
(Markus Klug, Germany) *in tch: rdn 2f out and kpt on fr 2f out: nvr gng pce to chal* **17/5**

**5** 12 **Apoleon (GER)**[51] 2667 7-9-0 0 FilipMinarik 6 77
(Frau Anna Schleusner-Fruhriep, Germany) *hld up in rr: trckd ldrs after 4f: rdn and outpcd over 2f out: wknd 1f out: eased last 100yds* **7/1**

2m 19.46s **5** Ran SP% **129.6**
PARI-MUTUEL (all including 10 euro stake): WIN 34 PLACE: 16, 14, SF: 81.
**Owner** Jens Schwarma **Bred** Gestut Gorlsdorf **Trained** Germany

# 4197 BATH (L-H)
Wednesday, July 5

**OFFICIAL GOING: Firm (10.4)**
Wind: virtually nil Weather: very warm

## 4488 RACEHORSE SYNDICATES ASSOCIATION NOVICE AUCTION STKS 5f 10y
**6:00** (6:00) (Class 6) 2-Y-O **£2,264** (£673; £336; £168) **Stalls** Centre

Form RPR

20 **1** **Connery (IRE)**[15] 3925 2-9-0 0 MartinDwyer 5 72+
(Sylvester Kirk) *trckd ldr: led wl over 1f out: edgd lft sn after: kpt on wl: readily* **13/8**[2]

3334 **2** ¾ **Aquadabra (IRE)**[7] 4204 2-8-9 71 JFEgan 2 60
(Mick Channon) *trckd ldrs: swtchd rt and rdn over 1f out: kpt on to go 2nd wl ins fnl f but nvr threatening to get on terms w wnr* **7/2**[3]

666 **3** ¾ **Funkadelic**[29] 3430 2-9-2 68 FranBerry 1 64
(Ben Haslam) *sn led: rdn and hdd wl over 1f out: sltly hmpd whn hld sn after: kpt on same pce fnl f* **16/1**

0426 **4** 5 **Pursuing The Dream (IRE)**[14] 3960 2-8-11 91 DougieCostello 4 40
(Jamie Osborne) *little awkwardly away: trckd ldrs: effrt but hanging lft fr 2f out: no ex and hld fnl f* **6/4**[1]

0 **5** 11 **Korak Boy (IRE)**[13] 3999 2-8-10 0 RobHornby 7
(Joseph Tuite) *sn pushed along: last of 5: outpcd over 2f out: nvr any threat* **40/1**

1m 0.72s (-1.78) **Going Correction** -0.40s/f (Firm) **5** Ran SP% **108.6**
Speed ratings (Par 92): **98,96,95,87,70**
CSF £7.42 TOTE £3.00: £1.10, £2.60; EX 7.10 Trifecta £31.10.
**Owner** N Simpson, Mrs T Burns & Partner **Bred** Rathasker Stud **Trained** Upper Lambourn, Berks

**FOCUS**
The two at the head of the market had performed creditably in a much higher grade at Royal Ascot last time, though with the favourite running a long way below that level, it's form to be dubious about. The race was won for the second year in succession by Sylvester Kirk.

## 4489 COLLECTION H'CAP 5f 160y
**6:30** (6:30) (Class 4) (0-80,81) 3-Y-O+ **£6,469** (£1,925; £962; £481) **Stalls** Centre

Form RPR

6236 **1** **Handytalk (IRE)**[16] 3919 4-9-11 **77** AdamKirby 2 86
(Rod Millman) *mde all: kpt on strly: rdn out* **4/1**[2]

0-54 **2** 1 ¼ **Case Key**[7] 4201 4-8-13 **72** (p) RayDawson(7) 1 77
(Michael Appleby) *trckd wnr: rdn 2f out: kpt on fnl f but a being hld by wnr* **10/1**

1-66 **3** 2 **Sfumato**[37] 3146 3-9-7 **79** TrevorWhelan 7 76
(Roger Charlton) *prom: rdn to chal over 2f out: drifted lft and hld over 1f out: kpt on same pce fnl f* **4/1**[2]

5434 **4** 1 ½ **September Issue**[11] 4080 4-9-11 **77** (p) RobertWinston 3 70
(Gay Kelleway) *in tch: rdn and hdwy over 1f out: kpt on same pce ins fnl f* **3/1**[1]

4-30 **5** 2 ½ **Secret Potion**[23] 3673 3-8-9 **67** SamHitchcott 6 51
(Ronald Harris) *trckd ldrs: rdn over 2f out: no ex ent fnl f* **40/1**

3-02 **6** ¾ **Royal Mezyan (IRE)**[18] 3834 6-10-1 **81** StevieDonohoe 5 64
(Henry Spiller) *in tch: rdn over 2f out: nt pce to chal: fdd ins fnl f* **13/2**[3]

0250 **7** 1 ½ **Silverrica (IRE)**[17] 3865 7-9-3 **74** GeorgiaCox(5) 8 52
(Malcolm Saunders) *in tch: rdn over 2f out: fdd ins fnl f* **7/1**

22-0 **8** 4 **Dyllan (IRE)**[16] 3903 4-9-8 **74** JimCrowley 4 39
(Ruth Carr) *slowly away: struggling over 2f out: a last* **7/1**

1m 9.04s (-2.16) **Going Correction** -0.40s/f (Firm)
**WFA** 3 from 4yo+ 6lb **8** Ran SP% **114.9**
Speed ratings (Par 105): **98,96,93,91,88 87,85,80**
CSF £43.09 CT £170.63 TOTE £5.40: £1.60, £2.60, £1.70; EX 49.30 Trifecta £348.80.
**Owner** Cantay Racing **Bred** Edmond Kinane & Donal Sweeney **Trained** Kentisbeare, Devon

**FOCUS**
Not the strongest of 0-80s with not one of these having won this season and the favourite searching for a first turf success.

## 4490 EXCELLO LAW MAIDEN STKS (PLUS 10 RACE) 1m
**7:00** (7:01) (Class 4) 3-Y-O **£5,822** (£1,732; £865; £432) **Stalls** Low

Form RPR

60 **1** **Balestra**[47] 2782 3-9-5 0 JimCrowley 3 82
(Charles Hills) *prom: carried wd on bnd over 5f out: sn rcvrd: led 2f out: rdn clr fnl f: styd on strly* **9/1**[3]

422 **2** 7 **Wonderfillo (IRE)**[30] 3394 3-9-5 74 (t[1]) SamHitchcott 2 66
(Paul Cole) *trckd ldrs: lft in ld on bnd over 5f out: hdd 2f out: sn rdn and hld by wnr: kpt on same pce fnl f* **5/1**[2]

-232 **3** ¾ **Black Trilby (IRE)**[18] 3836 3-9-5 84 (h) AdamKirby 1 64+
(Clive Cox) *led tl rn wd on bnd over 5f out: rdn to chse ldrs 2f out: wnt 3rd wl over 1f out: kpt on same pce fnl f* **1/4**[1]

06 **4** 1 ½ **Bringit (IRE)**[16] 3921 3-9-5 0 DougieCostello 5 61
(Jamie Osborne) *slowly away: cl 4th after 1f: rdn 2f out: sn swtchd rt: kpt on same pce fnl f* **50/1**

**5** *dist* **Little Miss Tango** 3-9-0 0 RobertWinston 4
(Roger Teal) *dwlt: looked to lose action leaving stalls: sn wl bhd* **50/1**

1m 39.99s (-0.81) **Going Correction** -0.30s/f (Firm) **5** Ran SP% **110.6**
Speed ratings (Par 102): **92,85,84,82,**
CSF £49.67 TOTE £17.10: £2.70, £1.70; EX 28.70 Trifecta £40.90.
**Owner** K Abdullah **Bred** Juddmonte Farms Ltd **Trained** Lambourn, Berks

**FOCUS**
A messy race and painful viewing for backers of the long odds-on favourite, who threw away his chance by failing to negotiate the bend. The level is fluid.

## 4491 BLAYTHWAYT PLATE H'CAP 1m
**7:30** (7:30) (Class 3) (0-90,85) 3-Y-O **£9,056** (£2,695; £1,346; £673) **Stalls** Low

Form RPR

1201 **1** **I'vegotthepower (IRE)**[19] 3780 3-9-5 **83** (v) JimCrowley 6 93
(Brian Meehan) *pressed ldr early: niggled along whn chsng ldr over 5f out: rdn to chal 2f out: narrow advantage ent fnl f: kpt on gamely: won on nod* **5/2**[1]

-621 **2** *nse* **Pillar Of Society (IRE)**[30] 3412 3-9-4 **82** SeanLevey 4 91
(Richard Hannon) *led: rdn 2f out: narrowly hdd ent fnl f: kpt on gamely: rallied cl home: lost on nod* **5/1**[3]

-040 **3** 6 **Ahlan Bil Zain (FR)**[25] 3592 3-9-2 **80** AdamKirby 3 75
(David Simcock) *trckd ldrs: rdn over 2f out: kpt on to go 3rd ins fnl f but nt pce of front pair* **8/1**

3261 **4** 1 **Pattie**[10] 4121 3-9-1 **79** 6ex JFEgan 2 72
(Mick Channon) *hld up in last pair: rdn and hdwy over 2f out: wnt 3rd over 1f out: no ex fnl f* **5/1**[3]

10-0 **5** *hd* **Seniority**[60] 2402 3-9-7 **85** PatCosgrave 5 77
(William Haggas) *stdd s: plld hrd in last pair: rdn to chse ldrs 2f out: kpt on same pce fnl f* **11/2**

-103 **6** 8 **Fujaira Bridge (IRE)**[22] 3700 3-9-3 **81** AndreaAtzeni 1 66
(Roger Varian) *trckd ldrs: rdn over 2f out: wknd ent fnl f* **3/1**[2]

1m 37.41s (-3.39) **Going Correction** -0.30s/f (Firm) **6** Ran SP% **113.4**
Speed ratings (Par 104): **104,103,97,96,96 88**
CSF £15.52 TOTE £2.80: £1.90, £2.80; EX 18.00 Trifecta £144.30.
**Owner** S E Sangster & Partner **Bred** D Farrington, P Gately, T Killarney **Trained** Manton, Wilts

**FOCUS**
A solid feature handicap and a lot to like about the performances of the first two home. The form could be rated a length better, but there are enough doubts for the time being.

## 4492 BATH RACECOURSE SUPPORTING RACING STAFF WEEK H'CAP 1m 2f 37y
**8:00** (8:00) (Class 5) (0-70,72) 3-Y-O+ **£2,911** (£866; £432; £216) **Stalls** Low

Form RPR
-560 **1** **X Rated (IRE)**[21] 3727 3-9-7 **72** JoeFanning 1 80
(Mark Johnston) *mde all: kpt on strly: pushed out* **9/2**[3]
000 **2** 2 ¼ **High Wells**[18] 3839 3-8-8 **59** (b[1]) MartinDwyer 5 62
(Seamus Durack) *hld up: hdwy over 2f out: sn rdn to chse wnr: kpt on for clr 2nd fnl f but nt pce to chal* **16/1**
6015 **3** 4 **Bayston Hill**[20] 3752 3-9-4 **69** LiamKeniry 8 64
(Mark Usher) *hld up in tch: hdwy over 2f out: sn rdn to chse wnr: nt pce to get on terms: no ex ins fnl f* **7/2**[2]
-030 **4** ½ **Daimochi (IRE)**[41] 3005 3-9-7 **72** AdamKirby 6 66
(Clive Cox) *chsd wnr: rdn over 2f out: lost 2nd whn edging lft over 1f out: kpt on same pce fnl f* **2/1**[1]
-350 **5** 2 ¾ **Harry Beau**[26] 3531 3-9-2 **67** SeanLevey 2 56
(Richard Hannon) *trckd ldrs: rdn over 2f out: fdd ins fnl f* **12/1**
2344 **6** 13 **Attain**[12] 4041 8-9-11 **69** EdwardGreatrex(3) 3 31
(Archie Watson) *hld up in tch: effrt over 2f out: wknd jst over 1f out* **6/1**
-405 **7** 2 ¾ **Aware (IRE)**[26] 3520 3-9-4 **69** (t) JimCrowley 4 26
(Charles Hills) *hld up in tch: effrt over 2f out: wknd over 1f out* **13/2**

2m 7.68s (-3.32) **Going Correction** -0.30s/f (Firm)
**WFA** 3 from 8yo 10lb **7** Ran SP% **114.9**
Speed ratings (Par 103): **101,99,96,95,93 83,80**
CSF £68.61 CT £279.76 TOTE £5.10: £2.20, £6.50; EX 94.60 Trifecta £418.20.
**Owner** Mark Johnston Racing Ltd **Bred** Mark Johnston Racing Ltd **Trained** Middleham Moor, N Yorks

**FOCUS**
An ordinary handicap in which the winner had the race sewn up from an early stage. The winner has been rated back to his 2yo form.

## 4493 DYRHAM FILLIES' H'CAP 1m 2f 37y
**8:30** (8:32) (Class 6) (0-60,60) 3-Y-O+ **£2,264** (£673; £336; £168) **Stalls** Low

Form RPR
0-34 **1** **Fanfair**[23] 3661 3-8-13 **55** SeanLevey 10 60
(Richard Hannon) *trckd ldrs: rdn to chal 2f out: kpt on wl to ld fnl 120yds: rdn out* **11/4**[1]
0420 **2** ½ **Sublime**[23] 3657 3-8-4 **46** (p) KieranO'Neill 7 50
(Rod Millman) *led: rdn whn strly chal over 2f out: drifted rt ent fnl f: no ex whn hdd fnl 100yds* **11/2**[3]
5064 **3** 1 ¼ **Tenby Two**[12] 4045 3-9-3 **59** JFEgan 6 61
(Mick Channon) *mid-div: rdn and hdwy 2f out: kpt on ins fnl f: wnt 3rd cl home* **4/1**[2]
056 **4** 1 **Bicolour (USA)**[15] 3945 3-9-1 **57** JoeFanning 3 59
(Mark Johnston) *trckd ldr: rdn and ev ch 2f out: sn hung lft: cl 3rd whn squeezed out ent fnl f: no ex whn losing 3rd cl home* **11/2**[3]
1040 **5** 2 ¾ **Sheer Intensity (IRE)**[13] 4010 4-9-7 **53** FranBerry 5 47
(David Evans) *s.i.s: hld up: sme hdwy 2f out: sn rdn: kpt on ins fnl f but nt pce to get on terms* **12/1**
0-66 **6** nk **Sunlit Waters**[64] 2281 4-9-6 **52** AdamKirby 2 45
(Tony Carroll) *hld up: hdwy 2f out: sn rdn: kpt on but nt pce to get involved* **8/1**
0-40 **7** 1 **Born To Please**[20] 3752 3-8-0 **49** NicolaCurrie(7) 9 41
(Mark Usher) *stdd at s: in last trio: rdn 2f out: little imp* **6/1**
00-0 **8** 3 **Paca Punch**[18] 3809 4-8-9 **46** oh1 MitchGodwin(5) 1 31
(John Flint) *trckd ldrs: rdn 2f out: wknd fnl f* **33/1**
0-00 **9** 58 **Embleton**[36] 3191 3-8-6 **48** MartinDwyer 8
(Charlie Wallis) *mid-div tl rn wd on bnd over 4f out: sn hung lft and wknd: eased fnl 2f* **25/1**

2m 11.01s (0.01) **Going Correction** -0.30s/f (Firm)
**WFA** 3 from 4yo 10lb **9** Ran SP% **117.3**
Speed ratings (Par 98): **87,86,85,84,82 82,81,79,32**
CSF £18.48 CT £60.40 TOTE £2.80: £1.10, £1.90, £1.80; EX 20.30 Trifecta £76.40.
**Owner** Theakston Stud Syndicate **Bred** Theakston Stud **Trained** East Everleigh, Wilts

**FOCUS**
A moderate affair, though a couple of these have the potential to do better.

## 4494 DJ & P H'CAP (BATH SUMMER STAYERS' SERIES QUALIFIER) 1m 3f 137y
**9:00** (9:00) (Class 6) (0-60,65) 3-Y-O+ **£2,264** (£673; £336; £168) **Stalls** Low

Form RPR
6432 **1** **Plato's Kode (IRE)**[12] 4045 3-9-2 **60** (tp) RobertWinston 11 73+
(Seamus Durack) *hld up: stdy prog fr 3f out: led ent fnl f: styd on wl: pushed out* **2/1**[1]
3052 **2** 3 **Eben Dubai (IRE)**[12] 4040 5-9-6 **52** MartinDwyer 5 59
(Tracey Barfoot-Saunt) *set str pce: drifted to centre over 2f out: rdn over 1f out: hdd ent fnl f: kpt on but no ex* **7/1**
231 **3** 1 ¼ **Hallingham**[12] 4040 7-10-0 **60** (v) LiamKeniry 7 65
(Ken Cunningham-Brown) *mid-div: smooth hdwy fr 4f out: rdn and ev ch over 1f out: no ex ins fnl f* **6/1**[3]
-011 **4** 3 **Grams And Ounces**[18] 3805 10-9-13 **59** (tp) TimmyMurphy 8 59
(Grace Harris) *mid-div: rdn over 2f out: styd on to go 4th ins fnl f but nvr threatened to get on terms* **9/1**
5365 **5** 1 ½ **Kiruna Peak (IRE)**[16] 3909 3-9-3 **61** (v) JFEgan 2 60
(Mick Channon) *chsd clr ldr: pushed along over 5f out: rdn over 2f out: fdd ins fnl f* **9/2**[2]
1031 **6** 6 **Av A Word**[8] 4177 3-9-7 **65** 6ex (p) GeorgeDowning 10 55
(Daniel Kubler) *chsd clr ldr: clsd on ldr 3f out: sn rdn: wknd fnl f* **6/1**[3]
0500 **7** ½ **Holyroman Princess**[23] 3657 3-8-3 **47** (v[1]) KieranO'Neill 6 36
(Rod Millman) *a towards rr* **16/1**
2415 **8** 1 **Powered (IRE)**[8] 4181 4-10-0 **60** FranBerry 4 46
(David Evans) *a towards rr* **14/1**

2m 28.26s (-2.34) **Going Correction** -0.30s/f (Firm)
**WFA** 3 from 4yo+ 12lb **8** Ran SP% **115.1**
Speed ratings (Par 101): **95,93,92,90,89 85,84,84**
CSF £16.76 CT £71.83 TOTE £3.10: £1.10, £3.60, £2.80; EX 18.30 Trifecta £75.50.
**Owner** Stephen Tucker **Bred** Old Carhue Stud **Trained** Upper Lambourn, Berkshire

**FOCUS**
A stronger race than most for the level. It was run at a strong early pace.
T/Plt: £406.10 to a £1 stake. Pool: £66,464.79 - 119.46 winning units. T/Qpdt: £80.30 to a £1 stake. Pool: £5,570.30 - 51.32 winning units. **Tim Mitchell**

# 4211 KEMPTON (A.W) (R-H)
Wednesday, July 5

**OFFICIAL GOING: Polytrack: standard to slow (watered)**
Wind: Nil Weather: Warm, clear

## 4495 JOCKEY CLUB SUPPORTING RACING STAFF WEEK APPRENTICE H'CAP 6f (P)
**6:10** (6:11) (Class 5) (0-75,75) 4-Y-O+ **£3,234** (£962; £481; £240) **Stalls** Low

Form RPR
1-23 **1** **Hackney Road**[21] 3729 4-9-6 **75** JoshuaBryan(3) 2 86+
(John Butler) *hld up in rr-div on inner: shkn up and tk clsr order over 2f out: rdn wl over 1f out: led 1f out: edgd lft to centre: kpt on wl ins fnl f* **5/2**[1]
0-15 **2** ½ **Nightingale Valley**[35] 3214 4-9-4 **75** WilliamCox(5) 8 83
(Stuart Kittow) *hld up in rr-div: c wd over 2f out: rdn w plenty to do wl over 1f out: kpt on wl ins fnl f: nvr nrr* **8/1**[3]
1550 **3** 1 ¾ **Dream Farr (IRE)**[28] 3454 4-9-8 **74** (t) JennyPowell 11 76+
(Ed Walker) *pressed clr ldr: shkn up and led over 1f out: hdd 1f out: kpt on one pce wl ins fnl f* **5/1**[2]
3045 **4** ½ **Hamish McGonagain**[26] 3532 4-9-4 **70** (p) GeorgeBuckell 6 71
(Jeremy Gask) *t.k.h in mid-div: rdn 2f out: styd on ent fnl f: didn't have pce of ldrs* **25/1**
1054 **5** nk **Whitecrest**[6] 4277 9-9-4 **73** JaneElliott(3) 5 73
(John Spearing) *settled in mid-div: rdn 2f out: kpt on one pce fnl f* **16/1**
1040 **6** ½ **Picket Line**[16] 3919 5-9-7 **73** PaddyPilley 9 71
(Geoffrey Deacon) *sltly squeezed up s and in rr: prog out wd over 2f out w plenty to do: nudged along over 1f out: kpt on fnl f: nvr nrr* **8/1**[3]
6365 **7** ½ **Kyllukey**[16] 3903 4-9-1 **70** RhiainIngram(3) 3 67
(Milton Bradley) *set early pce and clr w anther rival: hdd over 1f out: sn wknd* **11/1**
4444 **8** nk **Varsovian**[37] 3140 7-9-9 **75** (p[1]) LuluStanford 10 71
(Dean Ivory) *chsd ldrs: rdn over 2f out: ev ch over 1f out: kpt on one pce* **9/1**
0053 **9** ¾ **Fleckerl (IRE)**[23] 3666 7-9-2 **68** (p) PatrickO'Donnell 1 61
(Conor Dore) *a in rr: rdn 2f out: kpt on one pce* **8/1**[3]
25-0 **10** 1 ¼ **Beauden Barrett**[22] 3696 4-9-4 **73** (t) FinleyMarsh(3) 7 62
(Jeremy Gask) *early pce: sn taken bk and settled bhd ldrs: rdn 2f out: edgd rt and kpt on one pce tl wknd fnl f* **16/1**

1m 12.54s (-0.56) **Going Correction** +0.025s/f (Slow) **10** Ran SP% **112.5**
Speed ratings (Par 103): **104,103,101,100,99 99,98,98,97,95**
CSF £21.79 CT £93.01 TOTE £2.70: £1.20, £2.30, £2.00; EX 17.20 Trifecta £59.10.
**Owner** J Butler **Bred** Whatton Manor Stud **Trained** Newmarket, Suffolk
■ Stewards' Enquiry : Lulu Stanford two-day ban: used whip above permitted level (19-20 Jul)

**FOCUS**
A fair handicap, in which they went a good pace, and the closers came to the fore late on. It's been rated around the runner-up to the better view of her form.

## 4496 BRITISH STALLION STUDS EBF FILLIES' NOVICE STKS (PLUS 10 RACE) 7f (P)
**6:40** (6:42) (Class 5) 2-Y-O **£3,234** (£962; £481; £240) **Stalls** Low

Form RPR
322 **1** **Billesdon Brook**[17] 3868 2-9-0 **86** RyanMoore 9 87+
(Richard Hannon) *shaded ld: hdd after 2f and settled bhd ldrs: travelling best whn shkn up and led over 1f out: sn clr and only had to be kpt up to work ins fnl f* **8/15**[1]
**2** 6 **Last Enchantment (IRE)** 2-9-0 0 CharlesBishop 4 71
(Eve Johnson Houghton) *cl up: shkn up and led wl over 2f out: sn rdn: hdd over 1f out: kpt on one pce after: no ch w easy wnr* **14/1**
63 **3** 2 ¼ **Retained (FR)**[13] 4007 2-9-0 0 KierenFox 3 65
(John Best) *settled in rr on inner: rdn over 2f out: kpt on wl fr over 1f out* **33/1**
**4** 1 ¼ **It's Not Unusual** 2-8-11 0 KieranShoemark(3) 2 61
(Roger Charlton) *chsd ldrs on inner: ch whn rdn over 2f out: kpt on one pce after* **3/1**[2]
**5** 3 ½ **Shrewd Approach (IRE)** 2-9-0 0 HarryBentley 8 52
(Simon Crisford) *trckd ldrs: rdn wl over 3f out: one pce fr over 1f out* **14/1**
0 **6** 1 ¼ **Summer Thunder (USA)**[39] 3070 2-9-0 0 OisinMurphy 10 49
(Paul Cole) *cl up and led after 2f out: hdd 4f out but remained pressing ldr: shkn up ent 2f out: sn wknd* **10/1**[3]
40 **7** 3 ¼ **Mimram**[37] 3135 2-9-0 0 SteveDrowne 5 40
(Dean Ivory) *pushed along early to hold pl in rr-div: t.k.h wl over 4f out and carried rival wd: rdn over 2f out: no ex* **100/1**
66 **8** nk **Olive Mabel**[27] 3502 2-9-0 0 FrannyNorton 12 39
(Dean Ivory) *t.k.h early: taken bk to get cover in rr-div: carried four horses wd on bnd 4f out: rdn over 2f out: no ex* **66/1**
0 **9** 2 ¼ **Midnight Blue**[9] 4160 2-9-0 0 RyanPowell 6 33
(Sir Mark Prescott Bt) *a in rr and rn green* **66/1**
6 **10** 1 ¾ **Be Mindful (IRE)**[18] 3815 2-8-11 0 CallumShepherd(3) 11 28
(Charles Hills) *mid-div on outer: prog on bnd and c wd ent st: one pce fr over 1f out* **25/1**

1m 25.4s (-0.60) **Going Correction** +0.025s/f (Slow) **10** Ran SP% **123.4**
Speed ratings (Par 91): **104,97,94,93,89 87,84,83,81,79**
CSF £11.50 TOTE £1.30: £1.02, £3.50, £3.90; EX 15.10 Trifecta £108.20.
**Owner** Pall Mall Partners & Late R J McCreery **Bred** Stowell Hill Partners **Trained** East Everleigh, Wilts
■ Frolic and Little Poem were withdrawn. Prices at time of withdrawal 8-1 and 16-1. Rule 4 applies to all bets struck prior to withdrawal, but not SP. Deduction - 10p in the pound. New market formed.

**FOCUS**
An ordinary maiden, losing some interest when the well backed Frolic was withdrawn at the start, and the favourite won as she liked.

## 4497 100% PROFIT BOOST AT 32REDSPORT.COM MAIDEN FILLIES' STKS 1m 3f 219y(P)
**7:10** (7:13) (Class 5) 3-Y-O+ **£3,234** (£962; £481; £240) **Stalls** Centre

Form RPR
6- **1** **Erinyes (IRE)**[274] 7050 3-9-0 0 OisinMurphy 6 78+
(Archie Watson) *briefly led early: cl up: led wl over 5f out: rdn over 3f out w clr ld: kpt on wl tl edgd lft over 1f out: stuck on wl ins fnl f* **13/2**[3]
02 **2** 1 ¼ **Sileel (USA)**[24] 3615 3-9-0 0 (v) JosephineGordon 2 75
(Ed Dunlop) *led early tl hdd after 2f: styd cl up bhd ldrs on rail: rdn over 3f out: kpt on wl but nvr getting to wnr* **4/1**[1]

05 **3** *3 ½* **Miss Liguria**[46] 2834 3-9-0 0 ThomasBrown 14 69+
(Ed Walker) *missed break: in rr: rdn over 3f out: kpt on strly fr over 1f out: nvr nrr* **33/1**

**4** *1* **State Sovereignty**[39] 5-9-12 0 HarryBentley 13 67
(Michael Scudamore) *s.s and in rr: rdn over 3f out: kpt on wl fr over 1f out* **40/1**

0 **5** *½* **Lady Macha**[13] 4003 3-9-0 0 DanielMuscutt 8 67+
(Marco Botti) *settled in mid-div on inner: shkn up and prog over 3f out: kpt on one pce after* **10/1**

02 **6** *hd* **Mod**[26] 3542 3-8-11 0 GeorgeWood(3) 4 67+
(James Fanshawe) *chsd ldrs: niggled along at 1/2-way to hold pl: rdn over 3f out: kpt on one pce* **4/1**[1]

**7** *7* **Sonnet Rose (IRE)** 3-9-0 0 SaleemGolam 1 55
(Conrad Allen) *cl up bhd ldrs on inner: rdn over 3f out on inner: no ex fr over 2f out* **66/1**

6-0 **8** *3* **Button Up (IRE)**[41] 3007 3-9-0 0 (v1) RyanMoore 11 51
(Sir Michael Stoute) *sn settled in rr-div: rdn over 3f out: sn one pce* **9/2**[2]

05 **9** *4 ½* **Quay Point (IRE)**[37] 3145 4-9-12 0 LukeMorris 3 42
(Laura Mongan) *cl up bhd ldrs: rdn over 3f out and stl cl up: wknd qckly 2f out* **66/1**

60 **10** *15* **Shanandoa**[24] 3615 6-9-12 0 SteveDrowne 5 18
(Brian Barr) *settled in mid-div: n.m.r over 3f out: eased sn after* **100/1**

5 **11** *nk* **Reel Leisure (GR)**[98] 1420 4-9-12 0 (h) PatDobbs 9 18
(Amanda Perrett) *s.s: in rr on inner: rdn and fnd nil 3f out: sn eased* **40/1**

64 **12** *9* **Paris Rooftops (IRE)**[24] 3615 3-9-0 0 JamieSpencer 7 5
(Luca Cumani) *mid-div on outer: rdn over 3f out: no ex and eased fr over 2f out* **4/1**[1]

00 **13** *1 ¼* **Amber Morning**[35] 3209 3-8-11 0 KieranShoemark(3) 12 3
(Roger Charlton) *early spd fr wd draw and led after 3f: nt handle bnd hung lft and almost stopped on top of bnd into bk st: rdn to hold ld: hdd sn after: rdn over 4f out and sn lost pl: no ex in st and eased* **20/1**

**14** *50* **Notnowivorheadache**[1280] 8-9-5 0 RhiainIngram(7) 10
(Roger Ingram) *reluctant to load: missed break and a wl in rr: wl detached at 1/2-way: allowed to come home in own time fr wl over 5f out: t.o* **100/1**

2m 34.52s (0.02) **Going Correction** +0.025s/f (Slow)
**WFA** 3 from 4yo+ 12lb 14 Ran SP% **118.2**
Speed ratings (Par 100): **100,99,96,96,95 95,91,89,86,76 75,69,69,35**
CSF £30.49 TOTE £7.50: £2.50, £1.70, £8.70; EX 37.90 Trifecta £769.50.
**Owner** Al Asayl Bloodstock Ltd **Bred** Greenwood Lodge Farm Inc **Trained** Upper Lambourn, W Berks

**FOCUS**
A fair maiden and only two mattered in the closing stages. The runner-up has been rated to form.

## 4498 32RED H'CAP 1m 3f 219y(P)
**7:40** (7:44) (Class 3) (0-95,94) 4-Y-O+
**£7,470** (£2,236; £1,118; £559; £279; £140) **Stalls** Centre

Form RPR

1-13 **1** **Gibbs Hill (GER)**[47] 2804 4-9-7 **94** (b1) RyanMoore 7 109
(Roger Varian) *trckd ldrs: shkn up over 3f out to take clsr order: full of running and almost upsides over 2f out: sn rdn: led and qcknd clr over 1f out: pushed out fnl f: v easily* **10/11**[1]

1 **2** *7* **Zubayr (IRE)**[35] 3209 5-8-5 **83** MeganNicholls(5) 5 87
(Paul Nicholls) *pressed ldr on outer: t.k.h at 1/2-way wanting strer pce: shaded ld 4f out: rdn 2f out: wnr easily wnt by over 1f out: kpt on one pce after* **9/4**[2]

3000 **3** *1 ¾* **Top Beak (IRE)**[19] 3785 4-8-8 **84** (t) CharlieBennett(3) 8 85
(Hughie Morrison) *in rr: shkn up over 3f out and gd prog on inner: ev ch ent 2f out: kpt on wl but nt pce of front pair* **25/1**

6-20 **4** *4* **Sunblazer (IRE)**[39] 3067 7-9-2 **94** (t) JoshuaBryan(5) 3 89
(Kim Bailey) *pushed along early to get racing: mostly in last pair on outer: rdn 4f out: nt pce to go w ldrs: styd on in st* **25/1**

15-0 **5** *4* **Proctor**[19] 3785 4-8-9 **82** (b1) OisinMurphy 2 70
(Stuart Kittow) *chsd ldrs on inner: rdn wl over 3f out: one pce fr over 2f out* **50/1**

2-12 **6** *¾* **Regicide (IRE)**[42] 2959 4-8-13 **86** TomQueally 6 73
(James Fanshawe) *slow s: hld up in rr-div: rdn 3f out: no imp sn after* **10/1**

3311 **7** *1 ¼* **Pumblechook**[11] 4095 4-8-13 **86** HarryBentley 1 71
(Mark Johnston) *sn led: hdd 4f out: stl pressed ldr: rdn 3f out: no ex fr over 1f out and wknd* **9/1**[3]

2m 33.14s (-1.36) **Going Correction** +0.025s/f (Slow) 7 Ran SP% **111.9**
Speed ratings (Par 107): **105,100,99,96,93 93,92**
CSF £2.90 CT £20.21 TOTE £1.90: £1.40, £1.80; EX 5.90 Trifecta £35.20.
**Owner** Paul Smith **Bred** Gestut Gorlsdorf **Trained** Newmarket, Suffolk
■ Marmajuke Bay was withdrawn. Price at time of withdrawal 12-1. Rule 4 applies to all bets. Deduct 5p in the pound.

**FOCUS**
Not the most competitive handicap for the grade, the two market leaders coming to the fore, but an impressive winner. The runner-up has been rated close to his maiden win.

## 4499 32RED ON THE APP STORE H'CAP 1m 7f 218y(P)
**8:10** (8:10) (Class 3) (0-90,88) 4-Y-O+
**£7,470** (£2,236; £1,118; £559; £279; £140) **Stalls** Low

Form RPR

4/33 **1** **Clowance One**[7] 4216 5-8-10 **80** (b1) KieranShoemark(3) 4 89+
(Roger Charlton) *chsd ldr: shkn up and led over 4f out: kicked for home over 2f out: kpt on strly fr over 1f out: edgd rt ent fnl f: rdn out* **5/4**[1]

6-21 **2** *2* **King Calypso**[35] 3213 6-9-1 **82** OisinMurphy 1 86+
(Denis Coakley) *settled in mid-div: shkn up over 2f out: chsd ldr over 1f out: no ex nr fin* **9/4**[2]

0 **3** *2 ¼* **Age Of Wisdom (IRE)**[26] 3534 4-8-7 **77** NoelGarbutt(3) 5 78
(Gary Moore) *bmpd on both sides leaving stalls: hld up in last: rdn over 4f out: kpt on fr over 2f out: one pce fnl f* **40/1**

4-16 **4** *¾* **Grumeti**[48] 2770 9-9-2 **83** FergusSweeney 6 83
(Alan King) *settled in mid-div on outer: rdn 4f out: one pce fr over 2f out: nvr gng pce* **10/1**

0502 **5** *¾* **Lanceur (FR)**[28] 3459 8-8-13 **80** JosephineGordon 2 80
(William Stone) *in rr: rdn 4f out: kpt on one pce* **7/1**[3]

5211 **6** *2 ¼* **Multigifted**[25] 3574 4-8-2 **72** (t) GeorgeWood(3) 3 69
(Michael Madgwick) *settled bhd ldrs: rdn 3f out: kpt on one pce fnl f* **10/1**

200/ **7** *4 ½* **Taws**[89] 6271 6-9-1 **85** AaronJones(3) 9 76
(Rod Millman) *led and dictated slow pce: hdd over 4f out: nthing lft and wknd fr over 2f out* **16/1**

360/ **8** *3 ¾* **Handazan (IRE)**[579] 3252 8-9-4 **88** HectorCrouch(3) 7 75
(Ivan Furtado) *chsd ldrs on outer: rdn 4f out: wknd between horses 3f out: no ex and eased* **40/1**

3m 27.11s (-2.99) **Going Correction** +0.025s/f (Slow) 8 Ran SP% **116.7**
Speed ratings (Par 107): **108,107,105,105,105 104,101,99**
CSF £4.27 CT £62.54 TOTE £2.30: £1.10, £1.10, £7.00; EX 5.20 Trifecta £102.60.
**Owner** Seasons Holidays **Bred** Mrs S A J Kinsella-Hurley **Trained** Beckhampton, Wilts

**FOCUS**
A decent staying handicap. The runner-up has been rated close to form.

## 4500 32RED.COM H'CAP (JOCKEY CLUB GRASSROOTS FLAT SPRINT SERIES QUALIFIER) 6f (P)
**8:40** (8:42) (Class 5) (0-75,77) 3-Y-O **£3,234** (£962; £481; £240) **Stalls** Low

Form RPR

1203 **1** **Comprise**[23] 3673 3-9-7 **75** JamieSpencer 4 86
(Michael Bell) *mde all: slowed pce over 3f out: rdn 2f out: qcknd up smartly and sn clr: rdn out fnl f: comf* **7/2**[2]

5023 **2** *3 ¼* **Father McKenzie**[43] 2927 3-9-2 **75** JoshuaBryan(5) 3 75
(James Eustace) *chsd ldr on inner: rdn 2f out: edgd to centre: briefly threatened to cl ent fnl f: no ex fnl f* **11/2**[3]

5-31 **3** *½* **Blue On Blue (USA)**[71] 2071 3-9-9 **77** (h) RyanMoore 10 75+
(John Gosden) *in rr: rdn wl over 1f out w plenty to do: kpt on strly ins fnl f to take 3rd: nvr nrr* **2/1**[1]

0225 **4** *¾* **Kings Heart (IRE)**[14] 3971 3-8-9 **63** (h) SteveDrowne 1 59
(Mark Usher) *settled in mid-div: rdn 2f out: kpt on one pce fr over 1f out: lost 3rd 100yds out* **10/1**

232 **5** *½* **Monteamiata (IRE)**[32] 3331 3-9-4 **72** ThomasBrown 7 66
(Ed Walker) *tk fierce hold early in mid-div: rdn over 2f out: keeping on fnl f* **12/1**

6043 **6** *shd* **Kamra (USA)**[11] 4104 3-9-2 **75** (p) CliffordLee(5) 8 69
(Michael Herrington) *mid-div on outer: rdn 2f out: kpt on one pce* **16/1**

-532 **7** *1 ¼* **Nuzha**[13] 4011 3-8-12 **66** (p) LukeMorris 2 56
(Karen George) *mid-div: rdn 2f out: one pce* **12/1**

-552 **8** *½* **Malcolm The Pug (IRE)**[11] 4092 3-9-2 **70** TomMarquand 6 58
(Richard Hannon) *in rr: rdn over 2f out: no ex fr over 1f out* **14/1**

-005 **9** *4* **Silver Penny**[13] 4011 3-8-6 **60** (p) HarryBentley 5 36
(Jim Boyle) *chsd ldr on outer: rdn over 2f out: no ex and wknd fr over 1f out* **40/1**

0535 **10** *1 ¼* **Dandy Flame (IRE)**[29] 3424 3-9-1 **76** FinleyMarsh(7) 9 48
(Richard Hughes) *in rr: taken wd st and rdn 2f out: no imp* **16/1**

65-5 **11** *5* **Eskimo Bay (IRE)**[37] 3157 3-9-0 **71** HectorCrouch(3) 11 27
(Clive Cox) *in rr on outer: rdn v wd over 2f out: ducked rt 2f out: eased after* **20/1**

1m 13.02s (-0.08) **Going Correction** +0.025s/f (Slow) 11 Ran SP% **121.0**
Speed ratings (Par 100): **101,96,96,95,94 94,92,91,86,84 78**
CSF £24.03 CT £50.02 TOTE £4.30: £1.60, £2.20, £1.60; EX 26.40 Trifecta £134.20.
**Owner** The Royal Ascot Racing Club **Bred** Cheveley Park Stud Ltd **Trained** Newmarket, Suffolk

**FOCUS**
A competitive 3yo sprint handicap and a decisive winner. The runner-up has been rated close to form.

## 4501 32RED CASINO H'CAP (LONDON MILE SERIES QUALIFIER) 1m (P)
**9:10** (9:11) (Class 4) (0-80,82) 3-Y-O+ **£5,175** (£1,540; £769; £384) **Stalls** Low

Form RPR

1-4 **1** **Mr Minerals**[19] 3780 3-9-5 **80** ShaneKelly 9 91+
(Richard Hughes) *settled in mid-div: hdwy gng easily over 2f out: upsides ldrs on outer and shkn up over 1f out: led ent 1f out: nudged out ins fnl f and drew clr: easily* **2/1**[1]

030 **2** *4 ½* **Glorious Poet**[30] 3396 4-9-7 **73** LukeMorris 7 76
(John Spearing) *in rr: rdn over 2f out: keeping on one pce fr over 2f out: sixth ent 1f out: kpt on strly ins fnl f: tk 2nd post in bunch fin: no ch w wnr* **8/1**[3]

1-35 **3** *nse* **Hersigh**[22] 3700 3-9-4 **79** OisinMurphy 4 80
(Saeed bin Suroor) *led: rdn and strly pressed fr over 1f out: hdd ent fnl f: began to weaken 100yds out and lost 2nd post* **5/2**[2]

-610 **4** *nse* **Braztime**[40] 3031 3-9-3 **78** TomMarquand 1 79
(Richard Hannon) *chsd ldr on inner: rdn 2f out on heels of ldrs: kpt on ins fnl f and jst failed to pl in bunch fin* **16/1**

-000 **5** *shd* **Haulani (USA)**[19] 3780 3-8-9 **73** (t1) HectorCrouch(3) 5 74
(Philip Hide) *mid-div on inner: rdn 2f out and stuck to inner: kpt on fnl f and jst failed to pl in bunch fin* **16/1**

32-6 **6** *1 ¼* **Mighty Lady**[44] 2906 4-9-10 **76** JosephineGordon 11 76
(Robyn Brisland) *restless in stalls: missed break and in rr: darted to inner rail 2f out and rdn: kpt on ins fnl f: no ex fnl strides* **20/1**

0160 **7** *nk* **Ebbisham (IRE)**[21] 3718 4-9-1 **70** (p) CharlieBennett(3) 10 69
(Jim Boyle) *pressed ldr on outer: ev ch whn rdn 2f out: lost a few pls over 1f out: kpt on again ins fnl f* **25/1**

31-0 **8** *nse* **Daschas**[90] 1582 3-9-7 **82** (t) PatDobbs 8 79
(Amanda Perrett) *settled in rr-div: rdn in centre 2f out: one pce fr over 1f out: nt clrest run cl home and nudged out* **10/1**

6246 **9** *4 ½* **Tailor's Row (USA)**[30] 3388 3-9-5 **80** FrannyNorton 12 67
(Mark Johnston) *mid-div on outer: nvr really travelling: rdn over 4f out: hung rt into st: one pce after* **9/1**

4-00 **10** *7* **Multitask**[21] 3723 7-9-8 **74** TomQueally 6 46
(Gary Moore) *restrained into rr and t.k.h: rdn wl over 2f out: no ex and eased fnl f* **33/1**

1m 39.18s (-0.62) **Going Correction** +0.025s/f (Slow)
**WFA** 3 from 4yo+ 9lb 10 Ran SP% **115.4**
Speed ratings (Par 105): **104,99,99,99,99 98,97,97,93,86**
CSF £18.06 CT £42.23 TOTE £3.10: £1.30, £2.60, £1.30; EX 17.30 Trifecta £60.10.
**Owner** R P Gallagher **Bred** Bearstone Stud Ltd **Trained** Upper Lambourn, Berks

**FOCUS**
A decent handicap won in good style by a lightly raced 3yo. The runner-up helps set the standard, with the third and fourth close to form.

T/Jkpt: £2,000.00 to a £1 stake. Pool: £10,000 - 5.0 winning units. T/Plt: £6.90 to a £1 stake. Pool: £76,878.55 - 8,101.02 winning units. T/Qpdt: £5.20 to a £1 stake. Pool: £6,422.73 - 897.03 winning units. **Cathal Gahan**

# 3943 THIRSK (L-H)

Wednesday, July 5

**OFFICIAL GOING: Good (good to soft in places; 7.8)**

Wind: Nil Weather: Overcast

## 4502 RACING WELFARE RACING STAFF WEEK NOVICE AUCTION STKS (DIV I) 6f

**2:00** (2:01) (Class 5) 2-Y-O **£3,234** (£962; £481; £240) **Stalls** Centre

Form RPR

20 **1** **Trusting Friend (USA)**[36] 3187 2-9-2 0 KevinStott 5 78
(Kevin Ryan) *disp ld: rdn over 1f out: carried lft ins fnl f: def advantage fnl 110yds: edgd rt towards fin: kpt on gamely* **8/1**[3]

02 **2** ¾ **Arcavallo (IRE)**[16] 3895 2-9-0 0 PaulMulrennan 12 74
(Michael Dods) *disp ld: rdn over 1f out: edgd lft ins fnl f: hdd fnl 110yds: carried sltly rt towards fin and no ex* **7/4**[2]

2 **3** 1¾ **Elysee Star**[15] 3943 2-8-7 0 CamHardie 13 62
(Ben Haslam) *midfield: rdn and hdwy over 2f out: chsd ldrs over 1f out: styd on but no real imp ins fnl f* **8/1**[3]

6 **4** 2½ **Fink Hill (USA)**[47] 2786 2-9-1 0 DanielTudhope 9 64+
(Richard Guest) *racd keenly: hld up: rdn and hung lft fr over 2f out: hdwy over 1f out: nt trble ldrs: allowed to coast home towards fin* **6/4**[1]

30 **5** 2¼ **Aristodemus (IRE)**[54] 2590 2-8-13 0 DavidAllan 11 53
(Tim Easterby) *chsd ldrs: rdn over 2f out: styd on same pce ins fnl f* **25/1**

**6** 1 **Jaimie's Joy** 2-8-12 0 BarryMcHugh 3 49
(Tony Coyle) *racd keenly: sn dropped into midfield: rdn over 2f out: swtchd rt over 1f out: kpt on modly ins fnl f* **66/1**

**7** ½ **Viceroy Mac** 2-9-1 0 SamJames 2 51
(David Loughnane) *missed break: hld up: pushed along in midfield 1/2-way: rdn over 2f out: nvr able to trble ldrs* **33/1**

0 **8** 1¼ **Aliento**[30] 3398 2-8-8 0 JoeDoyle 1 40
(Ollie Pears) *racd keenly: chsd ldrs: rdn over 2f out: wknd 1f out* **100/1**

0 **9** ½ **Travel Lightly**[10] 4116 2-8-7 0 RachelRichardson(3) 8 41
(Tim Easterby) *hld up: rdn and outpcd over 2f out: nvr a threat* **50/1**

**10** 2 **Angie B (IRE)** 2-8-7 0 ShaneGray 10 32
(John Wainwright) *missed break: a bhd: sn outpcd: nvr a threat* **100/1**

50 **11** ¾ **Blue Havana (IRE)**[16] 3895 2-8-10 0 JasonHart 7 32
(John Quinn) *a towards rr: sn outpcd: nvr a threat* **22/1**

**12** 3 **Poppy Jag (IRE)** 2-8-10 0 PJMcDonald 6 23
(Kevin Frost) *midfield: rdn over 2f out: wknd over 1f out* **50/1**

1m 14.72s (2.02) **Going Correction** +0.175s/f (Good) **12 Ran SP% 117.1**

Speed ratings (Par 94): **93,92,89,86,83 82,81,79,79,76 75,71**

CSF £21.18 TOTE £8.50: £2.40, £1.02, £2.40; EX 28.00 Trifecta £83.20.

**Owner** Fergus Galvin **Bred** Hunter Valley Farm, S Sinatra Et Al **Trained** Hambleton, N Yorks

**FOCUS**

Race distances increased by 10yds for races 3, 4, 5 and 6. Division one of an ordinary novice, but definitely the stronger of the two legs.

## 4503 RACING WELFARE RACING STAFF WEEK NOVICE AUCTION STKS (DIV II) 6f

**2:30** (2:32) (Class 5) 2-Y-O **£3,234** (£962; £481; £240) **Stalls** Centre

Form RPR

4 **1** **Rockies Spirit**[12] 4049 2-8-12 0 PaulMulrennan 5 73
(Denis Quinn) *midfield: hdwy to trck ldrs 1/2-way: effrt to ld over 1f out: r.o ins fnl f: pushed out towards fin* **3/1**[2]

60 **2** 1¾ **Super Major (IRE)**[37] 3149 2-8-10 0 CallumRodriguez(5) 7 71
(Michael Dods) *racd keenly: a.p: rdn and ev ch 1f out: kpt on same pce fnl 110yds* **16/1**

3 **3** 2 **Raven's Raft (IRE)**[16] 3902 2-8-11 0 SilvestreDeSousa 9 61
(Michael Appleby) *led: rdn 2f out: hdd over 1f out: one pce and wl hld ins fnl f* **11/8**[1]

4 **4** ½ **Situation**[40] 3051 2-9-2 0 DanielTudhope 10 64
(Richard Guest) *in tch: rdn over 1f out: kpt on ins fnl f: nt pce to chal* **28/1**

4 **5** hd **Just For Fun**[16] 3902 2-8-8 0 BarryMcHugh 11 56
(Richard Fahey) *swtchd rt s to r alone on stands' side: chsd ldrs: hung lft and jnd main gp 1/2-way: rdn nt qckn over 1f out: kpt on ins fnl f* **9/1**[3]

**6** 2½ **Foxy Lady** 2-8-10 0 ShaneGray 6 50+
(Kevin Ryan) *no bttr than midfield tl rdn and outpcd 1/2-way: styd on fr over 1f out: nvr able to trble ldrs* **20/1**

3 **7** shd **Medici Oro**[34] 3237 2-9-0 0 TomEaves 12 54
(David Brown) *prom: rdn over 1f out: wknd ins fnl f* **9/1**[3]

60 **8** ½ **Plansina**[44] 2896 2-8-4 0 RachelRichardson(3) 3 45
(Tim Easterby) *sed awkwardly: hld up: rdn over 2f out: outpcd over 1f out* **80/1**

**9** 2¼ **Havana Heart** 2-8-10 0 KevinStott 2 42
(Ismail Mohammed) *wnt lft s: hld up in midfield: rdn and edgd rt ent fnl 2f: sn wknd* **16/1**

6 **10** 12 **Makofitwhatyouwill**[30] 3399 2-8-9 0 (t[1]) LewisEdmunds(5) 1 10
(Nigel Tinkler) *carried lft and hmpd s: in rr: outpcd 1/2-way: nvr a threat* **33/1**

**11** 53 **Fake News** 2-8-13 0 JamesSullivan 8
(David Barron) *hld up: eased whn smething amiss 2f out: virtually p.u: lame* **22/1**

1m 14.57s (1.87) **Going Correction** +0.175s/f (Good) **11 Ran SP% 115.6**

Speed ratings (Par 94): **94,91,89,88,88 84,84,83,80,64**

CSF £44.50 TOTE £4.40: £1.60, £4.60, £1.10; EX 54.10 Trifecta £172.40.

**Owner** J Mangan & D Quinn **Bred** The Red Mischief Partnership **Trained** Newmarket, Suffolk

**FOCUS**

The lesser of the two divisions.

## 4504 RACING UK DAY PASS JUST £10 (S) STKS 7f

**3:00** (3:02) (Class 6) 2-Y-O **£2,587** (£770; £384; £192) **Stalls** Low

Form RPR

0532 **1** **Give Em A Clump (IRE)**[12] 4054 2-9-0 60 (v[1]) SilvestreDeSousa 8 59
(David Evans) *trckd ldrs: led 2f out: rdn over 1f out: kpt on ins fnl f: hld on wl nr fin* **11/10**[1]

6 **2** ½ **Reel Mr Bond**[45] 2852 2-9-0 0 ShaneGray 5 58
(Kevin Ryan) *towards rr: pushed along 3f out: hdwy 2f out: trying to chal ins fnl f: r.o towards fin* **6/1**

4601 **3** 1 **Faradays Spark (IRE)**[12] 4054 2-9-6 62 TonyHamilton 2 61
(Richard Fahey) *trckd ldrs: rdn 2f out: trying to chal 1f out: styd on same pce towards fin* **4/1**[2]

00 **4** 2½ **Laydee Victoria (IRE)**[19] 3791 2-8-9 0 JoeDoyle 6 43
(Ollie Pears) *led for nrly 1f: chsd ldr: upsides gng wl over 2f out: rdn over 1f out: no ex fnl 150yds* **9/2**[3]

00 **5** 1¼ **Vallesa (IRE)**[16] 3902 2-8-9 0 TomEaves 1 40
(David Brown) *led after nrly 1f: rdn and hdd 2f out: one pce u.p fr over 1f out* **12/1**

00 **6** 5 **Abu Dhabi Doo**[44] 2890 2-8-9 0 BenCurtis 3 26
(K R Burke) *in rr: rdn 4f out: effrt over 2f out: sn no imp: wknd over 1f out* **28/1**

06 **7** 1¾ **Sunset Flyer**[7] 4199 2-8-9 0 LemosdeSouza 4 22
(Amy Murphy) *ref to settle: hld up in tch: swtchd rt over 2f out: nt qckning whn n.m.r and sltly hmpd over 1f out: sn dropped away and drifted lft* **100/1**

1m 30.82s (3.62) **Going Correction** +0.275s/f (Good) **7 Ran SP% 112.2**

Speed ratings (Par 92): **90,89,88,85,84 78,76**

CSF £8.03 TOTE £1.80: £1.10, £3.50; EX 10.00 Trifecta £31.30.There were no bids for the winner.

**Owner** Power Geneva Ltd & Partner **Bred** Pixies Syndicate **Trained** Pandy, Monmouths

**FOCUS**

Race distance increased by 10yds. The right horses came to the fore in this seller.

## 4505 FOLLOW @RACING_UK ON TWITTER H'CAP 6f

**3:30** (3:34) (Class 3) (0-95,96) 3-Y-O+ **£7,439** (£2,213; £1,106; £553) **Stalls** Centre

Form RPR

0002 **1** **Sir Billy Wright (IRE)**[29] 3424 6-9-2 **83** SilvestreDeSousa 6 91
(David Evans) *prom: rdn to ld over 1f out: drvn out and r.o ins fnl f* **6/1**[3]

-050 **2** ¾ **Bossipop**[17] 3861 4-9-0 **81** (b) DavidAllan 3 87
(Tim Easterby) *led: rdn and hdd over 1f out: kpt on u.p ins fnl f: hld fnl 75yds* **12/1**

1200 **3** 1¼ **King Robert**[49] 2736 4-9-10 **91** (v) ConnorBeasley 4 93
(Bryan Smart) *dipped at s: chsd ldrs: rdn and ev ch over 1f out: unable qck ins fnl f: kpt on same pce towards fin* **6/1**[3]

0400 **4** ½ **Clear Spring (IRE)**[32] 3324 9-9-0 **86** LewisEdmunds(5) 10 86
(John Spearing) *hld up: pushed along 1/2-way: hdwy over 1f out: styd on ins fnl f: no imp on front two* **5/1**[2]

-040 **5** shd **Laughton**[46] 2840 4-9-0 **81** ShaneGray 5 81
(Kevin Ryan) *dwlt: hld up: hdwy 2f out: rdn over 1f out: styd on ins fnl f: nvr able to mount serious chal* **14/1**

5010 **6** ¾ **Burnt Sugar (IRE)**[18] 3842 5-9-8 **89** PJMcDonald 9 86
(Roger Fell) *dwlt: hld up: rdn 2f out: kpt on ins fnl f: nvr able to trble ldrs* **8/1**

0004 **7** 1¾ **Giant Spark**[12] 4037 5-9-7 **88** JackGarritty 2 80
(Paul Midgley) *prom: rdn 2f out: wknd fnl f* **12/1**

4042 **8** ½ **Englishman**[3] 4411 7-9-1 **82** PaulMulrennan 11 72
(Milton Bradley) *chsd ldrs: rdn 2f out: sn lost pl: outpcd over 1f out: n.d after* **7/1**

1104 **9** hd **Wentworth Falls**[17] 3861 5-10-1 **96** PhillipMakin 8 85
(Geoffrey Harker) *in rr: rdn over 2f out: nvr a threat* **3/1**[1]

0-10 **10** 3½ **Zanetto**[17] 3861 7-9-7 **88** (p[1]) JasonHart 1 66
(John Quinn) *midfield: rdn and outpcd 2f out: bhd fnl f* **33/1**

1m 12.65s (-0.05) **Going Correction** +0.175s/f (Good) **10 Ran SP% 118.8**

Speed ratings (Par 107): **107,106,104,103,103 102,100,99,99,94**

CSF £76.93 CT £455.92 TOTE £4.90: £2.10, £3.30, £2.40; EX 75.00 Trifecta £881.90.

**Owner** Shropshire Wolves **Bred** Grangecon Stud **Trained** Pandy, Monmouths

■ Jaywalker (7-2) was withdrawn. Rule 4 applies to all bets struck prior to withdrawal, but not to SP bets. Deduction - 20p in the pound. New market formed.

**FOCUS**

It paid to race prominently in this useful sprint. The winner sets the standard, with the runner-up close to his best.

## 4506 JOHN HOPKINSON MEMORIAL H'CAP 7f

**4:00** (4:04) (Class 5) (0-70,69) 3-Y-O+ **£3,234** (£962; £481; £240) **Stalls** Low

Form RPR

-031 **1** **Mango Chutney**[16] 3912 4-9-6 **68** (p) PhillipMakin 5 77+
(John Davies) *midfield: nt clr run 2f out: hdwy whn swtchd rt over 1f out: led wl ins fnl f: r.o* **7/2**[1]

6022 **2** ½ **Kirkham**[15] 3949 4-9-5 **67** (p) JoeDoyle 11 74
(Julie Camacho) *trckd ldrs: chalng 2f out: led over 1f out: hdd wl ins fnl f: hld nr fin* **9/2**[2]

203 **3** 1¾ **Major Crispies**[37] 3136 6-9-7 **69** DanielTudhope 1 71
(David O'Meara) *t.k.h: trckd ldrs: nt clr run 2f out: big effrt over 1f out: styd on ins fnl f: nt trble front two* **16/1**

0-0 **4** nk **Donnelly's Rainbow (IRE)**[61] 2377 4-9-6 **68** DuranFentiman 8 69
(Rebecca Bastiman) *hld up: hdwy over 2f out: rdn to chal over 1f out: no ex fnl 75yds* **14/1**

5606 **5** shd **Ticks The Boxes (IRE)**[23] 3666 5-9-6 **68** (p) TomEaves 3 69
(John Wainwright) *midfield: effrt over 1f out: styd on ins fnl f: nvr able to mount serious chal* **25/1**

6630 **6** 2 **Ralphy Boy (IRE)**[16] 3899 8-9-5 **67** PaulMulrennan 4 63
(Alistair Whillans) *led: hdd after 2f: remained prom: led again over 2f out: hdd over 1f out: no ex fnl 100yds* **12/1**

1020 **7** nk **The Name's Paver**[16] 3912 4-9-2 **64** PatrickMathers 9 59
(Noel Wilson) *chsd ldrs: pushed along and lost pl 4f out: outpcd 3f out: styd on ins fnl f: no imp on front few* **12/1**

0044 **8** ¾ **Tellovoi (IRE)**[15] 3934 9-9-7 **69** (v) ConnorBeasley 2 62
(Richard Guest) *hld up: rdn over 2f out: one pce and no imp fnl f* **17/2**

1541 **9** shd **Tanawar (IRE)**[15] 3949 7-9-3 **65** (b) JamesSullivan 7 58
(Ruth Carr) *hld up: nt clr run 2f out: rdn over 1f out: one pce fnl f: nvr trbld ldrs* **8/1**

60-0 **10** 1½ **Relight My Fire**[35] 3203 7-8-13 **64** (p) RachelRichardson(3) 6 53
(Tim Easterby) *hld up: no bttr than midfield early: rdn on outer over 2f out: no imp on ldrs* **33/1**

3005 **11** 3 **Compton Park**[15] 3949 10-9-4 **66** (t) PJMcDonald 13 47
(Les Eyre) *in tch: rdn and wknd over 1f out* **12/1**

0030 **12** 9 **Hijran (IRE)**[35] 3203 4-9-2 **64** (p) SilvestreDeSousa 12 20
(Michael Appleby) *prom: led after 2f: rdn and hdd over 2f out: losing pl whn hmpd over 1f out: sn eased whn wl btn* **6/1**[3]

1m 28.52s (1.32) **Going Correction** +0.275s/f (Good) **12 Ran SP% 118.7**

Speed ratings (Par 103): **103,102,100,100,99 97,97,96,96,94 91,80**

CSF £18.50 CT £228.63 TOTE £3.60: £1.50, £2.00, £5.20; EX 19.10 Trifecta £161.90.

**Owner** The Sexy Fish Partnership **Bred** P Taylor **Trained** Piercebridge, Durham

**FOCUS**
Race distance increased by 10yds. A modest handicap but the right pair came to the fore. Another small pb from the runner-up.

## 4507 PAY AND WATCH RACING UK VIA MOBILE H'CAP 7f 218y
4:30 (4:31) (Class 2) (0-100,93) 3-Y-0 £12,602 (£3,772; £1,886; £944; £470) Stalls Low

Form RPR
-162 1 **Original Choice (IRE)**[21] 3713 3-9-4 **86** DanielTudhope 7 97
(William Haggas) *prom: led wl over 1f out: r.o ins fnl f: pushed out whn in command fnl 100yds* **5/4**[1]
-145 2 1 ¾ **Itsakindamagic**[25] 3578 3-9-2 **84** (t) PhillipMakin 3 91
(Andrew Balding) *ref to settle: hld up: nt clr run under 2f out: effrt to take 2nd sn after: kpt on u.p ins fnl f: hung lft and no imp on wnr fnl 100yds* **7/2**[2]
001 3 3 **Mutahaady (IRE)**[12] 4057 3-9-4 **89** JordanVaughan(3) 2 89
(K R Burke) *chsd ldrs: lost pl and outpcd 2f out: swtchd rt ins fnl f: rallied to take 3rd towards fin but no ch w front two* **20/1**
15 4 ¾ **Night Circus (IRE)**[60] 2401 3-9-11 **93** MartinLane 6 91
(Charlie Appleby) *hld up: rdn and hdwy over 2f out: chalng over 1f out: unable qck: kpt on same pce ins fnl f* **5/1**[3]
2-50 5 ¾ **Andok (IRE)**[46] 2824 3-9-3 **85** TonyHamilton 1 82
(Richard Fahey) *led: rdn and hdd wl over 1f out: one pce fnl f* **6/1**
5100 6 1 ¾ **Thomas Cranmer (USA)**[13] 3997 3-9-10 **92** PJMcDonald 4 85
(Mark Johnston) *prom: rdn and ev ch 2f out: wknd over 1f out* **14/1**

1m 41.89s (1.79) **Going Correction** +0.275s/f (Good) 6 Ran SP% **109.0**
Speed ratings (Par 106): **102,100,97,96,95 94**
CSF £5.38 TOTE £2.00: £1.40, £1.80; FX 6.40 Trifecta £46.50.
**Owner** A A Goodman **Bred** Ballybrennan Stud **Trained** Newmarket, Suffolk
**FOCUS**
Race distance increased by 10yds. A useful handicap, with the winner very much on the up. A length pb from the runner-up, with the fourth to the bare form of his Wood Ditton win.

## 4508 BREEDERS BACKING RACING EBF MAIDEN STKS 7f 218y
5:00 (5:01) (Class 5) 3-Y-0+ £3,881 (£1,155; £577; £288) Stalls Low

Form RPR
2-35 1 **El Cap (USA)**[34] 3262 3-9-5 78 PhillipMakin 7 92
(Sir Michael Stoute) *in tch: effrt over 2f out: led jst over 1f out: r.o wl to draw clr ins fnl 100yds: comf* **4/1**[3]
2-23 2 4 **Mathix (FR)**[45] 2857 3-9-5 79 (p[1]) DanielTudhope 5 83
(William Haggas) *prom: led 4f out: rdn over 2f out: hdd jst over 1f out: unable to go w wnr and no ch ins fnl 100yds* **2/1**[2]
2 3 1 ¾ **Tribal Conquest (IRE)**[53] 2632 3-9-5 0 MartinLane 4 79
(Charlie Appleby) *dwlt: hld up: hdwy 3f out: rdn and ev ch wl over 1f out: styng on same pce ins fnl f tl eased whn no ex fnl 75yds* **7/4**[1]
-242 4 7 **Envisaging (IRE)**[19] 3781 3-9-5 78 SilvestreDeSousa 8 63
(James Fanshawe) *racd keenly: hld up: tk clsr order after 2f: in tch: wnt 2nd over 3f out: rdn and chalng over 2f out: lost 2nd wl over 1f out: wknd ins fnl f* **4/1**[3]
5 5 **Ember's Glow** 3-9-5 0 CamHardie 3 51
(Jason Ward) *chsd ldrs: rdn over 2f out: sn lost pl: wknd over 1f out* **100/1**
0-0 6 8 **Canizay (IRE)**[32] 3342 3-9-5 0 TonyHamilton 6 33
(Roger Fell) *in rr: rdn over 2f out: lft bhd over 1f out: nvr a threat* **200/1**
0 7 5 **Simmo's Partytrick (IRE)**[12] 4055 4-10-0 0 SamJames 2 24
(Geoffrey Harker) *led: hdd 4f out: rdn and wknd over 2f out* **100/1**

1m 42.05s (1.95) **Going Correction** +0.275s/f (Good)
**WFA** 3 from 4yo 9lb 7 Ran SP% **112.2**
Speed ratings (Par 103): **101,97,95,88,83 75,70**
CSF £11.98 TOTE £5.00: £2.40, £1.70; EX 12.90 Trifecta £30.60.
**Owner** Flaxman Stables Ireland Ltd **Bred** Flaxman Holdings Limited **Trained** Newmarket, Suffolk
**FOCUS**
Race distance increased by 10yds. A fair maiden. The runner-up has been rated to form.

## 4509 "BEER FESTIVAL" EVENING RACING - TUESDAY 18TH JULY H'CAP 6f
5:30 (5:34) (Class 6) (0-65,65) 3-Y-0+ £2,911 (£866; £432; £216) Stalls Centre

Form RPR
-355 1 **Questo**[16] 3897 5-9-3 **58** BenCurtis 16 73
(Tracy Waggott) *in tch: led over 2f out: r.o wl to draw clr ins fnl f* **4/1**[1]
1265 2 4 ½ **Sea Of Green**[5] 4310 5-8-9 **57** (p) SeanMooney(7) 17 59
(Jim Goldie) *missed break: in rr: rdn and hdwy over 1f out: styd on to take 2nd fnl 150yds: nt trble wnr* **11/1**
02-0 3 1 **Le Manege Enchante (IRE)**[181] 80 4-9-3 **58** (p) PhillipMakin 6 57
(Derek Shaw) *midfield: rdn and hdwy over 2f out: styd on ins fnl f: nt pce of wnr* **33/1**
2443 4 ½ **Lucky Lodge**[20] 3758 7-9-9 **64** (v) CamHardie 3 61
(Antony Brittain) *hld up in midfield: hdwy 1/2-way: rdn and no imp on wnr over 1f out: kpt on same pce fnl 75yds* **12/1**
5003 5 1 **Bernie's Boy**[13] 4013 4-9-10 **65** (p) TonyHamilton 18 59
(Roger Fell) *racd alone on stands' side: handy: wl there 1/2-way: rdn 2f out: styd on same pce whn chsng ldrs ins fnl f* **16/1**
0005 6 ¾ **Gaelic Wizard (IRE)**[14] 3979 9-8-6 **52** GemmaTutty(5) 4 44
(Karen Tutty) *dwlt: hld up: hdwy over 1f out: kpt on u.p ins fnl f: one pce towards fin: nvr able to chal* **10/1**
-505 7 1 **Little Miss Lola**[10] 4122 3-8-11 **58** TomEaves 14 46
(Sally Haynes) *missed break: in rr: rdn and hdwy over 1f out: styd on ins fnl f: nt trble ldrs* **20/1**
-050 8 ¾ **Firesnake (IRE)**[34] 3265 4-9-2 **57** (p) KevinStott 15 44
(Lisa Williamson) *midfield: rdn over 2f out: one pce ins fnl f* **50/1**
3-00 9 1 ½ **Point Of Woods**[18] 3847 4-9-10 **65** JamesSullivan 20 47
(Tina Jackson) *hld up: hdwy 3f out: rdn and no imp on wnr over 1f out: no ex fnl 100yds* **20/1**
-045 10 hd **Bold Spirit**[30] 3402 6-9-2 **57** (vt) BarryMcHugh 5 38
(Declan Carroll) *led: rdn and hdd over 2f out: outpcd over 1f out: n.d after* **7/1**[2]
-553 11 1 ¼ **Mitchum**[27] 3488 8-9-8 **63** DavidAllan 8 41
(Ron Barr) *prom: rdn 2f out: kpt on same pce fr over 1f out* **20/1**
6640 12 1 **Wilde Extravagance (IRE)**[23] 3667 4-9-7 **62** JoeDoyle 2 37
(Julie Camacho) *dwlt: hld up: rdn and sme hdwy over 2f out: nvr able to trble ldrs* **12/1**
0000 13 nk **Be Bold**[23] 3666 5-9-10 **65** DuranFentiman 10 39
(Rebecca Bastiman) *chsd ldrs: rdn over 1f out: sn wknd* **33/1**
0006 14 2 **Etienne Gerard**[15] 3949 5-9-3 **63** (p) LewisEdmunds(5) 13 31
(Nigel Tinkler) *midfield: rdn and wknd over 2f out* **8/1**[3]
0-00 15 2 ¾ **Never Give In**[11] 4105 4-9-2 **62** (t) PhilDennis(5) 7 22
(John Weymes) *prom tl rdn and wknd over 2f out* **66/1**
00-0 16 2 ¾ **Princeofthequeen (USA)**[37] 3152 3-9-3 **64** (h) DanielTudhope 11 14
(David O'Meara) *in tch: rdn over 2f out: wknd over 1f out* **20/1**
5063 17 2 **Prazeres**[10] 4122 3-8-13 **60** PJMcDonald 1 4
(Les Eyre) *midfield: rdn over 2f out: wknd over 1f out* **8/1**[3]

1m 13.33s (0.63) **Going Correction** +0.175s/f (Good)
**WFA** 3 from 4yo+ 6lb 17 Ran SP% **121.8**
Speed ratings (Par 101): **102,96,94,94,92 91,90,89,87,87 85,84,83,81,77 73,71**
CSF £41.65 CT £1339.83 TOTE £4.90: £1.20, £2.70, £7.10, £2.60; EX 51.40 Trifecta £2676.20.
**Owner** John J Maguire **Bred** G Reed **Trained** Spennymoor, Co Durham
**FOCUS**
A moderate handicap that was turned into a rout by the favourite.
T/Plt: £25.20 to a £1 stake. Pool: £70,257.77 - 2,028.44 winning units. T/Qpdt: £12.40 to a £1 stake. Pool: £4,133.23 - 245.11 winning units. **Darren Owen**

4510 - 4511a (Foreign Racing) - See Raceform Interactive

# 3796 FAIRYHOUSE (R-H)
Wednesday, July 5

**OFFICIAL GOING: Good**

## 4512a IRISH STALLION FARMS EUROPEAN BREEDERS FUND BROWNSTOWN STKS (GROUP 3) (F&M) 7f
6:50 (6:51) 3-Y-0+
**£37,820** (£12,179; £4,166; £4,166; £1,282; £641)

RPR
1 **Realtra (IRE)**[32] 3334 5-9-8 105 ColinKeane 3 103+
(Roger Varian) *trckd ldrs in 3rd: short of room on inner 2f out: rdn to press ldr in 2nd ent fnl f: led fnl 150yds: kpt on wl clsng stages* **3/1**[2]
2 1 ¼ **Golden Stunner (IRE)**[18] 3843 4-9-8 107 ColmO'Donoghue 6 99
(Ralph Beckett) *led: strly pressed ent fnl f where edgd lft: hdd fnl 150yds: kpt on same pce in 2nd* **11/8**[1]
3 ½ **Asking (IRE)**[4] 4385 3-9-0 100 (t) AnaO'Brien 5 95+
(A P O'Brien, Ire) *racd in mid-div: clsr whn short of room appr fnl f: styd on wl fnl 100yds to dead-heat for 3rd cl home: nrst fin* **5/1**[3]
3 dht **Raymonda (USA)**[39] 3101 4-9-8 104 PatSmullen 4 98
(D K Weld, Ire) *sn trckd ldr in 2nd: travelled wl and almost on terms under 2f out: rdn and no imp in 3rd fnl 100yds: jnd for 3rd cl home* **16/1**
5 shd **Bumbasina (IRE)**[38] 3111 3-9-0 91 WJLee 8 94
(W McCreery, Ire) *chsd ldrs on outer in 4th: rdn and nt qckn ent fnl f: kpt on wl again clsng stages* **25/1**
6 1 ½ **Music Box (IRE)**[4] 4385 3-9-0 86 (h) SeamieHeffernan 1 90
(A P O'Brien, Ire) *slowly away: racd in rr for most: wnt 7th 1f out: kpt on wl clsng stages: nvr on terms* **7/1**
7 2 ¼ **Elusive Beauty (IRE)**[7] 4208 3-9-0 0 ShaneFoley 7 84
(K J Condon, Ire) *bit slowly away: racd towards rr on inner: rdn under 2f out: no imp appr fnl f: kpt on one pce* **16/1**

1m 28.4s (-2.10)
**WFA** 3 from 4yo+ 8lb 7 Ran SP% **111.9**
TF: R/GS/RM 31.20; R/GS/AS 11.00 CSF £7.16 TOTE £3.70: £1.60, £1.50; DF 7.90.
**Owner** Yasushi Kubota **Bred** Tom & Geraldine Molan **Trained** Newmarket, Suffolk
**FOCUS**
Rehana was a notable non-runner having been installed as favourite the night before. Golden Stunner inherited favouritism and appeared to get quick a cheap lead up front. The gallop did not appear overly strong and the entire field had some sort of chance 2f out.

4513 - 4516a (Foreign Racing) - See Raceform Interactive

# 4487 HAMBURG (R-H)
Wednesday, July 5

**OFFICIAL GOING: Turf: soft**

## 4517a GROSSER PREIS VON LOTTO HAMBURG - HAMBURGER FLIEGER-TROPHY (GROUP 3) (3YO+) (TURF) 6f
7:25 3-Y-0+ £27,350 (£10,256; £5,128; £2,564; £1,709)

RPR
1 **Millowitsch (GER)**[39] 3105 4-9-2 0 AndreasHelfenbein 2 106
(Markus Klug, Germany) *w ldr: rdn to ld 2f out: drvn and kpt on wl fnl f: drew clr last 100yds* **23/10**[2]
2 2 ¼ **Daring Match (GER)**[31] 3370 6-9-2 0 AlexanderPietsch 6 99
(J Hirschberger, Germany) *hld up towards rr of midfield: hdwy fr over 2f out: rdn and ev ch 1f out: hung lft 150yds out: kpt on: nt pce of wnr last 100yds* **105/10**
3 nse **Schang (GER)**[39] 3105 4-9-2 0 MichaelCadeddu 1 99
(P Vovcenko, Germany) *led: rdn and hdd 2f out: kpt on: nt pce of wnr last 100yds* **39/10**[3]
4 shd **Mc Queen (FR)**[14] 5-9-0 0 StephenHellyn 7 96
(Yasmin Almenrader, Germany) *hld up towards rr: rdn and kpt on wl fr 2f out: nrst fin* **7/1**
5 ¾ **Alwina (GER)**[17] 3882 3-8-7 0 MarcLerner 5 92
(Henk Grewe, Germany) *prom tl hmpd after 1 1/2f: trckd ldrs after: rdn over 2f out: outpcd appr fnl f: kpt on last 150yds* **84/10**
6 1 ¼ **Sanaadh**[437] 1669 4-9-2 0 EduardoPedroza 4 92
(A Wohler, Germany) *hld up in rr: rdn and gd hdwy fr under 2f out: chsd ldrs ent fnl f: wknd last 150yds* **11/5**[1]
7 2 ¼ **Forgino (GER)**[65] 6-9-0 0 AndraschStarke 3 83
(T Potters, Germany) *trckd ldrs: rdn and ev ch 1 1/2f out: wknd over 1f out* **54/10**

1m 13.38s (0.69)
**WFA** 3 from 4yo+ 6lb 7 Ran SP% **129.4**
PARI-MUTUEL (all including 10 euro stake): WIN 33 PLACE: 22, 36, SF: 401.
**Owner** Dr Alexandra Margarete Renz **Bred** Frau Dr Alexandra Margarete Renz **Trained** Germany

## 4422 HAMBURG (R-H)

Monday, July 3

**OFFICIAL GOING: Turf: soft**

### 4518a FRANZ-GUNTHER VON GAERTNER-GEDACHTNISRENNEN (GROUP 3) (3YO+ FILLIES & MARES) (TURF) 1m

6:55 3-Y-0+ £27,350 (£10,256; £5,128; £2,564; £1,709)

RPR

1 **Shy Witch (GER)**63 4-9-0 0 EduardoPedroza 2 106+
(H-J Groschel, Germany) *hld up towards rr: gd hdwy fr over 2f out: rdn under 2f out: led 100yds out: sn in command: readily* **6/1**3

2 1 3/4 **Wild Approach (GER)**39 4-9-0 0 WladimirPanov 1 102
(D Moser, Germany) *chsd ldr: rdn to ld over 2f out: hdd 100yds out: sn outpcd by wnr: kpt on* **224/10**

3 1/2 **Absolute Blast (IRE)**30 3319 5-9-2 0 OisinMurphy 8 103
(Archie Watson) *trckd ldrs: rdn 2f out: ev ch ins fnl f: no ex last 100yds* **6/5**1

4 1 3/4 **Flemish Duchesse (FR)**39 4-9-2 0 FilipMinarik 7 99
(Andreas Suborics, Germany) *led: rdn over 2f out: crossed to stands' side ent st: hdd 2f out: kpt on same pce* **26/5**2

5 3 **A Raving Beauty (GER)**28 4-9-2 0 (b) MarcLerner 9 92
(Andreas Suborics, Germany) *midfield: rdn and gd hdwy over 2f out: chsd ldr under 2f out: wknd last 150yds* **77/10**

6 nk **Djumay (GER)**44 3-8-7 0 AndreasHelfenbein 6 89
(Andreas Suborics, Germany) *midfield: rdn and outpcd over 2f out: kpt on steadily fnl f* **162/10**

7 7 **Vive Marie (GER)** 3-8-7 0 MaximPecheur 4 73
(J Hirschberger, Germany) *in rr: rdn after 3f: sme hdwy fr 2f out: wknd last 150yds: nvr a factor* **125/10**

8 2 **Intendantin (GER)**63 4-9-0 0 MichaelCadeddu 5 69
(Ferdinand J Leve, Germany) *a towards rr* **38/1**

9 11 **Sunny Belle (IRE)**37 3105 3-8-7 0 AndraschStarke 3 43
(P Schiergen, Germany) *midfield: lost pl 2f out: sn struggling* **8/1**

10 3/4 **Partyday (IRE)**39 4-9-0 0 BauyrzhanMurzabayev 10 41
(V Luka Jr, Czech Republic) *trckd ldrs: rdn and lost pl 2f out: sn struggling* **44/5**

1m 45.82s
**WFA** 3 from 4yo+ 9lb **10 Ran SP% 128.7**
PARI-MUTUEL (all including 10 euro stake): WIN 70 PLACE: 27, 39, 17; SF: 2161.
**Owner** Frau K Schwerdtfeger **Bred** Frau Karin Schwerdtfeger **Trained** Germany

## 3318 EPSOM (L-H)

Thursday, July 6

**OFFICIAL GOING: Good to firm (good in places; 7.7)**
Wind: Moderate, across becoming almost nil Weather: Fine, very warm

### 4519 WATCH RACING UK ANYWHERE H'CAP 1m 4f 6y

6:10 (6:11) (Class 5) (0-75,77) 4-Y-0+ £3,881 (£1,155; £577; £288) Stalls Centre

Form RPR

3403 1 **Star Of Lombardy (IRE)**15 3983 4-9-3 **71** JoeFanning 4 76
(Mark Johnston) *led 2f: trckd ldr: led again over 2f out and sent for home: rdn over 1f out: hld on wl* **7/2**2

000 2 1 **Wotabreeze (IRE)**33 3315 4-9-2 **70** JasonHart 2 73
(John Quinn) *trckd ldng pair: angled off rail to chse wnr 2f out: tried to chal fnl f: nt qckn and hld last 100yds* **8/1**3

4312 3 3 1/4 **Light Of Air (FR)**34 3308 4-9-7 **75** TimmyMurphy 5 73
(Gary Moore) *trckd ldrs: rdn over 2f out: no imp on first pair fr over 1f out: jst hld on for 3rd* **6/4**1

54/3 4 shd **Benbecula**23 3694 8-8-8 **67** (b) AliceMills(5) 1 65
(Richard Mitchell) *s.i.s: rcvrd to ld after 2f and sn 4 l clr: hdd over 2f out: sn btn but kpt on nr fin* **11/1**

22-6 5 hd **The Salmon Man**17 3920 5-9-2 **70** (p) PatDobbs 3 68
(Brendan Powell) *s.s: hld up in detached last: clsd 4f out: rdn 2f out: flashed tail: hanging and fnd little after* **10/1**

0546 6 1 1/2 **Castilo Del Diablo (IRE)**98 1457 8-9-4 **77** GeorgeBuckell(5) 6 74
(David Simcock) *hld up off the pce in 5th: rdn and no prog over 2f out: one pce no ch whn hmpd ins fnl f* **7/2**2

2m 38.96s (0.06) **Going Correction** -0.45s/f (Firm) **6 Ran SP% 113.0**
Speed ratings (Par 103): **81,80,78,78,77 76**
CSF £30.25 TOTE £3.90: £1.80, £3.90; EX 28.50.
**Owner** Paul Dean **Bred** Tom Darcy And Vincent McCarthy **Trained** Middleham Moor, N Yorks

**FOCUS**
Rail out 2 yards from 1m to winning post increasing advertised race distances as follows: Races 1, 4 and 5 by 10 yards, race 2 and 6 by 7 yards and race 3 by 4 yards. A fair middle-distance handicap. They went a muddling gallop on ground officially described as good to firm, good in places. The winner has been rated to her turf form.

### 4520 BRITISH STALLION STUDS EBF NOVICE MEDIAN AUCTION STKS 7f 3y

6:45 (6:45) (Class 5) 2-Y-0 £4,204 (£1,251; £625; £312) Stalls Low

Form RPR

6 1 **Sallab (IRE)**20 3783 2-9-2 0 TimmyMurphy 3 72+
(Richard Hannon) *trckd ldng trio: shkn up 2f out: angled arnd rivals fnl f: drvn and r.o to ld last strides* **4/1**3

5 2 nk **Shawwal**38 3135 2-8-13 0 KieranShoemark(3) 10 71
(John Gosden) *trckd ldng pair: chal fr 2f out tl led 1f out: rdn and kpt on: hdd last strides* **11/4**1

0 3 1/2 **Cheeky Rascal (IRE)**31 3390 2-9-2 0 KieranO'Neill 11 70
(Richard Hannon) *sn t.k.h fr wd draw and awkward downhill: 5th st: shkn up and nt qckn 2f out: styd on wl fnl f to take 3rd last strides* **9/1**

4 1/2 **Tiny Tempest (IRE)** 2-8-11 0 CharlesBishop 8 63
(Eve Johnson Houghton) *in tch in 7th: shkn up and prog 2f out: clsd on ldrs 1f out: no ex last 75yds* **14/1**

0 5 1 **Couldn't Could She**26 3576 2-8-11 0 JasonHart 9 61
(Adam West) *pressed ldr: upsides fr 1/2-way tl 1f out: one pce ins fnl f* **20/1**

6 shd **Doublet (IRE)** 2-9-2 0 JoeFanning 6 65
(Mark Johnston) *mde most: hrd pressed fr 3f out: hdd and one pce 1f out* **7/2**2

0 7 3 **Font Vert (FR)**20 3783 2-9-2 0 PatDobbs 2 57
(Ralph Beckett) *in tch: 6th st: rdn and no prog over 2f out: no hdwy over 1f out* **7/1**

0 8 3/4 **Galloping Hogan (IRE)**15 3965 2-9-2 0 RobertWinston 5 55
(Sylvester Kirk) *t.k.h: hld up in 8th: shkn up over 2f out: hanging sltly and no prog* **10/1**

00 9 16 **Final Rock**8 4213 2-8-9 0 ManuelFernandes(7) 4 12
(Sir Mark Prescott Bt) *a in last pair: t.o over 2f out* **50/1**

10 4 **The Naughty Step (IRE)** 2-9-2 0 JackMitchell 1
(Jim Boyle) *a in last pair: t.o over 2f out* **16/1**

1m 22.65s (-0.65) **Going Correction** -0.45s/f (Firm) **10 Ran SP% 119.8**
Speed ratings (Par 94): **85,84,84,83,82 82,78,77,59,55**
CSF £15.90 TOTE £4.00: £1.60, £1.50, £3.00; EX 14.50 Trifecta £105.40.
**Owner** Al Shaqab Racing **Bred** Athassel House Stud Ltd **Trained** East Everleigh, Wilts

**FOCUS**
Race distance increased 7 yards. An ordinary juvenile novice contest. They went a respectable gallop and the two horses with experience at the head of the betting flashed past the post together.

### 4521 FEDERATION OF BLOODSTOCK AGENTS H'CAP 6f 3y

7:15 (7:16) (Class 3) (0-95,91) 3-Y-0+
£7,470 (£2,236; £1,118; £559; £279; £140) Stalls High

Form RPR

-000 1 **Ashpan Sam**18 3861 8-9-6 **83** (p) WilliamCarson 5 92
(David W Drinkwater) *mde all: committed for home 1/2-way and sn at least 2 l ahd: drvn over 1f out: kpt on wl* **8/1**3

4232 2 3/4 **Storm Cry**6 4317 3-8-13 **82** JoeFanning 4 87
(Mark Johnston) *chsd ldrs: 4th st: shkn up 2f out: styd on to take 2nd last 100yds: clsd on wnr but unable to chal* **11/4**1

-061 3 1 1/4 **Farleigh Mac**24 3673 3-8-10 **79** RobHornby 6 80
(Andrew Balding) *taken down early: chsd wnr: rdn and no imp 2f out: one pce and lost 2nd last 100yds* **11/4**1

0010 4 1/2 **Reputation (IRE)**19 3842 4-10-0 **91** (v) JasonHart 2 91+
(John Quinn) *hmpd s: t.k.h and hld up: 6th st: rdn and no prog 2f out: styd on ins fnl f wout threatening* **11/2**2

0100 5 1 1/2 **Athassel**19 3808 8-9-0 **80** KieranShoemark(3) 9 76+
(David Evans) *dwlt: outpcd and detached in last: same thrght tl styd on wl fnl f: nrst fin* **20/1**

6125 6 3/4 **Taajub (IRE)**19 3834 10-8-9 **72** JackMitchell 8 65
(Peter Crate) *walked to post early: racd wd: in tch: 7th st: hanging and fnd nil whn asked for effrt 2f out* **25/1**

0602 7 3/4 **Highland Acclaim (IRE)**16 3946 6-9-5 **85** (h) JoshDoyle(3) 1 76
(David O'Meara) *awkward s then impeded: plld hrd and racd most awkwardly downhill: 5th st: no prog 2f out: sn btn* **11/2**2

3150 8 4 1/2 **Juan Horsepower**38 3146 3-9-0 **83** (p) KieranO'Neill 3 58
(Richard Hannon) *wnt sharply lft s: pushed up to chse ldng pair: rdn 2f out: wknd over 1f out* **8/1**3

1m 7.28s (-2.12) **Going Correction** -0.45s/f (Firm)
**WFA** 3 from 4yo+ 6lb **8 Ran SP% 114.9**
Speed ratings (Par 107): **96,95,93,92,90 89,88,82**
CSF £30.51 CT £76.73 TOTE £9.20: £2.60, £1.40, £1.40; EX 38.20.
**Owner** Advantage Chemicals Holdings Ltd **Bred** Advantage Chemicals Holdings Ltd **Trained** Hanley Castle, Worcs

**FOCUS**
Race distance increased 4 yards. The feature contest was a decent 6f handicap. They went a proper gallop and a course specialist dipped under standard time. The second and third have been rated pretty much to form.

### 4522 WATCH RACING UK ON YOUVIEW NOW H'CAP (JOCKEY CLUB GRASSROOTS FLAT MIDDLE DISTANCE QUALIFIER) 1m 2f 17y

7:50 (7:51) (Class 4) (0-80,82) 4-Y-0+ £5,175 (£1,540; £769; £384) Stalls Low

Form RPR

-421 1 **Silver Ghost (IRE)**25 3616 4-9-7 **80** CharlesBishop 6 88+
(Eve Johnson Houghton) *chsd clr ldng pair: clsd 3f out: rdn to ld 2f out: hrd drvn and pressed ins fnl f: hld on* **6/4**1

0132 2 nk **Berrahri (IRE)**30 3441 6-9-1 **74** RobertWinston 8 81
(John Best) *racd in 5th and off the pce: clsd and rdn over 2f out: chsd wnr over 1f out and edgd lft: chal ins fnl f: nt qckn last 50yds* **20/1**

-303 3 nk **Thundering Blue (USA)**62 2369 4-9-2 **75** PatDobbs 3 81+
(David Menuisier) *stdd s: hld up in last and long way off the pce: shkn up and swtchd to wd outside over 2f out: stl only 9th over 1f out: str run fnl f: too late* **14/1**

0231 4 1 3/4 **Tripartite (IRE)**19 3820 4-9-0 **73** AdamBeschizza 4 76
(Jeremy Gask) *racd off the pce in 6th: rdn over 2f out: no prog tl styd on jst over 1f out and tk 4th nr fin* **7/1**2

6041 5 1 1/4 **Jufn**20 3771 4-9-7 **80** (h) TrevorWhelan 2 80
(John Butler) *pressed ldr and sn 10 l clr of rest: c bk to rivals fr 3f out: lost pl over 1f out but stuck on quite wl* **14/1**

0-33 6 1/2 **Compton Mill**45 2893 5-9-6 **79** (t) TimmyMurphy 5 78
(Hughie Morrison) *chsd clr ldrs in 5th: rdn over 2f out: one pce after and nvr able to threaten seriously* **8/1**3

1430 7 1 3/4 **The Gay Cavalier**5 4365 6-8-10 **69** (t) JackMitchell 7 66
(John Ryan) *hld up in 9th: shkn up over 2f out: trying to cl on inner 1f out but no real threat whn hmpd and lost momentum* **11/1**

00 8 1/2 **Storm King**20 3790 8-9-6 **82** EdwardGreatrex(3) 11 77
(David C Griffiths) *led at str pce w one rival and pair sn 10 l clr: swung wd into st: c bk to rivals 3f out: hdd 2f out and steadily fdd* **7/1**2

40-5 9 3 3/4 **Ladurelli (IRE)**7 4254 5-9-5 **78** WilliamCarson 1 65
(Paul Cole) *hld up off the pce in 7th: rdn over 2f out: no great prog after: wknd fnl f* **9/1**

11-0 10 60 **Fort Jefferson**177 156 4-9-2 **75** RobHornby 9
(Andrew Balding) *hld up off the pce in 8th: dropped to last over 2f out and virtually p.u after* **14/1**

2m 3.95s (-5.75) **Going Correction** -0.45s/f (Firm) **10 Ran SP% 119.2**
Speed ratings (Par 105): **105,104,104,103,102 101,100,99,96,48**
CSF £38.10 CT £326.41 TOTE £2.40: £1.30, £3.80, £2.70; EX 36.70 Trifecta £411.70.
**Owner** Mrs Jennifer Simpson Racing **Bred** George Delahunt **Trained** Blewbury, Oxon


The Form Book Flat, Raceform Ltd, Newbury, RG14 5SJ

**FOCUS**
Race distance increased 10 yards. A decent handicap. They went a contested gallop and the clear favourite dipped under standard time. The fifth has been rated close to his Chepstow win.

## 4523 WATCH RACING UK ON SKY 432 H'CAP — 1m 113y
**8:20** (8:22) (Class 5) (0-75,77) 4-Y-0+ — **£3,881** (£1,155; £577; £288) **Stalls** Low

Form — RPR

520- **1** **Lord Reason**[280] 6889 5-9-3 **74** .... TimClark(3) 3 — 82
(John Butler) *mde all: dictated stdy pce tl booted on 3f out: hrd pressed fr over 1f out: hld on tenaciously* **14/1**

-510 **2** *shd* **Frank Bridge**[8] 4210 4-9-9 **77** .... CharlesBishop 4 — 84
(Eve Johnson Houghton) *trckd wnr: rdn 2f out: upsides fr over 1f out: nt qckn and jst hld last strides* **9/2**[2]

0403 **3** *3* **Matravers**[20] 3771 6-9-1 **69** .... PatDobbs 6 — 69
(Mary Hambro) *hld up disputing 5th: pushed along and effrt on inner over 2f out: shkn up and smuggled way through to take 3rd last 100yds: no ch w ldng pair* **7/1**

-240 **4** *nk* **Squire**[154] 516 6-9-7 **75** ....(t) AdamBeschizza 7 — 74
(Michael Attwater) *hld up disputing 5th: prog to chse ldng pair over 2f out: sn rdn: no imp over 1f out: lost 3rd last 100yds* **13/2**[3]

-061 **5** *1 1/2* **Galinthias**[27] 3521 5-9-1 **69** .... LouisSteward 5 — 65
(Simon Dow) *t.k.h: trckd ldng trio: rdn wl over 2f out and nt qckn: one pce and no threat after* **7/1**

4415 **6** *hd* **Live Dangerously**[16] 3940 7-8-2 **56** oh1 .... KieranO'Neill 9 — 51
(John Bridger) *taken down early: t.k.h and hld up in last: pushed along over 2f out: no prog tl passed two rivals nr fin: nvr involved* **12/1**

0-35 **7** *1/2* **Buckland Beau**[21] 3750 6-9-6 **74** .... MartinLane 8 — 68
(Charlie Fellowes) *hld up disputing 5th and trapped on outer: rdn over 2f out: no prog over 1f out: fdd ins fnl f* **3/1**[1]

2514 **8** *1* **Muthraab Aldaar (IRE)**[22] 3718 4-8-11 **65** .... JackMitchell 2 — 57
(Jim Boyle) *trckd ldng pair to over 2f out: sing to struggle whn hmpd over 1f out: no ch after* **9/2**[2]

1m 44.42s (-1.68) **Going Correction** -0.45s/f (Firm) — **8** Ran SP% **114.1**
Speed ratings (Par 103): **89,88,86,85,84 84,84,83**
CSF £75.24 CT £485.13 TOTE £14.80: £4.40, £1.60, £2.00; EX 83.70 Trifecta £705.00.
**Owner** Greenstead Hall Racing Ltd **Bred** Greenstead Hall Racing Ltd **Trained** Newmarket, Suffolk

**FOCUS**
Race distance increased 10 yards. A fair handicap. They went a modest gallop and the two horses on the lead dominated the finish. It's been rated a bit cautiously.

## 4524 EPSOM DOWNS SUPPORTING RACING STAFF WEEK H'CAP — 7f 3y
**8:50** (8:52) (Class 4) (0-85,87) 3-Y-0+ — **£5,175** (£1,540; £769; £384) **Stalls** Low

Form — RPR

-226 **1** **Pastoral Player**[20] 3777 10-9-13 **87** .... RobertWinston 8 — 94
(Hughie Morrison) *blindfold off late and slowly away: hld up in last: pushed along over 2f out: stl last over 1f out: str burst ins fnl f: led last stride* **8/1**

5535 **2** *nk* **Tavener**[19] 3833 5-8-13 **76** ....(p) EdwardGreatrex(3) 2 — 82
(David C Griffiths) *t.k.h: led: shkn up 2f out: hrd pressed ins fnl f: kpt on wl but hdd last stride* **10/1**

6551 **3** *nk* **Qeyaadah (IRE)**[12] 4103 4-9-5 **86** .... RayDawson(7) 4 — 91
(Michael Appleby) *trckd ldng trio: shkn up 2f out: chsd ldr jst over 1f out: edgd lft u.p after: str chal last 100yds: nt qckn and lost 2nd fnl strides* **7/2**[2]

6416 **4** *1/2* **Russian Soul (IRE)**[41] 3030 9-9-13 **87** ....(p) TimmyMurphy 1 — 91
(Jamie Osborne) *hld up in 5th: shkn up and no prog over 2f out: no imp ldrs after tl styd on ins fnl f: nrst fin but no threat* **8/1**

5013 **5** *3/4* **Noble Peace**[20] 3777 4-9-10 **87** .... KieranShoemark(3) 3 — 92+
(Henry Candy) *chsd ldng pair: nvr much room fr over 1f out then squeezed out jst ins fnl f: one pce after* **11/4**[1]

0302 **6** *1 1/4* **Fox Trotter (IRE)**[26] 3572 5-9-3 **84** .... JordanUys(7) 6 — 83
(Brian Meehan) *hld up in 8th: shkn up on inner 2f out: little rspnse: kpt on fnl f but no threat at all* **5/1**[3]

6106 **7** *hd* **Plucky Dip**[12] 4091 6-9-6 **80** .... JackMitchell 7 — 78
(John Ryan) *hld up in 7th: rdn 2f out: no prog and one pce after* **25/1**

0601 **8** *1/2* **In The Red (IRE)**[20] 3777 4-9-8 **82** .... WilliamCarson 5 — 79
(Martin Smith) *in tch in 6th: urged along wl over 2f out and no prog: one pce after* **8/1**

4115 **9** *1/2* **Sans Souci Bay**[42] 3000 3-9-2 **84** ....(b) KieranO'Neill 9 — 76
(Richard Hannon) *chsd wnr: rdn 2f out: lost 2nd jst over 1f out: wknd ins fnl f* **14/1**

1m 21.95s (-1.35) **Going Correction** -0.45s/f (Firm)
**WFA** 3 from 4yo+ 8lb — **9** Ran SP% **118.5**
Speed ratings (Par 105): **89,88,88,87,86 85,85,84,84**
CSF £86.56 CT £336.80 TOTE £9.90: £2.80, £3.80, £1.40; EX 85.10 Trifecta £571.60.
**Owner** The Pursuits Partnership **Bred** Whitsbury Manor Stud & Pigeon House Stud **Trained** East Ilsley, Berks

**FOCUS**
Race distance increased 7 yards. A decent handicap. They may have gone too hard up front and the veteran at the head of the weights managed another victory in pretty bizarre fashion. Ordinary form.
T/Plt: £186.80 to a £1 stake. Pool: £64,141.90. 250.62 winning units. T/Qpdt: £37.40 to a £1 stake. Pool: £5,977.91. 118.06 winning units. **Jonathan Neesom**

# 4081 HAYDOCK (L-H)
Thursday, July 6

**OFFICIAL GOING: Good to firm (8.9)**
Wind: Almost nil Weather: Cloudy

## 4525 STAY ON FIRE ON LEVEL FILLIES' H'CAP — 7f 212y
**2:00** (2:00) (Class 5) (0-75,77) 3-Y-0+ — **£3,557** (£1,058; £529; £264) **Stalls** Low

Form — RPR

-636 **1** **Trilliant (IRE)**[25] 3615 3-9-6 **76** .... PatCosgrave 4 — 88+
(Ed Walker) *stdd s: racd keenly: hld up: swtchd rt and hdwy 2f out: r.o ins fnl f to ld fnl 150yds: comf* **4/1**[3]

1161 **2** *2 1/4* **Miss Sheridan (IRE)**[17] 3900 3-9-3 **76** .... NathanEvans(3) 1 — 79
(Michael Easterby) *led: rdn over 1f out: hdd fnl 150yds: outpcd by wnr towards fin* **2/1**[1]

50-0 **3** *1 1/2* **Our Greta (IRE)**[37] 3171 3-8-11 **67** .... BenCurtis 5 — 67
(Michael Appleby) *hld up in rr: rdn over 2f out: no imp tl prog wl ins fnl f: gng on at fin* **16/1**

0-11 **4** *hd* **La Celebs Ville (IRE)**[27] 3540 4-9-11 **77** ....(p) PaddyPilley(5) 7 — 79
(Tom Dascombe) *chsd ldrs: rdn and ev ch fr 2f out: unable qck 1f out: styd on same pce ins fnl f* **3/1**[2]

1-00 **5** *1/2* **Conqueress (IRE)**[35] 3246 3-9-0 **70** ....(p[1]) RichardKingscote 3 — 68
(Tom Dascombe) *chsd ldr tl rdn 2f out: stl ev ch 1f out but unable qck: styd on same pce ins fnl f tl no ex towards fin* **10/1**

0252 **6** *nse* **Make On Madam (IRE)**[9] 4168 5-9-8 **69** ....(p) PJMcDonald 2 — 69
(Les Eyre) *in tch: u.p over 2f out: outpcd over 1f out: kpt on towards fin: nt pce to chal* **9/2**

1m 39.72s (-3.98) **Going Correction** -0.50s/f (Hard)
**WFA** 3 from 4yo+ 9lb — **6** Ran SP% **111.5**
Speed ratings (Par 100): **99,96,95,95,94 94**
CSF £12.27 CT £107.63 TOTE £4.80: £2.10, £1.30; EX 13.10 Trifecta £139.30.
**Owner** B E Nielsen **Bred** Bjorn Nielsen **Trained** Upper Lambourn, Berks

**FOCUS**
All races on Inner Home Straight. Distance increased by 9yds. After riding in the opener Nathan Evans said: "The ground is just on the quick side" and Pat Cosgrave said: "It is beautiful, it feels like good ground that has been watered." A fair handicap run at a nice gallop. The runner-up has been rated to form.

## 4526 PILKINGTON GLASS EBF STALLIONS NOVICE STKS (PLUS 10 RACE) — 6f
**2:30** (2:30) (Class 4) 2-Y-O — **£4,528** (£1,347; £673; £336) **Stalls** Centre

Form — RPR

**1** **Staxton** 2-9-2 0 .... DavidAllan 10 — 81
(Tim Easterby) *in rr: pushed along 2f out w work to do: hdwy over 1f out: rn ins fnl f to ld nr fin* **50/1**

01 **2** *hd* **Green Power**[44] 2926 2-9-8 0 .... BenCurtis 3 — 86
(John Gallagher) *led: rdn over 1f out: kpt on gamely ins fnl f: ct nr fin* **10/1**

1 **3** *1 1/4* **Green Fortune**[35] 3246 2-9-5 0 .... PatCosgrave 11 — 79
(William Haggas) *midfield: effrt over 2f out: hdwy over 1f out: styd on towards fin: nt pce to chal* **7/4**[1]

24 **4** *1/2* **Red Force One**[27] 3538 2-9-2 0 .... RichardKingscote 8 — 74
(Tom Dascombe) *a.p: rdn and edgd lft over 2f out: styd on same pce ins fnl f* **5/1**[3]

**5** *nk* **Wafeer (IRE)** 2-9-2 0 .... SeanLevey 4 — 73
(Richard Hannon) *hld up in midfield: hdwy over 1f out: styd on ins fnl f: nt quite get to winenr: no ex towards fin* **15/2**

5 **6** *1 1/2* **Vj Day (USA)**[49] 2769 2-9-2 0 .... JamieSpencer 9 — 69
(Kevin Ryan) *prom: rdn over 2f out: one pce ins fnl f* **4/1**[2]

00 **7** *3* **Admiral Spice (IRE)**[37] 3164 2-8-11 0 .... PaddyPilley(5) 2 — 59
(Tom Dascombe) *chsd ldrs: rdn over 2f out: wknd over 1f out* **66/1**

0 **8** *3/4* **Motabassim (IRE)**[21] 3746 2-9-2 0 .... GrahamLee 13 — 57
(Brian Meehan) *wnt rt s: in tch: rdn 2f out: wknd over 1f out: btn whn edgd lft ins fnl f* **40/1**

43 **9** *1/2* **The Right Choice (IRE)**[27] 3538 2-9-2 0 .... PaulHanagan 1 — 55
(Richard Fahey) *sn outpcd in rr: kpt on u.p ins fnl f: nvr a threat* **10/1**

0 **10** *nk* **Taifbalady (IRE)**[49] 2769 2-9-2 0 .... PJMcDonald 5 — 54
(Mark Johnston) *midfield: rdn over 2f out: wknd and edgd lft over 1f out* **20/1**

46 **11** *hd* **Arty But Poor**[10] 4160 2-9-2 0 .... KevinStott 6 — 53
(Oliver Greenall) *midfield: pushed along 1/2-way: green and outpcd over 2f out* **80/1**

**12** *3 3/4* **Hic Bibi** 2-8-11 0 .... TomEaves 12 — 36
(David Brown) *a in rr: outpcd over 1f out* **100/1**

1m 12.45s (-1.35) **Going Correction** -0.325s/f (Firm) — **12** Ran SP% **115.9**
Speed ratings (Par 96): **96,95,94,93,93 91,87,86,85,84 84,79**
CSF £467.21 TOTE £52.10: £13.10, £2.60, £1.20; EX 908.00 Trifecta £3688.70.
**Owner** Ontoawinner 10 & Partner **Bred** B & B Equine Limited **Trained** Great Habton, N Yorks

**FOCUS**
A fair novice event although there was a 50-1 winning newcomer. The second and thid have been rated close to form.

## 4527 ALUMINIUM DOORS AND WINDOWS CONTACT ALUFOLDDIRECT.CO.UK NURSERY H'CAP — 6f
**3:00** (3:00) (Class 5) 2-Y-O — **£3,557** (£1,058; £529; £264) **Stalls** Centre

Form — RPR

624 **1** **Our Man In Havana**[17] 3895 2-8-12 **69** .... RichardKingscote 14 — 73
(Tom Dascombe) *prom: rdn to ld over 1f out: r.o gamely ins fnl f: kpt finding towards fin* **2/1**[1]

645 **2** *nk* **Jim Rockford**[49] 2756 2-8-13 **70** .... DanielTudhope 11 — 73
(Ralph Beckett) *a.p: rdn and chalng fr over 1f out: r.o u.p ins fnl f: hld towards fin* **7/1**[2]

0610 **3** *1/2* **Magnus (IRE)**[16] 3929 2-9-2 **73** .... BenCurtis 8 — 74
(Tom Dascombe) *midfield: rdn and hung lft fr 2f out: hdwy over 1f out: chsd ldrs ins fnl f: styd on towards fin* **11/1**

010 **4** *1/2* **June Dog**[16] 3929 2-9-7 **78** .... SeanLevey 13 — 78
(Richard Hannon) *led: rdn and hdd over 1f out: continued to chal ins fnl f: no ex fnl 75yds* **8/1**[3]

450 **5** *2* **Shovel It On (IRE)**[29] 3467 2-8-6 **63** .... FrannyNorton 7 — 56
(David Evans) *in rr: rdn 2f out: hdwy over 1f out: styd on ins fnl f: nt pce to rch ldrs* **16/1**

626 **6** *2 3/4* **Shobrom (IRE)**[19] 3826 2-9-2 **73** .... PhillipMakin 6 — 58
(Richard Fahey) *midfield early: trckd ldrs 1/2-way: rdn over 1f out: one pce and unable to go w front few ins fnl f* **8/1**[3]

505 **7** *3* **I Am Dandy (IRE)**[34] 3283 2-8-0 **60** ow2 .... NathanEvans(3) 5 — 35
(James Ewart) *midfield: rdn over 2f out: no imp over 1f out: one pce ins fnl f* **33/1**

646 **8** *1* **Ventura Crest (IRE)**[17] 3895 2-8-1 **61** .... RachelRichardson(3) 9 — 33
(Tim Easterby) *chsd ldrs: rdn 2f out: wknd 1f out* **20/1**

560 **9** *nk* **Atalanta Queen**[22] 3712 2-8-9 **66** .... GrahamLee 12 — 37
(Brian Meehan) *hld up in midfield: rdn 2f out: wknd over 1f out* **28/1**

040 **10** *1 3/4* **New Empire**[14] 3993 2-9-1 **72** .... JamieSpencer 10 — 37+
(Peter Chapple-Hyam) *hld up: hung lft and no rspnse over 1f out: eased whn btn and looking uneasy ins fnl f* **12/1**

246 **11** *hd* **Thrifty**[42] 2988 2-8-7 **64** .... JamesSullivan 1 — 29
(Tim Easterby) *in rr: rdn over 2f out: no imp over 1f out: wl btn ins fnl f* **22/1**

053 **12** *7* **Bodybuilder**[25] 3622 2-8-12 **69** .... PatCosgrave 2 — 11
(Richard Hannon) *midfield: rdn over 2f out: wknd over 1f out* **8/1**[3]

1m 13.07s (-0.73) **Going Correction** -0.325s/f (Firm) — **12** Ran SP% **116.6**
Speed ratings (Par 94): **91,90,89,89,86 82,78,77,77,74 74,65**
CSF £14.27 CT £126.21 TOTE £2.80: £1.30, £2.50, £2.40; EX 20.80 Trifecta £163.20.
**Owner** John Abbey & Mike Nolan **Bred** Alvediston Stud & Partners **Trained** Malpas, Cheshire

**FOCUS**
This looked quite a competitive little nursery and so it proved. It's been rated around the first four.

## 4528 LONGINES IRISH CHAMPIONS WEEKEND EBF FILLIES' NOVICE STKS (PLUS 10 RACE) 6f 212y
**3:30** (3:30) (Class 4) 2-Y-O **£7,115** (£2,117; £1,058; £529) **Stalls** Low

Form RPR
5 **1** **Royal Parks**[23] 3697 2-9-0 0 DanielTudhope 8 82+
(James Tate) *mde all: shkn up and qcknd over 1f out: r.o strly to go clr ins fnl f* **5/2**[2]
**2** 3 ¼ **Akvavera** 2-9-0 0 RichardKingscote 4 73
(Ralph Beckett) *stdd s: hld up: hdwy over 2f out: wnt 2nd jst over 1f out: styd on ins fnl f: nt trble wnr: can improve* **5/1**[3]
4 **3** 2 **Falcon's Vision**[33] 3312 2-9-0 0 JamieSpencer 7 68
(David Simcock) *a.p: rdn over 1f out: sn outpcd by wnr: styd on same pce ins fnl f* **5/4**[1]
**4** 2 ¼ **Ryedale Encore** 2-9-0 0 DavidAllan 3 62
(Tim Easterby) *midfield: rdn over 2f out: sn outpcd: n.d after* **20/1**
**5** shd **Gamesters Icon** 2-9-0 0 ConnorBeasley 2 62
(Bryan Smart) *sluggish s: in rr and green: rdn 3f out: outpcd over 2f out: styd on ins fnl f: nt pce to trble ldrs* **33/1**
**6** ½ **Dalawyna (FR)** 2-9-0 0 KevinStott 1 60
(Kevin Ryan) *racd keenly: prom: rdn over 2f out: unable qck over 1f out: one pce fnl f* **12/1**
3 **7** 3 ½ **Fabella Bere (FR)**[28] 3483 2-9-0 0 BenCurtis 5 51
(K R Burke) *midfield: rdn and hung lft over 2f out: wknd over 1f out* **12/1**

1m 27.51s (-3.19) **Going Correction** -0.50s/f (Hard) 2y crse rec **7 Ran SP% 112.8**
Speed ratings (Par 93): **98,94,92,89,89 88,84**
CSF £14.95 TOTE £3.50: £1.60, £2.50; EX 18.10 Trifecta £39.80.
**Owner** Saeed Manana **Bred** Glebe Stud And Partners **Trained** Newmarket, Suffolk

**FOCUS**
Distance increased by 9yds. A decent fillies' novice run at a pretty steady gallop. The opening level is set around the third and seventh.

## 4529 TUFFX GLASS H'CAP 6f 212y
**4:00** (4:00) (Class 5) (0-75,75) 3-Y-O+ **£3,557** (£1,058; £529; £264) **Stalls** Low

Form RPR
-006 **1** **Groupie**[16] 3946 3-9-6 **75** JamesSullivan 6 81
(Tom Tate) *midfield: hdwy 2f out: led ins fnl f: r.o: in control towards fin* **12/1**
002- **2** ¾ **Manners Please**[217] 8174 3-9-2 **71** PhillipMakin 9 75
(Ralph Beckett) *midfield: hdwy over 1f out: chalng ins fnl f: hld and nt pce of wnr towards fin* **5/1**[2]
3004 **3** ½ **Captain Revelation**[27] 3540 5-9-9 **70** RichardKingscote 3 76
(Tom Dascombe) *prom: rdn over 3f out: outpcd over 2f out: rallied and styd on ins fnl f: gng on at fin* **4/1**[1]
4040 **4** 1 ½ **Deansgate (IRE)**[9] 4168 4-9-9 **70** (h) JoeDoyle 11 72
(Julie Camacho) *plld hrd: hld up: rdn over 2f out: swtchd rt wl over 1f out and hdwy after: styd on ins fnl f: nt rch ldrs* **6/1**[3]
2515 **5** ¾ **Magic Moments**[31] 3397 4-8-12 **59** DanielTudhope 7 59
(Alan King) *prom: led over 2f out: rdn over 1f out: hdd ins fnl f: no ex fnl 75yds* **4/1**[1]
1220 **6** nk **Rock Warbler (IRE)**[40] 3095 4-9-13 **74** (t) KevinStott 1 73
(Oliver Greenall) *midfield: hdwy over 2f out: chalng ins fnl f: no ex fnl 150yds* **7/1**
0515 **7** 1 ¼ **Passing Star**[23] 3696 6-9-11 **72** (tp) GeorgeDowning 10 67
(Daniel Kubler) *hld up: rdn over 2f out: kpt on ins fnl f: nvr able to trble ldrs* **10/1**
0-00 **8** 4 ½ **Redrosezorro**[35] 3243 3-8-1 **56** PatrickMathers 4 36
(Eric Alston) *led: rdn and hdd over 2f out: wknd over 1f out* **40/1**
5630 **9** 4 ½ **Baltic Prince (IRE)**[26] 3589 7-9-4 **70** PaddyPilley(5) 5 41
(Tony Carroll) *in tch: effrt over 2f out: wknd qckly 1f out* **16/1**
0006 **10** 2 ½ **Foresight (FR)**[60] 2428 4-9-6 **67** TomEaves 8 31
(Kevin Ryan) *hld up: rdn and outpcd over 2f out: nvr a threat* **20/1**

1m 26.59s (-4.11) **Going Correction** -0.50s/f (Hard)
**WFA** 3 from 4yo+ 8lb **10 Ran SP% 113.3**
Speed ratings (Par 103): **103,102,101,99,99 98,97,92,86,84**
CSF £68.99 CT £292.26 TOTE £11.00: £3.10, £2.30, £1.80; EX 90.90 Trifecta £492.90.
**Owner** T T Racing **Bred** John M Troy **Trained** Tadcaster, N Yorks

**FOCUS**
Distance increased by 9yds. Modest handicap form. The runner-up has been rated to the better view of his maiden form.

## 4530 DISTINCTION DOORS GROUND BREAKING NXT-GEN H'CAP 5f
**4:30** (4:31) (Class 4) (0-85,85) 3-Y-O **£6,469** (£1,925; £962; £481) **Stalls** Centre

Form RPR
0-50 **1** **Stoneyford Lane (IRE)**[26] 3584 3-8-10 **74** (p[1]) RoystonFfrench 3 80
(Steph Hollinshead) *in rr and outpcd: gd run ins fnl f: led towards fin: r.o* **17/2**
4520 **2** 1 **Merry Banter**[12] 4078 3-9-0 **85** ConnorMurtagh(7) 6 87
(Paul Midgley) *racd freely: led: rdn over 1f out: hdd and hld towards fin* **3/1**[2]
3102 **3** 1 ½ **Jack Flash (FR)**[15] 3982 3-9-4 **82** (h) PJMcDonald 5 79
(Les Eyre) *hld up in tch: effrt to take 2nd over 1f out: hung lft ins fnl f: sn lost 2nd: styd on same pce towards fin* **5/2**[1]
1245 **4** 1 **Rock Of America (USA)**[12] 4104 3-9-3 **81** DanielTudhope 4 74
(David O'Meara) *chsd ldrs: wnt 2nd over 2f out: rdn and lost 2nd over 1f out: one pce fnl 100yds* **3/1**[2]
6-01 **5** 1 **Harome (IRE)**[15] 3982 3-9-2 **80** TonyHamilton 1 70
(Roger Fell) *in tch: rdn and outpcd over 2f out: hung lft fr over 1f out: tried to keep on but no imp ins fnl f* **9/1**
1-00 **6** 2 ¼ **Foxcatcher**[23] 3692 3-8-7 **71** (b) SamHitchcott 2 53
(Clive Cox) *chsd ldr tl rdn over 2 fout: wknd ins fnl f* **8/1**[3]

59.96s (-0.84) **Going Correction** -0.325s/f (Firm) **6 Ran SP% 110.2**
Speed ratings (Par 102): **93,91,89,87,85 82**
CSF £32.68 TOTE £11.90: £4.40, £2.00; EX 47.30 Trifecta £131.40.
**Owner** Ocean Four **Bred** J C Bloodstock **Trained** Upper Longdon, Staffs

**FOCUS**
A decent sprint. The runner-up has been rated to form.

## 4531 SUPALITE TILED ROOF APPRENTICE TRAINING SERIES H'CAP (PART OF THE RACING EXCELLENCE INITIATIVE) 5f
**5:00** (5:01) (Class 5) (0-75,70) 3-Y-O+ **£3,557** (£1,058; £529; £264) **Stalls** Centre

Form RPR
0511 **1** **Foxy Boy**[9] 4174 3-9-9 **70** 6ex CallumRodriguez 2 81+
(Michael Dods) *in rr: hdwy wl over 1f out: r.o ins fnl f to get up nr post* **11/10**[1]
120 **2** hd **Razin' Hell**[146] 664 6-9-11 **67** (v) LewisEdmunds 13 76
(John Balding) *led: rdn over 1f out: drifted lft ins fnl f: hdd nr post* **9/1**
0650 **3** 2 ¼ **Toni's A Star**[43] 2962 5-8-10 **54** SophieRalston(2) 8 55
(Tony Carroll) *racd keenly: in tch: rdn over 1f out: kpt on ins fnl f: nt pce of ldrs* **22/1**
5-51 **4** nk **Eternalist**[16] 3944 4-9-3 **61** (h) SeanMooney(2) 5 61
(Jim Goldie) *prom: rdn over 1f out: unable qck ins fnl f: styd on same pce fnl 100yds* **6/1**[3]
0300 **5** ½ **Archimedes (IRE)**[21] 3758 4-9-7 **63** (tp) RowanScott 3 61
(David C Griffiths) *prom: rdn 2f out: one pce u.p fnl 150yds* **14/1**
-532 **6** 1 **Muatadel**[13] 4060 4-9-12 **70** BenSanderson(2) 4 64
(Roger Fell) *hld up in tch: rdn and no imp whn n.m.r and hmpd over 1f out: wl hld ins fnl f* **11/2**[2]
2300 **7** 2 **Spirit Of Zebedee (IRE)**[14] 4015 4-9-9 **65** JoshQuinn 6 52
(John Quinn) *hld up: rdn over 1f out: nvr able to trble ldrs* **20/1**
4026 **8** ½ **Bithynia (IRE)**[12] 4107 3-9-5 **66** (h) RobJFitzpatrick 10 49
(Christopher Kellett) *missed break: impr to chse ldrs over 3f out: rdn 2f out: edgd lft whn one pce over 1f out: n.d after* **25/1**
4405 **9** shd **Emjayem**[19] 3812 7-9-5 **65** MeganEllingworth(4) 1 50
(John Holt) *hld up: rdn and outpcd over 1f out: nvr able to trble ldrs* **25/1**
3130 **10** ½ **Mighty Zip (USA)**[5] 4337 5-9-6 **62** (p) KevinLundie 9 45
(Lisa Williamson) *in tch: rdn over 2f out: wknd over 1f out* **16/1**

1m 0.18s (-0.62) **Going Correction** -0.325s/f (Firm)
**WFA** 3 from 4yo+ 5lb **10 Ran SP% 116.6**
Speed ratings (Par 103): **91,90,87,86,85 84,81,80,80,79**
CSF £10.93 CT £139.60 TOTE £2.00: £1.02, £3.40, £5.00; EX 14.00 Trifecta £181.30.
**Owner** Sekura Group **Bred** Giles W Pritchard-Gordon (farming) Ltd **Trained** Denton, Co Durham

**FOCUS**
A modest enough sprint but the winner did well to land the hat-trick. A turf pb fom the runner-up.
T/Jkpt: Not won. T/Plt: £100.50 to a £1 stake. Pool: £70,285.24. 510.03 winning units. T/Qpdt: £30.80 to a £1 stake. Pool: £4,621.77. 110.84 winning units. **Darren Owen**

# 4251 NEWBURY (L-H)
Thursday, July 6

**OFFICIAL GOING: Good to firm (firm in places; 6.5)**
Wind: light breeze across Weather: sunny with some cloud

## 4532 FRONTIER APPRENTICE H'CAP 5f 34y
**5:55** (5:56) (Class 5) (0-70,72) 3-Y-O+ **£2,911** (£866; £432; £216) **Stalls** High

Form RPR
32-1 **1** **Madame Bounty (IRE)**[31] 3407 3-9-11 **72** JennyPowell 5 85+
(Ed Walker) *rrd leaving stalls and squeezed out sn after: bhd: smooth hdwy fr 3f out: led over 1f out: drifted rt: in command fnl f: readily* **4/1**[2]
4-42 **2** 1 **Our Lord**[10] 4148 5-9-0 **59** PaddyBradley(3) 10 68
(Michael Attwater) *mid-div: rdn and hdwy over 1 out: kpt on ins fnl f: wnt 2nd cl home* **8/1**
3150 **3** ¾ **Babyfact**[23] 3696 6-9-11 **70** KatherineGlenister(3) 7 76
(Malcolm Saunders) *trckd ldrs: rdn over 1f out: kpt on same pce fnl f* **10/1**
1131 **4** 1 ¾ **Major Valentine**[34] 3281 5-9-12 **71** BenRobinson(3) 11 71
(John O'Shea) *prom: led 2f out: sn rdn and hdd: no ex fnl f* **11/2**[3]
4512 **5** 1 ¼ **Lightoller (IRE)**[10] 4157 3-8-13 **65** (b) KeithQuinn(5) 1 59
(Mick Channon) *trckd ldrs: rdn and ev ch whn short of room over 1f out: kpt on same pce fnl f* **17/2**
3-3 **6** 1 ½ **Prominna**[43] 2967 7-9-2 **61** RhiainIngram(3) 6 51
(Tony Carroll) *mid-div: rdn 2f out: nvr any imp* **33/1**
-005 **7** ¾ **Lucky Clover**[19] 3811 6-8-11 **53** (p) GeorgiaCox 3 40
(Malcolm Saunders) *chsd ldrs: ch whn squeezed up jst over 1f out: fdd ins fnl f* **20/1**
0326 **8** nk **Deer Song**[16] 3942 4-8-10 **55** JaneElliott(3) 4 41
(John Bridger) *a towards rr* **33/1**
-132 **9** 2 **Swanton Blue (IRE)**[7] 4256 4-9-9 **70** RossaRyan(5) 9 49
(Ed de Giles) *led at str pce tl hdd 2f out: sn wknd* **2/1**[1]
1624 **10** 2 **Hurricane Alert**[12] 4093 5-8-10 **55** JoshuaBryan(3) 2 39
(Mark Hoad) *hld up: nt clr run over 1f out and again ent fnl f: no ch after* **25/1**

1m 1.38s (-0.02) **Going Correction** +0.10s/f (Good)
**WFA** 3 from 4yo+ 5lb **10 Ran SP% 113.9**
Speed ratings (Par 103): **104,102,101,98,96 94,92,92,89,85**
CSF £33.03 CT £293.35 TOTE £4.20: £1.40, £2.60, £2.60; EX 33.80 Trifecta £333.50.
**Owner** Paola Hewins Olivia Hoare **Bred** Mount Coote Partnership **Trained** Upper Lambourn, Berks

**FOCUS**
It had been a dry, hot day ahead of this evening meeting. Conditions were humid and sultry, with temperatures around 26C, although thunder storms were forecast. A decent apprentices' handicap to start but the pace collapsed and the first three came from off the pace. Fair form. The runner-up has been rated to form, and the third to her fast-ground best.

## 4533 CORNISH ORCHARDS EBF FILLIES' NOVICE STKS (PLUS 10 RACE) 6f
**6:25** (6:27) (Class 4) 2-Y-O **£4,851** (£1,443; £721; £360) **Stalls** High

Form RPR
**1** **Musical Art (IRE)** 2-9-0 0 FranBerry 6 82+
(Paul Cole) *trckd ldr: rdn to ld over 1f out: kpt in wl fnl f* **18/1**
**2** ¾ **Your Choice** 2-9-0 0 JohnFahy 8 80
(Laura Mongan) *led for 1f: trckd ldr: swtchd lft and rdn over 1f out: ev ch ent fnl f: kpt on wl: hld towards fin* **100/1**
4 **3** 3 ¾ **Golden Footsteps (IRE)**[23] 3687 2-9-0 0 LiamKeniry 11 69+
(Ed Walker) *mid-div: rdn over 1f out: kpt on ins fnl f: snatched 3rd fnl stride* **7/1**
4 **4** shd **Early Dawn**[23] 3697 2-9-0 0 HarryBentley 9 68
(Marco Botti) *trckd ldrs: rdn and v ch over 1f out: nt pce of front pair fnl f: lost 3rd fnl stride* **3/1**[1]
**5** nk **Chillala (IRE)** 2-9-0 0 (h[1]) StevieDonohoe 2 67
(Harry Dunlop) *led after 1f: drifted to stands' side rails and rdn 2f out: hdd over 1f out: no ex fnl f* **50/1**



The Form Book Flat, Raceform Ltd, Newbury, RG14 5SJ

6 ½ **Puchita (IRE)** 2-9-0 0 RyanMoore 7 66+
(Richard Hannon) *hld up towards rr: hmpd after 1f: rdn and hdwy over 1f out: kpt on ins fnl f but nt pce to get on terms* **6/1**³
7 ¾ **Sarshampla (IRE)** 2-9-0 0 OisinMurphy 1 64+
(David Simcock) *mid-div: hdwy 2f out: sn rdn to chal for 4th: fdd fnl 140yds* **7/2**²
8 shd **Hollywood Dream** 2-9-0 0 MartinDwyer 10 63+
(William Muir) *s.i.s: bhd: hmpd after 1f: hdwy ent fnl f: kpt on but no threat fnl f* **50/1**
03 9 nk **Little Miss Lilly**[19] 3815 2-9-0 0 AdamKirby 16 62
(Clive Cox) *mid-div: rdn 2f out: nvr any imp* **7/1**
10 nk **Wear It Well** 2-9-0 0 FergusSweeney 13 61
(Henry Candy) *rdn 2f out: a mid-div* **22/1**
11 ½ **Paint** 2-9-0 0 TomMarquand 12 60
(Richard Hannon) *mid-div: rdn 2f out: no imp* **16/1**
12 1 ½ **Cwynar** 2-9-0 0 SteveDrowne 5 55+
(Charles Hills) *towards rr: sme minor late prog: nvr any threat* **20/1**
13 2 ¼ **Sixties Secret** 2-9-0 0 JFEgan 15 49
(Mick Channon) *a towards rr* **50/1**
14 ½ **Counterfeit** 2-9-0 0 ShaneKelly 14 47
(Richard Hughes) *trckd ldrs: rdn over 2f out: wknd over 1f out* **12/1**
15 1 ¾ **Mystique** 2-8-11 0 CallumShepherd(3) 4 42
(Charles Hills) *towards rr of midfield: rdn over 2f out: wknd ent fnl f* **33/1**
16 2 ¼ **Ritha** 2-9-0 0 JimCrowley 3 35
(Richard Hannon) *mid-div tl wknd 2f out* **25/1**

1m 13.48s (0.48) **Going Correction** +0.10s/f (Good) **16** Ran SP% **128.1**
Speed ratings (Par 93): **100,99,94,93,93 92,91,91,91,90 90,88,85,84,82 79**
CSF £1247.63 TOTE £20.30: £6.00, £26.20, £2.40; EX 3099.80.
**Owner** Mrs Fitri Hay **Bred** Rathbarry Stud **Trained** Whatcombe, Oxon

**FOCUS**
A fair fillies' novices' sprint and the pace was genuine. The first two drew a little way clear of the remainder. The form should hold firm.

## 4534 FULLER'S LONDON PRIDE NOVICE STKS (PLUS 10 RACE) (C&G) 6f
**7:00** (7:00) (Class 4) 2-Y-O **£5,175** (£1,540; £769; £384) **Stalls** High

Form RPR
64 1 **Major Peirson (IRE)**[31] 3390 2-9-0 0 JFEgan 5 85+
(Jo Hughes) *mde all: kpt on strly to draw clr ent fnl f: comf* **9/1**
2 5 **Warsaan** 2-9-0 0 FranBerry 3 73+
(Owen Burrows) *hmpd leaving stalls: hld up: hdwy over 2f out: running on whn hmpd and snatched up ent fnl f: no ch after but kpt on wl to go 2nd nring fin* **8/1**
3 ½ **Alkhalifa (IRE)** 2-9-0 0 JimCrowley 8 69
(Brian Meehan) *trckd ldrs: chsd wnr ent fnl f: kpt on but nt pce to threaten: lost 2nd towards fin* **4/1**³
4 ¾ **Bobby's Charm (USA)** 2-9-0 0 PatCosgrave 1 66
(Robert Cowell) *trckd ldr: rn green whn rdn over 1f out: one pce fnl f* **13/2**
5 3 ¾ **Oliver Reed (IRE)** 2-9-0 0 SeanLevey 6 55
(Richard Hannon) *racd keenly: trckd ldrs: edgd lft over 2f out: sn rdn: nt qckn: fdd ins fnl f* **5/2**¹
6 2 **Bhodi (IRE)** 2-9-0 0 RyanMoore 7 49
(Sir Michael Stoute) *trckd ldrs: hung lft whn rdn over 1f out: wknd fnl f* **7/2**²
7 shd **Salsa Verde (IRE)** 2-8-11 0 CallumShepherd(3) 9 49
(Ed de Giles) *hld up last pair: rdn 2f out: nt pce to get involved: fdd ins fnl f* **25/1**
8 10 **Ocean Side** 2-9-0 0 TomMarquand 2 19
(Richard Hannon) *last trio: outpcd over 3f out: sn btn* **14/1**

1m 13.28s (0.28) **Going Correction** +0.10s/f (Good) **8** Ran SP% **115.8**
Speed ratings (Par 96): **102,95,94,93,88 86,85,72**
CSF £78.62 TOTE £11.30: £2.50, £2.70, £1.50; EX 89.70 Trifecta £481.90.
**Owner** Mrs C C Regalado-Gonzalez & Jo Hughes **Bred** Mrs C Regalado-Gonzalez **Trained** Lambourn, Berks

**FOCUS**
Some well-bred and expensive purchases were making their debuts in this sprint for novices, but the winner was the only one with previous experience and made all up the stands' rail. Fair form.

## 4535 LILLEMOR PENSER SILVER BAR H'CAP 1m 4f
**7:30** (7:32) (Class 3) (0-90,93) 3-Y-O **£9,703** (£2,887; £1,443; £721) **Stalls** Centre

Form RPR
0154 1 **Duke Of Bronte**[20] 3779 3-9-1 **81** OisinMurphy 5 89
(Rod Millman) *trckd ldrs: nt clrest of runs fr 2f out: qcknd up wl to ld jst ins fnl f: kpt on wl: pushed out* **10/1**
1-13 2 nk **Melting Dew**[27] 3528 3-9-3 **83** (v¹) RyanMoore 7 90
(Sir Michael Stoute) *rousted along on leaving stalls: sn pressing ldr: led 3f out: sn rdn: hdd jst ins fnl f: kpt on* **5/1**²
2121 3 shd **On To Victory**[8] 4221 3-9-13 **93** 6ex (h) TomMarquand 3 99
(Eve Johnson Houghton) *hld up last pair but in tch: swtchd rt and hdwy over 1f out: sn rdn: kpt on to chal ins fnl f: hld nring fin* **13/8**¹
16 4 1 **The Grand Visir**[41] 3032 3-9-5 **85** (p¹) PatCosgrave 4 91+
(William Haggas) *s.i.s: sn trcking ldrs: swtchd rt 2f out: sn rdn: kpt on but nt quite pce to chal* **7/1**
5-21 5 7 **Cross Step (USA)**[43] 2963 3-9-5 **85** (p) AdamKirby 8 83+
(Charlie Appleby) *trckd ldrs: rdn and ev ch 2f out: wknd ent fnl f* **13/2**³
1-04 6 1 ½ **Rosarno (IRE)**[28] 3505 3-9-0 **80** (bt) SilvestreDeSousa 6 71
(Charles Hills) *hld up: hdwy and effrt 2f out: sn wandered u.p: wknd over 1f out* **9/1**
4-31 7 ¾ **See Of Rome**[8] 4224 3-9-3 **83** 6ex ShaneKelly 2 73
(Richard Hughes) *led tl 3f out: sn rdn: wkng whn short of room over 1f out* **7/1**

2m 33.76s (-1.74) **Going Correction** -0.025s/f (Good) **7** Ran SP% **112.2**
Speed ratings (Par 104): **104,103,103,103,98 97,96**
CSF £56.23 CT £122.62 TOTE £7.80: £2.40, £2.90; EX 69.10 Trifecta £305.60.
**Owner** Perfect Match **Bred** Harts Farm Stud **Trained** Kentisbeare, Devon

**FOCUS**
Rail alignment added 35 yards to the official distance. A decent handicap run at an unsatisfactory early pace and it turned into something of a sprint. Not form to trust entirely. The third has been rated a bit below his Salisbury win.

## 4536 SEAFARERS EBF STALLIONS FILLIES' H'CAP 6f
**8:05** (8:07) (Class 4) (0-85,86) 3-Y-O+ **£5,983** (£1,780; £889; £444) **Stalls** High

Form RPR
0201 1 **Staintondale Lass (IRE)**[44] 2912 4-9-8 **86** FinleyMarsh(7) 3 98
(Ed Vaughan) *s.i.s: towards rr: gd hdwy whn swtchd lft 2f out: drifting rt whn ldng over 1f out: r.o wl: readily* **8/1**
1063 2 2 ¾ **Carolinae**[13] 4051 5-10-1 **86** StevieDonohoe 8 89+
(Charlie Fellowes) *hld up: hdwy 2f out: nt clr run jst over 1f out: kpt on wl to go 2nd fnl 150yds but nt pce of wnr* **11/2**³
033 3 nk **Belledesert**[8] 4201 4-9-12 **83** AdamKirby 9 85
(Steph Hollinshead) *mid-div: hdwy whn nt clr run jst over 1f out: kpt on wl ins fnl f* **4/1**²
1212 4 hd **Angel Of Darkness**[13] 4051 3-9-5 **85** CallumShepherd(3) 6 86+
(Charles Hills) *s.i.s: in tch: nt clr run over 2f out tl over 1f out: nt pce to get on terms whn gap appeared ent fnl f* **7/2**¹
3-31 5 2 ¼ **Carpe Diem Lady (IRE)**[20] 3773 4-9-6 **77** (v) RyanMoore 5 71
(Ralph Beckett) *trckd ldrs: led briefly 2f out: sn rdn: no ex fnl f* **7/2**¹
61 6 3 ¼ **Magic Approach**[114] 1192 3-8-3 **66** oh2 MartinDwyer 1 49
(David Simcock) *mid-div: hdwy for effrt in center 2f out: wknd ins fnl f* **33/1**
1624 7 1 ¾ **Mia Cara**[100] 1411 3-8-4 **67** (v) JFEgan 7 44
(David Evans) *trckd ldrs: rdn and ev ch 2f out: wknd fnl f* **22/1**
3611 8 hd **Jersey Breeze (IRE)**[13] 4043 4-9-3 **81** (v) KeithQuinn(7) 4 59
(Mick Channon) *wnt lft s: chsd ldrs: rdn and ev ch 2f out: sn short of room: wknd fnl f* **15/2**
-503 9 3 **Dainty Dandy (IRE)**[12] 4081 3-9-4 **81** (b) FranBerry 2 48
(Paul Cole) *racd keenly: led: steadily edgd to stands' side rails: hdd 2f out: sn wknd* **16/1**

1m 12.82s (-0.18) **Going Correction** +0.10s/f (Good)
**WFA** 3 from 4yo+ 6lb **9** Ran SP% **115.9**
Speed ratings (Par 102): **105,101,100,100,97 93,91,90,86**
CSF £51.66 CT £205.51 TOTE £8.00: £2.60, £2.10, £1.80; EX 47.20 Trifecta £228.90.
**Owner** A M Pickering **Bred** Ringfort Stud **Trained** Newmarket, Suffolk

**FOCUS**
A strong early pace and the first three home all came from off the pace. The form looks viable. The first two have been rated to form.

## 4537 OLIVER'S ISLAND H'CAP 1m (S)
**8:35** (8:39) (Class 5) (0-75,75) 3-Y-O **£3,234** (£962; £481; £240) **Stalls** High

Form RPR
-600 1 **Native Soldier (IRE)**[20] 3784 3-9-7 **75** (p¹) TomQueally 11 82+
(William Haggas) *hld up: hdwy 3f out: rdn 2f out: led jst over 1f out: drifted lft but r.o wl to assert fnl 140yds* **16/1**
0363 2 1 **Fastnet Spin (IRE)**[10] 4153 3-9-4 **72** (b) JFEgan 7 76
(David Evans) *hld up: hdwy over 2f out: rdn to chse ldrs wl over 1f out: ev ch ent fnl f: kpt on but no ex fnl 120yds* **14/1**
-516 3 shd **Zebulon (IRE)**[24] 3673 3-9-6 **74** SeanLevey 4 77
(Richard Hannon) *stdd s: mid-div: hdwy over 2f out: rdn and ev ch over 1f out: kpt on but no ex fnl 120yds* **12/1**
334 4 2 **Stararchitecture (IRE)**[28] 3485 3-9-7 **75** (bt¹) PatCosgrave 10 73
(William Haggas) *mid-div: rdn 2f out: kpt on ins fnl f: wnt 4th fnl 120yds* **8/1**
-450 5 3 **Milburn Jack**[20] 3784 3-9-5 **73** (p¹) AdamKirby 16 63
(Clive Cox) *prom: led narrowly over 2f out: sn rdn: hdd jst over 1f out: no ex* **16/1**
2-10 6 ½ **Evening Hill**[31] 3392 3-9-5 **73** ShaneKelly 2 61
(Richard Hughes) *hld up bhd: rdn 2f out: styd on fnl f: nvr any threat* **6/1**³
034 7 1 ½ **Tidal Watch (IRE)**[30] 3435 3-9-4 **72** FranBerry 8 56
(Jonjo O'Neill) *nvr bttr than mid-div* **20/1**
41-0 8 hd **Habbad (FR)**[62] 2361 3-9-7 **75** TomMarquand 6 59
(Richard Hannon) *led: rdn and narrowly hdd over 2f out: wknd ent fnl f* **10/1**
00-4 9 ½ **So Hoity Toity**[13] 4050 3-9-6 **74** SilvestreDeSousa 9 56
(Hughie Morrison) *trckd ldrs: rdn over 2f out: ev ch over 1f out tl ent fnl f: wknd* **4/1**¹
1364 10 nse **Revel**[20] 3784 3-9-6 **74** (t) OisinMurphy 12 56
(Stuart Williams) *trckd ldrs: rdn over 2f out: hld whn hmpd over 1f out: wknd* **13/2**
4550 11 1 ¾ **Olympic Legend (IRE)**[17] 3922 3-8-7 **64** CallumShepherd(3) 15 41
(Martin Bosley) *mid-div: rdn over 2f out: wknd over 1f out* **33/1**
-560 12 10 **Red Emperor (IRE)**[17] 3922 3-8-8 **62** (p¹) MartinDwyer 13 12
(Amanda Perrett) *sn rousted along and reminders: chsd ldrs: drvn over 3f out: wknd over 1f out* **33/1**
6004 13 2 ¼ **Know The Truth**[8] 4214 3-8-8 **67** JoshuaBryan(5) 1 11
(Andrew Balding) *wnt lft s: sn mid-div: rdn over 2f out: wknd over 1f out* **11/2**²

1m 39.6s (-0.10) **Going Correction** +0.10s/f (Good) **13** Ran SP% **120.0**
Speed ratings (Par 100): **104,103,102,100,97 97,95,95,95,95 93,83,81**
CSF £219.25 CT £2867.52 TOTE £12.90: £3.60, £3.10, £4.40; EX 274.00 Trifecta £2561.90.
**Owner** Mohamed Obaida **Bred** Rabbah Bloodstock Limited **Trained** Newmarket, Suffolk

**FOCUS**
A run-of-the-mill handicap and not a strongly-run affair, with the winner coming from off the pace. The form looks open to question. It's been rated around the runner-up.

## 4538 WILD RIVER H'CAP 1m 2f
**9:05** (9:05) (Class 5) (0-70,72) 4-Y-O+ **£3,234** (£962; £481; £240) **Stalls** Centre

Form RPR
-342 1 **Monsieur Glory**[19] 3820 4-9-8 **71** (v) PatCosgrave 8 79
(Tom Clover) *a.p: led wl over 2f out: kpt on strly ins fnl f: drvn out* **7/4**¹
1200 2 2 ¼ **Chelwood Gate (IRE)**[15] 3966 7-9-3 **66** (v) OisinMurphy 5 69
(Conor Dore) *hld up: hdwy over 2f out: sn rdn: swtchd lft into cl 3rd ent fnl f: kpt on to go 2nd fnl 120yds but nt pce of wnr* **16/1**
4-40 3 ½ **With Pleasure**[39] 648 4-9-5 **68** DanielMuscutt 7 70
(John Flint) *in tch: hdwy 4f out: chal 3f out: sn rdn: ev ch over 1f out: kpt on but no ex ins fnl f* **17/2**
5-12 4 2 **Thello**[12] 4082 5-9-7 **70** SteveDrowne 3 68
(Jo Hughes) *racd keenly: trckd ldrs: rdn 2f out: kpt on same pce fnl f* **9/2**³
00-0 5 ¾ **Silver Dixie (USA)**[21] 3753 7-9-5 **68** AdamKirby 4 65
(Peter Hedger) *hld up: rdn over 2f out: styd on fnl f but nvr gng pce to get involved* **6/1**
-661 6 8 **Golden Isles (IRE)**[12] 4088 4-8-6 **55** HarryBentley 6 36
(Heather Main) *racd keenly: led: hdd wl over 2f out: sn rdn: wknd over 1f out* **7/2**²
4536 7 ½ **Jersey Bull (IRE)**[108] 1283 5-8-13 **62** (h) LiamKeniry 10 42
(Michael Madgwick) *hld up: rdn wl over 2f out: nvr threatened* **28/1**
000- 8 11 **Prosecute (FR)**[259] 7486 4-9-9 **72** TomMarquand 9 30
(Ali Stronge) *trckd ldrs: rdn 2f out: sn btn* **25/1**

2m 9.59s (0.79) **Going Correction** -0.025s/f (Good) **8** Ran SP% **114.8**
Speed ratings (Par 103): **95,93,92,91,90 84,83,75**
CSF £33.14 CT £191.59 TOTE £2.50: £1.20, £2.50, £2.60; EX 29.80 Trifecta £155.30.
**Owner** J Collins & C Fahy **Bred** Crossfields Bloodstock Ltd **Trained** Newmarket, Suffolk

**FOCUS**
Rail alignment added 35 yards to the official distance. A modest handicap run at a dawdling early pace and despite turning into a sprint, they finished well strung out. The winner got first run and the form should not be taken at face value. The winner has been rated to the better view of his form, with the third and fourth to form.
T/Plt: £21,156.80 to a £1 stake Pool: £76,802.18. 2.65 winning units. T/Qpdt: £874.20 to a £1 stake. Pool: £7,607.91. 6.44 winning units. **Tim Mitchell**

## 4318 YARMOUTH (L-H)
Thursday, July 6

**OFFICIAL GOING: Good to firm (7.7) changing to soft after 1.50 (race 1)**
Wind: light, half against Weather: thunder storm until after race 1, thundery showers after

### 4539 BRITISH STALLION STUDS EBF NOVICE STKS (PLUS 10 RACE) 6f 3y
**1:50** (1:50) (Class 4) 2-Y-O **£4,657** (£1,386; £692; £346) **Stalls** Centre

Form RPR
20 1 **Hey Gaman**[12] 4068 2-9-2 0 ........ MartinHarley 3 99+
(James Tate) *mde all: pushed along and readily wnt clr over 1f out: in command and r.o wl fnl f: eased nr fin: unchal* **1/1**[1]
2 2 4 **Arbalet (IRE)**[19] 3846 2-9-2 0 ........ JosephineGordon 2 86+
(Hugo Palmer) *hld up in tch: swtchd rt and effrt to chse wnr 2f out: rdn and nt match pce of wnr over 1f out: styd on for clr 2nd ins fnl f* **6/4**[2]
3 11 **Johni Boxit** 2-9-2 0 ........ DanielMuscutt 4 51
(Gay Kelleway) *wnt rt s: in tch in rr: hdwy to chse ldrs 1/2-way: rdn 2f out: outpcd u.p over 1f out: no ch and battling for modest 3rd fnl f: kpt on* **80/1**
41 4 ½ **Gotti (USA)**[17] 3917 2-9-8 0 ........ GeraldMosse 1 55
(Jeremy Noseda) *hld up in tch: effrt to chse ldrs 2f out: outpcd u.p over 1f out: no ch and battling for modest 3rd fnl f: kpt on* **5/1**[3]
0 5 1½ **Elusive Bird**[36] 3215 2-8-11 0 ........ LiamJones 7 39
(Giles Bravery) *pushed rt s: chsd wnr: rdn over 2f out: lost pl 2f out and sn outpcd: wl hld 5th fnl f* **125/1**
5 6 10 **Expediate**[20] 3776 2-9-2 0 ........ LukeMorris 5 12
(Robert Cowell) *pushed rt s: chsd ldrs: rdn 1/2-way: dropped to rr 2f out: sn wl bhd: eased wl ins fnl f* **25/1**

1m 12.2s (-2.20) **Going Correction** -0.45s/f (Firm) 6 Ran SP% **112.5**
Speed ratings (Par 96): **96,90,76,75,73 60**
CSF £2.78 TOTE £1.90: £1.20, £1.10; EX 3.10 Trifecta £45.90.
**Owner** Sultan Ali **Bred** Rabbah Bloodstock Limited **Trained** Newmarket, Suffolk
**FOCUS**
The going was good to firm. They went a steady pace for this interesting contest with the field racing up the centre.

### 4540 188BET (S) STKS 1m 3y
**2:20** (2:20) (Class 6) 3-Y-O **£2,264** (£673; £336; £168) **Stalls** Centre

Form RPR
2033 1 **Glorvina (IRE)**[24] 3649 3-8-9 64 ........ AndreaAtzeni 4 59
(David O'Meara) *mde all: hld on wl u.p ins fnl f* **8/11**[1]
00 2 nk **Borntosin (IRE)**[57] 2521 3-9-0 0 ........ (t[1]) LukeMorris 3 63
(Marco Botti) *hld up in tch: effrt to press ldr over 1f out: ev ch fnl f: a hld* **13/2**[3]
-600 3 6 **Showdance Kid**[21] 3745 3-9-0 66 ........ MartinHarley 6 50
(K R Burke) *hld up in tch: swtchd rt 2f out: effrt and pressing ldrs over 1f out: btn 1f out: wknd* **5/2**[2]
-406 4 3 **Mungo Madness**[23] 3701 3-8-11 52 ........ ShelleyBirkett(3) 2 44
(Julia Feilden) *prom: struggling 2f out: sn btn* **18/1**
00-0 5 24 **Miss Island Ruler**[9] 4174 3-8-2 46 ........ AledBeech(7) 1
(Shaun Harris) *bhd 3f out: sn lost tch* **40/1**

1m 47.05s (6.45) **Going Correction** -0.45s/f (Firm) 5 Ran SP% **107.5**
Speed ratings (Par 98): **49,48,42,39,15**
CSF £5.76 TOTE £1.30: £1.10, £2.60; EX 4.80 Trifecta £7.30.The winner was bought in 4,000gns. Showdance Kid claimed by John Wainwright for £6,000.
**Owner** Nick Bradley Racing 1 **Bred** Liam Queally **Trained** Upper Helmsley, N Yorks
**FOCUS**
Racing was delayed for 30 minutes due to a heavy storm. The going was eased to soft, from good to firm, prior to the second race. An uncompetitive seller with the front two pulling a long way clear. A token rating has been put on the race through the third to this year's level, with the winner just off.

### 4541 JENNINGSBET H'CAP 1m 3y
**2:50** (2:50) (Class 5) (0-70,70) 3-Y-O+ **£2,911** (£866; £432; £216) **Stalls** Centre

Form RPR
-032 1 **Turning Gold**[13] 4050 3-8-10 61 ........ (b) LukeMorris 6 76
(Sir Mark Prescott Bt) *t.k.h: mde virtually all: rdn clr and in command over 1f out: styd on wl* **2/1**[1]
5062 2 3¾ **Sir Gnet (IRE)**[7] 4255 3-9-0 65 ........ (h) JosephineGordon 3 70
(Ed Dunlop) *in tch: rdn 3f out: chsd clr wnr over 1f out: no imp* **2/1**[1]
-662 3 1½ **Pacific Salt (IRE)**[13] 4047 4-9-4 67 ........ WilliamCox(7) 1 71
(Pam Sly) *in tch: effrt ent fnl 2f: 3rd and kpt on same pce fnl f* **8/1**[3]
5311 4 1¾ **Lunar Deity**[16] 3940 8-9-7 70 ........ (t) MillyNaseb(7) 4 70
(Stuart Williams) *in tch: effrt to chse wnr 2f out: 4th and no ex over 1f out: no imp and wl hld fnl f* **4/1**[2]
35-1 5 1 **Tan Arabiq**[180] 122 4-9-11 70 ........ AlistairRawlinson(3) 8 68
(Michael Appleby) *t.k.h: trckd ldrs: rdn ent fnl 2f: wknd fnl f* **20/1**
5-50 6 13 **Scarlet Thrush (IRE)**[114] 1195 3-9-0 65 ........ (b[1]) AndreaAtzeni 7 31
(Marco Botti) *w ldr tl 1/2-way: dropped to rr and n.m.r 2f out: sn bhd* **9/1**

1m 39.22s (-1.38) **Going Correction** -0.45s/f (Firm)
**WFA** 3 from 4yo+ 9lb 6 Ran SP% **112.5**
Speed ratings (Par 103): **88,84,82,81,80 67**
CSF £6.09 CT £23.24 TOTE £2.30: £1.60, £1.50; EX 7.70 Trifecta £24.90.
**Owner** Mrs Helen Jones **Bred** Cheveley Park Stud Ltd **Trained** Newmarket, Suffolk
**FOCUS**
Four withdrawals took some interest out of this handicap. It was run at a steady pace and the winner did it nicely. The third has been rated to his turf form.

### 4542 GROSVENOR CASINO MAGIC QUEEN TRIBUTE EVENING H'CAP 7f 3y
**3:20** (3:20) (Class 5) (0-70,72) 3-Y-O+ **£2,911** (£866; £432; £216) **Stalls** Centre

Form RPR
1602 1 **Alemaratalyoum (IRE)**[25] 3621 3-9-8 72 ........ LukeMorris 9 76
(Ed Dunlop) *hld up in tch in last trio: effrt 2f out: chsd ldrs 1f out: kpt on wl u.p to ld cl home* **3/1**[1]
5400 2 hd **Gunmaker (IRE)**[25] 3621 3-9-2 66 ........ MartinLane 6 69
(David Simcock) *stdd and wnt rt s: hld up in tch: effrt and clsng whn nt clr run jst over 1f out: hdwy u.p and lft in ld wl ins fnl f: hdd nr fin* **10/1**
2144 3 ½ **Anastazia**[22] 3730 5-9-12 68 ........ JoeyHaynes 10 72
(Paul D'Arcy) *chsd ldrs: rdn ent fnl 2f: ev ch wl ins fnl f: styd on same pce towards fin* **3/1**[1]
16 4 1 **Edged In Blue**[19] 3822 3-9-0 64 ........ MartinHarley 4 62
(K R Burke) *wnt rt s: t.k.h: chsd ldrs: rdn over 2f out: kpt on same pce ins fnl f* **5/1**[2]
-400 5 nk **Bay Watch (IRE)**[18] 3870 3-8-10 60 ........ (b[1]) ThomasBrown 8 58
(Andrew Balding) *t.k.h: led: rdn over 1f out: sn hanging bdly lft: hdd wl ins fnl f: eased towards fin* **20/1**
0304 6 nk **Aqua Libre**[30] 3441 4-9-13 69 ........ (t) JosephineGordon 3 69
(Philip McBride) *t.k.h: hld up wl in tch: effrt to chse ldrs over 1f out: styd on same pce ins fnl f* **11/2**[3]
5440 7 ¾ **De Vegas Kid (IRE)**[25] 3627 3-8-3 53 ........ JimmyQuinn 5 48
(Tony Carroll) *t.k.h: chsd ldr tl 2f out: sn lost pl: kpt on same pce ins fnl f* **8/1**
10-0 8 ¾ **He's My Boy (IRE)**[40] 3074 6-9-11 70 ........ (v) GeorgeWood(3) 7 66
(James Fanshawe) *dwlt and short of room leaving stalls: hld up in rr: effrt 2f out: no imp over 1f out: kpt on same pce ins fnl f* **12/1**

1m 27.93s (1.33) **Going Correction** -0.45s/f (Firm)
**WFA** 3 from 4yo+ 8lb 8 Ran SP% **114.7**
Speed ratings (Par 103): **74,73,73,72,71 71,70,69**
CSF £34.58 CT £97.17 TOTE £2.70: £1.20, £2.60, £1.30; EX 20.80 Trifecta £84.30.
**Owner** Mohammed Jaber **Bred** Ammerland Verwaltung Gmbh & Co Kg **Trained** Newmarket, Suffolk
**FOCUS**
The pace was steady for this fair handicap. It's been rated around the third.

### 4543 GREAT YARMOUTH RACECOURSE SUPPORTING RACING STAFF WEEK H'CAP 5f 42y
**3:50** (4:22) (Class 6) (0-60,61) 3-Y-O+ **£2,264** (£673; £336; £168) **Stalls** Centre

Form RPR
4000 1 **Cherry Kool**[13] 4053 4-9-8 58 ........ AndreaAtzeni 9 66
(Stuart Williams) *trckd ldrs: clsd and cantering upsides ldrs over 1f out: pushed ahd 1f out: sn wnt clr: easily* **7/4**[1]
0-00 2 3¼ **Proud Kate**[50] 2727 3-8-5 46 oh1 ........ (h) LiamJones 2 41
(Christine Dunnett) *swtchd rt after s: in tch in last pair: hdwy u.p over 1f out: edgd lft ins fnl f: styd on to go 2nd towards fin: no ch w wnr* **50/1**
0000 3 hd **Sakhee's Jem**[23] 3702 4-9-5 55 ........ DanielMuscutt 1 51
(Gay Kelleway) *chsd ldrs: shkn up 2f out: rdn over 1f out: carried lft jst ins fnl f: kpt on to go 3rd last stride: no ch w wnr* **4/1**[3]
0200 4 shd **Percy Toplis**[14] 4005 3-8-5 49 ........ (v) GeorgeWood(3) 4 43
(Christine Dunnett) *chsd ldr: rdn 1/2-way: drvn 2f out: unable qck over 1f out: chsd clr wnr 100yds out: kpt on same pce and lost 2 pls cl home* **13/2**
4006 5 2 **Popsilca**[10] 4157 3-8-11 52 ........ GeraldMosse 8 41
(Mick Quinn) *led: rdn and jnd by cantering wnr over 1f out: sn outpcd: lost 2nd and wknd fnl 100yds* **5/2**[2]
0000 6 6 **Willow Spring**[13] 4053 5-8-7 46 oh1 ........ TimClark(3) 7 21
(Denis Quinn) *stdd s: t.k.h: hld up in rr: effrt 2f out: sn btn: wknd fnl f* **7/1**

1m 3.31s (0.61) **Going Correction** -0.45s/f (Firm)
**WFA** 3 from 4yo+ 5lb 6 Ran SP% **112.7**
Speed ratings (Par 101): **77,71,71,71,68 58**
CSF £65.82 CT £313.28 TOTE £2.40: £1.60, £8.70; EX 44.30 Trifecta £175.90.
**Owner** B Piper & D Shekells **Bred** Old Mill Stud **Trained** Newmarket, Suffolk
**FOCUS**
A modest handicap but the winner did it well. The second and third suggest this is very limited form.

### 4544 MOULTON NURSERY OF ACLE H'CAP 1m 1f 21y
**4:20** (4:51) (Class 4) (0-80,80) 3-Y-O **£4,690** (£1,395; £697; £348) **Stalls** Low

Form RPR
350 1 **Voi**[14] 4003 3-8-10 69 ........ (t) GeraldMosse 2 72
(Conrad Allen) *taken down early: t.k.h: hld up in tch: effrt 2f out: clsd and rdn to chal 1f out: styd on u.p to ld wl ins fnl f: hld on wl* **20/1**
4-44 2 hd **Tamayef (IRE)**[22] 3727 3-9-4 77 ........ JosephineGordon 4 79
(Hugo Palmer) *t.k.h: led: rdn 2f out: hdd ins fnl f: kpt on gamely and ev ch after: jst hld towards fin* **3/1**[2]
1406 3 ½ **Millie's Kiss**[23] 3700 3-8-3 69 ........ MillyNaseb(7) 5 70
(Philip McBride) *chsd ldrs: effrt on inner 2f out: nt clr run and swtchd rt 1f out: styd on strly fnl 100yds: nt quite rch ldrs* **14/1**
3-21 4 ½ **Daira Prince (IRE)**[22] 3727 3-9-7 80 ........ AndreaAtzeni 6 80
(Roger Varian) *trckd ldrs: clsd to join ldr 2f: sn rdn: led ins fnl f: sn hdd and styd on same pce fnl 100yds* **1/1**[1]
041 5 8 **Star Gypsy (FR)**[30] 3435 3-9-7 80 ........ LukeMorris 1 62
(Luca Cumani) *chsd ldr: rdn over 2f out: sn dropped to rr: wknd over 1f out* **10/3**[3]

1m 58.1s (2.30) **Going Correction** +0.25s/f (Good) 5 Ran SP% **109.5**
Speed ratings (Par 102): **99,98,98,97,90**
CSF £75.98 TOTE £18.50: £6.50, £1.40; EX 84.00 Trifecta £224.40.
**Owner** B Homewood & Partner **Bred** Al Asayl Bloodstock Ltd **Trained** Newmarket, Suffolk
**FOCUS**
They went a steady pace for this fair handicap. The runner-up has been rated to his C&D latest, with the third close to form.

### 4545 188BET.CO.UK "HANDS AND HEELS" APPRENTICE H'CAP (PART OF THE RACING EXCELLENCE INITIATIVE) 1m 3f 104y
**4:50** (5:20) (Class 6) (0-60,66) 4-Y-O+ **£2,264** (£673; £336; £168) **Stalls** Low

Form RPR
6501 1 **Shining Romeo**[9] 4187 5-9-10 66 6ex ........ WilliamCox(3) 6 72
(Denis Quinn) *hld up in tch and travelling wl: clsd to ld wl over 1f out: pushed along and a doing enough ins fnl f* **10/11**[1]
6455 2 1¼ **Aumerle**[25] 3623 5-9-6 62 ........ (p[1]) NicolaCurrie(3) 1 66
(Shaun Lycett) *t.k.h: led for 1f: chsd ldr after tl led again 2f out: sn hdd: kpt on u.p but a hld* **16/1**
0-55 3 3 **Duke Of Sonning**[26] 3566 5-9-7 60 ........ (b) MillyNaseb 5 59
(Shaun Harris) *s.i.s: hdwy to ld after 2f: rdn and hdd 2f out: no ex 1f out: wknd fnl 100yds* **40/1**
0033 4 2½ **Saga Sprint (IRE)**[7] 4279 4-9-4 60 ........ GinaMangan(3) 3 56
(J R Jenkins) *bustled along early: in tch: effrt 2f out: 4th and no imp over 1f out* **8/1**[3]
5304 5 9 **Go On Gal (IRE)**[30] 3439 4-8-12 54 ........ TristanPrice(3) 2 36
(Julia Feilden) *t.k.h: w ldr for 2f: chsd ldrs tl rdn and struggling over 2f out: sn wknd* **5/1**[2]

/000 **6** *3 1/4* **Jeremy's Jet (IRE)**[26] 3575 6-8-13 **52** ............ AledBeech 4 29
(Tony Carroll) *t.k.h early: chsd ldrs for 2f: midfield after tl rdn and struggling 3f out: wl btn fnl 2f* **5/1**[2]

500 **7** *8* **Lagopus**[14] 4003 4-8-5 **49** ............ GeorgeBass(5) 7 13
(David Simcock) *hld up in rr: rdn 3f out: no rspnse and wl btn fnl 2f* **20/1**

2m 31.13s (2.43) **Going Correction** +0.25s/f (Good) 7 Ran SP% **109.9**
Speed ratings (Par 101): **101,100,97,96,89 87,81**
CSF £16.28 TOTE £1.70: £1.10, £6.10; EX 13.70 Trifecta £87.50.
**Owner** John Mangan **Bred** Newsells Park Stud **Trained** Newmarket, Suffolk

**FOCUS**
An uncompetitive handicap run at a steady pace. Straightforward form.
T/Plt: £15.30 to a £1 stake. Pool: £66,254.48. 3,149.09 winning units. T/Qpdt: £10.70 to a £1 stake. Pool: £4,271.11. 294.83 winning units. **Steve Payne**

4546 - 4553a (Foreign Racing) - See Raceform Interactive

## 4167 BEVERLEY (R-H)
Friday, July 7

**OFFICIAL GOING: Good to firm (good in places; 7.7)**
Wind: Light against Weather: Cloudy

### 4554 PARTY ON THE PASTURE (S) STKS 7f 96y
**6:10** (6:10) (Class 6) 3-Y-O+ **£1,678** (£1,678; £384; £192) **Stalls** Low

Form RPR
-064 **1** **Iberica Road (USA)**[13] 4105 4-9-2 69 ............ BenCurtis 7 60
(Grant Tuer) *mde all: rdn and strly pressed over 2f out: kpt on wl: jnd post* **7/2**[2]

2535 **1** *dht* **Chiswick Bey (IRE)**[29] 3487 9-9-7 71 ............ PaulHanagan 6 65
(Richard Fahey) *midfield: rdn and hdwy on outer over 1f out: styd on: jnd ldr line* **5/2**[1]

0300 **3** *nk* **I'm Super Too (IRE)**[17] 3935 10-8-11 52 ............(b) GemmaTutty(5) 5 59
(Karen Tutty) *hld up: briefly short of room over 1f out: hdwy appr fnl f: rdn and kpt on ins fnl f* **11/1**

6025 **4** *2* **Faintly (USA)**[34] 3344 6-9-2 61 ............(b) JamesSullivan 9 54
(Ruth Carr) *hld up: pushed along and hdwy 2f out: chsd ldrs ent fnl f: drvn and one pce fnl 110yds* **7/2**[2]

-000 **5** *2 1/2* **Zebedee Star**[43] 2989 3-8-3 45 ............ CamHardie 2 40
(Karen Tutty) *midfield: rdn and hdwy to chse ldrs 2f out: no ex ins fnl f* **50/1**

-000 **6** *nk* **Mercers Row**[10] 4174 10-8-9 51 ............(p) ConnorMurtagh(7) 3 47
(Michael Herrington) *prom: pressed ldr over 2f out: rdn over 1f out: wknd ins fnl f* **25/1**

0-00 **7** *5* **Eeny Mac (IRE)**[28] 3530 10-8-9 45 ............(p) SophieRalston(7) 8 35
(John Wainwright) *trckd ldrs: racd keenly: rdn over 2f out: wknd over 1f out* **50/1**

041 **8** *12* **Nonno Giulio (IRE)**[13] 4105 6-9-7 70 ............(p) PaulMulrennan 4 12
(Conor Dore) *dwlt: midfield: racd keenly and trckd ldrs 5f out: rdn over 2f out: wknd over 1f out* **9/2**[3]

0-50 **9** *13* **Italian Beauty (IRE)**[146] 677 5-8-8 64 ............ SammyJoBell(3) 1
(John Wainwright) *sn outpcd in rr: a bhd* **10/1**

1m 31.7s (-2.10) **Going Correction** -0.275s/f (Firm)
**WFA** 3 from 4yo+ 8lb 9 Ran SP% **116.4**
Speed ratings (Par 101): **101,101,100,98,95 95,89,75,60**
WIN: 1.20 Chiswick Bey, 2.20 Iberica Road; PL: 1.10 Chiswick Bey, Iberica Road, 3.50 I'm Super Too; EX: 5.30, 7.00; CSF: 6.32, 5.66; TC: ; TF: 53.60, 63.50;.Iberica Road was bought in for £6,500 by Mr Grant Tuer
**Owner** Grant Tuer **Bred** Haymarket Farm Llc **Trained** Birkby, N Yorks
**Owner** M J Macleod **Bred** Mrs Kay Egan **Trained** Musley Bank, N Yorks

**FOCUS**
The ground quickened up overnight to good to firm, good in places. The course was at its widest configuration and the distances were as advertised. A fair event of its type and one in which the gallop was reasonable. The third dictates the level.

### 4555 AUNT BESSIE'S EBF FILLIES' NOVICE STKS (PLUS 10 RACE) 5f
**6:40** (6:42) (Class 4) 2-Y-O **£5,040** (£1,508; £754; £377; £188) **Stalls** Low

Form RPR
6 **1** **Wirral Girl (IRE)**[29] 3482 2-9-0 0 ............ PaulHanagan 6 74+
(Richard Fahey) *mde all: pushed along over 1f out: kpt on wl to draw clr fnl f: comf* **3/1**[1]

213 **2** *2 1/2* **Our Little Pony**[21] 3791 2-9-0 63 ............ RobertWinston 14 65
(Lawrence Mullaney) *prom: rdn over 1f out: kpt on but sn no ch w wnr* **11/2**

55 **3** *1 1/4* **Moonlit Sands (IRE)**[27] 3557 2-9-0 0 ............ BenCurtis 5 61
(Brian Ellison) *in tch: rdn over 1f out: edgd rt jst ins fnl f: kpt on* **8/1**

**4** *1/2* **Ben My Chree** 2-9-0 0 ............ ConnorBeasley 2 61+
(Bryan Smart) *midfield: pushed along over 1f out: hmpd jst ins fnl f: kpt on: nrst fin* **12/1**

34 **5** *1/2* **Ce De Nullis (IRE)**[20] 3826 2-9-0 0 ............(h) LukeMorris 9 57
(Paul Midgley) *chsd ldrs: rdn 2f out: one pce* **5/1**[3]

**6** *nk* **Eller Brook** 2-9-0 0 ............ PaulMulrennan 7 56
(Michael Dods) *wnt lft s: midfield: pushed along over 3f out: kpt on same pce* **9/2**[2]

0 **7** *1 1/4* **Daffy Jane**[16] 3980 2-8-11 0 ............ RachelRichardson(3) 3 53
(Nigel Tinkler) *hld up: pushed along over 1f out: keeping on whn hmpd 110yds out* **33/1**

**8** *1/2* **Elnadim Star (IRE)** 2-9-0 0 ............ TomEaves 10 50+
(Kevin Ryan) *dwlt: hld up in rr: pushed along and sme hdwy on outer over 1f out: nvr threatened* **7/1**

**9** *shd* **Ideal Spirit** 2-8-7 0 ............ RussellHarris(7) 1 49
(Andrew Crook) *chsd ldrs: rdn 2f out: wknd ins fnl f* **40/1**

**10** *1 3/4* **Alaskan Beauty (IRE)** 2-9-0 0 ............ DavidAllan 8 43
(Tim Easterby) *dwlt and bmpd s: hld up: nvr threatened* **16/1**

**11** *2* **Little Monkey** 2-9-0 0 ............(p[1]) CamHardie 13 36
(Antony Brittain) *a in rr* **33/1**

1m 3.67s (0.17) **Going Correction** 0.0s/f (Good) 11 Ran SP% **120.7**
Speed ratings (Par 93): **98,94,92,91,90 89,87,87,86,84 80**
CSF £19.78 TOTE £4.00: £1.70, £1.30, £2.80; EX 22.20 Trifecta £118.70.
**Owner** Ms A Quinn **Bred** Sarah McCann **Trained** Musley Bank, N Yorks

**FOCUS**
Little strength in depth but an improved effort from the winner. Those attempting to come from off the pace were at a disadvantage. The runner-up more than backed up her recent good run in a valuable seller at York.

### 4556 JACKSON'S YORKSHIRE CHAMPION BREAD H'CAP 7f 96y
**7:10** (7:11) (Class 4) (0-80,79) 3-Y-O+ **£5,040** (£1,508; £754; £377; £188) **Stalls** Low

Form RPR
4550 **1** **Chupalla**[83] 1801 3-9-6 **79** ............ JoeFanning 9 83
(Mark Johnston) *dwlt: sn prom: led over 1f out: sn pushed along: edgd rt ent fnl f: rdn fnl 110yds: a doing enough: shade cosily* **20/1**

5-11 **2** *3/4* **Dan Troop**[31] 3434 3-9-3 **76** ............ PaulHanagan 4 78+
(Richard Fahey) *trckd ldrs: keen early: rdn to chal over 1f out: kpt on but a hld* **2/1**[1]

4143 **3** *nse* **Mon Beau Visage (IRE)**[13] 4085 4-10-0 **79** ............(p) PhillipMakin 7 84
(David O'Meara) *hld up in midfield: hdwy over 1f out: rdn and kpt on fnl f* **11/2**[3]

1350 **4** *1/2* **Proud Archi (IRE)**[19] 3862 3-9-6 **79** ............ PaulMulrennan 2 80
(Michael Dods) *trckd ldr: rdn over 1f out: kpt on same pce* **11/4**[2]

-060 **5** *2* **Mywayistheonlyway (IRE)**[25] 3652 4-9-10 **75** ............ BenCurtis 6 73
(Grant Tuer) *dwlt: hld up: rdn along over 2f out: kpt on fnl f: nvr threatened* **11/1**

0502 **6** *nk* **Florencio**[8] 4264 4-9-11 **76** ............(p) ConnorBeasley 1 73
(Roger Fell) *hld up in rr: rdn 2f out: nvr threatened* **14/1**

0-00 **7** *1 1/4* **Lawmaking**[18] 3919 4-10-0 **79** ............ RobertWinston 8 73
(Henry Spiller) *hld up: nvr threatened* **33/1**

2204 **8** *nk* **Adventureman**[7] 4298 5-8-11 **62** ............(p) JamesSullivan 5 55
(Ruth Carr) *led: rdn whn hdd over 1f out: stl cl up whn hmpd ent fnl f: wknd* **8/1**

0020 **9** *9* **Like No Other**[31] 3433 4-9-7 **75** ............(b) NathanEvans(3) 3 44
(Les Eyre) *midfield: rdn over 2f out: wknd fnl f* **12/1**

1m 31.7s (-2.10) **Going Correction** -0.275s/f (Firm)
**WFA** 3 from 4yo+ 8lb 9 Ran SP% **116.9**
Speed ratings (Par 105): **101,100,100,99,97 96,95,95,84**
CSF £61.08 CT £266.58 TOTE £22.20: £5.20, £1.20, £1.90; EX 100.70 Trifecta £808.90.
**Owner** Sheikh Hamdan bin Mohammed Al Maktoum **Bred** Darley **Trained** Middleham Moor, N Yorks

**FOCUS**
A reasonable handicap but a modest gallop meant those held up were at a big disadvantage and those bare facts may not be entirely reliable. The third helps set the standard.

### 4557 HIGHLAND LOVE H'CAP 1m 100y
**7:40** (7:40) (Class 5) (0-75,76) 3-Y-O **£3,780** (£1,131; £565; £283; £141) **Stalls** Low

Form RPR
5-24 **1** **Vaulted**[23] 3715 3-9-0 **67** ............ PaulHanagan 3 71
(Richard Fahey) *trckd ldr: pushed along to ld narrowly over 1f out: sn hung rt: rdn fnl f: kpt on* **10/3**[3]

6255 **2** *hd* **Hamster Jam (IRE)**[25] 3656 3-9-3 **70** ............ JoeFanning 1 73
(Mark Johnston) *led: rdn whn hdd over 1f out: remained cl up: kpt on but a jst hld* **15/2**

0311 **3** *1/2* **Brother McGonagall**[23] 3708 3-9-3 **70** ............ CamHardie 7 72+
(Tim Easterby) *hld up: rdn over 1f out: hdwy appr fnl f: kpt on* **3/1**[2]

1041 **4** *1 1/2* **Hajjam**[14] 4058 3-9-9 **76** ............(h) PhillipMakin 2 74
(David O'Meara) *dwlt: sn trckd ldr: rdn over 1f out: ct in pocket and n.m.r fr ent fnl f tl fnl 110yds: kpt on same pce* **5/2**[1]

4503 **5** *1/2* **George Reme (IRE)**[17] 3934 3-9-7 **74** ............(v) JasonHart 4 71
(John Quinn) *in tch: rdn 2f out: one pce* **3/1**[2]

1m 46.69s (-0.91) **Going Correction** -0.275s/f (Firm) 5 Ran SP% **113.4**
Speed ratings (Par 100): **93,92,92,90,90**
CSF £26.31 TOTE £2.70: £1.50, £2.40; EX 19.00 Trifecta £123.70.
**Owner** Cheveley Park Stud **Bred** Cheveley Park Stud Ltd **Trained** Musley Bank, N Yorks

**FOCUS**
A fair event but a muddling gallop meant that the whole field finished in a heap and this bare form doesn't look entirely reliable. Muddling form which has been rated cautiously.

### 4558 RACING AGAIN TOMORROW H'CAP (BEVERLEY MIDDLE DISTANCE SERIES) 1m 4f 23y
**8:10** (8:10) (Class 6) (0-60,59) 3-Y-O+ **£2,587** (£770; £384; £192) **Stalls** Low

Form RPR
6336 **1** **Cool Music (IRE)**[10] 4169 7-9-4 **53** ............(p) CamHardie 8 59
(Antony Brittain) *midfield: hdwy 3f out: rdn to ld narrowly appr fnl f: styd on* **9/1**

0025 **2** *1/2* **Midnight Warrior**[13] 4102 7-9-5 **54** ............(t) DavidAllan 11 59
(Ron Barr) *trckd ldrs: led 2f out: sn rdn: hdd appr fnl f: styd on but a hld* **12/1**

-606 **3** *1 1/4* **Chauvelin**[13] 4102 6-9-2 **51** ............(b) TomEaves 7 54
(Nigel Tinkler) *hld up: pushed along and gd hdwy over 1f out: chsd ldrs whn short of room 1f out tl fnl 75yds: kpt on* **20/1**

6052 **4** *hd* **Percy Verence**[13] 4102 4-9-5 **54** ............ BenCurtis 3 57
(Tracy Waggott) *trckd ldrs: lost pl over 4f out: hdwy and bk chsng ldrs 2f out: rdn and styd on same pce* **10/3**[2]

0215 **5** *1* **Diamond Runner (IRE)**[17] 3935 5-9-7 **56** ............(b) RobertWinston 6 57
(Lawrence Mullaney) *dwlt: hld up: gd hdwy over 1f out to chse ldrs ent fnl f: rdn and sn hung rt: no ex fnl 75yds* **3/1**[1]

50-3 **6** *9* **Aneedh**[31] 3436 7-9-3 **52** ............(p) GrahamLee 1 39
(Clive Mulhall) *midfield: rdn over 2f out: wknd over 1f out* **8/1**

0133 **7** *6* **Mrs Biggs**[32] 3405 5-8-13 **53** ............ PhilDennis(5) 4 30
(Declan Carroll) *led: 6f out: remained prom tl wknd 2f out* **7/2**[3]

054 **8** *1/2* **Fisherman's Blues (IRE)**[16] 3983 4-9-10 **59** ............ JamesSullivan 10 35
(Peter Niven) *stdd s: hld up: nvr threatened* **25/1**

0040 **9** *3 1/2* **Sehail (USA)**[9] 4217 4-9-6 **55** ............(b) LukeMorris 12 26
(George Peckham) *hld up: rdn over 4f out: sn btn* **25/1**

/400 **10** *2* **Tin Pan Alley**[17] 3935 9-9-9 **58** ............ ConnorBeasley 9 26
(David C Griffiths) *prom: led 6f out: rdn whn hdd 2f out: wknd* **12/1**

2m 36.69s (-3.11) **Going Correction** -0.275s/f (Firm) 10 Ran SP% **119.3**
Speed ratings (Par 101): **99,98,97,97,97 91,87,86,84,83**
CSF £109.88 CT £2090.66 TOTE £12.00: £2.90, £4.50, £5.00; EX 146.30.
**Owner** Antony Brittain **Bred** Mrs D M Solomon **Trained** Warthill, N Yorks

**FOCUS**
A moderate handicap but, although the gallop was reasonable, not too many got involved. Straightforward form rated around the first two.

## 4559 FERGUSON FAWSITT ARMS H'CAP 5f
**8:40** (8:41) (Class 6) (0-60,60) 3-Y-O+ **£2,587** (£770; £384; £192) **Stalls** Low

Form RPR
2313 1 **Dandilion (IRE)**[14] 4053 4-9-10 **60**....(t) LukeMorris 14 68
(Alex Hales) *dwlt: hld up in rr: bit short of room over 1f out: stl lot to do whn swtchd lft to outside appr fnl f: drvn and r.o strly: led post* **6/1**[2]
0600 2 *hd* **Sarabi**[32] 3384 4-9-10 **60**....(p) DavidAllan 5 67
(Scott Dixon) *midfield: rdn and hdwy over 2f out: chsd ldr jst ins fnl f: kpt on to ld 50yds out: hdd post* **8/1**[3]
5406 3 1 ½ **See Vermont**[10] 4174 9-9-8 **58**....(p) DuranFentiman 7 60
(Rebecca Bastiman) *midfield: rdn 2f out: hdwy appr fnl f: kpt on* **14/1**
1340 4 *nse* **Nuala Tagula (IRE)**[23] 3710 4-9-6 **56**....(t) JasonHart 4 58+
(John Quinn) *prom: led gng wl over 1f out: pushed along ent fnl f: rdn fnl 110yds: hdd 50yds out: wknd* **8/1**[3]
4006 5 3 ¼ **Groundworker (IRE)**[17] 3944 6-9-7 **57**....(t) JoeFanning 12 47
(Paul Midgley) *midfield towards outer: rdn over 2f out: chsd ldrs appr fnl f: no ex ins fnl f* **9/1**
0350 6 *nk* **Lady Joanna Vassa (IRE)**[18] 3915 4-9-0 **50**.... RobertWinston 6 39
(Richard Guest) *hld up: sme hdwy 2f out: short of room over 1f out tl ent fnl f: rdn and kpt on* **6/1**[2]
-300 7 *nk* **Emerald Secret (IRE)**[68] 2182 3-9-3 **58**....(p) PaulMulrennan 15 44
(Paul Midgley) *hld up towards outer: rdn over 1f out: kpt on fnl 110yds: nvr threatened* **25/1**
4300 8 2 **Jorvik Prince**[13] 4107 3-9-0 **55**....(b) SamJames 1 34
(Karen Tutty) *prom: led over 2f out: rdn whn hdd over 1f out: wknd ins fnl f* **17/2**
0-00 9 *hd* **Your Gifted (IRE)**[30] 3466 10-8-12 **48**....(v) TomEaves 2 28
(Lisa Williamson) *dwlt: hld up: nvr threatened* **50/1**
5040 10 ½ **Secret Asset (IRE)**[20] 3834 12-9-9 **59**....(v) KevinStott 8 37
(Lisa Williamson) *hld up: nvr threatened* **8/1**[3]
3504 11 1 **Thornaby Princess**[17] 3944 6-8-8 **47**....(p) NathanEvans(3) 10 22
(Colin Teague) *prom: rdn over 1f out: wknd fnl f* **16/1**
200- 12 4 **Miss Mayson**[224] 8097 3-8-12 **58**.... GemmaTutty(5) 11 16
(Karen Tutty) *chsd ldrs: rdn over 2f out: wknd over 1f out* **33/1**
3-00 13 *nk* **Peach Pavlova (IRE)**[16] 3979 3-9-3 **58**....(p¹) PaulHanagan 16 15
(Ann Duffield) *midfield on outside: rdn over 2f out: sn wknd* **20/1**
6600 14 1 **Young Tiger**[17] 3944 4-9-1 **51**.... JamesSullivan 13 6
(Tom Tate) *led on outer: hdd over 2f out: wknd over 1f out* **5/1**[1]

1m 3.6s (0.10) **Going Correction** 0.0s/f (Good)
**WFA** 3 from 4yo+ 5lb **14** Ran SP% **125.2**
Speed ratings (Par 101): **99,98,96,96,91 90,90,86,86,85 84,77,77,75**
CSF £53.62 CT £680.23 TOTE £6.80: £2.40, £2.10, £4.20; EX 36.40 Trifecta £386.10.
**Owner** The Golden Horse Racing Club **Bred** Ballyhane Stud **Trained** Edgcote, Northamptonshire

**FOCUS**
A strong pace teed things up for the winner, who is a progressive sprinter and may do better still. The third helps set the level.
T/Plt: £1,133.30 to a £1 stake. Pool: £52,476.87 - 33.80 winning units. T/Qpdt: £131.60 to a £1 stake. Pool: £4,127.80 - 23.20 winning units. **Andrew Sheret**

# 3999 CHELMSFORD (A.W) (L-H)
### Friday, July 7

**OFFICIAL GOING: Polytrack: standard**
Wind: virtually nil Weather: sunny and warm

## 4560 BET TOTEPLACEPOT AT BETFRED.COM NOVICE STKS (PLUS 10 RACE) 7f (P)
**6:00** (6:01) (Class 4) 2-Y-O **£7,115** (£2,117; £1,058; £529) **Stalls** Low

Form RPR
4 1 **Watheer**[19] 3868 2-8-13 0.... KieranShoemark(3) 1 75
(Marcus Tregoning) *hld up in tch in midfield: effrt on inner over 1f out: chsd wnr ent fnl f: styd on strly to ld towards fin* **11/10**[1]
05 2 ¾ **Barbarianatthegate**[16] 3965 2-9-2 0....(b) JosephineGordon 3 73
(Brian Meehan) *led: jnd over 3f out: drvn and fnd ex wl over 1f out: kpt on wl u.p tl hdd and one pce towards fin* **12/1**
3 3 ½ **Dark Liberty (IRE)** 2-8-11 0.... MartinDwyer 9 59+
(Simon Crisford) *s.i.s: in tch in rr: swtchd rt hdwy over 1f out: hdwy 1f out: styd on wl to go 3rd last strides: no threat to ldrs* **20/1**
0 4 *hd* **Mutafarrid (IRE)**[22] 3746 2-8-13 0.... EdwardGreatrex(3) 8 63
(Owen Burrows) *chsd ldrs: wnt 2nd over 4f out: jnd ldr 1/2-way: rdn and outpcd over 1f out: 3rd and one pce 1f out: lost 3rd last strides* **20/1**
5 1 **Ibn Al Emarat (IRE)** 2-9-2 0.... LiamKeniry 5 60
(David Simcock) *dwlt: in tch in rr and niggled along: hdwy over 1f out: kpt on ins fnl f: no threat to ldrs* **33/1**
40 6 *shd* **Move Over**[15] 4007 2-9-2 0.... KieranO'Neill 2 61
(Richard Hannon) *restless in stalls: chsd ldr tl over 4f out: struggling to qckn: edging rt and bumping rival over 1f out: wl hld and kpt on same pce ins fnl f* **14/1**
53 7 ½ **Global Wealth**[17] 3930 2-9-2 0.... MartinHarley 7 59
(Ed Dunlop) *in tch in midfield: effrt u.p over 2f out: unable qck and no imp fr over 1f out* **8/1**[3]
5 8 ½ **Rude Awakening**[15] 4007 2-9-2 0.... RyanPowell 6 57
(Sir Mark Prescott Bt) *midfield: pushed rt after 1f out: rdn over 2f out: outpcd and btn over 1f out: wl hld and kpt on same pce fnl f* **20/1**
53 9 1 ¼ **Chai Chai (IRE)**[13] 4083 2-8-11 0.... JoshuaBryan(5) 4 54
(Andrew Balding) *chsd ldrs: swtchd rt after 1f: effrt ent fnl 2f: unable qckn and bmpd over 1f out: wknd ins fnl f* **3/1**[2]
10 6 **Stormy Sand (IRE)** 2-9-2 0.... AntonioFresu 10 38
(Marco Botti) *pushed rt after 1f: in rr after: rdn and struggling 2f out: bhd fnl f* **20/1**

1m 26.98s (-0.22) **Going Correction** 0.0s/f (Stan) **10** Ran SP% **120.1**
Speed ratings (Par 96): **101,100,96,95,94 94,94,93,92,85**
CSF £15.06 TOTE £1.90: £1.02, £3.60, £4.50; EX 16.50 Trifecta £163.70.
**Owner** Hamdan Al Maktoum **Bred** Miss K Rausing **Trained** Whitsbury, Hants

**FOCUS**
The first two pulled clear in this novice event and a big gamble was landed. The pace looked decent but the time was 3.68 seconds slower than standard.

## 4561 BET TOTEEXACTA AT BETFRED.COM H'CAP 7f (P)
**6:30** (6:37) (Class 6) (0-60,62) 4-Y-O+ **£3,234** (£962; £481; £240) **Stalls** Low

Form RPR
-321 1 **Cainhoe Star**[7] 4323 4-9-7 **60** 6ex.... KieranO'Neill 2 75+
(Anthony Carson) *wl in tch in midfield: effrt and hdwy over 1f out: led 1f out: gng clr whn wnt rt ins fnl f: styd on wl: readily* **1/1**[1]
0002 2 3 ¼ **Flower Cup**[23] 3729 4-8-13 **57**.... LewisEdmunds(5) 3 63
(Chris Dwyer) *hld up in midfield: n.m.r over 2f out: swtchd rt and hdwy over 1f out: swtchd rt again and hdwy ins fnl f: wnt 2nd fnl 100yds: r.o but no ch w wnr* **7/1**[2]
3524 3 3 ¾ **Rosie Crowe (IRE)**[20] 3832 5-8-12 **51**....(v) TrevorWhelan 6 47
(Shaun Harris) *led for 2f: chsd ldrs: rdn 2f out: unable qck 1f out: outpcd by ldng pair: battled on to go 3rd last strides* **16/1**
0621 4 *nse* **Emily Goldfinch**[20] 3823 4-9-3 **56**.... DannyBrock 8 52
(Phil McEntee) *mostly chsd ldr: rdn and clsd to press ldr over 1f out: outpcd by ldng pair and battled for wl hld 3rd ins fnl f: kpt on* **14/1**
3044 5 *hd* **Caledonian Gold**[28] 3522 4-8-12 **51**....(b¹) RyanPowell 14 46
(Paul D'Arcy) *taken down early: chsd ldrs tl led after 2f: rdn over 1f out: hdd 1f out: sn outpcd and wl hld: plugged on same pce and lost 2 pls last strides* **25/1**
4530 6 1 **Tigserin (IRE)**[24] 3702 4-9-9 **62**.... PatCosgrave 9 55
(Giles Bravery) *hld up in last trio: effrt over 1f out: kpt on to pass btn rivals ins fnl f: nvr trbld ldrs* **20/1**
23U1 7 *nk* **Misu Pete**[16] 3971 5-9-1 **54**.... DanielMuscutt 10 46
(Mark Usher) *midfield: rdn over 1f out: kpt on same pce ins fnl f: nvr trbld ldrs* **10/1**[3]
2300 8 ½ **Broughtons Fancy**[28] 3522 4-8-13 **55**.... KieranShoemark(3) 1 45
(Gary Moore) *taken down early: chsd ldrs: unable qck u.p and nt clrest of runs over 1f out: wknd ins fnl f* **11/1**
4004 9 2 ½ **Overhaugh Street**[20] 3809 4-9-6 **59**....(v) JimCrowley 7 43
(Ed de Giles) *taken down early: towards rr: effrt swtchd rt over 1f out: no imp: nvr trbld ldrs* **12/1**
0-00 10 2 ¼ **Diamondsaretrumps (IRE)**[10] 4180 4-8-8 **47**....(t) JosephineGordon 5 25
(Phil McEntee) *a towards rr and nvr travelling wl: n.d* **50/1**
3062 11 ½ **Ambitious Icarus**[18] 3914 8-9-6 **59**....(b) JFEgan 11 35
(Richard Guest) *taken down early: t.k.h: hld up in midfield: effrt over 1f out: no hdwy: wknd fnl f* **14/1**
4046 12 6 **Knight Of The Air**[25] 3660 5-9-5 **58**.... LiamKeniry 4 18
(Joseph Tuite) *in rr: sme hdwy into midfield 4f out: rdn and struggling over 2f out: bhd fnl f* **25/1**
000- 13 74 **Indomitable Spirit**[116] 3624 5-9-4 **57**.... MartinHarley 15
(Martin Smith) *wd and sn dropped to rr: lost tch 2f out: t.o* **50/1**

1m 27.25s (0.05) **Going Correction** 0.0s/f (Stan) **13** Ran SP% **123.2**
Speed ratings (Par 101): **99,95,91,90,90 89,89,88,85,83 82,75,**
CSF £7.66 CT £77.43 TOTE £1.70: £1.10, £2.90, £4.70; EX 10.00 Trifecta £84.70.
**Owner** Hugh & Mindi Byrne & W H Carson **Bred** Cheveley Park Stud Ltd **Trained** Newmarket, Suffolk

**FOCUS**
They went a good pace and the hot favourite surged clear to complete a double. Paradise Found gave problems at the start and was withdrawn. The runner-up has been rated in line with her latest Yarmouth effort.

## 4562 BET TOTEQUADPOT AT BETFRED.COM MAIDEN STKS 7f (P)
**7:00** (7:08) (Class 5) 3-Y-O+ **£5,175** (£1,540; £769; £384) **Stalls** Low

Form RPR
1 **Golden Goal (IRE)** 3-9-5 0.... MartinLane 6 85+
(Saeed bin Suroor) *hld up wl in tch in midfield: rdn over 3f out: swtchd rt 2f out: styd on to chal 1f out: led ins fnl f: styd on wl and drew clr towards fin: readily* **13/8**[1]
2 2 ¼ **Subhaan** 3-9-5 0.... JimCrowley 4 79+
(Roger Varian) *chsd ldr: effrt over 1f out: pushed into ld 1f out: rdn and hdd ins fnl f: nt match pce of wnr but kpt on for clr 2nd* **9/4**[2]
-044 3 5 **Tesko Fella (IRE)**[11] 4152 3-9-2 64.... EdwardGreatrex(3) 1 65
(Luke McJannet) *chsd ldrs: rdn to ld on inner over 1f out: hdd 1f out: sn outpcd by ldng pair: kpt on same pce for clr 3rd ins fnl f* **16/1**
6 4 6 **Slow To Hand**[8] 4269 3-9-5 0.... DannyBrock 8 49
(William Jarvis) *in tch in ldng quintet: rdn over 3f out: outpcd over 1f out and sn wl btn: wnt modest 4th and plugged on ins fnl f* **20/1**
5 5 1 **St James's Park (IRE)**[30] 3456 4-9-13 0.... AntonioFresu 9 49
(Luke McJannet) *midfield but nvr on terms w ldrs: rdn and rn green 4f out: nvr trbld ldrs* **12/1**
00 6 6 **Allofmelovesallofu**[24] 3691 3-8-12 0.... FinleyMarsh(7) 3 30
(Ken Cunningham-Brown) *sn outpcd in rr: nvr on terms* **33/1**
03 7 *hd* **Good Bond**[20] 3825 5-9-10 0....(h¹) HectorCrouch(3) 2 32
(Linda Jewell) *rn green and sn outpcd in rr: n.d* **66/1**
8 3 ¼ **Afterburner** 3-9-5 0.... JosephineGordon 10 21
(Hugo Palmer) *rn green and sn outpcd in rr: n.d* **8/1**
54 9 *hd* **Mio Ragazzo**[29] 3493 3-9-5 0.... DanielMuscutt 11 20+
(Marco Botti) *racd keenly: led tl rdn and over 1f out: sn btn and fdd fnl f* **7/1**[3]
10 9 **Alternate Route** 3-9-5 0.... RyanPowell 5
(Sir Mark Prescott Bt) *v.s.a: v green and sn lost tch: t.o* **25/1**

1m 26.0s (-1.20) **Going Correction** 0.0s/f (Stan)
**WFA** 3 from 4yo+ 8lb **10** Ran SP% **119.1**
Speed ratings (Par 103): **106,103,97,90,89 82,82,78,78,68**
CSF £5.21 TOTE £2.20: £1.20, £1.10, £3.70; EX 6.10 Trifecta £38.10.
**Owner** Godolphin **Bred** Yeomanstown Stud **Trained** Newmarket, Suffolk

**FOCUS**
Two well-backed newcomers pulled clear in this maiden. It's been rated around the third.

## 4563 BET TOTETRIFECTA AT BETFRED.COM H'CAP 1m (P)
**7:30** (7:38) (Class 3) (0-90,90) 3-Y-O+ **£12,938** (£3,850; £1,924; £962) **Stalls** Low

Form RPR
-232 1 **Mutarabby (IRE)**[23] 3714 3-8-13 **87**.... KieranShoemark(3) 11 99+
(Saeed bin Suroor) *dwlt: hld up in tch towards rr: swtchd rt over 1f out: hdwy 1f out: str run ins fnl f to ld towards fin* **4/1**[2]
-511 2 ½ **Mukalal**[36] 3262 3-9-3 **88**.... JimCrowley 2 96+
(Marcus Tregoning) *t.k.h: pressed ldr tl led over 3f out: rdn over 1f out: clr ins fnl f: hdd and no ex towards fin* **13/8**[1]
1331 3 2 ¼ **Kenstone (FR)**[32] 3402 4-8-8 **75**....(p) JoshuaBryan(5) 9 80
(Adrian Wintle) *trckd ldrs: wnt 2nd 2f out: sn rdn: unable qck and styd on same pce ins fnl f* **16/1**

-561 **4** *nse* **North Creek**[23] 3723 4-9-5 **81**.................... MartinHarley 7 86
(Chris Wall) *t.k.h: trckd ldrs: effrt over 1f out: styd on same pce u.p ins fnl f* **14/1**

204 **5** *½* **Bunbury**[65] 2291 5-9-7 **90**....................(p[1]) FinleyMarsh(7) 13 94
(Richard Hughes) *stdd and dropped in bhd after s: effrt over 1f out: styd on wl ins fnl f: nvr trbld ldrs* **25/1**

-500 **6** *nk* **Via Serendipity**[15] 3997 3-9-3 **88**....................(t) JosephineGordon 8 89
(Hugo Palmer) *hld up in tch towards rr: rdn over 2f out: styd on ins fnl f: nvr trbld ldrs* **9/2**[3]

0040 **7** *nk* **Hammer Gun (USA)**[8] 4261 4-9-7 **83**....................(v) MartinLane 3 85
(Derek Shaw) *s.i.s: in rr: hdwy u.p 1f out: kpt on ins fnl f: nvr trbld ldrs* **16/1**

6305 **8** *½* **Bold Prediction (IRE)**[15] 4001 7-9-1 **82**.................... JennyPowell(5) 1 83
(Ed Walker) *led tl over 3f out: rdn ent fnl 2f: no ex u.p 1f out: wknd ins fnl f* **11/1**

30-0 **9** *1 ½* **Unforgiving Minute**[37] 3212 6-9-8 **87**.................... TimClark(3) 5 85
(John Butler) *t.k.h: hld up in midfield: effrt on inner over 1f out: kpt on ins fnl f: nvr threatened ldrs* **33/1**

0105 **10** *nk* **Pendo**[25] 3670 6-9-5 **81**.................... MartinDwyer 6 78
(John Best) *restless in stalls: in midfield tl hdwy to chse ldrs 4f out: unable qck u.p over 1f out: wknd ins fnl f* **16/1**

5031 **11** *6* **Wealth Tax**[15] 4001 4-8-11 **73**.................... JoeyHaynes 12 56
(Ed Dunlop) *wd: a towards rr: rdn over 2f out: swtchd rt wl over 1f out: no hdwy: bhd fnl f* **14/1**

065 **12** *2 ¾* **Beach Bar (IRE)**[15] 4017 6-9-6 **82**....................(h) TrevorWhelan 4 59
(Brendan Powell) *dwlt and niggled along leaving stalls: hld up in tch: rdn 2f out: sn outpcd and lost pl over 1f out: bhd fnl f* **66/1**

1m 37.85s (-2.05) **Going Correction** 0.0s/f (Stan)
**WFA** 3 from 4yo+ 9lb 12 Ran SP% **123.9**
Speed ratings (Par 107): **110,109,107,107,106 106,106,105,104,103 97,95**
CSF £11.21 CT £100.48 TOTE £4.90: £1.70, £1.30, £4.90; EX 13.60 Trifecta £81.60.
**Owner** Godolphin **Bred** Shadwell Estate Company Limited **Trained** Newmarket, Suffolk

**FOCUS**
The went a stop-start pace in this decent handicap and winner deserves extra credit for surging to victory from some way back. It's been rated around the third and fourth.

## 4564 TOTEPOOL RACECOURSE DEBIT CARD BETTING AVAILABLE H'CAP 1m (P)
**8:00** (8:05) (Class 4) (0-85,84) 3-Y-O **£7,439** (£2,213; £1,106; £553) **Stalls** Low

Form RPR

-030 **1** **Intimate Art (IRE)**[23] 3713 3-9-1 **83**.................... JoshuaBryan(5) 8 88
(Andrew Balding) *mde all: rdn over 1f out: edgd rt u.p ins fnl f: hld on gamely fnl 100yds: all out* **7/1**[3]

-260 **2** *shd* **Makaarim**[8] 4254 3-9-3 **83**.................... GeorgeWood(3) 7 87+
(Marco Botti) *hld up in last pair: effrt over 1f out: hdwy u.p ins fnl f: str chal towards fin: jst hld* **8/1**

-212 **3** *shd* **Ourmullion**[116] 1176 3-8-9 **72**.................... JosephineGordon 1 76
(John Butler) *in tch in midfield: hdwy u.p over 1f out: str chal 100yds out: kpt on but a jst hld after: lost 2nd last stride* **14/1**

63-5 **4** *1 ½* **Blushing Rose**[20] 3838 3-9-1 **78**.................... RyanMoore 5 79+
(Sir Michael Stoute) *short of room sn after s: hld up in tch in last pair: swtchd rt and effrt wl over 1f out: hdwy ins fnl f: styd on towards fin: nt rch ldrs* **6/5**[1]

1553 **5** *nk* **Tafaakhor (IRE)**[21] 3780 3-9-6 **83**....................(b[1]) JimCrowley 2 83
(Richard Hannon) *t.k.h: hld up in midfield: effrt to chse ldrs 1f out: styd on same pce ins fnl f* **7/2**[2]

5-12 **6** *shd* **Contentment**[18] 3900 3-9-1 **78**....................(t) PatCosgrave 4 78
(William Haggas) *t.k.h: chsd wnr: effrt and hung lft over 1f out: no ex and outpcd fnl 100yds* **10/1**

2152 **7** *1* **Toy Theatre**[90] 1625 3-8-5 **75**.................... RayDawson(7) 3 72
(Michael Appleby) *hld up in tch midfield: effrt over 1f out: dropped to rr and nt clr run jst over 1f out: swtchd rt and no imp fnl f* **25/1**

5-05 **8** *hd* **Plant Pot Power (IRE)**[35] 3303 3-9-7 **84**.................... KieranO'Neill 6 81
(Richard Hannon) *t.k.h: chsd ldng pair: effrt 2f out: hanging lft after: nt clr run and hmpd ins fnl f: sn rdn and no hdwy: wknd towards fin* **12/1**

1m 39.75s (-0.15) **Going Correction** 0.0s/f (Stan) 8 Ran SP% **118.6**
Speed ratings (Par 102): **100,99,99,98,98 97,96,96**
CSF £63.24 CT £780.43 TOTE £9.60: £2.20, £3.30, £2.50; EX 90.50 Trifecta £1048.10.
**Owner** Thurloe Thoroughbreds XXXIX **Bred** Mrs Clodagh McStay **Trained** Kingsclere, Hants

**FOCUS**
The pace was not very strong and there was a tight three-way finish in this handicap. It's been rated around the winner's penultimate C&D form.

## 4565 TOM AND VAL VICKERS MEMORIAL MAIDEN FILLIES' STKS 1m (P)
**8:30** (8:35) (Class 5) 3-5-Y-O **£5,175** (£1,540; £769; £384) **Stalls** Low

Form RPR

6 **1** **Labhay (IRE)**[42] 3039 3-9-0 0.................... PatCosgrave 3 82+
(William Haggas) *trckd ldrs: swtchd rt and chsd ldr over 1f out: clsd u.p to ld jst ins fnl f: kpt on wl: rdn out* **8/1**

4 **2** *nk* **Verity**[32] 3393 3-9-0 0.................... RyanMoore 4 81+
(Sir Michael Stoute) *led: rdn over 1f out: hdd ins fnl f: battled on wl u.p but a jst hld* **9/4**[2]

0- **3** *3 ¼* **Zafaranah (USA)**[251] 7695 3-9-0 0.................... AndreaAtzeni 7 73
(Roger Varian) *hld up wl in tch: nt clr run 2f out tl swtchd lft ins fnl f: lost any ch of threatening ldrs but styd on to go 3rd towards fin* **5/1**[3]

2-33 **4** *½* **Thafeera (USA)**[49] 2798 3-9-0 77....................(h) JimCrowley 6 72
(Charles Hills) *t.k.h: chsd ldng pair on outer: rdn over 1f out: 3rd and outpcd 1f out: plugged on same pce ins fnl f: lost 3rd towards fin* **7/4**[1]

23 **5** *1 ½* **Shankara (IRE)**[135] 862 3-9-0 0.................... JamieSpencer 9 68
(David Simcock) *hld up in rr: hdwy into midfield over 3f out: rdn to chse ldrs over 1f out: no ex 1f out: wknd ins fnl f* **10/1**

00- **6** *4* **Katabatika**[226] 8063 3-9-0 0.................... DavidProbert 5 59
(Hughie Morrison) *pressed ldr tl over 1f out: sn outpcd u.p: wknd ins fnl f* **28/1**

**7** *2* **Snowy Winter (USA)** 3-8-11 0.................... EdwardGreatrex(3) 8 54
(Archie Watson) *dwlt: in tch in rr: effrt and wd over 2f out: outpcd and btn over 1f out: wknd ins fnl f* **33/1**

6 **8** *½* **Beach Party**[30] 3456 3-9-0 0.................... HarryBentley 1 53
(Hughie Morrison) *hld up in tch in midfield: effrt and no hdwy over 1f out: wknd fnl f* **14/1**

5-6 **9** *4 ½* **Solitary Sister (IRE)**[20] 3824 3-8-9 0....................(t) JennyPowell(5) 2 42
(Richard Spencer) *dwlt and flashing tail leaving stalls: a towards rr: wknd over 1f out* **50/1**

0 **10** *2 ½* **Brave Tart**[22] 3748 3-8-7 0.................... MillyNaseb(7) 10 36
(Martin Smith) *midfield: dropped to rr over 3f out: wknd over 1f out* **125/1**

1m 40.64s (0.74) **Going Correction** 0.0s/f (Stan) 10 Ran SP% **119.8**
Speed ratings (Par 100): **96,95,92,91,90 86,84,83,79,76**
CSF £26.77 TOTE £9.80: £2.90, £1.60, £2.20; EX 34.30 Trifecta £280.40.
**Owner** Mohammed Jaber **Bred** Rabbah Bloodstock Limited **Trained** Newmarket, Suffolk

**FOCUS**
The favourite didn't really fire but the first two pulled some way clear in this maiden. The level is a bit fluid.

## 4566 CHELMSFORD CITY SUPPORTING RACING STAFF WEEK H'CAP 5f (P)
**9:00** (9:01) (Class 4) (0-80,80) 4-Y-O+ **£7,439** (£2,213; £1,106; £553) **Stalls** Low

Form RPR

4431 **1** **Saved My Bacon (IRE)**[15] 4005 6-8-12 **76**....................(h) LewisEdmunds(5) 4 85
(Chris Dwyer) *bhd: hdwy in centre jst over 1f out: str run ins fnl f to ld last strides* **5/1**[3]

0-0 **2** *hd* **Alsvinder**[64] 2341 4-9-6 **79**.................... JimCrowley 10 87+
(David O'Meara) *t.k.h: stdd s: hld up in tch towards rr: hdwy over 1f out: rdn to ld 100yds out: r.o u.p: hdd last strides* **18/1**

0320 **3** *1 ½* **Fredricka**[26] 3617 6-9-6 **79**....................(v) RenatoSouza 6 82
(Chris Dwyer) *t.k.h: hld up wl in tch in midfield: effrt to chse ldrs and hung lft jst over 1f out: kpt on same pce ins fnl f* **20/1**

6202 **4** *nse* **Excellent George**[36] 3231 5-9-6 **79**....................(t) HarryBentley 7 82
(Stuart Williams) *hld up in midfield: nt clr run over 1f out: swtchd rt 1f out: hdwy ins fnl f: styd on wl towards fin: nvr gng to rch ldrs* **9/2**[2]

5-02 **5** *nse* **Interlink (USA)**[7] 4310 4-8-10 **69**.................... JosephineGordon 2 72
(Michael Appleby) *hld up towards rr: switching rt over 1f out: hdwy and styd on wl ins fnl f: nt rch ldrs* **13/8**[1]

0155 **6** *½* **Brother Tiger**[16] 3967 8-9-7 **80**.................... JFEgan 5 81
(David C Griffiths) *led: rdn over 1f out: drvn and hdd 100yds out: wknd towards fin* **10/1**

120 **7** *1 ¼* **Zipedeedodah (IRE)**[10] 4182 5-9-4 **80**....................(t) KieranShoemark(3) 1 76
(Joseph Tuite) *chsd ldrs: effrt over 1f out: unable qck 1f out: wknd ins fnl f* **16/1**

000 **8** *¾* **New Road Side**[4] 4433 4-9-2 **75**....................(v) JamieSpencer 9 72
(Richard Guest) *chsd ldr: rdn over 1f out: nudged lft and lost 2nd 1f out: losing pl whn squeezed for room and hmpd ins fnl f: eased wl ins fnl f* **16/1**

33-0 **9** *1 ½* **Fang**[13] 4099 4-9-6 **79**.................... FranBerry 3 67
(William Jarvis) *hld up in midfield on inner: effrt over 1f out: no imp and kpt on same pce ins fnl f* **6/1**

5040 **10** *3* **Noble Act**[16] 3971 4-8-5 **64**.................... DannyBrock 11 41
(Phil McEntee) *a towards rr: struggling u.p over 1f out: bhd fnl f* **50/1**

1m 0.24s (0.04) **Going Correction** 0.0s/f (Stan) 10 Ran SP% **120.1**
Speed ratings (Par 105): **99,98,96,96,96 95,93,92,89,84**
CSF £92.82 CT £1704.16 TOTE £6.30: £1.60, £8.10, £4.10; EX 99.80 Trifecta £698.80.
**Owner** Mrs J Hughes & Mrs C Kemp **Bred** Kenneth Heelan **Trained** Newmarket, Suffolk

**FOCUS**
They went a decent pace and the first two came from some way back. A small pb from the winner.
T/Plt: £77.30 to a £1 stake. Pool: £61,263.84 - 578.06 winning units. T/Qpdt: £32.10 to a £1 stake. Pool: £5,863.78 - 134.80 winning units. **Steve Payne**

# 4339 DONCASTER (L-H)
Friday, July 7

**OFFICIAL GOING: Good to firm (8.1)**
Wind: Virtually nil Weather: Cloudy

## 4567 NORMANDIE STUD NOVICE STKS 6f 111y
**2:00** (2:02) (Class 5) 2-Y-O **£3,040** (£904; £452; £226) **Stalls** Low

Form RPR

**1** **Wasim (IRE)** 2-9-2 0.................... KevinStott 9 83
(Ismail Mohammed) *led: jnd and rdn along 1½f out: drvn and hdd narrowly ins fnl f: rallied to ld nr line* **33/1**

**2** *nse* **Nobleman's Nest** 2-9-2 0.................... HarryBentley 11 83
(Simon Crisford) *trckd ldrs: smooth hdwy over 2f out: cl up 1½f out:. sn chal: rdn 1f out: led ins fnl f: hdd nr line* **11/2**[2]

22 **3** *2 ¾* **Mutakatif (IRE)**[22] 3747 2-9-2 0.................... JimCrowley 10 75
(Charles Hills) *trckd ldng pair: hdwy to trck ldr 3f out: effrt to chal over 1f out: sn rdn and ev ch tl drvn and kpt on same pce ins fnl f* **4/7**[1]

**4** *½* **Picture No Sound (IRE)** 2-9-2 0.................... TonyHamilton 6 74+
(Richard Fahey) *hld up: hdwy wl over 2f out: chsd ldrs wl over 1f out: sn rdn: kpt on fnl f* **25/1**

**5** *4* **Dazzle Gold (USA)** 2-9-2 0.................... LukeMorris 12 63+
(Robert Cowell) *midfield: rdn along and hdwy over 2f out: drvn over 1f out: kpt on fnl f* **16/1**

**6** *½* **Muraadef** 2-9-2 0.................... GrahamLee 13 62
(Ed Dunlop) *trckd ldrs: pushed along over 2f out: sn rdn and grad wknd* **25/1**

**7** *½* **Jungle Room (USA)** 2-9-2 0.................... JamieSpencer 14 60+
(Kevin Ryan) *dwlt and towards rr: hdwy on outer over 2f out: styd on fnl f* **7/1**[3]

0 **8** *1 ¼* **Sandytown (IRE)**[88] 1673 2-9-2 0.................... ShaneGray 1 57
(Kevin Ryan) *dwlt and towards rr tl sme late hdwy* **25/1**

**9** *1* **She's Different (IRE)** 2-8-11 0.................... TomEaves 4 49
(Nigel Tinkler) *in tch: rdn along wl over 2f out: sn wknd* **66/1**

**10** *½* **Sunstorm** 2-9-2 0.................... OisinMurphy 8 53
(David Brown) *a towards rr* **40/1**

**11** *¾* **Bombshell Bay** 2-9-2 0.................... SeanLevey 2 51+
(Richard Hannon) *a towards rr* **16/1**

06 **12** *shd* **Thundercloud**[19] 3858 2-8-11 0.................... DavidAllan 5 45
(Scott Dixon) *chsd wnr: rdn along 3f out: sn wknd* **66/1**

**13** *3 ½* **Make Good (IRE)** 2-9-2 0.................... RobertWinston 3 41
(David Brown) *dwlt: a rr* **50/1**

1m 19.97s (0.07) **Going Correction** +0.10s/f (Good) 13 Ran SP% **125.2**
Speed ratings (Par 94): **103,102,99,99,94 94,93,92,90,90 89,89,85**
CSF £205.42 TOTE £49.70: £11.00, £2.10, £1.02; EX 437.90 Trifecta £2155.10.
**Owner** Ismail Mohammed **Bred** Floors Farming, S Roy & Admington Hall **Trained** Newmarket, Suffolk

**FOCUS**
The ground which had been watered to the tune of 4mm on the straight on Thursday and just shy of 1mm overnight. Jockeys confirmed that it was riding as per the official description. A decent novice event. They raced in one group down the centre, and nothing could get involved from the rear. High numbers came out on top. The opening level is fluid but the time was decent and it's been rated as good form.

## 4568 PAYZONE STARS MAIDEN FILLIES' STKS 7f 6y
**2:30** (2:31) (Class 5) 3-Y-O+ **£3,040** (£904; £452; £226) **Stalls** Low

Form RPR
1 **Lucky Lucrecia (IRE)** 3-9-0 0 DanielTudhope 4 76+
(William Haggas) *dwlt: hld up in rr: hdwy wl over 2f out: chsd ldrs wl over 1f out: chal appr fnl f: sn rdn and led last 120 yds* **5/2**[2]
2 ½ **Pretty Passe** 3-9-0 0 PaulHanagan 1 71+
(William Haggas) *t.k.h.: in tch: hdwy to trck ldrs over 2f out: effrt and green 11/2f out: sn rdn and styd on wl fnl f* **7/2**[3]
0-0 3 ½ **Ghaseedah**[27] 3595 3-9-0 0 (h) GrahamLee 7 70
(Simon Crisford) *trckd ldng pair: hdwy to chse ldr 2f out and sn cl up: rdn to dispute ld and ev ch ent fnl f: sn drvn and kpt on same pce* **16/1**
4-4 4 nk **South Sea Belle (IRE)**[78] 1905 3-9-0 0 KevinStott 2 69
(David Menuisier) *led: pushed along over 2f out: jnd and rdn over 1f out: drvn and hdd ins fnl f: kpt on same pce* **9/2**
5 4½ **Obeya** 3-9-0 0 HarryBentley 6 57
(Roger Varian) *trckd ldrs: hdwy wl over 2f out and sn pushed along: rdn wl over 1f out: sn one pce* **2/1**[1]
6 2 **Charlie's Dreamer** 3-9-0 0 LukeMorris 8 51
(Michael Appleby) *green and swvd bdly rt s: sn chsng ldrs: rdn along wl over 2f out: sn wknd* **22/1**
40 7 3¾ **Velvet Charm**[26] 3626 3-9-0 0 JamieSpencer 9 41
(Rae Guest) *dwlt: a towards rr* **25/1**
8 2 **Compass Rose (IRE)** 3-9-0 0 DavidAllan 5 36
(Scott Dixon) *green: a towards rr* **33/1**
0 9 10 **Rambling Queen (IRE)**[14] 4055 4-9-8 0 (t) JamesSullivan 3 12
(Brian Rothwell) *in tch: pushed along 1/2-way: rdn 3f out and sn wknd* **100/1**

1m 28.07s (1.77) **Going Correction** +0.10s/f (Good)
**WFA** 3 from 4yo 8lb **9 Ran SP% 120.3**
Speed ratings (Par 100): **93,92,91,91,86 84,79,77,66**
CSF £11.92 TOTE £3.00: £1.20, £1.40, £4.00; EX 13.90 Trifecta £128.00.
**Owner** Bernard Kantor **Bred** B Kantor (breeding) **Trained** Newmarket, Suffolk
**FOCUS**
A 1-2 for William Haggas in this ordinary fillies' maiden. It's been rated around the fourth.

## 4569 JOLLYS JEWELLERS MAIDEN STKS 1m 3f 197y
**3:05** (3:07) (Class 5) 3-Y-O+ **£3,040** (£904; £452; £226) **Stalls** Low

Form RPR
1 **Royal Associate** 3-9-2 0 MartinLane 12 87+
(Charlie Appleby) *prom: led after 21/2f: hdd 7 out and cl up: pushed along 4f out: rdn on inner 2f out: drvn to ld again ins fnl f: hld on gamely* **14/1**
2 2 ½ **Musaahim (USA)**[20] 3839 3-9-2 0 HarryBentley 9 86+
(Roger Varian) *trckd ldrs: hdwy over 3f out: cl up and rdn wl over 1f out: drvn to chal ent fnl f: no ex towards fin* **5/6**[1]
-622 3 3½ **Chief Craftsman**[19] 3860 3-9-2 78 JamieSpencer 8 80
(Luca Cumani) *prom: hdwy to ld wl over 2f out: rdn over 1f out: hdd and drvn ins fnl f: kpt on same pce* **3/1**[2]
5-4 4 4 **Percy B Shelley**[18] 3921 3-9-2 0 (t) GrahamLee 5 74+
(John Gosden) *chsd ldrs: pushed along 3f out: rdn over 2f out: kpt on one pce* **9/1**[3]
4 5 1 **Chartbuster (IRE)**[14] 4055 3-9-2 0 JoeDoyle 2 72
(Julie Camacho) *chsd ldrs: pushed along over 3f out: rdn over 2f out: sn one pce* **20/1**
3 6 3¼ **Helf (IRE)**[19] 3860 3-9-2 0 SeanLevey 1 67
(Richard Hannon) *led 21/2f: cl up: led again 7f out: pushed along over 3f out: hdd wl over 2f out and sn rdn: cl up and drvn wl over 1f out: sn wknd* **10/1**
7 hd **Grey Mist** 3-9-2 0 DavidAllan 11 66
(Tim Easterby) *s.i.s and green in rr: sme late hdwy* **66/1**
2 8 5 **Heron (USA)**[14] 4055 3-9-2 0 LukeMorris 7 58
(Hugo Palmer) *dwlt: midfield: hdwy and in tch 1/2-way: rdn along 4f out: sn outpcd and bhd* **11/1**
9 nk **Leodis (IRE)**[44] 5-10-0 0 JamesSullivan 6 57
(Tom Tate) *t.k.h: a towards rr* **50/1**
60 10 2½ **Dixon**[31] 3438 3-9-2 0 JoeyHaynes 10 54
(Mark H Tompkins) *chsd ldrs: rdn along over 3f out: sn wknd* **100/1**
04 11 1 **Titan**[8] 4274 3-9-2 0 PaulMulrennan 14 52
(Ed Dunlop) *t.k.h early: hld up: a towards rr* **50/1**
00 12 1 **Clearance**[8] 4274 3-9-2 0 ThomasBrown 13 51
(Mark H Tompkins) *a rr* **100/1**

2m 35.59s (0.69) **Going Correction** +0.10s/f (Good)
**WFA** 3 from 5yo 12lb **12 Ran SP% 125.8**
Speed ratings (Par 103): **101,100,98,95,95 92,92,89,89,87 86,86**
CSF £27.42 TOTE £16.40: £5.40, £1.02, £1.80; EX 42.60 Trifecta £120.90.
**Owner** Godolphin **Bred** Darley **Trained** Newmarket, Suffolk
**FOCUS**
Race run over an extra 12yds. Subsequent Group 3 winner Marmelo won this maiden easily last year. This edition should produce winners. It's been rated around the third.

## 4570 WIN BIGGER WITH BETFAIR CLASSIFIED STKS 7f 6y
**3:35** (3:35) (Class 3) 4-Y-O+ **£7,439** (£2,213; £1,106; £553) **Stalls** Low

Form RPR
-563 1 **Classic Seniority**[21] 3792 5-9-3 90 DanielTudhope 4 95
(Marjorie Fife) *trckd ldrs: effrt and nt clr run jst over 1f out: sn swtchd lft and rdn ent fnl f: styd on wl to ld towards fin* **7/1**
21-2 2 hd **Sun Lover**[21] 3792 4-9-3 89 HarryBentley 12 94
(Roger Varian) *trckd ldrs: hdwy over 2f out: rdn to ld jst over 1f out: drvn ins fnl f: hdd and no ex towards fin* **10/11**[1]
5-35 3 1½ **Lefortovo (FR)**[53] 2696 4-9-3 87 (p[1]) DougieCostello 11 90
(Jo Hughes) *hld up in tch: hdwy 2f out: rdn to chse ldrs ent fnl f: kpt on* **33/1**
415 4 shd **Takatul (USA)**[49] 2799 4-9-3 88 (b[1]) SteveDrowne 9 90
(Charles Hills) *trckd ldr: cl up 1/2-way: rdn to ld 2f out: hdd over 1f out: sn drvn: kpt on same pce* **12/1**
5050 5 nk **Eltezam (IRE)**[27] 3585 4-9-3 90 SeanLevey 14 89
(Richard Hannon) *led: pushed along 3f out: rdn and hdd 2f out: cl up: drvn ent fnl f: kpt on same pce* **12/1**
004 6 7 **Toofi (FR)**[27] 3585 6-9-3 89 RobertWinston 1 70
(John Butler) *dwlt: hld up in rr: hdwy 3f out: rdn along 2f out: sn outpcd* **6/1**[3]
00-5 7 7 **Claim The Roses (USA)**[8] 4261 6-9-3 90 PhillipMakin 3 52
(Ed Vaughan) *chsd ldng pair: rdn along 3f out: sn wknd* **11/2**[2]

1m 25.54s (-0.76) **Going Correction** +0.10s/f (Good) **7 Ran SP% 112.9**
Speed ratings (Par 107): **108,107,106,105,105 97,89**
CSF £13.49 TOTE £6.00: £2.50, £1.40; EX 14.90 Trifecta £197.60.
**Owner** HuggyMac Racing **Bred** E Cantillon, D Cantillon & A Driver **Trained** Stillington, N Yorks
**FOCUS**
A decent classified event, but it was weakened by a string of non-runners.

## 4571 CHESTERFIELD ESTATES/EBF STALLIONS BREEDING WINNERS FILLIES' H'CAP 1m 3f 197y
**4:10** (4:10) (Class 4) (0-85,84) 3-Y-O+ **£6,469** (£1,925; £962; £481) **Stalls** Low

Form RPR
315 1 **Pleasant Surprise (IRE)**[22] 3749 3-9-2 84 JamieSpencer 1 93+
(Luca Cumani) *stdd s and hld up in rr: smooth hdwy 3f out: led jst over 1f out: sn rdn and kpt on* **2/1**[1]
1-56 2 1 **Di Alta (IRE)**[34] 3341 3-8-9 77 ow2 ThomasBrown 7 83
(Ed Walker) *trckd ldrs: hdwy and cl up over 3f out: led 2f out and sn rdn: hdd jst over 1f out: drvn and kpt on fnl f* **8/1**
-013 3 ½ **Harebell (IRE)**[24] 3693 3-8-9 77 (h) HarryBentley 9 82
(Ralph Beckett) *hld up in tch: hdwy over 3f out: pushed along wl over 2f out: rdn over 1f out: kpt on fnl f* **5/2**[2]
0-43 4 1 **Melinoe**[45] 2921 3-8-5 73 LukeMorris 5 76
(Sir Mark Prescott Bt) *trckd ldr: cl up over 3f out: sn led and rdn: hdd 2f out: sn drvn and kpt on same pce* **13/2**[3]
3332 5 4 **Canny Style**[8] 4244 4-8-12 68 KevinStott 2 64
(Kevin Ryan) *trckd ldng pair: pushed along over 3f out: rdn over 2f out: drvn and wknd over 1f out* **13/2**[3]
6416 6 1½ **Perfect In Pink**[23] 3711 3-8-12 80 GrahamLee 4 75
(Mick Channon) *set stdy pce: pushed along 4f out: rdn and hdd 3f out: sn drvn and grad wknd* **9/1**
-053 7 1 **Island Flame (IRE)**[14] 4056 4-9-1 71 RobertWinston 3 63
(Richard Fahey) *hld up in tch: hdwy on inner over 3f out: rdn along over 2f out: sn wknd* **14/1**

2m 35.1s (0.20) **Going Correction** +0.10s/f (Good)
**WFA** 3 from 4yo 12lb **7 Ran SP% 116.3**
Speed ratings (Par 102): **103,102,102,101,98 97,97**
CSF £19.36 CT £41.67 TOTE £2.40: £1.50, £4.10; EX 20.10 Trifecta £79.50.
**Owner** Gerry Mordaunt & Partners **Bred** Dreaming Partnership **Trained** Newmarket, Suffolk
**FOCUS**
Race run over an additional 12yds. They didn't go much of a gallop until the home straight, but that didn't prevent the winner and third from coming from the back. The fifth time in six years that this has gone to a 3yo. The form makes sense rated around the third.

## 4572 BETFAIR EACH WAY EDGE H'CAP (DIV I) 1m 3f 197y
**4:40** (4:41) (Class 5) (0-70,72) 4-Y-O+ **£3,040** (£904; £452; £226) **Stalls** Low

Form RPR
1513 1 **Percys Princess**[39] 3148 6-8-12 65 JaneElliott[(5)] 8 71
(Michael Appleby) *trckd ldr: cl up over 5f out: slt ld 4f out: sn hdd: cl up and rdn on inner over 2f out: rallied to ld again jst over 1f out: edgd rt ins fnl f: hld on gamely* **9/1**
4202 2 nse **Luv U Whatever**[11] 4158 7-9-5 67 BarryMcHugh 5 73
(Marjorie Fife) *trckd ldrs: hdwy and cl up over 4f out: slt ld 31/2f out: rdn along over 2f out: hdd narrowly jst over 1f out: sn drvn and ev ch ins fnl f: jst hld* **9/4**[1]
4204 3 2¼ **Surround Sound**[13] 4102 7-8-10 61 (t) RachelRichardson[(3)] 7 63
(Tim Easterby) *dwlt and hld up in rr: hdwy wl over 2f out: rdn to chse ldrs on outer over 1f out: drvn and kpt on fnl f* **6/1**
-025 4 ¾ **Longside**[51] 2728 5-9-2 64 RyanTate 6 65
(James Eustace) *hld up in tch: hdwy 3f out: chsd ldng pair wl over 1f out and sn rdn: drvn and kpt ons ame pce fnl f* **3/1**[2]
5203 5 3¼ **All You (IRE)**[17] 3935 5-9-5 67 (v) PhillipMakin 4 63
(David O'Meara) *trckd ldrs on inner: pushed along and hdwy over 3f out: rdn along over 2f out: drvn and wknd wl over 1f out* **6/1**
0200 6 6 **Ice Galley (IRE)**[34] 3311 4-9-7 69 GrahamLee 3 55
(Philip Kirby) *led: pushed along 5f out: hdd and rdn 4f out: drvn 3f out and sn wknd* **9/2**[3]

2m 35.98s (1.08) **Going Correction** +0.10s/f (Good) **6 Ran SP% 112.5**
Speed ratings (Par 103): **100,99,98,97,95 91**
CSF £29.74 CT £132.13 TOTE £7.30: £3.40, £1.70; EX 34.20 Trifecta £113.80.
**Owner** C A Blyth **Bred** Norman A Blyth **Trained** Oakham, Rutland
**FOCUS**
Add 12yds to race distance. Moderate handicap form. It's been rated a bit cautiously, with the third to his latest form.

## 4573 BETFAIR EACH WAY EDGE H'CAP (DIV II) 1m 3f 197y
**5:10** (5:10) (Class 5) (0-70,70) 4-Y-O+ **£3,040** (£904; £452; £226) **Stalls** Low

Form RPR
055 1 **Sparte Quercus (IRE)**[18] 3921 4-9-7 70 GrahamLee 2 78+
(Ed Dunlop) *trckd ldrs: hdwy 3f out: chsd ldr 2f out: rdn to chal over 1f out: styd on to ld last 100 yds* **4/1**[3]
2522 2 ¾ **Boychick (IRE)**[28] 3547 4-9-5 68 ThomasBrown 5 75
(Ed Walker) *trckd ldr: hdwy and cl up 5f out: led 3f out: rdn along wl over 1f out: drvn ent fnl f: hdd and no ex last 100 yds* **11/4**[1]
5-25 3 2½ **Macksville (IRE)**[175] 218 4-8-13 62 RyanTate 9 65
(James Eustace) *hld up in tch: pushed along over 3f out: hdwy 2f out: rdn wl over 1f out: sn chsng ldng pair: drvn ins fnl; f: kpt on same pce* **11/4**[1]
0040 4 nse **Best Example (USA)**[22] 3753 5-9-1 67 ShelleyBirkett[(3)] 4 70
(Julia Feilden) *hld up in tch: hdwy 3f out: effrt and n.m.r 2f out: rdn to chse ldng pair jst over 1f out: drvn and kpt on same pce fnl f* **20/1**
1100 5 2¼ **Dunquin (IRE)**[31] 3432 5-9-6 69 LukeMorris 8 68
(John Mackie) *t.k.h: trckd ldng pair: effrt and n.m.r over 2f out: rdn along wl over 1f out: sn btn* **8/1**
5-64 6 2¾ **Goldslinger (FR)**[24] 3694 5-9-3 66 RobertWinston 1 61
(Dean Ivory) *led: pushed along over 4f out: hdd 3f out:. sn drvn and wknd fnl 2f* **7/2**[2]

2m 34.69s (-0.21) **Going Correction** +0.10s/f (Good) **6 Ran SP% 111.4**
Speed ratings (Par 103): **104,103,101,101,100 98**
CSF £15.13 CT £33.02 TOTE £4.20: £2.40, £1.30; EX 15.20 Trifecta £53.80.
**Owner** S F Hui **Bred** Daniel Chassagneux **Trained** Newmarket, Suffolk

**FOCUS**
Race run over an extra 12yds. Just ordinary form, but it was the quickest of the four C&D events. The runner-up has been rated to his AW form, with the third and fourth close to form.

## 4574 LYCETTS INSURANCE FILLIES' H'CAP 5f 3y
**5:40** (5:40) (Class 4) (0-80,80) 3-Y-O+ **£4,851** (£1,443; £721; £360) **Stalls** Low

Form RPR
-353 1 **Justice Lady (IRE)**[8] 4272 4-9-10 **78**................ ShaneKelly 3 84+
(David Elsworth) *stdd s and hld up in rr: smooth hdwy 2f out: swtchd lft wl over 1f out: effrt to chal ent fnl f: led last 50yds: cleverly* **15/8**[1]
3600 2 ½ **Rose Marmara**[32] 3401 4-9-4 **72**................(t) BarryMcHugh 4 76
(Brian Rothwell) *trckd ldrs: pushed along 2f out: rdn to chal over 1f out: drvn to take slt ld wl ins fnl f: hdd and no ex last 50yds* **12/1**
-650 3 shd **Savannah Beau**[7] 4305 5-9-1 **69**................(p) PhillipMakin 5 72
(Derek Shaw) *trckd ldrs: hdwy 2f out: rdn and n.m.r over 1f out: drvn to chal and ev ch ins fnl f: no ex towards fin* **14/1**
3214 4 shd **Penny Dreadful**[14] 4053 5-8-6 **67**................(p) RPWalsh(7) 2 70
(Scott Dixon) *trckd ldrs: hdwy and cl up 2f out: led 1 1/2f out: drvn and hdd wl ins fnl f: no ex* **15/2**
2124 5 1¾ **Berryessa (IRE)**[18] 3904 3-8-13 **72**................ StevieDonohoe 8 67
(Rae Guest) *trckd ldrs: pushed along and sltly outpcd wl over 1f out: rdn and chsd ldrs ent fnl f: sn drvn and kpt on same pce* **9/2**[3]
4153 6 3 **Yorkshiredebut (IRE)**[18] 3904 3-9-1 **74**................ JasonHart 6 58
(Paul Midgley) *trckd ldr: cl up 1/2-way: rdn along wl over 1f out: drvn and wknd ent fnl f* **4/1**[2]
15 7 3½ **Lydia's Place**[18] 3904 4-9-12 **80**................ SeanLevey 1 53
(Richard Guest) *led: rdn along 2f out: hdd 1 1/2f out: sn wknd* **6/1**
-064 8 7 **Broadhaven Honey (IRE)**[9] 4200 3-9-0 **73**................ GrahamLee 7 19
(Tony Carroll) *rrd s: sn cl up: rdn along over 2f out: wknd wl over 1f out* **25/1**

1m 0.15s (-0.35) **Going Correction** +0.10s/f (Good)
**WFA** 3 from 4yo+ 5lb **8** Ran SP% **117.2**
Speed ratings (Par 102): **106,105,105,104,102 97,91,80**
CSF £27.52 CT £251.19 TOTE £3.50: £1.90, £3.20, £3.30; EX 24.50 Trifecta £145.90.
**Owner** Robert Ng **Bred** Miss Audrey F Thompson **Trained** Newmarket, Suffolk

**FOCUS**
A fair fillies' sprint.
T/Jkpt: Not won. T/Plt: £26.70 to a £1 stake. Pool: £61,883.00 - 2,313.68 winning units. T/Qpdt: £7.50 to a £1 stake. Pool: £4,344.00 - 573.48 winning units. **Joe Rowntree**

# 4525 HAYDOCK (L-H)
Friday, July 7

**OFFICIAL GOING: Good to firm (9.0)**
Wind: Almost nil Weather: Overcast

## 4575 BETFRED FOLLOW US ON TWITTER H'CAP 1m 2f 42y
**5:50** (5:53) (Class 5) (0-70,71) 3-Y-O+ **£3,557** (£1,058; £529; £264) **Stalls** Centre

Form RPR
04-0 1 **Punkawallah**[63] 2366 3-9-0 **65**................(p¹) RichardKingscote 7 71
(Tom Dascombe) *midfield: u.p over 5f out: rdn over 4f out: hdwy 3f out: chalng fr 2f out: wanted to lug lft and led narrowly over 1f out: a hrd pressed: r.o u.p and jst did enough nr fin* **10/1**
-640 2 hd **Kuraka**[29] 3489 3-8-12 **66**................ JordanVaughan(3) 2 71
(K R Burke) *chsd ldrs: wnt 2nd 4f out: rdn to chal fr 2f out: r.o u.p thrght fnl f: jst hld* **5/1**[2]
4111 3 hd **Miningrocks (FR)**[8] 4279 5-9-9 **71**................ GerO'Neill(7) 8 75
(Declan Carroll) *sn led: rdn and hung rt fr 2f out: sn hrd pressed: hdd narrowly over 1f out: continued to chal ins fnl f: r.o u.p: edgd lft clsng stages: jst hld* **5/2**[1]
3005 4 nk **Sakurajima (IRE)**[8] 4255 3-8-10 **64**................(t) CallumShepherd(3) 6 68
(Charles Hills) *in rr: swtchd rt and hdwy over 2f out: swtchd lft whn chsng ldrs over 1f out: r.o u.p ins fnl f: clsd towards fin: jst hld* **11/2**[3]
5-06 5 shd **La Havrese (FR)**[27] 3560 6-9-1 **59**................ JoshDoyle(3) 10 62
(Lynn Siddall) *hld up: hdwy 3f out: rdn to chal fr 2f out: r.o u.p thrght fnl f: hld nr fin* **16/1**
5046 6 6 **Competition**[18] 3898 5-9-2 **60**................(t) AdamMcNamara(3) 4 51
(Brian Rothwell) *midfield: rdn 3f out: hdwy to chse ldrs over 2f out: one pce fr over 1f out* **22/1**
0202 7 1½ **Arithmetic (IRE)**[10] 4185 4-9-10 **65**................(p¹) JackGarritty 3 54
(Ruth Carr) *racd keenly: chsd ldrs: rdn over 2f out: sn trying to chal: one pce fr over 1f out* **5/1**[2]
0004 8 2¾ **King Of Paradise (IRE)**[22] 3740 8-8-9 **50**................ NeilFarley 13 33
(Eric Alston) *pushed along to ld early: chsd ldr after: lost 2nd 4f out: rdn and wknd over 3f out* **28/1**
005 9 nse **Arrowzone**[20] 3820 6-9-12 **67**................ FrannyNorton 5 50
(Kevin Frost) *hld up: no bttr than midfield: lost pl over 4f out: sn u.p: n.d after* **9/1**
10 4 **Twistsandturns (IRE)**[133] 909 6-9-0 **55**................ RoystonFfrench 9 31
(Declan Carroll) *hld up: rdn and outpcd 4f out: nvr a threat* **25/1**

2m 10.81s (-1.89) **Going Correction** -0.225s/f (Firm)
**WFA** 3 from 4yo+ 10lb **10** Ran SP% **113.9**
Speed ratings (Par 103): **98,97,97,97,97 92,91,89,89,85**
CSF £56.54 CT £164.42 TOTE £11.20: £2.10, £2.10, £1.20; EX 76.20 Trifecta £304.20.
**Owner** Laurence Bellman & Chasemore Farm **Bred** Chasemore Farm **Trained** Malpas, Cheshire

**FOCUS**
All races will run over the Inner Home Straight. Allowing for rail position on bends advertised race distances increase as follows: Races 1 and 6 by 31 yards; Races 3, 4 and 5 by 9 yards. An ordinary handicap. They went a decent gallop on watered, officially good to firm ground. They were kicking the top off the surface in the straight.

## 4576 BETFRED LIKE US ON FACEBOOK H'CAP 5f
**6:20** (6:24) (Class 5) (0-70,72) 3-Y-O **£3,557** (£1,058; £529; £264) **Stalls** Centre

Form RPR
0325 1 **Dundunah (USA)**[14] 4060 3-9-4 **67**................(t) DanielTudhope 10 76
(David O'Meara) *in tch: led over 1f out: edgd rt ins fnl f: r.o wl and drew away* **8/1**[3]
-302 2 2 **The Nazca Lines (IRE)**[13] 4104 3-9-9 **72**................(v) RichardKingscote 1 74
(John Quinn) *hld up: rdn and hdwy over 1f out: styd on ins fnl f: wnt 2nd fnl 110yds: nt trble wnr* **4/1**[2]
0-50 3 1¼ **Poet's Time**[46] 2898 3-8-2 **51** oh2................ FrannyNorton 8 48
(Tim Easterby) *in rr: rdn and hdwy over 1f out: styd on u.p ins fnl f: nt pce of wnr* **50/1**
3062 4 hd **Peachey Carnehan**[11] 4161 3-9-7 **70**................(b¹) RobertTart 4 67
(Michael Mullineaux) *sn bhd and outpcd: hdwy over 1f out: styd on ins fnl f: nt trble wnr* **25/1**
5111 5 shd **Foxy Boy**[1] 4531 3-8-10 **64**................ CallumRodriguez(5) 9 60
(Michael Dods) *sed awkwardly: hld up: hdwy over 2f out: styd on ins fnl f: no imp on wnr: hld nr fin* **10/11**[1]
0216 6 hd **Glyder**[20] 3812 3-8-13 **62**................ RoystonFfrench 5 58
(John Holt) *midfield: pushed along 2f out: hdwy 1f out: styd on ins fnl f: nt pce of wnr: hld nr fin* **10/1**
2-03 7 5 **Chickenfortea (IRE)**[43] 2993 3-8-13 **62**................ NeilFarley 6 40
(Eric Alston) *w ldr: led 2f out: hdd over 1f out: wknd fnl 110yds* **14/1**
2240 8 1 **Lambrini Legacy**[20] 3818 3-8-10 **59** ow2................(h) TomMarquand 2 33
(Lisa Williamson) *led: racd keenly: hdd 2f out: rdn and hung lft over 1f out: sn wknd* **50/1**
0164 9 nk **Who Told Jo Jo (IRE)**[23] 3719 3-9-4 **67**................(p) OisinMurphy 3 40
(Joseph Tuite) *chsd ldrs: rdn and losing grnd whn checked over 1f out: wknd after* **9/1**

59.99s (-0.81) **Going Correction** -0.225s/f (Firm) **9** Ran SP% **117.0**
Speed ratings (Par 100): **97,93,91,91,91 91,83,81,80**
CSF £40.09 CT £1509.12 TOTE £7.20: £2.10, £1.80, £9.10; EX 36.40 Trifecta £1245.70.
**Owner** Hamad Rashed Bin Ghedayer **Bred** Rf/Hf Mares Rule **Trained** Upper Helmsley, N Yorks

**FOCUS**
A fair 3yo sprint handicap. They went a decent gallop and the loose top surface after watering is having an effect on the times. The runner-up has been rated to this year's form.

## 4577 BETFRED TV EBF NOVICE STKS (PLUS 10 RACE) 6f 212y
**6:50** (6:53) (Class 4) 2-Y-O **£4,528** (£1,347; £673; £336) **Stalls** Low

Form RPR
1 **Mildenberger** 2-9-2 0................ FrannyNorton 7 79+
(Mark Johnston) *chsd ldr: rdn to chal over 1f out: led ins fnl f: r.o: in command towards fin* **3/1**[2]
46 2 1½ **Collateral (IRE)**[13] 4101 2-9-2 0................ OisinMurphy 4 75
(James Tate) *led: rdn whn pressed over 1f out: hdd ins fnl f: no ex towards fin* **11/4**[1]
3 2½ **Delph Crescent (IRE)** 2-9-2 0................ TonyHamilton 5 68+
(Richard Fahey) *sluggish s: hld up: hdwy 2f out: effrt to chse front two over 1f out: kpt on but no imp ins fnl f* **9/2**
4 3¾ **Shootingthe Breeze** 2-9-2 0................ RichardKingscote 3 58
(Tom Dascombe) *green on way to s: chsd ldrs: rdn over 2f out: one pce fr over 1f out* **7/2**[3]
5 1½ **Galactic (IRE)** 2-9-2 0................ TomMarquand 1 54
(Richard Hannon) *in rr: pushed along over 3f out: swtchd rt over 2f out: nvr able to trble ldrs* **12/1**
6 6 ½ **Drover**[16] 3973 2-9-2 0................ DougieCostello 9 53
(Keith Dalgleish) *hld up: rdn 2f out: nvr a threat* **14/1**
7 ¾ **Urban Soul (IRE)** 2-9-2 0................ DanielTudhope 8 51+
(James Bethell) *racd keenly: chsd ldrs wout cover: rdn and tried to chal 2f out: hung lft over 1f out: wknd fnl f* **14/1**

1m 28.89s (-1.81) **Going Correction** -0.225s/f (Firm) **7** Ran SP% **113.1**
Speed ratings (Par 96): **101,99,96,92,90 89,89**
CSF £11.43 TOTE £3.70: £1.80, £1.60; EX 11.00 Trifecta £49.80.
**Owner** Sheikh Hamdan bin Mohammed Al Maktoum **Bred** Godolphin **Trained** Middleham Moor, N Yorks

**FOCUS**
Race distance increased 9 yards. An ordinary juvenile novice contest. They went a respectable gallop but the loose surface proved tiring for most of these young horses. The opening level is fluid.

## 4578 BETFRED SUPER LEAGUE H'CAP 7f 212y
**7:20** (7:22) (Class 3) (0-95,95) 3-Y-O+ **£9,056** (£2,695; £1,346; £673) **Stalls** Low

Form RPR
4002 1 **Calder Prince (IRE)**[22] 3743 4-9-5 **86**................ RichardKingscote 5 95
(Tom Dascombe) *led early: chsd ldr: led over 2f out: edgd rt ins fnl f: drvn out and r.o* **7/2**[1]
-236 2 1¼ **Areen Heart (FR)**[36] 3232 3-8-10 **86**................ TonyHamilton 1 90+
(Richard Fahey) *racd keenly: trckd ldrs on inner: nt clr run fr 2f out tl swtchd rt over 1f out: wnt 2nd ent fnl f: styd on: no imp on wnr towards fin* **7/2**[1]
-443 3 ¾ **Midhmaar**[20] 3808 4-9-6 **87**................(b¹) OisinMurphy 6 91
(Owen Burrows) *racd keenly in midfield: rdn over 2f out: hdwy and big effrt over 1f out whn bmpd: styd on ins fnl f: no ex towards fin* **11/2**[3]
2431 4 3½ **Lincoln Rocks**[20] 3828 4-9-12 **93**................ DanielTudhope 2 89
(David O'Meara) *sn led: rdn and hdd over 2f out: one pce ins fnl f* **7/2**[1]
-335 5 ¾ **Alnashama**[20] 3837 5-9-5 **89**................ CallumShepherd(3) 7 83
(Charles Hills) *hld up: hdwy to chse ldrs over 2f out: no imp fr over 1f out: one pce after* **17/2**
5160 6 2¾ **Cote D'Azur**[16] 3963 4-10-0 **95**................ JackGarritty 3 83
(Les Eyre) *trckd ldrs: effrt to chal over 2f out: wknd over 1f out* **9/2**[2]
1104 7 8 **Theodorico (IRE)**[13] 4103 4-9-8 **89**................ DougieCostello 8 59
(David Loughnane) *midfield: rdn over 2f out and rdr dropped rein: sn wknd* **20/1**
0-00 8 2 **Accurate**[15] 4001 4-9-3 **84**................ GeorgeDowning 4 49
(Ian Williams) *hld up: rdn over 2f out: lft bhd fr over 1f out* **66/1**

1m 39.58s (-4.12) **Going Correction** -0.225s/f (Firm)
**WFA** 3 from 4yo+ 9lb **8** Ran SP% **117.0**
Speed ratings (Par 107): **111,109,109,105,104 102,94,92**
CSF £16.28 CT £66.53 TOTE £5.10: £1.70, £1.70, £2.30; EX 19.80 Trifecta £79.20.
**Owner** Peter Birbeck **Bred** Michael Pitt **Trained** Malpas, Cheshire

**FOCUS**
Race distance increased 9 yards. The feature contest was a good handicap. They went a decent gallop and one of the co-favourites won well from just off the pace. A small pb from the second, with the third helping to set the standard.

## 4579 BETFRED WATCH SKY SPORTS IN OUR SHOPS MAIDEN STKS 7f 212y
**7:50** (7:54) (Class 5) 3-Y-O+ **£3,557** (£1,058; £529; £264) **Stalls** Low

Form RPR
0-44 1 **Azaly (IRE)**[35] 3293 3-9-5 74................ RichardKingscote 2 77
(Owen Burrows) *w ldr: led again 6f out: rdn over 2f out: rdn whn pressed fr wl over 1f out: r.o gamely: fnd ex cl home* **9/2**[3]
60- 2 ½ **Reverend Jacobs**[286] 6777 3-9-5 0................ DanielTudhope 6 76
(William Haggas) *led for 2f: prom: chalng 2f out: upsides thrght fnl f: hld and no ex cl home* **9/4**[2]
4-2 3 ½ **Multicultural (IRE)**[98] 1471 3-9-0 0................ OisinMurphy 5 70
(James Tate) *trckd ldrs: effrt over 2f out: rdn and chalng fr over 1f out: r.o u.p ins fnl f: hld and styd on same pce cl home* **11/8**[1]

0 **4** 4 ½ **Dream Ballad (IRE)**[7] 4309 3-9-5 0..............................(t) JackMitchell 1 65
(Hugo Palmer) *missed break: sn trckd ldrs: rdn over 2f out: no imp and one pce ins fnl f* **25/1**

0 **5** 1 **Grey Diamond**[8] 4247 3-9-5 0........................ FrannyNorton 3 62
(Mark Johnston) *missed break: in rr: rdn 3f out: hung lft u.p over 2f out: nvr a threat* **22/1**

1m 42.09s (-1.61) **Going Correction** -0.225s/f (Firm) **5** Ran SP% **99.3**
Speed ratings (Par 103): **99,98,98,93,92**
CSF £11.82 TOTE £4.90: £1.80, £1.30; EX 13.90 Trifecta £19.50.
**Owner** Hamdan Al Maktoum **Bred** Rabbah Bloodstock Limited **Trained** Lambourn, Berks
■ Getna was withdrawn. Price at time of withdrawal 7-1. Rule 4 applies to all bets - deduction 10p in the pound.

**FOCUS**
Race distance increased 9 yards. A fair maiden. They went a modest gallop and the front-runner prevailed. The third has been rated close to form.

## 4580 BETFRED VISIT OUR SHOPS ON COURSE H'CAP 1m 2f 42y
8:20 (8:22) (Class 4) (0-80,82) 3-Y-O £5,822 (£1,732; £865; £432) **Stalls** Centre

Form RPR

1401 **1** **Teodoro (IRE)**[13] 4082 3-9-10 **82**..........................(h) RichardKingscote 1 93
(Tom Dascombe) *w ldr: led 7f out: rdn whn pressed 3f out: kpt on finding ins fnl f: game* **3/1**[1]

3134 **2** ½ **Carigrad (IRE)**[14] 4048 3-9-7 **79**.............................. JackMitchell 5 88
(Hugo Palmer) *trckd ldrs: prom 4f out: chalng fr 3f out: unable qck ins fnl f: hld fnl 50yds* **3/1**[1]

-542 **3** 3 ½ **Pirate Look (IRE)**[27] 3583 3-9-7 **79**.........................(p[1]) RobertTart 8 81
(Marco Botti) *prom on outer: rdn to chal 3f out: unable qck over 1f out: hung lft ins fnl f: kpt on same pce and no imp fnl 150yds* **7/1**

21 **4** 1 **Yaarmen (USA)**[14] 4052 3-9-5 **77**.............................. DanielTudhope 4 77
(William Haggas) *led: hdd 7f out: chalng 3f out: rdn over 2f out: kpt on same pce fr over 1f out: n.m.r ins fnl f whn no imp* **7/2**[2]

2504 **5** 1 ¼ **Plead**[11] 4155 3-9-7 **79**........................................ OisinMurphy 2 77
(Archie Watson) *s.i.s: hld up: hdwy over 4f out: rdn over 2f out: nvr able to chal: one pce over 1f out* **20/1**

0420 **6** 3 ¼ **Lunar Jet**[21] 3787 3-9-0 **72**.................................. JackGarritty 9 63
(John Mackie) *in rr: swtchd rt and hdwy over 2f out: sn chsd ldrs: hung lft whn no imp over 1f out: wknd ins fnl f* **12/1**

0232 **7** 1 ½ **Je Suis Charlie**[7] 4295 3-9-5 **77**.............................. LouisSteward 10 65
(Michael Bell) *racd keenly: in tch: rdn 3f out: wknd over 2f out* **5/1**[3]

300- **8** 18 **Riviere Argentee (FR)**[259] 7493 3-9-3 **78**............... JordanVaughan(3) 6 30
(K R Burke) *racd sltly worse than midfield: u.p 5f out: lft bhd fnl 3f* **50/1**

2m 10.65s (-2.05) **Going Correction** -0.225s/f (Firm) **8** Ran SP% **115.8**
Speed ratings (Par 102): **99,98,95,95,94 91,90,75**
CSF £12.35 CT £57.02 TOTE £3.00: £1.10, £1.50, £2.30; EX 15.60 Trifecta £87.80.
**Owner** Laurence Bellman & Caroline Ingram **Bred** John Connaughton **Trained** Malpas, Cheshire

**FOCUS**
Race distance increased 31 yards. A decent 3yo handicap. They went a respectable gallop and it is sound form. Another pb from the winner, with the third rated to his fast ground form.
T/Plt: £147.00 to a £1 stake. Pool: £62,677.75 - 311.23 winning units. T/Qpdt: £17.70 to a £1 stake. Pool: £4,630.58 - 193.18 winning units. **Darren Owen**

# 3834 SANDOWN (R-H)
Friday, July 7

**OFFICIAL GOING: Good to firm (firm in places)**
Wind: Almost nil Weather: Fine, hot

## 4581 JDX "CAN DO" H'CAP 5f 10y
1:50 (1:51) (Class 3) (0-95,95) 3-Y-O+
£9,337 (£2,796; £1,398; £699; £349; £175) **Stalls** Low

Form RPR

1341 **1** **Fethiye Boy**[9] 4200 3-8-3 **77** 6ex........................................ RyanPowell 3 82
(Ronald Harris) *mde al and sn 2 l clr: racd away fr far rail: rdn 2f out: hrd pressed on all sides fnl f: jst clung on* **11/1**

4450 **2** hd **Kasbah (IRE)**[42] 3034 5-9-5 **88**.......................................... JackMitchell 2 94
(Amanda Perrett) *prom against far rail: rdn to chse wnr jst over 1f out and sn chalng: upsides last 75yds: jst denied* **11/2**[2]

0050 **3** nse **Shamshon (IRE)**[51] 2736 6-9-4 **87**..........................(t) AndreaAtzeni 7 93
(Stuart Williams) *towards rr: rdn 2f out: prog fnl f: tk 3rd last 50yds and clsd on ldng pair: jst hld* **11/2**[2]

5504 **4** nk **Tomily (IRE)**[5] 4412 3-9-7 **95**........................................ RyanMoore 8 98
(Richard Hannon) *racd in last and detached by 1/2-way: appeared to hold no ch over 1f out: str prog ins fnl f: gng on at fin* **8/1**[3]

4515 **5** hd **Queen In Waiting (IRE)**[6] 4333 3-9-4 **92**........................ JamesDoyle 9 94
(Mark Johnston) *chsd wnr to jst over 1f out: styd pressing ldrs: nt qckn last 100yds and lost pls fnl strides* **4/1**[1]

1412 **6** 1 ¾ **Zac Brown (IRE)**[20] 3827 6-8-13 **82**......................(t) SilvestreDeSousa 4 80
(Charlie Wallis) *in tch: rdn 1/2-way: swtchd to outer over 1f out: one pce and nvr rchd ldrs* **4/1**[1]

215/ **7** nk **Direct Times (IRE)**[706] 4855 6-9-7 **90**.............................. TomQueally 5 87
(Peter Chapple-Hyam) *settled in last pair: rdn 2f out: one pce and no imp ldrs fnl f* **12/1**

5003 **8** nk **Seeking Magic**[22] 3757 9-8-13 **89**..............................(t) WilliamCox(7) 6 85
(Clive Cox) *taken down early: in tch and racd wdst of all: rdn 2f out: racd sltly awkwardly and one pce fr over 1f out* **10/1**

0-10 **9** ¾ **Love On The Rocks (IRE)**[41] 3092 4-9-5 **88**............(h) DavidProbert 10 81
(Charles Hills) *taken down early: t.k.h: prom: rdn to dispute 2nd over 1f out: wknd ins fnl f* **12/1**

1m 0.21s (-1.39) **Going Correction** -0.125s/f (Firm)
**WFA** 3 from 4yo+ 5lb **9** Ran SP% **114.7**
Speed ratings (Par 107): **106,105,105,105,104 102,101,101,99**
CSF £69.74 CT £374.30 TOTE £10.70: £2.70, £2.50, £2.30; EX 86.30 Trifecta £820.20.
**Owner** Mrs Ruth M Serrell **Bred** Longdon Stud Ltd **Trained** Earlswood, Monmouths

**FOCUS**
A useful sprint, there was a bunched finish with little between the first five. The runner-up has been rated close to his old turf form, with the third rated close to his best.

## 4582 ALLIED WORLD DRAGON STKS (LISTED RACE) 5f 10y
2:20 (2:20) (Class 1) 2-Y-O
£14,744 (£5,590; £2,797; £1,393; £699; £351) **Stalls** Low

Form RPR

2110 **1** **Havana Grey**[15] 3993 2-9-5 102.............................................. PJMcDonald 2 108
(K R Burke) *mde all: stretched clr 2f out: rdn over 1f out: styd on and unchal after but hung lft last 50yds* **3/1**[2]

12 **2** 1 ¼ **Roussel (IRE)**[17] 3929 2-9-2 0.............................................. JamesDoyle 9 100
(Charlie Appleby) *in tch on outer: prog to go 2nd 2f out but wnr sn skipped clr: rdn and kpt on fr over 1f out but nvr able to threaten* **5/4**[1]

12 **3** nk **To Wafij (IRE)**[56] 2577 2-9-2 0........................................ AndreaAtzeni 7 99
(Roger Varian) *w.w: effrt and prog wl over 1f out: rdn to dispute 2nd ins fnl f: styd on but nvr able to threaten wnr* **12/1**

10 **4** 5 **Formidable Kitt**[16] 3960 2-8-11 0.............................. RichardKingscote 5 76
(Tom Dascombe) *prom: chsd wnr over 3f out to 2f out: drvn and steadily wknd* **11/1**

201 **5** ¾ **Connery (IRE)**[2] 4488 2-9-2 0............................................ MartinDwyer 1 78
(Sylvester Kirk) *chsd wnr to over 3f out: rdn 2f out and sn outpcd: nvr on terms after* **16/1**

U25 **6** 1 ½ **Last Page**[17] 3929 2-9-2 94..............................................(p) JFEgan 3 73
(David Evans) *a in rr: outpcd and rdn 2f out: no ch over 1f out* **14/1**

00 **7** 4 **Ivy Leaguer**[17] 3925 2-9-2 0.............................................. TomQueally 6 58
(Brian Meehan) *hld up in last pair: pushed along and no prog 2f out no ch after: rdn and fnd nil fnl f* **100/1**

1241 **8** 3 ¾ **Rebel Assault (IRE)**[6] 4369 2-8-11 93.................... SilvestreDeSousa 8 40
(Mark Johnston) *racd on outer: rdn in rr 1/2-way: sn btn: wknd fnl f* **11/2**[3]

1m 0.59s (-1.01) **Going Correction** -0.125s/f (Firm) **8** Ran SP% **114.4**
Speed ratings (Par 102): **103,101,100,92,91 88,82,76**
CSF £7.11 TOTE £3.50: £1.60, £1.02, £3.30; EX 9.40 Trifecta £52.10.
**Owner** Global Racing Club & Mrs E Burke **Bred** Mickley Stud & Lady Lonsdale **Trained** Middleham Moor, N Yorks

**FOCUS**
Good Listed form and a taking performance from the winner. The winner has been rated as good as any previous winner of this race.

## 4583 LONGINES IRISH CHAMPIONS WEEKEND EBF NOVICE STKS (PLUS 10 RACE) 7f
2:50 (2:51) (Class 4) 2-Y-O £4,592 (£1,366; £683; £341) **Stalls** Low

Form RPR

4 **1** **Petrus (IRE)**[22] 3747 2-9-2 0.............................................. JamesDoyle 6 85
(Brian Meehan) *trckd ldng pair: shkn up to go 2nd 2f out: rdn and clsd fnl f to ld last 100yds: readily drew clr* **10/3**[2]

4 **2** 1 ¾ **Barford (IRE)**[18] 3908 2-9-2 0.............................................. PatCosgrave 5 80
(Pam Sly) *pressed ldr: led over 2f out: rdn fnl f: kpt on wl but hdd and outpcd last 100yds* **7/1**

**3** 5 **Trogon (IRE)** 2-9-2 0.................................................. CharlesBishop 8 67
(Mick Channon) *in tch: shkn up over 2f out: prog to take 3rd 1f out: no ch w ldng pair* **25/1**

**4** nk **Homerton** 2-9-2 0................................................................ TomQueally 4 66+
(Robyn Brisland) *trckd ldng pair: lost pl 2f out then hanging and rn green: n.m.r jst over 1f out: styd on last 150yds to press for 3rd* **25/1**

**5** 2 **Bathsheba Bay (IRE)** 2-9-2 0............................................ RyanMoore 1 61
(Richard Hannon) *led to over 2f out: steadily wknd over 1f out* **6/1**[3]

2 **6** 1 ½ **Master Of Wine (GER)**[21] 3783 2-9-2 0.......................... DavidProbert 2 57+
(Andrew Balding) *slowly away: a towards rr: rdn over 2f out and no prog: wl btn over 1f out* **11/10**[1]

**7** 1 **Amaretto** 2-9-2 0.............................................................. JackMitchell 9 54
(Jim Boyle) *racd wd towards rr: effrt 3f out: wknd wl over 1f out* **40/1**

U2 **8** nk **Rivas Rob Roy**[17] 3936 2-8-13 0.............................. HectorCrouch(3) 7 53
(John Gallagher) *t.k.h hld up bhd ldrs: rdn over 2f out: wknd over 1f out* **12/1**

**9** 1 ½ **Matewan (IRE)** 2-9-2 0........................................................ FranBerry 10 49
(Ian Williams) *s.i.s: a wl in rr: pushed along and no prog over 2f out* **33/1**

**10** 5 **Ahfad** 2-9-2 0............................................................ AdamBeschizza 3 35
(Stuart Williams) *mostly in last pair: struggling 3f out: sn bhd* **66/1**

1m 29.63s (0.13) **Going Correction** 0.0s/f (Good) **10** Ran SP% **119.7**
Speed ratings (Par 96): **99,97,91,90,88 86,85,85,83,78**
CSF £26.03 TOTE £4.30: £1.80, £2.10, £6.90; EX 23.40 Trifecta £332.30.
**Owner** G P M Morland **Bred** Timothy Nuttall **Trained** Manton, Wilts

**FOCUS**
Distance increased by 14yds. A fair maiden, the front two pulled clear.

## 4584 AMBANT GALA STKS (LISTED RACE) 1m 1f 209y
3:25 (3:25) (Class 1) 3-Y-O+
£20,982 (£7,955; £3,981; £1,983; £995; £499) **Stalls** Low

Form RPR

-325 **1** **Spark Plug (IRE)**[20] 3843 6-9-5 110..............................(p) RyanMoore 4 111
(Brian Meehan) *hld up in last trio: prog over 2f out: rdn to ld over 1f out: drvn and styd on stoutly fnl f* **4/1**[3]

-423 **2** 1 ¾ **Kidmenever (IRE)**[13] 4069 4-9-5 104................................ JamesDoyle 3 107
(Charlie Appleby) *trckd ldng pair tl moved up to join ldr after 4f: narrow ld wl over 2f out: hdd and nt qckn over 1f out: kpt on same pce after* **4/1**[3]

6-21 **3** hd **Jake's Hill**[29] 3506 3-8-9 89.............................................. CharlesBishop 2 108
(Eve Johnson Houghton) *won battle for ld but stdd pce after 2f: jnd after 4f: rdn 3f out and sn hdd: kpt on same pce u.p* **14/1**

-340 **4** 1 ¼ **Frankuus (IRE)**[14] 4029 3-8-9 106.............................. SilvestreDeSousa 7 105
(Mark Johnston) *racd on outer: trckd ldng trio: rdn over 2f out: wandered after and nt qckn: one pce fr over 1f out* **7/2**[2]

46-5 **5** 1 ¼ **Ayrad (IRE)**[13] 4069 6-9-5 109.............................................. AndreaAtzeni 6 102
(Roger Charlton) *pressed ldr for 4f: rdn over 2f out: steadily fdd over 1f out* **10/3**[1]

6601 **6** shd **Fanciful Angel (IRE)**[43] 2999 5-9-5 107........................ DanielMuscutt 1 101
(Marco Botti) *s.i.s: plld hrd and hld up in last: rdn over 2f out: wandered and no great prog* **13/2**

216- **7** 10 **Isomer (USA)**[346] 4732 3-8-9 99.............................................. DavidProbert 5 82
(Andrew Balding) *t.k.h: hld up in tch: rdn and wknd over 2f out: t.o* **14/1**

2m 5.74s (-4.76) **Going Correction** 0.0s/f (Good)
**WFA** 3 from 4yo+ 10lb **7** Ran SP% **112.0**
Speed ratings (Par 111): **119,117,117,116,115 115,107**
CSF £19.40 TOTE £3.60: £2.10, £2.20; EX 16.50 Trifecta £127.70.
**Owner** J L Day **Bred** Airlie Stud **Trained** Manton, Wilts

**FOCUS**
Distance increased by 14yds. A competitive Listed race and a strong effort from the winner, who was highest-rated. The form makes sense rated around the winner, second and fourth.

## 4585 BESSO H'CAP 1m 1f 209y
4:00 (4:02) (Class 2) (0-100,100) 3-Y-0+
£18,675 (£5,592; £2,796; £1,398; £699; £351) Stalls Low

Form RPR
20-2 1 **Euginio (IRE)**[79] 1886 3-9-4 **100** ........ AndreaAtzeni 4 104+
(Richard Hannon) *broke wl but t.k.h and hld up in last pair: pushed along over 2f out: prog on outer to ld 1f out: edgd rt after and hrd pressed: cajoled along and nudged runner-up nr fin: hld on* **5/4**[1]

5344 2 *hd* **Beardwood**[12] 4118 5-9-2 **88** ........ (p) SilvestreDeSousa 9 91
(Mark Johnston) *led 1f: trckd ldr: rdn to ld again 2f out: hdd 1f out: rallied wl and w wnr whn sltly impeded nr finsh: jst hld* **4/1**[2]

0303 3 *1* **Mutarakez (IRE)**[15] 4001 5-8-9 **88** ........ JordanUys[(7)] 5 89
(Brian Meehan) *hld up in last: promising prog whn nowhere to go 1f out: r.o whn in the clr last 140yds but too late to rch ldng pair* **8/1**[3]

-200 4 *1 3/4* **Grapevine (IRE)**[35] 3300 4-9-3 **89** ........ JamesDoyle 2 88
(Charles Hills) *sn trckd ldng pair: shkn up over 2f out: cl up but looked hld whn hmpd jst ins fnl f: swtchd lft and no prog after* **9/1**

0-00 5 *hd* **Pacify**[13] 4069 5-9-10 **96** ........ PatDobbs 6 94
(Ralph Beckett) *trckd ldng trio: shkn up over 2f out: jst losing pl whn squeezed out wl over 1f out: no ch after: kpt on again nr fin* **10/1**

0-55 6 *1/2* **Banish (USA)**[57] 2558 4-9-2 **88** ........ (bt) RyanMoore 1 84
(Hugo Palmer) *led after 1f: rdn 3f out: hdd 2f out: wknd fnl f* **14/1**

2m 8.31s (-2.19) **Going Correction** 0.0s/f (Good)
**WFA** 3 from 4yo+ 10lb 6 Ran SP% **101.3**
Speed ratings (Par 109): **108,107,107,105,105 105**
CSF £4.97 CT £15.75 TOTE £1.80: £1.10, £2.10; EX 5.50 Trifecta £16.50.
**Owner** Saleh Al Homaizi & Imad Al Sagar **Bred** Arkle Bloodstock **Trained** East Everleigh, Wilts
■ Berkshire was withdrawn. Price at time of withdrawal 15-2. Rule 4 applies to all bets - deduction 10p in the pound.
■ Stewards' Enquiry : James Doyle two-day ban: careless riding (Jul 21-22)
Andrea Atzeni three-day ban: careless riding (Jul 21-23)

**FOCUS**
Distance increased by 14yds. Decent handicap form, with the winner defying a mark of 100. It's been rated around the runner-up, with the third close to form.

## 4586 NIIT TECHNOLOGIES H'CAP 1m 6f
4:30 (4:32) (Class 4) (0-85,85) 3-Y-0+ £5,822 (£1,732; £865; £432) Stalls Low

Form RPR
-521 1 **UAE King**[23] 3717 3-8-13 **84** ........ AndreaAtzeni 3 95+
(Roger Varian) *prom early: dropped to 5th 9f out and pushed along briefly: prog on outer 3f out: drvn to ld wl over 1f out: kpt on wl fnl f* **5/4**[1]

31-1 2 *3/4* **Machine Learner**[20] 3840 4-9-13 **84** ........ RyanMoore 6 93+
(Joseph Tuite) *hld up and mostly in 4th: waiting for room 2f out tl tk 3rd over 1f out: rdn and styd on to take 2nd nr fin but too late to rch wnr* **5/1**[3]

/132 3 *3/4* **Sternrubin (GER)**[9] 4222 6-9-10 **81** ........ TomQueally 1 89
(Philip Hobbs) *led to over 9f out: trckd ldr: led again over 2f out gng strly: shkn up and hdd wl over 1f out: stuck on wl but a hld by wnr after: lost 2nd nr fin* **5/2**[2]

236 4 *5* **Orsino (IRE)**[37] 3209 3-8-3 **74** ........ JimmyQuinn 7 76
(Andrew Balding) *t.k.h early: trckd ldr 4f then racd in 3rd: rdn to chal over 2f out: wknd over 1f out* **6/1**

5450 5 *10* **Western Prince**[21] 3794 4-9-4 **75** ........ (h) SilvestreDeSousa 5 62
(Michael Appleby) *hld up: t.k.h after 3f and plld way into the ld over 9f out: hdd and btn over 2f out: eased over 1f out* **16/1**

6 *6* **Visandi (FR)**[87] 5-9-13 **84** ........ (t) FranBerry 4 63
(Jonjo O'Neill) *hld up in last: rdn and no rspnse over 2f out: eased whn no ch over 1f out* **50/1**

3m 3.39s (-1.11) **Going Correction** 0.0s/f (Good)
**WFA** 3 from 4yo+ 14lb 6 Ran SP% **111.8**
Speed ratings (Par 105): **103,102,102,99,93 90**
CSF £8.00 CT £12.84 TOTE £2.10: £1.40, £1.80; EX 7.60 Trifecta £13.70.
**Owner** Sheikh Mohammed Obaid Al Maktoum **Bred** Darley **Trained** Newmarket, Suffolk

**FOCUS**
Distance increased by 14yds. They went steady early before Western Prince injected some pace after about 4f. The right horses came to the fore and the form looks good. It's been rated on the positive side.

## 4587 CNA HARDY H'CAP (FOR LADY AMATEUR RIDERS) 1m
5:05 (5:05) (Class 4) (0-80,80) 4-Y-0+ £5,615 (£1,741; £870; £435) Stalls Low

Form RPR
6033 1 **Imperial State**[23] 3723 4-10-0 **78** ........ (vt[1]) MissJCooley[(5)] 2 87+
(George Scott) *hld up in 4th: quick move to ld over 2f out and sn at least 3 l clr: pushed out fr over 1f out and a holding on* **5/2**[1]

521 2 *3/4* **Honiara**[17] 3938 4-10-7 **80** ........ (b) MissPFuller 1 85
(Paul Cole) *trckd ldng pair to over 3f out then dropped to 5th: effrt over 2f out: rdn to chse wnr over 1f out: clsd fnl f but no imp nr fin* **4/1**[3]

251 3 *4 1/2* **Almanack**[68] 2178 7-9-6 **65** ........ MissSBrotherton 6 60
(Mark Pattinson) *pressed ldr: upsides over 3f out tl nt qckn and outpcd over 2f out: one pce after* **5/2**[1]

1440 4 *nk* **Rattle On**[11] 4165 4-8-11 **63** ........ (p) MissSStevens[(7)] 4 57
(Jim Boyle) *hld up in last pair: prog on outer over 3f out: chsd wnr over 2f out to over 1f out: fdd* **10/1**

0064 5 *3* **Peak Storm**[11] 4147 8-10-2 **75** ........ (vt) MissBrodieHampson 3 62
(John O'Shea) *hld up in last pair: lft bhd 3f out: no ch after* **20/1**

6-26 6 *shd* **Fashaak (IRE)**[51] 2730 4-10-5 **78** ........ MissGAndrews 5 65
(John Butler) *led to over 2f out: rdn and steadily wknd* **7/2**[2]

1m 43.58s (0.28) **Going Correction** 0.0s/f (Good) 6 Ran SP% **113.2**
Speed ratings (Par 105): **98,97,92,92,89 89**
CSF £13.06 TOTE £2.80: £1.50, £2.00; EX 10.10 Trifecta £31.10.
**Owner** The Harnage Partnership **Bred** Biddestone Stud Ltd **Trained** Newmarket, Suffolk
■ Stewards' Enquiry : Miss S Brotherton three-day ban; careless riding (22nd, 26th-27th July)

**FOCUS**
Distance increased by 14yds. A fair little lady riders' handicap and the winner won with more in hand than the result suggests. A small pb from the winner, and a small turf pb from the runner-up.
T/Plt: £59.20 to a £1 stake. Pool: £62,495.00 - 1,054.36 winning units. T/Qpdt: £11.00 to a £1 stake. Pool: £4,754.00 - 429.76 winning units. **Jonathan Neesom**

4588 - 4594a (Foreign Racing) - See Raceform Interactive

# 4677 DEAUVILLE (R-H)
Friday, July 7

**OFFICIAL GOING: Turf: good; polytrack: fast**

## 4595a PRIX MACHIAVELLIAN (MAIDEN) (UNRACED 2YO) (TURF) 5f
12:40 2-Y-0 £11,538 (£4,615; £3,461; £2,307; £1,153)

RPR
1 **Ken Colt (IRE)** 2-9-2 0 ........ IoritzMendizabal 6 85
(F Chappet, France) **6/4**[1]

2 *shd* **Evertogether (IRE)** 2-8-13 0 ........ AlexisBadel 4 82
(H-F Devin, France) **16/5**[3]

3 *5* **Elfend** 2-8-13 0 ........ CristianDemuro 1 64
(Rod Collet, France) **12/5**[2]

4 *1 1/2* **La Farfallina** 2-8-13 0 ........ GabrieleCongiu 2 58
(Frank Sheridan, Italy) **169/10**

5 *12* **Rue De Lille (FR)** 2-8-8 0 ........ MartinaHavelkova[(5)] 5 15
(I Endaltsev, Czech Republic) **188/10**

6 *5* **Formiga (IRE)** 2-8-13 0 ........ MickaelBarzalona 3
(Jose Santos) *dwlt: a in rr* **56/10**

59.0s (1.50) 6 Ran SP% **119.0**
PARI-MUTUEL (all including 1 euro stake): WIN 2.50 PLACE 1.60, 1.80 SF 7.40.
**Owner** Roy Racing Ltd **Bred** Stratford Place Stud **Trained** France

## 4596a PRIX DE CAEN (CONDITIONS) (2YO) (TURF) 6f
2:40 2-Y-0
£17,675 (£7,145; £5,264; £3,384; £2,068; £1,316)

RPR
1 **Contortioniste**[20] 2-8-13 0 ........ MaximeGuyon 7 91
(C Laffon-Parias, France) **23/10**[2]

2 *hd* **Simmy's Copshop**[17] 3929 2-8-13 0 ........ ChristopheSoumillon 1 90
(Richard Fahey) *hld up in midfield: tk clsr order over 2f out: rdn to ld under 2f out: kpt on wl: hdd cl home* **43/10**[3]

3 *1 1/2* **Cead Mile Failte (FR)**[29] 3515 2-8-9 0 ........ AntoineHamelin 4 82
(Matthieu Palussiere, France) **96/10**

4 *1 1/2* **Blue Tango (GER)**[14] 2-8-13 0 ........ AlexisBadel 8 81
(M Munch, Germany) **129/10**

5 *1 1/2* **Double Variance (FR)** 2-8-9 0 ........ CristianDemuro 2 73
(S Wattel, France) **77/10**

6 *2 1/2* **First Name Terms**[9] 2-8-13 0 ........ (b) EddyHardouin 6 69
(Matthieu Palussiere, France) **145/10**

7 *3/4* **Lili Du Sud (FR)**[14] 2-8-6 0 ........ MathieuPelletan 3 60
(Y Gourraud, France) **70/1**

8 *5* **Warren (FR)**[54] 2664 2-8-13 0 ........ TheoBachelot 5 52
(Y Barberot, France) **2/1**[1]

1m 10.83s (-0.17) 8 Ran SP% **118.5**
PARI-MUTUEL (all including 1 euro stake): WIN 3.30 PLACE 1.40, 1.50, 2.10 DF 6.60 SF 13.90.
**Owner** Wertheimer & Frere **Bred** Wertheimer & Frere **Trained** Chantilly, France

# 4554 BEVERLEY (R-H)
Saturday, July 8

**OFFICIAL GOING: Good to firm (watered; 7.9)**
Wind: Moderate against Weather: Fine & dry

## 4597 INDUSTRIAL RACKING SUPPLIES LTD NOVICE AUCTION STKS 7f 96y
1:40 (1:42) (Class 5) 2-Y-0 £3,881 (£1,155; £577; £288) Stalls Low

Form RPR
5 1 **Alfa McGuire (IRE)**[19] 3895 2-9-2 0 ........ GrahamLee 11 80
(Bryan Smart) *t.k.h: cl up: led 5f out: rdn clr ent fnl f: kpt on strly* **15/2**[3]

52 2 *4* **Iconic Sunset**[14] 4083 2-9-4 0 ........ LukeMorris 9 72
(James Tate) *in tch: hdwy 3f out: chsd ldrs 2f out: rdn and edgd rt appr fnl f: kpt on towards fin* **2/1**[2]

5001 3 *1 1/2* **Poet's Dawn**[11] 4167 2-9-7 77 ........ DavidAllan 3 71
(Tim Easterby) *led: hdd 5f out: cl up: pushed along over 2f out: rdn wl over 1f out: drvn and kpt on same pce fnl f* **13/8**[1]

4 *1 1/2* **Burnieboozle (IRE)** 2-9-2 0 ........ JackGarritty 10 63
(John Quinn) *midfield: hdwy on outer over 2f out: rdn wl over 1f out: styd on fnl f* **25/1**

5 5 *1/2* **Hogar Seguro (IRE)**[13] 4116 2-8-8 0 ........ SamJames 1 54
(David Loughnane) *dwlt and bhd: hdwy over 2f out: n.m.r and rdn over 1f out: sn swtchd rt to inner and styd on wl fnl f* **14/1**

3 6 *1* **Duke Of Freedom**[11] 4167 2-9-3 0 ........ PaulHanagan 5 60
(Ann Duffield) *t.k.h: trckd ldng pair: hdwy 3f out: rdn along wl over 1f out: drvn and wknd appr fnl f* **14/1**

0 7 *1/2* **Grimeford Lane (IRE)**[19] 3895 2-9-2 0 ........ PaulMulrennan 8 58
(Michael Dods) *midfield: effrt over 2f out: sn rdn along and n.d* **14/1**

6 8 *4 1/2* **Pearl's Calling (IRE)**[7] 4340 2-8-9 0 ........ PJMcDonald 7 40
(David Barron) *a towards rr* **14/1**

00 9 *1 1/2* **Progressive Jazz (IRE)**[63] 2403 2-9-1 0 ........ JordanVaughan[(3)] 2 46
(K R Burke) *trckd ldrs on inner: rdn along wl over 2f out: sn wknd* **50/1**

10 *2* **Surrender** 2-8-13 0 ........ DuranFentiman 4 36
(Tim Easterby) *dwlt: a rr* **33/1**

1m 32.95s (-0.85) **Going Correction** -0.20s/f (Firm) 10 Ran SP% **118.6**
Speed ratings (Par 94): **96,91,89,88,87 86,85,80,78,76**
CSF £22.98 TOTE £13.50: £2.80, £1.10, £1.10; EX 27.80 Trifecta £80.20.
**Owner** Alfa Site Services Ltd **Bred** O Costello & R Moorhead **Trained** Hambleton, N Yorks

**FOCUS**
All distances as advertised. Straightforward form rated around the second and third.

## 4598 PALLET RACKING EBF MAIDEN STKS (DIV I) 5f
2:15 (2:16) (Class 5) 2-Y-0 £3,881 (£1,155; £577; £288) Stalls Low

Form RPR
1 **Ghayadh** 2-9-5 0 ........ LouisSteward 8 80+
(Hugo Palmer) *trckd ldng pair: hdwy over 1f out: rdn to chal ent fnl f: led last 100 yds: kpt on wl* **8/1**

2 *3/4* **Regulator (IRE)** 2-9-5 0 ........ PaulHanagan 1 77+
(Richard Fahey) *midfield: green and pushed along on inner 1/2-way: effrt and nt clr run on inner over 1f out: swtchd lft and rdn ent fnl f: kpt on strly* **4/1**[3]

5 **3** ½ **Savalas (IRE)**[52] 2740 2-9-5 0 TomEaves 11 76
(Kevin Ryan) *cl up: rdn to ld over 1f out: drvn ins fnl f: hdd last 100 yds: no ex* **7/2**[2]

**4** 1¾ **Albert Street (IRE)** 2-9-5 0 GrahamLee 2 69
(Bryan Smart) *dwlt and towards rr: hdwy 2f out: nt clr run and swtchd lft over 1f out: rdn and kpt on wl fnl f* **22/1**

320 **5** 2 **Bath And Tennis (IRE)**[17] 3960 2-9-0 79 LukeMorris 4 57
(Sir Mark Prescott Bt) *trckd ldrs: n.m.r and sltly hmpd after 1f: effrt wl over 1f out: sn rdn and hung lft ent fnl f: sn drvn and kpt on same pce* **3/1**[1]

23 **6** 1 **Seyaady**[30] 3490 2-9-5 0 PJMcDonald 7 58
(Mark Johnston) *slt ld: rdn along 2f out: drvn and hdd jst over 1f out: wknd* **6/1**

**7** hd **Straffan (IRE)** 2-9-0 0 PhillipMakin 6 53+
(David O'Meara) *chsd ldrs whn hmpd after 1f: rdn along 1/2-way: n.d* **33/1**

0 **8** nk **Two Seas**[12] 4151 2-9-5 0 AndrewMullen 3 57
(George Peckham) *trckd ldrs: rdn along wl over 1f out: wkng whn sltly hmpd appr fnl f* **14/1**

0 **9** 2¼ **Magic Pulse (IRE)**[10] 4204 2-9-0 0 (t) KevinStott 13 44
(Ann Duffield) *wnt bdly lft s: a rr* **50/1**

05 **10** 1¾ **Billy Booth (IRE)**[14] 4074 2-9-5 0 DavidAllan 12 42
(Gay Kelleway) *a towards rr* **50/1**

00 **11** 6 **Bee Machine (IRE)**[27] 3622 2-9-5 0 NeilFarley 10 21
(Declan Carroll) *in tch: pushed along 2f out: sn rdn and wknd over 1f out* **50/1**

2 **12** nk **Roman River**[27] 3622 2-9-5 0 RobertWinston 9 20
(Martin Smith) *a towards rr* **10/1**

**13** 5 **Rock Hill (IRE)** 2-9-5 0 PaulMulrennan 5 2
(Paul Midgley) *dwlt: a rr* **33/1**

1m 3.04s (-0.46) **Going Correction** -0.20s/f (Firm) **13 Ran SP% 124.5**
Speed ratings (Par 94): **95,93,93,90,87 85,85,84,81,78 68,68,60**
CSF £39.76 TOTE £10.60: £3.20, £1.80, £2.20; EX 53.50 Trifecta £679.00.
**Owner** Al Shaqab Racing **Bred** Bobble Barn Stud **Trained** Newmarket, Suffolk
■ Stewards' Enquiry : Louis Steward three-day ban: careless riding (Jul 22-24)
Paul Hanagan caution: careless riding

**FOCUS**
They went quick up front in this modest 2yo maiden. The third has been rated as improving, and the fifth below form.

## 4599 PALLET RACKING EBF MAIDEN STKS (DIV II) 5f
**2:50** (2:53) (Class 5) 2-Y-O **£3,881** (£1,155; £577; £288) **Stalls** Low

Form RPR

**1** **That's A Surprise (IRE)** 2-9-5 0 BarryMcHugh 1 70+
(Tony Coyle) *hld up: smooth hdwy on inner over 1f out: shkn up to chal ent fnl f: sn led: readily* **5/1**[3]

0 **2** ¾ **Roundhay Park**[10] 4205 2-9-5 0 TomEaves 10 67+
(Nigel Tinkler) *hld up in tch: hdwy 2f out: nt clr run and swtchd lft jst over 1f out: rdn to chal and ev ch ins fnl f: kpt on* **33/1**

0 **3** 2½ **Hermana Santa (IRE)**[18] 3943 2-9-0 0 SamJames 8 53
(David Barron) *hld up in tch: hdwy 2f out: rdn along over 1f out: kpt on u.p fnl f* **16/1**

0 **4** ½ **Shades Of Mist**[16] 4014 2-9-5 0 KevinStott 5 56
(Ann Duffield) *led: rdn over 1f out: drvn and edgd lft ent fnl f: sn hdd and kpt on same pce* **25/1**

**5** ¾ **Rossall** 2-9-5 0 PaulMulrennan 3 57+
(Michael Dods) *trckd ldrs: effrt and nt clr run over 1f out: kpt on same pce* **15/8**[1]

0 **6** 1 **Orient Princess**[63] 2403 2-9-0 0 CamHardie 2 45
(Paul Midgley) *trckd ldrs: hdwy and cl up 2f out: rdn and ev ch over 1f out: edgd lft ent fnl f: wknd* **20/1**

00 **7** 2 **Rue Cambon (IRE)**[12] 4160 2-9-0 0 PaulHanagan 6 38
(George Peckham) *cl up: rdn along over 1f out: sn drvn and wknd* **25/1**

**8** ½ **Leaderofthepack** 2-9-5 0 GrahamLee 4 41
(Bryan Smart) *dwlt: a towards rr* **8/1**

030 **9** ¾ **Dark Hedges**[26] 3662 2-8-11 52 NathanEvans(3) 7 33
(Olly Williams) *chsd ldrs: rdn wl over 1f out: sn drvn and wknd* **33/1**

**10** 1 **Emphatic (IRE)** 2-9-5 0 LukeMorris 9 35
(Robert Cowell) *dwlt and wnt rt s: reminders and sn chsng ldrs: rdn along wl over 1f out: sn wknd* **9/4**[2]

**11** 7 **Crazy World** 2-9-5 0 NeilFarley 11
(Declan Carroll) *a towards rr* **12/1**

1m 4.52s (1.02) **Going Correction** -0.20s/f (Firm) **11 Ran SP% 125.2**
Speed ratings (Par 94): **83,81,77,77,75 74,71,70,69,67 56**
CSF £171.47 TOTE £8.10: £2.40, £8.80, £4.00; EX 222.80 Trifecta £1380.20.
**Owner** Tony Coyle **Bred** J M McGrath **Trained** Norton, N Yorks

**FOCUS**
The second division of the 2yo maiden. It was 1.48secs slower than the first.

## 4600 BEDDINGHEAVEN.CO.UK SUMMER DUVET SPECIALISTS H'CAP 5f
**3:25** (3:25) (Class 4) (0-85,87) 3-Y-O- **£7,876** (£2,357; £1,178; £590; £293) **Stalls** Low

Form RPR

4243 **1** **Stanghow**[7] 4333 5-9-11 83 CamHardie 12 92
(Antony Brittain) *prom: cl up 2f out: rdn to ld ent fnl f: sn drvn and jst hld on* **8/1**

2416 **2** nse **Signore Piccolo**[7] 4337 6-9-11 83 (h) PaulHanagan 15 91
(David Loughnane) *in tch on outer: hdwy 2f out: rdn over 1f out: styd on strly fnl f: jst failed* **8/1**

2266 **3** 1½ **Straightothepoint**[21] 3827 5-9-10 82 (p) TomEaves 9 85
(Bryan Smart) *led 1f: cl up: rdn to ld again over 1f out: drvn and hdd ent fnl f: kpt on same pce towards fin* **12/1**

4600 **4** 1¼ **Lexington Place**[14] 4079 7-9-3 75 JackGarritty 3 73
(Ruth Carr) *t.k.h: trckd ldrs: hdwy and nt clr run over 1f out: swtchd rt and rdn ins fnl f: no imp* **9/1**

5535 **5** nse **Aguerooo (IRE)**[24] 3707 4-9-4 76 (p) AndrewMullen 4 74
(Ollie Pears) *towards rr: hdwy 2f out: nt clr run over 1f out: sn rdn: kpt on towards fin* **16/1**

6004 **6** nk **First Bombardment**[7] 4379 4-9-4 76 PhillipMakin 7 73
(David O'Meara) *chsd ldrs: rdn along over 1f out: drvn and edgd rt ent fnl f: kpt on same pce* **7/1**

6001 **7** nk **Tarboosh**[16] 4015 4-9-5 77 LukeMorris 6 73
(Paul Midgley) *hld up towards rr: hdwy on outer over 1f out: sn rdn: styd on fnl f* **11/2**[2]

2100 **8** 1½ **Bosham**[17] 3967 7-9-4 79 (bt) NathanEvans(3) 5 69
(Michael Easterby) *chsd ldrs: rdn along wl over 1f out: hld whn n.m.r appr fnl f* **12/1**

1100 **9** shd **Excessable**[21] 3827 4-10-1 87 (t) DavidAllan 1 77
(Tim Easterby) *dwlt and rr: hdwy on inner 1/2-way: chsd ldrs wl over 1f out: sn rdn and wknd* **3/1**[1]

10-0 **10** 4½ **Robben Rainbow**[18] 3946 3-9-2 79 KevinStott 10 51
(David Barron) *a rr* **40/1**

1304 **11** hd **Oriental Relation (IRE)**[21] 3834 6-9-6 78 (b) BarryMcHugh 2 51
(James Given) *cl up: led after 2f: rdn 2f out: rdn and hdd over 1f out: sn wknd* **13/2**[3]

1m 2.06s (-1.44) **Going Correction** -0.20s/f (Firm)
**WFA** 3 from 4yo+ 5lb **11 Ran SP% 122.1**
Speed ratings (Par 105): **103,102,100,98,98 97,97,95,94,87 87**
CSF £73.42 CT £564.29 TOTE £7.30: £2.40, £2.70, £2.60; EX 76.70 Trifecta £597.90.
**Owner** Antony Brittain **Bred** Mel Brittain **Trained** Warthill, N Yorks

**FOCUS**
This was a fair sprint handicap. The winner has been rated to the better view of his form.

## 4601 DRIVE IN PALLET RACKING H'CAP 1m 100y
**4:00** (4:00) (Class 5) (0-70,73) 3-Y-O+ **£5,040** (£1,508; £754; £377; £188) **Stalls** Low

Form RPR

6101 **1** **Talent Scout (IRE)**[11] 4168 11-9-12 73 (p) GemmaTutty(5) 4 78
(Karen Tutty) *t.k.h: trckd ldr: effrt over 1f out: swtchd lft and rdn ent fnl f: lwed last 75 yds* **7/1**

-000 **2** ¾ **Ingleby Angel (IRE)**[10] 4210 8-9-8 64 KevinStott 7 67
(Colin Teague) *in tch: hdwy to trck ldrs 1/2-way: rdn over 1f out: drvn ins fnl f: kpt on wl towards fin* **10/1**

4245 **3** shd **Arcane Dancer (IRE)**[28] 3577 4-9-4 60 (p) RobertWinston 10 63
(Lawrence Mullaney) *trckd ldrs: hdwy to chse ldr 1/2-way: rdn to chal over 1f out: drvn and ev ch ins fnl f: no ex towards fin* **9/2**[2]

0345 **4** nk **Sooqaan**[9] 4262 6-8-9 51 oh3 CamHardie 2 53
(Antony Brittain) *in tch: hdwy wl over 1f out: sn rdn: drvn ent fnl f: kpt on wl towards fin* **11/1**

0440 **5** ¾ **Ellaal**[19] 3899 8-9-9 65 JackGarritty 9 66
(Ruth Carr) *sn led: pushed along 2f out: rdn over 1f out: drvn ent fnl f: hdd & wknd last 75 yds* **16/1**

6-04 **6** ½ **Pioneering (IRE)**[11] 4186 3-9-0 65 PhillipMakin 5 62
(David O'Meara) *towards rr: hdwy on outer over 2f out: rdn wl over 1f out: n.d* **5/1**[3]

6223 **7** nse **The Dukkerer (IRE)**[11] 4184 6-9-3 59 TomEaves 8 58
(James Given) *trckd ldrs: pushed along on inner wl over 2f out: rdn wl over 1f out: hld whn n.m.r over 1f out: wknd* **7/1**

0506 **8** 1 **Swiss Lait**[142] 757 6-8-7 54 RowanScott(5) 11 51
(Patrick Holmes) *a towards rr* **50/1**

1-50 **9** 8 **Getgo**[56] 2625 3-9-5 70 (b) PaulHanagan 3 54
(David Lanigan) *dwlt: a rr* **15/8**[1]

1m 45.37s (-2.23) **Going Correction** -0.20s/f (Firm)
**WFA** 3 from 4yo+ 9lb **9 Ran SP% 119.9**
Speed ratings (Par 103): **103,102,102,101,101 100,100,99,91**
CSF £77.08 CT £356.81 TOTE £6.90: £2.30, £3.00, £1.80; EX 73.10 Trifecta £207.50.
**Owner** Thoroughbred Homes Ltd **Bred** Johnston King **Trained** Osmotherley, N Yorks

**FOCUS**
A modest handicap, run at a fair pace. The winner has been rated back to his 2015 form, and the third close to form.

## 4602 PAUL MIDGLEY RACING H'CAP 7f 96y
**4:35** (4:36) (Class 5) (0-70,67) 3-Y-O **£3,881** (£1,155; £577; £288) **Stalls** Low

Form RPR

0120 **1** **Clear As A Bell (IRE)**[9] 4262 3-8-10 56 DavidAllan 1 66+
(Tim Easterby) *mde all: set stdy pce: qcknd 3f pout: rdn clr appr fnl f: kpt on strly* **3/1**[2]

350- **2** 1½ **Pantera Negra (IRE)**[308] 6130 3-9-5 65 PhillipMakin 4 70
(David Barron) *trckd ldrs: hdwy 2f out: rdn to chse wnr over 1f out: drvn ins fnl f: no imp* **6/1**

053 **3** 3¼ **Lord Kitten (USA)**[14] 4086 3-9-7 67 (b) PaulHanagan 5 64
(David Lanigan) *trckd ldrs: hdwy 2f out: rdn over 1f out: kpt on same pce fnl f* **5/1**[3]

50-0 **4** ½ **Leopard (IRE)**[94] 1552 3-9-0 63 JoshDoyle(3) 3 59
(Tony Coyle) *in tch on inner: hdwy 2f out: rdn wl over 1f out: sn no imp* **25/1**

04-4 **5** 2¼ **Pepys**[43] 3047 3-9-2 62 TomEaves 7 53
(Bryan Smart) *dwlt: bucking and rel to r for 1f and sn t.o: rapid hdwy to join field over 4f out: pushed along on outer wl over 2f out: rdn wl over 1f out: sn one pce* **5/2**[1]

6-05 **6** ¾ **Harvest Moon**[15] 4058 3-8-13 59 JackGarritty 8 48
(Richard Fahey) *t.k.h: trckd wnr: pushed along 3f out: rdn 2f out: sn wknd* **8/1**

604 **7** nk **Powercell (IRE)**[18] 3945 3-8-8 54 AndrewMullen 10 42
(Tim Easterby) *a towards rr* **25/1**

2500 **8** ½ **Hitchcock**[9] 4265 3-9-5 65 KevinStott 9 52+
(Kevin Ryan) *a towards rr* **6/1**

605 **9** 2¾ **Nightdress (IRE)**[38] 3206 3-8-5 51 (v[1]) BarryMcHugh 2 31
(Tony Coyle) *dwlt and rr whn hmpd after 150 yds: a bhd* **40/1**

1m 32.6s (-1.20) **Going Correction** -0.20s/f (Firm) **9 Ran SP% 120.1**
Speed ratings (Par 100): **98,96,92,92,89 88,88,87,84**
CSF £21.94 CT £90.18 TOTE £4.70: £1.60, £2.10, £1.40; EX 26.70 Trifecta £157.20.
**Owner** Habton Farms **Bred** Drumlin Bloodstock **Trained** Great Habton, N Yorks

**FOCUS**
An ordinary 3yo handicap in which winning form was very thin in the ground.

## 4603 COMPUTANET IT AND NETWORK SUPPORT SERVICES FILLIES' H'CAP 1m 1f 207y
**5:10** (5:11) (Class 5) (0-70,72) 3-Y-O **£5,040** (£1,508; £754; £377; £188) **Stalls** Low

Form RPR

22-2 **1** **Jive Talking (IRE)**[23] 3759 3-9-13 72 LouisSteward 4 80+
(Michael Bell) *hld up in tch: hdwy wl over 2f out: cl up wl over 1f out: rdn to ld appr fnl f: sn clr* **5/4**[1]

2232 **2** 2¼ **Greenview Paradise (IRE)**[7] 4332 3-9-6 65 JackGarritty 8 68
(Richard Fahey) *trckd ldr: cl up over 2f out: rdn to ld wl over 1f out: hdd appr fnl f: sn drvn and kpt on same pce* **6/1**

0042 **3** ½ **Rosemay (FR)**[11] 4172 3-9-7 66 (p[1]) PaulHanagan 5 68
(Iain Jardine) *hld up towards rr: hdwy over 2f out: chsd ldrs over 1f out: swtchd rt to inner and rdn: kpt on towards fin* **3/1**[2]

-043 **4** 2½ **Conistone**[38] 3207 3-8-12 57 TomEaves 2 54
(James Bethell) *trckd ldng pair: effrt over 2f out and sn rdn along: drvn over 1f out: sn one pce* **11/2**[3]

00-5 **5** ½ **Spanish Beauty**[11] 4171 3-8-4 49 AndrewMullen 3 45
(Ollie Pears) *rr: hdwy 3f out: chsd ldrs 2f out: sn rdn and kpt on one pce* **10/1**

6560 6 5 **Cosmic Sky**[29] 3543 3-8-2 **47**...(h) CamHardie 1 33
(Tim Easterby) *plld hrd: led: rdn along over 2f out: hdd wl over 1f out and sn wknd* **14/1**
0-00 7 16 **Thornton Mary**[47] 2902 3-7-12 **50** oh2 ow3... ZakWheatley(7) 7 4
(Brian Rothwell) *chsd ldrs on outer: rdn along over 3f out: sn wknd* **50/1**
2m 3.94s (-3.06) **Going Correction** -0.20s/f (Firm) **7** Ran SP% **116.8**
Speed ratings (Par 97): **104,102,101,99,99 95,82**
CSF £9.96 CT £19.41 TOTE £2.10: £1.40, £2.20; EX 9.70 Trifecta £18.60.
**Owner** Mrs B V Sangster **Bred** Inis Boffin Syndicate **Trained** Newmarket, Suffolk
**FOCUS**
A modest fillies' handicap, run at sound pace. It's been rated around the second and third.

## 4604 LONG SPAN SHELVING MAIDEN STKS 5f
**5:45** (5:50) (Class 5) 3-Y-O+ **£3,780** (£1,131; £565; £283; £141) **Stalls** Low

Form RPR
5- 1 **Flying Foxy**[252] 7689 3-9-0 0... KevinStott 3 71
(Michael Wigham) *trckd ldng pair on inner: swtchd lft and hdwy over 1f out: sn chsng ldr and rdn: drvn ins fnl f: kpt on wl to ld nr line* **8/1**
223- 2 hd **Jeany (IRE)**[291] 6641 3-9-0 67... TomEaves 6 70
(Bryan Smart) *qckly away and led: rdn along wl over 1f out: drvn ins fnl f: hdd nr line* **5/1**[3]
324- 3 3 ½ **Rapid Ranger**[249] 7748 3-9-2 73... JoshDoyle(3) 1 62
(David O'Meara) *trckd ldrs: hdwy wl over 1f out: sn rdn: kpt on fnl f* **5/2**[2]
6-42 4 ½ **Equiano Springs**[17] 3984 3-9-5 74... AndrewMullen 7 61
(Tom Tate) *sn trcking ldng pair: cl up 1/2-way: rdn wl over 1f out: drvn and wknd appr fnl f* **4/5**[1]
60 5 1 ½ **Fille The Force**[7] 4341 3-9-0 0... BarryMcHugh 4 50
(Scott Dixon) *in tch: rdn along wl over 1f out: sn drvn and no imp* **22/1**
0 6 ½ **Hamriyah**[47] 2887 3-9-5 0...(h) DavidAllan 2 53
(Tim Easterby) *rr tl sme late hdwy* **14/1**
5 7 2 ¾ **Quick Monet (IRE)**[5] 4448 4-9-3 0... AidenBlakemore(7) 5 46
(Shaun Harris) *a towards rr* **66/1**
06/ 8 5 **Time Continuum**[749] 3415 5-9-5 0... NeilFarley 8 23
(Eric Alston) *wnt lft s: chsd ldrs rdn along 1/2-way: sn wknd* **40/1**
1m 2.45s (-1.05) **Going Correction** -0.20s/f (Firm)
**WFA** 3 from 4yo+ 5lb **8** Ran SP% **126.9**
Speed ratings (Par 103): **100,99,94,93,90 90,85,77**
CSF £51.84 TOTE £11.30: £2.60, £1.90, £1.30; EX 65.60 Trifecta £230.90.
**Owner** Mrs Elizabeth Lloyd **Bred** Minster Stud **Trained** Newmarket, Suffolk
**FOCUS**
A run-of-the-mill sprint maiden. The runner-up has been rated to the better view of her form.
T/Plt: £293.70 to a £1 stake. Pool: £70,619.40 - 175.47 winning units. T/Qpdt: £91.80 to a £1 stake. Pool: £3,585.93 - 28.90 winning units. **Joe Rowntree**

# 4204 CARLISLE (R-H)
Saturday, July 8
**OFFICIAL GOING: Good to soft (soft in places; 6.8)**
Wind: Light, half against Weather: Sunny, warm

## 4605 RACING UK NOW ON TALK TALK TV APPRENTICE H'CAP (JOCKEY CLUB GRASSROOTS SPRINT SERIES QUALIFIER) 5f 193y
**6:00** (6:00) (Class 5) (0-70,72) 4-Y-O+ **£3,396** (£1,010; £505; £252) **Stalls** Low

Form RPR
0442 1 **Mr Orange (IRE)**[26] 3666 4-8-12 **66**...(p) HarrisonShaw(5) 7 75
(Paul Midgley) *cl up: rdn to ld over 1f out: edgd rt ins fnl f: hld on wl* **5/2**[1]
0001 2 1 ¼ **Cliff (IRE)**[17] 3979 7-8-11 **65**... FayeMcManoman(5) 2 70
(Nigel Tinkler) *hld up: hdwy over 1f out: effrt and ev ch ins fnl f: no ex nr fin* **4/1**[2]
5650 3 ¾ **Short Work**[21] 3845 4-9-3 **69**...(v) PatrickVaughan(3) 9 72
(David O'Meara) *hld up on outside: hdwy over 2f out: rdn and kpt on ins fnl f* **11/1**
6002 4 nk **Quick N Quirky (IRE)**[10] 4209 4-9-2 **70**...(p) RobertDodsworth(5) 6 72
(Tim Easterby) *hld up in tch: effrt and rdn over 1f out: kpt on ins fnl f: nt pce to chal* **5/1**[3]
660 5 1 ½ **Market Choice (IRE)**[5] 4433 4-9-9 **72**...(p[1]) CallumRodriguez 11 69
(Tracy Waggott) *led: rdn over 2f out: hdd over 1f out: outpcd fnl f* **7/1**
-415 6 3 ¾ **Ki Ki**[115] 1203 5-8-7 **63**... HarryRussell(7) 4 48
(Bryan Smart) *missed break: bhd: rdn and effrt whn drifted lft over 2f out: rdn: edgd rt and no imp fr wl over 1f out* **7/1**
4-05 7 1 ¾ **The Hooded Claw (IRE)**[28] 3567 6-9-1 **69**...(v[1]) ConnorMurtagh(5) 10 48
(Patrick Morris) *trckd ldrs: rdn over 2f out: wknd over 1f out* **8/1**
0-00 8 2 ½ **Sir Domino (FR)**[37] 3239 5-8-11 **65**... JamieGormley(5) 5 36
(Patrick Holmes) *trckd ldrs: rdn over 2f out: wknd over 1f out* **33/1**
0-00 9 ¾ **Mr Conundrum**[19] 3912 4-8-2 **51** oh5... RichardOliver 3 20
(Lynn Siddall) *hld up: rdn and outpcd wl over 2f out: sn btn* **50/1**
-060 10 hd **Reflation**[5] 4426 5-8-10 **59**...(p) MeganNicholls 8 27
(Patrick Holmes) *hld up bhd ldng gp: drvn along over 2f out: wknd over 1f out* **50/1**
1m 14.54s (0.84) **Going Correction** +0.25s/f (Good) **10** Ran SP% **116.5**
Speed ratings (Par 103): **104,102,101,100,98 93,91,88,87,87**
CSF £12.19 CT £93.51 TOTE £3.00: £1.30, £1.40, £2.90; EX 14.40 Trifecta £92.60.
**Owner** J Blackburn & A Turton **Bred** Rathbarry Stud **Trained** Westow, N Yorks
■ Stewards' Enquiry : Faye McManoman caution: careless riding
Robert Dodsworth caution: careless riding
**FOCUS**
All distances as advertised. No less than 19mm of rain had fallen in the preceding 48 hours ahead of this evening meeting. It had been dry and bright after a cloudy start, with temperatures around 18C and the ground appeared to be drying out. A modest apprentices' sprint handicap to start and the pace was adequate. The form should hold fast. The winner has been rated back to his best, with the runner-up to his latest.

## 4606 GLO AND GO TANNING LOUNGE NOVICE MEDIAN AUCTION STKS 5f
**6:30** (6:31) (Class 5) 2-Y-O **£3,396** (£1,010; £505; £252) **Stalls** Low

Form RPR
4 1 **Rumshak (IRE)**[22] 3789 2-9-2 0... PaulMulrennan 2 81+
(Michael Dods) *mde all: clr over 1f out: pushed out fnl f: comf* **2/1**[2]
05 2 5 **Magic Jazz (IRE)**[53] 2698 2-9-2 0... ShaneGray 3 64
(Kevin Ryan) *chsd ldrs: effrt and chsd (clr) wnr over 1f out: kpt on fnl f: no imp* **16/1**
02 3 2 ¼ **Charnock Richard**[29] 3523 2-9-2 0... GrahamLee 5 55
(David Brown) *t.k.h early: chsd wnr to over 1f out: kpt on same pce fnl f* **7/1**[3]
0 4 nk **Elements Quest (IRE)**[10] 4204 2-8-4 0... RussellHarris(7) 6 49
(K R Burke) *hld up in tch: rdn along over 2f out: no imp fnl f* **40/1**
3 5 1 ¾ **Onesarnieshort (FR)**[14] 4074 2-9-2 0... DanielTudhope 8 48
(David O'Meara) *prom: drvn and outpcd 2f out: n.d after* **9/1**
6 6 2 ½ **Panophobia**[46] 2926 2-9-2 0... TonyHamilton 4 39
(Richard Fahey) *hld up bhd ldng gp: rdn over 2f out: edgd rt and wknd over 1f out* **25/1**
3 7 1 ¼ **Weeton (IRE)**[10] 4204 2-9-2 0... ConnorBeasley 1 34
(Bryan Smart) *taken early to post: plld hrd in rr: rdn over 2f out: sn btn* **6/5**[1]
1m 2.27s (1.47) **Going Correction** +0.25s/f (Good) **7** Ran SP% **113.5**
Speed ratings (Par 94): **98,90,86,85,83 79,77**
CSF £31.87 TOTE £2.60: £1.30, £5.70; EX 32.90 Trifecta £117.40.
**Owner** Mrs C Dods & D Stone **Bred** Ballinacurra Stud Limited **Trained** Denton, Co Durham
**FOCUS**
An ordinary novices' sprint which very few got into and there was an all-the-way winner. The second, fifth and sixth are the keys to the form. The runner-up has been rated to his pre-race mark.

## 4607 CARLISLE SUPPORTING RACING STAFF WEEK H'CAP 5f
**7:00** (7:01) (Class 5) (0-70,73) 3-Y-O+ **£3,396** (£1,010; £505; £252) **Stalls** Low

Form RPR
-024 1 **Show Palace**[16] 4005 4-9-5 **63**... GrahamLee 6 71
(Jennie Candlish) *trckd ldrs: shkn up to ld appr fnl f: sn pushed clr: kpt on wl towards fin* **3/1**[2]
1115 2 ¾ **Deeds Not Words (IRE)**[9] 4256 6-9-13 **71**...(p) FrannyNorton 3 76+
(Michael Wigham) *hld up in tch: effrt and rdn over 1f out: chsd wnr ins fnl f: r.o* **15/8**[1]
0465 3 1 ¼ **Rose Eclair**[8] 4305 4-9-3 **61**...(p[1]) PaulMulrennan 5 62
(Tim Easterby) *chsd ldr: drvn and ch over 1f out: kpt on same pce ins fnl f* **3/1**[2]
1051 4 ½ **Bronze Beau**[5] 4428 10-10-1 **73** 6ex...(tp) ShaneGray 1 72
(Kristin Stubbs) *led: rdn and hdd appr fnl f: kpt on same pce* **8/1**
0-40 5 1 **Redarna**[108] 1308 3-8-8 **57**... JamesSullivan 4 50
(Dianne Sayer) *hld up: drvn along over 2f out: kpt on fnl f: nvr able to chal* **33/1**
5033 6 nse **Windforpower (IRE)**[18] 3944 7-9-1 **59**...(p) JasonHart 8 54
(Tracy Waggott) *prom: drvn along and outpcd 1/2-way: kpt on same pce fr over 1f out* **7/1**[3]
50-6 7 7 **First Rate**[37] 3238 4-9-6 **64**...(h[1]) DanielTudhope 7 34
(Marjorie Fife) *dwlt: bhd and outpcd: struggling fr 1/2-way* **20/1**
1m 2.39s (1.59) **Going Correction** +0.25s/f (Good)
**WFA** 3 from 4yo+ 5lb **7** Ran SP% **116.1**
Speed ratings (Par 103): **97,95,93,93,91 91,80**
CSF £9.36 CT £17.51 TOTE £4.00: £2.20, £1.40; EX 11.10 Trifecta £33.70.
**Owner** P and Mrs G A Clarke **Bred** M C Humby **Trained** Basford Green, Staffs
**FOCUS**
Not a strong sprint handicap for the class but the form has a solid feel. The winner has been rated back to his best.

## 4608 FABULOUS AT 50 H'CAP 1m 1f
**7:30** (7:31) (Class 5) (0-70,68) 4-Y-O+ **£3,396** (£1,010; £505; £252) **Stalls** Low

Form RPR
5-01 1 **Im Dapper Too**[29] 3530 6-9-1 **62**... SamJames 5 71+
(John Davies) *trckd ldrs: hdwy to ld over 2f out: rdn over 1f out: hld on wl fnl f* **3/1**[1]
2106 2 ¾ **Archipeligo**[7] 4358 6-9-0 **68**...(p) JamieGormley(7) 7 74
(Iain Jardine) *prom: rdn and chsd wnr over 1f out: kpt on ins fnl f* **17/2**
-644 3 ½ **Omotesando**[14] 4082 7-8-12 **62**... CharlieBennett(3) 3 67
(Oliver Greenall) *hld up in tch: drvn and outpcd over 2f out: rallied over 1f out: kpt on ins fnl f* **9/1**
66 4 ¾ **Indian Chief (IRE)**[43] 3050 7-9-5 **66**... DuranFentiman 8 69
(Rebecca Bastiman) *s.i.s: t.k.h: hld up: stdy hdwy and prom over 2f out: sn rdn: kpt on same pce ins fnl f* **15/2**
5603 5 2 ¼ **Eez Eh (IRE)**[19] 3898 4-9-1 **67**...(v) RowanScott(5) 4 65
(Keith Dalgleish) *t.k.h: hld up in tch: rdn over 2f out: no imp fr over 1f out* **7/1**
00 6 2 **Polar Forest**[9] 4260 7-9-7 **68**...(e) ConnorBeasley 9 62
(Richard Guest) *pressed ldr: rdn and ev ch over 2f out: wknd over 1f out* **18/1**
61 7 2 **Geordie George (IRE)**[30] 3487 5-9-1 **62**...(t) GrahamLee 2 52
(Rebecca Menzies) *t.k.h: hld up in tch: drvn along over 2f out: no imp over 1f out: sn btn* **7/2**[2]
6001 8 2 ¼ **Invictus (GER)**[11] 4185 5-9-7 **68**...(p) PaulMulrennan 1 53
(David Loughnane) *led to over 2f out: sn rdn and wknd* **5/1**[3]
1501 9 ¾ **Table Manners**[46] 2919 5-8-13 **63**... SammyJoBell(3) 6 46
(Wilf Storey) *bhd: struggling over 4f out: nvr on terms* **11/1**
1m 58.09s (0.49) **Going Correction** +0.25s/f (Good) **9** Ran SP% **122.3**
Speed ratings (Par 103): **107,106,105,105,103 101,99,97,97**
CSF £31.25 CT £215.56 TOTE £3.90: £1.50, £2.60, £3.20; EX 38.10 Trifecta £299.50.
**Owner** Christopher Davies **Bred** Christopher T Dawson **Trained** Piercebridge, Durham
**FOCUS**
An ordinary handicap and the early gallop was not strong, with the first two coming from just off the pace. They came up the centre of the track and the first four home finished close up. The runner-up has been rated to his recent AW form.

## 4609 RACING UK H'CAP 7f 173y
**8:00** (8:00) (Class 4) (0-80,75) 3-Y-O+ **£5,498** (£1,636; £817; £408) **Stalls** Low

Form RPR
-000 1 **Natajack**[20] 3862 3-8-8 **71**... ConnorMurtagh(7) 1 74+
(Richard Fahey) *trckd ldr: shkn up to ld over 1f out: rdn and hld on wl last 100yds* **9/4**[1]
0452 2 nk **Character Onesie (IRE)**[28] 3560 5-9-12 **73**... TonyHamilton 3 77
(Richard Fahey) *hld up in tch: rdn and hdwy over 1f out: chsd wnr ins fnl f: kpt on fin* **5/2**[2]
6062 3 ¾ **Framley Garth (IRE)**[31] 3450 5-9-5 **66**... DanielTudhope 4 68
(Patrick Holmes) *prom: drvn and outpcd over 2f out: rallied appr fnl f: r.o* **10/3**[3]
0-00 4 2 ½ **Lonely The Brave (IRE)**[8] 4290 3-9-5 **75**... FrannyNorton 6 70
(Mark Johnston) *trckd ldrs: effrt and rdn 2f out: outpcd ins fnl f* **11/2**
-000 5 1 **Jacob Black**[14] 4103 6-9-6 **67**...(t[1]) JasonHart 2 61
(Kenny Johnson) *led: rdn and hdd over 1f out: rallied: wknd ins fnl f* **25/1**
00-0 6 60 **Woody Bay**[21] 3845 7-10-0 **75**... DougieCostello 5
(Mark Walford) *hld up: drvn and struggling wl over 2f out: sn lost tch: t.o* **13/2**
1m 41.5s (1.50) **Going Correction** +0.25s/f (Good)
**WFA** 3 from 5yo+ 9lb **6** Ran SP% **115.0**
Speed ratings (Par 105): **102,101,100,98,97 37**
CSF £8.52 TOTE £3.30: £1.60, £1.50; EX 10.70 Trifecta £27.50.
**Owner** Nick Bradley Racing 28 **Bred** F Laing M Tuely W Tuely **Trained** Musley Bank, N Yorks

**FOCUS**
A modest handicap for the grade and the pace was light early on. A tight finish ensued with the Richard Fahey stablemates dominating. Fair form. The runner-up sets the standard, with the third to his recent form.

## 4610 RACINGUK.COM H'CAP 6f 195y
**8:30** (8:31) (Class 4) (0-85,89) 3-Y-O **£5,498** (£1,636; £817; £408) **Stalls** Low

Form RPR
1-50 **1** **Saint Equiano**[33] 3388 3-9-7 **82**........................................ PhillipMakin 2 87
(Keith Dalgleish) *hld up: rdn and hdwy over 1f out: styd on wl u.p to ld cl home* **15/2**
31 **2** *nk* **Raselasad (IRE)**[18] 3948 3-9-6 **81**........................... RoystonFfrench 6 85
(Tracy Waggott) *cl up: led 2f out: sn rdn: kpt on wl fnl f: hdd cl home* **22/1**
-214 **3** *nk* **Rutherford (IRE)**[39] 3167 3-9-0 **75**................................ ShaneGray 1 78
(Kevin Ryan) *cl up: rdn and outpcd over 2f out: rallied over 1f out: r.o ins fnl f* **12/1**
-021 **4** *1 1/4* **Parnassian (IRE)**[12] 4154 3-9-9 **89**.............................. CliffordLee(5) 3 89
(K R Burke) *hld up in tch: rdn over 2f out: hdwy over 1f out: r.o ins fnl f* **7/4**[1]
-535 **5** *3* **Fayez (IRE)**[20] 3862 3-9-5 **80**........................................ DanielTudhope 5 74
(David O'Meara) *led: rdn and hdd 2f out: wknd ins fnl f* **9/2**[2]
50-1 **6** *2 3/4* **Alfie's Angel (IRE)**[13] 4122 3-8-11 **72**......................... ConnorBeasley 8 57
(Bryan Smart) *prom on outside: drvn and outpcd over 2f out: n.d after* **13/2**[3]
0-05 **7** *4* **Captain Hawk**[24] 3715 3-8-8 **69**................................(p[1]) FrannyNorton 4 44
(Ian Williams) *plld hrd: prom: drvn and outpcd over 2f out: sn btn* **9/2**[2]
524 **8** *6* **Bob Maxwell (IRE)**[30] 3500 3-9-2 **77**............................ PaulMulrennan 7 36
(David Barron) *hld up: rdn and struggling over 2f out: btn wl over 1f out* **14/1**

1m 27.97s (0.87) **Going Correction** +0.25s/f (Good) **8** Ran SP% **116.5**
Speed ratings (Par 102): **105,104,104,102,99 96,91,84**
CSF £150.28 CT £1967.89 TOTE £9.30: £3.00, £5.30, £3.50; EX 135.90 Trifecta £1720.00.
**Owner** Paul & Clare Rooney **Bred** Usk Valley Stud **Trained** Carluke, S Lanarks
■ Stewards' Enquiry : Royston Ffrench two-day ban: used whip above permitted level (22-23 Jul)

**FOCUS**
A decent handicap and there was not much between the front three. This form looks viable. The third helps set the standard.

## 4611 ANDERSONS (DENTON HOLME) SAWMILLS CARLISLE MAIDEN STKS 1m 3f 39y
**9:00** (9:06) (Class 5) 3-Y-O+ **£3,396** (£1,010; £505; £252) **Stalls** High

Form RPR
23 **1** **Nadaitak**[38] 3209 3-9-3 0........................................ FrannyNorton 3 75+
(Sir Michael Stoute) *trckd ldrs: rdn over 2f out: rallied over 1f out: led ins fnl f: sn clr* **5/4**[1]
4 **2** *3 3/4* **Normandie Attack (FR)**[12] 4146 3-9-3 0........................ RobertTart 10 69+
(Charlie Fellowes) *hld up: rdn and outpcd over 3f out: gd hdwy on outside over 1f out: r.o strly under hands and heels riding fnl f: improve* **40/1**
24 **3** *1* **Circulation**[31] 3465 3-8-12 0........................................ PhillipMakin 6 62
(Ralph Beckett) *t.k.h early: cl up: wnt 2nd 1/2-way: led and rdn over 1f out: hdd ins fnl f: sn one pce* **7/4**[2]
0 **4** *nk* **Amazing Steps (IRE)**[19] 3921 3-9-3 0........................ PaulMulrennan 5 66+
(Charlie Fellowes) *hld up: pushed along and hdwy wl over 1f out: swtchd sharply rt to avoid veering rival ins fnl f: kpt on* **6/1**[3]
3 **5** *1 1/2* **Amazing Grazing (IRE)**[32] 3435 3-9-3 0........................ TomEaves 8 64
(Brian Ellison) *pressed ldrs: rdn and edgd lft 2f out: one pce whn veered rt ins fnl f* **16/1**
0 **6** *6* **Mick The Poser (IRE)**[39] 3191 3-9-3 41........................ JamesSullivan 9 54?
(Jennie Candlish) *hld up on outside: drvn along 3f out: outpcd fnl 2f* **100/1**
**7** *3/4* **Golden Jeffrey (SWI)**[34] 4-10-0 0.............................. GrahamLee 4 51
(Iain Jardine) *hld up midfield: rdn and outpcd over 3f out: btn fnl 2f* **12/1**
46 **8** *1/2* **Flowers Will Bloom (IRE)**[24] 3717 3-8-12 0........................ SamJames 7 47
(David O'Meara) *led: rdn over 2f out: hdd over 1f out: sn wknd* **20/1**
4 **9** *1/2* **Cold Shoulder**[32] 3427 3-9-3 0........................................ DougieCostello 2 51
(Andrew Balding) *hld up: drvn and outpcd over 2f out: sn btn* **14/1**
**10** *1 1/2* **Poppyinthepark**[234] 4-9-4 0.............................. CallumRodriguez(5) 1 42
(Richard Ford) *hld up: struggling wl over 2f out: sn btn* **50/1**

2m 27.29s (4.19) **Going Correction** +0.25s/f (Good)
**WFA** 3 from 4yo 11lb **10** Ran SP% **125.5**
Speed ratings (Par 103): **94,91,90,90,89 84,84,83,83,82**
CSF £73.09 TOTE £2.10: £1.10, £10.40, £1.10; EX 84.90 Trifecta £160.80.
**Owner** Hamdan Al Maktoum **Bred** Shadwell Estate Company Limited **Trained** Newmarket, Suffolk

**FOCUS**
An ordinary maiden run at a sound pace. Fair form. It's been rated around the fourth and fifth.
T/Plt: £183.00 to a £1 stake. Pool: £62,729.51 - 250.20 winning units. T/Qpdt: £46.70 to a £1 stake. Pool: £4,523.79 - 71.61 winning units. **Richard Young**

# 4575 HAYDOCK (L-H)
### Saturday, July 8

**OFFICIAL GOING: Good to firm (watered; 9.0)**
Wind: Faint breeze Weather: Warm, sunny intervals

## 4612 BET365 H'CAP 1m 6f
**2:05** (2:05) (Class 2) 3-Y-O
**£31,125** (£9,320; £4,660; £2,330; £1,165; £585) **Stalls** Low

Form RPR
4-21 **1** **Zenon (IRE)**[32] 3426 3-9-2 **87**........................................ RobertTart 4 98+
(John Gosden) *hld up: pushed along 4f out: last 3f out: drvn and hdwy 2f out: 2nd whn rdn 1f out: styd on strly to ld ins fnl f: won gng away* **7/2**[2]
6011 **2** *1 1/2* **Dominating (GER)**[22] 3788 3-8-4 **75**............................ FrannyNorton 8 83
(Mark Johnston) *hld up: hdwy 3f out: drvn 2f out: hdwy to ld over 1f out: rdn and hdd ins fnl f: r.o* **10/1**
1252 **3** *1* **Look My Way**[22] 3788 3-8-5 **76**.................................. JosephineGordon 6 83
(Andrew Balding) *chsd ldrs: hdwy 3f out: n.m.r 2f out: sn rdn: r.o strly to take 3rd ins fnl f* **16/1**
221 **4** *3/4* **Humble Hero (IRE)**[20] 3860 3-8-13 **84**............................ PatCosgrave 7 90
(William Haggas) *slowly away: in rr: hdwy 3f out: drvn 2f out: ev ch over 1f out: sn rdn: one pce* **11/4**[1]
2351 **5** *1* **Mistress Quickly (IRE)**[9] 4267 3-8-11 **82**........................ PatDobbs 2 87
(Ralph Beckett) *led: drvn over 2f out: rdn and hdd over 1f out: no ex* **12/1**
3162 **6** *1/2* **Cray (IRE)**[16] 4004 3-8-3 **74**..........................................(p) JamesSullivan 5 78
(James Bethell) *mid-div: pushed along 3f out: rdn 2f out: styd on fnl f* **28/1**
2510 **7** *3/4* **Never Surrender (IRE)**[16] 3998 3-9-3 **88**........................ JamieSpencer 3 91
(Charles Hills) *hld up in last: hdwy on outer 3f out: drvn 2f out: sn rdn and no imp* **14/1**
5111 **8** *nk* **Cribbs Causeway (IRE)**[8] 4319 3-8-8 **82**............ KieranShoemark(3) 9 84
(Roger Charlton) *chsd ldr: drvn over 2f out: rdn and wknd wl over 1f out* **9/1**
-131 **9** *3/4* **Jukebox Jive (FR)**[30] 3503 3-8-10 **86**..............................(t[1]) DavidEgan(5) 10 87
(Anthony Honeyball) *mid-div: hdwy to go 3rd 4f out: reminders 3f out: rdn 2f out: wknd* **9/1**
2040 **10** *1* **Mister Manduro (FR)**[15] 4032 3-9-7 **92**.................... RichardKingscote 1 92
(Mark Johnston) *trckd ldrs: pushed along 4f out: sn drvn: rdn over 1f out: fdd and eased* **5/1**[3]

3m 1.28s (-0.72) **Going Correction** -0.075s/f (Good) **10** Ran SP% **118.3**
Speed ratings (Par 106): **99,98,97,97,96 96,95,95,95,94**
CSF £39.20 CT £501.60 TOTE £5.60: £1.70, £3.40, £5.20; EX 48.10 Trifecta £749.70.
**Owner** Shirke Dhunjibhoy Desai Magnier & Tabor **Bred** V B Shirke, K N Dhunjibhoy & B M Desai **Trained** Newmarket, Suffolk

**FOCUS**
All races on stands' side Home Straight. After a dry few days the going was Good to Firm (9.0). After riding in the opener Josephine Gordon said: "The ground is quick" and Richard Kingscote and Pat Dobbs called it "Good to Firm" but Robert Tart said: "It is easy on top, there is give in it." The race distance was 1m 6f 38yds. A strong-looking 3yo staying handicap.

## 4613 BET365 LANCASHIRE OAKS (GROUP 2) (F&M) 1m 3f 175y
**2:40** (2:41) (Class 1) 3-Y-O+
**£52,740** (£19,995; £10,006; £4,984; £2,501; £1,255) **Stalls** Centre

Form RPR
1-12 **1** **The Black Princess (FR)**[51] 2765 4-9-5 107........................ RobertTart 1 108
(John Gosden) *hld up: hdwy whn n.m.r 2f out: sn in clr: str run to chal over 1f out: rdn ent fnl f: r.o wl to ld last 100yds* **3/1**[2]
15-1 **2** *1/2* **Abingdon (USA)**[13] 4119 4-9-5 110........................ RichardKingscote 6 107
(Sir Michael Stoute) *a handy: trckd ldr: tk clsr order 4f out: led 2f out: rdn over 1f out: r.o u.p but hdd last 100yds* **6/4**[1]
-113 **3** *1* **Ajman Princess (IRE)**[28] 3586 4-9-5 107........................ AndreaAtzeni 2 106
(Roger Varian) *mid-div: hdwy to trck ldrs gng wl 3f out: drvn into 2nd wl over 1f out: sn rdn: r.o one pce fnl f* **6/1**
3213 **4** *1 3/4* **Hertford Dancer**[16] 3995 3-8-7 105........................ HarryBentley 3 104
(John Gosden) *trckd ldrs: 3rd and drvn over 2f out: rdn over 1f out: lost pl and no ex fnl f* **5/1**[3]
0-44 **5** *nk* **Rich Legacy (IRE)**[16] 3995 3-8-7 103........................ DavidProbert 4 103
(Ralph Beckett) *t.k.h: hld up: hdwy on outer 3f out: drvn 2f out: rdn ent fnl f: one pce* **12/1**
6542 **6** *nk* **Lucy The Painter (IRE)**[13] 4119 5-9-5 93........................ DanielTudhope 7 102
(Ed de Giles) *hld up in last: pushed along in rr 2f out: rdn and sme hdwy over 1f out: one pce u.p fnl f* **33/1**
5-62 **7** *2 3/4* **Dubka**[28] 3586 4-9-5 102........................................ PatDobbs 8 97
(Sir Michael Stoute) *led: pushed along 3f out: hdd 2f out: wknd* **11/1**

2m 33.74s (-0.06) **Going Correction** -0.075s/f (Good)
**WFA** 3 from 4yo+ 12lb **7** Ran SP% **114.9**
Speed ratings (Par 115): **97,96,96,94,94 94,92**
CSF £8.00 TOTE £4.00: £2.00, £1.50; EX 9.50 Trifecta £42.40.
**Owner** R J H Geffen **Bred** Petra Bloodstock Agency Ltd **Trained** Newmarket, Suffolk

**FOCUS**
Race distance was 1m 3f 203yds. A decent renewal of this Group 2 was won by John Gosden for the seventh time in the last seven years. The winner and third have been rated to form.

## 4614 BET365 OLD NEWTON CUP H'CAP 1m 3f 175y
**3:15** (3:16) (Class 2) 4-Y-O+
**£62,250** (£18,640; £9,320; £4,660; £2,330; £1,170) **Stalls** Centre

Form RPR
5030 **1** **Dylan Mouth (IRE)**[42] 3090 6-9-10 **104**........................ HarryBentley 8 115
(Marco Botti) *hld up: weaved way through field to chal 2f out: led wl over 1f out: rdn and r.o wl fnl f* **25/1**
0610 **2** *2 1/4* **Soldier In Action (FR)**[15] 4033 4-9-10 **104**............ RichardKingscote 3 111
(Mark Johnston) *led tl hdd after 4f: remained prom: drvn and led again 2f out: hdd wl over 1f out: styd on wl ins fnl f* **9/1**
25-4 **3** *1 1/4* **Shraaoh (IRE)**[35] 3323 4-8-13 **93**........................................ AndreaAtzeni 7 98
(Sir Michael Stoute) *mid-div: hdwy on inner 4f out: rdn 2f out: sn 3rd and ev ch: styd on fnl f* **9/2**[1]
-104 **4** *1/2* **Blakeney Point**[42] 3073 4-8-12 **95**......................(p) KieranShoemark(3) 17 100+
(Roger Charlton) *hld up: hdwy 3f out: nt clr run 2f out: sn in clr: rdn and r.o strly fnl f* **25/1**
0240 **5** *nse* **Tawdeea**[28] 3594 5-9-6 **100**..........................................(v[1]) DanielTudhope 16 105
(David O'Meara) *mid-div: pushed along on outer 3f out: rdn 2f out: styd on strly fnl f: nvr nrr* **20/1**
-344 **6** *hd* **Fabricate**[59] 2519 5-9-1 **102**..................................(p) CameronNoble(7) 11 106
(Michael Bell) *hld up: hdwy on outer 3f out: drvn 2f out: hdwy and ch over 1f out: rdn and one pce* **16/1**
2221 **7** *1/2* **Kapstadt (FR)**[28] 3597 7-9-0 **94**........................................ FranBerry 4 97
(Ian Williams) *trckd ldrs: 4th 4f out: drvn 3f out: sn rdn: grad lost pl* **9/1**
1141 **8** *nk* **Big Country (IRE)**[22] 3790 4-9-4 **98**........................ JosephineGordon 18 101
(Michael Appleby) *chsd ldrs: 3rd 4f out: effrt and pushed along 3f out: 2nd 2f out: rdn and wknd 1f out* **5/1**[2]
1301 **9** *1/2* **Euchen Glen**[15] 4038 4-8-9 **89**........................................ JamesSullivan 1 91
(Jim Goldie) *hld up: effrt on inner 3f out: nt clr run 2f out: no ch after but r.o fnl fulong* **18/1**
6-03 **10** *3/4* **Carntop**[35] 3323 4-9-6 **100**..........................................(h) PatDobbs 5 101
(Ralph Beckett) *in rr: drvn 3f out: rdn 2f out: no hdwy* **16/1**
0-00 **11** *3/4* **Baydar**[15] 4033 4-9-4 **103**........................................ DavidEgan(5) 9 103
(Hugo Palmer) *mid-div: drvn over 2f out: rdn over 1f out: one pce* **20/1**
300- **12** *3/4* **Moonmeister (IRE)**[20] 3875 6-8-10 **90**........................(t) JamieSpencer 2 89
(A J Martin, Ire) *hld up: hdwy into mid-div 3f out: pushed along 2f out: rdn over 1f out and no further hdwy: eased* **10/1**
5125 **13** *1 1/4* **Brorocco**[36] 3300 4-8-10 **90**..........................................(h) DavidProbert 6 87
(Andrew Balding) *in rr: hdwy on inner 3f out: n.m.r over 3f out: rdn 2f out: no imp* **13/2**
4-11 **14** *3 3/4* **Toulson**[40] 3160 4-8-10 **90**........................................ CharlesBishop 14 81
(Eve Johnson Houghton) *trckd ldrs: rdn 2f out: grad lost tch* **6/1**[3]
2-00 **15** *5* **Cosmeapolitan**[52] 2735 4-8-12 **92**........................ DougieCostello 15 75
(Alan King) *hld up: effrt 2f out where n.m.r: drvn over 1f out: no imp* **28/1**

630 **16** *3 ¼* **Farquhar (IRE)**[16] 4002 6-8-11 **90** ow1............................(h) RobertTart 19 68
(Michael Appleby) *prom on outer: led after 4f: kicked 5 l clr 5f out: pushed along 3f out: rdn and hdd 2f out: spent force after* **33/1**

2m 29.39s (-4.41) **Going Correction** -0.075s/f (Good) **16** Ran SP% **132.2**
Speed ratings (Par 109): **111,109,108,108,108 108,107,107,107,106 106,105,104,102,99 96**
CSF £236.75 CT £1235.28 TOTE £36.10: £5.30, £2.90, £1.60, £6.00; EX 473.30 Trifecta £3132.20.
**Owner** Scuderia Effevi SRL **Bred** Azienda Agricola Mariano **Trained** Newmarket, Suffolk
■ Stewards' Enquiry : Andrea Atzeni caution: careless riding

**FOCUS**
Race distance was 1m 3f 203yds. An ultra-competitive handicap won with authority by the topweight who was recording his first win in Britain. The winner has been rated back to something like his best, while the fifth helps set the standard.

## 4615 BET365 CONDITIONS STKS 6f
**3:50** (3:50) (Class 2) 3-Y-0+ **£12,450** (£3,728; £1,864; £932; £466) **Stalls** High

Form RPR
0-20 **1** **Magical Memory (IRE)**[14] 4071 5-9-5 112........................ AndreaAtzeni 2 113
(Charles Hills) *trckd ldrs on stands' side: led gp 2f out: rdn to cl on runner-up ent fnl f: r.o wl: led nr fin* **13/8**[2]

-450 **2** *shd* **Kachy**[14] 4071 4-9-5 107............................................(t) RichardKingscote 4 112
(Tom Dascombe) *t.k.h: led and veered lft towards far rail after 2f: sn swtchd bk to centre of crse: clr ldr 1f out: rdn ins fnl f: hdd nr fin* **11/8**[1]

3011 **3** *4* **Pipers Note**[20] 3861 7-9-5 101...................................... JamesSullivan 6 99
(Ruth Carr) *trckd ldrs stands' side: rdn and ch 2f out: one pce* **5/1**[3]

3100 **4** *8* **Sutter County**[17] 3959 3-9-3 108...................................... FrannyNorton 3 77
(Mark Johnston) *racd stands' side: led tl hdd by runner-up after 2f: drvn and lft bhd fr 2f out* **10/1**

0450 **5** *5* **Mobsta (IRE)**[14] 4071 5-9-5 104..................................(v) CharlesBishop 5 58
(Mick Channon) *prom stands' side: rdn 2f out: wknd ent fnl f* **16/1**

1m 11.61s (-2.19) **Going Correction** -0.075s/f (Good)
**WFA** 3 from 4yo+ 6lb **5** Ran SP% **111.8**
Speed ratings (Par 109): **111,110,105,94,88**
CSF £4.33 TOTE £2.10: £1.50, £1.20; EX 3.80 Trifecta £8.30.
**Owner** Kennet Valley Thoroughbreds I **Bred** Wardstown Stud Ltd **Trained** Lambourn, Berks

**FOCUS**
A thrilling finish to this conditions sprint as the winner nailed the runaway leader on the line. The level is a bit fluid.

## 4616 BET365.COM H'CAP 6f
**4:25** (4:26) (Class 4) (0-80,82) 3-Y-0+ **£6,469** (£1,925; £962; £481) **Stalls** High

Form RPR
4312 **1** **Hart Stopper**[9] 4268 3-9-2 **76**........................................ JamieSpencer 13 87+
(Michael Bell) *dwlt: in rr: stl last 1/2-way: hdwy 2f out: pushed along over 1f out: led ins fnl f: hrd rdn to jst hold on* **4/1**[2]

4106 **2** *hd* **Scofflaw**[20] 3861 3-9-3 **80**........................................ AdamMcNamara(3) 2 90+
(Richard Fahey) *mid-div: pushed along and hdwy 2f out: swtchd rt: rdn and str run ins fnl f: jst failed* **20/1**

1113 **3** *1 ¾* **Meshardal (GER)**[14] 4099 7-9-6 **74**...........................(p) JamesSullivan 4 79
(Ruth Carr) *hld up: hdwy over 2f out: pushed along and led 1f out: sn rdn: hdd ins fnl f: no ex* **11/1**

04 **4** *1 ¼* **Sword Exceed (GER)**[21] 3814 3-9-4 **78**......................... FrannyNorton 3 78
(Ivan Furtado) *hld up: hdwy 2f out: rdn over 1f out: r.o ins fnl f* **14/1**

41 **5** *2 ¼* **Summerghand (IRE)**[17] 3970 3-9-1 **75**........................ DanielTudhope 5 68
(David O'Meara) *trckd ldrs: drvn 2f out: rdn and one pce fnl f* **7/2**[1]

1121 **6** *1 ¼* **The Armed Man**[18] 3946 4-8-12 **73**................................... PaulaMuir(7) 8 63
(Chris Fairhurst) *prom: led 2f out: rdn over 1f out: sn hdd & wknd* **8/1**[3]

3306 **7** *1 ½* **Dandyleekie (IRE)**[9] 4250 5-9-4 **75**.........................(p) ShelleyBirkett(3) 11 60
(David O'Meara) *mid-div: pushed along 2f out: rdn over 1f out: no imp* **20/1**

/000 **8** *nse* **Dr Doro (IRE)**[105] 1365 4-8-9 **63**............................(h) JosephineGordon 7 48
(Ian Williams) *led tl hdd 1/2-way: drvn and fdd 2f out* **66/1**

3231 **9** *nk* **Benjamin Thomas (IRE)**[28] 3568 3-9-4 **78**.....................(v) JasonHart 6 61
(John Quinn) *prom: drvn over 2f out: lost pl and rdn over 1f out: no ex* **9/1**

0660 **10** *½* **Newstead Abbey**[19] 3897 7-8-12 **66**...............................(p[1]) PatDobbs 10 48
(Michael Herrington) *hld up: drvn over 1f out: no impresssion* **50/1**

5524 **11** *3* **Full Intention**[28] 3584 3-9-8 **82**................................(v[1]) RichardKingscote 9 54
(Tom Dascombe) *chsd ldr tl wnt to far side and led 1/2-way: hdd and rdn 2f out: wknd ent fnl f* **4/1**[2]

-213 **12** *2* **Round The Island**[18] 3946 4-8-9 **68**......................... LewisEdmunds(5) 1 34
(Richard Whitaker) *mid-div: pushed along 1/2-way: rdn and sn lost tch* **10/1**

1m 12.28s (-1.52) **Going Correction** -0.075s/f (Good)
**WFA** 3 from 4yo+ 6lb **12** Ran SP% **120.4**
Speed ratings (Par 105): **107,106,104,102,99 98,96,96,95,94 90,88**
CSF £87.68 CT £843.37 TOTE £5.30: £2.00, £5.60, £2.40; EX 104.00 Trifecta £1034.90.
**Owner** Christopher Wright **Bred** Manor Farm Stud (rutland) **Trained** Newmarket, Suffolk

**FOCUS**
Runners all over the course in this decent handicap and the first three all came from the rear. The third helps set the standard.

## 4617 BET365 FILLIES' H'CAP 7f 37y
**5:00** (5:01) (Class 2) (0-100,95) 3-Y-0+ **£12,938** (£3,850; £1,924; £962) **Stalls** Low

Form RPR
0-01 **1** **Excellent Sounds**[20] 3869 4-8-10 **80**......................... CharlieBennett(3) 8 88
(Hughie Morrison) *chsd ldr: pushed along to chal over 1f out: led ent fnl f: hld on under hands and heels: being cl down at line* **9/1**

22-4 **2** *nk* **Aljuljalah (USA)**[33] 3395 4-10-0 **95**................................ AndreaAtzeni 9 102+
(Roger Varian) *hld up: drvn and hdwy 2f out: swtchd to outer to chal ent fnl f: rdn and r.o strly but nt rch wnr* **6/1**

4041 **3** *1 ¼* **Bint Arcano (FR)**[36] 3287 4-9-3 **84**................................ JoeDoyle 2 88
(Julie Camacho) *trckd ldrs on inner: 3rd 3f out: pushed along 2f out: rdn and r.o wl fnl f: snatched 3rd nr fin* **9/2**[3]

316 **4** *nse* **Moonwise (IRE)**[21] 3814 3-8-3 **78**................................... JimmyQuinn 1 79
(Ralph Beckett) *led: pushed along 2f out: hdd ent fnl f: rdn and no ex: lost 3rd nr fin* **7/1**

-216 **5** *1 ¾* **Highland Pass**[22] 3786 3-8-2 **77**............................. JosephineGordon 3 73
(Andrew Balding) *mid-div: pushed along 2f out: rdn over 1f out: one pce* **13/2**

400- **6** *1 ½* **Queensbrydge**[273] 7155 3-8-11 **86**............................. RichardKingscote 4 78
(Robyn Brisland) *hld up on inner: pushed along fnl 2 fs: no imp* **16/1**

-602 **7** *1* **Brogan**[24] 3715 3-8-6 **81**........................................... DavidProbert 5 70
(Tom Dascombe) *mid-div: drvn 2f out: rdn and wknd 1f out* **7/2**[1]

1-31 **8** *2 ½* **Roman Holiday (IRE)**[15] 4051 4-9-0 **81**........................(p) HarryBentley 6 67
(Ed Vaughan) *hld up: drvn along over 2f out: sn hrd rdn and no imp* **4/1**[2]

1m 30.41s (-2.29) **Going Correction** -0.075s/f (Good)
**WFA** 3 from 4yo+ 8lb **8** Ran SP% **116.4**
Speed ratings (Par 96): **110,109,108,108,106 104,103,100**
CSF £62.70 CT £280.11 TOTE £10.80: £2.90, £1.30, £1.90; EX 59.50 Trifecta £392.40.
**Owner** Helena Springfield Ltd **Bred** Meon Valley Stud **Trained** East Ilsley, Berks

**FOCUS**
Race distance 7f 58yds. A decent fillies handicap where the jockeys up front got the pace right. It's been rated around the third.

## 4618 CASH OUT AT BET365 H'CAP 1m 2f 100y
**5:30** (5:30) (Class 3) (0-95,91) 3-Y-0 **£12,938** (£3,850; £1,924; £962) **Stalls** Centre

Form RPR
1-2 **1** **Across Dubai**[67] 2284 3-9-1 **85**........................................ PatCosgrave 2 99+
(William Haggas) *settled in 4th: clsd on ldrs 2f out: wnt 2nd gng easily ent fnl f: shkn up and qcknd to ld 100yds out: comf* **15/8**[1]

1342 **2** *1* **Carigrad (IRE)**[1] 4580 3-8-9 **79**.................................. JosephineGordon 3 88
(Hugo Palmer) *led: 2 l clr 3f out: pushed along 2f out: 1 l clr and drvn ent fnl f: rdn and hdd last 100yds: no ex* **7/2**[3]

41- **3** *2 ¼* **Baashiq (IRE)**[267] 7329 3-8-13 **83**................................ AndreaAtzeni 4 88
(Roger Varian) *trckd ldr: tried to cl 2f out: sn drvn along: rdn 1f out: one pce fnl f* **5/2**[2]

13 **4** *1* **Hugin (IRE)**[24] 3713 3-9-0 **84**........................................ JamieSpencer 1 87
(David Simcock) *hld up in last: plenty to do 3f out: effrt and hdwy 2f out: swtchd ent fnl f: nt pce to chal* **7/2**[3]

0-65 **5** *6* **Hidden Steps**[59] 2523 3-9-3 **87**.......................................(h) DavidProbert 6 78
(Andrew Balding) . *racd in 3rd: pushed along 2f out: rdn over 1f out: wknd* **16/1**

2m 12.36s (-3.14) **Going Correction** -0.075s/f (Good) **5** Ran SP% **113.7**
Speed ratings (Par 104): **109,108,106,105,100**
CSF £9.12 TOTE £2.40: £1.40, £2.00; EX 6.70 Trifecta £20.60.
**Owner** Sheikh Juma Dalmook Al Maktoum **Bred** Rabbah Bloodstock Limited **Trained** Newmarket, Suffolk

**FOCUS**
Race distance increased by 21yds. An interesting 3yo handicap. They went a decent pace despite the small field. The runner-up has been rated similar to his run here the previous day.
T/Plt: £173.00 to a £1 stake. Pool: £146,480.06 - 617.99 winning units. T/Qpdt: £24.30 to a £1 stake. Pool: £9,432.50 - 286.10 winning units. **Keith McHugh**

# 4182 LEICESTER (R-H)
### Saturday, July 8
**OFFICIAL GOING: Good to firm (good in places; watered; 7.4)**
Wind: Nil Weather: Cloudy with sunny spells

## 4619 TAP'N'SHOWER BATHROOM PRODUCTS CLICK AND COLLECT SERVICE FILLIES' H'CAP 6f
**1:25** (1:27) (Class 5) (0-70,71) 3-Y-0+ **£4,528** (£1,347; £673; £336) **Stalls** High

Form RPR
1 **1** **Melonade**[106] 1349 3-9-3 **67**................................................ BenCurtis 4 75+
(David Barron) *hld up: plld hrd: early: hdwy over 2f out: rdn to ld over 1f out: edgd lft: styd on u.p* **3/1**[1]

50-0 **2** *1* **Seyasah (IRE)**[74] 2071 3-9-1 **65**........................................ TomQueally 2 69
(Chris Wall) *s.i.s: hld up: swtchd lft and hdwy over 1f out: sn rdn: styd on* **8/1**

-620 **3** *½* **Fabric**[39] 3171 3-9-6 **70**................................................ TomMarquand 7 72
(Richard Hannon) *s.i.s: hld up: hdwy over 1f out: rdn ins fnl f: styd on* **5/1**[2]

0636 **4** *½* **Manipura**[15] 4053 4-8-7 **51** oh1........................................(p) RyanPowell 9 53
(Derek Shaw) *plld hrd and prom: rdn over 2f out: styd on same pce wl ins fnl f* **14/1**

5113 **5** *½* **Nag's Wag (IRE)**[5] 4441 4-9-13 **71**.................................... LiamKeniry 11 71
(Conor Dore) *trckd ldrs: rdn and edgd lft over 1f out: edgd rt ins fnl f: styd on* **8/1**

06-5 **6** *¾* **Queens Royale**[24] 3719 3-8-10 **60**................................. DanielMuscutt 6 57
(Michael Appleby) *w ldr tl rdn over 2f out: styd on same pce ins fnl f* **17/2**

0-43 **7** *nk* **Miss Patience**[28] 3595 3-9-3 **67**..................................(h) FergusSweeney 8 63
(Peter Chapple-Hyam) *hld up in tch: plld hrd early: rdn over 1f out: carried hd high ins fnl f: nt trble ldrs* **7/1**[3]

0034 **8** *2 ¾* **Goadby**[24] 3728 6-8-7 **51** oh4........................................(v) RoystonFfrench 1 39
(John Holt) *led: rdn and hdd over 1f out: wknd ins fnl f* **20/1**

4523 **9** *4 ½* **Yorkshire Pudding**[17] 3984 3-8-12 **65**.............. RachelRichardson(3) 12 38
(Tim Easterby) *hld up: pushed along 1/2-way: nvr on terms* **10/1**

0030 **10** *4 ½* **Mad Rose (IRE)**[10] 4214 3-8-10 **65**...........................(p[1]) MitchGodwin(5) 5 23
(Jonathan Portman) *chsd ldrs: rdn over 2f out: hung lft and wknd over 1f out* **8/1**

1m 12.38s (-0.62) **Going Correction** -0.025s/f (Good)
**WFA** 3 from 4yo+ 6lb **10** Ran SP% **118.5**
Speed ratings (Par 100): **103,101,101,100,99 98,98,94,88,82**
CSF £27.98 CT £118.48 TOTE £2.90: £1.80, £4.10, £2.50; EX 35.30 Trifecta £414.50.
**Owner** Theakston Stud Syndicate & Partner **Bred** Theakston Stud **Trained** Maunby, N Yorks

**FOCUS**
There was not a great deal of depth to this 3yo handicap and it proved straightforward for the unbeaten favourite. The third has been rated close to her 2yo best, with the fourth to her recent best.

## 4620 TAP'N'SHOWER.COM BATHROOM PRODUCTS DELIVERED NEXT DAY (S) STKS 6f
**1:55** (1:57) (Class 5) 2-Y-0 **£3,234** (£962; £481; £240) **Stalls** High

Form RPR
6615 **1** **Milton Road**[22] 3791 2-9-2 68................................................ JFEgan 3 66
(Mick Channon) *racd keenly: a.p: led over 1f out: rdn out* **4/5**[1]

04 **2** *1 ¾* **Christmas Night**[22] 3791 2-8-12 0................................ RoystonFfrench 4 57
(Ollie Pears) *plld hrd and a.p: led 2f out: rdn and hdd over 1f out: styd on same pce wl ins fnl f* **5/2**[2]

**3** *2 ¼* **Casey Banter** 2-8-7 0........................................................ JoeyHaynes 1 45
(Julia Feilden) *s.s: sn pushed along in rr: hdwy to go 3rd over 1f out: nt trble ldrs* **16/1**

0602 **4** *5* **Roses In June (IRE)**[19] 3918 2-8-3 51 ow3............... GeorgiaDobie(7) 6 33
(J S Moore) *plld hrd: w ldrs: led wl over 2f out: hdd 2f out: wknd over 1f out* **6/1**[3]

06 **5** *4* **Gone To Sea (IRE)**[15] 4054 2-8-7 0.............................. PatrickMathers 7 18
(David Evans) *plld hrd: sn led: racd alone fnl 5f: hdd wl over 2f out: sn hung rt and wknd* **16/1**

0 **6** *3 ¼* **Lisbon Legend**[29] 3516 2-8-12 0 GeorgeDowning 5 13
(Tony Carroll) *plld hrd: w ldrs lost pl over 4f out: sn rdn: wknd over 2f out* **25/1**

1m 13.94s (0.94) **Going Correction** -0.025s/f (Good) **6** Ran SP% **114.0**
Speed ratings (Par 94): **92,89,86,80,74 70**
CSF £3.09 TOTE £1.70: £1.60, £1.20; EX 3.30 Trifecta £17.80.The winner was bought-in for 4,500 guineas.
**Owner** M Channon **Bred** M P Bishop **Trained** West Ilsley, Berks

**FOCUS**
The market proved a key guide to this weak seller. It's been rated around the winner.

## 4621 EBF STALLIONS / TAPNSHOWER.COM FILLIES' H'CAP 1m 2f
**2:30** (2:30) (Class 4) (0-80,83) 3-Y-0 **£7,561** (£2,263; £1,131; £566; £282) **Stalls** Low

Form RPR
6-01 **1** **Lady Bergamot (FR)**[35] 3342 3-8-8 73 GeorgeWood(3) 4 81+
(James Fanshawe) *prom: lost pl over 7f out: pushed along over 4f out: hdwy over 2f out: rdn to chse ldr and hung rt over 1f out: styd on to ld wl ins fnl f* **3/1**[1]

031 **2** *1* **Light Of Joy (USA)**[15] 4042 3-9-2 78 TomQueally 9 83
(David Lanigan) *hld up: hdwy u.p and hung rt fr over 1f out: r.o to go 2nd nr fin* **6/1**[3]

-601 **3** *nse* **Flying North**[12] 4155 3-9-7 83 TimmyMurphy 11 88
(Richard Hannon) *led 8f out: shkn up over 2f out: rdn and hdd wl ins fnl f* **6/1**[3]

-060 **4** *1* **Annie Fior (IRE)**[37] 3262 3-9-0 76 (h) JFEgan 5 79
(Denis Coakley) *prom: racd keenly: nt clr run and wnt 2nd over 6f out: rdn over 2f out: lost 2nd over 1f out: styd on same pce ins fnl f* **9/1**

6-53 **5** *1 ½* **Blind Faith (IRE)**[20] 3857 4-9-13 79 LiamKeniry 6 78+
(Luca Cumani) *hld up: nt clr run over 2f out: swtchd lft over 1f out: hung rt and r.o ins fnl f: nt rch ldrs* **7/1**

10-2 **6** *nk* **Squiggley**[22] 3771 4-9-8 74 FergusSweeney 12 72
(Henry Candy) *sn prom: rdn over 3f out: no ex wl ins fnl f* **8/1**

3066 **7** *1 ¾* **Rayaa**[16] 4010 4-9-1 67 (t) TomMarquand 3 62
(John Butler) *hld up: rdn over 2f out: sme hdwy u.p over 1f out: no ex ins fnl f* **25/1**

0225 **8** *9* **Heartstone (IRE)**[113] 1245 4-8-11 70 KatherineGlenister(7) 7 47
(David Evans) *hld up in tch: rdn over 2f out: wknd over 1f out* **33/1**

6332 **9** *¾* **Ghinia (IRE)**[25] 3683 6-9-6 72 RobHornby 8 47
(Pam Sly) *chsd ldrs: rdn over 2f out: wknd over 1f out* **11/2**[2]

2544 **10** *1 ½* **Auntie Barber (IRE)**[14] 4096 4-9-6 72 (t[1]) DanielMuscutt 10 44
(Stuart Williams) *stdd s: hld up: rdn over 1f out: nvr on terms* **10/1**

2-06 **11** *35* **The Jean Genie**[20] 3866 3-9-2 78 SamHitchcott 2
(Clive Cox) *mid-div: rdn over 3f out: wknd wl over 1f out: eased* **16/1**

/055 **12** *43* **Lahayeb**[19] 3905 5-9-8 81 RayDawson(7) 1
(Michael Appleby) *sn led: hdd 9f out: remained handy: rdn over 3f out: wknd over 2f out: eased* **50/1**

2m 6.13s (-1.77) **Going Correction** -0.025s/f (Good)
**WFA** 3 from 4yo+ 10lb **12** Ran SP% **126.3**
Speed ratings (Par 102): **106,105,105,104,103 102,101,94,93,92 64,30**
CSF £21.92 CT £108.26 TOTE £3.70: £1.30, £2.70, £2.00; EX 24.50 Trifecta £110.00.
**Owner** Andrew & Julia Turner **Bred** Sarl Elevage Du Haras De Bourgeauville **Trained** Newmarket, Suffolk

**FOCUS**
A fair fillies' handicap with a few of these likely to prove significantly better than their current marks. It's been rated around the third.

## 4622 H.A.C. PIPELINE SUPPLIES LTD H'CAP 7f
**3:05** (3:06) (Class 3) (0-95,93) 3-Y-O **£12,602** (£3,772; £1,886; £944; £470) **Stalls** High

Form RPR
22-2 **1** **Easy Tiger**[6] 4410 5-9-3 82 LiamKeniry 9 89
(Malcolm Saunders) *mde all: rdn over 1f out: edgd lft ins fnl f: styd on* **15/8**[1]

0663 **2** *1 ¼* **Twin Appeal (IRE)**[9] 4270 6-9-12 91 (b) BenCurtis 2 95
(David Barron) *hld up: hdwy 2f out: rdn over 1f out: r.o to go 2nd nr fin* **3/1**[2]

0502 **3** *nk* **Shyron**[127] 999 6-8-5 75 JaneElliott(5) 5 78
(George Margarson) *chsd ldrs: rdn over 2f out: r.o* **20/1**

0-06 **4** *shd* **Scottish Glen**[27] 3620 11-9-8 90 HectorCrouch(3) 10 93
(Patrick Chamings) *w wnr tl settled into 2nd 1/2-way: rdn over 1f out: styd on same pce wl ins fnl f* **12/1**

0103 **5** *2 ¾* **Welliesinthewater (IRE)**[9] 4264 7-9-10 89 (v) MartinLane 3 84
(Derek Shaw) *s.i.s: hld up: rdn over 2f out: edgd lft and styd on ins fnl f: nvr nrr* **14/1**

0000 **6** *nse* **Roll On Rory**[7] 4339 4-9-3 82 TomQueally 7 77
(Jason Ward) *n.m.r after s: hld up: rdn over 2f out: styd on ins fnl f: nvr nrr* **16/1**

3141 **7** *hd* **Art Echo**[7] 4339 4-8-13 78 (t) RoystonFfrench 6 73
(John Mackie) *prom: rdn over 2f out: no ex fnl f* **7/2**[3]

00-0 **8** *5* **Final Frontier (IRE)**[36] 3294 4-9-13 92 SamHitchcott 4 73
(Clive Cox) *hld up: rdn over 2f out: nvr on terms* **8/1**

1m 25.89s (-0.31) **Going Correction** -0.025s/f (Good) **8** Ran SP% **118.1**
Speed ratings (Par 107): **100,98,98,98,94 94,94,88**
CSF £7.92 CT £84.65 TOTE £3.00: £1.30, £1.40, £4.90; EX 11.30 Trifecta £106.60.
**Owner** Miss E J Tanner **Bred** D J Weston **Trained** Green Ore, Somerset

**FOCUS**
An ordinary race for the level with very few of these coming here in form. The winner has been rated to form.

## 4623 TAP'N'SHOWER SHOWROOM PRODUCTS AT TRADE PRICES H'CAP 1m 3f 179y
**3:40** (3:43) (Class 5) (0-70,72) 3-Y-0 **£4,528** (£1,347; £673; £336) **Stalls** Low

Form RPR
4435 **1** **Amelia Dream**[16] 4012 3-9-6 68 JFEgan 5 77
(Mick Channon) *hld up: hdwy and nt clr run over 1f out: rdn and r.o to ld wl ins fnl f* **12/1**

0-56 **2** *¾* **Uptown Funk (IRE)**[24] 3720 3-9-3 65 (p) TomQueally 13 73
(John Gosden) *s.i.s and pushed along early in rr: rdn over 2f out: hdwy u.p over 1f out: swtchd rt ins fnl f: r.o* **5/2**[2]

0-42 **3** *½* **Prosecution**[19] 3922 3-9-2 67 GeorgeWood(3) 4 74
(Hughie Morrison) *chsd ldrs: led over 1f out: sn rdn: hdd wl ins fnl f* **2/1**[1]

3-33 **4** *3 ¼* **Bolder Bob (IRE)**[15] 4036 3-9-7 69 BenCurtis 12 71
(David Barron) *sn prom: rdn over 2f out: no ex wl ins fnl f* **11/2**[3]

-343 **5** *1 ¼* **Amadeus Rox (FR)**[38] 3220 3-8-9 57 (p[1]) FergusSweeney 8 57
(Alan King) *chsd ldrs: lost pl over 10f out: hdwy over 8f out: chsd ldr over 2f out: rdn and hung rt fr over 1f out: styd on same pce fnl f* **14/1**

0006 **6** *2 ¾* **Gravity Wave (IRE)**[19] 3922 3-8-13 66 MitchGodwin(5) 11 67+
(Sylvester Kirk) *hld up: hdwy over 2f out: swtchd rt and nt clr run fr over 1f out tl hmpd ins fnl f: nt rcvr* **16/1**

6343 **7** *1 ¼* **Zamadance**[18] 3939 3-8-12 60 AntonioFresu 3 54
(Ed Dunlop) *led 11f out: rdn over 2f out: edgd rt and hdd over 1f out: wknd ins fnl f* **12/1**

6403 **8** *3* **Legato (IRE)**[30] 3489 3-9-3 65 LiamKeniry 2 54
(Tom Dascombe) *sn pushed along to chse ldrs: rdn over 3f out: wknd over 1f out* **10/1**

000- **9** *6* **Velvet Voice**[198] 8486 3-9-0 62 JoeyHaynes 10 41
(Mark H Tompkins) *hld up: effrt over 2f out: sn wknd* **28/1**

0-40 **10** *shd* **Inspector (IRE)**[24] 3717 3-9-6 68 (t[1]) JackMitchell 7 47
(Hugo Palmer) *hld up: hdwy over 2f out: nt clr run over 1f out: sn wknd* **20/1**

-000 **11** *3 ¼* **Whisper A Word (IRE)**[11] 4172 3-8-2 53 oh5 ow3 RachelRichardson(3) 6 27
(Tim Easterby) *led 1f: chsd ldr: rdn over 3f out: wknd over 2f out* **66/1**

0066 **12** *hd* **Navajo Grey (IRE)**[44] 2991 3-8-7 55 LiamJones 1 29
(Michael Appleby) *s.i.s: sn rcvrd into mid-div: lost pl over 8f out: rdn over 3f out: sn wknd* **50/1**

2m 32.28s (-1.62) **Going Correction** -0.025s/f (Good) **12** Ran SP% **126.0**
Speed ratings (Par 100): **104,103,103,101,100 98,97,95,91,91 89,89**
CSF £43.73 CT £91.25 TOTE £14.30: £3.00, £1.50, £1.30; EX 54.80 Trifecta £222.40.
**Owner** M Stewkesbury **Bred** Mervyn Stewkesbury **Trained** West Ilsley, Berks

**FOCUS**
They got racing from a relatively early stage here and it was the hold up horses that came to the fore. The fifth has been rated close to his recent low grade form.

## 4624 EBF BREEDERS BACKING RACING RATING RELATED MAIDEN STKS 7f
**4:15** (4:17) (Class 5) 3-Y-O **£4,528** (£1,347; £673; £336) **Stalls** High

Form RPR
-323 **1** **Cheerfilly (IRE)**[19] 3911 3-8-9 74 (p[1]) PaddyPilley(5) 5 79
(Tom Dascombe) *a.p: chsd ldr 4f out: nt clr run and swtchd rt 1/2-way: sn pushed along: led 2f out: sn hung rt and rdn: clr fnl f: eased nr fin* **5/1**[3]

-554 **2** *3* **Nibras Again**[26] 3673 3-9-0 72 TomMarquand 6 71
(Ismail Mohammed) *hld up in tch: rdn over 1f out: styd on same pce fnl f* **7/2**[2]

2324 **3** *nk* **Peach Melba**[9] 4248 3-9-0 75 JFEgan 2 70
(Mark Johnston) *led: crossed over to stands' side rail 1/2-way: rdn and hdd 2f out: no ex fnl f* **15/8**[1]

3-30 **4** *8* **The Lacemaker**[56] 2625 3-9-0 75 BenCurtis 3 48
(Ed Dunlop) *chsd ldr 3f: sn rdn: wknd wl over 1f out* **7/1**

2-22 **5** *1 ¾* **Nuncio**[21] 3824 3-9-0 73 GeorgeDowning 1 44
(Daniel Kubler) *hld up: pushed along over 4f out: rdn and wknd wl over 1f out* **6/1**

2224 **6** *17* **Wonder Of Dubai (IRE)**[32] 3443 3-8-7 72 (p[1]) TristanPrice(7) 4
(Michael Bell) *s.i.s: rdn 1/2-way: wknd over 2f out* **8/1**

1m 24.56s (-1.64) **Going Correction** -0.025s/f (Good) **6** Ran SP% **111.6**
Speed ratings (Par 100): **108,104,104,95,93 73**
CSF £22.28 TOTE £5.70: £2.70, £2.30; EX 22.70 Trifecta £67.60.
**Owner** Laurence Bellman **Bred** Airlie Stud & Mrs S M Rogers **Trained** Malpas, Cheshire
■ Accento was withdrawn. Price at time of withdrawal 16/1. Rule 4 does not apply.

**FOCUS**
An unusually competitive maiden with all of these rated within 3lb of each other. Only half the field gave their running, however. The runner-up has been rated close to form.

## 4625 H.A.C. GROUP OF COMPANIES H'CAP (DIV I) 1m 53y
**4:45** (4:47) (Class 6) (0-65,66) 3-Y-O+ **£3,234** (£962; £481; £240) **Stalls** Low

Form RPR
-345 **1** **Miss Osier**[39] 3175 3-9-2 62 (p[1]) TomQueally 11 67
(Rae Guest) *chsd ldr: rdn to ld over 1f out: styd on wl* **4/1**[2]

5350 **2** *1* **Sandy Shores**[19] 3922 3-9-2 62 (p[1]) TomMarquand 9 65
(Brian Meehan) *racd keenly: led at stdy pce tl qcknd 3f out: rdn and hdd over 1f out: styd on same pce wl ins fnl f* **9/1**

0666 **3** *1 ¾* **Clever Lady (IRE)**[22] 3774 3-7-11 46 oh1 NoelGarbutt(3) 7 45
(David Evans) *hld up: rdn and r.o to go 3rd nr fin: nt rch ldrs* **6/1**

6 **4** *½* **African Trader (USA)**[25] 3702 4-9-9 60 LiamKeniry 5 60
(Daniel Mark Loughnane) *hld up in tch: plld hrd: rdn over 1f out: styd on same pce ins fnl f* **11/2**[3]

0364 **5** *½* **Scent Of Power**[11] 4184 5-8-5 47 (t) JaneElliott(5) 3 46
(Barry Leavy) *trckd ldrs: plld hrd: rdn over 1f out: no ex ins fnl f* **4/1**[2]

1-20 **6** *2* **Ad Vitam (IRE)**[82] 1833 9-9-10 64 (bt) JordanVaughan(3) 8 58
(Suzzanne France) *hld up: plld hrd: shkn up over 1f out: nt trble ldrs* **16/1**

0001 **7** *1 ½* **Poor Duke (IRE)**[33] 3397 7-9-5 56 PaddyAspell 1 47
(Michael Mullineaux) *hld up: rdn over 2f out: no ex fnl f* **11/4**[1]

-000 **R** **Bold Grove**[12] 4149 5-8-9 46 oh1 (h) RobHornby 6
(Edward Bevan) *ref to r* **20/1**

1m 48.8s (3.70) **Going Correction** -0.025s/f (Good)
**WFA** 3 from 4yo+ 9lb **8** Ran SP% **117.0**
Speed ratings (Par 101): **80,79,77,76,76 74,72,**
CSF £40.28 CT £215.58 TOTE £4.30: £1.80, £3.70, £2.20; EX 40.90 Trifecta £327.00.
**Owner** Peter Saunders & Rae Guest **Bred** D Parisi, G Aletti & P Zambelli **Trained** Newmarket, Suffolk

**FOCUS**
A poor race and it was won in a time over 4secs slower than the second division. The first two home were sporting first-time cheekpieces. It's been rated around the first three.

## 4626 H.A.C. GROUP OF COMPANIES H'CAP (DIV II) 1m 53y
**5:15** (5:15) (Class 6) (0-65,67) 3-Y-O+ **£3,234** (£962; £481; £240) **Stalls** Low

Form RPR
5543 **1** **Valley Of Rocks (IRE)**[11] 4186 3-9-7 66 JFEgan 7 74
(Mark Johnston) *hld up: pushed along over 3f out: hdwy u.p over 1f out: hung rt and led wl ins fnl f: styd on* **6/4**[1]

0600 **2** *1 ½* **Shearian**[28] 3560 7-9-9 64 PhilDennis(5) 5 70
(Declan Carroll) *prom: rdn over 3f out: led over 1f out: hdd and unable qck wl ins fnl f* **13/2**

0000 **3** *2* **Imperial Link**[32] 3422 5-8-10 49 (v) EdwardGreatrex(3) 9 51
(John O'Shea) *sn pushed along to chse ldr: rdn and hung lft over 2f out: hung rt and lft ins fnl f: styd on* **10/1**

-450 **4** *½* **Salt Whistle Bay (IRE)**[25] 3700 3-9-8 67 TomQueally 10 66
(Rae Guest) *chsd ldrs: hung lft bnd over 6f out: rdn over 2f out: nt clr run 1f out: no ex towards fin* **11/2**[2]

356- **5** *nk* **Rock On Dandy (FR)**[263] 7454 3-9-3 62 (b) TomMarquand 2 60
(Harry Dunlop) *chsd ldrs: led 2f out: sn rdn and hdd: no ex ins fnl f* **16/1**

0461 **10** *15* **Spring Fling**[14] 4078 6-9-0 99 ........ SilvestreDeSousa 10 25
(Henry Candy) *a in last pair: hanging and wknd over 1f out: virtually p.u*
**14/1**

58.57s (-3.03) **Going Correction** -0.275s/f (Firm) course record
**WFA** 3 from 4yo+ 5lb **10** Ran SP% **114.3**
Speed ratings (Par 113): **113,107,103,101,99 99,98,95,95,71**
CSF £73.88 TOTE £2.70: £1.40, £6.70, £2.30; EX 65.30 Trifecta £418.10.

**Owner** Hamdan Al Maktoum **Bred** Ballyphilip Stud **Trained** Lambourn, Berks

**FOCUS**
A big performance from the winner, who lowered the track record, although he was allowed to dominate from a handy draw and a few of his rivals under-performed. The form has been rated at face value, with the runner-up rated to his Pattern race best over the past two years.

## 4636 CORAL CHALLENGE (H'CAP) 1m
**2:25** (2:25) (Class 2) 3-Y-0+
**£43,113** (£12,978; £6,489; £3,234; £1,624; £819) **Stalls** Low

Form RPR
-620 **1** **El Hayem (IRE)**[49] 2828 4-8-12 **92** ........ RyanMoore 10 101
(Sir Michael Stoute) *pushed along early and towards rr: stl there 3f out: rdn and prog towards outer 2f out: drvn and r.o to ld last 100yds: hld on wl* **8/1**[3]

0-00 **2** *nk* **Gm Hopkins**[17] 3963 6-9-10 **104** ........ JamesDoyle 7 112
(John Gosden) *dwlt: hld up in last pair: prog on outer 2f out: drvn to chal ins fnl f: pressed wnr last 100yds: a hld* **8/1**[3]

-500 **3** *1 ¼* **Muntazah**[14] 4069 4-9-9 **103** ........ DaneO'Neill 5 108
(Owen Burrows) *led: rdn 2f out: stl 2 l clr over 1f out: hdd and one pce last 100yds* **12/1**

3200 **4** *¾* **Hors De Combat**[17] 3963 6-9-8 **102** ........ OlivierPeslier 15 105
(Denis Coakley) *dwlt: towards rr: shkn up over 2f out and no prog: styd on fr jst over 1f out: nrst fin* **14/1**

03 **5** *½* **Manson**[122] 1079 4-9-1 **95** ........ GeraldMosse 13 97
(Dominic Ffrench Davis) *mostly in last pair: urged along wl over 2f out and no prog: kpt on fr over 1f out: nrst fin but n.d* **16/1**

1-21 **6** *nse* **Greenside**[21] 3837 6-9-5 **99** ........ MartinHarley 2 101+
(Henry Candy) *wl in tch on inner: effrt 2f out: rdn and pressing for a pl 1f out: one pce after* **7/2**[1]

2210 **7** *½* **Rusumaat (IRE)**[16] 3997 3-9-2 **105** ........ JimCrowley 11 104
(Mark Johnston) *hld up in midfield: prog 2f out to chse ldr briefly jst over 1f out: wknd ins fnl f* **8/1**[3]

2344 **8** *1 ¼* **Pactolus (IRE)**[28] 3597 6-8-4 **87** ........(tp) AaronJones(3) 1 85
(Stuart Williams) *cl up on inner: drvn to dispute 2nd pl jst over 1f out: wknd fnl f* **20/1**

0410 **9** *1 ¼* **Ripoll (IRE)**[23] 3750 4-8-0 **80** oh2 ........(t) KieranO'Neill 4 75+
(Sylvester Kirk) *hld up in last trio: tried to make prog on inner fr 2f out but nvr clrest of runs and unable to be involved* **40/1**

1420 **10** *2* **George William**[17] 3963 4-9-4 **98** ........ SeanLevey 6 89
(Richard Hannon) *trckd ldrs: shkn up and nt qckn 2f out: wknd fnl f* **13/2**[2]

0210 **11** *3 ¼* **Mythical Madness**[14] 4069 6-9-7 **101** ........(v) SilvestreDeSousa 9 84
(David O'Meara) *prom: chsd ldr 2f out to jst over 1f out: wknd qckly* **20/1**

-003 **12** *9* **Glory Awaits (IRE)**[21] 3837 7-8-10 **90** ........(b) StevieDonohoe 14 52
(David Simcock) *t.k.h: trckd ldr to 2f out: wknd qckly and eased: t.o* **33/1**

1-1 **13** *2* **Naval Warfare (IRE)**[60] 2505 3-8-6 **95** ........ OisinMurphy 17 51
(Andrew Balding) *pressed ldrs on wd outside to 2f out: wknd qckly and eased: t.o* **8/1**[3]

1m 39.21s (-4.09) **Going Correction** -0.30s/f (Firm)
**WFA** 3 from 4yo+ 9lb **13** Ran SP% **115.1**
Speed ratings (Par 109): **108,107,106,105,105 105,104,103,102,100 96,87,85**
CSF £61.67 CT £666.62 TOTE £8.20: £2.40, £2.70, £5.20; EX 74.60 Trifecta £923.80.

**Owner** Al Shaqab Racing **Bred** Denis Brosnan **Trained** Newmarket, Suffolk

**FOCUS**
A warm handicap, although last year's winner Secret Art and Hunt Cup second Blair House were notable non-runners. The first two came down the outside, while there was some congestion on the inner, and the time again dipped under the standard. The runner-up has been rated close to his best.

## 4637 CORAL DISTAFF (LISTED RACE) (FILLIES) 1m
**3:00** (3:00) (Class 1) 3-Y-O
**£20,982** (£7,955; £3,981; £1,983; £995; £499) **Stalls** Low

Form RPR
0130 **1** **Tisbutadream (IRE)**[17] 3964 3-9-0 97 ........ SilvestreDeSousa 7 98
(David Elsworth) *mde all: shkn up over 2f out: rdn over 1f out: v hrd pressed ins fnl f: fought on tenaciously* **7/2**[3]

-114 **2** *½* **Queen Of Time**[17] 3964 3-9-0 90 ........ JamesDoyle 3 97
(Henry Candy) *hld up in 4th: clsd over 1f out: disp 2nd ins fnl f and sn chalng strly: no imp last 50yds* **5/2**[1]

1650 **3** *½* **Dancing Breeze (IRE)**[17] 3964 3-9-0 87 ........ WilliamBuick 4 96
(John Gosden) *hld up in 6th: prog on outer 2f out: drvn to dispute 2nd ins fnl f and sn chalng strly: no ex last 75yds* **9/2**

4241 **4** *1* **Tai Hang Dragon (IRE)**[7] 4351 3-9-0 82 ........ SeanLevey 8 93
(Richard Hannon) *stdd s: hld up in last: effrt on outer over 1f out: rdn and styd on to take 4th last 100yds: too late to threaten* **16/1**

4-43 **5** *1* **Paco's Angel**[17] 3964 3-9-0 99 ........ ShaneKelly 6 91
(Richard Hughes) *trckd wnr: rdn wl over 1f out: lost 2nd and one pce fnl f* **3/1**[2]

1-13 **6** *½* **Pavillon**[37] 3262 3-9-0 86 ........ GeraldMosse 1 90
(Clive Cox) *t.k.h: trckd ldng pair: rdn wl over 1f out: nt qckn and lost pls fnl f* **7/1**

215- **7** *nk* **Soul Silver (IRE)**[259] 7547 3-9-0 88 ........ OisinMurphy 5 89
(David Simcock) *hld up in 5th: rdn 2f out: no prog over 1f out: one pce and no ch fnl f* **25/1**

1m 41.32s (-1.98) **Going Correction** -0.30s/f (Firm) **7** Ran SP% **116.2**
Speed ratings (Par 105): **97,96,96,95,94 93,93**
CSF £13.12 TOTE £4.50: £2.30, £1.80; EX 14.30 Trifecta £55.60.

**Owner** King Power Racing Co Ltd **Bred** J F Tuthill **Trained** Newmarket, Suffolk

**FOCUS**
This didn't look a strong Listed race beforehand, the winner was allowed to dominate and the seven runners were covered by under 4l at the line. The winner has been rated to form for now.

## 4638 CORAL-ECLIPSE (GROUP 1) (BRITISH CHAMPIONS SERIES) 1m 1f 209y
**3:35** (3:37) (Class 1) 3-Y-O+
**£283,550** (£107,500; £53,800; £26,800; £13,450; £6,750) **Stalls** Low

Form RPR
4-13 **1** **Ulysses (IRE)**[17] 3962 4-9-7 119 ........ JimCrowley 6 124+
(Sir Michael Stoute) *hld up in last pair: smooth prog on outer over 2f out: rdn to ld 1f out: pressed but r.o wl and abt a hd in front last 100yds tl nrly ct last stride* **8/1**

-121 **2** *nse* **Barney Roy**[18] 3927 3-8-11 120 ........ JamesDoyle 4 124+
(Richard Hannon) *hld up in midfield: rdn and prog jst over 2f out: drvn to chal fnl f: r.o wl but looked jst hld tl surged last strides: jst failed* **9/4**[2]

2-12 **3** *3 ½* **Desert Encounter (IRE)**[42] 3072 5-9-7 109 ........(h) SeanLevey 8 116
(David Simcock) *hld up in last: rdn and prog on outer 2f out: styd on to take 3rd last 100yds: no ch w ldng pair* **50/1**

12 **4** *1* **Cliffs Of Moher (IRE)**[35] 3322 3-8-11 117 ........(t) RyanMoore 1 115+
(A P O'Brien, Ire) *cl up: snatched up jst over 7f out and lost pl: rdn over 2f out: nt qckn and no imp ldrs over 1f out: tk 4th last stride* **7/4**[1]

-164 **5** *shd* **Eminent (IRE)**[35] 3322 3-8-11 116 ........ SilvestreDeSousa 3 115
(Martyn Meade) *t.k.h: w ldrs: rdn 3f out and inclined hd towards rival: chal and upsides 2f out: outpcd fnl f* **4/1**[3]

1612 **6** *¾* **Decorated Knight**[17] 3962 5-9-7 119 ........ OlivierPeslier 2 112
(Roger Charlton) *pressed ldr tl checked sltly jst over 7f out: styd handy: rdn to ld 2f out: hdd & wknd 1f out* **10/1**

3-20 **7** *2 ¼* **Lightning Spear**[18] 3924 6-9-7 120 ........ OisinMurphy 5 108
(David Simcock) *t.k.h: hld up in rr: shkn up and no prog 2f out: no ch* **25/1**

-200 **8** *½* **Salouen (IRE)**[15] 4029 3-8-11 107 ........ WilliamBuick 7 108
(Sylvester Kirk) *prom: trckd ldr after 3f: drvn to ld briefly over 2f out: wknd wl over 1f out* **33/1**

2446 **9** *½* **The Taj Mahal (IRE)**[7] 4387 3-8-11 112 ........(b) PBBeggy 9 107
(A P O'Brien, Ire) *led to over 2f out: steadily wknd* **50/1**

2m 3.49s (-7.01) **Going Correction** -0.30s/f (Firm)
**WFA** 3 from 4yo+ 10lb **9** Ran SP% **118.0**
Speed ratings (Par 117): **116,115,113,112,112 111,109,109,109**
CSF £26.47 CT £859.61 TOTE £10.40: £2.00, £1.30, £7.80; EX 39.10 Trifecta £1204.50.
**Owner** Flaxman Stables Ireland Ltd **Bred** Flaxman Stables Ireland Ltd **Trained** Newmarket, Suffolk
■ Stewards' Enquiry : James Doyle 10-day ban (additional five days deferred): excessive use of the whip (Jul 22-31)
P B Beggy eight-day ban: careless riding (22-29 Jul)
Silvestre De Sousa two-day ban: careless riding (Jul 22-23)

**FOCUS**
The first clash of 3yos and older horses in Group 1 company beyond a sprint trip in Britain this season, and one of each pulled clear with next to nothing separating them at the line. However, it was a rough race early on, with most of the runners bunched up through the first couple of furlongs, and judged on the winner and third this looks an ordinary Eclipse. It's been rated a shade below standard renewal.

## 4639 CORAL MARATHON (LISTED RACE) (REGISTERED AS THE ESHER STKS) 2m 50y
**4:10** (4:11) (Class 1) 4-Y-O+
**£20,982** (£7,955; £3,981; £1,983; £995; £499) **Stalls** Centre

Form RPR
-320 **1** **Nearly Caught (IRE)**[16] 3996 7-9-0 111 ........ JamesDoyle 4 110
(Hughie Morrison) *trckd clr ldng pair: rdn to cl 2f out: swtchd ins then lft between rivals over 1f out: drvn to ld jst ins fnl f: styd on wl* **6/4**[1]

00-1 **2** *¾* **Montaly**[59] 2525 6-9-0 102 ........ WilliamBuick 5 109
(Andrew Balding) *hld up in last pair: shkn up wl over 2f out: prog on outer to chal 1f out: nt qckn sn after: styd on but a hld by wnr* **9/2**[3]

01-0 **3** *1* **Alyssa**[42] 3090 4-8-9 102 ........ ShaneKelly 2 103
(Ralph Beckett) *led at gd pce and clr w one rival after 6f: rdn over 2f out as field clsd: hdd jst ins fnl f: kpt on but lost 2nd sn after* **8/1**

3-35 **4** *3* **Fun Mac (GER)**[14] 4073 6-9-0 103 ........(t) JimCrowley 6 104
(Hughie Morrison) *hld up in last pair: rdn over 2f out: kpt on same pce fr over 1f out and tk 4th nr fin* **13/2**

-251 **5** *1* **Oriental Fox (GER)**[14] 4073 9-9-0 105 ........ JoeFanning 3 103
(Mark Johnston) *pressed ldr and clr of rest after 6f: rdn to chal 2f out: lost 2nd and wknd over 1f out* **7/2**[2]

54-0 **6** *30* **Goldmember**[42] 3090 4-9-0 100 ........(t) OisinMurphy 1 67
(David Simcock) *t.k.h: trckd clr ldng pair: rdn over 2f out: sn wknd rapidly: virtually p.u ins fnl f* **14/1**

3m 29.51s (-9.19) **Going Correction** -0.30s/f (Firm) **6** Ran SP% **111.5**
Speed ratings (Par 111): **110,109,109,107,107 92**
CSF £8.44 TOTE £2.10: £1.20, £2.50; EX 8.10 Trifecta £47.80.
**Owner** A N Solomons **Bred** Irish National Stud **Trained** East Ilsley, Berks

**FOCUS**
This was a fair Listed race run at a solid enough-looking gallop. The runner-up confirmed his improved Chester Cup win, giving the fourth a bigger beating here.

## 4640 DOWNLOAD THE CORAL APP H'CAP 1m 1f 209y
**4:40** (4:41) (Class 4) (0-85,85) 3-Y-O **£6,469** (£1,925; £962; £481) **Stalls** Low

Form RPR
412 **1** **Archetype (FR)**[22] 3787 3-9-7 **85** ........ OisinMurphy 5 95
(Simon Crisford) *racd freely: mde all: pushed 2 l clr over 1f out: shkn up and kpt on wl fnl f* **5/1**[3]

14-2 **2** *¾* **Seafarer (IRE)**[24] 3727 3-8-4 **75** ........ TylerSaunders(7) 3 82
(Marcus Tregoning) *trckd ldng pair: effrt to chse wnr wl over 1f out but sn shkn up and no imp: styd on to cl last 100yds but nvr able to chal* **9/2**[2]

1-1 **3** *2 ½* **Frontispiece**[30] 3505 3-9-7 **85** ........ RyanMoore 4 87
(Sir Michael Stoute) *hld up in 4th: shkn up wl over 2f out: tk 3rd over 1f out but one pce and nvr able to threaten* **10/11**[1]

1 **4** *1 ¼* **African**[19] 3922 3-8-10 **74** ........ StevieDonohoe 2 74
(Charlie Fellowes) *hld up in last: shkn up over 2f out: one pce and nvr aa threat* **12/1**

0001 **5** *1 ¼* **Jupiter Light**[22] 3787 3-9-7 **85** ........(p[1]) WilliamBuick 6 82
(John Gosden) *trckd wnr: shkn up 2f out: sn lost 2nd and wknd tamely* **5/1**[3]

2m 6.66s (-3.84) **Going Correction** -0.30s/f (Firm) **5** Ran SP% **111.6**
Speed ratings (Par 102): **103,102,100,99,98**
CSF £26.54 TOTE £5.90: £2.20, £2.20; EX 27.30 Trifecta £84.20.
**Owner** Highclere Thoroughbred Racing-Wordsworth **Bred** E A R L Ecurie Du Grand Chene Haras **Trained** Newmarket, Suffolk

**FOCUS**
A decent handicap. The winner dictated from the front, and the time was over 3sec slower than Ulysses recorded in the Eclipse. It's been rated at face value for now, with the third to his latest C&D win.
T/Jkpt: Not Won. T/Plt: £116.20 to a £1 stake. Pool: £209,446.74 - 1,315.05 winning units. T/Qpdt: £33.50 to a £1 stake. Pool: £13,176.94 - 290.66 winning units. **Jonathan Neesom**

4641 - 4649a (Foreign Racing) - See Raceform Interactive

## 3605 BELMONT PARK (L-H)
Saturday, July 8

**OFFICIAL GOING: Dirt: fast; turf: firm**

### 4650a BELMONT OAKS INVITATIONAL STKS (GRADE 1) (3YO FILLIES) (TURF) — 1m 2f (T)
10:46 3-Y-O
**£434,959** (£150,406; £81,300; £52,845; £32,520; £24,390)

RPR

1 **New Money Honey (USA)**[30] 3-8-9 0 ...................... JavierCastellano 8 110
(Chad C Brown, U.S.A) *in tch: trckd ldrs over 3f out: rdn over 2f out: drvn to ld over 1f out: kpt on wl whn pressed clsng stages* **5/2**[2]

2 *nk* **Sistercharlie (IRE)**[20] 3881 3-8-9 0 ...................... JohnRVelazquez 11 109+
(Chad C Brown, U.S.A) *hld up in rr: stdy hdwy fr over 5f out: rdn over 2f out: styd on wl fr 1 1/2f out: pressed wnr clsng stages* **7/4**[1]

3 *1 ¾* **Uni**[58] 2560 3-8-9 0 ...................... IradOrtizJr 7 106
(Chad C Brown, U.S.A) *dwlt: hld up towards rr: rdn and gd hdwy fr 2f out: wnt 3rd 75yds out: no imp on front pair clsng stages* **79/10**

4 *½* **Daddys Lil Darling (USA)**[64] 2380 3-8-9 0 ...................... DylanDavis 10 105
(Kenneth McPeek, U.S.A) *in tch in midfield: rdn and kpt on fr 2 1/2f out: nvr gng pce to chal* **116/10**

5 *¾* **Grizzel (IRE)**[48] 3-8-9 0 ...................... DJMoran 4 103
(Michael J Doyle, Canada) *trckd ldrs: led 2 1/2f out: sn rdn: hdd over 1f out: wknd fnl f* **40/1**

6 *hd* **Beau Recall (IRE)**[21] 3-8-9 0 ...................... FlavienPrat 2 103+
(Simon Callaghan, U.S.A) *midfield: dropped towards rr 4 1/2f out: rdn and kpt on wl fr 2f out* **69/10**[3]

7 *1 ¼* **Coasted (USA)**[30] 3-8-9 0 ...................... JoelRosario 1 101
(Leah Gyarmati, U.S.A) *in tch in midfield: tk clsr order 3f out: rdn 2f out: wknd 1f out* **199/10**

8 *1* **Journey Home (USA)**[24] 3-8-9 0 ...................... EdgarSPrado 6 99
(H Graham Motion, U.S.A) *hld up towards rr: rdn and kpt on steadily on outer fr 2f out: n.d* **45/1**

9 *2* **Violet Blue (USA)**[35] 3-8-9 0 ...................... ManuelFranco 3 95
(James J Toner, U.S.A) *towards rr of midfield: rdn and outpcd over 2f out: sn no imp* **76/1**

10 *5* **Dynatail (USA)**[35] 3-8-9 0 ......................(b) LuisSaez 9 85
(Michael Dini, U.S.A) *led: rdn and hdd 2 1/2f out: wknd 1 1/2f out: eased ins fnl f* **206/10**

11 *8 ¼* **Key To My Heart (IRE)**[10] 4229 3-8-9 0 ...................... WayneLordan 5 68
(A P O'Brien, Ire) *w ldr: rdn 3f out: lost pl 2 1/2f out: sn wl btn* **123/10**

1m 59.89s (-1.40) **11** Ran SP% **119.6**
PARI-MUTUEL (all including 2 usd stake): WIN 7.00; PLACE (1-2) 3.30, 3.30; SHOW (1-2-3) 2.90, 2.80, 4.00; SF 21.20.
**Owner** e Five Racing Thoroughbreds **Bred** WinStar Farm LLC **Trained** USA

### 4652a BELMONT DERBY INVITATIONAL STKS (GRADE 1) (3YO) (TURF) — 1m 2f (T)
11:50 3-Y-O
**£528,455** (£178,861; £97,560; £65,040; £36,585; £26,829)

RPR

1 **Oscar Performance (USA)**[35] 3-8-10 0 ...................... JoseLOrtiz 4 114+
(Brian A Lynch, Canada) *mde all: rdn clr 2f out: kpt on strly* **11/2**[3]

2 *2* **Called To The Bar (IRE)**[46] 2947 3-8-10 0 ...................... MaximeGuyon 5 110
(Mme Pia Brandt, France) *trckd ldrs: rdn 2 1/2f out: wnt 2nd 1 1/2f out: kpt on wl: no imp on wnr* **68/10**

3 *¾* **Homesman (USA)**[16] 3998 3-8-10 0 ......................(b) IradOrtizJr 3 109+
(A P O'Brien, Ire) *midfield: tk clsr order 2 1/2f out: rdn and kpt on fr under 2f out* **118/10**

4 *nk* **Good Samaritan (USA)**[35] 3-8-10 0 ...................... JoelRosario 1 108+
(William Mott, U.S.A) *hld up in rr: stdy hdwy fr 2 1/2f out: rdn under 2f out: styd on fnl f: nrst fin* **56/10**

5 *1 ¼* **Yoshida (JPN)**[49] 3-8-10 0 ...................... JohnRVelazquez 7 105
(William Mott, U.S.A) *trckd ldrs: rdn 2f out: wknd last 75yds* **3/1**[1]

6 *hd* **Makarios (USA)**[35] 3-8-10 0 ...................... TylerGaffalione 8 105+
(Nicholas Zito, U.S.A) *towards rr of midfield: rdn 2 1/2f out: styd on last 150yds: n.d* **84/1**

7 *2 ½* **Whitecliffsofdover (USA)**[17] 3959 3-8-10 0 ......................(b) WayneLordan 10 100
(A P O'Brien, Ire) *midfield: rdn 2 1/2f out: outpcd under 2f out: sn no imp* **31/1**

8 *hd* **Big Score (USA)**[34] 3-8-10 0 ...................... FlavienPrat 9 100
(Tim Yakteen, U.S.A) *chsd ldr: rdn 2 1/2f out: wknd over 1f out* **207/10**

9 *nse* **Ticonderoga (USA)**[35] 3-8-10 0 ......................(b) JavierCastellano 2 100
(Chad C Brown, U.S.A) *a towards rr* **61/10**

10 *5 ¾* **Senior Investment (USA)**[28] 3610 3-8-10 0 ...................... DylanDavis 11 88
(Kenneth McPeek, U.S.A) *a towards rr* **36/1**

11 *1* **Arklow (USA)**[63] 3-8-10 0 ...................... MikeESmith 6 86
(Brad H Cox, U.S.A) *in tch in midfield: lost pl 2 1/2f out: sn wl btn* **23/5**[2]

2m 0.25s (-1.04) **11** Ran SP% **119.7**
PARI-MUTUEL (all including 2 usd stake): WIN 23.40; PLACE (1-2) 11.60, 13.40; SHOW (1-2-3) 5.60, 6.80, 3.00; SF 238.60.
**Owner** Amerman Racing Stables LLC **Bred** Mrs Jerry Amerman **Trained** Canada

4651 - 4652a (Foreign Racing) - See Raceform Interactive

## 1929 NANTES (R-H)
Saturday, July 8

**OFFICIAL GOING: Turf: good**

### 4653a GRAND PRIX ANJOU BRETAGNE (LISTED RACE) (4YO+) (TURF) — 1m
1:20 4-Y-O+ **£22,222** (£8,888; £6,666; £4,444; £2,222)

RPR

1 **Royal Julius (IRE)**[31] 4-8-13 0 ow2 ...................... TheoBachelot 8
(J Reynier, France) **8/5**[1]

2 *1 ½* **Maximum Aurelius (FR)**[225] 8117 4-9-2 0 ow1 ....... MickaelBarzalona 3
(F-H Graffard, France) **81/10**

3 *1 ½* **Black Max (FR)**[20] 3880 4-9-2 0 ow1 ...................... Pierre-CharlesBoudot 1
(H-A Pantall, France) **2/1**[2]

4 *¾* **Princess Gibraltar (FR)**[44] 4-9-3 0 ow1 ...................... StephanePasquier 4
(N Clement, France) **53/10**[3]

5 *3* **Flag Fen**[58] 4-8-13 0 ow2 ......................(b) FabriceVeron 2
(N Caullery, France) **58/10**

6 *5* **Huda (FR)**[273] 4-8-9 0 ow1 ...................... Jean-BaptisteHamel 5
(B Legros, France) **63/1**

P **Wowcha (IRE)**[27] 3632 4-8-9 0 ow1 ......................(b) HugoJourniac 6
(John Quinn) *nvr travelling and qckly detached: wl bhd whn p.u after 2f* **213/10**

1m 36.08s **7** Ran SP% **119.4**
PARI-MUTUEL (all including 1 euro stake): WIN: 2.60; PLACE: 1.20, 1.80, 1.30; DF: 11.70; SF: 19.50.
**Owner** Mme Jade Prescillia Angelini **Bred** Old Carhue Stud **Trained** France

### 4654a DERBY DE L'OUEST (LISTED RACE) (3YO) (TURF) — 1m 4f
1:50 3-Y-O **£23,504** (£9,401; £7,051; £4,700; £2,350)

RPR

1 **Fauguernon (FR)**[88] 3-9-3 0 ow1 ......................(b) JulienAuge 6 90
(C Ferland, France) **23/10**[1]

2 *snk* **Hipodamo De Mileto (FR)** 3-9-3 0 ow1(p)
Roberto-CarlosMontenegro 9 90
(J Calderon, Spain) **9/1**

3 *¾* **Vatican Hill (IRE)**[20] 3-9-3 0 ow1 ...................... AlexandreRoussel 1 89
(P Monfort, France) **144/10**

4 *1* **Not After Hours (FR)**[68] 3-9-0 0 ow1 ...................... Francois-XavierBertras 2 84
(F Rohaut, France) **14/5**[2]

5 *nk* **Royalickly (FR)**[46] 3-9-3 0 ow1 ...................... SebastienMartino 8 86
(S Gouvaze, France) **34/1**

6 *nk* **Cap Verite (IRE)**[56] 3-9-0 0 ow1 ...................... StephanePasquier 7 83
(N Clement, France) **56/10**

7 *8 ½* **Nullemont (IRE)**[22] 3804 3-9-0 0 ow1 ......................(p) MickaelForest 5 69
(C Ferland, France) **98/10**

8 *3* **Midnight Fair (IRE)**[30] 3-9-0 0 ow1 ...................... MickaelBarzalona 4 65
(H-A Pantall, France) *led: hdd after 2f: remained cl up on outer: 2nd whn niggled along to hold pl 3f out: rdn and no imp 1 1/2f out: wknd fnl f* **9/2**[3]

2m 29.79s (-5.21) **8** Ran SP% **118.6**
PARI-MUTUEL (all including 1 euro stake): WIN: 2.50 (coupled with Nullemont); PLACE: 1.90, 3.10, 3.60; DF: 13.30; SF: 21.60.
**Owner** Gerard Augustin-Normand **Bred** Mme G Forien & G Forien **Trained** France

## 4142 LES LANDES
Friday, July 7

**OFFICIAL GOING: Turf: firm**

### 4655a LA VERTE RUE H'CAP (TURF) — 5f 110y
6:30 (6:32) 3-Y-O+ **£1,780** (£640; £380)

RPR

1 **Swiss Cross**[10] 4176 10-10-12 0 ......................(tp) JemmaMarshall 78
(Phil McEntee) *trckd ldr: led 1f out: rdn clr* **8/11**[1]

2 *4* **Country Blue (FR)**[14] 4142 8-10-2 0 ......................(p) MattieBatchelor 54
(Mrs A Malzard, Jersey) *led: hdd 1f out: no ex* **13/8**[2]

3 *1* **Purley Queen (IRE)**[54] 2669 8-9-7 0 ...................... AliceMills 42
(Mrs C Gilbert, Jersey) *trckd ldrs: outpcd 1/2-way: kpt on to go 3rd 1f out* **9/4**[3]

4 *2* **Princess Kodia (IRE)**[14] 4-9-13 0 ...................... MrFTett 41
(Mrs A Malzard, Jersey) *trckd ldrs in 3rd: outpcd 1/2-way: wknd 1f out* **10/1**

5 *3 ½* **Ron's Ballad**[14] 4142 4-8-8 0 oh3 ow3 ...................... PhilipPrince 10
(K Kukk, Jersey) *outpcd: a bhd* **14/1**

.
**Owner** Steve Jakes **Bred** Lordship Stud **Trained** Newmarket, Suffolk

### 4656a "BUILDING AS BETTER WORLD" H'CAP (TURF) — 7f
7:05 (7:07) 3-Y-O+ **£1,780** (£640; £380)

RPR

1 **Brown Velvet**[14] 4143 5-9-9 0 ...................... AliceMills 47
(Mrs C Gilbert, Jersey) *trckd ldr in 2nd: led over 1f out: pushed out* **14/1**

2 *3* **Grey Panel (FR)**[14] 4143 9-10-2 0 ...................... JemmaMarshall 46
(T Le Brocq, Jersey) *led: hdd over 1f out: no ex* **5/2**[2]

3 *2 ½* **Justice Rock**[23] 3728 4-10-12 0 ......................(t) PaddyAspell 49
(Phil McEntee) *dwlt: hdwy over 4f out: kpt on one pce fnl 2f* **4/5**[1]

4 *1 ½* **Hawaiian Freeze**[14] 8-10-5 0 ......................(b) MarcGoldstein 38
(J Moon, Jersey) *trckd ldrs: sltly hmpd and dropped to last 3f out: kpt on one pce* **7/1**

5 *9* **First Cat**[14] 4143 10-9-12 0 ...................... PhilipPrince 7
(K Kukk, Jersey) *hld up: rdn 3f out: sn btn* **11/2**

6 *6* **Spanish Bounty**[14] 4142 12-10-11 0 ...................... MissMHooper 3
(Mrs A Malzard, Jersey) *trckd ldrs: wknd fr 2f out* **10/3**[3]

.
**Owner** La Vallette Ltd **Bred** D R Botterill **Trained** Jersey

## 4074 AYR (L-H)

Sunday, July 9

**OFFICIAL GOING: Good changing to good (good to soft in places) after race 1 (1.40)**

Wind: Fresh, half against Weather: Overcast

### 4657 BET TOTEPLACEPOT AT BETFRED.COM LONGINES IRISH CHAMPIONS EBF MAIDEN STKS — 1m 2f

**1:40** (1:41) (Class 5) 3-Y-0+ **£3,881** (£1,155; £577; £288) **Stalls** Low

Form RPR

3 **1** **Pouvoir Magique (FR)**[31] 3506 3-9-4 0 ........ JamesDoyle 1 90+
(John Gosden) *chsd ldr: sn clr of rest: shkn up to ld over 1f out: kpt on wl fnl f: comf* **1/12**[1]

**2** *1 ½* **Itsalonglongroad**[296] 6550 3-9-4 0 ........ (t[1]) JoeFanning 3 82
(John C McConnell, Ire) *led: rdn and hdd over 1f out: kpt on fnl f: nt rch wnr* **6/1**[2]

50 **3** *21* **Red Star Dancer (IRE)**[10] 4247 3-9-4 0 ........ JamesSullivan 2 40
(Linda Perratt) *hld up in tch: rdn over 2f out: hdwy to chse clr ldng pair over 1f out: no imp fnl f* **50/1**

0 **4** *shd* **Wee Bogus**[10] 4247 4-9-9 0 ........ RowanScott(5) 4 39
(Alistair Whillans) *hld up: rdn and outpcd over 3f out: rallied 2f out: sn no imp* **50/1**

55 **5** *½* **Hugoigo**[50] 2842 3-8-11 0 ........ SeanMooney(7) 5 39
(Jim Goldie) *s.i.s: hld up: drvn along 3f out: sn n.d* **33/1**

- **6** *8* **Anna's Legacy** 4-9-9 0 ........ PJMcDonald 6 17
(Jim Goldie) *chsd clr ldng pair: rdn over 3f out: wknd over 1f out* **25/1**[3]

2m 14.74s (2.74) **Going Correction** +0.275s/f (Good)
**WFA** 3 from 4yo 10lb **6** Ran SP% **117.3**
Speed ratings (Par 103): **100,98,82,81,81 75**
CSF £1.31 TOTE £1.10: £1.02, £2.00; EX 1.80 Trifecta £9.20.
**Owner** HRH Princess Haya Of Jordan **Bred** Mme Elisabeth Vidal **Trained** Newmarket, Suffolk

**FOCUS**
Inner rail out 4yds, add 12yds. The ground was changed to good, good to soft in places following this opening contest. This maiden only seriously concerned two horses, with the runner-up leading before the winner, who probably didn't have to match the form of his debut, got on top comfortably enough in the closing stages.

### 4658 BET TOTEEXACTA AT BETFRED.COM H'CAP — 1m 2f

**2:10** (2:11) (Class 4) (0-85,93) 3-Y-0+ **£5,498** (£1,636; £817; £408) **Stalls** Low

Form RPR

4212 **1** **Komodo (IRE)**[21] 3862 3-9-1 **82** ........ DanielTudhope 13 91
(Jedd O'Keeffe) *trckd ldrs: wnt 2nd 1/2-way: rdn over 2f out: rallied and led over 1f out: hld on wl fnl f* **2/1**[1]

1261 **2** *nk* **Lucent Dream (IRE)**[20] 3898 6-8-13 **70** ........ (t) JamesDoyle 5 78+
(John C McConnell, Ire) *dwlt: hld up: rdn along and effrt over 2f out: hdwy over 1f out: chsd wnr ins fnl f: kpt on* **8/1**

2313 **3** *1 ¼* **Royal Regent**[16] 4035 5-9-8 **82** ........ SammyJoBell(3) 4 87
(Lucy Normile) *t.k.h early: hld up: rdn over 2f out: hdwy over 1f out: kpt on fnl f: nrst fin* **8/1**

63 **4** *hd* **Konig Dax (GER)**[38] 3240 7-9-4 **75** ........ (t) TomEaves 6 80
(Alistair Whillans) *sn led: rdn and hdd over 1f out: kpt on same pce fnl f* **25/1**

3062 **5** *¾* **Mulligatawny (IRE)**[17] 4017 4-10-2 **87** ........ TonyHamilton 12 90
(Roger Fell) *hld up in tch: effrt and rdn 2f out: kpt on same pce fnl f* **12/1**

1121 **6** *1 ¾* **Gworn**[16] 4035 7-9-10 **81** ........ PJMcDonald 1 81+
(R Mike Smith) *hld up midfield: drvn along over 2f out: kpt on fnl f: nvr able to chal* **6/1**[3]

0-22 **7** *nk* **Throckley**[22] 3845 6-9-13 **84** ........ (t) SamJames 2 83
(John Davies) *early ldr: pressed ldr to 1/2-way: drvn and effrt over 2f out: kpt on same pce fnl f* **11/2**[2]

-406 **8** *¾* **Kodiac Khan (IRE)**[9] 4304 3-8-9 **76** ........ JoeFanning 8 75
(Mark Johnston) *prom: drvn over 2f out: outpcd appr fnl f* **12/1**

6665 **9** *hd* **Archie's Advice**[18] 3976 6-9-3 **74** ........ (p) GrahamLee 10 71
(Keith Dalgleish) *dwlt: hld up midfield on outside: effrt and hung lft 2f out: wknd ins fnl f* **28/1**

-640 **10** *1* **Bahama Moon (IRE)**[31] 3498 5-10-0 **85** ........ AndrewMullen 9 83
(David Barron) *hld up midfield: drvn and outpcd over 2f out: wknd over 1f out* **25/1**

000 **11** *½* **Spes Nostra**[6] 4430 9-9-2 **73** ........ (bt) DougieCostello 3 67
(Iain Jardine) *hld up: rdn and outpcd over 2f out: sn n.d* **80/1**

-605 **12** *3 ¼* **Salmon Sushi**[8] 4358 6-9-0 **71** ........ (h) DavidAllan 11 59
(Tim Easterby) *hld up: drvn along over 2f out: sn btn* **20/1**

2m 13.96s (1.96) **Going Correction** +0.275s/f (Good)
**WFA** 3 from 4yo+ 10lb **12** Ran SP% **117.7**
Speed ratings (Par 105): **103,102,101,101,101 99,99,98,98,97 97,94**
CSF £16.87 CT £108.42 TOTE £2.70: £1.50, £2.50, £2.60; EX 20.60 Trifecta £200.50.
**Owner** Geoff & Sandra Turnbull **Bred** Irish National Stud **Trained** Middleham Moor, N Yorks

**FOCUS**
Add 12yds. A fair handicap, although not much got involved.

### 4659 BET TOTEQUADPOT AT BETFRED.COM H'CAP (DIV I) — 1m 2f

**2:45** (2:55) (Class 6) (0-60,62) 3-Y-0+ **£2,587** (£770; £384; £192) **Stalls** Low

Form RPR

-031 **1** **Regal Mirage (IRE)**[18] 3977 3-8-8 **50** ........ DavidAllan 8 60
(Tim Easterby) *sn trcking ldr: rdn and clr of rest over 2f out: led ins fnl f: styd on strly* **4/1**[1]

**2** *nk* **Blankiedoodie**[316] 5903 4-9-0 **46** oh1 ........ PaulHanagan 1 54
(John C McConnell, Ire) *led after 1f: rdn and clr w wnr over 2f out: hdd ins fnl f: kpt on: hld nr fin* **13/2**

-036 **3** *4 ½* **Remember Rocky**[30] 3530 8-9-4 **57** ........ (b) ConnorMurtagh(7) 7 57
(Lucy Normile) *hld up midfield: effrt and rdn over 2f out: chsd clr ldng pair ins fnl f: r.o fin* **12/1**

0460 **4** *½* **Lopito De Vega (IRE)**[24] 3740 5-9-11 **62** ........ LewisEdmunds(5) 11 61
(David C Griffiths) *hld up: effrt whn nt clr run over 2f out: styd on fnl f: nvr rchd ldrs* **6/1**[3]

1500 **5** *1 ¼* **Mr Sundowner (USA)**[17] 4018 5-9-9 **55** ........ (t) DougieCostello 2 52
(Wilf Storey) *chsd ldrs: drvn along over 2f out: wknd ins fnl f* **11/1**

0550 **6** *1 ¼* **John Caesar (IRE)**[9] 4323 6-9-7 **53** ........ (tp) DanielTudhope 6 48
(Rebecca Bastiman) *hld up: rdn and effrt over 2f out: kpt on fnl f: no imp* **18/1**

3065 **7** *nk* **Let Right Be Done**[16] 4039 5-8-11 **46** ........ (b) SammyJoBell(3) 14 40
(Linda Perratt) *s.i.s: hld up: hdwy whn nt clr run over 2f out: rdn and no imp fr over 1f out* **25/1**

60/4 **8** *2 ¼* **Uriah Heep (FR)**[18] 3978 8-9-12 **58** ........ (p) PJMcDonald 12 48
(R Mike Smith) *dwlt: hld up on outside: rdn and effrt over 2f out: sn no imp: btn over 1f out* **12/1**

**9** *1 ½* **Mostawfee (IRE)**[76] 2051 4-9-6 **57** ........ (p) DMSimmonson(5) 9 45
(John James Feane, Ire) *hld up midfield: outpcd and edgd lft over 2f out: sn btn* **5/1**[2]

533 **10** *9* **Les Pecheurs (IRE)**[19] 3945 3-9-4 **60** ........ TomEaves 10 32
(James Ewart) *hld up midfield: drvn along over 3f out: sn wknd* **22/1**

6-05 **11** *7* **Harbour Belle**[34] 3404 3-8-12 **54** ........ PaulMulrennan 3 14
(Michael Dods) *prom tl rdn and wknd over 2f out* **25/1**

4-00 **12** *4 ½* **Silver Duke (IRE)**[44] 3048 6-9-8 **54** ........ (b) JamesSullivan 4 5
(Jim Goldie) *t.k.h: hld up: rdn and outpcd over 3f out: sn wknd* **40/1**

0-50 **13** *28* **Zacchetto (USA)**[16] 4055 3-9-0 **56** ........ JamesDoyle 13
(Mark Johnston) *led 1f: cl up tl rdn and wknd qckly 3f out: t.o* **10/1**

0560 **14** *82* **Whitchurch**[16] 4034 5-8-7 **46** oh1 ........ (p) JamieGormley(7) 5
(Iain Jardine) *hld up: drvn and struggling over 3f out: sn btn: eased whn no ch wl over 1f out* **33/1**

2m 14.13s (2.13) **Going Correction** +0.275s/f (Good)
**WFA** 3 from 4yo+ 10lb **14** Ran SP% **119.8**
Speed ratings (Par 101): **102,101,98,97,96 95,95,93,92,85 79,76,53,**
CSF £27.18 CT £292.75 TOTE £6.00: £2.70, £2.50, £3.60; EX 40.10 Trifecta £491.00.
**Owner** Ryedale Partners No 7 **Bred** Norelands, Lofts Hall & A Gold **Trained** Great Habton, N Yorks

**FOCUS**
Add 12yds. A moderate handicap and the first two pretty much had the race to themselves from some way out.

### 4660 BET TOTEQUADPOT AT BETFRED.COM H'CAP (DIV II) — 1m 2f

**3:15** (3:21) (Class 6) (0-60,59) 3-Y-0+ **£2,587** (£770; £384; £192) **Stalls** Low

Form RPR

0-04 **1** **Take A Turn (IRE)**[22] 3819 3-9-4 **59** ........ PaulMulrennan 9 64
(David Lanigan) *dwlt: hld up: hdwy and swtchd lft over 2f out: rdn and squeezed through to ld ins fnl f: kpt on strly* **11/2**[2]

0652 **2** *nk* **Never Say (IRE)**[29] 3564 4-9-0 **45** ........ (p) PaulHanagan 2 48
(Sam England) *hld up midfield: rdn and effrt 2f out: hdwy fnl f: edgd lft and tk 2nd nr fin* **9/1**[3]

006 **3** *nk* **Sakhalin Star (IRE)**[6] 4453 6-9-9 **54** ........ (e) ConnorBeasley 1 57
(Richard Guest) *in tch: hdwy to ld over 1f out: rdn and hdd ins fnl f: kpt on fin* **14/1**

5263 **4** *1* **Colour Contrast (IRE)**[16] 4034 4-9-6 **58** ........ (p) JamieGormley(7) 3 59
(Iain Jardine) *prom: hdwy and ev ch over 1f out: rdn and one pce ins fnl f* **3/1**[1]

0331 **5** *nk* **Haymarket**[16] 4034 8-9-8 **53** ........ PJMcDonald 12 54
(R Mike Smith) *led: rdn and hdd over 2f out: rallied: kpt on same pce fnl f* **3/1**[1]

-344 **6** *nk* **Joyful Star**[30] 3530 7-9-7 **52** ........ (p[1]) GrahamLee 10 52
(Fred Watson) *hld up: hdwy and edgd rt over 1f out: kpt on ins fnl f: nt pce to chal* **14/1**

4040 **7** *1 ¾* **Penelope Pitstop**[9] 4323 5-9-1 **46** ........ (p[1]) JamesSullivan 6 43
(Lee Smyth, Ire) *t.k.h: cl up: led over 2f out to over 1f out: no ex ins fnl f* **18/1**

000 **8** *shd* **Sir Runs A Lot**[20] 3898 5-10-0 **59** ........ AndrewMullen 11 56
(David Barron) *hld up midfield: drvn and edgd lft over 2f out: sn n.d* **25/1**

0050 **9** *½* **Naupaka**[33] 3431 3-8-5 **51** ........ (p) BenRobinson(5) 7 48
(Brian Ellison) *t.k.h: prom: rdn over 2f out: wknd over 1f out* **14/1**

0500 **10** *½* **Stardrifter**[16] 4039 5-9-7 **57** ........ LewisEdmunds(5) 13 52
(Linda Perratt) *hld up: rdn and edgd lft over 2f out: sn n.d* **10/1**

0604 **11** *13* **Jebulani**[32] 3449 7-8-7 **45** ........ (p) ConnorMurtagh(7) 8 17
(Barry Murtagh) *in tch on outside: rdn over 2f out: wknd wl over 1f out* **50/1**

/0-0 **12** *10* **Wolf Heart (IRE)**[16] 4034 9-8-11 **45** ........ SammyJoBell(3) 5
(Lucy Normile) *dwlt: hld up: struggling over 2f out: sn wknd* **33/1**

2m 14.7s (2.70) **Going Correction** +0.275s/f (Good)
**WFA** 3 from 4yo+ 10lb **12** Ran SP% **118.5**
Speed ratings (Par 101): **100,99,99,98,98 98,96,96,96,95 85,77**
CSF £53.44 CT £664.73 TOTE £7.20: £2.30, £2.30, £3.90; EX 58.10 Trifecta £768.00.
**Owner** 21st Century Farms Ltd **Bred** 21st Century Farms Ltd **Trained** Newmarket, Suffolk
■ Stewards' Enquiry : Graham Lee two-day ban; careless riding (23rd-24th Jul)
Paul Hanagan caution; careless riding

**FOCUS**
Add 12yds. The second leg of a moderate handicap, and this one set up for those who were waited with. Straightforward form.

### 4661 BET TOTETRIFECTA AT BETFRED.COM H'CAP — 1m

**3:50** (3:51) (Class 5) (0-75,77) 3-Y-0+ **£3,557** (£1,058; £529; £264) **Stalls** Low

Form RPR

0440 **1** **Zodiakos (IRE)**[22] 3845 4-10-0 **75** ........ (p) TonyHamilton 10 84
(Roger Fell) *pressed ldr: drvn to ld over 1f out: r.o wl fnl f* **15/2**

5333 **2** *1 ¼* **Abushamah (IRE)**[16] 4057 6-9-13 **74** ........ (p) JamesSullivan 6 80
(Ruth Carr) *s.i.s: hld up: rdn and plld out over 1f out: hdwy to chse wnr ins fnl f: kpt on fin* **4/1**[2]

-356 **3** *nk* **Royal Shaheen (FR)**[15] 4085 4-10-2 **77** ........ (v[1]) PaulMulrennan 3 82
(Alistair Whillans) *led at ordinary gallop: rdn and hdd over 1f out: lost 2nd ins fnl f: one pce* **9/2**[3]

40-0 **4** *1 ¾* **Dominannie (IRE)**[169] 360 4-8-13 **60** ........ JoeFanning 8 61
(Sally Haynes) *s.i.s: hld up: rdn and hdwy over 1f out: kpt on fnl f: nvr able to chal* **25/1**

5040 **5** *nk* **Crazy Tornado (IRE)**[22] 3833 4-9-4 **65** ........ (h) GrahamLee 5 66
(Keith Dalgleish) *hld up in tch: effrt and rdn 2f out: edgd lft: kpt on same pce fnl f* **11/1**

-000 **6** *2 ¾* **Argaki (IRE)**[11] 4210 7-8-11 **65** ........ CharlotteMcFarland(7) 7 59
(Keith Dalgleish) *hld up in tch: effrt on outside over 2f out: edgd lft and wknd over 1f out* **14/1**

1300 **7** *nse* **Newmarket Warrior (IRE)**[16] 4039 6-9-8 **69** ........ (p) TomEaves 1 63
(Iain Jardine) *s.i.s: hld up: shkn up and shortlived effrt 2f out: sn no imp* **18/1**

0322 **8** *hd* **Magistral**[16] 4039 7-9-9 **70** ........ (p) PJMcDonald 9 64
(R Mike Smith) *in tch: rdn over 2f out: wknd over 1f out* **11/4**[1]

-005 **9** *1 ¼* **Intiwin (IRE)**[16] 4035 5-8-11 **63** ........ LewisEdmunds(5) 2 54
(Linda Perratt) *hld up in tch: rdn along over 2f out: wknd over 1f out* **9/1**

0-00 **10** *4 ½* **Redvers (IRE)**[19] 3949 9-9-1 **62** ........ (p) PatrickMathers 4 43
(Noel Wilson) *trckd ldrs: rdn over 2f out: wknd over 1f out* **33/1**

1m 44.21s (0.41) **Going Correction** +0.275s/f (Good) **10** Ran SP% **113.7**
Speed ratings (Par 103): **108,106,106,104,104 101,101,101,100,95**
CSF £36.58 CT £154.72 TOTE £8.40: £2.40, £1.70, £1.90; EX 37.10 Trifecta £123.90.
**Owner** C Varley & R G Fell **Bred** Brian Walsh **Trained** Nawton, N Yorks

**FOCUS**
Add 12yds. A modest handicap and few got involved.

## 4662 TOTEPOOL RACECOURSE DEBIT CARD BETTING AVAILABLE H'CAP 1m
4:20 (4:20) (Class 3) (0-95,88) 3-Y-O+ £7,762 (£2,310; £1,154; £577) Stalls Low

Form RPR
2200 1 **Two For Two (IRE)**[31] 3498 9-10-0 88.........................(p) TonyHamilton 5 95
(Roger Fell) *hld up in last pl: rdn and hdwy on outside 2f out: led wl ins fnl f: drvn out* **7/1**
0136 2 *hd* **Finn Class (IRE)**[15] 4077 6-9-11 85.............................. PaulMulrennan 6 91
(Michael Dods) *in tch: effrt and hdwy to ld appr fnl f: hdd wl ins fnl f: kpt on* **3/1**[2]
-136 3 1 ¼ **Normandie Lady**[22] 3828 4-9-9 83.................................. PaulHanagan 4 86
(Richard Fahey) *hld up in tch: effrt and pushed along 2f out: kpt on ins fnl f: nt rch first two* **9/2**[3]
5-04 4 1 **Little Lady Katie (IRE)**[8] 4366 5-9-5 82.................. JordanVaughan(3) 3 82
(K R Burke) *cl up: led 2f out to appr fnl f: no ex last 100yds* **7/1**
00 5 2 ½ **Lavetta**[38] 3255 5-9-12 86.......................................... JoeFanning 2 81
(Sally Haynes) *plld hrd: cl up: rdn over 2f out: wknd fnl f* **14/1**
0344 6 4 ½ **Town Charter (USA)**[8] 4334 3-9-2 85............................. JamesDoyle 1 71
(Mark Johnston) *led at modest gallop: rdn and hdd 2f out: wknd fnl f* **13/8**[1]

1m 45.5s (1.70) **Going Correction** +0.275s/f (Good)
**WFA** 3 from 4yo+ 9lb 6 Ran SP% **112.9**
Speed ratings (Par 107): **102,101,100,99,97 92**
CSF £28.42 TOTE £8.10: £2.60, £2.00; EX 29.90 Trifecta £108.00.
**Owner** Fell & Kelvin **Bred** Patrick Fahey **Trained** Nawton, N Yorks

**FOCUS**
Add 12yds. The top weight was rated 7lb below the ceiling and the favourite disappointed; a weak race for the class.

## 4663 TOTEPOOL BETTING ON ALL UK RACING H'CAP 7f 50y
4:55 (4:55) (Class 5) (0-75,76) 3-Y-O+ £3,557 (£1,058; £529; £264) Stalls High

Form RPR
1 **Nothing To Lose (IRE)**[5] 4481 3-9-2 69......................... PaulHanagan 8 80
(John C McConnell, Ire) *hld up: gd hdwy on outside to ld over 1f out: pushed out fnl f: comf* **6/4**[1]
606- 2 1 ¾ **Inglorious**[274] 7140 3-8-5 63..............................(p) RowanScott(5) 11 69
(Keith Dalgleish) *t.k.h early: hld up in tch on outside: effrt and ev ch briefly over 1f out: sn pressing wnr: kpt on ins fnl f* **12/1**
-654 3 1 **Royal Duchess**[16] 4039 7-9-9 68.................................... JoeDoyle 10 74
(Lucy Normile) *hld up: effrt and angled rt over 1f out: kpt on fnl f: nt rch first two* **12/1**
0-20 4 1 ¼ **Destination Aim**[36] 3344 10-9-1 60................................ GrahamLee 5 63
(Fred Watson) *prom: effrt and rdn 2f out: kpt on same pce fnl f* **50/1**
1133 5 1 ¾ **Dark Crystal**[10] 4248 6-9-9 73.............................. LewisEdmunds(5) 4 72
(Linda Perratt) *hld up midfield: effrt and rdn over 2f out: kpt on same pce fr over 1f out* **12/1**
2652 6 1 ½ **Sea Of Green**[4] 4509 5-8-4 56..............................(p) SeanMooney(7) 6 51
(Jim Goldie) *hld up: rdn and outpcd over 2f out: rallied over 1f out: no imp fnl f* **16/1**
236 7 *shd* **Jay Kay**[27] 3652 8-9-6 70.................................... CliffordLee(5) 3 64
(K R Burke) *wore hood in paddock: led at decent gallop: rdn and hdd over 1f out: sn wknd* **8/1**[3]
1435 8 ¾ **Vallarta (IRE)**[15] 4080 7-10-0 73.............................. JamesSullivan 12 65
(Ruth Carr) *t.k.h: cl up tl rdn and wknd over 1f out* **20/1**
2431 9 9 **Dark Profit (IRE)**[16] 4039 5-10-3 76..........................(p) PaulMulrennan 2 45
(Keith Dalgleish) *hld up in tch: rdn over 2f out: wknd over 1f out* **5/2**[2]
4-00 10 2 ½ **Gun Case**[20] 3897 5-9-9 68................................(p) DougieCostello 7 31
(Alistair Whillans) *hld up: struggling over 2f out: sn btn* **20/1**
-163 11 1 **Control Centre (IRE)**[10] 4250 3-9-6 73.....................(p) BarryMcHugh 1 30
(Marjorie Fife) *chsd ldrs: rdn over 2f out: wknd over 1f out* **14/1**

1m 32.31s (-1.09) **Going Correction** +0.275s/f (Good)
**WFA** 3 from 5yo+ 8lb 11 Ran SP% **120.6**
Speed ratings (Par 103): **117,115,113,112,110 108,108,107,97,94 93**
CSF £148.30 CT £856.64 TOTE £2.30: £1.10, £12.90, £3.80; EX 141.60 Trifecta £2750.80.
**Owner** Rockview Racing Club **Bred** Rossenarra Bloodstock Limited **Trained** Stamullen, Co Meath

**FOCUS**
A modest handicap run at an overly strong pace.

## 4664 COLLECT TOTEPOOL WINNINGS AT BETFRED SHOPS AMATEUR RIDERS' H'CAP 5f
5:30 (5:31) (Class 6) (0-65,66) 4-Y-O+ £2,183 (£677; £338; £169) Stalls High

Form RPR
5052 1 **Perfect Words (IRE)**[10] 4246 7-10-5 56..................(p) MissBeckySmith 7 62
(Marjorie Fife) *chsd ldrs: effrt over 1f out: rdn to ld ins fnl f: kpt on strly* **11/4**[1]
000- 2 1 **Red Forever**[278] 7046 6-9-6 46 oh1...................... MissHelenCuthbert(3) 3 48
(Thomas Cuthbert) *led: shkn up over 1f out: hdd ins fnl f: kpt on same pce* **16/1**
1440 3 3 ¼ **Roy's Legacy**[17] 4005 8-10-13 64................................... MrsCBartley 6 55
(Shaun Harris) *trckd ldr to over 1f out: rdn and one pce fnl f* **10/1**
4402 4 3 ¼ **Dodgy Bob**[12] 4182 4-10-11 62............................(b) MissMMullineaux 8 41
(Michael Mullineaux) *hld up in tch: pushed along over 2f out: sn outpcd: no imp over 1f out* **5/1**[3]
4410 5 1 **Horsforth**[19] 3944 5-11-1 66..............................(b) MissJoannaMason 2 41
(Richard Guest) *chsd ldrs tl rdn and wknd over 1f out* **7/2**[2]
-060 6 ½ **Star Cracker (IRE)**[50] 2843 5-10-2 58....................(p) MissRHill(5) 4 32
(Jim Goldie) *s.v.s: bhd and struggling: nvr on terms* **7/2**[2]
5005 7 1 ¼ **Bond Bombshell**[17] 4015 4-10-7 65........................ MissCarlyScott(7) 1 34
(David O'Meara) *bhd on outside: struggling over 2f out: sn btn* **8/1**

1m 1.71s (2.31) **Going Correction** +0.275s/f (Good) 7 Ran SP% **113.9**
Speed ratings (Par 101): **92,90,85,80,78 77,75**
CSF £45.41 CT £382.97 TOTE £3.40: £2.10, £4.70; EX 48.00 Trifecta £356.30.
**Owner** Green Lane **Bred** Rathasker Stud **Trained** Stillington, N Yorks

**FOCUS**
A weak race.
T/Jkpt: Not won. T/Plt: £138.80 to a £1 stake. Pool: £69,288.00 - 498.84 winning units. T/Qpdt: £60.10 to a £1 stake. Pool: £5,499.00 - 91.40 winning units. **Richard Young**

# 3879 CHANTILLY (R-H)
Sunday, July 9

**OFFICIAL GOING: Turf: good**

## 4665a MOROCCO CUP PRIX CHLOE (GROUP 3) (3YO FILLIES) (TURF) 1m 1f
2:55 3-Y-O £34,188 (£13,675; £10,256; £6,837; £3,418)

RPR
1 **Ibiza (FR)**[27] 3681 3-8-13 0 ow2.................................. StephanePasquier 1 105+
(N Clement, France) *racd freely: cl up under restraint early: sn settled following ldr on inner: angled out and drvn to chse ldr 1 1/2f out: styd on wl and sustained chal fnl f: led 100yds out: qckly asserted* **124/10**
2 ¾ **Monroe Bay (IRE)**[21] 3881 3-8-13 0 ow2........(b) Pierre-CharlesBoudot 7 103
(P Bary, France) *sn led: drvn 2f out: rdn whn pressed wl over 1f out: rallied under sustained chal fr eventual wnr fnl f: hdd 100yds out: no ex* **3/1**[3]
3 ½ **Dallas Affair**[17] 4027 3-8-13 0 ow2.............................. AurelienLemaitre 4 102
(F Head, France) *racd keenly: fnd cover bhd ldrs: 3rd and styng on u.p over 1f out: nt quite pce to tackle front two* **5/2**[2]
4 *nk* **Beyond The Sea (USA)**[23] 3-8-13 0 ow2.................. VincentCheminaud 6 101
(A Fabre, France) *rdn patiently in rr: pushed along under 2 1/2f out but no immediate imp: last and rdn under 1 1/2f out: no hdwy til styd on fnl 150yds: nvr on terms* **119/10**
5 *shd* **Penny Lane (GER)**[47] 2945 3-8-13 0 ow2........................ GeraldMosse 2 101+
(F-H Graffard, France) *settled in fnl trio: drvn to try and get on terms 1 1/2f out: styd on at same pce fnl f: nvr trbld ldrs* **214/10**
6 *hd* **Silver Cape (FR)**[42] 3117 3-8-13 0 ow2.......................... EddyHardouin 3 101
(T Clout, France) *racd keenly: hld up in fnl trio: rdn and no imp 1 1/2f out: styd on ins fnl f: nt pce to get involved* **30/1**
7 *snk* **Wajnah (FR)**[57] 2644 3-8-13 0 ow2............................. CristianDemuro 5 100
(F Rohaut, France) *rowed along early: sn chsng ldr on outer: drvn but nt qckn over 2f out: lost pl 1 1/2f out: one pce fnl f* **7/5**[1]

1m 52.39s (1.29) 7 Ran SP% **118.1**
PARI-MUTUEL (all including 1 euro stake): WIN 13.40; PLACE 4.50, 2.90, SF 45.00.
**Owner** V Timoshenko & A Milovanov **Bred** V Timoshenko **Trained** Chantilly, France

## 4666a PRIX JEAN PRAT (GROUP 1) (3YO COLTS & FILLIES) (TURF) 1m
3:35 3-Y-O £195,350 (£78,153; £39,076; £19,521; £9,777)

RPR
1 **Thunder Snow (IRE)**[19] 3927 3-9-3 0 ow1......(p) ChristopheSoumillon 2 119+
(Saeed bin Suroor) *mde all: led single-file field: kicked clr under 1 1/2f out: rdn appr fnl f: styd on wl: unchal* **7/5**[2]
2 1 ¼ **Trais Fluors**[22] 3855 3-9-3 0 ow1.............................. VincentCheminaud 4 116+
(A Fabre, France) *w.w in 4th: angled out: shkn up and began to cl under 2f out: styd on fnl f: no ch w wnr* **11/10**[1]
3 1 ¼ **Gold Luck (FR)**[35] 3367 3-9-0 0 ow1.............................. MaximeGuyon 1 109
(F Head, France) *stmbld bdly leaving stalls: rcvrd qckly: chsd ldr: nt qckn whn scrubbed along 2f out: styd on same pce fnl f: lost 2nd 100yds out* **5/1**[3]
4 3 **Turf Laurel (IRE)**[21] 3881 3-9-0 0 ow1.......................... CristianDemuro 3 102
(S Kobayashi, France) *racd keenly: hld up in 3rd: rdn but nt qckn over 1 1/2f out: wl hld fnl f* **145/10**
5 *dist* **Lightupthenight**[6] 4456 3-9-0 0 ow1.................. Pierre-CharlesBoudot 5
(F-H Graffard, France) *planted in stalls: gave rest nrly a f s: a bhd: t.o* **154/10**

1m 38.78s (0.78) 5 Ran SP% **118.5**
PARI-MUTUEL (all including 1 euro stake): WIN 2.40; PLACE 1.10, 1.10, SF 3.50.
**Owner** Godolphin **Bred** Darley **Trained** Newmarket, Suffolk

**FOCUS**
Not a strong Group 1. A small field and a tactical affair, in which Christophe Soumillon took full advantage of an uncontested lead. The winner has been rated in line with his recent efforts.

4667 - 4676a (Foreign Racing) - See Raceform Interactive

# 4389 DEAUVILLE (R-H)
Wednesday, July 5

**OFFICIAL GOING: Turf: good; polytrack: standard**

## 4677a PRIX DE LA SOURCE (MAIDEN) (2YO FILLIES) (POLYTRACK) 6f 110y
11:25 2-Y-O £11,538 (£4,615; £3,461; £2,307; £1,153)

RPR
1 **Tantheem**[18] 2-9-2 0.................................................. AurelienLemaitre 5 90+
(F Head, France) **4/5**[1]
2 4 ½ **Marvellous Night (FR)**[29] 3445 2-8-13 0............ ClementLecoeuvre(3) 1 75
(H De Nicolay, France) **132/10**
3 ¾ **Shesgotthelot**[4] 4389 2-8-6 0...................... MmeAlexiaCeccarello(10) 6 73
(J S Moore) *wl into stride: settled in 2nd: rdn over 2f out: unable qck: styd on same pce fnl f* **25/1**
4 2 **Hot Zone (USA)** 2-9-2 0................................... ChristopheSoumillon 7 67
(J-C Rouget, France) **29/10**[2]
5 *snk* **Victoria's Angel (IRE)**[29] 3445 2-9-2 0............................ AlexisBadel 9 67
(H-F Devin, France) **61/10**[3]
6 5 **Dimaie (FR)** 2-8-11 0................................................ TheoBachelot 4 48
(Y Barberot, France) **40/1**
7 1 ¾ **Dream D'Ange (FR)** 2-8-11 0........................................ JulienAuge 8 43
(C Ferland, France) **102/10**
8 12 **Charming Ka (FR)** 2-8-7 0................................(b[1]) MlleAudeDuporte(4) 3 9
(H Fortineau, France) **85/1**

PARI-MUTUEL (all including 1 euro stake): WIN 1.80; PLACE 1.10, 2.30, 3.00; DF 11.10; SF 13.00.
**Owner** Hamdan Al Maktoum **Bred** Shadwell Estate Company Limited **Trained** France

## 4678a PRIX DU BOIS HUE (MAIDEN) (2YO COLTS & GELDINGS) (POLYTRACK) 6f 110y
11:55 2-Y-O £11,538 (£4,615; £3,461; £2,307; £1,153)

RPR
1 **Zanzi Win (FR)**[18] 2-9-2 0.................................................. GeraldMosse 7 75
(J-P Dubois, France) **31/10**[2]

2 shd **Belgrano (FR)**[71] 2-9-2 0 ...................................... ChristopheSoumillon 10 74
(C Lerner, France) **63/10**[3]

3 shd **Uther Pendragon (IRE)**[14] 3965 2-9-2 0................(p) IoritzMendizabal 4 74
(J S Moore) *qckly into stride: disp ld early: settled in 2nd: rdn to ld 2f out: drvn to maintain advantage over 1f out: strly pressed ins fnl f and hdd cl home* **67/10**

4 1 ¾ **Senoville (IRE)** 2-9-2 0 ................................................ CristianDemuro 2 69
(C Ferland, France) **19/10**[1]

5 nk **Premier Division (FR)** 2-9-2 0 .................................. AntoineHamelin 5 68
(Matthieu Palussiere, France) **228/10**

6 ¾ **Spirit Tango (FR)** 2-9-2 0 ........................................ StephanePasquier 8 66
(G Botti, France) **78/10**

7 1 ¼ **New Bresil (FR)** 2-8-11 0 ................................................ TheoBachelot 3 58
(S Wattel, France) **28/1**

8 ½ **Dancing Master (FR)** 2-8-11 0 ........................................ FabriceVeron 6 56
(E J O'Neill, France) **133/10**

9 hd **Meran (FR)**[52] 2664 2-9-2 0 .......................................... HugoJourniac 11 61
(M Nigge, France) **57/1**

10 5 **Poldina (FR)** 2-9-2 0 ............................................ Pierre-CharlesBoudot 1 47
(H-A Pantall, France) **189/10**

PARI-MUTUEL (all including 1 euro stake): WIN 4.10; PLACE 1.50, 1.80, 1.90; DF 11.30; SF 22.70.
**Owner** Ecurie Etoile NV **Bred** Haras De Grandcamp Earl **Trained** France

## 4679a PRIX DE LA CALONNE - FONDS EUROPEEN DE L'ELEVAGE (LISTED RACE) (4YO+ FILLIES & MARES) (POLYTRACK) 1m 1f 110y

1:35 4-Y-0+ **£20,512** (£8,205; £6,153; £4,102; £2,051)

RPR

1 **Syrita (FR)**[28] 4-8-11 0 ...................................................(p) OlivierPeslier 4 100+
(M Nigge, France) **134/10**

2 1 ½ **Astral Merit (FR)**[17] 3883 7-8-11 0 ...............................(b) FabriceVeron 6 97
(F Monnier, France) **51/10**[2]

3 shd **Ickymasho**[13] 4002 5-8-11 0 ............................................. TonyPiccone 5 97
(Jonathan Portman) *wl away: led: pushed along 3f out: drvn over 2f out: jnd and hdd 1f out: styd on ins fnl f* **71/10**

4 1 **Liwa Palace**[30] 4-8-11 0 ................................................. CristianDemuro 1 95
(Rod Collet, France) **153/10**

5 ¾ **Song Of Norway**[12] 6-8-11 0 ............................... Pierre-CharlesBoudot 7 93
(D De Watrigant, France) **66/10**[3]

6 snk **Desert Haze**[60] 2392 4-8-11 0 ............................... ChristopheSoumillon 2 93
(Ralph Beckett) *settled midfield: impr to 3rd after 2f: pushed along over 2f out: drvn over 1f out: unable qck ins fnl f and styd on one pce* **21/10**[1]

7 1 ¼ **Mint Julep (FR)**[17] 3883 4-8-11 0 ..................................... GeraldMosse 9 90
(J E Hammond, France) **51/10**[2]

8 3 **Westadora (IRE)**[338] 4-8-11 0 .................................. IoritzMendizabal 10 84
(J Reynier, France) **142/10**

9 10 **Hygrove Katie**[55] 4-8-11 0 ............................................. GuillaumeMillet 8 64
(J Reynier, France) **39/1**

10 6 **Endless Summer (ITY)**[94] 1530 4-8-11 0 ................ MickaelBarzalona 3 51
(M Guarnieri, Italy) **165/10**

1m 55.68s **10** Ran SP% **118.4**
PARI-MUTUEL (all including 1 euro stake): WIN 14.40; PLACE 3.50, 2.10, 2.60; DF 40.00; SF 81.10.
**Owner** Mme Christa Zass **Bred** Ctsse B De Tarragon & D Taylor **Trained** France

4680 - (Foreign Racing) - See Raceform Interactive

# 4657 AYR (L-H)

Monday, July 10

**OFFICIAL GOING: Good to soft (7.2)**
Wind: Breezy, half against on sprint course and in over 3f of home straight on races on the round course Weather: Cloudy, bright

## 4681 RACING UK NOW IN HD! EBF NOVICE STKS 6f

1:45 (1:46) (Class 5) 2-Y-0 **£3,881** (£1,155; £577; £288) **Stalls** High

Form RPR

10 1 **Another Batt (IRE)**[20] 3929 2-9-9 90 ............................ DanielTudhope 5 88
(George Scott) *mde all against stands' rail: shkn up and edgd lft over 1f out: kpt on strly fnl f* **5/6**[1]

5 2 1 ¼ **Cosa Nostra (IRE)**[25] 3754 2-9-2 0 .................................. TonyHamilton 7 77+
(Richard Fahey) *t.k.h: hld up in rr: rdn and hdwy over 1f out: kpt on wl under hands and heels riding last 150yds to take 2nd nr fin* **7/1**[3]

3 nk **Stormbringer** 2-9-2 0 ......................................................... MartinHarley 3 76+
(Kevin Ryan) *pressed wnr: rdn along over 1f out: kpt on same pce ins fnl f: lost 2nd nr fin* **5/2**[2]

0 4 7 **Cuillin Hills**[37] 3339 2-8-11 0 ........................................ RowanScott(5) 8 55
(Keith Dalgleish) *hld up: drvn and outpcd over 2f out: kpt on ins fnl f: nvr able to chal* **100/1**

5 ½ **Tight Lines** 2-8-11 0 ........................................................... JoeFanning 6 49
(Mark Johnston) *dwlt: sn prom: rdn over 2f out: wknd wl over 1f out* **20/1**

52 6 1 **Mable Lee (IRE)**[32] 3482 2-8-11 0 ........................................ TomEaves 9 46
(Iain Jardine) *trckd ldrs: drvn and outpcd 2f out: sn btn* **16/1**

7 2 **Remnant (IRE)** 2-8-11 0 ................................................... CliffordLee(5) 1 45
(K R Burke) *prominnet on outside: pushed along 1/2-way: wknd 2f out* **33/1**

1m 16.42s (4.02) **Going Correction** +0.60s/f (Yiel) 7 Ran SP% **110.2**
Speed ratings (Par 94): **97,95,94,85,84 83,80**
CSF £6.81 TOTE £1.70: £1.10, £3.20; EX 7.20 Trifecta £15.90.
**Owner** Excel Racing **Bred** J W Nicholson **Trained** Newmarket, Suffolk

**FOCUS**
After 8mm of rain in the past 24 hours, the going had been updated to good to soft (7.2). Jockeys variously described the ground as riding tacky, dead or good to soft after taking part in the first race. An okay novice stakes for the course with the first three all probably decent.

## 4682 RACING UK DAY PASS JUST £10 H'CAP 6f

2:15 (2:15) (Class 6) (0-60,60) 3-Y-0+ **£3,234** (£962; £481; £240) **Stalls** High

Form RPR

0606 1 **Racquet**[10] 4310 4-9-10 60 ................................................ JamesSullivan 6 68
(Ruth Carr) *hld up bhd ldng gp: hdwy over 1f out: rdn to ld ins fnl f: kpt on wl* **9/2**[2]

6330 2 ½ **Harbour Patrol (IRE)**[10] 4323 5-8-13 49 ow1 ...........(b) DanielTudhope 3 56
(Rebecca Bastiman) *trckd ldrs: hdwy to ld over 1f out: sn rdn and edgd rt: hdd ins fnl f: kpt on* **4/1**[1]

5235 3 1 ¼ **Ss Vega**[35] 3387 4-8-4 47 ........................................(p) ConnorMurtagh(7) 4 50
(Jim Goldie) *bhd and sn pushed along: hdwy to chse ldng pair over 1f out: rdn and kpt on fnl f: nt pce to chal* **9/2**[2]

344 4 3 ¼ **Bunce (IRE)**[11] 4246 9-9-7 57 ................................................ GrahamLee 7 50
(Linda Perratt) *bhd and sn pushed along: drvn over 2f out: kpt on fnl f: no imp* **12/1**

4-06 5 2 ¾ **Bahamian Sunshine**[16] 4110 4-8-7 46 oh1 .............(p) SammyJoBell(3) 8 31
(Lee Smyth, Ire) *led: rdn and hdd over 1f out: sn outpcd* **22/1**

1630 6 1 ¾ **Goninodaethat**[16] 4080 9-9-3 60 ................................ SeanMooney(7) 9 40
(Jim Goldie) *trckd ldrs tl rdn and wknd over 1f out* **12/1**

5006 7 ½ **Ershaad (IRE)**[10] 4323 5-8-10 46 oh1 ................................(b) NeilFarley 10 24
(Shaun Harris) *chsd ldrs: drvn along over 2f out: wknd over 1f out* **28/1**

0-50 8 3 **Hit The Lights (IRE)**[19] 3979 7-8-13 49 ...................(p) BarryMcHugh 13 18
(Marjorie Fife) *hld up: rdn and outpcd over 2f out: edgd lft and sn btn* **14/1**

315 9 1 ½ **Lackaday**[11] 4250 5-9-10 60 ...........................................(p) TonyHamilton 1 25
(Noel Wilson) *trckd ldrs: rdn over 2f out: wknd over 1f out* **5/1**[3]

-000 10 8 **Total Power**[28] 3666 4-9-4 59 ....................................(t[1]) BenRobinson(5) 5
(Brian Ellison) *dwlt: bhd and outpcd: drvn along over 2f out: sn n.d: btn over 1f out* **10/1**

00-0 11 15 **Brendan (IRE)**[35] 3383 4-8-13 49 ........................................ PJMcDonald 11
(Jim Goldie) *dwlt: hld up: drvn and outpcd over 2f out: sn btn* **33/1**

0005 12 22 **Warleggan (FR)**[6] 4479 3-8-4 46 oh1 ....................................(p[1]) JoeDoyle 2
(Linda Perratt) *bhd and drvn along: struggling 1/2-way: sn wknd: btn and eased fnl f* **100/1**

1m 16.48s (4.08) **Going Correction** +0.60s/f (Yiel)
**WFA** 3 from 4yo+ 6lb **12** Ran SP% **115.9**
Speed ratings (Par 101): **96,95,93,89,85 83,82,78,76,66 46,16**
CSF £21.53 CT £85.69 TOTE £6.10: £2.50, £1.70, £1.80; EX 23.60 Trifecta £109.50.
**Owner** Reach For The Moon & Mrs R Carr **Bred** P M Cunningham **Trained** Huby, N Yorks

**FOCUS**
A modest sprint handicap with the return to a Class 6 enough for the winner to get off the mark for his new stable. Straightforward form, with the winner to this year's mark.

## 4683 RACINGUK.COM/HD H'CAP 6f

2:45 (2:45) (Class 4) (0-85,87) 3-Y-0+ **£6,469** (£1,925; £962; £481) **Stalls** High

Form RPR

234 1 **Dark Defender**[9] 4343 4-9-6 82 ...............................(b) RowanScott(5) 2 92
(Keith Dalgleish) *mde all: rdn and clr over 1f out: kpt on wl fnl f: unchal* **15/2**

0064 2 1 ¼ **Kenny The Captain (IRE)**[11] 4250 6-8-12 72 .. RachelRichardson(3) 13 78
(Tim Easterby) *prom on nr side of gp: hdwy to chse wnr 1/2-way: sn rdn and edgd lft: kpt on ins fnl f* **6/1**[3]

4000 3 ¾ **Specialv (IRE)**[2] 4629 4-8-4 66 ..............................(p) BenRobinson(5) 4 70
(Brian Ellison) *dwlt: bhd: hdwy over 1f out: kpt on fnl f: nrst fin* **25/1**

-345 4 ½ **Holmeswood**[28] 3664 3-9-6 83 ....................................... PaulMulrennan 1 84
(Michael Dods) *prom: rdn and edgd lft over 1f out: kpt on same pce ins fnl f* **4/1**[2]

4064 5 ¾ **Tommy G**[16] 4079 4-8-12 76 ............................................ SeanMooney(7) 7 76+
(Jim Goldie) *hld up: rdn over 2f out: kpt on fnl f: nvr able to chal* **16/1**

-101 6 nk **Muscika**[35] 3386 3-9-7 84 ................................................ DanielTudhope 14 82
(David O'Meara) *hld up: rdn and edgd lft over 2f out: kpt on fnl f: no imp* **7/2**[1]

-225 7 2 ½ **Glengarry**[17] 4037 4-10-2 87 ........................................ ConnorBeasley 6 78
(Keith Dalgleish) *hld up on far side of gp: rdn and effrt over 2f out: no further imp appr fnl f* **8/1**

010 8 2 ¼ **Dragon King (IRE)**[9] 4343 5-9-9 85 ...............................(h) CliffordLee(5) 3 68
(Iain Jardine) *hld up: drvn over 2f out: sme hdwy over 1f out: sn no imp* **12/1**

-005 9 ¾ **Duke Cosimo**[9] 4343 7-9-4 75 .............................................. TomEaves 11 56
(Michael Herrington) *hld up: drvn along 2f out: sn no imp* **14/1**

0021 10 shd **Tatlisu (IRE)**[18] 4013 7-9-9 87 .................................. ConnorMurtagh(7) 10 68
(Richard Fahey) *prom: effrt and rdn over 2f out: wknd over 1f out* **12/1**

0146 11 2 **Merdon Castle (IRE)**[9] 4339 5-9-7 78 ...........................(e) JamesSullivan 8 52
(Ruth Carr) *hld up: rdn over 2f out: sn no imp: btn over 1f out* **16/1**

0/00 12 14 **Roaring Forties (IRE)**[24] 3792 4-9-11 82 .......................... DuranFentiman 9 12
(Rebecca Bastiman) *chsd ldrs: lost pl 1/2-way: sn struggling* **66/1**

-600 13 16 **Dawoodi**[17] 4039 3-8-4 67 oh1 ow1 .........................................(h[1]) JoeDoyle 12
(Linda Perratt) *chsd wnr to 1/2-way: sn rdn and wknd: t.o* **100/1**

1m 15.26s (2.86) **Going Correction** +0.60s/f (Yiel)
**WFA** 3 from 4yo+ 6lb **13** Ran SP% **119.5**
Speed ratings (Par 105): **104,102,101,100,99 99,95,92,91,91 89,70,49**
CSF £51.66 CT £1115.35 TOTE £9.40: £2.80, £2.40, £6.80; EX 73.80 Trifecta £3005.10.
**Owner** Prestige Thoroughbred Racing **Bred** Mrs C J Walker **Trained** Carluke, S Lanarks

**FOCUS**
Nothing got into this decent Class 4 sprint from the back and course form came good with three C&D winners finishing in the frame. The winner has been rated back to his best.

## 4684 FOLLOW @RACING_UK ON TWITTER H'CAP 1m 5f 26y

3:15 (3:15) (Class 5) (0-75,77) 4-Y-0+ **£3,881** (£1,155; £577; £288) **Stalls** Low

Form RPR

1 **Glenbank King (IRE)**[5] 4516 9-8-12 65 ...............................(b) GrahamLee 6 73
(Lee Smyth, Ire) *chsd ldrs: rdn and outpcd over 2f out: rallied and squeezed through over 1f out: styd on strly to ld post* **50/1**

2 shd **Guitar Pete (IRE)**[58] 5872 7-8-5 58 ........................................ JoeDoyle 10 65
(Nicky Richards) *hld up: stdy hdwy and in tch whn faltered bnd ent st: sn rcvrd: hdwy and ev ch over 1f out: rdn to ld ins fnl f: kpt on: hdd post* **3/1**[2]

/00- 3 1 ½ **Shamar (FR)**[10] 4328 9-8-10 63 .....................................(t) PJMcDonald 11 68
(R K Watson, Ire) *hld up: smooth hdwy on outside over 2f out: led and rdn over 1f out: hdd ins fnl f: kpt on same pce* **33/1**

0-00 4 2 **Transpennine Star**[24] 3794 4-9-7 74 .............................. PaulMulrennan 4 76
(Michael Dods) *chsd clr ldr: rdn over 2f out: lost 2nd wl over 1f out: sn one pce* **10/1**

5222 5 shd **Braes Of Lochalsh**[10] 4301 6-8-9 69 .........................(v) SeanMooney(7) 1 70
(Jim Goldie) *led at decent gallop: rdn and hdd over 1f out: sn one pce* **5/2**[1]

0326 6 1 ½ **Cosmic Tigress**[23] 3830 6-8-7 60 ............................................ JasonHart 9 59
(John Quinn) *hld up: drvn and outpcd over 2f out: no imp fr over 1f out* **16/1**

2133 7 2 ¾ **Jonny Delta**[37] 3338 10-8-2 55 ........................................ JamesSullivan 3 50
(Jim Goldie) *hld up: effrt and pushed along over 2f out: edgd lft: sn no imp* **9/1**

0/40 8 15 **Uriah Heep (FR)**[1] 4659 8-8-5 58 ...............................(p) DuranFentiman 7 31
(R Mike Smith) *missed break: hld up: drvn and outpcd over 3f out: sn btn* **25/1**

-043 **9** *19* **Torremar (FR)**[13] 4170 4-9-6 **73**........................(p) TomEaves 8 17
(Kevin Ryan) *prom tl rdn and wknd fr 3f out* **14/1**

0461 **10** *22* **Whitecliff Park (IRE)**[37] 3340 4-8-2 **55**........................(p) JoeFanning 5
(Brian Ellison) *missed break: hld up: rdn and struggling over 3f out: sn lost tch* **13/2**[3]

0-03 **11** *99* **Alphabetical Order**[10] 4301 9-9-10 **77**........................ DanielTudhope 12
(David O'Meara) *in tch: struggling 5f out: lost tch ent st: virtually p.u* **14/1**

2m 59.82s (5.82) **Going Correction** +0.25s/f (Good) **11** Ran SP% **114.0**
Speed ratings (Par 103): **92,91,91,89,89 88,87,77,66,52**
CSF £188.86 CT £5092.58 TOTE £27.80: £7.90, £1.80, £7.00; EX 157.10 Trifecta £6104.10.
**Owner** Victor Robinson **Bred** Victor Robinson **Trained** Magheralin, Co Down

**FOCUS**
Race distance 30yds further than advertised. A strangely run staying handicap with the favourite blazing a trail and the eventual winner rallying after looking beaten. Suspect form.

## 4685 RACINGUK.COM H'CAP 1m
**3:50** (3:50) (Class 4) (0-85,84) 3-Y-0+ **£6,469** (£1,925; £962; £481) **Stalls** Low

Form RPR

0-06 **1** **Le Chat D'Or**[28] 3651 9-9-13 **83**........................(bt) PaulMulrennan 9 92
(Michael Dods) *dwlt: hld up: effrt and hdwy over 1f out: led ins fnl f: edgd lft: pushed out* **8/1**

2421 **2** *nk* **Lamloom (IRE)**[17] 4036 3-8-13 **78**........................ DanielTudhope 4 84+
(David O'Meara) *t.k.h early: trckd ldrs: led gng wl over 2f out: rdn over 1f out: hdd ins fnl f: kpt on: hld cl home* **6/4**[1]

3054 **3** *1 ¾* **Timeless Art (IRE)**[28] 3651 4-9-7 **82**........................ CliffordLee(5) 5 86+
(K R Burke) *hld up: hdwy and ev ch over 1f out: rdn and one pce ins fnl f* **3/1**[2]

0-00 **4** *2* **Rock N Rolla (IRE)**[10] 4295 3-9-0 **79**........................(p) ConnorBeasley 7 77
(Keith Dalgleish) *led to over 3f out: ev ch over 2f out: kpt on same pce fnl f* **16/1**

3200 **5** *½* **Chaplin Bay (IRE)**[16] 4103 5-9-3 **73**........................(p) JamesSullivan 2 72
(Ruth Carr) *dwlt: hld up: rdn over 2f out: kpt on fnl f: nvr able to chal* **15/2**[3]

4646 **6** *½* **Byres Road**[86] 1788 4-9-9 **79**........................ JoeFanning 10 76
(Mark Johnston) *hld up in tch: rdn over 2f out: no imp fr over 1f out* **16/1**

-010 **7** *3 ¼* **Zeshov (IRE)**[12] 4210 6-9-8 **78**........................ DuranFentiman 1 68
(Rebecca Bastiman) *in tch: drvn along over 2f out: wknd over 1f out* **25/1**

1234 **8** *12* **Count Montecristo (FR)**[68] 2310 5-10-0 **84**........................ TomEaves 6 46
(Kevin Ryan) *pressed ldr: led over 3f out to over 2f out: wknd over 1f out* **17/2**

1m 45.17s (1.37) **Going Correction** +0.25s/f (Good)
**WFA** 3 from 4yo+ 9lb **8** Ran SP% **114.0**
Speed ratings (Par 105): **103,102,100,98,98 97,94,82**
CSF £20.34 CT £45.21 TOTE £8.20: £2.10, £1.20, £1.40; EX 26.30 Trifecta £104.70.
**Owner** Dr Anne J F Gillespie **Bred** Dr A Gillespie **Trained** Denton, Co Durham

**FOCUS**
Race distance 18yds further than advertised. A decent Class 4 run at a good pace with course form proving the key again. The winner has been rated to form.

## 4686 RACING UK PROFITS RETURNED TO RACING H'CAP 5f
**4:25** (4:25) (Class 3) (0-90,90) 3-Y-0+ **£9,703** (£2,887; £1,443; £721) **Stalls** High

Form RPR

0536 **1** **Showdaisy**[16] 4081 4-9-11 **87**........................(p) JasonHart 1 94
(Keith Dalgleish) *mde all: rdn over 1f out: edgd lft ins fnl f: hld on wl cl home* **12/1**

0340 **2** *hd* **Foxtrot Knight**[11] 4249 5-9-1 **77**........................ JamesSullivan 3 83
(Ruth Carr) *trckd ldrs: effrt and ev ch ins fnl f: kpt on: hld cl home* **22/1**

0560 **3** *½* **Lathom**[49] 2899 4-9-6 **82**........................(h[1]) DanielTudhope 5 86
(David O'Meara) *hld up: effrt and hdwy over 1f out: kpt on ins fnl f* **11/2**[3]

1113 **4** *½* **Royal Brave (IRE)**[37] 3337 6-9-5 **81**........................ PJMcDonald 10 84
(Rebecca Bastiman) *hld up: rdn and effrt 2f out: kpt on fnl f: nt pce to chal* **7/1**

0604 **5** *½* **Jack Dexter**[10] 4306 8-9-5 **88**........................ SeanMooney(7) 11 89+
(Jim Goldie) *hld up and bhd: effrt and pushed along over 1f out: kpt on fnl f: nvr rchd ldrs* **7/2**[1]

1354 **6** *¾* **Invincible Ridge (IRE)**[9] 4337 9-9-2 **78**........................ NeilFarley 2 76
(Eric Alston) *trckd ldrs: rdn and edgd lft over 1f out: outpcd ins fnl f* **12/1**

0300 **7** *nk* **Confessional**[10] 4306 10-9-10 **86**........................(e) PaulMulrennan 6 83
(Tim Easterby) *chsd ldrs: drvn and outpcd over 1f out: n.d after* **15/2**

0216 **8** *½* **My Name Is Rio (IRE)**[16] 4079 7-9-11 **87**........................ ConnorBeasley 8 82
(Michael Dods) *dwlt: sn pushed along in rr: drvn along 1/2-way: no imp over 1f out* **9/2**[2]

02 **9** *2 ½* **Rural Celebration**[16] 4078 6-10-0 **90**........................(p) TomEaves 9 77
(Kevin Ryan) *chsd wnr: rdn and edgd lft over 1f out: wknd fnl f* **13/2**

1m 1.47s (2.07) **Going Correction** +0.60s/f (Yiel)
**WFA** 3 from 4yo+ 5lb **9** Ran SP% **113.1**
Speed ratings (Par 107): **107,106,105,105,104 103,102,101,97**
CSF £233.05 CT £1607.40 TOTE £11.70: £3.30, £4.90, £2.00; EX 117.30 Trifecta £2255.50.
**Owner** Ronnie Docherty & Partner **Bred** Patricia Ann Scott-Dunn **Trained** Carluke, S Lanarks

**FOCUS**
A decent Class 3 where the winner had the run of the race but was very game, and she has been rated to her AW best.

## 4687 RACING UK APPRENTICE H'CAP (DIV I) 7f 50y
**4:55** (4:57) (Class 6) (0-60,62) 3-Y-0+ **£3,234** (£962; £481; £240) **Stalls** High

Form RPR

0650 **1** **Let Right Be Done**[1] 4659 5-8-7 **46**........................(b) LeanneFerguson(7) 12 52
(Linda Perratt) *v s.i.s: rcvrd and jnd pack after 2f: smooth hdwy on outside to ld over 1f out: rdn out fnl f* **13/2**[3]

-606 **2** *2* **Irvine Lady (IRE)**[130] 981 4-9-2 **48**........................(p) AdamMcNamara 8 49
(R Mike Smith) *mde most tl rdn and hdd over 1f out: kpt on same pce ins fnl f* **25/1**

6-66 **3** *1 ½* **Greengairs**[26] 3709 3-8-13 **60**........................(t[1]) CharlotteMcFarland(7) 7 54
(Keith Dalgleish) *midfield: effrt and pushed along 2f out: kpt on ins fnl f: nrst fin* **16/1**

5000 **4** *¾* **New Decade**[26] 3704 8-8-7 **46** oh1........................ SeanMooney(7) 10 41
(Jim Goldie) *hld up midfield on outside: effrt and pushed along over 2f out: kpt on fnl f: no imp* **20/1**

6-06 **5** *¾* **Red Shadow**[11] 4246 8-9-0 **46** oh1........................(v) ShelleyBirkett 4 40
(Alistair Whillans) *chsd ldrs: wnt 2nd over 3f out to over 2f out: kpt on same pce fnl f* **50/1**

0105 **6** *shd* **Blue Jacket (USA)**[51] 2843 6-9-11 **62**........................ ConnorMurtagh(5) 3 55
(Dianne Sayer) *t.k.h: trckd ldrs: effrt and rdn wl over 1f out: kpt on same pce fnl f* **3/1**[1]

0004 **7** *½* **Melaniemillie**[17] 4058 3-8-8 **48**........................ LewisEdmunds 2 37
(Ruth Carr) *hld up: pushed along and outpcd over 3f out: rallied fnl f: nrst fin* **4/1**[2]

0500 **8** *nk* **Naupaka**[1] 4660 3-8-8 **51**........................(p) BenRobinson(3) 11 39
(Brian Ellison) *s.i.s: hld up: rdn and outpcd over 2f out: sme late hdwy: nvr on terms* **17/2**

0536 **9** *shd* **New Delhi (IRE)**[6] 4473 3-9-4 **58**........................ RichardOliver 5 46
(Mark Johnston) *s.i.s: sn cl up: effrt and disp ld over 2f out to over 1f out: wknd ins fnl f* **12/1**

-043 **10** *5* **Captain Peaky**[40] 3196 4-9-7 **56**........................ PaulaMuir(3) 6 35
(Patrick Holmes) *chsd ldr to over 3f out: rdn and wknd 2f out* **4/1**[2]

1m 36.0s (2.60) **Going Correction** +0.25s/f (Good)
**WFA** 3 from 4yo+ 8lb **10** Ran SP% **113.0**
Speed ratings (Par 101): **95,92,91,90,89 89,88,88,88,82**
CSF £153.02 CT £2452.02 TOTE £7.30: £2.10, £4.00, £4.30; EX 167.30 Trifecta £3087.50.
**Owner** Ken McGarrity & Linda Perratt Racing Club **Bred** LAM Partnership **Trained** East Kilbride, S Lanarks

**FOCUS**
Race distance was 18yds further than advertised. A modest apprentice handicap, notable for jockey Leanne Ferguson's first winner.

## 4688 RACING UK APPRENTICE H'CAP (DIV II) 7f 50y
**5:30** (5:31) (Class 6) (0-60,62) 3-Y-0+ **£3,234** (£962; £481; £240) **Stalls** High

Form RPR

5020 **1** **Magic Journey (IRE)**[23] 3831 3-8-11 **54**........................ JoshQuinn(3) 11 61
(John Quinn) *hld up in tch on outside: hdwy to ld over 1f out: rdn and r.o wl fnl f* **15/2**[3]

6453 **2** *1 ¼* **Jessie Allan (IRE)**[11] 4263 6-8-7 **46** oh1........................ SeanMooney(7) 4 53
(Jim Goldie) *hld up: hdwy on outside 2f out: chsd wnr fnl f: kpt on fin* **10/1**

63-2 **3** *hd* **Yes You (IRE)**[10] 4302 3-8-13 **53**........................ AdamMcNamara 8 57
(Iain Jardine) *hld up: hdwy on ins 2f out: effrt and disp 2nd pl thrght fnl f: kpt on* **5/2**[1]

0-44 **4** *½* **Angel's Acclaim (IRE)**[71] 2180 3-9-8 **62**........................ LewisEdmunds 12 64
(Kevin Ryan) *hld up: rdn and edgd lft 2f out: kpt on ins fnl f* **4/1**[2]

0631 **5** *1 ¼* **Cyflymder (IRE)**[9] 4350 11-9-5 **51**........................ ShelleyBirkett 10 53
(David C Griffiths) *trckd ldrs: drvn along 2f out: one pce fnl f* **10/1**

0660 **6** *2 ½* **Peny Arcade**[11] 4263 3-8-13 **53**........................ CliffordLee 9 46
(Alistair Whillans) *hld up midfield: drvn and outpcd over 2f out: rallied fnl f: no imp* **16/1**

5000 **7** *¾* **Coral Princess (IRE)**[11] 4263 3-8-8 **48**........................ RowanScott 6 39
(Keith Dalgleish) *led to over 1f out: sn rdn and wknd* **8/1**

3420 **8** *1* **Monsieur Jimmy**[16] 4105 5-9-6 **57**........................ GerO'Neill(5) 2 49
(Declan Carroll) *t.k.h: trckd ldrs tl rdn and wknd over 1f out* **14/1**

-000 **9** *½* **Tael O' Gold**[23] 3831 3-8-1 **46** oh1........................(p) ConnorMurtagh(5) 1 33
(R Mike Smith) *prom tl rdn and wknd wl over 1f out* **40/1**

0442 **10** *9* **Secret City (IRE)**[23] 3832 11-8-12 **47**........................(b) BenRobinson(3) 7 15
(Rebecca Bastiman) *flyj. twice leaving stalls: bhd: rdn 1/2-way: struggling over 2f out: nvr on terms* **12/1**

0-00 **11** *8* **Charava (IRE)**[40] 3198 5-9-11 **60**........................(h[1]) PaulaMuir(3) 3 8
(Patrick Holmes) *hld up midfield on ins: struggling over 2f out: sn wknd* **28/1**

1m 34.57s (1.17) **Going Correction** +0.25s/f (Good)
**WFA** 3 from 5yo+ 8lb **11** Ran SP% **115.8**
Speed ratings (Par 101): **103,101,101,100,99 96,95,94,93,83 74**
CSF £78.94 CT £245.95 TOTE £8.80: £2.70, £2.90, £1.60; EX 86.40 Trifecta £412.30.
**Owner** J N Blackburn **Bred** Oghill House Stud & Jimmy Hyland **Trained** Settrington, N Yorks

**FOCUS**
Race distance 18yds further than advertised. The second division of the apprentice handicap saw the winner get off the mark.
T/Jkpt: Not Won. T/Plt: £236.80 to a £1 stake. Pool: £76,562.03 - 235.96 winning units T/Qpdt: £131.60 to a £1 stake. Pool: £6,434.28 - 36.17 winning units **Richard Young**

# 4013 RIPON (R-H)
Monday, July 10

**OFFICIAL GOING: Good (8.1; watered)**
Wind: Light, across in straight of nearly 5f Weather: Fine

## 4689 HAPPY BIRTHDAY SUSAN CAYGILL FILLIES' NOVICE AUCTION STKS (PLUS 10 RACE) 6f
**6:45** (6:47) (Class 5) 2-Y-0 **£3,234** (£962; £481; £240) **Stalls** High

Form RPR

**1** **Capomento (IRE)** 2-9-0 0........................ BenCurtis 6 82+
(Tom Dascombe) *racd off the pce: pushed along over 4f out: hdwy and swtchd rt jst after 1/2-way: rdn to chal over 1f out: r.o to ld wl ins fnl f: in command nr fin* **16/1**

5250 **2** *1* **Lady Anjorica (IRE)**[19] 3960 2-9-0 86........................ SilvestreDeSousa 5 79
(Keith Dalgleish) *w ldr: led over 2f out: rdn whn pressed over 1f out: hdd wl ins fnl f: no ex and eased nr fin* **8/13**[1]

**3** *6* **Me Before You (IRE)** 2-9-0 0........................ PhillipMakin 7 61+
(David O'Meara) *led: rdn and hdd over 2f out: stl ch over 1f out: unable to go w front two ins fnl f: no ex* **25/1**

**4** *½* **Miss Puddles (IRE)** 2-9-0 0........................ PaulHanagan 3 60
(Richard Fahey) *racd keenly and green: chsd ldrs: rdn over 2f out: kpt on same pce and no imp fr over 1f out* **17/2**[2]

16 **5** *4 ½* **Capla Dancer (IRE)**[49] 2890 2-9-4 0........................(h) JordanVaughan(3) 9 53
(K R Burke) *ponied to s: unruly bef r: s.i.s: sn trckd ldrs: rdn over 2f out: wkng whn edgd rt over 1f out* **9/1**[3]

4 **6** *4 ½* **Poppy Walton (IRE)**[20] 3943 2-9-0 0........................ AndrewMullen 8 33
(Ollie Pears) *in tch: pushed along over 4f out: wknd over 2f out* **9/1**[3]

5 **7** *nk* **Ladycammyofclare (IRE)**[12] 4199 2-9-0 0........................ FrannyNorton 1 32
(Mark Johnston) *in tch on outer w no cover: pushed along 1/2-way: wknd 2f out* **28/1**

**8** *8* **La Plusbelle** 2-9-0 0........................ JackGarritty 2 8
(Richard Fahey) *dwlt: sn pushed along and outpcd: a bhd* **12/1**

**9** *shd* **Lethal Lady** 2-8-9 0........................ CallumRodriguez(5) 4 7
(Michael Dods) *rn green: a outpcd and bhd* **20/1**

1m 11.69s (-1.31) **Going Correction** -0.225s/f (Firm) **9** Ran SP% **118.1**
Speed ratings (Par 91): **99,97,89,89,83 77,76,65,65**
CSF £26.55 TOTE £20.60: £4.60, £1.10, £4.80; EX 44.30 Trifecta £487.50.
**Owner** Deva Racing Casamento Partnership **Bred** Mr & Mrs T O'Brien **Trained** Malpas, Cheshire

**FOCUS**
A 6f novice contest in which they bet long odds bar the well-supported odds-on favourite. The first two were clear and they finished well strung out.

## 4690 SIS TRUSTED DELIVERY PARTNER H'CAP 1m
**7:15** (7:15) (Class 5) (0-70,69) 3-Y-O+ **£3,234** (£962; £481; £240) **Stalls** Low

Form RPR
-433 **1** **Racemaker**[32] 3499 3-9-5 **69** KevinStott 7 74
(Andrew Crook) *trckd ldrs: rdn over 2f out: chalng wl ins fnl f: styd on to ld nr fin* **5/1**[2]
0063 **2** *nk* **Hernando Torres**[14] 4165 9-9-4 **62** (tp) NathanEvans(3) 3 68
(Michael Easterby) *midfield: rdn and hdwy 2f out: styd on to ld fnl 150yds: hdd and hld nr fin* **20/1**
0412 **3** *3/4* **Beverley Bullet**[11] 4262 4-8-13 **59** (p) CallumRodriguez(5) 10 63
(Lawrence Mullaney) *midfield: nt clr run and swtchd lft wl over 2f out: effrt to chse ldrs over 1f out: no real imp tl styd on wl ins fnl 100yds: nrst fin* **15/2**
0-26 **4** *1/2* **Old China**[9] 4345 4-9-8 **63** (t[1]) SamJames 11 66
(John Davies) *chsd ldr: rdn over 2f out: led over 1f out: hdd fnl 150yds: no ex towards fin* **14/1**
2-13 **5** *1* **Clenymistra (IRE)**[19] 3977 3-8-12 **62** PhillipMakin 4 60
(David O'Meara) *chsd ldrs: rdn and swtchd lft over 1f out: kpt on u.p ins fnl f: one pce towards fin* **5/1**[2]
6040 **6** *4* **Rockliffe**[20] 3935 4-8-12 **53** PaulHanagan 1 41
(Micky Hammond) *towards rr: rdn 3f out: stdy hdwy over 2f out: one pce ins fnl f: unable to trble ldrs* **33/1**
0154 **7** *3/4* **Midlight**[10] 4019 5-9-0 **55** (t) JackGarritty 8 40
(Ruth Carr) *led: rdn and hdd over 1f out: wknd ins fnl f* **11/1**
-524 **8** *3 3/4* **Thornaby Nash**[30] 3560 6-9-8 **63** (p) ShaneGray 13 37
(Karen Tutty) *midfield: rdn over 2f out: sn outpcd: no imp after* **16/1**
-325 **9** *1 3/4* **Yensir**[12] 4210 4-9-12 **67** PaddyAspell 2 36
(Grant Tuer) *midfield: hdwy 5f out: effrt over 3f out: wknd over 1f out* **7/1**[3]
6000 **10** *1/2* **Nelson's Bay**[11] 4262 8-8-6 **50** SammyJoBell(3) 5 17
(Wilf Storey) *hld up: pushed along over 2f out: nvr a threat* **25/1**
0352 **11** *7* **So It's War (FR)**[21] 3899 6-9-10 **65** (p) SilvestreDeSousa 6 11
(Keith Dalgleish) *plld hrd: hld up in rr: u.p 4f out: nvr on terms: eased whn wl btn over 1f out* **3/1**[1]
100- **12** *2 3/4* **Arizona Sunrise**[280] 7007 4-9-8 **63** CamHardie 9 1
(Tina Jackson) *towards rr: pushed along 4f out: lft bhd fnl 2f* **100/1**
1m 39.29s (-2.11) **Going Correction** -0.10s/f (Good)
**WFA** 3 from 4yo+ 9lb **12** Ran SP% **116.0**
Speed ratings (Par 103): **106,105,104,104,103 99,98,94,93,92 85,82**
CSF £104.18 CT £757.68 TOTE £5.90: £1.90, £4.30, £2.20; EX 112.50 Trifecta £490.50.
**Owner** Mrs Helen Sinclair **Bred** R W K Lewis **Trained** Middleham Moor, N Yorks

**FOCUS**
Race run over an extra 8yds. Just an ordinary handicap run at a modest gallop and it paid to race handy. The first five were clear and the race has been rated around the 3rd/4th.

## 4691 SANLAM PRIVATE WEALTH AND GUESTS H'CAP 1m 4f 10y
**7:45** (7:47) (Class 4) (0-80,81) 3-Y-O **£5,175** (£1,540; £769; £384) **Stalls** Centre

Form RPR
641 **1** **Cape Coast**[15] 4117 3-9-7 **80** SilvestreDeSousa 2 93+
(Mark Johnston) *chsd ldrs: wnt 2nd 3f out: rdn to ld over 2f out: styd on gamely ins fnl f: in command fnl 100yds* **7/4**[1]
2221 **2** *2 1/4* **Kilowatt**[18] 4016 3-9-7 **80** DavidAllan 6 89
(Tim Easterby) *hld up: hdwy 3f out: rdn to chse ldrs over 2f out: wnt 2nd narrowly ins fnl f: sn no imp on wnr: continued to battle for 2nd* **9/2**[3]
4623 **3** *nse* **Tor**[21] 3909 3-8-9 **75** JamieGormley(7) 5 84
(Iain Jardine) *led: rdn and hdd over 2f out: lost 2nd narrowly ins fnl f: no imp on wnr after but battled for 2nd* **11/1**
41-2 **4** *4* **Crushed (IRE)**[22] 3859 3-8-11 **70** BenCurtis 1 73
(William Haggas) *racd keenly: chsd ldr to 3f out: one pce and n.d to front three over 1f out* **9/4**[2]
254 **5** *nk* **Romanor**[24] 3787 3-9-7 **80** (h) ThomasBrown 3 82
(Ed Walker) *in tch: rdn and one pce fr over 2f out* **12/1**
1-0 **6** *10* **High Waves (IRE)**[30] 3583 3-9-8 **81** (v[1]) KevinStott 4 67
(Saeed bin Suroor) *dwlt: hld up: rdn 3f out: edgd lft over 2f out: nvr able to trble ldrs: wknd over 1f out: eased whn btn ins fnl f* **8/1**
2m 33.42s (-3.28) **Going Correction** -0.10s/f (Good) **6** Ran SP% **112.5**
Speed ratings (Par 102): **106,104,104,101,101 94**
CSF £10.09 TOTE £2.30: £1.40, £2.10; EX 10.40 Trifecta £60.30.
**Owner** Ali Saeed **Bred** Mr & Mrs A E Pakenham **Trained** Middleham Moor, N Yorks

**FOCUS**
Race run over an extra 8yds. Quite an interesting handicap but run at something of a stop-start gallop. The winner landed quite a punt and is progressing well though the second favourite was disappointing.

## 4692 RIPON CATHEDRAL H'CAP 1m 1f 170y
**8:15** (8:16) (Class 3) (0-90,87) 3-Y-O- **£7,561** (£2,263; £1,131; £566; £282) **Stalls** Low

Form RPR
1614 **1** **Sands Chorus**[18] 4017 5-9-8 **86** SilvestreDeSousa 5 97
(James Given) *mde all: rdn over 2f out: styd on wl: eased cl home* **13/8**[1]
0625 **2** *2 1/4* **Mulligatawny (IRE)**[1] 4658 4-9-9 **87** TonyHamilton 1 92
(Roger Fell) *trckd ldrs: rdn to take 2nd over 2f out: no imp on wnr fr over 1f out: kpt on* **9/4**[2]
5001 **3** *1* **Sunglider (IRE)**[13] 4170 4-9-2 **80** (vt) BenCurtis 6 83+
(David O'Meara) *in rr: struggling to go pce 4f out: hdwy over 1f out: styd on ins fnl f: no imp on wnr: no ex towards fin* **10/1**
1314 **4** *4 1/2* **Energia Fox (BRZ)**[30] 3582 7-9-6 **84** PaulHanagan 3 78
(Richard Fahey) *chsd wnr tl over 3f out: rdn over 2f out: one pce over 1f out* **7/1**[3]
210- **5** *1 1/4* **Icefall (IRE)**[276] 7123 4-9-8 **86** DavidAllan 2 77
(Tim Easterby) *in tch: pushed along 3f out: nvr able to trble ldrs: wl hld over 1f out* **9/1**
6311 **6** *1/2* **Magic City (IRE)**[18] 4017 8-9-0 **85** HarrisonShaw(7) 4 75
(Michael Easterby) *chsd ldrs: 2nd over 3f out tl rdn over 2f out: wknd over 1f out* **8/1**
2m 2.5s (-2.90) **Going Correction** -0.10s/f (Good) **6** Ran SP% **111.6**
Speed ratings (Par 107): **107,105,104,100,99 99**
CSF £5.41 TOTE £1.90: £1.20, £2.10; EX 6.80 Trifecta £50.80.
**Owner** The Cool Silk Partnership **Bred** Worksop Manor Stud **Trained** Willoughton, Lincs

**FOCUS**
Race run over an extra 8yds. Just an ordinary gallop to this 1m2f handicap, but although the winner had the run of the race, there was no reason to think he was flattered. This was another race in which they finished quite well strung out.

## 4693 SIS TRADING SERVICES MAIDEN STKS 1m
**8:45** (8:45) (Class 5) 3-Y-O+ **£3,234** (£962; £481; £240) **Stalls** Low

Form RPR
6 **1** **Mooltazem (IRE)**[76] 2066 3-9-5 0 DaneO'Neill 1 80
(John Gosden) *trckd ldrs: rdn to ld 2f out: kpt on gamely ins fnl f: in control towards fin* **1/2**[1]
0 **2** *3/4* **Aclimatise**[10] 4309 3-9-5 0 FrannyNorton 7 78
(Mark Johnston) *in tch: hdwy 3f out: chalng over 1f out: unable qck ins fnl f: hld towards fin* **20/1**
3 **3** *4 1/2* **Kings Will Dream (IRE)**[32] 3500 3-9-5 0 PaulHanagan 6 68
(Micky Hammond) *hld up: hdwy 3f out: wnt 3rd and edgd rt over 1f out: kpt on ins fnl f: no imp on front two: nt knocked abt* **5/1**[3]
66 **4** *7* **Mark Of Excellence (IRE)**[8] 4409 3-9-5 0 (v[1]) SilvestreDeSousa 4 52
(Saeed bin Suroor) *racd keenly: led for 1f: chsd ldr tl led again 3f out: rdn and hdd 2f out: wknd 1f out* **4/1**[2]
00 **5** *2 1/4* **Simmo's Partytrick (IRE)**[5] 4508 4-10-0 0 AndrewMullen 5 49
(Geoffrey Harker) *led after 1f: hdd 3f out: wknd over 1f out* **100/1**
0 **6** *5* **Delegation**[50] 2857 3-9-5 0 DavidAllan 2 35
(Tim Easterby) *hld up: outpcd 2f out: nvr a threat* **33/1**
56 **7** *16* **Snoring**[16] 4106 3-9-5 0 SamJames 3
(John Davies) *racd keenly: stdd after 2f: hld up: outpcd over 2f out: sn lft bhd* **66/1**
1m 40.08s (-1.32) **Going Correction** -0.10s/f (Good)
**WFA** 3 from 4yo 9lb **7** Ran SP% **113.5**
Speed ratings (Par 103): **102,101,96,89,87 82,66**
CSF £15.27 TOTE £1.60: £1.10, £8.70; EX 13.60 Trifecta £33.70.
**Owner** Ms Hissa Hamdan Al Maktoum **Bred** Stonecross Stud **Trained** Newmarket, Suffolk

**FOCUS**
Race run over an extra 8yds. The pace was solid for this maiden. The winner built on his debut and the runner-up was a big improver.

## 4694 ST. AGNESGATE H'CAP 6f
**9:15** (9:16) (Class 5) (0-70,72) 3-Y-O **£3,234** (£962; £481; £240) **Stalls** High

Form RPR
-001 **1** **Kody Ridge (IRE)**[35] 3391 3-9-7 **67** (h) TonyHamilton 2 75
(Roger Fell) *w ldr: rdn to ld over 1f out: kpt on gamely towards fin* **12/1**
1102 **2** *3/4* **Mr Strutter (IRE)**[16] 4107 3-8-11 **62** (h) CallumRodriguez(5) 7 67
(John Quinn) *chsd ldrs: effrt over 1f out: chalng ins fnl f: no ex nr fin* **5/1**[2]
-055 **3** *3/4* **Haworth**[30] 3584 3-9-6 **66** KevinStott 1 69
(James Bethell) *hld up: hdwy over 2f out: styd on ins fnl f: nt pce to chal front two* **11/2**[3]
0-33 **4** *1/2* **Regal Decree**[71] 2182 3-8-9 **55** (p[1]) GrahamLee 4 56
(Jedd O'Keeffe) *midfield: rdn and hdwy over 2f out: chsd ldrs ins fnl f: kpt on* **9/1**
4-64 **5** *1/2* **Atrafan (IRE)**[10] 4302 3-8-10 **56** (p[1]) SilvestreDeSousa 11 56
(Alan Brown) *led: rdn and hung rt over 2f out: hdd over 1f out: hung rt whn no ex fnl 75yds* **7/1**
1260 **6** *shd* **Stubytuesday**[35] 3403 3-9-1 **64** NathanEvans(3) 8 63
(Michael Easterby) *midfield: pushed along 1/2-way: prog ins fnl f: styd on towards fin: nvr able to chal* **11/1**
0200 **7** *4 1/2* **Little Kingdom (IRE)**[16] 4107 3-8-10 **56** BenCurtis 3 41
(Tracy Waggott) *prom: rdn over 1f out: wknd ins fnl f* **16/1**
-002 **8** *3* **Chipping (IRE)**[16] 4080 3-9-12 **72** (p[1]) ConnorBeasley 6 47
(Michael Dods) *in rr: outpcd 4f out: nvr able to get on terms* **3/1**[1]
0640 **9** *2 1/4* **Party Tiger**[10] 4310 3-9-7 **67** (v[1]) PaulHanagan 10 35
(Richard Fahey) *in rr: pushed along 1/2-way: nvr on terms* **8/1**
-005 **10** *1/2* **Pavers Pride**[21] 3914 3-8-9 **55** PatrickMathers 9 22
(Noel Wilson) *stdd s: hld up in midfield: rdn and wknd over 2f out* **66/1**
6-50 **11** *10* **Mightaswellsmile**[42] 3152 3-8-13 **59** DavidAllan 5
(Ron Barr) *chsd ldrs tl rdn and wknd over 2f out* **40/1**
1m 11.57s (-1.43) **Going Correction** -0.225s/f (Firm) **11** Ran SP% **116.5**
Speed ratings (Par 100): **100,99,98,97,96 96,90,86,83,82 69**
CSF £70.36 CT £381.58 TOTE £12.60: £3.90, £2.10, £2.10; EX 92.00 Trifecta £400.10.
**Owner** Northern Marking Ltd & Partners **Bred** Tally-Ho Stud **Trained** Nawton, N Yorks

**FOCUS**
A run-of-the-mill sprint in which the winner did well from his wide draw, and he's getting closer to his 2yo best.
T/Plt: £37.10 to a £1 stake. Pool: £70,962.85 - 1393.73 winning units T/Qpdt: £10.90 to a £1 stake. Pool: £4,736.68 - 320.34 winning units **Darren Owen**

# 4440 WINDSOR (R-H)
Monday, July 10

**OFFICIAL GOING: Good to firm (good in places) changing to good to firm after race 4 (7:35)**
Wind: Fresh, behind Weather: Fine

## 4695 CALL STAR SPORTS ON 08000 521 321 APPRENTICE H'CAP 6f 12y
**6:05** (6:06) (Class 6) (0-65,67) 4-Y-O+ **£2,264** (£673; £336; £168) **Stalls** Low

Form RPR
-500 **1** **Cat Silver**[26] 3718 4-10-1 **67** (p[1]) PaddyPilley 8 74
(Roger Charlton) *trckd ldrs: led 2f out: edgd towards far rail fnl f: jst hld on* **11/2**[2]
6024 **2** *hd* **Atholblair Boy (IRE)**[10] 4310 4-9-12 **64** PhilDennis 13 70
(Nigel Tinkler) *wl in tch: prog 2f out: rdn to chse wnr jst over 1f out: styd on wl nr fin: jst failed* **6/1**[3]
-420 **3** *1 3/4* **Langley Vale**[31] 3532 8-9-5 **62** RossaRyan(5) 11 63
(Roger Teal) *taken down early: hld up in rr: prog on outer whn sltly impeded jst over 2f out: rdn to take 3rd fnl f: unable to chal* **14/1**
0520 **4** *hd* **Forever Yours (IRE)**[19] 3971 4-9-11 **63** LuluStanford 7 64
(Dean Ivory) *hld up wl in rr: prog against nr side rail 2f out: rdn and styd on: nrst fin* **5/1**[1]
4400 **5** *1 3/4* **Chetan**[11] 4256 5-9-4 **59** (tp) JoshuaBryan(3) 12 54
(Charlie Wallis) *taken down early: prom: rdn 1/2-way: nt pce to keep on terms fr 2f out* **8/1**
0060 **6** *hd* **Etienne Gerard**[5] 4509 5-9-4 **63** (p) FayeMcManoman(7) 1 58
(Nigel Tinkler) *in tch towards nr side: nudged along over 2f out: no imp ldrs after* **17/2**
0350 **7** *nk* **Blistering Dancer (IRE)**[30] 3569 7-8-7 **45** (b) MitchGodwin 6 39
(Tony Carroll) *spd to 1/2-way: lost pl u.p over 2f out* **33/1**

3215 **8** ¾ **Sir Geoffrey (IRE)**[30] 3563 11-8-7 **52**..........(b) JackOsborn(7) 3 44
(Scott Dixon) *v fast away: led and taken towards centre: hdd 3f out: grad fdd* **16/1**

3260 **9** ¾ **Deer Song**[4] 4532 4-9-0 **55**.......... JaneElliott(3) 2 44
(John Bridger) *chsd ldr: led 1/2-way to 2f out: wknd over 1f out* **18/1**

0253 **10** 2 **Doctor Parkes**[14] 4149 11-9-4 **59**.......... MillyNaseb(3) 5 42
(Natalie Lloyd-Beavis) *nvr beyond midfield: wknd over 1f out* **20/1**

3312 **11** nk **Frank Cool**[28] 3660 4-9-3 **55**.......... GeorgiaCox 14 37
(Tony Carroll) *hld up in midfield: prog whn drifted lft fr over 2f out: no hdwy 1f out: wknd and eased* **11/2**[2]

0150 **12** nk **Frangarry (IRE)**[35] 3385 5-9-4 **59**.......... KatherineGlenister(3) 4 41
(Alan Bailey) *towards rr: effrt u.p nr side over 2f out: no hdwy over 1f out: sn wknd* **14/1**

0000 **13** 8 **Tilly's Bridge**[68] 2294 4-8-2 **45**..........(p1) WilliamCox(5) 10 3
(Steve Woodman) *nvr beyond midfield: hanging and wknd rapidly over 1f out: t.o* **100/1**

0000 **14** 1 **Zerafino (BEL)**[42] 3137 4-8-2 **45**.......... AledBeech(5) 9
(Jimmy Fox) *s.i.s: outpcd: t.o* **100/1**

1m 11.11s (-1.89) **Going Correction** -0.275s/f (Firm) **14** Ran SP% **117.5**
Speed ratings (Par 101): **101,100,98,98,95 95,95,94,93,90 90,89,79,77**
CSF £30.58 CT £440.78 TOTE £4.90: £2.30, £2.30, £4.20; EX 32.00 Trifecta £487.10.
**Owner** Lady Rothschild **Bred** Carwell Equities Ltd **Trained** Beckhampton, Wilts
■ Stewards' Enquiry : Lulu Stanford 16-day ban (additional eight-days deferred): excessive use of the whip (Jul 21-Aug 5)

**FOCUS**
The bottom bend was fresher ground after becoming loose during the three-day meeting. A modest apprentice riders' handicap. They went a decent gallop on good to firm ground. It was noticeable how the sometimes favoured near rail was almost entirely shunned and the first five home were drawn seven or higher. The 2nd/3rd help pin the level.

## 4696 STARSPORTSBET.CO.UK EBF NOVICE STKS 6f 12y
6:35 (6:39) (Class 5) 2-Y-0 £2,911 (£866; £432; £216) Stalls Low

Form RPR

5 **1** **Peggy's Angel**[32] 3491 2-8-6 0.......... MitchGodwin(5) 5 73
(Jo Hughes) *t.k.h: hld up bhd ldrs: prog and squeezed through over 1f out: sn jnd ldr: disp ld after and jst prevailed* **9/2**[3]

**2** nse **Well Suited (IRE)** 2-9-2 0.......... HarryBentley 12 77
(Simon Crisford) *dwlt: sn chsd ldrs: rdn over 2f out whn hanging and rn green: clsd to ld jst over 1f out but sn jnd: jst pipped* **7/4**[1]

03 **3** ¾ **Iconic Knight (IRE)**[13] 4175 2-9-2 0.......... LiamKeniry 2 75
(Ed Walker) *hld up in rr but wl in tch: prog 2f out: rdn to chal jst over 1f out: kpt on same pce* **5/1**

**4** 1 ¾ **Gossip Column (IRE)** 2-9-2 0.......... DavidProbert 3 69
(Charles Hills) *mde most against nr side to over 1f out: outpcd after* **12/1**

45 **5** 2 ½ **Catapult**[31] 3516 2-9-2 0.......... PaoloSirigu 6 61
(Robert Eddery) *pressed ldng pair: led briefly over 1f out: wknd fnl f* **10/1**

0 **6** 3 ¼ **Spot Lite**[27] 3689 2-9-2 0.......... WilliamCarson 9 51+
(Rod Millman) *in tch in rr: fdd over 1f out* **25/1**

**7** 1 ¼ **Bezos (IRE)** 2-9-2 0.......... SeanLevey 4 47+
(Richard Hannon) *pressed ldr to over 1f out: wknd* **11/4**[2]

0 **8** 1 ¾ **Following Breeze (IRE)**[56] 2691 2-8-4 0.......... IsobelFrancis(7) 10 36
(Jim Boyle) *s.i.s: rcvrd out wd and on terms w ldrs 1/2-way: wknd over 1f out* **66/1**

**9** 3 ¾ **See The Tar (IRE)** 2-9-2 0.......... IrineuGoncalves 8 29
(Jo Hughes) *dwlt: tk fierce hold and hld up in last: lost tch 1/2-way: no ch after* **50/1**

1m 12.87s (-0.13) **Going Correction** -0.275s/f (Firm) **9** Ran SP% **122.0**
Speed ratings (Par 94): **89,88,87,85,82 77,76,73,68**
CSF £13.49 TOTE £5.30: £1.60, £1.20, £1.80; EX 15.00 Trifecta £67.70.
**Owner** Dalwhinnie Bloodstock Limited **Bred** Dalwhinnie Bloodstock **Trained** Lambourn, Berks
■ Yorbelucky was withdrawn. Price at time of withdrawal 10/3. Rule 4 applies to bets struck at board prices prior to withdrawal but not to SP bets - deduction 20p in the pound. New market formed

**FOCUS**
An ordinary juvenile novice contest. In contrast to the opener it helped to race handy towards the near side rail off a modest gallop. The winner has been rated in line with the lower end of the race average.

## 4697 BGC RACING COME ON ANDY CLAIMING STKS 1m 2f
7:05 (7:08) (Class 5) 3-Y-0 £2,911 (£866; £432; £216) Stalls Centre

Form RPR

3655 **1** **Kiruna Peak (IRE)**[5] 4494 3-9-0 61..........(v) CharlesBishop 4 66
(Mick Channon) *led after 2f: mde rest: hrd rdn over 2f out: clr over 1f out: kpt on* **11/4**[1]

-500 **2** 1 ¾ **See The Sea (IRE)**[22] 3864 3-8-5 64 ow1.......... RossaRyan(7) 3 61
(Richard Hannon) *hld up in last: impeded bnd over 5f out: rousted along over 3f out and hanging lft: prog over 2f out: styd on to take 2nd ins fnl f: unable to chal* **4/1**[2]

1000 **3** 2 ¼ **Alnasl (IRE)**[13] 4184 3-8-9 64..........(h) EdwardGreatrex(3) 6 56
(Archie Watson) *cl up: trckd wnr 3f out: rdn to chal over 2f out: fnd nil and btn wl over 1f out: lost 2nd ins fnl f* **8/1**

4621 **4** 6 **Chunkyfunkymonkey**[10] 4320 3-8-10 61.......... JackOsborn(7) 1 50
(John Ryan) *prog to chse ldng pair 1/2-way: rdn 3f out and sn outpcd: wknd wl over 1f out* **9/2**[3]

4433 **5** ½ **Log Off (IRE)**[6] 4462 3-8-7 55.......... JFEgan 2 39
(David Evans) *in tch in rr: shkn up 4f out: steadily wknd fnl 3f* **5/1**

-344 **6** 1 ¾ **Treagus**[13] 4172 3-9-1 56..........(p1) StevieDonohoe 5 44
(Charlie Fellowes) *led 2f: chsd wnr to 3f out: wknd* **7/1**

0526 **7** 23 **Niseko**[13] 4172 3-9-3 62..........(b) DougieCostello 7 2
(William Muir) *dwlt: in tch but racd awkwardly bnd over 5f out: shkn up 4f out: sn btn: eased over 1f out: t.o* **12/1**

2m 8.76s (0.06) **Going Correction** -0.125s/f (Firm) **7** Ran SP% **112.8**
Speed ratings (Par 100): **94,92,90,86,85 84,65**
CSF £13.45 TOTE £3.50: £2.10, £2.20; EX 14.80 Trifecta £116.50.
**Owner** M Channon **Bred** Kildaragh Stud **Trained** West Ilsley, Berks
■ Stewards' Enquiry : Dougie Costello two-day ban: careless riding (Jul 24-25)

**FOCUS**
A modest 3yo claimer.

## 4698 BGC RACING SUPORTS THAMES VALLEY AIR AMBULANCE H'CAP 1m 31y
7:35 (7:35) (Class 4) (0-80,82) 3-Y-0+ £4,690 (£1,395; £697; £348) Stalls Low

Form RPR

06-1 **1** **Sir Titan**[14] 4164 3-9-9 **82**.......... SteveDrowne 2 88+
(Marcus Tregoning) *trckd ldng pair: shkn up to cl over 2f out: led over 1f out: drvn out and hld on* **3/1**[1]

3414 **2** hd **Shifting Star (IRE)**[7] 4446 12-9-5 **69**..........(vt) WilliamCarson 4 74
(John Bridger) *led at gd pce: rdn over 2f out: hdd over 1f out: rallied last 100yds: jst hld* **11/1**

4652 **3** ½ **Fast Dancer (IRE)**[20] 3938 5-10-0 **78**..........(v) OisinMurphy 1 82
(Joseph Tuite) *hld up in tch: pushed along fr over 3f out: nvr clrest of runs fr over 2f out: drvn and styd on to take 3rd ins fnl f: jst unable to chal* **4/1**[2]

65 **4** 2 **Gilded Reflection**[47] 2952 4-10-0 **78**..........(b1) FranBerry 7 77
(Ralph Beckett) *stmbld s but chsd ldr: rdn wl over 2f out: lost 2nd sn after but styd cl up: fdd ins fnl f* **6/1**[3]

3632 **5** hd **Fastnet Spin (IRE)**[4] 4537 3-8-13 **72**..........(b) JFEgan 5 69
(David Evans) *dwlt: hld up in last: taken to outer and rdn 3f out: in tch 2f out: fdd fnl f* **4/1**[2]

012 **6** nse **Jumping Jack (IRE)**[7] 4446 3-9-2 **75**.......... ShaneKelly 6 72
(Richard Hughes) *dwlt: sn chsd ldrs: rdn 3f out: effrt on outer and in tch 2f out: fdd fnl f* **4/1**[2]

0110 **7** 14 **Mister Musicmaster**[23] 3808 8-9-7 **71**.......... DavidProbert 3 38
(Ron Hodges) *hld up in tch: rdn over 2f out: sn wknd: eased over 1f out: t.o* **20/1**

1m 42.52s (-2.18) **Going Correction** -0.125s/f (Firm)
**WFA** 3 from 4yo+ 9lb **7** Ran SP% **112.4**
Speed ratings (Par 105): **105,104,104,102,102 102,88**
CSF £34.86 TOTE £3.00: £2.10, £5.00; EX 32.90 Trifecta £111.70.
**Owner** Wedgewood Estates **Bred** Mrs Liza Judd **Trained** Whitsbury, Hants

**FOCUS**
A fair handicap. They went a decent gallop and it is sound form.

## 4699 STARSPREADS.COM H'CAP 1m 2f
8:05 (8:06) (Class 5) (0-75,76) 3-Y-0+ £2,911 (£866; £432; £216) Stalls Centre

Form RPR

6253 **1** **Russian Reward (IRE)**[17] 4041 5-9-11 **75**..........(p) JackMitchell 7 82
(Amanda Perrett) *trckd ldr after 3f: shkn up to chal 3f out: sustained battle after and drvn ahd ins fnl f: pushed along last strides and hld on* **15/2**

441 **2** hd **Marie Josephe**[21] 3921 3-9-2 **76**.......... ShaneKelly 9 84
(Richard Hughes) *led after 2f: rdn over 2f out and hrd pressed: hdd ins fnl f: kpt on wl nr fin* **9/4**[1]

124- **3** 1 ¾ **Captain Felix**[156] 5750 5-9-7 **71**.......... RyanTate 5 74
(James Eustace) *sn prom: chsd ldng pair after 4f: rdn wl over 2f out: kpt on but nvr quite able to chal* **8/1**

330 **4** 1 **Camakasi (IRE)**[11] 4257 6-9-7 **71**.......... TomMarquand 3 72
(Ali Stronge) *hld up wl in rr: rdn over 2f out: kpt on after on outer and tk 4th nr fin: n.d but did best of those hld up* **33/1**

13-5 **5** hd **Golden Nectar**[24] 3786 3-9-2 **76**.......... PatCosgrave 11 78
(Laura Mongan) *t.k.h: trckd ldrs: rdn over 2f out: no imp over 1f out: one pce* **15/2**

305 **6** 1 **Craftsmanship (FR)**[7] 4443 6-9-10 **74**.......... PaoloSirigu 1 75+
(Robert Eddery) *hld up wl in rr: no room to make prog against rail over 2f out: swtchd lft over 1f out: one reminder and passed rivals ins fnl f but too late to be involved* **12/1**

2236 **7** ½ **Essenaitch (IRE)**[29] 3616 4-8-13 **70**.......... KatherineGlenister(7) 6 68
(David Evans) *hld up in rr: rdn over 2f out: no real imp or prog: kpt on nr fin* **11/2**[3]

-056 **8** 1 **Gambit**[68] 2301 4-9-9 **73**.......... RichardKingscote 2 69
(Tom Dascombe) *t.k.h: led 2f: chsd ldrs after: no imp 2f out: wknd fnl f* **5/1**[2]

0000 **9** ½ **Lacan (IRE)**[45] 3030 6-9-8 **75**.......... CallumShepherd(3) 10 70
(Brett Johnson) *t.k.h: hld up in midfield: rdn over 2f out: no prog and wknd ins fnl f* **40/1**

5000 **10** ¾ **Ibazz**[16] 4085 4-9-9 **73**.......... GeorgeDowning 8 66
(Ian Williams) *hld up in last pair: rdn and no prog wl over 2f out* **66/1**

1-55 **11** ½ **Venutius**[21] 3920 10-9-9 **73**.......... DavidProbert 4 65
(Charles Hills) *in tch in midfield: rdn and no prog over 2f out: fdd over 1f out* **25/1**

2m 8.56s (-0.14) **Going Correction** -0.125s/f (Firm)
**WFA** 3 from 4yo+ 10lb **11** Ran SP% **115.9**
Speed ratings (Par 103): **95,94,93,92,92 91,91,90,90,89 89**
CSF £23.70 CT £141.32 TOTE £7.40: £1.80, £1.60, £2.50; EX 28.20 Trifecta £279.80.
**Owner** A D Spence **Bred** Times Of Wigan Ltd **Trained** Pulborough, W Sussex
■ Stewards' Enquiry : Jack Mitchell four-day ban: excessive use of the whip (Jul 25-27)

**FOCUS**
A fair handicap. They went a muddling gallop but the winner has been rated to his best since his early maidens.

## 4700 BGC RACING TEXT BGC TO 60777 MAIDEN STKS 1m 31y
8:35 (8:36) (Class 5) 3-4-Y-0 £2,911 (£866; £432; £216) Stalls Low

Form RPR

5-2 **1** **Big Tour (IRE)**[16] 4086 3-9-5 0.......... MartinLane 1 83+
(Saeed bin Suroor) *mde all: stretched on 3f out: rdn clr over 1f out: styd on wl* **5/4**[2]

3 **2** 3 ¾ **Hyperloop**[33] 3456 3-9-5 0.......... PatCosgrave 7 74+
(William Haggas) *t.k.h: trckd ldng pair: shkn up wl over 2f out: stl green and nt qckn wl over 1f out: kpt on to take 2nd nr fin* **1/1**[1]

0 **3** ¾ **Your Ladyship (IRE)**[32] 3506 3-9-0 0.......... PatDobbs 9 67
(Ralph Beckett) *pressed wnr: shkn up over 2f out: outpcd fr wl over 1f out: lost 2nd nr fin* **10/1**[3]

46 **4** 2 **Becuna (USA)**[31] 3542 3-9-0 0.......... DannyBrock 3 62+
(Michael Bell) *t.k.h: hld up in last: pushed along over 2f out: kpt on steadily to take 4th fnl f: likely to do bttr* **16/1**

**5** 1 **The Groove**[15] 4-10-0 0.......... TrevorWhelan 5 67
(Fergal O'Brien) *chsd ldrs: urged along 3f out: no prog whn edgd rt u.p over 1f out* **100/1**

06 **6** 2 **Pretty Obvious (FR)**[11] 4275 4-10-0 0.......... FranBerry 4 62
(Jonjo O'Neill) *hld up in tch: pushed along over 2f out: no ch whn hmpd over 1f out: one pce after* **33/1**

00- **7** 20 **Nordenfelt (IRE)**[465] 1184 4-10-0 0.......... GeorgeDowning 6 14
(Tony Newcombe) *s.i.s: in tch to 3f out: sn wknd: t.o* **150/1**

1m 45.38s (0.68) **Going Correction** -0.125s/f (Firm)
**WFA** 3 from 4yo 9lb **7** Ran SP% **114.0**
Speed ratings (Par 103): **91,87,86,84,83 81,61**
CSF £2.78 TOTE £2.00: £1.50, £1.10; EX 3.20 Trifecta £8.40.
**Owner** Godolphin **Bred** Rabbah Bloodstock Limited **Trained** Newmarket, Suffolk
■ Stewards' Enquiry : Trevor Whelan caution: careless riding

**FOCUS**
A fair maiden. They went a modest gallop and the second favourite completely dominated.

## 4701 BGC RACING £125 MEMBERSHIP H'CAP 1m 3f 99y
**9:05** (9:05) (Class 4) (0-85,85) 3-Y-O **£4,690** (£1,395; £697; £348) **Stalls** Centre

Form RPR

0133 **1** **Harebell (IRE)**[3] 4571 3-8-13 **77** PatDobbs 6 85
(Ralph Beckett) *hld up in last: prog over 3f out to chse ldr over 2f out: rdn to chal over 1f out: led last 100yds: styd on* **7/2**[3]

-311 **2** ¾ **Amlad (IRE)**[30] 3596 3-9-6 **84** OisinMurphy 5 90
(Ed Dunlop) *trckd ldr: led 3f out: edgd lft u.p whn pressed over 1f out: hdd last 100yds: kpt on* **11/4**[2]

-410 **3** 1 ½ **Wasatch Range**[52] 2784 3-9-7 **85** (b[1]) RobertTart 1 88
(John Gosden) *hld up in 4th: urged along and outpcd 3f out: rallied to chse ldng pair over 1f out: tried to cl u.p but one pce last 100yds* **9/4**[1]

4-35 **4** 3 ¼ **Berengaria (IRE)**[31] 3535 3-9-5 **83** RichardKingscote 2 80
(Mark Johnston) *led: pushed along 4f out: hdd 3f out: nt qckn and sn btn* **10/1**

1-60 **5** 3 ¼ **Azam**[52] 2784 3-9-6 **84** (p) HarryBentley 3 76
(John Gosden) *t.k.h: trckd ldrs: rdn and no rspnse over 2f out: sn btn* **11/4**[2]

2m 27.6s (-1.90) **Going Correction** -0.125s/f (Firm) **5** Ran SP% **115.4**
Speed ratings (Par 102): **101,100,99,97,94**
CSF £14.08 TOTE £4.60: £2.20, £1.40; EX 17.30 Trifecta £46.00.
**Owner** J H Richmond-Watson **Bred** J H Richmond-Watson **Trained** Kimpton, Hants

**FOCUS**
A decent middle-distance 3yo handicap. They went a respectable gallop and the winner is improving.
T/Plt: £33.60 to a £1 stake. Pool: £97,936.63 - 2124.2 winning units T/Qpdt: £8.50 to a £1 stake. Pool: £6,703.81 - 578.99 winning units **Jonathan Neesom**

4702 - 4708a (Foreign Racing) - See Raceform Interactive

# 4458 BRIGHTON (L-H)
Tuesday, July 11

**OFFICIAL GOING: Good to firm (watered) changing to good to firm (good in places) after race 1 (5.45) changing to good after race 4 (7.15)**
Wind: medium, against Weather: rain cleared, overcast until rain again race 3

## 4709 CALL STAR SPORTS ON 08000 521321 NOVICE STKS 6f 210y
**5:45** (5:47) (Class 5) 2-Y-O **£2,911** (£866; £432; £216) **Stalls** Centre

Form RPR

53 **1** **Wildnightinvegas (IRE)**[34] 3467 2-9-2 0 TomMarquand 1 73
(Richard Hannon) *chsd ldr tl 4f out: styd prom: effrt on inner to chal over 1f out: rdn to ld ins fnl f: styd on wl and pushed out fnl 75yds* **7/1**

3 **2** ¾ **Jazirat (IRE)**[14] 4183 2-9-2 0 (h) MartinLane 5 71
(Charlie Appleby) *sn led: rdn and hrd pressed over 1f out: hdd ins fnl f: styd on same pce after* **7/4**[1]

440 **3** 2 ¾ **Jo's Girl (IRE)**[18] 4028 2-8-11 75 DougieCostello 9 59
(Jamie Osborne) *in tch in last trio: rdn and hdwy over 1f out: wnt 3rd 100yds out: styd on but no threat to ldrs* **12/1**

0 **4** nk **Jaalboot**[42] 3187 2-9-2 0 JimCrowley 7 63
(Owen Burrows) *chsd ldrs: wnt 2nd 4f out tl dropped to 3rd and unable qck over 1f out: lost 3rd and wknd fnl 100yds* **3/1**[2]

00 **5** ½ **El Borracho (IRE)**[13] 4213 2-9-2 0 HarryBentley 8 61
(Simon Dow) *hld up in tch in midfield: effrt over 1f out: kpt on ins fnl f: nvr enough pce to threaten ldrs* **25/1**

00 **6** shd **Daffrah**[23] 3858 2-8-11 0 OisinMurphy 2 56
(James Tate) *hld up in tch in midfield: hdwy over 1f out: kpt on but no imp ins fnl f* **16/1**

0 **7** 4 ½ **Dark Blue (IRE)**[12] 4253 2-8-11 0 MartinDwyer 10 44
(Mick Channon) *dwlt: rn green and pushed along in last trio: rdn over 2f out: outpcd and wl hld over 1f out* **16/1**

0 **8** 15 **Honey Blossom**[28] 3697 2-8-4 0 GabrieleMalune(7) 4 3
(Mark H Tompkins) *plld hrd: chsd ldrs tl rdn and struggling 2f out: sn lost pl: wl bhd ins fnl f* **66/1**

**9** 5 **Sackeb** 2-9-2 0 JosephineGordon 3
(Hugo Palmer) *rn green: s.i.s: a in rr: lost tch over 1f out* **4/1**[3]

1m 24.19s (1.09) **Going Correction** +0.15s/f (Good) **9** Ran SP% **118.7**
Speed ratings (Par 94): **99,98,95,94,94 93,88,71,65**
CSF £20.23 TOTE £7.90: £1.90, £1.40, £2.50; EX 25.10 Trifecta £180.70.
**Owner** Cox, Galway, Barnett, Myerscough **Bred** Pat O'Rourke **Trained** East Everleigh, Wilts

**FOCUS**
Distance increased by 3yds. Rain turned the ground on the easy side. Ordinary novice form, with the 2nd helping to set the level.

## 4710 EARL KENDRICK BRIGHTON ONE YEAR CELEBRATION (S) H'CAP 5f 215y
**6:15** (6:17) (Class 6) (0-60,52) 3-Y-O+ **£2,264** (£673; £336; £168) **Stalls** Centre

Form RPR

0-62 **1** **Wild Flower (IRE)**[14] 4179 5-9-8 **50** KieranO'Neill 3 58
(Jimmy Fox) *mde all: rdn ent fnl 2f: sn hrd pressed and drvn ent fnl f: styd on wl u.p and forged ahd wl ins fnl f* **6/4**[1]

513 **2** 1 **Justice Rock**[4] 4656 4-9-8 **50** (t) OisinMurphy 1 55
(Phil McEntee) *trckd ldrs: shkn up and effrt over 1f out: rdn to chal ent fnl f: styd on same pce fnl 100yds: wnt 2nd cl home* **10/3**[2]

2532 **3** nk **Picansort**[19] 4008 10-9-10 **52** FergusSweeney 5 56
(Peter Crate) *stdd after s: hld up in rr: effrt on outer 2f out: rdn and hdwy to chal strly 1f out: no ex wl ins fnl f: wknd and lost 2nd towards fin* **8/1**

0060 **4** ¾ **Cooperess**[55] 2733 4-9-1 **50** (v) RossaRyan(7) 4 51
(John O'Shea) *hld up wl in tch: swtchd rt and effrt ent fnl 2f: rdn to press ldrs over 1f out: sltly outpcd and n.m.r jst ins fnl f: sn swtchd rt: kpt on towards fin* **9/2**[3]

63-3 **5** 8 **Triple Dream**[181] 171 12-9-5 **47** JosephineGordon 6 23
(Milton Bradley) *chsd wnr tl over 1f out: sn outpcd: wknd ins fnl f* **7/1**

-550 **6** nk **Verdi (IRE)**[15] 4157 3-8-9 **50** (p[1]) JackOsborn(7) 7 24
(John Ryan) *chsd ldrs: rdn over 2f out: outpcd over 1f out: wknd ins fnl f* **11/1**

1m 11.07s (0.87) **Going Correction** +0.15s/f (Good)
**WFA** 3 from 4yo+ 6lb **6** Ran SP% **113.2**
Speed ratings (Par 101): **100,98,98,97,86 86**
CSF £6.81 TOTE £2.20: £1.70, £2.10; EX 5.80 Trifecta £19.80.There was no bid for the winner.
**Owner** Mrs Sarah-Jane Fox **Bred** Peter Harms **Trained** Collingbourne Ducis, Wilts

**FOCUS**
Distance increased by 3yds. Lowly form.

## 4711 STARSPORTSBET.CO.UK FILLIES' H'CAP 6f 210y
**6:45** (6:45) (Class 5) (0-70,72) 3-Y-O+ **£2,911** (£866; £432; £216) **Stalls** Centre

Form RPR

1420 **1** **Andalusite**[32] 3522 4-9-3 **59** (v) FergusSweeney 8 64
(John Gallagher) *sn led and mde rest: rdn 2f out: hld on wl u.p whn pressed wl ins fnl f: rdn out* **6/1**

1465 **2** ½ **One Big Surprise**[17] 4093 5-9-9 **72** (p) FinleyMarsh(7) 6 76
(Richard Hughes) *hld up in tch in rr: clsd over 1f out: trckd wnr jst ins fnl f: sn swtchd rt and effrt to press wnr wl ins fnl f: kpt on but hld towards fin* **7/4**[1]

-500 **3** 3 ¾ **Chica De La Noche**[12] 4251 3-9-6 **70** JimCrowley 7 61
(Simon Dow) *t.k.h: chsd wnr for 1f: styd handy: effrt ent fnl 2f: drvn to chse ldrs over 1f out: no ex ins fnl f: outpcd fnl 100yds* **2/1**[2]

5-00 **4** ½ **Sparkle**[13] 4214 3-9-4 **68** JosephineGordon 5 57
(Ed Dunlop) *t.k.h: early: hld up in tch: effrt u.p to chse ldrs over 1f out: no ex and outpcd fnl 100yds* **9/2**[3]

0-00 **5** 2 ½ **Robin's Purse**[55] 2732 3-8-6 **56** MartinDwyer 4 38
(Charles Hills) *t.k.h: hdwy to chse wnr after 1f: rdn over 1f out: no ex and lost 2nd jst ins fnl f: wknd fnl 100yds* **10/1**

1m 23.61s (0.51) **Going Correction** +0.15s/f (Good)
**WFA** 3 from 4yo+ 8lb **5** Ran SP% **111.3**
Speed ratings (Par 100): **103,102,98,97,94**
CSF £17.17 TOTE £5.70: £1.60, £2.30; EX 15.70 Trifecta £35.80.
**Owner** The LAM Partnership **Bred** Pinnacle Bloodstock Ltd **Trained** Chastleton, Oxon

**FOCUS**
Distance increased by 3yds. Modest handicap form, with the winner rated to her best.

## 4712 BEND IT LIKE BISHOPS H'CAP 1m 3f 198y
**7:15** (7:16) (Class 4) (0-85,87) 4-Y-O+ **£4,690** (£1,395; £697; £348) **Stalls** High

Form RPR

5514 **1** **Pacharana**[10] 4364 4-9-5 **80** LukeMorris 5 89
(Luca Cumani) *broke wl: sn stdd and trckd ldrs: c nrest stands rail and effrt over 2f out: rdn to ld over 1f out: hung lft ins fnl f: hld on cl home: all out* **7/2**[2]

4-52 **2** hd **New World Power (JPN)**[21] 3947 4-9-6 **81** OisinMurphy 6 90
(David Simcock) *stdd s: hld up in rr: effrt in centre ent fnl 2f: chsd wnr 1f out: styd on strly u.p ins fnl f: jst hld* **11/8**[1]

3302 **3** 8 **Hepplewhite**[17] 4089 4-8-10 **71** (p) MartinDwyer 3 67
(William Muir) *sn led: rdn ent fnl 2f: hdd over 1f out: sn hung lft: lost 2nd and wknd fnl f* **9/2**[3]

6040 **4** 7 **Cape Discovery**[54] 2752 5-9-0 **82** FinleyMarsh(7) 4 67
(Richard Hughes) *hld up in tch: effrt over 2f out: 4th and btn over 1f out: sn wknd* **11/2**

1100 **5** 50 **General Hazard (IRE)**[13] 4206 4-9-4 **82** EdwardGreatrex(3) 1
(Archie Watson) *hld up in tch: clsd to trck ldrs 1/2-way: rdn over 2f out: dropped to last and btn over 1f out: virtually p.u ins fnl f* **6/1**

2m 36.19s (3.49) **Going Correction** +0.15s/f (Good) **5** Ran SP% **112.2**
Speed ratings (Par 105): **94,93,88,83,50**
CSF £8.99 TOTE £3.80: £1.50, £1.20; EX 9.40 Trifecta £19.30.
**Owner** S Stuckey **Bred** Stuart Stuckey **Trained** Newmarket, Suffolk

**FOCUS**
Distance increased by 3yds. The ground looked to have worsened by this stage and the winner of this fair handicap came more towards the stands' side.

## 4713 CYRIL LEONARD LTD H'CAP 7f 211y
**7:45** (7:45) (Class 6) (0-55,57) 3-Y-O+ **£2,264** (£673; £336; £168) **Stalls** Centre

Form RPR

4413 **1** **Luxford**[13] 4211 3-8-9 **52** MartinDwyer 10 62
(John Best) *chsd ldr tl led and racing against stands rail wl over 2f out: hld on wl u.p ins fnl f: rdn out* **9/4**[1]

5634 **2** ½ **Chough**[138] 881 3-8-6 **52** CharlieBennett(3) 6 60
(Hughie Morrison) *hld up in tch: clsd to press ldrs 2f out: rdn and chalng over 1f out: sustained effrt and c clr w wnr ins fnl f: a jst hld* **13/2**

3352 **3** 4 ½ **Lawfilly**[14] 4180 3-8-3 **53** (p) NicolaCurrie(7) 3 51
(Richard Hughes) *hld up in tch in last pair: clsd to chse ldrs and rdn over 1f out: 3rd and wknd ins fnl f* **7/2**[2]

5600 **4** ½ **George Baker (IRE)**[95] 1603 10-9-6 **57** HectorCrouch(3) 12 56
(George Baker) *hld up in tch in last pair: clsd to press ldrs 2f out: rdn over 1f out: no ex jst ins fnl f: wknd* **10/1**

1554 **5** nk **Jack Blane**[22] 3913 3-8-12 **55** GeorgeDowning 2 51
(Daniel Kubler) *in tch in midfield: effrt 2f out: unable qck u.p ent fnl f: wknd ins fnl f* **6/1**[3]

-053 **6** 8 **Captain Marmalade (IRE)**[14] 4180 5-8-12 **53** RossaRyan(7) 7 33
(Jimmy Fox) *dwlt: sn rcvrd and in tch in midfield: effrt 2f out: no imp u.p over 1f out: sn wknd* **6/1**[3]

0-60 **7** ½ **Lagertha (IRE)**[23] 3866 3-9-0 **57** (p[1]) JosephineGordon 1 34
(Hugo Palmer) *dwlt and bustled along early: sn rcvrd to chse ldrs: rdn over 2f out: lost pl and btn over 1f out: wknd fnl f* **8/1**

U55/ **8** 2 ½ **Almoqatel (IRE)**[668] 6303 5-8-12 **46** KieranO'Neill 4 19
(Natalie Lloyd-Beavis) *t.k.h: led tl wl over 2f out: sn rdn and lost pl over 1f out: wknd fnl f* **40/1**

1m 36.95s (0.95) **Going Correction** +0.15s/f (Good)
**WFA** 3 from 4yo+ 9lb **8** Ran SP% **117.5**
Speed ratings (Par 101): **101,100,96,95,95 87,86,84**
CSF £18.13 CT £50.78 TOTE £2.80: £1.10, £2.60, £1.50; EX 18.60 Trifecta £56.20.
**Owner** Stuart Mair, Wendy Bush & Steve Summers **Bred** Best Breeding **Trained** Oad Street, Kent

**FOCUS**
Distance increased by 3yds. The front pair came clear in this moderate handicap, with the winner having the benefit of the stands' rail late on.

## 4714 CALL STAR SPREADS ON 0808 2349709 H'CAP 6f 210y
**8:15** (8:16) (Class 6) (0-60,61) 3-Y-O **£2,264** (£673; £336; £168) **Stalls** Centre

Form RPR

5501 **1** **Tigerfish (IRE)**[29] 3661 3-8-9 **53** ow1 (p) JoshuaBryan(5) 1 60
(William Stone) *in tch in midfield: rdn to ld ent fnl f: styd on wl: rdn out* **9/2**[3]

-623 **2** 1 ½ **Fair Selene**[26] 3751 3-9-7 **60** (v) TomMarquand 5 63
(Heather Main) *hld up in tch: nt clr run over 1f out: hdwy to chse wnr 1f out: kpt on but a hld ins fnl f* **11/4**[2]

00-0 **3** 1 ¼ **Bradfield Magic (IRE)**[34] 3473 3-9-4 **60** CallumShepherd(3) 3 60
(Charles Hills) *stdd after s: hld up in tch in last pair: racing against stands rail and nt clr run 2f out: hdwy over 1f out: wnt 3rd ins fnl f: kpt on* **25/1**

6061 **4** 3 **Moonstone Rock**[21] 3937 3-9-4 **60**........................(b) CharlieBennett(3) 6 52
(Jim Boyle) *dwlt and pushed along early: in tch in rr: chsng ldrs u.p whn bmpd over 1f out: wknd ins fnl f* **7/1**

55-0 **5** 1 **Roman Legion (IRE)**[179] 209 3-9-6 **59**........................ JohnFahy 7 48
(Dean Ivory) *chsd ldrs: led over 1f out: sn hdd and no ex u.p: wknd ins fnl f* **16/1**

0060 **6** ½ **Beach Dancer (IRE)**[27] 3719 3-8-13 **52**........................ OisinMurphy 2 39
(William Knight) *taken down early: in tch in midfield: hdwy and ev ch u.p over 1f out: wknd ins fnl f* **7/1**

6443 **7** ¾ **Royal Peace (IRE)**[15] 4150 3-9-8 **61**........................(p1) KieranO'Neill 4 46
(Richard Hannon) *led tl rdn and hdd over 1f out: sn hung bdly lft: wknd fnl f* **5/2**[1]

0054 **8** 4 **Cherry Leyf**[24] 3818 3-9-0 **53**........................(t) JosephineGordon 8 28
(Stuart Williams) *chsd ldr: ev ch u.p over 1f out: sn no ex: wknd fnl f* **12/1**

1m 24.36s (1.26) **Going Correction** +0.15s/f (Good) **8 Ran SP% 115.8**
Speed ratings (Par 98): **98,96,94,91,90 89,88,84**
CSF £17.57 CT £280.33 TOTE £4.50: £1.10, £1.40, £6.40; EX 19.90 Trifecta £298.10.
**Owner** Miss Caroline Scott **Bred** Swordlestown Little **Trained** West Wickham, Cambs

**FOCUS**
Distance increased by 3yds. Visibility had worsened by this stage and, unlike in earlier contests, the centre-field runners fared best.

## 4715 STARSPREADS.COM H'CAP — 5f 215y
**8:45** (8:45) (Class 5) (0-75,76) 3-Y-O — **£2,911** (£866; £432; £216) **Stalls Centre**

Form — RPR

2222 **1** **Delfie Lane**[12] 4251 3-9-0 **74**........................(p) FinleyMarsh(7) 1 77
(Richard Hughes) *led tl 4f out: chsd ldr tl rdn to ld jst over 1f out: styd on wl and a jst holding chalr ins fnl f: rdn out* **6/4**[2]

20-4 **2** ½ **Maazel (IRE)**[17] 4104 3-9-9 **76**........................ HarryBentley 3 77
(Roger Varian) *trckd ldrs: swtchd lft and effrt over 1f out: ev ch 1f out: sustained chal and kpt on wl ins fnl f: a jst hld* **11/8**[1]

4456 **3** 2¼ **Whiteley (IRE)**[8] 4447 3-8-6 **59**........................ MartinDwyer 2 53
(Mick Channon) *t.k.h: chsd ldrs tl wnt 2nd 5f out: led 4f out: rdn wl over 1f out: hdd jst over 1f out: wknd ins fnl f* **7/2**[3]

330 **4** 16 **Prancelina (IRE)**[15] 4161 3-7-12 **58**........................(t1) MillyNaseb(7) 5
(Phil McEntee) *chsd wnr for 1f: dropped to last 1/2-way: rdn 2f out: sn struggling and wknd over 1f out* **16/1**

1m 12.06s (1.86) **Going Correction** +0.15s/f (Good) **4 Ran SP% 110.2**
Speed ratings (Par 100): **93,92,89,68**
CSF £4.03 TOTE £2.10; EX 2.10 Trifecta £3.60.
**Owner** Richard Hughes **Bred** Catridge Farm Stud **Trained** Upper Lambourn, Berks

**FOCUS**
Distance increased by 3yds. Racing stands' side, the two market leaders emerged late on.
T/Plt: £15.10 to a £1 stake. Pool: £74,376.92 - 3,579.04 winning units T/Qpdt: £6.70 to a £1 stake. Pool: £5,484.89 - 602.50 winning units **Steve Payne**

# 4433 PONTEFRACT (L-H)
Tuesday, July 11

**OFFICIAL GOING: Good to soft (good in places; watered; 7.4)**
Wind: Light across Weather: Heavy cloud and rain

## 4716 DIANNE NURSERY H'CAP — 6f
**2:10** (2:10) (Class 4) 2-Y-O — **£5,175** (£1,540; £769; £384) **Stalls Low**

Form — RPR

350 **1** **Areen Faisal (IRE)**[21] 3929 2-9-5 **76**........................ PhillipMakin 7 79
(Richard Fahey) *keen old: trckd ldng pair: hdwy 2f out: rdn over 1f out: led ins fnl f: sn drvn and kpt on* **5/1**

4362 **2** 1¼ **The Love Doctor (IRE)**[25] 3791 2-9-1 **72**........................ DanielTudhope 1 71+
(David Evans) *cl up on inner: led 2f out and sn rdn: hdd and drvn ins fnl f: kpt on u.p* **4/1**[3]

016 **3** 4½ **Another Day Of Sun (IRE)**[13] 4220 2-9-3 **74**.......... SilvestreDeSousa 2 60
(Mick Channon) *rdn along s and sn led: pushed along 1/2-way: rdn and hdd 2f out: drvn over 1f out: kpt on same pce* **5/2**[1]

4263 **4** 1¾ **Noble Manners (IRE)**[27] 3712 2-9-0 **71**........................ PJMcDonald 4 52
(Mark Johnston) *dwlt and sn rdn along in rr: hdwy 2f out: drvn over 1f out and sn no imp* **6/1**

063 **5** 11 **Monkey Magic**[36] 3399 2-8-5 **62**........................ PaulHanagan 3 10
(Nigel Tinkler) *chsd ldrs: rdn along over 2f out: sn outpcd* **16/1**

5312 **6** 1¾ **Collingham Park (IRE)**[19] 4014 2-9-7 **78**........................ GrahamLee 6 20
(Jedd O'Keeffe) *sn pushed along to chse ldrs: rdn wl over 2f out: sn btn* **3/1**[2]

1m 19.14s (2.24) **Going Correction** +0.275s/f (Good) **6 Ran SP% 110.4**
Speed ratings (Par 96): **96,94,88,86,71 69**
CSF £24.01 TOTE £5.60: £2.40, £2.20; EX 29.20 Trifecta £89.40.
**Owner** Sheikh Abdullah Almalek Alsabah **Bred** Mrs Mary Coonan **Trained** Musley Bank, N Yorks

**FOCUS**
There was 3mm of rain in the morning, following 1mm of rain overnight and 4mm on Monday, and the going was given as good to soft, good in places (GoingStick: 7.4). The rail was dolled out from the 6f marker to the winning post, adding approximately 8yds to all races. The front two got racing soon enough and that set things up for the winner, who had tracked them into the straight.

## 4717 SOCHALL SMITH CHARTERED ACCOUNTANTS H'CAP — 5f 3y
**2:40** (2:41) (Class 5) (0-75,75) 3-Y-O — **£3,881** (£1,155; £577; £288) **Stalls Low**

Form — RPR

4522 **1** **Sheepscar Lad (IRE)**[16] 4122 3-9-2 **70**........................ SilvestreDeSousa 1 79
(Nigel Tinkler) *hld up in rr: hdwy 3f out: chsd ldrs wl over 1f out: rdn to ld ins fnl f: kpt on strly* **5/4**[1]

5022 **2** 2½ **Lawless Louis**[15] 4159 3-9-7 **75**........................(v) DanielTudhope 8 74
(David O'Meara) *trckd ldrs: swtchd rt towards stands rail wl over 1f out: rdn and ch ent fnl f: sn drvn and kpt on same pce* **13/2**[3]

5125 **3** 2 **Lightoller (IRE)**[5] 4532 3-9-1 **69**........................(b) GrahamLee 2 61
(Mick Channon) *chsd ldng pair: rdn along wl over 1f out: n.m.r ent fnl f: sn drvn and kpt on same pce* **7/1**

-504 **4** 1¼ **Bay Station**[17] 4107 3-8-10 **64**........................ PJMcDonald 5 51
(Jason Ward) *chsd ldrs: rdn along wl over 1f out: drvn and no imp fnl f* **8/1**

100- **5** 1½ **Whiteandgold**[307] 6222 3-9-2 **70**........................ ConnorBeasley 7 52
(Bryan Smart) *towards rr: effrt on outer whn sltly hmpd and swtchd lft wl over 1f out: sn rdn and n.d* **33/1**

0132 **6** nse **Dapper Man (IRE)**[14] 4174 3-8-11 **65**........................(b) JamesSullivan 6 47
(Roger Fell) *t.k.h: cl up: disp ld 1/2-way: rdn to ld over 1f out: sn drvn and hdd ins fnl f: wknd* **5/1**[2]

4104 **7** ½ **Lady Cristal (IRE)**[11] 4305 3-9-1 **69**........................(p) BenCurtis 4 49
(K R Burke) *slt ld: rdn along 2f out: hdd over 1f out and sn wknd* **8/1**

1m 4.62s (1.32) **Going Correction** +0.275s/f (Good) **7 Ran SP% 112.1**
Speed ratings (Par 100): **100,96,92,90,88 88,87**
CSF £9.49 CT £39.48 TOTE £1.90: £1.30, £2.70; EX 9.30 Trifecta £36.50.
**Owner** Leeds Plywood And Doors Ltd **Bred** Stockvale Bloodstock Ltd **Trained** Langton, N Yorks

**FOCUS**
Race distance increased by 8yds. There was a good gallop on and that set things up nicely for the winner.

## 4718 WEATHERBYS GENERAL STUD BOOK ONLINE PIPALONG STKS (LISTED RACE) — 1m 6y
**3:10** (3:11) (Class 1) 4-Y-O+
**£22,684** (£8,600; £4,304; £2,144; £1,076; £540) **Stalls Low**

Form — RPR

4314 **1** **Lincoln Rocks**[4] 4578 4-9-0 **93**........................ DanielTudhope 6 101
(David O'Meara) *set stdy pce: c wd to home st and qcknd: rdn along on stands rail over 1f out: drvn ins fnl f: kpt on wl towards fin* **14/1**

-300 **2** nk **Dawn Of Hope (IRE)**[20] 3961 4-9-0 **108**........................ AndreaAtzeni 5 100
(Roger Varian) *trckd ldrs: hdwy 2f out: chsd ldrs over 1f out: rdn ent fnl f: sn drvn and ev ch ins fnl f: kpt on* **6/4**[1]

-320 **3** 1½ **Pirouette**[20] 3961 4-9-0 **105**........................ RobertWinston 8 96
(Hughie Morrison) *trckd ldrs: hdwy to trck wnr 3f out: rdn wl over 1f out: drvn ent fnl f: kpt on same pce* **3/1**[2]

0360 **4** ½ **Home Cummins (IRE)**[10] 4377 5-9-0 **90**........................(p) PaulHanagan 2 95
(Richard Fahey) *sn trcking wnr: pushed along over 2f out: rdn wl over 1f out: kpt on one pce* **8/1**

0-24 **5** 2¼ **Permission**[41] 3219 4-9-0 **93**........................ DanielMuscutt 3 90
(James Fanshawe) *trckd ldrs: rdn along over 2f out: drvn wl over 1f out: no imp* **10/3**[3]

405 **6** 6 **Coillte Cailin (IRE)**[20] 3981 7-9-0 **83**........................ PhillipMakin 4 76
(David O'Meara) *a towards rr* **66/1**

6605 **7** 6 **Summer Icon**[10] 4375 4-9-0 **94**........................ SilvestreDeSousa 7 62
(Mick Channon) *hld up in rr: effrt and sme hdwy on inner 2f out: sn rdn and n.d* **25/1**

1m 46.75s (0.85) **Going Correction** +0.275s/f (Good) **7 Ran SP% 111.2**
Speed ratings (Par 111): **106,105,104,103,101 95,89**
CSF £33.69 TOTE £12.60: £4.40, £1.10; EX 41.10 Trifecta £116.60.
**Owner** Peter Smith P C Coaches Limited **Bred** James Ortega Bloodstock **Trained** Upper Helmsley, N Yorks

■ Stewards' Enquiry : Andrea Atzeni four-day ban; used whip above the permitted level (Jul 25-28)
Daniel Tudhope two-day ban; used his whip above the permitted level (25th-26th July)

**FOCUS**
Race distance increased by 8yds. Something of a tactical affair, the winner dictating a modest gallop and holding off some much higher-rated rivals.

## 4719 KING RICHARD III H'CAP — 6f
**3:40** (3:40) (Class 3) (0-90,92) 3-Y-O+ — **£9,056** (£2,695; £1,346; £673) **Stalls Low**

Form — RPR

2215 **1** **Robero**[10] 4353 5-10-0 **90**........................ SilvestreDeSousa 11 101
(Michael Easterby) *racd wd: cl up: led wl over 2f out: c wd home turn to stands rail: rdn over 1f out: kpt on strly* **7/2**[1]

0002 **2** 2 **Mishaal (IRE)**[19] 4013 7-8-13 **75**........................ JoeDoyle 10 79
(Michael Herrington) *cl up: led after 1f: hdd wl over 2f out and sn pushed along: rdn wl over 1f out: kpt on u.p fnl f* **25/1**

-126 **3** nk **Magical Effect (IRE)**[26] 3757 5-9-4 **80**........................ JamesSullivan 8 83+
(Ruth Carr) *dwlt and hld up in rr: hdwy on stands rail wl over 1f out: sn rdn and styd on strly fnl f* **13/2**

00-1 **4** ½ **Avon Breeze**[8] 4435 8-9-7 **88** 6ex........................ LewisEdmunds(5) 1 89
(Richard Whitaker) *t.k.h: trckd ldrs early: lost pl and pushed along over 2f out: rdn along on inner wl over 1f out: kpt on wl u.p fnl f* **11/2**[3]

4453 **5** 1 **Cool Bahamian (IRE)**[22] 3919 6-9-5 **81**........................(b) CharlesBishop 3 79
(Eve Johnson Houghton) *trckd ldrs: pushed along over 2f out: rdn wl over 1f out: sn drvn and kpt on same pce* **7/1**

2010 **6** 1½ **Courier**[10] 4375 5-9-12 **88**........................ BarryMcHugh 5 81
(Marjorie Fife) *led 1f: prom: effrt to chse ldng pair wl over 1f out: sn rdn and grad wknd* **20/1**

5020 **7** 1 **Russian Realm**[11] 4327 7-9-8 **84**........................ RobertWinston 9 74
(Paul Midgley) *midfield: hdwy to chse ldrs over 2f out: rdn along wl over 1f out: sn drvn and wknd appr fnl f* **10/1**

140- **8** ¾ **Bamber Bridge (IRE)**[283] 6950 3-9-10 **92**........................ PaulMulrennan 4 79
(Michael Dods) *dwlt: a towards rr* **9/2**[2]

5600 **9** 2 **God Willing**[25] 3792 6-9-7 **83**........................ TomEaves 7 64
(Declan Carroll) *chsd ldrs: rdn along wl over 1f out: sn drvn and wknd* **11/1**

16-5 **10** 1 **Tigerwolf (IRE)**[77] 2054 4-9-5 **81**........................(v1) GrahamLee 6 59
(Mick Channon) *a rr* **12/1**

1m 17.44s (0.54) **Going Correction** +0.275s/f (Good)
**WFA** 3 from 4yo+ 6lb **10 Ran SP% 115.3**
Speed ratings (Par 107): **107,104,103,103,101 99,98,97,94,93**
CSF £92.84 CT £445.75 TOTE £3.60: £1.40, £7.00, £2.20; EX 90.10 Trifecta £677.80.
**Owner** Alan Zheng **Bred** Mrs P C Burton & Mr R J Lampard **Trained** Sheriff Hutton, N Yorks

**FOCUS**
Race distance increased by 8yds. They raced away from the inside rail and headed towards the stands' side in the straight. Not many got into it, the first two being up there the whole way, and the winner built on his Ascot form.

## 4720 BRIAN ELLISON RACING MAIDEN STKS — 1m 2f 5y
**4:10** (4:11) (Class 5) 3-Y-O+ — **£3,881** (£1,155; £577; £288) **Stalls Low**

Form — RPR

**1** **Walton Street** 3-9-4 0........................ JamesDoyle 2 86+
(Charlie Appleby) *hld up in tch: hdwy on inner wl over 2f out: green and rdn to ld wl over 1f out: sn swtchd rt to stands' rail: clr appr fnl f: readily* **15/8**[2]

5 **2** 1¾ **Roddy (IRE)**[18] 4055 3-9-4 0........................ JamesSullivan 3 75
(Tom Tate) *hld up in rr: pushed along and hdwy on inner wl over 1f out: rdn and styd on wl fnl f* **9/1**

00 **3** ½ **Precision**[33] 3506 3-9-4 0........................ PhillipMakin 4 74
(Sir Michael Stoute) *trckd ldr 3f: cl up: pushed along 2f out: rdn wl over 1f out: sn drvn and kpt on same pce* **7/4**[1]

62 **4** 4 **Broadway Dreams**[7] 4474 3-9-4 0........................ SilvestreDeSousa 6 69
(Marjorie Fife) *led: rdn along and hdd 2f out: drvn wl over 1f out: sn one pce* **4/1**[3]

53 **5** *1 ½* **Fire Leopard**[18] 4055 3-8-13 0....(h¹) DanielTudhope 7 61
(David O'Meara) *trckd ldrs: hdwy on outer 3f out: rdn along 2f out: sn drvn and wknd* **16/1**

5300 **6** *21* **Trade Route (IRE)**[18] 4050 3-9-4 69.... AndreaAtzeni 5 21
(David Elsworth) *prom: trckd ldr after 3f: pushed along 3f out: rdn over 2f out: sn wknd* **16/1**

2m 16.12s (2.42) **Going Correction** +0.275s/f (Good) **6** Ran SP% **112.9**
Speed ratings (Par 103): **101,99,99,96,94 78**
CSF £18.67 TOTE £2.70: £1.60, £4.50; EX 21.10 Trifecta £47.90.
**Owner** Godolphin **Bred** Darley **Trained** Newmarket, Suffolk
■ Stewards' Enquiry : Phillip Makin three-day ban; weighed out heavy (25th-27th July)

**FOCUS**
Race distance increased by 8yds. An easy win for the Godolphin newcomer, who outclassed his rivals and was allowed to coast home from half a furlong out. This has been rated around the 4th.

## 4721 PONTEFRACT SQUASH & LEISURE CLUB H'CAP 1m 6y
4:40 (4:40) (Class 5) (0-70,68) 3-Y-O £3,881 (£1,155; £577; £288) Stalls Low

Form RPR
061 **1** **Edgar Allan Poe (IRE)**[7] 4473 3-9-3 64 6ex.... DanielTudhope 6 75
(Rebecca Bastiman) *trckd ldr: hdwy and cl up 2f out: rdn to ld over 1f out: sn edgd rt to stands rail: clr ins fnl f* **15/8²**

3423 **2** *2 ¾* **Golconda Prince (IRE)**[12] 4276 3-9-3 64.... PaulHanagan 1 69
(Richard Fahey) *led: pushed along 2f out: wd st to stands rail: hdd and drvn over 1f out: kpt on same pce* **6/4¹**

063 **3** *5* **Kilbaha Lady (IRE)**[10] 4058 3-9-3 64.... SilvestreDeSousa 7 58
(Nigel Tinkler) *dwlt and hld up in rr: hdwy over 3f out: chsd ldrs 2f out: rdn wl over 1f out: sn no imp* **7/1³**

0000 **4** *1 ¾* **Foxy Rebel**[20] 3975 3-8-3 50.... JamesSullivan 2 39
(Ruth Carr) *trckd ldrs: effrt on inner 2f out: sn rdn and wandered over 1f out: drvn and hung lft and rt ins fnl f: one pce* **25/1**

0-24 **5** *1 ¾* **Hellomoto**[12] 4276 3-8-13 60....(p) ShaneGray 5 45
(Kevin Ryan) *hld up in rr: effrt over 2f out: sn rdn and n.d* **12/1**

0011 **6** *8* **Ching Ching Lor (IRE)**[42] 3191 3-9-1 62.... TomEaves 8 29
(Declan Carroll) *trckd ldrs: pushed along wl over 2f out: sn rdn and wknd wl over 1f out* **10/1**

1m 49.26s (3.36) **Going Correction** +0.275s/f (Good) **6** Ran SP% **107.9**
Speed ratings (Par 100): **94,91,86,84,82 74**
CSF £4.61 CT £10.70 TOTE £2.60: £1.60, £1.20; EX 5.10 Trifecta £18.60.
**Owner** I B Barker / P Bastiman **Bred** Paul, Ben & Charlie Cartan **Trained** Cowthorpe, N Yorks

**FOCUS**
Race distance increased by 8yds. A modest affair dominated by the big two in the market.

## 4722 PEOPLE'S HOLDINGS APPRENTICE H'CAP 1m 2f 5y
5:10 (5:11) (Class 5) (0-75,76) 3-Y-O+ £3,881 (£1,155; £577; £288) Stalls Low

Form RPR
4065 **1** **Mysterial**[14] 4169 7-8-13 67....(v¹) GerO'Neill(7) 10 75
(Declan Carroll) *t.k.h: set gd pce: pushed along and jnd over 2f out: sn hdd and rdn: wd st and rdr dropped whip wl over 1f out: rallied u.p fnl f: led nr fin: gamely* **12/1**

1313 **2** *nk* **Canberra Cliffs (IRE)**[45] 3094 3-9-5 76.... GeorgeWood 6 84+
(Don Cantillon) *keen t.k.h: trckd wnr: smooth hdwy and cl up over 2f out: sn led: rdn over 1f out: drvn ins fnl f: hdd nr fin* **9/4¹**

-036 **3** *11* **Hernandoshideaway**[12] 4260 5-9-10 74....(bt) CallumRodriguez(3) 2 61
(Michael Dods) *dwlt: sn trcking ldrs and plld hrd: chsd ldng pair over 2f out and sn rdn: drvn over 1f out: sn one pce* **7/2³**

5300 **4** *1* **House Of Commons (IRE)**[60] 2586 4-9-9 75.... RayDawson(5) 1 60
(Michael Appleby) *in tch: hdwy to chse ldrs 4f out: rdn along wl over 2f out: sn one pce* **17/2**

41 **5** *2 ¾* **Paddy's Rock (IRE)**[10] 4345 6-8-10 57....(p) NathanEvans 5 36
(Lynn Siddall) *dwlt and hld up in rr: hdwy 4f out: rdn along over 2f out: plugged on fr over 1f out* **10/1**

0-11 **6** *8* **Exclusive Waters (IRE)**[8] 4439 7-8-13 63 6ex.... LewisEdmunds(3) 3 27
(Tina Jackson) *in tch: hdwy to trck ldrs over 4f out: rdn along 3f out: sn outpcd and bhd* **11/4²**

2303 **7** *11* **Amber Mystique**[10] 4344 4-9-4 70.... JoshQuinn(5) 4 13
(Kristin Stubbs) *dwlt: a rr* **25/1**

320- **8** *14* **Ingleby Spring (IRE)**[293] 6684 5-8-7 61.... SebastianWoods(7) 7
(Richard Fahey) *prom: pushed along over 3f out: rdn wl over 2f out: sn drvn and wknd* **33/1**

2m 16.5s (2.80) **Going Correction** +0.275s/f (Good)
**WFA** 3 from 4yo+ 10lb **8** Ran SP% **113.8**
Speed ratings (Par 103): **99,98,89,89,86 80,71,60**
CSF £38.96 CT £117.30 TOTE £9.30: £2.40, £1.30, £1.50; EX 30.70 Trifecta £114.30.
**Owner** Mrs Sarah Bryan **Bred** Ladyswood, Canning Down & D Farrington **Trained** Malton, N Yorks

**FOCUS**
Race distance increased by 8yds. The first two finished well clear in a race that concerned only them from some way out, and the winner has been rated to this year's form.
T/Plt: £110.80 to a £1 stake. Pool: £74,737.93 - 492.25 winning units T/Qpdt: £17.20 to a £1 stake. Pool: £6,337.80 - 272.35 winning units **Joe Rowntree**

# 4447 WOLVERHAMPTON (A.W) (L-H)
Tuesday, July 11

**OFFICIAL GOING: Tapeta: standard**
Wind: light breeze across Weather: Overcast, showers, some heavy

## 4723 FOLLOW @ATTHERACES ON TWITTER H'CAP 6f 20y (Tp)
1:55 (2:00) (Class 6) (0-60,63) 3-Y-O+ £2,425 (£721; £360; £180) Stalls Low

Form RPR
4402 **1** **Bogsnog (IRE)**[15] 4162 7-9-4 54.... JackGarritty 2 61
(Ruth Carr) *trckd ldrs: 3rd 2f out: hdwy into 2nd and rdn over 1f out: r.o wl to ld wl ins fnl f: pressed by clsng runner-up but jst hld on nr fin* **5/1³**

0441 **2** *hd* **Tooty Fruitti**[8] 4448 3-9-7 63 6ex.... PatCosgrave 5 68
(Jo Hughes) *hld up: plenty to do on outer 2f out: hdwy over 1f out: r.o strly fnl f: clsng on wnr nr fin: jst failed* **9/2²**

-546 **3** *¾* **Mythical Spirit (IRE)**[20] 3971 3-9-4 60.... LukeMorris 9 63
(James Tate) *mid-div on outer: hdwy and rdn over 1f out: r.o to take 3rd ins fnl f* **4/1¹**

4 **4** *shd* **Mags Well (IRE)**[18] 4061 3-8-12 59.... CliffordLee(5) 8 62
(Edmond Daniel Linehan, Ire) *led: pushed along 2f out: kicked 2 l clr over 1f out: clsd down by wnr ent fnl f: sn rdn: hdd and lost 3 pls last 150yds* **9/1**

3544 **5** *¾* **Yorkshire Rover**[8] 4447 3-8-4 53....(p¹) ConnorMurtagh(7) 3 54
(David Brown) *hld up: effrt on outer 2f out: sn drvn: rdn over 1f out: r.o ins fnl f: nvr nrr* **4/1¹**

4500 **6** *¾* **Essaka (IRE)**[32] 3545 5-9-3 53.... DavidProbert 4 52
(Tony Carroll) *slowly away: hld up: hdwy and rdn over 1f out: one pce fnl f* **25/1**

4350 **7** *¾* **Atlanta Belle (IRE)**[71] 2235 3-9-4 60.... FranBerry 12 56
(Chris Wall) *chsd ldr: drvn in 2nd over 1f out: sn rdn: weakend fnl f* **8/1**

6053 **8** *9* **Bingo George (IRE)**[42] 3185 4-9-2 52....(t¹) AndrewMullen 1 22
(Mark Rimell) *trckd ldrs on inner: drvn 2f out: wknd wl over 1f out: eased* **14/1**

6450 **9** *11* **Zone In**[11] 4302 3-9-1 57....(p¹) TonyHamilton 13
(Roger Fell) *in rr: pushed along 2f out: sn lost tch* **20/1**

1m 14.46s (-0.04) **Going Correction** -0.125s/f (Stan)
**WFA** 3 from 4yo+ 6lb **9** Ran SP% **111.2**
Speed ratings (Par 101): **95,94,93,93,92 91,90,78,63**
CSF £26.22 CT £94.86 TOTE £6.70: £1.90, £1.80, £1.70; EX 26.80 Trifecta £84.30.
**Owner** Facts & Figures **Bred** J R Weston **Trained** Huby, N Yorks

**FOCUS**
A moderate sprint handicap rated around the principals.

## 4724 INVEST CITY OF WOLVERHAMPTON CLASSIFIED CLAIMING STKS 6f 20y (Tp)
2:25 (2:30) (Class 5) 3-Y-O+ £3,072 (£914; £456; £228) Stalls Low

Form RPR
0336 **1** **Favourite Treat (USA)**[11] 4293 7-9-4 70....(e) JackGarritty 3 74
(Ruth Carr) *racd in 3rd: pushed along and wnt 2nd 2f out: rdn over 1f out: led ent fnl f: sn clr: comf* **6/4¹**

0603 **2** *3* **Elusivity (IRE)**[19] 4009 9-8-7 62....(p) KatherineGlenister(7) 2 61
(Conor Dore) *led: 1 l clr 2f out: rdn and narrow ld 1f out: sn hdd by wnr and 3rd: r.o again to regain 2nd last 100yds* **14/1**

2323 **3** *1* **Pushkin Museum (IRE)**[10] 4337 6-9-5 68.... ConnorMurtagh(7) 1 70
(Patrick Morris) *trckd ldr: relegated to 3rd 2f out: rdn and wnt 2nd ent fnl f: wknd and lost 2nd last 100yds* **11/4²**

2-20 **4** *¾* **Arctic Angel (IRE)**[26] 3758 4-9-8 67....(h) TomQueally 6 64
(James Fanshawe) *hld up: drvn 2f out: rdn over 1f out: one pce* **3/1³**

-021 **5** *1* **Point North (IRE)**[40] 3258 10-9-8 70....(b) LukeMorris 7 61
(John Balding) *hld up: drvn along 2f out: rdn over 1f out: no imp* **15/2**

1m 13.74s (-0.76) **Going Correction** -0.125s/f (Stan)
**WFA** 3 from 4yo+ 6lb **5** Ran SP% **110.1**
Speed ratings (Par 103): **100,96,94,93,92**
CSF £21.08 TOTE £2.20: £1.50, £4.70; EX 21.80 Trifecta £51.20.There was no bid for the winner.
**Owner** Paul Saxton & The Bottom Liners **Bred** Fares Farm Inc **Trained** Huby, N Yorks

**FOCUS**
A modest claimer; straightforward form.

## 4725 SIGNAL 107 MORE OF YOUR MUSIC NOVICE AUCTION STKS 7f 36y (Tp)
2:55 (2:57) (Class 6) 2-Y-O £2,425 (£721; £360; £180) Stalls High

Form RPR
032 **1** **Mrs Teasdale**[17] 4090 2-8-11 72....(p¹) LukeMorris 9 68
(Archie Watson) *chsd ldr: rdn along 2f out: relegated to 3rd over 1f out: rallied u.p fnl f: led nr fin* **4/1²**

**2** *hd* **Oswald (IRE)** 2-9-2 0.... PatCosgrave 5 73
(Robyn Brisland) *trckd ldrs: pushed along 2f out: 2nd whn drvn over 1f out: rdn and led briefly wl ins fnl f: r.o: hdd nr fin* **11/2³**

6 **3** *½* **Danzan (IRE)**[20] 3965 2-9-2 0.... DavidProbert 8 71
(Andrew Balding) *led: kicked 2 l clr 2f out: 1 l ahd and rdn ent fnl f: no ex and ct by front two wl ins fnl f* **9/4¹**

00 **4** *8* **Four Fifty Three**[20] 3965 2-9-2 0.... ThomasBrown 1 52+
(Mark H Tompkins) *mid-div: rdn over 1f out: styd on to take 4th fnl f* **250/1**

**5** *1 ¾* **Sauchiehall Street (IRE)** 2-8-11 0.... MitchGodwin(5) 11 47+
(Sylvester Kirk) *hld up: pushed along and sme hdwy on outer 2f out: reminder 1f out: one pce* **6/1**

**6** *nse* **Uncovered** 2-9-2 0.... RichardKingscote 4 47
(Tom Dascombe) *mid-div: hdwy on outer into 4th 2f out: drvn over 1f out: no ex* **9/4¹**

0 **7** *½* **Bullseye Bullet**[36] 3390 2-9-2 0.... SteveDrowne 2 46
(Mark Usher) *hld up: pushed along 2f out: sn wknd* **150/1**

6 **8** *nk* **Odds On Oli**[12] 4259 2-9-2 0.... TonyHamilton 6 45
(Richard Fahey) *racd in rr: pushed along over 1f out: lost tch* **22/1**

06 **9** *2 ¼* **My Guy (IRE)**[77] 2052 2-9-2 0.... LiamKeniry 3 40
(J S Moore) *mid-div: pushed along and lost plcd 2f out: rdn over 1f out: fdd* **80/1**

0 **10** *6* **Maveway (IRE)**[43] 3156 2-8-11 0.... AndrewMullen 7 20
(David Evans) *trckd ldrs: pushed along and lost pl 2f out: wknd* **66/1**

**11** *hd* **Rum Ration** 2-9-2 0.... JoeyHaynes 10 25
(Mark H Tompkins) *a in rr: pushed along and wknd fr 2f out* **150/1**

1m 30.48s (1.68) **Going Correction** -0.125s/f (Stan) **11** Ran SP% **120.0**
Speed ratings (Par 92): **85,84,84,75,73 73,72,72,69,62 62**
CSF £26.46 TOTE £5.10: £1.50, £1.70, £1.40; EX 33.10 Trifecta £72.10.
**Owner** W J A Nash **Bred** Whatton Manor Stud **Trained** Upper Lambourn, W Berks

**FOCUS**
An ordinary race and steadily run, with the 1-2-3 racing 2-3-1 for much of the way and finishing clear of the others.

## 4726 WOLVERHAMPTON - VOTED BEST SMALL RACECOURSE (MIDLANDS) H'CAP (DIV I) 7f 36y (Tp)
3:25 (3:28) (Class 6) (0-60,60) 3-Y-O+ £2,425 (£721; £360; £180) Stalls High

Form RPR
503 **1** **Bell Heather (IRE)**[147] 729 4-9-5 60.... ConnorMurtagh(7) 3 69
(Patrick Morris) *trckd ldrs: 4th gng wl 2f out: hdwy into 2nd wl over 1f out: sn led: shkn up and 1 l clr ent fnl. r.o but being clsd down nr fin* **10/1**

-603 **2** *hd* **Loveatfirstsight**[15] 4162 4-9-9 57....(p¹) LiamJones 4 66
(Michael Attwater) *mid-div: hdwy into 4th over 1f out: rdn and r.o wl to take 2nd ent fnl f: clsng on wnr nr fin* **15/2**

0003 **3** *2* **Oakley Pride (IRE)**[36] 3391 3-8-13 60....(vt) CliffordLee(5) 2 61
(Gay Kelleway) *mid-div: drvn wl over 1f out: rdn and r.o to take 3rd ent fnl f* **11/1**

3050 **4** *4* **Provoking (USA)**[7] 4458 4-9-1 49.... FranBerry 8 43
(David Evans) *hld up: mod hdwy and drvn over 1f out: r.o one pce fnl f* **12/1**

0351 **5** *shd* **Viola Park**[15] 4162 3-9-2 58....(p) RyanPowell 6 49
(Ronald Harris) *prom: 2nd 2f out: rdn over 1f out: no ex ins fnl f* **10/3¹**

630 **6** *2 ½* **Cryptonite (IRE)**[30] 3624 3-9-3 59....(p) AndrewMullen 5 43
(Michael Appleby) *mid-div: rdn over 1f out: one pce fnl f* **11/2³**

-500 **7** *nse* **Men United (FR)**[171] 362 4-8-8 47.... KevinLundie(5) 7 36
(Roy Bowring) *t.k.h: led: 2 l clr 2f out: drvn and hdd over 1f out: rdn and no ex* **33/1**

0150 **8** *nk* **Fossa**[15] 4162 7-9-0 **51**..........(h) JordanVaughan(3) 10 38
(Mark Brisbourne) *hld up on outer: rdn wl over 1f out: no imp* **66/1**

0-46 **9** *17* **Silk Mill Blue**[22] 3897 3-9-0 **56**.......... FrannyNorton 1
(Richard Whitaker) *hld up: a bhd* **7/2**[2]

00-0 **10** *14* **Ciaras Cookie (IRE)**[182] 153 5-9-0 **48**..........(t) LiamKeniry 11
(Mandy Rowland) *slowly away: a in rr* **150/1**

0060 **11** *2 1/4* **Arize (IRE)**[48] 2962 4-9-10 **58**.......... PatCosgrave 9
(Jim Boyle) *chsd ldrs: 3rd 2f out: lost pl qckly and heavily eased* **8/1**

1m 28.69s (-0.11) **Going Correction** -0.125s/f (Stan)
**WFA** 3 from 4yo+ 8lb **11** Ran SP% **113.8**
Speed ratings (Par 101): **95,94,92,87,87 84,84,84,65,49 46**
CSF £79.76 CT £601.97 TOTE £10.50: £2.90, £2.40, £2.90; EX 82.00 Trifecta £448.30.
**Owner** Dr Marwan Koukash **Bred** Tinnakill Bloodstock & Joe Osborne **Trained** Prescot, Merseyside

**FOCUS**
A moderate handicap run at a good pace.

## 4727 WOLVERHAMPTON - VOTED BEST SMALL RACECOURSE (MIDLANDS) H'CAP (DIV II) 7f 36y (Tp)

**3:55** (3:58) (Class 6) (0-60,59) 3-Y-O+ **£2,425** (£721; £360; £180) **Stalls** High

Form RPR

5000 **1** **Beadlam (IRE)**[21] 3934 4-9-9 **56**..........(p[1]) TonyHamilton 6 66
(Roger Fell) *trckd ldr: hdwy to ld over 1f out: sn drvn 2 l clr: rdn ins fnl f: diminishing advantage but hld on under hand riding last 50yds* **33/1**

4233 **2** *nk* **Bruny Island (IRE)**[8] 4447 3-9-4 **59**..........(h) StevieDonohoe 5 67+
(Charlie Fellowes) *hld up: plenty to do 2f out: hdwy on inner over 1f out: rdn ins fnl f: r.o wl: too much to do* **1/1**[1]

5354 **3** *4 1/2* **Satchville Flyer**[10] 4339 6-9-10 **57**.......... FranBerry 9 55
(David Evans) *hld up: last 2f out: hdwy on inner wl over 1f out: rdn and rn to take 3rd ins fnl f* **7/1**[2]

0602 **4** *hd* **Black Truffle (FR)**[15] 4163 7-9-5 **52**.......... SteveDrowne 8 50
(Mark Usher) *mid-div: n.m.r over 1f out: rdn and hdwy ent fnl f: r.o* **12/1**

0056 **5** *1* **Jazz Legend (USA)**[14] 4179 4-9-3 **50**..........(h) JimmyQuinn 3 45
(Olly Murphy) *trckd ldrs: pushed along wl over 1f out: rdn and one pce fnl f* **8/1**[3]

0-60 **6** *1/2* **Kuiper Belt (USA)**[12] 4262 3-9-2 **57**.......... TomQueally 7 48
(David Lanigan) *hld up: rdn over 1f out: mod late hdwy* **9/1**

3605 **7** *3/4* **Camaradorie (IRE)**[28] 3701 3-9-0 **58**.......... SimonPearce(3) 1 47
(Lydia Pearce) *trckd ldrs: effrt on inner wl over 1f out: rdn and wknd ent fnl f* **18/1**

0031 **8** *2 1/4* **Zebelini (IRE)**[15] 4163 5-8-10 **48**.......... KevinLundie(5) 11 35
(Roy Bowring) *mid-div on outer: effrt 2f out: sn on heels of ldrs: rdn and wknd 1f out* **8/1**[3]

5440 **9** *2 1/4* **Little Indian**[55] 2732 7-9-5 **52**.......... LiamJones 10 33
(J R Jenkins) *hld up: drvn along over 1f out: no imp* **40/1**

2030 **10** *3/4* **National Service (USA)**[7] 4458 6-8-13 **46**..........(tp) PaddyAspell 4 25
(Clare Ellam) *mid-div: effrt and n.m.r over 1f out: no ch after* **50/1**

-000 **11** *1 3/4* **Molten Lava (IRE)**[27] 3723 5-9-4 **58**..........(b) PatrickVaughan(7) 2 33
(Christian Williams) *t.k.h: led: drvn and hdd over 1f out: wknd qckly* **40/1**

4000 **12** *nse* **Bridal March**[15] 4163 3-9-1 **56**..........(p) FrannyNorton 12 28
(John Mackie) *trckd ldrs: rdn and fdd wl over 1f out* **66/1**

1m 28.69s (-0.11) **Going Correction** -0.125s/f (Stan)
**WFA** 3 from 4yo+ 8lb **12** Ran SP% **118.5**
Speed ratings (Par 101): **95,94,89,89,88 87,86,84,81,80 78,78**
CSF £65.95 CT £293.21 TOTE £20.60: £7.10, £1.10, £2.40; EX 86.60 Trifecta £316.30.
**Owner** Smarty Socks Racing **Bred** Pipe View Stud **Trained** Nawton, N Yorks

**FOCUS**
The surprise winner, ignoring the free-running leader Molten Lava, was able to dominate the chasing pack and looked to pinch this. She took over at about the 2f the pole, and going off the on-screen timer she was around a second slower to that point than the leader in the first division, while the runner-up and third in this race were out the back and forced to wait until the straight to make their move.

## 4728 THANKS MICK SMITH FOR 15 YEARS SERVICE H'CAP 7f 36y (Tp)

**4:25** (4:28) (Class 5) (0-75,75) 3-Y-O+ **£3,234** (£962; £481; £240) **Stalls** High

Form RPR

554 **1** **The Yellow Bus**[70] 2285 4-9-2 **70**.......... DarraghKeenan(7) 10 79
(John Butler) *trckd ldrs: hdwy over 1f out: pushed along to ld ent fnl f: sn 1 l clr: kpt up to work to maintain advantage: readily* **16/1**

33-0 **2** *3/4* **Energia Flavio (BRZ)**[73] 2140 7-9-13 **74**..........(p) FranBerry 11 81+
(Patrick Morris) *hld up: last 2f out: swtchd to outer and hdwy wl over 1f out: rdn and r.o strly to take 2nd wl ins fnl f* **22/1**

5-00 **3** *3/4* **Beauden Barrett**[6] 4495 4-9-12 **73**..........(t[1]) DavidProbert 2 78
(Jeremy Gask) *hld up: drvn and hdwy over 1f out: sn rdn: r.o wl to take 3rd ins fnl f* **25/1**

-100 **4** *shd* **Dubai Art**[27] 3709 3-9-6 **75**.......... TonyHamilton 3 77
(Richard Fahey) *t.k.h: trckd ldrs: drvn to ld over 1f out: sn hdd by wnr: rdn and no ex* **8/1**[3]

-006 **5** *nk* **Northdown**[14] 4186 3-9-4 **73**..........(p) StevieDonohoe 8 74
(David Lanigan) *mid-div: hdwy over 1f out: rdn and r.o ins fnl f* **33/1**

-036 **6** *1 1/2* **Marbooh (IRE)**[21] 3934 4-9-12 **73**..........(vt[1]) SamJames 7 73
(David O'Meara) *mid-div: pushed along over 1f out: one pce* **12/1**

0432 **7** *hd* **Here's Two**[25] 3772 4-9-6 **67**.......... PatCosgrave 12 67
(Ron Hodges) *chsd ldrs on outer: pushed along 2f out: rdn and wknd 1f out* **20/1**

3055 **8** *nk* **Kachess**[17] 4081 3-9-1 **70**.......... RichardKingscote 9 66
(Tom Dascombe) *led: drvn and hdd over 1f out: no ex* **16/1**

63-2 **9** *1* **Narjes**[42] 3188 3-9-2 **71**..........(h) TomQueally 6 64
(James Fanshawe) *hld up: wd: drvn along on outer wl over 1f out: sn rdn: no imp* **1/1**[1]

4235 **10** *1/2* **Flying Fantasy**[14] 4185 5-9-5 **66**.......... WilliamBuick 4 61
(Michael Appleby) *hld up: pushed along 3f out: effrt on outside 2f out: sn rdn and no ex* **6/1**[2]

0040 **11** *1 1/4* **Mezmaar**[34] 3454 8-9-8 **69**..........(h) SteveDrowne 1 60
(Mark Usher) *hld up: rdn wl over 1f out: wknd* **12/1**

1000 **12** *15* **Harry Holland**[11] 4293 5-9-3 **64**.......... KevinStott 5 15
(Oliver Greenall) *chsd ldr: pushed along 3f out: drvn and wknd fr 2f out* **80/1**

1m 28.86s (0.06) **Going Correction** -0.125s/f (Stan)
**WFA** 3 from 4yo+ 8lb **12** Ran SP% **119.7**
Speed ratings (Par 103): **94,93,92,92,91 90,89,89,88,87 86,69**
CSF £330.43 CT £8590.69 TOTE £19.90: £4.30, £4.50, £6.20; EX 317.80 Trifecta £4389.70.
**Owner** Alex Percy **Bred** D Phelan **Trained** Newmarket, Suffolk

**FOCUS**
A fair handicap run at a steady pace, and the winner has been rated back to her early best.

## 4729 FOLLOW AT THE RACES ON INSTAGRAM MAIDEN FILLIES' STKS 1m 1f 104y (Tp)

**4:55** (4:56) (Class 5) 3-4-Y-O **£3,072** (£914; £456; £228) **Stalls** Low

Form RPR

426 **1** **Glittering Jewel (USA)**[37] 3366 3-9-0 **88**.......... WilliamBuick 4 77+
(Charlie Appleby) *mde all: kicked 2 l clr 2f out: sn wl in command: readily extended advantage ent fnl f: r.o wl under minimal hand riding: v easily* **1/9**[1]

4 **2** *4 1/2* **Alfa Queen (IRE)**[29] 3649 3-9-0 **0**.......... KevinStott 3 68
(Iain Jardine) *trckd ldrs: pushed along and wnt 2nd 2f out: sn rdn and r.o but no ch w wnr* **80/1**

**3** *3 1/4* **Jafetica** 3-9-0 **0**.......... TomQueally 7 61
(James Fanshawe) *t.k.h: mid-div: hdwy into 3rd wl over 1f out: drvn and rdn briefly ent fnl f: one pce* **9/2**[2]

65 **4** *7* **Princess Ophelia**[12] 4275 3-8-11 **0**.......... AlistairRawlinson(3) 5 46
(Michael Appleby) *hld up: hdwy 2f out: rdn over 1f out: one pce* **40/1**

0 **5** *2 1/2* **Chocolate Account (USA)**[11] 4300 3-9-0 **0**.......... AntonioFresu 2 41
(Ed Dunlop) *hld up: drvn along 2f out: no hdwy* **25/1**[3]

06 **6** *3/4* **Artic Nel**[12] 4274 3-9-0 **0**.......... StevieDonohoe 1 39
(Ian Williams) *a in rr: drvn 2f out: no imp* **100/1**

06 **7** *4 1/2* **Xylophone**[19] 4003 3-9-0 **0**.......... DavidProbert 6 30
(Archie Watson) *chsd wnr: passed for 2nd 2f out: sn wknd* **25/1**[3]

2m 0.82s (0.02) **Going Correction** -0.125s/f (Stan) **7** Ran SP% **120.5**
Speed ratings (Par 100): **94,90,87,80,78 78,74**
CSF £41.25 TOTE £1.10: £1.02, £15.80; EX 16.50 Trifecta £51.50.
**Owner** Godolphin **Bred** Darley **Trained** Newmarket, Suffolk

**FOCUS**
Not much of a contest.

## 4730 SIGNAL 107 MORE OF YOUR MUSIC H'CAP 1m 4f 51y (Tp)

**5:25** (5:25) (Class 5) (0-75,75) 3-Y-O+ **£3,072** (£914; £456; £228) **Stalls** Low

Form RPR

0000 **1** **Royal Reserve**[46] 3036 4-9-10 **74**.......... JoshDoyle(3) 7 82+
(David O'Meara) *hld up: hdwy and pushed along over 1f out: str run to ld ent fnl f: rdn and r.o wl* **22/1**

6-40 **2** *3/4* **Our Boy (IRE)**[36] 3392 3-8-13 **72**.......... FranBerry 4 79
(David Evans) *in rr: hdwy gng wl on inner over 1f out: rdn to take 2nd ent fnl f: r.o but a hld by wnr* **9/1**

325 **3** *1 1/2* **Waterville Dancer (IRE)**[95] 1607 3-9-2 **75**.......... RyanTate 3 79+
(Richard Hughes) *hld up: drvn along and hdwy wl over 1f out: rdn to take 3rd ins fnl f: nvr nrr* **8/1**

4262 **4** *3/4* **Many Waters (USA)**[35] 3425 3-9-1 **74**.......... DavidProbert 8 77
(Andrew Balding) *mid-div: hdwy over 1f out: rdn and one pce fnl f* **9/4**[1]

21 **5** *3* **Stepney**[77] 2062 3-8-12 **71**.......... PatCosgrave 6 69
(Robyn Brisland) *mid-div: pushed along over 1f out: reminder and no ex ent fnl f* **12/1**

0410 **6** *1* **Infiniti (IRE)**[14] 4187 4-8-6 **58**.......... JaneElliott(5) 10 54+
(Barry Leavy) *chsd ldr: led 3f out: pushed along and 2 l clr wl over 1f out: rdn and hdd ent fnl f: no ex* **25/1**

5434 **7** *2 3/4* **Touwari (IRE)**[13] 4202 3-8-12 **71**..........(b) RobertTart 12 63
(John Gosden) *led: hdd 3f out: sn drvn and wknd* **15/2**[3]

1600 **8** *1 3/4* **Smiley Bagel (IRE)**[28] 3683 4-9-8 **69**.......... RichardKingscote 2 57
(Ed Walker) *trckd ldrs: pushed along 3f out: rdn 2f out: wknd* **10/1**

2235 **9** *5* **Deep Challenger (IRE)**[24] 3817 5-9-11 **72**.......... WilliamBuick 11 52
(Jamie Osborne) *chsd ldrs: pushed along 3f out: drvn to take 3rd wl over 1f out: sn no ex and fdd* **5/1**[2]

6644 **10** *4 1/2* **Jack Of Diamonds (IRE)**[12] 4257 8-9-3 **69**..........(b) MitchGodwin(5) 9 42
(Roger Teal) *mid-div: drvn along 3f out: rdn and dropped to last 2f out: lost tch* **14/1**

40 **R** **Soiesauvage (FR)**[17] 4073 6-9-9 **70**..........(t) TrevorWhelan 1
(Sophie Leech) *planted feet and ref to leave stalls* **66/1**

2m 38.32s (-2.48) **Going Correction** -0.125s/f (Stan)
**WFA** 3 from 4yo+ 12lb **11** Ran SP% **113.4**
Speed ratings (Par 103): **103,102,101,101,99 98,96,95,92,89**
CSF £197.85 CT £1725.71 TOTE £23.70: £6.00, £3.30, £2.00; EX 222.10 Trifecta £1396.80.
**Owner** Royal Guinness Reserve Partnership **Bred** New England, Myriad & Watership Down **Trained** Upper Helmsley, N Yorks

**FOCUS**
A fair handicap and they looked to go fast enough, with the first three finishers coming from the last three places.
T/Jkpt: Not Won. T/Plt: £855.50 to a £1 stake. Pool: £84,613.51 - 72.20 winning units T/Qpdt: £295.40 to a £1 stake. Pool: £6,428.95 - 16.10 winning units **Keith McHugh**

# 4488 BATH (L-H)

Wednesday, July 12

**OFFICIAL GOING: Good to firm (9.2)**
Wind: light breeze Weather: warm, sunny intervals

## 4731 CREST NICHOLSON BATH RIVERSIDE H'CAP (BATH SUMMER SPRINT SERIES QUALIFIER) 5f 10y

**6:10** (6:10) (Class 6) (0-60,62) 3-Y-O+ **£2,264** (£673; £336; £168) **Stalls** Centre

Form RPR

0050 **1** **Lucky Clover**[6] 4532 6-9-3 **53**..........(p) DaneO'Neill 5 62
(Malcolm Saunders) *disp ld tl gained advantage on own over 1f out: 1 l clr ent fnl f: kpt up to work: r.o wl: comf* **7/1**[3]

0504 **2** *1 3/4* **Ask The Guru**[22] 3942 7-8-7 **48**..........(b) DavidEgan(5) 3 51
(Michael Attwater) *trckd ldrs: wnt 3rd 2f out: chsd wnr ent fnl f: rdn and r.o but no imp* **14/1**

5232 **3** *1 1/4* **Captain Ryan**[25] 3811 6-9-12 **62**.......... TimmyMurphy 2 64
(Geoffrey Deacon) *trckd ldrs: effrt on inner and hmpd over 1f out: sn in clr: rdn and r.o to take 3rd wl ins fnl f* **4/1**[1]

3010 **4** *hd* **Jaganory (IRE)**[13] 4256 5-9-3 **58**..........(p) LuluStanford(5) 7 55
(Christopher Mason) *mid-div: effrt on outer 2f out: rdn over 1f out: r.o ins fnl f* **8/1**

2635 **5** *2 1/4* **Mambo Spirit (IRE)**[48] 2995 13-9-10 **60**.......... MartinDwyer 4 49
(Tony Newcombe) *in rr: pushed along 2f out: n.m.r over 1f out: rdn and sme late hdwy whn in clr* **10/1**

4050 **6** *shd* **Tess Graham**[15] 4174 3-8-5 **46** oh1..........(p) RoystonFfrench 6 33
(Sarah Hollinshead) *mid-div: pushed along 2f out: rdn over 1f out: r.o one pce* **50/1**

6433 **7** *shd* **Mostashreqah**[16] 4148 4-8-10 **46** oh1..........(p) SilvestreDeSousa 9 35
(Milton Bradley) *disp ld tl rdn and wknd over 1f out* **9/1**

5030 **8** *shd* **Rat Catcher (IRE)**[8] 4458 7-8-10 **46** oh1....................(b) TomMarquand 1 34
(Lisa Williamson) *mid-div: pushed along over 2f out: rdn 1f out: no imp* **40/1**

6524 **9** *3 ½* **Double Spin**[39] 3313 3-9-6 **61**........................................ MartinLane 10 35
(Robert Cowell) *chsd ldrs: pushed along over 2f out: rdn and wknd appr fnl f* **10/1**

5431 **10** *1 ¼* **Staffa (IRE)**[20] 4009 4-9-5 **55**.................................... PatCosgrave 11 26+
(Denis Coakley) *rrd in stalls and v.s.a: a bhd* **9/2**[2]

4004 **11** *1 ¾* **Glam'Selle**[44] 3141 3-8-5 **46** oh1..............................(p) RyanPowell 12 9
(Ronald Harris) *mid-div on outer: rdn over 1f out: wknd* **40/1**

0530 **12** *4* **Three C's (IRE)**[12] 4302 3-9-3 **58**..................................(tp) FranBerry 8 7
(David Dennis) *in rr: drvn 3f out: rdn 2f out: no rspnse* **7/1**[3]

1m 0.18s (-2.32) **Going Correction** -0.20s/f (Firm)
**WFA** 3 from 4yo+ 5lb **12** Ran SP% **116.0**
Speed ratings (Par 101): **110,107,105,104,101 101,100,100,95,93 90,84**
CSF £97.31 CT £446.10 TOTE £8.30: £2.80, £4.10, £1.90; EX 124.10 Trifecta £417.90.
**Owner** Paul Nicholas & M S Saunders **Bred** Cobhall Court Stud **Trained** Green Ore, Somerset
■ Stewards' Enquiry : David Egan two-day ban: guilty of careless riding (Jul 26-27)

**FOCUS**
Despite 20mm of rain over the previous 24 hours the ground was still officially good to firm. A low-grade opener with the winner keeping out of the way of some of the trouble in behind.

## 4732 BRAKES H'CAP 5f 10y
**6:40** (6:40) (Class 4) (0-85,83) 3-Y-O+ **£6,469** (£1,925; £962; £481) **Stalls** Centre

Form RPR

5000 **1** **Union Rose**[27] 3741 5-9-11 **83**........................................ FranBerry 4 92
(Ronald Harris) *chsd ldrs: hdwy over 2f out: pushed along over 1f out: led ent fnl f: rdn and r.o wl to assert last 150yds* **7/1**

-331 **2** *2* **Trick Of The Light (IRE)**[40] 3278 3-8-12 **80**.................. DavidEgan[(5)] 2 80
(Roger Varian) *mid-div: pushed along over 1f out: rdn ent fnl f: r.o to take 2nd last 75yds* **5/4**[1]

660- **3** *nk* **Discreet Hero (IRE)**[291] 6793 4-9-10 **82**................(t) SilvestreDeSousa 1 85+
(Simon Crisford) *hld up on inner: sltly hmpd by 4th horse 1f out: sn in clr: r.o wl to take 3rd wl ins fnl f* **6/1**[3]

3411 **4** *½* **Fethiye Boy**[5] 4581 3-9-4 **81** 6ex.................................... RyanPowell 5 78
(Ronald Harris) *led: 1 l clr 2f out: drvn over 1f out: hdd ent fnl f: rdn and no ex* **7/2**[2]

-641 **5** *1 ¼* **Ginzan**[15] 4178 9-9-10 **82**............................................. PatCosgrave 6 76
(Malcolm Saunders) *hld up: pushed along 2f out: rdn wl over 1f out: no imp* **8/1**

40-3 **6** *1 ¼* **Shackled N Drawn (USA)**[24] 3865 5-9-2 **74**............... TomMarquand 3 64
(Peter Hedger) *trckd ldr: pushed along over 1f out: rdn and wknd ent fnl f* **16/1**

1m 0.31s (-2.19) **Going Correction** -0.20s/f (Firm)
**WFA** 3 from 4yo+ 5lb **6** Ran SP% **110.4**
Speed ratings (Par 105): **109,105,105,104,102 100**
CSF £15.80 TOTE £8.70: £3.00, £1.90; EX 19.80 Trifecta £100.50.
**Owner** Adrian Evans **Bred** Home Farm **Trained** Earlswood, Monmouths
■ Stewards' Enquiry : Ryan Powell two-day ban: careless riding (Jul 26-27)

**FOCUS**
A strongly run event saw the well-backed winner capitalise on his drop in the weights.

## 4733 BLUEFIN INSURANCE H'CAP (BATH SUMMER STAYERS' SERIES QUALIFIER) 1m 5f 11y
**7:10** (7:10) (Class 6) (0-60,62) 4-Y-O+ **£2,587** (£770; £384; £192) **Stalls** High

Form RPR

4226 **1** **Innoko (FR)**[36] 3428 7-9-5 **58**.........................................(h) PatCosgrave 6 65
(Robert Stephens) *hld up: hdwy 4f out: trckd ldrs 3f out: pushed along to ld 2f out: rdn and 3 l clr 1f out: pushed out ins fnl f: winning margin reduced nr fin* **6/1**[3]

/20- **2** *¾* **Londonia**[20] 7739 5-9-7 **60**..........................................(t) TomMarquand 10 65
(Graeme McPherson) *hld up last: pushed along and hdwy 3f out: 4th whn rdn over 1f out: sn wnt 3rd: r.o strly ins fnl f to take 2nd nr fin* **3/1**[2]

4412 **3** *½* **Hope Is High**[23] 3916 4-9-4 **57**................................ SilvestreDeSousa 4 61
(John Berry) *chsd clr ldr: tk clsr order 5f out: hdwy to ld over 3f out: rdn whn hdd 2f out: rallied: r.o ent fnl f: lost 2nd nr fin* **6/4**[1]

2333 **4** *6* **Halling's Wish**[15] 4181 7-9-9 **62**................................(b) TimmyMurphy 9 57
(Gary Moore) *mid-div: wnt 3rd 4f out: ev ch in 2nd 3f out: pushed along 2f out: rdn and wknd ent fnl f* **12/1**

0-31 **5** *5* **Wassail**[27] 3756 4-8-7 **49**........................................ CallumShepherd[(3)] 7 36
(Ed de Giles) *mid-div: hdwy over 3f out: sn drvn: rdn 2f out: one pce* **6/1**[3]

33-5 **6** *2 ¼* **Mr Lando**[28] 3724 8-9-1 **57**...................................... NoelGarbutt[(3)] 3 41
(Johnny Farrelly) *led: 6 l clr after 5f: much reduced ld 5f out: hdd over 3f out: drvn and wknd* **25/1**

5166 **7** *6* **Kay Sera**[56] 2722 9-9-0 **53**............................................ MartinDwyer 5 27
(Tony Newcombe) *hld up: effrt 5f out: chsng ldrs 3f out: rdn and wknd 2f out* **25/1**

505 **8** *16* **Skylark Lady (IRE)**[26] 3775 4-9-2 **55**.......................(p) CharlesBishop 2 4
(Nikki Evans) *racd in 3rd tl lost a pl 4f out: rdn and lost tch fr 3f out* **50/1**

2m 49.15s (-2.85) **Going Correction** -0.20s/f (Firm) **8** Ran SP% **110.9**
Speed ratings (Par 101): **100,99,99,95,92 91,87,77**
CSF £22.74 CT £38.25 TOTE £6.20: £1.90, £1.80, £1.10; EX 23.70 Trifecta £68.80.
**Owner** Threes Company **Bred** Marquise Soledad De Moratalla **Trained** Penhow, Newport

**FOCUS**
A modest staying handicap but the winner landed some market support on his first run for a new stable.

## 4734 VERNON LEE EIGHTIETH BIRTHDAY CELEBRATION H'CAP 1m 2f 37y
**7:40** (7:40) (Class 6) (0-60,59) 3-Y-O+ **£2,587** (£770; £384; £192) **Stalls** Low

Form RPR

0554 **1** **Henryhudsonbridge (USA)**[8] 4470 5-9-1 **55**............(bt) JordanUys[(7)] 6 60
(John Flint) *mid-div: hdwy 4f out: 3rd 2f out: drvn over 1f out: rdn and led ent fnl f: r.o: pressed nr fin: but hld on wl* **8/1**

-054 **2** *hd* **Eugenic**[32] 3575 6-8-12 **50**....................................... DavidEgan[(5)] 9 55
(Rod Millman) *mid-div: hdwy into 3rd 3f out: drvn 2f out: rdn over 1f out: ev ch ent fnl f: r.o but jst hld by wnr* **9/2**

5013 **3** *½* **Mamnoon (IRE)**[25] 3809 4-9-12 **59**...........................(b) FranBerry 3 63
(Roy Brotherton) *disp 2nd tl wnt tl wnt 2nd on own over 3f out: rdn 2f out: ev ch and kpt on u.p fnl f* **4/1**[3]

5050 **4** *nk* **Just Fred (IRE)**[25] 3805 4-8-12 **45**..........................(t) JimmyQuinn 4 48
(Neil Mulholland) *hld up: pushed along 3f out: hdwy 2f out: rdn ent fnl f: styd on: nrst fin* **33/1**

0522 **5** *nk* **Eben Dubai (IRE)**[7] 4494 5-9-5 **52**.............................. MartinDwyer 7 55
(Tracey Barfoot-Saunt) *led: 6 l clr 4f out: stl healthy ld 3f out: reduced ld and drvn 2f out: sn rdn: hdd ent fnl f: no ex* **5/2**[2]

0246 **6** *59* **Shirataki (IRE)**[23] 3916 9-8-10 **50**........................... MollyKing[(7)] 2
(Peter Hiatt) *slowly away: in rr: drvn over 3f out: sn rdn and lost tch: eased* **40/1**

0564 **7** *9* **Bicolour (USA)**[7] 4493 3-9-0 **57**........................... SilvestreDeSousa 1
(Mark Johnston) *disp 2nd tl over 3f out: sn rdn: wknd qckly: heavily eased* **9/4**[1]

2m 9.32s (-1.68) **Going Correction** -0.20s/f (Firm)
**WFA** 3 from 4yo+ 10lb **7** Ran SP% **114.0**
Speed ratings (Par 101): **98,97,97,97,96 49,42**
CSF £43.12 CT £165.90 TOTE £9.70: £3.10, £2.30; EX 50.00 Trifecta £377.10.
**Owner** J L Flint **Bred** Eureka Thoroughbred Farm **Trained** Kenfig Hill, Bridgend

**FOCUS**
A strong pace set by the eventual fifth and the first two home were patiently ridden.

## 4735 EDMUNDSON ELECTRICAL H'CAP 5f 160y
**8:10** (8:12) (Class 6) (0-55,56) 3-Y-O+ **£2,587** (£770; £384; £192) **Stalls** Centre

Form RPR

5504 **1** **Burauq**[8] 4467 5-8-7 **46** oh1..........................................(v) LuluStanford[(5)] 5 56
(Milton Bradley) *prom: sn trcking ldrs: hdwy to ld over 1f out: rdn ent fnl f: sn 2 l clr: r.o wl: readily* **11/2**[3]

6433 **2** *2* **Wedgewood Estates**[25] 3811 6-9-7 **55**....................... TomMarquand 8 59
(Tony Carroll) *mid-div: pushed along and hdwy 2f out: rdn and wnt 2nd ent fnl f: r.o but no imp on wnr* **4/1**[2]

0-00 **3** *½* **Angelito**[56] 2724 8-9-2 **50**............................................ MartinDwyer 1 52
(Tony Newcombe) *chsd ldrs: rdn 2f out: rdn and ev ch 1f out: r.o one pce fnl f* **11/2**[3]

-004 **4** *2 ¾* **Tally's Song**[16] 4149 4-8-12 **46** oh1............................(p) JimmyQuinn 15 39
(Grace Harris) *trckd ldrs: rdn over 1f out: styd on one pce* **16/1**

4656 **5** *1 ½* **Catalinas Diamond (IRE)**[16] 4148 9-8-7 **46** oh1........(t) DavidEgan[(5)] 13 34
(Pat Murphy) *hld up: hdwy and rdn 2f out: one pce fnl f* **6/1**

400 **6** *½* **Diamond Vine (IRE)**[8] 4467 9-8-12 **46**........................(p) FranBerry 14 32
(Ronald Harris) *in rr: rdn 2f out: mod late hdwy* **14/1**

0106 **7** *½* **Compton Prince**[8] 4467 8-9-7 **55**.....................(b) SilvestreDeSousa 6 40+
(Milton Bradley) *disp ld 2f: racd in 2nd tl wnt on 2f out: rdn and hdd over 1f out: wknd* **7/2**[1]

0-04 **8** *3 ¾* **Dawn Goddess**[25] 3825 3-8-7 **50**.............................. NoelGarbutt[(3)] 10 21
(Gary Moore) *hld up: drvn 3f out: no hdwy fnl 2f* **20/1**

306- **9** *nk* **Polkadot Princess (IRE)**[275] 7210 3-9-2 **56**.............. CharlesBishop 11 26
(Nikki Evans) *hld up: drvn 2f out: no imp* **20/1**

0-00 **10** *2* **She's Rosanna**[16] 4149 3-8-6 **46** oh1......................... RoystonFfrench 2 10+
(Steph Hollinshead) *disp ld 2f: tk over on own tl hdd 2f out: sn rdn and wknd* **25/1**

003 **11** *nk* **Jesse Tree (IRE)**[20] 4011 4-8-5 **46** oh1......................(t) WilliamCox[(7)] 12 10
(John Flint) *mid-div: pushed along 2f out: rdn 1f out: fdd* **20/1**

0000 **12** *9* **Mobley Chaos**[20] 4011 7-8-5 **46** oh1.........................(p) JordanUys[(7)] 16
(John Flint) *mid-div on outer: rdn 2f out: wknd qckly* **50/1**

1m 9.81s (-1.39) **Going Correction** -0.20s/f (Firm)
**WFA** 3 from 4yo+ 6lb **12** Ran SP% **119.9**
Speed ratings (Par 101): **101,98,97,94,92 91,90,85,85,82 82,70**
CSF £25.88 CT £129.75 TOTE £5.70: £1.90, £2.10, £2.50; EX 32.50 Trifecta £241.10.
**Owner** D Smith (saul) **Bred** Kirtlington Stud Ltd **Trained** Sedbury, Gloucs

**FOCUS**
A low-grade sprint run at a furious pace, the winner in a perfect position throughout and rated to his best in the last two years.

## 4736 WESTONBIRT H'CAP 1m
**8:40** (8:41) (Class 4) (0-85,85) 3-Y-O **£6,469** (£1,925; £962; £481) **Stalls** Low

Form RPR

0-62 **1** **Dowayla (IRE)**[21] 3981 3-9-7 **85**.................................. MartinLane 2 93
(Saeed bin Suroor) *disp ld 2f bef tk over on own: 1 l clr 2f out: drvn over 1f out: rdn to maintain advantage ent fnl f: r.o wl: comf* **5/2**[1]

3110 **2** *1* **Arctic Sea**[35] 3457 3-8-10 **74**........................................ FranBerry 1 79
(Paul Cole) *trckd ldrs: 3rd 3f out: pushed along 2f out: wnt 2nd appr fnl f: sn rdn and r.o but no imp on wnr* **4/1**[2]

0055 **3** *1 ½* **Rebel De Lope**[13] 4271 3-9-6 **84**................................ JimmyQuinn 7 86
(Charles Hills) *hld up: hdwy 2f out: rdn over 1f out: r.o to take 3rd ins fnl f* **6/1**

2530 **4** *¾* **Devil's Bridge (IRE)**[14] 4215 3-9-7 **85**...................... TomMarquand 3 85
(Richard Hannon) *mid-div: pushed along in 4th 2f out: rdn and briefly tk 2nd over 1f out: no ex ins fnl f* **5/1**[3]

-100 **5** *2 ½* **International Law**[28] 3713 3-8-13 **77**............................(p) DaneO'Neill 4 71
(Brian Meehan) *hld up: effrt and drvn 2f out: rdn over 1f out: no imp* **4/1**[2]

5106 **6** *5* **Gloriosus (USA)**[9] 4438 3-9-3 **81**......................... SilvestreDeSousa 6 70
(Mark Johnston) *disp ld 2f bef settled in 2nd: drvn and lost pl 2f out: sn rdn and wknd* **10/1**

1400 **7** *15* **Alkashaaf (USA)**[40] 3303 3-8-13 **80**..................(tp) GeorgeWood[(3)] 5 28
(Archie Watson) *a in rr: rdn and lost tch fr 3f out* **20/1**

1m 39.37s (-1.43) **Going Correction** -0.20s/f (Firm) **7** Ran SP% **113.4**
Speed ratings (Par 102): **99,98,96,95,93 88,73**
CSF £12.42 TOTE £3.10: £1.80, £2.20; EX 14.70 Trifecta £79.00.
**Owner** Godolphin **Bred** Darley **Trained** Newmarket, Suffolk

**FOCUS**
A small field for the 0-85 handicap but the progressive winner showed a willing attitude to repel all challengers.

## 4737 BRAKES MAIDEN FILLIES' STKS 1m
**9:10** (9:16) (Class 5) 3-Y-O+ **£2,911** (£866; £432) **Stalls** Low

Form RPR

244 **1** **Unified**[9] 4444 3-9-0 0.......................................... SilvestreDeSousa 5 75
(Clive Cox) *trckd ldr tl tk over after 1f: mde rest: pushed along and qcknd pce 3f out: 1 l clr 2f out: rdn over 1f out: chal by runner-up ent fnl f: hrd rdn and r.o: hld on by diminishing margin* **5/4**[2]

-5 **2** *hd* **Keeper's Choice (IRE)**[16] 4152 3-8-9 0......................... PaddyPilley[(5)] 4 74
(Denis Coakley) *led 1f: settled in 2nd tl relegated to 3rd 4f out: styd handy: hdwy and n.m.r between horses 2f out: rdn fnl f: r.o and clsng on wnr nr fin* **10/1**[3]

**3** *3 ¾* **Nadia Promise** 3-9-0 0............................................. PatCosgrave 6 65
(William Haggas) *hld up last tl wnt 2nd after 4f: drvn whn pce qcknd 3f out: rdn 2f out and sn dropped to last: position accepted ent fnl f* **8/13**[1]

1m 42.93s (2.13) **Going Correction** -0.20s/f (Firm)
**WFA** 3 from 6yo 9lb **3** Ran SP% **115.5**
Speed ratings (Par 100): **81,80,77**
CSF £8.58 TOTE £2.50; EX 7.00 Trifecta £5.90.
**Owner** Cheveley Park Stud **Bred** Whatton Manor Stud & Robert Cornelius **Trained** Lambourn, Berks
■ Orbit Light was withdrawn. Price at time of withdrawal 50-1. Rule 4 does not apply.

**FOCUS**
A small-field maiden in which the winner put her experience to good use.
T/Plt: £78.50 to a £1 stake. Pool: £82,942.01. 770.46 winning units. T/Qpdt: £21.20 to a £1 stake. Pool: £7,398.63. 257.86 winning units. **Keith McHugh**

3562 **CATTERICK** (L-H)
Wednesday, July 12
**OFFICIAL GOING: Good to soft (good in places; 8.1)**
Wind: Virtually nil Weather: Fine

## 4738 DINE AND VIEW MEDIAN AUCTION MAIDEN STKS 1m 4f 13y
2:10 (2:10) (Class 5) 3-4-Y-O £2,911 (£866; £432; £216) Stalls Low

Form RPR
55 1 **Uber Cool (IRE)**[28] 3717 3-9-2 0 MartinHarley 4 71
(Jane Chapple-Hyam) *in tch: pushed along and hdwy to chse ldr over 1f out: rdn to ld 110yds out: styd on pushed out* 5/4[1]
5003 2 1 **Ingleby Mackenzie**[9] 4449 3-9-2 59 GrahamLee 5 69
(Mick Channon) *trckd ldr: pushed along 4f out: led over 2f out: sn rdn: hdd 110yds out: one pce* 13/2[3]
500- 3 4 ½ **Piedita (IRE)**[267] 7441 3-8-11 68 LukeMorris 6 57
(Sir Mark Prescott Bt) *in tch: pushed along over 3f out: rdn over 2f out: sn one pce: edgd lft and hld in 3rd fr over 1f out* 13/8[2]
0 4 2 ½ **Golden Jeffrey (SWI)**[4] 4611 4-10-0 0 TomEaves 3 57
(Iain Jardine) *led: rdn whn hdd over 2f out: sn wknd* 9/1
2m 34.65s (-4.25) **Going Correction** -0.20s/f (Firm)
**WFA** 3 from 4yo 12lb 4 Ran SP% 105.9
Speed ratings (Par 103): **106,105,102,100**
CSF £8.58 TOTE £1.60; EX 6.70 Trifecta £10.80.
**Owner** Fiona and Ian Carmichael-Jennings **Bred** Albert Conneally **Trained** Dalham, Suffolk
**FOCUS**
All distances as advertised. After a dry night the going was given as good to soft, good in places. A modest maiden for older horses.

## 4739 ST TERESA'S HOSPICE FILLIES' NURSERY H'CAP 5f 212y
2:45 (2:45) (Class 4) 2-Y-O £4,204 (£1,251; £625; £312) Stalls Low

Form RPR
2104 1 **Faithful Promise**[34] 3482 2-9-0 75 PJMcDonald 8 77
(Mark Johnston) *hld up: rdn and hdwy on outer 2f out: chal strly ent fnl f: edgd ahd 75yds out: drvn all out* 9/1
044 2 nk **Dyson's Girl**[20] 4014 2-8-0 64 NathanEvans(3) 4 65
(Bryan Smart) *dwlt: sn trckd ldr: rdn to dispute ld ent fnl f: kpt on: hld nr fin* 6/1
434 3 nse **Reflect Alexander (IRE)**[11] 4361 2-9-7 82 JFEgan 2 83
(David Evans) *sn led: rdn over 1f out: jnd ent fnl f: kpt on: hld nr fin* 3/1[1]
2315 4 1 ¾ **Lexington Grace (IRE)**[13] 4252 2-8-4 70 (p[1]) RobJFitzpatrick(5) 6 66
(Richard Hannon) *hld up: pushed along and hdwy on inner to chse ldrs appr fnl f: rdn and one pce ins fnl f* 9/2
304 5 2 ¾ **Flo's Melody**[30] 3662 2-8-4 65 PaulHanagan 3 52
(Richard Fahey) *prom: rdn 2f out: wknd ins fnl f* 4/1[3]
045 6 1 ½ **Angel Force (IRE)**[39] 3333 2-8-0 61 oh8 PatrickMathers 5 44+
(David C Griffiths) *trckd ldrs: plld hrd and sddle sn slipped: wknd over 1f out* 40/1
4221 U **Mraseel (IRE)**[14] 4199 2-9-2 77 (p) MartinHarley 7 +
(James Tate) *jinked rt and uns rdr s* 7/2[2]
1m 14.22s (0.62) **Going Correction** -0.20s/f (Firm) 7 Ran SP% 112.1
Speed ratings (Par 93): **87,86,86,84,80 78,**
CSF £58.37 CT £199.67 TOTE £9.20: £3.90, £3.40; EX 68.50 Trifecta £248.90.
**Owner** Saeed Manana **Bred** Petches Farm Ltd **Trained** Middleham Moor, N Yorks
**FOCUS**
Drama at the start of a fair fillies' nursery, Mraseel unseating Martin Harley after getting a bump when leaving the stalls. There was a tight finish but the form looks solid, with the winner to her best.

## 4740 RACINGUK.COM CLAIMING STKS 5f
3:20 (3:21) (Class 6) 2-Y-O £2,264 (£673; £336; £168) Stalls Low

Form RPR
3540 1 **Just For The Craic (IRE)**[14] 4204 2-8-12 61 JamesSullivan 6 62
(Ruth Carr) *dwlt: hld up: rdn and hdwy over 1f out: led 110yds out: edgd lft: kpt on* 9/2[2]
050 2 ¾ **Kikini Bamalaam (IRE)**[48] 2988 2-8-10 0 ConnorBeasley 4 57
(Keith Dalgleish) *dwlt: hld up: rdn 2f out: hdwy appr fnl f: r.o: wnt 2nd nr fin* 16/1
030 3 hd **Placebo Effect (IRE)**[26] 3791 2-9-2 56 AndrewMullen 5 63
(Ollie Pears) *chsd ldrs: rdn over 1f out: hdwy and upsides 110yds out: one pce fnl 50yds: lost 2nd nr fin* 14/1
0531 4 1 ¾ **Tie Em Up Tel (IRE)**[23] 3918 2-9-3 67 JFEgan 9 61
(David Evans) *prom: rdn 2f out: led 1f out: hdd 110yds out: 3rd whn hmpd 75yds out: no ex* 5/4[1]
00 5 ½ **Free Spirited**[25] 3826 2-9-2 0 PaulHanagan 10 54
(Richard Fahey) *chsd ldrs: rdn 1/2-way: one pce* 7/1[3]
00 6 nk **Miss Mazzie**[26] 3791 2-8-5 0 NathanEvans(3) 7 45
(Michael Easterby) *outpcd in rr tl kpt on fnl f* 40/1
05 7 2 **Devil Or Angel**[47] 3029 2-9-1 0 LukeMorris 1 45
(Bill Turner) *prom: rdn and hung lft over 1f out: wknd fnl f* 9/1
0 8 1 ½ **Sovereign Katie (IRE)**[22] 3943 2-8-11 0 JoeDoyle 2 36
(Ollie Pears) *led: rdn 2f out: hdd 1f out: wknd* 33/1
0 9 1 **Little Monkey**[5] 4555 2-8-12 0 (p) CamHardie 3 33
(Antony Brittain) *hld up: nvr threatened* 40/1
0 10 3 **Tea Rattle**[9] 4440 2-8-13 0 DavidAllan 8 23
(Scott Dixon) *chsd ldrs: rdn 1/2-way: wknd over 1f out* 10/1
59.92s (0.12) **Going Correction** -0.175s/f (Firm) 10 Ran SP% 114.6
Speed ratings (Par 92): **92,90,90,87,86 86,83,80,79,74**
CSF £70.30 TOTE £4.80: £1.90, £4.90, £3.10; EX 64.20 Trifecta £337.90.The winner was claimed by Neil Mulholland for £3,000.
**Owner** Berry, Elsworth, Carr **Bred** Corrin Stud & Blackwater Bloodstock Ltd **Trained** Huby, N Yorks
**FOCUS**
A typically modest 2yo claimer run at a good pace, and the first two home came through late in the day. The 3rd helps set the opening level.

## 4741 LOOKERS VOLKSWAGEN H'CAP 7f 6y
3:55 (3:55) (Class 5) (0-75,75) 3-Y-O £2,911 (£866; £432; £216) Stalls Low

Form RPR
5214 1 **Our Charlie Brown**[18] 4075 3-9-4 72 JamesSullivan 4 77
(Tim Easterby) *trckd ldrs: pushed along over 1f out: led narrowly ins fnl f: sn drvn: hld on all out* 7/2[2]
2213 2 nse **Heir Of Excitement (IRE)**[12] 4290 3-9-7 75 ShaneGray 2 79
(Kevin Ryan) *prom: pushed along 2f out: rdn and upsides ins fnl f: kpt on* 11/4[1]
-000 3 1 ½ **Redrosezorro**[6] 4529 3-8-2 56 (h[1]) PatrickMathers 5 56
(Eric Alston) *in tch: rdn over 2f out: kpt on fnl f* 33/1
-543 4 ¾ **Lady In Question (IRE)**[13] 4268 3-9-4 72 (p[1]) PaulHanagan 7 70
(Richard Fahey) *hld up: rdn 2f out: kpt on fnl f: nrst fin* 11/4[1]
334 5 ¾ **Halawain (USA)**[17] 4122 3-9-6 74 PhillipMakin 1 70
(John Quinn) *led: rdn 2f out: hdd ins fnl f: sn wknd* 6/1[3]
0640 6 ½ **Kiribati**[16] 4144 3-8-9 63 (b[1]) PJMcDonald 3 58
(Mark Johnston) *dwlt: hld up in tch: rdn over 2f out: no imp* 10/1
0500 7 1 ¼ **Jumping Around (IRE)**[18] 4084 3-9-4 72 LukeMorris 6 63
(Ian Williams) *hld up: rdn over 2f out: edgd lft over 1f out: nvr threatened* 10/1
1m 25.23s (-1.77) **Going Correction** -0.20s/f (Firm) 7 Ran SP% 111.0
Speed ratings (Par 100): **102,101,100,99,98 97,96**
CSF £12.71 TOTE £4.20: £2.30, £1.40; EX 15.20 Trifecta £262.70.
**Owner** Ontoawinner, SDH Project Services Ltd 2 **Bred** North Bradon Stud & D R Tucker **Trained** Great Habton, N Yorks
**FOCUS**
A fair, competitive looking handicap run at an even pace.

## 4742 TURMERIC H'CAP (FOR THE TURMERIC CHALLENGE TROPHY) 1m 7f 189y
4:30 (4:30) (Class 4) (0-85,87) 3-Y-O+ £6,469 (£1,925; £962; £481) Stalls Low

Form RPR
1342 1 **Addicted To You (IRE)**[8] 4476 3-8-2 74 AndrewMullen 6 85+
(Mark Johnston) *sn led: mde rest: rdn clr over 1f out: styd on wl: comf* 11/10[1]
410- 2 4 **Project Bluebook (FR)**[86] 6561 4-9-11 80 JasonHart 2 85
(John Quinn) *trckd ldrs: rdn and lost pl 4f out: styd on fr over 1f out: wnt 2nd jst ins fnl f: no ch w wnr* 5/2[2]
513- 3 2 ½ **Tenzing Norgay**[314] 6050 4-10-0 83 (v) LukeMorris 4 85
(Sir Mark Prescott Bt) *hld up in tch: rdn and hdwy to chse ldr 2f out: lost 2nd jst ins fnl f: wknd* 7/1
0656 4 4 **General Allenby**[33] 3520 3-8-0 72 oh27 (be) CamHardie 5 70?
(Henry Tett) *trckd ldr: rdn along and lost pl 5f out: sn outpcd in 5th: plugged on again fr over 1f out* 200/1
032 5 5 **Hurricane Hollow**[34] 3501 7-9-4 73 BenCurtis 1 64
(David Barron) *led briefly: prom: rdn over 3f out: wknd over 1f out* 6/1[3]
/16- 6 4 ½ **Almost Gemini (IRE)**[125] 3149 8-9-4 73 (p) JamesSullivan 3 59
(Kenneth Slack) *a rr* 16/1
3m 31.55s (-0.45) **Going Correction** -0.20s/f (Firm)
**WFA** 3 from 4yo+ 17lb 6 Ran SP% 109.4
Speed ratings (Par 105): **93,91,89,87,85 83**
CSF £3.78 TOTE £1.90: £1.40, £1.30; EX 4.20 Trifecta £13.70.
**Owner** Markus Graff **Bred** M W Graff **Trained** Middleham Moor, N Yorks
**FOCUS**
A useful staying handicap taken in good style by a progressive 3yo.

## 4743 RACINGUK.COM H'CAP (DIV I) 7f 6y
5:05 (5:06) (Class 6) (0-65,65) 3-Y-O+ £2,264 (£673; £336; £168) Stalls Low

Form RPR
-033 1 **Carlovian**[21] 3979 4-8-6 46 (p) NathanEvans(3) 12 52
(Mark Walford) *midfield on outer: rdn and hdwy over 2f out: led ins fnl f: idled: edgd lft 50yds out: a doing enough* 11/4[1]
2364 2 nk **Grey Destiny**[16] 4165 7-9-8 59 CamHardie 6 64
(Antony Brittain) *slowly away: hld up: stl plenty to do over 1f out: r.o wl fnl f* 9/1
0035 3 hd **Bernie's Boy**[7] 4509 4-10-0 65 (p) TonyHamilton 9 70
(Roger Fell) *prom: rdn to ld appr fnl f: hdd ins fnl f: kpt on* 11/2[2]
0560 4 1 ¼ **Danot (IRE)**[23] 3912 5-9-6 57 (p) JackGarritty 4 58
(Jedd O'Keeffe) *trckd ldrs: bit short of room over 1f out: swtchd rt appr fnl f: rdn and kpt on: bit short of room 50yds out* 6/1[3]
-230 5 ½ **Broctune Papa Gio**[13] 4263 10-9-2 58 (b) CallumRodriguez(5) 3 58
(Gillian Boanas) *in tch: rdn 2f out: kpt on same pce fnl f* 13/2
0500 6 2 ¼ **Lukoutoldmakezebak**[23] 3912 4-8-9 46 oh1 PatrickMathers 1 40
(David Thompson) *dwlt: hld up: pushed along over 1f out: kpt on ins fnl f: nvr threatened* 33/1
3000 7 shd **Baby Helmet**[23] 3913 3-8-10 55 SamJames 10 46
(Karen Tutty) *chsd ldrs: rdn over 1f out: bit short of room ent fnl f: no ex ins fnl f* 22/1
0450 8 ¾ **Bold Spirit**[7] 4509 6-9-6 57 (vt) TomEaves 5 49
(Declan Carroll) *led: rdn over 2f out: hdd appr fnl f: wknd ins fnl f* 7/1
034 9 ¾ **Jennies Gem**[18] 4106 4-9-1 52 AndrewMullen 13 42
(Ollie Pears) *hld up: pushed along over 1f out: nvr threatened* 25/1
0500 10 1 ¼ **A Bit Of Ginger**[13] 4262 3-8-6 51 (p[1]) ShaneGray 11 34
(Ann Duffield) *in tch: pushed along whn short of room appr fnl f: wknd* 20/1
06-6 11 ½ **Arabela Dawn (IRE)**[44] 3150 3-8-8 53 JasonHart 7 35
(John Quinn) *midfield: pushed along over 2f out: wknd fnl f* 18/1
1m 25.1s (-1.90) **Going Correction** -0.20s/f (Firm)
**WFA** 3 from 4yo+ 8lb 11 Ran SP% 113.3
Speed ratings (Par 101): **102,101,101,100,99 96,96,95,95,93 93**
CSF £25.41 CT £128.30 TOTE £3.30: £1.50, £2.40, £2.00; EX 20.00 Trifecta £68.80.
**Owner** Profit Pony Racing **Bred** Bradmill Meats Ltd **Trained** Sherriff Hutton, N Yorks
**FOCUS**
The first division of a modest handicap and little separating the first three home.

## 4744 RACINGUK.COM H'CAP (DIV II) 7f 6y
5:35 (5:36) (Class 6) (0-65,67) 3-Y-O+ £2,264 (£673; £336; £168) Stalls Low

Form RPR
434 1 **The Stalking Moon (IRE)**[14] 4209 3-9-9 67 JasonHart 7 76+
(John Quinn) *in tch: pushed along and hdwy over 1f out: rdn to ld ins fnl f: kpt on: comf* 7/2[1]
4444 2 2 ¼ **Cupid's Arrow (IRE)**[13] 4265 3-9-1 59 JamesSullivan 5 61
(Ruth Carr) *led: rdn 2f out: hdd ins fnl f: one pce* 4/1[2]


The Form Book Flat, Raceform Ltd, Newbury, RG14 5SJ

0032 **3** 3/4 **Tom's Anna (IRE)**[23] 3906 7-8-10 **46** NathanEvans(3) 2 52
(Sean Regan) *chsd ldrs: rdn over 2f out: kpt on same pce* **8/1**
6224 **4** 3/4 **Cool Strutter (IRE)**[13] 4263 5-9-2 **57** GemmaTutty(5) 12 58
(Karen Tutty) *sn prom on outer: rdn over 2f out: edgd lft over 1f out: no ex ins fnl f* **7/1**
6040 **5** 1 1/2 **Leonard Thomas**[13] 4260 7-9-2 **52** (p) PaddyAspell 9 49
(Philip Kirby) *s.i.s: hld up: rdn over 1f out: kpt on fnl f: nvr threatened* **28/1**
4434 **6** 1 **Lucky Lodge**[7] 4509 7-10-0 **64** (v) CamHardie 6 59
(Antony Brittain) *hld up: pushed along whn hmpd over 1f out: kpt on ins fnl f* **10/1**
-006 **7** 1/2 **Ivors Involvement (IRE)**[21] 3979 5-8-9 **45** TomEaves 4 38
(Tina Jackson) *hld up in midfield: rdn over 2f out: one pce and nvr threatened* **33/1**
0004 **8** 1 3/4 **Albizu Campos**[33] 3525 3-8-1 **45** AndrewMullen 3 30
(Lawrence Mullaney) *hld up: pushed along over 1f out: nvr threatened* **10/1**
61-1 **9** 1 1/4 **Great Colaci**[25] 3831 4-9-5 **55** PaulHanagan 10 40
(Gillian Boanas) *in tch on outer: rdn 2f out: wknd fnl f* **5/1**[3]
-000 **10** 1/2 **Mulwith (IRE)**[12] 4303 3-8-8 **52** (b) PatrickMathers 8 32
(Scott Dixon) *prom: rdn over 3f out: wknd over 1f out* **100/1**
5300 **11** 1 1/2 **Hollywood Harry (IRE)**[13] 4265 3-8-10 **54** (p) GrahamLee 11 30
(Keith Dalgleish) *hld up: rdn over 2f out: sn btn* **25/1**

1m 25.03s (-1.97) **Going Correction** -0.20s/f (Firm)
**WFA** 3 from 4yo+ 8lb **11** Ran SP% **111.9**
Speed ratings (Par 101): **103,100,99,98,97 95,95,93,91,91 89**
CSF £15.78 CT £102.66 TOTE £4.30: £1.50, £1.60, £2.80; EX 19.10 Trifecta £121.40.
**Owner** D Ward **Bred** Norman Orminston **Trained** Settrington, N Yorks

**FOCUS**
A decisive winner of the second leg of a modest handicap.

## 4745 RACING AGAIN 19TH JULY H'CAP 5f 212y
**6:05** (6:05) (Class 5) (0-75,75) 3-Y-O **£2,911** (£866; £432; £216) **Stalls** Low

Form RPR
-030 **1** **Chickenfortea (IRE)**[5] 4576 3-8-8 **62** JasonHart 9 68
(Eric Alston) *mde all: pushed along over 1f out: rdn and kpt on fnl f* **6/1**[3]
0302 **2** 1 1/4 **Vintage Dream (IRE)**[9] 4428 3-8-6 **60** (b) PatrickMathers 2 61
(Noel Wilson) *prom: rdn 2f out: kpt on but a hld* **9/1**
0011 **3** nk **Kody Ridge (IRE)**[2] 4694 3-9-5 **73** 6ex (h) ConnorBeasley 5 73+
(Roger Fell) *hld up: pushed along over 2f out: rdn and hdwy over 1f out: kpt on fnl f* **5/4**[1]
3104 **4** hd **Kodicat (IRE)**[11] 4342 3-9-2 **70** TomEaves 7 69
(Kevin Ryan) *trckd ldrs: rdn 2f out: kpt on same pce* **10/1**
2203 **5** 2 1/4 **Springforth**[15] 4188 3-8-12 **66** TonyHamilton 4 57
(Richard Fahey) *dwlt: hld up: rdn along over 2f out: nvr threatened* **4/1**[2]
6000 **6** nse **Trick Of The Lyte (IRE)**[34] 3496 3-8-2 **56** CamHardie 8 47
(John Quinn) *midfield: rdn 2f out: wknd fnl f* **11/1**
356- **7** 3 1/2 **Quiet Moment (IRE)**[279] 7091 3-8-4 **63** RobJFitzpatrick(5) 1 41
(Ben Haslam) *trckd ldrs: pushed along and lost pl 3f out: wknd over 1f out* **16/1**

1m 11.46s (-2.14) **Going Correction** -0.20s/f (Firm) **7** Ran SP% **112.0**
Speed ratings (Par 100): **106,104,103,103,100 100,95**
CSF £54.27 CT £107.60 TOTE £7.70: £2.40, £2.60; EX 54.70 Trifecta £149.30.
**Owner** Brian Chambers **Bred** Seamus Finucane **Trained** Longton, Lancs

**FOCUS**
A fair handicap and not the strongest for the level.
T/Plt: £448.90 to a £1 stake. Pool: £39,361.77. 64 winning units. T/Qpdt: £20.30 to a £1 stake. Pool: £4,004.27. 145.28 winning units. **Andrew Sheret**

# 4495 KEMPTON (A.W) (R-H)
Wednesday, July 12

**OFFICIAL GOING: Polytrack: standard to slow**
Wind: Moderate, across (towards stands) Weather: Fine

## 4746 32RED ON THE APP STORE APPRENTICE H'CAP 7f (P)
**5:55** (5:58) (Class 4) (0-85,83) 4-Y-O+ **£5,175** (£1,540; £769; £384) **Stalls** Low

Form RPR
6-65 **1** **Human Nature (IRE)**[18] 4099 4-9-6 **80** (t) MillyNaseb(3) 2 87
(Stuart Williams) *mde all: hrd pressed fr 2f out: rdn and kpt on wl: a holding on ins fnl f* **8/1**
2300 **2** 1/2 **Kingsley Klarion (IRE)**[21] 3969 4-9-5 **76** RichardOliver 4 81+
(Mark Johnston) *s.i.s: prog fr rr on outer bnd 1/2-way: rdn over 2f out: styd on ins fnl f to take 2nd last strides: nt rch wnr* **8/1**
4364 **3** 1/2 **Childesplay**[19] 4051 6-9-2 **73** GeorgeBuckell 9 77
(Heather Main) *trckd wnr: rdn and nt qckn 2f out: styd pressing but a hld after: lost 2nd last strides* **8/1**
4030 **4** hd **Sarangoo**[13] 4251 9-9-3 **74** GeorgiaCox 6 77
(Malcolm Saunders) *trckd ldng pair: tried to chal 2f out: stl ch fnl f: kpt on same pce* **16/1**
3044 **5** nk **Mister Music**[14] 4215 8-9-2 **78** AledBeech(5) 7 81
(Tony Carroll) *hld up in last: rdn over 2f out: stl last jst ins fnl f: styd on last 100yds but too late to threaten* **9/2**[2]
000P **6** nk **Ejayteekay**[11] 4372 4-8-8 **72** TheodoreLadd(7) 8 74
(Hughie Morrison) *t.k.h: hld up in midfield: rdn 2f out: one pce and no imp ldrs after* **25/1**
145 **7** nse **Saleh (IRE)**[35] 3454 4-9-3 **77** PaddyBradley(3) 3 79
(Lee Carter) *sltly awkward s: wl in tch: prog 2f out: tried to chal on inner over 1f out: one pce fnl f* **4/1**[1]
036 **8** 1/2 **Professor**[13] 4270 7-9-9 **83** JoshuaBryan(3) 10 83
(Michael Attwater) *trckd ldrs: rdn 2f out: nt qckn over 1f out: one pce and lost pls ins fnl f* **5/1**[3]
6300 **9** 3/4 **Anonymous John (IRE)**[13] 4251 5-8-12 **72** KatherineGlenister(3) 5 70
(Dominic Ffrench Davis) *wl in tch in rr: rdn and no prog 2f out: one pce after* **7/1**

1m 26.08s (0.08) **Going Correction** +0.05s/f (Slow) **9** Ran SP% **110.4**
Speed ratings (Par 105): **101,100,99,99,99 98,98,98,97**
CSF £63.75 CT £458.44 TOTE £10.60: £3.00, £2.30, £2.60; EX 78.90 Trifecta £624.90.
**Owner** Enticknap, Reynolds & Watkins **Bred** Tally-Ho Stud **Trained** Newmarket, Suffolk
■ Arlecchino's Leap was withdrawn. Price at time of withdrawal 14-1. Rule 4 applies to all bets - deduction 5p in the pound.

**FOCUS**
The steady gallop saw those held up at a disadvantage. The 2nd/3rd/4th have been rated close to recent.

## 4747 RACING UK HD H'CAP 1m (P)
**6:25** (6:26) (Class 6) (0-65,63) 3-Y-O+ **£2,587** (£770; £384; £192) **Stalls** Low

Form RPR
1136 **1** **Dangerous Ends**[44] 3163 3-9-4 **63** JackMitchell 7 68
(Brett Johnson) *wl in tch: shkn up over 2f out: prog sn after: rdn to ld 1f out: pressed last 100yds but styd on wl* **13/8**[1]
4212 **2** 3/4 **Makhfar (IRE)**[16] 4165 6-9-12 **62** (p) SteveDrowne 8 67
(Mark Usher) *wl in tch on outer: shkn up over 2f out: prog over 1f out: tk 2nd last 100yds: styd on but a hld* **13/2**[2]
4-00 **3** 1 3/4 **Sir Compton**[13] 4251 4-9-9 **59** OisinMurphy 6 60
(Stuart Kittow) *trckd ldrs: rdn over 2f out: clsd over 1f out: chsd wnr briefly ins fnl f: outpcd last 100yds* **11/1**
0-06 **4** nk **Feel The Vibes**[27] 3751 3-9-3 **62** (b[1]) DanielMuscutt 11 60
(Michael Blanshard) *hld up towards rr: rdn over 2f out: prog through rivals over 1f out: rchd 4th 100yds out: no hdwy after* **40/1**
-666 **5** 2 **Mutineer**[11] 4350 3-9-4 **63** GeorgeDowning 9 56
(Daniel Kubler) *led after 1f and maintained ordinary pce: rdn over 2f out: hdd & wknd 1f out* **12/1**
0-40 **6** 1 1/4 **Presence Process**[35] 3457 3-9-2 **61** ShaneKelly 2 53
(Pat Phelan) *hld up towards rr: rdn over 2f out: trying to make prog whn hmpd over 1f out: no ch after: hung lft but kpt on fnl f* **8/1**[3]
3100 **7** 1 **Embankment**[42] 3208 8-9-4 **59** JoshuaBryan(5) 1 49
(Michael Attwater) *chsd ldrs: rdn over 2f out: no prog over 1f out: fdd fnl f* **14/1**
6050 **8** 1 **Rightway (IRE)**[31] 3616 6-9-6 **61** GeorgiaCox(5) 13 48+
(Tony Carroll) *s.i.s: rcvrd and chsd ldr after 2f: rdn over 2f out: stl upsides wl over 1f out: sn wknd* **16/1**
-350 **9** nk **McDelta**[27] 3753 7-9-8 **58** DougieCostello 5 45
(Geoffrey Deacon) *hld up in last trio: urged along over 3f out: effrt on inner 2f out: sn no prog* **10/1**
00-5 **10** 2 3/4 **Popeswood (IRE)**[58] 2676 5-9-6 **59** CharlieBennett(3) 3 39+
(Lee Carter) *taken down early: s.v.s: rcvrd and in tch in last pair: outpcd 3f out: no ch after* **25/1**
2630 **11** 1/2 **Secret Glance**[28] 3718 5-9-5 **60** LucyKBarry(5) 14 39
(Adrian Wintle) *restrained fr wd draw and hld up in last pair: outpcd 3f out: no ch after* **20/1**
-540 **12** 1 **Check 'Em Tuesday (IRE)**[23] 3912 4-9-7 **62** PaddyBradley(5) 4 39
(Daniel Mark Loughnane) *led for 1f at mod pce: chsd ldrs after: rdn over 2f out: wknd qckly over 1f out* **16/1**

1m 39.94s (0.14) **Going Correction** +0.05s/f (Slow)
**WFA** 3 from 4yo+ 9lb **12** Ran SP% **117.1**
Speed ratings (Par 101): **101,100,98,98,96 94,93,92,92,89 89,88**
CSF £11.12 CT £89.40 TOTE £2.10: £1.20, £1.90, £2.90; EX 11.10 Trifecta £79.60.
**Owner** Colin Westley **Bred** R S Cockerill (farms) Ltd **Trained** Epsom, Surrey

**FOCUS**
A modest handicap in which the gallop was only fair until picking up passing the interesection. The well-backed winner, who is unbeaten over this C&D, came down the centre in the last quarter mile. The 2nd helps set the form.

## 4748 32RED.COM H'CAP (LONDON MILE SERIES QUALIFIER) 1m (P)
**6:55** (6:57) (Class 5) (0-70,70) 3-Y-O **£3,234** (£962; £481; £240) **Stalls** Low

Form RPR
3145 **1** **Scala Regia (FR)**[24] 3870 3-8-11 **63** RosieJessop(3) 9 71
(Sir Mark Prescott Bt) *chsd ldr to over 3f out: sn urged along: responded wl to go 2nd again 2f out and led over 1f out: hrd pressed ins fnl f: hld on wl* **14/1**
1200 **2** hd **Badenscoth**[13] 4255 3-9-6 **69** (h) RobertWinston 5 76
(Dean Ivory) *hld up in last pair off decent pce: prog on outer jst over 2f out: tk 2nd 1f out: edgd rt but chal last 100yds: nt qckn last strides* **9/2**[2]
3004 **3** 1 3/4 **Rock N Roll Global (IRE)**[40] 3276 3-9-5 **68** ShaneKelly 7 71
(Richard Hughes) *stdd after s and hld up in last: prog on inner 2f out: tk 3rd jst ins fnl f: kpt on but wl hld whn swtchd lft 50yds out* **6/1**
000 **4** 2 1/2 **Mister Chow**[54] 2778 3-9-1 **67** HectorCrouch(3) 11 64
(Gary Moore) *prom: rdn to chse ldr over 3f out to 2f out: steadily fdd fnl f* **9/1**
-063 **5** 3/4 **Casado (IRE)**[20] 4006 3-8-11 **60** SteveDrowne 1 56
(John Best) *hld up in midfield: shkn up over 2f out: threatened to cl wl over 1f out: sn no prog* **4/1**[1]
2004 **6** 1/2 **Fiendish (USA)**[17] 4121 3-9-7 **70** JamesDoyle 10 64
(Mark Johnston) *led at gd pce: had most of rivals hrd at work 2f out: hdd and folded over 1f out* **12/1**
4030 **7** 1 **Do You Know (IRE)**[21] 3971 3-9-2 **65** (bt) AndreaAtzeni 3 57
(Marco Botti) *chsd ldrs: rdn over 2f out: no prog* **9/1**
300- **8** 3/4 **Beaconsfield**[224] 8159 3-9-1 **67** CharlieBennett(3) 4 57
(Hughie Morrison) *hld up in last trio: pushed along over 2f out: no great prog and nvr involved* **16/1**
3-30 **9** 1/2 **Settle Petal**[20] 4012 3-9-0 **63** OisinMurphy 8 52
(Pat Phelan) *towards rr: shkn up and no prog over 2f out* **33/1**
-163 **10** 3/4 **Altiko Tommy (IRE)**[43] 3173 3-9-5 **68** LiamKeniry 2 55
(George Baker) *chsd ldrs: rdn over 2f out: sn wknd* **5/1**[3]
0056 **11** 9 **Shamonix (IRE)**[14] 4211 3-7-13 **48** oh6 ow2 RichardOliver(5) 6 20
(Mark Usher) *in tch but racd wd: lost pl 3f out: last 2f out: t.o* **100/1**

1m 39.08s (-0.72) **Going Correction** +0.05s/f (Slow) **11** Ran SP% **113.3**
Speed ratings (Par 100): **105,104,103,100,99 99,98,97,97,96 87**
CSF £73.20 CT £423.66 TOTE £16.10: £3.90, £2.00, £2.90; EX 105.80 Trifecta £676.50.
**Owner** Cyril Humphris **Bred** Cyril Humphris **Trained** Newmarket, Suffolk

**FOCUS**
A modest handicap in which an ordinary gallop picked up early in the home straight. The winner raced towards the far rail in the straight.

## 4749 32RED/BRITISH STALLION STUDS EBF FILLIES' NOVICE STKS (PLUS 10 RACE) 6f (P)
**7:25** (7:28) (Class 5) 2-Y-O **£3,234** (£962; £481; £240) **Stalls** Low

Form RPR
**1** **Island Drive (IRE)** 2-9-0 0 DanielTudhope 2 78+
(William Haggas) *trckd ldrs gng wl: lft w fair bit to do whn ldr kicked clr over 1f out: prog to go 2nd jst over 1f out: clsd qckly to ld last 75yds: taking debut* **11/4**[2]
54 **2** 3/4 **Angel Islington (IRE)**[36] 3421 2-9-0 0 OisinMurphy 5 74
(Andrew Balding) *led: kicked 3 l clr wl over 1f out: styd on but hdd and readily outpcd last 75yds* **6/1**

3 2 ½ **Travelcard (USA)** 2-9-0 0 .......... JamesDoyle 4 67+
(Mark Johnston) *in tch in midfield: urged along over 2f out and sn outpcd: styd on wl fnl f to take 3rd last stride* **8/1**

3 4 hd **Downtown Mombasa (IRE)**[16] 4151 2-8-11 0 ....... EdwardGreatrex(3) 3 66
(Eve Johnson Houghton) *prom: rdn over 2f out: disp 2nd briefly over 1f out: sn outpcd: lost 3rd last stride* **4/1**[3]

50 5 2 ½ **That's My Girl (IRE)**[9] 4440 2-9-0 0 .......... KieranO'Neill 8 59
(Richard Hannon) *chsd ldr: rdn over 2f out: lost 2nd and wknd over 1f out* **33/1**

6 2 ½ **Catch The Pigeon** 2-9-0 0 .......... DougieCostello 6 51
(Ed de Giles) *nvr beyond midfield: shkn up and outpcd 2f out: fdd* **50/1**

7 1 ¾ **Pollyissimo** 2-9-0 0 .......... ShaneKelly 1 46
(Richard Hughes) *chsd ldrs: pushed along and outpcd 2f out: fdd* **50/1**

4 8 hd **Jane Rose (IRE)**[12] 4296 2-9-0 0 .......... SeanLevey 9 45
(Richard Hannon) *trckd ldng pair on outer: rdn over 2f out: wknd over 1f out* **2/1**[1]

0 9 2 ½ **Lady Of Authority**[16] 4151 2-9-0 0 .......... LiamKeniry 10 38
(Murty McGrath) *sltly awkward s: a towards rr: struggling over 2f out* **200/1**

00 10 ½ **Midnight Blue**[7] 4496 2-8-11 0 .......... RosieJessop(3) 7 36
(Sir Mark Prescott Bt) *a in rr: urged along and struggling 1/2-way* **100/1**

11 5 **Musical Dream** 2-9-0 0 .......... JimCrowley 11 21
(Sylvester Kirk) *wnt bdly lft s: a in rr and v green: hung lft over 2f out and ended against nr side rail* **10/1**

12 1 ¾ **Wotamadam** 2-9-0 0 .......... RobertWinston 12 16+
(Dean Ivory) *dwlt and carried bdly lft s: a bhd* **50/1**

1m 13.74s (0.64) **Going Correction** +0.05s/f (Slow) **12 Ran SP% 124.8**
Speed ratings (Par 91): **97,96,92,92,89 85,83,83,79,79 72,70**
CSF £20.60 TOTE £3.50: £1.80, £1.60, £2.00; EX 18.90 Trifecta £107.00.
**Owner** Clipper Logistics **Bred** Ken Lynch **Trained** Newmarket, Suffolk

**FOCUS**
Only fair form but the winner, who came down the centre, showed a good turn of foot to win with more in hand than the official margin suggests and she's a useful prospect.

## 4750 RACING UK H'CAP — 1m 7f 218y(P)
**7:55** (7:55) (Class 5) (0-75,74) 4-Y-0+ — **£3,234** (£962; £481; £240) **Stalls** Low

Form — RPR

40/0 1 **Authorized Too**[25] 3840 6-9-7 **74** .......... (p) JimCrowley 7 83+
(Noel Williams) *hld up in 7th: gd prog on outer 2f out: led jst over 1f out: shkn up and sn clr* **16/1**

5463 2 2 ¾ **Fitzwilly**[8] 4471 7-9-0 **67** .......... AndreaAtzeni 5 71
(Mick Channon) *hld up in 6th: shkn up over 2f out: prog over 1f out but wnr sn overtk him: styd on to take 2nd ins fnl f* **3/1**[2]

5-35 3 1 ½ **Pastoral Music**[14] 4222 4-9-2 **72** .......... (p[1]) CharlieBennett(3) 8 74
(Hughie Morrison) *trckd ldng trio: shkn up and prog to ld briefly over 1f out: sn outpcd by wnr: lost 2nd ins fnl f* **5/2**[1]

0/52 4 2 ¾ **Iniesta (IRE)**[32] 3574 6-8-10 **70** .......... FinleyMarsh(7) 6 69
(Fergal O'Brien) *trckd ldrs: rdn to chal and upsides 2f out to over 1f out: sn outpcd* **11/2**[3]

5444 5 2 **Southern States**[14] 4217 4-8-8 **61** .......... (e) KieranO'Neill 1 58
(Lydia Richards) *trckd ldng pair: urged along over 2f out: sn lost pl and btn* **6/1**

6 1 ¾ **Silver Sea**[131] 4-9-0 **67** .......... SteveDrowne 3 61
(Seamus Mullins) *hld up in last pair: shkn up over 2f out: mod prog 1f out: nvr a factor* **50/1**

7 2 **Lazio (IRE)**[267] 7453 4-9-2 **69** .......... DougieCostello 4 61
(Jamie Osborne) *trckd ldrs in 5th: rdn over 2f out: sn wknd* **12/1**

0322 8 2 ¼ **See And Be Seen**[14] 4217 7-8-12 **65** .......... (p) OisinMurphy 9 54
(Sylvester Kirk) *rousted to ld and set mod pce: tried to kick on 4f out: hdd & wknd qckly over 1f out* **6/1**

-430 9 16 **Henry Croft**[36] 3427 4-9-5 **72** .......... RobertWinston 2 42
(Tony Carroll) *a in last pair: wknd over 2f out: eased and t.o* **10/1**

3m 30.98s (0.88) **Going Correction** +0.05s/f (Slow) **9 Ran SP% 122.2**
Speed ratings (Par 103): **99,97,96,95,94 93,92,91,83**
CSF £67.55 CT £169.18 TOTE £14.10: £4.70, £1.60, £1.40; EX 68.30 Trifecta £257.30.
**Owner** Stonepoint Racing Club **Bred** Almagro De Actividades Commerciales **Trained** Blewbury, Oxon

**FOCUS**
Mainly exposed sorts in a fair handicap. The gallop was just an ordinary one but the winner showed a good turn of foot in the centre of the track. Form set around 2nd/3rd to recent.

## 4751 32RED H'CAP (LONDON MIDDLE DISTANCE SERIES QUALIFIER) — 1m 2f 219y(P)
**8:25** (8:26) (Class 4) (0-80,82) 3-Y-0+ — **£5,175** (£1,540; £769; £384) **Stalls** Low

Form — RPR

140 1 **Bush House (IRE)**[53] 2824 3-9-3 **79** .......... (b) JamesDoyle 3 89+
(Hugo Palmer) *trckd ldrs: hrd rdn wl over 2f out whn pce lifted: appeared to be struggling for pce but picked up over 1f out and led last 150yds: in command after and jst pushed out* **5/2**[1]

21-6 2 1 ¾ **St Malo (USA)**[46] 3091 4-10-3 **82** .......... (b[1]) AndreaAtzeni 2 88
(Roger Varian) *trckd ldrs on inner: rdn over 2f out whn pce lifted: clsd to ld over 1f out: hdd and outpcd last 150yds* **5/1**

31-0 3 ¾ **Graceful James (IRE)**[48] 3009 4-9-10 **75** .......... KieranO'Neill 5 79
(Jimmy Fox) *t.k.h: hld up in 6th: outpcd and rdn wl over 2f out: stl only 7th over 1f out: swtchd towards inner and styd on wl fnl f to take 3rd last strides* **40/1**

51 4 ½ **Distant (USA)**[20] 4003 3-9-0 **79** .......... KieranShoemark(3) 4 83
(Roger Charlton) *trckd ldrs: swift move to ld 3f out and upped the pce: nvr able to assert and hdd over 1f out: one pce after* **8/1**

1-13 5 nk **Rake's Progress**[37] 3392 3-8-11 **73** .......... GeraldMosse 1 76
(Heather Main) *led and dictated mod pce: hdd 3f out but styd on terms w ldr: outpcd fnl f* **11/4**[2]

0132 6 shd **Tom's Rock (IRE)**[14] 4216 4-10-3 **82** .......... DanielMuscutt 7 84
(John Butler) *t.k.h: hld up in last trio: nt wl plcd whn sprint sed 3f out: grad clsd u.p fr 2f out: kpt on same pce ins fnl f* **4/1**[3]

2160 7 6 **Choral Clan (IRE)**[65] 2477 6-9-9 **74** .......... JackMitchell 6 64
(Brendan Powell) *hld up in last trio: effrt on inner over 2f out: no prog over 1f out: sn wknd* **66/1**

4530 8 17 **Tangramm**[114] 1289 5-10-2 **81** .......... (p) RobertWinston 9 37
(Dean Ivory) *hld up in last trio: brief effrt on wd outside over 3f out: sn btn: t.o* **40/1**

341- 9 ¾ **Vincent's Forever**[34] 5768 4-10-3 **82** .......... (bt[1]) DougieCostello 8 37
(David Pipe) *pressed ldr but wd first 3f: lost 2nd 3f out: sn wknd: t.o* **25/1**

2m 20.94s (-0.96) **Going Correction** +0.05s/f (Slow)
**WFA** 3 from 4yo+ 11lb **9 Ran SP% 113.2**
Speed ratings (Par 105): **105,103,103,102,102 102,98,85,85**
CSF £14.64 CT £386.07 TOTE £2.90: £1.20, £1.50, £7.60; EX 15.40 Trifecta £488.50.
**Owner** W J and T C O Gredley **Bred** Camas Park, Lynch Bages & Summerhill **Trained** Newmarket, Suffolk

**FOCUS**
A useful-looking handicap in which a steady gallop picked up on the turn for home. The winner was another to race in the centre in the straight.

## 4752 32RED CASINO H'CAP — 6f (P)
**8:55** (8:57) (Class 4) (0-80,80) 3-Y-0+ — **£5,175** (£1,540; £769; £384) **Stalls** Low

Form — RPR

4-06 1 **Maakaasib**[32] 3584 3-9-7 **79** .......... (e) OisinMurphy 5 89
(Simon Crisford) *mde all: racd freely but hld together: hrd pressed fnl f: edgd lft nr fin but hld on wl* **7/2**[2]

-231 2 ½ **Hackney Road**[7] 4495 4-9-4 **75** .......... JoshuaBryan(5) 3 85
(John Butler) *trckd ldng trio: prog to take 2nd over 1f out and sn chalng: w wnr fnl f: edgd lft and nt qckn nr fin* **5/2**[1]

0310 3 1 ¾ **Showmethewayavrilo**[13] 4256 4-9-0 **69** .......... CharlieBennett(3) 8 73
(Malcolm Saunders) *pressed wnr: rdn over 1f out: sn lost 2nd: one pce fnl f* **20/1**

2625 4 ½ **Cappananty Con**[13] 4268 3-9-4 **76** .......... RobertWinston 1 77
(Dean Ivory) *t.k.h: trckd ldng pair: rdn to dispute 2nd over 1f out: one pce fnl f* **7/1**

6606 5 nk **Bring On A Spinner**[113] 1296 4-9-6 **75** .......... (v[1]) AaronJones(3) 2 76
(Stuart Williams) *trckd ldng trio: rdn and nt qckn wl over 1f out: no imp ldrs after* **20/1**

410 6 ½ **Fortitude (IRE)**[18] 4078 3-9-4 **76** .......... JamesDoyle 9 75+
(Hugo Palmer) *hld up in last pair: rdn on outer 2f out: kpt on fnl f: n.d but did best of those fr off the pce* **16/1**

2-11 7 1 ¼ **Madame Bounty (IRE)**[6] 4532 3-9-0 **72** .......... LiamKeniry 10 67
(Ed Walker) *hld up in midfield: effrt jst over 2f out: sn rdn and no imp ldrs* **9/2**[3]

15 8 nse **Alaadel**[32] 3572 4-9-11 **77** .......... JimCrowley 12 73+
(William Haggas) *dwlt: dropped in fr wdst draw and hld up in last pair: rdn and no prog 2f out: plugged on* **6/1**

1006 9 1 **Dutiful Son (IRE)**[35] 3471 7-10-0 **80** .......... JackMitchell 6 72
(Simon Dow) *hld up in rr: rdn 2f out: no imp ldrs after* **12/1**

0000 10 1 ¼ **Fairway To Heaven (IRE)**[13] 4251 8-9-0 **71** .......... PaddyBradley(5) 4 59
(Lee Carter) *dwlt: hld up in rr: rdn and no prog 2f out: sn btn* **33/1**

1m 12.95s (-0.15) **Going Correction** +0.05s/f (Slow)
**WFA** 3 from 4yo+ 6lb **10 Ran SP% 121.8**
Speed ratings (Par 105): **103,102,100,99,98 98,96,96,95,93**
CSF £12.98 CT £157.56 TOTE £4.30: £1.80, £1.60, £4.30; EX 18.10 Trifecta £212.70.
**Owner** Abdulla Al Mansoori **Bred** Newsells Park Stud **Trained** Newmarket, Suffolk
■ Porta Rosa was withdrawn. Price at time of withdrawal 66-1. Rule 4 does not apply.

**FOCUS**
A fair handicap but not a strong pace for a sprint and not surprisingly few figured. The winner came down the centre in the straight.
T/Jkpt: Not won. T/Plt: £250.20 to a £1 stake. Pool: £74,733.40. 218.01 winning units. T/Qpdt: £41.10 to a £1 stake. Pool: £7,491.91. 134.84 winning units. **Jonathan Neesom**

# 4346 LINGFIELD (L-H)
### Wednesday, July 12

**OFFICIAL GOING: Good to soft (7.1)**
Wind: Virtually nil Weather: Mainly sunny

## 4753 WIMBLEDON BETTING AT 188BET (S) STKS — 1m 2f
**2:25** (2:25) (Class 6) 3-Y-0+ — **£2,587** (£770; £384; £192) **Stalls** Low

Form — RPR

2220 1 **Hannington**[37] 3400 6-9-7 59 .......... (t) AlistairRawlinson(3) 2 65
(Michael Appleby) *trckd ldr: clsd and upsides over 2f out: rdn to ld wl over 1f out: styd on and in command ins fnl f: comf* **5/2**[3]

0-00 2 3 ¼ **Its A Sheila Thing**[27] 3760 4-9-0 43 .......... (h) GeorgeDowning 1 45
(Tony Carroll) *led: rdn and jnd over 2f out: hdd and drvn wl over 1f out: sn outpcd: wl hld in clr 2nd and kpt on same pce ins fnl f* **12/1**

666 3 2 ½ **Bizet (IRE)**[12] 4311 3-8-6 56 .......... (p) GeorgeWood(3) 3 47
(John Ryan) *hld up in rr: niggled along 5f out: struggling u.p 3f out: wl hld 3rd fnl 2f: nvr trbld ldrs* **7/4**[1]

03-0 4 9 **Port Paradise**[111] 1329 4-9-5 68 .......... (h) ShaneKelly 4 29
(William Jarvis) *hld up in 3rd: rdn and no rspnse 3f out: wl btn 4th and eased ins fnl f* **2/1**[2]

2m 13.45s (2.95) **Going Correction** +0.375s/f (Good)
**WFA** 3 from 4yo+ 10lb **4 Ran SP% 106.0**
Speed ratings (Par 101): **103,100,98,91**
CSF £21.69 TOTE £2.60; EX 26.80 Trifecta £73.20.There was no bid for the winner.
**Owner** From The Front Racing **Bred** Bearstone Stud Ltd **Trained** Oakham, Rutland

**FOCUS**
23mm of rainfall since the previous afternoon had turned the ground on the easy side. An uneventful seller rated around the winner.

## 4754 CTP 30TH ANNIVERSARY H'CAP — 1m 1f
**3:00** (3:00) (Class 6) (0-60,60) 3-Y-0 — **£2,587** (£770; £384; £192) **Stalls** Low

Form — RPR

0030 1 **Venetian Proposal (IRE)**[15] 4184 3-8-10 **49** .......... (p) KieranO'Neill 4 57+
(Zoe Davison) *in tch in midfield: rdn over 3f out: styd on to chse ldrs over 1f out: swtchd rt 1f out: led 100yds out: sn clr and r.o strly* **8/1**

-000 2 3 **Ronni Layne**[20] 4006 3-8-12 **51** .......... RobertTart 13 51
(Conrad Allen) *chsd ldr: rdn over 3f out: clsd to ld 2f out: rdr dropped whip over 1f out: hdd 100yds: immediately outpcd by wnr: kpt on same pce to hold 2nd* **20/1**

4000 3 1 **Accomplice**[16] 4150 3-9-6 **59** .......... RobHornby 9 57
(Michael Blanshard) *led: rdn 3f out: hdd 2f out: kpt on and styd chsng ldrs tl outpcd by wnr 100yds: keeping on same pce whn swtchd rt towards fin* **14/1**

2050 4 ½ **Never Folding (IRE)**[56] 2726 3-9-5 **58** .......... RobertWinston 2 55
(Seamus Durack) *taken down early and led rdrless to s: t.k.h: chsd ldrs: rdn over 2f out: pressing ldng air over 1f out: chsd ldr briefly 1f out: kpt on same pce after* **15/2**[3]

4-00 5 shd **Dancing Dragon (IRE)**[27] 3748 3-9-7 **60** .......... LiamKeniry 1 57
(George Baker) *chsd ldng pair: unable qck u.p over 2f out: rallied and kpt on again ins fnl f: no threat to wnr* **11/1**

0-03 6 nk **Henry Did It (IRE)**[30] 3657 3-8-13 **52** .......... ShaneKelly 10 48
(Tony Carroll) *stdd s: hld up in midfield: effrt over 2f out: rdn and switching rt over 1f out: keeping on but no threat to wnr whn nt clrest of runs ins fnl f* **5/1**[2]

6022 **7** *1 ½* **Whatalove**[16] 4150 3-8-5 **47**..........(h) GeorgeWood(3) 8 40
(Martin Keighley) *hld up in tch in last pair: effrt u.p over 2f out: nvr looked like clsng: plugged on ins fnl f: nvr trbld ldrs* **7/4**[1]

04 **8** *2 ¼* **Performance Art (IRE)**[22] 3939 3-8-9 **48**.......... SteveDrowne 7 37
(Seamus Mullins) *hld up in midfield: rdn 3f out: no imp whn nt clrest of runs over 1f out: wl hld after* **9/1**

00-0 **9** *4 ½* **French Silver (FR)**[13] 4274 3-8-7 **46** oh1.......... FrannyNorton 14 26
(Tony Carroll) *stdd and dropped in bhd after s: hld up in rr: pushed along over 2f out: no prog: nvr trbld ldrs* **25/1**

0-00 **10** *7* **Nip Down The Jug**[15] 4180 3-8-9 **48**.......... WilliamCarson 11 14
(Michael Attwater) *dropped in bhd after s: hld up in tch in last pair: rdn over 2f out: sn wl btn* **20/1**

1m 59.38s (2.78) **Going Correction** +0.375s/f (Good) **10** Ran SP% **114.3**
Speed ratings (Par 98): **102,99,98,98,97 97,96,94,90,84**
CSF £153.92 CT £2247.16 TOTE £9.30: £2.70, £5.20, £4.30; EX 149.70 Trifecta £3628.30.
**Owner** Mr & Mrs C Sowerby **Bred** John Browne **Trained** Hammerwood, E Sussex

**FOCUS**
Weak form, with little getting into it from off the pace, but the winner has been rated back to near her 2yo form.

## 4755 BRITISH GRAND PRIX BETTING AT 188BET H'CAP 1m 3f 133y
**3:35** (3:35) (Class 5) (0-70,71) 3-Y-O+ **£3,234** (£962; £481; £240) **Stalls** High

Form RPR

0-65 **1** **Jazzy (IRE)**[20] 4000 4-10-0 **70**..........(tp) TomQueally 8 79
(Martin Keighley) *hld up in midfield: clsd on ldrs over 4f out: rdn to chal 2f out: sustained chal u.p to ld ins fnl f: forged ahd towards fin* **14/1**

5343 **2** *¾* **Maroc**[33] 3537 4-9-11 **67**..........(p) RichardKingscote 9 75
(Nikki Evans) *chsd ldr and clr of field: clsd over 3f out: led over 2f out and sn edgd lft: hrd pressed 2f out: kpt on u.p: hdd ins fnl f: no ex towards fin* **11/1**

3-63 **3** *4* **Iballisticvin**[25] 3820 4-9-3 **64**.......... JoshuaBryan(5) 1 65
(Gary Moore) *chsd ldng pair for 2f: wnt 3rd again 6f out and grad clsd on ldrs: chsd ldrs and drvn over 1f out: no ex 1f out: outpcd fnl 100yds* **5/1**[3]

1452 **4** *hd* **Pete So High (GER)**[14] 4197 3-9-3 **71**..........(p) SeanLevey 4 73
(Richard Hannon) *led and sn clr: rdn and hdd over 2f out: kpt on u.p and styd chsng ldrs tl no ex 1f out: outpcd ins fnl f* **5/2**[2]

0-04 **5** *10* **Hard Toffee (IRE)**[56] 2728 6-10-1 **71**.......... RobertTart 6 56
(Conrad Allen) *stdd after s: hld up in last pair: clsd on ldrs 5f out: 5th and in tch whn rdn 3f out: sn struggling and wl btn over 1f out* **15/2**

3005 **6** *8* **Archangel Raphael (IRE)**[31] 3616 5-10-1 **71**.......... SteveDrowne 5 42
(Amanda Perrett) *hld up in midfield: rdn and dropped to last pair over 5f out: n.d after* **12/1**

05-3 **7** *½* **Hearty (IRE)**[51] 2909 4-9-9 **65**.......... LiamKeniry 3 36
(Richard Rowe) *dwlt: hld up in midfield: clsd on ldrs over 5th: effrt in 6th over 3f out: sn struggling: wknd wl over 1f out* **9/4**[1]

0000 **8** *34* **Fishergate**[50] 2914 4-8-13 **55**.......... FrannyNorton 7
(Richard Rowe) *s.i.s: hdwy to chse ldng pair after 2f tl 6f out: bhd 4f out: t.o* **66/1**

2m 34.12s (2.62) **Going Correction** +0.375s/f (Good)
**WFA** 3 from 4yo+ 12lb **8** Ran SP% **112.0**
Speed ratings (Par 103): **106,105,102,102,96 90,90,67**
CSF £147.64 CT £875.50 TOTE £11.10: £2.50, £2.50, £1.50; EX 112.90 Trifecta £378.30.
**Owner** Jazz Summers Racing **Bred** Ballyhane Stud **Trained** Condicote, Gloucs

**FOCUS**
The market leaders disappointed in this modest handicap, the front pair finishing clear.

## 4756 188BET.CO.UK H'CAP 2m 68y
**4:10** (4:11) (Class 6) (0-60,58) 4-Y-O+ **£2,587** (£770; £384; £192) **Stalls** Centre

Form RPR

350- **1** **Hiorne Tower (FR)**[230] 8084 6-9-7 **58**.......... RobertTart 12 64
(John Best) *hld up in rr: hdwy but stl plenty to do 4f out: clsng to chse ldrs whn pushed rt and impeded over 2f out: drvn to ld over 1f out: styd on strly and clr ins fnl f* **11/2**[3]

30-5 **2** *3 ¼* **Hermarna (IRE)**[49] 2964 4-9-1 **57**.......... GeorgiaCox(5) 10 59
(Neil King) *hld up in midfield: clsd 5f out: rdn to chse ldrs and swtchd rt over 2f out: ev ch over 1f out: outpcd by wnr and kpt on same pce in 2nd fnl f* **9/2**[1]

-055 **3** *1 ¾* **Esspeegee**[37] 3389 4-8-9 **46**..........(p) JimmyQuinn 2 46
(Alan Bailey) *t.k.h: chsd ldrs tl hdwy to chse ldr after 3f: led 6f out: rdn and clr w rival over 3f out: hdd over 1f out: sn outpcd: 3rd and kpt on same pce fnl f* **14/1**

2666 **4** *9* **Par Three (IRE)**[49] 2972 6-9-1 **52**..........(p) GeorgeDowning 13 41
(Tony Carroll) *midfield: hdwy to chse ldrs over 3f out: rdn over 3f out: unable qck and outpcd 2f out: wl hld 6th and whn swtchd lft 1f out: plugged on* **20/1**

4460 **5** *½* **Money Talks**[14] 4217 7-9-3 **54**..........(t) DanielMuscutt 11 43
(Michael Madgwick) *hld up in last pair: hdwy 5f out: in tch but unable qck u.p 3f out: sn outpcd and wl hld 2f out: plugged on* **5/1**[2]

4000 **6** *7* **Le Tissier**[27] 3756 4-8-12 **49**..........(p) RobHornby 1 29
(Michael Attwater) *midfield: rdn over 3f out: sn struggling and outpcd: wl btn fnl 2f* **14/1**

/0-0 **7** *2 ½* **Toptempo**[14] 4217 8-9-2 **53**.......... FergusSweeney 9 30
(Ralph J Smith) *hld up midfield: clsd 5f out: struggling u.p over 3f out: wl btn fnl 2f* **33/1**

-065 **8** *13* **Astrosecret**[40] 3292 4-8-11 **55**.......... GabrieleMalune(7) 6 17
(Mark H Tompkins) *midfield: dropped to rr over 4f out: sn lost tch: t.o* **40/1**

-004 **9** *2* **Honourable Knight (IRE)**[27] 3756 9-8-8 **45**.......... WilliamCarson 4 4
(Mark Usher) *chsd ldrs tl wnt 2nd 6f out: clr w ldr and ev ch over 3f out tl btn over 1f out: fdd and eased ins fnl f* **10/1**

0104 **10** *45* **Grand Facile**[11] 4346 5-9-5 **56**..........(b) TomQueally 7
(Gary Moore) *midfield: pushed along 12f out: sme prog on outer 1/2-way: lost tch over 3f out: t.o 2f out: eased* **14/1**

46/0 **11** *1 ¼* **Kalimantan (IRE)**[49] 2972 7-9-2 **53**.......... KieranO'Neill 3
(Tim Vaughan) *rn in snatches: chsd ldr for 3f: lost pl over 4f out: bhd and t.o fnl 2f: eased* **8/1**

4046 **P** **L'Ami De Rouge**[28] 3724 4-8-13 **50**.......... JackMitchell 8
(Ralph J Smith) *led tl 6f out: sn dropped out: t.o whn p.u and dismntd 4f out: burst blood vessel* **5/1**[2]

3m 42.62s (7.82) **Going Correction** +0.375s/f (Good) **12** Ran SP% **117.2**
Speed ratings (Par 101): **95,93,92,88,87 84,83,76,75,53 52,**
CSF £29.45 CT £332.08 TOTE £6.10: £1.80, £2.90, £4.60; EX 33.60 Trifecta £469.80.
**Owner** Mrs Jackie Jones **Bred** David Menuisier & Christiane Head Maarek **Trained** Oad Street, Kent
■ Stewards' Enquiry : Georgia Cox 2 day ban - guilty of careless riding (26/27 Jul)

**FOCUS**
Moderate staying form. The 2nd helps set the level.

## 4757 CTP CELEBRATION NOVICE AUCTION STKS 6f
**4:45** (4:45) (Class 5) 2-Y-O **£2,911** (£866; £432; £216) **Stalls** Centre

Form RPR

04 **1** **One For June (IRE)**[13] 4252 2-8-11 0.......... JamesDoyle 3 71
(William Haggas) *mde all: shkn up jst over 1f out: qcknd and asserted ins fnl f: r.o wl: eased towards fin: easily* **1/2**[1]

4 **2** *2 ¼* **Spanish Star (IRE)**[26] 3776 2-9-2 0.......... LiamKeniry 5 67
(Patrick Chamings) *stdd s: t.k.h: hld up in tch in rr: clsd and swtchd lft to press wnr over 1f out: edgd lft u.p ent fnl f: kpt on same pce ins fnl f* **4/1**[2]

0 **3** *hd* **Arden Pearl (IRE)**[25] 3821 2-8-11 0..........(h) JackMitchell 4 62
(Archie Watson) *taken down early: t.k.h: trckd wnr: rdn 2f out: 3rd and unable qck jst over 1f out: kpt on same pce ins fnl f* **16/1**

0 **4** *4* **Roman Spinner**[37] 3390 2-8-11 0..........(t) SeanLevey 2 50
(Rae Guest) *trckd ldng pair: rdn wl over 1f out: 4th and outpcd jst over 1f out: wl hld and kpt on same pce ins fnl f* **5/1**[3]

0 **5** *11* **Powerful Rose**[29] 3690 2-8-11 0.......... RobHornby 6 17
(Michael Blanshard) *wl in tch in 4th: dropped to last and rdn 2f out: sn outpcd: wknd fnl f* **40/1**

1m 15.71s (4.51) **Going Correction** +0.375s/f (Good) **5** Ran SP% **111.7**
Speed ratings (Par 94): **84,81,80,75,60**
CSF £2.97 TOTE £1.40: £1.02, £2.20; EX 3.00 Trifecta £9.90.
**Owner** Scotney/Symonds/Fisher Partnership **Bred** N O'Callaghan **Trained** Newmarket, Suffolk

**FOCUS**
Racing centre-field, this proved straightforward for the odds-on favourite.

## 4758 PLAY BLACKJACK AT 188BET NURSERY H'CAP 4f 217y
**5:15** (5:15) (Class 5) 2-Y-O **£2,911** (£866; £432; £216) **Stalls** Centre

Form RPR

0433 **1** **Firenze Rosa (IRE)**[25] 3821 2-8-9 **68**.......... KieranShoemark(3) 9 77
(John Bridger) *mde all: pushed along and asserted over 1f out: in command and r.o strly ins fnl f: readily* **11/2**[3]

0035 **2** *3 ½* **Terri Rules (IRE)**[30] 3655 2-8-0 **59** oh2 ow3.......... AaronJones(3) 1 55
(Julia Feilden) *chsd wnr: effrt and hung lft u.p over 1f out: sn outpcd by wnr but kpt on same pce for clr 2nd ins fnl f* **16/1**

032 **3** *1 ¼* **Zalshah**[11] 4349 2-9-7 **77**.......... SeanLevey 6 69
(Richard Hannon) *t.k.h: hld up in tch: clsd to trck ldrs 1/2-way: effrt but unable qck over 1f out: kpt on same pce ins fnl f* **6/4**[1]

006 **4** *1 ¼* **Hastenplace**[29] 3689 2-8-5 **61**..........(p[1]) KieranO'Neill 3 48
(Rod Millman) *dwlt: hld up in tch: effrt over 1f out: swtchd lft ins fnl f: wnt wl hld 4th and kpt on same pce fnl 100yds* **8/1**

2302 **5** *¾* **Autumn Lodge**[19] 4044 2-9-0 **70**..........(p[1]) LiamKeniry 5 55
(J S Moore) *t.k.h: hld up in tch: effrt over 1f out: sn rdn and unable qck: wknd ins fnl f* **9/1**

445 **6** *hd* **Data Protection**[40] 3277 2-8-0 **59**..........(b[1]) GeorgeWood(3) 8 43
(William Muir) *restless in stalls: in tch: rdn over 2f out: outpcd u.p over 1f out: wl hld and kpt on same pce ins fnl f* **6/1**

414 **7** *5* **Royal Liberty**[18] 4074 2-9-5 **75**.......... FrannyNorton 2 41
(Mark Johnston) *chsd ldrs: rdn 1/2-way: sn struggling and dropped to rr wl over 1f out: wknd fnl f* **5/1**[2]

59.88s (1.68) **Going Correction** +0.375s/f (Good) **7** Ran SP% **113.3**
Speed ratings (Par 94): **101,95,93,91,90 89,81**
CSF £80.51 CT £193.85 TOTE £6.00: £2.50, £6.70; EX 93.00 Trifecta £285.60.
**Owner** Mr & Mrs K Finch **Bred** Gervin Creaner **Trained** Liphook, Hants

**FOCUS**
A modest nursery but it produced a clear-cut winner.

## 4759 CRICKET BETTING AT 188BET MEDIAN AUCTION MAIDEN STKS 7f
**5:50** (5:52) (Class 6) 3-4-Y-O **£2,587** (£770; £384; £192) **Stalls** Centre

Form RPR

**1** **Bernardo O'Reilly** 3-9-1 0..........(h[1]) KieranShoemark(3) 3 84+
(Richard Spencer) *s.i.s: hld up in tch in rr: clsd over 2f out: led and rdn wl over 1f out: fnd ex and wnt clr 1f out: r.o strly: comf* **18/1**

3-03 **2** *6* **Joys Delight**[16] 4164 3-8-13 63.......... RichardKingscote 1 63
(Daniel Mark Loughnane) *mde most tl rdn and hdd wl over 1f out: outpcd by wnr over 1f out: wl hld and kpt on same pce ins fnl f: regained 2nd nr fin* **7/1**[3]

0- **3** *½* **Glenamoy Lad**[250] 7799 3-9-4 78.......... FrannyNorton 4 67
(Michael Wigham) *t.k.h: trckd ldrs: swtchd lft and jnd ldrs 2f out: rdn and nt match pce of wnr over 1f out: wknd ins fnl f: lost 2nd nr fin* **5/6**[1]

- **4** *1* **The Bear Can Fly** 3-8-13 0.......... WilliamCarson 6 59
(David Menuisier) *t.k.h: trckd ldrs tl jnd ldrs 1/2-way: rdn 2f out: sn outpcd: no ch w wnr and kpt on same pce ins fnl f* **25/1**

3 **5** *2 ¾* **Hydeandseek (FR)**[18] 4092 3-8-13 0.......... RobertTart 8 52
(John Best) *in tch in rr: rdn ent fnl 2f: sn outpcd: no ch and kpt on same pce fr over 1f out* **14/1**

5 **6** *hd* **Wardy (IRE)**[11] 4341 3-9-4 0.......... TomQueally 2 56
(Peter Chapple-Hyam) *t.k.h: w ldrs tl lost pl over 2f out: sn rdn: n.d over 1f out* **9/4**[2]

**7** *7* **Ventdanslesarbres** 3-8-13 0.......... TrevorWhelan 5 33
(George Baker) *s.i.s and wnt lft s: hld up in tch: clsd 3f out: rdn ent fnl 2f: sn outpcd and wknd: bhd ins fnl f* **33/1**

00-4 **8** *16* **Cadela Rica**[70] 2296 3-8-13 40..........(t[1]) FergusSweeney 7
(Gay Kelleway) *t.k.h: wl in tch: rdn ent fnl 2f: sn struggling: wl bhd and eased ins fnl f: t.o* **50/1**

1m 26.31s (3.01) **Going Correction** +0.375s/f (Good) **8** Ran SP% **118.5**
Speed ratings (Par 101): **97,90,89,88,85 85,77,58**
CSF £137.32 TOTE £17.10: £4.20, £2.30, £1.10; EX 138.20 Trifecta £227.10.
**Owner** Rebel Racing (2) **Bred** Chasemore Farm **Trained** Newmarket, Suffolk

**FOCUS**
A fairly weak maiden, with the favourite failing to run to anything like his mark, but still quite a taking winner. Not an easy race to put a figure on.

T/Plt: £15,426.80 to a £1 stake. Pool: £30,642.43. 1.45 winning units. T/Qpdt: £82.80 to a £1 stake. Pool: £5,058.89. 45.21 winning units. **Steve Payne**

# 4539YARMOUTH (L-H)

Wednesday, July 12

**OFFICIAL GOING: Good (7.1)**

Wind: Fresh, behind Weather: Cloudy with sunny spells

## 4760 BEST ODDS GUARANTEED AT 188BET NOVICE AUCTION STKS 5f 42y

**2:00** (2:00) (Class 5) 2-Y-O **£3,234** (£962; £481; £240) **Stalls** Centre

Form RPR
0214 **1** **Chatburn (IRE)**[32] 3556 2-9-7 82 DanielTudhope 3 80
(David O'Meara) *mde all: shkn up over 1f out: rdn out* **4/6**[1]
**2** *nk* **Fyre Cay (IRE)** 2-9-0 0 JamieSpencer 2 72
(Kevin Ryan) *a.p: shkn up over 1f out: rdn to chse wnr ins fnl f: r.o* **6/1**[3]
522 **3** 2 3/4 **Haveoneyerself (IRE)**[21] 3972 2-8-9 70 DarraghKeenan(7) 4 64
(John Butler) *chsd wnr: ev ch over 1f out: sn rdn: no ex wl ins fnl f* **3/1**[2]
**4** *shd* **Fortunate Vision** 2-8-12 0 JosephineGordon 1 60
(David Brown) *sn pushed along and rn green in rr: reminder 3f out: effrt over 1f out: styd on same pce fnl f* **16/1**

1m 1.64s (-1.06) **Going Correction** -0.30s/f (Firm) **4** Ran SP% **105.2**
Speed ratings (Par 94): **96,95,91,90**
CSF £4.68 TOTE £1.40; EX 6.50 Trifecta £7.90.
**Owner** David W Armstrong **Bred** Thomas Hassett **Trained** Upper Helmsley, N Yorks

**FOCUS**
A fair little juvenile novice contest. They went a respectable gallop on good ground and there was a tailwind on the straight course. This has been rated around the winner and 3rd.

## 4761 TICKET GIVEAWAYS AT 188BET FILLIES' H'CAP 1m 2f 23y

**2:35** (2:35) (Class 5) (0-70,72) 3-Y-0+ **£2,911** (£866; £432; £216) **Stalls** Low

Form RPR
-044 **1** **Three Duchesses**[24] 3859 3-9-2 **68** JamieSpencer 10 82
(Michael Bell) *hld up: swtchd rt and hdwy over 2f out: rdn to ld and hung lft wl over 1f out: sn clr: easily* **7/1**
5-06 **2** 6 **Ode To Glory**[12] 4320 3-8-6 **63** JaneElliott(5) 3 65
(Rae Guest) *chsd ldrs: rdn over 2f out: styd on same pce fnl f* **16/1**
4063 **3** *nk* **Millie's Kiss**[6] 4544 3-9-3 **69** DavidProbert 1 70
(Philip McBride) *hld up in tch: nt clr run over 2f out: rdn over 1f out: styd on to go 3rd nr fin* **9/2**[1]
-024 **4** *nk* **Poppy Time**[56] 2729 4-9-7 **63** RyanTate 2 63
(James Eustace) *hood removed late: s.i.s: hld up: nt clr run over 2f out: swtchd rt over 1f out: r.o to go 4th nr fin* **8/1**
6-03 **5** *hd* **Starlight Circus (IRE)**[12] 4319 3-8-12 **64** (b[1]) HarryBentley 6 64
(Marco Botti) *prom: chsd ldr over 8f out: rdn and ev ch 2f out: no ex fnl f* **13/2**
06-5 **6** 4 1/2 **Navajo Thunder (IRE)**[47] 3053 3-8-4 **56** ow1 LiamJones 5 47
(Michael Appleby) *chsd ldrs: rdn over 2f out: sn ev ch: wknd fnl f* **14/1**
1-06 **7** 5 **Marilyn**[50] 2929 3-9-4 **70** WilliamBuick 8 51
(Chris Wall) *hld up: hdwy over 3f out: rdn over 2f out: wknd over 1f out* **11/2**[3]
6031 **8** 1/2 **Katebird (IRE)**[15] 4171 3-9-6 **72** JoeFanning 4 52
(Mark Johnston) *sn led: rdn and hdd wl over 1f out: sn wknd* **5/1**[2]
16 **9** 1 3/4 **Enola (IRE)**[11] 4348 3-8-13 **65** AntonioFresu 7 42
(Ed Dunlop) *s.i.s: hld up: rdn over 3f out: wknd over 2f out* **16/1**
25-0 **10** 26 **Bianca Minola (FR)**[57] 2711 3-8-10 **62** JosephineGordon 9
(David Menuisier) *hld up: pushed along over 4f out: wknd 3f out* **12/1**

2m 7.56s (-2.94) **Going Correction** -0.30s/f (Firm)
**WFA** 3 from 4yo 10lb **10** Ran SP% **113.3**
Speed ratings (Par 100): **99,94,93,93,93 89,85,85,84,63**
CSF £108.65 CT £556.32 TOTE £7.60: £2.30, £4.90, £1.70; EX 124.50 Trifecta £513.30.
**Owner** Hon James Broughton **Bred** Barton Stud **Trained** Newmarket, Suffolk

**FOCUS**
A modest fillies' handicap. They went a modest gallop down the back into a headwind, with the tempo increasing in the straight.

## 4762 188BET.CO.UK H'CAP 1m 6f 17y

**3:10** (3:12) (Class 5) (0-75,76) 4-Y-0+ **£2,911** (£866; £432; £216) **Stalls** High

Form RPR
140- **1** **Avenue Des Champs**[412] 2605 5-8-10 **64** (p) JosephineGordon 3 69
(Jane Chapple-Hyam) *led 1f: chsd ldrs: led again wl over 2f out: rdn over 1f out: styd on* **7/2**[3]
0000 **2** 1/2 **Saved By The Bell (IRE)**[17] 4120 7-9-8 **76** (v) DanielTudhope 2 79
(David O'Meara) *racd keenly in 2nd tl rdn and hung lft fr over 3f out: nt run on* **15/8**[1]
2-36 **3** *nk* **Burning Heat (IRE)**[22] 616 4-9-1 **69** (p[1]) RyanTate 1 71
(James Eustace) *hld up: hdwy u.p over 1f out: styd on* **11/2**
0424 **4** 1 1/2 **Daisy Boy (IRE)**[18] 4095 6-9-5 **73** (t) JoeFanning 4 73
(Stuart Williams) *led after 1f: hdd wl over 2f out: sn rdn: nt clr run ins fnl f: styd on same pce towards fin* **5/2**[2]
6214 **5** 10 **Bracken Brae**[78] 2059 5-9-7 **75** JoeyHaynes 5 61
(Mark H Tompkins) *hld up: hdwy over 1f out: sn rdn: wknd fnl f* **12/1**

3m 4.24s (-3.36) **Going Correction** -0.30s/f (Firm) **5** Ran SP% **108.7**
Speed ratings (Par 103): **97,96,96,95,89**
CSF £10.20 TOTE £4.80: £2.20, £1.60; EX 13.50 Trifecta £40.70.
**Owner** The Tuesday Club **Bred** Grovewood Stud **Trained** Dalham, Suffolk

**FOCUS**
A muddling handicap. Once again the runners were wary of going too fast into the headwind down the back.

## 4763 188BET H'CAP 1m 1f 21y

**3:45** (3:45) (Class 3) (0-90,89) 3-Y-0+ **£7,246** (£2,168; £1,084; £542; £270) **Stalls** Low

Form RPR
-412 **1** **Rotherwick (IRE)**[23] 3905 5-9-10 **85** (t) DavidProbert 2 92
(Paul Cole) *hld up: hdwy over 1f out: rdn and r.o to ld wl ins fnl f* **15/2**
0-02 **2** 3/4 **Interconnection**[54] 2796 6-10-0 **89** (p) HarryBentley 8 95
(Ed Vaughan) *led at stdy pce tl qcknd over 3f out: rdn over 1f out: edgd rt and hdd wl ins fnl f* **9/2**[3]
1042 **3** *nk* **Morning Suit (USA)**[14] 4223 3-9-3 **88** JoeFanning 3 92
(Mark Johnston) *chsd ldrs: shkn up over 2f out: n.m.r and unable qck nr fin* **9/1**
1-32 **4** 1 3/4 **Dubara**[29] 3693 3-9-1 **86** JamieSpencer 6 86+
(Luca Cumani) *hld up: hdwy over 1f out: nt clr run ins fnl f: styd on same pce* **7/2**[1]
1-5 **5** 1/2 **Omeros**[28] 3713 3-8-12 **83** JosephineGordon 5 82
(Hugo Palmer) *racd keenly in 2nd pl: rdn 3f out: edgd lft: lost 2nd and no ex wl ins fnl f* **4/1**[2]
6610 **6** 1 1/2 **Bint Dandy (IRE)**[20] 4001 6-9-3 **83** (b) LewisEdmunds(5) 7 80
(Chris Dwyer) *prom: racd keenly: rdn over 2f out: styd on same pce fnl f* **16/1**
-625 **7** *nk* **Mikmak**[41] 3235 4-9-8 **83** (p) LouisSteward 4 79
(William Muir) *hld up: hdwy over 2f out: sn rdn: no ex fnl f* **25/1**
21-3 **U** **First Voyage (IRE)**[28] 3716 4-9-8 **83** (p) WilliamBuick 1
(Charlie Appleby) *edgd lft and uns rdr leaving stalls* **7/2**[1]

1m 53.99s (-1.81) **Going Correction** -0.30s/f (Firm)
**WFA** 3 from 4yo+ 10lb **8** Ran SP% **114.1**
Speed ratings (Par 107): **96,95,95,93,93 91,91,**
CSF £40.91 CT £308.92 TOTE £9.00: £2.20, £1.80, £2.50; EX 45.70 Trifecta £208.50.
**Owner** H R H Sultan Ahmad Shah **Bred** Brian O'Neill **Trained** Whatcombe, Oxon

**FOCUS**
The feature contest was a decent handicap. They went a modest gallop and one of the joint favourites unseated his rider leaving the stalls. The winner has been rated to his best since his 3yo days.

## 4764 READ SILVESTRE DE SOUSA AT 188BET MEDIAN AUCTION MAIDEN STKS 1m 3y

**4:20** (4:23) (Class 5) 3-Y-O **£3,234** (£962; £481; £240) **Stalls** Centre

Form RPR
-223 **1** **Cool Team (IRE)**[26] 3781 3-9-5 79 (tp) JosephineGordon 13 80
(Hugo Palmer) *hld up: hdwy over 3f out: rdn to ld 1f out: r.o* **6/4**[1]
5-3 **2** 1 **Working Class**[14] 4224 3-9-5 0 WilliamBuick 1 78
(Peter Chapple-Hyam) *chsd ldr: rdn and ev ch over 1f out: styd on same pce wl ins fnl f* **7/4**[2]
002 **3** 1 3/4 **Unit Of Assessment (IRE)**[37] 3393 3-9-5 74 HarryBentley 6 73
(William Knight) *led: rdn over 2f out: hdd 1f out: styd on same pce ins fnl f* **3/1**[3]
6 **4** 1 1/4 **Delilah Park**[35] 3472 3-9-0 0 DavidProbert 5 65
(Philip McBride) *hld up in tch: effrt over 2f out: no ex ins fnl f* **20/1**
05 **5** *hd* **Miss Pacific**[18] 4097 3-9-0 0 JoeFanning 3 65
(William Jarvis) *s.i.s: hld up: hdwy over 1f out: styd on same pce fnl f* **25/1**
0- **6** *nse* **Love Me Again**[252] 7763 3-9-0 0 StevieDonohoe 2 65
(Charlie Fellowes) *chsd ldrs: rdn and outpcd over 1f out: styd on towards fin* **20/1**
**7** 8 **Bamo Mc** 3-9-5 0 AntonioFresu 4 51
(Mike Murphy) *s.i.s: in rr and pushed along 1/2-way: sme hdwy u.p over 1f out: wknd fnl f* **50/1**
0 **8** 1 **Silken Moonlight**[32] 3555 3-8-7 0 RPWalsh(7) 11 43
(Scott Dixon) *s.i.s: in rr and pushed along over 3f out: n.d* **50/1**
00 **9** 4 1/2 **Hanningfield**[25] 3824 3-9-5 0 LouisSteward 8 37
(Michael Bell) *hld up: plld hrd: rdn and swtchd rt over 2f out: n.d* **66/1**
00-0 **10** 1/2 **I Dare To Dream**[73] 2182 3-8-9 46 (p[1]) JaneElliott(5) 7 31
(Lisa Williamson) *hld up: rdn over 2f out: n.d* **200/1**
0 **11** 3 **Poet's Quest**[126] 1083 3-9-0 0 LiamJones 10 24
(Dean Ivory) *prom: rdn over 2f out: sn wknd* **50/1**
00 **12** 2 **Brave Tart**[5] 4565 3-9-0 0 SaleemGolam 9 19
(Martin Smith) *prom over 5f* **200/1**

1m 37.78s (-2.82) **Going Correction** -0.30s/f (Firm) **12** Ran SP% **123.1**
Speed ratings (Par 100): **102,101,99,98,97 97,89,88,84,83 80,78**
CSF £4.25 TOTE £2.50: £1.10, £1.20, £1.30; EX 5.90 Trifecta £8.80.
**Owner** Lit Lung Lee **Bred** Ringfort Stud **Trained** Newmarket, Suffolk

**FOCUS**
An ordinary 3yo maiden. They went a respectable gallop and the favourite won well towards the near side from a high draw.

## 4765 OPEN GOLF BETTING AT 188BET H'CAP 1m 3y

**4:55** (4:55) (Class 6) (0-65,67) 3-Y-0+ **£2,264** (£673; £336; £168) **Stalls** Centre

Form RPR
0321 **1** **Turning Gold**[6] 4541 3-9-1 **67** 6ex (b) ManuelFernandes(7) 2 83+
(Sir Mark Prescott Bt) *sn w ldr: led over 6f out: clr fnl 3f: easily* **4/7**[1]
1P-0 **2** 8 **Ice Alert (IRE)**[12] 4311 4-10-0 **64** (t) JosephineGordon 6 64
(John Ryan) *chsd ldrs: pushed along and lost pl 1/2-way: hdwy u.p to go 2nd over 1f out: no ch w wnr* **28/1**
-020 **3** 5 **Jack Nevison**[12] 4298 4-9-7 **64** RayDawson(7) 3 53
(Michael Appleby) *chsd ldrs: pushed along 1/2-way: chsd wnr over 2f out tl rdn and wknd over 1f out* **15/2**[2]
54 **4** 1/2 **Touch The Clouds**[27] 3761 6-8-4 **45** LewisEdmunds(5) 8 32
(William Stone) *s.i.s: hld up: rdn over 2f out: styd on ins fnl f: nvr nrr* **14/1**
0530 **5** 2 1/4 **Dukes Meadow**[44] 3137 6-8-4 **47** RhiainIngram(7) 1 29
(Roger Ingram) *hld up: rdn over 2f out: n.d* **22/1**
3230 **6** 3/4 **Break The Silence**[12] 4298 3-8-3 **55** RPWalsh(7) 7 33
(Scott Dixon) *chsd ldrs: rdn and edgd lft over 2f out: wknd over 1f out* **12/1**
-000 **7** 3 3/4 **Seventii**[25] 3823 3-7-10 **48** DarraghKeenan(7) 9 18
(Robert Eddery) *hld up: rdn over 2f out: sn wknd* **28/1**
-050 **8** 1/2 **Penny Red**[28] 3721 3-9-4 **63** HarryBentley 5 32
(William Knight) *prom: pushed along and lost pl over 3f out: sn wknd* **9/1**[3]
45-2 **9** 4 **World Record (IRE)**[50] 2915 7-9-8 **58** DavidProbert 4 19
(Mick Quinn) *led: hdd over 6f out: chsd wnr tl rdn over 2f out: wknd over 1f out* **9/1**[3]

1m 34.56s (-6.04) **Going Correction** -0.30s/f (Firm)
**WFA** 3 from 4yo+ 9lb **9** Ran SP% **121.0**
Speed ratings (Par 101): **118,110,105,104,102 101,97,97,93**
CSF £27.95 CT £76.71 TOTE £1.50: £1.02, £4.20, £2.20; EX 24.70 Trifecta £145.50.
**Owner** Mrs Helen Jones **Bred** Cheveley Park Stud Ltd **Trained** Newmarket, Suffolk

**FOCUS**
A modest handicap. The odds-on favourite turned this into a procession.

## 4766 DAILY RACING SPECIALS AT 188BET H'CAP 7f 3y

**5:25** (5:25) (Class 6) (0-65,65) 3-Y-0+ **£2,264** (£673; £336; £168) **Stalls** Centre

Form RPR
1565 **1** **Daring Guest (IRE)**[15] 4186 3-9-1 **65** JaneElliott(5) 2 70
(George Margarson) *hld up: hdwy over 2f out: led over 1f out: sn rdn: r.o* **7/2**[2]
-000 **2** *hd* **Nellie's Dancer**[12] 4303 3-8-7 **52** (p) JosephineGordon 1 56
(Scott Dixon) *chsd ldrs: pushed along 1/2-way: rdn and ev ch fr over 1f out: r.o* **8/1**
1143 **3** 1 1/4 **Moi Aussie**[14] 4203 4-9-5 **63** RayDawson(7) 3 67
(Michael Appleby) *chsd ldr tl rdn to ld over 2f out: edgd rt over 1f out: styd on same pce ins fnl f* **5/2**[1]
2166 **4** *nk* **Commanche**[95] 1631 8-9-5 **61** (b) LewisEdmunds(5) 5 64
(Chris Dwyer) *hld up: rdn over 2f out: hdwy over 1f out: styd on* **7/1**

00P- **5** *2½* **Maddys Dream**[408] [2749] 4-9-10 **64**.............................. SimonPearce(3) 4 61
(Lydia Pearce) *hld up in tch: plld hrd: rdn over 1f out: styd on* **22/1**
3540 **6** *¾* **Gulland Rock**[11] [4350] 6-9-13 **64**....................................... DavidProbert 6 59
(Anthony Carson) *led: rdn and hdd over 2f out: no ex fr over 1f out* **9/2**[3]
0630 **7** *9* **Humour (IRE)**[28] [3728] 6-8-9 **46** oh1............................(vt) StevieDonohoe 7 16
(Christine Dunnett) *prom: rdn over 2f out: wknd over 1f out* **20/1**
2310 **8** *1½* **Alpha Tauri (USA)**[12] [4293] 11-8-9 **46** oh1......................... JoeyHaynes 8 12
(Charles Smith) *prom: rdn and ev ch over 2f out: wknd over 1f out* **9/1**
1m 23.53s (-3.07) **Going Correction** -0.30s/f (Firm)
**WFA** 3 from 4yo+ 8lb **8** Ran SP% **111.7**
Speed ratings (Par 101): **105,104,103,103,100 99,89,87**
CSF £29.80 CT £79.00 TOTE £4.20: £1.50, £2.50, £1.10; EX 20.70 Trifecta £26.40.
**Owner** John Guest Racing **Bred** Ringfort Stud **Trained** Newmarket, Suffolk
■ Stewards' Enquiry : Josephine Gordon 2 day ban - used whip above the permitted level (26/27 Jul)

**FOCUS**
A modest handicap. They went a respectable gallop on drying ground and it is sound form.
T/Plt: £58.00 to a £1 stake. Pool: £44,409.16. 558.53 winning units. T/Qpdt: £12.90 to a £1 stake. Pool: £5,685.11. 325.33 winning units. **Colin Roberts**

4767 - 4781a (Foreign Racing) - See Raceform Interactive

## [4454]MAISONS-LAFFITTE (R-H)
Wednesday, July 12

**OFFICIAL GOING: Turf: soft**

### 4782a PRIX SUN PRINCE (MAIDEN) (2YO COLTS & GELDINGS) (TURF) 5f 110y
2:20 2-Y-O **£11,538** (£4,615; £3,461; £2,307; £1,153)

RPR
**1** **Arecibo (FR)**[26] 2-9-2 0.................................................. MaximeGuyon 4 88
(C Laffon-Parias, France) **13/10**[1]
**2** *3½* **Global Passion (FR)**[26] [3782] 2-9-2 0.................. ChristopheSoumillon 5 76
(Charles Hills) *disp ld w wnr: rdn over 1f out: readily outpcd fnl f and sn wl hld in 2nd* **23/10**[2]
**3** *2* **Tadeem (IRE)**[25] 2-9-2 0.................................................. GeraldMosse 3 70
(J E Hammond, France) **14/5**[3]
**4** *2* **Varius (FR)**[25] 2-9-2 0.............................................. AurelienLemaitre 1 63
(M Nigge, France) **9/1**
**5** *30* **Artful Charlie (FR)** 2-8-11 0........................................ IoritzMendizabal 2
(E J O'Neill, France) **11/1**
1m 6.2s (-1.10) **5** Ran SP% **118.4**
PARI-MUTUEL (all including 1 euro stake): WIN 2.30; PLACE 1.20, 1.50; SF 5.10.
**Owner** Wertheimer & Frere **Bred** Wertheimer & Frere **Trained** Chantilly, France

### 4783a PRIX DE LIMAY (CLAIMER) (3YO) (TURF) 6f
2:55 3-Y-O **£9,829** (£3,931; £2,948; £1,965; £982)

RPR
**1** **Nuee Ardente (FR)**[39] [3355] 3-8-8 0......................... StephanePasquier 5 76
(K Borgel, France) **4/1**[2]
**2** *nk* **Sweeticon**[21] 3-8-8 0............................................... CristianDemuro 10 75
(Antonio Marcialis, Italy) **19/1**
**3** *nk* **Tan**[21] 3-9-2 0......................................................... DelphineSantiago(4) 13 82
(E J O'Neill, France) **43/10**[3]
**4** *nk* **Lord Cooper**[39] [3355] 3-9-1 0..................................(p) MickaelBarzalona 11 80
(Jose Santos) *midfield: u.p bef 1/2-way: kpt on wl and chal fnl f: jst hld in 4th nring fin* **15/2**
**5** *2* **Castle Dream (FR)**[103] 3-8-11 0.......................................... TonyPiccone 3 70
(K Borgel, France) **21/1**
**6** *1¼* **Esperitum (FR)**[26] 3-8-11 0......................................... AurelienLemaitre 9 66
(D & P Prod'Homme, France) **21/1**
**7** *1¾* **Rise Hit (FR)**[32] 3-9-1 0.................................... Pierre-CharlesBoudot 15 64
(H-A Pantall, France) **8/1**
**8** *¾* **Idroscalo (GER)**[40] [3310] 3-8-4 0.............................(b) MlleLauraGrosso(7) 12 54
(Antonio Marcialis, Italy) **36/1**
**9** *snk* **Larno (FR)**[21] 3-9-1 0.............................................. MaximeGuyon 14 61
(M Boutin, France) **33/10**[1]
**10** *½* **If I Say So**[11] 3-9-1 0...........................................(p) IoritzMendizabal 4 60
(M Boutin, France) **78/10**
**11** *6½* **Apero Time (FR)**[19] 3-8-2 0....................................... MlleLeaBails(9) 6 31
(D Windrif, France) **105/1**
**12** *11* **Groundskeeperwilly**[135] [956] 3-8-11 0............................. GabrieleCongiu 7
(Frank Sheridan, Italy) **67/1**
**13** *4½* **Saint Ferdinand (IRE)**[29] 3-8-6 0.............................. ClementLecoeuvre(5) 8
(E Lellouche, France) **30/1**
1m 11.0s (-2.40) **13** Ran SP% **118.8**
PARI-MUTUEL (all including 1 euro stake): WIN 5.00; PLACE 2.00, 4.90, 2.10; DF 42.30; SF 68.40.
**Owner** L Haegel **Bred** M Boutin, M Boutin & H Boutin **Trained** France

## [4605]CARLISLE (R-H)
Thursday, July 13

**OFFICIAL GOING: Good to firm (good in places; 8.0)**
Wind: Breezy, half against in over 2f of home straight Weather: Cloudy, bright

### 4784 BRITISH STALLION STUDS EBF MAIDEN STKS 7f 173y
1:30 (1:30) (Class 5) 3-4-Y-O **£3,881** (£1,155; £577; £288) **Stalls** Low

Form RPR
3 **1** **Kynren (IRE)**[13] [4309] 3-9-3 0.................................................. BenCurtis 3 71+
(David Barron) *mde all: rdn and hrd pressed whn blkd over 1f out: kpt on strly fnl f* **4/5**[1]
4363 **2** *1¾* **Arnarson**[42] [3259] 3-9-3 77.............................................. LukeMorris 4 66+
(Ed Dunlop) *pressed wnr: rdn and ev ch whn hung rt over 1f out: no ex ins fnl f* **7/4**[2]
**3** *1¾* **True Colors** 3-9-3 0......................................................... JackGarritty 2 62+
(Richard Fahey) *trckd ldrs: pushed along and effrt 2f out: checked briefly 1f out: kpt on same pce* **10/1**[3]
**4** *1¾* **Excellent Story** 3-9-3 0.................................................... PhillipMakin 7 58
(John Davies) *s.i.s and wnt lft s: t.k.h in rr: rdn over 2f out: hdwy over 1f out: no imp fnl f* **14/1**
00 **5** *1½* **Pipers Way**[33] [3568] 3-9-0 0........................................ AdamMcNamara(3) 1 54?
(Richard Fahey) *hld up in tch: drvn and outpcd 2f out: n.d after* **66/1**
00 **6** *hd* **Shine Baby Shine**[9] [4474] 3-8-12 0.......................................... PaddyAspell 5 49?
(Philip Kirby) *in tch: rdn and outpcd over 2f out: btn over 1f out* **100/1**
1m 46.0s (6.00) **Going Correction** 0.0s/f (Good) **6** Ran SP% **110.2**
Speed ratings (Par 103): **70,68,66,64,63 63**
CSF £2.28 TOTE £1.40: £1.10, £1.40; EX 2.60 Trifecta £8.30.
**Owner** Elliott Brothers & Peacock & Partner **Bred** Rathasker Stud **Trained** Maunby, N Yorks

**FOCUS**
After two dry days, the ground was described as good to firm, good in places (GoingStick: 8.0). The rail into the home straight was out 6yds, adding 18 yards to races 1, 2, 3 and 7. Distances for the rest were as advertised. Stalls: Inside all races. Add 18yds. An ordinary maiden in which the winner set a modest gallop for the first half of the race.

### 4785 RACINGUK.COM/DAYPASS H'CAP 7f 173y
2:00 (2:00) (Class 5) (0-75,76) 3-Y-O **£3,396** (£1,010; £505; £252) **Stalls** Low

Form RPR
4650 **1** **Ventura Secret (IRE)**[18] [4122] 3-8-8 **59**............... RachelRichardson(3) 3 65
(Tim Easterby) *t.k.h: pressed ldr: led over 1f out: rdn and r.o wl fnl f* **15/2**
6541 **2** *½* **Whatsthemessage (IRE)**[15] [4209] 3-9-7 **69**.................. AndrewMullen 1 74
(Keith Dalgleish) *t.k.h: led at ordinary gallop: rdn and hdd over 1f out: rallied: hld towards fin* **7/4**[1]
-502 **3** *1* **Savannah Moon (IRE)**[14] [4265] 3-9-3 **65**..........................(h[1]) KevinStott 4 68
(Kevin Ryan) *in tch: effrt and rdn wl over 1f out: edgd rt: kpt on ins fnl f: nt rch first two* **13/2**
2252 **4** *2½* **Mama Africa (IRE)**[14] [4276] 3-9-4 **66**.................................. BenCurtis 5 63
(David Barron) *t.k.h: hld up in tch: hdwy on outside over 1f out: outpcd ins fnl f* **9/4**[2]
-545 **5** *36* **Dream Team**[35] [3484] 3-9-5 **67**....................................(b[1]) PaulMulrennan 2
(Michael Dods) *t.k.h: trckd ldrs tl rdn and wknd fr 2f out: t.o* **5/1**[3]
1m 39.64s (-0.36) **Going Correction** 0.0s/f (Good) **5** Ran SP% **108.9**
Speed ratings (Par 100): **101,100,99,97,61**
CSF £20.65 TOTE £9.30: £2.60, £2.00; EX 28.30 Trifecta £192.30.
**Owner** Middleham Park Racing LXI & Partner **Bred** Audrey Frances Stynes **Trained** Great Habton, N Yorks

**FOCUS**
Add 18yds. The absence of top-weight Hajjam removed some interest from this handicap, but the winner relished the step up in trip. It was his best run this year but still well short of his 2yo best.

### 4786 RACING UK NOW ON TALK TALK FILLIES' NOVICE STKS (PLUS 10 RACE) 6f 195y
2:35 (2:35) (Class 5) 2-Y-O **£3,396** (£1,010; £505; £252) **Stalls** Low

Form RPR
1 **1** **Poetic Steps (FR)**[9] [4472] 2-9-4 0........................................ JoeFanning 2 81+
(Mark Johnston) *mde all: rdn over 1f out: styd on strly fnl f* **11/8**[1]
33 **2** *1¼* **Paramount Love**[25] [3858] 2-8-11 0......................... AdamMcNamara(3) 5 73
(Richard Fahey) *prom: effrt and chsd wnr over 1f out: kpt on ins fnl f: nt pce to chal* **11/4**[2]
401 **3** *½* **Seaella (IRE)**[27] [3791] 2-9-0 71.......................................... JasonHart 3 72
(John Quinn) *trckd ldrs: effrt and disp 2nd pl over 1f out: kpt on same pce ins fnl f* **5/1**[3]
**4** *nse* **Affina (IRE)** 2-9-0 0.......................................................... GrahamLee 6 72+
(Simon Crisford) *hld up: pushed along over 2f out: effrt and edgd rt over 1f out: sn one pce* **7/1**
634 **5** *5* **Deadly Reel (IRE)**[9] [4465] 2-9-0 0........................................ LukeMorris 4 58
(Archie Watson) *trckd wnr: rdn over 2f out: wknd over 1f out* **9/1**
00 **6** *4½* **Mountain Meadow**[25] [3858] 2-9-0 0.................................... JackGarritty 1 46
(Richard Fahey) *hld up: drvn and outpcd over 2f out: wknd wl over 1f out* **33/1**
1m 28.22s (1.12) **Going Correction** 0.0s/f (Good) **6** Ran SP% **110.9**
Speed ratings (Par 91): **93,91,91,90,85 80**
CSF £5.18 TOTE £2.10: £1.30, £1.70; EX 6.20 Trifecta £13.50.
**Owner** Kingsley Park 6 **Bred** Mark Johnston Racing Ltd **Trained** Middleham Moor, N Yorks

**FOCUS**
Add 18yds. A decent juvenile contest which produced a winner who looks sure to go on to much better things. The level is set around the 2nd/3rd.

### 4787 RACING UK H'CAP 5f
3:10 (3:12) (Class 4) (0-85,87) 3-Y-O+ **£5,498** (£1,636; £817; £408) **Stalls** Low

Form RPR
1132 **1** **El Hombre**[19] [4079] 3-9-4 **87**........................................ RowanScott(5) 6 92+
(Keith Dalgleish) *trckd ldrs: rdn 2f out: led ins fnl f: kpt on wl* **6/4**[1]
0230 **2** *nk* **Aprovado (IRE)**[12] [4337] 5-9-9 **82**..............................(p) AndrewMullen 3 88
(Michael Dods) *led: rdn over 1f out: hdd ins fnl f: rallied: hld nr fin* **22/1**
0502 **3** *nk* **Bossipop**[8] [4505] 4-9-8 **81**.............................................(b) PaulMulrennan 5 86
(Tim Easterby) *trckd ldrs: effrt on ins over 1f out: ev ch ins fnl f: kpt on: hld towards fin* **7/2**[2]
3006 **4** *3½* **Olivia Fallow (IRE)**[19] [4078] 5-9-10 **83**................................. GrahamLee 1 75
(Paul Midgley) *dwlt: hld up: rdn and effrt over 1f out: no imp ins fnl f* **6/1**
-362 **5** *1¼* **Fruit Salad**[13] [4305] 4-9-2 **75**.......................................(b[1]) JoeFanning 7 63
(James Bethell) *prom on outside: rdn and effrt over 1f out: wknd ins fnl f* **9/2**[3]
11-0 **6** *8* **Fast Act (IRE)**[52] [2899] 5-9-12 **85**.......................................... KevinStott 2 44
(Kevin Ryan) *pressed ldr: rdn over 2f out: wknd over 1f out* **9/1**
59.81s (-0.99) **Going Correction** 0.0s/f (Good)
**WFA** 3 from 4yo+ 5lb **6** Ran SP% **109.0**
Speed ratings (Par 105): **107,106,106,100,98 85**
CSF £32.23 CT £89.67 TOTE £2.00: £1.40, £4.40; EX 19.20 Trifecta £51.40.
**Owner** Weldspec Glasgow Limited **Bred** Mrs J McMahon **Trained** Carluke, S Lanarks

**FOCUS**
Ony a few runners, but a competitive sprint handicap which produced a rousing finish and a likeable winner. The 2nd sets the standard.

### 4788 BRITISH STALLION STUDS EBF FILLIES' H'CAP 5f 193y
3:45 (3:47) (Class 4) (0-80,82) 3-Y-O+ **£6,469** (£1,925; £962; £481) **Stalls** Low

Form RPR
0246 **1** **Maureb (IRE)**[20] [4154] 5-8-12 **64**..........................................(p) BarryMcHugh 2 71
(Tony Coyle) *mde all: rdn and edgd rt over 1f out: hld on wl fnl f* **12/1**
426 **2** *¾* **Rely On Me (IRE)**[29] [3716] 3-9-4 **81**.................................. JoshuaBryan(5) 4 85
(Andrew Balding) *chsd wnr thrght: effrt and drvn along over 1f out: kpt on ins fnl f* **11/4**[2]
6526 **3** *shd* **Sea Of Green**[4] [4663] 5-8-0 **59** oh3..............................(p) SeanMooney(7) 6 64
(Jim Goldie) *dwlt: hld up: effrt and rdn over 1f out: kpt on ins fnl f* **16/1**
0553 **4** *½* **Hamidans Girl (IRE)**[10] [4428] 3-8-8 **66**................................ AndrewMullen 7 68
(Keith Dalgleish) *in tch on outside: rdn and outpcd over 2f out: rallied fnl f: kpt on fin* **20/1**
-221 **5** *4½* **Dealer's Choice (IRE)**[19] [4092] 3-9-6 **78**.....................(p) PaulMulrennan 1 66
(Roger Varian) *chsd ldrs: rdn over 2f out: wknd over 1f out* **3/1**[3]

2322 **6** *1 1/2* **Storm Cry**[7] [4521] 3-9-10 **82** ............ JoeFanning 5 65
(Mark Johnston) *chsd ldrs: drvn over 2f out: edgd lft and wknd over 1f out* **9/4**[1]

5224 **7** *1 1/2* **Honeysuckle Lil (IRE)**[14] [4249] 5-9-3 **72** ..........(p) RachelRichardson(3) 3 51
(Tim Easterby) *t.k.h: hld up in tch: rdn over 2f out: wknd over 1f out* **8/1**

1m 12.55s (-1.15) **Going Correction** 0.0s/f (Good)
**WFA** 3 from 5yo 6lb 7 Ran SP% **111.9**
Speed ratings (Par 102): **107,106,105,105,99 97,95**
CSF £43.13 TOTE £11.20: £4.20, £2.10; EX 57.00 Trifecta £462.20.
**Owner** Gap Personnel & Tony Coyle **Bred** Lynn Lodge Stud **Trained** Norton, N Yorks

**FOCUS**
An ordinary sprint handicap which saw a dominant front-running display from the winner, who clearly loves this track.

## 4789 RACING UK NOW IN HD H'CAP — 5f 193y

**4:20** (4:21) (Class 6) (0-65,67) 3-Y-O+ **£2,911** (£866; £432; £216) **Stalls** Low

Form RPR

34 **1** **Ypres**[21] [4013] 8-9-3 **56** ............(p) KevinStott 11 66
(Jason Ward) *hld up: plenty to do bnd ent st: pushed along and gd hdwy to ld ins fnl f: sn clr* **8/1**

5060 **2** *2* **Willsy**[38] [3402] 4-9-4 **62** ............ GemmaTutty(5) 6 66
(Karen Tutty) *hld up in midfield: effrt and rdn 2f out: styd on fnl f to take 2nd towards fin: no ch w wnr* **15/2**[3]

-503 **3** *nk* **Picks Pinta**[24] [3912] 6-9-9 **62** ............(b) PaddyAspell 13 65
(John David Riches) *in tch: smooth hdwy to ld 2f out: rdn and hdd ins fnl f: kpt on same pce and lost 2nd towards fin* **12/1**

0056 **4** *hd* **Gaelic Wizard (IRE)**[8] [4509] 9-8-13 **52** ............(b1) SamJames 12 54
(Karen Tutty) *hld up: effrt on far side over 2f out: kpt on ins fnl f: nt pce to chal* **15/2**[3]

0134 **5** *1 3/4* **Searanger (USA)**[22] [3979] 4-9-6 **59** ............ PaulMulrennan 14 55
(Rebecca Menzies) *hld up in tch: smooth hdwy over 2f out: rdn over 1f out: kpt on same pce ins fnl f* **11/2**[1]

-000 **6** *shd* **Mr Conundrum**[5] [4605] 4-8-4 **46** ............ NathanEvans(3) 17 42
(Lynn Siddall) *hld up: rdn and hdwy over 1f out: kpt on fnl f: no imp* **40/1**

41-5 **7** *2* **Caeser The Gaeser (IRE)**[51] [2923] 5-9-11 **67**(p) RachelRichardson(3) 15 57
(Nigel Tinkler) *taken early to post: hld up: rdn over 2f out: sme hdwy over 1f out: sn no imp* **6/1**[2]

3506 **8** *nk* **Lady Joanna Vassa (IRE)**[6] [4559] 4-8-11 **50** ............ AndrewMullen 5 39
(Richard Guest) *led at str gallop: hung lft thrght: drifted lft and hdd 2f out: rdn and wknd appr fnl f* **16/1**

0005 **9** *nse* **Captain Scooby**[9] [4478] 11-8-8 **47** ............(b) LukeMorris 9 36
(Richard Guest) *dwlt: bhd: effrt and drvn over 1f out: sn no imp* **25/1**

0666 **10** *1/2* **Salvatore Fury (IRE)**[10] [4428] 7-9-8 **66** ............(v) RowanScott(5) 7 53
(Keith Dalgleish) *cl up: effrt whn carried lft over 2f out: rdn and wknd over 1f out* **10/1**

0053 **11** *2 1/2* **Whipphound**[29] [3704] 9-8-10 **49** ............(p) JackGarritty 10 28
(Ruth Carr) *midfield: drvn along over 2f out: wknd over 1f out* **10/1**

-660 **12** *13* **Mr Coco Bean (USA)**[33] [3561] 3-9-6 **65** ............ JoeFanning 2
(Ann Duffield) *chsd ldrs: drvn along over 2f out: wknd over 1f out* **15/2**[3]

0-00 **13** *nk* **Rainbow Chimes (IRE)**[16] [4172] 3-8-9 **54** ............ GrahamLee 4
(Ann Duffield) *prom: lost pl over 2f out: struggling whn n.m.r briefly wl over 1f out* **50/1**

062 **14** *2 1/4* **Spoken Words**[24] [3915] 8-8-7 **46** ............ PatrickMathers 16
(John David Riches) *in tch: drvn along over 2f out: sn lost pl* **28/1**

1m 13.39s (-0.31) **Going Correction** 0.0s/f (Good)
**WFA** 3 from 4yo+ 6lb 14 Ran SP% **119.5**
Speed ratings (Par 101): **102,99,98,98,96 96,93,93,93,92 89,71,71,68**
CSF £64.28 CT £745.88 TOTE £10.40: £3.40, £3.40, £4.00; EX 96.80 Trifecta £1625.30.
**Owner** Dante Yard Racing Club **Bred** Philip Graham Harvey **Trained** Middleham, N Yorks
■ Stewards' Enquiry : Nathan Evans two-day ban: used whip with his arm above shoulder height (Jul 27-28)

**FOCUS**
A fair sprint handicap which produced an eyecatching winner who swooped late and fast.

## 4790 RACING UK DAY PASS JUST £10 H'CAP — 1m 6f 32y

**4:50** (4:50) (Class 5) (0-75,75) 3-Y-O+ **£3,396** (£1,010; £505; £252) **Stalls** Low

Form RPR

1-61 **1** **Our Kylie (IRE)**[21] [4018] 5-8-10 **62** ............ BenRobinson(5) 4 68+
(Brian Ellison) *prom: drvn and outpcd over 3f out: rallied to ld over 2f out: drifted rt: idled and hrd pressed ins fnl f: jst hld on* **7/2**[3]

-013 **2** *nse* **Newt**[20] [4045] 3-8-6 **67** ............(p1) LukeMorris 7 73
(Sir Mark Prescott Bt) *led: flashed tail repeatedly: rdn and hdd 2f out: rallied and disp ld wl ins fnl f: jst hld* **1/1**[1]

4354 **3** *2 1/4* **Jan Smuts (IRE)**[40] [3340] 9-8-9 **59** ............(tp) NathanEvans(3) 1 61
(Wilf Storey) *in tch: hdwy and cl up 2f out: sn rdn: one pce ins fnl f* **16/1**

-004 **4** *14* **Transpennine Star**[3] [4684] 4-9-13 **74** ............ PaulMulrennan 2 56
(Michael Dods) *pressed ldr: drvn and ev ch over 3f out: wknd fr 2f out* **5/2**[2]

3m 7.81s (0.31) **Going Correction** 0.0s/f (Good)
**WFA** 3 from 4yo+ 14lb 4 Ran SP% **106.7**
Speed ratings (Par 103): **99,98,97,89**
CSF £7.37 TOTE £3.60; EX 8.90 Trifecta £20.40.
**Owner** Morecool & Cool Racing **Bred** Lynn Lodge Stud **Trained** Norton, N Yorks

**FOCUS**
Add 18yds. Not many runners, but a thrilling finish and worthy winner.
T/Plt: £89.40 to a £1 stake. Pool: £42,779.04 - 349.12 winning units. T/Qpdt: £44.70 to a £1 stake. Pool: £3,289.33 - 54.35 winning units. **Richard Young**

# 4567 DONCASTER (L-H)

Thursday, July 13

**OFFICIAL GOING: Good to firm (8.1)**
Wind: Moderate against Weather: Cloudy with sunny periods

## 4791 WE-FIT! WORKSOP'S INSULATED CONSERVATORY ROOFING SYSTEMS AMATEUR RIDERS' H'CAP — 2m 109y

**1:40** (1:40) (Class 5) (0-70,71) 4-Y-O+ **£2,807** (£870; £435; £217) **Stalls** Low

Form RPR

422 **1** **Wordiness**[9] [4471] 9-10-3 **64** ............ MrJFlook(5) 10 75
(David Evans) *hld up: hdwy over 6f out: trckd ldrs 4f out: led 3f out: rdn over 1f out: clr ent fnl f: kpt on strly* **5/1**[2]

0040 **2** *7* **Stormin Tom (IRE)**[26] [3830] 5-11-0 **70** ............ MrWEasterby 5 73
(Tim Easterby) *prom: cl up over 4f out: chsd wnr 2f out: rdn and edgd lft over 1f out: sn drvn and kpt on same pce* **8/1**

6-41 **3** *1 3/4* **Three Colours Red (IRE)**[29] [2059] 5-10-3 **64**(p) MrMorganWinstone(5) 7 65
(Robert Stephens) *trckd ldrs on outer: effrt 4f out: pushed along and hdwy over 2f out: rdn wl over 1f out: kpt on one pce* **6/1**[3]

-032 **4** *1/2* **Barizan (IRE)**[35] [3494] 11-10-10 **66** ............(bt) MrFinianMaguire 9 66
(Brendan Powell) *rr and sn pushed along: rdn along 12f out and again 1/2-way: tk clsr order over 5f out: rdn 3f out: drvn and chsd ldng pair over 1f out: one pce* **14/1**

-302 **5** *8* **Waiting For Richie**[27] [3794] 4-10-9 **70** ............ MrBJames(5) 3 60
(Tom Tate) *prom: trckd ldr after 6f: cl up over 4f out: chal 3f out: sn rdn and ev ch: drvn 2f out: sn wknd* **1/1**[1]

-055 **6** *15* **Art History (IRE)**[12] [4345] 9-9-4 **53** ............ MissCarlyScott(7) 8 25
(Philip Kirby) *rrd s and rel to r: t.o tl jnd field 1/2-way: rdn along over 3f out: nvr a factor* **20/1**

4031 **7** *3 1/2* **Tempuran**[16] [4181] 8-10-4 **65** ............(v) PoppyBridgwater(5) 11 33
(David Bridgwater) *led: pushed along over 4f out: hdd and rdn wl over 3f out: sn drvn and wknd* **11/1**

00-0 **8** *2* **Beaumont's Party (IRE)**[16] [4181] 10-9-5 **52** ............(b1) MissAPeck(5) 4 18
(Laura Morgan) *trckd ldrs on inner: cl up 1/2-way: rdn to ld briefly wl over 3f out: sn hdd & wknd qckly* **66/1**

3m 38.53s (-1.87) **Going Correction** -0.025s/f (Good) 8 Ran SP% **113.3**
Speed ratings (Par 103): **103,99,98,98,94 86,85,84**
CSF £43.23 CT £243.16 TOTE £5.80: £1.90, £2.70, £1.80; EX 49.80 Trifecta £94.80.
**Owner** Mrs E Evans **Bred** Juddmonte Farms Ltd **Trained** Pandy, Monmouths

**FOCUS**
Drying ground, officially good to firm all over. Rail movements added 12yds to the distance of race 1, a moderate staying handicap with a dominant winner. The time was 8.53sec outside standard.

## 4792 CLUGSTON CONSTRUCTION IRISH STALLION FARMS EBF MAIDEN STKS — 6f 2y

**2:10** (2:12) (Class 5) 2-Y-O **£3,234** (£962; £481; £240) **Stalls** High

Form RPR

33 **1** **James Garfield (IRE)**[23] [3929] 2-9-5 0 ............ OisinMurphy 4 90+
(George Scott) *trckd ldrs: cl up 1/2-way: led over 2f out: rdn clr appr fnl f: styd on strly* **1/3**[1]

**2** *6* **Bomad** 2-9-0 0 ............ LewisEdmunds(5) 8 70
(Derek Shaw) *dwlt and towards rr: hdwy wl over 2f out: rdn and chsd ldng pair over 1f out: kpt on fnl f: no ch w wnr* **100/1**

5 **3** *3/4* **Spray The Sea (IRE)**[14] [4259] 2-9-5 0 ............ ConnorBeasley 3 68
(Bryan Smart) *trckd ldrs: hdwy over 2f out: rdn to chse wnr wl over 1f out: sn drvn and kpt on same pce* **6/1**[2]

4 **4** *6* **Mont Kinabalu (IRE)**[50] [2948] 2-9-5 0 ............ ShaneGray 10 49
(Kevin Ryan) *trckd ldr: cl up 1/2-way: rdn along 2f out: sn drvn and wknd* **6/1**[2]

**5** *1 1/2* **Tarnemah (IRE)** 2-9-0 0 ............(h1) DanielTudhope 9 39
(George Peckham) *dwlt: green and sn pushed along in rr: rdn 1/2-way: hdwy wl over 1f out: swtchd lft ent fnl f: kpt on towards fin* **33/1**

**6** *1 1/4* **Technological** 2-9-5 0 ............ TomQueally 5 40
(George Margarson) *dwlt and in rr: hdwy over 2f out: rdn wl over 1f out: sn edgd rt and n.d* **33/1**

000 **7** *2 1/2* **Final Rock**[7] [4520] 2-9-5 0 ............(p1) RyanPowell 2 32
(Sir Mark Prescott Bt) *cl up: rdn along wl over 2f out: sn drvn and wknd* **100/1**

05 **8** *1/2* **Wiff Waff**[27] [3782] 2-9-2 0 ............(t) AaronJones(3) 11 30
(Stuart Williams) *led: rdn along 1/2-way: hdd jst over 2f out and sn wknd* **25/1**

6 **9** *3/4* **Squirrelheed**[19] [4074] 2-9-5 0 ............ PJMcDonald 7 28
(Richard Guest) *towards rr: rdn along wl over 2f out: n.d* **100/1**

**10** *1/2* **Shuhood (IRE)** 2-9-5 0 ............ TomMarquand 1 26
(Richard Hannon) *wnt lft s: sn chsng ldrs: cl up on outer over 3f out: rdn along wl over 2f out: sn wknd* **7/1**[3]

1m 13.06s (-0.54) **Going Correction** -0.05s/f (Good) 10 Ran SP% **128.8**
Speed ratings (Par 94): **101,93,92,84,82 80,77,76,75,74**
CSF £110.13 TOTE £1.20: £1.02, £16.70, £2.00; EX 74.90 Trifecta £844.00.
**Owner** W J and T C O Gredley **Bred** Stetchworth & Middle Park Studs Ltd **Trained** Newmarket, Suffolk
■ Crown of Cortez was withdrawn. Price at time of withdrawal was 20-1. Rule 4 does not apply.

**FOCUS**
Easy for the odds-on favourite, who has been rated close to his Royal Ascot form.

## 4793 BARTON STORAGE SYSTEMS MAIDEN STKS — 6f 2y

**2:45** (2:46) (Class 5) 3-Y-O+ **£2,911** (£866; £432; £216) **Stalls** High

Form RPR

**1** **Maid In India (IRE)** 3-9-0 0 ............ JamesSullivan 4 66
(Eric Alston) *t.k.h: in tch: hdwy 2f out: chsd ldrs over 1f out: swtchd lft and rdn ent fnl f: styd on wl to ld nr fin* **33/1**

03 **2** *nk* **Decision Maker (IRE)**[14] [4275] 3-9-2 0 ............ AlistairRawlinson(3) 1 70
(Roy Bowring) *led: hdd over 3f out: cl up and led again 1 1/2f out: sn rdn: drvn ins fnl f: hdd and no ex towards fin* **9/1**

440 **3** *1/2* **Chatoyer (FR)**[12] [4341] 3-9-5 0 ............(h1) TomMarquand 5 68
(Richard Hannon) *dwlt and hld up in rr: hdwy over 2f out: swtchd lft and rdn to chse ldrs over 1f out: drvn and edgd lft ins fnl f: styd on wl towards fin* **16/1**

0 **4** *3/4* **Katheefa (USA)**[85] [1889] 3-9-5 0 ............ PJMcDonald 3 66
(Charles Hills) *prom: cl up over 2f out: rdn to chal over 1f out: drvn and ev ch ent fnl f: kpt on same pce towards fin* **5/1**[3]

**5** *5* **My Angel** 0 0 0 0 ............ JoeDoyle 7 45
(Ollie Pears) *towards rr: hdwy 2f out: rdn over 1f out: kpt on fnl f* **50/1**

-204 **6** *3/4* **King Of Paris**[19] [4100] 3-9-5 77 ............(p1) DanielTudhope 6 48
(Roger Varian) *cl up on stands' rail: slt ld over 3f out: rdn along 2f out: sn hdd and drvn: wknd over 1f out* **10/11**[1]

**7** *1/2* **My Cherokee** 3-8-9 0 ............ CallumRodriguez(5) 2 41
(Michael Dods) *dwlt: green and a towards rr* **14/1**

5 **8** *2 1/4* **Roubles (USA)**[76] [2121] 3-9-0 0 ............(h1) TomQueally 8 34
(James Fanshawe) *awkward s: plld hrd and chsd ldrs: rdn along over 2f out: sn wknd* **4/1**[2]

0 **9** *1/2* **Snow Excuse**[80] [2033] 3-9-5 0 ............ ConnorBeasley 10 37
(Bryan Smart) *chsd ldrs: pushed along wl over 2f out: sn rdn and wknd* **33/1**

1m 13.55s (-0.05) **Going Correction** -0.05s/f (Good) 9 Ran SP% **119.4**
Speed ratings (Par 103): **98,97,96,95,89 88,87,84,83**
CSF £307.87 TOTE £33.60: £8.40, £2.80, £3.60; EX 242.20 Trifecta £1178.60.
**Owner** Con Harrington **Bred** C F Harrington **Trained** Longton, Lancs



The Form Book Flat, Raceform Ltd, Newbury, RG14 5SJ

**FOCUS**
The Group performers Strath Burn and Muthmir have won this maiden in recent seasons, but this is probably not form to get excited about, with the market leaders disappointing.

## 4794 YOUDAN TROPHY FOOTBALL YOUTH TOURNAMENT FILLIES' H'CAP 7f 213y(R)
**3:20** (3:21) (Class 4) (0-85,84) 3-Y-O+ **£5,175** (£1,540; £769; £384) **Stalls** Low

Form RPR
1-41 **1** **Tribute Act**[29] 3722 3-9-3 **82** TomQueally 8 91+
(James Fanshawe) *t.k.h: hld up in rr: hdwy 2f out: chsd ldrs jst over 1f out: shkn up to chal ins fnl f: qcknd to ld nr fin: readily* **1/1**[1]
1-36 **2** *hd* **Shenanigans (IRE)**[29] 3722 3-9-2 **81** DanielTudhope 5 89
(Roger Varian) *trckd ldrs: hdwy over 2f out: cl up over 1f out: rdn to chal jst over 1f out: slt ld ins fnl f: drvn: hdd and no ex nr fin* **7/2**[2]
2216 **3** *1 ¼* **Florenza**[12] 4375 4-10-0 **84** PJMcDonald 4 91
(Chris Fairhurst) *set stdy pce: qcknd wl over 2f out: rdn wl over 1f out: drvn and hdd ins fnl f: kpt on same pce* **11/1**
1-25 **4** *nk* **Panova**[20] 4051 3-9-5 **84** OisinMurphy 2 88
(Sir Michael Stoute) *hld up in tch: hdwy 2f out: rdn over 1f out: kpt on fnl f* **9/2**[3]
-403 **5** *1 ¾* **Fleeting Motion**[19] 4096 3-9-3 **82** TomMarquand 1 82
(Richard Hannon) *trckd ldr on inner: hdwy over 2f out: cl up and rdn over 1f out: drvn and wknd fnl f* **12/1**
6104 **6** *1 ½* **Braztime**[8] 4501 3-8-13 **78** CamHardie 3 75
(Richard Hannon) *trckd ldr: cl up 3f out: rdn along over 2f out: drvn over 1f out: grad wknd* **28/1**

1m 41.72s (2.02) **Going Correction** -0.025s/f (Good)
**WFA** 3 from 4yo 9lb **6** Ran SP% **109.9**
Speed ratings (Par 102): **88,87,86,86,84 83**
CSF £4.46 CT £19.04 TOTE £1.90: £1.20, £1.50; EX 5.30 Trifecta £23.90.
**Owner** Elite Racing Club **Bred** Elite Racing Club **Trained** Newmarket, Suffolk

**FOCUS**
The runners came down the middle of the straight in this fair fillies' handicap. It wasn't run at a great gallop.

## 4795 QUALITY CONSTRUCTION & SCAFFOLDING DONCASTER H'CAP 5f 3y
**3:55** (3:55) (Class 5) (0-75,76) 3-Y-O+ **£3,234** (£962; £481; £240) **Stalls** High

Form RPR
6060 **1** **Just Us Two (IRE)**[26] 3834 5-10-1 **76** (p) TomMarquand 5 84
(Robert Cowell) *wnt rt s: hld up: hdwy on outer 1/2-way: rdn to chal over 1f out: edgd lft ent fnl f: sn drvn to take slt ld: jst hld on* **5/1**[3]
1036 **2** *nse* **You're Cool**[41] 3295 5-9-1 **67** LewisEdmunds[(5)] 3 74
(John Balding) *trckd ldng pair: hdwy 2f out: rdn to take slt ld jst over 1f out: drvn and edgd lft ins fnl f: rallied gamely towards fin: jst failed* **3/1**[1]
3005 **3** *hd* **Archimedes (IRE)**[7] 4531 4-9-2 **63** (tp) RoystonFfrench 11 69
(David C Griffiths) *led 1f: cl up: rdn over 1f out: drvn ins fnl f: kpt on wl towards fin* **7/1**
6346 **4** *1 ¼* **Landing Night (IRE)**[29] 3707 5-9-12 **73** (tp) PJMcDonald 6 75
(Rebecca Menzies) *dwlt and sltly hmpd s: towards rr: hdwy wl over 2f out: rdn to chse ldrs over 1f out: drvn ins fnl f: no imp towards fin* **9/2**[2]
0033 **5** *nk* **Pearl Noir**[15] 4219 7-8-8 **62** (b) RPWalsh[(7)] 7 62
(Scott Dixon) *cl up: led after 1f: rdn wl over 1f out: drvn and hdd appr fnl f: grad wknd* **8/1**
0426 **6** *3 ¾* **K'Gari Spirit**[44] 3177 4-9-4 **65** (t) CamHardie 8 52
(Jeremy Gask) *chsd ldrs: rdn along wl over 1f out: sn wknd* **20/1**
1612 **7** *3 ¾* **Powerful Dream (IRE)**[20] 4043 4-9-5 **73** (p) RossaRyan[(7)] 9 46
(Ronald Harris) *a towards rr* **5/1**[3]
4030 **8** *19* **Twentysvnthlancers**[21] 4015 4-9-2 **63** (p) TomQueally 10
(Paul Midgley) *dwlt: in tch: rdn along wl over 2f out: sn wknd* **12/1**

59.34s (-1.16) **Going Correction** -0.05s/f (Good)
**WFA** 3 from 4yo+ 5lb **8** Ran SP% **112.6**
Speed ratings (Par 103): **107,106,106,104,104 98,92,61**
CSF £19.73 CT £103.52 TOTE £5.70: £1.80, £1.40, £2.50; EX 23.70 Trifecta £212.00.
**Owner** T W Morley **Bred** Andy Macdonald & Sarah Wigley **Trained** Six Mile Bottom, Cambs

**FOCUS**
A modest sprint handicap. The first two fought out a close finish down the centre of the track, having emerged from the two lowest stalls.

## 4796 DIRECT VALETING LTD H'CAP 1m 3f 197y
**4:25** (4:27) (Class 4) (0-85,87) 3-Y-O+ **£5,175** (£1,540; £769; £384) **Stalls** Low

Form RPR
-212 **1** **Kasperenko**[20] 4035 3-9-4 **87** (b[1]) TomQueally 6 98+
(David Lanigan) *hld up towards rr: smooth hdwy over 3f out: led on bit 2f out: shkn up ins fnl f: sn clr* **9/4**[2]
2463 **2** *2 ¾* **Chancery (USA)**[15] 4206 9-10-0 **85** (p) DanielTudhope 4 88
(David O'Meara) *hld up towards rr: pushed along over 3f out: hdwy on inner over 2f out: sn rdn: drvn and styd on fnl f: no ch w wnr* **6/1**[3]
-233 **3** *nk* **Sellingallthetime (IRE)**[12] 4380 6-9-1 **72** (p) TomMarquand 9 76
(Michael Appleby) *trckd ldrs: pushed along whn n.m.r: hmpd and lost pl 3f out: sn rdn: styd on u.p appr fnl f* **10/1**
2340 **4** *1* **Busy Street**[57] 2741 5-9-7 **78** NeilFarley 5 79
(Sally Haynes) *trckd ldrs: hdwy 3f out: sn cl up: rdn wl over 1f out: sn drvn and kpt on same pce* **25/1**
4121 **5** *2 ½* **Viewpoint (IRE)**[17] 4158 8-9-0 **74** AlistairRawlinson[(3)] 1 71
(Harriet Bethell) *trckd ldng pair on inner: effrt 3f out: pushed along 2f out: sn rdn to chse wnr: drvn over 1f out: grad wknd* **25/1**
5-21 **6** *½* **Beach Break**[41] 3286 3-8-10 **79** (b) PJMcDonald 7 77
(Ralph Beckett) *led: pushed along 3f out: rdn and hdd 2f out: sn drvn and wknd over 1f out* **6/4**[1]
-605 **7** *2 ¼* **Under Attack (IRE)**[23] 3947 4-9-5 **76** (h) JamesSullivan 8 69
(Ruth Carr) *trckd ldr: cl up 4f out: rdn along 3f out: sn drvn and wknd* **20/1**
0400 **8** *1 ¾* **Buonarroti (IRE)**[15] 4206 6-9-0 **78** GerO'Neill[(7)] 10 68
(Declan Carroll) *dwlt: hld up in rr: sme hdwy on outer over 3f out: sn rdn along and n.d* **12/1**

2m 32.75s (-2.15) **Going Correction** -0.025s/f (Good)
**WFA** 3 from 4yo+ 12lb **8** Ran SP% **114.3**
Speed ratings (Par 105): **106,104,103,103,101 101,99,98**
CSF £15.63 CT £108.45 TOTE £3.50: £1.30, £1.70, £1.90; EX 15.90 Trifecta £73.30.
**Owner** Ms Delaney, Black & Middleham Park L **Bred** Hillwood Thoroughbred Breeding Ltd **Trained** Newmarket, Suffolk

**FOCUS**
Race run over an additional 12yds. Fair handicap form. They raced down the centre in the straight with the first two coming from the rear.

## 4797 YOU-ARE-THE-REF.COM FILLIES' H'CAP 7f 6y
**4:55** (4:55) (Class 5) (0-75,75) 3-Y-O+ **£3,234** (£962; £481; £240) **Stalls** High

Form RPR
1352 **1** **Acadian Angel (IRE)**[10] 4437 3-9-4 **73** DanielTudhope 1 80
(John Quinn) *trckd ldrs: hdwy 2f out: rdn to chal ent fnl f: led last 100yds: kpt on wl towards fin* **7/4**[1]
-032 **2** *shd* **Totally Magic (IRE)**[24] 3911 5-8-9 **61** LewisEdmunds[(5)] 6 70
(Richard Whitaker) *trckd ldrs: swtchd rt and effrt to chal 2f out: rdn to ld jst over 1f out: drvn and edgd lft ins fnl f: hdd last 100yds: rallied towards fin: jst hld* **9/2**[2]
4403 **3** *2 ¼* **Art's Desire (IRE)**[15] 4214 3-8-6 **66** JennyPowell[(5)] 3 66
(Ed Walker) *s.i.s and lost several l at s: jnd field after 1f: hdwy over 2f out: rdn wl over 1f out: styd on wl fnl f* **6/1**
3-10 **4** *hd* **Qatari Riyals (IRE)**[56] 2757 3-9-4 **73** TomMarquand 5 72
(Richard Hannon) *led: pushed along 2f out: rdn and hdd appr fnl f: sn drvn and kpt on same pce* **16/1**
143- **5** *3* **Many A Tale**[307] 6292 3-9-6 **75** ShaneGray 7 66
(Ismail Mohammed) *hld up towards rr: effrt and sme hdwy over 2f out: sn rdn and n.d* **7/1**
4112 **6** *shd* **Dusky Maid (IRE)**[15] 4214 3-9-0 **69** JoeDoyle 2 60
(James Given) *cl up: disp ld 2f out: sn rdn: drvn appr fnl f: sn wknd* **5/1**[3]
4-40 **7** *½* **Nancy Hart**[62] 2587 3-8-12 **67** PJMcDonald 4 57
(Tom Dascombe) *cl up: rdn along 3f out: drvn 2f out and sn wknd* **16/1**

1m 26.73s (0.43) **Going Correction** -0.05s/f (Good)
**WFA** 3 from 4yo 8lb **7** Ran SP% **109.8**
Speed ratings (Par 100): **95,94,92,92,88 88,87**
CSF £8.83 CT £33.52 TOTE £2.40: £1.50, £2.40; EX 8.80 Trifecta £43.60.
**Owner** The Desperados **Bred** R Hannon & J Cullinan **Trained** Settrington, N Yorks

**FOCUS**
Ordinary fillies' form, but a small pb from the winner.
T/Plt: £355.90 to a £1 stake. Pool: £68,634.62 - 140.75 winning units. T/Qpdt: £307.70 to a £1 stake. Pool: £5,381.47 - 12.94 winning units. **Joe Rowntree**

# 4519 EPSOM (L-H)
Thursday, July 13

**OFFICIAL GOING: Good (good to soft in places; 6.7)**
Wind: Light, half against Weather: Fine

## 4798 WATCH RACING UK ON SKY 432 H'CAP 1m 2f 17y
**6:05** (6:06) (Class 5) (0-75,78) 3-Y-O **£3,881** (£1,155; £577; £288) **Stalls** Low

Form RPR
-451 **1** **Fair Power (IRE)**[9] 4462 3-9-10 **78** 6ex KieranShoemark[(3)] 2 84
(Sylvester Kirk) *pushed along in last early: gng bttr after 3f: prog to chse ldng pair over 2f out: rdn to cl over 1f out: styd on fnl f to ld last strides* **9/4**[1]
0-13 **2** *½* **Dream Machine (IRE)**[27] 3787 3-9-7 **72** LouisSteward 3 77
(Michael Bell) *trckd ldng pair: wnt 2nd st: rdn to chal 2f out and edgd lft: led jst ins fnl f: hdd last strides* **3/1**[3]
3022 **3** *1 ¾* **Celestation**[10] 4431 3-9-12 **77** SilvestreDeSousa 5 79
(Mark Johnston) *led: kicked on over 2f out: hrd pressed over 1f out: hdd and one pce jst ins fnl f* **5/2**[2]
-116 **4** *½* **Darkroom Angel**[48] 3033 3-9-5 **77** FinleyMarsh[(7)] 4 78
(Philip Hide) *chsd ldr to st: sn swtchd rt: outpcd in 4th 2f out: no ch after: kpt on again nr fin* **6/1**
0025 **5** *15* **Malt Teaser (FR)**[29] 3721 3-9-1 **66** RobertWinston 1 37
(John Best) *hld up in 4th: sltly checked and dropped to last 3f out: sn bhd* **6/1**

2m 9.8s (0.10) **Going Correction** +0.025s/f (Good) **5** Ran SP% **112.9**
Speed ratings (Par 100): **100,99,98,97,85**
CSF £9.57 TOTE £3.40: £1.90, £1.30; EX 9.30 Trifecta £23.60.
**Owner** Fairway Racing **Bred** Pitrizzia Partnership **Trained** Upper Lambourn, Berks
■ Stewards' Enquiry : Finley Marsh two-day ban: careless riding (Jul 27-28)

**FOCUS**
There was 25mm of rain overnight into Wednesday, but it had been dry since, and the going was given as good, good to soft in places (GoingStick: 6.7). The rail was out up to 7yds from the 1 mile point to the winning post, adding 22yds to all races of 1m+, and 7yds to 6f races. A fair contest.

## 4799 BRITISH STALLION STUDS EBF NOVICE STKS 6f 3y
**6:40** (6:41) (Class 5) 2-Y-O **£3,881** (£1,155; £432; £432) **Stalls** High

Form RPR
6 **1** **Chess Move (IRE)**[21] 4007 2-8-13 0 KieranShoemark[(3)] 5 76
(George Baker) *dwlt: sn cl up in 4th: rdn to chse ldng pair 2f out: clsd over 1f out: r.o to ld last 100yds: sn clr* **9/1**
6 **2** *1 ¾* **Diamond Express (IRE)**[26] 3807 2-8-4 0 FinleyMarsh[(7)] 3 66+
(Roger Teal) *hld up off the pce in 5th: hanging and no prog over 2f out: stl only 5th 1f out: r.o wl after to take 2nd last stride* **20/1**
62 **3** *hd* **Carouse (IRE)**[33] 3576 2-9-2 0 DavidProbert 2 71+
(Andrew Balding) *led: rdn and pressed over 1f out: hdd and one pce last 100yds* **4/7**[1]
03 **3** *dht* **Sorority**[21] 4014 2-8-11 0 SilvestreDeSousa 4 66+
(Mark Johnston) *pressed ldr: chal over 1f out: upsides whn wnr wnt past 100yds out: n.m.r briefly and one pce after* **5/1**[2]
6 **5** *2 ½* **Highland Mary**[74] 2173 2-8-11 0 HarryBentley 1 58
(Richard Hannon) *chsd ldng pair to 2f out: nt qckn over 1f out: one pce after* **6/1**[3]
**6** *6* **Quick Recovery** 2-8-11 0 WilliamCarson 6 40
(Jim Boyle) *dwlt: mostly in last and off the pce: no prog fnl 2f* **40/1**

1m 10.79s (1.39) **Going Correction** +0.025s/f (Good) **6** Ran SP% **111.8**
Speed ratings (Par 94): **91,88,88,88,85 77**
TF: CM/DE/C 263.50; CM/DE/S 340.20 CSF £138.77 TOTE £9.30: £3.10, £8.90; EX 161.60.
**Owner** Sir Alex Ferguson **Bred** Mrs Brenda Reilly **Trained** Manton, Wilts

**FOCUS**
Race distance increased by 7yds. A bit of an upset here, with the favourite below his best.

## 4800 WATCH RACING UK ON THE GO H'CAP 1m 113y
**7:15** (7:15) (Class 4) (0-85,85) 3-Y-O+ **£6,469** (£1,925; £962; £481) **Stalls** Low

Form RPR
2410 **1** **Pealer (GER)**[40] 3322 3-9-1 **85** (t) KieranShoemark[(3)] 2 102+
(John Gosden) *mde all at gd pce: rdn and wl in command over 1f out: styd on: unchal* **9/4**[2]

1024 **2** 2 1/2 **Native Prospect**49 3005 3-9-0 81 DavidProbert 1 89
(Andrew Balding) *chsd wnr: rdn and no imp over 2f out: wl hld after: kpt on* **6/5**1

2552 **3** 4 1/2 **Hamster Jam (IRE)**6 4557 3-8-3 70 SilvestreDeSousa 4 68
(Mark Johnston) *sn in 3rd: brought wd in st: rdn wl over 2f out: no prog and wl hld after* **3/1**3

043 **4** 28 **Harlequin Striker (IRE)**31 3670 5-9-10 81 RobertWinston 3 15
(Dean Ivory) *mostly in last: rdn and no rspnse over 3f out: wl btn after: heavily eased fnl f: t.o* **13/2**

1m 44.13s (-1.97) **Going Correction** +0.025s/f (Good)
**WFA** 3 from 5yo 10lb 4 Ran SP% **114.6**
Speed ratings (Par 105): **109,106,102,77**
CSF £5.76 TOTE £2.00; EX 5.80 Trifecta £8.50.
**Owner** Emma Capon, A Lloyd Webber & Rachel Hood **Bred** Stiftung Gestut Fahrhof **Trained** Newmarket, Suffolk

**FOCUS**
Race distance increased by 22yds. Just a small field, but there was plenty to like about the way the winner got the job done.

## 4801 LADIES' DERBY H'CAP (FOR LADY AMATEUR RIDERS) 1m 4f 6y
7:45 (7:49) (Class 4) (0-80,82) 4-Y-0+ £4,991 (£1,548; £773; £387) Stalls Centre

Form RPR

-361 **1** **Tapis Libre**26 3841 9-10-7 80 MissJoannaMason 4 87
(Jacqueline Coward) *pressed ldr: disp ld after 4f tl led 4f out: jnd wl over 2f out: gd battle w runner-up after: rdr had whip knocked out of hand over 1f out: narrow ld ins fnl f: hld on* **7/4**1

1-26 **2** shd **Whinging Willie (IRE)**40 3323 8-10-6 82 (v) MissHayleyMoore(3) 7 88
(Gary Moore) *hld up in last pair: swift prog to go 2nd st and jnd wnr wl over 2f out: gd battle after and clr of rest: jst denied* **7/4**1

2502 **3** 10 **Silver Quay (IRE)**98 1590 5-10-6 79 BryonyFrost 2 69
(Jimmy Frost) *hld up in 5th: prog over 3f out to take 3rd wl over 2f out: sn lft bhd by ldng pair* **14/1**

00 **4** 7 **Song Of Love (IRE)**27 3795 5-10-1 74 MrsCBartley 3 53
(Shaun Harris) *s.s: mostly in last: plugged on to take modest 4th over 1f out: no ch* **20/1**

0235 **5** 3 3/4 **Duke Of Yorkshire**14 4244 7-9-7 69 (p) MissEEasterby(3) 6 42
(Tim Easterby) *led: jnd after 4f: hdd 4f out: wknd ent st and sn bhd* **5/1**2

3360 **6** 14 **River Dart (IRE)**41 3308 5-10-2 75 MissPFuller 1 25
(Tony Carroll) *pressed ldr: disp after 4f to 5f out: wknd rapidly over 3f out: sn t.o: fin 7th: plcd 6th* **8/1**3

0653 **D** 1 1/2 **Turnbury**11 1698 6-8-11 63 oh3 ow2 (p) MrsDScott(7) 9
(Nikki Evans) *chsd ldng trio: in tch over 3f out: sn wknd: fin 6th: disqualified* **25/1**

2m 40.05s (1.15) **Going Correction** +0.025s/f (Good) 7 Ran SP% **115.8**
Speed ratings (Par 105): **97,96,90,85,83 72,82**
CSF £4.86 CT £28.93 TOTE £2.50: £1.60, £1.50; EX 7.00 Trifecta £29.60.
**Owner** Mrs Susan E Mason **Bred** Sedgecroft Stud **Trained** Dalby, North Yorks
■ Stewards' Enquiry : Mrs D Scott two-day ban: failed to weigh-in (Jul 27, 31)

**FOCUS**
Race distance increased by 22yds. The first two pulled well clear.

## 4802 WATCH RACING UK ANYWHERE H'CAP 1m 2f 17y
8:20 (8:21) (Class 5) (0-75,74) 4-Y-0+ £3,881 (£1,155; £577; £288) Stalls Low

Form RPR

1322 **1** **Berrahri (IRE)**7 4522 6-9-7 74 RobertWinston 2 83
(John Best) *trckd ldr after 4f: led 3f out: cajoled along and kpt on wl fnl 2f: drew clr 1f out* **11/8**1

3-64 **2** 3 1/2 **Transmitting**34 3519 4-8-12 65 (h) HarryBentley 4 67
(Ed Vaughan) *hld up in tch: 4th st: prog to chse wnr over 2f out: sn rdn and no imp: lost grnd fnl f but hld on for 2nd* **3/1**2

6-36 **3** 3/4 **East India**41 3308 5-9-6 73 TrevorWhelan 5 74
(George Baker) *hld up: 5th and pushed along in st: rdn over 2f out: no imp on ldrs but kpt on to take 3rd ins fnl f* **7/1**

4604 **4** 1/2 **Lopito De Vega (IRE)**4 4659 5-8-4 64 ow2 FinleyMarsh(7) 3 62
(David C Griffiths) *hld up in detached last: pushed along over 3f out: no real prog tl kpt on to take 4th ins fnl f* **7/2**3

-610 **5** 3/4 **Berkeley Vale**28 3753 6-8-13 66 (b) GeorgeDowning 1 64
(Roger Teal) *led 2f: 3rd st: rdn and one pce over 2f out: lost 2 pls ins fnl f* **8/1**

524 **6** 12 **Anton Chigurh**44 3168 8-9-2 69 (p) DavidProbert 6 43
(Nikki Evans) *led after 2f: hdd 3f out: sn wknd and bhd* **33/1**

2m 9.15s (-0.55) **Going Correction** +0.025s/f (Good) 6 Ran SP% **115.9**
Speed ratings (Par 103): **103,100,99,99,98 89**
CSF £6.07 TOTE £2.10: £1.40, £1.60; EX 6.30 Trifecta £19.70.
**Owner** White Turf Racing Uk **Bred** Kilnamoragh Stud **Trained** Oad Street, Kent
■ Stewards' Enquiry : Finley Marsh three-day ban: weighed in 2lb over (Jul 30, 31, Aug 4)

**FOCUS**
Race distance increased by 22yds. A comfortable success for the favourite, who did the rest for a turn of foot.

## 4803 WATCH RACING UK ON VIRGIN 536 H'CAP 6f 3y
8:50 (8:50) (Class 4) (0-85,89) 3-Y-0+ £5,175 (£1,540; £769; £384) Stalls High

Form RPR

6020 **1** **Highland Acclaim (IRE)**7 4521 6-9-12 85 (h) HarryBentley 1 93
(David O'Meara) *cl up: 4th st: chsd ldr 3f out: chal 2f out: narrow ld jst ins fnl f: jnd 100yds out: hld on wl* **3/1**1

0-60 **2** shd **Huntsmans Close**22 3967 7-9-13 86 (h) RobertWinston 8 93
(Robert Cowell) *wl in tch: 5th st: prog over 2f out: drvn to chal and w wnr 100yds out: nt qckn last strides* **7/1**

0001 **3** 2 1/4 **Ashpan Sam**7 4521 8-10-2 89 6ex (p) WilliamCarson 4 89
(David W Drinkwater) *mde most: rdn 2f out: hdd and no ex jst ins fnl f* **3/1**1

0321 **4** 1 3/4 **Pettochside**15 4219 8-9-5 85 KatherineGlenister(7) 2 79
(John Bridger) *in tch in rr: 7th on st: effrt on inner over 2f out: one pce and no imp on ldng trio over 1f out* **4/1**2

6060 **5** 1 1/4 **Red Stripes (USA)**12 4333 5-8-2 66 oh2 JaneElliott(5) 3 56
(Lisa Williamson) *in tch: 6th st: rdn wl over 2f out: no imp on ldrs after* **33/1**

-006 **6** 1 3/4 **Pour La Victoire (IRE)**49 3008 7-8-10 69 (b) GeorgeDowning 7 54
(Tony Carroll) *s.v.s: wl bhd in last most of way: styd on to pass 2 rivals ins fnl f* **14/1**

352 **7** 1 **Tavener**7 4524 5-9-3 76 (p) RoystonFfrench 10 57
(David C Griffiths) *pressed ldr on outer tl 3rd st: lost pl over 2f out: steadily wknd* **5/1**3

0003 **8** 1 1/2 **Monumental Man**16 4178 8-8-12 78 (p) FinleyMarsh(7) 5 55
(Michael Attwater) *prom: wnt 2nd briefly st: wknd over 2f out* **10/1**

1m 8.49s (-0.91) **Going Correction** +0.025s/f (Good)
**WFA** 3 from 5yo+ 6lb 8 Ran SP% **117.9**
Speed ratings (Par 105): **107,106,103,101,99 97,96,94**
CSF £25.62 CT £69.29 TOTE £4.00: £1.70, £3.10, £1.10; EX 26.70 Trifecta £136.00.
**Owner** Evan M Sutherland **Bred** Rathbarry Stud **Trained** Upper Helmsley, N Yorks

**FOCUS**
Race distance increased by 7yds. There was a disputed pace and that set things up for one of those who tracked the speed.
T/Plt: £518.10 to a £1 stake. Pool: £61,437.32 - 86.55 winning units. T/Qpdt: £8.00 to a £1 stake. Pool: £5,811.40 - 536.99 winning units. **Jonathan Neesom**

# 4532 NEWBURY (L-H)
Thursday, July 13

**OFFICIAL GOING: Good (6.2)**
Wind: light breeze half-across Weather: sunny with cloudy periods

## 4804 VISIT NEWBURY AMATEUR RIDERS' H'CAP 1m 2f
5:20 (5:21) (Class 5) (0-70,72) 3-Y-0+ £3,119 (£967; £483; £242) Stalls Centre

Form RPR

6-53 **1** **Hawridge Glory (IRE)**24 3922 3-9-6 58 MrPMillman 4 66
(Rod Millman) *mid-div: stdy hdwy fr over 3f out: rdn to ld over 1f out: edgd lft: kpt on* **7/2**1

32/0 **2** 1/2 **Milky Way (IRE)**32 3616 5-10-7 70 MissBeckyButler(7) 9 76
(Gary Moore) *mid-div: rdn and hdwy 2f out: disp 2nd ent fnl f: kpt on: hld nring fin* **5/1**3

-200 **3** 1/2 **Raj Balaraaj (GER)**14 4255 3-10-1 67 (p) MrSWalker 7 73
(George Baker) *in tch: rdn and hdwy over 2f out: ev ch briefly over 1f out: kpt on but no ex ins fnl f* **7/1**

0010 **4** 4 **Affair**19 4087 3-8-6 51 oh2 MissGDucker(7) 6 49
(Hughie Morrison) *led: sn clr: rdn and hdd over 2f out: kpt on same pce fnl f* **25/1**

-543 **5** 2 3/4 **Pack It In (IRE)**30 3683 4-10-9 70 (b) MissMO'Sullivan(5) 2 62
(Brian Meehan) *in tch: hdwy 4f out: rdn to ld over 2f out: hdd over 1f out: no ex fnl f* **15/2**

2416 **6** shd **Orithia (USA)**10 4442 3-9-13 65 MissSBrotherton 5 57
(Seamus Durack) *trckd ldrs: rdn 3f out: kpt on same pce fnl 2f* **4/1**2

0114 **7** 2 **Grams And Ounces**8 4494 10-9-10 59 (tp) MissCMBerry(7) 8 46
(Grace Harris) *hld up towards rr: rdn 3f out: no imp tl styd on fnl f* **16/1**

6040 **8** 3/4 **Pretty Jewel**28 3753 4-9-9 56 ow2 (h) DrMVoikhansky(7) 12 44
(Kevin Frost) *s.i.s: plld hrd and sn mid-div: rdn 3f out: hung lft over 2f out: nvr any imp* **25/1**

124 **9** 1/2 **Rum Swizzle**19 4089 5-11-2 72 MissPFuller 3 57
(Harry Dunlop) *trckd clr ldr: clsd on ldr 4f out: rdn and ev ch 3f out: wknd fnl f* **14/1**

0200 **10** 4 1/2 **Breakheart (IRE)**113 1298 10-9-2 51 oh3 (b) MrHGourdain(7) 10 27
(Andrew Balding) *s.i.s: a towards rr* **50/1**

20-6 **11** 2 **Wordismybond**28 3753 8-10-8 69 MrJamiePerrett(5) 1 41
(Brendan Powell) *a towards rr* **25/1**

0205 **12** hd **Ataman (IRE)**29 3718 5-10-8 71 (t) MrNathanHowie(7) 11 42
(Chris Wall) *a towards rr* **12/1**

2m 10.38s (1.58) **Going Correction** +0.15s/f (Good)
**WFA** 3 from 4yo+ 10lb 12 Ran SP% **116.9**
Speed ratings (Par 103): **99,98,98,95,92 92,91,90,90,86 84,84**
CSF £19.58 CT £116.69 TOTE £4.30: £1.80, £2.30, £2.80; EX 30.00 Trifecta £288.10.
**Owner** Eric Gadsden **Bred** Alan O'Flynn **Trained** Kentisbeare, Devon

**FOCUS**
Add 16yds. This was moderate and was a typical race of its type.

## 4805 MIRAGE SIGNS NOVICE AUCTION STKS (C&G) 6f
5:55 (5:56) (Class 5) 2-Y-0 £3,234 (£962; £481; £240) Stalls Centre

Form RPR

31 **1** **Luis Fernandez (USA)**52 2896 2-8-9 0 DavidEgan(5) 14 80+
(Kevin Ryan) *trckd ldr: rdn 2f out: led jst over 1f out: kpt on wl* **11/4**1

**2** 1 1/4 **Bombastic (IRE)** 2-8-11 0 CallumShepherd(3) 9 75
(Ed de Giles) *s.i.s: towards rr: hdwy 3f out: rdn 2f out: edgd lft: wnt 4th jst over 1f out: kpt on wl to chse wnr fnl 120yds but a being hld* **25/1**

**3** nse **He's Our Star (IRE)** 2-8-4 0 GeorgeWood(3) 1 68
(Ali Stronge) *towards rr: outpcd over 3f out: drifted towards stands' side fr over 2f out: hdwy over 1f out: r.o wl to chal for 2nd fnl f: a hld by wnr* **25/1**

3 **4** nk **Rainbow Jazz (IRE)**27 3776 2-8-9 0 SteveDrowne 4 69
(Mark Usher) *mid-div: pushed along 3f out: no imp tl hdwy over 1f out: sn rdn: kpt on wl ins fnl f* **11/1**

23 **5** 1 1/2 **Simpson (IRE)**21 3999 2-8-9 0 LiamKeniry 13 65
(Ed Walker) *trckd ldr: str chal over 2f out: rdn and ev ch ent fnl f: no ex fnl 100yds* **9/2**3

**6** nk **Character Witness (IRE)** 2-9-0 0 JackMitchell 2 69
(Roger Varian) *hld up towards rr: hdwy 2f out: rdn over 1f out: kpt on fnl f but nt quite pce to get on terms* **8/1**

**7** 2 3/4 **Choosey (IRE)** 2-8-9 0 FergusSweeney 10 56
(Henry Candy) *led: rdn whn strly chal fr over 2f out: hdd jst over 1f out: fdd fnl 120yds* **16/1**

00 **8** 1 3/4 **Rio Santos**30 3690 2-8-7 0 KieranO'Neill 6 48
(Rod Millman) *towards rr: rdn and hdwy over 1f out: sn swtchd lft: kpt on same pce fnl f* **100/1**

10 **9** hd **Optimum Time (IRE)**19 4068 2-9-2 0 CharlesBishop 3 57
(Eve Johnson Houghton) *chsd ldrs: rdn 2f out: wknd fnl f* **3/1**2

0 **10** 2 1/2 **Jazz Affair (IRE)**12 4367 2-8-11 0 DougieCostello 12 44
(Jamie Osborne) *mid-div: rdn over 2f out: wknd ent fnl f* **66/1**

**11** 3 1/4 **Rum Runner** 2-9-0 0 PatDobbs 7 37
(Richard Hannon) *a towards rr* **12/1**

000 **12** 2 **Mysaan (IRE)**27 3769 2-8-11 65 (p1) MartinDwyer 8 28
(Brian Meehan) *sn drvn along to chse ldrs: wknd fnl f* **20/1**

**13** 3 1/4 **Epsom Bounty** 2-8-4 0 CharlieBennett(3) 5 15
(Pat Phelan) *a towards rr* **66/1**

**14** 14 **Wiltons (FR)** 2-8-6 0 EdwardGreatrex(3) 11
(Harry Dunlop) *dwlt: a outpcd in rr* **50/1**

1m 14.03s (1.03) **Going Correction** +0.15s/f (Good) 14 Ran SP% **121.3**
Speed ratings (Par 94): **99,97,97,96,94 94,90,88,88,84 80,77,73,54**
CSF £80.93 TOTE £3.70: £1.70, £6.30, £6.70; EX 85.70 Trifecta £2001.50.
**Owner** Mrs R G Hillen **Bred** Castleton Lyons & Kilboy Estate **Trained** Hambleton, N Yorks

**FOCUS**
A bigger field than most novice races, though it featured only two previous winners and lacked depth.

## 4806 STALBRIDGE LINEN FILLIES' NOVICE AUCTION STKS (PLUS 10 RACE) 6f
**6:30** (6:31) (Class 5) 2-Y-O **£3,234** (£962; £481; £240) **Stalls** Centre

Form RPR
10 **1** **Electric Landlady (IRE)**[20] 4028 2-9-0 0........................ PatCosgrave 14 80
(Denis Coakley) *towards rr of midfield: rdn and hdwy fr 2f out: str run ins fnl f: led cl home* **9/2**[2]
2 **2** *nse* **Autumn Leaves**[30] 3689 2-8-6 0........................ HectorCrouch[(3)] 2 75
(Clive Cox) *in tch: tk cl order over 2f out: rdn to ld ent fnl f: kpt on: hdd fnl strides* **3/1**[1]
2 **3** *3/4* **Kareva**[13] 4312 2-9-0 0........................ JamieSpencer 15 78
(Charles Hills) *hld up towards rr: swtchd rt 2f out: rdn and hdwy over 1f out: kpt on ins fnl f to go 3rd fnl 75yds: clsng on front pair at fin* **5/1**[3]
**4** *1 3/4* **Escape The City** 2-8-4 0........................ CharlieBennett[(3)] 10 66+
(Hughie Morrison) *mid-div: hdwy over 2f out: rdn and ev ch jst ins fnl f: edgd lft: no ex fnl 100yds* **20/1**
63 **5** *2 1/4* **Sienna Says**[14] 4252 2-8-6 0........................ CallumShepherd[(3)] 11 61
(Tony Carroll) *trckd ldr: rdn to ld 2f out: edgd lft: hdd ent fnl f: no ex fnl 120yds* **12/1**
4 **6** *1 1/4* **Polly's Gold (IRE)**[10] 4440 2-8-11 0........................ ShaneKelly 9 59
(Richard Hughes) *towards rr of midfield: hdwy over 1f out where nt best of runs: kpt on fnl f but nt pce to get involved* **12/1**
1 **7** *5* **Boomerang Betty (IRE)**[17] 4151 2-9-7 0........................ DougieCostello 6 54
(Jamie Osborne) *trckd ldrs: rdn and ev ch 2f out: fdd ins fnl f* **7/1**
**8** *hd* **Titchy Digits** 2-8-2 0........................ DavidEgan[(5)] 12 39
(Michael Attwater) *towards rr: rdn over 2f out: styd on fnl f but nvr any threat* **150/1**
**9** *3/4* **Lamb Chop** 2-8-7 0........................ KieranO'Neill 16 37
(Rod Millman) *hmpd s: outpcd in rr: styd on ent fnl f but nvr any threat* **33/1**
**10** *3/4* **Hold Your Breath** 2-8-9 0........................ SteveDrowne 8 37
(Tony Carroll) *trckd ldr tl rdn over 2f out: wknd over 1f out* **66/1**
**11** *nse* **Deviate (IRE)** 2-8-11 0........................ RichardKingscote 4 39
(Tom Dascombe) *led: rdn and hdd 2f out: wknd fnl f* **14/1**
**12** *hd* **Amarone Red (IRE)** 2-8-11 0........................ LiamKeniry 1 38
(Tom Dascombe) *s.i.s: a towards rr* **50/1**
**13** *1* **Gainsay** 2-8-6 0........................ GeorgeWood[(3)] 3 33
(Jonathan Portman) *mid-div: rdn over 2f out: wknd fnl f* **25/1**
**14** *8* **Jedlitzka (IRE)** 2-8-9 0........................ JFEgan 7 9
(Mick Channon) *sn pushed along in mid-div: wknd ent fnl f* **25/1**
**15** *28* **Bhindi** 2-8-4 0........................ EdwardGreatrex[(3)] 5
(Eve Johnson Houghton) *s.i.s: sn mid-div: rdn 3f out: hung lft and bit wnt through mouth: wknd over 1f out* **20/1**

1m 12.8s (-0.20) **Going Correction** +0.15s/f (Good) **15** Ran SP% **118.7**
Speed ratings (Par 91): **107,106,105,103,100 98,92,92,91,90 89,89,88,77,40**
CSF £16.16 TOTE £6.00: £2.10, £1.60, £2.20; EX 21.60 Trifecta £95.00.
**Owner** Pmc Syndicate **Bred** Samuel William Ormsby **Trained** West Ilsley, Berks

**FOCUS**
The inaugural running of this fillies' only event was dominated by those towards the head of the market. The front three have been rated as improving.

## 4807 RELYON CLEANING NEWBURY H'CAP 1m
**7:05** (7:09) (Class 4) (0-85,86) 3-Y-O+ **£6,469** (£1,925; £962; £481) **Stalls** Centre

Form RPR
51 **1** **La Rav (IRE)**[30] 3691 3-9-5 **85**........................ JamieSpencer 5 95+
(Luca Cumani) *racd freely: sn led: styd on strly fnl f: rdn out* **15/8**[2]
1-41 **2** *3 1/4* **Mr Minerals**[8] 4501 3-9-6 **86** 6ex........................ ShaneKelly 2 88
(Richard Hughes) *trckd ldng trio: wnt cl 3rd 2f out: sn rdn: kpt on to go 2nd ins fnl f but nt pce to threaten wnr* **11/10**[1]
5003 **3** *1/2* **Kingston Kurrajong**[15] 4223 4-9-2 **78**........................(p[1]) DavidEgan[(5)] 6 81
(Michael Attwater) *trckd ldrs: racd keenly: wnt 2nd 3f out: rdn 2f out: kpt on but no ex fnl f* **12/1**
5312 **4** *3 1/2* **Traveller (FR)**[75] 2151 3-8-12 **78**........................(t) OisinMurphy 4 71
(Charles Hills) *trckd ldr: rdn 3f out: wknd fnl f* **5/1**[3]

1m 39.8s (1.10) **Going Correction** +0.15s/f (Good)
**WFA** 3 from 4yo+ 9lb **4** Ran SP% **106.8**
Speed ratings (Par 105): **100,96,96,92**
CSF £4.24 TOTE £2.40; EX 4.90 Trifecta £6.80.
**Owner** Simon Capon **Bred** Mrs Alison Lewis **Trained** Newmarket, Suffolk

**FOCUS**
Add 5yds. This race cut up badly beforehand and developed into a tactical affair. Jamie Spencer excelled from the front aboard the winner.

## 4808 ALDER RIDGE VINEYARD MAIDEN STKS 1m 2f
**7:35** (7:40) (Class 5) 3-Y-O **£3,234** (£962; £481; £240) **Stalls** Centre

Form RPR
**1** **White Desert (IRE)** 3-9-5 0........................(h[1]) WilliamBuick 10 77
(Charlie Appleby) *mid-div: pushed along and prog over 3f out: rdn 2f out: edging lft but kpt on ins fnl f: led fnl stride* **3/1**[2]
02 **2** *hd* **Love Conquers (JPN)**[24] 3921 3-9-0 0........................ OisinMurphy 9 71
(Ralph Beckett) *led: rdn wl over 1f out: 1 l up ent fnl f: kpt on but no ex whn hdd fnl stride* **15/2**
**3** *nse* **Saroog** 3-9-5 0........................ MartinDwyer 1 76
(Simon Crisford) *s.i.s: sn in tch: rdn over 2f out: kpt on wl fnl f: nrly snatched 2nd fnl stride* **25/1**
4 **4** *nk* **Luna Magic**[91] 1756 3-8-11 0........................ SimonPearce[(3)] 2 70
(Lydia Pearce) *trckd ldrs: rdn over 2f out: kpt on wl fnl f* **125/1**
4 **5** *hd* **Munthany (USA)**[26] 3839 3-9-5 0........................ DaneO'Neill 16 75
(Charles Hills) *pressed ldr: rdn over 2f out: kpt on w wnr ins fnl f: cl up but hld whn short of room cl home* **6/1**[3]
0- **6** *hd* **Ouja**[265] 7494 3-9-0 0........................ RobertTart 14 70
(John Gosden) *mid-div: rdn 3f out: hdwy over 1f out: kpt on wl fnl f* **11/8**[1]
**7** *6* **Rainbow Rising (FR)** 3-9-0 0........................ RichardKingscote 15 58
(David Menuisier) *s.i.s: towards rr: styd on fnl f: n.d* **66/1**
0- **8** *shd* **Oden**[215] 8305 3-9-5 0........................(p[1]) JackMitchell 11 62
(Roger Varian) *racd keenly: trckd ldrs: rdn over 2f out: wknd fnl f* **16/1**
**9** *3/4* **Section D'Or** 3-9-5 0........................ MartinLane 13 61
(David Menuisier) *hld up towards rr: sme minor prog u.p wl over 2f out: nvr threatened* **66/1**
0 **10** *1* **Captor**[40] 3342 3-9-5 0........................ DougieCostello 8 59
(David Simcock) *a towards rr* **20/1**
00 **11** *1* **Opera Queen**[25] 3866 3-9-0 0........................ LiamKeniry 4 52
(Andrew Balding) *nvr bttr than mid-div* **66/1**
**12** *3/4* **Lynique (IRE)** 3-9-0 0........................ PatCosgrave 6 50
(William Haggas) *s.i.s: sn mid-div: effrt 3f out: nvr threatened: wknd ent fnl f* **12/1**
**13** *47* **Breeze Up** 3-9-2 0........................ CallumShepherd[(3)] 3
(Ed de Giles) *s.i.s: a towards rr* **100/1**

2m 9.37s (0.57) **Going Correction** +0.15s/f (Good) **13** Ran SP% **121.6**
Speed ratings (Par 100): **103,102,102,102,102 102,97,97,96,95 95,94,56**
CSF £25.43 TOTE £4.00: £1.50, £2.00, £5.20; EX 25.10 Trifecta £153.20.
**Owner** Godolphin **Bred** Foursome Thoroughbreds, Muir & Waldron **Trained** Newmarket, Suffolk
■ Casemates Square was withdrawn. Price at time of withdrawal 125-1. Rule 4 does not apply.

**FOCUS**
Add 16yds. An informative maiden won last year by the hugely progressive Frontiersman. It was something of a slow-motion finish with the first six home covered by a little over a length.

## 4809 PARKWAY SHOPPING NEWBURY H'CAP 1m 5f 61y
**8:05** (8:09) (Class 5) (0-75,77) 3-Y-O+ **£3,234** (£962; £481; £240) **Stalls** Centre

Form RPR
0260 **1** **Takbeer (IRE)**[41] 3308 5-9-10 **71**........................(p) CharlesBishop 5 76
(Nikki Evans) *mde all: edgd off rails jst ins fnl f: styd on gamely: a holding on fnl 120yds* **50/1**
2316 **2** *1/2* **Flight Of Fantasy**[61] 2613 3-9-3 **77**........................ RichardKingscote 13 82
(Harry Dunlop) *chsd wnr thrght: rdn wl over 2f out: styd on but a being hld fnl f* **7/1**[3]
-323 **3** *nk* **Inconceivable (IRE)**[27] 3770 3-9-1 **75**........................ PatDobbs 7 80
(Ralph Beckett) *mid-div: pushed along and hdwy over 3f out: wnt 4th jst over 2f out: sn rdn: styd on ins fnl f* **11/2**[2]
-440 **4** *3/4* **Master Archer (IRE)**[29] 3720 3-9-0 **74**........................ TomQueally 12 78
(James Fanshawe) *hld up towards rr: hdwy fr 4f out: wnt 3rd over 2f out but sn hung lft u.p: styd on same pce fnl f* **11/2**[2]
-002 **5** *1/2* **Chocolate Box (IRE)**[28] 3752 3-8-12 **72**........................(p) JamieSpencer 10 75
(Luca Cumani) *mid-div: rdn and hdwy 3f out: wnt 5th wl over 1f out: sn edging lft: styd on same pce fnl f* **3/1**[1]
0-36 **6** *7* **Sheila's Fancy (IRE)**[37] 3427 3-8-6 **66**........................ JFEgan 15 59
(J S Moore) *mid-div: rdn whn outpcd over 3f out: styd on fr over 1f out but nvr any threat* **50/1**
5600 **7** *3/4* **Ban Shoof**[32] 3616 4-9-3 **67**........................ HectorCrouch[(3)] 8 58
(Gary Moore) *hld up towards rr: styd on u.p fnl 2f but nvr any danger* **33/1**
6250 **8** *10* **Tobacco Road (IRE)**[15] 4216 7-10-1 **76**........................(tp) OisinMurphy 3 52
(David Pipe) *hld up towards rr: rdn in midfield 3f out: no further imp: eased whn btn 1f out* **20/1**
1-52 **9** *2 1/4* **Nordic Combined (IRE)**[35] 3489 3-8-5 **68**........(p[1]) CallumShepherd[(3)] 1 41
(Brian Ellison) *trckd ldrs: rdn wl over 2f out: wknd over 1f out* **8/1**
6513 **10** *shd* **Gambol (FR)**[25] 3863 7-9-2 **63**........................(vt) StevieDonohoe 11 35
(Ian Williams) *hld up bhd: struggling in last over 3f out: nvr threatened to get involved* **33/1**
0-02 **11** *3/4* **Inn The Bull (GER)**[14] 4257 4-9-3 **69**........................(t) PaddyPilley[(5)] 16 40
(Alan King) *mid-div: rdn 3f out: wknd over 1f out* **12/1**
-002 **12** *9* **Onorina (IRE)**[30] 3694 5-9-6 **67**........................ PatCosgrave 14 24
(Jim Boyle) *mid-div: hdwy into 3rd over 4f out: rdn and hung lft over 2f out: sn wknd: eased whn btn over 1f out* **14/1**
-140 **13** *38* **Balancing Time**[32] 3616 4-10-0 **75**........................(p) MartinDwyer 2
(Amanda Perrett) *trckd ldrs: rdn 4f out: wknd over 2f out* **20/1**
66-6 **14** *1 1/4* **Lovely Story (IRE)**[80] 2041 6-9-12 **73**........................ DaneO'Neill 9
(Seamus Durack) *mid-div tl wknd and eased over 2f out* **20/1**

2m 52.9s (0.90) **Going Correction** +0.15s/f (Good)
**WFA** 3 from 4yo+ 13lb **14** Ran SP% **117.8**
Speed ratings (Par 103): **103,102,102,102,101 97,96,90,89,89 88,83,59,59**
CSF £344.92 CT £2259.57 TOTE £41.80: £11.90, £2.30, £1.90; EX 600.60 Trifecta £3721.90.
**Owner** Mrs Dawn Scott **Bred** Stourbank Stud **Trained** Pandy, Monmouths

**FOCUS**
Add 16yds. An ordinary race for the track and something of a boilover.

## 4810 KENNET SHOPPING CENTRE H'CAP 7f (S)
**8:40** (8:43) (Class 5) (0-75,77) 3-Y-O+ **£3,234** (£962; £481; £240) **Stalls** Centre

Form RPR
0-51 **1** **Madeleine Bond**[33] 3571 3-9-1 **75**........................ GeorgiaCox[(5)] 5 80+
(Henry Candy) *mid-div of nrside gp: drifted lft but hdwy 2f out: sn rdn: r.o wl to ld fnl 75yds: rdn out* **9/2**[3]
50-0 **2** *hd* **Cadeaux Boxer**[14] 4277 4-9-9 **70**........................(h[1]) JohnFahy 2 77
(Martin Smith) *overall ldr in centre tl over 2f out: sn rdn: ev ch over 1f out: led briefly fnl 120yds: kpt on* **50/1**
011- **3** *1/2* **Medicean El Diablo**[203] 8490 4-9-5 **66**........................ KieranO'Neill 1 72
(Jimmy Fox) *in centre pair: trckd ldr: rdn to chal over 1f out: led jst ins fnl f: hdd fnl 120yds: no ex* **12/1**
5-40 **4** *1 1/2* **Another Boy**[38] 3396 4-9-7 **73**........................ PatrickO'Donnell[(5)] 9 75
(Ralph Beckett) *led nrside gp: overall ldr over 2f out: rdn over 1f out: hdd jst ins fnl f: no ex* **11/1**
0044 **5** *1/2* **Diable D'Or (IRE)**[14] 4251 3-9-0 **72**........................ EdwardGreatrex[(3)] 3 70
(Eve Johnson Houghton) *nrside gp: trckd ldrs: rdn 2f out: kpt on but nt pce to chal fnl f* **7/2**[2]
-10P **6** *2 1/2* **Harbour Grey (IRE)**[26] 3847 3-9-8 **77**........................ SeanLevey 6 68
(Richard Hannon) *towards rr of nrside gp: rdn and hdwy over 1f out: kpt on same pce fnl f* **7/1**
3404 **7** *1/2* **Gramercy (IRE)**[19] 4091 10-9-11 **72**........................(v) StevieDonohoe 12 65
(Ian Williams) *hld up nrside gp: rdn over 2f out: nvr threatened* **33/1**
0265 **8** *1* **Glory Of Paris (IRE)**[15] 4215 3-9-7 **76**........................ OisinMurphy 4 63
(Rod Millman) *racd nrside: trckd ldr tl rdn over 2f out: fdd fnl f* **11/4**[1]
060- **9** *nk* **Operative**[321] 5832 4-9-9 **70**........................ DougieCostello 10 59
(Ed de Giles) *v awkward leaving stalls: a towards rr of nrside of gp* **33/1**
4460 **10** *nk* **Singing Sands (IRE)**[16] 4184 3-9-0 **69**........................ JamieSpencer 8 54
(Seamus Durack) *nrside gp: hld up: swtchd to centre 2f out: sn rdn: nt pce to get on terms: fdd fnl f* **14/1**
0113 **11** *10* **Papou Tony**[36] 3454 4-9-13 **74**........................ LiamKeniry 11 35
(George Baker) *chsd ldrs in nrside gp tl wknd 2f out* **16/1**

1m 27.11s (1.41) **Going Correction** +0.15s/f (Good)
**WFA** 3 from 4yo+ 8lb **11** Ran SP% **116.0**
Speed ratings (Par 103): **97,96,96,94,93 91,90,89,89,88 77**
CSF £212.37 CT £2512.76 TOTE £5.20: £1.60, £16.50, £3.10; EX 255.40 Trifecta £1633.50.
**Owner** Candy, Pritchard & Thomas **Bred** Hellwood Stud Farm **Trained** Kingston Warren, Oxon

**FOCUS**
Not a bad race for the level, with a few of these likely better than their current marks.
T/Plt: £170.50 to a £1 stake. Pool: £63,638.15 - 272.33 winning units. T/Qpdt: £23.40 to a £1 stake. Pool: £6,091.40 - 192.21 winning units. **Tim Mitchell**

# 4360 NEWMARKET (R-H)

Thursday, July 13

**OFFICIAL GOING: Good (stands' 7.3, centre 7.3, far side 7.2)**

Wind: light, behind Weather: light cloud, bright spells

## 4811 BAHRAIN TROPHY STKS (GROUP 3) 1m 5f

1:50 (1:53) (Class 1) 3-Y-O

**£56,710** (£21,500; £10,760; £5,360; £2,690; £1,350) **Stalls** Centre

Form RPR

-234 **1** **Raheen House (IRE)**[20] 4029 3-9-1 110 ........ JamieSpencer 1 109
(Brian Meehan) *lw: hld up in tch in midfield: effrt over 1f out: hdwy and chalng u.p over 1f out: drvn to ld jst ins fnl f: styd on* **7/2**[2]

-236 **2** *1* **Desert Skyline (IRE)**[20] 4032 3-9-1 100 ........ FranBerry 2 107
(David Elsworth) *broke wl: t.k.h: grad stdd bk into midfield after 2f: effrt to chse ldrs 3f out: pressed ldng pair and drvn over 1f out: chsd wnr wl ins fnl f: styd on but a hld* **11/1**

1010 **3** *½* **Sofia's Rock (FR)**[21] 3998 3-9-1 100 ........ SilvestreDeSousa 6 106
(Mark Johnston) *sn led: clr 8f out: rdn over 2f out: hrd pressed over 1f out: drvn and hdd jst ins fnl f: styd on same pce u.p after: lost 2nd wl ins fnl f* **20/1**

-140 **4** *6* **Tamleek (USA)**[21] 3994 3-9-1 107 ........ JimCrowley 4 97
(Saeed bin Suroor) *stdd s: sn chsng ldrs: c centre 8f out: effrt to chse ldr 3f out tl over 1f out: 4th and btn 1f out: wknd ins fnl f* **14/1**

1-15 **5** *1* **Wolf Country**[56] 2766 3-9-1 103 ........ WilliamBuick 8 96
(Charlie Appleby) *t.k.h: hld up in last pair: c centre 8f out: effrt 3f out: struggling to qckn whn nt clrest of runs over 2f out: 5th and btn over 1f out: wknd ins fnl f* **9/2**[3]

2140 **6** *1¼* **Face The Facts (IRE)**[20] 4032 3-9-1 90 ........ AdamKirby 9 94
(John Gosden) *awkward leaving stalls and s.i.s: hld up in rr: c centre 8f out: rdn 4f out: struggling and outpcd 3f out: n.d after: plugged on to pass btn rivals fnl f* **22/1**

1-10 **7** *3¼* **Crowned Eagle**[40] 3322 3-9-1 97 ........(p) AndreaAtzeni 7 89
(John Gosden) *chsd ldr after 2f: c centre 8f out: rdn and lost 2nd 3f out: sn struggling and outpcd: wknd over 1f out* **13/2**

05 **8** *3½* **Wisconsin (JPN)**[11] 4420 3-9-1 104 ........ RyanMoore 3 84
(A P O'Brien, Ire) *chsd ldr after 1f tl 2f: styd chsng ldrs tl rdn and lost pl 3f out: wl btn over 1f out: bhd and eased wl ins fnl f* **12/1**

-121 **9** *26* **Atty Persse (IRE)**[21] 3998 3-9-1 102 ........(p) JamesDoyle 5 72
(Roger Charlton) *lw: hld up in tch in midfield: effrt to chse ldrs 3f out: sn struggling and lost pl: wl bhd and heavily eased wl ins fnl f: t.o* **11/4**[1]

2m 44.74s (0.74) **Going Correction** +0.10s/f (Good) 9 Ran SP% **112.2**
Speed ratings (Par 110): **101,100,100,96,95 95,93,90,74**
CSF £39.87 TOTE £4.00: £1.50, £3.00, £3.90; EX 37.30 Trifecta £785.30.

**Owner** J L Day **Bred** Sunderland Holdings Inc **Trained** Manton, Wilts

**FOCUS**
Stands' side course used. Stalls on far side except 1m4f and 1m5f: centre. The ground was described as good by those who rode in the first, although James Doyle thought it was "tacky". Run at a good gallop courtesy of the third, those racing near to the stands' side came out on top, with the centre-field runners finishing well held, and three pulled clear.

## 4812 ARQANA JULY STKS (GROUP 2) (C&G) 6f

2:25 (2:28) (Class 1) 2-Y-O

**£45,368** (£17,200; £8,608; £4,288; £2,152; £1,080) **Stalls** High

Form RPR

4213 **1** **Cardsharp**[21] 3993 2-9-0 101 ........ JamesDoyle 3 110
(Mark Johnston) *racd in centre trio: in tch in midfield: effrt to chse ldrs 2f out: hung lft u.p but chalng over 1f out: drvn to ld jst ins fnl f: styd on to forge ahd wl ins fnl f: rdn out* **8/1**

30 **2** *1¾* **U S Navy Flag (USA)**[12] 4381 2-9-0 0 ........(bt) RyanMoore 8 105
(A P O'Brien, Ire) *led: rdn wl over 1f out: drvn and hdd jst ins fnl f: no ex and outpcd fnl 75yds* **10/1**

11 **3** *¾* **Rajasinghe (IRE)**[23] 3925 2-9-3 108 ........ StevieDonohoe 12 106
(Richard Spencer) *lw: taken down early: hld up in tch in midfield: effrt jst over 2f out: hdwy u.p to chse ldng 1f out: swtchd rt ins fnl f: styd on u.p to snatch 3rd last strides* **10/3**[2]

21 **4** *hd* **Invincible Army (IRE)**[20] 4049 2-9-0 0 ........ SilvestreDeSousa 11 102
(James Tate) *lw: w ldr: rdn ent fnl 2f: drvn and stl ev ch over tl no ex and btn ins fnl f: wknd towards fin and lost 3rd last strides* **3/1**[1]

61 **5** *2* **Alba Power (IRE)**[13] 4318 2-9-0 0 ........ JosephineGordon 7 96
(Hugo Palmer) *lw: hld up in tch in midfield: effrt jst over 2f out: hdwy over 1f out: nt clrest of runs and swtchd lft 1f out: kpt on same pce and no imp ins fnl f* **33/1**

01 **6** *½* **Enjazaat**[37] 3437 2-9-0 0 ........ JimCrowley 9 94
(Owen Burrows) *str: chsd ldrs: effrt ent fnl 2f: drvn and unable qck over 1f out: no imp and kpt on same pce ins fnl f* **14/1**

13 **7** *½* **Roland Rocks (IRE)**[14] 4266 2-9-0 0 ........(p[1]) GeraldMosse 10 93
(John Ryan) *cmpt: hld up in rr: effrt 2f out: sme hdwy u.p 1f out: kpt on ins fnl f: nvr trbld ldrs* **66/1**

421 **8** *nse* **Grand Koonta (IRE)**[12] 4367 2-9-0 83 ........ AdamKirby 2 93
(Clive Cox) *leggy: athletic: racd in centre trio: hld up in rr: effrt 2f out: no imp tl hdwy and styd on to pass btn horses ins fnl f: nvr trbld ldrs* **16/1**

110 **9** *2¾* **Denaar (IRE)**[23] 3925 2-9-0 95 ........ FrankieDettori 4 88
(Richard Hannon) *taken down early: stdd s: hld up in tch towards rr: swtchd rt and effrt over 2f out: no imp u.p over 1f out: wknd ins fnl f: eased towards fin* **14/1**

415 **10** *½* **It Dont Come Easy (IRE)**[21] 3993 2-9-0 96 ........ PaulHanagan 1 83
(Richard Fahey) *racd in centre trio: hld up in tch towards rr: effrt 2f out: sn no imp: wknd ins fnl f* **20/1**

141 **11** *3¼* **Sound And Silence**[23] 3929 2-9-0 104 ........(p) WilliamBuick 5 76
(Charlie Appleby) *lw: stdd s: t.k.h: hld up in tch in midfield: rdn ent fnl 2f: struggling and lost pl over 1f out: bhd and eased wl ins fnl f* **7/1**[3]

201 **12** *1¾* **Hey Gaman**[7] 4539 2-9-0 89 ........ MartinHarley 6 71
(James Tate) *t.k.h: chsd ldrs: rdn jst over 2f out: losing pl and nt that much room over 1f out: bhd and eased wl ins fnl f* **10/1**

1m 11.75s (-0.75) **Going Correction** +0.10s/f (Good) 12 Ran SP% **118.3**
Speed ratings (Par 106): **109,106,105,105,102 102,101,101,97,97 92,90**
CSF £83.80 TOTE £9.40: £2.80, £2.90, £1.80; EX 100.70 Trifecta £607.90.

**Owner** Sheikh Hamdan bin Mohammed Al Maktoum **Bred** Godolphin **Trained** Middleham Moor, N Yorks

**FOCUS**
The July Stakes has become an important 2yo event for sprinters again in recent seasons with top-class Shalaa winning in 2015 and Mehmas last year, but this season's race has been rated slightly below par, with concerns over the compressed finish and the 8th. After a messy start the majority kept far side and that proved the place to be inside the final furlong.

## 4813 BET365 H'CAP 6f

3:00 (3:01) (Class 2) (0-105,105) 3-Y-O

**£62,250** (£18,640; £9,320; £4,660; £2,330; £1,170) **Stalls** High

Form RPR

-215 **1** **Ekhtiyaar**[26] 3844 3-8-10 94 ........ JimCrowley 19 106+
(Roger Varian) *racd towards far side: in tch in midfield: clsd to trck ldrs and nt clr run jst over 1f out: swtchd lft 1f out: str chal ins fnl f: styd on wl to ld last strides* **13/2**[3]

46-3 **2** *hd* **Tommy Taylor (USA)**[84] 1901 3-8-11 95 ........ TomEaves 15 105
(Kevin Ryan) *lw: racd towards far side: stdd s: hld up in midfield: hdwy and rdn to chal over 1f out: drvn to ld 1f out: kpt on wl u.p: hdd last strides* **14/1**

16-3 **3** *½* **Ultimate Avenue (IRE)**[89] 1797 3-8-13 97 ........(t[1]) JamieSpencer 8 105
(Ed Walker) *racd centre tl wnt far side after 2f: stdd s: hld up in rr: clsd but nt clr run on far rail over 1f out: swtchd rt ins fnl f: r.o strly fnl 100yds: nt quite rch ldrs* **28/1**

4311 **4** *hd* **Golden Apollo**[26] 3844 3-8-9 93 ........ DavidAllan 12 100
(Tim Easterby) *racd centre tl wnt far side after 2f: in tch in midfield: effrt 2f out: shifting rt and hdwy u.p 1f out: styd on strly ins fnl f: nvr quite getting to ldrs* **6/1**[2]

-130 **5** *1¾* **Bacchus**[22] 3959 3-9-1 99 ........(p) JamesDoyle 10 101
(Brian Meehan) *racd centre tl wnt far side after 2f: in tch in midfield: rdn 1/2-way: hdwy u.p to chal jst over 1f out tl no ex ins fnl f: wknd towards fin* **12/1**

11-5 **6** *nk* **Love Dreams (IRE)**[26] 3836 3-8-7 91 ........ FrannyNorton 6 92
(Mark Johnston) *racd centre tl wnt far side after 2f: wl in tch in midfield: effrt 2f out: kpt on same pce u.p ins fnl f* **12/1**

1111 **7** *1½* **Goodwood Crusader (IRE)**[19] 4099 3-8-3 94 ........ FinleyMarsh[(7)] 7 90
(Richard Hughes) *racd centre tl wnt far side after 2f: in tch in midfield: sltly outpcd and lost pl whn nt clrest of runs and swtchd lft over 1f out: rdn and hdwy 1f out: kpt on ins fnl f: no threat to ldrs* **14/1**

4-00 **8** *¾* **Afandem (IRE)**[13] 4306 3-9-2 100 ........ JosephineGordon 18 94
(Hugo Palmer) *racd towards far side: chse ldr: rdn and ev ch over 1f out tl no ex ins fnl f: wknd towards fin* **50/1**

3241 **9** *hd* **Poet's Society**[14] 4272 3-8-5 89 ........ JFEgan 17 82
(Mark Johnston) *racd towards far side: chsd ldrs: effrt over 1f out: stl chsng ldrs whn squeezed for room and impeded jst ins fnl f: sn swtchd lft and styd on same pce after* **20/1**

4-50 **10** *¾* **Perfect Angel (IRE)**[26] 3844 3-8-11 95 ........ DavidProbert 1 86
(Andrew Balding) *racd alone nr stands' rail: midfield: rdn and drifting lft ent fnl 2f: hung lft and no imp over 1f out: wl hld and kpt on same pce ins fnl f* **20/1**

-400 **11** *¾* **Private Matter**[26] 3844 3-9-2 100 ........ TonyHamilton 16 88
(Richard Fahey) *racd towards far side: chsd ldrs: rdn over 1f out: unable qck and keeping on same pce whn pushed rt and hmpd ins fnl f: wl hld after* **50/1**

0331 **12** *nk* **Justanotherbottle (IRE)**[12] 4342 3-8-9 93 ........ PaulHanagan 20 80
(Declan Carroll) *racd towards far side: led: rdn over 1f out: hdd 1f out: wknd ins fnl f* **25/1**

-131 **13** *1¾* **Cartographer**[13] 4317 3-8-8 92 ........ SilvestreDeSousa 9 74
(Martyn Meade) *lw: racd centre tl wnt far side after 2f: in tch in midfield: rdn 2f out: lost pl u.p over 1f out and btn whn impeded ins fnl f: wknd* **11/2**[1]

5-11 **14** *1¼* **Unabated (IRE)**[12] 4353 3-9-6 104 ........(t) DanielMuscutt 2 82
(Marco Botti) *taken down early: racd centre tl wnt far side after 2f: swtchd lft after s and hld up towards rr: effrt over 1f out: no imp and drifting rt 1f out: wknd ins fnl f* **16/1**

-100 **15** *nse* **Victory Angel (IRE)**[20] 4030 3-8-8 92 ........(v[1]) AndreaAtzeni 3 69
(Roger Varian) *lw: restless in stalls: racd centre tl wnt far side after 2f: hld up in last quartet: effrt over 1f out: no imp u.p and sltly impeded ins fnl f: wknd* **16/1**

1-30 **16** *1* **Hyde Park**[21] 3997 3-8-12 96 ........ RyanMoore 14 70
(John Gosden) *racd centre tl wnt far side after 2f: wl in tch in midfield: lost pl u.p over 1f out: hmpd ent fnl f: wknd ins fnl f* **12/1**

-213 **17** *nk* **Mostahel**[68] 2400 3-8-9 93 ........ SeanLevey 5 66
(Richard Hannon) *racd centre tl wnt far side after 2f: in tch in midfield tl lost pl u.p over 1f out: bhd ins fnl f* **16/1**

0-10 **18** *½* **Danielsflyer (IRE)**[26] 3844 3-9-3 101 ........ AdamKirby 11 73
(David Barron) *racd centre tl wnt far side after 2f: hld up in rr: effrt but stl plenty to do whn hmpd over 1f out: lost any ch and n.d after* **33/1**

-156 **19** *1¾* **Brian The Snail (IRE)**[47] 3078 3-9-3 101 ........ WilliamBuick 4 67
(Richard Fahey) *racd centre tl wnt far side after 2f: hld up in rr: effrt over 1f out: no imp whn sltly impeded ent fnl f: wl bhd and eased towards fin* **14/1**

1m 11.72s (-0.78) **Going Correction** +0.10s/f (Good) 19 Ran SP% **127.4**
Speed ratings (Par 106): **109,108,108,107,105 105,103,102,101,100 99,99,97,95,95 94,93,92,90**
CSF £89.19 CT £2478.72 TOTE £6.70: £1.80, £4.30, £5.70, £2.10; EX 102.40 Trifecta £8732.70.

**Owner** Hamdan Al Maktoum **Bred** James Ortega Bloodstock **Trained** Newmarket, Suffolk

■ Stewards' Enquiry : Jamie Spencer caution: careless riding

**FOCUS**
A good-quality 3yo sprint, they merged into one group after a couple of furlongs, barring Perfect Angel who raced solo towards the stands' side, and the main action unfolded near to the far rail.

## 4814 PRINCESS OF WALES'S ARQANA RACING CLUB STKS (GROUP 2) 1m 4f

3:35 (3:35) (Class 1) 3-Y-O+

**£56,710** (£21,500; £10,760; £5,360; £2,690; £1,350) **Stalls** Centre

Form RPR

5136 **1** **Hawkbill (USA)**[11] 4423 4-9-2 115 ........(p) JamesDoyle 1 119
(Charlie Appleby) *swtg: mde all: rdn 2f out: hrd pressed and edging lft ins fnl f: styd on wl and a holding chalr ins fnl f: rdn out* **7/2**[2]

-412 **2** *¾* **Frontiersman**[41] 3299 4-9-2 117 ........(p[1]) WilliamBuick 5 118
(Charlie Appleby) *hld up in 4th: swtchd lft and effrt to chse wnr 2f out: chalng whn veered lft u.p 1f out: stened up and stl ev ch ins fnl f: kpt pressing but a looked hld: eased last strides* **5/4**[1]

16-2 **3** *3¾* **Algometer**[49] 3012 4-9-2 114 ........ AndreaAtzeni 4 112
(David Simcock) *hld up in 5th: effrt nrest stands' rail 2f out: wnt 3rd 1f out: styd on same pce and edgd lft ins fnl f* **7/1**[3]

1-10 **4** 2 **Western Hymn**[19] 4070 6-9-2 111 (p) AdamKirby 3 109
(John Gosden) *stdd s: hld up in rr: swtchd lft and effrt over 2f out: no imp u.p over 1f out: 4th and kpt on same pce ins fnl f* **14/1**

20-5 **5** 2 1/4 **Wings of Desire**[19] 4070 4-9-2 115 (p1) FrankieDettori 2 105
(John Gosden) *lw: chsd ldrs: effrt over 2f out: 3rd and unable qck over 1f out: wknd ins fnl f* **7/2**[2]

3100 **6** 11 **Muntahaa (IRE)**[19] 4070 4-9-2 113 JimCrowley 6 87
(John Gosden) *swtg: chsd ldrs and styd wd of rivals towards centre: rdn and lost 2nd 2f out: dropped to rr and wknd over 1f out* **16/1**

2m 31.0s (-1.90) **Going Correction** +0.10s/f (Good) **6** Ran SP% **113.9**
Speed ratings (Par 115): **110,109,107,105,104 96**
CSF £8.53 TOTE £4.70: £2.10, £1.40; EX 9.80 Trifecta £41.30.
**Owner** Godolphin **Bred** Helen K Groves Revokable Trust **Trained** Newmarket, Suffolk

**FOCUS**
It's a shame Poet's Word defected yet this was still a solid enough Group 2 event. They went a decent pace and the first pair finished clear of the remainder, giving Godolphin a 1-2.

## 4815 BRITISH STALLION STUDS EBF MAIDEN FILLIES' STKS (PLUS 10 RACE) 6f
**4:05** (4:06) (Class 2) 2-Y-O **£12,938** (£3,850; £1,924; £962) **Stalls** High

Form RPR

**1** **Spring Cosmos (IRE)** 2-9-0 0 WilliamBuick 2 82+
(Charlie Appleby) *str: lw: racd in centre: led gp and midfield overall tl hdwy to ld after 2f: mde rest: rdn over 1f out: styd on wl and in command ins fnl f: rdn out* **9/2**[2]

**2** 1 1/4 **Indicia** 2-9-0 0 PaulHanagan 6 79
(Charles Hills) *racd in centre: dwlt and wnt rt s: in tch in last pair: swtchd lft and hdwy jst over 2f out: rdn over 1f out: chsd wnr ins fnl f: kpt on wout threatening wnr* **20/1**

6 **3** 1/2 **Anna Nerium**[28] 3746 2-9-0 0 SeanLevey 11 77+
(Richard Hannon) *str: neat: racd towards far side: chsd ldrs tl led gp 2f out: sn rdn: kpt on same pce u.p ins fnl f* **12/1**

2 **4** nse **Fabulous Red**[13] 4296 2-9-0 0 JimmyQuinn 4 77
(Ed Dunlop) *w'like: ponied to s: racd in centre: midfield tl clsd to chse ldrs 1/2-way: rdn over 1f out: unable qck and styd on same pce ins fnl f* **7/1**

20 **5** 1/2 **Maybride**[22] 3960 2-9-0 0 RyanMoore 1 76
(Richard Fahey) *lw: racd in centre: midfield overall tl hdwy to chse wnr after 2f: rdn 2f out: unable qck ent fnl f: kpt on same pce and lost 3 pls ins fnl f* **2/1**[1]

**6** 1 **Lamya (GER)** 2-9-0 0 JimCrowley 13 73
(Richard Hannon) *str: racd towards far side: chsd ldrs: rdn over 1f out: unable qck u.p and btn jst ins fnl f: wknd towards fin* **7/1**

**7** hd **Wild Impala (FR)** 2-9-0 0 AndreaAtzeni 8 72
(John Gosden) *unf: racd towards far side: swtchd lft after s: in tch in midfield: effrt over 1f out: kpt on ins fnl f: no threat to ldrs* **14/1**

**8** 1/2 **Toomer** 2-9-0 0 MartinHarley 7 70
(Richard Hannon) *w'like: str: racd towards far side: hld up in tch in rr: swtchd rt and effrt 2f out: rdn and no imp over 1f out: kpt on same pce ins fnl f: nvr trbld ldrs* **50/1**

**9** 1 3/4 **Pulitzer** 2-9-0 0 JamesDoyle 9 65
(Hugo Palmer) *athletic: racd towards far side: t.k.h: trckd ldrs early tl dropped to midfield 1/2-way: rdn and unable qck over 1f out: wknd ins fnl f* **6/1**[3]

**9** dht **Amandine** 2-9-0 0 FranBerry 3 65+
(David Elsworth) *str: racd in centre: s.i.s and wnt rt leaving stalls: rn green: in tch in rr: rdn 2f out: sn drvn and unable qck: wknd ins fnl f* **14/1**

0 **11** 2 **Gold Eagle**[30] 3697 2-9-0 0 JosephineGordon 5 59
(Philip McBride) *leggy: racd towards far side: dropped towards rr 1/2-way: rdn and struggling 2f out: wknd ins fnl f* **33/1**

**12** 2 **She'sastorm (IRE)** 2-9-0 0 StevieDonohoe 12 53
(Henry Spiller) *leggy: racd towards far side: towards rr: rdn 2f out: sn struggling: wknd fnl f* **66/1**

**13** 16 **Shadow Seeker (IRE)** 2-9-0 0 JoeyHaynes 10 5
(Paul D'Arcy) *cmpt: racd towards far side: led for 2f: rdn and lost pl 2f out: bhd fnl f* **100/1**

1m 13.31s (0.81) **Going Correction** +0.10s/f (Good) **13** Ran SP% **124.0**
Speed ratings (Par 97): **98,96,95,95,94 93,93,92,90,90 87,85,63**
CSF £100.03 TOTE £5.40: £1.90, £5.80, £4.20; EX 105.80 Trifecta £1319.20.
**Owner** Godolphin **Bred** Wicklow Bloodstock Ireland Ltd **Trained** Newmarket, Suffolk

**FOCUS**
A useful fillies' maiden.

## 4816 JOHN DEERE H'CAP 5f
**4:35** (4:37) (Class 2) (0-100,100) 3-Y-O+ **£12,938** (£3,850; £1,924; £962) **Stalls** High

Form RPR

0503 **1** **Shamshon (IRE)**[6] 4581 6-9-1 87 (t) JimCrowley 5 95
(Stuart Williams) *hld up in tch in midfield: clsd and shkn up to chse ldrs 1f out: rdn to chal ins fnl f: r.o wl to ld cl home* **7/1**[3]

6556 **2** 1/2 **Top Boy**[12] 4343 7-8-9 81 (v) FrannyNorton 16 87
(Derek Shaw) *stdd s: hld up in rr: swtchd rt over 3f out: pushed along and hdwy over 1f out: rdn to ld ins fnl f: styd on tl hdd and no ex cl home* **33/1**

1243 **3** hd **A Momentofmadness**[22] 3967 4-9-5 91 (h) WilliamBuick 4 96
(Charles Hills) *taken down early: led: rdn wl over 1f out: kpt on wl u.p: hdd ins fnl f: kpt on but unable qck towards fin* **7/1**[3]

5526 **4** 1/2 **Soie D'Leau**[13] 4306 5-9-6 92 TonyHamilton 12 95
(Kristin Stubbs) *w ldrs: rdn and ev ch over 1f out: kpt on u.p tl unable qck towards fin* **14/1**

0003 **5** hd **Foxy Forever (IRE)**[26] 3834 7-8-9 81 (t) PaulHanagan 3 84
(Michael Wigham) *stdd s: hld up in rr: clsd jst over 1f out: nt clrest of runs and swtchd rt ins fnl f: r.o wl fnl 100yds: nt rch ldrs* **33/1**

-350 **6** 1/2 **Oh So Sassy**[32] 3625 7-9-2 88 FranBerry 1 89
(Chris Wall) *hld up in rr: hdwy over 1f out: rdn and kpt on wl ins fnl f: nt rch ldrs* **20/1**

4234 **7** 1/2 **Ice Age (IRE)**[11] 4411 4-9-0 86 (p1) JosephineGordon 7 85
(Eve Johnson Houghton) *lw: pressed ldr: rdn and ev ch over 1f out tl unable qck jst ins fnl f: outpcd wl ins fnl f* **6/1**[2]

600- **8** nk **King Of Rooks**[338] 5268 4-9-9 95 StevieDonohoe 15 93
(Henry Spiller) *t.k.h: hld up in tch in midfield: clsd over 1f out: nt clr run ent fnl f: hdwy ins fnl f: kpt on: nvr trbld ldrs* **50/1**

522 **9** 1/2 **Compas Scoobie**[14] 4272 4-8-12 84 (b) RyanMoore 9 80
(Roger Varian) *lw: hld up in tch towards rr: clsd over 1f out: kpt on same pce and no imp ins fnl f* **8/1**

1132 **10** 3/4 **Jumira Bridge**[19] 4098 3-9-6 97 AndreaAtzeni 6 89
(Roger Varian) *lw: trckd ldrs: effrt u.p over 1f out: unable qck 1f out: wknd ins fnl f* **10/3**[1]

0-23 **11** shd **Orvar (IRE)**[19] 4079 4-9-6 92 (p1) JamesDoyle 13 85
(Robert Cowell) *chsd ldrs: effrt over 1f out: unable qck u.p 1f out: wknd wl ins fnl f* **12/1**

0336 **12** 3/4 **Go Far**[33] 3593 7-9-12 98 (v) MartinHarley 8 89
(Alan Bailey) *midfield: u.p 2f out: no imp and kpt on same pce u.p fr over 1f out: short of room ins fnl f* **18/1**

5045 **13** 1/2 **Monsieur Joe (IRE)**[25] 3873 10-10-0 100 AdamKirby 14 89
(Paul Midgley) *midfield: effrt 2f out: chsng ldrs but unable qck u.p 1f out: wknd ins fnl f* **20/1**

0400 **14** 1 **Mont Kiara (FR)**[12] 4379 4-8-12 84 TomEaves 2 69
(Kevin Ryan) *taken down early: in tch in midfield: rdn over 1f out: sn struggling: wknd ins fnl f* **16/1**

58.36s (-0.74) **Going Correction** +0.10s/f (Good)
**WFA** 3 from 4yo+ 5lb **14** Ran SP% **116.3**
Speed ratings (Par 109): **109,108,107,107,106 105,105,104,103,102 102,101,100,98**
CSF £227.94 CT £1723.16 TOTE £7.80: £2.50, £9.10, £2.40; EX 278.30 Trifecta £2326.90.
**Owner** Mrs June Watts **Bred** Stonethorn Stud Farms Ltd **Trained** Newmarket, Suffolk
■ Poyle Vinnie was withdrawn. Price at time of withdrawal was 33-1. Rule 4 does not apply.

**FOCUS**
They shunned either rail in this decent sprint handicap and a strong pace suited the closers.

## 4817 ROBINSONS MERCEDES-BENZ SIR HENRY CECIL STKS (LISTED RACE) 1m
**5:05** (5:08) (Class 1) 3-Y-O
**£22,684** (£8,600; £4,304; £2,144; £1,076; £540) **Stalls** High

Form RPR

10 **1** **Beat The Bank**[22] 3959 3-9-3 106 JimCrowley 8 114
(Andrew Balding) *hld up wl in tch: effrt and rdn to chal over 1f out: led 1f out: r.o strly and drew clr ins fnl f: readily* **7/1**[3]

-165 **2** 3 **Forest Ranger (IRE)**[23] 3927 3-9-3 106 TonyHamilton 5 107
(Richard Fahey) *lw: t.k.h: trckd ldr: rdn and ev ch jst over 2f out: led over 1f out: hdd 1f out: kpt on but nt match pce of wnr ins fnl f* **8/1**

0-20 **3** 1 **D'bai (IRE)**[39] 3368 3-9-3 105 (p) WilliamBuick 6 105
(Charlie Appleby) *trckd ldrs: effrt ent fnl 2f: drvn and ev ch over 1f out: unable qck w wnr and kpt on same pce ins fnl f* **4/1**[2]

-502 **4** 2 1/2 **Larchmont Lad (IRE)**[54] 2830 3-9-3 107 RyanMoore 2 99
(Richard Hannon) *trckd ldrs: effrt to press ldrs 2f out: unable qck u.p over 1f out: outpcd but hld on to 4t ins fnl f* **7/1**[3]

2410 **5** 1/2 **Grey Britain**[21] 3994 3-9-6 99 GeraldMosse 7 101
(John Ryan) *led: rdn and tried to qckn jst over 2f out: hdd and outpcd over 1f out: wl hld and kpt on same pce ins fnl f* **25/1**

0-12 **6** 1/2 **Ronald R (IRE)**[21] 3997 3-9-3 104 AndreaAtzeni 3 97
(Michael Bell) *stdd s: hld up wl in tch: effrt ent fnl 2f: unable qck over 1f out and btn 1f out: kpt on same pce after* **5/2**[1]

1123 **7** hd **Tricorn (IRE)**[21] 3997 3-9-3 105 JamesDoyle 4 96
(John Gosden) *sn stdd bk towards rr: hld up wl in tch: swtchd rt 2f: sn rdn and unable qck: wl hld and plugged on same pce ins fnl f* **4/1**[2]

1-20 **8** 8 **Syphax (USA)**[56] 2766 3-9-3 106 TomEaves 1 78
(Kevin Ryan) *hld up wl in tch: effrt and bmpd 2f out: sn struggling and bhd 1f out: wknd ins fnl f* **20/1**

1m 37.86s (-2.14) **Going Correction** +0.10s/f (Good) **8** Ran SP% **113.3**
Speed ratings (Par 108): **114,113,112,109,109 108,108,100**
CSF £59.76 TOTE £7.80: £2.00, £2.40, £1.70; EX 62.30 Trifecta £340.40.
**Owner** King Power Racing Co Ltd **Bred** A S Denniff **Trained** Kingsclere, Hants

**FOCUS**
A good winner of this Listed contest. Good form for the level.
T/Jkpt: Not won. T/Plt: £262.60 to a £1 stake. Pool: £188,611.81 - 524.15 winning units. T/Qpdt: £36.60 to a £1 stake. Pool: £13,678.94 - 276.53 winning units. **Steve Payne**

4818 - 4821a (Foreign Racing) - See Raceform Interactive

# 4020 LEOPARDSTOWN (L-H)
Thursday, July 13

**OFFICIAL GOING: Good to firm**

## 4822a IRISH STALLION FARMS EBF "NASRULLAH" H'CAP (PREMIER HANDICAP) 1m 2f
**7:55** (7:55) 3-Y-O+
**£50,427** (£16,239; £7,692; £3,418; £1,709; £854)

RPR

**1** **Tandem**[60] 2658 8-9-10 99 PatSmullen 9 106
(D K Weld, Ire) *broke wl to ld briefly tl sn hdd and settled bhd ldrs: 3rd 1/2-way: impr gng best to ld over 1f out: sn rdn and kpt on wl u.p ins fnl f* **12/1**

**2** 3/4 **Ceol Na Nog (IRE)**[18] 4129 4-9-1 90 KevinManning 4 95
(J S Bolger, Ire) *trckd ldr: 2nd 1/2-way: pushed along into st and lost pl: rdn in 3rd over 1f out and clsd u.p into 2nd wl ins fnl f: a hld* **9/2**[2]

**3** 1/2 **Tennessee Wildcat (IRE)**[18] 4129 7-9-11 100 GaryCarroll 10 104+
(G M Lyons, Ire) *hld up towards rr: gng wl in 11th into st: hdwy on outer 1f out: rdn into 5th wl ins fnl f and r.o wl into nvr threatening 3rd cl home: nrst fin* **20/1**

**4** nk **Windsor Beach (IRE)**[46] 3114 5-9-5 94 (p) SeamieHeffernan 3 97
(J P Murtagh, Ire) *sn led: over 1 l clr at 1/2-way: pushed along into st and sn strly pressed: hdd u.p over 1f out and no imp on wnr in 3rd wl ins fnl f: denied 3rd cl home* **10/3**[1]

**5** hd **Speed Company (IRE)**[19] 4076 4-9-6 100 (h) KillianLeonard(5) 13 103
(John Quinn) *chsd ldrs: 4th 1/2-way: rdn in 4th under 2f out and no imp on wnr far side ins fnl f: denied 4th cl home* **12/1**

**6** shd **Le Vagabond (FR)**[25] 3875 5-9-6 95 WJLee 7 98+
(E J O'Grady, Ire) *hld up bhd ldrs: 5th 1/2-way: pushed along in 6th under 2f out and no imp on ldrs u.p ins fnl f: kpt on same pce* **10/1**

**7** 1 3/4 **The Moore Factor (IRE)**[17] 7165 4-8-13 88 WayneLordan 5 87
(A J Martin, Ire) *mid-div: gng wl in 7th into st: sn rdn and no imp on ldrs ent fnl f: kpt on same pce* **25/1**

**8** shd **Elleval (IRE)**[22] 3963 7-9-5 99 OisinOrr(5) 8 98
(David Marnane, Ire) *hld up in rr of mid-div: rdn in 9th 2f out and kpt on u.p ins fnl f: nvr nrr* **10/1**

**9** 1/2 **Elusive Heights (IRE)**[35] 3510 4-9-12 101 ColinKeane 12 99
(G M Lyons, Ire) *mid-div: 7th 3f out: gng wl into st: sme hdwy into 5th over 1f out where rdn: no ex ins fnl f and wknd clsng stages: eased fnl strides* **5/1**[3]

**10** 1 1/4 **Jaqen H'Ghar (IRE)**[13] 4329 4-9-8 97 (tp) DonnachaO'Brien 2 93
(Joseph Patrick O'Brien, Ire) *sn settled in rr: last at 1/2-way: rdn and no imp 2f out: kpt on one pce ins fnl f: nvr nrr* **14/1**

11 1 1/4 **Castle Guest (IRE)**[11] 4421 8-8-10 85..........................(t) ShaneFoley 11 78
(M Halford, Ire) *s.i.s and in rr early: hdwy bef 1/2-way to chse ldrs in 6th: impr into 5th fr 4f out: rdn in 5th 2f out and sn no ex: wknd over 1f out* **14/1**

12 1 3/4 **My Direction**[13] 4329 7-8-11 86.......................... DeclanMcDonogh 6 76
(Miss Ellmarie Holden, Ire) *mid-div early: pushed along in 10th over 3f out: rdn and no ex under 2f out: wknd to rr ins fnl f* **9/1**

2m 9.82s (1.62) **Going Correction** +0.40s/f (Good)
**WFA** 3 from 4yo+ 10lb **12** Ran SP% **123.4**
Speed ratings: **109,108,108,107,107 107,106,106,105,104 103,102**
CSF £68.02 CT £1107.08 TOTE £6.90: £2.40, £1.50, £5.00; DF 31.50 Trifecta £545.30.
**Owner** Bellamy Syndicate **Bred** Juddmonte Farms Ltd **Trained** Curragh, Co Kildare

**FOCUS**
A competitive contest in which it paid to be handy, with the first, second, fourth and fifth holding the top four positions for most of the race.

4823 - 4824a (Foreign Racing) - See Raceform Interactive

# OVREVOLL (R-H)
Thursday, July 13

**OFFICIAL GOING: Turf: good**

## 4825a OSLO CUP (GROUP 3) (3YO+) (TURF) 1m 4f
7:35 3-Y-O+ £28,195 (£14,097; £6,766; £4,511; £2,819)

RPR

1 1 1/4 **Giuseppe Piazzi (IRE)**[305] 6390 5-9-4 0.......................... OliverWilson 2 97
(Flemming Velin, Denmark) *hld up in fnl trio on outer: drvn and hdwy 2 1/2f out: chal 1f out: sustained run fnl f: a hld: fin 2nd: awrdd r* **11/2**

2 1 **Hurricane Red (IRE)**[24] 3923 7-9-6 0.......................... JacobJohansen 1 99
(Lennart Reuterskiold Jr, Sweden) *chsd ldng pair on inner: drvn and styd on 1 1/2f out: chal between horses 1f out: impeded and swtchd rt 120yds out: kpt on u.p: fin 3rd: plcd 2nd* **7/10**[1]

3 **Eye In The Sky (IRE)**[24] 3923 6-9-4 0..........................(b) CarlosLopez 7 97
(Niels Petersen, Norway) *disp ld on outer: hdd 4f out and pressed ldr: rdn to chal over 2f out: styd on to ld 1f out: edgd lft fnl 120yds and impeded Hurricane Red: styd on strly: fin 1st: plcd 3rd* **19/5**[2]

4 2 3/4 **Cockney Cracker (FR)**[274] 6-9-4 0.......................... Per-AndersGraberg 8 93
(Cathrine Witso Slettemark, Norway) *settled in fnl trio on inner: rdn and prog to ld over 2f out: hdd 1f out: one pce u.p fnl f* **163/10**

5 hd **Bokan (FR)**[256] 5-9-4 0.......................... Jan-ErikNeuroth 4 92
(Wido Neuroth, Norway) *disp ld on inner: kicked into outrt ld 4f out: rdn 2 1/2f out: hdd appr 2f out: wknd fnl f* **22/5**[3]

6 1 3/4 **Jubilance (IRE)**[24] 3923 8-9-4 0.......................... RafaeldeOliveira 3 89
(Bent Olsen, Denmark) *racd in rr: last and adrift 3 1/2f out: sme prog fr 1 1/2f out: wl hld fnl f* **38/1**

7 2 **Lord Divine (USA)**[24] 3923 4-9-4 0.......................... NelsonDeSouza 6 86
(Cathrine Erichsen, Norway) *racd keenly: restrained bhd ldng pair on outer: rdn and nt qckn over 2f out: sn btn* **147/10**

2m 33.0s (-1.10) **7** Ran SP% **128.3**

**Owner** Majken & Flemming Velin **Bred** Rockhart Trading Ltd **Trained** Denmark

# 4068 ASCOT (R-H)
Friday, July 14

**OFFICIAL GOING: Good (good to soft in places on round course; str 6.9, rnd 6.4)**
Wind: Moderate, across Weather: Fine but cloudy

## 4826 ARCADIS BRITISH EBF NOVICE STKS (PLUS 10 RACE) 6f
2:15 (2:17) (Class 3) 2-Y-O £9,056 (£2,695; £1,346; £673) Stalls High

Form RPR

03 1 **Lethal Lunch**[39] 3406 2-9-2 0.......................... TomMarquand 8 83
(Richard Hannon) *trckd ldrs: swtchd to r nr side and clsd to ld over 1f out: rdn and styd on wl fnl f* **20/1**

4 2 1 3/4 **Rebel Streak**[16] 4213 2-9-2 0.......................... DavidProbert 7 80+
(Andrew Balding) *towards rr: effrt over 2f out: making prog whn nt clr run over 1f out: r.o wl fnl f to take 2nd last strides* **6/1**

24 3 nk **Prince Ahwahnee**[32] 3668 2-9-2 0.......................... AdamKirby 4 77
(Clive Cox) *trckd ldrs: clsd to chal over 1f out: chsd wnr after and readily hld: lost 2nd last strides* **11/2**

4 nk **Mankind (FR)** 2-9-2 0.......................... HarryBentley 6 76
(George Scott) *dwlt: pushed along in last pair: swtchd to wd outside 2f out: rdn and prog over 1f out: kpt on same pce fnl f* **5/1**[3]

4 5 3 1/2 **Fighting Irish (IRE)**[45] 3164 2-9-2 0.......................... MartinHarley 3 68
(Harry Dunlop) *chsd ldrs: clsd to chal over 1f out: wknd fnl f* **15/2**

2 6 2 1/4 **Faraasah (IRE)**[34] 3591 2-9-2 0.......................... DaneO'Neill 2 59
(Brian Meehan) *wnt rt s: trckd ldr: pushed along and carried hd awkwardly fr 1/2-way: lost 2nd and wknd over 1f out* **5/2**[1]

7 8 **Prestbury Park (USA)** 2-9-2 0.......................... SilvestreDeSousa 5 35+
(Mark Johnston) *racd freely: led to over 1f out: wknd rapidly* **9/2**[2]

8 1 3/4 **Mister Maestro** 2-9-2 0.......................... TimmyMurphy 1 30
(Richard Hannon) *carried rt s: mostly in last: bhd over 1f out* **33/1**

1m 15.63s (1.13) **Going Correction** +0.275s/f (Good) **8** Ran SP% **112.6**
Speed ratings (Par 98): **103,100,100,99,95 92,81,79**
CSF £129.90 TOTE £17.30: £4.20, £2.00, £1.70; EX 102.00 Trifecta £689.60.
**Owner** The Rat Pack Partnership 2017 **Bred** Horizon Bloodstock Limited **Trained** East Everleigh, Wilts

**FOCUS**
After a couple of dry days the ground was given as predominately good, with jockeys after the first agreeing with the official description but stating there was still a bit of juice in it. No previous winners in this juvenile novice. The opening level is fluid.

## 4827 KNIGHTS 1759 NURSERY H'CAP 6f
2:50 (2:50) (Class 3) 2-Y-O £7,762 (£2,310; £1,154; £577) Stalls High

Form RPR

4124 1 **Rufus King**[22] 4020 2-9-9 94.......................... SilvestreDeSousa 4 100+
(Mark Johnston) *n.m.r s: racd in last tl prog on outer wl over 2f out: led over 1f out and hung lft: drvn out fnl f and continued to hang* **11/4**[1]

310 2 1 3/4 **Dragons Tail (IRE)**[24] 3929 2-9-4 89.......................... MartinHarley 3 90
(Tom Dascombe) *covered up bhd ldrs: plld out over 1f out but wnr already gone for home: rdn to take 2nd fnl f but limited rspnse and nvr threatened to chal* **11/4**[1]

210 3 1 1/2 **Joe's Spirit (IRE)**[34] 3556 2-8-7 78.......................... HarryBentley 5 74
(Michael Bell) *t.k.h early: in tch: effrt against rail 2f out: nvr that much room but styd on fnl f to take 3rd last strides* **5/1**[2]

3213 4 hd **Alaska (IRE)**[13] 4367 2-8-1 75.......................... GeorgeWood(3) 1 71
(Sylvester Kirk) *cl up: led 2f out to over 1f out: carried lft after: one pce fnl f* **6/1**[3]

030 5 2 3/4 **City Guest (IRE)**[24] 3929 2-7-9 71.......................... JaneElliott(5) 7 58
(George Margarson) *hld up in tch: nowhere to go on inner and swtchd sharply to outer 2f out: sn rdn and no prog* **11/1**

3121 6 1/2 **Queen Of Kalahari**[15] 4252 2-7-12 74.......................... DavidEgan(5) 6 61
(Charles Hills) *t.k.h: pressed ldr: stl upsides wl over 1f out: wknd sn after* **7/1**

5102 7 nk **Holdenhurst**[17] 4175 2-8-1 72.......................... LukeMorris 2 57
(Sylvester Kirk) *ledto 2f out: sn btn* **14/1**

1m 16.06s (1.56) **Going Correction** +0.275s/f (Good) **7** Ran SP% **111.8**
Speed ratings (Par 98): **100,97,95,95,91 91,90**
CSF £9.65 TOTE £3.30: £2.00, £1.70; EX 9.20 Trifecta £34.50.
**Owner** Garrett J Freyne Racing **Bred** Newsells Park Stud **Trained** Middleham Moor, N Yorks
■ Stewards' Enquiry : Silvestre De Sousa two-day ban: used whip in an incorrect place (Jul 28, 30)

**FOCUS**
Despite only seven runners in this nursery 23lb covered the field on official ratings. With class coming to the fore, the first four came home in racecard order.

## 4828 CLOSE BROTHERS PROPERTY FINANCE H'CAP 1m 5f 211y
3:25 (3:27) (Class 3) (0-95,96) 3-Y-O+ £9,703 (£2,887; £1,443; £721) Stalls Low

Form RPR

21-1 1 **Mount Moriah**[56] 2784 3-9-0 93.......................... HarryBentley 6 106+
(Ralph Beckett) *t.k.h: hld up in midfield: prog on wd outside over 2f out: shkn up to ld over 1f out: sn clr: pushed out* **6/4**[1]

2421 2 4 **Getback In Paris (IRE)**[35] 3534 4-9-13 92.......................... ShaneKelly 5 97
(Richard Hughes) *trckd ldrs: shkn up to ld 2f out: rdn and hdd over 1f out: no ch w wnr but hld on for 2nd* **5/1**[2]

6-00 3 nk **Shabeeb (USA)**[21] 4033 4-10-3 96..........................(p) DaneO'Neill 3 101
(Roger Varian) *dwlt: hld up in 6th: prog on inner to chal 2f out: kpt on same pce fr over 1f out* **8/1**

2201 4 1 **Marmajuke Bay**[30] 3716 4-9-9 88..........................(p) SteveDrowne 8 91
(Mark Usher) *trckd ldr to 6f out: styd cl up: rdn and nt qckn over 2f out: kpt on again at same pce fnl f* **14/1**

-232 5 1/2 **Rydan (IRE)**[35] 3534 6-9-4 86.......................... HectorCrouch(3) 4 88
(Gary Moore) *hld up in last pair: prog 3f out and on terms w ldrs 2f out: one pce u.p after* **11/1**

-422 6 3 **Jelly Monger (IRE)**[23] 3968 5-9-9 88.......................... SilvestreDeSousa 7 88
(Dominic Ffrench Davis) *hld up in last: effrt 3f out: sme prog to chse ldrs over 1f out: no hdwy after and eased last 100yds* **16/1**

6-54 7 13 **Parliamentarian (IRE)**[35] 3534 4-9-9 88..........................(b[1]) AdamKirby 1 68
(Charlie Appleby) *rdn to ld: hdd 5f out: led again over 3f out to 2f out: wknd qckly* **7/1**[3]

0415 8 1 **Mark Hopkins**[28] 3794 5-9-4 88.......................... DavidEgan(5) 9 67
(David Elsworth) *dwlt: rcvrd to press ldrs but trapped out wd and t.k.h: led 5f out to over 3f out: stl upsides jst over 2f out: sn wknd qckly* **8/1**

5500 9 41 **Calvinist**[22] 4002 4-9-8 87..........................(p) LukeMorris 2 8
(Ian Williams) *a in last trio: rdn and wknd over 5f out: sn t.o* **33/1**

3m 4.67s (3.67) **Going Correction** +0.275s/f (Good)
**WFA** 3 from 4yo+ 14lb **9** Ran SP% **115.2**
Speed ratings (Par 107): **100,97,97,96,96 94,87,86,63**
CSF £8.88 CT £44.78 TOTE £2.30: £1.20, £1.70, £2.60; EX 10.40 Trifecta £56.10.
**Owner** Norman Brunskill **Bred** Lady Bland And Newsells Park Stud Ltd **Trained** Kimpton, Hants

**FOCUS**
Race distance extended by 18yds. Not the strongest of staying events for the class and turned into a procession by the progressive winner. Sound form rated around the second, third and fourth as close to form.

## 4829 CUSHMAN & WAKEFIELD EBF "BREEDERS' SERIES' FILLIES" H'CAP (FOR THE JOHN TRAVERS MEMORIAL TROPHY) 1m 3f 211y
4:00 (4:02) (Class 3) (0-95,92) 3-Y-O+ £12,938 (£3,850; £1,924; £962) Stalls Low

Form RPR

134- 1 **Dawn Horizons**[259] 7669 4-9-7 85.......................... MartinHarley 1 94+
(William Haggas) *mde all: stretched on over 2f out: rdn over 1f out: styd on wl: unchal* **7/2**[3]

5-65 2 3 **Cliff Face (IRE)**[13] 4364 4-10-0 92.......................... LukeMorris 7 97
(Sir Mark Prescott Bt) *stdd fr wd draw and hld up in last pair: rdn and prog over 2f out: drvn to take 2nd ins fnl f: no threat to wnr* **14/1**

4123 3 1 **Nathania**[13] 4364 3-8-7 83.......................... ShaneKelly 3 87
(Richard Hughes) *t.k.h early: trckd ldrs: rdn to go 2nd over 2f out: no imp wnr after: lost 2nd ins fnl f* **6/1**

0/60 4 hd **Allumage**[49] 3033 5-8-13 82.......................... MitchGodwin(5) 6 85
(Sylvester Kirk) *taken down early: hld up in last pair: rdn and prog 2f out: nt qckn over 1f out: kpt on same pce to chal for 3rd nr fin* **16/1**

6-21 5 4 **Stoney Broke**[41] 3341 4-9-4 82.......................... DanielMuscutt 4 78
(James Fanshawe) *t.k.h early: hld up in 5th: rdn over 2f out: no real prog* **10/3**[2]

1-41 6 6 **Camerone (IRE)**[24] 3933 3-8-5 81.......................... HarryBentley 5 69
(Ralph Beckett) *t.k.h and trapped out wd: trckd ldrs: rdn over 3f out: sn lost pl and wknd* **2/1**[1]

632- 7 45 **Fashion Parade**[261] 7618 4-9-6 84.......................... SilvestreDeSousa 2
(Charles Hills) *t.k.h: chsd wnr to over 2f out: wknd rapidly and heavily eased: t.o* **10/1**

2m 35.31s (2.81) **Going Correction** +0.275s/f (Good)
**WFA** 3 from 4yo+ 12lb **7** Ran SP% **114.6**
Speed ratings (Par 107): **101,99,98,98,95 91,61**
CSF £48.60 TOTE £3.90: £2.10, £5.10; EX 42.30 Trifecta £255.90.
**Owner** A E Oppenheimer **Bred** Hascombe And Valiant Studs **Trained** Newmarket, Suffolk

**FOCUS**
15yds further than advertised. Not a vintage renewal of the feature, but an interesting race nonetheless. They looked to go a steady pace and the winner led all the way. The runner-up has been rated as running close to her AW best.

## 4830 LONG HARBOUR DEREK LUCIE-SMITH MEMORIAL H'CAP 6f
4:35 (4:37) (Class 3) (0-95,93) 3-Y-O+ £9,703 (£2,887; £1,443; £721) Stalls High

Form RPR

-225 1 **Lightning Charlie**[69] 2390 5-9-7 86.......................... SteveDrowne 9 94
(Amanda Perrett) *trckd nr side ldrs and racd cl nr side rail thrght: chsd ldr over 1f out: rdn and clsd to ld last 100yds: jst hld on* **16/1**

1004 **2** *shd* **Hakam (USA)**[52] 2943 5-10-0 **93**............................ SilvestreDeSousa 11 100
(Michael Appleby) *s.i.s: hld up nr side and racd against rail: prog 2f out: drvn to chal ins fnl f: w wnr last 100yds: jst denied* **10/1**

444 **3** *1* **Jordan Sport**[23] 3967 4-9-12 **91**....................................(h) MartinHarley 10 94
(David Simcock) *overall ldr nr side: dashed for home 2f out: drvn over 1f out: hdd and no ex last 100yds* **7/1**

0-63 **4** *2* **Hyperfocus (IRE)**[77] 2130 3-9-2 **87**............................ HarryBentley 7 83+
(Hugo Palmer) *taken down early and steadily: hld up in nr side gp gng wl: effrt whn nt clr run briefly 2f out: shkn up over 1f out: kpt on to take 4th ins fnl f: no ch* **8/1**

12/3 **5** *1* **Atletico (IRE)**[37] 3463 5-9-9 **88**............................ JackMitchell 1 82+
(Roger Varian) *trckd ldng pair in centre: led gp 2f out: wandered u.p and nt qckn over 1f out: one pce after* **9/2**[1]

0313 **6** *1 ½* **Boy In The Bar**[34] 3593 6-9-12 **91**...............................(b) LukeMorris 8 80
(Ian Williams) *chsd overall ldr nr side to 2f out: fdd u.p* **6/1**[3]

0012 **7** *½* **Major Pusey**[34] 3585 5-9-5 **84**............................ FergusSweeney 4 71
(John Gallagher) *led quartet in centre to 2f out: fdd* **12/1**

5503 **8** *shd* **Stellarta**[12] 4411 6-9-12 **91**............................ TomMarquand 3 78
(Michael Blanshard) *pushed along in last of centre gp: nvr on terms* **20/1**

2003 **9** *1 ¼* **Moonraker**[13] 4353 5-9-3 **87**............................ DavidEgan(5) 5 70
(Mick Channon) *t.k.h: hld up in last of nr side gp: shkn up on outer of gp 2f out: no prog* **5/1**[2]

5212 **10** *4 ½* **Patchwork**[14] 4313 3-8-10 **81**............................ ShaneKelly 6 49
(Richard Hughes) *t.k.h: trckd ldrs on nr side: rdn on outer of gp 2f out: wknd* **6/1**[3]

-130 **11** *3* **Little Palaver**[39] 3410 5-9-12 **91**............................ AdamKirby 2 50
(Clive Cox) *chsd ldr in centre to 1/2-way: sn rdn: wknd 2f out* **20/1**

1m 14.1s (-0.40) **Going Correction** +0.275s/f (Good)
**WFA** 3 from 4yo+ 6lb **11** Ran SP% **119.2**
Speed ratings (Par 107): **113,112,111,108,107 105,104,104,103,97 93**
CSF £168.95 CT £859.75 TOTE £17.70: £4.40, £2.70, £2.60; EX 151.90 Trifecta £2670.80.
**Owner** Lightning Charlie Partnership **Bred** J A E Hobby **Trained** Pulborough, W Sussex
■ Stewards' Enquiry : Silvestre De Sousa two-day ban: used whip above permitted level (Jul 31, Aug 4)
Adam Kirby caution: entered the wrong stall
Steve Drowne two-day ban: used whip above permitted level (Jul 28-30)

**FOCUS**
A wide-open, competitive sprint handicap. They were in two groups early and the highest three stalls occupied the places. The winner has been rated to his best.

## 4831 SAVILLS H'CAP 7f 213y(R)
**5:10** (5:11) (Class 3) (0-90,88) 3-Y-O **£9,703** (£2,887; £1,443; £721) **Stalls** Low

Form RPR

41 **1** **Addeybb (IRE)**[30] 3714 3-9-7 **88**............................ MartinHarley 7 98+
(William Haggas) *disp ld tl led wl over 1f out: drvn and jnd 100yds out: kpt on wl and hld on nr fin* **3/1**[2]

5314 **2** *nk* **Juanito Chico (IRE)**[34] 3592 3-9-6 **87**...................(h) SilvestreDeSousa 4 96
(William Jarvis) *t.k.h: hld up in last pair: swtchd out wd and gd prog wl over 1f out: rdn to join wnr last 100yds: nt qckn fnl strides* **2/1**[1]

6211 **3** *2* **Pastime**[15] 4265 3-8-10 **82**............................ DavidEgan(5) 6 86
(Gay Kelleway) *t.k.h: trckd ldrs: rdn over 2f out: disp 2nd briefly over 1f out: kpt on same pce after* **9/1**

1032 **4** *1 ½* **Abatement**[16] 4215 3-8-13 **80**............................ TomMarquand 5 81
(Roger Charlton) *trckd ldrs: shkn up over 2f out: nt qckn and no imp over 1f out: one pce after* **11/2**

0064 **5** *¾* **Poetic Force (IRE)**[14] 4290 3-8-7 **74**...............................(t) LukeMorris 3 73
(Tony Carroll) *trckd ldrs: rdn over 2f out: lost pl over 1f out: n.d after* **14/1**

3502 **6** *1 ½* **Mutawakked (IRE)**[20] 4084 3-9-1 **82**............................ DaneO'Neill 2 78
(Brian Meehan) *disp ld to wl over 1f out: wknd* **5/1**[3]

2406 **7** *2* **Shamrokh (IRE)**[27] 3838 3-9-2 **83**............................ AdamKirby 1 74
(Michael Appleby) *hld up in last pair: shkn up and no prog over 2f out: sn wknd* **20/1**

1m 42.47s (1.77) **Going Correction** +0.275s/f (Good) **7** Ran SP% **111.8**
Speed ratings (Par 104): **102,101,99,98,97 95,93**
CSF £8.98 TOTE £3.40: £1.90, £1.40; EX 10.00 Trifecta £43.90.
**Owner** Sheikh Ahmed Al Maktoum **Bred** Rabbah Bloodstock Limited **Trained** Newmarket, Suffolk

**FOCUS**
In a race extended by 11yds the front two fought out a good battle. Despite the small field this is probably decent 3yo handicap form. The third has been rated similar to his AW win.

## 4832 CMS REAL DEAL APPRENTICE H'CAP 1m (S)
**5:40** (5:41) (Class 4) (0-85,85) 4-Y-O+ **£6,469** (£1,925; £962; £481) **Stalls** High

Form RPR

351 **1** **Fire Tree (IRE)**[60] 2685 4-8-12 **77**............................ PaddyBradley(5) 5 85
(Charlie Fellowes) *racd in centre tl gps merged 1/2-way: wl in tch: shkn up and prog 2f out: pressed ldr 1f out: rdn to ld last 75yds: styd on* **5/2**[1]

0450 **2** *½* **Brilliant Vanguard (IRE)**[16] 4215 4-8-9 **76**.........(p[1]) SeamusCronin(7) 9 83
(Kevin Ryan) *pressed overall ldr nr side: led over 2f out and edgd rt towards centre: rdn wl over 1f out: kpt on but hdd last 75yds* **10/1**

0-00 **3** *½* **Balmoral Castle**[72] 2291 8-9-3 **84**............................ Pierre-LouisJamin(7) 6 90
(Jonathan Portman) *hld up in rr nr side: shkn up over 2f out: swtchd to centre over 1f out: styd on after and tk 3rd ins fnl f: nrst fin* **12/1**

1054 **4** *1 ½* **Zlatan (IRE)**[16] 4210 4-9-2 **79**...............................(p) DavidEgan(3) 7 81
(Ed de Giles) *trckd ldrs nr side: rdn and tried to chal over 1f out: fdd ins fnl f* **13/2**

0250 **5** *1 ¾* **Tomahawk Kid**[29] 3750 4-9-8 **82**............................ GeorgeWood 8 80
(Ian Williams) *trckd nr side ldrs: rdn and cl up over 1f out: fdd fnl f* **12/1**

6010 **6** *1* **In The Red (IRE)**[8] 4524 4-9-3 **82**............................ MillyNaseb(5) 3 78
(Martin Smith) *racd centre and styd on outer whn gps merged 1/2-way: shkn up over 1f out and plenty to do: no great prog* **14/1**

2262 **7** *1 ½* **Golden Wedding (IRE)**[29] 3750 5-9-10 **84**............................ EdwardGreatrex 4 77
(Eve Johnson Houghton) *led trio in centre to 2f out: wknd* **5/1**[3]

-035 **8** *2 ¾* **Archie (IRE)**[14] 4321 5-9-3 **82**............................ CameronNoble(5) 2 68
(Tom Clover) *s.s: swtchd to nr side and last of gp: swtchd to centre sn after 1/2-way: no prog and nvr on terms* **16/1**

0-41 **9** *9* **Mamillius**[27] 3816 4-9-11 **85**............................ HectorCrouch 10 51
(George Baker) *overall ldr nr side to over 2f out: wknd rapidly over 1f out* **4/1**[2]

1m 42.45s (1.65) **Going Correction** +0.275s/f (Good) **9** Ran SP% **115.6**
Speed ratings (Par 105): **102,101,101,99,97 96,95,92,83**
CSF £28.83 CT £255.66 TOTE £3.20: £1.20, £3.20, £3.80; EX 29.80 Trifecta £511.20.
**Owner** Never So Bold **Bred** Peter Reynolds & Robert Dore **Trained** Newmarket, Suffolk

**FOCUS**
A fair apprentice race. The runner-up has been rated to his better recent form.
T/Plt: £297.60 to a £1 stake. Pool: £79,460.83 - 194.91 winning units. T/Qpdt: £54.80 to a £1 stake. Pool: £6,045.07 - 81.62 winning units. **Jonathan Neesom**

# [4784] CARLISLE (R-H)
Friday, July 14

**OFFICIAL GOING: Good to firm (8.1)**
Wind: Fresh across Weather: Cloudy, rain after 3rd

## 4833 RACING UK NOW ON TALK TALK TV H'CAP (FOR LADY AMATEUR RIDERS) 7f 173y
**6:05** (6:05) (Class 5) (0-70,71) 4-Y-O+ **£3,275** (£1,015; £507; £254) **Stalls** Low

Form RPR

5043 **1** **Dark Confidant (IRE)**[11] 4451 4-9-1 **57**............................ MissEllaMcCain(7) 1 64
(Donald McCain) *midfield: rdn and hdwy over 1f out: styd on: led 50yds out* **7/1**

5055 **2** *¾* **Curzon Line**[25] 3899 8-10-5 **68**............................ MissJoannaMason 2 74
(Michael Easterby) *chsd clr ldng pair: rdn 2f out: led ent fnl f: hdd 50yds out: one pce* **15/8**[1]

0066 **3** *nk* **Ravenhoe (IRE)**[25] 3899 4-10-2 **70**............................ MissEmmaBedford(5) 3 75
(Mark Johnston) *dwlt: hld up: rdn 2f out: gd hdwy appr fnl f: kpt on* **8/1**

0142 **4** *1 ¼* **Kiwi Bay**[11] 4439 12-9-12 **68**............................ MissSEDods(7) 8 70
(Michael Dods) *dwlt: hld up: rdn along 2f out: kpt on fnl f: nrst fin* **4/1**[2]

-401 **5** *½* **Know Your Name**[11] 4453 6-9-12 **66** 6ex............................ MissAMcCain(5) 7 67
(Donald McCain) *midfield: rdn 2f out: one pce and nvr threatened* **5/1**[3]

10-0 **6** *3 ½* **Circuitous**[21] 4039 9-9-10 **59**...............................(v) MrsCBartley 5 52
(Keith Dalgleish) *led narrowly: rdn over 2f out: hdd ent fnl f: wknd* **22/1**

6240 **7** *2 ½* **Mustaqbal (IRE)**[11] 4439 5-10-1 **71**...............................(p) MissCADods(7) 10 58
(Michael Dods) *s.i.s: sn midfield: pushed along over 2f out: wknd over 1f out* **9/1**

3500 **8** *5* **Space War**[11] 4433 10-10-4 **67**............................ MissETodd 6 42
(Michael Easterby) *pressed ldr: rdn over 2f out: wknd over 1f out* **25/1**

1m 39.66s (-0.34) **Going Correction** +0.025s/f (Good) **8** Ran SP% **113.3**
Speed ratings (Par 103): **102,101,100,99,99 95,93,88**
CSF £20.16 CT £105.76 TOTE £6.50: £2.20, £1.10, £2.40; EX 35.80 Trifecta £162.50.
**Owner** D McCain Jnr **Bred** Rabbah Bloodstock Limited **Trained** Cholmondeley, Cheshire

**FOCUS**
Rail movements increase advertised distances by 18 yards in Races 1, 4, 5, 6 and 7. An ordinary handicap for lady amateur riders. They went an overly strong, contested gallop on good to firm ground. The winner has been rated to last year's AW form.

## 4834 EBF STALLIONS NOVICE STKS (PLUS 10 RACE) 5f 193y
**6:35** (6:36) (Class 4) 2-Y-O **£5,498** (£1,636; £817; £408) **Stalls** Low

Form RPR

3 **1** **Ingenuity**[16] 4205 2-9-2 0............................ JackGarritty 11 87+
(Jedd O'Keeffe) *led narrowly: rdn whn hdd appr fnl f: styd on: led again post* **3/1**[1]

**2** *nse* **Hey Jonesy (IRE)** 2-9-2 0............................ TomEaves 8 87+
(Kevin Ryan) *trckd ldrs: pushed along to ld appr fnl f: sn ¾ l up: rdn 110yds out: one pce and hdd post* **12/1**

3 **3** *5* **Phoenix Lightning (IRE)**[23] 3973 2-9-2 0............................ DavidNolan 3 70
(Richard Fahey) *dwlt: midfield: hdwy to trck ldrs 3f out: rdn over 1f out: one pce fnl f* **3/1**[1]

0 **4** *1 ¾* **Bibbidibobbidiboo (IRE)**[24] 3943 2-8-8 0............................ JordanVaughan(3) 4 59
(Ann Duffield) *trckd ldrs: rdn 2f out: sn one pce* **16/1**

6 **5** *1* **Mecca's Spirit (IRE)**[24] 3943 2-8-11 0............................ PaulMulrennan 2 56
(Michael Dods) *midfield: rdn over 2f out: no imp* **9/2**[3]

01 **6** *½* **Jackontherocks**[32] 3648 2-9-3 0............................ CallumRodriguez(5) 1 65
(Michael Dods) *hld up: rdn over 2f out: nvr threatened* **4/1**[2]

**7** *1 ½* **North Road Revue** 2-8-11 0............................ DavidAllan 10 49+
(Tim Easterby) *wnt lft s and slowly away: hld up: nvr threatened* **25/1**

4 **8** *½* **Kylie Rules**[36] 3495 2-8-11 0............................ FrannyNorton 6 48
(Ann Duffield) *pressed ldr: racd keenly: rdn 2f out: sn wknd* **18/1**

**9** *13* **Langtree Lane** 2-8-11 0............................ ConnorBeasley 7 5
(Bryan Smart) *slowly away: a rr* **18/1**

0 **10** *1 ½* **Bigdabog**[22] 4014 2-9-2 0............................ NeilFarley 9 5
(Eric Alston) *trckd ldrs: pushed along and lost pl 3f out: wknd 2f out and bhd* **80/1**

1m 12.78s (-0.92) **Going Correction** +0.025s/f (Good) **10** Ran SP% **117.4**
Speed ratings (Par 96): **107,106,100,97,96 95,93,93,75,73**
CSF £41.68 TOTE £3.10: £1.30, £3.50, £1.20; EX 32.60 Trifecta £177.30.
**Owner** Highbeck Racing **Bred** Aston Mullins Stud **Trained** Middleham Moor, N Yorks

**FOCUS**
An ordinary juvenile novice contest. They went a decent gallop and one of the joint-favourites came clear of the third with a promising newcomer. It's been rated as decent form for the grade.

## 4835 RACING UK ON BT TV H'CAP 5f
**7:05** (7:05) (Class 4) (0-80,81) 3-Y-O **£5,498** (£1,636; £817; £408) **Stalls** Low

Form RPR

3022 **1** **The Nazca Lines (IRE)**[7] 4576 3-8-13 **72**...............................(v) JackGarritty 4 77
(John Quinn) *in tch: gng wl whn bit short of room appr fnl f: sn swtchd lft to outer: rdn and r.o wl: led post* **5/1**[3]

6141 **2** *hd* **Intense Romance (IRE)**[14] 4305 3-9-1 **79**............ CallumRodriguez(5) 3 83
(Michael Dods) *chsd ldr: rdn to ld 1f out: kpt on but hdd post* **3/1**[2]

1430 **3** *nk* **Twizzell**[29] 3741 3-9-6 **79**............................ PJMcDonald 7 82
(K R Burke) *hld up in tch: rdn and hdwy over 1f out: ev ch ins fnl f: kpt on* **7/1**

-015 **4** *2 ¾* **Harome (IRE)**[8] 4530 3-9-7 **80**............................ ConnorBeasley 2 73
(Roger Fell) *led: rdn 2f out: edgd lft over 1f out: hdd 1f out: no ex ins fnl f* **10/1**

2030 **5** *4* **Hemingway (IRE)**[83] 1975 3-9-7 **80**...............................(p) TomEaves 1 59
(Kevin Ryan) *hld up: sn pushed along: nvr threatened* **8/1**

1-20 **6** *3* **Computable**[56] 2806 3-9-8 **81**............................ DavidAllan 6 49
(Tim Easterby) *stdd s: racd keenly and sn chsd ldr: rdn 2f out: wknd fnl f* **85/40**[1]

0200 **7** *¾* **Awesome Allan (IRE)**[13] 4333 3-9-6 **79**...............................(t) AndrewMullen 5 44
(David Evans) *prom: rdn over 2f out: wknd over 1f out* **14/1**

1m 0.51s (-0.29) **Going Correction** +0.025s/f (Good) **7** Ran SP% **113.0**
Speed ratings (Par 102): **103,102,102,97,91 86,85**
CSF £19.88 TOTE £5.30: £2.30, £1.10; EX 22.10 Trifecta £98.00.
**Owner** Ross Harmon **Bred** Rathasker Stud **Trained** Settrington, N Yorks

**FOCUS**
A fair 3yo sprint handicap. They went a proper gallop which suited the narrow winner. The winner has been rated to his late 2yo form.

## 4836 STELLA NURSERY H'CAP 6f 195y
**7:35** (7:37) (Class 5) 2-Y-O **£3,396** (£1,010; £505; £252) **Stalls** Low

Form RPR
3431 1 **Ventura Knight (IRE)**24 3930 2-9-7 **82** FrannyNorton 2 95+
(Mark Johnston) *mde all: pushed clr over 1f out: eased towards fin* **15/8**1
352 2 3 ½ **Star Of Zaam (IRE)**16 4205 2-8-10 **71** (p1) PJMcDonald 8 73
(K R Burke) *trckd ldrs: rdn 2f out: wnt 2nd 1f out: kpt on but no threat wnr* **3/1**3
332 3 1 ¾ **Move It Move It**15 4259 2-9-2 **77** PaulMulrennan 3 74
(Keith Dalgleish) *hld up: bit short of room 2f out and again over 1f out: angled lft into clr appr fnl f: rdn and kpt on same pce fnl f* **5/2**2
451 4 ¾ **Shazzab (IRE)**39 3390 2-8-13 **74** JackGarritty 5 69
(Richard Fahey) *hld up: rdn and sme hdwy 2f out: one pce fr appr fnl f* **7/1**
204 5 6 **Kheleyf's Girl**45 3187 2-8-5 **66** ConnorBeasley 6 45
(David Evans) *prom: racd keenly: rdn 2f out: wknd fnl f* **16/1**
0040 6 2 **Sam James (IRE)**32 3648 2-8-4 **65** (p1) AndrewMullen 1 39
(Iain Jardine) *trckd ldrs: rdn 3f out: wknd over 1f out* **33/1**
6006 7 2 ½ **Heavenly Pulse (IRE)**22 4014 2-7-7 **61** oh16 RPWalsh(7) 7 28
(Ann Duffield) *dwlt: hld up: rdn over 2f out: wknd over 1f out* **100/1**

1m 27.45s (0.35) **Going Correction** +0.025s/f (Good) **7** Ran SP% **110.7**
Speed ratings (Par 94): **99,95,93,92,85 83,80**
CSF £7.25 CT £12.24 TOTE £2.90: £1.50, £1.50; EX 8.90 Trifecta £18.70.
**Owner** Middleham Park Racing XXXVII **Bred** L K I Bloodstock Ltd **Trained** Middleham Moor, N Yorks

**FOCUS**
Race distance increased 18 yards. A fairly decent nursery handicap. The favourite gradually increased his own tempo in thoroughly dominant fashion. The second has been rated as matching his previous effort.

## 4837 RACING UK H'CAP 6f 195y
**8:10** (8:11) (Class 4) (0-80,79) 3-Y-O+ **£5,498** (£1,636; £817; £408) **Stalls** Low

Form RPR
4310 1 **Dark Profit (IRE)**5 4663 5-9-11 **76** (p) AndrewMullen 1 87
(Keith Dalgleish) *trckd ldr: rdn over 1f out: led ins fnl f: kpt on* **7/2**2
01-1 2 2 ½ **Big Storm Coming**27 3833 7-10-0 **79** TomEaves 6 83
(David Brown) *led: rdn over 1f out: hdd ins fnl f: one pce* **13/2**3
1534 3 2 **Champion Harbour (IRE)**14 4304 3-8-2 **61** FrannyNorton 4 57
(Richard Fahey) *hld up in tch: rdn over 1f out: kpt on same pce fnl f: wnt 3rd nr fin* **7/1**
4-12 4 hd **Call Me Grumpy (IRE)**21 4058 3-9-5 **78** PaulMulrennan 3 73
(Roger Varian) *trckd ldr: rdn over 2f out: sn one pce: no ex and lost 3rd towards fin* **4/5**1
4353 5 8 **Bush Beauty (IRE)**16 4209 6-9-0 **65** NeilFarley 2 41
(Eric Alston) *slowly away: a rr* **14/1**

1m 27.73s (0.63) **Going Correction** +0.025s/f (Good)
**WFA** 3 from 5yo+ 8lb **5** Ran SP% **110.3**
Speed ratings (Par 105): **97,94,91,91,82**
CSF £24.22 TOTE £3.70: £1.90, £2.90; EX 20.80 Trifecta £62.40.
**Owner** Weldspec Glasgow Limited **Bred** Mrs S M Rogers & Sir Thomas Pilkington **Trained** Carluke, S Lanarks

**FOCUS**
Race distance increased 18 yards. A fair handicap. They went a respectable gallop but the strong favourite proved disappointing. A clear pb from the winner, with the second rated to form.

## 4838 RACING UK IN HD H'CAP 1m 1f
**8:45** (8:45) (Class 5) (0-70,70) 3-Y-O **£3,396** (£1,010; £505; £252) **Stalls** Low

Form RPR
3113 1 **Brother McGonagall**7 4557 3-9-7 **70** DavidAllan 1 79
(Tim Easterby) *trckd ldr: rdn to chal over 1f out: edgd ahd ins fnl f: styd on wl* **6/4**1
5314 2 ½ **True Romance (IRE)**32 3665 3-9-6 **69** TomEaves 4 77
(James Given) *led: rdn 2f out: pressed over 1f out: hdd ins fnl f: styd on* **7/2**3
56-3 3 5 **Siyahamba (IRE)**29 3745 3-8-7 **56** ConnorBeasley 2 53
(Bryan Smart) *trckd ldr: rdn along over 3f out: outpcd over 1f out: plugged on ins fnl f* **9/1**
0-26 4 ¾ **Moonlight Blue (IRE)**25 3901 3-8-13 **67** (p1) CallumRodriguez(5) 3 62
(Michael Dods) *s.i.s: hld up: rdn over 2f out: one pce and nvr threatened* **25/1**
251 5 16 **Cliff Bay (IRE)**23 3975 3-9-5 **68** PaulMulrennan 5 45
(Keith Dalgleish) *racd keenly: hld up in tch: rdn over 2f out: wknd over 1f out* **2/1**2

1m 58.02s (0.42) **Going Correction** +0.025s/f (Good) **5** Ran SP% **109.4**
Speed ratings (Par 100): **99,98,94,93,79**
CSF £7.01 TOTE £2.10: £1.60, £1.40; EX 7.00 Trifecta £22.00.
**Owner** Reality Partnerships VI **Bred** J P Coggan **Trained** Great Habton, N Yorks

**FOCUS**
Race distance increased 18 yards. An ordinary little 3yo handicap. They went an, at best, respectable gallop, in pouring rain which hadn't as yet got into the ground significantly. The level is a bit fluid.

## 4839 RACING UK NOW IN HD H'CAP 1m 3f 39y
**9:20** (9:20) (Class 6) (0-60,62) 3-Y-O+ **£2,911** (£866; £432; £216) **Stalls** Low

Form RPR
4042 1 **Thorntoun Care**23 3978 6-9-12 **61** (p) CallumRodriguez(5) 1 69+
(Iain Jardine) *midfield: rdn and hdwy over 1f out: led 1f out: kpt on: pushed out towards fin* **11/4**1
6063 2 ½ **Chauvelin**7 4558 6-9-7 **51** (b) TomEaves 2 58
(Nigel Tinkler) *hld up: rdn and hdwy over 1f out: kpt on: wnt 2nd fnl 50yds* **11/1**
00-0 3 1 **Parkwarden (IRE)**21 2349 3-8-6 **47** FrannyNorton 7 54
(Chris Grant) *led: pushed along whn hdd 4f out: remained prom: rdn over 2f out: kpt on* **33/1**
5004 4 1 **Druid's Diamond**17 4169 4-9-5 **49** (p1) AndrewMullen 6 53
(Mark Walford) *trckd ldrs: racd keenly: rdn and lost pl over 2f out: kpt on ins fnl f* **8/1**3
-042 5 nk **Bollin Ted**17 4171 3-8-4 **45** DuranFentiman 9 49
(Tim Easterby) *prom: racd keenly: led 4f out: rdn over 2f out: hdd 1f out: one pce* **11/4**1
5430 6 shd **Mount Cheiron (USA)**21 4034 6-9-1 **45** PJMcDonald 8 48
(Richard Ford) *midfield: rdn and lost pl over 2f out: kpt on fnl f: nvr threatened* **14/1**
6005 7 1 ¾ **Thomas Crown (IRE)**17 4172 3-9-0 **55** ConnorBeasley 10 56
(Roger Fell) *hld up: rdn over 2f out: nvr threatened* **12/1**
000- 8 4 ½ **Rockabilly Riot (IRE)**12 8134 7-9-11 **55** DavidNolan 11 48
(Martin Todhunter) *trckd ldrs on outer: rdn over 2f out: wknd over 1f out* **20/1**
406 9 10 **Mystery Of War (IRE)**20 4097 3-9-3 **58** (p1) PaulMulrennan 3 35
(George Scott) *trckd ldrs: pushed along over 2f out: edgd rt over 1f out and wknd* **9/2**2

2m 31.48s (8.38) **Going Correction** +0.025s/f (Good)
**WFA** 3 from 4yo+ 11lb **9** Ran SP% **113.0**
Speed ratings (Par 101): **70,69,68,68,67 67,66,63,56**
CSF £34.17 CT £804.56 TOTE £3.80: £1.40, £2.20, £5.60; EX 17.90 Trifecta £1023.60.
**Owner** Alba-Eire Syndicate **Bred** W M Johnstone **Trained** Carrutherstown, D'fries & G'way

**FOCUS**
Race distance increased 18 yards. A modest middle-distance handicap. They went a particularly slow gallop and the winner, a well-backed joint-favourite, was one of only a few who settled into a rhythm. It's been rated as straightforward form around the principals.
T/Plt: £67.80 to a £1 stake. Pool: £47,342.67 - 509.32 winning units. T/Qpdt: £15.20 to a £1 stake. Pool: £3,211.60 - 156.6 winning units. **Andrew Sheret**

# 4465 CHEPSTOW (L-H)
Friday, July 14

**OFFICIAL GOING: Good to firm (good in places; 8.1)**
Wind: Light wind Weather: Sunny intervals

## 4840 COUNTY MARQUEES APPRENTICE H'CAP (PART OF THE RACING EXCELLENCE INITIATIVE) 1m 4f
**5:45** (5:46) (Class 5) (0-70,70) 4-Y-O+ **£3,234** (£962; £481; £240) **Stalls** Low

Form RPR
0-05 1 **Tobouggaloo**38 3428 6-8-12 **59** WilliamCox(3) 2 68
(Stuart Kittow) *hld up: hdwy into 4th 4f out: clsd on ldrs and reminder over 2f out: wnt 2nd over 1f out: pushed along ins fnl f: led last 50yds* **4/1**2
3-54 2 ½ **What A Scorcher**28 3770 6-9-7 **68** RossaRyan(3) 3 76
(Nikki Evans) *led: 4 l clr after 4f: 2 l clr 3f out: pushed along 2f out: rdn appr fnl f: r.o: ct last 50yds* **7/2**1
002 3 4 **Wotabreeze (IRE)**8 4519 4-9-12 **70** JoshQuinn 4 72
(John Quinn) *trckd ldrs: pushed along and wnt 2nd 2f out: sn rdn: lost 2nd over 1f out: no ex ins fnl f* **7/2**1
20-5 4 2 ¾ **Captain George (IRE)**29 1937 6-9-1 **62** (p) StephenCummins(3) 10 59
(Michael Blake) *mid-div: rdn over 2f out: styd on one pce ins fnl f* **9/1**
6005 5 1 ½ **Ring Eye (IRE)**10 4469 9-8-8 **52** (p) BenRobinson 8 47
(John O'Shea) *chsd ldr: reminders 2f out: sn rdn and wknd* **12/1**
-060 6 ¾ **Balmont Belle (IRE)**33 3628 7-8-7 **51** oh5 JaneElliott 7 45
(Barry Leavy) *in rr: last 4f out: sme hdwy 2f out: reminder over 1f out: one pce* **20/1**
4003 7 1 ¼ **Distant High**10 4470 6-8-9 **53** (v) KatherineGlenister 5 45
(Richard Price) *dwlt: hdwy 4f out: rdn 3f out: no ex* **5/1**3
3255 8 4 **Ceyhan**16 4202 5-9-5 **70** EmmaTaff(7) 9 55
(Jamie Osborne) *hld up: last and reminders over 2f out: no imp* **17/2**

2m 33.35s (-5.65) **Going Correction** -0.375s/f (Firm) **8** Ran SP% **114.1**
Speed ratings (Par 103): **103,102,100,98,97 96,95,93**
CSF £18.33 CT £52.59 TOTE £6.10: £1.40, £1.60, £1.70; EX 28.20 Trifecta £115.50.
**Owner** Dr G S Plastow **Bred** D R Tucker **Trained** Blackborough, Devon

**FOCUS**
The ground had dried out overnight and was riding quick. The only race on the card run over the round course. The runner-up set a decent gallop in this moderate apprentice handicap and the time was a respectable 3.35sec outside standard. It's been rated around the runner-up.

## 4841 FEEDER - THE HOMECOMING NOVICE STKS 5f 16y
**6:15** (6:16) (Class 5) 2-Y-O **£3,234** (£962; £481; £240) **Stalls** Centre

Form RPR
426 1 **Listen Alexander (IRE)**34 3611 2-8-11 0 CharlesBishop 6 79
(David Evans) *mde all on stands' rail: 1 l clr whn reminder 2f out: rdn over 1f out: r.o wl ins fnl f: nt fully extended* **11/4**2
5212 2 ¾ **May Remain**28 3776 2-9-5 77 WilliamCarson 4 84
(Paul Cole) *mid-div: hdwy into 2nd 2f out: drvn and tried to chal 1f out: r.o but hld fnl f* **3/1**3
4150 3 1 ¾ **Daddies Girl (IRE)**13 4361 2-8-12 79 LuluStanford(5) 8 76+
(Rod Millman) *in rr: niggled ins 1st f: outpcd w plenty to do 1/2-way: rdn and hdwy over 1f out: r.o to take 3rd ins fnl f* **10/3**
4 4 **Shaya (IRE)** 2-8-11 0 DavidProbert 2 56
(Simon Crisford) *chsd ldrs on outer: 3rd 2f out: losing grnd over 1f out: reminder and flashed tail three times ins fnl f: no ex* **9/4**1
0 5 3 ¼ **Istanbul Pasha (IRE)**16 4218 2-9-2 0 SaleemGolam 1 49
(David Evans) *in rr: last 1/2-way: drvn 2f out: rdn over 1f out: no imp* **25/1**
05 6 10 **Korak Boy (IRE)**9 4488 2-9-2 0 (b1) RobHornby 3 13
(Joseph Tuite) *chsd ldr: lost pl 1/2-way: sn rdn and wknd: eased fnl f* **66/1**

58.3s (-1.00) **Going Correction** -0.375s/f (Firm) **6** Ran SP% **110.9**
Speed ratings (Par 94): **93,91,89,82,77 61**
CSF £11.09 TOTE £3.20: £1.40, £1.60; EX 9.00 Trifecta £25.40.
**Owner** Noel O'Callaghan **Bred** Mountarmstrong Stud **Trained** Pandy, Monmouths

**FOCUS**
They all made for the stands' side in this decent little novice stakes. The time was quick. The winner has been rated near her latest Listed form.

## 4842 LABELS SHOPPING, ROSS ON WYE H'CAP 5f 16y
**6:45** (6:46) (Class 5) (0-70,70) 3-Y-O+ **£3,234** (£962; £481; £240) **Stalls** Centre

Form RPR
-302 1 **Glacier Point**13 4352 3-9-5 **70** (p1) DavidProbert 4 76
(Clive Cox) *led tl hdd after 1f: regained ld 2f out: drvn over 1f out: narrow ld ent fnl f: sn rdn: hld on wl cl home* **9/4**1
-630 2 nk **Compton Poppy**26 3865 3-9-4 **69** GeorgeDowning 6 74
(Tony Carroll) *chsd ldrs: hdwy to chal ldrs 2f out: wnt 2nd over 1f out: rdn ent fnl f: r.o but hld by wnr* **7/1**
5001 3 3 ½ **Quantum Dot (IRE)**18 4148 6-9-0 **63** (b) CallumShepherd(3) 8 57
(Ed de Giles) *led after 1f: drvn and hdd 2f out: rdn and relegated to 3rd wl over 1f out: no ex ins fnl f* **9/2**2
00-0 4 1 ¼ **Evening Starlight**185 161 4-9-3 **63** RyanTate 1 53
(Ron Hodges) *mid-div: rdn 2f out: one pce fnl f* **28/1**

335 **5** *nk* **Bonjour Steve**[15] 4278 6-8-12 **63**...............................(p) MitchGodwin(5) 5 52
(Richard Price) *hld up: last 1/2-way: rdn over 2f out: r.o one pce ins fnl f* **9/2**[2]

0-10 **6** *3* **Mad Endeavour**[35] 3532 6-9-6 **66**....................................(b) RobHornby 3 44
(Stuart Kittow) *mid-div: pushed along 1/2-way: losing pl whn reminders over 2f out: wknd fnl f* **6/1**[3]

2514 **7** *6* **Swendab (IRE)**[17] 4182 9-9-2 **67**...............................(b) BenRobinson(5) 2 23
(John O'Shea) *awkward and lost grnd leaving stalls: in rr: drvn 1/2-way: rdn 2f out: lost tch and eased fnl f* **13/2**

57.66s (-1.64) **Going Correction** -0.375s/f (Firm)
**WFA** 3 from 4yo+ 5lb **7** Ran SP% **110.7**
Speed ratings (Par 103): **98,97,91,89,89 84,75**
CSF £17.33 CT £60.72 TOTE £2.70: £1.80, £3.50; EX 19.40 Trifecta £68.90.
**Owner** Racegoers Club Owners Group **Bred** Whitsbury Manor Stud **Trained** Lambourn, Berks
■ Stewards' Enquiry : Ryan Tate two-day ban: careless riding (Jul 28-30)

**FOCUS**
Modest sprint form but the time was 0.44 quicker than standard, emphasising how fast the track was riding. The last three home blew their chances at the start. The level is fluid.

## 4843 OXBATHROOM PRODUCTS H'CAP 6f 16y
**7:15** (7:17) (Class 5) (0-70,70) 3-Y-O **£3,234** (£962; £481; £240) **Stalls** Centre

Form RPR

24-0 **1** **Sheikspear**[32] 3673 3-9-4 **70**.................................... CallumShepherd(3) 1 75
(Ed de Giles) *mde all: pushed along 2f out: narrow ld and rdn ent fnl f: hld on gamely u.p* **7/1**

40-0 **2** *nk* **Miss Anticipation (IRE)**[42] 3296 3-8-11 **65**.................. PaddyPilley(5) 4 69
(Roger Charlton) *mid-div: rdn and swtchd to stands' rail over 2f out: hdwy and wnt 2nd ent fnl furlong: sn ev ch: r.o: jst hld* **9/1**

0-13 **3** *½* **Zambezi Queen (IRE)**[21] 4046 3-9-4 **67**........................ DavidProbert 6 69
(Paul Cole) *prom: pushed along 2f out: rdn in cl 3rd 1f out: ev ch ent fnl f: r.o* **2/1**[1]

5520 **4** *½* **Malcolm The Pug (IRE)**[9] 4500 3-9-7 **70**...................... TimmyMurphy 2 70
(Richard Hannon) *hld up: hdwy 2f out: drvn and cl up 1f out: rdn and no ex wl ins fnl f* **4/1**[2]

0624 **5** *2½* **Peachey Carnehan**[7] 4576 3-9-3 **66**..........................(b) WilliamCarson 5 58
(Michael Mullineaux) *prom: drvn 2f out: rdn and lost pl over 1f out* **7/1**

0525 **6** *nk* **Bellevarde (IRE)**[17] 4188 3-8-9 **63**................................ MitchGodwin(5) 3 54
(Richard Price) *prom: 2nd 2f out: sn drvn along: rdn and lost pl over 1f out* **9/2**[3]

-000 **7** *3* **Herm (IRE)**[15] 4255 3-8-12 **61**.........................................(t) SteveDrowne 7 43
(David Evans) *in rr: chsd along 1/2-way: rdn over 2f out: no imp: eased* **12/1**

1m 9.57s (-2.43) **Going Correction** -0.375s/f (Firm) **7** Ran SP% **114.2**
Speed ratings (Par 100): **101,100,99,99,95 95,91**
CSF £65.35 TOTE £6.90: £2.70, £3.70; EX 76.10 Trifecta £514.80.
**Owner** Spear Family **Bred** Rosyground Stud **Trained** Ledbury, H'fords
■ Stewards' Enquiry : Paddy Pilley two-day ban: used whip above permitted level (Jul 28, 30)

**FOCUS**
A modest sprint handicap The winner has been rated close to his standout AW run, but the level is fluid.

## 4844 SILK SERIES LADY RIDERS' H'CAP 6f 16y
**7:50** (7:50) (Class 4) (0-80,80) 3-Y-O+ **£6,301** (£1,886; £943; £472; £235) **Stalls** Centre

Form RPR

0304 **1** **Oeil De Tigre (FR)**[13] 4373 6-9-1 **65**.......................... SophieRalston(5) 5 73
(Tony Carroll) *t.k.h: led: hdd by runner-up 2f out: drvn and rallied 1f out: rdn to regain ld 150yds out: r.o wl* **15/2**

-016 **2** *1* **Gold Hunter (IRE)**[20] 4099 7-10-4 **77**....................(p) MissJodieHughes 9 82
(Steve Flook) *prom: hdwy gng wl to ld 2f out: narrow advantage and rdn ent fnl f: hdd 150yds out: no ex* **9/2**[2]

1005 **3** *½* **Athassel**[8] 4521 8-10-2 **80**.......................................... MissEMacKenzie(5) 6 83
(David Evans) *racd in last: reminders 2f out: hdwy over 1f out: r.o wl to take 3rd ins fnl f: nvr nrr* **7/1**

6634 **4** *shd* **Indian Affair**[15] 4256 7-9-1 **65**................................(bt) KerrieRaybould(5) 7 68
(Milton Bradley) *prom early: sn settled in midfield: followed runner-up through 2f out: 3rd 1f out: pushed along and kpt on fnl f* **6/1**[3]

4024 **5** *3* **Dodgy Bob**[5] 4664 4-9-3 **62**...........................................(b) MissMMullineaux 1 55
(Michael Mullineaux) *chsd ldrs: rdn over 2f out: grad wknd* **6/1**[3]

0113 **6** *nk* **Kinglami**[11] 4426 8-9-12 **71**...................................(p) MissBrodieHampson 2 64
(John O'Shea) *hld up: plenty to do and rdn wl over 1f out: no imp* **15/2**

0101 **7** *1½* **Castlerea Tess**[18] 4149 4-9-5 **64**...........................(p) MissSBrotherton 8 52
(Sarah Hollinshead) *racd in cl 2nd: pushed along 2f out: sn lost pl and wknd* **9/4**[1]

1m 9.49s (-2.51) **Going Correction** -0.375s/f (Firm) **7** Ran SP% **113.6**
Speed ratings (Par 105): **101,99,99,98,94 94,92**
CSF £40.17 CT £246.62 TOTE £6.00: £1.90, £2.80; EX 50.90 Trifecta £895.10.
**Owner** A W Carroll **Bred** Jedburgh Stud & Madame Clody Norton **Trained** Cropthorne, Worcs

**FOCUS**
A modest handicap contested by a mix of amateur and apprentice jockeys. Not much between the first four at the line. The second has been rated to form.

## 4845 HICKS LOGISTIC FILLIES' H'CAP 1m 14y
**8:25** (8:26) (Class 5) (0-75,76) 3-Y-O+ **£3,234** (£962; £481; £240) **Stalls** Centre

Form RPR

2250 **1** **Heartstone (IRE)**[6] 4621 4-9-10 **70**................................ SteveDrowne 7 77
(David Evans) *trckd ldrs stands' side: hdwy 3f out: sn drvn: rdn 2f out: led wl over 1f out: 1 l clr ent fnl f: kpt on wl under hand riding last 150yds* **20/1**

0-06 **2** *½* **Delirium (IRE)**[17] 4184 3-7-9 **55** oh1...........................(p) JaneElliott(5) 8 59
(Ed de Giles) *hld up in stands' side gp: pushed along 3f out: hdwy whn moved towards centre of trck over 2f out: sn rdn: swtchd bk to stands' side and wnt 3rd 1f out: r.o wl to take 2nd ins fnl f: nrst fin* **14/1**

-005 **3** *2* **Zaria**[17] 4184 6-8-2 **55**............................................(p) KatherineGlenister(7) 2 56
(Richard Price) *led stands' side: pushed along and hdd in gp 3f out: rdn over 2f out: 4th ent fnl f: kpt on to take 3rd last 100yds* **10/1**

4241 **4** *1¼* **Carol (IRE)**[18] 4145 3-9-7 **76**...................................... SilvestreDeSousa 4 73
(Ed Dunlop) *prom stands' side: led that gp 3f out: led overall 2f out: sn rdn: hdd wl over 1f out: no ex fnl f: eased nr fin* **5/6**[1]

0-05 **5** *5* **Santafiora**[45] 3173 3-8-6 **66**........................................ PaddyPilley(5) 1 53
(Roger Charlton) *t.k.h: led and racd alone on far side: pushed along and swtchd to centre of trck 3f out: rdn and hdd 2f out: no ex approching fnl f* **9/2**[2]

6106 **6** *¾* **Harmonise**[20] 4096 3-9-5 **74**........................................ CharlesBishop 5 57
(Mick Channon) *prom stands' side: pushed along over 3f out: sn lost pl: rdn and wknd 2f out* **5/1**[3]

1m 32.74s (-3.46) **Going Correction** -0.375s/f (Firm)
**WFA** 3 from 4yo+ 9lb **6** Ran SP% **109.9**
Speed ratings (Par 100): **102,101,99,98,93 92**
CSF £224.80 CT £2772.49 TOTE £18.90: £7.30, £3.60; EX 134.80 Trifecta £449.10.
**Owner** R Kent **Bred** Lady Bamford **Trained** Pandy, Monmouths

**FOCUS**
The 1-2 came from the two highest stalls in this ordinary fillies' handicap. The time dipped inside the standard. The winner has been rated back to her maiden best.

## 4846 READ SILVESTRE DE SOUSA AT 188BET H'CAP 1m 14y
**9:00** (9:00) (Class 5) (0-70,72) 3-Y-O+ **£3,234** (£962; £481; £240) **Stalls** Centre

Form RPR

4311 **1** **Swilly Sunset**[10] 4459 4-9-13 **68** 6ex......................... SilvestreDeSousa 5 80
(Anthony Carson) *mid-div: hdwy 1/2-way: 2nd 3f out: drvn over 2f out: sn rdn: led 1f out: drew clr fnl f: eased last 50yds: comf* **5/4**[1]

-052 **2** *2¾* **Carcharias (IRE)**[10] 4459 4-9-4 **62**......................... CallumShepherd(3) 8 68
(Ed de Giles) *led: rdn 2f out: hdd 1f out: no ex ins fnl f* **7/1**

6232 **3** *1¾* **Fair Selene**[3] 4714 3-8-7 **60**.......................................(v) GeorgeWood(3) 2 59
(Heather Main) *rrd and lost several l leaving sing stalls: in rr tl hdwy 3f out: drvn 2f out: rdn over 1f out: r.o wl fnl f: tk 3rd cl home* **9/2**[3]

5-55 **4** *nk* **Pick A Little**[17] 4176 9-9-5 **65**.................................... MitchGodwin(5) 3 65
(Michael Blake) *mid-div: drvn over 2f out: 3rd and rdn 1f out: no ex ins fnl f: lost 3rd cl home* **16/1**

60-0 **5** *4½* **Primrose Place**[43] 3250 3-8-4 **54**.................................. KieranO'Neill 6 42
(David Evans) *hld up: hdwy over 2f out: sn rdn: one pce fnl f* **25/1**

0-06 **6** *hd* **Doctor Bong**[20] 3773 5-9-2 **57**.......................................(b) TrevorWhelan 4 47
(Grace Harris) *prom: rdn over 2f out: wknd over 1f out* **25/1**

0645 **7** *2* **Peak Storm**[7] 4587 8-9-12 **72**.................................(p) BenRobinson(5) 7 57
(John O'Shea) *hld up: drvn 3f out: rdn over 2f out: wknd* **20/1**

6451 **8** *2* **Chicago Star**[18] 4150 3-9-5 **69**...................................... CharlesBishop 10 47
(Mick Channon) *cl 2nd: pushed along and lost pl 3f out: rdn over 2f out: fdd* **7/2**[2]

1m 33.35s (-2.85) **Going Correction** -0.375s/f (Firm)
**WFA** 3 from 4yo+ 9lb **8** Ran SP% **115.7**
Speed ratings (Par 103): **99,96,94,94,89 89,87,85**
CSF £10.67 CT £29.68 TOTE £2.00: £1.10, £2.20, £1.50; EX 8.00 Trifecta £41.10.
**Owner** Alderson Carson Francis Hart **Bred** Aston House Stud **Trained** Newmarket, Suffolk

**FOCUS**
The first two drew clear in this modest handicap, the winner continuing to progress.
T/Plt: £10,006.50 to a £1 stake. Pool: £54,144.88 - 3.95 winning units. T/Qpdt: £1,423.10 to a £1 stake. Pool: £4,231.03 - 2.2 winning units. **Keith McHugh**

# 3826 MUSSELBURGH (R-H)
Friday, July 14

**OFFICIAL GOING: Good (good to firm in places; 6.6)**
Wind: Breezy, half against over 5f and in 4f of home straight on round course
Weather: Cloudy, bright

## 4847 100% RACING UK PROFITS BACK TO RACING H'CAP 5f 1y
**5:55** (5:57) (Class 6) (0-60,58) 3-Y-O+ **£3,234** (£962; £481; £240) **Stalls** High

Form RPR

3230 **1** **Culloden**[10] 4478 5-9-6 **57**.................................................(v) KevinStott 11 66
(Shaun Harris) *mde all against stands' rail: rdn over 1f out: hrd pressed ins fnl f: kpt on strly* **9/2**[3]

3423 **2** *nk* **Hadley**[43] 3256 4-8-11 **48**.......................................................(p) JasonHart 6 56
(Tracy Waggott) *wnt rt s: sn cl up: rdn over 1f out: ev ch ins fnl f: kpt on: hld nr fin* **7/2**[1]

4063 **3** *1½* **See Vermont**[7] 4559 9-9-0 **56**................................(p) RowanScott(5) 12 59
(Rebecca Bastiman) *dwlt: sn trcking ldrs: effrt and rdn 2f out: kpt on ins fnl f* **4/1**[2]

3223 **4** *shd* **Cheeni**[10] 4478 5-8-2 **46**...............................................(p) SeanMooney(7) 5 48
(Jim Goldie) *blkd s: hld up: rdn and hdwy over 1f out: kpt on fnl f: hld towards fin* **7/1**

444 **5** *6* **Bunce (IRE)**[4] 4682 9-9-6 **57**............................................... GrahamLee 2 38+
(Linda Perratt) *bhd: rdn and hdwy over 1f out: no imp fnl f* **9/1**

0-00 **6** *2¾* **Kylla**[15] 4246 4-8-3 **45**.................................................(b) PhilDennis(5) 10 16
(Shaun Harris) *trckd ldrs: hung rt and wknd wl over 1f out* **100/1**

6304 **7** *3¼* **Joysunny**[10] 4478 3-7-12 **47**...................................... JamieGormley(7) 8 4
(Jacqueline Coward) *chsd ldrs: drvn and lost pl over 1f out: sn btn* **10/1**

2440 **8** *1½* **Harpers Ruby**[10] 4479 7-8-8 **45**...................................... PaddyAspell 3 +
(Lynn Siddall) *cl up tl hung rt and wknd fr 2f out* **28/1**

-500 **9** *1¼* **Mr Enthusiastic**[25] 3915 3-8-3 **45**................................ PatrickMathers 1 +
(Noel Wilson) *midfield on outside: struggling over 2f out: sn btn* **50/1**

0430 **10** *3¼* **Storm Trooper (IRE)**[17] 4174 6-9-7 **58**.........................(p) JoeFanning 4 +
(Marjorie Fife) *blkd s: bhd on outside: struggling over 2f out: sn wknd* **13/2**

5050 **11** *¾* **Nefetari**[17] 4174 4-8-8 **45**..............................................(b) JamesSullivan 9
(Alan Brown) *bhd: struggling 1/2-way: btn over 1f out* **20/1**

1m 0.29s (-0.11) **Going Correction** +0.05s/f (Good)
**WFA** 3 from 4yo+ 5lb **11** Ran SP% **116.5**
Speed ratings (Par 101): **102,101,99,98,89 84,79,77,75,70 68**
CSF £19.79 CT £69.58 TOTE £5.60: £2.10, £1.40, £1.60; EX 27.50 Trifecta £93.00.
**Owner** Burflex (Scaffolding) Ltd **Bred** Burton Agnes Stud Co Ltd **Trained** Carburton, Notts

**FOCUS**
A low-grade sprint featuring mainly hard-to-win with types. The first four were clear and the form not strong. Straightforward low-grade form.

## 4848 BRITISH STALLION STUDS EBF NOVICE STKS 7f 33y
**6:25** (6:26) (Class 5) 2-Y-O **£3,234** (£962; £481; £240) **Stalls** Low

Form RPR

1 **1** **Cape Bunting (IRE)**[20] 4094 2-9-4 0.................................. JoeFanning 4 85+
(Mark Johnston) *pressed ldr: led 2f out: sn rdn and hung rt: kpt on wl to draw clr fnl f: readily* **5/6**[1]

03 **2** *5* **Queen's Sargent (FR)**[48] 3093 2-9-2 0.............................. KevinStott 2 68
(Kevin Ryan) *led at ordinary gallop: rdn and hdd 2f out: sn leant on by wnr: kpt on wl to hold on for 2nd pl cl home: no ch w wnr* **2/1**[2]

4 **3** *nse* **El Chapo**[14] 4297 2-9-2 0.............................................. PhillipMakin 5 68
(Richard Fahey) *t.k.h early: trckd ldrs: rdn 2f out: kpt on ins fnl f: no imp* **8/1**[3]

55 **4** *shd* **Northern Law (IRE)**[23] 3973 2-9-2 0 JasonHart 1 68
(John Quinn) *trckd ldrs: drvn and outpcd 2f out: rallied ins fnl f: nvr able to chal* **10/1**
**5** *5* **Mi Capricho (IRE)** 2-8-11 0 RowanScott(5) 3 55
(Keith Dalgleish) *s;owly into stride: hld up in last pl: drvn and outpcd over 2f out: btn over 1f out* **33/1**

1m 30.17s (1.17) **Going Correction** +0.05s/f (Good) **5** Ran SP% **111.0**
Speed ratings (Par 94): **95,89,89,89,83**
CSF £2.76 TOTE £1.60: £1.10, £1.30; EX 2.90 Trifecta £5.00.
**Owner** Sheikh Hamdan bin Mohammed Al Maktoum **Bred** Godolphin **Trained** Middleham Moor, N Yorks

**FOCUS**
Add 7yds. A 7f novice which was run at just an ordinary gallop so it developed into a bit of a sprint, but nevertheless an impressive winner. It's hard to rate the form higher than this at the moment.

## 4849 TILECRAFT AND DIMENSION CONDITIONS STKS 1m 4f 104y
**6:55** (6:55) (Class 2) 4-Y-0+ **£19,407** (£5,775; £2,886; £1,443) **Stalls** Low

Form RPR
1263 **1** **Chemical Charge (IRE)**[20] 4070 5-9-10 114 PhillipMakin 2 109+
(Ralph Beckett) *prom: smooth hdwy to ld 2f out: rdn clr ins fnl f: eased nr fin* **5/6**[1]
2016 **2** *2 ½* **Sir Chauvelin**[13] 4356 5-9-7 99 JamesSullivan 6 102
(Jim Goldie) *hld up: pushed along and hdwy wl over 1f out: chsd wnr fnl f: kpt on: nt pce to chal* **12/1**
6102 **3** *1 ¼* **Soldier In Action (FR)**[6] 4614 4-9-10 104 JoeFanning 5 103
(Mark Johnston) *led: jnd after 2f: rdn and hdd 2f out: lost 2nd and outpcd 1f out* **11/4**[2]
436P **4** *2 ½* **Maleficent Queen**[13] 4356 5-8-13 103 GrahamLee 1 88
(Keith Dalgleish) *t.k.h: hld up in tch: hdwy to chse ldrs whn edgd rt over 1f out: wknd ins fnl f* **13/2**[3]
3 **5** *4 ½* **Shearling**[19] 4119 4-8-13 0 JasonHart 4 81
(Brian Ellison) *chsd ldr 2f: cl up tl rdn and wknd fr 2f out* **14/1**
1330 **6** *1 ¼* **Jonny Delta**[4] 4684 10-9-4 55 SeanMooney 3 84?
(Jim Goldie) *dwlt: hdwy to press ldr after 2f: sn disputing ld: rdn and outpcd over 2f out: wknd wl over 1f out* **200/1**

2m 40.38s (-1.62) **Going Correction** +0.05s/f (Good) **6** Ran SP% **109.4**
Speed ratings (Par 109): **107,105,104,102,99 99**
CSF £11.74 TOTE £1.60: £1.10, £4.30; EX 9.20 Trifecta £19.30.
**Owner** Qatar Racing Limited **Bred** Viktor Timoshenko **Trained** Kimpton, Hants

**FOCUS**
Add 7yds. A valuable conditions event run at a medium gallop in which the winner had the best credentials. The rank outsider wasn't beaten that far so the whole form is slightly questionable. The runner-up has been rated to form.

## 4850 RACING UK PROFITS RETURNED TO RACING H'CAP 5f 1y
**7:25** (7:26) (Class 4) (0-80,81) 3-Y-0+ **£6,469** (£1,925; £962; £481) **Stalls** High

Form RPR
2200 **1** **Silvanus (IRE)**[13] 4337 12-9-9 77 GrahamLee 1 84
(Paul Midgley) *hld up: rdn and hdwy over 1f out: styd on strly fnl f to ld cl home* **8/1**
-111 **2** *nk* **Longroom**[41] 3337 5-9-8 81 PhilDennis(5) 6 87+
(Noel Wilson) *flyj. s: t.k.h: hld up in tch: smooth hdwy to ld wl over 1f out: rdn and edgd rt ins fnl f: kpt on: hdd cl home* **11/8**[1]
-205 **3** *½* **Economic Crisis (IRE)**[15] 4249 8-9-6 74 JamesSullivan 8 78
(Colin Teague) *prom: effrt and rdn over 1f out: kpt on ins fnl f* **22/1**
1103 **4** *1 ¾* **Kinloch Pride**[14] 4305 5-8-13 67 (p) PatrickMathers 3 65
(Noel Wilson) *prom on outside: drvn along 2f out: kpt on same pce ins fnl f* **6/1**[2]
-000 **5** *4* **Kibaar**[13] 4337 5-9-12 80 (p) KevinStott 2 63
(Kevin Ryan) *dwlt: hld up: rdn and hdwy over 1f out: no imp fnl f* **7/1**[3]
0010 **6** *8* **Desert Ace (IRE)**[13] 4379 6-9-7 75 (p) DougieCostello 7 30
(Iain Jardine) *led against stands' rail: rdn and hdd wl over 1f out: sn wknd* **8/1**
0000 **7** *2* **New Road Side**[7] 4566 4-9-7 75 (v) PhillipMakin 4 22+
(Richard Guest) *prom on outside: rdn over 2f out: outpcd whn hmpd and stmbld over 1f out: eased* **15/2**
-050 **8** *2 ¾* **Astrophysics**[11] 4428 5-9-3 71 PaddyAspell 5 8
(Lynn Siddall) *chsd ldrs: rdn and hung rt wl over 1f out: sn wknd* **16/1**

59.89s (-0.51) **Going Correction** +0.05s/f (Good) **8** Ran SP% **113.1**
Speed ratings (Par 105): **106,105,104,101,95 82,79,75**
CSF £19.03 CT £235.83 TOTE £8.80: £3.00, £1.10, £5.90; EX 23.70 Trifecta £171.70.
**Owner** Colin Alton **Bred** Barronstown Stud And Mrs T Stack **Trained** Westow, N Yorks

**FOCUS**
Just a fair sprint for the grade, but the pace was strong. The winner has been rated back to the level of his unlucky C&D form in May.

## 4851 NEVER MISS A RACE ON RACING UK H'CAP 7f 33y
**8:00** (8:01) (Class 5) (0-70,72) 3-Y-0+ **£5,175** (£1,540; £769; £384) **Stalls** Low

Form RPR
6-00 **1** **Echo Of Lightning**[13] 4339 7-9-11 72 (p) MeganNicholls(5) 4 82
(Brian Ellison) *chsd ldr: clr of rest after 3f: led gng wl over 1f out: rdn out fnl f* **10/1**
2140 **2** *2 ½* **Fine Example**[17] 4168 4-9-12 68 (b) KevinStott 8 71
(Kevin Ryan) *t.k.h: led: clr w wnr after 3f: rdn and hdd over 1f out: kpt on fnl f: nt pce of wnr* **9/2**[2]
06-2 **3** *nk* **Inglorious**[5] 4663 3-8-8 63 (p) RowanScott(5) 6 62
(Keith Dalgleish) *dwlt: sn prom: rdn and outpcd over 2f out: rallied over 1f out: edgd rt: kpt on ins fnl f* **13/8**[1]
6315 **4** *1 ¼* **Cyflymder (IRE)**[4] 4688 11-8-9 51 GrahamLee 3 50
(David C Griffiths) *prom: effrt and drvn along 2f out: kpt on same pce fnl f* **7/1**
5040 **5** *1* **Born To Finish (IRE)**[15] 4256 4-10-0 70 DougieCostello 5 66
(Jamie Osborne) *dwlt: hld up in tch: rdn and outpcd whn edgd rt wl over 1f out: sme late hdwy: n.d* **11/2**[3]
0430 **6** *¾* **Captain Peaky**[4] 4687 4-9-0 56 JoeFanning 2 50
(Patrick Holmes) *t.k.h: hld up in tch: rdn over 2f out: outpcd fr over 1f out* **12/1**
0000 **7** *1 ¼* **Slemy (IRE)**[17] 4168 6-9-12 68 JamesSullivan 1 59
(Ruth Carr) *stdd s: hld up: shortlived effrt on outside 2f out: sn btn* **10/1**

1m 29.3s (0.30) **Going Correction** +0.05s/f (Good)
**WFA** 3 from 4yo+ 8lb **7** Ran SP% **110.0**
Speed ratings (Par 103): **100,97,96,95,94 93,91**
CSF £49.92 CT £103.89 TOTE £12.20: £3.30, £1.60; EX 54.80 Trifecta £172.80.
**Owner** Victoria Greetham & Emily Beasley **Bred** Gracelands Stud **Trained** Norton, N Yorks

**FOCUS**
Add 7yds. A bit of a stop-start gallop to this ordinary 7f handicap in which the first two were the first two throughout. The runner-up has been rated close to his non-claiming form.

## 4852 FINEST COLLECTION OF RACING ON RACING UK H'CAP 1m 7f 217y
**8:35** (8:36) (Class 4) (0-80,78) 3-Y-0+ **£7,762** (£2,310; £1,154; £577) **Stalls** High

Form RPR
0112 **1** **Dominating (GER)**[6] 4612 3-8-8 75 JoeFanning 6 86+
(Mark Johnston) *trckd ldr: led gng wl over 2f out: rdn clr over 1f out: eased wl ins fnl f* **2/9**[1]
/33- **2** *1 ¾* **Yes Daddy (IRE)**[22] 8363 9-9-8 72 (bt[1]) PhillipMakin 3 75
(Robert Stephens) *hld up in tch: effrt and pushed along over 2f out: hdwy: edgd rt and chsd (clr) wnr over 1f out: kpt on fnl f: flattered by proximity to eased-down wnr* **10/1**[3]
1234 **3** *3* **Stoneham**[27] 3830 6-9-0 71 (h) JamieGormley(7) 2 70
(Iain Jardine) *dwlt: hld up: effrt on outside over 2f out: rdn and no imp appr fnl f* **6/1**[2]
-065 **4** *7* **Buyer Beware (IRE)**[27] 3830 5-9-6 70 DougieCostello 5 61
(Patrick Holmes) *led: rdn and hdd over 2f out: wknd over 1f out* **20/1**
1-00 **5** *5* **La Bacouetteuse (FR)**[32] 3663 12-8-11 64 (b) SammyJoBell(3) 4 49
(Iain Jardine) *chsd ldrs: drvn and outpcd over 2f out: sn wknd* **33/1**

3m 31.09s (-2.41) **Going Correction** +0.05s/f (Good)
**WFA** 3 from 4yo+ 17lb **5** Ran SP% **112.9**
Speed ratings (Par 105): **108,107,105,102,99**
CSF £3.73 TOTE £1.10: £1.02, £3.90; EX 3.50 Trifecta £6.90.
**Owner** A D Spence **Bred** Gestut Etzean **Trained** Middleham Moor, N Yorks

**FOCUS**
Add 7yds. A one-sided event with the odds-on favourite coming into it at the top of his form whereas his rivals weren't running to their best. It was run at a decent,even gallop. The runner-up has been rated to his winter AW form.

## 4853 RACINGUK.COM H'CAP 1m 4f 104y
**9:10** (9:11) (Class 6) (0-60,57) 4-Y-0+ **£3,234** (£962; £481; £240) **Stalls** Low

Form RPR
050/ **1** **Manomine**[20] 4113 8-9-3 53 JoeFanning 2 62
(R K Watson, Ire) *led 4f: cl up: regained ld over 2f out: rdn and styd on strly fnl f* **5/1**[2]
4-0 **2** *½* **Traditional Dancer (IRE)**[21] 4036 5-9-0 50 (b[1]) DougieCostello 8 58
(Iain Jardine) *cl up: effrt and pressed wnr over 2f out: edgd rt over 1f out: kpt on fnl f: hld nr fin* **4/1**[1]
5-53 **3** *4 ½* **Picture Painter (IRE)**[10] 4476 4-9-0 57 SeanMooney(7) 1 58
(Jim Goldie) *prom on ins: rdn over 2f out: chsd clr ldng pair over 1f out: sn no imp* **8/1**[3]
2066 **4** *1 ½* **Schmooze (IRE)**[15] 4244 8-9-0 50 KevinStott 7 49
(Linda Perratt) *dwlt: hld up: rdn over 2f out: kpt on fnl f: nvr able to chal* **25/1**
2664 **5** *nk* **New Abbey Angel (IRE)**[23] 3977 4-9-2 57 (v) RowanScott(5) 9 55
(Keith Dalgleish) *awkward s: t.k.h in rr: effrt and carried hd high on outside over 2f out: no imp fr over 1f out* **12/1**
6531 **6** *hd* **Adrakhan (FR)**[20] 4102 6-8-9 48 SammyJoBell(3) 4 46
(Wilf Storey) *hld up in tch: drvn and outpcd over 2f out: no imp fr over 1f out* **17/2**
42/4 **7** *¾* **Tropical Bachelor (IRE)**[13] 4345 11-9-0 50 JamesSullivan 5 47
(Ruth Carr) *hld up towards rr: drvn along wl over 2f out: sn no imp* **10/1**
32 **8** *1 ¾* **Miskin**[10] 4469 8-9-5 55 GrahamLee 6 49
(Robert Stephens) *t.k.h: w ldr: led after 4f to over 2f out: sn rdn and wknd* **4/1**[1]
0524 **9** *1 ¼* **Percy Verence**[7] 4558 4-9-4 54 JasonHart 3 49
(Tracy Waggott) *chsd ldrs: drvn along over 2f out: wknd over 1f out* **5/1**[2]

2m 45.88s (3.88) **Going Correction** +0.05s/f (Good) **9** Ran SP% **115.6**
Speed ratings (Par 101): **89,88,85,84,84 84,83,82,81**
CSF £25.36 CT £157.70 TOTE £5.40: £1.90, £2.10, £2.20; EX 35.10 Trifecta £401.90.
**Owner** W F Richardson **Bred** C R Mason **Trained** Killylea, Co Armagh

**FOCUS**
Add 7yds. A moderately-run affair in which it paid to race close to the pace with the first two, who were clear, racing in the first three from the outset. It is likely to prove ordinary form
T/Plt: £15.70 to a £1 stake. Pool: £39711,77 - 1838.12 winning units. T/Qpdt: £9.90 to a £1 stake. Pool: £2,933.08 - 217.36 winning units. **Richard Young**

# 4811 NEWMARKET (R-H)
Friday, July 14

**OFFICIAL GOING: Good changing to good to firm (good in places) after race 1 (1.50)**
Wind: medium, behind Weather: overcast

## 4854 BET365 H'CAP (SILVER BUNBURY CUP) 7f
**1:50** (1:52) (Class 2) 3-Y-0+
**£31,125** (£9,320; £4,660; £2,330; £1,165; £585) **Stalls** Low

Form RPR
3514 **1** **Parfait (IRE)**[23] 3959 3-9-9 100 (p) WilliamBuick 2 111
(John Gosden) *racd stands side: led gp and chsd overall ldr tl led over 1f out: sn rdn and clr 1f out: styd on wl: comf: 1st of 10 in gp* **5/2**[1]
-201 **2** *2* **Makzeem**[15] 4270 4-9-11 94 6ex RyanMoore 5 103
(Roger Charlton) *lw: racd stands side: hld up in rr: hdwy 2f out: nt clr run briefly over 1f out: sn swtchd lft and drvn: chsd wnr ins fnl f: styd on for clr 2nd: no imp on wnr: 2nd of 10 in gp* **15/2**[3]
11-3 **3** *1 ¾* **Fawaareq (IRE)**[76] 2142 4-9-10 93 JimCrowley 4 97
(Owen Burrows) *racd stands side: in tch in midfield: effrt over 1f out: hdwy and drvn to chse ldng pair ins fnl f: kpt on same pce after: 3rd of 10 in gp* **4/1**[2]
-000 **4** *1* **Swift Approval (IRE)**[68] 2433 5-9-9 92 (t[1]) FranBerry 10 93
(Stuart Williams) *racd stands side: chsd gp ldr and prom overall: effrt 2f out: chsd wnr over 1f out: unable qck w wnr: kpt on same pce and lost 2 pls ins fnl f: 4th of 10 in gp* **33/1**
2254 **5** *1 ½* **War Glory (IRE)**[48] 3089 4-9-8 91 SeanLevey 19 88
(Richard Hannon) *lw: racd in centre: t.k.h: chsd gp ldr and midfield overall: effrt to ld gp and chsd ldrs overall over 1f out: styd on same pce u.p ins fnl f: 1st of 7 in gp* **14/1**
3026 **6** *shd* **Fox Trotter (IRE)**[8] 4524 5-8-8 84 JordanUys(7) 18 81
(Brian Meehan) *racd in centre: stdd s: hld up in rr: clsd 2f out: shkn up and hdwy over 1f out: edgd lft u.p and styd on same pce ins fnl f: 2nd of 7 in gp* **25/1**



The Form Book Flat, Raceform Ltd, Newbury, RG14 5SJ

0-40 **7** *1* **Miracle Of Medinah**[62] 2606 6-9-8 **91** ............................ LiamKeniry 17 85
(Mark Usher) *racd in centre: hld up in rr: swtchd lft and effrt over 1f out: rdn and hdwy 1f out: kpt on ins fnl f: no threat to ldrs: 3rd of 7 in gp* **33/1**

4100 **8** *1¼* **Ripoll (IRE)**[6] 4636 4-8-9 **78** ............................(t) AntonioFresu 16 69
(Sylvester Kirk) *racd in centre: hld up in midfield overall: effrt 2f out: sme hdwy and hung lft 1f out: no imp ins fnl f: 4th of 7 in gp* **20/1**

4404 **9** *¾* **Shady McCoy (USA)**[15] 4270 7-9-5 **88** ............................ JamesDoyle 9 77
(Ian Williams) *racd stands side: in tch in midfield overall: effrt over 1f out: unable qck u.p ent fnl f: wknd ins fnl f: 5th of 10 in gp* **14/1**

0645 **10** *hd* **Tommy G**[4] 4683 4-8-8 **77** ............................ JoeyHaynes 6 65
(Jim Goldie) *racd stands side: stdd s: hld up towards rr: effrt 2f out: drvn and hdwy into midfield ent fnl f: no prog after: nvr trbld ldrs: 6th of 10 in gp* **25/1**

-522 **11** *hd* **Brigliadoro (IRE)**[14] 4321 6-9-5 **93** ............................ PaddyBradley(5) 3 81
(Philip McBride) *lw: racd stands side: hld up in rr: swtchd lft over 4f out: rdn over 2f out: sme modest hdwy 1f out: nvr threatening ldrs: 7th of 10 in gp* **16/1**

5220 **12** *1* **Majestic Moon (IRE)**[14] 4294 7-8-13 **85** ............................ ShelleyBirkett(3) 14 70
(Julia Feilden) *racd alone on far rail: overall ldr tl hdd over 1f out: sn btn and wknd ins fnl f* **50/1**

2560 **13** *½* **Dutch Uncle**[24] 3924 5-9-5 **88** ............................(p) OisinMurphy 8 72
(Robert Cowell) *racd stands side: hld up in midfield: effrt 2f out: no hdwy over 1f out: wknd ins fnl f: 8th of 10 in gp* **33/1**

1060 **14** *hd* **Gunmetal (IRE)**[34] 3593 4-9-10 **93** ............................ AndreaAtzeni 13 76
(Charles Hills) *racd in centre: led gp and chsd ldrs overall: rdn 2f out: lost pl over 1f out: wknd ins fnl f: 5th of 7 in gp* **20/1**

00-0 **14** *dht* **Funding Deficit (IRE)**[10] 4477 7-8-7 **76** ............................(h) JosephineGordon 1 59
(Jim Goldie) *racd stands side: hld up towards rr: no hdwy u.p over 1f out: wknd ins fnl f: 9th of 10 in gp* **50/1**

-353 **16** *½* **Lefortovo (FR)**[7] 4570 4-9-4 **87** ............................(p) JFEgan 15 69
(Jo Hughes) *racd in centre: hld up in midfield overall: rdn over 1f out: no imp and wknd ins fnl f: 6th of 7 in gp* **16/1**

1600 **17** *1¾* **Suzi's Connoisseur**[41] 3324 6-9-10 **93** ............................(v) GeraldMosse 12 70
(Stuart Williams) *rn wout declared tongue tie: racd in centre: hld up in midfield overall: effrt over 1f out: sn btn: wknd ins fnl f: 7th of 7 in gp* **20/1**

-000 **18** *1¼* **Stamp Hill (IRE)**[36] 3498 4-9-7 **90** ............................(p¹) TonyHamilton 11 64
(Richard Fahey) *racd stands side: hld up in midfield overall: rdn 2f out: lost pl over 1f out: bhd ins fnl f: 10th of 10 in gp* **22/1**

1m 22.89s (-2.81) **Going Correction** -0.15s/f (Firm)
**WFA** 3 from 4yo+ 8lb **18** Ran SP% **124.5**
Speed ratings (Par 109): **110,107,105,104,102 102,101,100,99,99 98,97,97,96,96 96,94,92**
CSF £17.09 CT £76.50 TOTE £3.10: £1.20, £2.20, £1.40, £7.80; EX 18.30 Trifecta £30.00.
**Owner** Godolphin **Bred** Mogeely Stud **Trained** Newmarket, Suffolk

**FOCUS**
Stands' side course used. Stalls: stands' side, except 1m2f: centre. It was dry overnight and the going was given as good (GoingStick: 7.8. Stands' side 7.9; centre 8.0; far side 7.8), but changed to good to firm, good in places after this first race. There was a bit of a tailwind. The field split into three groups, the largest, which contained the first four, racing on the stands' side, while a smaller group came up the centre, and Majestic Moon raced alone on the far rail. The third has been rated to form.

## 4855 DUCHESS OF CAMBRIDGE STKS (SPONSORED BY BET365) (GROUP 2) 6f
**2:25** (2:25) (Class 1) 2-Y-O

**£45,368** (£17,200; £8,608; £4,288; £2,152; £1,080) **Stalls** Low

Form RPR

01 **1** **Clemmie (IRE)**[12] 4418 2-9-0 0 ............................(t) RyanMoore 8 107
(A P O'Brien, Ire) *lw: in tch in midfield: effrt to chse ldrs 2f out: sn rdn: led 1f out: styd on strly and wnt clr fnl 100yds: rdn out* **11/8**[1]

12 **2** *1¾* **Nyaleti (IRE)**[20] 4068 2-9-0 0 ............................ WilliamBuick 2 102
(Mark Johnston) *mde most: rdn 2f out: hdd 1f out: no ex and outpcd by wnr fnl 100yds: hld on for 2nd wl ins fnl f* **7/4**[2]

503 **3** *½* **Mamba Noire (FR)**[12] 4418 2-9-0 0 ............................ AndreaAtzeni 9 100
(K J Condon, Ire) *stdd and dropped in bhd after s: hld up in last pair: effrt 2f out: hdwy to chse ldrs and swtchd lft 1f out: kpt on u.p to snatch 3rd last strides* **20/1**

534 **4** *nk* **Mistress Of Venice**[21] 4028 2-9-0 97 ............................ JimCrowley 4 99
(James Given) *w ldr: rdn and shifted lft 2f out: styd pressing ldrs tl no ex ins fnl f: styd on same pce and lost 3rd last strides* **11/1**

313 **5** *½* **Out Of The Flames**[23] 3960 2-9-0 96 ............................ OisinMurphy 1 98
(Richard Hannon) *trckd ldrs: pushed along 2f out: rdn ins fnl f: hung lft and styd on same pce after* **7/1**[3]

313 **6** *2* **So Hi Society (IRE)**[13] 4361 2-9-0 92 ............................ JamesDoyle 6 92
(Archie Watson) *w'like: niggled along leaving stalls: in tch in midfield: effrt 2f out: no imp u.p over 1f out: wl hld and kpt on same pce ins fnl f* **14/1**

0610 **7** *½* **Darkanna (IRE)**[23] 3960 2-9-0 91 ............................ BarryMcHugh 3 90
(Richard Fahey) *stdd s: hld up in tch in last pair: effrt over 1f out: edging lft and no imp 1f out: wl hld and kpt on same pce ins fnl f* **25/1**

02 **8** *5* **Cosmopolitan Queen**[16] 4213 2-9-0 0 ............................ FranBerry 7 75
(David Elsworth) *w'like: chsd ldrs: rdn ent fnl 2f: sn struggling and lost pl over 1f out: bhd and wknd ins fnl f* **50/1**

1m 10.34s (-2.16) **Going Correction** -0.15s/f (Firm) 2y crse rec **8** Ran SP% **116.5**
Speed ratings (Par 106): **108,105,105,104,103 101,100,93**
CSF £3.96 TOTE £2.30: £1.10, £1.10, £4.80; EX 4.90 Trifecta £45.40.
**Owner** Michael Tabor & Derrick Smith & Mrs John Magnier **Bred** Liberty Bloodstock **Trained** Cashel, Co Tipperary

**FOCUS**
An impressive performance from the winner, who lowered the 2yo course record, although the tailwind helped. They raced stands' side. The winner has been rated near the level of recent winners of this race.

## 4856 BET365 H'CAP 1m 2f
**3:00** (3:01) (Class 2) (0-105,103) 3-Y-O

**£43,575** (£13,048; £6,524; £3,262; £1,631; £819) **Stalls** Centre

Form RPR

2242 **1** **Marzouq (USA)**[28] 3780 3-8-8 **90** ............................ JFEgan 1 100
(Jeremy Noseda) *led tl over 8f out: chsd ldr: rdn and ev ch 2f out: sustained chal u.p to ld towards fin: forged ahd cl home* **6/1**[2]

2160 **2** *¾* **Oasis Charm**[22] 3998 3-8-6 **88** ............................(p¹) JosephineGordon 9 96
(Charlie Appleby) *t.k.h: hld up in midfield: clsd to trck ldrs 6f out: rdn to chal over 2f out: sustained effrt u.p to ld ent fnl f: hdd and no ex towards fin* **10/1**

3-11 **3** *1* **Atkinson Grimshaw (FR)**[48] 3068 3-8-0 **82** oh2 ............................ JimmyQuinn 11 88
(Andrew Balding) *aken down early: t.k.h: hdwy to ld over 8f out: rdn ent fnl 2f: hdd ent fnl f: no ex and styd on same pce ins fnl f* **12/1**

0145 **4** *½* **Leshlaa (USA)**[22] 3997 3-9-7 **103** ............................ OisinMurphy 4 108
(Saeed bin Suroor) *hld up in tch in midfield: clsd to trck ldrs 3f out: rdn and chalng 2f out: sustained chal tl no ex and btn ins fnl f: wknd towards fin* **7/1**

1111 **5** *nk* **Titi Makfi**[14] 4292 3-8-11 **93** ............................ RyanMoore 3 97
(Mark Johnston) *hld up in tch in midfield: effrt over 2f out: kpt on wl u.p ins fnl f: nvr getting on terms w ldrs* **13/2**[3]

1005 **6** *shd* **Cullingworth (IRE)**[13] 4376 3-8-1 **83** ............................ JoeyHaynes 2 87
(Richard Fahey) *hld up in tch in midfield: nt clr run and swtchd lft 2f out: hdwy u.p ent fnl f: kpt on wl fnl 100yds: nvr getting to ldrs* **33/1**

2126 **7** *1¼* **Speedo Boy (FR)**[22] 3994 3-9-4 **100** ............................ JamesDoyle 6 102
(Ian Williams) *lw: chsd ldrs tl 6f out: shuffled bk towards rr 3f out: nt clrest of runs over 1f out: rallied u.p 1f out: kpt on ins fnl f wout threatening ldrs* **8/1**

612 **8** *4* **Daawy (IRE)**[41] 3316 3-8-6 **88** ............................ AndreaAtzeni 5 82
(William Haggas) *chsd ldrs after 2f: rdn and shuffled bk over 2f out: nt clrest of runs 2f out: no hdwy u.p over 1f out: wknd ins fnl f* **4/1**[1]

5-00 **9** *1¼* **Medieval (IRE)**[22] 3997 3-9-0 **96** ............................(b) FranBerry 10 87
(Paul Cole) *stdd and awkward leaving stalls: hld up in rr: hdwy into midfield and rdn over 2f out: no imp and losing pl over 1f out: wknd ins fnl f* **25/1**

5322 **10** *4* **Monticello (IRE)**[14] 4316 3-8-8 **90** ............................ GeraldMosse 8 73
(Mark Johnston) *lw: hld up in tch in last trio: effrt 2f out: sn rdn and btn: wknd fnl f* **7/1**

1-40 **11** *2* **Colibri (IRE)**[22] 3997 3-8-11 **93** ............................ WilliamBuick 7 72
(Hugo Palmer) *in tch in midfield: rdn and dropped to rr 2f out: bhd fnl f* **11/1**

2m 2.34s (-3.16) **Going Correction** -0.15s/f (Firm) **11** Ran SP% **115.6**
Speed ratings (Par 106): **106,105,104,104,103 103,102,99,98,95 93**
CSF £63.57 CT £697.91 TOTE £6.30: £2.10, £3.20, £4.30; EX 72.60 Trifecta £1066.00.
**Owner** Naser Buresli **Bred** Nicholas Cimino **Trained** Newmarket, Suffolk
■ Stewards' Enquiry : J F Egan four-day ban: used whip above the permitted level (Jul 28,30,31, Aug 4)

**FOCUS**
This looked a good, open handicap but it proved hard to make up significant ground, with the third-placed finisher taking them along and the winner never far away. They raced stands' side. The form is set around the fourth and sixth for now.

## 4857 TATTERSALLS FALMOUTH STKS (GROUP 1) (BRITISH CHAMPIONS SERIES) 1m
**3:35** (3:36) (Class 1) 3-Y-O+

**£113,420** (£43,000; £21,520; £10,720; £5,380; £2,700) **Stalls** Low

Form RPR

0622 **1** **Roly Poly (USA)**[21] 4031 3-8-12 112 ............................(p) RyanMoore 3 114
(A P O'Brien, Ire) *mde all: rdn 2f out: kpt finding ex for mainly hands and heels riding: asserted ins fnl f: in command and idling towards fin: comf* **6/4**[1]

11- **2** *1¼* **Wuheida**[285] 6986 3-8-12 114 ............................ WilliamBuick 7 111
(Charlie Appleby) *lw: trckd ldrs: clsd to press wnr ent fnl 2f: rdn and chalng over 1f out tl unable to match pce of wnr ins fnl f: kpt on same pce fnl 100yds* **3/1**[2]

-111 **3** *½* **Arabian Hope (USA)**[27] 3843 3-8-12 108 ............................(h) JosephineGordon 4 110
(Saeed bin Suroor) *t.k.h: trckd ldrs: rdn 2f out: sltly outpcd over 1f out: rallied u.p to chse ldng pair ins fnl f: styng on towards fin: no threat to wnr* **13/2**

1-52 **4** *1½* **Sea Of Grace (IRE)**[62] 2644 3-8-12 109 ............................ AndreaAtzeni 1 107
(William Haggas) *lw: hld up in tch in rr: effrt 2f out: hdwy on outer over 1f out: kpt on same pce u.p ins fnl f* **9/2**[3]

-104 **5** *1¼* **Delectation**[26] 3882 3-8-12 106 ............................ EduardoPedroza 5 104
(A Wohler, Germany) *stdd s: t.k.h: hld up in tch in last pair: effrt jst over 2f out: keeping on same pce and no threat to wnr whn swtchd lft ins fnl f* **16/1**

0 **6** *2½* **Greta G (ARG)**[23] 3961 4-9-7 110 ............................ JimCrowley 6 100
(John Gosden) *pressed wnr tl 2f out: sn u.p and struggling to qckn: wknd ins fnl f* **14/1**

0420 **7** *1¼* **Opal Tiara (IRE)**[23] 3961 4-9-7 109 ............................ RonanWhelan 2 97
(Mick Channon) *trckd ldrs: rdn ent fnl 2f: sn outpcd and dropped to rr over 1f out: wknd fnl f* **25/1**

1m 36.01s (-3.99) **Going Correction** -0.15s/f (Firm)
**WFA** 3 from 4yo 9lb **7** Ran SP% **112.9**
Speed ratings (Par 117): **113,111,111,109,108 106,104**
CSF £5.94 TOTE £2.10: £1.40, £2.00; EX 6.30 Trifecta £25.70.
**Owner** Michael Tabor & Derrick Smith & Mrs John Magnier **Bred** Misty For Me Syndicate **Trained** Cashel, Co Tipperary

**FOCUS**
This looked just an ordinary Falmouth and the winner had the run of the race in front against the stands' rail. It's been rated a substandard renewal, with the runner-up rated a bit below her 2yo best.

## 4858 PRICE BAILEY NURSERY H'CAP 7f
**4:10** (4:10) (Class 2) 2-Y-O **£12,938** (£3,850; £1,924; £962) **Stalls** Low

Form RPR

524 **1** **Tangled (IRE)**[34] 3591 2-8-9 **77** ............................ SeanLevey 7 92+
(Richard Hannon) *lw: hld up wl in tch in midfield: effrt to chal over 1f out: rdn to ld 1f out: r.o strly and drew clr ins fnl f: comf* **13/2**[3]

6433 **2** *3½* **Uther Pendragon (IRE)**[9] 4678 2-8-2 **70** ............................(p) RyanPowell 12 76
(J S Moore) *leggy: pressed ldrs: ev ch u.p over 1f out: outpcd by wnr ins fnl f: kpt on and hld on for 2nd cl home* **33/1**

1550 **3** *½* **Gold Town**[20] 4068 2-9-9 **91** ............................(p) JamesDoyle 8 96
(Charlie Appleby) *hld up in tch in midfield: nt clrest of runs ent fnl 2f: shifting lft and hdwy u.p over 1f out: kpt on ins fnl f and pressing for 2nd cl home: no threat to wnr* **7/2**[1]

5442 **4** *shd* **Controversial Lady (IRE)**[15] 4252 2-7-7 **68** oh5 ............................ TinaSmith(7) 3 73
(J S Moore) *hld up wl in tch in midfield: rdn 2f out: nt clr run over 1f out: sn swtchd lft and hdwy 1f out: kpt on wl ins fnl f and pressing for 2nd cl home: no ch w wnr* **50/1**

11 **5** *2¼* **Guzman (IRE)**[41] 3339 2-8-13 **81** ............................ TonyHamilton 11 79
(Richard Fahey) *unf: lw: t.k.h: chsd ldrs tl wnt 2nd after 2f: rdn 2f out: n.m.r in 3rd and unable qck over 1f out: wknd ins fnl f* **10/1**

0521 **6** *nk* **Alifax**[14] 4291 2-8-5 **73** ............................ JoeyHaynes 4 70
(Jamie Osborne) *lw: trckd ldr for 2f: styd chsng ldrs: effrt 2f out: wanting to hang lft and no imp over 1f out: hmpd 1f out and wl hld after* **16/1**

410 **7** *shd* **Red Roman**[24] 3925 2-9-4 **86** ............................ AndreaAtzeni 6 83
(Charles Hills) *led: rdn ent fnl 2f: edging lft and hrd pressed over 1f out: hdd 1f out: no ex and wknd ins fnl f* **13/2**[3]

1120 **8** *1* **Starlight Mystery (IRE)**[21] 4028 2-9-5 **87**.............................. FranBerry 2 82
(Mark Johnston) *s.i.s: in rr: effrt in centre over 2f out: hdwy into midfield but no further prog over 1f out: wknd ins fnl f* **9/1**

U232 **9** *1 1/4* **Arabian Jazz (IRE)**[17] 4167 2-7-9 **70**............................ TristanPrice(7) 1 61
(Michael Bell) *cmpt: hld up towards rr: effrt over 1f out: sn rdn and no hdwy 1f out: nvr trbld ldrs* **10/1**

322 **10** *1* **Weellan**[15] 4258 2-8-6 **74**.............................................................. JFEgan 10 62
(John Quinn) *cmpt: t.k.h early: hld up in tch in midfield: rdn 2f out: sn outpcd and lost pl: wl btn 1f out* **11/1**

415 **11** *nk* **Elysium Dream**[20] 4068 2-9-3 **85**........................................ JimCrowley 9 73
(Richard Hannon) *lw: in tch in midfield: rdn 2f out: unable qck and lost pl over 1f out: wl btn ins fnl f* **5/1**[2]

033 **12** *9* **Merchant Marine (IRE)**[28] 3769 2-8-2 **70**.............(v) JosephineGordon 5 33
(Ralph Beckett) *short of room leaving stalls: a rr: lost tch over 1f out* **16/1**

1m 24.12s (-1.58) **Going Correction** -0.15s/f (Firm) **12** Ran SP% **118.7**
Speed ratings (Par 100): **103,99,98,98,95 95,95,94,92,91 91,80**
CSF £199.05 CT £890.06 TOTE £6.40: £2.40, £9.50, £1.80; EX 267.30 Trifecta £3308.80.
**Owner** Martin Hughes & Nick Robinson **Bred** Tally-Ho Stud **Trained** East Everleigh, Wilts

**FOCUS**
There looked a few potential improvers in this nursery but it maybe didn't turn out that strong a contest and nothing could live with the winner. They raced stands' side. The runner-up has been rated close to his recent Chelmsford/Deauville form.

## 4859 WEATHERBYS EBF STALLIONS MAIDEN STKS (PLUS 10 RACE) (DIV I) 7f
**4:45** (4:49) (Class 4) 2-Y-O **£6,469** (£1,925; £962; £481) **Stalls** Low

Form RPR

2 **1** **Being There (FR)**[29] 3746 2-9-0 0.................................... JamesDoyle 9 88
(Charlie Appleby) *str: lw: trckd ldrs: effrt to chal over 1f out: sn drvn and led 1f out: hld on gamely u.p ins fnl f: all out* **11/10**[1]

**2** *hd* **Doswell (USA)** 2-9-0 0.......................................................... RobertTart 11 87+
(John Gosden) *str: in tch in midfield: clsd to trck ldrs 3f out: rdn to chal over 1f out: kpt on wl u.p and sustained chal fnl f: jst hld* **20/1**

0 **3** *1* **Yaafour**[16] 4213 2-9-0 0.................................................... SeanLevey 8 85
(Richard Hannon) *athletic: lw: led: rdn ent fnl 2f: drvn and hdd 1f out: kpt on wl u.p tl no ex and outpcd fnl 50yds* **33/1**

2 **4** *nk* **Dukhan**[13] 4363 2-9-0 0.............................................. JosephineGordon 2 84+
(Hugo Palmer) *w'like: str: lw: t.k.h: hld up in tch: effrt but hanging lft over 1f out: hdwy but stl hanging 1f out: kpt on wl fnl 100yds: nvr quite getting on terms w ldrs* **3/1**[2]

**5** *nse* **Deja (FR)** 2-9-0 0.............................................................. GeraldMosse 6 84
(Jeremy Noseda) *lengthy: unf: trckd ldrs: effrt 2f out: unable qck over 1f out: styd on u.p ins fnl f: nvr quite enough pce to rch ldrs* **13/2**[3]

**6** *5* **Global Conqueror** 2-9-0 0............................................. AndreaAtzeni 1 70
(Simon Crisford) *athletic: lw: hld up in tch: rdn 2f out: swtchd lft and no imp over 1f out: wknd ins fnl f* **9/1**

**7** *4 1/2* **Parisian (IRE)** 2-9-0 0.................................................... OisinMurphy 7 58
(Ralph Beckett) *leggy: dwlt and rn green: in tch in rr: rdn 2f out: sn hung lft and wknd over 1f out* **16/1**

**8** *nk* **Boniface (IRE)** 2-9-0 0.................................................... PaoloSirigu 4 57
(Robert Eddery) *cmpt: hld up in tch in midfield: lost pl and dropped to rr 2f out: sn rdn and wl btn over 1f out: wknd* **66/1**

**9** *nse* **Chaparral Prince (IRE)** 2-9-0 0...................................... JimCrowley 3 57
(Charles Hills) *w'like: hld up in rr: switching lft and hdwy 3f out: rdn 2f out: sn outpcd and btn: wknd ins fnl f* **25/1**

**10** *2 3/4* **Insurgence** 2-9-0 0.......................................................... TomQueally 5 50
(James Fanshawe) *str: in tch in midfield: pushed along briefly 1/2-way: shkn up 2f out: sn outpcd and btn: wknd ins fnl f* **50/1**

1m 26.44s (0.74) **Going Correction** -0.15s/f (Firm) **10** Ran SP% **116.8**
Speed ratings (Par 96): **89,88,87,87,87 81,76,76,75,72**
CSF £31.80 TOTE £1.80: £1.10, £4.80, £7.30; EX 22.00 Trifecta £314.50.
**Owner** Godolphin **Bred** Dayton Investments Ltd **Trained** Newmarket, Suffolk

**FOCUS**
The first division of what is usually a strong maiden. However, this leg was a tactical affair, and the slower of the two by 1.71sec. The winner has been rated as improving a little on his debut effort.

## 4860 WEATHERBYS EBF STALLIONS MAIDEN STKS (PLUS 10 RACE) (DIV II) 7f
**5:20** (5:22) (Class 4) 2-Y-O **£6,469** (£1,925; £962; £481) **Stalls** Low

Form RPR

3 **1** **Global Giant**[20] 4094 2-9-0 0............................................ FranBerry 9 89
(Ed Dunlop) *leggy: bumping leaving stalls: hld up in tch in last pair: clsd and switching lft over 2f out: rdn to chal over 1f out: sustained duel w runner up fnl f: kpt on to wl to ld last stride* **7/1**[3]

2 **2** *shd* **Tribal Quest (USA)**[21] 4049 2-9-0 0.................................. MartinLane 6 89
(Charlie Appleby) *str: lw: trckd ldr: rdn to ld jst over 1f out: sustained duel w wnr fnl f: kpt on wl: hdd last stride* **11/4**[1]

236 **3** *2 3/4* **Bustam (IRE)**[20] 4068 2-9-0 89..........................(h) LiamKeniry 2 81
(John Quinn) *racd freely: led: hung lft 2f out: stl hanging and hdd jst over 1f out: outpcd ins fnl f* **11/2**[2]

6 **4** *3/4* **Magnificent**[29] 3747 2-9-0 0............................................ SeanLevey 4 79+
(Richard Hannon) *w'like: lw: hld up in tch in last pair: bmpd and pushed rt 2f out: nt clr run and swtchd lft jst over 1f out: 4th and kpt on ins fnl f: no threat to ldng pair* **20/1**

**5** *2 1/4* **Ibraz** 2-9-0 0.......................................................................... JimCrowley 8 73+
(Roger Varian) *athletic: in tch in midfield: pushed along 2f out: unable qck jst over 1f out: wknd ins fnl f* **8/1**

**6** *1* **Falcon Eye (IRE)** 2-9-0 0.................................................. JamesDoyle 10 71
(Charlie Appleby) *str: bumping leaving stalls: hld up in tch towards rr: hdwy over 2f out: no imp u.p and btn over 1f out: wknd ins fnl f* **11/4**[1]

**7** *6* **Taurean Dancer (IRE)** 2-9-0 0........................................ LouisSteward 1 54
(Michael Bell) *w'like: in tch in midfield: rdn and bmpd 2f out: sn struggling and outpcd whn edgd lft over 1f out: wknd fnl f* **50/1**

**8** *shd* **Drill** 2-9-0 0........................................................................ AndreaAtzeni 11 54
(Luca Cumani) *cmpt: bmpd s: sn swtchd rt and rn green in rr: pushed along 2f out: sn outpcd: wknd fnl f* **25/1**

06 **9** *3* **Hemingford (IRE)**[15] 4258 2-9-0 0............................ JosephineGordon 5 46
(Charlie Fellowes) *cmpt: chsd ldrs: rdn lost pl whn squeezed for room 2f out: wl hld whn pushed lft and then swtchd lft jst over 1f out: wknd ins fnl f* **66/1**

**10** *nk* **Al Ozzdi** 2-9-0 0................................................................. OisinMurphy 3 47
(Simon Crisford) *athletic: chsd ldr tl jst over 2f out: sn getting outpcd and edgd rt 2f out: lost pl and btn over 1f out: wl hld whn short of room and impeded 1f out: wknd* **7/1**[3]

**11** *nk* **Jetstream (IRE)** 2-9-0 0.......................................(t[1]) TomQueally 7 46
(Charles Hills) *leggy: stdd after s: hld up in tch in midfield: lost pl and short of room wl over 2f out: bhd and no rspnse to press 2f out: wknd fnl f* **33/1**

1m 24.73s (-0.97) **Going Correction** -0.15s/f (Firm) **11** Ran SP% **119.8**
Speed ratings (Par 96): **99,98,95,94,92 91,84,84,80,80 80**
CSF £25.90 TOTE £7.90: £2.30, £1.40, £1.60; EX 31.90 Trifecta £128.50.
**Owner** Dr Johnny Hon **Bred** M J & L A Taylor Llp **Trained** Newmarket, Suffolk

**FOCUS**
This was more strongly run and was the quicker of the two divisions by 1.71sec. The third has been rated in line with his debut form.

## 4861 CHELSEA WATERFRONT H'CAP 1m
**5:50** (5:50) (Class 3) (0-90,89) 3-Y-O+ **£9,703** (£2,887; £1,443; £721) **Stalls** Low

Form RPR

1-10 **1** **Mickey Rich**[48] 3077 3-9-1 **85**........................................ OisinMurphy 4 92
(Hughie Morrison) *led and dictated stdy gallop: rdn and qckdn 2f out: hrd pressed jst over 1f out: drvn ins fnl f: styd on strly and forged ahd wl ins fnl f* **11/4**[2]

3043 **2** *1* **Dr Julius No**[27] 3838 3-8-12 **89**................................ FinleyMarsh(7) 8 94
(Richard Hughes) *trckd ldrs: clsd to press ldr over 1f out: sn rdn and str chal ent fnl f: no ex and outpcd wl ins fnl f* **3/1**[3]

1 **3** *2* **Finishing Touch**[13] 4378 3-8-11 **81**................................ MartinLane 2 81
(Saeed bin Suroor) *trckd wnr: nt enough room on stands rail and dropped to 3rd over 1f out: swtchd lft and drvn 1f out: kpt on same pce ins fnl f* **9/4**[1]

1002 **4** *2 1/4* **Supersta**[15] 4270 6-9-11 **89**..............................(p) AlistairRawlinson(3) 6 85
(Michael Appleby) *stdd s: t.k.h: hld up in last pair: effrt on outer over 2f out: 4th and styd on same pce ins fnl f* **8/1**

-220 **5** *3 3/4* **Directorship**[29] 3750 11-9-4 **82**................................ CharlieBennett(3) 5 69
(Patrick Chamings) *stdd s: hld up wl in tch in midfield: effrt over 2f out: no imp and btn over 1f out: wknd ins fnl f* **16/1**

6/45 **6** *nk* **Groor**[26] 3857 5-9-8 **83**................................................ SeanLevey 1 70
(Mohamed Moubarak) *t.k.h: hld up in tch in midfield: rdn over 2f out: outpcd and btn over 1f out: wknd ins fnl f* **33/1**

1-5 **7** *1 1/4* **Time Zone**[87] 1859 3-9-5 **89**........................................ JamesDoyle 3 71
(Peter Chapple-Hyam) *stdd and dropped in bhd after s: hld up in rr: effrt ent fnl 2f: no hdwy and outpcd over 1f out: bhd fnl f* **9/1**

1m 40.02s (0.02) **Going Correction** -0.15s/f (Firm)
**WFA** 3 from 5yo+ 9lb **7** Ran SP% **112.4**
Speed ratings (Par 107): **93,92,90,87,84 83,82**
CSF £11.03 CT £20.09 TOTE £3.30: £1.80, £1.80; EX 10.10 Trifecta £41.50.
**Owner** Kerr-Dineen, Eason, Rothwell & Malpas **Bred** New England Stud, Myriad & T Vestey **Trained** East Ilsley, Berks

**FOCUS**
This was steadily run, the winner benefiting from an uncontested lead. The runner-up has been rated to form.
T/Jkpt: £3,475.00 to a £1 stake. Pool: £45,176.28 - 13.00 winning units. T/Plt: £42.50 to a £1 stake. Pool: £188,610.36 - 3,235.44 winning units. T/Qpdt: £43.50 to a £1 stake. Pool: £8,416.00 - 143.09 winning units. **Steve Payne**

# [4374]YORK (L-H)
### Friday, July 14

**OFFICIAL GOING: Good to firm (good in places; overall 7.4; home straight; far side 7.5, centre 7.4, stands' side 7.4)**
Wind: Fresh half against Weather: Cloudy and blustery

## 4862 IRISH EBF/ROA RACING POST OWNERS JACKPOT NOVICE STKS (PLUS 10 RACE) 5f 89y
**2:05** (2:05) (Class 3) 2-Y-O **£7,762** (£2,310; £1,154; £577) **Stalls** Low

Form RPR

12 **1** **One Minute (IRE)**[30] 3725 2-9-3 0.................................... PatCosgrave 3 90
(William Haggas) *mde all: rdn over 1f out: edgd lft ins fnl f: kpt on strly* **11/10**[1]

1 **2** *1 1/4* **Abel Handy (IRE)**[33] 3622 2-9-8 0.................................... TomEaves 8 91
(Declan Carroll) *cl up: effrt to chal over 1f out: sn rdn and kpt on* **7/1**

43 **3** *2 3/4* **Big Les (IRE)**[15] 4259 2-9-2 0...................................... JamieSpencer 5 75
(Karen McLintock) *trckd ldng pair: effrt 2f out and sn rdn: kpt on same pce ent fnl f* **5/1**[3]

00 **4** *4 1/2* **Daffy Jane**[7] 4555 2-8-8 0................................ RachelRichardson(3) 1 55
(Nigel Tinkler) *chsd ldrs: hdwy over 2f out: rdn along wl over 1f out: kpt on one pce* **66/1**

**5** *3* **Ganton Par** 2-8-13 0.......................................................... NathanEvans(3) 6 49
(Michael Easterby) *dwlt and rr: hdwy over 2f out: sn rdn: styd on fnl f* **16/1**

10 **6** *shd* **Pilkington**[22] 3993 2-9-8 0............................................ DanielTudhope 7 55
(David O'Meara) *towards rr: hdwy on outer 2f out: sn rdn and n.d* **9/2**[2]

04 **7** *1* **Peter Leonard**[33] 3622 2-9-2 0...................................... PaulHanagan 10 45
(Richard Fahey) *chsd ldrs: rdn along 2f out: grad wknd* **33/1**

66 **8** *1/2* **Where's Jeff**[13] 4359 2-8-9 0........................................ RyanTimby(7) 4 44
(Michael Easterby) *chsd ldrs: rdn along 1/2-way: sn wknd* **66/1**

50 **9** *1* **Mabo**[39] 3398 2-9-2 0........................................................ JackGarritty 2 40
(Richard Fahey) *dwlt: a rr* **20/1**

**10** *3 1/4* **Tiger Lyon (USA)** 2-8-13 0.............................................. TimClark(3) 9 29
(John Butler) *a towards rr* **16/1**

1m 4.39s (0.29) **Going Correction** +0.025s/f (Good) **10** Ran SP% **117.4**
Speed ratings (Par 98): **98,96,91,84,79 79,77,77,75,70**
CSF £9.27 TOTE £1.90: £1.02, £2.40, £2.00; EX 9.70 Trifecta £29.70.
**Owner** Abdulla Al Mansoori **Bred** Mubarak Al Naemi **Trained** Newmarket, Suffolk

**FOCUS**
Due to rail movement races 2 & 4 increased by 32yds. There was only 1.4mm of overnight rain and the going remained unchanged at good to firm, good in places. After riding in the opener Paul Hanagan and Jack Garritty said the ground was just on the quick side of good while Pat Cosgrave called it good. A novice event lacking in depth, and nothing got into it from off the pace, but the form looks solid. It's been rated around the third and fourth.

## 4863 UNIBET H'CAP 1m 3f 188y
**2:40** (2:40) (Class 2) (0-100,98) 3-Y-O+
**£12,450** (£3,728; £1,864; £932; £466; £234) **Stalls** Centre

Form RPR

0220 **1** **Mukhayyam**[16] 4206 5-8-13 **83**.......................................(p) DavidAllan 8 95
(Tim Easterby) *set gd pce: pushed along 3f out: rdn wl over 1f out: kpt on strly fnl f* **14/1**

2-36 **2** 1 ¾ **Mainstream**21 4033 4-10-0 **98**....................(h) StevieDonohoe 6 107
(Sir Michael Stoute) *awkward and wnt rt s: hld up in rr: tk clsr order 5f out: hdwy over 2f out: chsd wnr wl over 1f out: drvn and kpt on same pce fnl f* **7/2**2

5400 **3** 6 **Lustrous Light (IRE)**21 4033 4-10-0 **98**.................... PatDobbs 2 98
(Ralph Beckett) *trckd wnr: pushed along wl over 2f out: rdn wl over 1f out: sn drvn and kpt on one pce* **6/1**

0530 **4** ½ **Oasis Fantasy (IRE)**21 4033 6-9-11 **95**.................... JamieSpencer 5 94
(David Simcock) *hld up in rr: hdwy 3f out: rdn along over 2f out: kpt on fnl f* **6/1**

3442 **5** nk **Beardwood**7 4585 5-9-4 **88**....................(p) PJMcDonald 1 86
(Mark Johnston) *trckd ldrs: hdwy 3f out: rdn along 2f out: drvn wl over 1f out: grad wknd* **8/1**

-132 **6** 3 ¼ **Azari**13 4380 5-9-9 **93**.................... RichardKingscote 3 86
(Tom Dascombe) *hld up in rr: effrt over 3f out: sn rdn along and nvr a factor* **4/1**3

0 **7** nk **Night Of Glory**21 4032 3-8-11 **98**.................... JoshuaBryan(5) 7 92
(Andrew Balding) *rn in snatches: trckd ldng pair: reminders 1/2-way: pushed along over 4f out: rdn over 3f out: sn drvn and wknd* **11/4**1

2m 30.77s (-2.43) **Going Correction** +0.025s/f (Good)
**WFA** 3 from 4yo+ 12lb **7** Ran SP% **115.2**
Speed ratings (Par 109): **109,107,103,103,103 101,100**
CSF £63.17 CT £333.17 TOTE £13.40: £4.20, £2.30; EX 81.60 Trifecta £813.20.
**Owner** T A Scothern **Bred** Mrs James Wigan **Trained** Great Habton, N Yorks

**FOCUS**
Race distance increased by 32yds. A decent handicap and another all-the-way winner. The winner has been rated to last year's best, and the runner-up to form.

## 4864 UNIBET SUMMER STKS (GROUP 3) (F&M) 6f
**3:15** (3:16) (Class 1) 3-Y-0+
**£34,026** (£12,900; £6,456; £3,216; £1,614; £810) **Stalls** Centre

Form RPR

-605 **1** **Mystic Dawn (IRE)**48 3080 3-8-12 96.................... StevieDonohoe 11 108
(David Simcock) *hld up towards rr: hdwy 2f out: nt clr run and swtchd rt over 1f out: rdn to ld ent fnl f: sn drvn and hld on gamely towards fin* **20/1**

-503 **2** shd **Queen Kindly**20 4078 3-8-12 103.................... PaulHanagan 12 107
(Richard Fahey) *trckd ldrs: hdwy nr stands rail 2f out: rdn to chal ent fnl f: sn drvn and ev ch: jst hld* **11/2**2

1-01 **3** 5 **Eartha Kitt**28 3793 3-8-12 90....................(p) RichardKingscote 4 91+
(Tom Dascombe) *trckd ldrs towards inner: pushed along 2f out: n.m.r over 1f out: sn rdn and styd on fnl f* **7/1**3

0510 **4** shd **Buying Trouble (USA)**33 3632 4-9-4 97.................... AndrewMullen 14 91
(David Evans) *towards rr: hdwy 2f out: sn rdn along nr stands rail: styd on wl u.p fnl f* **20/1**

22-4 **5** 1 ¼ **Gheedaa (USA)**27 3835 3-8-12 92.................... PatDobbs 3 86+
(William Haggas) *dwlt and bhd: hdwy wl over 1f out: sn rdn and kpt on strly fnl f* **7/1**3

11 **6** ½ **Artistica (GER)**48 3105 3-9-1 103.................... FrannyNorton 2 88
(D Moser, Germany) *cl up towards centre: effrt 2f out: led briefly 11/2f out: sn rdn and hdd appr fnl f: sn drvn and one pce* **7/2**1

2234 **7** hd **Futoon (IRE)**20 4078 4-9-4 94.................... JoeDoyle 10 85
(Kevin Ryan) *slt ld centre: rdn along 2f out: hdd and drvn 11/2f out: grad wknd* **12/1**

20-0 **8** nk **Show Stealer**69 2390 4-9-4 91.................... MartinDwyer 1 84
(Rae Guest) *trckd ldrs on inner: cl up 2f out: sn rdn and edgd lft over 1f out: drvn and kpt on same pce fnl f* **33/1**

4105 **9** 1 **Equimou**20 4098 3-8-12 101.................... KieranShoemark 6 80
(Robert Eddery) *racd centre: cl up: rdn along wl over 1f out: grad wknd* **33/1**

12-0 **10** 2 **Gravity Flow (IRE)**48 3080 4-9-4 99.................... PatCosgrave 13 75
(William Haggas) *racd towards stands side: cl up: rdn along 2f out: sn wknd* **7/1**3

34 **11** 11 **Florida Times (IRE)**33 3632 3-8-12 93.................... DanielTudhope 15 38
(David O'Meara) *a rr* **14/1**

6 **12** 9 **Sugar Free (GER)**48 3080 4-9-4 100.................... RobertWinston 5 11
(D Moser, Germany) *chsd ldrs centre: rdn along over 2f out: sn wknd* **25/1**

3214 **13** ½ **Isabel's On It**16 4208 3-8-12 92.................... JamieSpencer 7 8
(William Haggas) *dwlt: t.k.h and sn chsng ldrs centre: rdn along 2f out: sn wknd* **8/1**

1m 10.84s (-1.06) **Going Correction** +0.025s/f (Good)
**WFA** 3 from 4yo+ 6lb **13** Ran SP% **119.8**
Speed ratings (Par 113): **108,107,101,101,99 98,98,98,96,94 79,67,66**
CSF £120.24 TOTE £29.20: £7.20, £2.10, £2.50; EX 217.60 Trifecta £1490.00.
**Owner** Al Asayl Bloodstock Ltd **Bred** Al Asayl Bloodstock Ltd **Trained** Newmarket, Suffolk

**FOCUS**
A competitive Group 3 sprint for fillies and mares, in which they went a good pace, the two principals pulling nicely clear close to the stands' rail. The runner-up has been rated to her best form since her peak 2yo run over this C&D.

## 4865 CAKEMARK H'CAP 1m 2f 56y
**3:45** (3:45) (Class 4) (0-85,86) 3-Y-0+ **£7,762** (£2,310; £1,154; £577) **Stalls** Low

Form RPR

-006 **1** **Novoman (IRE)**14 4322 3-9-0 **86**.................... GeorgiaCox(5) 5 99
(William Haggas) *t.k.h: trckd ldr on inner: hdwy to ld 3f out: rdn and qcknd clr wl over 1f out: kpt on strly* **4/1**2

-141 **2** 4 **Visitant**27 3845 4-9-9 **85**.................... LewisEdmunds(5) 4 89
(David Thompson) *hld up in rr: hdwy over 2f out and sn pushed along: rdn over 1f out: drvn and kpt on fnl f* **5/2**1

3464 **3** hd **In First Place**30 3713 3-8-11 **78**.................... PaulHanagan 9 83
(Richard Fahey) *in tch: hdwy wl over 2f out: rdn wl over 1f out: kpt on u.p fnl f* **9/1**

3403 **4** 2 ½ **Footlight**34 3558 4-9-0 **74**.................... AdamMcNamara(3) 8 73
(Richard Fahey) *trckd ldng pair: hdwy 4f out: cl up 3f out: rdn along over 2f out: drvn wl over 1f out: grad wknd* **25/1**

1454 **5** 1 ½ **Rockwood**13 4358 6-9-6 **77**....................(v) JamieSpencer 2 73
(Karen McLintock) *dwlt: hld up in rr: sme hdwy 3f out: rdn along over 2f out: sn drvn and n.d* **14/1**

1-02 **6** 1 ½ **Sound Bar**19 4118 3-9-1 **82**.................... PatDobbs 6 76
(Ralph Beckett) *led: pushed along 4f out: hdd 3f out: sn rdn and wknd* **5/1**3

3155 **7** 1 ½ **Mullarkey**28 3787 3-8-7 **74**.................... MartinDwyer 1 65
(John Best) *trckd ldrs on inner: hdwy over 3f out: rdn along over 2f out: sn drvn and wknd* **6/1**

3431 **8** 7 **Jacbequick**13 4380 6-9-11 **85**....................(b) JoshDoyle(3) 7 61
(David O'Meara) *dwlt and rr: swtchd wd to stands rail over 3f out: rdn along wl over 2f out: nvr a factor* **7/1**

2m 12.09s (-0.41) **Going Correction** +0.025s/f (Good)
**WFA** 3 from 4yo+ 10lb **8** Ran SP% **112.5**
Speed ratings (Par 105): **102,98,98,96,95 94,93,87**
CSF £13.94 CT £81.77 TOTE £4.90: £1.70, £1.30, £2.50; EX 15.50 Trifecta £116.30.
**Owner** Sheikh Ahmed Al Maktoum **Bred** Gerard Mullins **Trained** Newmarket, Suffolk

**FOCUS**
Race distance increased by 32yds. A competitive handicap for the grade and an impressive winner. The second and third have been rated to form.

## 4866 GARBUTT + ELLIOTT NURSERY H'CAP 5f
**4:20** (4:21) (Class 3) 2-Y-0 **£7,762** (£2,310; £1,154; £577) **Stalls** Low

Form RPR

5260 **1** **Marnie James**28 3789 2-8-3 **73**....................(t1) NathanEvans(3) 4 81
(Iain Jardine) *t.k.h: trckd ldr: effrt 2f out: sn rdn: led jst ins fnl f: kpt on wl* **20/1**

631 **2** 2 **Silver Starlight**23 3980 2-8-0 **70**.................... RachelRichardson(3) 6 71
(Tim Easterby) *dwlt: sn trcking ldrs: hdwy 2f out: rdn over 1f out: styd on to chse wnr ins fnl f: no imp* **7/1**

2132 **3** nk **Our Little Pony**7 4555 2-7-11 **67** oh4.................... NoelGarbutt(3) 2 67
(Lawrence Mullaney) *towards rr: rdn along and outpcd 1/2-way: hdwy wl over 1f out: styd on strly u.p fnl f* **12/1**

160 **4** ½ **Excellently Poised**24 3929 2-9-2 **83**....................(p1) DanielTudhope 8 81
(Bryan Smart) *chsd ldrs on outer: hdwy 2f out: rdn over 1f out: drvn and kpt on same pce fnl f* **7/2**2

0253 **5** 1 ½ **Shay C**42 3283 2-8-2 **69**.................... MartinDwyer 3 62
(Declan Carroll) *led: rdn along 2f out: hung rt over 1f out: hdd jst ins fnl f: wknd* **12/1**

3042 **6** ½ **Seen The Lyte (IRE)**23 3980 2-8-2 **69**.................... CamHardie 5 60
(John Quinn) *chsd ldr: rdn along 2f out: drvn and wknd over 1f out* **12/1**

6512 **7** 1 **Branscombe**18 4160 2-8-13 **80**.................... RichardKingscote 1 67
(Mark Johnston) *a towards rr* **4/1**3

110 **8** nk **Nine Below Zero**22 3993 2-9-9 **90**.................... PatDobbs 10 76
(Ralph Beckett) *dwlt and wnt rt s: hld up: a bhd* **9/4**1

6663 **9** 2 ½ **Funkadelic**9 4488 2-8-1 **68**.................... DuranFentiman 9 45
(Ben Haslam) *in tch on wd outside: rdn along 2f out: sn wknd* **10/1**

58.46s (-0.84) **Going Correction** +0.025s/f (Good) **9** Ran SP% **122.4**
Speed ratings (Par 98): **107,103,103,102,100 99,97,97,93**
CSF £161.29 CT £1793.32 TOTE £29.70: £6.00, £2.30, £2.50; EX 233.20 Trifecta £1402.70.
**Owner** James Property Ltd **Bred** Newsells Park Stud **Trained** Carrutherstown, D'fries & G'way

■ Almane was withdrawn. Price at time of withdrawal 9-1. Rule 4 applies to board prices prior to withdrawal - deduction 10p in the pound. New market formed.

**FOCUS**
This looked a decent nursery on paper, the whole field making their handicap debuts, but a couple of the market leaders underperformed and the form may not be reliable. It's been rated as straightforward form around the second and third.

## 4867 IRISH THOROUGHBRED MARKETING H'CAP 5f
**4:55** (4:56) (Class 3) (0-95,94) 3-Y-0+ **£11,644** (£3,465; £1,731; £865) **Stalls** Centre

Form RPR

1000 **1** **Excessable**6 4600 4-9-4 **87**.................... RachelRichardson(3) 12 95
(Tim Easterby) *trckd ldrs: effrt and nt clr run over 1f out: rdn ent fnl f: kpt on wl to ld last 50 yds* **20/1**

5215 **2** ½ **Coolfitch (IRE)**12 4412 3-9-3 **91**.................... JoshDoyle(3) 4 96
(David O'Meara) *dwlt: rr and sn swtchd rt towards stands side:. hld up: hdwy over 1f out: rdn and chsd ldrs ent fnl f: styd on wl towards fin* **11/1**

333 **3** ½ **Bashiba (IRE)**13 4379 6-9-0 **85**....................(t) LewisEdmunds(5) 13 90
(Nigel Tinkler) *hld up: hdwy towards stands side 2f out: rdn to ld appr fnl f: sn drvn: hdd and no ex last 50 yds* **15/2**3

2431 **4** ½ **Stanghow**6 4600 5-9-9 **89** 6ex.................... CamHardie 9 92
(Antony Brittain) *dwlt and towards rr: hdwy 2f out: rdn and edgd rt over 1f out: styd on u.p fnl f* **14/1**

-000 **5** hd **Move In Time**27 3829 9-10-0 **94**.................... DanielTudhope 10 99+
(David O'Meara) *hld up in tch: hdwy whn n.m.r 2f out: effrt whn nt clr run and hmpd over 1f out: swtchd lft and styd on strly towards fin* **12/1**

2400 **6** 1 ½ **East Street Revue**27 3829 4-9-12 **92**....................(b) DuranFentiman 2 89
(Tim Easterby) *chsd ldrs on inner: clsd up 2f out: sn rdn: drvn appr fnl f: kpt on same pce* **6/1**2

1042 **7** shd **Lucky Beggar (IRE)**13 4333 7-9-5 **88**.................... NathanEvans(3) 8 89+
(David C Griffiths) *chsd ldrs: pushed along whn hmpd over 1f out: sn rdn and styd on wl towards fin* **10/1**

5202 **8** shd **Merry Banter**8 4530 3-8-7 **85**.................... ConnorMurtagh(7) 7 79
(Paul Midgley) *racd centre: led: rdn along wl over 1f out: hdd appr fnl f: grad wknd* **14/1**

4626 **9** nk **Black Grass**13 4379 4-8-7 **80**.................... HarrisonShaw(7) 11 75
(Michael Easterby) *trckd ldr centre: pushed along 2f out: rdn and edgd rt over 1f out: sn drvn: edgd lft and wknd* **20/1**

5401 **10** ¾ **Tylery Wonder (IRE)**13 4379 7-9-4 **84**....................(v) PatDobbs 14 76
(Paul Midgley) *racd towards stands rail: prom: rdn along wl over 1f out: sn wknd* **12/1**

1000 **11** 2 ¼ **Desert Law (IRE)**12 4416 9-9-12 **92**.................... PaulHanagan 15 76
(Paul Midgley) *racd towards stands rail: hld up: hdwy 2f out: rdn over 1f out: sn wknd* **12/1**

23-0 **12** 1 ½ **Rosina**45 3183 4-8-10 **79**.................... AdamMcNamara(3) 6 58
(Ann Duffield) *a towards rr* **25/1**

-501 **13** 1 ¾ **Stoneyford Lane (IRE)**8 4530 3-8-9 **80** 6ex..........(p) RoystonFfrench 3 51
(Steph Hollinshead) *a rr: outpcd fr 1/2-way* **22/1**

011- **14** 2 ½ **Lapilli**317 6018 4-9-7 **87**.................... PatCosgrave 5 51
(William Haggas) *a towards rr: rdn along 2f out: sn outpcd* **7/2**1

58.5s (-0.80) **Going Correction** +0.025s/f (Good)
**WFA** 3 from 4yo+ 5lb **14** Ran SP% **119.8**
Speed ratings (Par 107): **107,106,105,104,104 101,101,101,101,99 96,93,91,87**
CSF £214.53 CT £1860.90 TOTE £22.70: £6.50, £3.40, £2.60; EX 316.20 Trifecta £1367.70.
**Owner** B Guerin & Habton Farms **Bred** Whitsbury Manor Stud **Trained** Great Habton, N Yorks

■ Stewards' Enquiry : Harrison Shaw three-day ban: careless riding (Jul 28-31)

**FOCUS**
A typically competitive big-field sprint for the track and they went a good pace throughout. The third helps set the standard.

## 4868 WINGATE CENTRE CHARITY SUPPORTED BY SUGRO APPRENTICE H'CAP 7f
**5:30** (5:30) (Class 3) (0-95,91) 3-Y-O **£7,762** (£2,310; £1,154; £577) **Stalls** Low

Form RPR

1321 **1** **Lualiwa**[13] 4334 3-9-5 **87** LewisEdmunds(3) 7 95
(Kevin Ryan) *qckly away and swtchd lft to inner rail: mde all: rdn wl over 1f out: kpt on strly fnl f* **9/2**[3]

1301 **2** 1 ½ **Derek Duval (USA)**[20] 4100 3-8-13 **78** (t) AaronJones 3 82
(Stuart Williams) *hld up in tch: hdwy over 2f out: rdn along wl over 1f out: drvn to chse wnr ins fnl f: sn no imp* **12/1**

0-00 **3** 1 ½ **Medici Banchiere**[27] 3844 3-9-9 **91** CliffordLee(3) 5 91
(K R Burke) *trckd wnr: pushed along 3f out: rdn 2f out: sn drvn and kpt on same pce* **14/1**

-060 **4** 1 ½ **Kreb's Cycle (IRE)**[6] 4634 3-9-1 **80** (p[1]) AdamMcNamara 6 76
(Ian Williams) *hmpd s: trckd ldrs on outer: pushed along 3f out: rdn 2f out: drvn over 1f out: kpt on same pce* **25/1**

1-1 **5** 5 **Pennsylvania Dutch**[34] 3584 3-9-2 **84** GeorgiaCox(3) 4 66
(William Haggas) *rrd and dwlt s: t.k.h: hld up: hdwy 3f out: chsd ldrs 2f out and sn rdn: drvn and wknd over 1f out* **5/2**[2]

0-11 **6** 9 **Silent Echo**[48] 3082 3-9-12 **91** KieranShoemark 1 49
(Roger Charlton) *t.k.h: trckd ldng pair on inner: pushed along 3f out: rdn over 2f out: sn btn* **2/1**[1]

102 **7** 30 **Sir Reginald Brown**[34] 3588 3-8-7 **77** ConnorMurtagh(5) 2
(Richard Fahey) *a rr: pushed along 3f out: sn rdn and outpcd: bhd and eased fnl 2f* **11/2**

1m 24.26s (-1.04) **Going Correction** +0.025s/f (Good) **7 Ran SP% 113.7**
Speed ratings (Par 104): **106,104,102,100,95 84,50**
CSF £53.49 TOTE £5.00: £2.20, £4.20; EX 49.00 Trifecta £473.60.
**Owner** Mrs Rosie Richer **Bred** M E Broughton **Trained** Hambleton, N Yorks

**FOCUS**
An interesting 3yo handicap, albeit not the strongest for the grade, and another front-running winner on the card. The second has been rated to his Newmarket win.
T/Plt: £896.80 to a £1 stake. Pool: £ - winning units. T/Qpdt: £180.80 to a £1 stake. Pool: £ - winning units. **Joe Rowntree**

4869 - 4877a (Foreign Racing) - See Raceform Interactive

# 4423 SAINT-CLOUD (L-H)
Friday, July 14

**OFFICIAL GOING: Turf: good**

## 4878a JUDDMONTE GRAND PRIX DE PARIS (GROUP 1) (3YO COLTS & FILLIES) (TURF) 1m 4f
**7:25** 3-Y-O **£293,025** (£117,230; £58,615; £29,282; £14,666)

RPR

**1** **Shakeel (FR)**[26] 3879 3-9-2 0 ChristopheSoumillon 4 114
(A De Royer-Dupre, France) *w.w in midfield on inner: 5th and travelling wl 3f out: niggled along to cl over 2f out: angled out to its pursuit of ldr 1 1/2f out: sn rdn and styd on wl: jnd ldr 110yds out: battled gamely: won on the nod* **57/10**

**2** nse **Permian (IRE)**[21] 4029 3-9-2 0 WilliamBuick 3 114
(Mark Johnston) *led after 1f: drvn over 2f out: styd on wl whn rdn 1 1/2f out: jnd 110yds out: rallied gamely u.p: lost out on the nod* **3/1**[1]

**3** 1 **Venice Beach (IRE)**[41] 3322 3-9-2 0 (p) SeamieHeffernan 1 112+
(A P O'Brien, Ire) *trckd ldrs: cl 4th and hrd rdn 1 1/2f out: styd on wl ins fnl f: nvr quite on terms* **28/1**

**4** 1 **Ice Breeze**[26] 3879 3-9-2 0 VincentCheminaud 5 111+
(P Bary, France) *settled towards rr on inner: rdn to cl 1 1/2f out: styd on fnl f: nrest at fin* **48/10**

**5** 1 **Falcon Wings**[26] 3879 3-9-2 0 (p) OlivierPeslier 9 109
(N Clement, France) *led: hdd after 1f: chsd ldr on outer: rdn wl over 2f out: kpt on at same pce* **229/10**

**6** ¾ **Parabellum (IRE)**[29] 3-9-2 0 MickaelBarzalona 10 108+
(A Fabre, France) *dwlt: w.w in rr: last and plenty to do 2 1/2f out: angled out and rdn but no immediate imp over 2f out: hdwy 1 1/2f out: kpt on ins fnl f: nvr nrr* **39/10**[2]

**7** snk **Orderofthegarter (IRE)**[22] 3994 3-9-2 0 (p) RyanMoore 8 108
(A P O'Brien, Ire) *w.w in fnl pair: drvn along appr 2f out: kpt on ins fnl f: nvr in contention* **23/5**[3]

**8** 3 **Mac Mahon (ITY)**[54] 2868 3-9-2 0 CristianDemuro 7 103
(Stefano Botti, Italy) *cl up: drvn 3f out but no imp: dropped away fnl f* **13/2**

**9** 1 **Spanish Steps (IRE)**[19] 4127 3-9-2 0 PBBeggy 6 101
(A P O'Brien, Ire) *settled towards rr on outer: 6th and pushed along 3f out: wl hld fnl f* **54/1**

2m 30.42s (-9.98) **9 Ran SP% 118.2**
PARI-MUTUEL (all including 1 euro stake): WIN 6.70; PLACE 2.40, 1.80, 3.70; DF 16.10; SF 40.00.
**Owner** H H Aga Khan **Bred** S.A. Aga Khan **Trained** Chantilly, France

**FOCUS**
Many top-class racehorses have landed this prize, with the likes of Bago, Rail Link (both 3yo winners of the Arc) and Flintshire among them since 2004. However, this renewal was a little unsatisfactory, with about half the field, mainly those held up, never making any impression after coming with their bids more towards the centre of the track than those who stayed closer to the inside. The fifth looks a fair guide to the form.

## 4879a PRIX MAURICE DE NIEUIL (GROUP 2) (4YO+) (TURF) 1m 6f
**8:00** 4-Y-O+ **£63,333** (£24,444; £11,666; £7,777; £3,888)

RPR

**1** **Talismanic**[40] 3369 4-9-0 0 MickaelBarzalona 4 115+
(A Fabre, France) *settled in midfield on inner: 5th and angled out appr fnl 2 1/2f: gd hdwy under 2f out: led 1 1/2f out and sn clr: styd on wl under driving fnl f: a in control* **21/10**[1]

**2** 1 ¼ **Marmelo**[56] 2803 4-9-0 0 ChristopheSoumillon 5 112+
(Hughie Morrison) *settled towards rr: 7th whn rdn to cl wl over 1 1/2f out: styd on wl u.p: wnt 2nd 110yds out: nvr on terms w wnr* **17/5**[2]

**3** ¾ **Sirius (GER)**[47] 3119 6-9-0 0 MaximeGuyon 8 111+
(Andreas Suborics, Germany) *w.w towards rr: drvn 2f out: hdwy on outer wl over 1 1/2f out: styd on wl fnl f: tk 3rd fnl stride* **67/10**[3]

**4** shd **Moonshiner (GER)**[26] 3884 4-9-0 0 Pierre-CharlesBoudot 7 111
(Jean-Pierre Carvalho, Germany) *prom on outer: cl 4th and drvn along under 2f out: styd on u.p: nt pce to chal: lost 3rd fnl stride* **26/1**

**5** 1 **Full Drago (ITY)**[26] 3884 4-9-3 0 CristianDemuro 6 113
(Stefano Botti, Italy) *led: rdn 2 1/2f out: hdd over 2f out: rallied gamely u.p: styd on same pce fnl f* **17/2**

**6** ¾ **Sweet Selection**[22] 3996 5-8-10 0 OlivierPeslier 9 105
(Hughie Morrison) *racd in midfield on outside of eventual wnr: 6th and scrubbed along 3f out: no imp tl styd on fr 1 1/2f out: nt pce to get involved* **91/10**

**7** 1 **Mille Et Mille**[64] 2559 7-9-0 0 FranckBlondel 10 107
(C Lerner, France) *chsd ldr: drvn to chal 2 1/2f out: led 2f over out: sn rdn and nt qckn: hdd over 1 1/2f out: grad dropped away fr over 1f out* **123/10**

**8** 1 ¾ **Canessar (FR)**[21] 4-9-0 0 AlexisBadel 2 105
(H-F Devin, France) *w.w towards rr: prog on inner under 3ff out: 5th and rdn under 2f out: wknd ins fnl f* **68/10**

**9** 2 **Tres Rock Glory (IRE)**[68] 2450 4-8-10 0 AurelienLemaitre 3 98
(F Head, France) *chsd ldrs on inner: drvn and no imp 2 1/2f out: lft bhd ins fnl 1 1/2f* **39/1**

**10** nk **Iraklion (GER)**[21] 5-9-0 0 MichaelCadeddu 1 102
(Christian Sprengel, Germany) *w.w in rr: scrubbed along and no imp 3f out: wl hld fnl f* **28/1**

2m 58.4s (-13.80) **10 Ran SP% 118.4**
PARI-MUTUEL (all including 1 euro stake): WIN 3.10; PLACE 1.30, 1.70, 1.70; DF 4.30; SF 12.90.
**Owner** Godolphin SNC **Bred** Darley **Trained** Chantilly, France

**FOCUS**
The first four and ninth have been rated to their marks.

# 4826 ASCOT (R-H)
Saturday, July 15

**OFFICIAL GOING: Good (good to soft in places on round course; str 7.4, rnd 6.9)**
Wind: Almost nil Weather: Overcast, drizzly

## 4880 RUDDY NOVICE AUCTION STKS (PLUS 10 RACE) (DIV I) 7f
**1:40** (1:44) (Class 4) 2-Y-O **£6,469** (£1,925; £962; £481) **Stalls** High

Form RPR

31 **1** **Curiosity (IRE)**[16] 4259 2-9-8 0 OisinMurphy 2 86+
(Hugo Palmer) *str: trckd ldrs: shkn up over 1f out: swtchd to nr side rail and drvn to press ldrs fnl f: r.o to ld last 50yds* **15/8**[1]

4 **2** ½ **Preacher Man (IRE)**[17] 4218 2-9-2 0 DougieCostello 5 79
(Jamie Osborne) *athletic: lw: t.k.h: hld up in last pair: smooth prog on outer over 2f out: shkn up to ld jst ins fnl f: sn drvn: hdd and outpcd last 50yds* **15/2**

**3** ½ **Jazeel (IRE)** 2-9-2 0 CharlesBishop 1 77+
(Mick Channon) *leggy: slowly away and swvd rt: rn green in last pair: pushed along over 2f out: prog on outer sn after: clsd on ldrs 1f out: rdn and styd on to take 3rd ins fnl f* **20/1**

0 **4** 1 **Snooker Jim**[15] 4291 2-9-2 0 RoystonFfrench 3 75
(Steph Hollinshead) *cmpt: lw: swvd rt s: sn w ldrs: disp ld after 2f tl led wl over 1f out: drvn and hdd jst ins fnl f: one pce* **50/1**

4 **5** 1 ¾ **Serjeant Painter**[19] 4151 2-8-9 0 TylerSaunders(7) 9 70
(Marcus Tregoning) *w'like: hld up in tch: pushed along 2f out: one pce and nvr rchd ldrs: can do bttr* **13/2**

3 **6** 1 **Jack Regan**[14] 4363 2-9-2 0 (t) DavidProbert 8 68
(Charles Hills) *athletic: lw: disp ld to over 2f out: steadily fdd* **7/2**[2]

6 **7** ¾ **Puchita (IRE)**[9] 4533 2-8-11 0 PatDobbs 6 61
(Richard Hannon) *unf: in tch in rr: trying to make prog but nt clr run 2f out tl swtchd sharply rt over 1f out: hanging and no hdwy after* **6/1**[3]

**8** 2 ¾ **Sotomayor** 2-9-2 0 DaneO'Neill 10 59
(Richard Hannon) *w'like: dwlt: in tch in rr: pushed along 3f out: no prog* **12/1**

05 **9** 2 **Colorado Dream**[17] 4218 2-9-2 0 (p) TrevorWhelan 4 53
(George Baker) *cmpt: disp ld to wl over 1f out: wknd qckly* **50/1**

1m 30.75s (3.15) **Going Correction** +0.25s/f (Good) **9 Ran SP% 112.8**
Speed ratings (Par 96): **92,91,90,89,87 86,85,82,80**
CSF £15.95 TOTE £2.70: £1.10, £2.40, £4.20; EX 19.30 Trifecta £167.30.
**Owner** H Moorhead, C Fahy & J Collins **Bred** M Phelan **Trained** Newmarket, Suffolk

**FOCUS**
Rain earlier in the day had not changed the official ground, all though the jockeys reported it was riding slow. The first division of a fair looking juvenile novice. They did not appear to go that fast early. The level will take time to settle.

## 4881 TOTESCOOP6 HERITAGE H'CAP 5f
**2:10** (2:16) (Class 2) 3-Y-O+
**£62,250** (£18,640; £9,320; £4,660; £2,330; £1,170) **Stalls** High

Form RPR

2-65 **1** **Danzeno**[21] 4072 6-9-10 **104** SilvestreDeSousa 15 114
(Michael Appleby) *dwlt: hld up in rr nr side: swtchd to outer of gp 1/2-way and prog sn after: rdn to ld over 1f out and hung lft: clr ins fnl f: eased last strides* **4/1**[1]

4034 **2** ¾ **Polybius**[21] 4072 6-9-8 **102** OisinMurphy 17 109+
(David Simcock) *lw: hld up in rr nr side: effrt whn nt clr run briefly over 1f out: gd prog after: r.o to take 2nd last 75yds: clsd on wnr but no threat* **7/1**[3]

0113 **3** 1 ½ **Pipers Note**[7] 4615 7-9-7 **101** JamesSullivan 12 103
(Ruth Carr) *pressed ldrs nr side: rdn whn carried lft over 1f out: chsd wnr fnl f but no imp: lost 2nd last 75yds* **16/1**

2-22 **4** shd **Lexington Abbey**[15] 4306 6-9-4 **98** (b) ShaneGray 14 100
(Kevin Ryan) *hld up in tch nr side: rdn whn sltly impeded over 1f out: styd on after but nvr pce to chal* **16/1**

6403 **5** 2 **Orion's Bow**[15] 4306 6-9-10 **104** BarryMcHugh 18 98
(Tim Easterby) *trckd overall ldr nr side: led 2f out to over 1f out: one pce after* **5/1**[2]

0620 **6** nse **Dougan**[13] 4411 5-8-9 **94** DavidEgan(5) 10 88
(David Evans) *lw: chsd ldrs in centre: rdn 2f out: kpt on wl fr over 1f out and did best of that gp but no ch* **25/1**

0420 **7** hd **Harry Hurricane**[21] 4072 5-9-6 **100** (b) TrevorWhelan 19 93
(George Baker) *hld up in tch nr side: rdn whn sltly impeded over 1f out: kpt on same pce* **14/1**

0-05 **8** 1 ¾ **Son Of Africa**[21] 4079 5-8-13 **93** DavidProbert 2 80
(Henry Candy) *s.s: wl in rr in centre: swtchd towards nr side 2f out: stl in rr over 1f out: kpt on fnl f* **22/1**

1456 **9** *shd* **Edward Lewis**[21] 4072 4-9-4 **101** .......... JoshDoyle(3) 6 88+
(David O'Meara) *hld up bhd ldrs in centre: gng wl 1/2-way: shkn up over 1f out and only one pce after* **7/1**[3]

6500 **10** *shd* **Naadirr (IRE)**[63] 2611 6-9-5 **99** .......... (v[1]) TimmyMurphy 9 85
(Kevin Ryan) *hld up in rr in centre: rdn 2f out: modest late prog: n.d* **28/1**

001- **11** *hd* **Green Door (IRE)**[387] 3573 6-9-6 **100** .......... (p) PatDobbs 11 86
(Robert Cowell) *led gp in centre but nt on terms: fdd over 1f out* **40/1**

-201 **12** *¾* **Doctor Sardonicus**[121] 1222 6-9-5 **99** .......... MartinHarley 8 82
(David Simcock) *prom in centre: rdn 2f out: fdd over 1f out* **40/1**

3-00 **13** *nk* **Squats (IRE)**[21] 4072 5-9-8 **102** .......... LiamJones 7 84
(William Haggas) *racd centre: nvr on terms w ldrs: no prog on wd outside over 1f out* **22/1**

1002 **14** *¾* **Royal Birth**[24] 3967 6-8-12 **95** .......... (t) AaronJones(3) 16 74
(Stuart Williams) *taken down early: chsd nr side ldrs tl wknd over 1f out* **8/1**

0410 **15** *4 ½* **Stepper Point**[28] 3829 8-8-12 **92** .......... (v) MartinDwyer 20 55
(William Muir) *lw: overall ldr nr side to 2f out: wkng whn hmpd over 1f out* **28/1**

1100 **16** *1 ½* **El Astronaute (IRE)**[28] 3829 4-8-12 **92** .......... JasonHart 4 50
(John Quinn) *racd centre: w ldrs over 3f out: sn wknd* **20/1**

2065 **17** *14* **Robot Boy (IRE)**[15] 4306 7-8-10 **95** .......... JoshuaBryan(5) 1 2
(David Barron) *restless bef stalls opened and completely missed break: allowed to complete in own time* **16/1**

1m 0.25s (-0.25) **Going Correction** +0.25s/f (Good)
**WFA** 3 from 4yo+ 5lb **17** Ran SP% **126.2**
Speed ratings (Par 109): **112,110,108,108,105 104,104,101,101,101 101,100,99,98,91 88,66**
CSF £28.28 CT £419.59 TOTE £4.70: £1.60, £2.20, £3.90, £3.40; EX 36.40 Trifecta £374.80.
**Owner** A M Wragg **Bred** Am Wragg **Trained** Oakham, Rutland
■ Lightscameraction was withdrawn. Price at time of withdrawal 25/1. Rule 4 does not apply.

**FOCUS**
A high-class and highly competitive sprint handicap that resulted in a comfortable victory for the top weight. As yesterday, those racing towards the stands' side dominated. The winner has been rated back to last year's form, with the third and fourth close to form.

## 4882 PLAYBOY CLUB LONDON H'CAP 1m 1f 212y
**2:40** (2:47) (Class 3) (0-95,97) 3-Y-0+ **£9,703** (£2,887; £1,443; £721) **Stalls** Low

Form RPR

11 **1** **Laraaib (IRE)**[50] 3042 3-9-4 **95** .......... DaneO'Neill 1 107+
(Owen Burrows) *lengthy: str: dwlt: sn trckd ldrs on inner: rdn and prog over 2f out: led over 1f out: sn clr: readily* **2/1**[1]

6421 **2** *2* **Banditry (IRE)**[15] 4316 5-9-13 **94** .......... SilvestreDeSousa 6 101
(Ian Williams) *lw: chsd ldng pair: drvn to cl over 2f out but wnr sn wnt past: styd on to take 2nd jst over 1f out: no threat* **9/2**[2]

1045 **3** *1 ¾* **Reaver (IRE)**[28] 3808 4-9-2 **83** .......... CharlesBishop 2 87
(Eve Johnson Houghton) *hld up in rr: rdn and prog over 2f out: styd on to take 3rd 1f out: nvr able to chal* **33/1**

6-20 **4** *nk* **Sinfonietta (FR)**[56] 2828 5-9-11 **92** .......... MartinLane 7 95
(David Menuisier) *swtg: wl in tch: rdn over 2f out: kpt on same pce fr over 1f out* **12/1**

16-1 **5** *1 ¼* **Angrywhitepyjamas (IRE)**[24] 3966 4-9-4 **85** .......... MartinDwyer 12 85
(William Muir) *sn chsd ldrs on outer fr wd draw: rdn wl over 2f out: nvr pce to chal but kpt on* **14/1**

600 **6** *½* **Repercussion**[51] 2999 4-9-10 **91** .......... DougieCostello 8 90
(Charlie Fellowes) *lw: trckd ldr: chal over 2f out: stl upsides over 1f out: wandered and nt qckn after: fdd fnl f* **20/1**

2-60 **7** *nk* **Saunter (FR)**[59] 2735 4-10-2 **97** .......... (p[1]) DavidProbert 4 96
(David Menuisier) *hld up in last pair: rdn over 2f out: hd at awkward angle and fnd little: kpt on fnl f but all too late* **10/1**[3]

3040 **8** *2* **Vettori Rules**[21] 4076 4-9-9 **90** .......... DanielMuscutt 3 85
(Gay Kelleway) *dwlt: hld up towards rr: rdn wl over 2f out: no prog and sn btn* **66/1**

30-1 **9** *3* **Nayel (IRE)**[26] 3905 5-9-9 **90** .......... (p) PatDobbs 5 79
(Richard Hannon) *led to over 1f out: wknd* **16/1**

3033 **10** *nk* **Mutarakez (IRE)**[8] 4585 5-9-0 **88** .......... JordanUys(7) 11 76
(Brian Meehan) *hld up in last pair: rdn wl over 2f out: no prog* **12/1**

-122 **11** *1 ½* **Burguillos**[29] 3790 4-10-0 **95** .......... MartinHarley 10 80
(Alan King) *hld up towards rr: tried to make prog on outer 1/2-way: no hdwy over 2f out: wknd over 1f out* **9/2**[2]

2m 11.11s (3.71) **Going Correction** +0.50s/f (Yiel)
**WFA** 3 from 4yo+ 10lb **11** Ran SP% **115.9**
Speed ratings (Par 107): **105,103,102,101,100 100,100,98,96,95 94**
CSF £10.08 CT £221.90 TOTE £2.50: £1.40, £1.70, £8.40; EX 11.10 Trifecta £332.40.
**Owner** Hamdan Al Maktoum **Bred** Shadwell Estate Company Limited **Trained** Lambourn, Berks
■ Pensax Boy was withdrawn. Price at time of withdrawal 25/1. Rule 4 does not apply.

**FOCUS**
Add 15yds. A good handicap but a decisive winner who could be a Group horse in the making. It's been rated around the second, third and fourth.

## 4883 TRANT ENGINEERING FILLIES' H'CAP 1m (S)
**3:15** (3:17) (Class 3) (0-90,90) 3-Y-0+ **£12,938** (£3,850; £1,924; £962) **Stalls** High

Form RPR

-331 **1** **Mittens**[14] 4366 3-9-2 **87** .......... DavidProbert 4 100+
(Sir Michael Stoute) *hld up in 5th: smooth prog over 2f out: pushed into the ld jst over 1f out: sn clr: v comf* **3/1**[1]

0-00 **2** *3 ¼* **Havre De Paix (FR)**[58] 2767 5-10-0 **90** .......... MartinLane 3 94
(David Menuisier) *led: rdn over 2f out: hdd jst over 1f out: no ch w wnr but hld on for 2nd* **20/1**

5121 **3** *¾* **Helfire**[23] 4010 4-8-10 **75** .......... CharlieBennett(3) 8 77+
(Hughie Morrison) *hld up in rr: shkn up over 2f out: prog over 1f out: r.o to take 3rd last 150yds: nvr nrr* **9/1**

312 **4** *4* **Tirania**[29] 3786 3-9-2 **87** .......... MartinHarley 5 78
(William Haggas) *athletic: lw: prom: wnt 2nd over 2f out and pressed ldr to over 1f out: wknd* **7/2**[2]

2614 **5** *1 ½* **Pattie**[10] 4491 3-8-8 **79** .......... SilvestreDeSousa 1 67
(Mick Channon) *hld up in rr: rdn over 2f out: tried to make prog on outer over 1f out: no hdwy after* **9/2**[3]

4363 **6** *2 ¼* **Yeah Baby Yeah (IRE)**[14] 4375 4-9-8 **84** .......... (p) MartinDwyer 6 68
(Gay Kelleway) *plld hrd: hld up towards rr: shkn up 2f out: no real prog* **16/1**

40 **7** *½* **Alexandrakollontai (IRE)**[11] 4475 7-9-0 **76** .......... (b) JamesSullivan 10 59
(Alistair Whillans) *nvr bttr than midfield: dropped to rr u.p 2f out: no ch after* **20/1**

0412 **8** *½* **Patching**[19] 4144 3-7-9 **71** oh3 .......... (v) DavidEgan(5) 9 51
(Giles Bravery) *pressed ldr: drvn and little rspnse wl over 2f out: sn lost pl and btn* **12/1**

24-3 **9** *¾* **Soldier's Girl (IRE)**[73] 2287 3-9-0 **85** .......... PatDobbs 7 63
(Richard Hannon) *dwlt and sltly awkward s: hld up in last pair: shkn up and no prog over 2f out* **15/2**

0021 **10** *¾* **Luna Bear**[22] 4050 3-8-2 **76** .......... NoelGarbutt(3) 2 53
(Gary Moore) *t.k.h: trckd ldrs: rdn wl over 2f out: wknd qckly over 1f out* **14/1**

1m 41.39s (0.59) **Going Correction** +0.25s/f (Good)
**WFA** 3 from 4yo+ 9lb **10** Ran SP% **116.9**
Speed ratings (Par 104): **107,103,103,99,97 95,94,94,93,92**
CSF £65.15 CT £490.26 TOTE £3.00: £1.50, £5.80, £3.10; EX 72.20 Trifecta £803.40.
**Owner** K Abdullah **Bred** Juddmonte Farms Ltd **Trained** Newmarket, Suffolk

**FOCUS**
This competitive fillies' handicap on paper was won in fine style by a progressive sort who looks up to Listed class at least. The level is hard to set.

## 4884 FRED COWLEY MBE MEMORIAL SUMMER MILE STKS (GROUP 2) 7f 213y(R)
**3:50** (3:53) (Class 1) 4-Y-0+
**£73,723** (£27,950; £13,988; £6,968; £3,497; £1,755) **Stalls** Low

Form RPR

3-52 **1** **Mutakayyef**[25] 3924 6-9-1 **120** .......... DaneO'Neill 3 121+
(William Haggas) *hld up: prog over 3f out: chsd clr ldr 2f out: clsd over 1f out: rdn to ld last 150yds: styd on wl and sn clr: dismntd after fin* **4/7**[1]

-525 **2** *3* **Kaspersky (IRE)**[25] 3924 6-9-1 **111** .......... MartinHarley 6 114
(Jane Chapple-Hyam) *led: drew 4 l clr over 3f out: rdn over 1f out: hdd and outpcd last 150yds* **14/1**

/10- **3** *1 ¼* **Hathal (USA)**[273] 7352 5-9-1 **112** .......... SilvestreDeSousa 4 111
(William Haggas) *trapped out wd: in tch: rdn over 2f out: kpt on to take 3rd over 1f out: no threat* **13/2**[3]

2424 **4** *1* **Gabrial (IRE)**[28] 3843 8-9-1 **111** .......... BarryMcHugh 5 109
(Richard Fahey) *dwlt: hld up in last pair: shkn up 2f out: prog over 1f out: tk 4th fnl f and kpt on but n.d* **20/1**

3111 **5** *2 ¾* **Sovereign Debt (IRE)**[42] 3320 8-9-4 **117** .......... JamesSullivan 7 106
(Ruth Carr) *hld up in last pair: shkn up and effrt on wd outside over 2f out: no imp ldrs over 1f out: fdd* **5/1**[2]

-325 **6** *3 ¾* **Firmament**[30] 3765 5-9-1 **109** .......... OisinMurphy 2 94
(David O'Meara) *trckd ldr to 2f out: sn wknd u.p* **12/1**

3165 **7** *3* **Zalamea (IRE)**[27] 3880 4-9-1 **102** .......... EddyHardouin 1 87
(Carina Fey, France) *w'like: mostly trckd ldng pair to over 2f out: fnd nil and wknd qckly* **50/1**

1m 41.6s (0.90) **Going Correction** +0.50s/f (Yiel) **7** Ran SP% **114.7**
Speed ratings (Par 115): **115,112,110,109,107 103,100**
CSF £10.82 TOTE £1.40: £1.10, £5.50; EX 10.60 Trifecta £43.10.
**Owner** Hamdan Al Maktoum **Bred** Cheveley Park Stud Ltd **Trained** Newmarket, Suffolk

**FOCUS**
Add 11yds. The feature race and a good class renewal of this mile Group 2. There was no obvious early pace but the winner proved his class. The runner-up has been rated to his best.

## 4885 RUDDY NOVICE AUCTION STKS (PLUS 10 RACE) (DIV II) 7f
**4:25** (4:26) (Class 4) 2-Y-0 **£6,469** (£1,925; £962; £481) **Stalls** High

Form RPR

**1** **Tigre Du Terre (FR)** 2-9-2 **0** .......... MartinHarley 9 91+
(Richard Hannon) *athletic: lw: hld up in last: quick prog jst over 2f out to ld over 1f out and racd nrest the rail: shkn up and sn drew clr: impressive debut* **14/1**

0 **2** *4 ½* **Cuban Heel**[30] 3747 2-9-2 **0** .......... DaneO'Neill 4 77
(Clive Cox) *athletic: slowly away and rn green early: sn in tch: prog on outer over 2f out: rdn to chal over 1f out: chsd wnr after: kpt on but no ch* **9/1**

**3** *2 ½* **Laugh A Minute** 2-9-2 **0** .......... SilvestreDeSousa 10 70
(Roger Varian) *tall: lw: hld up in tch: shkn up and prog 2f out: styd on to take 3rd last 100yds: no ch w wnr* **15/8**[1]

1 **4** *shd* **Christopher Wood (IRE)**[17] 4218 2-9-8 **0** .......... PatDobbs 3 76
(Ralph Beckett) *str: lw: led: rdn and hdd over 1f out: outpcd after* **9/4**[2]

03 **5** *1 ½* **Champs De Reves**[11] 4465 2-9-2 **0** .......... MartinDwyer 8 66
(Marcus Tregoning) *w'like: pressed ldr to over 2f out: shkn up and outpcd after* **13/2**[3]

5 **6** *shd* **Galactic (IRE)**[8] 4577 2-9-2 **0** .......... TimmyMurphy 7 66
(Richard Hannon) *cmpt: wl in tch in midfield: shkn up over 2f out: lft bhd over 1f out* **20/1**

**7** *¾* **Protected Guest** 2-9-2 **0** .......... DanielMuscutt 5 64
(George Margarson) *unf: scope: lw: slowly away and rn green in last pair: shkn up over 2f out: no prog* **33/1**

**8** *2 ½* **Freebe Rocks (IRE)** 2-9-2 **0** .......... DannyBrock 6 57
(Michael Bell) *cmpt: in tch in rr to 2f out: sn wknd* **14/1**

0 **9** *½* **Mr Large (IRE)**[11] 4465 2-9-2 **0** .......... DougieCostello 2 56
(Jamie Osborne) *leggy: prom: tk 2nd over 2f out: upsides ldr to over 1f out: wknd rapidly* **20/1**

1m 30.04s (2.44) **Going Correction** +0.25s/f (Good) **9** Ran SP% **114.7**
Speed ratings (Par 96): **96,90,88,87,86 86,85,82,81**
CSF £127.07 TOTE £14.00: £3.10, £2.50, £1.10; EX 136.10 Trifecta £642.50.
**Owner** Middleham Park Racing Cl **Bred** Erwan Le Pivert & Mme Annie Le Pivert **Trained** East Everleigh, Wilts

**FOCUS**
The second leg of this juvenile novice was run 0.71 secs faster than the first division. A surprise but quite impressive winner.

## 4886 WOODFORD RESERVE H'CAP 1m 3f 211y
**5:00** (5:02) (Class 2) (0-105,93) 3-Y-0
**£31,125** (£9,320; £4,660; £2,330; £1,165; £585) **Stalls** Low

Form RPR

1340 **1** **Bin Battuta**[23] 3998 3-9-7 **93** .......... (p[1]) MartinLane 6 105+
(Saeed bin Suroor) *hld up in last pair: rapid prog on outer over 2f out: edgd rt and jnd ldr over 1f out: hrd rdn to take narrow ld 150yds out: hld on* **7/2**[2]

6411 **2** *hd* **Cape Coast**[5] 4691 3-9-0 **86** 6ex .......... SilvestreDeSousa 8 97+
(Mark Johnston) *lw: led: drvn for home over 2f out: hung rt and lft over 1f out and sn jnd: narrowly hdd 150yds out: battled on wl but jst hld* **11/4**[1]

0331 **3** *1 ½* **Galactic Prince**[29] 3779 3-8-6 **78** .......... MartinDwyer 7 86
(Andrew Balding) *lw: t.k.h early: hld up in midfield: rdn and prog over 2f out: chsd ldng pair over 1f out: styd on wl but nvr able to chal* **8/1**

4-12 **4** *2 ¾* **Alfarris (FR)**[51] 2998 3-8-12 **84** .......... DaneO'Neill 9 88
(William Haggas) *hld up towards rr: rdn and prog over 2f out: chsd ldng trio over 1f out: kpt on same pce* **12/1**

1313 **5** 3 ¾ **Euro Nightmare (IRE)**[12] 4431 3-9-1 87........ JasonHart 11 85
(Keith Dalgleish) *pressed ldr: drvn over 2f out: lost 2nd and sltly impeded over 1f out: wknd* **12/1**

-132 **6** 1 **Melting Dew**[9] 4535 3-8-13 85........(v) DavidProbert 3 81
(Sir Michael Stoute) *s.i.s and rousted to get gng: mostly in last pair: rdn and no great prog over 2f out* **7/1**[3]

0161 **7** 1 **Mister Blue Sky (IRE)**[13] 4408 3-8-3 80........ MitchGodwin(5) 5 75
(Sylvester Kirk) *t.k.h early: trckd ldrs: rdn over 2f out: sn wknd* **20/1**

6230 **8** ½ **Bear Valley (IRE)**[14] 4376 3-9-5 91........ JFEgan 1 85
(Mark Johnston) *trckd ldng pair: rdn over 2f out: wknd over 1f out* **14/1**

3042 **9** nk **Society Red**[14] 4376 3-8-9 81........ JamesSullivan 10 75
(Richard Fahey) *t.k.h: trckd ldrs and trapped out wd: rdn and wknd 2f out* **14/1**

2m 35.99s (3.49) **Going Correction** +0.50s/f (Yiel) 9 Ran SP% **106.0**
Speed ratings (Par 106): **108,107,106,105,102 101,101,100,100**
CSF £11.40 CT £50.83 TOTE £3.70: £1.60, £1.50, £2.20; EX 11.90 Trifecta £99.80.
**Owner** Godolphin **Bred** Darley **Trained** Newmarket, Suffolk
■ Special Relation was withdrawn. Price at time of withdrawal 15/2. Rule 4 applies to all bets - deduction 10p in the pound.

**FOCUS**
Add 15yds. Another competitive 3yo handicap in which they went a reasonable gallop and the market leaders had it between them in the last furlong. This is form to take a positive view about.

## 4887 GL EVENTS UK H'CAP — 7f
**5:35** (5:36) (Class 4) (0-85,83) 3-Y-O+ **£8,086** (£1,804; £1,804; £601) **Stalls** High

Form RPR

0060 **1** **Cricklewood Green (USA)**[16] 4254 6-9-1 75........ MitchGodwin(5) 16 83
(Sylvester Kirk) *hld up: last tl prog over 2f out: weaved through jst over 1f out and drvn to chal ins fnl f: r.o to ld last 50yds* **8/1**[3]

2-53 **2** ½ **My Dad Syd (USA)**[28] 3847 5-9-6 75........(v) SilvestreDeSousa 9 82
(Ian Williams) *hld up in midfield gng wl: prog to chal 1f out: styd on but jst outpcd nr fin* **7/2**[1]

-104 **2** dht **Esprit De Corps**[33] 3664 3-9-3 80........ MartinHarley 6 84
(Roger Charlton) *lw: dwlt: hld up in rr: gd prog on wd outside over 2f out: rdn to ld 1f out: styd on but hdd last 50yds* **5/1**[2]

245 **4** 4 **Haraz (IRE)**[14] 4332 4-9-2 74........(b) JoshDoyle(3) 8 70
(David O'Meara) *t.k.h: hld up bhd ldrs: stl gng wl 2f out: shkn up and fnd nil over 1f out: one pce after* **16/1**

240- **5** shd **Titan Goddess**[226] 8178 5-9-4 73........ AntonioFresu 1 69
(Mike Murphy) *hld up in rr: rdn and struggling over 2f out: kpt on fr over 1f out on outer: nvr nrr* **33/1**

-604 **6** 1 **Madrinho (IRE)**[18] 4168 4-9-6 75........ BarryMcHugh 15 68
(Tony Coyle) *pressed ldr: led 2f out: edgd lft over 1f out: sn hdd & wknd* **9/1**

6045 **7** ½ **Fieldsman (USA)**[40] 3388 5-9-10 82........ ShelleyBirkett(3) 13 74
(David O'Meara) *hld up towards rr: shkn up 2f out: no real prog over 1f out: plugged on* **20/1**

265 **8** ½ **Until Midnight (IRE)**[31] 3723 7-8-9 67........(b[1]) AaronJones(3) 11 57
(Eugene Stanford) *wl plcd bhd ldrs: pushed along 2f out: edgd lft over 1f out and wknd sn after* **25/1**

-400 **9** nk **Mullionheir**[30] 3750 5-9-13 82........ MartinDwyer 3 71
(John Best) *lw: pressed ldr to 2f out: wknd over 1f out* **14/1**

22-1 **10** hd **Saluti (IRE)**[16] 4269 3-8-13 79........ GeorgeWood(3) 12 65+
(Amanda Perrett) *hld up in midfield: pushed along 2f out: trying to make prog against rail whn hmpd over 1f out: no ch after* **7/2**[1]

0000 **11** 2 **Outer Space**[15] 4293 6-9-13 82........ DougieCostello 14 70+
(Jamie Osborne) *hld up in rr: pushed along 2f out: no threat whn nt clr run on inner jst over 1f out and swtchd rt: no hdwy after* **25/1**

-026 **12** 4 **Little Miss Kodi (IRE)**[43] 3287 4-9-1 77........ TobyEley(7) 5 50
(Daniel Mark Loughnane) *led to 2f out: wknd qckly* **33/1**

3024 **13** ¼ **Inner Circle (IRE)**[27] 3862 3-9-1 78........ TimmyMurphy 7 47
(Richard Hannon) *prom to 2f out: wknd* **11/1**

63-0 **14** 116 **Anfaass (IRE)**[21] 4100 3-9-3 80........ JFEgan 2
(George Margarson) *plld hrd: hld up: lost action over 2f out and virtually p.u after* **20/1**

1m 28.51s (0.91) **Going Correction** +0.25s/f (Good)
**WFA** 3 from 4yo+ 8lb 14 Ran SP% **126.2**
Speed ratings (Par 105): **104,103,103,98,98 97,97,96,96,95 93,89,88,**
WIN: 9.80 Cricklewood Green; PL: 1.70 My Dad Syd, 2.70 Cricklewood Green, 2.20 Esprit De Corps; EX: 20.20, 34.00; CSF: 17.25, 22.81; TC: 82.65, 87.76; TF: 273.40, 354.50;.
**Owner** Chris Wright & Andy MacDonald **Bred** Stratford Place Stud **Trained** Upper Lambourn, Berks
■ Stewards' Enquiry : Barry McHugh 3 day ban - guilty of careless riding in that he allowed his mount to drift left-handed towards the rail without sufficient correction (30-31 Jul/4 Aug)

**FOCUS**
This competitive handicap was run over a second and a half faster than the quicker of the earlier juvenile maidens. The third has been rated to his best.
T/Plt: £28.30 to a £1 stake. Pool: £119,613.98 - 3,079.42 winning units T/Qpdt: £7.30 to a £1 stake. Pool: £7,246.22 - 732.72 winning units **Jonathan Neesom**

# 4332 CHESTER (L-H)
Saturday, July 15

**OFFICIAL GOING: Good (6.9)**
Wind: Moderate, half against in straight of over 1f Weather: Overcast

## 4888 STELLA ARTOIS/EBF STALLIONS NOVICE STKS (PLUS 10 RACE) — 5f 15y
**1:50** (1:50) (Class 4) 2-Y-O
**£6,225** (£1,864; £932; £466; £233; £117) **Stalls** Low

Form RPR

20 **1** **Gift In Time (IRE)**[23] 3993 2-9-2 0........ AdamBeschizza 8 80
(James Given) *rn green and towards rr: hdwy whn hung rt 3f out: rdn w work to do wl over 1f out: sn edgd lft: chsng ldrs and proging whn nt clr run and swtchd rt ins fnl f: r.o to ld nr fin* **4/1**

**2** nk **Ginbar (IRE)** 2-9-2 0........ FranBerry 1 79
(Tom Dascombe) *chsd ldrs: rdn and rn green over 1f out: r.o to ld ins fnl f: hdd nr fin* **7/2**[3]

6332 **3** 1 ¾ **Palmer (IRE)**[12] 4427 2-9-2 76........(p[1]) ConnorBeasley 3 73
(Bryan Smart) *disp ld: rdn and edgd lft over 1f out: sn def advantage: hdd ins fnl f: no ex fnl 75yds* **11/4**[2]

12 **4** 3 **Jasi (IRE)**[73] 2299 2-9-8 0........ PhillipMakin 2 68
(Richard Fahey) *disp ld: rdn whn bmpd over 1f out: sn hdd: no ex and fdd fnl 150yds* **5/2**[1]

45 **5** 1 **W G Grace (IRE)**[34] 3622 2-9-2 0........ FrannyNorton 4 59
(Mark Johnston) *towards rr: sn pushed along and outpcd: styd on ins fnl f: nvr gng pce to threaten* **17/2**

**6** 1 ½ **Go Sandy** 2-8-6 0........ JaneElliott(5) 5 48
(Lisa Williamson) *chsd ldrs: pushed along and lost pl 3f out: no imp after* **66/1**

**7** 13 **Graphite Girl (IRE)** 2-8-11 0........ RobHornby 6 1
(Tim Easterby) *dwlt: a outpcd and wl bhd* **20/1**

1m 2.35s (1.35) **Going Correction** +0.30s/f (Good) 7 Ran SP% **114.2**
Speed ratings (Par 96): **101,100,97,92,91 88,68**
CSF £18.33 TOTE £5.00: £2.20, £2.00; EX 20.90 Trifecta £44.10.
**Owner** The Cool Silk Partnership **Bred** Miss S Tolerton **Trained** Willoughton, Lincs

**FOCUS**
The rail between the 6f and 1.5f point had been moved out by 9 yards. It meant this actual race distance was 5f 45yds (+30yds). Probably a fair novice event to start the meeting off with. The third has been rated to his pre-race mark.

## 4889 MBNA MAKE GOOD STUFF HAPPEN FILLIES' H'CAP — 6f 17y
**2:25** (2:26) (Class 2) (0-100,93) 3-Y-O+
**£15,562** (£4,660; £2,330; £1,165; £582; £292) **Stalls** Low

Form RPR

-602 **1** **The Wagon Wheel (IRE)**[28] 3844 3-8-11 90........(b) ConnorMurtagh(7) 9 102
(Richard Fahey) *hld up in tch: hdwy on outer 3f out: rdn over 1f out: sn hung rt and led: ended on stands' rail: r.o wl and drew clr fnl 100yds* **10/1**

0-14 **2** 3 **Avon Breeze**[4] 4719 8-9-0 85........ CallumRodriguez(5) 6 88
(Richard Whitaker) *in tch: pushed along 2f out: nt clr run over 1f out: sn in clr and effrt: ev ch ins fnl f: nt pce of wnr fnl 100yds* **7/1**

-014 **3** ¾ **Turanga Leela**[29] 3793 3-8-12 84........(v) RyanPowell 1 84
(Ian Williams) *led: rdn over 1f out: sn hdd: styd on same pce fnl 100yds* **5/1**[3]

6131 **4** ½ **Rose Berry**[26] 3904 3-8-13 85........(h) AdamBeschizza 2 83
(Chris Dwyer) *chsd ldrs: effrt over 1f out: sn edgd sltly rt and ev ch: tail flashed for press: kpt on ins fnl f: no ex fnl 100yds* **9/2**[2]

4142 **5** nk **Southern Belle (IRE)**[29] 3793 4-9-13 93........ PhillipMakin 7 93+
(Robert Cowell) *missed break: racd keenly: hld up: nt clr run over 1f out: hdwy sn after: styng on whn nt clr run and snatched up ins fnl f: sn swtchd rt: kpt on towards fin but no ch* **8/1**

20-0 **6** 1 ¾ **Clear Water (IRE)**[22] 4051 4-9-8 88........ ConnorBeasley 8 80
(Michael Wigham) *missed break: in rr: nt clr run over 1f out: sn rdn: styng on whn nt clr run ins fnl f: nvr able to threaten* **33/1**

4431 **7** 2 **Pixeleen**[17] 4201 5-9-12 92........ FranBerry 4 78
(Malcolm Saunders) *chsd ldrs: rdn ent fnl 2f: one pce over 1f out: no imp after* **4/1**[1]

5155 **8** 3 ¼ **Queen In Waiting (IRE)**[8] 4581 3-9-5 91........ FrannyNorton 3 66
(Mark Johnston) *w ldr: ev ch 2f out: sn rdn: sn lost pl: wknd fnl 150yds: sn eased* **4/1**[1]

0-04 **9** 1 ½ **Hope Solo (IRE)**[12] 4435 3-8-13 85........ RobHornby 5 55
(Tim Easterby) *towards rr: outpcd wl over 1f out: nvr a threat* **20/1**

1m 14.92s (1.12) **Going Correction** +0.30s/f (Good)
**WFA** 3 from 4yo+ 6lb 9 Ran SP% **115.3**
Speed ratings (Par 96): **104,100,99,98,97 95,92,88,86**
CSF £77.68 CT £396.89 TOTE £12.60: £2.90, £2.00, £2.40; EX 92.10 Trifecta £567.80.
**Owner** T Proctor **Bred** Rathbarry Stud & Abbeylands Farm **Trained** Musley Bank, N Yorks

**FOCUS**
The rail between the 6f and 1.5f point had been moved out by 9 yards. It meant this actual race distance was 6f 54yds (+37yds). This had a strong look to it but the easy winner, drawn widest, ended up making her run down the stands' side, which makes the form a little hard to assess considering all her rivals finished more towards the inside. The runner-up has been rated close to her recent form, with the third to form.

## 4890 SPORTINGBET CITY PLATE STKS (LISTED RACE) — 7f 1y
**3:00** (3:03) (Class 1) 3-Y-O+
**£22,684** (£8,600; £4,304; £2,144; £1,076; £540) **Stalls** Low

Form RPR

4461 **1** **Viscount Barfield**[28] 3842 4-9-2 94........(h) RobHornby 9 109
(Andrew Balding) *hld up: nudged along 4f out: pushed along and hdwy over 2f out: r.o to ld ent fnl f: hld on gamely nr fin* **20/1**

1402 **2** hd **Jungle Cat (IRE)**[14] 4362 5-9-2 113........(b[1]) FrannyNorton 5 108
(Charlie Appleby) *trckd ldrs: wnt 2nd over 3f out: lost 2nd whn rdn and unable qck over 1f out: regained 2nd ins fnl f: rallied and rn towards fin: jst hld* **11/10**[1]

-320 **3** 2 ¼ **Jallota**[25] 3924 6-9-2 112........ FranBerry 2 102
(Charles Hills) *midfield: racd keenly and hdwy 3f out: chsd ldrs 2f out: unable qck over 1f out: wanted to lug lft and kpt on u.p ins fnl f: no imp on front two fnl 100yds* **10/3**[2]

**4** ¾ **Orangey Red (IRE)**[29] 3796 4-8-11 86........ JohnFahy 8 95
(W T Farrell, Ire) *in rr: rdn 2f out: hdwy whn nt clr run and swtchd rt over 1f out: swtchd lft whn proging 1f out: styd on tl one pce fnl 75yds* **33/1**

1343 **5** 1 ¾ **Salateen**[28] 3842 5-9-5 105........ PhillipMakin 10 98
(David O'Meara) *w ldr: led 5f out: rdn over 1f out: hdd ent fnl f: no ex fnl 150yds* **12/1**

1040 **6** 2 **Kool Kompany (IRE)**[25] 3924 5-9-5 112........ SteveDrowne 4 93
(Richard Hannon) *racd keenly in midfield: niggled along and lost pl 4f out: rdn and outpcd 2f out: tried to keep on 1f out: no imp and one pce after* **7/1**[3]

15-0 **7** 6 **Breakable**[79] 2115 6-8-11 95........ NeilFarley 3 69
(Tim Easterby) *trckd ldrs: rdn 2f out: wknd 1f out* **28/1**

-010 **8** 2 ½ **Sound Advice**[49] 3064 8-9-2 103........ ConnorBeasley 6 67
(Keith Dalgleish) *racd on outer in midfield: sme hdwy over 3f out: nvr able to chal: rdn over 2f out: wknd over 1f out* **20/1**

3-0 **9** 39 **Hillbilly Boy (IRE)**[64] 2568 7-9-2 105........ AdamBeschizza 7
(Tom Dascombe) *led: hdd 5f out: lost 2nd over 3f out: wknd qckly wl over 2f out: sn lft bhd* **9/1**

-300 **R** **Canny Kool**[14] 4353 5-9-2 92........ BenRobinson 1
(Brian Ellison) *ref to r: tk no part* **66/1**

1m 26.37s (-0.13) **Going Correction** +0.30s/f (Good) 10 Ran SP% **118.3**
Speed ratings (Par 111): **112,111,109,108,106 104,97,94,49,**
CSF £41.52 TOTE £25.90: £4.80, £1.10, £1.60; EX 63.40 Trifecta £298.60.
**Owner** David Brownlow **Bred** Rockwell Bloodstock **Trained** Kingsclere, Hants
■ Stewards' Enquiry : Franny Norton two-day ban: used whip above the permitted level (Jul 30-31)

**FOCUS**
The rail between the 6f and 1.5f point had been moved out by 9 yards. It meant this actual race distance was 7f 38yds (+37yds). A really good renewal of this race, with the first two in the betting alone holding solid form for this level and above, but it produced a surprise winner. The level is fluid.

## 4891 MANOR CAR HIRE H'CAP — 1m 6f 87y

**3:35** (3:36) (Class 3) (0-90,87) 3-Y-O

**£15,562** (£4,660; £2,330; £1,165; £582; £292) **Stalls** Low

Form RPR

-421 **1** **Hochfeld (IRE)**[14] 4336 3-9-4 **84** FrannyNorton 2 98
(Mark Johnston) *mde all: lugged out to the rt on bnd wl over 7f out: rdn over 1f out: qcknd clr ins fnl f: r.o strly* **13/8**[1]

2523 **2** *8* **Look My Way**[7] 4612 3-8-11 **77** RobHornby 5 80
(Andrew Balding) *chsd ldrs: rdn over 3f out: outpcd over 2f out: hung lft u.p over 1f out: kpt on ins fnl f: tk 2nd nr fin: no ch w wnr* **9/2**

-654 **3** *nk* **Mister Belvedere**[12] 4429 3-9-1 **86** CallumRodriguez(5) 1 89
(Michael Dods) *racd in 2nd pl: rdn over 2f out: unable qck over 1f out: unable to go w wnr and no ch ins fnl f: lost 2nd nr fin* **4/1**[3]

2131 **4** *2½* **Here And Now**[66] 2526 3-9-7 **87** PhillipMakin 6 86
(Ralph Beckett) *slowly away: hld up: pushed along and outpcd over 2f out: kpt on modly ins fnl f: nvr a threat* **5/2**[2]

1-03 **5** *1½* **Quinteo (IRE)**[12] 4450 3-8-11 **77** (b) AdamBeschizza 4 74
(Jo Hughes) *chsd ldrs: rdn 3f out: outpcd over 2f out: wl hld over 1f out* **28/1**

2203 **6** *16* **Tread Lightly**[16] 4247 3-8-2 **68** PaulQuinn 3 43
(Tim Easterby) *stdd s: hld up in rr: pushed along 4f out: lft bhd 3f out* **25/1**

3m 11.37s (4.37) **Going Correction** +0.30s/f (Good) 6 Ran SP% **112.1**
Speed ratings (Par 104): **99,94,94,92,91 82**
CSF £9.42 TOTE £2.20: £1.60, £3.20; EX 8.50 Trifecta £22.90.
**Owner** Sheikh Hamdan bin Mohammed Al Maktoum **Bred** Kenilworth House Stud **Trained** Middleham Moor, N Yorks

**FOCUS**
The rail between the 6f and 1.5f point had been moved out by 9 yards. It meant this actual race distance was 1m 6f 157yds (+70yds). With only one of these having run over the trip before, this was a step into the unknown for the majority of the field, although one got the impression the winner made his life much easier by dictating fractions to suit throughout. The time was pretty slow. The runner-up has been rated to his previous effort.

## 4892 WEST WAY NISSAN H'CAP — 6f 17y

**4:10** (4:13) (Class 4) (0-80,80) 3-Y-O

**£6,225** (£1,864; £932; £466; £233; £117) **Stalls** Low

Form RPR

4022 **1** **Boundsy (IRE)**[12] 4433 3-8-10 **76** ConnorMurtagh(7) 8 81
(Richard Fahey) *in tch: rdn over 1f out: r.o ins fnl f: led towards fin* **5/1**[3]

1510 **2** *nk* **Love Oasis**[12] 4435 3-9-4 **77** FrannyNorton 2 81
(Mark Johnston) *w ldr: rdn over 1f out: str chal ins fnl f: r.o: hld nr fin* **9/2**[2]

0002 **3** *hd* **The Amber Fort (USA)**[12] 4447 3-8-10 **69** JohnFahy 1 72
(David O'Meara) *led: rdn over 1f out: hdd narrowly wl ins fnl f: hld towards fin* **7/1**

0436 **4** *nk* **Kamra (USA)**[10] 4500 3-9-1 **74** (t[1]) AdamBeschizza 3 76
(Michael Herrington) *trckd ldrs: effrt on inner over 1f out: r.o to ld briefly wl ins fnl f: no ex nr fin* **11/1**

2-10 **5** *¾* **Tallinski (IRE)**[35] 3579 3-9-0 **78** BenRobinson(5) 9 78
(Brian Ellison) *trckd ldrs: rdn and unable qck over 1f out: styd on for press ins fnl f: nt pce of front quartet* **25/1**

3522 **6** *2¾* **Pepita (IRE)**[15] 4315 3-9-7 **80** SteveDrowne 7 71
(Richard Hannon) *midfield: kpt on u.p ins fnl f: no imp on ldrs* **10/1**

2400 **7** *¾* **Lambrini Legacy**[8] 4576 3-7-11 **61** oh6 (h) JaneElliott(5) 10 49
(Lisa Williamson) *racd keenly in tch: rdn over 1f out: kpt on same pce ins fnl f* **66/1**

-021 **8** *1* **Parys Mountain (IRE)**[24] 3974 3-9-6 **79** (h) FranBerry 6 64
(David Brown) *hld up: nt clr run 2f out: kpt on ins fnl f: nvr able to trble ldrs* **6/1**

2031 **9** *½* **Comprise**[10] 4500 3-9-4 **77** PhillipMakin 5 61
(Michael Bell) *midfield: rdn over 1f out: sn outpcd* **11/4**[1]

33-0 **10** *8* **Captain Sue (IRE)**[99] 1601 3-8-7 **66** RyanPowell 4 24
(Ian Williams) *in rr: outpcd 3f out: nvr able to get on terms* **25/1**

6033 **11** *shd* **Monks Stand (USA)**[14] 4342 3-9-3 **76** (p) RobHornby 12 34
(Tim Easterby) *midfield tl rdn and wknd over 1f out* **33/1**

43-5 **12** *6* **Somewhere Secret**[14] 4342 3-9-2 **75** NeilFarley 11 13
(Michael Mullineaux) *s.s: towards rr: hung bdly lft over 2f out: heavily eased over 1f out and bhd* **40/1**

1m 15.87s (2.07) **Going Correction** +0.30s/f (Good) 12 Ran SP% **120.3**
Speed ratings (Par 102): **98,97,97,96,95 92,91,89,89,78 78,70**
CSF £26.87 CT £164.33 TOTE £6.00: £2.00, £1.80, £2.30; EX 32.70 Trifecta £211.20.
**Owner** Kevin Mercer & Partner **Bred** Glenview House Stud **Trained** Musley Bank, N Yorks

**FOCUS**
The rail between the 6f and 1.5f point had been moved out by 9 yards. It meant this actual race distance was 6f 54yds (+37yds). A fair handicap. The second and third have been rated to their recent form.

## 4893 CSP AUDIO VISUAL H'CAP — 1m 2f 70y

**4:40** (4:42) (Class 4) (0-80,82) 4-Y-O+

**£6,225** (£1,864; £932; £466; £233; £117) **Stalls** High

Form RPR

000 **1** **Storm King**[9] 4522 8-9-10 **82** SteveDrowne 11 89
(David C Griffiths) *chsd ldrs: chalng 3 wd 3f out: led jst over 2f out: rdn whn jnd over 1f out: gamely fnd ex towards fin* **12/1**

0210 **2** *¾* **Theos Lolly (IRE)**[14] 4357 4-9-0 **79** ConnorMurtagh(7) 7 85
(Richard Fahey) *hld up: hdwy 4f out: rdn over 2f out: moved upsides and str chal over 1f out: no ex towards fin* **16/1**

5001 **3** *1½* **Age Of Elegance (IRE)**[26] 3910 5-8-11 **76** (p) CameronNoble(7) 8 79
(Roger Fell) *squeezed out s: hld up: hdwy over 3f out: chsd ldrs 2f out: edgd lft wl ins fnl f: nt pce to chal front two* **14/1**

-001 **4** *2½* **Cornborough**[29] 3153 6-8-10 **73** (p) CallumRodriguez(5) 4 71+
(Mark Walford) *midfield: lost pl whn waiting for run fr 2f out: nt clr run tl rdn and hdwy over 1f out: styd on ins fnl f: gng on at fin* **4/1**[2]

6352 **5** *1* **Save The Bees**[18] 4170 9-8-13 **78** GerO'Neill(7) 6 74
(Declan Carroll) *racd keenly in tch: rdn 2f out: kpt on same pce fr over 1f out* **5/1**[3]

0264 **6** *1¼* **Lord Franklin**[14] 4336 8-9-3 **75** NeilFarley 3 68
(Eric Alston) *chsd ldr: rdn and ev ch 2f out: unable qck over 1f out: kpt on same pce ins fnl f: no imp after* **16/1**

4540 **7** *1½* **Cape Banjo (USA)**[13] 4413 4-9-5 **77** PhillipMakin 5 67
(Ralph Beckett) *hld up: rdn and outpcd over 2f out: kpt on ins fnl f: nvr nrr* **10/1**

336 **8** *½* **Modernism**[35] 3580 8-9-7 **79** (p) FranBerry 9 68
(Ian Williams) *hld up: rdn over 2f out: nvr able to trble ldrs* **16/1**

35 **9** *shd* **Celtic Artisan (IRE)**[26] 3898 6-8-6 **69** (bt) MeganNicholls(5) 10 58
(Rebecca Menzies) *midfield: rdn 2f out: no imp: outpcd fnl f* **50/1**

0423 **10** *1¾* **Suitor**[14] 4357 5-9-0 **72** (p) FrannyNorton 1 57
(Brian Ellison) *chsd ldrs: rdn 2f out: wkng whn n.m.r over 1f out* **5/2**[1]

0141 **11** *4* **Amy Blair**[12] 4432 4-8-9 **67** (h) AdamBeschizza 2 44
(Keith Dalgleish) *racd keenly: led: hung rt and rn wd on bnd wl over 7f out: hdd jst over 2f out: wknd over 1f out: eased whn btn wl ins fnl f* **8/1**

2m 11.4s (0.20) **Going Correction** +0.30s/f (Good) 11 Ran SP% **119.4**
Speed ratings (Par 105): **111,110,109,107,106 105,104,103,103,102 99**
CSF £191.25 CT £2711.90 TOTE £17.80: £4.80, £6.30, £4.70; EX 176.10 Trifecta £3102.10 Part won..
**Owner** Eros Bloodstock **Bred** Norcroft Park Stud And D Laidlaw **Trained** Bawtry, S Yorks
■ Stewards' Enquiry : Connor Murtagh 2 day ban - used whip above the permitted level (30/31 Jul)

**FOCUS**
The rail between the 6f and 1.5f point had been moved out by 9 yards. It meant this actual race distance was 1m 2f 109yds (+39yds). Another solid handicap on the card, which was well run.

## 4894 FORWARD BUILDERS' SUPPLIES CELEBRATING 30 YEARS APPRENTICE H'CAP — 7f 127y

**5:10** (5:11) (Class 4) (0-80,81) 3-Y-O

**£6,225** (£1,864; £932; £466; £233; £117) **Stalls** Low

Form RPR

3 **1** **Kryptos**[21] 4097 3-9-4 **78** NicolaCurrie(7) 3 88+
(John Berry) *racd keenly: hld up: nt clr run over 1f out: hdwy whn swtchd lft ent fnl f: r.o ins fnl f: led towards fin* **11/1**

-050 **2** *¾* **Plant Pot Power (IRE)**[8] 4564 3-9-7 **81** RossaRyan(7) 5 87
(Richard Hannon) *trckd ldrs: led over 1f out: at least 2 l clr ins fnl f: edgd lft: hdd and no ex towards fin* **13/2**

3504 **3** *3¼* **Proud Archi (IRE)**[8] 4556 3-9-9 **79** CallumRodriguez(3) 1 78
(Michael Dods) *trckd ldrs: rdn over 1f out: kpt on same pce fnl 100yds* **3/1**[2]

0221 **4** *4* **Valentino Boy (IRE)**[15] 4290 3-9-1 **73** BenRobinson(5) 6 62
(Brian Ellison) *disp ld: rdn and def advantage 2f out: hdd over 1f out: wknd fnl 150yds* **2/1**[1]

4122 **5** *½* **Right Action**[15] 4290 3-9-6 **78** ConnorMurtagh(5) 4 66
(Richard Fahey) *racd keenly: hld up: rdn and outpcd over 2f out: rallied sn after: one pce over 1f out* **10/3**[3]

1406 **6** *3* **Blue Rocks**[15] 4290 3-8-2 **60** oh1 JaneElliott(5) 2 41
(Lisa Williamson) *racd keenly: disp ld tl rdn 2f out: wknd ins fnl f* **20/1**

2460 **7** *5* **Tailor's Row (USA)**[10] 4501 3-9-8 **78** RichardOliver(3) 7 48
(Mark Johnston) *a in rr: outpcd over 2f out: nvr a threat* **16/1**

1m 35.11s (1.31) **Going Correction** +0.30s/f (Good) 7 Ran SP% **113.7**
Speed ratings (Par 102): **105,104,101,97,96 93,88**
CSF £77.61 TOTE £13.90: £3.10, £3.40; EX 99.90 Trifecta £722.70.
**Owner** Tony Fordham **Bred** Juddmonte Farms Ltd **Trained** Newmarket, Suffolk

**FOCUS**
The rail between the 6f and 1.5f point had been moved out by 9 yards. It meant this actual race distance was 7f 164yds (+37yds). The winner of this looked most unlikely to get up about 1f out. The runner-up has been rated in line with his 2yo form.
T/Plt: £316.00 to a £1 stake. Pool: £68,693.86 - 158.66 winning units T/Qpdt: £37.40 to a £1 stake. Pool: £4,738.22 - 93.6 winning units **Darren Owen**

# 4472 HAMILTON (R-H)

Saturday, July 15

**OFFICIAL GOING: Good changing to good to soft after race 1 (6.05)**
Wind: Fresh, across Weather: Overcast, raining

## 4895 BB FOODSERVICE NOVICE AUCTION STKS (PLUS 10 RACE) (A £20,000 BB FOODSERVICE 2YO SERIES QUALIFIER) — 5f 7y

**6:05** (6:06) (Class 4) 2-Y-O

**£5,175** (£1,540; £769; £384) **Stalls** High

Form RPR

52 **1** **Camacho Chief (IRE)**[31] 3705 2-8-12 0 AndrewMullen 9 74+
(Michael Dods) *dwlt: hld up towards rr: gd hdwy against stands' rail over 1f out: led ins fnl f: rdn clr* **11/4**[1]

31 **2** *2¼* **Undercover Brother**[24] 3972 2-9-5 0 SamJames 2 73
(David O'Meara) *swtchd lft s: led: rdn over 1f out: edgd rt and hdd ins fnl f: kpt on same pce* **7/2**[2]

4 **3** *½* **Lina's Star (IRE)**[38] 3447 2-8-5 0 SammyJoBell(3) 5 60+
(Richard Fahey) *hld up: hdwy on outside wl over 1f out: kpt on ins fnl f: nrst fin* **10/1**

3125 **4** *1½* **Villa Tora**[24] 3972 2-9-0 77 JoeFanning 1 61
(Mark Johnston) *pressed ldr: rdn over 1f out: outpcd ins fnl f* **6/1**[3]

0 **5** *nk* **Savannah's Show**[96] 1673 2-8-11 0 DuranFentiman 8 57
(Richard Guest) *stdd s: hld up: pushed along and hdwy over 1f out: kpt on fnl f: nvr able to chal* **33/1**

**6** *½* **Spirit Power**[11] 4480 2-8-13 0 CamHardie 3 57+
(Joseph Patrick O'Brien, Ire) *in tch: rdn and edgd rt over 1f out: sn outpcd* **7/2**[2]

43 **7** *½* **Corton Lass**[12] 4427 2-8-4 0 RowanScott(5) 7 51
(Keith Dalgleish) *t.k.h: trckd ldrs: rdn and edgd rt 2f out: wknd fnl f* **15/2**

00 **8** *4½* **Ray Purchase**[11] 4472 2-9-2 0 JoeyHaynes 4 42
(Keith Dalgleish) *hld up: drvn and outpcd over 2f out: sn btn* **50/1**

44 **9** *1* **Situation**[10] 4503 2-8-9 0 BenSanderson(7) 10 38
(Richard Guest) *hung rt thrght: towards rr: drvn along over 2f out: sn struggling* **22/1**

00 **10** *9* **Westfield Wonder**[30] 3754 2-8-12 0 PaddyAspell 6 2
(Ronald Thompson) *bhd: rdn and struggling over 2f out: sn btn* **150/1**

1m 1.15s (1.15) **Going Correction** +0.20s/f (Good) 10 Ran SP% **116.2**
Speed ratings (Par 96): **98,94,93,91,90 89,89,81,80,65**
CSF £12.08 TOTE £3.80: £1.40, £1.70, £3.80; EX 15.30 Trifecta £135.50.
**Owner** Exors Of The Late Ron Davison **Bred** Doc Bloodstock **Trained** Denton, Co Durham

**FOCUS**
Rain on the day before the meeting and on race day itself left the ground as good (GoingStick 7.0). It was changed to good to soft after the first race following persistent rain in late afternoon. Stalls - 5f, 1m3f & 1m4f: stands' side. 6f: centre. 1m: inside. The rails were in their innermost position and race distances were as advertised. A fair juvenile contest which produced a winner who is clearly on the upgrade.

## 4896 SAS "THE POWER TO KNOW" H'CAP — 5f 7y
**6:35** (6:35) (Class 5) (0-70,74) 3-Y-0+ — **£4,528** (£1,347; £673; £336) **Stalls** High

Form — RPR

6012 **1** **Dutch Dream**[11] 4478 4-8-7 **51** oh1 ........ AndrewMullen 4 — 57
(Linda Perratt) *dwlt: sn in tch: effrt and edgd rt over 1f out: led ins fnl f: drvn out* — **9/2**[2]

0514 **2** *1* **Bronze Beau**[7] 4607 10-10-2 **74** ........(tp) SamJames 7 — 76
(Kristin Stubbs) *led against stands' rail: rdn along over 1f out: hdd ins fnl f: kpt on* — **5/1**[3]

6645 **3** *hd* **Compton River**[12] 4428 5-9-8 **66** ........ ConnorBeasley 1 — 67
(Bryan Smart) *disp ld: rdn along 2f out: kpt on same pce wl ins fnl f* — **7/1**

6000 **4** *3/4* **Dawoodi**[5] 4683 3-8-13 **65** ........ SammyJoBell(3) 6 — 62
(Linda Perratt) *t.k.h: trckd ldrs: effrt whn nt clr run over 1f out: edgd rt and kpt on fnl f* — **40/1**

0065 **5** *1 1/2* **Groundworker (IRE)**[8] 4559 6-8-11 **55** ........(t) JoeFanning 2 — 48
(Paul Midgley) *hld up: rdn and effrt over 1f out: no imp ins fnl f* — **9/2**[2]

5326 **6** *3/4* **Muatadel**[9] 4531 4-9-12 **70** ........ TonyHamilton 3 — 60
(Roger Fell) *hld up: rdn and effrt on outside over 2f out: no imp over 1f out* — **11/4**[1]

5530 **7** *4 1/2* **Mitchum**[10] 4509 8-9-2 **60** ........(p) DuranFentiman 5 — 34
(Ron Barr) *sn pushed along in rr: struggling 2f out: sn btn* — **20/1**

6660 **8** *2* **Salvatore Fury (IRE)**[2] 4789 7-9-1 **64** ........(v) RowanScott(5) 8 — 31
(Keith Dalgleish) *hld up: rdn over 2f out: wknd wl over 1f out* — **6/1**

1m 1.24s (1.24) **Going Correction** +0.20s/f (Good)
**WFA** 3 from 4yo+ 5lb — **8** Ran SP% **113.7**
Speed ratings (Par 103): **98,96,96,94,92 91,84,80**
CSF £26.85 CT £154.68 TOTE £5.20: £2.00, £1.50, £2.10; EX 15.10 Trifecta £76.20.
**Owner** B Jordan **Bred** Lark Copse Ltd **Trained** East Kilbride, S Lanarks

**FOCUS**
An ordinary handicap which went to an improving sprinter who may be able to defy another weight rise.

## 4897 SUNDAY MAIL H'CAP — 6f 6y
**7:05** (7:06) (Class 4) (0-80,81) 3-Y-0+ — **£6,469** (£1,925; £962; £481) **Stalls** Centre

Form — RPR

6222 **1** **Manshood (IRE)**[16] 4250 4-9-9 **75** ........(b) GrahamLee 5 — 86
(Paul Midgley) *hld up in tch: hdwy to ld appr fnl f: edgd lft: pushed out* — **3/1**[2]

2214 **2** *2* **Inexes**[33] 3652 5-9-13 **79** ........(p) CamHardie 7 — 84
(Marjorie Fife) *missed break: bhd and pushed along: hdwy on outside over 1f out: chsd wnr ins fnl f: r.o* — **7/2**[3]

0642 **3** *1 3/4* **Kenny The Captain (IRE)**[5] 4683 6-9-6 **72** ........ DuranFentiman 8 — 71
(Tim Easterby) *cl up against stands' rail: led over 2f out to over 1f out: outpcd ins fnl f* — **11/4**[1]

000 **4** *1* **Baron Run**[44] 3239 7-8-8 **60** oh3 ........ JoeyHaynes 2 — 56
(K R Burke) *cl up on outside: effrt and ev ch over 1f out: no ex ins fnl f* — **40/1**

2052 **5** *1 1/4* **Johnny Cavagin**[14] 4339 8-10-1 **81** ........(t) AndrewMullen 3 — 73
(Ronald Thompson) *cl up tl rdn and wknd appr fnl f* — **8/1**

0505 **6** *2* **Highly Sprung (IRE)**[17] 4201 4-9-10 **76** ........ JoeFanning 4 — 61
(Mark Johnston) *w ldrs: rdn 2f out: wknd ent fnl f* — **9/1**

0220 **7** *1 3/4* **Portland Street (IRE)**[26] 3897 4-9-1 **67** ........(b) ConnorBeasley 6 — 47
(Bryan Smart) *bhd: rdn and outpcd over 2f out: sn struggling* — **6/1**

1m 13.01s (0.81) **Going Correction** +0.20s/f (Good) — **7** Ran SP% **111.7**
Speed ratings (Par 105): **102,99,97,95,94 91,89**
CSF £13.25 CT £30.03 TOTE £3.60: £2.70, £2.40; EX 13.50 Trifecta £32.40.
**Owner** Taylor's Bloodstock Ltd **Bred** John McEnery **Trained** Westow, N Yorks

**FOCUS**
A fair sprint handicap which saw the winner break his duck at the tenth time of asking.

## 4898 DAILY RECORD H'CAP — 1m 4f 15y
**7:35** (7:36) (Class 4) (0-80,80) 3-Y-0+ — **£7,762** (£2,310; £1,154; £577) **Stalls** Low

Form — RPR

1614 **1** **Brimham Rocks**[30] 3752 3-9-2 **80** ........ GrahamLee 7 — 94+
(Ralph Beckett) *trckd ldr: led gng wl over 2f out: pushed out fnl f: readily* — **9/4**[1]

-102 **2** *3* **Kajaki (IRE)**[14] 4336 4-9-11 **77** ........(p) KevinStott 3 — 83
(Kevin Ryan) *led: rdn and hdd over 2f out: kpt on fnl f: nt pce of wnr* — **7/2**[3]

31 **3** *1 3/4* **Northwest Frontier (IRE)**[22] 4055 3-8-13 **77** ........ TonyHamilton 5 — 82+
(Richard Fahey) *hld up in tch: rdn and outpcd 3f out: rallied over 1f out: no imp* — **7/2**[3]

2201 **4** *3* **Breakwater Bay (IRE)**[12] 4436 3-8-6 **70** ........ AndrewMullen 4 — 69
(Tim Easterby) *chsd ldrs: drvn along over 2f out: outpcd and edgd rt wl over 1f out* — **8/1**

2 **5** *shd* **Ligeti (IRE)**[29] 3802 4-9-10 **76** ........(tp) JoeFanning 6 — 74
(Joseph Patrick O'Brien, Ire) *prom: effrt and drvn over 2f out: outpcd over 1f out* — **3/1**[2]

2m 39.72s (1.12) **Going Correction** +0.20s/f (Good)
**WFA** 3 from 4yo+ 12lb — **5** Ran SP% **111.3**
Speed ratings (Par 105): **104,102,100,98,98**
CSF £10.47 TOTE £2.90: £1.70, £2.00; EX 10.30 Trifecta £21.60.
**Owner** Mr and Mrs David Aykroyd **Bred** Mr & Mrs David Aykroyd **Trained** Kimpton, Hants

**FOCUS**
A decent middle-distance handicap and a progressive sort in the winner. The form should stand up.

## 4899 RACINGUK.COM H'CAP — 1m 3f 15y
**8:05** (8:06) (Class 5) (0-75,82) 3-Y-0+ — **£4,528** (£1,347; £673; £336) **Stalls** Low

Form — RPR

112 **1** **Archi's Affaire**[12] 4430 3-9-10 **82** ........ AndrewMullen 11 — 93
(Michael Dods) *trckd ldrs: edgd rt and led over 2f out: clr over 1f out: styd on strly* — **2/1**[1]

**2** *3 1/4* **Detailed (IRE)**[53] 2933 3-8-12 **70** ........ TonyHamilton 3 — 75
(Joseph Patrick O'Brien, Ire) *hld up in tch: rdn and outpcd over 2f out: rallied and chsd (clr) wnr over 1f out: kpt on fnl f: nt pce to chal* — **4/1**[3]

6253 **3** *1 3/4* **Kingthistle**[20] 4118 4-9-12 **73** ........(tp) GrahamLee 2 — 74
(Rebecca Menzies) *hld up in tch: effrt and pushed along over 2f out: kpt on fnl f: nt pce to chal* — **16/1**

0-54 **4** *nk* **Chinese Spirit (IRE)**[11] 4474 3-8-8 **66** ........ PaddyAspell 6 — 67
(R Mike Smith) *t.k.h: trckd ldrs: rdn and effrt over 2f out: kpt on same pce fnl f* — **12/1**

1062 **5** *nk* **Archipeligo**[7] 4608 6-9-1 **69** ........(p) JamieGormley(7) 10 — 69
(Iain Jardine) *hld up: effrt and rdn over 2f out: kpt on fnl f: no imp* — **11/1**

-543 **6** *nse* **Dark Intention (IRE)**[28] 3845 4-9-10 **76** ........(h) PatrickO'Donnell(5) 9 — 76+
(Lawrence Mullaney) *hld up: drvn and outpcd over 4f out: rallied wl over 1f out: kpt on fnl f: nvr on terms* — **7/2**[2]

5104 **7** *1* **Reinstorm**[12] 4430 3-8-0 **61** ........ SammyJoBell(3) 8 — 60
(Richard Fahey) *led to over 4f out: rallied and ch over 2f out: wknd fnl f* — **10/1**

63/0 **8** *1/2* **Sheriff Of Nawton (IRE)**[50] 3050 6-9-5 **73** ........ BenSanderson(7) 4 — 70
(Roger Fell) *dwlt: hld up: outpcd and hung rt over 3f out: struggling fnl 2f* — **33/1**

000 **9** *6* **Falcon's Fire (IRE)**[14] 4357 4-9-3 **69** ........(t[1]) RowanScott(5) 7 — 56
(Keith Dalgleish) *pressed ldr: led over 4f out to over 2f out: rdn and wknd over 1f out* — **20/1**

-400 **10** *3* **Tectonic (IRE)**[17] 4210 8-9-2 **63** ........(v) ConnorBeasley 5 — 45
(Keith Dalgleish) *dwlt: hld up: rdn and struggling over 3f out: sn wknd* — **28/1**

2m 25.51s (-0.09) **Going Correction** +0.20s/f (Good)
**WFA** 3 from 4yo+ 11lb — **10** Ran SP% **117.7**
Speed ratings (Par 103): **108,105,104,104,103 103,103,102,98,96**
CSF £9.76 CT £99.94 TOTE £3.10: £1.30, £2.20, £2.90; EX 12.00 Trifecta £94.40.
**Owner** D Neale **Bred** Miss K Rausing **Trained** Denton, Co Durham

**FOCUS**
What seemed quite a competitive handicap was turned into a procession by the winner. Both he and the runner-up should be worth following.

## 4900 HAMILTON ADVERTISER H'CAP — 1m 68y
**8:35** (8:36) (Class 6) (0-60,61) 3-Y-0+ — **£3,234** (£962; £481; £240) **Stalls** Low

Form — RPR

/600 **1** **Cline**[16] 4263 4-9-6 **54** ........(p[1]) KevinStott 3 — 62
(Kevin Ryan) *mde all: shkn up over 1f out: kpt on strly fnl f* — **12/1**

0-01 **2** *3/4* **Belisa (IRE)**[16] 4263 3-9-4 **61** ........ DavidNolan 1 — 65
(Ivan Furtado) *trckd ldrs: effrt and wnt 2nd over 2f out: kpt on fnl f* — **2/1**[1]

2453 **3** *2 1/4* **Arcane Dancer (IRE)**[7] 4601 4-9-7 **60** ........(p) RowanScott(5) 10 — 61
(Lawrence Mullaney) *hld up on ins: effrt and rdn over 2f out: kpt on fnl f: nvr able to chal* — **7/1**[3]

**4** *3* **Templemary Boy (IRE)**[27] 3876 4-9-0 **48** ........ SamJames 6 — 43
(Paul W Flynn, Ire) *s.i.s: hld up: rdn 3f out: hdwy over 1f out: kpt on fnl f: no imp* — **25/1**

0000 **5** *1/2* **Coral Princess (IRE)**[5] 4688 3-8-5 **48** ........ JoeyHaynes 2 — 40
(Keith Dalgleish) *prom: rdn along over 2f out: outpcd fr over 1f out* — **10/1**

5000 **6** *nk* **Stardrifter**[6] 4660 5-9-6 **57** ........ SammyJoBell(3) 7 — 50
(Linda Perratt) *s.i.s: hld up: rdn along over 2f out: hdwy on outside over 1f out: kpt on fnl f: no imp* — **22/1**

**7** *nk* **Pronounced (IRE)**[7] 4647 3-8-9 **52** ........(b) TonyHamilton 8 — 42
(Joseph Patrick O'Brien, Ire) *t.k.h early: hld up midfield: drvn along 3f out: no imp fr over 1f out: btn fnl f* — **7/2**[2]

5-60 **8** *3 1/2* **Breaking Free**[68] 2455 3-8-7 **50** ........ DuranFentiman 12 — 33
(John Quinn) *t.k.h: hld up on outside: drvn over 2f out: edgd rt and wknd over 1f out* — **40/1**

1355 **9** *hd* **Kerry Icon**[42] 3343 4-8-10 **51** ........(h) JamieGormley(7) 9 — 35
(Iain Jardine) *prom: rdn and effrt over 2f out: wknd over 1f out* — **14/1**

5003 **10** *nk* **Palindrome (USA)**[73] 2313 4-9-0 **48** ........(b) AndrewMullen 11 — 32
(Ronald Thompson) *hld up: stmbld and pushed along 4f out: sn n.d: btn fnl 2f* — **25/1**

5244 **11** *8* **Kensington Palace (IRE)**[26] 3912 4-9-8 **56** ........ CamHardie 14 — 22
(Marjorie Fife) *hld up: rdn along over whn drifted lft over 2f out: sn btn* — **12/1**

-000 **12** *7* **Pennington**[39] 3431 3-8-12 **55** ........(v[1]) JoeFanning 5 — 4
(Mark Johnston) *pressed wnr to over 2f out: sn rdn and lost pl* — **20/1**

1m 48.9s (0.50) **Going Correction** +0.20s/f (Good)
**WFA** 3 from 4yo+ 9lb — **12** Ran SP% **118.4**
Speed ratings (Par 101): **105,104,102,99,98 98,97,94,94,93 85,78**
CSF £33.80 CT £193.08 TOTE £14.50: £3.80, £1.20, £2.80; EX 53.90 Trifecta £272.40.
**Owner** Bernard Cloney **Bred** Cheveley Park Stud Ltd **Trained** Hambleton, N Yorks

**FOCUS**
An ordinary handicap landed in taking style by the all-the-way winner. The runner-up is progressive so the form looks solid. The third and fourth help pin the opening level.

## 4901 RACING UK ON SKY 432 FILLIES' H'CAP — 1m 68y
**9:05** (9:05) (Class 5) (0-75,75) 3-Y-0+ — **£4,528** (£1,347; £673; £336) **Stalls** Low

Form — RPR

0/ **1** **Jackie Ellis (IRE)**[16] 4284 6-8-12 **59** ........ SamJames 7 — 65
(Paul W Flynn, Ire) *trckd ldr: rdn and led ent fnl f: hld on wl towards fin* — **5/1**

**2** *3/4* **Sweetasever (IRE)**[8] 4591 3-9-1 **71** ........ TonyHamilton 6 — 73
(Joseph Patrick O'Brien, Ire) *hld up in tch: effrt 2f out: chsd wnr ins fnl f: kpt on* — **7/2**[2]

0550 **3** *1/2* **Invermere**[14] 4375 4-9-11 **75** ........ SammyJoBell(3) 1 — 79
(Richard Fahey) *trckd ldrs: effrt and pushed along whn n.m.r over 1f out to ins fnl f: kpt on* — **11/4**[1]

2205 **4** *1 3/4* **Forever A Lady (IRE)**[16] 4248 4-10-0 **75** ........ GrahamLee 5 — 74
(Keith Dalgleish) *led at modest gallop: rdn along 2f out: hdd ent fnl f: outpcd last 100yds* — **11/4**[1]

02 **5** *2 1/2* **Duck Egg Blue (IRE)**[16] 4248 3-8-8 **71** ........(p) PaulaMuir(7) 4 — 62
(Patrick Holmes) *t.k.h: prom on outside: rdn over 2f out: wknd over 1f out* — **4/1**[3]

1m 50.16s (1.76) **Going Correction** +0.20s/f (Good)
**WFA** 3 from 4yo+ 9lb — **5** Ran SP% **112.2**
Speed ratings (Par 100): **99,98,97,96,93**
CSF £22.50 TOTE £6.30: £2.30, £1.60; EX 25.30 Trifecta £71.30.
**Owner** Miss C Howes **Bred** Edmond Kinane & Donal Sweeney **Trained** Colehill, Co Longford

**FOCUS**
Not the most competitive of fillies' handicaps, but the winner saw it out well.
T/Plt: £26.10 to a £1 stake. Pool: £68,413.13 - 1,909.71 winning units T/Qpdt: £6.30 to a £1 stake. Pool: £5,755.65 - 667.64 winning units **Richard Young**

4854 **NEWMARKET** (R-H)
Saturday, July 15

**OFFICIAL GOING: Good to firm (8.3)**
Wind: Light across Weather: Overcast

## 4902 ROSSDALES EBF STALLIONS MAIDEN FILLIES' STKS (PLUS 10 RACE) 7f
**1:45** (1:45) (Class 4) 2-Y-O **£6,469** (£1,925; £962; £481) **Stalls** Low

| Form | | | | RPR |
|---|---|---|---|---|
| | 1 | | **Poetic Charm** 2-9-0 0 WilliamBuick 1 (Charlie Appleby) *hld up: nt clr run over 2f out: hdwy over 1f out: shkn up to ld and edgd lft ins fnl f: r.o* **3/1**2 | 87+ |
| | 2 | 1 | **Sizzling (IRE)**15 4325 2-9-0 0 RyanMoore 10 (A P O'Brien, Ire) *prom: pushed along over 2f out: rdn and edgd rt over 1f out: sn ev ch: styd on same pce towards fin* **6/4**1 | 82 |
| 04 | 3 | hd | **Juliet Capulet (IRE)**16 4253 2-9-0 0 (p) SeanLevey 4 (John Gosden) *chsd ldrs: led over 1f out: sn rdn and hung lft: styd on same pce ins fnl f* **12/1** | 82 |
| | 4 | 1 | **Jousi** 2-9-0 0 JosephineGordon 7 (Hugo Palmer) *trckd ldrs: shkn up and nt clr run over 1f out: sn ev ch: styd on same ins fnl f* **16/1** | 79+ |
| 6 | 5 | nk | **Fleeting Freedom**37 3491 2-9-0 0 JimmyQuinn 13 (Alan Bailey) *hld up: hdwy and nt clr run over 1f out: styd on: nt trble ldrs* **66/1** | 78 |
| | 6 | nk | **Roulette** 2-9-0 0 LouisSteward 3 (Michael Bell) *s.i.s: hld up: rdn over 2f out: hmpd over 1f out: r.o ins fnl f: nvr nrr* **33/1** | 79+ |
| 0 | 7 | 1 | **The Mums**16 4253 2-8-11 0 KieranShoemark(3) 9 (John Gosden) *chsd ldr: upsides and pushed along 3f out: ev ch over 1f out: no ex ins fnl f* **33/1** | 75 |
| | 8 | 1 1/2 | **Quargent (USA)** 2-9-0 0 JamieSpencer 8 (Jeremy Noseda) *hld up: shkn up: hdwy and nt clr run over 1f out: wknd ins fnl f* **6/1**3 | 71+ |
| 42 | 9 | 1 3/4 | **One Second**15 4297 2-9-0 0 JimCrowley 2 (Mark Johnston) *chsd ldrs: led 1/2-way: rdn and hdd over 1f out: sn hung lft: wknd fnl f* **13/2** | 66 |
| | 10 | hd | **Janabiya** 2-9-0 0 HarryBentley 12 (George Peckham) *chsd ldrs: rdn over 2f out: wknd over 1f out* **66/1** | 65 |
| 5 | 11 | 1/2 | **Queen Adelaide**14 4363 2-9-0 0 KieranO'Neill 6 (John Ryan) *chsd ldrs: rdn 1/2-way: wknd over 1f out* **100/1** | 64 |
| | 12 | 3/4 | **Bessie Warfield** 2-9-0 0 ShaneKelly 14 (Luca Cumani) *prom: racd keenly: stdd and lost pl 5f out: drvn along and outpcd 1/2-way: hung rt over 2f out: n.d after* **50/1** | 62 |
| | 13 | nk | **Tricksy Spirit** 2-9-0 0 PaulHanagan 5 (Mick Channon) *hld up: hdwy over 2f out: hung lft and wknd over 1f out* **100/1** | 61 |
| 5 | 14 | 7 | **Sukhovey (USA)**16 4253 2-9-0 0 TomEaves 11 (Michael Attwater) *led to 1/2-way: wknd over 1f out* **66/1** | 42 |

1m 26.0s (0.30) **Going Correction** +0.025s/f (Good) **14 Ran SP% 120.5**
Speed ratings (Par 93): **99,97,97,96,96 95,94,92,90,90 90,89,88,80**
CSF £7.60 TOTE £3.80: £1.60, £1.30, £3.40; EX 10.50 Trifecta £73.60.
**Owner** Godolphin **Bred** Godolphin **Trained** Newmarket, Suffolk

**FOCUS**
Racing middle-to-stands' side, this looked a good fillies' maiden with the right horses coming to the fore. The fifth is an early candidate for rating the race around.

## 4903 SPA AT BEDFORD LODGE HOTEL EBF STALLIONS FILLIES' H'CAP 7f
**2:15** (2:17) (Class 2) (0-100,98) 3-Y-O **£15,562** (£4,660; £2,330; £1,165; £582; £292) **Stalls** Low

| Form | | | | RPR |
|---|---|---|---|---|
| 3313 | 1 | | **Inshiraah (FR)**15 4313 3-8-3 **80** KieranO'Neill 1 (George Peckham) *hld up in tch: rdn to ld over 1f out: sn hung lft: styd on* **7/1** | 92 |
| -120 | 2 | nk | **Gymnaste (IRE)**24 3964 3-8-12 **89** RyanMoore 10 (John Gosden) *hld up: hdwy 2f out: rdn and ev ch fr over 1f out: edgd lft ins fnl f: styd on* **11/4**1 | 100 |
| 3-20 | 3 | 3 | **On Her Toes (IRE)**24 3964 3-9-7 **98** WilliamBuick 8 (William Haggas) *hld up in tch: rdn over 2f out: styd on same pce ins fnl f* **7/2**2 | 101 |
| 50-0 | 4 | nk | **Marie Of Lyon**24 3964 3-8-9 **86** PaulHanagan 4 (Richard Fahey) *prom: led and hung rt over 2f out: rdn and hdd over 1f out: styd on same pce ins fnl f* **14/1** | 88 |
| 11-0 | 5 | 1 1/4 | **Tropical Rock**63 2623 3-8-8 **85** HarryBentley 7 (Ralph Beckett) *hld up: hdwy u.p over 1f out: styd on same pce ins fnl f* **8/1** | 84 |
| 210 | 6 | 4 1/2 | **Cheval Blanche (USA)**24 3964 3-8-4 **86** LuluStanford(5) 5 (Michael Bell) *racd keenly: led: rdn and hdd over 2f out: wknd fnl f* **4/1**3 | 73 |
| 0000 | 7 | 1 1/2 | **Island Vision (IRE)**22 4051 3-8-10 **87** JamieSpencer 2 (David Simcock) *hld up: pushed along 1/2-way: swtchd rt over 2f out: rdn and hung lft over 1f out: nvr on terms* **33/1** | 70 |
| 4500 | 8 | 1/2 | **Miss Infinity (IRE)**17 4208 3-8-13 **90** (b1) PJMcDonald 6 (Mark Johnston) *chsd ldr tl rdn and hmpd over 2f out: wknd over 1f out* **33/1** | 71 |
| -332 | 9 | 1 3/4 | **Alouja (IRE)**35 3595 3-8-2 **79** JosephineGordon 3 (Hugo Palmer) *chsd ldrs: hmpd over 2f out: wknd over 1f out* **11/1** | 56 |

1m 24.3s (-1.40) **Going Correction** +0.025s/f (Good) **9 Ran SP% 113.4**
Speed ratings (Par 103): **109,108,105,104,103 98,96,96,94**
CSF £26.06 CT £78.36 TOTE £8.30: £2.20, £1.50, £1.40; EX 30.30 Trifecta £110.70.
**Owner** Fawzi Abdulla Nass **Bred** Jean-Philippe Dubois **Trained** Newmarket, Suffolk

**FOCUS**
Few landes a serious blow in this good-quality fillies' handicap. It was run at a sound pace and the first pair drew clear down the middle. It's been rated an up-to-standard renewal, with the fourth and fifth close to form.

## 4904 BET365 MILE H'CAP 1m
**2:50** (2:52) (Class 2) (0-100,100) 3-Y-O **£18,675** (£5,592; £2,796; £1,398; £699; £351) **Stalls** Low

| Form | | | | RPR |
|---|---|---|---|---|
| 2020 | 1 | | **Medahim (IRE)**23 3997 3-9-1 **94** SeanLevey 8 (Richard Hannon) *hld up: hdwy over 1f out: sn edgd rt: rdn to ld ins fnl f: r.o* **12/1** | 104+ |
| 3502 | 2 | 1 1/2 | **Masham Star (IRE)**11 4475 3-9-7 **100** PJMcDonald 10 (Mark Johnston) *led: rdn over 1f out: hdd ins fnl f: styd on same pce* **8/1**3 | 106 |
| 3-50 | 3 | 1 1/2 | **Maths Prize**23 3997 3-8-8 **90** KieranShoemark(3) 7 (Roger Charlton) *hld up: hdwy over 2f out: chsd wnr briefly over 1f out: sn rdn: styd on same pce ins fnl f* **12/1** | 93 |
| 4110 | 4 | 3/4 | **Afaak**23 3997 3-8-13 **92** JimCrowley 4 (Charles Hills) *chsd wnr: rdn over 2f out: lost 2nd over 1f out: styd on same pce fnl f* **3/1**1 | 93 |
| 1025 | 5 | 1 1/2 | **Hajaj (IRE)**13 4408 3-8-2 **81** JosephineGordon 3 (Charlie Fellowes) *hld up: hdwy and nt clr run over 1f out: sn rdn and hung lft: styd on same pce ins fnl f* **16/1** | 78 |
| -310 | 6 | 2 | **The Statesman**14 4376 3-8-2 **81** oh1 KieranO'Neill 9 (Ian Williams) *chsd ldrs: pushed along over 3f out: rdn over 1f out: wknd fnl f* **20/1** | 74 |
| 2212 | 7 | 1/2 | **Mountain Angel (IRE)**42 3317 3-8-5 **84** HarryBentley 2 (Roger Varian) *chsd ldrs: rdn over 2f out: wknd over 1f out* **4/1**2 | 76 |
| -240 | 8 | shd | **Executive Force**23 3997 3-9-3 **96** WilliamBuick 5 (William Haggas) *dwlt: hld up: effrt over 1f out: sn wknd* **8/1**3 | 87 |
| 160- | 9 | 1 3/4 | **Lost At Sea**266 7544 3-9-1 **99** CliffordLee(5) 6 (K R Burke) *hld up in tch: shkn up over 2f out: wknd over 1f out* **25/1** | 86 |
| -110 | 10 | 2 3/4 | **City Of Joy**23 3997 3-9-1 **94** RyanMoore 1 (Sir Michael Stoute) *s.s and wnt rt s: hld up: shkn up over 2f out: wknd over 1f out: eased* **4/1**2 | 75+ |

1m 38.66s (-1.34) **Going Correction** +0.025s/f (Good) **10 Ran SP% 117.1**
Speed ratings (Par 106): **107,105,104,103,101 99,99,99,97,94**
CSF £104.76 CT £828.71 TOTE £13.40: £3.70, £2.70, £2.90; EX 105.10 Trifecta £1095.70.
**Owner** Al Shaqab Racing **Bred** Paul McEnery **Trained** East Everleigh, Wilts

**FOCUS**
A decent 3yo handicap, they raced centre-field. The runner-up has been rated to the better view of his form.

## 4905 BET365 BUNBURY CUP H'CAP 7f
**3:25** (3:26) (Class 2) 3-Y-O+ **£74,700** (£22,368; £11,184; £5,592; £2,796; £1,404) **Stalls** Low

| Form | | | | RPR |
|---|---|---|---|---|
| 4044 | 1 | | **Above The Rest (IRE)**28 3842 6-8-10 **101** (h) CliffordLee(5) 19 (David Barron) *hld up in tch: pushed along over 2f out: rdn and edgd rt over 1f out: r.o to ld wl ins fnl f* **12/1** | 110 |
| -560 | 2 | 1/2 | **Sir Dancealot (IRE)**24 3959 3-8-12 **106** JimmyQuinn 20 (David Elsworth) *s.i.s: hld up: racd keenly: hdwy over 1f out: sn rdn: r.o* **16/1** | 111 |
| 4442 | 3 | nk | **Steady Pace**21 4072 4-9-4 **104** JosephineGordon 15 (Saeed bin Suroor) *chsd ldrs: led over 4f out: rdn: edgd rt and hdd wl ins fnl f* **7/1**3 | 111 |
| 44-0 | 4 | 3/4 | **Tony Curtis**49 3069 4-9-2 **102** SeanLevey 12 (Richard Hannon) *hld up: in tch: shkn up over 1f out: r.o* **33/1** | 107 |
| 2151 | 5 | 1 1/4 | **Robero**4 4719 5-8-11 **97** 6ex TomQueally 3 (Michael Easterby) *led: hdd over 4f out: chsd ldr: rdn over 2f out: lost 2nd over 1f out: styd on same pce wl ins fnl f* **11/1** | 99 |
| 3-50 | 6 | 1/2 | **Von Blucher (IRE)**24 3963 4-8-13 **99** (t) PJMcDonald 14 (Rebecca Menzies) *hld up: swtchd rt over 1f out: r.o ins fnl f: nt rch ldrs* **33/1** | 99 |
| 1311 | 7 | nk | **Gossiping**51 3003 5-8-10 **96** ShaneKelly 7 (Gary Moore) *hld up in tch: rdn over 2f out: styd on u.p* **8/1** | 95 |
| 0662 | 8 | 1/2 | **Mutawathea**28 3842 6-8-10 **101** (p) LewisEdmunds(5) 10 (Simon Crisford) *prom: rdn over 2f out: styd on same pce fnl f* **8/1** | 99 |
| -215 | 9 | 3/4 | **Tabarrak (IRE)**24 3963 4-9-11 **111** RyanMoore 1 (Richard Hannon) *trckd ldrs: rdn over 2f out: edgd lft and no ex fnl f* **13/2**2 | 107 |
| 0010 | 10 | 3/4 | **Withernsea (IRE)**24 3963 6-8-11 **97** PaulHanagan 11 (Richard Fahey) *chsd ldrs: rdn over 2f out: wknd ins fnl f* **25/1** | 91 |
| 0-00 | 11 | 1/2 | **Boomshackerlacker (IRE)**24 3963 7-9-0 **100** (p) RichardKingscote 16 (George Baker) *chsd ldrs: rdn over 1f out: wknd ins fnl f* **28/1** | 93 |
| 2060 | 12 | 2 | **Kadrizzi (FR)**13 4411 4-8-9 **95** (v1) HarryBentley 13 (Dean Ivory) *mid-div: rdn over 2f out: wknd fnl f* **33/1** | 82 |
| 3000 | 13 | nk | **Donncha (IRE)**13 4410 6-8-10 **99** KieranShoemark(3) 18 (Robert Eddery) *hld up: pushed along over 2f out: rdn and hung rt over 1f out: wknd fnl f* **16/1** | 86 |
| -500 | 14 | 3 1/4 | **Bossy Guest (IRE)**24 3963 5-9-3 **103** AdamKirby 17 (Mick Channon) *wnt lft s and rel to r: sn pushed along in rr: rdn and hung lft over 2f out: n.d* **16/1** | 81 |
| 0665 | 15 | nk | **Holiday Magic (IRE)**35 3585 6-8-8 **94** TomEaves 5 (Michael Easterby) *hld up: rdn over 2f out: wknd over 1f out* **25/1** | 71 |
| /-03 | 16 | 1 1/4 | **Tashweeq (IRE)**24 3963 4-9-6 **106** JimCrowley 9 (John Gosden) *hld up: rdn and wknd over 1f out* **4/1**1 | 80 |
| 45-0 | 17 | nk | **Buckstay (IRE)**21 4072 7-9-8 **108** (b1) JamieSpencer 8 (Peter Chapple-Hyam) *hld up: shkn up over 2f out: a in rr* **25/1** | 81 |
| 1004 | 18 | 1/2 | **Sutter County**7 4615 3-9-0 **108** WilliamBuick 4 (Mark Johnston) *hld up: pushed along 1/2-way: rdn: edgd rt and wknd over 1f out* **20/1** | 76 |

1m 23.78s (-1.92) **Going Correction** +0.025s/f (Good)
**WFA** 3 from 4yo+ 8lb **18 Ran SP% 130.3**
Speed ratings (Par 109): **111,110,110,109,107 107,106,106,105,104 104,101,101,97,97 95,95,95**
CSF £181.56 CT £939.49 TOTE £14.30: £2.60, £4.10, £2.10, £7.80; EX 280.20 Trifecta £2832.60.
**Owner** Laurence O'Kane **Bred** J C Carr **Trained** Maunby, N Yorks

**FOCUS**
Another fiercely competitive Bunbury Cup on paper. They kept to the middle of the course but didn't go all that quick early on. Strong handicap form. It's been rated around the third close to his Wokingham form.

## 4906 BET365 SUPERLATIVE STKS (GROUP 2) 7f
**4:00** (4:00) (Class 1) 2-Y-O **£45,368** (£17,200; £8,608; £4,288; £2,152; £1,080) **Stalls** Low

| Form | | | | RPR |
|---|---|---|---|---|
| | 1 | | **Gustav Klimt (IRE)**13 4414 2-9-1 0 (t) RyanMoore 6 (A P O'Brien, Ire) *chsd ldrs: hmpd and lost pl over 2f out: swtchd lft and hdwy over 1f out: r.o gamely to ld wl ins fnl f* **5/6**1 | 110+ |
| 10 | 2 | hd | **Nebo (IRE)**25 3925 2-9-1 0 JimCrowley 4 (Charles Hills) *chsd ldrs: led over 2f out: sn edgd lft: rdn over 1f out: hung lft and hdd wl ins fnl f* **10/1** | 104 |
| 1 | 3 | 1/2 | **Great Prospector (IRE)**30 3754 2-9-1 0 PaulHanagan 7 (Richard Fahey) *s.i.s: hld up: hdwy over 1f out: sn rdn: edgd rt ins fnl f: r.o* **12/1** | 103 |

101 **4** ¾ **Zaman**[12] 4434 2-9-1 95 AdamKirby 1 101
(Charlie Appleby) *prom: jnd ldr 5f out: led 1/2-way: rdn and hdd over 2f out: styd on* **14/1**

2 **5** ¾ **Zaaki**[39] 3437 2-9-1 0 TomQueally 5 99
(Mohamed Moubarak) *stdd s: hld up: racd keenly: hdwy u.p over 1f out: nt clr run ins fnl f: styd on same pce* **66/1**

1 **6** ½ **Finniston Farm**[50] 3037 2-9-1 0 RichardKingscote 8 97
(Tom Dascombe) *sn led: hdd 1/2-way: edgd rt over 2f out: idden and ev ch fr over 1f out tl styd on same pce wl ins fnl f* **7/1[3]**

1 **7** ¾ **Bullington Bandit (IRE)**[30] 3746 2-9-1 0 (p) JosephineGordon 2 95
(Jane Chapple-Hyam) *hld up: effrt over 2f out: styd on same pce fnl f* **20/1**

01 **8** 1½ **Etefaaq (IRE)**[16] 4266 2-9-1 0 SeanLevey 10 91
(Richard Hannon) *prom: rdn and ev ch fr over 1f out tl wknd wl ins fnl f* **33/1**

145 **9** 2¾ **Aqabah (USA)**[25] 3925 2-9-1 104 WilliamBuick 3 84
(Charlie Appleby) *hld up: hdwy over 2f out: sn rdn: wknd fnl f* **5/1[2]**

51 **10** ½ **Maksab (IRE)**[18] 4183 2-9-1 0 PJMcDonald 9 82
(Mick Channon) *prom tl rdn and wknd over 1f out* **33/1**

1m 25.39s (-0.31) **Going Correction** +0.025s/f (Good) 10 Ran SP% **119.3**
Speed ratings (Par 106): **102,101,101,100,99 98,98,96,93,92**
CSF £10.33 TOTE £1.70: £1.10, £2.60, £3.10; EX 9.60 Trifecta £74.70.
**Owner** Mrs John Magnier & Michael Tabor & Derrick Smith **Bred** Orpendale, Chelston & Wynatt **Trained** Cashel, Co Tipperary

**FOCUS**
Not the strongest of Group 2s in truth, but hard not to be taken with the winner, who overcame a troubled run to justify short odds. He's been rated value for a few lengths extra.

## 4907 DARLEY JULY CUP STKS (GROUP 1) (BRITISH CHAMPIONS SERIES & GLOBAL SPRINT CHALLENGE) 6f
**4:35** (4:37) (Class 1) 3-Y-O+
**£283,550** (£107,500; £53,800; £26,800; £13,450; £6,750) **Stalls** Low

Form RPR

-212 **1** **Harry Angel (IRE)**[22] 4030 3-9-0 118 AdamKirby 6 122
(Clive Cox) *w ldr: shkn up to ld and qcknd over 1f out: rdn and edgd rt ins fnl f: r.o* **9/2[3]**

6-03 **2** 1¼ **Limato (IRE)**[21] 4071 5-9-6 120 HarryBentley 1 118
(Henry Candy) *prom: rdn over 1f out: r.o to go 2nd wl ins fnl f: nt rch wnr* **4/1[2]**

3-10 **3** ½ **Brando**[59] 2737 5-9-6 116 TomEaves 4 116
(Kevin Ryan) *hld up: rdn and r.o wl ins fnl f: nt rch ldrs* **28/1**

1-11 **4** shd **Caravaggio (USA)**[22] 4030 3-9-0 122 RyanMoore 2 115
(A P O'Brien, Ire) *hld up: shkn up over 2f out: edgd lft over 1f out: rdn and r.o ins fnl f: nt rch ldrs* **10/11[1]**

0-40 **5** nk **Intelligence Cross (USA)**[22] 4030 3-9-0 104 (bt) PBBeggy 3 114
(A P O'Brien, Ire) *led: qcknd over 2f out: rdn and hdd over 1f out: styd on same pce wl ins fnl f* **100/1**

-00U **6** ½ **Growl**[21] 4071 5-9-6 109 PaulHanagan 9 113
(Richard Fahey) *hld up: pushed along and hdwy over 1f out: edgd rt: styd on same pce wl ins fnl f* **50/1**

5502 **7** 1¼ **Intisaab**[14] 4354 6-9-6 108 (p) WilliamBuick 7 109
(David O'Meara) *chsd ldrs: rdn over 2f out: edgd rt and no ex ins fnl f* **66/1**

1-51 **8** 1 **The Tin Man**[21] 4071 5-9-6 117 TomQueally 10 106
(James Fanshawe) *hld up: shkn up over 2f out: rdn and edgd rt over 1f out: no ex ins fnl f* **7/1**

2130 **9** ½ **Mr Lupton (IRE)**[27] 3867 4-9-6 112 JamieSpencer 8 104
(Richard Fahey) *s.i.s: hld up: shkn up over 1f out: nvr on terms* **66/1**

-212 **10** nk **Tasleet**[21] 4071 4-9-6 116 (p) JimCrowley 5 103
(William Haggas) *trckd ldrs: racd keenly: rdn over 1f out: wknd ins fnl f* **9/1**

1m 11.25s (-1.25) **Going Correction** +0.025s/f (Good)
**WFA** 3 from 4yo+ 6lb 10 Ran SP% **122.4**
Speed ratings (Par 117): **109,107,106,106,106 105,103,102,101,101**
CSF £23.73 CT £478.33 TOTE £5.80: £1.40, £1.40, £5.00; EX 24.40 Trifecta £284.90.
**Owner** Godolphin **Bred** Cbs Bloodstock **Trained** Lambourn, Berks

**FOCUS**
A mouth-watering July Cup with the principals from the Diamond Jubilee taking on the first two home in the Commonwealth Cup. The field went a solid pace down the middle, but it was a pretty messy finish behind the winner. The bare form takes some believing, with the front-running fifth not beaten far. The sixth and seventh also limit the form.

## 4908 JOHN BANKS RENAULT SPORT TROPHY H'CAP 1m 4f
**5:05** (5:12) (Class 3) (0-90,89) 3-Y-O+ **£9,703** (£2,887; £1,443; £721) **Stalls** Centre

Form RPR

4-11 **1** **Quloob**[36] 3520 3-9-0 87 JimCrowley 11 99+
(Owen Burrows) *s.i.s: hld up: hdwy over 3f out: rdn to chse ldr over 1f out: led ins fnl f: styd on wl* **3/1[2]**

-205 **2** 1¾ **Batts Rock (IRE)**[35] 3594 4-9-8 83 (p[1]) JamieSpencer 1 91
(Michael Bell) *chsd ldrs: shkn up to ld over 2f out: rdn and hung lft fr over 1f out: hdd ins fnl f: styd on same pce* **8/1**

-416 **3** 2¼ **Sporting Times**[16] 4254 3-8-9 82 PJMcDonald 5 88
(Ed Dunlop) *hld up in tch: rdn over 2f out: sn ev ch: styd on same pce fnl f* **10/1**

-2P5 **4** 3½ **Plutocracy (IRE)**[14] 4370 7-10-0 89 (p) AdamKirby 10 88
(Gary Moore) *hld up: hdwy over 1f out: wknd wl ins fnl f* **33/1**

3126 **5** 4½ **Panko (IRE)**[17] 4206 4-9-7 82 HarryBentley 3 74
(Ed de Giles) *chsd ldr tl led 1/2-way: hdd over 3f out: sn rdn: wknd over 1f out* **12/1**

1 **6** 1 **Silken Dancer**[68] 2476 3-8-12 85 WilliamBuick 2 76
(Charlie Appleby) *led to 1/2-way: led again over 3f out: sn hung lft: hdd over 2f out: wknd over 1f out* **5/4[1]**

621 **7** ½ **Opposition**[29] 3795 4-9-10 85 RyanMoore 6 74
(Ed Dunlop) *hld up: shkn up over 3f out: wknd over 1f out* **13/2[3]**

-336 **8** ½ **Apres Midi (IRE)**[20] 4118 4-9-3 78 RichardKingscote 9 67
(K R Burke) *prom: rdn over 2f out: wknd over 1f out* **33/1**

2m 31.61s (-1.29) **Going Correction** +0.025s/f (Good)
**WFA** 3 from 4yo+ 12lb 8 Ran SP% **116.6**
Speed ratings (Par 107): **105,103,102,100,97 96,96,95**
CSF £27.73 CT £210.54 TOTE £4.30: £1.30, £1.70, £2.60; EX 21.90 Trifecta £162.90.
**Owner** Hamdan Al Maktoum **Bred** Shadwell Estate Company Limited **Trained** Lambourn, Berks

**FOCUS**
A useful handicap, it predictably went to one of the 3yos. The runner-up has been rated as improving a little.

T/Plt: £375.70 to a £1 stake. Pool: £179,564.60 - 348.82 winning units T/Qpdt: £133.00 to a £1 stake. Pool: £10,841.92 - 60.3 winning units **Colin Roberts**

# [4218] SALISBURY (R-H)
Saturday, July 15

**OFFICIAL GOING: Good to firm (good in places; 8.3)**
Wind: light breeze against Weather: cloudy

## 4909 BATHWICK TYRES EBF NOVICE STKS (PLUS 10 RACE) 6f 213y
**5:50** (5:50) (Class 4) 2-Y-O **£4,043** (£1,203; £601; £300) **Stalls** Low

Form RPR

0 **1** **Beringer**[17] 4218 2-8-9 0 FinleyMarsh(7) 1 78
(Alan King) *trckd ldrs: led over 2f out: rdn clr over 1f out: r.o strly* **16/1**

35 **2** 2½ **Coastal Drive**[15] 4297 2-9-2 0 OisinMurphy 3 71
(Richard Hannon) *mid-div: hdwy over 3f out: ev ch whn wandered u.p 2f out: sn hld by wnr but kpt on fnl f* **7/2[2]**

06 **3** hd **General Zoff**[33] 3668 2-8-11 0 JoshuaBryan(5) 2 71
(William Muir) *led: rdn and hdd over 2f out: kpt on same pce fnl f* **20/1**

**4** 1 **Groveman** 2-8-13 0 CallumShepherd(3) 10 68+
(Charles Hills) *s.i.s: towards rr: stdy hdwy fr 2f out: kpt on ins fnl f but nt pce to get on terms* **13/2**

0 **5** ½ **Strategic (IRE)**[19] 4151 2-9-2 0 ShaneKelly 8 67+
(Richard Hannon) *trckd ldrs: rdn over 2f out: trying to mount chal whn bdly squeezed out sn after: kpt on ins fnl f but no ch after* **5/1[3]**

**6** nk **Marble Bar** 2-8-13 0 HectorCrouch(3) 12 66+
(Henry Candy) *hld up towards rr: rdn and hdwy 2f out: kpt on same pce fnl f* **8/1**

**7** 1½ **Blackheath** 2-9-2 0 LiamKeniry 5 62
(Ed Walker) *s.i.s: racd keenly towards rr: hdwy 3f out: rdn 2f out: nt pce to threaten: no ex fnl 100yds* **10/1**

2 **8** 2¾ **Camomile Lawn (IRE)**[17] 4212 2-8-8 0 KieranShoemark(3) 7 49+
(Ralph Beckett) *mid-div: hdwy over 3f out: effrt over 2f out: nt pce to chal: wknd fnl f* **15/8[1]**

**9** nse **Raven's Song (IRE)** 2-8-11 0 WilliamCarson 4 49
(Harry Dunlop) *mid-div: pushed along over 3f out: nvr threatened: wknd ent fnl f* **33/1**

0 **10** 3¾ **Sixties Secret**[9] 4533 2-8-11 0 GeorgeDowning 6 39
(Mick Channon) *squeezed up sn after s: sn mid-div: rdn over 2f out: nvr threatened: wknd ent fnl f* **33/1**

00 **11** 44 **Mullion Star**[68] 2473 2-8-13 0 TimClark(3) 9
(Michael Madgwick) *chsd ldrs tl rdn wl over 3f out: sn wknd: t.o* **200/1**

**12** 77 **Amenhotepthethird** 2-8-13 0 NoelGarbutt(3) 11
(Mark Gillard) *slowly away: v green: sn t.o* **150/1**

1m 28.66s (0.06) **Going Correction** -0.05s/f (Good) 12 Ran SP% **124.9**
Speed ratings (Par 96): **97,94,93,92,92 91,90,87,86,82 32,**
CSF £73.58 TOTE £18.10: £4.40, £1.60, £5.20; EX 91.60 Trifecta £2013.00.
**Owner** L Field, B Cognet, N Farrell, J Spack **Bred** Aiden Murphy **Trained** Barbury Castle, Wilts

**FOCUS**
An inch of rain had fallen on the course during Tuesday and Wednesday but nothing of any significance subsequently. The stalls were situated on the far side for this pretty routine opening novice stakes, in which few featured. The opening level is fluid.

## 4910 TONY BROWN'S 75TH BIRTHDAY H'CAP 6f
**6:20** (6:20) (Class 5) (0-75,78) 3-Y-O+ **£3,396** (£1,010; £505; £252) **Stalls** Low

Form RPR

5350 **1** **Dandy Flame (IRE)**[10] 4500 3-8-12 74 FinleyMarsh(7) 7 81
(Richard Hughes) *mde all: kpt on gamely: rdn out* **10/1**

0545 **2** 1¼ **Whitecrest**[10] 4495 9-9-8 71 WilliamCarson 5 75
(John Spearing) *mid-div: hdwy 2f out: sn rdn: kpt on gamely to go 2nd ins fnl f but a being hld by wnr* **16/1**

0-60 **3** ½ **Field Of Vision (IRE)**[29] 3777 4-9-5 75 SophieScardifield(7) 4 77
(Joseph Tuite) *stdd s: last: swtchd lft 2f out: stl last ent fnl f: fin strly: wnt 3rd cl home* **16/1**

-403 **4** 1 **Coastal Cyclone**[16] 4251 3-9-1 75 JoshuaBryan(5) 1 73
(Harry Dunlop) *chsd ldrs: rdn to chse wnr 2f out: nt quite pce to get on terms: no ex whn losing 2 pls fnl 75yds* **5/2[1]**

0502 **5** 1 **Procurator (IRE)**[11] 4468 3-9-9 78 OisinMurphy 6 73
(Richard Hannon) *mid-div: rdn over 2f out: kpt on fnl f but nt pce to threaten* **3/1[2]**

1320 **6** nk **Swanton Blue (IRE)**[9] 4532 4-9-6 72 CallumShepherd(3) 9 67
(Ed de Giles) *chsd wnr: rdn over 2f out: one pce fnl f* **5/1**

-315 **7** 1¼ **Carpe Diem Lady (IRE)**[9] 4536 4-10-0 77 (v) PatDobbs 2 68
(Ralph Beckett) *chsd ldrs: rdn over 2f out: nt pce to chal: no ex ins fnl f* **9/2[3]**

3200 **8** 4½ **Raffle King (IRE)**[49] 3085 3-9-2 71 CharlesBishop 3 47
(Mick Channon) *hld up last pair: rdn over 2f out: nvr threatened: wknd fnl f* **12/1**

1m 14.47s (-0.33) **Going Correction** -0.05s/f (Good)
**WFA** 3 from 4yo+ 6lb 8 Ran SP% **117.0**
Speed ratings (Par 103): **100,98,97,96,95 94,92,86**
CSF £153.75 CT £2525.57 TOTE £10.10: £2.70, £4.00, £3.70; EX 140.60 Trifecta £1530.70.
**Owner** Terence Wood **Bred** Limestone & Tara Studs **Trained** Upper Lambourn, Berks

**FOCUS**
Stalls far side. As generously run a race as was always likely, but the pace up front never collapsed and the winner made all, granting Finley Marsh a rapid-fire double in the process.

## 4911 CPA SCAFFOLDING MAIDEN STKS 6f 213y
**6:50** (6:52) (Class 5) 3-Y-O+ **£3,881** (£1,155; £577; £288) **Stalls** Low

Form RPR

**1** **Robin Weathers (USA)** 3-9-5 0 DanielMuscutt 3 84
(William Haggas) *trckd ldrs: rdn 2f out: kpt on strly to dispute fnl 120yds: won on nod* **9/2[2]**

**2** nse **Killay** 3-9-0 0 CharlesBishop 10 78
(Eve Johnson Houghton) *wnt lft s: sn pressing ldr: rdn over 1f out: narrow ld jst ins fnl f: jnd fnl 120yds: kpt on gamely: lost on nod* **9/1[3]**

**3** 2¼ **Island Of Life (USA)** 3-9-0 0 OisinMurphy 2 72
(Saeed bin Suroor) *led: rdn and strly chal fr over 2f out: narrowly hdd jst ins fnl f: no ex fnl 120yds* **1/1[1]**

**4** ½ **Romina** 3-9-0 0 ShaneKelly 7 70
(Richard Hughes) *trckd ldrs: rdn 2f out: nt pce to chal but kpt on fnl 120yds* **9/1[3]**

**5** 1¼ **Ristretto (USA)** 3-9-0 0 PatDobbs 9 67
(Ralph Beckett) *in tch: rdn over 2f out: nt pce to get on terms* **9/2[2]**

**6** 9 **O'Connor (IRE)** 4-9-13 0 WilliamCarson 5 51
(Rod Millman) *sltly hmpd s: last pair: effrt 3f out: wknd jst over 1f out* **16/1**



The Form Book Flat, Raceform Ltd, Newbury, RG14 5SJ

0 7 6 **Henriqua**[38] 3456 3-8-7 0 .......... FinleyMarsh(7) 1 27
(Denis Coakley) *sn struggling in last pair: wknd 2f out* 25/1

0 8 8 **Lookintomyeyes**[81] 2066 3-9-0 0 .......... (t) SaleemGolam 4 5
(Mrs Ilka Gansera-Leveque) *trckd ldrs tl rdn and wknd over 2f out* 33/1

1m 27.65s (-0.95) **Going Correction** -0.05s/f (Good)
**WFA** 3 from 4yo+ 8lb 8 Ran SP% **119.0**
Speed ratings (Par 103): **103,102,100,99,98 88,81,72**
CSF £45.89 TOTE £5.20: £1.90, £2.80, £1.10; EX 40.50 Trifecta £111.80.
**Owner** St Albans Bloodstock Limited **Bred** Andrew Stone **Trained** Newmarket, Suffolk

**FOCUS**
Stalls on far side. A decent-looking maiden stakes, in which newcomers locked out the frame. The opening level is fluid.

## 4912 TOTAL DECOR LTD H'CAP 1m
**7:20** (7:25) (Class 4) (0-80,80) 3-Y-O+ **£5,175** (£1,540; £769; £384) **Stalls** Low

Form RPR

3414 1 **Exceeding Power**[30] 3750 6-9-6 75 .......... GeorgeWood(3) 8 83
(Martin Bosley) *last pair but in tch: hdwy 3f out: rdn to ld over 1f out: kpt on wl whn in command fnl f* 4/1[3]

42-1 2 ¾ **Harbour Rock**[29] 3781 3-9-5 80 .......... OisinMurphy 1 84
(David Simcock) *last pair but in tch: tk clsr order 3f out: sn rdn: no further imp tl r.o ent fnl f: fin strly to go 2nd towards fin clsng qckly on wnr* 11/8[1]

-240 3 1 ¾ **Wannabe Friends**[16] 4254 4-9-11 77 .......... ShaneKelly 7 79+
(Richard Hughes) *sn led: rdn over 2f out: hdd over 1f out: sn hld: no ex fnl 100yds* 5/1

541- 4 2 ¾ **Mamdood (IRE)**[252] 7812 3-9-4 79 .......... DaneO'Neill 2 73
(Richard Hannon) *chsd ldrs: rdn over 2f out: sn one pce* 7/2[2]

6026 5 9 **British Embassy (IRE)**[15] 4294 5-9-7 78 .......... (p) JoshuaBryan(5) 4 60
(Bill Turner) *prom: rdn over 2f out: sn hld: eased whn btn fnl f* 16/1

5363 D 56 **Zamalight**[11] 4460 3-8-12 76 .......... (h) KieranShoemark(3) 5
(Amanda Perrett) *chsd ldrs tl lost pl qckly u.p 4f out: sn eased: fin 6th btn 70 ¼ l. Disqualified after jockey failed to weigh in.* 12/1

1m 43.05s (-0.45) **Going Correction** -0.05s/f (Good)
**WFA** 3 from 4yo+ 9lb 6 Ran SP% **114.6**
Speed ratings (Par 105): **100,99,97,94,85 29**
CSF £10.28 CT £26.93 TOTE £4.70: £1.90, £1.20; EX 11.90 Trifecta £43.70.
**Owner** The Chalfonts **Bred** Rabbah Bloodstock Limited **Trained** Chalfont St Giles, Bucks

**FOCUS**
Stalls far side. This rather fell into the lap of the most exposed runner in the field.

## 4913 BATHWICK TYRES H'CAP 1m 4f 5y
**7:50** (7:52) (Class 5) (0-75,77) 3-Y-O+ **£3,396** (£1,010; £505; £252) **Stalls** Low

Form RPR

2435 1 **Koeman**[17] 4221 3-8-12 71 .......... JFEgan 5 79
(Mick Channon) *trckd ldrs: led over 2f out: sn rdn: styd on wl* 11/2

3-32 2 2 ¾ **Balashakh (USA)**[120] 1239 3-9-1 74 .......... (h[1]) OisinMurphy 8 78
(David Simcock) *hld up: hdwy fr over 2f out: sn rdn: styd on to go 2nd ins fnl f but no threat to wnr* 9/2[2]

5013 3 ¾ **Cotton Club (IRE)**[17] 4222 6-9-12 73 .......... WilliamCarson 4 74
(Rod Millman) *trckd ldrs: rdn and ev ch 2f out: tl over 1f out: no ex ins fnl f* 10/1

0-21 4 5 **Solo Mission**[26] 3901 3-9-2 75 .......... (p) DanielMuscutt 1 69
(William Haggas) *hld up: rdn and hdwy fr 3f out: wnt 4th over 1f out: nvr quite threatened: one pce fnl f* 6/4[1]

5232 5 3 ¾ **Prerogative (IRE)**[17] 4224 3-9-4 77 .......... (p) PatDobbs 7 65
(Richard Hannon) *led for 1f: trckd ldr tl rdn over 2f out: fdd ins fnl f* 5/1[3]

5-53 6 1 ¼ **Zoffanist (IRE)**[17] 4197 3-8-3 62 .......... (b[1]) MartinDwyer 2 48
(Amanda Perrett) *awkwardly away: sn racing keenly: led after 1f: rn wd on loop: rdn and hdd 2f out: wknd ent fnl f* 9/1

145- 7 12 **Midnight Mood**[278] 7223 4-8-12 59 .......... LiamKeniry 6 25
(Dominic Ffrench Davis) *trckd ldrs: pushed along over 4f out: wknd over 2f out* 25/1

2m 34.4s (-3.60) **Going Correction** -0.05s/f (Good)
**WFA** 3 from 4yo+ 12lb 7 Ran SP% **113.2**
Speed ratings (Par 103): **110,108,107,104,101 101,93**
CSF £29.52 CT £238.81 TOTE £6.70: £2.80, £2.60; EX 32.10 Trifecta £183.90.
**Owner** Taplin & Bunney Partnership **Bred** B V Sangster **Trained** West Ilsley, Berks

**FOCUS**
Stalls stands side. A fair event for the grade, but another in which it proved hard to make a telling contribution from the rear.

## 4914 PARTY CONTINUES AT THE CHAPEL NIGHTCLUB H'CAP 1m 1f 201y
**8:20** (8:22) (Class 6) (0-60,62) 3-Y-O **£3,234** (£962; £481; £240) **Stalls** Low

Form RPR

-050 1 **Lyrica's Lion (IRE)**[12] 4446 3-8-10 54 .......... DavidEgan(5) 6 62
(Michael Attwater) *trckd ldrs: narrow ld 3f out: sn rdn: wandered sltly u.p: styd on wl fnl f* 20/1

3044 2 ¾ **Famous Dynasty (IRE)**[14] 4348 3-9-3 56 .......... DanielMuscutt 9 63
(Michael Blanshard) *mid-div: smooth hdwy over 3f out: chal gng best sn after: edgd lft u.p over 2f out: ev ch ent fnl f: styd on but no ex* 11/4[1]

0450 3 4 **Crystal Secret**[14] 4348 3-8-3 47 .......... (v[1]) MitchGodwin(5) 3 46
(John Bridger) *hld up: hdwy over 3f out: drifted lft u.p over 2f out: styd on to go 3rd fnl f but nt pce to get on terms* 12/1

0002 4 1 ¾ **High Wells**[10] 4492 3-9-8 61 .......... (b) OisinMurphy 4 57
(Seamus Durack) *slowly away: last trio: hdwy over 4f out: rdn over 3f out: nt pce to mount chal and sn hld in 3rd: no ex fnl f* 11/4[1]

0-06 5 17 **Socrates**[27] 3870 3-9-7 60 .......... GeorgeDowning 5 24
(Daniel Kubler) *trckd ldr: rdn w ch 3f out: wknd over 1f out* 16/1

4400 6 1 ¾ **Cecilator**[27] 3864 3-9-4 57 .......... (b[1]) DougieCostello 10 17
(Noel Williams) *mid-div: rn wd on the loop: rdn 3f out: nvr threatened: wknd 2f out* 33/1

000 7 10 **Bombero (IRE)**[30] 3755 3-9-2 58 .......... CallumShepherd(3) 1
(Ed de Giles) *trckd ldrs: led v briefly over 3f out: sn rdn: wknd 2f out* 7/2[2]

000- 8 28 **Miriam Violet**[207] 8467 3-8-7 46 oh1 .......... (t[1]) MartinDwyer 2 +
(Paul Henderson) *led tl over 3f out: sn wknd: eased whn btn 2f out* 25/1

055 9 3 ½ **Estrellada**[22] 4042 3-9-6 59 .......... SilvestreDeSousa 7
(Mick Channon) *hld up last: short-lived effrt over 3f out: sn btn: eased fnl 2f* 5/1[3]

2m 9.06s (-0.84) **Going Correction** -0.05s/f (Good) 9 Ran SP% **117.3**
Speed ratings (Par 98): **101,100,97,95,82 80,72,50,47**
CSF £74.55 CT £717.13 TOTE £15.90: £4.40, £1.20, £3.00; EX 73.30 Trifecta £414.30.
**Owner** Ricki Vaughan **Bred** Schneider Adolf **Trained** Epsom, Surrey

**FOCUS**
Stalls on far side. A muddling affair, with the field stretched by Miriam Violet's strong pace initially but all stacked up again by the half-mile pole. The runner-up has been rated to form.

## 4915 BRITISH STALLION STUDS EBF "LADIES' EVENING" FILLIES' H'CAP 1m 1f 201y
**8:50** (8:50) (Class 3) (0-95,89) 3-Y-O+ **£9,056** (£2,695; £1,346; £673) **Stalls** Low

Form RPR

1 1 **Standing Rock (IRE)**[30] 3748 3-8-8 82 .......... KieranShoemark(3) 3 93+
(John Gosden) *hld up: pushed along 4f out: hdwy over 3f out: shkn up to ld over 1f out: hld on a shade cosily* 6/4[1]

-521 2 nk **Billesdon Bess**[32] 3693 3-8-13 84 .......... PatDobbs 5 92
(Richard Hannon) *led: rdn whn jnd fr wl over 2f out: hdd over 1f out: rallied v gamely ins fnl f: kpt on* 5/1[2]

-043 3 ¾ **Sagely (IRE)**[23] 4002 4-10-0 89 .......... SilvestreDeSousa 2 94
(Ed Dunlop) *mid-div: hdwy over 2f out: sn rdn: str chal for cl 2nd ent fnl f: no ex cl home* 10/1

20/0 4 2 **Uele River**[70] 2392 5-9-11 89 .......... GeorgeWood(3) 10 90
(Henry Candy) *trckd ldr: chal over 3f out: rdn to dispute wl over 2f out: hdd over 1f out: no ex fnl 100yds* 16/1

-314 5 ½ **Turning The Table (IRE)**[47] 3158 4-9-13 88 .......... OisinMurphy 1 88
(David Simcock) *hld up: sme prog 3f out: sn rdn: nt pce to get involved but styd on fnl f* 8/1[3]

2160 6 nk **Prosper**[24] 3964 3-9-2 87 .......... (b[1]) JackMitchell 4 87
(Roger Varian) *trckd ldrs: rdn whn v sltly hmpd over 1f out: kpt on same pce* 8/1[3]

204- 7 5 **Miss Minuty**[234] 8076 5-8-7 75 .......... FinleyMarsh(7) 6 64
(Jeremy Scott) *hld up: sme hdwy 2f out: sn rdn: wknd fnl f* 14/1

4-01 8 1 ¼ **Hadeeqa (IRE)**[51] 3007 3-8-12 83 .......... DaneO'Neill 9 71
(Simon Crisford) *slowly away: sn in tch: wnt 4th 6f out: rdn over 2f out: wknd over 1f out* 8/1[3]

21-4 9 8 **Brief Visit**[105] 1504 4-9-8 83 .......... DavidProbert 7 54
(Andrew Balding) *mid-div: rdn over 2f out: wknd over 1f out* 14/1

2m 7.71s (-2.19) **Going Correction** -0.05s/f (Good)
**WFA** 3 from 4yo+ 10lb 9 Ran SP% **118.3**
Speed ratings (Par 104): **106,105,105,103,103 102,98,97,91**
CSF £9.22 CT £56.89 TOTE £2.40: £1.10, £1.80, £2.70; EX 12.00 Trifecta £89.70.
**Owner** Rachel Hood & Mrs P Shanahan **Bred** P A Byrne **Trained** Newmarket, Suffolk

**FOCUS**
Stalls on inner. The evening's feature, and certainly the most taking winner on the whole card despite a bunch finish.
T/Plt: £5,047.70 to a £1 stake. Pool: £66,727.18 - 9.65 winning units T/Qpdt: £27.10 to a £1 stake. Pool: £7,515.32 - 205.16 winning units **Tim Mitchell**

# 4862 YORK (L-H)
Saturday, July 15

**OFFICIAL GOING: Good (good to firm in places; 7.2)**
Wind: Moderate behind Weather: Cloudy

## 4916 JOHN SMITH'S RACING H'CAP 7f 192y
**1:55** (1:55) (Class 2) (0-105,105) 3-Y-O+
**£15,562** (£4,660; £2,330; £1,165; £582; £292) **Stalls** Low

Form RPR

P121 1 **Chiefofchiefs**[17] 4215 4-8-9 86 .......... (p[1]) StevieDonohoe 7 94+
(Charlie Fellowes) *hld up in rr: hdwy wl over 2f out: swtchd rt and rdn over 1f out: styd on strly fnl f to ld nr fin* 8/1[3]

6-04 2 ½ **Arcanada (IRE)**[163] 538 4-9-9 105 .......... PaddyPilley(5) 2 112
(Tom Dascombe) *cl up on inner: led 2 1/2f out: rdn clr wl over 1f out: drvn ins fnl f: hdd and no ex nr fin* 11/1

-400 3 hd **Kings Gift (IRE)**[23] 3994 3-9-0 100 .......... PaulMulrennan 6 104
(Michael Dods) *trckd ldrs: hdwy over 2f out: rdn over 1f out: drvn to chse ldr ins fnl f: kpt on towards fin* 8/1[3]

0601 4 hd **Just Hiss**[14] 4377 4-8-11 91 .......... (p) RachelRichardson(3) 10 97
(Tim Easterby) *slt ld: pushed along 3f out: sn hdd and rdn: drvn over 1f out: kpt on wl u.p fnl f* 9/1

5500 5 nk **First Selection (SPA)**[21] 4072 4-9-7 98 .......... (e[1]) GrahamLee 13 103
(Simon Crisford) *trckd ldng pair on outer: hdwy and cl up 3f out: rdn over 2f out: drvn wl over 1f out: kpt on u.p fnl f* 33/1

1-3P 6 ½ **Weekend Offender (FR)**[11] 4475 4-8-12 89 .......... KevinStott 14 93+
(Kevin Ryan) *dwlt and towards rr: pushed along and hdwy on outer over 2f out: rdn and edgd lft over 1f out: drvn and styd on wl fnl f* 6/1[1]

6632 7 nk **Twin Appeal (IRE)**[7] 4622 6-9-0 91 .......... (b) AndrewMullen 3 94
(David Barron) *trckd ldrs: hdwy over 2f out: rdn over 1f out: drvn and kpt on same pce fnl f* 25/1

0305 8 ½ **Sir Roderic (IRE)**[17] 4223 4-9-2 93 .......... (p[1]) DanielTudhope 8 96
(Rod Millman) *hld up in midfield: hdwy wl over 2f out: chsd ldrs and rdn over 1f out: styng on whn n.m.r ent fnl f: sn drvn and no imp* 20/1

1-04 9 1 ½ **Firnas**[15] 4316 4-9-4 95 .......... (p[1]) JamesDoyle 12 94+
(Charlie Appleby) *dwlt and rr tl styd on fr over 2f out: n.d* 13/2[2]

0544 10 nk **General Macarthur (USA)**[13] 4410 4-9-1 92 .......... (t) AndreaAtzeni 5 90
(David Simcock) *hld up in midfield: sme hdwy wl over 2f out: sn rdn and n.d* 10/1

3633 11 1 ½ **Qaffaal (USA)**[16] 4261 6-8-11 91 .......... NathanEvans(3) 1 86
(Michael Easterby) *trckd ldrs on inner: hdwy 3f out: rdn along over 2f out: drvn wl over 1f out: grad wknd* 20/1

6-04 12 shd **One Word More (IRE)**[16] 4261 7-9-2 93 .......... (h) DavidAllan 9 88
(Tim Easterby) *dwlt and rr: rdn along over 2f out and sme late hdwy* 11/1

52-0 13 6 **Abe Lincoln (USA)**[24] 3963 4-9-8 99 .......... (t[1]) GeraldMosse 11 80
(Jeremy Noseda) *in tch: pushed along 3f out:. rdn over 2f out and sn wknd* 13/2[2]

-221 14 10 **Constantino (IRE)**[16] 4261 4-9-3 94 .......... (b) TonyHamilton 15 52
(Richard Fahey) *trckd ldrs: pushed along 3f out: rdn over 2f out: sn wknd and rr whn eased fnl f* 11/1

1m 37.56s (-1.44) **Going Correction** +0.05s/f (Good)
**WFA** 3 from 4yo+ 9lb 14 Ran SP% **123.6**
Speed ratings (Par 109): **109,108,108,108,107 107,107,106,105,104 103,103,97,87**
CSF £90.79 CT £742.84 TOTE £8.70: £2.70, £4.00, £3.40; EX 114.00 Trifecta £2065.60.
**Owner** Mervyn Ayers **Bred** Executive Bloodlines **Trained** Newmarket, Suffolk
■ Stewards' Enquiry : Stevie Donohoe caution: careless riding

**FOCUS**
Rail movements increase advertised distances as follows: Race 1 by 28 yards; Race 2, 3 and 6 by 32 yards. A good handicap. They went a respectable gallop on ground officially described as good, good to firm in places. A pb from the second, with the fifth in line with his better form in Britain.

## 4917 JOHN SMITH'S SILVER CUP STKS (LISTED RACE) 1m 5f 188y
**2:30** (2:30) (Class 1) 3-Y-O+ **£28,355** (£10,750; £5,380; £2,680; £1,345) **Stalls** Low

Form RPR

/0-1 **1** **Rare Rhythm**22 4033 5-9-6 105 JamesDoyle 4 115
(Charlie Appleby) *sn trcking ldr: hdwy to ld on inner rail 3f out: jnd and rdn 2f out: drvn over 1f out: edgd rt ins fnl f: styd on gamely to draw clr last 100 yds* **9/4**2

2-32 **2** 2 ¾ **Barsanti (IRE)**21 4070 5-9-6 116 AndreaAtzeni 2 112
(Roger Varian) *trckd ldng pair: hdwy 3f out: chal 2f out: rdn over 1f out: drvn and ev ch ent fnl f: sn edgd rt and ev ch tl no ex last 100 yds* **1/1**1

-600 **3** 1 ¾ **Clever Cookie**14 4356 9-9-6 108 (p) GrahamLee 7 109
(Peter Niven) *hld up in rr: hdwy over 2f out: rdn wl over 1f out: styd on fnl f* **14/1**

13-5 **4** 2 ¼ **Platitude**14 4360 4-9-6 107 DanielTudhope 1 106
(Sir Michael Stoute) *hld up in tch: hdwy 3f out: rdn to chse ldng pair 2f out: swtchd rt and drvn over 1f out: sn one pce* **8/1**3

4/3 **5** 3 ½ **High Jinx (IRE)**57 2803 9-9-6 111 DavidAllan 5 101
(Tim Easterby) *led: pushed along 4f out: rdn and hdd 3f out: sn drvn and grad wknd* **8/1**3

3m 0.79s (0.59) **Going Correction** +0.05s/f (Good) **5 Ran SP% 109.7**
Speed ratings (Par 111): **100,98,97,96,94**
CSF £4.85 TOTE £2.70: £1.50, £1.10; EX 4.30 Trifecta £26.20.
**Owner** Godolphin **Bred** Highclere Stud And Floors Farming **Trained** Newmarket, Suffolk

**FOCUS**
Race distance increased 32 yards. A good quality Listed contest. They went a respectable gallop and an improving gelding turned the favourite away from over 1f out. The third has been rated to this year's form for now.

## 4918 58TH JOHN SMITH'S CUP H'CAP 1m 2f 56y
**3:05** (3:05) (Class 2) 3-Y-O+
**£124,500** (£37,280; £18,640; £9,320; £4,660; £2,340) **Stalls** Low

Form RPR

1564 **1** **Ballet Concerto**24 3963 4-9-3 **102** JamesDoyle 11 109
(Sir Michael Stoute) *trckd ldrs: hdwy 3f out: cl up 2f out: rdn over 1f out: drvn ins fnl f: kpt on wl to ld last 50 yds* **8/1**

1410 **2** ¾ **Big Country (IRE)**7 4614 4-8-7 **99** 5ex RayDawson(7) 4 105
(Michael Appleby) *in tch: hdwy over 2f out: chsd ldrs over 1f out: rdn ent fnl f: styd on wl towards fin* **7/1**3

4230 **3** *nk* **Mistiroc**22 4033 6-9-0 **99** (v) GrahamLee 16 104
(John Quinn) *t.k.h: cl up on inner: hdwy over 2f out: rdn to dispute ld over 1f out: drvn and ev ch ins fnl f: no ex towards fin* **50/1**

6-15 **4** *nse* **UAE Prince (IRE)**63 2604 4-8-12 **97** AndreaAtzeni 20 102
(Roger Varian) *t.k.h: trckd ldrs: hdwy to ld 2f out: rdn over 1f out: drvn ins fnl f: hdd and no ex last 50 yds* **13/2**2

104- **5** *hd* **Mr Garcia**301 6557 4-8-10 **95** JackGarritty 13 100+
(Richard Fahey) *hld up in rr: hdwy 3f out: swtchd to outer and rdn wl over 1f out: styd on strly fnl f* **14/1**

6020 **6** 1 ¼ **Eddystone Rock (IRE)**22 4033 5-9-0 **99** (h) RobertTart 1 101
(John Best) *hld up in midfield: effrt on inner and n.m.r over 2f out: sn rdn and styd on wl fnl f* **20/1**

64-3 **7** *nk* **Victory Bond**58 2767 4-9-3 **102** PatCosgrave 17 103+
(William Haggas) *hld up in rr: hdwy on wd outside over 2f out: sn rdn and kpt on fnl f* **6/1**1

2410 **8** ½ **Another Touch**24 3963 4-9-5 **104** TonyHamilton 19 104
(Richard Fahey) *hld up in rr: swtchd wd and hdwy over 2f out: sn rdn and kpt on fnl f* **33/1**

3-30 **9** *nk* **Central Square (IRE)**21 4069 5-9-8 **107** JackMitchell 8 107
(Roger Varian) *hld up in rr: effrt and nt clr run wl over 2f out: sn swtchd rt and rdn: kpt on fnl f* **16/1**

10-6 **10** *shd* **Scarlet Dragon**21 4069 4-9-10 **109** (h) TomMarquand 10 109
(Eve Johnson Houghton) *hld up: hdwy and n.m.r over 2f out: effrt and nt clr run over 1f out: sn rdn and kpt on same pce* **10/1**

2-60 **11** ¾ **Erik The Red (FR)**59 2735 5-8-12 **97** (p1) KevinStott 7 95
(Kevin Ryan) *t.k.h in midfield: hdwy 3f out: chsd ldrs 2f out: sn rdn and wknd appr fnl f* **16/1**

0010 **12** 1 **Master Carpenter (IRE)**22 4033 6-9-3 **105** AdamMcNamara(3) 15 101
(Rod Millman) *midfield: hdwy 3f out: chsd ldrs 2f out: sn rdn: drvn and wknd appr fnl f* **12/1**

0-44 **13** 1 ¼ **Dark Red (IRE)**51 2999 5-8-10 **95** PaulMulrennan 3 89
(Ed Dunlop) *trckd ldrs on inner: effrt and n.m.r over 2f out: sn rdn and wknd wl over 1f out* **25/1**

1-05 **14** ½ **Sixties Groove (IRE)**22 4033 4-8-13 **98** (p) GeraldMosse 14 91+
(Jeremy Noseda) *hld up in midfield: hdwy on outer 3f out: chsd ldrs and rdn 2f out: sn edgd lft: drvn and wknd over 1f out* **8/1**

1501 **15** 1 **Snoano**21 4069 5-9-8 **107** 5ex DavidAllan 6 98
(Tim Easterby) *hld up: hdwy 3f out: sn rdn along over 2f out: n.d* **20/1**

1000 **16** ¾ **Bravery (IRE)**24 3963 4-9-5 **104** (h) DanielTudhope 9 93
(David O'Meara) *a towards rr* **33/1**

4002 **17** *nk* **Majeed**21 4069 7-9-1 **100** FergusSweeney 5 89
(David Simcock) *stdd s: hld up: a towards rr* **14/1**

5030 **18** 1 ¼ **Dragon Mall (USA)**21 4069 4-9-2 **101** (be1) StevieDonohoe 21 87
(David Simcock) *dwlt: a rr* **25/1**

1210 **19** 24 **Briardale (IRE)**16 4261 5-9-1 **100** DavidNolan 18 38
(James Bethell) *t.k.h: sn led: set stdy pce: rdn along and qcknd 3f out: hdd 2f out and sn wknd* **33/1**

/600 **20** 11 **Tumbaga (USA)**21 4069 6-8-12 **100** EdwardGreatrex(3) 22 16
(Saeed bin Suroor) *t.k.h: cl up: chal 3f out: rdn along over 2f out: sn wknd* **40/1**

2m 10.16s (-2.34) **Going Correction** +0.05s/f (Good) **20 Ran SP% 134.7**
Speed ratings (Par 109): **111,110,110,110,109 108,108,108,108,108 107,106,105,105,104 103,103,102,83,74**
CSF £60.45 CT £2736.83 TOTE £9.40: £2.60, £2.30, £10.40, £2.30; EX 82.50 Trifecta £3688.50 Part won..
**Owner** Saeed Suhail **Bred** Meon Valley Stud **Trained** Newmarket, Suffolk

**FOCUS**
Race distance increased 32 yards. The feature contest was a typically competitive renewal of a good quality heritage handicap. There was a bunched finish off a disappointing pace and it therefore helped to race prominently. The third sets the standard and also rather limits the form.

## 4919 JOHN SMITH'S NOVICE MEDIAN AUCTION STKS (PLUS 10 RACE) 6f
**3:40** (3:41) (Class 3) 2-Y-O **£7,762** (£2,310; £1,154; £577) **Stalls** Low

Form RPR

4 **1** **Ulshaw Bridge (IRE)**16 4259 2-9-2 0 DanielTudhope 11 84
(James Bethell) *trckd ldrs: hdwy 2f out: rdn to chal ent fnl f: led last 100 yds: kpt on strly* **12/1**

3 **2** 1 ¾ **Midnight Wilde**21 4090 2-9-2 0 GeraldMosse 8 79
(John Ryan) *towards rr: hdwy on outer 2f out: rdn over 1f out: styd on wl fnl f* **20/1**

01 **3** ¾ **Encrypted**17 4213 2-9-8 0 JamesDoyle 3 83
(Hugo Palmer) *wnt rt s: t.k.h: led: rdn over 1f out: drvn ins fnl f: hdd last 100 yds: kpt on same pce* **11/4**2

21 **4** 2 **Royal Household**29 3776 2-9-8 0 TomMarquand 5 77
(Richard Hannon) *t.k.h: cl up: rdn along 2f out: wknd over 1f out* **5/2**1

4 **5** *hd* **Collateral Beauty**20 4116 2-8-11 0 JackGarritty 4 65+
(Richard Fahey) *bmpd s: t.k.h: green: awkward and j. path after 100 yds: chsd ldrs: rdn along 2f out: styd on wl fnl f* **20/1**

33 **6** *hd* **Magic Mark**29 3789 2-8-13 0 JordanVaughan(3) 7 69
(K R Burke) *cl up: rdn wl over 1f out: drvn and wknd appr fnl f* **6/1**3

**7** 2 ¼ **Sands Of Mali (FR)** 2-9-2 0 DavidNolan 2 64
(Richard Fahey) *trckd ldrs: effrt on inner and n.m.r wl over 1f out: sn rdn and one pce after* **7/1**

02 **8** 2 ½ **Lyrical Pursuit**14 4359 2-8-8 0 NathanEvans(3) 9 50
(Michael Easterby) *a towards rr* **33/1**

**9** 1 **Push N'Pull (IRE)** 2-8-13 0 AdamMcNamara(3) 6 52
(Richard Fahey) *a towards rr* **14/1**

4 **10** *hd* **Foxrush Take Time (FR)**14 4374 2-9-2 0 PatCosgrave 10 51
(Richard Guest) *dwlt: a rr* **50/1**

**11** *hd* **Lucky Lucky Man (IRE)** 2-9-2 0 PatrickMathers 1 51
(Richard Fahey) *chsd ldrs: bmpd at path after 100 yds rdn along wl over 2f out: sn wknd* **9/1**

1m 11.82s (-0.08) **Going Correction** +0.05s/f (Good) **11 Ran SP% 120.8**
Speed ratings (Par 98): **102,99,98,96,95 95,92,89,87,87 87**
CSF £233.00 TOTE £13.50: £3.30, £5.40, £1.40; EX 246.90 Trifecta £2822.30 Part won..
**Owner** Geoffrey Van Cutsem & Partners **Bred** Camas Park & Lynch Bages **Trained** Middleham Moor, N Yorks

**FOCUS**
A decent juvenile novice contest. They went a respectable gallop and a 6lb penalty anchored the second favourite in the final furlong.

## 4920 JOHN SMITH'S CITY WALLS STKS (LISTED RACE) 5f
**4:15** (4:17) (Class 1) 3-Y-O+
**£28,355** (£10,750; £5,380; £2,680; £1,345; £675) **Stalls** Centre

Form RPR

0-05 **1** **Take Cover**25 3926 10-9-1 111 DavidAllan 12 113
(David C Griffiths) *mde virtually all: rdn wl over 1f out: drvn ins fnl f: kpt on gamely towards fin* **9/2**1

4105 **2** ½ **Final Venture**14 4354 5-9-4 108 PaulMulrennan 7 114
(Paul Midgley) *cl up: disp ld 2f out: rdn and ev ch over 1f out: drvn ent fnl f: kpt on same pce towards fin* **14/1**

-000 **3** *nk* **Cotai Glory**25 3926 5-9-1 110 JamesDoyle 11 110
(Charles Hills) *hld up: hdwy 2f out: rdn to chse ldrs over 1f out: drvn and styd on wl fnl f* **7/1**3

5111 **4** 2 ¼ **Judicial (IRE)**25 3932 5-9-1 107 (e) JoeDoyle 1 102
(Julie Camacho) *in tch: hdwy on outer 2f out: rdn to chse ldrs over 1f out: drvn and kpt on fnl f* **9/2**1

2660 **5** ½ **Ornate**14 4354 4-9-1 105 (h) AndreaAtzeni 9 100
(Robert Cowell) *chsd ldng pair: rdn along 2f out: drvn over 1f out: kpt on same pce* **20/1**

3203 **6** *nse* **Goldream**7 4635 8-9-1 110 (p) PatCosgrave 3 100
(Robert Cowell) *dwlt and rr: hdwy 2f out: rdn over 1f out: styd on fnl f* **11/2**2

301 **7** *nse* **Encore D'Or**24 3967 5-9-1 105 JackGarritty 4 100
(Robert Cowell) *chsd ldrs: hdwy 2f out: rdn over 1f out: sn drvn and kpt on same pce* **25/1**

041 **8** *hd* **Out Do**21 4072 8-9-1 104 (v) DanielTudhope 8 99
(David O'Meara) *hld up: hdwy over 2f out: rdn to chse ldrs over 1f out: kpt on same pce fnl f* **10/1**

3-32 **9** 1 **Bounce**49 3080 4-8-10 95 FergusSweeney 6 93
(Henry Candy) *a towards rr* **8/1**

2113 **10** 1 **Copper Knight (IRE)**28 3835 3-8-10 101 RachelRichardson 10 90
(Tim Easterby) *chsd ldrs: rdn wl over 1f out: sn drvn and wknd* **9/1**

122 **11** 4 **Kyllang Rock (IRE)**36 3539 3-8-10 107 (p1) GeraldMosse 2 75
(James Tate) *chsd ldrs: rdn wl over 1f out: sn drvn and wknd* **10/1**

57.26s (-2.04) **Going Correction** +0.05s/f (Good)
**WFA** 3 from 4yo+ 5lb **11 Ran SP% 118.8**
Speed ratings (Par 111): **118,117,116,113,112 112,112,111,110,108 102**
CSF £69.74 TOTE £5.00: £2.00, £4.70, £2.30; EX 64.80 Trifecta £479.70.
**Owner** Norcroft Park Stud **Bred** Norcroft Park Stud **Trained** Bawtry, S Yorks

**FOCUS**
A good quality Listed sprint won last year by the subsequent Group 1 Prix De L'Abbaye winner Marsha. One of the joint-favourites made virtually all at a strong tempo towards the near side. The winner has been rated close to his best.

## 4921 JOHN SMITH'S STAYERS' H'CAP 2m 56y
**4:45** (4:46) (Class 3) (0-95,93) 4-Y-O+ **£9,703** (£2,887; £1,443; £721) **Stalls** Low

Form RPR

4411 **1** **Theydon Grey**29 3794 4-8-12 **89** GeorgiaCox(5) 1 98+
(William Haggas) *set stdy pce: qcknd over 3f out: pushed along over 2f out: rdn wl over 1f out: strly chal ent fnl f: carried hd high but styd on gamely towards fin* **5/2**2

2402 **2** *nk* **Byron Flyer**35 3594 6-9-4 **90** JamesDoyle 10 98+
(Ian Williams) *trckd ldrs: hdwy 3f out: chsd wnr over 1f out: sn rdn to chal: drvn and ev ch ins fnl f: no ex towards fin* **7/4**1

160/ **3** 1 ¼ **Edge Of Sanity (IRE)**801 2004 8-9-7 **93** (t) PaulMulrennan 2 99
(Iain Jardine) *trckd ldrs: hdwy on inner 3f out: cl up over 2f out: rdn wl over 1f out: ev ch: drvn ins fnl f: kpt on same pce towards fin* **20/1**

6305 **4** 3 ½ **Gabrial's King (IRE)**14 4355 8-9-2 **88** DavidNolan 6 90
(Richard Fahey) *trckd ldrs: hdwy over 3f out: rdn along 2f out: drvn over 1f out: sn one pce* **14/1**

-611 **5** 1 1/4 **Great Fighter**[28] 3830 7-8-8 **85**........................(v) PhilDennis(5) 8 86
(Jim Goldie) *hld up in rr: hdwy over 3f out: rdn to chse ldrs 2f out: sn drvn and no imp appr fnl f* **4/1**[3]

2000 **6** 1 1/4 **Purple Rock (IRE)**[17] 4206 5-8-7 **82**........................(t) NathanEvans(3) 5 81+
(Michael Easterby) *trckd ldrs: hdwy over 3f out: rdn along on outer to chse ldrs 2f out: drvn over 1f out: sn wknd* **20/1**

010 **7** 1 1/4 **Perfect Summer (IRE)**[24] 3968 7-8-4 **76**..................(v) PatrickMathers 9 74
(Ian Williams) *trckd wnr: cl up over 3f out: sn rdn and wknd* **20/1**

0144 **8** 3/4 **Gabrial's Star**[14] 4338 8-8-10 **85**........................(v) AdamMcNamara(3) 4 82
(Richard Fahey) *hld up in tch: pushed along over 3f out: rdn wl over 2f out: sn btn* **12/1**

005/ **9** 21 **Mawaqeet (USA)**[363] 8124 8-8-11 **83**............................ TomMarquand 7 54
(Michael Appleby) *a rr: rdn along and outpcd fnl 3f* **33/1**

3m 43.22s (8.72) **Going Correction** +0.05s/f (Good) **9** Ran SP% **116.5**
Speed ratings (Par 107): **80,79,79,77,76 76,75,75,64**
CSF £6.87 CT £67.53 TOTE £3.20: £1.20, £1.10, £3.80; EX 9.10 Trifecta £84.30.
**Owner** The Going Grey Partnership **Bred** Pinnacle Bloodstock Ltd **Trained** Newmarket, Suffolk

**FOCUS**
Race distance increased 32 yards. A fairly good staying handicap. The second favourite gamely dictated his own increasing tempo in the straight off a modest pace. The fourth has been rated close to his recent form.

## 4922 JOHN SMITH'S NURSERY H'CAP 6f
**5:15** (5:15) (Class 2) 2-Y-O **£9,703** (£2,887; £1,443; £721) **Stalls** Low

Form RPR

621 **1** **Mr Wagyu (IRE)**[23] 4014 2-8-8 **73**............................ TomMarquand 7 77
(John Quinn) *in tch on outer: hdwy 2f out: rdn to chal ent fnl f: drvn and kpt on wl to ld towards fin* **4/1**[2]

011 **2** nk **John Kirkup**[17] 4204 2-9-7 **86**............................ PaulMulrennan 2 89
(Michael Dods) *trckd ldrs: hdwy 2f out: cl up over 1f out: sn rdn: drvn to ld ins fnl f: hdd and no ex towards fin* **9/2**[3]

430 **3** 3/4 **The Right Choice (IRE)**[9] 4526 2-8-3 **68**............................ PatrickMathers 6 69
(Richard Fahey) *dwlt and rr: pushed along 2f out: rdn over 1f out: kpt on wl fnl f* **6/1**

0456 **4** 1/2 **Angel Force (IRE)**[3] 4739 2-7-13 **67** oh12 ow2......(h[1]) NathanEvans(3) 4 66
(David C Griffiths) *led: rdn along 2f out: drvn over 1f out: hdd ins fnl f: kpt on same pce* **18/1**

4211 **5** 1/2 **Jedi Master (IRE)**[39] 3430 2-9-1 **83**........................ AdamMcNamara(3) 1 81
(Richard Fahey) *chsd ldrs: rdn along and sltly outpcd 2f out: swtchd rt and drvn ent fnl f: kpt on towards fin* **7/2**[1]

054 **6** 1/2 **Contribute**[21] 4094 2-8-3 **68**............................(b[1]) RyanTate 5 64
(Martyn Meade) *cl up: chal over 2f out: rdn wl over 1f out ev ch: drvn ins fnl f and wknd last 100 yds* **7/1**

6452 **7** 7 **Jim Rockford**[9] 4527 2-8-8 **73**............................ AndreaAtzeni 3 48
(Ralph Beckett) *cl up: rdn along over 2f out: sn drvn and wknd* **7/2**[1]

1m 12.03s (0.13) **Going Correction** +0.05s/f (Good) **7** Ran SP% **114.7**
Speed ratings (Par 100): **101,100,99,98,98 97,88**
CSF £22.34 TOTE £4.90: £2.40, £2.80; EX 18.40 Trifecta £74.20.
**Owner** The New Century Partnership **Bred** Danny O'Sullivan **Trained** Settrington, N Yorks

**FOCUS**
A decent nursery handicap. They went a respectable gallop and an improving colt grabbed the spoils.
T/Jkpt: Not Won. T/Plt: £98.40 to a £1 stake. Pool: £190,714.94 - 1,413.91 winning units T/Qpdt: £15.10 to a £1 stake. Pool: £11,102.45 - 541.39 winning units **Joe Rowntree**

4923 - 4924a (Foreign Racing) - See Raceform Interactive

# 4414 CURRAGH (R-H)
Saturday, July 15

**OFFICIAL GOING: Good to firm**

## 4925a TOTE SCURRY H'CAP (PREMIER HANDICAP) 6f 63y
**4:20** (4:20) 3-Y-O+
**£50,427** (£16,239; £7,692; £3,418; £1,709; £854) **Stalls** Centre

RPR

**1** **Tithonus (IRE)**[13] 4416 6-9-0 **90**............................(bt) GaryHalpin(3) 12 99+
(Denis Gerard Hogan, Ire) *broke wl to sn ld: narrow advantage at 1/2-way: rdn 2f out and sn edgd sltly lft: kpt on wl u.p ins fnl f: all out* **10/1**

**2** 1/2 **Snap Shots (IRE)**[35] 3585 5-9-4 **91**..................(p) DeclanMcDonogh 17 98+
(Tony Coyle) *wnt sltly lft s: w ldrs: cl 2nd at 1/2-way: sn pushed along and n.m.r on inner u.p 1 1/2f out: sn swtchd rt and kpt on ins fnl f: a hld* **7/1**[3]

**3** 1/2 **Celebration**[13] 4416 4-9-7 **94**............................ ColinKeane 5 99
(G M Lyons, Ire) *in rr of mid-div: 9th 1/2-way: hdwy far side over 2f out to chse ldrs u.p over 1f out: kpt on same pce in 3rd clsng stages: nt trble wnr* **7/1**[3]

**4** 3/4 **Ma Fee Heela (FR)**[15] 4327 3-8-3 **89**..................(p[1]) SeanDavis(7) 2 91
(M D O'Callaghan, Ire) *hld up towards rr: hdwy in 15th after 1/2-way to chse ldrs u.p far side over 1f out: kpt on same pce in 4th clsng stages: nt trble wnr* **9/1**

**5** 1 1/4 **Rattling Jewel**[13] 4416 5-9-3 **90**............................(p) KevinManning 13 89
(Miss Nicole McKenna, Ire) *chsd ldrs: 3rd 1/2-way: rdn 1f out and no ex u.p in 3rd ins fnl f: kpt on same pce in 5th clsng stages: jst hld 5th* **20/1**

**6** hd **Rivellino**[9] 4548 7-8-9 **82**............................ RonanWhelan 16 80
(Adrian McGuinness, Ire) *cl up early: 4th 1/2-way: rdn 1 1/2f out and no imp on ldrs ins fnl f: kpt on same pce: jst hld for 5th* **33/1**

**7** shd **George Bowen (IRE)**[30] 3757 5-9-10 **97**............................ WJLee 3 95+
(Richard Fahey) *in rr of mid-div: gng wl in 12th after 1/2-way: n.m.r 2f out: swtchd rt 1f out and r.o clsng stages: nvr nrr* **6/1**[2]

**8** shd **Gin In The Inn (IRE)**[35] 3593 4-9-4 **91**............................ ChrisHayes 4 89+
(Richard Fahey) *hld up towards rr: 14th 1/2-way: sme hdwy far side under 2f out where n.m.r bhd horses: swtchd rt ins fnl f and kpt on same pce: nvr trbld ldrs* **16/1**

**9** nk **Sors (IRE)**[13] 4416 5-9-1 **93**............................ KillianLeonard(5) 14 90
(Andrew Slattery, Ire) *prom tl sn settled bhd ldrs: 5th 1/2-way: rdn over 2f out and sn no ex: wknd fnl f* **25/1**

**10** 1 **Shepherd's Purse**[20] 4125 5-8-10 **83**............................ ShaneFoley 11 77
(Joseph G Murphy, Ire) *hld up in tch: 6th 1/2-way: rdn after 1/2-way and no ex over 1f out: sn wknd* **16/1**

**11** shd **Rapid Applause**[49] 3097 5-8-12 **88**............................ ShaneBKelly(3) 9 81
(M D O'Callaghan, Ire) *mid-div: 7th 1/2-way: rdn 2f out and no ex u.p ent fnl f: wknd* **12/1**

**12** 1/2 **Maarek**[13] 4416 10-9-11 **98**............................ SeamieHeffernan 15 90+
(Miss Evanna McCutcheon, Ire) *dwlt and towards rr early: tk clsr order in rr of mid-div after 1f: 10th 1/2-way: n.m.r bhd horses fr under 2f out: rdn and no ex ins fnl f* **25/1**

**13** hd **Big Time (IRE)**[69] 2433 6-9-7 **99**............................(v) OisinOrr(5) 1 90
(Kevin Ryan) *towards rr: last at 1/2-way: pushed along after 1/2-way and no imp u.p ent fnl f: kpt on one pce* **14/1**

**14** 1 1/4 **Master Speaker (IRE)**[14] 4382 7-9-8 **95**..............(bt) ColmO'Donoghue 7 82+
(Martin Hassett, Ire) *dwlt: w.w in rr early: 16th 1/2-way: n.m.r 2f out and sltly hmpd on inner: no imp after* **20/1**

**15** 1/2 **Tobacco Bay (IRE)**[14] 4385 3-8-6 **85**............................ WayneLordan 8 69
(J P Murtagh, Ire) *hld up: 11th 1/2-way: pushed along over 2f out and no imp ins fnl f: wknd clsng stages* **11/1**

**16** 2 1/4 **Normandy Barriere (IRE)**[21] 4072 5-9-12 **99**.................... PatSmullen 6 77
(Nigel Tinkler) *hld up: sme hdwy in 13th after 1/2-way: n.m.r between horses under 2f out and sn chekced: no imp after and eased wl ins fnl f* **11/2**[1]

**17** 3 3/4 **G Force (IRE)**[21] 4072 6-9-4 **98**............................(p) DannySheehy(7) 10 64
(Adrian Paul Keatley, Ire) *sltly awkward s: settled in mid-div: 8th 1/2-way: rdn after 1/2-way and wknd towards rr 2f out: eased ins fnl f* **16/1**

1m 14.25s (-4.85) **Going Correction** -0.775s/f (Hard)
**WFA** 3 from 4yo+ 6lb **17** Ran SP% **134.3**
Speed ratings: **101,100,99,98,97 96,96,96,96,94 94,93,93,92,91 88,83**
CSF £80.00 CT £565.23 TOTE £15.50: £3.00, £2.10, £1.90, £2.60; DF 132.90 Trifecta £587.60.
**Owner** T & M Racing Partnership **Bred** K N Dhunjibhoy & B M Desai **Trained** Cloughjordan, Co Tipperary

**FOCUS**
Not many if any horses achieve back-to-back premier sprint handicaps over five and six furlongs respectively in the space of a fortnight and such an accolade does not even begin to describe the versatility of the winner. He is a no-nonsense sprinter, who is maybe even a shade lazy, but he really fights in a finish and is effective over five, six and seven furlongs. The 2nd/4th/6th set the standard.

## 4926a JEBEL ALI SILVER JUBILEE ANGLESEY STKS (GROUP 3) 6f 63y
**4:50** (4:51) 2-Y-O **£32,777** (£10,555; £5,000; £2,222; £1,111) **Stalls** Centre

RPR

**1** **Actress (IRE)**[9] 4680 2-9-0 0............................ SeamieHeffernan 2 104
(A P O'Brien, Ire) *cl up bhd ldrs far side tl disp ld gng wl fr 1/2-way: led gng best over 1f out: pushed out ins fnl f and kpt on wl: comf* **7/1**

**2** 1 3/4 **Theobald (IRE)**[23] 4021 2-9-3 0............................ KevinManning 3 102
(J S Bolger, Ire) *led and disp tl pushed along between horses in cl 3rd fr 1/2-way: rdn over 2f out and no imp on wnr u.p ent fnl f: kpt on same pce in 2nd wl ins fnl f: nt trble wnr* **10/3**[2]

**3** 1/2 **Brother Bear (IRE)**[25] 3925 2-9-3 106........................ ColmO'Donoghue 5 100
(Mrs John Harrington, Ire) *led and disp: rdn 2f out and hdd u.p over 1f out where edgd sltly lft: no imp on wnr ins fnl f: kpt on same pce in 3rd clsng stages* **9/10**[1]

**4** 4 3/4 **Commander Grigio (IRE)**[14] 4386 2-9-3 100.................... ChrisHayes 6 89
(J A Stack, Ire) *chsd ldrs: 4th 1/2-way: rdn under 2f out and n.m.r nr side over 1f out where checked sltly: sn swtchd and no imp on ldrs: kpt on one pce in 4th wl ins fnl f* **9/2**[3]

**5** 1/2 **Guessthebill (IRE)**[56] 2845 2-9-3 0............................ PatSmullen 4 85
(J P Murtagh, Ire) *in rr thrght: pushed along after 1/2-way and no imp on ldrs u.p over 1f out: kpt on one pce ins fnl f* **16/1**

1m 14.26s (-4.84) **Going Correction** -0.775s/f (Hard) **5** Ran SP% **112.3**
Speed ratings: **101,98,98,91,91**
CSF £30.10 TOTE £8.00: £2.80, £1.60; DF 28.20 Trifecta £62.40.
**Owner** Michael Tabor & Derrick Smith & Mrs John Magnier **Bred** Lynch Bages Ltd **Trained** Cashel, Co Tipperary
■ Stewards' Enquiry : Colm O'Donoghue one-day ban: careless riding

**FOCUS**
A small field but a race that was run not without incident. The winner was good value for her near 2l success and was impressive.

## 4927a FRIARSTOWN STUD SAPPHIRE STKS (GROUP 2) 5f
**5:20** (5:22) 3-Y-O+
**£60,512** (£19,487; £9,230; £4,102; £2,051; £1,025) **Stalls** Centre

RPR

**1** **Caspian Prince (IRE)**[28] 3829 8-9-8 110...............(t) DeclanMcDonogh 6 116
(Tony Coyle) *broke wl to ld and wnt sltly rt s: over 1 l clr at 1/2-way: reduced advantage after 1/2-way: rdn and strly pressed over 1f out: hdd narrowly ins fnl f tl rallied clsng stages to regain ld fnl stride* **10/1**

**2** shd **Marsha (IRE)**[25] 3926 4-9-5 116............................ LukeMorris 3 113+
(Sir Mark Prescott Bt) *settled bhd ldr and racd keenly early: jnd for 2nd bef 1/2-way: rdn in 2nd 1 1/2f out and led narrowly ins fnl f: all out wl ins fnl f where strly pressed and hdd fnl stride* **1/2**[1]

**3** 2 1/2 **Ardhoomey (IRE)**[25] 3926 5-9-8 110............................(t) ColinKeane 2 107
(G M Lyons, Ire) *hooded to load: hld up in rr: sme hdwy far side over 1f out: rdn in 3rd ins fnl f and no imp on ldrs: kpt on same pce clsng stages to jst hold 3rd* **5/1**[2]

**4** hd **Hit The Bid**[13] 4416 3-9-3 107............................ LeighRoche 5 104+
(D J Bunyan, Ire) *chsd ldrs: tk clsr order at 1/2-way: rdn nr side 1 1/2f out and no imp on ldrs u.p in 4th ins fnl f: kpt on same pce clsng stages: jst hld for 3rd* **15/2**[3]

**5** 1 3/4 **Spirit Quartz (IRE)**[13] 4416 9-9-8 104............................ ChrisHayes 1 100
(Barry John Murphy, Ire) *hooded to load: settled bhd ldrs: rdn 2f out and sn lost tch: one pce in 5th ins fnl f* **33/1**

**6** 3 1/2 **Alphabet**[27] 3873 3-9-0 95............................(t) SeamieHeffernan 4 82
(A P O'Brien, Ire) *chsd ldrs tl disp 2nd bef 1/2-way: rdn in 3rd after 1/2-way and no ex 1 1/2f out: sn wknd to rr and eased wl ins fnl f* **16/1**

57.15s (-5.75) **Going Correction** -0.775s/f (Hard)
**WFA** 3 from 4yo+ 5lb **6** Ran SP% **113.0**
Speed ratings: **115,114,110,110,107 102**
CSF £15.95 TOTE £10.40: £3.20, £1.02; DF 18.30 Trifecta £44.30.
**Owner** Stephen Louch **Bred** Ballygallon Stud Limited **Trained** Norton, N Yorks
■ Stewards' Enquiry : Luke Morris two-day ban: used whip above shoulder height

**FOCUS**
A bit of a surprise in the end as the favourite was outbattled a bit, but credit to the winner for the attitude he displayed and he posted a small pb.

## 4928a DARLEY IRISH OAKS (GROUP 1) (FILLIES) 1m 4f
**5:55** (5:56) 3-Y-O
**£194,871** (£64,957; £30,769; £13,675; £6,837; £3,418)

RPR

**1** **Enable**[43] 3301 3-9-0 120............................ FrankieDettori 6 121+
(John Gosden) *settled bhd ldr in 2nd: impr gng wl to ld over 2f out where pushed along: sn rdn and qckned clr: styd on strly to assert ins fnl f: eased cl home: easily* **2/5**[1]

2 5 1/2 **Rain Goddess (IRE)**[13] 4419 3-9-0 110 ..................(t) SeamieHeffernan 2 112
(A P O'Brien, Ire) *on toes befhand: sn led: disp 3rd at 1/2-way: hdwy 4th into st: impr into 2nd and rdn 2f out: no imp on easy wnr u.p ent fnl f: kpt on same pce* **7/1**[3]

3 2 **Eziyra (IRE)**[37] 3511 3-9-0 106 ..........................................(h) PatSmullen 3 109
(D K Weld, Ire) *in rr of mid-div early: 7th 1/2-way: hdwy 2f out to chse ldrs: rdn in 3rd under 2f out and no imp on easy wnr ent fnl f: kpt on same pce* **20/1**

4 1 1/4 **Coronet**[23] 3995 3-9-0 108 .................................................. OlivierPeslier 9 107+
(John Gosden) *hld up towards rr: racd keenly early: last at 1/2-way: pushed along in rr into st and sme hdwy on outer 2f out: wnt 4th ins fnl f and kpt on clsng stages: nvr trbld ldrs* **6/1**[2]

5 2 1/2 **Aurora Butterfly (IRE)**[17] 4208 3-9-0 93 ..............................(h[1]) WJLee 1 103
(W McCreery, Ire) *in rr early: tk clsr order in 9th after 1f: hdwy in 8th under 3f out and impr between horses 2f out where n.m.r: rdn to dispute 4th over 1f out and sn no ex: one pce in 5th wl ins fnl f* **66/1**

6 1 1/4 **Alluringly (USA)**[23] 3995 3-9-0 106 .................................... WayneLordan 8 101
(A P O'Brien, Ire) *in rr of mid-div early: 6th 1/2-way: pushed along on outer in 6th under 3f out: sn rdn and no ex disputing 4th over 1f out: one pce after* **16/1**

7 2 **Intricately (IRE)**[13] 4419 3-9-0 108 ............................ DonnachaO'Brien 5 98
(Joseph Patrick O'Brien, Ire) *hld up in tch: 5th 1/2-way: pushed along in 5th into st: sn rdn bhd ldrs on outer and no ex between horses over 1f out: sn wknd* **20/1**

8 5 **Bean Feasa**[24] 3964 3-9-0 101 ......................................(t) KevinManning 10 90
(J S Bolger, Ire) *chsd ldrs: racd keenly early: disp 3rd at 1/2-way: pushed along in 3rd into st and sn no ex u.p: wknd 2f out* **33/1**

9 3/4 **Bengala (FR)**[27] 3874 3-9-0 94 ..............................(h[1]) DeclanMcDonogh 4 89
(John M Oxx, Ire) *broke wl to ld: over 2 l clr at 1/2-way: pressed clly into st: rdn and hdd over 2f out: wknd* **33/1**

10 7 1/2 **Naughty Or Nice (IRE)**[23] 3995 3-9-0 99 ......................... ColinKeane 7 77
(John M Oxx, Ire) *w.w towards rr: niggled along briefly in 8th at 1/2-way: rdn and no imp over 2f out: wknd: eased ins fnl f* **16/1**

2m 32.13s (-6.37) **Going Correction** -0.125s/f (Firm) **10** Ran SP% **126.9**
Speed ratings: **116,112,111,110,108 107,106,103,102,97**
CSF £4.20 CT £34.79 TOTE £1.40: £1.02, £1.50, £3.30; DF 4.40 Trifecta £27.20.
**Owner** K Abdullah **Bred** Juddmonte Farms Ltd **Trained** Newmarket, Suffolk

**FOCUS**
A performance of pure class from the winner, cementing the suspicion that she could be the best middle-distance 3yo around. The 4th helps set the level in line with her latest, with the 2nd/3rd fully entitled to small pbs up in trip. The winner posted the best figure in this race since Sariska (123).

4929 - 4933a (Foreign Racing) - See Raceform Interactive

## 4923 CURRAGH (R-H)
Sunday, July 16

**OFFICIAL GOING: Good to firm**

### 4934a KILBOY ESTATE STKS (GROUP 2) (F&M) 1m 1f
3:10 (3:10) 3-Y-O+
**£57,991** (£18,675; £8,846; £3,931; £1,965; £982)

RPR

1 **Elizabeth Browning (IRE)**[18] 4229 3-9-0 92 .........(t) SeamieHeffernan 2 105
(A P O'Brien, Ire) *dwlt: w.w in rr: last at 1/2-way: hdwy on outer fr 2f out to chse ldrs u.p over 1f out: r.o wl to ld wl ins fnl f* **12/1**

2 1 3/4 **Wilamina (IRE)**[46] 3219 4-9-9 99 .............................. ColmO'Donoghue 4 102+
(Martyn Meade) *sn disp tl hdd after 1f and settled bhd ldrs: 3rd 1/2-way: rdn in 3rd over 2f out and ev ch almost on terms ins fnl f: no imp on wnr in 2nd clsng stages* **8/1**

3 1 1/2 **Laganore (IRE)**[14] 4419 5-9-9 105 ..................................... ColinKeane 7 99+
(A J Martin, Ire) *got upset in stalls briefly: dwlt and towards rr: travelling wl in 6th into st: hdwy 2f out: sn swtchd rt and rdn almost on terms fnl side 1f out: no imp on wnr u.p in 3rd wl ins fnl f* **3/1**[2]

4 nk **Turret Rocks (IRE)**[14] 4419 4-9-9 107 ........................... KevinManning 1 99+
(J S Bolger, Ire) *chsd ldrs tl impr to ld after 1f: rdn and pressed clly under 3f out: hdd u.p ins fnl f and wknd into 4th clsng stages* **7/4**[1]

5 7 **Pocketfullofdreams (FR)**[14] 4419 3-9-0 97 ......................... RyanMoore 6 83
(A P O'Brien, Ire) *sn led and disp tl settled in 2nd after 1f: cl 2nd at 1/2-way: rdn almost on terms under 2f out and no ex over 1f out: wknd into 5th and eased ins fnl f* **11/2**[3]

6 2 1/2 **Absolute Blast (IRE)**[13] 4518 5-9-9 102 ......................... LukeMorris 5 79
(Archie Watson) *hld up in tch: niggled along in 4th bef 1/2-way: rdn into st and no ex 2f out: sn wknd* **7/1**

7 15 **Sea Swift (IRE)**[6] 4707 4-9-9 99 .......................................(h) PatSmullen 3 47
(D K Weld, Ire) *broke wl to ld briefly tl sn hdd and settled bhd ldrs: 5th 1/2-way: pushed along over 2f out and sn dropped to rr: eased fr under 2f out* **14/1**

1m 49.29s (-5.61) **Going Correction** -0.30s/f (Firm)
**WFA** 3 from 4yo+ 9lb **7** Ran SP% **114.7**
Speed ratings: **112,110,109,108,102 100,87**
CSF £100.93 TOTE £14.40: £6.00, £3.40; DF 110.50 Trifecta £729.50.
**Owner** China Horse Club International Ltd & Mrs John Magn **Bred** Desert Star Phoenix Jvc **Trained** Cashel, Co Tipperary

**FOCUS**
A turn-up here, with the outsider of the O'Brien stable coming with a wet sail in the final furlong. The leaders were racing a fair way out and had little left to offer late on. The runner-up, rated to her best, helps set the standard for now.

### 4935a QATAR AIRWAYS MINSTREL STKS (GROUP 2) 7f
3:45 (3:47) 3-Y-O+
**£60,512** (£19,487; £9,230; £4,102; £2,051; £1,025)

RPR

1 **Spirit Of Valor (USA)**[25] 3959 3-9-1 114 ......................(bt) RyanMoore 8 117+
(A P O'Brien, Ire) *broke wl to ld: narrow advantage at 1/2-way: jnd briefly after 1/2-way: regained ld fr 2f out where pushed along: drvn clr 1f out and styd on wl: comf* **5/2**[1]

2 1 3/4 **So Beloved**[15] 4371 7-9-8 108 ....................................(h) DanielTudhope 1 115
(David O'Meara) *settled in mid-div: 5th 1/2-way: stl gng wl under 2f out: rdn and r.o wl ins fnl f to snatch 2nd fnl stride: nt trble wnr* **20/1**

3 shd **Stormy Antarctic**[15] 4371 4-9-8 0 ............................ JamieSpencer 3 115
(Ed Walker) *chsd ldrs in 4th early: 6th 1/2-way: tk clsr order bhd ldrs in 4th over 2f out: rdn into 2nd ins fnl f and no imp on wnr clsng stages: denied 2nd fnl stride* **7/1**[3]

4 1 1/2 **Gordon Lord Byron (IRE)**[15] 4382 9-9-8 112 ............................ WJLee 4 111
(T Hogan, Ire) *trckd ldr: cl 2nd at 1/2-way: disp ld briefly after 1/2-way: rdn in 2nd under 2f out and sn no imp on wnr: kpt on same pce in 4th wl ins fnl f: jst hld 4th* **16/1**

5 nse **Cougar Mountain (IRE)**[26] 3924 6-9-8 112 ..........(tp) DonnachaO'Brien 5 111
(A P O'Brien, Ire) *towards rr: 8th 1/2-way: rdn 2f out and r.o wl clsng stages: jst failed for 4th* **10/1**

6 shd **Dutch Connection**[26] 3924 5-9-8 114 ................................. JamesDoyle 6 110
(Charles Hills) *trckd ldrs: cl 3rd at 1/2-way: rdn 2f out and no imp on wnr ent fnl f: sn wknd* **5/2**[1]

7 1/2 **Mubtasim (IRE)**[25] 3959 3-9-1 109 ..............................(p[1]) PatCosgrave 7 106
(William Haggas) *settled in mid-div early: 7th 1/2-way: rdn disputing 6th over 1f out and sn no ex: one pce ins fnl f* **6/1**[2]

8 1 **Flight Risk (IRE)**[15] 4383 6-9-8 113 ................................ KevinManning 9 106
(J S Bolger, Ire) *w.w in rr: last at 1/2-way: pushed along under 2f out and no imp ent fnl f: kpt on one pce: nvr a factor* **12/1**

9 1 3/4 **Peace Envoy (FR)**[26] 3927 3-9-1 106 ......................... SeamieHeffernan 2 104+
(A P O'Brien, Ire) *towards rr early tl tk clsr order in 4th at 1/2-way: rdn disputing 2nd far side ins fnl f and no ex bhd ldrs whn squeezed for room ins fnl 100yds: hmpd and eased rt down clsng stages* **25/1**

1m 24.56s (-6.24) **Going Correction** -0.65s/f (Hard)
**WFA** 3 from 4yo+ 7lb **9** Ran SP% **115.2**
Speed ratings: **109,107,106,105,105 105,104,103,101**
CSF £60.47 TOTE £2.80: £1.02, £4.40, £2.30; DF 60.50 Trifecta £273.30.
**Owner** Smith/Magnier/Tabor/Stonestreet Stables **Bred** Nursery Place **Trained** Cashel, Co Tipperary

**FOCUS**
A clever ride by Ryan Moore but he was helped by the fact that nothing else wanted the lead early on, so he got a soft enough time of it, allowing him to save something for the finish. Several raced keenly in behind as a consequence. The winner has been rated in line with the better view of his Ascot form.

4936 - 4938a (Foreign Racing) - See Raceform Interactive

## 3636 COLOGNE (R-H)
Sunday, July 16

**OFFICIAL GOING: Turf: good**

### 4939a MEILEN TROPHY (GROUP 2) (3YO+) (TURF) 1m
3:45 3-Y-O+
**£34,188** (£13,247; £6,837; £3,418; £2,136)

RPR

1 **Dragon Lips (GER)**[21] 4130 3-8-8 0 ................................... MarcLerner 9 108
(Andreas Suborics, Germany) *racd alone towards outside rail: cut in to ins rail and led after 3f: led all but one towards stands' rail turning for home 3f out: hdd narrowly 2f out: sn rdn and rallied to ld over 1 1/2f out: styd on wl fnl f: drvn out* **56/10**[3]

2 1 **Wonnemond (GER)**[21] 4130 4-9-2 0 .................... BayarsaikhanGanbat 4 108
(S Smrczek, Germany) *settled in midfield: lost plcd and drvn 3 1/2f out: last and rdn under 2 1/2f out: styd on u.p fr 1 1/2f out: run flattened out last 50yds* **73/10**

3 nse **Millowitsch (GER)**[11] 4517 4-9-2 0 ......................... AndreasHelfenbein 5 108+
(Markus Klug, Germany) *led on ins rail: chsd ldr after 3f: drvn to ld narrowly 2f out: rdn and hdd over 1 1/2f out: styd on same pce fnl f* **29/10**[2]

4 1 1/2 **Diplomat (GER)**[27] 3923 6-9-2 0 ...................................... StephenHellyn 3 104+
(Mario Hofer, Germany) *chsd ldrs on inner: dropped towards rr 1/2-way: drvn over 2f out: styd on wl over 1f out: run petered out last 50yds* **208/10**

5 nk **Pas De Deux (GER)**[318] 6067 7-9-5 0 .............................. MaximPecheur 8 107
(Yasmin Almenrader, Germany) *chsd ldrs: rdn and nt qckn 2f out: styd on at same pice fnl f* **99/10**

6 nk **Degas (GER)**[52] 3019 4-9-2 0 ...............................................(b) MartinSeidl 7 103
(Markus Klug, Germany) *cl up on outer: rdn and n.m.r under 2f out: styd on same pce u.p* **56/10**[3]

7 3 1/2 **Poetic Dream (IRE)**[56] 2869 3-8-11 0 ........................... EduardoPedroza 6 96
(A Wohler, Germany) *w.w in fnl trio: rdn and effrt 2f out: wl hld fr over 1f out* **8/5**[1]

8 2 1/4 **Nordico (GER)**[98] 1661 6-9-2 0 ...................................(b) AlexanderPietsch 2 90
(Mario Hofer, Germany) *w.w in rr: hdwy down centre of crse ins fnl 3f: rdn and no further imp under 2f out: dropped away fnl f* **35/1**

9 hd **Aufsteiger (FR)**[36] 3613 3-8-8 0 ..................................... AndraschStarke 1 87
(P Schiergen, Germany) *racd in fnl pair: last and drvn over 2 1/2f out: short-lived effrt 1 1/2f out: sn rdn and btn* **139/10**

1m 34.1s (-4.29)
**WFA** 3 from 4yo+ 8lb **9** Ran SP% **129.7**
PARI-MUTUEL (all including 10 euro stake): WIN 66 PLACE: 23, 18, 16; SF: 490.
**Owner** Stall Lintec **Bred** Stall Parthenaue **Trained** Germany

**FOCUS**
The runner-up helps set the standard.

## 2941 JAGERSRO (R-H)
Sunday, July 16

**OFFICIAL GOING: Dirt: standard**

### 4940a ZAWAWI CUP (GROUP 3) (3YO+) (DIRT) 6f (D)
3:37 3-Y-O+
**£53,191** (£17,730; £8,865; £5,319; £3,546)

RPR

1 **Land's End (DEN)** 5-9-6 0 ................................ AlexandreDosSantos 15 96
(Francisco Castro, Sweden) *racd in midfield on outer: drvn to cl under 2f out: str run to ld 150yds out: sn clr: won easing down* **9/1**[3]

2 1 1/2 **Ikc Dragon Heart (USA)**[54] 2943 7-9-6 0 ................(b) JacobJohansen 8 92
(Lennart Reuterskiold Jr, Sweden) *hld up in fnl trio: began to cl on outer 2 1/2f out: styd on wl fnl f: no ch w wnr* **125/10**

3 1/2 **Gunvald (USA)**[54] 2942 4-9-6 0 ..........................................(b) KevinStott 6 90
(Fredrik Reuterskiold, Sweden) *settled towards rr of midfield: 12th and pushed along under 2 1/2f out: styd on wl fr 1 1/2f out: nvr able to chal* **23/5**[2]

4 nk **Spykes Bay (USA)**[54] 2943 8-9-6 0 ......................... MartinRodriguez 14 89
(Vanja Sandrup, Sweden) *broke wl and led fr wd draw: drvn clr 2f out: hdd fnl 150yds: no ex* **175/10**

5 1 1/4 **Over The Ocean (USA)**[54] 2943 7-9-6 0 ............. Per-AndersGraberg 11 85
(Niels Petersen, Norway) *racd in midfield: hdwy 2f out: styd on at same pce* **171/10**

6 3 **Tinnitus (IRE)**[27] 4-9-6 0 MarkLarsen 12 75
(Niels Petersen, Norway) *w.w towards rr: rdn and clsd 1 1/2f out: kpt on fnl f: nvr in contention* **169/10**
7 1 1/4 **Only Bacan (CHI)**[54] 2943 4-9-6 0 (b) RafaeldeOliveira 2 71
(Francisco Castro, Sweden) *chsd ldr on inner: rdn and no imp 1 1/2f out: wknd ins fnl f* **33/1**
8 1 **No Comment (DEN)**[27] 4-9-6 0 NelsonDeSouza 1 68
(Bent Olsen, Denmark) *prom towards inner: rdn and wknd wl over 1 1/2f out* **34/1**
9 hd **Solamente Vos (ARG)** 4-9-6 0 ElioneChaves 7 68
(Fredrik Reuterskiold, Sweden) *chsd ldr in centre: drvn tohold pl 2f out: rdn and no imp 1 1/2f out: wknd fnl f* **119/10**
10 1 1/2 **Honeymoon Honey (USA)**[1107] 6-9-6 0 ValmirDeAzeredo 3 63
(Katharina Stenefeldt, Sweden) *racd in fnl trio: moved into midfield bef 1/2-way: sn drvn and no hdwy: wl hld ins fnl 1 1/2f* **211/10**
11 3 **Saving Kenny (IRE)**[27] 7-9-6 0 MrFredrikJanetzky 5 53
(Roy Arne Kvisla, Sweden) *outpcd in rr: nvr able to get involved* **211/10**
12 nse **Tertian (SWE)** 5-9-6 0 CarlosLopez 13 53
(Niels Petersen, Norway) *prom on outer: drvn and nt qckn wl over 2f out: wknd appr fnl f* **177/10**
13 2 1/2 **Ambiance (IRE)**[308] 6-9-6 0 ShaneKarlsson 9 45
(Katharina Stenefeldt, Sweden) *chsd ldng trio: lost pl 2f out: sn btn* **57/1**
14 8 **Staring At The Sea (IRE)**[245] 6-9-6 0 Jan-ErikNeuroth 10 19
(Wido Neuroth, Norway) *w.w in midfield: rdn and wknd ins last 2f* **166/10**
15 2 **Kimberella**[15] 4354 7-9-6 0 OliverWilson 4 13
(Richard Fahey) *sltly outpcd early: towards rr: scrubbed along 1/2-way but no imp: a bhd* **33/20**[1]

1m 11.9s **15** Ran SP% **124.9**

**Owner** Stald Seaside **Bred** Stutteri Hjortebo **Trained** Sweden

## 4782 MAISONS-LAFFITTE (R-H)

Sunday, July 16

**OFFICIAL GOING: Turf: good**

### 4941a PRIX EUGENE ADAM (GRAND PRIX DE MAISONS-LAFFITTE) (GROUP 2) (3YO) (ROUND) (TURF) 1m 2f (S)

**2:45** 3-Y-0 **£63,333** (£24,444; £11,666; £7,777; £3,888)

RPR

1 **Finche**[34] 3680 3-9-0 0 VincentCheminaud 1 111
(A Fabre, France) *chsd ldr: shkn up to ld ins fnl 2f out: drvn 1f out: jnd ent fnl f: rallied to ld 100yds out: on top in fnl 50yds* **98/10**
2 1/2 **Afandem (FR)**[34] 3680 3-9-0 0 FrankieDettori 5 110
(J-C Rouget, France) *chsd ldrs on outer: clsd 3rd and clsng 2f out: rdn to press ldr 1 1/2f out: upsides whn rdn ent fnl f: hdd 100yds out: kpt on under driving* **5/2**[1]
3 1 1/4 **Avilius**[82] 2074 3-9-0 0 MickaelBarzalona 6 107
(A Fabre, France) *settled in fnl pair: last and pushed along over 3f out: prog appr 2f out: rdn to chse ldrs over 1f out: styd on: tk 3rd fnl strides* **66/10**
4 hd **Volfango (IRE)**[53] 3-9-0 0 AurelienLemaitre 4 107
(F Head, France) *hld up towards rr on outer: last and pushed along over 2f out: clsd on outer sn after: styd on u.p fnl f: tk 4th fnl stride: nvr threatened ldrs* **29/10**[2]
5 shd **Phelps Win (FR)**[70] 2448 3-9-0 0 Pierre-CharlesBoudot 2 106
(H-A Pantall, France) *racd keenly: hld up wl bhd ldrs: lost pl 1/2-way: began to cl 2f out: chsd ldrs over 1f out: kpt on same pce u.p dropped two pls cl home* **3/1**[3]
6 2 1/2 **Amore Hass (IRE)**[56] 2868 3-9-0 0 CristianDemuro 3 101
(Stefano Botti, Italy) *hld up towards rr on inner: drvn and clsd to chsd ldr between horses 2f out: rdn and nt qckn over 1f out: grad dropped away in fnl f* **41/1**
7 1 3/4 **Berdibek (FR)**[30] 3-9-0 0 ChristopheSoumillon 8 98
(M Delzangles, France) *stdd fr wd draw: w.w in rr: clsd on inner tl nt clr run wl over 2f out: again blocked 1 1/2f out: stdd: dropped to last and angled out over 1f fr home: unable to get bk in contention and eased* **87/10**
8 3 1/2 **Back On Board (IRE)**[56] 2868 3-9-0 0 FabioBranca 7 91
(Stefano Botti, Italy) *led: drifted rt on to ins rail 2f out: hdd ins fnl 2f out: wknd wl over 1f out* **28/1**

2m 5.0s (2.60) **8** Ran SP% **117.8**
PARI-MUTUEL (all including 1 euro stake): WIN 10.80; PLACE 2.70, 1.40, 2.20; DF 14.60; SF 24.20.
**Owner** K Abdullah **Bred** Juddmonte Farms Ltd **Trained** Chantilly, France

**FOCUS**
The third has been rated to the better view of his latest effort.

### 4942a PRIX MESSIDOR (GROUP 3) (3YO+) (STRAIGHT) (TURF) 1m

**4:10** 3-Y-0+ **£34,188** (£13,675; £10,256; £6,837; £3,418)

RPR

1 **Taareef (USA)**[28] 3880 4-9-4 0 IoritzMendizabal 3 119+
(J-C Rouget, France) *w.w in fnl pair on inner: clsd to chse 3l ldr bef 1/2-way: rdn and styd on to ld wl over 1f out: styd on fnl f: readily* **21/10**[2]
2 2 **Al Wukair (IRE)**[71] 2399 3-8-10 0 FrankieDettori 6 112+
(A Fabre, France) *dwlt: slow to stride: sn settled towards rr: hdwy 1 1/2f out: chsd ldr fnl f: nvr on terms* **7/10**[1]
3 2 **Attendu (FR)**[18] 4234 4-9-2 0 OlivierPeslier 4 108
(C Laffon-Parias, France) *chsd ldng pair: rdn to cl 1 1/2f out: kpt on at same pce fnl f: nvr able to chal* **8/1**[3]
4 1 1/2 **Shutterbug (FR)**[29] 3856 5-9-2 0 (b) AntoineHamelin 1 104
(M Figge, Germany) *led on inner: hdd wl over 1f out: plugged on at one pce* **176/10**
5 3/4 **Wireless (FR)**[53] 2977 6-9-2 0 TheoBachelot 2 103
(V Luka Jr, Czech Republic) *missed break: racd in rr: drvn and no imp 2f out: kpt on ins fnl f wout ever being involved* **97/10**
6 hd **Mankib**[63] 2666 3-8-8 0 AurelienLemaitre 7 100
(F Head, France) *cl up on outer: lost plcd 3f out: rdn and btn fnl f* **28/1**

1m 34.86s (-7.44)
**WFA** 3 from 4yo+ 8lb **6** Ran SP% **120.4**
PARI-MUTUEL (all including 1 euro stake): WIN 2.80; PLACE 1.20, 1.10, SF 5.20.
**Owner** Hamdan Al Maktoum **Bred** Dixiana Farms Llc **Trained** Pau, France

**FOCUS**
The winner backed up his big last-time-out performance and looks to be knocking on Group 1 company now.

## SAINT-MALO (L-H)

Sunday, July 16

**OFFICIAL GOING: Turf: good**

### 4943a PRIX DE LA CHALOTAIS (CLAIMER) (3YO) (TURF) 1m 1f

**5:40** 3-Y-0 **£5,555** (£2,222; £1,666; £1,111; £555)

RPR

1 **Cropus (FR)**[13] 3-9-0 0 MllePaulineDominois(4) 7 72
(R Le Gal, France) **29/10**[1]
2 3 1/2 **Gormlaith (FR)**[14] 3-8-11 0 (b) JeromeClaudic 6 58
(P Monfort, France) **78/10**
3 nk **Vanisia (FR)** 3-8-8 0 MickaelForest 6 54
(C Lotoux, France) **144/10**
4 nse **Numeration (FR)**[42] 3-8-11 0 (b) EmmanuelEtienne 11 57
(Alex Fracac, France) **51/10**[3]
5 1 3/4 **Evalya Senora (FR)**[13] 4455 3-9-1 0 JeromeCabre 4 58
(Y Barberot, France) **168/10**
6 1 3/4 **Minimiss (FR)**[14] 3-8-9 0 ow1 (p) MorganDelalande 10 48
(Mme S Adet, France) **35/1**
7 1 **Brise De Mer (FR)**[30] 3781 3-9-4 0 HugoJourniac 2 55
(George Baker) *chsd ldr: drvn and nt qckn 2 1/2f out: lft bhd by ldrs: rdn and kpt on at same pce fnl f* **19/5**[2]
8 4 1/2 **Dankara (FR)** 3-8-8 0 (p) FlorentGavilan(3) 12 38
(E Leray, France) **72/1**
9 4 1/2 **Saphir Chop (FR)** 3-8-11 0 (p) WilliamsSaraiva 13 29
(Mme S Adet, France) **44/1**
10 nse **Douceur Angevine (FR)** 3-8-11 0 ChristopherGrosbois 8 29
(J-F Doucet, France) **216/10**
11 1 **Casou (FR)**[191] 3-8-11 0 FabriceVeron 9 27
(L Gadbin, France) **47/1**
12 8 **Flash Flower (FR)** 3-8-9 0 TristanBaron(6) 3 14
(H-A Pantall, France) **29/1**
13 3 1/2 **Panos (FR)**[41] 3-9-1 0 SylvainRuis 1 7
(Henk Grewe, Germany) **11/2**

PARI-MUTUEL (all including 1 euro stake): WIN 3.90; PLACE 1.30, 1.70, 1.70; DF 4.30; SF 12.90.
**Owner** Marc-Elie Uzan **Bred** Scea Haras De Saint Pair **Trained** France

4944 - 4954a (Foreign Racing) - See Raceform Interactive

## 3515 DIEPPE (R-H)

Tuesday, July 11

**OFFICIAL GOING: Turf: good to soft**

### 4955a PRIX MAX DE BETHUNE (CLAIMER) (4YO+) (TURF) 5f 110y

**12:25** 4-Y-0+ **£6,410** (£2,564; £1,923; £1,282; £641)

RPR

1 **O Dee**[13] 4233 5-9-5 0 MickaelBarzalona 7
(Jose Santos) *mde all: rdn 2f out: kpt on strly against rail and drew clr fnl f: comf* **32/5**[3]
2 4 1/2 **Alkhor**[20] 4-9-4 0 StephanePasquier 6
(J Phelippon, France) **10/1**
3 1 **King David (FR)**[12] 9-9-4 0 EddyHardouin 10
(M Boutin, France) **17/2**
4 shd **Agnes Champ (FR)**[13] 11-8-11 0 (b) MrHugoBoutin 4
(M Boutin, France) **20/1**
5 hd **Mr Chuckles (IRE)**[31] 3569 4-9-1 0 (p) AlexisBadel 5
(Mme G Rarick, France) **15/2**
6 1/2 **Bellcanto (GER)**[62] 5-9-8 0 AlexanderPietsch 1
(J Hirschberger, Germany) **9/2**[2]
7 2 1/2 **Xenophanes (IRE)**[12] 7-8-10 0 GuillaumeNugou(8) 15
(M Boutin, France) **82/1**
8 3/4 **Poet's Rock (FR)**[51] 4-8-13 0 JeromeMoutard(5) 2
(J-M Lefebvre, France) **27/1**
9 1 1/2 **Akbulat**[396] 3120 4-8-11 0 (b) FabriceVeron 16
(A Savujev, Czech Republic) **37/1**
10 hd **Munazan (FR)**[2042] 9-8-11 0 JeffersonSmith 8
(Jan Keppens, Belgium) **51/1**
11 3 **Elsie's Indian (FR)**[238] 7-9-1 0 TonyPiccone 9
(E Kurdu, Germany) **11/1**
12 3 1/2 **Mignolino (IRE)**[44] 5-9-1 0 (b) StephaneBreux 13
(R Roels, Germany) **34/1**
13 1 3/4 **Flicka's Boy**[13] 4233 5-8-13 0 (b) TristanBaron(5) 12
(P Monfort, France) **79/1**
14 11 **Alyce (IRE)**[691] 5574 4-8-10 0 DelphineSantiago(5) 3
(N Branchu, France) **50/1**
15 6 **Duquesa Penguin**[84] 5-9-2 0 (b) Pierre-CharlesBoudot 14
(D & P Prod'Homme, France) **14/5**[1]
16 11 **Irish Ilie (FR)**[408] 4-9-1 0 StephaneLaurent 11
(Mlle G Gadbled, France) **97/1**

PARI-MUTUEL (all including 1 euro stake): WIN 7.40; PLACE 2.80, 3.60, 3.30; DF 30.50; SF 59.00.
**Owner** Jose Santos Racing Ltd **Bred** Lofts Hall Stud & B Sangster **Trained** Upper Lambourn, Berks

4681
# AYR (L-H)
Monday, July 17

**OFFICIAL GOING: Good (7.8)**
Wind: Breezy, half against on sprint course and in over 3f of home straight on round course Weather: Fine, dry

## 4956 WESTERN HOUSE NOVICE AUCTION STKS (PLUS 10 RACE) 7f 50y
**2:00** (2:00) (Class 4) 2-Y-O **£4,269** (£1,270; £634; £317) **Stalls** High

Form RPR

22 **1** **Poet's Prince**[26] 3973 2-9-2 0 JoeFanning 2 75+
(Mark Johnston) *trckd ldr: led over 2f out: rdn over 1f out: styd on strly to draw clr ins fnl f* **2/1**[2]

00 **2** 2 ¼ **Grimeford Lane (IRE)**[9] 4597 2-8-13 0 ConnorBeasley 7 66
(Michael Dods) *t.k.h: trckd ldrs: effrt and chsd wnr appr fnl f: kpt on: nt pce to chal* **22/1**

1 **3** ¾ **French Flyer (IRE)**[23] 4074 2-9-4 0 PaulMulrennan 8 70
(Michael Dods) *hld up in tch: stdy hdwy to trck ldrs over 2f out: rdn and outpcd over 1f out: r.o same pce ins fnl f* **5/4**[1]

**4** ½ **Firby (IRE)** 2-8-12 0 PJMcDonald 6 62+
(James Bethell) *s.i.s: hld up: pushed along over 2f out: hdwy and edgd lft over 1f out: kpt on fnl f: nvr able to chal* **14/1**

05 **5** ½ **Gabrial The Devil (IRE)**[23] 4101 2-9-2 0 PhillipMakin 4 65
(David O'Meara) *led: rdn and hdd appr fnl f: rallied: outpcd fnl f* **10/1**

0 **6** 7 **Mountain Approach (IRE)**[52] 3037 2-9-1 0 PaulHanagan 5 47
(Richard Fahey) *hld up on ins: drvn and outpcd over 2f out: btn over 1f out* **7/1**[3]

0 **7** nk **Toohottotouch**[28] 3908 2-8-7 0 CallumRodriguez(5) 3 43
(Michael Dods) *dwlt: t.k.h and sn cl up: drvn and outpcd over 2f out: sn wknd* **40/1**

0 **8** 7 **Barney George**[26] 3973 2-9-2 0 TomEaves 1 29
(Iain Jardine) *missed break: bhd: struggling over 2f out: sn wknd* **66/1**

1m 33.41s (0.01) **Going Correction** +0.075s/f (Good) **8** Ran SP% **114.3**
Speed ratings (Par 96): **102,99,98,98,97 89,89,81**
CSF £44.48 TOTE £2.80: £1.40, £4.30, £1.02; EX 33.80 Trifecta £94.20.
**Owner** J David Abell **Bred** Jointsense Limited **Trained** Middleham Moor, N Yorks

**FOCUS**
No rain in the previous 24 hours; drying conditions. Inner rail out 6yds/top bend out 8yds, add 24yds to this race distance. An ordinary novice. The form is rated around the winner to his mark.

## 4957 POLYFLOR H'CAP 7f 50y
**2:30** (2:30) (Class 4) (0-85,86) 3-Y-O+ **£5,498** (£1,636; £817; £408) **Stalls** High

Form RPR

2514 **1** **Be Kool (IRE)**[16] 4377 4-8-13 81 (v) BenRobinson(5) 2 88
(Brian Ellison) *t.k.h: trckd ldr: rdn over 2f out: rallied and led over 1f out: drvn out fnl f* **5/4**[1]

2502 **2** 1 ¼ **Strong Steps**[17] 4293 5-9-5 82 JamesSullivan 5 86
(Jim Goldie) *in tch: effrt and rdn 2f out: chsd wnr ins fnl f: r.o* **7/2**[3]

5116 **3** nk **Luis Vaz De Torres (IRE)**[37] 3565 5-9-8 85 (h) PaulHanagan 4 88
(Richard Fahey) *t.k.h: trckd ldrs: effrt and chal over 1f out: no ex ins fnl f* **4/1**

2002 **4** 1 ¼ **Heir To A Throne (FR)**[17] 4294 4-9-8 85 ShaneGray 1 85
(Kevin Ryan) *led at ordinary gallop: rdn over 2f out: hdd over 1f out: outpcd fnl f* **3/1**[2]

1m 32.23s (-1.17) **Going Correction** +0.075s/f (Good)
**WFA** 3 from 4yo+ 7lb **4** Ran SP% **111.7**
Speed ratings (Par 105): **109,107,107,105**
CSF £6.08 TOTE £1.30; EX 7.70 Trifecta £23.30.
**Owner** Miss Jessica J Bell **Bred** E Lonergan **Trained** Norton, N Yorks

**FOCUS**
Add 24yds. Only four runnners, but still a competitive enough race. The race is rated around the runner-up to his recent form.

## 4958 WEMYSS BAY HOLIDAY PARK H'CAP 6f
**3:00** (3:00) (Class 5) (0-70,72) 3-Y-O+ **£3,557** (£1,058; £529; £264) **Stalls** Low

Form RPR

5263 **1** **Sea Of Green**[4] 4788 5-8-7 56 (p) SeanMooney(7) 3 66
(Jim Goldie) *hld up: rdn and hdd over 1f out: led ins fnl f: kpt on strly* **9/2**[2]

4-10 **2** 2 **Duncan Of Scotland (IRE)**[12] 4514 4-9-5 64 (b) ShaneBKelly(3) 6 67
(Lee Smyth, Ire) *awkward s: hdwy to dispute ld after 1f: rdn over 1f out: kpt on wl fnl f to take 2nd last stride* **10/3**[1]

0-06 **3** nse **Circuitous**[3] 4833 9-9-3 59 (v) TomEaves 7 62
(Keith Dalgleish) *w ldrs: rdn over 2f out: chsd wnr ins fnl f: no ex and lost 2nd last stride* **16/1**

6306 **4** ¾ **Goninodaethat**[7] 4682 9-8-13 60 CallumRodriguez(5) 8 61
(Jim Goldie) *w ldrs: drvn along and outpcd wl over 1f out: r.o ins fnl f* **20/1**

0003 **5** ½ **Specialv (IRE)**[7] 4683 4-9-2 63 (p) BenRobinson(5) 9 62
(Brian Ellison) *dwlt: bhd and outpcd: rdn and hdwy over 1f out: r.o fnl f: nrst fin* **9/2**[2]

3600 **6** nk **Danish Duke (IRE)**[16] 4343 6-9-11 67 (p) JamesSullivan 4 65
(Ruth Carr) *in tch: smooth hdwy to ld over 1f out: rdn and hdd ins fnl f: sn btn* **15/2**

3060 **7** ½ **Dandyleekie (IRE)**[9] 4616 5-9-9 72 (b) PatrickVaughan(7) 5 68
(David O'Meara) *in tch: drvn and outpcd wl over 1f out: btn fnl f* **13/2**[3]

0-63 **8** nse **Cool Run Girl (IRE)**[13] 4479 3-8-2 49 oh1 JoeDoyle 2 44
(Iain Jardine) *hld up: stdy hdwy wl over 1f out: sn drvn and outpcd: btn ins fnl f* **25/1**

-040 **9** 1 ½ **Lotara**[30] 3827 5-8-13 58 AdamMcNamara(3) 11 49
(Jim Goldie) *hld up: rdn along over 2f out: wknd over 1f out* **18/1**

1-00 **10** nk **Desperados Destiny**[37] 3584 3-9-11 72 (p[1]) PaulMulrennan 1 62
(Michael Dods) *led to over 1f out: sn rdn and wknd* **8/1**

1m 14.36s (1.96) **Going Correction** +0.075s/f (Good)
**WFA** 3 from 4yo+ 5lb **10** Ran SP% **115.4**
Speed ratings (Par 103): **89,86,86,85,84 84,83,83,81,81**
CSF £19.66 CT £219.14 TOTE £4.90: £1.70, £1.10, £5.80; EX 21.30 Trifecta £325.80.
**Owner** James Callow **Bred** Frank Brady **Trained** Uplawmoor, E Renfrews
■ Stewards' Enquiry : Sean Mooney two-day ban: used whip above permitted level (Jul 31, Aug 4)

**FOCUS**
A modest sprint handicap. The winner confirmed her improved latest Carlisle form, doing best of those from the rear.

## 4959 SUNDRUM CASTLE HOLIDAY PARK H'CAP 1m 2f
**3:30** (3:30) (Class 5) (0-75,77) 3-Y-O+ **£3,557** (£1,058; £529; £264) **Stalls** Low

Form RPR

2612 **1** **Lucent Dream (IRE)**[8] 4658 6-9-9 70 (t) PaulHanagan 5 79+
(John C McConnell, Ire) *hld up towards rr: stdy hdwy whn hmpd and stmbld bnd over 3f out: sn rcvrd and impr to ld over 1f out: drvn out* **7/4**[1]

000 **2** 1 ½ **Zealous (IRE)**[17] 4304 4-9-9 70 PJMcDonald 8 76
(Sally Haynes) *hld up: hdwy on outside 3f out: effrt and ev ch over 1f out: kpt on same pce ins fnl f* **20/1**

-316 **3** 4 **Rubis**[25] 4018 4-8-11 61 AdamMcNamara(3) 6 59
(Richard Fahey) *in tch: edgd rt over 3f out: drvn and outpcd 2f out: styd on fnl f: nt rch first two* **6/1**[3]

4632 **4** nk **Gerry The Glover (IRE)**[16] 4358 5-9-11 77 (p) BenRobinson(5) 7 74
(Brian Ellison) *s.i.s: hld up: effrt and edgd lft over 2f out: hdwy over 1f out: kpt on fnl f: no imp* **7/2**[2]

634 **5** 3 ½ **Konig Dax (GER)**[8] 4658 7-10-0 75 (t) TomEaves 3 65
(Alistair Whillans) *sn led: rdn and hrd pressed over 2f out: hdd over 1f out: sn wknd* **10/1**

0363 **6** 3 ½ **Hernandoshideaway**[6] 4722 5-9-13 74 (tp) PaulMulrennan 2 57
(Michael Dods) *plld hrd: early ldr: cl up: chal over 2f out: rdn and wknd over 1f out* **8/1**

000 **7** 1 **Spes Nostra**[8] 4658 9-9-3 69 (b) LewisEdmunds(5) 1 50
(Iain Jardine) *hld up in tch: drvn and outpcd over 2f out: sn btn* **25/1**

5025 **8** hd **Powerful Love (IRE)**[14] 4430 3-8-13 69 (v[1]) JoeFanning 4 51
(Mark Johnston) *chsd ldrs: drvn and struggling over 2f out: hung lft and sn wknd* **15/2**

2m 10.62s (-1.38) **Going Correction** +0.075s/f (Good)
**WFA** 3 from 4yo+ 9lb **8** Ran SP% **113.4**
Speed ratings (Par 103): **108,106,103,103,100 97,96,96**
CSF £39.73 CT £175.01 TOTE £2.40: £1.30, £4.80, £2.00; EX 28.00 Trifecta £206.50.
**Owner** Ms Caroline Ahearn **Bred** Roland H Alder **Trained** Stamullen, Co Meath

**FOCUS**
Add 24yds. The pace looked overly strong, with the first two finishers coming from out the back. The winner is improving.

## 4960 SANDYLANDS CARAVAN PARK H'CAP 1m
**4:00** (4:01) (Class 5) (0-75,77) 3-Y-O+ **£3,557** (£1,058; £529; £264) **Stalls** Low

Form RPR

3563 **1** **Royal Shaheen (FR)**[8] 4661 4-10-3 77 (v) PJMcDonald 9 85
(Alistair Whillans) *pressed ldr: led over 2f out: rdn and edgd lft over 1f out: veered rt ins fnl f: sn corrected and kpt on wl* **9/4**[1]

0352 **2** 1 ¾ **Billy Bond**[25] 4019 5-8-10 56 (b) PaulHanagan 3 60
(Richard Fahey) *hld up in tch: hdwy on outside to chse wnr over 1f out: checked ins fnl f: kpt on same pce* **6/1**

0002 **3** ¾ **Ingleby Angel (IRE)**[9] 4601 8-9-4 64 (p) KevinStott 7 66
(Colin Teague) *t.k.h: prom: effrt and rdn over 2f out: kpt on ins fnl f: nrst fin* **7/2**[2]

0-04 **4** hd **Dominannie (IRE)**[8] 4661 4-9-0 60 JoeFanning 8 62
(Sally Haynes) *s.i.s: hld up: hdwy over 2f out: rdn and kpt on same pce fnl f* **8/1**

0010 **5** 3 ¼ **Reinforced**[24] 4039 4-9-5 65 (tp) ConnorBeasley 1 60
(Michael Dods) *t.k.h: cl up: effrt and drvn along 2f out: wknd fnl f* **9/2**[3]

0000 **6** ½ **Sikandar (IRE)**[18] 4260 5-9-1 66 (t) BenRobinson(5) 10 59
(Brian Ellison) *t.k.h: hld up: drvn along over 2f out: edgd lft and sn no imp* **16/1**

4405 **7** 2 **Ellaal**[9] 4601 8-9-3 63 JamesSullivan 2 52
(Ruth Carr) *led at ordinary gallop: rdn and hdd over 2f out: wknd over 1f out* **8/1**

1m 42.6s (-1.20) **Going Correction** +0.075s/f (Good)
**WFA** 3 from 4yo+ 8lb **7** Ran SP% **113.6**
Speed ratings (Par 103): **109,107,106,106,103 102,100**
CSF £15.98 CT £45.02 TOTE £2.90: £2.30, £2.70; EX 15.10 Trifecta £46.40.
**Owner** Frank Lowe **Bred** SF Bloodstock LLC **Trained** Newmill-On-Slitrig, Borders

**FOCUS**
Add 24yds. An ordinary handicap. The race is rated a bit cautiously, the winner to this year's form.

## 4961 PARKDEAN RESORTS GLASGOW FAIR H'CAP 1m
**4:30** (4:31) (Class 2) (0-100,94) 3-Y-O+
**£15,562** (£4,660; £2,330; £1,165; £582; £292) **Stalls** Low

Form RPR

-341 **1** **Century Dream (IRE)**[17] 4299 3-9-5 93 (t) GrahamLee 13 101+
(Simon Crisford) *trckd ldr: led gng wl over 2f out: pushed along over 1f out: kpt on wl fnl f: comf* **6/5**[1]

6432 **2** ¾ **Truth Or Dare**[16] 4377 6-9-3 86 AdamMcNamara(3) 6 93
(James Bethell) *hld up: hdwy on outside over 2f out: effrt and chsd wnr fnl f: r.o fin* **6/1**[2]

3110 **3** hd **Nicholas T**[13] 4475 5-9-10 90 JamesSullivan 4 96+
(Jim Goldie) *hld up: nt clr run briefly over 2f out: effrt and plld out fnl f: r.o fin* **6/1**[2]

-552 **4** 1 ½ **King's Pavilion (IRE)**[19] 4207 4-9-8 88 PaulMulrennan 7 91
(David Barron) *prom: effrt and drvn along 2f out: kpt on same pce fnl f* **9/1**

6500 **5** ¾ **Al Khan (IRE)**[17] 4293 8-9-3 88 (p) LewisEdmunds(5) 14 89
(Kevin Ryan) *chsd ldrs: effrt and drvn along 2f out: kpt on same pce fnl f* **33/1**

623 **6** ¾ **Testa Rossa (IRE)**[16] 4358 7-8-9 82 (b) SeanMooney(7) 10 82
(Jim Goldie) *hld up on outside: rdn and outpcd 2f out: no imp fnl f* **16/1**

-122 **7** nk **Sophie P**[23] 4077 4-10-0 94 PJMcDonald 5 93
(R Mike Smith) *chsd ldrs: rdn over 2f out: wknd over 1f out* **7/1**[3]

2000 **8** 1 ½ **Moonlightnavigator (USA)**[16] 4377 5-9-4 84 JasonHart 12 79
(John Quinn) *led: hdd over 2f out: rdn and wknd over 1f out* **14/1**

1m 42.79s (-1.01) **Going Correction** +0.075s/f (Good)
**WFA** 3 from 4yo+ 8lb **8** Ran SP% **112.0**
Speed ratings (Par 109): **108,107,107,105,104 104,103,102**
CSF £8.26 CT £30.05 TOTE £2.00: £1.10, £1.50, £1.70; EX 9.20 Trifecta £40.10.
**Owner** Abdullah Saeed **Bred** Rabbah Bloodstock Limited **Trained** Newmarket, Suffolk

**FOCUS**
Add 24yds. A useful handicap even with all the non-runners. The progressive winner dominated but will have tougher tasks from here.

## 4962 CREATING AMAZING MEMORIES APPRENTICE H'CAP 1m 5f 26y
**5:00** (5:01) (Class 6) (0-65,67) 3-Y-O+ **£2,587** (£770; £384; £192) **Stalls** Low

Form RPR
-502 **1** **Question Of Faith**[37] 3566 6-8-8 **50**.......................... SeamusCronin(5) 6 61
(Martin Todhunter) *hld up: hdwy over 2f out: shkn up and led 1f out: drifted lft: r.o strly* **8/1**

0411 **2** 1 ¾ **Donnachies Girl (IRE)**[18] 4244 4-9-6 **64**.................... RhonaPindar(7) 2 72
(Alistair Whillans) *led: shkn up and hdd 1f out: carried lft: kpt on same pce last 100yds* **10/3**[1]

005 **3** 1 **Easy Wind**[30] 3824 3-8-5 **56**................................ ManuelFernandes(3) 11 65+
(Sir Mark Prescott Bt) *t.k.h early: prom on outside: pushed along over 2f out: outpcd and hung lft over 1f out: r.o ins fnl f* **4/1**[2]

646 **4** nk **Vindicator (IRE)**[24] 4036 3-9-3 **65**..............................(p[1]) BenRobinson 5 73
(Michael Dods) *hld up midfield: pushed along over 2f out: kpt on fnl f: nvr able to chal* **15/2**

53-4 **5** 1 **Bodacious Name (IRE)**[48] 3180 3-8-6 **54**....................... JoshQuinn 12 61
(John Quinn) *hld up midfield: effrt on outside over 2f out: kpt on fnl f: nt pce to chal* **7/1**[3]

2- **6** ¾ **Bell Of The Ball (IRE)**[30] 4194 7-9-3 **54**..................... PatrickVaughan 1 57
(Liam Lennon, Ire) *pressed ldr: ev ch to over 1f out: rdn and outpcd ins fnl f* **10/1**

-356 **7** 2 **Royal Cosmic**[14] 4436 3-8-2 **50**................................(b[1]) ConnorMurtagh 8 52
(Richard Fahey) *t.k.h: trckd ldrs: effrt wl over 1f out: wknd ins fnl f* **20/1**

0664 **8** 1 ¾ **Schmooze (IRE)**[3] 4853 8-8-0 **50**......................... LeanneFerguson(5) 10 47
(Linda Perratt) *hld up: pushed along over 2f out: kpt on fnl f: no imp* **20/1**

665 **9** 1 ¼ **Nuova Scuola**[48] 3182 4-8-4 **46**...............................(v[1]) SeanMooney(5) 9 41
(Jim Goldie) *trckd ldrs: rdn over 2f out: wknd over 1f out* **40/1**

0-3 **10** ¾ **Ruth Melody (IRE)**[12] 4516 5-9-7 **61**........................ AndrewBreslin(3) 4 55
(Lee Smyth, Ire) *in tch on ins: effrt over 2f out: wknd over 1f out* **15/2**

5-66 **11** ½ **Sepal (USA)**[18] 4248 4-9-11 **67**...............................(h) JamieGormley(5) 7 60
(Iain Jardine) *hld up: pushed along over 2f out: sn no imp: btn over 1f out* **14/1**

4302 **12** 3 ¾ **Thackeray**[35] 3654 10-8-9 **46** oh1......................................... PaulaMuir 3 33
(Chris Fairhurst) *hld up: shortlived effrt on outside wl over 2f out: sn wknd* **25/1**

3m 0.78s (6.78) **Going Correction** +0.15s/f (Good)
**WFA** 3 from 4yo+ 11lb 12 Ran SP% **121.8**
Speed ratings (Par 101): **85,83,83,83,82 82,80,79,78,78 78,75**
CSF £34.11 CT £127.41 TOTE £9.10: £3.10, £1.60, £1.80; EX 37.50 Trifecta £401.60.
**Owner** K Fitzsimons & G Fell **Bred** Sir Robert Ogden **Trained** Orton, Cumbria
■ Seamus Cronin's first winner in Britain, following one in Ireland.

**FOCUS**
Add 42yds. A modest but competitive staying handicap. The winner essentially just ran to form.
T/Plt: £6.70 to a £1 stake. Pool: £82,623.96. 8,936.15 winning units. T/Qpdt: £3.60 to £1 stake. Pool: £5,692.05. 1,1577.88 winning units. **Richard Young**

# FFOS LAS (L-H)
### Monday, July 17

**OFFICIAL GOING: Good (6.9)**
Wind: light breeze, partly behind them up the straight Weather: fine

## 4963 BET TOTEPLACEPOT AT BETFRED.COM NOVICE AUCTION STKS 7f 80y(R)
**2:15** (2:18) (Class 5) 2-Y-O **£3,881** (£1,155; £577; £288) **Stalls** Low

Form RPR
53 **1** **Liva (IRE)**[13] 4466 2-9-1 0............................................................ JFEgan 5 69
(David Evans) *trckd ldrs on outer: rdn to ld wl over 1f out: drvn and styd on fnl f: hld on as runner-up clsd* **11/4**[2]

00 **2** hd **Coal Stock (IRE)**[13] 4465 2-9-2 0.................................... SteveDrowne 8 70
(David Evans) *dropped in s and hld up in last: pushed along 3f out: clsd and swtchd rt over 1f out: rdn and r.o wl: fnl f: jst hld* **40/1**

30 **3** 1 **We Are The World**[23] 4068 2-9-1 0................................ OisinMurphy 2 66
(Archie Watson) *wnt to post early: cl up: rdn to ld over 2f out: hdd wl over 1f out: drvn and kpt on: unable qck ins fnl f: lost 2nd towards fin* **4/6**[1]

00 **4** 2 ¼ **Show Of Force**[18] 4252 2-8-11 0.............................. KieranShoemark 3 57
(Jonathan Portman) *settled in tch in 5th: drvn 2f out: sn wnt 3rd: one pce fnl f* **10/1**[3]

5 **5** 10 **Sauchiehall Street (IRE)**[6] 4725 2-9-1 0......................... DaneO'Neill 7 36
(Sylvester Kirk) *s.i.s: t.k.h and sn chsng ldrs: rdn over 2f out: wknd appr fnl f* **14/1**

**6** 8 **American Ruby (USA)** 2-8-11 0.......................................... LiamKeniry 4 12
(Mark Johnston) *racd green in rr and niggled along at times: drvn 3f out: bhd fnl 2f* **11/1**

054 **7** 3 **Jaffar**[20] 4167 2-8-13 68...............................................(be) DougieCostello 1 7
(Scott Dixon) *led tl rdn and hdd over 2f out: sn wknd: eased fnl f* **33/1**

1m 32.8s (-0.80) **Going Correction** -0.075s/f (Good) 7 Ran SP% **116.1**
Speed ratings (Par 94): **101,100,99,97,85 76,73**
CSF £88.31 TOTE £3.80: £2.30, £14.20; EX 68.10 Trifecta £247.80.
**Owner** Simon Munir & Isaac Souede **Bred** Brook Stud Bloodstock Ltd **Trained** Pandy, Monmouths

**FOCUS**
An ordinary race. The first four finished clear with the form rated around the first two.

## 4964 BET TOTEEXACTA AT BETFRED.COM MAIDEN STKS 6f
**2:45** (2:48) (Class 5) 3-Y-O+ **£2,911** (£866; £432; £216) **Stalls** Centre

Form RPR
54-0 **1** **Paradwys (IRE)**[17] 4305 3-9-0 72...............................(p[1]) OisinMurphy 6 75
(Archie Watson) *mde virtually all: rdn 2f out: edgd lft 1f out: drvn and wl in command fnl f* **9/4**[2]

2- **2** 4 ½ **Waqt (IRE)**[409] 2874 3-9-5 0.................................................. DaneO'Neill 7 66
(Marcus Tregoning) *in tch: niggled along over 3f out: rdn 2f out: nt clr run and swtchd rt over 1f out: r.o to to go 2nd ins fnl f: no threat to wnr* **6/5**[1]

0-5 **3** 1 ¼ **Mishari**[18] 4269 3-9-5 0.................................................... KieranShoemark 1 62
(David Lanigan) *trckd ldrs: rdn 3f out: hung lft 2f out: chsd wnr over 1f out but little imp: lost 2nd ins fnl f* **11/2**[3]

0- **4** 2 **Assertor**[297] 6733 3-9-0 0.................................................. GeorgeDowning 5 50
(Tony Carroll) *chsd ldrs: drvn and unable qck 2f out: kpt on same pce* **50/1**

60- **5** shd **The Night Before**[283] 7122 3-9-5 0.................................. AdamBeschizza 3 55
(Robert Cowell) *trckd wnr tl rdn and lost 2nd over 1f out: one pce* **7/1**

0000 **6** 1 ¾ **Marettimo (IRE)**[9] 4633 3-9-2 60............................ CallumShepherd(3) 4 49
(Charles Hills) *trckd ldrs: pushed along 1/2-way: hung lft 2f out: sn wknd* **10/1**

**7** 45 **Nitro** 3-9-5 0...................................................................... TrevorWhelan 2
(Roy Brotherton) *s.s and a wl bhd: t.o* **100/1**

1m 9.95s (-0.05) **Going Correction** -0.075s/f (Good) 7 Ran SP% **116.2**
Speed ratings (Par 103): **97,91,89,86,86 84,24**
CSF £5.49 TOTE £3.40: £1.50, £1.50; EX 6.90 Trifecta £17.10.
**Owner** Mrs Julie Martin And David R Martin **Bred** Clarecastle Stud Ltd **Trained** Upper Lambourn, W Berks

**FOCUS**
Racing stands' side, the right horses came to the fore with the winner much the best. Weak maiden form, the winner rated to a better view of her 2yo form.

## 4965 BET TOTEQUADPOT AT BETFRED.COM H'CAP 5f
**3:15** (3:18) (Class 4) (0-80,77) 3-Y-O+ **£5,175** (£1,540; £769; £384) **Stalls** Centre

Form RPR
1314 **1** **Major Valentine**[11] 4532 5-9-6 **71**................................ TomMarquand 9 80
(John O'Shea) *chsd ldrs: rdn over 1f out: led ins fnl f: r.o* **2/1**[1]

35-4 **2** 1 ¼ **The Daley Express (IRE)**[21] 4159 3-9-4 **73**.................. SamHitchcott 7 77
(Ronald Harris) *chsd ldrs: drvn and edgd lft 2f out: ev ch fnl f tl unable qck and hld nr fin* **10/1**

1200 **3** ½ **Zipedeedodah (IRE)**[10] 4566 5-9-6 **71**...........................(t) OisinMurphy 8 74
(Joseph Tuite) *towards rr: drvn over 1f out: r.o to chse ldrs ins fnl f: wnt 3rd nr fin* **6/1**

2144 **4** ¾ **Penny Dreadful**[10] 4574 5-8-9 **67**..................................(p) RPWalsh(7) 4 67
(Scott Dixon) *chsd ldrs: led over 3f out: rdn 1/2-way: hdd ins fnl f: no ex* **5/1**[3]

265 **5** 2 ¾ **Hollander**[16] 4368 3-9-4 **73**........................................... KieranShoemark 2 62
(William Muir) *hld up: rdn and clsd 2f out: one pce fnl f* **7/1**

3543 **6** nk **Satchville Flyer**[6] 4727 6-9-5 **77**........................... KatherineGlenister(7) 6 66
(David Evans) *hld up in last: drvn 1/2-way: modest late hdwy* **3/1**[2]

5140 **7** 1 **Swendab (IRE)**[3] 4842 9-9-2 **67**......................................(b) TimmyMurphy 3 53
(John O'Shea) *led over 1f: rdn and lost 2nd over 1f out: wknd fnl f* **16/1**

/31- **8** 3 ¾ **Mysterious Glance**[292] 6879 4-9-4 **72**................... CallumShepherd(3) 1 44
(Sarah Hollinshead) *in tch: rdn wl over 1f out: wknd fnl f* **20/1**

57.27s (-1.03) **Going Correction** -0.075s/f (Good)
**WFA** 3 from 4yo+ 4lb 8 Ran SP% **121.5**
Speed ratings (Par 105): **105,103,102,101,96 96,94,88**
CSF £25.32 CT £105.99 TOTE £2.40: £1.20, £3.00, £1.90; EX 27.00 Trifecta £162.80.
**Owner** Pete Smith **Bred** J R Salter **Trained** Elton, Gloucs

**FOCUS**
A modest sprint in which the winner continued his progress.

## 4966 BET TOTETRIFECTA AT BETFRED.COM H'CAP 1m 6f (R)
**3:45** (3:49) (Class 5) (0-75,75) 3-Y-O+ **£3,881** (£1,155; £577; £288) **Stalls** Low

Form RPR
-064 **1** **Nabhan**[15] 3574 5-9-11 **72**..........................................(t[1]) TimmyMurphy 2 79+
(Bernard Llewellyn) *hld up: hdwy on outer over 2f out: led over 1f out: drvn clr fnl f: readily* **6/1**

0636 **2** 2 ¼ **Moojaned (IRE)**[13] 4471 6-8-6 **60**.................................. JordanUys(7) 4 63
(John Flint) *led and t.k.h: jnd and drvn 3f out: hdd over 1f out: styd on u.p* **6/1**

-332 **3** ¾ **African Beat (IRE)**[14] 4450 3-8-9 **75**.................... StephenCummins(7) 5 79
(Richard Hughes) *hld up and racd keenly: tk clsr order 1/2-way: hdwy over 2f out: rdn and swtchd rt over 1f out: r.o: wnt 3rd cl home* **7/4**[1]

536/ **4** hd **Smooth Operator**[317] 6148 5-9-4 **65**.......................... KieranShoemark 1 67
(Mark Pitman) *trckd ldrs: rdn over 2f out: kpt on to dispute 2nd ins fnl f tl nr fin* **12/1**

32-6 **5** 4 **Kaisan**[37] 3574 4-9-7 **68**...........................................................(t[1]) LiamKeniry 8 64
(Bernard Llewellyn) *cl up: rdn to chal 3f out: unable qck: wknd fnl f* **20/1**

03-0 **6** ½ **Ettihadi (IRE)**[45] 3291 3-9-0 **73**........................................ OisinMurphy 6 70
(Tim Vaughan) *chsd ldrs: rdn over 3f out: wkng whn sltly hmpd over 1f out* **4/1**[2]

0/0- **7** 3 ¼ **Ayla's Emperor**[39] 7274 8-8-13 **60**.................................(p) TomMarquand 7 51
(John Flint) *in rr: drvn on ins 3f out: no imp* **14/1**

1-40 **8** 1 ½ **Sunny Future (IRE)**[51] 3086 11-9-12 **73**.............................. DaneO'Neill 3 62
(Malcolm Saunders) *hld up: rdn and nt clr run over 2f out: sn swtchd rt: wknd over 1f out* **5/1**[3]

3m 5.05s (1.25) **Going Correction** -0.075s/f (Good)
**WFA** 3 from 4yo+ 12lb 8 Ran SP% **120.7**
Speed ratings (Par 103): **93,91,91,91,88 88,86,85**
CSF £44.01 CT £90.66 TOTE £7.20: £1.60, £2.10, £1.40; EX 54.60 Trifecta £150.10.
**Owner** Gethyn Mills & Alex James **Bred** Rabbah Bloodstock Limited **Trained** Fochriw, Caerphilly
■ Stewards' Enquiry : Stephen Cummins caution: careless riding

**FOCUS**
No great gallop on in what was a pretty modest handicap. They finished quite compressed and it probably didn't take much winning.

## 4967 TOTEPOOL RACECOURSE DEBIT CARD BETTING AVAILABLE H'CAP 1m 3f 209y(R)
**4:15** (4:22) (Class 6) (0-55,56) 3-Y-O+ **£2,264** (£673; £336; £168) **Stalls** Low

Form RPR
65-5 **1** **Rowlestonerendezvu**[20] 4187 4-9-3 **48**...................... GeorgeDowning 5 59+
(Tony Carroll) *midfield: hdwy over 2f out: led wl over 1f out: edgd lft u.p ins fnl f: drvn out* **7/1**[2]

5-4 **2** ½ **Perla Blanca (USA)**[96] 1726 3-8-6 **55**...................... TylerSaunders(7) 6 66+
(Marcus Tregoning) *hld up: gd hdwy 4f out: led 3f out: drvn and hdd wl over 1f out: swtchd rt ins fnl f: styd on towards fin* **5/4**[1]

6-50 **3** 11 **Masterfilly (IRE)**[159] 627 3-8-13 **55**................................ LiamKeniry 3 50
(Ed Walker) *midfield: nt clr run 2f out: sn swtchd rt to wd outside: styd on to go modest 3rd nr fin but nvr a threat to front two* **11/1**

06 **4** nk **Petrify**[15] 3805 7-9-11 **56**..................................................(tp) PaddyAspell 10 48
(Bernard Llewellyn) *s.s: in rr: hdwy 4f out: rdn over 2f out: carried lft over 1f out: wnt mod 3rd appr fnl f tl nr fin* **20/1**

20/0 **5** 1 ¼ **Garcon De Soleil**[34] 3694 4-9-5 **50**.................................. DaneO'Neill 12 40
(Michael Blanshard) *hld up towards rr: stdy hdwy on outer over 2f out: rdn and edgd lft over 1f out: disp mod 3rd fnl f* **25/1**

-666 **6** 9 **Sunlit Waters**[12] 4493 4-9-6 **51**.................................. TrevorWhelan 14 27
(Tony Carroll) *t.k.h: prom: rdn over 2f out: lost mod 3rd appr fnl f: wknd* **20/1**

040- **7** 2 ¼ **Cougar Kid (IRE)**[50] 8497 6-9-1 **46**.............................(p) TomMarquand 13 18
(John O'Shea) *towards rr: rdn 5f out: styd on fnl f* **16/1**

3012 **8** 5 **Filament Of Gold (USA)**[30] 3805 6-9-10 **55**...........(p) KieranShoemark 2 19
(Roy Brotherton) *chsd ldrs: rdn 3f out: wknd over 1f out* **7/1**[2]

0245 **9** *2 ½* **Golden Muscade (USA)**[30] 3805 4-9-7 **52**.................. SteveDrowne 11 12
(Brian Barr) *chsd ldrs: hdwy into 2nd after 2f: rdn 3f out: wknd wl over 1f out* **9/1**[3]

40 **10** *2 ½* **Avocet (USA)**[20] 4187 4-9-4 **49**................................(b[1]) AdamBeschizza 8
(Julia Feilden) *led 2f: styd prom: rdn over 2f out: grad wknd* **25/1**

000- **11** *7* **Quina Brook (IRE)**[249] 7896 4-9-3 **51**........................ CharlieBennett(3) 9
(Daniel Mark Loughnane) *in rr: rdn 4f out: wknd 3f out* **33/1**

0-00 **12** *2* **Think So (IRE)**[35] 3657 3-8-5 **47**.................................. JFEgan 4
(Mark Johnston) *midfield: rdn over 3f out: sn wknd: eased wl over 1f out* **7/1**[2]

/200 **13** *1* **Leonardo (GER)**[56] 2909 5-9-7 **52**.................................. TimmyMurphy 7
(Mark Pitman) *tooo t.k.h: chsd ldrs tl led after 2f: hdd 3f out: sn wknd* **11/1**

2m 34.33s (-3.07) **Going Correction** -0.075s/f (Good)
**WFA** 3 from 4yo+ 11lb **13** Ran SP% **134.7**
Speed ratings (Par 101): **107,106,99,99,98 92,90,87,85,84 79,78,77**
CSF £17.06 CT £113.04 TOTE £8.50: £2.20, £1.40, £3.50; EX 27.80 Trifecta £231.50.
**Owner** The Rowlestone Racing Club **Bred** G E Amey **Trained** Cropthorne, Worcs

**FOCUS**
Run at a steady gallop, two drew a long way clear and they could be a pair of fillies to keep on side. A weak race overall.

## 4968 TOTEPOOL BETTING ON ALL UK RACING H'CAP 1m (R)
**4:45** (4:51) (Class 6) (0-60,61) 3-Y-O+ **£2,587** (£770; £384; £192) **Stalls** Low

Form RPR

03U5 **1** **Captain Sedgwick (IRE)**[21] 4150 3-8-2 **45**........................ JimmyQuinn 5 52+
(John Spearing) *midfield: hdwy 4f out: led jst over 2f out: drvn out* **7/1**[3]

0-35 **2** *2* **Mordoree (IRE)**[46] 3250 3-8-12 **55**.................................. SamHitchcott 9 57
(Clive Cox) *chsd ldrs: rdn 3f out: chsd wnr over 1f out: styd on* **6/1**[2]

2322 **3** *¾* **Mowhoob**[30] 3809 7-9-5 **54**.............................................. DougieCostello 10 57
(Brian Barr) *midfield: rdn 3f out: hdwy 2f out: styd on wl u.p* **9/1**

5505 **4** *1 ¼* **Cloud Nine (FR)**[30] 3809 4-9-2 **51**................................ KieranShoemark 8 52
(Tony Carroll) *s.i.s: sn midfield: rdn 3f out: nt run on over 1f out: styd on fnl f* **11/1**

5405 **5** *2 ¼* **Rocket Ronnie (IRE)**[14] 4453 7-8-12 **47**........................(b) SteveDrowne 4 42
(Brian Barr) *s.i.s: towards rr: drvn and sme hdwy 3f out: styd on fnl f* **10/1**

-500 **6** *1 ½* **Edge (IRE)**[19] 4203 6-9-3 **52**............................................(b) TimmyMurphy 7 43
(Bernard Llewellyn) *rdn along early to chse ldrs: rdn over 2f out: one pce fnl f* **10/1**

000 **7** *4 ½* **Jump Around**[72] 2408 3-7-9 **45**......................................(t[1]) RPWalsh(7) 12 24
(Ali Stronge) *dwlt and rdn along in rr: drvn 3f out: modest prog fnl f* **33/1**

3515 **8** *2 ½* **Viola Park**[6] 4726 3-9-1 **58**..................................................(p) LiamKeniry 2 31
(Ronald Harris) *cl up: rdn and ev ch over 2f out: wknd over 1f out* **6/1**[2]

066 **9** *1* **Aladdin Sane (IRE)**[42] 3394 3-9-4 **61**.............................. TomMarquand 3 32
(Brian Meehan) *chsd ldrs: rdn over 3f out: wknd 2f out* **8/1**

64 **10** *1 ½* **African Trader (USA)**[9] 4625 4-9-7 **59**.................... CharlieBennett(3) 6 28
(Daniel Mark Loughnane) *drvn over 3f out: a in rr* **8/1**

6663 **11** *1 ¼* **Clever Lady (IRE)**[9] 4625 3-8-5 **48** ow3.......................... JFEgan 1 12
(David Evans) *led narrowly: rdn and hdd jst over 2f out: sn wknd* **4/1**[1]

0000 **12** *3 ¾* **A Definite Diamond**[21] 4148 4-8-10 **45**.......................... TrevorWhelan 11 3
(Grace Harris) *midfield on outer: rdn 4f out: wknd 3f out* **100/1**

040- **13** *8* **Red Douglas**[254] 7819 3-8-9 **52**........................................ AdamBeschizza 13
(Scott Dixon) *chsd ldng pair: rdn over 3f out: wknd over 2f out* **33/1**

1m 40.49s (-0.51) **Going Correction** -0.075s/f (Good)
**WFA** 3 from 4yo+ 8lb **13** Ran SP% **126.7**
Speed ratings (Par 101): **99,97,96,95,92 91,86,84,83,81 80,76,68**
CSF £49.14 CT £347.39 TOTE £9.10: £3.00, £2.50, £2.70; EX 64.50 Trifecta £705.70.
**Owner** Personal Racehorse Owners 3 **Bred** Yeomanstown Stud **Trained** Kinnersley, Worcs
■ Belgravian was withdrawn. Price at time of withdrawal 12-1. Rule applies to all bets - deduction 5p in the pound.
■ Stewards' Enquiry : Jimmy Quinn two-day ban: careless riding (Jul 31, Aug 4)

**FOCUS**
Moderate handicap form, two of the 3yos came to the fore. The third helps with the level.

## 4969 COLLECT TOTEPOOL WINNINGS AT BETFRED SHOPS H'CAP (DIV I) 7f 80y(R)
**5:15** (5:22) (Class 6) (0-55,57) 3-Y-O+ **£2,264** (£673; £336; £168) **Stalls** Low

Form RPR

3046 **1** **The Special One (IRE)**[54] 2976 4-9-3 **50**....................(t) TomMarquand 7 55
(Ali Stronge) *hld up: rdn over 2f out: swtchd rt and hdwy over 1f out: r.o to ld post* **11/2**[2]

4404 **2** *shd* **Spare Parts (IRE)**[13] 4458 3-8-9 **49**.......................... SamHitchcott 5 51
(Charles Hills) *chsd ldrs: rdn over 3f out: led and edgd lft over 1f out: kpt on u.p: hdd post* **9/2**[1]

600- **3** *1 ½* **Lady Gwhinnyvere (IRE)**[258] 7748 3-8-5 **45**.................... JimmyQuinn 2 43
(John Spearing) *in rr: rdn over 2f out: stl plenty to do 1f out: r.o wl: wnt 3rd cl home* **25/1**

0-40 **4** *nk* **Tally's Son**[41] 3423 3-8-12 **52**.......................................... DougieCostello 9 50
(Grace Harris) *chsd ldrs: drvn over 2f out: kpt on same pce fnl f* **7/1**

-004 **5** *hd* **Kath's Boy (IRE)**[19] 4211 3-7-12 **45**.............................. AledBeech(7) 10 42
(Tony Carroll) *midfield: rdn to chse ldrs over 2f out: one pce fnl f* **6/1**[3]

006- **6** *½* **Indiana Dawn**[210] 8457 4-9-7 **54**...................................... LiamKeniry 12 53
(Robert Stephens) *towards rr: rdn and hdwy on outer over 2f out: unable qck fnl f* **10/1**

4044 **7** *¾* **Kingstreet Lady**[24] 4043 4-9-5 **52**...................................... JFEgan 6 49
(Richard Price) *midfield: clsd 3f out: rdn 2f out: ev ch 1f out: wknd fnl f* **9/2**[1]

50-0 **8** *2 ½* **Leith Bridge**[159] 622 5-9-1 **48**.......................................... SteveDrowne 11 39
(Mark Usher) *in rr: drvn over 2f out: modest heaway fnl f* **12/1**

0-05 **9** *1 ¼* **Swan Serenade**[30] 3810 3-8-6 **49**.............................. CharlieBennett(3) 1 34
(Jonathan Portman) *trckd ldrs: rdn 2f out: losing pl whn hmpd over 1f out: wknd* **12/1**

6600 **10** *½* **Lakeski**[17] 4298 3-8-10 **50**................................................(p[1]) AdamBeschizza 3 33
(Scott Dixon) *chsd clr ldr: drvn and lost 2nd over 2f out: n.m.r over 1f out: wknd fnl f* **16/1**

0040 **11** *hd* **Overhaugh Street**[10] 4561 4-9-7 **57**........................(v) CallumShepherd(3) 8 43+
(Ed de Giles) *led: 7 l clr 4f out: rdn over 2f out: hdd over 1f out: wknd* **9/2**[1]

0-00 **12** *8* **Zorlu (IRE)**[45] 3280 4-8-12 **45**........................................(v) TrevorWhelan 4 11
(John O'Shea) *awkward s: sn midfield: drvn 3f out: wknd 2f out* **40/1**

1m 32.62s (-0.98) **Going Correction** -0.075s/f (Good)
**WFA** 3 from 4yo+ 7lb **12** Ran SP% **133.4**
Speed ratings (Par 101): **102,101,100,99,99 99,98,95,93,93 93,83**
CSF £34.66 CT £623.44 TOTE £6.50: £2.30, £2.10, £10.80; EX 46.20 Trifecta £1863.20.
**Owner** BGC Racing **Bred** Barouche Stud Ireland Ltd **Trained** Eastbury, Berks

**FOCUS**
Lowly handicap form, but they did go a good gallop. The form is rated cautiously around the principals.

## 4970 COLLECT TOTEPOOL WINNINGS AT BETFRED SHOPS H'CAP (DIV II) 7f 80y(R)
**5:45** (5:48) (Class 6) (0-55,57) 3-Y-O+ **£2,264** (£673; £336; £168) **Stalls** Low

Form RPR

3U10 **1** **Misu Pete**[10] 4561 5-9-7 **54**..................................................(p) OisinMurphy 3 61
(Mark Usher) *chsd ldrs: rdn over 2f out: hmpd and swtchd rt over 1f out: r.o to ld nr fin* **9/2**[3]

000 **2** *nk* **Tallulah's Quest (IRE)**[42] 3394 3-8-12 **52**.................... AdamBeschizza 6 55
(Julia Feilden) *hld up: hdwy on outer 3f out: led over 1f out: sn drvn and r.o: hdd nr fin* **6/1**

4400 **3** *2* **De Vegas Kid (IRE)**[11] 4542 3-8-10 **50**........................ GeorgeDowning 2 48
(Tony Carroll) *bmpd s: towards rr: hdwy on inner over 2f out: nt clr run over 1f out: r.o u.p fnl f: clsng towards fin* **4/1**[2]

522 **4** *½* **Hungarian Rhapsody**[110] 1432 3-9-3 **57**...................... DougieCostello 4 54
(Jamie Osborne) *chsd ldrs: rdn 2f out: hung rt over and sltly outpcd 1f out: styd on fnl f* **7/2**[1]

-066 **5** *1 ¾* **Doctor Bong**[3] 4846 5-9-10 **57**........................................(b) TrevorWhelan 11 53
(Grace Harris) *chsd ldr: rdn and sltly hmpd over 1f out: wknd ins fnl f* **5/1**

3000 **6** *1 ¾* **Toolatetodelegate**[30] 3819 3-8-9 **49**.............................. TomMarquand 1 38
(Brian Barr) *bmpd s: chsd ldrs: rdn over 2f out: swtchd rt over 1f out: one pce fnl f* **33/1**

-040 **7** *2 ½* **Coachella (IRE)**[19] 4211 3-8-6 **49** ow1...................... CallumShepherd(3) 5 31
(Ed de Giles) *midfield: rdn whn nt clr run over 2f out: one pce and no imp* **6/1**

0240 **8** *1* **Greyfriarschorista**[55] 2916 10-8-10 **50**............(bt) KatherineGlenister(7) 9 33
(David Evans) *led and sn several l clr: drvn over 2f out: hdd over 1f out: grad wknd* **6/1**

0300 **9** *1 ½* **National Service (USA)**[6] 4727 6-8-12 **45**....................(tp) PaddyAspell 7 24
(Clare Ellam) *hld up towards rr: effrt on outer whn carried rt over 1f out: no real imp* **33/1**

4-00 **10** *2 ¾* **Jungle George**[172] 415 3-7-12 **45**.................................. RPWalsh(7) 10 15
(Scott Dixon) *s.i.s: midfield: hdwy 4f out: drvn over 2f out: grad wknd* **33/1**

0-40 **11** *1 ½* **Sniper Viper**[45] 3309 3-8-5 **45**........................................(b) JimmyQuinn 8 11
(Daniel Kubler) *dwlt and wnt rt s: rdn 3f out: a in rr* **33/1**

1m 32.6s (-1.00) **Going Correction** -0.075s/f (Good)
**WFA** 3 from 5yo+ 7lb **11** Ran SP% **131.7**
Speed ratings (Par 101): **102,101,99,98,96 94,91,90,89,85 84**
CSF £34.95 CT £120.62 TOTE £6.40: £2.20, £2.70, £2.20; EX 52.00 Trifecta £185.40.
**Owner** The Mark Usher Racing Club **Bred** A C M Spalding **Trained** Upper Lambourn, Berks

**FOCUS**
Like division one this was pretty open and several had their chance. The winner is rated to his AW level.
T/Plt: £41.40 to a £1 stake. Pool: £67,148.58. 1,183.18 winning units. T/Qpdt: £6.70 to a £1 stake. Pool: £6,934.25. 756.53 winning units. **Richard Lowther**

# 4695 WINDSOR (R-H)
Monday, July 17

**OFFICIAL GOING: Good to firm (good in places; 8.0)**
Wind: Almost nil Weather: Fine, warm

## 4971 SKY BET APPRENTICE H'CAP 1m 2f
**5:50** (5:54) (Class 6) (0-60,62) 3-Y-O+ **£2,264** (£673; £336; £168) **Stalls** Centre

Form RPR

3262 **1** **Epsom Secret**[25] 4006 3-8-10 **54**.................................. PaddyBradley(3) 4 61
(Pat Phelan) *hld up in midfield: rdn and swtchd lft to outer 2f out: clsd u.p over 1f out: led ins fnl f: kpt on* **7/1**[3]

56-5 **2** *½* **Rock On Dandy (FR)**[9] 4626 3-9-0 **60**........................(b) WilliamCox(5) 2 66
(Harry Dunlop) *prom: chal against rail over 3f out: led jst over 2f out to ins fnl f: kpt on u.p* **9/1**

4003 **3** *¾* **Secret Soul**[14] 4442 3-9-7 **62**.......................................(v) PatrickO'Donnell 15 67
(Ralph Beckett) *prom: rdn to chal and upsides fr 2f out on outer: no ex ins fnl f* **9/4**[1]

4040 **4** *3* **Nouvelle Ere**[32] 3761 6-9-5 **56**..........................................(t) RossaRyan(5) 1 54
(Tony Carroll) *broke wl: led: rdn and hdd jst over 2f out: fdd fnl f* **20/1**

-620 **5** *1 ½* **Permanent**[34] 3701 3-9-2 **60**..........................................(p) RayDawson(3) 9 56
(Daniel Kubler) *towards rr: rdn 3f out: kpt on fr over 1f out: nvr nrr but n.d* **16/1**

0456 **6** *¾* **Kilim**[24] 4040 4-8-11 **50**..................................................(t) NicolaCurrie(7) 5 44
(John Berry) *hld up in midfield: lost pl and in rr 4f out: nvr on terms after but kpt on against rail fnl f* **20/1**

-400 **7** *½* **Russian Regard (IRE)**[30] 3819 3-8-9 **57**.......... Pierre-LouisJamin(7) 10 51
(Jonathan Portman) *trckd ldrs: rdn over 2f out: no imp wl over 1f out: fdd* **12/1**

-530 **8** *1* **Dark Phantom (IRE)**[46] 3251 6-9-3 **49**...................... GeorgiaCox 13 40
(Eve Johnson Houghton) *pressed ldr to 3f out: wknd over 1f out* **16/1**

4600 **9** *½* **Neptune Star**[41] 3423 3-7-12 **46**................................ DarraghKeenan(7) 3 37
(Michael Easterby) *free to post: dwlt: t.k.h and hld up in rr: pushed along over 3f out: modest late prog* **13/2**[2]

0-0 **10** *2* **Hi Milady (IRE)**[46] 3246 3-9-5 **60**.................................. PaddyPilley 6 47
(Dominic Ffrench Davis) *hld up in last trio: urged along 4f out: no real prog* **25/1**

0360 **11** *3 ¾* **Dr Goodhead (FR)**[19] 4214 3-9-3 **58**.............................. DavidEgan 11 38
(Charles Hills) *in tch in midfield: rdn wl over 2f out: wknd qckly on outer wl over 1f out* **8/1**

1040 **12** *2 ½* **Caribbean Spring (IRE)**[9] 4627 4-9-7 **56**.................... JaneElliott(3) 14 30
(George Margarson) *hld up in last: detached 4f out: pushed along and no prog* **16/1**

0000 **13** *6* **Zerafino (BEL)**[7] 4695 4-8-7 **46** oh1................................ TinaSmith(7) 12 9
(Jimmy Fox) *a in rr: wknd 3f out* **100/1**

2m 9.04s (0.34) **Going Correction** -0.025s/f (Good)
**WFA** 3 from 4yo+ 9lb **13** Ran SP% **117.4**
Speed ratings (Par 101): **97,96,96,93,92 91,91,90,90,88 85,83,78**
CSF £64.29 CT £187.69 TOTE £7.40: £2.60, £2.50, £1.10; EX 52.00 Trifecta £107.30.
**Owner** Epsom Racegoers No 3 **Bred** Ermyn Lodge Stud Limited **Trained** Epsom, Surrey

**FOCUS**
Rail on straight moved back in to open straight to full width. There was a fair pace on in this moderate handicap for apprentice riders. The winner built on her latest fair effort.

## 4972 SKY BET BRITISH STALLION STUDS EBF MAIDEN STKS 5f 21y
**6:20** (6:20) (Class 5) 2-Y-O £2,911 (£866; £432; £216) Stalls Low

Form RPR
0 1 **Golden Salute (IRE)**16 4367 2-9-0 0 DavidProbert 2 76+
(Andrew Balding) *trckd ldrs: clsd towards outer wl over 1f out: rdn to ld 150yds out: styd on wl* **4/1**2
2 ¾ **Global Rose (IRE)** 2-9-0 0 FranBerry 8 73
(Gay Kelleway) *hld up in 7th: prog 1/2-way: chsd ldng pair jst over 1f out: styd on and tk 2nd last stride* **12/1**
54 3 *nse* **Expecting**28 3917 2-9-5 0 WilliamBuick 9 78
(Charles Hills) *pressed ldr: led 2f out and off the rail: drvn and hdd 150yds out: kpt on but lost 2nd last stride* **11/4**1
4 4 ½ **Awesometank** 2-9-0 0 PatCosgrave 4 57+
(William Haggas) *hld up wl in rr: pushed along and styd on wl fr over 1f out: nvr nrr* **9/2**3
60 5 ¾ **Glamorous Rocket (IRE)**21 4160 2-9-0 0 ShaneKelly 7 54
(Ronald Harris) *led: styd against nr side rail and hdd 2f out: wknd over 1f out* **100/1**
3022 6 1 ¼ **Airshow**13 4466 2-9-5 73 (h) AdamKirby 1 55
(Rod Millman) *prom to 2f out: steadily wknd* **11/4**1
7 1 ¾ **Alaskan Bay (IRE)** 2-9-0 0 MartinDwyer 6 43
(Rae Guest) *t.k.h: hld up in rr: pushed along over 2f out: no ch but kpt on steadily* **25/1**
3 8 *shd* **Avenging Red (IRE)**24 4044 2-9-5 0 RoystonFfrench 3 48
(Adam West) *towards rr: dropped to last and outpcd 1/2-way: urged along and kpt on fnl f* **28/1**
00 9 4 ½ **Mossketeer**31 3782 2-9-5 0 RobertTart 10 32
(John Best) *a towards rr: struggling fr 2f out* **33/1**
06 10 1 ¼ **Summer Thunder (USA)**12 4496 2-9-0 0 DanielMuscutt 11 22
(Paul Cole) *chsd ldrs to 1/2-way: sn wknd u.p* **20/1**
11 1 ½ **Calvin's Gal (IRE)** 2-9-0 0 (h1) AntonioFresu 5 17
(Luke McJannet) *pushed along in midfield bef 1/2-way: wknd 2f out* **66/1**
1m 0.32s (0.02) **Going Correction** -0.025s/f (Good) **11** Ran SP% **116.7**
Speed ratings (Par 94): **98,96,96,89,88 86,83,83,76,74 71**
CSF £45.19 TOTE £5.20: £1.50, £3.30, £1.30; EX 70.40 Trifecta £221.20.
**Owner** The Hot To Trot Syndicate-Golden Salute **Bred** Max Morris **Trained** Kingsclere, Hants
**FOCUS**
Not a bad 2yo maiden with the principals coming clear down the middle late on. The form will take time to settle.

## 4973 EBF STALLIONS NOVICE STKS 6f 12y
**6:50** (6:52) (Class 5) 2-Y-O £2,911 (£866; £432; £216) Stalls Low

Form RPR
1 **Tip Two Win** 2-9-2 0 DavidProbert 7 89+
(Roger Teal) *hld up in last pair: prog 2f out: shkn up and clsd qckly to ld jst ins fnl f: rn green but sn drew rt away* **20/1**
2 3 ½ **Zyzzyva (FR)** 2-9-2 0 JackMitchell 1 78
(Robyn Brisland) *broke wl but sn in midfield: prog against rail 2f out: led jst over 1f out to jst ins fnl f: styd on but readily outpcd* **3/1**2
15 3 3 ½ **Running Cloud (IRE)**19 4220 2-9-9 0 CharlesBishop 5 73
(Eve Johnson Houghton) *pushed along early: sn chsd ldrs: rdn to chal and upsides 2f out to over 1f out: qckly outpcd after* **11/10**1
4 3 ¼ **Fiery Breath** 2-9-2 0 PatCosgrave 4 56
(Robert Eddery) *pressed ldr: led 2f out to jst over 1f out: wknd* **9/1**
5 *shd* **Rustang (FR)** 2-9-2 0 ShaneKelly 8 56
(Richard Hughes) *hld up in last pair: pushed along over 2f out: nvr on terms but kpt on fnl f: nt disgracd* **12/1**
505 6 1 ¾ **Cruel Clever Cat**20 4175 2-8-8 55 HectorCrouch(3) 6 45
(John Gallagher) *sn led: shkn up and hdd 2f out: wknd jst over 1f out* **25/1**
7 2 ¾ **Expelled** 2-9-2 0 DanielMuscutt 2 41
(James Fanshawe) *chsd ldrs: pushed along 1/2-way: wknd jst over 2f out* **7/1**3
0 8 4 ½ **Spring Romance (IRE)**70 2473 2-9-2 0 AdamKirby 3 27
(Dean Ivory) *pressed ldrs: rdn on outer 1/2-way: wknd qckly 2f out* **20/1**
1m 13.26s (0.26) **Going Correction** -0.025s/f (Good) **8** Ran SP% **116.2**
Speed ratings (Par 94): **97,92,87,83,83 80,77,71**
CSF £78.85 TOTE £16.90: £4.00, £1.50, £1.10; EX 111.10 Trifecta £448.80.
**Owner** Mrs Anne Cowley **Bred** Mrs Anne Cowley **Trained** Great Shefford, Berks
**FOCUS**
Not a bad novice event, and the winner could be worth a try in a higher grade.

## 4974 SKY BET WINDSOR SPRINT SERIES H'CAP (SKY BET WINDSOR SPRINT SERIES QUALIFIER) 5f 21y
**7:20** (7:20) (Class 3) (0-95,94) 3-Y-O+ £7,246 (£2,168; £1,084; £542; £270) Stalls Low

Form RPR
-100 1 **Love On The Rocks (IRE)**10 4581 4-9-5 87 (h) WilliamBuick 2 96
(Charles Hills) *plld hrd: hld up in 6th: gd prog against rail over 1f out: rdn to ld jst ins fnl f: styd on wl* **7/1**
-340 2 1 **Spring Loaded (IRE)**37 3593 5-9-10 92 ShaneKelly 6 97
(Paul D'Arcy) *hld up in last: followed wnr through against rail over 1f out: pushed along and styd on to take 2nd last 100yds: nvr threatened to chal* **5/1**2
1000 3 1 ½ **Majestic Hero (IRE)**15 4416 5-9-8 90 AdamKirby 5 90
(Ronald Harris) *chsd ldr: led over 1f out to jst ins fnl f: outpcd after* **12/1**
3255 4 ½ **Dark Shot**15 4411 4-9-3 90 JoshuaBryan(5) 8 88
(Andrew Balding) *chsd ldrs: rdn and tried to chal over 1f out: one pce fnl f* **11/8**1
0411 5 ½ **Super Julius**13 4464 3-8-13 85 (p) CharlesBishop 1 80
(Eve Johnson Houghton) *chsd ldrs: rdn and ch over 1f out: one pce after* **5/1**2
0-05 6 3 **Musical Comedy**18 4272 6-8-8 76 AntonioFresu 4 61
(Mike Murphy) *chsd ldrs early but lost pl bef 1/2-way: struggling in rr over 1f out* **28/1**
4100 7 2 **Stepper Point**2 4881 8-9-10 92 (v) MartinDwyer 7 70
(William Muir) *led to over 1f out: wknd qckly* **6/1**3
59.51s (-0.79) **Going Correction** -0.025s/f (Good)
**WFA** 3 from 4yo+ 4lb **7** Ran SP% **113.4**
Speed ratings (Par 107): **105,103,101,100,99 94,91**
CSF £40.58 CT £411.70 TOTE £6.10: £2.70, £2.90; EX 35.40 Trifecta £355.30.
**Owner** The Chriselliam Partnership **Bred** Mount Coote New England Barton & Myriad **Trained** Lambourn, Berks
**FOCUS**
This feature sprint handicap was a good-quality affair. The first two came from the rear and the runner-up sets the level, rated to his turf best.

## 4975 SKY BET HORSERACING CASH OUT FILLIES' H'CAP 1m 31y
**7:50** (7:50) (Class 4) (0-80,79) 3-Y-O+ £4,690 (£1,395; £697; £348) Stalls Low

Form RPR
0561 1 **Sayem**16 4372 3-9-2 75 PatCosgrave 4 85
(Ed Walker) *hld up in 4th: prog to chse ldr over 1f out: rdn to cl and led last 100yds: sn clr* **5/1**3
00-0 2 2 ¾ **High On Love (IRE)**31 3786 3-9-4 77 RobertTart 2 81
(Charlie Fellowes) *racd freely: led: 5 l clr bef 1/2-way: c bk fr 2f out: hdd and no ex last 100yds* **9/1**
3-54 3 1 **Blushing Rose**10 4564 3-9-5 78 WilliamBuick 6 80
(Sir Michael Stoute) *hld up disputing 5th: effrt on outer over 2f out: drvn into 3rd fnl f: kpt on same pce after* **5/2**1
4-00 4 1 ½ **Fire Palace**75 2293 3-8-10 74 DavidEgan(5) 1 72
(Robert Eddery) *hld up in 6th: rdn over 2f out: no real imp on ldrs* **14/1**
-532 5 ¾ **Angel's Quest (FR)**23 4096 3-9-3 76 ShaneKelly 5 73
(Richard Hughes) *propped after s: t.k.h and sn rcvrd to chse ldr: rdn and no great imp over 2f out: lost 2nd and btn over 1f out* **7/2**2
3132 6 2 **Canberra Cliffs (IRE)**6 4722 3-9-0 76 GeorgeWood(3) 9 68
(Don Cantillon) *chsd ldng pair to 2f out: steadily wknd* **5/2**1
-400 7 2 ¼ **Dynamic Girl (IRE)**29 3869 4-9-1 66 FranBerry 3 55
(Brendan Powell) *restrained sn after s and hld up in last: shuffled along over 2f out: no prog and nvr remotely involved* **50/1**
1m 43.1s (-1.60) **Going Correction** -0.025s/f (Good)
**WFA** 3 from 4yo 8lb **7** Ran SP% **114.7**
Speed ratings (Par 102): **107,104,103,101,101 99,96**
CSF £47.78 CT £137.68 TOTE £5.80: £2.40, £3.60; EX 42.30 Trifecta £192.90.
**Owner** B Greenwood, I Dodds-Smith & R Hatter **Bred** Saleh Al Homaizi & Imad Al Sagar **Trained** Upper Lambourn, Berks
**FOCUS**
A fair fillies' handicap run at a decent pace. The winner built on her previous C&D win.

## 4976 SKY BET BEST ODDS GUARANTEED H'CAP 1m 2f
**8:20** (8:21) (Class 4) (0-85,85) 4-Y-O+ £4,690 (£1,395; £697; £348) Stalls Centre

Form RPR
1210 1 **Celebration Day (IRE)**25 4002 4-9-2 85 DavidEgan(5) 1 93
(Simon Crisford) *t.k.h: led at mod pce: rdn and hdd jst over 2f out: led again over 1f out: drvn and kpt on* **5/2**2
6-13 2 2 **Hollywood Road (IRE)**18 4254 4-9-3 84 (b) GeorgeWood(3) 3 88
(Don Cantillon) *hld up in tch: rdn and no prog 3f out: hdwy u.p 2f out: kpt on fnl f to take 2nd last stride* **13/8**1
0043 3 *hd* **Calvados Spirit**14 4443 4-9-7 85 (h) MartinDwyer 2 89
(William Muir) *t.k.h: trckd ldng pair tl wnt 2nd over 3f out: led 2f out: rdn and fnd little in front: hdd over 1f out: lost 2nd last stride* **4/1**3
05/4 4 2 ½ **Ogbourne Downs**28 3920 7-8-11 75 DavidProbert 4 74
(Ben Pauling) *s.s: hld up in last: prog on outer 2f out: rdn and little rspnse over 1f out* **14/1**
0-06 5 1 ½ **Udogo**14 4443 6-8-7 76 ow1 JennyPowell(5) 6 72
(Brendan Powell) *chsd ldr to over 3f out: lost pl u.p and btn wl over 1f out* **33/1**
00-2 6 ¾ **Classic Villager**26 3966 5-9-2 80 (h) AdamKirby 5 74
(Dean Ivory) *hld up in tch: shkn up 3f out: no prog and btn wl over 1f out* **11/2**
2m 9.72s (1.02) **Going Correction** -0.025s/f (Good) **6** Ran SP% **111.7**
Speed ratings (Par 105): **94,92,92,90,89 88**
CSF £6.90 CT £13.65 TOTE £3.20: £1.60, £1.60; EX 6.60 Trifecta £17.10.
**Owner** Mohammed Al Nabouda **Bred** Rabbah Bloodstock Limited **Trained** Newmarket, Suffolk
**FOCUS**
This wasn't a bad handicap. They went an ordinary pace and it paid to be handy. This rates a pb from the winner.
T/Plt: £191.90 to a £1 stake. Pool: £88,240.93. 335.65 winning units. T/Qpdt: £90.10 to a £1 stake. Pool: £6,123.66. 50.24 winning units. **Jonathan Neesom**

# 4723 WOLVERHAMPTON (A.W) (L-H)
Monday, July 17

**OFFICIAL GOING: Tapeta: standard**
Wind: Light, across Weather: Fine

## 4977 FCL GLOBAL FORWARDING NOVICE AUCTION STKS 6f 20y (Tp)
**5:40** (5:41) (Class 6) 2-Y-O £3,072 (£914; £456; £228) Stalls Low

Form RPR
0251 1 **Amazing Alice**25 3999 2-9-2 79 (p) LukeMorris 5 81
(Archie Watson) *mde all: shkn up over 1f out: clr fnl f* **5/6**1
6 2 2 ¼ **Tranquil Soul**28 3902 2-8-7 0 HarryBentley 7 64
(David Lanigan) *hld up: hdwy over 1f out: r.o to go 2nd wl ins fnl f: no ch w wnr* **9/1**
3 1 ¾ **Sancerre (IRE)** 2-8-5 0 RyanTate 8 57
(Sylvester Kirk) *prom: chsd wnr over 4f out: rdn and hung lft over 1f out: no ex ins fnl f* **25/1**
025 4 ½ **Lady Alavesa**47 3210 2-8-5 64 JosephineGordon 4 55
(Gay Kelleway) *hld up: rdn over 2f out: hung lft and r.o ins fnl f: nvr nrr* **13/2**3
0 5 1 ½ **Grand Acclaim (IRE)**34 3689 2-8-10 0 WilliamCarson 3 55
(Harry Dunlop) *prom: rdn over 2f out: edgd lft over 1f out: no ex fnl f* **40/1**
00 6 ½ **Bullseye Bullet**6 4725 2-8-10 0 KieranO'Neill 1 54
(Mark Usher) *sn pushed along and prom: rdn and edgd lft over 1f out: styd on same pce* **125/1**
620 7 2 ½ **Storm Doris (IRE)**68 2522 2-8-5 54 RyanPowell 2 41
(James Unett) *chsd wnr tl over 4f out: remained handy: rdn and wknd over 1f out* **28/1**
8 1 **Saxonroad Boy (USA)** 2-9-0 0 TonyHamilton 9 46+
(Richard Fahey) *s.s: outpcd* **16/1**
9 14 **Society Secret (IRE)** 2-9-2 0 RichardKingscote 6 4+
(Tom Dascombe) *s.s: outpcd* **4/1**2
1m 15.94s (1.44) **Going Correction** +0.125s/f (Slow) **9** Ran SP% **114.3**
Speed ratings (Par 92): **95,92,89,89,87 86,83,81,63**
CSF £8.95 TOTE £1.60: £1.10, £2.40, £6.00; EX 9.10 Trifecta £140.60.
**Owner** C R Hirst **Bred** Home Farm **Trained** Upper Lambourn, W Berks

**FOCUS**
A fair juvenile novice auction contest. They went a respectable gallop on standard Tapeta and the favourite proved thoroughly dominant. The winner is the best guide to the form.

## 4978 FCL GLOBAL FORWARDING MAKING LOGISTICS PERSONAL H'CAP 1m 5f 219y (Tp)
**6:10** (6:11) (Class 6) (0-60,60) 3-Y-O **£2,587** (£770; £384; £192) **Stalls** Low

Form RPR
-642 **1** **Sheriff Garrett (IRE)**$^{48}$ 3180 3-9-2 **55**..........................(p$^{1}$) DavidAllan 10 65+
(Tim Easterby) *chsd ldrs: hmpd wl over 1f out: nt clr run sn after: rdn to ld ins fnl f: styd on wl* **7/1**$^{2}$
1453 **2** 3 ¼ **Padleyourowncanoe**$^{46}$ 3261 3-9-6 **59**..........................(b) LukeMorris 8 62
(Daniel Mark Loughnane) *hld up: hdwy over 4f out: rdn and hung rt over 1f out: ev ch ins fnl f: styd on same pce* **11/1**
-406 **3** 2 ½ **Arcadian Sea (IRE)**$^{21}$ 4156 3-9-2 **55**.................... RichardKingscote 11 55
(William Jarvis) *chsd ldr tl led over 4f out: hdd 3f out: sn rdn: ev ch ins fnl f: wknd towards fin* **15/2**$^{3}$
1214 **4** ½ **Dyna Might**$^{14}$ 4436 3-9-7 **60**..........................(p) AndrewMullen 7 59
(Ollie Pears) *sn pushed along to go prom: led 3f out: rdn and edgd rt over 1f out: hdd ins fnl f: wknd towards fin* **12/1**
604- **5** 1 ¼ **Kozier (GER)**$^{292}$ 6875 3-8-10 **56**.................... FinleyMarsh$^{(7)}$ 3 53
(Alan King) *s.i.s: in rr whn hmpd after 1f: pushed along over 3f out: swtchd rt over 1f out: r.o ins fnl f: nt trble ldrs* **9/2**$^{1}$
5600 **6** ¾ **Netley Abbey**$^{44}$ 3326 3-8-3 **49**..........................(p) RhiainIngram$^{(7)}$ 5 45
(Karen George) *hld up: nt clr run wl over 3f out: styd on fr over 1f out: nt trble ldrs* **40/1**
0644 **7** ¾ **Astrostorm**$^{47}$ 3220 3-8-11 **50**.................... JoeyHaynes 9 45
(Mark H Tompkins) *hld up: rdn over 5f out: hdwy over 1f out: no ex fnl f* **33/1**
-344 **8** 2 **All About The Pace**$^{25}$ 4012 3-8-13 **52**.................... KieranO'Neill 6 44
(Mark Usher) *prom: rdn over 2f out: wknd fnl f* **15/2**$^{3}$
-305 **9** 1 ¾ **Percy Thrower (IRE)**$^{51}$ 3087 3-9-7 **60**.................... MartinHarley 1 50
(Charles Hills) *hld up: rdn whn hmpd over 2f out: nvr on terms* **17/2**
-403 **10** ¾ **Curtsy (IRE)**$^{48}$ 3180 3-9-5 **58**.................... FrannyNorton 2 47
(Hughie Morrison) *hld up: racd keenly: nt clr run over 2f out: nvr on terms* **9/2**$^{1}$
660 **11** 30 **Act Swiftly (IRE)**$^{33}$ 3720 3-8-10 **49**..........................(b$^{1}$) JohnFahy 12
(J S Moore) *s.i.s and given reminders after s: hdwy over 11f out: rdn and wknd over 3f out* **66/1**
00-5 **12** 18 **You Look Different**$^{20}$ 4173 3-8-10 **49**.................... CamHardie 4
(Antony Brittain) *hld up: rdn 7f out: bhd fnl 5f* **125/1**
3505 **13** 1 ½ **Spirit Of Rome (IRE)**$^{42}$ 3405 3-9-3 **56**..........(p$^{1}$) JosephineGordon 13
(James Bethell) *led: hdd over 4f out: sn rdn: wknd wl over 2f out* **14/1**

3m 4.72s (-3.28) **Going Correction** -0.275s/f (Stan) 13 Ran SP% **113.3**
Speed ratings (Par 98): **98,96,94,94,93 93,92,91,90,90 73,62,62**
CSF £75.98 CT £591.03 TOTE £6.80: £2.40, £3.20, £3.10; EX 76.20 Trifecta £705.80.
**Owner** Ontoawinner 10 & Partner 4 **Bred** Eimear Mulhern **Trained** Great Habton, N Yorks

**FOCUS**
A modest 3yo handicap. They went a muddling stop-start gallop and the first four horses home raced prominently throughout. The winner is rated back to his 2yo form.

## 4979 FCL GLOBAL FORWARDING H'CAP 6f 20y (Tp)
**6:40** (6:42) (Class 4) (0-80,82) 3-Y-O+ **£4,851** (£1,443; £721; £360) **Stalls** Low

Form RPR
225 **1** **Desert Rain (IRE)**$^{66}$ 2572 3-9-1 **76**..........(v$^{1}$) EdwardGreatrex$^{(3)}$ 7 82
(Saeed bin Suroor) *sn led: rdn over 1f out: jst hld on* **3/1**$^{2}$
1 **2** shd **Samarmadi**$^{16}$ 4341 3-9-3 **75**.................... JosephineGordon 2 80+
(Hugo Palmer) *s.i.s: in rr and drvn along over 3f out: r.o wl ins fnl f: nt quite rch wnr* **11/8**$^{1}$
3650 **3** 1 **Kyllukey**$^{12}$ 4495 4-9-1 **68**..........................(p$^{1}$) FrannyNorton 9 71
(Milton Bradley) *led early: chsd wnr: shkn up over 1f out: styd on* **20/1**
1556 **4** hd **Brother Tiger**$^{10}$ 4566 8-9-12 **79**..........................(p$^{1}$) DavidAllan 8 81
(David C Griffiths) *hld up: rdn over 1f out: r.o ins fnl f: nt rch ldrs* **14/1**
4344 **5** nk **September Issue**$^{12}$ 4489 4-9-9 **76**..........................(p) LukeMorris 5 77
(Gay Kelleway) *prom: rdn over 1f out: r.o* **11/2**$^{3}$
0530 **6** ½ **Fleckerl (IRE)**$^{12}$ 4495 7-9-0 **67**..........................(p) MartinHarley 1 67
(Conor Dore) *s.i.s: hld up: r.o ins fnl f: nvr nrr* **28/1**
2250 **7** 1 **French**$^{17}$ 4310 4-8-12 **65**..........................(p) CamHardie 4 62
(Antony Brittain) *chsd ldrs: rdn over 1f out: styd on same pce ins fnl f* **12/1**
3005 **8** 1 ¾ **Seamster**$^{9}$ 4629 10-8-12 **72**..........................(t) CameronNoble$^{(7)}$ 3 63
(David Loughnane) *hld up: hdwy over 3f out: rdn over 1f out: no ex ins fnl f* **10/1**

1m 15.36s (0.86) **Going Correction** +0.125s/f (Slow)
**WFA** 3 from 4yo+ 5lb 8 Ran SP% **114.1**
Speed ratings (Par 105): **99,98,97,97,96 96,94,92**
CSF £7.46 CT £64.60 TOTE £4.20: £1.50, £1.30, £3.40; EX 9.60 Trifecta £114.40.
**Owner** Godolphin **Bred** Darley **Trained** Newmarket, Suffolk

**FOCUS**
The feature contest was a decent sprint handicap. They went a respectable gallop and the uneasy favourite got going just too late. The winner progressed and the third is the key to the form.

## 4980 FCLGF.COM CLASSIFIED CLAIMING STKS 1m 4f 51y (Tp)
**7:10** (7:10) (Class 6) 3-Y-O+ **£2,425** (£721; £360; £180) **Stalls** Low

Form RPR
66-0 **1** **Howardian Hills (IRE)**$^{20}$ 4187 4-9-6 54..........................(p$^{1}$) LukeMorris 11 61
(Victor Dartnall) *led over 10f out: clr over 6f out tl over 3f out: pushed clr again over 2f out: rdn over 1f out: kpt on* **33/1**
0-55 **2** 1 **Frozon**$^{14}$ 4439 4-9-3 52..........................(h) DavidAllan 7 56
(Brian Ellison) *hld up in tch: hdwy on outer to chse wnr over 2f out: rdn over 1f out: styd on* **15/2**
5656 **3** 3 ¼ **Yasir (USA)**$^{21}$ 4165 9-9-6 58.................... MartinHarley 10 54
(Conor Dore) *s.i.s: hld up: rdn and r.o ins fnl f: wnt 3rd post: nt rch ldrs* **13/2**$^{3}$
000 **4** nk **Sevilla**$^{54}$ 2956 4-9-6 58.................... KieranO'Neill 12 54
(Olly Murphy) *hld up: hdwy over 1f out: rdn to go 3rd 1f out: edgd lft ins fnl f: styd on: lost 3rd post* **4/1**$^{2}$
34-5 **5** 2 ¾ **Medieval Bishop (IRE)**$^{21}$ 4158 8-8-10 52..........(p) TobyEley$^{(7)}$ 6 46
(Tony Forbes) *s.i.s: hld up: rdn over 2f out: r.o ins fnl f: nvr nrr* **28/1**
0040 **6** ¾ **Alshan Fajer**$^{47}$ 3208 7-9-10 60.................... TonyHamilton 8 52
(J R Jenkins) *hld up: rdn over 3f out: r.o ins fnl f: nvr on terms* **12/1**
54/6 **7** 4 **Dalgig**$^{13}$ 4470 7-9-1 54.................... CamHardie 3 37
(Jennie Candlish) *prom: racd keenly: rdn over 2f out: wknd over 1f out* **33/1**
145 **8** 3 ½ **Monologue (IRE)**$^{84}$ 2022 4-9-6 55..........................(t$^{1}$) RobHornby 5 36
(Neil Mulholland) *hld up: effrt over 2f out: wknd over 1f out* **6/4**$^{1}$
-006 **9** 10 **Walking In Rhythm (IRE)**$^{65}$ 2626 4-8-13 54.................... FinleyMarsh$^{(7)}$ 4 20
(Barry Leavy) *chsd ldrs: rdn over 3f out: wknd over 2f out* **50/1**
6522 **10** 13 **Never Say (IRE)**$^{8}$ 4660 4-9-3 42..........................(p) AndrewMullen 2
(Sam England) *led: hdd over 10f out: chsd wnr tl rdn over 2f out: wknd over 1f out* **11/1**

2m 41.42s (0.62) **Going Correction** +0.125s/f (Slow) **10** Ran SP% **112.4**
Speed ratings (Par 101): **102,101,99,98,97 96,93,91,84,76**
CSF £248.10 TOTE £16.20: £4.20, £2.40, £2.40; EX 99.90 Trifecta £686.10.
**Owner** Mrs C Carter & V Dartnall **Bred** J Beckett **Trained** Brayford, Devon

**FOCUS**
A modest middle-distance claimer. The shock winner increased the tempo after 2f and dominated thereafter. He had every chance on his form here early last year. The first two were clear.

## 4981 FCL GLOBAL FORWARDING MEDIAN AUCTION MAIDEN STKS 1m 1f 104y (Tp)
**7:40** (7:41) (Class 6) 3-4-Y-O **£2,425** (£721; £360; £180) **Stalls** Low

Form RPR
5 **1** **Fools And Kings**$^{16}$ 4347 3-9-5 0.................... LukeMorris 2 71
(Robyn Brisland) *a.p: chsd ldr over 3f out: shkn up to ld over 1f out: rdn and edgd lft ins fnl f: styd on* **10/1**
3-24 **2** 1 ¼ **Golden Wolf (IRE)**$^{82}$ 2092 3-8-12 75.................... FinleyMarsh$^{(7)}$ 5 69
(Richard Hughes) *sn led: racd keenly: shkn up: hung rt and hdd over 1f out: sn rdn: styd on same pce wl ins fnl f* **6/4**$^{1}$
36 **3** 1 **Josh The Plod (IRE)**$^{16}$ 4347 3-8-12 0.................... JasonWatson$^{(7)}$ 1 67
(Andrew Balding) *dwlt: pushed along in rr early: hmpd over 7f out: hdwy over 4f out: rdn over 1f out: styd on* **25/1**
2 **4** 4 ½ **Lewinsky (IRE)**$^{25}$ 4003 3-9-0 0.................... JosephineGordon 7 54
(Hugo Palmer) *s.i.s: hld up: pushed along 1/2-way: hdwy u.p over 1f out: nt trble ldrs* **2/1**$^{2}$
6 **5** 2 ¾ **Swaffham Bulbeck (IRE)**$^{32}$ 3755 3-9-5 0.................... HarryBentley 4 53
(Ed Vaughan) *prom: rdn and hung rt over 1f out: wknd fnl f* **7/2**$^{3}$
0-06 **6** 4 ½ **Fire Empress**$^{49}$ 3137 4-9-9 45..........................(h) RyanPowell 3 41
(James Unett) *pushed along towards rr early: hld up: rdn and wknd over 1f out* **100/1**
006- **7** 5 **The Batham Boy (IRE)**$^{310}$ 6314 3-9-5 51.................... WilliamCarson 8 35
(Daniel Mark Loughnane) *s.i.s: a in rr* **100/1**
004 **8** 12 **Kimene**$^{25}$ 4003 3-9-0 65.................... RichardKingscote 6 7
(William Stone) *sn chsng ldr: rdn and lost 2nd over 3f out: wknd over 2f out* **20/1**

2m 1.21s (0.41) **Going Correction** +0.125s/f (Slow)
**WFA** 3 from 4yo 9lb 8 Ran SP% **115.2**
Speed ratings (Par 101): **103,101,101,97,94 90,86,75**
CSF £25.40 TOTE £8.90: £2.20, £1.10, £5.40; EX 28.90 Trifecta £199.80.
**Owner** Paul Hancock **Bred** Mrs D O'Brien **Trained** Newmarket, Suffolk

**FOCUS**
An ordinary maiden which lacked depth. They went a respectable gallop but once again it paid to be prominent.

## 4982 FCLGF.COM H'CAP 1m 142y (Tp)
**8:10** (8:10) (Class 6) (0-60,62) 3-Y-O+ **£2,425** (£721; £360; £180) **Stalls** Low

Form RPR
3000 **1** **Cat Royale (IRE)**$^{47}$ 3208 4-9-12 **60**..........................(p) DannyBrock 7 69
(John Butler) *sn led: hdd over 6f out: chsd ldr tl shkn up to ld over 2f out: rdn out* **8/1**$^{3}$
0645 **2** 1 ¼ **Life Of Luxury**$^{21}$ 4163 4-9-7 **55**.................... WilliamCarson 5 62
(Mark Brisbourne) *led early: chsd ldrs: rdn to chse wnr over 1f out: styd on u.p* **10/1**
-060 **3** nk **Anna Medici**$^{112}$ 1401 3-8-7 **50**.................... LukeMorris 2 55
(Sir Mark Prescott Bt) *prom: rdn over 3f out: sn outpcd: rallied over 1f out: hung rt ins fnl f: r.o* **5/1**$^{2}$
11 **4** 1 **Society Ranger (IRE)**$^{38}$ 3550 4-9-7 **62**..........(p) GearoidBrouder$^{(7)}$ 6 66
(S M Duffy, Ire) *hld up: rdn over 2f out: r.o ins fnl f: nt rch ldrs* **6/4**$^{1}$
5 nk **Love To Rock (IRE)**$^{20}$ 4195 4-9-2 **50**..........(b$^{1}$) MarkGallagher 3 53
(Adrian Paul Keatley, Ire) *hld up: hdwy over 1f out: nt clr run ins fnl f: styd on* **20/1**
-000 **6** 1 ½ **Rock Of Monaco**$^{18}$ 4263 4-8-12 **46**..........................(b) CamHardie 8 46+
(Antony Brittain) *hood removed late: dwlt and edgd rt s: hld up: hdwy over 1f out: nt rch ldrs* **20/1**
0040 **7** 1 **Greyjoy (IRE)**$^{27}$ 3939 3-7-10 **46** oh1.................... ShariqMohd$^{(7)}$ 11 43
(Sylvester Kirk) *hld up: hung rt: hdwy over 5f out: rdn over 2f out: no ex fnl f* **25/1**
0060 **8** 1 ¼ **Tawfeer**$^{34}$ 3703 3-8-10 **53**..........................(p) RyanPowell 12 48
(James Unett) *s.i.s: hdwy over 7f out: led over 6f out: rdn and hdd over 2f out: wknd fnl f* **100/1**
0046 **9** shd **Rising Sunshine (IRE)**$^{30}$ 3809 4-8-12 **46** oh1..........(b) DavidAllan 13 42
(Milton Bradley) *chsd ldrs: rdn over 2f out: wknd ins fnl f* **16/1**
5056 **10** nk **Pivotal Dream (IRE)**$^{20}$ 4180 4-8-12 **46** oh1.................... KieranO'Neill 4 41
(Mark Brisbourne) *hld up: pushed along over 3f out: swtchd rt over 1f out: nvr on terms* **16/1**
6-05 **11** 7 **Whitstable Pearl (IRE)**$^{31}$ 3772 4-9-0 **48**..........(p$^{1}$) SaleemGolam 1 29
(Sophie Leech) *prom: hmpd after 1f: nt clr run over 5f out: rdn over 2f out: wknd over 1f out* **66/1**
0-02 **12** 3 ¼ **Star Links (USA)**$^{14}$ 4453 11-8-12 **46** oh1..........(b) MartinHarley 10 21
(John Butler) *hld up: a in rr: shkn up and wknd over 2f out* **8/1**$^{3}$
0000 **13** 9 **Genuine Approval (IRE)**$^{21}$ 4165 4-9-10 **61**.................... TimClark$^{(3)}$ 9 18
(John Butler) *hmpd s: sn bhd* **50/1**

1m 52.18s (2.08) **Going Correction** +0.125s/f (Slow)
**WFA** 3 from 4yo+ 9lb 13 Ran SP% **117.6**
Speed ratings (Par 101): **95,93,93,92,92 91,90,89,89,88 82,79,71**
CSF £77.73 CT £444.63 TOTE £8.20: £2.10, £3.10, £2.50; EX 110.80 Trifecta £602.40.
**Owner** Whiterok Ltd **Bred** Kellsgrange Stud & Ruskerne Ltd **Trained** Newmarket, Suffolk

**FOCUS**
A modest handicap. They went a muddling gallop and the evening's theme of success for those ridden prominently continued.

## 4983 FCL PERSONALISED GLOBAL FREIGHT SOLUTIONS H'CAP 7f 36y (Tp)
**8:40** (8:42) (Class 5) (0-75,77) 3-Y-O **£3,234** (£962; £481; £240) **Stalls** High

Form RPR
1-05 **1** **Phalaborwa**$^{29}$ 3869 3-9-9 **77**.................... HarryBentley 5 87
(Ed Vaughan) *chsd ldr tl rdn to ld over 1f out: styd on* **8/1**
-103 **2** 1 ¼ **Nostalgie**$^{48}$ 3189 3-9-9 **77**.................... MartinHarley 9 84
(James Tate) *chsd ldrs: rdn and ev ch ins fnl f: styd on same pce* **14/1**
0023 **3** 1 ½ **The Amber Fort (USA)**$^{2}$ 4892 3-8-12 **69**.................... JoshDoyle$^{(3)}$ 2 72
(David O'Meara) *chsd ldrs: rdn over 1f out: edgd lft ins fnl f: styd on same pce* **5/2**$^{2}$
6021 **4** ½ **Alemaratalyoum (IRE)**$^{11}$ 4542 3-9-6 **74**.................... LukeMorris 6 76
(Ed Dunlop) *hld up: hdwy u.p over 2f out: nt rch ldrs* **6/1**$^{3}$

0445 **5** *1* **Diable D'Or (IRE)**[4] 4810 3-9-1 **72**....................(p[1]) EdwardGreatrex(3) 10 71
(Eve Johnson Houghton) *hld up: shkn up over 1f out: r.o ins fnl f: nt trble ldrs* **12/1**

200 **6** *shd* **Red Gunner**[30] 3814 3-9-4 **75**.................................... ShelleyBirkett(3) 11 74
(David O'Meara) *hld up: r.o ins fnl f: nvr nrr* **66/1**

2332 **7** *nk* **Bruny Island (IRE)**[6] 4727 3-8-5 **59**......................(h) JosephineGordon 1 57
(Charlie Fellowes) *hld up in tch: plld hrd: shkn up over 1f out: no ex ins fnl f* **2/1**[1]

306 **8** *1* **Cryptonite (IRE)**[6] 4726 3-8-5 **59**...................................... DannyBrock 3 54
(Michael Appleby) *sn led: clr over 5f out tl over 2f out: rdn and hdd over 1f out: no ex ins fnl f* **33/1**

-620 **9** *½* **Casina Di Notte (IRE)**[24] 4050 3-9-7 **75**..................(p[1]) FrannyNorton 4 72
(Marco Botti) *s.i.s: hld up: running on whn nt clr run wl ins fnl f: eased* **18/1**

6100 **10** *½* **El Torito (IRE)**[18] 4251 3-9-2 **75**..............................(v[1]) PaddyBradley(5) 7 67
(Jim Boyle) *hld up: rdn over 2f out: wknd fnl f* **66/1**

546- **11** *45* **Tullinahoo (IRE)**[261] 7690 3-8-8 **62**.................................... CamHardie 8
(Denis Coakley) *hld up: rdn and wknd over 2f out* **150/1**

1m 28.39s (-0.41) **Going Correction** +0.125s/f (Slow) **11** Ran SP% **113.5**
Speed ratings (Par 100): **107,105,103,103,102 102,101,100,99,99 47**
CSF £107.34 CT £365.50 TOTE £7.40: £2.10, £2.60, £1.40; EX 92.80 Trifecta £426.20.
**Owner** A E Oppenheimer **Bred** Hascombe And Valiant Studs **Trained** Newmarket, Suffolk

**FOCUS**
A fair 3yo handicap and the best time on the card. They went a decent gallop but once again those who raced prominently did best. The form is rated through the third.
T/Jkpt: Not won. T/Plt: £79.50 to a £1 stake. Pool: £77,356.75. 710.28 winning units. T/Qpdt: £18.10 to a £1 stake. Pool: £5,873.97. 239.78 winning units. **Colin Roberts**

4984 - 4987a (Foreign Racing) - See Raceform Interactive

# VICHY
Monday, July 17

**OFFICIAL GOING: Turf: soft**

## 4988a PRIX MADAME JEAN COUTURIE (LISTED RACE) (3YO FILLIES) (TURF) 1m 2f
**1:20** 3-Y-O **£23,504** (£9,401; £7,051; £4,700; £2,350)

RPR

**1** **Araaja (IRE)**[31] 3-8-13 0 ow2...................................... MickaelBarzalona 2 95
(A De Watrigant, France) **29/10**[1]

**2** *nk* **Golden Legend (FR)**[35] 3681 3-8-13 0 ow2...................... AlexisBadel 7 95
(H-F Devin, France) **39/10**[3]

**3** *½* **Dream Awhile (USA)**[51] 3103 3-8-13 0 ow2....... ChristopheSoumillon 4 94
(J-C Rouget, France) **19/5**[2]

**4** *nk* **Indian Blessing**[32] 3749 3-8-13 0 ow2.......................... FranckBlondel 1 93
(Ed Walker) *wl into stride: settled bhd ldr: pushed along over 2f out: rdn over 1f out: styd on one pce fnl f* **155/10**

**5** *nk* **Viola Da Terra (FR)**[31] 3-8-13 0 ow2............................ MaximeGuyon 3 92
(F-H Graffard, France) **41/10**

**6** *nk* **Baltic Duchess (IRE)**[35] 3681 3-8-13 0 ow2...... Pierre-CharlesBoudot 6 92
(A Fabre, France) **93/10**

**7** *nk* **Clear For Take Off**[41] 3-8-13 0 ow2......................... AurelienLemaitre 8 91
(F Head, France) **79/10**

**8** *2 ½* **Haya Of Fortune (FR)**[29] 3881 3-8-13 0 ow2................. TheoBachelot 5 86
(N Leenders, France) **185/10**

1m 57.1s (-11.50) **8** Ran SP% **118.6**
PARI-MUTUEL (all including 1 euro stake): WIN 3.90; PLACE 1.40, 1.40, 1.60; DF 8.20; SF 14.60.
**Owner** OTI Management Pty Ltd **Bred** Rathregan Stud **Trained** France

# 4731 BATH (L-H)
Tuesday, July 18

**OFFICIAL GOING: Firm (10.2)**
Wind: light, behind Weather: warm

## 4989 TRAVIS PERKINS WAVIN H'CAP (BATH SUMMER STAYERS SERIES QUALIFIER) 1m 3f 137y
**2:00** (2:01) (Class 5) (0-70,71) 3-Y-O+ **£4,204** (£1,251; £625; £312) **Stalls** Low

Form RPR

4435 **1** **Cubswin (IRE)**[15] 4450 3-9-3 **70**...................................... AndreaAtzeni 3 76
(Roger Charlton) *mde all: qcknd pce over 2f out: kpt on wl: rdn out* **2/1**[2]

4321 **2** *2* **Plato's Kode (IRE)**[13] 4494 3-8-12 **65**..................(tp) RobertWinston 1 68
(Seamus Durack) *hld up bhd ldng trio: tk clsr order 3f out: chsd wnr over 1f out: nt pce to get on terms* **6/4**[1]

4524 **3** *nse* **Pete So High (GER)**[6] 4755 3-9-4 **71**..................(p) TomMarquand 5 74
(Richard Hannon) *trckd ldr: chal 3f out tl rdn wl over 1f out: kpt pressing for 2nd but nt pce of wnr fnl f* **7/2**[3]

6421 **4** *10* **Pondering**[17] 4347 3-8-10 **66**.............................(v) EdwardGreatrex(3) 2 53
(Eve Johnson Houghton) *trckd ldr: pushed along over 4f out: rdn 3f out: wknd ent fnl f* **6/1**

2m 31.49s (0.89) **Going Correction** -0.025s/f (Good)
**WFA** 3 from 4yo 11lb **4** Ran SP% **109.8**
Speed ratings (Par 103): **96,94,94,87**
CSF £5.48 TOTE £2.90; EX 5.70 Trifecta £11.30.
**Owner** Mrs Diane Engelhardt **Bred** Mrs D Engelhardt & Wellsummers Farm **Trained** Beckhampton, Wilts

**FOCUS**
A modest handicap run at a steady gallop and the winner had the run of things. The form is around the winner's best maiden runs.

## 4990 HALL'S DISMANTLING AND REMOVAL LTD FILLIES' H'CAP 5f 160y
**2:30** (2:30) (Class 5) (0-70,70) 3-Y-O+ **£3,234** (£962; £481; £240) **Stalls** Centre

Form RPR

-533 **1** **Coronation Cottage**[20] 4200 3-8-12 **64**..................... CharlieBennett(3) 6 69
(Malcolm Saunders) *disp ld: overall ldr over 1f out: sn rdn: kpt on wl* **5/2**[2]

-353 **2** *¾* **Island Cloud**[22] 4157 3-9-0 **66**.................................. GeorgeWood(3) 5 68
(Heather Main) *hld up: hdwy over 2f out: sn rdn: wnt 3rd over 1f out: kpt on into 2nd ent fnl f but a being hld by wnr* **2/1**[1]

1200 **3** *¾* **Little Miss Daisy**[78] 2235 3-9-2 **65**................................ MartinDwyer 1 64
(William Muir) *hld up: hdwy over 1f out: sn rdn: kpt on into 3rd fnl 120yds: no ex nring fin* **16/1**

065- **4** *1 ¾* **Grand Myla (IRE)**[301] 6658 3-9-6 **69**................................(p) ShaneKelly 2 63
(Gary Moore) *disp ld tl rdn over 1f out: no ex fnl f* **16/1**

0-04 **5** *2* **Evening Starlight**[4] 4842 4-8-12 **63**............................. FinleyMarsh(7) 4 51
(Ron Hodges) *hld up: swtchd rt and hdwy over 1f out: wknd ins fnl f* **7/1**

3-41 **6** *7* **Bella Alissa**[31] 3806 3-9-7 **70**..........................................(p) AndreaAtzeni 7 33
(Robert Cowell) *chsd ldrs: rdn over 2f out: nt quite pce to chal: wknd fnl f* **3/1**[3]

4000 **7** *4* **Silver Springs (IRE)**[34] 3728 4-8-0 **51** oh6................. RhiainIngram(7) 3
(Roger Ingram) *prom for 1f: chsd ldrs: rdn wl over 2f out: wknd ent fnl f* **66/1**

1m 8.72s (-2.48) **Going Correction** -0.55s/f (Hard)
**WFA** 3 from 4yo 5lb **7** Ran SP% **112.7**
Speed ratings (Par 100): **94,93,92,89,87 77,72**
CSF £7.67 TOTE £3.40: £1.50, £1.70; EX 8.80 Trifecta £52.30.
**Owner** Pat Hancock & Eric Jones **Bred** Eric Jones, Pat Hancock **Trained** Green Ore, Somerset

**FOCUS**
The market leaders came to the fore in this modest fillies' sprint. The jockey's claim helped the winner.

## 4991 AFI-UPLIFT NURSERY H'CAP 5f 10y
**3:00** (3:00) (Class 5) 2-Y-O **£4,204** (£1,251; £625; £312) **Stalls** Centre

Form RPR

3342 **1** **Aquadabra (IRE)**[13] 4488 2-8-13 **68**................................ AndreaAtzeni 3 72
(Mick Channon) *little slowly away: sn mid-div: hdwy whn nt clr run and swtchd rt 2f out: led over 1f out: edgd lft: r.o: rdn out* **5/2**[1]

501 **2** *nk* **Dreamboat Annie**[25] 4044 2-8-10 **65**............................... SteveDrowne 2 68
(Mark Usher) *chsd ldrs: chalng whn bmpd sltly 2f out: sn rdn: kpt on wl for str chal ins fnl f: hld nring fin* **12/1**

000 **3** *2 ¼* **Ivy Leaguer**[11] 4582 2-9-2 **71**.......................................... TomMarquand 1 65
(Brian Meehan) *chsd ldrs: rdn 2f out: kpt on but nt pce of front pair fnl f* **20/1**

1450 **4** *hd* **Diamond Pursuit**[17] 4361 2-9-1 **70**..........................(b[1]) DougieCostello 5 64
(Jo Hughes) *slowly away: sn nudged along towards rr: hdwy over 1f out: nt clrest of runs but kpt on ins fnl f* **12/1**

554 **5** *shd* **Llamrei**[20] 4199 2-8-3 **58**.................................... JosephineGordon 6 51
(Jo Hughes) *mid-div: rdn over 2f out: no imp whn nt clr run briefly ent fnl f: r.o wl fnl 120yds* **20/1**

050 **6** *hd* **Laura Knight (IRE)**[20] 4212 2-8-9 **64**.............................. DavidProbert 7 56
(Gary Moore) *in tch: hdwy over 2f out: sn rdn: kpt on same pce fnl f* **10/1**

0064 **7** *nk* **Hastenplace**[6] 4758 2-8-3 **61**.................................(b[1]) GeorgeWood(3) 10 52
(Rod Millman) *pressed ldr: rdn to ld briefly over 1f out: hld whn sltly hmpd by wnr sn after: no ex ins fnl f* **7/1**[2]

050 **8** *nse* **Cove Beach**[19] 4252 2-8-8 **63**.....................................(b[1]) SamHitchcott 4 54
(Paul Cole) *led: rdn 2f out: hdd over 1f out: no ex fnl 120yds* **20/1**

3025 **9** *2 ¼* **Autumn Lodge**[6] 4758 2-9-1 **70**.......................................... ShaneKelly 9 53
(J S Moore) *hld up: rdn 2f out: nt pce to get involved* **8/1**[3]

0104 **10** *2 ¼* **June Dog**[12] 4527 2-9-9 **78**................................................ SeanLevey 8 52
(Richard Hannon) *hld up: effrt over 2f out: nvr threatened: wknd ent fnl f* **5/2**[1]

1m 1.06s (-1.44) **Going Correction** -0.55s/f (Hard) **10** Ran SP% **119.5**
Speed ratings (Par 94): **89,88,84,84,84 84,83,83,79,76**
CSF £35.98 CT £398.43 TOTE £3.40: £1.10, £3.10, £5.90; EX 23.70 Trifecta £447.90.
**Owner** Insignia Racing **Bred** Rathasker Stud **Trained** West Ilsley, Berks

**FOCUS**
Modest nursery form, although they did go a good, fast pace. The winner is rated back to her best.

## 4992 DRIBUILD LTD H'CAP 5f 160y
**3:30** (3:30) (Class 3) (0-95,95) 3-Y-O **£9,703** (£2,887; £1,443; £721) **Stalls** Centre

Form RPR

6322 **1** **Open Wide (USA)**[22] 4154 3-8-10 **84**..........................(b[1]) MartinDwyer 7 90
(Amanda Perrett) *slowly away: last: swtchd to center over 2f out: r.o wl fnl f led cl home: pushed out* **4/1**[3]

6214 **2** *nk* **Arzaak (IRE)**[36] 3672 3-8-10 **84**...............................(b) JosephineGordon 6 89
(Chris Dwyer) *led: rdn over 2f out: kpt on: hdd cl home* **14/1**

6-60 **3** *hd* **Barrington (IRE)**[27] 3959 3-9-7 **95**................................(t) OisinMurphy 4 99
(Charles Hills) *trckd ldrs: chal 2f out: sn rdn: kpt on w wnr towards fin* **8/1**

2-12 **4** *1 ½* **Yalawin (IRE)**[50] 3159 3-9-1 **89**.......................................... AndreaAtzeni 5 88
(Roger Varian) *trckd ldrs: swtchd lft for effrt over 1f out: nt quite pce to chal: no ex fnl 120yds* **6/4**[1]

5044 **5** *nk* **Tomily (IRE)**[11] 4581 3-9-6 **94**................................................ SeanLevey 1 92
(Richard Hannon) *in tch: nt best of runs whn swtchd rt over 1f out: nt pce to get on terms whn clr* **6/1**

1022 **6** *2* **Mr Pocket (IRE)**[21] 4178 3-8-9 **83**.........................................(t) FranBerry 2 74
(Paul Cole) *prom: rdn over 2f out: kpt chsng ldrs tl no ex ins fnl f* **7/2**[2]

1m 8.5s (-2.70) **Going Correction** -0.55s/f (Hard) **6** Ran SP% **114.3**
Speed ratings (Par 104): **96,95,95,93,92 90**
CSF £52.76 TOTE £4.90: £2.10, £5.50; EX 55.10 Trifecta £252.40.
**Owner** George Materna & John McInerney **Bred** Moyglare Stud **Trained** Pulborough, W Sussex

**FOCUS**
Fair sprinting form. The winner had shaped as if capable of better in the past.

## 4993 BIRD IN HAND SALTFORD H'CAP (BATH SUMMER SPRINT SERIES QUALIFIER) 5f 10y
**4:00** (4:01) (Class 5) (0-70,70) 3-Y-O+ **£4,204** (£1,251; £625; £312) **Stalls** Centre

Form RPR

0053 **1** **Archimedes (IRE)**[5] 4795 4-9-2 **61**..............................(tp) OisinMurphy 4 70
(David C Griffiths) *mde all: rdn over 1f out: kpt on wl* **15/8**[1]

-222 **2** *1 ½* **Secret Agent**[20] 4198 3-9-3 **69**.................................(p[1]) GeorgeWood(3) 5 72
(William Muir) *trckd wnr: rdn over 1f out: kpt on but nt pce to chal* **11/4**[2]

1503 **3** *nse* **Babyfact**[12] 4532 6-9-11 **70**...................................... JosephineGordon 2 74
(Malcolm Saunders) *chsd ldrs: rdn 2f out: kpt on ins fnl f: nrly snatched 2nd cl home* **11/4**[2]

1602 **4** *2 ¾* **Go Amber Go**[22] 4149 5-9-2 **66**..................................... LuluStanford(5) 3 60
(Rod Millman) *trckd wnr: rdn 2f out: drifted sltly lft: nt pce to chal: fdd fnl 120yds* **5/1**[3]

4050 **5** *4* **Emjayem**[12] 4531 7-9-3 **62**............................................(p) LiamKeniry 1 42
(John Holt) *s.i.s: last but in tch: rdn over 2f out: nvr threatened: fdd fnl f* **16/1**

59.93s (-2.57) **Going Correction** -0.55s/f (Hard)
**WFA** 3 from 4yo+ 4lb **5** Ran SP% **110.7**
Speed ratings (Par 103): **98,95,95,91,84**
CSF £7.36 TOTE £2.30: £1.10, £2.50; EX 7.10 Trifecta £13.70.
**Owner** Ladies And The Tramps **Bred** Paddy Twomey & Irish National Stud **Trained** Bawtry, S Yorks

**FOCUS**
Modest form, they finished in betting order. The winner repeated his latest form.

## 4994 DRIBUILD SUPPORTS TOGETHER FOR SHORT LIVES H'CAP 1m 5f 11y
**4:30** (4:30) (Class 5) (0-70,70) 3-Y-O+ **£4,204** (£1,251; £625; £312) **Stalls** High

Form RPR
0-21 **1** **Imphal**[25] 4045 3-8-4 **64**....................(p) TylerSaunders(7) 1 77+
(Marcus Tregoning) *racd freely: mde all: shkn up 2f out: styd on strly to assert fnl f* **4/6**[1]
20-2 **2** 4 ½ **Londonia**[6] 4733 5-9-4 **60**....................(t) OisinMurphy 4 64
(Graeme McPherson) *trckd ldrs: rdn over 2f out: styd on to go 2nd towards fin but no threat to wnr* **2/1**[2]
1062 **3** ¾ **Becca Campbell (IRE)**[15] 4442 4-9-11 **70**..........(p) EdwardGreatrex(3) 2 73
(Eve Johnson Houghton) *trckd wnr: rdn to chal briefly over 2f out: hld ent fnl f: no ex whn lost 2nd towards fin* **8/1**[3]
0643 **4** 13 **Tenby Two**[13] 4493 3-8-6 **59**.................... RyanTate 3 50
(Mick Channon) *trckd ldrs: rdn over 3f out: nt pce to get on terms. wknd ent fnl f and eased* **20/1**

2m 48.61s (-3.39) **Going Correction** -0.025s/f (Good)
**WFA** 3 from 4yo+ 11lb **4 Ran SP% 109.2**
Speed ratings (Par 103): **109,106,105,97**
CSF £2.28 TOTE £1.50; EX 2.30 Trifecta £4.00.
**Owner** Mrs M E Slade **Bred** G S Bishop **Trained** Whitsbury, Hants

**FOCUS**
An ordinary race that played out as expected, with a winner on the up. The second and third are rated close to form.
T/Plt: £260.80 to a £1 stake. Pool: £68,388.64 - 191.36 winning units T/Qpdt: £39.10 to a £1 stake. Pool: £5,214.95 - 98.48 winning units **Tim Mitchell**

# 4597 BEVERLEY (R-H)
Tuesday, July 18

**OFFICIAL GOING: Good to firm (watered; 7.9)**
Wind: Moderate behind Weather: Fine & dry

## 4995 RACING UK NOVICE AUCTION STKS (DIV I) 5f
**2:15** (2:16) (Class 5) 2-Y-O **£3,881** (£1,155; £577; £288) **Stalls** Low

Form RPR
0 **1** **Cameo Star (IRE)**[29] 3895 2-8-13 0.................... PaulHanagan 8 71
(Richard Fahey) *towards rr: pushed along 1/2-way: hdwy wl over 1f out: swtchd lft and rdn to chal ins fnl f: kpt on wl to ld towards fin* **9/2**[3]
3 **2** 1 ¼ **Johni Boxit**[12] 4539 2-8-9 0.................... DanielMuscutt 3 63
(Gay Kelleway) *cl up: rdn to take slt ld appr fnl f: sn drvn: hdd and no ex towards fin* **8/1**
26 **3** hd **Tember**[20] 4204 2-8-13 0.................... PJMcDonald 6 66
(David Barron) *chsd ldrs: hdwy 2f out: swtchd rt to inner over 1f out: sn rdn to chal and ev ch: drvn and kpt on same pce ins fnl f* **5/2**[1]
6 **4** 1 ¼ **Foxy Lady**[13] 4503 2-8-8 0.................... ShaneGray 5 57+
(Kevin Ryan) *dwlt and rr: hdwy 2f out: rdn over 1f out: styd on wl fnl f* **16/1**
4 **5** 1 ¾ **Ben My Chree**[11] 4555 2-8-6 0.................... ConnorBeasley 1 48
(Bryan Smart) *slt ld: rdn along wl over 1f out: hdd appr fnl f: sn drvn and wknd* **3/1**[2]
30 **6** 1 **Medici Oro**[13] 4503 2-8-11 0.................... KieranShoemark 7 50
(David Brown) *towards rr: rdn along 2f out: kpt on fnl f* **8/1**
**7** ¾ **Magic Ship (IRE)** 2-9-2 0.................... AndrewMullen 9 52
(Ollie Pears) *cl up on outer: pushed along over 2f out: rdn wl over 1f out: grad wknd* **25/1**
**8** 4 ½ **Geesala Brave (IRE)** 2-9-2 0.................... JasonHart 2 36
(John Quinn) *dwlt and wnt rt s: green and sn outpcd in rr* **7/1**

1m 1.91s (-1.59) **Going Correction** -0.575s/f (Hard) **8 Ran SP% 116.2**
Speed ratings (Par 94): **89,87,86,84,81 80,79,71**
CSF £40.56 TOTE £5.70: £2.80, £2.40, £1.10; EX 42.50 Trifecta £167.20.
**Owner** Let's Go Racing 2 **Bred** Mrs P O'Rourke **Trained** Musley Bank, N Yorks

**FOCUS**
Good to firm (watered), with the course at its widest configuration to allow for fresh ground. Race distances as advertised. An ordinary-looking novice auction race. The winner improved from his debut.

## 4996 RACING UK NOVICE AUCTION STKS (DIV II) 5f
**2:45** (2:46) (Class 5) 2-Y-O **£3,881** (£1,155; £577; £288) **Stalls** Low

Form RPR
02 **1** **Roundhay Park**[10] 4599 2-9-2 0.................... TomEaves 8 71
(Nigel Tinkler) *trckd ldrs: hdwy on inner wl over 1f out: nt clr run and swtchd lft jst over 1f out: rdn ent fnl f: styd on wl to ld last 50 yds* **7/2**[2]
5 **2** nk **Wensley**[14] 4472 2-8-13 0.................... PJMcDonald 2 67
(James Bethell) *trckd ldng pair: n.m.r and swtchd lft to outer jst over 1f over 1f out: sn rdn and ev ch. kpt on* **9/4**[1]
04 **3** ¾ **Curzon (IRE)**[27] 3972 2-9-2 0.................... DanielTudhope 4 67
(David O'Meara) *slt ld on inner: rdn along 11/2f out: drvn ent fnl f: hdd and no ex last 50 yds* **8/1**
0 **4** 1 ¾ **Mendali**[50] 3149 2-8-9 0.................... DavidAllan 5 54
(David C Griffiths) *cl up: rdn and ev ch over 1f out: drvn ent fnl f: kpt on same pce* **66/1**
0 **5** ½ **Leaderofthepack**[10] 4599 2-8-9 0.................... ConnorBeasley 1 52
(Bryan Smart) *towards rr: pushed along 1/2-way: rdn wl over 1f out: kpt on fnl f* **16/1**
**6** hd **Dandy's Beano (IRE)** 2-8-8 0.................... ShaneGray 7 52
(Kevin Ryan) *dwlt: towards rr t.k.h: hdwy wl over 1f out: swtchd rt and rdn appr fnl f: kpt on* **7/1**[3]
6 **7** 1 ¼ **Jaimie's Joy**[13] 4502 2-8-9 0.................... BarryMcHugh 9 47
(Tony Coyle) *chsd ldng pair: rdn along wl over 1f out: drvn appr fnl f: hld whn sltly hmpd ent fnl f* **8/1**
**8** 4 ½ **Aislin Moon (IRE)** 2-8-4 0.................... JoeFanning 6 26
(Les Eyre) *dwlt: a towards rr* **7/1**[3]
**9** 21 **Cavendish Place** 2-8-9 0.................... KieranShoemark 3
(David Brown) *dwlt: sn rdn along in rr: green and outpcd fr 3f out* **9/1**

1m 2.88s (-0.62) **Going Correction** -0.575s/f (Hard) **9 Ran SP% 117.6**
Speed ratings (Par 94): **81,80,79,76,75 75,73,66,32**
CSF £12.05 TOTE £4.00: £1.20, £1.20, £2.20; EX 14.20 Trifecta £61.00.
**Owner** Leeds Plywood And Doors Ltd **Bred** James Munroe **Trained** Langton, N Yorks

**FOCUS**
A slower time than the first division but there looked more depth to this. The winner's effort was in keeping with his C&D debut.

## 4997 MALCOLM GREENSLADE DONCASTER LVA STALWART MEMORIAL H'CAP 5f
**3:15** (3:16) (Class 6) (0-60,62) 3-Y-O+ **£2,587** (£770; £384; £192) **Stalls** Low

Form RPR
3353 **1** **Roaring Rory**[21] 4174 4-9-4 **61**....................(p) SeamusCronin(7) 1 68
(Ollie Pears) *trckd ldr on inner: swtchd lft and rdn to chal jst over 1f out: sn drvn: kpt on to ld last 100 yds* **9/4**[1]
3040 **2** nk **Joysunny**[4] 4847 3-8-6 **46**.................... ShaneGray 2 51
(Jacqueline Coward) *led: rdn along 11/2f out: jnd and drvn ent fnl f: hdd last 100 yds: no ex* **10/1**
2004 **3** 2 ¼ **Tinsill**[14] 4479 6-8-10 **46** oh1....................(p) AndrewMullen 4 44
(Nigel Tinkler) *hld up: hdwy on inner 2f out: effrt and nt clr run over 1f out: sn rdn and kpt on fnl f* **14/1**
230 **4** hd **Maggi May (IRE)**[14] 4478 3-8-11 **51**.................... KieranShoemark 3 47
(David Brown) *cl up: rdn wl over 1f out: ev ch tl drvn and kpt on same pce fnl f* **11/2**[2]
4500 **5** shd **La Haule Lady**[14] 4479 3-8-8 **48**.................... CamHardie 14 44
(Paul Midgley) *dwlt and swtchd rt s: towards rr: hdwy wl over 1f out: rdn and styd on strly fnl f* **33/1**
0056 **6** hd **Six Of The Best**[14] 4478 5-8-10 **46** oh1.................... ConnorBeasley 8 42
(Bryan Smart) *cl up on outer: rdn along and ev ch 11/2f out: sn drvn and grad wknd* **25/1**
0000 **7** 1 ½ **Be Bold**[13] 4509 5-9-10 **60**....................(b) DanielTudhope 9 51
(Rebecca Bastiman) *t.k.h: chsd ldrs: hdwy 2f out: rdn over 1f out: kpt on same pce fional f* **13/2**[3]
6005 **8** nk **George Bailey (IRE)**[48] 3201 5-8-10 **46** oh1.................... TomEaves 5 36
(Suzzanne France) *chsd ldrs: rdn along wl over 1f out: sn no imp* **10/1**
0056 **9** ¾ **Harbour Lightning**[29] 3915 3-9-2 **56**....................(p[1]) PatrickMathers 7 42+
(Noel Wilson) *rrd and dwlt s: towards rr: hdwy 2f out: rdn over 1f out: kpt on fnl f* **9/1**
0446 **10** 1 **Little Cupcake**[14] 4458 6-8-10 **46** oh1....................(v) DannyBrock 10 29+
(Denis Quinn) *towards rr: hmpd after 2f: sme hdwy on outer 2f out: rdn over 1f out: n.d* **20/1**
3000 **11** hd **Spirit Of Zebedee (IRE)**[12] 4531 4-9-12 **62**.................... JasonHart 11 45+
(John Quinn) *chsd ldrs towards outer: rdn along 2f out: sn drvn and wknd* **7/1**
0003 **12** 2 **Miss Pepper (IRE)**[19] 4246 3-8-3 **46** oh1....................(h) SammyJoBell(3) 13 20+
(Paul Midgley) *dwlt: t.k.h: a towards rr* **33/1**
6060 **13** 3 ¾ **Whispering Wolf**[48] 3202 4-8-7 **46** oh1.................... JordanVaughan(3) 12 8+
(Suzzanne France) *in tch on wd outside: rdn along 2f out: sn wknd* **33/1**

1m 1.75s (-1.75) **Going Correction** -0.575s/f (Hard)
**WFA** 3 from 4yo+ 4lb **13 Ran SP% 124.3**
Speed ratings (Par 101): **91,90,86,86,86 86,83,83,82,80 80,76,70**
CSF £25.57 CT £228.98 TOTE £3.20: £1.30, £3.40, £4.20; EX 29.70 Trifecta £368.40.
**Owner** Ownaracehorse Ltd (ownaracehorse.co.uk) **Bred** R S Hoskins & Hermes Services **Trained** Norton, N Yorks

**FOCUS**
A modest sprint. The 1-2-3-4 were drawn 1-2-4-3, and with the runner-up making the pace not much got involved.

## 4998 132ND YEAR OF THE WATT MEMORIAL H'CAP 2m 32y
**3:45** (3:45) (Class 4) (0-85,87) 3-Y-O+
**£6,225** (£1,864; £932; £466; £233; £117) **Stalls** Low

Form RPR
-422 **1** **Corpus Chorister (FR)**[17] 4338 4-9-11 **82**.................... KevinStott 4 90
(David Menuisier) *mde virtually all: pushed along over 2f out: rdn clr over 1f out: kpt on strly* **5/2**[1]
0605 **2** 3 **Angel Gabrial (IRE)**[17] 4338 8-10-0 **85**.................... PaulHanagan 6 89
(Richard Fahey) *hld up in rr: hdwy 4f out: pushed along and clsng whn rdr dropped reins over 2f out: gd hdwy over 1f out: styng on wl on inner whn hmpd ent fnl f: kpt on same pce after* **7/2**[3]
-164 **3** 1 **Grumeti**[13] 4499 9-9-11 **82**....................(p) KieranShoemark 2 85
(Alan King) *trckd ldng pair on inner: pushed along over 2f out: rdn and edgd lft jst over 1f out: drvn and edgd rt ent fnl f: sn one pce* **4/1**
6132 **4** 4 **La Fritillaire**[23] 4120 5-8-9 **66**.................... AndrewMullen 7 64
(James Given) *trckd ldng pair: pushed along wl over 2f out: rdn wl over 1f out: sn drvn and one pce* **7/1**
0330 **5** 2 ½ **The Blues Master (IRE)**[18] 4307 3-8-0 **72**.................... JoeFanning 1 69
(Mark Johnston) *trckd wnr: effrt and cl up 3f out: rdn along over 2f out: sn drvn and wknd* **10/3**[2]
33-0 **6** 65 **Highland Castle**[18] 728 9-10-2 **87**....................(t) NeilFarley 5 4
(Lucinda Egerton) *hld up in rr: pushed along 5f out: rdn 4f out: sn outpcd and bhd* **100/1**
00-4 **P** **Waterclock (IRE)**[66] 2032 8-8-9 **66** oh1....................(v) PJMcDonald 3
(Micky Hammond) *trckd ldrs on inner: pushed along after 5f: rdn along 1/2-way: sn lost action and p.u 7f out: fatally injured* **20/1**

3m 28.62s (-11.18) **Going Correction** -0.375s/f (Firm) course record
**WFA** 3 from 4yo+ 15lb **7 Ran SP% 112.1**
Speed ratings (Par 105): **112,110,110,108,106 74,**
CSF £11.05 TOTE £3.40: £2.00, £2.20; EX 12.10 Trifecta £30.80.
**Owner** Clive Washbourn **Bred** Mme Elisabeth Erbeya **Trained** Pulborough, W Sussex

**FOCUS**
A useful staying handicap. The winner is rated similar to Chester latest.

## 4999 RACING UK IN GLORIOUS HD H'CAP 7f 96y
**4:15** (4:15) (Class 5) (0-75,75) 3-Y-O+ **£3,780** (£1,131; £565; £283; £141) **Stalls** Low

Form RPR
0605 **1** **Mywayistheonlyway (IRE)**[11] 4556 4-9-6 **72**.................... PhilDennis(5) 13 80
(Grant Tuer) *t.k.h: trckd ldr: hdwy and cl up over 2f out: rdn to ld 11/2f out: drvn ins fnl f: hld on gamely* **16/1**
33 **2** nse **Major Crispies**[13] 4506 6-9-7 **68**.................... DanielTudhope 6 76
(David O'Meara) *trckd ldrs: swtchd lft to outer and hdwy 2f out: rdn to chal ent fnl f: sn drvn and ev ch: no ex nr fin* **6/1**[2]
-165 **3** 2 ¼ **Keepup Kevin**[25] 4050 3-9-3 **71**.................... RobHornby 10 70
(Pam Sly) *trckd ldrs: hdwy over 2f out: rdn wl over 1f out: drvn and kpt on same pce fnl f* **4/1**[1]
1011 **4** ¾ **Talent Scout (IRE)**[10] 4601 11-9-9 **75**....................(p) GemmaTutty(5) 12 75
(Karen Tutty) *sn led: pushed along and jnd over 2f out: rdn and hdd 11/2f out: sn drvn and grad wknd* **10/1**[3]

2003 **5** 1/2 **Tadaawol**[24] 4105 4-9-11 **72**..........(p) TonyHamilton 2 71
(Roger Fell) *chsd ldrs: rdn along on inner 2f out: drvn over 1f out: no imp* **10/1**[3]

5035 **6** 2 **George Reme (IRE)**[11] 4557 3-9-4 **72**..........(v) JasonHart 9 62
(John Quinn) *dwlt: t.k.h towards rr: hdwy on inner wl over 1f out: sn rdn and kpt on fnl f* **10/1**[3]

3352 **7** 3/4 **Amood (IRE)**[18] 4304 6-9-9 **70**..........(p) KieranShoemark 1 61+
(Simon West) *t.k.h: in tch: hdwy to go cl up over 5f out: rdn along over 2f out: wknd over 1f out* **4/1**[1]

0-56 **8** shd **Dot Green (IRE)**[10] 4631 4-9-12 **73**.......... JoeyHaynes 8 64
(Mark H Tompkins) *rrd s: a rr* **33/1**

6212 **9** 1 1/2 **Full Of Promise**[15] 4438 4-9-7 **68**.......... PaulHanagan 4 55
(Richard Fahey) *nvr bttr than midfield* **4/1**[1]

0-00 **10** 1 **Relight My Fire**[13] 4506 7-8-11 **61**..........(p) RachelRichardson(3) 7 45
(Tim Easterby) *towards rr: hdwy on outer 3f out: rdn along 2f out: n.d* **20/1**

5410 **11** 1 3/4 **Tanawar (IRE)**[13] 4506 7-9-4 **65**..........(b) JackGarritty 11 44
(Ruth Carr) *t.k.h: hld up: a towards rr* **25/1**

01-0 **12** 5 **Traveltalk (IRE)**[18] 4310 3-8-12 **66**..........(p) MartinLane 5 29
(Brian Ellison) *a rr* **25/1**

1m 30.91s (-2.89) **Going Correction** -0.375s/f (Firm)
**WFA** 3 from 4yo+ 7lb **12** Ran SP% **122.8**
Speed ratings (Par 103): **101,100,98,97,96 94,93,93,91,90 88,83**
CSF £108.18 CT £477.98 TOTE £19.90: £4.50, £2.20, £1.80; EX 165.30 Trifecta £760.80.
**Owner** ARC Racing Yorkshire X **Bred** M Duffy **Trained** Birkby, N Yorks

**FOCUS**
The pace was steady so it paid to be handy. The winner is rated back to his 3yo best.

## 5000 IRISHBIGRACETRENDS.COM H'CAP 1m 100y
**4:45** (4:45) (Class 4) (0-80,80) 3-Y-O+ **£5,040** (£1,508; £754; £377; £188) **Stalls** Low

Form RPR

-404 **1** **Mont Royal (FR)**[28] 3949 3-8-8 **68**.......... AndrewMullen 7 72+
(Ollie Pears) *hld up in rr: hdwy 2f out: chsd ldrs over 1f out: sn rdn: swtchd lft ent fnl f: sn drvn and styd on strly to ld nr line* **12/1**

0525 **2** hd **Pumaflor (IRE)**[57] 2884 5-9-7 **80**.......... PatrickVaughan(7) 5 85
(David O'Meara) *prom: hdwy over 2f out: sn cl up: led over 1f out: sn rdn and edgd rt: drvn and edgd lft ins fnl f: hdd nr line* **5/1**[2]

1433 **3** nk **Mon Beau Visage (IRE)**[11] 4556 4-10-0 **80**..........(p) DanielTudhope 8 84
(David O'Meara) *hld up in tch: hdwy over 2f out: chsd ldr ent fnl f: sn swtchd rt and rdn to chal: drvn and ev ch last 50 yds: no ex nr line* **4/1**[1]

0340 **4** 1/2 **Worlds His Oyster**[20] 4207 4-10-0 **80**..........(v) JasonHart 6 83
(John Quinn) *hld up in tch: hdwy on inner wl over 1f out: rdn and n.m.r ent fnl f: styd on wl towards fin* **11/2**[3]

11-6 **5** 2 1/4 **Big Time Dancer (IRE)**[20] 4210 4-9-1 **67**.......... MartinLane 4 65
(Brian Ellison) *cl up: rdn along wl over 1f out: sn drvn and wknd ent fnl f* **4/1**[1]

2526 **6** 3/4 **Make On Madam (IRE)**[12] 4525 5-9-7 **73**.......... PJMcDonald 1 69
(Les Eyre) *t.k.h: sn led: rdn along over 2f out: drvn and hdd over 1f out: grad wknd* **12/1**

20-1 **7** 1 **Lord Reason**[12] 4523 5-9-9 **78**.......... TimClark(3) 2 72
(John Butler) *trckd ldrs: hdwy 3f out: rdn along wl over 1f out: drvn and wknd appr fnl f* **11/1**

5431 **8** 3 1/4 **Valley Of Rocks (IRE)**[10] 4626 3-8-10 **70**.......... JoeFanning 3 54
(Mark Johnston) *hld up in rr: effrt and sme hdwy on outer over 2f out: sn rdn and n.d* **4/1**[1]

1m 44.22s (-3.38) **Going Correction** -0.375s/f (Firm)
**WFA** 3 from 4yo+ 8lb **8** Ran SP% **115.8**
Speed ratings (Par 105): **101,100,100,100,97 97,96,92**
CSF £71.47 CT £287.18 TOTE £13.70: £3.50, £2.00, £1.40; EX 78.40 Trifecta £459.90.
**Owner** Mrs Z Wentworth **Bred** Dr Vet Gerard Samain **Trained** Norton, N Yorks
■ Stewards' Enquiry : Patrick Vaughan two-day ban; used whip above permitted level (Aug 4-5)

**FOCUS**
A fair handicap, rated around the second, third and fourth.

## 5001 RACING AGAIN NEXT MONDAY EVENING H'CAP 1m 1f 207y
**5:15** (5:16) (Class 6) (0-65,65) 3-Y-O £2,587 (£770; £384; £192) **Stalls** Low

Form RPR

0425 **1** **Bollin Ted**[4] 4839 3-8-2 **46** oh1.......... DuranFentiman 9 62+
(Tim Easterby) *trckd ldrs: smooth hdwy on outer 2f out: led appr fnl f: sn rdn clr: readily* **6/1**[3]

-135 **2** 7 **Clenymistra (IRE)**[8] 4690 3-9-4 **62**.......... DanielTudhope 10 65
(David O'Meara) *trckd ldng pair: hdwy over 2f out: rdn to chal over 1f out and ev ch: drvn ent fnl f: kpt on same pce* **3/1**[1]

-451 **3** 1 3/4 **Shambra (IRE)**[57] 2902 3-9-7 **65**.......... TonyHamilton 2 65
(Roger Fell) *trckd ldrs: led after 2f: rdn along over 2f out: drvn wl over 1f out: hdd appr fnl f: kpt on same pce* **13/2**

2035 **4** nk **Knightsbridge Liam (IRE)**[15] 4436 3-8-4 **55**.......... HarrisonShaw(7) 6 54
(Michael Easterby) *hld up towards rr: hdwy on inner over 2f out: nt clr run wl over 1f out and again appr fnl f: sn rdn and kpt on* **9/1**

-006 **5** hd **Moonlight Silver**[42] 3425 3-9-5 **63**.......... PhillipMakin 3 62
(William Muir) *prom: trckd ldng pair after 3f: pushed along wl over 2f out: rdn wl over 1f out: sn drvn and kpt on same pce* **8/1**

-550 **6** 1/2 **Pitch High (IRE)**[36] 3657 3-8-7 **54**.......... ShelleyBirkett(3) 7 52
(Julia Feilden) *sn led: hdd after 2f: trckd ldr: hdwy to chal over 2f out: sn rdn and ev ch tl hld whn sltly hmpd appr fnl f* **33/1**

0-50 **7** 3 3/4 **Seebring (IRE)**[19] 4265 3-9-0 **58**..........(p) MartinLane 4 49
(Brian Ellison) *trckd ldrs on inner: hdwy wl over 2f out: rdn along wl over 1f out: sn wknd* **20/1**

0-04 **8** 1 1/2 **Babamunchkin**[53] 3053 3-9-7 **65**.......... LouisSteward 1 53+
(Michael Bell) *dwlt and rr: sme hdwy on wd outside over 2f out: sn rdn and n.d* **7/2**[2]

633 **9** 1/2 **Kilbaha Lady (IRE)**[7] 4721 3-9-1 **64**..........(t) LewisEdmunds(5) 8 51
(Nigel Tinkler) *hld up: a towards rr* **10/1**

-460 **10** 6 **Petit Filous**[21] 4171 3-9-3 **61**.......... KevinStott 5 36
(Giles Bravery) *a rr* **16/1**

2m 4.39s (-2.61) **Going Correction** -0.375s/f (Firm) **10** Ran SP% **118.6**
Speed ratings (Par 98): **95,89,88,87,87 87,84,83,82,77**
CSF £24.79 CT £123.49 TOTE £7.80: £2.30, £1.50, £1.90; EX 30.30 Trifecta £139.80.
**Owner** Habton Farms **Bred** Habton Farms **Trained** Great Habton, N Yorks

**FOCUS**
A weak race, but an emphatic winner and straightforward form.

## 5002 DOROTHY LAIRD MEMORIAL TROPHY LADY RIDERS' H'CAP (PRO-AM LADIES RACE) 1m 1f 207y
**5:45** (5:49) (Class 6) (0-65,71) 4-Y-O+ **£2,587** (£770; £384; £192) **Stalls** Low

Form RPR

0000 **1** **Graceful Act**[10] 4627 9-9-2 **46** oh1..........(p) MissSBrotherton 9 54
(Ron Barr) *trckd ldng pair: hdwy to ld jst over 2f out: rdn clr appr fnl f: kpt on* **33/1**

0001 **2** 1 1/2 **Royal Reserve**[7] 4730 4-10-13 **71** 6ex.......... ShelleyBirkett 4 76
(David O'Meara) *hld up towards rr: hdwy over 2f out: rdn to chse ldrs over 1f out: drvn and kpt on fnl f* **11/4**[1]

-651 **3** 1/2 **Diamonds A Dancing**[10] 4627 7-10-0 **63**..........(h) MissAMcCain(5) 8 67
(Donald McCain) *trckd ldrs: hdwy 2f out: rdn over 1f out: kpt on fnl f* **9/2**[2]

3003 **4** 1 1/2 **I'm Super Too (IRE)**[11] 4554 10-9-13 **57**..........(b) GemmaTutty 11 58
(Karen Tutty) *t.k.h: hld up towards rr: hdwy into midfield 1/2-way: chsd ldrs over 2f out: rdn over 1f out: kpt on fnl f* **12/1**

6050 **5** 4 1/2 **Candesta (USA)**[15] 4446 7-9-12 **56**.......... SammyJoBell 10 49
(Julia Feilden) *in tch: hdwy 3f out: rdn to chse ldrs wl over 1f out: sn drvn and no imp fnl f* **14/1**

0033 **6** 1 1/4 **Spinart**[10] 4627 4-10-8 **66**..........(p[1]) MissGAndrews 13 56
(Pam Sly) *t.k.h: chsd ldrs on outer: rdn along over 2f out: drvn wl over 1f out: sn one pce* **9/2**[2]

6460 **7** 1 **Inspector Norse**[10] 4627 6-9-8 **52**..........(p) MissEEasterby 12 41
(Tim Easterby) *in tch: pushed along over 3f out: rdn over 2f out: sn no imp* **14/1**

0541 **8** 2 3/4 **Lean On Pete (IRE)**[21] 4160 8-10-2 **60**.......... MissCWalton 5 43
(Ollie Pears) *trckd ldr: led 6f out: rdn along over 2f out: sn hdd and drvn: wknd appr fnl f* **7/1**[3]

0-60 **9** 2 1/4 **American Hustle (IRE)**[29] 3912 5-9-13 **57**.......... MissLWilson 3 36
(Brian Ellison) *a towards rr* **12/1**

505- **10** 1 1/4 **Euro Mac**[266] 7602 5-9-8 **52**.......... RachelRichardson 6 29
(Neville Bycroft) *led: hdd 6f out: cl up: rdn along over 2f out: drvn and wknd over 1f out* **20/1**

230 **11** 2 **Royal Holiday (IRE)**[43] 3402 10-10-7 **65**..........(p) MissBeckySmith 7 38
(Marjorie Fife) *a towards rr* **12/1**

030- **12** 1 3/4 **Belle Peinture (FR)**[308] 6438 6-8-11 **46** oh1.......... MissEmilyBullock(5) 2 16
(Alan Lockwood) *dwlt: a rr* **66/1**

2m 4.52s (-2.48) **Going Correction** -0.375s/f (Firm) **12** Ran SP% **121.1**
Speed ratings (Par 101): **94,92,92,91,87 86,85,83,81,80 79,77**
CSF £123.68 CT £516.01 TOTE £43.90: £8.50, £1.40, £1.80; EX 238.30 Trifecta £2813.80.
**Owner** D Thomson **Bred** Mayden Stud, J A And D S Dewhurst **Trained** Seamer, N Yorks

**FOCUS**
A modest handicap. The form is rated at face value around the first four.
T/Jkpt: Not Won. T/Plt: £87.70 to a £1 stake. Pool: £77,269.12 - 642.88 winning units T/Qpdt: £33.50 to a £1 stake. Pool: £5,689.55 - 125.54 winning units **Joe Rowntree**

# 4502 THIRSK (L-H)
Tuesday, July 18

**OFFICIAL GOING: Good to firm (watered; 8.7)**
Wind: Fresh across Weather: Fine

## 5003 DABBLEBET - "FIRST ACCA ON US" APPRENTICE MAIDEN STKS 7f 218y
**6:10** (6:12) (Class 5) 3-Y-O+ **£3,234** (£962; £481; £240) **Stalls** Low

Form RPR

02 **1** **Aclimatise**[8] 4693 3-9-2 0.......... RichardOliver(3) 8 81
(Mark Johnston) *prom: rdn to ld wl over 1f out: strly pressed appr fnl f: kpt on wl* **11/4**[2]

5222 **2** 1 **Spinnaka (IRE)**[17] 4378 3-8-7 78.......... GabrieleMalune(7) 7 74
(Luca Cumani) *in tch: pushed along and hdwy over 2f out: rdn to chal strly appr fnl f: one pce fnl 50yds* **4/6**[1]

53 **3** 6 **Infamous Lawman (IRE)**[17] 4332 3-9-0 0.......... BenRobinson(5) 6 65
(Brian Ellison) *trckd ldrs: pushed along and outpcd 3f out: plugged on to go modest 3rd ins fnl f* **5/1**[3]

04 **4** 1 1/2 **Golden Jeffrey (SWI)**[6] 4738 4-9-10 0.......... CallumRodriguez(3) 5 63+
(Iain Jardine) *midfield on inner: pushed along over 2f out: one pce and nvr threatened* **12/1**

**5** 2 1/2 **Stolen Angel (IRE)** 3-9-2 0.......... PhilDennis(3) 3 56
(Antony Brittain) *racd keenly: sn led: rdn along whn hdd wl over 1f out: wknd* **25/1**

5 **6** 2 **Danny Mc D**[41] 3448 4-9-6 0.......... JamieGormley(7) 2 53
(Iain Jardine) *hld up: pushed along over 2f out: nvr threatened* **40/1**

**7** nk **Budarri**[179] 4-9-10 0.......... CliffordLee(3) 4 52
(Stuart Coltherd) *s.i.s: hld up in midfield: pushed along over 2f out: sn btn* **100/1**

**8** 3/4 **Rownak (IRE)**[155] 4-9-10 0.......... MeganNicholls(3) 11 51
(Brian Ellison) *slowly away: hld up: pushed along over 2f out: nvr threatened* **28/1**

0 **9** 23 **Compass Rose (IRE)**[11] 4568 3-8-7 0.......... ManuelFernandes(7) 9
(Scott Dixon) *dwlt: midfield on outer: rdn over 2f out: wknd over 1f out and bhd* **100/1**

1m 40.21s (0.11) **Going Correction** +0.025s/f (Good)
**WFA** 3 from 4yo 8lb **9** Ran SP% **122.7**
Speed ratings (Par 103): **100,99,93,91,89 87,86,85,62**
CSF £5.18 TOTE £4.80: £1.50, £1.02, £1.20; EX 7.90 Trifecta £19.70.
**Owner** Mark Johnston Racing Ltd **Bred** Longview Stud & Bloodstock Ltd **Trained** Middleham Moor, N Yorks

**FOCUS**
The watered ground was given as good to firm (GoingStick: 8.7) The rail on the 'Away' (Stables) bend was dolled out by about 6 metres, increasing distances for races over 1m4f+ by 20yds. An ordinary maiden in which the first two finished clear. There was no depth to it and the level of form is shaky behind the first two.

## 5004 ANDERSON BARROWCLIFF (S) STKS 5f
**6:40** (6:41) (Class 6) 3-5-Y-O **£2,587** (£770; £384; £192) **Stalls** High

Form RPR

1135 **1** **Nag's Wag (IRE)**[10] 4619 4-9-7 69.......... PaulMulrennan 4 63
(Conor Dore) *prom: rdn to ld narrowly over 1f out: strly pressed thrght fnl f: jst hld on* **11/4**[3]

6526 **2** nse **Semana Santa**[87] 1980 4-8-11 69.......... SamJames 3 53
(David Barron) *prom: pushed along over 1f out: rdn and upsides thrght fnl f: jst failed* **2/1**[1]

4232 **3** *¾* **Hadley**[4] 4847 4-9-2 48 ....................(p) JasonHart 1 55
(Tracy Waggott) *sn led: rdn whn hdd over 1f out: remained w ev ch tl no ex towards fin* **5/2**[2]

6600 **4** *3¾* **Chip Or Pellet**[21] 4174 4-9-2 44 .................... TomEaves 6 42
(Paul Midgley) *hld up in tch: rdn over 1f out: one pce and no threat ldng trio* **14/1**

3000 **5** *nk* **Emerald Secret (IRE)**[11] 4559 3-8-7 56 ....................(p) CamHardie 5 35
(Paul Midgley) *slowly away: hld up in rr: pushed along over 1f out: kpt on ins fnl f: nrst fin* **14/1**

40-0 **6** **Chevalier Du Lac (IRE)**[15] 4447 3-8-5 60 .......... KatherineGlenister(7) 7 29
(Conor Dore) *hld up: rdn 2f out: wknd fnl f* **16/1**

0-00 **7** *4½* **King Of Castilla**[19] 4246 3-8-10 50 ow1 ..............(b) AdamMcNamara(3) 2 14
(Colin Teague) *in tch: rdn along 1/2-way: wknd over 1f out* **66/1**

59.51s (-0.09) **Going Correction** +0.025s/f (Good)
**WFA** 3 from 4yo 4lb **7** Ran SP% **109.3**
Speed ratings (Par 101): **101,100,99,93,93 88,81**
CSF £7.84 TOTE £3.30: £1.70, £1.50; EX 9.30 Trifecta £15.80.There was no bid for the winner.
**Owner** Mrs Jennifer Marsh **Bred** Mrs Ann Foley & Mr William Neville **Trained** Hubbert's Bridge, Lincs

**FOCUS**
The first three came clear in this ordinary seller. A negative view has been taken of the form.

## 5005 WEATHERBYS RACING BANK H'CAP 1m 4f 8y
**7:10** (7:10) (Class 5) (0-75,75) 3-Y-O+ **£3,557** (£1,058; £529; £264) **Stalls** High

Form RPR

3-66 **1** **Hayward Field (IRE)**[40] 3501 4-9-2 **63** .................... PatrickMathers 8 70
(Noel Wilson) *hld up: rdn and gd hdwy on outer over 2f out: led over 1f out: styd on wl* **80/1**

-006 **2** *2¼* **Correggio**[21] 4169 7-8-11 **58** .................... PJMcDonald 9 61
(Micky Hammond) *hld up: angled rt to outer over 2f out: sn hdwy: rdn to chse ldr over 1f out: styd on but a hld* **8/1**[3]

000 **3** *2¼* **Sir Runs A Lot**[9] 4660 5-8-12 **59** .................... AndrewMullen 10 58
(David Barron) *hld up in tch: rdn and hdwy to chse ldr 2f out: one pce ins fnl f* **12/1**

3/00 **4** *shd* **Sheriff Of Nawton (IRE)**[3] 4899 6-9-12 **73** .................... TonyHamilton 1 72
(Roger Fell) *midfield: hdwy to trck ldr 3f out: short of room and lost pl 2f out: kpt on ins fnl f* **11/1**

5064 **5** *2½* **Good Time Ahead (IRE)**[26] 4016 3-8-4 **62** .................... PaddyAspell 2 58
(Philip Kirby) *chsd ldr: rdn over 2f out: edgd lft 2f out: wknd fnl f* **20/1**

0651 **6** *nse* **Mysterial**[7] 4722 7-8-13 **67** ....................(v) GerO'Neill(7) 6 62
(Declan Carroll) *led: racd keenly: rdn over 2f out: hdd over 1f out: sn wknd* **15/8**[2]

1445 **7** *6* **Blushing Red (FR)**[32] 3788 3-9-1 **73** .................... PaulMulrennan 3 60
(Ed Dunlop) *stmbld sltly s: racd keenly in tch: plld way up to trck ldr 8f out: pushed along and already losing pl whn short of room 2f out: wknd* **5/4**[1]

2m 35.01s (-1.19) **Going Correction** +0.025s/f (Good)
**WFA** 3 from 4yo+ 11lb **7** Ran SP% **112.4**
Speed ratings (Par 103): **104,102,101,100,99 99,95**
CSF £585.96 CT £8033.63 TOTE £41.80: £8.40, £2.60; EX 377.20 Trifecta £4396.90 Part won..
**Owner** Marwood Racing Limited **Bred** Selective Syndicate **Trained** Marwood, Co Durham

**FOCUS**
Race distance increased by 20yds. A messy race pace-wise, Mysterial going off too fast, and Blushing Red racing keen early and then going in pursuit too soon. That set things up for the closers, who had run at a more even gallop. The form is rated cautiously, with the market 1-2 not running their races.

## 5006 DABBLEBET MAIDEN STKS 5f
**7:40** (7:41) (Class 5) 3-4-Y-O **£3,234** (£962; £481; £240) **Stalls** High

Form RPR

5-22 **1** **Liquid (IRE)**[73] 2405 3-9-6 77 .................... TomEaves 7 56
(David Barron) *dwlt but sn led: mde rest: rdn over 1f out: drvn fnl f: hung bdly lft fnl 75yds and reduced advantage nr fin* **4/7**[1]

5- **2** *hd* **Canford Bay (IRE)**[368] 4371 3-9-6 0 .................... AndrewMullen 8 55
(Antony Brittain) *prom: racd keenly: rdn and hung lft fr over 1f out: kpt on: hmpd crossing line* **10/1**[3]

406 **3** *hd* **Our Place In Loule**[34] 3710 4-9-10 48 .................... PatrickMathers 5 55
(Noel Wilson) *chsd ldrs: rdn 2f out: carried lft appr fnl f: kpt on* **12/1**

45 **4** *2¼* **Melrose Girl**[27] 3984 3-9-1 0 .................... ConnorBeasley 1 41
(Bryan Smart) *hld up: rdn along 1/2-way: kpt on ins fnl f* **12/1**

6 **5** *1¼* **Angelou**[161] 612 3-9-1 0 .................... DanielTudhope 2 36
(David O'Meara) *hld up on outer: rdn and hdwy 2f out: chsd ldrs appr fnl f: wknd ins fnl f* **13/2**[2]

50 **6** *8* **Kodiac Pearl (IRE)**[56] 2924 3-9-1 0 .................... JoeFanning 3 8
(Robert Cowell) *in tch: rdn 2f out: sn wknd* **12/1**

**7** *12* **Fintry Flyer** 3-8-8 0 ....................(h[1]) SeanMooney(7) 9
(Jim Goldie) *v.s.a: a wl bhd* **40/1**

59.39s (-0.21) **Going Correction** +0.025s/f (Good)
**WFA** 3 from 4yo 4lb **7** Ran SP% **111.6**
Speed ratings (Par 103): **102,101,101,97,95 82,63**
CSF £6.88 TOTE £1.40: £1.02, £5.60; EX 7.80 Trifecta £35.00.
**Owner** Ron Hull **Bred** Cooneen Stud **Trained** Maunby, N Yorks
■ Stewards' Enquiry : Andrew Mullen caution; careless riding

**FOCUS**
Weak maiden form judged by the performance of the third.

## 5007 WEATHERBYS BANK FOREIGN EXCHANGE FILLIES' H'CAP 7f
**8:10** (8:11) (Class 5) (0-70,73) 3-Y-O+ **£3,557** (£1,058; £529; £264) **Stalls** Low

Form RPR

3-22 **1** **Rosy Ryan (IRE)**[18] 4298 7-9-1 **55** .................... JoeDoyle 11 62
(Tina Jackson) *trckd ldrs: rdn to chal appr fnl f: kpt on: led towards fin* **6/1**[3]

0040 **2** *shd* **Melaniemillie**[8] 4687 3-8-2 **49** oh1 .................... DuranFentiman 10 53
(Ruth Carr) *prom: rdn to ld 2f out: strly pressed fr appr fnl f: kpt on but hdd towards fin* **40/1**

0322 **3** *¾* **Totally Magic (IRE)**[5] 4797 5-9-2 **61** .................... LewisEdmunds(5) 2 66+
(Richard Whitaker) *hld up: angled to outer 2f out: sn rdn and hdwy: kpt on fnl f* **9/4**[1]

-624 **4** *½* **Halinka (IRE)**[22] 4144 3-9-7 **68** ....................(p[1]) HarryBentley 4 68
(Roger Varian) *trckd ldrs: rdn over 1f out: kpt on same pce* **13/2**

5230 **5** *1¾* **Yorkshire Pudding**[10] 4619 3-8-12 **62** ...........(b[1]) RachelRichardson(3) 8 58
(Tim Easterby) *hld up: hdwy on outer over 2f out: rdn over 1f out: one pce fnl f* **20/1**

6240 **6** *½* **Mia Cara**[12] 4536 3-9-4 **65** .................... AndrewMullen 9 59
(David Evans) *keen in midfield: bit short of room over 2f out: rdn over 1f out: one pce* **20/1**

341 **7** *hd* **The Stalking Moon (IRE)**[6] 4744 3-9-12 **73** 6ex .............. JasonHart 13 67
(John Quinn) *midfield on outside: hdwy to trck ldrs over 2f out: rdn over 1f out: wknd ins fnl f* **11/4**[2]

3353 **8** *1* **Cabal**[25] 4059 10-9-8 **62** ....................(b) DavidAllan 7 56
(Geoffrey Harker) *s.i.s: hld up up: rdn along over 2f out: one pce and nvr threatened* **10/1**

2-66 **9** *hd* **Lovely Acclamation (IRE)**[27] 3970 3-9-7 **68** .............. PaulMulrennan 1 59
(Ismail Mohammed) *midfield on inner: pushed along 2f out: angled rt off rail over 1f out: nvr threatened* **20/1**

F0-5 **10** *6* **Nellie Deen (IRE)**[123] 1237 4-9-1 **55** ....................(p) TonyHamilton 6 32
(Roger Fell) *led: rdn whn hdd 2f out: wknd appr fnl f* **28/1**

000 **11** *4* **Maid In Brittain**[18] 4309 3-8-3 **50** .................... CamHardie 3 14
(Antony Brittain) *a towards rr* **66/1**

-253 **12** *10* **Circulate**[166] 520 3-9-4 **65** .................... PatCosgrave 5 2
(Tom Clover) *dwlt: sn in tch: rdn along over 3f out: wknd over 1f out* **33/1**

1m 26.67s (-0.53) **Going Correction** +0.025s/f (Good)
**WFA** 3 from 4yo+ 7lb **12** Ran SP% **118.8**
Speed ratings (Par 100): **104,103,103,102,100 99,99,98,98,91 86,75**
CSF £227.47 CT £710.47 TOTE £6.70: £2.00, £9.30, £1.90; EX 344.00 Trifecta £1197.70.
**Owner** H L Thompson **Bred** Roger A Ryan **Trained** Liverton, Cleveland

**FOCUS**
The pace wasn't that strong and it was an advantage to race handily. A small step up from the winner on her recent form.

## 5008 DOWNLOAD THE DABBLEBET APP H'CAP 2m 13y
**8:40** (8:41) (Class 5) (0-70,72) 4-Y-O+ **£3,234** (£962; £481; £240) **Stalls** Centre

Form RPR

3541 **1** **Vercingetorix (IRE)**[12] 3389 6-9-4 **72** ....................(p) JamieGormley(7) 8 77
(Iain Jardine) *sn led: pushed along whn hdd over 4f out: rdn over 3f out: dropped to 3rd over 1f out: rallied fnl f: led again 110yds out* **3/1**[1]

0/1- **2** *½* **Italian Riviera**[174] 7592 8-9-0 **61** ....................(h) PaulMulrennan 10 65+
(Kenneth Slack) *dwlt and swtchd lft s: hld up in rr: pushed along and stl lot to do over 3f out: rdn and gd hdwy 2f out: styd on strly: gaining at fin* **3/1**[1]

64-5 **3** *¾* **Mcvicar**[137] 525 8-8-9 **56** ....................(p) SamJames 2 59
(John Davies) *prom: led over 4f out: rdn over 3f out: pressed over 1f out: hdd 110yds out: one pce* **14/1**

004 **4** *nk* **Celtic Power**[19] 4244 5-8-2 **49** ....................(v) CamHardie 6 52
(Jim Goldie) *in tch: rdn over 2f out: styd on* **16/1**

2225 **5** *½* **Stoneboat Bill**[37] 3628 5-8-11 **63** .................... PhilDennis(5) 7 65
(Declan Carroll) *hld up in rr: stl lot to do 3f out: rdn and hdwy 2f out: styd on fnl f* **13/2**[3]

6-04 **6** *¾* **Byronegetonefree**[13] 4018 6-8-4 **51** .................... PatrickMathers 5 52
(Stuart Coltherd) *midfield: hdwy to trck ldr over 5f out: rdn over 3f out: chal over 1f out: wknd ins fnl f* **25/1**

3543 **7** *½* **Jan Smuts (IRE)**[5] 4790 9-8-9 **59** ....................(tp) SammyJoBell(3) 4 60
(Wilf Storey) *midfield: rdn over 2f out: one pce and nvr threatened* **10/1**

-045 **8** *hd* **Carthage (IRE)**[17] 4357 6-9-2 **68** .................... BenRobinson(5) 3 68
(Brian Ellison) *slowly away: sn midfield: rdn and outpcd over 3f out: plugged on fnl f* **10/1**

5240 **9** *4* **Percy Verence**[4] 4853 4-8-6 **53** .................... JoeFanning 9 48
(Tracy Waggott) *hld up: rdn over 3f out: wknd over 1f out* **6/1**[2]

1403 **10** *1¼* **Cavalieri (IRE)**[38] 3566 7-9-0 **61** ....................(tp) KevinStott 1 55
(Philip Kirby) *midfield: rdn over 3f out: wknd 2f out* **20/1**

3m 33.97s (5.67) **Going Correction** +0.025s/f (Good) **10** Ran SP% **117.0**
Speed ratings (Par 103): **86,85,85,85,84 84,84,84,82,81**
CSF £11.09 CT £107.99 TOTE £3.80: £1.20, £1.80, £4.50; EX 13.90 Trifecta £109.30.
**Owner** Graeme Slesser **Bred** M Henochsberg & Madame D Ades-Hazan **Trained** Carruthertown, D'fries & G'way

**FOCUS**
Race distance increased by 20yds. A modest staying handicap. It was slowly run and the form is rated cautiously.

## 5009 CAROL & LEE BINNEY 25TH WEDDING ANNIVERSARY H'CAP 7f 218y
**9:10** (9:13) (Class 5) (0-75,75) 3-Y-O **£3,234** (£962; £481; £240) **Stalls** Low

Form RPR

0-22 **1** **Breanski**[27] 3975 3-9-1 **69** .................... DanielTudhope 4 75
(David O'Meara) *trckd ldr: pushed along to chal over 2f out: rdn over 1f out: led narrowly 1f out: styd on wl: asserted fnl 75yds* **13/8**[1]

-520 **2** *2* **Spirit Of Belle**[33] 3745 3-8-11 **72** ....................(v[1]) KatherineGlenister(7) 6 73
(David Evans) *trckd ldr: led narrowly over 2f out: sn rdn: hdd 1f out: no ex fnl 75yds* **6/1**

0-36 **3** *½* **Doria Road (USA)**[20] 4214 3-8-10 **64** .................... KevinStott 3 64
(Kevin Ryan) *dwlt: hld up in tch: hdwy to trck ldrs over 2f out: rdn and edgd lft over 1f out: kpt on fnl f* **7/1**

0320 **4** *½* **The Eagle's Nest (IRE)**[30] 3862 3-9-1 **72** .............. AdamMcNamara(3) 1 71
(Richard Fahey) *trckd ldrs: rdn over 2f out: one pce* **5/2**[2]

024 **5** *8* **Right About Now (IRE)**[22] 4164 3-9-7 **75** .................... PaulMulrennan 5 55
(Ismail Mohammed) *hld up: rdn along over 2f out: wknd over 1f out* **5/1**[3]

260- **6** *33* **Dream On Dreamer (IRE)**[298] 6741 3-8-12 **66** ............ AndrewMullen 2
(Antony Brittain) *racd keenly: led: rdn whn hdd over 2f out: wknd* **33/1**

1m 39.6s (-0.50) **Going Correction** +0.025s/f (Good) **6** Ran SP% **113.1**
Speed ratings (Par 100): **103,101,100,100,92 59**
CSF £12.15 TOTE £1.90: £1.20, £3.30; EX 13.50 Trifecta £39.70.
**Owner** Mrs P Good **Bred** Mrs P Good **Trained** Upper Helmsley, N Yorks
■ Stewards' Enquiry : Katherine Glenister caution; careless riding

**FOCUS**
A fair contest and the winner looks to be going the right way. The next two ran to form.
T/Plt: £115.60 to a £1 stake. Pool: £61,308.16 - 386.94 winning units T/Qpdt: £80.80 to a £1 stake. Pool: £4,670.33 - 42.76 winning units **Andrew Sheret**

5010 - 5014a (Foreign Racing) - See Raceform Interactive



The Form Book Flat, Raceform Ltd, Newbury, RG14 5SJ

# 4738 CATTERICK (L-H)

Wednesday, July 19

**OFFICIAL GOING: Good to firm (good in places; 8.9)**

Wind: light behind Weather: Cloudy

## 5015 EBF FILLIES' NOVICE STKS (PLUS 10 RACE) 5f

**2:05** (2:06) (Class 5) 2-Y-O **£2,911** (£866; £432; £216) **Stalls** Low

Form RPR

343 **1** **Reflect Alexander (IRE)**[7] 4739 2-9-0 82 DaneO'Neill 3 84
(David Evans) *mde all: pushed along over 1f out: kpt on wl* **4/5**[1]

4 **2** 1 ½ **May Girl**[35] 3725 2-8-7 0 JonathanFisher(7) 1 77
(Robert Cowell) *trckd ldrs: pushed along to chse ldr over 1f out: kpt on wl but a hld* **20/1**

0 **3** 7 **Cherry Oak (IRE)**[11] 4628 2-9-0 0 GrahamLee 8 51
(Ben Haslam) *chsd ldrs towards outer: rdn 1/2-way: one pce* **33/1**

6 **4** shd **Rema Al Kuwait (IRE)**[28] 3980 2-9-0 0 PhillipMakin 11 51
(David O'Meara) *prom: pushed along and outpcd 2f out: one pce fnl f* **14/1**

0 **5** 1 **Ideal Spirit**[12] 4555 2-8-7 0 RussellHarris(7) 2 47
(Andrew Crook) *midfield: pushed along over 1f out: kpt on ins fnl f* **50/1**

6 **6** 1 ¾ **What Do You Think (IRE)**[24] 4116 2-9-0 0 PaulMulrennan 4 41
(Michael Dods) *chsd ldrs: rdn 1/2-way: wknd ins fnl f* **6/1**[2]

300 **7** hd **Dark Hedges**[11] 4599 2-8-7 49 ConnorMurtagh(7) 9 40
(Olly Williams) *midfield on outer: rdn 1/2-way: sn edgd rt: nvr threatened* **125/1**

00 **8** ¾ **Your Just Desserts (IRE)**[42] 3460 2-9-0 0 BarryMcHugh 7 38
(Micky Hammond) *hld up: nvr threatened* **125/1**

**9** ¾ **Cool Baby** 2-9-0 0 TomEaves 6 35
(Robert Cowell) *rn green in rr tl sme late hdwy* **9/1**[3]

**10** 1 ¼ **Sandie Gem** 2-9-0 0 JackGarritty 12 31+
(Richard Fahey) *swtchd lft s: midfield: pushed along 1/2-way: wknd ins fnl f* **10/1**

05 **11** 2 ½ **Lil Gem (IRE)**[41] 3482 2-9-0 0 PJMcDonald 5 22
(Keith Dalgleish) *a towards rr* **14/1**

58.62s (-1.18) **Going Correction** -0.30s/f (Firm) **11** Ran SP% **113.5**

Speed ratings (Par 91): **97,94,83,83,81 78,78,77,76,74 70**

CSF £24.28 TOTE £1.60: £1.02, £6.40, £7.00; EX 17.60 Trifecta £220.70.

**Owner** Noel O'Callaghan **Bred** C Farrell **Trained** Pandy, Monmouths

**FOCUS**

It was dry overnight and the watered ground was given as good to firm, good in places (GoingStick: 8.9). All distances as advertised. An ordinary maiden, in which the winner stood out on paper. The first two finished well clear.

## 5016 RACINGUK.COM (S) STKS 5f 212y

**2:40** (2:40) (Class 6) 3-Y-O+ **£2,264** (£673; £336; £168) **Stalls** Low

Form RPR

1345 **1** **Searanger (USA)**[6] 4789 4-9-6 59 PJMcDonald 4 65
(Rebecca Menzies) *dwlt: hld up: pushed along and hdwy on inner over 1f out: kpt on: led towards fin* **11/4**[2]

-640 **2** ½ **Deben**[32] 3832 4-8-11 50 CliffordLee(3) 3 57
(John Weymes) *midfield: rdn and hdwy 2f out: led ins fnl f: kpt on: hdd towards fin* **20/1**

6044 **3** 1 ¾ **Manatee Bay**[15] 4477 7-9-0 71 (p) PatrickMathers 1 52
(Noel Wilson) *chsd ldrs: rdn over 2f out: kpt on* **13/8**[1]

6040 **4** nse **Spike (IRE)**[30] 3914 4-9-0 51 (b) PaulMulrennan 2 52
(Donald McCain) *led: rdn 2f out: hdd ins fnl f: wknd fnl 110yds* **12/1**

0006 **5** 1 ½ **Mercers Row**[12] 4554 10-8-7 50 (p) ConnorMurtagh(7) 6 47
(Michael Herrington) *hld up: rdn 2f out: kpt on ins fnl f: nvr threatened* **20/1**

4500 **6** 2 ½ **Bold Spirit**[7] 4743 6-9-0 55 (vt) DanielTudhope 7 39
(Declan Carroll) *midfield: rdn 2f out: one pce: eased towards fin* **3/1**[3]

5000 **7** 7 **A Bit Of Ginger**[7] 4743 3-8-4 51 (b[1]) ShaneGray 9 10
(Ann Duffield) *chsd ldr: rdn over 2f out: wknd over 1f out* **25/1**

0060 **8** ½ **Zaytoon (IRE)**[30] 3906 4-9-0 41 (p[1]) AndrewMullen 8 15
(Micky Hammond) *a rr* **125/1**

-006 **9** hd **Roman Times (IRE)**[15] 4479 4-8-9 52 (p) TomEaves 5 9
(Colin Teague) *chsd ldrs: sn pushed along: wknd 2f out* **66/1**

1m 11.52s (-2.08) **Going Correction** -0.30s/f (Firm)

**WFA** 3 from 4yo+ 5lb **9** Ran SP% **113.1**

Speed ratings (Par 101): **101,100,98,97,95 92,83,82,82**

CSF £56.31 TOTE £4.10: £1.40, £4.50, £1.10; EX 47.00 Trifecta £142.50.No bid for the winner

**Owner** ICM Racing & John Dance **Bred** Phoenix Rising Farms **Trained** Mordon, Durham

**FOCUS**

There was plenty of pace on in this seller. The race is rated around the winner's form this year.

## 5017 ALAN TIPPLING LIFETIME IN RACING AWARD FILLIES' H'CAP (QUALIFIER CATTERICK 12F SERIES) 1m 4f 13y

**3:15** (3:15) (Class 5) (0-70,74) 3-Y-O+ **£3,234** (£962; £481; £240) **Stalls** Low

Form RPR

0441 **1** **Three Duchesses**[7] 4761 3-9-9 74 6ex LouisSteward 3 87+
(Michael Bell) *hld up: smooth hdwy on outer over 3f out: led gng wl over 1f out: nudged clr ins fnl f* **1/1**[1]

3361 **2** 5 **Cool Music (IRE)**[12] 4558 7-9-2 56 (p) CamHardie 5 57
(Antony Brittain) *trckd ldr: rdn over 2f out: kpt on same pce and no ch wnr fnl f* **8/1**[3]

4513 **3** ¾ **Shambra (IRE)**[1] 5001 3-9-0 65 TonyHamilton 2 66
(Roger Fell) *led: rdn over 2f out: hdd over 1f out: one pce* **3/1**[2]

-600 **4** ½ **Silver Gleam (IRE)**[41] 3489 3-8-0 51 oh1 DuranFentiman 1 51
(Chris Fairhurst) *dwlt: midfield: rdn over 2f out: styd on fnl f* **25/1**

-060 **5** 2 ¼ **Russian Royale**[51] 3155 7-9-6 60 PJMcDonald 4 55
(Micky Hammond) *trckd ldr: rdn over 2f out: wknd fnl f* **12/1**

0003 **6** 1 **Fillydelphia (IRE)**[20] 4244 6-8-5 52 (h) PaulaMuir(7) 9 46
(Patrick Holmes) *slowly away: hld up: nvr threatened* **14/1**

-005 **7** 2 ½ **Chionodoxa**[49] 3207 3-8-0 54 oh6 ow3 RachelRichardson(3) 8 45?
(Tim Easterby) *trckd ldr: rdn over 2f out: wknd over 1f out* **28/1**

5-66 **8** 9 **Pennerley**[28] 3983 4-9-1 55 PaulHanagan 7 30
(Micky Hammond) *midfield: rdn over 2f out: wknd over 1f out* **14/1**

2m 35.12s (-3.78) **Going Correction** -0.30s/f (Firm)

**WFA** 3 from 4yo+ 11lb **8** Ran SP% **114.4**

Speed ratings (Par 100): **100,96,96,95,94 93,92,86**

CSF £10.07 CT £18.89 TOTE £1.90: £1.02, £2.30, £1.30; EX 8.60 Trifecta £21.70.

**Owner** Hon James Broughton **Bred** Barton Stud **Trained** Newmarket, Suffolk

**FOCUS**

This proved very easy for the well-treated winner. The form is rated around the second and third.

## 5018 5TH REGIMENT ROYAL ARTILLERY H'CAP 5f 212y

**3:50** (3:50) (Class 4) (0-85,86) 3-Y-O+ **£6,469** (£1,925; £962; £481) **Stalls** Low

Form RPR

1133 **1** **Meshardal (GER)**[11] 4616 7-9-2 74 (p) JackGarritty 2 83
(Ruth Carr) *trckd ldrs: rdn to chal appr fnl f: led 75yds out: kpt on* **3/1**[2]

5102 **2** ½ **Love Oasis**[4] 4892 3-9-0 77 PJMcDonald 6 83
(Mark Johnston) *prom: rdn 2f out: led narrowly 1f out: hdd 75yds out: one pce* **3/1**[2]

2663 **3** 1 ¾ **Straightothepoint**[11] 4600 5-9-9 81 (p) ConnorBeasley 4 82
(Bryan Smart) *led narrowly: rdn 2f out: hdd 1f out: no ex fnl 75yds* **7/2**[3]

1062 **4** 3 ¼ **Scofflaw**[11] 4616 3-9-7 84 PaulHanagan 8 74
(Richard Fahey) *hld up: racd keenly: rdn 2f out: kpt on ins fnl f: nvr threatened* **5/2**[1]

0004 **5** ¾ **Pea Shooter**[27] 4015 8-9-3 75 TomEaves 5 64
(Brian Ellison) *dwlt: sn trckd ldrs: rdn over 2f out: wknd fnl f* **16/1**

0-00 **6** 3 ½ **Robben Rainbow**[11] 4600 3-8-12 75 AndrewMullen 7 51
(David Barron) *hld up: rdn over 2f out: nvr threatened* **66/1**

-100 **7** 1 ¾ **Zanetto**[14] 4505 7-10-0 86 JasonHart 1 58
(John Quinn) *hld up: rdn over 2f out: wknd over 1f out* **22/1**

1m 11.07s (-2.53) **Going Correction** -0.30s/f (Firm)

**WFA** 3 from 4yo+ 5lb **7** Ran SP% **112.5**

Speed ratings (Par 105): **104,103,101,96,95 91,88**

CSF £12.02 CT £31.11 TOTE £3.70: £1.90, £2.50; EX 14.80 Trifecta £37.90.

**Owner** The Hollinbridge Partnership & Ruth Carr **Bred** Gestut Hofgut Heymann **Trained** Huby, N Yorks

**FOCUS**

A fair sprint but few got into it. The winner's best run since 2015.

## 5019 RACING WELFARE MEDIAN AUCTION MAIDEN STKS 7f 6y

**4:20** (4:22) (Class 6) 3-5-Y-O **£2,264** (£673; £336; £168) **Stalls** Low

Form RPR

345 **1** **Khitaamy (IRE)**[28] 3970 3-9-5 73 DaneO'Neill 6 65+
(Ed Dunlop) *led: hdd over 5f out: remained prom: rdn to chal strly over 1f out: led 75yds out: kpt on* **6/5**[1]

02 **2** ½ **Dandys Denouement**[29] 3948 3-9-5 0 TomEaves 8 63+
(Brian Ellison) *prom: led over 5f out: rdn 2f out: strly pressed over 1f out: hdd 75yds out: one pce towards fin* **9/4**[2]

0-00 **3** 4 ½ **Kulgri**[58] 2897 3-9-0 42 JoeDoyle 4 46
(Kevin Ryan) *trckd ldrs: rdn over 2f out: sn outpcd by ldng pair* **40/1**

06 **4** hd **Hamriyah**[11] 4604 3-9-5 0 (h) DavidAllan 7 50
(Tim Easterby) *midfield: rdn over 2f out: kpt on same pce* **9/1**

50-0 **5** 1 ½ **Outfox**[90] 1913 3-9-0 63 ConnorBeasley 1 41
(Bryan Smart) *hld up: rdn 3f out: bit short of room over 1f out: kpt on ins fnl f* **11/2**[3]

-000 **6** 1 **Diamond Avalanche (IRE)**[32] 3832 4-9-12 46 (p) JackGarritty 3 47
(Patrick Holmes) *trckd ldrs: rdn over 2f out: wknd over 1f out* **25/1**

0 **7** 4 **Monsieur Mel**[23] 4164 3-9-5 0 CamHardie 2 33
(Antony Brittain) *slowly away: hld up: nvr threatened* **20/1**

06 **8** 3 **Delegation**[9] 4693 3-9-2 0 RachelRichardson(3) 5 25
(Tim Easterby) *dwlt: a rr* **25/1**

1m 25.14s (-1.86) **Going Correction** -0.30s/f (Firm)

**WFA** 3 from 4yo 7lb **8** Ran SP% **116.5**

Speed ratings (Par 101): **98,97,92,92,90 89,84,81**

CSF £3.90 TOTE £2.00: £1.10, £1.40, £7.00; EX 4.90 Trifecta £95.80.

**Owner** Hamdan Al Maktoum **Bred** Yeomanstown Stud **Trained** Newmarket, Suffolk

**FOCUS**

An ordinary maiden dominated by the front pair. The third helps pin the level.

## 5020 RACING UK NOW ON TALKTALK TV H'CAP 5f

**4:55** (4:55) (Class 5) (0-75,77) 3-Y-O **£3,234** (£962; £481; £240) **Stalls** Low

Form RPR

1536 **1** **Yorkshiredebut (IRE)**[12] 4574 3-9-7 72 (p[1]) PaulMulrennan 3 80
(Paul Midgley) *mde all: pushed along 2f out: rdn clr ins fnl f: easily* **2/1**[2]

00-3 **2** 4 ½ **Liberatum**[26] 4060 3-8-13 64 JackGarritty 4 56
(Ruth Carr) *chsd ldr: rdn 2f out: kpt on but no ch wnr fnl f* **9/2**[3]

**3** 1 ¾ **Caesar's Comet (IRE)**[33] 3798 3-9-4 69 GrahamLee 2 55
(Paul Midgley) *dwlt: hld up in tch: rdn 1/2-way: one pce and nvr threatened* **7/1**

1-51 **4** 8 **Wadood (IRE)**[19] 4324 3-9-12 77 (h) PhillipMakin 1 45
(Robert Cowell) *chsd ldr: rdn 1/2-way: wknd over 1f out* **5/4**[1]

57.48s (-2.32) **Going Correction** -0.30s/f (Firm) **4** Ran SP% **108.5**

Speed ratings (Par 100): **106,98,96,83**

CSF £10.37 TOTE £2.60; EX 9.20 Trifecta £26.60.

**Owner** Taylor's Bloodstock Ltd **Bred** Yasmeena Partnership **Trained** Westow, N Yorks

**FOCUS**

Just the four runners but they finished well strung out and the time was good. The winner was not an obvious improver based on her profile.

## 5021 BETFAIR "NOVICE" AMATEUR RIDERS' H'CAP 1m 4f 13y

**5:25** (5:26) (Class 6) (0-65,66) 4-Y-O+ **£2,183** (£677; £338; £169) **Stalls** Low

Form RPR

0632 **1** **Swansway**[11] 4627 4-11-7 65 MrWJMilburn 6 73
(Michael Easterby) *midfield: in tch over 3f out: rdn and hdwy on outer 2f out: styd on: led 25yds out* **4/1**[2]

5650 **2** 1 ¼ **King Of The Celts (IRE)**[29] 3935 9-11-2 63 (p) MissJGillam(3) 11 69
(Tim Easterby) *led: rdn and pressed 2f out: no ex and hdd 25yds out* **16/1**

113 **3** 1 **Tonto's Spirit**[19] 3978 5-10-13 60 (h) MissAMSlack(3) 10 64+
(Kenneth Slack) *prom: pushed along over 2f out: one pce* **9/2**[3]

5513 **4** 1 ¼ **Miss Tree**[15] 4469 6-10-11 55 MrTGreenwood 3 57
(John Quinn) *trckd ldrs: rdn to chal 2f out: no ex ins fnl f* **7/2**[1]

0320 **5** 2 ¼ **Gabrial The Terror (IRE)**[155] 727 7-11-0 58 MrMEnnis 4 57
(Patrick Morris) *slowly away: hld up in rr: stl plenty to do whn bit short of room 3f out: styd on fnl 2f: nrst fin* **16/1**

0-04 **6** 2 **Sherman McCoy**[37] 3654 11-10-10 54 MrBillyGarritty 7 50
(Marjorie Fife) *midfield: rdn over 2f out: styd on fnl f* **12/1**

524- **7** hd **Magnolia Ridge (IRE)**[10] 8091 7-10-0 47 (p) MrMHaigh(3) 5 42+
(Mark Walford) *hld up: rdn 2f out: styd on fnl f: nrst fin* **22/1**

0-40 **8** ½ **Arabian Oasis**[18] 4358 5-11-4 65 (p) MissCarlyScott(3) 9 59
(Philip Kirby) *hld up in midfield: pushed along over 2f out: kpt on fnl f: nvr threatened* **33/1**

0-36 **9** ½ **Gabrial The Duke (IRE)**[18] 4338 7-11-8 66 (v) MissAMcCain 1 60
(Patrick Morris) *prom: rdn over 2f out: wknd over 1f out* **14/1**

0/5- **10** 1 1/4 **Tawseef (IRE)**[19] 6724 9-10-13 **57**.................... MissEllaMcCain 15 49
(Donald McCain) *midfield: rdn along over 3f out: sn struggling* **8/1**
0000 **11** 3/4 **Buthelezi (USA)**[74] 2386 9-11-5 **66**.................... MrMWBrown(3) 12 56
(Brian Ellison) *hld up: nvr threatened* **12/1**
655/ **12** 5 **Volcanic Jack (IRE)**[19] 3331 9-10-2 **46** oh1.......... MrRomainClavreul 2 28
(Michael Chapman) *in tch: rdn over 3f out: sn wknd* **100/1**
60-0 **13** 6 **Fledermaus (IRE)**[27] 4018 7-9-13 **46** oh1..............(t) MissBJohnson(3) 8 19
(Tina Jackson) *a towards rr* **80/1**
0-06 **14** nk **Python**[35] 3706 5-9-13 **46** oh1.................... MrJCummins(3) 13 18
(Andrew Crook) *a towards rr* **100/1**
62-6 **15** 6 **Bob's Boy**[54] 3028 4-10-12 **59**....................(bt) MrHMyddelton(3) 14 22
(Oliver Greenall) *midfield on outer: rdn 3f out: sn wknd* **40/1**
2m 37.38s (-1.52) **Going Correction** -0.30s/f (Firm) **15** Ran SP% **118.3**
Speed ratings (Par 101): **93,92,91,90,89 87,87,87,87,86 85,82,78,78,74**
CSF £61.89 CT £301.87 TOTE £4.80: £1.80, £5.60, £1.80; EX 78.50 Trifecta £323.00.
**Owner** W H & Mrs J A Tinning **Bred** Pontchartrain Stud **Trained** Sheriff Hutton, N Yorks
■ A winner for Will Milburn on his first Flat ride.
**FOCUS**
A moderate affair. Nothing got into it from the back half of the field. The winner is fully entitled to rate this high.
T/Plt: £12.60 to a £1 stake. Pool: £51,953.89 - 3008.17 winning units T/Qpdt: £8.90 to a £1 stake. Pool: £2,953.74 - 244.4 winning units **Andrew Sheret**

# 4753 LINGFIELD (L-H)
## Wednesday, July 19

**OFFICIAL GOING: Turf course - good changing to good to soft after race 1 (2:15); all-weather - polytrack: standard**
Wind: light to medium, half behind Weather: overcast, light rain at times

## 5022 READ SILVESTRE DE SOUSA AT 188BET MAIDEN FILLIES' STKS 1m 3f 133y
**2:15** (2:18) (Class 5) 3-4-Y-O **£2,911** (£866; £432; £216) **Stalls** High

Form RPR
-332 **1** **So Sleek**[33] 3770 3-8-12 77.................... JamieSpencer 12 79
(Luca Cumani) *hld up in tch in midfield: rdn and hdwy over 2f out: drvn to ld over 1f out: styd on wl u.p ins fnl f* **11/4**[1]
45 **2** 1 **Nathalie**[31] 3866 3-8-12 0.................... DanielMuscutt 7 77
(James Fanshawe) *hld up in tch in midfield: effrt over 2f out: hdwy and rdn to chse ldrs over 1f out: wnt 2nd and pressing wnr ins fnl f: styd on but a hld* **5/1**[3]
5 **3** 1 1/2 **Tarte Tropezienne (IRE)**[38] 3615 3-8-12 0.................... PatCosgrave 8 75
(William Haggas) *hld up in midfield: effrt and hdwy over 1f out: chsd ldrs and swtchd lft over 1f out: nt clr run on inner ins fnl f: squeezed through to go 3rd wl ins fnl f: nvr able to threaten ldrs: eased cl home* **4/1**[2]
03-5 **4** 1 1/2 **Fashion Theory**[82] 2131 3-8-12 76....................(p[1]) WilliamBuick 4 73
(Charlie Appleby) *chsd ldrs tl wnt 2nd 7f out: rdn to ld 2f out: drvn and hdd over 1f out: no ex u.p jst ins fnl f: lost 3rd and wknd wl ins fnl f* **11/4**[1]
**5** 1/2 **Sula Island** 3-8-12 0.................... FergusSweeney 11 72
(Alan King) *dwlt: hld up in last pair: pushed along and hdwy over 2f out: chsd ldrs whn rn green and edgd lft 1f out: kpt on same pce ins fnl f* **50/1**
2-23 **6** 12 **Lady Valdean**[21] 4232 3-8-12 74.................... SilvestreDeSousa 3 58
(Jose Santos) *led: rdn over 2f out: hdd 2f out: sn struggling and lost pl over 1f out: wknd fnl f: eased towards fin* **6/1**
06 **7** 3 1/4 **Dukinta (IRE)**[19] 4300 3-8-12 0....................(b) JosephineGordon 6 47
(Hugo Palmer) *chsd ldr tl 7f out: reminder over 5f out: rdn and unable qck over 2f out: lost pl wl over 1f out: wknd fnl f* **25/1**
**8** nk **Kirkland Forever** 3-8-12 0.................... MartinDwyer 10 46
(Brendan Powell) *hld up in last quartet: rdn 3f out: no hdwy and sn outpcd: wknd over 1f out* **66/1**
60 **9** shd **Percipio**[31] 3866 3-8-9 0.................... CallumShepherd(3) 2 46
(Alan King) *stdd after s: hld up in last pair: rdn wl over 2f out: no hdwy and sn btn: wknd over 1f out* **100/1**
**10** 22 **Koubba (IRE)** 4-9-9 0....................(t[1]) LiamKeniry 5 9
(Neil Mulholland) *chsd ldrs: rdn 3f out: sn btn and lost pl: wl bhd fnl f: t.o* **100/1**
6 **11** 19 **Beauchamp Rose**[16] 4449 3-8-12 0.................... StevieDonohoe 9
(Charlie Fellowes) *a towards rr and nvr gng wl: lost tch 4f out: t.o* **100/1**
2m 32.66s (1.16) **Going Correction** +0.225s/f (Good)
**WFA** 3 from 4yo 11lb **11** Ran SP% **114.6**
Speed ratings (Par 100): **105,104,103,102,102 94,91,91,91,76 64**
CSF £16.19 TOTE £3.30: £1.30, £1.90, £1.50; EX 16.10 Trifecta £51.00.
**Owner** Lordship Stud **Bred** Fittocks Stud & Arrow Farm & Stud **Trained** Newmarket, Suffolk
■ Sampaquita was withdrawn.Price at time of withdrawal 100/1. Rule 4 does not apply
**FOCUS**
No less than 5.6mm of rain had fallen overnight, turning the ground to Good for this mixed card. Overcast and cooler than of late, with temperatures around 19C and the chance of showers. The going changed to Good to Soft after this first race. A modest fillies' maiden and the pace was adequate. This form should prove worthy, rated around the winner, second and fourth.

## 5023 FOLLOW US ON TWITTER AT 188BET H'CAP 1m 2f
**2:50** (2:50) (Class 6) (0-60,59) 3-Y-O+ **£2,587** (£770; £384; £192) **Stalls** Low

Form RPR
-341 **1** **Fanfair**[14] 4493 3-9-3 **59**.................... SeanLevey 5 67
(Richard Hannon) *hld up in midfield: effrt 3f out: clsd on ldr 2f out: rdn to ld over 1f out: edgd lft u.p ins fnl f: kpt on and a jst holding on towards fin* **15/2**
000- **2** hd **Retribution**[238] 8074 3-9-3 **59**.................... TomQueally 9 67
(David Lanigan) *dwlt: hld up in last quartet: pushed along and effrt over 2f out hdwy to chse ldrs u.p over 1f out: chsd wnr 100yds out: styd on and clsng towards fin: nvr quite getting to wnr* **10/1**
4156 **3** 2 3/4 **Live Dangerously**[13] 4523 7-9-8 **55**.................... WilliamCarson 3 57
(John Bridger) *stdd after s: t.k.h: hld up in tch in rr: effrt on outer over 2f out: hdwy and drvn to chse ldrs over 1f out: kpt on same pce ins fnl f: wnt 3rd towards fin* **16/1**
1352 **4** 3/4 **Buzz Lightyere**[15] 4461 4-9-8 **55**.................... SilvestreDeSousa 2 56
(Philip Hide) *chsd ldrs tl chsd clr ldr over 3f out: clsd u.p to ld over 1f out sn hdd and swtchd lft 1f out: no ex ins fnl f: wknd wl ins fnl f* **7/4**[1]
2023 **5** 3/4 **Betsalottie**[15] 4461 4-9-9 **56**.................... LukeMorris 7 55
(John Bridger) *chsd ldrs: effrt 3f out: chsd ldrs but unable qck u.p 1f out: kpt on same pce ins fnl f: eased towards fin* **4/1**[2]
1155 **6** 7 **Street Art (IRE)**[20] 4279 5-9-8 **55**....................(bt) ShaneKelly 8 42
(Mike Murphy) *led: wnt clr over 3f out: rdn over 2f out: hdd over 1f out and sn btn: wknd ins fnl f* **40/1**
0001 **7** 1 1/2 **About Glory**[37] 3657 3-9-2 **58**....................(b) TomMarquand 6 43
(Richard Hannon) *s.i.s: hld up in tch in last quartet: rdn 3f out: no imp u.p over 2f out: wl btn over 1f out* **6/1**[3]
1106 **8** 12 **Master Of Heaven**[15] 4461 4-9-8 **55**.................... PatCosgrave 10 17
(Jim Boyle) *chsd ldr tl over 3f out: lost pl and btn over 2f out: bhd fnl f* **14/1**
600 **9** 1 3/4 **Shanandoa**[14] 4497 6-9-12 **59**.................... SteveDrowne 4 18
(Brian Barr) *stdd and wnt lft s: hld up in tch in last quartet: rdn over 2f out: sn btn and bhd over 1f out* **25/1**
1200 **10** 21 **Etaad (USA)**[57] 2914 6-9-7 **57**....................(b) HectorCrouch(3) 1
(Gary Moore) *in tch in midfield: lost pl 3f out: bhd and eased over 1f out* **33/1**
2m 10.72s (0.22) **Going Correction** +0.225s/f (Good)
**WFA** 3 from 4yo+ 9lb **10** Ran SP% **113.3**
Speed ratings (Par 101): **108,107,105,105,104 98,97,88,86,69**
CSF £75.70 CT £1156.36 TOTE £6.90: £2.40, £3.30, £4.40; EX 101.10 Trifecta £1071.40.
**Owner** Theakston Stud Syndicate **Bred** Theakston Stud **Trained** East Everleigh, Wilts
**FOCUS**
A very modest handicap but competitive for the class, and 3yos finished 1-2. The pace was ordinary.

## 5024 DAILY RACING SPECIALS AT 188BET H'CAP 1m 3f 133y
**3:25** (3:25) (Class 5) (0-70,72) 3-Y-O+ **£2,911** (£866; £432; £216) **Stalls** High

Form RPR
15 **1** **Mam'Selle (IRE)**[40] 3531 3-9-5 **72**.................... PatCosgrave 4 85
(William Haggas) *chsd ldrs: clr in ldng trio and waiting for gap 3f out: pushed along and qcknd to ld over 2f out: clr and in command over 1f out: styd on readily: comf* **10/3**[2]
2503 **2** 4 1/2 **Zorba The Greek**[20] 4267 5-10-0 **70**....................(h) HarryBentley 8 75
(Ed Vaughan) *hld up in last trio: hdwy to chse clr ldng trio 3f out: styd on to chse clr wnr and hung lft jst over 1f out: kpt on same pce and no imp ins fnl f* **7/2**[3]
0022 **3** 1 1/4 **Theglasgowwarrior**[20] 4267 3-8-12 **65**.................... WilliamBuick 9 69
(Michael Bell) *chsd ldr: rdn and ev ch 3f out: outpcd and chsng clr wnr over 2f out: lost 2nd jst over 1f out and kpt on same pce after* **9/4**[1]
4204 **4** nk **Bamako Du Chatelet (FR)**[36] 3685 6-10-0 **70**...(b[1]) RichardKingscote 5 72
(Ian Williams) *hld up in midfield: n.m.r on downhill over 3f out: effrt 3f out: hdwy 2f out: kpt on steadily fr over 1f out: no threat to wnr* **11/1**
0-05 **5** 6 **Silver Dixie (USA)**[13] 4538 7-9-9 **65**....................(p) CharlesBishop 7 58
(Peter Hedger) *s.i.s: hld up in last trio: pushed along over 2f out: nvr trbld ldrs* **25/1**
0-52 **6** 5 **Bermondsey Belle (IRE)**[18] 4347 3-8-12 **65**.................... DavidProbert 1 50
(Lucy Wadham) *led: rdn and hrd pressed 3f out: hdd and outpcd over 2f out: wknd over 1f out: wl btn and eased wl ins fnl f* **9/2**
6660 **7** 2 **Al Jawza**[54] 3024 3-8-12 **65**.................... SeanLevey 6 47
(Richard Hannon) *hld up in tch in midfield: rdn and struggling 3f out: sn edging lft and wl btn: wknd over 1f out* **14/1**
323- **8** 8 **Unsuspected Girl (IRE)**[266] 7609 4-9-7 **68**.......... RachealKneller(5) 2 36
(Brian Barr) *s.i.s: hld up in last trio: swtchd lft and effrt over 2f out: no hdwy and sn btn: bhd fnl f* **50/1**
5360 **9** 19 **Jersey Bull (IRE)**[13] 4538 5-9-4 **60**....................(h) LiamKeniry 3
(Michael Madgwick) *midfield tl dropped to rr u.p over 2f out: sn lost tch: eased ins fnl f: t.o* **100/1**
2m 34.07s (2.57) **Going Correction** +0.225s/f (Good)
**WFA** 3 from 4yo+ 11lb **9** Ran SP% **116.0**
Speed ratings (Par 103): **100,97,96,95,91 88,87,81,69**
CSF £15.40 CT £30.95 TOTE £4.10: £1.30, £1.30, £1.40; EX 16.90 Trifecta £42.30.
**Owner** Highclere Thoroughbred Racing - TS Eliot **Bred** Roundhill Stud & C & M Murphy **Trained** Newmarket, Suffolk
**FOCUS**
An ordinary handicap run at a modest early pace. They finished strung out and the winner did this nicely, showing a clear pb.

## 5025 RACING WELFARE H'CAP 2m 68y
**4:00** (4:00) (Class 5) (0-75,77) 3-Y-O+ **£2,911** (£866; £432; £216) **Stalls** Low

Form RPR
4255 **1** **Ayr Of Elegance**[32] 3840 5-10-0 **73**.................... RichardKingscote 6 78
(Philip Hide) *stdd and dropped in bhd after s: hld up in rr: hdwy to trck ldrs on downhill run 4f out: jnd ldr and wnt clr 3f out: led over 1f out: rdn to assert 1f out: kpt on wl* **11/2**[3]
4632 **2** 2 1/4 **Fitzwilly**[7] 4750 7-9-7 **66**.................... SilvestreDeSousa 4 68
(Mick Channon) *chsd ldrs: wnt 2nd 10f out tl led over 3f out: rdn and wnt clr w wnr 3f out: hdd over 1f out: no ex u.p 1f out: kpt on same pce ins fnl f* **15/8**[2]
4-43 **3** 3/4 **Oxford Blu**[33] 3788 3-8-3 **63**....................(p[1]) LukeMorris 3 66
(Sir Mark Prescott Bt) *t.k.h: in tch: dropped to rr and rdn over 4f out: rallied 3f out: chsd ldng pair wl over 1f out: kpt on but nvr a threat to wnr* **7/4**[1]
3220 **4** 2 1/4 **See And Be Seen**[7] 4750 7-9-6 **65**....................(p) RenatoSouza 5 64
(Sylvester Kirk) *hld up in tch: effrt in 3rd 3f out: 4th and no imp over 1f out: keeping on same pce and hld whn nt clrest of runs wl ins fnl f: eased towards fin* **14/1**
2206 **5** 3 **Ulysses (GER)**[33] 3788 3-8-11 **71**....................(b) PatDobbs 1 68
(Ralph Beckett) *chsd ldr tl 10f out: styd chsng ldrs tl lost pl and n.m.r downhill run over 3f out: rdn 3f out: kpt on same pce and no imp after* **8/1**
0/5- **6** 20 **Linguine (FR)**[52] 1914 7-10-4 **77**....................(b) KieranShoemark 2 57
(Seamus Durack) *led tl over 3f out: sn struggling and dropped to rr 3f out: lost tch over 1f out* **16/1**
3m 39.91s (5.11) **Going Correction** +0.225s/f (Good)
**WFA** 3 from 5yo+ 15lb **6** Ran SP% **110.2**
Speed ratings (Par 103): **96,94,94,93,91 81**
CSF £15.67 TOTE £4.40: £1.70, £1.40; EX 15.00 Trifecta £26.60.
**Owner** W F Davis **Bred** W F Davis **Trained** Findon, W Sussex
**FOCUS**
A staying handicap which was run at a modest pace. The form is modest, but the first two close to form.

## 5026 INJURED JOCKEYS FUND/EBF FILLIES' NOVICE STKS (PLUS 10 RACE) 6f 1y(P)
**4:30** (4:31) (Class 5) 2-Y-O **£2,911** (£866; £432; £216) **Stalls** Low

Form RPR
3 **1** **Travelcard (USA)**[7] 4749 2-9-0 0.................... RichardKingscote 9 74
(Mark Johnston) *dwlt:sn bustled along and hdwy to join ldr over 4f out: rdn 2f out: sustained chal u.p and forged ahd towards fin: rdn out* **11/4**[2]

0 **2** *nk* **Misty Spirit**[16] 4440 2-9-0 0 ........ FranBerry 6 73
(David Elsworth) *led and set stdy gallop: jnd over 4f out: rdn over 1f out: kpt on wl u.p tl hdd and no ex towards fin* **8/1**

2160 **3** *1 1/4* **Get Even**[39] 3611 2-9-7 0 ........ JFEgan 1 77
(Jo Hughes) *t.k.h: chsd ldr tl over 4f out: effrt on inner over 1f out: nt clr run 1f out tl swtchd rt ins fnl f: kpt on wl ins fnl f: unable to get bk on terms* **7/2**[3]

40 **4** *2 1/2* **Jan's Joy**[16] 4440 2-8-11 0 ........(t[1]) AaronJones(3) 5 62
(Stuart Williams) *taken down early: t.k.h: early: chsd ldrs: shkn up over 1f out: outpcd ent fnl f and hld whn sltly impeded ins fnl f: kpt on same pce after* **28/1**

**5** *nk* **Forever In Love** 2-9-0 0 ........ WilliamBuick 2 61+
(Sir Michael Stoute) *t.k.h: hld up in tch in midfield: swtchd rt over 2f out: effrt and rn green bnd 2f out: kpt on same pce fr over 1f out* **9/4**[1]

5 **6** *2 3/4* **Graffitista (IRE)**[19] 4312 2-9-0 0 ........ SilvestreDeSousa 8 53+
(George Scott) *t.k.h: hld up in tch in midfield: pushed rt over 2f out: sn rdn: no imp and kpt on same pce fr over 1f out* **11/2**

00 **7** *6* **Lady Of Authority**[7] 4749 2-9-0 0 ........ ShaneKelly 7 35
(Murty McGrath) *swtchd lft after s: hld up in last trio: rdn and struggling over 2f out: sn outpcd and n.d fnl 2f* **100/1**

**8** *hd* **Equilibrium** 2-9-0 0 ........ KieranShoemark 3 34
(Robert Eddery) *t.k.h: hld up in tch in last trio: effrt and pushed along 2f out: sn outpcd and wknd over 1f out* **22/1**

**9** *3 1/2* **Spirit Of Ishy** 2-9-0 0 ........ TomQueally 4 24
(Stuart Kittow) *sn in rr and rn green: wl bhd fnl 2f* **33/1**

1m 13.39s (1.49) **Going Correction** +0.075s/f (Slow) **9** Ran SP% **117.9**
Speed ratings (Par 91): **93,92,90,87,87 83,75,75,70**
CSF £24.39 TOTE £3.50: £1.20, £2.60, £1.40; EX 27.20 Trifecta £92.10.
**Owner** Sheikh Hamdan bin Mohammed Al Maktoum **Bred** Godolphin **Trained** Middleham Moor, N Yorks

**FOCUS**
Probably a decent fillies' novices' race and winners should come from this, although the bare form was limited.

## 5027 188BET H'CAP 5f 6y(P)
**5:05** (5:06) (Class 6) (0-60,62) 3-Y-0+ **£2,587** (£770; £384; £192) **Stalls** High

Form RPR

5042 **1** **Ask The Guru**[7] 4731 7-8-12 **48** ........(b) KierenFox 6 54
(Michael Attwater) *mde all: clr 1/2-way: rdn over 1f out: reduced ld ins fnl f but nvr gng to be ct: rdn out* **7/2**[2]

031 **2** *3/4* **Camino**[29] 3942 4-8-10 **46** ........ MartinLane 4 49
(Andi Brown) *stdd s: hld up in rr: clsd on inner jst over 2f out: 4th and swtchd rt wl over 1f out: hdwy u.p to chse clr wnr ins fnl f: styd on and clsng on wnr fnl 75yds: nvr quite getting to wnr* **9/2**[3]

4412 **3** *2* **Tooty Fruitti**[8] 4723 3-9-5 **59** ........ JFEgan 9 54
(Jo Hughes) *dwlt: t.k.h: in tch in midfield on outer: hdwy to chse wnr ent fnl 2f: sn rdn: kpt on but nvr getting on terms w wnr: lost 2nd ins fnl f* **13/8**[1]

6644 **4** *nk* **Barnsdale**[40] 3545 4-8-3 **46** oh1 ........ MeganEllingworth(7) 1 41
(John Holt) *chsd ldr tl ent fnl 2f: rdn wl over 1f out: kpt on same pce u.p ins fnl f* **25/1**

1345 **5** *1 3/4* **Mercers**[23] 4157 3-9-8 **62** ........ ShaneKelly 8 50
(Peter Crate) *taken down early: hld up in last pair: swtchd rt and clsd over 2f out: effrt over 1f out: hung lft u.p and no imp 1f out: kpt on same pce ins fnl f* **7/2**[2]

2546 **6** *3/4* **Pharoh Jake**[27] 4009 9-9-3 **53** ........ WilliamCarson 3 39
(John Bridger) *short of room and snatched up sn after s: in tch in midfield: rdn 2f out: no imp and kpt on same pce fr over 1f out* **8/1**

00-0 **7** *16* **Sea My Diamond (IRE)**[16] 4445 3-8-6 **46** oh1 ........ KieranO'Neill 7
(Mark Hoad) *chsd ldrs but sn rdn along: lost pl qckly over 2f out: bhd fnl 2f* **80/1**

59.03s (0.23) **Going Correction** +0.075s/f (Slow)
**WFA** 3 from 4yo+ 4lb **7** Ran SP% **116.9**
Speed ratings (Par 101): **101,99,96,96,93 92,66**
CSF £20.32 CT £34.43 TOTE £4.90: £2.20, £2.10; EX 25.30 Trifecta £58.30.
**Owner** Canisbay Bloodstock **Bred** Redmyre Bloodstock & Tweenhills Stud **Trained** Epsom, Surrey

**FOCUS**
A run-of-the-mill sprint handicap for the grade, which very few got into. Ordinary form.

## 5028 OPEN GOLF BETTING AT 188BET H'CAP 6f 1y(P)
**5:35** (5:36) (Class 6) (0-65,65) 3-Y-0 **£2,587** (£770; £384; £192) **Stalls** Low

Form RPR

-333 **1** **Seprani**[22] 4179 3-9-3 **61** ........(h) JosephineGordon 4 66+
(Marco Botti) *broke wl: sn stdd bk to chse ldrs: effrt on inner to chse ldr 2f out: led 1f out: sn clr and r.o strly: readily* **3/1**[2]

0365 **2** *2* **Baby Gal**[29] 3941 3-8-12 **59** ........ CharlieBennett(3) 2 57
(Jim Boyle) *hld up in tch in midfield: effrt and swtchd rt over 1f out: styd on to chse wnr wl ins fnl f: r.o but no threat to wnr* **8/1**

6030 **3** *2 1/2* **Sixties Habana**[21] 4211 3-8-9 **53** ........ JFEgan 1 44
(Pat Phelan) *sn pushed along to press ldr: lost 2nd and rdn 2f out: kpt on same pce u.p fr over 1f out* **5/1**

3603 **4** *1/2* **Billy's Boots**[27] 4008 3-8-9 **53** ........ KierenFox 5 42
(J R Jenkins) *led: rdn and hrd pressed over 1f out: hdd 1f out: sn outpcd and wknd wl ins fnl f* **16/1**

5531 **5** *2 3/4* **Zavikon**[23] 4157 3-9-7 **65** ........ ShaneKelly 6 46+
(Richard Hughes) *s.i.s and rousted along early: bdly hmpd and snatched up after 1f: effrt on outer ent bnd 2f out: hmpd gain and swtchd rt wl over 1f out: no imp after* **5/2**[1]

2254 **6** *1* **Kings Heart (IRE)**[14] 4500 3-9-4 **62** ........(h) SteveDrowne 3 42
(Mark Usher) *hld up in tch in midfield: bdly hmpd and snatched up after 1f out: effrt and swtchd rt over 1f out: no imp after* **7/2**[3]

0650 **7** *2 1/2* **Texas Wedge**[16] 4447 3-8-6 **50** ........(p) MartinDwyer 9 20
(William Muir) *dropped in bhd after s: detached in last: pushed along after 2f: rdn over 2f out: swtchd lft and no hdwy over 1f out: n.d* **25/1**

-000 **8** *1 3/4* **Embleton**[14] 4493 3-7-13 **46** ........(v[1]) NoelGarbutt(3) 7 11
(Charlie Wallis) *chsd ldrs: rdn and struggling whn hung rt bnd 2f out: sn lost pl: bhd ins fnl f* **66/1**

1m 11.8s (-0.10) **Going Correction** +0.075s/f (Slow) **8** Ran SP% **114.8**
Speed ratings (Par 98): **103,100,97,96,92 91,88,85**
CSF £27.23 CT £115.77 TOTE £3.50: £1.50, £2.10, £1.60; EX 29.30 Trifecta £121.70.
**Owner** Book 3 Partnership **Bred** Rabbah Bloodstock Limited **Trained** Newmarket, Suffolk
■ Stewards' Enquiry : Kieren Fox 3 day ban - guilty of careless riding in that he allowed his mount to drift left (4-6 Aug)

**FOCUS**
A lowly sprint handicap which the winner took with ease. It was a rough race early.
T/Plt: £54.90 to a £1 stake. Pool: £67,732.02 - 899.34 winning units T/Qpdt: £10.90 to a £1 stake. Pool: £5,570.20 - 377.85 winning units **Steve Payne**

# 4634 SANDOWN (R-H)
Wednesday, July 19

**OFFICIAL GOING: Good (round 7.2, sprint 7.0)**
Wind: Fresh, against Weather: Fine but cloudy, humid

## 5029 WATCH RACING UK ON BT TV H'CAP 5f 10y
**6:05** (6:05) (Class 4) (0-85,85) 3-Y-0 **£5,822** (£1,732; £865; £432) **Stalls** High

Form RPR

-151 **1** **Ocelot**[32] 3812 3-8-8 **72** ........ TomMarquand 6 87
(Robert Cowell) *urged along after 1f and struggling to keep up in last pl: prog on outer 2f out: drvn to ld 1f out: sn clr and styd on wl* **10/1**

1340 **2** *3 1/2* **Erissimus Maximus (FR)**[51] 3146 3-9-1 **79** ........(b) SilvestreDeSousa 4 81
(Chris Dwyer) *pushed along in 5th pl after 2f: effrt u.p over 1f out but wnr sn shot past: kpt on fnl f on outer to take 2nd last strides* **11/4**[1]

2215 **3** *nk* **Fair Cop**[23] 4154 3-9-2 **80** ........ DavidProbert 7 81
(Andrew Balding) *cl up on outer: chsd ldr 2f out: led briefly jst over 1f out: sn outpcd by wnr: lost 2nd last strides* **11/2**

431 **4** *1 3/4* **Tahoo (IRE)**[17] 4412 3-9-6 **84** ........ OisinMurphy 3 79
(K R Burke) *pushed up to ld and set gd pce: hdd & wknd jst over 1f out* **10/3**[2]

2461 **5** *2 3/4* **Blitz**[44] 3411 3-9-3 **84** ........ HectorCrouch(3) 2 69
(Clive Cox) *racd against rail: chsd ldr to 2f out: wkng whn impeded jst ins fnl f* **4/1**[3]

1164 **6** *2* **Ascot Day (IRE)**[25] 4098 3-9-7 **85** ........ JimCrowley 1 63
(David Simcock) *racd against rail: chsd ldrs in 4th: rdn and no prog 2f out: wknd over 1f out* **5/1**

1m 2.68s (1.08) **Going Correction** +0.275s/f (Good) **6** Ran SP% **110.9**
Speed ratings (Par 102): **102,96,95,93,88 85**
CSF £36.56 TOTE £8.90: £4.10, £1.80; EX 40.10 Trifecta £245.00.
**Owner** Manor Farm Stud (rutland) **Bred** Manor Farm Stud & Mrs A J Ralli **Trained** Six Mile Bottom, Cambs

**FOCUS**
Round course on innermost configuration with all distances as advertised. 6mm of overnight rain saw the going downgraded prior to racing and it looked to have got into the surface. Predictably this fair 3yo sprint handicap was run at a strong early tempo. The race is rated around the runner-up to C&D form.

## 5030 WOLSELEY NOVICE AUCTION STKS 7f
**6:35** (6:36) (Class 5) 2-Y-0 **£3,881** (£1,155; £577; £288) **Stalls** Low

Form RPR

5 **1** **Finsbury Park**[16] 4452 2-8-7 0 ........ GeorgeWood(3) 9 75
(Robyn Brisland) *trckd ldrs: prog to go 2nd 2f out: rdn to ld jst over 1f out: drvn out and hld on* **10/1**

0 **2** *nk* **Macaque**[21] 4218 2-9-2 0 ........ DavidProbert 1 80
(Andrew Balding) *trckd ldrs: rdn 2f out: styd on to take 2nd 1f out: edgd lft sn after: clsd on wnr nr fin but a hld* **5/1**[3]

61 **3** *1 1/2* **Simply Breathless**[36] 3690 2-8-11 0 ........ SamHitchcott 12 71
(Clive Cox) *chsd ldrs on outer: rdn over 2f out: prog over 1f out: tk 3rd jst ins fnl f: nvr able to chal* **8/1**

**4** *1/2* **Guvenor's Choice (IRE)** 2-9-0 0 ........(t[1]) JimCrowley 8 73+
(K R Burke) *s.v.s: detached in last to 1/2-way: pushed along and prog 2f out: nt clr run briefly ins fnl f: styd on wl nr fin: one to nte* **16/1**

03 **5** *nk* **Cheeky Rascal (IRE)**[13] 4520 2-9-2 0 ........ TomMarquand 10 74
(Richard Hannon) *in tch in 8th: shkn up over 2f out: prog over 1f out: kpt on fnl f: nt pce to threaten* **11/2**

**6** *1/2* **Great Vizier** 2-9-0 0 ........ CharlesBishop 13 70+
(Eve Johnson Houghton) *dwlt: wl in rr: pushed along 3f out: prog 2f out: kpt on steadily fnl f: fair debut* **25/1**

42 **7** *3* **Groundnut**[36] 3690 2-8-10 0 ........ RichardKingscote 6 58
(Jonathan Portman) *prom: chsd ldr briefly over 2f out: steadily wknd over 1f out* **4/1**[2]

2 **8** *1/2* **Dance To Paris**[37] 3662 2-8-9 0 ........ OisinMurphy 5 56
(Lucy Wadham) *chsd ldr to over 2f out: steadily wknd over 1f out* **3/1**[1]

400 **9** *3 1/4* **Go Bananas**[28] 3960 2-8-9 62 ........ SilvestreDeSousa 3 47
(Brian Meehan) *led at gd pce: kicked on over 2f out: hdd jst over 1f out: wknd qckly fnl f and eased* **16/1**

00 **10** *3/4* **Amiirah**[49] 3210 2-8-5 0 ........ LukeMorris 11 41
(John Gallagher) *a wl in rr: pushed along and no prog 1/2-way* **150/1**

6 **11** *1 3/4* **Champs Inblue**[33] 3776 2-8-10 0 ........ FergusSweeney 7 41
(Pat Phelan) *a wl in rr: rn green and no prog 3f out* **50/1**

**12** *3 1/2* **Secratario (FR)** 2-8-9 0 ........ FinleyMarsh(7) 2 38
(Richard Hughes) *dwlt: a wl in rr: nvr a factor* **33/1**

00 **13** *7* **Jazz Affair (IRE)**[6] 4805 2-9-2 0 ........ DougieCostello 4 19
(Jamie Osborne) *chsd ldr: wknd qckly over 2f out: bhd fnl f* **66/1**

1m 31.85s (2.35) **Going Correction** +0.30s/f (Good) **13** Ran SP% **119.9**
Speed ratings (Par 94): **98,97,95,95,95 94,91,90,86,85 83,79,71**
CSF £58.18 TOTE £12.90: £3.70, £2.20, £2.60; EX 94.00 Trifecta £954.10.
**Owner** Franconson Partners **Bred** Maze Rattan Limited **Trained** Newmarket, Suffolk

**FOCUS**
Not a bad novice event, best rated around the penalised third.

## 5031 PIPE CENTER H'CAP 7f
**7:05** (7:08) (Class 5) (0-70,71) 3-Y-0 **£3,881** (£1,155; £577; £288) **Stalls** Low

Form RPR

U-31 **1** **Harba (IRE)**[29] 3931 3-9-6 **68** ........ PatCosgrave 9 87
(William Haggas) *sn trckd ldng pair: quick move to ld over 2f out and sn clr: in n.d at all after: rdn out fnl f* **2/1**[1]

550- **2** *7* **Captain Pugwash (IRE)**[203] 8557 3-9-4 **66** ........ LiamKeniry 11 66
(Henry Spiller) *in tch in midfield: prog on outer 2f out: drvn to chse clr wnr jst ins fnl f: no imp and jst hld on for 2nd* **16/1**

0061 **3** *shd* **Dragon Dream (IRE)**[21] 4211 3-8-6 **61** ........ RhiainIngram(7) 8 63
(Roger Ingram) *trckd ldrs in 5th: nt clr run 2f out and again over 1f out whn swtchd lft: rdn and styd on fnl f: nrly snatched 2nd* **20/1**

-106 **4** *1/2* **Moonshine Dancer**[22] 4188 3-8-10 **65** ........(h) PatrickVaughan(7) 13 64
(Christian Williams) *hld up in rr: swtchd to inner and effrt over 2f out: nt clr run briefly over 1f out: squeezed through on inner and kpt on to press for a pl nr fin* **50/1**

2116 **5** *3/4* **Pass The Cristal (IRE)**[29] 3937 3-9-3 **65** ........ DougieCostello 7 62
(William Muir) *hld up in midfield: prog over 2f out: drvn to press for a pl over 1f out: one pce ins fnl f* **12/1**

-300 **6** *1 1/4* **Inlawed**[16] 4446 3-9-4 **66** ........ RichardKingscote 14 59
(Ed Walker) *chsd ldrs: rdn to chse wnr 2f out but no ch: lost 2nd and wknd jst ins fnl f* **8/1**[3]

0-66 **7** *2 ¾* **Junoesque**[41] 3507 3-8-12 **60**........................ FergusSweeney 6 46
(John Gallagher) *hld up in last trio: shkn up over 2f out: plugged on fr over 1f out: nvr really involved* **12/1**

0130 **8** *3 ½* **Beepeecee**[18] 4350 3-8-10 **65**........................(p) FinleyMarsh(7) 10 41
(Richard Hughes) *slowly away: mostly in last: shkn up over 2f out: no great prog* **10/1**

4505 **9** *shd* **Milburn Jack**[13] 4537 3-9-9 **71**........................(b[1]) AdamKirby 4 47
(Clive Cox) *chsd ldr to over 2f out: wandered and wknd wl over 1f out* **11/4**[2]

6-40 **10** *14* **Eternal Dream**[18] 4347 3-9-1 **63**........................ OisinMurphy 2
(William Knight) *led at str pce: hdd over 2f out: wkng whn hmpd on inner over 1f out: t.o* **12/1**

1m 30.98s (1.48) **Going Correction** +0.30s/f (Good) **10** Ran SP% **115.9**
Speed ratings (Par 100): **103,95,94,94,93 92,88,84,84,68**
CSF £36.58 CT £503.84 TOTE £2.80: £1.40, £4.00, £3.70; EX 36.20 Trifecta £405.40.
**Owner** Al Shaqab Racing **Bred** Summerville Bloodstock Investments **Trained** Newmarket, Suffolk

**FOCUS**
This modest 3yo handicap proved one-way traffic for the easy winner. The form is taken at face value.

## 5032 ROBERT DYAS H'CAP 1m

**7:40** (7:41) (Class 3) (0-90,91) 3-Y-O+ **£8,092** (£2,423; £1,211; £605; £302) **Stalls** Low

Form RPR

21-0 **1** **Make Time (IRE)**[88] 1959 3-9-2 **91**........................ JimCrowley 2 106
(David Menuisier) *hld up in 4th: shkn up and prog over 2f out: rdn to ld over 1f out: sn clr: pushed out last 75yds* **11/10**[1]

1351 **2** *6* **Selection (FR)**[35] 3730 4-9-2 **83**........................(p[1]) SilvestreDeSousa 4 86
(William Haggas) *trckd ldr: shkn up to chal over 2f out: upsides tl wnr wnt by over 1f out: no ch after but kpt on to win battle for 2nd* **3/1**[2]

5141 **3** *hd* **Captain Courageous (IRE)**[25] 4085 4-9-8 **89**........ RichardKingscote 1 91
(Ed Walker) *hld up in detached last: rdn and no prog over 2f out: styd on fr over 1f out: nrly snatched 2nd* **5/1**[3]

00-2 **4** *½* **Ginger Jack**[26] 4057 10-9-9 **90**........................ JFEgan 5 91
(Jo Hughes) *led: rdn and jnd over 2f out: hdd over 1f out and no ch w wnr after: kpt on but lost 2 pls nr fin* **12/1**

3604 **5** *30* **Volatile**[23] 4154 3-9-2 **91**........................ LukeMorris 3 21
(James Tate) *t.k.h: trckd ldng pair to over 2f out: wknd rapidly: t.o* **8/1**

1m 45.62s (2.32) **Going Correction** +0.30s/f (Good)
**WFA** 3 from 4yo+ 8lb **5** Ran SP% **108.1**
Speed ratings (Par 107): **100,94,93,93,63**
CSF £4.39 TOTE £1.90: £1.30, £1.30; EX 4.60 Trifecta £11.70.
**Owner** Gail Brown Racing (VII) **Bred** Kildaragh Stud **Trained** Pulborough, W Sussex

**FOCUS**
This good-quality handicap was run at a fair enough pace and it saw another impressive winner on the night. He built on his impressive maiden win.

## 5033 NUFFIELD HEALTH H'CAP 1m 1f 209y

**8:10** (8:12) (Class 4) (0-80,81) 3-Y-O **£5,822** (£1,732; £865; £432) **Stalls** Low

Form RPR

0-13 **1** **Eynhallow**[33] 3778 3-9-10 **81**........................ KieranShoemark 4 97
(Roger Charlton) *stdd s: hld up in last: gd prog on outer to chse ldr 2f out: drvn to cl and led jst over 1f out: styd on wl after* **13/8**[1]

51-0 **2** *2 ¾* **Buzz (FR)**[65] 2690 3-9-7 **78**........................ AdamKirby 6 88
(Hughie Morrison) *hld up in tch: prog to dispute 2nd 2f out: drvn to cl on ldr along w wnr over 1f out: styd on but readily outpcd fnl f* **8/1**

-214 **3** *4 ½* **Okool (FR)**[53] 3068 3-9-10 **81**........................ JimCrowley 7 82
(Owen Burrows) *t.k.h: hld up in tch: rdn over 2f out: kpt on fr over 1f out to take 3rd ins fnl f: no ch w ldng pair* **3/1**[2]

5510 **4** *1 ½* **Chance To Dream (IRE)**[41] 3504 3-9-5 **76**........................ KierenFox 8 74
(John Best) *t.k.h: hld up in last pair: rdn and stl in last 2f out: kpt on u.p after* **14/1**

1611 **5** *6* **Sir Plato (IRE)**[23] 4153 3-9-7 **78**........................ OisinMurphy 2 64
(Rod Millman) *led: kicked 3 l clr over 2f out: hrd rdn and hung lft over 1f out: sn hdd & wknd qckly* **7/1**[3]

1130 **6** *3* **Rita's Man (IRE)**[16] 4443 3-9-3 **74**........................ SilvestreDeSousa 3 54
(Richard Hannon) *trckd ldr 2f: rdn over 2f out: wkng whn impeded wl over 1f out* **11/1**

-613 **7** *5* **Mouille Point**[23] 4155 3-9-7 **78**........................ SeanLevey 5 51
(Richard Hannon) *hld up bhd ldrs: shkn up and no rspnse over 2f out: wknd and eased over 1f out* **11/1**

1005 **8** *nk* **International Law**[7] 4736 3-9-6 **77**........................(b[1]) TomMarquand 9 46
(Brian Meehan) *t.k.h: trckd ldr after 2f to 2f out: wknd qckly* **20/1**

2m 11.16s (0.66) **Going Correction** +0.30s/f (Good) **8** Ran SP% **114.8**
Speed ratings (Par 102): **109,106,103,102,97 94,90,90**
CSF £15.68 CT £36.08 TOTE £2.40: £1.10, £2.40, £1.50; EX 19.40 Trifecta £76.90.
**Owner** Exors Of The Late Rj McCreery & Partners **Bred** Stowell Hill Ltd & D Ludlow **Trained** Beckhampton, Wilts

**FOCUS**
A decent 3yo handicap. It was run at an uneven pace but the form is strong. Another step up from the winner.

## 5034 WATCH RACING UK ANYWHERE H'CAP 1m 6f

**8:40** (8:43) (Class 5) (0-70,72) 3-Y-O **£3,881** (£1,155; £577; £288) **Stalls** Low

Form RPR

-402 **1** **Padrinho (IRE)**[65] 2686 3-9-2 **65**........................ KierenFox 6 76
(John Best) *trckd ldrs in 4th: prog to ld wl over 2f out: drvn and wandered in front but clr over 1f out: kpt on wl* **6/1**[3]

3-03 **2** *4 ½* **Sussex Ranger (USA)**[23] 4156 3-9-6 **72**........................ HectorCrouch(3) 3 75
(Gary Moore) *racd in 5th but pushed along at times: drvn 3f out: styd on fr 2f out: tk 2nd last strides* **7/2**[2]

5255 **3** *hd* **Gee Sixty Six**[55] 2998 3-9-2 **65**........................ JoeyHaynes 4 68
(Mark H Tompkins) *blindfold off late and slowly away: hld up in last: rdn and prog on outer over 2f out: chsd wnr over 1f out: no imp after: lost 2nd last strides* **14/1**

6-54 **4** *2 ¼* **Magic Beans**[53] 3087 3-8-9 **61**........................ CharlieBennett(3) 10 61
(Hughie Morrison) *hld up in 6th: rdn and rt qckn wl over 2f out: kpt on fr over 1f out: no ch* **6/1**[3]

00-0 **5** *¾* **Leapt**[18] 4347 3-9-4 **67**........................(h[1]) ShaneKelly 1 66
(Richard Hughes) *hld up in last pair: rdn 3f out: no prog and sn adrift: plugged on fr over 1f out* **20/1**

0-52 **6** *1* **Veiled Secret (IRE)**[41] 3503 3-9-7 **70**........................(p[1]) LukeMorris 2 67
(Sir Mark Prescott Bt) *free to post: t.k.h: trckd ldng pair: urged along and no rspnse 3f out: struggling and no imp ldrs after* **1/1**[1]

4-36 **7** *5* **Avantgardist (GER)**[41] 3503 3-8-13 **67**........................(b[1]) PaddyBradley(5) 9 57
(Pat Phelan) *pushed up to ld after 2f but sn stdd pce: hdd 8f out: chal 3f out: chsd wnr sn after to over 1f out: wknd qckly* **33/1**

-000 **8** *16* **Pushjockeypush**[37] 3657 3-8-3 **52**........................(t) RoystonFfrench 7 20
(Stuart Williams) *led 2f: led again 8f out: hdd & wknd wl over 2f out: t.o* **25/1**

3m 13.7s (9.20) **Going Correction** +0.30s/f (Good) **8** Ran SP% **119.0**
Speed ratings (Par 100): **85,82,82,81,80 80,77,68**
CSF £27.80 CT £287.92 TOTE £6.60: £1.90, £1.60, £3.60; EX 29.90 Trifecta £139.00.
**Owner** Simon Malcolm **Bred** Simon Malcolm **Trained** Oad Street, Kent

**FOCUS**
There was a messy pace on in this modest 3yo staying handicap. The race is rated around the runner-up, to form.
T/Jkpt: Part Won. Pool: £13,047.36 - 0.5 winning unit. T/Plt: £111.20 to a £1 stake. Pool: £76,450.75 - 501.78 winning units T/Qpdt: £16.50 to a £1 stake. Pool: £6,492.25 - 290.1 winning units **Jonathan Neesom**

# 4760 YARMOUTH (L-H)

### Wednesday, July 19

**OFFICIAL GOING: Good (good to soft in places; 7.0)**
Wind: Fresh across Weather: Fine

## 5035 SILK SERIES LADY RIDERS' H'CAP (PRO-AM LADY JOCKEYS SERIES) 6f 3y

**5:45** (5:47) (Class 4) (0-85,85) 3-Y-O+ **£6,469** (£1,925; £962; £481) **Stalls** Centre

Form RPR

3121 **1** **Hart Stopper**[11] 4616 3-9-12 **81**........................ HayleyTurner 1 87+
(Michael Bell) *stdd s: hld up: hdwy and swtchd lft over 1f out: shkn up to ld wl ins fnl f: rdn out* **6/4**[1]

-542 **2** *½* **Case Key**[14] 4489 4-9-9 **73**........................(p) MissSBrotherton 7 78
(Michael Appleby) *trckd ldrs: led over 1f out: rdn and hdd wl ins fnl f: styd on* **13/2**[3]

2200 **3** *1 ¾* **Majestic Moon (IRE)**[5] 4854 7-10-6 **84**........................ ShelleyBirkett 2 83
(Julia Feilden) *led: rdn and hdd wl over 1f out: styd on same pce ins fnl f* **6/1**[2]

4021 **4** *½* **Vimy Ridge**[22] 4182 5-9-6 **75**........................(t) MissJCooley(5) 6 73
(Alan Bailey) *hld up in tch: racd keenly: led wl over 1f out: sn hdd: n.m.r and no ex wl ins fnl f* **7/1**

4510 **5** *1 ¼* **Diamond Lady**[25] 4099 6-10-5 **83**........................ JaneElliott 3 77
(William Stone) *chsd ldr tl pushed along over 2f out: no ex wl ins fnl f* **15/2**

1-00 **6** *3 ½* **Syrian Pearl**[34] 3757 6-10-7 **85**........................ GeorgiaCox 4 68
(Chris Wall) *s.s: hld up: rdn over 1f out: nvr on terms* **13/2**[3]

1060 **7** *hd* **Plucky Dip**[13] 4524 6-10-1 **79**........................ LucyKBarry 5 61
(John Ryan) *hld up: rdn over 2f out: nvr on terms* **25/1**

1m 12.8s (-1.60) **Going Correction** -0.05s/f (Good)
**WFA** 3 from 4yo+ 5lb **7** Ran SP% **109.1**
Speed ratings (Par 105): **108,107,105,104,102 98,97**
CSF £10.45 TOTE £1.90: £1.30, £2.90; EX 9.80 Trifecta £55.00.
**Owner** Christopher Wright **Bred** Manor Farm Stud (rutland) **Trained** Newmarket, Suffolk
■ Stewards' Enquiry : Lucy K Barry five-day ban: used whip when out of contention (Aug 2-6)

**FOCUS**
The going was good, good to soft in places. A fair handicap run at a sound pace. The form is rated around the runner-up to his best.

## 5036 BAZUKA / EBF NOVICE STKS (PLUS 10 RACE) 7f 3y

**6:15** (6:17) (Class 4) 2-Y-O **£4,528** (£1,347; £673; £336) **Stalls** Centre

Form RPR

**1** **The Last Emperor** 2-9-2 0........................ AndreaAtzeni 4 78+
(Roger Varian) *s.i.s: hdwy over 5f out: shkn up to ld over 1f out: r.o* **10/3**[1]

**2** *½* **Radio Source (IRE)** 2-9-2 0........................ RyanMoore 2 76+
(Sir Michael Stoute) *led: j. path over 5f out: sn hdd: chsd ldr tl led again 2f out: shkn up and hdd over 1f out: styd on* **9/1**

**3** *2* **Ship Of The Fen** 2-9-2 0........................ JamieSpencer 1 71
(Martyn Meade) *hld up: hdwy 1/2-way: ev ch 2f out: shkn up over 1f out: edgd rt and styd on same pce ins fnl f* **9/2**[3]

**4** *1 ¾* **Bajan Gold (IRE)** 2-9-2 0........................ AdamBeschizza 6 66
(Stuart Williams) *hld up: hdwy over 1f out: styd on same pce ins fnl f* **40/1**

**5** *1* **Baghdad (FR)** 2-9-2 0........................ StevieDonohoe 5 64
(Charlie Fellowes) *chsd ldr: led over 5f out: rdn and hdd 2f out: no ex ins fnl f* **4/1**[2]

**6** *½* **Global Wonder (IRE)** 2-9-2 0........................ MartinHarley 8 65
(Ed Dunlop) *hld up: plld hrd: nt clr run over 1f out: r.o ins fnl f: nvr nrr* **8/1**

**7** *½* **Verstappen (IRE)** 2-9-2 0........................ DanielMuscutt 7 61
(Marco Botti) *hld up: shkn up over 1f out: nvr on terms* **14/1**

**8** *1 ¼* **Dark Spec** 2-9-2 0........................ RobHornby 9 58
(Pam Sly) *sn chsng ldrs: pushed along 1/2-way: hmpd over 2f out: wknd over 1f out* **25/1**

**9** *½* **Adulate** 2-9-2 0........................ JamesDoyle 3 56
(Hugo Palmer) *trckd ldrs: plld hrd: hmpd over 5f out: lost pl over 4f out: effrt and swtchd rt over 2f out: wknd fnl f* **9/2**[3]

1m 28.32s (1.72) **Going Correction** -0.05s/f (Good) **9** Ran SP% **113.5**
Speed ratings (Par 96): **88,87,85,83,82 81,80,79,78**
CSF £33.40 TOTE £3.90: £1.50, £2.60, £1.70; EX 20.40 Trifecta £78.90.
**Owner** Sheikh Mohammed Obaid Al Maktoum **Bred** Wellsummers Farm **Trained** Newmarket, Suffolk

**FOCUS**
The pace was steady for this interesting contest, which was contested by newcomers. The front two pulled clear and look useful, but there are no race averages to compare the form to.

## 5037 DIOMED DEVELOPMENT H'CAP 1m 2f 23y

**6:45** (6:46) (Class 2) (0-100,100) 3-Y-O+ **£11,971** (£3,583; £1,791; £896; £446) **Stalls** Low

Form RPR

0010 **1** **Good Omen**[27] 3998 3-8-12 **93**........................ JamieSpencer 1 98
(David Simcock) *hld up: hdwy 3f out: rdn over 1f out: r.o u.p to ld ins fnl f* **15/8**[1]

2100 **2** *¾* **Petite Jack**[26] 4033 4-9-7 **93**........................ JackMitchell 7 96
(Archie Watson) *a.p: chsd ldr over 4f out: rdn over 2f out: led over 1f out: hdd ins fnl f: styd on* **20/1**

1250 **3** *nk* **Brorocco**[11] 4614 4-9-3 **89**........................(h) ThomasBrown 8 91
(Andrew Balding) *s.i.s: hld up: plld hrd: hdwy over 5f out: led on bit over 3f out: rdn over 1f out: hdd ins fnl f: eased whn hld nr fin* **4/1**[3]

0404 **4** *nse* **Law And Order (IRE)**[19] 4322 3-9-5 **100**........................ MartinHarley 6 103
(James Tate) *chsd ldrs: lost pl over 5f out: rallied over 1f out: r.o* **11/2**

6603 **5** *1 ¾* **Great Hall**[18] 4370 7-9-10 **96**........................ JamesDoyle 2 94
(Mick Quinn) *led: hdd over 3f out: sn rdn: styd on same pce fnl f* **10/1**

-664 **6** *shd* **Basil Berry**[19] 4321 6-9-8 **94** TrevorWhelan 4 92
(Chris Dwyer) *chsd ldr over 5f: nt clr run and lost pl over 3f out: styd on ins fnl f* **33/1**

00/2 **7** *shd* **First Flight (IRE)**[39] 3597 6-9-12 **98** AndreaAtzeni 5 96
(Heather Main) *s.i.s: hld up: pushed along over 2f out: styd on ins fnl f: nt trble ldrs* **7/2**[2]

2m 14.09s (3.59) **Going Correction** +0.60s/f (Yiel)
**WFA** 3 from 4yo+ 9lb **7** Ran SP% **109.2**
Speed ratings (Par 109): **109,108,108,108,106 106,106**
CSF £37.15 CT £121.51 TOTE £2.70: £1.80, £5.40; EX 33.50 Trifecta £173.90.
**Owner** Mrs Q J Guo **Bred** Hascombe And Valiant Studs **Trained** Newmarket, Suffolk

**FOCUS**
A decent handicap. They went a steady pace and it produced an exciting, compressed finish. The winner was back to his penultimate Doncaster form.

## 5038 4HEAD MAIDEN FILLIES' STKS 7f 3y
**7:15** (7:16) (Class 5) 3-Y-O+ **£2,911** (£866; £432; £216) **Stalls** Centre

Form RPR

30 **1** **UAE Queen**[38] 3626 3-9-0 0 AndreaAtzeni 2 73+
(Roger Varian) *mde all: qcknd over 2f out: shkn up over 1f out: r.o wl* **2/1**[2]

**2** *2 ¼* **Chalky (IRE)** 3-9-0 0 JackMitchell 6 67
(Martyn Meade) *s.i.s: hld up: hdwy over 1f out: r.o to go 2nd nr fin: nt trble wnr* **14/1**

55 **3** *nk* **Zilza (IRE)**[21] 4214 3-9-0 64 (t) SaleemGolam 1 66
(Conrad Allen) *disp 2nd to 1/2-way: rdn and swtchd lft over 1f out: styd on* **25/1**

? **4** *shd* **Pretty Passe**[12] 4568 3-9-0 0 RyanMoore 4 66
(William Haggas) *trckd wnr to 1/2-way: sn pushed along: rdn and hung lft over 1f out: styd on towards fin* **6/5**[1]

235 **5** *2 ¼* **Shankara (IRE)**[12] 4565 3-9-0 72 JamieSpencer 3 60
(David Simcock) *s.i.s: hdwy over 4f out: chsd wnr 1/2-way: ev ch 2f out: sn rdn: no ex ins fnl f* **6/1**[3]

5325 **6** *5* **Ocean Temptress**[19] 4313 3-9-0 58 StevieDonohoe 5 46
(John Ryan) *hld up: pushed along over 2f out: sn wknd* **12/1**

1m 26.78s (0.18) **Going Correction** -0.05s/f (Good) **6** Ran SP% **111.3**
Speed ratings (Par 100): **96,93,93,92,90 84**
CSF £27.06 TOTE £2.90: £1.30, £4.70; EX 21.70 Trifecta £285.50.
**Owner** Sheikh Mohammed Obaid Al Maktoum **Bred** Fittocks Stud **Trained** Newmarket, Suffolk

**FOCUS**
The pace was steady for this uncompetitive maiden. The winner did it comfortably and the form is rated around the third.

## 5039 AEROPAK H'CAP 7f 3y
**7:50** (7:51) (Class 5) (0-70,72) 3-Y-O+ **£2,911** (£866; £432; £216) **Stalls** Centre

Form RPR

301 **1** **Golden Guest**[15] 4463 3-8-11 **66** JaneElliott(5) 1 71
(George Margarson) *hld up in tch: shkn up to ld 1f out: rdn and edgd rt ins fnl f: styd on* **7/1**

0-14 **2** *hd* **In Ken's Memory**[56] 2973 4-9-8 **72** RayDawson(7) 10 79
(Michael Appleby) *racd alone on stands' side rail for much of the trip: w ldrs: led over 2f out: rdn and hung lft over 1f out: sn hdd: ev ch ins fnl f: rdr bec unbalanced towards fin: styd on* **5/1**[2]

1320 **3** *1 ½* **Caledonia Laird**[30] 3912 6-8-11 **61** (b[1]) NicolaCurrie(7) 4 64
(Jo Hughes) *hld up: nt clr run over 1f out: r.o ins fnl f: wnt 3rd nr fin: nt rch ldrs* **8/1**

616 **4** *nk* **Wahiba (GER)**[49] 3216 4-9-12 **69** AndreaAtzeni 8 71
(Marco Botti) *led: rdn and hdd over 2f out: no ex wl ins fnl f* **9/2**[1]

3046 **5** *2* **Aqua Libre**[13] 4542 4-9-5 **67** DavidEgan(5) 9 64
(Philip McBride) *dwlt: hdwy over 5f out: rdn over 1f out: styd on same pce ins fnl f* **5/1**[2]

2440 **6** *1* **Widnes**[58] 2895 3-9-5 **69** (h[1]) RobertTart 7 60
(Alan Bailey) *s.i.s: hld up: rdn over 2f out: styd on ins fnl f: nvr nrr* **11/2**[3]

4-00 **7** *hd* **Ubla (IRE)**[165] 570 4-9-5 **62** MartinHarley 6 56
(Jane Chapple-Hyam) *trckd ldrs: rdn over 1f out: nt clr run and no ex ins fnl f* **9/1**

0413 **8** *1 ½* **Soaring Spirits (IRE)**[22] 4176 7-9-12 **69** (p) RobertWinston 2 59
(Dean Ivory) *w ldrs: ev ch over 2f out: sn rdn: wknd and eased wl ins fnl f* **10/1**

60-0 **9** *5* **Fever Few**[82] 2124 8-9-3 **63** SimonPearce(3) 3 39
(Chris Wall) *racd keenly: prom: ev ch 2f out: sn rdn: wknd fnl f* **22/1**

1m 25.66s (-0.94) **Going Correction** -0.05s/f (Good)
**WFA** 3 from 4yo+ 7lb **9** Ran SP% **113.9**
Speed ratings (Par 103): **103,102,101,100,98 97,97,95,89**
CSF £41.28 CT £287.51 TOTE £5.60: £2.20, £2.00, £2.30; EX 45.10 Trifecta £196.40.
**Owner** John Guest Racing **Bred** P A & M J Reditt & Catridge Stud **Trained** Newmarket, Suffolk

**FOCUS**
This was competitive enough for the grade. They were spread across the track and the winner built on his Brighton win.

## 5040 FREEDERM H'CAP 6f 3y
**8:20** (8:26) (Class 6) (0-55,57) 3-Y-O **£2,264** (£673; £336; £168) **Stalls** Centre

Form RPR

5445 **1** **Yorkshire Rover**[8] 4723 3-9-5 **53** JamieSpencer 9 62
(David Brown) *hld up: hdwy over 1f out: rdn to ld ins fnl f: r.o u.p* **5/1**[2]

00-0 **2** *hd* **Canadian Royal**[43] 3438 3-9-9 **57** (t) AdamBeschizza 7 65
(Stuart Williams) *hld up: hdwy 2f out: led over 1f out: sn rdn: hdd ins fnl f: r.o u.p* **5/1**[2]

4004 **3** *2 ¾* **African Girl**[36] 3703 3-8-11 **48** SimonPearce(3) 11 49
(Lydia Pearce) *chsd ldrs: lost pl over 3f out: hdwy and nt clr run and swtchd lft over 1f out: styd on* **7/1**[3]

046 **4** *1 ¾* **Shyarch**[56] 2970 3-9-7 **55** RyanPowell 8 50
(George Margarson) *s.i.s: pushed along in rr: nt clr run over 1f out: r.o ins fnl f: nvr nrr* **16/1**

3056 **5** *¾* **Tea El Tee (IRE)**[63] 2734 3-8-11 **50** (p) DavidEgan(5) 3 43
(Gay Kelleway) *prom: racd keenly: rdn over 2f out: no ex ins fnl f* **10/1**

-012 **6** *nk* **Iron Lady (IRE)**[26] 4046 3-9-7 **55** JamesDoyle 12 47
(William Muir) *led: rdn and hdd over 2f out: no ex ins fnl f* **11/4**[1]

2004 **7** *nk* **Percy Toplis**[13] 4543 3-9-0 **48** (b[1]) TrevorWhelan 14 39
(Christine Dunnett) *chsd ldr tl led over 2f out: rdn and hdd over 1f out: no ex ins fnl f* **33/1**

6000 **8** *2 ¼* **Nonnie And Norny**[36] 3701 3-8-12 **46** oh1 StevieDonohoe 6 30
(Shaun Harris) *chsd ldrs: rdn over 2f out: wknd wl over 1f out* **100/1**

036- **9** *¾* **Sweet Sienna**[251] 7884 3-9-1 **49** RobertWinston 13 31
(Dean Ivory) *trckd ldrs: rdn over 2f out: wknd fnl f* **20/1**

-002 **10** *3 ¼* **Proud Kate**[13] 4543 3-8-12 **46** oh1 (h) LiamJones 5 18
(Christine Dunnett) *hld up in tch: plld hrd: n.m.r and lost pl 4f out: rdn and wknd over 1f out* **33/1**

3105 **11** *4 ½* **Sadieroseclifford (IRE)**[15] 4458 3-9-5 **53** KevinStott 4 12
(Giles Bravery) *hld up in tch: rdn over 2f out: wknd over 1f out* **5/1**[2]

1m 13.41s (-0.99) **Going Correction** -0.05s/f (Good) **11** Ran SP% **115.8**
Speed ratings (Par 98): **104,103,100,97,96 96,95,92,91,87 81**
CSF £28.70 CT £175.45 TOTE £5.80: £1.80, £2.00, £2.30; EX 34.60 Trifecta £253.70.
**Owner** Browns Boy's **Bred** Mrs Brown's Boys **Trained** Averham Park, Notts

**FOCUS**
An open handicap that produced an exciting finish.

## 5041 IBULEVE H'CAP 5f 42y
**8:50** (8:53) (Class 5) (0-70,70) 3-Y-O **£2,911** (£866; £432; £216) **Stalls** Centre

Form RPR

-502 **1** **Cool Breeze (IRE)**[26] 4053 3-8-3 **52** JimmyQuinn 1 61+
(David Simcock) *hld up: racd keenly: hdwy over 1f out: led ins fnl f: r.o wl* **7/2**[3]

1354 **2** *1 ¼* **Midnightly**[19] 4324 3-9-2 **70** (t) DavidEgan(5) 6 74
(Rae Guest) *chsd ldrs: led 2f out: rdn over 1f out: hdd ins fnl f: styd on same pce* **9/2**

1143 **3** *½* **Wild Approach (IRE)**[23] 4159 3-9-6 **69** JamieSpencer 7 71
(Robert Cowell) *led 3f: rdn and ev ch over 1f out: styd on same pce ins fnl f* **10/3**[2]

0402 **4** *¾* **Miss Rosina (IRE)**[19] 4324 3-8-5 **59** JaneElliott(5) 3 59
(George Margarson) *chsd ldr: rdn and ev ch over 1f out: no ex wl ins fnl f* **15/2**

0540 **5** *nk* **Cherry Leyf**[8] 4714 3-7-11 **53** (t) MillyNaseb(7) 2 51
(Stuart Williams) *chsd ldrs: rdn over 1f out: kpt on* **25/1**

4105 **6** *2 ¼* **Secret Strategy (IRE)**[22] 4178 3-9-4 **70** ShelleyBirkett(3) 5 60
(Julia Feilden) *hld up: rdn over 1f out: nt clr run ins fnl f: nt trble ldrs* **9/1**

5-1 **7** *1 ½* **Flying Foxy**[11] 4604 3-9-6 **69** KevinStott 8 54
(Michael Wigham) *hld up: pushed along 1/2-way: rdn over 1f out: nvr on terms* **3/1**[1]

1m 1.93s (-0.77) **Going Correction** -0.05s/f (Good) **7** Ran SP% **114.1**
Speed ratings (Par 100): **104,102,101,100,99 95,93**
CSF £19.45 CT £55.77 TOTE £3.80: £1.90, £2.20; EX 19.00 Trifecta £71.80.
**Owner** Khalifa Dasmal **Bred** K A Dasmal **Trained** Newmarket, Suffolk

**FOCUS**
The pace was sound for this fair handicap, which is rated around the second and fourth.
T/Plt: £125.90 to a £1 stake. Pool: £67,703.12 - 392.54 winning units T/Qpdt: £59.40 to a £1 stake. Pool: £5,131.99 - 63.9 winning units **Colin Roberts**

5042 - 5045a (Foreign Racing) - See Raceform Interactive

# 5014 VICHY
Wednesday, July 19

**OFFICIAL GOING: Turf: good to soft**

## 5046a GRAND PRIX DE VICHY (GROUP 3) (3YO+) (TURF) 1m 2f
**8:10** 3-Y-O+ **£34,188** (£13,675; £10,256; £6,837; £3,418)

RPR

**1** **Best Fouad (FR)**[25] 4115 6-9-2 0 ChristopheSoumillon 112
(F Rohaut, France) **9/5**[2]

**2** *1* **Garlingari (FR)**[32] 3856 6-9-2 0 (p) RonanThomas 110
(Mme C Barande-Barbe, France) **13/10**[1]

**3** *nk* **Qurbaan (USA)**[53] 3104 4-9-2 0 Francois-XavierBertras 109
(F Rohaut, France) **19/5**[3]

**4** *4 ½* **Porsenna (IRE)**[26] 7-9-2 0 (p) GuillaumeMillet 100
(F Vermeulen, France) **8/1**

**5** *nk* **Subway Dancer (IRE)**[81] 2169 5-9-2 0 RadekKoplik 100
(Z Koplik, Czech Republic) **45/1**

**6** *8 ½* **Raseed**[81] 2169 4-9-2 0 AurelienLemaitre 83
(F Head, France) **229/10**

2m 5.38s (-3.22) **6** Ran SP% **117.5**
PARI-MUTUEL (all including 1 euro stake): WIN 2.80 PLACE 1.40, 1.20 SF 5.10.
**Owner** LG Bloodstock **Bred** M Mouni **Trained** Sauvagnon, France

# 4840 CHEPSTOW (L-H)
Thursday, July 20

**OFFICIAL GOING: Good (good to soft in places; watered; 7.0)**
Wind: Light wind Weather: Sunny intervals, mild

## 5047 OPEN GOLF BETTING AT 188BET NOVICE MEDIAN AUCTION STKS (DIV I) 6f 16y
**1:50** (1:52) (Class 6) 2-Y-O **£2,587** (£770; £384; £192) **Stalls** Centre

Form RPR

3252 **1** **Demons Rock (IRE)**[19] 4335 2-9-2 75 LiamKeniry 7 75
(Tom Dascombe) *mde all: narrow ld whn runner-up veered lft 2f out: sn 3 l clr: rdn ent fnl f: kpt up to work to maintain advantage: comf* **9/4**[1]

**2** *3 ¼* **Music Society (IRE)** 2-8-11 0 MitchGodwin(5) 3 67+
(Sylvester Kirk) *prom: cl 2nd whn veered lft to far rail 2f out: sn reminder and bmpd into rail over 1f out: rdn and rcvrd momentum fnl f: r.o* **3/1**[2]

0 **3** *1 ¼* **Bezos (IRE)**[10] 4696 2-9-2 0 KieranO'Neill 5 62
(Richard Hannon) *prom: ev ch whn pushed along 2f out: sn rdn: one pce fnl f* **7/2**[3]

**4** *shd* **Dan's Dream** 2-8-11 0 JFEgan 10 56
(Mick Channon) *trckd ldrs: effrt 3f out: 4th 2f out: drvn over 1f out: no ex fnl f* **5/1**

**5** *3 ¼* **Mouchee (IRE)** 2-9-2 0 DavidProbert 4 51
(David Evans) *mid-div: drvn 2f out: reminder over 1f out: no imp* **10/1**

50 **6** *2 ¼* **Rude Awakening**[13] 4560 2-9-2 0 RyanPowell 6 45
(Sir Mark Prescott Bt) *in rr: pushed along 3f out: one pce fnl 2f* **16/1**

**7** *8* **Tulane (IRE)** 2-9-2 0 TimmyMurphy 1 21
(Richard Phillips) *slowly away: in rr: pushed along 2f out: mod hdwy fnl f* **50/1**

00 **8** *½* **Bib And Tucker**[20] 4291 2-9-2 0 PatCosgrave 8 19
(David Brown) *mid-div: rdn and lost pl wl over 2f out: fdd* **25/1**

9 5 **Ruby Sound** 2-8-11 0 RoystonFfrench 2
(Steph Hollinshead) *reluctant to enter stalls: in rr: pushed along 2f out: no rspnse* **66/1**

1m 11.5s (-0.50) **Going Correction** -0.05s/f (Good) 9 Ran SP% **116.9**
Speed ratings (Par 92): **101,96,95,94,90 87,76,76,69**
CSF £9.17 TOTE £2.80: £1.10, £1.70, £1.50; EX 10.40 Trifecta £41.00.
**Owner** The Famous Five Partnership **Bred** James & Geoff Mulcahy **Trained** Malpas, Cheshire
■ Silvington was withdrawn. Rule 4 does not apply.

**FOCUS**
Race distances as advertised. The ground had eased slightly following a bit of rain and Liam Keniry, who won the opener, thought the official description was fair. This was a modest novice event, effectively a maiden. The bulk of the field raced down the centre, but the runner-up ended up on the far rail. It was the quicker division by 0.6sec. The winner is rated just to his mark.

## 5048 OPEN GOLF BETTING AT 188BET NOVICE MEDIAN AUCTION STKS (DIV II) 6f 16y
**2:20** (2:21) (Class 6) 2-Y-O **£2,587** (£770; £384; £192) **Stalls** Centre

Form RPR
256 **1** **She Believes (IRE)**[21] 4253 2-8-11 74 LiamKeniry 4 72
(Sylvester Kirk) *mid-div: hdwy over 2f out: reminder over 1f out: clsd on ldrs ent fnl f: rdn and r.o wl: led last few strides* **11/4**[1]

44 **2** *shd* **Kimifive (IRE)**[22] 4220 2-9-2 0 FranBerry 7 77
(Joseph Tuite) *prom: led over 2f out: drvn over 1f out: rdn and r.o ins fnl f: hdd last few strides* **4/1**[2]

54 **3** *¾* **Ragstone View (IRE)**[21] 4266 2-9-2 0 ShaneKelly 9 74
(Richard Hughes) *prom: led 1/2-way: hdd over 2f out: rdn and stl ev ch 1f out: r.o fnl f* **11/4**[1]

0 **4** *1 ¼* **Fenagh (IRE)**[42] 3491 2-8-8 0 EdwardGreatrex(3) 5 66+
(David Loughnane) *rousted along to keep in tch first f: in rr and struggling 1/2-way: drvn 2f out: rdn and hdwy appr fnl f: r.o wl: nvr nrr* **25/1**

**5** *1 ½* **Surfa Rosa** 2-9-2 0 TimmyMurphy 1 66
(Richard Hannon) *in rr: hdwy and in tch 1/2-way: sn pushed along: rdn over 1f out: kpt on* **20/1**

6 **6** *nk* **Lady Marigold (IRE)**[33] 3821 2-8-11 0 CharlesBishop 3 60
(Eve Johnson Houghton) *trckd ldrs: pushed along over 2f out: rdn wl over 1f out: one pce* **17/2**

6 **7** *2* **Swissal (IRE)**[24] 4151 2-9-2 0 DaneO'Neill 6 59
(David Dennis) *led: hdd 1/2-way: sn pushed along: rdn over 1f out: no ex* **8/1**[3]

6 **8** *½* **Time For Wine (IRE)**[31] 3917 2-8-11 0 JFEgan 8 53
(David Evans) *prom: rdn over 2f out: wknd ent fnl f* **9/1**

**9** *14* **Redtedd** 2-9-2 0 MartinDwyer 2 16
(Tom Dascombe) *slowly away: in rr: pushed along and lost tch over 2f out* **16/1**

1m 12.1s (0.10) **Going Correction** -0.05s/f (Good) 9 Ran SP% **119.5**
Speed ratings (Par 92): **97,96,95,94,92 91,89,88,69**
CSF £14.37 TOTE £3.40: £1.20, £1.60, £1.40; EX 17.40 Trifecta £49.60.
**Owner** Marchwood Recycling Ltd **Bred** Ringfort Stud **Trained** Upper Lambourn, Berks

**FOCUS**
The slower division by 0.6sec, and similarly ordinary form, with Liam Keniry winning both legs. The winner came more down the middle than the next two home. The form is rated around the front trio.

## 5049 BEST ODDS GUARANTEED AT 188BET H'CAP 1m 14y
**2:55** (2:56) (Class 5) (0-75,77) 3-Y-O+ **£3,234** (£962; £481; £240) **Stalls** Centre

Form RPR
3513 **1** **Fantasy Queen**[16] 4468 4-9-4 65 CharlesBishop 7 73
(Eve Johnson Houghton) *chsd ldrs: hdwy into 3rd 3f out: pushed along over 2f out: rdn and led over 1f out: r.o wl fnl f* **7/2**[2]

4156 **2** *1 ½* **Black Dave (IRE)**[21] 4251 7-8-9 63 KatherineGlenister(7) 3 67
(David Evans) *cl up as ldr set fast pce: led 3f out: rdn 2f out: hdd over 1f out: kpt on fnl f* **8/1**

3610 **3** *1 ¼* **Intensical (IRE)**[22] 4207 6-10-2 77 (p) DavidNolan 4 78
(Ivan Furtado) *trckd ldrs: pushed along in 4th 3f out: sn rdn: hdwy to go 3rd over 1f out: one pce fnl f* **5/1**

1451 **4** *1 ½* **Admirable Art (IRE)**[44] 3422 7-10-0 75 JFEgan 6 73
(Tony Carroll) *hld up: effrt and rdn 2f out: 4th 1f out: no ex* **4/1**[3]

6000 **5** *3* **Canford Tor (IRE)**[21] 4255 3-8-10 65 (b[1]) DaneO'Neill 2 54
(Henry Candy) *slowly away and lost 5 l: effrt to latch on to pack 1/2-way: drvn over 2f out: sn rdn and wknd: eased* **12/1**

05-4 **6** *nk* **Eastern Lady (IND)**[21] 4279 4-9-2 68 (t) MitchGodwin(5) 1 58
(Richard Price) *in rr: effrt and drvn 3f out: rdn over 2f out: no imp* **25/1**

0522 **7** *3 ½* **Carcharias (IRE)**[6] 4846 4-8-12 62 CallumShepherd(3) 8 44
(Ed de Giles) *led at fast pce: hdd and drvn 3f out: sn lost pl: rdn and wknd* **9/4**[1]

1m 36.87s (0.67) **Going Correction** -0.05s/f (Good)
**WFA** 3 from 4yo+ 8lb 7 Ran SP% **112.3**
Speed ratings (Par 103): **94,92,91,89,86 86,82**
CSF £29.68 CT £137.01 TOTE £3.90: £1.90, £4.60; EX 29.40 Trifecta £116.00.
**Owner** Mrs Zara Campbell-Harris **Bred** Mrs Z C Campbell-Harris **Trained** Blewbury, Oxon

**FOCUS**
The runners came down the centre. This proved a true test at the trip as the runner-up and the beaten favourite contested the pace, clear of the remainder. The form is rated around the runner-up.

## 5050 188BET.CO.UK H'CAP 7f 16y
**3:25** (3:27) (Class 6) (0-55,55) 3-Y-O+ **£2,587** (£770; £384; £192) **Stalls** Centre

Form RPR
3302 **1** **Harbour Patrol (IRE)**[10] 4682 5-9-0 48 (b) DavidProbert 12 60
(Rebecca Bastiman) *in rr: prog 3f out: led 2f out: drvn 1f out: rdn and drifted lft ent fnl f: r.o* **6/1**[3]

3523 **2** *1 ¾* **Lawfilly**[9] 4713 3-8-12 53 (p) ShaneKelly 8 57
(Richard Hughes) *hld up: pushed along 3f out: effrt and n.m.r 2f out: hdwy and rdn ent fnl f: fashed tail: r.o wl to take 2nd cl home* **15/2**

0201 **3** *nse* **Magic Journey (IRE)**[10] 4688 3-8-13 54 PatCosgrave 4 58
(John Quinn) *trckd ldrs: hdwy and rdn over 1f out: sn in 2nd pl: rdn and one pce fnl f: lost 3rd cl home* **11/4**[1]

00-0 **4** *2* **She's Zoff (IRE)**[29] 3975 3-8-8 49 RyanPowell 3 48
(John Quinn) *prom: pushed along 2f out: rdn and ev ch 1f out: one pce* **50/1**

0-65 **5** *hd* **Prince Of Cardamom (IRE)**[85] 2095 5-8-13 54 (p) JordanUys(7) 10 56
(Jonathan Geake) *led: rdn and hdd 2f out: one pce fnl f* **12/1**

6502 **6** *2 ¾* **Altaira**[120] 1298 6-9-3 51 WilliamCarson 13 45
(Tony Carroll) *in rr: hdwy 2f out: rdn over 1f out: styd on fnl f* **12/1**

4420 **7** *¾* **Secret City (IRE)**[10] 4688 11-8-13 47 (b) RoystonFfrench 2 40
(Rebecca Bastiman) *in rr: drvn 3f out: hdwy u.p 2f out: r.o fnl f* **25/1**

-405 **8** *1* **Royal Melody**[24] 4162 3-8-7 53 MitchGodwin(5) 7 40
(Heather Main) *trckd ldrs: drvn over 1f out: no imp* **14/1**

3165 **9** *½* **Everkyllachy (IRE)**[41] 3536 3-9-0 55 (b) LiamKeniry 9 41
(J S Moore) *mid-div: effrt 1/2-way: prom gng wl 2f out: drvn over 1f out: wknd* **9/1**

4042 **10** *5* **Spare Parts (IRE)**[3] 4969 3-8-8 49 SamHitchcott 5 22
(Charles Hills) *prom: drvn and wknd in last 2f* **4/1**[2]

0-6 **11** *3* **Angelical Eve (IRE)**[84] 2112 3-9-0 55 SteveDrowne 6 20
(George Baker) *mid-div: pushed along 3f out: rdn 2f out: sn lost pl: eased* **25/1**

0504 **12** *6* **Provoking (USA)**[9] 4726 4-9-0 48 (v[1]) JFEgan 1
(David Evans) *prom: drvn and wknd 3f out* **10/1**

0530 **13** *½* **Bingo George (IRE)**[9] 4723 4-9-4 52 FranBerry 14
(Mark Rimell) *mid-div: hdwy 1/2-way: drvn over 2f out: wknd 1f out* **25/1**

0000 **14** *5* **The Perfect Show**[24] 4149 4-8-9 50 (b) KerrieRaybould(7) 17
(Milton Bradley) *slowly away: hdwy 1/2-way: ev ch 3f out: drvn and wknd qckly* **66/1**

0/0- **15** *2 ¾* **Blackadder**[396] 346 5-8-10 47 EdwardGreatrex(3) 11
(Mark Gillard) *prom tl lost pl 1/2-way: sn rdn and fdd* **100/1**

1m 23.63s (0.43) **Going Correction** -0.05s/f (Good)
**WFA** 3 from 4yo+ 7lb 15 Ran SP% **129.8**
Speed ratings (Par 101): **95,93,92,90,90 87,86,85,84,79 75,68,68,62,59**
CSF £51.75 CT £161.68 TOTE £8.10: £2.40, £2.90, £1.40; EX 46.80 Trifecta £163.40.
**Owner** Mrs P Bastiman **Bred** Kilfrush Stud **Trained** Cowthorpe, N Yorks

**FOCUS**
Low-grade handicap form. Four of the first seven represented a pair of Yorkshire-based stables. Those close up help to confirm the straightforward standard.

## 5051 GET 1/4 ODDS AT 188BET H'CAP 6f 16y
**4:00** (4:02) (Class 4) (0-80,82) 3-Y-O+ **£5,175** (£1,540; £769; £384) **Stalls** Centre

Form RPR
2210 **1** **Bahamian Dollar**[19] 4343 4-9-5 80 KatherineGlenister(7) 1 86
(David Evans) *prom: drvn to chal 2f out: 2nd over 1f out: rdn and led ent fnl f: chal last 100yds: hld on wl on nr fin* **9/2**[3]

0613 **2** *hd* **Farleigh Mac**[14] 4521 3-9-6 79 DavidProbert 8 83
(Andrew Balding) *prom: led 2f out: pushed along over 1f out: rdn and hdd ent fnl f: rallied last 100yds: jst hld* **2/1**[1]

3241 **3** *¾* **Morache Music**[17] 4441 9-9-9 77 (p) LiamKeniry 6 80
(Patrick Chamings) *hld up: last 1/2-way: hdwy 2f out: rdn 1f out: fin wl: nvr nrr* **10/1**

355 **4** *¾* **Bonjour Steve**[6] 4842 6-8-4 63 (p) MitchGodwin(5) 3 64
(Richard Price) *trckd ldrs: drvn 2f out: hdwy over 1f out: sn rdn: r.o one pce fnl f* **18/1**

0546 **5** *1 ¼* **Munfallet (IRE)**[16] 4477 6-10-0 82 PatCosgrave 5 79
(David Brown) *led: swtchd to stands' rail after 2f: rdn and hdd 2f out: one pce* **10/3**[2]

3103 **6** *nk* **Showmethewayavrilo**[8] 4752 4-9-1 69 DaneO'Neill 2 65
(Malcolm Saunders) *chsd ldrs: pushed along 2f out: rdn over 1f out: no ex* **8/1**

-150 **7** *3 ½* **Cinque Port**[69] 2567 3-9-4 77 ShaneKelly 4 60
(Richard Hughes) *hld up: drvn over 2f out: no imp* **12/1**

1500 **8** *½* **Juan Horsepower**[14] 4521 3-9-8 81 (p) KieranO'Neill 7 63
(Richard Hannon) *mid-div: drvn 2f out: wknd* **16/1**

0002 **9** *19* **Vincentti (IRE)**[17] 4441 7-9-0 68 (p) SamHitchcott 9
(Ronald Harris) *mid-div: drvn and lost pl 3f out: fdd qckly* **25/1**

1m 11.02s (-0.98) **Going Correction** -0.05s/f (Good)
**WFA** 3 from 4yo+ 5lb 9 Ran SP% **117.5**
Speed ratings (Par 105): **104,103,102,101,100 99,95,94,69**
CSF £14.17 CT £86.61 TOTE £4.90: £1.30, £1.60, £2.80; EX 19.00 Trifecta £106.30.
**Owner** Shropshire Wolves **Bred** Burns Farm Stud **Trained** Pandy, Monmouths

**FOCUS**
They came down the stands' side in this fair handicap. The winner found a bit more on his recent form.

## 5052 188BET H'CAP 5f 16y
**4:30** (4:32) (Class 6) (0-55,57) 3-Y-O+ **£2,587** (£770; £384; £192) **Stalls** Centre

Form RPR
6503 **1** **Toni's A Star**[14] 4531 5-9-1 54 AliceMills(5) 13 62
(Tony Carroll) *hld up: hdwy 2f out: reminder 1f out: pushed along to ld wl ins fnl f: cosily* **6/1**[3]

0501 **2** *nk* **Lucky Clover**[8] 4731 6-9-9 57 6ex (p) DaneO'Neill 10 64
(Malcolm Saunders) *prom: rdn and led ent fnl f: r.o but sn hdd and hld* **9/4**[1]

5455 **3** *½* **David's Beauty (IRE)**[24] 4148 4-9-5 53 (p) PatCosgrave 11 58
(Brian Baugh) *prom: led over 2f out: rdn over 1f out: hdd ent fnl f: no ex* **11/2**[2]

6606 **4** *½* **Rebel Heart**[33] 3818 3-9-2 54 (v) WilliamCarson 12 56
(Bill Turner) *hld up: hdwy over 2f out: sn rdn: r.o ins fnl f* **12/1**

6022 **5** *¾* **Minty Jones**[16] 4479 8-8-9 46 (v) EdwardGreatrex(3) 2 47+
(Michael Mullineaux) *chsd ldrs: hdwy and drvn 2f out: rdn over 1f out: no ex* **15/2**

4330 **6** *1* **Mostashreqah**[8] 4731 4-8-5 46 oh1 (p) KatherineGlenister(7) 9 43
(Milton Bradley) *prom: 4th and pushed along over 2f out: rdn over 1f out: one pce* **10/1**

660 **7** *1 ¾* **Celerity (IRE)**[24] 4148 3-8-8 46 oh1 (v) JFEgan 5 36
(David Evans) *led: hdd over 2f out: sn rdn and one pce* **25/1**

0044 **8** *hd* **Tally's Song**[8] 4735 4-8-12 46 oh1 (p) MartinDwyer 16 36
(Grace Harris) *in rr: pushed along 1/2-way: rdn over 1f out: no imp* **16/1**

5540 **9** *nk* **Ginger Truffle**[16] 4458 3-8-9 47 JohnFahy 8 35
(Brett Johnson) *slowly away: drvn 1/2-way: mod late hdwy* **8/1**

3653 **10** *1* **Hot Stuff**[56] 2995 4-9-7 55 DavidProbert 1 40
(Tony Carroll) *chsd ldrs: pushed along 1/2-way: rdn over 1f out: no imp* **9/1**

-000 **11** *1 ½* **She's Rosanna**[8] 4735 3-8-8 46 oh1 (t[1]) RoystonFfrench 3 25
(Steph Hollinshead) *hld up: rdn 2f out: no imp* **33/1**

-000 **12** *17* **Wilspa's Magic (IRE)**[44] 3422 4-8-12 46 KieranO'Neill 7
(Ron Hodges) *mid-div: pushed along and lost pl 1/2-way: wknd qckly: eased* **50/1**

59.63s (0.33) **Going Correction** -0.05s/f (Good)
**WFA** 3 from 4yo+ 4lb 12 Ran SP% **124.7**
Speed ratings (Par 101): **95,94,93,92,91 90,87,87,86,84 82,55**
CSF £20.62 CT £83.62 TOTE £7.30: £2.10, £1.70, £1.90; EX 26.20 Trifecta £130.50.
**Owner** A Star Recruitment Ltd **Bred** Paul Green **Trained** Cropthorne, Worcs

**FOCUS**
They were spread right across the track in this very modest sprint. The winner came down the centre, with the next three on the stands' side, high numbers dominating. Straightforward form.

## 5053 PLAY ROULETTE AT 188BET H'CAP 1m 2f
5:05 (5:06) (Class 5) (0-70,71) 3-Y-O+ £3,234 (£962; £481; £240) Stalls Low

Form RPR
1433 1 **Avocadeau (IRE)**[27] 4040 6-9-0 **54**.....(t[1]) MartinDwyer 4 61
(Stuart Kittow) *led at sedate gallop: grad wound up pce fr 4f out: pushed along 2f out: rdn over 1f out: 1 l clr ent fnl f: extended advantage: comf* 13/2
-106 2 1 3/4 **Evening Hill**[14] 4537 3-9-8 **71**..... ShaneKelly 7 74
(Richard Hughes) *mid-div hdwy 3f out: pushed along and ev ch over 2f out: rdn in 3rd over 1f out: r.o fnl f: snatched 2nd nr fin* 7/4[1]
3063 3 shd **Challow (IRE)**[21] 4255 3-9-3 **66**..... LiamKeniry 5 69
(Sylvester Kirk) *cl 2nd: pushed along over 2f out: rdn over 1f out: lost grnd on wnr ent fnl f: hdd for 2nd nr fin* 4/1[2]
335 4 shd **Frantical**[34] 3771 5-9-2 **56**.....(p) WilliamCarson 1 58
(Tony Carroll) *trckd ldrs: drvn 2f out: rdn over 1f out: r.o ins fnl f* 8/1
4033 5 3/4 **Matravers**[14] 4523 6-10-0 **68**..... TimmyMurphy 6 68
(Mary Hambro) *mid-div: plld out to chal wl over 1f out: sn rdn: no imp* 6/1[3]
050 6 10 **Arrowzone**[13] 4575 6-9-11 **65**..... RyanPowell 3 45
(Kevin Frost) *in rr: bustled along 4f out: drvn 3f out: wknd* 25/1
044/ 7 7 **Be Seeing You**[10] 8239 6-9-4 **65**.....(bt) WilliamCox(7) 8 31
(Trevor Wall) *slowly away: in rr: drvn 4f out: sn lost tch* 33/1
2m 8.94s (-1.66) **Going Correction** -0.05s/f (Good)
**WFA** 3 from 5yo+ 9lb 7 Ran SP% **101.9**
Speed ratings (Par 103): **104,102,102,102,101 93,88**
CSF £14.46 CT £34.93 TOTE £4.80: £2.90, £1.50; EX 13.20 Trifecta £49.60.
**Owner** Mrs S Clapp & Mrs L Sharpe **Bred** Wiji Bloodstock & Ceka Ltd **Trained** Blackborough, Devon
■ Ski Blast was withdrawn. Price at time of withdrawal 7-1. Rule 4 applies to all bets. Deduction - 10p in the pound.
**FOCUS**
The first race of the day on the round course, and the winner dictated from the front. It may pay not to interpret the form too literally. The winner built on his spring form.

## 5054 BOXING BETTING AT 188BET APPRENTICE H'CAP 1m 4f
5:35 (5:36) (Class 6) (0-65,65) 4-Y-O+ £2,587 (£770; £384; £192) Stalls Low

Form RPR
-051 1 **Tobougaloo**[6] 4840 6-9-0 **65** 6ex..... WilliamCox(7) 2 75+
(Stuart Kittow) *trckd ldrs: n.m.r and briefly snatched up 5f out: plld out to chal over 2f out: sn led gng wl: rdn over 1f out: wnt lft and hmpd runner-up ent fnl f: stened up and qckly c clr: readily* 10/11[1]
0024 2 2 1/2 **St Andrews (IRE)**[37] 3698 4-8-8 **52**.....(t[1]) AdamMcNamara 3 58
(Ian Williams) *trckd ldr: led over 3f out: rdn over 2f out: sn hdd: trying to rally whn hmpd ent fnl f: no ex* 5/1[3]
1043 3 2 1/2 **Pour L'Amour (IRE)**[23] 4169 4-9-7 **65**..... CharlieBennett 4 66
(Daniel Mark Loughnane) *hld up in last: pushed along 3f out: rdn over 2f out: hdwy appr fnl f: r.o to take 3rd nr fin* 7/2[2]
0-43 4 1/2 **Ocean Gale**[23] 4187 4-8-6 **50**..... CallumShepherd 5 50
(Richard Price) *racd in 3rd: wnt cl 2nd 3f out: drvn over 2f out: sn lft bhd by front two: rdn over 1f out: one pce fnl f: lost 3rd nr fin* 5/1[3]
00-0 5 54 **Arthur's Queen (FR)**[16] 4469 6-8-5 **49**..... EdwardGreatrex 1
(Carroll Gray) *led: drvn and hdd over 3f out: sn rdn and wknd: heavily eased* 33/1
2m 36.69s (-2.31) **Going Correction** -0.05s/f (Good) 5 Ran SP% **110.9**
Speed ratings (Par 101): **105,103,101,101,65**
CSF £6.01 TOTE £1.90: £1.10, £2.10; EX 7.10 Trifecta £14.50.
**Owner** Dr G S Plastow **Bred** D R Tucker **Trained** Blackborough, Devon
■ Stewards' Enquiry : William Cox 2 day ban - guilty of careless riding in that he allowed his mount to shift left away from the whip (4/5 Aug)
**FOCUS**
They went a decent pace for the first section of this minor apprentice handicap before it slowed as they approached the home turn. The winner won well but it's hard to be too positive about the form.
T/Jkpt: Not Won. T/Plt: £10.90 to a £1 stake. Pool: £74,496.79 - 4,979.76 winning units. T/Qpdt: £9.90 to a £1 stake. Pool: £4,836.76 - 358.98 winning units. **Keith McHugh**

# 4791 DONCASTER (L-H)
Thursday, July 20

**OFFICIAL GOING: Good (good to soft in places; watered; 7.5)**
Wind: Moderate against Weather: Sunny

## 5055 NAPOLEONS CASINOS & RESTAURANTS SHEFFIELD APPRENTICE H'CAP 5f 3y
5:40 (5:40) (Class 5) (0-70,72) 3-Y-O+ £2,911 (£866; £432; £216) Stalls Low

Form RPR
3266 1 **Muatadel**[5] 4896 4-9-9 **70**..... BenSanderson(3) 1 77
(Roger Fell) *prom: effrt 2f out: rdn to ld 1 1/2f out: edgd rt ins fnl f: kpt on* 4/1[3]
-000 2 3/4 **Point Of Woods**[15] 4509 4-9-4 **62**..... ConnorMurtagh 6 66
(Tina Jackson) *hld up in tch: hdwy 2f out: rdn and ev ch ins fnl f: kpt on same pce towards fin* 7/1
0050 3 shd **Bond Bombshell**[11] 4664 4-9-7 **65**.....(p) PatrickVaughan 3 69
(David O'Meara) *hld up in rr: hdwy wl over 1f out: rdn to chal ins fnl f and ev ch: kpt on same pce towards fin* 16/1
2164 4 3/4 **Oriental Splendour (IRE)**[17] 4433 5-10-0 **72**..... BenRobinson 4 73
(Ruth Carr) *trckd ldrs: effrt 2f out: rdn over 1f out: kpt on same pce* 5/2[1]
0531 5 3/4 **Archimedes (IRE)**[2] 4993 4-9-6 **67** 6ex.....(tp) ManuelFernandes(3) 5 66
(David C Griffiths) *sn led: pushed along over 2f out: hdd and rdn 1 1/2f out: wknd ent fnl f* 11/4[2]
504 6 1 1/2 **Kiringa**[31] 3903 4-8-8 **57**..... JonathanFisher(5) 8 50
(Robert Cowell) *trckd ldrs: pushed along over 2f out: rdn over 1f out: sn no imp* 8/1
4403 7 shd **Roy's Legacy**[11] 4664 8-9-1 **64**..... SebastianWoods(5) 10 57
(Shaun Harris) *cl up: rdn along over 2f out: sn drvn and wknd over 1f out* 20/1
1m 1.95s (1.45) **Going Correction** +0.375s/f (Good)
**WFA** 3 from 4yo+ 4lb 7 Ran SP% **109.5**
Speed ratings (Par 103): **103,101,101,100,99 96,96**
CSF £28.68 CT £364.68 TOTE £4.60: £2.10, £4.90; EX 33.00 Trifecta £255.90.
**Owner** R G Fell **Bred** Lofts Hall Stud & B Sangster **Trained** Nawton, N Yorks

**FOCUS**
An ordinary sprint handicap for apprentices and the for is unlikely to be strong. A small pb from the winner.

## 5056 TRENT REFRACTORIES EBF MAIDEN FILLIES' STKS (PLUS 10 RACE) 7f 6y
6:10 (6:12) (Class 5) 2-Y-O £2,911 (£866; £432; £216) Stalls Low

Form RPR
1 **Laurens (FR)** 2-9-0 0..... PJMcDonald 6 83+
(K R Burke) *dwlt: hld up towards rr: smooth hdwy 1/2-way: trckd ldrs over 2f out: rdn to ld 1 1/2f out: edgd rt ins fnl f: kpt on wl* 9/2[3]
2 nk **Exhort** 2-9-0 0..... PatrickMathers 9 81+
(Richard Fahey) *trckd ldrs: hdwy over 2f out: sn cl up: rdn to chal over 1f out: swtchd lft ins fnl f: kpt on wl towards fin* 16/1
42 3 2 3/4 **Sultanaa**[19] 4340 2-9-0 0..... SilvestreDeSousa 2 74
(Ismail Mohammed) *towards rr: stdy hdwy wl over 2f out: chsd ldrs over 1f out: sn rdn and kpt on same pce fnl f* 7/2[2]
52 4 1/2 **Tig Tog (IRE)**[21] 4253 2-9-0 0..... SeanLevey 1 73
(Richard Hannon) *towards rr: hdwy 3f out: chsd ldrs on inner wl over 1f out: sn rdn and kpt on same pce* 7/2[2]
5 4 **Shaherezada (IRE)** 2-9-1 0 ow1..... AdamKirby 16 63
(Clive Cox) *dwlt and wnt rt at s: green and sn pushed along in rr: hdwy wl over 1f out: kpt on fnl f* 25/1
6 hd **Rayna's World (IRE)** 2-9-0 0..... TomEaves 10 62+
(Philip Kirby) *dwlt and hld up in rr: hdwy over 2f out: rdn over 1f out: kpt on fnl f* 100/1
7 1 1/2 **Piccola Collina (IRE)** 2-9-0 0..... WilliamBuick 14 58+
(Charlie Appleby) *midfield: hdwy and in tch over 2f out: green and sn rdn along: kpt on fnl f* 9/4[1]
23 8 2 **Vodka Pigeon**[20] 4312 2-9-0 0..... RichardKingscote 8 53
(Tom Dascombe) *prom: rdn along over 2f out: grad wknd* 9/1
000 9 1 **Elixsoft (IRE)**[44] 3430 2-8-7 **50**..... BenSanderson(7) 15 50
(Roger Fell) *cl up: rdn to take slt ld jst over 2f out: hdd 1 1/2f out: sn drvn: edgd lft and wknd* 100/1
00 10 3 1/4 **Milan Reef (IRE)**[36] 3712 2-9-0 0..... SamJames 13 42
(David Loughnane) *chsd ldrs on outer: rdn along over 2f out: sn wknd* 100/1
0 11 1 1/2 **Miss Perception**[25] 4116 2-9-0 0..... MartinHarley 3 38
(Tom Dascombe) *in tch on inner: pushed along 3f out: rdn over 2f out: sn one pce* 66/1
12 1 **Lucky Reset** 2-9-0 0..... SaleemGolam 12 35
(David Evans) *dwlt: a towards rr* 66/1
5 13 1 1/2 **Princess Jessica (FR)**[21] 4273 2-8-7 0..... ConnorMurtagh(7) 5 31
(Richard Fahey) *in tch: rdn along over 2f out: sn wknd* 66/1
0 14 2 1/2 **Madame Jo Jo**[25] 4116 2-8-11 0..... CliffordLee(3) 11 25
(Sarah Hollinshead) *led: rdn along and hdd jst over 2f out: sn wknd* 150/1
0 15 3 1/2 **Headwear (IRE)**[32] 3858 2-9-0 0..... PhillipMakin 4 16
(David Brown) *chsd ldrs on inner: rdn along wl over 2f out: sn wknd* 66/1
1m 28.72s (2.42) **Going Correction** +0.375s/f (Good) 15 Ran SP% **122.7**
Speed ratings (Par 91): **101,100,97,96,92 92,90,88,87,83 81,80,78,75,71**
CSF £72.37 TOTE £5.30: £1.70, £4.40, £1.60; EX 85.60 Trifecta £347.90.
**Owner** John Dance **Bred** Bloodstock Agency Ltd **Trained** Middleham Moor, N Yorks
**FOCUS**
Quite an interesting maiden for juvenile fillies. The early pace wasn't overly strong and the finish was fought out by two newcomers. The form is taken at face value around the third and fourth.

## 5057 ERIC WILSON MEMORIAL FILLIES' NURSERY H'CAP 6f 2y
6:40 (6:41) (Class 4) 2-Y-O £4,204 (£1,251; £625; £312) Stalls Low

Form RPR
066 1 **Song Of Summer**[20] 4296 2-8-0 **65**..... JimmyQuinn 5 66
(Archie Watson) *hld up: hdwy 2f out: rdn to chal ent fnl f: kpt on wl to ld nr fin* 7/1[3]
4510 2 nk **Silca Mistress**[19] 4361 2-8-6 **71**..... SilvestreDeSousa 4 72+
(Mick Channon) *trckd ldrs: hdwy 2f out: n.m.r and swtchd lft to inner over 1f out: sn rdn: slt ld ins fnl f: drvn and hdd towards fin* 5/2[1]
453 3 nk **Miss Mo Brown Bear (IRE)**[22] 4212 2-8-6 **71**..... TomMarquand 3 70
(Richard Hannon) *t.k.h: cl up: disp ld 1/2-way: rdn and ev ch ent fnl f: sn drvn and kpt on same pce towards fin* 7/1[3]
553 4 3/4 **Moonlit Sands (IRE)**[13] 4555 2-8-3 **68**..... PatrickMathers 1 65
(Brian Ellison) *trckd ldrs on inner: hdwy to ld 2f out: rdn over 1f out: drvn and hdd ins fnl f: kpt on same pce* 10/1
210 5 hd **Miss Bar Beach (IRE)**[27] 4028 2-9-9 **88**..... ConnorBeasley 7 84
(Keith Dalgleish) *t.k.h: trckd ldrs: hdwy over 2f out: rdn and ev ch over 1f out: hld whn n.m.r ins fnl f* 4/1[2]
325 6 9 **Donny Belle**[33] 3826 2-8-7 **72**..... JosephineGordon 6 41
(David Brown) *cl up: rdn along over 2f out: sn drvn and wknd* 8/1
210 7 4 **Miss Dd (IRE)**[19] 4361 2-8-10 **75**.....(p) RichardKingscote 2 32
(Tom Dascombe) *led: pushed along 1/2-way: rdn and hdd 2f out: sn wknd* 4/1[2]
1m 16.01s (2.41) **Going Correction** +0.375s/f (Good) 7 Ran SP% **113.8**
Speed ratings (Par 93): **98,97,97,96,95 83,78**
CSF £24.62 TOTE £7.30: £2.80, £3.10; EX 30.50 Trifecta £202.50.
**Owner** Al Asayl Bloodstock Ltd **Bred** Al Asayl Bloodstock Ltd **Trained** Upper Lambourn, W Berks
**FOCUS**
A 6f nursery for fillies in which five were virtually in line abreast crossing the line. The runner-up had no luck through the race and was an unlucky loser. It has to rate as ordinary form.

## 5058 SAINT GOBAIN WEBER NOVICE STKS (PLUS 10 RACE) 6f 2y
7:15 (7:17) (Class 4) 2-Y-O £4,204 (£1,251; £625; £312) Stalls Low

Form RPR
0 1 **Make Good (IRE)**[13] 4567 2-9-2 0..... PhillipMakin 8 78
(David Brown) *trckd ldng pair: hdwy 2f out and sn cl up: rdn to ld ins fnl f: kpt on strly* 33/1
2 2 1/2 **Beatbox Rhythm (IRE)** 2-9-2 0..... PJMcDonald 4 71
(K R Burke) *led: pushed along and jnd wl over 1f out: rdn and hdd ins fnl f: sn edgd rt and kpt on same pce* 10/3[3]
6 3 1/2 **Divine Intuition (IRE)**[37] 3690 2-9-2 0..... SeanLevey 9 69
(Richard Hannon) *t.k.h: trckd ldr: pushed along 2f out: rdn wl over 1f out: kpt on u.p fnl f* 11/4[2]
4 1 3/4 **Hippeia (IRE)** 2-8-11 0..... ConnorBeasley 3 59
(Jedd O'Keeffe) *in tch: green and pushed along over 2f out: rdn and kpt on fnl f* 16/1
4 5 1/2 **Shootingthe Breeze**[13] 4577 2-9-2 0..... RichardKingscote 7 62
(Tom Dascombe) *in tch: pushed along 1/2-way: rdn along 2f out: sn no imp* 9/4[1]

0 **6** 4 1/2 **She's Different (IRE)**[13] 4567 2-8-11 0 TomEaves 1 44
(Nigel Tinkler) *dwlt: a towards rr* **20/1**
**7** 12 **Stark Reality (IRE)** 2-8-11 0 SilvestreDeSousa 6 8
(Nigel Tinkler) *a towards rr* **12/1**
**8** 2 **Smugglers Top** 2-9-2 0 MartinHarley 2 7
(Tom Dascombe) *dwlt: a in rr* **8/1**

1m 15.97s (2.37) **Going Correction** +0.375s/f (Good) **8** Ran SP% **112.9**
Speed ratings (Par 96): **99,95,95,92,92 86,70,67**
CSF £136.95 TOTE £29.00: £5.00, £1.40, £1.30; EX 40.60 Trifecta £715.10.
**Owner** J C Fretwell **Bred** Ivan And Mrs Eileen Heanen **Trained** Averham Park, Notts

**FOCUS**
A race won last year by Blue Point but there looked nothing of his calibre this time, in fact it looked a pretty ordinary contest and not a race likely to throw many future winners.

## 5059 FRENCHGATE FASHION H'CAP 7f 6y
**7:50** (7:50) (Class 3) (0-90,91) 3-Y-O+ **£7,439** (£2,213; £1,106; £553) **Stalls** Low

Form RPR
3103 **1** **Firefright (IRE)**[12] 4634 3-9-3 **85** WilliamBuick 7 93+
(Jeremy Noseda) *t.k.h: trckd ldrs: pushed along 2f out: hdwy to ld over 1f out: rdn and qcknd clr ent fnl f: readily* **5/4**[1]
0053 **2** 2 1/4 **Athassel**[6] 4844 8-9-5 **80** PJMcDonald 3 85
(David Evans) *hld up: hdwy over 2f out: chsd ldrs over 1f out: sn swtchd lft and rdn: styd on to chse wnr ins fnl f: no imp* **14/1**
5-51 **3** 1 **Redgrave (IRE)**[20] 4311 3-8-13 **81** (h) SilvestreDeSousa 10 80
(Charles Hills) *hld up in tch: hdwy on wd outside over 1f out: rdn to chse ldrs ent fnl f: sn edgd lft and no imp* **4/1**[2]
3005 **4** 1/2 **Sakhee's Return**[26] 4103 5-9-5 **80** (t) DavidAllan 6 81
(Tim Easterby) *dwlt: sn trcking ldrs: hdwy to chal 2f out: sn ev ch: rdn over 1f out and kpt on same pce fnl f* **5/1**[3]
5-00 **5** 1 1/4 **Tukhoom (IRE)**[19] 4339 4-9-0 **75** JoeDoyle 2 73
(Michael Herrington) *prom: hdwy and cl up over 2f out: rdn wl over 1f out: wknd appr fnl f* **10/1**
4-00 **6** 3/4 **Zaeem**[155] 736 8-9-4 **79** JosephineGordon 4 74
(Ivan Furtado) *set stdy pce: rdn and qcknd over 2f out: drvn and hdd over 1f out: sn wknd* **33/1**
1021 **7** 1 1/4 **Explain**[20] 4294 5-9-13 **88** (p) TomEaves 5 80
(Ruth Carr) *hld up and bhd: hdwy 2f out: rdn wl over 1f out: n.d* **10/1**
0-00 **8** 3 **Farlow (IRE)**[19] 4353 9-9-9 **87** SammyJoBell(3) 8 71
(Richard Fahey) *cl up: rdn along wl over 2f out: sn wknd* **16/1**

1m 28.62s (2.32) **Going Correction** +0.375s/f (Good)
**WFA** 3 from 4yo+ 7lb **8** Ran SP% **114.8**
Speed ratings (Par 107): **101,98,97,96,95 94,93,89**
CSF £21.66 CT £57.86 TOTE £2.00: £1.10, £3.60, £1.50; EX 17.50 Trifecta £70.00.
**Owner** Mrs Susan Roy **Bred** Mighty Universe Ltd **Trained** Newmarket, Suffolk

**FOCUS**
Quite a valuable 7f handicap but the pace was ordinary and the majority were exposed sorts. The winner is rated to his best, the runner-up to his best.

## 5060 YESSS ELECTRICAL DAVE BARBER MEMORIAL H'CAP 1m 2f 43y
**8:20** (8:22) (Class 4) (0-85,84) 4-Y-O+ **£4,851** (£1,443; £721; £360) **Stalls** Low

Form RPR
-436 **1** **Desert Way (IRE)**[23] 4170 4-9-0 **77** PJMcDonald 9 87
(Rebecca Menzies) *dwlt: hld up towards rr: hdwy on outer 3f out: chsd ldrs 2f out: rdn and edgd lft over 1f out: drvn to ld ent fnl f: kpt on strly* **25/1**
0050 **2** 3 1/2 **Parish Boy**[19] 4336 5-9-1 **78** JosephineGordon 4 81
(David Loughnane) *dwlt: hld up towards rr: hdwy over 3f out: rdn to chse ldrs wl over 1f out: drvn and kpt on fnl f* **20/1**
-243 **3** 1/2 **Lexington Law (IRE)**[44] 3427 4-9-6 **83** TomMarquand 8 85
(Alan King) *hld up in tch: hdwy 3f out: sn trcking ldrs: effrt and nt clr run over 1f out: sn rdn and kpt on fnl f* **8/1**
1-3U **4** 2 1/2 **First Voyage (IRE)**[8] 4763 4-9-6 **83** (p) WilliamBuick 7 80
(Charlie Appleby) *trckd ldr: hdwy and cl up over 3f out: led 2f out: sn rdn: drvn and hdd ent fnl f: wknd* **2/1**[1]
2333 **5** 1 **Sellingallthetime (IRE)**[7] 4796 6-8-9 **72** (p) SilvestreDeSousa 6 67
(Michael Appleby) *trckd ldrs: pushed along over 3f out: rdn over 2f out: sn drvn and one pce* **7/2**[2]
3144 **6** nk **Energia Fox (BRZ)**[10] 4692 7-9-0 **84** ConnorMurtagh(7) 1 78
(Richard Fahey) *trckd ldrs: hdwy 4f out: cl up 3f out: rdn and ev ch wl over 1f out: drvn and wknd appr fnl f* **12/1**
-211 **7** 2 1/2 **Vernatti**[51] 3168 4-9-4 **81** RobHornby 5 70
(Pam Sly) *led: pushed along 3f out: rdn and hdd 2f out: sn drvn and wknd* **9/2**[3]
4120 **8** 1 **Boycie**[21] 4254 4-8-9 **79** TinaSmith(7) 3 66
(Richard Hannon) *hld up: hdwy 4f out: trckd ldrs 3f out: effrt over 2f out: sn rdn and wknd over 1f out* **7/1**

2m 12.61s (3.21) **Going Correction** +0.375s/f (Good) **8** Ran SP% **113.6**
Speed ratings (Par 105): **102,99,98,96,96 95,93,92**
CSF £414.36 CT £4299.49 TOTE £16.30: £4.40, £4.00, £2.10; EX 213.20 Trifecta £1610.60.
**Owner** Titanium Racing Club **Bred** J H Richmond-Watson **Trained** Mordon, Durham

**FOCUS**
Add 18 yards to the official distance. Just an ordinary handicap run at a solid gallop in which the hold-up horses dominated the finish. The winner is rated back to her best.

## 5061 EVANS HALSHAW RENAULT CROSSOVER EVENT H'CAP 1m 3f 197y
**8:50** (8:51) (Class 5) (0-70,72) 3-Y-O **£2,911** (£866; £432; £216) **Stalls** Low

Form RPR
0032 **1** **Ingleby Mackenzie**[8] 4738 3-9-1 **62** SilvestreDeSousa 5 64
(Mick Channon) *t.k.h: trckd ldr: hdwy 3f out: cl up 2f out and sn rdn: drvn over 1f out: styd on u.p to ld nr fin* **15/8**[1]
62-2 **2** 1/2 **American History (USA)**[174] 437 3-9-11 **72** (b) PhillipMakin 10 73
(William Muir) *led: styd on far rail early in home st: swtchd rt to join field in centre and stl gng wl: rdn over 1f out: drvn ins fnl f: rdr dropped reins 100yds out: hdd nr fin* **13/2**[3]
-050 **3** 1/2 **Trautmann (IRE)**[23] 4171 3-8-9 **56** AndrewMullen 6 56
(Daniel Mark Loughnane) *hld up: hdwy over 3f out: trckd ldrs over 2f out: sn rdn: drvn to chse ldg pair over 1f out: kpt on wl towards fin* **25/1**
-400 **4** 1 3/4 **Two Dollars (IRE)**[31] 3909 3-9-6 **67** (h[1]) PJMcDonald 8 64
(William Jarvis) *hld up: hdwy 3f out: rdn along to chse ldrs 2f out: sn drvn and no imp fnl f* **8/1**
0-15 **5** 15 **London Master**[65] 2711 3-9-4 **65** AdamBeschizza 7 38
(Chris Wall) *trckd ldg pair: pushed along 3f out: rdn over 2f out: sn drvn and wknd* **3/1**[2]

533 **6** 26 **Temir Kazyk**[113] 1420 3-9-7 **68** AndreaAtzeni 1
(David Simcock) *trckd ldg pair on inner: pushed along 4f out: rdn over 3f out: sn btn and eased* **3/1**[2]

2m 39.97s (5.07) **Going Correction** +0.375s/f (Good) **6** Ran SP% **113.1**
Speed ratings (Par 100): **98,97,97,96,86 68**
CSF £14.87 CT £222.84 TOTE £2.70: £1.30, £2.30; EX 13.70 Trifecta £146.50.
**Owner** M Channon **Bred** Mike Channon Bloodstock Ltd **Trained** West Ilsley, Berks

**FOCUS**
Run over 18 yards further than advertised. A stop-start gallop with the first two being the first two throughout, the first four were clear and overall likely to be weakish form. The second looks the best guide.
T/Plt: £967.80 to a £1 stake. Pool: £77,881.35 - 58.74 winning units. T/Qpdt: £150.90 to a £1 stake. Pool: £8,241.80 - 40.41 winning units. **Joe Rowntree**

# 4798 EPSOM (L-H)
### Thursday, July 20

**OFFICIAL GOING: Good to soft (6.7)**
Wind: Fresh, against, becoming half against Weather: Cloudy becoming fine

## 5062 BET TOTEPLACEPOT AT BETFRED.COM APPRENTICE H'CAP 1m 113y
**6:00** (6:00) (Class 5) (0-75,77) 4-Y-O+ **£3,881** (£1,155; £577; £288) **Stalls** Low

Form RPR
105- **1** **Midnight Whistler (USA)**[282] 7245 5-9-11 **73** (p) GeorgeWood 1 79
(Martyn Meade) *trckd ldr: led on inner 2f out: drvn and narrow advantage after: hld on* **7/2**[2]
0-24 **2** nk **Chosen Character (IRE)**[26] 4085 9-9-8 **77** (vt) ElishaWhittington(7) 8 82
(Tom Dascombe) *mde most to 2f out: pressed wnr after: urged along and kpt on ins fnl f: jst hld* **6/1**[3]
332 **3** 6 **Stosur (IRE)**[28] 4010 6-9-12 **74** (b) KieranShoemark 5 65
(Gay Kelleway) *chsd ldng pair: rdn and lft bhd by them fr 2f out: clung on for 3rd* **3/1**[1]
0663 **4** 1 **Ravenhoe (IRE)**[6] 4833 4-9-5 **70** RichardOliver(3) 3 59
(Mark Johnston) *dwlt: sn in 4th: rdn over 2f out: lft bhd by ldng pair sn after: one pce* **7/2**[2]
4404 **5** 3/4 **Rattle On**[13] 4587 4-8-11 **62** (p) PaddyBradley(3) 6 49
(Jim Boyle) *hld up in last pair: shkn up and effrt over 2f out: readily lft bhd by ldng pair sn after: fdd ins fnl f* **7/1**
-035 **6** nse **Ede's The Mover**[28] 4010 4-8-0 **55** oh1 SophieRalston(7) 7 42
(Pat Phelan) *hld up in last pair: outpcd 3f out: no ch after: pushed along and kpt on ins fnl f* **7/1**

1m 47.98s (1.88) **Going Correction** +0.25s/f (Good) **6** Ran SP% **108.7**
Speed ratings (Par 103): **101,100,95,94,93 93**
CSF £22.38 CT £60.92 TOTE £4.20: £2.20, £2.30; EX 20.10 Trifecta £91.20.
**Owner** Sefton Lodge (Thoroughbred Racing) **Bred** Kirk Wycoff & Deby Wycoff **Trained** Newmarket, Suffolk

**FOCUS**
All race distances as advertised. After a further 3mm of rain during the morning the going was changed to good to soft. A fair apprentice handicap in which it paid to race handy, the front two being up there throughout.

## 5063 BRITISH STALLION STUDS EBF MAIDEN STKS 7f 3y
**6:30** (6:30) (Class 5) 2-Y-O **£3,881** (£1,155; £577; £288) **Stalls** Low

Form RPR
6 **1** **Doublet (IRE)**[14] 4520 2-9-5 0 FrannyNorton 7 81
(Mark Johnston) *mde all: shkn up 2f out: styd on wl and asserted over 1f out* **10/3**[2]
**2** 2 **Algam (IRE)** 2-9-5 0 TomQueally 6 76+
(Richard Hannon) *dwlt: sn pushed up to press wnr: shkn up to chal 2f out: rn green and hld 1f out: jst hld on for 2nd* **8/1**[3]
032 **3** shd **Dichato (USA)**[21] 4266 2-9-5 **83** KieranShoemark 5 76+
(John Gosden) *racd in 4th: rdn wl over 2f out and hanging: no prog tl kpt on to take 3rd ins fnl f and nrly snatched 2nd* **4/5**[1]
4 **4** 1 1/4 **Arrogant (IRE)**[27] 4044 2-9-2 0 HollieDoyle(3) 1 72
(Jose Santos) *chsd ldng pair: rdn and no imp 2f out: one pce after and lost 3rd ins fnl f* **50/1**
U20 **5** 5 **Rivas Rob Roy**[13] 4583 2-9-2 0 HectorCrouch(3) 4 59
(John Gallagher) *hld up: 6th st: rdn over 2f out: sn no prog and btn* **16/1**
00 **6** 2 1/2 **Font Vert (FR)**[14] 4520 2-9-0 0 DavidEgan(5) 2 53
(Ralph Beckett) *hld up: 5th st: jst pushed along fr over 2f out and steadily wknd* **11/1**
66 **7** 19 **Erastus**[55] 3025 2-9-5 0 CharlesBishop 3
(Mick Channon) *dwlt: a last: wknd over 2f out: t.o* **20/1**

1m 25.35s (2.05) **Going Correction** +0.25s/f (Good) **7** Ran SP% **110.7**
Speed ratings (Par 94): **98,95,95,94,88 85,63**
CSF £27.46 TOTE £4.60: £1.90, £3.20; EX 27.10 Trifecta £54.40.
**Owner** Sheikh Hamdan bin Mohammed Al Maktoum **Bred** T & B Jones **Trained** Middleham Moor, N Yorks

**FOCUS**
An interesting maiden and the winner was never headed.

## 5064 BET TOTEQUADPOT AT BETFRED.COM H'CAP 7f 3y
**7:00** (7:00) (Class 4) (0-85,86) 3-Y-O+ **£6,469** (£1,925; £962; £481) **Stalls** Low

Form RPR
5102 **1** **Frank Bridge**[14] 4523 4-9-9 **80** CharlesBishop 4 91
(Eve Johnson Houghton) *trckd ldr: rdn to chal 2f out: narrow ld fnl f: all out and jst hld on* **5/2**[1]
2361 **2** shd **Handytalk (IRE)**[15] 4489 4-9-11 **82** OisinMurphy 7 92
(Rod Millman) *led: hrd pressed and shkn up 2f out: narrowly hdd and drvn fnl f: kpt on wl: jst failed* **3/1**[2]
0304 **3** 2 1/2 **Sarangoo**[8] 4746 9-8-12 **74** GeorgiaCox(5) 2 77
(Malcolm Saunders) *hld up in 5th: nt handle downhill that wl: rdn over 2f out: nvr on terms w ldng pair but kpt on fnl f* **5/1**[3]
-651 **4** hd **Human Nature (IRE)**[8] 4746 4-9-2 **80** (t) MillyNaseb(7) 1 83
(Stuart Williams) *cl up: 3rd on st: rdn over 2f out: one pce and no imp on ldrs after* **3/1**[2]
0-00 **5** 3 **Carnival King (IRE)**[61] 2833 5-9-10 **86** (b) DavidEgan(5) 5 81
(Amy Murphy) *pressed ldrs on outer tl 4th and rdn st: sn struggling u.p: wl btn 2f out* **14/1**
450 **6** 6 **Saleh (IRE)**[8] 4746 4-9-1 **77** PaddyBradley(5) 6 55
(Lee Carter) *hld up: a last: lost tch 3f out: pushed along and no prog after* **11/1**

1m 24.02s (0.72) **Going Correction** +0.25s/f (Good)
**WFA** 3 from 4yo+ 7lb **6** Ran SP% **110.2**
Speed ratings (Par 105): **105,104,102,101,98 91**
CSF £9.86 CT £30.50 TOTE £2.90: £2.00, £2.20; EX 12.50 Trifecta £51.60.

**Owner** John Dyer **Bred** Catherine Dyer **Trained** Blewbury, Oxon
**FOCUS**
A decent handicap and the pace held up.

## 5065 J F DAUGHTERS, PRESTIGE WATCHES & PAWNBROKERS H'CAP 1m 4f 6y
**7:35** (7:35) (Class 5) (0-75,77) 3-Y-O+ **£3,881** (£1,155; £577; £288) **Stalls** Centre

Form RPR
-341 **1** **Ya Jammeel**[16] 4470 4-9-8 **69**.......... CharlesBishop 6 80+
(Mick Channon) *led 1f and again after 3f: drvn 3 l clr 3f out: maintained advantage after: unchal* **11/4**[2]
4344 **2** 3 ¾ **Really Super**[31] 3909 3-9-4 **76**..........(b[1]) OisinMurphy 5 81
(Ralph Beckett) *led after 1f tl after 3f: chsd wnr: rdn and nt qckn wl over 2f out: kpt on same pce after and nvr able to cl the gap* **15/8**[1]
4031 **3** 7 **Star Of Lombardy (IRE)**[14] 4519 4-10-0 **75**.......... FrannyNorton 4 68
(Mark Johnston) *chsd ldng pair tl 4th st: sn drvn: n.d fnl 2f: tk 3rd again nr fin* **9/2**[3]
056 **4** ½ **Craftsmanship (FR)**[10] 4699 6-9-6 **72**.......... DavidEgan(5) 3 64
(Robert Eddery) *cl up: wnt 3rd st: rdn to dispute 2nd 2f out: hung rt over 1f out: wknd after and lost 3rd nr fin* **8/1**
005 **5** 92 **Sputnik Planum (USA)**[22] 4224 3-8-13 **71**.......... TomQueally 7
(David Lanigan) *nt gng wl bef 1/2-way: sn lost tch: t.o whn virtually p.u 2f out* **9/2**[3]
2m 42.95s (4.05) **Going Correction** +0.25s/f (Good)
**WFA** 3 from 4yo+ 11lb 5 Ran SP% **108.9**
Speed ratings (Par 103): **96,93,88,88,27**
CSF £8.14 TOTE £3.40: £1.90, £1.40; EX 8.30 Trifecta £30.30.
**Owner** M Channon **Bred** Rabbah Bloodstock Limited **Trained** West Ilsley, Berks
**FOCUS**
A fair handicap and a decisive winner.

## 5066 BET TOTEEXACTA AT BETFRED.COM H'CAP 1m 2f 17y
**8:10** (8:11) (Class 4) (0-80,82) 3-Y-O+ **£5,175** (£1,540; £769; £384) **Stalls** Low

Form RPR
3033 **1** **Thundering Blue (USA)**[14] 4522 4-9-10 **76**.......... KieranShoemark 4 87
(David Menuisier) *trckd ldr after 2f: pushed along to chal over 2f out: led wl over 1f out: styd on strly and drew clr: readily* **9/4**[2]
-006 **2** 4 ½ **First Up (IRE)**[54] 3077 3-9-7 **82**.......... JFEgan 2 85
(Jeremy Noseda) *trckd ldr 2f: styd cl up: rdn to chal and upsides 2f out: chsd wnr after but readily outpcd* **13/8**[1]
2204 **3** 3 ¼ **War At Sea (IRE)**[18] 4408 3-9-3 **78**..........(h) OisinMurphy 1 75
(David Simcock) *t.k.h: hld up in 4th: shkn up and no imp on ldrs over 2f out: tk modest 3rd ins fnl f* **10/3**[3]
5-46 **4** 1 **White Tower (IRE)**[22] 4223 3-9-5 **80**.......... FrannyNorton 5 75
(Mark Johnston) *led: rdn and hdd wl over 1f out: wknd* **14/1**
5050 **5** 17 **Akamanto (IRE)**[48] 3291 3-8-8 **72**.......... HollieDoyle(3) 3 33
(Richard Hannon) *in tch in last tl pushed along and wknd over 3f out: t.o* **8/1**
2m 11.3s (1.60) **Going Correction** +0.25s/f (Good)
**WFA** 3 from 4yo 9lb 5 Ran SP% **109.7**
Speed ratings (Par 105): **103,99,96,96,82**
CSF £6.28 TOTE £3.00: £1.50, £1.20; EX 7.40 Trifecta £12.20.
**Owner** Mrs Gay Jarvis **Bred** Dr Tom Castoldi **Trained** Pulborough, W Sussex
**FOCUS**
A decent handicap run at an even pace.

## 5067 BET TOTETRIFECTA AT BETFRED.COM H'CAP 1m 113y
**8:40** (8:41) (Class 5) (0-70,72) 3-Y-O **£3,881** (£1,155; £577; £288) **Stalls** Low

Form RPR
0-62 **1** **Lord Clenaghcastle (IRE)**[16] 4463 3-9-7 **72**.......... HectorCrouch(3) 7 83
(Gary Moore) *settled in 6th: outpcd and pushed along ent st: prog to go 3rd over 2f out: rdn to chse ldr over 1f out: styd on to ld last 100yds* **7/1**
3502 **2** 2 **Sandy Shores**[12] 4625 3-9-1 **63**..........(b[1]) CharlesBishop 3 69
(Brian Meehan) *led: dashed 4 l clr ent st: drvn 3f out: kpt on but hdd last 100yds* **10/1**
0331 **3** 2 ½ **Ashazuri**[32] 3870 3-8-12 **67**..........(h) Pierre-LouisJamin(7) 4 67
(Jonathan Portman) *dwlt: racd in 7th: outpcd and pushed along ent st: prog u.p on outer over 2f out: styd on on fnl f to take 3rd last strides* **13/2**
0253 **4** ¾ **Peloton**[19] 4347 3-9-0 **67**.......... PaddyBradley(5) 1 66
(Pat Phelan) *chsd ldr: 4 l down ent st but clr of rest: sn rdn: no imp and lost 2nd over 1f out: lost 3rd last strides* **10/3**[2]
-042 **5** 1 ¼ **Lesanti**[33] 3823 3-7-13 **52**.......... DavidEgan(5) 6 48
(Ed de Giles) *settled in 6th: outpcd ent st: sn rdn: nvr able to make any significant prog* **3/1**[1]
4503 **6** ¾ **Crystal Secret**[5] 4914 3-8-2 **50** oh3..........(v) KieranO'Neill 8 44
(John Bridger) *pushed up to chse ldng pair but forced to r wd: outpcd and rdn ent st: sn lost pl and btn* **14/1**
0614 **7** 10 **Moonstone Rock**[9] 4714 3-8-12 **60**..........(b) TomQueally 5 31
(Jim Boyle) *s.s: mostly in last: bhd and struggling st: nvr a factor* **20/1**
4401 **8** 15 **Pinnata (IRE)**[24] 4144 3-9-4 **69**..........(t) AaronJones(3) 2 5
(Stuart Williams) *chsd ldng pair: outpcd ent st: sn rdn and wknd rapidly: t.o* **4/1**[3]
1m 46.72s (0.62) **Going Correction** +0.25s/f (Good) 8 Ran SP% **114.4**
Speed ratings (Par 100): **107,105,103,102,101 100,91,78**
CSF £73.22 CT £478.50 TOTE £7.30: £2.10, £2.20, £2.00; EX 44.90 Trifecta £232.00.
**Owner** Michael Baldry **Bred** D McCarthy **Trained** Lower Beeding, W Sussex
**FOCUS**
A modest handicap run at a good pace.
T/Plt: £170.70 to a £1 stake. Pool: £59,674.34 - 255.09 winning units. T/Qpdt: £9.40 to a £1 stake. Pool: £5,565.46 - 434.43 winning units. **Jonathan Neesom**

# 4895 HAMILTON (R-H)
Thursday, July 20

**OFFICIAL GOING: Good (6.7)**
Wind: Breezy, across Weather: Overcast

## 5068 BRITISH STALLION STUDS EBF NOVICE STKS (PLUS 10 RACE) (£20,000 BB FOODSERVICE 2YO SERIES QUAL) 5f 7y
**2:00** (2:01) (Class 4) 2-Y-O **£5,175** (£1,540; £769; £384) **Stalls** High

Form RPR
0023 **1** **Jive Lady (IRE)**[12] 4628 2-8-11 **75**.......... JoeFanning 3 77
(Mark Johnston) *bmpd s: sn swtchd lft and mde all against stands' rail: shkn up and qckd clr over 1f out: kpt on strly fnl f: unchal* **2/1**[2]
4 **2** 4 **Albert Street (IRE)**[12] 4598 2-9-2 0.......... ConnorBeasley 5 68
(Bryan Smart) *dwlt: sn trcking wnr: rdn 1/2-way: kpt on same pce fr over 1f out* **6/5**[1]
35 **3** 4 **Onesarnieshort (FR)**[12] 4606 2-9-2 0.......... DanielTudhope 4 56
(David O'Meara) *wnt rt and bmpd wnr s: chsd clr ldng pair: rdn 1/2-way: outpcd fr over 1f out* **5/1**[3]
04 **4** 2 ¼ **Elements Quest (IRE)**[12] 4606 2-8-8 0.......... JordanVaughan(3) 2 41
(K R Burke) *sn bhd on outside: drvn and outpcd after 2f: no imp after* **16/1**
**5** 10 **Le Gros Serpant (IRE)** 2-8-11 0.......... RowanScott(5) 1 10
(Keith Dalgleish) *s.v.s: t.o thrght* **12/1**
1m 0.64s (0.64) **Going Correction** +0.075s/f (Good) 5 Ran SP% **109.0**
Speed ratings (Par 96): **97,90,84,80,64**
CSF £4.68 TOTE £2.40: £1.80, £1.10; EX 4.60 Trifecta £10.20.
**Owner** John Brown & Megan Dennis **Bred** Airlie Stud **Trained** Middleham Moor, N Yorks
**FOCUS**
Largely dry and overcast, with temperatures around 17C for this afternoon meeting. No less than 4.2mm of rain had fallen overnight and the going was described as Good. Not a strong novices' sprint to start and they finished strung out. The winner did it nicely enough, however, and showed improved form.

## 5069 WATCH RACING UK IN HD H'CAP 5f 7y
**2:30** (2:30) (Class 6) (0-60,62) 3-Y-O+ **£3,234** (£962; £481; £240) **Stalls** High

Form RPR
6216 **1** **Kodimoor (IRE)**[40] 3563 4-9-6 **57**..........(bt) JoeFanning 10 63
(Christopher Kellett) *mde all against stands' rail: rdn and drifted rt over 1f out: kpt on wl fnl f: unchal* **9/2**[3]
5033 **2** 1 ¼ **Picks Pinta**[7] 4789 6-9-6 **62**..........(b) LewisEdmunds(5) 4 65
(John David Riches) *dwlt and n.m.r s: hld up: hdwy over 2f out: effrt whn checked over 1f out: kpt on wl fnl f to take 2nd nr fin: nt rch wnr* **15/8**[1]
0-01 **3** nk **Camanche Grey (IRE)**[16] 4478 6-8-13 **55**.......... RobJFitzpatrick(5) 1 55
(Ben Haslam) *prom on outside: effrt and chsd wnr over 1f out: kpt on same pce ins fnl f: lost 2nd nr fin* **4/1**[2]
450- **4** 1 ¾ **Lydiate Lady**[205] 8541 5-9-2 **53**.......... PaulMulrennan 9 47
(Eric Alston) *wnt bdly rt s: hung rt thrght: t.k.h and sn chsng ldrs: rdn and one pce over 1f out* **15/2**
-503 **5** ¾ **Poet's Time**[13] 4576 3-8-5 **49**.......... RachelRichardson(3) 2 39
(Tim Easterby) *hld up: pushed along over 2f out: hdwy fnl f: nvr able to chal* **9/1**
0606 **6** 1 **Star Cracker (IRE)**[11] 4664 5-9-7 **58**..........(p) DanielTudhope 7 46+
(Jim Goldie) *carried rt s: hld up in tch: rdn over 2f out: outpcd over 1f out* **6/1**
-060 **7** ½ **Trulove**[29] 3977 4-8-8 **45**..........(p[1]) JoeDoyle 8 31+
(John David Riches) *hmpd s: chsd ldrs tl rdn: edgd rt and wknd over 1f out* **66/1**
0300 **8** 1 ½ **Rat Catcher (IRE)**[8] 4731 7-8-8 **45**..........(b) CamHardie 3 26
(Lisa Williamson) *taken early to post: blkd s: sn towards rr: struggling 1/2-way: sn btn* **33/1**
1m 1.04s (1.04) **Going Correction** +0.075s/f (Good)
**WFA** 3 from 4yo+ 4lb 8 Ran SP% **113.4**
Speed ratings (Par 101): **94,92,91,88,87 85,85,82**
CSF £13.13 CT £35.82 TOTE £5.90: £1.70, £1.10, £1.40; EX 14.50 Trifecta £39.70.
**Owner** Blythe Stables Llp **Bred** Tally-Ho Stud **Trained** Lathom, Lancs
**FOCUS**
An ordinary handicap run at a modest pace. Not for the first time, the stands' rail draw was advantageous and the winner was in command early after a runner on his inside veered right, causing a concertina effect. The form is open to question, but the winner's Catterick success could be rated this high.

## 5070 RACING UK CLUB DAY HERE TODAY H'CAP 6f 6y
**3:05** (3:05) (Class 5) (0-70,71) 3-Y-O+ **£4,528** (£1,347; £673; £336) **Stalls** Centre

Form RPR
3-23 **1** **Yes You (IRE)**[10] 4688 3-8-1 **53**.......... NathanEvans(3) 1 59
(Iain Jardine) *hld up centre: shkn up and hdwy over 2f out: led and hrd pressed appr fnl f: kpt on wl* **3/1**[3]
3200 **2** hd **Dark Forest**[22] 4210 4-9-10 **68**..........(p) BarryMcHugh 2 74
(Marjorie Fife) *cl up centre: effrt and chal over 1f out: kpt on fnl f: jst hld* **6/1**
5-41 **3** 1 ¾ **Metisian**[20] 4303 3-9-5 **68**.......... GrahamLee 3 69+
(Jedd O'Keeffe) *in tch centre: pushed along and hdwy to chal over 1f out: one pce whn n.m.r briefly ins fnl f* **9/4**[1]
6354 **4** 1 **Buccaneers Vault (IRE)**[45] 3401 5-9-13 **71**.......... PaulMulrennan 5 68
(Paul Midgley) *trckd ldr stands' side: effrt and edgd rt over 1f out: kpt on same pce ins fnl f* **11/4**[2]
6300 **5** 3 **Top Of The Bank**[12] 4629 4-9-12 **70**..........(p) JoeFanning 7 58
(Kristin Stubbs) *cl up stands' rail: rdn and led briefly over 1f out: wknd ins fnl f* **10/1**
420 **6** 12 **Quiet Warrior (IRE)**[20] 4310 6-8-9 **60**.......... HarrisonShaw(7) 4 9
(Michael Easterby) *led centre to over 1f out: sn rdn and wknd* **14/1**
1m 12.2s **Going Correction** +0.075s/f (Good)
**WFA** 3 from 4yo+ 5lb 6 Ran SP% **112.5**
Speed ratings (Par 103): **103,102,100,99,95 79**
CSF £20.80 TOTE £4.20: £1.70, £3.00; EX 21.70 Trifecta £55.00.
**Owner** Taco Partners **Bred** Tower Place Bloodstock **Trained** Carrutherstown, D'fries & G'way
**FOCUS**
Not a strong race for the class but the tempo was solid. Four raced up the centre of the track and two raced stands' side, but the first three home came up the middle. The form is rated around the runner-up.

## 5071 RACING UK H'CAP 1m 5f 16y
**3:35** (3:35) (Class 4) (0-85,90) 3-Y-O+ **£7,762** (£2,310; £1,154; £577) **Stalls** High

Form RPR
6233 **1** **Tor**[10] 4691 3-8-1 **75**.......... JamieGormley(7) 5 87
(Iain Jardine) *mde all at modest gallop: rdn 2f out: styd on wl fnl f* **9/2**[2]
4211 **2** 1 ¼ **Hochfeld (IRE)**[5] 4891 3-9-9 **90** 6ex.......... JoeFanning 3 100
(Mark Johnston) *trckd wnr: effrt and pushed along 2f out: edgd rt: kpt on same pce ins fnl f* **4/9**[1]
3235 **3** 6 **Warp Factor (IRE)**[17] 4429 4-9-10 **80**.......... TadhgO'Shea 4 79
(John Patrick Shanahan, Ire) *in tch: stdy hdwy over 2f out: rdn and no imp over 1f out* **13/2**[3]
0001 **4** 2 ¾ **Be Perfect (USA)**[17] 4429 8-10-2 **86**..........(p) JackGarritty 2 81
(Ruth Carr) *pressed ldrs: rdn and outpcd over 2f out: btn over 1f out* **20/1**
2m 47.52s (-6.38) **Going Correction** -0.175s/f (Firm)
**WFA** 3 from 4yo+ 11lb 4 Ran SP% **105.5**
Speed ratings (Par 105): **112,111,107,105**
CSF £6.86 TOTE £6.00; EX 9.70 Trifecta £15.70.
**Owner** I Wilson **Bred** Iain Wilson **Trained** Carrutherstown, D'fries & G'way

**FOCUS**
Rail alignment on loop was out two yards, adding five yards to the official distance. The tempo was sensible, they quickened from 3.5f out and the first two drew a little way clear. The form should hold fast, the runner-up close to his Chester latest.

## 5072 WELCOME TO RACING UK CLUB MEMBERS H'CAP 1m 1f 35y
**4:10** (4:13) (Class 4) (0-85,83) 3-Y-O+ **£7,762** (£2,310; £1,154; £577) **Stalls** Low

Form RPR
6520 **1** **Mohab**[19] 4377 4-9-5 **81**......(p) SeamusCronin(7) 7 90
(Kevin Ryan) *hld up in last pl: pushed along and hdwy over 2f out: led over 1f out: kpt on strly fnl f* **6/1**

232 **2** *2* **Desert Ruler**[66] 2685 4-9-4 **73**...... JackGarritty 3 78
(Jedd O'Keeffe) *t.k.h: sn prom: stdy hdwy over 2f out: rdn and effrt over 1f out: chsd wnr ins fnl f: kpt on: nt pce to chal* **2/1**[1]

1-06 **3** *nk* **Rashford's Double (IRE)**[63] 2755 3-9-3 **81**...... BarryMcHugh 2 84
(Richard Fahey) *pressed ldr: effrt and ev ch over 2f out to over 1f out: chsd wnr to ins fnl f: no ex* **11/1**

-412 **4** *4 ½* **Fivehundredmiles (IRE)**[43] 3451 4-9-5 **74**......(b) TadhgO'Shea 4 68
(John Patrick Shanahan, Ire) *prom: effrt and pushed along over 2f out: edgd rt and outpcd over 1f out: btn fnl f* **3/1**[2]

5601 **5** *1 ¾* **X Rated (IRE)**[15] 4492 3-9-0 **78**...... JoeFanning 1 70
(Mark Johnston) *led at ordinary gallop: hrd pressed over 2f out: hdd over 1f out: sn wknd* **7/2**[3]

0434 **6** *2 ¼* **Hidden Rebel**[17] 4431 5-10-0 **83**...... PaulMulrennan 6 69
(Alistair Whillans) *reluctant to enter stalls: s.i.s: t.k.h and sn prom: rdn and outpcd over 2f out: sn btn* **8/1**

1m 56.82s (-2.88) **Going Correction** -0.175s/f (Firm)
**WFA** 3 from 4yo+ 9lb **6** Ran SP% **114.3**
Speed ratings (Par 105): **105,103,102,98,97 95**
CSF £18.96 TOTE £6.70: £3.10, £1.60; EX 21.00 Trifecta £103.10.
**Owner** Mrs J Ryan **Bred** Chasemore Farm **Trained** Hambleton, N Yorks

**FOCUS**
Rail alignment on loop was out two yards, adding five yards to the official distance. Not a strong race for the grade but truly-run. The winner came from off the pace, and had taken a big drop in the weights.

## 5073 RACING UK HD ON SKY 432 MAIDEN AUCTION STKS 1m 68y
**4:40** (4:41) (Class 5) 3-Y-O **£3,881** (£1,155; £577; £288) **Stalls** Low

Form RPR
0 **1** **Snowy Winter (USA)**[13] 4565 3-9-0 0......(t[1]) PaulMulrennan 5 64+
(Archie Watson) *in tch: hdwy over 2f out: drvn over 1f out: led ins fnl f: kpt on strly* **8/1**[3]

-046 **2** *1* **Pioneering (IRE)**[12] 4601 3-9-5 63...... DanielTudhope 1 67
(David O'Meara) *in tch: hdwy over 1f out: rdn to chal ins fnl f: kpt on: hld nr fin* **15/8**[2]

0325 **3** *1 ½* **Somnambulist**[16] 4474 3-9-5 74......(h) GrahamLee 6 64
(Keith Dalgleish) *pressed ldr: led and edgd rt over 1f out: hdd ins fnl f: sn outpcd* **6/5**[1]

6-45 **4** *1 ¼* **Princess Nearco (IRE)**[17] 4432 3-9-0 63...... DougieCostello 2 56
(Patrick Holmes) *hld up on ins: rdn and outpcd over 2f out: rallied over 1f out: no imp fnl f* **9/1**

5 **5** *1 ½* **Ember's Glow**[15] 4508 3-9-5 0...... CamHardie 3 57
(Jason Ward) *led: rdn and hdd over 1f out: wknd ins fnl f* **40/1**

503 **6** *4* **Red Star Dancer (IRE)**[11] 4657 3-9-0 0...... LewisEdmunds(5) 4 48
(Linda Perratt) *hld up: drvn and outpcd over 2f out: sn wknd* **16/1**

1m 47.46s (-0.94) **Going Correction** -0.175s/f (Firm) **6** Ran SP% **109.7**
Speed ratings (Par 100): **97,96,94,93,91 87**
CSF £22.41 TOTE £8.10: £3.90, £1.80; EX 23.50 Trifecta £64.50.
**Owner** Boadicea Bloodstock **Bred** Darley **Trained** Upper Lambourn, W Berks

**FOCUS**
Rail alignment on loop was out two yards, adding five yards to the official distance. A weak maiden auction event but the pace was fair and an improver scored in a tight finish. The form is rated around the runner-up.

## 5074 RACING UK PROFITS RETURNED TO RACING H'CAP 1m 68y
**5:15** (5:15) (Class 6) (0-60,61) 3-Y-O+ **£3,234** (£962; £481; £240) **Stalls** Low

Form RPR
3315 **1** **Haymarket**[11] 4660 8-9-5 **53**...... DanielTudhope 3 59
(R Mike Smith) *led: rdn over 2f out: hdd over 1f out: edgd lft and regained ld ins fnl f: gamely* **3/1**[2]

4002 **2** *hd* **Catastrophe**[17] 4432 4-9-7 **55**......(p[1]) JackGarritty 2 61
(John Quinn) *t.k.h early: trckd ldrs: rdn to ld over 1f out: hdd ins fnl f: rallied: hld nr fin* **7/1**

0006 **3** *1 ½* **Stardrifter**[5] 4900 5-9-4 **57**...... LewisEdmunds(5) 8 59
(Linda Perratt) *hld up: rdn and hdd over 2f out: kpt on fnl f: nt rch first two* **9/1**

006 **4** *4 ¼* **The King's Steed**[31] 3906 4-8-7 **46** oh1...... RobJFitzpatrick(5) 4 38
(Micky Hammond) *cl up: rdn over 2f out: outpcd over 1f out: btn fnl f* **13/2**[3]

46 **5** *hd* **Leven (IRE)**[16] 4476 3-9-1 **57**...... TadhgO'Shea 9 47
(John Patrick Shanahan, Ire) *s.i.s: hld up on outside: effrt and pushed along over 2f out: edgd rt and no imp fr over 1f out* **12/1**

620 **6** *3 ½* **Kelpie Spirit (IRE)**[31] 3913 3-8-6 **53**...... PhilDennis(5) 12 35
(John Weymes) *hld up towards rr: rdn along over 3f out: no imp fr 2f out* **20/1**

0406 **7** *nk* **Rockliffe**[10] 4690 4-9-5 **53**...... PaulMulrennan 10 36
(Micky Hammond) *hld up in rr: drvn along wl over 2f out: sn no imp: btn over 1f out* **33/1**

-600 **8** *1 ¼* **Indian Giver**[29] 3978 9-8-7 **46**......(p) CallumRodriguez(5) 1 26
(John David Riches) *hld up in midfield on ins: drvn and outpcd over 2f out: sn btn* **12/1**

4550 **9** *3 ½* **The Bard's Advice**[76] 2374 3-9-4 **60**...... GrahamLee 5 34
(Keith Dalgleish) *in tch: rdn 3f out: wknd wl over 1f out* **33/1**

6001 **10** *hd* **Cline**[5] 4900 4-9-5 **60** 6ex......(p) SeamusCronin(7) 6 32
(Kevin Ryan) *sn prom: rdn over 2f out: wknd over 1f out* **2/1**[1]

1m 47.56s (-0.84) **Going Correction** -0.175s/f (Firm)
**WFA** 3 from 4yo+ 8lb **10** Ran SP% **120.2**
Speed ratings (Par 101): **97,96,95,91,90 87,87,85,82,82**
CSF £24.76 CT £175.54 TOTE £4.20: £1.50, £2.10, £3.00; EX 21.30 Trifecta £143.30.
**Owner** Ewan Ross **Bred** J Breslin **Trained** Galston, E Ayrshire

**FOCUS**
Rail alignment on loop was out two yards, adding five yards to the official distance. A modest handicap where the front three drew a little way clear of the remainder. The form looks viable, but it's hard to race the rate much higher.
T/Plt: £99.90 to a £1 stake. Pool: £44,680.19 - 326.21 winning units. T/Qpdt: £54.00 to a £1 stake. Pool: £2,669.98 - 36.56 winning units. **Richard Young**

# 4619 LEICESTER (R-H)
### Thursday, July 20

**OFFICIAL GOING: Good (7.6)**
Wind: Light half-behind Weather: Cloudy

## 5075 BREEDERS BACKING RACING EBF MAIDEN STKS 1m 2f
**2:10** (2:11) (Class 5) 3-Y-O **£5,175** (£1,540; £769; £384) **Stalls** Low

Form RPR
222- **1** **Calibration (IRE)**[290] 7016 3-9-5 87...... OisinMurphy 1 90+
(Martyn Meade) *mde virtually all: set stdy pce tl qcknd over 2f out: hung lft and pushed clr fr over 1f out* **4/5**[1]

-30 **2** *7* **Nathan**[62] 2783 3-9-5 0...... FergusSweeney 3 75
(Alan King) *hld up: hdwy to chse wnr over 3f out: hung lft fr over 2f out: styd on same pce fr over 1f out* **15/8**[2]

05 **3** *10* **Grey Diamond**[13] 4579 3-9-5 0...... SilvestreDeSousa 2 62
(Mark Johnston) *trckd ldrs: rdn over 2f out: wknd over 1f out* **14/1**

0 **4** *11* **Seaside Dreamer**[48] 3293 3-9-5 0...... DannyBrock 6 33
(Michael Bell) *chsd wnr tl rdn over 3f out: wknd 2f out* **50/1**

6 **5** *5* **My Name Is Jeff**[33] 3839 3-9-5 0...... AdamBeschizza 7 23
(Julia Feilden) *prom tl rdn and wknd over 2f out* **40/1**

**6** *21* **Warm Oasis** 3-9-5 0...... DanielMuscutt 4
(James Fanshawe) *s.s: rn green in rr: pushed along over 4f out: wknd over 3f out* **9/1**[3]

0-0 **7** *1 ¾* **Here I Go Again (IRE)**[18] 4409 3-9-5 0......(h) TrevorWhelan 5
(Christine Dunnett) *hld up: plld hrd: pushed along over 4f out: wknd over 3f out* **250/1**

2m 9.73s (1.83) **Going Correction** +0.05s/f (Good) **7** Ran SP% **111.8**
Speed ratings (Par 100): **94,88,80,71,67 50,49**
CSF £2.34 TOTE £1.60: £1.10, £1.50; EX 2.80 Trifecta £9.50.
**Owner** Sefton Lodge (Thoroughbred Racing) **Bred** Ennistown Stud **Trained** Newmarket, Suffolk

**FOCUS**
A fairly decent 3yo maiden, but lacking depth. The form is taken at face value. They went a respectable gallop on officially good ground, and were knocking the top off the surface. The winning time, and the winning jockey Oisin Murphy, suggested it was riding on the easier side of that description.

## 5076 GAULBY (S) STKS 7f
**2:45** (2:45) (Class 6) 3-Y-O **£3,234** (£962; £481; £240) **Stalls** High

Form RPR
4504 **1** **Major Cornwallis (IRE)**[35] 3751 3-9-1 60...... TonyHamilton 2 65
(Richard Fahey) *hld up: hdwy over 2f out: rdn to ld ins fnl f: r.o* **11/4**[2]

605- **2** *¾* **Supreme Power (IRE)**[245] 7981 3-9-1 63...... SilvestreDeSousa 6 65+
(Philip McBride) *stdd s: hld up: racd keenly: nt clr run over 2f out: sn outpcd: rallied u.p over 1f out: hung rt and r.o to go 2nd nr fin* **7/4**[1]

0300 **3** *½* **Do You Know (IRE)**[8] 4748 3-8-10 65......(t) AndreaAtzeni 3 57
(Marco Botti) *a.p: rdn to ld over 1f out: edgd rt and hdd ins fnl f: styd on same pce* **7/4**[1]

6-00 **4** *2 ¾* **Garth Rockett**[24] 4150 3-9-1 45...... OisinMurphy 4 55
(Brendan Powell) *prom: chsd ldr 5f out: led 1/2-way: rdn: edgd rt and hdd over 1f out: no ex ins fnl f* **33/1**

5000 **5** *6* **Naupaka**[10] 4687 3-8-5 51......(p) BenRobinson(5) 1 34
(Brian Ellison) *sn pushed along in rr: rdn over 2f out: nvr on terms* **14/1**[3]

0-05 **6** *11* **Miss Island Ruler**[14] 4540 3-8-5 46......(b) PaddyPilley(5) 7
(Shaun Harris) *w ldr 2f: remained handy tl rdn and wknd over 2f out* **100/1**

0-00 **7** *7* **Red Bordeaux (FR)**[21] 4275 3-9-1 48...... GeorgeDowning 5
(Tony Carroll) *led to 1/2-way: sn rdn: wknd 2f out* **50/1**

1m 26.11s (-0.09) **Going Correction** +0.05s/f (Good) **7** Ran SP% **112.0**
Speed ratings (Par 98): **102,101,100,97,90 78,70**
CSF £7.62 TOTE £3.40: £1.50, £1.30; EX 9.20 Trifecta £17.10.Supreme Power was sold to Mr David Tate for £8000
**Owner** Middleham Park Racing XLIII **Bred** M S & C S Griffiths **Trained** Musley Bank, N Yorks

**FOCUS**
A modest 3yo seller. They went a decent gallop and it is sound form for the grade with the winner rated to his recent level.

## 5077 THISTLETON GAP H'CAP 1m 53y
**3:15** (3:15) (Class 4) (0-80,80) 3-Y-O+ **£6,469** (£1,925; £962; £481) **Stalls** Low

Form RPR
-214 **1** **Daira Prince (IRE)**[14] 4544 3-9-6 **80**...... AndreaAtzeni 3 88+
(Roger Varian) *trckd ldrs: stdd and lost pl 6f out: hdwy over 2f out: shkn up to ld ins fnl f: r.o wl* **11/10**[1]

3232 **2** *2 ½* **Mr Tyrrell (IRE)**[54] 3062 3-9-5 **79**...... RyanMoore 1 81
(Richard Hannon) *sn led: qcknd over 2f out: rdn and edgd rt over 1f out: hdd ins fnl f: styd on same pce* **11/4**[2]

4522 **3** *nk* **Character Onesie (IRE)**[12] 4609 5-9-7 **73**...... TonyHamilton 2 76
(Richard Fahey) *prom: rdn over 2f out: sn outpcd: styd on towards fin* **7/2**[3]

3540 **4** *nk* **Armagnac (IRE)**[17] 4446 3-8-8 **68**...... OisinMurphy 4 69
(Michael Bell) *s.i.s: sn chsng ldr: rdn over 1f out: styd on same pce ins fnl f* **7/1**

1m 47.1s (2.00) **Going Correction** +0.05s/f (Good)
**WFA** 3 from 5yo 8lb **4** Ran SP% **109.0**
Speed ratings (Par 105): **92,89,89,88**
CSF £4.41 TOTE £1.80; EX 3.50 Trifecta £4.90.
**Owner** Sheikh Mohammed Obaid Al Maktoum **Bred** Castlemartin Sky & Skymarc Farm **Trained** Newmarket, Suffolk

**FOCUS**
The feature contest was a fairly decent handicap. They went an, at best, respectable gallop and the favourite produced a second handicap win of the summer. He progressed again.

## 5078 EBF STALLIONS BREEDING WINNERS FILLIES' H'CAP 7f
**3:50** (3:50) (Class 4) (0-85,85) 3-Y-O+ **£6,301** (£1,886; £943; £472; £235) **Stalls** High

Form RPR
3231 **1** **Cheerfilly (IRE)**[12] 4624 3-8-9 **78**......(p) PaddyPilley(5) 3 85
(Tom Dascombe) *s.i.s: sn prom: led and qcknd 1/2-way: rdn clr over 1f out: comf* **9/4**[2]

4100 **2** *2 ¾* **Bahamian Bird**[40] 3577 4-9-7 **78**...... TonyHamilton 1 81
(Richard Fahey) *hld up: hdwy over 1f out: rdn and r.o to go 2nd wl ins fnl f: no ch w wnr* **10/1**

-021 **3** *½* **Limelite (IRE)**[35] 3751 3-8-8 **72**...... SilvestreDeSousa 2 71
(Richard Hannon) *prom: chsd wnr 1/2-way: rdn and hung lft over 1f out: styd on same pce fnl f* **3/1**[3]

1-43 **4** 2 ¾ **Parlance (IRE)**[20] 4317 3-9-7 **85** RyanMoore 4 76
(Sir Michael Stoute) *racd keenly: led to 1/2-way: shkn up over 2f out: styng on same pce whn nt clr run over 1f out* **13/8**[1]

4652 **5** 7 **One Big Surprise**[9] 4711 5-8-8 **72** (p) FinleyMarsh(7) 6 47
(Richard Hughes) *chsd ldr 2f: lost pl 4f out: rdn over 2f out: sn wknd* **14/1**

1m 25.77s (-0.43) **Going Correction** +0.05s/f (Good)
**WFA** 3 from 4yo+ 7lb 5 Ran SP% **109.6**
Speed ratings (Par 102): **104,100,100,97,89**
CSF £21.72 TOTE £2.80: £1.40, £3.20; EX 19.90 Trifecta £71.20.
**Owner** Laurence Bellman **Bred** Airlie Stud & Mrs S M Rogers **Trained** Malpas, Cheshire

**FOCUS**
A decent fillies' handicap. The second favourite won readily in the quickest comparative time on the card so far. Her previous C&D win was potentially this good.

## 5079 COLD OVERTON NURSERY H'CAP 7f
**4:20** (4:22) (Class 5) 2-Y-0 **£4,528** (£1,347; £673; £336) **Stalls** High

Form RPR

4311 **1** **Ventura Knight (IRE)**[6] 4836 2-10-0 **88** 6ex SilvestreDeSousa 3 93+
(Mark Johnston) *led: hdd over 5f out: led again 1/2-way: shkn up over 1f out: styd on wl* **8/15**[1]

662 **2** ½ **Ferik (IRE)**[16] 4465 2-9-1 **75** StevieDonohoe 8 79
(David Evans) *w ldrs: led over 5f out: hdd 1/2-way: remained handy: rdn over 2f out: nt clr run and swtchd rt over 1f out: r.o to go 2nd wl ins fnl f* **9/1**

031 **3** 2 ¼ **Shaheen (IRE)**[26] 4101 2-9-1 **75** (t) JasonHart 4 73
(John Quinn) *plld hrd and prom: chsd wnr over 2f out: rdn and ev ch over 1f out: no ex wl ins fnl f* **7/1**[2]

6103 **4** ¾ **Magnus (IRE)**[14] 4527 2-8-10 **75** PaddyPilley(6) 6 71
(Tom Dascombe) *chsd ldrs: pushed along 1/2-way: rdn over 2f out: styd on same pce fnl f* **17/2**

316 **5** ½ **Ventura Dragon (IRE)**[48] 3297 2-9-1 **75** TonyHamilton 7 70
(Richard Fahey) *hld up: nt clr run over 2f out: rdn over 1f out: edgd rt: nt trble ldrs* **8/1**[3]

405 **6** 13 **Inuk (IRE)**[19] 4349 2-8-0 **60** oh3 JimmyQuinn 1 21
(Richard Hughes) *wnt rt s: plld hrd and sn prom: rdn over 2f out: wknd over 1f out* **28/1**

1m 26.65s (0.45) **Going Correction** +0.05s/f (Good) 6 Ran SP% **112.8**
Speed ratings (Par 94): **99,98,95,95,94 79**
CSF £6.38 CT £17.24 TOTE £1.40: £1.10, £4.40; EX 7.10 Trifecta £21.10.
**Owner** Middleham Park Racing XXXVII **Bred** L K I Bloodstock Ltd **Trained** Middleham Moor, N Yorks

**FOCUS**
A decent nursery handicap. The odds-on favourite made most at an increasing tempo but this is rated no better than his previous win.

## 5080 KUBE EXHIBITION CENTRE H'CAP 1m 3f 179y
**4:55** (4:56) (Class 6) (0-60,61) 4-Y-O+ **£3,234** (£962; £481; £240) **Stalls** Low

Form RPR

2254 **1** **Tyrsal (IRE)**[23] 4185 6-9-3 **56** PaddyPilley(5) 14 66+
(Clifford Lines) *hld up: hdwy over 2f out: led over 1f out: rdn clr ins fnl f* **8/1**

4-00 **2** 4 **Annoushka**[20] 4323 4-8-11 **50** (t[1]) AdamBeschizza 13 49
(Mrs Ilka Gansera-Leveque) *plld hrd and prom: jnd ldr 10f out: led over 6f out: rdn and hdd over 1f out: styd on same pce fnl f* **33/1**

1250 **3** ¾ **Albert Boy (IRE)**[19] 4345 4-9-1 **61** FinleyMarsh(7) 4 58
(Scott Dixon) *led 1f: remained handy: rdn over 1f out: styd on same pce fnl f* **10/1**

544 **4** 1 ½ **Touch The Clouds**[8] 4765 6-8-2 **46** oh1 JaneElliott(5) 2 41
(William Stone) *hld up: hdwy and nt clr run over 1f out: r.o: nt trble ldrs* **20/1**

450 **5** 1 ¼ **The Juggler**[40] 3575 4-8-10 **49** MartinLane 9 42
(William Knight) *prom: rdn to chse ldr over 3f out: no ex fnl f* **14/1**

2043 **6** 2 ¼ **Surround Sound**[13] 4572 7-9-7 **60** (p) DavidAllan 11 49
(Tim Easterby) *s.s: hld up: rdn over 2f out: nvr nrr* **5/1**[2]

0031 **7** ¾ **Dove Mountain (IRE)**[16] 4461 6-9-2 **60** (bt) JoshuaBryan(5) 3 48
(Olly Murphy) *dwlt: hld up: hdwy over 2f out: rdn and hung rt over 1f out: wknd fnl f* **5/2**[1]

-445 **8** ¾ **Flying Power**[12] 4630 9-8-8 **47** PaddyAspell 1 34
(John Norton) *hld up in tch: rdn over 2f out: wknd fnl f* **16/1**

1364 **9** 2 ¼ **Star Ascending (IRE)**[23] 4187 5-9-3 **56** (p) KevinStott 7 39
(Jennie Candlish) *hld up: hdwy over 3f out: rdn over 2f out: wknd fnl f* **11/2**[3]

0650 **10** 3 ½ **Astrosecret**[8] 4756 4-9-2 **55** JoeyHaynes 8 33
(Mark H Tompkins) *mid-div: pushed along over 5f out: rdn over 2f out: wknd over 1f out: nt clr run ins fnl f* **66/1**

6552 **11** 6 **Yul Finegold (IRE)**[23] 4187 7-9-1 **54** AndrewMullen 12 22
(Conor Dore) *led after 1f: hdd over 6f out: chsd ldr tl over 3f out: rdn over 2f out: wknd over 1f out* **16/1**

-013 **12** 29 **Theydon Girls**[37] 3699 4-8-7 **53** JoshQuinn(7) 10
(Peter Charalambous) *hld up: plld hrd: hdwy over 8f out: wknd 3f out* **7/1**

2m 34.97s (1.07) **Going Correction** +0.05s/f (Good) 12 Ran SP% **121.0**
Speed ratings (Par 101): **98,95,94,93,93 91,91,90,89,86 82,63**
CSF £253.31 CT £2666.42 TOTE £10.00: £2.90, £7.70, £2.80; EX 164.40 Trifecta £1660.30.
**Owner** Prima Racing Partnership **Bred** Daniel Furini **Trained** Exning, Suffolk

**FOCUS**
A modest middle-distance handicap. They went a respectable gallop and a previous course winner produced a convincing victory. This is not far off last year's best.

## 5081 SUTTON APPRENTICE H'CAP 6f
**5:30** (5:30) (Class 6) (0-65,64) 3-Y-O+ **£3,234** (£962; £481; £240) **Stalls** High

Form RPR

0565 **1** **Jazz Legend (USA)**[9] 4727 4-8-8 **50** (h) DarraghKeenan(5) 9 55
(Olly Murphy) *hld up in tch: rdn over 1f out: hung rt ins fnl f: r.o to ld nr fin* **3/1**[3]

4004 **2** ½ **Quintus Cerialis (IRE)**[17] 4441 5-8-12 **49** (tp) RhiainIngram 6 53
(Karen George) *s.s: outpcd: hdwy over 1f out: led ins fnl f: sn rdn: hdd nr fin* **25/1**

4-04 **3** ½ **One Too Many (IRE)**[20] 4303 3-9-8 **64** FinleyMarsh 8 65
(David Brown) *trckd ldrs: rdn over 1f out: styd on* **9/4**[1]

5050 **4** ½ **Monarch Maid**[34] 3774 6-9-6 **62** MollyKing(5) 1 63
(Peter Hiatt) *w ldrs: led over 1f out: rdn and hdd ins fnl f: styd on same pce* **15/2**

3-00 **5** nk **Q Cee**[83] 2120 4-9-7 **61** RossaRyan(3) 4 61
(Eugene Stanford) *hld up: hdwy and nt clr run over 1f out: sn rdn: styd on same pce ins fnl f* **11/4**[2]

6032 **6** 7 **Elusivity (IRE)**[9] 4724 9-9-8 **62** (p) GabrieleMalune(3) 5 41
(Conor Dore) *w ldr tl led over 4f out: rdn and hdd over 1f out: wknd fnl f* **9/1**

2466 **7** 12 **Generalyse**[23] 4182 8-9-8 **59** (p) JoshuaBryan 7 2
(Anabel K Murphy) *led: hdd over 4f out: rdn over 2f out: wknd over 1f out* **14/1**

1m 12.73s (-0.27) **Going Correction** +0.05s/f (Good)
**WFA** 3 from 4yo+ 5lb 7 Ran SP% **114.7**
Speed ratings (Par 101): **103,102,101,101,100 91,75**
CSF £66.52 CT £197.76 TOTE £3.40: £2.00, £7.80; EX 50.40 Trifecta £239.50.
**Owner** Olly Murphy Racing Club **Bred** Two Hearts Farm LLC & Four Legacy LLC **Trained** Wilmcote, Warks

**FOCUS**
A modest handicap for apprentice riders, and an unconvincing field overall. A horse towards the head of the betting came through late to win in a good time for the grade.
T/Plt: £54.00 to a £1 stake. Pool: £43,256.08 - 584.21 winning units. T/Qpdt: £45.10 to a £1 stake. Pool: £2,580.55 - 42.28 winning units. **Colin Roberts**

5082 - 5086a (Foreign Racing) - See Raceform Interactive

# 4818 LEOPARDSTOWN (L-H)
Thursday, July 20

**OFFICIAL GOING: Good to yielding**

## 5087a ICON MELD STKS (GROUP 3) 1m 1f
**8:00** (8:00) 3-Y-O+ **£31,769** (£10,230; £4,846; £2,153; £1,076)

RPR

**1** **Moonlight Magic**[18] 4417 4-9-9 112 (t) KevinManning 3 115
(J S Bolger, Ire) *chsd ldr: pushed along in 2nd fr 3f out: rdn 1 1/2f out and clsd u.p to strly press ldr wl ins fnl f: kpt on best to ld cl home: all out* **5/1**[3]

**2** hd **Deauville (IRE)**[30] 3924 4-9-12 119 DonnachaO'Brien 4 117
(A P O'Brien, Ire) *attempted to make all: over 1 l clr at 1/2-way: pressed clly into st and sn pushed along: rdn over 1f out and all out wl ins fnl f where strly pressed: hdd cl home* **4/5**[1]

**3** 4 ½ **Tennessee Wildcat (IRE)**[7] 4822 7-9-9 100 GaryCarroll 1 105+
(G M Lyons, Ire) *settled in rr: last at 1/2-way: hdwy into 4th 1 1/2f out: rdn ins fnl f and r.o into 3rd cl home: nvr trbld clr ldrs* **20/1**

**4** nk **Brendan Brackan (IRE)**[42] 3510 8-9-9 112 ColinKeane 2 104
(G M Lyons, Ire) *chsd ldrs in 3rd: tk clsr order bhd ldrs stl in 3rd appr st: rdn under 2f out and no imp on ldrs ent fnl f: one pce after and dropped to 4th cl home* **5/1**[3]

**5** 4 **The Grey Gatsby (IRE)**[18] 4417 6-9-9 116 (v[1]) PatSmullen 5 96
(D K Weld, Ire) *dismntd bef s and loaded wout rdr: hld up in 4th: tk clsr order stl in 4th over 2f out: sn rdn and no imp in rr 1 1/2f out: one pce after* **9/2**[2]

1m 58.8s (4.70) **Going Correction** +0.375s/f (Good) 5 Ran SP% **111.8**
Speed ratings: **94,93,89,89,86**
CSF £9.76 TOTE £5.30: £2.20, £1.02; DF 8.90 Trifecta £50.00.
**Owner** Godolphin **Bred** Darley **Trained** Coolcullen, Co Carlow

**FOCUS**
The rain certainly played a part in the outcome of this race as it blunted the favourite a little and inconvenienced the winner a bit less. The winner sets the standard to his best form.

## 5088a IRISH STALLION FARMS EBF STANERRA STKS (LISTED RACE) 1m 6f
**8:30** (8:30) 3-Y-O+
**£27,735** (£8,931; £4,230; £1,880; £940; £470)

RPR

**1** **Wild Irish Rose (IRE)**[15] 4515 3-8-11 89 SeamieHeffernan 3 97+
(A P O'Brien, Ire) *w.w towards rr: 7th 1/2-way: c wd into st and prog into 5th under 2f out: sn rdn and r.o wl fr over 1f out to ld cl home: readily* **7/4**[1]

**2** ½ **Wingingit (IRE)**[26] 4111 3-8-11 85 ColinKeane 5 96+
(Noel Meade, Ire) *dwlt sltly and towards rr early: 5th 1/2-way: gng wl in 5th 3f out and impr into 3rd 1 1/2f out where rdn: clsd u.p to ld briefly wl ins fnl f tl hdd cl home* **4/1**[2]

**3** 3 ¼ **Tilly's Chilli (IRE)**[26] 4111 3-8-11 88 ColmO'Donoghue 9 91
(Mrs John Harrington, Ire) *settled bhd ldr in 2nd: tk clsr order into st and disp ld under 2f out: rdn to ld over 1f out: all out and hdd u.p wl ins fnl f: no ex in 3rd clsng stages: jst hld 3rd* **11/2**[3]

**4** shd **Moorside**[30] 3928 4-9-9 93 PatSmullen 7 89+
(Charles Hills) *chsd ldrs: racd keenly early: 4th 1/2-way: pushed along in 3rd into st and sn lost pl: rdn in 4th 1 1/2f out and sn no imp on ldrs u.p in 5th: r.o again into 4th wl ins fnl f: jst failed for 3rd* **10/1**

**5** 2 ¾ **Zamira (IRE)**[32] 3875 4-9-9 82 WJLee 4 85
(W McCreery, Ire) *sn led: 2 l clr at 1/2-way: pushed along and pressed clly into st: sn rdn and jnd: hdd u.p over 1f out: wknd ins fnl f* **7/1**

**6** 2 ½ **Tara Dylan (IRE)**[7] 4823 5-9-9 81 GaryCarroll 2 82
(Thomas Mullins, Ire) *cl up tl sn settled bhd ldrs: 6th 1/2-way: gng wl in 6th 3f out: nt clr run on inner briefly appr st: sn rdn and no imp on ldrs u.p in 6th 1 1/2f out: one pce after* **8/1**

**7** 7 ½ **Ruby Gates (IRE)**[67] 2660 4-9-9 70 WayneLordan 1 71
(Joseph Patrick O'Brien, Ire) *hld up: last at 1/2-way: pushed along in rr over 4f out and no imp u.p into st: one pce fnl 2f* **33/1**

**8** 2 ¾ **Ringside Humour (IRE)**[32] 3875 5-9-9 93 (t) KevinManning 8 67
(J S Bolger, Ire) *chsd ldrs: 3rd 1/2-way: pushed along over 3f out and sn lost pl: wknd u.p in 4th fr under 3f out: eased in rr ins fnl f* **10/1**

3m 3.65s (2.65) **Going Correction** +0.375s/f (Good)
**WFA** 3 from 4yo+ 12lb 8 Ran SP% **116.5**
Speed ratings: **107,106,104,104,103 101,97,95**
CSF £8.95 TOTE £2.60: £1.02, £1.40, £1.90; DF 8.10 Trifecta £28.90.
**Owner** Mrs Magnier & M Tabor & D Smith & Mrs A M O'Brien **Bred** Whisperview Trading Ltd **Trained** Cashel, Co Tipperary

**FOCUS**
A pretty ordinary Listed race if based on ratings, two handicappers emerged as the two best in the race and perhaps they can progress enough to be of genuine stakes class. Wild Irish Rose has taken decent steps forward on her last few starts.

5089 - (Foreign Racing) - See Raceform Interactive

## 5046 VICHY

Thursday, July 20

**OFFICIAL GOING: Turf: soft**

### 5090a PRIX DES REVES D'OR - JACQUES BOUCHARA (LISTED RACE) (2YO) (TURF) 5f

1:50 2-Y-0 £25,641 (£10,256; £7,692; £5,128; £2,564)

RPR

1 **Rioticism (FR)**[29] 3960 2-8-13 0 AntoineHamelin 2 96
(Matthieu Palussiere, France) **158/10**

2 ½ **Rimini (FR)**[27] 2-9-2 0 JulienAuge 8 97
(C Ferland, France) **16/5**[2]

3 shd **Haddaf (IRE)**[19] 4359 2-9-2 0 ChristopheSoumillon 5 97
(James Tate) *settled bhd ldrs: impr to dispute ld over 2f out: rdn to ld over 1f out: drvn and hdd wl ins fnl f* **11/5**[1]

4 1¾ **Double Variance (FR)**[13] 4596 2-8-13 0 TheoBachelot 9 88
(S Wattel, France) **127/10**

5 ¾ **Beautiful Destiny (IRE)**[8] 2-8-13 0 ClementLecoeuvre 4 85
(Matthieu Palussiere, France) **149/10**

6 nk **Kentish Waltz (IRE)**[34] 2-8-13 0 FabriceVeron 1 84
(E J O'Neill, France) **22/5**[3]

7 3 **Mister Five Euros (FR)**[53] 2-9-2 0 TonyPiccone 7 76
(F Chappet, France) **71/10**

8 1½ **Evabienchope (FR)**[119] 1335 2-8-13 0 AnthonyCrastus 3 68
(P Sogorb, France) **66/10**

58.0s **8 Ran SP% 118.6**

PARI-MUTUEL (all including 1 euro stake): WIN 8.20; PLACE 2.40, 1.50, 1.70; DF 28.70; SF 63.50.

**Owner** Mrs Theresa Marnane **Bred** Haras D'Haspel **Trained** France

**FOCUS**

The third is rated up 2lb on his domestic form.

## 5068 HAMILTON (R-H)

Friday, July 21

**OFFICIAL GOING: Good (7.5)**

Wind: Breezy, half behind on sprint course and in 5f of home straight on races on round track Weather: Overcast

### 5091 CONTRAFLOW LTD 30TH ANNIVERSARY APPRENTICE H'CAP 1m 68y

5:45 (5:45) (Class 5) (0-70,71) 4-Y-0+ £3,881 (£1,155; £577; £288) Stalls Low

Form RPR

0632 1 **Hernando Torres**[11] 4690 9-8-11 62 (tp) NathanEvans(3) 3 73
(Michael Easterby) *mde all: set stdy pce: pushed along and drew clr fr 2f out: eased nr fin: unchal* **5/2**[1]

5545 2 4½ **Bollihope**[18] 4446 5-9-7 69 CliffordLee 4 70
(Richard Guest) *t.k.h: led after 1f: ev ch 3f out: rdn and kpt on same pce fr over 1f out* **7/2**[2]

5351 3 nk **Chiswick Bey (IRE)**[14] 4554 9-9-1 71 SebastianWoods(8) 2 71
(Richard Fahey) *hld up in last pl in slowly run r: pushed along over 2f out: kpt on fr over 1f out: nvr able to chal* **15/2**

0023 4 2½ **Ingleby Angel (IRE)**[4] 4960 8-9-2 64 (v[1]) ShelleyBirkett 6 58
(Colin Teague) *s.i.s: hld up in tch: pushed along over 2f out: rallied over 1f out: wknd ins fnl f* **7/2**[2]

0623 5 ½ **Framley Garth (IRE)**[13] 4609 5-9-0 65 PaulaMuir(3) 7 58
(Patrick Holmes) *in tch on outside: effrt and cl up over 3f out: sn rdn: wknd over 1f out* **5/1**[3]

0100 6 ¾ **Rioja Day (IRE)**[28] 4034 7-8-1 55 (b) SeanMooney(6) 1 46
(Jim Goldie) *t.k.h: chsd wnr 1f: cl up: drvn and outpcd wl over 3f out: btn fnl 2f* **12/1**

1m 46.77s (-1.63) **Going Correction** -0.20s/f (Firm) **6 Ran SP% 109.1**

Speed ratings (Par 103): **100,95,95,92,92 91**

CSF £10.73 TOTE £2.50: £1.50, £1.50; EX 10.30 Trifecta £27.60.

**Owner** Clive Sigsworth **Bred** Mrs J A Chapman & Mrs Shelley Dwyer **Trained** Sheriff Hutton, N Yorks

**FOCUS**

Race distance increased by 5yds in races 1, 5, 6 & 7. The going was good ahead of the opener and winning jockey, Nathan Evans, said: "It's dried out from yesterday when it was a little dead. I would say it's good now". A modest handicap in which the winner dictated a slow gallop. He's rated to his best since last summer.

### 5092 BB FOODSERVICE EBF NOVICE STKS (PLUS 10 RACE) (A £20,000 BB FOODSERVICE 2YO SERIES QUALIFIER) 6f 6y

6:20 (6:21) (Class 4) 2-Y-0 £5,175 (£1,540; £769; £384) Stalls High

Form RPR

3 1 **Han Solo Berger (IRE)**[32] 3895 2-9-2 0 PaulMulrennan 1 79
(Keith Dalgleish) *w ldr: rdn to ld ins fnl f: edgd lft: hld on wl u.p cl home* **15/8**[2]

3 2 nse **Clubbable**[26] 4116 2-8-11 0 PaulHanagan 3 74
(Richard Fahey) *dwlt: t.k.h and sn prom: rdn and outpcd wl over 1f out: rallied to press wnr ins fnl f: kpt on wl: jst hld* **3/1**[3]

02 3 5 **Austin Powers (IRE)**[17] 4472 2-9-2 0 JoeFanning 4 68
(Mark Johnston) *t.k.h: led: rdn along over 1f out: hdd ins fnl f: sn checked and outpcd* **7/4**[1]

4 2½ **Black Friday** 2-9-2 0 TomEaves 2 56
(Karen McLintock) *dwlt: sn prom on outside: pushed along over 2f out: wknd over 1f out* **9/1**

5 19 **Retirement Beckons** 2-9-2 0 ShaneGray 5 +
(Linda Perratt) *v noisy and green in paddock: s.v.s: t.o thrght* **50/1**

1m 12.21s (0.01) **Going Correction** -0.20s/f (Firm) **5 Ran SP% 108.1**

Speed ratings (Par 96): **91,90,84,80,55**

CSF £7.53 TOTE £2.70: £1.10, £1.50; EX 6.50 Trifecta £10.90.

**Owner** Thats My Boys **Bred** Irish National Stud **Trained** Carluke, S Lanarks

**FOCUS**

A small novice sprint in which they went fast, and the first two came clear to force a photo. Tricky form to pin, and it could be worth a few lengths better.

### 5093 JOHN SMITH'S EXTRA SMOOTH H'CAP 6f 6y

6:50 (6:51) (Class 4) (0-85,87) 3-Y-0+ £7,762 (£2,310; £1,154; £577) Stalls Centre

Form RPR

0000 1 **Glenrowan Rose (IRE)**[18] 4435 4-9-12 85 ConnorBeasley 1 98+
(Keith Dalgleish) *sn crossed over to r against stands' rail: mde all: pushed along 2f out: drew clr fnl f: eased towards fin* **16/1**

3302 2 4 **Harwoods Volante (IRE)**[17] 4477 6-9-11 84 SamJames 4 84
(David O'Meara) *pressed wnr cl to stands' rail: rdn over 2f out: kpt on same pce fnl f* **13/2**

6-21 3 1¾ **Gilmer (IRE)**[27] 4080 6-9-6 79 TomEaves 3 74
(James Ewart) *cl up in centre: drvn along 2f out: kpt on same pce fnl f* **6/1**[3]

0100 4 ¾ **Khelman (IRE)**[21] 4294 7-9-9 82 PaulHanagan 5 74
(Richard Fahey) *in tch centre: drvn over 2f out: no imp fr over 1f out* **14/1**

2211 5 ½ **Hee Haw (IRE)**[22] 4250 3-9-2 80 LeighRoche 6 70
(Paul Midgley) *chsd ldrs jst away fr stands' side duo: drvn and effrt over 1f out: sn no imp: btn ins fnl f* **7/4**[1]

4402 6 nk **Eccleston**[20] 4343 6-10-0 87 (b[1]) DanielTudhope 2 77
(David O'Meara) *dwlt: bhd centre: drvn along 1/2-way: no imp fr over 1f out* **2/1**[2]

1m 10.64s (-1.56) **Going Correction** -0.20s/f (Firm)

**WFA** 3 from 4yo+ 5lb **6 Ran SP% 109.9**

Speed ratings (Par 105): **102,96,94,93,92 92**

CSF £105.13 TOTE £16.00: £5.80, £2.50; EX 109.10 Trifecta £394.80.

**Owner** Weldspec Glasgow Limited **Bred** Tipper House Stud **Trained** Carluke, S Lanarks

**FOCUS**

A tight sprint handicap, although the winner made all in storming clear up the favoured stands' rail. She's rated to her handicap best.

### 5094 JOHN SMITH'S SCOTTISH STEWARDS' CUP H'CAP 6f 6y

7:20 (7:23) (Class 2) (0-105,100) 3-Y-0+

£21,165 (£6,337; £3,168; £1,584; £792; £397) Stalls Centre

Form RPR

5631 1 **Classic Seniority**[14] 4570 5-9-2 90 (p) DanielTudhope 6 100
(Marjorie Fife) *dwlt: sn cl up in centre: effrt and pushed along over 1f out: led ins fnl f: kpt on strly: 1st of 6 in gp* **16/1**

2341 2 1¼ **Dark Defender**[11] 4683 4-8-9 88 6ex (b) RowanScott(5) 5 94
(Keith Dalgleish) *overall ldr in centre: rdn over 1f out: hdd ins fnl f: kpt on same pce: 2nd of 6 in gp* **28/1**

01-2 3 ¾ **Six Strings**[41] 3592 3-8-8 87 PaulHanagan 2 90
(Richard Fahey) *hld up centre: rdn and hdwy over 1f out: kpt on ins fnl f: nvr able to chal: 3rd of 6 in gp* **9/1**

6045 4 hd **Jack Dexter**[11] 4686 8-8-7 88 SeanMooney(7) 8 91
(Jim Goldie) *prom in stands' side gp: hdwy and led that gp over 1f out: edgd rt and kpt on same pce ins fnl f: 1st of 8 in gp* **14/1**

5304 5 1¼ **Get Knotted (IRE)**[20] 4353 5-9-8 96 (p) PaulMulrennan 9 95
(Michael Dods) *sn pushed along in rr on outside of stands' side gp: rdn and hdwy appr fnl f: no imp last 100yds: 2nd of 8 in gp* **15/2**[3]

2220 6 1 **Muntadab (IRE)**[27] 4072 5-9-11 99 (p[1]) HarryBentley 15 95+
(Roger Fell) *w ldr stands' side: rdn over 2f out: edgd rt and one pce fr over 1f out: 3rd of 8 in gp* **5/1**[2]

2003 7 1 **King Robert**[16] 4505 4-9-2 90 (v) ConnorBeasley 13 83
(Bryan Smart) *in tch stands' side gp: effrt and rdn over 2f out: no imp over 1f out: 4th of 8 in gp* **16/1**

5561 8 2 **Flying Pursuit**[28] 4037 4-8-13 90 (p) RachelRichardson(3) 11 76
(Tim Easterby) *chsd stands' side ldrs: rdn over 2f out: edgd rt and wknd over 1f out: 5th of 8 in gp* **12/1**

2100 9 nk **Rich And Famous (USA)**[55] 3092 3-8-13 92 JoeFanning 7 76
(Mark Johnston) *cl up centre: drvn along over 2f out: wknd appr fnl f: 4th of 6 in gp* **20/1**

-003 10 ½ **Red Pike (IRE)**[33] 3861 6-9-3 91 TomEaves 10 75
(Bryan Smart) *led stands' side gp to over 1f out: sn struggling: 6th of 8 in gp* **14/1**

1541 11 shd **Sharp Defence (USA)**[17] 4477 3-9-2 95 TadhgO'Shea 3 77
(John Patrick Shanahan, Ire) *cl up in centre: drvn along over 2f out: wknd over 1f out: 5th of 6 in gp* **9/1**

133- 12 ½ **Hoof It**[286] 7156 10-9-9 100 NathanEvans(3) 14 82
(Michael Easterby) *bhd stands' side: drvn along over 2f out: sn no imp: btn over 1f out: 7th of 8 in gp* **10/1**

6431 13 nse **War Department (IRE)**[22] 4264 4-9-4 95 (v) CliffordLee(3) 4 77
(Keith Dalgleish) *dwlt: bhd centre: short-lived effrt over 2f out: sn btn: last of six in gp* **33/1**

4120 14 8 **Naggers (IRE)**[19] 4416 6-9-10 98 LeighRoche 12 54
(Paul Midgley) *bhd on outside of stands' side gp: drvn along over 2f out: sn btn: eased over 1f out: last of 8 in gp* **4/1**[1]

1m 10.11s (-2.09) **Going Correction** -0.20s/f (Firm)

**WFA** 3 from 4yo+ 5lb **14 Ran SP% 121.5**

Speed ratings (Par 109): **105,103,102,102,100 99,97,95,94,94 93,93,93,82**

CSF £413.32 CT £2548.40 TOTE £18.70: £5.20, £9.00, £2.40; EX 401.60 Trifecta £2065.00.

**Owner** HuggyMac Racing **Bred** E Cantillon, D Cantillon & A Driver **Trained** Stillington, N Yorks

**FOCUS**

A cracking renewal of this valuable sprint handicap featuring a host of improving types. The stands' rail wasn't as favoured as earlier on the card in this bigger field, as those on the fresher ground more towards the far side came out best. The winner built on his progress last year.

### 5095 BRITISH STALLION STUDS EBF GLASGOW STKS (LISTED RACE) 1m 3f 15y

7:55 (7:55) (Class 1) 3-Y-0

£23,818 (£9,030; £4,519; £2,251; £1,129; £567) Stalls Low

Form RPR

0-11 1 **Defoe (IRE)**[20] 4376 3-9-5 104 HarryBentley 5 112+
(Roger Varian) *chsd ldrs: effrt and wnt 2nd over 2f out: rdn and edgd rt over 1f out: led ins fnl f: styd on strly* **5/4**[1]

3404 2 1½ **Frankuus (IRE)**[14] 4584 3-9-5 104 (b[1]) JoeFanning 6 107
(Mark Johnston) *t.k.h: led and sn clr: rdn over 2f out: hdd ins fnl f: kpt on same pce* **5/1**[3]

136 3 1¼ **Call To Mind**[28] 4029 3-9-5 109 PaulHanagan 2 105
(William Haggas) *chsd clr ldr: drvn along and lost 2nd over 2f out: sn outpcd: kpt on ins fnl f: no imp* **85/40**[2]

3135 4 7 **Euro Nightmare (IRE)**[6] 4886 3-9-0 87 PaulMulrennan 1 88
(Keith Dalgleish) *hld up: pushed along and effrt over 2f out: no imp fr over 1f out* **16/1**

40 **5** 3 1/4 **Twin Star (IRE)**[29] 3998 3-9-5 99.......................................... TomEaves 3 87
(Andrew Balding) *stdd s: hld up: pushed along and effrt 3f out: wknd fr 2f out* **14/1**

-520 **6** 13 **Fierce Impact (JPN)**[28] 4032 3-9-5 98......................(b[1]) DanielTudhope 7 73
(David Simcock) *hld up: pushed along and effrt on outside over 2f out: edgd rt and wknd wl over 1f out* **20/1**

2m 19.17s (-6.43) **Going Correction** -0.20s/f (Firm) 6 Ran SP% **110.4**
Speed ratings (Par 108): **115,113,113,107,105 96**
CSF £7.74 TOTE £1.80: £1.10, £2.40; EX 7.30 Trifecta £12.80.
**Owner** Sheikh Mohammed Obaid Al Maktoum **Bred** Darley **Trained** Newmarket, Suffolk

**FOCUS**
Race distance increased by 5yds. A really good Listed event won by a trio of subsequent Group 1 winners during the last six years. The runner-up set a blistering gallop and they first three came clear in a good time, suggesting the form is decent. Defoe continues to progress, with the runner-up to form.

## 5096 ROUTE 74 TRUCKSTOP H'CAP 1m 3f 15y
**8:25** (8:25) (Class 5) (0-70,69) 3-Y-O+ **£3,881** (£1,155; £577; £288) **Stalls** Low

Form RPR

0311 **1** **Regal Mirage (IRE)**[12] 4659 3-8-2 56 6ex........... RachelRichardson(3) 8 68+
(Tim Easterby) *chsd clr ldr: stdy hdwy over 3f out: led over 2f out: pushed out fnl f: comf* **5/2**[2]

6640 **2** 3 3/4 **Schmooze (IRE)**[4] 4962 8-8-9 50.................................... PaulHanagan 6 55
(Linda Perratt) *sn pushed along in rr: plenty to do over 4f out: rdn and gd hdwy over 2f out: chsd wnr 1f out: sn one pce* **28/1**

000 **3** 2 1/4 **Falcon's Fire (IRE)**[6] 4899 4-10-0 69..........................(t) PaulMulrennan 4 70
(Keith Dalgleish) *hld up: pushed along over 3f out: hdwy to chse ldrs 2f out: kpt on same pce fnl f* **14/1**

1333 **4** 2 **Bonnie Arlene (IRE)**[18] 4439 3-9-4 69.............................. JoeFanning 5 68
(Mark Johnston) *sn in tch on outside: hdwy to chse wnr 2f out to 1f out: sn rdn and wknd* **2/1**[1]

2634 **5** 10 **Colour Contrast (IRE)**[12] 4660 4-8-10 58............(b[1]) JamieGormley(7) 3 39
(Iain Jardine) *t.k.h: led and clr: rdn and hdd over 2f out: wknd over 1f out* **4/1**[3]

3234 **6** 3 1/2 **Archibelle**[17] 4476 3-8-13 67.......................................... NathanEvans(3) 7 43
(R Mike Smith) *hld up in tch: drvn and outpcd over 4f out: hung lft over 3f out: sn btn* **10/1**

40 **7** 6 **Mr Davies**[60] 2892 3-9-3 68.................................................. TomEaves 2 34
(David Brown) *prom: outpcd 4f out: struggling fnl 3f* **14/1**

62-0 **8** 18 **Optima Petamus**[157] 727 5-9-11 66............................ DanielTudhope 1
(Patrick Holmes) *hld up in tch: drvn and outpcd over 3f out: sn struggling: t.o* **10/1**

2m 21.51s (-4.09) **Going Correction** -0.20s/f (Firm)
**WFA** 3 from 4yo+ 10lb 8 Ran SP% **116.9**
Speed ratings (Par 103): **106,103,101,100,92 90,86,72**
CSF £66.86 CT £832.41 TOTE £2.90: £1.30, £4.80, £3.50; EX 49.60 Trifecta £259.20.
**Owner** Ryedale Partners No 7 **Bred** Norelands, Lofts Hall & A Gold **Trained** Great Habton, N Yorks

**FOCUS**
Add five yards to race distance. An ordinary handicap in which they went fast, and the first four came clear. The winner recorded a hat-trick and continues to progress.

## 5097 JOHN SMITH'S H'CAP 1m 1f 35y
**8:55** (8:55) (Class 5) (0-70,69) 3-Y-O+ **£3,881** (£1,155; £577; £288) **Stalls** Low

Form RPR

1410 **1** **Amy Blair**[6] 4893 4-9-12 67..........................................(h) ConnorBeasley 8 79+
(Keith Dalgleish) *t.k.h: mde all: sn wl clr: rdn 2f out: kpt on gamely fnl f: unchal* **7/2**[3]

0625 **2** 1 3/4 **Archipeligo**[6] 4899 6-9-7 69......................................(p) JamieGormley(7) 4 75
(Iain Jardine) *in tch chsng gp: hdwy to chse (clr) wnr over 2f out: sn rdn along: kpt on fnl f: nt rch wnr* **10/3**[2]

4 **3** nk **Indian Chief (IRE)**[13] 4608 7-9-11 66........................... DanielTudhope 5 71
(Rebecca Bastiman) *hld up: stdy hdwy 3f out: effrt and rdn wl over 1f out: kpt on same pce fnl f* **5/2**[1]

0063 **4** 7 **Stardrifter**[1] 5074 5-9-2 57.............................................. TomEaves 7 47
(Linda Perratt) *hld up in tch: rdn along and effrt over 2f out: wknd over 1f out* **12/1**

2515 **5** 5 **Cliff Bay (IRE)**[7] 4838 3-9-4 68..................................... PaulMulrennan 1 46
(Keith Dalgleish) *t.k.h: chsd (clr) wnr to over 2f out: rdn and wknd wl over 1f out* **4/1**

3000 **6** 7 **Bahamian C**[13] 4627 6-9-3 58..........................................(t) PaulHanagan 6 21
(Richard Fahey) *bhd: struggling over 4f out: nvr on terms* **11/1**

11-0 **7** 5 **Galilee Chapel (IRE)**[18] 4430 8-9-7 69...................(b) RhonaPindar(7) 2 21
(Alistair Whillans) *hld up: struggling over 3f out: sn wknd* **25/1**

1m 56.92s (-2.78) **Going Correction** -0.20s/f (Firm)
**WFA** 3 from 4yo+ 9lb 7 Ran SP% **113.7**
Speed ratings (Par 103): **104,102,102,95,91 85,80**
CSF £15.41 CT £33.04 TOTE £3.80: £1.90, £2.00; EX 18.60 Trifecta £50.50.
**Owner** J Fyffe **Bred** Summertree Stud **Trained** Carluke, S Lanarks

**FOCUS**
Race distance increased by 5yds. A modest handicap and another good pace set by the winner. The first three came clear but the bare form is modest.
T/Plt: £624.20 to a £1 stake. Pool: £53,233.29 - 62.25 winning units T/Qpdt: £165.30 to a £1 stake. Pool: £5,094.15 - 22.80 winning units **Richard Young**

# 4612 HAYDOCK (L-H)
### Friday, July 21

**OFFICIAL GOING: Good to firm (firm in places) racing abandoned after race 3 (2.55) due to a fatal injury to a stalls handler.**
Wind: strong, gusty winds (behind in home straight) Weather: overcast

## 5098 BEST BETTING SITES AT BETTINGSITES.LTD.UK H'CAP 5f
**1:50** (1:53) (Class 4) (0-80,82) 3-Y-O+ **£5,822** (£1,732; £865; £432) **Stalls** High

Form RPR

0035 **1** **Foxy Forever (IRE)**[8] 4816 7-9-12 80.........................(t) FrannyNorton 13 88
(Michael Wigham) *reluctant to load: hld up: hdwy 2f out: pushed along over 1f out: str run fnl f: r.o wl to ld last few strides* **5/1**[3]

2620 **2** nk **Midnight Malibu (IRE)**[20] 4379 4-9-12 80.......................... DavidAllan 6 87
(Tim Easterby) *prom: led over 1f out: drvn ent fnl f: reminders and 1 l clr 150 yds out: r.o: hdd last few strides* **11/2**

3464 **3** 2 1/2 **Landing Night (IRE)**[8] 4795 5-9-2 73.......................(tp) CliffordLee(3) 11 71
(Rebecca Menzies) *prom: led after 1f: hdd over 1f out: sn rdn: one pce fnl f* **7/1**

5603 **4** 1 1/4 **Lathom**[11] 4686 4-10-0 82...............................................(v) DanielTudhope 4 76
(David O'Meara) *slowly away: effrt 1/2-way: rdn and hdwy ent fnl f: r.o wl to take 4th cl home* **4/1**[2]

0605 **5** nk **Red Stripes (USA)**[8] 4803 5-8-3 64................................ JordanUys(7) 10 56
(Lisa Williamson) *prom: pushed along 2f out: rdn and no ex ent fnl f* **33/1**

3402 **6** 2 1/4 **Foxtrot Knight**[11] 4686 5-9-9 77........................................ JackGarritty 2 61
(Ruth Carr) *chsd ldrs: pushed along 2f out: rdn and one pce fr over 1f out* **13/2**

202 **7** 2 1/2 **Razin' Hell**[15] 4531 6-8-12 71.......................(v) LewisEdmunds(5) 8 46
(John Balding) *led tl hdd after 1f: remained prom: rdn and lost pl over 1f out* **7/2**[1]

022 **8** 1 **Cruise Tothelimit (IRE)**[44] 3466 9-8-6 65........(t) CallumRodriguez(5) 12 37
(Patrick Morris) *racd alone on stands' side: chsd ldrs: drvn 2f out: wknd* **18/1**

0556 **9** 2 1/2 **Ballesteros**[20] 4333 8-9-3 78...................................... ConnorMurtagh(7) 3 41
(Richard Fahey) *slowly away: lost several l and sn pushed along: drvn 3f out: no imp: position accepted* **20/1**

57.38s (-3.42) **Going Correction** -1.125s/f (Hard) course record 9 Ran SP% **113.1**
Speed ratings (Par 105): **82,81,77,75,75 71,67,65,61**
CSF £31.86 CT £191.71 TOTE £5.30: £2.20, £2.00, £3.00; EX 37.50 Trifecta £280.20.
**Owner** D Hassan, J Cullinan **Bred** Tally-Ho Stud **Trained** Newmarket, Suffolk

**FOCUS**
Races run on the inner home straight. Conditions were quite blustery with the wind mainly behind the runners up the straight. This ordinary sprint handicap was weakened by no fewer than seven non-runners, all due to the ground. There was a contested pace and Foxy Forever lowered the 5f course record, breaking the previous best set by Sole Power in 2011. He's rated in line with this year's form. Winning jockey Franny Norton said: "It's quick ground but there was a strong wind in behind all the way," and Danny Tudhope said: "It's good to firm and they're just kicking the top off slightly."

## 5099 BRITISH STALLION STUDS EBF NOVICE STKS (PLUS 10 RACE) 6f
**2:20** (2:24) (Class 4) 2-Y-O **£4,592** (£1,366; £683; £341) **Stalls** High

Form RPR

0 **1** **Prestbury Park (USA)**[7] 4826 2-9-2 0............................ FrannyNorton 5 84+
(Mark Johnston) *mde all: 1 l clr 2f out: reminders over 1f out: kpt up to work and extended advantage fnl f: comf* **9/2**

**2** 2 1/4 **Diamond Set** 2-9-2 0.............................................. RichardKingscote 1 74+
(Tom Dascombe) *a chsng wnr: 1 l bhd 2f out: rdn over 1f out: r.o ins fnl f but wl hld* **5/2**[1]

0 **3** 3/4 **Viceroy Mac**[16] 4502 2-9-2 0................................................ SamJames 8 71
(David Loughnane) *hld up: pushed along and hdwy 2f out: rdn over 1f out: r.o to take 3rd ins fnl f* **28/1**

**4** 1 3/4 **Humble Gratitude** 2-9-2 0.............................................. MartinHarley 7 66
(K R Burke) *trckd ldrs: pushed along in 3rd 2f out: sn rdn: no ex and lost 3rd fnl f* **7/2**[3]

**5** 3 1/2 **Saisons D'Or (IRE)** 2-9-2 0............................................... GrahamLee 3 55
(Jedd O'Keeffe) *in rr: niggled after 2f: pushed along over 2f out: sn given reminders: styd on one pce ent fnl f* **14/1**

031 **6** 6 **Quayside**[22] 4245 2-9-8 77................................................ JackGarritty 2 41+
(Richard Fahey) *stmbld leaving stalls: sn rcvrd but racd in rr: hdwy to chse ldrs 1/2-way: drvn over 2f out: rdn and wknd 2f out: eased* **3/1**[2]

63 **7** 1 **Billiebrookedit (IRE)**[66] 2706 2-9-2 0........................... RoystonFfrench 4 32
(Steph Hollinshead) *trckd ldrs: drvn 2f out: wknd quicky* **11/1**

1m 10.58s (-3.22) **Going Correction** -1.125s/f (Hard) 2y crse rec 7 Ran SP% **112.4**
Speed ratings (Par 96): **76,73,72,69,65 57,55**
CSF £15.61 TOTE £4.60: £2.50, £1.40; EX 18.60 Trifecta £193.50.
**Owner** Sheikh Hamdan bin Mohammed Al Maktoum **Bred** Godolphin **Trained** Middleham Moor, N Yorks

**FOCUS**
Last year's winner South Seas went on to win the Solario and finish second in a French Group 1. Another quick time for this novice event, breaking the 2yo track record. The winner can likely rate a good deal higher.

## 5100 SIMON LANDI BORN TO RUN H'CAP 6f
**2:55** (2:57) (Class 4) (0-85,86) 3-Y-O **£5,822** (£1,732; £865; £432) **Stalls** High

Form RPR

2112 **1** **Merlin**[27] 4100 3-9-8 86...................................................... MartinHarley 1 97+
(Michael Bell) *mde all: 2 l clr 2f out: pushed along to extend advantage over 1f out: coasted home ins fnl f: v easily* **1/1**[1]

1116 **2** 3 1/2 **Black Isle Boy (IRE)**[39] 3664 3-9-8 86.......................... DanielTudhope 5 84
(David O'Meara) *a chsng wnr: 2 l bhd 2f out: drvn along over 1f out: reminder ent fnl f as wnr plld clr: r.o under hand riding to keep 2nd fnl f* **85/40**[2]

0603 **3** 1/2 **Letmestopyouthere (IRE)**[25] 4154 3-9-2 85........... LewisEdmunds(5) 7 81
(David Evans) *settled in 3rd: pushed along 2f out: rdn wl over 1f out: one pce fnl f* **4/1**[3]

-005 **4** 4 **Glorious Rocket**[34] 3814 3-8-10 74.................................... GrahamLee 4 58
(David Barron) *t.k.h: hld up in last: niggled along over 2f out: shkn up 1f out: no imp* **12/1**

1m 10.04s (-3.76) **Going Correction** -1.125s/f (Hard) 4 Ran SP% **109.7**
Speed ratings (Par 102): **80,75,74,69**
CSF £3.46 TOTE £1.80; EX 3.30 Trifecta £6.10.
**Owner** The Queen **Bred** The Queen **Trained** Newmarket, Suffolk

**FOCUS**
Another race run quicker than standard. The order barely changed and the form is limited, but the winner impressed.

## 5101 ROA/RACING POST OWNERS JACKPOT H'CAP 1m 2f 42y
(3:30) (Class 5) (0-70,) 3-Y-O £

## 5102 FREE BETS AT BETFREEBETS.UK H'CAP 1m 6f
(4:05) (Class 4) (0-85,) 3-Y-O £

## 5103 RACING UK NOW ON TALK TALK MAIDEN STKS 7f 212y
(4:35) (Class 5) 3-Y-O+ £

## 5104 HAYDOCK PARK TRAINING SERIES APPRENTICE H'CAP (PART OF THE RACING EXCELLENCE INITIATIVE) 7f 212y
(5:05) (Class 5) (0-75,) 4-Y-O+ £

T/Plt: £7.50 to a £1 stake. Pool: £61,752.05 - 5,995.37 winning units T/Qpdt: £1.20 to a £1 stake. Pool: £4,378.95 - 2,671.86 winning units **Keith McHugh**

## 4804 NEWBURY (L-H)

Friday, July 21

**OFFICIAL GOING: Good to soft (good in places; 5.6)**

Wind: blustery, medium, across Weather: light cloud

### 5105 UPHAM BREWERY EBF NOVICE STKS (PLUS 10 RACE) (DIV I) 7f (S)

1:40 (1:49) (Class 4) 2-Y-O £6,469 (£1,925; £962; £481) Stalls Centre

Form RPR

1 1 **Mildenberger**[14] 4577 2-9-8 0 OisinMurphy 7 95+
(Mark Johnston) *mde all: shkn up ent fnl 2f: rdn and asserted jst over 1f out: styd on strly and drew clr ins fnl f: readily* 4/1[3]

2 5 **Ode To Autumn** 2-9-2 0 KieranShoemark 6 77+
(John Gosden) *stdd after s: hld up in tch in midfield: shkn up and effrt ent fnl 2f: wnt 2nd but wnr gng clr 1f out: kpt on to hold 2nd but nvr matching pce of wnr* 8/1

3 3 1 **Al Jellaby**[23] 4218 2-9-2 0 AdamKirby 3 74
(Clive Cox) *t.k.h: trckd ldrs: effrt ent fnl 2f: rdn to chse wnr over 1f out tl 1f out: outpcd by wnr and kpt on same pce ins fnl f* 7/2[2]

4 hd **Dubhe** 2-9-2 0 WilliamBuick 1 74+
(Charlie Appleby) *dwlt: hld up in tch: dropped towards rr and pushed along after 2f: swtchd lft and effrt 2f out: hdwy over 1f out and wnt 4th ins fnl f: styd on steadily to press for 3rd cl home: no threat to wnr* 3/1[1]

0 5 1 ¾ **Motown Mick (IRE)**[91] 1941 2-9-2 0 KieranO'Neill 4 69
(Richard Hannon) *chsd wnr: rdn jst over 2f out: lost 2nd over 1f out and btn 4th 1f out: wknd ins fnl f* 33/1

0 6 2 ¾ **Bombshell Bay**[14] 4567 2-9-2 0 TomMarquand 8 62
(Richard Hannon) *trckd ldrs: rdn over 2f out: unable qck and lost pl over 1f out: wknd ins fnl f* 50/1

6 7 ½ **Letsbe Avenue (IRE)**[20] 4363 2-9-2 0 SeanLevey 10 61
(Richard Hannon) *t.k.h: hld up in tch in last pair: rdn and effrt over 1f out: no imp u.p jst over 1f out: wknd ins fnl f* 25/1

8 1 ¾ **Wings Of Gold (IRE)** 2-9-2 0 JimCrowley 11 57
(Saeed bin Suroor) *hld up in tch in tch: shkn up ent fnl 2f: no imp and btn over 1f out: wl hld whn nt clrest of runs jst ins fnl f: wknd* 7/2[2]

9 hd **Carlini (IRE)** 2-9-2 0 SilvestreDeSousa 9 59+
(Brian Meehan) *stdd s and t.k.h early: hld up in tch towards rr: shkn up 2f out: rdn and no hdwy over 1f out: btn and rdr looking down ins fnl f: sn wknd and eased towards fin* 14/1

10 10 **Rockwell Lloyd (IRE)** 2-9-2 0 CharlesBishop 5 31
(Mick Channon) *sn dropped towards rr and rdn: reminders after 2f out: last and lost tch ent fnl 2f* 66/1

11 7 **Quick Breath** 2-9-2 0 TrevorWhelan 2
(Jonathan Portman) *in tch in midfield tl lost pl qckly 2f out: wl bhd ins fnl f: t.o* 150/1

1m 26.97s (1.27) **Going Correction** +0.125s/f (Good) 11 Ran SP% **118.1**
Speed ratings (Par 96): **97,91,90,89,87 84,84,82,81,70 62**
CSF £34.84 TOTE £4.70: £1.50, £2.50, £1.40; EX 39.40 Trifecta £154.00.
**Owner** Sheikh Hamdan bin Mohammed Al Maktoum **Bred** Godolphin **Trained** Middleham Moor, N Yorks

**FOCUS**
Race distances as advertised. The first division of a fairly decent juvenile novice contest. There was a false start with stall 11 not opening for Wings Of Gold. The remainder covered about three furlongs before returning to the start. They then went a respectable gallop on ground officially described as good to soft, good in places. An emphatic winner who built on his debut.

### 5106 UPHAM BREWERY EBF NOVICE STKS (PLUS 10 RACE) (DIV II) 7f (S)

2:10 (2:19) (Class 4) 2-Y-O £6,469 (£1,925; £962; £481) Stalls Centre

Form RPR

2 1 **Stage Magic (IRE)**[36] 3742 2-9-2 0 WilliamBuick 3 86+
(Charlie Appleby) *mde all: shkn up wl over 1f out: rdn and asserted ent fnl f: styd on strly and drew clr fnl f: eased nr fin: easily* 8/11[1]

1 2 4 ½ **Albishr (IRE)**[27] 4083 2-9-8 0 TomMarquand 1 79
(Richard Hannon) *chsd ldrs: rdn to chse wnr 2f out tl over 1f out: sn drvn and unable qck: no ch w wnr and kpt on same pce u.p to go 2nd again fnl 75yds* 8/1[3]

3 ½ **He's Amazing (IRE)** 2-9-2 0 AdamKirby 10 72+
(Clive Cox) *rn green: s.i.s: rousted along early and reminder sn after s: in tch towards rr: rdn 2f out: hdwy to go 4th 1f out: styd on steadily to go 3rd towards fin: no ch w wnr* 20/1

4 4 ¾ **Metatrons Cube (IRE)**[20] 4363 2-9-2 0 SilvestreDeSousa 7 70
(Charles Hills) *dwlt and short of room leaving stalls: sn rcvrd and in tch in midfield: clsd to trck ldrs 1/2-way: rdn to chse wnr over 1f out: unable qck and btn 1f out: lost 2nd and wknd fnl 75yds* 10/1

5 4 **Nebuchadnezzar (FR)** 2-9-2 0 FergusSweeney 4 60+
(Alan King) *hld up in tch in last quartet: effrt 2f out: rdn and 7th over 1f out: no ch w wnr but kpt on steadily ins fnl f* 50/1

3 6 ½ **Mosalim (IRE)**[21] 4318 2-9-2 0 RobertWinston 9 59
(William Haggas) *t.k.h: hld up wl in tch in midfield: rdn 2f out: outpcd and hung lft ent fnl f: wknd* 8/1[3]

0 7 ½ **Lucky's Dream**[36] 3746 2-9-2 0 JFEgan 8 57
(David Evans) *t.k.h: chsd wnr tl 2f out: sn outpcd and lost pl u.p: wknd ins fnl f* 100/1

8 1 **Elsaakb (USA)** 2-9-2 0 JimCrowley 6 55
(John Gosden) *in tch in last trio: effrt and reminder 2f out: sn outpcd: wl hld and plugged on same pce ins fnl f* 6/1[2]

0 9 5 **Glacier (IRE)**[36] 3747 2-9-2 0 SeanLevey 2 42
(Richard Hannon) *in tch in midfield: rdn 2f out: sn struggling and lost pl: wknd fnl f* 33/1

10 10 **Universal Command** 2-9-2 0 KieranShoemark 5 17
(Roger Charlton) *rn green: s.i.s: in tch in rr: hdwy into midfield 1/2-way: lost pl and in rr whn rdn 2f out: sn struggling and btn: wl bhd and eased wl ins fnl f* 20/1

1m 27.45s (1.75) **Going Correction** +0.125s/f (Good) 10 Ran SP% **118.9**
Speed ratings (Par 96): **95,89,89,88,83 83,82,81,75,64**
CSF £6.92 TOTE £1.60: £1.10, £2.20, £4.30; EX 8.80 Trifecta £118.00.
**Owner** Godolphin **Bred** Paul & Billy McEnery **Trained** Newmarket, Suffolk

**FOCUS**
The second division of a fairly decent juvenile novice contest. They went a modest gallop and the winning time was marginally slower.

### 5107 BET365 EBF FILLIES' NOVICE STKS (PLUS 10 RACE) 6f

2:40 (2:51) (Class 4) 2-Y-O £6,469 (£1,925; £962; £481) Stalls Centre

Form RPR

1 **Mayyasah (USA)** 2-9-0 0 SeanLevey 11 85+
(Richard Hannon) *t.k.h: trckd ldrs: effrt to press ldrs over 1f out: rdn and qcknd to ld ins fnl f: r.o strly: comf* 12/1

2 2 ½ **Mushahadaat (IRE)** 2-9-0 0 JimCrowley 8 76+
(Brian Meehan) *chsd ldr tl rdn to ld over 1f out: hdd ins fnl f: nt match pce of wnr and kpt on same pce to hold 2nd fnl 100yds* 9/4[1]

3 ¾ **Lady Dancealot (IRE)** 2-9-0 0 PatDobbs 10 73+
(David Elsworth) *wl in tch in midfield: effrt to chse ldrs whn nt clrest of runs and swtchd rt jst over 1f out: hdwy u.p to chse ldng pair 100yds out: kpt on but no threat to wnr* 7/1[3]

4 ¾ **Daybreak** 2-9-0 0 OisinMurphy 12 71+
(Hughie Morrison) *hld up in tch in midfield: hdwy to chse ldrs and rdn over 1f out: battling for 3rd and kpt on same pce and no imp on wnr fnl 100yds* 12/1

5 ½ **Elation (IRE)** 2-9-0 0 SilvestreDeSousa 4 70+
(Roger Varian) *slipped leaving stalls: s.i.s: off the pce in last pair:grad rcvrd and tagged onto bk of field 1/2-way: pushed along over 1f out: sme hdwy whn nt clr run ins fnl f: swtchd lft and styd on wl fnl 100yds* 10/3[2]

40 6 ¾ **Jane Rose (IRE)**[9] 4749 2-9-0 0 TomMarquand 14 67
(Richard Hannon) *t.k.h: hld up in tch in midfield: effrt 2f out: drvn and unable qck over 1f out: styd on same pce ins fnl f* 20/1

7 2 ½ **Maygold** 2-9-0 0 ThomasBrown 2 60
(Ed Walker) *hld up in tch in rr of main gp: pushed along and hdwy into midfield over 1f out: rdn 1f out: no imp and kpt on same pce ins fnl f* 16/1

3362 8 hd **Kodiac Express (IRE)**[23] 4199 2-9-0 70 RobertWinston 3 59
(Mike Murphy) *t.k.h: chsd ldrs: rdn and chal over 1f out tl no ex and btn ins fnl f: fdd fnl 100yds* 8/1

00 9 ¾ **Shoyd**[22] 4252 2-9-0 0 KieranO'Neill 9 57
(Richard Hannon) *led tl rdn and hdd over 1f out: sn struggling and lost pl: wknd ins fnl f* 66/1

10 1 ¾ **Lady Of The Court (IRE)** 2-9-0 0 JohnFahy 6 52
(J S Moore) *s.i.s: off the pce in rr: clsd 1/2-way: rdn 2f out: n.d but plugged on to pass btn rivals ins fnl f* 100/1

0 11 nk **Choral Music**[34] 3815 2-9-0 0 PaddyAspell 1 51
(Jonathan Portman) *in tch in midfield: rdn 2f out: sn struggling and lost pl over 1f out: wknd fnl f* 66/1

12 4 ½ **Jean Paget (IRE)** 2-9-0 0 JFEgan 5 37
(Mick Channon) *in tch in midfield: rdn 1/2-way: lost pl u.p 2f out: bhd and wknd fnl f* 16/1

13 1 **Fanciful Miss** 2-9-0 0 AdamKirby 7 34
(Tom Dascombe) *in tch in midfield: rdn 2f out: sn struggling and lost pl over 1f out: bhd and wknd fnl f* 25/1

1m 13.4s (0.40) **Going Correction** +0.125s/f (Good) 13 Ran SP% **117.2**
Speed ratings (Par 93): **102,98,97,96,96 95,91,91,90,88 87,81,80**
CSF £37.11 TOTE £12.50: £3.40, £1.50, £2.80; EX 49.40 Trifecta £544.40.
**Owner** Al Shaqab Racing **Bred** Martin Schwartz **Trained** East Everleigh, Wilts

**FOCUS**
A fair juvenile fillies' novice contest. They went a decent gallop and it was a particularly promising debut from the winner.She should be up to contesting good races.

### 5108 AJC PREMIER FILLIES' H'CAP 1m 5f 61y

3:15 (3:26) (Class 3) (0-95,88) 3-Y-O+ £16,172 (£4,812; £2,405; £1,202) Stalls Centre

Form RPR

3515 1 **Mistress Quickly (IRE)**[13] 4612 3-8-11 82 PatDobbs 5 93+
(Ralph Beckett) *shifted lft sn after s:led for 1f out: chsd ldr after tl clsd to ld 2f out: sn shkn up and qcknd clr: in command and kpt on wl ins fnl f: comf* 7/2[1]

1-33 2 2 ¼ **Notice (IRE)**[30] 3968 4-9-7 81 JimCrowley 8 85
(David Simcock) *stdd after s: hld up in last pair: shkn up and effrt 2f out: 5th and swtchd rt over 1f out: styd on u.p ins fnl f to go 2nd towards fin: no threat to wnr* 4/1[2]

-434 3 nk **Melinoe**[14] 4571 3-7-13 73 HollieDoyle(3) 1 79
(Sir Mark Prescott Bt) *impeded sn after s: hld up in midfield: rdn and hdwy to chse ldrs over 2f out: kpt on u.p to chse wnr wl ins fnl f: nvr getting on terms w wnr and lost 2nd towards fin* 5/1

3162 4 2 **Flight Of Fantasy**[8] 4809 3-8-6 77 KieranO'Neill 7 80
(Harry Dunlop) *led after 1f: rdn over 2f out: hdd 2f out: unable to match pce of wnr and edgd rt 1f out: kpt on same pce after: lost 2 pls wl ins fnl f and eased nr fin* 9/2[3]

4226 5 2 **Jelly Monger (IRE)**[7] 4828 5-10-0 88 OisinMurphy 3 86
(Dominic Ffrench Davis) *hld up in midfield: hdwy on inner 3f out: rdn and chsng ldrs 2f out: unable qck and hung lft 1f out: plugged on same pce ins fnl f* 16/1

4-10 6 2 **St Mary's**[41] 3580 4-9-2 83 WilliamCox(7) 6 78
(Andrew Balding) *hld up in last trio: effrt 3f out: kpt on same pce and no imp fnl 2f: nvr trbld ldrs* 25/1

-015 7 hd **Renfrew Street**[75] 2426 4-9-6 80 AdamKirby 2 74
(Mark Johnston) *impeded sn after s: chsd ldng trio: rdn 4f out: lost pl and btn 2f out: wknd ins fnl f* 33/1

-104 8 2 ½ **Admiral's Sunset**[23] 4206 4-9-7 81 WilliamBuick 10 72
(Hughie Morrison) *chsd ldng pair: rdn 4f out: hung lft: lost pl and btn 2f out: wknd fnl f* 11/2

2134 9 20 **Fire Jet (IRE)**[21] 4301 4-9-10 84 SilvestreDeSousa 4 45
(John Mackie) *stdd s: hld up in last pair: effrt over 2f out: sn btn and eased fr wl over 1f out* 8/1

2m 50.94s (-1.06) **Going Correction** +0.125s/f (Good)
**WFA** 3 from 4yo+ 11lb 9 Ran SP% **116.2**
Speed ratings (Par 104): **108,106,106,105,103 102,102,101,88**
CSF £17.71 CT £69.51 TOTE £4.30: £1.90, £1.70, £1.90; EX 18.20 Trifecta £113.20.
**Owner** Mrs M E Slade **Bred** Rockhart Trading Ltd **Trained** Kimpton, Hants

■ Sure To Explore was withdrawn. Price at time of withdrawal 12-1. Rule 4 applies to board prices prior to withdrawal but not to SP bets - deduction 5p in the pound. New market formed.

■ Stewards' Enquiry : Pat Dobbs 3 day ban - guilty of careless riding in that he had manoeuvred left towards the rail when not clear (4-6 Aug)

**FOCUS**
A decent staying fillies' handicap. They went a proper gallop and the favourite ran out a good winner. She did it a bit more decisively than the bare form.

## 5109 BATHWICK TYRES ROSE BOWL STKS (LISTED RACE) 6f
**3:50** (4:03) (Class 1) 2-Y-O
**£14,461** (£5,482; £2,743; £1,366; £685; £344) **Stalls** Centre

Form RPR
515 **1** **Madeline (IRE)**28 4028 2-8-9 95 SilvestreDeSousa 1 103+
(Roger Varian) *hld up in tch in last trio: rdn over 2f out: hdwy to chal wandered u.p over 1f out: led ins fnl f: sn asserted but rn green in front and edgd rt: wl in command at fin* **13/8**1

10 **2** *2 1/4* **Natural (IRE)**28 4028 2-8-9 0 OisinMurphy 2 96
(Richard Hannon) *trckd ldrs: clsd to join ldrs 2f out: rdn to ld over 1f out: hdd ins fnl f: no ex and outpcd by wnr fnl 100yds* **13/2**3

101 **3** *2 3/4* **Another Batt (IRE)**11 4681 2-9-0 90 KieranShoemark 5 93
(George Scott) *in tch in midfield: effrt 2f out: wnt 3rd 1f out: edgd rt and no imp ins fnl f: clr 3rd and styd on same pce fnl 100yds* **5/1**2

1302 **4** *2 3/4* **Simmy's Copshop**14 4596 2-9-0 93 PatDobbs 4 85
(Richard Fahey) *hld up in last pair: effrt 2f out: shifting lft and hdwy over 1f out: keeping on but no threat to ldrs whn short of room ins fnl f: wnt 4th wl ins fnl f* **8/1**

641 **5** *1/2* **Major Peirson (IRE)**15 4534 2-9-0 82 JFEgan 9 83+
(Jo Hughes) *chsd ldrs: rdn 2f out: unable qck u.p over 1f out: wknd ins fnl f* **25/1**

4261 **6** *1* **Listen Alexander (IRE)**7 4841 2-8-9 0 CharlesBishop 6 75
(David Evans) *chsd ldr: rdn and ev ch 2f out tl unable qck over 1f out: lost 3rd and btn 1f out: wknd ins fnl f* **40/1**

21 **7** *3 3/4* **Looks A Million**43 3502 2-8-9 0 JimCrowley 8 64
(Joseph Tuite) *sn led: rdn 2f out: sn hdd and lost pl: wknd fnl f* **16/1**

12 **8** *6* **Way Of Wisdom**61 2852 2-9-0 0 WilliamBuick 3 51
(Charlie Appleby) *hld up in tch in last pair: shkn up ent fnl 2f: no imp and outpcd over 1f out: bhd and eased wl ins fnl f* **13/2**3

322 **9** *27* **Jellmood**21 4318 2-9-0 90 AdamKirby 7
(Marco Botti) *t.k.h: wl in tch in midfield tl lost pl 2f out: wl bhd and virtually p.u ins fnl f: t.o* **12/1**

1m 12.36s (-0.64) **Going Correction** +0.125s/f (Good) **9** Ran SP% **112.4**
Speed ratings (Par 102): **109,106,102,98,98 96,91,83,47**
CSF £11.95 TOTE £2.50: £1.40, £2.00, £1.50; EX 12.70 Trifecta £34.30.
**Owner** Sheikh Mohammed Obaid Al Maktoum **Bred** Manfred Wurtenberger **Trained** Newmarket, Suffolk

**FOCUS**
A good-quality juvenile Listed contest won in 2014 by subsequent dual Group 1 winner Limato. The favourite won this contest decisively off a decent tempo, building on her Ascot from. The third helps set the opening level.

## 5110 BATHWICK TYRES H'CAP 2m 2f
**4:25** (4:31) (Class 3) (0-95,91) 3-Y-O+ **£7,762** (£2,310; £1,154; £577) **Stalls** Centre

Form RPR
1310 **1** **Jukebox Jive (FR)**13 4612 3-8-6 86 (t) JFEgan 1 95
(Anthony Honeyball) *mde all: rdn 4f out: jnd by runner up 3f out: forged ahd u.p over 1f out: almost 2 l ahd 1f out: advantage grad being reduced fnl 100yds: jst lasted home: all out: v gamely* **13/8**1

1133 **2** *shd* **Aurora Gray**26 4120 4-8-13 79 CharlieBennett(3) 6 87
(Hughie Morrison) *trckd ldng pair fr 14f out tl jnd wnr and travelling best 3f out: rdn 2f out: sn drvn and little rspnse: almost 2 l down 1f out: plugged on u.p and grad clsd fnl 100yds: jst hld* **6/1**3

2330 **3** *10* **Champagne Champ**20 4356 5-10-0 91 (p) OisinMurphy 5 88
(Rod Millman) *in tch tl hdwy to chse ldr 12f out tl unable qck u.p 3f out: wknd over 1f out* **2/1**2

3110 **4** *4* **Pumblechook**16 4498 4-9-8 85 AdamKirby 4 78
(Mark Johnston) *chsd ldr tl 12f out: in tch in 4th after: rdn briefly 7f out: effrt 4f out: no ex 3f out: wknd over 1f out* **6/1**3

/0-0 **5** *46* **Cousin Khee**20 4380 10-9-1 78 JimCrowley 3 20
(Hughie Morrison) *sn in rr: detached 12f out: rdn 9f out: nvr getting bk on terms after: eased over 2f out: t.o* **14/1**

3m 58.99s
**WFA** 3 from 4yo+ 17lb **5** Ran SP% **106.7**
CSF £10.67 TOTE £2.70: £1.50, £2.00; EX 8.40 Trifecta £16.00.
**Owner** R W Huggins **Bred** Ronald Wallace Huggins **Trained** Mosterton, Dorset

**FOCUS**
Only the fourth race run over this trip at the track. A good staying handicap won in its inaugural running last year by subsequent Cesarewitch and Group 3 Sagaro Stakes winner Sweet Selection. They went a respectable gallop and the front-runner proved thoroughly game. Only two ran their race and the second sets the standard.

## 5111 R & M ELECTRICAL GROUP H'CAP 7f (S)
**4:55** (5:04) (Class 5) (0-75,76) 3-Y-O+ **£3,234** (£962; £481; £240) **Stalls** Centre

Form RPR
0222 **1** **World Power (IRE)**32 3896 3-9-5 73 JimCrowley 9 80
(Paul Cole) *hld up in rr: rdn and hdwy over 2f out: drvn to chse ldrs over 1f out: edging rt but styd on wl under pressue to ld wl ins fnl f* **7/1**

-306 **2** *3/4* **Dance Teacher (IRE)**22 4255 3-9-0 68 PatDobbs 2 73
(Ralph Beckett) *led: rdn jst over 1f out: hung rt ins fnl f: hdd and no ex wl ins fnl f* **4/1**1

4-01 **3** *2 3/4* **Sheikspear**7 4843 3-9-8 76 6ex AdamKirby 5 77+
(Ed de Giles) *chsd ldrs tl hdwy to chse ldr over 2f out: drvn over 1f out: kpt on same pce u.p: hld in 3rd whn short of room wl ins fnl f: eased towards fin* **6/1**3

040- **4** *1 1/4* **Hedging (IRE)**290 7033 3-9-0 68 CharlesBishop 3 62
(Eve Johnson Houghton) *hld up in tch in midfield: rdn over 2f out: unable qck over 1f out: 4th and kpt on same pce u.p ins fnl f* **17/2**

0-02 **5** *shd* **Cadeaux Boxer**8 4810 4-9-9 70 (h) JohnFahy 7 67
(Martin Smith) *chsd ldr tl over 2f out: outpcd u.p over 1f out: wl hld edging lft and kpt on same pce ins fnl f* **11/2**2

252 **6** *4 1/2* **Bounty Pursuit**35 3773 5-9-1 67 MitchGodwin(5) 8 52
(Michael Blake) *hld up in tch in midfield: effrt over 2f out: drvn and no ex u.p over 1f out: wknd ins fnl f* **11/1**

-506 **7** *7* **Big Chill (IRE)**18 4446 5-9-4 68 (h1) CharlieBennett(3) 10 34
(Patrick Chamings) *hld up in midfield: rdn over 2f out: sn struggling and btn over 1f out: wknd fnl f* **12/1**

3505 **8** *3/4* **Harry Beau**16 4492 3-8-8 65 HollieDoyle(3) 6 26
(Richard Hannon) *chsd ldrs: rdn over 2f out: sn struggling and lost pl 2f out: wknd over 1f out* **11/1**

-500 **9** *16* **Tifl**141 986 4-9-2 63 TomMarquand 1
(Heather Main) *a towards rr: struggling u.p 3f out: sn bhd* **50/1**

-106 **P** **Mutoondresdashorse**22 4268 3-9-7 75 (bt1) OisinMurphy 4
(Paul Cole) *stdd s: hld up in last trio: effrt jst over 2f out: sn btn: lost action and heavily eased over 1f out: p.u and dismntd ins fnl f* **6/1**3

1m 27.45s (1.75) **Going Correction** +0.125s/f (Good)
**WFA** 3 from 4yo+ 7lb **10** Ran SP% **113.3**
Speed ratings (Par 103): **95,94,91,89,89 84,76,75,57,**
CSF £34.07 CT £181.70 TOTE £7.50: £2.40, £1.80, £2.10; EX 39.30 Trifecta £159.00.
**Owner** P F I Cole Ltd **Bred** Churchtown House Stud & Liam Butler **Trained** Whatcombe, Oxon

**FOCUS**
A fair handicap. They went an, at best, respectable gallop and the favourite didn't quite see it out. He's the best guide to the form.

## 5112 OAKLEY COACHBUILDERS APPRENTICE H'CAP 6f
**5:25** (5:28) (Class 5) (0-75,75) 4-Y-O+ **£3,234** (£962; £481; £240) **Stalls** Centre

Form RPR
0331 **1** **Champagne Bob**17 4467 5-8-6 60 JonathanFisher(5) 5 68
(Richard Price) *chsd ldr tl rdn to ld over 1f out: edgd lft u.p ins fnl f: styd on strly to draw clr fnl 100yds* **9/4**2

-603 **2** *2 1/2* **Field Of Vision (IRE)**6 4910 4-9-5 75 SophieScardifield(7) 1 75
(Joseph Tuite) *hld up in 4th: clsd to press ldng pair ent fnl 2f: rdn and ev ch over 1f out: carried lft ins fnl f: no ex and outpcd fnl 100yds* **15/8**1

3041 **3** *2 1/2* **Oeil De Tigre (FR)**7 4844 6-9-3 71 6ex SophieRalston(5) 2 63
(Tony Carroll) *chsd ldng pair tl dropped to last and swtchd rt over 2f out: effrt on stands rail to chse ldng pair jst over 1f out: kpt on same pce ins fnl f* **15/8**1

06/6 **4** *10* **Sexy Legs**71 2548 5-9-5 68 (t1) GabrieleMalune 3 28
(Lucinda Egerton) *sn led: rdn and hdd over 1f out: sn dropped to rr and btn: wknd fnl f* **14/1**3

1m 14.27s (1.27) **Going Correction** +0.125s/f (Good) **4** Ran SP% **107.0**
Speed ratings (Par 103): **96,92,89,76**
CSF £6.68 TOTE £2.60; EX 6.90 Trifecta £8.00.
**Owner** M F Oseman **Bred** London Thoroughbred Services Ltd **Trained** Ullingswick, H'fords

**FOCUS**
A fair little handicap for apprentice riders, the winner running to his Chepstow mark. They went a respectable gallop.
T/Plt: £12.90 to a £1 stake. Pool: £78,405.38 - 4,434.04 winning units T/Qpdt: £5.50 to a £1 stake. Pool: £5,789.85 - 769.94 winning units **Steve Payne**

# 4902 NEWMARKET (R-H)
Friday, July 21

**OFFICIAL GOING: Good (good to soft in places)**
Wind: Fresh half behind Weather: Fine

## 5113 FLY LONDON SOUTHEND AIRPORT TO PERPIGNAN FILLIES' H'CAP (JC GRASSROOTS MIDDLE DISTANCE SERIES) 1m 2f
**5:35** (5:35) (Class 5) (0-75,77) 3-Y-O+ **£3,881** (£1,155; £577; £288) **Stalls** Centre

Form RPR
4342 **1** **Glenys The Menace (FR)**29 4012 3-8-11 67 KierenFox 7 77
(John Best) *wnt rt s: chsd ldrs: wnt 2nd over 5f out: led and hung lft over 2f out: rdn over 1f out: hung rt ins fnl f: styd on: hung lft nr fin* **3/1**1

515 **2** *1 3/4* **Twenty Times (IRE)**35 3779 3-9-7 77 ShaneKelly 5 84+
(Richard Hughes) *hld up: hdwy: nt clr run and swtchd lft over 2f out: rdn over 1f out: styd on to go 2nd wl ins fnl f: nt rch wnr* **3/1**1

6322 **3** *1 1/4* **Safira Menina**102 1684 5-9-7 75 MillyNaseb(7) 1 78
(Martin Smith) *prom: chsd wnr over 2f out: rdn over 1f out: styd on same pce ins fnl f* **12/1**

0216 **4** *5* **Carducci**28 4050 3-9-6 76 RyanMoore 3 70
(Richard Hannon) *hld up: hmpd after 1f: pushed along over 3f out: swtchd lft and hdwy over 1f out: sn rdn: no imp fnl f* **9/2**3

4/6- **5** *3* **Duchy**470 1289 4-10-0 75 JamieSpencer 6 62
(Michael Bell) *s.i.s: hld up: swtchd lft over 2f out: hdwy over 1f out: hung rt and wknd ins fnl f* **14/1**

0-12 **6** *7* **Trulee Scrumptious**21 4311 8-9-1 69 (v) JoshQuinn(7) 8 42
(Peter Charalambous) *led: clr 8f out tl over 4f out: rdn and hdd over 2f out: wknd over 1f out* **4/1**2

52 **7** *1 1/4* **Della Valle (GER)**20 4344 4-9-5 66 AntonioFresu 2 37
(Mike Murphy) *hld up: hdwy over 2f out: rdn and wknd over 1f out* **16/1**

5440 **8** *20* **Auntie Barber (IRE)**13 4621 4-9-6 70 (t) AaronJones(3) 4
(Stuart Williams) *chsd ldr over 4f: remained handy tl rdn and wknd over 2f out* **16/1**

2m 9.38s (3.88) **Going Correction** +0.225s/f (Good)
**WFA** 3 from 4yo+ 9lb **8** Ran SP% **114.3**
Speed ratings (Par 100): **93,91,90,86,84 78,77,61**
CSF £11.96 CT £91.40 TOTE £3.80: £1.40, £1.60, £3.00; EX 13.10 Trifecta £128.70.
**Owner** Curtis, Malt & Jenkins **Bred** Haras D'Etreham & Mr Georges Lugon **Trained** Oad Street, Kent

**FOCUS**
Far side course in use for all races, except 1m2f: centre. The course had dried out slightly from its overnight good to soft, and the meeting started in dry conditions also. Rail movements added 21yds to just this opening fillies' handicap, run at a very generous pace.The winner had shaped as if capable of better on the AW latest.

## 5114 FLY LONDON SOUTHEND AIRPORT TO MILAN FILLIES' NOVICE STKS (PLUS 10 RACE) 7f
**6:10** (6:11) (Class 5) 2-Y-O **£3,881** (£1,155; £577; £144; £144) **Stalls** High

Form RPR
1 **1** **Quivery (USA)**33 3858 2-9-7 0 JamieSpencer 9 81+
(Jeremy Noseda) *trckd ldrs: lost pl 1/2-way: swtchd rt over 2f out: hdwy sn after: rdn to ld and hung lft fr over 1f out: drvn out* **8/11**1

**2** *3/4* **Dixieland Diva (USA)** 2-9-0 0 RobHornby 10 72
(Andrew Balding) *chsd ldrs: pushed along and outpcd over 1f out: rallied ins fnl f: r.o: edgd rt towards fin* **20/1**

4 **3** *2* **Ruysch (IRE)**20 4340 2-9-0 0 LukeMorris 1 67
(Ed Dunlop) *chsd ldr: rdn over 2f out: ev ch over 1f out: styd on same pce ins fnl f* **14/1**

06 **4** *1/2* **Polar Light**23 4212 2-9-0 0 ShaneKelly 7 65
(David Elsworth) *chsd ldrs: rdn and ev ch over 1f out: styd on same pce ins fnl f* **33/1**

0 **4** *dht* **Ruby's Gem**20 4363 2-9-0 0 SilvestreDeSousa 8 65+
(Philip McBride) *hld up: rdn and swtchd rt over 1f out: r.o ins fnl f: nvr nrr* **25/1**

3 **6** *2 1/4* **Dark Liberty (IRE)**14 4560 2-9-0 0 MartinDwyer 4 59
(Simon Crisford) *s.i.s: plld hrd: hdwy over 5f out: rdn over 2f out: hung lft over 1f out: hmpd sn after: wknd ins fnl f* **9/2**2

7 ½ **Eastern Sunrise** 2-9-0 0 RyanMoore 5 58
(Richard Hannon) *s.i.s: hld up: hdwy 2f out: hmpd over 1f out: wknd ins fnl f* **8/1**

66 8 13 **Red Snapper**[21] 4312 2-8-7 0 MillyNaseb(7) 6 23
(William Stone) *led: rdn and hdd over 1f out: sn hung rt: hung lft and wknd ins fnl f* **100/1**

9 11 **Forest Dragon** 2-9-0 0 WilliamBuick 3
(Hugo Palmer) *s.s: hld up: rdn over 2f out: wknd over 1f out* **6/1**[3]

1m 29.01s (3.31) **Going Correction** +0.225s/f (Good) **9** Ran SP% **120.7**
Speed ratings (Par 91): **90,89,86,86,86 83,83,68,55**
CSF £24.01 TOTE £1.60: £1.10, £4.60, £3.40; EX 18.90 Trifecta £152.30.
**Owner** Marc Keller **Bred** Elm Tree Farm Llc **Trained** Newmarket, Suffolk

**FOCUS**
A muddling pace in this potentially fair novices' event and they all got in each other's way a little racing down the centre early on, but the winner certainly looks useful. The amount of depth to this race is questionable.

## 5115 FLY LONDON SOUTHEND AIRPORT TO LYON H'CAP 1m
**6:40** (6:41) (Class 4) (0-85,85) 3-Y-O **£5,175** (£1,540; £769; £384) **Stalls** High

Form RPR

5535 1 **Tafaakhor (IRE)**[14] 4564 3-9-5 **83** (b) DaneO'Neill 6 88
(Richard Hannon) *hld up in tch: rdn to ld over 1f out: hung lft ins fnl f: styd on u.p* **16/1**

1-05 2 1 ½ **Sterling Silva (IRE)**[64] 2755 3-9-2 **80** WilliamBuick 7 82
(Richard Hannon) *hmpd s: chsd ldrs: ev ch fr over 2f out: rdn over 1f out: no ex wl ins fnl f* **20/1**

-601 3 1 **Angel Down**[21] 4313 3-8-10 **81** FinleyMarsh(7) 2 81
(Henry Candy) *prom: led over 2f out: rdn and hdd over 1f out: nt clr run ins fnl f: styd on same pce* **4/1**[3]

511 4 ½ **Rigoletto (SWI)**[22] 4271 3-9-7 **85** JamieSpencer 3 84+
(Luca Cumani) *hld up: nt clr run fr over 2f out tl swtchd rt over 1f out: sn rdn: styd on: nt trble ldrs* **9/4**[1]

4320 5 4 **Arsenio Lupin**[46] 3412 3-8-12 **76** (t) SilvestreDeSousa 4 65
(Denis Quinn) *hld up: plld hrd: hdwy and nt clr run over 1f out: sn rdn: no ex ins fnl f* **13/2**

2200 6 4 **Spirit Of Sarwan (IRE)**[34] 3836 3-8-10 **74** AdamBeschizza 1 54
(Julia Feilden) *s.i.s: hld up: hrd rdn over 2f out: wknd fnl f* **50/1**

3211 7 7 **Turning Gold**[9] 4765 3-8-11 **75** 6ex (b) LukeMorris 8 39
(Sir Mark Prescott Bt) *sn led: shkn up over 3f out: rdn and hdd over 2f out: edgd rt and wknd over 1f out* **11/4**[2]

2221 8 3 ½ **Time's Arrow (IRE)**[31] 3945 3-9-3 **81** RyanMoore 5 37
(Sir Michael Stoute) *chsd ldr tl pushed along 3f out: wkng whn hmpd over 1f out: eased* **9/1**

1m 41.19s (1.19) **Going Correction** +0.225s/f (Good) **8** Ran SP% **113.4**
Speed ratings (Par 102): **103,101,100,100,96 92,85,81**
CSF £273.89 CT £1533.64 TOTE £18.50: £3.30, £3.70, £1.40; EX 85.70 Trifecta £534.90.
**Owner** Hamdan Al Maktoum **Bred** Ms Ashley O'Leary **Trained** East Everleigh, Wilts

**FOCUS**
A bit of a messy event and possibly not form in which to place maximum store. The winner is rated to his AW best, and the second to his 2yo form.

## 5116 FLY LONDON SOUTHEND AIRPORT TO PRAGUE BRITISH STALLION STUDS EBF CONDITIONS STKS 5f
**7:10** (7:10) (Class 3) 3-Y-O+ **£9,056** (£2,695; £1,346; £673) **Stalls** High

Form RPR

6605 1 **Ornate**[6] 4920 4-9-5 **105** (h) RyanMoore 2 110
(Robert Cowell) *racd alone stands' side of centre: prom: shkn up to ld over 1f out: qcknd clr wl ins fnl f* **7/2**[3]

0450 2 4 **Monsieur Joe (IRE)**[8] 4816 10-9-5 **100** DaneO'Neill 3 96
(Paul Midgley) *chsd ldr in centre tl led that gp 2f out: sn rdn: styd on same pce ins fnl f* **12/1**

2036 3 ¾ **Goldream**[6] 4920 8-9-5 **110** (p) LukeMorris 5 93
(Robert Cowell) *racd centre: chsd ldrs: rdn 1/2-way: no ex wl ins fnl f* **5/2**[1]

5/60 4 hd **Tropics (USA)**[33] 3867 9-9-5 **103** RobertWinston 7 92
(Dean Ivory) *hld up in centre: pushed along and hdwy over 1f out: styd on same pce wl ins fnl f* **11/1**

1300 5 1 ¼ **Duke Of Firenze**[27] 4072 8-9-9 **109** JamieSpencer 4 92
(David C Griffiths) *racd centre: hld up: rdn over 1f out: nt trble ldrs* **3/1**[2]

00 6 nk **Lightscameraction (IRE)**[20] 4333 5-9-5 **94** (b) DanielMuscutt 8 87
(Gay Kelleway) *racd alone on far side: led and sn clr tl rdn and hung rt wl over 1f out: sn hdd: wknd ins fnl f* **22/1**

3006 7 2 **Willytheconqueror (IRE)**[13] 4635 4-9-5 **104** MartinDwyer 6 79
(William Muir) *led main gp in centre tl rdn 2f out: wknd fnl f* **9/2**

59.05s (-0.05) **Going Correction** +0.225s/f (Good)
**WFA** 3 from 4yo+ 4lb **7** Ran SP% **114.3**
Speed ratings (Par 107): **109,102,101,101,99 98,95**
CSF £42.79 TOTE £3.80: £1.90, £3.60; EX 44.70 Trifecta £142.40.
**Owner** Cheveley Park Stud **Bred** Cheveley Park Stud Ltd **Trained** Six Mile Bottom, Cambs

**FOCUS**
All of those to stand their ground coveted adjusted RPRs of between 106 and 123, so this was better than many weekday evening conditions events. The pace was good. The form is rated a bit cautiously, the winner close to his best.

## 5117 EBF FILLIES' H'CAP 6f
**7:45** (7:46) (Class 3) (0-95,93) 3-Y-O+ **£12,938** (£3,850; £1,924; £962) **Stalls** High

Form RPR

531 1 **Raven's Lady**[21] 4315 3-9-1 **88** GeorgeWood(3) 10 99
(Marco Botti) *chsd ldrs: led over 1f out: sn rdn: jst hld on* **11/2**[2]

1 2 nk **Clon Coulis (IRE)**[32] 3896 3-8-13 **83** JamieSpencer 8 93+
(David Barron) *awkward s: hld up: nt clr run 2f out: hdwy over 1f out: rdn and r.o wl ins fnl f: nt quite rch wnr* **9/2**[1]

1-00 3 2 ¾ **Summer Chorus**[27] 4099 4-9-5 **84** JimmyQuinn 12 86
(Andrew Balding) *hld up: shkn up and hdwy over 1f out: sn edgd rt: drvn and styd on same pce wl ins fnl f* **16/1**

1302 4 2 ¾ **Quench Dolly**[19] 4407 3-9-9 **93** FergusSweeney 6 85
(John Gallagher) *led: rdn and hdd over 1f out: wknd wl ins fnl f* **7/1**

2011 5 ½ **Staintondale Lass (IRE)**[15] 4536 4-9-7 **93** FinleyMarsh(7) 3 85
(Ed Vaughan) *s.s: hld up: swtchd rt over 2f out: rdn and r.o ins fnl f: nvr nrr* **10/1**

0432 6 ¾ **Partitia**[18] 4435 3-9-1 **85** RyanMoore 11 73
(Sir Michael Stoute) *chsd ldrs: rdn over 1f out: wknd ins fnl f* **7/1**

333 7 2 **Belledesert**[15] 4536 4-9-4 **83** AdamBeschizza 5 66
(Steph Hollinshead) *chsd ldr tl rdn over 2f out: edgd rt over 1f out: wknd fnl f* **12/1**

2124 8 1 ¼ **Angel Of Darkness**[15] 4536 3-9-1 **85** SilvestreDeSousa 7 63
(Charles Hills) *slowly in to stride: hld up: hdwy 1/2-way: rdn and hung lft over 1f out: wknd fnl f* **6/1**[3]

0436 9 hd **Reedanjas (IRE)**[21] 4305 3-7-13 **74** DavidEgan(5) 4 51
(Gay Kelleway) *hld up: hdwy 1/2-way: sn rdn: wknd fnl f* **66/1**

0-5 10 hd **Tilly Trotter (IRE)**[18] 4435 3-9-0 **84** ShaneKelly 2 61
(Declan Carroll) *hld up in tch: plld hrd: nt clr run 2f out: wknd over 1f out* **33/1**

-020 11 ¾ **Poet's Princess**[40] 3632 3-9-4 **88** RobertWinston 9 62
(Hughie Morrison) *s.i.s: hld up: hdwy 2f out: rdn and hung lft over 1f out: wknd fnl f* **7/1**

0-46 12 ¾ **Guishan**[162] 639 7-9-8 **87** LukeMorris 1 60
(Michael Appleby) *chsd ldrs: rdn over 2f out: wknd fnl f* **33/1**

1m 12.48s (-0.02) **Going Correction** +0.225s/f (Good)
**WFA** 3 from 4yo+ 5lb **12** Ran SP% **115.4**
Speed ratings (Par 104): **109,108,104,101,100 99,96,95,95,94 93,92**
CSF £29.19 CT £372.98 TOTE £5.80: £2.10, £2.20, £4.80; EX 36.50 Trifecta £500.60.
**Owner** Heart of the South Racing & Partner **Bred** Rabbah Bloodstock Limited **Trained** Newmarket, Suffolk

**FOCUS**
A well-stocked fillies' handicap, and with the two market leaders finishing comfortably clear at the end of a well-run affair the form looks pretty credible. The first two finished clear and are on the upgrade.

## 5118 FLY LONDON SOUTHEND AIRPORT TO DUBROVNIK MAIDEN FILLIES' STKS 1m
**8:15** (8:17) (Class 5) 3-Y-O+ **£3,881** (£1,155; £577; £288) **Stalls** High

Form RPR

1 **Pretty Asset (IRE)** 3-9-0 0 WilliamBuick 2 86+
(Charlie Appleby) *s.i.s: hld up: hdwy to chse ldr over 3f out: led over 2f out: shkn up over 1f out: r.o wl* **6/5**[1]

6- 2 2 ¼ **Awfaa (IRE)**[274] 7484 3-9-0 0 DaneO'Neill 7 80+
(Sir Michael Stoute) *hld up in tch: chsd wnr over 1f out: sn rdn: styd on same pce ins fnl f* **8/1**[3]

322- 3 3 **Song Maker**[276] 7441 3-9-0 82 (p[1]) JamieSpencer 3 73
(Charlie Appleby) *led: rdn and hdd over 2f out: edgd rt over 1f out: no ex fnl f* **9/4**[2]

5 4 2 **Obeya**[14] 4568 3-9-0 0 SilvestreDeSousa 6 68
(Roger Varian) *trckd ldrs: wnt 2nd 1/2-way tl rdn over 2f out: nt clr run over 1f out: wknd ins fnl f* **9/1**

5220 5 2 **Tibibit**[153] 811 4-9-8 68 LukeMorris 4 65
(Henry Tett) *s.i.s: hld up: outpcd over 3f out: n.d after* **40/1**

50 6 15 **Shimmering Light**[21] 4300 3-9-0 0 RyanMoore 8 27
(Michael Bell) *hld up: hdwy over 3f out: eased fnl 2f* **9/1**

05 7 4 **Chocolate Account (USA)**[10] 4729 3-9-0 0 AntonioFresu 1 18
(Ed Dunlop) *chsd ldr to 1/2-way: rdn and wknd over 2f out* **50/1**

1m 41.49s (1.49) **Going Correction** +0.225s/f (Good)
**WFA** 3 from 4yo 8lb **7** Ran SP% **111.7**
Speed ratings (Par 100): **101,98,95,93,91 76,72**
CSF £11.30 TOTE £2.00: £1.40, £3.40; EX 10.80 Trifecta £23.60.
**Owner** Godolphin **Bred** Kenilworth House Stud **Trained** Newmarket, Suffolk

**FOCUS**
Not too many played a meaningful role in this fillies' maiden, which was run at a modest early gallop and won in a time 0.3 seconds slower than the earlier 0-85 event. An impressive winner but the level of the form is a bit fluid.

## 5119 FLY LONDON SOUTHEND AIRPORT TO VENICE H'CAP 7f
**8:45** (8:46) (Class 5) (0-75,73) 4-Y-O+ **£3,881** (£1,155; £577; £288) **Stalls** High

Form RPR

210 1 **Whispered Kiss**[18] 4446 4-8-13 **65** ShaneKelly 11 75
(Mike Murphy) *led duo towards far side: overall ldr to 1/2-way: stl up w the pce: rdn over 1f out: led wl ins fnl f: r.o* **14/1**

6214 2 shd **Emily Goldfinch**[14] 4561 4-8-4 **56** DannyBrock 1 65
(Phil McEntee) *chsd ldrs towards stands' side: led that gp over 4f out: overall ldr 1/2-way: rdn and hung lft fr over 2f out: hdd wl ins fnl f: r.o* **8/1**

5321 3 2 ½ **Robbie Roo Roo**[23] 4214 4-8-5 **57** (vt) AdamBeschizza 2 59
(Mrs Ilka Gansera-Leveque) *chsd ldrs: towards stands' side: outpcd over 2f out: rallied ins fnl f: r.o* **4/1**[2]

4150 4 hd **African Blessing**[32] 3899 4-9-5 **71** JamieSpencer 12 73
(David Barron) *trckd wnr towards far side: rdn over 2f out: r.o* **7/2**[1]

1664 5 hd **Commanche**[9] 4766 8-8-9 **61** (b) SilvestreDeSousa 9 62
(Chris Dwyer) *led towards stands' side to 1/2-way: remained handy: rdn over 2f out: styd on same pce u.p ins fnl f* **8/1**

4300 6 nk **The Gay Cavalier**[15] 4522 6-9-2 **68** (t[1]) JackMitchell 5 68
(John Ryan) *s.s: outpcd towards stands' side: r.o wl ins fnl f: nrst fin* **8/1**

0436 7 ½ **Tulip Dress**[28] 4047 4-8-6 **63** JaneElliott(5) 8 62
(Anthony Carson) *hld up towards stands' side: hdwy over 2f out: rdn over 1f out: no ex wl ins fnl f* **9/1**

410 8 ½ **Nonno Giulio (IRE)**[14] 4554 6-8-10 **67** (p) DavidEgan(5) 10 65
(Conor Dore) *chsd ldrs towards stands' side: rdn over 2f out: styd on same pce fnl f* **28/1**

2321 9 1 ½ **Strictly Carter**[24] 4179 4-8-8 **60** RobertTart 7 54
(Alan Bailey) *racd towards stands' side: hld up in tch: rdn over 2f out: no ex fnl f* **8/1**

0042 10 2 **Good Luck Charm**[24] 4176 8-8-6 **72** (v) RyanMoore 3 60
(Gary Moore) *racd towards stands' side: hld up: shkn up over 2f out: n.d* **15/2**[3]

1m 26.81s (1.11) **Going Correction** +0.225s/f (Good) **10** Ran SP% **118.5**
Speed ratings (Par 103): **102,101,99,98,98 98,97,97,95,93**
CSF £123.12 CT £551.73 TOTE £14.70: £3.50, £3.20, £1.80; EX 182.40 Trifecta £2162.00 Part won..
**Owner** D Ellison, B Olkowicz, C Speller **Bred** T Ellison, B Olkowicz And C Speller **Trained** Westoning, Beds

**FOCUS**
A modest finale and a peculiar spectacle, with horses scattered all over the extremities of the track from an early stage, but it was nonetheless won in a time 2.2 seconds faster than the earlier fillies' novice event. The first two are both rated as running pbs.

T/Plt: £321.10 to a £1 stake. Pool: £75,264.09 - 171.06 winning units T/Qpdt: £219.00 to a £1 stake. Pool: £6,328.82 - 21.38 winning units **Colin Roberts**



The Form Book Flat, Raceform Ltd, Newbury, RG14 5SJ

# 4627 NOTTINGHAM (L-H)

Friday, July 21

**OFFICIAL GOING: Good to soft (7.0)**

Wind: Fresh half against Weather: Cloudy

## 5120 BETTINGGODS.COM EBF MAIDEN STKS 6f 18y

**2:00** (2:03) (Class 5) 2-Y-O £3,234 (£962; £481; £240) **Stalls** Centre

Form RPR

20 1 **First Drive**[23] 4212 2-9-0 0 LouisSteward 5 72+
(Michael Bell) *trckd ldrs: n.m.r and swtchd lft over 1f out: rdn ins fnl f: styd on strly to ld towards fin: hung bdly lft nr line* **7/2**[3]

2 ½ **Barig Al Thumama** 2-9-5 0 DanielMuscutt 4 74
(Marco Botti) *dwlt: hld up in rr: hdwy over 2f out: chal over 1f out: rdn and ev ch whn n.m.r and hmpd ins fnl f: hmpd again nr line* **15/2**

0 3 shd **Pheidippides**[25] 4151 2-9-5 0 PatCosgrave 3 73
(Tom Clover) *trckd ldng pair: hdwy and cl up over 2f out: led wl over 1f out: jnd and rdn 1f out: drvn and edgd lft ins fnl f: hdd towards fin: hmpd nr line* **11/4**[2]

4 4 hd **Picture No Sound (IRE)**[14] 4567 2-9-5 0 TonyHamilton 1 73
(Richard Fahey) *hld up in rr: swtchd lft to outer and pushed along over 2f out: rdn to chal over 1f out: ev ch ins fnl f: sn edgd rt and then sltly hmpd: hld whn hmpd nr line* **7/4**[1]

00 5 2½ **Moakkad**[29] 4014 2-9-5 0 DavidProbert 2 65
(Mark Johnston) *trckd ldr: hdwy and cl up wl over 2f out: rdn wl over 1f out: grad wknd appr fnl f* **25/1**

05 6 6 **Sausage Fingers**[21] 4291 2-9-5 0 FranBerry 7 47
(Tom Dascombe) *led: pushed along wl over 2rf out: rdn and hdd wl over 1f out: sn wknd* **12/1**

1m 16.48s (1.78) **Going Correction** -0.075s/f (Good) 6 Ran SP% **108.6**
Speed ratings (Par 94): **85,84,84,83,80 72**
CSF £26.49 TOTE £3.90: £2.30, £4.30; EX 20.10 Trifecta £63.00.
**Owner** The Queen **Bred** The Queen **Trained** Newmarket, Suffolk

**FOCUS**
Outer track used and all distances as advertised. Rain earlier in the week had resulted in Good to Soft going which led to a number of withdrawals. The best winner of this maiden in recent years was Dream Ahead, but this race looked unlikely to throw up anything of that class. Things got rough in the closing stages and a blanket would have covered the first four. The form is rated a bit negatively.

## 5121 BETTINGGODS.COM FREE RACING TIPS NURSERY H'CAP 6f 18y

**2:30** (2:30) (Class 5) 2-Y-O £3,881 (£1,155; £577; £288) **Stalls** Centre

Form RPR

6151 1 **Milton Road**[13] 4620 2-9-4 69 GeorgeDowning 6 72
(Mick Channon) *hld up in rr: hdwy over 2f out: chal over 1f out: rdn to ld ent fnl f: drvn and edgd lft last 100 yds: kpt on* **7/1**

0050 2 nk **Rock On Bertie (IRE)**[21] 4297 2-8-2 53 (p) JoeDoyle 10 55
(Nigel Tinkler) *cl up: led over 3f out: rdn along over 1f out: drvn and hdd ent fnl f: carried lft last 100 yds: kpt on* **8/1**

463 3 1½ **Shania Says (IRE)**[23] 4213 2-8-12 68 DavidEgan(5) 5 66
(Tony Carroll) *trckd ldrs: effrt 2f out: pushed along and n.m.r over 1f out: sn rdn and kpt fnl f* **6/1**[3]

535 4 2¼ **Global Exceed**[52] 3187 2-8-10 61 FranBerry 4 52
(Ed Dunlop) *dwlt: sn trcking ldrs: hdwy 1/2-way: cl up over 2f out: rdn wl over 1f out: sn ev ch: drvn and wknd fnl f* **7/2**[2]

022 5 2½ **Gangland**[27] 4101 2-9-6 71 TonyHamilton 8 54
(Richard Fahey) *t.k.h: trckd ldng pair: pushed along 2f out: sn rdn and wknd over 1f out* **7/2**[2]

064 6 nk **Owen The Law**[41] 3570 2-8-6 57 AndrewMullen 2 39
(David Evans) *led: hdd over 3f out: cl up: rdn wl over 1f out: drvn and wknd appr fnl f* **14/1**

423 7 10 **Porchy Party (IRE)**[46] 3390 2-9-4 72 CallumShepherd(3) 3 24
(Tom Dascombe) *t.k.h: trckd ldng pair: pushed along 2f out: sn rdn and wknd* **10/3**[1]

1m 15.07s (0.37) **Going Correction** -0.075s/f (Good) 7 Ran SP% **112.1**
Speed ratings (Par 94): **94,93,91,88,85 84,71**
CSF £57.35 CT £353.00 TOTE £7.10: £2.20, £5.50; EX 58.50 Trifecta £396.20.
**Owner** M Channon **Bred** M P Bishop **Trained** West Ilsley, Berks

**FOCUS**
The runners came up the centre this time and this nursery was run 1.41 secs faster than the opening maiden. The most experienced pair dominated. Straightforward, ordinary form.

## 5122 FREE RACING TIPS FROM BETTINGGODS.COM H'CAP 6f 18y

**3:05** (3:07) (Class 5) (0-70,72) 3-Y-O £3,234 (£962; £481; £240) **Stalls** Centre

Form RPR

3-21 1 **Zumran**[21] 4302 3-9-2 70 DavidEgan(5) 4 81
(Philip McBride) *dwlt: sn trcking ldng pair: swtchd rt and hdwy to ld wl over 1f out: rdn and qcknd clr ent fnl f: readily* **6/4**[2]

313 2 3 **Fantasy Keeper**[41] 3584 3-9-9 72 TomQueally 2 73
(Michael Appleby) *trckd ldr: cl up over 2f out: sn rdn and ev ch: drvn over 1f out: kpt on same pce* **11/10**[1]

2600 3 1½ **Stringybark Creek**[46] 3403 3-8-10 59 GeorgeDowning 1 56
(Mick Channon) *trckd ldrs: effrt 2f out and sn pushed along: rdn over 1f out: kpt on fnl f* **14/1**

-000 4 1¾ **Allux Boy (IRE)**[28] 4058 3-9-1 64 AndrewMullen 5 55
(Nigel Tinkler) *led: rdn along over 2f out: hdd wl over 1f out: sn wknd* **8/1**[3]

-456 5 hd **Cool Echo**[155] 764 3-9-1 64 (p[1]) TonyHamilton 6 54
(J R Jenkins) *dwlt: hld up: effrt and sme hdwy 2f out: sn rdn and n.d* **33/1**

1m 14.29s (-0.41) **Going Correction** -0.075s/f (Good) 5 Ran SP% **108.3**
Speed ratings (Par 100): **99,95,93,90,90**
CSF £3.35 TOTE £2.20: £1.10, £1.60; EX 3.40 Trifecta £9.80.
**Owner** Martin Percival & Mrs C E Percival **Bred** Boyce Bloodstock & Mrs C E Percival **Trained** Newmarket, Suffolk

**FOCUS**
A fair 3yo sprint but the time was 0.78 secs faster than the quicker of the two earlier juvenile contests. The winner is on the upgrade and the second was close to form.

## 5123 PICK A WINNER WITH BETTINGGODS.COM H'CAP 6f 18y

**3:40** (3:40) (Class 3) (0-95,95) 3-Y-O+ £9,703 (£2,887; £1,443; £721) **Stalls** Centre

Form RPR

0030 1 **Seeking Magic**[14] 4581 9-9-4 87 (t) RyanTate 4 94
(Clive Cox) *sn led: rdn along and hdd over 1f out: drvn ent fnl f: rallied wl to ld again nr fin* **5/1**

0025 2 nk **Lexington Times (IRE)**[17] 4477 5-8-11 80 TonyHamilton 8 86
(Ruth Carr) *dwlt and hld up in rr: hdwy wl over 1f out: chsd ldng pair ent fnl f: sn chal and ev ch: rdn and nt qckn nr fin* **3/1**[1]

00-0 3 ½ **Shamsaya (IRE)**[35] 3793 3-8-12 86 PatCosgrave 7 89
(Simon Crisford) *trckd ldr: hdwy and cl up 2f out: rdn to ld over 1f out: drvn ins fnl f: hdd and no ex nr fin* **4/1**[3]

0021 4 1¼ **Sir Billy Wright (IRE)**[16] 4505 6-8-13 87 DavidEgan(5) 1 87
(David Evans) *trckd ldrs: pushed along 2f out: rdn over 1f out: drvn and edgd rt fnl f: no imp* **7/2**[2]

0040 5 4½ **Giant Spark**[16] 4505 5-9-2 85 DougieCostello 3 71
(Paul Midgley) *in tch: hdwy over 2f out: sn pushed along: rdn wl over 1f out: n.d* **7/1**

0420 6 1¾ **Englishman**[16] 4505 7-9-0 83 JosephineGordon 2 63
(Milton Bradley) *awkward s: sn chsng ldrs: rdn along 2f out: sn drvn and btn* **15/2**

1m 13.11s (-1.59) **Going Correction** -0.075s/f (Good)
**WFA** 3 from 5yo+ 5lb 6 Ran SP% **108.2**
Speed ratings (Par 107): **107,106,105,104,98 95**
CSF £18.73 CT £56.18 TOTE £7.10: £2.70, £1.60; EX 21.70 Trifecta £81.30.
**Owner** The Seekers **Bred** R, J D & M R Bromley Gardner **Trained** Lambourn, Berks

**FOCUS**
The feature contest and a good-class sprint handicap, but weakened by the absence of the two top weights. It produced a close finish. Unsurprisingly the time was over a second faster the preceding 3yo contest. The form is rated around the runner-up.

## 5124 BETTINGGODS.COM "BEAT THE BOOKIES" MAIDEN FILLIES' STKS (PLUS 10 RACE) 1m 2f 50y

**4:15** (4:15) (Class 5) 3-Y-O £3,234 (£962; £481; £240) **Stalls** Low

Form RPR

42 1 **Frosting**[17] 4460 3-9-0 0 PatCosgrave 6 80
(William Haggas) *mde all: rdn and qcknd over 2f out: drvn and kpt on strly fnl f* **11/1**

32- 2 nk **Sea Tide**[261] 7762 3-9-0 0 (t) JosephineGordon 1 81+
(Hugo Palmer) *in tch on inner: swtchd rt and hdwy wl over 2f out: effrt whn nt clr run and hmpd wl over 1f out: squeezed through and rdn over 1f out: styd on strly ins fnl f: nt quite rch wnr* **2/1**[2]

3 3 1 **Mahabba (IRE)**[33] 3866 3-9-0 0 FranBerry 7 77
(Luca Cumani) *trckd wnr: hdwy and cl up 3f out: rdn along wl over 1f out: drvn and kpt on fnl f* **15/8**[1]

05 4 ¾ **Saniyaat**[21] 4300 3-9-0 0 (v) AndrewMullen 3 76
(George Peckham) *trckd ldrs on inner: hdwy 3f out: rdn along 2f out: drvn over 1f out: kpt on same pce* **16/1**

0 5 4 **Line Of Beauty**[33] 3866 3-9-0 0 TimmyMurphy 8 68
(Simon Crisford) *trckd ldrs: hdwy on outer over 3f out: rdn along 2f out and sn edgd lft: drvn and wknd over 1f out* **25/1**

022 6 2 **Sileel (USA)**[16] 4497 3-9-0 78 (v) StevieDonohoe 5 64
(Ed Dunlop) *trckd ldrs: pushed along wl over 2f out: rdn wl over 1f out: grad wknd* **11/2**[3]

0 7 1½ **Rainbow Rising (FR)**[8] 4808 3-9-0 0 DougieCostello 2 61
(David Menuisier) *dwlt: a towards rr* **33/1**

8 nk **Miss Nouriya** 3-9-0 0 (t[1]) DanielMuscutt 9 61
(Marco Botti) *hld up towards rr: effrt and sme hdwy over 3f out: sn rdn along and n.d* **12/1**

9 ½ **Udzungwa Forest** 3-9-0 0 TomQueally 4 60
(Henry Candy) *a towards rr* **50/1**

2m 12.34s (-1.96) **Going Correction** -0.575s/f (Hard) 9 Ran SP% **114.2**
Speed ratings (Par 97): **84,83,82,82,79 77,76,76,75**
CSF £32.60 TOTE £9.90: £2.80, £1.20, £1.10; EX 22.10 Trifecta £90.50.
**Owner** Cheveley Park Stud **Bred** Cheveley Park Stud Ltd **Trained** Newmarket, Suffolk

**FOCUS**
A few interesting types in this 3yo fillies' maiden but something of a messy contest that turned into a sprint in the straight. The runner-up looked unlucky but the form is taken at face value.

## 5125 RATEDBOOKIES.COM H'CAP 1m 75y

**4:45** (4:45) (Class 4) (0-85,83) 3-Y-O+ £5,175 (£1,540; £769; £384) **Stalls** Centre

Form RPR

2041 1 **See The Master (IRE)**[17] 4468 3-9-1 78 SamHitchcott 3 85+
(Clive Cox) *sn led: hdd over 4f out: led again 3f out: rdn wl over 1f out: kpt on strly fnl f* **11/4**[1]

213- 2 1½ **Ehtiraas**[305] 6628 4-10-0 83 FranBerry 5 87
(Owen Burrows) *dwlt: hld up in rr: hdwy on wd outside 2f out: rdn to chse ldrs over 1f out: drvn and kpt on fnl f* **7/2**[2]

2303 3 ½ **Madroos**[23] 4210 4-9-3 79 HarrisonShaw(7) 1 82
(Michael Easterby) *trckd ldrs on inner: hdwy 3f out: rdn wl over 1f out: kpt on same pce fnl f* **9/2**[3]

0006 4 nk **Roll On Rory**[13] 4622 4-9-10 79 TomQueally 2 81
(Jason Ward) *chsd ldng pair: hdwy 3f out: rdn wl over 1f out: sn drvn and kpt on same pce* **18/1**

1363 5 2¼ **Normandie Lady**[12] 4662 4-9-11 83 AdamMcNamara(3) 7 80
(Richard Fahey) *rdn along s and towards rr: hdwy over 3f out: chsd ldrs over 2f out: sn rdn and no imp* **6/1**

2210 6 ½ **Palmerston**[34] 3837 4-9-13 82 JosephineGordon 4 78
(Michael Appleby) *t.k.h: trckd wnr: hdwy to ld over 4f out: hdd 3f out and sn rdn along: drvn wl over 1f out: sn wknd* **5/1**

0626 7 1¾ **Mutamid**[23] 4215 5-9-11 83 HectorCrouch(3) 6 75
(Ismail Mohammed) *in tch: effrt over 3f out and sn pushed along: : rdn over 2f out: sn drvn and btn* **12/1**

1m 44.77s (-4.23) **Going Correction** -0.575s/f (Hard)
**WFA** 3 from 4yo+ 8lb 7 Ran SP% **111.0**
Speed ratings (Par 105): **98,96,96,95,93 92,91**
CSF £11.73 TOTE £2.80: £1.70, £2.00; EX 12.40 Trifecta £50.20.
**Owner** Mr And Mrs P Hargreaves **Bred** Amanda Brudenell & Anthea Gibson Fleming **Trained** Lambourn, Berks

**FOCUS**
A tightly knit mile handicap on paper but the winner is progressing and made all. The third and fourth are rated close to this year's form.

## 5126 GEEKYGAMBLER.COM H'CAP 1m 75y

**5:15** (5:18) (Class 6) (0-65,67) 3-Y-O+ £2,587 (£770; £384; £192) **Stalls** Centre

Form RPR

6623 1 **Pacific Salt (IRE)**[15] 4541 4-9-11 65 CallumShepherd(3) 11 72
(Pam Sly) *led 2f: cl up: led again 2f out: sn rdn: drvn ins fnl f: kpt on* **8/1**

0-44 2 ½ **Heart Of Gold**[22] 4255 3-9-0 64 DavidEgan(5) 3 68
(William Muir) *cl up on inner: led after 2f: rdn along over 2f out: sn hdd: cl up and drvn over 1f out: ev ch ins fnl f: no ex towards fin* **6/1**[2]

4123 3 ½ **Beverley Bullet**[11] 4690 4-9-5 **59**....................(p) JoshDoyle(3) 8 64
(Lawrence Mullaney) *t.k.h: prom: chsd ldng pair 3f out: rdn along wl over 1f pout: drvn and kpt on fnl f* **11/2**[1]
0253 4 2 **Size Matters**[21] 4298 3-8-11 **56**.................... DougieCostello 7 54+
(Mark Walford) *dwlt and rr: hdwy 1/2-way: in tch 3f out: rdn along to chse ldrs 2f out: sn drvn and kpt on same pce* **11/2**[1]
3626 5 ½ **Fantasy Gladiator**[40] 3628 11-9-11 **62**....................(p) AndrewMullen 2 61+
(Michael Appleby) *towards rr: hdwy on wd outside 3f out: in tch and sltly hmpd over 2f out: sn rdn and kpt on fnl f* **7/1**[3]
-500 6 ¾ **Getgo**[13] 4601 3-9-7 **66**....................(b) StevieDonohoe 14 62
(David Lanigan) *hld up in midfield: hdwy 3f out: rdn to chse ldrs 2f out: drvn and edgd lft over 1f out: kpt on same pce* **12/1**
0440 7 ½ **Tellovoi (IRE)**[16] 4506 9-9-11 **67**....................(p[1]) BenRobinson(5) 4 64
(Richard Guest) *dwlt: rapid hdwy to chse ldrs after 1f: rdn along over 2f out: drvn wl over 1f out: grad wknd* **20/1**
6002 8 ½ **Shearian**[13] 4626 7-9-9 **65**.................... PhilDennis(5) 6 60
(Declan Carroll) *midfield: hdwy 3f out: rdn along to chse ldrs 2f out: sn drvn and no imp* **14/1**
0323 9 ¾ **Tom's Anna (IRE)**[9] 4744 7-8-6 **46**.................... NoelGarbutt(3) 10 40
(Sean Regan) *t.k.h: chsd ldrs: rdn along over 2f out: sn btn* **12/1**
416 10 1 ¼ **Rey Loopy (IRE)**[22] 4265 3-8-12 **62**.................... RobJFitzpatrick(5) 9 51
(Ben Haslam) *hld up towards rr: hdwy on inner to chse ldrs 3f out: rdn over 2f out: sn wknd* **8/1**
-052 11 3 ¼ **Duchess Of Fife**[24] 4186 3-9-6 **65**....................(b[1]) JosephineGordon 15 47
(William Knight) *chsd ldrs: rdn along on outer 3f out: sn drvn and edgd rt over 2f out: sn wknd* **11/1**
/0-0 12 14 **Southview Lady**[191] 176 5-8-9 **46** oh1.................... RyanTate 13
(Sean Regan) *a rr* **66/1**
4/6- 13 1 ¾ **Prince Jai**[134] 1115 4-9-6 **57**....................(p) FranBerry 1 6
(Ian Williams) *a rr* **33/1**

1m 45.15s (-3.85) **Going Correction** -0.575s/f (Hard)
**WFA** 3 from 4yo+ 8lb **13 Ran SP% 119.4**
Speed ratings (Par 101): **96,95,95,93,92 91,91,90,90,88 85,71,69**
CSF £54.44 CT £302.54 TOTE £9.10: £2.60, £2.60, £1.80; EX 74.50 Trifecta £566.70.
**Owner** D L Bayliss & G A Libson **Bred** Tally-Ho Stud **Trained** Thorney, Cambs

**FOCUS**
This moderate handicap was run 0.38 secs slower than the preceding contest, although the pace held up well and the first three were always prominent. The winner is rated back to his mark.
T/Plt: £165.40 to a £1 stake. Pool: £49,605.13 - 218.84 winning units T/Qpdt: £6.00 to a £1 stake. Pool: £4,598.94 - 559.99 winning units **Joe Rowntree**

# 4716 PONTEFRACT (L-H)
Friday, July 21

**OFFICIAL GOING: Good to firm (8.6)**
Wind: Light across Weather: Cloudy

## 5127 COUNTRYWIDE FREIGHT NOVICE AUCTION STKS (PLUS 10 RACE) 6f
**6:30** (6:31) (Class 4) 2-Y-O **£4,528** (£1,347; £673; £336) **Stalls Low**

Form RPR
63 1 **Danzan (IRE)**[10] 4725 2-8-11 0.................... DavidProbert 13 96
(Andrew Balding) *sn prom on outer: pushed along to ld over 1f out: styd on strly to draw clr* **7/1**
6241 2 10 **Our Man In Havana**[15] 4527 2-9-3 74.................... RichardKingscote 1 72
(Tom Dascombe) *led: rdn over 2f out: hdd over 1f out: one pce and sn no ch wnr* **11/4**[1]
4 3 1 **Life For Rent**[60] 2882 2-8-13 0.................... DavidAllan 12 65
(Tim Easterby) *chsd ldrs: rdn over 2f out: one pce* **16/1**
23 4 shd **Wahoo**[53] 3149 2-8-6 0.................... CallumRodriguez(5) 10 63+
(Michael Dods) *dwlt: sn midfield on outer: rdn over 2f out: styd on fnl f* **3/1**[2]
35 5 shd **Sinaloa (IRE)**[76] 2382 2-9-2 0.................... TonyHamilton 6 67
(Richard Fahey) *chsd ldrs: rdn over 2f out: one pce* **16/1**
4313 6 2 **Armed Response**[17] 4472 2-9-5 80.................... JackGarritty 11 64
(Jedd O'Keeffe) *midfield: rdn and sme hdwy over 2f out: no ex ins fnl f* **9/2**[3]
7 nk **Powerful Society (IRE)** 2-8-1 0.................... ConnorMurtagh(7) 9 53
(Richard Fahey) *midfield: pushed along and outpcd over 2f out: kpt on ins fnl f* **20/1**
4 8 nk **Burnieboozle (IRE)**[13] 4597 2-8-11 0.................... JasonHart 7 55
(John Quinn) *midfield on inner: rdn along over 2f out: no imp* **20/1**
40 9 ½ **Foxrush Take Time (FR)**[6] 4919 2-8-11 0.................... KevinLundie(5) 3 58
(Richard Guest) *hld up: pushed along 2f out: kpt on ins fnl f* **50/1**
06 10 6 **Sandama (IRE)**[17] 4472 2-8-3 0.................... SammyJoBell(3) 2 30
(Richard Fahey) *a towards rr* **25/1**
60 11 1 ¾ **Squirrelheed**[8] 4792 2-8-13 0.................... JoeDoyle 8 32
(Richard Guest) *dwlt: a towards rr* **100/1**
4 12 nk **Birdette (IRE)**[23] 4205 2-8-11 0.................... FrannyNorton 5 29
(Mark Johnston) *trckd ldrs: rdn 3f out: wknd 2f out* **9/1**

1m 17.76s (0.86) **Going Correction** +0.10s/f (Good) **12 Ran SP% 120.4**
Speed ratings (Par 96): **98,84,83,83,83 80,80,79,78,70 68,68**
CSF £25.54 TOTE £6.20: £2.00, £1.40, £4.50; EX 24.20 Trifecta £241.90.
**Owner** B Greenwood/ R Homburg & Partner **Bred** Colin Kennedy **Trained** Kingsclere, Hants
■ Stewards' Enquiry : Connor Murtagh 2 day ban - guilty of careless riding in that allowed his mount to drift left (4/5 Aug)

**FOCUS**
Add 8yds to race distance. A novice auction event in which the first three were in the first three throughout, the winner trotted up and the majority of the others are likely to be handicappers. The form makes sense in behind the winner.

## 5128 TOTEPOOL SUPPORTS JACK BERRY HOUSE MAIDEN AUCTION STKS (PLUS 10 RACE) 1m 4f 5y
**7:00** (7:01) (Class 4) 3-Y-O **£5,175** (£1,540; £769; £384) **Stalls Low**

Form RPR
624 1 **Mancini**[23] 4224 3-9-5 73.................... RichardKingscote 2 77
(Jonathan Portman) *led narrowly: rdn over 2f out: hdd narrowly over 1f out: styd on to ld again towards fin* **4/9**[1]
42 2 nk **Count Simon (IRE)**[26] 4117 3-9-5 0.................... DavidProbert 5 76
(Andrew Balding) *pressed ldr: pushed into narrow ld over 1f out: rdn ins fnl f: one pce and hdd towards fin* **7/2**[2]
0 3 21 **Grey Mist**[14] 4569 3-9-5 0.................... DavidAllan 6 54
(Tim Easterby) *hld up: rdn and hdwy to chse ldrs 3f out: wknd fnl 2f* **7/1**[3]
4 70 **Seirios (IRE)** 3-9-0 0.................... PaddyBradley(5) 4
(Jane Chapple-Hyam) *hld up: rdn over 4f out: sn wknd and t.o* **12/1**

2m 39.86s (-0.94) **Going Correction** +0.10s/f (Good) **4 Ran SP% 111.7**
Speed ratings (Par 102): **107,106,92,46**
CSF £2.49 TOTE £1.40; EX 2.70 Trifecta £4.60.
**Owner** Laurence Bellman **Bred** Mrs James Wigan **Trained** Upper Lambourn, Berks

**FOCUS**
Add 8yds to race distance. A four-runner older-horse maiden in which the pace was decent and only two got involved. The winner is rated to form.

## 5129 BETFRED SUPPORTS JACK BERRY HOUSE H'CAP 5f 3y
**7:35** (7:35) (Class 3) (0-95,94) 3-Y-O+
**£9,337** (£2,796; £1,398; £699; £349; £175) **Stalls Low**

Form RPR
-142 1 **Avon Breeze**[6] 4889 8-8-12 **85**.................... LewisEdmunds(5) 7 94
(Richard Whitaker) *midfield: pushed along and outpcd over 2f out: swtchd rt to outside appr fnl f: r.o strly: edgd lft 110yds out: led 50yds out* **9/2**[3]
-062 2 1 **Powerallied (IRE)**[20] 4337 4-9-2 **84**.................... TonyHamilton 3 89
(Richard Fahey) *led narrowly: rdn appr fnl f: kpt on but hdd 50yds out* **9/1**
460 3 1 ¾ **Gamesome (FR)**[34] 3829 6-9-7 **89**.................... GrahamLee 5 88
(Paul Midgley) *chsd ldrs: rdn 2f out: kpt on same pce fnl f* **7/2**[1]
6500 4 1 ¾ **Sandra's Secret (IRE)**[20] 4379 4-8-9 **77**.................... JasonHart 6 69
(Les Eyre) *pressed ldr: rdn 2f out: wknd fnl 110yds* **20/1**
0420 5 ½ **Lucky Beggar (IRE)**[7] 4867 7-9-6 **88**.................... DavidProbert 11 79
(David C Griffiths) *prom towards outer: rdn 2f out: no ex fnl f* **9/1**
3040 6 1 ½ **Oriental Relation (IRE)**[13] 4600 6-8-8 **76**....................(v) JoeDoyle 1 61
(James Given) *midfield: rdn over 2f out: one pce and nvr threatened* **9/1**
2410 7 5 **Poet's Society**[8] 4813 3-9-3 **89**.................... FrannyNorton 10 55
(Mark Johnston) *midfield: rdn over 2f out: wknd appr fnl f* **5/1**
2250 8 1 ½ **Rasheeq (IRE)**[21] 4306 4-9-8 **90**.................... DavidAllan 8 52
(Tim Easterby) *hld up: pushed along over 2f out: wknd over 1f out* **4/1**[2]

1m 3.18s (-0.12) **Going Correction** +0.10s/f (Good)
**WFA** 3 from 4yo+ 4lb **8 Ran SP% 111.8**
Speed ratings (Par 107): **104,102,99,96,96 93,85,83**
CSF £41.91 CT £154.26 TOTE £5.10: £1.70, £2.20, £1.60; EX 50.60 Trifecta £184.90.
**Owner** Grange Park Racing II & Partner **Bred** Hellwood Stud Farm **Trained** Scarcroft, W Yorks

**FOCUS**
Add 8yds to race distance. Mainly exposed sorts in this sprint, but the pace was sound and the winner continues in good form. The winner is rated back to her 2016 form.

## 5130 ALAMO BUSINESS SYSTEMS H'CAP 1m 6y
**8:05** (8:07) (Class 3) (0-95,94) 3-Y-O+ **£7,762** (£2,310; £1,154; £577) **Stalls Low**

Form RPR
-045 1 **Crowning Glory (FR)**[48] 3319 4-9-8 **93**.................... GeorgiaCox(5) 7 102
(Ralph Beckett) *hld up: pushed along over 2f out: hdwy on outer over 1f out: rdn to ld ins fnl f: styd on* **6/1**
-510 2 1 ¼ **Red Tea**[41] 3589 4-9-9 **89**.................... DavidProbert 9 95
(Peter Hiatt) *hld up in tch: chsd ldrs over 2f out: rdn over 1f out: wnt 2nd ins fnl f: kpt on* **14/1**
5364 3 1 **Spring Offensive (IRE)**[27] 4077 5-9-3 **90**.................... ConnorMurtagh(7) 6 94
(Richard Fahey) *in tch: trckd ldrs gng wl 2f out: rdn to ld appr fnl f: hdd ins fnl f: no ex* **4/1**[2]
-241 4 2 ¾ **Destroyer**[18] 4438 4-9-1 **81**.................... DougieCostello 1 78
(Tom Tate) *chsd ldrs: rdn over 2f out: wknd ins fnl f* **9/2**[3]
6141 5 ¾ **Sands Chorus**[11] 4692 5-9-12 **92** 6ex.................... RichardKingscote 3 88
(James Given) *prom: rdn 2f out: wknd ins fnl f* **7/2**[1]
0423 6 nk **Morning Suit (USA)**[9] 4763 3-9-0 **88**.................... FrannyNorton 2 81
(Mark Johnston) *s.i.s: outpcd in rr tl kpt on ins fnl f* **9/2**[3]
1606 7 3 ¾ **Cote D'Azur**[14] 4578 4-10-0 **94**.................... JasonHart 4 80
(Les Eyre) *led: racd keenly: rdn 2f out: hdd appr fnl f: wknd and eased* **8/1**

1m 44.44s (-1.46) **Going Correction** +0.10s/f (Good)
**WFA** 3 from 4yo+ 8lb **7 Ran SP% 110.6**
Speed ratings (Par 107): **111,109,108,106,105 104,101**
CSF £75.18 CT £356.94 TOTE £6.20: £2.90, £4.50; EX 67.50 Trifecta £473.40.
**Owner** The Eclipse Partnership **Bred** Car Colston Hall Stud **Trained** Kimpton, Hants

**FOCUS**
Add 8yds to race distance. They went hard in front and it paid to come from off the pace, so the overall form may prove misleading. However, it's been taken at face value.

## 5131 YACHT LONDON CUP MAIDEN H'CAP 1m 2f 5y
**8:35** (8:39) (Class 5) (0-70,70) 3-Y-O+ **£3,234** (£962; £481; £240) **Stalls Low**

Form RPR
0-03 1 **Mr C (IRE)**[24] 4172 3-8-2 **53** oh2 ow2.................... JoeDoyle 7 59
(Ollie Pears) *midfield on outer: hdwy to trck ldrs 3f out: pushed along to chal appr fnl f: rdn to ld narrowly 75yds out: kpt on* **14/1**[3]
2064 2 hd **Akkadian Empire**[18] 4432 3-9-4 **69**....................(h) DavidNolan 11 74
(Iain Jardine) *hld up in midfield: hdwy on outer over 2f out: rdn to ld narrowly appr fnl f: hdd 75yds out: kpt on* **14/1**[3]
3 1 **Epitaph (IRE)**[56] 3059 3-9-3 **68**.................... AlistairRawlinson 5 71
(Michael Appleby) *midfield: rdn over 1f out: kpt on fnl f* **4/1**[2]
4505 4 nk **Satish**[22] 4260 4-9-11 **67**....................(b) PhillipMakin 9 68+
(David O'Meara) *s.i.s: hld up in rr: racd keenly: stl plenty to do appr fnl f: r.o ins fnl f: nrst fin* **16/1**
0622 5 nk **Sir Gnet (IRE)**[15] 4541 3-9-2 **67**....................(h) DavidProbert 10 69
(Ed Dunlop) *hld up in rr: racd keenly: pushed along and hdwy on outer 2f out: rdn to chse ldrs appr fnl f: no ex fnl 75yds* **4/1**[2]
-506 6 ¾ **Broughtons Knight**[20] 4365 3-9-1 **66**.................... StevieDonohoe 4 66+
(Henry Spiller) *hld up in midfield: rdn ent fnl f: swtchd lft ins fnl f: kpt on same pce* **4/1**[2]
00-0 7 5 **Shakabula (IRE)**[73] 2507 3-8-4 **60** ow3.................... BenRobinson(5) 6 50
(Brian Ellison) *trckd ldrs: rdn 2f out: wknd ins fnl f* **33/1**
246/ 8 1 ¾ **Vodka Wells (FR)**[15] 5270 7-9-7 **63**....................(p) DougieCostello 8 49
(Rebecca Menzies) *prom: rdn 2f out: wknd ins fnl f* **20/1**
-405 9 2 ¼ **Almunther (IRE)**[29] 4019 4-9-5 **61**.................... JasonHart 3 42
(Micky Hammond) *dwlt: sn trckd ldrs racing keenly: rdn 2f out: wknd fnl f* **20/1**
0-32 10 4 **Luminous**[24] 4173 3-9-5 **70**....................(h) GrahamLee 1 57
(Simon Crisford) *led: racd keenly: rdn whn hdd appr fnl f: wknd* **11/4**[1]

2m 15.27s (1.57) **Going Correction** +0.10s/f (Good)
**WFA** 3 from 4yo+ 9lb **10 Ran SP% 118.3**
Speed ratings (Par 103): **97,96,96,95,95 94,90,89,87,84**
CSF £189.03 CT £938.26 TOTE £13.50: £3.20, £2.90, £1.50; EX 202.50 Trifecta £363.50.
**Owner** A M Caygill **Bred** J O'Haire **Trained** Norton, N Yorks



The Form Book Flat, Raceform Ltd, Newbury, RG14 5SJ

**FOCUS**
Add 8yds to race distance. A moderately-run maiden handicap in which the first six were clear. Many were fairly exposed, and the form won't be strong. An improved effort from the winner.

## 5132 JOHN NIXON SUPPORTS JACK BERRY HOUSE H'CAP 6f
9:05 (9:09) (Class 5) (0-75,77) 3-Y-O+ £3,234 (£962; £481; £240) Stalls Low

Form RPR
4421 1 **Mr Orange (IRE)**13 4605 4-9-6 69..........(p) DougieCostello 11 78
(Paul Midgley) *midfield on outer: pushed along and hdwy 2f out: rdn to ld appr fnl f: kpt on* **7/1**

1-03 2 1 1/2 **Perfect Symphony (IRE)**18 4433 3-9-5 73..........(p) KevinStott 2 76
(Kevin Ryan) *trckd ldrs: rdn to chal ent fnl f: kpt on but a hld* **6/1**3

00-0 3 1 3/4 **Kommander Kirkup**22 4277 6-9-7 70.......... PhillipMakin 12 68
(Michael Herrington) *hld up: rdn and hdwy on outer over 1f out: kpt on fnl f: wnt 3rd towards fin* **33/1**

-300 4 nk **Gloriux**20 4341 3-8-13 70..........(p1) CallumShepherd(3) 5 66
(Charles Hills) *chsd ldrs: rdn 2f out: one pce fnl f: lost 3rd towards fin* **22/1**

0450 5 3/4 **Royal Connoisseur (IRE)**20 4343 6-9-5 75.......... ConnorMurtagh(7) 7 70
(Richard Fahey) *hld up: sn pushed along: kpt on fnl f: nvr threatened* **20/1**

0-16 6 1/2 **Alfie's Angel (IRE)**13 4610 3-9-4 72.......... GrahamLee 4 64
(Bryan Smart) *midfield: sn pushed along: brielf short of room appr fnl f: one pce ins fnl f and nvr threatened* **7/1**

0022 7 6 **Mishaal (IRE)**10 4719 7-9-12 75.......... JoeDoyle 3 49
(Michael Herrington) *pressed ldr: rdn 2f out: wknd fnl f* **7/2**2

-163 8 2 **Grinty (IRE)**18 4437 3-9-0 73.......... CallumRodriguez(5) 10 40
(Michael Dods) *dwlt: hld up: sn pushed along: a towards rr* **14/1**

341 9 1 1/4 **Ypres**8 4789 8-8-13 62 6ex..........(p) CamHardie 13 26
(Jason Ward) *dwlt: a in rr* **25/1**

5530 10 5 **Yeeoow (IRE)**22 4277 8-9-9 75..........(p) JordanVaughan(3) 8 23
(K R Burke) *led narrowly: rdn over 2f out: hdd appr fnl f: wknd* **25/1**

0113 11 hd **Kody Ridge (IRE)**9 4745 3-9-5 73 6ex..........(h) TonyHamilton 9 19
(Roger Fell) *pressed ldr: rdn over 2f out: wknd over 1f out: eased* **10/1**

5542 12 24 **Nibras Again**13 4624 3-9-4 72..........(p1) StevieDonohoe 1
(Ismail Mohammed) *chsd ldrs: rdn and wknd over 2f out: eased* **3/1**1

1m 17.45s (0.55) **Going Correction** +0.10s/f (Good)
**WFA** 3 from 4yo+ 5lb 12 Ran SP% **122.0**
Speed ratings (Par 103): **100,98,95,95,94 93,85,82,74,74 74,42**
CSF £46.40 CT £1339.07 TOTE £5.90: £2.40, £2.30, £11.10; EX 50.90 Trifecta £2137.90 Part won..
**Owner** J Blackburn & A Turton **Bred** Rathbarry Stud **Trained** Westow, N Yorks

**FOCUS**
Add 8yds to race distance. A competitive sprint in which most were exposed sorts runat a very strong gallop which suited the hold-up horses. The runner-up is the best guide, with the market 1-2 disappointing.
T/Plt: £643.70 to a £1 stake. Pool: £70,893.95 - 80.39 winning units T/Qpdt: £86.50 to a £1 stake. Pool: £5,977.44 - 51.10 winning units **Andrew Sheret**

# 5098 HAYDOCK (L-H)
Saturday, July 22

**OFFICIAL GOING: Good (good to firm in places) changing to good after race 1 (5.55)**
Wind: Negligible Weather: Cloudy, occasional sunny spells, warm

## 5134 BETFRED SUPPORTS JACK BERRY HOUSE FILLIES' H'CAP 5f
5:55 (5:59) (Class 5) (0-70,72) 3-Y-O+ £3,557 (£1,058; £529; £264) Stalls High

Form RPR
3603 1 **Teepee Time**19 4448 4-8-2 50 oh3..........(b) PhilDennis(5) 12 59
(Michael Mullineaux) *racd in 2nd stands' side: drvn and led ent fnl f: sn 1 l clr: hld on by diminishing margin* **25/1**

035 2 nk **Oriental Lilly**32 3948 3-8-8 62.......... SeanMooney(7) 3 69+
(Jim Goldie) *hld up: looking for room 2f out: swtchd and pushed along over 1f out: hdwy and rdn fnl f: r.o strly: clsng on wnr nr fin* **16/1**

600- 3 1 1/4 **Ayresome Angel**267 7660 4-9-9 66.......... DavidNolan 4 70
(John Mackie) *led: pushed along and hdd ent fnl f: rdn and no ex* **12/1**

6002 4 1/2 **Rose Marmara**15 4574 4-9-12 72..........(t) AdamMcNamara(3) 9 74
(Brian Rothwell) *in rr: effrt 1/2-way: rdn over 2f out: styd on ins fnl f: tk 4th nr fin* **5/1**3

5044 5 hd **Bay Station**11 4717 3-9-0 61..........(p1) KevinStott 6 61
(Jason Ward) *mid-div: drvn 2f out: sn reminders: one pce fnl f: lost 4th nr fin* **8/1**

4653 6 3 3/4 **Rose Eclair**14 4607 4-9-0 60..........(p) RachelRichardson(3) 2 47
(Tim Easterby) *mid-div: drvn 2f out: no imp* **11/4**1

0550 7 shd **Kachess**11 4728 3-9-7 68..........(v) RichardKingscote 10 54
(Tom Dascombe) *trckd ldrs: pushed along over 2f out: reminders over 1f out: wknd ent fnl f* **4/1**2

6503 8 nk **Savannah Beau**15 4574 5-9-12 69..........(v1) TomEaves 7 55
(Derek Shaw) *hld up: drvn over 1f out: no rspnse* **9/1**

2166 9 1/2 **Glyder**15 4576 3-9-0 61.......... RoystonFfrench 1 44
(John Holt) *chsd ldrs: drvn 2f out: rdn over 1f out: wknd* **6/1**

58.19s (-2.61) **Going Correction** -0.325s/f (Firm)
**WFA** 3 from 4yo+ 4lb 9 Ran SP% **116.2**
Speed ratings (Par 100): **107,106,104,103,103 97,97,96,95**
CSF £366.83 CT £4987.57 TOTE £26.40: £6.50, £2.10, £2.60; EX 530.80 Trifecta £1562.30.
**Owner** G Cornes **Bred** Brook Stud Bloodstock Ltd **Trained** Alpraham, Cheshire
■ Stewards' Enquiry : Sean Mooney caution: careless riding

**FOCUS**
All races run over the Inner home straight. Rail movements increase advertised distances as follows: Race 2 by 38 yards; Races 3, 4 and 6 by 16 yards and Race 5 by 49 yards. A modest fillies' sprint handicap, with the surprise winner back to her best. They went a decent gallop on good ground. They were kicking the top off the surface in places but the winning time concurs with that ground assessment.

## 5135 BETFRED GREAT VALUE EVERY DAY H'CAP 1m 2f 42y
6:30 (6:30) (Class 5) (0-75,77) 4-Y-O+ £3,557 (£1,058; £529; £264) Stalls Centre

Form RPR
0014 1 **Cornborough**7 4893 6-9-0 73..........(p) CallumRodriguez(5) 12 81
(Mark Walford) *hld up: hdwy on outer 3f out: pushed along 2f out: clsd on ldrs over 1f out: drvn and r.o wl to ld last 50yds* **13/8**1

-044 2 nk **Outback Blue**18 4468 4-8-10 71..........(vt1) KatherineGlenister(7) 4 78
(David Evans) *mid-div: hdwy gng wl 3f out: n.m.r 2f out: sn swtchd: prog to ld ent fnl f: rdn and r.o: hdd last 50yds* **10/1**

-030 3 2 1/4 **Saxo Jack (FR)**36 3795 7-9-0 75..........(t) RossaRyan(7) 11 78
(Sophie Leech) *in rr: hdwy on inner 3f out: pushed along 2f out: rdn in 3rd and ev ch 1f out: one pce fnl f* **9/1**

2-02 4 3 3/4 **Scottish Summit (IRE)**33 3910 4-9-3 71.......... SamJames 7 66
(Geoffrey Harker) *prom: led 2f out: rdn wl over 1f out: hdd ent fnl f: no ex* **10/1**

-114 5 1 1/2 **La Celebs Ville (IRE)**16 4525 4-9-9 77..........(p) RichardKingscote 10 69
(Tom Dascombe) *chsd ldrs: wnt 2nd 1/2-way: pushed along 2f out: lost pl and rdn over 1f out: one pce fnl f* **4/1**3

-000 6 6 **Street Poet (IRE)**21 4358 4-8-11 65.......... TomEaves 13 45
(Michael Herrington) *led: pushed along 3f out: hdd 2f out: fdd* **16/1**

6044 7 8 **Lopito De Vega (IRE)**9 4802 5-8-8 61 ow1..........(p1) DavidAllan 3 26
(David C Griffiths) *mid-div: relegated to last 3f out: sn rdn: wknd and eased* **7/2**2

2m 10.78s (-1.92) **Going Correction** -0.325s/f (Firm) 7 Ran SP% **114.4**
Speed ratings (Par 103): **94,93,91,88,87 82,76**
CSF £19.30 CT £113.10 TOTE £2.30: £1.80, £4.40; EX 17.30 Trifecta £120.20.
**Owner** Cornborough Racing Club **Bred** Mr & Mrs A E Pakenham **Trained** Sherriff Hutton, N Yorks

**FOCUS**
Race distance increased by 38 yards. A fair handicap. The tempo increased in the straight and the favourite got up in the nick of time. He still has a bit of mileage compared with his jumps form.

## 5136 BETFRED TV EBF NOVICE STKS (PLUS 10 RACE) 6f 212y
7:00 (7:00) (Class 4) 2-Y-O £4,528 (£1,347; £673; £336) Stalls Low

Form RPR
1 1 **Veejay (IRE)**24 4220 2-9-5 0.......... RobHornby 3 84+
(Mick Channon) *hld up: hdwy on outer 3f out: pushed along 2f out: sn jnd ldrs: rdn and led 1f out: pushed out to assert nr fin* **3/1**2

2 1/2 **Al Barg (IRE)** 2-9-2 0.......... DaneO'Neill 2 80+
(Richard Hannon) *trckd ldrs: n.m.r 3f out: sn swtchd and pushed along: hdwy to chal ldrs over 1f out: sn ev ch: r.o wl ins fnl f: jst hld nr fin* **9/2**

1 3 hd **Wasim (IRE)**15 4567 2-9-8 0.......... KevinStott 8 85
(Ismail Mohammed) *disp ld tl settled in 2nd after 1 f: gng wl 3f out: pushed along 2f out: drvn and ev ch 1f out: rdn and kpt on wl fnl f* **9/4**1

42 4 4 1/2 **Knight In Armour (IRE)**22 4291 2-9-2 0.......... JoeFanning 1 67
(Mark Johnston) *disp ld tl led after 1 f: drvn over 2f out: rdn and hdd 1f out: one pce and btn whn n.m.r ins fnl f* **10/3**3

0 5 11 **Hic Bibi**16 4526 2-8-11 0.......... DavidAllan 7 34
(David Brown) *chsd ldrs: ev ch 3f out: pushed along 2f out: sn lost pl: fdd* **25/1**

6 1 1/2 **Floreat Floreat (IRE)** 2-9-2 0.......... RichardKingscote 5 35
(Tom Dascombe) *slowly away: in rr: reminder over 2f out: no imp* **7/1**

1m 27.6s (-3.10) **Going Correction** -0.325s/f (Firm) 6 Ran SP% **113.4**
Speed ratings (Par 96): **104,103,103,98,85 83**
CSF £16.96 TOTE £4.00: £1.60, £2.80; EX 17.20 Trifecta £41.90.
**Owner** John & Zoe Webster **Bred** Messrs Billy McEnery & Paul McEnery **Trained** West Ilsley, Berks

**FOCUS**
Race distance increased by 16 yards. A decent juvenile novice contest. An early-pace duel between the third and the fourth compromised their chances and the overall winning time.

## 5137 BETFRED FOLLOW US ON TWITTER CONDITIONS STKS 6f 212y
7:30 (7:30) (Class 3) 3-Y-O+ £9,056 (£2,695; £1,346) Stalls Low

Form RPR
4022 1 **Jungle Cat (IRE)**7 4890 5-9-9 113..........(b) WilliamBuick 7 116
(Charlie Appleby) *hld up: niggled briefly over 2f out: gd hdwy on outer over 1f out: led appr fnl f: kpt up to work and c clr: easily* **8/13**1

40-4 2 5 **Ibn Malik (IRE)**21 4362 4-9-5 108.......... DaneO'Neill 4 99
(Charles Hills) *led: pushed along 2f out: sn drvn: rdn and hdd jst over 1f out: no ex ins fnl f* **7/4**2

1365 3 11 **That Is The Spirit**23 4264 6-9-5 101.......... DanielTudhope 2 82
(David O'Meara) *chsd ldr: pushed along 2f out: reminder and lost 2nd over 1f out: no ex: eased fnl f* **8/1**3

1m 25.86s (-4.84) **Going Correction** -0.325s/f (Firm) course record 3 Ran SP% **109.4**
Speed ratings (Par 107): **114,108,95**
CSF £2.05 TOTE £1.50; EX 1.90 Trifecta £1.90.
**Owner** Godolphin **Bred** Darley **Trained** Newmarket, Suffolk

**FOCUS**
Race distance increased by 16 yards. The feature race was a good quality little conditions contest. They went a decent gallop and the odds-on favourite confirmed his superiority. He's rated to his best.

## 5138 BETFRED LIKE US ON FACEBOOK H'CAP 1m 6f
8:00 (8:00) (Class 4) (0-80,82) 4-Y-O+ £5,822 (£1,732; £865; £432) Stalls Low

Form RPR
41-2 1 **Stamford Raffles**21 4365 4-9-6 82.......... PaddyBradley(5) 9 92+
(Jane Chapple-Hyam) *racd in 2nd: pushed along to ld 2f out: drvn and narrow advantage over 1f out: rdn ent fnl f: r.o wl: on top last 100yds* **11/4**1

2154 2 1 1/4 **On Fire**36 3794 4-9-3 74..........(p) DanielTudhope 3 82
(James Bethell) *led: pushed along and hdd 2f out: rdn and rallied ent fnl f: r.o but hld last 100yds* **11/4**1

1653 3 4 **Royal Flag**21 4338 7-8-7 69.......... BenRobinson(5) 1 71
(Brian Ellison) *t.k.h: trckd ldrs: drvn on inner 3f out: rdn in 3rd 2f out: kpt on one pce fnl f* **10/1**

221 4 1 3/4 **Wordiness**9 4791 9-8-13 70.......... DaneO'Neill 6 70
(David Evans) *hld up in last: effrt on outer over 2f out: rdn over 1f out: tk 4th ins fnl f* **8/1**3

4534 5 1/2 **Peterhouse (USA)**23 4267 5-9-4 75.......... KevinStott 7 74
(Jason Ward) *mid-div: pushed along over 2f out: sn rdn and wknd* **4/1**2

3131 6 1 **Zenafire**21 4338 8-8-13 73..........(p) SammyJoBell(3) 11 71
(Sarah Hollinshead) *5th early: hld up to take clsr order 1/2-way: pushed along 3f out: drvn over 2f out: rdn wl over 1f out: fdd* **4/1**2

3m 10.78s **Going Correction** -0.325s/f (Firm) 6 Ran SP% **113.5**
Speed ratings (Par 105): **61,60,58,57,56 56**
CSF £10.67 CT £62.75 TOTE £4.00: £1.80, £1.80; EX 11.00 Trifecta £68.40.
**Owner** Mrs Jane Chapple-Hyam **Bred** C A Cyzer **Trained** Dalham, Suffolk

**FOCUS**
Race distance increased by 49 yards. A fairly decent handicap. They went a sedate gallop and the joint-favourites came clear from prominent pitches. The winner built on his reappearance promise.

## 5139 BETFRED SUPER LEAGUE H'CAP 7f 212y
**8:30** (8:30) (Class 5) (0-75,76) 3-Y-O **£3,557** (£1,058; £529; £264) **Stalls** Low

Form RPR

-216 **1** **Wigan Warrior**[28] 4084 3-9-6 **74**.......................................... TomEaves 4 80
(David Brown) *mid-div: 4th gng wl 2f out: plld out 2f out: hdwy and rdn over 1f out: r.o strly fnl f: led last 75yds* **12/1**

415 **2** ½ **Jumira Prince (IRE)**[28] 4084 3-9-6 **74**........................(b[1]) JackMitchell 5 79
(Roger Varian) *t.k.h: hdwy to ld 2f out: sn drvn: rdn fnl f: r.o: hdd 75yds out* **13/8**[1]

655 **3** 1 **Mac O'Polo (IRE)**[26] 4164 3-8-10 **64**.............. RichardKingscote 3 67
(Tom Dascombe) *in rr: last 1/2-way: hdwy on outer over 2f out: pushed along over 1f out: sn rdn: r.o wl to take 3rd ins fnl f: nvr nrr* **8/1**

-005 **4** 1¼ **Conqueress (IRE)**[16] 4525 3-8-9 **68**....................(p) JaneElliott(5) 12 68
(Tom Dascombe) *pushed along to ld fr wd draw: sn 4 l clr: given breather and 1 l clr 4f out: drvn and hdd 2f out: rdn and tried to rally tl no ex ins fnl f* **14/1**

20 **5** ¾ **Thornton**[22] 4309 3-9-4 **72**.......................................... PaulMulrennan 2 70
(Michael Dods) *hld up: trcking ldrs 2f out: rdn over 1f out: styd on one pce fnl f* **6/1**[3]

1-00 **6** 2 **Habbad (FR)**[16] 4537 3-9-4 **72**.................................. TimmyMurphy 7 65
(Richard Hannon) *mid-div: hdwy 3f out: sn ev ch: pushed along over 2f out: rdn wl over 1f out: one pce* **7/1**

5202 **7** 3 **Spirit Of Belle**[4] 5009 3-9-4 **72**...........................(v) DanielTudhope 11 62
(David Evans) *prom: drvn and ev ch 2f out: wknd appr fnl f* **7/2**[2]

0410 **8** 8 **Best Of My Love (IRE)**[24] 4208 3-9-8 **76**...................... RobHornby 9 44
(Mick Channon) *mid-div: drvn over 2f out: sn rdn and wknd: eased fnl f* **16/1**

1m 41.35s (-2.35) **Going Correction** -0.325s/f (Firm) **8** Ran SP% **118.5**
Speed ratings (Par 100): **98,97,96,95,94 92,89,81**
CSF £33.23 CT £176.08 TOTE £12.30: £2.90, £1.10, £2.70; EX 49.20 Trifecta £359.00.
**Owner** Peter Onslow & David H Brown **Bred** Peter Onslow **Trained** Averham Park, Notts

**FOCUS**
Race distance increased by 16 yards. A fair 3yo handicap. They went a respectable gallop and it is sound form, the first three all improving a bit.
T/Plt: £317.70 to a £1 stake. Pool: £70,553.64 - 162.07 winning units. T/Qpdt: £9.30 to a £1 stake. Pool: £7,351.14 - 579.57 winning units. **Keith McHugh**

# 5022 LINGFIELD (L-H)
Saturday, July 22

**OFFICIAL GOING: Soft (good to soft in places) changing to soft after race 1 (5.45)**
Weather: Showers early, clearing up

## 5140 READ SILVESTRE DE SOUSA AT 188BET H'CAP 1m 2f
**5:45** (5:45) (Class 5) (0-75,77) 4-Y-O+ **£2,911** (£866; £432; £216) **Stalls** Low

Form RPR

0505 **1** **Michael's Mount**[21] 4336 4-9-8 **74**...............................(b) LukeMorris 4 84
(Ed Dunlop) *bhd ldrs on outer: travelling wl over 3f out: shkn up and prog to ld 2f out: sn rdn: 3 l up over 1f out: began to weaken ins fnl f: hld on* **9/4**[1]

2-33 **2** ¾ **Singapore Sling**[30] 4019 4-9-6 **72**...............................(h) TomQueally 3 80
(James Fanshawe) *bhd ldrs on rail: nt handled bnd on ent st and lost grnd: shkn up over 3f out: rdn over 2f out: began to keep on strly fr over 1f out: clsng on wnr ins fnl f: jst hld nr fin* **4/1**

5032 **3** 5 **Zephyros (GER)**[18] 3753 6-8-10 **65**........................ HectorCrouch(3) 7 64
(David Bridgwater) *sluggish s and pushed along to pressed ldr on outer: rdn over 2f out where led marginally: sn hdd & wknd: no ex fr ent fnl f* **3/1**[2]

4231 **4** 2½ **Glens Wobbly**[29] 4041 9-9-3 **74**................................ PaddyPilley(5) 1 69
(Jonathan Geake) *narrowly led on rail: shkn up over 3f out: rdn wl over 2f out: narrowly hdd over 2f out: wknd after fr over 1f out* **7/1**

2-66 **5** 1¼ **Mighty Lady**[17] 4501 4-9-9 **75**.................................... TomMarquand 6 67
(Robyn Brisland) *hld up in rr: shkn up over 3f out: and wnt wd on turn into st: sn rdn: no imp sn after* **7/2**[3]

2m 15.61s (5.11) **Going Correction** +0.50s/f (Yiel) **5** Ran SP% **110.5**
Speed ratings (Par 103): **99,98,94,92,91**
CSF £11.44 TOTE £2.90: £1.80, £2.40; EX 9.70 Trifecta £20.90.
**Owner** Miltil Consortium **Bred** Southill Stud **Trained** Newmarket, Suffolk

**FOCUS**
Race distances as advertised. The going was soft (good to soft) ahead of the opener, a modest handicap in which they went a fair gallop in the ground.

## 5141 GET 1/4 ODDS AT 188BET MAIDEN STKS 1m 3f 133y
**6:15** (6:16) (Class 5) 3-Y-O+ **£2,911** (£866; £432; £216) **Stalls** High

Form RPR

40 **1** **Thistimenextyear**[52] 3209 3-8-12 0............................ JennyPowell(5) 6 81
(Richard Spencer) *sn led: increased advantage after 4f: 5 l advantage 5f out: c bk to chsng gp over 3f out: rdn over 2f out and wnt clr: ld reduced fnl f: pushed out fnl 100yds* **8/1**[3]

42 **2** 1¾ **Normandie Attack (FR)**[14] 4611 3-9-3 0.................. StevieDonohoe 2 77
(Charlie Fellowes) *racd in mid-div and niggled along at times: prog to chse ldr 4f out: rdn over 2f out: kpt on wl ins fnl f: but nvr getting to wnr* **4/1**[2]

042 **3** 8 **Kazawi**[46] 3427 3-9-3 80........................................ KieranShoemark 1 64
(Roger Charlton) *broke wl: hld up bhd ldr on rail: shkn up and taken off rail over 3f out: rdn over 2f out and no rspnse one pce fr over 1f out* **4/7**[1]

36 **4** 10 **Helf (IRE)**[15] 4569 3-9-3 0........................................ TomMarquand 7 48
(Richard Hannon) *chsd ldr: shkn up over 2f out: no ex over 1f out: hands and heels fnl f* **4/1**[2]

**5** ¾ **Monar Lad (IRE)**[20] 5-9-9 0...................................... MitchGodwin(5) 4 46
(Dai Burchell) *s.s and wl bhd in last: nvr involved* **40/1**

**6** 53 **Royal Hall (FR)**[145] 5-9-11 0.................................... HectorCrouch(3) 5
(Gary Moore) *s.s: a in rr: t.o fr over 3f out* **16/1**

00 **7** 3¼ **Volturnus**[23] 4274 3-9-3 0.......................................... DougieCostello 3
(Jamie Osborne) *a in last trio: struggling fr 6f out: wl bhd ent st: t.o* **80/1**

0 **8** 6 **Desi Daru (IRE)**[23] 4274 5-10-0 0.................................. SaleemGolam 8
(Conrad Allen) *racd in 2nd: wknd qckly fr 6f out: sn struggling: t.o* **33/1**

2m 39.11s (7.61) **Going Correction** +0.50s/f (Yiel)
**WFA** 3 from 5yo 11lb **8** Ran SP% **127.3**
Speed ratings (Par 103): **94,92,87,80,80 45,42,38**
CSF £44.17 TOTE £11.70: £2.70, £1.30, £1.02; EX 88.30 Trifecta £146.10.
**Owner** Rebel Racing (2) **Bred** Brook Stud Bloodstock Ltd **Trained** Newmarket, Suffolk

**FOCUS**
The going was changed to soft ahead of the second race, an uncompetitive maiden in which they finished well strung out.

## 5142 188BET.CO.UK H'CAP 1m 6f
**6:45** (6:47) (Class 6) (0-65,67) 3-Y-O+ **£2,587** (£770; £384; £192) **Stalls** Low

Form RPR

-454 **1** **Our Cilla**[27] 4117 3-7-7 **48** oh3...................................(b) MillyNaseb(7) 8 58+
(Julia Feilden) *hmpd at s and pushed sideways: lost grnd: hld up in rr: stealthy prog fr wl off the pce 4f out: shkn up and tk clsr order in centre fr 3f out: sn rdn: ld over 1f out: bounded clr fnl 150yds: readily* **20/1**

0553 **2** 6 **Esspeegee**[10] 4756 4-8-10 **46**...................................(p) JimmyQuinn 3 46
(Alan Bailey) *led early tl settled bhd ldrs: rdn and led wl over 3f out: hdd wl over 2f out: kpt on again to take 2nd over 1f out: no imp on easy wnr fnl 150yds* **4/1**[1]

6000 **3** 4½ **Ban Shoof**[9] 4809 4-9-11 **64**................................(p) HectorCrouch(3) 9 58
(Gary Moore) *mid-div on outer: tk clsr order wl over 3f out and rdn to chse ldr wl over 2f out: led narrowly wl over 1f out: sn hdd on both sides: wknd after* **4/1**[1]

-266 **4** 11 **Haldaw**[61] 2892 3-8-11 **64**........................................ DavidEgan(5) 4 46
(Mick Channon) *chsd ldr on rail: lost a few pls wl over 6f out: n.m.r bhd ldrs on turn into st: sn rdn: one pce after* **4/1**[1]

040 **5** 10 **Titan**[15] 4569 3-9-1 **63**.................................................. LukeMorris 7 32
(Ed Dunlop) *wnt rt s and hmpd wnr: cl up tl taken away fr gp to jst off nr side rail after 4f: c bk across to gp wl over 6f out and racd jst off ldr: led over 5f out: rdn and hdd over 3f out: sn hld* **11/2**[2]

-006 **6** 6 **Kitsey (IRE)**[35] 3819 3-8-9 **57**................................. TomMarquand 2 18
(Richard Hannon) *mid-div: sltly hmpd early on: being niggled along bef 1/2-way: rdn wl over 3f out: no ex and pushed out fr 2f out* **6/1**[3]

6000 **7** 12 **Navajo Star (IRE)**[67] 2705 3-8-0 **48** oh1.........................(v[1]) KieranO'Neill 5
(Michael Appleby) *t.k.h and sn led: settled bttr after 3f: rdn over 5f out and hdd: wknd over 3f out: drifted rt u.p over 2f out: pushed out* **14/1**

0-06 **8** 2¾ **Bed Of Diamonds**[67] 2711 3-7-11 **48** oh3..................... NoelGarbutt(3) 6
(Adam West) *a towards rr: nvr involved* **9/1**

0006 **9** 2¾ **Fast Play (IRE)**[43] 3547 5-10-3 **67**...............................(b) DougieCostello 1 3
(Conor Dore) *mid-div: rdn 5f out: sn hld* **14/1**

3m 14.77s (4.77) **Going Correction** +0.50s/f (Yiel)
**WFA** 3 from 4yo+ 12lb **9** Ran SP% **117.8**
Speed ratings (Par 101): **106,102,100,93,88 84,77,76,74**
CSF £100.34 CT £397.27 TOTE £21.90: £4.20, £1.60, £1.80; EX 109.60 Trifecta £1525.60.
**Owner** Mrs C T Bushnell **Bred** Meon Valley Stud **Trained** Exning, Suffolk

**FOCUS**
A moderate staying handicap, in which they went a fair pace, setting things up for the closers. The first three came clear down the middle of the home straight.

## 5143 INDEPENDENT CATERING NURSERY H'CAP 6f
**7:15** (7:16) (Class 5) 2-Y-O **£2,911** (£866; £432; £216) **Stalls** Centre

Form RPR

313 **1** **Tulip Fever**[24] 4199 2-9-2 **75**.................................... GeorgiaCox(5) 10 77+
(William Haggas) *sn led on rail and t.k.h: hdd wl over 3f out: shkn up ent 2f out: sn rdn: led over 1f out: in control ins fnl f and nudged out fnl 110yds: cosily* **6/5**[1]

064 **2** hd **Brockey Rise (IRE)**[21] 4335 2-8-5 **64**........................ DavidEgan(5) 7 62
(David Evans) *chsd ldrs: rdn wl over 1f out: kpt on ins fnl f to cl on eased wnr nr fin* **8/1**[3]

005 **3** 1 **Hope And Glory (IRE)**[44] 3502 2-8-3 **57**........................ KieranO'Neill 2 52
(Tom Dascombe) *racd in centre tl c across 4f out and sn led: shkn up 2f out: hdd over 1f out and sn edgd lft: one pce ins fnl f* **12/1**

665 **4** 11 **Ventura Gold (IRE)**[19] 4427 2-9-0 **68**............................ JackGarritty 5 30
(Richard Fahey) *hld up on rail bhd ldrs: shkn up over 2f out and sn rdn: no ex fr over 1f out: wknd fnl f* **8/1**[3]

500 **5** 5 **Starboy (IRE)**[42] 3590 2-8-13 **67**........................(p[1]) SilvestreDeSousa 4 14
(George Scott) *racd in last on outside: briefly outpcd and shkn up over 3f out: lft bhd and eased fr over 1f out* **15/8**[2]

1m 14.34s (3.14) **Going Correction** +0.50s/f (Yiel) **5** Ran SP% **110.2**
Speed ratings (Par 94): **99,98,97,82,76**
CSF £11.15 TOTE £1.90: £1.10, £3.50; EX 10.80 Trifecta £42.70.
**Owner** Mrs Deborah June James **Bred** Mrs D J James **Trained** Newmarket, Suffolk

**FOCUS**
An interesting nursery and the first three came clear.

## 5144 L & R 5TH ANNIVERSARY/EBF NOVICE STKS 7f
**7:45** (7:46) (Class 5) 2-Y-O **£2,911** (£866; £432; £216) **Stalls** Centre

Form RPR

212 **1** **Indomeneo**[19] 4452 2-9-6 78........................................ JackGarritty 7 81
(Richard Fahey) *early ldr: hder after 1f: pressed ldr fr over 2f out: shkn up and led over 1f out: wnt clr ins fnl f: eased nr fin: impressive* **13/8**[1]

4 **2** 3¼ **Jupiter**[21] 4367 2-9-2 0............................................ FergusSweeney 1 67
(Henry Candy) *led after 1f: shkn up over 2f out: rdn 2f out: hdd over 1f out: kpt on: no match for wnr ins fnl f* **6/1**[3]

05 **3** 2¼ **Far Dawn**[32] 3930 2-9-2 0............................................ RyanPowell 3 61
(Simon Crisford) *chsd ldrs on outer: rdn over 2f out: kpt on one pce* **20/1**

00 **4** ½ **Dark Blue (IRE)**[11] 4709 2-8-11 0................................ CharlesBishop 5 55
(Mick Channon) *bhd ldr on rail: rdn over 2f out: front pair wnt clr over 1f out: kpt on one pce* **16/1**

10 **5** 1 **Boomerang Betty (IRE)**[9] 4806 2-9-4 0........................ DougieCostello 2 60
(Jamie Osborne) *t.k.h in rr: rdn over 2f out: lft bhd by front pair fr 2f out: kpt on fnl f* **7/1**

**6** 8 **General Marius (IRE)** 2-9-2 0................................ SilvestreDeSousa 4 38+
(Roger Varian) *missed break and in last: rn green: nt handle path: swtchd to outer 3f out: niggled along: no rspnse and pushed out after* **7/4**[2]

0 **7** 18 **Wiltons (FR)**[9] 4805 2-9-2 0............................................ LukeMorris 6
(Harry Dunlop) *in rr-div on rail: struggling and shkn up fr 4f out: rdn over 3f out: sn hld* **50/1**

1m 28.13s (4.83) **Going Correction** +0.50s/f (Yiel) **7** Ran SP% **113.8**
Speed ratings (Par 94): **92,88,85,85,84 74,54**
CSF £11.94 TOTE £2.40: £1.20, £2.90; EX 10.40 Trifecta £83.90.
**Owner** Middleham Park Racing LX **Bred** Hungerford Park Stud **Trained** Musley Bank, N Yorks



The Form Book Flat, Raceform Ltd, Newbury, RG14 5SJ

**FOCUS**
An uncompetitive novice in which experience told. They came up the stands' rail at a sedate tempo, and the positions didn't change much throughout.

## 5145 188BET H'CAP 7f
**8:15** (8:17) (Class 6) (0-65,65) 3-Y-O+ **£2,587** (£770; £384; £192) **Stalls** Centre

Form RPR

-034 **1** **Arctic Flower (IRE)**[21] 4350 4-8-5 **47**.......................... MitchGodwin(5) 9 55
(John Bridger) *pressed ldr three wd off rail: rdn wl over 2f out: led ent 2f out: kpt on wl fnl 110yds: hld on nr fin* **8/1**[3]

0-40 **2** *nk* **Bryght Boy**[22] 4298 4-9-8 **59**..............................(p[1]) ThomasBrown 5 66
(Ed Walker) *hld up in rr: shkn up and gd prog over 2f out: edgd rt 1f out: rdn jst ins fnl f: kpt on wl ins fnl 100yds: nt get to wnr* **7/1**[2]

3154 **3** *1 3/4* **Cyflymder (IRE)**[8] 4851 11-8-10 **50**......................... EdwardGreatrex(3) 7 53
(David C Griffiths) *hld up in rr-div: rdn over 2f out: ev ch in centre 1f out: kpt on* **9/1**

-034 **4** *2 1/4* **Easy Code**[22] 4311 4-10-0 **65**................................. SilvestreDeSousa 6 62+
(William Haggas) *restless in stalls: prom bhd wnr: rdn over 2f out: kpt on and carried sltly rt 1f out: one pce afterm: jst hld 4th* **6/4**[1]

3000 **5** *nse* **Corporal Maddox**[23] 4251 10-9-9 **60**.....................(p) LukeMorris 10 57
(Ronald Harris) *settled bhd ldrs: shkn up 3f out: rdn over 2f out kpt on ins fnl f: jst failed for 4th* **22/1**

-655 **6** *1 1/4* **Prince Of Cardamom (IRE)**[2] 5050 5-8-12 **54**........(p) PaddyPilley(5) 12 48
(Jonathan Geake) *pressed ldr: rdn over 2f out: drifted off rail over 1f out: no ex after* **11/1**

6000 **7** *3 1/4* **Luduamf (IRE)**[59] 2968 3-8-10 **54**.................................. TomMarquand 8 37
(Richard Hannon) *in rr-div: rdn along over 3f out: hld fr over 1f out* **25/1**

-006 **8** *3 1/4* **Morello (IRE)**[22] 4302 3-8-8 **57**............................... GeorgiaCox(5) 1 32
(Henry Candy) *styd in centre bhd gp ldr: shkn up 3f out: rdn over 2f out: kpt on wl and ev ch over 1f out: one pce fnl f* **12/1**

5-00 **9** *1 1/4* **Double Dutch**[97] 1818 3-8-2 **46** oh1............................... KieranO'Neill 11 18
(John Butler) *squeezed up s: in rr on rail: rdn over 2f out: no ex over 1f out* **28/1**

4330 **10** *3* **Bookmaker**[21] 4350 7-8-12 **54**.....................................(p) DavidEgan(5) 15 21
(John Bridger) *bhd ldrs: rdn over 2f out: kpt on tl wknd ins fnl f* **11/1**

3500 **11** *6* **Blistering Dancer (IRE)**[12] 4695 7-8-9 **46** oh1.........(p) WilliamCarson 2
(Tony Carroll) *styd in centre: overall ldr ent 4f out: rdn 3f out: hdd ent 2f out: sn wknd* **28/1**

-100 **12** *15* **Olympic Duel (IRE)**[59] 2961 4-9-8 **59**............................. RyanPowell 13
(Peter Hiatt) *led on rail: hdd ent 4f out: wknd sn after* **20/1**

0-50 **13** *8* **Popeswood (IRE)**[10] 4747 5-9-9 **60**.........................(b[1]) CharlesBishop 14
(Lee Carter) *mid-div: bec unbalance wl over 2f out: sn eased* **14/1**

1m 27.0s (3.70) **Going Correction** +0.50s/f (Yiel)
**WFA** 3 from 4yo+ 7lb **13** Ran SP% **124.5**
Speed ratings (Par 101): **98,97,95,93,93 91,87,84,82,79 72,55,46**
CSF £61.03 CT £525.14 TOTE £8.30: £2.50, £2.20, £2.40; EX 80.20 Trifecta £507.40.
**Owner** Mr & Mrs K Finch **Bred** B Kennedy **Trained** Liphook, Hants

**FOCUS**
A big field for this moderate handicap, but not many in-form types, and the first three pulled away from the pack down the centre (two runners went down the far side but were well beaten). The form doesn't look up to much.

## 5146 OPEN GOLF BETTING AT 188BET AMATEUR RIDERS' H'CAP 6f
**8:45** (8:50) (Class 6) (0-60,58) 3-Y-O+ **£2,495** (£774; £386; £193) **Stalls** Centre

Form RPR

3423 **1** **Sweet Pursuit**[18] 4467 3-10-1 **50**............................. MissJoannaMason 9 63+
(Rod Millman) *disp ld: led over 2f out: rdn over 1f out: pressed by runner-up 1f out: asserted ins fnl f and wnt clr fnl 110yds* **7/4**[1]

40-0 **2** *3 3/4* **Time Medicean**[35] 3811 11-10-7 **58**............................... MissSAColl(7) 10 61
(Tony Carroll) *chsd ldrs: t.k.h: travelling strly over 2f out: ev ch being pushed along 1f out: edgd lft and no ex fnl 110yds* **11/1**

0500 **3** *5* **Multi Quest**[38] 3728 5-9-13 **48**.............................(b) MissEMacKenzie(5) 5 36
(John E Long) *cl up in centre: rdn over 2f out: ev ch over 1f out: sn one pce and wknd out of contention: stuck on to hold 3rd* **12/1**

4540 **4** *1 3/4* **Limerick Lord (IRE)**[121] 1325 5-10-1 **45**.........................(p) MrRBirkett 2 28
(Julia Feilden) *racd in centre chsng ldrs: rdn over 2f out: no qckn 2f out: plugged on* **9/1**

5-00 **5** *2* **Portrush Storm**[155] 784 12-9-8 **45**.......................... MissSPeacock(7) 12 22
(Ray Peacock) *s.s: in rr: rdn over 3f out: kpt on one pce past btn horses fr over 1f out* **66/1**

2530 **6** *1 3/4* **Doctor Parkes**[12] 4695 11-10-8 **57**................................ MrWillPettis(5) 3 29
(Natalie Lloyd-Beavis) *hld up in mid-div in centre: rdn 3f out: one pce fr over 1f out* **20/1**

6254 **7** *1 3/4* **All Or Nothin (IRE)**[75] 2469 8-10-3 **52**...................... MissMBryant(5) 15 18
(Paddy Butler) *narrowly led: hdd over 2f out: sn wknd* **10/1**

5114 **8** *nk* **Concur (IRE)**[19] 4426 4-10-10 **54**...............................(tp) MrPMillman 11 19
(Rod Millman) *hld up bhd ldrs: rdn over 2f out: no rspnse and wknd wl over 1f out* **11/4**[2]

006 **9** *1 3/4* **Diamond Vine (IRE)**[10] 4735 9-9-12 **45**....................(p) MrConorOrr(3) 14 5
(Ronald Harris) *in rr: rdn over 3f out: kpt on one pce* **16/1**

1500 **10** *1* **Frangarry (IRE)**[12] 4695 5-10-8 **57**........................(h[1]) MissJCooley(5) 6 14
(Alan Bailey) *s.s: in rr: rdn over 2f out: sn wknd* **8/1**[3]

1m 14.05s (2.85) **Going Correction** +0.50s/f (Yiel)
**WFA** 3 from 4yo+ 5lb **10** Ran SP% **121.4**
Speed ratings (Par 101): **101,96,89,87,84 82,79,79,76,75**
CSF £24.21 CT £189.73 TOTE £2.60: £1.60, £2.70, £3.30; EX 22.30 Trifecta £159.10.
**Owner** Always Hopeful Partnership **Bred** Tom Chadney & Peter Green **Trained** Kentisbeare, Devon

**FOCUS**
A low-grade sprint handicap in which the favourite was a convincing winner.
T/Plt: £26.60 to a £1 stake. Pool: £69,570.17 - 1,902.29 winning units. T/Qpdt: £10.90 to a £1 stake. Pool: £5,979.85 - 403.76 winning units. **Cathal Gahan**

# [5105]NEWBURY (L-H)
Saturday, July 22

**OFFICIAL GOING: Soft (5.1)**
Wind: Virtually nil Weather: Rain

## 5147 BATHWICK TYRES H'CAP 7f (S)
**1:50** (1:52) (Class 2) (0-110,106) 3-Y-O+ **£16,172** (£4,812; £2,405; £1,202) **Stalls** Centre

Form RPR

2100 **1** **Rusumaat (IRE)**[14] 4636 3-9-2 **105**.................................... JimCrowley 6 111
(Mark Johnston) *mde all: rdn over 1f out: hrd pressed and bmpd ins fnl f: battled on wl u.p to hold towards fin: all out: v gamely* **6/1**[3]

-006 **2** *nk* **Remarkable**[31] 3963 4-9-8 **104**.................................(b) FrankieDettori 2 112
(John Gosden) *hld up in tch in midfield: rdn 3f out: hdwy u.p to chse ldrs 2f out: chal jst over 1f out: hung rt ins fnl f: kpt on but hld towards fin* **11/4**[1]

0-04 **3** *1 1/4* **Johnny Barnes (IRE)**[21] 4390 5-9-5 **101**............................ AdamKirby 4 105
(John Gosden) *hld up in tch in last pair: hdwy to trck ldrs jst over 2f out: effrt to press ldrs and rdn ent fnl f: ev ch whn nudged rt ins fnl f: no ex and wknd towards fin* **13/2**

2400 **4** *6* **Executive Force**[7] 4904 3-8-7 **96**................................... PaulHanagan 3 79
(William Haggas) *chsd wnr tl wl over 1f out: sn u.p and outpcd in 4th 1f out: wknd ins fnl f* **8/1**

430 **5** *4 1/2* **Straight Right (FR)**[29] 4030 3-9-3 **106**.......................... OisinMurphy 9 76
(Andrew Balding) *bmpd s: dropped in and hld up wl in tch in rr: effrt ent fnl 2f: 5th and no imp over 1f out: wknd ins fnl f* **11/2**[2]

4-60 **6** *1/2* **Majeste**[71] 2569 3-8-8 **97**................................................. TomMarquand 8 65
(Richard Hannon) *chsd ldrs: rdn over 2f out: sn struggling and lost pl ent fnl 2f: wl btn over 1f out* **25/1**

6411 **7** *nk* **Realize**[35] 3808 7-9-0 **96**.........................................(t) RyanMoore 7 66
(David Simcock) *hld up wl in tch in midfield: effrt ent fnl 2f: sn struggling and outpcd: wl btn over 1f out* **7/1**

4160 **8** *19* **Omran**[30] 3997 3-8-8 **97**...........................................(t[1]) LukeMorris 5 7
(Marco Botti) *wl in tch in midfield: rdn over 2f out: sn lost pl and bhd 2f out: wknd over 1f out and eased ins fnl f* **7/1**

1m 29.44s (3.74) **Going Correction** +0.825s/f (Soft)
**WFA** 3 from 4yo+ 7lb **8** Ran SP% **109.6**
Speed ratings (Par 109): **111,110,109,102,97 96,96,74**
CSF £20.94 CT £101.36 TOTE £5.90: £1.90, £1.20, £2.10; EX 21.80 Trifecta £123.70.
**Owner** Hamdan Al Maktoum **Bred** J C Bloodstock **Trained** Middleham Moor, N Yorks

**FOCUS**
Race distances as advertised. The opener confirmed that the wet conditions would play a considerable role, several of these not giving their running. Frankie Dettori and Paul Hanagan confirmed that it was riding soft. The winner made all in this decent handicap, the field racing centre to stands' side. The first three were clear and the form is rated around the runner-up.

## 5148 BET365 STKS (LISTED RACE) (REGISTERED AS THE STEVENTON STAKES) 1m 2f
**2:25** (2:25) (Class 1) 3-Y-O+ **£20,982** (£7,955; £3,981; £1,983; £995) **Stalls** Centre

Form RPR

-032 **1** **What About Carlo (FR)**[21] 4370 6-9-4 102.................. CharlesBishop 5 111
(Eve Johnson Houghton) *pressed ldr and travelled strly: led over 2f out: rdn over 1f out: styd on wl in command fnl f: rdn out* **5/2**[1]

0-60 **2** *2 3/4* **Arthenus**[28] 4070 5-9-4 105...........................................(p) TomQueally 8 106
(James Fanshawe) *hld up in tch: clsd to trck wnr jst over 2f out: effrt over 1f out: sn drvn and styd on same pce ins fnl f* **13/2**

21-0 **3** *4 1/2* **Best Of Days**[29] 4029 3-8-9 110........................................(t) OisinMurphy 1 98
(Hugo Palmer) *s.i.s: in tch: trckd ldrs 7f out: effrt in 3rd 2f out: unable qck u.p over 1f out: wknd ins fnl f* **5/2**[1]

-030 **4** *9* **Thikriyaat (IRE)**[21] 4362 4-9-4 111................................(p[1]) JimCrowley 6 79
(Sir Michael Stoute) *stdd s: hld up in tch in rr: effrt 3f out: sn u.p and btn: no ch fnl 2f* **3/1**[2]

0350 **5** *5* **Restorer**[28] 4069 5-9-4 102............................................... MartinDwyer 4 69
(William Muir) *led tlover 2f out: sn u.p and btn 4th 2f out: wknd* **5/1**[3]

2m 12.78s (3.98) **Going Correction** +0.675s/f (Yiel)
**WFA** 3 from 4yo+ 9lb **5** Ran SP% **112.1**
Speed ratings (Par 111): **111,108,105,98,94**
CSF £18.45 TOTE £2.80: £1.60, £2.30; EX 12.70 Trifecta £46.30.
**Owner** Anthony Pye-Jeary **Bred** Earl Haras Du Logis & J Ince **Trained** Blewbury, Oxon

■ Mount Logan was withdrawn. Price at the time of withdrawal 11-4. Rule 4 applies to bets struck prior to the withdrawal but not to SP bets. Deduction 25p in the pound. New market formed.

**FOCUS**
Favourite Mount Logan was withdrawn after getting loose before the start. Ordinary Listed form. They shunned the inside in the home straight. Improvement from the winner with the second close to his British best, but only they ran their races.

## 5149 BET365 HACKWOOD STKS (GROUP 3) 6f
**3:00** (3:01) (Class 1) 3-Y-O+
**£34,026** (£12,900; £6,456; £3,216; £1,614; £810) **Stalls** Centre

Form RPR

-201 **1** **Magical Memory (IRE)**[14] 4615 5-9-7 112...................... FrankieDettori 6 114
(Charles Hills) *hld up in tch in midfield: clsd to trck ldr 2f out: rdn to ld over 1f out: r.o wl and a in command ins fnl f: pushed out nr fin* **3/1**[1]

-500 **2** *1 1/4* **Perfect Angel (IRE)**[9] 4813 3-8-13 92........................... MartinDwyer 3 106
(Andrew Balding) *hld up in tch in midfield: trckd wnr through over 2f out: rdn to press wnr ent fnl f: kpt on same pce u.p ins fnl f* **20/1**

0-30 **3** *1 3/4* **Lady Macapa**[70] 2623 4-9-4 97.........................................(h) AdamKirby 8 101
(Clive Cox) *trckd ldr tl led 2f out: rdn and hdd over 1f out: unable qck w ldng pair 1f out: kpt on same pce ins fnl f* **20/1**

-140 **4** *2* **Raucous**[28] 4072 4-9-7 104..........................................(tp) PaulHanagan 5 98
(William Haggas) *taken down early: in tch in rr of main gp: effrt over 2f out: hdwy over 1f out: 4th and kpt on same pce ins fnl f* **5/1**[3]

0-10 **5** *1 3/4* **Perfect Pasture**[21] 4354 7-9-7 109...................................(v) SeanLevey 11 92
(Michael Easterby) *chsd ldrs: rdn 2f out: edgd lft and unable qck over 1f out: wl hld and kpt on same pce ins fnl f* **14/1**

5020 **6** *1 3/4* **Intisaab**[7] 4907 6-9-7 108..........................................(p) DanielTudhope 12 87
(David O'Meara) *hld up in tch in rr of main gp: effrt 2f out: no imp over 1f out: wl hld: edging lft and plugged on same pce ins fnl f* **8/1**

0-40 **7** *1/2* **Gifted Master (IRE)**[119] 1373 4-9-7 109.........................(b) OisinMurphy 10 85
(Hugo Palmer) *led tl 2f out: sn u.p and lost pl: wknd ins fnl f* **8/1**

0521 **8** *3/4* **Koropick (IRE)**[21] 4354 3-9-5 109...................................... JackMitchell 9 85
(Hugo Palmer) *squeezed for room leaving stalls: chsd ldrs: swtchd lft and effrt ent fnl 2f: no ex and lost pl ent fnl f: wknd* **12/1**

1210 **9** *7* **Visionary (IRE)**[29] 4030 3-9-2 101.................................... LukeMorris 2 59
(Robert Cowell) *s.i.s: nvr gng wl in rr: n.d* **8/1**

4166 **10** *7* **Tupi (IRE)**[28] 4071 5-9-7 108............................................. RyanMoore 7 38
(Richard Hannon) *sn dropped to last pair and nt travelling wl: rdn 1/2-way: lost tch over 1f out: eased wl ins fnl f* **9/2**[2]

1m 15.86s (2.86) **Going Correction** +0.825s/f (Soft)
**WFA** 3 from 4yo+ 5lb **10** Ran SP% **117.1**
Speed ratings (Par 113): **113,111,109,106,104 101,101,100,90,81**
CSF £67.77 TOTE £3.10: £1.20, £4.10, £5.90; EX 55.90 Trifecta £1562.30.
**Owner** Kennet Valley Thoroughbreds I **Bred** Wardstown Stud Ltd **Trained** Lambourn, Berks

**FOCUS**
This Group 3 was won by The Tin Man last season. The field came over towards the stands' side but the first four home were the four who raced furthest towards the centre. Magical Memory is rated close to his best, with the runner-up key to the form.

## 5150 WEATHERBYS SUPER SPRINT STKS 5f 34y
**3:35** (3:38) (Class 2) 2-Y-O

**£122,925** (£52,275; £24,600; £14,750; £9,825; £7,375) **Stalls** Centre

Form RPR

122 **1** **Bengali Boys (IRE)**[54] 3149 2-8-7 85.......................... BarryMcHugh 13 100
(Richard Fahey) *racd in centre: chsd ldrs: rdn and qcknd to ld over 1f out: r.o strly and drew wl clr fnl f: readily: 1st of 10 in gp* **12/1**

4310 **2** *6* **Declarationoflove (IRE)**[32] 3929 2-8-9 79.................... OisinMurphy 12 80
(Tom Clover) *racd in centre: rr of gp and midfield overall: hdwy u.p ent fnl f: styd on wl to go 2nd last strides: no ch w wnr: 2nd of 10 in gp* **20/1**

1422 **3** *nk* **Maggies Angel (IRE)**[21] 4361 2-8-6 95........................ PaulHanagan 11 76+
(Richard Fahey) *racd in centre: midfield overall: effrt 2f out: unable to match pce of wnr over 1f out: wnt 2nd ins fnl f: no imp: lost 2nd last strides: 3rd of 10 in gp* **9/4**[1]

1120 **4** *1* **Corinthia Knight (IRE)**[32] 3929 2-8-7 89........................ LukeMorris 17 74+
(Archie Watson) *racd stands side: chsd gp ldr tl led gp after 1f: chsd ldrs overall: rdn 2f out: drvn over 1f out: no ch w wnr: hung lft and kpt on same pce ins fnl f: 1st of 9 in gp* **8/1**[2]

4264 **5** *1* **Pursuing The Dream (IRE)**[17] 4488 2-8-5 89.......... PatrickMathers 18 68
(Jamie Osborne) *racd in centre: swtchd lft sn after s: rr of gp: rdn 1/2-way: hdwy 2f out: chsd clr wnr 1f out: hung lft and no imp: lost pls ins fnl f: 4th of 10 in gp* **33/1**

220 **6** *nk* **Mother Of Dragons (IRE)**[31] 3960 2-8-0 82.................... JimmyQuinn 3 62
(Joseph Tuite) *racd far side: led gp and chsd ldrs overall: rdn 2f out: outpcd by wnr over 1f out: pressing for wl hld 2nd 1f out: kpt on same pce: 1st of 4 in gp: 5th of 10 in gp* **12/1**

23 **7** *1* **Three Little Birds**[24] 4220 2-8-2 72.................................. KieranO'Neill 8 60
(Sylvester Kirk) *racd in centre: overall ldr tl rdn and hdd over 1f out: sn outpcd and btn: wknd ins fnl f* **33/1**

335 **8** *nse* **Glaceon (IRE)**[24] 4212 2-8-11 71......................................... SeanLevey 2 69
(Richard Hannon) *racd far side: chsd gp ldr and midfield overall: effrt 2f out: unable qck over 1f out: wl hld and kpt on same pce ins fnl f: 2nd of 4 in gp* **40/1**

31 **9** *shd* **Lynn's Memory**[16] 4680 2-8-8 0.................................. KieranShoemark 1 66
(Joseph Patrick O'Brien, Ire) *racd far side: midfield overall: effrt 2f out: no imp and outpcd over 1f out: wl hld and kpt on same pce ins fnl f: 3rd of 4 in gp* **25/1**

2 **10** *½* **Falabelle (IRE)**[24] 4204 2-8-5 0............................................ ShaneGray 4 61
(Kevin Ryan) *racd in centre: midfield overall: rdn 2f out: outpcd u.p over 1f out: wl hld but kpt on u.p ins fnl f: 6th of 10 in gp* **16/1**

132 **11** *1 ¼* **Inviolable Spirit (IRE)**[57] 3051 2-8-9 78......................... ConnorBeasley 10 61
(Richard Fahey) *racd in centre: chsd ldrs: u.p and unable qck 2f out: lost pl and wl btn over 1f out: plugged on ins fnl f: 7th of 10 in gp* **40/1**

2502 **12** *¾* **Lady Anjorica (IRE)**[12] 4689 2-8-4 84..............(p) SilvestreDeSousa 9 53
(Keith Dalgleish) *racd in centre: hmpd after 1f: rr of gp: swtchd rt and rdn 1/2-way: no ch w wnr: plugged on ins fnl f: 8th of 10 in gp* **9/1**[3]

323 **13** *nse* **Zalshah**[10] 4758 2-8-13 77.................................................. RyanMoore 6 62
(Richard Hannon) *racd far side: swtchd lft far side: rr of gp and midfield overall: effrt 2f out: no imp u.p over 1f out: wl btn fnl f: 4th of 4 in gp* **20/1**

105 **14** *nse* **Debutante's Ball (IRE)**[21] 4391 2-8-1 0.......................... RyanPowell 20 50+
(J S Moore) *racd stands side: midfield of gp but nvr on terms w overall ldrs: effrt ent fnl 2f: no imp and wl btn over 1f out: 2nd of 9 in gp* **12/1**

622 **15** *1* **Hello Girl**[33] 3902 2-8-1 70................................................. PaoloSirigu 15 46
(Dean Ivory) *racd in centre: chsd ldrs: rdn pressing ldrs ent fnl 2f: sn outpcd and btn over 1f out: wknd ins fnl f: 9th of 10 in gp* **25/1**

451 **16** *5* **Danehill Desert (IRE)**[38] 3705 2-8-7 75.......................... SammyJoBell 22 34+
(Richard Fahey) *racd stands side: hld up in rr: effrt 2f out: no imp and sn wl btn: n.d: 3rd of 9 in gp* **66/1**

532 **17** *3* **Onefootinparadise**[24] 4220 2-8-0 73.................................. CamHardie 16 16+
(Philip McBride) *racd stands side: swtchd rt after s: midfield in gp but nvr on terms w ldrs: effrt 2f out: sn outpcd and wl btn: wknd: 4th of 9 in gp* **25/1**

2015 **18** *4* **Connery (IRE)**[15] 4582 2-8-8 86...................................... MartinDwyer 24 10+
(Sylvester Kirk) *racd stands side: chsd gp ldrs but midfield overall: rdn 1/2-way: sn struggling: lost pl wl btn over 1f out: wknd: 5th of 9 in gp* **25/1**

120 **19** *1 ¼* **Requinto Dawn (IRE)**[73] 2522 2-8-9 84............................ ShaneKelly 19 6+
(Richard Fahey) *racd stands side: hmpd sn after s: hld up in rr: effrt ent fnl 2f: no hdwy and sn btn: wknd: 6th of 9 in gp* **25/1**

1020 **20** *1 ¼* **Holdenhurst**[8] 4827 2-8-7 70........................................... MitchGodwin 21 +
(Sylvester Kirk) *racd stands side: led gp for 1f: midfield overall: rdn 1/2-way: sn struggling: wknd over 1f out: 7th of 9 in gp* **100/1**

11 **21** *4 ½* **Time Trail**[58] 2987 2-8-8 81........................................... AndrewMullen 23 +
(Michael Dods) *racd stands side: t.k.h: hld up in midfield of gp: rdn jst over 2f out: sn btn: wl bhd ins fnl f: 8th of 9 in gp* **16/1**

041 **22** *1 ¼* **One For June (IRE)**[10] 4757 2-8-5 72................................ LiamJones 5
(William Haggas) *racd in centre: midfield overall: rdn over 2f out: sn struggling and lost pl: wl bhd ins fnl f: 10th of 10 in gp* **20/1**

3154 **23** *3 ¼* **Lexington Grace (IRE)**[10] 4739 2-8-6 68..................(b[1]) HollieDoyle 25 +
(Richard Hannon) *racd stands side: bhd: lost tch u.p 2f out: wl bhd fnl f: 9th of 9 in gp* **66/1**

1m 4.05s (2.65) **Going Correction** +0.825s/f (Soft) **23** Ran SP% **135.0**
Speed ratings (Par 100): **111,101,100,99,97 97,95,95,95,94 92,91,91,91,89 81,76,70,68,66 59,57,52**
CSF £241.67 TOTE £14.20: £4.70, £6.60, £1.70; EX 346.60 Trifecta £1607.80.
**Owner** A Tattersall **Bred** N Hartery **Trained** Musley Bank, N Yorks

**FOCUS**
A weaker than average edition of this valuable sales race, but an impressive, wide-margin winner who rates a big improver. The field split into three groups and the pace was among the ten-strong bunch in the centre, which is where the first three came from. The time was just under five seconds outside standard.

## 5151 BET365 NOVICE STKS (PLUS 10 RACE) (C&G) 6f
**4:10** (4:19) (Class 4) 2-Y-O **£4,690** (£1,395; £697; £348) **Stalls** Centre

Form RPR

3 **1** **Alkhalifa (IRE)**[16] 4534 2-9-0 0.......................................... JimCrowley 9 81+
(Brian Meehan) *mde all: jnd and rdn over 1f out: drvn ent fnl f: edgd lft u.p and sustained duel w chalr ins fnl f: styd on and forged ahd towards fin* **4/1**[3]

5 **2** *½* **Oliver Reed (IRE)**[16] 4534 2-9-0 0.......................................... RyanMoore 2 80+
(Richard Hannon) *hld up in midfield: effrt to chse ldrs 2f out: rdn and str chal over 1f out: sustained duel w wnr and carried lft ins fnl f: kpt on wl: jst outpcd towards fin* **3/1**[1]

**3** *4 ½* **Bullingdon** 2-9-0 0........................................................... SeanLevey 1 66
(Richard Hannon) *hld up in tch: swtchd lft and pushed along jst over 2f out: outpcd by ldng pair in 5th over 1f out: styd on steadily to go 3rd wl ins fnl f: no threat to ldng pair* **14/1**

1 **4** *1 ¾* **Ghayadh**[14] 4598 2-9-6 0............................................... FrankieDettori 10 67
(Hugo Palmer) *pressed wnr tl rdn and outpcd in 3rd over 1f out: wknd ins fnl f* **7/2**[2]

00 **5** *5* **Manco Inca (IRE)**[99] 1767 2-9-0 0.................................... OisinMurphy 4 46
(Joseph Tuite) *wnt lft s: hld up in tch in midfield: effrt jst over 2f out: hung lft and no imp over 1f out: wknd ins fnl f* **50/1**

4 **6** *1 ½* **Global Academy (IRE)**[54] 3149 2-9-0 0.......................(b[1]) FranBerry 11 41
(Gay Kelleway) *stdd s: t.k.h: sn trcking ldrs: rdn ent fnl 2f: 4th and outpcd over 1f out: wknd fnl f* **12/1**

**7** *¾* **City Gent** 2-9-0 0............................................................... ShaneKelly 3 39
(Ralph Beckett) *rn green in rr of main gp: rdn 1/2-way: outpcd and btn 2f out: no ch whn hung lft u.p over 1f out* **8/1**

0 **8** *6* **Salsa Verde (IRE)**[16] 4534 2-9-0 0.................................... PaulHanagan 6 21
(Ed de Giles) *bmpd s: hld up in tch in midfield: rdn over 2f out: sn lost pl: wl bhd fnl f* **20/1**

**9** *2* **Helvetian** 2-9-0 0..................................................... SilvestreDeSousa 8 15
(Mick Channon) *v s.i.s: rn green in rr: lost tch over 1f out* **5/1**

0 **10** *7* **Mountain Peak**[26] 4151 2-9-0 0.......................................... LiamKeniry 7
(Ed Walker) *bmpd s: hld up in tch in midfield: shkn up 2f out: lost pl qckly and btn over 1f out: wl bhd fnl f* **25/1**

1m 18.95s (5.95) **Going Correction** +0.825s/f (Soft) **10** Ran SP% **119.9**
Speed ratings (Par 96): **93,92,86,84,77 75,74,66,63,54**
CSF £16.61 TOTE £5.10: £1.60, £1.50, £3.70; EX 18.00 Trifecta £157.80.
**Owner** Hamdan Al Maktoum **Bred** Denis Noonan **Trained** Manton, Wilts

**FOCUS**
A race that should produce winners. The first two drew clear, ending up further towards the far side than the others, with both taking a step forward from their debut.

## 5152 EBF BREEDERS' SERIES FILLIES' H'CAP 1m (S)
**4:45** (4:46) (Class 2) (0-100,95) 3-Y-O+ **£18,675** (£5,592; £2,796; £1,398) **Stalls** Centre

Form RPR

15-0 **1** **Soul Silver (IRE)**[14] 4637 3-8-13 **88**.................................. OisinMurphy 2 95
(David Simcock) *trckd ldng pair: effrt to chal jst over 1f out: drvn to ld ins fnl f: styd on wl: rdn out* **9/2**[3]

3141 **2** *¾* **Lincoln Rocks**[11] 4718 4-10-0 **95**...................................... JimCrowley 3 102
(David O'Meara) *led: jnd 2f out: rdn over 1f out: drvn and hdd ins fnl f: edgd lft but kpt on u.p: no ex and jst outpcd towards fin* **5/4**[1]

136 **3** *7* **Pavillon**[14] 4637 3-8-11 **86**.......................................... SilvestreDeSousa 4 75
(Clive Cox) *stdd s: t.k.h: hld up in rr: effrt ent fnl 2f: hung lft u.p over 1f out: no ch w ldng pair ins fnl f: wnt modest 3rd towards fin* **2/1**[2]

-305 **4** *½* **Zest (IRE)**[56] 3101 4-9-11 **92**..........................................(v[1]) AdamKirby 6 82
(James Fanshawe) *t.k.h: trckd ldr: swtchd lft and clsd to join ldr 2f out: rdn over 1f out: sn struggling and btn 3rd 1f out: wknd ins fnl f* **6/1**

1m 48.05s (8.35) **Going Correction** +0.825s/f (Soft)
**WFA** 3 from 4yo 8lb **4** Ran SP% **110.2**
Speed ratings (Par 96): **91,90,83,82**
CSF £10.81 TOTE £6.20; EX 11.40 Trifecta £22.90.
**Owner** Qatar Racing Limited **Bred** Lisieux Stud & Irish National Stud **Trained** Newmarket, Suffolk

**FOCUS**
A disappointing turnout for this valuable prize. They raced in Indian file, the runner-up bringing the field over to the stands' rail. The runner-up is the best guide.

## 5153 GRUNDON RECYCLING H'CAP 1m 4f
**5:20** (5:20) (Class 4) (0-85,84) 3-Y-O

**£6,225** (£1,864; £932; £466; £233; £117) **Stalls** Centre

Form RPR

61 **1** **Intellect (IRE)**[23] 4274 3-9-3 **80**........................................ RyanMoore 6 95+
(Sir Michael Stoute) *mde all: shkn up and readily wnt clr ent fnl f: styd on strly: easily* **11/4**[1]

4351 **2** *9* **Amelia Dream**[14] 4623 3-8-9 **72**................................. SilvestreDeSousa 4 73
(Mick Channon) *hld up in tch in last pair: effrt 3f out: drvn over 2f out: kpt on steadily to go 2nd ins fnl f: no ch w wnr* **15/2**

2341 **3** *3 ¼* **Wefait (IRE)**[26] 4156 3-9-3 **80**......................................... SeanLevey 8 76
(Richard Hannon) *chsd ldrs: 4th and rdn 4f out: chsd clr wnr wl over 1f out: no imp: kpt on but lost 2nd ins fnl f* **7/1**

0-32 **4** *nk* **Munstead Star**[54] 3145 3-9-0 **77**...................................... OisinMurphy 2 72
(Andrew Balding) *hld up in tch in midfield: chsd ldrs 4f out: rdn over 3f out: battling for 2nd but no ch w wnr wl over 1f out: kpt on* **11/2**[3]

2301 **5** *12* **Star Maker**[21] 4348 3-8-11 **74**........................................... JimCrowley 3 50
(Sylvester Kirk) *t.k.h: chsd wnr: rdn over 2f out: lost 2nd and wl btn wl over 1f out: sn wknd: eased ins fnl f* **7/1**

0-21 **6** *7* **Knight Destroyer (IRE)**[46] 3428 3-9-0 **77**............................ FranBerry 7 42
(Jonjo O'Neill) *t.k.h: hld up in tch in midfield: effrt over 3f out: no imp u.p and btn over 2f out: wl btn whn wnt lft and eased over 1f out* **3/1**[2]

130 **7** *37* **Harlow**[76] 2437 3-9-7 **84**.................................................(h) AdamKirby 1
(Hugo Palmer) *hld up in rr: rdn 4f out: sn btn: wl bhd and eased fnl 2f: t.o* **10/1**

2m 43.15s (7.65) **Going Correction** +0.675s/f (Yiel) **7** Ran SP% **112.9**
Speed ratings (Par 102): **101,95,92,92,84 79,55**
CSF £22.91 CT £128.43 TOTE £3.10: £1.90, £2.90; EX 17.50 Trifecta £160.50.
**Owner** Highclere T'Bred Racing - Thomas Hardy **Bred** Duncan A McGregor **Trained** Newmarket, Suffolk

**FOCUS**
This was run on the worst of the ground. There were five last-time-out winners in this fair handicap, but only one counted. They finished well strung out behind Intellect, who took a big step up.

T/Jkpt: Not won. T/Plt: £1,013.40 to a £1 stake. Pool: £170,627.46 - 112.90 winning units
T/Qpdt: £183.30 to a £1 stake. Pool: £9,860.89 - 39.80 winning units **Steve Payne**

# [5113]NEWMARKET (R-H)

Saturday, July 22

**OFFICIAL GOING: Soft**
Wind: Light behind Weather: Showers

## 5154 LETTERGOLD FILLIES' NOVICE AUCTION STKS (PLUS 10 RACE) 7f
**2:05** (2:07) (Class 5) 2-Y-O £3,881 (£1,155; £577; £288) **Stalls** High

Form RPR
1 **1** **Capla Temptress (IRE)**[31] 3965 2-8-12 0 DavidEgan(5) 6 90
(Marco Botti) *hld up in tch: led over 2f out: rdn clr ins fnl f* **10/3**[1]
**2** *3 1/2* **La Diva** 2-8-12 0 HarryBentley 5 76+
(Roger Varian) *hld up: hdwy over 2f out: rdn over 1f out: styd on same pce ins fnl f* **8/1**
1 **3** *1 1/2* **Bambino Lola**[28] 4090 2-8-13 0 RoystonFfrench 12 74
(Adam West) *prom: racd keenly: rdn and ev ch over 1f out: no ex ins fnl f* **4/1**[2]
**4** *3/4* **Shepherd Market (IRE)** 2-8-10 0 DavidProbert 10 69+
(Clive Cox) *prom: lost pl over 5f out: hdwy over 2f out: shkn up over 1f out: hung lft and wknd ins fnl f* **10/1**
63 **5** *4 1/2* **Lucifugous (IRE)**[22] 4291 2-8-7 0 PJMcDonald 3 54
(Stuart Williams) *trckd ldrs: nt clr run wl over 1f out: sn rdn: hung lft and wknd* **13/2**[3]
0 **6** *2 1/4* **Richenza (FR)**[23] 4253 2-9-0 0 PatDobbs 1 56
(Ralph Beckett) *sn prom: rdn over 1f out: wknd fnl f* **8/1**
001 **7** *4 1/2* **Show Of Force**[5] 4963 2-8-7 0 GeorgeWood(3) 7 41
(Jonathan Portman) *chsd ldr: ev ch over 2f out: sn rdn: wknd over 1f out* **20/1**
03 **8** *1 1/2* **Gemologist (IRE)**[21] 4340 2-8-9 0 WilliamBuick 9 36
(Mark Johnston) *chsd ldrs: pushed along 1/2-way: wknd over 2f out* **7/1**
0 **9** *hd* **She'sastorm (IRE)**[9] 4815 2-8-12 0 StevieDonohoe 4 38
(Henry Spiller) *sn led: rdn and hdd over 2f out: hung lft and wknd over 1f out* **40/1**
0 **10** *2 3/4* **Tricksy Spirit**[7] 4902 2-8-11 0 JFEgan 11 30
(Mick Channon) *uns rdr to post: chsd ldrs: rdn and hung lft over 2f out: sn wknd* **14/1**
0 **11** *5* **Jedlitzka (IRE)**[9] 4806 2-8-10 0 GrahamLee 2 17
(Mick Channon) *sn outpcd* **66/1**

1m 28.25s (2.55) **Going Correction** +0.40s/f (Good) 11 Ran SP% **115.6**
Speed ratings (Par 91): **101,97,95,94,89 86,81,79,79,76 70**
CSF £29.30 TOTE £4.00: £1.60, £2.50, £1.90; EX 30.10 Trifecta £146.80.
**Owner** Capla Developments & Les Boyer **Bred** Pier House Stud **Trained** Newmarket, Suffolk

**FOCUS**
Far side course used. Stalls: 1m2f & 1m4f: centre; remainder: far side. There was 8mm of rain overnight and the going was given as soft (GoingStick: 6.5). The rail on the bend into the home straight had been repositioned, increasing the distance of the 1m2f and 1m4f races by 21yds. This looked competitive but they finished quite well strung out on the soft ground. A step forward from the winner, the form rated around the recent race averages.

## 5155 BETBRIGHT APHRODITE STKS (LISTED RACE) (F&M) 1m 4f
**2:40** (2:42) (Class 1) 3-Y-O+
£20,982 (£7,955; £3,981; £1,983; £995; £499) **Stalls** Centre

Form RPR
3-21 **1** **God Given**[43] 3542 3-8-5 79 GeorgeWood 8 105
(Luca Cumani) *plld hrd and prom: led 2f out: sn rdn: hung lft fnl f: styd on wl* **7/1**[3]
1-26 **2** *1* **Isabel De Urbina (IRE)**[50] 3301 3-8-5 98 JFEgan 6 103
(Ralph Beckett) *chsd ldr over 2f: remained handy: rdn over 3f out: hung lft over 1f out: chsd wnr fnl f: no ex nr fin* **5/1**[1]
60-1 **3** *2* **More Mischief**[22] 4308 5-9-5 102 GrahamLee 11 102
(Jedd O'Keeffe) *prom: chsd ldr over 9f out: led over 2f out: sn hdd: rdn over 1f out: styd on same pce fnl f* **11/2**[2]
215 **4** *1 3/4* **Apphia (IRE)**[30] 3995 3-8-5 102 JosephineGordon 1 97
(Hugo Palmer) *prom: racd keenly: rdn over 2f out: styd on same pce fr over 1f out* **8/1**
0-52 **5** *1/2* **Capricious Cantor (IRE)**[34] 3883 4-9-2 95 DavidProbert 4 95
(Ed Dunlop) *sn led: rdn and hdd over 2f out: no ex fnl f* **33/1**
53-0 **6** *3/4* **Skiffle**[76] 2432 4-9-2 103 WilliamBuick 12 94
(Charlie Appleby) *hld up: hdwy over 3f out: rdn over 2f out: nt clr run over 1f out: wknd ins fnl f* **7/1**[3]
1-21 **7** *1 1/2* **High Hopes**[42] 3558 4-9-2 94 JamieSpencer 3 92
(David Simcock) *dwlt: hld up: swtchd lft and hdwy over 2f out: rdn over 1f out: wknd ins fnl f* **5/1**[1]
1-22 **8** *3 3/4* **Gallifrey**[21] 4364 3-8-5 83 PJMcDonald 2 87
(Lucy Wadham) *hld up: hmpd over 8f out: rdn over 2f out: n.d* **12/1**
1 **9** *1 3/4* **Adjective**[59] 2971 4-9-2 73 MartinHarley 9 83
(James Fanshawe) *hld up: hdwy over 4f out: rdn over 2f out: sn wknd* **66/1**
-130 **10** *1/2* **Serenada**[30] 3995 3-8-5 100 HarryBentley 5 83
(Roger Varian) *hld up: rdn over 2f out: sn wknd* **7/1**[3]
15-5 **11** *1/2* **Return Ace**[42] 3586 5-9-2 93 DanielMuscutt 10 81
(James Fanshawe) *hld up: hdwy over 3f out: rdn and wknd over 1f out* **16/1**

2m 35.98s (3.08) **Going Correction** +0.65s/f (Yiel)
**WFA** 3 from 4yo+ 11lb 11 Ran SP% **115.3**
Speed ratings (Par 111): **115,114,113,111,111 111,110,107,106,106 105**
CSF £41.06 TOTE £8.20: £2.50, £2.30, £2.40; EX 48.00 Trifecta £297.30.
**Owner** St Albans Bloodstock Limited **Bred** St Albans Bloodstock Llp **Trained** Newmarket, Suffolk

**FOCUS**
Race distance increased by 21yds. An ordinary Listed race, with the third the best guide to the form. Big improvement from God Given.

## 5156 BETBRIGHT CASINO H'CAP (JOCKEY CLUB GRASSROOTS SPRINT SERIES QUALIFIER) 6f
**3:15** (3:16) (Class 4) (0-80,82) 3-Y-O+ £5,175 (£1,540; £769; £384) **Stalls** High

Form RPR
-612 **1** **Curious Fox**[43] 3532 4-9-12 79 DavidProbert 9 88+
(Anthony Carson) *dwlt: hld up: hdwy over 2f out: led over 1f out: rdn out* **11/2**[3]
4535 **2** *1 3/4* **Cool Bahamian (IRE)**[11] 4719 6-9-12 79 (v) RobertWinston 5 81
(Eve Johnson Houghton) *chsd ldr: overall ldr over 2f out: rdn: edgd rt and hdd wl over 1f out: styd on same pce ins fnl f* **4/1**[2]
0000 **3** *nk* **Consulting**[28] 4099 4-8-11 67 (vt) AaronJones(3) 4 68
(Stuart Williams) *led tl swtchd to r alone on stands' side rail 5f out: stl up w the pce: overall ldr wl over 1f out: sn rdn: hung lft and hdd: styd on same pce ins fnl f* **33/1**
1020 **4** *3/4* **Tricky Dicky**[21] 4343 4-9-7 74 PJMcDonald 8 73
(Olly Williams) *prom: racd keenly: rdn over 2f out: styd on same pce ins fnl f* **11/2**[3]
31-3 **5** *3/4* **Fivetwoeight**[35] 3814 3-9-7 79 DanielMuscutt 6 74
(Peter Chapple-Hyam) *trckd ldrs: racd keenly: rdn over 1f out: no ex ins fnl f* **6/1**
5320 **6** *2 1/4* **Ventura Blues (IRE)**[21] 4385 3-9-9 81 (p1) PatDobbs 3 69
(Richard Hannon) *hld up: rdn over 2f out: nt trble ldrs* **4/1**[2]
-451 **7** *10* **Stanhope**[23] 4268 3-9-10 82 (v) PatCosgrave 2 38
(Mick Quinn) *led overall 5f out: rdn: hung lft and hdd over 2f out: wknd fnl f* **11/4**[1]

1m 14.94s (2.44) **Going Correction** +0.40s/f (Good)
**WFA** 3 from 4yo+ 5lb 7 Ran SP% **114.7**
Speed ratings (Par 105): **99,96,96,95,94 91,77**
CSF £27.74 CT £659.83 TOTE £5.60: £2.30, £2.70; EX 24.00 Trifecta £511.40.
**Owner** Carson, Francis, Ghauri & Percy **Bred** Minster Stud **Trained** Newmarket, Suffolk

**FOCUS**
The 3yos proved disappointing in this sprint handicap despite featuring prominently in the market. The form is rated around the second.

## 5157 BETBRIGHT RECALL H'CAP 1m
**3:50** (3:50) (Class 2) (0-105,103) 3-Y-O+
£28,012 (£8,388; £4,194; £2,097; £1,048; £526) **Stalls** High

Form RPR
2152 **1** **Ballard Down (IRE)**[30] 4001 4-9-0 93 (v) HarryBentley 12 105
(William Knight) *trckd ldrs: led over 1f out: rdn clr fnl f: eased nr fin* **16/1**
450 **2** *3 1/2* **Master The World (IRE)**[31] 3963 6-9-5 103 (p) DavidEgan(5) 14 107
(David Elsworth) *hld up: hdwy over 2f out: rdn to chse wnr over 1f out: styd on same pce ins fnl f* **5/1**[3]
5-01 **3** *3* **Zwayyan**[42] 3589 4-8-12 91 PatCosgrave 11 88
(William Haggas) *hld up: hdwy over 2f out: rdn and nt clr run over 1f out: styd on same pce* **9/2**[2]
4354 **4** *1/2* **Temple Church (IRE)**[21] 4376 3-8-11 98 RobertWinston 7 92
(Hughie Morrison) *chsd ldrs: rdn and ev ch over 1f out: hung lft and no ex ins fnl f* **4/1**[1]
5022 **5** *3 3/4* **Masham Star (IRE)**[7] 4904 3-9-0 101 PJMcDonald 9 86
(Mark Johnston) *led: hdd over 5f out: led again over 3f out: rdn and hdd over 1f out: wkng whn nt clr run ins fnl f* **11/2**
0-P0 **6** *3 1/4* **Raising Sand**[63] 2828 5-9-1 94 DougieCostello 10 74
(Jamie Osborne) *s.i.s: hld up: rdn and hung lft over 1f out: nvr trbld ldrs* **40/1**
0446 **7** *5* **Highland Colori (IRE)**[18] 4475 9-9-1 94 (v) DavidProbert 2 62
(Andrew Balding) *chsd ldrs: rdn over 2f out: hung lft and wknd over 1f out* **16/1**
4041 **8** *nse* **Examiner (IRE)**[24] 4223 6-9-3 96 (t) JamieSpencer 3 64
(Stuart Williams) *hld up: shkn up and wknd over 1f out* **14/1**
0004 **9** *3/4* **Dream Walker (FR)**[22] 4293 8-8-8 92 (t) BenRobinson(5) 5 59
(Brian Ellison) *hld up: rdn 1/2-way: wknd 2f out* **33/1**
04-3 **10** *7* **Knight Owl**[62] 2855 7-8-11 93 GeorgeWood(3) 4 43
(James Fanshawe) *trckd ldrs: rdn over 2f out: wknd over 1f out* **12/1**
5000 **11** *5* **Bossy Guest (IRE)**[7] 4905 5-9-7 100 JFEgan 8 39
(Mick Channon) *hung lft s and rel to r: a bhd* **14/1**
2-10 **12** *nk* **Manchego**[64] 2784 3-8-1 88 oh3 ow1 JosephineGordon 6 24
(Hugo Palmer) *w ldr tl led over 5f out: hdd over 3f out: rdn over 2f out: wknd over 1f out* **11/1**
-010 **13** *12* **Secret Art (IRE)**[58] 3014 7-9-1 94 WilliamBuick 1
(William Knight) *s.i.s: hld up: rdn and wknd over 2f out* **25/1**

1m 40.02s (0.02) **Going Correction** +0.40s/f (Good)
**WFA** 3 from 4yo+ 8lb 13 Ran SP% **120.6**
Speed ratings (Par 109): **115,111,108,108,104 101,96,95,95,88 83,82,70**
CSF £93.63 CT £352.98 TOTE £17.20: £4.10, £2.10, £2.10; EX 119.00 Trifecta £816.40.
**Owner** Angmering Park Thoroughbreds I **Bred** D Harron, Ederidge Ltd & Glenvale Stud **Trained** Patching, W Sussex

**FOCUS**
A good handicap in which the principals raced towards the far rail. The winner has progressed since being visored.

## 5158 BETBRIGHT MAIDEN STKS 7f
**4:25** (4:31) (Class 5) 3-Y-O+ £3,881 (£1,155; £577; £288) **Stalls** High

Form RPR
5 **1** **Dark Magic**[40] 3669 3-9-5 0 RobertWinston 7 75+
(Dean Ivory) *hld up: nt clr run over 2f out: hdwy over 1f out: shkn up to ld ins fnl f: r.o: comf* **9/4**[2]
4222 **2** *2* **Buxted Dream (USA)**[35] 3825 3-9-5 82 JamieSpencer 2 69
(Luca Cumani) *sn led: rdn and hung rt wl over 1f out: hung lft jst over 1f out: hdd ins fnl f: styd on same pce* **4/6**[1]
0 **3** *nk* **Just Surprise Me (IRE)**[46] 3438 4-9-12 0 (t) PatCosgrave 5 72+
(Mohamed Moubarak) *trckd ldrs: nt clr run over 2f out: hmpd over 1f out: nt clr run and swtchd rt ins fnl f: r.o* **25/1**
4 **4** *1 1/4* **Mohsen**[31] 3984 3-9-5 0 DavidProbert 4 65
(Marcus Tregoning) *s.i.s: hld up: rdn over 1f out: r.o towards fin: nt trble ldrs* **7/1**[3]
004 **5** *1 1/2* **Dream Start**[23] 4269 3-9-0 57 (t) JosephineGordon 6 56
(John Ryan) *prom: chsd ldr 2f out: sn rdn: no ex ins fnl f* **16/1**
0 **6** *4* **Lady Prima**[101] 1727 3-9-0 0 AntonioFresu 1 45
(Mike Murphy) *racd keenly in 2nd pl tl rdn 2f out: wknd fnl f* **25/1**

1m 29.25s (3.55) **Going Correction** +0.40s/f (Good)
**WFA** 3 from 4yo 7lb 6 Ran SP% **116.8**
Speed ratings (Par 103): **95,92,92,90,89 84**
CSF £4.32 TOTE £3.40: £1.90, £1.10; EX 5.20 Trifecta £49.30.
**Owner** Heather & Michael Yarrow **Bred** Lordship Stud **Trained** Radlett, Herts
■ Stewards' Enquiry : Jamie Spencer caution: careless riding

**FOCUS**
An ordinary maiden in which the favourite found one to beat him again. Little depth to this.

## 5159 BETBRIGHT H'CAP 7f
**5:00** (5:00) (Class 3) (0-90,92) 3-Y-O+ £7,762 (£2,310; £1,154; £577) **Stalls** High

Form RPR
1-56 **1** **Love Dreams (IRE)**[9] 4813 3-9-9 91 PJMcDonald 8 106
(Mark Johnston) *chsd ldr: led 2f out: rdn clr and flashed tail fnl f* **7/4**[1]

0006 **2** *5* **Mountain Rescue (IRE)**[23] 4261 5-9-8 **83**...................... HarryBentley 7 88
(Chris Wall) *led: hdd over 4f out: rdn edgd rt and ev ch 2f out: no ex fnl f* **9/2**[3]

5654 **3** *4 ½* **Mazyoun**[14] 4634 3-9-6 **88**........................................(b) JosephineGordon 9 78
(Hugo Palmer) *chsd ldrs: rdn over 2f out: wknd fnl f* **7/2**[2]

5513 **4** *1 ½* **Qeyaadah (IRE)**[16] 4524 4-9-4 **86**..................... RayDawson(7) 4 75
(Michael Appleby) *edgd rt s: swtchd to stands' side to r alone sn after s: up w the pce: led over 4f out: rdn and hung lft over 2f out: sn hdd: wknd fnl f* **6/1**

3-00 **5** *½* **Anfaass (IRE)**[7] 4887 3-8-12 **80**............................................... JFEgan 5 65
(George Margarson) *chsd ldrs: rdn over 2f out: wknd fnl f* **16/1**

520 **6** *17* **Ghalib (IRE)**[50] 3294 5-10-0 **89**.......................................(bt) WilliamBuick 2 33
(Amy Murphy) *hld up: rdn 1/2-way: wknd and eased over 1f out* **10/1**

0046 **7** *9* **Toofi (FR)**[15] 4570 6-9-13 **88**...................................... RobertWinston 3 9
(John Butler) *hmpd s: hld up and a in rr: eased wl over 1f out* **9/1**

1m 27.28s (1.58) **Going Correction** +0.40s/f (Good)
**WFA** 3 from 4yo+ 7lb **7** Ran SP% **116.0**
Speed ratings (Par 107): **106,100,95,93,92 73,63**
CSF £10.28 CT £24.76 TOTE £2.70: £1.50, £2.30; EX 9.30 Trifecta £29.90.
**Owner** Crone Stud Farms Ltd **Bred** John O'Connor **Trained** Middleham Moor, N Yorks

**FOCUS**
They finished well strung out here. The 1-2 were always the front pair and the form is rated around the runner-up, close to his turf best.

## 5160 BETFINDER BY BETBRIGHT H'CAP 1m 2f
5:35 (5:35) (Class 3) (0-90,91) 3-Y-O **£7,762** (£2,310; £1,154) **Stalls** Centre

Form RPR
11 **1** **Contango (IRE)**[22] 4295 3-9-6 **82**.............................. DavidProbert 6 94
(Andrew Balding) *disp ld tl settled into 2nd over 8f out: led on bit 2f out: shkn up and c readily clr fnl f* **11/10**[1]

4641 **2** *11* **Ray's The Money (IRE)**[28] 4084 3-9-7 **83**...............(v) JamieSpencer 3 82
(Michael Bell) *hld up: hdwy to chse wnr over 1f out: wknd and eased ins fnl f* **4/1**[3]

0-12 **3** *17* **Valcartier (IRE)**[20] 4408 3-10-1 **91**.............................. WilliamBuick 7 53+
(John Gosden) *disp ld tl wnt on over 8f out: shkn up and hdd 2f out: sn edgd rt and wknd: eased* **11/8**[2]

2m 12.25s (6.75) **Going Correction** +0.65s/f (Yiel) **3** Ran SP% **109.7**
Speed ratings (Par 104): **99,90,76**
CSF £5.15 TOTE £1.90; EX 7.10 Trifecta £4.30.
**Owner** Kennet Valley Thoroughbreds XII **Bred** Thomas Hassett **Trained** Kingsclere, Hants

**FOCUS**
Race distance increased by 21yds. Just the three runners in the end, and the winner proved much too good for his two rivals. It's hard to know what he achieved here.
T/Plt: £98.00 to a £1 stake. Pool: £101,245.43 - 753.61 winning units. T/Qpdt: £19.20 to a £1 stake. Pool: £5,796.60 - 222.56 winning units. **Colin Roberts**

# 4689 RIPON (R-H)
Saturday, July 22

**OFFICIAL GOING: Soft**
Wind: Virtually Nil Weather: Sunny

## 5161 DOBSONS GASKETS (S) STKS 6f
2:20 (2:20) (Class 6) 2-Y-O **£3,234** (£962; £481; £240) **Stalls** High

Form RPR
0303 **1** **Placebo Effect (IRE)**[10] 4740 2-9-0 60........................ FrannyNorton 7 66
(Ollie Pears) *trckd ldrs: pushed along to ld ent fnl f: kpt on rdn out* **9/4**[1]

5600 **2** *2 ¾* **Atalanta Queen**[16] 4527 2-8-2 63.............................(b[1]) JordanUys(7) 6 53
(Brian Meehan) *pressed ldrs: rdn 2f out: one pce and sn hld by wnr fnl f* **3/1**[2]

004 **3** *1 ¾* **Laydee Victoria (IRE)**[17] 4504 2-8-9 53........................ JoeDoyle 9 48
(Ollie Pears) *led narrowly: rdn over 2f out: hdd ent fnl f: no ex* **7/2**[3]

00 **4** *2* **Sixties Secret**[7] 4909 2-8-9 0............................................ BenCurtis 3 42
(Mick Channon) *midfield: sn pushed along: kpt on same pce* **7/2**[3]

00 **5** *7* **Kathy**[21] 4335 2-8-9 0................................................................ DavidAllan 4 21
(Scott Dixon) *hld up: sn pushed along: nvr threatened* **20/1**

006 **6** *2 ½* **Abu Dhabi Doo**[17] 4504 2-8-6 43...........................(v[1]) JordanVaughan(3) 2 13
(K R Burke) *hld up: rdn over 2f out: edgd rt over 1f out and wknd* **14/1**

0060 **7** *1* **Heavenly Pulse (IRE)**[8] 4836 2-9-0 41.........................(b[1]) JoeyHaynes 1 15
(Ann Duffield) *racd alone centre: chsd ldrs: rdn over 2f out: wknd over 1f out* **33/1**

00 **8** *14* **St Helens Gate (IRE)**[82] 2222 2-8-9 0................................ TomEaves 5
(Rebecca Menzies) *a in rr* **50/1**

1m 15.23s (2.23) **Going Correction** +0.15s/f (Good) **8** Ran SP% **116.5**
Speed ratings (Par 92): **91,87,85,82,73 69,68,49**
CSF £9.29 TOTE £2.80: £1.10, £1.10, £1.40; EX 6.20 Trifecta £15.10.No bid for winner.
**Owner** Timothy O'Gram, Keith West & Ollie Pears **Bred** Hawaiian Dream Partnership **Trained** Norton, N Yorks

**FOCUS**
Plenty of rain around in the morning and the official going was changed from good to soft prior to the first of seven races. A weak seller, in which three of the runners were sporting first-time headgear. The winner built slightly on his latest effort.

## 5162 MICK GIBBONS MEMORIAL EBF NOVICE STKS (PLUS 10 RACE) 5f
2:55 (2:57) (Class 4) 2-Y-O **£5,175** (£1,540; £769; £384) **Stalls** High

Form RPR
5 **1** **Bow Belles**[93] 1909 2-8-11 0........................................ DavidAllan 1 72
(Tim Easterby) *trckd ldrs on outer: pushed along to ld 1f out: kpt on wl pushed out* **14/1**

64 **2** *1 ¾* **Arizona Mist (IRE)**[14] 4628 2-8-11 0........................ PaulMulrennan 10 69+
(Simon Crisford) *chsd ldrs: pushed along 2f out: wnt 2nd ins fnl f: kpt on but no threat wnr* **6/1**[3]

0 **3** *1 ¾* **Alaskan Beauty (IRE)**[15] 4555 2-8-11 0........................ JasonHart 11 60
(Tim Easterby) *chsd ldrs: rdn 2f out: kpt on ins fnl f* **28/1**

00 **4** *1 ¼* **Lady Lintera (IRE)**[86] 2105 2-8-11 0............................ NeilFarley 12 55
(Ann Duffield) *in tch: rdn over 2f out: kpt on ins fnl f* **100/1**

**5** *nk* **Royal Diplomat (IRE)**[106] 1611 2-9-2 0........................ TonyHamilton 7 59
(Richard Fahey) *led narrowly: rdn 2f out: hdd 1f out: wknd fnl 110yds* **3/1**[2]

1 **6** *hd* **Moseeb (IRE)**[21] 4374 2-9-5 0........................ EdwardGreatrex(3) 5 64
(Saeed bin Suroor) *w ldr: rdn 2f out: hung rt appr fnl f: wknd ins fnl f* **1/1**[1]

66 **7** *nk* **Panophobia**[14] 4606 2-8-13 0........................ AdamMcNamara(3) 3 57+
(Richard Fahey) *hld up in midfield: sn pushed along: kpt on ins fnl f* **50/1**

**8** *5* **Navarra Princess (IRE)** 2-8-11 0........................ TomEaves 6 34
(Don Cantillon) *a towards rr* **20/1**

05 **9** *nk* **Laith Alareen**[36] 3789 2-9-2 0...........................................(t) PhillipMakin 4 38
(David O'Meara) *w ldr: rdn over 2f out: wknd over 1f out* **12/1**

50 **10** *3 ¼* **Burn Some Dust (IRE)**[23] 4259 2-9-2 0.............................. BenCurtis 2 27
(Brian Ellison) *a in rr* **50/1**

**11** *7* **Bowgey Man** 2-8-13 0........................................... NathanEvans(3) 8 1
(Michael Easterby) *dwlt: a in rr* **25/1**

1m 1.16s (1.16) **Going Correction** +0.15s/f (Good) **11** Ran SP% **120.6**
Speed ratings (Par 96): **96,93,90,88,87 87,87,79,78,73 62**
CSF £91.43 TOTE £19.90: £4.10, £2.20, £8.00; EX 106.90 Trifecta £2764.30.
**Owner** The Hecklers **Bred** Tibthorpe Stud **Trained** Great Habton, N Yorks

**FOCUS**
This was run at a suicidal early pace and played very much into the hands of the closers. They finished quite compressed and this was probably an ordinary renewal.

## 5163 SKY BET GO-RACING-IN-YORKSHIRE SUMMER FESTIVAL H'CAP 1m 1f 170y
3:30 (3:30) (Class 4) (0-85,87) 3-Y-O+ **£6,931** (£2,074; £1,037; £519; £258) **Stalls** Low

Form RPR
6252 **1** **Mulligatawny (IRE)**[12] 4692 4-10-3 **87**.....................(p[1]) TonyHamilton 3 94
(Roger Fell) *mde all: pushed along over 1f out: kpt on* **3/1**[2]

4310 **2** *1 ¼* **Jacbequick**[8] 4865 6-9-11 **84**........................................(p) JoshDoyle(3) 1 88
(David O'Meara) *trckd ldr: pushed along and bit short of room on inner over 1f out: kpt on ins fnl f* **5/1**

0223 **3** *4 ½* **Celestation**[9] 4798 3-8-12 **77**........................................ FrannyNorton 4 73
(Mark Johnston) *trckd ldrs: rdn over 2f out: wknd ins fnl f* **4/1**[3]

6400 **4** *1 ½* **Bahama Moon (IRE)**[13] 4658 5-9-13 **83**.............................. BenCurtis 5 75
(David Barron) *hld up: rdn and hdwy over 2f out: wknd ins fnl f* **9/1**

0361 **5** *3* **Aelius**[14] 4633 3-8-1 **69**..................................... NathanEvans(3) 2 56
(Michael Easterby) *dwlt hld up: rdn along 3f out: wknd over 1f out* **5/2**[1]

1526 **6** *3 ¼* **Prying Pandora (FR)**[31] 3981 4-9-3 **80**................... ConnorMurtagh(7) 7 59
(Richard Fahey) *trckd ldr: rdn over 2f out: wknd over 1f out* **9/1**

0150 **7** *21* **Marmion**[18] 4476 5-9-1 **71**.......................................(h) PhillipMakin 8 7
(Les Eyre) *hld up: rdn over 3f out: wknd over 2f out and eased* **25/1**

2m 6.46s (1.06) **Going Correction** +0.25s/f (Good)
**WFA** 3 from 4yo+ 9lb **7** Ran SP% **114.1**
Speed ratings (Par 105): **105,104,100,99,96 94,77**
CSF £18.23 CT £59.47 TOTE £3.10: £1.90, £2.70; EX 9.90 Trifecta £41.90.
**Owner** Middleham Park Racing Li & Partner **Bred** Pat O'Rourke **Trained** Nawton, N Yorks

**FOCUS**
Race distance increased by 8yds. A fair handicap and a dominant performance from the top weight under an excellent front-running ride. He was closely matched with the second on their June 22 form here.

## 5164 RIPON BELL-RINGER H'CAP 1m 4f 10y
4:05 (4:07) (Class 2) (0-100,98) 3-Y-O+
**£15,562** (£4,660; £2,330; £1,165; £582; £292) **Stalls** Centre

Form RPR
2201 **1** **Mukhayyam**[8] 4863 5-9-4 **88**.......................................(p) DavidAllan 4 98
(Tim Easterby) *trckd ldr: led 10f out: mde rest: rdn over 2f out: briefly pressed 2f out: wandered appr fnl f: styd on wl* **4/1**

5622 **2** *3 ½* **Fleeting Visit**[24] 4206 4-9-0 **84**.......................................(p) JohnFahy 1 88
(Eve Johnson Houghton) *led for 2f: trckd ldr: rdn to chal 2f out: no ex fnl f* **3/1**[1]

5543 **3** *4* **Sennockian Star**[19] 4429 7-9-4 **88**.............................. FrannyNorton 2 86
(Mark Johnston) *midfield on inner: rdn over 3f out: plugged on to go modest 3rd ins fnl f* **10/1**

130- **4** *½* **Henry Smith**[270] 7594 5-8-8 **83**..............................(be) LewisEdmunds(5) 8 80
(John Weymes) *prom: rdn over 3f out: wknd fnl f* **28/1**

2110 **5** *2 ¼* **Jaameh (IRE)**[21] 4356 4-10-0 **98**.............................. DaneO'Neill 5 92
(Mark Johnston) *in tch: rdn over 3f out: wknd over 1f out* **10/3**[2]

2124 **6** *nse* **Kensington Star**[21] 4355 4-9-4 **88**.......................................(p) JasonHart 6 82
(Keith Dalgleish) *dwlt: hld up: rdn over 3f out: sn btn* **7/2**[3]

424- **7** *2* **Mustaaqeem (USA)**[339] 5552 5-9-4 **88**.............................. TonyHamilton 3 78
(Richard Fahey) *a in rr* **8/1**

1500 **8** *9* **Corton Lad**[21] 4356 7-9-1 **90**.......................................(tp) RowanScott(5) 7 66
(Keith Dalgleish) *trckd ldrs on outer: rdn over 3f out: wknd* **28/1**

2m 37.29s (0.59) **Going Correction** +0.25s/f (Good) **8** Ran SP% **117.4**
Speed ratings (Par 109): **108,105,103,102,101 101,99,93**
CSF £16.96 CT £109.72 TOTE £4.70: £1.60, £1.20, £2.50; EX 23.00 Trifecta £120.20.
**Owner** T A Scothern **Bred** Mrs James Wigan **Trained** Great Habton, N Yorks

**FOCUS**
Race distance increased by 8yds. A solid renewal of this feature handicap and they came home at long intervals behind the game all-the-way winner. He's rated to a better view of his old form.

## 5165 VW VAN CENTRE (WEST YORKSHIRE) H'CAP 1m
4:40 (4:41) (Class 4) (0-85,87) 3-Y-O+ **£6,931** (£2,074; £1,037; £519; £258) **Stalls** Low

Form RPR
0260 **1** **Shouranour (IRE)**[24] 4207 7-9-8 **83**..............................(b) JoshDoyle(3) 6 90
(Alan Brown) *trckd ldrs: rdn to chse ldr over 1f out: led 110yds out: styd on* **10/1**

2362 **2** *½* **Areen Heart (FR)**[15] 4578 3-9-7 **87**..............................(h) PhillipMakin 4 91
(Richard Fahey) *led: pushed along 2f out: rdn appr fnl f: hdd 110yds out: one pce* **6/4**[1]

4500 **3** *2 ½* **Rousayan (IRE)**[24] 4207 6-9-8 **83**..............................(h) ShelleyBirkett(3) 5 83
(David O'Meara) *midfield: pushed along and hdwy to go 3rd over 1f out: rdn and edgd rt: sn one pce* **15/2**

3446 **4** *½* **Town Charter (USA)**[13] 4662 3-9-3 **83**.............................. FrannyNorton 3 80
(Mark Johnston) *hld up: pushed along and bit short of room on inner 3f out: angled lft over 1f out: styd on fnl f: nrst fin* **13/2**[3]

2-12 **5** *½* **Torrid**[51] 3255 6-9-9 **84**.............................................. NathanEvans(3) 2 82
(Michael Easterby) *trckd ldrs: rdn over 2f out: sn one pce* **11/4**[2]

-305 **6** *6* **Hitman**[19] 4438 4-9-2 **74**.............................................. DuranFentiman 8 58
(Rebecca Bastiman) *hld up: rdn over 2f out: wknd fnl f* **11/1**

02-0 **7** *11* **Planetaria (IRE)**[24] 4210 4-9-3 **80**.............................. LewisEdmunds(5) 7 39
(John Weymes) *prom: rdn over 2f out: wknd over 1f out* **14/1**

1m 41.69s (0.29) **Going Correction** +0.25s/f (Good)
**WFA** 3 from 4yo+ 8lb **7** Ran SP% **115.9**
Speed ratings (Par 105): **108,107,105,104,104 98,87**
CSF £26.27 CT £124.09 TOTE £11.80: £4.70, £1.80; EX 22.80 Trifecta £143.90.
**Owner** David Lumley **Bred** His Highness The Aga Khan's Studs S C **Trained** Yedingham, N Yorks



The Form Book Flat, Raceform Ltd, Newbury, RG14 5SJ

**FOCUS**
Race distance increased by 8yds. This lacked recent winners but was competitive with all bar one of the runners rated 80 or above. The winner is rated to last year's form.

## 5166 RUTH GIBBONS' FAMILY H'CAP 1m 4f 10y
5:15 (5:15) (Class 4) (0-80,79) 3-Y-O+ £6,301 (£1,886; £943; £472; £235) Stalls Centre

Form RPR
54 1 **Indy (IRE)**[44] 3497 6-9-7 72 JasonHart 8 85+
(John Quinn) *trckd ldrs: led 4f out: rdn clr 2f out: eased fnl 50yds* 5/1[3]
00 2 3 **Tamayuz Magic (IRE)**[24] 4206 6-9-11 79 NathanEvans(3) 3 84
(Michael Easterby) *trckd ldrs: rdn 3f out: kpt on but no ch easy wnr* 9/1
41 3 hd **Starplex**[18] 4474 7-9-7 77 RowanScott(5) 4 82
(Keith Dalgleish) *dwlt: hld up: pushed along and hdwy 3f out: rdn 2f out: kpt on same pce* 4/1[2]
6-61 4 2 1/4 **Roar (IRE)**[21] 4365 3-9-2 78 BenCurtis 7 80
(Brian Ellison) *w ldr: rdn along 4f out: outpcd by wnr over 2f out: wknd ins fnl f* 11/10[1]
000 5 7 **Foresee (GER)**[21] 4336 4-9-5 70 FrannyNorton 6 60
(Tony Carroll) *midfield: rdn 4f out: lost pl whn briefly short of room over 3f out: wknd* 25/1
6-00 6 3/4 **The Twisler**[170] 519 5-9-13 78 TrevorWhelan 5 67
(Neil Mulholland) *dwlt: hld up: hdwy on wd outside over 4f out: rdn over 3f out: wknd fnl 2f* 9/1
53/0 7 7 **Parole (IRE)**[49] 3315 5-9-2 67 TonyHamilton 2 45
(Tim Easterby) *led: rdn whn hdd 4f out: sn wknd* 16/1
2m 38.0s (1.30) **Going Correction** +0.25s/f (Good)
**WFA** 3 from 4yo+ 11lb 7 Ran SP% **114.0**
Speed ratings (Par 105): **105,103,102,101,96 96,91**
CSF £47.23 CT £196.11 TOTE £5.20: £2.10, £4.60; EX 31.90 Trifecta £151.80.
**Owner** White Rose Racing **Bred** Maurice Burns **Trained** Settrington, N Yorks

**FOCUS**
Race distance increased by 8yds. The expected match between the two last-time-out winners failed to materialise as Indy raced clear on his first try at the distance. He's rated back to his latter 2016 form.

## 5167 PLAY SPORTING-LIFE PICK 7 FOR FREE TOMORROW MAIDEN H'CAP 6f
5:50 (5:51) (Class 5) (0-70,70) 3-Y-O+ £3,881 (£1,155; £577; £288) Stalls High

Form RPR
5022 1 **Granny Roz**[28] 4106 3-8-13 62 BenCurtis 14 69
(David Barron) *mde all: pushed clr 2f out: rdn out ins fnl f* 4/1[1]
3-00 2 1 1/2 **Twilight Spirit**[22] 4303 3-8-10 59 FrannyNorton 6 62
(Tony Carroll) *hld up: hdwy whn bit short of room on inner over 2f out: sn swtchd rt to outer 2f out: rdn to chse wnr appr fnl f: kpt on but a hld* 11/2[2]
5534 3 2 1/2 **Hamidans Girl (IRE)**[9] 4788 3-9-2 65 JasonHart 4 60
(Keith Dalgleish) *hld up: rdn along 1/2-way: hdwy over 1f out: kpt on fnl f* 4/1[1]
0000 4 4 **Flying Onsite (FR)**[22] 4303 3-7-11 53 oh5 ow2(e[1]) FayeMcManoman(7) 7 36
(Nigel Tinkler) *dwlt: outpcd in rr tl kpt on fr over 1f out: wnt modest 4th ins fnl f* 33/1
24-3 5 4 **Rapid Ranger**[14] 4604 3-9-4 70 JoshDoyle(3) 13 41
(David O'Meara) *chsd ldr: rdn over 2f out: wknd fnl f* 11/2[2]
0-0 6 1 1/2 **Mighty Bond**[38] 3710 5-8-5 52 oh5 ow1 JordanVaughan(3) 5 20
(Tracy Waggott) *sn prom: rdn over 2f out: wknd fnl f* 16/1
6030 7 3 3/4 **Tagur (IRE)**[22] 4302 3-8-11 65 (p) LewisEdmunds(5) 1 20
(Kevin Ryan) *chsd ldrs on outside: rdn over 2f out: wknd over 1f out* 4/1[1]
0630 8 3 **Prazeres**[17] 4509 3-8-8 60 (p) NathanEvans(3) 10 6
(Les Eyre) *midfield: rdn 1/2-way: wknd over 1f out* 11/1
6500 9 16 **Ryedale Rio (IRE)**[19] 4453 4-8-7 51 oh3 (b) DuranFentiman 3
(Tim Easterby) *chsd ldrs: lost pl over 3f out: sn wknd and bhd* 10/1[3]
1m 13.27s (0.27) **Going Correction** +0.15s/f (Good)
**WFA** 3 from 4yo+ 5lb 9 Ran SP% **117.0**
Speed ratings (Par 103): **104,102,98,93,88 86,81,77,55**
CSF £26.48 CT £94.31 TOTE £4.40: £1.60, £2.10, £1.50; EX 29.00 Trifecta £95.70.
**Owner** M Rozenbroek **Bred** The Kathryn Stud **Trained** Maunby, N Yorks

**FOCUS**
These had yet to win a race between them from a combined 82 starts. Modest form with the runner-up near her mark.
T/Plt: £676.40 to a £1 stake. Pool: £63,921.98 - 68.98 winning units. T/Qpdt: £41.80 to a £1 stake. Pool: £4,486.31 - 79.35 winning units. **Andrew Sheret**

5168 - 5175a (Foreign Racing) - See Raceform Interactive

# 4955 DIEPPE (R-H)
Saturday, July 22

**OFFICIAL GOING: Turf: soft**

## 5176a PRIX OSCAR WILDE (H'CAP) (4YO+) (TURF) 5f 110y
5:40 4-Y-O+ £6,837 (£2,735; £2,051; £1,367; £683)

RPR
1 **Whipper Snapper (FR)**[23] 7-9-4 0 ChristopheSoumillon 7 64
(J-V Toux, France) 67/10
2 2 1/2 **Xenophanes (IRE)**[11] 4955 7-9-0 0 AdrienMoreau 6 52
(M Boutin, France) 72/1
3 3/4 **Silent Romance (FR)**[23] 4-9-7 0 (b[1]) GeraldMosse 5 57
(J E Hammond, France) 48/10[1]
4 hd **Range Of Knowledge (IRE)**[42] 4-10-7 0 (p) FabriceVeron 1 70
(E J O'Neill, France) 66/10[3]
5 1 1/2 **Agnes Champ (FR)**[11] 4955 11-9-2 0 (b) CesarPasserat 10 46
(M Boutin, France) 153/10
6 snk **Intibaah**[24] 4219 7-10-10 0 (b) TheoBachelot 4 67
(George Baker) 92/10
7 2 1/2 **Sayeuri**[55] 5-9-0 0 AntoineHamelin 2 35
(Frank Sheridan, Italy) 183/10
8 1 **King David (FR)**[11] 4955 9-10-0 0 Pierre-CharlesBoudot 3 46
(M Boutin, France) 94/10
9 1 3/4 **Kolokol (IRE)**[73] 10-8-3 0 ow1 (b) AlexisBadel 11 15
(M Cesandri, France) 28/1
10 9 1/2 **Majik Charly (FR)**[23] 5-8-10 0 (b) MaximeGuyon 13
(T Castanheira, France) 94/10
11 1 **Tenorio (FR)**[23] 4-8-8 0 (b) AurelienLemaitre 14
(Mlle V Dissaux, France) 14/1
12 3/4 **Rhythm Of Life (GER)**[23] 8-9-0 0 (b) SebastienMaillot 12
(G Bernaud, Belgium) 215/10
13 12 **Renounce (FR)**[23] 6-8-7 0 (b) AntoineCoutier 15
(D De Waele, France) 61/10[2]
14 3 **Ghor (FR)**[23] 9-9-3 0 (b) MickaelBarzalona 16
(R Roels, Germany) 38/1
P **Cracker'star (FR)**[24] 4233 4-8-0 0 Dimitrilbouth 9
(C Plisson, France) 65/1

PARI-MUTUEL (all including 1 euro stake): WIN 7.70; PLACE 2.50, 6.70, 2.10; DF 92.10; SF 182.80.
**Owner** Jean-Vincent Toux **Bred** Haras D'Ecouves **Trained** France

5177 - 5178a (Foreign Racing) - See Raceform Interactive

# 4101 REDCAR (L-H)
Sunday, July 23

**OFFICIAL GOING: Good to firm (8.9)**
Wind: Light against Weather: Cloudy, steady rain after 5th

## 5179 GET THE SKY BET ADVANTAGE EBF NOVICE STKS (DIV I) 7f
2:00 (2:01) (Class 5) 2-Y-O £3,396 (£1,010; £505; £252) Stalls Centre

Form RPR
22 1 **Arbalet (IRE)**[17] 4539 2-9-2 0 JosephineGordon 7 88+
(Hugo Palmer) *dwlt: sn chsd ldrs: pushed along to ld appr fnl f: kpt on wl: comf* 8/11[1]
052 2 3 1/2 **Barbarianatthegate**[16] 4560 2-9-2 79 (b) OisinMurphy 5 74
(Brian Meehan) *led narrowly: rdn whn hdd over 2f out: remained cl up: kpt on but no ch wnr fnl f* 5/1[3]
54 3 2 1/4 **Knowing Glance (IRE)**[22] 4359 2-9-2 0 PaulHanagan 3 68
(Richard Fahey) *s.i.s: hld up: keen early: pushed along 2f out: sme hdwy over 1f out: kpt on wl fnl f: wnt 3rd post* 9/1
14 4 nse **Falmouth Light (FR)**[26] 4183 2-9-9 0 PJMcDonald 9 75
(Mark Johnston) *pressed ldr: led over 2f out: sn rdn: hdd appr fnl f: wknd ins fnl f: lost 3rd post* 9/2[2]
5 5 1/2 **Tebay (IRE)**[25] 4205 2-9-2 0 PaulMulrennan 2 66+
(Michael Dods) *racd keenly in midfield: pushed along over 2f out: one pce and edgd lft ins fnl f* 12/1
0 6 6 **Jaycols Star**[23] 4291 2-8-13 0 JordanVaughan(3) 1 51
(Philip Kirby) *wnt lft s: sn midfield: pushed along over 3f out: wknd over 1f out* 40/1
0 7 4 1/2 **Angie B (IRE)**[18] 4502 2-8-11 0 TomEaves 10 33
(John Wainwright) *hld up: nvr threatened* 200/1
0 8 1/2 **Crazy World**[15] 4599 2-9-2 0 DanielTudhope 8 37
(Declan Carroll) *midfield: rdn along 3f out: wknd over 1f out* 40/1
9 2 1/4 **Gardinia** 2-8-8 0 RachelRichardson(3) 6 26
(Tim Easterby) *hld up: rdn along over 3f out: sn btn* 40/1
0 10 21 **David Fallow**[31] 4014 2-9-2 0 CamHardie 4
(Paul Midgley) *trckd ldrs: plld hrd early: rdn over 3f out: wknd and bhd* 150/1
1m 24.11s (-0.39) **Going Correction** -0.05s/f (Good) 10 Ran SP% **118.9**
Speed ratings (Par 94): **100,96,93,93,92 85,80,80,77,53**
CSF £4.87 TOTE £1.70: £1.02, £1.80, £1.80; EX 5.00 Trifecta £19.30.
**Owner** V I Araci **Bred** Ms Mags Durkan **Trained** Newmarket, Suffolk

**FOCUS**
It was dry overnight and the going was given as good to firm (GoingStick: 8.9). All distances as advertised. A nice performance from the winner, who drew clear for an easy win in the end. He was value for a good bit extra.

## 5180 GET THE SKY BET ADVANTAGE EBF NOVICE STKS (DIV II) 7f
2:30 (2:35) (Class 5) 2-Y-O £3,396 (£1,010; £505; £252) Stalls Centre

Form RPR
5 1 **Tight Lines**[13] 4681 2-8-11 0 JoeFanning 4 83+
(Mark Johnston) *trckd ldrs: led gng wl over 2f out: pushed clr over 1f out: easily* 5/2[1]
2 3 3/4 **Glacier Fox** 2-9-2 0 AndrewMullen 5 76+
(Tom Tate) *s.i.s: sn chsd ldrs: pushed along over 2f out: wnt 2nd appr fnl f: kpt on but no ch wnr* 15/2
00 3 5 **Hamba Moyo (IRE)**[26] 4167 2-8-11 0 (p[1]) DavidAllan 1 57
(Tim Easterby) *chsd ldrs: rdn over 2f out: wknd fnl f* 40/1
0 4 6 **Molly Mayhem (IRE)**[24] 4258 2-8-11 0 TonyHamilton 3 41
(Richard Fahey) *trckd ldrs: rdn over 2f out: wknd over 1f out* 7/2[2]
5 1 1/4 **Nunnery Lane** 2-8-13 0 NathanEvans(3) 9 42
(Michael Easterby) *hld up in tch: pushed along over 2f out: wknd over 1f out* 16/1
0 6 7 **Lethal Lady**[13] 4689 2-8-6 0 CallumRodriguez(5) 6 19
(Michael Dods) *led: rdn whn hdd over 2f out: wknd* 25/1
7 1/2 **Echo (IRE)** 2-9-2 0 JackGarritty 2 22+
(Jedd O'Keeffe) *slowly away: bucked and sn wl bhd: minor late hdwy* 7/2[2]
8 2 3/4 **Charming Power (IRE)** 2-9-2 0 NeilFarley 7 15
(Ann Duffield) *in tch: rdn over 2f out: wknd* 18/1
9 6 **Mydadsared** 2-9-2 0 BarryMcHugh 8
(Tony Coyle) *hld up: rdn over 3f out: wknd and bhd* 7/1[3]
1m 24.76s (0.26) **Going Correction** -0.05s/f (Good) 9 Ran SP% **114.7**
Speed ratings (Par 94): **96,91,86,79,77 69,69,66,59**
CSF £21.95 TOTE £3.60: £1.50, £1.70, £7.90; EX 24.60 Trifecta £505.90.
**Owner** The Duke Of Roxburghe & D Burke **Bred** Floors Farming And Dominic Burke **Trained** Middleham Moor, N Yorks

**FOCUS**
This looked the weaker of the two divisions on paper, and the time was 0.65sec slower than the first leg. They finished well strung out and the winner has been given some credit.

## 5181 RACING UK NOW LIVE ON YOUVIEW 231 H'CAP 1m 1f
3:00 (3:01) (Class 6) (0-60,60) 3-Y-O+ £2,911 (£866; £432; £216) Stalls Low

Form RPR
5005 1 **Mr Sundowner (USA)**[14] 4659 5-9-3 54 (t) SammyJoBell(3) 2 60
(Wilf Storey) *hld up in midfield: pushed along and hdwy over 2f out: led 1f out: kpt on* 5/1[1]
0001 2 3/4 **Graceful Act**[5] 5002 9-9-3 51 6ex (p) DavidAllan 7 56
(Ron Barr) *midfield: pushed along and hdwy over 2f out: chsd ldr jst ins fnl f: kpt on* 6/1[2]
5540 3 3/4 **Lozah**[34] 3911 4-9-10 58 TonyHamilton 14 61
(Roger Fell) *slowly away: hld up: rdn and hdwy on outer 2f out: kpt on ins fnl f* 8/1
2230 4 3/4 **The Dukkerer (IRE)**[15] 4601 6-9-11 59 TomEaves 4 61
(James Given) *trckd ldrs: rdn to ld narrowly over 1f out: hdd 1f out: one pce* 13/2[3]

3454 **5** 3/4 **Sooqaan**[15] 4601 6-9-3 **51** ..... CamHardie 6 53
(Antony Brittain) *in tch: pushed along whn short of room over 1f out: kpt on ins fnl f: nrst fin* **6/1**[2]

0000 **6** *nk* **Nelson's Bay**[13] 4690 8-8-10 **47** ..... NathanEvans(3) 3 46
(Wilf Storey) *hld up: rdn and sme hdwy on inner 2f out: one pce fnl f* **16/1**

-005 **7** *nk* **Pindaric**[47] 3431 3-8-4 **54** ..... ConnorMurtagh(7) 1 53
(Alan Lockwood) *slowly away: hld up: rdn 2f out: kpt on ins fnl f* **13/2**[3]

30-0 **8** 1 1/4 **Cosmic Dust**[38] 3760 4-8-7 **46** ..... PhilDennis(5) 10 42
(Richard Whitaker) *trckd ldrs: rdn and ev ch over 1f out: wknd ins fnl f* **22/1**

-000 **9** 1 3/4 **Dylan's Storm (IRE)**[33] 3934 5-9-2 **50** .....(p) PaulMulrennan 13 43
(Peter Niven) *prom: rdn to ld over 2f out: hdd over 1f out: wknd fnl f* **33/1**

0 **10** 8 **Twistsandturns (IRE)**[16] 4575 6-8-12 **53** ..... GerO'Neill(7) 16 30
(Declan Carroll) *trckd ldrs on outer: rdn 3f out: wknd over 1f out* **16/1**

040- **11** 4 **Snappydresser**[332] 5803 4-9-2 **50** ..... RobertWinston 9 19
(Chris Grant) *led: rdn whn hdd over 2f out: sn wknd: eased fnl f* **33/1**

6-56 **P** **Navajo Thunder (IRE)**[11] 4761 3-8-3 **53** ..... RayDawson(7) 11
(Michael Appleby) *midfield: rdn over 3f out: wnt wrong and p.u over 2f out* **7/1**

1m 55.02s (2.02) **Going Correction** -0.15s/f (Firm)
**WFA** 3 from 4yo+ 9lb **12** Ran SP% **117.5**
Speed ratings (Par 101): **85,84,83,83,82 82,81,80,79,72 68,**
CSF £33.23 CT £238.64 TOTE £4.40: £1.40, £2.60, £2.70; EX 47.00 Trifecta £218.90.
**Owner** W Storey **Bred** Hunter Valley Farm Et Al **Trained** Muggleswick, Co Durham
■ Stewards' Enquiry : Nathan Evans two-day ban: used whip with his arm above shoulder height (Aug 6-7)

**FOCUS**
A low-grade handicap. They went steady early but the pace lifted in the straight. The winner is rated to this year's best form.

## 5182 WATCH RACING UK ON BT TV H'CAP 7f
**3:30** (3:32) (Class 5) (0-70,72) 3-Y-O **£3,396** (£1,010; £505; £252) **Stalls** Centre

Form RPR

1201 **1** **Clear As A Bell (IRE)**[15] 4602 3-8-13 **61** ..... DavidAllan 7 69+
(Tim Easterby) *prom: led 5f out: rdn over 2f out: kpt on fnl f: hld on towards fin* **6/1**[2]

3605 **2** *nk* **Darvie**[23] 4303 3-8-8 **56** ..... SamJames 15 62
(David Barron) *hld up: rdn over 2f out: angled lft and stl plenty to do over 1f out: r.o wl fnl f: gaining at fin* **14/1**

-334 **3** *hd* **Regal Decree**[13] 4694 3-8-6 **54** .....(p) PaulHanagan 12 60
(Jedd O'Keeffe) *midfield: rdn and hdwy to chse ldr over 1f out: kpt on* **13/2**[3]

500 **4** 1 **Channel Packet**[65] 2794 3-9-0 **62** ..... AlistairRawlinson 2 65
(Michael Appleby) *chsd ldrs: rdn over 2f out: kpt on* **25/1**

0553 **5** 3 1/2 **Haworth**[13] 4694 3-9-4 **66** ..... DanielTudhope 9 60
(James Bethell) *midfield: pushed along whn short of room over 1f out: one pce fnl f* **7/2**[1]

0020 **6** 1/2 **Chipping (IRE)**[13] 4694 3-9-10 **72** .....(p) ConnorBeasley 8 64
(Michael Dods) *midfield: rdn over 2f out: one pce* **8/1**

5000 **7** 2 3/4 **Hitchcock**[15] 4602 3-8-13 **61** .....(b[1]) KevinStott 1 46
(Kevin Ryan) *slowly away: hld up: hdwy to trck ldrs 4f out: rdn over 2f out: wknd ins fnl f* **12/1**

460 **8** 2 1/2 **Silk Mill Blue**[12] 4726 3-8-4 **55** .....(b[1]) NathanEvans(3) 11 33
(Richard Whitaker) *chsd ldrs: rdn over 2f out: wknd fnl f* **20/1**

-645 **9** 1 1/2 **Atrafan (IRE)**[13] 4694 3-8-7 **55** ..... BenCurtis 13 29
(Alan Brown) *hld up: rdn over 2f out: nvr threatened* **9/1**

-532 **10** *nk* **Roys Dream**[34] 3897 3-9-7 **69** ..... TonyHamilton 10 42
(Paul Collins) *chsd ldrs: rdn over 2f out: wknd appr fnl f* **13/2**[3]

0000 **11** 3/4 **Baby Helmet**[11] 4743 3-8-3 **51** ..... DuranFentiman 3 22
(Karen Tutty) *led: hdd 5f out: remained prom tl wknd over 2f out* **33/1**

-000 **12** 1 3/4 **Thornton Mary**[15] 4603 3-8-2 **51** oh6 ..... CamHardie 14 16
(Brian Rothwell) *hld up: rdn over 3f out: sn btn* **100/1**

0003 **13** 4 1/2 **Redrosezorro**[11] 4741 3-8-7 **55** .....(h) PatrickMathers 17 9
(Eric Alston) *hld up in midfield: rdn over 2f out: sn wknd* **25/1**

50-0 **14** 9 **Prince Of Clappers**[26] 4186 3-8-6 **57** ..... RachelRichardson(3) 6
(Tim Easterby) *dwlt: a towards rr* **40/1**

0-00 **15** 7 **Zarkavon**[23] 4302 3-8-3 **52** oh6 ow1 .....(v[1]) AndrewMullen 4
(John Wainwright) *hld up: rdn over 2f out: wknd and eased* **125/1**

1m 23.5s (-1.00) **Going Correction** -0.05s/f (Good) **15** Ran SP% **118.3**
Speed ratings (Par 100): **103,102,102,101,97 96,93,90,89,88 87,85,80,70,62**
CSF £79.20 CT £582.92 TOTE £7.70: £2.10, £4.50, £2.50; EX 103.20 Trifecta £901.20.
**Owner** Habton Farms **Bred** Drumlin Bloodstock **Trained** Great Habton, N Yorks

**FOCUS**
A modest but competitive affair. Straightforward form.

## 5183 RACING UK NOW ON TALKTALK TV CLASSIFIED CLAIMING STKS 1m 2f 1y
**4:00** (4:00) (Class 6) 3-Y-O+ **£2,911** (£866; £432; £216) **Stalls** Low

Form RPR

1424 **1** **Kiwi Bay**[9] 4833 12-9-1 67 ..... CallumRodriguez(5) 2 72
(Michael Dods) *hld up in midfield: keen early: pushed along and hdwy 3f out: rdn to ld 2f out: kpt on to draw clr fnl f* **11/4**[2]

2201 **2** 3 1/2 **Hannington**[11] 4753 6-8-11 59 .....(t) RayDawson(7) 1 63
(Michael Appleby) *trckd ldrs: rdn to ld over 3f out: hdd 2f out: rdr dropped whip over 1f out: one pce fnl f* **13/2**[3]

0200 **3** *shd* **Dutch Artist (IRE)**[26] 4168 5-9-10 75 .....(p) DanielTudhope 8 69
(David O'Meara) *prom: brought wd st: rdn over 3f out: one pce* **13/2**[3]

3446 **4** 3/4 **Attain**[18] 4492 8-8-13 68 ..... EdwardGreatrex(3) 7 60
(Archie Watson) *in tch: rdn over 3f out: plugged on fnl f* **13/2**[3]

6516 **5** 1 1/2 **Mysterial**[5] 5005 7-8-11 72 ..... GerO'Neill(7) 5 59
(Declan Carroll) *led: rdn whn hdd over 3f out: sn outpcd and no threat after* **7/4**[1]

2002 **6** 10 **Chelwood Gate (IRE)**[17] 4538 7-9-5 66 .....(v) PaulMulrennan 4 41
(Conor Dore) *hld up: hdwy 3f out: rdn over 2f out: wknd over 1f out* **12/1**

56/0 **7** 31 **In The House (IRE)**[39] 3724 5-9-4 52 .....(t[1]) NeilFarley 3
(Lucinda Egerton) *dwlt: hld up: rdn 4f out: sn bhd: eased and t.o* **100/1**

2m 5.32s (-1.78) **Going Correction** -0.15s/f (Firm) **7** Ran SP% **111.7**
Speed ratings (Par 101): **101,98,98,97,96 88,63**
CSF £19.74 TOTE £4.30: £2.10, £3.00; EX 19.90 Trifecta £101.00.
**Owner** Kiwi Racing **Bred** Templeton Stud **Trained** Denton, Co Durham

**FOCUS**
A modest contest, rated around the pair.

## 5184 SKY BET GO-RACING-IN-YORKSHIRE SUMMER FESTIVAL H'CAP 5f 217y
**4:30** (4:31) (Class 4) (0-85,84) 3-Y-O+ **£6,469** (£1,925; £962; £481) **Stalls** Centre

Form RPR

056 **1** **Highly Sprung (IRE)**[8] 4897 4-9-1 **73** ..... JoeFanning 6 79
(Mark Johnston) *trckd ldr: led narrowly over 2f out: rdn over 1f out: hld on wl* **11/2**[3]

1016 **2** 1/2 **Muscika**[13] 4683 3-9-7 **84** ..... DanielTudhope 2 87
(David O'Meara) *dwlt: sn trckd ldr: upsides over 2f out: pushed along over 1f out: drvn ins fnl f: edgd lft 110yds out: kpt on* **8/11**[1]

0050 **3** *shd* **Duke Cosimo**[13] 4683 7-9-2 **74** ..... TomEaves 8 78
(Michael Herrington) *hld up: pushed along and hdwy over 1f out: rdn and ev ch ins fnl f: carried lft 110yds out: kpt on* **10/1**

0010 **4** 6 **Zapper Cass (FR)**[19] 4477 4-9-6 **81** .....(t[1]) JoshDoyle(3) 3 66
(Tony Coyle) *hld up in tch: rdn 2f out: wknd ins fnl f* **9/2**[2]

0-00 **5** 3/4 **Funding Deficit (IRE)**[9] 4854 7-8-8 **73** .....(h) SeanMooney(7) 4 55
(Jim Goldie) *hld up in tch: rdn 2f out: wknd ins fnl f* **12/1**

025/ **6** 56 **Stone Of Folca**[809] 1989 9-8-12 **70** .....(h) NeilFarley 1
(Lucinda Egerton) *led: hdd over 2f out: wknd and eased* **50/1**

1m 10.7s (-1.10) **Going Correction** -0.05s/f (Good)
**WFA** 3 from 4yo+ 5lb **6** Ran SP% **110.2**
Speed ratings (Par 105): **105,104,104,96,95 20**
CSF £9.62 CT £33.92 TOTE £5.50: £2.10, £1.50; EX 11.90 Trifecta £40.40.
**Owner** Douglas Livingston **Bred** Patrick J Moloney **Trained** Middleham Moor, N Yorks

**FOCUS**
There was a good battle between the first three here. The winner and third were both on good marks.

## 5185 REDCAR CRICKET CLUB FILLIES' H'CAP 7f 219y
**5:00** (5:02) (Class 5) (0-75,75) 3-Y-O+ **£3,396** (£1,010; £505; £252) **Stalls** Centre

Form RPR

400 **1** **Alexandrakollontai (IRE)**[8] 4883 7-9-7 **73** .....(b) RowanScott(5) 12 86
(Alistair Whillans) *stmbld and wnt rt s: hld up in rr: rapid hdwy to ld over 2f out: rdn over 1f out: kpt on* **16/1**

3223 **2** 2 3/4 **Totally Magic (IRE)**[5] 5007 5-8-12 **64** ..... LewisEdmunds(5) 9 70
(Richard Whitaker) *led narrowly: hdd over 2f out: sn rdn: one pce ins fnl f* **4/1**[2]

021 **3** 1/2 **Flourishing**[22] 4332 3-9-6 **75** ..... OisinMurphy 4 77
(Sir Michael Stoute) *prom: keen early: pushed along over 2f out: rdn over 1f out: one pce ins fnl f* **6/4**[1]

0436 **4** 2 **Someone Exciting**[25] 4209 4-8-9 **56** ..... PatrickMathers 8 55
(David Thompson) *midfield: rdn and outpcd over 2f out: kpt on ins fnl f* **18/1**

-241 **5** 1 1/4 **Vaulted**[16] 4557 3-9-0 **69** ..... PaulHanagan 2 62+
(Richard Fahey) *hld up: hdwy to trck ldrs over 2f out: sn rdn: edgd lft and wknd ins fnl f* **6/1**[3]

00-2 **6** 3/4 **Connemera Queen**[30] 4059 4-9-7 **68** ..... RobertWinston 6 61
(Chris Grant) *hld up: racd keenly: rdn over 2f out: nvr threatened* **11/1**

-000 **7** 2 3/4 **Lil Sophella (IRE)**[36] 3828 8-9-12 **73** ..... DanielTudhope 7 59
(Patrick Holmes) *dwlt: hld up in tch: rdn and outpcd 2f out: nvr threatened* **14/1**

-400 **8** 2 3/4 **Nancy Hart**[10] 4797 3-8-9 **64** .....(p[1]) PJMcDonald 5 41
(Tom Dascombe) *trckd ldrs: rdn over 2f out: wknd over 1f out* **50/1**

0001 **9** *nk* **Beadlam (IRE)**[12] 4727 4-9-1 **62** .....(p) TonyHamilton 1 40
(Roger Fell) *trckd ldrs: rdn over 2f out: wknd fnl f* **25/1**

5455 **10** 3 1/4 **Beatbybeatbybeat**[26] 4168 4-9-4 **65** .....(v) CamHardie 13 34
(Antony Brittain) *trckd ldrs: rdn over 2f out: wknd over 1f out* **25/1**

50-2 **11** 1 **Pantera Negra (IRE)**[15] 4602 3-8-11 **66** ..... BenCurtis 10 30
(David Barron) *pressed ldr: rdn over 2f out: wknd* **12/1**

1m 37.65s (1.05) **Going Correction** -0.05s/f (Good)
**WFA** 3 from 4yo+ 8lb **11** Ran SP% **117.8**
Speed ratings (Par 100): **92,89,88,86,85 84,82,79,78,75 74**
CSF £77.95 CT £159.74 TOTE £20.60: £5.40, £1.90, £1.20; EX 106.40 Trifecta £642.10.
**Owner** Chris Spark & William Orr **Bred** Sean O'Sullivan **Trained** Newmill-On-Slitrig, Borders

**FOCUS**
A fair handicap. The form is rated around the runner-up.

## 5186 GO RACING IN YORKSHIRE FUTURE STARS APPRENTICE H'CAP 1m 5f 218y
**5:30** (5:30) (Class 5) (0-70,71) 4-Y-O+ **£3,396** (£1,010; £505; £252) **Stalls** Low

Form RPR

0252 **1** **Midnight Warrior**[16] 4558 7-8-9 **55** .....(t) JamieGormley(3) 1 61
(Ron Barr) *trckd ldr: led over 3f out: styd on fnl f: led nr fin* **10/3**[1]

-544 **2** *nk* **Jan De Heem**[37] 3795 7-9-1 **58** ..... ConnorMurtagh 3 63
(Tina Jackson) *hld up: stdy hdwy fr 4f out: rdn to ld over 1f out: sn 2l up: wandered lft and rt ins fnl f and hdd nr fin* **6/1**

-056 **3** 2 1/4 **Ingleby Hollow**[34] 3907 5-9-12 **69** .....(p) PatrickVaughan 5 71
(David O'Meara) *led: rdn whn hdd over 3f out: plugged on* **8/1**

5316 **4** 1/2 **Adrakhan (FR)**[9] 4853 6-8-7 **50** oh2 ..... JaneElliott 7 51
(Wilf Storey) *hld up in rr: rdn over 3f out: stl last ent fnl f: styd on* **8/1**

-533 **5** *nse* **Picture Painter (IRE)**[9] 4853 4-8-9 **55** ..... SeanMooney(3) 9 56
(Jim Goldie) *in tch: dropped to midfield over 5f out: rdn 4f out: plugged on fnl f* **5/1**[3]

5436 **6** *hd* **London Glory**[22] 4357 4-9-0 **60** .....(b) ManuelFernandes(3) 8 61
(David Thompson) *midfield: smooth hdwy over 3f out: led over 2f out: sn rdn: hdd over 1f out: edgd lft: no ex fnl 110yds* **4/1**[2]

2-00 **7** 3/4 **Maple Stirrup (IRE)**[130] 1197 5-8-12 **55** .....(p) PaulaMuir 6 55
(Patrick Holmes) *trckd ldrs: rdn and lost pl over 4f out: no threat after* **33/1**

220 **8** 1 1/4 **Serenity Now (IRE)**[41] 3663 9-9-11 **71** ..... RossaRyan(3) 2 69
(Brian Ellison) *hld up: rdn over 3f out: nvr threatened* **15/2**

3m 4.77s (0.07) **Going Correction** -0.15s/f (Firm) **8** Ran SP% **111.0**
Speed ratings (Par 103): **93,92,91,91,91 91,90,89**
CSF £22.06 CT £139.38 TOTE £3.80: £1.40, £1.60, £2.60; EX 19.60 Trifecta £64.30.
**Owner** K Trimble **Bred** Tarworth Bloodstock Investments Ltd **Trained** Seamer, N Yorks

**FOCUS**
A modest contest thrown away by the runner-up. The winner is rated to form, with little solid in the race.
T/Jkpt: Part won. £9,269.00 to a £1 stake. Pool: £18,537.30 - 0.50 winning units T/Plt: £55.80 to a £1 stake. Pool: £95,538.23 - 1,249.00 winning units T/Qpdt: £22.20 to a £1 stake. Pool: £5,855.62 - 194.75 winning units **Andrew Sheret**

5187 - 5193a (Foreign Racing) - See Raceform Interactive

## 5177 DEL MAR (L-H)

Sunday, July 23

**OFFICIAL GOING: Dirt: fast; turf: firm**

### 5194a TVG SAN DIEGO H'CAP (GRADE 2 HANDICAP) (3YO+) (DIRT) 1m 110y

2:10 3-Y-0+ £146,341 (£48,780; £29,268; £14,634; £4,878)

RPR

1 **Accelerate (USA)**29 4-8-5 0 (b1) VictorEspinoza 1 117
(John W Sadler, U.S.A) 78/10[2]

2 8 1/2 **Donworth (USA)**29 5-8-4 0 MarioGutierrez 4 97
(Doug O'Neill, U.S.A) 248/10

3 2 1/2 **Cat Burglar (USA)**29 7-8-6 0 (b) RafaelBejarano 5 94
(Bob Baffert, U.S.A) 18/1[3]

4 4 1/4 **Arrogate (USA)**120 1380 4-9-0 0 MikeESmith 3 92
(Bob Baffert, U.S.A) 1/20[1]

5 19 3/4 **El Huerfano (USA)**35 5-8-3 0 (b) EvinARoman 2 38
(Peter Miller, U.S.A) 31/1

1m 42.15s 5 Ran SP% 118.9

**Owner** Hronis Racing LLC **Bred** Mike Abraham **Trained** USA

**FOCUS**

A major shock, and not form to take seriously.

## 4941 MAISONS-LAFFITTE (R-H)

Sunday, July 23

**OFFICIAL GOING: Turf: good to soft**

### 5195a PRIX ROBERT PAPIN (GROUP 2) (2YO) (TURF) 5f 110y

1:35 2-Y-0 £63,333 (£24,444; £11,666; £7,777; £3,888)

RPR

1 **Unfortunately (IRE)**20 4434 2-9-2 0 (v1) TonyPiccone 1 110
(K R Burke) *racd in fnl pair: drvn to take clsr order 2f out: jnd ldrs towards inner appr 1f out: edgd lft onto rail ins fnl f: sn led and asserted last 75yds* 102/10

2 1/2 **Frozen Angel (IRE)**31 3993 2-9-2 0 RichardKingscote 3 108
(Tom Dascombe) *pressed ldr on inner: led wl bef 1/2-way: jnd either side appr 1f out: styd on wl u.p: no ex fnl 75yds* 83/10

3 shd **Heartache**32 3960 2-8-13 0 GeraldMosse 5 105
(Clive Cox) *bmpd by horse outside leaving stalls and bec unbalanced and lit up: racd keenly: hld up bhd ldr: drvn to cl 2f out: jnd ldrs on outer appr 1f out: styd on gamely u.p: no ex late on* 4/5[1]

4 3/4 **High Dream Milena (FR)**36 2-8-13 0 Pierre-CharlesBoudot 2 105+
(Mme C Head-Maarek, France) *niggled along in rr: rdn and styd on 1 1/2f out: nt clr run and snatched up ins fnl f: kpt on again wout getting bk on terms* 9/2[2]

5 4 1/2 **Ipompieridiviggiu (ITY)**28 4131 2-9-2 0 CristianDemuro 6 91
(Il Cavallo In Testa, Italy) *wnt lft s and bmpd Heartache: led: hdd wl bef 1/2-way and remained cl up: rdn and wknd over 1f out* 73/10

6 3/4 **De Bruyne Horse**22 4386 2-9-2 0 ChristopheSoumillon 4 88
(Richard Hannon) *chsd ldrs: outpcd and drvn under 2f out: sn lost pl: wl hld fnl f* 66/10[3]

1m 4.5s (-2.80) 6 Ran SP% 118.6

PARI-MUTUEL (all including 1 euro stake): WIN: 11.20; PLACE: 4.40, 4.40; SF: 55.00.

**Owner** J Laughton & Mrs E Burke **Bred** Tally-Ho Stud **Trained** Middleham Moor, N Yorks

### 5196a PRIX DE BAGATELLE (LISTED RACE) (3YO FILLIES) (STRAIGHT) (TURF) 1m

2:45 3-Y-0 £23,504 (£9,401; £7,051; £4,700; £2,350)

RPR

1 **Esquisse**30 3-8-11 0 MaximeGuyon 1 104
(A Fabre, France) 58/10[2]

2 1 3/4 **Ettisaal**56 3117 3-8-11 0 AurelienLemaitre 11 100
(F Head, France) 13/10[1]

3 1/2 **Limited Edition (FR)**20 4456 3-8-11 0 TonyPiccone 3 99
(E Lellouche, France) 242/10

4 1/2 **Flower Fashion (FR)**43 3612 3-8-11 0 StephanePasquier 8 98
(N Clement, France) 61/10[3]

5 1/2 **Thrust Home (IRE)**55 3-8-11 0 (p) Pierre-CharlesBoudot 7 97
(Y Durepaire, France) 115/10

6 1 1/2 **Tikitiki (FR)**30 3-8-11 0 CristianDemuro 5 93
(Mlle J Soudan, France) 31/1

7 shd **Shes Ranger (IRE)**20 4456 3-8-11 0 AlexisBadel 2 93
(H-F Devin, France) 222/10

8 1 3/4 **Arazza (GER)**35 3882 3-8-11 0 AntoineHamelin 6 89
(J Hirschberger, Germany) 77/10

9 2 **Maytime (FR)**31 4027 3-8-11 0 MickaelBarzalona 12 84
(C Ferland, France) 192/10

10 1/2 **Tai Hang Dragon (IRE)**15 4637 3-8-11 0 RichardKingscote 4 83
(Richard Hannon) *chsd ldrs towards centre of trck: rdn and no imp under 2f fr home: wknd fnl f* 207/10

11 10 **Westit**31 4027 3-8-11 0 OlivierPeslier 10 60
(C Laffon-Parias, France) 228/10

12 12 **Honeymoon Trip (FR)**31 4027 3-8-11 0 JoseLuisMartinez 9 32
(L A Urbano-Grajales, France) 48/1

1m 34.72s (-7.58) 12 Ran SP% 119.0

PARI-MUTUEL (all including 1 euro stake): WIN: 5.30; PLACE: 2.20, 1.30, 4.00; DF: 8.00; SF: 21.30.

**Owner** Wertheimer & Frere **Bred** Wertheimer & Frere **Trained** Chantilly, France

### 5198a PRIX DU CARROUSEL (LISTED RACE) (4YO+) (TURF) 1m 7f 110y

4:10 4-Y-0+ £22,222 (£8,888; £6,666; £4,444; £2,222)

RPR

1 **Fun Mac (GER)**15 4639 6-9-0 0 (b) OlivierPeslier 6 96
(Hughie Morrison) *mde all: drvn whn pressed 1 1/2f out: rdn and styd on wl fnl f: hld on gamely* 96/10

2 nse **Vent De Force**59 3011 6-9-0 0 ChristopheSoumillon 1 96
(Hughie Morrison) *w.w in midfield on inner: drvn to chse ldrs 1 1/2f out: angled out and styd on wl u.p fnl f: jst failed* 155/10

3 hd **Travelling Man**30 4-9-6 0 AurelienLemaitre 3 102
(F Head, France) 21/10[1]

4 hd **Matauri Jewel (IRE)**27 4-8-10 0 VincentCheminaud 10 92
(M Delzangles, France) 127/10

5 1/2 **Tuvalu**21 5-9-0 0 Pierre-CharlesBoudot 7 95
(J-M Osorio, Spain) 107/10

6 shd **Line Des Ongrais (FR)**27 6-8-10 0 MorganDelalande 8 91
(P Chemin & C Herpin, France) 154/10

7 1 1/2 **Galiteo (FR)**24 4-9-0 0 MaximeGuyon 9 93
(Mme Pia Brandt, France) 43/10[2]

8 12 **Lord George (IRE)**22 4356 4-9-0 0 CristianDemuro 5 80
(James Fanshawe) *w.w towards rr: outpcd and scrubbed along wl over 1 1/2f out: bhd fnl f* 155/10

9 nk **Now We Can**44 3553 8-9-0 0 StephanePasquier 2 80
(N Clement, France) 23/5[3]

10 4 **San Salvador (GER)**70 2667 4-9-6 0 MickaelBarzalona 4 81
(Andreas Suborics, Germany) 156/10

3m 22.99s 10 Ran SP% 118.5

PARI-MUTUEL (all including 1 euro stake): WIN: 10.60; PLACE: 2.80, 3.30, 1.50; DF: 40.00; SF: 117.10.

**Owner** Mrs Angela McAlpine & Partners **Bred** Gestut Gorlsdorf **Trained** East Ilsley, Berks

**FOCUS**

A bunch finish, and a 1-2 for Hughie Morrison.

5197 - 5199a (Foreign Racing) - See Raceform Interactive

## 4655 LES LANDES

Sunday, July 23

**OFFICIAL GOING: Turf: good**

### 5200a RAVENSCROFT H'CAP SPRINT 5f 110y

3:05 (3:05) 3-Y-0+ £1,780 (£640; £380)

RPR

1 **National Service (USA)**6 4970 6-9-8 0 (tp) PaddyAspell 51
(Clare Ellam) *pressed ldr in 2nd: wnt on 2f out: rdn clr* 7/4[2]

2 4 **Country Blue (FR)**16 4655 8-10-12 0 (p) MattieBatchelor 56
(Mrs A Malzard, Jersey) *led: rdn and hdd 2f out: no ex* 7/4[2]

3 hd **Ron's Ballad**16 4655 4-8-12 0 AndrewElliott 27
(K Kukk, Jersey) *chsd ldrs: kpt on one pce fnl f* 12/1[3]

4 1 1/2 **Princess Kodia (IRE)**16 4655 4-10-8 0 MrFTett 46
(Mrs A Malzard, Jersey) *chsd ldrs: 3rd fr 4f out tl lost pl fnl f* 14/1

5 1 1/2 **Purley Queen (IRE)**16 4655 8-10-3 0 AliceMills 36
(Mrs C Gilbert, Jersey) *chsd ldrs thrght but a in last* 11/8[1]

**Owner** Matt Watkinson **Bred** Three Chimneys Farm Llc **Trained** Market Drayton, Shropshire

### 5201a BUILDING A BETTER WORLD H'CAP 1m 100y

4:15 (4:15) 3-Y-0+ £1,780 (£640; £380)

RPR

1 **Order Of Service**36 3833 7-10-12 0 MarcGoldstein 69
(Shaun Harris) *reluctant to line up: disp ld: wnt on over 3f out: drifted rt and pushed out fnl f* 2/1[2]

2 1 **Brown Velvet**16 4656 5-8-9 0 AliceMills 36
(Mrs C Gilbert, Jersey) *trckd ldrs: 6th into st: kpt on wl fnl f: nvr nrr* 15/2

3 3/4 **First Cat**16 4656 10-8-10 0 oh2 ow5 AndrewElliott 35
(K Kukk, Jersey) *hld up: 8th into st kpt on wl fnl f despite hanging lft* 12/1

4 4 **Hard To Handel**30 5-10-9 0 (h) PaddyAspell 54
(Mrs A Malzard, Jersey) *disp ld: rdn & hdd over 3f out: stl 2nd into st: wknd fnl f* 6/4[1]

5 3/4 **Grey Panel (FR)**16 4656 9-8-11 0 JemmaMarshall 26
(T Le Brocq, Jersey) *trckd ldrs: 4th into st and ev ch: one pce fnl f* 7/2[3]

6 2 **Pas D'Action**328 9-9-9 0 MrFTett 34
(Mrs A Malzard, Jersey) *trckd ldrs: 5th into st and ev ch: wknd fnl f* 15/2

7 1 **Mendacious Harpy (IRE)**30 6-9-9 0 (p) MattieBatchelor 31
(Mrs A Malzard, Jersey) *hld up and racd keenly: rdn into st: kpt on one pce* 4/1

8 1/2 **Chapeau Bleu (IRE)**42 5-9-8 0 PhilipPrince 29
(Mrs C Gilbert, Jersey) *trckd ldrs: racd wd: wnt 3rd fr over 5f out: wknd fr over 1f out* 6/1

9 9 **Larch (IRE)**315 5-8-5 0 oh12 MissMHooper
(Mrs A Malzard, Jersey) *hld up: a in last: n.d* 20/1

**Owner** Burflex (Scaffolding) Ltd **Bred** Cheveley Park Stud Ltd **Trained** Carburton, Notts

## 4956 AYR (L-H)

Monday, July 24

**OFFICIAL GOING: Good (good to firm in places; 7.8)**

Wind: Light, half against in sprints and in over 3f of home straight in races on the round course Weather: Sunny, warm

### 5202 RACINGUK.COM NOVICE STKS 6f

1:55 (1:56) (Class 5) 2-Y-0 £3,881 (£1,155; £577; £288) **Stalls** Centre

Form RPR

2 1 **Regulator (IRE)**16 4598 2-9-2 0 PaulHanagan 6 81+
(Richard Fahey) *wnt rt s: pressed ldr on nr side of gp: led over 2f out: rdn over 1f out: kpt on strly fnl f* 4/5[1]

235 2 2 1/4 **Tough Remedy (IRE)**26 4204 2-9-2 75 PJMcDonald 7 74
(Keith Dalgleish) *dwlt and checked s: hld up: hdwy on nr side of gp: hdwy 2f out: rdn and chsd wnr 1f out: kpt on: nt pce to chal* 13/2[3]

5 3 2 **Rossall**16 4599 2-9-2 0 PaulMulrennan 9 68
(Michael Dods) *trckd ldrs: effrt and rdn over 1f out: edgd lft and one pce ins fnl f* 7/1

0 4 2 1/4 **Jungle Room (USA)**17 4567 2-9-2 0 KevinStott 3 61+
(Kevin Ryan) *t.k.h early: prom on far side of gp: effrt and pressed wnr over 1f out: wknd ins fnl f* 10/3[2]

5 2 1/4 **Indian Admiral** 2-9-2 0 .................. FrannyNorton 2 55
(Mark Johnston) *prom: rn green and sn drvn along: outpcd 1/2-way: plugged on fnl f: no imp* **14/1**

66 6 3/4 **Drover**[17] 4577 2-9-2 0 .................. GrahamLee 1 52
(Keith Dalgleish) *led to over 2f out: rdn and wknd over 1f out* **50/1**

7 5 **Lady Cashmere (IRE)** 2-8-6 0 .................. RowanScott(5) 4 32
(Alistair Whillans) *hld up in tch: drvn and struggling over 3f out: wknd fnl 2f* **66/1**

0 8 4 1/2 **Oriental Power**[66] 2771 2-8-11 0 .................. CallumRodriguez(5) 5 24
(Jim Goldie) *t.k.h: hld up in tch: rdn and outpcd over 2f out: sn wknd* **100/1**

1m 13.63s (1.23) **Going Correction** +0.075s/f (Good) 8 Ran SP% **115.6**
Speed ratings (Par 94): **94,91,88,85,82 81,74,68**
CSF £6.96 TOTE £1.60: £1.02, £1.80, £1.70; EX 6.50 Trifecta £16.20.
**Owner** Cheveley Park Stud **Bred** Karis Bloodstock Ltd & Rathbarry Stud **Trained** Musley Bank, N Yorks

**FOCUS**
A fair little novice and the favourite won nicely.

## 5203 COASTAL GETAWAY OFFER AT WESTERN HOUSE HOTEL H'CAP 6f
**2:30** (2:30) (Class 6) (0-65,65) 3-Y-O+ **£2,911** (£866; £432; £216) **Stalls** Centre

Form RPR

2234 1 **Cheeni**[10] 4847 5-8-8 46 .................. PJMcDonald 7 52
(Jim Goldie) *hld up: rdn and hdwy over 1f out: chsd wnr ent fnl f: kpt on strly to ld cl home* **11/2[3]**

3064 2 hd **Goninodaethat**[7] 4958 9-9-2 59 .................. CallumRodriguez(5) 6 64
(Jim Goldie) *led: rdn clr over 1f out: edgd lft ins fnl f: kpt on: hdd cl home* **10/1**

4650 3 1 1/4 **Insurplus (IRE)**[40] 3704 4-9-5 57 .................. PatrickMathers 10 59
(Jim Goldie) *hld up on nr side of gp: rdn and hdwy 2f out: kpt on wl fnl f: nrst fin* **10/1**

2631 4 1 1/4 **Sea Of Green**[7] 4958 5-9-6 65 6ex .................. (p) SeanMooney(7) 1 63
(Jim Goldie) *hld up in tch towards far side of gp: rdn and effrt 2f out: kpt on same pce fnl f* **10/3[2]**

6061 5 5 **Racquet**[14] 4682 4-9-12 64 .................. PaulHanagan 8 47
(Ruth Carr) *chsd ldrs: effrt and wnt 2nd over 2f out to ent fnl f: sn wknd* **2/1[1]**

-063 6 2 3/4 **Circuitous**[7] 4958 9-9-1 58 .................. (v) RowanScott(5) 11 33
(Keith Dalgleish) *prom on nr side of gp: drvn along over 2f out: wknd over 1f out* **7/1**

0050 7 3 1/2 **Warleggan (FR)**[14] 4682 3-7-13 45 .................. (p) SammyJoBell(3) 2 8
(Linda Perratt) *chsd ldr to over 2f out: rdn and wknd over 1f out* **80/1**

0300 8 6 **Little Belter (IRE)**[61] 2949 5-8-9 47 .................. (v) GrahamLee 9
(Keith Dalgleish) *hld up: rdn over 2f out: sn no imp: btn over 1f out* **33/1**

-630 9 5 **Cool Run Girl (IRE)**[7] 4958 3-8-5 48 .................. FrannyNorton 4
(Iain Jardine) *hld up: pushed along wl over 1f out: sn no imp and rdr sn looking down: eased* **11/1**

1m 13.08s (0.68) **Going Correction** +0.075s/f (Good)
**WFA** 3 from 4yo+ 5lb 9 Ran SP% **115.0**
Speed ratings (Par 101): **98,97,96,94,87 84,79,71,64**
CSF £58.56 CT £539.64 TOTE £5.30: £1.70, £3.10, £2.70; EX 44.70 Trifecta £433.30.
**Owner** Mrs Camille Macdonald **Bred** Johayro Investments Ltd **Trained** Uplawmoor, E Renfrews

**FOCUS**
A clean-sweep for the Jim Goldie runners, the handler responsible for the first four home. This has been rated around the front pair.

## 5204 FINEST COLLECTION OF RACING ON RACING UK H'CAP 5f
**3:05** (3:05) (Class 4) (0-85,87) 3-Y-O+ **£5,498** (£1,636; £817; £408) **Stalls** Centre

Form RPR

3454 1 **Holmeswood**[14] 4683 3-9-7 82 .................. PaulMulrennan 5 91
(Michael Dods) *trckd ldrs: shkn up and hdwy over 1f out: led ins fnl f: edgd lft and pushed out: comf* **6/4[1]**

0106 2 1 **Desert Ace (IRE)**[10] 4850 6-9-3 74 .................. (p) DavidNolan 9 80
(Iain Jardine) *led at decent gallop: rdn along over 1f out: edgd lft and hdd ins fnl f: kpt on: hld nr fin* **16/1**

1134 3 1/2 **Royal Brave (IRE)**[14] 4686 6-9-10 81 .................. PJMcDonald 4 85
(Rebecca Bastiman) *hld up in tch: effrt and rdn over 1f out: kpt on ins fnl f: nrst fin* **7/2[3]**

0004 4 6 **Dawoodi**[9] 4896 3-8-1 65 .................. SammyJoBell(3) 8 47
(Linda Perratt) *missed break: outpcd and bhd: sme hdwy over 1f out: kpt on fnl f: nvr able to chal* **33/1**

1305 5 1 1/4 **Suwaan (IRE)**[42] 3653 3-8-8 69 .................. PaulHanagan 3 46
(Ruth Carr) *t.k.h: pressed ldr to over 1f out: sn rdn and wknd* **7/1**

1-06 6 3/4 **Fast Act (IRE)**[11] 4787 5-9-12 83 .................. KevinStott 11 58
(Kevin Ryan) *sn pushed along towards rr: edgd lft over 2f out: sn no imp: btn over 1f out* **20/1**

0-02 7 2 3/4 **Sahreej (IRE)**[24] 4327 4-8-11 75 .................. DannySheehy(7) 6 41
(Adrian Paul Keatley, Ire) *chsd ldrs: rdn over 2f out: wknd over 1f out* **3/1[2]**

58.65s (-0.75) **Going Correction** +0.075s/f (Good)
**WFA** 3 from 4yo+ 4lb 7 Ran SP% **113.3**
Speed ratings (Par 105): **109,107,106,97,95 93,89**
CSF £27.39 CT £73.62 TOTE £2.30: £1.40, £7.70; EX 25.30 Trifecta £75.20.
**Owner** David W Armstrong **Bred** Highfield Farm Llp **Trained** Denton, Co Durham

**FOCUS**
An ordinary sprint, but improved form from the winner.

## 5205 QTS LADIES NIGHT ON 12 AUGUST H'CAP 7f 50y
**3:40** (3:40) (Class 6) (0-65,65) 3-Y-O+ **£2,587** (£770; £384; £192) **Stalls** High

Form RPR

0 1 **Cosy Club (IRE)**[18] 4552 3-8-4 55 .................. DannySheehy(7) 1 59
(Adrian Paul Keatley, Ire) *mde all: rdn over 1f out: hld on wl towards fin* **16/1**

2013 2 nse **Magic Journey (IRE)**[4] 5050 3-9-0 58 .................. KevinStott 10 62
(John Quinn) *hld up midfield on outside: effrt and rdn 2f out: chsd wnr fnl f: edgd lft and kpt on wl towards fin: jst hld* **5/2[1]**

4532 3 nk **Jessie Allan (IRE)**[14] 4688 6-8-3 47 .................. SeanMooney(7) 14 53
(Jim Goldie) *hld up: hdwy over 1f out: rdn and kpt on wl fnl f: nrst fin* **12/1**

-663 4 2 3/4 **Greengairs**[14] 4687 3-9-0 58 .................. (tp) PaulMulrennan 5 54
(Keith Dalgleish) *trckd ldrs: effrt and rdn 2f out: kpt on same pce fnl f* **16/1**

0200 5 2 **The Name's Paver**[19] 4506 4-9-12 63 .................. PatrickMathers 8 57
(Noel Wilson) *trckd ldrs: rdn over 2f out: wknd fnl f* **12/1**

01 6 shd **Let Right Be Done**[14] 4687 5-8-13 50 .................. (b) GrahamLee 11 44
(Linda Perratt) *t.k.h early: hld up in tch: n.m.r over 2f out and over 1f out: shkn up ins fnl f: nvr nrr* **20/1**

6-23 7 hd **Inglorious**[10] 4851 3-9-1 64 .................. (p) RowanScott(5) 13 55
(Keith Dalgleish) *dwlt: hld up: rdn and hdwy over 1f out: kpt on fnl f: nvr able to chal* **5/1[2]**

0-00 8 2 **Declamation (IRE)**[31] 4039 7-9-1 52 .................. PJMcDonald 2 41
(Alistair Whillans) *pressed ldr: rdn and ev ch over 2f out: wknd over 1f out* **5/1[2]**

0000 9 2 3/4 **Slemy (IRE)**[10] 4851 6-10-0 65 .................. DavidNolan 7 47
(Ruth Carr) *dwlt and swtchd lft s: hld up: rdn along over 2f out: sn no imp: btn over 1f out* **16/1**

6062 10 2 **Irvine Lady (IRE)**[14] 4687 4-8-5 47 .................. (p) KevinLundie(5) 9 24
(R Mike Smith) *prom on outside: drvn along over 2f out: wknd over 1f out* **20/1**

00-4 11 2 3/4 **Mallymkun**[20] 4467 5-9-7 58 .................. FrannyNorton 6 28
(David Loughnane) *taken early to post: t.k.h: hld up in tch: drvn over 2f out: sn lost pl* **7/1[3]**

1m 32.24s (-1.16) **Going Correction** +0.025s/f (Good)
**WFA** 3 from 4yo+ 7lb 11 Ran SP% **117.0**
Speed ratings (Par 101): **107,106,106,103,101 101,100,98,95,93 89**
CSF £55.66 CT £514.19 TOTE £22.90: £5.70, £1.30, £2.40; EX 75.30 Trifecta £842.70.
**Owner** Ontoawinner Syndicate/Adrian P Keatley **Bred** J Yeomans, B McGarvey & A Everard **Trained** Friarstown, Co. Kildare

**FOCUS**
Race distance increased by 24yds. No surprise to see the 3yos come to the fore in this modest handicap, and straightforward form around the 2nd/3rd recent C&D run.

## 5206 NEVER MISS A RACE ON RACING UK H'CAP 1m
**4:10** (4:11) (Class 6) (0-65,67) 3-Y-O+ **£2,587** (£770; £384; £192) **Stalls** Low

Form RPR

0405 1 **Crazy Tornado (IRE)**[15] 4661 4-9-13 63 .................. (h) GrahamLee 2 72
(Keith Dalgleish) *hld up in tch on outside: swept into ld over 2f out: pushed along adn edgd lft over 1f out: rdn and faltered ins fnl f: kpt on* **11/2[3]**

0363 2 3/4 **Remember Rocky**[15] 4659 8-8-13 56 .................. (b) ConnorMurtagh(7) 4 63
(Lucy Normile) *hld up midfield: effrt on outside and chsd (clr) wnr over 2f out: edgd lft over 1f out: kpt on fnl f: hld nr fin* **9/2[2]**

-000 3 5 **Gun Case**[15] 4663 5-9-12 67 .................. (p) RowanScott(5) 7 63
(Alistair Whillans) *missed break: bhd: hdwy on outside wl over 1f out: kpt on fnl f: no imp* **12/1**

0006 4 4 **Argaki (IRE)**[15] 4661 7-9-6 63 .................. CharlotteMcFarland(7) 1 50
(Keith Dalgleish) *hld up: shkn up over 2f out: kpt on fnl f: nvr on terms* **8/1**

5 2 **Quiet Company**[20] 4481 3-8-0 51 .................. DannySheehy(7) 11 31
(Adrian Paul Keatley, Ire) *hld up midfield: drvn and outpcd 3f out: no imp fr 2f out* **16/1**

0443 6 1/2 **Tesko Fella (IRE)**[17] 4562 3-9-6 64 .................. PJMcDonald 5 43
(Ruth Carr) *prom: effrt and drvn along over 2f out: wknd over 1f out* **4/1[1]**

1006 7 2 1/2 **Rioja Day (IRE)**[3] 5091 7-9-0 55 .................. (b) CallumRodriguez(5) 9 30
(Jim Goldie) *hld up towards rr: drvn and outpcd 3f out: n.d after* **9/1**

0004 8 1 1/2 **New Decade**[14] 4687 8-8-2 45 .................. SeanMooney(7) 6 17
(Jim Goldie) *hld up: drvn along wl over 2f out: sn n.d* **20/1**

-360 9 nk **Royal Icon**[21] 4432 3-9-4 62 .................. (p[1]) KevinStott 3 31+
(Kevin Ryan) *led at decent gallop: rdn and hdd over 2f out: wknd over 1f out* **8/1**

0000 10 nk **Tael O' Gold**[14] 4688 3-8-1 45 .................. (b[1]) FrannyNorton 12 13+
(R Mike Smith) *w ldr: drvn and outpcd over 2f out: sn wknd* **40/1**

004 11 12 **Swiftee (IRE)**[25] 4262 4-9-3 53 .................. (b) DavidNolan 8
(Ivan Furtado) *chsd ldrs: drvn and outpcd over 2f out: sn wknd* **9/1**

1m 41.35s (-2.45) **Going Correction** +0.025s/f (Good)
**WFA** 3 from 4yo+ 8lb 11 Ran SP% **116.6**
Speed ratings (Par 101): **113,112,107,103,101 100,98,96,96,96 84**
CSF £30.17 CT £291.98 TOTE £5.70: £2.00, £1.60, £4.10; EX 22.20 Trifecta £171.00.
**Owner** Ken McGarrity **Bred** Celbridge Estates Ltd **Trained** Carluke, S Lanarks
■ Stewards' Enquiry : Connor Murtagh two-day ban: excessive use of whip (Aug 7-8)

**FOCUS**
Race distance increased by 24yds. The front two came clear in what was a moderate handicap run at an overly strong pace.

## 5207 RACING UK H'CAP 1m 2f
**4:40** (4:40) (Class 4) (0-80,82) 3-Y-O+
**£5,291** (£1,584; £792; £396; £198; £99) **Stalls** Low

Form RPR

3216 1 **Maulesden May (IRE)**[23] 4344 4-9-6 71 .................. GrahamLee 6 75
(Keith Dalgleish) *trckd ldrs: drvn along over 2f out: led over 1f out: hld on gamely fnl f* **16/1**

1216 2 1/2 **Gworn**[15] 4658 7-9-9 81 .................. ConnorMurtagh(7) 7 84
(R Mike Smith) *s.i.s: hld up: effrt on outside over 1f out: rdn and kpt on fnl f: tk 2nd cl home* **5/2[1]**

3133 3 nse **Royal Regent**[15] 4658 5-10-0 82 .................. SammyJoBell(3) 2 85
(Lucy Normile) *t.k.h: trckd ldrs: rdn and outpcd 2f out: rallied and ev ch ins fnl f: kpt on: hld nr fin* **3/1[2]**

236 4 3/4 **Testa Rossa (IRE)**[7] 4961 7-9-10 82 .................. (b) SeanMooney(7) 3 83
(Jim Goldie) *in tch: rdn and outpcd over 2f out: rallied fnl f: kpt on fin* **8/1**

-354 5 shd **Berengaria (IRE)**[14] 4701 3-9-7 81 .................. PJMcDonald 8 83
(Mark Johnston) *led at stdy pce: rdn and hdd over 2f out: rallied and ev ch ins fnl f: no ex towards fin* **9/2[3]**

223 6 hd **Jamacho**[46] 3485 3-8-10 75 .................. BenRobinson(5) 9 77
(Brian Ellison) *pressed ldr: led over 2f out to over 1f out: rallied: no ex wl ins fnl f* **5/1**

5560 7 3 1/4 **Eastern Dragon (IRE)**[98] 1832 7-9-5 77 .................. (p) JamieGormley(7) 1 71
(Iain Jardine) *dwlt: hld up: drvn and outpcd over 2f out: wknd over 1f out* **25/1**

2m 12.5s (0.50) **Going Correction** +0.025s/f (Good)
**WFA** 3 from 4yo+ 9lb 7 Ran SP% **109.3**
Speed ratings (Par 105): **99,98,98,97,97 97,95**
CSF £51.18 CT £143.08 TOTE £12.40: £5.00, £1.70; EX 48.90 Trifecta £236.70.
**Owner** The County Set (Two) **Bred** Yeomanstown Stud **Trained** Carluke, S Lanarks

**FOCUS**
Race distance increased by 24yds. No real gallop on here and it resulted in a bunched finish. Muddling form.

## 5208 RACING UK PROFITS RETURNED TO RACING APPRENTICE H'CAP 1m 5f 26y
**5:10** (5:10) (Class 5) (0-75,75) 4-Y-O+ **£3,557** (£1,058; £529; £264) **Stalls** Low

Form RPR

1/0- 1 **Kashmiri Sunset**[288] 7195 6-9-9 75 .................. (tp) JamieGormley(3) 5 81+
(Iain Jardine) *hld up in tch: effrt on outside over 1f out: rdn to ld ins fnl f: kpt on wl* **13/2**

2225 **2** *nk* **Braes Of Lochalsh**[14] 4684 6-9-3 **69**.......................(p) SeanMooney(3) 2 74
(Jim Goldie) *sn chsng ldr: rdn along over 2f out: rallied fnl f: kpt on to take 2nd pl cl home* **5/2**[1]

4205 **3** *shd* **Bridey's Lettuce (IRE)**[41] 3685 5-8-13 **65**........... ManuelFernandes(3) 7 70
(Ivan Furtado) *led: rdn over 2f out: hdd ins fnl f: rallied: hld nr fin* **11/2**[3]

1423 **4** *2 ¼* **Monaco Rose**[23] 4336 4-9-12 **75**.............................(h[1]) ConnorMurtagh 1 77
(Richard Fahey) *chsd ldr early: prom: pushed along over 2f out: rallied over 1f out: no imp fnl f* **5/2**[1]

0246 **5** *shd* **Itlaaq**[24] 4301 11-9-7 **75**..........................................(t) HarrisonShaw(5) 6 76
(Michael Easterby) *hld up: stdy hdwy whn nt clr run over 2f out: effrt over 1f out: no imp fnl f* **12/1**

1-24 **6** *10* **Buzz Boy (ITY)**[49] 3389 4-8-7 **56**.................................(b) DannySheehy 4 42
(Adrian Paul Keatley, Ire) *in tch on outside: stdy hdwy over 4f out: rdn over 2f out: wknd over 1f out* **9/2**[2]

2m 59.38s (5.38) **Going Correction** +0.025s/f (Good) **6** Ran SP% **111.7**
Speed ratings (Par 103): **84,83,83,82,82 76**
CSF £22.85 TOTE £6.10: £3.30, £1.70; EX 19.80 Trifecta £122.90.
**Owner** Paul & Clare Rooney **Bred** K F Fallon **Trained** Carrutherstown, D'fries & G'way

**FOCUS**
Race distance increased by 42yds. Another race ending in a tight finish. Again, muddling form.
T/Plt: £87.60 to a £1 stake. Pool: £89,443.23 - 744.71 winning units. T/Qpdt: £21.70 to a £1 stake. Pool: £7,615.84 - 258.82 winning units. **Richard Young**

## 4995 BEVERLEY (R-H)
### Monday, July 24

**OFFICIAL GOING: Good to soft**
Wind: Strong across Weather: Heavy cloud and blustery

### 5209 PLAY SPORTING LIFE PICK 7 FOR FREE NOW MAIDEN H'CAP 2m 32y
**5:55** (5:56) (Class 6) (0-65,67) 3-Y-O **£2,587** (£770; £384; £192) **Stalls Low**

Form RPR
00-3 **1** **Piedita (IRE)**[12] 4738 3-9-8 **66**............................................ LukeMorris 7 72+
(Sir Mark Prescott Bt) *trckd ldrs on inner: hdwy and squeezed through over 3f out: chsd ldng pair over 2f out: rdn along on inner and led jst over 1f out: drvn out* **4/1**[2]

000 **2** *2 ½* **Astroshadow**[40] 3720 3-8-2 **46** oh1................................ JoeyHaynes 11 49
(Mark H Tompkins) *t.k.h early: hld up towards rr: hdwy over 3f out: chsd ldrs 2f out: sn rdn: drvn and kpt on to chse wnr ins fnl f: no imp towards fin* **66/1**

6630 **3** *2 ½* **Nothing Compares**[55] 3180 3-8-6 **50**................................ JoeFanning 9 50
(Mark Johnston) *trckd ldrs: hdwy 3f out: effrt on outer wl over 1f out and sn rdn: drvn and kpt on same pce fnl f* **7/1**[3]

4302 **4** *1 ¼* **Laureate**[35] 3909 3-9-9 **67**.................................................... JasonHart 10 65
(Mark Johnston) *sn led: pushed along over 3f out: rdn over 2f out: drvn and hdd jst over 1f out: kpt on same pce* **3/1**[1]

6564 **5** *hd* **General Allenby**[12] 4742 3-8-6 **50**.................................(be) CamHardie 4 48
(Henry Tett) *hld up in rr: hdwy 3f out: rdn along 2f out: sn drvn and kpt on appr fnl f* **10/1**

000- **6** *1 ¾* **Legalized**[238] 8130 3-8-7 **51**............................................ AndrewMullen 1 47
(James Given) *hld up and bhd: hdwy 7f out: rdn along wl over 2f out: plugged on: nvr nr ldrs* **25/1**

6663 **7** *2 ¾* **Bizet (IRE)**[12] 4753 3-8-1 **52**.........................................(p) JackOsborn(7) 8 45
(John Ryan) *hld up and bhd: sme hdwy 3f out: sn rdn and n.d* **25/1**

0050 **8** *2* **Thomas Crown (IRE)**[10] 4839 3-8-9 **53**.......................... ConnorBeasley 6 43
(Roger Fell) *prom: cl up after 3f: pushed along 3f out: rdn over 2f out: drvn wl over 1f out: sn wknd* **16/1**

0050 **9** *½* **Chionodoxa**[5] 5017 3-8-0 **46** oh1 ow1................... RachelRichardson(3) 3 37
(Tim Easterby) *in tch: on inner: pushed along 4f out: rdn 3f out: sn outpcd* **14/1**

-050 **10** *57* **Sambuca Nera**[45] 3542 3-8-4 **48**............................................ JoeDoyle 2
(James Given) *trckd ldng pair: pushed along over 4f out: rdn whn hmpd over 3f out: sn drvn and wknd: bhd and eased fnl 2f* **20/1**

-303 **11** *6* **Black Prince (FR)**[36] 3864 3-8-9 **53**.......................................(t) JFEgan 5
(Anthony Honeyball) *midfield: hdwy on outer 1/2-way: in tch over 4f out: rdn along whn hmpd over 3f out: sn drvn and wknd: bhd and eased fnl 2f* **3/1**[1]

-400 **12** *16* **Inspector (IRE)**[16] 4623 3-9-7 **65**...............................(tp) OisinMurphy 12 +
(Hugo Palmer) *trckd ldrs: pushed along whn hmpd over 3f out: sn rdn and wknd: bhd and eased fnl 2f* **16/1**

3m 45.99s (6.19) **Going Correction** +0.375s/f (Good) **12** Ran SP% **124.0**
Speed ratings (Par 98): **99,97,96,95,95 94,93,92,92,63 60,52**
CSF £270.08 CT £1842.56 TOTE £4.40: £1.80, £13.00, £2.40; EX 285.30 Trifecta £6703.20.
**Owner** Mrs Carmen Frubeck & Denford Stud **Bred** D J & Mrs Brown **Trained** Newmarket, Suffolk
■ Stewards' Enquiry : Luke Morris six-day ban: careless riding (Aug 7-12)

**FOCUS**
All distances as advertised. A maiden handicap for three-year-olds over 2m. It was a bit of a stop-start pace but ended up a fair test, though there was trouble on the turn for home. The form is unlikely to be strong.

### 5210 CARNIVAL NIGHT FILLIES' NOVICE STKS (PLUS 10 RACE) 5f
**6:25** (6:29) (Class 5) 2-Y-O **£3,881** (£1,155; £577; £288) **Stalls Low**

Form RPR
1 **1** **Special Purpose (IRE)**[23] 4349 2-9-7 0.......................... OisinMurphy 4 88+
(William Haggas) *cl up: led over 1f out: sn rdn and clr ins fnl f: kpt on strly* **4/9**[1]

**2** *3 ¼* **Gold Stone** 2-9-0 0................................................................ TomEaves 1 69
(Kevin Ryan) *dwlt: sn trcking ldrs on inner: hdwy over 2f out: rdn to chse wnr ent fnl f: kpt on: no imp* **12/1**[3]

3 **3** *2 ¼* **Me Before You (IRE)**[14] 4689 2-9-0 0......................... DanielTudhope 2 61
(David O'Meara) *slt ld on inner: rdn along 2f out: hdd over 1f out: sn drvn and kpt on same pce* **4/1**[2]

00 **4** *½* **Excellent Times**[29] 4116 2-9-0 0........................................ DavidAllan 11 59
(Tim Easterby) *cl up on outer: rdn along and outpcd wl over 1f out: kpt on u.p fnl f* **28/1**

0 **5** *1 ½* **Lady Sandy (IRE)**[24] 4296 2-9-0 0....................................... BenCurtis 12 54
(David Barron) *towards rr: hdwy wl over 1f out: sn rdn and styd on fnl f* **25/1**

004 **6** *¾* **Daffy Jane**[10] 4862 2-8-11 0................................... RachelRichardson(3) 3 51
(Nigel Tinkler) *chsd ldrs: rdn along 2f out: sn drvn and kpt on one pce* **20/1**

**7** *½* **Sitsi** 2-9-0 0........................................................................ ConnorBeasley 5 49
(Bryan Smart) *cl up: rdn along wl over 1f out: wknd appr fnl f* **50/1**

**8** *1 ½* **Babylon Lane** 2-9-0 0.......................................................... AndrewMullen 8 44
(Michael Dods) *towards rr: rdn along 1/2-way: no hdwy* **14/1**

4 **9** *nk* **Show Princess**[44] 3562 2-9-0 0............................................ LukeMorris 6 43
(Michael Appleby) *chsd ldrs: rdn along over 2f out: sn wknd* **66/1**

0 **10** *9* **Lady Grand**[34] 3943 2-9-0 0.............................................. TonyHamilton 9 10
(Richard Fahey) *wnt lft s: a towards rr* **33/1**

**11** *1 ¼* **Honey Gg** 2-8-9 0.......................................................... PhilDennis(5) 10 6
(Declan Carroll) *hmpd s: a rr* **66/1**

**12** *nk* **Siena Flyer (IRE)** 2-9-0 0................................................... JackGarritty 7 5
(Jedd O'Keeffe) *a towards rr* **40/1**

1m 5.02s (1.52) **Going Correction** +0.175s/f (Good) **12** Ran SP% **126.0**
Speed ratings (Par 91): **94,88,85,84,82 80,80,77,77,62 60,60**
CSF £7.47 TOTE £1.40: £1.10, £2.80, £1.50; EX 9.20 Trifecta £18.00.
**Owner** Qatar Racing Limited **Bred** Epona Bloodstock Ltd **Trained** Newmarket, Suffolk

**FOCUS**
Not much strength in depth in the novice event in which they bet double digits bar two. But a nice step forward from the winner with 3rd-6th suggesting this level is sensible.

### 5211 JAIMIE KERR MEMORIAL H'CAP 5f
**6:55** (6:59) (Class 5) (0-75,75) 3-Y-O+ **£3,780** (£1,131; £565; £283; £141) **Stalls Low**

Form RPR
0006 **1** **Musharrif**[59] 3052 5-9-7 **75**.............................................. PhilDennis(5) 13 86
(Declan Carroll) *hld up in rr: gd hdwy on outer 2f out: rdn and str run ent fnl f: led last 110 yds* **12/1**

0500 **2** *2 ¼* **Astrophysics**[10] 4850 5-9-6 **69**........................................ PaddyAspell 12 72
(Lynn Siddall) *hld up in midfield: hdwy 2f out: chsd ldrs over 1f out: sn rdn to chal: ev ch ins fnl f: sn drvn: kpt on same pce* **50/1**

5066 **3** *?* **One Boy (IRE)**[35] 3903 6-9-6 **69**...................................... OisinMurphy 6 65
(Paul Midgley) *in tch: hdwy wl over 1f out: rdn to ld ins fnl f: sn drvn: hdd last 110yds: kpt on same pce* **12/1**

3024 **4** *½* **Jack Luey**[45] 3524 10-9-5 **71**.......................................(b) NathanEvans(3) 2 65
(Lawrence Mullaney) *prom: effrt wl over 1f out: rdn along whn nt clr run 1f out: sdrvn and kpt on last 100 yds* **9/2**[2]

0046 **5** *1 ½* **First Bombardment**[16] 4600 4-9-11 **74**........................... DanielTudhope 5 63
(David O'Meara) *trckd ldrs: hdwy 2f out: rdn to chal 11/2f out and ev ch tl drvn ent fnl f and kpt on same pce* **4/1**[1]

6022 **6** *shd* **Flash City (ITY)**[25] 4278 9-9-6 **69**..................................... JackGarritty 14 57
(Ruth Carr) *t.k.h: prom on outer: cl up 2f out: rdn to ld over 1f out: drvn and hdd ins fnl f: kpt on same pce* **20/1**

5355 **7** *¾* **Aguerooo (IRE)**[16] 4600 4-9-11 **74**............................(p) AndrewMullen 15 59
(Ollie Pears) *dwlt and swtchd rt s: in rr: rdn along 2f out: swtchd lft towards outer and drvn over 1f out: kpt on fnl f* **12/1**

0221 **8** *nse* **The Nazca Lines (IRE)**[10] 4835 3-9-8 **75**........................(v) JasonHart 8 59
(John Quinn) *midfield: effrt 2f out: sn rdn and nt mnuch room over 1f out: n.d* **6/1**[3]

2461 **9** *nk* **Maureb (IRE)**[11] 4788 5-9-4 **67**..................................(p) BarryMcHugh 7 51
(Tony Coyle) *a towards rr* **8/1**

1404 **10** *1 ¾* **Crosse Fire**[25] 4278 5-9-1 **64**.............................................. DavidAllan 10 42
(Scott Dixon) *qckly away and led: hdd over 3f out: cl up rdn wl over 1f out: hld whn n.m.r and hmpd appr fnl f* **12/1**

1203 **11** *shd* **Classic Pursuit**[27] 4182 6-9-3 **66**................................ RoystonFfrench 11 44
(Michael Appleby) *dwlt and rr: hdwy over 1f out: nt clr run appr fnl f: n.d* **22/1**

5142 **12** *2 ½* **Bronze Beau**[9] 4896 10-9-11 **74**.......................................(tp) ShaneGray 1 43
(Kristin Stubbs) *cl up: led over 3f out: rdn along and hdd over 1f out: sn wknd* **14/1**

-000 **13** *shd* **Bapak Asmara (IRE)**[20] 4477 5-9-12 **75**...........................(p) TomEaves 9 43
(Kevin Ryan) *a towards rr* **16/1**

5015 **14** *1 ½* **Thatcherite (IRE)**[27] 4174 9-9-2 **65**............................(t) DuranFentiman 3 28
(Tony Coyle) *a towards rr* **20/1**

00-5 **15** *3 ½* **Whiteandgold**[13] 4717 3-9-0 **67**...................................... ConnorBeasley 4 16
(Bryan Smart) *chsd ldrs on inner: rdn along 2f out: sn wknd* **25/1**

1m 4.09s (0.59) **Going Correction** +0.175s/f (Good)
**WFA** 3 from 4yo+ 4lb **15** Ran SP% **126.6**
Speed ratings (Par 103): **102,98,95,94,92 91,90,90,90,87 87,83,82,80,74**
CSF £542.49 CT £7334.47 TOTE £14.50: £4.00, £13.60, £4.50; EX 809.00.
**Owner** Ray Flegg & John Bousfield **Bred** Mr & Mrs J Davis & P Mitchell B'Stock **Trained** Malton, N Yorks

**FOCUS**
A competitive sprint in which most were fully exposed and the first two were drawn high and came quite wide from off the strong gallop. The form may not prove reliable.

### 5212 GEORGE KILBURN MEMORIAL H'CAP 1m 1f 207y
**7:25** (7:25) (Class 5) (0-70,72) 3-Y-O+ **£3,780** (£1,131; £565; £283; £141) **Stalls Low**

Form RPR
4323 **1** **Snookered (IRE)**[21] 4432 3-8-11 **64**...................... AdamMcNamara(3) 7 73
(Richard Fahey) *a.p: cl up 1/2-way: effrt 2f out: rdn to ld jst over 1f out: drvn ins fnl f: kpt on gamely towards fin* **9/2**[3]

2003 **2** *nk* **Strummer (IRE)**[25] 4260 4-9-3 **63**.........................(p) LewisEdmunds(5) 5 70
(Kevin Ryan) *hld up: hdwy over 2f out: trckd ldrs over 1f out: rdn to chal ent fnl f: sn drvn and ev ch tl no ex nr fin* **13/2**

0310 **3** *6* **Katebird (IRE)**[12] 4761 3-9-8 **72**.......................................... JoeFanning 6 68
(Mark Johnston) *cl up: rdn to ld 2f out: hdd and drvn jst over 1f out: kpt on same pce* **9/2**[3]

2322 **4** *1 ¾* **Greenview Paradise (IRE)**[16] 4603 3-9-1 **65**................ TonyHamilton 4 58
(Richard Fahey) *slt ld: rdn along and hdd 2f out: drvn over 1f out: grad wknd* **10/3**[1]

**5** *hd* **Bal De Rio (FR)**[248] 4-10-3 **72**............................................... BenCurtis 1 64
(Brian Ellison) *trckd ldrs on inner: rdn along over 2f out: drvn wl over 1f out and sn wknd* **4/1**[2]

6420 **6** *6* **Perceived**[25] 4260 5-10-0 **69**............................................. CamHardie 9 49
(Antony Brittain) *hld up: effrt and sme hdwy on outer over 2f out: sn rdn and btn* **12/1**

0120 **7** *25* **Bromance**[27] 4170 4-9-6 **61**.......................................(p) DanielTudhope 2
(Peter Niven) *t.k.h early: hld up in rr: effrt 3f out: rdn along over 2f out: sn btn and eased* **6/1**

2m 9.36s (2.36) **Going Correction** +0.375s/f (Good)
**WFA** 3 from 4yo+ 9lb **7** Ran SP% **114.8**
Speed ratings (Par 103): **105,104,99,98,98 93,73**
CSF £33.39 CT £138.43 TOTE £5.50: £2.20, £4.00; EX 24.10 Trifecta £130.70.
**Owner** Kristian Strangeway **Bred** Michael Burke **Trained** Musley Bank, N Yorks

**FOCUS**
A fair gallop to this 1m2f handicap. The winner raced close up and the second came from behind. The form is slightly hard to assess with several running below their best.

## 5213 RICHARD AND CAROL HUDSON H'CAP 7f 96y
7:55 (7:55) (Class 4) (0-85,86) 3-Y-0+ £6,301 (£1,886; £943; £472; £235) Stalls Low

Form RPR
3642 1 **El Principe**[21] 4426 4-8-6 67 ....(t) JaneElliott(5) 1 74
(Les Eyre) *mde all: rdn over 1f out: drvn ins fnl f: kpt on gamely* 8/1
-501 2 ¾ **Saint Equiano**[16] 4610 3-9-7 84 .... PhillipMakin 7 86
(Keith Dalgleish) *hld up in tch: hdwy over 2f out: rdn over 1f out: drvn and ev ch ins fnl f: kpt on same pce towards fin* 4/1[2]
0525 3 ½ **Sovereign Bounty**[30] 4085 5-9-9 79 .... TomEaves 5 83
(Jedd O'Keeffe) *hld up in tch: hdwy 2f out: rdn and n.m.r jst ins fnl f: swtchd rt and drvn: kpt on* 8/1
3312 4 nk **Navarone (IRE)**[30] 4075 3-9-1 78 .... TonyHamilton 10 78
(Richard Fahey) *trckd ldrs: hdwy to chse wnr wl over 1f out: drvn ent fnl f:* 11/2[3]
/000 5 nk **Roaring Forties (IRE)**[14] 4683 4-9-7 77 .... DanielTudhope 11 79
(Rebecca Bastiman) *hld up in rr: styd nr inner rail in home st: hdwy 2f out: rdn over 1f out: kpt on wl fnl f* 50/1
2-02 6 ¾ **Muirsheen Durkin**[26] 4210 3-9-7 84 ....(p) JoeDoyle 6 81
(Neville Bycroft) *hld up towards rr: hdwy ion outer 2f out: rdn to chse ldrs jst over 1f out: drvn and edgd rt ins fnl f: no imp* 7/4[1]
2005 7 ½ **Chaplin Bay (IRE)**[14] 4685 5-9-2 72 ....(p) JackGarritty 4 71
(Ruth Carr) *dwlt: hld up: effrt over 2f out: rdn along wl over 1f out: drvn and kpt on fnl f* 8/1
4600 8 1¾ **Tailor's Row (USA)**[9] 4894 3-8-12 75 .... JoeFanning 2 66
(Mark Johnston) *prom: rdn along wl over 2f out: sn wknd* 16/1
0114 9 nk **Talent Scout (IRE)**[6] 4999 11-9-0 75 ....(p) GemmaTutty(5) 12 68
(Karen Tutty) *cl up: rdn along 2f out: sn wknd* 16/1

1m 35.97s (2.17) **Going Correction** +0.375s/f (Good)
**WFA** 3 from 4yo+ 7lb **9** Ran SP% **118.8**
Speed ratings (Par 105): **102,101,100,100,99 99,98,96,96**
CSF £41.25 CT £273.22 TOTE £9.00: £2.30, £1.50, £2.40; EX 49.80 Trifecta £446.60.
**Owner** M Rozenbroek **Bred** Mrs Irene Clifford **Trained** Catwick, N Yorks

**FOCUS**
A moderately run affair in which the winner had the run of the race and the two market leaders were both too keen, so the form has a bit of a shaky look about it. A small pb from the winner.

## 5214 SKY BET GO-RACING-IN-YORKSHIRE SUMMER FESTIVAL H'CAP 7f 96y
8:25 (8:26) (Class 6) (0-65,65) 3-Y-0+ £2,587 (£770; £384; £192) Stalls Low

Form RPR
4533 1 **Arcane Dancer (IRE)**[9] 4900 4-9-9 60 ....(p[1]) DanielTudhope 16 66
(Lawrence Mullaney) *midfield: hdwy over 2f out: rdn wl over 1f out: chsd ldng pair ent fnl f: sn drvn: styd on wl to ld nr fin* 5/1[2]
4200 2 hd **Monsieur Jimmy**[14] 4688 5-8-11 55 .... GerO'Neill(7) 6 61
(Declan Carroll) *rr: hdwy 3f out: effrt on wd outside wl over 1f out: sn rdn: drvn ent fnl f: ev ch tl no ex nr fin* 22/1
-000 3 1 **Relight My Fire**[6] 4999 7-9-10 61 ....(b) DavidAllan 12 64
(Tim Easterby) *sn led and set str pce: wl clr 1/2-way: rdn over 1f out: drvn ins fnl f: wknd last 100 yds: hdd nr fin* 11/1
20-0 4 ¾ **Ingleby Spring (IRE)**[13] 4722 5-9-2 60 .... SebastianWoods(7) 14 61
(Richard Fahey) *rr: hdwy 2f out: chsd ldrs and rdn over 1f out: swtchd rt and drvn ent fnl f: styd on wl towards fin* 25/1
0-00 5 ½ **Mayfield Boy**[62] 2919 6-9-4 55 .... CamHardie 11 55
(Antony Brittain) *chsd clr ldr: rdn over 2f out: drvn over 1f out: wknd fnl f* 33/1
5240 6 3¼ **Thornaby Nash**[14] 4690 6-9-11 62 ....(p) TomEaves 13 55
(Karen Tutty) *chsd ldrs: hdwy 2f out: sn rdn: drvn and no imp appr fnl f* 22/1
4630 7 shd **False Id**[24] 4298 4-9-10 61 ....(t) BarryMcHugh 1 53
(Marjorie Fife) *chsd ldrs: rdn along over 2f out: sn drvn and kpt on same pce* 13/2[3]
3520 8 3¼ **So It's War (FR)**[14] 4690 6-10-0 65 ....(b) PhillipMakin 4 50
(Keith Dalgleish) *dwlt and rr: hdwy over 3f out: chsd ldrs 2f out and sn rdn: drvn over 1f out: sn no imp* 8/1
0034 9 2 **I'm Super Too (IRE)**[6] 5002 10-9-1 57 ....(b) GemmaTutty(5) 2 37
(Karen Tutty) *dwlt: a towards rr* 8/1
36/5 10 4½ **Media World (IRE)**[34] 3945 4-9-9 60 .... JoeDoyle 10 29
(Julie Camacho) *a towards rr* 25/1
5243 11 nk **Rosie Crowe (IRE)**[17] 4561 5-9-0 51 ....(v) LukeMorris 3 20
(Shaun Harris) *chsd ldng pair: rdn wl over 2f out: sn drvn and wknd* 12/1
1433 12 nk **Moi Aussie**[12] 4766 4-9-5 63 .... RayDawson(7) 7 31
(Michael Appleby) *chsd ldrs: rdn along over 2f out: sn wknd* 8/1
-264 13 22 **Old China**[14] 4690 4-9-11 62 .... SamJames 8
(John Davies) *chsd ldrs: rdn along over 2f out: sn wknd and eased* 7/2[1]

1m 36.16s (2.36) **Going Correction** +0.375s/f (Good)
**WFA** 3 from 4yo+ 7lb **13** Ran SP% **120.9**
Speed ratings (Par 101): **101,100,99,98,98 94,94,90,88,83 82,82,57**
CSF £110.56 CT £1056.29 TOTE £5.70: £2.30, £6.00, £4.30; EX 127.20 Trifecta £2219.50.
**Owner** S Rimmer **Bred** Eimear Mulhern & Abbeville Stud **Trained** Great Habton, N Yorks
■ Justice Pleasing was withdrawn. Price at time of withdrawal 12-1. Rule 4 applies to all bets - deduction 5p in the pound.

**FOCUS**
A strongly run event in which few featured and the pacesetter was caught only well inside the final furlong. Straightforward form with the winner's level pretty well established.

## 5215 RACING AGAIN NEXT TUESDAY H'CAP 1m 1f 207y
8:55 (8:57) (Class 6) (0-55,55) 3-Y-0+ £2,587 (£770; £384; £192) Stalls Low

Form RPR
4251 1 nk **Bollin Ted**[6] 5001 3-8-11 51 6ex .... DuranFentiman 11 60
(Tim Easterby) *trckd ldr: hdwy to ld 2f out: drvn and hdd jst ins fnl f: ev ch whn carried bdly lft and hmpd ins fnl f: rallied wl towards fin. Finished 2nd plcd 1st* 6/4[1]
0044 2 **Druid's Diamond**[10] 4839 4-9-1 49 ....(h[1]) NathanEvans(3) 5 55
(Mark Walford) *trckd ldrs: hdwy 2f out: rdn over 1f out: led ins jst ins fnl f: sn drvn and hung persistently lft: jst hld on fin 1st plcd 2nd* 8/1[3]
5506 3 nk **John Caesar (IRE)**[15] 4659 6-9-7 52 ....(tp) DanielTudhope 12 57
(Rebecca Bastiman) *midfield: hdwy wl over 2f out: rdn to chal on outer ent fnl f: ev ch whn carried bdly lft and hmpd: kpt pon towards fin* 16/1
-531 4 3¾ **Lady Of York**[30] 4087 3-8-10 50 ....(h[1]) JoeyHaynes 9 49
(Alan Bailey) *chsd ldng pair: hdwy 2f out: rdn and ev ch over 1f out: drvn and kpt on same pce fnl f* 9/2[2]
05-0 5 ¾ **Euro Mac**[6] 5002 5-9-7 52 .... JoeDoyle 13 48
(Neville Bycroft) *hld up in rr: hdwy wl over 2f out: rdn wl over 1f out: kpt on fnl f* 25/1
6343 6 nk **Outlaw Torn (IRE)**[39] 3761 8-9-7 52 ....(e) ConnorBeasley 10 48
(Richard Guest) *chsd ldrs: rdn along over 2f out: drvn over 1f out: kpt on same pce* 16/1
6000 7 hd **Neptune Star**[7] 4971 3-8-6 46 .... ShaneGray 1 42
(Michael Easterby) *hld up in rr: hdwy over 2f out: rdn wl over 1f out: kpt on u.p fnl f* 20/1
5060 8 2½ **Swiss Lait**[16] 4601 6-9-6 51 .... JackGarritty 8 42
(Patrick Holmes) *led: rdn along and hdd 2f out: drvn over 1f out: grad wknd* 50/1
50-0 9 2 **Little Pippin**[25] 4262 4-9-3 48 .... BarryMcHugh 15 35
(Tony Coyle) *stdd and swtchd rt s: hld up: a towards rr* 25/1
-000 10 14 **Bad Girl Caoimhe (IRE)**[163] 684 4-9-10 55 .... PhillipMakin 2 15
(Marjorie Fife) *a towards rr* 20/1
2-06 11 1 **Judicious**[34] 3935 10-9-9 54 ....(p) SamJames 14 12
(Geoffrey Harker) *hld up towards rr: hdwy 1/2-way: rdn along over 2f out: sn wknd* 16/1
0340 12 3¾ **Jennies Gem**[12] 4743 4-9-5 50 .... AndrewMullen 6 1
(Ollie Pears) *t.k.h: trckd ldrs: rdn along over 2f out: sn wknd* 20/1
-500 13 4 **Zacchetto (USA)**[15] 4659 3-9-1 55 .... JoeFanning 7
(Mark Johnston) *midfield: rdn along 3f out: sn wknd* 20/1
5-10 14 3 **St Dunstan (IRE)**[20] 4470 4-9-10 55 ....(v) JasonHart 3
(John Quinn) *chsd ldrs on inner: rdn along over 3f out: sn wknd* 20/1
0006 15 3½ **Rock Of Monaco**[7] 4982 4-9-1 46 .... CamHardie 4
(Antony Brittain) *a rr* 25/1

2m 10.83s (3.83) **Going Correction** +0.375s/f (Good)
**WFA** 3 from 4yo+ 9lb **15** Ran SP% **124.2**
Speed ratings (Par 101): **98,99,98,95,94 94,94,92,90,79 78,75,72,70,67**
CSF £10.95 CT £152.59 TOTE £2.40: £1.10, £2.20, £5.80; EX 17.30 Trifecta £169.20.
**Owner** Neil Arton & Partner **Bred** Habton Farms **Trained** Great Habton, N Yorks
■ Stewards' Enquiry : Nathan Evans three-day ban: careless riding (Aug 8-10)

**FOCUS**
A low-grade handicap in which most were exposed and they bet long odds bar four. The first three finished clear but the first-past-the post hung markedly left and carried the second and third with him and the first two places were reversed.
T/Jkpt: Not won. T/Plt: £3,136.70 to a £1 stake. Pool: £84,004.01 - 19.55 winning units. T/Qpdt: £603.80 to a £1 stake. Pool: £7,311.14 - 8.96 winning units. **Joe Rowntree**

# 4971 WINDSOR (R-H)
Monday, July 24

**OFFICIAL GOING: Good to soft**
Wind: Light, behind Weather: Cloudy becoming bright

## 5216 BOYZONE HERE ON AUGUST 26TH FILLIES' NOVICE AUCTION STKS (PLUS 10 RACE) 6f 12y
6:15 (6:16) (Class 4) 2-Y-O £3,946 (£1,174; £586; £293) Stalls Low

Form RPR
1 **Villa Savina (IRE)** 2-8-11 0 .... SamHitchcott 7 69
(Clive Cox) *led against rail: drvn and hdd over 1f out: kpt on but hld whn lft in ld last strides* 7/1
0 2 ½ **Bhindi**[11] 4806 2-8-11 0 .... CharlesBishop 12 68
(Eve Johnson Houghton) *in tch: prog to chse ldng pair wl over 1f out: clsd to chal ins fnl f: might have won but carried bdly lft last 50yds: fin 3rd: promoted to 2nd* 33/1
62 3 nk **Sweet Vixen**[25] 4273 2-8-13 0 .... PatCosgrave 14 69
(Tom Clover) *trckd wnr after 1f: rdn to ld over 1f out: hrd pressed ins fnl f: hung bdly lft last 50yds and hdd fnl strides: fin 2nd: disqualified and plcd 3rd* 9/2[3]
4 4 hd **Escape The City**[11] 4806 2-8-9 0 .... CharlieBennett(3) 9 67
(Hughie Morrison) *chsd ldrs: shkn up and nt qckn 2f out: no imp after tl styd on last 150yds: gaining at fin* 9/4[1]
5 4½ **Ortiz** 2-8-13 0 .... HarryBentley 4 54+
(Henry Candy) *s.i.s and sn wl in rr: urged along 1/2-way: kpt on fr over 1f out but n.d* 7/2[2]
6 6 shd **Catch The Pigeon**[12] 4749 2-8-8 0 .... CallumShepherd(3) 5 52
(Ed de Giles) *slowest away and bhd first f: rcvrd into midfield by 1/2-way: nvr able to rch ldrs but kpt on: nt disgracd* 22/1
7 1½ **Zapateado** 2-8-11 0 .... ShaneKelly 10 47
(Richard Hughes) *t.k.h: trckd wnr 1f: chsd ldng pair to wl over 1f out: wknd* 20/1
8 ¾ **Compton Grace** 2-8-11 0 .... RobHornby 8 45
(Mick Channon) *nvr beyond midfield: rdn and no prog sn after 1/2-way* 33/1
04 9 2¾ **Fusion Central (IRE)**[54] 3210 2-8-13 0 .... TomMarquand 11 39
(Richard Hannon) *chsd ldrs to 1/2-way: sn outpcd and btn* 14/1
0 10 hd **Lamb Chop**[11] 4806 2-8-13 0 .... WilliamCarson 3 38+
(Rod Millman) *nvr bttr than midfield: urged along and no prog 1/2-way* 16/1
11 2 **Dolydaydream** 2-8-11 0 .... FergusSweeney 2 30+
(Pat Phelan) *a struggling and wl in rr* 100/1
050 12 ¾ **Raven's Girl**[30] 4090 2-8-10 43 .... GeorgeWood(3) 15 30+
(Michael Madgwick) *v.s.i.s: a in rr* 200/1
0 13 shd **Anna Briggs**[54] 3210 2-8-12 0 .... DavidProbert 1 29+
(Michael Blanshard) *a wl in rr: nvr a factor* 50/1
0 14 6 **Arachina (IRE)**[25] 4253 2-8-12 0 .... FranBerry 6 11
(Harry Dunlop) *a in rr: bhd over 1f out* 80/1

1m 13.6s (0.60) **Going Correction** +0.25s/f (Good) **14** Ran SP% **115.9**
Speed ratings (Par 93): **106,104,105,104,98 98,96,95,91,91 88,87,87,79**
CSF £221.03 TOTE £7.70: £2.30, £7.60; EX 294.40 Trifecta £2793.00.
**Owner** Mrs David Egan **Bred** John B Hughes **Trained** Lambourn, Berks
■ Stewards' Enquiry : Pat Cosgrave four-day ban: careless riding (Aug 7-10)

**FOCUS**
Rail on straight moved back in to open straight to full width. An ordinary juvenile fillies' novice contest. They went a decent gallop on good to soft ground.

## 5217 EBF STALLIONS BREEDING WINNERS FILLIES' H'CAP 1m 3f 99y
6:45 (6:45) (Class 4) (0-80,78) 3-Y-O+ £6,301 (£1,886; £943; £472; £235) Stalls Centre

Form RPR
-562 1 **Di Alta (IRE)**[17] 4571 3-9-4 78 .... ThomasBrown 8 84+
(Ed Walker) *trckd ldng pair: shkn up 3f out: clsd on outer 2f out: rdn to ld 1f out: styd on* 2/1[2]

2-21 **2** 3/4 **Jive Talking (IRE)**[16] 4603 3-9-3 **77**........................ JamieSpencer 7 81+
(Michael Bell) *hld up in last pair: rdn 3f out: prog u.p wl over 1f out: styd on to take 2nd nr fin: unable to chal* **13/8**[1]

6551 **3** 3/4 **Kiruna Peak (IRE)**[14] 4697 3-7-11 **62**........................ DavidEgan(5) 4 65
(Mick Channon) *led: styd against rail in st: kicked on 3f out: rdn 2f out: hdd and one pce 1f out* **5/1**[3]

35-3 **4** 1 **Kath's Legacy**[91] 2028 4-9-6 **73**........................ EdwardGreatrex(3) 5 73
(Ben De Haan) *trckd ldr: chal over 2f out: stl upsides jst over 1f out: fnd little and lost pl fnl f* **12/1**

15-5 **5** 1 3/4 **Kind Of Beauty (IRE)**[41] 3693 3-9-3 **77**........................ WilliamBuick 1 75
(Hugo Palmer) *trckd ldng pair: shkn up 3f out: nt qckn 2f out: no prog and btn over 1f out* **8/1**

**6** 6 **Geoffrey's Girl (FR)**[81] 4-9-11 **75**........................(h[1]) AdamBeschizza 3 63
(Richard Rowe) *slowly away: in tch in last pair tl wknd jst over 2f out* **25/1**

2m 31.67s (2.17) **Going Correction** +0.25s/f (Good)
**WFA** 3 from 4yo 10lb **6** Ran SP% **110.7**
Speed ratings (Par 102): **102,101,100,100,98 94**
CSF £5.47 CT £11.34 TOTE £2.50: £1.60, £1.60; EX 6.90 Trifecta £18.10.
**Owner** Robert Ng **Bred** Robert Ng **Trained** Upper Lambourn, Berks

**FOCUS**
A fair middle-distance fillies' handicap. They went a muddling gallop but the two form principals still came to the fore.

## 5218 SKY BET BEST ODDS GUARANTEED H'CAP 1m 2f
**7:15** (7:15) (Class 5) (0-75,76) 3-Y-0+ **£2,911** (£866; £432; £216) **Stalls** Centre

Form RPR
1142 **1** **Fast And Hot (IRE)**[28] 4147 4-9-6 **74**........................(b) RossaRyan(7) 9 85+
(Richard Hannon) *trckd ldrs: on terms 3f out: led wl over 1f out: sn clr: rdn out* **10/1**

0-26 **2** 2 1/4 **Squiggley**[16] 4621 4-9-12 **73**........................ DaneO'Neill 12 78
(Henry Candy) *chsd ldrs: shkn up wl over 2f out: prog after and styd on to take 2nd ins fnl f: no ch to threaten wnr* **7/1**[3]

005 **3** 1 3/4 **Haulani (USA)**[19] 4501 3-9-0 **73**........................(tp) HectorCrouch(3) 10 76
(Philip Hide) *hld up in last trio: prog and shkn up over 2f out: styd on fr over 1f out to take 3rd ins fnl f* **12/1**

1062 **4** 2 1/4 **Evening Hill**[4] 5053 3-9-1 **71**........................ ShaneKelly 4 69
(Richard Hughes) *led 3f: trckd ldr: led again 3f out to wl over 1f out: wknd fnl f* **7/1**[3]

-425 **5** 2 1/2 **Hernandes (FR)**[24] 4295 3-9-3 **73**........................ LiamKeniry 8 66
(Ed Walker) *hld up in last trio: pushed along 3f out: no ch whn rdn over 1f out: plugged on but nvr involved* **6/1**[2]

3-56 **6** 1 1/2 **Blaze Of Hearts (IRE)**[42] 3670 4-10-0 **75**........................ HarryBentley 5 64
(Dean Ivory) *chsd ldrs: rdn in 4th pl 3f out: no prog 2f out: sn wknd* **16/1**

-050 **7** nk **Balgair**[24] 4311 3-8-7 **68**........................ MitchGodwin(5) 11 57
(Jonathan Portman) *trapped out wd early: in tch: rdn 3f out: no imp ldrs over 2f out: wandered over 1f out* **20/1**

354 **8** 6 **Sea Sovereign (IRE)**[36] 3860 4-10-0 **75**........................ TimmyMurphy 2 51+
(Mark Pitman) *dwlt: sn chsd ldrs: no room on inner over 6f and lost pl: shkn up 4f out: no prog 3f out: no ch whn trapped bhd wkng rival over 1f out and lost more grnd* **8/1**

2100 **9** 8 **Solajan (IRE)**[47] 3457 3-9-5 **75**........................ AdamKirby 6 36
(Ed Dunlop) *plld hrd: hld up in last: effrt on outer over 3f out: wknd qckly over 2f out* **25/1**

3-13 **10** 3 3/4 **Outcrop (IRE)**[66] 2784 3-9-6 **76**........................ RobertWinston 1 30
(Hughie Morrison) *t.k.h: w ldr: led after 3f to 3f out: sn wknd: eased over 1f out* **2/1**[1]

2m 10.79s (2.09) **Going Correction** +0.25s/f (Good)
**WFA** 3 from 4yo+ 9lb **10** Ran SP% **115.0**
Speed ratings (Par 103): **101,99,97,96,94 92,92,87,81,78**
CSF £77.10 CT £852.64 TOTE £8.80: £2.70, £2.50, £3.40; EX 35.40 Trifecta £600.70.
**Owner** Derek And Jean Clee **Bred** D D & Mrs J P Clee **Trained** East Everleigh, Wilts

**FOCUS**
A fair handicap. They went a muddling gallop again and it proved hard to make up ground from off the pace.

## 5219 SKY BET WINDSOR SPRINT SERIES H'CAP (A QUALIFIER FOR THE WINDSOR SPRINT SERIES FINAL) 5f 21y
**7:45** (7:47) (Class 3) (0-90,90) 3-Y-0 **£7,246** (£2,168; £1,084; £542; £270) **Stalls** Low

Form RPR
2/35 **1** **Atletico (IRE)**[10] 4830 5-9-9 **87**........................ AndreaAtzeni 2 98+
(Roger Varian) *in tch in 5th: shkn up and prog over 1f out: led 130yds out: sn in command: readily* **8/11**[1]

6-03 **2** 1 1/4 **Wiley Post**[25] 4278 4-8-2 **71**........................(b) DavidEgan(5) 4 77
(Tony Carroll) *disp ld against rail tl def advantage wl over 1f out: rdn and hdd 130yds out: kpt on but no ch w wnr* **25/1**

3214 **3** 1 **Pettochside**[11] 4803 8-9-1 **84**........................ MitchGodwin(5) 9 86
(John Bridger) *disp ld to wl over 1f out: one pce u.p after* **7/1**[2]

0001 **4** 1/2 **Union Rose**[12] 4732 5-9-11 **89**........................ ShaneKelly 6 90
(Ronald Harris) *broke wl but stdd bhd ldrs: rdn 2f out: kpt on same pce and nvr able to threaten* **10/1**

30/0 **5** 1 **Secondo (FR)**[22] 4411 7-9-9 **87**........................ FranBerry 7 84
(Joseph Tuite) *hld up in last pair: cajoled along fr 2f out: no real prog* **7/1**[2]

3226 **6** 2 1/4 **The Big Lad**[37] 3834 5-8-7 **78**........................ NicolaCurrie(7) 5 67
(Richard Hughes) *hld up in last pair: rdn and no prog 2f out: wl btn over 1f out* **16/1**

0003 **7** 4 **Majestic Hero (IRE)**[7] 4974 5-9-12 **90**........................ AdamKirby 10 65
(Ronald Harris) *chsd ldrs on outer: rdn 2f out: wknd qckly jst over 1f out* **8/1**[3]

1m 0.54s (0.24) **Going Correction** +0.25s/f (Good) **7** Ran SP% **112.8**
Speed ratings (Par 107): **108,106,104,103,102 98,92**
CSF £22.06 CT £79.19 TOTE £1.60: £1.20, £6.30; EX 22.80 Trifecta £93.30.
**Owner** A D Spence **Bred** Tally-Ho Stud **Trained** Newmarket, Suffolk

**FOCUS**
The feature contest was a decent 5f handicap. The odds-on favourite outclassed these opponents in the quickest comparative winning time on the card so far.

## 5220 SKY BET HORSERACING CASH OUT MAIDEN STKS 1m 2f
**8:15** (8:18) (Class 5) 3-4-Y-0 **£2,911** (£866; £432; £216) **Stalls** Centre

Form RPR
33- **1** **Al Mayda (USA)**[242] 8081 3-9-0 0........................(t) HarryBentley 11 80
(Hugo Palmer) *mde all: drew clr 3f out: pushed along over 1f out: rdn out nr fin as runner-up clsd* **12/1**

**2** 1/2 **Fujaira Prince (IRE)** 3-9-5 0........................ AndreaAtzeni 7 84+
(Roger Varian) *chsd ldrs: off the bridle bef 1/2-way: prog u.p over 2f out: tk 2nd fnl f: clsd on wnr nr fin: jst hld* **12/1**

**3** 2 1/4 **Hats Off To Larry** 3-9-5 0........................ CharlesBishop 1 79
(Mick Channon) *chsd ldrs: rdn 3f out: prog 2f out to chse clr wnr jst over 1f out: kpt on one pce and sn lost 2nd* **13/2**[3]

3 **4** 3 3/4 **Graphite (IRE)**[22] 4409 3-9-5 0........................ FranBerry 10 72
(David Simcock) *t.k.h: trckd ldrs: rdn 3f out: clsd on outer 2f out: ch of a pl jst over 1f out: rn green and fdd* **12/1**

**5** 3 **Circuit Judge** 3-9-5 0........................ DavidProbert 14 66
(William Knight) *trckd wnr to 3f out: stl disputing 2nd over 1f out: wknd fnl f* **100/1**

**6** 1/2 **Adjacent** 3-9-5 0........................ AdamKirby 4 65+
(Charlie Appleby) *towards rr: pushed along over 3f out: sme prog over 2f out: nvr a threat* **11/4**[2]

5 **7** 1 1/2 **Outofthequestion**[25] 4274 3-9-5 0........................ FergusSweeney 2 62
(Alan King) *t.k.h: hld up in midfield: rdn and prog over 2f out: tried to cl on ldrs over 1f out: wknd fnl f* **50/1**

00 **8** nse **Murchison River**[66] 2783 3-9-5 0........................ DaneO'Neill 9 61
(Henry Candy) *chsd ldrs: pushed along and wknd wl over 2f out* **80/1**

5 **9** nse **The Groove**[14] 4700 4-10-0 0........................(t) TrevorWhelan 3 60
(Fergal O'Brien) *racd in 3rd: chsd wnr 3f out to jst over 1f out: wknd qckly* **150/1**

3 **10** nse **Abel Tasman**[171] 552 3-9-5 0........................ RichardKingscote 16 61
(Ed Walker) *stdd s: hld up in last trio: wl bhd over 3f out: sme prog fr 2f out: nt entirely disgraced* **16/1**

0 **11** 1 3/4 **Raining Stars**[54] 3209 3-9-5 0........................ TomQueally 8 58
(James Fanshawe) *wl in rr: lft bhd over 3f out: shkn up over 2f out: nvr on terms* **66/1**

**12** hd **Clearly** 3-9-0 0........................ RobertTart 12 52
(John Gosden) *green preliminaries: dwlt: mostly in last trio: passed a couple over 2f out but no prog after* **16/1**

50 **13** 8 **Reel Leisure (GR)**[19] 4497 4-9-9 0........................ ShaneKelly 15 35
(Amanda Perrett) *in tch in midfield tl wknd qckly 3f out* **200/1**

4 **14** 2 **Seinfeld**[20] 4460 3-9-5 0........................ StevieDonohoe 13 37
(David Simcock) *a in rr: urged along over 4f out: sn no ch* **100/1**

02 **15** 1/2 **Stormy Blues**[25] 4274 3-9-5 0........................(t) WilliamBuick 5 36
(Charlie Appleby) *a towards rr: bhd over 2f out* **15/8**[1]

**16** 7 **Sky Eagle (IRE)** 3-9-5 0........................ ThomasBrown 6 22
(Ed Walker) *sn detached in last: t.o 1/2-way: lost no further grnd but didn't make any* **25/1**

2m 10.05s (1.35) **Going Correction** +0.25s/f (Good)
**WFA** 3 from 4yo 9lb **16** Ran SP% **121.3**
Speed ratings (Par 103): **104,103,101,98,96 96,94,94,94,94 93,93,86,85,84 79**
CSF £145.42 TOTE £13.50: £3.20, £3.40, £3.00; EX 138.40 Trifecta £1608.30.
**Owner** Al Shaqab Racing **Bred** Riverbend Farm **Trained** Newmarket, Suffolk

**FOCUS**
A fair maiden. They went an, at best, respectable gallop and once again it paid to be prominent.

## 5221 LADIES EVENING HERE 31ST JULY H'CAP 1m 31y
**8:45** (8:45) (Class 5) (0-75,75) 3-Y-0+ **£2,911** (£866; £432; £216) **Stalls** Low

Form RPR
6313 **1** **Dragons Voice**[43] 3627 3-9-5 **74**........................ RichardKingscote 7 80+
(Philip Hide) *trckd ldng pair: shkn up over 2f out: led wl over 1f out: drvn and styd on wl* **7/4**[1]

044 **2** 1 1/2 **Stanley (GER)**[48] 3433 6-10-0 **75**........................ FranBerry 2 79
(Jonjo O'Neill) *wl in tch: prog over 2f out: rdn to chse wnr jst over 1f out: kpt on but nvr able to cl* **9/2**[2]

5452 **3** shd **Bollihope**[3] 5091 5-9-8 **69**........................ RobertWinston 6 73
(Richard Guest) *t.k.h early: hld up: shkn up 3f out: prog fr 2f out: styd on to press for 2nd nr fin* **14/1**

4102 **4** 1 1/2 **Snow Squaw**[23] 4372 3-8-13 **73**........................(p[1]) DavidEgan(5) 3 72
(David Elsworth) *t.k.h: hld up: rdn and trying to make prog whn nt clr run against nr side rail wl over 1f out: swtchd and kpt on fnl f but no ch to chal* **5/1**[3]

4142 **5** 1 **Shifting Star (IRE)**[14] 4698 12-9-9 **70**........................(vt) WilliamCarson 10 68
(John Bridger) *led: drvn over 2f out: hdd wl over 1f out and sn lost pl: kpt on again nr fin* **11/1**

302 **6** 1 3/4 **Glorious Poet**[19] 4501 4-9-12 **73**........................ KierenFox 8 67
(John Spearing) *hld up in last: pushed along wl over 3f out: effrt on outer over 2f out: no prog over 1f out: eased last 75yds* **9/2**[2]

000 **7** 2 3/4 **Topology**[25] 4251 4-9-10 **71**........................(b[1]) LiamKeniry 9 59
(Joseph Tuite) *t.k.h: trckd ldr: upsides gng easily over 2f out: shkn up and fnd nil over 1f out and wknd* **25/1**

00-0 **8** 5 **Beaconsfield**[12] 4748 3-8-5 **63**........................ CharlieBennett(3) 4 37
(Hughie Morrison) *chsd ldrs: lost pl 3f out: wknd 2f out* **12/1**

1m 46.35s (1.65) **Going Correction** +0.25s/f (Good)
**WFA** 3 from 4yo+ 8lb **8** Ran SP% **115.9**
Speed ratings (Par 103): **101,99,99,97,96 95,92,87**
CSF £9.88 CT £83.27 TOTE £2.60: £1.30, £2.10, £3.40; EX 11.00 Trifecta £100.30.
**Owner** Heart Of The South Racing **Bred** Parry, Stratton, Steele-Mortimer **Trained** Findon, W Sussex

**FOCUS**
A fair handicap. They recorded the slowest comparative winning time on the card but the well-backed favourite still won cosily.
T/Plt: £180.20 to a £1 stake. Pool: £111,251.86 - 45056 winning units. T/Qpdt: £60.10 to a £1 stake. Pool: £9,286.44 - 114.23 winning units. **Jonathan Neesom**

5222 - 5238a (Foreign Racing) - See Raceform Interactive

# 4560 CHELMSFORD (A.W) (L-H)
Tuesday, July 25

**OFFICIAL GOING: Polytrack: standard**
Wind: virtually nil Weather: bright and sunny

## 5239 JULIE VICKERS MEMORIAL RACE APPRENTICE H'CAP 7f (P)
**6:00** (6:00) (Class 6) (0-60,61) 3-Y-0+ **£3,234** (£962; £481; £240) **Stalls** Low

Form RPR
0603 **1** **Anna Medici**[8] 4982 3-8-6 **50**........................ ManuelFernandes(5) 8 59+
(Sir Mark Prescott Bt) *rdn along and sn dropped to rr of main gp: hdwy u.p over 1f out: chsng ldrs and swtchd rt ins fnl f: styd on to ld wl ins fnl f: sn in command and eased towards fin* **3/1**[1]

-600 **2** 1 1/4 **Breaking Free**[10] 4900 3-8-8 **47**........................ LewisEdmunds 5 50
(John Quinn) *rr of main gp: swtchd rt and hdwy u.p over 1f out: styd on wl ins fnl f: wnt 2nd last strides: nvr getting to wnr* **9/2**[2]

0445 **3** nk **Caledonian Gold**[18] 4561 4-8-11 **50**........................(b) OliverDaykin(7) 3 55
(Paul D'Arcy) *taken down early: t.k.h: chsd ldrs: wnt 2nd over 2f out: clsd qckly to ld over 1f out: sn pushed along: hdd and no ex wl ins fnl f: lost 2nd last strides* **7/1**

6024 **4** 1 **Black Truffle (FR)**[14] 4727 7-8-13 **52**........................(e) NicolaCurrie(7) 9 54
(Mark Usher) *chsd ldrs: effrt u.p on inner over 1f out: styd on to chse ldr 1f out: kpt on same pce and lost 2 pls wl ins fnl f* **8/1**

40 **5** ½ **Lady Morel (IRE)**[122] 1367 3-8-12 **56**.................. StephenCummins(5) 6 54
(Joseph Tuite) *chsd ldr for 1f: settled bk and hld up in tch in midfield: effrt over 1f out: chsd ldrs 1f out: kpt on same pce ins fnl f* **14/1**

6406 **6** 1¾ **Kiribati**[13] 4741 3-9-7 **60**..............................................(b) RichardOliver 4 53
(Mark Johnston) *chsd ldrs: bmpd after 1f: hdwy to ld over 4f out and sn wnt clr: rdn and hdd over 1f out: sn btn and wknd ins fnl f* **6/1**

0000 **7** 3½ **Cookie Ring (IRE)**[35] 3935 6-8-12 **47**..........................(p) PaulaMuir(3) 2 34
(Patrick Holmes) *s.i.s: wl off the pce in last pair: swtchd rt and effrt on outer bnd wl over 1f out: sme hdwy over 1f out: nvr trbld ldrs* **16/1**

6300 **8** 1¾ **Humour (IRE)**[13] 4766 6-9-1 **47**..................................(v) PaddyPilley 12 29
(Christine Dunnett) *towards rr of main gp: reminder 4f out: sme prog u.p over 1f out: nvr trbld ldrs* **20/1**

4430 **9** 10 **Royal Peace (IRE)**[14] 4714 3-9-3 **61**........................(p) RossaRyan(5) 11 13
(Richard Hannon) *led tl over 4f out: lost pl over 2f out: and towards rr whn drvn wl over 1f out: sn wknd* **5/1**[3]

0000 **10** 5 **Artsteelwork**[46] 3545 3-8-0 **46** oh1......................... DarraghKeenan(7) 10
(John Butler) *sn wl off the pce in last pair: n.d* **50/1**

0400 **11** 1 **Noble Act**[18] 4566 4-9-8 **61**...................................... JonathanFisher(7) 7
(Phil McEntee) *rousted along early: hdwy to chse ldr after 1f tl 5f out: steadily lost pl: towards rr 2f out: sn wknd and wl bhd fnl f* **16/1**

0-00 **12** 5 **Golden Harbour (FR)**[42] 3695 3-8-2 **46**...................(bt[1]) WilliamCox(5) 1
(Brian Barr) *chsd ldrs: wnt 2nd over 3f out tl over 2f out: sn struggling and lost pl: bhd fnl f* **25/1**

1m 27.08s (-0.12) **Going Correction** -0.05s/f (Stan)
**WFA** 3 from 4yo+ 7lb **12** Ran SP% **126.7**
Speed ratings (Par 101): **98,96,96,95,94 92,88,86,75,69 68,62**
CSF £16.96 CT £94.51 TOTE £4.00: £2.10, £2.20, £1.80; EX 26.10 Trifecta £168.40.
**Owner** Neil Greig **Bred** W N Greig **Trained** Newmarket, Suffolk

**FOCUS**
This modest handicap was run at a sound pace which suited the closers.

## 5240 HAVANA CLUB 3 YEAR OLD RUM NOVICE STKS (PLUS 10 RACE) 6f (P)
**6:30** (6:30) (Class 4) 2-Y-O **£7,115** (£2,117; £1,058; £529) **Stalls** Centre

Form RPR

13 **1** **Green Fortune**[19] 4526 2-9-5 0....................................(p[1]) PatCosgrave 1 84
(William Haggas) *taken down early: trckd ldng pair: rdn 2f out: clsd but nt clr run over 1f out: swtchd rt and squeezed through ent fnl f: r.o u.p to ld wl ins fnl f: sn in command* **11/10**[1]

2511 **2** 1 **Amazing Alice**[8] 4977 2-9-3 79......................................(p) OisinMurphy 4 79
(Archie Watson) *led: rdn over 1f out: drvn 1f out: hdd and no ex wl ins fnl f* **5/4**[2]

16 **3** 2¼ **Tunes Of Glory**[22] 4452 2-9-8 0.......................................... LukeMorris 5 77
(Sir Mark Prescott Bt) *sn pressing ldr: rdn wl over 1f out: drvn and unable qck whn nudged rt ent fnl f: outpcd fnl 150yds* **12/1**[3]

2 **4** 1½ **Bomad**[12] 4792 2-8-11 0............................................. LewisEdmunds(5) 2 67
(Derek Shaw) *rn green: v.s.a: sn rcvrd and t.k.h in last pair: rdn and unable qck over 1f out: kpt on same pce fnl f* **12/1**[3]

62 **5** ¾ **Goldenground (IRE)**[33] 3999 2-9-2 0.......................... StevieDonohoe 3 65
(Henry Spiller) *in tch in last pair: outpcd and rdn along over 3f out: rallied over 1f out: rdn and no imp ins fnl f* **20/1**

1m 13.54s (-0.16) **Going Correction** -0.05s/f (Stan) **5** Ran SP% **112.2**
Speed ratings (Par 96): **99,97,94,92,91**
CSF £2.83 TOTE £1.80: £1.10, £1.20; EX 2.70 Trifecta £8.10.
**Owner** Saleh Al Homaizi & Imad Al Sagar **Bred** Saleh Al Homaizi & Imad Al Sagar **Trained** Newmarket, Suffolk
■ Stewards' Enquiry : Pat Cosgrave caution: careless riding

**FOCUS**
A truly run contest which was dominated by the market leaders.

## 5241 BARENTSZ GIN CHALLENGE H'CAP 6f (P)
**7:00** (7:01) (Class 3) (0-95,95) 3-Y-O+ **£16,172** (£4,812; £2,405; £1,202) **Stalls** Centre

Form RPR

6026 **1** **Mazzini**[24] 4353 4-9-4 **90**............................................(p[1]) GeorgeWood(3) 5 108+
(James Fanshawe) *mde all: shkn up and readily qcknd clr over 1f out: r.o strly: heavily eased towards fin: unchal* **11/4**[2]

1050 **2** 4½ **Sign Of The Kodiac (IRE)**[52] 3321 4-9-11 **94**.................. LukeMorris 7 97
(James Given) *chsd wnr: rdn wl over 1f out: drvn and unable to match pce of wnr over 1f out: no ch w wnr but battled on gamely u.p to hold 2nd ins fnl f* **7/1**

1001 **3** ½ **Udontdodou**[34] 3969 4-9-10 **93**.................................... ConnorBeasley 13 94+
(Richard Guest) *taken down early: t.k.h: hld up towards rr: effrt over 1f out: hdwy u.p 1f out: wnt 3rd 100yds out: styd on but no ch w wnr* **5/2**[1]

0600 **4** 1½ **Kadrizzi (FR)**[10] 4905 4-9-9 **92**..............................(vt[1]) RobertWinston 10 89
(Dean Ivory) *rousted along leaving stalls: sn chsng ldrs and t.k.h: effrt over 1f out: unable qck and kpt on same pce ins fnl f* **6/1**[3]

0060 **5** ¾ **Dutiful Son (IRE)**[13] 4752 7-8-6 **78**................................ JackDuern(3) 8 72
(Simon Dow) *hld up in tch in midfield: effrt over 1f out: no ch w wnr but kpt on ins fnl f* **25/1**

5564 **6** ¾ **Brother Tiger**[8] 4979 8-8-10 **79**...........................................(p) DavidAllan 2 71
(David C Griffiths) *broke wl enough: sn stdd bk and hld up towards rr: rdn and hdwy over 1f out: nvr on terms w wnr and kpt on same pce ins fnl f* **10/1**

4164 **7** 1½ **Russian Soul (IRE)**[19] 4524 9-9-10 **93**......................(p) DougieCostello 9 80
(Jamie Osborne) *dwlt and swtchd lft after s: hld up in rr: effrt over 1f out: no ch w wnr but kpt on to pass btn rivals fnl f* **16/1**

2206 **8** ½ **Upavon**[26] 4272 7-9-2 **88**................................................(t) AaronJones(3) 1 73
(Stuart Williams) *chsd ldrs: rdn over 1f out: unable qck and sn outpcd: wknd fnl f* **14/1**

4314 **9** 2 **Stanghow**[11] 4867 5-9-5 **88**............................................... CamHardie 4 67
(Antony Brittain) *restless in stalls and stmbld as stalls opened: hld up in tch in rr: effrt over 1f out: no imp and sn outpcd: wl btn fnl f* **12/1**

65- **10** nk **Leader Writer (FR)**[119] 5-9-12 **95**............................. StevieDonohoe 11 73
(Henry Spiller) *chsd ldng pair: impeded wl over 3f out: lost pl u.p and wl btn over 1f out: wknd ins fnl f* **16/1**

4515 **11** 10 **Captain Lars (SAF)**[110] 1586 7-9-0 **83**............................(v) MartinLane 6 29
(Derek Shaw) *hld up towards rr: hung rt 4f out: v wd: dropped to rr and eased 3f out: wl bhd after* **25/1**

1m 11.36s (-2.34) **Going Correction** -0.05s/f (Stan)
**WFA** 3 from 4yo+ 5lb **11** Ran SP% **124.9**
Speed ratings (Par 107): **113,107,106,104,103 102,100,99,97,96 83**
CSF £24.37 CT £56.09 TOTE £3.50: £1.40, £2.30, £1.80; EX 19.40 Trifecta £55.00.
**Owner** Mr & Mrs P Hopper, Mr & Mrs M Morris **Bred** Jan & Peter Hopper **Trained** Newmarket, Suffolk

■ Maakaasib was withdrawn. Price at time of withdrawal 9/2. Rule 4 applies to bets struck at board prices prior to withdrawal but not to SP bets - deduction 15p in the pound. New market formed

**FOCUS**
A competitive handicap run at a sound pace.

## 5242 COCA COLA ZERO SUGAR CHALLENGE H'CAP 1m (P)
**7:30** (7:36) (Class 4) (0-80,81) 3-Y-O **£8,086** (£2,406; £1,202; £601) **Stalls** Low

Form RPR

2002 **1** **Badenscoth**[13] 4748 3-8-11 **73**........................................ JackDuern(3) 4 84
(Dean Ivory) *taken down early: short of room and impeded sn after s: sn rcvrd to trck ldrs: rdn to ld over 1f out: sn clr and r.o wl: readily* **12/1**

-424 **2** 3¾ **Music Lesson**[24] 4351 3-8-13 **72**..................................(b[1]) OisinMurphy 6 74
(Hughie Morrison) *t.k.h: hld up in last trio: effrt over 1f out: styd on wl u.p ins fnl f to go 2nd towards fin: no ch w wnr* **25/1**

61 **3** ½ **Mooltazem (IRE)**[15] 4693 3-9-5 **78**................................. JimCrowley 5 79
(John Gosden) *hld up in tch in midfield: swtchd rt and effrt over 1f out: styd on u.p ins fnl f: wnt 3rd towards fin: no ch w wnr* **2/1**[1]

01 **4** hd **Important Mission (USA)**[25] 4309 3-9-3 **81**.................. GeorgiaCox(5) 8 81+
(William Haggas) *hld up in tch in last pair: effrt and forced v wd bnd wl over 1f out: hdwy over 1f out: edging lft and wnt 2nd wl ins fnl f: no imp and lost 2 pls towards fin* **2/1**[1]

1520 **5** 1½ **Toy Theatre**[18] 4564 3-9-1 **74**............................................. TomQueally 1 71
(Michael Appleby) *led: drifted rt and rdn bnd wl over 1f out: hdd over 1f out and sn outpcd by wnr: lost 2nd wl ins fnl f: sn wknd* **40/1**

1451 **6** ½ **Scala Regia (FR)**[13] 4748 3-8-9 **68**................................(p[1]) LukeMorris 2 64
(Sir Mark Prescott Bt) *chsd ldr: carried rt and rdn bnd wl over 1f out: sn drvn and unable qck: keeping on same pce and wl hld whn squeezed for room ins fnl f* **10/1**

2410 **7** 1½ **Favourite Royal (IRE)**[27] 4209 3-9-5 **78**..............(p[1]) RobertWinston 9 70
(Eve Johnson Houghton) *dwlt: hld up in rr: effrt over 1f out: nvr getting on terms and wl hld whn nt clr run and swtchd rt wl ins fnl f* **16/1**

2123 **8** shd **Ourmullion**[18] 4564 3-9-0 **73**............................................. KierenFox 7 65
(John Best) *in tch in midfield on outer: urged along and clsd to chse ldrs over 2f out: carried rt bnd wl over 1f out: sn lost pl u.p: wknd fnl f* **9/1**[3]

4014 **9** 3¾ **Cyrus Dallin**[25] 4313 3-9-7 **80**........................................(h) MartinDwyer 3 63
(William Muir) *t.k.h: hld up in midfield: effrt over 1f out: sn drvn and no imp: bhd and wknd fnl f* **8/1**[2]

1m 38.15s (-1.75) **Going Correction** -0.05s/f (Stan) **9** Ran SP% **116.7**
Speed ratings (Par 102): **106,102,101,101,100 99,98,97,94**
CSF £264.88 CT £850.94 TOTE £13.40: £3.30, £4.40, £1.10; EX 260.40 Trifecta £2522.30.
**Owner** Peter J Skinner **Bred** Peter J Skinner **Trained** Radlett, Herts
■ Stewards' Enquiry : Georgia Cox two-day ban: careless riding (Aug 8-9)

**FOCUS**
An interesting handicap run at a steady pace.

## 5243 HILLS PROSPECT SIMPLY THE BEST MAIDEN STKS 1m (P)
**8:00** (8:05) (Class 4) 3-Y-O+ **£8,086** (£2,406; £1,202; £601) **Stalls** Low

Form RPR

**1** **High End** 3-9-5 0........................................................ JosephineGordon 5 85+
(Saeed bin Suroor) *rn green: chsd ldrs: shkn up 1/2-way: sn rdn: kpt on and styd chsng ldrs: n.m.r and swtchd rt 1f out: sn chalng: r.o wl to ld last strides* **5/4**[1]

32 **2** hd **Hyperloop**[15] 4700 3-9-5 0................................................ PatCosgrave 7 84
(William Haggas) *led: rdn over 1f out: drvn and hrd pressed ins fnl f: styd on: hdd last strides* **7/2**[3]

6 **3** 1½ **Ancient Foe**[24] 4332 3-9-5 0............................................ DavidProbert 2 81
(Andrew Balding) *hld up in tch in midfield: effrt to chse ldrs over 1f out: drvn and cl 3rd jst ins fnl f: kpt on same pce fnl 100yds* **8/1**

2 **4** 2 **Subhaan**[18] 4562 3-9-5 0.................................................... JimCrowley 8 76
(Roger Varian) *dwlt: sn rcvrd to chse ldr: effrt u.p over 1f out: unable qck and lost 2nd whn n.m.r jst ins fnl f: wknd fnl 100yds* **2/1**[2]

0-0 **5** 3¼ **Scooness**[99] 1830 3-9-5 0................................................... TomQueally 4 68
(James Fanshawe) *hld up wl in tch in midfield: shkn up and outpcd over 1f out: rdn jst over 1f out: sn btn and wknd ins fnl f* **25/1**

0 **6** 2¾ **Section D'Or**[12] 4808 3-9-5 0............................................ MartinLane 3 62
(David Menuisier) *hld up in tch in midfield: effrt 2f out: sn u.p and outpcd: wknd fnl f* **33/1**

55 **7** 2 **St James's Park (IRE)**[18] 4562 4-9-13 0........................ AntonioFresu 1 60
(Luke McJannet) *t.k.h: hld up in last trio: effrt but no imp whn drifted rt over 1f: swtchd bk lft and no imp jst ins fnl f: sn wknd* **50/1**

0 **8** 1½ **Alternate Route**[18] 4562 3-9-5 0...................................... LukeMorris 6 54
(Sir Mark Prescott Bt) *dwlt: in tch in last pair: rdn over 3f out: struggling ent fnl 2f: wknd over 1f out* **50/1**

1m 40.08s (0.18) **Going Correction** -0.05s/f (Stan)
**WFA** 3 from 4yo 8lb **8** Ran SP% **121.8**
Speed ratings (Par 105): **97,96,95,93,90 87,85,83**
CSF £6.51 TOTE £2.20: £1.30, £1.40, £2.20; EX 7.70 Trifecta £20.60.
**Owner** Godolphin **Bred** Watership Down Stud **Trained** Newmarket, Suffolk

**FOCUS**
Not a bad maiden. They went a steady pace and the winner looks above average.

## 5244 POMMERY CHAMPAGNE H'CAP 2m (P)
**8:30** (8:33) (Class 6) (0-65,67) 4-Y-O+ **£3,234** (£962; £481; £240) **Stalls** Low

Form RPR

0053 **1** **Woofie (IRE)**[27] 4217 5-9-2 **60**........................................ OisinMurphy 4 66
(Laura Mongan) *mde all: rdn over 1f out: drvn ins fnl f: jst hld on: all out* **5/2**[2]

00-0 **2** shd **Desktop**[40] 3756 5-8-10 **54**................................................... CamHardie 8 60
(Antony Brittain) *stdd and dropped in bhd after s: hld up in last pair: rdn and hdwy jst over 2f out: chsd clr wnr 1f out: styd on wl u.p fnl 100yds: jst failed* **16/1**

3025 **3** ¾ **Topalova**[82] 2332 4-8-4 **48**................................................. JoeyHaynes 2 53
(Mark H Tompkins) *hld up in last pair: sltly impeded and swtchd rt over 2f out: effrt over 1f out: styd on strly ins fnl f: nvr quite getting to ldng pair* **10/1**

-133 **4** ¾ **King Olav (UAE)**[24] 4346 12-9-2 **65**............................... GeorgiaCox(5) 5 69
(Tony Carroll) *midfield: clsd and carried rt over 2f out: styd on u.p to chse ldrs 1f out: kpt on same pce ins fnl f* **10/1**

40-0 **5** 3 **Tayaar (IRE)**[114] 1519 4-9-1 **59**....................................... StevieDonohoe 1 59
(John Ryan) *hld up in midfield: effrt u.p over 1f out: no imp and styd on same pce ins fnl f* **20/1**

0-05 **6** 3¾ **Byron Blue (IRE)**[9] 988 8-8-2 **46** oh1............................(t) JimmyQuinn 7 42
(Brian Barr) *dwlt: rcvrd to chse wnr after 1f: rdn and ev ch 3f out tl outpcd 2f out: lost 2nd 1f out and wknd ins fnl f* **8/1**

0/63 **7** 3 **Wintour Leap**[14] 3724 6-9-1 **59**.......................................(p[1]) LukeMorris 6 51
(Robert Stephens) *hld up in last trio: rdn over 3f out: dropped to rr 2f out: n.d after* **6/1**[3]

163 **P** **Mishko (IRE)**[47] 3494 6-9-9 **67**.......................................... JimCrowley 3
(Steve Gollings) *chsd ldng pair: 5 l 3rd whn lost action and eased over 2f out: p.u and dismntd 1f out* **15/8**[1]

3m 31.9s (1.90) **Going Correction** -0.05s/f (Stan) **8** Ran SP% **117.6**
Speed ratings (Par 101): **93,92,92,92,90 88,87,**
CSF £42.42 CT £349.82 TOTE £3.00: £1.20, £4.50, £2.80; EX 47.90 Trifecta £306.00.
**Owner** Mrs P J Sheen **Bred** James F Hanly **Trained** Epsom, Surrey

**FOCUS**
Not a great race for the grade, rated around the balance of the front three.

## 5245 UB40 PLAYING HERE 12TH AUGUST H'CAP 7f (P)
**9:00** (9:02) (Class 4) (0-85,87) 3-Y-O+ **£8,086** (£2,406; £1,202; £601) **Stalls** Low

Form RPR

1 **1** **Golden Goal (IRE)**[18] 4562 3-9-3 **81**................................... MartinLane 7 88+
(Saeed bin Suroor) *t.k.h: trckd ldrs: rdn ent fnl 2f: hdwy to ld jst ins fnl f: hld on u.p towards fin: drvn out* **5/4**[1]

650 **2** nk **Until Midnight (IRE)**[10] 4887 7-9-7 **78**...........................(b) JoeyHaynes 5 85
(Eugene Stanford) *hld up in tch in midfield: effrt over 1f out: hdwy u.p 1f out: chsd wnr ins fnl f: styd on to press wnr but hld towards fin* **50/1**

1213 **3** 1 1/2 **Dark Side Dream**[34] 3969 5-8-12 **76**.......................... MillyNaseb(7) 11 79
(Chris Dwyer) *w ldr: rdn and ev ch over 1f out tl no ex jst ins fnl f: kpt on same pce fnl 100yds* **20/1**

5614 **4** hd **North Creek**[18] 4563 4-9-10 **81**.......................................... MartinHarley 2 83
(Chris Wall) *chsd ldrs: effrt over 1f out: hung lft 1f out: styd on u.p fnl 100yds: nt enough pce to rch wnr* **7/1**

2350 **5** 1 1/4 **Flying Fantasy**[14] 4728 5-8-9 **66** oh2......................... JosephineGordon 9 65
(Michael Appleby) *led: rdn over 1f out: drvn and hdd jst ins fnl f: no ex and wknd fnl 100yds* **50/1**

0000 **6** 1/2 **Outer Space**[10] 4887 6-10-2 **87**...................................... DougieCostello 3 85
(Jamie Osborne) *hld up in tch in last pair: hdwy into midfield over 1f out: shkn up 1f out: styd on ins fnl f: nvr trbld ldrs* **25/1**

31-4 **7** 3/4 **Al Reeh (IRE)**[55] 3211 3-9-2 **80**........................................ LukeMorris 1 73
(Marco Botti) *in tch in midfield: effrt 2f out: hung lft over 1f out: swtchd righ and drvn 1f out: no imp ins fnl f* **9/2**[3]

6-61 **8** 3 3/4 **Etikaal**[61] 3000 3-9-7 **85**.....................................................(p) JimCrowley 4 68
(Simon Crisford) *hld up in tch in midfield: swtchd rt and effrt over 1f out: keeping on but nt looking like getting on terms whn nt clr run 1f out: no imp after* **10/3**[2]

25-4 **9** 3 1/4 **Rouge Nuage (IRE)**[22] 4451 7-9-9 **80**........................... JimmyQuinn 10 57
(Conrad Allen) *t.k.h: hld up in tch towards rr: effrt over 1f out: no imp and sn outpcd: wknd ins fnl f* **50/1**

1-24 **10** 1 3/4 **Coronation Day**[75] 2548 4-9-12 **83**.................................. DavidAllan 8 55
(James Tate) *chsd ldrs tl lost pl u.p over 1f out: bhd and wknd ins fnl f* **16/1**

0301 **11** 2 **Joey's Destiny (IRE)**[22] 4451 7-9-10 **81**........................... CamHardie 12 48
(Antony Brittain) *stdd and dropped in bhd after s: hld up in tch in rr: effrt u.p over 1f out: no hdwy: wknd ins fnl f* **33/1**

1m 25.25s (-1.95) **Going Correction** -0.05s/f (Stan)
**WFA** 3 from 4yo+ 7lb **11** Ran SP% **121.5**
Speed ratings (Par 105): **109,108,106,106,105 104,103,99,95,93 91**
CSF £103.85 CT £923.79 TOTE £2.00: £1.20, £9.80, £3.70; EX 96.10 Trifecta £2471.30.
**Owner** Godolphin **Bred** Yeomanstown Stud **Trained** Newmarket, Suffolk

**FOCUS**
A fair handicap run at a steady pace.
T/Jkpt: £16,707.60. Pool: £16,707.60 - 1 winning unit T/Plt: £44.70 to a £1 stake. Pool: £80,306.02 - 1309.9 winning units T/Qpdt: £19.40 to a £1 stake. Pool: £7,412.45 - 282.58 winning units **Steve Payne**

# 4963 FFOS LAS (L-H)
Tuesday, July 25

**OFFICIAL GOING: Good to soft (6.7)**
Wind: light breeze, partly against them in the home straight Weather: fine

## 5246 DOWNLOAD THE FREE AT THE RACES APP NOVICE STKS (PLUS 10 RACE) 7f 80y(R)
**2:00** (2:01) (Class 4) 2-Y-O **£5,175** (£1,540; £769; £384) **Stalls** Low

Form RPR

62 **1** **Rhosneigr (IRE)**[28] 4183 2-9-2 0...................................... SteveDrowne 4 74
(Charles Hills) *hld up and racd keenly: rdn and hdwy 2f out: swtchd rt over 1f out: hung lft and r.o ins fnl f: led post* **5/2**[1]

406 **2** hd **Move Over**[18] 4560 2-9-2 71........................................(b[1]) TomMarquand 5 74
(Richard Hannon) *led: drvn and hrd pressed 2f out: kpt on wl u.p: hdd post* **5/1**[3]

5 **3** 3/4 **Shrewd Approach (IRE)**[20] 4496 2-8-11 0......................... RyanPowell 8 67
(Simon Crisford) *s.i.s: sn chsng ldr: rdn to chal 2f out and ev ch tl unable qck towards fin* **12/1**

002 **4** 1 1/4 **Coal Stock (IRE)**[8] 4963 2-9-2 0..................................... ShaneKelly 6 69
(David Evans) *chsd ldrs: rdn qwl over 2f out: carried rt over 1f out: drvn and unable qck fnl f* **7/2**[2]

**5** 3/4 **Mail Order** 2-8-11 0.......................................................... FrannyNorton 2 62
(Mark Johnston) *chsd ldrs on ins: pushed along over 3f out: kpt on: nt pce to chal* **7/2**[2]

00 **6** 3 **Mafeking**[43] 3679 2-9-2 0................................................. FranBerry 1 60
(Harry Dunlop) *hld up: rdn 3f out: hung rt over 1f out: no imp* **12/1**

56 **7** shd **Master Grey (IRE)**[27] 4218 2-9-2 0.................................. WilliamCarson 7 59
(Rod Millman) *s.i.s: in tch in midfield: rdn over 2f out: one pce an no imp* **6/1**

**8** 5 **Miss Condi** 2-8-8 0........................................................ EdwardGreatrex(3) 3 42
(Martin Keighley) *s.i.s: in rr: effrt on outer over 2f out: no real imp: hung lft and wknd ins fnl f* **50/1**

1m 36.87s (3.27) **Going Correction** +0.225s/f (Good) **8** Ran SP% **121.3**
Speed ratings (Par 96): **90,89,88,87,86 83,83,77**
CSF £16.65 TOTE £3.10: £1.20, £2.00, £3.70; EX 14.90 Trifecta £122.40.
**Owner** Julie Martin & David R Martin & Partner **Bred** Lismacue Mare Syndicate **Trained** Lambourn, Berks

**FOCUS**
Ordinary juvenile form, with the winner probably just below form in getting off the mark.

## 5247 FREE TIPS DAILY ON ATTHERACES.COM/EBF MAIDEN STKS 7f 80y(R)
**2:30** (2:32) (Class 5) 3-Y-O+ **£3,881** (£1,155; £577; £288) **Stalls** Low

Form RPR

6420 **1** **Bumptious**[48] 3454 4-9-7 75........................................(p[1]) TomMarquand 4 78
(Ismail Mohammed) *trckd ldr: led gng wl 2f out: drvn and pressed over 1f out: r.o u.p: jst hld on* **11/10**[1]

03- **2** nse **Harvest Wind (IRE)**[262] 7818 3-9-5 0.............................. SamHitchcott 2 80
(Clive Cox) *chsd ldrs: rdn over 2f out: pressed wnr over 1f out: nt qckn u.p fnl f tl r.o cl home: jst hld* **2/1**[2]

4 **3** 7 **Astone Man (FR)**[50] 3407 3-9-5 0................................. GeorgeDowning 7 62
(Tony Carroll) *hld up towards rr: rdn over 2f out: sn outpcd by ldrs: styd on to go modest 3rd ins fnl f* **14/1**

00 **4** 1 3/4 **D'Waterside**[47] 3493 3-9-2 0..................................... EdwardGreatrex(3) 3 57
(David Loughnane) *led :rdn over 2f out: hdd 2f out: sn no ch w ldng pair: wknd and lost modest 3rd ins fnl f* **33/1**

**5** 1 1/2 **Mooroverthebridge** 3-8-9 0.................................... JennyPowell(5) 5 48
(Grace Harris) *s.i.s: hld up: swtchd lft and effrt wl over 2f out: one pce and no further imp over 1f out* **33/1**

60 **6** 2 1/4 **Beach Party**[18] 4565 3-9-0 0.................................................. LiamKeniry 1 43
(Hughie Morrison) *trckd ldrs: rdn over 2f out: wknd over 1f out* **14/1**

6665 **7** 3/4 **Hisar (IRE)**[22] 4444 3-9-5 69..........................................(p) ShaneKelly 8 46
(Ronald Harris) *dropped in and hld up: rdn on outer over 2f out: one pce and no imp* **7/1**[3]

**8** 1/2 **Thechampagnesonice**[175] 4-9-7 0........................... KieranShoemark 6 42
(Ed de Giles) *t.k.h early: midfield: rdn and nt clr run over 2f out: sn dropped to rr: wknd appr fnl f* **12/1**

1m 33.92s (0.32) **Going Correction** +0.225s/f (Good)
**WFA** 3 from 4yo 7lb **8** Ran SP% **120.4**
Speed ratings (Par 103): **107,106,98,96,95 92,91,91**
CSF £3.69 TOTE £1.80: £1.10, £1.30, £2.70; EX 4.10 Trifecta £25.40.
**Owner** Abdulla Al Mansoori **Bred** Swettenham Stud **Trained** Newmarket, Suffolk

**FOCUS**
A modest maiden that saw the big two in the market draw well clear.

## 5248 FOLLOW @ATTHERACES ON TWITTER H'CAP 7f 80y(R)
**3:00** (3:05) (Class 5) (0-75,77) 3-Y-O+ **£3,234** (£962; £481; £240) **Stalls** Low

Form RPR

1 **1** **Nothing To Lose (IRE)**[5] 5086 3-9-2 75.............. CallumShepherd(3) 7 83+
(John C McConnell, Ire) *t.k.h in midfield: hdwy 3f out: drvn: carried hd to one side and led over 1f out: idled briefly ins fnl f but a holding runner-up* **13/8**[1]

3243 **2** 3/4 **Peach Melba**[17] 4624 3-9-3 73......................................... FrannyNorton 9 79
(Mark Johnston) *led: 4 l clr 3f out: rdn 2f out: hdd over 1f out: kpt on but a being hld* **3/1**[2]

-000 **3** 1 1/4 **Hidden Oasis (IRE)**[26] 4256 6-9-4 67................................. FranBerry 2 73
(Jonjo O'Neill) *s.i.s: hld up: rdn over 3f out: swtchd rt over 1f out: styd on to go 3rd ins fnl f: nrst fin* **8/1**

43-5 **4** 1 1/4 **Many A Tale**[12] 4797 3-9-3 73...................................... TomMarquand 3 73
(Ismail Mohammed) *chsd ldrs: rdn over 3f out: unable qck: in hld 3rd over 1f out tl ins fnl f* **10/1**

5436 **5** 4 **Satchville Flyer**[8] 4965 6-10-0 77.............................. KieranShoemark 1 69
(David Evans) *t.k.h: hld up: rdn over 3f out: edgd rt over 2f out: kpt on one pce and no real imp* **16/1**

02-2 **6** 4 1/2 **Manners Please**[19] 4529 3-9-2 72...................................... PatDobbs 8 49
(Ralph Beckett) *chsd ldrs: briefly in 2nd over 2f out: sn drvn: wknd fnl f* **9/2**[3]

420 **7** 4 **Highway One (USA)**[40] 3748 3-9-5 75............................. TrevorWhelan 5 42
(George Baker) *reluctant to load: s.s: in rr: drvn wl over 2f out: wknd 2f out* **10/1**

00 **8** 5 **Mr Andros**[38] 3820 4-8-13 67....................................(p[1]) JennyPowell(5) 6 24
(Brendan Powell) *chsd ldr: rdn 3f out: lost 2nd over 2f out: grad wknd: eased 1f out* **50/1**

1m 33.22s (-0.38) **Going Correction** +0.225s/f (Good)
**WFA** 3 from 4yo+ 7lb **8** Ran SP% **118.4**
Speed ratings (Par 103): **111,110,108,107,102 97,93,87**
CSF £6.88 CT £30.16 TOTE £2.20: £1.10, £1.60, £2.50; EX 7.40 Trifecta £49.90.
**Owner** Rockview Racing Club **Bred** Rossenarra Bloodstock Limited **Trained** Stamullen, Co Meath

**FOCUS**
A modest handicap, but the right horses came to the fore.

## 5249 VISIT ATTHERACES.COM H'CAP (DIV I) 1m 2f (R)
**3:30** (3:32) (Class 6) (0-60,62) 3-Y-O+ **£2,264** (£673; £336; £168) **Stalls** Low

Form RPR

354 **1** **Frantical**[5] 5053 5-9-8 56...................................(p) WilliamCarson 7 61
(Tony Carroll) *hld up: rdn 4f out: hdwy 3f out: drvn to ld ins fnl f: idled but jst doing enough* **7/1**[3]

0003 **2** 3/4 **Alnasl (IRE)**[15] 4697 3-9-0 60................................(h) EdwardGreatrex(3) 2 65
(Archie Watson) *led: rdn 2f out: drvn: hdd and edgd rt ins fnl f: unable qck* **8/1**

5-00 **3** 1 3/4 **Bianca Minola (FR)**[13] 4761 3-9-1 58....................(p[1]) KieranShoemark 5 60
(David Menuisier) *disp 2nd: rdn over 3f out: hung lft over 2f out: n.m.r in cl 3rd ins fnl f: nt qckn* **12/1**

6536 **4** 3 **Turnbury**[12] 4801 6-9-10 58...........................................(p) CharlesBishop 4 53
(Nikki Evans) *chsd ldrs: rdn 3f out: one pce fnl 2f* **20/1**

2 **5** 5 **Blankiedoodie**[16] 4659 4-9-4 52.......................................... ShaneKelly 1 38
(John C McConnell, Ire) *disp 2nd: drvn over 3f out: losing pl whn hmpd over 2f out: wknd over 1f out* **6/5**[1]

000 **6** 2 **Beast**[33] 4006 3-8-12 55................................................ TomMarquand 9 39
(Lee Carter) *chsd ldrs: rdn over 3f out: grad weakned fnl 2f* **5/2**[2]

0005 **7** 1 3/4 **Go On Mayson**[29] 4144 3-9-3 60..................................... TimmyMurphy 8 40
(Christian Williams) *hld up in last: rdn 3f out: one pce and little imp fnl 2f* **25/1**

6-65 **8** 2 **Beatisa**[157] 814 3-9-5 62..................................................... LiamKeniry 3 39
(Ed Walker) *hld up: rdn 4f out: wknd over 2f out* **20/1**

0-05 **9** 3 1/4 **Primrose Place**[11] 4846 3-8-5 51................................(t) HollieDoyle(3) 6 22
(David Evans) *towards rr: rdn over 3f out: wknd wl over 1f out* **14/1**

2m 10.97s (1.57) **Going Correction** +0.225s/f (Good)
**WFA** 3 from 4yo+ 9lb **9** Ran SP% **125.4**
Speed ratings (Par 101): **102,101,100,97,93 92,90,89,86**
CSF £64.61 CT £681.77 TOTE £10.40: £2.10, £2.80, £4.60; EX 43.50 Trifecta £523.60.
**Owner** J M Wall **Bred** L J Vaessen **Trained** Cropthorne, Worcs

**FOCUS**
The first division of a moderate handicap and the winner has been rated back to last year's best.

## 5250 VISIT ATTHERACES.COM H'CAP (DIV II) 1m 2f (R)
**4:00** (4:01) (Class 6) (0-60,61) 3-Y-O+ **£2,264** (£673; £336; £168) **Stalls** Low

Form RPR
0063 1 **Sakhalin Star (IRE)**16 4660 6-9-5 **53**...(e) ShaneKelly 3 59
(Richard Guest) *wnt to post early: trckd ldrs: led 2f out: sn drvn: hdd 1f out: rallied to ld last strides* **9/2**3
-403 2 *nk* **Weardiditallgorong**73 2615 5-9-4 **57**...(b) MitchGodwin(5) 4 62
(Des Donovan, Ire) *trckd ldrs tl lost pl 1/2-way: stdy hdwy 3f out: drvn and wandered over 1f out: led narrowly 1f out: hdd last strides* **3/1**2
- 3 ½ **Phebes Dream (IRE)**399 3502 4-8-12 **49**...(h) CallumShepherd(3) 8 54
(John C McConnell, Ire) *hld up: hdwy 3f out: rdn and nt qckn wl over 1f out: r.o towards fin* **11/4**1
0405 4 3 ¼ **Sheer Intensity (IRE)**20 4493 4-9-4 **52**... SteveDrowne 6 51
(David Evans) *midfield: rdn over 2f out: sn outpcd by ldrs: styd on fnl f* **12/1**
00-6 5 ½ **Katabatika**18 4565 3-9-4 **61**... PatDobbs 1 60
(Hughie Morrison) *hld up: rdn 3f out: no imp tl styd on fnl f* **11/4**1
000 6 *nk* **Queen Beatrice**23 4409 3-9-0 **57**... FranBerry 9 55
(William Muir) *trckd ldr 3f: styd prom: rdn 2f out: no ex and lost 3 pls fnl f* **14/1**
0-00 7 3 ¼ **Hi Milady (IRE)**8 4971 3-9-3 **60**...(b) LiamKeniry 5 52
(Dominic Ffrench Davis) *led: drvn over 2f out: hdd 2f out: wknd appr fnl f* **20/1**
0-00 8 23 **Hellarious**104 1723 4-8-12 **46** oh1...(t) SamHitchcott 2
(Geoffrey Deacon) *plld hrd towards rr: hdwy into 2nd after 3f: rdn 3f out: sn wknd: t.o* **33/1**

2m 12.28s (2.88) **Going Correction** +0.225s/f (Good)
**WFA** 3 from 4yo+ 9lb **8 Ran SP% 118.6**
Speed ratings (Par 101): **97,96,96,93,93 93,90,72**
CSF £19.21 CT £44.41 TOTE £8.70: £1.60, £1.60, £1.40; EX 15.20 Trifecta £53.50.
**Owner** Bamboozelem **Bred** Sig Massimo Parri **Trained** Ingmanthorpe, W Yorks

**FOCUS**
This looked the lesser of the two divisions and it paid to race handily. It's been rated around the runner-up to best of last year and the winner to the best of this.

## 5251 DOWNLOAD THE ATTHERACES APP FOR IPAD H'CAP 2m (R)
**4:30** (4:31) (Class 4) (0-80,78) 4-Y-O+ **£5,175** (£1,540; £769; £384) **Stalls** Low

Form RPR
0/01 1 **Authorized Too**13 4750 6-9-7 **78**...(p) FergusSweeney 6 82+
(Noel Williams) *hld up in tch: no run 3f out tl swtchd rt wl over 1f out: drvn and r.o to ld nr fin* **5/2**1
0641 2 ½ **Nabhan**8 4966 5-9-7 **78** 6ex...(tp) TimmyMurphy 8 80
(Bernard Llewellyn) *hld up: tk clsr order 1/2-way: trckd ldrs travelling strly fr 4f out: rdn to ld 110 yds out: hdd nr fin* **4/1**2
020- 3 ½ **Norab (GER)**15 6279 6-9-5 **76**...(b) KieranShoemark 2 77
(Bernard Llewellyn) *led: drvn 3f out: kpt on wl: hdd 110 yds out: unable qck* **8/1**
630- 4 5 **Spice Fair**136 7732 10-9-5 **76**... LiamKeniry 1 71
(Mark Usher) *s.s: hld up: rdn and clsd 3f out: sn hung lft: styd on on same pce* **7/1**
053 5 *shd* **Entihaa**29 4158 9-8-7 **67**... HollieDoyle(3) 5 62
(Dai Burchell) *trckd ldrs: wnt 2nd 5f out: rdn over 2f out: lost 2nd appr fnl f: wknd* **4/1**2
5-04 6 2 ¾ **Lady Makfi (IRE)**56 3190 5-9-3 **74**... ShaneKelly 7 66
(Johnny Farrelly) *dwlt: hld up in last: tried to cl but no run 3f out tl wl over 1f out: rdn and no imp* **14/1**
12/0 7 2 ¼ **Dire Straits (IRE)**55 3213 6-8-11 **68**...(tp) FranBerry 4 57
(Stuart Kittow) *midfield: losing pl whn hmpd on ins over 4f out: rdn 3f out: wknd over 1f out* **16/1**
12- 8 1 **Sporty Yankee (USA)**27 7332 4-9-4 **75**...(p) TomMarquand 3 63
(Martin Keighley) *chsd ldrs: lost 2nd 5f out: drvn 3f out: wknd over 1f out* **6/1**3

3m 40.72s (10.72) **Going Correction** +0.225s/f (Good) **8 Ran SP% 119.0**
Speed ratings (Par 105): **82,81,81,79,78 77,76,75**
CSF £13.21 CT £70.83 TOTE £3.40: £1.10, £1.90, £2.90; EX 14.90 Trifecta £63.10.
**Owner** Stonepoint Racing Club **Bred** Almagro De Actividades Commerciales **Trained** Blewbury, Oxon

**FOCUS**
Reasonable form for the grade, with the front three clear.

## 5252 FOLLOW AT THE RACES ON INSTAGRAM H'CAP 5f
**5:00** (5:03) (Class 6) (0-60,62) 3-Y-O+ **£2,587** (£770; £384; £192) **Stalls** Centre

Form RPR
-000 1 **Your Gifted (IRE)**18 4559 10-8-13 **45**...(v) TomMarquand 5 52
(Lisa Williamson) *hld up in tch: drvn to chse ldr over 1f out: r.o to ld towards fin* **18/1**
600 2 ½ **Celerity (IRE)**5 5052 3-8-6 **45**...(b) HollieDoyle(3) 6 49
(David Evans) *chsd ldrs: led 2f out: sn drvn: edgd rt early ins fnl f: sn hung lft: hdd towards fin* **5/1**1
0000 3 2 ¼ **Royal Normandy**29 4148 5-8-10 **45**...(b) EdwardGreatrex(3) 10 42
(Grace Harris) *towards rr: sn pushed along: drvn 1/2-way: r.o wl fnl f: wnt 3rd nr fin* **6/1**2
0002 4 *hd* **Monsieur Paddy**32 4142 4-9-10 **56**... GeorgeDowning 8 52
(Tony Carroll) *hld up: rdn 2f out: r.o fnl f and briefly in hld 3rd* **8/1**
0050 5 *hd* **Captain Scooby**12 4789 11-8-13 **45**...(b) ShaneKelly 7 41
(Richard Guest) *dwlt: detached in last and rdn along: stl only one bhd him 1f out: r.o wl* **6/1**2
0050 6 1 ¾ **Diminutive (IRE)**21 4467 5-9-0 **46**...(p) TrevorWhelan 11 35
(Grace Harris) *chsd ldrs: drvn 2f out: hld in 3rd 1f out: wknd* **5/1**1
040 7 2 ½ **Glam'Selle**13 4731 3-8-9 **45**...(b1) FrannyNorton 4 24
(Ronald Harris) *chsd ldrs: rdn and unable qck 2f out: wknd ins fnl f* **12/1**
00 8 1 **Candelaria**21 4467 4-10-2 **62**... FranBerry 3 39
(Jonjo O'Neill) *led: hdd 2f out: sn drvn: wknd fnl f* **9/1**
6 9 ½ **Flying Expectation (ITY)**20 4514 3-8-9 **50**...(p1) MitchGodwin(5) 9 24
(Des Donovan, Ire) *trckd ldrs: rdn over 1f out: wknd fnl f* **7/1**3
0400 10 2 ¼ **Secret Asset (IRE)**18 4559 12-9-2 **55**...(v) JordanUys(7) 2 22
(Lisa Williamson) *rdn along early: cl up: drvn over 1f out: wknd fnl f* **6/1**2
000- 11 7 **Bills Delight**379 4195 3-8-9 **45**... WilliamCarson 1
(Bill Turner) *a towards rr: drvn 1/2-way: lost tch wl over 1f out* **33/1**

59.28s (0.98) **Going Correction** +0.225s/f (Good)
**WFA** 3 from 4yo+ 4lb **11 Ran SP% 125.7**
Speed ratings (Par 101): **101,100,96,96,95 93,89,87,86,83 71**
CSF £112.95 CT £639.71 TOTE £24.90: £6.60, £2.30, £2.50; EX 191.50 Trifecta £2583.20.
**Owner** Anthony Thomas Sykes **Bred** Rathasker Stud **Trained** Saighton, Cheshire

**FOCUS**
Lowly sprint form.

## 5253 AT THE RACES H'CAP 6f
**5:30** (5:33) (Class 5) (0-75,77) 3-Y-O+ **£3,881** (£1,155; £577; £288) **Stalls** Centre

Form RPR
5-42 1 **The Daley Express (IRE)**8 4965 3-9-5 **73**... FrannyNorton 1 86+
(Ronald Harris) *hld up: clsd gng wl 2f out: swtchd lft over 1f out: let down to ld 150yds out: r.o strly* **7/2**2
2234 2 2 ¾ **Del Parco**27 4198 3-9-7 **75**...(t1) SamHitchcott 3 77
(Clive Cox) *hld up: drvn 2f out: r.o fnl f: wnt 2nd nr fin: no ch w wnr* **7/2**2
3-36 3 *nk* **Prominna**19 4532 7-8-11 **60**... GeorgeDowning 5 62
(Tony Carroll) *chsd ldng pair: drvn to ld appr fnl f: hdd 150yds out: qckly outpcd by wnr: lost 2nd nr fin* **8/1**
-044 4 ¾ **Abiento (IRE)**63 2927 3-9-5 **73**... LiamKeniry 2 72
(Ed Walker) *hld up bhd ldrs: carried sltly lft over 1f out: drvn and kpt on same pce* **3/1**1
2000 5 3 **Awesome Allan (IRE)**11 4835 3-9-6 **77**...(t) HollieDoyle(3) 6 66
(David Evans) *taken steadily to post: led: rdn 2f out: hdd appr fnl f: sn fdd: sddle slipped* **7/1**3
4034 6 1 ¼ **Coastal Cyclone**10 4910 3-9-7 **75**...(v1) FranBerry 4 60
(Harry Dunlop) *taken steadily to post: cl up: rdn and ev ch over 1f out: wknd fnl f* **3/1**1

1m 10.71s (0.71) **Going Correction** +0.225s/f (Good)
**WFA** 3 from 7yo 5lb **6 Ran SP% 118.1**
Speed ratings (Par 103): **104,100,99,98,94 93**
CSF £17.09 TOTE £4.20: £2.00, £2.00; EX 16.00 Trifecta £76.60.
**Owner** The W H O Society **Bred** Allevamento Ficomontanino Srl **Trained** Earlswood, Monmouths

**FOCUS**
Average form but the winner did it well.
T/Plt: £20.00 to a £1 stake. Pool: £81,690.71 - 2973.81 winning units T/Qpdt: £8.50 to a £1 stake. Pool: £6,503.91 - 561.56 winning units **Richard Lowther**

# 4847 MUSSELBURGH (R-H)
Tuesday, July 25

**OFFICIAL GOING: Good to firm (watered; 7.6)**
Wind: Light, across Weather: Overcast

## 5254 100% RACING UK PROFITS BACK TO RACING H'CAP 1m 208y
**2:15** (2:15) (Class 6) (0-60,61) 3-Y-O+ **£2,587** (£770; £384; £192) **Stalls** Low

Form RPR
3151 1 **Haymarket**5 5074 8-9-3 **59** 6ex... SeamusCronin(7) 3 65
(R Mike Smith) *pressed ldr: led after 2f: rdn and hrd pressed fr 2f out: styd on gamely ins fnl f* **9/2**1
3550 2 2 ¼ **Kerry Icon**10 4900 4-8-12 **50**...(h) SammyJoBell(3) 8 51
(Iain Jardine) *in tch: hdwy and disp ld over 1f out to ins fnl f: kpt on same pce last 75yds* **9/1**
0005 3 ½ **Coral Princess (IRE)**10 4900 3-8-2 **46**... JoeFanning 11 45
(Keith Dalgleish) *hld up in midfield: smooth hdwy on outside to press ldrs over 2f out: rdn and edgd rt over 1f out: kpt on same pce* **15/2**
16 4 1 ¾ **Let Right Be Done**1 5205 5-9-1 **50**...(b) AndrewMullen 12 47
(Linda Perratt) *hld up midfield: effrt and pushed along over 2f out: no imp fr over 1f out* **12/1**
6000 5 ¾ **Indian Giver**5 5074 9-8-9 **47** ow1...(b) AdamMcNamara(3) 6 42
(John David Riches) *hld up in tch: rdn over 2f out: edgd rt and outpcd over 1f out* **25/1**
6645 6 *hd* **New Abbey Angel (IRE)**11 4853 4-9-1 **55**...(v) RowanScott(5) 5 50
(Keith Dalgleish) *slowly away: sn midfield: pushed along and carried hd high over 2f out: no further imp over 1f out* **9/1**
0006 7 1 **Nelson's Bay**2 5181 8-8-12 **47**... NathanEvans 9 40
(Wilf Storey) *dwlt: hld up: drvn along over 2f out: sme late hdwy: nvr on terms* **16/1**
5101 8 1 ¼ **Symbolic Star (IRE)**26 4262 5-9-4 **60**...(p) ConnorMurtagh(7) 7 50
(Barry Murtagh) *dwlt: hld up in rr: pushed along over 2f out: nvr rchd ldrs* **7/1**3
2040 9 2 ½ **Adventureman**18 4556 5-9-12 **61**...(p) JackGarritty 4 46
(Ruth Carr) *led 2f: cl up: ev ch and rdn over 2f ou: wknd over 1f out* **11/2**2
5 10 5 **Love To Rock (IRE)**8 4982 4-8-8 **50**...(b) DannySheehy(7) 2 25
(Adrian Paul Keatley, Ire) *t.k.h early: trckd ldrs: rdn and edgd rt over 2f out: wknd over 1f out* **7/1**3
0340 11 3 **Frontline Phantom (IRE)**32 4034 10-8-10 **48**... CliffordLee(3) 13 17
(K R Burke) *hld up towards rr: drvn along over 2f out: sn wknd: eased fnl f* **25/1**
-000 12 ¾ **Silver Duke (IRE)**16 4659 6-9-3 **52**...(b) DanielTudhope 10 19
(Jim Goldie) *dwlt: hld up: struggling over 2f out: sn btn: eased fnl f* **20/1**

1m 51.8s (-2.10) **Going Correction** -0.10s/f (Good)
**WFA** 3 from 4yo+ 9lb **12 Ran SP% 116.4**
Speed ratings (Par 101): **105,103,102,101,100 100,99,98,95,91 88,88**
CSF £42.68 CT £297.20 TOTE £4.60: £2.00, £3.40, £3.00; EX 38.50 Trifecta £344.00.
**Owner** Ewan Ross **Bred** J Breslin **Trained** Galston, E Ayrshire

**FOCUS**
The going was given as good to firm (GoingStick: 7.6) and jockeys reported it to be on the quick side after the first. The rail on the bottom bend was dolled out 2yds, adding 7yds to all races other than the 5f sprints. It was tough to challenge from too far back in this moderate handicap. The 2nd helps set the level.

## 5255 IRISH STALLION FARMS EBF NOVICE MEDIAN AUCTION STKS 7f 33y
**2:45** (2:45) (Class 5) 2-Y-O **£3,234** (£962; £481; £240) **Stalls** Low

Form RPR
5 1 **Myboyhenry (IRE)**62 2948 2-8-13 0... CliffordLee(3) 2 78+
(K R Burke) *t.k.h: trckd ldrs: effrt whn hung lft and outpcd wl over 1f out: stened and rallied to ld ins fnl f: kpt on strly* **3/1**3
61 2 1 ¾ **Footsteps Forever (IRE)**30 4116 2-9-4 0... JoeFanning 3 75
(Mark Johnston) *t.k.h early: disp ld: led over 1f out to ins fnl f: kpt on same pce* **5/4**1
04 3 ¾ **Hello My Sunshine**26 4258 2-9-2 0... GrahamLee 5 71
(Karen McLintock) *trckd ldrs on outside: hdwy to chal over 1f out: kpt on same pce ins fnl f* **20/1**
34 4 3 **Here In The Dark**26 4245 2-9-2 0... PaulMulrennan 4 63
(Keith Dalgleish) *hld up in tch: outpcd whn checked wl over 1f out: sn edgd rt: no imp fnl f* **10/1**

5432 **5** ¾ **Dontgiveuponbob**[24] 4374 2-9-2 77 .................................. PaulHanagan 1 61
(Richard Fahey) *t.k.h early: mde most to over 1f out: wknd ins fnl f* **5/2**[2]

1m 29.43s (0.43) **Going Correction** -0.10s/f (Good) **5** Ran SP% **111.9**
Speed ratings (Par 94): **93,91,90,86,85**
CSF £7.35 TOTE £3.20: £1.70, £1.20; EX 8.50 Trifecta £53.80.
**Owner** Mrs M Gittins **Bred** Jim McDonald **Trained** Middleham Moor, N Yorks

**FOCUS**
Race distance increased by 7yds. A fair novice race but the level is a bit fluid.

## 5256 ARTHUR MCKAY SERVEST H'CAP 5f 1y
**3:15** (3:16) (Class 4) (0-80,81) 3-Y-O+ **£5,175** (£1,540; £769; £384) **Stalls** Low

Form RPR
1343 **1** **Royal Brave (IRE)**[1] 5204 6-9-8 **81** .................................. RowanScott(5) 4 89
(Rebecca Bastiman) *trckd ldrs: effrt and rdn over 1f out: led wl ins fnl f: drvn out* **5/2**[1]

2052 **2** *nk* **Pearl Acclaim (IRE)**[22] 4448 7-8-12 **66** .................................. NathanEvans 3 73
(David C Griffiths) *led: rdn over 1f out: hdd wl ins fnl f: kpt on* **9/2**[2]

2001 **3** 1 ¼ **Silvanus (IRE)**[11] 4850 12-9-12 **80** .................................. GrahamLee 1 82
(Paul Midgley) *trckd ldrs: effrt and drvn along over 1f out: kpt on same pce ins fnl f* **11/2**

2454 **4** ¾ **Rock Of America (USA)**[19] 4530 3-9-8 **80** .................. DanielTudhope 2 79
(David O'Meara) *dwlt: t.k.h: hld up on outside: drvn and edgd rt wl over 1f out: kpt on same pce ins fnl f* **9/2**[2]

10U0 **5** ½ **Paddy Power (IRE)**[24] 4379 4-9-10 **81** .................. SammyJoBell(3) 5 79
(Richard Fahey) *prom: rdn whn nt clr run briefly over 1f out: kpt on same pce ins fnl f* **5/1**[3]

2053 **6** 2 **Economic Crisis (IRE)**[11] 4850 8-9-6 **74** .................. PaulMulrennan 6 65
(Colin Teague) *pressed ldr to over 1f out: sn rdn: wknd fnl f* **7/1**

58.78s (-1.62) **Going Correction** -0.175s/f (Firm)
**WFA** 3 from 4yo+ 4lb **6** Ran SP% **109.5**
Speed ratings (Par 105): **105,104,102,101,100 97**
CSF £13.12 CT £49.49 TOTE £2.90: £1.70, £2.60; EX 14.40 Trifecta £59.60.
**Owner** James Edgar & William Donaldson **Bred** M Fahy **Trained** Cowthorpe, N Yorks

**FOCUS**
A fair sprint.

## 5257 RACING UK PROFITS RETURNED TO RACING H'CAP 1m 4f 104y
**3:45** (3:45) (Class 6) (0-60,61) 4-Y-O+ **£2,587** (£770; £384; £192) **Stalls** Low

Form RPR
3306 **1** **Jonny Delta**[11] 4849 10-9-2 **54** .................................. DanielTudhope 1 64
(Jim Goldie) *mde all: sn 3 l clr: rdn and drifted lft appr fnl f: drvn and hld on wl towards fin* **7/2**[3]

5021 **2** ½ **Question Of Faith**[8] 4962 6-8-5 **50** .................................. SeamusCronin(7) 3 59
(Martin Todhunter) *missed break: hld up: hdwy on outside 3f out: chsd wnr appr fnl f: kpt on: hld nr fin* **3/1**[2]

4000 **3** 1 ¼ **Tectonic (IRE)**[10] 4899 8-9-9 **61** ..................................(v) JoeFanning 2 68
(Keith Dalgleish) *dwlt: hld up: stdy hdwy over 2f out: effrt and prom appr fnl f: kpt on same pce last 100yds* **20/1**

3266 **4** 3 ¾ **Cosmic Tigress**[15] 4684 6-9-7 **59** .................................. JasonHart 6 60
(John Quinn) *cl up: chsd wnr 1/2-way: rdn over 2f out: lost 2nd and no ex appr fnl f* **15/2**

-046 **5** 2 ¼ **Byronegetonefree**[7] 5008 6-8-13 **51** .................................. PatrickMathers 8 49
(Stuart Coltherd) *hld up in tch: drvn along over 2f out: wknd appr fnl f* **12/1**

4-02 **6** 5 **Traditional Dancer (IRE)**[11] 4853 5-9-1 **53** ..................(b) TomEaves 7 43
(Iain Jardine) *dwlt: hld up in tch: stdy hdwy 4f out: sn drvn: edgd rt and wknd over 1f out* **13/8**[1]

6650 **7** 6 **Nuova Scuola**[8] 4962 4-8-8 **46** ..................................(v) NathanEvans 4 26
(Jim Goldie) *chsd wnr to 1/2-way: cl up tl outpcd 4f out: hung lft and wknd over 2f out* **33/1**

00-0 **8** 75 **Spokesperson (USA)**[116] 1469 9-8-10 **48** .................................. GrahamLee 5
(Fred Watson) *bhd: struggling over 4f out: lost tch and eased fnl 2f* **40/1**

2m 40.32s (-1.68) **Going Correction** -0.10s/f (Good) **8** Ran SP% **114.9**
Speed ratings (Par 101): **101,100,99,97,95 92,88,38**
CSF £14.23 CT £179.51 TOTE £5.00: £1.60, £1.90, £4.80; EX 15.20 Trifecta £106.80.
**Owner** Johnnie Delta Racing **Bred** Miss Gill Quincey **Trained** Uplawmoor, E Renfrews

**FOCUS**
Race distance increased by 7yds. This was dominated throughout by the winner, who took them along at a good clip.

## 5258 BRUCE STEVENSON INSURANCE BROKERS H'CAP 7f 33y
**4:15** (4:15) (Class 5) (0-70,71) 3-Y-O+ **£3,234** (£962; £481; £240) **Stalls** Low

Form RPR
-204 **1** **Destination Aim**[16] 4663 10-9-2 **58** .................................. GrahamLee 2 67
(Fred Watson) *trckd ldrs: effrt and rdn over 2f out: led ent fnl f: drvn out* **10/1**

1402 **2** 1 **Fine Example**[11] 4851 4-9-12 **68** ..................................(b) KevinStott 4 74
(Kevin Ryan) *led at modest gallop: rdn over 1f out: hdd ent fnl f: rallied: kpt on same pce towards fin* **4/1**[2]

412 **3** ½ **Whatsthemessage (IRE)**[12] 4785 3-9-7 **70** .................. AndrewMullen 5 72
(Keith Dalgleish) *t.k.h: in tch: effrt and rdn over 2f out: edgd rt over 1f out: kpt on same pce ins fnl f* **7/1**

332 **4** 1 ½ **Major Crispies**[7] 4999 6-9-12 **68** ..................................(t) DanielTudhope 1 69
(David O'Meara) *hld up on ins: stdy hdwy to trck ldrs whn ct in pocket over 1f out: cajoled along ent fnl f: sn no ex* **7/4**[1]

-454 **5** 4 **Flinty Fell (IRE)**[38] 3833 4-9-5 **66** .................................. RowanScott(5) 7 56
(Keith Dalgleish) *hld up: rdn and outpcd over 2f out: rallied fnl f: nvr able to chal* **6/1**[3]

0005 **6** 2 ½ **Sunnua (IRE)**[22] 4431 4-9-9 **65** .................................. PaulHanagan 6 48
(Richard Fahey) *bhd: struggling after 3f: sme late hdwy: nvr on terms* **13/2**

4056 **7** 2 ½ **Fire Diamond**[81] 2369 4-9-12 **68** ..................................(p) PaulMulrennan 10 44
(Tom Dascombe) *hld up on outside: hdwy and prom over 2f out: sn rdn: wknd over 1f out* **25/1**

306 **8** *nse* **Captain Peaky**[11] 4851 4-8-11 **53** .................................. JasonHart 12 29
(Patrick Holmes) *trckd ldr: rdn and edgd lft over 2f out: edgd rt and wknd over 1f out* **33/1**

1m 28.05s (-0.95) **Going Correction** -0.10s/f (Good)
**WFA** 3 from 4yo+ 7lb **8** Ran SP% **112.4**
Speed ratings (Par 103): **101,99,99,97,93 90,87,87**
CSF £47.97 CT £299.38 TOTE £11.30: £3.70, £1.90, £2.00; EX 62.80 Trifecta £375.20.
**Owner** F Watson **Bred** Darley **Trained** Sedgefield, Co Durham

**FOCUS**
Race distance increased by 7yds. Not a strongly run race and it was an advantage to be handy.

## 5259 NEVER MISS A RACE ON RACING UK H'CAP 1m 7f 217y
**4:45** (4:45) (Class 4) (0-80,79) 4-Y-O+ **£5,175** (£1,540; £769; £384) **Stalls** High

Form RPR
113 **1** **Sebastian's Wish (IRE)**[38] 3830 4-9-6 **78** .................................. JoeFanning 6 86+
(Keith Dalgleish) *trckd ldr: led gng wl over 2f out: pushed out fnl f: comf* **4/6**[1]

0402 **2** 1 ½ **Stormin Tom (IRE)**[12] 4791 5-8-9 **70** .................. RachelRichardson(3) 5 74
(Tim Easterby) *led at ordinary gallop: rdn and hdd over 2f out: rallied: kpt on same pce ins fnl f* **6/1**[3]

3600 **3** 1 **Wor Lass**[24] 4357 9-8-13 **76** .................................. RowanScott(5) 2 79
(Donald Whillans) *trckd ldrs: rdn and edgd lft over 2f out: sn outpcd: rallied ins fnl f: nt rch first two* **16/1**

2343 **4** 1 ¾ **Stoneham**[11] 4852 6-8-5 **70** ..................................(h) JamieGormley(7) 3 71
(Iain Jardine) *hld up: rdn along and outpcd over 2f out: kpt on fnl f: no imp* **7/2**[2]

5430 **5** 7 **Jan Smuts (IRE)**[7] 5008 9-8-2 **60** oh3..................(tp) NathanEvans 4 52
(Wilf Storey) *hld up in tch: drvn and outpcd over 2f out: sn n.d: btn over 1f out* **12/1**

3m 30.24s (-3.26) **Going Correction** -0.10s/f (Good) **5** Ran SP% **110.1**
Speed ratings (Par 105): **104,103,102,101,98**
CSF £5.22 TOTE £1.30: £1.10, £2.80; EX 5.10 Trifecta £24.70.
**Owner** Two Goldfish & A Balloon **Bred** Gestut Schlenderhan **Trained** Carluke, S Lanarks

**FOCUS**
Race distance increased by 7yds. Few got into this, the first two merely switching positions at the finish.

## 5260 FINEST COLLECTION OF RACING ON RACING UK H'CAP 5f 1y
**5:15** (5:15) (Class 6) (0-60,61) 3-Y-O+ **£2,587** (£770; £384; £192) **Stalls** High

Form RPR
0633 **1** *nse* **See Vermont**[11] 4847 9-9-10 **55** ..................................(b[1]) DuranFentiman 5 62
(Rebecca Bastiman) *trckd ldrs: effrt and pushed along whn nt clr run appr fnl f: sn swtchd rt: carried rt ins fnl f: kpt on wl cl home: fin 2nd: awrdd r* **6/1**

063 **2** **Our Place In Loule**[7] 5006 4-9-3 **48** .................................. PatrickMathers 4 54
(Noel Wilson) *trckd ldr: led and rdn whn edgd sltly lft appr fnl f: edgd rt ins fnl f: sn hrd pressed: hld on wl cl home: fin first: demoted to 2nd* **9/4**[2]

0-00 **3** 1 ½ **Brendan (IRE)**[15] 4682 4-9-0 **45** .................................. NathanEvans 1 45
(Jim Goldie) *t.k.h: trckd ldrs: drvn along 2f out: kpt on ins fnl f: nt pce of first two* **28/1**

0503 **4** *nk* **Bond Bombshell**[5] 5055 4-10-2 **61** .................................. DanielTudhope 6 60
(David O'Meara) *led: rdn and hdd whn edgd sltly rt appr fnl f: one pce last 100yds* **15/8**[1]

620 **5** *nk* **Spoken Words**[12] 4789 8-8-12 **46** ..................(p) AdamMcNamara(3) 3 44
(John David Riches) *in tch: drvn along 2f out: outpcd ins fnl f* **20/1**

**6** 1 ¼ **Olaudah**[27] 4226 3-8-9 **51** .................................. DannySheehy(7) 2 44
(Adrian Paul Keatley, Ire) *prom on outside: drvn along over 2f out: wknd ins fnl f* **4/1**[3]

59.46s (-0.94) **Going Correction** -0.175s/f (Firm)
**WFA** 3 from 4yo+ 4lb **6** Ran SP% **108.0**
Speed ratings (Par 101): **99,100,97,97,96 94**
CSF £18.39 TOTE £9.90: £2.10, £1.50; EX 16.70 Trifecta £111.80.
**Owner** John Smith **Bred** Oakhill Stud **Trained** Cowthorpe, N Yorks
■ Stewards' Enquiry : Duran Fentiman two-day ban: used whip without allowing his mount time to respond (Aug 8-9)

**FOCUS**
There was a tight finish to this weak sprint and it went to a stewards inquiry.
T/Plt: £33.00 to a £1 stake. Pool: £76,468.33 - 1688.6 winning units T/Qpdt: £9.50 to a £1 stake. Pool: £5,447.08 - 421.14 winning units **Richard Young**

# 5120 NOTTINGHAM (L-H)
Tuesday, July 25

**OFFICIAL GOING: Good to soft (soft in places)**
Wind: Light against Weather: Fine

## 5261 32RED CASINO RACING EXCELLENCE TRAINING SERIES APPRENTICE H'CAP 1m 2f 50y
**5:50** (5:50) (Class 6) (0-65,66) 4-Y-O+ **£2,587** (£770; £384; £192) **Stalls** Low

Form RPR
40-0 **1** **Champagne Rules**[84] 2272 6-8-8 **47** .................................. BenRobinson 2 53
(Sharon Watt) *s.i.s: racd keenly and sn prom: led 3f out: rdn and hung rt over 1f out: edgd lft ins fnl f: styd on* **20/1**

6-34 **2** 1 ¼ **Castle Talbot (IRE)**[25] 4320 5-9-11 **64** ..................................(p) DavidEgan 8 68
(Tom Clover) *hld up: hdwy 4f out: rdn to chse wnr 2f out: styd on* **5/1**[3]

642 **3** ¾ **Transmitting**[12] 4802 4-9-10 **63** ..................................(h) FinleyMarsh 3 65
(Ed Vaughan) *s.i.s: sn chsng ldrs: shkn up over 1f out: styd on* **5/2**[1]

0053 **4** 1 ¼ **Zaria**[11] 4845 6-9-0 **53** ..................................(p) KatherineGlenister 6 53
(Richard Price) *hld up: hdwy over 3f out: swtchd rt over 2f out: rdn over 1f out: styd on same pce fnl f* **8/1**

444 **5** 2 ½ **Touch The Clouds**[5] 5080 6-8-7 **46** oh1 .................................. JaneElliott 5 42
(William Stone) *plld hrd and prom: wnt 2nd 9f out: led over 3f out: sn hdd: rdn over 1f out: no ex fnl f* **15/2**

2120 **6** 3 ¼ **Indigo Princess**[36] 3906 4-9-12 **65** .................................. RayDawson 10 55
(Michael Appleby) *broke wl: sn stdd and lost pl: hld up: shkn up over 1f out: nt trble ldrs* **12/1**

2020 **7** *hd* **Arithmetic (IRE)**[18] 4575 4-9-12 **65** ..................(p) CallumRodriguez 1 54
(Ruth Carr) *chsd ldr 1f: remained handy: pushed along over 2f out: wknd over 1f out* **9/2**[2]

4500 **8** 1 ¼ **Karam Albaari (IRE)**[27] 4217 9-9-5 **63** ..................(v) GinaMangan(5) 7 50
(J R Jenkins) *s.i.s: hld up: rdn over 1f out: nvr on terms* **33/1**

0641 **9** 9 **Iberica Road (USA)**[18] 4554 4-9-13 **66** .................................. PatrickVaughan 4 37
(Grant Tuer) *led: hdd over 3f out: rdn and wknd over 1f out* **8/1**

0000 **10** 8 **Harry Holland**[14] 4728 5-9-0 **58** ..................(b) SebastianWoods(5) 9 15
(Oliver Greenall) *hld up: pushed along over 3f out: wknd over 2f out* **66/1**

2m 14.89s (0.59) **Going Correction** 0.0s/f (Good) **10** Ran SP% **114.3**
Speed ratings (Par 101): **97,96,95,94,92 89,89,88,81,75**
CSF £113.47 CT £343.01 TOTE £23.60: £7.50, £2.50, £1.10; EX 183.90 Trifecta £643.50.
**Owner** Rosey Hill Partnership **Bred** Heather Raw **Trained** Brompton-on-Swale, N Yorks

**FOCUS**
Outer track. Rail set out 2 yards on home bend, adding 6 yards to Races 1, 5, 6 and 7. A modest handicap for apprentice riders. The 2nd/3rd set a straightforward level.

## 5262 32RED.COM NOVICE AUCTION STKS — 5f 8y
**6:20** (6:20) (Class 5) 2-Y-O — **£3,234** (£962; £481; £240) **Stalls** Centre

| Form | Pos | Dist | Horse / Comment | Jockey | SP | RPR |
|---|---|---|---|---|---|---|
| 2122 | 1 | | **May Remain**[11] 4841 2-9-9 80 (Paul Cole) *chsd ldrs: shkn up and nt clr run over 1f out: rdn to ld ins fnl f: r.o* | PJMcDonald 7 | 2/1[2] | 84 |
| 2 | 2 | 1 ¼ | **Ginbar (IRE)**[10] 4888 2-9-2 0 (Tom Dascombe) *led: rdn and hung lft over 1f out: hdd ins fnl f: styd on same pce* | RichardKingscote 5 | 8/11[1] | 73 |
| 645 | 3 | 2 ¾ | **The Golden Cue**[50] 3406 2-9-2 62 (Steph Hollinshead) *w ldr tl rdn over 1f out: styd on same pce fnl f* | AdamBeschizza 1 | 25/1 | 63 |
| 45 | 4 | nk | **Just For Fun**[20] 4503 2-8-11 0 (Richard Fahey) *sn pushed along in rr: styd on fr over 1f out: nvr nrr* | TonyHamilton 4 | 14/1[3] | 57 |
| 05 | 5 | ¾ | **Savannah's Show**[10] 4895 2-8-11 0 (Richard Guest) *trckd ldrs: swtchd lft 1/2-way: rdn over 1f out: hung lft and wknd ins fnl f* | JFEgan 6 | 20/1 | 54 |
| 04 | 6 | 3 | **Shades Of Mist**[17] 4599 2-9-2 0 (Ann Duffield) *hld up: outpcd 1/2-way: nvr on terms after* | AdamKirby 2 | 40/1 | 48 |
| 60 | 7 | nk | **Odds On Oli**[14] 4725 2-9-2 0 (Richard Fahey) *s.s: pushed along in rr: nvr on terms* | DavidNolan 3 | 50/1 | 47 |

1m 1.33s (-0.17) **Going Correction** -0.075s/f (Good) — **7 Ran SP% 110.9**
Speed ratings (Par 94): **98,96,91,91,89 85,84**
CSF £3.49 TOTE £3.10: £1.30, £1.10; EX 4.60 Trifecta £23.10.
**Owner** PJL Racing Wright Asprey Meyrick Wilcock **Bred** The Ultimate Best Partnership **Trained** Whatcombe, Oxon

**FOCUS**
A fair juvenile novice auction sprint. They went a decent gallop and the two horses at the head of the betting came to the fore. Straightforward form.

## 5263 £10 FREE AT 32RED.COM H'CAP — 5f 8y
**6:50** (6:51) (Class 5) (0-75,75) 3-Y-O+ — **£3,234** (£962; £481; £240) **Stalls** Centre

| Form | Pos | Dist | Horse / Comment | Jockey | SP | RPR |
|---|---|---|---|---|---|---|
| 0513 | 1 | | **Sitar**[25] 4324 3-8-12 67 (h) (James Fanshawe) *trckd ldrs: rdn to ld ins fnl f: r.o* | DanielMuscutt 6 | 9/2[3] | 76 |
| 3021 | 2 | 1 ¼ | **Glacier Point**[11] 4842 3-9-6 75 (p) (Clive Cox) *led: qcknd 1/2-way: rdn and hung lft over 1f out: hdd ins fnl f: styd on same pce* | AdamKirby 7 | 7/2[2] | 79 |
| 0241 | 3 | 1 ¾ | **Show Palace**[17] 4607 4-9-2 67 (Jennie Candlish) *s.i.s: hld up: plld hrd: hdwy and nt clr run 2f out: rdn ins fnl f: styd on same pce* | DavidNolan 5 | 5/2[1] | 66 |
| 6004 | 4 | 1 ½ | **Lexington Place**[17] 4600 7-9-8 73 (Ruth Carr) *s.i.s: outpcd: r.o ins fnl f: nvr nrr* | JamesSullivan 2 | 6/1 | 66 |
| 31-0 | 5 | 3 | **Ace Master**[26] 4277 9-9-1 71 (b) (Roy Bowring) *w ldrs tl rdn 1/2-way: hung lft and wknd over 1f out* | KevinLundie(5) 1 | 20/1 | 54 |
| -444 | 6 | ½ | **Primanora**[55] 3216 4-8-6 64 (Michael Appleby) *w ldrs to 1/2-way: rdn: hung lft and wknd over 1f out* | RayDawson(7) 4 | 6/1 | 45 |
| 5506 | 7 | 4 | **Burning Thread (IRE)**[27] 4219 10-9-0 70 (b) (David Elsworth) *prom: sn pushed along: outpcd 1/2-way: wknd over 1f out* | DavidEgan(5) 3 | 14/1 | 36 |

1m 0.66s (-0.84) **Going Correction** -0.075s/f (Good)
**WFA** 3 from 4yo+ 4lb — **7 Ran SP% 109.0**
Speed ratings (Par 103): **103,101,98,95,91 90,83**
CSF £18.57 TOTE £4.50: £2.00, £1.80; EX 19.10 Trifecta £39.20.
**Owner** Manor Farm Stud & John Rose **Bred** Manor Farm Stud (rutland) **Trained** Newmarket, Suffolk
■ Stewards' Enquiry : Ray Dawson two-day ban: used whip down the shoulder (Aug 8-9)

**FOCUS**
A fair sprint handicap. They went a decent gallop and it is sound form under the conditions.

## 5264 PLAY JURASSIC WORLD AT 32RED H'CAP — 6f 18y
**7:20** (7:21) (Class 4) (0-80,82) 3-Y-O+ — **£5,175** (£1,540; £769; £384) **Stalls** Centre

| Form | Pos | Dist | Horse / Comment | Jockey | SP | RPR |
|---|---|---|---|---|---|---|
| 21-5 | 1 | | **Dark Power (IRE)**[23] 4407 3-9-7 76 (t[1]) (Clive Cox) *racd keenly and sn w ldrs: rdn to ld over 1f out: sn hung rt: r.o wl* | AdamKirby 2 | 4/1[2] | 94+ |
| 0002 | 2 | 3 ½ | **Cosmic Chatter**[34] 3974 7-9-9 73 (p) (Ruth Carr) *sn pushed along in rr: hdwy over 1f out: chsd wnr fnl f: no imp* | JamesSullivan 1 | 12/1 | 81 |
| 3322 | 3 | 2 ¼ | **Dirchill (IRE)**[24] 4341 3-9-4 73 (David Barron) *led: hdd over 3f out: sn hung lft: rdn over 2f out: styd on same pce fnl f* | BenCurtis 6 | 3/1[1] | 73 |
| 3311 | 4 | nse | **Champagne Bob**[4] 5112 5-8-3 60 (Richard Price) *w ldr tl led over 3f out: rdn and hdd over 1f out: sn hung lft: wknd ins fnl f* | KatherineGlenister(7) 5 | 4/1[2] | 61 |
| 142 | 5 | ¾ | **King Of Spin**[36] 3919 4-9-11 82 (t) (Richard Hughes) *awkward s: sn prom: rdn and nt clr run over 1f out: wknd ins fnl f* | FinleyMarsh(7) 4 | 3/1[1] | 80 |
| 3226 | 6 | 2 | **Storm Cry**[12] 4788 3-9-13 82 (Mark Johnston) *chsd ldrs: rdn over 2f out: wknd fnl f* | PJMcDonald 3 | 6/1[3] | 73 |

1m 14.72s (0.02) **Going Correction** -0.075s/f (Good)
**WFA** 3 from 4yo+ 5lb — **6 Ran SP% 112.0**
Speed ratings (Par 105): **96,91,88,88,87 84**
CSF £45.75 TOTE £4.40: £2.20, £4.20; EX 46.80 Trifecta £254.80.
**Owner** Alan G Craddock **Bred** Guy O'Callaghan **Trained** Lambourn, Berks

**FOCUS**
A fairly decent sprint handicap. They went a contested gallop and the pace collapsed to a degree.

## 5265 32RED H'CAP — 1m 75y
**7:50** (7:50) (Class 4) (0-80,81) 3-Y-O+ — **£5,175** (£1,540; £769; £384) **Stalls** Centre

| Form | Pos | Dist | Horse / Comment | Jockey | SP | RPR |
|---|---|---|---|---|---|---|
| 2214 | 1 | | **Al Nafoorah**[24] 4372 3-9-4 75 (Ed Dunlop) *hld up: hdwy over 1f out: shkn up to ld ins fnl f: rdn out* | PJMcDonald 7 | 11/4[2] | 83+ |
| 4212 | 2 | 1 ¼ | **Lamloom (IRE)**[15] 4685 3-9-10 81 (David O'Meara) *racd keenly: led rdn over 1f out: hdd ins fnl f: styd on same pce towards fin* | DavidNolan 2 | 11/8[1] | 86 |
| 1130 | 3 | 1 ¾ | **Roman De Brut (IRE)**[25] 4304 5-9-7 77 (Daniel Mark Loughnane) *prom: chsd ldr 7f out: rdn and ev ch fr over 2f out tl no ex wl ins fnl f* | RayDawson(7) 3 | 8/1 | 80 |
| 0001 | 4 | 2 ¼ | **Natajack**[17] 4609 3-9-1 72 (Richard Fahey) *chsd ldr over 1f: remained handy: pushed along over 2f out: swtchd rt over 1f out: no ex ins fnl f* | TonyHamilton 1 | 4/1[3] | 68 |
| 6050 | 5 | 1 ½ | **Under Attack (IRE)**[12] 4796 4-9-9 72 (b[1]) (Ruth Carr) *prom: rdn over 2f out: nt clr run wl over 1f out: styd on same pce* | JamesSullivan 5 | 12/1 | 66 |

1m 46.91s (-2.09) **Going Correction** 0.0s/f (Good)
**WFA** 3 from 4yo+ 8lb — **5 Ran SP% 107.6**
Speed ratings (Par 105): **110,108,107,104,103**
CSF £6.62 TOTE £3.60: £1.90, £1.30; EX 5.90 Trifecta £23.40.
**Owner** Mohammed Jaber **Bred** Aston Mullins Stud **Trained** Newmarket, Suffolk

**FOCUS**
Raced distance increased by 6 yards. A fairly decent handicap. They went a proper gallop and a change of tactics saw the second favourite successfully come from last to first in the second half of the straight.

## 5266 32RED.COM H'CAP — 1m 75y
**8:20** (8:26) (Class 6) (0-60,60) 3-Y-O — **£2,587** (£770; £384; £192) **Stalls** Centre

| Form | Pos | Dist | Horse / Comment | Jockey | SP | RPR |
|---|---|---|---|---|---|---|
| -352 | 1 | | **Mordoree (IRE)**[8] 4968 3-9-2 55 (p[1]) (Clive Cox) *hld up: pushed along and hdwy on outer over 2f out: rdn to ld and hung lft 1f out: styd on u.p* | AdamKirby 8 | 7/4[1] | 63 |
| 0003 | 2 | ¾ | **Accomplice**[13] 4754 3-9-5 58 (Michael Blanshard) *chsd ldrs: led over 1f out: sn rdn and hdd: styd on same pce towards fin* | RobHornby 3 | 14/1 | 64 |
| -400 | 3 | ½ | **Born To Please**[20] 4493 3-8-9 48 (Mark Usher) *hld up in tch: plld hrd early: pushed along 5f out: rdn over 2f out: nt clr run over 1f out: r.o wl towards fin* | KieranO'Neill 12 | 12/1 | 54 |
| 6-56 | 4 | 1 ¾ | **Queens Royale**[17] 4619 3-9-5 58 (Michael Appleby) *hld up: hdwy over 2f out: rdn over 1f out: styd on same pce ins fnl f* | TonyHamilton 4 | 7/1[3] | 59 |
| 0002 | 5 | shd | **Ronni Layne**[13] 4754 3-8-12 51 (Conrad Allen) *sn led: hdd over 5f out: remained handy: led again over 2f out: rdn and hdd over 1f out: no ex ins fnl f* | RobertTart 2 | 8/1 | 52 |
| 6342 | 6 | ½ | **Chough**[14] 4713 3-8-13 55 (Hughie Morrison) *chsd ldrs: rdn over 2f out: no ex ins fnl f* | CharlieBennett(3) 6 | 11/4[2] | 55 |
| 400 | 7 | 4 | **Velvet Charm**[18] 4568 3-9-2 60 (Rae Guest) *s.s: hld up: rdn over 2f out: n.d* | DavidEgan(5) 7 | 16/1 | 51 |
| 0004 | 8 | 5 | **Foxy Rebel**[14] 4721 3-8-8 47 (Ruth Carr) *prom: hung rt after 1f: led over 5f out: rdn and hdd over 2f out: wknd over 1f out: eased* | JamesSullivan 11 | 25/1 | 26 |
| 0560 | 9 | 1 ½ | **Shamonix (IRE)**[13] 4748 3-8-0 46 oh1 (Mark Usher) *chsd ldrs tl wknd over 2f out* | TheodoreLadd(7) 13 | 50/1 | 22 |

1m 48.62s (-0.38) **Going Correction** 0.0s/f (Good) — **9 Ran SP% 112.7**
Speed ratings (Par 98): **101,100,99,98,97 97,93,88,86**
CSF £27.74 CT £226.68 TOTE £2.60: £1.10, £2.50, £3.70; EX 27.50 Trifecta £182.10.
**Owner** Wood Hall Stud Limited **Bred** Old Carhue Stud **Trained** Lambourn, Berks
■ Nyx (50/1) and Dusty Bin (14/1) were withdrawn. Rule 4 applies to bets struck at board prices prior to withdrawal but not to SP bets - deduction 5p in the pound. New market formed.

**FOCUS**
Raced distance increased by 6 yards. A modest 3yo handicap. They went a respectable gallop and the well-backed favourite ran out a game winner, posting a small pb.

## 5267 32RED SPORT H'CAP — 1m 6f
**8:50** (8:51) (Class 6) (0-60,62) 4-Y-O+ — **£2,587** (£770; £384; £192) **Stalls** Low

| Form | Pos | Dist | Horse / Comment | Jockey | SP | RPR |
|---|---|---|---|---|---|---|
| 050 | 1 | | **Quay Point (IRE)**[20] 4497 4-8-9 48 (Laura Mongan) *mde all: rdn clr over 1f out: eased wl ins fnl f* | JohnFahy 3 | 20/1 | 60+ |
| 5110 | 2 | 3 | **Incus**[25] 4301 4-9-1 59 (Ed de Giles) *plld hrd and prom: rdn to chse wnr over 2f out: styd on same pce fnl f* | DavidEgan(5) 4 | 3/1[1] | 65 |
| -253 | 3 | ½ | **Macksville (IRE)**[18] 4573 4-9-8 61 (p[1]) (James Eustace) *hld up: hdwy over 2f out: rdn over 1f out: r.o: nt rch ldrs* | RyanTate 13 | 9/2[2] | 66 |
| 6-64 | 4 | 1 ¾ | **Art Scholar (IRE)**[36] 3907 10-9-0 60 (Michael Appleby) *hld up: rdn over 2f out: hdwy over 1f out: nvr nrr* | RayDawson(7) 11 | 12/1 | 63 |
| -235 | 5 | hd | **Lady Natasha (IRE)**[21] 4476 4-9-7 60 (K R Burke) *hld up: rdn and hdwy over 1f out: nvr on terms* | PJMcDonald 16 | 8/1 | 63 |
| 0040 | 6 | ¾ | **Honourable Knight (IRE)**[13] 4756 9-8-7 46 oh1 (Mark Usher) *chsd ldrs: rdn to chse wnr over 3f out tl over 2f out: no ex fnl f* | KieranO'Neill 6 | 25/1 | 48 |
| 0304 | 7 | 1 ¾ | **Tingo In The Tale (IRE)**[17] 4627 8-8-8 52 (p) (Tony Forbes) *hld up: styd on appr fnl f: nvr nrr* | JaneElliott(5) 15 | 8/1 | 52 |
| 415 | 8 | ½ | **Paddy's Rock (IRE)**[14] 4722 6-9-4 57 (p) (Lynn Siddall) *chsd ldrs: lost pl 10f out: hdwy over 3f out: sn rdn: wknd over 1f out* | PaddyAspell 1 | 14/1 | 56 |
| -065 | 9 | 2 | **Rob's Legacy**[9] 3698 4-8-7 46 oh1 (Shaun Harris) *hld up in tch: rdn over 3f out: wknd wl over 1f out* | AdamBeschizza 10 | 66/1 | 42 |
| 5606 | 10 | 5 | **Absolute Angel**[52] 3340 6-9-0 53 (p[1]) (Peter Niven) *hld up in tch: rdn over 3f out: wknd wl over 1f out* | DavidNolan 5 | 18/1 | 43 |
| 0003 | 11 | 4 ½ | **Sir Runs A Lot**[7] 5005 5-9-3 56 (David Barron) *mid-div: lost pl 8f out: in rr whn hung lft fr over 4f out* | BenCurtis 8 | 7/1[3] | 40 |
| -005 | 12 | 3 ¾ | **Barbary Prince**[24] 4346 5-8-7 46 oh1 (Shaun Harris) *prom: pushed along over 4f out: wknd over 2f out* | JoeDoyle 14 | 66/1 | 25 |
| 4610 | 13 | 2 ¾ | **Whitecliff Park (IRE)**[15] 4684 4-8-8 52 (b[1]) (Brian Ellison) *s.s and rel to r: hdwy into mid-div over 9f out: drvn along over 4f out: sn wknd* | BenRobinson(5) 12 | 12/1 | 28+ |
| 6030 | 14 | 53 | **Mr Standfast**[40] 3756 4-8-8 47 (Alan Phillips) *prom: jnd wnr over 10f out tl over 4f out: wknd 3f out* | RobHornby 7 | 50/1 | |

3m 9.48s (2.48) **Going Correction** 0.0s/f (Good) — **14 Ran SP% 118.8**
Speed ratings (Par 101): **92,90,90,89,88 88,87,87,86,83 80,78,76,46**
CSF £76.11 CT £330.38 TOTE £33.50: £8.90, £1.50, £1.90; EX 144.60 Trifecta £1205.90.
**Owner** Mrs Jackie Cornwell **Bred** Mrs J A Cornwell **Trained** Epsom, Surrey

**FOCUS**
Raced distance increased by 6 yards. A modest staying contest won in thoroughly convincing fashion by a handicap debutante.

T/Plt: £29.30 to a £1 stake. Pool: £62,386.61 - 1550.8 winning units T/Qpdt: £21.60 to a £1 stake. Pool: £4,641.45 - 158.73 winning units **Colin Roberts**


The Form Book Flat, Raceform Ltd, Newbury, RG14 5SJ

## 4115 COMPIEGNE (L-H)

Tuesday, July 25

**OFFICIAL GOING: Turf: soft**

### 5268a PRIX DU RU DE BERNE (CLAIMER) (3YO FILLIES) (TURF) 1m

12:10 3-Y-O £8,119 (£3,247; £2,435; £1,623; £811)

RPR

1 **Ettu**[51] 3-9-1 0......(b) TheoBachelot 3 63
(S Wattel, France) **6/1**[3]

2 1 1/4 **Numeration (FR)**[9] 4943 3-8-8 0......(b) ClementLecoeuvre(3) 7 57
(Alex Fracas, France) **68/10**

3 shd **Bubble Bath**[22] 4455 3-9-2 0...... FranckBlondel 2 61
(M Pimbonnet, France) **2/1**[1]

4 snk **Undiscovered Angel (FR)**[26] 4288 3-9-1 0...... TonyPiccone 9 60
(K R Burke) *led: rdn and hdd 2f out: kpt on gamely u.p after but hld in 4th nring fin* **15/2**

5 2 **Parin**[22] 4455 3-8-6 0...... JeromeMoutard(5) 8 51
(W Mongil, Germany) **9/1**

6 nk **Wood Avens (FR)**[23] 3-8-11 0...... Pierre-CharlesBoudot 5 51
(H-A Pantall, France) **78/10**

7 6 **Winwhip (FR)**[49] 3-9-1 0...... RonanThomas 1 41
(P Adda, France) **32/1**

8 12 **Miss Osier**[17] 4625 3-8-11 0......(p) MaximeGuyon 6 9
(Rae Guest) *trckd ldr: rdn early in st: no ex fnl 2f: wknd: eased and dropped to last: t.o* **4/1**[2]

1m 41.69s **8** Ran SP% **116.6**

PARI-MUTUEL (all including 1 euro stake): WIN 7.00; PLACE 2.10, 2.20, 1.20; DF 23.90; SF 40.00.

**Owner** Salabi Racing & T De La Heronniere **Bred** Widden Stud Australia Pty Ltd **Trained** France

### 5269a PRIX DE VIGNEMONT (CONDITIONS) (4YO+) (TURF) 1m

1:20 4-Y-0+ £11,965 (£4,786; £3,589; £2,393; £1,196)

RPR

1 **London Protocol (FR)**[22] 4454 4-8-11 0......(p) TonyPiccone 3 86
(K R Burke) **7/1**

2 3/4 **Prince Apache**[64] 4-9-0 0...... DelphineSantiago(4) 6 91
(Andreas Suborics, Germany) **14/1**

3 1 1/4 **Kiwi Green Suite (BRZ)**[261] 4-8-11 0 ow1...... ChristopheSoumillon 11 81
(D Smaga, France) **48/10**[2]

4 hd **Al Erayg (IRE)**[22] 4454 4-9-0 0...... CristianDemuro 5 84
(F-H Graffard, France) **9/5**[1]

5 5 **Le Juge (IRE)**[22] 4454 4-9-4 0...... MllePaulineDominois(4) 2 80
(A Fabre, France) **5/1**[3]

6 2 **Incitator (FR)**[436] 2281 4-8-11 0...... AlexisBadel 8 65
(Mme M Bollack-Badel, France) **15/1**

7 snk **Atlantik Cup (GER)**[96] 1920 4-8-11 0...... AntoineHamelin 4 64
(A Kleinkorres, Germany) **15/2**

8 2 1/2 **Zermatta (CAN)**[304] 4-8-8 0...... VincentCheminaud 7 55
(J Baudron, France) **19/1**

9 3/4 **Le Depute (FR)**[133] 5-8-6 0...... JeromeMoutard(5) 10 57
(Ecurie Saint Simeon, Belgium) **31/1**

10 2 1/2 **Malak El Hawa (FR)**[142] 7-8-11 0...... MickaelBerto 1 51
(P Lenogue, France) **54/1**

1m 41.95s **10** Ran SP% **116.7**

PARI-MUTUEL (all including 1 euro stake): WIN 8.00; PLACE 2.60, 3.80, 2.60; DF 40.00; SF 64.10.

**Owner** Ontoawinner, R Mckeown & E Burke **Bred** Gerard Rollain **Trained** Middleham Moor, N Yorks

## 4989 BATH (L-H)

Wednesday, July 26

**OFFICIAL GOING: Good (good to soft in places; 8.2)**

Wind: Light wind Weather: Cloudy, mild

### 5270 BRITISH STALLION STUDS EBF NOVICE STKS (PLUS 10 RACE) 5f 10y

**2:10** (2:10) (Class 4) 2-Y-O £4,269 (£1,270; £634; £317) **Stalls** Centre

Form RPR

01 1 **Golden Salute (IRE)**[9] 4972 2-8-10 0...... WilliamCox(7) 1 79
(Andrew Balding) *trckd ldrs: hdwy to ld over 1f out: sn rdn: chal by runner-up ins fnl f: briefly hdd: r.o wl to regain advantage and assert last 50yds* **5/4**[1]

2 hd **Little Boy Blue** 2-8-11 0...... JoshuaBryan(5) 4 77
(Bill Turner) *chsd ldrs tl briefly outpcd after 2f: sn regained contact w pack: hdwy and pushed along 2f out: reminders over 1f out: jnd wnr ins fnl f: led briefly: r.o but hdd and jst hld last 50yds* **40/1**

325 3 2 **White Feather**[48] 3515 2-8-11 0......(p[1]) MitchGodwin(5) 2 70
(Jo Hughes) *prom: drvn 2f out: rdn over 1f out: styd on one pce fnl f* **4/1**[3]

3421 4 1 1/4 **Aquadabra (IRE)**[8] 4991 2-9-3 68...... SilvestreDeSousa 5 67
(Mick Channon) *led: pushed along 2f out: hdd over 1f out: sn rdn and no ex* **2/1**[2]

5 3/4 **Zumurud (IRE)** 2-9-2 0...... DaneO'Neill 3 63
(Charles Hills) *in rr but in tch: drvn 2f out: reminders over 1f out: no imp* **13/2**

1m 3.12s (0.62) **Going Correction** +0.175s/f (Good) **5** Ran SP% **113.6**

Speed ratings (Par 96): **102,101,98,96,95**

CSF £36.84 TOTE £2.00: £1.20, £6.10; EX 45.00 Trifecta £114.10.

**Owner** The Hot To Trot Syndicate-Golden Salute **Bred** Max Morris **Trained** Kingsclere, Hants

**FOCUS**

Steady rain through the morning saw the ground change to good, good to soft in places. Not the strongest of novice events but a good finish and the winner was picking up a handy bonus in the process.

### 5271 RAINBOW CASINO BRISTOL H'CAP (BATH SUMMER SPRINT SERIES QUALIFIER) 5f 160y

**2:40** (2:41) (Class 5) (0-70,72) 3-Y-0+ £2,911 (£866; £432; £216) **Stalls** Centre

Form RPR

5033 1 **Babyfact**[8] 4993 6-9-12 70...... DaneO'Neill 2 84+
(Malcolm Saunders) *mde all: 2 l clr 2f out: rdn over 1f out: kpt up to work and in command fnl f: comf* **9/2**[2]

0050 2 2 3/4 **Seamster**[9] 4979 10-9-7 72......(t) CameronNoble(7) 13 77
(David Loughnane) *prom: hdwy to go 3rd 2f out: sn drvn: rdn over 1f out: chsd wnr ent fnl f: no imp* **10/1**

0406 3 hd **Picket Line**[21] 4495 5-9-13 71......(p[1]) TimmyMurphy 4 75
(Geoffrey Deacon) *mid-div: effrt and drvn 2f out: hdwy over 1f out: r.o to take 3rd ins fnl f* **16/1**

-504 4 1/2 **Storm Melody**[18] 4629 4-9-13 71...... FranBerry 10 74
(Jonjo O'Neill) *mid-div: pushed along 2f out: rdn over 1f out: r.o fnl f* **3/1**[1]

5006 5 1 **Essaka (IRE)**[15] 4723 5-8-8 55...... CallumShepherd(3) 3 54
(Tony Carroll) *hld up: effrt 2f out and briefly n.m.r: rdn 1f out: r.o* **20/1**

5204 6 1/2 **Malcolm The Pug (IRE)**[12] 4843 3-9-5 68...... TomMarquand 1 65
(Richard Hannon) *chsd ldr: 2 l down and pushed along 2f out: sn rdn: no ex appr fnl f* **5/1**[3]

0104 7 1/2 **Jaganory (IRE)**[14] 4731 5-8-9 58......(p) MitchGodwin(5) 11 54
(Christopher Mason) *mid-div: rdn 2f out: one pce fnl f* **16/1**

2-11 8 shd **Debonaire David**[23] 4447 3-9-9 72......(t) ShaneKelly 6 67
(Richard Hughes) *rrd leaving stalls and lost several l: sn rcvrd into midfield: pushed along 2f out: one pce fr over 1f out* **7/1**

5041 9 nk **Burauq**[14] 4735 5-8-0 51......(v) KatherineGlenister(7) 9 46
(Milton Bradley) *trckd ldrs: drvn 2f out: rdn over 1f out: wknd* **11/1**

5000 10 1 1/2 **Divine Call**[27] 4256 10-8-7 51 oh4......(b) FrannyNorton 5 41
(Milton Bradley) *in rr: pushed along 2f out: rdn over 1f out: fdd* **33/1**

060 11 2 1/2 **Diamond Vine (IRE)**[4] 5146 9-8-7 51 oh6......(p) SamHitchcott 8 32
(Ronald Harris) *in rr: drvn over 2f out: no imp* **66/1**

0400 12 7 **Overhaugh Street**[9] 4969 4-8-13 57...... SilvestreDeSousa 12 15
(Ed de Giles) *prom: pushed along and lost pl 1/2-way: eased fnl 2f* **12/1**

1m 10.92s (-0.28) **Going Correction** +0.175s/f (Good)

**WFA** 3 from 4yo+ 5lb **12** Ran SP% **118.4**

Speed ratings (Par 103): **108,104,104,103,102 101,100,100,100,98 94,85**

CSF £48.17 CT £675.69 TOTE £5.80: £1.90, £2.90, £4.90; EX 46.80 Trifecta £480.70.

**Owner** Mrs Ginny Nicholas **Bred** M S Saunders And Chris Scott **Trained** Green Ore, Somerset

**FOCUS**

A run-of-the-mill sprint handicap but an impressive display from the front-running winner.

### 5272 RAINBOW CASINO BIRMINGHAM H'CAP 5f 160y

**3:10** (3:10) (Class 4) (0-80,80) 3-Y-O £6,469 (£1,925; £962; £481) **Stalls** Centre

Form RPR

-305 1 **Secret Potion**[21] 4489 3-8-5 64...... SamHitchcott 1 73
(Ronald Harris) *chsd ldr in 1st f: sn led: mde rest: pushed along 2f out: drvn in narrow ld over 1f out: rdn and r.o wl to pull clr ins fnl f: on top last 100yds* **16/1**

1022 2 1 3/4 **Love Oasis**[7] 5018 3-9-5 78...... FrannyNorton 2 81
(Mark Johnston) *led in 1st f: sn hdd and settled in 2nd: pushed along in cl 2nd 2f out: rdn and ev ch 1f out: struggling to keep tabs on wnr ins fnl f: btn last 100yds* **5/2**[2]

6132 3 1 3/4 **Farleigh Mac**[6] 5051 3-9-0 78...... JoshuaBryan(5) 3 75
(Andrew Balding) *trckd ldrs: hdwy and ev ch in cl 3rd 2f out: sn drvn: rdn over 1f out: one pce fnl f* **10/11**[1]

-505 4 nse **Big Lachie**[51] 3411 3-9-4 77...... ShaneKelly 4 74
(Daniel Mark Loughnane) *trckd ldrs: pushed along 2f out: rdn over 1f out: styd on fnl f but jst hld for 3rd nr fin* **20/1**

3006 5 11 **Sayesse**[30] 4154 3-9-7 80...... SilvestreDeSousa 5 41
(Mick Channon) *in rr: outpcd early and sn pushed along: rdn 2f out: no imp: eased over 1f out* **9/2**[3]

1m 11.96s (0.76) **Going Correction** +0.175s/f (Good) **5** Ran SP% **109.8**

Speed ratings (Par 102): **101,98,96,96,81**

CSF £54.67 TOTE £15.90: £6.30, £1.80; EX 54.60 Trifecta £124.50.

**Owner** RHS Ltd, R Fox, P Charter **Bred** Llety Farms **Trained** Earlswood, Monmouths

**FOCUS**

A small field for this 0-80 and a surprise winner, albeit there was no fluke about the performance. The winning time was over a second slower than Babyfact recorded in the previous race.

### 5273 RAINBOW CASINOS CARDIFF FILLIES' H'CAP 1m 3f 137y

**3:40** (3:40) (Class 3) (0-90,86) 3-Y-O-£7,246 (£2,168; £1,084; £542; £270) **Stalls** Low

Form RPR

5141 1 **Pacharana**[15] 4712 4-9-11 83...... KieranShoemark 4 97+
(Luca Cumani) *trckd ldrs: hdwy 3f out: pushed along to ld 2f out: drew 3 l clr over 1f out: extended advantage thrght fnl f: easily* **4/1**[3]

52-2 2 8 **Silver Link (IRE)**[23] 4449 3-8-8 77...... ShaneKelly 6 79
(Marcus Tregoning) *chsd ldr: chal and ev ch 2f out: sn lft bhd by wnr: rdn over 1f out: styd on alongside 3rd ins fnl f: won battle for 2nd cl home* **5/2**[2]

3442 3 hd **Really Super**[6] 5065 3-8-7 76......(b) SilvestreDeSousa 2 78
(Ralph Beckett) *t.k.h: led: 3 l clr and given breather 4f out: pushed along 3f out: drvn and hdd 2f out: sn lft bhd by wnr: rdn wl over 1f out: kpt on alongside runner-up fnl f: lost battle for 2nd cl home* **5/4**[1]

41 4 1 3/4 **Sure To Explore (IRE)**[40] 3770 3-8-8 77...... MartinDwyer 5 76
(William Muir) *racd in last: hdwy into 4th over 3f out: sn pushed along: drvn and no ex fnl 2f* **15/2**

-416 5 23 **Stockhill Diva**[25] 4370 7-10-0 86...... FranBerry 1 47
(Brendan Powell) *racd in 4th: relegated to last over 3f out: sn drvn and lost tch: eased over 1f out* **16/1**

2m 30.11s (-0.49) **Going Correction** +0.175s/f (Good)

**WFA** 3 from 4yo+ 11lb **5** Ran SP% **110.7**

Speed ratings (Par 104): **108,102,102,101,86**

CSF £14.35 TOTE £4.00: £2.00, £1.40; EX 19.80 Trifecta £25.20.

**Owner** S Stuckey **Bred** Stuart Stuckey **Trained** Newmarket, Suffolk

**FOCUS**
Race distance increased by 5yds. The feature event on the card produced a career-best display from a filly whose progress since handicapping has been a credit to her trainer. The pace set by the eventual third looked strong.

## 5274 RAINBOW CASINO ABERDEEN H'CAP (BATH SUMMER STAYERS' SERIES QUALIFIER) 1m 6f

**4:10** (4:10) (Class 5) (0-70,65) 4-Y-O+ **£2,911** (£866; £432; £216) **Stalls** Centre

Form RPR

1033 **1** **Desert Cross**[18] 4630 4-9-6 **64** FranBerry 7 71
(Jonjo O'Neill) *hld up: smooth hdwy to chal 3f out: led gng wl over 1f out: sn nudged along: rdn and 1 l clr ent fnl f: pushed out to hold off fast-fining runner-up* **11/4**[2]

261 **2** *nk* **Innoko (FR)**[14] 4733 7-9-4 **62** (h) SilvestreDeSousa 5 68
(Robert Stephens) *hld up: hdwy to chse ldrs 2f out: rdn into 3rd over 1f out: r.o u.p to take 2nd ins fnl f: clsng on wnr nr fin* **11/8**[1]

0-54 **3** *¾* **Captain George (IRE)**[12] 4840 6-8-11 **60** MitchGodwin(5) 2 65
(Michael Blake) *mid-div: pushed along and hdwy to ld 3f out: rdn 2f out: hdd over 1f out: kpt on but lost 2nd ins fnl f* **6/1**[3]

3334 **4** *10* **Halling's Wish**[14] 4733 7-9-2 **60** (p[1]) ShaneKelly 8 52
(Gary Moore) *hld up in rr: pushed along 3f out: sn no ch w first three: tk 4th ins fnl f* **7/1**

-000 **5** *1 ¾* **Bohemian Rhapsody (IRE)**[50] 3428 8-8-11 **60** (p) JennyPowell(5) 6 49
(Brendan Powell) *chsd ldr: led jst over 3f out: almost immediately hdd: rdn and wknd* **25/1**

025/ **6** *1 ¾* **Shot In The Dark (IRE)**[578] 5689 8-8-1 **48** NoelGarbutt(3) 4 35
(Jonathan Geake) *trckd ldrs: drvn over 3f out: lost pl and rdn 2f out: one pce* **33/1**

365- **7** *23* **Meetings Man (IRE)**[300] 6892 10-9-7 **65** (p) TomMarquand 1 22
(Ali Stronge) *led: drvn and hdd jst over 3f out: fdd and eased* **12/1**

3m 10.28s (6.48) **Going Correction** +0.175s/f (Good) 7 Ran SP% **110.0**
Speed ratings (Par 103): **88,87,87,81,80 79,66**
CSF £6.34 CT £16.80 TOTE £3.30: £1.50, £1.60; EX 7.20 Trifecta £25.00.
**Owner** P Hickey **Bred** W T , R T & N S Whittle **Trained** Cheltenham, Gloucs

**FOCUS**
Race distance increased by 5yds. A staying handicap run at a good pace saw three pull clear of the remainder. Straightforward form around the front two.

## 5275 RAINBOW BRISTOL POKER H'CAP 1m 2f 37y

**4:40** (4:41) (Class 5) (0-70,67) 3-Y-O **£2,911** (£866; £432; £216) **Stalls** Low

Form RPR

5002 **1** **See The Sea (IRE)**[16] 4697 3-8-9 **62** (p[1]) RossaRyan(7) 7 71
(Richard Hannon) *mde all: kicked on 3f out: drvn 2f out: rdn and over 1 l clr 1f out: r.o wl to extend advantage ins fnl f: readily* **9/2**[3]

5513 **2** *2 ½* **Kiruna Peak (IRE)**[2] 5217 3-9-2 **62** (v) CharlesBishop 3 66
(Mick Channon) *slowly away: qckly rcvrd to r in mid-div: pushed along and hdwy into 2nd 2f out: sn rdn: one pce and lost grnd on wnr fnl f* **3/1**[1]

-062 **3** *1 ¼* **Ode To Glory**[14] 4761 3-8-12 **63** JaneElliott(5) 5 65
(Rae Guest) *hld up: hdwy 3f out: 3rd and rdn 2f out: r.o one pce fnl f* **4/1**[2]

6040 **4** *1 ½* **Delannoy**[18] 4633 3-9-3 **63** (p) KieranShoemark 8 62
(Eve Johnson Houghton) *chsd ldr: pushed along 3f out: drvn and lost pl over 2f out: one pce* **8/1**

060 **5** *1 ½* **Upended**[51] 3394 3-9-3 **63** FranBerry 2 59
(Chris Wall) *hld up: pushed along over 3f out: rdn 2f out: no imp* **11/1**

0442 **6** *6* **Famous Dynasty (IRE)**[11] 4914 3-9-0 **60** DanielMuscutt 1 45
(Michael Blanshard) *trckd ldrs: pushed along 2f out: sn rdn and lost pl: wknd* **3/1**[1]

600 **7** *2* **Singing Sands (IRE)**[13] 4810 3-9-7 **67** ShaneKelly 4 48
(Seamus Durack) *slowly away: hld up: last and rdn 2f out: no rspnse: eased* **14/1**

2m 13.2s (2.20) **Going Correction** +0.175s/f (Good) 7 Ran SP% **114.3**
Speed ratings (Par 100): **98,96,95,93,92 87,86**
CSF £18.37 CT £57.54 TOTE £4.60: £2.30, £1.90; EX 19.10 Trifecta £65.50.
**Owner** Middleham Park Racing XXIX **Bred** James Doyle **Trained** East Everleigh, Wilts

**FOCUS**
Race distance increased by 5yds. A modest event which saw two of the seven runners miss the break badly, the runner-up doing well to finish as close as she did in the circumstances.

## 5276 RAINBOW CASINOS OPEN 24/7 H'CAP 1m

**5:10** (5:10) (Class 4) (0-80,78) 3-Y-O+ **£4,690** (£1,395; £697; £348) **Stalls** Low

Form RPR

6523 **1** **Fast Dancer (IRE)**[16] 4698 5-10-0 **78** FranBerry 3 87
(Joseph Tuite) *hld up: hdwy 2f out: pushed along to ld over 1f out: rdn and r.o wl to go clr ent fnl f: comf* **3/1**[1]

0544 **2** *2 ¼* **Zlatan (IRE)**[12] 4832 4-9-11 **78** (p) CallumShepherd(3) 7 82
(Ed de Giles) *trckd ldrs: hdwy gng wl 2f out: 2nd and rdn ent fnl f: r.o but wl hld by wnr* **7/2**[2]

-403 **3** *2 ¼* **With Pleasure**[20] 4538 4-9-3 **67** DanielMuscutt 8 66
(John Flint) *chsd ldr: led 2f out: rdn and hdd over 1f out: one pce fnl f* **8/1**

0265 **4** *½* **British Embassy (IRE)**[11] 4912 5-9-6 **75** (p) JoshuaBryan(5) 6 73
(Bill Turner) *led: pushed along and hdd 2f out: rdn and one pce ent fnl f* **8/1**

135 **5** *4 ½* **King Oswald (USA)**[42] 3730 4-8-13 **63** (t[1]) MartinDwyer 4 50
(James Unett) *hld up in last: hdwy over 2f out: sn drvn: no imp* **11/1**

0-50 **6** *2 ½* **Ladurelli (IRE)**[20] 4522 5-9-12 **76** SamHitchcott 5 57
(Paul Cole) *hld up: effrt and drvn 3f out: rdn 2f out: no imp* **5/1**

1100 **7** *1 ½* **Mister Musicmaster**[16] 4698 8-9-6 **70** DaneO'Neill 1 48
(Ron Hodges) *hld up: drvn 3f out: no imp last 2f: eased* **20/1**

5156 **8** *nk* **Waves (IRE)**[41] 3759 3-8-11 **69** CharlesBishop 2 44
(Eve Johnson Houghton) *prom: drvn and lost pl 2f out: reminders over 1f out: no ex* **9/2**[3]

1m 41.73s (0.93) **Going Correction** +0.175s/f (Good)
**WFA** 3 from 4yo+ 8lb 8 Ran SP% **117.4**
Speed ratings (Par 105): **102,99,97,97,92 90,88,88**
CSF £14.09 CT £76.64 TOTE £3.70: £1.30, £1.80, £2.50; EX 15.80 Trifecta £74.80.
**Owner** Alan & Christine Bright **Bred** Limetree Stud **Trained** Lambourn, Berks

**FOCUS**
Race distance increased by 5yds. Not a strong race for the grade but a taking performance from the winner in a race run at a good pace.
T/Plt: £74.30 to a £1 stake. Pool: £64,552.48 - 633.52 winning units. T/Qpdt: £9.10 to a £1 stake. Pool: £4,798.69 - 390.22 winning units. **Keith McHugh**

# 5015 CATTERICK (L-H)

Wednesday, July 26

**OFFICIAL GOING: Soft**
Wind: Fresh behind Weather: Overcast, shower after 2nd

## 5277 SPORTING LIFE PICK 7 STARTS NOW (S) STKS 7f 6y

**2:00** (2:01) (Class 6) 2-Y-O **£2,264** (£673; £336; £168) **Stalls** Low

Form RPR

3031 **1** **Placebo Effect (IRE)**[4] 5161 2-9-7 60 AndrewMullen 3 63
(Ollie Pears) *dwlt: sn in tch: pushed along to ld over 1f out: rdn and edgd rt ent fnl f: kpt on* **11/4**[2]

00 **2** *1 ¼* **Mr Carbonator**[40] 3791 2-9-1 0 PaulHanagan 7 54
(Richard Fahey) *prom: rdn to ld over 2f out: hdd over 1f out: kpt on fnl f* **7/1**[3]

05 **3** *nk* **Shovel It On (IRE)**[20] 4527 2-9-1 61 PJMcDonald 5 53
(David Evans) *hld up: pushed along 1/2-way: brought towards stands' rail in st: rdn and hdwy over 1f out: kpt on* **6/4**[1]

006 **4** *nk* **Miss Mazzie**[14] 4740 2-8-10 49 NathanEvans 1 47
(Michael Easterby) *trckd ldrs: rdn over 2f out: ev ch in centre over 1f out: one pce ins fnl f* **20/1**

0600 **5** *2* **Heavenly Pulse (IRE)**[4] 5161 2-8-8 41 SebastianWoods(7) 6 47
(Ann Duffield) *dwlt: sn chsd ldrs on outer: rdn over 2f out: wknd ins fnl f* **80/1**

60 **6** *4* **Pearl's Calling (IRE)**[18] 4597 2-8-10 0 BenCurtis 4 32
(David Barron) *hld up: rdn over 2f out: nvr threatened* **10/1**

5 **7** *8* **One Drunken Night**[45] 3619 2-8-12 0 CliffordLee(3) 2 17
(Gay Kelleway) *led: rdn whn hdd over 2f out: sn wknd* **22/1**

643 **P** **Society's Dream (IRE)**[56] 3200 2-8-10 50 JoeFanning 8
(K R Burke) *prom: lost action after 1f and eased: p.u and dismntd* **7/1**[3]

1m 32.56s (5.56) **Going Correction** +0.50s/f (Yiel) 8 Ran SP% **111.1**
Speed ratings (Par 92): **88,86,86,85,83 79,69,**
CSF £20.55 TOTE £2.60: £1.10, £2.10, £1.30; EX 23.80 Trifecta £72.10.Winner was bought in for £6,500. Mr Carbonator was claimed by Mr P Kirby for £7,000. Shovel It On was the subject of a friendly claim by Mr P D Evans for £7000
**Owner** Timothy O'Gram, Keith West & Ollie Pears **Bred** Hawaiian Dream Partnership **Trained** Norton, N Yorks

**FOCUS**
Distance increased by 6yds. An ordinary seller, they came stands' side.

## 5278 SUPPORT THE YORKSHIRE AIR AMBULANCE EBF NOVICE STKS 5f 212y

**2:30** (2:30) (Class 5) 2-Y-O **£2,911** (£866; £432; £216) **Stalls** Low

Form RPR

3522 **1** **Star Of Zaam (IRE)**[12] 4836 2-8-13 71 (p) CliffordLee(3) 9 71
(K R Burke) *trckd ldrs: upsides gng wl over 1f out: led jst ins fnl f: kpt on pushed out* **11/10**[1]

**2** *¾* **Northern Angel (IRE)** 2-8-11 0 JasonHart 5 62
(John Quinn) *trckd ldrs: pushed along over 2f out: kpt on fnl f: wnt 2nd fnl 75yds* **8/1**[3]

5 **3** *½* **Sunbreak (IRE)**[61] 3025 2-9-2 0 PJMcDonald 10 65
(Mark Johnston) *sn led: rdn over 2f out: hdd jst ins fnl f: one pce: lost 2nd fnl 75yds* **11/4**[2]

0 **4** *1 ¼* **Optimickstickhill**[26] 4296 2-8-11 0 DavidAllan 2 57
(Scott Dixon) *trckd ldrs: rdn over 2f out: ev ch over 1f out: no ex ins fnl f* **20/1**

36 **5** *1* **Duke Of Freedom**[18] 4597 2-9-2 0 GrahamLee 7 59
(Ann Duffield) *midfield: rdn along over 1f out: kpt on ins fnl f* **33/1**

**6** *nk* **By Royal Approval (IRE)** 2-9-2 0 DougieCostello 4 58
(Michael Appleby) *s.i.s: hld up in rr: rdn over 2f out: kpt on ins fnl f* **40/1**

**7** *shd* **The Auld Hoose (IRE)** 2-9-2 0 PaulHanagan 1 57
(Richard Fahey) *midfield: pushed along over 2f out: kpt on ins fnl f* **9/1**

5 **8** *2 ¼* **Le Gros Serpant (IRE)**[6] 5068 2-8-11 0 RowanScott(5) 3 51
(Keith Dalgleish) *dwlt: hld up: sn pushed along: nvr threatened* **33/1**

50 **9** *4* **Ladycammyofclare (IRE)**[16] 4689 2-8-11 0 JoeFanning 6 34+
(Mark Johnston) *prom: rdn over 2f out: wknd fnl f* **20/1**

**10** *15* **Arabellas Fortune** 2-8-11 0 PaulMulrennan 8
(James Ewart) *dwlt: a in rr: eased fr over 1f out* **40/1**

1m 17.38s (3.78) **Going Correction** +0.50s/f (Yiel) 10 Ran SP% **115.7**
Speed ratings (Par 94): **94,93,92,90,89 88,88,85,80,60**
CSF £9.51 TOTE £1.80: £1.10, £2.30, £1.10; EX 11.10 Trifecta £31.40.
**Owner** Hambleton Racing Ltd III & E Burke **Bred** Sonia Brannigan **Trained** Middleham Moor, N Yorks

**FOCUS**
Distance increased by 6yds. Ordinary novice form.

## 5279 WATCH RACING UK ON BT TV NURSERY H'CAP 7f 6y

**3:00** (3:00) (Class 5) 2-Y-O **£2,911** (£866; £432; £216) **Stalls** Low

Form RPR

4024 **1** **Go Now Go Now (IRE)**[32] 4101 2-8-13 **66** PJMcDonald 4 67
(Mark Johnston) *led after 1f: mde rest: rdn over 2f out: strly pressed thrght fnl f: hld on wl* **7/2**[2]

303 **2** *nk* **Crownthorpe**[57] 3187 2-9-2 **69** TonyHamilton 2 69
(Richard Fahey) *chsd ldrs: rdn 2f out: chal ins fnl f: kpt on* **9/2**[3]

6013 **3** *½* **Faradays Spark (IRE)**[21] 4504 2-8-9 **62** PaulHanagan 1 61
(Richard Fahey) *hld up: sn pushed along: styd on fnl f: nrst fin* **5/1**

4013 **4** *hd* **Seaella (IRE)**[13] 4786 2-9-2 **74** LewisEdmunds(5) 3 74
(John Quinn) *trckd ldrs: pushed along and bit short of room over 1f out: rdn and kpt on ins fnl f* **2/1**[1]

440 **5** *hd* **Situation**[11] 4895 2-8-12 **68** CliffordLee(3) 5 66
(Richard Guest) *led for 1f: remained cl up: rdn over 2f out: no ex fnl 75yds* **33/1**

3565 **6** *nk* **Felisa**[42] 3712 2-9-0 **67** AndrewMullen 7 64
(David Evans) *hld up in tch: rdn over 2f out: sme hdwy over 1f out: kpt on same pce fnl f* **8/1**

305 **7** *2 ½* **Aristodemus (IRE)**[21] 4502 2-8-4 **60** RachelRichardson(3) 6 51
(Tim Easterby) *trckd ldrs: racd keenly: rdn over 2f out: wknd fnl f* **12/1**

1m 31.8s (4.80) **Going Correction** +0.50s/f (Yiel) 7 Ran SP% **112.1**
Speed ratings (Par 94): **92,91,91,90,90 90,87**
CSF £18.74 TOTE £3.90: £1.80, £2.50; EX 22.40 Trifecta £116.10.
**Owner** Paul & Clare Rooney **Bred** Gerry Ross **Trained** Middleham Moor, N Yorks

**FOCUS**
Distance increased by 6yds. A modest nursery and they finished well bunched.

## 5280 AUGUST 18TH IS LADIES' EVENING CLAIMING STKS 7f 6y
**3:30** (3:32) (Class 6) 3-4-Y-0 **£2,264** (£673; £336; £168) **Stalls** Low

| Form | | | | RPR |
|---|---|---|---|---|
| 353 | 1 | | **Bernie's Boy**[14] 4743 4-8-12 65..............(p) BenSanderson(7) 8 (Roger Fell) *mde all: rdn over 1f out: kpt on* **5/1** | 72 |
| 2-00 | 2 | 3/4 | **Dyllan (IRE)**[21] 4489 4-9-9 71.............. JamesSullivan 3 (Ruth Carr) *dwlt sltly but sn prom: rdn 2f out: one pce and a hld* **14/1** | 74 |
| 1203 | 3 | 1 1/4 | **Ancient Astronaut**[18] 4629 4-9-10 77..............(h) JasonHart 5 (John Quinn) *early reminders: sn in tch: rdn to chse ldrs over 1f out: one pce* **9/4**[1] | 72 |
| 0035 | 4 | 2 | **Tadaawol**[8] 4999 4-9-8 72..............(p) TonyHamilton 6 (Roger Fell) *hld up in tch: rdn over 2f out: one pce and nvr threatened* **4/1**[3] | 65 |
| 0033 | 5 | 1 1/2 | **Oakley Pride (IRE)**[15] 4726 3-8-8 60..............(vt) CliffordLee(3) 4 (Gay Kelleway) *dwlt: hld up: rdn over 2f out: nvr threatened* **11/1** | 54 |
| -004 | 6 | 8 | **Lonely The Brave (IRE)**[18] 4609 3-8-12 73.............. PJMcDonald 2 (Mark Johnston) *chsd ldrs: rdn and lost pl over 2f out: wknd over 1f out* **11/4**[2] | 35 |

1m 29.31s (2.31) **Going Correction** +0.50s/f (Yiel)
**WFA** 3 from 4yo 7lb **6** Ran SP% **109.1**
Speed ratings (Par 101): **106,105,103,101,99 90**
CSF £59.99 TOTE £5.00: £2.20, £4.30; EX 65.10 Trifecta £325.60.The winner was claimed by Mr I J Jardine for £10,000.
**Owner** R G Fell **Bred** Mrs Eleanor Kent **Trained** Nawton, N Yorks
**FOCUS**
Distance increased by 6yds. The market leaders didn't live up to expectations in a race where it paid to race prominently. The runner-up looks the key form horse.

## 5281 SKY BET GO-RACING-IN-YORKSHIRE SUMMER FESTIVAL H'CAP 5f
**4:00** (4:01) (Class 4) (0-85,91) 3-Y-0+ **£6,469** (£1,925; £962; £481) **Stalls** Low

| Form | | | | RPR |
|---|---|---|---|---|
| 0001 | 1 | | **Glenrowan Rose (IRE)**[5] 5093 4-10-4 91 6ex.............. ConnorBeasley 6 (Keith Dalgleish) *mde all: rdn over 1f out: kpt on: comf* **2/1**[1] | 102+ |
| 4643 | 2 | 2 1/4 | **Landing Night (IRE)**[5] 5098 5-8-13 72..............(tp) PJMcDonald 4 (Rebecca Menzies) *dwlt: hld up: rdn 2f out: kpt on to go 2nd ins fnl f: no ch w wnr* **10/3**[3] | 74 |
| 30-2 | 3 | 1 1/2 | **Fumbo Jumbo (IRE)**[25] 4379 4-9-6 84.............. CallumRodriguez(5) 2 (Michael Dods) *chsd ldr: rdn 2f out: no ex and ins fnl f* **5/2**[2] | 81 |
| 0064 | 4 | 4 1/2 | **Olivia Fallow (IRE)**[13] 4787 5-9-8 81..............(v[1]) GrahamLee 7 (Paul Midgley) *prom: rdn over 2f out: wknd over 1f out* **7/1** | 61 |
| 0300 | 5 | 9 | **Indian Pursuit (IRE)**[23] 4433 4-8-7 66 oh2.............. JasonHart 1 (John Quinn) *chsd ldrs: rdn over 2f out: wknd over 1f out* **8/1** | 14 |

1m 0.54s (0.74) **Going Correction** +0.275s/f (Good) **5** Ran SP% **108.6**
Speed ratings (Par 105): **105,101,99,91,77**
CSF £8.64 TOTE £2.20: £2.00, £1.70; EX 10.20 Trifecta £20.30.
**Owner** Weldspec Glasgow Limited **Bred** Tipper House Stud **Trained** Carluke, S Lanarks
**FOCUS**
Distance as advertised. A fair sprint that was dominated by the top weight.

## 5282 NEVER MISS A RACE ON RACING UK H'CAP (DIV I) 5f 212y
**4:30** (4:30) (Class 6) (0-60,64) 3-Y-0+ **£2,264** (£673; £336; £168) **Stalls** Low

| Form | | | | RPR |
|---|---|---|---|---|
| 4442 | 1 | | **Cupid's Arrow (IRE)**[14] 4744 3-9-5 60.............. JamesSullivan 5 (Ruth Carr) *trckd ldrs: pushed along to ld appr fnl f: rdn out ins fnl f: edgd lft fnl 75yds* **5/4**[1] | 65 |
| 0340 | 2 | 1 3/4 | **Goadby**[18] 4619 6-8-6 47..............(v) RichardOliver(5) 4 (John Holt) *hld up: rdn over 2f out: hdwy appr fnl f: kpt on* **12/1** | 47 |
| 0060 | 3 | nk | **Jess**[133] 1200 4-9-2 52..............(p) TomEaves 10 (Kevin Ryan) *in tch on outside: brought towards stands' rail st: rdn 2f out: kpt on fnl f* **50/1** | 51 |
| 0500 | 4 | 1 | **Firesnake (IRE)**[21] 4509 4-8-13 54..............(v) CallumRodriguez(5) 9 (Lisa Williamson) *midfield: rdn over 2f out: kpt on same pce* **16/1** | 50 |
| 0065 | 5 | 3/4 | **Mercers Row**[7] 5016 10-8-7 50.............. SeamusCronin(7) 2 (Michael Herrington) *dwlt: hld up: rdn and sme hdwy over 1f out: kpt on fnl f: nvr threatened* **12/1** | 44 |
| 0006 | 6 | 1 | **Trick Of The Lyte (IRE)**[14] 4745 3-8-12 53.............. JasonHart 11 (John Quinn) *hld up: rdn 2f out: nvr threatened* **9/1**[3] | 43 |
| 2150 | 7 | 2 | **Sir Geoffrey (IRE)**[16] 4695 11-8-10 51..............(b) LewisEdmunds(5) 8 (Scott Dixon) *sn led: rdn over 2f out: hdd over 1f out: sn wknd* **10/1** | 36 |
| 3150 | 8 | 3/4 | **Lackaday**[16] 4682 5-9-9 59..............(p) PatrickMathers 7 (Noel Wilson) *prom: rdn over 2f out: led over 1f out: hdd appr fnl f: wknd* **13/2**[2] | 41 |
| 0404 | 9 | 20 | **Spike (IRE)**[7] 5016 4-9-1 51..............(b) PaulMulrennan 1 (Donald McCain) *midfield: rdn over 2f out: wknd over 1f out and eased* **13/2**[2] | |

1m 16.49s (2.89) **Going Correction** +0.50s/f (Yiel)
**WFA** 3 from 4yo+ 5lb **9** Ran SP% **113.4**
Speed ratings (Par 101): **100,97,97,95,94 93,90,89,63**
CSF £17.58 CT £494.40 TOTE £1.90: £1.10, £3.50, £5.70; EX 22.50 Trifecta £597.80.
**Owner** Miss Vanessa Church **Bred** Liam Foley **Trained** Huby, N Yorks
**FOCUS**
Distance increased by 6yds. Moderate sprinting form but a nice performance from the winner.

## 5283 NEVER MISS A RACE ON RACING UK H'CAP (DIV II) 5f 212y
**5:00** (5:00) (Class 6) (0-60,60) 3-Y-0+ **£2,264** (£673; £336; £168) **Stalls** Low

| Form | | | | RPR |
|---|---|---|---|---|
| 0000 | 1 | | **Be Bold**[8] 4997 5-9-10 60..............(b) ConnorBeasley 10 (Rebecca Bastiman) *chsd ldrs: rdn to ld over 1f out: kpt on* **13/2** | 68 |
| 6402 | 2 | 1 | **Deben**[7] 5016 4-8-11 50.............. CliffordLee(3) 7 (John Weymes) *in tch on outer: hdwy 2f out: rdn to chse ldr appr fnl f: kpt on* **9/2**[2] | 55 |
| 0530 | 3 | 2 | **Whipphound**[13] 4789 9-8-11 47..............(p) JamesSullivan 11 (Ruth Carr) *hld up: rdn and hdwy over 1f out: kpt on fnl f* **5/1**[3] | 46 |
| 060 | 4 | 1 1/2 | **Cryptonite (IRE)**[9] 4983 3-8-10 58..............(b[1]) RayDawson(7) 2 (Michael Appleby) *dwlt: hld up: hdwy into midfield 1/2-way: rdn to chse ldrs 2f out: no ex ins fnl f* **8/1** | 52 |
| 5006 | 5 | nk | **Bold Spirit**[7] 5016 6-9-0 55..............(vt) PhilDennis(5) 3 (Declan Carroll) *led narrowly: rdn whn hdd over 1f out: grad wknd* **9/1** | 49 |
| 0-50 | 6 | 3 3/4 | **Nellie Deen (IRE)**[8] 5007 4-9-5 55..............(p) TonyHamilton 5 (Roger Fell) *pressed ldrs: rdn over 2f out: wknd fnl f* **33/1** | 37 |
| 0265 | 7 | 1 | **Misu Moneypenny**[27] 4246 4-9-3 53..............(p) DavidAllan 8 (Scott Dixon) *hld up: nvr threatened* **12/1** | 32 |
| 0006 | 8 | 1 3/4 | **Diamond Avalanche (IRE)**[7] 5019 4-8-10 46..............(v[1]) JoeFanning 9 (Patrick Holmes) *a outpcd in rr* **22/1** | 20 |
| -503 | 9 | 1 1/4 | **Kroy**[51] 3403 3-9-2 57..............(p) AndrewMullen 4 (Ollie Pears) *midfield: pushed along whn bmpd 3f out: lost pl and sn btn* **11/4**[1] | 26 |
| 0005 | 10 | 3 | **Emerald Secret (IRE)**[8] 5004 3-9-1 56..............(p) GrahamLee 1 (Paul Midgley) *in tch: rdn over 2f out: wknd over 1f out* **22/1** | 16 |

1m 15.56s (1.96) **Going Correction** +0.50s/f (Yiel)
**WFA** 3 from 4yo+ 5lb **10** Ran SP% **115.3**
Speed ratings (Par 101): **106,104,102,100,99 94,93,90,89,85**
CSF £34.53 CT £158.96 TOTE £6.90: £2.50, £1.80, £1.80; EX 40.20 Trifecta £247.90.
**Owner** Ms M Austerfield **Bred** Simon Balding **Trained** Cowthorpe, N Yorks
**FOCUS**
Distance increased by 6yds. Perhaps just the lesser of the two divisions, but the winner has been rated near his best.

## 5284 CATTERICKBRIDGE.CO.UK APPRENTICE TRAINING SERIES H'CAP (PART OF THE RACING EXCELLENCE INITIATIVE) 1m 4f 13y
**5:30** (5:31) (Class 6) (0-65,71) 4-Y-0+ **£2,264** (£673; £336; £168) **Stalls** Low

| Form | | | | RPR |
|---|---|---|---|---|
| 3325 | 1 | | **Canny Style**[19] 4571 4-9-9 67.............. SeamusCronin(5) 11 (Kevin Ryan) *trckd ldrs: led 2f out: rdn and strly pressed fnl f: hld on wl* **9/2**[3] | 72 |
| 34-6 | 2 | nk | **Angel In The Snow**[41] 3756 4-8-8 47.............. BenRobinson 8 (Brian Ellison) *in tch: hdwy 2f out: rdn to chal strly fnl f: kpt on but hld* **4/1**[2] | 52 |
| 00-0 | 3 | 1/2 | **Almutamarred (USA)**[55] 3252 5-8-13 52.............. KevinLundie 4 (David Brown) *midfield: hdwy to chse ldrs over 1f out: rdn and kpt on* **50/1** | 56 |
| 3250 | 4 | 3 1/2 | **Yensir**[16] 4690 4-9-13 66.............. PatrickVaughan 6 (Grant Tuer) *midfield towards outer: racd quite keenly: rdn and hdwy over 1f out: no ex fnl f* **15/2** | 65 |
| 0466 | 5 | 1/2 | **Competition**[19] 4575 5-9-2 58..............(t) JamieGormley(3) 7 (Brian Rothwell) *midfield: rdn over 2f out: no imp* **14/1** | 56 |
| 6502 | 6 | 1 1/2 | **King Of The Celts (IRE)**[7] 5021 9-9-5 63..............(p) HannahWorrall(5) 9 (Tim Easterby) *led: rn wd on bnd over 8f out and hdd: trckd ldr: rdn over 2f out: wknd over 1f out* **12/1** | 59 |
| 6321 | 7 | 1/2 | **Swansway**[7] 5021 4-9-13 71 6ex.............. HarrisonShaw(5) 10 (Michael Easterby) *in tch: rdn over 2f out: wknd fnl f* **3/1**[1] | 66 |
| 0036 | 8 | 1/2 | **Fillydelphia (IRE)**[7] 5017 6-8-13 52..............(h) PaulaMuir 5 (Patrick Holmes) *hld up in midfield: pushed along over 2f out: nvr threatened* **20/1** | 47 |
| 0200 | 9 | 1 1/4 | **Cockney Boy**[58] 3143 4-9-0 53.............. RayDawson 1 (Michael Appleby) *prom: led over 8f out: rdn whn hdd 2f out: wknd over 1f out* **25/1** | 46 |
| -046 | 10 | 6 | **Sherman McCoy**[7] 5021 11-8-10 54.............. RyanTimby(5) 2 (Marjorie Fife) *a in rr* **14/1** | 38 |
| 65-0 | 11 | 7 | **Cloud Monkey (IRE)**[105] 1716 7-10-0 67.............. CallumRodriguez 3 (Martin Todhunter) *a in rr* **9/1** | 40 |

2m 46.08s (7.18) **Going Correction** +0.50s/f (Yiel) **11** Ran SP% **116.5**
Speed ratings (Par 101): **96,95,95,93,92 91,91,91,90,86 81**
CSF £22.11 CT £793.47 TOTE £5.20: £1.80, £1.80, £8.20; EX 30.60 Trifecta £666.60.
**Owner** Hambleton Racing Ltd XXXVII **Bred** Biddestone Stud Ltd **Trained** Hambleton, N Yorks
**FOCUS**
Distance increased by 6yds. Two of the market leaders came to the fore in this moderate handicap.
T/Plt: £61.10 to a £1 stake. Pool: £61,389.02 - 732.54 winning units. T/Qpdt: £45.90 to a £1 stake. Pool: £3,164.33 - 51.0 winning units. **Andrew Sheret**

# 5075 LEICESTER (R-H)
Wednesday, July 26

**OFFICIAL GOING: Soft**
Wind: Fresh behind Weather: Cloudy

## 5285 BETFAIR NOVICE AMATEUR RIDERS' H'CAP 7f
**5:45** (5:45) (Class 6) (0-60,59) 4-Y-0+ **£2,495** (£774; £386; £193) **Stalls** High

| Form | | | | RPR |
|---|---|---|---|---|
| 0331 | 1 | | **Carlovian**[14] 4743 4-10-10 48..............(p) MrWJMilburn 14 (Mark Walford) *chsd ldrs: pushed along and hung rt fr 2f out: led over 1f out: styd on* **7/2**[1] | 55 |
| 5604 | 2 | 1 3/4 | **Danot (IRE)**[14] 4743 5-11-0 55..............(p) MissACawley(3) 3 (Jedd O'Keeffe) *a.p: jnd ldr over 4f out: led over 2f out: rdn and hdd over 1f out: styd on same pce wl ins fnl f* **5/1**[2] | 58 |
| -005 | 3 | 1 3/4 | **Jacksonfire**[30] 4149 5-10-7 45..............(p) MrLewisStones 11 (Michael Mullineaux) *prom: pushed along 1/2-way: outpcd over 2f out: rallied u.p over 1f out: r.o to go 3rd wl ins fnl f: nt rch ldrs* **16/1** | 44 |
| 000- | 4 | 1 1/2 | **Nightswift**[249] 8039 5-10-9 50.............. MissEmmaYardley(3) 7 (James Evans) *hld up: rdn over 2f out: styd on fr over 1f out: nt rch ldrs* **16/1** | 45 |
| 004 | 5 | 1/2 | **Baron Run**[11] 4897 7-11-2 57.............. MrJCummins(3) 13 (K R Burke) *led: rdn and hdd over 2f out: wknd wl ins fnl f* **20/1** | 51 |
| -644 | 6 | 1 | **Tommy's Secret**[42] 3731 7-11-4 56..............(p) MissAmyTaylor 1 (Jane Chapple-Hyam) *sn outpcd: styd on fr over 1f out: nt trble ldrs* **13/2** | 47 |
| 0431 | 7 | 7 | **Dark Confidant (IRE)**[12] 4833 4-11-7 59.............. MissEllaMcCain 6 (Donald McCain) *chsd ldr 2f: remained handy: rdn 1/2-way: wknd 2f out* **15/2** | 33 |
| 000 | 8 | nk | **Tilsworth Lukey**[50] 3438 4-10-7 45.............. PoppyBridgwater 5 (J R Jenkins) *hld up: pushed along over 4f out: hdwy 1/2-way: rdn and wknd wl over 1f out* **66/1** | 18 |
| 1553 | 9 | nk | **Intimately**[22] 4459 4-11-3 58.............. MrScottSainsbury(3) 2 (Jonathan Portman) *s.s: hld up: rdn over 2f out: n.d* **6/1**[3] | 30 |
| 4-30 | 10 | 10 | **Munaawib**[23] 4453 9-11-4 59..............(bt) MissSPeacock(3) 4 (Ray Peacock) *prom tl rdn and wknd over 2f out* **50/1** | 6 |
| 00 | 11 | nk | **Keene's Pointe**[63] 2961 7-10-11 52..............(p) MrSHawkins(3) 8 (Steph Hollinshead) *s.s and rel to r: a bhd* **16/1** | + |
| 6053 | 12 | 5 | **Kingfisher Girl**[26] 4323 4-10-7 45..............(tp) MrJamesKendrick 9 (Michael Appleby) *hld up: pushed along 1/2-way: rdn and wkng whn hung rt over 2f out* **10/1** | |

1m 27.82s (1.62) **Going Correction** +0.175s/f (Good) **12** Ran SP% **113.2**
Speed ratings (Par 101): **97,95,93,91,90 89,81,80,80,69 69,63**
CSF £18.78 CT £244.92 TOTE £3.70: £1.60, £2.40, £4.60; EX 19.20 Trifecta £521.60.
**Owner** Profit Pony Racing **Bred** Bradmill Meats Ltd **Trained** Sherriff Hutton, N Yorks

**FOCUS**
6mm of rain hit the track in the morning which led to an official description of soft. A race for amateur riders' who had ridden less than three winners at the start of the season and, typical of such a race, it is weak form.

## 5286 MEDBOURNE (S) STKS 1m 53y
6:15 (6:18) (Class 6) 3-Y-O £2,587 (£770; £384; £192) Stalls Low

Form RPR
033 1 **Dreamofdiscovery (IRE)**65 2902 3-8-12 58....................(p1) JoeDoyle 2 60
(Julie Camacho) *trckd ldrs: led on bit over 2f out: rdn over 1f out: styd on u.p: edgd lft towards fin* 9/4[2]
6434 2 nk **Tenby Two**8 4994 3-8-7 59.................... BenCurtis 3 54
(Mick Channon) *sn pushed along in rr: hdwy over 3f out: rdn and ev ch fr over 2f out: nt run on* 6/4[1]
-506 3 11 **Scarlet Thrush (IRE)**20 4541 3-8-4 62.................... GeorgeWood(3) 5 30
(Marco Botti) *chsd ldr: stmbld over 5f out: rdn over 3f out: wknd 2f out* 7/2[3]
6000 4 3/4 **Flawed Diamond (FR)**27 4289 3-8-7 51....................(v1) JoeyHaynes 1 28
(K R Burke) *led: clr over 3f out: rdn and hdd over 2f out: wknd over 1f out* 8/1
60 5 7 **Oscar Ranger (IRE)**25 4341 3-8-5 0....................(b1) ConnorMurtagh(7) 4 18
(Richard Fahey) *difficult to load into the stalls: s.i.s: hld up: drvn along over 4f out: wknd over 3f out* 16/1

1m 48.86s (3.76) **Going Correction** +0.50s/f (Yiel) 5 Ran SP% 110.0
Speed ratings (Par 98): **101,100,89,88,81**
CSF £6.03 TOTE £2.90: £1.20, £1.50; EX 5.40 Trifecta £12.60.There was no bid for the winner
**Owner** Ridge Ahkong Caine & Camacho **Bred** Palmerston Bloodstock Ltd **Trained** Norton, N Yorks

**FOCUS**
Little in the way of convincing form and, with three trying headgear for the first-time, this was weak even by selling race standards. It's been rated around the winner.

## 5287 TOM CRIBB H'CAP 1m 3f 179y
6:45 (6:46) (Class 4) (0-85,87) 4-Y-O+ £5,175 (£1,540; £769; £384) Stalls Low

Form RPR
-336 1 **Compton Mill**20 4522 5-8-11 78.................... CharlieBennett(3) 6 87
(Hughie Morrison) *hld up: hdwy 1/2-way: rdn to ld over 1f out: edgd rt ins fnl f: styd on wl* 4/1[2]
002 2 2 **Deinonychus**27 4279 6-8-0 67.................... GeorgeWood(3) 8 73
(Michael Appleby) *racd keenly: led 1f: remained w ldr tl settled into 2nd pl over 7f out: led again over 3f out: rdn and hdd over 1f out: styd on same pce ins fnl f* 14/1
-045 3 1/2 **William Hunter**74 2603 5-9-7 85.................... FergusSweeney 1 90
(Alan King) *hld up in tch: nt clr run over 3f out: rdn and ev ch over 1f out: styd on same pce ins fnl f* 7/1[3]
4632 4 3/4 **Chancery (USA)**13 4796 9-9-7 85....................(p) DavidNolan 3 89
(David O'Meara) *hld up: rdn over 2f out: styd on fr over 1f out: nt clr run towards fin: nt rch ldrs* 12/1
6010 5 nk **Swaheen**28 4206 5-9-3 81.................... JoeDoyle 2 84
(Julie Camacho) *prom: rdn over 2f out: kpt on* 17/2
-522 6 1/2 **New World Power (JPN)**15 4712 4-9-5 83.................... OisinMurphy 5 86
(David Simcock) *s.i.s: hld up: rdn over 2f out: styd on appr fnl f: nt rch ldrs* 11/4[1]
0400 7 22 **Vettori Rules**11 4882 4-9-8 86.................... TomQueally 10 53
(Gay Kelleway) *racd keenly: prom: led over 7f out: rdn and hdd over 3f out: wknd over 1f out* 40/1
6 8 1 3/4 **Visandi (FR)**19 4586 5-9-2 80.................... JackGarritty 4 45
(Jonjo O'Neill) *pushed along to ld after 1f: hdd over 7f out: remained handy: rdn over 3f out: wknd over 2f out* 50/1
-030 9 4 1/2 **Silca Star**28 4216 4-8-10 74 ow1.................... RobertTart 9 31
(Alan King) *unruly in stalls: s.i.s: hld up: pushed along and hdwy over 3f out: rdn and wknd over 2f out* 9/1

2m 38.13s (4.23) **Going Correction** +0.50s/f (Yiel) 9 Ran SP% 98.5
Speed ratings (Par 105): **105,103,103,102,102 102,87,86,83**
CSF £41.95 CT £234.55 TOTE £4.80: £2.10, £3.20, £1.80; EX 51.10 Trifecta £256.70.
**Owner** M T Bevan **Bred** M E Broughton **Trained** East Ilsley, Berks
■ Zzore was withdrawn. Price at time of withdrawal was 6-1. Rule 4 applies to all bets. Deduction - 10p in the pound.

**FOCUS**
No more than a fair handicap.

## 5288 THISTLETON GAP H'CAP 7f
7:20 (7:21) (Class 4) (0-80,81) 3-Y-O+ £6,301 (£1,886; £943; £472; £235) Stalls High

Form RPR
0111 1 **Pursuing Steed**27 4251 3-9-3 76.................... CharlieBennett(3) 9 82+
(Hughie Morrison) *hld up: hdwy over 1f out: sn chsng ldr: rdn and r.o to ld post* 2/1[1]
0326 2 shd **Flyboy (IRE)**32 4103 4-9-6 76....................(b) ConnorMurtagh(7) 3 84
(Richard Fahey) *s.i.s: hld up: hdwy over 2f out: rdn to ld over 1f out: hdd post* 5/1[2]
0414 3 3/4 **Hajjam**19 4557 3-9-5 75....................(h) DavidNolan 2 78
(David O'Meara) *chsd ldrs: rdn over 1f out: edgd rt: r.o* 8/1[3]
0222 4 1/2 **Kirkham**21 4506 4-9-5 68....................(p) JoeDoyle 11 72
(Julie Camacho) *hld up in tch: rdn over 1f out: edgd rt ins fnl f: r.o* 11/1
1504 5 3 3/4 **African Blessing**5 5119 4-9-8 71.................... BenCurtis 8 66
(David Barron) *chsd ldr tl rdn over 2f out: sn outpcd: swtchd rt over 1f out: r.o ins fnl f* 8/1[3]
0104 6 shd **Zapper Cass (FR)**3 5184 4-10-1 81....................(t) JoshDoyle(3) 5 75
(Tony Coyle) *s.i.s: hld up: hdwy u.p over 1f out: no ex ins fnl f* 16/1
1460 7 3/4 **Merdon Castle (IRE)**16 4683 5-10-0 77....................(e) JackGarritty 7 70
(Ruth Carr) *prom: hmpd and lost pl 4f out: rdn over 2f out: n.d after* 40/1
401 8 shd **Warsaw Road (IRE)**39 3824 3-9-4 77.................... GeorgeWood(3) 4 66
(Luca Cumani) *prom: racd keenly: rdn over 2f out: wknd fnl f* 8/1[3]
2-00 9 nk **Tadaany (IRE)**67 2838 5-10-0 77.................... OisinMurphy 6 68
(David O'Meara) *led: rdn and hdd over 1f out: wknd fnl f* 10/1
0052 10 3/4 **Sophisticated Heir (IRE)**23 4451 7-9-10 73.................... DougieCostello 1 63
(Kevin Frost) *chsd ldrs: shkn up over 2f out: wknd over 1f out* 66/1
4150 11 4 **Jet Setter (IRE)**26 4290 3-8-11 67.................... GeorgeDowning 10 43
(Tony Carroll) *hld up: rdn over 2f out: n.d* 28/1

1m 25.97s (-0.23) **Going Correction** +0.175s/f (Good)
**WFA** 3 from 4yo+ 7lb 11 Ran SP% 114.0
Speed ratings (Par 105): **108,107,107,106,102 102,101,101,100,99 95**
CSF £10.75 CT £65.30 TOTE £2.60: £1.20, £1.60, £3.10; EX 14.00 Trifecta £87.20.
**Owner** Caveat Emptor Partnership **Bred** A E Smith And Co **Trained** East Ilsley, Berks

**FOCUS**
Plenty held chances in this fair handicap. They went a good pace and eventually elected to come down the centre.

## 5289 BREEDERS BACKING RACING EBF MAIDEN STKS 5f
7:50 (7:51) (Class 5) 3-Y-O+ £4,528 (£1,347; £673; £336) Stalls High

Form RPR
2 1 **Indian Raj**25 4368 3-9-5 0.................... OisinMurphy 5 70+
(Stuart Williams) *s.i.s: sn prom: shkn up to ld over 1f out: pushed out* 2/7[1]
0565 2 2 3/4 **Tea El Tee (IRE)**7 5040 3-8-12 50....................(v1) CameronNoble(7) 4 60
(Gay Kelleway) *w ldr tl led 1/2-way: rdn and hdd over 1f out: styd on same pce ins fnl f* 25/1
-404 3 nk **Tawaafoq**60 3085 3-9-5 69.................... FrannyNorton 6 59
(Mick Quinn) *racd alone on stands' side: led to 1/2-way: sn hung rt: rdn over 1f out: no ex ins fnl f* 3/1[2]
4 23 **Swing Time (IRE)** 3-9-5 0.................... JasonHart 3
(Eric Alston) *rn green and hung rt thrght: chsd ldr: lost pl over 3f out: sn bhd* 11/1[3]
5 9 **Tina Teaspoon** 3-8-11 0.................... AaronJones(3) 1
(Derek Shaw) *s.s: outpcd* 50/1

1m 1.32s (1.32) **Going Correction** +0.175s/f (Good) 5 Ran SP% 116.9
Speed ratings (Par 103): **96,91,91,54,39**
CSF £12.08 TOTE £1.20: £1.10, £6.70; EX 8.60 Trifecta £12.30.
**Owner** D A Shekells **Bred** Old Mill Stud & S Williams & J Parry **Trained** Newmarket, Suffolk

**FOCUS**
Weak form and things went to plan for the short-priced favourite.

## 5290 MELTON MOWBRAY FILLIES' H'CAP 1m 2f
8:20 (8:24) (Class 5) (0-70,71) 4-Y-O+ £3,234 (£962; £481; £240) Stalls Low

Form RPR
0651 1 **Inflexiball**25 4344 5-8-9 58.................... FrannyNorton 1 66
(John Mackie) *trckd ldr 4f: remained handy: wnt 2nd again over 3f out: led over 2f out: rdn and hung lft fr over 1f out: styd on gamely* 4/1[2]
0660 2 shd **Rayaa**18 4621 4-9-2 65....................(t) TomQueally 8 72
(John Butler) *hld up: hdwy over 2f out: ev ch fr over 1f out: sn rdn: carried lft ins fnl f: styd on* 7/2[1]
00P6 3 1 1/4 **Ejayteekay**14 4746 4-9-5 71.................... CharlieBennett(3) 3 75
(Hughie Morrison) *s.i.s: hld up: hdwy over 5f out: swtchd lft over 2f out: rdn and nt clr run over 1f out: styd on* 6/1[3]
3443 4 2 1/4 **Angelical (IRE)**32 4088 4-8-11 60....................(p) DougieCostello 11 60
(Daniel Mark Loughnane) *hld up: rdn over 2f out: r.o ins fnl f: nt rch ldrs* 7/1
30-0 5 shd **Enchanted Moment**18 4627 5-7-12 54....................(p) DarraghKeenan(7) 10 54
(Olly Murphy) *s.i.s: hld up: hdwy over 2f out: rdn over 1f out: no ex ins fnl f* 10/1
0003 6 1 3/4 **Imperial Link**18 4626 5-8-2 51 oh3....................(v) JimmyQuinn 4 47
(John O'Shea) *led: qcknd over 3f out: rdn and hdd over 2f out: edgd lft and no ex ins fnl f* 14/1
5131 7 7 **Percys Princess**19 4572 6-8-13 67.................... JaneElliott(5) 7 49
(Michael Appleby) *chsd ldrs: lost pl 6f out: hdwy and hung rt fr over 4f out: wknd 3f out* 7/1
3005 8 3 **Sister Dude**22 4470 4-8-9 63.................... MitchGodwin(5) 6 39
(Jonathan Portman) *prom: chsd ldr 6f out tl rdn over 3f out: wknd over 1f out* 14/1
5-26 9 20 **Dora's Field (IRE)**57 3168 4-9-7 70....................(p1) OisinMurphy 5 6
(Stuart Kittow) *hld up: plld hrd: hdwy over 5f out: rdn and wknd over 2f out* 8/1

2m 13.11s (5.21) **Going Correction** +0.50s/f (Yiel) 9 Ran SP% 115.0
Speed ratings (Par 100): **99,98,97,96,96 94,89,86,70**
CSF £18.35 CT £82.34 TOTE £4.60: £1.80, £1.50, £2.10; EX 18.80 Trifecta £64.70.
**Owner** Derbyshire Racing II **Bred** Derbyshire Racing **Trained** Church Broughton , Derbys
■ Dream Voice was withdrawn. Price at time of withdrawal 33-1. Rule 4 does not apply.

**FOCUS**
A tight finish to this modest fillies' handicap, with the winner showing a good attitude to hold off the gamble of the race.

## 5291 MOLYNEUX H'CAP 6f
8:50 (8:51) (Class 5) (0-70,68) 3-Y-O £3,234 (£962; £481; £240) Stalls High

Form RPR
0-36 1 **Gaval**51 3403 3-9-2 63.................... BenCurtis 7 74+
(David Barron) *chsd ldr: rdn to ld 1f out: r.o* 11/2
506 2 2 **Deciding Vote**25 4341 3-8-6 56.................... GeorgeWood(3) 4 60
(Chris Wall) *chsd ldrs: rdn over 2f out: r.o to go 2nd nr fin* 9/1
0301 3 1/2 **Chickenfortea (IRE)**14 4745 3-9-5 66.................... JasonHart 2 68
(Eric Alston) *led: rdn and hdd 1f out: styd on same pce ins fnl f* 9/2[3]
6245 4 nk **Peachey Carnehan**12 4843 3-9-1 65....................(v) CharlieBennett(3) 8 66
(Michael Mullineaux) *hld up: rdn 1/2-way: hdwy u.p over 1f out: nt rch ldrs* 25/1
0022 5 2 3/4 **Majestic Stone (IRE)**26 4303 3-8-8 55....................(v) JoeDoyle 1 47
(Julie Camacho) *chsd ldrs: rdn over 2f out: wknd ins fnl f* 3/1[2]
0-02 6 1 1/2 **Canadian Royal**7 5040 3-8-10 57....................(t) OisinMurphy 5 44
(Stuart Williams) *hld up: rdn over 1f out: wknd fnl f* 2/1[1]
1460 7 shd **Brother In Arms (IRE)**38 3870 3-9-2 63.................... GeorgeDowning 6 50
(Tony Carroll) *hld up: rdn 1/2-way: n.d* 25/1

1m 13.45s (0.45) **Going Correction** +0.175s/f (Good) 7 Ran SP% 109.6
Speed ratings (Par 100): **104,101,100,100,96 94,94**
CSF £47.75 CT £221.06 TOTE £6.10: £3.10, £4.30; EX 57.30 Trifecta £218.40.
**Owner** Bearstone Stud Limited **Bred** Bearstone Stud Ltd **Trained** Maunby, N Yorks

**FOCUS**
Mainly modest 3yos in this sprint handicap, but the front two are unexposed.
T/Jkpt: £6,666.60 to a £1 stake. Pool: £10,000.00 - 1.50 winning units. T/Plt: £25.00 to a £1 stake. Pool: £65,073.09 - 1,900.10 winning units. T/Qpdt: £9.20 to a £1 stake. Pool: £5,717.67 - 455.17 winning units. **Colin Roberts**

## 5140 LINGFIELD (L-H)
Wednesday, July 26

**OFFICIAL GOING: Turf course - good to soft (soft in places; 7.0) changing to soft (good to soft in places) after race 1 (2.20); all-weather course - polytrack: standard**
Wind: light, half behind Weather: light cloud, light rain races 6 and 7

### 5292 READ SILVESTRE DE SOUSA AT 188BET NOVICE AUCTION STKS 7f
**2:20** (2:21) (Class 6) 2-Y-O £2,264 (£673; £336; £168) **Stalls** Centre

Form RPR
1 **Regimented (IRE)** 2-9-0 0 KieranO'Neill 7 73
(Richard Hannon) *racd in centre: prom in gp and chsd ldrs overall: ev ch 2f out: edgd rt over 1f out: clr w rival 1f out: flashed tail u.p but rn to ld wl ins fnl f: pushed out: 1st of 8 in gp* **25/1**

5 2 ¾ **Sarstedt**[22] 4466 2-9-0 0 FergusSweeney 12 72
(Henry Candy) *racd stands' side: chsd ldrs overall: effrt to chal 2f out: led and carried rt over 1f out: clr w wnr and drvn 1f out: hdd and styd on same pce ins fnl f: 1st of 6 in gp* **4/1**[3]

05 3 5 **Giovanni Medici**[22] 4465 2-9-2 0 RobertWinston 1 61
(Seamus Durack) *prom in gp and chsd ldrs overall: effrt 2f out: chsd clr ldng pair ent fnl f: no imp but kpt on for clr 3rd ins fnl f: 2nd of 8 in gp* **20/1**

5324 4 3 ½ **Zabaletaswansong (GER)**[35] 3965 2-9-2 72 SeanLevey 13 52
(Richard Hannon) *racd stands' side: w ldr tl led over 2f out: drvn and hdd over 1f out: 4th and btn 1f out: wknd ins fnl f: 2nd of 6 in gp* **11/4**[2]

0 5 1 ¼ **Secratario (FR)**[7] 5030 2-8-9 0 FinleyMarsh(7) 10 49
(Richard Hughes) *racd in centre: awkward as stalls opened: swtchd rt to r stands' side: in rr: rdn 3f out: sme hdwy over 1f out: kpt on ins fnl f: nvr trbld ldrs: 3rd of 6 in gp* **66/1**

6 hd **Mirror Magic** 2-8-5 0 ow1 PaddyPilley(5) 5 43+
(Geoffrey Deacon) *racd in centre: midfield overall: rdn 3f out: nvr on terms w ldrs but modest hdwy over 1f out: wl hld and kpt on same pce ins fnl f: 4th of 8 in gp* **50/1**

60 7 1 **Headline Act**[37] 3902 2-8-8 0 EdwardGreatrex(3) 3 41
(Archie Watson) *racd in centre: prom in gp and chsd ldrs overall: rdn and losing pl whn wandered jst over 2f out: wknd over 1f out: 5th of 8 in gp* **33/1**

2 8 2 ½ **Oswald (IRE)**[15] 4725 2-8-12 0 LukeMorris 15 36
(Robyn Brisland) *racd stands' side: led tl over 2f out: sn u.p and struggling: wl btn over 1f out: wknd fnl f: 4th of 6 in gp* **5/2**[1]

0 9 5 **The Naughty Step (IRE)**[20] 4520 2-9-0 0 PatCosgrave 2 25
(Jim Boyle) *racd in centre: s.i.s: nvr bttr than midfield: struggling over 2f out: sn btn and wknd over 1f out: 6th of 8 in gp* **80/1**

10 5 **Peveril Point (IRE)** 2-8-12 0 LouisSteward 8 11
(Henry Tett) *racd in centre: s.i.s: wl off the pce in rr: n.d: 6th of 8 in gp* **200/1**

34 11 1 ¾ **Rainbow Jazz (IRE)**[13] 4805 2-9-0 0 SteveDrowne 14 9
(Mark Usher) *racd stands' side: a towards rr of gp: struggling over 2f out: wknd over 1f out: 5th of 6 in gp* **5/1**

6 12 ½ **Uncovered**[15] 4725 2-8-12 0 RichardKingscote 6 5
(Tom Dascombe) *racd in centre: prom in gp and chsd ldrs overall: rdn and lost pl over 2f out: sn btn and wknd over 1f out: 7th of 8 in gp* **16/1**

13 6 **Rocus (IRE)** 2-9-0 0 LiamKeniry 11
(Mark Usher) *racd in centre: s.i.s: a off the pce in rr: n.d: 8th of 8 in gp* **50/1**

0 14 1 **Rum Ration**[15] 4725 2-8-12 0 JoeyHaynes 9
(Mark H Tompkins) *racd in centre: sn swtchd rt to r stands' side: lost pl 3f out: bhd fnl 2f: 6th of 6 in gp* **200/1**

1m 25.62s (2.32) **Going Correction** +0.175s/f (Good) 14 Ran SP% **117.0**
Speed ratings (Par 92): **93,92,86,82,81 80,79,76,71,65 63,62,55,54**
CSF £116.23 TOTE £29.90: £6.10, £1.70, £4.50; EX 328.60 Trifecta £5754.80.
**Owner** Mason Brown Partnership **Bred** J P Keappock **Trained** East Everleigh, Wilts

**FOCUS**
There had been 3mm of rain in the morning and the going on the turf course was given as good to soft, soft in places (GoingStick: 7.0), but that was quickly changed to soft, good to soft in places after the first race. The gamble on the runner-up was foiled by a Richard Hannon-trained newcomer. It seemed more a case of which horses handled the ground than where they raced.

### 5293 GET 1/4 ODDS AT 188BET CLAIMING STKS 6f
**2:50** (2:51) (Class 6) 2-Y-O £2,264 (£673; £336; £168) **Stalls** Centre

Form RPR
6002 1 **Atalanta Queen**[4] 5161 2-8-2 63 (b) JordanUys(7) 2 59
(Brian Meehan) *mde virtually all: pushed along and asserted over 1f out: r.o strly and drew clr ins fnl f: readily* **5/2**[2]

406 2 5 **Cranworth Phoenix**[45] 3619 2-8-1 54 HollieDoyle(3) 4 39
(Brian Barr) *w wnr tl rdn and unable qck over 1f out: hung lft and plugged on same pce ins fnl f* **18/1**

6024 3 1 ¾ **Roses In June (IRE)**[18] 4620 2-8-5 51 LukeMorris 3 35
(J S Moore) *in tch in rr: effrt and swtchd lft 2f out: outpcd by wnr over 1f out: wl hld and plugged on same pce ins fnl f: wnt 3rd cl home* **8/1**

5314 4 hd **Tie Em Up Tel (IRE)**[14] 4740 2-8-11 66 JFEgan 1 40
(David Evans) *awkward leaving stalls: trckd ldrs: effrt and reminder 2f out: outpcd and drifted rt over 1f out: wl hld and plugged on same pce ins fnl f: lost 3rd cl home* **10/11**[1]

056 5 4 ½ **Sausage Fingers**[5] 5120 2-8-10 0 (p[1]) PaddyPilley(5) 5 31
(Tom Dascombe) *trckd ldrs: rdn wl over 2f out: struggling and btn over 1f out: wknd fnl f* **7/1**[3]

1m 13.53s (2.33) **Going Correction** +0.175s/f (Good) 5 Ran SP% **109.8**
Speed ratings (Par 92): **91,84,82,81,75**
CSF £35.33 TOTE £3.40: £1.50, £4.30; EX 38.20 Trifecta £130.30.The winner was claimed by Mr Michael Appleby for £9000
**Owner** Jonathan Harvey **Bred** R T Dunne **Trained** Manton, Wilts

**FOCUS**
An ordinary race taken apart by the winner.

### 5294 PAUL KELLEWAY MEMORIAL CLASSIFIED STKS 7f 135y
**3:20** (3:20) (Class 3) 3-Y-O+ £7,246 (£2,168; £1,084; £542; £270) **Stalls** Centre

Form RPR
-125 1 **Khamaary (IRE)**[27] 4270 3-8-10 90 JimCrowley 2 99+
(Mark Johnston) *racd in centre: mde all: gng best 2f out: sn pushed along and readily asserted: clr and r.o wl ins fnl f: easily* **2/1**[1]

0030 2 3 ¾ **Glory Awaits (IRE)**[18] 4636 7-9-7 89 (v) JamieSpencer 5 94
(David Simcock) *racd in centre: chsd wnr: rdn over 2f out: unable qck over 1f out: clr 2nd but wl hld whn edgd lft ins fnl f* **9/1**

0120 3 1 ¾ **Black Bess**[54] 3307 4-9-4 87 PatCosgrave 3 87
(Jim Boyle) *racd in centre: t.k.h: hld up wl in tch: effrt 2f out: sn drvn and unable qck over 1f out: wl hld 3rd and kpt on same pce ins fnl f* **10/1**

3-10 4 2 ¼ **Bahamadam**[28] 4208 3-8-7 89 EdwardGreatrex(3) 1 80
(Eve Johnson Houghton) *racd in centre: t.k.h: hld up in tch: rdn over 2f out: outpcd and wl hld whn drifted rt over 1f out: plugged on ins fnl f* **10/1**

-620 5 ¾ **Graphite Storm**[60] 3077 3-8-10 88 HectorCrouch(3) 4 81
(Clive Cox) *racd in centre: dwlt: t.k.h: effrt 2f out: sn u.p and struggling: wknd fnl f* **11/4**[2]

0305 6 1 **Ice Slice (IRE)**[41] 3743 6-9-7 90 RyanTate 6 81
(James Eustace) *swtchd rt to r alone on stands' side: in tch in midfield: rdn over 2f out: outpcd and btn whn hung lft 1f out: wknd fnl f* **7/2**[3]

1m 31.09s (-1.21) **Going Correction** +0.175s/f (Good)
**WFA** 3 from 4yo+ 8lb 6 Ran SP% **110.4**
Speed ratings (Par 107): **113,109,107,105,104 103**
CSF £19.47 TOTE £2.20: £1.40, £3.40; EX 11.70 Trifecta £40.40.
**Owner** Hamdan Al Maktoum **Bred** Shadwell Estate Company Limited **Trained** Middleham Moor, N Yorks

**FOCUS**
A tight race on paper but the unexposed winner came away for a comfortable success.

### 5295 PAUL BLACKMORE 70TH BIRTHDAY OLD TIMER FILLIES' H'CAP 6f
**3:50** (3:58) (Class 5) (0-70,72) 3-Y-O+ £2,911 (£866; £432; £216) **Stalls** Centre

Form RPR
325 1 **Monteamiata (IRE)**[21] 4500 3-9-10 **72** LiamKeniry 3 79
(Ed Walker) *travelled strly and pressed ldr tl shkn up to ld over 1f out: rdn and styd on wl ins fnl f: rdn out* **4/1**[2]

3652 2 1 **Baby Gal**[7] 5028 3-8-11 **59** PatCosgrave 5 63
(Jim Boyle) *hld up in tch in midfield: effrt over 1f out: styd on u.p ins fnl f to go 2nd last strides: nvr quite getting on terms w wnr* **7/2**[1]

1403 3 hd **Flowing Clarets**[25] 4352 4-9-4 **61** WilliamCarson 1 65
(John Bridger) *led: rdn and hdd over 1f out: drvn and styd on same pce ins fnl f: lost 2nd last strides* **5/1**[3]

5452 4 ¾ **Whitecrest**[11] 4910 9-10-1 **72** LukeMorris 4 74
(John Spearing) *chsd ldng pair: rdn 2f out: drvn and unable qck over 1f out: styd on same pce u.p ins fnl f* **11/2**

616 5 4 **Magic Approach**[20] 4536 3-9-0 **62** JamieSpencer 6 50
(David Simcock) *reluctant to go to post and led rdrless to s: hld up in tch in last trio: effrt over 1f out: rdn and no imp 1f out: wknd ins fnl f: eased towards fin* **10/1**

000 6 ½ **Posh Bounty**[28] 4214 6-9-4 **68** (h) JordanUys(7) 9 55
(Paul Burgoyne) *stdd s: t.k.h: hld up in tch in last trio: effrt 2f out: hung lft u.p and no hdwy over 1f out: wknd ins fnl f* **25/1**

0315 7 hd **East Coast Lady (IRE)**[26] 4317 5-9-9 **69** HollieDoyle(3) 7 56+
(William Stone) *v.s.a: grad rcvrd and clsd on to bk of field after 2f: rdn over 2f out: sn struggling: outpcd and wl hld over 1f out* **7/2**[1]

0050 8 4 ½ **Silver Penny**[21] 4500 3-8-0 **55** (v[1]) IsobelFrancis(7) 2 26
(Jim Boyle) *hld up in tch in midfield: effrt 2f out: hung lft and lost pl over 1f out: wknd fnl f* **20/1**

1m 11.9s (0.70) **Going Correction** +0.175s/f (Good)
**WFA** 3 from 4yo+ 5lb 8 Ran SP% **114.2**
Speed ratings (Par 100): **102,100,100,99,94 93,93,87**
CSF £18.36 CT £70.82 TOTE £3.50: £1.40, £1.70, £1.80; EX 15.30 Trifecta £88.20.
**Owner** Kingsdown Racing Club **Bred** Kildaragh Stud **Trained** Upper Lambourn, Berks

**FOCUS**
They all came up the centre of the track this time.

### 5296 188BET (S) H'CAP 1m 2f (P)
**4:20** (4:22) (Class 6) (0-60,60) 4-Y-O+ £2,264 (£673; £336; £168) **Stalls** Low

Form RPR
-050 1 **Gold Merlion (IRE)**[18] 4627 4-9-6 **59** HarryBentley 7 68+
(Mark Johnston) *chsd ldrs: effrt over 1f out: str run to ld jst ins fnl f: sn clr and r.o strly: readily* **12/1**

0004 2 3 ¾ **Sevilla**[9] 4980 4-9-5 **58** KieranO'Neill 2 60
(Olly Murphy) *t.k.h: led: rdn over 1f out: drvn and hdd jst ins fnl f: outpcd by wnr: kpt on to hold 2nd cl home* **13/8**[1]

100 3 nse **Gunner Moyne**[74] 2615 5-9-4 **60** (v) HectorCrouch(3) 9 62
(Gary Moore) *hld up in tch towards rr: hdwy over 3f out: effrt 2f out: chsd clr ldng trio 1f out: styd on to go 3rd nr fin: no threat to wnr* **8/1**[3]

-400 4 ½ **Russian Ranger (IRE)**[30] 4165 4-9-7 **60** (b[1]) RichardKingscote 3 61
(Jonathan Portman) *t.k.h: chsd ldr after 2f: effrt and swtchd lft over 1f out: sn pressing ldr tl outpcd by wnr jst ins fnl f: kpt on same pce after* **11/2**[2]

3-00 5 3 **Solid Justice (IRE)**[22] 4461 6-8-7 **46** oh1 (v) DannyBrock 6 41
(Mark Pattinson) *hld up in tch in midfield: effrt jst over 2f out: no imp u.p over 1f out: wknd ins fnl f* **8/1**[3]

2660 6 2 ½ **Fairy Mist (IRE)**[29] 4180 10-8-7 **46** oh1 (v) WilliamCarson 11 37
(John Bridger) *stdd and dropped in bhd after s: hld up in rr: rdn over 3f out: no imp: swtchd rt over 1f out: no ch but styd on ins fnl f* **25/1**

-002 7 nse **Its A Sheila Thing**[14] 4753 4-8-7 **46** oh1 (h) LukeMorris 4 36
(Tony Carroll) *t.k.h: chsd ldr for 2f: styd chsng ldrs: unable qck and outpcd over 1f out: wknd fnl f* **10/1**

-020 8 ¾ **Star Links (USA)**[9] 4982 11-8-6 **48** oh1 ow2 (v[1]) TimClark(3) 10 37
(John Butler) *dwlt and rousted along early: hdwy into midfield on outer 6f out: u.p and struggling over 2f out: wl btn fnl 2f* **14/1**

0000 9 1 ¾ **Silver Lining (IRE)**[29] 4177 5-8-7 **46** oh1 JimmyQuinn 1 32
(Mark Hoad) *in tch in midfield: effrt on inner over 2f out: outpcd u.p 2f out: wknd over 1f out* **66/1**

5004 10 4 **Schottische**[23] 4453 7-8-13 **55** (b) HollieDoyle(3) 5 33
(Alan Bailey) *rousted along early: a towards rr: rdn 3f out: sn struggling and no ch fnl 2f* **9/1**

030 P **Good Bond**[19] 4562 5-8-11 **50** (h) SaleemGolam 8
(Linda Jewell) *in tch in midfield: lost pl 5f out: bhd and rdn 3f out: bhd and eased 1f out: p.u and dismntd nr fin* **40/1**

2m 5.56s (-1.04) **Going Correction** -0.075s/f (Stan) 11 Ran SP% **116.9**
Speed ratings (Par 101): **101,98,97,97,95 93,93,92,91,87**
CSF £31.28 CT £174.48 TOTE £13.50: £2.90, £1.60, £2.80; EX 42.70 Trifecta £330.90.Winner was bought in for 3,600gns
**Owner** Kingsley Park 7 - Ready To Run **Bred** Peter McGlynn **Trained** Middleham Moor, N Yorks

**FOCUS**
This was run at a good gallop, and not bad form for the grade.

## 5297 CRICKET BETTING AT 188BET H'CAP 5f 6y(P)
**4:50** (4:52) (Class 6) (0-65,66) 3-Y-O+ **£2,264** (£673; £336; £168) **Stalls** High

Form RPR

6010 1 **Red Invader (IRE)**[71] 2700 7-9-12 **64**.................. LiamKeniry 4 71+
(John Butler) *stdd after s: trckd ldrs tl wnt clsr to press ldr on inner over 1f out: shkn to ld jst ins fnl f: sn rdn and readily wnt clr: comf* **5/2**[1]

30-5 2 1 ¾ **Regal Miss**[34] 4009 5-8-12 **57**.................. FinleyMarsh(7) 2 58
(Patrick Chamings) *led: rdn over 1f out: hdd jst ins fnl f: sn outpcd by wnr but kpt on for clr 2nd* **6/1**

5630 3 1 ¾ **Billyoakes (IRE)**[58] 3140 5-10-0 **66**..................(p) LukeMorris 3 60
(Charlie Wallis) *chsd ldr tl over 1f out: sn drvn and unable qck: styd on same pce ins fnl f* **5/1**

5323 4 nk **Picansort**[15] 4710 10-9-11 **63**..................(b) RobertWinston 7 56
(Peter Crate) *dwlt: hld up in last pair: effrt on inner over 1f out: nt clr run and hmpd 1f out: kpt on but no threat to wnr after* **4/1**[2]

-003 5 1 ¼ **Gaia Princess (IRE)**[22] 4458 3-9-1 **60**.................. HectorCrouch(3) 6 48
(Gary Moore) *hld up in tch in midfield: effrt over 1f out: no imp and hung lft 1f out: wknd ins fnl f* **6/1**

4310 6 1 ¼ **Staffa (IRE)**[14] 4731 4-9-3 **55**.................. PatCosgrave 8 39
(Denis Coakley) *stdd s: hld up in last pair: c wd and effrt wl over 1f out: no imp and bhd ins fnl f* **9/2**[3]

59.32s (0.52) **Going Correction** -0.075s/f (Stan)
**WFA** 3 from 4yo+ 4lb **6 Ran SP% 112.0**
Speed ratings (Par 101): **92,89,86,85,83 81**
CSF £17.61 CT £67.57 TOTE £3.40: £2.30, £3.20; EX 19.80 Trifecta £71.50.
**Owner** Sterling Racing **Bred** Tally-Ho Stud **Trained** Newmarket, Suffolk

**FOCUS**
A modest sprint that wasn't run at a strong gallop, so those held up were at a disadvantage.

## 5298 188BET.CO.UK H'CAP 1m 4f (P)
**5:20** (5:20) (Class 5) (0-75,77) 3-Y-O **£2,911** (£866; £432; £216) **Stalls** Low

Form RPR

4351 1 **Koeman**[11] 4913 3-9-7 **75**.................. JFEgan 4 82
(Mick Channon) *sn trcking ldng pair: nt clr run over 2f out: swtchd rt and effrt wl over 1f out: wnt 2nd jst ins fnl f: sn chalng: r.o wl to ld towards fin* **4/1**[2]

-025 2 ¾ **Footman (GER)**[30] 4156 3-9-2 **77**.................. FinleyMarsh(7) 6 83
(Richard Hughes) *chsd ldr after 1f tl rdn to ld over 1f out: hrd pressed ins fnl f: hdd and styd on same pce towards fin* **13/2**[3]

5-42 3 2 ¾ **Perla Blanca (USA)**[9] 4967 3-8-2 **56** oh1.................. RoystonFfrench 5 57+
(Marcus Tregoning) *hld up in tch in rr of main gp: effrt and forced to swtchd wd wl over 1f out: hdwy ins fnl f: r.o wl fnl 100yds to snatch 3rd on post: no threat to ldng pair* **3/1**[1]

603 4 nse **Pioneertown (IRE)**[41] 3755 3-9-5 **73**.................. LukeMorris 3 74
(Sir Mark Prescott Bt) *racd keenly: led: rdn and hdd over 1f out: unable qck u.p: kpt on same pce ins fnl f: lost 3rd on post* **3/1**[1]

10-0 5 nk **First Quest (USA)**[42] 3727 3-9-6 **74**..................(t[1]) MartinHarley 1 75
(Ed Dunlop) *hld up in tch in midfield: effrt 2f out: drvn and unable qck over 1f out: styd on same pce u.p ins fnl f* **16/1**

0324 6 1 ¾ **Chaparrachik (IRE)**[40] 3788 3-9-4 **72**.................. RichardKingscote 9 70
(Amanda Perrett) *trckd ldng trio: rdn over 2f out: unable qck and outpcd over 1f out: wl hld and kpt on same pce ins fnl f* **13/2**[3]

2621 7 1 ¾ **Epsom Secret**[9] 4971 3-8-2 **56** oh2.................. KieranO'Neill 8 51
(Pat Phelan) *chsd ldr early: stdd bk and hld up in tch in midfield after 1f: effrt ent fnl 2f: no imp u.p over 1f out: wknd ins fnl f* **20/1**

023 8 42 **Oxford Don**[100] 1840 3-9-2 **70**.................. PatCosgrave 2
(David Simcock) *s.i.s: a in rr: reminders over 4f out: drvn and lost tch 3f out: t.o* **12/1**

2m 30.49s (-2.51) **Going Correction** -0.075s/f (Stan) **8 Ran SP% 115.0**
Speed ratings (Par 100): **105,104,102,102,102 101,100,72**
CSF £30.21 CT £87.98 TOTE £4.40: £1.60, £1.90, £1.50; EX 30.90 Trifecta £127.80.
**Owner** Taplin & Bunney Partnership **Bred** B V Sangster **Trained** West Ilsley, Berks

**FOCUS**
A fair handicap.
T/Plt: £272.10 to a £1 stake. Pool: £73,950.27 - 198.35 winning units. T/Qpdt: £17.90 to a £1 stake. Pool: £6,467.22 - 266.17 winning units. **Steve Payne**

# 5029 SANDOWN (R-H)
## Wednesday, July 26

**OFFICIAL GOING: Round course - good to soft (6.4); sprint course - soft (good to soft in places; 5.5)**
Wind: Quite fresh, against Weather: Overcast

## 5299 VISIT RACINGUK.COM APPRENTICE H'CAP (JC GRASSROOTS FLAT MIDDLE DISTANCE SERIES QUALIFIER) 1m 1f 209y
**6:00** (6:00) (Class 5) (0-70,70) 4-Y-O+ **£3,881** (£1,155; £577; £288) **Stalls** Low

Form RPR

2000 1 **Breakheart (IRE)**[13] 4804 10-8-0 **51** oh4.........(v) KayleighStephens(7) 10 57+
(Andrew Balding) *hld up in last pair: stdy prog on outer over 3f out: led over 2f out gng easily: looked in command fnl f: nudged along and jst hld on* **40/1**

3006 2 shd **The Gay Cavalier**[5] 5119 6-9-5 **68**..................(t) JackOsborn(5) 6 72
(John Ryan) *hld up in rr: rdn wl over 2f out: last and gng nowhere wl over 1f out: prog fnl f: r.o to take 2nd nr fin and clsd rapidly on wnr: jst failed* **17/2**

3122 3 ¾ **Sir Jack**[39] 3813 4-9-5 **63**.................. PaddyPilley 7 66
(Tony Carroll) *trckd ldng pair: rdn to chal over 2f out: nt qckn after and lost pl over 1f out: styd on again ins fnl f to take 3rd last strides* **3/1**[1]

2-60 4 nk **Archimento**[86] 2233 4-9-12 **70**..................(t[1]) AdamMcNamara 3 72
(Philip Hide) *trckd ldr: rdn to chal over 2f out: chsd wnr to over 1f out: kpt on u.p* **9/2**[3]

1550 5 hd **Roy Rocket (FR)**[27] 4257 7-9-6 **69**.................. NicolaCurrie(5) 4 71
(John Berry) *trckd ldrs: effrt over 2f out: rdn to chse wnr over 1f out: kpt on but a hld: lost pls nr fin* **20/1**

1313 6 2 ½ **Miss Inga Sock (IRE)**[29] 4185 5-9-8 **66**.................. EdwardGreatrex 8 63
(Eve Johnson Houghton) *hld up towards rr: effrt on outer over 2f out: tried to cl over 1f out: fdd ins fnl f* **7/2**[2]

5435 7 ½ **Pack It In (IRE)**[13] 4804 4-9-12 **70**..................(b) JordanUys 9 66
(Brian Meehan) *t.k.h: racd wd: wl in tch: on terms w ldrs over 2f out: sn lost pl and drvn: n.d fnl f* **6/1**

6440 8 2 ½ **Jack Of Diamonds (IRE)**[15] 4730 8-9-8 **66**..................(b) PaddyBradley 2 57
(Roger Teal) *trckd ldrs: chal on inner over 2f out: wknd over 1f out* **8/1**

1000 9 nse **Embankment**[14] 4747 8-9-1 **59**.................. GeorgeBuckell 1 50
(Michael Attwater) *led at stdy pce: hdd over 2f out: steadily wknd* **33/1**

00 10 3 ¼ **Hong Kong Joe**[27] 4257 7-8-4 **51** oh5..................(p[1]) AledBeech(3) 5 35
(Lydia Richards) *s.v.s: ct up w field after 3f: no prog over 2f out: wknd after* **66/1**

2m 16.69s (6.19) **Going Correction** +0.575s/f (Yiel) **10 Ran SP% 113.0**
Speed ratings (Par 103): **98,97,97,97,96 94,94,92,92,89**
CSF £330.01 CT £1342.61 TOTE £33.50: £3.10, £2.60, £2.40; EX 556.70 Trifecta £1633.50.
**Owner** I A Balding **Bred** Littleton Stud **Trained** Kingsclere, Hants

**FOCUS**
The Round Course rail was out 3 yards from the 1m point to the winning post, adding 20 yards to all Round Course distances. The opener was a modest but competitive event and it saw a fairytale start for Kayleigh Stephens, winning on her first ride. The pace didn't look overly quick early.

## 5300 WATCH RACING UK ON SKY 432 H'CAP 1m
**6:35** (6:36) (Class 4) (0-85,86) 3-Y-O+ **£5,822** (£1,732; £865; £432) **Stalls** Low

Form RPR

-146 1 **Almoreb (IRE)**[18] 4634 3-9-5 **82**.................. JimCrowley 6 88+
(Richard Hannon) *w ldr: led wl over 1f out and sent for home: move nt decisive and hrd pressed sn after: drvn and fnd enough to assert last 100yds* **7/4**[1]

0033 2 ½ **Kingston Kurrajong**[13] 4807 4-9-9 **78**..................(p) AdamBeschizza 2 85
(Michael Attwater) *trckd ldrs: rdn to chal over 1f out: pressed wnr hrd despite being sltly tight for room: no ex last 100yds* **7/1**[3]

1452 3 1 **Itsakindamagic**[21] 4507 3-9-9 **86**..................(t) DavidProbert 5 89
(Andrew Balding) *t.k.h: hld up in last pair: gng wl whn prog 2f out: cajoled along 1f out and little rspnse: kpt on to take 3rd nr fin but nvr gng to chal* **2/1**[2]

434 4 1 ¼ **Harlequin Striker (IRE)**[13] 4800 5-9-10 **79**.................. RobertWinston 3 82
(Dean Ivory) *led at mod pce: urged along over 2f out: hdd wl over 1f out: kpt on despite being short of room at times after: lost 3rd nr fin* **14/1**

0445 5 1 ½ **Mister Music**[14] 4746 8-9-8 **77**.................. AdamKirby 4 76
(Tony Carroll) *hld up in last pair: bmpd along fr 2f out: nvr threatened to rch chalng position* **7/1**[3]

6003 6 3 ½ **Dubai's Secret**[26] 4293 4-10-0 **83**.................. SeanLevey 7 74
(David Brown) *t.k.h: trckd ldrs: rdn 2f out: wknd over 1f out* **10/1**

-000 7 12 **Multitask**[21] 4501 7-8-13 **68**.................. LouisSteward 8 33
(Gary Moore) *t.k.h: racd wd: in tch: jnd ldrs 1/2-way: wknd rapidly jst over 2f out: t.o* **50/1**

1m 48.11s (4.81) **Going Correction** +0.575s/f (Yiel)
**WFA** 3 from 4yo+ 8lb **7 Ran SP% 112.4**
Speed ratings (Par 105): **98,97,96,95,93 90,78**
CSF £14.14 CT £25.24 TOTE £2.80: £1.20, £3.10; EX 15.20 Trifecta £34.80.
**Owner** Hamdan Al Maktoum **Bred** Stowell Park Stud **Trained** East Everleigh, Wilts

**FOCUS**
The Round Course rail was out 3 yards from the 1m point to the winning post, adding 20 yards to this race distance. The betting had this between the two 3yos lining up and one of them proved successful. Once again the pace only increased heading up the home straight.

## 5301 BRITISH STALLION STUDS EBF MAIDEN STKS 7f
**7:10** (7:13) (Class 5) 2-Y-O **£3,881** (£1,155; £577; £288) **Stalls** Low

Form RPR

1 **Red Mist** 2-9-5 **0**.................. SilvestreDeSousa 5 82+
(Simon Crisford) *t.k.h: sn hld up bhd ldrs: prog on outer over 2f out: shkn up to ld over 1f out: narrowly hdd fnl f: rn green but rallied to ld again last 50yds* **6/4**[1]

5 2 shd **Bathsheba Bay (IRE)**[19] 4583 2-9-5 **0**.................. SeanLevey 8 82
(Richard Hannon) *hld up in rr: prog on outer over 2f out: rdn to chal over 1f out: narrow ld fnl f: hdd and jst hld last 50yds* **8/1**[3]

3 3 ¼ **Blue Laureate** 2-9-5 **0**.................. AdamKirby 9 74
(Clive Cox) *racd wd: in tch: prog to chse ldr 3f out to wl over 1f out: one pce after* **25/1**

4 1 ¾ **Bold Reason (GER)** 2-9-5 **0**.................. FrankieDettori 4 69+
(John Gosden) *led: pushed along and hdd over 1f out: steadily fdd* **3/1**[2]

0 5 2 ½ **Sotomayor**[11] 4880 2-9-5 **0**.................. JimCrowley 7 63
(Richard Hannon) *dwlt: hld up in last: lft bhd over 2f out: reminder and sme prog over 1f out: n.d but kpt on steadily* **10/1**

6 ½ **Wax And Wane** 2-9-2 **0**.................. JordanVaughan(3) 2 62+
(K R Burke) *hld up: shkn up wl over 2f out: n.d but plugged on fr over 1f out* **12/1**

7 7 **Petra's Pony (IRE)** 2-8-12 **0**.................. JordanUys(7) 3 44
(Brian Meehan) *dwlt: tk fierce hold: hld up bhd ldrs: wknd over 2f out* **50/1**

0 8 1 ¼ **Ahfad**[19] 4583 2-9-5 **0**.................. AdamBeschizza 10 41
(Stuart Williams) *trckd ldr to 3f out: wknd* **100/1**

1m 33.16s (3.66) **Going Correction** +0.575s/f (Yiel) **8 Ran SP% 99.7**
Speed ratings (Par 94): **102,101,98,96,93 92,84,83**
CSF £10.26 TOTE £2.20: £1.10, £1.60, £3.60; EX 9.90 Trifecta £70.30.
**Owner** Sheikh Ahmed Al Maktoum **Bred** Godolphin **Trained** Newmarket, Suffolk
■ Sam Gold was withdrawn. Price at time of withdrawal was 5-1. Rule 4 applies to all bets. Deduction - 15p in the pound.
■ Stewards' Enquiry : Sean Levey 2 day ban - used whip above the permitted level (9/10 Aug)

**FOCUS**
The Round Course rail was out 3 yards from the 1m point to the winning post, adding 20 yards to this race distance. Some good horses have won this recently, namely Best Of Days (2016) and Cymric (2015), the first named a Group 2 winner as a juvenile and the latter Group 1-placed at the same age, so this winner might end up well above average.

## 5302 RACING UK PROFITS RETURNED TO RACING H'CAP 7f
**7:40** (7:42) (Class 3) (0-95,90) 3-Y-O+
**£8,092** (£2,423; £1,211; £605; £302; £152) **Stalls** Low

Form RPR

0266 1 **Fox Trotter (IRE)**[12] 4854 5-9-2 **82**.................. JimCrowley 6 91
(Brian Meehan) *hld up in last: shkn up and stl there 2f out: gd prog on outer after to chse ldr 1f out: styd on wl to ld last 50yds* **5/2**[2]

-002 2 hd **Sultan Baybars**[18] 4634 3-9-2 **89**..................(b) SilvestreDeSousa 2 95
(Roger Varian) *led: set alight over 2f out: drvn at least 2 l clr over 1f out: kpt on u.p against rail but hdd last 50yds* **11/10**[1]

0360 3 4 **Professor**[14] 4746 7-9-2 **82**..................(p[1]) LukeMorris 1 81
(Michael Attwater) *t.k.h: trckd ldng pair: rdn over 2f out: disp 2nd briefly jst over 1f out: fdd ins fnl f* **12/1**

-064 4 1 ¼ **Scottish Glen**[18] 4622 11-9-6 **89**.................. HectorCrouch(3) 4 84
(Patrick Chamings) *settled in 4th: rdn over 2f out: tried to make prog over 1f out but sn hld: fdd fnl f* **10/1**



The Form Book Flat, Raceform Ltd, Newbury, RG14 5SJ

1006 **5** 1 **Thomas Cranmer (USA)**21 4507 3-9-3 **90**.................... WilliamBuick 3 80
(Mark Johnston) *chsd ldr: rdn over 2f out: lost 2nd and wknd fnl f* **15/2**3

5600 **6** nk **Dutch Uncle**12 4854 5-9-5 **85**...............................(p) AdamKirby 5 77
(Robert Cowell) *dwlt: hld up in 5th: bmpd along and no prog 2f out: reminders over 1f out: nvr in it* **16/1**

1m 31.48s (1.98) **Going Correction** +0.575s/f (Yiel)
**WFA** 3 from 5yo+ 7lb 6 Ran SP% **110.6**
Speed ratings (Par 107): **111,110,106,104,103 103**
CSF £5.44 TOTE £3.40: £1.40, £1.20; EX 6.20 Trifecta £34.90.
**Owner** Mrs Sheila Tucker **Bred** Edmond Kent **Trained** Manton, Wilts

**FOCUS**
The Round Course rail was out 3 yards from the 1m point to the winning post, adding 20 yards to this race distance. A small field but it was run at a strong gallop.

## 5303 WATCH RACING UK ON VIRGIN 536 H'CAP 1m 6f
**8:10** (8:12) (Class 4) (0-85,87) 4-Y-0+ **£5,822** (£1,732; £865; £432) **Stalls** Low

Form RPR
-415 **1** **West Drive (IRE)**28 4206 4-9-6 **84**.......................(p) SilvestreDeSousa 5 92
(Roger Varian) *in tch: rdn wl over 2f out: prog on outer after: led over 1f out: kpt on u.p* **5/2**1

210- **2** 1 **Slunovrat (FR)**290 7195 6-9-7 **85**.............................. KevinStott 7 91
(David Menuisier) *trckd ldr to 7f out and again wl over 2f out: drvn to ld wl over 1f out: sn hdd and nt qckn: kpt on after but readily hld* **5/2**1

13-3 **3** 1 **Tenzing Norgay**14 4742 4-9-5 **83**...............................(p) LukeMorris 2 87
(Sir Mark Prescott Bt) *dwlt: mostly in last pair: pushed along briefly 1/2-way: rdn and no prog 3f out: plugged on fr 2f out to take 3rd nr fin* **6/1**3

/331 **4** ¾ **Clowance One**21 4499 5-9-7 **85**...........................(b) KieranShoemark 1 88
(Roger Charlton) *led to 6f out and again over 4f out: drvn over 2f out and sn hung rt into rail: hdd wl over 1f out: nt qckn* **11/4**2

1060 **5** 4 ½ **Captain Peacock**25 4370 4-9-6 **84**....................(b1) RichardKingscote 4 82
(William Knight) *hld up in tch: rdn and no prog over 2f out: wknd over 1f out* **16/1**

6000 **6** 27 **Warrior Of Light (IRE)**25 4370 6-9-9 **87**......................... AdamKirby 3 49
(Brendan Powell) *nt gng wl in last and str reminder after 3f: prog after and taken wd in bk st: led 6f out to over 4f out: sn drvn: wknd wl over 2f out: t.o* **33/1**

3m 10.22s (5.72) **Going Correction** +0.575s/f (Yiel) 6 Ran SP% **106.9**
Speed ratings (Par 105): **106,105,104,104,101 86**
CSF £8.12 TOTE £3.10: £1.10, £1.90; EX 10.30 Trifecta £41.40.
**Owner** H R H Sultan Ahmad Shah **Bred** Airlie Stud **Trained** Newmarket, Suffolk

**FOCUS**
The Round Course rail was out 3 yards from the 1m point to the winning post, adding 20 yards to this race distance. Another competitive handicap.

## 5304 WALL STREET JOURNAL H'CAP 5f 10y
**8:40** (8:43) (Class 4) (0-80,82) 3-Y-0+ **£5,966** (£1,876; £1,010) **Stalls** Low

Form RPR
-260 **1** **Bahamian Sunrise**61 3021 5-9-1 **75**......................(b) HectorCrouch(3) 2 80
(John Gallagher) *racd against rail: mde all and sn 3 l clr: c bk to rivals 2f out: rdn over 1f out and a finding enough after* **3/1**3

520- **2** 1 ¼ **Francisco**312 6583 5-9-9 **80**................................................ AdamKirby 4 81
(Tony Carroll) *chsd wnr: pushed along to cl 2f out: rdn and no imp fr over 1f out* **7/4**1

5010 **3** ½ **Stoneyford Lane (IRE)**12 4867 3-9-2 **77**...............(p) RoystonFfrench 3 75
(Steph Hollinshead) *racd in 3rd: rdn to cl on ldng pair 2f out: kpt on but readily hld fnl f* **2/1**2

006 **U** **Seve**55 3231 5-9-10 **81**...............................................(t) AdamBeschizza 1
(Karen George) *dismntd and led to post: rel to r whn stalls opened then rrd and uns rdr* **13/2**

1m 4.59s (2.99) **Going Correction** +0.725s/f (Yiel)
**WFA** 3 from 4yo+ 4lb 4 Ran SP% **108.0**
Speed ratings (Par 105): **105,103,102,**
CSF £8.54 TOTE £3.80; EX 9.20 Trifecta £17.00.
**Owner** Caveat Emptor Partnership **Bred** Mel Roberts & Ms Nicola Meese **Trained** Chastleton, Oxon

**FOCUS**
A four-runner race soon became three when Seve lost his rider emerging from the stalls.
T/Plt: £70.10 to a £1 stake. Pool: £83,911.33 - 872.77 winning units. T/Qpdt: £10.40 to a £1 stake. Pool: £6,090.35 - 432.96 winning units. **Jonathan Neesom**

5305 - 5307a (Foreign Racing) - See Raceform Interactive

# 4641 NAAS (L-H)
### Wednesday, July 26

**OFFICIAL GOING: Good**

## 5308a YEOMANSTOWN STUD DARK ANGEL EBF STKS (LISTED RACE) (F&M) 6f
**7:30** (7:33) 3-Y-0+
**£30,256** (£9,743; £4,615; £2,051; £1,025; £512)

RPR
**1** **Only Mine (IRE)**25 4382 4-9-8 104.................................... GaryCarroll 13 107+
(Joseph G Murphy, Ire) *broke wl on stands' side and sn crossed towards far side to press ldr in 2nd: led 1/2-way and rdn clr over 1f out: styd on wl fnl f: advantage reduced cl home* **9/4**1

**2** 1 **Music Box (IRE)**9 4986 3-9-0 93.............................. SeamieHeffernan 7 99+
(A P O'Brien, Ire) *t.k.h to chse ldrs: 4th at 1/2-way: wnt 3rd ent fnl f: styd on wl clsng stages into 2nd on line* **8/1**

**3** hd **Rehana (IRE)**59 3110 3-9-5 106......................................... PatSmullen 9 103
(M Halford, Ire) *sn trckd ldrs in 3rd: clsr in 2nd over 2f out: nt qckn w ldr appr fnl f: kpt on same pce and ct on line for 2nd* **7/2**2

**4** 2 **Smoulder**45 3632 3-9-0 83.....................................(h) ColmO'Donoghue 4 92
(A P O'Brien, Ire) *bit slowly away and racd in rr: rdn and prog on far side over 1f out: kpt on wl into 4th fnl 100yds: nvr nrr* **50/1**

**5** hd **Peticoatgovernment (IRE)**25 4382 4-9-5 95......................... WJLee 2 92
(W McCreery, Ire) *chsd ldrs: 6th at 1/2-way: rdn and no imp appr fnl f: kpt on same pce* **9/1**

**6** ½ **Pious Alexander (IRE)**27 4280 3-9-0 88.........(h1) DeclanMcDonogh 10 90
(Edward Lynam, Ire) *bit slowly away and racd towards rr: styd on wl fnl f: nvr nrr* **20/1**

**7** hd **Asking (IRE)**9 4986 3-9-0 101..................................(t) DonnachaO'Brien 1 89
(A P O'Brien, Ire) *chsd ldrs: 5th at 1/2-way: rdn in 3rd appr fnl f: sn no imp: wknd fnl 100yds* **6/1**3

**8** 2 ½ **Mur Hiba (IRE)**12 4872 3-9-0 95..................................(t1) KevinManning 6 81
(M D O'Callaghan, Ire) *hld up: rdn under 2f out: kpt on one pce fnl f: nvr on terms* **14/1**

**9** 5 **Go Kart (IRE)**14 4771 4-9-5 93..................................(v) RonanWhelan 12 66
(P J Prendergast, Ire) *racd in mid-div on stands' side: pushed along and nt qckn over 1f out: wknd fnl f* **25/1**

**10** nk **Old Time Waltz (USA)**9 4986 3-9-1 84 ow1......(bt) EmmetMcNamara 3 65
(A P O'Brien, Ire) *sn rdn to ld: hdd 1/2-way: wknd over 1f out* **40/1**

**11** 5 ½ **Carolinae**20 4536 5-9-5 86............................................ StevieDonohoe 5 47
(Charlie Fellowes) *racd in mid-div to 1/2-way: sn rdn and dropped towards rr: detached ent fnl f* **10/1**

1m 11.14s (-2.06)
**WFA** 3 from 4yo+ 5lb 11 Ran SP% **117.2**
CSF £19.27 TOTE £3.00: £1.60, £2.10, £1.40; DF 21.00 Trifecta £78.60.
**Owner** Mrs C C Regalado-Gonzalez **Bred** Mrs C L Weld **Trained** Fethard, Co Tipperary
■ Alphabet was withdrawn. Price at time of withdrawal 14-1. Rule 4 applies to all bets. Deduct 5p in the pound.

**FOCUS**
A performance of some authority from the winner which would mark her out as an improving filly and one that can step up further in grade. The fourth and sixth limit the form.

5309 - 5312a (Foreign Racing) - See Raceform Interactive

# 5055 DONCASTER (L-H)
### Thursday, July 27

**OFFICIAL GOING: Soft (6.8)**
Wind: Moderate against Weather: Cloudy with sunny periods and showers

## 5313 PLAY SPORTING LIFE PICK 7 FOR FREE NOW H'CAP 1m 3f 197y
**5:45** (5:49) (Class 4) (0-80,80) 4-Y-0+ **£4,851** (£1,443; £721; £360) **Stalls** Low

Form RPR
-602 **1** **The New Pharaoh (IRE)**26 4345 6-9-1 **74**.......................... DavidAllan 1 81
(Chris Wall) *trckd ldrs: hdwy over 3f out: chal 2f out: rdn to ld jst over 1f out: drvn and edgd lft ins fnl f: kpt on strly* **9/4**1

2323 **2** ½ **Prendergast Hill (IRE)**41 3785 5-9-4 **80**............(p) CallumShepherd(3) 5 85
(Ed de Giles) *trckd ldr: cl up 4f out: led over 3f out: jnd 2f out and sn rdn: hdd jst over 1f out: sn drvn and kpt on* **4/1**2

/004 **3** ½ **Sheriff Of Nawton (IRE)**9 5005 6-8-11 **70**.................. TonyHamilton 4 75
(Roger Fell) *hld up in midfield: hdwy over 4f out: trckd ldrs over 2f out: rdn to chal ent fnl f: sn drvn and ev ch whn n.m.r on inner: kpt on* **10/1**

4000 **4** 5 **Buonarroti (IRE)**14 4796 6-9-2 **75**.................................(t1) TomEaves 8 71
(Declan Carroll) *hld up in rr: hdwy 3f out: chsd ldrs 2f out: sn rdn and no imp fnl f* **9/1**

0010 **5** 3 **Auxiliary**24 4430 4-8-12 **71**..........................................(p) JamesSullivan 9 63
(Patrick Holmes) *trckd ldrs: hdwy over 3f out: rdn over 2f out: drvn wl over 1f out: sn one pce* **25/1**

-030 **6** 1 ¼ **Alphabetical Order**17 4684 9-9-4 **77**.......................... DanielTudhope 6 67
(David O'Meara) *hld up towards rr: hdwy 3f out: rdn along over 2f out: drvn wl over 1f out: n.d* **12/1**

0502 **7** 3 ¾ **Parish Boy**7 5060 5-9-5 **78**............................................ PaulMulrennan 3 62
(David Loughnane) *dwlt: sn in midfield: hdwy 4f out: pushed along 3f out: rdn to chse ldrs jst over 2f out: sn drvn and btn* **13/2**3

2006 **8** 3 ½ **Ice Galley (IRE)**20 4572 4-8-9 **68** ow1.........................(p1) GrahamLee 2 46
(Philip Kirby) *trckd ldng pair: pushed along 4f out: rdn 3f out: sn drvn and wknd* **40/1**

/456 **9** 16 **Groor**13 4861 5-9-6 **79**..................................................... SaleemGolam 7 31
(Mohamed Moubarak) *dwlt and hld up towards rr: hdwy towards inner over 3f out: chsd ldrs jst over 2f out: sn rdn and wknd* **50/1**

24-5 **10** 17 **Warrior Prince**36 3966 4-9-2 **75**................................... PJMcDonald 12
(Ed Dunlop) *a towards rr* **8/1**

2420 **11** 14 **Bluff Crag**69 2785 4-8-11 **70**........................................ ShaneKelly 11
(Richard Hughes) *led: rdn along over 3f out: sn hdd & wknd* **16/1**

2m 42.94s (8.04) **Going Correction** +0.80s/f (Soft) 11 Ran SP% **116.1**
Speed ratings (Par 105): **105,104,104,101,99 98,95,93,82,71 62**
CSF £10.39 CT £73.93 TOTE £3.00: £1.70, £2.70, £2.50; EX 12.60 Trifecta £98.90.
**Owner** Ms Aida Fustoq **Bred** Deerfield Farm **Trained** Newmarket, Suffolk
■ Stewards' Enquiry : David Allan two-day ban: guilty of careless riding (Aug 10-11)

**FOCUS**
Course railed out about 6yds from 1m2f to where the round joins the straight. Race distance increased by 18yds. This modest handicap was run at a sound pace and the principals came well clear.

## 5314 TERRY BELLAS MEMORIAL NOVICE STKS (PLUS 10 RACE) 7f 6y
**6:15** (6:15) (Class 4) 2-Y-O **£4,204** (£1,251; £625; £312) **Stalls** High

Form RPR
4 **1** **Dark Acclaim (IRE)**33 4083 2-9-2 0.......................... DanielMuscutt 5 89+
(Marco Botti) *t.k.h: trckd ldng pair: hdwy and cl up over 2f out: led wl over 1f out: sn rdn clr: green and idled ins fnl f: readily* **13/2**

**2** 3 ¾ **Qaroun** 2-9-2 0................................................................ TedDurcan 6 80+
(Sir Michael Stoute) *hld up on heels of ldrs: effrt over 2f out: swtchd lft and rdn over 1f out: styd on to chse wnr ins fnl f: sn no imp* **7/2**3

51 **3** 1 ¾ **Alfa McGuire (IRE)**19 4597 2-9-5 0........................ ConnorBeasley 3 78
(Bryan Smart) *led 1f: cl up: pushed along over 2f out: rdn wl over 1f out: sn drvn and kpt on same pce* **15/8**2

5 **4** 2 **Wafeer (IRE)**21 4526 2-9-2 0....................................... DaneO'Neill 1 70
(Richard Hannon) *dwlt: t.k.h and led after 1f: pushed along over 2f out: rdn and hdd wl over 1f out: drvn and wknd appr fnl f* **7/4**1

6 **5** 5 **The Fettler (IRE)**27 4297 2-9-2 0................................ DavidNolan 2 58
(Kevin Frost) *trckd ldrs: pushed along 3f out: rdn over 2f out: sn outpcd* **50/1**

1m 29.92s (3.62) **Going Correction** +0.425s/f (Yiel) 5 Ran SP% **108.7**
Speed ratings (Par 96): **96,91,89,87,81**
CSF £27.67 TOTE £7.30: £2.60, £2.20; EX 35.00 Trifecta £92.10.
**Owner** Middleham Park Racing Cxxi & Partners **Bred** Elite Racing Club **Trained** Newmarket, Suffolk

**FOCUS**
This didn't look a bad novice event. It was run at a fair pace on the stands' side.

## 5315 POLYPIPE MAIDEN STKS 7f 6y
**6:45** (6:50) (Class 5) 3-Y-0+ **£2,911** (£866; £432; £216) **Stalls** High

Form RPR
00 **1** **Wasm**76 2584 3-9-5 0.................................................. TonyHamilton 8 75+
(Roger Fell) *hld up in rr: swtchd lft to outer and hdwy wl over 2f out: chsd ldrs over 1f out: led jst ins fnl f: readily* **10/1**

0- **2** 1 ¼ **Sunday Prospect (FR)**375 4423 3-9-5 0......................... PJMcDonald 9 70
(K R Burke) *hld up in tch: pushed along and hdwy over 2f out: rdn over 1f out: styd on wl fnl f* **14/1**

2 **3** ½ **Raawy**[28] 4269 3-9-5 0 DaneO'Neill 7 69
(Simon Crisford) *hld up in tch: hdwy over 2f out: chsd ldng pair over 1f out: sn rdn: chal and ev ch ent fnl f: sn drvn and kpt on same pce* **6/4**[1]

2403 **4** ½ **Wannabe Friends**[12] 4912 4-9-12 77 ShaneKelly 5 71
(Richard Hughes) *cl up: led after 1f: rdn clr wl over 1f out: drvn ent fnl f: sn hdd and kpt on same pce* **9/4**[2]

**5** ½ **Gorham's Cave** 3-9-5 0 SilvestreDeSousa 4 67
(Roger Varian) *trckd ldrs: hdwy 1/2-way: chsd ldr wl over 2f out: rdn wl over 1f out: drvn appr fnl f: kpt on same pce* **3/1**[3]

- **6** ¾ **Chosen World** 3-9-5 0 JoeDoyle 1 65
(Julie Camacho) *in tch: pushed along wl over 2f out: rdn to chse ldrs 2f out: sn drvn and kpt on same pce* **25/1**

4/- **7** 13 **Pound Note**[703] 5688 5-9-7 0 PhilDennis(5) 2 35
(Michael Mullineaux) *led 1f: cl up: pushed along 1/2-way: rdn wl over 2f out: sn wknd* **100/1**

50 **8** 3 ¼ **Quick Monet (IRE)**[19] 4604 4-9-5 0 (e[1]) AidenBlakemore(7) 6 27
(Shaun Harris) *chsd ldrs: rdn 3f out: sn wknd* **200/1**

1m 30.5s (4.20) **Going Correction** +0.425s/f (Yiel)
**WFA** 3 from 4yo+ 7lb **8 Ran SP% 116.9**
Speed ratings (Par 103): **93,91,91,90,89 89,74,70**
CSF £132.66 TOTE £11.60: £2.70, £3.50, £1.02; EX 43.80 Trifecta £217.30.
**Owner** Nick Bradley Racing 12 & Partner **Bred** Highclere Stud And Floors Farming **Trained** Nawton, N Yorks
■ Crucial Response was withdrawn. Price at time of withdrawal 150/1. Rule 4 does not apply.
**FOCUS**
A modest maiden, run at a sound pace.

## 5316 SKY BET GO-RACING-IN-YORKSHIRE SUMMER FESTIVAL H'CAP 6f 2y
**7:20** (7:22) (Class 4) (0-80,79) 3-Y-O **£4,851** (£1,443; £721; £360) **Stalls** High

Form RPR

0111 **1** **Kaeso**[49] 3496 3-9-0 72 TomEaves 9 77+
(Nigel Tinkler) *hld up in rr: hdwy 2f out: chsd ldrs on outer over 1f out: chal ins fnl f: sn rdn and qcknd to ld last 75 yds* **3/1**[1]

-122 **2** ½ **Marseille (IRE)**[26] 4342 3-9-1 73 JoeDoyle 7 76
(Julie Camacho) *trckd ldrs: smooth hdwy over 1f out: rdn to take slt ld ins fnl f: hdd and no ex last 75 yds* **3/1**[1]

035 **3** ½ **Jessinamillion**[27] 4309 3-9-1 73 PJMcDonald 6 75
(James Bethell) *dwlt and rr: hdwy 2f out: chsd ldrs over 1f out: rdn and ev ch ent fnl f: sn drvn and kpt on* **10/1**[3]

3-50 **4** nk **Somewhere Secret**[12] 4892 3-8-12 75 (h[1]) PhilDennis(5) 1 76
(Michael Mullineaux) *trckd ldng pair: hdwy over 2f out: rdn and ev ch over 1f out: drvn ins fnl f: kpt on same pce towards fin* **33/1**

-016 **5** ¾ **Coral Sea**[27] 4317 3-9-5 77 (h) SilvestreDeSousa 3 75+
(Charles Hills) *trckd ldrs: pushed along over 2f out: rdn wl over 1f out: hld whn n.m.r appr fnl f* **6/1**[2]

-210 **6** 1 **Black Salt**[28] 4265 3-9-1 73 BenCurtis 2 68
(David Barron) *cl up: led after 2f: rdn along 2f out: drvn over 1f out: hdd ent fnl f: grad wknd* **16/1**

415 **7** ½ **Summerghand (IRE)**[19] 4616 3-9-3 75 DanielTudhope 5 69
(David O'Meara) *hld up in tch: hdwy on outer and cl up 2f out: rdn wl over 1f out: drvn and wknd ent fnl f* **3/1**[1]

032 **8** 2 ½ **Decision Maker (IRE)**[14] 4793 3-8-12 70 AlistairRawlinson 8 56
(Roy Bowring) *t.k.h: led 2f: cl up: rdn along over 2f out: sn drvn and wknd over 1f out* **11/1**

1m 17.26s (3.66) **Going Correction** +0.425s/f (Yiel) **8 Ran SP% 115.5**
Speed ratings (Par 102): **92,91,90,90,89 87,87,83**
CSF £11.88 CT £78.21 TOTE £4.40: £1.90, £1.40, £2.10; EX 15.50 Trifecta £102.40.
**Owner** M Webb **Bred** Sir Eric Parker **Trained** Langton, N Yorks
**FOCUS**
There was a bunched finish down the middle but this rates fair sprinting form.

## 5317 BRITISH STALLION STUDS EBF FILLIES' H'CAP 7f 6y
**7:50** (7:51) (Class 3) (0-90,89) 3-Y-O+ **£9,056** (£2,695; £1,346; £673) **Stalls** High

Form RPR

0413 **1** **Bint Arcano (FR)**[19] 4617 4-9-9 84 JoeDoyle 7 93
(Julie Camacho) *trckd ldng pair: smooth hdwy 2f out and sn cl up: led over 1f out: sn rdn and kpt on strly* **4/1**[3]

0-24 **2** 2 **Peak Princess (IRE)**[28] 4271 3-8-13 84 HollieDoyle(3) 4 85
(Richard Hannon) *hld up towards rr: hdwy 2f out: rdn over 1f out: drvn to chse wnr ins fnl f: sn edgd lft and no imp* **7/2**[2]

0015 **3** ¾ **Savannah Slew**[29] 4208 3-9-5 87 (b) PaulMulrennan 3 86
(James Given) *dwlt and hld up in rr: hdwy on inner over 2f out: rdn to chal over 1f out: drvn and kpt on same pce fnl f* **3/1**[1]

0106 **4** 1 ¼ **Courier**[16] 4719 5-9-12 87 BarryMcHugh 5 86
(Marjorie Fife) *led: pushed along 2f out and sn jnd: rdn and hdd over 1f out: drvn and kpt on one pce fnl f* **9/1**

-044 **5** 4 **Little Lady Katie (IRE)**[18] 4662 5-9-2 80 JordanVaughan(3) 1 68
(K R Burke) *trckd ldrs: hdwy 3f out: rdn along over 2f out: drvn and wknd over 1f out* **7/2**[2]

1612 **6** ½ **Miss Sheridan (IRE)**[21] 4525 3-8-9 77 CamHardie 2 61
(Michael Easterby) *cl up: rdn along wl over 2f out: drvn and wknd wl over 1f out: sn edgd rt and in rr* **15/2**

1m 30.77s (4.47) **Going Correction** +0.425s/f (Yiel)
**WFA** 3 from 4yo+ 7lb **6 Ran SP% 111.2**
Speed ratings (Par 104): **91,88,87,86,81 81**
CSF £17.85 TOTE £4.90: £2.00, £2.30; EX 21.50 Trifecta £53.20.
**Owner** G B Turnbull Ltd **Bred** Rabbah Bloodstock Limited **Trained** Norton, N Yorks
**FOCUS**
They went a solid pace down the centre in this good-quality sprint handicap for fillies.

## 5318 PEGLER YORKSHIRE H'CAP 6f 2y
**8:20** (8:21) (Class 5) (0-70,72) 4-Y-O+ **£2,911** (£866; £432; £216) **Stalls** High

Form RPR

661 **1** **Muatadel**[7] 5055 4-9-5 68 TonyHamilton 10 78
(Roger Fell) *trckd ldrs: smooth hdwy 2f out: led over 1f out: rdn ins fnl f: sn jnd and drvn: kpt on strly* **15/2**

3544 **2** ¾ **Buccaneers Vault (IRE)**[7] 5070 5-9-5 71 (v) SammyJoBell(3) 13 78
(Paul Midgley) *prom: effrt over 1f out: rdn to chal ins fnl f: ev ch tl drvn and no ex last 75 yds* **8/1**

0602 **3** 2 ¾ **Willsy**[14] 4789 4-8-8 62 GemmaTutty(5) 12 60
(Karen Tutty) *rr: pushed along 1/2-way: rdn 2f out: hdwy over 1f out: styd on strly fnl f* **8/1**

2-03 **4** shd **Le Manege Enchante (IRE)**[22] 4509 4-8-8 57 (p) TomEaves 11 55
(Derek Shaw) *dwlt and towards rr: sn swtchd and smooth hdwy over 3f out: chsd ldrs on inner 2f out: rdn over 1f out: drvn ent fnl f: kpt on same pce* **25/1**

4346 **5** nk **Lucky Lodge**[15] 4744 7-8-13 62 (v) CamHardie 14 59
(Antony Brittain) *towards rr: pushed along and hdwy 2f out: rdn over 1f out: styd on u.p fnl f* **25/1**

6232 **6** 1 **Burtonwood**[40] 3812 5-8-12 66 (p) CallumRodriguez(5) 1 60
(Julie Camacho) *cl up: chal 2f out: sn rdn and ev ch: drvn and wknd ent fnl f* **11/1**

0600 **7** 1 ¼ **Dandyleekie (IRE)**[10] 4958 5-9-9 72 (b) DanielTudhope 8 68
(David O'Meara) *hld up towards rr: sme hdwy 2f out: sn rdn along and no imp fnl f* **11/2**[2]

4345 **8** hd **Willbeme**[24] 4426 9-9-1 64 (t) JasonHart 3 53
(Simon West) *led: rdn along 2f out: drvn and hdd over 1f out: grad wknd* **16/1**

006- **9** 5 **Run With Pride (IRE)**[338] 5736 7-8-9 63 LewisEdmunds(5) 4 36
(Derek Shaw) *chsd ldrs: rdn along wl over 2f out: sn wknd* **8/1**

0-03 **10** 4 **Kommander Kirkup**[6] 5132 6-9-7 70 PaulMulrennan 2 31
(Michael Herrington) *midfield: hdwy to chse ldrs 1/2-way: rdn along over 2f out: sn drvn and wknd* **7/1**[3]

0242 **11** 7 **Athollblair Boy (IRE)**[17] 4695 4-9-3 66 SilvestreDeSousa 9 4
(Nigel Tinkler) *chsd ldrs: pushed along 1/2-way: sn rdn and wknd* **4/1**[1]

1m 17.66s (4.06) **Going Correction** +0.425s/f (Yiel) **11 Ran SP% 114.9**
Speed ratings (Par 103): **89,88,84,84,83 82,80,80,73,68 59**
CSF £64.69 CT £489.39 TOTE £7.30: £2.50, £3.00, £2.80; EX 45.40 Trifecta £606.40.
**Owner** R G Fell **Bred** Lofts Hall Stud & B Sangster **Trained** Nawton, N Yorks
**FOCUS**
A run-of-the-mill sprint handicap. Only two mattered from the furlong marker.

## 5319 1STSECURITYSOLUTIONS.CO.UK H'CAP 1m 2f 43y
**8:55** (8:56) (Class 5) (0-70,71) 3-Y-O **£2,911** (£866; £432; £216) **Stalls** Low

Form RPR

1666 **1** **Lightly Squeeze**[19] 4632 3-9-8 71 (p) GrahamLee 11 83
(Philip Hide) *trckd ldng pair: hdwy over 3f out: led over 2f out: rdn over 1f out: drvn ins fnl f: kpt on strly* **9/1**

630 **2** 2 ¼ **Entangling (IRE)**[107] 1692 3-9-6 69 SilvestreDeSousa 3 77+
(Chris Wall) *hld up in rr: hdwy on wd outside 3f out: chsd ldrs wl over 1f out: sn rdn and styd on to chse wnr ins fnl f: sn drvn and no imp* **4/1**[1]

025 **3** 4 **Duck Egg Blue (IRE)**[22] 4901 3-9-1 71 PaulaMuir(7) 10 71
(Patrick Holmes) *chsd ldr: hdwy and cl up over 3f out: effrt 2f out: sn rdn: drvn over 1f out: kpt on one pce* **25/1**

5023 **4** 3 ¾ **Savannah Moon (IRE)**[14] 4785 3-9-2 65 (h) KevinStott 7 58
(Kevin Ryan) *led and sn clr: pushed along over 3f out: rdn and hdd over 2f out: sn drvn and kpt on one pce* **8/1**

243 **5** 1 ½ **Circulation**[19] 4611 3-9-7 70 PatDobbs 4 60
(Ralph Beckett) *hld up in rr: hdwy 3f out: rdn 2f out: drvn over 1f out: nvr nr ldrs* **4/1**[1]

506- **6** nk **Lenoire**[241] 8130 3-8-13 62 AlistairRawlinson 9 52
(Michael Appleby) *midfield: hdwy on outer over 4f out: chsd ldrs wl over 2f out: sn rdn and n.d* **18/1**

4-66 **7** nse **Fleetfoot Jack (IRE)**[42] 3745 3-9-0 63 (p[1]) DanielTudhope 6 53
(David O'Meara) *awkward after s: hld up towards rr: hdwy over 4f out: rdn along to chse ldrs 3f out: drvn 2f out and n.d* **5/1**[3]

00-6 **8** 3 ¼ **Indian Vision (IRE)**[98] 1914 3-8-6 55 PJMcDonald 5 39
(Micky Hammond) *in tch: hdwy to chse ldrs over 4f out: rdn along 3f out: sn drvn and wknd* **14/1**

006 **9** 10 **Shine Baby Shine**[14] 4784 3-8-2 51 oh1 PaddyAspell 1 16
(Philip Kirby) *a towards rr* **50/1**

565 **10** 9 **Circling Vultures**[65] 2921 3-8-10 59 CamHardie 8
(Antony Brittain) *a towards rr* **28/1**

1463 **11** 9 **Four Wishes**[36] 3975 3-9-1 64 DavidAllan 2
(Tim Easterby) *chsd ldrs on inner: pushed along 4f out: rdn 3f out: sn drvn and wknd* **9/2**[2]

2m 21.41s (12.01) **Going Correction** +0.80s/f (Soft) **11 Ran SP% 117.1**
Speed ratings (Par 100): **83,81,78,75,73 73,73,70,62,55 48**
CSF £44.02 CT £881.28 TOTE £11.30: £3.00, £2.00, £6.00; EX 56.30 Trifecta £539.30.
**Owner** Wong Yu On **Bred** Highbury Stud Ltd **Trained** Findon, W Sussex
**FOCUS**
Race distance increased by 18yds. An ordinary 3yo handicap and another race where two came clear.
T/Jkpt: Not Won. T/Plt: £141.90 to a £1 stake. Pool: £86,078.54 - 442.75 winning units T/Qpdt: £20.50 to a £1 stake. Pool: £8,135.07 - 292.77 winning units **Joe Rowntree**

# 5147 NEWBURY (L-H)
### Thursday, July 27

**OFFICIAL GOING: Soft (good to soft in places; 5.5) changed to soft after race 3 (6.30)**
Wind: light, against Weather: bright spells, showers earlier and from race 4

## 5320 PREMIER FOOD COURTS AMATEUR RIDERS' H'CAP 1m 5f 61y
**5:30** (5:30) (Class 5) (0-70,70) 3-Y-O+ **£3,119** (£967; £483; £242) **Stalls** Centre

Form RPR

0666 **1** **Firestorm (GER)**[19] 4627 6-9-9 51 oh3 MissCWalton 4 56
(Richard Ford) *s.i.s: sn rcvrd and hld up in tch in last pair: stdy hdwy 4f out: trckd ldrs 2f out: pushed along to chal ent fnl f: rdn to ld 100yds out: r.o* **10/1**

00-2 **2** nk **Meyandi**[80] 2468 3-9-11 64 MissAnnaHesketh 7 71
(Andrew Balding) *t.k.h: early: sn led: hdd after 2f and chsd ldr: rdn to ld 2f out: sn drvn hdd 100yds out: kpt on but a jst hld* **5/2**[1]

4443 **3** 1 ¼ **Take Two**[69] 2785 8-10-3 66 MrJBrace(7) 8 69
(Alex Hales) *awkward leaving stalls and slowly away: sn rcvrd and in tch towards rr: hdwy to chse 5f out: upsides ldrs and travelling strly over 2f out: rdn over 1f out: no ex ins fnl f: wknd towards fin* **7/1**[3]

006- **4** shd **Manny Owens (IRE)**[95] 7775 5-10-4 65 (t) MissAMcCain(5) 5 68
(Jonjo O'Neill) *trckd ldrs: effrt 2f out: hung lft 1f out: kpt on ins fnl f* **14/1**

2022 **5** 2 ¾ **Luv U Whatever**[20] 4572 7-10-12 68 MissBeckySmith 9 67
(Marjorie Fife) *chsd ldrs tl led after 2f: rdn over 2f out: hdd 2f out: 4th and outpcd 1f out: wknd ins fnl f* **4/1**[2]

-430 **6** 10 **Art Of Swing (IRE)**[46] 3616 5-10-13 69 MrRBirkett 1 53
(Gary Moore) *hld up in tch in midfield: clsd to chse ldrs and effrt on inner 2f out: sn outpcd u.p: wknd fnl f* **7/1**[3]

3315 **7** 6 **Party Royal**[42] 3753 7-10-7 63 (p) MrDHDunsdon 2 38
(Nick Gifford) *hld up in tch towards rr: effrt 3f out: sn struggling and outpcd: n.d fnl 2f* **18/1**

6005 **8** 4 ½ **Elusive Cowboy (USA)**[20] 4257 4-10-12 68 MrSWalker 3 36
(Chris Gordon) *hld up in tch: rdn over 3f out: sn struggling and dropped to rr: n.d fnl 2f* **16/1**

24-4 **9** 1 3/4 **Jersey Jewel (FR)**[54] 3325 5-10-9 **70**.................. MissCAGreenway(5) 6 35
(Tom Dascombe) *led early: sn hdd and stdd bk into midfield: clsd to trck ldr 4f out: rdn and lost pl over 2f out: wknd wl over 1f out* **7/1**[3]
3m 7.63s (15.63) **Going Correction** +0.95s/f (Soft)
**WFA** 3 from 4yo+ 11lb **9** Ran SP% **113.0**
Speed ratings (Par 103): **89,88,88,87,86 80,76,73,72**
CSF £34.49 CT £188.69 TOTE £12.50: £3.10, £1.30, £2.30; EX 55.10 Trifecta £328.50.
**Owner** Matt Watkinson **Bred** Gestut Etzean **Trained** Garstang, Lancs

**FOCUS**
There had been 3.4mm of rain over the previous 24 hours, and the going was given as soft, good to soft in places (GoingStick: 5.5), although it was changed to soft all round after the third race. All race distances were as advertised. A modest heat.

## 5321 COMPTON BEAUCHAMP ESTATES LTD EBF NOVICE STKS (PLUS 10 RACE) 6f
**6:00** (6:00) (Class 4) 2-Y-O **£4,269** (£1,270; £634; £317) **Stalls** Centre

Form RPR
03 **1** **Tathmeen (IRE)**[34] 4049 2-9-2 0........................................ JimCrowley 3 83+
(Richard Hannon) *mde all and travelled strly: shkn up and readily asserted over 1f out: in n.d fnl f: v easily* **4/6**[1]
0 **2** 6 **Qayes**[47] 3590 2-9-2 0............................................ MartinLane 7 63
(John Gosden) *t.k.h: hld up in tch in last pair: clsd 3f out: effrt to chse wnr 2f out: sn outpcd: wl hld 2nd and kpt on same pce ins fnl f* **7/2**[2]
**3** 1 1/4 **Lady Of Petra** 2-8-11 0............................................. JosephineGordon 2 54
(Eve Johnson Houghton) *hld up in tch in last pair: clsd to chse ldrs over 2f out: 3rd and outpcd over 1f out: wl hld and kpt on same pce ins fnl f* **9/1**
**4** 3 1/4 **Achianna (USA)** 2-8-11 0............................................. WilliamCarson 1 45
(Rod Millman) *chsd wnr tl 2f out: sn rdn and lost pl: hung rt and wknd 1f out* **25/1**
6 **5** 6 **Reverberation**[70] 2756 2-9-2 0........................................ MartinDwyer 4 32
(Sylvester Kirk) *t.k.h: chsd ldng pair tl rdn: lost pl and dropped to rr over 2f out: bhd over 1f out* **13/2**[3]
1m 17.7s (4.70) **Going Correction** +1.025s/f (Soft) **5** Ran SP% **109.4**
Speed ratings (Par 96): **109,101,99,95,87**
CSF £3.22 TOTE £1.50: £1.02, £2.30; EX 3.00 Trifecta £11.10.
**Owner** Hamdan Al Maktoum **Bred** Shadwell Estate Company Limited **Trained** East Everleigh, Wilts

**FOCUS**
This proved straightforward for the odds-on winner.

## 5322 STEVE MCNALLY LIFETIME IN RACING NURSERY H'CAP 6f
**6:30** (6:31) (Class 5) 2-Y-O **£3,881** (£1,155; £577; £288) **Stalls** Centre

Form RPR
505 **1** **That's My Girl (IRE)**[15] 4749 2-8-5 **62**.......................... KieranO'Neill 6 63
(Richard Hannon) *sn rdn along in rr: hung rt and hdwy on stands rail over 1f out: chal and hung lft u.p ins fnl f: styd on to ld 50yds out: gng away at fin* **16/1**
2134 **2** 1 1/2 **Alaska (IRE)**[13] 4827 2-8-13 **75**.................................. MitchGodwin(5) 2 71
(Sylvester Kirk) *hung lft thrght: hld up in tch: clsd to trck ldrs 1/2-way: ev ch 2f out: sn rdn: led ins fnl f: hdd 50yds out: outpcd and hung lft towards fin* **7/2**[2]
343 **3** nk **Story Minister (IRE)**[31] 4160 2-9-1 **72**...................... RichardKingscote 3 67
(Tom Dascombe) *t.k.h: chsd ldr tl led 2f out: hung rt over 1f out: edgd bk lft and hdd ins fnl f: outpcd fnl 50yds* **8/1**
4533 **4** 1 3/4 **Miss Mo Brown Bear (IRE)**[7] 5057 2-9-0 **71**.................... SeanLevey 1 61
(Richard Hannon) *hld up in tch: trckd ldrs over 2f out: rdn to chal over 1f out tl no ex ins fnl f: wknd fnl 75yds* **5/2**[1]
3622 **5** 1 **The Love Doctor (IRE)**[16] 4716 2-9-1 **72**...................(v[1]) JimCrowley 4 59
(David Evans) *led: rdn over 2f out: hdd 2f out: no ex u.p over 1f out: wknd ins fnl f* **5/2**[1]
5120 **6** 42 **Branscombe**[13] 4866 2-9-7 **78**........................................ WilliamBuick 5
(Mark Johnston) *chsd ldrs: rdn to chal ent fnl 2f tl lost pl qckly jst over 1f out: sn eased and virtually p.u ins fnl f: t.o* **6/1**[3]
1m 19.05s (6.05) **Going Correction** +1.025s/f (Soft) **6** Ran SP% **110.6**
Speed ratings (Par 94): **100,98,97,95,93 37**
CSF £68.18 TOTE £13.70: £4.30, £1.80; EX 90.10 Trifecta £432.90.
**Owner** J S Threadwell & J Botton **Bred** Ms C Peddie **Trained** East Everleigh, Wilts

**FOCUS**
The going was changed to soft all round after this race. An ordinary nursery, rated cautiously around those close up.

## 5323 SNOWS PEUGEOT H'CAP 1m 2f
**7:05** (7:05) (Class 4) (0-85,85) 3-Y-O **£6,469** (£1,925; £962; £481) **Stalls** Centre

Form RPR
-135 **1** **Rake's Progress**[15] 4751 3-8-4 **73**................................ DavidEgan(5) 7 85
(Heather Main) *mde all: rdn over 1f out: edgd rt 1f out: styd on strly and drew clr fnl 100yds: rdn out* **8/1**
5-21 **2** 2 3/4 **Big Tour (IRE)**[17] 4700 3-9-4 **82**........................................ MartinLane 5 89
(Saeed bin Suroor) *chsd ldrs: clsd to trck ldrs and nt clrest of run ent fnl 2f: hdwy to chse wnr over 1f out: drvn and 1 l down 1f out: hung rt and no ex u.p ins fnl f: outpcd fnl 100yds* **11/2**
6-16 **3** 2 1/2 **Music Seeker (IRE)**[54] 3317 3-9-6 **84**............................ RyanTate 8 86
(James Eustace) *dwlt: sn rcvrd and in tch in midfield: effrt over 2f out: hdwy u.p 1f out: styd on ins fnl f to snatch 3rd on post: nvr threatening ldng pair* **9/2**[3]
2461 **4** nse **Bedouin (IRE)**[19] 4632 3-9-0 **78**.....................(b) JamieSpencer 1 80
(Luca Cumani) *hld up in tch in last pair: effrt 3f out: swtchd rt 2f out and hdwy u.p over 1f out: styd on to go 3rd wl ins fnl f: nvr threatening ldng pair: lost 3rd on post* **7/1**
41-3 **5** 3/4 **Baashiq (IRE)**[19] 4618 3-9-5 **83**........................................ JimCrowley 6 84
(Roger Varian) *t.k.h: chsd ldrs: effrt over 2f out: 3rd and no ex u.p 1f out: wknd ins fnl f* **10/3**[1]
5312 **6** 1 3/4 **Pilgrim's Treasure (USA)**[28] 4254 3-9-7 **85**...............(p) WilliamBuick 4 82
(Charlie Appleby) *rousted along leaving stalls: in tch in midfield: effrt over 2f out: no imp u.p over 1f out: wknd ins fnl f* **7/2**[2]
6013 **7** 3 **Flying North**[19] 4621 3-9-7 **85**........................................ TimmyMurphy 9 76
(Richard Hannon) *t.k.h: chsd wnr tl over 1f out: sn lost pl: wknd ins fnl f* **20/1**
-460 **8** 1 3/4 **Jackhammer (IRE)**[27] 4322 3-9-5 **83**.....................(h) RichardKingscote 3 71
(William Knight) *stdd s: hld up in rr: effrt 3f out: no imp: nvr trbld ldrs* **20/1**
2m 14.27s (5.47) **Going Correction** +0.95s/f (Soft) **8** Ran SP% **112.0**
Speed ratings (Par 102): **116,113,111,111,111 109,107,105**
CSF £49.09 CT £221.10 TOTE £7.80: £2.00, £1.70, £2.10; EX 33.00 Trifecta £258.50.
**Owner** Coxwell Partnership **Bred** Mr & Mrs A E Pakenham **Trained** Kingston Lisle, Oxon

**FOCUS**
An interesting handicap but few got into it, the winner dominating from the front.

## 5324 ZENERGI FILLIES' H'CAP 1m (S)
**7:35** (7:37) (Class 4) (0-80,84) 3-Y-O+ **£4,690** (£1,395; £697; £348) **Stalls** Centre

Form RPR
4425 **1** **Seduce Me**[38] 3900 3-9-3 **77**........................................(p) JimCrowley 4 92
(K R Burke) *hld up in tch: clsd to trck ldrs 3f out: swtchd rt over 2f out: led 2f out: rdn and readily asserted jst over 1f out: wl clr ins fnl f: easily* **8/1**
61-4 **2** 8 **Medicean Ballet (IRE)**[41] 3786 3-9-2 **76**.................... FergusSweeney 3 73
(Henry Candy) *pressed ldrs: rdn 3f out: outpcd by wnr jst over 1f out: no ch w wnr and battling for placings fnl f: wnt 2nd fnl 50yds* **11/2**[3]
13 **3** 3/4 **Finishing Touch**[13] 4861 3-9-7 **81**...............................(t[1]) MartinLane 2 76
(Saeed bin Suroor) *w ldrs tl led after 3f: rdn 3f out: drvn and hdd 2f out: outpcd by wnr jst over 1f out: no ch w wnr after: lost wl hld 2nd fnl 50yds* **2/1**[1]
2311 **4** 3 1/4 **Cheerfilly (IRE)**[7] 5078 3-9-5 **84** 6ex..........................(p) PaddyPilley(5) 5 71
(Tom Dascombe) *pressed ldrs: rdn 3f out: outpcd by wnr jst over 1f out: no ch w wnr 1f out: wknd ins fnl f* **9/4**[2]
0-20 **5** 17 **Salamah (IRE)**[36] 3964 3-9-6 **80**.................................. WilliamBuick 6 28
(Michael Bell) *led for 3f: rdn and lost pl 1/2-way: bhd 2f out: eased ins fnl f* **8/1**
10 **6** 116 **Hidden Charms (IRE)**[44] 3693 3-8-12 **72**.......................... JamieSpencer 1
(David Simcock) *stdd s: a rr: lost tch 1/2-way: virtually p.u fnl 2f: t.o* **8/1**
1m 47.32s (7.62) **Going Correction** +1.025s/f (Soft) **6** Ran SP% **112.8**
Speed ratings (Par 102): **102,94,93,90,73**
CSF £49.97 TOTE £8.60: £3.10, £2.70; EX 39.70 Trifecta £134.70.
**Owner** Ontoawinner, R Mckeown & E Burke **Bred** Jeremy Green And Sons **Trained** Middleham Moor, N Yorks

**FOCUS**
A well-run handicap.

## 5325 EVENTS BAR MANAGEMENT FILLIES' H'CAP 6f
**8:05** (8:08) (Class 4) (0-80,81) 3-Y-O+ **£4,690** (£1,395; £697; £348) **Stalls** Centre

Form RPR
2005 **1** **Jule In The Crown**[40] 3822 3-9-8 **81**.............................. TomMarquand 6 90
(Richard Hannon) *t.k.h: hld up in tch in midfield: swtchd lft and effrt wl over 1f out: rdn to chal ins fnl f: r.o wl to ld towards fin* **7/1**[3]
5256 **2** nk **Bellevarde (IRE)**[13] 4843 3-8-2 **61**............................ JosephineGordon 2 69
(Richard Price) *trckd ldrs: rdn to ld over 1f out: drew clr w wnr ins fnl f: kpt on wl tl hdd and no ex towards fin* **9/1**
3560 **3** 7 **Pretty Bubbles**[38] 3919 8-9-12 **80**..........................(v) FergusSweeney 1 68
(J R Jenkins) *in tch in last trio: clsd to trck ldrs 2f out: rdn to chal over 1f out tl no ex ins fnl f: wknd fnl 100yds* **20/1**
-211 **4** 1 3/4 **Zumran**[6] 5122 3-8-12 **76** 6ex............................................ DavidEgan(5) 9 58
(Philip McBride) *chsd ldrs: rdn over 2f out: drvn and no imp over 1f out: wknd ins fnl f* **2/1**[1]
-304 **5** 2 1/2 **The Lacemaker**[19] 4624 3-9-0 **73**................................(b[1]) JamieSpencer 4 47
(Ed Dunlop) *stdd and bmpd s: hld up in last pair: effrt 2f out: sn outpcd and btn: wknd fnl f* **14/1**
-321 **6** 1 1/2 **Beck And Call**[40] 3822 3-8-13 **77**.................................... GeorgiaCox(5) 3 47+
(Henry Candy) *chsd ldr: sddle slipped after 2f: cl up but rdr unable to offer meaningful assistance: led ent fnl 2f: hdd over 1f out: 4th and btn ent fnl f: wknd ins fnl f* **11/4**[2]
10P6 **7** 5 **Harbour Grey (IRE)**[14] 4810 3-9-2 **75**............................ SeanLevey 5 30
(Richard Hannon) *wnt lft and bmpd s: hld up in tch in last pair: short lived effrt over 1f out: sn wknd: burst blood vessel* **17/2**
331 **8** 8 **Think Fashion (IRE)**[45] 3669 3-9-5 **78**........................(p) WilliamBuick 10 9
(Brian Meehan) *t.k.h: led tl ent fnl 2f: sn lost pl u.p: bhd and eased ins fnl f* **8/1**
1m 18.76s (5.76) **Going Correction** +1.025s/f (Soft)
**WFA** 3 from 8yo 5lb **8** Ran SP% **115.6**
Speed ratings (Par 102): **102,101,92,89,86 84,77,67**
CSF £67.83 CT £1205.77 TOTE £8.90: £2.40, £2.10, £3.80; EX 67.40 Trifecta £447.50.
**Owner** M Stewkesbury **Bred** Mervyn Stewkesbury **Trained** East Everleigh, Wilts

**FOCUS**
The first two pulled clear of the rest in this fillies' sprint.

## 5326 MATTHEW FEDRICK FARRIERY H'CAP 7f (S)
**8:40** (8:41) (Class 5) (0-75,75) 3-Y-O+ **£3,234** (£962; £481; £240) **Stalls** Centre

Form RPR
3643 **1** **Childesplay**[15] 4746 6-9-7 **73**........................................ DavidEgan(5) 5 84
(Heather Main) *chsd ldr tl rdn to ld over 1f out: sn clr and r.o wl: readily* **8/1**
1232 **2** 5 **Lucky Louie**[70] 2763 4-9-8 **69**........................................(p) JimCrowley 1 67
(Roger Teal) *hld up in tch in last pair: effrt 2f out: rdn over 1f out: styd on to chse clr wnr ins fnl f: kpt on but nvr a threat to wnr* **4/1**[2]
5503 **3** 2 1/4 **Dream Farr (IRE)**[22] 4495 4-9-8 **74**.............................(t) JennyPowell(5) 3 66
(Ed Walker) *led tl rdn and hdd over 1f out: sn outpcd: wknd ins fnl f* **6/1**
-050 **4** 1 1/2 **Captain Hawk**[19] 4610 3-8-13 **67**.................................(p) StevieDonohoe 4 52
(Ian Williams) *t.k.h: hld up in tch: lost pl and dropped to rr u.p 2f out: rallied to pass btn rivals ins fnl f: no ch w wnr* **10/1**
4002 **5** 1 1/4 **Gunmaker (IRE)**[21] 4542 3-8-13 **67**.............................. JamieSpencer 7 49
(David Simcock) *stdd s: hld up in last pair: swtchd lft and clsd to chse ldrs 2f out: rdn and no hdwy over 1f out: wknd ins fnl f* **9/2**[3]
030 **6** 3 **Mulsanne Chase**[33] 4097 3-9-4 **72**................................... SteveDrowne 2 46
(Brian Barr) *in tch in midfield: rdn over 2f out: sn struggling and btn over 1f out: wknd fnl f* **25/1**
12 **7** 19 **Samarmadi**[10] 4979 3-9-7 **75**........................................ JosephineGordon 6
(Hugo Palmer) *chsd ldrs: rdn 3f out: lost pl u.p 2f out: bhd and eased ins fnl f* **7/4**[1]
1m 34.47s (8.77) **Going Correction** +1.025s/f (Soft)
**WFA** 3 from 4yo+ 7lb **7** Ran SP% **112.9**
Speed ratings (Par 103): **90,84,81,80,78 75,53**
CSF £38.67 TOTE £8.20: £2.90, £2.00; EX 35.60 Trifecta £191.30.
**Owner** Wetumpka Racing & Andrew Knott **Bred** J P M Main **Trained** Kingston Lisle, Oxon

**FOCUS**
They didn't go that quick early and it looked an advantage to race handily.
T/Plt: £2,336.20 to a £1 stake. Pool: £59,782.42 - 18.68 winning units T/Qpdt: £405.20 to a £1 stake. Pool: £6,106.70 - 11.15 winning units **Steve Payne**

# 5299 SANDOWN (R-H)

Thursday, July 27

**OFFICIAL GOING: Round course - good to soft (6.5); sprint course - soft (good to soft in places; 5.5)**

Wind: Fresh, against Weather: Fine but cloudy, rain during races 4 & 5

## 5327 BRITISH STALLION STUDS EBF MAIDEN FILLIES' STKS (PLUS 10 RACE) 5f 10y

**2:00** (2:00) (Class 5) 2-Y-O **£3,881** (£1,155; £577; £288) **Stalls** Low

Form RPR

42 1 **May Girl**[8] 5015 2-9-0 0 JimCrowley 9 71
(Robert Cowell) *unf: racd off the rail: disp ld tl def advantage wl over 1f out: drvn fnl f: hld on wl nr fin* **7/1**

65 2 *hd* **Highland Mary**[14] 4799 2-9-0 0 SeanLevey 3 70
(Richard Hannon) *chsd ldng pair: rdn over 1f out: clsd u.p fnl f: tk 2nd last 100yds: jst hld nr fin* **14/1**

2 3 *hd* **Global Rose (IRE)**[10] 4972 2-9-0 0 FranBerry 2 70
(Gay Kelleway) *w'like: racd against rail: disp ld to wl over 1f out: sn rdn: lost 2nd last 100yds but kpt on wl towards fin* **2/1**[1]

0 4 *3* **Comselle**[76] 2563 2-9-0 0 OisinMurphy 6 59
(Stuart Kittow) *a abt same pl: pushed along over 1f out: no imp ldrs but nt disgracd* **66/1**

2 5 *shd* **Princess Keira (IRE)**[19] 4628 2-9-0 0 FrannyNorton 7 58
(Mick Quinn) *w'like: disp 3rd pl tl over 1f out: one pce fnl f* **3/1**[3]

6 *1 1/2* **Rachael's Rocket (IRE)** 2-8-7 0 GeorgiaDobie(7) 4 53
(J S Moore) *cmpt: v s.i.s: detached in last: shkn up 2f out and sed to make gd prog against rail over 1f out: n.m.r and hanging into rail after: nt persevered w whn no ch after* **80/1**

7 *hd* **Dutch Desire** 2-9-0 0 WilliamBuick 1 52+
(William Haggas) *cmpt: dwlt: mostly in last trio: pushed along wl over 1f out: nvr on terms but kpt on ins fnl f* **11/4**[2]

0 8 *2 3/4* **Counterfeit**[21] 4533 2-9-0 0 KieranShoemark 8 42
(Richard Hughes) *str: in tch disputing 5th and racd wd: shkn up 2f out: fdd* **25/1**

9 *5* **Violet Beauregarde** 2-9-0 0 MartinHarley 5 24
(Harry Dunlop) *leggy: s.i.s: mostly in last trio: shkn up 2f out: wknd fnl f* **66/1**

1m 4.81s (3.21) **Going Correction** +0.50s/f (Yiel) **9** Ran SP% **112.2**
Speed ratings (Par 91): **94,93,93,88,88 86,85,81,73**
CSF £89.57 TOTE £7.10: £1.90, £3.40, £1.10; EX 50.30 Trifecta £213.40.
**Owner** Bottisham Heath Stud **Bred** Bottisham Heath Stud **Trained** Six Mile Bottom, Cambs

**FOCUS**
This looked a decent juvenile race, and it was taken by the filly drawn the widest.

## 5328 RACINGUK.COM H'CAP 1m 6f

**2:30** (2:30) (Class 3) (0-95,89) 3-Y-O **£8,092** (£2,423; £1,211; £605; £302) **Stalls** Low

Form RPR

-531 1 **Joshua Reynolds**[27] 4314 3-9-3 85 (b) AdamKirby 3 97+
(John Gosden) *t.k.h and pressed ldr after 2f: led over 2f out and sent for home: hanging rt and racing awkwardly fr over 1f out but a enough of a ld to hold on* **15/8**[1]

231 2 *3/4* **Nadaitak**[19] 4611 3-9-0 82 JimCrowley 5 91
(Sir Michael Stoute) *hld up and last to 5f out: pushed along 4f out: prog and drvn over 2f out: chsd wnr over 1f out: grad clsd fnl f: nvr quite got there* **7/2**[2]

2364 3 *4* **Orsino (IRE)**[20] 4586 3-8-5 73 JimmyQuinn 4 76
(Andrew Balding) *lw: chsd ldr 2f: styd cl up: drvn over 2f out: wnt 2nd again briefly wl over 1f out: sn one pce and btn* **14/1**[3]

1541 4 *9* **Duke Of Bronte**[21] 4535 3-9-2 84 OisinMurphy 1 74
(Rod Millman) *lw: in tch: dropped to last and struggling 5f out: no prog over 2f out: wknd over 1f out* **7/2**[2]

2160 5 *19* **Janszoon**[35] 3998 3-9-7 89 (b) WilliamBuick 2 53
(Charlie Appleby) *led: shkn up and hdd over 2f out: wknd qckly wl over 1f out: eased and t.o* **7/2**[2]

3m 7.31s (2.81) **Going Correction** +0.20s/f (Good) **5** Ran SP% **108.1**
Speed ratings (Par 104): **99,98,96,91,80**
CSF £8.31 TOTE £2.30: £1.50, £2.40; EX 9.00 Trifecta £41.40.
**Owner** Castle Down Racing & Rachel Hood **Bred** Meon Valley Stud **Trained** Newmarket, Suffolk

**FOCUS**
The round course rail was out 3 yards from the 1m point to the winning post, adding 20 yards to this race distance. Only one of these didn't seem overly fancied in the betting, strongly suggesting this was a tight race to break down before the off.

## 5329 LONGINES IRISH CHAMPIONS WEEKEND EBF STALLIONS STAR STKS (LISTED RACE) 7f

**3:05** (3:06) (Class 1) 2-Y-O

**£17,013** (£6,450; £3,228; £1,608; £807; £405) **Stalls** Low

Form RPR

16 1 **Tajaanus (IRE)**[26] 4361 2-9-0 0 JimCrowley 1 97
(Richard Hannon) *hld up in midfield: shkn up 2f out: prog and rdn over 1f out: chsd ldr jst ins fnl f: clsd to ld last strides: jst hld on* **8/1**[2]

1 2 *nse* **Capomento (IRE)**[17] 4689 2-9-0 0 RichardKingscote 9 97
(Tom Dascombe) *w'like: hld up towards rr: prog on outer over 1f out: clsd w wnr ins fnl f: styd on wl to take 2nd last strides: jst failed* **14/1**

3221 3 *nk* **Billesdon Brook**[22] 4496 2-9-0 87 SeanLevey 6 96
(Richard Hannon) *lw: trckd ldng pair: led gng strly 2f out: committed for home over 1f out: styd on but hdd last strides* **5/2**[1]

3136 4 *1 3/4* **So Hi Society (IRE)**[13] 4855 2-9-0 92 MartinDwyer 5 92
(Archie Watson) *hld up in midfield: rdn and prog 2f out: disp 2nd over 1f out to jst ins fnl f: kpt on same pce after and hld in 4th whn squeezed for room nr fin* **8/1**[2]

0 5 *1/2* **Whitefountainfairy (IRE)**[34] 4028 2-9-0 0 OisinMurphy 10 91+
(Andrew Balding) *dropped in fr wd draw and hld up in last pair: waiting for room over 2f out: prog over 1f out but hanging rt after: kpt on fnl f but nvr able to threaten* **14/1**

41 6 *5* **Ellthea (IRE)**[49] 3482 2-9-0 0 CliffordLee 3 78
(K R Burke) *cmpt: reluctant to enter stalls: towards rr: plld out wd and shkn up over 2f out but no rspnse: wl adrift over 1f out: consented to run on last 100yds* **16/1**

11 7 *nk* **Cape Bunting (IRE)**[13] 4848 2-9-0 88 WilliamBuick 8 78
(Mark Johnston) *athletic: won skirmish for ld after 1f: rdn and hdd 2f out: kpt on in 2nd pl tl wknd qckly fnl f* **5/2**[1]

51 8 *1 1/4* **Royal Parks**[21] 4528 2-9-0 0 MartinHarley 4 74
(James Tate) *led 1f: trckd ldrs: rdn 2f out: sn wknd* **14/1**

315 9 *1/2* **Elizabeth Bennet (IRE)**[26] 4361 2-9-0 85 FrannyNorton 7 73
(Charles Hills) *pressed ldr after 1f and racd on inner: lost pl 2f out: sn wknd* **10/1**[3]

4140 10 *9* **Campion**[26] 4361 2-9-0 80 TomMarquand 2 51
(Richard Hannon) *a in last pair: wknd 2f out* **50/1**

1m 30.76s (1.26) **Going Correction** +0.20s/f (Good) **10** Ran SP% **116.3**
Speed ratings (Par 102): **100,99,99,97,97 91,90,89,88,78**
CSF £113.04 TOTE £8.90: £2.20, £3.70, £1.70; EX 94.30 Trifecta £585.60.
**Owner** Hamdan Al Maktoum **Bred** Shadwell Estate Company Limited **Trained** East Everleigh, Wilts

**FOCUS**
The round course rail was out 3 yards from the 1m point to the winning post, adding 20 yards to this race distance. A competitive race for the level, with the winner posting a pb and the 4th helping to set the level along with the race averages.

## 5330 WATCH RACING UK ANYWHERE H'CAP 1m 1f 209y

**3:40** (3:40) (Class 4) (0-85,87) 3-Y-O+ **£5,822** (£1,732; £865; £432) **Stalls** Low

Form RPR

4211 1 **Silver Ghost (IRE)**[21] 4522 4-9-12 83 CharlesBishop 5 97
(Eve Johnson Houghton) *trckd ldr: led wl over 2f out: clr over 1f out: rdn and styd on strly fnl f: quite impressive* **3/1**[2]

-131 2 *3* **Eynhallow**[8] 5033 3-9-2 87 6ex PaddyPilley(5) 6 96+
(Roger Charlton) *lw: hld up in last pair: shkn up and prog over 2f out: chsd wnr 1f out but 4 l down: styd on but no significant imp* **4/6**[1]

-001 3 *5* **High Draw (FR)**[56] 3274 4-9-2 73 MartinHarley 8 71
(K R Burke) *led at gd pce and styd away fr inner rail: rdn and hdd wl over 2f out: no ch w wnr after: lost 2nd 1f out: fdd but hld on for 3rd* **16/1**

-622 4 *1 3/4* **Inke (IRE)**[76] 2575 5-9-7 78 WilliamCarson 3 73
(Jim Boyle) *chsd ldng pair: rdn and no imp over 2f out: fdd over 1f out* **20/1**

6250 5 *1 3/4* **Mikmak**[15] 4763 4-9-10 81 (p) MartinDwyer 2 72
(William Muir) *chsd ldng pair: rdn over 2f out: wknd over 1f out* **16/1**

-160 6 *nk* **Caponova (IRE)**[42] 3744 4-9-11 82 RichardKingscote 4 72
(Tom Dascombe) *hld up in last: shkn up over 2f out: nvr a factor but keeping on bttr than sme at fin* **14/1**

-326 7 *1* **Artful Rogue (IRE)**[29] 4216 6-9-11 82 JimCrowley 7 70
(Amanda Perrett) *lw: hld up in midfield: rdn and no prog over 2f out: wl btn after* **8/1**[3]

1124 8 *6* **Start Seven**[124] 1361 5-9-12 83 DougieCostello 1 59
(Jamie Osborne) *t.k.h: hld up in midfield: shkn up 3f out: sn wl btn* **33/1**

2m 11.13s (0.63) **Going Correction** +0.20s/f (Good)
**WFA** 3 from 4yo+ 9lb **8** Ran SP% **122.2**
Speed ratings (Par 105): **105,102,98,97,95 95,94,89**
CSF £5.74 CT £27.47 TOTE £4.10: £1.20, £1.10, £4.00; EX 6.00 Trifecta £42.10.
**Owner** Mrs Jennifer Simpson Racing **Bred** George Delahunt **Trained** Blewbury, Oxon

**FOCUS**
The round course rail was out 3 yards from the 1m point to the winning post, adding 20 yards to this race distance. Punters only seemed to want to know about two of these, and they were first and second, but not in the order most expected.

## 5331 PADDOCK FILLIES' H'CAP 1m 1f 209y

**4:10** (4:15) (Class 5) (0-75,77) 3-Y-O **£3,881** (£1,155; £577; £288) **Stalls** Low

Form RPR

4214 1 **Pondering**[9] 4989 3-8-10 66 (v) EdwardGreatrex(3) 3 74
(Eve Johnson Houghton) *hld up towards rr: rdn and prog over 2f out: chsd ldr jst over 1f out: styd on to ld last 150yds: drvn out* **14/1**

2624 2 *1* **Many Waters (USA)**[16] 4730 3-9-7 74 (v[1]) OisinMurphy 4 80
(Andrew Balding) *pushed up to chse ldrs: rdn over 2f out: clsd w wnr over 1f out: chal ins fnl f: jst outpcd last 100yds* **7/2**[2]

5-41 3 *2 3/4* **Paradise Cove**[45] 3649 3-9-7 74 WilliamBuick 9 75+
(William Haggas) *lw: led: styd away fr inner in bk st but racd nr it in home st: skipped clr 3f out: rdn over 1f out: worn down last 150yds* **9/4**[1]

0-40 4 *7* **So Hoity Toity**[21] 4537 3-9-6 73 AdamKirby 2 60
(Hughie Morrison) *reluctant to enter stalls: chsd ldng pair: wnt 2nd over 3f out: sn rdn: no imp ldr and lost 2nd jst over 1f out: wknd and fin tired* **10/1**

-522 5 *3 1/2* **Tomorrow Mystery**[162] 737 3-9-6 73 DougieCostello 1 53
(Jamie Osborne) *hld up in midfield: effrt on inner whn nt clr run over 2f out: and lost pl: no ch after: plugged on to pass a few nr fin* **14/1**

3501 6 *nk* **Voi**[21] 4544 3-9-3 70 (t) FranBerry 7 49
(Conrad Allen) *hld up in last: effrt on inner over 2f out: sn no prog and btn* **10/1**

1046 7 *1* **Braztime**[14] 4794 3-9-10 77 SeanLevey 13 54
(Richard Hannon) *lw: a in rr: rdn and no prog 3f out* **16/1**

0301 8 *1/2* **Venetian Proposal (IRE)**[15] 4754 3-8-2 55 (p) KieranO'Neill 5 31
(Zoe Davison) *hld up towards rr: rdn on outer 3f out: no prog and btn 2f out* **14/1**

464 9 *14* **Becuna (USA)**[17] 4700 3-8-13 66 LouisSteward 11 14
(Michael Bell) *lw: sn restrained into 5th: rdn over 2f out and no prog: wknd wl over 1f out: eased fnl f* **14/1**

5-25 10 *35* **Beyond Recall**[43] 3727 3-9-5 72 KieranShoemark 12
(Luca Cumani) *chsd ldr to over 3f out: wknd qckly: virtually p.u over 1f out* **7/1**[3]

2m 13.02s (2.52) **Going Correction** +0.20s/f (Good) **10** Ran SP% **116.2**
Speed ratings (Par 97): **97,96,94,88,85 85,84,84,72,44**
CSF £62.47 CT £155.32 TOTE £21.90: £3.90, £1.60, £1.60; EX 95.30 Trifecta £401.70.
**Owner** Eden Racing Club **Bred** Aston House Stud **Trained** Blewbury, Oxon

**FOCUS**
The round course rail was out 3 yards from the 1m point to the winning post, adding 20 yards to this race distance. The three non-runners weren't that short in the market when taken out, so the race looked as competitive as it did at the declaration stage.

## 5332 ROA/RACING POST OWNERS JACKPOT H'CAP 1m

**4:45** (4:45) (Class 5) (0-75,74) 3-Y-O **£3,881** (£1,155; £577; £288) **Stalls** Low

Form RPR

6231 1 **Finale**[28] 4276 3-9-5 72 AdamKirby 5 85+
(Hughie Morrison) *trckd ldr 2f: styd cl up: led over 2f out: idled and hanging rt fr over 1f out: edgd into runner-up 100yds out: jst prevailed* **11/10**[1]

6161 2 *shd* **Kyllachys Tale (IRE)**[28] 4255 3-9-4 71 OisinMurphy 2 81
(Roger Teal) *led: rdn and hdd over 2f out: rallied u.p over 1f out: jnd wnr and impeded 100yds out: jst pipped* **7/2**[3]

3-63 3 *2 1/4* **Funky Footsteps (IRE)**[26] 4372 3-9-3 70 (p[1]) CharlesBishop 1 75
(Eve Johnson Houghton) *t.k.h early: trckd ldrs: rdn 3f out: sn outpcd: tk 3rd 1f out: styd on after and nrst fin* **11/4**[2]

2200 **4** *9* **Testbourne (IRE)**[23] 4474 3-9-1 **68** MartinHarley 4 52
(K R Burke) *trckd ldr after 2f to 3f out: tried to chal over 2f out: rdn and no rspnse wl over 1f out: sn wknd* **25/1**

6402 **5** *12* **My Illusionist**[31] 4164 3-9-7 **74** KieranShoemark 3 31
(Harry Dunlop) *lw: a last: rdn and btn 3f out: sn wl bhd* **10/1**

1m 46.61s (3.31) **Going Correction** +0.20s/f (Good) 5 Ran SP% **109.4**
Speed ratings (Par 100): **91,90,88,79,67**
CSF £5.21 TOTE £1.80: £1.10, £2.40; EX 5.20 Trifecta £3.00.
**Owner** T D Rootes & O F Waller **Bred** Shutford Stud **Trained** East Ilsley, Berks

**FOCUS**
The round course rail was out 3 yards from the 1m point to the winning post, adding 20 yards to this race distance. Two came away from the remainder but the winner needed to survive a stewards' inquiry.

## 5333 LUBRICATORS H'CAP 7f
**5:15** (5:17) (Class 5) (0-75,77) 3-Y-0+ **£3,881** (£1,155; £577; £288) **Stalls** Low

Form RPR

-404 **1** **Another Boy**[14] 4810 4-9-5 **71** (p) PatrickO'Donnell(5) 2 79
(Ralph Beckett) *lw: mde all: styd away fr inner in st: had rivals at work over 2f out: shkn up over 1f out: drvn fnl f: ld dwindled but a holding on* **9/2**[3]

53-4 **2** *½* **Bengal Lancer**[28] 4268 3-9-2 **70** FranBerry 1 73
(Ian Williams) *chsd ldng pair: rdn over 2f out: disp 2nd fr over 1f out: clsd on wnr fnl f but a jst hld* **9/2**[3]

0214 **3** *shd* **Alemaratalyoum (IRE)**[10] 4983 3-9-6 **74** AdamKirby 7 77
(Ed Dunlop) *lw: hld up in 5th: rdn over 2f out: prog to dispute 2nd over 1f out: clsd on wnr fnl f but a hld* **9/4**[1]

2360 **4** *2 ¼* **Jay Kay**[18] 4663 8-9-4 **68** (h) CliffordLee(3) 8 68
(K R Burke) *trckd ldng trio: rdn and nt qckn over 2f out: kpt on again fnl f but nvr able to threaten* **10/3**[2]

0000 **5** *¾* **Fairway To Heaven (IRE)**[15] 4752 8-9-1 **67** PaddyBradley(5) 5 65
(Lee Carter) *chsd wnr: rdn over 2f out: lost 2nd over 1f out: steadily fdd* **25/1**

4216 **6** *½* **Duke Of North (IRE)**[65] 2917 5-9-2 **70** IsobelFrancis(7) 4 67
(Jim Boyle) *s.s: t.k.h and hld up in 6th: effrt on wd outside over 2f out: hanging rt and racd awkwardly after: nvr able to land a blow* **8/1**

00-0 **7** *10* **Prosecute (FR)**[21] 4538 4-9-9 **70** TomMarquand 6 40
(Ali Stronge) *rrd s and slowly away: a last: rdn 3f out: sn btn* **25/1**

1m 31.71s (2.21) **Going Correction** +0.20s/f (Good)
**WFA** 3 from 4yo+ 7lb 7 Ran SP% **109.0**
Speed ratings (Par 103): **95,94,94,91,90 90,78**
CSF £22.46 CT £50.33 TOTE £4.80: £2.30, £3.20; EX 28.00 Trifecta £74.10.
**Owner** Mrs Philip Snow & Partners **Bred** Mrs P Snow & Partners **Trained** Kimpton, Hants

**FOCUS**
The round course rail was out 3 yards from the 1m point to the winning post, adding 20 yards to this race distance. Probably just a modest contest but it was run at a decent pace.
T/Plt: £13.30 to a £1 stake. Pool: £78,140.82 - 4,261.69 winning units T/Qpdt: £3.70 to a £1 stake. Pool: £5,121.57 - 1,004.47 winning units **Jonathan Neesom**

# 5035 YARMOUTH (L-H)
Thursday, July 27

**OFFICIAL GOING: Good to firm (7.5)**
Wind: Fresh across Weather: Cloudy

## 5334 READ SILVESTRE DE SOUSA AT 188BET NOVICE AUCTION STKS (PLUS 10 RACE) 6f 3y
**1:40** (1:41) (Class 4) 2-Y-0 **£4,528** (£1,347; £673; £336) **Stalls** Centre

Form RPR

2 **1** *nk* **Fyre Cay (IRE)**[15] 4760 2-8-12 0 JamieSpencer 3 70
(Kevin Ryan) *racd centre: prom: rdn over 1f out: r.o to go 2nd nr fin: fin 2nd: awrdd r* **4/6**[1]

2264 **2** *nk* **Take Shelter**[40] 3821 2-8-11 77 LukeMorris 8 68
(James Tate) *racd alone on stands' side: sn overall ldr: rdn over 1f out: hdd wl ins fnl f: r.o: fin 3rd: plcd 2nd* **11/4**[2]

**3** *½* **Merkava** 2-8-9 0 GeorgeWood(3) 2 67
(Robyn Brisland) *racd centre: chsd ldrs: led that gp over 2f out tl rdn over 1f out: styd on: fin 4th: plcd 3rd* **20/1**

4 **4** *nk* **Dorcas**[86] 2258 2-8-7 0 SilvestreDeSousa 4 61
(James Given) *racd centre: hld up: pushed along and hdwy over 2f out: rdn over 1f out: styd on: n.m.r towards fin: fin 5th: plcd 4th* **13/2**[3]

**5** *1 ¼* **Agent Of Fortune** 2-8-4 0 RoystonFfrench 7 54
(Christine Dunnett) *s.s: in rr: shkn up over 1f out: r.o: nt rch ldrs: fin 6th: plcd 5th* **250/1**

0 **6** *1* **Moremoneymoreparty (IRE)**[23] 4472 2-8-7 0 AdamBeschizza 5 54
(Richard Guest) *racd keenly: led centre gp over 3f: rdn over 1f out: no ex ins fnl f: fin 7th: plcd 6th* **28/1**

0633 **D** **Millie's Kiss**[15] 4761 3-8-5 0 ow1 JFEgan 6 47+
(Philip McBride) *rn mstkenly instead of 2yo Mandarin Princess: racd centre: chsd ldrs: rdn to ld that gp over 1f out: edgd rt and led overall wl ins fnl f: r.o: fin 1st: subsequently disqualified and plcd last* **50/1**

1m 12.76s (-1.64) **Going Correction** -0.475s/f (Firm) 7 Ran SP% **110.6**
Speed ratings (Par 96): **90,90,89,89,87 86,91**
Dividends relate to official race day result CSF £81.11 TOTE £43.90: £13.40, £1.10; EX 91.20 Trifecta £277.00.
**Owner** Fyre Partners **Bred** L Wright **Trained** Hambleton, N Yorks

**FOCUS**
An average novice in which plenty had their chance and it went to a 50-1 newcomer. That doesn't tell the whole story, though, as we learnt after the race that the first past the post was actually a 3yo who had been due to run in the 3.15. The second past the post didn't need to improve to win.

## 5335 GET 1/4 ODDS AT 188BET MAIDEN FILLIES' STKS 6f 3y
**2:10** (2:15) (Class 5) 3-4-Y-0 **£3,234** (£962; £481; £240) **Stalls** Centre

Form RPR

-334 **1** **Thafeera (USA)**[20] 4565 3-9-0 75 DavidProbert 5 89
(Charles Hills) *w ldr tl led over 4f out: shkn up over 1f out: r.o wl* **5/2**[2]

64- **2** *3 ½* **Dream Of Joy (IRE)**[280] 7484 3-9-0 0 SilvestreDeSousa 4 78
(Roger Varian) *led: hdd over 4f out: remained handy: chsd wnr over 2f out: rdn over 1f out: no ex ins fnl f* **5/4**[1]

3463 **3** *4 ½* **Omneeya**[24] 4445 3-8-12 69 ow1 (t[1]) MarcMonaghan(3) 6 64
(Marco Botti) *hld up: hdwy over 2f out: rdn over 1f out: hung lft and wknd ins fnl f* **13/2**

**4** *2* **Counter Spirit (IRE)** 3-9-0 0 StevieDonohoe 8 57
(Ismail Mohammed) *hld up in tch: outpcd 2f out: r.o ins fnl f* **16/1**

2 **5** *nk* **Charleston Belle**[24] 4445 3-9-0 0 PatCosgrave 2 56
(Giles Bravery) *hld up: hdwy 2f out: wknd fnl f* **11/2**[3]

0 **6** *15* **Here's The Deal**[24] 4445 3-8-9 0 JaneElliott(5) 9
(Lisa Williamson) *prom: rdn over 3f out: wknd over 2f out* **150/1**

**7** *4 ½* **Eureka Springs** 4-8-12 0 JordanUys(7) 3
(Lisa Williamson) *w ldrs tl hung lft and wknd over 2f out* **100/1**

1m 10.98s (-3.42) **Going Correction** -0.475s/f (Firm)
**WFA** 3 from 4yo 5lb 7 Ran SP% **109.3**
Speed ratings (Par 100): **103,98,92,89,89 69,63**
CSF £5.43 TOTE £2.70: £1.90, £1.10; EX 6.00 Trifecta £15.00.
**Owner** Hamdan Al Maktoum **Bred** Shadwell Farm LLC **Trained** Lambourn, Berks

■ All Good was withdrawn. Price at time of withdrawal 12/1. Rule 4 applies to all bets - deduction 5p in the pound.
■ Stewards' Enquiry : Marc Monaghan 3 day ban - weighed in at 9st having weighed out at 8st 12lb (10-12 Aug)

**FOCUS**
An ordinary maiden dominated by the market leaders.

## 5336 ASL GROUP H'CAP 1m 2f 23y
**2:40** (2:49) (Class 6) (0-60,62) 3-Y-0+ **£2,264** (£673; £336; £168) **Stalls** Low

Form RPR

3436 **1** **Outlaw Torn (IRE)**[3] 5215 8-9-4 **52** (e) RobHornby 2 58
(Richard Guest) *a.p: rdn to ld ins fnl f: r.o* **10/1**

2541 **2** *nk* **Tyrsal (IRE)**[7] 5080 6-9-11 **62** 6ex HollieDoyle(3) 9 67
(Clifford Lines) *hld up: hdwy over 2f out: edgd lft fr over 1f out: rdn and ev ch ins fnl f: r.o* **5/2**[1]

0-02 **3** *2 ¼* **Broughtons Admiral**[40] 3819 3-9-1 **58** PatCosgrave 3 60
(Henry Spiller) *s.i.s: hld up: rdn over 2f out: r.o ins fnl f: wnt 3rd post: nt rch ldrs* **10/3**[2]

-000 **4** *shd* **Dor's Law**[168] 636 4-9-7 **55** RobertWinston 6 56
(Dean Ivory) *led: rdn over 1f out: hdd ins fnl f: styd on same pce* **25/1**

/00- **5** *1* **Navajo Storm (IRE)**[556] 243 4-9-1 **54** JaneElliott(5) 16 54
(Michael Appleby) *chsd ldrs: wnt 2nd over 2f out: rdn and ev ch ins fnl f: hmpd sn after: styd on same pce* **33/1**

0400 **6** *1 ½* **Ripper Street (IRE)**[19] 4626 3-8-6 **49** (h) JFEgan 12 46
(Christine Dunnett) *hld up in tch: rdn over 2f out: edgd lft over 1f out: no ex ins fnl f* **50/1**

6652 **7** *hd* **Sunshineandbubbles**[155] 865 4-9-8 **56** (p) LukeMorris 11 52
(Daniel Mark Loughnane) *w ldr 3f: remained handy: rdn over 2f out: hung lft over 1f out: styd on same pce* **22/1**

0005 **8** *nk* **Justice Frederick (IRE)**[19] 4633 3-9-3 **60** (t) JoeyHaynes 4 57
(Paul D'Arcy) *hld up: hdwy over 3f out: sn rdn: nt clr run over 1f out: styd on towards fin* **12/1**

3-00 **9** *nk* **Lady Nahema (IRE)**[58] 3172 4-9-3 **54** GeorgeWood(3) 13 49
(Martin Bosley) *chsd ldrs: lost pl over 6f out: rdn over 2f out: n.d after* **28/1**

3430 **10** *nk* **Zamadance**[19] 4623 3-9-2 **59** (b[1]) SilvestreDeSousa 10 54
(Ed Dunlop) *hld up: swtchd rt 3f out: rdn over 1f out: nt trble ldrs* **7/2**[3]

45-0 **11** *1* **Midnight Mood**[12] 4913 4-9-9 **57** LiamKeniry 1 49
(Dominic Ffrench Davis) *hld up: effrt and nt clr run over 2f out: nvr on terms* **16/1**

0000 **12** *3 ½* **Pushjockeypush**[8] 5034 3-8-9 **52** (t) RoystonFfrench 7 39
(Stuart Williams) *hld up in tch: rdn over 3f out: wknd over 1f out* **50/1**

064 **13** *3 ¾* **Book Of Dust**[30] 4173 3-9-0 **57** (v[1]) DavidProbert 14 36
(Giles Bravery) *hld up: hdwy to join ldr 7f out: rdn and lost 2nd over 2f out: wknd over 1f out* **50/1**

2m 7.96s (-2.54) **Going Correction** -0.225s/f (Firm)
**WFA** 3 from 4yo+ 9lb 13 Ran SP% **117.0**
Speed ratings (Par 101): **101,100,98,98,98 96,96,96,96,96 95,92,89**
CSF £32.34 CT £102.30 TOTE £10.50: £2.20, £1.30, £1.70; EX 41.50 Trifecta £187.30.
**Owner** J Toes & J O'Loan **Bred** Derek Veitch & Rory O'Brien **Trained** Ingmanthorpe, W Yorks

**FOCUS**
Moderate handicap form. The winner has been rated close to his best from the last few years in a straightforward race.

## 5337 188BET.CO.UK H'CAP 1m 1f 21y
**3:15** (3:16) (Class 5) (0-75,75) 3-Y-0+ **£2,911** (£866; £432; £216) **Stalls** Low

Form RPR

6214 **1** **Chunkyfunkymonkey**[17] 4697 3-7-12 **61** JackOsborn(7) 1 70
(John Ryan) *mde all: clr fr 7f out: shkn up over 1f out: styd on wl* **4/1**[3]

-506 **2** *3 ¾* **Ski Blast**[27] 4298 6-9-6 **67** LukeMorris 3 69
(Ivan Furtado) *prom: rdn over 2f out: swtchd rt over 1f out: styd on to go 2nd wl ins fnl f: no ch w wnr* **11/2**

00 **3** *1 ¼* **Billy Roberts (IRE)**[19] 4631 4-10-0 **75** RobertWinston 6 74
(Richard Guest) *racd keenly: trckd wnr who wnt clr 7f out: shkn up over 2f out: no imp and lost 2nd wl ins fnl f* **7/1**

1443 **4** *1 ¼* **Anastazia**[21] 4542 5-9-7 **68** (h[1]) JoeyHaynes 2 65
(Paul D'Arcy) *s.i.s: hld up: pushed along over 4f out: hdwy over 2f out: no imp fnl f* **11/4**[2]

0564 **5** *9* **Craftsmanship (FR)**[7] 5065 6-9-11 **72** SilvestreDeSousa 7 59
(Robert Eddery) *chsd ldrs: rdn over 2f out: wknd and eased over 1f out* **7/4**[1]

1m 53.93s (-1.87) **Going Correction** -0.225s/f (Firm)
**WFA** 3 from 4yo+ 9lb 5 Ran SP% **110.9**
Speed ratings (Par 103): **99,95,94,93,85**
CSF £24.55 TOTE £3.50: £2.00, £2.40; EX 18.20 Trifecta £81.40.
**Owner** Jon A Thompson **Bred** Mrs Fiona Shaw **Trained** Newmarket, Suffolk

**FOCUS**
A modest handicap that went to the sole 3yo, who slipped the field under a fine ride.

## 5338 MARTIN FOULGER MEMORIAL H'CAP 5f 42y
**3:50** (3:50) (Class 4) (0-80,79) 3-Y-0 **£4,690** (£1,395; £697; £348) **Stalls** Centre

Form RPR

3402 **1** **Erissimus Maximus (FR)**[8] 5029 3-9-7 **79** (b) SilvestreDeSousa 4 87
(Chris Dwyer) *led: shkn up 1/2-way: rdn over 1f out: hdd ins fnl f: rallied gamely to ld towards fin* **11/8**[1]

3251 **2** *hd* **Dundunah (USA)**[20] 4576 3-9-1 **73** (t) HarryBentley 3 80
(David O'Meara) *trckd ldrs: rdn to ld ins fnl f: hdd towards fin* **5/2**[2]

1433 **3** *¾* **Wild Approach (IRE)**[8] 5041 3-8-11 **69** (h[1]) LukeMorris 2 74
(Robert Cowell) *w wnr: rdn and ev ch over 1f out: unable qck towards fin* **9/2**[3]

10-6 **4** *4 ½* **Loving**[26] 4342 3-9-6 **78** PatCosgrave 5 67
(William Haggas) *hld up: shkn up over 1f out: styd on same pce fnl f* **11/2**

0040 **5** *2 ¼* **Percy Toplis**[8] 5040 3-8-2 **60** oh12 (b) RoystonFfrench 1 41
(Christine Dunnett) *chsd ldrs tl rdn and wknd over 1f out* **66/1**

0- 6 2¾ **Terrific Feeling (IRE)**36 3-9-0 72 JFEgan 6 43
(Dominic Ffrench Davis) *hld up: shkn up: edgd rt and wknd over 1f out*
**33/1**

1m 1.87s (-0.83) **Going Correction** -0.475s/f (Firm) **6** Ran SP% **108.7**
Speed ratings (Par 102): **87,86,85,78,74 70**
CSF £4.65 TOTE £2.10: £1.30, £1.40; EX 4.80 Trifecta £11.10.
**Owner** P Venner **Bred** Derek Clee **Trained** Newmarket, Suffolk

**FOCUS**
An ordinary race but a likeable effort from the favourite.

## 5339 188BET H'CAP (DIV I) 6f 3y
**4:25** (4:25) (Class 6) (0-60,62) 3-Y-0+ **£2,264** (£673; £336; £168) **Stalls** Centre

Form RPR
-552 1 **Defining Moment**40 3818 3-9-2 56 DavidProbert 4 63+
(Rae Guest) *hld up: shkn up and hdwy over 1f out: rdn to ld wl ins fnl f: r.o: comf*
**5/1**2

0464 2 ¾ **Shyarch**8 5040 3-8-10 55 JaneElliott(5) 3 60
(George Margarson) *pushed along in rr: hdwy over 1f out: rdn and ev ch ins fnl f: r.o*
**8/1**

0022 3 shd **Flower Cup**20 4561 4-9-10 59 (b) SilvestreDeSousa 11 64
(Chris Dwyer) *s.i.s: sn trcking ldrs: nt clr run 2f out: sn swtchd lft: rdn to ld 1f out: hdd wl ins fnl f*
**11/4**1

6450 4 nk **Nicky Baby (IRE)**35 4006 3-9-4 58 (b1) RobertWinston 1 61
(Dean Ivory) *hld up: hdwy over 2f out: rdn and ev ch ins fnl f: unable qck towards fin*
**20/1**

532 5 nk **Agnethe (IRE)**44 3703 3-9-8 62 JoeyHaynes 7 64
(Paul D'Arcy) *hld up: hdwy over 3f out: rdn to ld over 1f out: sn hdd: no ex nr fin*
**5/1**2

5 6 1¾ **My Girl Maisie (IRE)**27 4302 3-9-2 56 LiamKeniry 8 53+
(Richard Guest) *prom: lost pl over 3f out: nt clr run over 1f out: sn rdn: styd on*
**13/2**3

4005 7 2¾ **Chetan**17 4695 5-9-8 57 (bt) LukeMorris 10 46
(Charlie Wallis) *led: rdn: hung lft and hdd over 1f out: wknd ins fnl f* **7/1**

00 8 1¼ **Innstigator**27 4303 3-9-2 56 AdamBeschizza 9 40
(Ralph J Smith) *chsd ldrs: nt clr run over 2f out: rdn over 1f out: sn wknd*
**25/1**

5003 9 3 **Multi Quest**5 5146 5-8-13 48 (b) RyanPowell 6 23
(John E Long) *w ldr tl rdn over 2f out: wknd over 1f out* **16/1**

0/0- 10 10 **Big City Boy (IRE)**569 46 9-8-8 46 (vt) GeorgeWood(3) 5
(Phil McEntee) *w ldr tl rdn over 2f out: wknd over 1f out* **66/1**

1m 12.34s (-2.06) **Going Correction** -0.475s/f (Firm)
**WFA** 3 from 4yo+ 5lb **10** Ran SP% **112.9**
Speed ratings (Par 101): **94,93,92,92,92 89,86,84,80,67**
CSF £42.05 CT £133.16 TOTE £6.00: £1.90, £4.20, £1.20; EX 61.90 Trifecta £276.90.
**Owner** Derek J Willis **Bred** Derek J Willis **Trained** Newmarket, Suffolk

**FOCUS**
Division one of a moderate sprint.

## 5340 188BET H'CAP (DIV II) 6f 3y
**4:55** (4:56) (Class 6) (0-60,59) 3-Y-0+ **£2,264** (£673; £336; £168) **Stalls** Centre

Form RPR
-235 1 **Wotadoll**29 4211 3-9-0 54 RobertWinston 2 60
(Dean Ivory) *mde all: qcknd over 2f out: rdn over 1f out: styd on* **7/4**1

0620 2 ½ **Ambitious Icarus**20 4561 8-9-8 57 (h) LiamKeniry 5 63
(Richard Guest) *hld up: hrd rdn over 1f out: r.o u.p ins fnl f: nt quite rch wnr*
**9/1**

0003 3 hd **Sakhee's Jem**21 4543 4-9-0 54 JaneElliott(5) 9 59
(Gay Kelleway) *a.p: chsd wnr 4f out: rdn and ev ch whn buckle c undone and rdr dropped rein over 1f out: r.o*
**10/1**

6364 4 ½ **Manipura**19 4619 4-9-1 50 (p) RyanPowell 4 53
(Derek Shaw) *s.i.s: hld up: rdn over 1f out: r.o ins fnl f* **5/1**3

4563 5 1¼ **Whiteley (IRE)**16 4715 3-9-2 56 JFEgan 7 55
(Mick Channon) *racd keenly in 2nd pl tl 4f out: remained handy: rdn over 1f out: styd on same pce ins fnl f*
**7/2**2

066 6 ½ **Malaysian Boleh**57 3201 7-9-4 53 (v) DavidProbert 8 51
(Phil McEntee) *hld up: rdn over 1f out: nt trble ldrs* **8/1**

5050 7 9 **Torment**58 3177 4-9-10 59 LukeMorris 3 30
(Charlie Wallis) *plld hrd and prom: rdn over 2f out: wknd over 1f out* **12/1**

1m 14.0s (-0.40) **Going Correction** -0.475s/f (Firm)
**WFA** 3 from 4yo+ 5lb **7** Ran SP% **113.1**
Speed ratings (Par 101): **83,82,82,81,79 79,67**
CSF £18.10 CT £121.12 TOTE £2.60: £1.50, £3.80; EX 17.70 Trifecta £133.60.
**Owner** David C Mead **Bred** David C Mead **Trained** Radlett, Herts

**FOCUS**
Probably the lesser of the two divisions, but another unexposed 3yo winner.

## 5341 TED JACKSON A LIFETIME IN RACING H'CAP 7f 3y
**5:25** (5:25) (Class 5) (0-70,74) 3-Y-0+ **£2,911** (£866; £432; £216) **Stalls** Centre

Form RPR
-311 1 **Harba (IRE)**8 5031 3-9-12 74 6ex FrankieDettori 4 83+
(William Haggas) *led 1f: trckd ldr: shkn up to ld over 1f out: sn edgd rt: pushed out: comf*
**4/7**1

3620 2 ½ **Still Waiting**23 4463 3-9-0 62 DavidProbert 3 69
(William Jarvis) *a.p: rdn to chse wnr ins fnl f: r.o* **20/1**

-142 3 1¾ **In Ken's Memory**8 5039 4-9-10 72 RayDawson(7) 6 77
(Michael Appleby) *racd alone on stands' side: up w the pce: rdn and ev ch over 1f out: styd on same pce ins fnl f*
**5/1**2

5204 4 2 **Forever Yours (IRE)**17 4695 4-9-8 63 RobertWinston 1 63
(Dean Ivory) *hld up in tch: rdn over 1f out: no ex ins fnl f* **10/1**

4400 5 ¾ **Tellovoi (IRE)**6 5126 9-9-5 67 (v) WilliamCox(7) 5 65
(Richard Guest) *dwlt: rcvrd to ld 6f out: rdn and hdd over 1f out: no ex fnl f*
**16/1**

5651 6 5 **Daring Guest (IRE)**15 4766 3-9-2 69 JaneElliott(5) 7 50
(George Margarson) *hld up: pushed along over 2f out: nt trble ldrs* **9/1**3

4100 7 7 **Nonno Giulio (IRE)**6 5119 6-9-12 67 (p) TomQueally 2 32
(Conor Dore) *s.s: a in rr: wknd over 1f out* **66/1**

1m 25.37s (-1.23) **Going Correction** -0.475s/f (Firm)
**WFA** 3 from 4yo+ 7lb **7** Ran SP% **111.5**
Speed ratings (Par 103): **88,87,85,83,82 76,68**
CSF £14.11 CT £32.47 TOTE £1.40: £1.10, £9.10; EX 11.20 Trifecta £37.30.
**Owner** Al Shaqab Racing **Bred** Summerville Bloodstock Investments **Trained** Newmarket, Suffolk

**FOCUS**
Pretty modest form, but a progressive winner.
T/Plt: £43.40 to a £1 stake. Pool: £61,747.32 - 1,036.81 winning units T/Qpdt: £16.90 to a £1 stake. Pool: £4,851.01 - 212.11 winning units **Colin Roberts**

5342 - 5343a (Foreign Racing) - See Raceform Interactive

# 5083 LEOPARDSTOWN (L-H)
Thursday, July 27

**OFFICIAL GOING: Good**

## 5344a JOCKEY CLUB OF TURKEY SILVER FLASH STKS (GROUP 3) (FILLIES) 7f
**6:55** (6:55) 2-Y-0 **£30,256** (£9,743; £4,615; £2,051; £1,025)

RPR
1 **Happily (IRE)**27 4325 2-9-0 0 (t) RyanMoore 3 105+
(A P O'Brien, Ire) *dwlt sltly: sn settled bhd ldrs in 3rd: tk clsr order into st and pushed along on outer to ld over 1f out: drvn clr and styd on strly ins fnl f: easily*
**8/11**1

2 5 **Shalailah (IRE)**27 4325 2-9-0 0 (t) ColinKeane 4 92
(G M Lyons, Ire) *hld up towards rr: disp 4th at 1/2-way: pushed along into st and impr into 3rd fr 1f out where rdn: kpt on into 2nd wl ins fnl f: nt trble easy wnr*
**20/1**

3 1¼ **Dawn Delivers**11 4932 2-9-0 0 KevinManning 6 89
(J S Bolger, Ire) *prom tl sn settled bhd ldr: 2nd 1/2-way: rdn to dispute ld briefly between horses 1 1/2f out tl sn hdd and no ch w easy wnr: kpt on same pce in 3rd wl ins fnl f*
**7/1**

4 1¾ **Golden Spell**11 4933 2-9-0 93 ShaneFoley 2 84
(J P Murtagh, Ire) *prom tl sn settled bhd ldrs: disp 4th at 1/2-way: pushed along into st and n.m.r briefly: rdn 1f out and no imp on ldrs: kpt on one pce in 4th wl ins fnl f*
**11/2**3

5 2¾ **Easter Lily (IRE)**14 4818 2-9-0 0 DonnachaO'Brien 5 77
(A P O'Brien, Ire) *chsd ldrs tl rapid hdwy to sn ld: over 1 l clr at 1/2-way: pushed along and reduced advantage under 2f out: hdd 1 1/2f out and wknd to rr ins fnl f: eased wl ins fnl f*
**7/2**2

1m 28.99s (0.29) **Going Correction** +0.125s/f (Good) **5** Ran SP% **112.8**
Speed ratings: **103,97,95,93,90**
CSF £16.71 TOTE £1.70: £1.02, £7.50; DF 14.10 Trifecta £48.90.
**Owner** Derrick Smith & Mrs John Magnier & Michael Tabor **Bred** Orpendale And Chelston Ireland **Trained** Cashel, Co Tipperary

**FOCUS**
A tactical contest, but an impressive winner.

## 5345a JRA TYROS STKS (GROUP 3) 7f
**7:30** (7:31) 2-Y-0
**£30,256** (£9,743; £4,615; £2,051; £1,025; £512)

RPR
1 **The Pentagon (IRE)**12 4923 2-9-3 0 RyanMoore 3 106
(A P O'Brien, Ire) *chsd ldrs: 3rd 1/2-way: hung lft briefly under 2f out: rdn in 3rd over 1f out and clsd u.p to ld ins fnl f: styd on wl to assert clsng stages*
**4/11**1

2 1¾ **Theobald (IRE)**12 4926 2-9-3 0 KevinManning 6 101
(J S Bolger, Ire) *prom tl sn settled bhd ldr: 2nd 1/2-way: pushed along into st: sn rdn and lost pl briefly u.p ins fnl f: kpt on wl in 2nd clsng stages: nt match wnr*
**4/1**2

3 ½ **Would Be King (IRE)**25 4414 2-9-3 97 ColinKeane 1 100
(G M Lyons, Ire) *w.w in rr early: 4th 1/2-way: pushed along in 4th into st and hdwy far side u.p ins fnl f: kpt on wl in 3rd clsng stages: nt trble wnr*
**8/1**3

4 ¾ **Burgundy Boy (IRE)**17 4702 2-9-3 0 GaryCarroll 4 98
(Ms Sheila Lavery, Ire) *hld up bhd ldrs in 5th early: last at 1/2-way: rdn over 2f out and u.p in 5th over 1f out: r.o into nvr threatening 4th clsng stages: nvr trbld ldrs*
**33/1**

5 1¼ **Berkeley Square (IRE)**21 4551 2-9-3 0 SeamieHeffernan 2 95
(A P O'Brien, Ire) *sn led: 1 l clr at 1/2-way: stl gng wl into st: rdn 1 1/2f out and hdd u.p ins fnl f: wknd between horses into 5th clsng stages* **16/1**

6 3¾ **Red Persian (IRE)**35 4020 2-9-3 85 RonanWhelan 5 85
(P J Prendergast, Ire) *chsd ldrs: 5th 1/2-way: rdn on outer into st and sn no ex u.p in rr: wknd and eased ins fnl f: lost a shoe in running* **33/1**

1m 28.05s (-0.65) **Going Correction** +0.125s/f (Good) **6** Ran SP% **116.2**
Speed ratings: **108,106,105,104,103 98**
CSF £2.43 TOTE £1.20: £1.02, £1.80; DF 2.70 Trifecta £5.20.
**Owner** Derrick Smith & Mrs John Magnier & Michael Tabor **Bred** Barronstown Stud **Trained** Cashel, Co Tipperary

**FOCUS**
A more workmanlike than impressive performance from the winner, who has been rated to the same level as his maiden rout, but it certainly identified him as a middle-distance horse.

5346 - 5348a (Foreign Racing) - See Raceform Interactive

# 4880 ASCOT (R-H)
Friday, July 28

**OFFICIAL GOING: Good to soft (stands' side 7.1, centre 7.1, far side 6.9, round 6.3)**
Wind: Moderate, half against Weather: Cloudy

## 5349 JOHN GUEST BRITISH EBF FILLIES' NOVICE STKS (PLUS 10 RACE) 7f
**1:40** (1:40) (Class 4) 2-Y-0 **£6,469** (£1,925; £962; £481) **Stalls** Centre

Form RPR
4 1 **Jousi**13 4902 2-9-0 0 JosephineGordon 3 81+
(Hugo Palmer) *leggy: sltly awkward s: sn trckd ldng trio: shkn up and clsd to ld wl over 1f out: styd on wl fnl f*
**4/1**3

2 1 **Give And Take** 2-9-0 0 PatCosgrave 9 79+
(William Haggas) *athletic: s.i.s: hld up in last pair: gng strly 3f out: prog 2f out: rdn to chse wnr ins fnl f: styd on but no imp nr fin*
**20/1**

3 1 **Expressiy (FR)** 2-9-0 0 (h1) AdamKirby 1 76+
(Charlie Appleby) *w'like: dwlt: sn rcvrd to chse ldr: led over 2f out to wl over 1f out: kpt on same pce*
**7/2**2

2 4 ½ **Indicia**15 4815 2-9-0 0 RyanMoore 5 75
(Charles Hills) *tall: lw: wl in tch: shkn up to chal jst over 2f out: one pce over 1f out*
**3/1**1

0 5 2 **Mahaarat**29 4253 2-9-0 0 JimCrowley 7 70
(Sir Michael Stoute) *str: trckd ldng pair: shkn up over 2f out: lost pl sn after: no prog over 1f out*
**9/2**

6 nse **Lady Momoka (IRE)** 2-9-0 0 SilvestreDeSousa 8 70
(Roger Varian) *athletic: lw: wl in tch: outpcd over 2f out: kpt on same pce fnl f*
**8/1**



The Form Book Flat, Raceform Ltd, Newbury, RG14 5SJ

7 hd **Stream Song** 2-9-0 0 KieranShoemark 2 69
(John Gosden) *cmpt: bit bkwd: dwlt: hld up in last pair: shkn up and prog fr 3f out to chal and upsides 2f out: wknd over 1f out* **10/1**

8 1 1/4 **Lady Godiva (IRE)** 2-9-0 0 SeanLevey 6 66
(Richard Hannon) *hld up towards rr: nt clr run briefly over 2f out: no prog over 1f out* **25/1**

0 9 2 **Ritha**22 4533 2-8-11 0 HollieDoyle(3) 10 61
(Richard Hannon) *cmpt: led to over 2f out: sn lost pl and btn* **66/1**

1m 31.84s (4.24) **Going Correction** +0.475s/f (Yiel) 9 Ran SP% **115.7**
Speed ratings (Par 93): **94,92,91,91,88 88,88,87,84**
CSF £79.56 TOTE £4.80: £1.60, £3.80, £1.80; EX 94.80 Trifecta £313.30.
**Owner** Saleh Al Homaizi & Imad Al Sagar **Bred** Saleh Al Homaizi & Imad Al Sagar **Trained** Newmarket, Suffolk

**FOCUS**
All distances as advertised. Silvestre De Sousa described the ground as being "on the slow side". A decent fillies' novice.

## 5350 ANDERS FOUNDATION BRITISH EBF CROCKER BULTEEL MAIDEN STKS (PLUS 10 RACE) (C&G) 6f
**2:10** (2:12) (Class 2) 2-Y-O

**£12,450** (£3,728; £1,864; £932; £466; £234) **Stalls** Centre

Form RPR

1 **Mythical Magic (IRE)** 2-9-0 0 AdamKirby 7 88+
(Charlie Appleby) *lengthy: str: coltish preliminaries: prom: trckd ldr over 2f out: pushed into the ld jst over 1f out: shkn up and readily drew away* **11/8**1

2 2 1/4 **No I'm Easy (IRE)** 2-9-0 0 RichardKingscote 4 81
(Tom Dascombe) *str: led: shkn up over 1f out: sn hdd and one pce* **12/1**

3 1/2 **Merlin Magic** 2-9-0 0 SilvestreDeSousa 8 80+
(David Elsworth) *unf: dwlt: hld up in tch: effrt 2f out: shkn up and kpt on fnl f: nrst fin* **8/1**

4 1 **Strategist (IRE)** 2-9-0 0 RyanMoore 6 77
(William Haggas) *athletic: trckd ldrs: tried to cl on ldng pair over 1f out: one pce fnl f* **4/1**2

5 1 1/2 **Global Art** 2-9-0 0 FranBerry 1 72
(Ed Dunlop) *cmpt: bit bkwd: slowly away: in tch in rr: shkn up and no prog 2f out* **10/1**

6 1/2 **Lord Vetinari** 2-9-0 0 DavidProbert 5 71
(Andrew Balding) *w'like: lengthy: s.i.s: in tch in rr: shkn up and no prog over 2f out* **16/1**

7 4 **G Eye Joe** 2-9-0 0 LukeMorris 2 59
(James Given) *neat: lw: chsd ldr to over 2f out: sn rdn and wknd* **9/2**3

1m 17.51s (3.01) **Going Correction** +0.475s/f (Yiel) 7 Ran SP% **114.1**
Speed ratings (Par 100): **98,95,94,93,91 90,85**
CSF £19.70 TOTE £2.20: £1.50, £4.40; EX 19.20 Trifecta £93.00.
**Owner** Godolphin **Bred** Peter Kelly And Ms Wendy Daly **Trained** Newmarket, Suffolk

**FOCUS**
A decent maiden for newcomers and quite a taking winner. The level is fluid.

## 5351 JOHN GUEST BROWN JACK H'CAP 1m 7f 209y
**2:45** (2:45) (Class 2) (0-100,99) 3-Y-O+

**£18,675** (£5,592; £2,796; £1,398; £699; £351) **Stalls** Low

Form RPR

5211 1 **UAE King**21 4586 3-8-4 **90** SilvestreDeSousa 7 103+
(Roger Varian) *lw: t.k.h early: hld up in 5th: shkn up and hanging jst over 2f out: suddenly surged forward to ld jst over 1f out: sn clr: drvn out* **6/5**1

0400 2 4 1/2 **Mister Manduro (FR)**20 4612 3-8-4 **90** JoeFanning 4 96
(Mark Johnston) *lw: led 1f: trckd ldrs after: rdn over 2f out: chalng whn wnr shot past over 1f out: wnt 2nd ins fnl f and styd on but no ch* **9/4**2

4150 3 3 1/2 **Mark Hopkins**14 4828 5-8-11 **87** DavidEgan(5) 6 87
(David Elsworth) *led after 1f: rdn and hrd pressed over 2f out: hdd and outpcd over 1f out* **8/1**3

004 4 shd **Desert God (IND)**27 4370 5-9-11 **96** ShaneKelly 5 96
(Richard Hughes) *prog to trck ldr after 4f: chal over 2f out: rdn to ld over 1f out but finding little: sn hdd and btn* **16/1**

40-0 5 3 1/4 **Wolfcatcher (IRE)**38 3928 5-9-4 **89** (tp) FranBerry 1 85
(Ian Williams) *t.k.h: trckd ldrs: styd against ins rail in st: rdn over 2f out: wknd over 1f out* **14/1**

4060 6 16 **Gavlar**27 4356 6-9-4 **92** (v) CallumShepherd(3) 2 69
(William Knight) *hld up in last trio: rdn on outer 4f out: wknd 3f out: t.o* **25/1**

000 7 10 **Cosmelli (ITY)**27 4356 4-10-0 **99** (b) AdamKirby 8 64
(Gay Kelleway) *hld up in last trio: rdn and tried to make prog over 3f out: wknd over 2f out: t.o* **20/1**

2050 8 22 **Isharah (USA)**70 2788 4-9-8 **93** RyanMoore 3 31
(Mark Johnston) *dwlt: in tch in last trio: pushed along 5f out: wknd over 3f out: sn t.o* **16/1**

3m 34.04s (5.04) **Going Correction** +0.575s/f (Yiel)
**WFA** 3 from 4yo+ 15lb 8 Ran SP% **114.4**
Speed ratings (Par 109): **110,107,106,105,104 96,91,80**
CSF £3.94 CT £12.93 TOTE £1.90: £1.02, £1.50, £2.60; EX 4.80 Trifecta £19.40.
**Owner** Sheikh Mohammed Obaid Al Maktoum **Bred** Darley **Trained** Newmarket, Suffolk

**FOCUS**
The pace steadied a fair way out in what was a useful staying handicap and the 3yo pair predictably dominated. The fourth has been rated to his British debut figure for now.

## 5352 CARRAIG INSURANCE BRITISH EBF VALIANT STKS (LISTED RACE) (F&M) 7f 213y(R)
**3:20** (3:21) (Class 1) 3-Y-O+

**£34,026** (£12,900; £6,456; £3,216; £1,614; £810) **Stalls** Low

Form RPR

-203 1 **On Her Toes (IRE)**13 4903 3-8-7 97 JoeFanning 10 103
(William Haggas) *trckd ldr fr wd draw: rdn to ld jst over 1f out: styd on and a holding rivals* **8/1**

3203 2 1/2 **Pirouette**17 4718 4-9-1 102 (b1) RobertWinston 4 104
(Hughie Morrison) *trckd ldng pair: waiting for a gap 2f out: tried to chal between them jst over 1f out: styd on to take 2nd nr fin but a hld* **8/1**

1301 3 nk **Tisbutadream (IRE)**20 4637 3-8-7 97 SilvestreDeSousa 9 101
(David Elsworth) *lw: wl away fr wd draw: led at mod pce: rdn jst over 2f out: hdd jst over 1f out: kpt on but lost 2nd nr fin* **8/1**

-200 4 1/2 **Urban Fox**55 3319 3-8-7 101 (b1) LukeMorris 6 100
(James Tate) *t.k.h: hld up in 5th: rdn to press ldrs over 1f out: nt qckn u.p last 150yds* **25/1**

3311 5 hd **Mittens**13 4883 3-8-7 97 DavidProbert 7 100+
(Sir Michael Stoute) *lw: trapped out wd in midfield: rdn 2f out: kpt on wl fnl f but nvr able to threaten* **3/1**2

203- 6 1 1/4 **Nathra (IRE)**308 6749 4-9-1 108 FrankieDettori 3 102+
(John Gosden) *hld up towards rr: shkn up to try to make prog on inner wl over 1f out: keeping on but no ch of winning whn rn out of room last 100yds and eased* **11/4**1

-206 7 shd **Materialistic**28 4308 4-9-1 96 (p1) AdamKirby 5 99
(Luca Cumani) *lw: hld up in last pair: rdn on outer 2f out: styd on but nvr any ch to threaten* **25/1**

-122 8 4 1/2 **Golden Stunner (IRE)**23 4512 4-9-1 107 PatDobbs 8 88
(Ralph Beckett) *trapped out wd bhd ldrs: rdn 2f out: wknd over 1f out* **11/2**3

2124 9 nk **Rebel Surge (IRE)**27 4375 4-9-1 90 (p) StevieDonohoe 1 88
(Richard Spencer) *hld up in last pair: rdn and no prog over 2f out: sn wknd* **80/1**

3-1 10 2 3/4 **Whispering Bell (IRE)**26 4409 3-8-7 89 (h) KieranShoemark 2 79
(John Gosden) *leggy: t.k.h: hld up in midfield: wknd 2f out* **12/1**

1m 43.87s (3.17) **Going Correction** +0.575s/f (Yiel)
**WFA** 3 from 4yo 8lb 10 Ran SP% **117.0**
Speed ratings (Par 111): **107,106,106,105,105 104,104,99,99,96**
CSF £69.24 TOTE £9.10: £2.20, £2.80, £2.40; EX 78.20 Trifecta £589.20.
**Owner** Cheveley Park Stud **Bred** Knocklong House Stud **Trained** Newmarket, Suffolk

**FOCUS**
A useful Listed event but there was a lack of pace and those racing prominently were at an advantage. It's been rated as ordinary Listed form, with the runner-up helping to set the standard.

## 5353 JOHN GUEST H'CAP 1m 3f 211y
**3:55** (3:55) (Class 2) (0-105,104) 3-Y-O+

**£18,675** (£5,592; £2,796; £1,398; £699; £351) **Stalls** Low

Form RPR

2430 1 **Gawdawpalin (IRE)**55 3323 4-8-12 **88** MartinDwyer 11 95
(Sylvester Kirk) *racd wd in midfield: prog over 2f out: clsd w others but edgd rt and caused interference to others: led jst over 1f out: drvn out* **11/1**

1300 2 1 1/4 **Red Galileo**35 4033 6-9-6 **101** DavidEgan(5) 4 106
(Saeed bin Suroor) *lw: trckd ldrs: rdn and tried to cl on inner over 2f out: short of room briefly over 1f out but sn in 3rd: swtchd off rail 100yds out and styd on to take 2nd last strides* **7/1**2

-001 3 nk **King Bolete (IRE)**27 4370 5-9-12 **102** (p) JackMitchell 10 107
(Roger Varian) *led 1f: trckd ldr: led over 3f out and dashed for home: drvn 2f out: hdd jst over 1f out: one pce after and lost 2nd last strides* **8/1**3

-600 4 1/2 **Saunter (FR)**13 4882 4-9-5 **95** DavidProbert 8 99
(David Menuisier) *hld up in rr: rdn and prog over 2f out: hanging and racd awkwardly after but kpt on to take 4th ins fnl f: nrst fin* **8/1**3

3-12 5 2 3/4 **Appeared**35 4033 5-10-0 **104** SilvestreDeSousa 7 108+
(Roger Varian) *t.k.h: hld up in tch: rdn and prog over 2f out: disputing 2nd whn carried rt and bmpd over 1f out: lost momentum and fdd* **2/1**1

2405 6 2 1/2 **Tawdeea**20 4614 5-9-10 **100** (v) AdamKirby 3 96
(David O'Meara) *slowly away: detached in last and nt gng wl: stl last 3f out: eventually kpt on fnl 2f: n.d* **9/1**

5-10 7 1 1/4 **Fidaawy**56 3300 4-9-8 **98** JimCrowley 9 100+
(Sir Michael Stoute) *trckd ldrs: rdn and prog over 2f out: disputing 2nd whn bmpd then squeezed out over 1f out: lost all ch and eased* **8/1**3

1446 8 6 **Galapiat**47 3637 4-10-0 **104** RyanMoore 6 88
(Mark Johnston) *lw: wl in tch: rdn over 2f out: sn wknd* **8/1**3

5433 9 9 **Sennockian Star**6 5164 7-8-12 **88** JoeFanning 1 58
(Mark Johnston) *trckd ldng pair to over 2f out: wknd qckly* **20/1**

6123 10 12 **Noble Gift**28 4316 7-9-6 **99** CallumShepherd(3) 5 50
(William Knight) *urged along to ld after 1f: hdd over 3f out: sn wknd: t.o* **33/1**

26/ 11 2 3/4 **Seaport**487 1130 6-9-10 **100** RobertWinston 2 46
(Seamus Durack) *dwlt: hld up in last pair: effrt 3f out: sn no prog and wknd qckly: t.o* **66/1**

2m 36.68s (4.18) **Going Correction** +0.575s/f (Yiel) 11 Ran SP% **117.8**
Speed ratings (Par 109): **109,108,107,107,105 104,103,99,93,85 83**
CSF £84.62 CT £659.03 TOTE £14.90: £4.10, £2.30, £2.70; EX 94.60 Trifecta £1450.50.
**Owner** H Balasuriya **Bred** L Queally **Trained** Upper Lambourn, Berks
■ Stewards' Enquiry : Martin Dwyer 10-day ban: careless riding (Aug 11-20)

**FOCUS**
A good-quality middle-distance handicap that went to the bottom one, although he did cause marked interference to three runners, including the second home. The runner-up has been rated to his 2015 form, with the third to form.

## 5354 NEPTUNE INVESTMENT MANAGEMENT H'CAP 5f
**4:25** (4:26) (Class 2) 3-Y-O+

**£28,012** (£8,388; £4,194; £2,097; £1,048; £526) **Stalls** Centre

Form RPR

0454 1 **Jack Dexter**7 5094 8-8-6 **87** WilliamCarson 1 98
(Jim Goldie) *trckd ldrs gng wl: rdn to cl over 1f out: led jst ins fnl f: drvn clr* **5/1**2

2143 2 1 1/2 **Pettochside**4 5219 8-8-0 **84** HollieDoyle(3) 9 90
(John Bridger) *chsd ldrs: rdn wl over 1f out: styd on ins fnl f to take 2nd last strides* **11/1**

5264 3 shd **Soie D'Leau**15 4816 5-8-11 **92** JoeFanning 5 98
(Kristin Stubbs) *trckd ldr: rdn to chal over 1f out: upsides jst ins fnl f: nt qckn w wnr after: lost 2nd last strides* **15/2**3

1130 4 1 1/2 **Copper Knight (IRE)**13 4920 3-8-13 **101** RachelRichardson(3) 7 100
(Tim Easterby) *led: rdn over 1f out: hdd and no ex jst ins fnl f* **8/1**

5562 5 1 1/4 **Top Boy**15 4816 7-7-12 **82** (v) AaronJones(3) 15 78
(Derek Shaw) *hld up in last of quartet towards nr side: rdn and no prog 2f out: styd on fnl f to grab 5th last strides* **16/1**

5031 6 1/2 **Shamshon (IRE)**15 4816 6-8-9 **90** (t) JimCrowley 8 84
(Stuart Williams) *blindfold off late and slowly away: wl in rr: rdn 2f out: kpt on fr over 1f out: nrst fin but no ch* **7/2**1

0650 7 shd **Robot Boy (IRE)**13 4881 7-8-9 **95** (h1) CallumRodriguez(5) 10 89
(David Barron) *chsd ldr in quartet towards nr side: drvn sn after 1/2-way: tried to make prog over 1f out: no hdwy fnl f* **12/1**

2000 8 2 1/4 **Exceed The Limit**37 3967 4-8-7 **88** (p) MartinDwyer 4 73
(Robert Cowell) *in tch in midfield: rdn and struggling 2f out: no ch after* **33/1**

-000 9 7 **Afandem (IRE)**15 4813 3-8-10 **98** CharlieBennett(3) 6 57
(Hugo Palmer) *a struggling in rr: bhd over 1f out* **8/1**

1360 **10** ½ **Verne Castle**[105] 1772 4-9-4 **99**....................(h) DavidProbert 13 57
(Andrew Balding) *chsd ldrs in quartet towards nr side: rdn 2f out: wknd qckly sn after* **50/1**

4502 **11** 1¼ **Monsieur Joe (IRE)**[7] 5116 10-9-1 **96**.................... RobertWinston 2 50
(Paul Midgley) *chsd ldrs but u.p to do so early on: wknd 2f out: eased* **14/1**

2152 **12** 5 **Coolfitch (IRE)**[14] 4867 3-8-5 **93**.................... ShelleyBirkett(3) 11 28
(David O'Meara) *s.v.s: a in rr: brief effrt 2f out: sn wknd* **9/1**

-000 **13** 10 **Just Glamorous (IRE)**[38] 3926 4-9-10 **105**.................... ShaneKelly 12 5
(Ronald Harris) *led quartet towards nr side and on terms: wknd rapidly wl over 1f out: t.o* **25/1**

1m 1.42s (0.92) **Going Correction** +0.475s/f (Yiel)
**WFA** 3 from 4yo+ 4lb **13** Ran SP% **120.2**
Speed ratings (Par 109): **111,108,108,106,104 103,103,99,88,87 85,77,61**
CSF £58.62 CT £431.65 TOTE £5.10: £1.90, £4.10, £2.70; EX 65.40 Trifecta £585.50.
**Owner** J Fyffe & J S Goldie **Bred** Jim Goldie **Trained** Uplawmoor, E Renfrews

**FOCUS**
Two of the older runners came to the fore in what was a useful sprint. The runner-up has been rated as running a small pb, with the third to this year's form.

## 5355 CHELSEA THOROUGHBREDS OCTOBER CLUB CHARITY FILLIES' H'CAP 5f
**4:55** (4:58) (Class 4) (0-85,87) 3-Y-O+ **£6,469** (£1,925; £962; £481) **Stalls** Centre

Form RPR

1412 **1** **Intense Romance (IRE)**[14] 4835 3-8-12 **80**.......... CallumRodriguez(5) 7 90
(Michael Dods) *lw: w ldr in gp towards nr side: overall ldr wl over 1f out and stl gng strly: drvn and styd on wl fnl f* **5/1**[3]

5030 **2** 1¾ **Savannah Beau**[6] 5134 5-8-7 **69**....................(v) AaronJones(3) 6 74
(Derek Shaw) *n.m.r s: sn chsd ldrs in gp towards nr side: rdn wl over 1f out: styd on fnl f to take 2nd last strides* **20/1**

6202 **3** shd **Midnight Malibu (IRE)**[7] 5098 4-9-4 **80**.............. RachelRichardson(3) 8 85
(Tim Easterby) *led gp towards nr side to 2f out: chsd wnr after: no imp fnl f: lost 2nd last strides* **5/2**[1]

3531 **4** nk **Justice Lady (IRE)**[21] 4574 4-9-8 **81**.................... ShaneKelly 1 85
(David Elsworth) *sn swtchd to gp towards nr side and chsd ldrs: rdn over 1f out to dispute 2nd: kpt on same pce fnl f* **9/2**[2]

3-15 **5** 1¼ **Cosmopolitan Girl (IRE)**[34] 4078 4-10-0 **87**.................... FranBerry 5 86
(Robert Cowell) *n.m.r s: in tch in rr towards nr side: rdn 2f out: kpt on fr over 1f out but nvr able to rch ldrs* **13/2**

6110 **6** ¾ **Jersey Breeze (IRE)**[22] 4536 4-9-8 **81**....................(v) CharlesBishop 3 77
(Mick Channon) *overall ldr in centre tl wl over 1f out: fdd u.p* **12/1**

1314 **7** 3¼ **Rose Berry**[13] 4889 3-9-7 **84**....................(h) JoeFanning 9 68
(Chris Dwyer) *chsd ldrs towards nr side: wknd over 1f out* **5/1**[3]

4360 **8** 2¼ **Reedanjas (IRE)**[7] 5117 3-8-11 **74**.................... MartinDwyer 4 50
(Gay Kelleway) *wnt lft s: chsd ldr in centre: u.p 1/2-way: sn wknd* **33/1**

1-40 **9** 8 **Dandyman Port (IRE)**[8] 5086 3-9-10 **87**.................... DavidProbert 2 34
(Des Donovan, Ire) *s.v.s: last of the trio racing in centre and a bhd: drvn and wandering over 1f out* **16/1**

1m 2.0s (1.50) **Going Correction** +0.475s/f (Yiel)
**WFA** 3 from 4yo+ 4lb **9** Ran SP% **114.7**
Speed ratings (Par 102): **107,104,104,103,101 100,95,91,78**
CSF £96.01 CT £306.20 TOTE £5.40: £1.90, £5.30, £1.30; EX 96.90 Trifecta £372.30.
**Owner** Hugh Malcolm Linsley **Bred** John O'Connor **Trained** Denton, Co Durham

**FOCUS**
A fair handicap, the 3yo filly winning with a bit in hand. They split into two early before merging late on. The fourth has been rated close to form.
T/Jkpt: Not won. T/Plt: £519.90 to a £1 stake. Pool: £80,646.00 - 155.11 winning units T/Qpdt: £96.70 to a £1 stake. Pool: £7,618.00 - 78.76 winning units **Jonathan Neesom**

# 5047 CHEPSTOW (L-H)
Friday, July 28

**OFFICIAL GOING: Soft**
Wind: blustery and variable Weather: rain

## 5356 BATHWICK TYRES CARDIFF FILLIES' NOVICE AUCTION STKS (PLUS 10 RACE) 6f 16y
**5:50** (5:51) (Class 5) 2-Y-O **£3,234** (£962; £481; £240) **Stalls** Centre

Form RPR

4 **1** **Double Reflection**[57] 3237 2-8-11 0.................... CliffordLee(3) 3 73
(K R Burke) *trckd ldrs: rdn to ld over 2f out: drvn out to hold runner-up fnl f* **5/1**[2]

46 **2** ½ **Polly's Gold (IRE)**[15] 4806 2-8-7 0.................... FinleyMarsh(7) 1 72
(Richard Hughes) *chsd ldrs: shkn up over 1f out: sn chsng wnr: edgd lft and r.o fnl f: jst hld* **13/2**[3]

23 **3** 2¼ **Kareva**[15] 4806 2-9-0 0.................... LukeMorris 5 65
(Charles Hills) *in tch: clsd to trck ldrs 1/2-way: ev ch 2f out: drvn and hung lft over 1f out: sn lost 2nd: styd on same pce* **1/2**[1]

**4** hd **Lope De Loop (IRE)** 2-9-0 0.................... SteveDrowne 6 64
(David Evans) *cl up: racd keenly: rdn over 2f out: one pce* **33/1**

**5** 2¼ **Claramara (IRE)** 2-9-0 0.................... FrannyNorton 2 59
(Mark Johnston) *in rr and sn outpcd: hdwy u.p fr 1/2-way: no further imp fnl f* **14/1**

66 **6** 4 **Catch The Pigeon**[4] 5216 2-9-0 0.................... RobHornby 7 46
(Ed de Giles) *racd on stands' side a little apart fr the others: in tch: drvn over 2f out: wknd over 1f out* **14/1**

00 **7** 21 **Bucks Frizz (IRE)**[25] 4440 2-9-0 0.................... SeanLevey 4
(David Evans) *led tl hdd over 2f out: wknd qckly: t.o* **50/1**

1m 15.93s (3.93) **Going Correction** +0.65s/f (Yiel) **7** Ran SP% **114.9**
Speed ratings (Par 91): **99,98,95,95,92 86,58**
CSF £37.02 TOTE £6.00: £2.50, £3.30; EX 37.70 Trifecta £56.10.
**Owner** Ontoawinner, SDH, James Pak & E Burke **Bred** M J Benton **Trained** Middleham Moor, N Yorks

**FOCUS**
The going was soft on a rainy night. They went a decent pace in this opening novice event and the hot favourite was turned over. The level is fluid.

## 5357 BYERLEY STUD FILLIES' H'CAP 7f 16y
**6:20** (6:21) (Class 5) (0-70,69) 3-Y-O+ **£3,234** (£962; £481; £240) **Stalls** Centre

Form RPR

320 **1** **Here's Two**[17] 4728 4-9-12 **67**.................... KieranO'Neill 8 74
(Ron Hodges) *cl up: rdn over 2f out: drvn and edgd rt over 1f out: kpt on u.p to ld fnl 110 yds* **3/1**[1]

2406 **2** 1¼ **Mia Cara**[10] 5007 3-9-3 **65**....................(v) SteveDrowne 1 66
(David Evans) *led: rdn over 1f out: kpt on gamely: hdd and unable qck fnl 110 yds* **5/1**[3]

0604 **3** ½ **Cooperess**[17] 4710 4-8-2 **50** oh1....................(v) FinleyMarsh(7) 6 53
(John O'Shea) *hld up: drvn over 1f out: hdwy and edgd lft fnl f: styd on to go 3rd towards fin* **7/1**

0-00 **4** nk **Suni Dancer**[169] 640 6-8-10 **51**.................... GeorgeDowning 3 53
(Tony Carroll) *hld up: hdwy to chse ldrs 1/2-way: rdn 2f out: kpt on: lost 3rd towards fin* **20/1**

06-6 **5** ½ **Indiana Dawn**[11] 4969 4-8-8 **54**.................... JoshuaBryan(5) 7 55
(Robert Stephens) *chsd ldrs: drvn over 2f out: wandered over 1f out: styd on same pce* **8/1**

523 **6** 2¼ **Characterized**[32] 4145 3-9-6 **68**.................... TimmyMurphy 4 60
(Geoffrey Deacon) *in tch: clsd to chse ldrs 3f out: shkn up 2f out: drvn and wknd fnl f* **4/1**[2]

0-03 **7** ¾ **Bradfield Magic (IRE)**[17] 4714 3-8-10 **58**.................... LukeMorris 5 48
(Charles Hills) *chsd ldrs: drvn 3f out: unable qck: grad wknd fnl f* **4/1**[2]

0-60 **8** 8 **Oddsocks (IRE)**[169] 640 5-8-9 **50** oh5.................... FrannyNorton 10 22
(Tony Carroll) *hld up: rdn over 3f out: lost tch 2f out* **50/1**

0006 **9** 1¾ **Posh Bounty**[2] 5295 6-9-6 **68**....................(h) JordanUys(7) 9 35
(Paul Burgoyne) *wnt to post early: t.k.h: sn chsng ldrs: lost pl 1/2-way: drvn: hung lft and lost tch over 1f out: eased fnl f* **16/1**

1m 27.92s (4.72) **Going Correction** +0.65s/f (Yiel)
**WFA** 3 from 4yo+ 7lb **9** Ran SP% **117.9**
Speed ratings (Par 100): **99,97,97,96,96 93,92,83,81**
CSF £18.68 CT £98.38 TOTE £4.20: £2.00, £1.80, £2.50; EX 21.70 Trifecta £152.50.
**Owner** K Corcoran, C E Weare, R J Hodges **Bred** D R Tucker **Trained** Charlton Mackrell, Somerset

**FOCUS**
The first two were always prominent in this steadily-run handicap and the hold-up performers couldn't land a major blow. They raced centre to far side. The winner has been rated to her best level since last year's best effort, which was also on soft ground.

## 5358 BATHWICK TYRES H'CAP 7f 16y
**6:50** (6:52) (Class 5) (0-75,74) 3-Y-O **£3,234** (£962; £481; £240) **Stalls** Centre

Form RPR

2432 **1** **Peach Melba**[3] 5248 3-9-6 **73**.................... FrannyNorton 3 81
(Mark Johnston) *mde all: shkn up 2f out: taken lft to r on rail over 1f out: in command whn rdn out towards fin* **8/11**[1]

6325 **2** 2 **Fastnet Spin (IRE)**[18] 4698 3-9-5 **72**....................(b) SteveDrowne 4 74
(David Evans) *s.s: in tch in last: shkn up 3f out: chsd wnr 2f out: swtchd rt over 1f out: drvn and r.o fnl f: a being hld* **3/1**[2]

006 **3** 3 **Used To Be**[29] 4247 3-8-12 **68**.................... CliffordLee(3) 5 62
(K R Burke) *taken to post steadily: trckd ldng pair: drvn 2f out: no ex 1f out* **5/1**[3]

1660 **4** 7 **Ashwaq**[28] 4298 3-9-2 **69**....................(b[1]) SeanLevey 2 45
(Richard Hannon) *t.k.h: trckd wnr: rdn over 2f out: lost 2nd 2f out: wknd qckly* **7/1**

1m 27.55s (4.35) **Going Correction** +0.65s/f (Yiel) **4** Ran SP% **112.1**
Speed ratings (Par 100): **101,98,95,87**
CSF £3.39 TOTE £1.60; EX 2.20 Trifecta £4.90.
**Owner** Lowther Racing & Partner **Bred** Lowther Racing **Trained** Middleham Moor, N Yorks

**FOCUS**
They ended up on the far side in this small-field event and the odds-on favourite made all to score with authority from the clear second. The runner-up has been rated close to this year's form.

## 5359 BATHWICK CAR & VAN HIRE H'CAP 1m 14y
**7:20** (7:21) (Class 5) (0-70,71) 3-Y-O+ **£3,234** (£962; £481; £240) **Stalls** Centre

Form RPR

2323 **1** **Fair Selene**[14] 4846 3-8-12 **61**.................... LukeMorris 2 68
(Heather Main) *chsd ldrs: drvn to chal 2f out: sn led narrowly: edgd rt appr fnl f: jst hdd 100yds out: rallied u.p to ld post* **6/1**

6321 **2** shd **Hernando Torres**[7] 5091 9-9-6 **64**....................(tp) CliffordLee(3) 5 73
(Michael Easterby) *trckd ldr tl led over 3f out: rdn over 2f out: sn jnd: hdd narrowly over 1f out: jst led again 100yds out: hdd post* **3/1**[2]

021 **3** 2½ **Flood Defence (IRE)**[28] 4298 3-9-3 **66**.................... AdamBeschizza 8 67
(Chris Wall) *hld up: rdn and hdwy 3f out: pressed ldng pair 2f out: sn one pce and hld* **6/4**[1]

6450 **4** 7 **Peak Storm**[14] 4846 8-9-5 **67**....................(t[1]) FinleyMarsh(7) 1 54
(John O'Shea) *hld up: rdn over 2f out: no imp on ldrs: wnt mod 4th 1f out* **12/1**

1562 **5** 1½ **Black Dave (IRE)**[8] 5049 7-9-1 **63**.................... KatherineGlenister(7) 6 46
(David Evans) *t.k.h: led tl drvn and hdd over 3f out: wknd wl over 1f out* **5/1**[3]

003 **6** nse **Sir Compton**[16] 4747 4-9-3 **58**....................(p[1]) SeanLevey 7 41
(Stuart Kittow) *trckd ldrs: rdn and lost pl over 2f out: wknd over 1f out* **8/1**

1m 41.3s (5.10) **Going Correction** +0.65s/f (Yiel)
**WFA** 3 from 4yo+ 8lb **6** Ran SP% **114.8**
Speed ratings (Par 103): **100,99,97,90,88 88**
CSF £24.90 CT £40.30 TOTE £6.00: £1.70, £2.00; EX 25.80 Trifecta £46.50.
**Owner** Andrew Knott, Mrs Penelope Toll, Mr Lloyd **Bred** P And Mrs A G Venner **Trained** Kingston Lisle, Oxon

■ Stewards' Enquiry : Luke Morris two-day ban: used whip above shoulder height (Aug 13-14)

**FOCUS**
This was weakened by several withdrawals but the winner battled really well to narrowly deny a last-time-out winner. The runner-up and third have been rated to form.

## 5360 BATHWICK TYRES NEWPORT H'CAP 5f 16y
**7:50** (7:51) (Class 5) (0-70,72) 3-Y-O+ **£3,234** (£962; £481; £240) **Stalls** Centre

Form RPR

1136 **1** **Kinglami**[14] 4844 8-9-12 **70**....................(p) LukeMorris 7 77
(John O'Shea) *towards rr: rdn 1/2-way: sn clsd: kpt on to ld 110 yds out: drvn out* **9/2**[3]

0502 **2** nk **Seamster**[2] 5271 10-9-7 **72**....................(t) RossaRyan(7) 1 78
(David Loughnane) *s.i.s: sn chsng ldrs: n.m.r over 1f out: r.o and ev ch ins fnl f: jst hld* **3/1**[2]

2 **3** 1¾ **Spirit Of Rosanna**[48] 3573 5-9-4 **62**....................(tp) AdamBeschizza 3 62
(Steph Hollinshead) *led: qckly tk field over to far side: rdn 2f out: kpt on wl: hdd 110 yds out: no ex* **9/4**[1]

6302 **4** 1 **Compton Poppy**[14] 4842 3-9-10 **72**.................... GeorgeDowning 4 68
(Tony Carroll) *trckd ldrs: rdn 2f out: sn ev ch: no ex fnl 100 yds* **3/1**[2]

0225 **5** ¾ **Minty Jones**[8] 5052 8-8-4 **51** oh5....................(v) EdwardGreatrex(3) 5 46
(Michael Mullineaux) *prom: rdn over 2f out: unable qck and hld fnl f* **7/1**



The Form Book Flat, Raceform Ltd, Newbury, RG14 5SJ

1400 **6** *11* **Swendab (IRE)**[11] 4965 9-9-8 **66**....................(b) TimmyMurphy 2 26
(John O'Shea) *sed a little awkwardly: in last after 1f: shkn up and lost tch 2f out* **22/1**

1m 1.98s (2.68) **Going Correction** +0.65s/f (Yiel)
**WFA** 3 from 5yo+ 4lb **6** Ran SP% **115.8**
Speed ratings (Par 103): **104,103,100,99,97 80**
CSF £19.05 TOTE £5.40: £2.50, £1.70; EX 23.90 Trifecta £54.90.
**Owner** Pete Smith & Phil Hart Racing **Bred** Cheveley Park Stud Ltd **Trained** Elton, Gloucs

**FOCUS**
They raced on the far side in this handicap and there was a tight finish. The runner-up has been rated close to his best since the spring.

## 5361 BATHWICK TYRES BRIGEND H'CAP 2m
**8:20** (8:20) (Class 6) (0-60,60) 3-Y-0+ **£2,587** (£770; £384; £192) **Stalls** Low

Form RPR
000 **1** **Tsundoku (IRE)**[17] 3575 6-9-0 **46**.................... JohnFahy 1 56
(Alexandra Dunn) *sn led: mde rest: set stdy pce tl qcknd 4f out: hung lft over 2f out: edgd rt over 1f out: styd on wl: eased towards fin* **5/1**[3]

0053 **2** *1 ¼* **Easy Wind**[11] 4962 3-8-9 **56**.................... LukeMorris 6 65
(Sir Mark Prescott Bt) *t.k.h early: midfield: drvn over 4f out: styd on to go 2nd over 1f out: kpt on and clsng on eased wnr towards fin* **1/1**[1]

2400 **3** *2 ½* **Riptide**[24] 4471 11-9-11 **57**.................... SamHitchcott 10 61
(Michael Scudamore) *towards rr tl hdwy to chse wnr after 4f: lost 2nd and outpcd by ldrs 4f out: styd on u.p to go 3rd nr fin* **20/1**

6-66 **4** *nk* **Aristocracy**[52] 3436 6-9-4 **50**.................... TrevorWhelan 12 53
(Fergal O'Brien) *chsd wnr 4f: styd prom: drvn 4f out: kpt on same pce: in hld 3rd 100 yds out tl nr fin* **16/1**

4030 **5** *1 ¼* **Curtsy (IRE)**[11] 4978 3-8-11 **58**.................... SeanLevey 2 62
(Hughie Morrison) *broke wl: t.k.h and chsd ldrs: rdn to go 2nd 4f out: no imp on wnr fr 2f out: wknd and lost 3 pls fnl f* **7/2**[2]

/0-0 **6** *6* **Ayla's Emperor**[11] 4966 8-9-7 **60**....................(p) JordanUys(7) 3 54
(John Flint) *chsd ldrs: rdn 4f out: one pce and hld fnl 3f* **20/1**

0-60 **7** *12* **Put The Boot In (IRE)**[93] 1698 5-8-11 **50**.................... RossaRyan(7) 11 30
(Nikki Evans) *hld up: detached last and rdn over 4f out: passed btn rivals late* **50/1**

621/ **8** *½* **Torero**[60] 7099 8-9-3 **54**.................... JoshuaBryan(5) 4 33
(Alan Phillips) *hld up: rdn 5f out: no ch fnl 3f* **25/1**

0055 **9** *1 ½* **Ring Eye (IRE)**[14] 4840 9-9-1 **50**.................... EdwardGreatrex(3) 8 28
(John O'Shea) *hld up: hdwy 5f out: chsng ldrs and rdn 3f out: wknd over 1f out* **8/1**

51/0 **10** *59* **Storming Harry**[30] 4217 5-9-6 **52**.................... RobHornby 13
(Robin Dickin) *dwlt: t.k.h and hdwy into midfield after 2f: rdn 4f out: sn wknd: eased 1f out: t.o* **20/1**

3m 51.66s (12.76) **Going Correction** +0.775s/f (Yiel)
**WFA** 3 from 5yo+ 15lb **10** Ran SP% **126.0**
Speed ratings (Par 101): **99,98,97,96,96 93,87,87,86,56**
CSF £10.58 CT £102.92 TOTE £6.80: £1.60, £1.40, £4.30; EX 15.00 Trifecta £260.00.
**Owner** Dave Arthur & W B B **Bred** Iona Equine **Trained** West Buckland, Somerset

**FOCUS**
They went a stop-start gallop and the winner dominated. It's been rated around the third, fourth and fifth.

## 5362 SHIPYARD BREWERY H'CAP 1m 4f
**8:50** (8:50) (Class 6) (0-65,66) 3-Y-0+ **£2,587** (£770; £384; £192) **Stalls** Low

Form RPR
1140 **1** **Grams And Ounces**[15] 4804 10-9-9 **59**....................(tp) TimmyMurphy 11 64
(Grace Harris) *hld up: hdwy after 5f: chsd ldrs 3f out: rdn to go 2nd 2f out: led appr fnl f: all out* **6/1**[3]

-646 **2** *½* **Goldslinger (FR)**[21] 4573 5-9-11 **64**.................... JackDuern(3) 9 68
(Dean Ivory) *led: clr after 3f: 10 l up ent st over 4f out: rdn over 3f out: hdd appr fnl f: kpt on* **4/1**[1]

500/ **3** *nk* **Whipcrackaway (IRE)**[127] 172 8-9-4 **54**.................... JohnFahy 10 58
(Peter Hedger) *hld up in last: rdn and hdwy over 3f out: styd on fnl 2f: clsng towards fin* **12/1**

30 **4** *2 ½* **Bishop Of Bling (IRE)**[29] 4260 4-10-2 **66**.................... LukeMorris 15 66
(Chris Wall) *t.k.h towards rr: hdwy after 4f: chsd clr ldr 4f out: lost 2nd 2f out: one pce fnl f* **9/2**[2]

0/ **5** *6* **Flannery (IRE)**[34] 4066 6-8-11 **52**....................(t) MitchGodwin(5) 5 43
(Tim Vaughan) *chsd ldrs: rdn over 3f out: grad wknd fnl 2f* **4/1**[1]

-603 **6** *10* **Sark (IRE)**[32] 4147 4-10-2 **66**.................... SteveDrowne 3 42
(David Evans) *midfield: effrt and clsd on ins over 3f out: wknd over 2f out* **9/2**[2]

23-0 **7** *1* **Red Dragon (IRE)**[43] 3753 7-9-4 **54**.................... KieranO'Neill 8 29
(Michael Blanshard) *chsd ldrs: rdn 4f out: wknd 2f out* **16/1**

4566 **8** *3 ½* **Kilim**[11] 4971 4-8-7 **50**....................(t) NicolaCurrie(7) 12 19
(John Berry) *hld up towards rr: drvn 3f out: no rspnse and sn lost tch* **16/1**

0-53 **9** *66* **Everlasting Sea**[32] 4146 3-8-13 **60**.................... RobHornby 14
(Stuart Kittow) *t.k.h: sn chsng ldr who wnt clr: rdn and lost 2nd over 4f out: sn wknd: eased 2f out: t.o* **6/1**[3]

2m 47.34s (8.34) **Going Correction** +0.775s/f (Yiel)
**WFA** 3 from 4yo+ 11lb **9** Ran SP% **124.4**
Speed ratings (Par 101): **103,102,102,100,96 90,89,87,43**
CSF £32.79 CT £291.39 TOTE £5.40: £1.80, £1.70, £3.80; EX 26.50 Trifecta £568.60.
**Owner** Grace Harris Racing **Bred** Brook Stud Bloodstock Ltd **Trained** Shirenewton, Monmouthshire

**FOCUS**
There were plenty of non-runners but the leader set a strong gallop and there was an exciting finish in this handicap.
T/Plt: £222.80 to a £1 stake. Pool: £60,985.57 - 199.81 winning units T/Qpdt: £16.60 to a £1 stake. Pool: £5,998.62 - 266.18 winning units **Richard Lowther**

# 5154 NEWMARKET (R-H)
Friday, July 28

**OFFICIAL GOING: Good to soft (6.8)**
Wind: light to medium, across Weather: overcast, light rain from 6

## 5363 FLY LONDON SOUTHEND AIRPORT TO PERPIGNAN H'CAP 1m
**5:35** (5:36) (Class 5) (0-75,75) 3-Y-0+ **£3,881** (£1,155; £577; £288) **Stalls** High

Form RPR
-000 **1** **Lawmaking**[21] 4556 4-10-0 **75**.................... LiamKeniry 4 85
(Henry Spiller) *trckd ldrs: effrt to chal over 1f out: sn drew clr w runner up and sustained duel after: drvn ahd wl ins fnl f: hld on wl towards fin* **20/1**

3-20 **2** *hd* **Capton**[43] 3750 4-10-0 **75**.................... FergusSweeney 3 84
(Henry Candy) *led: rdn wl over 1f out: sn hrd pressed and drew clr w wnr: sustained duel w wnr after: hdd wl ins fnl f: battled bk but hld towards fin* **5/1**[3]

-000 **3** *4* **Ubla (IRE)**[9] 5039 4-8-10 **62**.................... DavidEgan(5) 5 61
(Jane Chapple-Hyam) *t.k.h: trckd ldrs tl stdd bk to last pair 5f out: hdwy 2f out: rdn to chse ldrs over 1f out: sn outpcd and wknd ins fnl f* **12/1**

2100 **4** *¾* **Oud Metha Bridge (IRE)**[67] 2894 3-9-6 **75**.................... MartinHarley 8 71
(Ed Dunlop) *hld up in tch in midfield: effrt u.p 2f out: chsd ldrs but unable qck over 1f out: wknd ins fnl f* **16/1**

05-1 **5** *4 ½* **Midnight Whistler (USA)**[8] 5062 5-9-9 **73**....................(p) GeorgeWood(3) 1 60
(Martyn Meade) *chsd ldr: rdn over 2f out: lost pl and btn whn edgd lft over 1f out: wl btn fnl f* **10/3**[2]

3211 **6** *nk* **Cainhoe Star**[21] 4561 4-9-8 **69**.................... SilvestreDeSousa 2 56
(Anthony Carson) *hld up wl in tch in midfield: rdn over 2f out: edgd lft u.p and no imp over 1f out: wl hld fnl f* **6/4**[1]

4523 **7** *3 ¾* **Bollihope**[4] 5221 5-9-8 **69**.................... DougieCostello 7 47
(Richard Guest) *stdd s: hld up in tch in rr: effrt and carried lft over 1f out: no imp: bhd and eased wl ins fnl f* **7/1**

1m 41.57s (1.57) **Going Correction** +0.35s/f (Good)
**WFA** 3 from 4yo+ 8lb **7** Ran SP% **110.6**
Speed ratings (Par 103): **106,105,101,101,96 96,92**
CSF £107.61 CT £1210.19 TOTE £18.60: £6.80, £2.80; EX 122.10 Trifecta £1399.00.
**Owner** Marchwood Aggregates **Bred** Juddmonte Farms Ltd **Trained** Newmarket, Suffolk

**FOCUS**
Stands' side course. Stalls: far Side, except 1m4f: centre. A bit of an upset in this fair handicap with the big two in the market running well below expectations. The winning time, which 5.37secs slower standard, suggests the rain has got into the ground. The runner-up has been rated as improving.

## 5364 FLY LONDON SOUTHEND AIRPORT TO MILAN MAIDEN STKS 1m 4f
**6:10** (6:12) (Class 5) 3-4-Y-O **£3,881** (£1,155; £577; £288) **Stalls** Centre

Form RPR
2 **1** **Festival Of Ages (USA)**[44] 3717 3-9-3 0.................... AdamKirby 2 91+
(Charlie Appleby) *t.k.h early: hld up in tch in midfield: hdwy to trck ldrs 4f out: led 3f out: drvn and pressed over 1f out: hdd wl ins fnl f: battled bk u.p to ld again towards fin* **2/1**[1]

**2** *½* **Kohinur** 3-8-12 0.................... JosephineGordon 7 85+
(Hugo Palmer) *stdd s: t.k.h: wl in tch in midfield: effrt to chse wnr wl over 2f out: styd on u.p and chalng ent fnl f: led ins fnl f: hdd and no ex towards fin* **25/1**

**3** *2* **Gold Star** 3-9-3 0.................... SilvestreDeSousa 4 87+
(Saeed bin Suroor) *hld up in tch towards rr: rdn 4f out: hdwy to chse ldrs 2f out: chsd ldng pair u.p 1f out: kpt on but nvr enough pce to get on terms* **3/1**[2]

0-6 **4** *1 ½* **Ouja**[15] 4808 3-8-12 0.................... KieranShoemark 11 79
(John Gosden) *stdd s: t.k.h early: hld up in tch in midfield: effrt to chse ldrs over 2f out: wandered u.p over 1f out: 4th and styd on same pce ins fnl f* **8/1**

3 **5** *2 ¾* **Tinker Tailor (IRE)**[76] 2632 4-9-4 0.................... DavidEgan(5) 5 74
(Denis Quinn) *t.k.h: hld up in tch in midfield: swtchd rt and effrt 3f out: 5th and no imp whn edgd lft over 1f out: kpt on same pce ins fnl f* **33/1**

4424 **6** *7* **Turnpike Trip**[30] 4221 3-9-3 80.................... FergusSweeney 12 69
(Henry Candy) *stdd s: hld up in tch in midfield: reminder ent fnl 2f: sn outpcd: wknd over 1f out* **16/1**

22 **7** *hd* **Musaahim (USA)**[21] 4569 3-9-3 0.................... JimCrowley 8 68
(Roger Varian) *chsd ldrs tl wnt 2nd after 3f: led 5f out tl hdd and rdn 3f out: sn lost pl: wknd over 1f out* **7/2**[3]

6223 **8** *3 ¼* **Chief Craftsman**[21] 4569 3-9-0 78.................... GeorgeWood(3) 1 63
(Luca Cumani) *chsd ldr for 3f: styd chsng ldrs: ev ch 5f out tl unable qck u.p 3f out: sn lost pl: wknd over 1f out* **9/1**

00 **9** *nk* **Captor**[15] 4808 3-9-3 0.................... DougieCostello 9 63
(David Simcock) *stdd s: t.k.h: hld up in last pair: nudged along over 2f out: sn outpcd and wl btn over 1f out* **66/1**

0 **10** *10* **Quite Sharp**[28] 4300 3-8-12 0.................... MartinHarley 10 42
(Charlie Fellowes) *hld up in last pair: rdn and struggling 3f out: sn bhd* **66/1**

0 **11** *19* **Sonnet Rose (IRE)**[23] 4497 3-8-12 0.................... SaleemGolam 6 11
(Conrad Allen) *stdd s: t.k.h in midfield: rdn and lost pl qckly over 3f out: sn bhd: t.o* **150/1**

0 **12** *46* **The Iron Factor (USA)**[41] 3839 3-9-3 0....................(t) DannyBrock 3
(Phil McEntee) *led tl 5f out: sn u.p and dropped out: t.o fnl 2f* **150/1**

2m 36.08s (3.18) **Going Correction** +0.45s/f (Yiel)
**WFA** 3 from 4yo 11lb **12** Ran SP% **118.6**
Speed ratings (Par 103): **107,106,105,104,102 97,97,95,95,88 76,45**
CSF £61.72 TOTE £2.80: £1.20, £5.40, £1.90; EX 61.40 Trifecta £229.00.
**Owner** Godolphin **Bred** Darley **Trained** Newmarket, Suffolk

**FOCUS**
An informative maiden, featuring a host of well bred individuals. The 'right' horses came to the fore in what appeared testing conditions.

## 5365 FLY LONDON SOUTHEND AIRPORT TO LYON NOVICE MEDIAN AUCTION STKS (PLUS 10 RACE) 6f
**6:40** (6:42) (Class 4) 2-Y-O **£3,946** (£1,174; £586; £293) **Stalls** High

Form RPR
2 **1** **Nobleman's Nest**[21] 4567 2-9-2 0.................... JimCrowley 12 83+
(Simon Crisford) *chsd ldr tl led 2f out: sn rdn and qcknd over 1f out: clr and r.o wl ins fnl f: pushed out* **5/4**[1]

**2** *1 ½* **Can't Explain** 2-8-11 0.................... LouisSteward 13 74+
(Michael Bell) *hld up in tch in midfield: effrt 2f out: chsd ldrs and rdn over 1f out: chsd wnr ins fnl f: styd on for clr 2nd but nvr threatening wnr* **33/1**

03 **3** *1 ½* **Yaafour**[14] 4859 2-9-2 0.................... TomMarquand 9 74
(Richard Hannon) *t.k.h: led tl hdd and rdn 2f out: unable qck over 1f out: lost 2nd and kpt on same pce ins fnl f* **8/1**

6 **4** *nk* **Character Witness (IRE)**[15] 4805 2-9-2 0.................... SilvestreDeSousa 4 73
(Roger Varian) *hld up in tch in midfield: effrt 2f out: drvn over 1f out: 4th and kpt on same pce ins fnl f: nvr getting on terms w wnr* **12/1**

0 **5** *2 ¼* **Stormy Sand (IRE)**[21] 4560 2-8-13 0.................... GeorgeWood(3) 2 66
(Marco Botti) *t.k.h: chsd ldrs: rdn 2f out: unable qck over 1f out: wknd ins fnl f* **50/1**

**6** *1 ¼* **Roseau City** 2-8-6 0.................... DavidEgan(5) 7 58
(David Elsworth) *s.i.s: rn green and pushed along in rr early: clsd and travelling bttr after 2f: rdn again over 2f out: no ch w wnr but hdwy and styd on steadily ins fnl f* **66/1**

7 nk **Desert Mountain (IRE)** 2-9-2 0 MartinLane 10 62
(Saeed bin Suroor) *in tch in midfield: clsd to chse ldrs 3f out: rdn 2f out: unable qck and lost pl over 1f out: wknd ins fnl f* **7/1**[3]

8 1 1/4 **Exprompt (FR)** 2-9-2 0 JosephineGordon 6 58
(Hugo Palmer) *s.i.s: hld up in last quartet: pushed along and sme hdwy but nvr on terms w ldrs whn hung lft over 1f out: no imp after: wknd ins fnl f* **14/1**

0 9 nk **Dark Freedom (IRE)**[41] 3846 2-9-2 0 MartinHarley 3 57
(Charles Hills) *chsd ldrs: rdn 2f out: sn struggling and lost pl over 1f out: wknd fnl f* **40/1**

4 10 hd **Mankind (FR)**[14] 4826 2-9-2 0 AdamKirby 8 56
(George Scott) *hld up in tch in midfield: lost pl and rdn 2f out: no threat to ldrs after: wknd fnl f* **7/2**[2]

0 11 2 1/2 **Freebe Rocks (IRE)**[13] 4885 2-9-2 0 DannyBrock 11 49
(Michael Bell) *stdd after s: hld up in tch in last quartet: effrt 2f out: sn struggling and wl btn 1f out* **33/1**

00 12 shd **Mountain Peak**[6] 5151 2-9-2 0 LiamKeniry 5 49
(Ed Walker) *stdd after s: hld up in tch in last quartet: rdn over 1f out: sn btn and wknd fnl f* **100/1**

1m 14.83s (2.33) **Going Correction** +0.35s/f (Good) **12** Ran SP% **117.4**
Speed ratings (Par 96): **98,96,94,93,90 88,88,86,86,86 82,82**
CSF £61.31 TOTE £2.00: £1.10, £7.70, £1.90; EX 56.10 Trifecta £326.50.
**Owner** Mrs P Good **Bred** Mrs P Good **Trained** Newmarket, Suffolk

**FOCUS**
This lacked depth and proved easy picking for Gimcrack Stakes entry Nobleman's Rest. The level is a bit fluid, with the third below his recent start.

## 5366 FLY LONDON SOUTHEND AIRPORT TO PRAGUE NURSERY H'CAP 7f
**7:10** (7:10) (Class 4) 2-Y-O **£4,528** (£1,347; £673; £336) **Stalls** High

Form RPR

2634 1 **Noble Manners (IRE)**[17] 4716 2-8-12 **69** JimCrowley 9 77
(Mark Johnston) *dwlt: in tch in last trio: hdwy and followed wnr through on far rail 2f out: rdn to chse wnr ent fnl f: styd on wl u.p to ld cl home* **7/2**[1]

510 2 nk **Di Fede (IRE)**[34] 4068 2-9-4 **75** PatDobbs 7 82
(Ralph Beckett) *hld up wl in tch in midfield: clsd to ld wl over 1f out: sn rdn and kicked clr over 1f out: drvn ins fnl f: kpt on but worn down and hdd cl home* **9/1**[3]

004 3 5 **Isoletta**[36] 4007 2-8-10 **67** LiamKeniry 2 62
(Ed Walker) *t.k.h: hld up in tch in midfield: effrt 2f out: sme hdwy to chse clr ldng pair jst ins fnl f: sn hung lft and no imp: kpt on same pce for clr 2nd* **10/1**

2103 4 6 **Joe's Spirit (IRE)**[14] 4827 2-9-0 **78** TristanPrice(7) 8 58
(Michael Bell) *t.k.h: sn trcking ldrs: clsd to ld and bmpd 2f out: sn rdn: hdd and outpcd over 1f out: wknd fnl f* **7/2**[1]

530 5 3/4 **Global Wealth**[21] 4560 2-9-0 **71** JosephineGordon 6 49
(Ed Dunlop) *dwlt: in tch in last pair but nvr looked to be travelling wl in enough: effrt u.p over 2f out: no imp over 1f out: sn wknd* **9/2**[2]

0163 6 4 1/2 **Another Day Of Sun (IRE)**[17] 4716 2-9-1 **72**.....(v[1]) SilvestreDeSousa 5 39
(Mick Channon) *chsd ldr: ev ch whn edgd rt and bmpd rival 2f out: sn outpcd and btn: no ch whn eased ins fnl f* **9/2**[2]

063 7 3/4 **General Zoff**[13] 4909 2-9-2 **73** DougieCostello 3 38
(William Muir) *in tch in last trio: effrt 2f out: sn struggling and btn: wknd fnl f* **14/1**

405 8 9 **Situation**[2] 5279 2-8-11 **68**(p[1]) KieranShoemark 4 10
(Richard Guest) *restless in stalls: t.k.h and sn led: hdd and rdn 2f out: sn dropped out and bhd: eased ins fnl f* **16/1**

1m 28.04s (2.34) **Going Correction** +0.35s/f (Good) **8** Ran SP% **112.4**
Speed ratings (Par 96): **100,99,93,87,86 81,80,69**
CSF £34.29 CT £285.75 TOTE £4.10: £1.50, £2.50, £2.00; EX 30.00 Trifecta £227.30.
**Owner** Abdulla Al Mansoori **Bred** Jim McCormack **Trained** Middleham Moor, N Yorks

**FOCUS**
A competitive nursery and a strong staying performance from Noble Manners on her first try at the distance.

## 5367 FLY LONDON SOUTHEND AIRPORT TO BUDAPEST FILLIES' H'CAP (LONDON MILE SERIES QUALIFIER) 1m
**7:40** (7:41) (Class 5) (0-70,71) 3-Y-O+ **£3,881** (£1,155; £577; £288) **Stalls** High

Form RPR

00-3 1 **Oh It's Saucepot**[70] 2794 3-8-11 **60** TedDurcan 7 70
(Chris Wall) *trckd ldrs: clsd and rdn to chal 2f out: sustained chal u.p and styd on wl ins fnl f: to ld cl home* **9/2**[1]

055 2 nk **Miss Pacific**[16] 4764 3-9-2 **65** SilvestreDeSousa 5 74
(William Jarvis) *hld up in tch towards rr: swtchd lft to r along on far rail 1/2-way: rdn and ev ch 2f out: sustained chal to ld jst ins fnl f: kpt on: hdd and no ex cl home* **6/1**[3]

035 3 1 **Drumochter**[27] 4378 3-9-2 **65** PatCosgrave 6 72
(Charles Hills) *led: rdn 2f out: drvn and hdd jst ins fnl f: no ex and styd on same pce fnl 100yds* **11/2**[2]

4360 4 3 3/4 **Tulip Dress**[7] 5119 4-9-3 **63** JaneElliott(5) 4 63
(Anthony Carson) *hld up in tch: hdwy over 2f out: rdn to chse ldrs 2f out st unable qck and outpcd 1f out: wknd ins fnl f* **10/1**

33-5 5 1 3/4 **Miss Fay (IRE)**[36] 4003 3-9-6 **69**(v) AdamKirby 9 63
(Michael Bell) *s.i.s and rousted along early: in tch in rr: swtchd rt and effrt u.p over 2f out: no imp and hld whn hung lft 1f out: plugged on same pce ins fnl f* **10/1**

553 6 nk **Zilza (IRE)**[9] 5038 3-9-1 **64**(t) JimCrowley 2 58
(Conrad Allen) *t.k.h: chsd ldr tl ent fnl 2f: outpcd and btn over 1f out: wl hld and plugged on same pce ins fnl f* **6/1**[3]

003 7 1/2 **Street Marie (USA)**[25] 4444 3-8-12 **61** KieranShoemark 3 54
(John Gosden) *t.k.h: trckd ldrs: rdn jst over 2f out: lost pl u.p over 1f out: wl hld and plugged on same pce ins fnl f* **7/1**

0314 8 2 **Prize Diva**[28] 4319 3-9-1 **69**(p) DavidEgan(5) 1 57
(David Elsworth) *in tch: rdn over 2f out: sn struggling and lost pl: bhd and wknd ins fnl f* **9/2**[1]

1m 43.77s (3.77) **Going Correction** +0.35s/f (Good)
**WFA** 3 from 4yo 8lb **8** Ran SP% **111.0**
Speed ratings (Par 100): **95,94,93,89,88 87,87,85**
CSF £29.45 CT £144.06 TOTE £4.80: £1.60, £2.00, £2.10; EX 28.20 Trifecta £132.80.
**Owner** The Eight Of Diamonds **Bred** Mrs C J Walker **Trained** Newmarket, Suffolk
■ Stewards' Enquiry : Ted Durcan two-day ban: used whip above permitted level (11-12 Aug)

**FOCUS**
A moderate level but it featured some unexposed fillies' with the potential to do better.

## 5368 FLY LONDON SOUTHEND AIRPORT TO DUBROVNIK H'CAP 1m 4f
**8:10** (8:13) (Class 3) (0-95,88) 3-Y-O **£9,056** (£2,695; £1,346; £673) **Stalls** Centre

Form RPR

164 1 **The Grand Visir**[22] 4535 3-9-4 **85** PatCosgrave 4 98
(William Haggas) *mde all: rdn 3f out: kpt on finding ex for press and forged ahd ent fnl f: styd on wl u.p and a doing enough ins fnl f* **11/4**[2]

31 2 3/4 **Petitioner (IRE)**[44] 3720 3-8-11 **78** KieranShoemark 1 89
(Roger Charlton) *t.k.h: disp 2nd tl dropped to 3rd 5f out: rdn ent fnl 3f: outpcd over 2f out: hung lft but rallied u.p over 1f out: wnt 2nd and pressing wnr 150yds out: kpt on but a hld* **10/3**[3]

6-24 3 7 **Sable Island (IRE)**[25] 4450 3-8-12 **79** TedDurcan 5 81
(Sir Michael Stoute) *stdd and dropped in bhd after s: hld up in tch in rr: rdn ent fnl 3f: outpcd over 2f out: no threat to ldrs after: wnt 3rd ins fnl f: no imp and sn eased* **11/1**

31 4 8 **Pouvoir Magique (FR)**[19] 4657 3-9-7 **88** FrankieDettori 3 84
(John Gosden) *t.k.h: disp 2nd tl chsd wnr 5f out: rdn and chal over 2f out tl no ex and btn ent fnl f: lost 2nd 150yds: sn fdd and eased fnl 100yds* **1/1**[1]

2m 38.56s (5.66) **Going Correction** +0.45s/f (Yiel) **4** Ran SP% **108.1**
Speed ratings (Par 104): **99,98,93,88**
CSF £11.44 TOTE £3.30; EX 11.20 Trifecta £20.00.
**Owner** Saleh Al Homaizi & Imad Al Sagar **Bred** Qatar B'Stock, Ecurie Monceaux & Skymarc **Trained** Newmarket, Suffolk

**FOCUS**
A disappointing turn out numerically for this feature and it led to a tactical affair. Two of the runners held St Leger entries. The form has been rated on the positive side.

## 5369 FLY LONDON SOUTHEND AIRPORT TO VENICE H'CAP 7f
**8:40** (8:41) (Class 4) (0-85,84) 3-Y-O+ **£5,175** (£1,540; £769; £384) **Stalls** High

Form RPR

41- 1 **Yellowhammer**[272] 7696 3-8-13 **76** KieranShoemark 2 85+
(Roger Charlton) *stdd and dropped in after s: t.k.h: hld up in tch in last pair: nt clr run and swtchd rt over 2f out: hdwy to chse ldrs 1f out: str chal ins fnl f: styd on wl u.p to ld on post* **7/2**[1]

2113 2 nse **Pastime**[14] 4831 3-9-5 **82** JosephineGordon 3 90
(Gay Kelleway) *hld up in tch in midfield: clsd to chse ldr 2f out: sn rdn and ev ch ent fnl f: led ins fnl f: kpt on wl u.p: hdd on post* **4/1**[2]

3040 3 1 **Ower Fly**[27] 4339 4-9-10 **83**(b[1]) HollieDoyle(3) 8 91
(Richard Hannon) *led: rdn and edgd rt over 1f out: hrd pressed ent fnl f: hdd ins fnl f: no ex and outpcd towards fin* **7/1**

6106 4 4 1/2 **Bint Dandy (IRE)**[16] 4763 6-9-12 **82**(b) SilvestreDeSousa 4 78
(Chris Dwyer) *chsd ldrs: effrt ent fnl 2f: unable qck u.p over 1f out: wknd ins fnl f* **13/2**

0416 5 1 1/4 **Artscape**[29] 4277 5-9-6 **76** AdamKirby 5 69
(Dean Ivory) *t.k.h: hld up wl in tch in midfield: effrt 2f out: no ex u.p over 1f out: wknd ins fnl f* **6/1**[3]

0020 6 2 1/2 **Palawan**[34] 4091 4-10-0 **84** DougieCostello 1 70
(Jamie Osborne) *hld up in last pair: effrt and hung lft 2f out: sn outpcd and n.d fr over 1f out* **20/1**

1-00 7 1 **Gabrielle**[144] 1066 4-8-8 **67** GeorgeWood(3) 6 50
(Dr Jon Scargill) *t.k.h early: hld up wl in tch in midfield: rdn ent fnl 2f: sn struggling and outpcd over 1f out: wknd fnl f* **28/1**

40-5 8 hd **Titan Goddess**[13] 4887 5-9-2 **72** ShaneKelly 7 55
(Mike Murphy) *dwlt and bustled along leaving stalls: sn rcvrd to chse ldr: rdn and lost 2nd 2f out: sn struggling and lost pl: wknd fnl f* **4/1**[2]

1m 28.38s (2.68) **Going Correction** +0.35s/f (Good)
**WFA** 3 from 4yo+ 7lb **8** Ran SP% **110.6**
Speed ratings (Par 105): **98,97,96,91,90 87,86,86**
CSF £16.35 CT £86.15 TOTE £3.80: £1.70, £1.50, £2.20; EX 9.00 Trifecta £92.00.
**Owner** Lady Rothschild **Bred** Kincorth Investments Inc **Trained** Beckhampton, Wilts

**FOCUS**
A wide open handicap with only three points separating the first six in the betting. It was run in near darkness in heavy rain. The third has been rated to his recent form.
T/Plt: £363.50 to a £1 stake. Pool: £62,586.69 - 125.66 winning units T/Qpdt: £24.90 to a £1 stake. Pool: £6,810.35 - 202.20 winning units **Steve Payne**

# 5003 THIRSK (L-H)
## Friday, July 28

**OFFICIAL GOING: Good to soft**
Wind: Fresh half behind Weather: Cloudy

## 5370 SPORTING LIFE PICK 7 STARTS NOW EBF NOVICE STKS 5f
**1:20** (1:22) (Class 5) 2-Y-O **£3,234** (£962; £481; £240) **Stalls** Centre

Form RPR

53 1 **Savalas (IRE)**[20] 4598 2-9-2 0 TomEaves 5 79
(Kevin Ryan) *stdd s: sn trckd ldrs: rdn 2f out: kpt on to ld 25yds out* **11/4**[2]

41 2 1/2 **Rumshak (IRE)**[20] 4606 2-9-6 0 PaulMulrennan 4 81
(Michael Dods) *led: pushed along 2f out: rdn and strly pressed appr fnl f: hdd 25yds out: one pce* **5/6**[1]

5 3 2 **Mr Greenlight**[27] 4374 2-9-2 0 DavidAllan 6 70
(Tim Easterby) *prom: rdn to chal strly appr fnl f: no ex fnl 75yds* **10/1**

03 4 nk **Hermana Santa (IRE)**[20] 4599 2-8-11 0 SamJames 10 64
(David Barron) *chsd ldrs: rdn 2f out: one pce* **40/1**

0 5 1/2 **Rock Hill (IRE)**[20] 4598 2-9-2 0 GrahamLee 7 67
(Paul Midgley) *chsd ldrs: rdn 2f out: one pce* **150/1**

6 1/2 **Kyllachy Dragon (IRE)** 2-9-2 0 DavidNolan 3 65+
(Iain Jardine) *hld up: pushed along 2f out: kpt on ins fnl f: nrst fin* **66/1**

6 7 1 1/4 **Eller Brook**[21] 4555 2-8-11 0 ConnorBeasley 9 56
(Michael Dods) *midfield: sn pushed along: in tch over 1f out: no ex fnl 110yds* **25/1**

8 3 1/2 **Havana Mariposa** 2-8-11 0 BenCurtis 1 43
(K R Burke) *wnt lft s: hld up: nvr threatened* **20/1**

01 9 3/4 **Cameo Star (IRE)**[10] 4995 2-9-6 0 PaulHanagan 8 50
(Richard Fahey) *dwlt: hld up: pushed along 3f out: nvr threatened* **7/1**[3]

10 1 1/2 **Marconi** 2-9-2 0 PhillipMakin 2 40
(John Davies) *s.i.s: a rr* **200/1**

65 11 3 1/2 **Stopwatch**[44] 3705 2-9-2 0 AndrewMullen 11 28
(Karen McLintock) *hld up: rdn 1/2-way: wknd over 1f out* **100/1**

1m 0.51s (0.91) **Going Correction** +0.30s/f (Good) **11** Ran SP% **117.5**
Speed ratings (Par 94): **104,103,100,99,98 97,95,90,89,86 81**
CSF £5.17 TOTE £3.40: £1.40, £1.10, £3.00; EX 5.60 Trifecta £30.50.
**Owner** Mrs Angie Bailey **Bred** Tally-Ho Stud **Trained** Hambleton, N Yorks

■ Stewards' Enquiry : Paul Mulrennan two-day ban: used whip above permitted level (11-12 Aug)

**FOCUS**

There had been about 1.5mm of rain over the previous 24 hours and the going was given as good to soft. The market principals came to the fore in this novice race. It's been rated around the first two.

## 5371 BRITISH STALLION STUDS EBF FILLIES' NOVICE STKS (PLUS 10 RACE) (DIV I) 7f

**1:50** (1:52) (Class 4) 2-Y-O **£4,269** (£1,270; £634; £317) **Stalls** Low

Form RPR

4 **1** **Affina (IRE)**[15] 4786 2-9-0 0 GrahamLee 4 79
(Simon Crisford) *mde most: pressed thrght: pushed along 2f out: drvn ins fnl f: hld on wl* **4/1**[2]

2 **2** *hd* **Akvavera**[22] 4528 2-9-0 0 PhillipMakin 6 78
(Ralph Beckett) *trckd ldrs: rdn 2f out: pushed along to chal strly appr fnl f: rdn ins fnl f: kpt on but a jst hld* **6/4**[1]

**3** *1 1/4* **Voicemail** 2-9-0 0 DanielTudhope 8 75
(James Tate) *w ldr: led briefly 5f out: rdn 2f out: one pce fnl 110yds* **16/1**

40 **4** *3 1/2* **Kylie Rules**[14] 4834 2-9-0 0 ShaneGray 9 66+
(Ann Duffield) *chsd ldrs: pushed along over 2f out: one pce in modest 4th fr over 1f out* **150/1**

4 **5** *4 1/2* **Ryedale Encore**[22] 4528 2-9-0 0 DavidAllan 12 55+
(Tim Easterby) *midfield: rdn along over 2f out: one pce and nvr threatened* **20/1**

5 **6** *1 3/4* **Zoffinia (IRE)**[27] 4340 2-9-0 0 PaulHanagan 10 51+
(Richard Fahey) *hld up: pushed along over 2f out: sme late hdwy: nvr threatened* **10/1**

35 **7** *1* **Marsh Storm (IRE)**[0C] 2299 2-9-0 0 PJMcDonald 1 48+
(K R Burke) *midfield: pushed along over 2f out: wknd over 1f out* **28/1**

5 **8** *1 1/4* **Gamesters Icon**[22] 4528 2-9-0 0 ConnorBeasley 2 45+
(Bryan Smart) *slowly away: hld up: nvr threatened* **33/1**

0 **9** *1* **Forest Dragon**[7] 5114 2-9-0 0 LouisSteward 3 42
(Hugo Palmer) *trckd ldrs: rdn over 2f out: wknd over 1f out* **9/1**

0 **10** *hd* **Gift Of Loulins**[29] 4258 2-9-0 0 BarryMcHugh 7 42
(Tony Coyle) *hld up: nvr threatened* **150/1**

0 **11** *11* **Salty Sugar**[62] 3070 2-9-0 0 (p[1]) RobertTart 11 14
(John Gosden) *dwlt: hld up: rdn over 3f out: sn btn: eased ins fnl f* **9/2**[3]

1m 29.23s (2.03) **Going Correction** +0.20s/f (Good) **11** Ran SP% **115.6**

Speed ratings (Par 93): **96,95,94,90,85 83,82,80,79,79 66**

CSF £9.79 TOTE £4.40: £1.80, £1.10, £4.30; EX 11.40 Trifecta £123.90.

**Owner** Sheikh Juma Dalmook Al Maktoum **Bred** Max Morris **Trained** Newmarket, Suffolk

**FOCUS**

They didn't go that quick early and few got into it. The runner-up has been rated close to her debut effort.

## 5372 BRITISH STALLION STUDS EBF FILLIES' NOVICE STKS (PLUS 10 RACE) (DIV II) 7f

**2:20** (2:23) (Class 4) 2-Y-O **£4,269** (£1,270; £634; £317) **Stalls** Low

Form RPR

043 **1** **Juliet Capulet (IRE)**[13] 4902 2-9-0 81 (p) RobertTart 11 87+
(John Gosden) *prom on outer: led 5f out: mde rest: pushed along over 2f out: rdn over 1f out: kpt on wl to draw clr ins fnl f* **4/5**[1]

**2** *3 1/2* **Crown Vallary (FR)** 2-8-11 0 JordanVaughan(3) 2 78
(K R Burke) *trckd ldrs: chal 2f out: rdn over 1f out: edgd lft ent fnl f: no ex fnl 75yds* **33/1**

65 **3** *1 1/2* **Fleeting Freedom**[13] 4902 2-9-0 0 JimmyQuinn 7 75+
(Alan Bailey) *hld up in midfield: pushed along and hdwy 2f out: wnt 3rd over 1f out: rdn and kpt on fnl f* **9/2**[2]

0 **4** *4 1/2* **Tell Me (IRE)**[45] 3697 2-9-0 0 (v[1]) GrahamLee 4 63
(Simon Crisford) *midfield: pushed along and hdwy to chse ldrs over 2f out: wknd over 1f out* **18/1**

**5** *1 1/2* **Mafdet** 2-9-0 0 ConnorBeasley 8 60
(Bryan Smart) *hld up: kpt on ins fnl f: nrst fin* **50/1**

**6** *3/4* **Yamuna River** 2-9-0 0 DavidAllan 1 58
(James Tate) *led narrowly: hdd 5f out: trckd ldr: rdn over 2f out: wknd over 1f out* **16/1**

64 **7** *3 1/4* **Fastalong (IRE)**[28] 4291 2-9-0 0 DuranFentiman 12 50
(Tim Easterby) *hld up: nvr threatened* **14/1**

**8** *nse* **Cum Spiro Spero (IRE)** 2-9-0 0 BarryMcHugh 9 49
(Tony Coyle) *dwlt: a towards rr* **100/1**

**9** *4* **Ventura Royal (IRE)** 2-9-0 0 DanielTudhope 3 39
(David O'Meara) *dwlt: sn trckd ldrs: rdn over 2f out: sn wknd* **8/1**[3]

**10** *nk* **Stripey** 2-9-0 0 PaulHanagan 5 39
(Richard Fahey) *awkward s: hld up in midfield: pushed along over 3f out: wknd over 1f out* **12/1**

00 **11** *2 1/4* **Travel Lightly**[23] 4502 2-9-0 0 JamesSullivan 6 33
(Tim Easterby) *midfield: rdn over 2f out: wknd over 1f out* **125/1**

1m 29.57s (2.37) **Going Correction** +0.20s/f (Good) **11** Ran SP% **117.0**

Speed ratings (Par 93): **94,90,88,83,81 80,76,76,72,71 69**

CSF £41.82 TOTE £1.70: £1.10, £8.30, £1.50; EX 39.60 Trifecta £135.10.

**Owner** Cheveley Park Stud **Bred** Yeomanstown Stud **Trained** Newmarket, Suffolk

**FOCUS**

The winning time was 0.34sec slower than the first division. The winner has been rated to her latest form.

## 5373 JW 4X4 NORTHALLERTON NURSERY H'CAP 6f

**2:55** (2:56) (Class 3) 2-Y-O **£6,469** (£1,925; £962; £481) **Stalls** Centre

Form RPR

6312 **1** **Silver Starlight**[14] 4866 2-9-5 72 DavidAllan 8 74
(Tim Easterby) *trckd ldrs: rdn 2f out: edgd lft ins fnl f: led 75yds out: kpt on* **4/1**[3]

054 **2** *1/2* **Reinbeau Prince**[38] 3930 2-9-0 67 PaulHanagan 1 68
(Richard Fahey) *led narrowly: rdn over 2f out: hdd 75yds out: one pce* **12/1**

040 **3** *1* **Admiral Rooke (IRE)**[30] 4204 2-9-1 68 PaulMulrennan 9 66
(Michael Dods) *hld up: rdn over 2f out: hdwy over 1f out: kpt on fnl f: wnt 3rd towards fin* **9/1**

0442 **4** *1/2* **Dyson's Girl**[16] 4739 2-8-11 64 ConnorBeasley 4 60
(Bryan Smart) *chsd ldrs: rdn over 2f out: chal ent fnl f: no ex fnl 110yds: lost 3rd towaerds fin* **6/1**

0635 **5** *1 1/4* **Monkey Magic**[17] 4716 2-8-6 59 AndrewMullen 7 51
(Nigel Tinkler) *w ldr: rdn over 2f out: wknd fnl 110yds* **22/1**

6211 **6** *1 1/2* **Mr Wagyu (IRE)**[13] 4922 2-9-7 74 JasonHart 6 62
(John Quinn) *chsd ldrs: rdn over 2f out: wknd ins fnl f* **11/4**[1]

500 **7** *1/2* **Mabo**[14] 4862 2-9-3 70 TonyHamilton 2 56
(Richard Fahey) *slowly away: hld up: rdn over 2f out: nvr threatened* **18/1**

0044 **8** *nk* **Archie Perkins (IRE)**[29] 4273 2-8-12 65 TomEaves 3 50
(Nigel Tinkler) *dwlt: hld up: rdn over 2f out: nvr threatened* **25/1**

5102 **9** *4 1/2* **Silca Mistress**[8] 5057 2-9-2 69 GrahamLee 5 41
(Mick Channon) *trckd ldrs: rdn over 2f out: wknd fnl f* **10/3**[2]

1m 14.68s (1.98) **Going Correction** +0.30s/f (Good) **9** Ran SP% **115.2**

Speed ratings (Par 98): **98,97,96,95,93 91,91,90,84**

CSF £50.58 CT £411.14 TOTE £4.80: £1.80, £3.80, £2.90; EX 56.70 Trifecta £373.10.

**Owner** Reality Partnerships I **Bred** Mrs Fiona Denniff **Trained** Great Habton, N Yorks

**FOCUS**

A competitive nursery.

## 5374 BUY ONLINE DISCOUNT AT THIRKRACECOURSE.NET (S) H'CAP 7f

**3:30** (3:31) (Class 6) (0-65,64) 3-Y-O **£2,587** (£770; £384; £192) **Stalls** Low

Form RPR

5606 **1** **Cosmic Sky**[20] 4603 3-8-1 47 (h) SammyJoBell(3) 4 55
(Tim Easterby) *prom: rdn over 1f out: led ins fnl f: kpt on* **9/1**

0402 **2** *1 3/4* **Melaniemillie**[10] 5007 3-8-4 47 JamesSullivan 16 50
(Ruth Carr) *prom: led gng wl over 2f out: rdn over 1f out: hdd ins fnl f: no ex* **4/1**[2]

0005 **3** *2 1/4* **Zebedee Star**[21] 4554 3-8-2 45 CamHardie 10 43
(Karen Tutty) *midfield: hdwy over 2f out: rdn to chse ldrs over 1f out: edgd lft and one pce ins fnl f* **28/1**

0-04 **4** *1 1/4* **She's Zoff (IRE)**[8] 5050 3-8-6 49 PJMcDonald 13 43+
(John Quinn) *dwlt: sn midfield on outer: rdn and hdwy 2f out: kpt on* **7/2**[1]

0004 **5** *3 3/4* **Flying Onsite (FR)**[6] 5167 3-8-3 46 (be[1]) JoeDoyle 7 31
(Nigel Tinkler) *trckd ldrs: rdn over 2f out: wknd over 1f out* **7/1**

0-00 **6** *2 1/2* **I Dare To Dream**[1b] 4764 3-7-9 45 (p) JamieGormley(7) 6 23+
(Lisa Williamson) *awkward s and slowly away: hld up: sme hdwy on outside over 1f out: nvr threatened* **66/1**

0-06 **7** *nse* **Canizay (IRE)**[23] 4508 3-8-2 45 PatrickMathers 3 23
(Roger Fell) *trckd ldrs: rdn over 2f out: sn outpcd and btn* **16/1**

2035 **8** *nse* **Springforth**[16] 4745 3-9-7 64 TonyHamilton 12 42
(Richard Fahey) *trckd ldrs: rdn over 2f out: wknd fnl f* **9/2**[3]

6050 **9** *2* **Nightdress (IRE)**[20] 4602 3-8-6 49 DuranFentiman 1 22
(Tony Coyle) *slowly away: hld up: nvr threatened* **66/1**

0040 **10** *2 1/4* **Albizu Campos**[16] 4744 3-8-2 45 (v[1]) AndrewMullen 5 12
(Lawrence Mullaney) *a towards rr* **12/1**

206 **11** *1* **Kelpie Spirit (IRE)**[8] 5074 3-8-5 53 PhilDennis(5) 11 17
(John Weymes) *hld up in midfield: rdn over 2f out: wknd over 1f out* **12/1**

-000 **12** *3* **King Of Castilla**[10] 5004 3-8-7 50 (b) JimmyQuinn 15 6
(Colin Teague) *hld up: rdn over 2f out: sn wknd* **100/1**

0-06 **13** *1 3/4* **Chevalier Du Lac (IRE)**[10] 5004 3-9-3 60 PaulMulrennan 14 12
(Conor Dore) *a towards rr* **28/1**

4250 **14** *11* **Panther In Pink (IRE)**[24] 4473 3-8-4 47 (h) ShaneGray 9
(Ann Duffield) *led: rdn whn hdd over 2f out: wknd* **16/1**

1m 28.56s (1.36) **Going Correction** +0.20s/f (Good) **14** Ran SP% **120.9**

Speed ratings (Par 98): **100,98,95,94,89 86,86,86,84,81 80,77,75,62**

CSF £43.96 CT £1019.86 TOTE £10.00: £3.70, £1.80, £8.20; EX 59.10 Trifecta £1042.50.

**Owner** Reality Partnerships VII **Bred** Milldown Stud & Trickledown Stud **Trained** Great Habton, N Yorks

**FOCUS**

The first two were prominent throughout.

## 5375 SAMMY LANE FILLIES' H'CAP 6f

**4:05** (4:05) (Class 5) (0-70,71) 3-Y-O+ **£3,234** (£962; £481; £240) **Stalls** Centre

Form RPR

4156 **1** **Ki Ki**[20] 4605 5-9-5 62 ConnorBeasley 10 69
(Bryan Smart) *in tch: rdn and hdwy over 1f out: led 110yds out: kpt on* **11/2**[2]

0352 **2** *3/4* **Oriental Lilly**[6] 5134 3-9-0 62 DanielTudhope 7 66
(Jim Goldie) *hld up: rdn and hdwy over 1f out: kpt on: wnt 2nd towards fin* **6/4**[1]

1044 **3** *1/2* **Kodicat (IRE)**[16] 4745 3-9-7 69 TomEaves 5 71
(Kevin Ryan) *chsd clr ldr: rdn and clsd over 1f out: led narrowly ins fnl f: hdd 110yds out: no ex and lost 2nd towards fin* **13/2**[3]

2305 **4** *1 1/4* **Yorkshire Pudding**[10] 5007 3-9-0 62 (b) DavidAllan 8 60
(Tim Easterby) *in tch: rdn over 2f out: kpt on same pce* **13/2**[3]

U0-0 **5** *1/2* **Lexington Sky (IRE)**[99] 1913 3-9-9 71 TonyHamilton 2 68
(Roger Fell) *hld up: rdn 2f out: kpt on ins fnl f: nrst fin* **8/1**

56-0 **6** *2* **Quiet Moment (IRE)**[16] 4745 3-8-11 59 (b[1]) GrahamLee 4 49
(Ben Haslam) *racd alone far side: led and sn clr: rdn and reduced advantage appr fnl f: hdd ins fnl f: wknd* **33/1**

-520 **7** *nk* **Magical Molly Joe**[126] 1348 3-9-2 64 BenCurtis 3 53
(David Barron) *hld up: rdn 2f out: nvr threatened* **20/1**

526- **8** *4* **Dandy Bird (IRE)**[285] 7380 3-9-6 68 JoeDoyle 6 45
(Julie Camacho) *chsd clr ldr: rdn 2f out: wknd over 1f out* **12/1**

3100 **9** *1 3/4* **Dusty Blue**[25] 4433 5-9-2 66 RyanTimby(7) 9 38
(Michael Easterby) *hld up: rdn over 2f out: wknd and bhd over 1f out* **16/1**

1m 14.12s (1.42) **Going Correction** +0.30s/f (Good)

**WFA** 3 from 5yo 5lb **9** Ran SP% **114.4**

Speed ratings (Par 100): **102,101,100,98,98 95,94,89,87**

CSF £13.98 CT £54.92 TOTE £5.60: £1.70, £1.10, £2.10; EX 16.20 Trifecta £71.80.

**Owner** B Smart **Bred** Mrs P A Clark **Trained** Hambleton, N Yorks

**FOCUS**

A modest sprint. The runner-up has been rated to her latest effort, with the third, fourth and fifth close to their marks.

## 5376 LADIES' DAY SATURDAY 9TH SEPTEMBER BOOK NOW H'CAP 7f

**4:35** (4:38) (Class 4) (0-80,82) 3-Y-O **£5,175** (£1,540; £769; £384) **Stalls** Low

Form RPR

-210 **1** **Aimez La Vie (IRE)**[40] 3869 3-9-3 75 PaulHanagan 5 84
(Richard Fahey) *midfield: gd hdwy on outer 2f out: rdn to ld appr fnl f: kpt on wl* **12/1**

355 **2** *3/4* **Fayez (IRE)**[20] 4610 3-9-6 78 DanielTudhope 10 85
(David O'Meara) *hld up: midfield 1/2-way: pushed along and hdwy to chse ldr appr fnl f: kpt on wl but a hld* **6/1**[3]

1225 **3** *3 1/4* **Right Action**[13] 4894 3-9-5 77 TonyHamilton 9 75
(Richard Fahey) *rrd s: hld up in rr: pushed along and bit clsr over 2f out: swtchd rt to outer over 1f out: sn rdn: kpt on: wnt 3rd 50yds out* **8/1**

6501 **4** *1 1/4* **Ventura Secret (IRE)**[15] 4785 3-8-3 61 DuranFentiman 12 56+
(Tim Easterby) *pressed ldr: led 2f out: sn rdn: hdd appr fnl f: wknd fnl 110yds* **17/2**

-412 **5** *1 1/4* **Mulzim**[59] 3173 3-9-5 77 DaneO'Neill 6 68
(Ed Dunlop) *in tch: hdwy 2f out: rdn to chal over 1f out: wknd ins fnl f* **9/2**[1]

-004 6 1 3/4 **Rock N Rolla (IRE)**[18] 4685 3-9-5 77......................(p) ConnorBeasley 11 64
(Keith Dalgleish) *dwlt: sn chsd ldrs: rdn over 2f out: wknd fnl f* 5/1[2]
5043 7 hd **Proud Archi (IRE)**[13] 4894 3-9-7 79............................. PaulMulrennan 4 68
(Michael Dods) *trckd ldrs: short of room 2f out and shuffled bk: rdn and no imp fnl f* 7/1
8 3 3/4 **Pecheurs De Perles (IRE)**[108] 1709 3-9-10 82................ DavidNolan 7 58
(Iain Jardine) *hld up: pushed along over 2f out: bit short of room and swtchd lft over 1f out: nvr threatened* 8/1
3-00 9 7 **Heavenly Angel**[40] 3869 3-8-12 70.................................. JamesSullivan 1 27
(Ruth Carr) *led narrowly: rdn whn hdd 2f out: wknd* 20/1
0061 10 10 **Groupie**[22] 4529 3-9-6 78................................................ AndrewMullen 2 8
(Tom Tate) *hld up: pushed along over 2f out: sn wknd and bhd* 12/1

1m 28.14s (0.94) **Going Correction** +0.20s/f (Good) **10** Ran SP% **114.5**
Speed ratings (Par 102): **102,101,97,96,94 92,92,88,80,68**
CSF £80.80 CT £615.83 TOTE £14.00: £3.50, £2.80, £2.40; EX 103.20 Trifecta £489.10.
**Owner** Mr & Mrs N Wrigley **Bred** Lynn Lodge Stud And Foxtale Farm **Trained** Musley Bank, N Yorks

■ Hemingway was withdrawn. Price at time of withdrawal 14-1. Rule 4 applies to board prices prior to withdrawal but not to SP bets - deductions 5p in the pound. New market formed.

**FOCUS**
This was run at a good pace and it set up for the closers. The runner-up has been rated to his 2yo best.

## 5377 SKY BET GO-RACING-IN-YORKSHIRE SUMMER FESTIVAL "HANDS N HEELS" APPRENTICE H'CAP 5f
**5:05** (5:05) (Class 6) (0-65,65) 3-Y-O+ **£2,587** (£770; £384; £192) **Stalls** Centre

Form RPR
2301 1 **Culloden**[14] 4847 5-9-9 60.........................(v) ManuelFernandes 5 66
(Shaun Harris) *led: pushed along whn hdd narrowly appr fnl f: kpt on to ld again nr fin* 13/2
0002 2 nk **Point Of Woods**[8] 5055 4-9-11 62........................(p[1]) JamieGormley 4 67
(Tina Jackson) *sn chsd ldrs: pushed along to ld narrowly appr fnl f: edgd rt ins fnl f: hdd nr fin* 9/2[2]
0-32 3 hd **Liberatum**[9] 5020 3-9-6 64........................................ SeamusCronin(3) 11 67
(Ruth Carr) *midfield: pushed along and hdwy over 1f out: kpt on wl* 5/2[1]
1326 4 3 **Dapper Man (IRE)**[17] 4717 3-9-9 64...........................(b) BenSanderson 8 56
(Roger Fell) *prom: pushed along 2f out: no ex fnl f* 5/1[3]
50-4 5 nk **Lydiate Lady**[8] 5069 5-9-2 53.................................................. GerO'Neill 6 45
(Eric Alston) *slowly away: sn rcvrd to chse ldrs: pushed along and outpcd over 1f out: no threat after* 7/1
0505 6 2 1/2 **Captain Scooby**[3] 5252 11-8-9 46 oh1.............................(b) WilliamCox 7 29
(Richard Guest) *slowly away: outpcd in rr tl minor late hdwy* 7/1
0043 7 3/4 **Tinsill**[10] 4997 6-8-4 46 oh1.........................................(p) ZakWheatley(5) 13 27
(Nigel Tinkler) *hld up: pushed along over 2f out: nvr threatened* 14/1
0-00 8 3 1/4 **Imperial Legend (IRE)**[25] 4428 8-10-0 65.............(p) GabrieleMalune 3 34
(Alan Brown) *prom: pushed along over 2f out: wknd over 1f out* 18/1
4206 9 6 **Quiet Warrior (IRE)**[8] 5070 6-9-6 60.............................. RyanTimby(3) 9 7
(Michael Easterby) *hld up: pushed along 1/2-way: sn wknd and bhd* 25/1

1m 0.94s (1.34) **Going Correction** +0.30s/f (Good)
**WFA** 3 from 4yo+ 4lb **9** Ran SP% **117.5**
Speed ratings (Par 101): **101,100,100,95,94 90,89,84,74**
CSF £36.52 CT £94.21 TOTE £5.60: £2.00, £1.70, £2.00; EX 36.00 Trifecta £115.60.
**Owner** Burflex (Scaffolding) Ltd **Bred** Burton Agnes Stud Co Ltd **Trained** Carburton, Notts

**FOCUS**
An ordinary 'hands and heels' sprint. It's been rated around the first three.
T/Plt: £20.10 to a £1 stake. Pool: £40,876 - 2,029.86 winning units T/Qpdt: £11.30 to a £1 stake. Pool: £2,780.00 - 244.66 winning units **Andrew Sheret**

# 4916 YORK (L-H)
## Friday, July 28

**OFFICIAL GOING: Good (good to soft in places) changing to good to soft after race 2 (6.30)**
Wind: Moderate behind Weather: Heavy cloud and showers

## 5378 THINK AS ONE APPRENTICE H'CAP 1m 177y
**6:00** (6:00) (Class 4) (0-80,79) 3-Y-O **£7,762** (£2,310; £1,154; £577) **Stalls** Low

Form RPR
4643 1 **In First Place**[14] 4865 3-8-13 78.......................... SebastianWoods(7) 9 86
(Richard Fahey) *hld up in rr: gd hdwy on outer wl over 2f out: led 11/2f out: sn rdn and hung lft: clr ins fnl f: styd on* 9/2[2]
-221 2 2 **Breanski**[10] 5009 3-9-0 75 6ex.................................. PatrickVaughan(3) 5 79
(David O'Meara) *hld up towards rr: hdwy on inner over 2f out: chsd wnr over 1f out: drvn ins fnl f: no imp towards fin* 11/2[3]
4-56 3 2 1/2 **Mount Rock**[51] 3465 3-9-1 73......................................... MeganNicholls 6 72
(Michael Easterby) *trckd ldrs: hdwy 3f out: cl up and rdn whn n.m.r and hmpd over 1f out: kpt on same pce after* 12/1
042 4 10 **Rinaria (IRE)**[33] 4121 3-8-7 72...............................(t[1]) PatrickO'Hanlon(7) 4 50
(K R Burke) *t.k.h: cl up: led over 4f out: pushed along 3f out: rdn 2f out: hdd and sltly hmpd 11/2f out: sn wknd* 8/1
1131 5 2 1/4 **Brother McGonagall**[14] 4838 3-8-11 76.............. RobertDodsworth(7) 3 49
(Tim Easterby) *cl up: disp ld 5f out: rdn along 3f out: rdn over 2f out: sn btn* 4/1[1]
0-03 6 6 **Our Greta (IRE)**[22] 4525 3-8-5 66.................................. RayDawson(3) 1 27
(Michael Appleby) *chsd ldrs: pushed along over 3f out: rdn wl over 2f out: sn wknd* 10/1
03-0 7 1 **Buccaneers Cove (IRE)**[95] 2035 3-8-2 63............. ConnorMurtagh(3) 2 22
(Richard Fahey) *cl up on inner: slt ld 6f out: pushed along and hdd over 4f out: rdn over 3f out: sn drvn and wknd* 8/1
2063 8 8 **Zehrah (IRE)**[20] 4633 3-8-12 70.................................. LewisEdmunds 7 12
(Simon Crisford) *plld hrd on outer and sn led: hdd 6f out: chsd ldrs and rdn along 4f out: wknd 3f out* 9/2[2]

1m 49.5s (-2.50) **Going Correction** +0.15s/f (Good) **8** Ran SP% **110.8**
Speed ratings (Par 102): **117,115,113,104,102 96,95,88**
CSF £27.41 CT £261.55 TOTE £4.70: £1.60, £2.00, £2.70; EX 30.30 Trifecta £310.40.
**Owner** CBWS & Partner **Bred** Trebles Holford Farm Thoroughbreds **Trained** Musley Bank, N Yorks
■ Stewards' Enquiry : Sebastian Woods caution: careless riding

**FOCUS**
All distances as advertised. A 61-80 handicap for apprentices run on ground officially described as good, good to soft in places. They went hard here and those who raced close to the strong pace paid the penalty. The first three were clear. The runner-up has been rated as improving again.

## 5379 IRISH THOROUGHBRED MARKETING H'CAP 6f
**6:30** (6:33) (Class 4) (0-80,86) 4-Y-O+ **£7,762** (£2,310; £1,154; £577) **Stalls** Centre

Form RPR
0252 1 **Lexington Times (IRE)**[7] 5123 5-9-7 80..................(p[1]) JamesSullivan 11 89
(Ruth Carr) *hld up in rr: hdwy wl over 1f out: rdn ent fnl f: styd on wl to ld last 50 yds* 13/2[1]
-033 2 3/4 **Pomme De Terre (IRE)**[27] 4343 5-9-7 80.................(b) PaulMulrennan 7 87
(Michael Dods) *cl up centre: chal over 2f out: led wl over 1f out: rdn clr ent fnl f: hdd and no ex last 50 yds* 7/1[2]
5005 3 1 3/4 **B Fifty Two (IRE)**[27] 4379 8-9-1 74............................(bt) BarryMcHugh 2 75
(Marjorie Fife) *chsd ldrs towards far side: rdn and hdwy over 1f out: drvn and kpt on fnl f* 8/1[3]
0012 4 nk **Cliff (IRE)**[20] 4605 7-7-13 65................................ FayeMcManoman(7) 20 65+
(Nigel Tinkler) *racd towards stands rail: hld up in rr: hdwy on wd outside wl over 1f out: sn rdn and styd on wl fnl f* 20/1
6000 5 2 **God Willing**[17] 4719 6-9-0 80...........................................(b) GerO'Neill(7) 15 74
(Declan Carroll) *hld up towards rr: hdwy 2f out: rdn over 1f out: styd on fnl f* 14/1
6032 6 1 **Field Of Vision (IRE)**[7] 5112 4-9-2 75............................ OisinMurphy 9 65
(Joseph Tuite) *towards rr far side: hdwy 2f out: sn rdn and styd on wl fnl f* 12/1
3600 7 1 **Meandmyshadow**[46] 3666 9-8-7 66......................................(b) CamHardie 4 53
(Alan Brown) *chsd ldng pair: rdn along wl over 1f out: sn drvn and grad wknd* 33/1
0450 8 1 1/4 **Fieldsman (USA)**[13] 4887 5-9-7 80.............................. DanielTudhope 19 63
(David O'Meara) *racd towards stands side: hld up towards rr: hdwy 2f out: sn rdn and kpt on fnl f* 8/1[3]
2454 9 hd **Haraz (IRE)**[13] 4887 4-8-11 73.......................................(v) JoshDoyle(3) 1 56
(David O'Meara) *dwlt and bhd far side: hdwy wl over 1f out: rdn and kpt on fnl f* 14/1
0403 10 3/4 **Bogart**[69] 2837 8-9-7 80.............................................(tp) TomEaves 14 60
(Kevin Ryan) *racd towards stands side: chsd ldrs: rdn wl over 1f out: sn drvn and wknd* 12/1
31-0 11 1 1/2 **Jameerah**[69] 2840 4-9-5 78............................................. ConnorBeasley 8 53
(Bryan Smart) *in tch towards far side: rdn along over 2f out: grad wknd* 16/1
0000 12 3/4 **See The Sun**[27] 4379 6-8-13 72.........................................(p) DavidAllan 13 45
(Tim Easterby) *qckly away and swtchd lft to centre: led: rdn along 2f out: sn hdd and drvn: grad wknd* 10/1
0053 13 1 **Another Wise Kid (IRE)**[24] 4477 9-9-7 80...................... GrahamLee 17 50
(Paul Midgley) *racd towards stands side: chsd ldrs: rdn along wl over 2f out: sn wknd* 20/1
0405 14 1 1/2 **Laughton**[23] 4505 4-9-7 80................................................ ShaneGray 18 45
(Kevin Ryan) *racd towards stands side: hld up: hdwy over 2f out: sn rdn and n.d* 12/1
0005 15 1 1/4 **Kibaar**[14] 4850 5-9-4 77...................................................(p) KevinStott 5 38
(Kevin Ryan) *nvr bttr than midfield* 12/1
-025 16 2 1/2 **Interlink (USA)**[21] 4566 4-8-5 71.............................. RayDawson(7) 12 24
(Michael Appleby) *in tch centre: rdn along wl over 2f out: sn wknd* 20/1
34-3 17 1 **General Alexander (IRE)**[99] 1915 4-8-12 76........(p) BenRobinson(5) 10 26
(Brian Ellison) *chsd ldrs centre: rdn along wl over 2f out: sn wknd* 20/1

1m 12.03s (0.13) **Going Correction** +0.20s/f (Good) **17** Ran SP% **129.1**
Speed ratings (Par 105): **107,106,103,103,100 99,97,96,96,95 93,92,90,88,87 83,82**
CSF £48.44 CT £398.89 TOTE £7.50: £2.10, £2.00, £2.20, £5.10; EX 47.50 Trifecta £113.00.
**Owner** Middleham Park Racing C **Bred** Ruskerne Ltd **Trained** Huby, N Yorks

**FOCUS**
Exposed sorts in this 6f handicap which was run at a strong gallop, few got involved and there didn't appear to be any marked draw bias. The winner has been rated to his recent form, and the runner-up close to his best.

## 5380 BEST ONE AND XTRA LOCAL NOVICE MEDIAN AUCTION STKS (PLUS 10 RACE) 7f
**7:00** (7:02) (Class 3) 2-Y-O **£7,762** (£2,310; £1,154; £577) **Stalls** Low

Form RPR
1 **Wells Farhh Go (IRE)** 2-9-2 0........................................... DavidAllan 3 86+
(Tim Easterby) *dwlt and keen in rr: swtchd rt to outer and gd hdwy wl over 1f out: rdn and styd on strly fnl f: led last 50 yds* 16/1
3 2 2 1/4 **Laugh A Minute**[13] 4885 2-9-2 0...................................... HarryBentley 10 80+
(Roger Varian) *trckd ldrs: hdwy on outer over 2f out: rdn to ld wl over 1f out: drvn ins fnl f: hdd last 50 yds: no ex* 2/1[1]
3 3 1/2 **Pacific Fleet (USA)**[34] 4101 2-9-2 0............................ DanielMuscutt 11 79
(Archie Watson) *t.k.h: sn led: pushed along over 2f out: rdn and hdd wl over 1f out: drvn and kpt on fnl f* 11/2[3]
1 4 3/4 **Fortune's Pearl (IRE)**[24] 4465 2-9-8 0............................ OisinMurphy 5 83
(Andrew Balding) *trckd ldrs: effrt 2f out: sn rdn and n.m.r wl over 1f out: kpt on same pce* 3/1[2]
5 1 1/4 **Dubai Empire (FR)** 2-9-2 0................................................ JasonHart 8 74
(John Quinn) *wnt rt s: keen in rr whn hung rt bnd over 4f out: pushed along 3f out: kpt on fnl 2f* 14/1
36 6 nk **Jack Regan**[13] 4880 2-9-2 0........................................... PaulHanagan 7 73
(Charles Hills) *trckd ldrs: rdn along over 2f out: drvn over 1f out: kpt on same pce* 13/2
0 7 2 1/2 **Urban Soul (IRE)**[21] 4577 2-9-2 0.................................. PJMcDonald 1 67
(James Bethell) *trckd ldrs: hdwy 3f out: rdn over 2f out: sn drvn and wknd* 20/1
33 8 1 3/4 **Astraea**[41] 3846 2-8-11 0................................................. CamHardie 6 57
(Michael Easterby) *trckd ldr: pushed along 3f out: sn rdn and wknd 2f out* 12/1
0 9 1 3/4 **Duggary**[25] 4452 2-9-2 0................................................... DavidNolan 9 58
(Kevin Frost) *t.k.h: a towards rr* 66/1
0 10 9 **Prediction (IRE)**[86] 2299 2-9-2 0...................................... TomEaves 2 36
(Kevin Ryan) *dwlt: t.k.h: a rr* 16/1

1m 28.13s (2.83) **Going Correction** +0.15s/f (Good) **10** Ran SP% **119.4**
Speed ratings (Par 98): **89,86,85,85,83 83,80,78,76,66**
CSF £49.46 TOTE £19.50: £4.50, £1.30, £2.20; EX 67.30 Trifecta £422.40.
**Owner** S A Heley & Partner **Bred** Ms Maria Marron **Trained** Great Habton, N Yorks

**FOCUS**
the ground was changed to good to soft after the previous race. This wouldn't be the strongest of York maidens but the winner was quite impressive.

## 5381 BRITISH STALLION STUDS EBF LYRIC FILLIES' STKS (LISTED RACE) 1m 2f 56y
**7:30** (7:30) (Class 1) 3-Y-0+
**£28,355** (£10,750; £5,380; £2,680; £1,345; £675) **Stalls** Low

Form RPR
6-34 **1** **Entsar (IRE)**[28] 4308 4-9-4 95 (p1) PaulHanagan 9 108
(William Haggas) *trckd ldr: wd st towards stands side: rdn to ld 2f out: drvn ins fnl f: kpt on wl towards fin* **7/1**
1133 **2** 1 1/4 **Ajman Princess (IRE)**[20] 4613 4-9-7 107 HarryBentley 6 109
(Roger Varian) *trckd ldrs: hdwy on inner 3f out: cl up 2f out: sn rdn and ev ch whn edgd rt over 1f out: drvn to chse wnr ins fnl f: no imp* **4/1[2]**
0-10 **3** 1 1/4 **Playful Sound**[58] 3219 4-9-4 99 DanielTudhope 7 104
(Sir Michael Stoute) *trckd ldrs: hdwy and cl up 3f out: rdn along 2f out and sn sltly outpcd : drvn and n.m.r over 1f out: kpt on u.p fnl f* **7/2[1]**
-463 **4** 1 **Very Dashing**[28] 4308 4-9-4 100 PhillipMakin 3 102
(Ralph Beckett) *dwlt: t.k.h ion tch: hdwy 3f out: rdn to chse ldrs 2f out: drvn and kpt on same pce fnl f* **8/1**
13-4 **5** 1 3/4 **Rosental**[66] 2946 5-9-4 102 JamieSpencer 2 98
(Luca Cumani) *hld up ion tch: hdwy on inner 3f out: chsd ldrs 2f out: sn rdn and no imp* **9/2[3]**
-035 **6** 1/2 **Aim To Please (FR)**[37] 3961 4-9-4 106 PJMcDonald 8 97
(K R Burke) *dwlt: hld up in rr: hdwy wl over 2f out: sn rdn along and n.d* **9/2[3]**
6410 **7** 2 3/4 **Reachforthestars (IRE)**[36] 3998 3-8-9 91 SamJames 1 93
(David O'Meara) *led: rdn along 3f out: hdd 2f out: drvn and hld whn n.m.r over 1f out: sn wknd* **16/1**
1220 **8** 10 **Sophie P**[11] 4961 4-9-4 94 PaulMulrennan 10 73
(R Mike Smith) *hld up: a towards rr* **25/1**
3-44 **9** 4 1/2 **Pure Art**[33] 4119 4-9-4 99 GrahamLee 5 65
(Ralph Beckett) *chsd ldrs: rdn along 3f out: sn wknd* **20/1**

2m 11.2s (-1.30) **Going Correction** +0.15s/f (Good)
**WFA** 3 from 4yo+ 9lb 9 Ran SP% **116.7**
Speed ratings (Par 108): **111,110,109,108,106 106,104,96,92**
CSF £35.53 TOTE £7.60: £2.40, £1.60, £1.70; EX 39.00 Trifecta £179.10.
**Owner** Al Shaqab Racing **Bred** Manister House Stud **Trained** Newmarket, Suffolk

**FOCUS**
A Listed race for fillies and mares though not the strongest of races of its type. It was a stop-start gallop for the leader set off pretty fast but slowed it down turning for home.

## 5382 TOM PARSONS MEMORIAL H'CAP 7f 192y
**8:00** (8:02) (Class 3) (0-95,94) 3-Y-0+ **£8,086** (£2,406; £1,202; £601) **Stalls** Low

Form RPR
00-0 **1** **Lord Of The Rock (IRE)**[118] 1492 5-9-10 **90** PaulMulrennan 2 98
(Michael Dods) *hld up: hdwy over 3f out: chsd ldrs 2f out: rdn to ld 11/2f out: drvn ins fnl f: kpt on wl towards fin* **17/2**
3604 **2** 1/2 **Home Cummins (IRE)**[17] 4718 5-9-10 **90** (p) PaulHanagan 5 97
(Richard Fahey) *trckd ldng pair: wd st towards stands side and hdwy 3f out: chal 2f out: rdn over 1f out and ev ch tl drvn ins fnl f and no ex towards fin* **7/1[3]**
0021 **3** 1 1/4 **Calder Prince (IRE)**[21] 4578 4-9-5 **90** PaddyPilley(5) 13 95
(Tom Dascombe) *trckd ldr: wd st to stands rail: cl up 3f out: rdn along 2f out: drvn and ev ch over 1f out: kpt on same pce fnl f* **11/2[2]**
1003 **4** 3/4 **Boots And Spurs**[27] 4377 8-8-11 **82** (v) GeorgeBuckell(5) 1 85
(Scott Dixon) *chsd ldrs: hdwy centre 3f out: rdn along 2f out: drvn over 1f out: kpt on same pce* **14/1**
0624 **5** nk **Innocent Touch (IRE)**[42] 3790 6-9-12 **92** TonyHamilton 10 95
(Richard Fahey) *trckd ldrs: wd to stands rail home turn: rdn along over 2f out: drvn over 1f out: kpt on one same pce* **8/1**
1- **6** 1 **Kharbetation (IRE)**[363] 4895 4-9-13 **93** DanielTudhope 8 94+
(David O'Meara) *led: styd centre home st: rdn along and jnd over 2f out: hdd 11/2f out: sn drvn and grad wknd* **7/2[1]**
1114 **7** 1/2 **Gulf Of Poets**[24] 4475 5-9-10 **90** CamHardie 4 90
(Michael Easterby) *chsd ldrs: wd st: rdn along over 2f out: sn drvn and no imp* **14/1**
000 **8** 2 1/2 **Instant Attraction (IRE)**[27] 4377 6-9-10 **90** JackGarritty 14 85
(Jedd O'Keeffe) *nvr bttr than midfield* **10/1**
2001 **9** 1 3/4 **Two For Two (IRE)**[19] 4662 9-9-10 **90** (p) ConnorBeasley 6 82
(Roger Fell) *a towards rr* **14/1**
0005 **10** 4 **Gabrial's Kaka (IRE)**[28] 4293 7-9-0 **83** AdamMcNamara(3) 11 67
(Richard Fahey) *dwlt: a rr* **20/1**

1m 38.77s (-0.23) **Going Correction** +0.15s/f (Good) 10 Ran SP% **105.6**
Speed ratings (Par 107): **107,106,105,104,104 103,102,100,98,94**
CSF £52.04 CT £233.44 TOTE £9.00: £2.70, £2.20, £2.10; EX 64.70 Trifecta £400.80.
**Owner** Tony Fordham **Bred** Geoff & Sandra Turnbull **Trained** Denton, Co Durham
■ Candelisa was withdrawn. Price at time of withdrawal 11-2. Rule 4 applies to all bets - deduction 15p in the pound.

**FOCUS**
A fair handicap run on deteriorating ground. The gallop was a fair one and they fanned out across the track in the straight. The winner has been rated back to form, the runner-up helps to set the standard, the third was confirming his recent Haydock win, and the fourth has been rated to his recent best.

## 5383 SKY BET GO-RACING-IN-YORKSHIRE SUMMER FESTIVAL H'CAP 5f 89y
**8:30** (8:31) (Class 4) (0-85,87) 3-Y-0 **£7,762** (£2,310; £1,154; £577) **Stalls** Centre

Form RPR
5-12 **1** **Dakota Gold**[67] 2899 3-10-0 **87** ConnorBeasley 3 99
(Michael Dods) *dwlt and rr: hdwy 1/2-way: chsd ldrs wl over 1f out: sn rdn and styd on to ld ins fnl f* **5/2[1]**
1541 **2** 3/4 **Batten The Hatches**[34] 4104 3-9-13 **86** (b) BenCurtis 7 95
(David Barron) *qckly away and led: rdn and edgd lft jst over 1f out: drvn and hdd ins fnl f: edgd lft to far rail and kpt on towards fin* **9/2[3]**
4303 **3** 2 1/2 **Twizzell**[14] 4835 3-9-6 **79** PJMcDonald 8 79
(K R Burke) *racd towards stands side: prom: rdn over 1f out: drvn ent fnl f: kpt on same pce* **8/1**
5221 **4** 1 3/4 **Sheepscar Lad (IRE)**[17] 4717 3-8-13 **77** LewisEdmunds(5) 2 71
(Nigel Tinkler) *t.k.h: chsd ldrs: rdn wl over 1f out: sn drvn and one pce* **4/1[2]**
-253 **5** 1 3/4 **Monte Cinq (IRE)**[142] 1090 3-9-5 **78** (h1) TomEaves 1 66
(Jason Ward) *prom: rdn along 2f out: sn drvn and grad wknd* **33/1**
1560 **6** 1 **Impart**[27] 4333 3-9-10 **86** JoshDoyle(3) 10 71
(David O'Meara) *racd towards stands side: hld up: hdwy 2f out: rdn wl over 1f out: sn no imp* **8/1**
1162 **7** 1/2 **Black Isle Boy (IRE)**[7] 5100 3-9-13 **86** HarryBentley 9 69
(David O'Meara) *hld up in tch: hdwy over 2f out: rdn wl over 1f out: sn btn* **7/1**
-445 **8** 3 1/4 **Night Law**[25] 4437 3-9-0 **73** (h) TonyHamilton 11 44
(Richard Fahey) *a rr* **20/1**
-165 **9** 3 **Savannah's Dream**[49] 3526 3-9-7 **80** DanielTudhope 5 41
(David O'Meara) *a rr* **10/1**

1m 4.98s (0.88) **Going Correction** +0.20s/f (Good) 9 Ran SP% **118.3**
Speed ratings (Par 102): **100,98,94,92,89 87,86,81,76**
CSF £14.17 CT £79.43 TOTE £3.40: £1.50, £1.80, £2.50; EX 16.60 Trifecta £129.30.
**Owner** Doug Graham & The Late Ron Davison **Bred** Redgate Bstock & Peter Bottowley Bstock **Trained** Denton, Co Durham

**FOCUS**
A competitive sprint run at a sound gallop and though not many featured the form should prove sound. The first two have been rated on the positive side.
T/Plt: £45.30 to a £1 stake. Pool: £99,598.30 - 1,604.09 winning units T/Qpdt: £10.50 to a £1 stake. Pool: £8,057.07 - 565.33 winning units **Joe Rowntree**

5384 - 5390a (Foreign Racing) - See Raceform Interactive

# 5349 ASCOT (R-H)
### Saturday, July 29

**OFFICIAL GOING: Good to soft (soft in places on round course) changing to soft after race 4 (3.35)**
Wind: Almost nil Weather: Overcast, raining after race 2 onwards

## 5391 PRINCESS MARGARET JUDDMONTE STKS (GROUP 3) (FILLIES) 6f
**1:50** (1:52) (Class 1) 2-Y-0
**£28,355** (£10,750; £5,380; £2,680; £1,345; £675) **Stalls** Centre

Form RPR
122 **1** **Nyaleti (IRE)**[15] 4855 2-9-0 101 RyanMoore 1 110+
(Mark Johnston) *trckd ldr and clr of rest: shkn up to ld 2f out: sn clr: rdn and styd on strly fnl f: impressive* **2/1[1]**
111 **2** 5 **Dance Diva**[28] 4361 2-9-0 99 PaulHanagan 7 95
(Richard Fahey) *athletic: lengthy: chsd ldrs: pushed along sn after 1/2-way: styd on wl to take 2nd ins fnl f but absolutely no ch w wnr* **9/4[2]**
1 **3** 1 3/4 **Musical Art (IRE)**[23] 4533 2-9-0 0 FranBerry 5 90
(Paul Cole) *cmpt: towards rr: shkn up and no prog over 2f out: nvr any ch but styd on wl fnl f to snatch 3rd last stride* **12/1**
1 **4** shd **Spring Cosmos (IRE)**[16] 4815 2-9-0 0 WilliamBuick 3 89
(Charlie Appleby) *lw: hld up: prog 1/2-way: rdn and no imp on ldrs 2f out: kpt on fnl f to press for 3rd last strides* **6/1[3]**
2410 **5** nk **Rebel Assault (IRE)**[22] 4582 2-9-0 93 DavidProbert 4 89
(Mark Johnston) *v fast away: led and clr w wnr: hdd 2f out and immediately lft bhd: lost 2nd ins fnl f and 2 more pls last strides* **25/1**
5125 **6** 2 **Neola**[38] 3960 2-9-0 92 GrahamLee 2 83
(Mick Channon) *chsd clr ldng pair: shkn up over 2f out: wknd over 1f out* **8/1**
5344 **7** nk **Mistress Of Venice**[15] 4855 2-9-0 99 JimCrowley 6 82
(James Given) *stdd s: hld up in last pair: rdn over 2f out: no prog and wl btn after* **15/2**

1m 14.62s (0.12) **Going Correction** +0.45s/f (Yiel) 7 Ran SP% **112.8**
Speed ratings (Par 101): **117,110,108,107,107 104,104**
CSF £6.54 TOTE £2.50: £1.60, £1.80; EX 6.40 Trifecta £66.50.
**Owner** 3 Batterhams and A Reay **Bred** SF Bloodstock LLC **Trained** Middleham Moor, N Yorks

**FOCUS**
The track was at full width, with distances as advertised. William Buick, Jim Crowley and Fran Berry thought it was soft after the first, while Ryan Moore said it was "probably good to soft". Not the deepest of Group 3s and the decisive winning favourite stood out on form. The winner has been rated in line with the best winner of this in the last 20 years.

## 5392 PORSCHE H'CAP 1m (S)
**2:25** (2:27) (Class 2) 3-Y-0
**£28,012** (£8,388; £4,194; £2,097; £1,048; £526) **Stalls** Centre

Form RPR
-203 **1** **D'bai (IRE)**[16] 4817 3-9-7 **105** (b1) WilliamBuick 3 115
(Charlie Appleby) *lw: hld up in midfield: nvr clrest of passages fr 3f out but gd prog over 1f out to chse ldr fnl f: drvn to ld last 100yds* **8/1**
4101 **2** nk **Pealer (GER)**[16] 4800 3-8-8 **92** (t) FrankieDettori 6 101
(John Gosden) *t.k.h: cl up: trckd ldr over 2f out: rdn to ld over 1f out: hdd last 100yds: styd on but hld* **7/1**
1415 **3** 2 1/4 **Fire Brigade**[29] 4322 3-8-0 **84** HayleyTurner 5 88
(Michael Bell) *lw: hld up in last trio: swtchd briefly over 2f out and prog sn after: drvn and r.o fnl f to take 3rd last strides* **9/1**
3142 **4** hd **Juanito Chico (IRE)**[15] 4831 3-8-7 **91** (h) SilvestreDeSousa 2 94+
(William Jarvis) *t.k.h: hld up in last trio: prog wl over 2f out and taken to far side where racd on own: chsd ldng pair fnl f: kpt on but lost 3rd last strides* **5/1[2]**
0225 **5** 3/4 **Masham Star (IRE)**[7] 5157 3-9-2 **100** FranBerry 7 102
(Mark Johnston) *swtg: trckd ldr: led 3f out: hdd and fdd over 1f out* **20/1**
3411 **6** 1 1/2 **Century Dream (IRE)**[12] 4961 3-9-0 **98** (t) RyanMoore 1 96
(Simon Crisford) *hld up towards rr: sme prog over 3f out: rdn 2f out: one pce and no imp after* **4/1[1]**
0056 **7** shd **Cullingworth (IRE)**[15] 4856 3-8-0 **84** oh1 RoystonFfrench 12 82
(Richard Fahey) *hld up in last trio: urged along and struggling 3f out: drvn and kpt on fr 2f out: nvr nrr* **25/1**
1252 **8** 3 1/4 **Mustarrid (IRE)**[29] 4299 3-8-10 **94** JimCrowley 9 84
(Richard Hannon) *t.k.h: hld up in midfield: shkn up over 2f out: no prog and wl btn over 1f out* **11/2[3]**
-241 **9** 1 3/4 **Alwahsh (IRE)**[44] 3755 3-8-3 **87** (p) PaulHanagan 10 73
(William Haggas) *led to 3f out: sn lost pl and btn* **8/1**
1-10 **10** 1/2 **Naval Warfare (IRE)**[21] 4636 3-8-11 **95** OisinMurphy 8 80
(Andrew Balding) *lw: trckd ldng pair to 3f out: sn btn* **14/1**
-063 **11** nk **Rashford's Double (IRE)**[9] 5072 3-7-11 **84** oh3 HollieDoyle(3) 11 69
(Richard Fahey) *in tch: urged along 3f out: sn struggling and btn* **40/1**
4004 **12** hd **Executive Force**[7] 5147 3-8-7 **91** MartinDwyer 4 75
(William Haggas) *prom: chsd ldr 3f out to over 2f out: wknd qckly* **18/1**

1m 41.88s (1.08) **Going Correction** +0.45s/f (Yiel) 12 Ran SP% **119.8**
Speed ratings (Par 106): **112,111,109,109,108 107,106,103,101,101 101,100**
CSF £62.32 CT £523.22 TOTE £9.40: £2.90, £2.40, £2.30; EX 75.80 Trifecta £840.40.
**Owner** Godolphin **Bred** Lodge Park Stud **Trained** Newmarket, Suffolk

**FOCUS**
A good 3yo handicap in which they raced middle to far side. A clear pb from the winner, with the third rated to form.

## 5393 GIGASET INTERNATIONAL STKS (HERITAGE H'CAP) 7f
**3:00** (3:03) (Class 2) 3-Y-0+

**£93,375** (£27,960; £13,980; £6,990; £3,495; £1,755) **Stalls** Centre

Form RPR

0000 **1** **Stamp Hill (IRE)**[15] 4854 4-8-5 **90**............................(b[1]) PaulHanagan 14 102
(Richard Fahey) *racd in centre: trckd ldrs: cruising whn chalng 2f out: led over 1f out: rdn out and kpt on fnl f whn drifted towards far side* **50/1**

0110 **2** *1 ¼* **Mjjack (IRE)**[28] 4383 3-8-2 **94**.................................... RoystonFfrench 26 100
(K R Burke) *t.k.h: pressed ldr in centre: rdn to chal 2f out: styd on to win battle for 2nd fnl f but no threat to wnr* **25/1**

0100 **3** *1* **Withernsea (IRE)**[14] 4905 6-8-12 **97**............................. GeraldMosse 17 103
(Richard Fahey) *pressed ldr in centre: overall ldr briefly wl over 1f out: one pce fnl f* **22/1**

-043 **4** *¾* **Johnny Barnes (IRE)**[7] 5147 5-9-2 **101**..................... WilliamBuick 20 105+
(John Gosden) *hld up wl in rr in centre: stl jst abt last over 2f out: rapid prog over 1f out: storming run to take 4th last strides: no ch to chal* **25/1**

3256 **5** *nse* **Firmament**[14] 4884 5-9-10 **109**........................................ OisinMurphy 25 113+
(David O'Meara) *hld up towards rr in centre: rdn 2f out: styd on wl fr over 1f out: nvr rchd ldrs* **33/1**

2012 **6** *½* **Makzeem**[15] 4854 4-8-6 **91**..................................... SilvestreDeSousa 1 94
(Roger Charlton) *trckd ldrs towards far side: nt qckn wl over 1f out: styd on again ins fnl f and tk 4th briefly* **11/2[1]**

-002 **7** *¾* **Havre De Paix (FR)**[14] 4883 5-8-5 **90**........................... MartinDwyer 18 91
(David Menuisier) *overall ldr in centre: stl led whn gps jnd over 2f out: hdd sn after: fdd* **20/1**

4040 **8** *nk* **Shady McCoy (USA)**[15] 4854 7-8-3 **88**.......................... RyanPowell 10 88+
(Ian Williams) *lw: awkward s: hld up in last pair in gp towards far side: nt clr run over 2f out: prog over 1f out: styd on: nvr pce to rch ldrs* **50/1**

01-1 **9** *1* **Flaming Spear (IRE)**[198] 199 5-9-2 **101**..................... RobertWinston 8 98
(Kevin Ryan) *lw: trckd ldrs towards far side: cruising bhd them over 2f out: shkn up and rather limited rspnse over 1f out* **9/1**

532 **10** *nk* **Mount Tahan (IRE)**[80] 2518 5-8-8 **93**............................... JoeDoyle 22 90
(Kevin Ryan) *swtg: rrd bdly s: racd centre: chsd ldrs: drvn 2f out: no imp over 1f out: fdd ins fnl f* **33/1**

0062 **11** *hd* **Remarkable**[7] 5147 4-9-5 **104**......................................(b) FrankieDettori 9 103+
(John Gosden) *racd towards far side: hld up in rr: nt clr run over 1f out: coaxed along and styd on fnl f but racd awkwardly and nvr a threat* **8/1[3]**

0106 **12** *hd* **Burnt Sugar (IRE)**[24] 4505 5-8-3 **88**.............................. JoeyHaynes 6 84
(Roger Fell) *chsd ldrs far side: chal and rt on terms 2f out: nt qckn over 1f out: wknd fnl f* **40/1**

4541 **13** *1 ½* **Jack Dexter**[1] 5354 8-8-3 **91** 3ex................................... HollieDoyle(3) 19 83
(Jim Goldie) *t.k.h: hld up towards rr in centre: no prog 2f out: kpt on fr over 1f out: n.d* **12/1**

1103 **14** *1 ½* **Nicholas T**[12] 4961 5-8-5 **90**............................................. KieranO'Neill 5 78
(Jim Goldie) *hld up wl in rr towards far side: drvn and no prog over 2f out: jst abt last over 1f out: kpt on fnl f but nvr in it* **40/1**

1-33 **15** *nk* **Fawaareq (IRE)**[15] 4854 4-8-8 **93**..................................... JimCrowley 7 80
(Owen Burrows) *trckd ldng pair towards far side: chal gng easily jst over 2f out: wknd tamely over 1f out* **11/1**

-300 **16** *shd* **Yuften**[38] 3963 6-9-5 **104**.............................................. KieranShoemark 16 91
(Roger Charlton) *hld up in rr in centre: effrt 3f out and sme prog: no hdwy over 1f out* **20/1**

-000 **17** *nk* **Squats (IRE)**[14] 4881 5-9-3 **102**........................................... AdamKirby 4 88
(William Haggas) *led gp towards far side for 2f: styd cl up: chal and on terms 2f out: sn wknd* **25/1**

3050 **18** *nk* **Sir Roderic (IRE)**[14] 4916 4-8-8 **93**............................... WilliamCarson 2 78
(Rod Millman) *hld up in rr towards far side: rdn and no real prog fr 2f out* **40/1**

4611 **19** *¾* **Viscount Barfield**[14] 4890 4-8-12 **97** 3ex...................(h) DavidProbert 28 80
(Andrew Balding) *racd centre: nvr beyond midfield: rdn and no prog 2f out* **10/1**

-200 **20** *1 ¼* **Big Time (IRE)**[14] 4925 6-9-0 **99**....................................(p) GrahamLee 12 79
(Kevin Ryan) *lw: chsd ldrs towards far side: no prog 2f out: fdd* **66/1**

0004 **21** *nk* **Swift Approval (IRE)**[15] 4854 5-8-0 **92**........................(t) MillyNaseb(7) 3 71
(Stuart Williams) *racd in gp towards far side: taken to r alone against far rail sn after 1/2-way: struggling 2f out* **40/1**

3110 **22** *1 ½* **Fastnet Tempest (IRE)**[38] 3963 4-9-0 **99**..................(b[1]) RyanMoore 24 74
(William Haggas) *lw: t.k.h: hld up in midfield in centre: rdn and no prog 2f out: sn bhd* **7/1[2]**

3110 **23** *1 ¼* **Gossiping**[14] 4905 5-8-11 **96**............................................. ShaneKelly 15 68
(Gary Moore) *lw: squeezed out s: racd centre and a towards rr: shkn up and no prog 2f out: wknd* **16/1**

0441 **24** *shd* **Above The Rest (IRE)**[14] 4905 6-9-2 **104** 3ex...........(h) CliffordLee(3) 27 76
(David Barron) *chsd ldrs in centre over 4f: wknd wl over 1f out* **20/1**

5-00 **25** *4* **Buckstay (IRE)**[14] 4905 7-9-8 **107**...................................(p) FranBerry 21 68
(Peter Chapple-Hyam) *s.s: racd centre: a wl in rr and nvr able to make prog* **50/1**

0000 **26** *1 ¾* **Heaven's Guest (IRE)**[42] 3842 7-8-9 **94**.................. StevieDonohoe 11 51
(Richard Fahey) *led gp towards far side after 2f to 2f out: wknd rapidly* **33/1**

0060 **27** *¾* **Top Score**[38] 3959 3-8-9 **108**...................................(v[1]) CameronNoble(7) 23 60
(Saeed bin Suroor) *s.v.s: qckly rcvrd into midfield in centre: wknd rapidly 2f out* **33/1**

1m 28.89s (1.29) **Going Correction** +0.45s/f (Yiel)
**WFA** 3 from 4yo+ 7lb **27** Ran SP% **139.1**
Speed ratings (Par 109): **110,108,107,106,106 105,105,104,103,103 103,102,101,99,99 98,98,98,97,95 95,93,92,92,87 85,84**
CSF £1023.00 CT £24473.74 TOTE £112.90: £16.20, £8.50, £8.50, £5.80; EX 3209.50 TRIFECTA Not won..
**Owner** Merchants and Missionaries **Bred** Ms Ellen O'Neill **Trained** Musley Bank, N Yorks

**FOCUS**
Always a competitive handicap, they split into two groups before merging at around halfway. They went a pretty steady gallop, though, considering the big field, and the main action unfolded more towards the far side, with it going to one of the complete outsiders. The third helps set the standard.

## 5394 KING GEORGE VI AND QUEEN ELIZABETH STKS (SPONSORED BY QIPCO) (GROUP 1) (BRITISH CHAMPIONS SERIES) 1m 3f 211y
**3:35** (3:39) (Cla£852,155 (£247,250; £123,740; £61,640; £30,935; £15,525) **Stalls** Low

3111 **1** **Enable**[14] 4928 3-8-7 122............................................... FrankieDettori 7 128
(John Gosden) *t.k.h: trckd ldr: clsd to ld wl over 2f out: sn qcknd clr: shkn up over 1f out and r.o strly: impressive* **5/4[1]**

-131 **2** *4 ½* **Ulysses (IRE)**[21] 4638 4-9-7 121......................................... JimCrowley 8 123
(Sir Michael Stoute) *hld up in rr: smooth prog over 3f out to trck wnr over 2f out: sn unable to live w her but clr of rest: hld on to 2nd nr fin* **9/1**

5-61 **3** *¾* **Idaho (IRE)**[35] 4070 4-9-7 118............................................ SeamieHeffernan 3 122
(A P O'Brien, Ire) *swtg: trckd ldrs: rdn and lost pl over 3f out: prog again over 2f out: chsd clr ldng pair over 1f out: styd on* **8/1**

-011 **4** *4* **Highland Reel (IRE)**[38] 3962 5-9-7 123............................. RyanMoore 4 116
(A P O'Brien, Ire) *swtg: racd wd: prom: rdn 3f out: sn outpcd and btn: plugged on bravely fr over 1f out* **9/2[2]**

3251 **5** *2 ¼* **Benbatl**[37] 3994 3-8-10 114...........................................(t) OisinMurphy 1 113
(Saeed bin Suroor) *hld up in midfield: prog over 3f out: rdn and no imp on ldrs over 2f out: wknd steadily* **14/1**

-123 **6** *6* **Desert Encounter (IRE)**[21] 4638 5-9-7 114....................(h) SeanLevey 9 102
(David Simcock) *lw: t.k.h: hld up in rr: rdn and lft bhd fr 3f out: tk remote 6th u.p 1f out and all out to hold that pl nr fin* **33/1**

-324 **7** *shd* **My Dream Boat (IRE)**[27] 4423 5-9-7 114........................(p) AdamKirby 6 102
(Clive Cox) *t.k.h early: hld up towards rr: drvn and no prog 3f out: wl btn after: plugged on ins fnl f and nrly snatched remote 6th* **16/1**

00-4 **8** *2* **Maverick Wave (USA)**[35] 4069 6-9-7 102......................... GrahamLee 10 99
(John Gosden) *led: clr after 3f: hdd & wknd wl over 2f out* **100/1**

3-10 **9** *11* **Jack Hobbs**[38] 3962 5-9-7 123...........................................(b) WilliamBuick 2 81
(John Gosden) *trckd ldrs: prog to chal and w wnr wl over 2f out: wnt out like a light sn after: virtually p.u fnl f* **11/2[3]**

**10** *4 ½* **Sixties Song (ARG)**[65] 4-9-3 119......................................... GeraldMosse 5 70
(Alfredo F Gaitan Dassie, Argentina) *w'like: t.k.h early: hld up in last pair: wknd 3f out: t.o* **33/1**

2m 36.22s (3.72) **Going Correction** +0.90s/f (Soft)
**WFA** 3 from 4yo+ 11lb **10** Ran SP% **118.5**
Speed ratings (Par 117): **123,120,119,116,115 111,111,109,102,99**
CSF £13.98 CT £68.43 TOTE £2.10: £1.30, £2.70, £2.10; EX 14.70 Trifecta £71.10.
**Owner** K Abdullah **Bred** Juddmonte Farms Ltd **Trained** Newmarket, Suffolk

**FOCUS**
This was run in driving rain (ground changed to soft afterwards) and the front-running Maverick Wave, who hugged the inside rail, was ignored by the others, with most of them shunning the fence for much of the way. However, it still seemed a fair enough test in the circumstances and the winner was superb. It's been rated at face value, with the runner-up close to his Eclipse figure. The third has been rated to the better view of his 3yo form.

## 5395 WOOLDRIDGE GROUP PAT EDDERY STKS (LISTED RACE) (FORMERLY THE WINKFIELD STAKES) 7f
**4:10** (4:14) (Class 1) 2-Y-0

**£17,013** (£6,450; £3,228; £1,608; £807; £405) **Stalls** Centre

Form RPR

21 **1** **Raydiance**[50] 3538 2-9-3 0................................................. JimCrowley 2 100
(K R Burke) *cmpt: stdd s: hld up in last pair: prog wl over 2f out: rdn to ld over 1f out: edgd lft ins fnl f and jnd: fnd ex last 75yds* **7/1**

1013 **2** *nk* **Another Batt (IRE)**[8] 5109 2-9-3 94.............................. FrankieDettori 5 99
(George Scott) *led to over 2f out: styd cl up: rdn and rallied over 1f out: wnt 2nd ins fnl f and sn jnd wnr: no ex last 75yds* **9/1**

615 **3** *2 ¼* **Alba Power (IRE)**[16] 4812 2-9-3 97..................................... AdamKirby 1 94
(Hugo Palmer) *trckd ldrs: moved up to chal 2f out: pressed wnr over 1f out: nt qckn and dropped to 3rd ins fnl f* **12/1**

1 **4** *¾* **Tigre Du Terre (FR)**[14] 4885 2-9-3 0.................................. RyanMoore 3 92+
(Richard Hannon) *str: lw: hld up in last pair: outpcd in last and shkn up wl over 2f out: prog wl over 1f out: one pce fnl f* **7/4[1]**

11 **5** *¾* **Ghost Serge (IRE)**[15] 4876 2-9-3 99.................................. OisinMurphy 4 90
(Archie Watson) *w'like: sltly awkward s: trckd ldr: led over 2f out to over 1f out: losing pl whn short of room sn after: fdd* **9/2[2]**

21 **6** *½* **Being There (FR)**[15] 4859 2-9-3 0..................................... WilliamBuick 7 89
(Charlie Appleby) *trckd ldrs: shkn up over 2f out: hanging and nt qckn after: n.d* **11/2[3]**

3111 **7** *14* **Ventura Knight (IRE)**[9] 5079 2-9-3 93...................... SilvestreDeSousa 6 54+
(Mark Johnston) *in tch tl wknd over 2f out: t.o* **7/1**

1m 31.95s (4.35) **Going Correction** +0.45s/f (Yiel) **7** Ran SP% **112.6**
Speed ratings (Par 102): **93,92,90,89,88 87,71**
CSF £63.57 TOTE £8.00: £3.40, £3.90; EX 50.90 Trifecta £421.20.
**Owner** Ontoawinner 14 & Mrs E Burke **Bred** Hungerford Park Stud **Trained** Middleham Moor, N Yorks

■ Stewards' Enquiry : Adam Kirby caution: careless riding

**FOCUS**
Not the strongest of Listed races. The winner has been rated to par for the grade.

## 5396 LONGINES H'CAP (FOR LADY AMATEUR RIDERS) 7f
**4:45** (4:47) (Class 3) (0-90,96) 3-Y-0+ **£8,110** (£2,515; £1,257; £629) **Stalls** Centre

Form RPR

4330 **1** **Georgian Bay (IRE)**[27] 4410 7-10-5 **85**.............................(v) MsKWalsh 5 94
(K R Burke) *trckd ldrs: clsd against far rail and rdn 2f out: drvn to ld 1f out: hld on wl* **5/1[1]**

055 **2** *nk* **Bertiewhittle**[43] 3792 9-10-9 **89**................................ MissJoannaMason 1 97
(David Barron) *dwlt: hld up in rr: stdy prog over 2f out: brought to chal over 1f out: pressed wnr fnl f: outbattled* **13/2[3]**

6450 **3** *½* **Tommy G**[15] 4854 4-9-9 **75**............................................. MissCWalton 14 82+
(Jim Goldie) *prom and racd on nr side of gp: urged along fr 2f out: drifted across the crse towards far side after: styd on fnl f: a hld* **8/1**

0331 **4** *1* **Imperial State**[22] 4587 4-9-11 **82**..............................(vt) MissJCooley(5) 8 86
(George Scott) *trckd ldrs: led towards far side wl over 1f out: hdd and no ex 1f out* **11/2[2]**

6311 **5** *2* **Classic Seniority**[8] 5094 5-11-2 **96**............................ MissBeckySmith 11 95
(Marjorie Fife) *lw: prom in centre: effrt u.p 2f out: drifted towards far side after: nvr quite able to chal and fdd ins fnl f* **13/2[3]**



The Form Book Flat, Raceform Ltd, Newbury, RG14 5SJ

1040 **6** *shd* **Theodorico (IRE)**[22] 4578 4-10-4 **87**...................... MissABO'Connor(3) 2 86
(David Loughnane) *lw: racd towards far side thrght and on own to 1/2-way: sn overall ldr: hdd u.p wl over 1f out and sn btn: plugged on again nr fin* **14/1**

0024 **7** *4 1/2* **Supersta**[15] 4861 6-10-6 **89**.................................(p) MissHayleyMoore(3) 3 76
(Michael Appleby) *slowly away: wl in rr: passed rivals to rch midfield over 1f out but nowhere nr ldrs after* **8/1**

-000 **8** *1 1/2* **Farlow (IRE)**[9] 5059 9-10-3 **83**.................................. MissEmmaSayer 10 66
(Richard Fahey) *wl in rr: bhd over 2f out: kpt on into midfield over 1f out but nowhere nr ldrs after* **14/1**

0532 **9** *3/4* **Athassel**[9] 5059 8-9-9 **80**........................................ MissEMacKenzie(5) 7 61
(David Evans) *chsd ldrs: struggling u.p over 2f out: fdd* **20/1**

2003 **10** *1 3/4* **Majestic Moon (IRE)**[10] 5035 7-10-3 **83**.......................... MissGAndrews 4 60
(Julia Feilden) *led main gp to wl over 2f out: wknd u.p* **12/1**

02-6 **11** *7* **Dark Alliance (IRE)**[77] 2608 6-9-12 **78**........................... MissJWalton 6 36
(Adrian Paul Keatley, Ire) *chsd ldrs 4f: sn wknd and bhd fnl 2f* **16/1**

-000 **12** *1 1/4* **Accurate**[22] 4578 4-9-12 **78**........................................... MissADeniel 15 33
(Ian Williams) *a wl in rr: t.o 2f out* **33/1**

0245 **13** *1/2* **Dodgy Bob**[15] 4844 4-9-5 **71** oh11..........................(p) MissMMullineaux 9 25
(Michael Mullineaux) *in tch 4f: wknd rapidly: t.o* **50/1**

4043 **14** *8* **Just An Idea (IRE)**[27] 4412 3-9-11 **84**.......................... MissAnnaHesketh 12 14
(Harry Dunlop) *rrd s and slowly away: rcvrd to chse ldrs: wknd rapidly over 2f out: t.o* **16/1**

1m 33.1s (5.50) **Going Correction** +0.45s/f (Yiel)
**WFA** 3 from 4yo+ 7lb **14** Ran SP% **123.4**
Speed ratings (Par 107): **86,85,85,83,81 81,76,74,73,71 63,62,61,52**
CSF £37.04 CT £271.01 TOTE £5.20: £2.10, £2.30, £2.80; EX 27.50 Trifecta £206.20.
**Owner** Market Avenue Racing Club & Mrs E Burke **Bred** Old Carhue & Graeng Bloodstock **Trained** Middleham Moor, N Yorks
■ Stewards' Enquiry : Ms K Walsh 11-day ban: excessive use of whip

**FOCUS**
A useful handicap and the action unfolded centre-to-far side, with the winner showing a good attitude nearest to the far rail. The runner-up helps set the standard, while the third has been rated to form.

## 5397 CANISBAY BLOODSTOCK H'CAP 1m 3f 211y
**5:20** (5:21) (Class 3) (0-90,88) 3-Y-0+ **£9,703** (£2,887; £1,443; £721) **Stalls** Low

Form RPR

1 **1** **Royal Associate**[22] 4569 3-9-1 **86**.................................... WilliamBuick 6 99+
(Charlie Appleby) *unf: scope: led 1f: trckd ldrs after: rdn 3f out: prog to take 2nd 2f out and led over 1f out: idled in front and looked vulnerable whn pressed jst ins fnl f: picked up again and sn in command* **2/1**[1]

43-5 **2** *1* **Niblawi (IRE)**[34] 4118 5-10-0 **88**.................................. RobertWinston 15 98
(Neil Mulholland) *lw: hld up wl in rr: cajoled along and gd prog on outer over 2f out: tk 2nd and pressed wnr fnl f: styd on but readily hld nr fin* **11/1**

321 **3** *2* **Dark Pearl (IRE)**[33] 4146 3-8-10 **81**.................................. LiamKeniry 14 89
(Ed Walker) *str: lw: t.k.h: hld up in midfield: prog wl over 2f out: drvn to take 3rd 1f out: styd on but unable to chal* **11/4**[2]

-403 **4** *5* **Ravenous**[27] 4413 6-8-10 **77**............................................ WilliamCox(7) 2 76
(Luke Dace) *led after 1f: 5 l clr 1/2-way: drvn 2f out: hdd and fdd over 1f out* **20/1**

0130 **5** *3 1/2* **Gaelic Tiger**[26] 4429 4-10-0 **88**........................................(p) AdamKirby 11 81
(David O'Meara) *sn chsd ldrs: rdn over 2f out: sn wknd* **28/1**

4060 **6** *3/4* **Shamrokh (IRE)**[15] 4831 3-8-10 **81**.............................. AlistairRawlinson 13 74
(Michael Appleby) *hld up wl in rr: stl there 3f out but gng bttr than many: rdn and tried to make prog 2f out: tk modest 6th nr fin but nvr in it* **50/1**

0-02 **7** *3/4* **Zambeasy**[27] 4413 6-9-6 **80**................................................ GrahamLee 12 71
(Philip Hide) *wl in tch on outer: rdn and nt qckn over 2f out: no prog after: wknd over 1f out* **12/1**

45/4 **8** *2* **Castlelyons (IRE)**[31] 4216 5-10-0 **88**.................................(t[1]) JohnFahy 1 76
(Robert Stephens) *lw: chsd ldr after 1f to 2f out: wknd* **20/1**

1125 **9** *1/2* **Mutadaffeq (IRE)**[36] 4038 4-10-0 **88**................................ RyanMoore 16 75
(David O'Meara) *racd wdst of all for most of r: in tch: rdn 3f out: no real prog 2f out: wknd* **8/1**[3]

004/ **10** *nk* **Zaidiyn (FR)**[469] 7732 7-9-9 **83**...................................... SaleemGolam 10 69
(Brian Ellison) *stdd s: hld up wl in rr: drvn and tried to make prog over 2f out: sn no hdwy* **33/1**

3101 **11** *14* **Spinners Ball (IRE)**[31] 4216 4-9-1 **80**........................ MitchGodwin(5) 8 44
(Sylvester Kirk) *chsd ldrs: rdn and wknd wl over 2f out: bhd fnl f* **16/1**

5000 **12** *16* **Calvinist**[15] 4828 4-9-8 **82**..................................................(t) RyanPowell 5 20
(Ian Williams) *a wl in rr: detached in last fr 1/2-way: t.o* **33/1**

-304 **13** *6* **Barwick**[26] 4457 9-9-13 **87**.................................................. GeraldMosse 4 16
(George Baker) *dwlt: rcvrd to chse ldrs: wknd rapidly wl over 2f out: t.o* **12/1**

622 **14** *10* **Alcatraz (IRE)**[72] 2752 5-9-5 **79**...........................................(tp) FranBerry 7
(George Baker) *s.s: a wl in rr: wknd over 3f out: t.o* **10/1**

2m 43.23s (10.73) **Going Correction** +0.90s/f (Soft)
**WFA** 3 from 4yo+ 11lb **14** Ran SP% **130.6**
Speed ratings (Par 107): **100,99,98,94,92 91,91,90,89,89 80,69,65,58**
CSF £26.04 CT £68.46 TOTE £2.80: £1.60, £4.70, £1.70; EX 34.40 Trifecta £115.80.
**Owner** Godolphin **Bred** Darley **Trained** Newmarket, Suffolk

**FOCUS**
A decent, competitive handicap and all bar the front-running fourth avoided the inside rail for most of the way.
T/Jkpt: Not Won. T/Plt: £3,244.40 to a £1 stake. Pool: £230,446.73 - 51.85 winning units. T/Qpdt: £696.10 to a £1 stake. Pool: £14,864.61 - 15.80 winning units. **Jonathan Neesom**

# 4888 CHESTER (L-H)
Saturday, July 29

**OFFICIAL GOING: Good to soft (6.2)**
Wind: Light across Weather: Showers

## 5398 STELLA ARTOIS NOVICE MEDIAN AUCTION STKS (PLUS 10 RACE) 5f 15y
**2:00** (2:03) (Class 4) 2-Y-0
**£6,225** (£1,864; £932; £466; £233; £117) **Stalls** Low

Form RPR

4 **1** **Miss Puddles (IRE)**[19] 4689 2-8-9 0 ow1............. AdamMcNamara(3) 1 84
(Richard Fahey) *disp ld tl wnt on over 1f out: sn rdn clr* **10/3**[2]

023 **2** *3* **Charnock Richard**[21] 4606 2-9-2 76................................. FrannyNorton 6 77
(David Brown) *chsd ldrs: rdn over 1f out: r.o to go 2nd ins fnl f* **11/2**

204 **3** *5* **Big Time Maybe (IRE)**[51] 3490 2-9-2 76................. RichardKingscote 3 59
(Tom Dascombe) *w wnr tl rdn over 1f out: wknd ins fnl f* **4/1**[3]

32 **4** *nk* **Johni Boxit**[11] 4995 2-8-11 0................................... JoshuaBryan(5) 4 58
(Gay Kelleway) *sn pushed along in rr: styd on ins fnl f: nvr nrr* **8/1**

1 **5** *3* **Buridan (FR)**[47] 3668 2-9-8 0..............................................(b[1]) PatDobbs 5 53+
(Richard Hannon) *s.i.s: in rr: rdn over 1f out: nvr on terms* **6/4**[1]

06 **6** *4* **Orient Princess**[21] 4599 2-8-11 0.......................................... JasonHart 8 28
(Paul Midgley) *wnt rt s: hdwy over 3f out: rdn and wknd over 1f out* **40/1**

0 **7** *2 1/2* **Lady Ensign**[43] 3791 2-8-8 0................................... JordanVaughan(3) 2 19
(Mark Brisbourne) *prom: sn pushed along: wknd 2f out* **150/1**

**8** *1 1/2* **Mariah's Melody (IRE)** 2-8-11 0..................................(h[1]) ShaneGray 9 13
(Lisa Williamson) *wnt rt s: outpcd* **150/1**

6 **9** *nk* **Go Sandy**[14] 4888 2-8-6 0............................................... JaneElliott(5) 7 12
(Lisa Williamson) *sn pushed along in rr: lost tch 1/2-way* **33/1**

1m 2.67s (1.67) **Going Correction** +0.425s/f (Yiel) **9** Ran SP% **116.3**
Speed ratings (Par 96): **103,98,90,89,84 78,74,72,71**
CSF £21.87 TOTE £5.90: £2.10, £1.90, £1.20; EX 28.50 Trifecta £104.10.
**Owner** Richard Fahey Ebor Racing Club Ltd **Bred** Sherbourne Lodge **Trained** Musley Bank, N Yorks

**FOCUS**
The running rail had been returned to the very inside, meaning all race distances were as advertised. Hard to know what to make of this form quite yet and the winner made all from stall 1. The runner-up helps set a straightforward standard.

## 5399 MBNA GOOD STUFF FILLIES' H'CAP 7f 127y
**2:35** (2:35) (Class 4) (0-85,85) 3-Y-0+
**£6,225** (£1,864; £932; £466; £233; £117) **Stalls** Low

Form RPR

2143 **1** **Rutherford (IRE)**[21] 4610 3-8-10 **75**................................ ShaneGray 6 83
(Kevin Ryan) *pushed along to ld 7f out: rdn clr over 2f out: jst hld on* **4/1**[2]

-212 **2** *1/2* **Shaaqaaf (IRE)**[28] 4366 3-9-6 **85**....................................... KieranFox 8 95+
(John Gosden) *sn pushed along in rr: rdn: hdwy and nt clr run over 1f out: sn chsng wnr: r.o wl ins fnl f* **3/1**[1]

3535 **3** *6* **Bush Beauty (IRE)**[15] 4837 6-8-9 **66** oh2.......................... NeilFarley 5 61
(Eric Alston) *s.i.s: swtchd rt over 2f out: hdwy on outer over 1f out: sn rdn: styd on same pce fnl f* **10/1**

4152 **4** *6* **Alpine Dream (IRE)**[28] 4375 4-9-6 **77**............................(b) JasonHart 7 58
(Tim Easterby) *s.i.s: hdwy 4f out: rdn and hmpd over 1f out: sn wknd* **11/2**[3]

-015 **5** *3 3/4* **Vice Versa**[59] 3217 3-8-12 **77**.........................................(v[1]) FrannyNorton 1 48
(Sir Michael Stoute) *s.i.s: sn pushed along and prom: rdn and lost pl over 3f out: wkng whn nt clr run over 2f out* **3/1**[1]

031 **6** *5* **Bell Heather (IRE)**[18] 4726 4-8-9 **73**..................... ConnorMurtagh(7) 4 34
(Patrick Morris) *led early: chsd ldrs: drvn and lost pl 4f out: wknd over 2f out* **12/1**

4000 **7** *2 1/4* **Maggie Pink**[28] 4375 8-8-10 **74**........................................ RayDawson(7) 3 30
(Michael Appleby) *s.i.s: hdwy to chse wnr over 6f out: rdn over 2f out: hung rt wl over 1f out: sn wknd* **7/1**

1m 35.8s (2.00) **Going Correction** +0.425s/f (Yiel)
**WFA** 3 from 4yo+ 8lb **7** Ran SP% **114.7**
Speed ratings (Par 102): **107,106,100,94,90 85,83**
CSF £16.52 CT £110.31 TOTE £4.70: £3.10, £1.90; EX 17.70 Trifecta £139.00.
**Owner** Mrs Angie Bailey & K&j Bloodstock Ltd **Bred** Eimear Mulhern & Abbeville Stud **Trained** Hambleton, N Yorks
■ Stewards' Enquiry : Shane Gray caution: careless riding

**FOCUS**
This looked competitive even with three runners coming out. The winner has been rated to the better view of her form.

## 5400 SEBASTIAN ARTOIS APPRENTICE H'CAP 7f 127y
**3:10** (3:10) (Class 3) (0-90,92) 3-Y-0
**£12,450** (£3,728; £1,864; £932; £466; £234) **Stalls** Low

Form RPR

-112 **1** **Dan Troop**[22] 4556 3-9-1 **77**........................................ ConnorMurtagh(3) 2 96
(Richard Fahey) *trckd ldrs: nt clr run over 2f out: led over 1f out: rdn clr* **7/2**[2]

1621 **2** *7* **Original Choice (IRE)**[24] 4507 3-10-5 **92**......................... GeorgiaCox 1 95+
(William Haggas) *hld up: nt clr run over 2f out: hdwy over 1f out: wnt 2nd and hung lft ins fnl f: no ch w wnr* **2/1**[1]

0502 **3** *1 3/4* **Plant Pot Power (IRE)**[14] 4894 3-9-7 **85**...................... RossaRyan(5) 5 84
(Richard Hannon) *hld up in tch: nt clr run over 2f out tl over 1f out: carried lft ins fnl f: styd on same pce* **13/2**

5205 **4** *1* **Toy Theatre**[4] 5242 3-8-12 **74**....................................... RayDawson(3) 8 71
(Michael Appleby) *hld up: hdwy over 2f out: rdn over 1f out: no ex fnl f* **33/1**

5434 **5** *2 1/4* **Lady In Question (IRE)**[17] 4741 3-8-11 **70**.................... RichardOliver 7 62
(Richard Fahey) *prom: chsd wnr over 2f out: rdn and ev ch wl over 1f out: wknd fnl f* **20/1**

0301 **6** *6* **Intimate Art (IRE)**[22] 4564 3-9-4 **80**............................... JoshuaBryan(3) 4 58
(Andrew Balding) *sn pushed along in rr: rdn over 2f out: nvr nrr* **6/1**

-621 **7** *nk* **Armandihan (IRE)**[79] 2547 3-9-8 **81**.......................(p[1]) LewisEdmunds 3 58
(Kevin Ryan) *chsd ldr tl led 4f out: rdn and hdd over 1f out: wknd fnl f* **11/2**[3]

2141 **8** *2 3/4* **Our Charlie Brown**[17] 4741 3-8-9 **75**................. RobertDodsworth(7) 10 46
(Tim Easterby) *hld up: hdwy over 2f out: rdn and wknd over 1f out* **16/1**

0430 **9** *10* **Arc Royal**[29] 4290 3-9-5 **78**..............................................(p[1]) PaddyPilley 9 26
(Tom Dascombe) *sn pushed along to ld: hdd 4f out: rdn over 2f out: nt clr run and wknd over 1f out* **20/1**

650 **10** *4* **Something Brewing (FR)**[28] 4377 3-8-8 **72**.....(b) ManuelFernandes(5) 6 11
(Iain Jardine) *s.i.s: outpcd* **28/1**

1m 34.97s (1.17) **Going Correction** +0.425s/f (Yiel) **10** Ran SP% **120.4**
Speed ratings (Par 104): **111,104,102,101,99 93,92,89,79,75**
CSF £10.73 CT £44.44 TOTE £4.10: £1.40, £2.10, £2.10; EX 13.40 Trifecta £64.50.
**Owner** Mrs Janis Macpherson **Bred** Liam Sheridan **Trained** Musley Bank, N Yorks

**FOCUS**
A useful looking handicap for apprentices, but the home bend got a little messy and the second and third found trouble when making their bids. The level is hard to pin down.

## 5401 ANS MAIDEN FILLIES' STKS 1m 4f 63y
**3:45** (3:45) (Class 4) 3-Y-0+
**£6,225** (£1,864; £932; £466; £233; £117) **Stalls** Low

Form RPR

33 **1** **What A Home (IRE)**[29] 4300 3-9-1 0.............................. FrannyNorton 3 85+
(William Haggas) *s.i.s: hld up: hdwy 1/2-way: slipped wl over 2f out: hmpd sn after: shkn up over 1f out: r.o to ld wl ins fnl f: comf* **11/10**[1]

35 **2** *1 1/4* **Shearling**15 4849 4-9-12 0 JasonHart 1 76
(Brian Ellison) *led: hdd 10f out: chsd ldr tl led again 5f out: rdn over 1f out: hdd and unable qck wl ins fnl f* **7/2**3

053 **3** *2* **Miss Liguria**24 4497 3-8-10 0 JennyPowell(5) 7 74
(Ed Walker) *chsd ldrs: wnt 2nd over 2f out: rdn over 1f out: no ex wl ins fnl f* **16/1**

640 **4** *16* **Paris Rooftops (IRE)**24 4497 3-9-1 73 RichardKingscote 5 48
(Luca Cumani) *hld up in tch: rdn over 4f out: wknd wl over 2f out* **8/1**

2346 **5** *2 1/2* **Archibelle**8 5096 3-8-8 65 ConnorMurtagh(7) 10 44
(R Mike Smith) *broke wl sn stdd and lost pl: hld up: hung lft 8f out: hmpd over 2f out: nvr on terms* **20/1**

-324 **6** *8* **Munstead Star**7 5153 3-8-10 77 JoshuaBryan(5) 4 32
(Andrew Balding) *chsd ldr: led 10f out: hdd 5f out: chsd ldr tl rdn wl over 2f out: sn wknd* **3/1**2

**7** *12* **Sturdy Dawn**753 7-9-7 0 (h1) JaneElliott(5) 6 11
(Michael Mullineaux) *sn pushed along in rr: hmpd 8f out: bhd fr 1/2-way* **100/1**

\- **8** *73* **Romann Angel**219 8-9-7 0 PhilDennis(5) 9
(Michael Mullineaux) *hld up in tch: rdn and lost pl over 7f out: sn bhd* **100/1**

0500 **S** **Penny Red**17 4765 3-8-8 60 RossaRyan(7) 2
(Nikki Evans) *s.i.s: sn prom: 3rd and rdn whn slipped up over 2f out* **25/1**

2m 42.21s (3.71) **Going Correction** +0.425s/f (Yiel)
**WFA** 3 from 4yo+ 11lb **9** Ran SP% **122.4**
Speed ratings (Par 102): **104,103,101,91,89 84,76,27,**
CSF £5.54 TOTE £2.10: £1.10, £1.50, £3.30; EX 5.40 Trifecta £24.70.
**Owner** Sunderland Holding Inc **Bred** Tullpark Ltd **Trained** Newmarket, Suffolk

**FOCUS**
This maiden was run at what seemed a solid tempo, and their was drama of the final bend when one of the runners came down. The level is a bit fluid.

## 5402 CHALICE H'CAP 5f 15y
**4:20** (4:32) (Class 3) (0-95,93) 3-Y-0+
**£12,450** (£3,728; £1,864; £932; £466; £234) **Stalls** Low

Form RPR

3000 **1** **Confessional**19 4686 10-8-11 83 (e) LewisEdmunds(5) 3 93
(Tim Easterby) *a.p: rdn over 1f out: r.o to ld wl ins fnl f* **6/1**3

0000 **2** *3/4* **Blithe Spirit**28 4333 6-9-0 81 JasonHart 2 88
(Eric Alston) *sn led: rdn and edgd rt over 1f out: hdd and unable qck wl ins fnl f* **7/2**1

601 **3** *nk* **Reflektor (IRE)**28 4333 4-9-7 93 PaddyPilley(5) 7 99
(Tom Dascombe) *sn chsng ldr: rdn and edgd lft over 1f out: styd on* **8/1**

4514 **4** *3/4* **Orient Class**28 4333 6-9-0 88 ConnorMurtagh(7) 8 91
(Paul Midgley) *chsd ldrs: rdn to go 2nd over 1f out: sn hung lft: ev ch wl ins fnl f: no ex towards fin* **18/1**

0013 **5** *3/4* **Ashpan Sam**16 4803 8-9-1 87 (p) PhilDennis(5) 1 88
(David W Drinkwater) *chsd ldrs: rdn 1/2-way: hmpd over 1f out: nt clr run ins fnl f: styd on* **8/1**

4162 **6** *shd* **Signore Piccolo**21 4600 6-9-4 85 (h) RichardKingscote 4 85
(David Loughnane) *s.i.s: hdwy 1/2-way: nt clr run fr over 1f out: styd on* **9/2**2

0622 **7** *1/2* **Powerallied (IRE)**8 5129 4-9-0 84 AdamMcNamara(3) 9 82+
(Richard Fahey) *mid-div: rdn over 1f out: swtchd rt and r.o ins fnl f: nt rch ldrs* **12/1**

3031 **8** *1 3/4* **Normal Equilibrium**28 4337 7-8-10 77 FrannyNorton 10 69
(Ivan Furtado) *prom: shkn up over 1f out: styd on same pce ins fnl f* **20/1**

3310 **9** *nk* **Justanotherbottle (IRE)**16 4813 3-9-8 93 NeilFarley 6 83
(Declan Carroll) *hld up in tch: rdn 1/2-way: nt trble ldrs* **12/1**

603 **10** *3/4* **Gamesome (FR)**8 5129 6-9-6 87 (p1) KierenFox 12 75
(Paul Midgley) *s.i.s: hld up: rdn over 1f out: nvr on terms* **18/1**

0-40 **11** *1/2* **Mayleaf Shine (IRE)**35 4078 3-9-3 88 PatDobbs 5 73
(Iain Jardine) *unruly in stalls: a in rr* **16/1**

5560 **12** *2 1/4* **Ballesteros**8 5098 8-8-9 76 ShaneGray 13 54
(Richard Fahey) *sn pushed along and a in rr* **40/1**

06 **13** *1* **Lightscameraction (IRE)**8 5116 5-9-6 92 (b) JoshuaBryan(5) 11 67
(Gay Kelleway) *sn pushed along in rr: rdn 1/2-way: wknd over 1f out* **33/1**

1m 2.07s (1.07) **Going Correction** +0.425s/f (Yiel)
**WFA** 3 from 4yo+ 4lb **13** Ran SP% **118.8**
Speed ratings (Par 107): **108,106,106,105,103 103,102,100,99,98 97,94,92**
CSF £26.47 CT £172.70 TOTE £6.50: £2.30, £1.40, £3.00; EX 30.00 Trifecta £254.90.
**Owner** Bearstone Stud Limited **Bred** Bearstone Stud Ltd **Trained** Great Habton, N Yorks

**FOCUS**
With plenty of known front runners drawn well in low stalls, this was always going to be run at a strong gallop. The winner has been rated to this year's form, with the third close to his C&D latest.

## 5403 STELLA ARTOIS 4% H'CAP 1m 5f 84y
**4:55** (4:58) (Class 4) (0-80,80) 4-Y-0+
**£6,225** (£1,864; £932; £466; £233; £117) **Stalls** Low

Form RPR

3221 **1** **Berrahri (IRE)**16 4802 6-9-6 79 KierenFox 13 90
(John Best) *sn chsng ldr: led over 8f out: rdn over 1f out: styd on wl* **8/1**

1022 **2** *2 1/2* **Kajaki (IRE)**14 4898 4-8-13 77 (p) LewisEdmunds(5) 11 83
(Kevin Ryan) *led: hdd over 9f out: chsd wnr tl 6f out: rdn to go 2nd again over 1f out: styd on same pce fnl f* **3/1**1

4234 **3** *3 1/2* **Monaco Rose**5 5208 4-9-2 75 (h) FrannyNorton 5 76
(Richard Fahey) *prom: rdn over 3f out: styd on same pce fnl f* **7/2**2

1316 **4** *3/4* **Zenafire**7 5138 8-8-9 73 (p) JaneElliott(5) 8 73
(Sarah Hollinshead) *mid-div: rdn over 3f out: hdwy over 2f out: styd on same pce fnl f* **12/1**

2102 **5** *1 1/4* **Theos Lolly (IRE)**14 4893 4-9-0 80 ConnorMurtagh(7) 15 78+
(Richard Fahey) *hld up: hdwy over 1f out: sn rdn and edgd lft: nt trble ldrs* **14/1**

4-53 **6** *shd* **Mcvicar**11 5008 8-7-11 61 oh5 (p) RichardOliver(5) 6 59
(John Davies) *hld up: rdn over 4f out: styd on fr over 1f out: nvr on terms* **25/1**

0551 **7** *2 1/2* **Sparte Quercus (IRE)**22 4573 4-9-0 73 RichardKingscote 10 67
(Ed Dunlop) *prom: chsd wnr 6f out tl rdn over 1f out: wknd fnl f* **6/1**3

0023 **8** *1 3/4* **Wotabreeze (IRE)**15 4840 4-8-13 72 JasonHart 1 63
(John Quinn) *prom: rdn over 2f out: wknd fnl f* **12/1**

-316 **9** *hd* **Belabour**43 3794 4-9-2 80 JoshuaBryan(5) 2 71
(Mark Brisbourne) *chsd ldrs: rdn over 2f out: wkng whn nt clr run over 1f out* **20/1**

0201 **10** *3/4* **Airton**28 4357 4-9-3 79 AdamMcNamara(3) 12 69
(James Bethell) *hld up: rdn over 2f out: n.d* **12/1**

360 **11** *10* **Modernism**14 4893 8-9-4 77 (p) PatDobbs 7 52
(Ian Williams) *hld up: hdwy u.p over 3f out: wknd over 2f out* **22/1**

0000 **12** *1* **Buthelezi (USA)**10 5021 9-7-11 63 RobertDodsworth(7) 9 37
(Brian Ellison) *s.i.s: hld up: rdn over 2f out: a in rr* **33/1**

00-0 **13** *8* **My Fantasea (IRE)**200 154 4-8-13 72 RyanTate 4 34
(David Evans) *s.i.s: hdwy into mid-div over 11f out: rdn and wknd over 2f out* **40/1**

-360 **14** *19* **Gabrial The Duke (IRE)**10 5021 7-8-4 63 (v) ShaneGray 3
(Patrick Morris) *s.s: sn drvn along in rr: lost tch fnl 5f* **33/1**

2m 59.29s (6.59) **Going Correction** +0.425s/f (Yiel) **14** Ran SP% **123.6**
Speed ratings (Par 105): **96,94,92,91,91 91,89,88,88,87 81,81,76,64**
CSF £30.37 CT £104.34 TOTE £10.10: £3.00, £1.90, £1.80; EX 43.20 Trifecta £191.50.
**Owner** White Turf Racing Uk **Bred** Kilnamoragh Stud **Trained** Oad Street, Kent

**FOCUS**
A prominent position proved an advantage in this staying handicap. Another pb from the winner, with the second and third running similar to their 1m4f form here on July 1.

## 5404 STELLA ARTOIS CIDRE H'CAP 1m 2f 70y
**5:25** (5:29) (Class 4) (0-80,80) 3-Y-O
**£6,225** (£1,864; £932; £466; £233; £117) **Stalls** High

Form RPR

3421 **1** **Glenys The Menace (FR)**8 5113 3-9-0 73 KierenFox 9 86+
(John Best) *hld up: hdwy 2f out: shkn up to ld and n.m.r over 1f out: styd on strly* **7/1**

60-2 **2** *4* **Reverend Jacobs**22 4579 3-8-12 76 GeorgiaCox(5) 3 82+
(William Haggas) *chsd ldrs: pushed along over 2f out: rdn and ev ch over 1f out: styd on same pce ins fnl f* **15/8**1

3 **3** *2* **Epitaph (IRE)**8 5131 3-8-9 68 RyanTate 1 70
(Michael Appleby) *sn pushed along and prom: lost pl after 1f: hdwy u.p over 2f out: styd on same pce fnl f* **9/1**

-026 **4** *1/2* **Sound Bar**15 4865 3-9-7 80 (b1) PatDobbs 7 81
(Ralph Beckett) *hld up: hdwy over 3f out: rdn and hung lft over 1f out: no ex fnl f* **12/1**

3321 **5** *5* **Alexander M (IRE)**41 3859 3-8-12 71 FrannyNorton 6 63
(Mark Johnston) *prom: chsd ldr over 2f out: rdn and ev ch over 1f out: wknd ins fnl f* **5/1**2

5034 **6** *3 1/2* **Critical Thinking (IRE)**29 4295 3-7-12 62 JaneElliott(5) 8 47
(Kevin Frost) *chsd ldr over 8f out: led over 3f out: rdn and hdd over 1f out: wknd ins fnl f* **25/1**

0050 **7** *5* **International Law**10 5033 3-9-0 73 (b) JasonHart 10 48
(Brian Meehan) *s.s: a in rr* **33/1**

-515 **8** *2 3/4* **Desert Dream**56 3336 3-9-7 80 (p1) RichardKingscote 4 50
(Sir Michael Stoute) *led 1f: chsd ldrs: edgd rt 8f out: rdn and wknd over 2f out* **13/2**

-442 **9** *9* **Tamayef (IRE)**23 4544 3-8-13 77 JoshuaBryan(5) 2 30
(Hugo Palmer) *led after 1f: rdn and hdd over 3f out: wknd over 2f out* **6/1**3

5141 **10** *12* **Metronomic (IRE)**32 4172 3-8-5 64 ShaneGray 5
(Peter Niven) *plld hrd and prom: hmpd: stmbld and lost pl 8f out: wknd and eased over 3f out* **33/1**

2m 17.19s (5.99) **Going Correction** +0.425s/f (Yiel) **10** Ran SP% **119.0**
Speed ratings (Par 102): **93,89,88,87,83 81,77,74,67,58**
CSF £21.57 CT £121.57 TOTE £10.00: £2.70, £1.40, £2.50; EX 29.70 Trifecta £194.00.
**Owner** Curtis, Malt & Jenkins **Bred** Haras D'Etreham & Mr Georges Lugon **Trained** Oad Street, Kent

■ Stewards' Enquiry : Jane Elliott three-day ban: careless riding (Aug 12-14)

**FOCUS**
A competitive handicap to finish the meeting. The runner-up has been rated as improving.
T/Plt: £21.20 to a £1 stake. Pool: £70,404.84 - 2,423.84 winning units. T/Qpdt: £5.00 to a £1 stake. Pool: £4,435.24 - 651.93 winning units. **Colin Roberts**

# 5292 LINGFIELD (L-H)
Saturday, July 29

**OFFICIAL GOING: Soft (good to soft in places; 6.9) changing to soft after race 1 (5.30)**
Wind: Light Weather: Showers

## 5405 BOXING BETTING AT 188BET H'CAP 1m 3f 133y
**5:30** (5:34) (Class 6) (0-60,59) 3-Y-0+ **£2,587** (£770; £384; £192) **Stalls** High

Form RPR

360- **1** **Hermosa Vaquera (IRE)**221 8468 7-9-1 49 (p) HectorCrouch(3) 6 56
(Gary Moore) *settled bhd ldrs on outer: shkn up over 3f out and led wl over 2f out: sn rdn and pressed by runner-up: asserted ent fnl f: rdn out fnl 110yds* **9/1**

-001 **2** *2 1/2* **Ablaze**28 4346 3-8-10 55 EdwardGreatrex(3) 7 59
(Laura Mongan) *cl up w ldr: rdn over 2f out and pressed wnr: styd on tl no ex ent fnl f: no ex fnl 110yds* **11/8**1

5500 **3** *2 1/2* **Galuppi**109 1699 6-9-3 48 (v) SamHitchcott 5 47
(J R Jenkins) *in rr on outer: rdn over 2f out: kpt on fr over 1f out past btn horses: no ch w ldng pair* **14/1**

-063 **4** *2 1/2* **Lemon Drop**75 2679 3-8-3 52 (b) IsobelFrancis(7) 3 48
(Jim Boyle) *s.s: settled in rr: rdn over 2f out: kpt on one pce* **5/1**2

000- **5** *shd* **Rod Of Iron**320 6406 4-9-0 45 KieranO'Neill 10 40
(Michael Madgwick) *early spd: settled in rr-div on inner: lost pl over 4f out: shuffled along fr over 2f out: nvr involved* **25/1**

6050 **6** *6* **Megalala (IRE)**35 4087 16-8-9 47 MillyNaseb(7) 8 32
(John Bridger) *sn led: shkn up over 3f out and wknd: no ex fr over 2f out and hdd: sn wknd* **13/2**3

-504 **7** *1 1/4* **Montycristo**32 4177 4-9-8 53 (b) DougieCostello 1 36
(Philip Hide) *t.k.h early: chsd ldr on rail: rdn over 3f out: sn hld* **7/1**

0-00 **8** *nse* **French Silver (FR)**17 4754 3-7-10 45 AledBeech(7) 4 29
(Tony Carroll) *mid-div on inner: rdn over 3f out: sn hld* **20/1**

2m 38.07s (6.57) **Going Correction** +0.40s/f (Good)
**WFA** 3 from 4yo+ 11lb **8** Ran SP% **109.9**
Speed ratings (Par 101): **94,92,90,89,88 84,84,84**
CSF £19.42 CT £133.72 TOTE £8.70: £2.30, £1.40, £3.20; EX 27.80 Trifecta £268.90.
**Owner** Michael Baldry **Bred** James Burns And A Moynan **Trained** Lower Beeding, W Sussex

■ Rianna Star was withdrawn. Price at time of withdrawal 15-2. Rule 4 applies to all bets. Deduction - 10p in the pound.


The Form Book Flat, Raceform Ltd, Newbury, RG14 5SJ

**FOCUS**
Only one of these was rated within 11lb of the ceiling rating for the grade, so this is weak form, even for this lowly level. Conditions sorted these out and they finished strung out. The going was changed to soft all round after this opener. The winner hasn't been rated this high since 2015.

## 5406 PROFESSOR BRIAN NEVILLE H'CAP 1m 6f
**6:00** (6:00) (Class 5) (0-70,72) 3-Y-O **£2,911** (£866; £432; £216) **Stalls** Low

Form RPR
-032 **1** **Sussex Ranger (USA)**[10] 5034 3-9-8 **72**.................... HectorCrouch(3) 3 79
(Gary Moore) *in rr and racd on and off the bit: prog wl over 3f out wd: sn rdn and picked up wl in centre: led ent 2f out: kpt on wl over 1f out: idled last 150yds: rdn out* **4/1**[3]

0-05 **2** *1 ¼* **Leapt**[10] 5034 3-9-4 **65**..........................................................(h) ShaneKelly 5 69
(Richard Hughes) *hld up: shkn up wl over 3f out and travelled wl trcking ldrs over 2f out: sn rdn and pressed wnr: edgd lft over 1f out: kpt on ins fnl f: no ex fnl 100yds* **11/1**

4063 **3** *9* **Arcadian Sea (IRE)**[12] 4978 3-8-8 **55**...................... SilvestreDeSousa 8 46
(William Jarvis) *led after 3f: shkn up 5f out: rdn over 3f out: hdd ent 2f out: sn lft bhd by ldng pair: plugged on* **11/4**[2]

6122 **4** *2 ¼* **The Secrets Out**[33] 4156 3-8-9 **56**..................................(h) KieranO'Neill 7 44
(Luke Dace) *t.k.h for first half of r: shkn up over 4f out: rdn over 3f out: sn no ex: plugged on after* **9/2**

5522 **5** *13* **Duke's Girl**[45] 3711 3-9-7 **68**............................................. LouisSteward 2 38
(Michael Bell) *t.k.h to post: settled in mid-div: shkn up over 3f out and travelled wl onto heels of ldrs: rdn over 2f out: fnd nil and no ex fr over 1f out* **5/2**[1]

4004 **6** *1 ¾* **Two Dollars (IRE)**[9] 5061 3-9-4 **65**.............................(h) DougieCostello 1 33
(William Jarvis) *in rr on inner: niggled along fr over 5f out: rdn over 3f out: sn hld: t.o* **14/1**

6630 **7** *15* **Bizet (IRE)**[5] 5209 3-8-5 **52**..................................................(b) DannyBrock 4
(John Ryan) *s.s: shkn up to make prog and chsd ldr after 4f: shkn up 5f out: sn struggling and lost pl fr over 3f out: t.o* **20/1**

2664 **8** *29* **Haldaw**[7] 5142 3-9-0 **61**.............................................. SamHitchcott 6
(Mick Channon) *shkn up to ld: hdd after 3f: chsd ldrs on inner: struggling over 5f out: sn dropped bk: t.o fr 3f out* **20/1**

3m 9.9s (-0.10) **Going Correction** +0.40s/f (Good) **8** Ran SP% **117.9**
Speed ratings (Par 100): **116,115,110,108,101 100,91,75**
CSF £48.03 CT £138.81 TOTE £5.30: £1.80, £2.80, £1.10; EX 35.10 Trifecta £327.70.
**Owner** The Tongdean Partnership **Bred** Paul Knapper & Tcr Ranch **Trained** Lower Beeding, W Sussex

**FOCUS**
A few of these came into this in decent form and the gallop looked fairly even given the conditions, so this probably wouldn't be bad form for the grade even though the favourite disappointed. The front two came clear in the final furlong.

## 5407 GET 1/4 ODDS AT 188BET H'CAP 2m 68y
**6:30** (6:30) (Class 5) (0-70,69) 4-Y-O+ **£2,911** (£866; £432; £216) **Stalls** Low

Form RPR
50-1 **1** **Hiorne Tower (FR)**[17] 4756 6-8-11 **62**......................... HectorCrouch(3) 8 68+
(John Best) *tk v t.k.h most of way: shkn up and c wd wl over 3f out: travelling powerfully in centre 2f out: led over 1f out: rdn out ins fnl f: easily* **8/11**[1]

0-00 **2** *1* **Toptempo**[17] 4756 8-7-13 **50**............................................ HollieDoyle(3) 3 53
(Ralph J Smith) *s.s and in last: struggling over 5f out: 6 l last 4f out: rdn wl over 3f out and began to cl: chsd ldr fr over 1f out: stuck on wl ins fnl f: no ch w easy wnr* **16/1**

4445 **3** *1 ¾* **Southern States**[17] 4750 4-8-12 **60**........................... SilvestreDeSousa 2 61
(Lydia Richards) *chsd ldr: niggled along over 3f out: led 3f out: rdn over 2f out: plugged on ins fnl f and jst hld 3rd* **4/1**[2]

-564 **4** *shd* **Mazalto (IRE)**[48] 3618 4-9-2 **69**.................................... PaddyBradley(5) 1 70
(Pat Phelan) *racd in 3rd: rdn over 3f out: kpt on one pce fr over 1f out and jst hld for 3rd post* **4/1**[2]

0 **5** *29* **Lazio (IRE)**[17] 4750 4-9-3 **65**.......................................... DougieCostello 6 31
(Jamie Osborne) *led: shkn up over 3f out: sn rdn: hdd wl 3f out: wknd qckly after: t.o* **10/1**[3]

3m 46.99s (12.19) **Going Correction** +0.40s/f (Good) **5** Ran SP% **112.9**
Speed ratings (Par 103): **85,84,83,83,69**
CSF £13.95 TOTE £1.60: £1.10, £5.00; EX 15.80 Trifecta £41.10.
**Owner** Mrs Jackie Jones **Bred** David Menuisier & Christiane Head Maarek **Trained** Oad Street, Kent

**FOCUS**
They went steady here, resulting in a few of these racing freely, notably market leader Hiorne Tower, but it didn't stop him getting the job done. The winner has been rated back to his best.

## 5408 GEORGE DALLIGAN NOVICE STKS 4f 217y
**7:00** (7:01) (Class 5) 2-Y-O **£2,911** (£866; £432; £216) **Stalls** Centre

Form RPR
543 **1** **Ragstone View (IRE)**[9] 5048 2-9-2 77................................ ShaneKelly 3 67
(Richard Hughes) *led: hdd over 2f out: rdn over 1f out and chsd ldr: kpt on wl between horses and led 110yds: wl on top at fin* **4/9**[1]

0530 **2** *½* **Bodybuilder**[23] 4527 2-8-13 69........................................ HollieDoyle(3) 8 65
(Richard Hannon) *pressed ldr: rdn over 1f out: ev ch ins fnl f kpt on to take 2nd fnl 75yds* **4/1**[2]

**3** *½* **Aegean Legend** 2-9-2 0.................................................... KieranO'Neill 9 63
(John Bridger) *in rr: shkn up and prog on nrside fr 2f out: sn rdn: kpt on wl to take 3rd nr fin: nvr nrr* **16/1**

0 **4** *nk* **Jean Paget (IRE)**[8] 5107 2-8-11 0............................ SilvestreDeSousa 2 57
(Mick Channon) *s.s: prog and led over 2f out: sn rdn: kpt on wl and drifted to rail ins fnl f: hdd over 110yds out: lost 2nd 75yds out and dropped to 4th nr fin* **6/1**[3]

00 **5** *4 ½* **Watch Tan**[26] 4440 2-8-8 0.............................................. HectorCrouch(3) 5 41
(George Baker) *tk fierce hold early chsng ldrs: no ex fr over 1f out and wknd* **14/1**

06 **6** *4 ½* **Lisbon Legend**[21] 4620 2-9-2 0........................................... JimmyQuinn 4 30
(Tony Carroll) *chsd ldrs: shkn up over 2f out: wknd fr over 1f out* **33/1**

000 **7** *2* **Mullion Star**[14] 4909 2-9-2 27.......................................(v[1]) SamHitchcott 1 23
(Michael Madgwick) *pressed ldrs: shkn up over 2f out: losing pl fr 2f out: sn no ex* **40/1**

1m 0.67s (2.47) **Going Correction** +0.35s/f (Good) **7** Ran SP% **121.5**
Speed ratings (Par 94): **94,93,92,91,84 77,74**
CSF £3.06 TOTE £1.30: £1.10, £2.80; EX 3.30 Trifecta £15.00.
**Owner** Gallagher Bloodstock Limited **Bred** Peter Henley **Trained** Upper Lambourn, Berks

**FOCUS**
A modest little maiden which presented a golden opportunity for Ragstone View to get off the mark, but he made very hard work of this and only pulled it out of the fire late on.

## 5409 YOUNG EPILEPSY MEDIAN AUCTION MAIDEN STKS 7f
**7:30** (7:32) (Class 6) 3-5-Y-O **£2,587** (£770; £384; £192) **Stalls** Centre

Form RPR
5-32 **1** **Working Class**[17] 4764 3-9-5 77.............................. SilvestreDeSousa 4 77
(Peter Chapple-Hyam) *cl up w ldrs on outer: shkn up 2f out and briefly hmpd rival: led wl over 1f out: sn rdn: asserted ins fnl f and wnt clr* **1/2**[1]

-4 **2** *4* **The Bear Can Fly**[17] 4759 3-9-0 0..................................... TomMarquand 5 62
(David Menuisier) *chsd ldrs between horses: rdn over 2f out: no imp tl kpt on under hands and heels ins fnl f to take 2nd nr fin* **5/1**[3]

-225 **3** *¾* **Nuncio**[21] 4624 3-9-5 73................................................................ FranBerry 7 66
(Daniel Kubler) *chsd ldrs: shkn up over 3f: briefly checked 2f out: kpt on one pce* **3/1**[2]

02 **4** *2 ½* **Violet's Lads (IRE)**[33] 4152 3-9-0 0................................ KieranO'Neill 8 54
(Brett Johnson) *led: racd awkward: hung rt over 3f out: hung lft wl over 2f out: sn hdd: hmpd rival 2f: drifted lft and one pce after: lost two pls nr fin* **10/1**

35 **5** *2 ½* **Hydeandseek (FR)**[17] 4759 3-8-11 0.......................... HectorCrouch(3) 6 48
(John Best) *s.s: rdn along over 3f out: plugged on under hands and heels fr over 1f out* **16/1**

0000 **6** *8* **Secret Willow**[31] 4211 3-9-5 44........................................ SamHitchcott 3 33
(John E Long) *pressed ldrs on outer: rdn over 2f out: sn wknd* **66/1**

00- **7** *hd* **Giveitsomeginger**[316] 6534 3-9-0 0................................ DougieCostello 2 27
(Jo Hughes) *a in rr: pushed along over 3f out: no ex fr over 2f out: pushed out after* **25/1**

00 **8** *8* **Henriqua**[14] 4911 3-9-0 0.................................................... ShaneKelly 9 7
(Denis Coakley) *chsd ldrs: rdn over 3f out: wknd fr 2f out* **50/1**

600 **9** *5* **Moorea**[112] 1624 3-9-0 0.............................................. MitchGodwin(5) 1
(John Bridger) *a in rr: struggling over 3f out: sn hld* **66/1**

1m 25.63s (2.33) **Going Correction** +0.35s/f (Good) **9** Ran SP% **132.1**
Speed ratings (Par 101): **100,95,94,91,88 79,79,70,64**
CSF £4.72 TOTE £1.40: £1.02, £1.60, £1.20; EX 5.70 Trifecta £11.40.
**Owner** M Venus & W Prosser **Bred** R Chennells **Trained** Newmarket, Suffolk

**FOCUS**
Not much depth to this maiden and the clear form choice came away in the final furlong to win comfortably.

## 5410 RON EAGLE WELL DONE STEAKS H'CAP 7f
**8:00** (8:04) (Class 6) (0-55,55) 3-Y-O+ **£2,587** (£770; £384; £192) **Stalls** Centre

Form RPR
0341 **1** **Arctic Flower (IRE)**[7] 5145 4-8-9 **49**........................... HectorCrouch(3) 6 58
(John Bridger) *mde all: rdn over 3f out: kpt on wl fr over 1f out: rdn out cl home to hold on* **5/2**[1]

1563 **2** *shd* **Live Dangerously**[10] 5023 7-9-4 **55**.................................. KieranO'Neill 5 64
(John Bridger) *chsd ldrs: shkn up over 2f out: sn rdn and prog to chse clr ldr over 1f out: shuffled along ins fnl f: gaining qckly last 50yds: jst hld* **9/2**[2]

1543 **3** *9* **Cyflymder (IRE)**[7] 5145 11-8-9 **49**............................. EdwardGreatrex(3) 4 36
(David C Griffiths) *in rr: rdn along over 3f out: no imp tl styd on fr over 1f out: kpt on to take 3rd nr fin* **6/1**[3]

2540 **4** *nk* **All Or Nothin (IRE)**[7] 5146 8-8-13 **50**............................... DannyBrock 12 36
(Paddy Butler) *disp ld on rail: rdn over 3f out: kpt on one pce and began to weaken ins fnl f: lost 3rd nr fin* **25/1**

2640 **5** *¾* **Kristoff (IRE)**[66] 2961 4-8-6 **46** oh1...........................(p) CharlieBennett(3) 8 30
(Jim Boyle) *chsd ldr: rdn over 3f out: kpt on one pce ins fnl f* **33/1**

0000 **6** *1* **Luduamf (IRE)**[7] 5145 3-8-4 **51**.......................................... HollieDoyle(3) 3 29
(Richard Hannon) *towards rr: rdn 3f out: plugged on fr over 1f out* **7/1**

-040 **7** *½* **Dawn Goddess**[17] 4735 3-8-3 **47**...................................... JimmyQuinn 10 24
(Gary Moore) *chsd ldrs: j. path: rdn over 3f out: sn lost pl and one pce fr over 1f out* **33/1**

0040 **8** *2 ½* **Hurricane Rock**[28] 4350 4-8-13 **55**............................... PaddyBradley(5) 1 29
(Simon Dow) *a in rr: rdn over 3f out: plugged on fr over 1f out* **12/1**

00-6 **9** *2 ½* **Joshlee (IRE)**[37] 4006 3-8-10 **54**.....................................(b[1]) ShaneKelly 2 19
(Richard Hughes) *chsd ldrs on outer: rdn over 3f out: sn wknd* **20/1**

0002 **10** *14* **Tallulah's Quest (IRE)**[12] 4970 3-8-11 **55**.................... AdamBeschizza 7
(Julia Feilden) *mid-div: rdn over 3f out: wknd qckly fr 2f out* **7/1**

00 **11** *4* **Leith Bridge**[12] 4969 5-8-9 **46**................................(v[1]) SilvestreDeSousa 9
(Mark Usher) *chsd ldr on rail: rdn over 3f out: eased fr 2f out* **12/1**

060 **12** *65* **Golden Eye**[31] 4211 3-8-6 **55**........................................ MitchGodwin(5) 11
(Sylvester Kirk) *a in rr: struggling wl over 3f out: t.o* **8/1**

1m 25.22s (1.92) **Going Correction** +0.35s/f (Good)
**WFA** 3 from 4yo+ 7lb **12** Ran SP% **127.0**
Speed ratings (Par 101): **103,102,92,92,91 90,89,86,83,67 63,**
CSF £13.76 CT £64.63 TOTE £3.30: £1.50, £2.10, £2.20; EX 17.30 Trifecta £62.50.
**Owner** Mr & Mrs K Finch **Bred** B Kennedy **Trained** Liphook, Hants

**FOCUS**
Run of the mill low-grade form but the front two, stablemates from John Bridger's yard, pulled a long way clear and remain in good heart. The first two have been rated near their best of recent times.

## 5411 188BET H'CAP 7f
**8:30** (8:31) (Class 5) (0-70,69) 3-Y-O **£2,911** (£866; £432; £216) **Stalls** Centre

Form RPR
4504 **1** **Salt Whistle Bay (IRE)**[21] 4626 3-9-3 **65**................. SilvestreDeSousa 6 76
(Rae Guest) *chsd ldrs: shkn up over 2f out: rdn sn after: kpt on wl and led over 1f out: pushed out ins fnl f: comf* **5/4**[1]

00-0 **2** *1 ½* **Vibes (IRE)**[61] 3163 3-9-7 **69**.......................................... DougieCostello 1 75
(Jamie Osborne) *hld up bhd ldrs and t.k.h: shkn up and tk clsr order over 2f out: rdn 2f out: briefly pressed wnr over 1f out: hld ins fnl f* **20/1**

0303 **3** *3 ¼* **Sixties Habana**[10] 5028 3-8-4 **52**...................................... KieranO'Neill 5 50
(Pat Phelan) *led: shkn up over 3f out and sn rdn: hdd over 1f out: one pce after* **4/1**[2]

2546 **4** *2 ¼* **Kings Heart (IRE)**[10] 5028 3-8-12 **60**.................................(h) ShaneKelly 4 52
(Mark Usher) *chsd ldrs: rdn over 2f out: no ex fr over 1f out* **9/2**[3]

1-00 **5** *1 ¾* **Traveltalk (IRE)**[11] 4999 3-9-3 **65**.....................................(p) BenCurtis 7 52
(Brian Ellison) *a in rr: rdn over 3f out: no imp fr over 2f out* **11/2**

00-6 **6** *1* **Silver Mist**[114] 1580 3-8-2 **50** oh5........................................ JimmyQuinn 3 35
(Sylvester Kirk) *a in rr: rdn over 3f out: sn hld* **20/1**

1300 **7** *¾* **Beepeecee**[10] 5031 3-8-8 **63**.................................(p) StephenCummins(7) 2 46
(Richard Hughes) *chsd ldrs: rdn over 2f out: sn wknd: no ex fr over 1f out* **10/1**

1m 26.11s (2.81) **Going Correction** +0.35s/f (Good) **7** Ran SP% **116.6**
Speed ratings (Par 100): **97,95,91,89,87 85,85**
CSF £31.15 TOTE £2.10: £1.40, £5.30; EX 31.10 Trifecta £112.80.

**Owner** The Hightailers & Rae Guest **Bred** Shortgrove Manor Stud **Trained** Newmarket, Suffolk
**FOCUS**
Not a particularly competitive 0-70 with most of the runners having something to prove on once count or another. The runner-up has been rated back to his debut form.
T/Plt: £8.20 to a £1 stake. Pool: £73,170.38 - 6,457.95 winning units. T/Qpdt: £1.90 to a £1 stake. Pool: £7,341.48 - 2,839.66 winning units. **Cathal Gahan**

# [4353]NEWCASTLE (A.W) (L-H)
Saturday, July 29

**OFFICIAL GOING: Tapeta: standard**
Wind: Breezy; half against on straight course and in over 3f of home straight on round course Weather: Cloudy; bright

## 5412 COLLINGWOOD INSURANCE COMPANY NOVICE AUCTION STKS (PLUS 10 RACE) 7f 14y (Tp)
1:25 (1:26) (Class 4) 2-Y-O £6,469 (£1,925; £962; £481) Stalls Centre

Form RPR
6 1 **Aussie Wind**[29] 4291 2-8-11 0 DavidEgan(5) 6 83+
(Hugo Palmer) *cl up: led over 2f out: sn hrd pressed: hld on gamely ins fnl f* 5/2[2]
5 2 ¾ **Ibn Al Emarat (IRE)**[22] 4560 2-9-2 0 JoeFanning 1 81
(David Simcock) *dwlt: hld up: smooth hdwy on outside and ev ch over 1f out: rdn and edgd lft ins fnl f: one pce last 75yds* 5/1[3]
20 3 nk **Highlight Reel (IRE)**[35] 4068 2-9-2 0 JamieSpencer 8 80
(Michael Bell) *hld up bhd ldng gp: smooth hdwy and disp ld over 1f out: sn rdn: one pce last 100yds* 13/8[1]
4 1¼ **Bungee Jump (IRE)** 2-8-11 0 ConnorBeasley 5 72+
(Kevin Ryan) *missed break: t.k.h in rr: shkn up and hdwy over 1f out: kpt on fnl f: nrst fin* 25/1
43 5 6 **El Chapo**[15] 4848 2-9-2 0 PatrickMathers 2 60
(Richard Fahey) *cl up: faltered and outpcd over 2f out: no imp fr over 1f out* 10/1
61 6 4½ **Byron's Choice**[31] 4205 2-9-8 0 AndrewMullen 3 54
(Michael Dods) *t.k.h: prom: drvn and outpcd over 2f out: n.d after* 5/1[3]
0 7 ½ **La Plusbelle**[19] 4689 2-8-8 0 SammyJoBell(3) 9 42
(Richard Fahey) *hld up in tch: drvn and outpcd over 2f out: sn wknd* 66/1
0 8 1 **El Bertie (IRE)**[70] 2816 2-9-2 0 CamHardie 4 44
(Tim Easterby) *led at stdy pce: rdn and hdd over 2f out: sn wknd* 50/1
1m 30.53s (4.33) **Going Correction** +0.375s/f (Slow) 8 Ran SP% 116.4
Speed ratings (Par 96): **90,89,88,87,80 75,74,73**
CSF £15.59 TOTE £3.30: £1.50, £1.90, £1.10; EX 17.80 Trifecta £40.20.
**Owner** Nick Bradley Racing 43 & Partner **Bred** Lady Juliet Tadgell **Trained** Newmarket, Suffolk
**FOCUS**
A fair novice event run at a steady pace, the tempo increasing from the two-furlong-pole. The third sets a tentative level.

## 5413 COLLINGWOOD CONVICTED DRIVER INSURANCE H'CAP 2m 56y (Tp)
1:55 (1:57) (Class 6) (0-60,62) 4-Y-O+ £3,234 (£962; £481; £240) Stalls Low

Form RPR
0/ 1 **Banff (IRE)**[20] 5048 4-8-11 50 ow3 (p) JamieSpencer 1 56+
(Olly Murphy) *hld up: hdwy and prom 1/2-way: led over 2f out: sn rdn: styd on wl fnl f* 8/11[1]
0465 2 1¼ **Byronegetonefree**[4] 5257 6-8-6 50 RowanScott(5) 5 54
(Stuart Coltherd) *trckd ldrs: drvn and outpcd 2f out: rallied to chse wnr wl ins fnl f: r.o: nt pce to chal* 10/1
2241 3 1¼ **Highway Robber**[45] 3706 4-8-11 53 SammyJoBell(3) 8 56
(Wilf Storey) *mounted on crse and taken early to post: hld up in tch: hdwy and disp ld over 2f out: lost 2nd and one pce ins fnl f* 7/1[2]
0030 4 1½ **Stanarley Pic**[44] 3756 6-9-4 57 JoeFanning 2 58
(Sally Haynes) *t.k.h: led 1f: chsd ldrs: drvn and outpcd 2f out: kpt on same pce ins fnl f* 20/1
545 5 1 **Toast Of London**[26] 4449 4-8-10 49 CamHardie 10 49
(Antony Brittain) *t.k.h: sn cl up: rdn and outpcd over 2f out: no imp fr over 1f out* 33/1
044 6 1½ **Celtic Power**[11] 5008 5-8-3 49 (b[1]) SeanMooney(7) 6 47
(Jim Goldie) *hld up: stdy hdwy over 4f out: drvn and outpcd over 2f out: kpt on fnl f: no imp* 9/1[3]
-005 7 nk **La Bacouetteuse (FR)**[15] 4852 12-9-9 62 (b) AndrewMullen 9 59
(Iain Jardine) *hld up: rdn and outpcd over 2f out: n.d after* 40/1
-060 8 2½ **Python**[10] 5021 5-8-7 46 oh1 PaddyAspell 3 40
(Andrew Crook) *hld up in midfield: drvn and outpcd over 2f out: sn wknd* 100/1
5/00 9 4 **Dizoard**[24] 3706 7-8-0 46 oh1 (h) JamieGormley(7) 11 36
(Iain Jardine) *cl up: led after 1f to over 2f out: rdn and wknd wl over 1f out* 33/1
4366 10 1 **London Glory**[6] 5186 4-9-7 60 (b) PatrickMathers 4 48
(David Thompson) *hld up bhd ldng gp: struggling over 2f out: sn btn* 7/1[2]
046/ P **Dubai Celebrity**[29] 5051 5-9-9 62 ConnorBeasley 7
(Chris Grant) *hld up: drvn along and outpcd whn broke down and p.u wl over 1f out* 25/1
3m 40.36s (5.16) **Going Correction** +0.375s/f (Slow) 11 Ran SP% 119.9
Speed ratings (Par 101): **102,101,100,100,99 98,98,97,95,94**
CSF £8.40 CT £34.69 TOTE £1.60: £1.02, £3.00, £2.10; EX 10.60 Trifecta £36.90.
**Owner** Mary Shalvey & Aiden Murphy **Bred** Highfort Stud **Trained** Wilmcote, Warks
**FOCUS**
A modest staying handicap. The second and third are among those who set the opening level.

## 5414 COLLINGWOOD TAXI INSURANCE / EBFSTALLIONS.COM FILLIES' H'CAP 1m 4f 98y (Tp)
2:30 (2:31) (Class 4) (0-85,83) 4-Y-O+ £8,086 (£2,406; £1,202; £601) Stalls High

Form RPR
4112 1 **Donnachies Girl (IRE)**[12] 4962 4-8-4 66 CamHardie 4 75
(Alistair Whillans) *hld up bhd ldng gp: pushed along over 4f out: drvn and outpcd over 2f out: rallied over 1f out: styd on wl to ld cl home* 8/1
-215 2 shd **Stoney Broke**[15] 4829 4-9-6 82 DanielMuscutt 7 90
(James Fanshawe) *hld up: stdy hdwy 1/2-way: rdn to ld ent fnl f: kpt on: hdd cl home* 7/4[1]
2252 3 1¼ **High On Light**[39] 3933 4-8-6 73 DavidEgan(5) 5 79
(David Barron) *cl up: led over 2f out: edgd rt over 1f out: hdd ent fnl f: kpt on same pce* 6/1[3]
3132 4 hd **Cape Peninsular**[28] 4357 4-9-7 83 AndrewMullen 2 88
(James Tate) *trckd ldrs: effrt and ch over 1f out: kpt on same pce ins fnl f* 3/1[2]
332- 5 3¼ **Bybrook**[276] 7627 4-8-13 75 JamieSpencer 1 75
(David Simcock) *hld up on ins: effrt and drvn along over 2f out: no imp over 1f out* 8/1
4436 6 6 **Marsh Pride**[28] 4364 5-9-1 82 RowanScott(5) 8 72
(K R Burke) *t.k.h: hld up: rdn and outpcd over 2f out: sn btn* 10/1
0313 7 5 **Star Of Lombardy (IRE)**[9] 5065 4-8-13 75 JoeFanning 3 57
(Mark Johnston) *led to over 2f out: sn rdn and wknd* 14/1
2m 40.85s (-0.25) **Going Correction** +0.375s/f (Slow) 7 Ran SP% 113.6
Speed ratings (Par 102): **115,114,114,113,111 107,104**
CSF £22.21 CT £90.98 TOTE £6.00: £2.70, £1.90; EX 29.10 Trifecta £91.60.
**Owner** Mrs Karen Spark **Bred** Darley **Trained** Newmill-On-Slitrig, Borders
**FOCUS**
A decent fillies' handicap and the form looks solid. The third and fourth help set the standard.

## 5415 COLLINGWOOD LEARNER DRIVER INSURANCE "BEESWING" H'CAP 7f 14y (Tp)
3:05 (3:07) (Class 3) (0-95,92) 3-Y-O+ £16,172 (£4,812; £2,405; £1,202) Stalls Centre

Form RPR
3402 1 **Northgate Lad (IRE)**[28] 4353 5-9-7 90 BenRobinson(5) 1 99
(Brian Ellison) *mde all: set ordinary gallop: rdn over 1f out: r.o wl fnl f* 6/1[3]
1140 2 ½ **Horroob**[37] 3997 3-9-0 90 DavidEgan(5) 3 95
(Roger Varian) *trckd ldrs: effrt and pressed wnr over 1f out: drvn and kpt on same pce wl ins fnl f* 7/4[1]
2321 3 1¼ **Horsted Keynes (FR)**[29] 4321 7-10-0 92 JamieSpencer 10 96+
(David Simcock) *hld up and bhd: shkn up and gd hdwy over 1f out: chsd ldrs ins fnl f: kpt on same pce nr fin* 7/1
3520 4 hd **Amood (IRE)**[11] 4999 6-9-3 81 (p) AndrewMullen 5 85
(Simon West) *hld up: stdy hdwy over 2f out: effrt and rdn appr fnl f: one pce last 100yds* 14/1
5026 5 2 **Florencio**[22] 4556 4-9-4 82 (p) ConnorBeasley 13 80
(Roger Fell) *hld up: hdwy and pushed along 2f out: no imp fnl f* 22/1
4464 6 3½ **Town Charter (USA)**[7] 5165 3-8-10 81 JoeFanning 6 67
(Mark Johnston) *hld up in midfield: effrt on outside over 2f out: no imp fr over 1f out: btn fnl f* 12/1
3022 7 1¼ **Harwoods Volante (IRE)**[8] 5093 6-9-3 84 JoshDoyle(3) 11 70
(David O'Meara) *t.k.h: prom: rdn over 2f out: wknd fnl f* 25/1
5022 8 ½ **Strong Steps**[12] 4957 5-9-4 82 PatrickMathers 7 66
(Jim Goldie) *hld up in midfield: drvn and outpcd over 2f out: n.d after* 14/1
-213 9 2¼ **Gilmer (IRE)**[8] 5093 6-8-8 79 (p[1]) JamieGormley(7) 12 57
(James Ewart) *hld up: drvn and struggling over 2f out: sn btn* 33/1
2445 10 1 **Inaam (IRE)**[29] 4304 4-9-0 81 SammyJoBell(3) 4 56
(Richard Fahey) *in tch on outside: struggling over 2f out: wknd wl over 1f out* 16/1
1035 11 ½ **Welliesinthewater (IRE)**[21] 4622 7-9-10 88 (v) CamHardie 8 62
(Derek Shaw) *hld up in tch: rdn over 2f out: wknd over 1f out* 33/1
050 12 1¾ **Gothic Empire (IRE)**[43] 3792 5-9-9 87 DanielMuscutt 2 56
(James Fanshawe) *chsd ldrs: rdn over 2f out: wknd wl over 1f out* 5/1[2]
1m 28.59s (2.39) **Going Correction** +0.375s/f (Slow)
**WFA** 3 from 4yo+ 7lb 12 Ran SP% 120.8
Speed ratings (Par 107): **101,100,99,98,96 92,91,90,87,86 86,84**
CSF £16.44 CT £78.01 TOTE £5.90: £1.80, £1.30, £2.00; EX 17.20 Trifecta £63.50.
**Owner** Mrs J A Martin **Bred** Frank Moynihan **Trained** Norton, N Yorks
**FOCUS**
A valuable AW handicap, albeit not the strongest for the grade. They went an ordinary pace and it paid to race handily, the winner never being headed. The third has been rated close to form.

## 5416 COLLINGWOOD FLEET INSURANCE H'CAP 6f (Tp)
3:40 (3:43) (Class 4) (0-85,85) 3-Y-O £8,086 (£2,406; £1,202; £601) Stalls Centre

Form RPR
1646 1 **Ascot Day (IRE)**[10] 5029 3-9-2 85 GeorgeBuckell(5) 8 96
(David Simcock) *hld up: gd hdwy on nr side of gp over 1f out: led ins fnl f: rdn out* 16/1
0221 2 hd **Boundsy (IRE)**[14] 4892 3-8-11 78 SammyJoBell(3) 3 88
(Richard Fahey) *cl up: led after 2f: rdn and hdd ins fnl f: kpt on: hld nr fin* 11/2
3312 3 2¼ **Trick Of The Light (IRE)**[17] 4732 3-8-11 80 DavidEgan(5) 4 83
(Roger Varian) *prom: effrt and rdn over 1f out: kpt on same pce ins fnl f* 3/1[1]
0310 4 4 **Comprise**[14] 4892 3-9-5 83 JamieSpencer 6 73
(Michael Bell) *cl up: effrt and ev ch over 1f out: rdn and wknd ins fnl f* 10/3[2]
-105 5 1¼ **Tallinski (IRE)**[14] 4892 3-8-9 78 BenRobinson(5) 1 64
(Brian Ellison) *led 2f: cl up: effrt and drvn over 1f out: wknd fnl f* 12/1
0154 6 4 **Harome (IRE)**[15] 4835 3-9-1 79 ConnorBeasley 7 52
(Roger Fell) *t.k.h early: chsd ldrs: drvn along over 2f out: wknd over 1f out* 16/1
0554 7 3½ **Lord Cooper**[17] 4783 3-8-13 77 (tp) JoeFanning 2 39
(Jose Santos) *in tch on far side of gp: rdn over 2f out: wknd over 1f out* 8/1
120 8 ¾ **Archer's Arrow (USA)**[59] 3211 3-8-13 80 (v[1]) JoshDoyle(3) 5 40
(Saeed bin Suroor) *dwlt: hld up: stdy hdwy 1/2-way: rdn and wknd wl over 1f out* 4/1[3]
1m 13.79s (1.29) **Going Correction** +0.375s/f (Slow) 8 Ran SP% 114.0
Speed ratings (Par 102): **106,105,102,97,95 90,85,84**
CSF £100.12 CT £344.36 TOTE £15.30: £3.70, £1.80, £1.30; EX 119.10 Trifecta £709.70.
**Owner** Ahmed Jaber **Bred** Rabbah Bloodstock Limited **Trained** Newmarket, Suffolk
**FOCUS**
A decent 3yo handicap and the front two fought out a close finish. The level is a bit fluid, but the third has been rated to his latest effort.

## 5417 COLLINGWOOD YOUNG DRIVER INSURANCE SILK SERIES LADY RIDERS' H'CAP (PRO-AM LADY RIDERS RACE) 1m 2f 42y (Tp)
4:15 (4:15) (Class 4) (0-80,82) 3-Y-O+ £6,469 (£1,925; £962; £481) Stalls High

Form RPR
6252 1 **Archipeligo**[8] 5097 6-9-12 70 (p) MrsCBartley 11 77
(Iain Jardine) *hld up in midfield: smooth hdwy over 2f out: led over 1f out: drifted rt ins fnl f: kpt on wl* 14/1
0006 2 ½ **Sikandar (IRE)**[12] 4960 5-9-0 63 (tp) MissEllaMcCain(5) 8 70+
(Brian Ellison) *hld up: hdwy over 2f out: effrt and chsng wnr whn carried rt and blkd ins fnl f: no ex nr fin* 50/1
0012 3 ¾ **Royal Reserve**[11] 5002 4-10-2 79 MissCarlyScott(5) 3 86+
(David O'Meara) *hld up: hdwy far rail over 2f out: effrt whn nt clr run and swtchd rt over 1f out: styd on strly fnl f: nt rch first two* 10/1

0530 **4** 1 ½ **Island Flame (IRE)**[22] 4571 4-9-11 **69**............................ SammyJoBell 7 70
(Richard Fahey) *hld up: pushed along 3f out: hdwy over 1f out: kpt on same pce ins fnl f* **10/1**

-124 **5** ½ **Thello**[23] 4538 5-9-7 **70**............................ NicolaCurrie(5) 5 70
(Jo Hughes) *t.k.h: chsd ldrs: hdwy to ld over 2f out: rdn and hdd over 1f out: sn outpcd* **9/1**

3644 **6** 1 **Lac Leman (GER)**[28] 4357 6-9-13 **76**....................(h) MissAMcCain(5) 10 74
(Pauline Robson) *hld up: hdwy on outside over 3f out: effrt and pushed along 2f out: sn outpcd* **9/2**[2]

101 **7** hd **Auspicion**[28] 4358 5-10-2 **74**............................ MissSBrotherton 9 72
(Tom Tate) *hld up: hdwy on outside over 2f out: shkn up over 1f out: sn no imp* **9/4**[1]

364 **8** 2 ½ **Testa Rossa (IRE)**[5] 5207 7-10-5 **82**....................(b) MissRHill(5) 2 75
(Jim Goldie) *in tch: rdn over 2f out: sn outpcd: n.d after* **9/1**

5002 **9** 3 ¼ **Steel Helmet (IRE)**[30] 4263 3-8-7 **60**............................ MissAWaugh 4 47
(Brian Ellison) *hld up in tch: effrt over 2f out: wknd wl over 1f out* **16/1**

2355 **10** 2 ¼ **Duke Of Yorkshire**[16] 4801 7-9-9 **67**....................(p) MissEEasterby 1 49
(Tim Easterby) *led to 1/2-way: cl up tl rdn and wknd fr 2f out* **20/1**

4400 **11** 3 ¾ **Green Light**[28] 4355 6-10-9 **81**....................(b) MissLWilson 6 55
(Brian Ellison) *hld up: drvn and outpcd wl over 2f out: sn btn* **20/1**

13-0 **12** 8 **The Resdev Way**[98] 1976 4-10-6 **78**............................ ShelleyBirkett 12 36
(David O'Meara) *pressed ldr: led and qcknd 1/2-way: hdd over 2f out: sn wknd* **8/1**[3]

2m 13.44s (3.04) **Going Correction** +0.375s/f (Slow)
**WFA** 3 from 4yo+ 9lb **12** Ran SP% **122.3**
Speed ratings (Par 105): **102,101,101,99,99 98,98,96,93,92 89,82**
CSF £598.94 CT £7119.60 TOTE £15.00: £4.10, £14.10, £2.40; EX 819.70 TRIFECTA Not won..
**Owner** Top Of The Hill Racing Club **Bred** Dachel Stud **Trained** Carrutherstown, D'fries & G'way
■ Stewards' Enquiry : Mrs C Bartley two-day ban: careless riding

**FOCUS**
A fair handicap for lady riders and a bit of late drama. The winner has been rated back to his early 2016 form.

## 5418 COLLINGWOOD SHORT TERM LEARNER DRIVER INSURANCE H'CAP (DIV I) 5f (Tp)

**4:50** (4:51) (Class 6) (0-55,57) 3-Y-O+ **£3,234** (£962; £481; £240) **Stalls** Centre

Form RPR

6202 **1** **Ambitious Icarus**[2] 5340 8-9-9 **57**....................(v1) ConnorBeasley 11 66
(Richard Guest) *hld up: shkn up and gd hdwy over 1f out: kpt on wl to ld towards fin* **9/2**[2]

3404 **2** ½ **Nuala Tagula (IRE)**[22] 4559 4-9-3 **56**....................(t) DavidEgan(5) 4 63
(John Quinn) *dwlt: sn in tch: smooth hdwy and wnt between horses to ld over 1f out: sn rdn: kpt on fnl f: hdd and no ex towards fin* **6/1**[3]

-013 **3** 2 ¼ **Camanche Grey (IRE)**[9] 5069 6-8-9 **48**.................. RobJFitzpatrick(5) 5 47
(Ben Haslam) *hld up in tch: effrt and rdn over 1f out: edgd lft and kpt on same pce ins fnl f* **10/1**

5021 **4** ½ **Cool Breeze (IRE)**[10] 5041 3-9-4 **56**............................ JamieSpencer 9 52
(David Simcock) *hld up and bhd: stdy hdwy 2f out: rdn and edgd lft ins fnl f: kpt on same pce* **7/4**[1]

0060 **5** nse **Roman Times (IRE)**[10] 5016 4-8-13 **47**....................(p) PatrickMathers 7 44
(Colin Teague) *chsd ldrs: drvn along over 2f out: kpt on same pce fnl f* **33/1**

5035 **6** nk **Poet's Time**[9] 5069 3-8-9 **47**............................ CamHardie 13 42
(Tim Easterby) *dwlt: bhd: pushed along 1/2-way: hdwy over 1f out: kpt on fnl f: nvr able to chal* **20/1**

300 **7** 3 ¾ **A J Cook (IRE)**[77] 2628 7-8-7 **46**....................(p) RowanScott(5) 10 29
(Ron Barr) *sn pushed along towards rr: kpt on fnl f: nvr able to chal* **25/1**

5300 **8** shd **Three C's (IRE)**[17] 4731 3-8-12 **55**....................(vt1) BenRobinson(5) 2 36
(David Dennis) *midfield: drvn over 2f out: outpcd wl over 1f out* **20/1**

0500 **9** nk **Nefetari**[15] 4847 4-8-5 **46** oh1....................(b) TristanPrice(7) 6 27
(Alan Brown) *pressed ldr to over 1f out: wknd ins fnl f* **50/1**

06 **10** 2 ¼ **Mighty Bond**[7] 5167 5-8-12 **46**............................ JoeFanning 8 19
(Tracy Waggott) *hld up: hung lft thrght: wknd over 1f out: sn eased* **16/1**

0655 **11** 3 **Mercers Row**[3] 5282 10-9-0 **48**............................ AndrewMullen 12 10
(Michael Herrington) *bhd: rdn along over 2f out: sn struggling* **16/1**

2-23 **12** 1 ½ **Luv U Always**[169] 667 3-8-8 **53**....................(p1) JamieGormley(7) 3 9
(Iain Jardine) *led at str gallop: rdn and hdd over 1f out: sn btn: eased fnl f* **13/2**

1m 1.28s (1.78) **Going Correction** +0.375s/f (Slow)
**WFA** 3 from 4yo+ 4lb **12** Ran SP% **121.3**
Speed ratings (Par 101): **100,99,95,94,94 94,88,88,87,84 79,76**
CSF £30.20 CT £267.17 TOTE £5.40: £1.90, £1.60, £2.40; EX 28.80 Trifecta £249.10.
**Owner** ABS Metals & Waste **Bred** L T Roberts **Trained** Ingmanthorpe, W Yorks

**FOCUS**
The first leg of a moderate handicap. The winner has been rated close to this year's best. The winner has been rated close to the best of last year's form.

## 5419 COLLINGWOOD SHORT TERM LEARNER DRIVER INSURANCE H'CAP (DIV II) 5f (Tp)

**5:25** (5:25) (Class 6) (0-55,56) 3-Y-O+ **£3,234** (£962; £481; £240) **Stalls** Centre

Form RPR

6004 **1** **Chip Or Pellet**[11] 5004 4-9-5 **52**............................ JoeFanning 8 58
(Paul Midgley) *trckd ldrs: shkn up to ld over 1f out: edgd lft ins fnl f: kpt on strly* **8/1**

2323 **2** ¾ **Hadley**[11] 5004 4-8-13 **51**....................(p) BenRobinson(5) 2 54
(Tracy Waggott) *w ldr: rdn over 1f out: wnt 2nd ins fnl f: r.o* **5/1**[2]

5300 **3** nk **Mitchum**[14] 4896 8-9-4 **56**....................(p) RowanScott(5) 4 58
(Ron Barr) *led at decent gallop: rdn and hdd over 1f out: rallied: lost 2nd ins fnl f: one pce* **25/1**

-630 **4** 1 ½ **Digital Revolution**[26] 4447 3-9-0 **51**............................ CamHardie 3 47
(Antony Brittain) *prom: drvn along over 2f out: rallied fnl f: kpt on* **25/1**

0653 **5** 1 ¾ **Henrietta's Dream**[29] 4303 3-8-2 **46**....................(b) JamieGormley(7) 6 36
(John Wainwright) *bhd and outpcd: detached 1/2-way: gd hdwy fnl f: kpt on strly* **33/1**

5060 **6** ¾ **Lady Joanna Vassa (IRE)**[16] 4789 4-9-1 **48**............ ConnorBeasley 12 36
(Richard Guest) *in tch: drvn along over 2f out: rallied: one pce fnl f* **11/2**[3]

06-2 **7** nk **Vecheka (IRE)**[58] 3256 6-9-4 **54**....................(t1) JoshDoyle(3) 9 41
(Kenny Johnson) *bhd and sn pushed along: hdwy over 1f out: kpt on: nvr able to chal* **9/1**

6034 **8** ½ **Billy's Boots**[10] 5028 3-9-0 **51**............................ PaddyAspell 5 35
(J R Jenkins) *in tch: lost pl 1/2-way: n.d after* **16/1**

0034 **9** nk **Vaux (IRE)**[36] 4060 3-8-7 **49**............................ RobJFitzpatrick(5) 13 32
(Ben Haslam) *rrd in stalls: bhd: drvn along 1/2-way: wknd over 1f out* **14/1**

0430 **10** 1 **Tinsill**[1] 5377 6-8-7 **45**....................(p) DavidEgan(5) 11 25
(Nigel Tinkler) *bhd and sn pushed along: sme hdwy over 1f out: sn btn* **9/1**

6000 **11** 3 ½ **Young Tiger**[22] 4559 4-9-2 **49**............................ AndrewMullen 1 17
(Tom Tate) *in tch: rdn over 2f out: wknd over 1f out* **5/1**[2]

304 **12** 7 **Maggi May (IRE)**[11] 4997 3-8-13 **50**............................ JamieSpencer 7
(David Brown) *bhd: struggling over 2f out: btn and eased fnl f* **4/1**[1]

1m 1.22s (1.72) **Going Correction** +0.375s/f (Slow)
**WFA** 3 from 4yo+ 4lb **12** Ran SP% **123.0**
Speed ratings (Par 101): **101,99,99,96,94 92,92,91,91,89 83,72**
Not won. Pool of £916.58 carried forward. CSF £48.67 CT £997.04 TOTE £9.70: £3.00, £1.90, £7.70; EX 68.80 Trifecta £1347.90.
**Owner** S Duncan **Bred** L T Roberts **Trained** Westow, N Yorks

**FOCUS**
The second division of a moderate handicap looked stronger than first division. The winner has been rated to his pre-race best.
T/Plt: £53.80 to a £1 stake. Pool: £71,210.17 - 966.16 winning units T/Qpdt: £23.50 to a £1 stake. Pool: £3,970.99 - 124.58 winning units **Richard Young**

# 5363 NEWMARKET (R-H)

Saturday, July 29

**OFFICIAL GOING: Good to soft (7.1)**
Wind: light, across Weather: light cloud, light rain races 6 and 7

## 5420 ADNAMS SOUTHWOLD BITTER EBF STALLIONS NOVICE STKS (PLUS 10 RACE) 7f

**2:15** (2:16) (Class 4) 2-Y-O **£4,528** (£1,347; £673; £336) **Stalls** High

Form RPR

63 **1** **Anna Nerium**[16] 4815 2-8-11 0............................ TomMarquand 1 78
(Richard Hannon) *wnt rt s: sn w ldrs: rdn and ev ch 2f out: led over 1f out: forged ahd ins fnl f: hrd pressed towards fin: jst hld on* **6/1**[3]

**2** nse **Al Hajar (IRE)** 2-9-2 0............................ MartinLane 4 83+
(Charlie Appleby) *hld up wl in tch in midfield: hdwy to press ldrs whn rn green and flashed tail u.p over 1f out: hung lft 1f out: rallied ins fnl f to chse wnr wl ins fnl f: styd on strly: jst failed* **1/1**[1]

**3** 1 ¾ **Jawwaal** 2-9-2 0............................ DaneO'Neill 2 78+
(John Gosden) *s.i.s: sn rcvrd and hld up wl in tch: effrt to chal wl over 1f out: sn drvn: no ex ins fnl f: wknd towards fin* **8/1**

0 **4** ½ **Game Player (IRE)**[64] 3037 2-9-2 0............................ AndreaAtzeni 5 77
(Roger Varian) *led and set stdy gallop: rdn 2f out: hdd over 1f out: no ex u.p ins fnl f: outpcd fnl 150yds* **3/1**[2]

**5** 1 ½ **I'm A Star (IRE)** 2-9-2 0............................ AdamBeschizza 8 73
(Stuart Williams) *stdd s: hld up in tch in rr: pushed along over 1f out: hdwy ins fnl f: kpt on wl fnl 100yds: nvr trbld ldrs* **66/1**

4 **6** nk **Groveman**[14] 4909 2-9-2 0............................ TomQueally 7 72
(Charles Hills) *hld up wl in tch in midfield: effrt 2f out: switching rt and nt clrest of runs over 1f out: rdn and kpt on same pce ins fnl f* **12/1**

**7** ¾ **Wilson (IRE)** 2-8-9 0............................ GabrieleMalune(7) 3 70
(Luca Cumani) *wnt rt and rn green leaving stalls: sn pressing ldr: rdn 2f out: unable qck and outpcd over 1f out: wknd ins fnl f* **40/1**

**8** 2 **Slipstream (IRE)** 2-9-2 0............................ HarryBentley 6 65
(George Scott) *hld up wl in tch in midfield: rdn and unable qck over 1f out: lost pl and bhd 1f out: wknd ins fnl f* **16/1**

1m 30.52s (4.82) **Going Correction** +0.375s/f (Good) **8** Ran SP% **117.9**
Speed ratings (Par 96): **87,86,84,84,82 82,81,79**
CSF £12.84 TOTE £7.20: £1.80, £1.10, £2.20; EX 16.60 Trifecta £63.10.
**Owner** Exors Of The Late R J McCreery **Bred** Stowell Hill Ltd **Trained** East Everleigh, Wilts

**FOCUS**
Stands' side course. Stalls: far side, except 1m2f: centre. A fair juvenile novice contest. They went an initially modest gallop on good to soft ground. The winner has been rated to her latest run.

## 5421 ADNAMS BROADSIDE H'CAP 1m 2f

**2:50** (2:50) (Class 3) (0-95,94) 3-Y-O+ **£9,056** (£2,695; £1,346; £673) **Stalls** Centre

Form RPR

-042 **1** **Anythingtoday (IRE)**[26] 4443 3-8-11 **86**....................(p1) JosephineGordon 5 95
(Hugo Palmer) *hld up in tch in last trio: effrt over 1f out: hdwy to chse ldrs 1f out: styd on u.p to ld wl ins fnl f: rdn out* **4/1**[2]

-005 **2** ½ **Pacify**[22] 4585 5-10-0 **94**............................ HarryBentley 6 101
(Ralph Beckett) *hld up in tch in midfield: swtchd lft and effrt wl over 1f out: drvn to chal 1f out: kpt on wl u.p ins fnl f* **4/1**[2]

-440 **3** nk **Dark Red (IRE)**[14] 4918 5-9-12 **92**............................ AntonioFresu 1 98
(Ed Dunlop) *chsd ldrs: effrt to ld 2f out: drvn and edgd lft over 1f out: kpt on wl u.p tl hdd and no ex wl ins fnl f* **9/1**

-110 **4** 1 ½ **Toulson**[21] 4614 4-9-10 **90**............................ CharlesBishop 8 93
(Eve Johnson Houghton) *chsd ldr: effrt over 2f out: sn chalng tl unable qck and outpcd jst over 1f out: rallied and styd on again fnl 100yds* **10/3**[1]

-246 **5** hd **Ay Ay (IRE)**[112] 1621 3-9-0 **89**............................ DaneO'Neill 7 92
(David Elsworth) *hld up in tch in last trio: swtchd lft and effrt wl over 1f out: drvn to chse ldrs 1f out: kpt on same pce ins fnl f* **16/1**

6035 **6** ¾ **Great Hall**[10] 5037 7-10-0 **94**............................ TomQueally 9 95
(Mick Quinn) *wl in tch in midfield: clsd and ev ch whn rdn 2f out: edgd lft and unable qck ent fnl f: hld and kpt on same pce ins fnl f* **20/1**

2-40 **7** ¾ **Awake My Soul (IRE)**[49] 3597 8-9-11 **91**............................ TomEaves 3 91
(Tom Tate) *led: rdn and hdd 2f out: unable qck and lost pl jst over 1f out: hld and kpt on same pce ins fnl f* **10/1**

64 **8** 4 ½ **Storm Rock**[31] 4223 5-9-8 **88**............................ MartinHarley 10 82
(Harry Dunlop) *t.k.h: hld up in tch in midfield: clsd to chal 2f out: struggling to qckn and jst getting outpcd whn squeezed for room 1f out: nt rcvr and wknd ins fnl f* **16/1**

5412 **9** 1 **Tyrsal (IRE)**[2] 5336 6-8-9 **75** oh11............................ JimmyQuinn 2 64
(Clifford Lines) *stdd s: hld up in tch in last trio: effrt 2f out: rdn and no imp over 1f out: wknd ins fnl f* **50/1**

1-62 **10** 9 **St Malo (USA)**[17] 4751 4-9-1 **81**....................(v1) AndreaAtzeni 4 52
(Roger Varian) *in tch in midfield: rdn 2f out: sn outpcd and dropped to rr: bhd ins fnl f* **11/2**[3]

2m 8.69s (3.19) **Going Correction** +0.375s/f (Good)
**WFA** 3 from 4yo+ 9lb **10** Ran SP% **116.0**
Speed ratings (Par 107): **102,101,101,100,100 99,98,95,94,87**
CSF £20.31 CT £135.53 TOTE £4.50: £1.60, £1.70, £2.70; EX 22.10 Trifecta £122.50.
**Owner** MPH Racing - II **Bred** T Whitehead **Trained** Newmarket, Suffolk

**FOCUS**
A good handicap. They went a respectable gallop and the joint second-favourites came to the fore. The level is a bit fluid.

## 5422 ADNAMS GHOST SHIP FILLIES' H'CAP 7f
**3:25** (3:25) (Class 2) (0-100,94) 3-Y-O+ **£12,938** (£3,850; £1,924; £962) **Stalls** High

Form RPR
3131 1 **Inshiraah (FR)**[14] 4903 3-8-13 **86** HarryBentley 7 101
(George Peckham) *hld up wl in tch: effrt and qcknd to ld over 1f out: sn rdn and wl clr ins fnl f: r.o strly: readily* **9/4**[2]
1310 2 4 ½ **Cartographer**[16] 4813 3-9-5 **92** JosephineGordon 4 95
(Martyn Meade) *t.k.h: pressed ldr: rdn and ev ch 2f out tl unable qck w wnr ent fnl f: chsd clr wnr and styd on same pce fnl 150yds* **9/2**[3]
0-04 3 ½ **Marie Of Lyon**[14] 4903 3-8-10 **83** JackGarritty 6 85
(Richard Fahey) *led: rdn and hdd over 1f out: unable qck w wnr ent fnl f: wl hld 3rd and kpt on same pce fnl 100yds* **7/1**
5-00 4 1 ¼ **Breakable**[14] 4890 6-9-13 **93** TomQueally 1 95
(Tim Easterby) *pressed ldng pair: rdn 2f out: outpcd u.p over 1f out: wl hld 4th and plugged on same pce ins fnl f* **25/1**
3636 5 1 ¾ **Yeah Baby Yeah (IRE)**[14] 4883 4-9-3 **83** TomEaves 5 80
(Gay Kelleway) *stdd s: hld up in rr: effrt 2f out: no imp over 1f out: nvr trbld ldrs* **33/1**
-011 6 ½ **Excellent Sounds**[21] 4617 4-9-1 **84** CharlieBennett(3) 2 80
(Hughie Morrison) *hld up wl in tch: clsd to trck ldrs 3f out: unable qck over 1f out: wknd ins fnl f* **9/1**
1202 7 9 **Gymnaste (IRE)**[14] 4903 3-9-7 **94** AndreaAtzeni 3 72
(John Gosden) *stdd s: t.k.h: hld up in tch: effrt 2f out: no imp u.p over 1f out: wknd fnl f* **15/8**[1]

1m 26.56s (0.86) **Going Correction** +0.375s/f (Good)
**WFA** 3 from 4yo+ 7lb **7** Ran SP% **113.0**
Speed ratings (Par 96): **110,104,104,102,100 100,90**
CSF £12.53 TOTE £3.10: £1.70, £2.50; EX 13.00 Trifecta £72.40.
**Owner** Fawzi Abdulla Nass **Bred** Jean-Philippe Dubois **Trained** Newmarket, Suffolk

**FOCUS**
A good fillies' handicap. They went a respectable gallop and it is sound form. The runner-up has been rated a bit off her penultimate 6f win here.

## 5423 ADNAMS SOLE STAR H'CAP 6f
**4:00** (4:01) (Class 2) (0-105,105) 3-Y-O
**£28,012** (£8,388; £4,194; £2,097; £1,048; £526) **Stalls** High

Form RPR
4233 1 **The Feathered Nest (IRE)**[26] 4435 3-7-11 **84** oh1..(p1) AaronJones(3) 3 92
(Richard Fahey) *hld up in tch in rr of main gp: swtchd rt and hdwy over 1f out: str run u.p ins fnl f to ld last strides* **14/1**
1223 2 nk **Scorching Heat**[36] 4037 3-8-0 **84** JimmyQuinn 14 91
(Andrew Balding) *pressed ldrs: rdn and ev ch over 1f out: drvn to ld ent fnl f: kpt on wl u.p ins fnl f: hdd last strides* **5/1**[1]
1305 3 nse **Bacchus**[16] 4813 3-9-1 **99** (p) TomQueally 1 106
(Brian Meehan) *hld up in tch towards rr of main gp: rdn and hdwy 2f out: chal and hung lft ent fnl f: kpt on u.p ins fnl f* **14/1**
12-3 4 nk **Nobly Born**[27] 4407 3-8-13 **97** AndreaAtzeni 9 103
(John Gosden) *in tch in midfield: ev ch and rdn 2f out: drvn jst over 1f out: kpt on u.p ins fnl f* **5/1**[1]
201 5 1 ¾ **Eqtiraan (IRE)**[41] 3867 3-9-7 **105** DaneO'Neill 7 105
(Richard Hannon) *hld up in tch: effrt 2f out: hdwy u.p over 1f out: kpt on same pce u.p ins fnl f* **16/1**
-634 6 ½ **Hyperfocus (IRE)**[15] 4830 3-8-2 **86** JosephineGordon 13 85
(Hugo Palmer) *taken down early: t.k.h: hld up in tch in midfield: effrt 2f out: drvn and chsd ldrs 1f out: kpt on same pce ins fnl f* **12/1**[3]
4000 7 ½ **Private Matter**[16] 4813 3-8-12 **96** JackGarritty 8 93+
(Richard Fahey) *chsd ldr: ev ch 2f out: stl ev ch whn pushed lft and hmpd jst over 1f out: kpt on same pce ins fnl f* **25/1**
-100 8 nk **Danielsflyer (IRE)**[16] 4813 3-9-2 **100** BenCurtis 2 96+
(David Barron) *hld up in tch: effrt whn pushed lft and hmpd over 1f out: kpt on ins fnl f: nvr getting on terms w ldrs* **25/1**
3114 9 shd **Golden Apollo**[16] 4813 3-8-11 **95** TomMarquand 12 91
(Tim Easterby) *t.k.h: hld up in tch in midfield: effrt 2f out: drvn and no imp 1f out: kpt on same pce ins fnl f: nvr trbld ldrs* **5/1**[1]
1211 10 ½ **Hart Stopper**[10] 5035 3-8-0 **84** DannyBrock 11 78
(Michael Bell) *hld up in tch in midfield: effrt over 1f out: sn drvn and no imp 1f out: no imp fnl f: nvr trbld ldrs* **10/1**[2]
1000 11 1 ½ **Rich And Famous (USA)**[8] 5094 3-8-6 **90** HarryBentley 6 80
(Mark Johnston) *led: rdn 2f out: hdd whn pushed lft and bdly hmpd jst over 1f out: nt rcvr and no ch after* **16/1**
214- 12 nk **Waqaas**[366] 4798 3-8-12 **96** MartinHarley 5 85
(Charles Hills) *t.k.h: hld up in tch in midfield: effrt over 1f out: no imp whn nt clr run and hmpd jst over 1f out: no ch after* **33/1**
6-32 13 shd **Tommy Taylor (USA)**[16] 4813 3-9-2 **100** TomEaves 4 88
(Kevin Ryan) *hld up in tch towards rr of main gp: effrt wl over 1f out: hdwy whn squeezed for room and bdly hmpd jst over 1f out: nt rcvr and no ch after* **5/1**[1]
0100 14 4 **Smokey Lane (IRE)**[28] 4334 3-9-0 **98** MartinLane 10 73
(Christian Williams) *rrd as stalls: ducked lft and unruly leaving stall: v.s.a: n.d* **50/1**

1m 13.72s (1.22) **Going Correction** +0.375s/f (Good) **14** Ran SP% **121.1**
Speed ratings (Par 106): **106,105,105,105,102 102,101,101,100,100 98,97,97,92**
CSF £80.42 CT £1050.56 TOTE £15.50: £3.80, £1.90, £4.10; EX 94.60 Trifecta £1708.40.
**Owner** R A Fahey **Bred** Airlie Stud **Trained** Musley Bank, N Yorks
■ Stewards' Enquiry : Tom Queally seven-day ban: careless riding (Aug 12-18)

**FOCUS**
The feature contest was a good quality 3yo sprint handicap. They seemed to go fast enough given the conditions in quite a rough race and a horse from well off the pace narrowly landed the spoils in a thrilling four-way go.

## 5424 ADNAMS MOSAIC EBF STALLIONS CONDITIONS STKS (PLUS 10 RACE) 6f
**4:30** (4:30) (Class 3) 2-Y-O **£9,056** (£2,695; £1,346) **Stalls** High

Form RPR
2010 1 **Hey Gaman**[16] 4812 2-9-3 89 MartinHarley 2 104
(James Tate) *mde all: rdn 2f out: asserted over 1f out and in command whn edgd lft ins fnl f: eased towards fin* **3/1**[2]
122 2 5 **Roussel (IRE)**[22] 4582 2-9-3 102 MartinLane 3 89
(Charlie Appleby) *hld up in tch in 3rd: effrt 2f out: rdn and chsd wnr over 1f out: no imp: wl hld and kpt on same pce ins fnl f* **8/15**[1]
6101 3 5 **Billy Dylan (IRE)**[28] 4335 2-9-5 89 TomMarquand 1 76
(Richard Hannon) *trckd wnr: rdn 2f out: dropped to 3rd and btn over 1f out: wknd ins fnl f* **9/2**[3]

1m 13.59s (1.09) **Going Correction** +0.375s/f (Good) **3** Ran SP% **108.4**
Speed ratings (Par 98): **107,100,93**
CSF £5.24 TOTE £4.40; EX 7.50 Trifecta £6.10.
**Owner** Sultan Ali **Bred** Rabbah Bloodstock Limited **Trained** Newmarket, Suffolk

**FOCUS**
A good quality little juvenile conditions contest won in 2010 by high-class miler Excelebration. They went a respectable gallop given the small field and easy underfoot conditions. The runner-up and third appeared to run below their best.

## 5425 ADNAMS INNOVATION H'CAP 1m
**5:05** (5:07) (Class 3) (0-90,89) 3-Y-O+ **£7,762** (£2,310; £1,154; £577) **Stalls** High

Form RPR
6212 1 **Pillar Of Society (IRE)**[24] 4491 3-9-3 **86** TomMarquand 6 93
(Richard Hannon) *mde all and sn wl clr: rdn ent fnl f: drvn ins fnl f: tiring fnl 100yds but a jst gng to last home: all out* **7/2**[2]
1 2 ½ **Don't Give Up**[52] 3456 3-9-6 **89** MartinLane 4 95+
(Saeed bin Suroor) *hld up in 4th: effrt in 3rd wl over 2f out: drvn over 1f out: chsd wnr ins fnl f: styd on u.p but nvr quite getting to wnr* **7/4**[1]
-212 3 hd **To Dibba**[29] 4322 3-9-1 **84** AndreaAtzeni 1 89+
(Roger Varian) *racd off the pce in 3rd: chsd clr wnr over 2f out: sn rdn: 3rd and styd on u.p ins fnl f: nvr quite getting to wnr* **7/4**[1]
4502 4 1 ¾ **Brilliant Vanguard (IRE)**[15] 4832 4-9-3 **78** (p) TomEaves 3 81
(Kevin Ryan) *stdd s: hld up off the pce in rr: effrt in 4th 2f out: drvn ent fnl f: styd on and swtchd rt towards fin: nvr getting on terms w wnr* **16/1**[3]
3611 5 17 **Showboating (IRE)**[31] 4210 9-9-10 **85** MartinHarley 2 49
(John Balding) *t.k.h: hld up off the pce in 5th: effrt ent fnl 2f: sn outpcd and wknd over 1f out* **16/1**[3]
-464 6 5 **White Tower (IRE)**[9] 5066 3-8-8 **77** HarryBentley 5 28
(Mark Johnston) *chsd clr wnr: rdn 3f out: lost pl over 2f out and sn bhd: wknd over 1f out* **20/1**

1m 41.25s (1.25) **Going Correction** +0.375s/f (Good)
**WFA** 3 from 4yo+ 8lb **6** Ran SP% **111.5**
Speed ratings (Par 107): **108,107,107,105,88 83**
CSF £9.93 TOTE £4.40: £1.80, £1.80; EX 12.80 Trifecta £31.40.
**Owner** Mrs J Wood **Bred** Jas Linnane, J Moore & B Gardiner **Trained** East Everleigh, Wilts

**FOCUS**
A decent handicap. It was a proper test at the trip under the conditions.

## 5426 ADNAMS EAST COAST VODKA H'CAP 5f
**5:40** (5:40) (Class 4) (0-85,87) 3-Y-O+ **£5,175** (£1,540; £769; £384) **Stalls** High

Form RPR
220 1 **Compas Scoobie**[16] 4816 4-9-5 **83** (v1) AndreaAtzeni 1 91+
(Roger Varian) *stdd s: hld up in tch in last pair: pushed along and clsd to press ldrs ent fnl f: edgd lft u.p but drvn to ld 100yds out: styd on and a doing enough after* **4/1**[2]
5105 2 nk **Diamond Lady**[10] 5035 6-9-4 **82** AdamBeschizza 3 89
(William Stone) *in tch in last pair: rdn and hdwy to chse ldrs whn nt clrest of runs jst over 1f out: rdn to ld ins fnl f: styd on u.p but a jst hld after* **10/1**
0120 3 1 ¾ **Major Pusey**[15] 4830 5-9-6 **84** JosephineGordon 4 85
(John Gallagher) *chsd ldrs: rdn ent fnl 2f: drvn over 1f out: styd on same pce ins fnl f* **5/2**[1]
62-0 4 ¾ **Apricot Sky**[28] 4379 7-9-2 **80** BenCurtis 8 78
(Brian Ellison) *hld up in tch in midfield: effrt to press ldrs over 1f out: drvn to ld 1f out: sn hdd and no ex: wknd wl ins fnl f* **8/1**
3506 5 ½ **Oh So Sassy**[16] 4816 7-9-9 **87** HarryBentley 2 83
(Chris Wall) *hld up in tch in midfield: effrt u.p to chse ldrs jst over 1f out: no ex and wknd wl ins fnl f* **4/1**[2]
4126 6 2 **Zac Brown (IRE)**[22] 4581 6-9-1 **82** (t) CharlieBennett(3) 7 71
(Charlie Wallis) *w ldr: rdn to ld over 1f out: hdd and no ex 1f out: sn wknd* **8/1**
140 7 ½ **Elysian Flyer (IRE)**[27] 4416 5-9-4 **82** TomQueally 6 69
(Paul Midgley) *led tl rdn and hdd over 1f out: sn lost pl: wknd ins fnl f* **11/2**[3]

1m 0.25s (1.15) **Going Correction** +0.375s/f (Good) **7** Ran SP% **115.3**
Speed ratings (Par 105): **105,104,101,100,99 96,95**
CSF £42.56 CT £118.91 TOTE £4.40: £2.40, £5.50; EX 42.90 Trifecta £222.70.
**Owner** Michael Hill **Bred** Aston Mullins Stud **Trained** Newmarket, Suffolk

**FOCUS**
A decent sprint handicap. They went a contested pace and a confirmed hold-up horse got on top in the closing stages. The runner-up has been rated to her old best.
T/Plt: £244.90 to a £1 stake. Pool: £67,778.21 - 201.96 winning units. T/Qpdt: £103.20 to a £1 stake. Pool: £3,163.55 - 22.67 winning units. **Steve Payne**

# 4909 SALISBURY (R-H)
Saturday, July 29

**OFFICIAL GOING: Soft (good to soft in places)**
Wind: almost nil Weather: heavy rain

## 5427 PARTY CONTINUES AT THE CHAPEL NIGHTCLUB "CARNARVON" H'CAP (FOR GENTLEMAN AMATEUR RIDERS) 1m
**5:15** (5:18) (Class 5) (0-70,69) 3-Y-O+ **£3,275** (£1,015; £507; £254) **Stalls** Low

Form RPR
0400 1 **Pretty Jewel**[16] 4804 4-9-13 **54** DrMVoikhansky(7) 1 64
(Kevin Frost) *s.i.s: detached in last: hdwy whn swtchd lft fr over 3f out: led over 1f out: sn in command: styd on wl* **25/1**
-531 2 2 ½ **Hawridge Glory (IRE)**[16] 4804 3-10-6 **62** MrPMillman 9 64
(Rod Millman) *trckd ldrs: led wl over 2f out: hdd over 1f out: sn rdn and hld: styd on same pce* **2/1**[1]
3500 3 2 **McDelta**[17] 4747 7-10-2 **57** MrMSJohnson(7) 3 57
(Geoffrey Deacon) *chsd ldrs: rdn wl over 2f out: chsng ldng pair whn edgd lft jst over 1f out: kpt on same pce* **10/1**
6105 4 ½ **Berkeley Vale**[16] 4802 6-11-3 **65** (p) MrHHunt 8 64
(Roger Teal) *hld up in last pair: struggling 4f out: plenty to do and no imp: stl in last pair 2f out: kpt on wl fnl f: nvr threatened ldrs* **8/1**
5006 5 1 ¾ **Edge (IRE)**[12] 4968 6-10-2 **50** (b) MrJordanWilliams 2 44
(Bernard Llewellyn) *mid-div: rdn wl over 2f out: sn one pce* **14/1**
0-60 6 hd **Wordismybond**[16] 4804 8-10-13 **66** MrJamiePerrett(5) 10 60
(Brendan Powell) *awkward leaving stalls: mid-div: rdn over 2f out: sn one pce* **25/1**

2360 **7** ½ **Essenaitch (IRE)**[19] 4699 4-11-1 **68**.................................... MrJFlook(5) 5 61
(David Evans) *prom nrest far side: led 4f out tl wl over 2f out: wknd ent fnl f* **4/1**[3]

-020 **8** 2¾ **Pink Ribbon (IRE)**[44] 3753 5-11-7 **69**.......................(p) MrAlexFerguson 6 56
(Sylvester Kirk) *led for 4f: chsd ldrs tl wknd over 1f out* **12/1**

**9** 22 **Born On The Clyde (IRE)**[99] 1955 3-9-12 **54** ow2............ MrSWalker 7
(John Patrick Shanahan, Ire) *s.i.s: sn in tch: struggling 4f out: sn btn: t.o* **7/2**[2]

1m 48.48s (4.98) **Going Correction** +0.575s/f (Yiel)
**WFA** 3 from 4yo+ 8lb **9** Ran SP% **117.8**
Speed ratings (Par 103): **98,95,93,93,91 91,90,87,65**
CSF £76.82 CT £561.45 TOTE £26.80: £5.60, £1.70, £2.90; EX 121.70 Trifecta £1423.50.
**Owner** Dr Misha Voikhansky **Bred** Highland Thoroughbred Ltd **Trained** Market Drayton, Shropshire
■ Stewards' Enquiry : Mr Jordan Williams two-day ban: excessive use of whip (Aug 13,15)

**FOCUS**
Rain earlier in the afternoon had eased the ground to Good to Soft (soft in places). A modest field for this amateur riders' handicap and a surprise result. The winner has been rated back to her best, with the runner-up to his latest.

## 5428 BHQMS LTD 20TH ANNIVERSARY MAIDEN STKS 1m 1f 201y
**5:45** (5:48) (Class 5) 3-Y-O+ **£3,881** (£1,155; £577; £288) **Stalls** Low

Form RPR

23 **1** **Torcello (IRE)**[25] 4474 3-9-5 0.......................................... RobHornby 13 82
(Andrew Balding) *trckd ldrs: led over 1f out: styd on wl: rdn out* **5/2**[2]

0 **2** 1 **Star Story**[297] 7074 3-8-9 0.................................. PatrickO'Donnell(5) 8 75
(Ralph Beckett) *mid-div: hdwy 5f out: rdn 3f out: chsd wnr over 1f out: kpt on ins fnl f: hld towards fin* **11/1**

44 **3** 1¼ **Persistence (IRE)**[65] 3007 3-9-0 0...................................... SeanLevey 1 73+
(Ralph Beckett) *led for 2f: travelled strly: nt clr run whn swtchd rt over 1f out: sn rdn: styd on to go 3rd towards fin but nt pce to get on terms* **5/1**[3]

3 **4** ½ **Saroog**[16] 4808 3-9-5 0....................................................... MartinDwyer 7 76
(Simon Crisford) *trckd ldrs: led over 3f out: rdn and hdd over 1f out: sn one pce* **2/1**[1]

**5** 1½ **Ancient Longing** 3-9-0 0......................................... KieranShoemark 11 68
(Roger Charlton) *s.i.s: towards rr: stdy prog fr over 3f out: styd on fnl f but nt pce to get on terms* **5/1**[3]

5 **6** 9 **Monar Lad (IRE)**[7] 5141 5-10-0 0................................ TimmyMurphy 10 54
(Dai Burchell) *mid-div: hdwy 4f out: effrt 3f out: wknd over 1f out* **150/1**

0 **7** 4½ **Koubba (IRE)**[10] 5022 4-9-4 0....................................(t) LucyKBarry(5) 14 40
(Neil Mulholland) *hld up towards rr: rdn over 3f out: nvr any imp on ldrs* **50/1**

4 **8** 25 **Pequeninha**[48] 3626 3-9-0 0.......................................... StevieDonohoe 4
(David Simcock) *mid-dvision: rdn 3f out: sn wknd* **14/1**

6 **9** ½ **Royal Hall (FR)**[7] 5141 5-9-11 0.................................(p[1]) NoelGarbutt(3) 9
(Gary Moore) *mid-div: struggling 4f out: wknd 3f out* **50/1**

0 **10** hd **Breeze Up**[16] 4808 3-9-2 0....................................... CallumShepherd(3) 3
(Ed de Giles) *mid-div tl hung bdly rt over 3f out: sn bhd* **50/1**

**11** nk **Bubbles Arcade**[22] 5-9-9 0............................................. WilliamCarson 2
(Rod Millman) *led tl jst over 3f out: wknd over 2f out* **20/1**

**12** 44 **What A Welcome** 3-9-5 0.................................................. JoeyHaynes 12
(Eric Wheeler) *a towards rr: bhd fnl 3f* **100/1**

2m 12.7s (2.80) **Going Correction** +0.575s/f (Yiel)
**WFA** 3 from 4yo+ 9lb **12** Ran SP% **122.5**
Speed ratings (Par 103): **111,110,109,108,107 100,96,76,76,76 76,40**
CSF £30.09 TOTE £3.40: £1.80, £3.80, £2.30; EX 37.70 Trifecta £170.40.
**Owner** Mick and Janice Mariscotti **Bred** Rathasker Stud **Trained** Kingsclere, Hants

**FOCUS**
Apart from a pair of hurdlers and a bumper winner, a field of mainly inexperienced sorts in this maiden. They again came up the stands' side in the straight. The winner has been rated back to his debut form, with the third and fourth close to form.

## 5429 GEORGE SMITH HORSEBOXES H'CAP 5f
**6:15** (6:18) (Class 6) (0-65,65) 3-Y-O+ **£3,234** (£962; £481; £240) **Stalls** Low

Form RPR

422 **1** **Our Lord**[23] 4532 5-9-8 **61**.................................................... RobHornby 8 74
(Michael Attwater) *trckd ldr: led over 1f out: r.o strly: rdn out* **4/1**[2]

222 **2** 3 **Tidal's Baby**[54] 3397 8-9-6 **59**....................................... GeorgeDowning 9 61
(Tony Carroll) *mid-div: rdn and hdwy jst over 1f out: kpt on to chse wnr fnl 100yds but nvr threatened to get on terms* **8/1**

-060 **3** 1¼ **John Joiner**[28] 4352 5-9-4 **57**.......................................... CharlesBishop 5 55
(Peter Hedger) *mid-div: hdwy over 3f out: rdn to chse wnr over 1f out: nt pce to mount chal: no ex whn lost 2nd fnl 100yds* **11/1**

0000 **4** 1 **Bushwise (IRE)**[44] 3758 4-8-9 **48**................................(p) MartinDwyer 10 42
(Milton Bradley) *towards rr of midfield: rdn 2f out: no imp tl kpt on ins fnl f: snatched 4th fnl stride* **20/1**

-520 **5** nse **Incentive**[50] 3536 3-9-6 **63**.........................................(p[1]) KieranShoemark 4 56
(Stuart Kittow) *trckd ldrs: hrd rdn 2f out: kpt on same pce* **14/1**

0205 **6** 1 **Flying Sakhee**[42] 3823 4-8-13 **52**................................ WilliamCarson 12 42
(John Bridger) *trckd ldrs: rdn over 2f out: sn one pce* **16/1**

5434 **7** ½ **Pride Of Angels**[28] 4368 4-9-12 **65**.................................... JimCrowley 3 53
(Gary Moore) *hld up towards rr: rdn over 1f out: little imp* **7/1**[3]

2323 **8** ¾ **Captain Ryan**[17] 4731 6-9-9 **62**...................................... TimmyMurphy 2 48
(Geoffrey Deacon) *travelled wl in tch: wnt 3rd over 1f out: sn rdn: wknd fnl 140yds* **9/1**

0000 **9** nse **The Perfect Show**[9] 5050 4-8-0 **46** oh1...........(v[1]) KatherineGlenister(7) 6 31
(Milton Bradley) *s.i.s: towards rr of midfield: effrt over 2f out: nvr threatened ldrs* **50/1**

11 **10** 2½ **Wee Jock (IRE)**[25] 4479 3-9-0 **57**.............................. RoystonFfrench 13 32
(John Patrick Shanahan, Ire) *propped leaving stalls: led: rdn and hdd over 1f out: sn wknd* **3/1**[1]

1640 **11** 1¾ **Who Told Jo Jo (IRE)**[22] 4576 3-9-8 **65**........................ OisinMurphy 1 34
(Joseph Tuite) *a towards rr* **10/1**

1m 3.24s (2.24) **Going Correction** +0.575s/f (Yiel)
**WFA** 3 from 4yo+ 4lb **11** Ran SP% **115.3**
Speed ratings (Par 101): **105,100,98,96,96 94,94,92,92,88 86**
CSF £33.91 CT £285.25 TOTE £4.20: £1.30, £2.40, £3.10; EX 37.20 Trifecta £307.50.
**Owner** Mrs M S Teversham **Bred** Mrs Monica Teversham **Trained** Epsom, Surrey
■ Kings Academy was withdrawn. Price at time of withdrawal 14-1. Rule 4 applies to all bets. Deduction - 5p in the pound.

**FOCUS**
A low-grade sprint handicap but a clear-cut winner. The runner-up helps set the level.

## 5430 BATHWICK TYRES EBF MAIDEN STKS (PLUS 10 RACE) 6f
**6:45** (6:46) (Class 4) 2-Y-O **£4,043** (£1,203; £601; £300) **Stalls** Low

Form RPR

45 **1** **Fighting Irish (IRE)**[15] 4826 2-9-5 0............................ StevieDonohoe 9 73
(Harry Dunlop) *a.p: rdn to ld over 1f out: kpt on wl* **9/2**[2]

0 **2** ¾ **Livingstones Quest (IRE)**[31] 4218 2-9-5 0..................... OisinMurphy 3 71
(Rod Millman) *in tch: rdn over 2f out: chsd wnr ent fnl f: drifted lft but kpt on wl: hld towards fin* **16/1**

0 **3** 2¼ **Paint**[23] 4533 2-9-0 0............................................................... SeanLevey 2 59
(Richard Hannon) *in tch: rdn 2f out: wnt 3rd ent fnl f: kpt on but nt pce to get on terms w front pair* **7/2**[1]

5 **4** 1¼ **Blazing Beryl (IRE)**[42] 3815 2-9-0 0............................. CharlesBishop 8 55
(Brian Meehan) *led: rdn and hdd over 1f out: no ex ins fnl f* **7/2**[1]

**5** 1¼ **Hidden Affair** 2-9-5 0...................................................... FergusSweeney 4 57+
(Henry Candy) *s.i.s: sn in tch: rdn over 2f out: kpt on but nt pce to get involved* **6/1**[3]

234 **6** 1¾ **Joegogo (IRE)**[46] 3689 2-9-5 72....................................... SteveDrowne 6 51
(David Evans) *prom: rdn over 2f out: ev ch over 1f out: wknd ins fnl f* **9/2**[2]

06 **7** ¾ **Spot Lite**[19] 4696 2-9-5 0................................................. WilliamCarson 7 49
(Rod Millman) *s.i.s: in last pair: hdwy over 2f out: sn rdn: wknd ins fnl f* **40/1**

03 **8** 1 **Bezos (IRE)**[9] 5047 2-8-12 0............................................... TinaSmith(7) 11 46
(Richard Hannon) *s.i.s: sn in tch: effrt over 2f out: wknd ins fnl f* **10/1**

5 **9** 11 **Mouchee (IRE)**[9] 5047 2-9-5 0........................................ TimmyMurphy 5 13
(David Evans) *in tch tl wknd over 2f out* **16/1**

1m 18.57s (3.77) **Going Correction** +0.575s/f (Yiel) **9** Ran SP% **118.4**
Speed ratings (Par 96): **97,96,93,91,89 87,86,85,70**
CSF £74.45 TOTE £5.20: £2.00, £4.10, £1.70; EX 51.40 Trifecta £587.60.
**Owner** Daniel Macauliffe & Anoj Don **Bred** Kilcarn Stud **Trained** Lambourn, Berks

**FOCUS**
This juvenile maiden has thrown up a number of Group and Listed winners in the last ten years, but some interest was lost when a couple were withdrawn, including the forecast favourite. The winner has been rated to his debut form.

## 5431 OAKWOODS MAIDEN STKS 6f
**7:15** (7:15) (Class 5) 3-Y-O+ **£3,881** (£1,155; £577; £288) **Stalls** Low

Form RPR

3 **1** **Yabrave**[108] 1727 3-8-12 0...................................... CameronNoble(7) 2 91+
(Roger Varian) *trckd ldrs: led over 1f out: sn in command: readily* **5/2**[2]

2 **2** 1¼ **Killay**[14] 4911 3-9-0 0...................................................... CharlesBishop 3 79
(Eve Johnson Houghton) *led: rdn and hdd over 1f out: sn hld by wnr but kpt on ins fnl f* **11/10**[1]

**3** 4½ **Majboor (IRE)** 3-9-5 0........................................................ LiamKeniry 1 70
(Dominic Ffrench Davis) *hld up: hdwy over 2f out: sn rdn: wnt 3rd jst ins fnl f: kpt on but nt pce to get on terms* **16/1**

03 **4** 1¼ **Noble Masterpiece**[38] 3970 3-9-5 0............................. StevieDonohoe 7 66
(Sir Michael Stoute) *trckd ldrs: rdn 2f out: kpt on same pce fnl f* **3/1**[3]

**5** 4 **Suit Of Lights (IRE)** 3-9-2 0........................................... TimClark(3) 8 53
(Henry Tett) *wnt lft s: bhd: sme minor late prog: n.d* **33/1**

06- **6** 4 **Secret Striker**[259] 7935 5-9-2 0............................... CallumShepherd(3) 6 36
(Ken Cunningham-Brown) *in tch: effrt over 2f out: wknd over 1f out* **33/1**

**7** 2¼ **Spitfire Limited** 3-9-0 0................................................ FergusSweeney 4 28
(George Baker) *dwlt: a towards rr* **14/1**

-0 **8** 14 **Blackadder**[9] 5050 5-9-3 40.................................................. JordanUys(7) 5
(Mark Gillard) *prom tl 3f out* **50/1**

1m 17.48s (2.68) **Going Correction** +0.575s/f (Yiel)
**WFA** 3 from 4yo+ 5lb **8** Ran SP% **121.6**
Speed ratings (Par 103): **105,103,97,95,90 85,82,63**
CSF £5.99 TOTE £3.20: £1.10, £1.10, £4.50; EX 5.60 Trifecta £38.50.
**Owner** Sheikh Ahmed Al Maktoum **Bred** Carmel Stud **Trained** Newmarket, Suffolk

**FOCUS**
Limited experience amongst the runners in this older horse maiden and the time was 1.09 secs faster than the preceding juvenile contest. The level is fluid, but the runner-up has been rated close to her fluid debut figure.

## 5432 SGS HEATING & ELECTRICAL LTD H'CAP 1m 6f 44y
**7:45** (7:46) (Class 5) (0-75,77) 3-Y-O+ **£3,396** (£1,010; £505; £252) **Stalls** Far side

Form RPR

5 **1** **Moabit (GER)**[25] 4471 5-9-7 **73**.............................(t) MeganNicholls(5) 11 83
(Paul Nicholls) *mid-div: hdwy to dispute 2nd over 6f out: led over 2f out: shkn up fnl f: styd on wl* **8/1**

3253 **2** 1¾ **Waterville Dancer (IRE)**[18] 4730 3-8-10 **76**................ FinleyMarsh(7) 3 85
(Richard Hughes) *trckd ldrs early: lost pl whn dropped to 5th over 5f out: hdwy over 2f out: chsd wnr ent fnl f: styd on but a being hld* **3/1**[2]

3233 **3** 8 **Inconceivable (IRE)**[16] 4809 3-9-3 **76**...................... KieranShoemark 12 75
(Ralph Beckett) *racd keenly: trckd clr ldr: led over 3f out: rdn and hdd over 2f out: no ex fnl f* **5/2**[1]

5621 **4** 2½ **Rahmah (IRE)**[25] 4470 5-9-8 **69**.................................... TimmyMurphy 8 63
(Geoffrey Deacon) *mid-div: plenty to do in last quartet over 3f out: hdwy over 2f out: wnt 4th over 1f out: styd on but nvr threatened to rch ldrs* **12/1**

4/34 **5** 8 **Benbecula**[23] 4519 8-8-13 **65**.........................................(b) AliceMills(5) 2 48
(Richard Mitchell) *led: sn clr: rdn and hdd over 3f out where kpt to r alone on far side: wknd over 1f out* **25/1**

402- **6** 11 **Lord Huntingdon**[70] 3557 4-10-2 **77**............................ FergusSweeney 1 46
(Alan King) *hld up towards rr: sme prog 3f out but nvr threatened to get on terms w ldrs* **8/1**

06 **7** 3½ **Tyrolean**[46] 3682 4-9-9 **70**................................................... OisinMurphy 9 35
(Seamus Durack) *mid-div: rdn 3f out: nvr any imp* **25/1**

13 **8** 4 **What Wonders Weave (IRE)**[26] 4430 3-9-1 **74**............ TadhgO'Shea 6 35
(John Patrick Shanahan, Ire) *hld up towards rr: nvr on terms* **11/2**[3]

0554 **9** 2 **Ivanhoe**[21] 4630 7-9-1 **62**.................................................(b) RobHornby 7 19
(Michael Blanshard) *chsd ldrs: rdn over 3f out: sn wknd* **14/1**

6 **10** 7 **Silver Sea**[17] 4750 4-9-3 **64**.............................................. SteveDrowne 13 12
(Seamus Mullins) *hld up bhd: nvr on terms* **50/1**

03 **11** 17 **Age Of Wisdom (IRE)**[24] 4499 4-9-11 **75**..................... NoelGarbutt(3) 5 1
(Gary Moore) *hld up: nvr on terms* **12/1**

3m 18.8s (11.40) **Going Correction** +0.575s/f (Yiel)
**WFA** 3 from 4yo+ 12lb **11** Ran SP% **122.9**
Speed ratings (Par 103): **90,89,84,83,78 72,70,67,66,62 53**
CSF £33.21 CT £80.91 TOTE £8.30: £3.10, £1.50, £1.70; EX 39.90 Trifecta £132.50.
**Owner** Owners Group 014 **Bred** Gestut Am Schlossgarten Gbr **Trained** Ditcheat, Somerset

**FOCUS**
This competitive staying handicap was run at a strong early pace and became attritional, with a jumper coming out on top. The winner is a 131 hurdler and has been rated in line with that.

## 5433 BATHWICK TYRES H'CAP 6f 213y
**8:15** (8:16) (Class 4) (0-85,83) 3-Y-O £7,762 (£2,310; £1,154; £577) **Stalls** Centre

Form RPR
2-10 **1** **Saluti (IRE)**[14] 4887 3-9-2 **79** JimCrowley 4 83+
(Amanda Perrett) *trckd ldrs: rdn over 2f out: chal ent fnl f: led fnl 75yds: kpt on* **9/4**[1]
1150 **2** *nk* **Sans Souci Bay**[23] 4524 3-9-4 **81** (b) TimmyMurphy 3 84
(Richard Hannon) *led: swtchd to r on stands' side rails 4f out: rdn ent fnl f: hdd fnl 75yds: hld nring fin* **8/1**
1 **3** *3* **Bernardo O'Reilly**[17] 4759 3-9-6 **83** (h) StevieDonohoe 1 78
(Richard Spencer) *s.i.s: last of 5: rdn 3f out: kpt on to go 3rd ent fnl f but nt pce to get on terms* **9/2**[3]
-052 **4** *1 3/4* **Sterling Silva (IRE)**[8] 5115 3-9-5 **82** SeanLevey 5 73
(Richard Hannon) *prom for 3f: rdn to chse ldr 3f out: fdd ins fnl f* **4/1**[2]
4262 **5** *1* **Rely On Me (IRE)**[16] 4788 3-9-4 **81** OisinMurphy 6 69
(Andrew Balding) *stmbld leaving stalls: sn prom: rdn to chse ldr 3f out: fdd fnl f* **9/4**[1]

1m 33.23s (4.63) **Going Correction** +0.575s/f (Yiel) **5 Ran SP% 110.8**
Speed ratings (Par 102): **96,95,92,90,89**
CSF £19.77 TOTE £2.70: £1.30, £3.00; EX 18.30 Trifecta £66.50.
**Owner** J E Bodie & Partners **Bred** J Hanly **Trained** Pulborough, W Sussex

**FOCUS**
The feature contest and a competitive 3yo sprint on paper despite the small field. The runner-up is the key to the form.
T/Plt: £155.10 to a £1 stake. Pool: £58,431.56 - 274.96 winning units. T/Qpdt: £19.10 to a £1 stake. Pool: £8,019.52 - 310.01 winning units. **Tim Mitchell**

# 5378 YORK (L-H)
Saturday, July 29

**OFFICIAL GOING: Good to soft (6.5)**
Wind: Moderate across

## 5434 WIN £100K FOR FREE AT SPORTINGLIFE.COM/PICK7 NOW H'CAP 7f
**2:05** (2:05) (Class 2) (0-105,105) 3-Y-O+
£15,562 (£4,660; £2,330; £1,165; £582; £292) **Stalls** Low

Form RPR
3045 **1** **Get Knotted (IRE)**[8] 5094 5-9-3 **94** (p) PaulMulrennan 8 103
(Michael Dods) *hld up in rr: swtchd rt to outer 3f out: smooth hdwy over 2f out: chal on bit over 1f out: rdn to ld ins fnl f: sn edgd lft and clr* **4/1**[2]
0100 **2** *1 3/4* **Fingal's Cave (IRE)**[28] 4377 5-9-0 **91** DanielTudhope 2 95
(Philip Kirby) *t.k.h: in tch: n.m.r and shuffled bk to rr 3f out: swtchd rt to outer and hdwy over 2f out: rdn over 1f out: styd on wl fnl f* **14/1**
-506 **3** *1/2* **Von Blucher (IRE)**[14] 4905 4-9-6 **97** (t) PJMcDonald 10 100
(Rebecca Menzies) *prom: cl up on outer 1/2-way: led over 2f out: jnd and rdn over 1f out: hdd ins fnl f: kpt on same pce* **10/1**
6320 **4** *2 1/4* **Twin Appeal (IRE)**[14] 4916 6-8-9 **91** (b) CallumRodriguez(5) 7 88
(David Barron) *hld up in rr: hdwy 3f out: rdn along 2f out: chsd ldrs over 1f out: sn no imp* **7/1**
5413 **5** *2 1/2* **Battered**[42] 3836 3-8-8 **92** (p) DavidAllan 1 79
(William Haggas) *chsd ldrs on inner and sn pushed along: rdn along and outpcd over 3f out: drvn wl over 1f out: plugged on one pce* **15/8**[1]
-556 **6** *1 1/2* **Right Touch**[30] 4264 7-9-6 **97** TonyHamilton 6 83
(Richard Fahey) *trckd ldrs on outer: pushed along wl over 2f out: rdn wl over 1f out: no imp* **16/1**
1312 **7** *1 1/4* **Starlight Romance (IRE)**[28] 4334 3-8-6 **90** BarryMcHugh 5 69
(Richard Fahey) *led 1f: cl up: pushed along 3f out: rdn over 2f out: sn wknd* **9/2**[3]
0065 **8** *2* **Aardwolf (USA)**[25] 4475 3-8-3 **90** GeorgeWood(3) 11 64
(Mark Johnston) *t.k.h: prom: led after 1f: pushed along 3f out: rdn and hdd over 2f out: sn wknd* **20/1**
5005 **9** *3/4* **Al Khan (IRE)**[12] 4961 8-8-10 **87** (p) KevinStott 3 62
(Kevin Ryan) *trckd ldrs on inner: pushed along 3f out: rdn over 2f out: sn drvn and wknd* **25/1**
2/0- **10** *3/4* **Start Time (IRE)**[534] 536 4-9-1 **92** JamesSullivan 9 65
(Paul Midgley) *t.k.h: trckd ldrs: pushed along 3f out: rdn over 2f out: sn wknd* **25/1**

1m 24.71s (-0.59) **Going Correction** +0.125s/f (Good)
**WFA** 3 from 4yo+ 7lb **10 Ran SP% 119.6**
Speed ratings (Par 109): **108,106,105,102,100 98,96,94,93,92**
CSF £57.95 CT £534.44 TOTE £4.20: £1.40, £4.00, £3.00; EX 57.90 Trifecta £883.00.
**Owner** D Neale **Bred** Rossenarra Bloodstock Limited **Trained** Denton, Co Durham

**FOCUS**
The going was good to soft ahead of the opener, a nice handicap in which they went a fair pace, suiting those ridden patiently. The winner has been rated close to his best, with the runner-up to form.

## 5435 SKY BET DASH H'CAP 6f
**2:40** (2:41) (Class 2) (0-105,104) 3-Y-O+
£31,125 (£9,320; £4,660; £2,330; £1,165; £585) **Stalls** Centre

Form RPR
5610 **1** **Flying Pursuit**[8] 5094 4-8-7 **90** (p) RachelRichardson(3) 1 102
(Tim Easterby) *racd towards far side: cl up: led over 2f out: rdn clr wl over 1f out: kpt on wl* **12/1**
-100 **2** *2* **Al Qahwa (IRE)**[28] 4353 4-9-3 **97** DanielTudhope 2 102
(David O'Meara) *racd centre: trckd ldrs: hdwy 2f out: sn rdn and kpt on wl fnl f* **9/1**
2500 **3** *1 1/4* **Rasheeq (IRE)**[8] 5129 4-8-8 **88** DavidAllan 4 89+
(Tim Easterby) *stmbld bdly s and towards rr: racd towards far side: hdwy 1/2-way: rdn wl over 1f out: kpt on wl fnl f* **8/1**[3]
00-0 **4** *1/2* **Teruntum Star (FR)**[28] 4353 5-8-12 **92** (p[1]) KevinStott 9 92
(Kevin Ryan) *awkward s: sn cl up towards stands' side: rdn along over 1f out: drvn ins fnl f: kpt on same pce* **20/1**
6206 **5** *shd* **Dougan**[14] 4881 5-8-8 **93** CallumRodriguez(5) 5 92
(David Evans) *trckd ldrs centre: effrt 2f out: sn rdn and edgd lft over 1f out: drvn and kpt on fnl f* **9/1**
2340 **6** *1/2* **Futoon (IRE)**[15] 4864 4-8-5 **92** SeamusCronin(7) 18 90
(Kevin Ryan) *in tch stands' side: hdwy over 2f out: rdn to chse ldrs over 1f out: kpt on same pce fnl f* **12/1**
0232 **7** *1 1/4* **Snap Shots (IRE)**[14] 4925 5-9-0 **94** (p) BarryMcHugh 11 88
(Tony Coyle) *towards rr centre: rdn along and hdwy wl over 1f out: kpt on fnl f* **7/1**[2]
0005 **8** *1* **Move In Time**[15] 4867 9-9-0 **94** DavidNolan 15 84
(David O'Meara) *racd towards stands' side: hld up in rr: hdwy wl over 1f out: sn rdn and kpt on fnl f* **14/1**
4505 **9** *1* **Mobsta (IRE)**[21] 4615 5-9-8 **102** TedDurcan 3 89
(Mick Channon) *racd far side: towards rr: rdn along and hdwy over 1f out: n.d* **12/1**
6310 **10** *3/4* **George Bowen (IRE)**[14] 4925 5-9-1 **95** TonyHamilton 12 79
(Richard Fahey) *towards rr: hdwy in centre wl over 1f out: sn rdn and kpt on fnl f* **7/1**[2]
650- **11** *2* **Hoofalong**[294] 7156 7-9-2 **96** (h) NathanEvans 17 74
(Michael Easterby) *awkward s: racd towards stands' side: a towards rr* **16/1**
1042 **12** *3/4* **Jaywalker (IRE)**[84] 2381 6-8-10 **90** DuranFentiman 14 65
(Rebecca Bastiman) *racd towards stands' side: led: hdd over 2f out and sn rdn: drvn over 1f out: sn wknd* **16/1**
2206 **13** *2 1/4* **Muntadab (IRE)**[8] 5094 5-9-3 **97** (p) PJMcDonald 13 65
(Roger Fell) *chsd ldrs towards stands' side: rdn along 2f out: sn wknd* **11/2**[1]
-500 **14** *hd* **Nameitwhatyoulike**[28] 4354 8-9-6 **100** PaulMulrennan 19 67
(Bryan Smart) *racd stands' side: chsd ldrs: rdn along over 2f out: sn wknd* **16/1**
0-06 **15** *3* **Clear Water (IRE)**[14] 4889 4-8-4 **87** GeorgeWood(3) 10 44
(Michael Wigham) *midfield centre: rdn along over 2f out: sn wknd* **33/1**

1m 11.48s (-0.42) **Going Correction** +0.125s/f (Good)
**WFA** 3 from 4yo+ 5lb **15 Ran SP% 126.6**
Speed ratings (Par 109): **107,104,102,102,101 101,99,98,96,95 93,92,89,88,84**
CSF £121.05 CT £647.42 TOTE £12.70: £4.20, £3.70, £3.70; EX 123.60 Trifecta £1059.20.
**Owner** Ontoawinner, M Hulin & Partner **Bred** Crossfields Bloodstock Ltd **Trained** Great Habton, N Yorks
■ Stewards' Enquiry : Seamus Cronin three-day ban: careless riding (Aug 12-14)

**FOCUS**
A wide-open renewal of this valuable sprint handicap, but turned into a procession by the well-ridden winner. The winner has been rated to the better view of his C&D form last year, while the runner-up has been rated close to form.

## 5436 SKY BET YORK STKS (GROUP 2) 1m 2f 56y
**3:15** (3:15) (Class 1) 3-Y-O+
£68,052 (£25,800; £12,912; £4,830; £4,830; £1,620) **Stalls** Low

Form RPR
-242 **1** **Success Days (IRE)**[27] 4417 5-9-3 114 (t) ShaneFoley 3 115
(K J Condon, Ire) *mde all: set ordinary gallop: rdn and qcknd over 2f out: drvn over 1f out: edgd rt wl ins fnl f: hld on gamely* **3/1**[1]
0646 **2** *nse* **Mondialiste (IRE)**[42] 3843 7-9-3 108 DanielTudhope 7 114
(David O'Meara) *hld up in rr: hdwy on wd outside 3f out: chal over 1f out: rdn ins fnl f: edgd lft and ev ch: jst hld* **12/1**
10-3 **3** *1 1/4* **Hathal (USA)**[14] 4884 5-9-3 112 PatCosgrave 2 112
(William Haggas) *hld up in tch: hdwy 2f out: rdn to chse ldrs ent fnl f: styng on whn sltly checked last 100yds: drvn and kpt on* **4/1**[2]
-300 **4** *1 3/4* **Central Square (IRE)**[14] 4918 5-9-3 105 JackMitchell 6 108
(Roger Varian) *trckd ldrs: pushed along 3f out: rdn along and sltly outpcd 2f out: drvn and kpt on fnl f* **9/1**
4-30 **4** *dht* **Victory Bond**[14] 4918 4-9-3 102 PhillipMakin 1 108
(William Haggas) *trckd wnr on inner: hdwy 3f out: cl up 2f out: sn rdn and ev ch: drvn ent fnl f: grad wknd* **4/1**[2]
4240 **6** *2 1/4* **Elbereth**[35] 4069 6-9-0 107 PJMcDonald 5 101
(Andrew Balding) *trckd wnr: hdwy and cl up 3f out: rdn along over 2f out: sn drvn and wknd over 1f out* **8/1**[3]
6-23 **7** *5* **Algometer**[16] 4814 4-9-3 114 PaulMulrennan 8 94
(David Simcock) *chsd ldrs on outer: hdwy and cl up 3f out: rdn along over 2f out: sn drvn and wknd* **4/1**[2]

2m 10.59s (-1.91) **Going Correction** +0.125s/f (Good) **7 Ran SP% 113.8**
Speed ratings (Par 115): **112,111,110,109,109 107,103**
CSF £38.57 TOTE £3.10: £1.50, £4.20; EX 30.90 Trifecta £115.70.
**Owner** Robert Ng **Bred** Robert Ng & Dermot Farrington **Trained** Rathbride, Co Kildare
■ Stewards' Enquiry : Shane Foley six-day ban: excessive use of whip (Aug 12-17)

**FOCUS**
Race distance increased by 11yds. A fair renewal of this Group 2. The winner set a steady tempo and just held on. The dead-heating fourth Central Square has been rated to his recent form.

## 5437 GET THE SKY BET ADVANTAGE NOVICE MEDIAN AUCTION STKS (PLUS 10 RACE) 6f
**3:50** (3:50) (Class 3) 2-Y-O £7,762 (£2,310; £1,154; £577) **Stalls** High

Form RPR
2 **1** **Hey Jonesy (IRE)**[15] 4834 2-9-2 0 KevinStott 2 93+
(Kevin Ryan) *mde all: rdn over 1f out: kpt on strly* **11/8**[1]
1 **2** *2 3/4* **Staxton**[23] 4526 2-9-8 0 DavidAllan 5 91
(Tim Easterby) *trckd ldrs: hdwy to chse wnr over 2f out: rdn and ch over 1f out: sn drvn and kpt on same pce* **5/2**[2]
4 **3** *6* **The Throstles**[26] 4452 2-9-2 0 DavidNolan 6 67
(Kevin Frost) *chsd wnr: pushed along over 2f: sn rdn and kpt on one pce* **14/1**
0 **4** *2* **Push N'Pull (IRE)**[14] 4919 2-9-2 0 BarryMcHugh 1 61
(Richard Fahey) *in tch on outer: green and pushed along bef 1/2-way: sn outpcd and bhd: rdn and kpt on fr over 1f out* **12/1**
4 **5** *3/4* **Fiery Breath**[12] 4973 2-9-2 0 PhillipMakin 7 59
(Robert Eddery) *chsd ldrs: rdn 2f out: sn wknd* **12/1**
**6** *4* **Barefoot Baby (IRE)** 2-8-11 0 TonyHamilton 4 42
(Richard Fahey) *green: dwlt and a towards rr* **5/1**[3]
**7** *6* **Fitzrovia** 2-9-2 0 DanielTudhope 8 29
(Ed de Giles) *dwlt and in rr: hdwy and in tch 1/2-way: green and pushed along over 2f out: sn wknd* **14/1**

1m 12.52s (0.62) **Going Correction** +0.125s/f (Good) **7 Ran SP% 116.1**
Speed ratings (Par 98): **100,96,88,85,84 79,71**
CSF £5.12 TOTE £2.00: £1.50, £1.80; EX 4.40 Trifecta £29.40.
**Owner** Pallister Racing **Bred** Ms Alice Fitzgerald **Trained** Hambleton, N Yorks

| | | | | |
|---|---|---|---|---|
| | 4 | 13 | **Little Jo** 3-9-5 0 ...... GrahamLee 11 (Chris Grant) *dwlt and rr: hdwy on outer over 2f out: rdn along wl over 1f out: kpt on: nvr a factor* **33/1** | 39 |
| 0 | 5 | 1 1/2 | **Good Man (IRE)**[30] 4309 4-9-13 0 ...... (p[1]) DougieCostello 9 (Karen McLintock) *chsd ldrs: rdn along over 2f out: sn drvn and wknd* **66/1** | 38 |
| 56 | 6 | 1 3/4 | **Danny Mc D**[12] 5003 4-9-6 0 ...... JamieGormley(7) 7 (Iain Jardine) *bhd: sme hdwy on inner wl over 1f out: nvr a factor* **66/1** | 34 |
| 4 | 7 | shd | **Excellent Story**[17] 4784 3-9-5 0 ...... PhillipMakin 4 (John Davies) *chsd ldrs on inner: rdn along over 2f out: sn drvn and wknd* **25/1** | 31 |
| | 8 | 2 1/2 | **Pantera** 3-9-0 0 ...... DanielTudhope 10 (David O'Meara) *cl up: rdn along 3f out: wknd 2f out* **10/1** | 21 |
| | 9 | 10 | **Zihaam**[55] 3413 3-9-5 0 ...... TonyHamilton 3 (Roger Fell) *dwlt: a rr* **7/1**[2] | 3 |
| 4-5 | 10 | 6 | **Tuscany (IRE)**[47] 3691 3-9-5 0 ...... JamieSpencer 5 (Paul Cole) *chsd ldrs: rdn along over 2f out: sn wknd* **8/1**[3] | |
| | 11 | 6 | **Callaloo** 3-8-11 0 ...... JoshDoyle(3) 8 (Tony Coyle) *dwlt: a rr* **50/1** | |

1m 48.36s (2.46) **Going Correction** +0.325s/f (Good)
**WFA** 3 from 4yo 8lb **11** Ran SP% **136.0**
Speed ratings (Par 103): **100,99,95,82,81 79,79,76,66,60 54**
CSF £15.05 TOTE £16.80: £2.50, £1.10, £3.90; EX 33.90 Trifecta £207.50.
**Owner** The Golden Cuckoo **Bred** Steven Nolan **Trained** Middleham, N Yorks

**FOCUS**
The red-hot favourite set a high standard in this maiden but was found wanting in the end.

## 5459 FLY HIGH FAYE NICKELS H'CAP 5f 3y
**5:00** (5:00) (Class 5) (0-70,71) 3-Y-O+ £4,528 (£1,347; £673; £336) **Stalls** Low

| Form | | | | RPR |
|---|---|---|---|---|
| 4040 | 1 | | **Crosse Fire**[6] 5211 5-9-7 **64** ...... (v[1]) DavidAllan 1 (Scott Dixon) *cl up on inner: led over 3f out: rdn clr appr fnl f: kpt on strly* **7/1**[3] | 73 |
| 5002 | 2 | 2 3/4 | **Astrophysics**[6] 5211 5-9-12 **69** ...... PaddyAspell 4 (Lynn Siddall) *trckd ldrs: effrt on inner and n.m.r over 1f out: swtchd rt and rdn ent fnl f: chsd wnr: sn drvn and no imp* **7/1**[3] | 68 |
| 1644 | 3 | 3/4 | **Oriental Splendour (IRE)**[10] 5055 5-10-0 **71** ...... JamesSullivan 8 (Ruth Carr) *towards rr: gd hdwy on inner 2f out: rdn to chse wnr over 1f out: sn drvn and kpt on same pce* **6/1**[2] | 67+ |
| -413 | 4 | 1 3/4 | **Metisian**[10] 5070 3-9-7 **68** ...... DavidNolan 11 (Jedd O'Keeffe) *towards rr: hdwy towards inner 2f out: rdn to chse ldrs over 1f out: drvn and kpt on fnl f* **9/2**[1] | 57+ |
| 0-00 | 5 | nk | **Knockamany Bends (IRE)**[46] 3710 7-8-7 **50** oh4 ...... (p) AndrewMullen 3 (John Wainwright) *trckd ldng pair: rdn to chse wnr 2f out: drvn and edgd lft over 1f out: kpt on same pce* **33/1** | 39 |
| 2030 | 6 | 1 | **Classic Pursuit**[6] 5211 6-9-9 **66** ...... RoystonFfrench 9 (Michael Appleby) *dwlt and rr: hdwy on inner wl over 1f out: sn rdn and kpt on: n.d* **20/1** | 51+ |
| 4553 | 7 | 3 1/2 | **David's Beauty (IRE)**[10] 5052 4-8-10 **53** ...... (p) LukeMorris 14 (Brian Baugh) *towards rr: sme hdwy 2f out: sn rdn and nvr a factor* **20/1** | 26 |
| 5126 | 8 | 4 | **Jacob's Pillow**[27] 4433 6-9-10 **67** ...... (p) DanielTudhope 5 (Rebecca Bastiman) *chsd ldrs: rdn along 2f out: sn drvn and wknd* **7/1**[3] | 25 |
| 0663 | 9 | 1 1/2 | **One Boy (IRE)**[6] 5211 6-9-12 **69** ...... PaulMulrennan 13 (Paul Midgley) *a towards rr* **12/1** | 22 |
| 0244 | 10 | 1 | **Jack Luey**[6] 5211 10-9-9 **71** ...... (b) LewisEdmunds(5) 7 (Lawrence Mullaney) *midfield: rdn along over 2f out: sn wknd* **9/2**[1] | 20 |
| 0-2 | 11 | 7 | **Jabbarockie**[57] 3313 4-9-12 **69** ...... JasonHart 6 (Eric Alston) *racd wd: qckly away and led: hdd and stmbld jst over 3f out: rdn along 2f out: sn wknd* **12/1** | |
| 3022 | 12 | 6 | **Vintage Dream (IRE)**[18] 4745 3-8-13 **60** ...... (b) PatrickMathers 10 (Noel Wilson) *chsd ldrs: rdn along over 2f out: sn wknd* **14/1** | |

1m 5.46s (2.16) **Going Correction** +0.325s/f (Good)
**WFA** 3 from 4yo+ 4lb **12** Ran SP% **122.7**
Speed ratings (Par 103): **95,90,89,86,86 84,78,72,70,68 57,47**
CSF £55.94 CT £324.34 TOTE £9.00: £3.10, £2.70, £2.30; EX 69.60 Trifecta £558.90.
**Owner** Paul J Dixon & Darren Lucas **Bred** Dr A Gillespie **Trained** Babworth, Notts

**FOCUS**
A modest sprint won in decisive fashion.
T/Jkpt: Not won. T/Plt: £139.30 to a £1 stake. Pool: £101,207.00 - 726.32 winning units. T/Qpdt: £19.10 to a £1 stake. Pool: £8,995.00 - 470.48 winning units. **Joe Rowntree**

# 5448 DEAUVILLE (R-H)
Sunday, July 30
**OFFICIAL GOING: Turf: good; polytrack: standard**

## 5460a PRIX ROTHSCHILD (GROUP 1) (3YO+ FILLIES & MARES) (STRAIGHT) (TURF) 1m (R)
**2:55** 3-Y-O+ **£146,512** (£58,615; £29,307; £14,641; £7,333)

| | | | RPR |
|---|---|---|---|
| 1 | | **Roly Poly (USA)**[16] 4857 3-8-9 0 ...... (p) RyanMoore 7 (A P O'Brien, Ire) *led gp of five towards centre of trck: merged w stands' side gp after 3f to dispute ld: led 2 1/2f out and shkn up: pressed thrght fnl 1 1/2f: r.o gamely to repel chalrs* **16/5**[2] | 114 |
| 2 | snk | **Via Ravenna (IRE)**[32] 4234 3-8-9 0 ...... VincentCheminaud 8 (A Fabre, France) *hld up in rr of centre gp: towards rr whn gps merged after 3f: began to cl but bhd wall of horses 2 1/2f out: drvn through gap 1 1/2f out: 4th and rdn appr fnl f: styd on wl: nvr quite on terms* **155/10** | 114+ |
| 3 | shd | **Siyoushake (IRE)**[42] 3880 5-9-3 0 ...... StephanePasquier 6 (F Head, France) *trckd ldrs towards centre: cl up on outer whn gps merged after 3f: cl 3rd and drvn 2f out: rdn and styd on to chal ent fnl f: r.o but no ex cl home* **17/1** | 115 |
| 4 | snk | **Qemah (IRE)**[39] 3961 4-9-3 0 ...... CristianDemuro 3 (J-C Rouget, France) *racd keenly: hld up in rr of stands' side gp: remained in fnl pair whn gps merged after 3f: drvn and hdwy over 2f out: 5th and styng on 1f out: kpt on wl fnl f: nvr nrr* **19/10**[1] | 115+ |
| 5 | 1 1/4 | **Persuasive (IRE)**[323] 6352 4-9-3 0 ...... FrankieDettori 4 (John Gosden) *chsd ldrs stands' side: settled in midfield whn gps merged after 3f: a little outpcd and rdn more than 1 1/2f out: styd on ins fnl f: nt pce to chal* **69/10** | 112 |
| 6 | 1 1/4 | **Usherette (IRE)**[39] 3961 5-9-3 0 ...... MickaelBarzalona 1 (A Fabre, France) *led gp of five on stands' rail: disp ld whn gps merged after 3f: hdd 2 1/2f out: sn drvn and rallied to press ldr: kpt on at same pce fnl f* **19/5**[3] | 109 |
| 7 | nse | **Furia Cruzada (CHI)**[39] 3961 6-9-3 0 ...... (h) AlexisBadel 2 (S Kobayashi, France) *racd in fnl pair stands' side: chsd ldrs whn gps merged after 3f: outpcd and drvn wl over 2f out: kpt on at one pce* **76/1** | 109 |
| 8 | hd | **Dame Du Roi (IRE)**[27] 4456 3-8-9 0 ...... MaximeGuyon 10 (F Head, France) *hld up in fnl pair of centre gp: remained in fnl pair whn gps merged after 3f: drvn to cl over 1 1/2f out: one pce u.p fnl f* **132/10** | 107 |
| 9 | 4 | **Realtra (IRE)**[25] 4512 5-9-3 0 ...... Pierre-CharlesBoudot 9 (Roger Varian) *cl up towards centre: midfield on outer whn gps merged after 3f: effrt to chse ldrs over 2f out: rdn and wknd ins last 1 1/2f* **32/1** | 100 |
| 10 | 2 | **Arabian Hope (USA)**[16] 4857 3-8-10 0 ow1 ...... (h) ChristopheSoumillon 5 (Saeed bin Suroor) *trckd ldr stands' side: cl 3rd after 3f: drvn and lost pl 2f out: wknd fnl f* **26/1** | 94 |

1m 36.45s (-4.35)
**WFA** 3 from 4yo+ 8lb **10** Ran SP% **118.5**
PARI-MUTUEL (all including 1 euro stake): WIN 4.20; PLACE 2.30, 4.70, 4.10; DF 40.00; SF 53.10.
**Owner** Michael Tabor & Derrick Smith & Mrs John Magnier **Bred** Misty For Me Syndicate **Trained** Cashel, Co Tipperary

**FOCUS**
This looked a really strong race prior to the off, but those placed can be used to hold the form down. Two of the 3yos came home first and second. The second, third, seventh and eighth limit the form.

## 5461a PRIX DE CABOURG (GROUP 3) (2YO) (TURF) 6f
**3:35** 2-Y-O **£34,188** (£13,675; £10,256; £6,837; £3,418)

| | | | RPR |
|---|---|---|---|
| 1 | | **Tantheem**[25] 4677 2-8-10 0 ...... MickaelBarzalona 6 (F Head, France) *mde all: led and dropped ins to rail after 1f: drvn over 1 1/2f out: styd on strly u.p fnl f* **11/5**[2] | 105 |
| 2 | 3 1/2 | **Darkanna (IRE)**[16] 4855 2-8-10 0 ...... AlexisBadel 1 (Richard Fahey) *chsd ldr on inner: drvn and styd on over 1f out: wnt 2nd fnl 110yds: no ch w wnr* **124/10** | 94 |
| 3 | 1/2 | **Mister Picnic (FR)**[50] 3611 2-9-0 0 ...... Francois-XavierBertras 7 (D Guillemin, France) *racd keenly: hld up in midfield on outer: rdn and clsd 1 1/2f out: chsd ldr into fnl f: kpt on at same pce* **53/10**[3] | 97 |
| 4 | 1 | **Debutante's Ball (IRE)**[8] 5150 2-8-10 0 ...... (p) TonyPiccone 2 (J S Moore) *w.w in fnl pair: styd on u.p fr over 1f out: nvr nrr* **231/10** | 90 |
| 5 | 1/2 | **Over Reacted (FR)**[42] 2-8-10 0 ...... Pierre-CharlesBoudot 4 (F Chappet, France) *racd keenly: hld up in fnl trio: tk clsr order whn rdn 1 1/2f out: one pce fnl f* **77/10** | 88 |
| 6 | 5 | **Contortioniste**[23] 4596 2-9-0 0 ...... MaximeGuyon 5 (C Laffon-Parias, France) *racd keenly: chsd ldr under restraint: rdn and no imp fr 1 1/2f out: wknd fnl f* **2/1**[1] | 77 |
| 7 | 1 1/4 | **Blue Tango (GER)**[23] 4596 2-9-0 0 ...... AntoineHamelin 3 (M Munch, Germany) *racd keenly: hld up in midfield: rdn and btn ins last 2f* **205/10** | 73 |
| 8 | 1 1/4 | **Frizzanto (FR)**[28] 2-9-0 0 ...... CristianDemuro 8 (Mario Hofer, Germany) *drvn sn after leaving stalls: sn outpcd in rr: rdn along to chse ldrs wl over 2f out: sn btn: bhd fnl f* **89/10** | 70 |

1m 10.85s (-0.15) **8** Ran SP% **118.3**
PARI-MUTUEL (all including 1 euro stake): WIN 3.20; PLACE 1.70, 2.90, 1.80; DF 24.20; SF 36.50.
**Owner** Hamdan Al Maktoum **Bred** Shadwell Estate Company Limited **Trained** France

**FOCUS**
The winner has been rated to the race average.

5462 - (Foreign Racing) - See Raceform Interactive

# 4396 MONMOUTH PARK (L-H)
Sunday, July 30
**OFFICIAL GOING: Dirt: fast; turf: firm**

## 5463a BETFAIR.COM HASKELL INVITATIONAL STKS (GRADE 1) (3YO) (DIRT) 1m 1f
**10:47** (10:47) 3-Y-O **£487,804** (£162,601; £81,300; £48,780; £24,390; £8,130)

| | | | RPR |
|---|---|---|---|
| 1 | | **Girvin (USA)**[36] 3-8-6 0 ...... RobbyAlbarado 7 (Joe Sharp, U.S.A) *w.w in fnl pair wl off pce: gd hdwy sn after 1/2-way: cl 7th on outer but styng on fr 2f out: r.o u.p fnl f: led post* **92/10** | 116+ |
| 2 | nse | **McCraken (USA)**[42] 3-8-6 0 ...... BrianJosephHernandezJr 5 (Ian Wilkes, U.S.A) *w.w towards rr: gd hdwy on outer after 1/2-way: virtually upsides ldrs 2f out: sustained run to ld 1 1/2f out: styd on u.p fnl f: hdd post* **73/10** | 116 |
| 3 | 1/2 | **Practical Joke (USA)**[22] 4648 3-8-6 0 ...... JoelRosario 4 (Chad C Brown, U.S.A) *chsd ldrs: 5 l 4th bef 1/2-way: tk clsr order travelling wl 3f out: cl 6th and pushed along 2f out: r.o u.p fnl f: nvr quite on terms and effrt flattened out cl home* **22/5**[3] | 115+ |
| 4 | 4 3/4 | **Irish War Cry (USA)**[50] 3610 3-8-6 0 ...... RajivMaragh 1 (H Graham Motion, U.S.A) *broke wl and led: hdd after 1f: cl 3rd after 3f and clr of 4th: drvn between horses to ld 2f out: hdd 1 1/2f out: wknd fnl f* **23/10**[2] | 105 |
| 5 | 3 | **Timeline (USA)**[42] 3-8-6 0 ...... JavierCastellano 3 (Chad C Brown, U.S.A) *dwlt: rcvrd to go 3rd after 2f: jnd ldr between horses after 3f: pressed new ldr 2f out: sn rdn and no ex: wknd fnl f* **19/10**[1] | 99 |
| 6 | 1/2 | **Battle Of Midway (USA)**[36] 3-8-6 0 ...... FlavienPrat 2 (Jerry Hollendorfer, U.S.A) *dwlt: rcvrd qckly to ld on inner after 1f: jnd after 3f: drvn and hdd 2f out: sn rdn and nt qckn: dropped away fr over 1f out* **73/10** | 98 |
| 7 | 1 1/2 | **Hence (USA)**[22] 3-8-6 0 ...... PacoLopez 6 (Steven Asmussen, U.S.A) *settled in fnl pair: last but in tch after 1/2-way: sn rdn and no prog: plugged on u.p late but nvr in contention* **198/10** | 94 |

PARI-MUTUEL (all including 2 usd stake): WIN 20.40; PLACE (1-2) 9.20, 7.20; SHOW (1-2-3) 4.80, 4.40, 3.80; SF 154.80.
**Owner** Brad Grady **Bred** Bob Austin & John Witte **Trained** USA

## 2246 MUNICH (L-H)
Sunday, July 30

**OFFICIAL GOING: Turf: good**

### 5464a GROSSER DALLMAYR-PREIS - BAYERISCHES ZUCHTRENNEN (GROUP 1) (3YO+) (TURF) 1m 2f
**2:40** 3-Y-0+ **£85,470** (£25,641; £12,820; £5,982; £2,564)

RPR

1 **Iquitos (GER)**[29] 4392 5-9-6 0 DanielePorcu 2 117+
(H-J Groschel, Germany) *hld up in fnl pair: hdwy on inner 2 1/2f out: rdn to chal 1 1/2f out: led over 1f out and styd on wl: drvn out* **59/10**

2 1 1/2 **Best Solution (IRE)**[37] 4029 3-8-11 0 GeraldMosse 9 114
(Saeed bin Suroor) *chsd ldng gp early: sn chsng ldr: drvn to ld appr 2f out: hdd over 1f out: styd on but a hld by wnr* **111/10**

3 2 3/4 **Potemkin (GER)**[50] 3609 6-9-6 0 EduardoPedroza 1 108
(A Wohler, Germany) *w.w midfield on inner: angled out and nt clr run 3f fr home: sn rdn to chse ldng trio over 1f out: one pce fnl f: nvr trbld ldrs* **33/10**[2]

4 nk **Enjoy Vijay (GER)**[28] 4422 3-8-11 0 AndraschStarke 4 108
(P Schiergen, Germany) *w.w in rr: drvn and began to cl over 1 1/2f out: styd on ins fnl f: nvr nrr* **16/5**[1]

5 2 3/4 **Noor Al Hawa (FR)**[35] 4130 4-9-6 0 JozefBojko 6 101
(A Wohler, Germany) *w.w midfield on outer: drvn to hold pl 2f out: kpt on at one pce: wl hld fnl f* **76/10**

6 2 1/2 **Prize Money**[36] 4070 4-9-6 0 OisinMurphy 7 96
(Saeed bin Suroor) *nudged along in midfield: 9th and drvn 2 1/2f out: rallied u.p ins last 2f: no further imp over 1f out: wl hld fnl f* **49/10**[3]

7 3 **Wild Chief (GER)**[35] 4130 6-9-6 0 AlexanderPietsch 3 90
(J Hirschberger, Germany) *hld up towards rr: hdwy 2 1/2f out: 3rd and drvn 1 1/2f out: wknd over 1f out* **81/10**

8 6 **Air Pilot**[28] 4417 8-9-6 0 HarryBentley 10 78
(Ralph Beckett) *cl up on outer: 4th and drvn but no imp 2 1/2f out: lost pl 1 1/2f out: wknd appr fnl f* **157/10**

9 1 1/4 **Boscaccio (GER)**[35] 4130 4-9-6 0 DennisSchiergen 11 76
(Christian Sprengel, Germany) *sn led: hdd appr 2f out: wknd u.p ins fnl 1 1/2f* **269/10**

10 1 3/4 **Palace Prince (GER)**[35] 4130 5-9-6 0 (p) FilipMinarik 5 72
(Jean-Pierre Carvalho, Germany) *chsd ldrs: outpcd and drvn fr 3f out: wknd over 1 1/2f out* **174/10**

11 19 **Parviz (IRE)**[28] 4422 3-8-11 0 MarcLerner 6 35
(Waldemar Hickst, Germany) *settled towards rr on outer: btn whn eased ins fnl 2f* **193/10**

2m 5.12s (-3.85)
**WFA** 3 from 4yo+ 9lb **11** Ran SP% **129.3**
PARI-MUTUEL (all including 10 euro stake): WIN 69 PLACE: 21, 37, 18; SF: 1171.
**Owner** Stall Mulligan **Bred** Frau Dr Erika Buhmann **Trained** Germany

## 5202 AYR (L-H)
Monday, July 31

**OFFICIAL GOING: Good to soft (good in places; 7.2)**
Wind: Breezy, half against on straight sprint course and in over 3f of home straight on round course Weather: Overcast

### 5465 RACING UK EBF NOVICE STKS 7f 50y
**1:30** (1:30) (Class 5) 2-Y-O **£3,557** (£1,058; £529; £264) **Stalls** High

Form RPR

1 **New Show (IRE)** 2-9-2 0 TomEaves 5 80+
(Kevin Ryan) *s.i.s: hld up in last pl: smooth hdwy over 2f out: led over 1f out: sn pushed along and green: ears pricked and asserted last 100yds: improve* **7/1**[3]

52 2 1 1/2 **Cosa Nostra (IRE)**[21] 4681 2-9-2 0 TonyHamilton 3 75
(Richard Fahey) *trckd ldrs: wnt 2nd over 4f out: effrt and disp ld over 2f out to over 1f out: kpt on same pce ins fnl f* **7/4**[2]

04 3 6 **Cuillin Hills**[21] 4681 2-8-11 0 RowanScott(5) 1 60
(Keith Dalgleish) *in tch: rdn and outpcd over 2f out: rallied fnl f: tk 3rd nr fin: no ch w first two* **33/1**

2363 4 1/2 **Bustam (IRE)**[17] 4860 2-9-2 87 JasonHart 4 59
(John Quinn) *plld hrd: led: hrd pressed over 2f out: hdd over 1f out: wknd fnl f* **1/1**[1]

5 5 31 **Mi Capricho (IRE)**[17] 4848 2-9-2 0 PaulMulrennan 2
(Keith Dalgleish) *t.k.h: w ldr 2f: cl up: rdn and outpcd over 2f out: sn wknd: t.o* **20/1**

1m 33.2s (-0.20) **Going Correction** -0.025s/f (Good) **5** Ran SP% **106.6**
Speed ratings (Par 94): **100,98,91,90,55**
CSF £18.47 TOTE £6.90: £2.60, £1.10; EX 19.40 Trifecta £145.20.
**Owner** Jaber Abdullah **Bred** Rabbah Bloodstock Limited **Trained** Hambleton, N Yorks

**FOCUS**
After riding in the first race the consensus from jockeys was that the going was dead or tacky. There's also a headwind. This was run over an additional 18yds. The favourite was desperately disappointing but the winner looks useful. It's been rated at face value.

### 5466 WEMYSS BAY HOLIDAY PARK H'CAP (DIV I) 7f 50y
**2:00** (2:00) (Class 6) (0-65,67) 3-Y-0+ **£2,911** (£866; £432; £216) **Stalls** High

Form RPR

5026 1 **Miss Goldsmith (IRE)**[27] 4474 4-9-5 56 PJMcDonald 8 65
(Rebecca Menzies) *prom: hdwy to ld over 2f out: rdn over 1f out: edgd lft and kpt on strly ins fnl f* **14/1**

0132 2 1 1/2 **Magic Journey (IRE)**[7] 5205 3-9-0 58 JasonHart 12 60
(John Quinn) *pressed ldr: chal gng wl over 2f out: rdn over 1f out: kpt on same pce ins fnl f* **3/1**[1]

-065 3 1 **Red Shadow**[21] 4687 8-8-4 46 oh1 (v) RowanScott(5) 10 49
(Alistair Whillans) *hld up midfield: hdwy on outside over 2f out: rdn over 1f out: kpt on fnl f: nt rch first two* **66/1**

5323 4 1 1/4 **Jessie Allan (IRE)**[7] 5205 6-8-3 47 SeanMooney(7) 2 47
(Jim Goldie) *t.k.h: hld up midfield: effrt and rdn on outside over 2f out: kpt on fnl f: no imp* **6/1**[3]

5155 5 1 1/2 **Cliff Bay (IRE)**[10] 5097 3-9-9 67 (h[1]) PaulMulrennan 6 60+
(Keith Dalgleish) *s.i.s: hld up: effrt on outside over 2f out: kpt on fnl f: nvr able to chal* **18/1**

4100 6 1 1/4 **Tanawar (IRE)**[13] 4999 7-9-13 64 (b) JamesSullivan 4 57
(Ruth Carr) *in tch: rdn along over 2f out: outpcd fr over 1f out* **28/1**

64 7 shd **Let Right Be Done**[6] 5254 5-8-13 50 (b) PaulHanagan 11 43
(Linda Perratt) *hld up: stdy hdwy on outside over 2f out: rdn and edgd lft wl over 1f out: sn no imp: btn fnl f* **12/1**

2002 8 1/2 **Monsieur Jimmy**[7] 5214 5-8-13 55 PhilDennis(5) 5 46
(Declan Carroll) *t.k.h: hld up towards rr: effrt whn nt clr run briefly over 2f out: sn rdn and no imp* **11/1**

0105 9 1 3/4 **Reinforced**[14] 4960 4-10-0 65 (tp) AndrewMullen 13 52
(Michael Dods) *t.k.h early: led and sn crossed to ins rail: rdn and hdd over 2f out: wknd over 1f out* **9/1**

2353 10 1/2 **Ss Vega**[21] 4682 4-8-3 47 ConnorMurtagh(7) 3 33
(Jim Goldie) *towards rr: drvn along 4f out: no imp fr over 2f out* **9/1**

-544 11 shd **Chinese Spirit (IRE)**[16] 4899 3-9-0 65 SeamusCronin(7) 7 47
(R Mike Smith) *hld up: effrt and swtchd lft whn bdly hmpd over 2f out: nt rcvr* **9/2**[2]

0-02 12 6 **Newspeak (IRE)**[41] 3945 5-9-2 53 (v) GrahamLee 1 23
(Fred Watson) *chsd ldrs: rdn and edgd lft over 2f out: sn wknd* **33/1**

1m 32.94s (-0.46) **Going Correction** -0.025s/f (Good)
**WFA** 3 from 4yo+ 7lb **12** Ran SP% **113.3**
Speed ratings (Par 101): **101,99,98,96,95 93,93,92,90,90 90,83**
CSF £52.63 CT £2696.60 TOTE £18.90: £3.80, £1.60, £14.00; EX 73.00 Trifecta £4070.00.
**Owner** West Coast Racing & Partner **Bred** G Devlin **Trained** Mordon, Durham

**FOCUS**
Race run over an additional 18yds. The principals were always prominent in this low-grade handicap, which was slightly the quicker division. The winner only had to repeat this year's best to win.

### 5467 WEMYSS BAY HOLIDAY PARK H'CAP (DIV II) 7f 50y
**2:30** (2:30) (Class 6) (0-65,66) 3-Y-0+ **£2,911** (£866; £432; £216) **Stalls** High

Form RPR

-405 1 **Redarna**[23] 4607 3-8-11 55 JamesSullivan 1 65
(Dianne Sayer) *t.k.h: hld up midfield: hdwy over 2f out: led and edgd lft ins fnl f: kpt on wl towards fin* **20/1**

545 2 nk **Jack Blane**[20] 4713 3-8-10 54 (p[1]) JoeFanning 4 63+
(Keith Dalgleish) *prom: smooth hdwy to ld wl over 1f out: sn pushed along: edgd lft and hdd ins fnl f: kpt on: hld nr fin* **5/1**[2]

3021 3 2 3/4 **Harbour Patrol (IRE)**[11] 5050 5-9-4 55 (b) DanielTudhope 3 60
(Rebecca Bastiman) *dwlt: hld up: hdwy 2f out: chsd clr ldng pair ins fnl f: r.o: nt pce to chal* **7/2**[1]

0-00 4 1 1/4 **Pipe Dreamer**[73] 2792 3-8-3 47 oh1 ow1 (p[1]) ShaneGray 6 46
(Kevin Ryan) *hld up: rdn over 2f out: styd on wl fnl f: nvr able to chal* **40/1**

6634 5 1 1/2 **Greengairs**[7] 5205 3-9-0 58 (tp) PaulMulrennan 9 53
(Keith Dalgleish) *trckd ldrs: effrt over 2f out: outpcd fnl f* **8/1**

306 6 nk **Ralphy Boy (IRE)**[26] 4506 8-10-0 65 (p) PJMcDonald 12 63
(Alistair Whillans) *t.k.h: led: hdd over 2f out: rallied: outpcd fnl f* **12/1**

6503 7 hd **Insurplus (IRE)**[7] 5203 4-9-6 57 PatrickMathers 7 54
(Jim Goldie) *hld up in tch: rdn along and outpcd over 2f out: rallied ins fnl f: no imp* **8/1**

0332 8 3/4 **Picks Pinta**[11] 5069 6-9-7 63 (b) LewisEdmunds(5) 8 58
(John David Riches) *hld up midfield on outside: effrt and pushed along over 2f out: no imp over 1f out* **12/1**

0634 9 nk **Stardrifter**[10] 5097 5-9-2 56 SammyJoBell(3) 10 50
(Linda Perratt) *hld up: rdn on outside over 2f out: no imp fr over 1f out* **16/1**

0040 10 nk **New Decade**[7] 5206 8-8-2 46 oh1 (p) SeanMooney(7) 5 40
(Jim Goldie) *pressed ldr: led over 2f out to over 1f out: edgd lft: wknd fnl f* **25/1**

4-00 11 1 3/4 **Centre Haafhd**[144] 1106 6-8-9 46 oh1 (p) AndrewMullen 11 35
(Kenneth Slack) *in tch: drvn and outpcd over 2f out: n.d after* **40/1**

646 12 3 **Fortuities (IRE)**[28] 4432 3-9-8 66 GrahamLee 2 45
(Jedd O'Keeffe) *t.k.h: in tch: drvn and outpcd over 2f out: sn wknd* **9/1**

5343 13 12 **Champion Harbour (IRE)**[17] 4837 3-9-1 59 PaulHanagan 13 8
(Richard Fahey) *stdd s: hld up: struggling over 2f out: lost tch over 1f out* **7/1**[3]

1m 33.1s (-0.30) **Going Correction** -0.025s/f (Good)
**WFA** 3 from 4yo+ 7lb **13** Ran SP% **118.4**
Speed ratings (Par 101): **100,99,96,95,93 93,92,91,91,91 89,85,72**
CSF £112.85 CT £373.05 TOTE £20.10: £5.40, £2.50, £1.50; EX 131.10 Trifecta £883.70.
**Owner** Mrs Dianne Sayer **Bred** A H Bennett **Trained** Hackthorpe, Cumbria

**FOCUS**
Race run over an additional 18yds. This time three of the first four came from the rear, and the first two finished a little way clear. It was slightly slower than the first division.

### 5468 PARKDEAN RESORTS H'CAP 1m 7f
**3:00** (3:01) (Class 4) (0-85,83) 3-Y-0+ **£6,469** (£1,925; £962; £481) **Stalls** Low

Form RPR

214- 1 **Dubawi Fifty**[227] 8399 4-9-10 79 GrahamLee 8 89
(Karen McLintock) *hld up: smooth hdwy to press ldr over 2f out: rdn to ld over 1f out: kpt on strly fnl f* **14/1**

2331 2 1 1/2 **Tor**[11] 5071 3-8-4 79 JamieGormley(7) 3 86
(Iain Jardine) *led: rdn and qcknd over 2f out: hdd over 1f out: rallied: hld towards fin* **9/4**[2]

6003 3 3 1/4 **Wor Lass**[6] 5259 9-9-2 76 RowanScott(5) 5 79
(Donald Whillans) *hld up in tch: smooth hdwy and disp 2nd pl over 2f out: sn drvn along: one pce fr over 1f out* **20/1**

1440 4 15 **Gabrial's Star**[16] 4921 8-9-11 83 (b) AdamMcNamara(3) 7 68
(Richard Fahey) *missed break: hld up: rdn and outpcd over 3f out: no imp fr 2f out* **25/1**

2252 5 1 3/4 **Braes Of Lochalsh**[7] 5208 6-9-0 69 (p) JamesSullivan 2 52
(Jim Goldie) *trckd ldrs: wnt 2nd over 4f out to over 2f out: sn rdn and wknd* **11/2**[3]

6445 6 1 **Silva Eclipse**[31] 4301 4-9-9 78 (b[1]) PaulMulrennan 6 60
(Jedd O'Keeffe) *tk keen: drvn along bnd over 3f out: rallied: wknd fr 2f out* **11/2**[3]

000/ 7 28 **New Youmzain (FR)**[760] 3501 8-9-1 70 AndrewMullen 1 18
(Lucy Normile) *bhd: detached after 5f: nvr on terms* **100/1**

3421 P **Addicted To You (IRE)**[19] 4742 3-8-12 80 JoeFanning 4
(Mark Johnston) *chsd ldr to over 4f out: drvn and sn struggling: lost tch whn p.u and dismntd ins fnl f* **15/8**[1]

3m 22.87s (2.47) **Going Correction** -0.025s/f (Good)
**WFA** 3 from 4yo+ 13lb **8** Ran SP% **112.6**
Speed ratings (Par 105): **92,91,89,81,80 80,65,**
CSF £44.43 CT £641.43 TOTE £12.00: £3.00, £1.30, £3.50; EX 52.50 Trifecta £438.60.
**Owner** Paul & Clare Rooney **Bred** Hesmonds Stud Ltd **Trained** Ingoe, Northumberland

**FOCUS**
This was run over an extra 33yds. It was a truly run race thanks to the runner-up, and only the first three passed the stamina test. The third has been rated to her recent best.

## 5469 SANDYLANDS CARAVAN PARK H'CAP 1m
**3:30** (3:31) (Class 4) (0-80,82) 3-Y-0+ **£6,469** (£1,925; £962; £481) **Stalls** Low

Form RPR

0220 **1** **Strong Steps**[2] 5415 5-10-3 **82**........................................ PatrickMathers 1 90
(Jim Goldie) *hld up in tch: effrt and rdn over 1f out: led ins fnl f: kpt on strly* **17/2**

4051 **2** 3/4 **Crazy Tornado (IRE)**[7] 5206 4-9-4 **69** 6ex......................(h) GrahamLee 5 75
(Keith Dalgleish) *hld up midfield: effrt and rdn over 1f out: edgd lft and chsd wnr ins fnl f: r.o: hld nr fin* **13/2**[3]

0100 **3** 3/4 **Zeshov (IRE)**[21] 4685 6-9-11 **76**.................................... DanielTudhope 6 80
(Rebecca Bastiman) *cl up: hdwy to ld over 2f out: rdn and edgd lft over 1f out: hdd and no ex ins fnl f* **11/1**

4545 **4** 1 **Rockwood**[17] 4865 6-9-10 **75**........................................(v) TonyHamilton 3 77
(Karen McLintock) *hld up: effrt and hdwy whn nt clr run over 1f out: sn swtchd lft: edgd lft and kpt on ins fnl f: no imp* **10/1**

3332 **5** 2 **Abushamah (IRE)**[22] 4661 6-9-9 **74**............................(p) JamesSullivan 9 71
(Ruth Carr) *hld up: rdn over 2f out: kpt on fnl f: nvr able to chal* **6/1**[2]

5631 **6** 1 1/4 **Royal Shaheen (FR)**[14] 4960 4-10-2 **81**.......................(v) PJMcDonald 11 76
(Alistair Whillans) *hld up in tch: effrt and rdn over 2f out: outpcd fnl f* **5/1**[1]

/40- **7** 4 **Coreczka (IRE)**[18] 4820 6-9-2 **67**......................................... BenCurtis 7 52
(Miss Clare Louise Cannon, Ire) *in tch on outside: effrt and pushed along 2f out: wknd fnl f* **11/1**

1335 **8** 1 1/2 **Dark Crystal**[22] 4663 6-9-2 **72**.................................. LewisEdmunds(5) 2 54
(Linda Perratt) *trckd ldrs: effrt and ch over 2f out: wknd appr fnl f* **9/1**

0300 **9** 2 3/4 **Shah Of Armaan (IRE)**[77] 2685 4-9-6 **71**........................(p) TomEaves 4 47
(Kevin Ryan) *led to over 2f out: rdn and wknd wl over 1f out* **33/1**

0/05 **10** 1/2 **Belle De Lawers**[73] 2787 6-9-13 **78**................................... JoeFanning 12 52
(James Bethell) *hld up: rdn over 2f out: edgd lft and sn wknd* **9/1**

2-00 **11** 6 **Planetaria (IRE)**[9] 5165 4-9-7 **77**.................................... PhilDennis(5) 10 38
(John Weymes) *pressed ldr: rdn and ev ch over 2f out: wknd over 1f out* **80/1**

3220 **12** 6 **Magistral**[22] 4661 7-9-4 **69**...............................................(p) PaulHanagan 8 16
(R Mike Smith) *bhd: struggling over 3f out: sn btn* **17/2**

1m 44.03s (0.23) **Going Correction** -0.025s/f (Good) 12 Ran SP% **115.3**
Speed ratings (Par 105): **97,96,95,94,92 91,87,85,83,82 76,70**
CSF £61.05 CT £623.33 TOTE £7.10: £2.80, £2.10, £3.20; EX 54.50 Trifecta £760.60.
**Owner** Mrs M Craig & G Adams **Bred** Exors Of The Late J Ellis **Trained** Uplawmoor, E Renfrews

**FOCUS**
Add 18yds to advertised race distance. Ordinary handicap form, plenty of these still in with a shout in the latter stages. The third has been rated close to form.

## 5470 WESTERN HOUSE H'CAP 1m 2f
**4:00** (4:01) (Class 3) (0-95,92) 3-Y-0+ **£9,380** (£2,791; £1,394; £697) **Stalls** Low

Form RPR

1354 **1** **Euro Nightmare (IRE)**[10] 5095 3-9-0 **87**............................ GrahamLee 3 98
(Keith Dalgleish) *pressed ldr: led gng wl over 2f out: rdn over 1f out: kpt on wl fnl f* **5/2**[1]

-3P6 **2** 1/2 **Weekend Offender (FR)**[16] 4916 4-9-11 **89**....................... TomEaves 8 99
(Kevin Ryan) *reluctant to enter stalls: hld up in last pl: smooth hdwy on outside to press wnr over 1f out: sn rdn and edgd both ways: kpt on: hld nr fin* **5/2**[1]

2162 **3** 6 **Gworn**[7] 5207 7-9-3 **81**.......................................................... PJMcDonald 5 79
(R Mike Smith) *prom: rdn and outpcd 2f out: plugged on fnl f: no ch w first two* **7/2**[3]

2521 **4** 3/4 **Mulligatawny (IRE)**[9] 5163 4-10-0 **92**.........................(p) TonyHamilton 4 89
(Roger Fell) *led at modest gallop: hdd over 2f out: outpcd over 1f out: sn btn* **3/1**[2]

4034 **5** 6 **Footlight**[17] 4865 4-8-9 **73** oh1............................................ PaulHanagan 1 58
(Richard Fahey) *t.k.h: trckd ldrs: drvn and outpcd over 2f out: sn wknd* **12/1**

2m 16.64s (4.64) **Going Correction** -0.025s/f (Good)
**WFA** 3 from 4yo+ 9lb 5 Ran SP% **112.1**
Speed ratings (Par 107): **80,79,74,74,69**
CSF £9.23 TOTE £3.60: £1.50, £1.80; EX 10.80 Trifecta £39.20.
**Owner** J S Morrison **Bred** Miss Annmarie Burke **Trained** Carluke, S Lanarks

**FOCUS**
This was run over an extra 18 yards. Perhaps not the strongest race for the grade, but the pace was solid. The runner-up has been rated close to the better view of his form.

## 5471 SUNDRUM CASTLE HOLIDAY PARK H'CAP 6f
**4:30** (4:31) (Class 4) (0-85,85) 3-Y-0+ **£7,115** (£2,117; £1,058; £529) **Stalls** Centre

Form RPR

1004 **1** **Khelman (IRE)**[10] 5093 7-9-8 **81**......................................... PaulHanagan 6 89
(Richard Fahey) *prom in chsng gp: rdn to ld over 1f out: sn hrd pressed: kpt on strly last 100yds* **8/1**

0210 **2** 1 1/4 **Tatlisu (IRE)**[21] 4683 7-9-5 **85**.................................... ConnorMurtagh(7) 2 89
(Richard Fahey) *hld up: smooth hdwy on far side of gp: chal gng wl over 1f out: rdn and one pce wl ins fnl f* **7/2**[1]

0035 **3** 1 1/4 **Specialv (IRE)**[14] 4958 4-8-7 **66** oh1.................................(p) BenCurtis 5 66
(Brian Ellison) *missed break: hld up: hdwy over 2f out: rdn over 1f out: edgd lft and kpt on ins fnl f: nt rch first two* **11/2**[3]

6314 **4** 1 1/2 **Sea Of Green**[7] 5203 5-8-0 **66** oh5..............................(p) SeanMooney(7) 7 61
(Jim Goldie) *prom: rdn along 2f out: outpcd fnl f* **9/1**

2302 **5** 3/4 **Aprovado (IRE)**[18] 4787 5-9-6 **84**.........................(p) CallumRodriguez(5) 4 77
(Michael Dods) *t.k.h: led: rdn and hdd over 1f out: btn ins fnl f* **7/2**[1]

2130 **6** 4 1/2 **Gilmer (IRE)**[2] 5415 6-9-6 **79**................................................(p) TomEaves 3 57
(James Ewart) *hld up: rdn and outpcd over 2f out: sn wknd* **4/1**[2]

0044 **7** 1/2 **Dawoodi**[7] 5204 3-7-13 **66** oh1.......................................(h) SammyJoBell(3) 8 42
(Linda Perratt) *dwlt: t.k.h and sn trcking ldr: rdn and wknd appr fnl f* **28/1**

1005 **8** 2 1/2 **Zylan (IRE)**[41] 3946 5-9-9 **82**............................................ TonyHamilton 1 51
(Roger Fell) *hld up: drvn and struggling over 2f out: sn btn* **9/1**

1m 14.75s (2.35) **Going Correction** +0.525s/f (Yiel)
**WFA** 3 from 4yo+ 5lb 8 Ran SP% **114.4**
Speed ratings (Par 105): **105,103,101,99,98 92,92,88**
CSF £36.16 CT £169.89 TOTE £7.70: £2.30, £1.70, £1.70; EX 41.90 Trifecta £264.80.
**Owner** Morebrooke Ltd **Bred** Oghill House Stud & Jimmy Hyland **Trained** Musley Bank, N Yorks

**FOCUS**
Race distance as advertised. A 1-2 for Richard Fahey in this fair sprint handicap. The winner has been rated to his non-claiming best.

## 5472 CREATING AMAZING MEMORIES APPRENTICE H'CAP 5f
**5:00** (5:01) (Class 6) (0-60,61) 3-Y-0+ **£2,911** (£866; £432; £216) **Stalls** Centre

Form RPR

6050 **1** **Hot Hannah**[50] 3624 3-9-7 **61**.............................................. BenRobinson 7 69
(Michael Dods) *mde all: rdn wl over 1f out: hld on gamely fnl f* **11/1**

666 **2** nk **Boogie Babe**[147] 1064 3-8-6 **50**................................ SebastianWoods(4) 2 57+
(Richard Fahey) *dwlt and bhd: hdwy and angled rt 2f out: str run fnl f to take 2nd nr fin: jst hld* **18/1**

6066 **3** 1/2 **Star Cracker (IRE)**[11] 5069 5-9-5 **55**................................(p) KevinLundie 6 61
(Jim Goldie) *hld up midfield: hdwy far side of gp wl over 1f out: chsd wnr ins fnl f tl no ex nr fin* **9/1**

0521 **4** 1 1/2 **Perfect Words (IRE)**[22] 4664 7-9-5 **59**....................(p) HarrisonShaw(4) 8 60
(Marjorie Fife) *prom: effrt and drvn along 2f out: kpt on same pce ins fnl f* **4/1**[2]

2341 **5** 1 1/2 **Cheeni**[7] 5203 5-9-0 **52** 6ex...........................................(p) SeanMooney(2) 1 47
(Jim Goldie) *hld up: stdy hdwy over 2f out: rdn over 1f out: kpt on same pce fnl f* **3/1**[1]

0642 **6** nk **Goninodaethat**[7] 5203 9-9-9 **59**.................................... ConnorMurtagh 4 53
(Jim Goldie) *cl up: effrt and drvn along wl over 1f out: outpcd ins fnl f* **5/1**

0121 **7** 3/4 **Dutch Dream**[16] 4896 4-9-0 **54**................................ LeanneFerguson(4) 5 46
(Linda Perratt) *dwlt: bhd and outpcd: hdwy and edgd lft over 1f out: kpt on fnl f: no imp* **9/2**[3]

-006 **8** 2 1/4 **Kylla**[17] 4847 4-8-8 **46** oh1.........................................(b) BenSanderson(2) 10 29
(Shaun Harris) *dwlt and bmpd s: hld up midfield: rdn and edgd rt 2f out: wknd fnl f* **100/1**

44 **9** 1 1/2 **Lizzy's Dream**[42] 3915 9-8-10 **46** oh1.................................. JoshQuinn 13 24
(Rebecca Bastiman) *chsd ldrs: rdn over 2f out: wknd over 1f out* **12/1**

0000 **10** 2 **Tael O' Gold**[7] 5206 3-8-4 **46** oh1..............................(b) JamieGormley(2) 12 16
(R Mike Smith) *bmpd s: bhd: drvn along over 2f out: sn wknd* **33/1**

0600 **11** 6 **Trulove**[11] 5069 4-8-8 **46** oh1......................................(p) SeamusCronin(2) 9
(John David Riches) *chsd ldrs tl rdn and wknd wl over 1f out* **50/1**

1m 1.76s (2.36) **Going Correction** +0.525s/f (Yiel)
**WFA** 3 from 4yo+ 4lb 11 Ran SP% **117.0**
Speed ratings (Par 101): **102,101,100,98,95 95,94,90,88,85 75**
CSF £187.83 CT £1855.40 TOTE £10.60: £3.20, £5.80, £2.60; EX 174.60 Trifecta £1700.60.
**Owner** J A Knox and Mrs M A Knox **Bred** J A And M A Knox **Trained** Denton, Co Durham
■ Stewards' Enquiry : Ben Sanderson one-day ban: failed to weigh out at correct weight

**FOCUS**
Race distance as advertised. A very modest sprint handicap. Limited form.
T/Plt: £264.70 to a £1 stake. Pool: £55,910.00 - 211.21 winning units. T/Qpdt: £54.30 to a £1 stake. Pool: £6,200.00 - 114.03 winning units. **Richard Young**

# 5216 WINDSOR (R-H)
Monday, July 31

**OFFICIAL GOING: Good (good to soft in places)**
Wind: Fresh, behind Weather: Fine

## 5473 SILK SERIES LADY RIDERS' H'CAP (FOR PRO-AM LADY RIDERS) 6f 12y
**5:35** (5:35) (Class 4) (0-80,82) 3-Y-0+ **£6,469** (£1,925; £962; £481) **Stalls** Low

Form RPR

3501 **1** **Dandy Flame (IRE)**[16] 4910 3-9-12 **78**........................... NicolaCurrie(5) 2 85
(Richard Hughes) *mde all against nr side rail: rdn over 1f out: kpt on wl* **5/1**[2]

-056 **2** 1/2 **Musical Comedy**[14] 4974 6-10-3 **73**.................................... JennyPowell 1 79
(Mike Murphy) *hld up bhd ldrs: shkn up 2f out: n.m.r over 1f out but sn chsd wnr: rdn and kpt on but a hld* **15/2**

4106 **3** 3/4 **Fortitude (IRE)**[19] 4752 3-10-0 **75**.............................. JosephineGordon 4 78+
(Hugo Palmer) *trckd ldrs: checked briefly over 2f out: rdn to press ldrs on outer jst over 1f out: kpt on* **3/1**[1]

0226 **4** 2 3/4 **Mr Pocket (IRE)**[13] 4992 3-10-7 **82**..............................(bt) HayleyTurner 9 76
(Paul Cole) *t.k.h: hld up: prog gng wl 1/2-way: edgd rt over 2f out but sn chsd wnr: hung rt over 1f out and lost 2nd: sn rdn and fnd nil* **3/1**[1]

6344 **5** 3/4 **Indian Affair**[17] 4844 7-9-3 **64**.................................(bt) KerrieRaybould(5) 5 56
(Milton Bradley) *hld up in last: outpcd after 2f: no ch over 1f out: passed two rivals fnl f* **13/2**[3]

5000 **6** 4 1/2 **Juan Horsepower**[11] 5051 3-10-4 **79**..............................(p) HollieDoyle 8 56
(Richard Hannon) *chsd wnr to 2f out: losing pl whn hmpd over 1f out* **5/1**[2]

000- **7** 3 3/4 **Zebs Lad (IRE)**[294] 7211 5-9-2 **58** oh1...................(p) MissJodieHughes 7 24
(Nikki Evans) *dwlt sltly but sn pressed ldng pair: sing to lose pl whn checked over 2f out: wknd* **66/1**

1m 12.1s (-0.90) **Going Correction** -0.025s/f (Good)
**WFA** 3 from 5yo+ 5lb 7 Ran SP% **109.9**
Speed ratings (Par 105): **105,104,103,99,98 92,87**
CSF £37.87 CT £121.26 TOTE £6.00: £2.40, £3.70; EX 43.20 Trifecta £162.00.
**Owner** Terence Wood **Bred** Limestone & Tara Studs **Trained** Upper Lambourn, Berks

**FOCUS**
The rail was out 6yds in the straight to move off worn ground. There was 20mm of rain on Saturday but it had been dry since. This was a competitive sprint handicap.

## 5474 NEW LEAF FINANCIAL SERVICES MAIDEN STKS 5f 21y
**6:05** (6:05) (Class 5) 2-Y-O **£2,911** (£866; £432; £216) **Stalls** Low

Form RPR

0305 **1** **City Guest (IRE)**[17] 4827 2-9-0 69.............................. JaneElliott(5) 2 74
(George Margarson) *chsd ldng pair: shkn up to go 2nd over 1f out: styd on fnl f to ld last 50yds* **5/2**[2]

46 **2** 1 1/4 **Global Academy (IRE)**[9] 5151 2-9-5 0................................(b) FranBerry 1 70
(Gay Kelleway) *sn led and clr against nr side rail: 5 l up 1/2-way: rdn over 1f out: wknd and hdd last 50yds* **3/1**[3]

64 **3** 5 **Dream Prospect**[27] 4466 2-9-5 0........................................ AndreaAtzeni 5 52
(Roger Charlton) *free to post: chsd clr ldr: rdn 2f out: lost 2nd over 1f out and wl btn after* **11/10**[1]

05 **4** 4 1/2 **Istanbul Pasha (IRE)**[17] 4841 2-9-5 0............................. SaleemGolam 3 35
(David Evans) *stdd s: hld up in last and sn wl outpcd: pushed along 2f out: tk 4th fnl f: nvr in it* **16/1**

00 **5** 4 1/2 **Spring Romance (IRE)**[14] 4973 2-9-2 0............................. JackDuern(3) 4 19
(Dean Ivory) *sn outpcd by ldng trio: nvr on terms: wknd fnl f* **25/1**

1m 1.07s (0.77) **Going Correction** -0.025s/f (Good) 5 Ran SP% **110.9**
Speed ratings (Par 94): **92,90,82,74,67**
CSF £10.38 TOTE £2.90: £1.50, £1.50; EX 10.00 Trifecta £13.40.
**Owner** John Guest Racing **Bred** Tom McDonald **Trained** Newmarket, Suffolk

**FOCUS**
This only seriously concerned the first three. It's been rated as straightforward form.

## 5475 LAVENDER GREEN FLOWERS H'CAP 1m 2f
6:40 (6:42) (Class 4) (0-85,87) 3-Y-O+ £4,690 (£1,395; £697; £348) Stalls Centre

Form RPR
3360 1 Apres Midi (IRE)[16] 4908 4-9-6 76 HarryBentley 3 81
(K R Burke) *in tch: rdn to chse clr ldr 3f out: looked hld tl clsd qckly fnl f to ld last 75yds: jst hld on* 4/1[3]
6015 2 shd X Rated (IRE)[11] 5072 3-8-13 78 AndreaAtzeni 4 82
(Mark Johnston) *in tch tl outpcd in last 4f out and pushed along: sed to stay on over 2f out: tk 3rd over 1f out: clsd qckly w wnr to chal 75yds out: jst failed* 5/1
1421 3 1 Fast And Hot (IRE)[7] 5218 4-9-3 80 6ex (b) TinaSmith(7) 1 82
(Richard Hannon) *awkward s but led: drew clr after 4f: 8 l up 3f out: looked like winning tl tied up bdly ins fnl f and hdd last 75yds* 5/2[2]
-003 4 7 Western Duke (IRE)[77] 2690 3-9-8 87 PatDobbs 2 76
(Ralph Beckett) *chsd clr ldr to 3f out: sn rdn: wknd wl over 1f out* 5/4[1]
2m 9.44s (0.74) **Going Correction** +0.025s/f (Good)
**WFA** 3 from 4yo 9lb 4 Ran SP% **109.7**
Speed ratings (Par 105): **98,97,97,91**
CSF £20.84 TOTE £6.60; EX 16.70 Trifecta £47.40.
**Owner** Mrs Melba Bryce **Bred** B V Sangster **Trained** Middleham Moor, N Yorks

**FOCUS**
A muddling race; the early pace looked steady before the third-placed finisher opened up a big lead, only to be caught late on, and there was little more than a length separating the first three at the line. Add to that, the favourite bombed out. The level is a bit fluid.

## 5476 JIM ALFIN HEINZ 57 NOVICE STKS (PLUS 10 RACE) 6f 12y
7:15 (7:16) (Class 4) 2-Y-O £3,946 (£1,174; £586; £293) Stalls Low

Form RPR
2 1 Al Barg (IRE)[9] 5136 2-9-2 0 SeanLevey 6 82+
(Richard Hannon) *t.k.h: trckd ldrs: wnt 2nd over 2f out: shkn up to ld wl over 1f out: rdn out and kpt on* 4/5[1]
60 2 1 1/4 Time For Wine (IRE)[11] 5048 2-8-11 0 FranBerry 1 73
(David Evans) *led against nr side rail but pressed: rdn and hdd wl over 1f out: kpt on wl to hold 2nd pl after* 33/1
1 3 1 Tip Two Win[14] 4973 2-9-8 0 DavidProbert 3 81
(Roger Teal) *trckd ldrs: nt clr run briefly over 2f out and sn taken to outer: rdn to go 3rd over 1f out: kpt on same pce after* 5/2[2]
0 4 5 Wear It Well[25] 4533 2-8-11 0 DaneO'Neill 2 55
(Henry Candy) *hld up bhd ldrs: pushed along over 2f out: already outpcd whn nt clr run over 1f out: tk 4th fnl f but no imp after* 12/1
0 5 3 Adulate[12] 5036 2-9-2 0 AndreaAtzeni 7 51
(Hugo Palmer) *w ldr to over 2f out: wknd qckly* 12/1
6 nk River Rule 2-8-11 0 HarryBentley 5 45
(Stuart Williams) *pushed along in 6th 1/2-way and nt on terms: nvr a threat* 50/1
7 7 Usher 2-9-2 0 KieranShoemark 4 29
(Roger Charlton) *sn pushed along in last and nvr gng the pce* 10/1[3]
1m 12.45s (-0.55) **Going Correction** -0.025s/f (Good) 7 Ran SP% **113.5**
Speed ratings (Par 96): **102,100,99,92,88 87,78**
CSF £32.73 TOTE £1.70: £1.10, £5.20; EX 33.70 Trifecta £86.70.
**Owner** Al Shaqab Racing **Bred** D G Hardisty Bloodstock **Trained** East Everleigh, Wilts

**FOCUS**
The bare form looks limited judged on the second, who had the run of the race, but some of these should be able to rate higher. The third has been rated near his debut win.

## 5477 ROYAL OAK PALEY STREET H'CAP 1m 3f 99y
7:50 (7:50) (Class 5) (0-70,72) 4-Y-O+ £2,911 (£866; £432; £216) Stalls Centre

Form RPR
5222 1 Boychick (IRE)[24] 4573 4-9-5 68 JamieSpencer 6 75
(Ed Walker) *trckd ldrs: rdn to chal over 2f out: edgd rt u.p after: led jst over 1f out: continued to edge rt and hld on* 2/1[1]
3432 2 nk Maroc[19] 4755 4-9-6 69 (p) CharlesBishop 8 75
(Nikki Evans) *led: rdn 3f out: edgd lft over 2f out and over 1f out: hdd sn after: kpt on u.p and sltly impeded ins fnl f* 11/2[3]
304 3 1 1/4 Camakasi (IRE)[21] 4699 6-9-7 70 HarryBentley 4 74
(Ali Stronge) *dwlt: hld up in last pair: rdn and prog on wd outside over 2f out: kpt on to take 3rd ins fnl f: nvr able to chal* 10/1
6535 4 nk Cordite (IRE)[29] 4413 6-9-1 69 (h) PaddyBradley(5) 9 72
(Jim Boyle) *t.k.h: trckd ldr 4f: styd cl up: rdn wl over 2f out: trying to cl on ldng pair against nr side rail whn briefly short of room 150yds out: kpt on same pce* 6/1
6362 5 4 Moojaned (IRE)[14] 4966 6-8-4 60 JordanUys(7) 10 59
(John Flint) *prom: trckd ldr after 4f: upsides over 3f out tl nt qckn wl over 1f out and then squeezed out sn after: wknd* 7/1
24-3 6 3 Captain Felix[21] 4699 5-9-8 71 RyanTate 7 63
(James Eustace) *hld up towards rr: shkn up over 3f out: in tch bhd ldrs 2f out: sn wknd* 9/2[2]
520 7 1 1/2 Della Valle (GER)[10] 5113 4-9-2 65 AntonioFresu 2 54
(Mike Murphy) *wl in tch: rdn and struggling 3f out: n.d after* 20/1
0-00 8 1/2 Tatawu (IRE)[68] 2956 5-8-7 56 KieranO'Neill 1 45
(Peter Hiatt) *dwlt: hld up in last pair: lost tch 4f out: no ch after: plugged on* 33/1
-065 9 3/4 Udogo[14] 4976 6-9-4 72 JennyPowell(5) 3 59
(Brendan Powell) *in tch in midfield: urged along over 3f out: no prog 2f out: sn wknd qckly* 50/1
030- 10 1 1/2 Heezararity[446] 2151 9-9-4 67 LiamKeniry 5 52
(Jonathan Geake) *sweating: dwlt: nvr bttr than 7th: shkn up over 2f out: wknd over 1f out* 33/1
2m 28.76s (-0.74) **Going Correction** +0.025s/f (Good) 10 Ran SP% **115.4**
Speed ratings (Par 103): **103,102,101,101,98 96,95,95,94,93**
CSF £12.39 CT £88.11 TOTE £2.20: £1.30, £1.70, £3.50; EX 14.00 Trifecta £83.90.
**Owner** Laurence Bellman **Bred** Lynch Bages Ltd **Trained** Upper Lambourn, Berks

**FOCUS**
A modest but competitive handicap. The runner-up has been rated to the balance of his form.

## 5478 BGC SUPPORTS SILENT VOICES SANCTUARY H'CAP 1m 31y
8:20 (8:20) (Class 5) (0-75,74) 3-Y-O £2,911 (£866; £432; £216) Stalls Centre

Form RPR
4-35 1 Fastar (IRE)[88] 2330 3-9-6 73 DaneO'Neill 4 79
(Brian Meehan) *hld up in 4th: clsd on outer 2f out and rdn: drvn to ld jst 1f out: hld on nr fin* 9/2[3]
3-32 2 hd Know Your Limit (IRE)[93] 2145 3-9-6 73 JamieSpencer 6 78
(Ed Walker) *trckd ldr: rdn to ld 2f out: hdd u.p 1f out: kpt on but jst hld* 6/4[1]
0510 3 1 1/2 Lyric Harmony (IRE)[37] 4096 3-9-7 74 PatDobbs 3 76
(Giles Bravery) *trckd ldrs: rdn over 2f out: trying to chal between ldng pair whn short of room jst over 1f out: kpt on same pce fnl f* 7/1
5163 4 1/2 Zebulon (IRE)[25] 4537 3-9-7 74 SeanLevey 5 74
(Richard Hannon) *hld up in last: shkn up and stl last 2f out: n.m.r clsd over 1f out but nvr pce fnl f to mount a chal* 11/4[2]
0520 5 1 1/2 Duchess Of Fife[10] 5126 3-8-12 65 (v) HarryBentley 2 62
(William Knight) *led at mod pce: tried to kick on 3f out: hdd and nt qckn 2f out: steadily fdd* 13/2
1m 46.7s (2.00) **Going Correction** +0.025s/f (Good) 5 Ran SP% **110.7**
Speed ratings (Par 100): **91,90,89,88,87**
CSF £11.84 TOTE £5.30: £2.30, £1.20; EX 10.70 Trifecta £52.30.
**Owner** Biddestone Racing Partnership XVIII **Bred** Ringfort Stud **Trained** Manton, Wilts

**FOCUS**
A fair 3yo handicap. It's been rated around the runner-up to the better view of his form.
T/Plt: £401.10 to a £1 stake. Pool: £81,048.99 - 147.50 winning units. T/Qpdt: £29.50 to a £1 stake. Pool: £8,631.53 - 215.94 winning units. **Jonathan Neesom**

# 4977 WOLVERHAMPTON (A.W) (L-H)
Monday, July 31

**OFFICIAL GOING: Tapeta: standard**
Wind: Light behind Weather: Cloudy with sunny spells

## 5479 WOLVERHAMPTON VOTED BEST SMALL RACECOURSE (MIDLANDS) NURSERY H'CAP 5f 21y (Tp)
5:45 (5:45) (Class 6) 2-Y-O £2,425 (£721; £360; £180) Stalls Low

Form RPR
236 1 Seyaady[23] 4598 2-9-7 71 JimCrowley 2 73+
(Mark Johnston) *trckd ldrs: rdn over 1f out: r.o to ld wl ins fnl f* 11/8[1]
4230 2 nk Porchy Party (IRE)[10] 5121 2-9-6 70 (p[1]) RichardKingscote 8 71
(Tom Dascombe) *chsd ldr: rdn over 1f out: r.o* 11/2[3]
430 3 nk Zain Smarts (IRE)[42] 3917 2-8-6 61 DavidEgan(5) 7 61
(David Evans) *led: rdn over 1f out: hdd and unable qck wl ins fnl f* 16/1
0426 4 1/2 Seen The Lyte (IRE)[17] 4866 2-9-4 68 OisinMurphy 4 66
(John Quinn) *chsd ldrs: rdn over 1f out: r.o* 9/2[2]
0352 5 1/2 Terri Rules (IRE)[19] 4758 2-8-9 59 AdamBeschizza 5 55
(Julia Feilden) *hld up: pushed along and hdwy over 1f out: r.o: nt rch ldrs* 14/1
2423 6 nk Auntie Pam (IRE)[59] 3306 2-9-5 69 (p) MartinHarley 1 64
(Tom Dascombe) *prom: rdn over 1f out: r.o* 11/1
3045 7 2 1/4 Flo's Melody[19] 4739 2-8-13 63 JackGarritty 3 50
(Richard Fahey) *hld up: rdn and swtchd rt over 1f out: nt rch ldrs* 9/1
050 8 2 1/4 Laith Alareen[9] 5162 2-9-3 67 (t) PhillipMakin 9 46
(David O'Meara) *s.i.s: hld up: hung lft over 2f out: nvr on terms* 25/1
500 9 6 Butterfly Spirit[52] 3516 2-8-2 52 FrannyNorton 6 9
(Michael Attwater) *dwlt: outpcd* 33/1
1m 1.21s (-0.69) **Going Correction** -0.175s/f (Stan) 9 Ran SP% **113.3**
Speed ratings (Par 92): **98,97,97,96,95 94,91,87,78**
CSF £8.80 CT £81.65 TOTE £2.20: £1.10, £1.90, £4.90; EX 10.30 Trifecta £91.50.
**Owner** Hamdan Al Maktoum **Bred** Shadwell Estate Company Limited **Trained** Middleham Moor, N Yorks

**FOCUS**
They went a decent pace in this nursery and the unexposed winner justified strong support. It's been rated as straightforward form.

## 5480 DOWNLOAD THE AT THE RACES APP NOVICE STKS 5f 21y (Tp)
6:15 (6:15) (Class 5) 2-Y-O £3,072 (£914; £456; £228) Stalls Low

Form RPR
0 1 Deviate (IRE)[18] 4806 2-8-11 0 RichardKingscote 7 66
(Tom Dascombe) *sn led: shkn up over 1f out: rdn out* 12/1
30 2 nk Ghepardo[83] 2502 2-8-11 0 TomMarquand 5 65
(Richard Hannon) *a.p: chsd wnr over 3f out: rdn over 1f out: r.o* 16/1
433 3 shd Qaaraat[66] 3025 2-9-2 79 JimCrowley 3 70
(Ed Dunlop) *chsd ldr tl over 3f out: remained handy: rdn over 1f out: ev ch ins fnl f: r.o* 6/4[1]
0 4 nse Lucky Lucky Man (IRE)[16] 4919 2-9-2 0 DavidNolan 4 69
(Richard Fahey) *sn pushed along towards rr: hdwy 1/2-way: rdn over 1f out: r.o* 16/1
4 5 nk Bobby's Charm (USA)[25] 4534 2-9-2 0 PatCosgrave 2 68+
(Robert Cowell) *s.i.s and n.m.r s: in rr: rdn over 1f out: r.o wl ins fnl f: nt rch ldrs* 15/8[2]
1 6 hd Pranceabootthetoon (IRE)[34] 4175 2-8-13 0 JackOsborn(7) 1 72
(John Ryan) *prom: rdn over 1f out: r.o* 6/1[3]
7 14 Goldakoya 2-8-4 0 TobyEley(7) 6 12
(Daniel Mark Loughnane) *s.s: outpcd* 100/1
1m 1.68s (-0.22) **Going Correction** -0.175s/f (Stan) 7 Ran SP% **109.5**
Speed ratings (Par 94): **94,93,93,93,92 92,70**
CSF £157.75 TOTE £9.20: £4.70, £6.60; EX 75.90 Trifecta £364.30.
**Owner** The Hot To Trot Syndicate - Deviate **Bred** Carrigbeg Stud & David Powell **Trained** Malpas, Cheshire

**FOCUS**
There was a bunch finish and a surprise winner in this novice event. It's been rated cautiously.

## 5481 AUTUMN MUSIC LIVE AT WOLVERHAMPTON RACECOURSE H'CAP 6f 20y (Tp)
6:50 (6:52) (Class 5) (0-75,75) 3-Y-O+ £3,234 (£962; £481; £240) Stalls Low

Form RPR
6254 1 Cappananty Con[19] 4752 3-9-4 75 RobertWinston 2 84
(Dean Ivory) *s.i.s: hld up: racd keenly: hdwy over 1f out: rdn to ld ins fnl f: r.o* 4/1[1]
4364 2 nk Kamra (USA)[16] 4892 3-9-3 74 (tp) JimCrowley 1 82
(Michael Herrington) *chsd ldrs: rdn over 1f out: ev ch ins fnl f: r.o* 7/1
046 3 2 Miracle Garden[33] 4201 5-9-7 73 (p) StevieDonohoe 7 76
(Ian Williams) *chsd ldrs: rdn and nt clr run over 1f out: styd on* 14/1
215 4 hd Spirit Of Wedza (IRE)[28] 4433 5-9-3 69 JoeDoyle 4 71
(Julie Camacho) *led: rdn and edgd rt over 1f out: hdd ins fnl f: styd on same pce* 15/2
3361 5 nk Favourite Treat (USA)[20] 4724 7-9-4 70 (e) JackGarritty 10 71
(Ruth Carr) *prom: chsd ldr over 2f out: rdn and edgd rt over 1f out: styd on same pce ins fnl f* 11/2[3]

0060 **6** ½ **Rockley Point**[32] 4256 4-9-1 **72** DavidEgan(5) 13 71
(Paul D'Arcy) *broke wl: sn pushed along and lost pl: hdwy over 1f out: rdn and ev ch ins fnl f: styd on same pce* **25/1**

0010 **7** 2¼ **Picture Dealer**[65] 3074 8-9-5 **74** SimonPearce(3) 3 66
(Lydia Pearce) *s.i.s: hld up: hdwy over 1f out: sn rdn: no ex ins fnl f* **18/1**

2466 **8** *nse* **Gold Club**[41] 3941 6-9-3 **69** (t[1]) PatCosgrave 5 61
(Tom Clover) *sn mid-div: hdwy and nt clr run over 1f out: no ex ins fnl f* **9/2**[2]

5150 **9** *nk* **Passing Star**[25] 4529 6-9-3 **69** (tp) GeorgeDowning 12 60
(Daniel Kubler) *s.i.s: sn pushed along in rr: rdn over 1f out: nvr nrr* **14/1**

4440 **10** 2½ **Varsovian**[26] 4495 7-9-7 **73** JohnFahy 6 56
(Dean Ivory) *s.s: nvr on terms* **16/1**

3250 **11** 2¼ **Extrasolar**[40] 3974 7-9-4 **70** (p) PhillipMakin 8 46
(Geoffrey Harker) *s.i.s: hld up: rdn over 1f out: nvr on terms* **12/1**

6503 **12** 3½ **Kyllukey**[14] 4979 4-9-2 **68** (p) FrannyNorton 11 33
(Milton Bradley) *chsd ldrs: rdn over 2f out: wknd fnl f* **20/1**

0100 **13** 2¾ **Krystallite**[31] 4305 4-9-3 **69** OisinMurphy 9 25
(Scott Dixon) *chsd ldr: rdn over 2f out: wknd and eased fnl f* **40/1**

1m 13.42s (-1.08) **Going Correction** -0.175s/f (Stan)
**WFA** 3 from 4yo+ 5lb **13** Ran SP% **121.0**
Speed ratings (Par 103): **100,99,96,96,96 95,92,92,92,88 85,81,77**
CSF £31.50 CT £376.51 TOTE £3.70: £1.60, £2.30, £4.70; EX 28.60 Trifecta £485.90.
**Owner** Jim Biggane, John Waterfall & Dean Ivory **Bred** Miss H Botterill & Mr D R Botterill **Trained** Radlett, Herts

**FOCUS**
They went a good pace and the winner justified favouritism under a hold-up ride.

## 5482 JOIN BLACK COUNTRY CHAMBER OF COMMERCE H'CAP 7f 36y (Tp)
**7:25** (7:25) (Class 6) (0-65,65) 4-Y-0+ **£2,425** (£721; £360; £180) **Stalls** High

Form RPR

0344 **1** **Easy Code**[9] 5145 4-9-6 **64** PatCosgrave 12 76+
(William Haggas) *s.i.s: hld up: nt clr run wl over 1f out: hdwy sn after: rdn to ld wl ins fnl f: r.o* **5/2**[1]

6001 **2** 1 **Himalayan Queen**[48] 3702 4-9-7 **65** RichardKingscote 1 73
(William Jarvis) *trckd ldrs: hmpd over 4f out: rdn and ev ch wl ins fnl f: edgd lft and styd on same pce towards fin* **11/2**[2]

6032 **3** 2½ **Loveatfirstsight**[20] 4726 4-8-11 **60** (p) DavidEgan(5) 8 62
(Michael Attwater) *awkward s: hld up: plld hrd: hdwy over 1f out: nt clr run sn after: r.o to go 3rd nr fin* **5/2**[1]

/6-0 **4** *hd* **Prince Jai**[10] 5126 4-8-8 **52** (p) StevieDonohoe 5 53
(Ian Williams) *led: tk a false step over 4f out: rdn over 1f out: hdd and no ex wl ins fnl f* **25/1**

-346 **5** *shd* **Quite A Story**[35] 4149 5-9-1 **62** CharlieBennett(3) 10 63
(Patrick Chamings) *hld up: hdwy over 1f out: sn rdn and edgd lft: r.o* **12/1**

500 **6** 1½ **Langham**[47] 3729 4-9-4 **62** (p) AlistairRawlinson 3 59
(Michael Appleby) *hld up in tch: shkn up and edgd rt over 1f out: styd on same pce ins fnl f* **20/1**

4021 **7** ¾ **Bogsnog (IRE)**[20] 4723 7-8-13 **57** JackGarritty 7 52
(Ruth Carr) *chsd ldr 6f out: rdn and ev ch fr over 1f out tl wknd wl ins fnl f* **15/2**[3]

00 **8** 1 **Keene's Pointe**[5] 5285 7-8-8 **52** (p) RoystonFfrench 6 45
(Steph Hollinshead) *prom: hmpd over 4f out: rdn over 2f out: wknd fnl f* **25/1**

1500 **9** 3½ **Fossa**[20] 4726 7-8-6 **50** FrannyNorton 9 34
(Mark Brisbourne) *hld up: plld hrd: hdwy over 5f out: shkn up over 1f out: wknd ins fnl f* **33/1**

4-04 **10** ½ **Wahaab (IRE)**[191] 363 6-9-6 **64** TomMarquand 4 47
(Sophie Leech) *prom: racd keenly: nt clr run and lost pl 6f out: rdn and wknd over 1f out* **18/1**

0006 **11** 5 **Mr Conundrum**[18] 4789 4-8-5 **49** PaddyAspell 11 20
(Lynn Siddall) *hld up: a in rr* **66/1**

1m 28.88s (0.08) **Going Correction** -0.175s/f (Stan) **11** Ran SP% **114.1**
Speed ratings (Par 101): **92,90,88,87,87 85,85,83,79,79 73**
CSF £14.79 CT £37.47 TOTE £3.10: £1.30, £1.30, £2.00; EX 16.20 Trifecta £36.50.
**Owner** A R Legal Partnership **Bred** Usk Valley Stud **Trained** Newmarket, Suffolk

**FOCUS**
A modest handicap. The winner has been rated back near last year's best.

## 5483 CELEBRATE CHRISTMAS AT WOLVERHAMPTON RACECOURSE H'CAP 1m 4f 51y (Tp)
**8:00** (8:00) (Class 6) (0-65,65) 4-Y-0+ **£2,425** (£721; £360; £180) **Stalls** Low

Form RPR

600 **1** **Brandon Castle**[30] 4336 5-9-4 **62** (t[1]) OisinMurphy 5 71+
(Archie Watson) *trckd ldrs: racd keenly: swtchd rt over 2f out: hrd rdn fr over 1f out: r.o to ld nr fin* **9/4**[1]

064- **2** *hd* **Shoofly (IRE)**[110] 1745 4-9-2 **60** AlistairRawlinson 7 69
(David Harry Kelly, Ire) *chsd ldr tl led over 3f out: rdn over 1f out: hdd nr fin* **5/1**[3]

6443 **3** *nk* **Omotesando**[23] 4608 7-8-13 **62** MeganNicholls(5) 6 71
(Oliver Greenall) *a.p: chsd ldr over 2f out: ev ch fr over 1f out: sn rdn: styd on* **8/1**

0/ **4** 2 **Konig Hall**[25] 4066 9-9-0 **58** (p) ShaneKelly 8 63+
(Anthony McCann, Ire) *hld up in tch: rdn over 1f out: styd on same pce ins fnl f* **9/2**[2]

0433 **5** 4 **Pour L'Amour (IRE)**[11] 5054 4-9-4 **65** CharlieBennett(3) 9 64
(Daniel Mark Loughnane) *hld up: rdn over 1f out: r.o ins fnl f: nvr nrr* **9/1**

3640 **6** 1¼ **Star Ascending (IRE)**[11] 5080 5-8-11 **55** (p) TomQueally 2 52
(Jennie Candlish) *hld up: hdwy over 1f out: sn rdn: wknd ins fnl f* **14/1**

6563 **7** 1 **Yasir (USA)**[14] 4980 9-8-7 **58** KatherineGlenister(7) 10 53
(Conor Dore) *s.s: hld up: rdn over 1f out: nvr on terms* **25/1**

3000 **8** 1¾ **Handsome Dan (IRE)**[105] 1257 11-9-5 **63** (p[1]) DougieCostello 11 56
(Sarah Hollinshead) *hld up: rdn over 1f out: n.d* **50/1**

4150 **9** *nk* **Powered (IRE)**[26] 4494 4-9-1 **59** JimCrowley 3 51
(David Evans) *s.s: a in rr* **16/1**

5410 **10** 6 **Lean On Pete (IRE)**[13] 5002 8-9-5 **63** FrannyNorton 4 45
(Ollie Pears) *led: hdd over 3f out: sn rdn: wknd fnl f* **14/1**

0 **11** 7 **Ballyfarsoon (IRE)**[100] 1985 6-8-13 **57** (v) StevieDonohoe 1 38
(Ian Williams) *hld up: pushed along over 5f out: nvr on terms* **20/1**

0060 **12** *nk* **Fast Play (IRE)**[9] 5142 5-9-5 **63** (b) MartinHarley 12 43
(Conor Dore) *hld up in tch: rdn over 2f out: sn wknd* **66/1**

2m 36.0s (-4.80) **Going Correction** -0.175s/f (Stan) **12** Ran SP% **118.0**
Speed ratings (Par 101): **109,108,108,107,104 103,103,102,101,97 97,96**
CSF £12.42 CT £77.57 TOTE £3.00: £1.30, £1.30, £2.60; EX 14.90 Trifecta £92.80.
**Owner** C R Hirst **Bred** Barry Walters **Trained** Upper Lambourn, W Berks

**FOCUS**
Two heavily backed runners filled the first couple of places in this handicap.

## 5484 VISIT ATTHERACES.COM H'CAP 1m 142y (Tp)
**8:30** (8:33) (Class 4) (0-85,83) 3-Y-0+ **£4,851** (£1,443; £721; £360) **Stalls** Low

Form RPR

3135 **1** **Glorious Artist (IRE)**[86] 2385 3-9-1 **82** CallumShepherd(3) 2 91
(Charles Hills) *chsd ldr: rdn to ld over 1f out: r.o wl* **18/1**

6-12 **2** 2½ **Pushaq (IRE)**[17] 4870 4-9-11 **80** (h) ShaneKelly 1 84
(Anthony McCann, Ire) *hdwy over 6f out: nt clr run over 1f out: sn rdn: r.o to go 2nd nr fin* **6/1**[3]

344 **3** *nse* **Toga Tiger (IRE)**[34] 4170 10-9-9 **78** RichardKingscote 7 82
(Daniel Mark Loughnane) *hld up: hdwy over 1f out: r.o to go 3rd nr fin* **20/1**

315- **4** *nk* **Dubai Elegance**[259] 7956 3-9-2 **80** OisinMurphy 10 82
(Saeed bin Suroor) *s.i.s: rcvrd to chse ldr over 7f out: rdn over 1f out: no ex towards fin* **8/1**

1341 **5** *shd* **Excel Again**[31] 4304 3-9-5 **83** MartinHarley 8 85+
(James Tate) *chsd ldrs: shkn up and hung rt over 2f out: sn outpcd: rallied ins fnl f: r.o* **2/1**[1]

0062 **6** *shd* **First Up (IRE)**[11] 5066 3-9-4 **82** JimCrowley 6 84
(Jeremy Noseda) *hld up: hdwy over 2f out: rdn over 1f out: r.o* **5/2**[2]

2340 **7** 1¼ **Count Montecristo (FR)**[21] 4685 5-9-13 **82** (p[1]) KevinStott 3 82
(Kevin Ryan) *led: rdn and edgd rt wl over 1f out: sn hdd: no ex ins fnl f* **17/2**

4-30 **8** 1¾ **Soldier's Girl (IRE)**[16] 4883 3-9-5 **83** TomMarquand 5 78
(Richard Hannon) *hld up: hdwy over 2f out: sn rdn: wknd ins fnl f* **16/1**

2106 **9** 6 **Palmerston**[10] 5125 4-9-12 **81** DougieCostello 9 63
(Michael Appleby) *hld up: rdn over 1f out: nvr on terms* **33/1**

3010 **10** 3¼ **Idol Deputy (FR)**[93] 2163 11-9-0 **74** (p) RachealKneller(5) 4 49
(James Bennett) *hld up: rdn and wknd over 1f out* **66/1**

1m 46.93s (-3.17) **Going Correction** -0.175s/f (Stan)
**WFA** 3 from 4yo+ 9lb **10** Ran SP% **118.2**
Speed ratings (Par 105): **107,104,104,104,104 104,103,101,96,93**
CSF £121.75 CT £2260.84 TOTE £23.70: £4.40, £1.80, £4.60; EX 179.80 Trifecta £2057.40 Part won..
**Owner** Kangyu International Racing (HK) Limited **Bred** N Hartery **Trained** Lambourn, Berks

**FOCUS**
They went a stop-start gallop and the hold-up performers couldn't land a blow.

## 5485 UNIVERSITY OF WOLVERHAMPTON RACING MAIDEN H'CAP 1m 142y (Tp)
**9:00** (9:02) (Class 6) (0-65,65) 3-Y-0+ **£2,425** (£721; £360; £180) **Stalls** Low

Form RPR

2004 **1** **Prancing Oscar (IRE)**[27] 4473 3-9-5 **65** OisinMurphy 8 71
(Ben Haslam) *sn led: rdn over 1f out: jst hld on* **6/1**[3]

6665 **2** *nk* **Mutineer**[19] 4747 3-9-0 **60** GeorgeDowning 5 65
(Daniel Kubler) *a.p: rdn over 1f out: n.m.r and chsd wnr ins fnl f: r.o* **16/1**

6452 **3** ¾ **Life Of Luxury**[14] 4982 4-9-6 **57** WilliamCarson 6 62
(Mark Brisbourne) *led early: settled to trck ldrs: rdn over 1f out: r.o* **10/1**

3202 **4** *hd* **Dream Magic (IRE)**[62] 3175 3-9-2 **65** CharlieBennett(3) 9 68
(Daniel Mark Loughnane) *sn chsng wnr: rdn over 1f out: hung lft and no ex ins fnl f* **14/1**

-064 **5** 2¾ **Feel The Vibes**[19] 4747 3-9-0 **60** (b) DanielMuscutt 1 58+
(Michael Blanshard) *hld up: hdwy over 1f out: nt trble ldrs* **12/1**

0-04 **6** *nse* **Leopard (IRE)**[23] 4602 3-8-12 **61** (h[1]) JoshDoyle(3) 3 58+
(Tony Coyle) *hld up: plld hrd: hdwy over 1f out: nt trble ldrs* **33/1**

4033 **7** 1 **Art's Desire (IRE)**[18] 4797 3-9-5 **65** RichardKingscote 12 60+
(Ed Walker) *hld up: rdn over 1f out: nvr nrr* **7/2**[1]

0533 **8** ½ **Lord Kitten (USA)**[23] 4602 3-9-5 **65** TomQueally 11 59
(David Lanigan) *hld up: rdn over 2f out: n.d* **13/2**

654 **9** *nse* **Princess Ophelia**[20] 4729 3-9-3 **63** AlistairRawlinson 4 57
(Michael Appleby) *prom: rdn over 1f out: no ex fnl f* **66/1**

-032 **10** *nse* **Joys Delight**[19] 4759 3-9-4 **64** ShaneKelly 13 58
(Daniel Mark Loughnane) *hld up: styng on whn nt clr run ins fnl f: nvr nrr* **33/1**

005- **11** 1¾ **Nargiza (USA)**[250] 8074 3-9-1 **64** GeorgeWood(3) 7 54
(Chris Wall) *hld up: hdwy on outer over 2f out: sn rdn: wknd fnl f* **16/1**

-230 **12** ¾ **Inglorious**[7] 5205 3-9-4 **64** (v[1]) JimCrowley 2 53
(Keith Dalgleish) *hld up: a in rr* **4/1**[2]

053 **13** ½ **Grey Diamond**[11] 5075 3-9-4 **64** FrannyNorton 10 52
(Mark Johnston) *s.i.s: pushed along in rr: nvr on terms* **12/1**

1m 50.62s (0.52) **Going Correction** -0.175s/f (Stan)
**WFA** 3 from 4yo 9lb **13** Ran SP% **120.1**
Speed ratings (Par 101): **90,89,89,88,86 86,85,85,85,84 83,82,82**
CSF £97.50 CT £955.52 TOTE £7.50: £3.20, £5.50, £2.20; EX 107.70 Trifecta £1404.90 Part won..
**Owner** Middleham Park Racing XVIII **Bred** Fontstown Stud **Trained** Middleham Moor, N Yorks

**FOCUS**
The first two were always prominent in this steadily-run handicap. A minor pb from the winner, with the third rated near his latest form.
T/Jkpt: Part won. £25,423.10 to a £1 stake. T/Plt: £3,288.00 to a £1 stake. Pool: £87,516.55 - 19.43 winning units. T/Qpdt: £98.90 to a £1 stake. Pool: £10,072.36 - 75.36 winning units.
**Colin Roberts**

# GALWAY (R-H)
Monday, July 31
**OFFICIAL GOING: Flat course - soft; hurdle course - yielding**

## 5488a CONNACHT HOTEL (Q.R.) H'CAP 2m 179y
**7:40** (7:40) (70-100,95) 4-Y-0+
**£50,427** (£16,239; £7,692; £3,418; £1,709; £854)

RPR

**1** **Whiskey Sour (IRE)**[59] 7371 4-10-10 **84** MrAMcMahon(7) 3 91+
(W P Mullins, Ire) *mid-div: gd hdwy on outer fr over 2f out to chse ldrs in 3rd into st and led gng best on outer ins fnl f: pushed out nr fin: easily* **16/1**

**2** 2¾ **Swamp Fox (IRE)**[11] 7708 5-11-1 **87** (b) MrJCBarry(5) 7 90
(Joseph G Murphy, Ire) *w.w in rr of mid-div: prog on outer gng wl over 4f out: rdn in cl 2nd into st and no imp on easy wnr u.p in 3rd wl ins fnl f: kpt on into 2nd fnl strides* **5/1**[1]

**3** *hd* **Lagostovegas (IRE)**[12] 5045 5-11-8 **89**........................ MrPWMullins 15 92
(W P Mullins, Ire) *chsd ldrs: tk clsr order bhd ldrs gng wl under 3f out and led over 2f out: sn rdn and strly pressed: hdd ins fnl f and sn no ch w easy wnr: denied 2nd fnl strides: jst hld 3rd* **6/1**[2]

**4** *nse* **Digeanta (IRE)**[15] 4937 10-11-9 **90**....................................(t) MsKWalsh 9 93+
(W P Mullins, Ire) *hld up towards rr: prog fr over 2f out to chse ldrs into st where rdn: kpt on u.p in 4th wl ins fnl f: jst failed for 3rd: nrst fin* **25/1**

**5** *1 ¾* **Miles To Memphis (IRE)**[16] 4929 8-10-13 **85**............(t) MsLO'Neill(5) 19 86
(Mrs Denise Foster, Ire) *hld up in tch: rdn in 4th over 2f out and no imp on easy wnr u.p in 4th ins fnl f: one pce clsng stages* **16/1**

**6** *hd* **Hidden Cyclone (IRE)**[61] 6594 12-11-8 **89**......................(p) MrBO'Neill 8 90
(John Joseph Hanlon, Ire) *dwlt and pushed along in rr early: last at 1/2-way: hdwy over 2f out: r.o wl u.p in 11th over 1f out: nvr nrr* **16/1**

**7** *¾* **Sweet Company (IRE)**[31] 4329 6-10-12 **82**.........(t[1]) MrSClements(3) 12 82
(A J Martin, Ire) *hooded to load: in rr of mid-div: prog to chse ldrs 2f out: rdn in 6th into st and no ex ent fnl f: one pce after* **6/1**[2]

**8** *½* **Benkei (IRE)**[3] 5388 7-11-8 **92**........................................ MrDGLavery(3) 2 91
(H Rogers, Ire) *hld up in tch: n.m.r on inner under 3f out and dropped to mid-div over 2f out: pushed along in 10th appr st and kpt on one pce fr over 1f out* **10/1**

**9** *nk* **St Lawrence Gap (IRE)**[38] 4067 5-11-1 **85**................ MrDLQueally(3) 1 84
(Eoin Doyle, Ire) *chsd ldrs: rdn over 2f out and no ex in 8th appr st: one pce after* **20/1**

**10** *¾* **Shinghari (IRE)**[12] 5045 5-10-11 **85**........................(p[1]) MrPJCawley(7) 14 83
(Denis Gerard Hogan, Ire) *hld up in tch: rdn in 5th over 2f out and sn no ex: wknd fnl f* **22/1**

**11** *7* **Sir Ector (USA)**[20] 3602 10-11-1 **85**.......................... MrNMcParlan(3) 4 75
(Miss Nicole McKenna, Ire) *nvr bttr than mid-div: rdn in 14th and no imp under 3f out: kpt on one pce fnl 2f* **33/1**

**12** *nk* **Automated**[53] 3513 6-11-2 **83**.............................................(p) MrJJCodd 20 73
(Gordon Elliott, Ire) *w.w towards rr: 19th 1/2-way: tk clsr order under 3f out: rdn in 13th into st and no imp: kpt on one pce ins fnl f* **8/1**[3]

**13** *hd* **Rashaan (IRE)**[17] 2354 5-10-13 **87**.................................. MrRDeegan(7) 6 77
(Colin Kidd, Ire) *chsd ldrs: disp ld over 3f out and sn led briefly: rdn and hdd over 2f out: sn wknd* **10/1**

**14** *5 ½* **Wonder Laish**[51] 3602 5-11-7 **88**....................... MrDerekO'Connor 5 72
(C Byrnes, Ire) *mid-div: pushed along 2f out and sn no ex: wknd 1f out: sn eased* **8/1**[3]

**15** *6 ½* **Powersbomb (IRE)**[21] 4708 7-10-13 **87**.....................(h) MrEMahon(7) 16 64
(Brian M McMahon, Ire) *w ldrs and led narrowly after 2f: jnd over 3f out and sn hdd: wknd over 2f out: eased 1 1/2f out* **12/1**

**16** *1 ¼* **Elishpour (IRE)**[171] 669 7-10-11 **83**........................(t) MrTHamilton(5) 10 58
(Alan Fleming, Ire) *in rr of mid-div best: rdn and no imp under 3f out* **33/1**

**17** *5 ½* **Ezanak (IRE)**[102] 1918 4-11-5 **89**.........................(b[1]) MrFinianMaguire(3) 17 58
(D K Weld, Ire) *hld up towards rr: tk clsr order after 1/2-way: rdn in mid-div over 3f out and sn wknd* **33/1**

**18** *6 ½* **Argus (IRE)**[76] 7538 5-11-2 **86**............................(h) MissKHarrington(3) 11 48
(Alexandra Dunn) *w ldrs and led narrowly after 1f tl hdd after 2f: disp ld briefly over 3f out: rdn and hdd over 2f out: wknd* **33/1**

**19** *10* **Zafayan (IRE)**[30] 4388 6-11-7 **95**....................................(v) MrDSinnott(7) 13 46
(D K Weld, Ire) *mid-div: rdn and no ex over 3f out: sn wknd* **33/1**

**20** *1 ¼* **Winter Lion (IRE)**[58] 3349 7-11-1 **85**......................(bt) MrRPQuinlan(3) 18 35
(Matthew J Smith, Ire) *a bhd: sltly impeded towards rr bef 1/2-way: rdn over 4f out and no imp: wknd* **50/1**

3m 52.77s **20** Ran SP% **140.6**
CSF £95.86 CT £572.71 TOTE £17.70: £4.30, £1.70, £2.00, £6.30; DF 120.90 Trifecta £1118.30.
**Owner** Luke McMahon **Bred** Airlie Stud **Trained** Muine Beag, Co Carlow

**FOCUS**
A terrific race for Willie Mullins. The winner had never run beyond 1m2f on the Flat before.

5489 - (Foreign Racing) - See Raceform Interactive

## CLAIREFONTAINE (R-H)
Monday, July 31

**OFFICIAL GOING: Turf: good**

### 5490a PRIX ASMODEE (PRIX DES COSMOS) (CLAIMER) (4YO+) (TURF) 1m
**2:20** (2:20) 4-Y-0+ **£9,829** (£3,931; £2,948; £1,965; £982)

RPR

**1** **Dylan Dancing (IRE)**[29] 4-9-0 0........................... DelphineSantiago(4) 8 86
(C Le Veel, France) **59/10**

**2** *1 ½* **Mangusto (FR)**[29] 4-9-4 0..................................... ChristopheSoumillon 6 87
(M Delcher Sanchez, France) **43/10**[2]

**3** *nk* **Lotus Garden (FR)**[40] 6-8-11 0.......................................... IoritzMendizabal 1 79
(F Chappet, France) **137/10**

**4** *1 ¼* **Palang (USA)**[94] 5-9-1 0................................................ EddyHardouin 10 80
(Andreas Suborics, Germany) **13/2**

**5** *shd* **Admire Fuji (IRE)**[24] 7-8-11 0................................... RaphaelMarchelli 11 76
(D De Waele, France) **216/10**

**6** *hd* **Yume (FR)**[22] 6-9-1 0...................................................(b) AntoineHamelin 7 79
(C Lerner, France) **18/5**[1]

**7** *1 ¾* **Hout Bay (FR)**[81] 4-8-11 0..................................... ClementLecoeuvre(4) 9 75
(Mario Hofer, Germany) **8/1**

**8** *nk* **Crepusculedesdieux (FR)**[26] 6-9-1 0..........................(p) GeraldMosse 3 75
(P Sobry, France) **56/10**[3]

**9** *1 ¼* **Enduring Power (IRE)**[341] 5765 4-9-1 0........................ MickaelBarzalona 2 72
(Jo Hughes) *wl into stride: led early: hdd after 1f but remained cl up: pushed along over 2f out: rdn over 1f out: grad wknd* **243/10**

**10** *2 ½* **Line Drummer (FR)**[77] 2696 7-8-10 0.................. MlleLauraGrosso(8) 5 65
(J Reynier, France) **142/10**

**11** *snk* **Rockyl (IRE)**[40] 5-8-7 0........................................ MlleAlisonMassin(4) 4 58
(D De Waele, France) **80/1**

1m 35.7s **11** Ran SP% **117.7**
PARI-MUTUEL (all including 1 euro stake): WIN 6.90; PLACE 2.70, 2.20, 2.60; DF 16.50; SF 40.00.
**Owner** Christian Le Veel **Bred** Knockainey Stud **Trained** France

## 5209 BEVERLEY (R-H)
Tuesday, August 1

**OFFICIAL GOING: Good to soft (soft in places; 6.7)**
Wind: Fresh against Weather: Cloudy with showers

### 5492 COMPLETE THE COURSE FOR ANTIBIOTIC RESEARCH UK EBF NOVICE STKS 7f 96y
**2:00** (2:01) (Class 5) 2-Y-O **£3,881** (£1,155; £577; £288) **Stalls** Low

Form RPR

1 **1** **Codicil**[34] 4212 2-9-4 0........................................................ RyanPowell 5 77
(Sir Mark Prescott Bt) *trckd clr ldr: pushed along 2f out: rdn over 1f out: styd on strly fnl f to ld nr fin* **13/2**

**2** *nk* **Morning Wonder (IRE)** 2-9-2 0.......................................... TomEaves 6 74+
(Kevin Ryan) *chsd ldrs: pushed along over 2f out: rdn and green over 1f out: swtchd lft to outer ent fnl f: sn rdn and fin strly* **10/1**

3220 **3** *nk* **Weellan**[18] 4858 2-9-2 72.................................................... PhillipMakin 4 73
(John Quinn) *led and sn clr : rdn over 1f out: drvn and edgd lft ins fnl f: hdd and no ex nr fin* **9/4**[2]

1 **4** *1 ½* **International Man**[45] 3846 2-9-9 0.................................. PaulHanagan 2 76
(Richard Fahey) *chasded ldrs: pushed along and hdwy 2f out: rdn over 1f out: swtchd rt to inner and drvn ins fnl f: kpt on same pce towards fin* **13/8**[1]

0 **5** *3 ½* **Cum Spiro Spero (IRE)**[4] 5372 2-8-11 0.......................... BarryMcHugh 1 56
(Tony Coyle) *towards rr: hdwy over 2f out: rdn wl over 1f out: drvn and no imp fnl f* **50/1**

0013 **6** *1 ¾* **Poet's Dawn**[24] 4597 2-9-3 75.................................. RachelRichardson(3) 9 60
(Tim Easterby) *chsd ldng pair: hdwy over 2f out: rdn wl over 1f out: sn drvn and wknd* **6/1**[3]

0 **7** *6* **Echo (IRE)**[9] 5180 2-9-2 0............................................... JackGarritty 7 41
(Jedd O'Keeffe) *dwlt: green and a bhd* **20/1**

**8** *8* **Troop** 2-9-2 0......................................................................... ShaneGray 8 21
(Ann Duffield) *dwlt: green and a bhd* **33/1**

0 **9** *1 ½* **Charming Power (IRE)**[9] 5180 2-9-2 0.............................. GrahamLee 3 17
(Ann Duffield) *a towards rr* **50/1**

1m 36.21s (2.41) **Going Correction** +0.35s/f (Good) **9** Ran SP% **117.2**
Speed ratings (Par 94): **100,99,99,97,93 91,84,75,73**
CSF £65.76 TOTE £6.90: £2.20, £2.80, £1.60; EX 65.50 Trifecta £305.20.
**Owner** Cheveley Park Stud **Bred** Cheveley Park Stud Ltd **Trained** Newmarket, Suffolk

**FOCUS**
Race distance increased by 7yds. After a dry morning the official going was changed to good to soft, soft in places. An interesting novice and the form is worth keeping an eye on. It's been rated at face value.

### 5493 HOLDERNESS PONY CLUB (S) H'CAP (BEVERLEY MIDDLE DISTANCE SERIES) 1m 4f 23y
**2:35** (2:35) (Class 6) (0-65,65) 3-Y-0+ **£2,587** (£770; £384; £192) **Stalls** Low

Form RPR

2053 **1** **Bridey's Lettuce (IRE)**[8] 5208 5-9-7 **65**............... ManuelFernandes(7) 8 73+
(Ivan Furtado) *mde all: sn clr: rdn wl over 1f out: drifted lft ins fnl f: kpt on* **9/4**[1]

3612 **2** *6* **Cool Music (IRE)**[13] 5017 7-9-5 **56**..................................(p) CamHardie 2 55
(Antony Brittain) *trckd ldrs: hdwy over 2f out: rdn to chse wnr wl over 1f out: sn drvn. no imp fnl f* **4/1**[3]

064 **3** *½* **Petrify**[15] 4967 7-9-4 **55**............................................(tp) DanielMuscutt 6 53
(Bernard Llewellyn) *dwlt and towards rr: hdwy over 2f out: rdn wl over 1f out: drvn and kpt on fnl f* **10/1**

3-45 **4** *shd* **Taste The Wine (IRE)**[14] 2712 11-9-0 **51**..........................(tp) BenCurtis 3 49
(Bernard Llewellyn) *hld up in midfield: hdwy on outer 2f out: rdn wl over 1f out: drvn and kpt on fnl f* **8/1**

-025 **5** *3 ¼* **Moon Over Rio (IRE)**[41] 3978 6-8-13 **55**................. MeganNicholls(5) 1 48
(Ben Haslam) *trckd ldng pair: pushed along over 2f out: sn rdn: drvn wl over 1f out: one pce* **7/2**[2]

050- **6** *2 ¼* **Heaven Scent**[8] 6424 4-9-1 **52**.......................................(p) PaulMulrennan 9 42
(Donald McCain) *chsd wnr: rdn along wl over 2f out: sn drvn and grad wknd over 1f out* **16/1**

0500 **7** *¾* **Thomas Crown (IRE)**[8] 5209 3-8-7 **54** ow1..............(p) ConnorBeasley 7 44
(Roger Fell) *hld up: sme hdwy to chse ldrs over 4f out: rdn along wl over 2f out: sn wknd* **6/1**

0-00 **8** *8* **Strikemaster (IRE)**[139] 1197 11-8-9 **46** oh1.................. JamesSullivan 5 23
(Lee James) *a rr* **50/1**

2m 42.78s (2.98) **Going Correction** +0.35s/f (Good)
**WFA** 3 from 4yo+ 10lb **8** Ran SP% **115.3**
Speed ratings (Par 101): **104,100,99,99,97 95,95,90**
CSF £11.54 CT £73.35 TOTE £3.30: £1.40, £1.60, £2.00; EX 12.70 Trifecta £77.50.
**Owner** J Melo **Bred** Limestone & Tara Studs **Trained** Wiseton, Nottinghamshire

**FOCUS**
Race distance increased by 7yds. A modest selling handicap and an all-the-way winner.

### 5494 CHRIS GRAY 70TH BIRTHDAY CELEBRATIONS NOVICE AUCTION STKS 5f
**3:10** (3:11) (Class 5) 2-Y-O **£3,881** (£1,155; £577; £288) **Stalls** Low

Form RPR

022 **1** **Arcavallo (IRE)**[27] 4502 2-8-12 76.................................. PaulMulrennan 7 75
(Michael Dods) *mde all: rdn over 1f out: kpt on strly fnl f* **5/4**[1]

43 **2** *2 ½* **Lina's Star (IRE)**[17] 4895 2-8-7 0.................................... PaulHanagan 9 61
(Richard Fahey) *wnt lft s and rr: hdwy 2f out: chsd ldrs over 1f out: swtchd rt and drvn ent fnl f: kpt on* **15/2**[3]

0 **3** *shd* **Choosey (IRE)**[19] 4805 2-9-2 0........................................ DaneO'Neill 2 70
(Henry Candy) *wnt rt s: cl up: rdn and ev ch over 1f out: drvn and edgd lft ins fnl f: kpt on same pce* **2/1**[2]

4 **4** *1 ¼* **Fortunate Vision**[20] 4760 2-8-9 0........................................ TomEaves 8 58
(David Brown) *sn trcking ldrs on outer: hdwy over 2f out: rdn and ev ch over 1f out: sn drvn and kpt on same pce* **20/1**

**5** *1* **Biddy Brady (USA)** 2-8-8 0.............................. RachelRichardson(3) 5 57
(Tim Easterby) *towards rr: hdwy over 2f out: effrt on inner to chse ldrs over 1f out: sn rdn and no imp fnl f* **14/1**

**6** *hd* **Canford's Joy (IRE)** 2-9-2 0.............................................. ShaneGray 6 61
(Ann Duffield) *hld up: pushed along: green and sltly outpcd wl over 1f out: kpt on fnl f* **50/1**

0 **7** *¾* **Aislin Moon (IRE)**[14] 4996 2-7-13 0................................. JaneElliott(5) 1 46
(Les Eyre) *midfield: hdwy 1/2-way: chsd ldrs wl over 1f out: sn rdn and wknd appr fnl f* **25/1**

45 **8** *4* **Ben My Chree**[14] 4995 2-8-7 0 ConnorBeasley 3 35
(Bryan Smart) *t.k.h: trckd ldrs: pushed along over 2f out: sn rdn and wknd* **20/1**

**9** *8* **Racing Radio (IRE)** 2-8-12 0 BenCurtis 4 11
(David Barron) *trckd ldrs: green and pushed along over 3f out: sn lost pl and bhd* **20/1**

1m 5.7s (2.20) **Going Correction** +0.30s/f (Good) 9 Ran SP% **116.3**
Speed ratings (Par 94): **94,90,89,87,86 85,84,78,65**
CSF £10.40 TOTE £2.00: £1.10, £1.90, £1.30; EX 8.80 Trifecta £21.50.
**Owner** P Appleton & Mrs Anne Elliott **Bred** Nicola And Eleanor Kent **Trained** Denton, Co Durham

**FOCUS**
An ordinary novice. Straightforward form.

## 5495 ROBERTA MARSHALL MEMORIAL H'CAP 5f
**3:45** (3:47) (Class 5) (0-75,81) 3-Y-O+ **£3,780** (£1,131; £565; £283; £141) **Stalls** Low

Form RPR

0010 **1** **Tarboosh**[24] 4600 4-9-12 **77** CamHardie 5 93+
(Paul Midgley) *t.k.h: trckd ldrs: smooth hdwy to ld over 1f out: rdn and qcknd clr ins fnl f* **6/1**[3]

0336 **2** *3 ½* **Windforpower (IRE)**[24] 4607 7-8-4 **60** ow2 (p) BenRobinson(5) 3 61
(Tracy Waggott) *cl up: rdn to chal wl over 1f out: sn ev ch: drvn and kpt on same pce fnl f* **16/1**

1115 **3** *¾* **Foxy Boy**[25] 4576 3-9-7 **75** PaulMulrennan 2 72
(Michael Dods) *led: rdn along 2f out: drvn and hdd over 1f out: kpt on same pce* **5/2**[2]

0061 **4** *hd* **Musharrif**[8] 5211 5-9-11 **81** 6ex PhilDennis(5) 9 79
(Declan Carroll) *hld up towards rr: hdwy on outer 1/2-way: rdn to chse ldng trio and edgd rt over 1f out: sn drvn and kpt on same pce* **6/4**[1]

1130 **5** *5* **Kody Ridge (IRE)**[11] 5132 3-9-4 **72** (h) TonyHamilton 7 51
(Roger Fell) *cl up on outer: rdn along over 2f out: drvn wl over 1f out: sn wknd* **6/1**[3]

-006 **6** *1 ½* **Robben Rainbow**[13] 5018 3-9-2 **70** BenCurtis 1 43
(David Barron) *chsd ldrs on inner: rdn along over 2f out: sn wknd* **10/1**

1m 4.53s (1.03) **Going Correction** +0.30s/f (Good)
**WFA** 3 from 4yo+ 3lb 6 Ran SP% **112.1**
Speed ratings (Par 103): **103,97,96,95,87 85**
CSF £82.29 CT £297.77 TOTE £5.20: £2.10, £5.50; EX 57.20 Trifecta £230.10.
**Owner** The Guys & Dolls & Sandfield Racing **Bred** Landmark Racing Limited **Trained** Westow, N Yorks

**FOCUS**
A fair handicap run at an even pace. The runner-up has been rated close to his recent form.

## 5496 WILFORD WATTS MEMORIAL H'CAP 1m 100y
**4:20** (4:20) (Class 4) (0-85,87) 3-Y-O+ **£6,301** (£1,886; £943; £472; £235) **Stalls** Low

Form RPR

4401 **1** **Zodiakos (IRE)**[23] 4661 4-9-11 **78** (p) TonyHamilton 7 86
(Roger Fell) *trckd ldr: hdwy and cl up 2f out: rdn to ld jst over 1f out: drvn ins fnl f: hld on gamely* **6/1**[3]

-351 **2** *nk* **El Cap (USA)**[27] 4508 3-9-13 **87** PhillipMakin 6 93
(Sir Michael Stoute) *trckd ldrs: hdwy on outer 2f out: rdn over 1f out: drvn to chal ins fnl f: no ex towards fin* **13/8**[1]

4004 **3** *1 ½* **Bahama Moon (IRE)**[10] 5163 5-10-0 **81** BenCurtis 5 85
(David Barron) *led: rdn along over 2f out: hdd 11/2f out: sn drvn: kpt on u.p ins fnl f* **5/1**[2]

5266 **4** *shd* **Make On Madam (IRE)**[14] 5000 5-8-12 **70** (h) JaneElliott(5) 1 74
(Les Eyre) *t.k.h early: trckd ldrs on inner: hdwy 2f out: chal over 1f out: rdn and ev ch ent fnl f: sn drvn and no ex last 100 yds* **16/1**

-500 **5** *hd* **Off Art**[73] 2838 7-9-3 **70** JamesSullivan 3 73
(Tim Easterby) *hld up in tch: hdwy over 2f out: chsd ldrs and swtchd rt over 1f out: rdn and ch ent fnl f: sn drvn and kpt on same pce* **6/1**[3]

5223 **6** *¾* **Character Onesie (IRE)**[12] 5077 5-9-6 **73** (b[1]) PaulHanagan 2 74
(Richard Fahey) *dwlt and rr: hdwy 2f out: rdn wl over 1f out: kpt on u.p fnl f* **5/1**[2]

4310 **7** *½* **Valley Of Rocks (IRE)**[14] 5000 3-8-10 **70** FrannyNorton 4 69
(Mark Johnston) *dwlt: hld up towards rr: hdwy over 2f out: rdn wl over 1f out: sn drvn and wknd* **12/1**

1m 49.26s (1.66) **Going Correction** +0.35s/f (Good)
**WFA** 3 from 4yo+ 7lb 7 Ran SP% **113.6**
Speed ratings (Par 105): **105,104,103,103,102 102,101**
CSF £16.00 TOTE £7.20: £3.10, £1.40; EX 21.80 Trifecta £90.30.
**Owner** C Varley & R G Fell **Bred** Brian Walsh **Trained** Nawton, N Yorks

**FOCUS**
Race distance increased by 7yds. A decent handicap, albeit not the strongest for the level. The third has been rated close to his form under similar conditions.

## 5497 ROA/RACING POST OWNERS JACKPOT H'CAP 7f 96y
**4:55** (4:56) (Class 5) (0-70,73) 3-Y-O+ **£3,780** (£1,131; £565; £283; £141) **Stalls** Low

Form RPR

-221 **1** **Rosy Ryan (IRE)**[14] 5007 7-9-1 **59** JoeDoyle 4 68
(Tina Jackson) *hld up in rr: hdwy wl over 2f out: chsd ldrs over 1f out: rdn ent fnl f: styd on wl to ld nr fin* **13/2**[3]

0003 **2** *½* **Relight My Fire**[8] 5214 7-8-11 **58** (p) RachelRichardson(3) 2 66
(Tim Easterby) *chsd ldrs on inner: hdwy 3f out: rdn to chal over 1f out: drvn to ld last 100 yds: hdd and no ex nr fin* **6/1**[2]

6421 **3** *hd* **El Principe**[8] 5213 4-9-10 **73** 6ex (t) JaneElliott(5) 8 80
(Les Eyre) *set gd pce: pushed along and jnd wl over 1f out: rdn and hdd jst over 1f out: edgd lft ins fnl f: kpt on wl towards fin* **11/2**[1]

0354 **4** *½* **Tadaawol**[6] 5280 4-9-12 **70** (p) TonyHamilton 7 76
(Roger Fell) *hld up in rr: hdwy 2f out: rdn over 1f out: drvn and styd on wl fnl f* **10/1**

0105 **5** *¾* **Mr Cool Cash**[32] 4298 5-9-10 **68** ConnorBeasley 6 72
(Richard Guest) *trckd ldrs: hdwy over 2f out: chal wl over 1f out: rdn to ld appr fnl f: drvn: edgd rt and hdd last 100 yds: wknd towards fin* **6/1**[2]

0355 **6** *½* **Fidelma Moon (IRE)**[29] 4451 5-8-13 **57** RoystonFfrench 13 60
(Tracy Waggott) *chsd ldng pair on outer: hdwy and wd st towards stands side: cl up 2f out: sn rdn and ev ch tl drvn and wknd appr fnl f* **33/1**

3642 **7** *2 ¼* **Grey Destiny**[20] 4743 7-9-2 **60** CamHardie 10 57
(Antony Brittain) *dwlt and hld up in rr: hdwy over 2f out: sn rdn and kpt on appr fnl f: nrst fin* **16/1**

10 **8** *hd* **Geordie George (IRE)**[24] 4608 5-9-3 **61** (t[1]) GrahamLee 5 57
(Rebecca Menzies) *in tch: pushed along and hdwy 3f out: rdn 2f out: sn drvn and wknd* **8/1**

-005 **9** *2 ½* **Mayfield Boy**[8] 5214 6-8-11 **55** JamesSullivan 9 44
(Antony Brittain) *chsd ldr:. cl up 3f out: rdn along over 2f out: sn wknd* **9/1**

3522 **10** *1 ½* **Billy Bond**[15] 4960 5-8-12 **56** (b) PaulHanagan 1 41
(Richard Fahey) *dwlt: a towards rr* **6/1**[2]

0020 **11** *4 ½* **Shearian**[11] 5126 7-9-1 **64** PhilDennis(5) 3 37
(Declan Carroll) *in tch on inner: rdn along over 2f out: sn wknd* **20/1**

5666 **12** *8* **Popsies Joy (IRE)**[35] 4168 4-9-0 **58** DuranFentiman 12 9
(Tim Easterby) *chsd ldrs on outer: rdn along 3f out: sn wknd* **20/1**

1m 35.51s (1.71) **Going Correction** +0.35s/f (Good) 12 Ran SP% **120.1**
Speed ratings (Par 103): **104,103,103,102,101 101,98,98,95,93 88,79**
CSF £44.71 CT £236.93 TOTE £7.60: £2.40, £2.50, £1.90; EX 45.90 Trifecta £220.30.
**Owner** H L Thompson **Bred** Roger A Ryan **Trained** Liverton, Cleveland
■ Stewards' Enquiry : Rachel Richardson 4 day ban - used her whip above the permitted level (15-18 Aug)

**FOCUS**
Race distance increased by 7yds. A fair handicap and several were in with a chance throughout the final furlong. The fourth has been rated close to form.

## 5498 LADY JANE BETHELL MEMORIAL H'CAP (FOR LADY AMATEUR RIDERS) (DIV I) 1m 1f 207y
**5:30** (5:30) (Class 6) (0-65,66) 3-Y-O+ **£2,495** (£774; £386; £193) **Stalls** Low

Form RPR

06 **1** **Polar Forest**[24] 4608 7-11-0 **66** (e) MissJoannaMason 2 73+
(Richard Guest) *led: hdd 1/2-way: cl up: led again over 3f out: rdn wl over 1f out: kpt on wl fnl f* **3/1**[2]

5063 **2** *¾* **John Caesar (IRE)**[8] 5215 6-10-0 **52** (p) MrsCBartley 1 58
(Rebecca Bastiman) *trckd ldrs: hdwy to chse wnr 3f out: rdn over 1f out: drvn and kpt on fnl f* **5/2**[1]

040 **3** *nse* **Decima (IRE)**[82] 2547 3-9-11 **60** MissEEasterby(3) 5 67
(Michael Easterby) *t.k.h: trckd ldrs: pushed along and sltly outpcd 2f out: rdn over 1f out: styd on wl fnl f* **12/1**

3330 **4** *1 ¾* **Hussar Ballad (USA)**[31] 4336 8-10-3 **62** MissJGillam(7) 3 65
(Antony Brittain) *in tch: hdwy 3f out: rdn to chse ldrs over 2f pout: drvn over 1f out: kpt on same pce fnl f* **20/1**

2460 **5** *¾* **Warfare**[53] 3537 8-10-9 **66** MissHDukes(5) 6 67
(Tim Fitzgerald) *dwlt and rr: hdwy and wd st: rdn over 2f out: swtchd rt to join field over 1f out: kpt on u.p fnl f* **10/1**[3]

-050 **6** *shd* **Cadmium**[29] 4439 6-9-11 **49** MissBeckySmith 4 50
(Micky Hammond) *hld up in rr: hdwy over 2f out: rdn wl over 1f out: kpt on fnl f* **10/1**[3]

3163 **7** *¾* **Rubis**[15] 4959 4-10-2 **61** MissFMcSharry(7) 7 61
(Richard Fahey) *chsd ldrs: hdwy 3f out: rdn over 2f out: drvn over 1f out: kpt on one pce* **5/2**[1]

30-0 **8** *13* **Belle Peinture (FR)**[14] 5002 6-9-2 **45** (b) MissEmilyBullock(5) 9 21
(Alan Lockwood) *cl up: led 1/2-way: hdd over 3f out and sn rdn along: wknd 2f out* **33/1**

2m 11.93s (4.93) **Going Correction** +0.35s/f (Good)
**WFA** 3 from 4yo+ 8lb 8 Ran SP% **115.7**
Speed ratings (Par 101): **94,93,93,91,91 91,90,80**
CSF £11.12 CT £76.61 TOTE £4.10: £1.30, £1.30, £2.90; EX 12.80 Trifecta £94.70.
**Owner** Alfa Site Services Ltd/Mrs Alison Guest **Bred** Worksop Manor Stud **Trained** Ingmanthorpe, W Yorks

**FOCUS**
Race distance increased by 7yds. A modest handicap. It's been rated as straightforward form, with the second to his recent effort.

## 5499 LADY JANE BETHELL MEMORIAL H'CAP (FOR LADY AMATEUR RIDERS) (DIV II) 1m 1f 207y
**6:00** (6:00) (Class 6) (0-65,66) 3-Y-O+ **£2,495** (£774; £386; £193) **Stalls** Low

Form RPR

43 **1** **Indian Chief (IRE)**[11] 5097 7-10-12 **66** MrsCBartley 1 74+
(Rebecca Bastiman) *hld up towards rr: hdwy 2f out: swtchd wd and chsd ldrs over 1f out: rdn and styd on strly to ld last 100 yds* **13/8**[1]

5026 **2** *1 ½* **King Of The Celts (IRE)**[6] 5284 9-10-7 **64** (p) MissEEasterby(3) 9 67
(Tim Easterby) *trckd ldr: hdwy over 2f out: rdn wl over 1f out: led ent fnl f: hdd and no ex last 100 yds* **7/1**

0060 **3** *1 ¾* **Ivors Involvement (IRE)**[20] 4744 5-9-5 **45** MissPFuller 3 45
(Tina Jackson) *led: clr 4f out: rdn along 2f out: drvn over 1f out: hdd ent fnl f: grad wknd* **9/1**

5330 **4** *½* **Les Pecheurs (IRE)**[23] 4659 3-9-9 **57** (h[1]) MissBeckySmith 4 57
(James Ewart) *chsd ldrs: hdwy on inner over 2f out: rdn wl over 1f out: drvn and kpt on same pce fnl f* **20/1**

0012 **5** *½* **Graceful Act**[9] 5181 9-9-10 **50** (p) MissSBrotherton 2 48
(Ron Barr) *chsd ldrs: hdwy 3f out: rdn wl over 1f out: sn drvn and kpt on one pce* **6/1**[3]

0631 **6** *3 ¾* **Sakhalin Star (IRE)**[7] 5250 6-10-5 **59** 6ex (e) MissJoannaMason 7 50
(Richard Guest) *in tch: n.m.r and hmpd over 4f out: chsd ldrs 3f out: rdn along 2f out: sn drvn and no imp* **7/2**[2]

-660 **7** *hd* **Patent**[47] 3760 4-9-8 **53** (p) MissAMcCain(5) 8 44
(Peter Niven) *dwlt: a rr* **10/1**

0065 **8** *3 ½* **Port Lairge**[64] 2255 7-9-7 **52** MissJCooley(5) 6 37
(Michael Chapman) *dwlt: a rr* **22/1**

2m 11.13s (4.13) **Going Correction** +0.35s/f (Good)
**WFA** 3 from 4yo+ 8lb 8 Ran SP% **115.3**
Speed ratings (Par 101): **97,95,94,94,93 90,90,87**
CSF £13.91 CT £78.90 TOTE £3.10: £1.60, £2.40, £2.60; EX 15.20 Trifecta £116.70.
**Owner** Castle Construction (NE) Ltd **Bred** Paget Bloodstock **Trained** Cowthorpe, N Yorks

**FOCUS**
Race distance increased by 7yds. The second division of a modest handicap and a slightly quicker time than the first leg. Straightforward form.
T/Plt: £51.10 to a £1 stake. Pool: £55,719.34 - 794.59 winning units. T/Qpdt: £18.30 to a £1 stake. Pool: £4,189.65 - 168.99 winning units. **Joe Rowntree**

# 3776 GOODWOOD (R-H)

## Tuesday, August 1

**OFFICIAL GOING: Good (good to soft in places on straight course; 7.2)**
Wind: light to medium, across Weather: light cloud, bright spells

## 5500 MATCHBOOK BETTING EXCHANGE H'CAP — 1m 1f 197y
**1:50** (1:50) (Class 2) 4-Y-0+
**£31,125** (£9,320; £4,660; £2,330; £1,165; £585) **Stalls** Low

Form RPR
3446 **1** *hd* **Fabricate**[24] 4614 5-9-4 **102**...(p) AdamKirby 6 111
(Michael Bell) *wl in tch in midfield: effrt wl over 1f out: drvn and str chal ins fnl f: ev ch whn bmpd and pushed lft wl ins fnl f: rallied cl home: nt quite rcvr and jst hld: fin 2nd: awrdd the r* **20/1**

4403 **2** **Dark Red (IRE)**[3] 5421 5-8-8 **92**... OisinMurphy 2 101
(Ed Dunlop) *chsd ldr for 2f: styd chsng ldrs: effrt to chal ent fnl f: drvn to ld ins fnl f: hung bdly lft: bmpd nrest chalr wl ins fnl f: hld on: fin 1st: disqualified and plcd 2nd* **12/1**

1-10 **3** *¾* **Khairaat (IRE)**[38] 4069 4-9-5 **103**... JimCrowley 16 110
(Sir Michael Stoute) *stdd after s: hld up in tch in last trio: rdn and hdwy over 1f out: str run ins fnl f to chal 75yds out: intimated and wnt lft towards fin: no imp cl home* **7/1**[3]

-154 **4** *1 ¼* **UAE Prince (IRE)**[17] 4918 4-8-13 **97**... AndreaAtzeni 15 104+
(Roger Varian) *hld up in tch in last trio: stl towards rr and looking for run whn swtchd rt over 1f out: hdwy 1f out: str run to chse ldrs ins fnl f whn forced to switch lft arnd ldrs 100yds out: kpt on* **6/1**[2]

1230 **5** *¾* **Noble Gift**[4] 5353 7-8-12 **99**... CallumShepherd(3) 10 102
(William Knight) *taken down early: sn pushed up to ld: rdn ent fnl 2f: hdd briefly wl over 1f out: sn battled bk and led again over 1f out: hdd ins fnl f: no ex and outpcd fnl 100yds* **66/1**

5304 **6** *nk* **Oasis Fantasy (IRE)**[18] 4863 6-8-9 **93**...(p[1]) JamieSpencer 3 95
(David Simcock) *hld up in tch in midfield: hdwy and edging out lft over 1f out: swtchd rt ins fnl f: styd on u.p fnl 100yds: nvr getting on terms w ldrs* **10/1**

04-5 **7** *1 ½* **Mr Garcia**[17] 4918 4-8-11 **95**... RyanMoore 12 98+
(Richard Fahey) *chsd ldrs: upsides ldr ent fnl 2f: rdn to ld wl over 1f out: sn hdd but ev ch after: stl pressing ldrs but looked to be jst getting outpcd whn bdly squeezed and hmpd ins fnl f: eased after* **9/2**[1]

0206 **8** *hd* **Eddystone Rock (IRE)**[17] 4918 5-9-1 **99**...(h) KierenFox 5 98
(John Best) *t.k.h: hld up towards rr: nt clr run and swtchd lft over 1f out: stl nt enough room tl swtchd rt ins fnl f: styd on wl fnl 100yds: nvr trbld ldrs* **11/1**

0000 **9** *nse* **Bravery (IRE)**[17] 4918 4-9-3 **101**... DanielTudhope 8 100
(David O'Meara) *hld up in tch in midfield: swtchd lft and effrt over 2f out: no imp over 1f out: kpt on same pce ins fnl f* **33/1**

/04- **10** *½* **Eye Of The Storm (IRE)**[437] 2465 7-9-2 **100**... PatDobbs 4 98
(Amanda Perrett) *dwlt: sn rcvrd and in tch in midfield: effrt but nt clrest of runs over 1f out: no imp u.p 1f out: kpt on same pce ins fnl f* **33/1**

-000 **11** *hd* **Baydar**[24] 4614 4-9-3 **101**... JosephineGordon 18 99+
(Hugo Palmer) *hld up in tch in last trio: effrt on inner whn nt clr run and bdly hmpd over 1f out: sn swtchd lft: swtchd rt again wl ins fnl f: kpt on towards fin: nvr trbld ldrs* **16/1**

0321 **12** *nk* **What About Carlo (FR)**[10] 5148 6-9-10 **108**... CharlesBishop 9 105
(Eve Johnson Houghton) *hld up towards rr: nt clr run 2f out tl ent fnl f: styd on fnl 150yds: nvr trbld ldrs* **14/1**

0-01 **13** *nk* **Murad Khan (FR)**[30] 4410 4-9-5 **103**...(h) JamesDoyle 11 99
(Hugo Palmer) *taken down early: hld up in tch in midfield on outer: rdn and nudged lft over 2f out: no imp u.p over 1f out: wl hld and kpt on same pce ins fnl f* **9/1**

4-46 **14** *¾* **Abdon**[66] 3069 4-9-7 **105**...(p[1]) FrankieDettori 7 100
(Sir Michael Stoute) *t.k.h: chsd ldrs tl wnt 2nd after 2f tl 2f out: lost pl u.p ent fnl f: btn and eased ins fnl f* **12/1**

0015 **15** *6* **Speed Company (IRE)**[19] 4822 4-9-1 **99**...(h) JasonHart 1 82
(John Quinn) *hld up in tch in midfield: effrt on inner whn nt clr run and bdly hmpd over 1f out: nt rcvr: wl hld and eased ins fnl f* **25/1**

1/0- **16** *3 ¼* **Tha'ir (IRE)**[558] 283 7-9-4 **102**... LukeMorris 13 78
(Michael Appleby) *hld up in tch in midfield: effrt 2f out: keeping on same pce whn hmpd over 1f out: sn dropped to rr and btn: bhd and eased wl ins fnl f* **25/1**

2m 7.79s (-0.31) **Going Correction** +0.175s/f (Good) **16** Ran SP% **120.2**
Speed ratings (Par 109): **107,108,107,106,105 105,104,104,104,103 103,103,102,102,97 94**
CSF £226.45 CT £1863.37 TOTE £22.00: £3.80, £2.60, £2.10, £1.80; EX 270.20 Trifecta £6370.40.
**Owner** The Queen **Bred** The Queen **Trained** Newmarket, Suffolk
■ Stewards' Enquiry : Oisin Murphy eight-day ban; careless riding (Aug 15th-22nd)

**FOCUS**
Dry overnight and a dry day, although not especially warm, and the ground was good, good to soft in places. Lower bend out 5yds at the 6f marker to the winning post. Top bend out 3yds. Add 10yds to this race distance. A decent handicap to open the meeting, although it proved hard to make up significant ground, and the stewards were needed. The first past the post has been rated close to his old best.

## 5501 QATAR VINTAGE STKS (GROUP 2) — 7f
**2:25** (2:27) (Class 1) 2-Y-0
**£113,420** (£43,000; £21,520; £10,720; £5,380; £2,700) **Stalls** Low

Form RPR
1 **1** **Expert Eye**[47] 3747 2-9-1 0... AndreaAtzeni 7 116+
(Sir Michael Stoute) *str: lw: travelled strly in midfield: hdwy over 3f out: led wl over 2f out: sn had evthing off bridle: qcknd clr wl over 1f out: impressive* **7/4**[1]

1014 **2** *4 ½* **Zaman**[17] 4906 2-9-1 101...(b[1]) WilliamBuick 1 104
(Charlie Appleby) *pressed ldr: led over 3f out tl rdn wl over 2f out: sn outpcd by wnr but kpt on wl for 2nd* **8/1**

11 **3** *¾* **Mildenberger**[11] 5105 2-9-1 96... JamesDoyle 5 102+
(Mark Johnston) *tall: on toes: sltly awkwardly away: trckd ldrs: rdn 3f out: kpt on ins fnl f but nt pce to get on terms: snatched 3rd fnl stride* **7/2**[2]

331 **4** *hd* **James Garfield (IRE)**[19] 4792 2-9-1 99... OisinMurphy 4 102
(George Scott) *lw: trckd ldrs: rdn wl over 2f out: chsd ldng pair 2f out but nt pce to get on terms: kpt on: lost 3rd fnl stride* **12/1**

**5** *2 ½* **Seahenge (USA)**[24] 4641 2-9-1 0... RyanMoore 3 95
(A P O'Brien, Ire) *str: lw: little slowly away: sn mid-div: pushed along over 3f out: hdwy to chal for 3rd briefly 2f out: sn one pce* **4/1**[3]

311 **6** *4 ½* **Curiosity (IRE)**[17] 4880 2-9-1 86... JosephineGordon 8 83
(Hugo Palmer) *trckd ldrs: rdn wl over 2f out: nt pce to chal: wknd ins fnl f* **33/1**

130 **7** *3 ¼* **Roland Rocks (IRE)**[19] 4812 2-9-1 94... JamieSpencer 6 75
(John Ryan) *hld up towards rr: rdn wl over 2f out: nt pce to get involved* **66/1**

51 **8** *4* **Finsbury Park**[13] 5030 2-9-1 0... LukeMorris 9 64
(Robyn Brisland) *w'like: hld up towards rr: rdn and hdwy over 3f out: nvr threatened: wknd over 1f out* **100/1**

**9** *1 ¼* **Cold Stare (IRE)**[18] 4876 2-9-1 102... FabriceVeron 10 61
(E J O'Neill, France) *leggy: led tl rdn over 3f out: wknd over 2f out* **16/1**

61 **10** *8* **Sallab (IRE)**[26] 4520 2-9-1 0... FrankieDettori 2 40
(Richard Hannon) *athletic: nvr travelling: a detached in last (sddle slipped)* **25/1**

1m 26.97s (-0.03) **Going Correction** +0.175s/f (Good) **10** Ran SP% **112.5**
Speed ratings (Par 106): **107,101,101,100,97 92,89,84,83,73**
CSF £15.70 TOTE £2.60: £1.20, £2.30, £1.60; EX 15.50 Trifecta £59.00.
**Owner** K Abdullah **Bred** Juddmonte Farms Ltd **Trained** Newmarket, Suffolk

**FOCUS**
Add 15yds. Perhaps not the strongest of Group 2s, but it was run at a reasonable pace and the favourite ran out a most impressive winner. The winner has been rated up with the better winners of this race.

## 5502 QATAR LENNOX STKS (GROUP 2) — 7f
**3:00** (3:02) (Class 1) 3-Y-0+
**£170,130** (£64,500; £32,280; £16,080; £8,070; £4,050) **Stalls** Low

Form RPR
-353 **1** **Breton Rock (IRE)**[31] 4362 7-9-3 112... AndreaAtzeni 15 116
(David Simcock) *in rr: effrt to cl and rn into heels of rivals over 1f out: sn swtchd lft and nudged way out: hdwy 1f out: storming run u.p ins fnl f to ld towards fin* **50/1**

0-11 **2** *½* **Home Of The Brave (IRE)**[31] 4362 5-9-3 115...(t) JamesDoyle 1 114
(Hugo Palmer) *lw: sn led and racd keenly: rdn ent fnl 2f: drvn and hdd ent fnl f: battled on gamely u.p and led again wl ins fnl f: hdd and no ex towards fin* **4/1**[2]

-030 **3** *shd* **Suedois (FR)**[38] 4071 6-9-3 112... DanielTudhope 6 113
(David O'Meara) *t.k.h: trckd ldrs: effrt and nt clr run over 1f out: swtchd lft 1f out: hdwy u.p ins fnl f: r.o strly to snatch 3rd on post* **25/1**

-032 **4** *nse* **Limato (IRE)**[17] 4907 5-9-3 118... HarryBentley 8 113
(Henry Candy) *broke wl: stdd bk and hld up in tch in midfield: effrt to chal wl over 1f out: drvn to ld and edgd rt jst over 1f out: kpt on u.p tl hdd wl ins fnl f: kpt on same pce: lost 2 pls nr fin* **3/1**[1]

3342 **5** *½* **So Beloved**[16] 4935 7-9-3 111...(h) AdamKirby 3 112
(David O'Meara) *lw: t.k.h: hld up in tch in midfield on inner: clsd but nt clr run over 1f out: swtchd lft 1f out: styd on wl fnl 100yds: nvr quite getting to ldrs* **50/1**

1-60 **6** *nk* **Aclaim (IRE)**[38] 4071 4-9-3 114... FrankieDettori 2 111+
(Martyn Meade) *trckd ldrs: nt clr run over 1f out: swtchd lft and nudged way out jst ins fnl f: styd on wl 100yds: nvr quite getting on terms w ldrs* **9/1**

1255 **7** *nse* **Dream Castle**[41] 3959 3-8-11 112... OisinMurphy 5 109
(Saeed bin Suroor) *rring in stalls: hld up in tch in midfield: effrt and nudged lft over 1f out: hdwy u.p 1f out: styd on wl ins fnl f* **5/1**[3]

3203 **8** *1 ¾* **Jallota**[17] 4890 6-9-3 110... FranBerry 12 106
(Charles Hills) *hld up in last pair: effrt 2f out: clsd but nt clrest of runs over 1f out: swtchd lft 1f out: hdwy ins fnl f: styd on but nvr threatening ldrs* **100/1**

16-4 **9** *½* **Librisa Breeze**[38] 4071 5-9-3 113... RobertWinston 14 110+
(Dean Ivory) *stdd and swtchd rt after s: nt clr run 2f out: enough room and clsd over 1f out: effrt whn squeezed for room and hmpd jst ins fnl f: nvr threatening after: hmpd again and eased wl ins fnl f* **7/1**

0621 **10** *1* **Spirit Of Valor (USA)**[16] 4935 3-9-0 116...(bt) RyanMoore 10 103+
(A P O'Brien, Ire) *chsd ldr: pushed along to chal 2f out: drvn and stl chalng over 1f out: jst getting outpcd whn nudged and hmpd jst ins fnl f: nt rcvr and eased ins fnl f* **7/1**

2130 **11** *¾* **Oh This Is Us (IRE)**[42] 3924 4-9-3 109... SeanLevey 9 100
(Richard Hannon) *hld up in tch towards rr: effrt whn sltly impeded over 1f out: no imp u.p 1f out: wl hld and kpt on same pce ins fnl f* **33/1**

0221 **12** *½* **Jungle Cat (IRE)**[10] 5137 5-9-3 113...(b) WilliamBuick 11 99
(Charlie Appleby) *hld up in tch in last trio: effrt wl over 1f out: no imp over 1f out: wl hld whn edgd rt u.p jst ins fnl f* **20/1**

2523 **13** *2 ¼* **Stormy Antarctic**[16] 4935 4-9-3 112... JamieSpencer 13 93
(Ed Walker) *racd keenly: chsd ldrs: rdn and losing pl whn squeezed for room and swtchd lft jst over 1f out: wknd and bhd ins fnl f* **20/1**

1m 26.62s (-0.38) **Going Correction** +0.175s/f (Good)
**WFA** 3 from 4yo+ 6lb **13** Ran SP% **117.9**
Speed ratings (Par 115): **109,108,108,108,107 107,107,105,104,103 102,102,99**
CSF £228.85 TOTE £51.60: £12.10, £1.80, £5.70; EX 480.60 Trifecta £8133.30.
**Owner** John Cook **Bred** George Kent **Trained** Newmarket, Suffolk

**FOCUS**
Add 15yds. A good, competitive Group 2 but some of these found trouble and if you ran the race again you'd probably get a different result. The second has been rated close to form.

## 5503 QATAR GOODWOOD CUP STKS (GROUP 1) (BRITISH CHAMPIONS SERIES) — 2m
**3:35** (3:36) (Class 1) 3-Y-0+
**£296,593** (£112,445; £56,274; £28,032; £14,068; £7,060) **Stalls** Low

Form RPR
-121 **1** **Stradivarius (IRE)**[39] 4032 3-8-8 100... AndreaAtzeni 5 118
(John Gosden) *towards rr of mid-div: weaved way through and hdwy fr over 3f out: led jst over 1f out: styd on strly: rdn out* **6/1**[2]

-411 **2** *1 ¾* **Big Orange**[40] 3996 6-9-7 121...(p) FrankieDettori 11 116
(Michael Bell) *lw: led: rdn whn hdd jst over 1f out: styd on but no ex fnl 100yds* **6/4**[1]

2362 **3** *3 ½* **Desert Skyline (IRE)**[19] 4811 3-8-8 101...(p[1]) DavidProbert 13 112
(David Elsworth) *hld up towards rr: hdwy over 3f out: rdn over 2f out: chsd ldng pair wl over 1f out: edgd rt: styd on but nt pce to get on terms* **14/1**

0-42 **4** *3 ½* **Wicklow Brave**[30] 4420 8-9-7 115... JimCrowley 7 108
(W P Mullins, Ire) *hld up towards rr: hdwy over 3f out: rdn over 2f out: styd on but nt pce to threaten: wnt 4th fnl 120yds* **8/1**[3]

1-34 **5** *¾* **She Is No Lady**[40] 3996 5-9-4 110... JamesDoyle 10 104
(Ralph Beckett) *s.i.s: sn mid-div: hdwy over 4f out: rdn in 4th 2f out: styd on but nt pce to threaten: lost 4th fnl 120yds* **33/1**

20-5 **6** ¾ **Pallasator**$^{90}$ 2288 8-9-7 113 OisinMurphy 9 106
(Sir Mark Prescott Bt) *hld up bhd: hdwy over 2f out: sn rdn: styd on wl fnl f but nvr threatening to get on terms* **25/1**

-336 **7** ½ **Sheikhzayedroad**$^{40}$ 3996 8-9-7 116 (h) MartinHarley 12 105
(David Simcock) *trckd ldr: rdn over 3f out: nt pce to chal: no ex ent fnl f* **10/1**

3203 **8** ½ **US Army Ranger (IRE)**$^{38}$ 4073 4-9-7 110 (h$^{1}$) RyanMoore 16 105
(A P O'Brien, Ire) *.in tch: rdn over 3f out: sn one pce* **8/1**$^{3}$

-106 **9** 3 ¼ **Sweet Selection**$^{18}$ 4879 5-9-4 105 (b) AdamKirby 8 98
(Hughie Morrison) *hld up towards rr: rdn over 3f out: sme late prog but little imp on ldrs* **33/1**

3520 **10** 1 **Prince Of Arran**$^{40}$ 3996 4-9-7 107 StevieDonohoe 3 100
(Charlie Fellowes) *mid-div: rdn over 3f out: wknd over 1f out* **33/1**

-221 **11** 3 ¼ **Higher Power**$^{31}$ 4356 5-9-7 110 TomQueally 14 96
(James Fanshawe) *lw: mid-div: rdn over 3f out: wknd over 1f out* **20/1**

4/35 **12** 5 **High Jinx (IRE)**$^{17}$ 4917 9-9-7 110 DavidAllan 1 90
(Tim Easterby) *s.i.s: rcvrd to midfield after 3f: wknd over 3f out* **66/1**

41-4 **13** 2 **Qewy (IRE)**$^{38}$ 4073 7-9-7 107 (p) WilliamBuick 4 87
(Charlie Appleby) *lw: trckd ldr: rdn 3f out: wknd 2f out* **16/1**

2515 **14** 30 **Oriental Fox (GER)**$^{24}$ 4639 9-9-7 105 JoeFanning 2 51
(Mark Johnston) *trckd ldrs tl wknd 4f out* **50/1**

3m 25.47s (-3.53) **Going Correction** +0.175s/f (Good)
**WFA** 3 from 4yo+ 13lb **14** Ran SP% **119.0**
Speed ratings (Par 117): **115,114,112,110,110 109,109,109,107,107 105,103,102,87**
CSF £14.05 TOTE £6.20: £2.20, £1.10, £4.60; EX 18.10 Trifecta £183.70.
**Owner** B E Nielsen **Bred** Bjorn Nielsen **Trained** Newmarket, Suffolk

**FOCUS**
Add 10yds. Group 1 status now for the Goodwood Cup, and it was run at a good gallop early, before the favourite steadied it once establishing the lead. The form looks strong, with the right pair coming to the fore. The runner-up has been rated slightly below his best.

## 5504 IRISH THOROUGHBRED MARKETING EBF MAIDEN STKS (PLUS 10 RACE) (C&G) 6f
**4:10** (4:11) (Class 2) 2-Y-O **£16,172** (£4,812; £2,405; £1,202) **Stalls** High

Form RPR

**1** **Thechildren'strust (IRE)** 2-9-0 0 HectorCrouch 2 82
(Gary Moore) *tall: stdd: swtchd lft and impeded sn after s: hdwy to chse ldrs after 1f: effrt and ev ch over 1f out: edgd lft u.p ins fnl f: kpt on to ld wl ins fnl f: hld on last strides* **100/1**

42 **2** shd **Rebel Streak**$^{18}$ 4826 2-9-0 0 DavidProbert 3 82
(Andrew Balding) *athletic: racd keenly: led and dictated stdy gallop: rdn and qcknd wl over 1f out: drvn and hdd ins fnl f: battled bk wl towards fin: jst hld* **4/1**$^{2}$

2 **3** hd **Bombastic (IRE)**$^{19}$ 4805 2-9-0 0 DanielTudhope 5 81
(Ed de Giles) *w'like: coltish: t.k.h: pressed ldr : rdn and ev ch over 1f out: edgd lft ins fnl f: styd on u.p wl ins fnl f: clsng steadily on ldng pair cl home* **12/1**

2 **4** ½ **Alrahaal (IRE)**$^{60}$ 3305 2-9-0 0 JimCrowley 4 80
(Marcus Tregoning) *str: lw: dwlt: sn rcvrd and in tch in midfield: clsd to chse ldrs 2f out: effrt over 1f out: ev ch u.p ins fnl f: kpt on but no imp towards fin* **9/1**

52 **5** ¾ **Oliver Reed (IRE)**$^{10}$ 5151 2-9-0 0 SeanLevey 13 79+
(Richard Hannon) *athletic: t.k.h: hld up in tch in midfield: clsd to chse ldrs over 1f out: swtchd rt and effrt ent fnl f: kpt on u.p but no imp fnl 100yds* **10/1**

2 **6** 1 ¼ **Algam (IRE)**$^{12}$ 5063 2-9-0 0 FrankieDettori 9 77+
(Richard Hannon) *athletic: lw: wnt lft and bmpd rival sn after s: t.k.h: hld up in tch in rr: swtchd lft 1/2-way: nt clr run on stands rail 2f out: pushed along and hdwy over 1f out: kpt on ins fnl f wout threatening ldrs* **8/1**$^{3}$

**7** 1 ¼ **Lake Volta (IRE)** 2-9-0 0 JamesDoyle 7 70
(Mark Johnston) *neat: chsd ldrs early: wl in tch in midfield after: effrt 2f out: unable qck u.p over 1f out: wknd ins fnl f* **12/1**

22 **8** shd **Tribal Quest (USA)**$^{18}$ 4860 2-9-0 0 WilliamBuick 8 70+
(Charlie Appleby) *hld up in midfield: stmbld sltly over 4f out: swtchd rt ent fnl 2f: effrt whn pushed lft over 1f out: wnt rt again ins fnl f: kpt on but nvr threatened ldrs* **7/4**$^{1}$

35 **9** ¾ **George (IRE)**$^{63}$ 3164 2-9-0 0 PatDobbs 12 68
(Sylvester Kirk) *unf: chsd ldrs: rdn and unable qck over 1f out: drvn and btn 1f out: wknd ins fnl f* **33/1**

**10** 5 **The Great Dandini (IRE)** 2-9-0 0 OisinMurphy 14 53+
(Seamus Durack) *w'like: hld up in tch in midfield: effrt 2f out: rn green and hung rt over 1f out: sn outpcd and btn: wknd ins fnl f* **100/1**

5 **11** 1 ¾ **Baghdad (FR)**$^{13}$ 5036 2-9-0 0 StevieDonohoe 10 47
(Charlie Fellowes) *w'like: bmpd sn after s: hld up towards rr: swtchd rt and effrt 2f out: sn outpcd: rn green and hung rt: wl hld whn bdly hmpd ins fnl f* **33/1**

**12** 3 ¼ **Princely** 2-9-0 0 RyanMoore 11 38
(Richard Hannon) *cmpt: chsd ldrs: rdn ent fnl 2f: sn struggling and lost pl: wknd and bhd ins fnl f* **12/1**

**13** nk **Makambe (IRE)** 2-9-0 0 FranBerry 6 37
(Charles Hills) *w'like: bit bkwd: sn towards rr: bhd and struggling whn rn green and hung lft over 2f out: wl bhd whn bdly hmpd ins fnl f* **50/1**

**P** **Hell Of A Band** 2-9-0 0 ShaneKelly 1
(Richard Hughes) *tall: stdd and swtchd lft after s: plld hrd in rr: hdwy into midfield over 3f out: pushed rt over 1f out: effrt whn wnt lft sn after and lost action: p.u and dismntd jst ins fnl f (fatally injured)* **80/1**

1m 12.88s (0.68) **Going Correction** -0.10s/f (Good) **14** Ran SP% **120.7**
Speed ratings (Par 100): **91,90,90,89,88 87,85,85,84,77 75,71,70,**
CSF £471.49 TOTE £58.90: £16.00, £1.70, £3.30; EX 913.00 Trifecta £12860.30.
**Owner** Ashley Head **Bred** N Bradley **Trained** Lower Beeding, W Sussex

**FOCUS**
A valuable maiden but the pace was steady, it proved hard to make significant ground, the first four were drawn 2-3-5-4 (horse from stall 1 was pulled up), and there was a shock winner, so this seems likely to prove muddling form. Pre-race form and the race average suggests the form is at least as good as rated.

## 5505 NEW & LINGWOOD H'CAP 5f
**4:45** (4:48) (Class 2) (0-105,104) 4-Y-O+**£19,407** (£5,775; £2,886; £1,443) **Stalls** High

Form RPR

1000 **1** **El Astronaute (IRE)**$^{17}$ 4881 4-8-8 91 JasonHart 9 99
(John Quinn) *mde all: edgd sltly rt but kpt on strly: jst hld on: all out* **33/1**

2433 **2** shd **A Momentofmadness**$^{19}$ 4816 4-8-9 92 (h) HarryBentley 6 99
(Charles Hills) *taken down early: pressed wnr thrght: rdn and ev ch fr 2f out: kpt on strly: jst failed* **7/1**$^{3}$

01-0 **3** 1 **Green Door (IRE)**$^{17}$ 4881 6-9-1 98 (v) JamieSpencer 8 101
(Robert Cowell) *trckd ldng pair thrght: swtchd rt for effrt 2f out: kpt on but nt quite pce to mount chal* **22/1**

0300 **4** ½ **Poyle Vinnie**$^{38}$ 4072 7-9-2 99 AlistairRawlinson 14 100+
(Michael Appleby) *taken down early: hld up towards rr: swtchd rt 2f out: hdwy sn after: r.o fnl f* **50/1**

/351 **5** ½ **Atletico (IRE)**$^{8}$ 5219 5-8-10 93 6ex AndreaAtzeni 12 92
(Roger Varian) *lw: in tch: rdn whn swtchd rt 2f out: kpt on same pce fnl f* **9/2**$^{1}$

1432 **6** hd **Pettochside**$^{4}$ 5354 8-7-13 85 oh1 HollieDoyle$^{(3)}$ 10 84+
(John Bridger) *towards rr: hdwy ent fnl f: r.o wl but no threat* **16/1**

0014 **7** 1 ¼ **Union Rose**$^{8}$ 5219 5-8-6 89 SamHitchcott 4 83
(Ronald Harris) *chsd ldrs: rdn over 2f out: kpt on tl no ex fnl 100yds* **28/1**

0110 **8** shd **Line Of Reason (IRE)**$^{24}$ 4635 7-9-7 104 OisinMurphy 7 98
(Paul Midgley) *hld up: nt clr run 2f out: kpt on but no ch fnl f* **16/1**

4200 **9** ¾ **Harry Hurricane**$^{17}$ 4881 5-9-2 99 (b) PatCosgrave 2 90
(George Baker) *mid-div: hdwy over 2f out: sn rdn: nt quite pce to get on terms: fdd fnl 120yds* **6/1**$^{2}$

0001 **9** dht **Confessional**$^{3}$ 5402 10-8-1 89 6ex (e) DavidEgan$^{(5)}$ 1 80
(Tim Easterby) *nvr bttr than mid-div* **12/1**

-612 **11** nk **Vibrant Chords**$^{67}$ 3034 4-8-13 96 TomMarquand 15 86
(Henry Candy) *a towards rr* **9/1**

1001 **12** 2 **Love On The Rocks (IRE)**$^{15}$ 4974 4-8-5 91 (h) CallumShepherd$^{(3)}$ 11 74
(Charles Hills) *taken down early: awkward leaving stalls: hld up: swtchd rt over 1f out: sn rdn: nvr threatened* **25/1**

4060 **13** shd **Boom The Groom (IRE)**$^{38}$ 4072 6-9-5 102 AdamKirby 3 85
(Tony Carroll) *taken down early: mid-div: effrt 2f out: fdd fnl f* **9/1**

2554 **14** ½ **Dark Shot**$^{15}$ 4974 4-8-7 90 DavidProbert 5 71
(Andrew Balding) *lw: hld up towards rr: rdn wl over 1f out: no imp* **6/1**$^{2}$

4502 **15** 1 ¼ **Kasbah (IRE)**$^{25}$ 4581 5-8-6 89 JoeFanning 13 65
(Amanda Perrett) *mid-div: rdn 2f out: wknd fnl f* **33/1**

57.47s (-2.73) **Going Correction** -0.10s/f (Good) **15** Ran SP% **118.2**
Speed ratings (Par 109): **117,116,115,114,113 113,111,111,109,109 109,106,106,105,103**
CSF £232.44 CT £5168.51 TOTE £38.30: £9.90, £3.00, £6.90; EX 385.80 Trifecta £5764.80.
**Owner** Ross Harmon & Mrs S Quinn **Bred** T Jones **Trained** Settrington, N Yorks

**FOCUS**
A useful sprint, it paid to race handily and those nearer to the stands' rail were favoured. The winner has been rated to the better view of his form.

## 5506 SMARTER BETS WITH MATCHBOOK BETTING EXCHANGE FILLIES' H'CAP 1m
**5:15** (5:21) (Class 3) (0-95,97) 3-Y-O+ **£16,172** (£4,812; £2,405; £1,202) **Stalls** Low

Form RPR

-362 **1** **Shenanigans (IRE)**$^{19}$ 4794 3-8-11 84 AndreaAtzeni 2 93+
(Roger Varian) *hld up in tch in midfield: effrt to chse ldrs over 1f out: styd on strly to ld wl ins fnl f: sn in command and r.o wl* **15/2**

1412 **2** 1 ¼ **Lincoln Rocks**$^{10}$ 5152 4-10-3 97 DanielTudhope 3 104
(David O'Meara) *chsd ldr: effrt 2f out: clsd to ld and drifted lft 1f out: drvn and hdd wl ins fnl f: kpt on same pce after* **12/1**

-010 **3** ½ **Hadeeqa (IRE)**$^{17}$ 4915 3-8-8 81 (h$^{1}$) HarryBentley 6 86
(Simon Crisford) *short of room and shuffled bk to rr sn after s: hdwy into midfield on inner 5f out: effrt over 2f out: hdwy u.p over 1f out: swtchd lft ins fnl f: styd on strly u.p to snatch 3rd last strides* **20/1**

-121 **4** nk **Ghadaayer (IRE)**$^{38}$ 4096 3-8-11 84 JimCrowley 5 88
(Sir Michael Stoute) *hld up in tch in midfield: effrt 2f out: hdwy u.p to chse ldrs 1f out: kpt on but nt match pce of wnr wl ins fnl f* **6/1**$^{3}$

1 **5** 1 ½ **Pretty Asset (IRE)**$^{11}$ 5118 3-9-1 88 WilliamBuick 10 89+
(Charlie Appleby) *str: lw: hld up in tch in midfield: effrt over 1f out: sme hdwy u.p 1f out: kpt on same pce ins fnl f* **11/2**$^{2}$

5-01 **6** nk **Soul Silver (IRE)**$^{10}$ 5152 3-9-5 92 OisinMurphy 4 92
(David Simcock) *stmbld leaving stalls: hld up in tch in midfield: effrt 2f out: nt clrest of runs over 1f out tl sme hdwy ent fnl f: styd on u.p ins fnl f: nvr threatened ldrs* **20/1**

15-1 **7** ½ **Amabilis**$^{61}$ 3233 3-9-7 94 RyanMoore 13 93+
(Ralph Beckett) *swtchd rt after s: hld up in rr: effrt 2f out: nt clrest of runs tl hdwy u.p 1f out: styd on ins fnl f: nvr trbld ldrs* **10/1**

5325 **8** ½ **Angel's Quest (FR)**$^{15}$ 4975 3-8-0 76 HollieDoyle$^{(3)}$ 7 74
(Richard Hughes) *chsd ldrs: rdn 2f out: unable qck over 1f out and btn 1f out: wknd ins fnl f* **16/1**

5611 **9** nk **Sayem**$^{15}$ 4975 3-8-9 82 JamieSpencer 11 79+
(Ed Walker) *lw: swtchd rt and dropped in bhd after s: effrt over 1f out: sn swtchd lft and hdwy 1f out: swtchd lft again ins fnl f: styd on u.p fnl 100yds: nvr trbld ldrs* **9/1**

1164 **10** ½ **Darkroom Angel**$^{19}$ 4798 3-8-4 77 JoeFanning 1 73
(Philip Hide) *led: rdn wl over 1f out: hdd 1f out: sn btn and wknd ins fnl f* **16/1**

2141 **11** ½ **Al Nafoorah**$^{7}$ 5265 3-8-8 81 6ex DavidProbert 12 76
(Ed Dunlop) *t.k.h: hld up in midfield on outer: effrt 2f out: no imp u.p over 1f out: wl hld ins fnl f* **16/1**

00-6 **12** 4 ½ **Queensbrydge**$^{24}$ 4617 3-8-11 84 LukeMorris 8 68
(Robyn Brisland) *chsd ldrs: rdn 2f out: unable qck and lost pl over 1f out: bhd whn hung rt 1f out: wknd ins fnl f* **40/1**

-411 **13** 18 **Tribute Act**$^{19}$ 4794 3-9-0 87 TomQueally 9 30+
(James Fanshawe) *str: stdd after s: t.k.h: hld up towards rr: effrt 3f out but immediately wanting to hang lft: rdn and no imp 2f out: hanging bdly and eased 1f out* **7/2**$^{1}$

1m 39.54s (-0.36) **Going Correction** +0.175s/f (Good)
**WFA** 3 from 4yo 7lb **13** Ran SP% **120.1**
Speed ratings (Par 104): **108,106,106,105,104 104,103,103,102,102 101,97,79**
CSF £92.39 CT £1739.24 TOTE £8.00: £2.60, £3.90, £5.90; EX 84.80 Trifecta £1861.70.
**Owner** Ann Black,M Al Qatami & K M Al Mudhaf **Bred** Ringfort Stud **Trained** Newmarket, Suffolk

**FOCUS**
Add 15yds. A decent fillies' handicap. The runner-up, rated to the better view of her form, helps set the standard.

T/Jkpt: Not won. T/Plt: £795.50 to a £1 stake. Pool: £337,757.30 - 309.91 winning units. T/Qpdt: £191.30 to a £1 stake. Pool: £21,142.60 - 81.75 winning units. **Steve Payne & Tim Mitchell**

# 5334 YARMOUTH (L-H)

Tuesday, August 1

**OFFICIAL GOING: Good to firm (good in places; 7.4)**

Wind: Fresh against Weather: Cloudy with sunny spells

## 5507 GOODWOOD FESTIVAL BETTING AT 188BET NOVICE AUCTION STKS 7f 3y

**1:40** (1:41) (Class 6) 2-Y-O **£2,587** (£770; £384; £192) **Stalls** Centre

Form RPR

32 **1** **Midnight Wilde**17 4919 2-9-0 0 SilvestreDeSousa 10 77+
(John Ryan) *prom: led over 5f out: shkn up over 1f out: styd on wl: comf* **30/100**1

**2** *1 ½* **Azezati (IRE)** 2-8-11 0 DougieCostello 9 67+
(David Simcock) *s.s: hld up: swtchd rt and hdwy wl over 1f out: rdn to chse wnr ent fnl f: sn hung lft: styd on* **6/1**2

**3** *1* **Harbour Vision** 2-9-2 0 KieranShoemark 5 69
(David Brown) *hld up: racd keenly: hdwy over 2f out: rdn over 1f out: styd on same pce ins fnl f* **18/1**

004 **4** *2 ¾* **Four Fifty Three**21 4725 2-8-12 53 JoeyHaynes 4 58
(Mark H Tompkins) *led: hdd over 5f out: chsd wnr tl rdn over 1f out: no ex ins fnl f* **28/1**

04 **5** *hd* **Roman Spinner**20 4757 2-8-9 0 (t) MartinDwyer 3 54
(Rae Guest) *hld up: hdwy over 1f out: styd on same pce ins fnl f* **12/1**

0 **6** *2 ½* **Kentucky Blueblood (USA)**62 3210 2-8-7 0 AdamBeschizza 11 46+
(Richard Guest) *hld up: rdn over 2f out: nvr on terms* **10/1**3

3 **7** *shd* **Casey Banter**24 4620 2-8-0 0 MillyNaseb(7) 2 45
(Julia Feilden) *plld hrd and prom: rdn over 1f out: wknd fnl f* **14/1**

**8** *3* **Pammi** 2-8-7 0 RyanTate 7 37
(Anthony Carson) *hld up in tch: pushed along 1/2-way: rdn and wknd over 1f out* **22/1**

0 **9** *1 ¼* **Gas Monkey**32 4291 2-8-9 0 ShelleyBirkett(3) 8 39
(Julia Feilden) *plld hrd and prom: rdn and wknd over 1f out* **28/1**

1m 28.09s (1.49) **Going Correction** -0.10s/f (Good) **9** Ran SP% **131.2**
Speed ratings (Par 92): **87,85,84,81,80 77,77,74,72**
CSF £3.59 TOTE £1.20: £1.02, £2.10, £3.80; EX 4.10 Trifecta £20.30.
**Owner** Jon A Thompson **Bred** P A & M J Reditt & Catridge Stud **Trained** Newmarket, Suffolk

**FOCUS**

The official ground dried out to good to firm, good in places ahead of the opener, an uncompetitive novice in which the market leader dominated. The form can be rated around the fourth.

## 5508 GET 1/4 ODDS AT 188BET H'CAP 1m 3f 104y

**2:15** (2:15) (Class 6) (0-65,66) 4-Y-O+ **£2,264** (£673; £336; £168) **Stalls** Low

Form RPR

501 **1** **The Detainee**28 4469 4-9-0 58 (p) TrevorWhelan 4 66
(Neil Mulholland) *sn chsng ldrs: led 2f out: sn rdn and hung lft: styd on gamely* **11/2**2

4123 **2** *hd* **Hope Is High**20 4733 4-8-12 56 SilvestreDeSousa 1 64
(John Berry) *s.i.s and rdr lost iron briefly s: hld up: swtchd rt over 3f out: hdwy over 2f out: chsd wnr and edgd lft over 1f out: rdn and ev ch ins fnl f: styd on* **11/8**1

0404 **3** *2 ¼* **Best Example (USA)**25 4573 5-9-4 65 ShelleyBirkett(3) 7 70
(Julia Feilden) *hld up: hdwy and n.m.r over 1f out: shkn up ins fnl f: styd on same pce* **14/1**

1322 **4** *5* **Strictly Art (IRE)**35 4181 4-8-12 61 JoshuaBryan(5) 3 57
(Alan Bailey) *chsd ldrs: rdn over 2f out: nt clr run over 1f out: wknd fnl f* **8/1**

4552 **5** *8* **Aumerle**26 4545 5-9-4 62 (p) KieranShoemark 5 46
(Shaun Lycett) *chsd ldr: rdn and ev ch 2f out: hmpd and wknd over 1f out* **8/1**

4-46 **6** *1 ½* **Three Loves (IRE)**28 4469 4-8-2 49 (t1) AaronJones(3) 2 30
(Stuart Williams) *hld up: rdn over 4f out: sme hdwy on inner over 2f out: wknd over 1f out* **7/1**3

-002 **7** *13* **Annoushka**12 5080 4-8-6 50 (t) AdamBeschizza 6 10
(Mrs Ilka Gansera-Leveque) *led: plld hrd: rdn and hdd 2f out: hmpd and wknd over 1f out* **12/1**

6460 **R** **Sandy Cove**30 1519 6-9-8 66 (p1) RyanTate 8
(James Eustace) *ref to r* **16/1**

2m 24.62s (-4.08) **Going Correction** -0.25s/f (Firm) **8** Ran SP% **112.5**
Speed ratings (Par 101): **104,103,102,98,92 91,82,**
CSF £13.00 CT £97.67 TOTE £5.90: £1.90, £1.10, £3.00; EX 16.30 Trifecta £76.80.
**Owner** Crowd Racing Partnership **Bred** Overbury Stallions Ltd & Dukes Stud **Trained** Limpley Stoke, Wilts

**FOCUS**

A competitive little handicap for the grade. A muddling pace, but the first four came clear. The runner-up has been rated a fraction higher than her recent efforts.

## 5509 188BET.CO.UK H'CAP 1m 2f 23y

**2:50** (2:50) (Class 6) (0-65,65) 3-Y-O+ **£2,264** (£673; £336; £168) **Stalls** Low

Form RPR

000 **1** **Free Forum (IRE)**98 2066 3-8-13 58 SilvestreDeSousa 6 69+
(David Simcock) *s.i.s: hld up: hdwy and nt clr run over 1f out: rdn to ld ins fnl f: r.o* **9/2**2

5006 **2** *1* **Getgo**11 5126 3-9-4 63 (b) MartinLane 9 69
(David Lanigan) *s.i.s: hld up: hdwy over 1f out: rdn ins fnl f: r.o to go 2nd post* **7/1**

2-12 **3** *nse* **Seven Clans (IRE)**192 351 5-9-13 64 (b) JFEgan 1 69
(Neil Mulholland) *chsd ldrs: nt clr run over 2f out: rdn and ev ch ins fnl f: styd on* **6/1**3

00-2 **4** *¾* **Retribution**13 5023 3-9-5 64 TedDurcan 5 69
(David Lanigan) *chsd ldrs: led 2f out: sn rdn: hdd ins fnl f: styd on same pce* **5/4**1

0553 **5** *1 ¾* **Sexy Secret**56 3440 6-8-11 51 (p) SimonPearce(3) 3 51
(Lydia Pearce) *led: qcknd over 3f out: hdd 2f out: sn rdn: no ex ins fnl f* **10/1**

/0-3 **6** *shd* **Appease**124 1456 8-8-6 46 oh1 ShelleyBirkett(3) 4 46
(Julia Feilden) *chsd ldrs: lost pl over 6f out: hdwy over 2f out: rdn over 1f out: styd on same pce fnl f* **14/1**

400 **7** *7* **Mr Davies**11 5096 3-9-6 65 (v1) KieranShoemark 7 53
(David Brown) *w ldr to 1/2-way: rdn over 3f out: sn hung lft: wknd over 1f out* **25/1**

2m 8.55s (-1.95) **Going Correction** -0.25s/f (Firm)
**WFA** 3 from 5yo+ 8lb **7** Ran SP% **109.0**
Speed ratings (Par 101): **97,96,96,95,94 94,88**
CSF £31.82 CT £169.96 TOTE £5.10: £2.30, £3.10; EX 39.90 Trifecta £177.70.
**Owner** Mrs Doreen Tabor **Bred** Churchtown House Stud **Trained** Newmarket, Suffolk

**FOCUS**

A moderate handicap. They didn't go much of a gallop and finished close-up.

## 5510 188BET H'CAP 1m 3y

**3:25** (3:26) (Class 5) (0-75,77) 3-Y-O+ **£2,911** (£866; £432; £216) **Stalls** Centre

Form RPR

6200 **1** **Casina Di Notte (IRE)**15 4983 3-9-4 74 (p) MarcMonaghan(3) 3 80
(Marco Botti) *hld up: rdr dropped whip bef 1/2-way: hdwy over 2f out: shkn up to ld and edgd rt over 1f out: pushed out* **6/1**

4120 **2** *hd* **Patching**17 4883 3-9-0 67 (b1) JFEgan 4 72
(Giles Bravery) *chsd ldr tl led over 3f out: rdn and hdd over 1f out: ev ch ins fnl f: styd on* **4/1**2

-350 **3** *1* **Buckland Beau**26 4523 6-9-12 72 SilvestreDeSousa 6 76
(Charlie Fellowes) *hld up in tch: rdn over 1f out: sn ev ch: no ex towards fin* **11/4**1

41 **4** *½* **The Yellow Bus**21 4728 4-9-10 73 TimClark(3) 8 76
(John Butler) *hld up: hdwy over 2f out: rdn over 1f out: styd on* **8/1**

1355 **5** *1 ¾* **King Oswald (USA)**6 5276 4-9-3 63 (tp) MartinDwyer 7 62
(James Unett) *hld up: hdwy over 2f out: rdn and ev ch over 1f out: no ex ins fnl f* **5/1**3

50 **6** *8* **Celtic Artisan (IRE)**17 4893 6-9-7 67 (bt) DougieCostello 9 47
(Rebecca Menzies) *led over 4f: sn rdn: wknd over 1f out* **20/1**

1-12 **7** *7* **Phosphorescence (IRE)**48 3718 7-9-9 76 (b) FletcherYarham(7) 5 40
(George Scott) *s.i.s: sn prom: rdn and wknd over 2f out* **4/1**2

1m 38.99s (-1.61) **Going Correction** -0.10s/f (Good)
**WFA** 3 from 4yo+ 7lb **7** Ran SP% **113.5**
Speed ratings (Par 103): **104,103,102,102,100 92,85**
CSF £29.55 CT £80.05 TOTE £6.20: £3.00, £2.60; EX 31.20 Trifecta £125.60.
**Owner** Les Boyer Partnership **Bred** John T Heffernan & Grainne Dooley **Trained** Newmarket, Suffolk

**FOCUS**

Several with plenty to prove in this moderate handicap and they went a good gallop. The runner-up was backing up her recent form.

## 5511 GALWAY FESTIVAL BETTING AT 188BET H'CAP (DIV I) 7f 3y

**4:00** (4:00) (Class 6) (0-60,62) 3-Y-O+ **£2,264** (£673; £336; £168) **Stalls** Centre

Form RPR

6031 **1** **Anna Medici**7 5239 3-8-7 52 RosieJessop(3) 5 65+
(Sir Mark Prescott Bt) *s.i.s: hdwy over 4f out: led 1/2-way: shkn up and edgd lft over 1f out: styd on wl* **5/4**1

5423 **2** *3 ½* **Masquerade Bling (IRE)**99 2017 3-9-2 58 RobHornby 6 60
(Daniel Mark Loughnane) *hld up: hdwy over 2f out: rdn to chse wnr and edgd lft over 1f out: styd on same pce ins fnl f* **15/2**

/564 **3** *hd* **Monsieur Royale**69 2976 7-8-10 46 JackMitchell 1 49
(Clive Drew) *hld up: hdwy over 2f out: rdn over 1f out: styd on* **8/1**

0060 **4** *1 ½* **Ershaad (IRE)**22 4682 5-8-7 46 oh1 (b) CharlieBennett(3) 4 45
(Shaun Harris) *led to 1/2-way: rdn over 1f out: no ex ins fnl f* **16/1**

6645 **5** *3* **Commanche**11 5119 8-9-10 60 (b) SilvestreDeSousa 8 51
(Chris Dwyer) *prom: racd keenly: rdn over 1f out: wknd ins fnl f* **7/2**2

0P-5 **6** *8* **Maddys Dream**20 4766 4-9-9 62 SimonPearce(3) 3 32
(Lydia Pearce) *chsd ldrs: pushed along 1/2-way: rdn and wknd over 1f out* **7/1**3

600- **7** *11* **Charlie Chaplin (GER)**253 8046 3-9-2 58 PaoloSirigu 11
(Robert Eddery) *s.i.s: sn prom: rdn over 2f out: wknd over 1f out* **20/1**

60-0 **R** **Hollywood Style**207 89 3-8-4 46 oh1 MartinDwyer 9
(Brendan Powell) *ref to r* **50/1**

1m 27.3s (0.70) **Going Correction** -0.10s/f (Good)
**WFA** 3 from 4yo+ 6lb **8** Ran SP% **114.6**
Speed ratings (Par 101): **92,88,87,86,82 73,60,**
CSF £11.61 CT £54.43 TOTE £2.30: £1.10, £1.90, £2.30; EX 13.00 Trifecta £67.00.
**Owner** Neil Greig **Bred** W N Greig **Trained** Newmarket, Suffolk

**FOCUS**

A weak handicap dominated by the favourite who came clear. They action unfolded more towards the far side of centre. The third has been rated to his best.

## 5512 GALWAY FESTIVAL BETTING AT 188BET H'CAP (DIV II) 7f 3y

**4:30** (4:31) (Class 6) (0-60,62) 3-Y-O+ **£2,264** (£673; £336; £168) **Stalls** Centre

Form RPR

004 **1** **Garth Rockett**12 5076 3-8-10 52 (p1) MartinDwyer 8 62
(Brendan Powell) *chsd ldrs 6f out: shkn up to ld over 1f out: drvn out* **16/1**

5011 **2** *2 ¼* **Tigerfish (IRE)**21 4714 3-8-11 58 (p) JoshuaBryan(5) 10 62
(William Stone) *prom: rdn to chse wnr over 1f out: styd on same pce ins fnl f* **11/4**2

-630 **3** *¾* **Bo Selecta (IRE)**161 848 3-9-6 62 LiamKeniry 4 64
(Richard Spencer) *hld up: hdwy over 2f out: rdn over 1f out: styd on same pce ins fnl f* **7/1**

52 **4** *2 ½* **The Happy Hammer (IRE)**49 3702 11-8-10 46 JoeyHaynes 1 43
(Eugene Stanford) *hld up: hdwy over 1f out: sn rdn: no ex ins fnl f* **5/2**1

050- **5** *1* **Noneedtotellme (IRE)**222 8499 4-8-10 46 oh1 JFEgan 5 41
(James Unett) *hld up: rdn over 2f out: nt trble ldrs* **16/1**

2430 **6** *1* **Rosie Crowe (IRE)**8 5214 5-8-12 51 (v) CharlieBennett(3) 3 43
(Shaun Harris) *led 1f: chsd ldrs: rdn over 1f out: styd on same pce* **7/2**3

000 **7** *¾* **Hanningfield**20 4764 3-8-7 49 DannyBrock 7 37
(Michael Bell) *s.i.s: hld up: rdn over 2f out: n.d* **16/1**

-400 **8** *½* **Refuse Colette (IRE)**48 3728 8-9-5 55 WilliamCarson 9 43
(Mick Quinn) *led 6f out: rdn and hdd over 1f out: wknd fnl f* **10/1**

1m 26.12s (-0.48) **Going Correction** -0.10s/f (Good)
**WFA** 3 from 4yo+ 6lb **8** Ran SP% **116.7**
Speed ratings (Par 101): **98,95,94,91,90 89,88,88**
CSF £61.28 CT £350.16 TOTE £19.80: £3.80, £1.10, £2.50; EX 69.40 Trifecta £397.10.
**Owner** Philip Banfield **Bred** P Banfield **Trained** Upper Lambourn, Berks

**FOCUS**

Several improvers made this low-grade handicap interesting enough, though they didn't go a great gallop and plenty held a chance a furlong out.

## 5513 SHIRLEY GILL MEMORIAL H'CAP 6f 3y

**5:00** (5:01) (Class 3) (0-95,95) 3-Y-O+ **£7,439** (£2,213; £1,106; £553) **Stalls** Centre

Form RPR

1000 **1** **Victory Angel (IRE)**19 4813 3-9-3 90 SilvestreDeSousa 7 104+
(Roger Varian) *prom: led wl over 1f out: pushed clr: comf* **4/1**1

-040 **2** *2 ½* **Gulliver**45 3844 3-9-2 89 (vt1) JackMitchell 3 93+
(Hugo Palmer) *s.i.s and sn pushed along in rr: rdn over 1f out: r.o wl ins fnl f: no ch w wnr* **5/1**3

-602 **3** *3 ½* **Huntsmans Close**19 4803 7-9-6 89 (h) GeorgeDowning 9 83
(Robert Cowell) *prom: rdn to chse wnr over 1f out tl no ex wl ins fnl f* **11/1**

-603 **4** 3/4 **Barrington (IRE)**[14] 4992 3-9-8 **95**................................(t) SteveDrowne 2 85
(Charles Hills) *hld up: rdn over 2f out: styd on fr over 1f out: nt trble ldrs* **13/2**

0201 **5** 3/4 **Highland Acclaim (IRE)**[19] 4803 6-9-6 **89**....................(h) SamJames 6 78
(David O'Meara) *led: rdn and hdd wl over 1f out: wknd ins fnl f* **8/1**

-006 **6** 3/4 **Syrian Pearl**[13] 5035 6-8-13 **82**........................................ TedDurcan 8 69
(Chris Wall) *hld up: rdn over 2f out: nvr on terms* **8/1**

2000 **7** 2 3/4 **Captain Colby (USA)**[38] 4072 5-9-12 **95**...........(h[1]) RichardKingscote 10 73
(Ed Walker) *hld up: shkn up over 2f out: a in rr* **9/2**[2]

-664 **8** 3/4 **Rosabelle**[32] 4315 3-8-8 **84**.......................................(h[1]) RosieJessop(3) 5 58
(Alan Bailey) *chsd ldrs: rdn over 2f out: wknd fnl f* **12/1**

3-00 **9** 9 **Fang**[25] 4566 4-8-7 **76**............................................ MartinDwyer 4 23
(William Jarvis) *w ldr over 3f: sn rdn: wknd over 1f out* **10/1**

1m 11.03s (-3.37) **Going Correction** -0.10s/f (Good)
**WFA** 3 from 4yo+ 4lb **9** Ran SP% **115.5**
Speed ratings (Par 107): **118,114,110,109,108 107,103,102,90**
CSF £23.98 CT £204.24 TOTE £4.10: £1.80, £2.50, £2.60; EX 32.60 Trifecta £429.70.
**Owner** Ziad A Galadari **Bred** Max Morris **Trained** Newmarket, Suffolk

**FOCUS**
The feature race was a good sprint handicap and they went a strong pace, suiting those ridden patiently.

## 5514 EXTRA PLACE RACES AT 188BET H'CAP 5f 42y
**5:35** (5:40) (Class 5) (0-70,70) 3-Y-0+ **£2,911** (£866; £432; £216) **Stalls** Centre

Form RPR

0164 **1** **Annie Salts**[38] 4081 4-9-6 **66**..................................(h) SilvestreDeSousa 2 76+
(Chris Dwyer) *hld up: hdwy 1/2-way: led over 1f out: shkn up ins fnl f: r.o: comf* **3/1**[2]

6405 **2** 1 3/4 **Racing Angel (IRE)**[39] 4053 5-9-4 **64**.......................... WilliamCarson 6 67
(Mick Quinn) *hld up in tch: rdn over 1f out: hung lft and styd on same pce ins fnl f* **7/2**[3]

145 **3** 1 3/4 **Noah Amor (IRE)**[40] 4013 4-9-9 **69**.................................... SamJames 4 66
(David O'Meara) *racd keenly in 2nd: rdn over 1f out: styd on same pce fnl f* **4/1**

1351 **4** 1 1/4 **Nag's Wag (IRE)**[14] 5004 4-9-9 **69**...................................... LiamKeniry 5 62
(Conor Dore) *prom: pushed along 1/2-way: rdn and nt clr run over 1f out: n.d after* **7/1**

054 **5** 4 **Powerful Wind (IRE)**[40] 4009 8-9-0 **60**.................(t) RichardKingscote 1 39
(Charlie Wallis) *led: rdn and hdd over 1f out: wknd ins fnl f* **12/1**

0556 **6** 7 **Bahamian Heights**[24] 4629 6-9-10 **70**......................(h) AdamBeschizza 3 24
(Robert Cowell) *unruly to post: s.s: outpcd* **5/2**[1]

1m 1.19s (-1.51) **Going Correction** -0.10s/f (Good) **6** Ran SP% **116.0**
Speed ratings (Par 103): **108,105,102,100,94 82**
CSF £14.48 TOTE £3.30: £2.10, £1.80; EX 15.30 Trifecta £51.30.
**Owner** Mrs Shelley Dwyer **Bred** D R Botterill **Trained** Newmarket, Suffolk

**FOCUS**
A tight little sprint handicap and they didn't hang around. The runner-up has been rated close to this year's form.
T/Plt: £49.70 to a £1 stake. Pool: £55,253.88 - 810.75 winning units. T/Qpdt: £35.80 to a £1 stake. Pool: £3,574.60 - 73.75 winning units. **Colin Roberts**

5515 - 5516a (Foreign Racing) - See Raceform Interactive

# 5486 GALWAY (R-H)
Tuesday, August 1

**OFFICIAL GOING: Flat course - yielding; jumps course - good**

## 5517a COLM QUINN BMW MILE H'CAP (PREMIER HANDICAP) 1m 123y
**7:40** (7:40) 3-Y-0+
**£60,512** (£19,487; £9,230; £4,102; £2,051; £1,025)

RPR

**1** **Riven Light (IRE)**[32] 4329 5-9-0 **92**........................ DeclanMcDonogh 10 101
(W P Mullins, Ire) *hld up towards rr: hdwy into mid-div under 2f out: sn swtchd rt in 8th and nt clr run: swtchd lft bhd ldrs ins fnl f and sn qcknd between horses where n.m.r to ld fnl 100yds: styd on wl* **7/2**[1]

**2** 1 1/2 **Hibou**[28] 4475 4-9-2 **94**..........................................................(b) DavidNolan 8 100
(Iain Jardine) *in tch and pushed along early: 7th 1/2-way: gng wl in 5th 2f out: effrt ins fnl f where hmpd and lost sme momentum: kpt on again into 2nd cl home: nt trble wnr* **16/1**

**3** 1 1/4 **Dream Walker (FR)**[10] 5157 8-8-12 **90**.................................(t) WJLee 17 93+
(Brian Ellison) *hld up in rr: gd hdwy fr over 2f out to chse ldrs ins fnl f where n.m.r and rdn in 7th: r.o wl to snatch 3rd fnl stride: nrst fin* **25/1**

**4** hd **Turbine (IRE)**[17] 4924 4-8-11 **89**............................(tp) SeamieHeffernan 9 92
(Denis Gerard Hogan, Ire) *chsd ldrs: 4th 1/2-way: impr into 2nd fr 2f out: rdn to ld narrowly briefly ins fnl f: hdd fnl 100yds and no imp on wnr: one pce in 3rd cl home: denied 3rd fnl stride* **16/1**

**5** hd **Windsor Beach (IRE)**[19] 4822 5-8-11 **94**................(b) DenisLinehan(5) 3 96
(J P Murtagh, Ire) *disp early tl settled in cl 2nd after 1f: led over 2f out: sn rdn and hdd ins fnl f: wknd clsng stages* **7/1**[2]

**6** 1 1/4 **Baraweez (IRE)**[31] 4377 7-8-9 **94**................................... SeanDavis(7) 11 94
(Brian Ellison) *chsd ldrs: 5th 1/2-way: rdn bhd ldrs in 6th into st and no ex wl ins fnl f: one pce clsng stages* **8/1**[3]

**7** 2 **Mizaah (IRE)**[31] 4384 4-9-5 **97**.......................................(vt[1]) ChrisHayes 13 92
(Kevin Prendergast, Ire) *mid-div: rdn in 7th over 2f out and no imp on ldrs ins fnl f: kpt on one pce* **12/1**

**8** shd **Marshall Jennings (IRE)**[47] 3765 5-9-9 **101**........... ColmO'Donoghue 4 96
(Mrs John Harrington, Ire) *chsd ldrs: 3rd 1/2-way: pushed along bhd ldrs into st: sn rdn and u.p in 3rd ins fnl f where bdly hmpd: no imp and eased after* **16/1**

**9** 1 1/4 **Tandem**[19] 4822 8-9-12 **104**................................................ PatSmullen 12 96
(D K Weld, Ire) *mid-div: 8th 1/2-way: pushed along under 2f out and no imp whn sltly hmpd over 1f out: eased ins fnl f* **12/1**

**10** 2 1/4 **Tony The Gent (IRE)**[31] 4384 4-9-6 **98**......................... GaryCarroll 18 85
(G M Lyons, Ire) *w.w towards rr: sme hdwy in 15th fr 2f out: kpt on one pce ins fnl f* **10/1**

**11** nk **Stipulate**[46] 3790 8-8-11 **89**.......................................... GaryHalpin(3) 5 79
(Brian Ellison) *s.i.s and in rr: pushed along in 14th over 2f out and no imp 1f out where nt clr run: kpt on one pce* **12/1**

**12** nk **Sands Chorus**[11] 5130 5-9-0 **92**.................................... KevinManning 1 78
(James Given) *on toes befhand: disp early tl led narrowly after 1f: pushed along after 1/2-way and hdd over 2f out: wknd into st* **25/1**

**13** 2 1/4 **Red Avenger (USA)**[9] 5190 7-8-13 **91**............................ ConorHoban 14 72
(Damian Joseph English, Ire) *mid-div: 9th 1/2-way: pushed along after 1/2-way and u.p in 10th appr st: wknd fnl f* **66/1**

**14** 1 **Examiner (IRE)**[10] 5157 6-9-5 **97**...................................(t) ShaneFoley 15 76
(Stuart Williams) *hld up: pushed along under 3f out and no imp in rr appr st: rdn briefly over 1f out where nt clr run and sn eased: nvr involved* **33/1**

**15** 8 **Gold Spinner (IRE)**[32] 4330 3-8-13 **98**............................. ColinKeane 2 60
(G M Lyons, Ire) *in rr of mid-div: 10th 1/2-way: rdn into st and sn nt clr run on inner 1f out where eased* **12/1**

**16** 1 1/2 **Fuwairt (IRE)**[47] 3743 5-8-11 **89**.................................(t[1]) WayneLordan 7 47
(Gavin Cromwell, Ire) *s.i.s: towards rr early: pushed along in mid-div after 1/2-way and checked on inner over 2f out: n.m.r between horses into st: wknd and eased fnl f* **10/1**

**17** 1 1/2 **Secret Wizard (IRE)**[14] 5011 4-8-12 **90**........................ RonanWhelan 16 45
(Ms Sheila Lavery, Ire) *in rr of mid-div: 11th 1/2-way: rdn over 2f out and u.p whn short of room 1f out where eased* **16/1**

**18** 4 1/2 **Geological (IRE)**[6] 5311 5-9-1 **98**......................... DonaghO'Connor(5) 6 43
(Damian Joseph English, Ire) *chsd ldrs: 6th 1/2-way: pushed along 3f out and sn wknd: eased in rr fnl f* **40/1**

1m 48.56s
**WFA** 3 from 4yo+ 8lb **18** Ran SP% **132.9**
CSF £65.26 CT £1335.22 TOTE £4.50: £1.50, £3.10, £6.80, £3.40; DF 73.40 Trifecta £3492.50.
**Owner** Mrs S Ricci **Bred** Stilvi Compania Financiera Sa **Trained** Muine Beag, Co Carlow

**FOCUS**
A second big-race win of the week on the Flat for champions jumps trainer Willie Mullins. The ex-French Riven Light had to survive a stewards' enquiry. British-trained runners took second and third places.

## 5518a CAULFIELD INDUSTRIAL H'CAP 1m 123y
**8:10** (8:11) (50-70,71) 4-Y-0+ **£8,423** (£2,611; £1,244; £560; £218)

RPR

**1** **Serefeli (IRE)**[24] 4646 5-9-12 **68**..................................................(t) WJLee 3 74
(Peter Fahey, Ire) *hld up in tch: hdwy in 8th fr over 2f out: rdn ent fnl f and r.o wl to ld ins fnl 100yds* **4/1**[1]

**2** 1/2 **Usa (IRE)**[8] 5226 10-9-5 **66**.......................................... DanielRedmond(5) 9 71
(S J Mahon, Ire) *chsd ldrs: racd keenly early: 4th 1/2-way: rdn in 4th over 2f out and clsd u.p into 2nd wl ins fnl f: kpt on wl wout matching wnr clsng stages* **12/1**

**3** nk **Zippy**[20] 4769 4-9-5 **66**............................................... DonaghO'Connor(5) 8 70
(J F Levins, Ire) *w ldrs and led after 1f: rdn ins fnl f and hdd u.p ins fnl 100yds: no imp on wnr in 3rd clsng stages* **9/1**[3]

**4** 3/4 **Atlas (IRE)**[49] 1480 4-9-11 **67**.......................................(b[1]) LeighRoche 14 70+
(Denis Gerard Hogan, Ire) *hld up towards rr: pushed along and prog on outer 2f out: wd into st: r.o wl u.p nr side ins fnl f to snatch 4th on line: nrst fin* **8/1**[2]

**5** hd **Guanabara Bay (IRE)**[4] 5387 4-10-1 **71** 6ex.......... DeclanMcDonogh 1 73+
(Adrian McGuinness, Ire) *dwlt and racd keenly early: sn settled in rr of mid-div: hdwy fr 2f out to chse ldrs 1f out where nt clr run briefly: kpt on into 4th clsng stages: denied 4th on line* **12/1**

**6** hd **Military Hill (IRE)**[33] 4285 4-9-13 **69**..........................(b) RonanWhelan 10 71+
(Adrian McGuinness, Ire) *hld up: rdn in rr of mid-div over 2f out and wd into st: sme late hdwy fr over 1f out: nvr nrr* **16/1**

**7** 3/4 **Mountain Fox (IRE)**[15] 4985 4-9-13 **69**........................... NGMcCullagh 5 69
(F Oakes, Ire) *prom tl sn settled bhd ldrs: 3rd 1/2-way: rdn bhd ldrs over 2f out and no ex ent fnl f: sn wknd* **16/1**

**8** nse **Prove The Point (IRE)**[47] 3766 4-9-13 **69**.....................(t) GaryCarroll 12 69
(Michael Mulvany, Ire) *in tch: pushed along in 6th over 2f out and no ex ins fnl f: one pce clsng stages* **20/1**

**9** 1/2 **Colonel Maximus (IRE)**[28] 4482 4-9-8 **67**................(t[1]) GaryHalpin(3) 11 66
(Gordon Elliott, Ire) *sn trckd ldr: rdn in 2nd over 2f out and no ex ins fnl f: wknd clsng stages* **12/1**

**10** nse **Essenaitch (IRE)**[3] 5427 4-9-12 **68**............................ DonnachaO'Brien 7 67+
(David Evans) *in rr of mid-div: sme hdwy under 2f out: wd into st: rdn over 1f out and kpt on ins fnl f: nvr nrr* **14/1**

**11** 1 1/2 **Rosenborg Rider (IRE)**[8] 5225 4-9-7 **68**............................ OisinOrr(5) 6 64
(Adrian McGuinness, Ire) *hld up in tch: pushed along in 5th over 2f out and no ex u.p over 1f out: wknd ins fnl f* **25/1**

**12** 1/2 **Il Piccolo Grande (IRE)**[10] 5174 4-9-12 **68**.....................(h) ColinKeane 4 62
(G M Lyons, Ire) *towards rr: tk clsr order into st: no ex over 1f out: one pce after* **10/1**

**13** 3/4 **Miss Ballygally (IRE)**[22] 4703 7-9-9 **65**.......................(t) ConorHoban 2 58
(Mark Michael McNiff, Ire) *hld up: rdn in rr of mid-div into st and sn no ex: one pce fnl f* **20/1**

**14** 1/2 **Paved With Gold (IRE)**[10] 5174 4-9-8 **64**........................ ShaneFoley 18 56
(John Joseph Murphy, Ire) *hld up towards rr: sme hdwy on outer 2f out: sn rdn and no ex over 1f out* **33/1**

**15** nk **County Show**[15] 4985 4-9-3 **64**..................................(t[1]) KillianLeonard(5) 17 55
(Joseph G Murphy, Ire) *towards rr for most: rdn over 1f out and no imp: one pce clsng stages* **25/1**

**16** 1 **Storm Ranger (IRE)**[10] 5174 5-10-0 **70**............................ ChrisHayes 13 59
(Patrick J Flynn, Ire) *dwlt and settled in rr: tk clsr order fr 1/2-way: rdn in rr of mid-div 2f out and sn wknd* **8/1**[2]

**17** 3/4 **So Sensible (IRE)**[24] 4646 6-10-0 **70**............................ PatSmullen 16 57
(Tracey Collins, Ire) *prom tl sn settled bhd ldrs: rdn in 7th over 2f out and no ex into st: wknd and eased fnl f* **10/1**

**18** 15 **California Lad**[47] 3766 4-9-9 **70**.........................(v) ConorMcGovern(5) 15 24
(F Birrane, Ire) *chsd ldrs: 5th 1/2-way: rdn and wknd over 2f out* **50/1**

1m 51.09s **18** Ran SP% **134.0**
CSF £52.27 CT £437.82 TOTE £5.00: £1.60, £2.30, £2.30, £2.40; DF 49.60 Trifecta £244.90.
**Owner** Unidentified Partnership **Bred** H H The Aga Khan's Stud's S C **Trained** Monasterevln, Co. Kildare

**FOCUS**
A competitive handicap, with a very narrow weight-range, only 7lb between top and bottom.

## 5519a CAULFIELDINDUSTRIAL.COM H'CAP 7f
**8:40** (8:41) (50-80,80) 4-Y-0+ **£7,897** (£2,448; £1,166; £525; £205)

RPR

**1** **Knockmaole Boy (IRE)**[23] 6496 5-9-8 **74**.......................(t) LeighRoche 1 79
(Gordon Elliott, Ire) *cl up early tl sn settled bhd ldrs: gng wl into st and wnt 2nd fr 1 1/2f out: rdn to ld ins fnl f and kpt on wl clsng stages: readily* **6/1**[3]

**2** 1/2 **Allegio (IRE)**[15] 4985 4-9-13 **79**................................ SeamieHeffernan 13 83
(Denis Gerard Hogan, Ire) *chsd ldrs tl impr to ld after 2f: stl gng wl into st: rdn and hdd ins fnl f: no imp on wnr clsng stages* **10/1**

**3** 1 1/4 **Hasselnott**[28] 4482 4-9-3 **74**................................ DonaghO'Connor(5) 3 75+
(J F Levins, Ire) *chsd ldrs: rdn over 1f out and no imp on wnr u.p in 3rd ins fnl f: kpt on same pce* **4/1**[1]

4 ¾ **Avalanche**[15] 4985 8-9-5 **71** WayneLordan 10 70
(T J O'Mara, Ire) *mid-div: tk clsr order on outer 2f out: wd into st: no imp on wnr u.p in 4th ins fnl f: kpt on same pce* **18/1**

5 ¾ **Midnitemudcrabs (IRE)**[9] 5190 4-9-4 **73** GaryHalpin(3) 4 70
(John James Feane, Ire) *in rr of mid-div: hdwy 2f out to chse ldrs u.p far side 1f out: kpt on same pce in 5th wl ins fnl f: nvr trbld ldrs* **10/1**

6 ½ **Beau Satchel**[45] 3852 7-9-6 **72** (t) DeclanMcDonogh 8 67
(Adrian McGuinness, Ire) *mid-div: tk clsr order gng wl into st: nt clr run 1f out: kpt on in 6th wl ins fnl f: nvr trbld ldrs* **9/2**[2]

7 ½ **Cappadocia (IRE)**[38] 4110 7-9-3 **69** RonanWhelan 12 63+
(John James Feane, Ire) *in rr of mid-div: tk clsr order gng wl under 2f out: nt clr run 1f out: sme late hdwy wl ins fnl f: nvr nrr* **25/1**

8 hd **Grainne's Dream (IRE)**[14] 5012 4-9-5 **71** PatSmullen 16 64+
(W P Mullins, Ire) *in rr of mid-div: pushed along over 2f out: tk clsr order and rdn over 1f out: no ex and one pce ins fnl f* **6/1**[3]

9 nk **Athassel**[3] 5396 8-10-0 **80** DonnachaO'Brien 14 73+
(David Evans) *in rr of mid-div: rdn 2f out and no imp ins fnl f where short of room briefly: kpt on clsng stages* **25/1**

10 shd **Northern Surprise (IRE)**[30] 4415 6-9-7 **73** WJLee 2 65
(Timothy Doyle, Ire) *hld up towards rr: 14th appr st: nt clr run ins fnl f: kpt on one pce clsng stages* **14/1**

11 1½ **Roibeard (IRE)**[24] 4646 4-9-9 **75** (t) GaryCarroll 6 63
(Eamonn O'Connell, Ire) *in rr of mid-div: rdn over 1f out where nt clr run briefly: kpt on one pce ins fnl f* **14/1**

12 1¾ **Dance Alone**[26] 4548 4-9-6 **72** (t) ShaneFoley 5 55
(Damian Joseph English, Ire) *hooded to load: broke wl to ld tl hdd after 2f: rdn in 2nd over 2f out and no ex into st: wknd over 1f out* **33/1**

13 1½ **Mo Henry**[6] 5307 5-8-11 **70** (v) DannySheehy(7) 9 49
(Adrian Paul Keatley, Ire) *sltly awkward s: chsd ldrs: rdn disputing 3rd 2f out and no ex bhd ldrs into st: wknd over 1f out* **20/1**

14 1 **Honor Oak (IRE)**[16] 4936 5-9-10 **76** ChrisHayes 7 53
(T Hogan, Ire) *chsd ldrs: rdn and no ex into st: sn wknd and eased* **10/1**

15 ¾ **Free Code (IRE)**[12] 5085 6-9-6 **77** (p) DenisLinehan(5) 11 52
(Eugene M O'Sullivan, Ire) *dwlt and pushed along towards rr early: rdn and no imp over 2f out: nvr a factor* **50/1**

16 shd **Sbraase**[6] 5310 6-8-8 **70** (p) SeanKirrane(10) 15 44
(J F Levins, Ire) *s.i.s and detached in rr: no imp appr st: kpt on one pce ins fnl f: nvr a factor* **25/1**

1m 29.97s (-1.63) **16** Ran SP% **133.8**
Pick Six @46,666.60 CSF £66.04 CT £294.10 TOTE £6.80: £1.80, £2.40, £1.40, £4.00; DF 69.00 Trifecta £287.70.
**Owner** Twenty Times Two Syndicate **Bred** John Byrne **Trained** Longwood, Co Meath

**FOCUS**
Five last-time out winners clashed here, including the eventual winner who had looked potentially well handicapped having gained back-to-back wins over hurdles. It's been rated around the balance of the first three.
T/Jkpt: @6,672.60. Pool: @190,646.54 T/Plt: @185.40. Pool: @70,764.80 **Brian Fleming**

## 5460 DEAUVILLE (R-H)
Tuesday, August 1
**OFFICIAL GOING: Turf: good; polytrack: standard**

### 5520a PRIX BISTROT FERNAND A TROUVILLE (PRIX DU VIEUX PONT) (CONDITIONS) (2YO) (TURF) 7f 110y
11:10 2-Y-0
**£17,675** (£7,145; £5,264; £3,384; £2,068; £1,316)

RPR

1 **Masterpiece (FR)**[41] 2-8-9 0 VincentCheminaud 5 77
(A Fabre, France) **4/5**[1]

2 snk **Uther Pendragon (IRE)**[18] 4858 2-8-9 0 (p) TonyPiccone 1 77
(J S Moore) *wl into stride: led early: pushed along and hung lft over 2f out: rdn to hold advantage over 1f out: styd on ins fnl f: hdd cl home* **77/10**

3 shd **Zanzi Win (FR)**[27] 4678 2-8-13 0 GeraldMosse 2 80
(J-P Dubois, France) **59/10**[3]

4 2 **Day Of Rest (FR)**[38] 4090 2-8-9 0 MaximeGuyon 6 72
(George Baker) *settled bhd ldr: carried lft over 2f out: rdn over 1f out: wknd ins fnl f* **99/10**

5 snk **Monargent (FR)**[41] 2-8-13 0 Pierre-CharlesBoudot 4 75
(F-H Graffard, France) **16/5**[2]

6 7 **Varius (FR)**[20] 4782 2-8-9 0 AurelienLemaitre 3 55
(M Nigge, France) **269/10**

1m 35.62s (7.22) **6** Ran SP% **118.1**
PARI-MUTUEL (all including 1 euro stake): WIN 1.80; PLACE 1.20, 2.60; SF 8.40.
**Owner** Ballymore Thoroughbred Ltd **Bred** Dayton Investments Ltd **Trained** Chantilly, France

### 5521a PRIX LA FLAMBEE (PRIX DE BONNEBOSQ) (CLAIMER) (3YO) (POLYTRACK) 6f 110y
12:10 3-Y-0 **£11,538** (£4,615; £3,461; £2,307; £1,153)

RPR

1 **Fongani (FR)**[52] 3-8-9 0 (b) ClementLecoeuvre(4) 2 85
(Simone Brogi, France) **46/1**

2 shd **Highest Rockeur**[33] 3-8-11 0 ThierryThulliez 3 83
(P Bary, France) **15/2**

3 1¼ **Sivinsk (FR)**[33] 4289 3-8-6 0 JeromeMoutard(5) 4 79
(Simone Brogi, France) **47/10**[3]

4 shd **Morigane Forlonge (FR)**[18] 3-9-1 0 CristianDemuro 5 83
(A Giorgi, Italy) **41/1**

5 1¼ **Carlton Choice (IRE)**[36] 3-9-5 0 (b) MlleMarylineEon(5) 1 84
(Louis Baudron, France) **146/10**

6 hd **Swanning Around (IRE)**[273] 3-8-11 0 TonyPiccone 6 75
(Matthieu Palussiere, France) **57/1**

7 nse **High One (FR)**[30] 4425 3-8-13 0 MathieuPelletan(5) 12 82
(P Demercastel, France) **26/1**

8 ¾ **Ucel (IRE)**[33] 4289 3-9-2 0 (b) ChristopheSoumillon 10 78
(F Chappet, France) **31/5**

9 1 **World Power (IRE)**[11] 5111 3-8-8 0 StephanePasquier 7 67
(Paul Cole) *dwlt: in rr early: pushed along over 2f out: rdn and no rspnse over 1f out: nvr a factor* **17/5**[2]

10 ¾ **Spirit De Cerisy (FR)**[18] 3-9-4 0 EddyHardouin 8 74
(Matthieu Palussiere, France) **18/1**

11 ¾ **Alliance Secrete (FR)**[36] 3-9-1 0 (p) MaximeGuyon 9 69
(T Castanheira, France) **33/10**[1]

12 2½ **Deimos (FR)**[78] 2697 3-8-11 0 FranckBlondel 11 58
(K Borgel, France) **127/10**

PARI-MUTUEL (all including 1 euro stake): WIN 47.00; PLACE 10.60, 2.60, 2.00; DF 155.10; SF 251.50.
**Owner** Alain Jathiere **Bred** Guy Pariente Holding **Trained** France

### 5522a PRIX DE TOURGEVILLE (LISTED RACE) (3YO COLTS & GELDINGS) (TURF) (ROUND) 1m (R)
1:50 3-Y-0 **£23,504** (£9,401; £7,051; £4,700; £2,350)

RPR

1 **Farshad (GER)**[114] 1660 3-8-13 0 (b) ClementLecoeuvre 5 108+
(Henk Grewe, Germany) **134/10**

2 3½ **Bay Of Poets (IRE)**[40] 3994 3-8-13 0 CristianDemuro 1 100+
(Charlie Appleby) *settled in midfield: sn 20 l bhd clr ldr: rdn to chse ldr over 2f out: styd on into 2nd over 1f out: no ch w wnr* **157/10**

3 ¾ **Empire Of The Star (FR)**[30] 4425 3-8-13 0 ChristopheSoumillon 7 98+
(A Wohler, Germany) **7/2**[3]

4 1¼ **Argentic (FR)**[30] 4425 3-8-13 0 MaximeGuyon 2 95+
(F Head, France) **63/10**

5 2½ **Mask Of Time (IRE)**[44] 3879 3-9-3 0 Pierre-CharlesBoudot 3 94+
(A Fabre, France) **16/5**[2]

6 1¾ **Glen Shiel**[50] 3680 3-8-13 0 MickaelBarzalona 6 86+
(A Fabre, France) *settled in rr: pushed along over 3f out: sn no imp and eased ins fnl f* **9/5**[1]

7 1¼ **Roc Angel (FR)**[34] 4235 3-8-13 0 TonyPiccone 4 83+
(F Chappet, France) **91/10**

1m 41.13s (0.33) **7** Ran SP% **118.3**
PARI-MUTUEL (all including 1 euro stake): WIN 14.40; PLACE 4.90, 4.80; SF 93.50.
**Owner** Darius Racing **Bred** Darius Racing **Trained** Germany

### 5523a PRIX LA FOLIE DOUCE BY BARRIERE DEAUVILLE (PRIX DE BRETONCELLES) (CLAIMER) (3YO) (POLYTRACK) 1m 4f 110y
2:55 3-Y-0 **£9,829** (£3,931; £2,948; £1,965; £982)

RPR

1 **Vecellio (IRE)**[29] 3-9-1 0 ThierryThulliez 2 68
(G Botti, France) **27/10**[1]

2 snk **Norilsk (FR)**[71] 3-9-1 0 JulienGuillochon 7 68
(Y Barberot, France) **3/1**[2]

3 shd **Maison D'Or (IRE)**[8] 5235 3-9-1 0 (b) MathieuPelletan 8 68
(Robert Collet, France) **28/1**

4 3 **Sweet Bay (FR)**[318] 3-8-8 0 (p) RichardJuteau 10 56
(N Leenders, France) **226/10**

5 shd **Chicissime (FR)**[41] 3-8-8 0 AlexisLarue 4 56
(J-P Gauvin, France) **47/10**[3]

6 ½ **Augustini (FR)**[41] 3-8-11 0 StephaneLaurent 6 58
(H De Nicolay, France) **44/1**

7 1½ **Hold Me Tight (IRE)**[45] 3819 3-8-11 0 FrankPanicucci 11 56
(J S Moore) *racd in rr of midfield: nudged along to go 6th 5f out: shkn up and ev ch turning in: rdn and outpcd 1f out: no ex* **142/10**

8 6 **Chancellor (FR)** 3-8-11 0 (b) EnzoCorallo 9 46
(C Ferland, France) **93/10**

9 1¼ **Shazain (FR)**[91] 3-9-1 0 YohannBourgois 3 48
(M Rolland, France) **109/10**

10 2 **Quinteo (IRE)**[17] 4891 3-9-1 0 (b) GuillaumeTrolleyDePrevaux 5 45
(Jo Hughes) *led after 100yds: hdd ins 3f out: continued to r promly tl rdn along and lost position 2f out: wknd fnl 2f* **113/10**

11 ½ **Micolys (FR)**[29] 4455 3-9-1 0 (p) ThomasHuet 1 44
(J-M Lefebvre, France) **17/1**

PARI-MUTUEL (all including 1 euro stake): WIN 3.70; PLACE 1.70, 1.50, 4.20; DF 5.40; SF 11.30.
**Owner** Eledy Srl & G Botti **Bred** Messers Mark Hanly & James Hanly **Trained** France

## 5500 GOODWOOD (R-H)
Wednesday, August 2
**OFFICIAL GOING: Good to soft (7.4) changing to soft after race 1 (1.50)**
Wind: medium, across Weather: heavy and persistent rain, moderate visibility

### 5524 MATCHBOOK BETTING EXCHANGE GOODWOOD H'CAP 2m 4f 134y
1:50 (1:51) (Class 2) (0-100,99) 3-Y-0+
**£31,125** (£9,320; £4,660; £2,330; £1,165; £585) Stalls Far side

Form RPR

3/66 1 **Cool Sky**[46] 3840 8-8-2 **80** JosephineGordon 18 88
(Ian Williams) *hld up in midfield: effrt 4f out: gd hdwy to chal over 1f out: drifted rt and led ins fnl f: styd on wl: rdn out* **25/1**

1332 2 1¼ **Aurora Gray**[12] 5110 4-8-4 **82** SilvestreDeSousa 6 89
(Hughie Morrison) *hld up in midfield: effrt and hdwy 4f out: styd on to ld over 1f out: hdd ins fnl f: styd on same pce fnl 100yds* **13/2**[2]

0430 3 3½ **Arthur Mc Bride (IRE)**[39] 4073 8-8-5 **83** (t) HarryBentley 12 87
(Nigel Twiston-Davies) *mde most tl rdn and hdd wl over 3f out: kpt on u.p and stl ev ch tl no ex 1f out: outpcd fnl 100yds: eased nr fin* **9/1**

00/0 4 3½ **Taws**[15] 4499 6-8-5 **83** (p) JFEgan 13 84
(Rod Millman) *wl in tch in midfield: clsd to chse ldrs 10f out: rdn 4f out: stl chsng ldrs whn nt clrest of runs over 1f out: sn outpcd and btn 1f out: kpt on same pce ins fnl f* **9/1**

4131 5 ¾ **Denmead**[56] 3459 4-7-10 **79** DavidEgan(5) 8 79+
(John Butler) *chsd ldrs: clsd to join ldrs over 4f out tl led over 3f out: drvn and hdd over 1f out: no ex and wknd ins fnl f* **16/1**

-114 6 7 **Frederic**[38] 4120 6-8-10 **88** GrahamLee 3 82+
(Keith Dalgleish) *hld up towards rr and travelled strly: clsd 4f out: nt clrest of runs jst over 3f out: effrt ent fnl 2f: no imp u.p and wl hld over 1f out* **14/1**

0250 7 3 **Suegioo (FR)**[32] 4356 8-9-7 **99** (p) TonyHamilton 10 90
(Richard Fahey) *niggled along in last pair: hdwy u.p to pass stragglers and midfield over 2f out: plugged but nvr threatened ldrs* **14/1**

-546 8 1 **Guard of Honour (IRE)**[39] 4073 6-8-11 **89** (b) PatCosgrave 17 79
(George Baker) *t.k.h: hld up in midfield: effrt over 4f out: sn struggling and outpcd 4f out: n.d after* **20/1**

/33- **9** 3 **Golden Doyen (GER)**[38] 6919 6-8-1 **79**..........................(p) LukeMorris 1 66
(Philip Hobbs) *chsd ldrs: rdn over 5f out: struggling u.p and lost pl over 4f out: no ch fnl 2f* **9/1**

6411 **10** 4 ½ **Hawkerland (IRE)**[29] 4471 4-7-11 **78**.......................... GeorgeWood(3) 4 61
(Marcus Tregoning) *t.k.h: wl in tch in midfield: rdn 4f out: sn struggling and wl hld 2f out: fdd over 1f out* **11/2**[1]

1-66 **11** 4 **Star Rider**[43] 3928 5-9-2 **94**..............................................(p) AdamKirby 2 74
(Hughie Morrison) *t.k.h: hld up in midfield: rdn and lost pl 4f out: n.d after* **15/2**[3]

1300 **12** 1 **October Storm**[32] 4355 4-8-0 **78** oh2............................. NathanEvans 11 57
(Mick Channon) *hld up in midfield: effrt over 4f out: sn struggling: no ch over 2f out* **10/1**

4211 **13** 21 **Akavit (IRE)**[38] 4120 5-7-9 **78** oh2............................. JaneElliott(5) 16 38
(Ed de Giles) *w ldr: rdn over 4f out: outpcd and struggling 4f out: lost pl 3f out: wl bhd fnl f: t.o* **16/1**

334 **14** 2 ½ **Red Rannagh (IRE)**[31] 4413 4-8-2 **80**.......................(h) FrannyNorton 14 38
(David Simcock) *t.k.h: hld up in rr: lost tch over 3f out: t.o* **16/1**

-204 **15** 41 **Sunblazer (IRE)**[28] 4498 7-8-9 **92** ow2.......................(t) JoshuaBryan(5) 5 13
(Kim Bailey) *hld up in last trio: lost tch over 3f out: t.o* **50/1**

4m 48.04s (17.04) **Going Correction** +1.125s/f (Soft) **15** Ran SP% **121.1**
Speed ratings (Par 109): **112,111,110,108,108 105,104,104,103,101 100,99,91,90,75**
CSF £177.46 CT £1608.04 TOTE £25.70: £6.00, £1.70, £4.10; EX 199.90 Trifecta £2344.40.
**Owner** Norte Sur Partnership **Bred** Miss K J Keir **Trained** Portway, Worcs

**FOCUS**
The rail on the lower bend was dolled out 5yds from the 6f marker to the winning post. The top bend was dolled out 3yds. Race distance increased by 10yds. 15mm of rain turned the ground soft and the time of this opener was the slowest this decade by some way. They appeared to go a reasonable gallop for this marathon handicap and, with the ground having deteriorated, it proved a thorough test. The winner has been rated back to his old best.

## 5525 BETTER ODDS WITH MATCHBOOK BETTING EXCHANGE H'CAP 1m 3f 218y

**2:25** (2:32) (Class 2) (0-105,105) 3-Y-O

**£46,687** (£13,980; £6,990; £3,495; £1,747; £877) **Stalls** High

Form RPR

1-23 **1** **Londinium**[33] 4295 3-8-0 **84**.................................................. JoeFanning 5 95
(Mark Johnston) *trckd ldrs: led over 2f out: drifted lft fnl f: styd on strly: rdn out* **9/1**

1213 **2** 1 ½ **On To Victory**[27] 4535 3-8-13 **97**...............................(h) TomMarquand 12 106
(Eve Johnson Houghton) *mid-div: hdwy fr 3f out: rdn to dispute 2nd over 2f out: styd on fnl f but nt pce to get on terms w wnr* **11/2**[2]

-331 **3** 1 ¼ **Winston C (IRE)**[30] 4450 3-7-11 **86**................................. DavidEgan(5) 8 93
(Michael Bell) *mid-div: hdwy over 3f out: rdn to dispute 2nd over 2f out: styd on same pce ins fnl f* **16/1**

2022 **4** 2 ½ **First Nation**[41] 3998 3-8-12 **96**........................................... JamesDoyle 4 99
(Charlie Appleby) *hld up towards rr: hdwy fr 3f out: rdn to chal for 2nd 2f out: styd on tl no ex ins fnl f* **10/1**

1223 **5** 3 **Secret Advisor (FR)**[40] 4032 3-8-12 **96**........................ WilliamBuick 13 94
(Charlie Appleby) *trckd ldrs: rdn over 3f out: sn hld: one pce fnl 2f* **5/1**[1]

2112 **6** 4 **Hochfeld (IRE)**[13] 5071 3-8-8 **92**................................ SilvestreDeSousa 6 84
(Mark Johnston) *trckd ldrs: lost pl over 4f out: rdn over 3f out: styd on fnl 2f but nvr threatened to get bk on terms* **7/1**[3]

3313 **7** 2 ½ **Galactic Prince**[18] 4886 3-8-0 **84** oh4.............................. JimmyQuinn 3 72
(Andrew Balding) *s.i.s: last pair: hdwy 3f out: rdn to chse ldrs over 2f out: wknd ent fnl f* **10/1**

3112 **8** 3 ¾ **Amlad (IRE)**[23] 4701 3-8-2 **86**........................................... LukeMorris 11 68
(Ed Dunlop) *hld up towards rr: rdn and sme prog into midfield 3f out: no further imp fnl 2f* **25/1**

5100 **9** 1 **Never Surrender (IRE)**[25] 4612 3-8-3 **87**.................(p[1]) FrannyNorton 2 67
(Charles Hills) *s.i.s: a towards rr* **25/1**

6141 **10** ½ **Brimham Rocks**[18] 4898 3-8-5 **89**................................. HarryBentley 14 68
(Ralph Beckett) *mid-div: hdwy 3f out: sn rdn: wknd 2f out* **10/1**

-155 **11** 7 **Wolf Country**[20] 4811 3-9-5 **103**....................................... AdamKirby 1 71
(Charlie Appleby) *led: kicked on wl over 3f out: hdd over 2f out: sn wknd* **10/1**

4511 **12** 16 **Fair Power (IRE)**[20] 4798 3-7-11 **84** oh2....................... AaronJones(3) 7 27
(Sylvester Kirk) *trckd ldrs: rdn over 3f out: sn wknd* **50/1**

1404 **13** 5 **Tamleek (USA)**[20] 4811 3-9-7 **105**...............................(p[1]) JimCrowley 10 40
(Saeed bin Suroor) *a towards rr* **20/1**

0103 **14** 8 **Sofia's Rock (FR)**[20] 4811 3-9-2 **100**............................... RyanMoore 9 22
(Mark Johnston) *trckd ldrs: struggling 4f out: sn wknd* **10/1**

2m 47.38s (8.98) **Going Correction** +1.125s/f (Soft) **14** Ran SP% **120.3**
Speed ratings (Par 106): **115,114,113,111,109 106,105,102,102,101 97,86,83,77**
CSF £55.33 CT £796.53 TOTE £10.00: £3.00, £2.20, £5.30; EX 67.10 Trifecta £1992.30.
**Owner** Sheikh Hamdan bin Mohammed Al Maktoum **Bred** Darley **Trained** Middleham Moor, N Yorks

**FOCUS**
Race distance increased by 10yds. Invariably a strong handicap, but how reliable a form guide it will prove given the ground conditions is difficult to tell. It's been rated around the race average.

## 5526 BOMBAY SAPPHIRE MOLECOMB STKS (GROUP 3) 5f

**3:00** (3:02) (Class 1) 2-Y-O

**£42,532** (£16,125; £8,070; £4,020; £2,017; £1,012) **Stalls** High

Form RPR

1101 **1** **Havana Grey**[26] 4582 2-9-1 **109**........................................ PJMcDonald 10 109
(K R Burke) *mde all: rdn over 1f out: styd on strly u.p ins fnl f: gng away at fin* **7/2**[2]

214 **2** 1 ¾ **Invincible Army (IRE)**[20] 4812 2-9-1 **103**......................... MartinHarley 1 103
(James Tate) *dwlt: in rr early: hdwy after 2f: trckd ldrs 2f out: effrt over 1f out and drvn to press wnr 1f out: kpt on same pce ins fnl f* **5/2**[1]

123 **3** nse **To Wafij (IRE)**[26] 4582 2-9-1 **101**.................................... AndreaAtzeni 12 103
(Roger Varian) *in tch in midfield: swtchd lft and effrt over 1f out: rdn to chse ldng pair 1f out: kpt on ins fnl f: nvr enough pce to threaten wnr* **8/1**

610 **4** 4 ½ **Wings Of The Rock (IRE)**[42] 3960 2-8-12 **75**..............(h[1]) LukeMorris 5 83
(Scott Dixon) *stdd and wnt lft s: hld up in tch: trckd ldrs after 2f: effrt over 1f out: unable qck 1f out: wknd ins fnl f* **40/1**

1221 **5** 1 ¼ **May Remain**[8] 5262 2-9-1 **80**.................................................. FranBerry 8 82
(Paul Cole) *s.i.s: in rr: clsd and swtchd rt ent fnl 2f: hdwy into midfield but no further hdwy over 1f out: wl hld and kpt on same pce ins fnl f* **16/1**

4150 **6** ½ **It Dont Come Easy (IRE)**[20] 4812 2-9-1 **96**.................. TonyHamilton 6 80
(Richard Fahey) *bmpd s: pressed wnr: pushed along and hung rt 2f out: lost 2nd and btn ent fnl f: wknd ins fnl f* **12/1**

130 **7** 2 ½ **Koditime (IRE)**[41] 3993 2-9-1 **91**..................................(b[1]) AdamKirby 9 71
(Clive Cox) *in tch towards rr: effrt over 1f out: sn outpcd and btn: wknd fnl f* **15/2**

1100 **8** 2 ¾ **Denaar (IRE)**[20] 4812 2-9-1 **93**........................................... FrankieDettori 4 61
(Richard Hannon) *taken down early: hld up in tch in midfield: effrt over 1f out: sn drifting rt and outpcd: wknd fnl f* **6/1**[3]

013 **9** 1 ½ **Encrypted**[18] 4919 2-9-1 **84**................................................ JamesDoyle 11 56+
(Hugo Palmer) *chsd ldrs for 2f: steadily lost pl: towards rr and rdn 2f out: sn struggling: wknd fnl f* **14/1**

4331 **10** 14 **Firenze Rosa (IRE)**[21] 4758 2-8-12 **78**....................... KieranShoemark 7 2
(John Bridger) *chsd ldrs: rdn and struggling 1/2-way: lost pl and wl bhd ins fnl f* **25/1**

1m 0.89s (0.69) **Going Correction** +0.525s/f (Yiel) **10** Ran SP% **114.5**
Speed ratings (Par 104): **115,112,112,104,102 102,98,93,91,68**
CSF £12.38 TOTE £4.00: £1.60, £1.50, £2.40; EX 14.40 Trifecta £50.60.
**Owner** Global Racing Club & Mrs E Burke **Bred** Mickley Stud & Lady Lonsdale **Trained** Middleham Moor, N Yorks

**FOCUS**
Three important non-runners weakened this event and it was run in miserable conditions, but the right horses did come to the fore, with the first three clear. The winner has been rated as repeating his previous form.

## 5527 QATAR SUSSEX STKS (GROUP 1) (BRITISH CHAMPIONS SERIES) 1m

**3:35** (3:39) (Class 1) 3-Y-O+

**£560,200** (£213,300; £106,800; £53,300; £26,700; £13,400) **Stalls** Low

Form RPR

4-13 **1** **Here Comes When (IRE)**[32] 4371 7-9-8 **110**................(h) JimCrowley 5 118
(Andrew Balding) *trckd ldrs: tk narrow advantage wl over 1f out: sn strly pressed and drvn: hld on wl: all out* **20/1**

-311 **2** nk **Ribchester (IRE)**[43] 3924 4-9-8 **125**................................ WilliamBuick 6 117
(Richard Fahey) *led: rdn and hdd wl over 1f out: edgd rt: short of room and looking hld whn eased v briefly disputing cl 3rd ent fnl f: r.o again whn in the clr fnl 150yds: fin wl but a being hld* **8/13**[1]

-200 **3** ¾ **Lightning Spear**[25] 4638 6-9-8 **117**.................................. OisinMurphy 1 116
(David Simcock) *trckd ldrs: chal over 2f out: rdn over 1f out: ev ch ent fnl f: kpt on but no ex towards fin* **8/1**[3]

13-2 **4** 1 ½ **Zelzal (FR)**[45] 3880 4-9-8 **119**........................................... FrankieDettori 7 113
(J-C Rouget, France) *in tch: hdwy but nt clr run jst over 2f out tl over 1f out: rdn and ev ch ent fnl f: no ex fnl 120yds* **4/1**[2]

4500 **5** ½ **Toscanini (IRE)**[43] 3924 5-9-8 **110**................................... JamesDoyle 2 111
(Richard Fahey) *slowly away: in last pair but in tch: rdn over 2f out: nvr gng pce to get involved* **66/1**

4452 **6** 1 ¼ **Lancaster Bomber (USA)**[43] 3927 3-9-1 **118**.................. RyanMoore 3 107
(A P O'Brien, Ire) *trckd ldrs: pushed along to mount chal over 2f out: rdn and hld over 1f out: fdd fnl f* **8/1**[3]

0406 **7** ½ **Kool Kompany (IRE)**[18] 4890 5-9-8 **110**......................... AndreaAtzeni 9 107
(Richard Hannon) *hld up last but in tch: outpcd over 2f out: kpt on ins fnl f but nvr threatened to get involved* **40/1**

1m 46.11s (6.21) **Going Correction** +1.125s/f (Soft)
**WFA** 3 from 4yo+ 7lb **7** Ran SP% **112.8**
Speed ratings (Par 117): **113,112,111,110,109 108,108**
CSF £32.42 CT £119.60 TOTE £20.40: £6.90, £1.10; EX 38.80 Trifecta £145.40.
**Owner** Mrs Fitri Hay **Bred** Old Carhue & Graeng Bloodstock **Trained** Kingsclere, Hants

**FOCUS**
Race distance increased by 15yds. Extreme conditions, and a turn-up to this Group 1. Ability to handle the ground was the only factor, and on the whole this is probably form to put in the bin. The third has been rated close to his Lockinge form.

## 5528 MARKEL INSURANCE MAIDEN FILLIES' STKS (PLUS 10 RACE) 6f

**4:10** (4:11) (Class 2) 2-Y-O **£16,172** (£4,812; £2,405; £1,202) **Stalls** High

Form RPR

**1** **Threading (IRE)** 2-9-0 **0**................................................... WilliamBuick 6 96+
(Mark Johnston) *hld up in tch in midfield: clsd to join ldrs and travelling strly 2f: shkn up and led jst over 1f out: sn rdn clr and r.o strly: eased towards fin: v easily* **12/1**

2 **2** 6 **Your Choice**[27] 4533 2-9-0 **0**............................................... JohnFahy 10 77
(Laura Mongan) *chsd ldrs: rdn and ev ch 2f out: led briefly over 1f out: sn hdd and outpcd by wnr: no ch w wnr but kpt on to hold 2nd ins fnl f* **8/1**

0 **3** 2 ¼ **Pulitzer**[20] 4815 2-9-0 **0**..................................................... JamesDoyle 8 70+
(Hugo Palmer) *hld up in tch and travelled strly: clsd to join ldrs 2f out: rdn and unable qck w wnr over 1f out: wl hld 3rd and kpt on same pce ins fnl f* **11/1**

0 **4** 1 ¼ **Hollywood Dream**[27] 4533 2-9-0 **0**................................... FranBerry 5 67
(William Muir) *towards rr: clsd to trck ldrs over 2f out: rdn 2f out: unable qck w wnr over 1f out: wl hld in 4th and kpt on same pce ins fnl f* **20/1**

**5** 1 **Revived** 2-9-0 **0**............................................................ DanielTudhope 16 64+
(Michael Bell) *hld up in tch in midfield: clsd to trck ldrs and nt clr run 2f out: rdn over 1f out: sn outpcd and btn: wl hld and plugged on same pce fnl f* **11/1**

**6** 1 **Naqaawa (IRE)** 2-9-0 **0**.................................................... AndreaAtzeni 4 61+
(Owen Burrows) *s.i.s: in rr: clsd 1/2-way: pushed along and outpcd over 2f out: no ch and carried rt over 1f out: swtchd bk lft 1f out: styd on to pass btn rivals fnl f* **14/1**

3 **7** 1 ¼ **Lady Dancealot (IRE)**[12] 5107 2-9-0 **0**............................. PatDobbs 7 57+
(David Elsworth) *hld up towards rr: clsd to chse ldrs and travelling wl over 2f out swtchd rt 2f out: sn rdn and btn: wknd fnl f* **6/1**[2]

60 **8** shd **Puchita (IRE)**[18] 4880 2-9-0 **0**....................................... TomMarquand 17 56+
(Richard Hannon) *s.i.s: rn green and wl off the pce in rr: hung rt 1/2-way: styd on to pass btn rival fr over 1f out: n.d* **33/1**

2 **9** 6 **Last Enchantment (IRE)**[28] 4496 2-9-0 **0**................... CharlesBishop 12 38+
(Eve Johnson Houghton) *pressed ldr tl led over 2f out: rdn and hdd over 1f out: sn btn and wknd: eased ins fnl f* **16/1**

0 **10** 1 ½ **Toomer**[20] 4815 2-9-0 **0**....................................................... SeanLevey 9 34+
(Richard Hannon) *in tch in midfield: pushed along jst over 2f out: sn outpcd and btn: wknd over 1f out: eased wl ins fnl f* **16/1**

**11** ¾ **Dizzy G (IRE)** 2-9-0 **0**...................................................... PJMcDonald 18 32+
(K R Burke) *chsd ldrs: rdn over 2f out: sn struggling and hung lft: stl hanging and wknd over 1f out: eased wl ins fnl f* **16/1**

2 **12** 3 ½ **Mushahadaat (IRE)**[12] 5107 2-9-0 **0**................................. JimCrowley 20 21+
(Brian Meehan) *led tl hung rt and hdd over 2f out: stl hanging and sn dropped out: eased ins fnl f* **3/1**[1]

**13** 3 ¼ **Foxtrot Lady** 2-9-0 **0**.......................................................... LiamKeniry 15 11+
(Andrew Balding) *s.i.s: a rr: lost tch 2f out: eased wl ins fnl f* **20/1**

0 **14** 2 ¼ **Royal Wave**[46] 3815 2-9-0 **0**.............................................. HarryBentley 11 5
(William Knight) *in tch in midfield: rdn and hung rt over 2f out: sn btn and dropped out: wl bhd and eased ins fnl f* **50/1**

4 **15** *1 ¼* **Supersymmetry (IRE)**[55] 3491 2-9-0 0................. RichardKingscote 19 1
(Tom Dascombe) *chsd ldrs tl 1/2-way: sn rdn and lost pl: wl bhd and eased ins fnl f* **7/1**[3]

1m 16.96s (4.76) **Going Correction** +0.525s/f (Yiel) **15** Ran SP% **126.0**
Speed ratings (Par 97): **89,81,78,76,75 73,72,71,63,61 60,56,51,48,47**
CSF £104.69 TOTE £10.50: £3.50, £4.30, £3.70; EX 159.80 Trifecta £1151.60.

**Owner** Sheikh Hamdan bin Mohammed Al Maktoum **Bred** Darley **Trained** Middleham Moor, N Yorks

**FOCUS**
What had looked a pretty open fillies' maiden was turned into a rout by an impressive debut winner.

## 5529 EBF BREEDERS' SERIES FILLIES' H'CAP 1m 1f 197y
**4:45** (4:51) (Class 2) (0-105,101) 3-Y-O+
**£18,675** (£5,592; £2,796; £1,398; £699; £351) **Stalls** Low

Form RPR

5212 **1** **Billesdon Bess**[18] 4915 3-8-2 **86**........................ HollieDoyle(3) 6 97
(Richard Hannon) *mde all: kpt on gamely: rdn out* **7/1**

1115 **2** *1* **Titi Makfi**[19] 4856 3-8-12 **93**........................ JamesDoyle 3 102
(Mark Johnston) *trckd ldrs: rdn to chse wnr 2f out: kpt on but a being hld fnl f* **4/1**[2]

41-1 **3** *¾* **Indulged**[74] 2817 4-9-1 **91**........................ GeorgeWood(3) 11 98
(James Fanshawe) *trckd ldrs tl lost pl over 5f out: hdwy 3f out: sn rdn: kpt on into 3rd over 1f out but nt quite pce to get on terms fnl f* **9/2**[3]

-112 **4** *1 ¾* **White Chocolate (IRE)**[33] 4292 3-8-4 **85**................ JosephineGordon 9 89+
(David Simcock) *hld up: hdwy 3f out: sn rdn: kpt on same pce fnl 2f* **11/4**[1]

3-06 **5** *3 ¾* **Skiffle**[11] 5155 4-10-0 **101**........................(p[1]) WilliamBuick 16 97
(Charlie Appleby) *mid-div: dropped to last pair over 5f out: hdwy over 2f out: rdn to chse ldrs over 1f out: wknd fnl f* **15/2**

4411 **6** *11* **Three Duchesses**[14] 5017 3-7-13 **85**........................ DavidEgan(5) 4 60
(Michael Bell) *mid-div: last pair over 5f out: hdwy 3f out: sn rdn: wknd over 1f out* **12/1**

3145 **7** *6* **Turning The Table (IRE)**[18] 4915 4-9-0 **87**................ RyanMoore 5 49
(David Simcock) *racd keenly in tch: hdwy 3f out: effrt 2f out: sn wknd* **10/1**

12-0 **8** *13* **Lady Perignon**[31] 4410 4-8-9 **82** oh3........................ OisinMurphy 8 18
(Andrew Balding) *trckd wnr: chal 3f out tl rdn 2f out: sn wknd* **25/1**

-115 **9** *6* **La Casa Tarifa (IRE)**[92] 2268 3-8-2 **83**........................ JoeFanning 14 8
(Mark Johnston) *hld up: hdwy 6f out: chal 3f out: sn rdn: wknd over 1f out* **20/1**

2m 19.36s (11.26) **Going Correction** +1.125s/f (Soft)
**WFA** 3 from 4yo+ 8lb **9** Ran SP% **114.5**
Speed ratings (Par 96): **99,98,97,96,93 84,79,69,64**
CSF £34.82 CT £140.29 TOTE £7.50: £2.40, £1.70, £1.80; EX 32.40 Trifecta £180.60.

**Owner** Pall Mall Partners & Partners **Bred** Stowell Hill Partners **Trained** East Everleigh, Wilts

**FOCUS**
Race distance as advertised. This looked a competitive heat but the winner made every yard. The third has been rated to form.

## 5530 CANTOR FITZGERALD H'CAP 7f
**5:50** (5:51) (Class 3) (0-95,95) 3-Y-O+ **£16,172** (£4,812; £2,405; £1,202) **Stalls** Low

Form RPR

4322 **1** **Truth Or Dare**[16] 4961 6-9-4 **87**........................ DanielTudhope 5 96
(James Bethell) *hld up in tch in midfield 5f out: in ld and clr ins fnl f: r.o wl: comf* **6/1**[3]

0135 **2** *1 ½* **Noble Peace**[27] 4524 4-9-4 **87**........................ HarryBentley 14 92
(Henry Candy) *hld up in last quartet: effrt to r on stands rail over 3f out: racing on stands rail and chsng wnr ins fnl f: kpt on* **11/1**

2545 **3** *2 ¾* **War Glory (IRE)**[19] 4854 4-9-5 **91**........................ HollieDoyle(3) 4 89
(Richard Hannon) *chsd ldng pair 5f out: 3rd and hld ins fnl f: wknd towards fin* **7/2**[1]

-000 **4** *1* **Medieval (IRE)**[19] 4856 3-9-3 **92**........................(b) FranBerry 7 85
(Paul Cole) *hld up in tch in last quartet 5f out: 4th and hld ins fnl f: wknd towards fin* **8/1**

5410 **5** *nk* **Goring (GER)**[35] 4207 5-9-2 **85**........................ JohnFahy 8 80
(Eve Johnson Houghton) *hld up in tch in midfield 5f out: 5th and hld ins fnl f: wknd towards fin* **14/1**

1163 **6** *10* **Luis Vaz De Torres (IRE)**[16] 4957 5-9-1 **84**..............(h) TonyHamilton 6 53
(Richard Fahey) *hld up in tch in last pair 5f out: wl hld in midfield ins fnl f* **25/1**

0250 **7** *¾* **The Warrior (IRE)**[46] 3837 5-9-6 **89**........................(e) SteveDrowne 11 56
(Amanda Perrett) *hld up in midfield 5f out: wl hld ins fnl f* **20/1**

3-16 **8** *½* **Ifwecan**[32] 4362 6-9-9 **95**........................ NoelGarbutt(3) 13 60
(Martin Smith) *chsd ldr 5f out: wl hld in midfield ins fnl f* **14/1**

60-0 **9** *6* **Lost At Sea**[18] 4904 3-9-6 **95**........................(p[1]) RichardKingscote 12 43
(K R Burke) *t.k.h: hld up in tch in midfield 5f out: wl bhd ins fnl f: eased towards fin* **14/1**

-204 **10** *3 ¼* **Sinfonietta (FR)**[18] 4882 5-9-8 **91**........................ WilliamBuick 17 32
(David Menuisier) *chsd ldng trio 4f out: wl bhd ins fnl f: eased towards fin* **9/2**[2]

4216 **11** *½* **Medburn Dream**[31] 4410 4-9-10 **93**........................ JFEgan 9 33
(Paul Henderson) *in ld 5f out: wl bhd ins fnl f: eased towards fin* **12/1**

-0 **12** *1* **Cenotaph (USA)**[18] 4924 5-9-7 **90**........................ RyanMoore 18 27
(A P O'Brien, Ire) *hld up in rr 5f out: wl bhd ins fnl f: eased towards fin* **8/1**

1m 33.36s (6.36) **Going Correction** +1.125s/f (Soft)
**WFA** 3 from 4yo+ 6lb **12** Ran SP% **121.5**
Speed ratings (Par 107): **108,106,103,102,101 90,89,88,81,78 77,76**
CSF £72.42 CT £274.14 TOTE £7.40: £2.50, £3.20, £1.70; EX 75.60 Trifecta £522.30.

**Owner** J A Tabet **Bred** D G Hardisty Bloodstock **Trained** Middleham Moor, N Yorks

**FOCUS**
Race distance increased by 15yds. A race hit by non-runners, visibility was poor and they only came back into view inside the last furlong. The runner-up has been rated close to form.

T/Jkpt: Not Won. T/Plt: £190.70 to a £1 stake. Pool: £344,782.28 - 1,319.68 winning units
T/Qpdt: £13.50 to a £1 stake. Pool: £23,101.80 - 1,261.83 winning units
**Steve Payne & Tim Mitchell**

# 5285 LEICESTER (R-H)
Wednesday, August 2

**OFFICIAL GOING: Good (8.4)**
Wind: Fresh behind Weather: Overcast turning to rain after race 4

## 5531 BRITISH STALLION STUDS EBF NOVICE STKS (PLUS 10 RACE) 6f
**5:55** (5:56) (Class 4) 2-Y-O **£4,528** (£1,347; £673; £336) **Stalls** High

Form RPR

**1** **Tabdeed** 2-9-2 0........................ DavidProbert 7 92+
(Owen Burrows) *s.i.s: hld up: hdwy over 2f out: swtchd rt over 1f out: shkn up to ld and edgd lft ins fnl f: r.o wl: readily* **14/1**

42 **2** *2 ¼* **Yafta**[39] 4094 2-9-2 0........................ DaneO'Neill 6 81
(Richard Hannon) *led: rdn over 1f out: hdd and unable qck ins fnl f* **11/10**[1]

0 **3** *1 ¾* **Amandine**[20] 4815 2-8-11 0........................ ShaneKelly 4 71
(David Elsworth) *chsd ldr: rdn and ev ch over 1f out: styd on same pce ins fnl f* **10/1**

14 **4** *5* **Ghayadh**[11] 5151 2-9-8 0........................ LouisSteward 1 67
(Hugo Palmer) *w ldrs: rdn and ev ch over 1f out: wknd fnl f* **10/3**[2]

03 **5** *3 ¼* **Viceroy Mac**[12] 5099 2-9-2 0........................ SamJames 8 51
(David Loughnane) *prom: pushed along 1/2-way: outpcd fr over 2f out: hung rt over 1f out* **22/1**

**6** *2 ½* **Authentic Art** 2-9-2 0........................ MartinLane 9 44
(Ralph Beckett) *s.i.s: outpcd* **10/1**

**7** *7* **Enzo (IRE)** 2-8-11 0........................ JennyPowell(5) 2 23
(Ed Walker) *w ldrs tl rdn and wknd over 2f out* **9/2**[3]

1m 10.74s (-2.26) **Going Correction** -0.55s/f (Hard) **7** Ran SP% **118.1**
Speed ratings (Par 96): **93,90,87,81,76 73,64**
CSF £31.56 TOTE £11.10: £5.10, £1.50; EX 36.70 Trifecta £226.10.

**Owner** Hamdan Al Maktoum **Bred** Red House Stud & Ketton Ashwell Ltd **Trained** Lambourn, Berks

**FOCUS**
Not a bad novice event and the runner-up gives it a sound look.

## 5532 PAT AND PETE WOODCOCK DIAMOND ANNIVERSARY (S) STKS 1m 2f
**6:30** (6:30) (Class 6) 3-Y-O **£3,234** (£962; £481; £240) **Stalls** Low

Form RPR

0505 **1** **Akamanto (IRE)**[13] 5066 3-9-2 70........................ DaneO'Neill 4 66+
(Richard Hannon) *chsd ldrs: wnt 2nd over 4f out: shkn up to ld over 1f out: sn hrd rdn: hung lft wl ins fnl f: styd on* **9/2**[3]

4342 **2** *½* **Tenby Two**[7] 5286 3-8-11 57........................ BenCurtis 7 60+
(Mick Channon) *pushed along early in rr then hld up and plld hrd: hdwy on outer over 2f out: rdn and edgd rt over 1f out: chsd wnr ins fnl f: nt qckn towards fin* **2/1**[1]

363 **3** *2 ½* **Josh The Plod (IRE)**[16] 4981 3-8-9 73........................ JasonWatson(7) 6 61
(Andrew Balding) *s.i.s: hld up: hdwy 1/2-way: rdn over 1f out: styd on same pce ins fnl f* **9/4**[2]

00 **4** *3* **Iley Boy**[49] 3720 3-8-13 0........................ HectorCrouch(3) 2 55
(John Gallagher) *trckd ldrs: racd keenly: rdn over 2f out: styd on same pce fr over 1f out* **50/1**

4060 **5** *3 ¾* **Mystery Of War (IRE)**[19] 4839 3-9-2 55........................ TedDurcan 3 48
(George Scott) *led after 1f: qcknd over 3f out: rdn and hdd over 1f out: wknd ins fnl f* **25/1**

6062 **6** *hd* **California Cliffs (IRE)**[51] 3657 3-8-11 56........................ DavidProbert 1 43
(Rae Guest) *sn led: hdd after 1f: chsd ldr to 1/2-way: remained handy: rdn over 2f out: wknd fnl f* **5/1**

5336 **7** *1* **Temir Kazyk**[13] 5061 3-8-11 68........................ GeorgeBuckell(5) 5 46
(David Simcock) *hld up: rdn over 2f out: wknd over 1f out* **12/1**

4064 **8** *½* **Mungo Madness**[27] 4540 3-8-13 52........................ ShelleyBirkett(3) 8 45
(Julia Feilden) *hld up: effrt and nt clr run over 2f out: wknd over 1f out* **33/1**

2m 9.8s (1.90) **Going Correction** +0.15s/f (Good) **8** Ran SP% **115.4**
Speed ratings (Par 98): **98,97,95,93,90 90,89,88**
.The winner was bought by R.M. Smith for 10,000 guineas. Tenby Two was claimed by Mr Neil Mulholland for £8,000.\n\x\x

**Owner** Michael Pescod **Bred** Nanallac Stud **Trained** East Everleigh, Wilts

**FOCUS**
An ordinary 3yo seller. It was run at a fair pace and the first two came clear. The winner did not need to quite match his best pre-race form to win.

## 5533 JOULES CELEBRATION FILLIES' H'CAP 1m 2f
**7:05** (7:06) (Class 4) (0-80,80) 3-Y-O+ **£6,469** (£1,925; £962; £481) **Stalls** Low

Form RPR

0-10 **1** **Curlew River**[84] 2520 3-9-6 **80**........................ FrannyNorton 7 89
(Mark Johnston) *led at stdy pce over 8f out: qcknd over 2f out: shkn up and hdd wl ins fnl f: sn led again: styd on wl* **5/1**[3]

-335 **2** *shd* **Italian Heiress**[32] 4365 3-9-0 **77**........................ HectorCrouch(3) 9 85
(Clive Cox) *trckd ldrs: wnt 2nd 6f out: rdn over 1f out: led wl ins fnl f: sn hdd: styd on* **4/1**[2]

-426 **3** *2 ½* **Cotinga**[32] 4336 3-9-0 **74**........................ DavidProbert 8 77
(Ralph Beckett) *hld up: racd keenly: hdwy over 2f out: rdn over 1f out: styd on same pce ins fnl f: eased whn hld nr fin* **5/2**[1]

6602 **4** *1 ¾* **Rayaa**[7] 5290 4-8-13 **65**........................(t) LouisSteward 5 64
(John Butler) *hld up: pushed along and hdwy over 1f out: sn rdn: styd on same pce ins fnl f* **4/1**[2]

1-40 **5** *1 ¾* **Brief Visit**[18] 4915 4-10-0 **80**........................ RobHornby 1 75
(Andrew Balding) *s.i.s: hld up: effrt over 2f out: styd on same pce fr over 1f out* **10/1**

-514 **6** *1 ¾* **Meshaykh (IRE)**[37] 4153 3-9-4 **78**........................ TedDurcan 6 71
(Sir Michael Stoute) *hld up in tch: hung rt and rdn over 1f out: sn outpcd* **6/1**

00-0 **7** *15* **Riviere Argentee (FR)**[26] 4580 3-9-1 **75**........................ BenCurtis 3 38
(K R Burke) *led. hdd over 8f out: chsd wnr tl 6f out: remained handy tl rdn and wknd over 1f out* **33/1**

2m 10.19s (2.29) **Going Correction** +0.15s/f (Good)
**WFA** 3 from 4yo 8lb **7** Ran SP% **111.6**
Speed ratings (Par 102): **96,95,93,92,91 89,77**
CSF £23.88 CT £59.24 TOTE £5.20: £2.60, £2.40; EX 25.30 Trifecta £70.70.

**Owner** Sheikh Hamdan bin Mohammed Al Maktoum **Bred** Darley **Trained** Middleham Moor, N Yorks

■ Stewards' Enquiry : Hector Crouch 2 day ban - used his whip above the permitted level (16/17 Aug)


The Form Book Flat, Raceform Ltd, Newbury, RG14 5SJ

**FOCUS**
This fair fillies' handicap was run at an uneven pace and the first pair was always up there.

## 5534 EBF STALLIONS FILLIES' NOVICE MEDIAN AUCTION STKS (PLUS 10 RACE) 6f
**7:40** (7:44) (Class 5) 2-Y-O **£4,528** (£1,347; £673; £336) **Stalls** High

Form RPR
02 **1** **Misty Spirit**[14] 5026 2-8-12 0 ShaneKelly 3 74+
(David Elsworth) *mde all: rdn over 1f out: hung rt ins fnl f: styd on wl* **5/1**[3]
6 **2** *2 ½* **Isabella Mayson**[34] 4252 2-8-12 0 MartinLane 14 66
(Stuart Kittow) *s.i.s: hdwy over 4f out: outpcd over 2f out: rallied over 1f out: edgd rt and styd on to go 2nd nr fin* **12/1**
45 **3** *½* **Collateral Beauty**[18] 4919 2-8-12 0 JackGarritty 8 64
(Richard Fahey) *chsd wnr: rdn and swtchd rt over 1f out: styd on same pce ins fnl f* **3/1**[1]
00 **4** *1 ½* **Gold Eagle**[20] 4815 2-8-12 0 DavidProbert 7 60
(Philip McBride) *hld up: nt clr run over 2f out: hdwy over 1f out: no imp ins fnl f* **12/1**
4 **5** *nk* **Tiny Tempest (IRE)**[27] 4520 2-8-9 0 EdwardGreatrex(3) 10 59
(Eve Johnson Houghton) *chsd ldrs: rdn over 2f out: styd on same pce fr over 1f out* **7/2**[2]
**6** *5* **Dandiesque (IRE)** 2-8-12 0 FrannyNorton 11 44+
(Richard Hannon) *s.i.s: hld up: pushed along and hdwy over 1f out: wknd ins fnl f* **8/1**
**7** *2 ¼* **Harbour Seal** 2-8-12 0 StevieDonohoe 13 37
(Henry Spiller) *uns rdr to post: s.i.s: hld up: rdn over 1f out: nvr on terms* **26/1**
**8** *½* **Chloellie** 2-8-5 0 GinaMangan(7) 6 35
(J R Jenkins) *hld up: hdwy over 2f out: rdn over 1f out: sn wknd* **66/1**
**9** *2 ¼* **Chickpea** 2-8-12 0 LouisSteward 2 29
(Michael Bell) *s.i.s: hdwy and hung rt over 4f out: rdn and wknd over 1f out* **6/1**
**10** *1 ¾* **Astrojewel** 2-8-12 0 JoeyHaynes 12 23
(Mark H Tompkins) *sn pushed along in rr: sme hdwy 1/2-way: sn outpcd* **50/1**
**11** *nk* **Helen Sherbet** 2-8-12 0 BenCurtis 9 22
(K R Burke) *s.i.s: outpcd* **12/1**
0 **12** *nk* **Raise A Little Joy**[30] 4440 2-8-9 0 ShelleyBirkett(3) 4 22
(J R Jenkins) *chsd ldrs: rdn over 2f out: wknd over 1f out* **66/1**
00 **13** *2* **Headwear (IRE)**[13] 5056 2-8-12 0 TedDurcan 5 16
(David Brown) *prom over 3f* **50/1**
**14** *64* **Night Air** 2-8-5 0 TobyEley(7) 1
(Derek Shaw) *sn hung rt and outpcd* **66/1**

1m 12.03s (-0.97) **Going Correction** -0.55s/f (Hard) 14 Ran SP% **124.6**
Speed ratings (Par 91): **84,80,80,78,77 70,67,67,64,61 61,61,58,**
CSF £63.82 TOTE £5.80: £2.00, £3.10, £1.70; EX 57.30 Trifecta £288.70.
**Owner** Lordship Stud **Bred** Crossfields Bloodstock Ltd **Trained** Newmarket, Suffolk

**FOCUS**
A modest novice event for fillies. It's been rated as straightforward form.

## 5535 HEINEKEN H'CAP 6f
**8:10** (8:11) (Class 5) (0-70,69) 3-Y-O+ **£3,881** (£1,155; £577; £288) **Stalls** High

Form RPR
-361 **1** **Gaval**[7] 5291 3-9-8 **69** 6ex BenCurtis 8 82+
(David Barron) *mde all: rdn over 1f out: edgd lft u.p ins fnl f: styd on wl* **11/10**[1]
0053 **2** *4* **Jacksonfire**[7] 5285 5-8-4 **50** oh5 (p) EdwardGreatrex(3) 5 52
(Michael Mullineaux) *a.p: rdn 1/2-way: chsd wnr over 1f out: no ex wl ins fnl f* **7/1**
3644 **3** *1 ½* **Manipura**[6] 5340 4-8-7 **50** (p) RyanPowell 1 48
(Derek Shaw) *s.i.s: hld up: hdwy over 2f out: sn rdn: styd on to go 3rd nr fin* **6/1**[3]
-106 **4** *hd* **Mad Endeavour**[19] 4842 6-9-8 **65** (b) MartinLane 9 62
(Stuart Kittow) *chsd wnr: rdn over 2f out: hung rt and lost 2nd over 1f out: no ex ins fnl f* **10/1**
5306 **5** *5* **Fleckerl (IRE)**[16] 4979 7-9-9 **66** (p) RobertWinston 3 51
(Conor Dore) *s.i.s: shkn up: hdwy and hung rt over 1f out: nvr trbld ldrs* **5/1**[2]
-440 **6** *6* **Diamond Indulgence**[167] 761 4-8-3 **53** oh3 ow3 (h) TobyEley(7) 7 17
(Derek Shaw) *prom: rdn over 3f out: wknd over 2f out* **25/1**
0042 **7** *10* **Quintus Cerialis (IRE)**[13] 5081 5-8-9 **52** ow2 (tp) TedDurcan 10
(Karen George) *dwlt: outpcd* **12/1**
600 **8** *2 ¼* **Allen's Folly**[105] 1887 4-8-4 **50** oh5 ShelleyBirkett(3) 2
(Peter Hiatt) *prom over 3f* **33/1**

1m 10.95s (-2.05) **Going Correction** -0.55s/f (Hard)
**WFA** 3 from 4yo+ 4lb 8 Ran SP% **114.6**
Speed ratings (Par 103): **91,85,83,83,76 68,55,52**
CSF £9.50 CT £32.88 TOTE £2.10: £1.10, £2.30, £1.90; EX 9.70 Trifecta £37.10.
**Owner** Bearstone Stud Limited **Bred** Bearstone Stud Ltd **Trained** Maunby, N Yorks

**FOCUS**
A moderate sprint handicap in which they again came stands' side.

## 5536 SHANGTON H'CAP 1m 53y
**8:40** (8:41) (Class 6) (0-65,66) 3-Y-O **£3,234** (£962; £481; £240) **Stalls** Low

Form RPR
-012 **1** **Belisa (IRE)**[18] 4900 3-9-6 **64** DavidNolan 10 70+
(Ivan Furtado) *chsd ldrs: led over 6f out: hung lft over 5f out: sn hdd: remained handy: rdn to ld over 1f out: edgd rt: r.o* **11/4**[1]
5506 **2** *1 ½* **Pitch High (IRE)**[15] 5001 3-8-5 **52** ShelleyBirkett(3) 3 54
(Julia Feilden) *w ldr tl over 6f out: remained handy: rdn and ev ch over 1f out: styd on same pce wl ins fnl f* **20/1**
0545 **3** *1 ½* **Time To Sea (IRE)**[33] 4320 3-9-7 **65** RobertWinston 11 63
(John Butler) *hld up: rdn over 2f out: hdwy over 1f out: sn hung rt: styd on u.p to go 3rd wl ins fnl f* **3/1**[2]
-660 **4** *1* **Lovely Acclamation (IRE)**[15] 5007 3-9-5 **66** HectorCrouch(3) 2 62
(Ismail Mohammed) *led: hdd over 6f out: led again 5f out: rdn and hdd over 1f out: no ex ins fnl f* **14/1**
5420 **5** *2 ¼* **Madam Prancealot (IRE)**[60] 3327 3-8-3 **50** EdwardGreatrex(3) 5 41
(Karen George) *hld up: hdwy over 2f out: sn rdn: styd on same pce ins fnl f* **25/1**
000- **6** *¾* **Unonothinjonsnow**[278] 7659 3-8-2 **46** oh1 RoystonFfrench 4 35
(Richard Guest) *plld hrd and prom: rdn over 1f out: no ex fnl f* **10/1**
2524 **7** *2* **Mama Africa (IRE)**[20] 4785 3-9-7 **65** BenCurtis 1 49
(David Barron) *hld up: nt clr run over 2f out: nvr trbld ldrs* **9/2**[3]
664 **8** *hd* **Mark Of Excellence (IRE)**[23] 4693 3-8-11 **55** PatCosgrave 9 39
(Saeed bin Suroor) *hld up in tch: plld hrd: rdn and hung rt over 1f out: wknd fnl f* **5/1**
0065 **9** *4* **Northdown**[22] 4728 3-9-5 **63** (p) StevieDonohoe 7 38
(David Lanigan) *s.i.s: hld up: plld hrd: rdn over 2f out: wknd over 1f out* **16/1**

1m 46.36s (1.26) **Going Correction** +0.15s/f (Good) 9 Ran SP% **116.8**
Speed ratings (Par 98): **99,97,96,95,92 92,90,89,85**
CSF £58.81 CT £178.27 TOTE £3.40: £1.40, £4.30, £1.40; EX 57.80 Trifecta £246.50.
**Owner** John L Marriott & Albert L Marriott **Bred** Zalim Bifov **Trained** Wiseton, Nottinghamshire

**FOCUS**
An ordinary 3yo handicap.
T/Plt: £24.40 to a £1 stake. Pool: £58,841.54 - 1,753.61 winning units T/Qpdt: £10.60 to a £1 stake. Pool: £5,869.97 - 406.61 winning units **Colin Roberts**

# 5179 REDCAR (L-H)
Wednesday, August 2

**OFFICIAL GOING: Good to soft (7.7)**
Wind: Moderate behind Weather: Cloudy

## 5537 RACINGUK.COM/JOIN BRITISH EBF NOVICE STKS 5f 217y
**2:00** (2:04) (Class 5) 2-Y-O **£3,234** (£962; £481; £240) **Stalls** Centre

Form RPR
3 **1** **Stormbringer**[23] 4681 2-9-2 0 (p[1]) TomEaves 8 83+
(Kevin Ryan) *cl up: led after 1f: pushed clr wl over 1f out: rdn and kpt on strly fnl f* **11/10**[1]
5334 **2** *2* **Miss Mo Brown Bear (IRE)**[6] 5322 2-8-4 71 (p[1]) ConnorMurtagh(7) 2 68
(Richard Hannon) *led 1f: cl up: rdn along 2f out: drvn over 1f out: kpt on u.p fnl f* **9/2**[2]
13 **3** *1 ¼* **Havana Star (IRE)**[68] 3051 2-9-6 0 KevinStott 7 73
(Kevin Ryan) *in tch: hdwy 1/2-way: chsd ldrs 2f out: sn rdn and kpt on u.p fnl f* **13/2**[3]
0 **4** *1 ¼* **Geesala Brave (IRE)**[15] 4995 2-9-2 0 JackGarritty 9 66
(John Quinn) *towards rr: hdwy over 3f out: chsd ldrs over 2f out and sn rdn along: kpt on u.p fnl f* **33/1**
**5** *1 ½* **Arctic Treasure (IRE)** 2-9-2 0 DavidNolan 13 61+
(Richard Fahey) *towards rr: hdwy over 2f out: rdn along and styd on appr fnl f* **14/1**
16 **6** *¾* **Our Kid (IRE)**[35] 4205 2-9-6 0 PaulHanagan 4 63
(Richard Fahey) *chsd ldrs: rdn along over 2f out: drvn wl over 1f out: sn wknd* **12/1**
66 **7** *2* **What Do You Think (IRE)**[14] 5015 2-8-11 0 PaulMulrennan 1 48
(Michael Dods) *towards rr: hdwy over 2f out: sn rdn and kpt on: n.d* **25/1**
0 **8** *1 ¼* **North Road Revue**[19] 4834 2-8-11 0 DavidAllan 3 44
(Tim Easterby) *towards rr: pushed along over 2f out: sn rdn and kpt on: n.d* **14/1**
0 **9** *1 ¾* **Cavendish Place**[15] 4996 2-9-2 0 PhillipMakin 5 44
(David Brown) *cl up: rdn along wl over 2f out: sn drvn and wknd* **100/1**
0 **10** *4 ½* **Smugglers Top**[13] 5058 2-9-2 0 BenCurtis 6 30
(Tom Dascombe) *dwlt: a rr* **66/1**
0 **11** *3* **Saxonroad Boy (USA)**[16] 4977 2-8-13 0 AdamMcNamara(3) 14 21
(Richard Fahey) *rr: rdn along 1/2-way: sn bhd* **40/1**
**12** *½* **Time Exposed (IRE)** 2-8-8 0 JordanVaughan(3) 15 15
(K R Burke) *rr: rdn along 1/2-way: sn bhd* **33/1**
00 **13** *9* **French Silk**[51] 3662 2-8-11 0 RoystonFfrench 11
(Chris Fairhurst) *chsd ldrs: edgd rt and racd wd bef 1/2-way: sn rdn and wknd over 2f out* **200/1**

1m 10.13s (-1.67) **Going Correction** -0.225s/f (Firm) 13 Ran SP% **115.3**
Speed ratings (Par 94): **102,99,97,96,94 93,90,88,86,80 76,75,63**
CSF £5.14 TOTE £1.90: £1.02, £1.80, £2.30; EX 6.40 Trifecta £19.10.
**Owner** Charles Wentworth **Bred** Riva Royale Partnership **Trained** Hambleton, N Yorks

**FOCUS**
Dry overnight and a blustery day, with the ground given as just 'good to soft'. The first year this has been run as a novice event and two previous winners took their chance. It's not strong form, but it should be reliable and the winner did it well. The second and third set the level.

## 5538 RACING UK CLUB DAY HERE TODAY MAIDEN STKS 7f
**2:35** (2:41) (Class 5) 3-Y-O+ **£3,234** (£962; £481; £240) **Stalls** Centre

Form RPR
44 **1** **Caridade (USA)**[32] 4378 3-9-0 0 KevinStott 7 81+
(Kevin Ryan) *sn led: rdn and qcknd clr over 1f out: kpt on strly* **13/8**[1]
55 **2** *6* **Ember's Glow**[13] 5073 3-9-5 0 CamHardie 9 70
(Jason Ward) *trckd ldrs: hdwy 3f out: rdn along 2f out: drvn and kpt on fnl f: no ch w wnr* **40/1**
54 **3** *2 ¾* **Obeya**[12] 5118 3-9-0 0 JackMitchell 12 57
(Roger Varian) *prom: chsd wnr 2f out: sn rdn: drvn over 1f out and kpt on same pce* **6/1**[3]
02- **4** *½* **Sureyoutoldme (IRE)**[279] 7648 3-9-5 0 JamesSullivan 15 61
(Ruth Carr) *trckd ldrs: hdwy 3f out: rdn along 2f out: kpt on same pce* **17/2**
**5** *¾* **Teomaria** 3-8-11 0 CliffordLee(3) 1 54
(K R Burke) *trckd ldrs: pushed along over 2f out: sn rdn and kpt on same pce* **9/2**[2]
**6** *½* **Betty Grable (IRE)** 3-9-0 0 PaulMulrennan 6 53
(Wilf Storey) *in tch: hdwy to chse ldrs 3f out: rdn along over 2f out: kpt on same pce* **20/1**
**7** *3* **Mr Slicker (FR)** 3-9-5 0 BenCurtis 10 50
(Tom Dascombe) *chsd ldrs on inner: rdn along wl over 2f out: sn drvn and grad wknd* **14/1**
5 **8** *¾* **My Angel**[20] 4793 3-9-0 0 AndrewMullen 13 43
(Ollie Pears) *dwlt and towards rr: rdn along over 2f out: n.d* **25/1**
5 **9** *¾* **Stolen Angel (IRE)**[15] 5003 3-9-5 0 (h[1]) PhillipMakin 14 46
(Antony Brittain) *in tch: rdn along wl over 2f out: sn wknd* **22/1**
05-2 **10** *nk* **Supreme Power (IRE)**[13] 5076 3-9-5 63 RoystonFfrench 3 45
(Tracy Waggott) *dwlt: a towards rr* **17/2**
0 **11** *5* **Precious Rock (IRE)**[34] 4247 3-9-5 0 JackGarritty 11 31
(Jedd O'Keeffe) *a towards rr* **25/1**
0/ **12** *7* **Jay Em Gee (IRE)**[646] 7515 4-9-11 0 ConnorBeasley 5 14
(Bryan Smart) *prom: rdn along 3f out: sn drvn and wknd* **50/1**
605- **13** *9* **Kirkby's Phantom**[336] 6025 3-9-0 40 PatrickMathers 16
(Colin Teague) *a rr* **250/1**

1m 22.22s (-2.28) **Going Correction** -0.225s/f (Firm)
**WFA** 3 from 4yo 6lb 13 Ran SP% **119.9**
Speed ratings (Par 103): **104,97,94,93,92 92,88,87,86,86 80,72,62**
CSF £98.77 TOTE £2.40: £1.30, £12.10, £2.40; EX 62.80 Trifecta £326.60.

**Owner** Hambleton Racing Ltd XVIII & CN Farm Ltd **Bred** Darley **Trained** Hambleton, N Yorks
■ My Cherokee, Budarri and Tap On The Bar were withdrawn. Prices at time of withdrawal 20/1,100/1 and 125/1 respectively. Rule 4 does not apply.
**FOCUS**
They took an age to load, there were three withdrawals at the start and a number of these were in the stalls for at least five minutes. All the money poured in for the front two in the market and the favourite proved the money on her was well placed. The winner has been rated to the better view of her debut C&D form.

## 5539 WATCH RACING UK ON BT TV (S) STKS 1m 2f 1y
**3:10** (3:10) (Class 6) 3-Y-O+ **£2,897** (£855; £427) **Stalls** Low

Form RPR
3636 **1** **Hernandoshideaway**[16] 4959 5-9-6 72........................(t) PaulMulrennan 6 67+
(Michael Dods) *t.k.h: hld up in rr: hdwy 4f out: cl up over 2f out: sn led: rdn and hdd narrowly ent fnl f: drvn and rallied to ld again last 50 yds* **10/11**[1]
4222 **2** *nk* **Bling King**[42] 3977 8-9-6 61................................................(p) DavidAllan 7 66
(Geoffrey Harker) *chsd clr ldr: hdwy 3f out: cl up over 2f out: rdn to chal over 1f out: slt ld ent fnl f: sn drvn: hdd and no ex last 50 yds* **5/2**[2]
236- **3** *11* **Le Deluge (FR)**[9] 7321 7-9-6 66.........................................(t) TomEaves 5 46
(Micky Hammond) *led and sn clr: pushed along 3f out: jnd over 2f out: sn hdd and plodded on same pce* **11/2**[3]
5006 **4** *9* **Lukoutoldmakezebak**[21] 4743 4-9-6 39..................(h[1]) PatrickMathers 1 30
(David Thompson) *rr: sme hdwy 3f out: sn rdn along and nvr a factor* **33/1**
04 **5** *3 1/4* **Wee Bogus**[24] 4657 4-9-1 0............................................ RowanScott[(5)] 4 24
(Alistair Whillans) *chsd ldng pair: pushed along 4f out: rdn 3f out: sn outpcd and bhd* **12/1**
2500 **6** *10* **Panther In Pink (IRE)**[5] 5374 3-8-7 47............................(p) ShaneGray 3 2
(Ann Duffield) *t.k.h: hld up: rdn along 4f out: sn outpcd and bhd* **20/1**

2m 7.71s (0.61) **Going Correction** +0.10s/f (Good)
**WFA** 3 from 4yo+ 8lb **6** Ran SP% **111.7**
Speed ratings (Par 101): **101,100,91,84,82 74**
CSF £3.32 TOTE £1.80: £1.20, £1.10; EX 3.90 Trifecta £8.50.The winner was claimed by Amanda Mooney for £7,000.
**Owner** D C Batey & Foster Watson **Bred** Miss K Rausing **Trained** Denton, Co Durham
**FOCUS**
The rain came before this weak seller. It's been given a token rating through the runner-up.

## 5540 RACING UK PROFITS RETURNED TO RACING H'CAP 1m 2f 1y
**3:45** (3:46) (Class 5) (0-75,77) 3-Y-O+ **£3,234** (£962; £481; £240) **Stalls** Low

Form RPR
3525 **1** **Save The Bees**[18] 4893 9-9-10 77................................(b) GerO'Neill[(7)] 7 83
(Declan Carroll) *led and clr: pushed along over 2f out: sn rdn and edgd lft: drvn and hdd 1f out: rallied to ld again last 100 yds* **7/1**
-030 **2** *1/2* **Quoteline Direct**[30] 4439 4-9-0 60..............................(h) PaulMulrennan 3 65
(Micky Hammond) *hld up: hdwy on inner over 3f out: n.m.r 2f out: sn swtchd rt and rdn to chal: led narrowly 1f out and sn drvn: hdd and no ex last 100 yds* **20/1**
5054 **3** *1/2* **Satish**[12] 5131 4-9-7 67....................................................(b) PhillipMakin 11 71
(David O'Meara) *dwlt and hld up in rr: hdwy 3f out: chsd ldrs wl over 1f out: sn rdn: styng on whn nt clr run and swtchd rt ins fnl f: kpt on wl towards fin* **11/1**
3142 **4** *1 1/4* **True Romance (IRE)**[19] 4838 3-9-6 74................................ TomEaves 2 77
(James Given) *trckd ldrs: chsd wnr 1/2-way: rdn along 2f out: drvn over 1f out: kpt on same pce* **7/2**[1]
002 **5** *2* **Zealous (IRE)**[16] 4959 4-9-6 73.................................. DarraghKeenan[(7)] 1 71
(Sally Haynes) *trckd ldrs: hdwy 4f out: rdn along over 2f out: drvn wl over 1f out: sn one pce* **4/1**[2]
533 **6** *1 3/4* **Infamous Lawman (IRE)**[15] 5003 3-8-10 69............. BenRobinson[(5)] 9 64
(Brian Ellison) *chsd ldrs: rdn along on outer 4f out: drvn over 2f out: plodded on one pce* **6/1**[3]
6035 **7** *1* **Eez Eh (IRE)**[25] 4608 4-9-6 66.................................(b[1]) ConnorBeasley 10 58
(Keith Dalgleish) *hld up in rr: effrt 3f out: sn rdn along and n.d* **10/1**
1514 **8** *hd* **Bit Of A Quirke**[30] 4439 4-9-6 66.................................... PaulHanagan 5 58
(Mark Walford) *prom: rdn along 3f out: drvn 2f out: sn wknd* **4/1**[2]
0005 **9** *7* **Jacob Black**[25] 4609 6-9-2 62.................................(t) AndrewMullen 6 40
(Kenny Johnson) *a rr* **66/1**
00-0 **10** *27* **Arizona Sunrise**[23] 4690 4-8-11 57.................................... CamHardie 8
(Tina Jackson) *chsd ldrs: rdn along over 3f out: sn wknd and bhd whn eased wl over 1rf out* **50/1**

2m 7.42s (0.32) **Going Correction** +0.10s/f (Good)
**WFA** 3 from 4yo+ 8lb **10** Ran SP% **114.6**
Speed ratings (Par 103): **102,101,101,100,98 97,96,96,90,69**
CSF £132.12 CT £1515.46 TOTE £8.10: £2.40, £6.10, £3.00; EX 195.70 Trifecta £1604.70.
**Owner** Steve Ryan **Bred** S P Ryan **Trained** Malton, N Yorks
**FOCUS**
A good pace set by the winner in this modest handicap. The first two have been rated to their recent form.

## 5541 RACING UK STRAIGHT-MILE SERIES H'CAP (QUALIFIER FOR THE RACING UK STRAIGHT MILE SERIES FINAL) 7f 219y
**4:20** (4:21) (Class 4) (0-85,84) 3-Y-O **£6,469** (£1,925; £962; £481) **Stalls** Centre

Form RPR
134 **1** **Hugin (IRE)**[25] 4618 3-9-7 84.......................................... JamieSpencer 3 94+
(David Simcock) *trckd ldrs: hdwy over 2f out: rdn to ld over 1f out: kpt on strly* **5/4**[1]
6000 **2** *2* **Tailor's Row (USA)**[9] 5213 3-8-12 75................................ AndrewMullen 4 79
(Mark Johnston) *cl up: chal 2f out: rdn and hung bdly lft over 1f out: drvn and kpt on fnl f* **33/1**
05-3 **3** *1 1/4* **Portledge (IRE)**[179] 577 3-8-9 72....................................... PaulHanagan 8 73
(James Bethell) *wnt rt s: hld up in rr: hdwy over 2f out: rdn to chse ldrs and swtchd lft over 1f out: drvn and kpt on fnl f* **9/1**
2132 **4** *nse* **Heir Of Excitement (IRE)**[21] 4741 3-9-0 77....................... ShaneGray 7 77
(Kevin Ryan) *trckd ldrs on outer: hdwy over 2f out: rdn along wl over 1f out: sn drvn and kpt on fnl f* **4/1**[2]
312 **5** *nse* **Raselasad (IRE)**[25] 4610 3-9-5 82................................ RoystonFfrench 2 84+
(Tracy Waggott) *t.k.h early: cl up: trckd ldng pair 1/2-way: effrt whn nt clr run and hmpd over 1f out: sn rdn and kpt on fnl f* **11/2**[3]
-055 **6** *2 1/2* **Maldonado (FR)**[25] 4631 3-8-5 75.................................. HarrisonShaw[(7)] 5 69
(Michael Easterby) *hld up in tch: pushed along wl over 2f out: rdn wl over 1f out: no hdwy* **25/1**
5304 **7** *3 1/2* **Devil's Bridge (IRE)**[21] 4736 3-9-4 84............(p[1]) RachelRichardson[(3)] 1 68
(Richard Hannon) *led: rdn along 2f out: sn drvn and hdd: hld whn hmpd over 1f out: wknd after* **6/1**

1m 35.31s (-1.29) **Going Correction** -0.225s/f (Firm) **7** Ran SP% **110.9**
Speed ratings (Par 102): **97,95,93,93,93 91,87**
CSF £43.64 CT £254.73 TOTE £2.00: £1.20, £7.00; EX 33.80 Trifecta £204.90.
**Owner** Steffen Norris **Bred** Glenvale Stud **Trained** Newmarket, Suffolk
**FOCUS**
A few unexposed types in this 3yo handicap, but it's still no more than fair form. The runner-up has been rated close to his turf best.

## 5542 WATCH RACING UK ANYWHERE H'CAP (DIV I) 5f 217y
**4:55** (4:56) (Class 6) (0-60,64) 3-Y-O+ **£2,749** (£818; £408; £204) **Stalls** Centre

Form RPR
0564 **1** **Gaelic Wizard (IRE)**[20] 4789 9-8-11 51....................(b) GemmaTutty[(5)] 5 58
(Karen Tutty) *rr and pushed along 1/2-way: swtchd rt and hdwy over 2f out: chsd ldrs over 1f out: rdn to ld ins fnl f: kpt on strly* **15/2**
6536 **2** *1 1/4* **Rose Eclair**[11] 5134 4-9-7 59..............................(p) RachelRichardson[(3)] 3 62
(Tim Easterby) *led: rdn wl over 1f out: drvn ent fnl f: sn hdd: kpt on* **9/2**[2]
045 **3** *1/2* **Tango Sky (IRE)**[49] 3704 8-9-7 56..............................(p) PaulMulrennan 8 58
(Paul Midgley) *trckd ldrs: hdwy 2f out: rdn to chal over 1f out: ev ch: drvn ent fnl f: kpt on same pce towards fin* **8/1**
3000 **4** *1/2* **A J Cook (IRE)**[4] 5418 7-8-6 46....................................(p) RowanScott[(5)] 10 46
(Ron Barr) *rrd s: sn in tch: hdwy to chse ldrs 2f out: rdn over 1f out: ev ch tl drvn ent fnl f and and kpt on same pce* **20/1**
0001 **5** *2 3/4* **Be Bold**[7] 5283 5-10-1 64 6ex.......................................(b) ConnorBeasley 6 56
(Rebecca Bastiman) *chsd ldrs: rdn along wl over 1f out: sn drvn and grad wknd* **3/1**[1]
5300 **6** *1* **Bingo George (IRE)**[13] 5050 4-9-1 50............................ PaulHanagan 12 39
(Mark Rimell) *towards rr: hdwy 2f out: rdn over 1f out: styd on wl fnl f* **25/1**
0505 **7** *1* **Emjayem**[15] 4993 7-9-3 59.......................................... MeganEllingworth[(7)] 7 45
(John Holt) *cl up: rdn along 2f out: grad wknd* **40/1**
0604 **8** *1/2* **Cryptonite (IRE)**[7] 5283 3-9-5 58...........................(b) AlistairRawlinson 1 42
(Michael Appleby) *cl up: rdn along 2f out: sn drvn and wknd appr fnl f* **7/1**[3]
0-00 **9** *4 1/2* **Le Laitier (FR)**[43] 3949 6-9-6 55...................................... DavidAllan 11 26
(Scott Dixon) *chsd ldrs: rdn along wl over 1f out: sn drvn and wknd* **12/1**
6300 **10** *3/4* **Cool Run Girl (IRE)**[9] 5203 3-8-7 46............................ AndrewMullen 2 14
(Iain Jardine) *in tch towards inner: rdn along over 2f out: sn wknd* **25/1**
-005 **11** *1/2* **Knockamany Bends (IRE)**[3] 5459 7-8-11 46.........(p) BarryMcHugh 13 13
(John Wainwright) *swtchd rt s and racd alone nr stands rail: prom: rdn over 2f out: sn wknd* **14/1**
000- **12** *1* **Royboy**[223] 8496 4-8-10 45.................................................. TomEaves 14 9
(Bryan Smart) *dwlt: a rr* **50/1**
00-0 **13** *1 1/4* **Tilly Devine**[33] 4302 3-8-6 45......................................... PatrickMathers 4 5
(Scott Dixon) *chsd ldrs on inner: rdn along over 2f out: sn wknd* **16/1**
5-00 **14** *1* **Clubland (IRE)**[58] 3397 8-9-4 58................................. KevinLundie[(5)] 15 16
(Roy Bowring) *racd wd: chsd ldrs: rdn along over 2f out: sn drvn and wknd* **16/1**

1m 10.34s (-1.46) **Going Correction** -0.225s/f (Firm)
**WFA** 3 from 4yo+ 4lb **14** Ran SP% **121.5**
Speed ratings (Par 101): **100,98,97,97,93 92,90,90,84,83 82,81,79,78**
CSF £39.14 CT £286.05 TOTE £8.80: £2.80, £2.00, £2.80; EX 85.90 Trifecta £567.00.
**Owner** Grange Park Racing (Tutty Trio) **Bred** Mrs Mary Gallagher **Trained** Osmotherley, N Yorks
**FOCUS**
They spread right across the course in the first division of this moderate sprint handicap. It's been rated around the balance of the second, third and fourth.

## 5543 WATCH RACING UK ANYWHERE H'CAP (DIV II) 5f 217y
**5:30** (5:35) (Class 6) (0-60,60) 3-Y-O+ **£2,749** (£818; £408; £204) **Stalls** Centre

Form RPR
-231 **1** **Yes You (IRE)**[13] 5070 3-8-8 55.................................... JamieGormley[(7)] 1 62+
(Iain Jardine) *hld up in tch towards far side: hdwy 2f out: rdn over 1f out: styd on to ld ins fnl f: edgd rt and kpt on* **13/8**[1]
0606 **2** *3/4* **Etienne Gerard**[23] 4695 5-9-7 60........................(p) LewisEdmunds[(3)] 14 66
(Nigel Tinkler) *racd towards stands side: in tch on outer: hdwy 2f out: rdn to ld over 1f out: drvn and edgd lft ins fnl f:. sn hdd : kpt on* **12/1**
454 **3** *1 1/4* **Melrose Girl**[15] 5006 3-9-5 59.......................................... ConnorBeasley 11 60
(Bryan Smart) *t.k.h: hld up in midfield: hdwy 2f out: rdn over 1f out: kpt on u.p fnl f* **33/1**
060 **4** *3/4* **Mighty Bond**[4] 5418 5-8-10 46..................................(p[1]) RoystonFfrench 13 46
(Tracy Waggott) *cl up: led jst over 2f out: sn rdn and hdd over 1f out: drvn and kpt on same pce fnl f* **40/1**
6400 **5** *1* **Wilde Extravagance (IRE)**[28] 4509 4-9-9 59.................(p[1]) JoeDoyle 10 56
(Julie Camacho) *dwlt and towards rr: hdwy to chse ldrs over 2f out: rdn over 1f out: kpt on same pce fnl f* **12/1**
3003 **6** *2* **Mitchum**[4] 5419 8-9-1 56................................................(p) PhilDennis[(5)] 9 47
(Ron Barr) *chsd ldrs: rdn along 2f out: sn drvn and grad wknd* **9/1**
5303 **7** *1/2* **Whipphound**[7] 5283 9-8-11 47.......................................(p) JamesSullivan 7 36
(Ruth Carr) *chsd ldrs: rdn along 2f out: sn wknd* **8/1**[3]
451 **8** *nk* **Searanger (USA)**[14] 5016 4-9-3 58................................ RowanScott[(5)] 2 46
(Rebecca Menzies) *towards rr far side: hdwy over 2f out: sn rdn and n.d* **4/1**[2]
4200 **9** *nk* **Secret City (IRE)**[13] 5050 11-8-10 46 oh1...................(b) DuranFentiman 3 33
(Rebecca Bastiman) *a towards rr* **25/1**
064 **10** *1/2* **Hamriyah**[14] 5019 3-9-5 59..................................................(h) DavidAllan 8 44
(Tim Easterby) *dwlt: a rr* **14/1**
5000 **11** *nse* **Men United (FR)**[22] 4726 4-8-5 46 oh1......................... KevinLundie[(5)] 5 32
(Roy Bowring) *racd centre: led: rdn along and hdd over 2f out: sn drvn and wknd* **22/1**
0603 **12** *1/2* **Jess**[7] 5282 4-9-2 52.........................................................(p) TomEaves 15 36
(Kevin Ryan) *prom: centre: rdn along over 2f out: sn drvn and wknd* **22/1**

1m 9.99s (-1.81) **Going Correction** -0.225s/f (Firm)
**WFA** 3 from 4yo+ 4lb **12** Ran SP% **119.2**
Speed ratings (Par 101): **103,102,100,99,98 95,94,94,93,93 93,92**
CSF £21.50 CT £491.61 TOTE £2.70: £1.20, £3.30, £6.60; EX 26.70 Trifecta £335.60.
**Owner** Taco Partners **Bred** Tower Place Bloodstock **Trained** Carrutherstown, D'fries & G'way
**FOCUS**
They got racing a long way out here. On paper this looked slightly stronger than the first division and - although still moderate form - they were slightly quicker. It's been rated around the balance of the principals.

## 5544 BETFAIR NOVICE AMATEUR RIDERS' H'CAP 7f 219y
**6:05** (6:11) (Class 6) (0-65,66) 4-Y-O+ **£2,651** (£822; £410; £205) **Stalls** Centre

Form RPR
4050 **1** **Ellaal**[16] 4960 8-11-3 61............................................(p) MissEmilyBullock 10 68
(Ruth Carr) *cl up: led over 2f out: rdn over 1f out: kpt on wl* **16/1**
0300 **2** *1 1/4* **Rebel State (IRE)**[40] 4034 4-10-9 56........................(p) MissACawley[(3)] 2 60
(Jedd O'Keeffe) *towards rr: hdwy 3f out: chsd ldrs 2f out: rdn over 1f out: kpt on fnl f* **10/1**

1000 **3** ½ **Nonno Giulio (IRE)**[6] 5341 6-11-6 **64**..........................(p) MissJCooley 7 67
(Conor Dore) *led: rdn along and hdd over 2f out: hung lft and rt over 1f out: kpt on same pce* **25/1**
2305 **4** 1¾ **Broctune Papa Gio**[21] 4743 10-10-12 **56**....................(b) MrWJMilburn 6 55
(Gillian Boanas) *chsd ldrs: rdn along 2f out: sn drvn and no imp fnl f* **11/1**
0-04 **5** 1½ **Ingleby Spring (IRE)**[9] 5214 5-11-2 **60**.......................... MrBillyGarritty 1 56
(Richard Fahey) *towards rr: pushed along and hdwy 3f out: rdn 2f out: kpt on fnl f* **9/2**[2]
4015 **6** ¾ **Know Your Name**[19] 4833 6-11-8 **66**........................... MissAMcCain 13 60
(Donald McCain) *hld up towards rr: swtchd markedly lft to far rail 1/2-way: hdwy wl over 2f out: rdn wl over 1f out: kpt on fnl f* **14/1**
2406 **7** ¾ **Thornaby Nash**[9] 5214 6-11-4 **62**.............................(p) MissLMPinchin 8 54
(Karen Tutty) *chsd ldrs: rdn along 2f out: drvn over 1f out: grad wknd* **8/1**
0-00 **8** 2½ **Fledermaus (IRE)**[14] 5021 7-9-13 **46** oh1.............(t) MissBJohnson[(3)] 16 32
(Tina Jackson) *sn outpcd and wl bhd 1/2-way: styd on fnl 2f* **80/1**
0-00 **9** ½ **Southview Lady**[12] 5126 5-9-13 **46** oh1............... MissMDabrowski[(3)] 14 31
(Sean Regan) *chsd ldrs towards stands side: rdn along over 2f out: sn wknd* **66/1**
2244 **10** *hd* **Cool Strutter (IRE)**[21] 4744 5-10-9 **56**....................... MissACollier[(3)] 17 41
(Karen Tutty) *chsd ldrs centre: rdn along 3f out: sn drvn and wknd* **8/1**
30 **11** 1¼ **Green Howard**[42] 3977 9-11-2 **60**.......................(b) MrJamesKendrick 5 42
(Rebecca Bastiman) *sn outpcd and bhd tl sme late hdwy* **4/1**[1]
0000 **12** 8 **Dylan's Storm (IRE)**[10] 5181 5-10-3 **50**..............(p) MissFMcSharry[(3)] 11 13
(Peter Niven) *dwlt: a rr* **28/1**
-040 **13** 5 **Sexton Blake (IRE)**[99] 2053 4-10-12 **56**...........................(p) MrTGillard 4 8
(John Norton) *chsd ldrs: rdn along over 2f out: wkng whn n.m.r over 1f out* **66/1**
0-00 **14** 10 **Breton Blues**[40] 4056 7-10-2 **46** oh1.......................(p) MissEllaMcCain 12
(Fred Watson) *dwlt and swtchd rt to stands rail: a bhd* **66/1**
4005 **R** **Tellovoi (IRE)**[6] 5341 9-11-4 **65**...................................(h) MrSASmith[(3)] 3
(Richard Guest) *Refused to r* **6/1**[3]
1m 37.18s (0.58) **Going Correction** -0.225s/f (Firm) **15** Ran SP% **117.7**
Speed ratings (Par 101): **88,86,86,84,83 82,81,79,78,78 77,69,64,54,**
CSF £156.95 CT £4031.46 TOTE £15.70: £4.70, £3.80, £6.00; EX 240.30 Trifecta £3694.00.
**Owner** The Bottom Liners & Paul Saxton **Bred** W And R Barnett Ltd **Trained** Huby, N Yorks

**FOCUS**
Typically weak form and it proved difficult to get into it from off the pace. The winner has been rated to this year's best.
T/Plt: £30.70 to a £1 stake. Pool: £50,159.75 - 1,192.64 winning units T/Qpdt: £15.30 to a £1 stake. Pool: £2,535.22 - 122.10 winning units **Joe Rowntree**

## 5327 SANDOWN (R-H)
### Wednesday, August 2

**OFFICIAL GOING: Round course - good to soft (soft in places, 6.4); sprint course - soft (heavy in places, 4.9)**
Wind: Moderate, half against Weather: Overcast, intermittent showers

### 5545 RACINGUK.COM APPRENTICE H'CAP 1m
**5:45** (5:45) (Class 5) (0-70,67) 3-Y-O **£3,881** (£1,155; £577; £288) **Stalls** Low

Form RPR
4003 **1** **Born To Please**[8] 5266 3-8-0 **48**.................................... NicolaCurrie[(7)] 9 56
(Mark Usher) *hld up towards rr: styd far side st: rdn and prog over 2f out: chsd ldr over 1f out: led last 150yds: kpt on wl* **8/1**
0613 **2** 1 **Dragon Dream (IRE)**[14] 5031 3-9-1 **61**...................... RhiainIngram[(5)] 2 67
(Roger Ingram) *hld up bhd ldrs: c towards centre st: prog over 2f out: rdn to ld wl over 1f out: hdd and one pce last 150yds* **8/1**
-660 **3** 1¼ **Junoesque**[14] 5031 3-9-0 **58**......................................(p[1]) PaddyPilley[(3)] 7 61
(John Gallagher) *lw: led 1f out: styd far side st and led again 3f out to wl over 1f out: kpt on same pce* **16/1**
5022 **4** 1 **Sandy Shores**[13] 5067 3-9-4 **64**...................................(b) JordanUys[(5)] 10 65
(Brian Meehan) *prom: chalng whn c towards nr side in st: drvn 2f out and edgd bk towards far side: kpt on one pce u.p* **11/2**[2]
3313 **5** 2½ **Ashazuri**[13] 5067 3-9-5 **67**.......................................(h) Pierre-LouisJamin[(7)] 3 62
(Jonathan Portman) *towards rr: styd far side st: rdn over 2f out: plugged on fr over 1f out but nvr pce to threaten* **6/1**[3]
0425 **6** 3¼ **Lesanti**[13] 5067 3-8-11 **52**............................................ CallumShepherd 12 39
(Ed de Giles) *led after 1f: styd far side in st: hdd 3f out: steadily wknd fnl 2f* **7/1**
4131 **7** 3¼ **Luxford**[22] 4713 3-8-8 **56**................................................ LeviWilliams[(7)] 6 36
(John Best) *sn stdd and hld up in 9th: c centre st: pushed along over 2f out and no real prog: eased whn no ch fnl f* **11/4**[1]
60-0 **8** 1 **Noble Ballad**[201] 210 3-9-2 **60**............................ PatrickO'Donnell[(3)] 11 38
(Ralph Beckett) *chsd ldrs: c towards nr side in st: no prog over 2f out: wknd over 1f out* **8/1**
060 **9** *nk* **Desert Song**[35] 4224 3-8-13 **57**..................................... PaddyBradley[(3)] 5 34
(Pat Phelan) *detached in last pair: c towards nr side in st and sn no prog* **25/1**
5404 **10** 1¼ **Armagnac (IRE)**[13] 5077 3-9-5 **67**.................................. TristanPrice[(7)] 1 41
(Michael Bell) *t.k.h: hld up bhd ldrs: c centre st: effrt and rdn over 2f out: sn wknd* **8/1**
5600 **11** 12 **Shamonix (IRE)**[8] 5266 3-8-4 **48** oh3............................ MitchGodwin[(3)] 4
(Mark Usher) *a detached in last: t.o* **33/1**
1m 49.47s (6.17) **Going Correction** +0.90s/f (Soft) **11** Ran SP% **126.0**
Speed ratings (Par 100): **105,104,102,101,99 96,92,91,91,90 78**
CSF £75.79 CT £1045.61 TOTE £11.90: £4.50, £1.80, £6.40; EX 125.20 Trifecta £896.20.
**Owner** The Mark Usher Racing Club **Bred** P H Davies **Trained** Upper Lambourn, Berks

**FOCUS**
A soggy day in Esher, with 6mm of rain up to 3.30pm leading to an easing of the going from the morning's published description. Rail movements added 22 yards to all contests, including this moderate opener for apprentices. The third has been rated close to this year's form.

### 5546 RACING UK PROFITS RETURNED TO RACING NURSERY H'CAP 5f 10y
**6:20** (6:21) (Class 5) (0-75,73) 2-Y-O **£3,881** (£1,155; £577; £288) **Stalls** High

Form RPR
6453 **1** **The Golden Cue**[8] 5262 2-8-10 **62**.............................. AdamBeschizza 2 70
(Steph Hollinshead) *racd nr far rail: mde all: rdn clr over 1f out: in n.d after: comf* **9/2**[3]
534 **2** 5 **Gold Filigree (IRE)**[68] 3023 2-9-7 **73**.................................... PatDobbs 6 63
(Richard Hughes) *lw: carried sltly lft s: hld up in 4th and swtchd to far rail after 1f: rdn to chse wnr over 1f out: no imp after* **7/2**[2]
633 **3** 1½ **Shania Says (IRE)**[12] 5121 2-9-1 **67**........................... GeorgeDowning 3 52
(Tony Carroll) *prom but off the rail: chsd wnr after 2f to over 1f out: n.d after* **11/2**
5056 **4** 5 **Cruel Clever Cat**[16] 4973 2-7-8 **53**.............................. RhiainIngram[(7)] 5 20
(John Gallagher) *wnt lft s: chsd wnr 2f: rdn over 2f out: sn struggling* **16/1**
5230 **5** 5 **Spoof**[54] 3516 2-9-7 **73**......................................................... TomQueally 4 22
(Charles Hills) *restless stalls and awkward s: hld up in last pair: checked after 1f and then t.k.h: swtchd to outer and effrt over 2f out: sn rdn and wknd* **8/1**
1511 **6** 25 **Milton Road**[12] 5121 2-9-6 **72**........................... SilvestreDeSousa 7
(Mick Channon) *carried sltly lft s: racd on outer: struggling after 2f: sn bhd: eased over 1f out and t.o* **6/4**[1]
1m 7.01s (5.41) **Going Correction** +0.95s/f (Soft) **6** Ran SP% **112.8**
Speed ratings (Par 94): **94,86,83,75,67 27**
CSF £20.59 TOTE £5.70: £2.30, £1.70; EX 19.70 Trifecta £70.80.
**Owner** The Golden Cue Partnership **Bred** D R Botterill **Trained** Upper Longdon, Staffs

**FOCUS**
Likely not as strong a piece of form as it might have been with the favourite bombing, but an engaging piece of successful front-running nonetheless.

### 5547 BRITISH STALLION STUDS EBF NOVICE STKS 7f
**6:55** (6:55) (Class 5) 2-Y-O **£3,881** (£1,155; £577; £288) **Stalls** Low

Form RPR
4 **1** **Connect**[47] 3783 2-9-2 0........................................... AdamKirby 6 90+
(Clive Cox) *tall: green: mde all and stretched field: pressed 2f out: rdn over 1f out and sn drew clr: v readily* **5/2**[2]
210 **2** 6 **Westerland**[39] 4068 2-9-9 84........................................... FrankieDettori 7 82
(John Gosden) *str: taken steadily to post: trckd ldng pair tl chsd wnr 1/2-way: rdn to try to chal over 2f out: fnd little and brushed aside over 1f out* **4/6**[1]
**3** 1¾ **La La Land (IRE)** 2-9-2 0.......................................... DougieCostello 2 71+
(Jamie Osborne) *athletic: slowly away: hld up in last pair early: shkn up 3f out: stl only 6th whn rdn over 1f out: styd on to take 3rd nr fin* **14/1**
**4** ¾ **Ledham (IRE)** 2-9-2 0.................................................. PatDobbs 8 69+
(Sir Michael Stoute) *lengthy: bit bkwd: in tch: chsd ldng pair over 2f out: shkn up and no imp over 1f out: fdd and lost 3rd nr fin* **7/1**[3]
56 **5** 2¼ **Galactic (IRE)**[18] 4885 2-9-2 0...................................... SeanLevey 10 63
(Richard Hannon) *chsd wnr to 1/2-way: shkn up over 2f out: steadily wknd* **20/1**
**6** 3 **Manor Park** 2-9-2 0............................................... FergusSweeney 1 56
(Alan King) *str: bit bkwd: in tch: shkn up and outpcd over 2f out: wknd over 1f out* **20/1**
0 **7** 6 **Stockings Lane (IRE)**[47] 3769 2-9-2 0......................... AdamBeschizza 9 41
(Steph Hollinshead) *w'like: hld up in last trio: no prog over 2f out: bhd after* **50/1**
**8** 7 **Surrey Blaze (IRE)** 2-9-2 0.......................................... OisinMurphy 4 23
(Joseph Tuite) *w'like: bit bkwd: swtg: s.s: a bhd in last* **12/1**
1m 33.52s (4.02) **Going Correction** +0.90s/f (Soft) **8** Ran SP% **126.9**
Speed ratings (Par 94): **113,106,104,103,100 97,90,82**
CSF £4.99 TOTE £3.30: £1.10, £1.02, £3.40; EX 4.50 Trifecta £28.80.
**Owner** A D Spence **Bred** D J Weston **Trained** Lambourn, Berks

**FOCUS**
Add 22 yards. An interesting novice event run at a good pace in the conditions, and there'll be winners to come from among the beaten horses.

### 5548 VISIT RACINGUK.COM H'CAP 1m
**7:25** (7:25) (Class 3) (0-90,90) 3-Y-O-**£8,092** (£2,423; £1,211; £605; £302) **Stalls** Low

Form RPR
1021 **1** **Frank Bridge**[13] 5064 4-9-8 **84**................................. CharlesBishop 6 95
(Eve Johnson Houghton) *hld up in 4th: smooth prog to trck ldr over 2f out: shkn up to ld over 1f out: styd on strly and drew clr* **6/1**
0411 **2** 4½ **See The Master (IRE)**[12] 5125 3-9-0 **83**....................... SamHitchcott 4 83
(Clive Cox) *lw: trckd ldr: led 3f out: rdn and hdd over 1f out: kpt on but no ch w wnr* **13/8**[1]
0524 **3** 3¾ **Sterling Silva (IRE)**[4] 5433 3-8-13 **82**............................. SeanLevey 3 73
(Richard Hannon) *lw: trckd ldng pair: rdn over 2f out and sn lft bhd: plugged on same pce fr over 1f out* **11/2**[3]
-503 **4** 9 **Maths Prize**[18] 4904 3-9-7 **90**..................................(p) KieranShoemark 1 60
(Roger Charlton) *hld up in last: shkn up over 2f out: no prog and sn btn: wknd and eased fnl f* **9/4**[2]
1-50 **5** 3¾ **Time Zone**[19] 4861 3-9-2 **85**.................................. SilvestreDeSousa 2 47
(Peter Chapple-Hyam) *t.k.h: led to 3f out: sn wknd: heavily eased over 1f out* **7/1**
1m 47.74s (4.44) **Going Correction** +0.90s/f (Soft)
**WFA** 3 from 4yo 7lb **5** Ran SP% **111.0**
Speed ratings (Par 107): **113,108,104,95,92**
CSF £16.42 TOTE £7.30: £2.40, £1.60; EX 12.40 Trifecta £39.10.
**Owner** John Dyer **Bred** Catherine Dyer **Trained** Blewbury, Oxon

**FOCUS**
Add 22 yards. A fair feature event, and with a thriving winner beating a hat-trick seeking favourite the form looks solid. The winning time was over 1.7 seconds faster than that of the earlier apprentice handicap. A clear pb from the winner, with the runner-up rated close to form.

### 5549 OLLY MURS HERE ON 10TH AUGUST FILLIES' H'CAP 1m 1f
**7:55** (7:55) (Class 5) (0-75,76) 3-Y-O+ **£3,881** (£1,155; £577; £288) **Stalls** Centre

Form RPR
3334 **1** **Bonnie Arlene (IRE)**[12] 5096 3-8-13 **68**.................... SilvestreDeSousa 5 74
(Mark Johnston) *lw: dwlt: hld up in last: rdn 3f out and looked to be struggling: racd nrr stands' rail and prog u.p over 2f out: chsd ldr over 1f out: styd on relentlessly to ld last 75yds* **11/4**[1]
2164 **2** ½ **Carducci**[12] 5113 3-9-6 **75**......................................... SeanLevey 4 80
(Richard Hannon) *trckd ldr: led wl over 2f out: shkn up wl over 1f out and looked in command: kpt on fnl f but worn down last 75yds* **4/1**[2]
53-5 **3** 2¼ **Great Court (IRE)**[93] 2227 3-9-6 **75**............................ AndreaAtzeni 3 75
(Roger Varian) *hld up in 5th: rdn and nt qckn over 2f out: kpt on fr over 1f out to take 3rd fnl f: no imp after* **5/1**
654 **4** 2 **Gilded Reflection**[23] 4698 4-10-1 **76**............................(b) FranBerry 6 72
(Ralph Beckett) *lw: t.k.h: hld up in 4th: rdn to dispute 2nd 2f out to over 1f out: fdd* **9/2**[3]
5-34 **5** 2¼ **Kath's Legacy**[9] 5217 4-9-12 **73**..................................... OisinMurphy 1 64
(Ben De Haan) *led: tk field wd in bk st in to centre in home st: hdd wl over 2f out: steadily wknd u.p over 1f out* **4/1**[2]
/6-5 **6** 2¼ **Duchy**[12] 5113 4-9-11 **72**................................................ AdamKirby 2 59
(Michael Bell) *trckd ldng pair: rdn over 2f out: wandered and no rspnse: wknd over 1f out* **10/1**
2m 6.03s (10.33) **Going Correction** +0.90s/f (Soft)
**WFA** 3 from 4yo 8lb **6** Ran SP% **110.6**
Speed ratings (Par 100): **90,89,87,85,83 81**
CSF £13.45 TOTE £3.70: £1.70, £2.10; EX 14.50 Trifecta £78.10.
**Owner** Paul Dean **Bred** Tinnakill Bloodstock **Trained** Middleham Moor, N Yorks

**FOCUS**
Add 22 yards. A really tight betting heat with no genuine standout candidate, and a good effort in the saddle to wrest the spoils. A length pb from the winner, with the third rated to her maiden form.

## 5550 FOLLOW @RACING_UK ON TWITTER NOW H'CAP 1m 6f
8:25 (8:25) (Class 4) (0-80,78) 3-Y-O £5,822 (£1,732; £865; £432) Stalls Low

Form RPR
003 1 **Precision**22 4720 3-9-4 **75** AndreaAtzeni 1 84+
(Sir Michael Stoute) *lw: t.k.h: trckd ldr: shkn up over 2f out: led over 1f out: edgd rt and bmpd runner-up jst ins fnl f: sn hdd: drvn and rallied to ld last 75yds: won gng away* **2/1**1
4404 2 1 **Master Archer (IRE)**20 4809 3-9-3 **74** (p1) TomQueally 5 81
(James Fanshawe) *hld up in last: clsd in centre over 2f out: rdn to chal over 1f out: bmpd jst ins fnl f but sn led: hdd and nt qckn last 75yds* **7/2**
4021 3 2 1/2 **Padrinho (IRE)**14 5034 3-9-2 **73** KierenFox 6 77
(John Best) *lw: t.k.h: led: c to nr side in st: rdn over 2f out: hdd and no ex over 1f out* **5/2**2
1624 4 5 **Flight Of Fantasy**12 5108 3-9-7 **78** AdamKirby 4 75
(Harry Dunlop) *trckd ldng pair: rdn 2f out: sn dropped to last and wknd* **11/4**3
3m 24.32s (19.82) **Going Correction** +0.90s/f (Soft) 4 Ran SP% **110.8**
Speed ratings (Par 102): **79,78,77,74**
CSF £9.12 TOTE £2.40; EX 16.50 Trifecta £28.10.
**Owner** Highclere Thoroughbred Racing - Lord Byron **Bred** Stilvi Compania Financiera Sa **Trained** Newmarket, Suffolk

**FOCUS**
Add 22 yards. A fair little stayers' handicap and a decent pace on throughout, despite the small field.
T/Plt: £154.10 to a £1 stake. Pool: £50,914.91 - 241.05 winning units T/Qpdt: £9.80 to a £1 stake. Pool: £7,716.59 - 582.13 winning units **Jonathan Neesom**

5551 - 5554a (Foreign Racing) - See Raceform Interactive

5062

# EPSOM (L-H)
Thursday, August 3

**OFFICIAL GOING: Good to soft (soft in places)**
Wind: Strong, half against Weather: Fine but cloudy

## 5555 STEVE DONOGHUE APPRENTICE H'CAP 1m 2f 17y
5:50 (5:51) (Class 5) (0-70,72) 4-Y-O+ £3,881 (£1,155; £577; £288) Stalls Low

Form RPR
3136 1 **Miss Inga Sock (IRE)**8 5299 5-9-3 **66** GeorgiaCox(3) 4 71
(Eve Johnson Houghton) *dwlt: hld up in last pair: prog 3f out to chse ldr 2f out: clsd to chal last 100yds: won on the nod* **11/4**2
0501 2 nse **Gold Merlion (IRE)**8 5296 4-9-2 **65** 6ex RichardOliver(3) 2 70
(Mark Johnston) *led: 3 l clr 3f out: rdn 2f out: kpt on wl whn chal ins fnl f: btn on the nod* **5/1**3
5505 3 3 **Roy Rocket (FR)**8 5299 7-9-2 **69** NicolaCurrie(7) 1 68
(John Berry) *dwlt: chsd clr ldng pair: wnt 2nd 3f out to 2f out: one pce after* **6/1**
0062 4 1 1/4 **The Gay Cavalier**8 5299 6-9-1 **68** (t) JackOsborn(7) 7 64
(John Ryan) *dwlt: hld up in last pair: shkn up and nt qckn 3f out: no imp on ldrs after* **5/2**1
2-50 5 1 1/4 **Gannicus**36 2913 6-9-3 **66** (t) JennyPowell(3) 5 60
(Brendan Powell) *chsd clr ldng pair: shkn up and nt qckn 3f out: no imp after* **8/1**
0000 6 12 **Lacan (IRE)**24 4699 6-9-12 **72** CallumShepherd 6 42
(Brett Johnson) *t.k.h: trckd ldr and hanging rt: clr of rest whn hung bdly rt bnd over 3f out: sn lost 2nd and btn: bhd fnl f* **7/1**
2m 14.76s (5.06) **Going Correction** +0.475s/f (Yiel) 6 Ran SP% **109.8**
Speed ratings (Par 103): **98,97,95,94,93 83**
CSF £15.82 CT £68.01 TOTE £2.90: £1.70, £1.70; EX 11.10 Trifecta £46.40.
**Owner** The Ascot Colts & Fillies Club **Bred** R F Johnson Houghton **Trained** Blewbury, Oxon

**FOCUS**
There was 13mm of rain during Wednesday afternoon and evening, but it was a blustery day and the going was given as good to soft, soft places in the back straight (GoingStick: 5.7). The rail was out up to 6yds from the mile marker to the winning post, adding 20yds to all races of 1m+ and 15yds to the 7f races. A modest handicap. The winner has been rated back to her best.

## 5556 WATCH RACING UK ON SKY 432 H'CAP 1m 4f 6y
6:25 (6:28) (Class 5) (0-75,75) 4-Y-O+ £4,528 (£1,347; £673; £336) Stalls Centre

Form RPR
3411 1 **Ya Jammeel**14 5065 4-9-6 **74** CharlesBishop 8 86+
(Mick Channon) *mde all: shkn up and drew clr wl over 2f out: maintained gallop after: unchal* **10/11**1
3023 2 3 1/2 **Hepplewhite**23 4712 4-9-1 **69** (p) DougieCostello 2 73
(William Muir) *chsd wnr to 1/2-way and again 3f out: sn rdn and no imp: kpt on* **8/1**
0623 3 1 1/4 **Becca Campbell (IRE)**16 4994 4-9-2 **70** (p) TomQueally 3 72
(Eve Johnson Houghton) *in tch pushed along in 5th st: rdn over 2f out: wnt 3rd wl over 1f out: kpt on one pce after* **6/1**3
3223 4 5 **Safira Menina**13 5113 5-9-7 **75** TomMarquand 6 69
(Martin Smith) *in tch: 4th st: rdn over 2f out: no prog over 1f out: wknd fnl f* **9/2**2
36/4 5 17 **Smooth Operator**17 4966 5-8-7 **64** GeorgeWood(3) 7 31
(Mark Pitman) *prom: chsd wnr 1/2-way to 3f out: sn wknd: wl bhd over 1f out* **16/1**
3111 6 46 **Rail Dancer**71 2956 5-9-7 **75** (p) JimCrowley 4
(Richard Rowe) *a last: rdn 5f out: lost tch 3f out: sn t.o: eased fnl 2f* **14/1**
2m 46.38s (7.48) **Going Correction** +0.475s/f (Yiel) 6 Ran SP% **108.5**
Speed ratings (Par 103): **94,91,90,87,76 45**
CSF £8.17 CT £23.47 TOTE £1.70: £1.10, £3.80; EX 9.10 Trifecta £27.60.
**Owner** M Channon **Bred** Rabbah Bloodstock Limited **Trained** West Ilsley, Berks

**FOCUS**
Race distance increased by 20yds. This proved straightforward for the odds-on favourite. The runner-up helps set the standard.

## 5557 CROWN PAINTS EBF NOVICE STKS 7f 3y
6:55 (6:57) (Class 5) 2-Y-O £3,881 (£1,155; £577; £288) Stalls Low

Form RPR
61 1 **Doublet (IRE)**14 5063 2-9-9 0 SilvestreDeSousa 2 87+
(Mark Johnston) *mde all: pushed along 3f out: edgd rt fr 2f out: styd on wl and in command fnl f* **5/6**1
4 2 2 3/4 **Guvenor's Choice (IRE)**15 5030 2-9-2 0 (t) MartinHarley 4 73
(K R Burke) *dwlt: chsd ldng trio: sltly awkward downhill over 4f out: shkn up over 2f out: chsd wnr over 1f out and tried to cl: no imp fnl f* **13/8**2
00 3 1 **Motabassim (IRE)**28 4526 2-9-2 0 JimCrowley 5 70
(Brian Meehan) *chsd wnr: reminder over 2f out: lost 2nd over 1f out: wl hld after but kpt on steadily* **18/1**
06 4 14 **Bombshell Bay**13 5105 2-9-2 0 TomMarquand 1 34
(Richard Hannon) *chsd ldng pair to 3f out: sn wknd* **8/1**3
0 5 13 **Lady Maldiva (IRE)**40 4090 2-8-8 0 GeorgeWood(3) 8
(Jose Santos) *immediately detached in last: shkn up briefly 3f out: eased whn t.o over 2f out but lost no further grnd* **50/1**
1m 26.19s (2.89) **Going Correction** +0.475s/f (Yiel) 5 Ran SP% **111.0**
Speed ratings (Par 94): **102,98,97,81,66**
CSF £2.45 TOTE £1.70: £1.10, £1.10; EX 2.60 Trifecta £9.20.
**Owner** Sheikh Hamdan bin Mohammed Al Maktoum **Bred** T & B Jones **Trained** Middleham Moor, N Yorks

**FOCUS**
Race distance increased by 15yds. Another all-the-way winner.

## 5558 BRITISH EBF FIFINELLA FILLIES' H'CAP 7f 3y
7:30 (7:30) (Class 4) (0-80,77) 3-Y-O+ £6,469 (£1,925; £962; £481) Stalls Low

Form RPR
0165 1 **Coral Sea**7 5316 3-9-7 **77** (h) JimCrowley 4 84+
(Charles Hills) *hld up in last: gd prog on outer 2f out: hanging lft but clsd qckly to ld 150yds out: sn clr* **7/2**1
152 2 1 1/2 **Nightingale Valley**29 4495 4-9-13 **77** TomQueally 1 82
(Stuart Kittow) *trckd ldrs: 5th st: prog to chse ldr wl over 1f out: trying to cl whn wnr shot past ins fnl f then short of room: tk 2nd nr fin* **7/2**1
4201 3 1/2 **Andalusite**23 4711 4-8-12 **62** (v) FergusSweeney 6 66
(John Gallagher) *t.k.h: led over 5f out: 3 l clr over 2f out: rdn over 1f out: worn down 150yds out and sn dropped to 3rd* **6/1**3
3003 4 5 **Very Honest (IRE)**30 4464 4-9-8 **75** CallumShepherd(3) 7 66
(Brett Johnson) *chsd ldng trio: rdn over 2f out: stl pressing for a pl over 1f out: sn wknd* **14/1**
536 5 3 **Zilza (IRE)**6 5367 3-9-0 **70** (t1) SilvestreDeSousa 5 50
(Conrad Allen) *hld up in 6th: drvn and no rspnse over 2f out: no prog after* **9/2**2
300 6 3/4 **Settle Petal**22 4748 3-7-12 **61** SophieRalston(7) 2 39
(Pat Phelan) *t.k.h: led over 1f: chsd ldr to wl over 1f out: sn wknd* **14/1**
5040 7 3/4 **Porto Ferro (IRE)**36 4214 3-8-4 **63** GeorgeWood(3) 8 39
(Dr Jon Scargill) *hld up in 7th: shkn up and no prog 3f out: btn after* **8/1**
4000 8 1 1/2 **Dynamic Girl (IRE)**17 4975 4-8-8 **63** (h) JennyPowell(5) 3 37
(Brendan Powell) *chsd ldng pair to over 2f out: wknd sn after* **15/2**
1m 25.61s (2.31) **Going Correction** +0.475s/f (Yiel)
**WFA** 3 from 4yo 6lb 8 Ran SP% **113.1**
Speed ratings (Par 102): **105,103,102,97,93 92,91,90**
CSF £15.28 CT £69.84 TOTE £3.70: £1.60, £1.50, £2.00; EX 11.40 Trifecta £45.60.
**Owner** P Winkworth **Bred** Peter Winkworth **Trained** Lambourn, Berks

**FOCUS**
Race distance increased by 15yds. A fair handicap and a good performance from the winner. The third has been rated to form.

## 5559 CHANTILLY H'CAP 1m 113y
8:00 (8:02) (Class 4) (0-80,83) 3-Y-O+ £5,175 (£1,540; £769; £384) Stalls Low

Form RPR
4251 1 **Seduce Me**7 5324 3-9-7 **83** 6ex (p) JimCrowley 1 92
(K R Burke) *hld up in last: stdy prog on outer 2f out: shkn up to ld 150yds out: sn clr: readily* **13/8**1
5252 2 3 1/4 **Pumaflor (IRE)**16 5000 5-9-13 **81** (p) SilvestreDeSousa 6 83
(David O'Meara) *led: kicked on wl over 2f out: hdd and readily outpcd last 150yds* **11/4**2
-031 3 2 **Fit For The Job (IRE)**31 4446 5-9-8 **76** (p) FranBerry 2 73
(Jonjo O'Neill) *hld up in 4th: prog on outer over 2f out: shkn up to take 2nd briefly over 1f out: nt qckn sn after and fdd tamely* **4/1**3
2322 4 2 3/4 **Mr Tyrrell (IRE)**14 5077 3-9-3 **79** TomMarquand 3 70
(Richard Hannon) *chsd ldng pair: pushed along over 3f out: wnt 2nd over 2f out to over 1f out: fdd* **10/1**
545 5 5 **Romanor**24 4691 3-9-2 **78** (t1) PatCosgrave 4 58
(Ed Walker) *chsd ldr to over 2f out: wknd* **5/1**
1m 48.79s (2.69) **Going Correction** +0.475s/f (Yiel)
**WFA** 3 from 5yo+ 8lb 5 Ran SP% **110.5**
Speed ratings (Par 105): **107,104,102,99,95**
CSF £6.37 TOTE £2.40: £1.20, £1.60; EX 6.60 Trifecta £16.20.
**Owner** Ontoawinner, R Mckeown & E Burke **Bred** Jeremy Green And Sons **Trained** Middleham Moor, N Yorks

**FOCUS**
Race distance increased by 20yds. A cosy win for the favourite. The second has been rated close to his non-claiming best.

## 5560 WATCH RACING UK ON BT TV H'CAP 7f 3y
8:30 (8:31) (Class 5) (0-75,75) 3-Y-O £3,881 (£1,155; £577; £288) Stalls Low

Form RPR
05-5 1 **Dourado (IRE)**86 2506 3-9-6 **74** DavidProbert 1 79
(Patrick Chamings) *trckd ldng pair: shkn up to take 2nd over 1f out and sn chalng: rdn to ld last 100yds: styd on* **7/2**2
2310 2 1/2 **Benjamin Thomas (IRE)**26 4616 3-9-7 **75** (v) SilvestreDeSousa 3 78
(John Quinn) *led but pressed: rdn 2f out: kpt on but hdd and no ex last 100yds* **11/10**1
-006 3 5 **Habbad (FR)**12 5139 3-9-1 **69** (p1) TomMarquand 7 59
(Richard Hannon) *dwlt: hld up in last: rdn and no prog over 2f out: tk modest 3rd last strides* **7/1**
1000 4 1/2 **El Torito (IRE)**17 4983 3-9-7 **75** PatCosgrave 4 63
(Jim Boyle) *wl away but unable to ld: pressed ldr: rdn over 2f out: lost 2nd over 1f out: wknd fnl f and lost 3rd last strides* **11/1**
3011 5 1/2 **Golden Guest**15 5039 3-8-11 **70** JaneElliott(5) 6 57
(George Margarson) *hld up in 4th: pushed along and no prog wl over 2f out: no ch fr wl over 1f out: plugged on* **4/1**3
1m 26.44s (3.14) **Going Correction** +0.475s/f (Yiel) 5 Ran SP% **110.7**
Speed ratings (Par 100): **101,100,94,94,93**
CSF £7.89 TOTE £4.30: £1.90, £1.20; EX 9.70 Trifecta £29.30.
**Owner** Mrs Alexandra J Chandris **Bred** Canice M Farrell Jnr **Trained** Baughurst, Hants

**FOCUS**
Race distance increased by 15yds. A fair contest and the race set up nicely for the winner. The winner has been rated back to his best.
T/Plt: £9.90 to a £1 stake. Pool: £57,843.16 - 4,252.44 winning units. T/Qpdt: £3.10 to a £1 stakes. Pool: £5,429.41 - 1,267.73 winning units. **Jonathan Neesom**

# 5246 FFOS LAS (L-H)

Thursday, August 3

**OFFICIAL GOING: Heavy**

Wind: quite a strong crosswind in the home straight Weather: overcast and drizzling

## 5561 HEINEKEN NOVICE AUCTION STKS 6f

5:35 (5:38) (Class 5) 2-Y-O £3,881 (£1,155; £577; £288) Stalls Centre

Form RPR

1 **Greeneyedafghan** 2-9-2 0 MartinDwyer 2 69+
(William Muir) *hld up: sn outpcd and pushed along in last: clsd 2f out: kpt on to ld 110yds out: pushed out* **9/2**

4 2 1 3/4 **Lope De Loop (IRE)**[6] 5356 2-8-11 0 SteveDrowne 3 59
(David Evans) *cl up: rdn over 1f out: led jst ins fnl f: hdd 110yds out: unable qck* **9/4[2]**

00 3 1 1/2 **Moremoneymoreparty (IRE)**[7] 5334 2-8-11 0 ShaneKelly 4 55
(Richard Guest) *led: rdn 2f out: hdd jst ins fnl f: no ex* **16/1**

62 4 2 3/4 **Diamond Express (IRE)**[21] 4799 2-8-4 0 FinleyMarsh(7) 5 46
(Roger Teal) *trckd ldrs: rdn and unable qck 2f out: wknd fnl f* **13/8[1]**

33 5 1 **Silvington**[35] 4273 2-9-2 0 GeorgeDowning 1 48
(Daniel Mark Loughnane) *chsd ldrs: drvn and edgd lft over 2f out: wknd over 1f out* **4/1[3]**

1m 19.49s (9.49) **Going Correction** +1.425s/f (Soft) 5 Ran SP% **112.9**
Speed ratings (Par 94): **93,90,88,85,83**
CSF £15.36 TOTE £5.00: £2.10, £1.50; EX 15.10 Trifecta £98.50.
**Owner** J O'Mulloy & K Jeffery **Bred** D J Weston **Trained** Lambourn, Berks

**FOCUS**
After 11mm of rain the going was eased to heavy, from soft, heavy in places. They went a sensible pace in the conditions and the winner did it nicely. It's been rated around the runner-up.

## 5562 HEINEKEN NURSERY H'CAP 7f 80y(R)

6:10 (6:12) (Class 6) (0-65,64) 2-Y-O £2,587 (£770; £384; £192) Stalls Low

Form RPR

0254 1 **Lady Alavesa**[17] 4977 2-9-5 62 MartinDwyer 7 64
(Gay Kelleway) *s.i.s: hld up in tch in last: hdwy 3f out: rdn to ld appr fnl f: sn hrd pressed and hung lft: jst hld on* **11/4[2]**

400 2 shd **Foxrush Take Time (FR)**[13] 5127 2-9-4 61 ShaneKelly 2 63
(Richard Guest) *hld up bhd ldrs: clsd gng wl over 1f out: rdn and ev ch fnl f: jst hld* **3/1[3]**

0000 3 2 3/4 **Mysaan (IRE)**[21] 4805 2-9-5 62 (b) JackMitchell 1 57
(Brian Meehan) *led: rdn and hdd over 2f out: outpcd over 1f out: styd on to go 3rd ins fnl f* **9/2**

000 4 1 3/4 **Rio Santos**[21] 4805 2-8-11 54 WilliamCarson 4 45
(Rod Millman) *trckd ldrs: wnt 2nd 4f out: led over 2f out: sn rdn: hdd appr fnl f: grad wknd* **6/1**

0642 5 2 **Brockey Rise (IRE)**[12] 5143 2-9-7 64 TimmyMurphy 3 51
(David Evans) *trckd ldr over 3f: styd prom: rdn and ev ch 2f out: wknd fnl f* **9/4[1]**

1m 44.16s (10.56) **Going Correction** +1.425s/f (Soft) 5 Ran SP% **114.9**
Speed ratings (Par 92): **96,95,92,90,88**
CSF £11.83 TOTE £4.40: £1.70, £2.00; EX 16.20 Trifecta £56.80.
**Owner** Rioja Racing **Bred** A C M Spalding **Trained** Exning, Suffolk

**FOCUS**
Not a strong handicap. It was run at a fair pace in the conditions which suited the closers. The winner has been rated in line with her Leicester figure.

## 5563 HEINEKEN MAIDEN STKS 1m 3f 209y(R)

6:40 (6:47) (Class 5) 3-Y-O+ £3,234 (£962; £481; £240) Stalls Low

Form RPR

1 **Catcher On The Go (IRE)**[42] 7-10-0 0 SamHitchcott 1 82
(Evan Williams) *s.i.s and chsd along early: hld up: rdn in 5th 4f out: hdwy 3f out: led narrowly 2f out: styd on to assert fnl f* **12/1**

2532 2 1 1/4 **Waterville Dancer (IRE)**[5] 5432 3-9-4 76 ShaneKelly 8 81
(Richard Hughes) *trckd ldr: rdn and ev ch 2f out: kpt on same pce and hld fnl f* **6/4[1]**

-224 3 16 **Steaming (IRE)**[59] 3408 3-9-4 80 KieranShoemark 9 55
(Ralph Beckett) *led: drvn and wandered over 2f out: sn hdd: wknd over 1f out: hld mod 3rd* **9/4[2]**

6- 4 2 1/4 **Wine List**[286] 7503 3-9-4 0 LiamKeniry 7 52
(Andrew Balding) *trckd ldrs: rdn over 2f out: sn wknd* **11/4[3]**

- 5 13 **In Dreams** 3-9-4 0 JackMitchell 4 31
(Brian Meehan) *uns rdr and rn loose bef s: hld up: clsd into 4th and rdn 4f out: wknd 2f out* **14/1**

0 6 34 **The Last Melon**[45] 3921 5-9-9 0 (h) RachealKneller(5) 10
(James Bennett) *hld up: rdn 5f out: wknd over 3f out: t.o* **100/1**

7 28 **Cable Car**[351] 6-10-0 0 WilliamCarson 6
(John Flint) *s.i.s: urged along and chsd ldrs after 1f: rdn and wknd over 4f out: racd alone on ins in st: t.o* **25/1**

2m 52.18s (14.78) **Going Correction** +1.425s/f (Soft)
**WFA** 3 from 5yo+ 10lb 7 Ran SP% **116.6**
Speed ratings (Par 103): **107,106,95,94,85 62,44**
CSF £31.66 TOTE £12.70: £3.60, £1.10; EX 42.60 Trifecta £80.50.
**Owner** T Hywel Jones Racing **Bred** Michael Woodlock And Seamus Kennedy **Trained** Llancarfan, Vale Of Glamorgan

■ Flooded and Jumbo's Boy were withdrawn. Prices at time of withdrawal 100/1 and 18/1. Rule 4 does not apply.

■ Stewards' Enquiry : Shane Kelly two-day ban: used whip with arm above shoulder height (Aug 17-18)

**FOCUS**
Not a great maiden run at a steady pace. The front two pulled a long way clear.

## 5564 HEINEKEN H'CAP 6f

7:15 (7:19) (Class 4) (0-80,79) 3-Y-O+ £5,175 (£1,540; £769; £384) Stalls Centre

Form RPR

1361 1 **Kinglami**[6] 5360 8-9-9 76 6ex (p) TimmyMurphy 2 84
(John O'Shea) *hld up: clsd 2f out: drvn to ld ins fnl f: edgd rt: jst hld on* **7/1**

150 2 nse **Alaadel**[22] 4752 4-9-8 75 (t[1]) DaneO'Neill 1 83
(William Haggas) *s.i.s: sn trcking ldrs: rdn over 2f out: chal appr fnl f: r.o u.p: jst failed* **2/1[2]**

554 3 hd **Bonjour Steve**[14] 5051 6-8-4 62 ow1 (p) MitchGodwin(5) 5 69
(Richard Price) *trckd ldr: led over 1f out: sn rdn: hdd ins fnl f: r.o u.p* **6/1[3]**

3203 4 9 **Fredricka**[27] 4566 6-9-12 79 (v) RenatoSouza 3 59
(Ivan Furtado) *hld up and racd keenly: drvn 2f out: wknd over 1f out* **12/1**

1036 5 nk **Showmethewayavrilo**[14] 5051 4-9-2 69 LiamKeniry 4 48
(Malcolm Saunders) *led and got over to stands' rail: rdn 2f out: sn hdd: wknd appr fnl f* **6/1[3]**

-421 6 1/2 **The Daley Express (IRE)**[9] 5253 3-9-8 79 6ex SamHitchcott 6 56
(Ronald Harris) *t.k.h: trckd ldrs: rdn and nt clr run over 1f out: grad wknd fnl f* **7/4[1]**

1m 18.67s (8.67) **Going Correction** +1.425s/f (Soft)
**WFA** 3 from 4yo+ 4lb 6 Ran SP% **118.5**
Speed ratings (Par 105): **99,98,98,86,86 85**
CSF £22.87 TOTE £7.70: £2.90, £1.40; EX 25.20 Trifecta £212.70.
**Owner** Pete Smith & Phil Hart Racing **Bred** Cheveley Park Stud Ltd **Trained** Elton, Gloucs

■ Stewards' Enquiry : Timmy Murphy 6 day ban - used his whip above the permitted level and in an incorrect place (17-22 Aug)

**FOCUS**
A fair handicap run at a sensible pace.

## 5565 FOSTERS H'CAP 1m 2f (R)

7:45 (7:48) (Class 6) (0-65,67) 3-Y-O £3,234 (£962; £481; £240) Stalls Low

Form RPR

-356 1 **Eolian**[46] 3864 3-9-7 65 (p) LiamKeniry 7 74+
(Andrew Balding) *chsd ldr and sme way clr of others: rdn and clsd over 2f out: led over 1f out: drvn and styd on wl* **11/4[1]**

3440 2 5 **It's How We Roll (IRE)**[31] 4446 3-9-1 64 (b) JoshuaBryan(5) 8 64
(John Spearing) *chsd ldng pair who were sme way clr: rdn in 3rd over 2f out: styd on to go 2nd 150yds out: no imp on wnr* **4/1[2]**

004 3 3 1/2 **Mister Chow**[22] 4748 3-9-9 67 TimmyMurphy 3 61
(Gary Moore) *chsd ldng pair who were sme way clr: rdn over 3f out and sn lost tch w ldrs: mod 5th 1f out: styd on: wnt 3rd nr fin* **13/2[3]**

0032 4 2 1/4 **Alnasl (IRE)**[9] 5249 3-8-13 60 (h) EdwardGreatrex(3) 6 50
(Archie Watson) *led and clr w one other: rdn 2f out: wandered and hdd over 1f out: wknd and lost 2 pls fnl f* **11/4[1]**

1005 5 1 1/4 **Broad Appeal**[45] 3922 3-9-0 63 (h[1]) MitchGodwin(5) 4 50
(Jonathan Portman) *hld up: rdn 3f out and sme hdwy into 4th: wknd over 1f out* **7/1**

3060 6 11 **Angel Of Rome (IRE)**[31] 4442 3-9-4 62 (b[1]) ShaneKelly 1 30
(Richard Hughes) *hld up: rdn 3f out: sn wknd* **16/1**

065 7 8 **Moonlight Silver**[16] 5001 3-9-3 61 (h[1]) MartinDwyer 5 14
(William Muir) *t.k.h early: hld up: drvn 3f out: sn wknd* **8/1**

2m 24.25s (14.85) **Going Correction** +1.425s/f (Soft) 7 Ran SP% **116.2**
Speed ratings (Par 98): **97,93,90,88,87 78,72**
CSF £14.44 CT £64.80 TOTE £3.70: £1.90, £2.20; EX 15.50 Trifecta £74.00.
**Owner** C C Buckley **Bred** Hunscote House Farm Stud **Trained** Kingsclere, Hants

**FOCUS**
This was competitive enough for the grade.

## 5566 KRONENBOURG H'CAP 2m (R)

8:15 (8:16) (Class 4) (0-80,81) 4-Y-O+ £5,175 (£1,540; £769; £384)

Form RPR

1 1 **Rolling Maul (IRE)**[16] 4202 9-8-13 73 JoshuaBryan(5) 84
(Peter Bowen) *hld up in tch in last: smooth hdwy 3f out: shkn up to ld appr fnl f: styd on strly: comf* **11/10[1]**

-106 2 4 **St Mary's**[13] 5108 4-9-5 81 WilliamCox(7) 87
(Andrew Balding) *trckd ldr tl relegated a pl after 3f: led and bmpd 2f out: sn rdn: hdd appr fnl f: qckly outpcd by comfortable wnr* **7/4[2]**

30-4 3 4 1/2 **Spice Fair**[9] 5251 10-9-7 76 LiamKeniry 77?
(Mark Usher) *trckd ldrs: hdwy to ld after 4f: bmpd and hdd 2f out: one pce and hld over 1f out* **7/2[3]**

2-65 4 24 **Kaisan**[17] 4966 4-8-11 66 (tp) KieranShoemark 38
(Bernard Llewellyn) *led and set stdy pce: flashed tail several times and hdd after 4f: styd cl up: rdn 3f out: wknd and hung lft 2f out: t.o* **10/1**

4m 1.8s (31.80) **Going Correction** +1.425s/f (Soft) 4 Ran SP% **115.3**
Speed ratings (Par 105): **77,75,72,60**
CSF £3.65 TOTE £2.00; EX 3.70 Trifecta £5.60.
**Owner** Roddy Owen & Paul Fullagar **Bred** Rathmore Stud **Trained** Little Newcastle, Pembrokes

**FOCUS**
A fair staying handicap despite the small field.

## 5567 STRONGBOW H'CAP 5f

8:45 (8:47) (Class 6) (0-60,60) 3-Y-O+ £2,587 (£770; £384; £192) Stalls Centre

Form RPR

002/ 1 **New Identity (IRE)**[47] 3849 6-9-1 54 (p) ShaneKelly 5 63+
(W J Martin, Ire) *hld up: hdwy whn nt clr run over 1f out: sn swtchd lft: r.o wl u.p to ld wl ins fnl f* **3/1[1]**

0606 2 nk **Lady Joanna Vassa (IRE)**[5] 5419 4-8-9 48 (v[1]) SamHitchcott 8 53
(Richard Guest) *cl up: led over 3f out tl over 2f out: rdn to ld again again 1f out: hdd wl ins fnl f* **5/1[2]**

5056 3 1/2 **Captain Scooby**[6] 5377 11-8-2 46 oh1 (v[1]) KevinLundie(5) 3 49
(Richard Guest) *s.i.s: in rr: rdn 1/2-way: stl only 8th 1f out: r.o wl: wnt 3rd nr fin* **8/1**

363 4 3/4 **Prominna**[9] 5253 7-9-7 60 GeorgeDowning 1 60
(Tony Carroll) *chsd ldrs: led over 2f out: drvn over 1f out: hdd 1f out: no ex: lost 3rd nr fin* **3/1[1]**

0440 5 1/2 **Tally's Song**[14] 5052 4-8-4 46 oh1 (p) EdwardGreatrex(3) 11 45
(Grace Harris) *chsd ldrs: rdn 1/2-way: unable qck fnl f* **11/1**

0-54 6 3 1/4 **Shelneverwalkalone**[75] 2819 3-9-3 59 KieranShoemark 7 45
(Ivan Furtado) *led over 1f: styd prom: drvn 2f out: wknd over 1f out* **6/1[3]**

0506 7 1/2 **Diminutive (IRE)**[9] 5252 5-8-8 47 ow1 (p) JohnFahy 2 32
(Grace Harris) *towards rr: rdn and clsd 2f out: wknd fnl f* **8/1**

0-40 8 3 **Charlie Victor**[90] 2362 3-8-12 54 LiamKeniry 9 27
(Malcolm Saunders) *hld up: rdn 2f out: wknd over 1f out* **16/1**

6500 9 3 1/4 **Texas Wedge**[15] 5028 3-8-5 47 (p) MartinDwyer 6 9
(William Muir) *prom: rdn over 2f out: wknd appr fnl f* **20/1**

1m 4.04s (5.74) **Going Correction** +1.425s/f (Soft)
**WFA** 3 from 4yo+ 3lb 9 Ran SP% **122.2**
Speed ratings (Par 101): **111,110,109,108,107 102,101,96,91**
CSF £19.37 CT £113.79 TOTE £4.00: £1.60, £1.70, £2.80; EX 20.20 Trifecta £109.90.
**Owner** Stephen McGuinness **Bred** Micheal D Ryan **Trained** Enniscorthy, Co Wexford

■ Stewards' Enquiry : Sam Hitchcott 2 day ban - used his whip above the permitted level (17/18 Aug)

**FOCUS**
The pace was sound for this modest handicap. The second and third offer perspective to the level of the form.

T/Plt: £101.90 to a £1 stake. Pool: £60,409.01 - 432.55 winning units. T/Qpdt: £16.70 to a £1 stake. Pool: £6,551.51 - 288.59 winning units. **Richard Lowther**

# 5524 GOODWOOD (R-H)

Thursday, August 3

**OFFICIAL GOING: Soft (heavy in places; 5.8)**

Wind: strong, gusty, half against Weather: cloudy, breezy

## 5568 MATCHBOOK BETTING EXCHANGE H'CAP 1m 1f 197y

**1:50** (1:51) (Class 2) 3-Y-0

**£31,125** (£9,320; £4,660; £2,330; £1,165; £585) **Stalls** Low

Form RPR

0101 **1** **Good Omen**[15] 5037 3-9-1 **96** JamieSpencer 11 107+
(David Simcock) *edgy: s.i.s and bustled along early: in rr: clsd to far rail to trck ldrs and travelling wl over 2f out: pushed along to chal over 1f out: rdn to ld ins fnl f: styd on wl* **8/1**

1-13 **2** *1 ¼* **Frontispiece**[26] 4640 3-7-13 **85** DavidEgan(5) 18 93
(Sir Michael Stoute) *in tch in last quartet but niggled along: hdwy 4f out: styd far side and led over 2f out: drvn over 1f out: hdd and styd on same pce ins fnl f* **7/1**[3]

411 **3** *1 ½* **Addeybb (IRE)**[20] 4831 3-8-12 **93** RyanMoore 13 98
(William Haggas) *str: lw: hld up in tch in midfield: styd far side and ev ch over 3f out: rdn over 2f out: no ex and outpcd ins fnl f* **11/2**[2]

4105 **4** *shd* **Grey Britain**[21] 4817 3-9-4 **99** GeraldMosse 7 104
(John Ryan) *led: c centre over 3f out: rdn and hdd over 2f out: rallied u.p ent fnl f: edgd rt and kpt on ins fnl f* **12/1**

3213 **5** *3 ¼* **Hold Sway (IRE)**[56] 3505 3-8-6 **87** (p) SilvestreDeSousa 5 85
(Charlie Appleby) *lw: towards rr: c centre over 3f out: chsng ldrs and rdn over 2f out: carried rt and no imp over 1f out: wl hld and plugged on same pce ins fnl f* **9/2**[1]

6412 **6** *hd* **Ray's The Money (IRE)**[12] 5160 3-7-13 **83** (v) AaronJones(3) 8 81
(Michael Bell) *s.i.s: hld up in rr: styd far side over 3f out: clsd to chse ldrs over 2f out: nt clrest of runs over 1f out: effrt 1f out: no imp: wl hld and plugged on same pce ins fnl f* **25/1**

4121 **7** *4* **Archetype (FR)**[26] 4640 3-8-10 **91** OisinMurphy 15 81
(Simon Crisford) *t.k.h: chsd ldrs: c centre over 3f out: effrt u.p over 2f out: hung rt and btn over 1f out: wknd ins fnl f* **14/1**

4236 **8** *shd* **Morning Suit (USA)**[13] 5130 3-8-7 **88** PJMcDonald 3 78
(Mark Johnston) *niggled along in midfield: lost pl and pushed along 1/2-way: rdn and gd hdwy on inner over 4f out: styd far side and ev ch u.p 3f out: lost pl over 1f out: wknd ins fnl f* **20/1**

5123 **9** *4 ½* **Emenem**[33] 4376 3-8-8 **89** JFEgan 6 70
(Simon Dow) *hld up in midfield: c centre over 3f out: effrt to chse ldrs u.p over 2f out: hung rt and btn over 1f out: wknd ins fnl f* **14/1**

0420 **10** *nk* **Society Red**[19] 4886 3-8-0 **81** PatrickMathers 9 61
(Richard Fahey) *chsd ldrs: c centre over 3f out: effrt u.p over 2f out: no ex and btn over 1f out: wknd fnl f* **14/1**

4102 **11** *1 ¼* **Rumpole**[38] 4153 3-8-0 **81** KieranO'Neill 4 59
(Hughie Morrison) *chsd ldrs: wnt 2nd over 4f out: c centre over 3f out: lost pl u.p over 2f out: bhd ent fnl f: wknd* **11/1**

4003 **12** *12* **Kings Gift (IRE)**[19] 4916 3-9-5 **100** PaulMulrennan 14 54
(Michael Dods) *hld up in midfield: c centre over 3f out: swtchd rt and effrt over 2f out: sn outpcd: wknd over 1f out: eased wl ins fnl f* **11/1**

3220 **13** *10* **Monticello (IRE)**[20] 4856 3-8-7 **88** JoeFanning 12 22
(Mark Johnston) *chsd ldr tl over 4f out: c centre and lost pl over 3f out: bhd 2f out: eased ins fnl f* **16/1**

2m 10.4s (2.30) **Going Correction** +0.85s/f (Soft) 13 Ran SP% **116.0**

Speed ratings (Par 106): **124,123,121,121,119 118,115,115,112,111 110,101,93**

CSF £61.15 CT £336.63 TOTE £6.90: £2.20, £2.80, £1.90; EX 81.40 Trifecta £466.10.

**Owner** Mrs Q J Guo **Bred** Hascombe And Valiant Studs **Trained** Newmarket, Suffolk

**FOCUS**

Lower bend dolled out to the 3f marker. In complete contrast to the previous day it was dry and windy. There was fresh ground from last 3.5f in the straight and the top bend on the far rail, with the going officially described as soft, heavy in places prior to racing. It was predictably hard work in the opener with a headwind to boot. There was a difference of opinion as to the best ground once the runners turned for home in this classy 3yo handicap. That resulted in a messy race and the far side was the place to be, but it's hard to knock the form. The runner-up and third help pin this at the bottom end of the race averages.

## 5569 MARKEL INSURANCE FILLIES' STKS (REGISTERED AS THE LILLIE LANGTRY) (GROUP 3) 1m 6f

**2:25** (2:26) (Class 1) 3-Y-0+

**£56,710** (£21,500; £10,760; £5,360; £2,690; £1,350) **Stalls** Low

Form RPR

2-40 **1** **Endless Time (IRE)**[42] 3996 5-9-6 110 (p[1]) WilliamBuick 1 109
(Charlie Appleby) *hld up in tch in midfield: clsd and nt clr run over 2f out: sn swtchd lft: hdwy u.p to chse ldng trio over 1f out: styd on strly ins fnl f to ld last strides* **5/2**[1]

-620 **2** *nk* **Dubka**[26] 4613 4-9-6 102 RyanMoore 4 108
(Sir Michael Stoute) *trckd ldrs: nt clr run over 2f out: sn swtchd lft and forced way out to chse ldr: rdn to ld over 1f out: hrd pressed ent fnl f: kpt on gamely u.p: hdd and no ex last strides* **13/2**[3]

-111 **3** *nk* **Melodic Motion (IRE)**[33] 4364 3-8-9 100 OisinMurphy 10 107
(Ralph Beckett) *lw: chsd ldng trio: effrt to press ldrs 2f out: ev ch u.p over 1f out: kpt on wl u.p: kpt on same pce towards fin* **11/2**[2]

1162 **4** *¾* **Natural Scenery**[33] 4356 4-9-6 105 (p) JimCrowley 8 106
(Saeed bin Suroor) *lw: hld up in tch in midfield: clsd to chse ldrs ent fnl 2f: rdn to chal over 1f out: kpt on u.p tl no ex wl ins fnl f: jst outpcd towards fin* **9/1**

0-1 **5** *2 ¼* **Wild Irish Rose (IRE)**[14] 5088 3-8-10 93 ow1 SeamieHeffernan 6 104
(A P O'Brien, Ire) *w'like: swtg: hld up in tch in last quartet: clsd into midfield whn pushed lft and hmpd jst over 2f out: trying to rally and swtchd rt over 1f out: kpt on but no imp ins fnl f* **7/1**

P1-0 **6** *8* **Diamonds Pour Moi**[83] 2571 4-9-6 105 DavidProbert 7 92
(Ralph Beckett) *lw: led: rdn and hdd over 1f out: sn outpcd and btn: wknd ins fnl f* **9/1**

-445 **7** *¾* **Rich Legacy (IRE)**[26] 4613 3-8-9 103 HarryBentley 12 91
(Ralph Beckett) *hld up in tch in last pair: effrt on outer ent fnl 2f: no imp and outpcd whn hung rt over 1f out: wknd fnl f* **16/1**

34-1 **8** *9* **Dawn Horizons**[20] 4829 4-9-6 92 PatCosgrave 5 78
(William Haggas) *chsd ldr tl bmpd: jostled and lost pl jst over 2f out: wl btn over 1f out: wknd* **10/1**

330- **9** *1 ¾* **Harlequeen**[350] 5586 4-9-6 109 SilvestreDeSousa 2 76
(Mick Channon) *taken down early: t.k.h: stdd bk to last trio after 2f: effrt on outer over 2f out: sn struggling: bhd over 1f out* **12/1**

5426 **10** *11* **Lucy The Painter (IRE)**[26] 4613 5-9-6 93 DougieCostello 3 60
(Ed de Giles) *hld up in tch in last pair: swtchd lft and effrt wl over 2f out: sn struggling and btn: wl bhd and eased ins fnl f: t.o* **33/1**

3m 14.11s (10.51) **Going Correction** +0.85s/f (Soft)

**WFA** 3 from 4yo+ 11lb 10 Ran SP% **115.4**

Speed ratings (Par 110): **103,102,102,102,100 96,95,90,89,83**

CSF £18.34 TOTE £3.20: £1.50, £2.30, £2.10; EX 19.70 Trifecta £78.30.

**Owner** Godolphin **Bred** Mabaki Investments **Trained** Newmarket, Suffolk

**FOCUS**

This competitive Group 3 for fillies was run at a fair pace. It got rough 2f out and threw up a thrilling four-way finish, with the far side favoured once more. The runner-up has been rated to the better view of her Haydock second.

## 5570 QATAR RICHMOND STKS (GROUP 2) (C&G) 6f

**3:00** (3:00) (Class 1) 2-Y-0

**£113,420** (£43,000; £21,520; £10,720; £5,380; £2,700) **Stalls** High

Form RPR

31 **1** **Barraquero (IRE)**[30] 4466 2-9-0 0 WilliamBuick 3 110
(Brian Meehan) *athletic: lw: racd in centre: hld up in tch in last pair: clsd and rdn to chal over 1f out: drvn to ld ins fnl f: r.o wl* **4/1**[3]

102 **2** *1 ¼* **Nebo (IRE)**[19] 4906 2-9-0 104 JimCrowley 1 106
(Charles Hills) *racd in centre: chsd ldrs: effrt to chal over 1f out: rdn to ld 1f out: hdd and styd on same pce ins fnl f* **3/1**[2]

2131 **3** *2 ¼* **Cardsharp**[21] 4812 2-9-3 110 JamesDoyle 2 102
(Mark Johnston) *racd in centre: chsd ldr tl rdn to ld over 1f out: sn drvn and hdd 1f out: wl hld 3rd and styd on same pce ins fnl f* **2/1**[1]

010 **4** *2 ¼* **Etefaaq (IRE)**[19] 4906 2-9-0 92 FrankieDettori 6 93
(Richard Hannon) *racd in centre: hld up in tch in midfield: effrt u.p but no imp over 1f out: wl hld and styd on same pce ins fnl f: snatched 4th last strides* **16/1**

012 **5** *hd* **Green Power**[28] 4526 2-9-0 87 BenCurtis 4 92
(John Gallagher) *str: racd in centre: led tl rdn and hdd over 1f out: sn outpcd and btn 4th 1f out: wknd ins fnl f* **16/1**

212 **6** *nse* **Headway**[44] 3925 2-9-0 107 PatCosgrave 9 92+
(William Haggas) *lw: racd along nr stands' rail: pressed ldng pair: rdn ent fnl 2f: sn struggling and outpcd over 1f out: wknd ins fnl f* **4/1**[3]

10 **7** *2 ¾* **Bullington Bandit (IRE)**[19] 4906 2-9-0 0 (p) StevieDonohoe 10 84
(Jane Chapple-Hyam) *racd in centre: swtchd rt after s: hld up in rr: effrt ent fnl f: sn struggling and outpcd: wl btn 1f out* **22/1**

1m 15.42s (3.22) **Going Correction** +0.45s/f (Yiel) 7 Ran SP% **114.4**

Speed ratings (Par 106): **96,94,91,88,88 88,84**

CSF £16.45 TOTE £4.30: £2.20, £2.00; EX 14.90 Trifecta £45.20.

**Owner** Manton Thoroughbreds II **Bred** Helen Smith & Sally Mullen **Trained** Manton, Wilts

**FOCUS**

The placed horses give this year's Richmond a sound look. Not that surprisingly those nearest the far side came out best. The second has been rated to his Superlative form and the third below his July Stakes win.

## 5571 QATAR NASSAU STKS (GROUP 1) (BRITISH CHAMPIONS SERIES) (F&M) 1m 1f 197y

**3:35** (3:39) (Class 1) 3-Y-0+

**£340,260** (£129,000; £64,560; £32,160; £16,140; £8,100) **Stalls** Low

Form RPR

2111 **1** **Winter (IRE)**[41] 4031 3-8-13 119 RyanMoore 6 118+
(A P O'Brien, Ire) *swtg: t.k.h: trckd ldng pair: clsd to chse ldr and swtchd lft 2f out: rdn to ld 1f out: sn asserted and r.o wl ins fnl f: quite comf* **10/11**[1]

10-1 **2** *1 ½* **Blond Me (IRE)**[77] 2765 5-9-7 110 OisinMurphy 9 113
(Andrew Balding) *broke wl: sn stdd bk and t.k.h in last pair: effrt 2f out: chsd ldng pair jst over 1f out: styd on u.p to go 2nd last strides: nvr seriously threatening wnr* **16/1**

5-10 **3** *nk* **Sobetsu**[62] 3301 3-8-13 113 WilliamBuick 2 113
(Charlie Appleby) *led and dictated stdy gallop: rdn and qcknd ent fnl 2f: hdd over 1f out: kpt on but nt match pce of wnr ins fnl f: lost 2nd last strides* **6/1**[3]

1033 **4** *1 ¼* **Hydrangea (IRE)**[41] 4031 3-8-13 111 (p) SeamieHeffernan 4 111
(A P O'Brien, Ire) *swtg: dwlt: rcvrd to chse ldr after 1f: lost 2nd and rdn 2f out: wandered rt u.p over 1f out: styd on same pce ins fnl f* **10/1**

113- **5** *½* **So Mi Dar**[305] 6988 4-9-7 114 FrankieDettori 3 109
(John Gosden) *swtg: on toes: t.k.h: broke wl: sn stdd bk and hld up wl in tch in midfield: effrt on inner 2f out: kpt on same pce fnl f* **4/1**[2]

1-44 **6** *½* **Queen's Trust**[43] 3962 4-9-7 118 JimCrowley 7 108
(Sir Michael Stoute) *hld up in tch in rr: effrt on outer over 1f out: no imp and kpt on same pce ins fnl f* **8/1**

2m 11.79s (3.69) **Going Correction** +0.85s/f (Soft)

**WFA** 3 from 4yo+ 8lb 6 Ran SP% **112.8**

Speed ratings (Par 117): **119,117,117,116,116 115**

CSF £17.48 CT £58.78 TOTE £1.70: £1.20, £3.90; EX 15.00 Trifecta £69.40.

**Owner** Mrs John Magnier & Michael Tabor & Derrick Smith **Bred** Laddies Poker Two Syndicate **Trained** Cashel, Co Tipperary

**FOCUS**

Hit by non-runners, with no obvious pacesetter this year's Nassau was run at an uneven tempo, causing most to take a keen hold, and it's muddling Group 1 form. The third and fourth have been rated close to form.

## 5572 TELEGRAPH NURSERY H'CAP 7f

**4:10** (4:11) (Class 2) 2-Y-0 **£16,172** (£4,812; £2,405; £1,202) **Stalls** Low

Form RPR

2213 **1** **Billesdon Brook**[7] 5329 2-9-3 **87** SeanLevey 4 98+
(Richard Hannon) *hld up in midfield: looking for room and barging match over 2f out: nt clr run tl swtchd lft and in the clr 1f out but stl lots to do: rdn hands and heels and hdwy ins fnl f: str burst fnl 100yds: led last strides* **10/3**[1]

035 **2** *hd* **Cheeky Rascal (IRE)**[15] 5030 2-8-3 **73** KieranO'Neill 13 74
(Richard Hannon) *w'like: w ldrs tl rdn to ld wl over 1f out: hdd ent fnl f: kpt on wl u.p and led again wl ins fnl f: hdd last strides* **16/1**

5216 **3** *nk* **Alifax**[20] 4858 2-8-2 **72** PatrickMathers 14 72
(Jamie Osborne) *hld up in tch in last quartet: rdn and hdwy on outer to chal over 1f out: drvn to ld ent fnl f: kpt on wl u.p tl hdd and no ex wl ins fnl f* **33/1**

2115 **4** *hd* **Jedi Master (IRE)**[19] 4922 2-8-9 **82** AdamMcNamara(3) 12 82
(Richard Fahey) *w'like: lw: hld up in tch in last quartet: rdn and hdwy on outer 2f out: chsd ldrs 1f out: kpt on wl u.p ins fnl f* **16/1**

020 5 nk **Cosmopolitan Queen**[20] 4855 2-8-3 **78** DavidEgan(5) 1 77
(David Elsworth) *neat: led: rdn and hdd wl over 1f out: stl chsng ldrs and hung lft 1f out: swtchd rt and rallied ins fnl f: kpt on towards fin* **7/1**[3]

1200 6 ½ **Starlight Mystery (IRE)**[20] 4858 2-9-1 **85** SilvestreDeSousa 6 85+
(Mark Johnston) *lw: hld up in last quartet: clsd whn nt clr run and swtchd lft 2f out: hdwy on outer over 1f out: chsng ldrs whn edgd rt and swtchd lft ins fnl f: kpt on towards fin: nvr quite getting to ldrs* **10/1**

530 7 ½ **Chai Chai (IRE)**[27] 4560 2-8-4 **74** JimmyQuinn 9 72
(Andrew Balding) *hld up in tch in midfield: nt clr run and swtchd lft 2f out: carried rt and hmpd over 1f out: shifting rt and hdwy 1f out: kpt on ins fnl f: nvr quite getting to ldrs* **33/1**

214 8 2¼ **Royal Household**[19] 4919 2-8-7 **80** HollieDoyle(3) 15 73
(Richard Hannon) *sn off the pce in last: clsd but nt clr run on inner over 2f out: swtchd lft and rdn over 1f out: kpt on ins fnl f: nvr threatened ldrs* **20/1**

4344 9 1¼ **Central City (IRE)**[42] 3999 2-8-8 **78** JosephineGordon 17 66
(Hugo Palmer) *cmpt: hld up in tch in midfield: rdn 2f out: hung rt and no imp 1f out: kpt on same pce ins fnl f* **33/1**

11 10 ¾ **Veejay (IRE)**[12] 5136 2-8-11 **81** RobHornby 7 74+
(Mick Channon) *angular: hld up in tch in last quartet: clsd on inner but nt clr run ent fnl 2f tl swtchd lft and in the clr jst ins fnl f: no ch w ldrs but styd on fnl 100yds* **11/2**[2]

006 11 3½ **Devil's Cowboy (IRE)**[41] 4049 2-8-0 **70** RoystonFfrench 10 47
(Charles Hills) *t.k.h: chsd ldrs: rdn and edgd rt over 2f out: lost pl and btn over 1f out: wknd ins fnl f* **33/1**

11 12 2 **Poetic Steps (FR)**[21] 4786 2-9-0 **84** PJMcDonald 3 56
(Mark Johnston) *w'like: chsd ldrs: rdn wl over 2f out: lost pl and btn over 1f out: wknd fnl f* **7/1**[3]

221 13 3½ **Poet's Prince**[17] 4956 2-8-9 **79** JoeFanning 16 42
(Mark Johnston) *unf: lw: t.k.h: w ldrs: rdn and edgd rt over 2f out: lost pl and edgd rt over 1f out: wknd fnl f* **11/1**

522 14 4½ **Barbarianatthegate**[11] 5179 2-8-9 **79** (b) OisinMurphy 2 31
(Brian Meehan) *cmpt: chsd ldrs: rdn and losing pl whn bmpd and hmpd over 2f out: bhd 1f out* **25/1**

1m 32.38s (5.38) **Going Correction** +0.85s/f (Soft) **14** Ran SP% **113.0**
Speed ratings (Par 100): **103,102,102,102,101 101,100,98,96,95 91,89,85,80**
CSF £46.07 CT £1090.00 TOTE £3.80: £1.70, £4.50, £8.00; EX 60.00 Trifecta £2506.50.
**Owner** Pall Mall Partners & Late R J McCreery **Bred** Stowell Hill Partners **Trained** East Everleigh, Wilts

■ Tangled was withdrawn. Price at time of withdrawal 15/2. Rule 4 applies to all bets - deduction 10p in the pound.

**FOCUS**
Race distance increased 15yds. No great gallop on here and a rather messy race, with several of the runners meeting trouble and the field finishing in a bunch. The winner did exceptionally well over severe trouble. Straightforward form rated around the second to the fifth.

## 5573 VICTORIA RACING CLUB EBF BRITISH STALLION STUDS MAIDEN FILLIES' STKS (PLUS 10 RACE) 7f
**4:45** (4:45) (Class 2) 2-Y-O **£16,172** (£4,812; £2,405; £1,202) **Stalls** Low

Form RPR
6 1 **Roulette**[19] 4902 2-9-0 0 JamesDoyle 1 78+
(Michael Bell) *lw: mde all: gng best ent fnl 2f: rdn over 1f out: 2 l clr 1f out: drvn ins fnl f: reduced advantage towards fin: a holding on: drvn out* **1/1**[1]

2 nk **Ripley (IRE)** 2-9-0 0 WilliamBuick 3 77+
(Charles Hills) *unf: chsd ldng pair: effrt over 2f out: rdn to chse wnr 1f out: styd on wl u.p fnl 100yds: clsng on wnr towards fin* **5/1**[3]

3 1¼ **Ann Without An E** 2-9-0 0 JFEgan 6 74+
(Mick Channon) *leggy: s.i.s and rn green early: hld up in tch in last pair: effrt over 2f out: hdwy over 1f out: kpt on ins fnl f: nvr quite enough pce to rch ldrs* **17/2**

4 hd **Zilara (IRE)** 2-9-0 0 PatDobbs 8 74+
(Ralph Beckett) *unf: swtg: on toes: hld up in tch in last pair: rdn over 2f out: sn outpcd: rallied 1f out: kpt on wl ins fnl f: nvr threatened ldrs* **8/1**

0 5 1¼ **Titchy Digits**[21] 4806 2-9-0 0 DavidEgan 5 71
(Michael Attwater) *leggy: t.k.h: hld up wl in tch in midfield: rdn over 2f out: chsd wnr and edgd rt wl over 1f out: lost 2nd 1f out: wknd wl ins fnl f* **20/1**

6 16 **Miss Paris** 2-9-0 0 SilvestreDeSousa 4 31
(Charles Hills) *str: chsd wnr: rdn over 2f out: lost 2nd wl over 1f out and losing pl whn sltly short of room over 1f out: bhd and eased ins fnl f* **9/2**[2]

1m 34.07s (7.07) **Going Correction** +0.85s/f (Soft) **6** Ran SP% **111.2**
Speed ratings (Par 97): **93,92,91,91,89 71**
CSF £6.24 TOTE £1.80: £1.30, £2.20; EX 6.60 Trifecta £24.40.
**Owner** W J and T C O Gredley **Bred** Stetchworth & Middle Park Studs Ltd **Trained** Newmarket, Suffolk

■ Stewards' Enquiry : William Buick 2 day ban - used his whip above the permitted level (17/18 Aug)

**FOCUS**
Race distance increased 15yds. A race weakened by the absence of Magical, the winner had the run of it and just did enough. It's hard to rate the form higher, with five in a heap at the finish.

## 5574 TATLER H'CAP 5f
**5:20** (5:20) (Class 3) (0-95,93) 3-Y-O
**£15,562** (£4,660; £2,330; £1,165; £582; £292) **Stalls** High

Form RPR
3024 1 **Quench Dolly**[13] 5117 3-9-2 **93** GeorgeBuckell(5) 8 104
(John Gallagher) *on toes: racd in centre: t.k.h: hld up in tch in rr: swtchd rt effrt nr far rail over 1f out: qcknd to ld ins fnl f: sn clr and r.o strly: readily* **10/3**[1]

2153 2 3 **Fair Cop**[15] 5029 3-8-7 **79** DavidProbert 5 79+
(Andrew Balding) *lw: racd in centre: trckd ldrs and travelled strly: led over 1f out: sn rdn and kicked clr: hdd ins fnl f: no ch w wnr but kpt on for clr 2nd* **11/2**[3]

061 3 2¾ **Maakaasib**[22] 4752 3-8-12 **84** (e) OisinMurphy 4 74
(Simon Crisford) *lw: racd in centre: stdd s: hld up in tch in rr: hdwy 1/2-way: effrt to chse ldr ent fnl f: sn hung rt and no imp: 3rd and wknd fnl 100yds* **7/1**

4121 4 hd **Intense Romance (IRE)**[6] 5355 3-9-0 **86** 6ex ConnorBeasley 10 76
(Michael Dods) *lw: racd in centre: hld up in tch: effrt whn nt clr run over 1f out: swtchd lft and barging match w rival over 1f out: styd on u.p ins fnl f: no ch w ldrs* **9/2**[2]

4100 5 1½ **Poet's Society**[13] 5129 3-9-2 **88** WilliamBuick 7 72
(Mark Johnston) *racd in centre: chsd ldrs: rdn and ev ch ent fnl 2f: sn outpcd: wknd ins fnl f* **13/2**

5361 6 2 **Yorkshiredebut (IRE)**[15] 5020 3-8-6 **78** (p) JosephineGordon 9 55
(Paul Midgley) *taken down early: racd in centre: led gp and chsd overall ldr tl led 2f out: sn rdn and hdd: outpcd whn edgd lft ent fnl f: wknd ins fnl f* **14/1**

2100 7 1½ **Megan Lily (IRE)**[33] 4333 3-9-0 **89** AdamMcNamara(3) 13 61
(Richard Fahey) *on toes: racd in centre: t.k.h: hld up in tch: effrt 2f out: no imp whn barging match w rival over 1f out: wknd ins fnl f* **10/1**

-110 8 11 **Carlton Frankie**[47] 3844 3-9-4 **90** SilvestreDeSousa 12 22
(Michael Easterby) *racd alone nr stands' rail: overall ldr tl hung rt towards centre and hdd 2f out: sn btn: wknd and bhd ins fnl f* **11/2**[3]

1m 0.8s (0.60) **Going Correction** +0.45s/f (Yiel) **8** Ran SP% **113.6**
Speed ratings (Par 104): **113,108,103,103,101 97,95,77**
CSF £21.47 CT £118.74 TOTE £3.90: £1.50, £2.20, £2.20; EX 23.20 Trifecta £137.00.
**Owner** Quench Racing Partnership **Bred** Mrs R J Gallagher **Trained** Chastleton, Oxon

**FOCUS**
Racing down the centre, the winner ended up nearer the far side and got well on top late. Ordinary sprint form. The winner has been rated in keeping with the better view of her form.
T/Jkpt: £6,676.30 to a £1 stake. Pool: £33,381.82 - 5 winning units. T/Plt: £32.30 to a £1 stake. Pool: £261,440.30 - 5,900.01 winning units. T/Qpdt: £15.70 to a £1 stake. Pool: £15,974.39 - 750.88 winning units. **Steve Payne**

# 5261 NOTTINGHAM (L-H)
### Thursday, August 3

**OFFICIAL GOING: Soft changing to heavy after race 2 (2.45)**
Wind: Strong against Weather: Sunny periods and showers

## 5575 MYRACING.COM FOR FREE NOTTINGHAM TIPS EBF FILLIES' NOVICE STKS (PLUS 10 RACE) 5f 8y
**2:10** (2:11) (Class 5) 2-Y-O **£3,234** (£962; £481; £240) **Stalls** High

Form RPR
1 **Crotchet** 2-9-0 0 JackGarritty 5 78+
(Richard Fahey) *hld up towards rr on inner: hdwy over 2f out: swtchd lft to outer and chsd ldrs over 1f out: rdn to chal ins fnl f: kpt on wl to ld nr fin* **5/1**[3]

6 2 ½ **Dandy's Beano (IRE)**[16] 4996 2-9-0 0 KevinStott 1 76+
(Kevin Ryan) *trckd ldrs: hdwy and cl up 2f out: led jst over 1f out: rdn ins fnl f: hdd and no ex nr fin* **7/1**

0 3 4 **Maygold**[13] 5107 2-9-0 0 RichardKingscote 6 62+
(Ed Walker) *dwlt: sn trcking ldrs: smooth hdwy 2f out and sn cl up: ev ch over 1f out: sn rdn and kpt on same pce* **5/1**[3]

4 shd **Harmonica** 2-9-0 0 LukeMorris 2 62+
(Sir Mark Prescott Bt) *dwlt: green and sn rdn along in rr: outpcd and wl detached 1/2-way: styd on fr wl over 1f out* **12/1**

03 5 2¾ **Cherry Oak (IRE)**[15] 5015 2-9-0 0 GrahamLee 4 52
(Ben Haslam) *a towards rr* **33/1**

30 6 1¼ **Three Little Birds**[12] 5150 2-8-9 72 MitchGodwin(5) 8 47
(Sylvester Kirk) *trckd ldr: cl up 2f out: rdn to ld briefly over 1f out: sn hdd and drvn: wknd fnl f* **7/2**[2]

6 7 5 **Kandy Kove (IRE)**[26] 4628 2-9-0 0 (h1) AdamBeschizza 3 29
(Robert Cowell) *led: pushed along over 2f out: rdn and hdd wl over 1f out: sn wknd* **10/1**

2206 8 2¾ **Mother Of Dragons (IRE)**[12] 5150 2-9-0 80 FranBerry 7 19
(Joseph Tuite) *prom: rdn along 2f out: sn wknd* **11/4**[1]

1m 5.99s (4.49) **Going Correction** +0.825s/f (Soft) **8** Ran SP% **114.4**
Speed ratings (Par 91): **97,96,89,89,85 83,75,70**
CSF £39.53 TOTE £6.30: £1.90, £2.10, £1.80; EX 29.60 Trifecta £369.60.
**Owner** Cheveley Park Stud **Bred** Cheveley Park Stud Ltd **Trained** Musley Bank, N Yorks

**FOCUS**
Outer Track. The rail was set out 4 yards on both bends adding 12 yards to races 3, 4 and 5, and 24 yards to race 7. Probably just a fair novice event, with the less-exposed types coming to the fore.

## 5576 MYRACING.COM EBF NOVICE STKS 6f 18y
**2:45** (2:46) (Class 5) 2-Y-O **£3,234** (£962; £481; £240) **Stalls** High

Form RPR
0 1 **Sands Of Mali (FR)**[19] 4919 2-9-2 0 PaulHanagan 5 99+
(Richard Fahey) *racd centre: cl up: led wl over 2f out: rdn and hdd narrowly jst over 1f out: led again ins fnl f: sn edgd lft and styd on strly* **5/1**[3]

31 2 3¾ **Eirene**[34] 4296 2-9-4 0 RobertWinston 7 90
(Dean Ivory) *racd centre: trckd ldrs: hdwy and cl up 2f out: rdn to take narrow advantage jst over 1f out: drvn and hdd ins fnl f: kpt on* **2/1**[2]

3 13 **Captain Jameson (IRE)** 2-9-2 0 JasonHart 6 49
(John Quinn) *trckd ldrs: hdwy 2f out: sn rdn and kpt on one pce* **20/1**

1 4 ¾ **Island Drive (IRE)**[22] 4749 2-9-4 0 DanielTudhope 3 49
(William Haggas) *racd centre: trckd ldrs: pushed along 2f out: sn rdn and btn* **13/8**[1]

5 7 **Ferrier** 2-8-11 0 (h1) LukeMorris 4 21
(Sir Mark Prescott Bt) *a towards rr* **16/1**

33 6 ½ **Raven's Raft (IRE)**[29] 4503 2-8-11 0 AlistairRawlinson 8 19
(Michael Appleby) *racd towards stands' rail: led: pushed along 1/2-way: sn hdd and rdn: wknd wl over 1f out* **14/1**

7 11 **Charles Fox** 2-9-2 0 DanielMuscutt 1
(James Fanshawe) *sn outpcd and a bhd* **16/1**

1m 21.43s (6.73) **Going Correction** +0.825s/f (Soft) **7** Ran SP% **111.3**
Speed ratings (Par 94): **88,83,65,64,55 54,40**
CSF £14.59 TOTE £6.00: £2.70, £1.40; EX 15.50 Trifecta £225.00.
**Owner** The Cool Silk Partnership **Bred** Simon Urizzi **Trained** Musley Bank, N Yorks

■ Redtedd was withdrawn. Price at time of withdrawal 50/1. Rule 4 does not apply.

**FOCUS**
Three dominated the market for the second novice event on the card, this one over a furlong further than the previous one.

## 5577 @MYRACINGTIPS FOLLOW US ON TWITTER MEDIAN AUCTION MAIDEN STKS 1m 75y
**3:20** (3:21) (Class 6) 3-4-Y-O **£2,587** (£770; £384; £192) **Stalls** Centre

Form RPR
65 1 **Swaffham Bulbeck (IRE)**[17] 4981 3-9-6 0 AdamBeschizza 7 72+
(Ed Vaughan) *t.k.h: trckd ldrs: hdwy over 2f out: effrt to chal over 1f out: rdn to ld ins fnl f: kpt on* **13/2**[2]

65 2 ¾ **Ididitforyoooo (IRE)**[47] 3839 3-9-6 0 KierenFox 8 68+
(Brian Meehan) *t.k.h early: in tch: pushed along 3f out: rdn along 2f out: swtchd lft and drvn over 1f out: styd on ins fnl f* **9/2**[1]

3 **3** *1* **Glenn Coco**[35] 4269 3-9-6 0............................................ DanielMuscutt 6 66
(Stuart Williams) *t.k.h: cl up: led 2f out: rdn over 1f out: drvn and hdd ins fnl f: kpt on same pce* **12/1**

56 **4** *1 ½* **Long Socks**[50] 3714 3-9-6 0............................................ FranBerry 2 63
(Alan King) *t.k.h early: hld up in tch: hdwy on inner over 2f out: rdn wl over 1f out: no imp fnl f* **8/1**[3]

0-6 **5** *shd* **Love Me Again**[22] 4764 3-9-1 0.................................. DanielTudhope 10 58
(Charlie Fellowes) *trckd ldrs on outer: hdwy and cl up 3f out: rdn along 2f out: drvn over 1f out: kpt on same pce* **9/2**[1]

3 **6** *½* **True Colors**[21] 4784 3-9-6 0............................................ JackGarritty 1 62
(Richard Fahey) *trckd ldr on inner: effrt to dispute ld 3f out and sn rdn along: drvn wl over 1f out: grad wknd* **9/2**[1]

0 **7** *2 ½* **Afterburner**[27] 4562 3-9-6 0............................................ LukeMorris 4 56
(Hugo Palmer) *led: rdn along 3f out: hdd 2f out: sn edgd lft and wknd* **18/1**

**8** *nk* **Saradani Bay** 3-9-6 0............................................ DavidAllan 15 55
(Rae Guest) *towards rr: hdwy on outer 1/2-way: chsd ldrs over 3f out: rdn along over 2f out: sn drvn and wknd* **25/1**

**9** *nk* **The Lady Rules** 3-9-1 0............................................ SaleemGolam 13 50
(Mrs Ilka Gansera-Leveque) *dwlt: a in rr* **50/1**

6 **10** *1 ¾* **Big Bad Lol (IRE)**[31] 4444 3-9-6 0.......................... RichardKingscote 14 51
(Ed Walker) *hld up: a in rr* **11/1**

06 **11** *nk* **Lady Prima**[12] 5158 3-9-1 0.......................................... AlistairRawlinson 9 45
(Mike Murphy) *a towards rr* **66/1**

0 **12** *5* **Bamo Mc**[22] 4764 3-9-6 0............................................ AntonioFresu 12 39
(Mike Murphy) *dwlt: a bhd* **50/1**

**13** *18* **Steady (IRE)** 3-9-1 0............................................ TrevorWhelan 5
(Dan Skelton) *dwlt: sn in tch on inner: rdn along over 3f out: sn wknd* **16/1**

1m 58.93s (9.93) **Going Correction** +0.925s/f (Soft) **13** Ran SP% **115.4**
Speed ratings (Par 101): **87,86,85,83,83 83,80,80,80,78 78,73,55**
CSF £33.74 TOTE £7.10: £2.60, £2.40, £2.60; EX 36.10 Trifecta £392.20.
**Owner** Ballymore Downunder Syndicate **Bred** John O'Mahony **Trained** Newmarket, Suffolk

**FOCUS**
Outer Track. The rail was set out 4 yards on both bends adding 12 yards to this race. A really ordinary race of its type and the going was changed to heavy before the off.

## 5578 @MYRACINGTIPS JOIN 235,000 RACING ENTHUSIASTS H'CAP 1m 75y
**3:55** (3:56) (Class 5) (0-75,79) 3-Y-0+ **£3,234** (£962; £481; £240) **Stalls** Centre

Form RPR

0310 **1** **Wealth Tax**[27] 4563 4-9-12 **73**............................................ GrahamLee 4 85+
(Ed Dunlop) *t.k.h early: trckd ldrs: smooth hdwy on outer over 2f out: led over 1f out: rdn clr fnl f* **10/1**

-423 **2** *3* **Prosecution**[26] 4623 3-8-11 **68**.................................. CharlieBennett(3) 2 71
(Hughie Morrison) *trckd ldrs: pushed along over 2f out: sltly outpcd and rdn wl over 1f out: styd on to chse wnr ins fnl f: no imp* **2/1**[1]

0021 **3** *1* **Badenscoth**[9] 5242 3-9-8 **79** 6ex.................................. JackDuern(3) 3 80
(Dean Ivory) *trckd ldrs: hdwy on inner over 3f out: sn pushed along: led 2f out and sn rdn: hdd over 1f out: sn drvn and kpt on same pce* **7/2**[2]

-044 **4** *1 ½* **Dominannie (IRE)**[17] 4960 4-8-12 **59**.................................. DavidAllan 6 58
(Sally Haynes) *cl up: pushed along 3f out: rdn over 2f out: drvn wl over 1f out: kpt on same pce* **10/1**

2003 **5** *2 ½* **Dutch Artist (IRE)**[11] 5183 5-10-0 **75**..........................(p) DanielTudhope 1 68
(David O'Meara) *led: rdn along 3f out: hdd 2f out: sn drvn and wknd* **7/1**

0003 **6** *nk* **Hidden Oasis (IRE)**[9] 5248 6-9-6 **67**..........................(p) FranBerry 5 59
(Jonjo O'Neill) *dwlt and in rr: effrt 3f out: rdn along 2f out: sn drvn and no imp* **4/1**[3]

0234 **7** *6* **Ingleby Angel (IRE)**[13] 5091 8-9-2 **63**.................................. TomEaves 9 42
(Colin Teague) *hld up: a in rr* **20/1**

1m 55.79s (6.79) **Going Correction** +0.925s/f (Soft)
**WFA** 3 from 4yo+ 7lb **7** Ran SP% **111.0**
Speed ratings (Par 103): **103,100,99,97,95 94,88**
CSF £28.67 CT £81.98 TOTE £10.60: £4.30, £1.40; EX 34.30 Trifecta £85.80.
**Owner** Mhs Partners & E Dunlop **Bred** Barry Walters **Trained** Newmarket, Suffolk

**FOCUS**
Outer Track. The rail was set out 4 yards on both bends adding 12 yards to this race. Nothing more than a fair handicap. The third has been rated a bit below his AW win.

## 5579 MYRACING.COM FREE BETS & TIPS H'CAP 1m 2f 50y
**4:30** (4:30) (Class 4) (0-85,82) 3-Y-0+ **£5,175** (£1,540; £769; £384) **Stalls** Low

Form RPR

022 **1** **Deinonychus**[8] 5287 6-8-13 **67**............................................ LukeMorris 4 73
(Michael Appleby) *trckd ldng pair: hdwy on outer 3f out: sn cl up: chal 2f out: rdn to ld over 1f out: edgd lft ins fnl f: kpt on* **11/4**[2]

0-33 **2** *1 ½* **Azzir (IRE)**[49] 3744 5-9-3 **74**.................................. CliffordLee(3) 3 76
(K R Burke) *hld up: hdwy over 3f out: pushed along to chse ldng pair 2f out: sn rdn: drvn to chse wnr ins fnl f: no imp towards fin* **6/4**[1]

2433 **3** *1 ¼* **Lexington Law (IRE)**[14] 5060 4-10-0 **82**.................................. FranBerry 2 82
(Alan King) *led 2f: cl up: led again 3f out: rdn over 2f out: hdd over 1f out: sn drvn and edgd lft: one pce* **3/1**[3]

3103 **4** *7* **Katebird (IRE)**[10] 5212 3-8-10 **72**.................................. FrannyNorton 1 59
(Mark Johnston) *trckd ldr: led after 2f: pushed along 4f out: hdd 3f out: sn rdn along and wknd fnl 2f* **5/1**

2m 22.05s (7.75) **Going Correction** +0.925s/f (Soft)
**WFA** 3 from 4yo+ 8lb **4** Ran SP% **108.3**
Speed ratings (Par 105): **106,104,103,98**
CSF £7.27 TOTE £3.10; EX 7.10 Trifecta £8.30.
**Owner** I R Hatton **Bred** Howdale Bloodstock Ltd **Trained** Oakham, Rutland

**FOCUS**
Outer Track. The rail was set out 4 yards on both bends adding 12 yards to this race. Tactics were always going to play a part in these conditions and the winner got going at the right time to collect the victory. The winner has been rated to his recent form.

## 5580 MYRACING.COM FOR GLORIOUS GOODWOOD TIPS H'CAP 5f 8y
**5:05** (5:07) (Class 5) (0-75,77) 3-Y-0+ **£3,234** (£962; £481; £240) **Stalls** High

Form RPR

2413 **1** **Show Palace**[9] 5263 4-9-2 **67**............................................ GrahamLee 6 77
(Jennie Candlish) *hld up in rr: swtchd rt towards stands' side and hdwy over 2f out: chal on bit over 1f out: rdn to ld ins fnl f* **7/2**[1]

00-3 **2** *1 ¼* **Ayresome Angel**[12] 5134 4-9-0 **65**.................................. DavidNolan 3 70
(John Mackie) *racd centre: led: rdn along and jnd over 1f out: drvn and hdd ins fnl f: kpt on same pce towards fin* **10/1**

3141 **3** *4* **Major Valentine**[17] 4965 5-9-5 **75**.................................. BenRobinson(5) 8 66
(John O'Shea) *racd towards stands' side: prom: chsd ldr 1/2-way: rdn and edgd lft wl over 1f out: sn rdn and hung lft 1f out: drvn and kpt on one pce* **7/2**[1]

4026 **4** *nk* **Foxtrot Knight**[13] 5098 5-9-12 **77**.................................. JamesSullivan 1 67
(Ruth Carr) *dwlt: sn trcking ldrs: hdwy and n.m.r over 1f out: sltly hmpd 1f out: sn rdn and one pce* **7/1**

540 **5** *2 ¼* **Casterbridge**[35] 4249 5-9-7 **72**..........................(h) NeilFarley 5 53
(Eric Alston) *chsd ldrs centre: rdn along 2f out: sn no imp* **5/1**[3]

4030 **6** *2 ¼* **Roy's Legacy**[14] 5055 8-8-7 **61**.................................. CharlieBennett(3) 2 34
(Shaun Harris) *chsd ldrs centre: rdn along 2f out: sn wknd* **20/1**

260 **7** *5* **Bithynia (IRE)**[28] 4531 3-8-10 **64**.................................. FrannyNorton 7 18
(Christopher Kellett) *in tch: rdn along over 2f out: sn btn* **14/1**

0-11 **8** *¾* **Rainbow Orse**[35] 4278 5-9-12 **77**..........................(p) LukeMorris 4 30
(Robert Cowell) *chsd ldng pair centre: rdn along over 2f out: sn wknd* **9/2**[2]

1m 5.21s (3.71) **Going Correction** +0.825s/f (Soft)
**WFA** 3 from 4yo+ 3lb **8** Ran SP% **112.3**
Speed ratings (Par 103): **103,101,94,94,90 86,78,77**
CSF £37.62 CT £129.99 TOTE £4.80: £1.70, £3.00, £1.60; EX 36.50 Trifecta £201.90.
**Owner** P and Mrs G A Clarke **Bred** M C Humby **Trained** Basford Green, Staffs

**FOCUS**
This looked a decent race for the level and it was run at a good pace. Two came clear.

## 5581 MYRACING.COM H'CAP 2m
**5:40** (5:40) (Class 6) (0-65,67) 3-Y-0 **£3,234** (£962; £481; £240) **Stalls** Low

Form RPR

3-45 **1** **Bodacious Name (IRE)**[17] 4962 3-8-9 **53**.................................. JasonHart 10 66+
(John Quinn) *hld up in midfield: stdy hdwy to trck ldrs 5f out: swtchd lft towards inner over 3f out: sn prom: smooth effrt to ld wl over 1f out: styd on strly: readily* **7/1**

5645 **2** *2 ¼* **General Allenby**[10] 5209 3-8-6 **50**..........................(be) KierenFox 2 55
(Henry Tett) *trckd ldrs: hdwy on inner home turn and led over 4f out: rdn along wl over 2f out: drvn: hdd and edgd lft wl over 1f out: kpt on u.p fnl f: no ch w wnr* **14/1**

4541 **3** *5* **Our Cilla**[12] 5142 3-8-4 **55**..........................(b) MillyNaseb(7) 7 54
(Julia Feilden) *hld up and bhd: stdy hdwy 5f out: chsd ldrs on inner 3f out: rdn along over 2f out: drvn whn sltly hmpd wl over 1f out: one pce after* **11/2**[3]

1522 **4** *19* **Maori Bob (IRE)**[34] 4314 3-9-7 **65**.................................. LouisSteward 6 41
(Michael Bell) *hld up in tch: hdwy to trck ldrs over 6f out: effrt over 3f out and sn pushed along: rdn over 2f out: sn wknd* **15/8**[1]

-433 **5** *28* **Oxford Blu**[15] 5025 3-9-5 **63**..........................(b) LukeMorris 4 6
(Sir Mark Prescott Bt) *led: rdn along and wd st to centre: hdd over 4f out: sn drvn and wknd* **4/1**[2]

2065 **6** *4* **Ulysses (GER)**[15] 5025 3-9-9 **67**..........................(b) PaulHanagan 3 5
(Ralph Beckett) *sn cl up: rdn along and wd st: drvn along over 3f out: sn wknd* **8/1**

000 **7** *5* **Clearance**[27] 4569 3-8-6 **50**.................................. JoeyHaynes 8
(Mark H Tompkins) *hld up: hdwy and in tch over 6f out: rdn along 5f out: sn outpcd and bhd fnl 3f* **20/1**

6303 **8** *3* **Nothing Compares**[10] 5209 3-8-6 **50**.................................. FrannyNorton 9
(Mark Johnston) *trckd ldrs: pushed along 7f out: sn lost pl and bhd fnl 4f* **10/1**

6500 **9** *3* **Company Trader (IRE)**[56] 3489 3-8-4 **48**..........................(b[1]) PaddyAspell 1
(Sharon Watt) *chsd ldrs: rdn along over 6f out: sn lost pl and bhd: t.o fnl 3f* **66/1**

3m 49.79s (15.29) **Going Correction** +0.925s/f (Soft) **9** Ran SP% **115.8**
Speed ratings (Par 98): **98,96,94,84,70 68,66,64,63**
CSF £98.73 CT £579.26 TOTE £8.20: £2.40, £2.00, £2.40; EX 97.40 Trifecta £1581.80 Part won..
**Owner** Excelsior Racing Ltd **Bred** Jude Doherty **Trained** Settrington, N Yorks

**FOCUS**
Outer Track. The rail was set out 4 yards on both bends adding 24 yards to this race. Three pulled miles clear of the remainder in this proper test. It's been rated cautiously.
T/Plt: £320.00 to a £1 stake. Pool: £45,929.03 - 104.75 winning units. T/Qpdt: £39.70 to a £1 stake. Pool: £3,789.85 - 70.51 winning units. **Joe Rowntree**

# 5551 GALWAY (R-H)
Thursday, August 3

**OFFICIAL GOING: Flat course - soft; jumps course - yielding**

## 5582a GUINNESS DRAUGHT H'CAP 1m 98y
**2:50** (2:51) 4-Y-0+ **£10,529** (£3,264; £1,555; £700; £273)

RPR

**1** **Remarkable Lady (IRE)**[10] 5225 4-9-4 **87**..........................(tp) SeanDavis(7) 14 93+
(H Rogers, Ire) *racd in mid-div: pushed along in 6th 3f out: wnt 3rd off home turn: pushed out on wl to ld fnl 150yds* **16/1**

**2** *1 ½* **Cairdiuil (IRE)**[17] 4985 11-8-4 **66** oh4.................................. RoryCleary 6 69
(I Madden, Ire) *chsd clr ldr in 2nd: clsr over 2f out: led appr fnl f tl hdd fnl 150yds: kpt on same pce* **25/1**

**3** *1 ¼* **Tribal Path (IRE)**[8] 5310 7-9-6 **82**..........................(t) ShaneFoley 9 82
(Damian Joseph English, Ire) *led and sn clr: 4 l advantage at 1/2-way: ld reduced over 2f out: hdd appr fnl f: kpt on same pce in 3rd* **11/1**

**4** *hd* **Ace Of Diamonds (IRE)**[120] 1567 4-9-3 **79**.................................. PatSmullen 18 79+
(D K Weld, Ire) *racd in mid-div: pushed along and clsr 5th 1f out: kpt on wl into 4th clsng stages: nvr nrr* **14/1**

**5** *½* **Nebulla**[220] 1018 5-9-7 **83**.................................. GaryCarroll 5 82+
(James Leavy, Ire) *racd in mid-div: swtchd lft appr home turn: wnt 6th ent fnl f: kpt on wl into 5th cl home: nvr nrr* **33/1**

**6** *hd* **Be Kool (IRE)**[17] 4957 4-9-4 **85**..........................(v) DonaghO'Connor(5) 13 83
(Brian Ellison) *chsd ldrs in 3rd: rdn and no imp ent fnl f in 4th: dropped to 6th cl home* **10/1**

**7** *1 ¼* **Spruce Meadows (IRE)**[19] 4929 4-9-9 **88**..........................(p) GaryHalpin(3) 4 83
(John James Feane, Ire) *racd in rr of mid-div: rdn and plenty to do over 2f out: wnt 10th 1f out: kpt on wl into 7th clsng stages: nvr on terms* **9/1**

**8** *1 ¾* **Dinkum Diamond (IRE)**[16] 5011 9-9-4 **85**.................................. KillianLeonard(5) 10 76
(Andrew Slattery, Ire) *racd in rr of mid-div: prog on outer home turn: kpt on wl fnl f: nvr on terms* **20/1**

**9** *shd* **Roibeard (IRE)**[2] 5519 4-8-10 **75**..........................(t) RobbieDowney(3) 16 66
(Eamonn O'Connell, Ire) *racd towards rr: swtchd off rails home turn: styd on strly ins fnl f: nvr nrr* **25/1**

**10** *1* **Clonard Street**[32] 4421 5-8-12 **79**..........................(t) TomMadden(5) 11 68
(A J Martin, Ire) *racd towards rr: rdn and sme prog ent fnl f: nvr nrr* **7/1**[2]

**11** *1 ½* **Aussie Valentine (IRE)**[33] 4384 6-9-13 **89**........(tp) ColmO'Donoghue 12 74
(P D Deegan, Ire) *chsd ldrs: rdn in 6th under 3f out: no imp over 1f out: sn no ex* **10/1**

12 ½ **Collision Course (IRE)**[12] 5174 4-9-3 **79**.......................... ChrisHayes 8 63
(A Oliver, Ire) *nvr bttr than mid-div: rdn and no imp home turn: kpt on one pce* **8/1**[3]
13 1 ½ **Elm Grove (IRE)**[32] 4421 5-9-13 **89**.......................... WJLee 15 70
(W McCreery, Ire) *racd in rr for most: rdn and modest hdwy 2f out: kpt on one pce fr over 1f out: nvr on terms* **20/1**
14 3 ½ **Total Demolition (IRE)**[27] 4590 5-9-0 **76**.......................... ConorHoban 2 49
(J Larkin, Ire) *bit slowly away: racd towards rr for most: modest late hdwy wout ever threatening* **20/1**
15 ½ **Snoozing Indian**[10] 5225 5-9-1 **77**.......................... WayneLordan 17 48
(T J O'Mara, Ire) *chsd ldrs: rdn in 5th 3f out: wknd over 1f out* **40/1**
16 3 ¾ **Fountain (IRE)**[19] 4924 4-9-11 **87**..........................(p[1]) KevinManning 3 50
(J S Bolger, Ire) *nvr bttr than mid-div: rdn and no imp home turn: eased ins fnl f* **20/1**
17 nk **Knockmaole Boy (IRE)**[2] 5519 5-9-4 **80** 6ex........(t) DeclanMcDonogh 7 42
(Gordon Elliott, Ire) *chsd ldrs on inner: pushed along in 7th 3f out: wknd appr fnl f: sn eased* **3/1**[1]
18 4 ½ **Beau Et Sublime (FR)**[32] 4421 7-8-12 **74**..........................(t) ColinKeane 1 26
(A J Martin, Ire) *a towards rr: rdn and no imp 3f out: sn dropped to rr* **16/1**

1m 50.18s (-0.02) **18** Ran SP% **135.7**
CSF £390.43 CT £4721.38 TOTE £18.10: £3.60, £7.20, £2.70, £2.60; DF 863.40.
**Owner** Nap Racing Syndicate **Bred** Miss Ciara Doyle **Trained** Ardee, Co. Louth

**FOCUS**
The softening ground shouldn't have been in the winner's favour, which suggested that conditions might have been a bit better than the official description. The runner-up has been rated back to form.

5583 - 5584a (Foreign Racing) - See Raceform Interactive

## 5490 CLAIREFONTAINE (R-H)
Thursday, August 3

**OFFICIAL GOING: Turf: good**

### 5585a PRIX DES PAQUERETTES (CLAIMER) (2YO FILLIES) (TURF) 7f
**12:10** (12:10) 2-Y-O **£8,119** (£3,247; £2,435; £1,623; £811)

RPR
1 **Palya (FR)**[33] 4389 2-9-8 0..........................(b) AntoineHamelin 12 84
(Matthieu Palussiere, France) **74/10**[3]
2 5 **Joan Jet (FR)**[22] 2-8-11 0.......................... AlexisBadel 13 60
(H-F Devin, France) **9/1**
3 1 **Espaldinha (FR)**[49] 2-8-11 0.......................... TheoBachelot 4 57
(Y Barberot, France) **12/1**
4 1 ½ **Jugeotte (FR)**[38] 4166 2-9-4 0..........................(b) ChristopheSoumillon 1 60
(F Doumen, France) **9/2**[2]
5 ½ **Controversial Lady (IRE)**[20] 4858 2-8-8 0.. MmeAlexiaCeccarello(10) 9 59
(J S Moore) **6/4**[1]
6 1 ¼ **Filrine (FR)** 2-8-11 0.......................... MickaelBerto 11 49
(Jean-Raymond Breton, France) **74/1**
7 shd **First Pond (FR)**[43] 2-8-4 0.......................... AlexisPouchin(7) 6 48
(Y Gourraud, France) **54/1**
8 4 **Vida Loca (FR)**[37] 4196 2-9-1 0.......................... MickaelBarzalona 5 42
(M Boutin, France) **15/2**
9 nk **Scarlett Chope (FR)**[49] 2-8-6 0..........................(p) JessyJolivet(5) 7 37
(R Le Gal, France) **16/1**
10 snk **Lucky Rock (FR)** 2-8-11 0.......................... JulienGuillochon 3 37
(J Merienne, France) **88/1**
11 1 ½ **Miss Milliner**[37] 4196 2-8-6 0.......................... GuillaumeTrolleyDePrevaux(5) 2 33
(Jo Hughes) **73/1**
12 5 **Pif D'Avril (FR)**[37] 4196 2-8-10 0.......................... MlleAlisonMassin(5) 10 24
(F-X De Chevigny, France) **72/1**
13 8 **Fileva (IRE)** 2-8-11 0.......................... CristianDemuro 8
(A Giorgi, Italy) **13/1**

1m 25.2s **13** Ran SP% **119.6**
PARI-MUTUEL (all including 1 euro stake): WIN 8.40; PLACE 2.80, 3.10, 3.60; DF 38.10; SF 75.30.
**Owner** Mrs Theresa Marnane **Bred** Ecurie Euroling **Trained** France

## 5270 BATH (L-H)
Friday, August 4

**OFFICIAL GOING: Good to soft (good in places; 7.9)**
Wind: light against Weather: sunny periods

### 5586 MARSTONS MAIDEN AUCTION STKS 5f 160y
**5:30** (5:31) (Class 5) 2-Y-O **£4,528** (£1,347; £673; £336) **Stalls** Centre

Form RPR
0 1 **Helvetian**[13] 5151 2-8-13 0.......................... DavidEgan(5) 1 82
(Mick Channon) *little slowly away: sn rcvrd to ld: kpt on wl whn strly chal fr 2f out: hld on: rdn out* **6/1**
5 2 nk **Swing Out Sister (IRE)**[27] 4628 2-8-13 0.......................... SamHitchcott 6 76
(Clive Cox) *trckd wnr: chal 2f out: sn rdn: ev ch fnl f: kpt on but hld nring fin* **2/1**[1]
42 3 3 ¼ **Spanish Star (IRE)**[23] 4757 2-9-1 0.......................... LiamKeniry 5 67
(Patrick Chamings) *hld up: hdwy over 2f out: rdn to chal ldng pair over 1f out: no ex ins fnl f* **9/1**
30 4 6 **Avenging Red (IRE)**[18] 4972 2-8-11 0.......................... RoystonFfrench 3 43
(Adam West) *pressed wnr tl rdn over 2f out: sn hld: wknd ent fnl f* **20/1**
3 5 nk **He's Our Star (IRE)**[22] 4805 2-8-11 0.......................... DavidProbert 2 42
(Ali Stronge) *in tch: rdn over 2f out: chal: wknd ent fnl f* **9/4**[2]
624 6 2 ½ **Diamond Express (IRE)**[1] 5561 2-8-8 0.......................... JohnFahy 8 31
(Roger Teal) *trckd ldrs on outer: effrt over 2f out: wknd over 1f out* **11/2**[3]
7 12 **Courteous Crown** 2-8-8 0.......................... TomMarquand 4
(Richard Hannon) *s.i.s: sn in tch: effrt over 2f out: sn wknd* **12/1**
8 4 ½ **Western Dynamisme (FR)** 2-7-13 0.......................... RhiainIngram(7) 9
(Harry Dunlop) *in tch tl outpcd 3f out* **50/1**

1m 12.29s (1.09) **Going Correction** +0.15s/f (Good) **8** Ran SP% **118.2**
Speed ratings (Par 94): **98,97,93,85,84 81,65,59**
CSF £19.13 TOTE £6.60: £1.70, £1.30, £2.60; EX 24.70 Trifecta £115.70.
**Owner** Box 41 **Bred** Whitsbury Manor Stud **Trained** West Ilsley, Berks

**FOCUS**
Add 5yds to race distance. Not a bad little maiden in which the front three came clear, and the form has a solid feel to it given the front two were both strong in the market. Most of the field came down the middle. The third has been rated to form.

### 5587 KINGSTONE PRESS APPLE CLASSIC H'CAP 5f 10y
**6:05** (6:05) (Class 4) (0-80,81) 4-Y-0+ **£6,469** (£1,925; £962; £481) **Stalls** Centre

Form RPR
3445 1 **September Issue**[18] 4979 4-8-12 **75**..........................(p) DavidEgan(5) 6 84
(Gay Kelleway) *led: rdn and narrowly hdd ent fnl f: rallied to regain ld fnl 100yds: drvn out* **10/3**[1]
5022 2 nk **Seamster**[7] 5360 10-8-5 **70**..........................(t) LauraCoughlan(7) 10 78
(David Loughnane) *sn trckd ldrs: rdn into narrow advantage ent fnl f: hdd fnl 100yds: kpt on but no ex* **4/1**[2]
1106 3 2 ½ **Jersey Breeze (IRE)**[7] 5355 4-9-9 **81**..........................(v) RobHornby 8 80
(Mick Channon) *chsd ldrs: sltly outpcd wl over 2f out: kpt on to go 3rd ent fnl f but nt pce to get on terms* **7/1**
6120 4 2 ¼ **Powerful Dream (IRE)**[22] 4795 4-9-0 **72**..........................(p) DavidProbert 11 63
(Ronald Harris) *in tch on outer: swtchd to stands' side and rdn wl over 2f out: one pce fnl f* **12/1**
2024 5 hd **Excellent George**[28] 4566 5-9-7 **79**..........................(t) TomMarquand 9 69
(Stuart Williams) *in tch :hdwy over 2f out: sn rdn: one pce fnl f* **6/1**[3]
2500 6 ¾ **Silverrica (IRE)**[30] 4489 7-8-11 **72**.......................... CharlieBennett(3) 4 59
(Malcolm Saunders) *trckd ldrs: rdn over 2f out: wknd fnl f* **9/1**
6664 7 2 **Waseem Faris (IRE)**[37] 4219 8-9-4 **79**..........................(b[1]) HectorCrouch(3) 12 59
(Ken Cunningham-Brown) *sn prom: rdn over 2f out: wknd ent fnl f* **7/1**
2160 8 ¾ **Air Of York (IRE)**[55] 3573 5-8-7 **65**.......................... JohnFahy 2 43
(John Flint) *a last trio: nvr threatened to get involved* **25/1**
5315 9 1 ¼ **Archimedes (IRE)**[15] 5055 4-8-8 **66**..........................(tp) RoystonFfrench 5 39
(David C Griffiths) *squeezed up leaving stalls: a last trio* **8/1**
3060 10 ½ **Big Amigo (IRE)**[35] 4310 4-8-9 **67**.......................... SamHitchcott 1 38
(Daniel Mark Loughnane) *a towards rr* **25/1**

1m 2.23s (-0.27) **Going Correction** +0.15s/f (Good) **10** Ran SP% **118.9**
Speed ratings (Par 105): **108,107,103,99,99 98,95,94,92,91**
CSF £16.87 CT £86.64 TOTE £3.80: £1.50, £1.70, £2.20; EX 17.80 Trifecta £115.80.
**Owner** Short, Moore, Buy & Kerr **Bred** Bearstone Stud Ltd **Trained** Exning, Suffolk

**FOCUS**
Add 5yds to race distance. Relatively sound 0-80 sprint handicap form give the front two pulled clear. The in-form runner-up looks a solid marker. The runner-up has been rated to his recent form.

### 5588 FROME SCAFFOLDING GROUP H'CAP (BATH SUMMER SPRINT SERIES QUALIFIER) 5f 10y
**6:35** (6:36) (Class 4) (0-80,77) 3-Y-O **£5,822** (£1,732; £865; £432) **Stalls** Centre

Form RPR
0103 1 **Stoneyford Lane (IRE)**[9] 5304 3-9-7 **77**..........................(p) RoystonFfrench 3 84
(Steph Hollinshead) *outpcd in 6th early but in wl tch: hdwy 2f out: drifted lft fnl f: r.o strly: led fnl 60yds* **7/1**
1342 2 1 **Jashma (IRE)**[37] 4200 3-8-13 **69**.......................... ShaneKelly 6 72
(Richard Hughes) *led: drifted lft u.p ent fnl f: hdd fnl 60yds: no ex* **9/2**[2]
1253 3 ¾ **Lightoller (IRE)**[24] 4717 3-8-7 **68**..........................(v) DavidEgan(5) 4 68
(Mick Channon) *prom whn squeezed up after 1f: chsd ldrs: keeping on whn short of room ent fnl f: sn swtchd rt: kpt on cl home but hld* **6/1**[3]
3051 4 1 ¼ **Secret Potion**[9] 5272 3-9-0 **70** 6ex.......................... SamHitchcott 2 68
(Ronald Harris) *pressed ldr: rdn w ev ch whn short of room and snatched up ent fnl f: kpt on but hld after* **9/2**[2]
2222 5 1 ¾ **Secret Agent**[17] 4993 3-8-6 **69**..........................(p) CameronNoble(7) 5 59
(William Muir) *chsd ldrs: rdn over 2f out: ch over 1f out: no ex fnl f* **3/1**[1]
5331 6 9 **Coronation Cottage**[17] 4990 3-8-8 **67**.......................... CharlieBennett(3) 1 24+
(Malcolm Saunders) *prom early: rdn to chse ldrs whn sltly outpcd wl over 2f out: keeping on and looked as though she was abt to mount str chal whn v bdly hmpd ent fnl f: no ch after and eased* **3/1**[1]

1m 2.81s (0.31) **Going Correction** +0.15s/f (Good) **6** Ran SP% **113.1**
Speed ratings (Par 102): **103,101,100,98,95 81**
CSF £38.06 TOTE £7.70: £3.40, £2.50; EX 38.60 Trifecta £189.20.
**Owner** Ocean Four **Bred** J C Bloodstock **Trained** Upper Longdon, Staffs
■ Stewards' Enquiry : Shane Kelly six-day ban; careless riding (19th-24th Aug)

**FOCUS**
Add 5yds to race distance. A weak 0-80 given only one of the runners had an official rating above 70. Three horses had their chances severely impeded by the errant Jashma who hung right across to the inside rail. It's been rated as straightforward form around the second and third.

### 5589 KINGSTONE PRESS SWEET APPLE DYRHAM VASE H'CAP 1m 2f 37y
**7:10** (7:10) (Class 4) (0-80,80) 3-Y-O **£7,762** (£2,310; £1,154; £577) **Stalls** Low

Form RPR
-302 1 **Nathan**[15] 5075 3-9-5 **78**.......................... FergusSweeney 1 88+
(Alan King) *hld up last pair: hdwy over 2f out: shkn up to ld jst oer 1f out: styd on wl: readily* **7/2**[2]
4-22 2 ½ **Seafarer (IRE)**[27] 4640 3-9-0 **80**.......................... TylerSaunders(7) 2 89+
(Marcus Tregoning) *hld up last pair: hdwy in center 2f out: drifted lft but styd on into 2nd ins fnl f: kpt on towards fin but a being hld* **9/4**[1]
0604 3 1 ½ **Annie Fior (IRE)**[27] 4621 3-8-12 **76**..........................(h) DavidEgan(5) 3 82
(Denis Coakley) *racd keenly: sn disputing ld: outrt ldr 6f out: rdn and hdd jst over 1f out: edgd rt and no ex ins fnl f* **5/1**[3]
1-00 4 ¾ **Pivoine (IRE)**[57] 3504 3-9-7 **80**.......................... StevieDonohoe 4 85
(Sir Michael Stoute) *trckd ldrs: rdn wl over 2f out: styd on fnl f but nt quite pce to mount chal* **7/2**[2]
2320 5 ½ **Je Suis Charlie**[28] 4580 3-9-5 **78**.......................... LouisSteward 5 82
(Michael Bell) *trckd ldrs: rdn and ev ch over 1f out: no ex ins fnl f* **5/1**[3]
0023 6 5 **Unit Of Assessment (IRE)**[23] 4764 3-9-1 **74**.......................... DavidProbert 6 68
(William Knight) *led: jnd after 1f: hdd 6f out: trckd ldr: rdn and ev ch over 1f out: wknd ins fnl f* **14/1**

2m 12.0s (1.00) **Going Correction** +0.15s/f (Good) **6** Ran SP% **115.2**
Speed ratings (Par 102): **102,101,100,99,99 95**
CSF £12.26 TOTE £5.20: £2.30, £1.70; EX 11.70 Trifecta £45.60.
**Owner** Normandie Stud Ltd **Bred** Normandie Stud Ltd **Trained** Barbury Castle, Wilts

**FOCUS**
A competitive little race of its type and the winner looks a horse to follow in the short term. It's been rated around the third.

### 5590 KINGSTONE PRESS WILD BERRY CHASE H'CAP (BATH SUMMER STAYERS' SERIES QUALIFIER) 2m 1f 24y
**7:40** (7:40) (Class 5) (0-70,71) 4-Y-0+ **£4,528** (£1,347; £673; £336) **Stalls** Centre

Form RPR
4033 1 **With Pleasure**[9] 5276 4-9-4 **67**.......................... DanielMuscutt 13 74+
(John Flint) *mid-div: travelling wl whn nt clr run jst over 2f out: swtchd rt: hdwy over 1f out: fin strly: led fnl stride* **9/1**

-334 **2** *hd* **Tyrell (IRE)**[31] 4471 4-9-8 **71**....................(b) FergusSweeney 8 76
(Alan King) *led: rdn over 2f out: sn strly chal: jnd ins fnl f: edgd ahd nring fin: hdd fnl stride* **7/2**[1]

612 **3** *hd* **Innoko (FR)**[9] 5274 7-8-13 **62**....................(h) LiamKeniry 6 67
(Robert Stephens) *mid-div: hdwy into 3rd 6f out: rdn for str chal 2f out: disp ld ins fnl f: no ex whn hdd cl home* **6/1**[2]

-353 **4** *½* **Pastoral Music**[23] 4750 4-9-4 **70**.................... CharlieBennett(3) 10 74
(Hughie Morrison) *trckd ldrs: rdn whn tight for room over 1f out: ev ch ins fnl f: kpt on but no ex cl home* **6/1**[2]

0320 **5** *½* **Spiritoftomintoul**[36] 4244 8-9-1 **64**....................(t) ShaneKelly 12 68
(Tony Carroll) *s.i.s: rcvrd to midfield after 2f: rdn and hdwy to chse ldrs over 2f out: styd on same pce fnl f* **20/1**

6322 **6** *hd* **Fitzwilly**[16] 5025 7-8-12 **66**.................... DavidEgan(5) 5 69
(Mick Channon) *mid-div: rdn whn outpcd wl over 2f out: hdwy over 1f out where nt clrest of runs: styd on fnl f* **7/2**[1]

3- **7** *¾* **Rolanna (IRE)**[28] 1993 5-8-2 **51**....................(p) RoystonFfrench 11 54
(W J Martin, Ire) *trckd ldr: rdn over 2f out: nt clr run and swtchd rt over 1f out: styd on same pce fnl f* **13/2**[3]

-600 **8** *nk* **Daghash**[27] 4630 8-9-2 **65**.................... TomMarquand 3 67
(Stuart Kittow) *hld up towards rr: rdn wl over 2f out: styd on fnl f but nt pce to get on terms* **16/1**

6/ **9** *4½* **Lake Shore Drive (IRE)**[38] 1941 5-8-10 **59**.................... StevieDonohoe 2 56
(Johnny Farrelly) *hld up last pair: outpcd 3f out: styd on but nvr gng pce to get involved* **16/1**

-400 **10** *21* **Sunny Future (IRE)**[18] 4966 11-9-7 **70**....................(h) RobertWinston 4 44
(Malcolm Saunders) *hld up bhd: effrt on outer 3f out: nvr threatened: wknd jst over 1f out: eased* **12/1**

3m 56.69s (4.79) **Going Correction** +0.15s/f (Good) **10** Ran SP% **120.6**
Speed ratings (Par 103): **94,93,93,93,93 93,92,92,90,80**
CSF £42.03 CT £211.51 TOTE £11.90: £3.40, £1.30, £2.50; EX 54.80 Trifecta £284.80.
**Owner** Burnham P & D ltd **Bred** Rabbah Bloodstock Limited **Trained** Kenfig Hill, Bridgend
■ Stewards' Enquiry : Liam Keniry four-day ban; used whip above the permitted level (18th-21st Aug)
David Egan two-day ban; careless riding (18th-19th Aug)

**FOCUS**
A wide open staying handicap on paper and, having gone what appeared an even enough gallop, they finished in a big heap.

## 5591 MYRACING.COM VISIT FOR HORSE RACING TIPS FILLIES' H'CAP 1m
**8:10** (8:11) (Class 4) (0-80,79) 3-Y-0+ **£7,115** (£2,117; £1,058; £529) **Stalls** Low

Form RPR

-511 **1** **Madeleine Bond**[22] 4810 3-8-13 **78**.................... NicolaCurrie(7) 8 86+
(Henry Candy) *trckd ldr: rdn over 2f out: led ent fnl f: kpt on wl to assert fnl 120yds* **2/1**[1]

323 **2** *1¾* **Stosur (IRE)**[15] 5062 6-9-3 **73**....................(b) DavidEgan(5) 3 78
(Gay Kelleway) *led: rdn and narrowly hdd over 2f out: ev ch ent fnl f: kpt on but no ex fnl 120yds* **8/1**

2501 **3** *1½* **Heartstone (IRE)**[21] 4845 4-9-4 **72**.................... HectorCrouch(3) 2 74
(David Evans) *trckd ldrs: led over 2f out: sn rdn: hdd ent fnl f: sn no ex* **9/1**

3206 **4** *1¼* **Ventura Blues (IRE)**[13] 5156 3-9-7 **79**....................(p) TomMarquand 6 77
(Richard Hannon) *hld up: rdn over 2f out: styd on fnl f but nt pce to threaten* **13/2**

6145 **5** *3½* **Pattie**[20] 4883 3-9-6 **78**.................... RobHornby 1 68
(Mick Channon) *dwlt: last trio: hdwy whn bmpd 4f out: rdn to chse ldrs over 2f out: swtchd rt over 1f out: fdd fnl f* **9/2**[3]

4-33 **6** *nk* **Stellar Surprise**[34] 4366 3-9-7 **79**....................(t[1]) DanielMuscutt 5 68
(Stuart Williams) *s.i.s: last pair: rdn and sme prog over 2f out: nvr threatened: wknd fnl f* **7/2**[2]

06-6 **7** *2* **Lenoire**[8] 5319 3-8-4 **62**.................... RoystonFfrench 4 46
(Michael Appleby) *trckd ldrs: rdn over 2f out: hld over 1f out: wknd fnl f* **20/1**

6360 **8** *3* **Miss M (IRE)**[111] 1790 3-8-4 **65** ow3.................... CharlieBennett(3) 7 42
(William Muir) *trckd ldrs: rdn over 2f out: hld whn edgd lft over 1f out: wknd* **20/1**

1m 41.75s (0.95) **Going Correction** +0.15s/f (Good)
**WFA** 3 from 4yo+ 7lb **8** Ran SP% **117.7**
Speed ratings (Par 102): **101,99,97,96,93 92,90,87**
CSF £19.77 CT £116.11 TOTE £2.60: £1.10, £2.00, £2.30; EX 23.60 Trifecta £115.50.
**Owner** Candy, Pritchard & Thomas **Bred** Hellwood Stud Farm **Trained** Kingston Warren, Oxon

**FOCUS**
A soundly-run fillies' event and although up in trip, Madeline Bond saw it out strongly to complete the hat-trick. The runner-up has been rated to her recent level for now.
T/Plt: £65.10 to a £1 stake. Pool: £56,551.64 - 633.70 winning units. T/Qpdt: £13.40 to a £1 stake. Pool: £5,445.07 - 300.44 winning units. **Tim Mitchell**

# 5568 GOODWOOD (R-H)
Friday, August 4

**OFFICIAL GOING: Soft (6.3)**
Wind: strong, half against Weather: bright spells, breezy

## 5592 BETFRED GLORIOUS STKS (GROUP 3) 1m 3f 218y
**1:50** (1:50) (Class 1) 4-Y-0+
**£56,710** (£21,500; £10,760; £5,360; £2,690; £1,350) **Stalls** High

Form RPR

2-12 **1** **Poet's Word (IRE)**[85] 2553 4-9-1 113.................... RyanMoore 8 116+
(Sir Michael Stoute) *hld up wl in tch in 4th: effrt to chal ent fnl 2f: led and edgd rt over 1f out: forged ahd ins fnl f: styd on wl: rdn out* **7/4**[1]

-312 **2** *1½* **Second Step (IRE)**[34] 4360 6-9-1 110.................... JamieSpencer 4 113
(Roger Charlton) *lw: dwlt and urged along briefly leaving stall: swtchd lft and sn rcvrd to chse ldr: rdn to led 2f out: sn hdd and carried rt over 1f out: kpt on same pce ins fnl f* **10/3**[2]

0-60 **3** *nk* **Scarlet Dragon**[20] 4918 4-9-1 108....................(h) HollieDoyle 5 112
(Eve Johnson Houghton) *stdd and dropped in bhd after s: t.k.h: hld up off the pce in 5th: clsd and in tch 1/2-way: swtchd lft and effrt over 2f out: chsd ldng pair over 1f out: kpt on u.p* **9/2**

5010 **4** *5* **Snoano**[20] 4918 5-9-1 105.................... DavidAllan 3 104
(Tim Easterby) *trckd ldng pair tl nt clr run over 2f out: sn swtchd lft and effrt 2f out: 4th and no imp over 1f out: plugged on same pce fnl f* **14/1**

0-11 **5** *1¼* **Lord Yeats**[34] 4360 4-9-1 108.................... PJMcDonald 2 102
(Jedd O'Keeffe) *led: rdn and hdd 2f out: sn outpcd and btn 5th over 1f out: plugged on same pce ins fnl f* **7/2**[3]

0020 **6** *6* **Majeed**[20] 4918 7-9-1 102.................... OisinMurphy 7 93
(David Simcock) *stdd s: hld up in rr: struggling 4f: no ch after* **25/1**

2m 42.6s (4.20) **Going Correction** +0.50s/f (Yiel) **6** Ran SP% **110.4**
Speed ratings (Par 113): **106,105,104,101,100 96**
CSF £7.52 TOTE £2.20: £1.40, £2.00; EX 7.20 Trifecta £19.90.
**Owner** Saeed Suhail **Bred** Woodcote Stud Ltd **Trained** Newmarket, Suffolk

**FOCUS**
Fresh ground was used on the lower bend, and race distances were as advertised. Drying conditions, the heavy patches removed from the official description, and the riders reported it was really hard work. Ryan Moore described the ground simply as "bad", while Oisin Murphy said: "It's holding and tacky". This was a bit of a messy race according to Moore, Lord Yeats dictating a stop-start pace, and the time was 9.6sec outside the standard. It wasn't a strong race for the grade, weakened by the defection of Frontiersman, and only the first three produced their true running. Straightforward form, with the second and third rated to marks.

## 5593 BONHAMS THOROUGHBRED STKS (GROUP 3) 1m
**2:25** (2:25) (Class 1) 3-Y-O
**£56,710** (£21,500; £10,760; £5,360; £2,690; £1,350) **Stalls** Low

Form RPR

101 **1** **Beat The Bank**[22] 4817 3-9-1 112.................... RyanMoore 4 116
(Andrew Balding) *lw: t.k.h: hld u wl in tch in midfield: nt clr run and swtchd lft 2f out: gap opened and qcknd through to ld ent fnl f: r.o strly to draw clr ins fnl f: readily* **7/4**[1]

1-01 **2** *3* **Make Time (IRE)**[16] 5032 3-9-1 103.................... AndreaAtzeni 9 109
(David Menuisier) *lw: trckd ldng pair: effrt to chal 2f out: led and edgd lft over 1f out: hdd ent fnl f: outpcd by wnr and battling for 2nd ins fnl f: kpt on* **5/2**[2]

1652 **3** *nk* **Forest Ranger (IRE)**[22] 4817 3-9-1 106.................... TonyHamilton 7 108
(Richard Fahey) *lw: pressed ldr tl pushed into ld jst over 2f out: rdn and hdd over 1f out: outpcd by wnr and battling for 2nd ins fnl f: kpt on* **13/2**

0410 **4** *1¼* **Solomon's Bay (IRE)**[44] 3959 3-9-1 108.................... SilvestreDeSousa 8 105
(Roger Varian) *sn stdd bk to last pair: effrt on outer 2f out: styd on same pce u.p fnl f* **14/1**

0-20 **5** *¾* **Escobar (IRE)**[44] 3959 3-9-1 106....................(p[1]) JamesDoyle 10 104
(Hugo Palmer) *t.k.h: stdd bk to rr after 1f: clsd and nt clr run over 1f out: gap opened and sme hdwy u.p ent fnl f: styd on same pce ins fnl f* **12/1**

2-33 **6** *8* **Zainhom (USA)**[71] 3013 3-9-1 106.................... JimCrowley 5 85
(Sir Michael Stoute) *swtg: led and set stdy gallop: rdn and hdd 2f out: lost pl and btn over 1f out: wknd fnl f* **5/1**[3]

1m 40.83s (0.93) **Going Correction** +0.50s/f (Yiel) **6** Ran SP% **109.3**
Speed ratings (Par 110): **115,112,111,110,109 101**
CSF £5.93 TOTE £2.30: £1.60, £1.60; EX 6.40 Trifecta £25.30.
**Owner** King Power Racing Co Ltd **Bred** A S Denniff **Trained** Kingsclere, Hants

**FOCUS**
Some key non-runners here and not a strong Group 3 as a result, but no doubting the winner's superiority over those remaining. The pace was a steady one. The runner-up has been rated as improving on his handicap latest.

## 5594 BETFRED MILE H'CAP 1m
**3:00** (3:02) (Class 2) 3-Y-0+
**£93,375** (£27,960; £13,980; £6,990; £3,495; £1,755) **Stalls** Low

Form RPR

4502 **1** **Master The World (IRE)**[13] 5157 6-9-7 **103**....................(p) RyanMoore 3 113
(David Elsworth) *on toes: t.k.h: hld up in tch in midfield: hdwy on inner over 1f out: styd on u.p to ld 100yds out: r.o wl: rdn out* **6/1**[2]

4-04 **2** *¾* **Tony Curtis**[20] 4905 4-9-6 **102**.................... SeanLevey 6 110
(Richard Hannon) *hld up in tch in midfield: nt clr run and swtchd lft over 1f out: hdwy u.p 1f out: edging rt but styd on strly ins fnl f: snatched 2nd last stride* **14/1**

-060 **3** *shd* **Birchwood (IRE)**[41] 4072 4-9-6 **102**.................... JamieSpencer 2 110
(Richard Fahey) *t.k.h: chsd ldrs: hdwy to trck ldng pair and travelling wl over 1f out: swtchd lft and chal ent fnl f: drvn to ld and edgd rt jst ins fnl f: hdd 100yds out: kpt on: lost 2nd last stride* **16/1**

1003 **4** *¾* **Withernsea (IRE)**[6] 5393 6-9-1 **97**.................... TonyHamilton 7 103
(Richard Fahey) *lw: t.k.h: chsd ldrs early tl stdd bk into midfield after 2f: hdwy to chse ldrs and nt clrest of runs jst over 1f out: kpt on u.p ins fnl f* **12/1**

-040 **5** *¾* **One Word More (IRE)**[20] 4916 7-8-11 **93**....................(h) DavidAllan 10 97+
(Tim Easterby) *hld up in rr: stl in rr 2f out: swtchd rt and hdwy over 1f out: styng on and forced to switch lft ins fnl f: styd on strly fnl 100yds: nt rch ldrs* **25/1**

2255 **6** *1¼* **Masham Star (IRE)**[6] 5392 3-8-8 **97**.................... PJMcDonald 18 97
(Mark Johnston) *lw: chsd ldr tl rdn to ld 2f out: drvn and hrd pressed ent fnl f: hdd jst ins fnl f: sn carried rt and no ex: wknd wl ins fnl f* **12/1**

0031 **7** *nse* **Zhui Feng (IRE)**[44] 3963 4-9-10 **106**....................(p) MartinDwyer 4 107
(Amanda Perrett) *led: hdd and rdn 2f out: kpt on u.p tl no ex and btn jst ins fnl f: wknd wl ins fnl f* **14/1**

-000 **8** *nse* **Boomshackerlacker (IRE)**[20] 4905 7-9-2 **98**.......(p) FergusSweeney 15 100+
(George Baker) *t.k.h: hld up in tch in rr: hdwy towards inner to chse ldrs whn n.m.r jst over 1f out: keeping on whn nt clr of run and swtchd rt ins fnl f: kpt on but no hope of getting on terms w ldrs after* **33/1**

2100 **9** *nse* **Mythical Madness**[27] 4636 6-9-5 **101**....................(v) DanielTudhope 20 102
(David O'Meara) *hld up in tch towards rr on outer: effrt and squeezed through jst over 1f out: styd on strly ins fnl f: nvr threatened ldrs* **50/1**

124- **10** *nk* **Mustashry**[324] 6482 4-9-9 **105**.................... JimCrowley 8 105
(Sir Michael Stoute) *stdd s: hld up in tch towards rr: nt clr run over 1f out: hdwy u.p 1f out: styd on ins fnl f: nvr trbld ldrs* **14/1**

12-2 **11** *¾* **Blair House (IRE)**[44] 3963 4-9-6 **102**....................(b) WilliamBuick 9 101
(Charlie Appleby) *lw: hld up wl in tch in midfield: effrt u.p but no imp over 1f out: keeping on same pce but btn whn squeezed for room ins fnl f* **5/1**[1]

-216 **12** *1* **Greenside**[27] 4636 6-9-3 **99**.................... MartinHarley 11 95
(Henry Candy) *t.k.h: hld up in midfield: short of room and swtchd to outer after 2f: effrt 2f out: no imp over 1f out: kpt on same pce fnl f* **9/1**

-002 **13** *shd* **Gm Hopkins**[27] 4636 6-9-8 **104**.................... AndreaAtzeni 1 100+
(John Gosden) *lw: hld up in tch in rr: nt clr run ent fnl 2f: swtchd lft and hdwy but stl plenty to do 1f out: keeping on but no hope of getting to ldrs whn squeezed for room and hmpd ins fnl f: no ch after* **13/2**[3]

0500 **14** *5* **Sir Roderic (IRE)**[6] 5393 4-8-11 **93**....................(t[1]) WilliamCarson 17 78
(Rod Millman) *hld up in midfield: swtchd lft and effrt u.p over 2f out: no imp over 1f out: wknd fnl f* **33/1**

1100 **15** *2½* **Gossiping**[6] 5393 5-9-0 **96**....................(v[1]) ShaneKelly 22 75+
(Gary Moore) *lw: t.k.h: hld up in midfield but nvr settled: hdwy to chse ldrs after 2f: lost pl and squeezed for room over 1f out: eased fnl f* **28/1**

5005 **16** *6* **First Selection (SPA)**[20] 4916 4-9-2 **98**........................(e) GrahamLee 13 63
(Simon Crisford) *t.k.h: hld up in midfield but nvr settled: swtchd lft and hdwy after 2f out: chsd ldrs 1/2-way tl lost pl over 1f out: eased fnl f* **28/1**

2110 **17** *1 ½* **G K Chesterton (IRE)**[44] 3963 4-9-3 **99**...................(b[1]) JamesDoyle 14 61
(Charlie Appleby) *t.k.h: chsd ldrs: rdn 2f out: sn struggling: hung rt and lost pl over 1f out: wknd and eased ins fnl f* **17/2**

1m 41.34s (1.44) **Going Correction** +0.50s/f (Yiel)
**WFA** 3 from 4yo+ 7lb **17** Ran SP% **124.7**
Speed ratings (Par 109): **112,111,111,110,109 108,108,108,108,107 107,106,106,101,98 92,91**
CSF £82.45 CT £855.81 TOTE £6.80: £1.80, £3.30, £4.90, £3.00; EX 92.00 Trifecta £1251.10.
**Owner** K Quinn/ C Benham **Bred** A Hanahoe **Trained** Newmarket, Suffolk
■ Stewards' Enquiry : David Allan caution; careless riding

**FOCUS**
Another competitive edition of this valuable handicap, although non-runners meant a slightly smaller field than usual. There was plenty of scrimmaging early on as they didn't go a great pace, and an inside draw proved key with the first four home coming out of the bottom six stalls. The winner has been rated back to the level he reached in this race last year.

## 5595 QATAR KING GEORGE STKS (GROUP 2) 5f
**3:35** (3:35) (Class 1) 3-Y-O+
**£176,991** (£67,101; £33,581; £16,728; £8,395; £4,213) **Stalls** High

Form RPR

3-11 **1** **Battaash (IRE)**[27] 4635 3-8-13 115...................................... JimCrowley 1 125
(Charles Hills) *swtg: taken down early: trckd ldrs and travelled strly: clsd to trck ldr 1/2-way: rdn and led over 1f out: rdn and qcknd clr ins fnl f: r.o strly: impressive* **9/2[3]**

0-22 **2** *2 ¼* **Profitable (IRE)**[45] 3926 5-9-2 116.................................... JamesDoyle 5 118
(Clive Cox) *lw: hld up in tch: hdwy to chse ldrs whn squeezed for room 2f out: swtchd lft and rallied u.p over 1f out: chsd clr wnr ins fnl f: kpt on but no threat to wnr* **9/4[1]**

-132 **3** *¾* **Marsha (IRE)**[20] 4927 4-8-13 115........................................ LukeMorris 7 112
(Sir Mark Prescott Bt) *lw: hld up in midfield: effrt 2f out: 4th and nt clr run 1f out: swtchd lft ins fnl f: styd on to go 3rd wl ins fnl f: no threat to wnr* **9/2[3]**

-051 **4** *¾* **Take Cover**[20] 4920 10-9-2 111............................................. DavidAllan 3 113
(David C Griffiths) *on toes: taken down early and led to s: led: rdn and hdd over 1f out: sn outpcd by wnr: lost 2nd ins fnl f: lost 3rd and wknd wl ins fnl f* **10/1**

0260 **5** *1 ¼* **Washington DC (IRE)**[45] 3926 4-9-2 110....................(bt[1]) RyanMoore 4 108
(A P O'Brien, Ire) *hld up in midfield: effrt and hanging rt over 1f out: swtchd lft and kpt on ins fnl f: no ch w wnr* **4/1[2]**

220 **6** *¾* **Kyllang Rock (IRE)**[20] 4920 3-8-13 107.......................... MartinHarley 2 104
(James Tate) *taken down early: outpcd in last trio: clsd and nt clrest of runs ent fnl f: kpt on u.p ins fnl f: nvr trbld ldrs* **33/1**

1052 **7** *1* **Final Venture**[20] 4920 5-9-2 112...................................... OisinMurphy 11 102
(Paul Midgley) *taken down early: trckd ldrs: effrt over 1f out: sn outpcd and wknd ins fnl f* **16/1**

10/4 **8** *2 ½* **Glass Office**[47] 3867 7-9-2 105...................................... JamieSpencer 9 93
(David Simcock) *stdd and swtchd rt s: outpcd in rr: n.d* **40/1**

1510 **9** *shd* **Priceless**[45] 3926 4-9-2 109................................................ AdamKirby 12 92
(Clive Cox) *pressed ldrs tl 1/2-way: lost pl u.p over 1f out: wknd fnl f* **20/1**

4502 **10** *½* **Kachy**[27] 4615 4-9-2 107.........................................(t) RichardKingscote 8 91
(Tom Dascombe) *pressed ldr tl 1/2-way: sn struggling and lost pl over 1f out: wknd fnl f* **25/1**

0-45 **11** *¾* **Ardad (IRE)**[48] 3835 3-8-13 104..................................... FrankieDettori 10 87
(John Gosden) *on toes: sn outpcd in last trio: hung rt 1/2-way: n.d* **20/1**

58.51s (-1.69) **Going Correction** +0.20s/f (Good)
**WFA** 3 from 4yo+ 3lb **11** Ran SP% **120.9**
Speed ratings (Par 115): **121,117,116,115,113 111,110,106,106,105 104**
CSF £14.42 TOTE £5.30: £2.00, £1.20, £1.60; EX 17.20 Trifecta £61.00.
**Owner** Hamdan Al Maktoum **Bred** Ballyphilip Stud **Trained** Lambourn, Berks

**FOCUS**
Racing far side, this rates strong sprinting form and the winner was most impressive. The runner-up has been rated close to form.

## 5596 BETFRED MOBILE NURSERY H'CAP 6f
**4:10** (4:10) (Class 2) 2-Y-O **£16,172** (£4,812; £2,405; £1,202) **Stalls** High

Form RPR

4100 **1** **Red Roman**[21] 4858 2-8-6 **85**........................................... HarryBentley 10 88
(Charles Hills) *swtg: mde all: rdn over 1f out: asserting whn hung lft 1f out: sn stened and styd on wl ins fnl f: rdn out* **11/2[2]**

0400 **2** *1 ¼* **New Empire**[29] 4527 2-7-11 **79** oh8...........................(b[1]) NoelGarbutt[(3)] 5 78
(Peter Chapple-Hyam) *wnt lft s: hld up in tch: effrt and swtchd lft over 1f out: sn edging bk rt and hdwy 1f out: styd on u.p ins fnl f: wnt 2nd nr fin: nvr getting on terms w wnr* **66/1**

201 **3** *½* **Gift In Time (IRE)**[20] 4888 2-8-3 **82**................................ LukeMorris 3 80
(James Given) *chsd ldrs: effrt to chse wnr wl over 1f out: hung lft u.p and unable qck jst ins fnl f: kpt on same pce after: lost 2nd nr fin* **3/1[1]**

161 **4** *½* **Holy Tiber (IRE)**[36] 4273 2-8-0 **79** oh1............................ JoeyHaynes 8 75
(George Scott) *tall: stdd after s: t.k.h: hld up in tch: effrt over 1f out:edgd rt u.p and hdwy ins fnl f: kpt on wl under hands and heels riding fnl 100yds: nvr getting on terms w wnr* **13/2[3]**

623 **5** *nk* **Carouse (IRE)**[22] 4799 2-8-7 **86** ow2............................ OisinMurphy 6 81
(Andrew Balding) *w'like: trckd ldrs tl lost pl and rdn 2f out: rallied u.p 1f out: kpt on ins fnl f: no threat to wnr* **11/2[2]**

0316 **6** *nk* **Quayside**[14] 5099 2-7-11 **79** oh2................................ AaronJones[(3)] 4 73
(Richard Fahey) *str: lw: w wnr tl wl over 1f out: 3rd and no ex u.p 1f out: wknd wl ins fnl f* **8/1**

1241 **7** *3 ¾* **Rufus King**[21] 4827 2-9-10 **103**................................ SilvestreDeSousa 7 86
(Mark Johnston) *athletic: t.k.h: hld up in tch towards rr: effrt 2f out: nt clrest of runs over 1f out: sn rdn and no imp: btn and eased ins fnl f* **3/1[1]**

033 **8** *2* **Iconic Knight (IRE)**[25] 4696 2-8-0 **79** oh5......................... RyanPowell 9 56
(Ed Walker) *cmpt: lw: stdd s: t.k.h: hld up in tch: urged along 2f out: sn hung lft and outpcd over 1f out: wl btn 1f out* **25/1**

5 **9** *hd* **Royal Diplomat (IRE)**[13] 5162 2-8-1 **80**..................... PatrickMathers 12 57
(Richard Fahey) *str: lw: t.k.h: chsd ldrs tl lost pl u.p over 1f out: wknd ins fnl f* **16/1**

1m 14.42s (2.22) **Going Correction** +0.20s/f (Good) **9** Ran SP% **116.4**
Speed ratings (Par 100): **93,91,90,90,89 89,84,81,81**
CSF £267.27 CT £1296.47 TOTE £5.90: £2.00, £9.80, £1.50; EX 265.20 Trifecta £1310.30.
**Owner** John C Grant & The Hon R J Arculli **Bred** Mrs F S Williams **Trained** Lambourn, Berks

**FOCUS**
Not an especially strong nursery. The runners made their way over towards the far side, although the winner ended up in the centre after veering left. The first three had all contested Group races at Royal Ascot. The fourth, fifth and sixth have been rated close to form.

## 5597 L'ORMARINS QUEENS PLATE OAK TREE STKS (GROUP 3) (F&M) 7f
**4:40** (4:42) (Class 1) 3-Y-O+
**£45,368** (£17,200; £8,608; £4,288; £2,152; £1,080) **Stalls** Low

Form RPR

/1-0 **1** **Al Jazi (IRE)**[41] 4071 4-9-3 108........................................ FrankieDettori 6 111+
(F Rohaut, France) *warm: hld up wl in tch in midfield: effrt to chse ldr jst over 1f out: rdn and qcknd to ld ins fnl f: sn in command and eased cl home: easily* **9/4[1]**

211- **2** *1 ¼* **Eternally**[307] 6939 4-9-3 101................................................ JamesDoyle 8 106
(John Gosden) *lw: led: rdn and qcknd 2f out: drvn ent fnl f: hdd and outpcd by wnr ins fnl f: jst hld 2nd cl home* **9/2[2]**

-116 **3** *hd* **Tomyris**[42] 4031 3-8-11 104............................................ AndreaAtzeni 16 103
(Roger Varian) *hld up in tch in midfield: effrt 2f out: hdwy on outer over 1f out: styd on wl ins fnl f to press for 2nd cl home: no ch w wnr* **7/1**

6-2 **4** *1 ¼* **Wild Approach (GER)**[32] 4518 4-9-3 98......................... JamieSpencer 1 102
(D Moser, Germany) *chsd ldrs: effrt u.p and edgd rt over 1f out: edgd lft and styd on same pce ins fnl f* **11/1**

0-20 **5** *nk* **Same Jurisdiction (SAF)**[44] 3961 6-9-3 100.................. AdamKirby 14 101
(Ed Dunlop) *stdd and dropped in bhd after s: hld up in tch in last pair: effrt over 1f out: styd on ins fnl f: no ch w wnr* **66/1**

1-1 **6** *hd* **Sainted**[34] 4375 4-9-3 91................................................ JimCrowley 15 103+
(William Haggas) *t.k.h: hld up in tch in last trio: clsd and nt clr run over 1f out: sn swtchd lft: styd on ins fnl f: no ch w wnr* **6/1[3]**

0-12 **7** *nse* **Bletchley**[37] 4208 3-8-11 100........................................... OisinMurphy 2 99
(Ralph Beckett) *hld up in tch in midfield: nt enough room on inner over 1f out: gap opened 1f out: kpt on ins fnl: nvr any ch of threatening ldrs* **9/1**

6130 **8** *1 ¼* **Asking (IRE)**[9] 5308 3-8-11 100...................................(t) RyanMoore 3 97+
(A P O'Brien, Ire) *hld up in tch in last trio: nt clr run over 1f out: lost any ch: eventually swtchd lft and kpt on same pce ins fnl f* **9/1**

42-1 **9** *1 ¼* **Tundra**[48] 3825 3-8-11 75...................................... SilvestreDeSousa 13 92
(Roger Varian) *tall: lw: chsd ldrs: effrt 2f out: unable qck and lost pl 1f out: wknd ins fnl f* **50/1**

5002 **10** *1 ½* **Perfect Angel (IRE)**[13] 5149 3-8-11 100......................... MartinDwyer 12 88
(Andrew Balding) *trckd ldr: effrt and tried to chal 2f out: lost pl over 1f out: and sn btn: wknd ins fnl f* **14/1**

1m 29.29s (2.29) **Going Correction** +0.50s/f (Yiel)
**WFA** 3 from 4yo+ 6lb **10** Ran SP% **114.2**
Speed ratings (Par 113): **106,104,104,102,102 102,102,100,99,97**
CSF £11.67 TOTE £2.80: £1.30, £1.70, £2.10; EX 13.20 Trifecta £70.10.
**Owner** Al Shaqab Racing **Bred** Skymarc Farm **Trained** Sauvagnon, France

**FOCUS**
Seven non-runners, but still a good race and the runner-up ensured there was a reasonable gallop. Sound form. The runner-up has been rated close to form, while the third helps set the standard.

## 5598 BETFRED SUPPORTS JACK BERRY HOUSE H'CAP 1m 3f 44y
**5:15** (5:20) (Class 3) (0-90,90) 3-Y-O
**£15,562** (£4,660; £2,330; £1,165; £582; £292) **Stalls** Low

Form RPR

1 **1** **Walton Street**[24] 4720 3-9-1 **84**.................................... WilliamBuick 2 97+
(Charlie Appleby) *tall: lw: dwlt and pushed along early: hld up in last pair: hdwy on outer 2f out: clsng and edging rt over 1f out: led ins fnl f: styd on wl: rdn out* **7/2[2]**

-231 **2** *2* **Londinium**[2] 5525 3-9-7 **90** 6ex.................................... OisinMurphy 5 99
(Mark Johnston) *hld up in tch in midfield: clsd to trck ldrs over 2f out: rdn to chal 2f out: led over 1f out: hdd and styd on same pce ins fnl f* **2/1[1]**

-310 **3** *2 ¼* **See Of Rome**[29] 4535 3-9-1 **84**................................... JamieSpencer 6 89
(Richard Hughes) *hld up in midfield: pushed along briefly after 2f: hdwy and edgd lft u.p 2f out: swtchd rt and clsd over 1f out: wnt 3rd ins fnl f: no imp fnl 100yds* **10/1**

1510 **4** *1* **Shymkent**[43] 3998 3-9-7 **90**....................................... DanielTudhope 4 94
(David O'Meara) *hld ip in last trio: clsd whn nt clr run and hmpd 2f out: swtchd lft and rallied over 1f out: styd on wl ins fnl f: no threat to ldrs* **14/1**

-563 **5** *1* **Count Calabash (IRE)**[33] 4408 3-9-5 **88**.................. CharlesBishop 11 90
(Eve Johnson Houghton) *chsd ldr for 1f: styd chsng ldrs tl clsd to press ldr over 3f out: led over 2f out: drvn and hdd over 1f out: wknd ins fnl f* **25/1**

**6** *3* **Reshoun (FR)**[39] 3-9-4 **87**............................................ JimCrowley 14 84
(Ian Williams) *str: hld up in tch in midfield: effrt and edgd lft u.p 2f out: no imp over 1f out: wknd ins fnl f* **33/1**

2-1 **7** *1 ½* **Opinionate**[202] 237 3-8-12 **81**...................................... AndreaAtzeni 12 76
(Amanda Perrett) *lengthy: lw: stdd s: hld up in last trio: clsd whn squeezed for room and hmpd 2f out: no threat to ldrs and kpt on same pce fr over 1f out* **11/1**

2300 **8** *8* **Bear Valley (IRE)**[20] 4886 3-9-7 **90**.............................. PJMcDonald 13 76
(Mark Johnston) *chsd ldrs: rdn 3f out: lost pl and btn over 1f out: fdd 1f out: eased wl ins fnl f* **16/1**

0013 **9** *3* **Swiftsure (IRE)**[34] 4365 3-9-5 **88**................................. RyanMoore 1 65
(Sir Michael Stoute) *hld up in midfield: short lived effrt 2f out: sn wl btn and eased ins fnl f* **8/1[3]**

-215 **10** *12* **Cross Step (USA)**[29] 4535 3-9-2 **85**.......................(p) JamesDoyle 10 43
(Charlie Appleby) *led for 2f: chsd clr ldr tl clsd to ld again over 3f out: rdn and hdd over 2f out: sn dropped out: bhd and eased fnl f* **20/1**

161- **11** *21* **Star Of The East (IRE)**[314] 6791 3-8-12 **81**.......... SilvestreDeSousa 7 6
(Mark Johnston) *in tch in midfield: effrt over 2f out: sn wnt rt and eased: t.o* **25/1**

0-41 **12** *4* **Tuff Rock (USA)**[56] 3533 3-9-0 **83**.......................(b[1]) PatCosgrave 9
(Ed Walker) *plld hrd: hld up in midfield: nt settle and dashed up to ld after 2f: sn clr: hdd over 3f out: sn dropped out: bhd and eased fnl 2f* **11/1**

2m 29.81s (3.31) **Going Correction** +0.50s/f (Yiel) **12** Ran SP% **120.4**
Speed ratings (Par 104): **107,105,103,103,102 100,99,93,91,82 67,64**
CSF £10.46 CT £65.19 TOTE £4.70: £1.90, £1.30, £2.90; EX 13.90 Trifecta £116.40.
**Owner** Godolphin **Bred** Darley **Trained** Newmarket, Suffolk

**FOCUS**
A decent handicap, won last year by Poet's Word who took the Group 3 Glorious Stakes earlier on this card. It was run at a reasonable gallop. The third and fourth have been rated in line with the race averages.
T/Jkpt: Not won. T/Plt: £26.20 to a £1 stake. Pool: £327,549.93 - 9,103.25 winning units. T/Qpdt: £14.80 to a £1 stake. Pool: £21,086.54 - 1,054.09 winning units. **Steve Payne**

# [5254]MUSSELBURGH (R-H)

Friday, August 4

**OFFICIAL GOING: Good to soft (good in places) changing to soft after race 2 (6.10)**

Wind: Breezy, half against in sprints and in over 3f of home straight on round course Weather: Overcast, raining

## 5599 ALL NEW RACINGUK.COM AMATEUR RIDERS' H'CAP — 1m 5f

5:40 (5:40) (Class 5) (0-70,68) 4-Y-O+ £3,119 (£967; £483; £242) Stalls Low

Form / RPR

3251 **1** **Canny Style**[9] 5284 4-10-13 67 MissJoannaMason 2 75
(Kevin Ryan) *prom: hdwy to ld over 2f out: rdn over 1f out: r.o wl* **13/8**[1]

4500 **2** ¾ **In Focus (IRE)**[46] 3899 6-9-11 51 (h[1]) MissEmmaSayer 5 57
(Dianne Sayer) *awkward s: t.k.h: hld up: hdwy on outside to ld after 3f: hdd over 2f out: sn pushed along and rallied: kpt on same pce last 100yds* **20/1**

2521 **3** shd **Midnight Warrior**[12] 5186 7-10-1 55 (t) MissSBrotherton 3 61
(Ron Barr) *w ldr 2f: cl up: rdn and outpcd 2f out: rallied and edgd lft over 1f out: styd on wl fnl f* **15/2**

0436 **4** 2¼ **Surround Sound**[15] 5080 7-10-5 59 (p) MrWEasterby 6 61
(Tim Easterby) *dwlt and checked s: hld up: stdy hdwy over 2f out: rdn and no imp over 1f out* **17/2**

003 **5** 2¼ **Falcon's Fire (IRE)**[14] 5096 4-10-13 67 (t) MrsCBartley 1 66
(Keith Dalgleish) *hld up on ins: outpcd over 4f out: rallied on ins over 2f out: effrt whn nt clr run briefly over 1f out: hung lft and sn no imp* **7/1**[3]

2664 **6** ¾ **Cosmic Tigress**[10] 5257 6-10-2 59 MrBLynn(3) 4 57
(John Quinn) *in tch: shortlived effrt on outside over 2f out: sn outpcd: n.d after* **13/2**[2]

5335 **7** 1 **Picture Painter (IRE)**[12] 5186 4-9-10 55 (p[1]) MissRHill(5) 8 51
(Jim Goldie) *tok t.k.h: led 3f: cl up tl rdn and wknd fr 2f out* **10/1**

4464 **8** 3½ **Attain**[12] 5183 8-11-0 68 MrSWalker 7 59
(Archie Watson) *prom: pushed along over 5f out: rallied: wknd over 2f out* **15/2**

2m 56.55s (4.55) **Going Correction** +0.45s/f (Yiel) 8 Ran SP% **111.8**
Speed ratings (Par 103): **104,103,103,102,100 100,99,97**
CSF £36.26 CT £189.63 TOTE £2.20: £1.30, £4.80, £1.60; EX 40.80 Trifecta £257.30.
**Owner** Hambleton Racing Ltd XXXVII **Bred** Biddestone Stud Ltd **Trained** Hambleton, N Yorks

**FOCUS**
All distances as advertised. A moderately-run handicap for amateur riders which developed into a bit of a sprint up the straight, and those who raced prominently were favoured. The third has been rated close to form.

## 5600 IRISH STALLIONS FARMS EBF NOVICE STKS — 7f 33y

6:10 (6:11) (Class 5) 2-Y-O £3,234 (£962; £481; £240) Stalls Low

Form / RPR

51 **1** **Myboyhenry (IRE)**[10] 5255 2-9-3 0 CliffordLee(3) 9 80+
(K R Burke) *t.k.h: mde all: shkn up and qcknd over 1f out: kpt on wl fnl f* **9/4**[2]

33 **2** ¾ **Phoenix Lightning (IRE)**[21] 4834 2-9-2 0 PaulHanagan 4 72
(Richard Fahey) *s.i.s: hld up in last pl: hdwy and rdn over 1f out: chsd wnr ins fnl f: kpt on strly towards fin* **7/2**[3]

**3** 1¾ **Baileys Excelerate (FR)** 2-9-2 0 JoeFanning 1 68+
(Mark Johnston) *trckd ldrs: effrt and rdn 2f out: wnt 2nd briefly 1f out: one pce* **5/1**

04 **4** ½ **Bibbidibobbidiboo (IRE)**[21] 4834 2-8-11 0 ShaneGray 6 61
(Ann Duffield) *chsd wnr: rdn 2f out: outpcd fr 1f out* **33/1**

462 **5** 3¼ **Collateral (IRE)**[28] 4577 2-9-2 78 JamesSullivan 3 58
(James Tate) *trckd ldrs: rdn over 2f out: wknd over 1f out* **2/1**[1]

**6** 3¾ **Out Last** 2-8-6 0 RowanScott(5) 5 44
(Keith Dalgleish) *hld up: shortlived effrt on outside over 2f out: wknd over 1f out* **22/1**

6 **7** 6 **American Ruby (USA)**[18] 4963 2-8-11 0 JasonHart 2 29
(Mark Johnston) *prom tl rdn and wknd over 2f out* **28/1**

1m 31.52s (2.52) **Going Correction** +0.45s/f (Yiel) 7 Ran SP% **113.7**
Speed ratings (Par 94): **103,102,100,99,95 91,84**
CSF £10.36 TOTE £2.20: £2.00, £1.80; EX 9.90 Trifecta £35.70.
**Owner** Mrs M Gittins **Bred** Jim McDonald **Trained** Middleham Moor, N Yorks

**FOCUS**
A 7f juvenile novice run at just an ordinary gallop in which the winner defied a big market drift to win his second race over C&D a shade cosily. The winner has been rated to form, while the runner-up and fourth help set the standard.

## 5601 WISE BETTING AT RACINGUK.COM H'CAP — 7f 33y

6:45 (6:45) (Class 5) (0-75,79) 3-Y-O+ £3,234 (£962; £481; £240) Stalls Low

Form / RPR

410 **1** **The Stalking Moon (IRE)**[17] 5007 3-9-6 74 JasonHart 1 80
(John Quinn) *led 1f: trckd ldrs: led over 2f out: rdn and edgd lft ins fnl f: hld on wl* **11/4**[1]

0005 **2** 1¼ **Roaring Forties (IRE)**[11] 5213 4-10-1 77 JoeFanning 7 82
(Rebecca Bastiman) *s.i.s: hld up in last pl: effrt and hdwy on outside over 1f out: chsd wnr ins fnl f: r.o* **11/1**[3]

-001 **3** 2¾ **Echo Of Lightning**[21] 4851 7-9-10 77 (p) MeganNicholls(5) 6 75
(Brian Ellison) *t.k.h: cl up: effrt and ev ch briefly over 2f out: sn chsng wnr: no ex and lost 2nd ins fnl f* **5/1**[2]

4-45 **4** nk **Pepys**[27] 4602 3-8-8 62 ConnorBeasley 3 57
(Bryan Smart) *cl up: drvn and ev ch briefly over 2f out: kpt on same pce fnl f* **5/1**[2]

0552 **5** 1 **Curzon Line**[21] 4833 8-9-6 68 NathanEvans 2 63
(Michael Easterby) *hld up in tch: effrt and pushed along over 2f out: no imp fr over 1f out* **5/1**[2]

0046 **6** 4½ **Rock N Rolla (IRE)**[7] 5376 3-9-9 77 (b[1]) PaulMulrennan 5 58
(Keith Dalgleish) *t.k.h: led after 1f: rdn over 3f out: hdd over 2f out: btn whn hung lft over 1f out* **11/4**[1]

1m 31.84s (2.84) **Going Correction** +0.45s/f (Yiel)
**WFA** 3 from 4yo+ 6lb 6 Ran SP% **111.7**
Speed ratings (Par 103): **101,99,96,96,94 89**
CSF £32.36 TOTE £3.10: £1.40, £4.70; EX 22.50 Trifecta £65.00.
**Owner** D Ward Racing **Bred** Norman Orminston **Trained** Settrington, N Yorks

**FOCUS**
The going was changed to soft before this race. This was a strongly-run handicap in which the first two were clear but the form is unlikely to prove anything special. The third has been rated close to his previous best soft ground figures.

## 5602 BERNARD HUNTER MOBILE CRANES H'CAP — 5f 1y

7:20 (7:20) (Class 3) (0-90,91) 3-Y-O+ £8,409 (£2,502; £1,250; £625) Stalls High

Form / RPR

20 **1** **Rural Celebration**[25] 4686 6-9-10 90 (v) TomEaves 12 97
(Kevin Ryan) *prom: hdwy to ld over 1f out: drvn and hrd pressed fnl f: hld on gamely towards fin* **12/1**

-400 **2** hd **Mayleaf Shine (IRE)**[6] 5402 3-9-5 88 (h[1]) NathanEvans 3 93
(Iain Jardine) *hld up: effrt whn nt clr run briefly over 1f out: kpt on wl fnl f to take 2nd cl home: jst hld* **14/1**

0-23 **3** nk **Fumbo Jumbo (IRE)**[9] 5281 4-9-4 84 ConnorBeasley 13 89
(Michael Dods) *cl up: drvn and ev ch over 1f out: sn chsng wnr: kpt on fnl f: no ex and lost 2nd cl home* **7/2**[1]

6034 **4** nk **Lathom**[14] 5098 4-8-13 82 (v) JoshDoyle(3) 7 86
(David O'Meara) *hld up: rdn and hdwy over 1f out: kpt on fnl f: nrst fin* **8/1**

0000 **5** 1½ **Desert Law (IRE)**[21] 4867 9-9-9 89 PaulMulrennan 5 88
(Paul Midgley) *hld up in tch: effrt and drvn along over 1f out: no ex last 100yds* **7/1**

0536 **6** 2¼ **Economic Crisis (IRE)**[10] 5256 8-8-8 74 JamesSullivan 8 65
(Colin Teague) *hld up midfield on outside: rdn along over 2f out: no imp fr over 1f out* **25/1**

4010 **7** ½ **Tylery Wonder (IRE)**[21] 4867 7-9-4 84 (b) DougieCostello 10 73
(Paul Midgley) *led at str gallop: hdd over 1f out: sn wknd* **11/1**

1550 **8** 3 **Queen In Waiting (IRE)**[20] 4889 3-9-8 91 JoeFanning 9 68
(Mark Johnston) *prom on outside: rdn over 2f out: wknd over 1f out* **11/2**[2]

-02 **9** nk **Alsvinder**[28] 4566 4-9-2 82 DavidNolan 2 59
(David O'Meara) *dwlt: hld up on outside: hung rt and pushed along over 2f out: sn wknd* **12/1**

2-04 **10** nk **Apricot Sky**[6] 5426 7-8-9 80 BenRobinson(5) 6 56
(Brian Ellison) *sat down as stalls opened: bhd: rdn along over 2f out: no imp over 1f out* **13/2**[3]

16- **11** shd **Rozy Boys**[244] 8209 3-8-13 87 RowanScott(5) 11 62
(David Barron) *dwlt: bhd: struggling 1/2-way: sn btn* **12/1**

1m 0.9s (0.50) **Going Correction** +0.275s/f (Good)
**WFA** 3 from 4yo+ 3lb 11 Ran SP% **116.5**
Speed ratings (Par 107): **107,106,106,105,103 99,98,94,93,93 93**
CSF £166.70 CT £728.73 TOTE £15.10: £3.80, £4.40, £1.90; EX 144.30 Trifecta £1061.10.
**Owner** Hambleton Racing Ltd - Two Chances **Bred** J A And M A Knox **Trained** Hambleton, N Yorks

**FOCUS**
A competitive sprint run at a strong pace, and the first five were clear. The third has been rated to form.

## 5603 25 YEARS OF THE SCOTTISH SENIOR OPEN NURSERY H'CAP — 5f 1y

7:50 (7:50) (Class 5) (0-75,76) 2-Y-O £3,234 (£962; £481; £240) Stalls High

Form / RPR

521 **1** **Camacho Chief (IRE)**[20] 4895 2-9-7 75 PaulMulrennan 4 85+
(Michael Dods) *prom: sn pushed along: bk on bridle and gd hdwy to ld 1f out: edgd lft and sn clr: readily* **9/4**[1]

4264 **2** 2¾ **Seen The Lyte (IRE)**[4] 5479 2-9-0 68 JasonHart 1 66
(John Quinn) *prom: hdwy to chal over 1f out: rdn and kpt on ins fnl f: no ch w ready wnr* **11/2**

043 **3** 2 **Curzon (IRE)**[17] 4996 2-9-0 68 DavidNolan 8 59
(David O'Meara) *sn outpcd and bhd: hdwy over 1f out: kpt on fnl f: nvr able to chal* **11/1**

0232 **4** 1¼ **Charnock Richard**[6] 5398 2-9-8 76 TomEaves 3 62
(David Brown) *chsd clr ldr: hdwy to ld briefly over 1f out: wknd ins fnl f* **4/1**[2]

0650 **5** 1¼ **Lord Of The Glen**[53] 3648 2-8-5 59 (p) NathanEvans 5 41
(Jim Goldie) *dwlt: bhd and outpcd: hdwy over 1f out: nvr able to chal* **16/1**

502 **6** 2 **Kikini Bamalaam (IRE)**[23] 4740 2-8-2 56 JoeFanning 7 31
(Keith Dalgleish) *bhd and sn outpcd: hung rt 1/2-way: btn over 1f out* **5/1**[3]

2535 **7** 3¾ **Shay C**[21] 4866 2-8-8 67 PhilDennis(5) 9 28
(Declan Carroll) *led at str gallop: rdn and hdd over 1f out: sn wknd* **13/2**

550 **8** 1½ **Holmfirst**[49] 3791 2-8-0 54 oh5 JamesSullivan 11 10
(Paul Midgley) *towards rr: drvn and struggling 1/2-way: sn btn* **28/1**

1m 2.07s (1.67) **Going Correction** +0.275s/f (Good) 8 Ran SP% **113.8**
Speed ratings (Par 94): **97,92,89,87,85 82,76,73**
CSF £14.79 CT £110.75 TOTE £2.50: £1.10, £2.30, £3.70; EX 14.90 Trifecta £145.30.
**Owner** Exors Of The Late Ron Davison **Bred** Doc Bloodstock **Trained** Denton, Co Durham

**FOCUS**
A strongly-run nursery with a progressive winner and a race in which they finished well strung out. The runner-up has been rated close to form.

## 5604 BOOGIE IN THE MORNING H'CAP — 1m 208y

8:20 (8:21) (Class 5) (0-70,72) 3-Y-O £3,234 (£962; £481; £240) Stalls Low

Form / RPR

0-20 **1** **Pantera Negra (IRE)**[12] 5185 3-9-3 66 NathanEvans 8 73
(David Barron) *trckd ldrs: rdn to ld over 1f out: kpt on wl fnl f* **16/1**

4232 **2** ¾ **Golconda Prince (IRE)**[24] 4721 3-9-2 65 PaulHanagan 10 71
(Richard Fahey) *t.k.h early: led: rdn over 2f out: hdd over 1f out: rallied: hld nr fin* **3/1**[2]

2300 **3** 1½ **Inglorious**[4] 5485 3-8-10 64 (v) RowanScott(5) 9 67
(Keith Dalgleish) *s.i.s: hld up on outside: stdy hdwy and cl up over 2f out: rdn and edgd rt over 1f out: no ex ins fnl f* **12/1**

01 **4** nk **Snowy Winter (USA)**[15] 5073 3-8-13 62 (t) PaulMulrennan 2 64
(Archie Watson) *trckd ldrs: pushed along 3f out: rallied: one pce fr over 1f out* **4/1**[3]

2214 **5** 2¾ **Valentino Boy (IRE)**[20] 4894 3-9-4 72 BenRobinson(5) 3 68
(Brian Ellison) *t.k.h: pressed ldr: rdn and ev ch over 2f out to over 1f out: wknd ins fnl f* **11/4**[1]

0053 **6** shd **Coral Princess (IRE)**[10] 5254 3-8-2 51 oh5 JoeFanning 4 47
(Keith Dalgleish) *hld up: effrt and pushed along over 2f out: no imp over 1f out* **7/1**

0-02 **7** shd **Twiggy**[67] 3142 3-9-4 67 (h) DavidNolan 1 63
(Iain Jardine) *hld up: pushed along over 2f out: sn no imp: hld whn hung lft ins fnl f* **7/1**

1m 58.44s (4.54) **Going Correction** +0.45s/f (Yiel) 7 Ran SP% **110.2**
Speed ratings (Par 100): **97,96,95,94,92 92,92**
CSF £59.09 CT £573.27 TOTE £16.80: £5.20, £1.90; EX 58.70 Trifecta £518.70.
**Owner** D G Pryde **Bred** Lynch Bages & Camas Park Stud **Trained** Maunby, N Yorks



The Form Book Flat, Raceform Ltd, Newbury, RG14 5SJ

**FOCUS**
A moderately-run affair with several taking a keen grip early. The form is unlikely to be anything special. It's been rated around the runner-up to his Pontefract latest.

## 5605 BET AT RACINGUK.COM H'CAP 5f 1y
8:50 (8:50) (Class 6) (0-65,66) 3-Y-0+ £2,587 (£770; £384; £192) Stalls High

Form RPR
3011 1 **Culloden**[7] 5377 5-9-2 61 .....(v) ManuelFernandes(7) 2 69
(Shaun Harris) *cl up: led after 1f: mde rest: hrd pressed fnl f: hld on wl towards fin* 9/4[1]
4042 2 ¾ **Nuala Tagula (IRE)**[6] 5418 4-9-4 56 .....(t) JasonHart 6 61
(John Quinn) *chsd ldrs: hdwy over 1f out: ev ch and rdn ent fnl f: one pce last 75yds* 9/4[1]
40 3 1 ¼ **Lizzy's Dream**[4] 5472 9-8-7 45 ..... ConnorBeasley 1 46
(Rebecca Bastiman) *bhd and outpcd: hdwy on outside over 1f out: kpt on fnl f: nt rch first two* 6/1[3]
2161 4 1 **Kodimoor (IRE)**[15] 5069 4-9-10 62 .....(bt) JoeFanning 9 59
(Christopher Kellett) *led 1f: pressed ldr: rdn and ev ch over 1f out: no ex ins fnl f* 9/2[2]
-230 5 2 ¼ **Luv U Always**[6] 5418 3-8-12 53 ..... TomEaves 3 41
(Iain Jardine) *dwlt: t.k.h in rr: pushed along 2f out: sn no imp* 28/1
-003 6 3 ¾ **Brendan (IRE)**[10] 5260 4-8-7 45 ..... JamesSullivan 8 20
(Jim Goldie) *hld up in tch: outpcd over 2f out: btn over 1f out* 10/1
0050 7 5 **Emerald Secret (IRE)**[9] 5283 3-8-13 54 .....(b[1]) PaulMulrennan 7 10
(Paul Midgley) *in tch early: sn outpcd and pushed along: struggling fr 1/2-way* 12/1

1m 1.86s (1.46) **Going Correction** +0.275s/f (Good)
**WFA** 3 from 4yo+ 3lb 7 Ran SP% 114.2
Speed ratings (Par 101): **99,97,95,94,90 84,76**
CSF £7.21 CT £24.92 TOTE £2.80: £1.80, £1.90; EX 8.60 Trifecta £29.20.
**Owner** Burflex (Scaffolding) Ltd **Bred** Burton Agnes Stud Co Ltd **Trained** Carburton, Notts

**FOCUS**
A good gallop to this low-grade sprint handicap in which the winner completed a hat-trick but the form isn't strong. A length pb from the winner, with the runner-up rated close to form.
T/Plt: £141.70 to a £1 stake. Pool: £48,709.67 - 250.82 winning units. T/Qpdt: £40.50 to a £1 stake. Pool: £4,107.89 - 74.91 winning units. **Richard Young**

# 5420 NEWMARKET (R-H)
Friday, August 4

**OFFICIAL GOING: Good (good to soft in places)**
Wind: light breeze Weather: hot and sunny; 22 degrees

## 5606 FLY LONDON SOUTHEND AIRPORT TO PERPIGNAN H'CAP 6f
5:20 (5:25) (Class 5) (0-75,76) 3-Y-0 £3,881 (£1,155; £577; £288) Stalls High

Form RPR
0-3 1 **Glenamoy Lad**[23] 4759 3-9-7 75 .....(t) FrannyNorton 2 82+
(Michael Wigham) *uns rdr bef loading: racd in last pl on far rails tl swtchd rt and drvn over 1f out: str run on outer to ld cl home* 7/1[3]
2562 2 ½ **Bellevarde (IRE)**[8] 5325 3-8-7 61 ..... JosephineGordon 5 66
(Richard Price) *led: rdn and tried to qckn over 2f out: looked probable wnr and drvn ins fnl f: one pce and ct nr fin* 2/1[1]
-005 3 shd **Anfaass (IRE)**[13] 5159 3-9-8 76 ..... FranBerry 4 80
(George Margarson) *prom: rdn over 2f out: ev ch 100yds out: nt qckn after* 7/1[3]
-110 4 1 **Debonaire David**[9] 5271 3-9-4 72 .....(t) KieranShoemark 3 73
(Richard Hughes) *racd keenly on outside: pressed ldrs: hrd drvn over 2f out: remained in contention tl no ex fnl 100yds* 7/1[3]
2-50 5 ½ **Fareeq**[35] 4313 3-9-5 76 .....(t) LewisEdmunds(3) 6 75
(Charlie Wallis) *towards rr: rdn and brief oeffrt over 2f out: no ex ins fnl f* 20/1
03-0 6 1 **Norwegian Highness (FR)**[66] 3171 3-9-5 73 ..... TimmyMurphy 7 69
(Kevin Ryan) *taken down early: stdd s: plld hrd: chsd ldrs: rdn and nt qckn over 1f out* 16/1
0-21 7 1 **Peace Dreamer (IRE)**[41] 4106 3-9-7 75 ..... GeorgeDowning 1 68
(Robert Cowell) *jnd ldr after 2f: rdn over 1f out: wknd ins fnl f* 5/2[2]

1m 14.48s (1.98) **Going Correction** +0.175s/f (Good) 7 Ran SP% 110.0
Speed ratings (Par 100): **93,92,92,90,90 88,87**
CSF £19.82 TOTE £6.00: £2.90, £1.60; EX 21.80 Trifecta £104.70.
**Owner** V Healy **Bred** Mrs T A Foreman **Trained** Newmarket, Suffolk

**FOCUS**
Far side course. Stalls: far side, apart from 1m2f and 1m4f: centre. There was 6mm of rain on Wednesday, but it had been largely dry since then and the going was given as good, good to soft in places (GoingStick: 7.2). The re-positioning of the bend into the home straight increased the distance of the 1m2f and 1m4f races by 19yds. The early pace wasn't that strong but the winner came from last to first. The winner has been rated back to his Irish 2yo form, with the runner-up close to her recent form.

## 5607 FLY LONDON SOUTHEND AIRPORT TO MILAN FILLIES' H'CAP 1m 4f
5:55 (5:55) (Class 5) (0-70,72) 3-Y-0+ £3,881 (£1,155; £577; £288) Stalls Centre

Form RPR
40-5 1 **Kerrera**[83] 2615 4-9-5 60 ..... FranBerry 3 70
(Paul Webber) *trckd ldrs: effrt gng wl 4f out: led wl over 1f out: rdn and in command thrght fnl f: styd on stoutly* 6/1
5-51 2 3 ½ **Rowlestonerendezvu**[18] 4967 4-9-2 57 ..... GeorgeDowning 5 61
(Tony Carroll) *settled towards rr: prog to press ldrs 3f out: rdn to go 2nd over 1f out: outstyd by wnr fnl 100yds* 9/2[3]
240 3 2 ½ **Tapdancealltheway**[72] 2963 3-9-2 67 ..... SteveDrowne 4 68
(Amanda Perrett) *chsd ldrs: clsd 5f out: led 4f out: sn rdn: hdd wl over 1f out: plugged on same pce ins fnl f* 8/1
000 4 10 **Melanna (IRE)**[62] 3311 6-9-5 63 ..... LewisEdmunds(3) 7 47
(Richard Ford) *sn led: hdd 6f out: rdn 4f out: stl ev ch 2f out: dropped out qckly over 1f out* 3/1[1]
2116 5 2 **Multigifted**[30] 4499 4-10-0 72 .....(t) GeorgeWood(3) 8 53
(Michael Madgwick) *racd freely: clsd up: pushed along 4f out: fdd over 2f out* 6/1
5-46 6 3 ½ **Eastern Lady (IND)**[15] 5049 4-9-2 64 .....(t) JonathanFisher(7) 6 39
(Richard Price) *t.k.h: sn prom: 2nd 4f out: rdn and lost pl 3f out: t.o fnl f* 25/1
335 7 3 ¾ **Dalavida (FR)**[139] 1259 3-8-8 64 ..... GeorgeBuckell(5) 1 34
(David Simcock) *t.k.h in last: lost tch over 3f out: t.o over 1f out* 14/1
6-45 8 88 **Star Of Doha**[59] 3425 3-9-4 69 ..... JosephineGordon 2
(Ralph Beckett) *plld hrd: cl up: led 6f out: hung bdly lft and ended up on far side: rdn and hdd 4f out: dropped out rapidly: t.o and virtually p.u 1f out* 4/1[2]

2m 35.22s (2.32) **Going Correction** +0.175s/f (Good)
**WFA** 3 from 4yo+ 10lb 8 Ran SP% 113.4
Speed ratings (Par 100): **99,96,95,88,87 84,82,23**
CSF £32.47 CT £215.95 TOTE £5.80: £1.90, £1.50, £2.70; EX 28.90 Trifecta £193.30.
**Owner** Mrs Gwen Thomas **Bred** Millsec Limited **Trained** Mollington, Oxon

**FOCUS**
Race distance increased by 19yds. They finished well strung out here. It's been rated to the better view of the runner-up's form.

## 5608 FLY LONDON SOUTHEND AIRPORT TO LYON EBF NOVICE STKS (PLUS 10 RACE) 6f
6:25 (6:25) (Class 4) 2-Y-0 £4,528 (£1,347; £673; £336) Stalls High

Form RPR
1 **Crossing The Line** 2-8-11 0 ..... JimmyQuinn 3 73+
(Andrew Balding) *plld hrd in 3rd pl: swtchd rt over 1f out: rdn to ld ins fnl f: hrd pressed but hld on wl cl home* 9/1
2 nk **Gabr** 2-9-2 0 ..... TedDurcan 5 77+
(Sir Michael Stoute) *lost 6 l s: bhd: pushed along and effrt over 1f out: styd on strly ins fnl f: jst failed: promising* 7/2[2]
2 3 1 ¾ **Warsaan**[29] 4534 2-9-2 0 ..... DaneO'Neill 1 72+
(Owen Burrows) *dwlt: t.k.h and sn rcvrd to press ldrs: hrd drvn 2f out: nt qckn fnl 100yds* 6/5[1]
4 4 hd **Gossip Column (IRE)**[25] 4696 2-9-2 0 ..... FranBerry 4 71
(Charles Hills) *cl 2nd tl led over 2f out: sn rdn: hdd ins fnl f: nt qckn last 100yds* 6/1[3]
53 5 3 ½ **Sunbreak (IRE)**[9] 5278 2-9-2 0 ..... FrannyNorton 6 61
(Mark Johnston) *led: drvn and hdd over 2f out: fdd fnl 120yds* 13/2
6 1 ¼ **Georgian Manor (IRE)** 2-9-2 0 ..... JosephineGordon 2 57
(Sir Michael Stoute) *rn green: sn last and drvn along: outpcd thrght but stl plugging on ins fnl f* 14/1

1m 14.54s (2.04) **Going Correction** +0.175s/f (Good) 6 Ran SP% 112.0
Speed ratings (Par 96): **93,92,90,90,85 83**
CSF £39.73 TOTE £10.50: £3.90, £2.00; EX 48.10 Trifecta £103.30.
**Owner** Sheikh Juma Dalmook Al Maktoum **Bred** Mrs F S Williams **Trained** Kingsclere, Hants

**FOCUS**
Not a bad novice race, and the first two both ran with promise for the future. It's been rated around the fourth and fifth.

## 5609 FLY LONDON SOUTHEND AIRPORT TO PRAGUE H'CAP 1m 2f
7:00 (7:00) (Class 3) (0-90,92) 3-Y-0+ £7,762 (£2,310; £1,154; £577) Stalls Centre

Form RPR
2-1 1 **Game Starter (IRE)**[41] 4097 3-9-2 90 .....(p[1]) SilvestreDeSousa 2 107+
(Saeed bin Suroor) *mde all: rdn over 1f out: fnd plenty and wl in command after* 4/5[1]
2503 2 4 ½ **Brorocco**[16] 5037 4-9-9 89 .....(h) JimmyQuinn 5 96
(Andrew Balding) *taken down early: hld ip in last pce: effrt on outside over 2f out: rdn and tried to chal 1f out: one pced and sn no match for wnr* 9/2[2]
1412 3 2 ¾ **Visitant**[21] 4865 4-9-5 85 ..... JamesDoyle 7 87
(David Thompson) *chse ldrs: drvn and outpcd 2f out: plugged on to take mod 3rd cl home* 6/1[3]
0432 4 1 **Dr Julius No**[21] 4861 3-8-11 92 ..... StephenCummins(7) 3 93
(Richard Hughes) *t.k.h in 3rd pl: effrt 3f out: sn rdn: wknd ins fnl f: lost 3rd cl home* 8/1
2004 5 4 **Grapevine (IRE)**[28] 4585 4-9-8 88 ..... WilliamBuick 6 80
(Charles Hills) *racd keenly: towards rr: rdn over 2f out: no rspnse and btn over 1f out* 16/1
6300 6 4 ½ **Farquhar (IRE)**[27] 4614 6-9-8 88 .....(h) LukeMorris 8 71
(Michael Appleby) *pressed ldr on outer: rdn and lost pl over 2f out: sn racing awkwardly* 20/1

2m 5.58s (0.08) **Going Correction** +0.175s/f (Good)
**WFA** 3 from 4yo+ 8lb 6 Ran SP% 109.8
Speed ratings (Par 107): **106,102,100,99,96 92**
CSF £4.43 CT £10.58 TOTE £1.50: £1.10, £1.90; EX 4.70 Trifecta £11.40.
**Owner** Godolphin **Bred** Darley **Trained** Newmarket, Suffolk

**FOCUS**
Race distance increased by 19yds. A decent handicap won by a promising sort. The fourth has been rated close to form.

## 5610 FLY LONDON SOUTHEND AIRPORT TO BUDAPEST H'CAP 7f
7:30 (7:30) (Class 4) (0-85,86) 4-Y-0+ £5,175 (£1,540; £769; £384) Stalls High

Form RPR
0062 1 **Mountain Rescue (IRE)**[13] 5159 5-9-6 83 ..... JamesDoyle 11 96+
(Chris Wall) *pressed ldng pair: drvn to ld over 1f out: 3 l clr 120yds out: eased cl home* 11/4[1]
-003 2 2 **Summer Chorus**[14] 5117 4-9-7 84 ..... JimmyQuinn 9 91
(Andrew Balding) *dwlt: in rr tl 1/2-way: gd prog 2f out: rdn to go 2nd ins fnl f: kpt on but no match for wnr* 7/1[2]
3163 3 2 **Ross Raith Rover**[32] 4446 4-8-4 67 .....(p) PaoloSirigu 6 69
(Robert Eddery) *outpcd in rr tl 1/2-way: rdn and hdwy 2f out: wnt 3rd ins fnl f: no ch w wnr* 25/1
5134 4 1 **Qeyaadah (IRE)**[13] 5159 4-9-6 86 ..... GeorgeWood(3) 7 85
(Michael Appleby) *a abt same pl: drvn over 1f out: nt qckn after* 8/1[3]
1410 5 1 ¼ **Art Echo**[27] 4622 4-9-1 78 .....(t) LukeMorris 12 74
(John Mackie) *midfield: rdn and effrt on outer 2f out: edgd lft and no ex 1f out* 14/1
4360 6 4 **Lagenda**[37] 4207 4-9-1 81 .....(p) LewisEdmunds(3) 4 66
(Kevin Ryan) *w ldrr and gng a str pce tl rdn over 1f out: sn wknd* 8/1[3]
5615 7 nse **Thaqaffa (IRE)**[59] 3441 4-9-5 82 ..... JosephineGordon 8 67
(Amy Murphy) *led narrowly at str pce: rdn and hdd over 1f out: sn btn* 33/1
5023 8 6 **Shyron**[27] 4622 6-8-7 75 ..... JaneElliott(5) 3 44
(George Margarson) *chsd ldrs: rdn and racing awkwardly 1/2-way: sn struggling* 16/1
0600 9 2 ¾ **Plucky Dip**[16] 5035 6-8-5 75 ..... JackOsborn(7) 1 36
(John Ryan) *rr and sn drvn: nvr gng wl: t.o* 50/1
33-2 10 nse **Mr Bossy Boots (IRE)**[202] 235 6-9-9 86 .....(t) SteveDrowne 2 47
(Amanda Perrett) *rr and sn rdn: nvr gng wl: struggling 1/2-way: t.o* 20/1
-532 11 2 **My Dad Syd (USA)**[20] 4887 5-9-0 77 .....(v) SilvestreDeSousa 5 33
(Ian Williams) *prom: rdn and lost pl over 2f out: eased and t.o* 11/4[1]

0053 **12** 3 **Young John (IRE)**[55] 3567 4-9-3 **80**.............................. AntonioFresu 10 28
(Mike Murphy) *swvd bdly rt s and rdr unbalanced: continued t.o* **20/1**

1m 24.64s (-1.06) **Going Correction** +0.175s/f (Good) **12** Ran SP% **118.9**
Speed ratings (Par 105): **113,110,108,107,105 101,101,94,91,91 88,85**
CSF £20.98 CT £410.89 TOTE £4.00: £1.60, £2.50, £7.80; EX 24.00 Trifecta £448.60.
**Owner** ValueRacingClub.co.uk **Bred** Lady Richard Wellesley **Trained** Newmarket, Suffolk

**FOCUS**
This was run at a good gallop. The runner-up has been rated to last year's C&D form.

## 5611 FLY LONDON SOUTHEND AIRPORT TO DUBROVNIK MAIDEN STKS 1m

**8:00** (8:06) (Class 5) 3-Y-O+ **£3,881** (£1,155; £577; £288) **Stalls** High

Form RPR

**1** **Mountain Hunter (USA)** 3-9-5 0.............................. SilvestreDeSousa 3 88+
(Saeed bin Suroor) *chsd ldrs: effrt 2f out: rdn to ld over 1f out: rn green and edgd lft but kpt on resolutely whn in command cl home* **11/8**[1]

50 **2** 1 ¾ **Dawaaleeb (USA)**[81] 2681 3-9-5 0.............................. DaneO'Neill 9 83
(Charles Hills) *led or disp ld tl rdn and hdd over 1f out: styd on in wl hld 2nd fnl 100yds* **16/1**

0 **3** ½ **Casement (IRE)**[88] 2476 3-9-5 0.............................. KieranShoemark 1 82
(Roger Charlton) *cl up and t.k.h: rdn and in last of four gng clr over 1f out: no imp and rn green but kpt on wl fnl 100yds* **9/1**[3]

252 **4** 2 **Euqranian (USA)**[33] 4409 3-9-0 79.............................. JamesDoyle 13 72
(Jeremy Noseda) *t.k.h: prom: rdn and disp ld over 2f out tl over 1f out: no ex ins fnl f* **5/2**[2]

**5** 8 **Kunani (USA)** 3-9-5 0..............................(b[1]) WilliamBuick 2 59
(John Gosden) *pressed ldrs tl drvn and fdd tamely over 1f out* **11/1**

0-0 **6** ½ **Discovered (IRE)**[104] 1961 3-9-5 0.............................. TrevorWhelan 8 57+
(Roger Charlton) *bhd early: passed btn horses fnl 2f: nvr nr ldrs* **50/1**

0-4 **7** ½ **Girl Squad**[205] 168 3-8-7 0.............................. AarronMiller[(7)] 11 51
(William Jarvis) *dwlt: in last after 3f: edging rt after: nvr on terms* **66/1**

3 **8** nk **Scribbler**[62] 3329 3-9-0 0.............................. AdamBeschizza 14 51
(Rae Guest) *chsd ldrs tl rdn and outpcd wl over 2f out* **14/1**

04 **9** 7 **Good Business (IRE)**[33] 4409 3-9-0 0.............................. JFEgan 7 35
(Jeremy Noseda) *rdn 1/2-way: no ch after: t.o* **66/1**

4 **10** ½ **Wannabe Like You**[41] 4097 3-9-5 0.............................. PatCosgrave 6 38
(William Haggas) *led rnd dismntd at s: a bhd: t.o* **16/1**

03 **11** 5 **Just Surprise Me (IRE)**[13] 5158 4-9-12 0..............................(t) FranBerry 4 28
(Mohamed Moubarak) *led or disp ld tl over 2f out: lost pl rapidly: t.o* **33/1**

64 **12** 4 **Slow To Hand**[28] 4562 3-9-5 0.............................. DannyBrock 5 18
(William Jarvis) *cl up: rdn 1/2-way: sn struggling: eased and t.o* **100/1**

**13** 2 ¾ **Timely Arrival** 3-9-5 0.............................. SteveDrowne 10 11
(Amanda Perrett) *chsd ldrs to 1/2-way: sn rdn and btn: eased and t.o* **12/1**

00 **14** ½ **Nevasca (IRE)**[77] 2798 3-9-2 0..............................(h[1]) SimonPearce[(3)] 12 10
(Lydia Pearce) *wnt rt s: a labouring in last trio: t.o fnl 2f* **100/1**

1m 39.4s (-0.60) **Going Correction** +0.175s/f (Good)
**WFA** 3 from 4yo 7lb **14** Ran SP% **125.0**
Speed ratings (Par 103): **110,108,107,105,97 97,96,96,89,88 83,79,77,76**
CSF £28.70 TOTE £2.30: £1.10, £3.90, £2.80; EX 29.40 Trifecta £206.00.
**Owner** Godolphin **Bred** Darley **Trained** Newmarket, Suffolk

**FOCUS**
A fair maiden, and the first four finished well clear. The fourth has been rated a bit below form.

## 5612 FLY LONDON SOUTHEND AIRPORT TO VENICE H'CAP 6f

**8:30** (8:31) (Class 3) (0-90,91) 3-Y-O+ **£7,762** (£2,310; £1,154; £577) **Stalls** High

Form RPR

4000 **1** **Mont Kiara (FR)**[22] 4816 4-9-5 **80**.............................. HarryBentley 4 89
(Kevin Ryan) *taken down early: steadied s: racd in last pl for over 4f: swtchd rt and gd prog 1f out: wanting to hang rt u.p but sustained str run to ld cl home* **5/1**[2]

4004 **2** 1 ¼ **Clear Spring (IRE)**[30] 4505 9-9-9 **84**.............................. LukeMorris 3 89
(John Spearing) *pressed ldrs: effrt 2f out: drvn to ld over 1f out: hdd and no ex fnl 50yds* **9/1**

0240 **3** 2 **Ice Lord (IRE)**[36] 4270 5-9-12 **87**.............................. FranBerry 6 86
(Chris Wall) *bhd: rdn and prog over 1f out: wnt 3rd but nt qckn ins fnl f* **13/2**

5150 **4** 2 ¾ **Captain Lars (SAF)**[10] 5241 8-9-5 **83**..............................(v) AaronJones[(3)] 8 73
(Derek Shaw) *taken down early: t.k.h: prom: w ldr 2f out tl drvn over 1f out: fdd fnl 100yds* **40/1**

1031 **5** 2 ½ **Firefright (IRE)**[15] 5059 3-9-12 **91**.............................. WilliamBuick 5 72
(Jeremy Noseda) *pressed ldrs: rdn and effrt over 2f out: wknd over 1f out* **2/1**[1]

0222 **6** nk **Love Oasis**[9] 5272 3-9-0 **79**.............................. FrannyNorton 7 59
(Mark Johnston) *prom: jnd ldr 1/2-way tl rdn over 1f out: wknd ins fnl f* **13/2**

5100 **7** shd **Zamjar**[41] 4099 3-9-2 **81**..............................(b) JosephineGordon 1 61
(Ed Dunlop) *towards rr: rdn and btn over 1f out* **16/1**

0030 **8** 3 ½ **Moonraker**[21] 4830 5-9-10 **85**.............................. JFEgan 2 54
(Mick Channon) *plld hrd and prom: ev ch 2f out: fdd over 1f out* **11/2**[3]

441 **9** 4 ½ **Swiss Cross**[28] 4655 10-8-10 **71**..............................(tp) SilvestreDeSousa 9 26
(Phil McEntee) *w ldr to 1/2-way: sn rdn and lost pl: heavily eased 1f out* **18/1**

1m 12.47s (-0.03) **Going Correction** +0.175s/f (Good)
**WFA** 3 from 4yo+ 4lb **9** Ran SP% **115.6**
Speed ratings (Par 107): **107,105,102,99,95 95,95,90,84**
CSF £49.19 CT £295.99 TOTE £5.80: £1.60, £3.00, £2.40; EX 54.30 Trifecta £318.90.
**Owner** JCG Chua & CK Ong 1 **Bred** Guy Pariente Holding Sprl **Trained** Hambleton, N Yorks

**FOCUS**
Not a bad sprint handicap. The runner-up has been rated close to this year's form.
T/Plt: £99.10 to a £1 stake. Pool: £50,195.12 - 369.41 winning units. T/Qpdt: £22.60 to a £1 stake. Pool: £4,326.66 - 141.64 winning units. **Iain Mackenzie**

# 5370 THIRSK (L-H)

### Friday, August 4

**OFFICIAL GOING: Good to soft (7.4)**
Wind: Fresh behind Weather: Sunshine and Cloud

## 5613 PROJECT MANAGEMENT SCOTLAND (S) STKS 6f

**1:40** (1:42) (Class 6) 2-Y-O **£2,587** (£770; £384; £192) **Stalls** Centre

Form RPR

3144 **1** **Tie Em Up Tel (IRE)**[9] 5293 2-9-5 66.............................. JFEgan 1 63
(David Evans) *mde all: rdn over 2f out: pressed ent fnl f: kpt on and in command fnl 110yds* **3/1**[2]

**2** 2 **Silverlight (IRE)** 2-8-9 0.............................. PaddyAspell 6 47
(Philip Kirby) *dwlt: hld up: smooth hdwy over 2f out: pushed along to chal ent fnl f: one pce fnl 110yds* **18/1**

060 **3** hd **Sandama (IRE)**[14] 5127 2-8-10 0 ow1.............................. JackGarritty 7 47
(Richard Fahey) *trckd ldr: rdn 2f out: one pce* **5/1**

00 **4** 2 ½ **Angie B (IRE)**[12] 5179 2-8-9 0.............................. CamHardie 2 39
(John Wainwright) *in tch on outer: rdn along 3f out: one pce* **50/1**

6005 **5** 4 **Heavenly Pulse (IRE)**[9] 5277 2-8-7 39.............................. SebastianWoods[(7)] 3 32
(Ann Duffield) *trckd ldr: rdn over 2f out: wknd over 1f out* **22/1**

23 **6** 6 **Time For Treacle**[42] 4054 2-8-9 58.............................. TomEaves 4 9
(Ben Haslam) *dwlt: sn prom: pushed along and lost pl over 2f out: wknd over 1f out* **10/3**[3]

04 **7** ¾ **Jean Paget (IRE)**[6] 5408 2-8-9 0.............................. PaulHanagan 5 7
(Mick Channon) *dwlt: hld up in tch: rdn over 2f out: sn no hdwy: wknd and eased ins fnl f* **15/8**[1]

1m 15.11s (2.41) **Going Correction** +0.20s/f (Good) **7** Ran SP% **111.1**
Speed ratings (Par 92): **91,88,88,84,79 71,70**
CSF £48.36 TOTE £3.00: £1.60, £6.90; EX 37.60 Trifecta £167.20.There was no bid for the winner.
**Owner** Power Geneva Ltd & Partner **Bred** Albert Ennis **Trained** Pandy, Monmouths

**FOCUS**
After a dry night the going was good to soft. A modest seller run at a steady pace. It's been rated around the winner.

## 5614 BRITISH STALLION STUDS EBF FILLIES' NURSERY H'CAP 5f

**2:10** (2:10) (Class 4) 2-Y-O **£6,469** (£1,925; £962; £481) **Stalls** Centre

Form RPR

526 **1** **Mable Lee (IRE)**[25] 4681 2-8-6 **66**.............................. NathanEvans 3 70
(Iain Jardine) *trckd ldrs: rdn 2f out: led jst ins fnl f: kpt on* **13/2**

3121 **2** ¾ **Silver Starlight**[7] 5373 2-9-1 **78** 6ex.............................. RachelRichardson[(3)] 4 79
(Tim Easterby) *trckd ldrs: rdn appr fnl f: kpt on* **10/3**[2]

3131 **3** 1 ¾ **Tulip Fever**[13] 5143 2-9-0 **79**.............................. GeorgiaCox[(5)] 5 74
(William Haggas) *hld up: racd quite keenly: rdn and edgd lft 2f out: kpt on ins fnl f: wnt 3rd fnl 75yds* **2/1**[1]

4424 **4** nk **Dyson's Girl**[7] 5373 2-8-4 **64**.............................. PaulHanagan 1 58
(Bryan Smart) *wnt sltly lft s sn prom: rdn 2f out: no ex fnl 110yds* **9/2**[3]

110 **5** 3 ¼ **Time Trail**[13] 5150 2-9-7 **81**.............................. PaulMulrennan 2 63
(Michael Dods) *led: pushed along 2f out: hdd jst ins fnl f: wknd* **15/2**

4214 **6** 1 ¼ **Aquadabra (IRE)**[9] 5270 2-8-13 **73**.............................. BenCurtis 6 51
(Mick Channon) *hld up: rdn 2f out: edgd lft over 1f out: wknd ins fnl f* **10/1**

1m 0.5s (0.90) **Going Correction** +0.20s/f (Good) **6** Ran SP% **108.8**
Speed ratings (Par 93): **100,98,96,95,90 88**
CSF £26.36 TOTE £8.40: £3.70, £1.30; EX 26.50 Trifecta £80.20.
**Owner** Dunedin Castle Rock Partnership **Bred** Tower Place Bloodstock **Trained** Carrutherstown, D'fries & G'way

**FOCUS**
An interesting handicap run at a fair pace. The winner has been rated to form.

## 5615 TOMRODS STEEL STOCKHOLDERS NURSERY H'CAP 5f

**2:45** (2:45) (Class 3) 2-Y-O **£6,469** (£1,925; £962; £481) **Stalls** Centre

Form RPR

0112 **1** **John Kirkup**[20] 4922 2-9-7 **86**.............................. PaulMulrennan 2 92
(Michael Dods) *dwlt sltly: hld up in tch: pushed along 1/2-way: led appr fnl f: rdn and edgd lft: kpt on* **5/4**[1]

5641 **2** 1 ½ **Angel Force (IRE)**[6] 5440 2-8-4 **69** 6ex..............................(h) NathanEvans 5 70
(David C Griffiths) *pressed ldr: rdn to ld over 1f out: hdd appr fnl f: hung lft and no ex fnl 75yds* **2/1**[2]

3323 **3** 1 ¼ **Palmer (IRE)**[20] 4888 2-8-10 **75**..............................(p) ConnorBeasley 1 71
(Bryan Smart) *hld up in tch: rdn 2f out: one pce and nvr threatened* **7/2**[3]

1254 **4** nk **Villa Tora**[20] 4895 2-8-10 **75**.............................. AndrewMullen 4 70
(Mark Johnston) *led narrowly: rdn whn hdd over 1f out: no ex fnl f* **14/1**

1m 0.38s (0.78) **Going Correction** +0.20s/f (Good) **4** Ran SP% **106.7**
Speed ratings (Par 98): **101,98,96,96**
CSF £3.92 TOTE £1.90; EX 4.30 Trifecta £5.40.
**Owner** Mrs Suzanne Kirkup & Kevin Kirkup **Bred** W M Lidsey **Trained** Denton, Co Durham

**FOCUS**
Not a bad contest despite the small field. It was run at a decent pace and the improving winner did it nicely. The runner-up has been rated similar to her York latest.

## 5616 BREEDERS BACKING RACING EBF CONDITIONS STKS 7f

**3:20** (3:20) (Class 3) 3-Y-O+ **£9,056** (£2,695; £1,346; £673) **Stalls** Low

Form RPR

-504 **1** **Mitchum Swagger**[55] 3587 5-9-4 106..............................(p[1]) TomQueally 3 103+
(David Lanigan) *hld up: pushed along over 2f out: rdn and hdwy over 1f out: led 1f out: edgd lft but kpt on to draw clr fnl 110yds* **6/4**[1]

05 **2** 2 ½ **Lavetta**[26] 4662 5-8-13 84.............................. BenCurtis 5 91
(Sally Haynes) *trckd ldrs: rdn to chal 2f out: kpt on same pce fnl f* **25/1**

3653 **3** nk **That Is The Spirit**[13] 5137 6-9-4 100.............................. PhillipMakin 7 95
(David O'Meara) *led: rdn and pressed fr 2f out: hdd 1f out: one pce* **8/1**

320 **4** ½ **Mount Tahan (IRE)**[6] 5393 5-9-4 93.............................. KevinStott 4 94
(Kevin Ryan) *rrd s and slowly away: hld up in rr: rdn and hdwy on outer over 1f out: kpt on same pce fnl f* **10/3**[2]

0100 **5** 4 ½ **Sound Advice**[20] 4890 8-9-4 102.............................. DougieCostello 2 82
(Keith Dalgleish) *midfield: rdn over 2f out: wknd ins fnl f* **14/1**

-466 **6** ½ **Sea Fox (IRE)**[90] 2402 3-8-12 96..............................(t) JFEgan 6 78
(David Evans) *midfield: rdn over 3f out: sn struggling* **5/1**[3]

5-50 **7** 1 ¼ **George Dryden (IRE)**[41] 4072 5-9-4 98.............................. ConnorBeasley 1 77
(Ann Duffield) *trckd ldr: rdn over 2f out: wknd over 1f out* **8/1**

1m 28.11s (0.91) **Going Correction** +0.325s/f (Good)
**WFA** 3 from 5yo+ 6lb **7** Ran SP% **112.5**
Speed ratings (Par 107): **107,104,103,103,98 97,96**
CSF £40.22 TOTE £2.10: £1.30, £12.00; EX 51.70 Trifecta £281.90.
**Owner** Paul Dean & The Mitchum Swagger P'Ship **Bred** Peter Webb & Peter Lay **Trained** Newmarket, Suffolk

**FOCUS**
Add 20yds to race distance. A decent conditions event run at a sound pace. It's been rated around the second, third and fourth.

## 5617 JW 4X4 NORTHALLERTON H'CAP (DIV I) 1m 4f 8y

**3:55** (3:59) (Class 6) (0-65,66) 3-Y-O **£2,911** (£866; £432; £216) **Stalls** Low

Form RPR

6464 **1** **Vindicator (IRE)**[18] 4962 3-9-4 **65**..............................(p) AdamMcNamara[(3)] 6 80
(Michael Dods) *hld up: pushed along over 4f out: rdn and gd hdwy 2f out: led 110yds out: styd on wl* **4/1**[2]

6421 **2** *1 ½* **Sheriff Garrett (IRE)**[18] 4978 3-9-1 **62**............(p) RachelRichardson(3) 3 75
(Tim Easterby) *led: 3 l up on bit 4f out: pushed along and reduced advantage over 2f out: rdn whn hdd 110yds out: one pce* **10/3**[1]

535 **3** *2 ¾* **Fire Leopard**[24] 4720 3-9-8 **66**......................(h) PhillipMakin 4 74
(David O'Meara) *midfield: hdwy over 3f out: rdn to chse ldr over 2f out: no ex ins fnl f* **9/2**[3]

6-33 **4** *6* **Siyahamba (IRE)**[21] 4838 3-8-10 **54**.............................. JackGarritty 8 53
(Bryan Smart) *dwlt: sn chsd ldr: rdn 3f out: wknd fnl f* **9/1**

0-00 **5** *1 ¼* **Shakabula (IRE)**[14] 5131 3-8-11 **55**................................... BenCurtis 9 52
(Brian Ellison) *trckd ldrs: rdn over 3f out: wknd over 1f out* **14/1**

6004 **6** *hd* **Silver Gleam (IRE)**[16] 5017 3-8-5 **49**..................... DuranFentiman 1 45
(Chris Fairhurst) *hld up in rr: rdn and hdd over 3f out: wknd fnl f* **20/1**

6-65 **7** *22* **My Brother Mike (IRE)**[163] 864 3-9-3 **61**...................... TomQueally 10 22
(Kevin Frost) *trckd ldrs: rdn over 3f out: sn wknd* **20/1**

0000 **8** *½* **Thornton Mary**[12] 5182 3-8-2 **46** oh1.............................. CamHardie 7
(Brian Rothwell) *midfield: rdn over 3f out: wknd* **100/1**

5-46 **9** *5* **Mister Moosah (IRE)**[96] 2186 3-9-5 **63**.............................. NeilFarley 5 15
(Micky Hammond) *a towards rr* **20/1**

2144 **10** *22* **Dyna Might**[18] 4978 3-9-2 **60**........................................(p) AndrewMullen 2
(Ollie Pears) *trckd ldrs: rdn over 3f out: wknd and eased* **4/1**[2]

0060 **11** *9* **What's Up Walter**[51] 3708 3-8-2 **46** oh1......................... PaddyAspell 11
(Philip Kirby) *midfield: rdn 5f out: sn wknd and bhd* **50/1**

2m 40.25s (4.05) **Going Correction** +0.325s/f (Good) **11** Ran SP% **115.2**
Speed ratings (Par 98): **99,98,96,92,91 91,76,76,72,58 52**
CSF £16.12 CT £61.63 TOTE £5.20: £1.50, £1.60, £2.00; EX 21.10 Trifecta £119.30.
**Owner** Pat & Gary Cahill **Bred** Gearoid Cahill **Trained** Denton, Co Durham

**FOCUS**
Add 20yds to race distance. The pace was strong for this open handicap. The third has been rated to her maiden form.

## 5618 JW 4X4 NORTHALLERTON H'CAP (DIV II) 1m 4f 8y
**4:30** (4:30) (Class 6) (0-65,65) 3-Y-O **£2,911** (£866; £432; £216) **Stalls** Low

Form RPR

4063 **1** **Tewafeedj**[38] 4171 3-9-1 **59**................................................... KevinStott 1 65
(Kevin Ryan) *mde all: rn wd on bnd 9f out: rdn over 2f out: pressed over 1f out: styd on wl* **7/1**

0321 **2** *1* **Ingleby Mackenzie**[15] 5061 3-9-3 **64**.................. AdamMcNamara(3) 7 68
(Mick Channon) *trckd ldr: rdn over 2f out: chal over 1f out: kpt on fnl f* **11/4**[1]

1352 **3** *nk* **Clenymistra (IRE)**[17] 5001 3-9-4 **62**................................ PhillipMakin 10 66
(David O'Meara) *hld up: gd hdwy on outer over 2f out: rdn to chse ldrs over 1f out: kpt on same pce ins fnl f* **11/2**

454 **4** *1 ¾* **Princess Nearco (IRE)**[15] 5073 3-8-10 **61**...................... PaulaMuir(7) 8 62
(Patrick Holmes) *s.i.s: hld up in rr: pushed along and stl in last 3f out: edgd lft but hdwy over 1f out: kpt on fnl f: nrst fin* **16/1**

5066 **5** *hd* **Broughtons Knight**[14] 5131 3-9-7 **65**................................ MartinLane 2 66
(Henry Spiller) *in tch: rdn over 2f out: one pce fnl f* **5/1**[3]

-041 **6** *7* **Take A Turn (IRE)**[26] 4660 3-9-4 **62**................................ TomQueally 6 52
(David Lanigan) *midfield: in tch 4f out: rdn over 2f out: wknd fnl f* **9/2**[2]

5000 **7** *1 ½* **Thomas Crown (IRE)**[3] 5493 3-8-4 **55** ow2............ BenSanderson(7) 5 42
(Roger Fell) *trckd ldrs: rdn over 3f out: wknd 2f out* **16/1**

0-55 **8** *2 ¼* **Spanish Beauty**[27] 4603 3-8-3 **47**................................ AndrewMullen 4 31
(Ollie Pears) *midfield on inner: rdn 3f out: sn wknd* **11/1**

0500 **9** *1* **Circuit**[36] 4263 3-7-13 **46** oh1.......................................(t) SammyJoBell(3) 3 28
(Wilf Storey) *a towards rr* **33/1**

2m 42.28s (6.08) **Going Correction** +0.325s/f (Good) **9** Ran SP% **112.4**
Speed ratings (Par 98): **92,91,91,89,89 85,84,82,82**
CSF £25.70 CT £112.91 TOTE £7.60: £2.10, £1.20, £2.30; EX 30.80 Trifecta £193.70.
**Owner** H M K Al Mehairi **Bred** Hamad Mohammed Bin Kadfoor Al Mehairi **Trained** Hambleton, N Yorks
■ Stewards' Enquiry : Martin Lane caution; careless riding

**FOCUS**
Add 20yds to race distance. The second division of this moderate handicap was run at a steady pace. The runner-up helps set the standard.

## 5619 BOOK NOW FOR LADIES' DAY SATURDAY 9TH SEPTEMBER MAIDEN STKS 5f
**5:00** (5:02) (Class 5) 3-4-Y-O **£3,234** (£962; £481; £240) **Stalls** Centre

Form RPR

0050 **1** **Pavers Pride**[25] 4694 3-9-2 51................................ AdamMcNamara(3) 2 65
(Noel Wilson) *prom: rdn 2f out: kpt on: led narrowly 50yds out* **50/1**

**2** *hd* **Nuns Walk** 3-9-0 0........................................................... DuranFentiman 3 59
(Tim Easterby) *dwlt: in tch: pushed along and hdwy to chse ldrs over 1f out: rdn and ev ch ins fnl f: kpt on* **20/1**

20 **3** *nk* **Jabbarockie**[5] 5459 4-9-8 69................................................... NeilFarley 9 64
(Eric Alston) *led: rdn 2f out: hdd 50yds out: one pce* **9/2**[2]

4-35 **4** *2 ¼* **Rapid Ranger**[13] 5167 3-9-2 67................................ ShelleyBirkett(3) 4 55
(David O'Meara) *chsd ldrs: rdn 2f out: no ex ins fnl f* **8/1**[3]

5-2 **5** *2 ¼* **Canford Bay (IRE)**[17] 5006 3-9-5 0.............................. AndrewMullen 5 47
(Antony Brittain) *stdd s: hld up in tch racing keenly: rdn and hung lft over 1f out: wknd ins fnl f* **11/4**[1]

00 **6** *3* **Snow Excuse**[22] 4793 3-9-5 0.............................................(t) JackGarritty 6 36
(Bryan Smart) *dwlt: hld up: sn pushed along: nvr threatened* **80/1**

**7** *5* **Redeeming** 3-9-2 0................................................. RachelRichardson(3) 1 18
(Eric Alston) *hld up: rdn 3f out: wknd over 1f out* **25/1**

0 **8** *3 ¾* **Fintry Flyer**[17] 5006 3-9-0 0............................................ SaleemGolam 10
(Jim Goldie) *a outpcd in rr* **80/1**

1m 0.46s (0.86) **Going Correction** +0.20s/f (Good)
**WFA** 3 from 4yo 3lb **8** Ran SP% **69.0**
Speed ratings (Par 103): **101,100,100,96,93 88,80,74**
CSF £261.73 TOTE £29.70: £6.50, £3.60, £1.10; EX 429.00 Trifecta £1115.30.
**Owner** G J Paver **Bred** Mrs C K Paver **Trained** Marwood, Co Durham
■ Creek Walk and Silently were withdrawn. Prices at time of withdrawal 5-4f and 16-1 respectively. Rule 4 applies to all bets - deduction 40p in the pound.

**FOCUS**
There was drama prior to the off as the well-backed favourite Creek Walk reared in the stalls and had to be withdrawn. He kicked Tom Queally, the jockey of Silently who was also taken out. They went an honest pace for this uncompetitive maiden. The level is fluid.

## 5620 GO RACING IN YORKSHIRE FUTURE STARS APPRENTICE H'CAP (GO RACING IN YORKSHIRE FUTURE STARS) 6f
**5:35** (5:36) (Class 5) (0-70,67) 3-Y-O+ **£3,234** (£962; £481; £240) **Stalls** Centre

Form RPR

6006 **1** **Danish Duke (IRE)**[18] 4958 6-9-10 **65**....................(p) SeamusCronin(2) 6 75
(Ruth Carr) *mde all: rdn 2f out: kpt on* **4/1**[1]

0022 **2** *2* **Point Of Woods**[7] 5377 4-9-9 **62**....................................(p) JoshQuinn 4 66
(Tina Jackson) *dwlt: sn chsd ldrs: rdn over 2f out: kpt on* **4/1**[1]

6065 **3** *½* **Ticks The Boxes (IRE)**[30] 4506 5-10-0 **67**....................(p) GerO'Neill 5 69
(John Wainwright) *in tch: rdn 2f out: edgd rt over 1f out: kpt on ins fnl f* **6/1**[2]

010- **4** *1* **Gypsy Major**[238] 8287 5-9-9 **62**........................................(v) JordanUys 3 61
(John Weymes) *hld up: hdwy 3f out: rdn 2f out: chsd ldr over 1f out: one pce ins fnl f* **33/1**

-506 **5** *1 ¼* **Nellie Deen (IRE)**[9] 5283 4-8-11 **52**....................(b[1]) BenSanderson(2) 1 47
(Roger Fell) *wnt lft s: sn prom: rdn over 2f out: edgd lft over 1f out: no ex ins fnl f* **12/1**

6003 **6** *nk* **Stringybark Creek**[14] 5122 3-8-10 **57**...................... LenkaHelmecka(4) 2 50
(Mick Channon) *prom: rdn over 2f out: no ex fnl f* **20/1**

-034 **7** *1 ½* **Le Manege Enchante (IRE)**[8] 5318 4-9-2 **57**................... TobyEley(2) 7 46
(Derek Shaw) *dwlt: hld up: rdn 3f out: nvr threatened ldrs* **8/1**[3]

2326 **8** *hd* **Burtonwood**[8] 5318 5-9-11 **66**.................................(p) JamieGormley(2) 8 54
(Julie Camacho) *prom: rdn over 2f out: already lost pl and btn whn sltly hmpd appr fnl f* **8/1**[3]

1-50 **9** *nse* **Caeser The Gaeser (IRE)**[22] 4789 5-9-10 **65**(p) FayeMcManoman(2) 11 53
(Nigel Tinkler) *chsd ldrs towards outer: rdn over 2f out: wknd over 1f out* **10/1**

3144 **10** *3* **Sea Of Green**[4] 5471 5-9-8 **61**.........................................(p) KevinLundie 10 40
(Jim Goldie) *hld up: nvr threatened* **6/1**[2]

0600 **11** *3* **Reflation**[27] 4605 5-9-0 **53**................................................(p) PaulaMuir 9 22
(Patrick Holmes) *a towards rr* **66/1**

1m 13.73s (1.03) **Going Correction** +0.20s/f (Good)
**WFA** 3 from 4yo+ 4lb **11** Ran SP% **116.8**
Speed ratings (Par 103): **101,98,97,96,94 94,92,92,91,87 83**
CSF £18.59 CT £95.32 TOTE £4.70: £1.90, £2.00, £1.90; EX 19.40 Trifecta £82.30.
**Owner** Michael Hill **Bred** Dean Harron & Ciaran Conroy **Trained** Huby, N Yorks

**FOCUS**
A truly run handicap. The runner-up and third have been rated close to their recent form.
T/Plt: £119.60 to a £1 stake. Pool: £46,082.89 - 281.06 winning units. T/Qpdt: £6.40 to a £1 stake. Pool: £4,317.04 - 499.15 winning units. **Andrew Sheret**

5621 - 5625a (Foreign Racing) - See Raceform Interactive

# 5520 DEAUVILLE (R-H)
Friday, August 4

**OFFICIAL GOING: Polytrack: standard; turf: good to soft**

## 5626a PRIX D'AUQUAINVILLE (MAIDEN) (2YO COLTS & GELDINGS) (TURF) 6f
**12:40** 2-Y-O **£11,538** (£4,615; £3,461; £2,307; £1,153)

RPR

**1** **Diamond Vendome (FR)**[24] 2-9-2 0.................................. JulienAuge 4 83
(C Ferland, France) **7/5**[1]

**2** *hd* **True Romance (FR)** 2-8-11 0....................................... MaximeGuyon 3 77
(F-H Graffard, France) **8/1**

**3** *¾* **Louis D'Or (IRE)**[26] 2-8-10 0.................................. JeromeMoutard(6) 5 80
(T Castanheira, France) **11/5**[2]

**4** *1 ½* **Dragon's Teeth (IRE)**[38] 4196 2-9-2 0.......................(b[1]) TheoBachelot 7 76
(Jo Hughes) *led: drvn whn pressed wl over 1 1/2f out: hdd appr fnl f: one pce u.p* **127/10**

**5** *5 ½* **Grand Daddy**[26] 2-9-2 0........................................ ChristopheSoumillon 6 59
(P Bary, France) **18/5**[3]

**6** *1 ¾* **Petrus (FR)** 2-9-2 0............................................................ AnthonyCrastus 2 54
(Cedric Rossi, France) **135/10**

1m 10.62s (-0.38) **6** Ran SP% **120.0**
PARI-MUTUEL (all including 1 euro stake): WIN 2.40; PLACE 1.40, 2.90; SF 12.10.
**Owner** Guy Pariente **Bred** Guy Pariente Holding **Trained** France

## 5627a PRIX DE BAVENT (CLAIMER) (2YO COLTS & GELDINGS) (TURF) 6f
**1:10** 2-Y-O **£11,538** (£4,615; £3,461; £2,307; £1,153)

RPR

**1** **Wooldix (FR)**[59] 3444 2-8-11 0........................................... MaximeGuyon 4 70
(C Escuder, France) **13/10**[1]

**2** *1* **Autumn Lodge**[17] 4991 2-8-11 0........................................ TonyPiccone 3 67
(J S Moore) *w ldrs: drvn to ld wl over 1 1/2f out: hdd ins fnl f: kpt on u.p* **18/5**[2]

**3** *1 ½* **Le King (FR)** 2-8-8 0................................... MlleLauraPoggionovo(10) 2 70
(J-M Capitte, France) **9/2**

**4** *1 ¼* **Chante Blu (FR)**[106] 1919 2-8-11 0........................ VincentCheminaud 5 59
(A Giorgi, Italy) **97/10**

**5** *1* **Captain Kissinger**[93] 2292 2-8-11 0....................(b[1]) MickaelBarzalona 1 56
(Jo Hughes) *w ldrs: drvn and nt qckn over 1 1/2f out: dropped away ins fnl f* **4/1**[3]

**6** *nk* **Belobog (FR)**[37] 2-8-11 0.............................................. EddyHardouin 6 55
(M Boutin, France) **183/10**

1m 12.16s (1.16) **6** Ran SP% **117.9**
PARI-MUTUEL (all including 1 euro stake): WIN 2.30; PLACE 1.50, 2.00; SF 8.20.
**Owner** Mohamed Chahbani **Bred** Sarl Winning Bloodstock Agency **Trained** France

## 5628a PRIX D'HUDIMESNIL (CONDITIONS) (4YO+) (POLYTRACK) 6f 110y
**1:40** 4-Y-O+ **£14,102** (£5,641; £4,230; £2,820; £1,410)

RPR

**1** **Ross (IRE)**[132] 1373 5-9-6 0......................................... AndraschStarke 7 107
(P Schiergen, Germany) **27/10**[2]

**2** *2* **Gold Vibe (IRE)**[44] 4-9-0 0................................. ChristopheSoumillon 6 95
(P Bary, France) **19/10**[1]

**3** *½* **Walec**[44] 5-9-0 0.................................................................. CristianDemuro 4 94
(P Sogorb, France) **19/2**

**4** *hd* **Yeah Baby Yeah (IRE)**[6] 5422 4-8-10 0...................(p) UmbertoRispoli 8 89
(Gay Kelleway) *w.w towards rr: shkn up and hdwy appr 1 1/2f out: styd on fnl f: nvr nrr* **199/10**

**5** *¾* **City Money (IRE)**[83] 2643 5-9-3 0................................. StephanePasquier 5 94
(M Delcher Sanchez, France) **56/10**[3]

**6** *1 ½* **Bohemien (IRE)**[30] 4-9-0 0................................................ TonyPiccone 1 87
(Alain Couetil, France) **114/10**

**7** *1* **Narnia Dawn (IRE)**[70] 4-8-10 0............................................. AlexisBadel 9 80
(F-H Graffard, France) **123/10**

**8** *½* **Daring Lion (GER)**[419] 4-9-3 0.......................................... AntoineHamelin 3 86
(A Kleinkorres, Germany) **94/10**

9 9 **Engaging Smile**[54] 3957 5-8-10 0 ................................ EddyHardouin 2 52
(J Moon, Jersey) **56/1**

PARI-MUTUEL (all including 1 euro stake): WIN 3.70; PLACE 1.50, 1.30, 2.00; DF 4.20; SF 9.50.
**Owner** Stall Domstadt **Bred** Dr T Grewe **Trained** Germany

## 5629a PRIX D'HEROUVILLE (CLAIMER) (2YO FILLIES) (TURF) 6f
**3:50** 2-Y-O **£11,538** (£4,615; £3,461; £2,307; £1,153)

RPR

1 **Lili Du Sud (FR)**[10] 2-9-3 0 ................................ MathieuPelletan(5) 9 79
(Y Gourraud, France) **18/5**[3]

2 hd **Rachael's Rocket (IRE)**[8] 5327 2-8-11 0 ........................ TonyPiccone 5 67
(J S Moore) *led: hdd narrowly wl over 2f out: sltly outpcd and rdn wl over 1f out: rdr stopped riding and rchd down to off-side iron ins fnl f: styd on str last 125yds: jst failed* **151/10**

3 snk **Money Sister** 2-9-4 0 ................................(p) CristianDemuro 8 74
(Francesco Santella, Italy) **27/1**

4 shd **Bombetta (FR)**[11] 5232 2-9-4 0 ........................(p) ChristopheSoumillon 1 74
(N Caulliery, France) **33/10**[2]

5 ¾ **Oona (FR)**[19] 2-8-11 0 ................................ AnthonyCrastus 7 64
(P Sogorb, France) **5/2**[1]

6 1 ¼ **Occhiobello (FR)** 2-8-11 0 ................................ VincentCheminaud 6 61
(Robert Collet, France) **147/10**

7 ½ **Shesgotthelot**[30] 4677 2-8-2 0 ........................ MmeAlexiaCeccarello(9) 4 59
(J S Moore) *chsd ldr on inner: outpcd and drvn appr 2f out: kpt on again fnl 150yds* **58/10**

8 2 ½ **Diamond Pursuit**[17] 4991 2-9-1 0 ........................(b) MickaelBarzalona 2 56
(Jo Hughes) *wl in tch bhd ldrs: lost pl and drvn wl over 2f out: wl hld fnl f* **108/10**

9 dist **Laureva Chope (FR)**[19] 2-8-11 0 ................................ JulienAuge 3
(A Chopard, France) **19/1**

1m 12.23s (1.23) **9** Ran SP% **117.9**
PARI-MUTUEL (all including 1 euro stake): WIN 4.60; PLACE 2.50, 4.60, 6.80; DF 44.10; SF 67.50.
**Owner** J-L Pelletan & Y Gourraud **Bred** Sci Cercy **Trained** France

# 5313 DONCASTER (L-H)
## Saturday, August 5

**OFFICIAL GOING: Good to soft (good in places) changing to good after race 1 (2:10)**
Wind: Strong half against Weather: Fine & dry

## 5630 THOMPSONS ACTING FOR UNISON H'CAP 1m 3f 197y
**2:10** (2:10) (Class 4) (0-85,85) 3-Y-O **£5,175** (£1,540; £769; £384) **Stalls** Low

Form RPR

51 1 **Great White Shark (FR)**[36] 4300 3-9-4 **82** .................. DanielMuscutt 3 88+
(James Fanshawe) *trckd ldng pair:. hdwy over 3f out: slt ld wl over 2f out: rdn over 1f out: kpt on fnl f* **13/8**[1]

6543 2 ½ **Mister Belvedere**[21] 4891 3-9-2 **85** ........................ CallumRodriguez(5) 6 90
(Michael Dods) *led at sedate pce for 11/2f: sn hdd and trckd ldrs: hdwy 4f out: cl up 3f out: chal over 2f out: rdn wl over 1f out: ev ch: drvn ent fnl f: kpt on wl towards fini* **4/1**[3]

021 3 1 ¼ **Key Bid**[77] 2841 3-9-3 **81** ................................................(p) WilliamBuick 5 84
(Charlie Appleby) *cl up: led after 11/2f: hdd after 4f: cl up on inner: pushed along over 3f out: rdn over 1f out: drvn over 1f out: kpt on same pce* **11/4**[2]

3413 4 hd **Wefait (IRE)**[14] 5153 3-8-13 **80** ................................ HollieDoyle(3) 2 83
(Richard Hannon) *t.k.h early: hld up in rr: hdwy over 3f out: effrt and hung lft wl over 1f out: sn drvn : kpt on same pce* **5/1**

402 5 11 **Our Boy (IRE)**[25] 4730 3-8-11 **75** ................................ TomQueally 4 60+
(David Evans) *plld hrd: hld up: rapid hdwy and cl up after 2f : led after 4f: pushed along over 3f out: sn hdd & wknd fnl 2f* **11/1**

0-00 6 5 **Riviere Argentee (FR)**[3] 5533 3-8-11 **75** .................(p[1]) AndrewMullen 1 52
(K R Burke) *hld up in rr: rdn along wl over 3f out: sn outpcd* **50/1**

2m 39.08s (4.18) **Going Correction** +0.425s/f (Yiel) **6** Ran SP% **111.7**
Speed ratings (Par 102): **103,102,101,101,94 91**
CSF £8.43 TOTE £2.30: £1.40, £2.20; EX 9.10 Trifecta £30.20.
**Owner** Malcolm C Denmark **Bred** Mme Anne-Marie D'Estainville Gedik **Trained** Newmarket, Suffolk

**FOCUS**
The ground was good to soft, good in places (GoingStick: 7.5). The round course was railed out 6yds from 1m2f until the round course joins the straight, adding 18yds to races 1, 3 and 5. The stalls on the straight course were in the centre, and they were on the inside on the round course. They went slowly early on, but this was a fair middle-distance handicap won by a filly who should continue to improve. The second, third and fourth have been rated to their handicap form.

## 5631 UNISON DEFENDING YOUR NHS NOVICE AUCTION STKS (PLUS 10 RACE) 7f 6y
**2:45** (2:46) (Class 4) 2-Y-O **£4,204** (£1,251; £625; £312) **Stalls** Centre

Form RPR

1 **Narcos (IRE)** 2-9-2 0 ................................................ DavidNolan 3 81+
(Richard Fahey) *hld up: hdwy wl over 2f out: chal over 1f out: rdn to ld ent fnl f: kpt on strly* **9/1**

01 2 1 ¼ **Make Good (IRE)**[16] 5058 2-9-3 0 ................................ WilliamBuick 4 79
(David Brown) *trckd ldrs: hdwy 3f out: led wl over 1f out: sn rdn: hdd and drvn ent fnl f: kpt on* **6/1**[3]

3 1 **Moxy Mares** 2-8-11 0 ................................................ GeorgeDowning 12 70
(Daniel Mark Loughnane) *dwlt and rr: hdwy 1/2-way: swtchd lft and effrt whn hung lft 2f out: sn rdn: styd on wl appr fnl f* **50/1**

4 1 ½ **Amazing Michele (FR)** 2-8-11 0 ................................ DanielMuscutt 7 67+
(Richard Fahey) *dwlt and towards rr: hdwy 3f out: rdn along to chse ldrs 2f out: kpt on same pce appr fnl f* **14/1**

4 5 1 **Firby (IRE)**[19] 4956 2-8-9 0 ................................ AndrewMullen 5 62
(James Bethell) *trckd ldrs: hdwy 3f out: chsd ldng pair 2f out: rdn wl over 1f out: kpt on same pce* **7/1**

6 3 **Faadhel (GER)** 2-9-2 0 ................................................ JackMitchell 13 61+
(Roger Varian) *midfield: hdwy on outer 3f out: in tch and rdn along wl over 1f out: no imp fnl f* **4/1**[2]

5 7 ½ **Perfect Hustler (USA)**[35] 4367 2-9-2 0 ................................ SamHitchcott 15 60
(Jeremy Noseda) *dwlt: sn midfield: hdwy on outer 3f out: rdn along 2f out: kpt on same pce* **10/1**

8 2 **Wasim (IRE)**[14] 5136 2-9-8 0 ................................................ KevinStott 1 61
(Ismail Mohammed) *led: sn clr: rdn along over 2f out: hdd wl over 1f out: sn wknd* **5/2**[1]

6 9 1 ½ **Viking Way (IRE)**[37] 4273 2-8-6 0 ................................ PhilDennis(5) 8 46
(Olly Williams) *trckd ldng pair: hdwy 1/2-way: pushed along wl over 2f out: sn rdn and grad wknd* **66/1**

10 1 **Dream Mount (IRE)** 2-8-10 0 ................................ MarcMonaghan(3) 10 45
(Marco Botti) *a towards rr* **16/1**

11 ½ **Bertog** 2-8-13 0 ................................................ TomQueally 6 44
(John Mackie) *a towards rr* **40/1**

12 1 ½ **Normandy Blue** 2-8-11 0 ................................................ BarryMcHugh 14 38
(Richard Fahey) *a towards rr* **20/1**

0 13 3 ¾ **Gardinia**[13] 5179 2-8-5 0 ................................ RachelRichardson(3) 9 25
(Tim Easterby) *chsd ldrs: rdn along 3f out: sn wknd* **66/1**

14 6 **Airplane (IRE)** 2-8-9 0 ................................................ NeilFarley 11 11
(Tim Easterby) *chsd ldr: pushed along 1/2-way: sn rdn and wknd* **40/1**

1m 28.08s (1.78) **Going Correction** +0.05s/f (Good) **14** Ran SP% **121.6**
Speed ratings (Par 96): **91,89,88,86,85 82,81,79,77,76 75,74,69,63**
CSF £60.11 TOTE £10.40: £3.10, £2.10, £11.70; EX 75.30 Trifecta £3453.30 Part Won..
**Owner** Merchants and Missionaries **Bred** Western Eyes Partnership **Trained** Musley Bank, N Yorks

**FOCUS**
Plenty of newcomers in this juvenile contest and the winner was one of them. He looks useful and ought to stay further. The runner-up has been rated to form.

## 5632 UNISON AND LV LIVERPOOL VICTORIA CAR INSURANCE MAIDEN STKS 1m 2f 43y
**3:20** (3:21) (Class 5) 3-Y-O **£2,911** (£866; £432; £216) **Stalls** Low

Form RPR

23 1 **Tribal Conquest (IRE)**[31] 4508 3-9-5 0 ................................ WilliamBuick 4 91+
(Charlie Appleby) *prom on inner: hdwy to ld over 2f out: rdn clr over 1f out: readily* **13/8**[1]

52 2 4 ½ **Roddy (IRE)**[25] 4720 3-9-5 0 ................................ AndrewMullen 10 80
(Tom Tate) *hmpd s and towards rr: hdwy to join ldrs after 2f : sn trcking ldr on outer: effrt over 2f out and ev ch: rdn along wl over 1f out: chsd wnr: sn no imp* **5/2**[2]

0-0 3 1 ¾ **Oden**[23] 4808 3-9-5 0 ................................................(p) JackMitchell 12 77
(Roger Varian) *trckd ldrs: hdwy over 3f out: rdn along 2f out: sn drvn and kpt on same pce* **11/1**

44 4 3 **Luna Magic**[23] 4808 3-8-11 0 ................................(h[1]) SimonPearce(3) 9 66
(Lydia Pearce) *wnt rt s: sn led: pushed along over 3f out: rdn and hdd over 2f out: drvn wl over 1f out: grad wknd* **20/1**

45 5 5 **Chartbuster (IRE)**[29] 4569 3-9-5 0 ................................ DavidNolan 11 62
(Julie Camacho) *hld up: hdwy over 4f out: rdn to chse ldrs over 2f out: sn drvn and one pce* **14/1**

6 2 ¾ **Golden Set** 3-9-0 0 ................................................ TomQueally 1 51+
(James Fanshawe) *hld up in rr: pushed along 3f out: hdwy wl over 1f out: kpt on fnl f: nrst fin* **12/1**

34 7 hd **Graphite (IRE)**[12] 5220 3-9-5 0 ................................ SamHitchcott 8 56
(David Simcock) *t.k.h: in tch: hdwy over 4f out: chsd ldrs 3f out: sn rdn along and wknd wl over 1f out* **7/1**[3]

P 8 shd **War Brigade (FR)**[52] 3717 3-9-5 0 ................................ DanielMuscutt 7 56
(David Simcock) *hld up in rr: sme hdwy over 2f out: sn rdn and kpt on fnl f* **25/1**

03 9 1 ½ **Grey Mist**[15] 5128 3-9-2 0 ................................ RachelRichardson(3) 3 53
(Tim Easterby) *chsd ldrs: rdn along 3f out: sn wknd* **25/1**

-600 10 10 **Just Heather (IRE)**[55] 3627 3-9-0 37 ........................(p[1]) GeorgeDowning 5 29
(John Wainwright) *a rr* **150/1**

60- 11 3 ¼ **Quiet Weekend**[323] 6535 3-9-5 0 ................................(t[1]) KevinStott 6 28
(James Bethell) *a towards rr* **25/1**

2m 15.15s (5.75) **Going Correction** +0.425s/f (Yiel) **11** Ran SP% **118.8**
Speed ratings (Par 100): **94,90,89,86,82 80,80,80,78,70 68**
CSF £5.23 TOTE £2.30: £1.20, £1.20, £3.30; EX 6.70 Trifecta £47.80.
**Owner** Godolphin **Bred** Rabbah Bloodstock Limited **Trained** Newmarket, Suffolk

**FOCUS**
Add 18yds. An ordinary maiden, but the winner looks the type to go on to better things now connections have found his trip. It's been rated slightly positively.

## 5633 UNISON ESSENTIAL COVER WHEREVER YOU WORK CONDITIONS STKS 6f 2y
**3:55** (3:55) (Class 3) 3-Y-O+ **£9,337** (£2,796; £1,398; £699) **Stalls** Centre

Form RPR

-400 1 **Gifted Master (IRE)**[14] 5149 4-9-2 105 ........................(b) WilliamBuick 5 113
(Hugo Palmer) *cl up: led over 4f out: rdn clr over 1f out: kpt on strly* **7/4**[1]

1300 2 3 ½ **Mr Lupton (IRE)**[21] 4907 4-9-6 110 ................................ DavidNolan 1 106
(Richard Fahey) *dwlt and rr: hdwy over 2f out: rdn wl over 1f out: drvn to chse wnr fnl f: no imp* **7/4**[1]

403- 3 2 ¼ **Global Applause**[322] 6572 3-8-12 103 ................................ TomQueally 4 94
(Ed Dunlop) *trckd ldng pair: pushed along over 2f out: rdn wl over 1f out: kpt on same pce* **5/1**[3]

300- 4 15 **Mattmu**[413] 3385 5-8-13 108 ................................(p) RachelRichardson(3) 2 47
(Tim Easterby) *slt ld: hdd over 4f out: cl up: rdn along over 2f out: sn drvn and wknd* **9/2**[2]

1m 12.28s (-1.32) **Going Correction** +0.05s/f (Good)
**WFA** 3 from 4yo+ 4lb **4** Ran SP% **107.6**
Speed ratings (Par 107): **110,105,102,82**
CSF £4.95 TOTE £2.30; EX 4.10 Trifecta £10.20.
**Owner** Dr Ali Ridha **Bred** Tally-Ho Stud **Trained** Newmarket, Suffolk

**FOCUS**
Only four runners, but a decent sprint which saw the very useful winner return to something approaching his best. He enjoyed the run of the race, however.

## 5634 UNISON ERIC ROBERTS MEMORIAL H'CAP 1m 2f 43y
**4:30** (4:32) (Class 2) (0-100,98) 3-Y-O+
**£12,450** (£3,728; £1,864; £932; £466; £234) **Stalls** Low

Form RPR

-600 1 **Erik The Red (FR)**[21] 4918 5-9-10 **94** ........................(p) KevinStott 6 105
(Kevin Ryan) *hld up: hdwy 4f out: cl up over 2f out: rdn to ld over 1f out: drvn out* **11/4**[1]

-231 2 1 ½ **Another Eclipse (IRE)**[32] 4460 3-8-6 **84** ........................ SamHitchcott 10 93
(David Simcock) *hld up in rr: hdwy on inner 3f out: rdn to ld 2f out: hdd over 1f out: drvn fnl f: kpt on* **7/2**[2]

-412 3 4 ½ **Al Destoor**[33] 4429 7-9-7 **91** ................................................(t) DavidNolan 5 90
(Jennie Candlish) *trckd ldrs: hdwy 4f out: cl up over 2f out: sn rdn: kpt on same pce* **9/1**

-013 **4** *nk* **Zwayyan**[14] 5157 4-9-7 **91**........(p[1]) WilliamBuick 9 89
(William Haggas) *hld up towards rr: hdwy on wd outside 3f out: rdn to chse ldrs wl over 1f out: drvn and kpt on same pce appr fnl f* **11/4**[1]

4-16 **5** *4 1/2* **Pensax Boy**[38] 4207 5-8-13 **83**........ GeorgeDowning 4 72
(Daniel Mark Loughnane) *chsd ldrs: rdn along over 4f out: drvn over 2f out: sn btn* **20/1**

6014 **6** *1 3/4* **Just Hiss**[21] 4916 4-9-4 **91**........(p) RachelRichardson(3) 2 77
(Tim Easterby) *chsd clr ldr: hdwy 3f out: led briefly wl over 2f out: sn rdn and hdd: wknd qckly* **8/1**[3]

-650 **7** *14* **Al Hamdany (IRE)**[77] 2824 3-9-0 **92**........ DanielMuscutt 3 51
(Marco Botti) *chsd ldrs: rdn along over 3f out: sn wknd* **16/1**

455 **8** *5* **Berkshire (IRE)**[56] 3597 6-10-0 **98**........(b) TomQueally 1 46
(Paul Cole) *plld hrd: led and sn clr: jnd 3f out: hdd wl over 2f out and wknd qckly* **12/1**

2m 11.17s (1.77) **Going Correction** +0.425s/f (Yiel)
**WFA** 3 from 4yo+ 8lb **8** Ran SP% **115.0**
Speed ratings (Par 109): **109,107,104,103,100 98,87,83**
CSF £12.61 CT £74.50 TOTE £2.90: £1.40, £1.40, £2.70; EX 14.90 Trifecta £128.10.
**Owner** F Gillespie **Bred** E A R L Guy Pariente Holding **Trained** Hambleton, N Yorks

**FOCUS**
Add 18yds. A quite competitive handicap won by a horse who clearly likes this track. The form looks solid enough. The winner has been rated to the best view of his form.

## 5635 UNISON SUPPORTING YOUR COMMUNITY FILLIES' H'CAP 6f 2y
**5:05** (5:05) (Class 5) (0-70,70) 3-Y-0+ **£3,234** (£962; £481; £240) **Stalls** Centre

Form RPR
1 **1** **Maid In India (IRE)**[23] 4793 3-9-3 **65**........ NeilFarley 10 77+
(Eric Alston) *in tch: hdwy 1/2-way: led 11/2f out: rdn ins fnl f: kpt on wl towards fin* **9/2**[1]

0-02 **2** *3/4* **Seyasah (IRE)**[28] 4619 3-9-4 **66**........ TomQueally 7 72
(Chris Wall) *dwlt and rr: hdwy on inner over 2f out: chsd ldrs over 1f out: rdn to chal ent fnl f: sn drvn and ev ch: no ex last 50 yds* **8/1**

000 **3** *1 1/4* **Naralsaif (IRE)**[35] 4341 3-8-3 **51** oh5........(v[1]) AndrewMullen 11 53
(Derek Shaw) *in tch: hdwy on wd outside and cl up over 2f: rdn wl over 1f out: drvn and edgd lft ins fnl f: kpt on* **66/1**

5262 **4** *1 3/4* **Semana Santa**[18] 5004 4-9-5 **66**........ HollieDoyle(3) 9 63
(David Barron) *dwlt and rr: hdwy over 2f out: rdn over 1f out: styd on wl fnl f* **12/1**

0400 **5** *nk* **Lotara**[19] 4958 5-8-4 **55**........ SeanMooney(7) 1 51
(Jim Goldie) *midfield: hdwy to chse ldrs 2f out: sn rdn and kpt on same pce* **16/1**

3 **6** *hd* **Spirit Of Rosanna**[8] 5360 5-9-4 **62**........(bt) WilliamBuick 5 58
(Steph Hollinshead) *wnt lft s: led: rdn along 2f out: hdd 11/2f out: sn drvn and grad wknd* **5/1**[2]

306- **7** *2 3/4* **Vote**[291] 7440 3-9-6 **68**........ RyanTate 3 54
(James Eustace) *sltly hmpd s: chsd ldrs: rdn along over 2f out: sn wknd* **12/1**

4-02 **8** *3* **Penny Pot Lane**[75] 2883 4-9-8 **69**........ LewisEdmunds(3) 4 46
(Richard Whitaker) *hmpd s: chsd ldrs: rdn along over 2f out: sn drvn and wknd* **5/1**[2]

2240 **9** *nk* **Honeysuckle Lil (IRE)**[23] 4788 5-9-9 **70**........(p) RachelRichardson(3) 2 46
(Tim Easterby) *chsd ldrs: cl up 1/2-way: rdn over 2f out: sn drvn and wknd* **6/1**[3]

-430 **10** *1* **Miss Patience**[28] 4619 3-9-3 **65**........(h) JackMitchell 6 37
(Peter Chapple-Hyam) *chsd ldrs: rdn along wl over 2f out: sn wknd* **9/1**

0-05 **11** *5* **Lexington Sky (IRE)**[8] 5375 3-9-7 **69**........ DavidNolan 8 25
(Roger Fell) *a towards rr* **9/1**

1m 13.2s (-0.40) **Going Correction** +0.05s/f (Good)
**WFA** 3 from 4yo+ 4lb **11** Ran SP% **119.7**
Speed ratings (Par 100): **104,103,101,99,98 98,94,90,90,88 82**
CSF £41.39 CT £2104.29 TOTE £5.10: £1.90, £2.60, £13.20; EX 48.20 Trifecta £1795.10.
**Owner** Con Harrington **Bred** C F Harrington **Trained** Longton, Lancs

**FOCUS**
A fair sprint handicap which produced a winner who looks destined to go on to better things.

## 5636 UNISON CAMPAIGNING FOR PUBLIC SERVICES H'CAP 5f 3y
**5:35** (5:36) (Class 5) (0-70,71) 3-Y-0 **£3,234** (£962; £481; £240) **Stalls** Centre

Form RPR
2454 **1** **Peachey Carnehan**[10] 5291 3-8-13 **64**........(v) PhilDennis(5) 2 70
(Michael Mullineaux) *dwlt and rr: hdwy on wd outside over 2f out: rdn to chse ldrs over 1f out: chal ins fnl f: sn drvn and edgd rt: led last 75 yds* **12/1**

0221 **2** *1/2* **Granny Roz**[14] 5167 3-9-4 **67**........ RachelRichardson(3) 4 71
(David Barron) *led: rdn along wl over 1f out: hung bdly rt to stands rail ent fnl f: drvn and hdd last 75 yds: kpt on* **6/4**[1]

0304 **3** *nse* **Angel Palanas**[33] 4428 3-8-6 **59**........(p) RussellHarris(7) 3 63
(K R Burke) *chsd ldr: rdn along 2f out: drvn ent fnl f and ev ch: kpt on same pce last 100 yds* **11/1**

-104 **4** *1/2* **Qatari Riyals (IRE)**[23] 4797 3-9-8 **71**........ HollieDoyle(3) 1 73
(Richard Hannon) *chsd ldrs: rdn along wl over 1f out:. drvn and kpt on fnl f* **4/1**[3]

3522 **5** *1 1/2* **Oriental Lilly**[8] 5375 3-8-12 **65**........ SeanMooney(7) 5 62+
(Jim Goldie) *dwlt and rr: hdwy wl over 1f out: sn rdn and kpt on fnl f* **5/2**[2]

60-5 **6** *1* **The Night Before**[19] 4964 3-8-12 **58**........ TomQueally 6 51
(Robert Cowell) *trckd ldr: hdwy 2f out and sn cl up: rdn over 1f out: drvn and kpt on same pce fnl f* **12/1**

6535 **7** *3 3/4* **Henrietta's Dream**[7] 5419 3-8-2 **48** oh2........(b) AndrewMullen 7 28
(John Wainwright) *cjhased ldrs: rdn along 2f out: sn outpcd* **25/1**

1m 0.82s (0.32) **Going Correction** +0.05s/f (Good) **7** Ran SP% **116.1**
Speed ratings (Par 100): **99,98,98,97,94 93,87**
CSF £31.52 TOTE £13.90: £4.20, £1.40; EX 46.90 Trifecta £222.50.
**Owner** Keith Jones **Bred** J M Duggan & The Late T Duggan **Trained** Alpraham, Cheshire

**FOCUS**
An ordinary sprint handicap which saw the winner come from last to first. The third has been rated to this year's form.

T/Plt: £143.10 to a £1 stake. Pool: £76,787.65 - 391.46 winning units T/Qpdt: £16.80 to a £1 stake. Pool: £5,245.66 - 230.23 winning units. **Joe Rowntree**

# 5592 GOODWOOD (R-H)
Saturday, August 5

**OFFICIAL GOING: Soft (good to soft in places; 6.7)**
Wind: light to medium, half against, changing to half behind race 4 Weather: sunny spells, heavy shower before racing

## 5637 QATAR STEWARDS' SPRINT H'CAP (CONSOLATION RACE FOR THE QATAR STEWARDS' CUP) 6f
**1:50** (1:51) (Class 2) 3-Y-0+
**£46,687** (£13,980; £6,990; £3,495; £1,747; £877) **Stalls** High

Form RPR
2232 **1** **Scorching Heat**[7] 5423 3-8-9 **84**........ OisinMurphy 12 93+
(Andrew Balding) *travelled strly thrght: chsd ldrs: clsd on bridle over 1f out: rdn to ld ins fnl f: a doing enough after: rdn out* **9/2**[1]

4503 **2** *3/4* **Tommy G**[7] 5396 4-8-0 **76**........ DavidEgan(5) 18 84
(Jim Goldie) *swtg: chsd ldrs: rdn 2f out: hdwy u.p 1f out: chsd wnr 100yds out: kpt on wl but a hld* **14/1**

-050 **3** *1* **Son Of Africa**[21] 4881 5-9-8 **93**........ MartinHarley 3 98
(Henry Candy) *lw: hld up in last quartet: effrt and hdwy over 1f out: clsng whn nt clrest of runs 1f out: kpt on wl u.p ins fnl f: nt rch ldrs* **12/1**

3431 **4** *hd* **Royal Brave (IRE)**[11] 5256 6-9-2 **87** 6ex........ DanielTudhope 2 91
(Rebecca Bastiman) *lw: hld up in rr: effrt over 1f out: gd hdwy u.p 1f out: styd on wl ins fnl f: nt rch ldrs* **25/1**

5030 **5** *nk* **Stellarta**[22] 4830 6-9-6 **91**........ DavidProbert 9 94
(Michael Blanshard) *hld up in midfield: effrt over 1f out: hdwy to chse ldrs ins fnl f: kpt on but nvr threatening wnr* **33/1**

3100 **6** *1 3/4* **George Bowen (IRE)**[7] 5435 5-9-10 **95**........(v) JackGarritty 5 93
(Richard Fahey) *hld up in last quartet: hdwy and drifting rt over 1f out: nt clrest of runs and swtchd lft 1f out: kpt on same pce ins fnl f* **14/1**

4205 **7** *3/4* **Lucky Beggar (IRE)**[15] 5129 7-9-3 **88**........ SilvestreDeSousa 8 86+
(David C Griffiths) *taken down early and led to post: led tl over 2f out: rdn and ev ch whn carried rt over 1f out: hmpd 1f out: wknd ins fnl f* **16/1**

4105 **8** *1/2* **Goring (GER)**[3] 5530 5-9-0 **85**........ JohnFahy 17 79
(Eve Johnson Houghton) *squeezed for room leaving stalls: hld up in midfield: effrt 2f out: kpt on u.p ins fnl f: nvr getting on terms w ldrs* **20/1**

6021 **9** *hd* **The Wagon Wheel (IRE)**[21] 4889 3-9-0 **96** 6ex.(b) ConnorMurtagh(7) 16 88
(Richard Fahey) *lw: bmpd leaving stalls: sn rcvrd and w ldr tl led over 2f out: hung rt over 1f out: hdd ins fnl f: sn btn and wknd fnl 100yds* **10/1**[3]

1-23 **10** *1 1/4* **Six Strings**[15] 5094 3-8-12 **87**........ TonyHamilton 20 75
(Richard Fahey) *lw: hld up in midfield: drvn and outpcd wl over 1f out: no threat to ldrs kpt on same pce u.p fr over 1f out* **12/1**

4326 **11** *nk* **Pettochside**[4] 5505 8-8-11 **85**........ HectorCrouch(3) 14 73
(John Bridger) *bmpd s: sn chsng ldrs: drvn wl over 1f out: unable qck u.p: wknd ins fnl f* **14/1**

5003 **12** *1/2* **Rasheeq (IRE)**[7] 5435 4-9-5 **90**........ DavidAllan 10 76
(Tim Easterby) *hld up in midfield: lost pl and dropped to rr 2f out: sn drvn and modest hdwy 1f out: no threat to ldrs but kpt on ins fnl f* **10/1**[3]

2002 **13** *nk* **Gin In The Inn (IRE)**[6] 5457 4-9-6 **91**........ RyanMoore 4 76
(Richard Fahey) *racd alone towards far rail: hld up in last quartet: effrt over 1f out: no imp: wl hld and eased wl ins fnl f* **6/1**[2]

1110 **14** *1 1/2* **Goodwood Crusader (IRE)**[23] 4813 3-8-12 **94**........ FinleyMarsh(7) 7 74
(Richard Hughes) *midfield tl lost pl and dropped to rr 2f out: n.d after and wl btn whn swtchd lft over 1f out* **10/1**[3]

2251 **15** *1/2* **Lightning Charlie**[22] 4830 5-9-7 **92** 6ex........ SteveDrowne 19 71
(Amanda Perrett) *hld up in midfield: rdn 2f out: sn struggling and lost pl over 1f out: wknd fnl f* **20/1**

2221 **16** *3/4* **Manshood (IRE)**[21] 4897 4-8-10 **81** 6ex........(b) AndreaAtzeni 21 58
(Paul Midgley) *swtg: hld up in midfield: effrt u.p ent fnl 2f: sn struggling and lost pl over 1f out: bhd ins fnl f* **12/1**

1m 13.17s (0.97) **Going Correction** +0.325s/f (Good)
**WFA** 3 from 4yo+ 4lb **16** Ran SP% **125.0**
Speed ratings (Par 109): **106,105,103,103,103 100,99,99,98,97 96,96,95,93,92 91**
CSF £66.14 CT £760.92 TOTE £5.30: £1.80, £3.80, £3.30, £4.70; EX 55.60 Trifecta £890.20.
**Owner** Qatar Racing Limited **Bred** Dukes Stud & Overbury Stallions Ltd **Trained** Kingsclere, Hants
■ L C Saloon was withdrawn. Price at time of withdrawal 50/1. Rule 4 does not apply
■ Stewards' Enquiry : Connor Murtagh three-day ban; careless riding (19th-21st Aug)

**FOCUS**
All distances as advertised. Clerk of the course Seamus Buckley left the going description of soft, good to soft in places following the opening race. Steve Drowne said the ground was "very hard work", while David Probert said it was "verging on heavy". Martin Harley did say, though, that the rain before the first "100 per cent helped" the runners get through the ground. The action unfolded down the centre in what was a competitive sprint, as one would expect for a consolation Stewards' Cup, and the 3yo winner was well backed. A small pb from the runner-up, with the fourth running as well as ever.

## 5638 QATAR SUMMER H'CAP 1m 6f
**2:25** (2:26) (Class 2) 3-Y-0+
**£62,250** (£18,640; £9,320; £4,660; £2,330; £1,170) **Stalls** Low

Form RPR
1023 **1** **Soldier In Action (FR)**[22] 4849 4-9-10 **106**........ SilvestreDeSousa 2 114
(Mark Johnston) *mid-div: hdwy 3f out: sn rdn: cl 5th ent fnl f: str run fnl 100yds: led fnl stride* **11/1**

1044 **2** *hd* **Blakeney Point**[28] 4614 4-8-13 **95**........ KieranShoemark 11 102
(Roger Charlton) *lw: hld up towards rr: hdwy fr 3f out: sn rdn: chal over 1f out: led jst ins fnl f: styd on wl: hdd fnl stride* **12/1**

4212 **3** *shd* **Getback In Paris (IRE)**[22] 4828 4-8-10 **92**........ ShaneKelly 8 99
(Richard Hughes) *lw: cl up: wnt 3rd 6f out: chal 3f out: sn rdn: disputing cl 3rd ent fnl f: ev ch fnl 100yds: styd on wl* **11/2**[1]

-015 **4** *3/4* **My Reward**[35] 4356 5-8-12 **94**........ DavidAllan 10 100
(Tim Easterby) *led: rdn to qckn pce jst over 3f out: sn strly chal but hld on gamely to advantage: hdd jst ins fnl f: styd on but no ex fnl 75yds* **16/1**

1105 **5** *1 1/2* **Jaameh (IRE)**[14] 5164 4-9-1 **97**........ JimCrowley 6 101
(Mark Johnston) *trckd ldr: chal 3f out: sn rdn: stl ev ch ent fnl f: no ex fnl 140yds* **11/1**

3-54 **6** *2 3/4* **Platitude**[21] 4917 4-9-9 **105**........ AndreaAtzeni 7 105
(Sir Michael Stoute) *hld up towards rr: hdwy 3f out: sn rdn: styd on but nt pce to get involved* **8/1**[3]

0162 **7** *3/4* **Sir Chauvelin**[22] 4849 5-9-3 **99**........ DanielTudhope 5 98
(Jim Goldie) *hld up towards rr: hdwy over 3f out: sn rdn: styd on same pce fnl 2f* **14/1**

-030 **8** ½ **Carntop**[28] 4614 4-9-4 **100** HarryBentley 14 98
(Ralph Beckett) *mid-div: swtchd lft 3f out: sn rdn: hdwy over 2f out: styd on but nt pce to get involved* **20/1**

3-21 **9** ¾ **Saigon City**[78] 2797 7-9-2 **98** PatCosgrave 9 95
(Declan Carroll) *cl up tl outpcd 3f out: no threat after* **6/1**[2]

3-50 **10** 1½ **Cleonte (IRE)**[46] 3928 4-9-1 **97** (p[1]) LiamKeniry 4 92
(Andrew Balding) *mid-div: outpcd and lost pl over 3f out: no threat after* **25/1**

-362 **11** 7 **Mainstream**[22] 4863 4-9-4 **100** (h) RyanMoore 1 85
(Sir Michael Stoute) *s.i.s: bhd: rdn over 2f out: nvr any imp* **6/1**[2]

034- **12** shd **Felix Mendelssohn (IRE)**[70] 3102 6-8-11 **93** (t) FranBerry 12 78
(Joseph Patrick O'Brien, Ire) *a towards rr* **10/1**

5-43 **13** 2¼ **Shraaoh (IRE)**[28] 4614 4-8-11 **93** (p[1]) FrankieDettori 13 75
(Sir Michael Stoute) *trckd ldr: chal 3f out: sn rdn: wknd wl over 1f out* **8/1**[3]

3m 10.25s (6.65) **Going Correction** +0.425s/f (Yiel) 13 Ran SP% **120.8**
Speed ratings (Par 109): **98,97,97,97,96 94,94,94,93,92 88,88,87**
CSF £138.05 CT £815.80 TOTE £11.50: £3.30, £3.90, £2.10; EX 209.60 Trifecta £1534.60.
**Owner** A D Spence **Bred** Randolf Peters **Trained** Middleham Moor, N Yorks

**FOCUS**
This high-quality staying handicap looked wide open. It was run at a fair pace and saw a tight finish towards the far side. The third and fourth help set the standard.

## 5639 QATAR GORDON STKS (GROUP 3) 1m 3f 218y
**3:00** (3:02) (Class 1) 3-Y-O **£56,710** (£21,500; £10,760; £5,360; £2,690) **Stalls** High

Form RPR

-133 **1** **Crystal Ocean**[43] 4029 3-9-1 112 RyanMoore 1 116
(Sir Michael Stoute) *swtg: trckd ldng pair: gng best over 2f out: rdn and qcknd to ld over 1f out: drifted rt but clr 1f out: r.o strly: comf* **6/4**[1]

3102 **2** 3½ **Khalidi**[43] 4029 3-9-1 114 FrankieDettori 4 110
(John Gosden) *hld up in 4th: swtchd lft and effrt to chal wl over 2f out: led wl over 1f out: sn hdd and unable to match pce of wnr: wl hld and kpt on same pce fnl f* **9/4**[2]

1-11 **3** 1 **Mount Moriah**[22] 4828 3-9-1 102 HarryBentley 2 109
(Ralph Beckett) *lw: led and set stdy gallop: rdn and qcknd ent fnl 3f: drvn and hdd wl over 1f out: outpcd by wnr over 1f out: 3rd and kpt on same pce fnl f: eased towards fin* **10/3**[3]

-213 **4** 1¼ **Jake's Hill**[29] 4584 3-9-1 104 CharlesBishop 3 107
(Eve Johnson Houghton) *trckd ldr: rdn wl over 2f out: outpcd and dropped to rr over 1f out: no ch w wnr and kpt on same pce after* **16/1**

1-21 **5** 1¾ **Across Dubai**[28] 4618 3-9-1 95 PatCosgrave 5 104
(William Haggas) *lw: hld up in rr: effrt over 2f out: 4th and no imp 1f out: wknd ins fnl f* **9/1**

2m 42.94s (4.54) **Going Correction** +0.425s/f (Yiel) 5 Ran SP% **109.7**
Speed ratings (Par 110): **101,98,98,97,96**
CSF £5.10 TOTE £2.20: £1.30, £1.50; EX 5.30 Trifecta £8.50.
**Owner** Sir Evelyn De Rothschild **Bred** Southcourt Stud **Trained** Newmarket, Suffolk

**FOCUS**
This looked a match between the King Edward second and third and they duly dominated, with the impressive winner reversing Ascot form. The pace as just a steady one. The fourth has been rated to his Sandown figure.

## 5640 QATAR STEWARDS' CUP H'CAP (HERITAGE HANDICAP) 6f
**3:35** (3:36) (Class 2) 3-Y-O+
**£155,625** (£46,600; £23,300; £11,650; £5,825; £2,925) **Stalls** High

Form RPR

1240 **1** **Lancelot Du Lac (ITY)**[42] 4072 7-9-5 **104** (h) FrankieDettori 15 113
(Dean Ivory) *on toes: taken down early: led centre gp: swtchd to far side and overall ldr 3f out: rdn wl over 1f out: kpt on strly fnl f* **25/1**

-624 **2** ¾ **Aeolus**[35] 4354 6-9-4 **103** (p[1]) PatCosgrave 12 110
(Ed Walker) *racd centre: mid-div: hdwy 2f out: nt clr run over 1f out: r.o strly fnl f: snatched 2nd fnl stride* **16/1**

-021 **3** nse **Upstaging**[34] 4411 5-8-10 **100** 6ex (p) DavidEgan(5) 7 106
(Paul Cole) *trckd ldr on far side: rdn over 2f out: r.o ins fnl f: wnt 2nd briefly nring fin: kpt on* **25/1**

00U6 **4** hd **Growl**[21] 4907 5-9-3 **109** (p) ConnorMurtagh(7) 8 115
(Richard Fahey) *chsd ldrs in centre: rdn to chse wnr ent fnl f: sn drifted lft: kpt on* **7/1**[2]

41-0 **5** ¾ **Shanghai Glory (IRE)**[42] 4072 4-9-2 **101** FranBerry 3 104
(Charles Hills) *trckd ldr on far side: rdn whn sltly outpcd over 2f out: swtchd off rails ins fnl f: kpt on wl fnl 120yds* **14/1**

33-0 **6** hd **Hoof It**[15] 5094 10-9-1 **100** NathanEvans 4 103
(Michael Easterby) *led on far side tl 3f out: sn rdn: kpt on same pce fnl f* **20/1**

-651 **7** ¾ **Danzeno**[21] 4881 6-9-11 **110** 6ex SilvestreDeSousa 16 110
(Michael Appleby) *hld up towards rr of centre gp: rdn over 1f out: r.o strly ins fnl f but nvr threatening to get involved* **7/1**[2]

2156 **8** shd **Solar Flair**[35] 4354 5-9-4 **103** HarryBentley 6 103
(William Knight) *chsd ldrs on far side: rdn over 2f out: kpt on same pce fnl f* **40/1**

2-03 **9** ¾ **Donjuan Triumphant (IRE)**[98] 2150 4-9-7 **106** (h) DavidProbert 20 104
(Andrew Balding) *lw: hld up towards rr on nrside: hdwy jst over 1f out: kpt on ins fnl f but nvr threatening to get involved* **20/1**

3115 **10** nse **Classic Seniority**[7] 5396 5-8-11 **96** 6ex (p) WilliamCarson 10 93
(Marjorie Fife) *racd centre: mid-div: rdn 3f out: kpt on but nt pce to get on terms* **33/1**

0320 **11** nk **Eastern Impact (IRE)**[42] 4072 6-9-4 **103** (p[1]) JackGarritty 11 100
(Richard Fahey) *racd centre: trckd ldrs: rdn 2f out: fdd ins fnl f* **20/1**

1404 **12** ½ **Raucous**[14] 5149 4-9-5 **104** (bt) JimCrowley 26 99
(William Haggas) *s.i.s: racd nrside: towards rr: rdn and hdwy over 1f out: kpt on fnl f but no ch* **14/1**

0206 **13** ½ **Intisaab**[14] 5149 6-9-6 **108** (p) ShelleyBirkett(3) 1 101
(David O'Meara) *s.i.s: racd far side: nvr bttr than mid-div* **25/1**

3-63 **14** shd **Projection**[42] 4072 4-9-6 **105** KieranShoemark 27 98+
(Roger Charlton) *on toes: taken down early: hld up towards rr on nrside: hdwy over 3f out: sn rdn: nvr threatened: wknd fnl 120yds* **11/1**

2126 **15** hd **Stake Acclaim (IRE)**[34] 4411 5-8-13 **98** RobertWinston 14 90
(Dean Ivory) *chsd ldrs in centre gp: rdn and ev ch 2f out: wknd ent fnl f* **33/1**

3005 **16** nk **Duke Of Firenze**[15] 5116 8-9-10 **109** DavidAllan 13 100
(David C Griffiths) *racd centre: hld up towards rr: hdwy over 2f out into midfield: sn rdn: wknd fnl f* **40/1**

3004 **17** nk **Poyle Vinnie**[4] 5505 7-9-0 **99** AlistairRawlinson 18 89
(Michael Appleby) *taken down early: racd centre: hld up towards rr: rdn 2f out: sme late prog: n.d* **28/1**

4560 **18** ½ **Edward Lewis**[21] 4881 4-8-13 **101** JoshDoyle(3) 22 90
(David O'Meara) *racd nrside: towards rr: sme hdwy 4f out: rdn over 2f out: no further imp* **33/1**

2000 **19** nk **Harry Hurricane**[4] 5505 5-9-1 **100** FergusSweeney 19 88
(George Baker) *racd nrside: a towards rr* **50/1**

3360 **20** hd **Go Far**[23] 4816 7-8-8 **98** (v) JoshuaBryan(5) 21 85
(Alan Bailey) *led nrside gp but overall midfield: rdn and hdwy over 2f out: hung lft over 1f out: wknd ent fnl f* **66/1**

1560 **21** ½ **Brian The Snail (IRE)**[23] 4813 3-8-12 **101** (b[1]) TonyHamilton 2 86
(Richard Fahey) *racd far side: mid-div: rdn over 3f out: nvr any imp: wknd ent fnl f* **16/1**

5602 **22** ½ **Sir Dancealot (IRE)**[21] 4905 3-8-12 **101** RyanMoore 24 84
(David Elsworth) *lw: slowly away: swtchd to centre gp sn after s: hld up bhd: pushed along 3f out: no imp whn nt clr run 2f out: no ch after* **5/1**[1]

1002 **23** ¾ **Al Qahwa (IRE)**[7] 5435 4-8-12 **97** DanielTudhope 9 79
(David O'Meara) *chsd ldrs in centre: pushed along whn hmpd and lost pl over 2f out: no ch after: snatched up again whn hmpd jst ins fnl f* **9/1**[3]

-105 **24** 5 **Perfect Pasture**[14] 5149 7-9-10 **109** (v) AndreaAtzeni 17 75
(Michael Easterby) *racd centre mid-div tl over 2f out* **33/1**

5050 **25** ¾ **Mobsta (IRE)**[7] 5435 5-9-5 **104** MartinDwyer 23 67
(Mick Channon) *racd nrside: hmpd s: a towards rr* **33/1**

0-00 **26** 30 **Outback Traveller (IRE)**[42] 4072 6-9-3 **102** (v[1]) MartinHarley 28
(Robert Cowell) *racd nrside: hld up towards rr: eased whn appeared to lose action wl over 1f out* **25/1**

1m 12.28s (0.08) **Going Correction** +0.325s/f (Good)
**WFA** 3 from 4yo+ 4lb 26 Ran SP% **141.3**
Speed ratings (Par 109): **112,111,110,110,109 109,108,108,107,107 106,106,105,105,105 104,104,103,103,102 102,101,100,93**
CSF £353.38 CT £9838.22 TOTE £28.10: £5.80, £5.20, £5.40, £2.60; EX 762.20 Trifecta £13230.70 Part Won..
**Owner** Michael & Heather Yarrow **Bred** Elektra Di Fausto Martellozzo & C Sas **Trained** Radlett, Herts

■ Stewards' Enquiry : Frankie Dettori four-day ban: careless riding (Aug 19-22)

**FOCUS**
A classy edition of the Stewards' Cup. The pace was all on the far side, causing the field to head that way, and it proved hard to make up ground from behind. Those drawn low were at a distinct advantage. The winner has been rated to his turf best.

## 5641 QATAR EBF STALLIONS MAIDEN STKS (PLUS 10 RACE) 7f
**4:10** (4:13) (Class 2) 2-Y-O **£19,407** (£5,775; £2,886; £1,443) **Stalls** Low

Form RPR

**1** **Dee Ex Bee** 2-9-0 0 SilvestreDeSousa 8 93+
(Mark Johnston) *athletic: lw: mde all: urged along 3f: drvn and kpt finding ex whn pressed 2f out: forged ahd ins fnl f: styd on strly: rdn out* **5/2**[1]

52 **2** 2¼ **Bathsheba Bay (IRE)**[10] 5301 2-9-0 0 RyanMoore 14 87
(Richard Hannon) *lw: chsd ldrs: effrt to press wnr wl over 1f out: sn wnt clr w wnr: no ex u.p ins fnl f: outpcd fnl 150yds* **5/2**[1]

**3** 4½ **Capital Flight (IRE)** 2-9-0 0 FranBerry 3 79+
(Paul Cole) *athletic: hld up in last quartet: nt clr run on inner and shuffled bk to last 2f out: swtchd lft over 1f out: weaving through and hdwy over 1f out: styd on wl to go 3rd wl ins fnl f: no ch w ldng pair* **16/1**

44 **4** ½ **Rogue**[51] 3746 2-9-0 0 MartinHarley 5 74
(Richard Hannon) *cmpt: trckd ldr tl 2f out: 3rd and outpcd over 1f out: battling for wl hld 3rd fnl f: plugged on but lost 3rd wl ins fnl f* **9/2**[2]

42 **5** ½ **Preacher Man (IRE)**[21] 4880 2-9-0 0 DougieCostello 12 73
(Jamie Osborne) *t.k.h: hld up in last trio: swtchd rt and hdwy 2f out: no imp u.p over 1f out: battling for wl hld 3rd and plugged on same pce ins fnl f* **8/1**[3]

**6** 1¾ **Power Of Darkness** 2-9-0 0 JimCrowley 1 68
(Marcus Tregoning) *unf: dwlt: hld up in last pair: effrt 2f out: rdn and hdwy into midfield jst over 1f out: nvr on terms w ldrs and kpt on same pce fnl f* **9/1**

3 **7** 2¾ **Trogon (IRE)**[29] 4583 2-9-0 0 CharlesBishop 10 61
(Mick Channon) *w'like: wl in tch in midfield: rdn over 2f out: sn struggling and outpcd 2f out: wknd over 1f out* **16/1**

5 **8** shd **Rustang (FR)**[19] 4973 2-9-0 0 ShaneKelly 7 61
(Richard Hughes) *w'like: t.k.h: hld up wl in tch in midfield: lost pl and sltly impeded 2f out: sn wknd and drifted rt* **33/1**

**9** 2¼ **Sing Out Loud (IRE)** 2-9-0 0 HectorCrouch 11 55
(Gary Moore) *w'like: stdd s: hld up in last trio: effrt ent fnl 2f: sn btn and wknd* **25/1**

00 **10** 3½ **Galloping Hogan (IRE)**[30] 4520 2-9-0 0 MartinDwyer 2 46
(Sylvester Kirk) *leggy: t.k.h: in tch in midfield on inner: hmpd after 1f: wandering and lost pl jst over 2f out: sn wknd and bhd over 1f out* **50/1**

**11** 2¾ **The Lamplighter (FR)** 2-9-0 0 PatCosgrave 13 39
(George Baker) *w'like: hld up in midfield on outer: rdn 2f out: sn edgd rt and wknd: bhd fnl f* **50/1**

1m 28.62s (1.62) **Going Correction** +0.425s/f (Yiel) 11 Ran SP% **118.9**
Speed ratings (Par 100): **107,104,99,98,98 96,93,92,90,86 83**
CSF £8.11 TOTE £3.20: £1.40, £1.30, £4.50; EX 9.00 Trifecta £133.70.
**Owner** Sheikh Hamdan bin Mohammed Al Maktoum **Bred** Godolphin **Trained** Middleham Moor, N Yorks

■ King Of The Sand was withdrawn. Price at time of withdrawal 20/1. Rule 4 does not apply

**FOCUS**
The big two dominated this maiden, with the experienced runner-up no match for the highly promising newcomer. The first two have been rated around the better race standard.

## 5642 QATAR H'CAP 7f
**4:45** (4:45) (Class 2) (0-105,103) 3-Y-O
**£18,675** (£5,592; £2,796; £1,398; £699; £351) **Stalls** Low

Form RPR

4135 **1** **Battered**[7] 5434 3-8-9 **91** (b[1]) SilvestreDeSousa 6 101
(William Haggas) *plld hrd: hld up in midfield: effrt over 1f out: hdwy and edgd rt ent fnl f: chsd wnr 1f out: styd on wl u.p to ld last strides* **7/2**[2]

6-11 **2** hd **Sir Titan**[26] 4698 3-8-2 **84** HayleyTurner 2 93
(Marcus Tregoning) *t.k.h: led after 1f and dictated stdy gallop: rdn wl over 1f out: drvn ins fnl f: kpt on wl: hdd last strides* **7/1**

0201 **3** 2¾ **Medahim (IRE)**[21] 4904 3-9-4 **100** FrankieDettori 4 102+
(Richard Hannon) *stdd after s: hld up in tch in last pair: effrt whn hung rt over 1f out: squeezed for room and hmpd 1f out: stl hanging and swtchd lft ins fnl f: r.o to go 3rd towards: no threat to ldng pair* **7/2**[2]

6543 **4** ½ **Mazyoun**[14] 5159 3-8-0 **87** (b) DavidEgan(5) 1 88
(Hugo Palmer) *stdd after s: t.k.h: hld up in tch in midfield: effrt and hdwy on inner over 1f out: kpt on same pce and no imp fnl f* **6/1**[3]

-101 **5** *shd* **Aventinus (IRE)**55 3620 3-8-6 **88** HarryBentley 5 89
(Hugo Palmer) *led for 1f: chsd ldr: effrt over 2f out: struggling to qckn over 1f out: lost 2nd 1f out: kpt on same pce ins fnl f* **8/1**
016- **6** *hd* **Colonel Frank**276 7764 3-8-2 **84** JoeyHaynes 3 84
(Ed Walker) *trckd ldrs: effrt ent fnl 2f: struggling to qckn whn carried rt and hmpd 1f out: styd on same pce ins fnl f* **20/1**
-410 **7** *2* **Taamol (IRE)**45 3959 3-9-7 **103** JimCrowley 7 98
(Sir Michael Stoute) *swtg: stdd s and dropped in bhd: effrt 2f out: no imp and edging rt over 1f out: wl hld and onepced fnl f* **11/4**1
1m 28.2s (1.20) **Going Correction** +0.425s/f (Yiel) 7 Ran SP% **113.8**
Speed ratings (Par 106): **110,109,106,106,105 105,103**
CSF £27.39 TOTE £3.80: £2.30, £2.90; EX 35.80 Trifecta £117.40.
**Owner** B Haggas **Bred** Coln Valley Stud **Trained** Newmarket, Suffolk
■ Stewards' Enquiry : Silvestre De Sousa caution; careless riding

**FOCUS**
This rates sound handicap form, despite it being run at a steady pace.

## 5643 QATAR APPRENTICE H'CAP 1m 1f 11y
**5:20** (5:21) (Class 3) (0-90,90) 3-Y-0+ **£16,172** (£4,812; £2,405; £1,202) **Stalls** Low

Form RPR
001 **1** **Storm King**21 4893 8-9-8 **85** EdwardGreatrex 16 96
(David C Griffiths) *broke v qckly: led for 1f: pressed ldr tl led again 3f out: edgd rt u.p over 1f out: forged ahd ins fnl f: styd on and a doing enough: rdn out* **25/1**
21 **2** *½* **Born To Be Alive (IRE)**61 3383 3-9-5 **90** CliffordLee 4 100+
(K R Burke) *athletic: lw: hld up in tch in midfield: effrt 2f out: hdwy u.p over 1f out: chsd wnr ins fnl f: styd on and clsng towards fin: nvr quite getting to wnr* **5/2**1
0034 **3** *2 ¾* **Boots And Spurs**8 5382 8-9-2 **82** (v) PaddyPilley(3) 13 86
(Scott Dixon) *chsd ldrs: effrt ent fnl 2f: unable qck over 1f out: styd on same pce and no imp ins fnl f* **25/1**
-022 **4** *hd* **Interconnection**24 4763 6-9-6 **90** (p) StephenCummins(7) 1 94
(Ed Vaughan) *rousted along leaving stalls and hdwy to ld 1f out: hdd 3f out: sn rdn and styd pressing ldrs: cl 3rd but struggling to qckn whn squeezed for room and hmpd ent fnl f: kpt on same pce after* **12/1**
3116 **5** *nk* **Magic City (IRE)**26 4692 8-9-8 **85** NathanEvans 6 88
(Michael Easterby) *hld up in tch in midfield: swtchd rt 3f out: hdwy on inner to chal over 1f out tl no ex ins fnl f: wknd and lost 3 pls fnl 100yds* **20/1**
4121 **6** *½* **Rotherwick (IRE)**24 4763 5-9-8 **88** (t) MitchGodwin(3) 8 90
(Paul Cole) *hld up in tch in midfield: trying to cl whn nt clr run 2f: effrt u.p whn n.m.r ent fnl f: drvn and kpt on same pce ins fnl f* **11/1**
5231 **7** *½* **Fast Dancer (IRE)**10 5276 5-9-3 **83** DavidEgan(3) 9 84
(Joseph Tuite) *t.k.h: hld up in last trio: swtchd lft and effrt 2f out: hdwy u.p over 1f out: kpt on ins fnl f: nvr trbld ldrs* **14/1**
3643 **8** *1 ¼* **Spring Offensive (IRE)**15 5130 5-9-8 **90** ConnorMurtagh(5) 11 88
(Richard Fahey) *hld up in tch in midfield: effrt 2f out: no imp u.p whn swtchd lft 1f out: kpt on same pce ins fnl f* **16/1**
511 **9** *2* **Fire Tree (IRE)**22 4832 4-9-1 **81** GeorgiaCox(3) 12 75
(Charlie Fellowes) *lw: hld up in midfield: effrt whn squeezed for room wl over 1f out: sn drvn and no hdwy: wknd ins fnl f* **10/1**3
0106 **10** *½* **In The Red (IRE)**22 4832 4-9-4 **81** HectorCrouch 17 74
(Martin Smith) *chsd ldrs: rdn ent fnl 2f: unable qck and lost pl over 1f out: wknd ins fnl f and eased towards fin* **20/1**
-003 **11** *¾* **Balmoral Castle**22 4832 8-9-1 **85** Pierre-LouisJamin(7) 7 77
(Jonathan Portman) *hld up in midfield: swtchd lft and effrt on outer over 2f out: no imp over 1f out: wl hld fnl f* **16/1**
316R **12** *3* **Retrieve (AUS)**13 4158 10-8-12 **82** TinaSmith(7) 15 67
(Carroll Gray) *bustled along early: nvr travelling towards rr: drvn over 2f out: sn outpcd and wknd over 1f out* **40/1**
-300 **13** *1 ½* **Bancnuanaheireann (IRE)**72 2999 10-9-13 **90** AlistairRawlinson 2 72
(Michael Appleby) *hld up towards rr: effrt u.p over 2f out: sn struggling: wknd over 1f out* **33/1**
2360 **14** *¾* **Morning Suit (USA)**2 5568 3-9-0 **88** RichardOliver(3) 14 69
(Mark Johnston) *hld up towards rr: rdn wl over 2f out: sn struggling and btn: bhd over 1f out* **20/1**
0415 **15** *nk* **Jufn**30 4522 4-9-2 **79** (h) TimClark 3 59
(John Butler) *hld up in last trio: effrt over 2f out: no hdwy u.p 2f out: bhd and eased ins fnl f* **16/1**
131- **16** *shd* **You're Hired**326 6456 4-9-13 **90** KieranShoemark 5 70
(Amanda Perrett) *chsd ldrs: pushed along 2f out: sn rdn and btn: eased ins fnl f* **6/1**2
-045 **17** *½* **Storm Ahead (IRE)**34 4410 4-9-4 **88** TylerSaunders(7) 10 67
(Marcus Tregoning) *t.k.h: hld up in rr: effrt effrt ent fnl 2f: no imp: bhd 1f out* **6/1**2
1m 57.5s (1.20) **Going Correction** +0.425s/f (Yiel)
**WFA** 3 from 4yo+ 8lb 17 Ran SP% **133.9**
Speed ratings (Par 107): **111,110,108,107,107 107,106,105,103,103 102,100,98,98,97 97,97**
CSF £87.84 CT £1727.13 TOTE £23.20: £3.60, £1.30, £5.10, £3.00; EX 231.00 Trifecta £5597.10.
**Owner** Eros Bloodstock **Bred** Norcroft Park Stud And D Laidlaw **Trained** Bawtry, S Yorks

**FOCUS**
An ordinary handicap, it went to an outsider who got first run on the favourite. Those who raced prominently were favoured, so the runner-up should have his effort upgraded. The third helps set the standard.
T/Jkpt: Not Won. T/Plt: £160.80 to a £1 stake. Pool £301,770.79 - 1369.72 winning units. T/Qpdt: £19.90 to a £1 stake. Pool: £19,689.98 - 729.96 winning units. **Steve Payne & Tim Mitchell**

# 5091 HAMILTON (R-H)
Saturday, August 5
**OFFICIAL GOING: Good to soft (soft in places; 6.2)**
Wind: Breezy, across Weather: Fine, dry

## 5644 BB FOODSERVICE NURSERY H'CAP (A £20,000 BB FOODSERVICE 2YO SERIES QUALIFIER) 6f 6y
**6:00** (6:02) (Class 4) (0-80,75) 2-Y-0 **£5,175** (£1,540; £769; £384) **Stalls** High

Form RPR
052 **1** **Magic Jazz (IRE)**28 4606 2-9-2 **70** JoeDoyle 3 75
(Kevin Ryan) *mde all against stands' rail: rdn and edgd rt ins fnl f: hld on gamely towards fin* **9/4**2
355 **2** *nk* **Sinaloa (IRE)**15 5127 2-9-0 **71** AdamMcNamara(3) 1 72
(Richard Fahey) *trckd ldrs: drvn and sltly outpcd wl over 1f out: rallied appr fnl f: ev ch wl ins fnl f: one pce towards fin* **8/1**
5221 **3** *5* **Star Of Zaam (IRE)**10 5278 2-9-0 **71** (p) JordanVaughan(3) 4 70+
(K R Burke) *missed break: bhd: hdwy and prom over 2f out: rdn and outpcd over 1f out: n.d after* **11/8**1
023 **4** *¾* **Austin Powers (IRE)**15 5092 2-9-7 **75** JoeFanning 2 59
(Mark Johnston) *w wnr: rdn along and effrt over 1f out: wknd ins fnl f* **3/1**3
1m 15.28s (3.08) **Going Correction** +0.40s/f (Good) 4 Ran SP% **109.0**
Speed ratings (Par 96): **95,94,87,86**
CSF £16.40 TOTE £2.90; EX 24.90 Trifecta £27.90.
**Owner** Hambleton Racing Xxxi & Partner **Bred** Golden Vale Stud **Trained** Hambleton, N Yorks

**FOCUS**
There had been plenty of rain around; approximately 13mm had fallen in the preceding three days and a further 1mm during the afternoon. Sharp showers were forecast for this evening card, which started in sunshine with a temperature of 16C. A fair nursery for the paucity of runners and they went no great pace, so the form is open to question. The runner-up has been rated to his debut form.

## 5645 AVIA SIGNS "FROM CONCEPT TO COMPLETION" MAIDEN STKS 6f 6y
**6:30** (6:31) (Class 5) 3-Y-0+ **£4,528** (£1,347; £673; £336) **Stalls** High

Form RPR
3223 **1** **Dirchill (IRE)**11 5264 3-9-6 72 JoeFanning 4 76
(David Barron) *t.k.h early: cl up against stands' rail: led over 2f out: pushed clr fnl f: comf* **1/1**1
5343 **2** *4* **Hamidans Girl (IRE)**14 5167 3-9-1 64 GrahamLee 3 58
(Keith Dalgleish) *trckd ldrs: wnt 2nd over 2f out: effrt and rdn over 1f out: outpcd fnl f* **4/1**3
**3** *5* **Equitation** 3-8-13 0 CameronNoble(7) 5 47
(Roger Varian) *dwlt: hld up: shkn up over 2f out: rdn to chse ldrs over 1f out: edgd rt: wknd ins fnl f* **7/4**2
0500 **4** *30* **Warleggan (FR)**12 5203 3-9-6 39 (p1) JoeDoyle 1
(Linda Perratt) *led to over 2f out: sn rdn and wknd: eased whn no ch fnl f* **40/1**
1m 13.89s (1.69) **Going Correction** +0.40s/f (Good) 4 Ran SP% **108.8**
Speed ratings (Par 103): **104,98,92,52**
CSF £5.36 TOTE £1.80; EX 3.60 Trifecta £5.20.
**Owner** Elliott Brothers & Peacock & Partner **Bred** Castlefarm Stud **Trained** Maunby, N Yorks

**FOCUS**
A very modest maiden and while a visually impressive winner, the pace was not strong and the form does not hold much weight. The winner has been rated to form.

## 5646 ANDRAIL LTD H'CAP 6f 6y
**7:00** (7:01) (Class 4) (0-80,80) 3-Y-0+ **£7,762** (£2,310; £1,154; £577) **Stalls** High

Form RPR
1260 **1** **Jacob's Pillow**6 5459 6-8-13 **67** (p) ConnorBeasley 6 78
(Rebecca Bastiman) *mde all against stands' rail: pushed along 2f out: drew clr fnl f: readily* **6/1**
5050 **2** *4 ½* **Royal Connoisseur (IRE)**6 5457 6-9-2 **73** AdamMcNamara(3) 2 70
(Richard Fahey) *in tch: effrt and rdn 2f out: chsd (clr) wnr ins fnl f: kpt on: no imp* **4/1**3
605 **3** *½* **Market Choice (IRE)**28 4605 4-9-1 **69** (p) JoeFanning 5 64
(Tracy Waggott) *t.k.h: trckd ldrs: effrt and chsd wnr over 1f out: hung rt: no ex and lost 2nd ins fnl f* **11/2**
3611 **4** *½* **Kinglami**2 5564 8-9-6 **79** 6ex (p) BenRobinson(5) 1 72
(John O'Shea) *hld up on outside: stdy hdwy over 2f out: rdn over 1f out: sn no imp* **11/4**2
4010 **5** *2 ¼* **Souls In The Wind (IRE)**37 4248 3-9-3 **75** RoystonFfrench 4 60
(John Patrick Shanahan, Ire) *s.i.s: bhd: drvn and outpcd over 2f out: sn btn* **12/1**
2115 **6** *4* **Hee Haw (IRE)**15 5093 3-9-8 **80** GrahamLee 3 52
(Paul Midgley) *t.k.h early: chsd wnr: rdn over 2f out: wknd over 1f out* **5/2**1
1m 13.99s (1.79) **Going Correction** +0.40s/f (Good)
**WFA** 3 from 4yo+ 4lb 6 Ran SP% **112.6**
Speed ratings (Par 105): **104,98,97,96,93 88**
CSF £29.82 TOTE £7.10: £3.60, £2.60; EX 36.10 Trifecta £199.60.
**Owner** Miss Rebecca Bastiman **Bred** Lael Stables **Trained** Cowthorpe, N Yorks

**FOCUS**
Fairly weak for the grade and there was an all-the-way winner, with the stands' side again the place to be. The winner has been rated to his early 2016 form for now.

## 5647 BRITISH STALLION STUDS EBF SOBA CONDITIONS STKS 5f 7y
**7:30** (7:31) (Class 3) 3-Y-0+
**£9,960** (£2,982; £1,491; £745; £372; £187) **Stalls** Centre

Form RPR
0011 **1** **Glenrowan Rose (IRE)**10 5281 4-8-10 97 GrahamLee 2 93+
(Keith Dalgleish) *mde all: swtchd lft sn after s: rdn over 1f out: kpt on wl fnl f* **2/1**2
0360 **2** *¾* **Alpha Delphini**28 4635 6-9-8 110 (p) ConnorBeasley 5 102
(Bryan Smart) *trckd ldrs: drvn and wnt 2nd over 1f out: kpt on ins fnl f* **15/8**1
400 **3** *2 ½* **Elysian Flyer (IRE)**7 5426 5-9-1 81 JoeDoyle 3 86
(Paul Midgley) *hld up: hdwy on outside over 1f out: r.o ins fnl f: nt pce to chal* **22/1**
2006 **4** *2 ¼* **Taexali (IRE)**56 3585 4-9-1 93 RoystonFfrench 6 78
(John Patrick Shanahan, Ire) *hld up in tch: drvn along over 2f out: no imp fr over 1f out* **7/1**
3412 **5** *3 ¼* **Dark Defender**15 5094 4-8-10 90 (b) RowanScott(5) 4 66
(Keith Dalgleish) *cl up: drvn along over 2f out: wknd ins fnl f* **9/2**3
5110 **6** *1 ¼* **Henley**35 4379 5-8-10 83 BenRobinson(5) 7 62
(Tracy Waggott) *pressed ldr tl rdn and wknd fr over 1f out* **9/1**
1m 0.81s (0.81) **Going Correction** +0.40s/f (Good) 6 Ran SP% **113.1**
Speed ratings (Par 107): **109,107,103,100,95 93**
CSF £6.28 TOTE £2.50: £1.60, £1.40; EX 7.00 Trifecta £36.10.
**Owner** Weldspec Glasgow Limited **Bred** Tipper House Stud **Trained** Carluke, S Lanarks

**FOCUS**
A decent conditions sprint and run at an honest pace for the conditions. The market proved correct with the top two fighting it out. Solid form. The third is the key to the form.

## 5648 BUILDING CRAFTSMEN DUMFRIES H'CAP 1m 3f 15y
**8:00** (8:01) (Class 5) (0-70,72) 3-Y-0+ **£4,528** (£1,347; £673; £336) **Stalls** Low

Form RPR
005 **1** **Taxmeifyoucan (IRE)**20 4307 3-9-5 **70** (v1) GrahamLee 4 83
(Keith Dalgleish) *prom: rdn over 2f out: rallied and edgd rt over 1f out: led last 75yds: hld on wl* **9/2**3

431 2 nk **Indian Chief (IRE)**[4] 5499 7-10-2 **72** 6ex.................. ConnorBeasley 10 84
(Rebecca Bastiman) *rn wout off hind shoe: dwlt: hld up: smooth hdwy on outside over 2f out: rdn to ld ent fnl f: hdd last 75yds: hld cl home* **7/2**[2]
-660 3 4 ½ **Sepal (USA)**[19] 4962 4-9-7 **63**.............................. JoeFanning 1 67
(Iain Jardine) *led: rdn over 2f out: hdd ent fnl f: kpt on same pce* **14/1**
400- 4 3 ¼ **Eyreborn (IRE)**[297] 7284 3-8-8 **64**..............................(h[1]) RowanScott(5) 2 63
(Keith Dalgleish) *hld up: drvn and outpcd over 3f out: rallied over 1f out: kpt on fnl f: nt pce to chal* **25/1**
3422 5 ½ **Henpecked**[30] 4260 7-10-2 **72**..............................(p) JasonHart 5 70
(Alistair Whillans) *hld up: rdn over 3f out: rallied whn nt clr run and swtchd rt wl over 1f out: edgd rt: no imp fnl f* **9/1**
1 6 1 ½ **Mistiness (IRE)**[59] 3449 6-9-0 **59**..............................(b) RobbieDowney(3) 6 54
(Keith Henry Clarke, Ire) *prom: hdwy on outside over 2f out: drvn and outpcd fnl f* **5/2**[1]
0234 7 1 ¼ **Savannah Moon (IRE)**[9] 5319 3-8-13 **64**..............................(h) JoeDoyle 9 58
(Kevin Ryan) *hld up: drvn along over 2f out: no imp fr over 1f out* **10/1**
0423 8 2 ½ **Rosemay (FR)**[28] 4603 3-8-10 **66**.............................. BenRobinson(5) 3 56
(Iain Jardine) *chsd ldrs: rdn and ev ch over 2f out: wknd over 1f out* **7/1**
465 9 9 **Leven (IRE)**[16] 5074 3-8-4 **55**.............................. RoystonFfrench 8 29
(John Patrick Shanahan, Ire) *pressed ldr: drvn along over 2f out: wknd over 1f out* **16/1**

2m 28.65s (3.05) **Going Correction** +0.35s/f (Good)
**WFA** 3 from 4yo+ 9lb **9** Ran SP% **117.0**
Speed ratings (Par 103): **102,101,98,96,95 94,93,91,85**
CSF £20.95 CT £205.08 TOTE £5.50: £1.80, £1.30, £4.00; EX 23.50 Trifecta £351.70.
**Owner** Straightline Bloodstock **Bred** E Lonergan **Trained** Carluke, S Lanarks

**FOCUS**
Add 13 yards to the official distance of this modest handicap, which was devoid of pace, particularly early on. Two in-form horses fought out the finish and drew a little way clear of the third. The runner-up has been rated a bit below last year's best.

## 5649 GAS CALL SERVICES H'CAP 1m 1f 35y
**8:30** (8:32) (Class 6) (0-60,60) 3-Y-0+ **£3,234** (£962; £481; £240) **Stalls** Low

Form RPR
-000 1 **Riponian**[37] 4244 7-9-2 **50**..............................(t) JoeFanning 9 58
(Susan Corbett) *mde all: shkn up and clr over 1f out: sn shkn up: kpt on wl fnl f: unchal* **28/1**
0022 2 2 **Catastrophe**[16] 5074 4-9-9 **57**.............................. JasonHart 3 61
(John Quinn) *hld up on ins: rdn and hdwy over 2f out: edgd rt and chsd wnr over 1f out: kpt on: nt pce to chal* **5/1**[3]
00 3 2 ¾ **Green Howard**[3] 5544 9-9-12 **60**..............................(b) ConnorBeasley 5 60
(Rebecca Bastiman) *t.k.h: hld up: stdy hdwy over 2f out: rdn and kpt on fnl f: nt rch first two* **9/2**[2]
0-00 4 1 **Little Pippin**[12] 5215 4-8-12 **46**.............................. BarryMcHugh 1 42
(Tony Coyle) *hld up: rdn and hdwy over 2f out: kpt on fnl f: no imp* **14/1**
0030 5 ¾ **Palindrome (USA)**[21] 4900 4-8-12 **46** oh1..............................(b) JoeDoyle 2 40
(Ronald Thompson) *in tch: smooth hdwy to chse wnr over 2f out to over 1f out: edgd lft and sn outpcd* **12/1**
-030 6 1 **Hellavashock**[43] 4034 4-8-12 **51**.............................. RowanScott(5) 8 43
(Alistair Whillans) *s.i.s: hld up: rdn over 3f out: rallied over 1f out: kpt on fnl f: nrst fin* **11/1**
6345 7 9 **Colour Contrast (IRE)**[15] 5096 4-9-3 **58**..............................(v[1]) JamieGormley(7) 7 31
(Iain Jardine) *hld up on outside: rdn along 3f out: hung rt and outpcd 2f out: sn btn* **11/2**
0600 8 nk **Swiss Lait**[12] 5215 6-8-12 **49**..............................(p) JordanVaughan(3) 10 22
(Patrick Holmes) *chsd ldrs: wnt 2nd 4f out to over 2f out: sn rdn and wknd* **33/1**
-642 9 6 **Devil's Guard (IRE)**[32] 4473 3-8-11 **53**..............................(v) GrahamLee 4 13
(Keith Dalgleish) *t.k.h: in tch: rdn and outpcd 3f out: sn wknd* **11/4**[1]
0 10 4 **Born On The Clyde (IRE)**[7] 5427 3-8-10 **52**.......(b[1]) RoystonFfrench 11 4
(John Patrick Shanahan, Ire) *chsd wnr to 4f out: struggling fr 3f out* **25/1**
3304 11 1 ¾ **Les Pecheurs (IRE)**[4] 5499 3-8-8 **57**..............................(h) DanielleMooney(7) 6 5
(James Ewart) *hld up: struggling over 3f out: sn btn* **14/1**

2m 1.14s (1.44) **Going Correction** +0.35s/f (Good)
**WFA** 3 from 4yo+ 8lb **11** Ran SP% **116.5**
Speed ratings (Par 101): **107,105,102,101,101 100,92,92,86,83 81**
CSF £159.18 CT £766.02 TOTE £21.00: £4.70, £1.60, £2.30; EX 229.70 Trifecta £281.20.
**Owner** Girsonfield Racing Club **Bred** W B Imison **Trained** Otterburn, Northumberland

**FOCUS**
Add 13 yards to the official distance. Not a strong handicap for the grade and the winner made all. The form looks suspect. The winner has been rated back to his September C&D form, with the second to his recent form.

## 5650 MACGREGOR FLOORING CO LTD H'CAP 1m 68y
**9:00** (9:01) (Class 5) (0-75,75) 3-Y-0+ **£4,528** (£1,347; £673; £336) **Stalls** Low

Form RPR
4016 1 **Set In Stone (IRE)**[33] 4431 3-9-1 **73**.............................. RowanScott(5) 8 82
(John Patrick Shanahan, Ire) *hld up: smooth hdwy on outside over 2f out: rdn: edgd rt and led over 1f out: kpt on strly fnl f* **6/1**[3]
3350 2 2 **Dark Crystal**[5] 5469 6-9-12 **72**.............................. JoeDoyle 1 77
(Linda Perratt) *hld up midfield: effrt over 2f out: chsd wnr ins fnl f: r.o* **10/1**
6650 3 1 ½ **Archie's Advice**[27] 4658 6-9-12 **72**.............................. GrahamLee 2 74
(Keith Dalgleish) *hld up on ins: pushed along over 2f out: hdwy over 1f out: edgd lft and kpt on ins fnl f: no imp* **8/1**
640- 4 2 ¾ **Timia**[197] 339 4-9-0 **63**.............................. RobbieDowney(3) 4 58
(Keith Henry Clarke, Ire) *chsd ldrs: effrt and ev ch briefly over 1f out: rdn and outpcd ins fnl f* **33/1**
-003 5 ¾ **Beauden Barrett**[25] 4728 4-9-12 **72**..............................(t) JasonHart 9 66
(John Quinn) *s.i.s: hld up: rdn 3f out: rallied over 1f out: sn no imp* **16/1**
4124 6 ½ **Fivehundredmiles (IRE)**[16] 5072 4-10-0 **74**..........(b) RoystonFfrench 5 66
(John Patrick Shanahan, Ire) *hld up towards rr: drvn along 3f out: hdwy over 1f out: sn no imp* **15/2**
4101 7 1 **Amy Blair**[15] 5097 4-9-12 **72**..............................(h) ConnorBeasley 3 62
(Keith Dalgleish) *led: rdn over 2f out: hdd over 1f out: wknd ins fnl f* **4/1**[1]
234 8 ¾ **Spiritofhayton (IRE)**[157] 970 3-9-5 **72**.............................. BarryMcHugh 11 59
(David Barron) *s.i.s: hld up: rdn over 3f out: sme late hdwy: nvr rchd ldrs* **20/1**
3556 9 hd **Fidelma Moon (IRE)**[4] 5497 5-8-6 **57**.............................. BenRobinson(5) 12 45
(Tracy Waggott) *pressed ldr: drvn along over 2f out: edgd lft and wknd over 1f out* **17/2**
0515 10 2 ¾ **Heatongrad (IRE)**[45] 3975 3-9-2 **72**.............................. AdamMcNamara(3) 6 53
(Richard Fahey) *prom: drvn over 2f out: wknd wl over 1f out* **5/1**[2]
6235 11 ¾ **Framley Garth (IRE)**[15] 5091 5-9-1 **64**..............................(p[1]) JordanVaughan(3) 7 44
(Patrick Holmes) *s.i.s: bhd: struggling over 4f out: no imp fnl 2f* **12/1**
2330 12 3 ½ **Celestation**[7] 5439 3-9-8 **75**.............................. JoeFanning 10 46
(Mark Johnston) *midfield: drvn and outpcd over 2f out: sn wknd: eased whn btn ins fnl f* **12/1**

1m 50.44s (2.04) **Going Correction** +0.35s/f (Good)
**WFA** 3 from 4yo+ 7lb **12** Ran SP% **122.4**
Speed ratings (Par 103): **103,101,99,96,96 95,94,93,93,90 90,86**
CSF £67.15 CT £501.46 TOTE £7.20: £2.50, £3.90, £3.40; EX 73.90 Trifecta £541.70.
**Owner** Thistle Bloodstock Limited **Bred** Thistle Bloodstock Limited **Trained** Kells, Co Kilkenny

**FOCUS**
Add 13 yards to the official distance. Quite competitive for the grade, with nine of the field all within 3lb of the ceiling. A fair pace and the form should hold firm. A pb from the winner, with the third rated to his recent form.
T/Plt: £300.50 to a £1 stake. Pool: £64,101.67 - 155.67 winning units T/Qpdt: £25.90 to a £1 stake. Pool: £6,796.45 - 193.45 winning units **Richard Young**

# 5405 LINGFIELD (L-H)
Saturday, August 5

**OFFICIAL GOING: Soft (good to soft in places) changing to good to soft (soft in places) after race 4 (6.45)**
Wind: Almost nil Weather: Fine

## 5651 JIMMY COLEMANS 75TH BIRTHDAY APPRENTICE H'CAP 7f 135y
**5:15** (5:16) (Class 6) (0-65,65) 4-Y-0+ **£2,587** (£770; £384; £192) **Stalls** Centre

Form RPR
3411 1 **Arctic Flower (IRE)**[7] 5410 4-9-1 **54**.............................. JordanUys 4 59
(John Bridger) *pressed ldr: led 5f out: rdn 2f out: jnd ins fnl f: kpt on gamely towards fin* **15/8**[1]
4045 2 ½ **Rattle On**[16] 5062 4-8-13 **60**..............................(p) IsobelFrancis(8) 6 64
(Jim Boyle) *hld up in last trio: prog 3f out: chsd wnr 2f out: chal and upsides ins fnl f: nt qckn nr fin* **16/1**
0625 3 ½ **King Of Swing**[61] 3396 4-9-9 **65**..............................(h) FinleyMarsh(3) 9 68
(Richard Hughes) *awkward s: hld up in last trio against rail: pushed along over 2f out: prog over 1f out: styd on wl last 100yds and gaining at fin but too late* **3/1**[3]
266 4 ½ **Welsh Inlet (IRE)**[32] 4459 9-8-13 **57**.............................. SophieRalston(5) 1 58
(John Bridger) *trckd ldrs: gng strly over 2f out: shkn up over 1f out: limited rspnse and nvr cl enough to chal* **14/1**
0463 5 hd **Masarzain (IRE)**[101] 2082 4-9-7 **63**.............................. WilliamCox(3) 10 64
(Archie Watson) *trckd ldrs: disp 2nd 2f out: sn hanging and nt qckn: kpt on same pce fnl f* **11/4**[2]
0004 6 2 **Bushwise (IRE)**[7] 5429 4-8-7 **46**..............................(p) MillyNaseb 2 42
(Milton Bradley) *hld up in last trio and racd wdst of all: no prog whn hung across towards far side 2f out: nvr a threat* **18/1**
6405 7 2 **Kristoff (IRE)**[7] 5410 4-8-2 **46** oh1.............................. NicolaCurrie(5) 7 37
(Jim Boyle) *trckd ldrs: rdn over 2f out: no prog and btn over 1f out* **20/1**
513 8 7 **Almanack**[29] 4587 7-9-12 **65**.............................. RhiainIngram 5 40
(Mark Pattinson) *racd against rail: led to 5f out: chsd wnr to 2f out: wknd rapidly* **10/1**

1m 34.09s (1.79) **Going Correction** +0.15s/f (Good) **8** Ran SP% **118.1**
Speed ratings (Par 101): **97,96,96,95,95 93,91,84**
CSF £35.78 CT £90.75 TOTE £2.50: £1.40, £3.30, £1.40; EX 28.20 Trifecta £94.80.
**Owner** Mr & Mrs K Finch **Bred** B Kennedy **Trained** Liphook, Hants

**FOCUS**
There was 4mm of rain earlier in the day and the going was described as soft, good to soft in places (GoingStick: 7.3). The early gallop was fairly steady. The winner has been rated back to her best.

## 5652 GOODWOOD FESTIVAL BETTING AT 188BET H'CAP 1m 3f 133y
**5:45** (5:47) (Class 5) (0-70,72) 3-Y-0+ **£2,911** (£866; £432; £216) **Stalls** High

Form RPR
-633 1 **Iballisticvin**[24] 4755 4-9-9 **62**.............................. TrevorWhelan 6 69
(Gary Moore) *trckd ldng pair: smooth prog to ld 2f out: sn rdn: hrd pressed ins fnl f: hld on* **3/1**[2]
60-2 2 hd **Astute Boy (IRE)**[35] 4348 3-8-11 **67**.............................. FinleyMarsh(7) 1 73
(Ed Vaughan) *trckd ldr to over 2f out: shkn up and effrt sn after but wnr already gone: racing awkwardly over 1f out but tk 2nd fnl f: chal last 100yds: nt qckn last strides* **8/11**[1]
06-0 3 2 ½ **Ravenswood**[103] 2042 4-8-13 **52**.............................. RobHornby 7 54
(Patrick Chamings) *hld up in last: pushed along 3f out and then hanging lft: no imp tl styd on fnl f to take 3rd nr fin* **14/1**
364 4 2 **Helf (IRE)**[14] 5141 3-9-9 **72**.............................. TomMarquand 2 70
(Richard Hannon) *led: shkn up and hdd 2f out: sn btn and wknd fnl f* **7/1**[3]
0634 5 2 ½ **Lemon Drop**[7] 5405 3-7-10 **52**..............................(p[1]) IsobelFrancis(7) 5 46
(Jim Boyle) *dwlt: in tch: pushed along and fdd fnl 2f* **10/1**

2m 38.42s (6.92) **Going Correction** +0.50s/f (Yiel)
**WFA** 3 from 4yo+ 10lb **5** Ran SP% **111.2**
Speed ratings (Par 103): **96,95,94,92,91**
CSF £5.68 TOTE £3.60: £2.20, £1.10; EX 7.40 Trifecta £39.10.
**Owner** Scuderia Vita Bella **Bred** Houghton-Barrons Partnership **Trained** Lower Beeding, W Sussex

**FOCUS**
Some good race riding from Trevor Whelan looked to play a part in this result. The winner has been rated to form, and the fourth to his modest maiden form.

## 5653 GALWAY FESTIVAL BETTING AT 188BET H'CAP 1m 2f
**6:15** (6:20) (Class 6) (0-60,59) 3-Y-0+ **£2,587** (£770; £384; £192) **Stalls** Low

Form RPR
0-40 1 **Mirimar (IRE)**[51] 3755 3-9-4 **59**..............................(h[1]) AdamBeschizza 3 67+
(Ed Vaughan) *trckd ldrs: shkn up over 2f out: prog over 1f out: drvn to ld last 150yds: styd on* **11/4**[2]
00-0 2 1 **Velvet Voice**[28] 4623 3-9-4 **59**.............................. DougieCostello 8 65
(Mark H Tompkins) *reluctant to enter stalls: sn prom: led after 4f: rdn over 2f out: jnd over 1f out: kpt on but hdd and outpcd last 150yds* **20/1**
3010 3 ¾ **Venetian Proposal (IRE)**[9] 5331 3-9-0 **55**..................(p) KieranO'Neill 6 59
(Zoe Davison) *a in ldng trio: urged along 4f out: rdn to press ldr over 2f out: upsides over 1f out tl wnr wnt past 150yds out: nt qckn* **6/1**
0453 4 2 ¼ **Loving Your Work**[37] 4257 6-9-11 **58**.............................. ShaneKelly 5 57
(Ken Cunningham-Brown) *hld up in midfield: gng bttr than many 3f out: coaxed along after: tk 4th fnl f but nt on terms: no imp whn reminders nr fin* **5/1**[3]
0235 5 2 ¼ **Betsalottie**[17] 5023 4-9-8 **55**.............................. WilliamCarson 13 49
(John Bridger) *led 4f: chsd ldr to over 2f out: lost pl over 1f out: wknd fnl f* **5/2**[1]

4054 **6** *1* **Sheer Intensity (IRE)**[11] 5250 4-8-11 **51**................ GabrieleMalune(7) 2 43
(David Evans) *hld up in last quartet: pushed along and no prog 3f out: rdn and plugged on fr ovost pler 1f out: nvr a factor* **14/1**

0100 **7** *2* **London Grammar (IRE)**[65] 3250 3-9-0 **55**..................... DavidProbert 9 44
(Ralph J Smith) *hld up in last quartet: rdn 3f out: sme prog 2f out but w no great enthusiasm: no hdwy fnl f* **12/1**

0050 **8** *2 1/4* **Our Kim (IRE)**[36] 4320 3-8-10 **51**.............................. DannyBrock 4 36
(Mohamed Moubarak) *rrd s: rcvrd to chse ldrs after 3f: urged along 4f out: wknd over 2f out* **25/1**

0060 **9** *shd* **Coup De Vent**[42] 4087 6-8-12 **45**.............................(be) TrevorWhelan 12 28
(John O'Shea) *hld up in last: pushed along and no prog 3f out: nvr a factor* **40/1**

-000 **10** *6* **Secret Look**[59] 3468 7-9-10 **57**.................................. TomMarquand 1 28
(Richard Phillips) *t.k.h: hld up in last quartet: pushed along and no prog 3f out: wknd 2f out* **25/1**

2m 13.57s (3.07) **Going Correction** +0.50s/f (Yiel)
**WFA** 3 from 4yo+ 8lb **10** Ran SP% **115.4**
Speed ratings (Par 101): **107,106,105,103,102 101,99,97,97,92**
CSF £60.38 CT £308.17 TOTE £3.70: £1.60, £4.70, £2.00; EX 62.10 Trifecta £346.50.
**Owner** Ballymore Downunder Syndicate **Bred** William Flood **Trained** Newmarket, Suffolk
■ Everdina was withdrawn. Price at time of withdrawal 16/1. Rule 4 does not apply
■ Stewards' Enquiry : Adam Beschizza six-day ban; used his whip above the permitted level (19th-22nd Aug)

**FOCUS**
A moderate handicap. The third has been rated close to her penultimate win here.

## 5654 CORE GROUP EBF NOVICE STKS 4f 217y
**6:45** (6:45) (Class 5) 2-Y-O **£3,234** (£962; £481; £240) **Stalls** Centre

Form RPR

0 **1** **Sarshampla (IRE)**[30] 4533 2-8-11 0................................ AndreaAtzeni 1 78+
(David Simcock) *hld up in last: stdy prog on outer 1/2-way: pushed into ld jst ins fnl f: v comf* **11/8**[1]

3230 **2** *1 1/2* **Zalshah**[14] 5150 2-9-2 77................................................ TomMarquand 3 74
(Richard Hannon) *cl up: trckd ldr 1/2-way: shkn up to ld over 1f out: hdd jst ins fnl f: styd on but no match for wnr* **2/1**[2]

3 **3** *4* **Diamond Dougal (IRE)**[106] 1934 2-9-2 0...................... CharlesBishop 5 60
(Mick Channon) *chsd ldr to 1/2-way: rdn 2f out: lft bhd over 1f out: tk modest 3rd nr fin* **13/2**

605 **4** *nk* **Glamorous Rocket (IRE)**[19] 4972 2-8-11 54................. DavidProbert 2 54
(Ronald Harris) *led: rdn 2f out: hdd & wknd over 1f out: lost 3rd nr fin* **25/1**

**5** *11* **Littlelordconford (IRE)** 2-9-2 0..................................... FranBerry 4 19
(Richard Spencer) *in tch to 1/2-way: rn green and wknd: sn bhd* **5/1**[3]

58.69s (0.49) **Going Correction** +0.15s/f (Good) **5** Ran SP% **109.3**
Speed ratings (Par 94): **102,99,93,92,75**
CSF £4.31 TOTE £2.00: £1.40, £1.20; EX 3.90 Trifecta £10.50.
**Owner** Sheikh Juma Dalmook Al Maktoum **Bred** Dermot Kelly **Trained** Newmarket, Suffolk

**FOCUS**
After this race the going was changed to good to soft, soft in places. A fair novice, and a nice performance from the winner. The fourth has been rated to form.

## 5655 EXTRA PLACE RACES AT 188BET NOVICE MEDIAN AUCTION STKS 7f 135y
**7:15** (7:19) (Class 6) 2-Y-O **£2,587** (£770; £384; £192) **Stalls** Centre

Form RPR

3 **1** **Jazeel (IRE)**[21] 4880 2-9-2 0......................................... CharlesBishop 9 71+
(Mick Channon) *mde all against rail: rdn 2f out: drifted lft fr over 1f out: drvn out and kpt on* **1/1**[1]

**2** *1 1/4* **Ambient (IRE)** 2-9-2 0................................................ AndreaAtzeni 11 68+
(Roger Varian) *trckd ldng pair: wnt 2nd 2f out: rdn to try to chal over 1f out: kpt on same pce* **6/1**[3]

00 **3** *1* **Mr Large (IRE)**[21] 4885 2-9-2 0.................................. DougieCostello 2 66
(Jamie Osborne) *in tch in 6th: pushed along and prog jst over 2f out: drifted lft fnl f but styd on steadily to take 3rd last 50yds* **25/1**

6 **4** *1 1/2* **Garden Oasis**[35] 4367 2-9-2 0........................................ TedDurcan 1 62
(Sir Michael Stoute) *chsd ldng quartet: shkn up over 2f out: one pce fr over 1f out* **11/4**[2]

**5** *2* **Rosedale Topping (IRE)** 2-8-11 0................................... FranBerry 8 52+
(Ed Vaughan) *dwlt: off the pce in rr: pushed along over 2f out: n.d but kpt on steadily over 1f out: nt disgracd* **16/1**

**6** *3/4* **Becky Sharp** 2-8-11 0.................................................. ShaneKelly 6 55+
(Jim Boyle) *t.k.h: trckd wnr to 2f out: shkn up after: cl 5th but hld whn bdly hmpd 75yds out and eased* **40/1**

0 **7** *2 1/4* **Rockwell Lloyd (IRE)**[15] 5105 2-9-2 0........................... RobHornby 5 50
(Mick Channon) *chsd ldng trio on outer tl wknd 2f out* **33/1**

00 **8** *2 1/2* **Ahfad**[10] 5301 2-9-2 0.............................................. AdamBeschizza 4 44
(Stuart Williams) *nvr bttr than 7th and nvr on terms w ldrs: no prog 2f out* **66/1**

**9** *1* **Kiss Me Daily (FR)** 2-8-11 0.......................................... DavidProbert 7 37
(Ralph Beckett) *dwlt: a wl off the pce in rr: pushed along and no prog over 2f out* **13/2**

0 **10** *1* **Bunch Of Thyme (IRE)**[120] 1604 2-9-2 0..............(p[1]) WilliamCarson 12 39
(Bill Turner) *reminder after 3f: sn struggling in rr* **50/1**

**11** *1/2* **Free Talkin** 2-8-11 0.................................................. SteveDrowne 3 33
(Michael Attwater) *dwlt: a wl off the pce in last pair* **33/1**

1m 34.88s (2.58) **Going Correction** +0.15s/f (Good) **11** Ran SP% **125.8**
Speed ratings (Par 92): **93,91,90,89,87 86,84,81,80,79 79**
CSF £8.14 TOTE £1.90: £1.10, £2.10, £5.70; EX 9.50 Trifecta £92.90.
**Owner** Abdullatif M Al-Abdulrazzaq **Bred** Mrs Joan Murphy **Trained** West Ilsley, Berks

**FOCUS**
The first three raced in line on the rail for a long way.

## 5656 USPGA GOLF AT 188BET H'CAP 7f
**7:45** (7:48) (Class 5) (0-75,73) 3-Y-O+ **£2,911** (£866; £432; £216) **Stalls** Centre

Form RPR

0-02 **1** **Vibes (IRE)**[7] 5411 3-9-4 **70**.......................................... DougieCostello 3 79
(Jamie Osborne) *mde all: 3 l clr after 3f: shkn up and drew rt away over 2f out: eased last 75yds* **7/2**[3]

0245 **2** *8* **Right About Now (IRE)**[18] 5009 3-9-4 **73**................ HectorCrouch(3) 6 61
(Ismail Mohammed) *chsd ldrs: rdn and no prog over 2f out: no ch whn nt clr run jst ins fnl f: styd on after to snatch modest 2nd last stride* **13/2**

3522 **3** *shd* **Getna (USA)**[40] 4145 3-9-6 **72**.................................... TomMarquand 4 60
(Richard Hannon) *chsd ldrs: shkn up and no prog over 2f out: kpt on one pce to chal for modest 2nd nr fin* **5/2**[2]

13-0 **4** *nse* **Luang Prabang (IRE)**[99] 2120 4-9-6 **66**........................ TedDurcan 5 56
(Chris Wall) *chsd wnr and clr of rest bef 1/2-way: rdn and no imp over 2f out: no ch after: lost 2 pls last strides* **8/1**

5044 **5** *1 1/2* **Storm Melody**[10] 5271 4-9-10 **70**..................................... FranBerry 2 56
(Jonjo O'Neill) *hld up in 5th: rdn on outer over 2f out: sn no real prog* **2/1**[1]

500 **6** *13* **Popeswood (IRE)**[14] 5145 5-8-9 **60**.....................(b) PaddyBradley(5) 1 12
(Lee Carter) *taken down early: rel to r and reminders: ct up at bk of field after 3f: wknd 3f out: eased and t.o* **25/1**

1m 25.01s (1.71) **Going Correction** +0.15s/f (Good)
**WFA** 3 from 4yo+ 6lb **6** Ran SP% **112.4**
Speed ratings (Par 103): **96,86,86,86,84 70**
CSF £25.53 TOTE £4.00: £2.00, £2.40; EX 16.60 Trifecta £52.40.
**Owner** Ian Barratt, Stephen Short & Adam Signy **Bred** Mrs C Hartery **Trained** Upper Lambourn, Berks

**FOCUS**
The winner routed his rivals from the front. The form has been rated cautiously.

## 5657 GET 1/4 ODDS AT 188BET H'CAP 6f
**8:15** (8:19) (Class 6) (0-65,65) 3-Y-O+ **£2,587** (£770; £384; £192) **Stalls** Centre

Form RPR

4231 **1** **Sweet Pursuit**[14] 5146 3-8-13 **56**..................................... LukeMorris 7 68+
(Rod Millman) *trckd ldrs: prog over 2f out: led wl over 1f out: urged along fnl f but wl in command* **4/5**[1]

5315 **2** *2 1/4* **Zavikon**[17] 5028 3-9-8 **65**................................................. ShaneKelly 5 69
(Richard Hughes) *hld up in midfield: prog over 2f out: rdn to chse wnr over 1f out: kpt on but no real imp* **7/2**[2]

000 **3** *1* **Fantasy Justifier (IRE)**[32] 4467 6-9-7 **60**..................... DavidProbert 9 62
(Ronald Harris) *hld up in rr: rdn and prog 2f out: styd on to take 3rd 1f out: nvr able to threaten* **11/1**

5404 **4** *4* **All Or Nothin (IRE)**[7] 5410 8-8-3 **49**........................... JordanUys(7) 1 39
(Paddy Butler) *chsd ldrs on outer: rdn 2f out: no imp over 1f out: wknd fnl f* **12/1**

2056 **5** *1/2* **Flying Sakhee**[7] 5429 4-8-11 **50**.................................. WilliamCarson 2 39
(John Bridger) *prom: disp 2nd pl over 2f out: wknd over 1f out* **7/1**[3]

0500 **6** *1 3/4* **Torment**[9] 5340 4-8-11 **55**.....................................(b[1]) JoshuaBryan(5) 3 38
(Charlie Wallis) *spd on outer: led after 2f: rdn and hdd wl over 1f out: wknd* **20/1**

000 **7** *nk* **Candelaria**[11] 5252 4-9-5 **58**........................................... FranBerry 6 40
(Jonjo O'Neill) *hld up in last: pushed along and sme prog 2f out: nvr involved and fdd fnl f* **20/1**

0660 **8** *9* **Classic Flyer**[52] 3728 5-8-13 **52**..............................(v) TrevorWhelan 11 7
(Christine Dunnett) *in tch tl wknd over 2f out* **33/1**

0/4- **9** *17* **Special Code (IRE)**[538] 579 5-8-11 **50**........................... DannyBrock 8
(Paddy Butler) *fast away: led 2f: wknd rapidly 1/2-way: t.o* **50/1**

1m 11.71s (0.51) **Going Correction** +0.15s/f (Good)
**WFA** 3 from 4yo+ 4lb **9** Ran SP% **120.7**
Speed ratings (Par 101): **102,99,97,92,91 89,88,76,54**
CSF £3.75 CT £18.87 TOTE £1.60: £1.10, £1.60, £2.70; EX 5.00 Trifecta £25.80.
**Owner** Always Hopeful Partnership **Bred** Tom Chadney & Peter Green **Trained** Kentisbeare, Devon

**FOCUS**
A modest sprint, but the winner is at the top of her game at the moment. The runner-up has been rated to his penultimate Windsor win.
T/Plt: £27.30 to a £1 stake. Pool: £53,118.92 - 1416.53 winning units T/Qpdt: £21.80 to a £1 stake. Pool: £5,857.13 - 198.82 winning units **Jonathan Neesom**

# 5606 NEWMARKET (R-H)
Saturday, August 5

**OFFICIAL GOING: Good to soft changing to soft after race 1 (2.05)**
Wind: light breeze Weather: very changeable including sun and rain; 16 degrees

## 5658 BRITISH STALLION STUDS EBF CHALICE STKS (LISTED RACE) 1m 4f
**2:05** (2:07) (Class 1) 3-Y-O+
**£22,684** (£8,600; £4,304; £2,144; £1,076; £540) **Stalls** Centre

Form RPR

212- **1** **To Eternity**[352] 5587 4-9-5 100........................................ JamesDoyle 14 108
(John Gosden) *mde all: only one to keep to stands rails after home turn whn rest elected centre positions: clr and in command over 2f out: r.o strly: v enterprising ride* **5/1**[2]

3151 **2** *6* **Pleasant Surprise (IRE)**[29] 4571 3-8-9 92................... JamieSpencer 3 100
(Luca Cumani) *stdy prog up centre fr 4f out to ld that bunch over 1f out: rdn and edgd rt after: nvr nr wnr* **7/1**

0-10 **3** *nk* **Fleur Forsyte**[51] 3749 3-8-9 79.................................(h[1]) GeorgeWood 15 99
(James Fanshawe) *dwlt: hdwy in centre 4f out: rdn over 2f out: 3rd but no imp fnl f* **40/1**

-262 **4** *6* **Isabel De Urbina (IRE)**[14] 5155 3-8-9 100........................ JFEgan 16 90
(Ralph Beckett) *midfield in centre bunch: effrt 3f out: rdn to ld them over 2f out but wnr already clr: wknd and lost pl over 1f out* **11/4**[1]

0/2- **5** *1 3/4* **Groovejet**[142] 6951 6-9-5 97.......................................... JennyPowell 2 86
(Richard Spencer) *bhd: rdn and hdwy on far rails 3f out: plugged on but nvr looked like chalng* **33/1**

2154 **6** *1* **Apphia (IRE)**[14] 5155 3-8-9 100................................... JosephineGordon 9 85
(Hugo Palmer) *pressed ldr of centre bunch after 3f: rdn 3f out: wknd 2f out: wandering whn tired after* **9/1**

-512 **7** *1 3/4* **Ebbesbourne (IRE)**[51] 3749 3-8-9 92.............................(h) TedDurcan 7 83
(Sir Michael Stoute) *t.k.h: prom tl drvn over 2f out: sn struggling* **13/2**[3]

-525 **8** *shd* **Capricious Cantor (IRE)**[14] 5155 4-9-5 93..................... AntonioFresu 6 81
(Ed Dunlop) *chsd ldrs: rdn 3f out: sn struggling* **20/1**

-504 **9** *2 1/4* **Moorside**[16] 5088 4-9-5 91............................................. AdamKirby 12 78
(Charles Hills) *led all bar wnr after being swtchd to centre of crse home turn: drvn and hdd over 2f out: sn lost pl* **20/1**

-132 **10** *hd* **Singyoursong (IRE)**[66] 3219 4-9-5 97..........................(h) SeanLevey 8 78
(David Simcock) *stdd s: wl bhd: rdn and btn 3f out: plugging on ins fnl f* **9/1**

6-1 **11** *3 1/2* **Erinyes (IRE)**[31] 4497 3-8-9 79.................................... TomMarquand 1 73
(Archie Watson) *t.k.h: chsd ldrs: drvn 3f out: sn wknd: t.o* **33/1**

35 **12** *15* **Tinker Tailor (IRE)**[8] 5364 4-9-5 0..............................(t) KieranO'Neill 11 48
(Denis Quinn) *taken down v early: slowly away: t.o 3f out* **100/1**

-652 **13** *4 1/2* **Cliff Face (IRE)**[22] 4829 4-9-5 93................................. LukeMorris 10 41
(Sir Mark Prescott Bt) *bhd: rdn and wandering and struggling over 3f out: sn heavily eased* **16/1**

621- 14 20 **Hestina (FR)**[14] 7669 4-9-5 89 (t) TrevorWhelan 13 9
(Dan Skelton) *towards rr: struggling bdly 4f out: t.o over 2f out: heavily eased* 28/1

2m 34.03s (1.13) **Going Correction** +0.275s/f (Good)
**WFA** 3 from 4yo+ 10lb 14 Ran SP% **117.3**
Speed ratings (Par 111): **107,103,102,98,97 96,95,95,94,94 91,81,78,65**
CSF £35.63 TOTE £5.40: £1.90, £2.30, £12.90; EX 32.70 Trifecta £2465.00.
**Owner** Lady Bamford **Bred** Lady Bamford **Trained** Newmarket, Suffolk

**FOCUS**
Far side course used. Stalls on stands' side, except 1m4f: centre. Add 19 yards to race distance. John Egan said of the ground: "It's slow and chopped up," and Sean Levey said: "It's soft." This looked a competitive Listed race, but there was an easy winner. She was the only one to race down the stands' side, the rest of the jockeys opting for the centre. The winner has been rated up with the better winners of this.

## 5659 BRITISH EBF FILLIES' NURSERY H'CAP 6f
**2:40** (2:40) (Class 2) 2-Y-O

**£24,900** (£7,456; £3,728; £1,864; £932; £468) **Stalls** Low

Form RPR
052 1 **Hunni**[33] 4440 2-8-1 72 KieranO'Neill 4 77
(Tom Clover) *pressed ldr: rdn 1/2-way: led 150yds out: hld on gamely* 16/1

1041 2 ½ **Faithful Promise**[24] 4739 2-8-6 77 PJMcDonald 2 80
(Mark Johnston) *led: drvn over 1f out: hdd 150yds out: tried to rally but edgd lft and a hld* 8/1

023 3 1½ **Queen Penn**[35] 4374 2-8-0 74 AaronJones(3) 1 73+
(Richard Fahey) *a same pl: drvn and tried to chal over 1f out but kpt hanging bdly lft fnl f and ended up nr far rails* 10/1

4150 4 1¼ **Elysium Dream**[22] 4858 2-9-0 85 SeanLevey 3 80
(Richard Hannon) *pressed ldrs: rdn over 1f out: kpt on same pce and no threat* 13/2

332 5 nk **Paramount Love**[23] 4786 2-8-4 75 (p1) PatrickMathers 8 69
(Richard Fahey) *chsd ldrs: rdn wl over 1f out: no imp after* 9/2[2]

1256 6 ¾ **Neola**[7] 5391 2-9-7 92 JFEgan 9 84
(Mick Channon) *bhd: rdn and effrt on outer wl over 1f out: nvr got in a blow* 4/1[1]

201 7 ½ **First Drive**[15] 5120 2-8-5 76 JosephineGordon 5 66
(Michael Bell) *pressed ldrs: rdn wl over 1f out: kpt on same pce after: btn 1f out* 7/1

524 8 ¾ **Tig Tog (IRE)**[16] 5056 2-8-7 78 TomMarquand 6 66
(Richard Hannon) *midfield: drvn 2f out: n.d after: btn 1f out* 6/1[3]

5320 9 1½ **Onefootinparadise**[14] 5150 2-8-2 73 LukeMorris 7 56
(Philip McBride) *stdd s: t.k.h in rr: drvn over 2f out: nvr on terms* 8/1

1m 13.53s (1.03) **Going Correction** +0.275s/f (Good) 9 Ran SP% **115.5**
Speed ratings (Par 97): **104,103,101,99,99 98,97,96,94**
CSF £137.00 CT £1354.02 TOTE £20.20: £4.90, £2.80, £3.10; EX 196.40 Trifecta £4512.10 Part Won..
**Owner** The Hunni Partnership **Bred** R G & Alison Percival & Rosie Bowers **Trained** Newmarket, Suffolk

**FOCUS**
The official going description became Soft before this race, a valuable event of its type. The first four came out of the four lowest stalls with the stands' rail clearly the place to be, although the third home ended up on the far side.

## 5660 NEWMARKET EQUINE HOSPITAL EBF FILLIES' NOVICE STKS (PLUS 10 RACE) 7f
**3:15** (3:16) (Class 4) 2-Y-O **£4,528** (£1,347; £673; £336) **Stalls** Low

Form RPR
04 1 **Dathanna (IRE)**[52] 3712 2-9-0 0 (h) JamesDoyle 2 80
(Charlie Appleby) *pressed ldr on stand side rail: rdn to ld 2f out: edgd clr fnl 100yds: cosily* 7/4[1]

40 2 1¼ **Amourice (IRE)**[35] 4361 2-8-9 0 (h1) PaddyBradley(5) 7 77
(Jane Chapple-Hyam) *led and racd freely: drvn and hdd 2f out: ev ch 100yds out but no match for wnr after* 16/1

3 1 **Frolic** 2-9-0 0 LukeMorris 4 74
(Sir Mark Prescott Bt) *pressed ldrs: 3rd and rdn and edgd lft over 1f out: kpt on same pce and no imp after* 9/1

4 ¾ **Tivoli (IRE)** 2-9-0 0 RobertTart 10 72+
(John Gosden) *bhd: rdn and effrt over 2f out: styd on ins fnl fulrong: snatched wl hld 4th* 4/1[2]

5 hd **Dark Rose Angel (IRE)** 2-9-0 0 JamieSpencer 1 72
(Simon Crisford) *settled towards rr: rdn and effrt over 2f out: 4th and no imp ins fnl f* 7/1[3]

43 6 5 **Ruysch (IRE)**[15] 5114 2-9-0 0 PJMcDonald 5 59
(Ed Dunlop) *chsd ldrs: drvn over 2f out: btn over 1f out* 10/1

7 ¾ **Rozanne (IRE)** 2-9-0 0 JFEgan 11 57
(Jeremy Noseda) *midfield: pushed along 2f out: one pce and no imp after* 16/1

8 hd **Casima** 2-9-0 0 (h1) AdamKirby 8 56
(Clive Cox) *a bhd: rdn and outpcd over 2f out* 16/1

0 9 12 **Eastern Sunrise**[15] 5114 2-9-0 0 SeanLevey 3 25
(Richard Hannon) *stdd s: t.k.h and prom tl drvn and fdd over 2f out: t.o and eased 1f out* 16/1

10 4½ **Allegramente** 2-9-0 0 TedDurcan 9 14
(Sir Michael Stoute) *lost 6 l s: rdn and rn green in last pl: t.o and eased 1f out* 12/1

5 11 1 **Tarnemah (IRE)**[23] 4792 2-9-0 0 AntonioFresu 6 11
(George Peckham) *cl up tl drvn and fdd over 2f out: t.o and eased 1f out* 50/1

1m 27.96s (2.26) **Going Correction** +0.275s/f (Good) 11 Ran SP% **121.1**
Speed ratings (Par 93): **98,96,95,94,94 88,87,87,73,68 67**
CSF £35.49 TOTE £2.40: £1.20, £4.50, £2.90; EX 37.50 Trifecta £350.60.
**Owner** Godolphin **Bred** Godolphin **Trained** Newmarket, Suffolk

**FOCUS**
Again, the winner raced on the stands' rail. There were some promising performances behind her.

## 5661 MALCOLM ROXBURGH RETIREMENT H'CAP 7f
**3:50** (3:50) (Class 3) (0-90,91) 3-Y-O **£7,762** (£2,310; £1,154; £577) **Stalls** Low

Form RPR
-331 1 **Mojito (IRE)**[28] 4634 3-9-7 88 JamesDoyle 6 97+
(William Haggas) *sn led fr outside draw and worked over to bag stand side rail after 1f: travelled best: pushed 2 l clr 1f out and in command after* 5/6[1]

-543 2 2¼ **Perfect Madge (IRE)**[36] 4315 3-9-4 85 AdamKirby 4 87
(Kevin Ryan) *dwlt: towards rr tl rdn and effrt over 2f out: swtchd lft and wnt 2nd 1f out: a hld after* 25/1

0-26 3 ¾ **Musawaat**[64] 3303 3-9-6 87 DaneO'Neill 5 87
(Charles Hills) *pressed ldrs: drvn over 2f out. 3rd and no imp fnl f* 5/1[3]

042 4 1½ **Esprit De Corps**[21] 4887 3-9-1 82 JamieSpencer 2 78
(Roger Charlton) *lost 5 l s: bhd tl short-lived effrt in centre 2f out: nvr landed a blow* 9/2[2]

3012 5 hd **Derek Duval (USA)**[22] 4868 3-8-10 80 (t) AaronJones(3) 3 76
(Stuart Williams) *taken down early: settled in 4th pl: pushed along and outpcd 2f out: edgd lft ins fnl f* 8/1

-606 6 1¼ **Majeste**[14] 5147 3-9-10 91 SeanLevey 1 84
(Richard Hannon) *w wnr for 1f: drvn over 2f out: outpcd over 1f out* 16/1

1m 26.83s (1.13) **Going Correction** +0.275s/f (Good) 6 Ran SP% **110.2**
Speed ratings (Par 104): **104,101,100,98,98 97**
CSF £22.96 TOTE £1.50: £1.10, £3.90; EX 15.80 Trifecta £58.30.
**Owner** Fiona and Ian Carmichael-Jennings **Bred** Earl Ecurie Du Grand Chene **Trained** Newmarket, Suffolk

**FOCUS**
A decent little handicap.

## 5662 EUF RUBY ANNIVERSARY H'CAP 7f
**4:25** (4:25) (Class 2) (0-110,105) 3-Y-O+**£16,172** (£4,812; £2,405; £1,202) **Stalls** Low

Form RPR
0040 1 **Swift Approval (IRE)**[7] 5393 5-8-12 91 oh2 (t) LukeMorris 5 99
(Stuart Williams) *chsd ldrs: hrd drvn over 2f out: little rspnse tl wl ins fnl f: led fnl 50yds: all out* 16/1

3435 2 ¾ **Salateen**[21] 4890 5-9-12 105 AdamKirby 4 111
(David O'Meara) *pressed ldr: drvn and chal 2f out: led 1f out: looked wnr tl idled u.p and ct cl home* 3/1[2]

-561 3 3 **Love Dreams (IRE)**[14] 5159 3-9-1 100 PJMcDonald 2 96
(Mark Johnston) *led: drvn 2f out: hdd 1f out: wknd fnl 100yds* 10/11[1]

3213 4 1½ **Horsted Keynes (FR)**[7] 5415 7-8-13 92 JamieSpencer 6 86
(David Simcock) *stdd s: chsd ldrs: rdn 2f out: fnd little and no imp after* 6/1[3]

2100 5 10 **Normandy Barriere (IRE)**[21] 4925 5-9-5 98 JosephineGordon 3 77
(Nigel Tinkler) *chsd ldrs: rdn 1/2-way: sn struggling: eased 1f out* 8/1

1m 26.4s (0.70) **Going Correction** +0.275s/f (Good)
**WFA** 3 from 5yo+ 6lb 5 Ran SP% **108.7**
Speed ratings (Par 109): **107,106,102,101,89**
CSF £60.17 TOTE £16.20: £5.20, £1.60; EX 55.80 Trifecta £141.60.
**Owner** JLM Racing **Bred** Mrs Jean Brennan **Trained** Newmarket, Suffolk

**FOCUS**
A valuable little handicap, but not a strong race for the grade.

## 5663 MARITIME CARGO SERVICES H'CAP 1m 4f
**5:00** (5:01) (Class 4) (0-85,87) 4-Y-O+ **£5,175** (£1,540; £769; £384) **Stalls** Centre

Form RPR
-360 1 **Amazing Red (IRE)**[56] 3594 4-9-8 86 PJMcDonald 12 94
(Ed Dunlop) *settled towards rr: effrt on outside 3f out: drvn to chal 1f out: sustained run to ld fnl 100yds* 13/2

1-21 2 ¾ **Stamford Raffles**[14] 5138 4-9-2 85 PaddyBradley(5) 8 92+
(Jane Chapple-Hyam) *pressed ldr: led 2f out: sn drvn: hdd 100yds out: kpt on to regain 2nd cl home* 6/1[3]

0611 3 nk **C'Est No Mour (GER)**[34] 4413 4-9-0 78 SeanLevey 10 84
(Peter Hedger) *pressed ldrs: wnt prom 4f out: tk 2nd 2f out: sn drvn: ev ch 100yds out: nt qckn and lost 2nd cl home* 4/1[2]

2325 4 1¼ **Rydan (IRE)**[22] 4828 6-9-7 85 (v) TimmyMurphy 3 89
(Gary Moore) *settled towards rr: effrt and looked gng wl 3f out: chsd ldrs over 1f out: no imp and wl hld after* 8/1

1113 5 1½ **Lugano**[43] 4038 4-9-9 87 LukeMorris 9 89
(Sir Mark Prescott Bt) *led at modest pce: pushed along 3f out: drvn and hdd 2f out: btn whn hung lft 1f out* 5/2[1]

1326 6 4½ **Tom's Rock (IRE)**[24] 4751 4-9-4 82 JosephineGordon 4 77
(John Butler) *t.k.h in last pl: rdn 3f out: nvr rchd ldrs: edgd lft fnl f* 8/1

-332 7 12 **Singapore Sling**[14] 5140 4-8-8 75 (h) GeorgeWood(3) 1 51
(James Fanshawe) *t.k.h: prom: lost pl 1/2-way: fnd nil after: t.o fnl f but drvn out* 8/1

5466 8 27 **Castilo Del Diablo (IRE)**[30] 4519 8-8-10 74 JamieSpencer 13 6
(David Simcock) *prom: rdn and lost pl 4f out: t.o and eased 1f out* 25/1

2m 38.72s (5.82) **Going Correction** +0.275s/f (Good) 8 Ran SP% **113.4**
Speed ratings (Par 105): **91,90,90,89,88 85,77,59**
CSF £44.09 CT £175.10 TOTE £6.20: £2.30, £2.00, £1.70; EX 40.50 Trifecta £146.30.
**Owner** The Hon R J Arculli **Bred** Foursome Thoroughbreds, Muir & Waldron **Trained** Newmarket, Suffolk

**FOCUS**
Race run over an additional 19 yards. A fair handicap and there's a solid look to the form. The time was 4.69sec slower than the opening fillies' Listed race. The fourth has been rated to his recent form.

## 5664 FEDERATION OF BLOODSTOCK AGENTS H'CAP 1m
**5:30** (5:32) (Class 4) (0-80,82) 3-Y-O+ **£5,175** (£1,540; £769; £384) **Stalls** Low

Form RPR
101 1 **Whispered Kiss**[15] 5119 4-9-4 70 AntonioFresu 6 86
(Mike Murphy) *prom: led 2f out: 2 l clr 1f out: pushed along and readily increased advantage after* 14/1

441 2 4½ **Azaly (IRE)**[29] 4579 3-9-4 77 DaneO'Neill 4 82
(Owen Burrows) *chsd ldrs: rdn over 2f out: wnt 2nd over 1f out: in vain pursuit of wnr after* 11/2[3]

31 3 1 **Whosyourhousemate**[137] 1293 3-9-7 80 LukeMorris 2 83
(Ed Vaughan) *chsd ldrs: drvn over 2f out: no imp on ldng pair fnl f* 12/1

0604 4 1¾ **Kreb's Cycle (IRE)**[22] 4868 3-9-3 76 (p) JamesDoyle 13 75
(Ian Williams) *prom: drvn 2f out: outpcd by wnr 1f out and wl hld after* 5/1[2]

-040 5 ½ **Oasis Spear**[54] 3670 5-9-11 80 GeorgeWood(3) 8 79
(Chris Wall) *towards rr: rdn 1/2-way: wnt rt 2f out: no prog tl styd on ins fnl f:snatched wl hld 5th cl home* 16/1

2122 6 nk **Lamloom (IRE)**[11] 5265 3-9-8 81 AdamKirby 10 78
(David O'Meara) *racd freely in ld: rdn and hdd 2f out: fdd ins fnl f* 10/3[1]

3004 7 nk **House Of Commons (IRE)**[25] 4722 4-9-4 73 AaronJones(3) 9 70
(Michael Appleby) *prom: rdn 3f out: wknd over 1f out* 16/1

1633 8 1¼ **Ross Raith Rover**[1] 5610 4-8-12 67 (p) CallumShepherd(3) 3 61
(Robert Eddery) *bhd: drvn over 2f out: nvr nr ldrs* 7/1

0543 9 1 **Timeless Art (IRE)**[26] 4685 4-10-2 82 (e1) PJMcDonald 7 74
(K R Burke) *a towards rr: rdn and btn 2f out* 6/1

-005 **10** *nk* **Tukhoom (IRE)**[16] 5059 4-9-6 **72**..............................(h[1]) TimmyMurphy 11 63
(Michael Herrington) *a bhd: rdn and struggling 2f out* **14/1**

1-56 **11** *18* **Kitten's Johnstown (USA)**[34] 4408 3-9-7 **80**.................... SeanLevey 5 29
(Kevin Ryan) *dwlt: bhd: hrd rdn 1/2-way: t.o and eased 1f out* **25/1**

1m 39.7s (-0.30) **Going Correction** +0.275s/f (Good)
**WFA** 3 from 4yo+ 7lb **11** Ran SP% **118.6**
Speed ratings (Par 105): **112,107,106,104,104 103,103,102,101,101 83**
CSF £89.95 CT £969.52 TOTE £11.80: £3.20, £2.20, £2.90; EX 110.30 Trifecta £412.10.
**Owner** D Ellison, B Olkowicz, C Speller **Bred** T Ellison, B Olkowicz And C Speller **Trained** Westoning, Beds

**FOCUS**
Fair handicap form. The whole field raced down the centre, but the first three home came from a group of five who raced closer to the stands' side than the others. The second and third have been rated to the better view of their maiden form.
T/Plt: £1,050.90 to a £1 stake. Pool: £96,458.23 - 67 winning units. T/Qpdt: £37.00 to a £1 stake. Pool: £5,668.04 - 113.19 winning units. **Iain Mackenzie**

## 5613 THIRSK (L-H)
### Saturday, August 5

**OFFICIAL GOING: Good (good to soft in places; 7.8)**
Wind: Fresh across Weather: Cloudy

## 5665 KEEP CALM - MISS SMITH'S GETTING HITCHED! EBF NOVICE STKS (PLUS 10 RACE) 5f
**2:15** (2:20) (Class 4) 2-Y-O **£5,175** (£1,540; £769; £384) **Stalls** Centre

Form RPR

12 **1** **Abel Handy (IRE)**[22] 4862 2-9-8 0.............................. TomEaves 11 89+
(Declan Carroll) *mde all: rdn over 1f out: kpt on wl* **5/4**[1]

53 **2** *1 ¾* **Rossall**[12] 5202 2-9-2 0.............................. PaulMulrennan 4 75
(Michael Dods) *prom: rdn 2f out: kpt on but a hld* **9/2**[2]

51 **3** *2 ½* **Bow Belles**[14] 5162 2-9-3 0.............................. JamesSullivan 3 67
(Tim Easterby) *racd alone far side: prom: pushed along 2f out: rdn 1f out: kpt on same pce* **6/1**[3]

**4** *½* **Ghost** 2-8-11 0.............................. JasonHart 10 59
(John Quinn) *trckd ldrs: pushed along 2f out: kpt on same pce* **20/1**

**5** *2 ¼* **Dangerous Lady** 2-8-11 0.............................. DuranFentiman 13 51+
(Tim Easterby) *dwlt: sn midfield: pushed along over 2f out: kpt on same pce* **25/1**

05 **6** *hd* **Rock Hill (IRE)**[8] 5370 2-9-2 0.............................. GrahamLee 8 55
(Paul Midgley) *chsd ldrs: pushed along over 2f out: outpcd over 1f out* **25/1**

0 **7** *1 ½* **Navarra Princess (IRE)**[14] 5162 2-8-11 0................ StevieDonohoe 14 45
(Don Cantillon) *hld up: pushed along 2f out: kpt on ins fnl f* **66/1**

0 **8** *2* **Magic Ship (IRE)**[18] 4995 2-9-2 0.............................. JoeDoyle 6 42
(Ollie Pears) *trckd ldrs racing keenly: restrained into midfield 3f out: pushed along and outpcd 2f out: no threat after* **40/1**

0 **9** *½* **Graphite Girl (IRE)**[21] 4888 2-8-11 0.............................. CamHardie 5 36
(Tim Easterby) *hld up: pushed along 1/2-way: nvr threatened* **66/1**

**10** *1 ½* **Kodi Beach** 2-9-2 0.............................. BenCurtis 2 35
(David Barron) *hld up: sn rdn along: edgd lft 2f out: nvr threatened* **14/1**

50 **11** *nk* **Le Gros Serpant (IRE)**[10] 5278 2-8-11 0.................... RowanScott(5) 7 34
(Keith Dalgleish) *a towards rr* **100/1**

**12** *hd* **Flere Imsaho (IRE)** 2-9-2 0.............................. RichardKingscote 9 33
(Tom Dascombe) *dwlt: sn midfield: rdn along 2f out: wknd* **17/2**

00 **13** *7* **Lady Grand**[12] 5210 2-8-11 0..............................(h[1]) PaulHanagan 1 3
(Richard Fahey) *a towards rr* **33/1**

59.54s (-0.06) **Going Correction** +0.025s/f (Good) **13** Ran SP% **115.9**
Speed ratings (Par 96): **101,98,94,93,89 89,87,83,83,80 80,79,68**
CSF £5.61 TOTE £2.10: £1.10, £1.80, £2.00; EX 8.80 Trifecta £20.90.
**Owner** F Gillespie **Bred** Mr & Mrs G Middlebrook **Trained** Malton, N Yorks
■ Lady Sandy was withdrawn. Price at time of withdrawal 33/1. Rule 4 does not apply

**FOCUS**
Race distances were increased by 20yds in races 2, 3, 4, 5 and 6. The going was good (good to soft in places) ahead of the opener, after which Paul Hanagan described the ground as "tacky". A well-contested novice in which the majority raced down the centre.

## 5666 MARK BROWN 50TH BIRTHDAY CELEBRATION H'CAP 7f 218y
**2:50** (2:51) (Class 5) (0-70,71) 3-Y-O **£3,234** (£962; £481; £240) **Stalls** Low

Form RPR

123 **1** **Whatsthemessage (IRE)**[11] 5258 3-9-7 **70**........................ GrahamLee 5 79
(Keith Dalgleish) *prom: rdn to chal strly over 1f out: led narrowly jst ins fnl f: kpt on wl* **4/1**[1]

5240 **2** *nk* **Mama Africa (IRE)**[3] 5536 3-8-11 **65**..........................(p[1]) JaneElliott(5) 10 73
(David Barron) *led: rdn and strly pressed over 1f out: hdd jst ins fnl f: kpt on wl* **12/1**

2534 **3** *3* **Size Matters**[15] 5126 3-8-7 **56**.............................. DuranFentiman 13 57
(Mark Walford) *trckd ldrs: rdn 2f out: one pce fnl f* **13/2**[3]

6330 **4** *1* **Kilbaha Lady (IRE)**[18] 5001 3-8-10 **62**..................(t) LewisEdmunds(3) 6 61+
(Nigel Tinkler) *dwlt: hld up: rdn over 2f out: r.o wl fnl f: nrst fin* **25/1**

660 **5** *1* **Fleetfoot Jack (IRE)**[9] 5319 3-8-12 **61**..................(p) RichardKingscote 7 58+
(David O'Meara) *hld up in rr: rdn over 2f out: r.o wl fnl f: nrst fin* **14/1**

3054 **6** *shd* **Yorkshire Pudding**[8] 5375 3-8-11 **60**..................(b) FrannyNorton 4 57
(Tim Easterby) *trckd ldrs: rdn along 2f out: no ex fnl f* **16/1**

2415 **7** *½* **Vaulted**[13] 5185 3-9-6 **69**.............................. PaulHanagan 14 64
(Richard Fahey) *dwlt: hld up: pushed along and hdwy 2f out: rdn and one pce fnl f* **11/2**[2]

4436 **8** *nk* **Tesko Fella (IRE)**[12] 5206 3-9-0 **63**.............................. JamesSullivan 3 58
(Ruth Carr) *midfield: rdn over 2f out: no imp* **18/1**

0116 **9** *½* **Ching Ching Lor (IRE)**[25] 4721 3-8-13 **62**.............................. TomEaves 15 56
(Declan Carroll) *midfield towards outer: rdn and hdwy to chse ldrs over 2f out: wknd ins fnl f* **28/1**

-363 **10** *1 ½* **Doria Road (USA)**[18] 5009 3-9-0 **63**.............................. ShaneGray 9 53
(Kevin Ryan) *hld up in midfield: rdn over 2f out: wknd over 1f out* **14/1**

0356 **11** *½* **George Reme (IRE)**[18] 4999 3-9-8 **71**..............................(p) JasonHart 12 60
(John Quinn) *midfield: rdn over 2f out: wknd fnl f* **10/1**

666 **12** *¾* **Super Ruby**[58] 3493 3-8-7 **56** ow2.............................. MartinLane 2 43
(K R Burke) *dwlt: hld up: nvr threatened* **40/1**

205 **13** *½* **Thornton**[14] 5139 3-9-7 **70**.............................. PaulMulrennan 8 56
(Michael Dods) *prom: rdn over 2f out: wknd fnl f* **15/2**

0462 **14** *3* **Pioneering (IRE)**[16] 5073 3-9-2 **65**.............................. PhillipMakin 11 44
(David O'Meara) *in tch: rdn 3f out: sn wknd* **10/1**

-030 **15** *18* **Orientelle**[47] 3913 3-8-3 **52**.............................. CamHardie 1
(Richard Whitaker) *hld up: rdn along 4f out: wknd over 2f out* **40/1**

1m 43.08s (2.98) **Going Correction** +0.35s/f (Good) **15** Ran SP% **123.0**
Speed ratings (Par 100): **99,98,95,94,93 93,93,92,92,90 90,89,89,86,68**
CSF £51.84 CT £319.03 TOTE £4.80: £1.70, £4.10, £3.20; EX 64.20 Trifecta £695.50.
**Owner** Ronnie Docherty **Bred** Lynn Lodge Stud **Trained** Carluke, S Lanarks

**FOCUS**
Race distance increased by 20yds. A competitive handicap for the grade, but they didn't go fast and those near the pace were favoured. The winner has been rated back to her best.

## 5667 BET TOTEQUADPOT AT BETFRED.COM H'CAP 1m 4f 8y
**3:25** (3:26) (Class 4) (0-80,80) 3-Y-O+ **£5,175** (£1,540; £769; £384) **Stalls** High

Form RPR

551 **1** **Uber Cool (IRE)**[24] 4738 3-9-0 **76**.............................. PaulMulrennan 1 86
(Jane Chapple-Hyam) *midfield inner: hdwy 3f out: swtchd lft 2f out: sn pushed along to chal: led 1f out: sn rdn: styd on: all out* **9/2**[3]

313 **2** *shd* **Northwest Frontier (IRE)**[21] 4898 3-9-1 **77**.................. PaulHanagan 7 86
(Richard Fahey) *hld up: rn wd on bnd 10f out: pushed along 5f out: rdn and hdwy on outer 2f out: chsd ldrs ent fnl f: styd on wl fnl 110yds: jst failed* **3/1**[1]

02 **3** *2 ¼* **Tamayuz Magic (IRE)**[14] 5166 6-9-13 **79**.............................. CamHardie 9 83
(Michael Easterby) *in tch: rdn to ld 2f out: hdd 1f out: no ex fnl 110yds* **12/1**

0006 **4** *4 ½* **Purple Rock (IRE)**[21] 4921 5-9-7 **80**..........................(t) HarrisonShaw(7) 5 77
(Michael Easterby) *midfield: rdn over 2f out: wknd ins fnl f* **16/1**

25 **5** *4* **Hurricane Hollow**[24] 4742 7-8-13 **70**.............................. JaneElliott(5) 11 60
(David Barron) *trckd ldr: rdn over 2f out: wknd fnl f* **11/1**

1-21 **6** *7* **King's Coinage (IRE)**[51] 3752 3-8-11 **73**.................... JamesSullivan 6 53
(Ruth Carr) *hld up in midfield: rdn over 2f out: wknd over 1f out* **7/2**[2]

1133 **7** *shd* **Miningrocks (FR)**[6] 5455 5-9-1 **74**.............................. GerO'Neill(7) 10 53
(Declan Carroll) *rrd s but sn led: rdn 3f out: hdd 2f out: wknd appr fnl f* **9/2**[3]

5600 **8** *2 ½* **Eastern Dragon (IRE)**[12] 5207 7-9-1 **74**................(p) JamieGormley(7) 8 49
(Iain Jardine) *dwlt: a towards rr* **33/1**

5-55 **9** *shd* **Kind Of Beauty (IRE)**[12] 5217 3-8-13 **75**......................(p[1]) BenCurtis 4 51
(Hugo Palmer) *trckd ldrs: rdn 3f out: sn wknd* **16/1**

2m 37.97s (1.77) **Going Correction** +0.35s/f (Good)
**WFA** 3 from 4yo+ 10lb **9** Ran SP% **114.3**
Speed ratings (Par 105): **108,107,106,103,100 96,96,94,94**
CSF £18.20 CT £149.59 TOTE £5.40: £1.80, £1.40, £2.60; EX 22.30 Trifecta £125.00.
**Owner** Fiona and Ian Carmichael-Jennings **Bred** Albert Conneally **Trained** Dalham, Suffolk
■ Stewards' Enquiry : Paul Hanagan two-day ban; used his whip above the permitted level (20th-21th Aug)

**FOCUS**
Race distance increased by 20yds. A competitive handicap with a host of improving 3yos, and the form looks solid as they went a good pace and the first two pulled away from the third. It's been rated around the third.

## 5668 TOTEPOOL THIRSK SUMMER CUP H'CAP 7f 218y
**4:00** (4:03) (Class 3) (0-90,90) 3-Y-O+ **£12,591** (£12,591; £2,886; £1,443) **Stalls** Low

Form RPR

2163 **1** **Florenza**[23] 4794 4-9-4 **84**.............................. TomEaves 12 93
(Chris Fairhurst) *led: pushed along over 2f out: drvn over 1f out: strly pressed fnl 110yds: kpt on: jnd line* **40/1**

0000 **1** *dht* **Moonlightnavigator (USA)**[19] 4961 5-9-2 **82**.................... JasonHart 8 91
(John Quinn) *dwlt: sn trckd ldrs: rdn over 2f out: chal strly fnl 110yds: kpt on: jnd ldr line* **20/1**

1211 **3** *2 ¾* **Chiefofchiefs**[21] 4916 4-9-8 **88**..............................(p) StevieDonohoe 14 91+
(Charlie Fellowes) *hld up on outer: rdn over 2f out: hdwy over 1f out: kpt on wl fnl f* **9/4**[1]

0010 **4** *1* **Two For Two (IRE)**[8] 5382 9-9-10 **90**..........................(p) JamesSullivan 15 90
(Roger Fell) *dropped in s and hld up in rr: rdn over 2f out: sme hdwy on outer over 1f out: r.o wl fnl f: nrst fin* **28/1**

4011 **5** *hd* **Zodiakos (IRE)**[4] 5496 4-8-11 **84** 6ex..................(p) BenSanderson(7) 13 84
(Roger Fell) *trckd ldrs on outer: rdn over 2f out: kpt on same pce* **8/1**[2]

5003 **6** *nk* **Rousayan (IRE)**[14] 5165 6-9-2 **82**..............................(h) PhillipMakin 2 81
(David O'Meara) *midfield on inner: rdn over 1f out: kpt on same pce fnl f* **12/1**

451- **7** *1* **Severus (GER)**[21] 4924 7-9-7 **87**..............................(p[1]) MartinLane 7 84
(Des Donovan, Ire) *hld up: rdn over 2f out: kpt on ins fnl f* **14/1**

3204 **8** *nse* **Twin Appeal (IRE)**[7] 5434 6-9-5 **90**..........................(b) JaneElliott(5) 17 87
(David Barron) *trckd ldrs: rdn over 2f out: lost pl and bit short of room appr fnl f: kpt on ins fnl f* **12/1**

5253 **9** *shd* **Sovereign Bounty**[12] 5213 5-9-0 **80**.............................. DuranFentiman 10 77
(Jedd O'Keeffe) *trckd ldrs: rdn over 2f out: wknd fnl 110yds* **20/1**

-220 **10** *nk* **Throckley**[27] 4658 6-9-4 **84**..............................(t) SamJames 11 80
(John Davies) *prom: rdn over 2f out: wknd ins fnl f* **14/1**

0-24 **11** *1 ¼* **Ginger Jack**[17] 5032 10-9-9 **89**.............................. RichardKingscote 18 82
(Jo Hughes) *prom towards outer: rdn over 2f out: wknd ins fnl f* **14/1**

125 **12** *1 ¼* **Torrid**[14] 5165 6-9-3 **83**.............................. CamHardie 5 73
(Michael Easterby) *hld up in midfield: rdn over 2f out: no imp* **25/1**

5524 **13** *nk* **King's Pavilion (IRE)**[19] 4961 4-9-7 **87**.............................. BenCurtis 1 76
(David Barron) *dwlt: hld up: rdn over 2f out: nvr threatened* **14/1**

431 **14** *shd* **Carnageo (FR)**[38] 4207 4-9-5 **85**..............................(b) PaulHanagan 6 74
(Richard Fahey) *dwlt: sn midfield: rdn 2f out: wknd ins fnl f* **9/1**[3]

1362 **15** *½* **Finn Class (IRE)**[27] 4662 6-9-6 **86**.............................. PaulMulrennan 9 74
(Michael Dods) *hld up in midfield: rdn over 2f out: short of room ins fnl f: nvr threatened* **10/1**

6115 **16** *1 ¼* **Showboating (IRE)**[7] 5425 9-9-5 **85**.............................. FrannyNorton 4 70
(John Balding) *dwlt: a towards rr* **50/1**

0024 **17** *hd* **Heir To A Throne (FR)**[19] 4957 4-9-4 **84**.............................. ShaneGray 3 69
(Kevin Ryan) *midfield: rdn 3f out: wknd over 1f out* **25/1**

1m 41.7s (1.60) **Going Correction** +0.35s/f (Good) **17** Ran SP% **128.1**
Speed ratings (Par 107): **106,106,103,102,102 101,100,100,100,100 99,97,97,97,96 95,95**
WIN: F £23.60, M £13.60; PLACE: F £5.80, M £5.20, C £1.30, TFT £5.20; EX: F/M £1,139.80, M/F £878.80; TRIFECTA: F/M/C £1,816.80, M/F/C £1,816.80; CF: F/M £343.83, M/F £327.38; TRICAST: F/M/C £1,280.38, M/F/C £1256.97 TRIFECTA Part Won..
**Owner** 980 Racing **Bred** 980 Racing **Trained** Middleham, N Yorks
**Owner** Malcolm Walker **Bred** Highfield Farm **Trained** Settrington, N Yorks

**FOCUS**
Race distance increased by 20yds. A competitive renewal of this valuable handicap, featuring plenty of in-form runners and there was a thrilling finish. They didn't go a mad pace. Moonlightnavigator has been rated close to form.

## 5669 PETER BELL MEMORIAL H'CAP — 7f
**4:35** (4:35) (Class 3) (0-90,91) 3-Y-O+ **£8,086** (£2,406; £1,202; £601) **Stalls** Low

Form — RPR

0406 **1** **Theodorico (IRE)**[7] 5396 4-9-8 **86** ........ BenCurtis 3 — 94
(David Loughnane) *midfield: rdn over 2f out: hdwy over 1f out: chal fnl f: led 110yds out: kpt on* **10/1**

1060 **2** *nk* **Burnt Sugar (IRE)**[7] 5393 5-9-9 **87** ........ PaulHanagan 5 — 94
(Roger Fell) *dwlt: hld up in rr: pushed along over 2f out: gd hdwy over 1f out: chal fnl 110yds out: rdn and kpt on* **6/1**[2]

2601 **3** *1 ¾* **Shouranour (IRE)**[14] 5165 7-9-8 **86** ........(b) SamJames 10 — 88
(Alan Brown) *chsd ldrs: rdn over 2f out: led narrowly over 1f out: hdd 110yds out: edgd lft and no ex* **11/1**

5012 **4** *1 ¼* **Saint Equiano**[12] 5213 3-9-2 **86** ........ PhillipMakin 4 — 83
(Keith Dalgleish) *midfield: pushed along over 2f out: hdwy appr fnl f: rdn and one pce ins fnl f* **9/2**[1]

40-0 **5** *1* **Bamber Bridge (IRE)**[25] 4719 3-9-6 **90** ........ PaulMulrennan 8 — 84
(Michael Dods) *hld up in midfield: rdn over 2f out: kpt on ins fnl f: nvr threatened* **9/1**

3552 **6** *¾* **Fayez (IRE)**[8] 5376 3-8-10 **80** ........ FrannyNorton 9 — 72
(David O'Meara) *hld up: pushed along over 2f out: kpt on ins fnl f: nvr threatened* **13/2**[3]

0552 **7** *1 ¼* **Bertiewhittle**[7] 5396 9-9-8 **91** ........ JaneElliott(5) 11 — 82+
(David Barron) *dwlt: hld up: nvr threatened* **10/1**

-026 **8** *hd* **Muirsheen Durkin**[12] 5213 3-9-0 **84** ........(p) RichardKingscote 2 — 72
(Neville Bycroft) *chsd ldrs: rdn over 2f out: wknd fnl f* **6/1**[2]

0210 **9** *nk* **Explain**[16] 5059 5-9-10 **88** ........(p) JamesSullivan 1 — 77
(Ruth Carr) *hld up in midfield: pushed along over 2f out: nvr threatened* **16/1**

0005 **10** *shd* **God Willing**[8] 5379 6-9-0 **78** ........(b) TomEaves 12 — 67
(Declan Carroll) *led: rdn over 2f out: hdd over 1f out: wknd fnl f* **10/1**

0054 **11** *4 ½* **Sakhee's Return**[16] 5059 5-9-1 **79** ........(t) DuranFentiman 6 — 56
(Tim Easterby) *trckd ldrs: rdn over 2f out: wknd appr fnl f* **14/1**

/0-0 **12** *8* **Start Time (IRE)**[7] 5434 4-9-12 **90** ........ CamHardie 7 — 45
(Paul Midgley) *trckd ldrs: rdn 3f out: wknd over 1f out* **50/1**

1m 28.24s (1.04) **Going Correction** +0.35s/f (Good)
**WFA** 3 from 4yo+ 6lb — **12** Ran SP% **120.2**
Speed ratings (Par 107): **108,107,105,104,103 102,100,100,100,100 94,85**
CSF £69.92 CT £694.30 TOTE £12.80: £3.20, £2.50, £3.40; EX 82.60 Trifecta £1534.80.
**Owner** Mike And Eileen Newbould **Bred** J S Bolger & John Corcoran **Trained** Market Drayton, Shropshire
■ Stewards' Enquiry : Ben Curtis two-day ban; used his whip above the permitted level (19th-20th Aug)

**FOCUS**
Race distance increased by 20yds. An average handicap. They went a strong gallop, suiting those coming from behind. The winner has been rated back to his best.

## 5670 BREEDERS BACKING RACING EBF MAIDEN STKS — 7f 218y
**5:10** (5:12) (Class 4) 3-Y-O+ **£5,175** (£1,540; £769; £384) **Stalls** Low

Form — RPR

4- **1** **Isabella (IRE)**[277] 7740 3-9-0 0 ........ PhillipMakin 4 — 85
(David O'Meara) *mde all: pushed along over 1f out: rdn and edgd lft ent fnl f: kpt on* **5/1**[3]

35 **2** *¾* **Noble Conquest (FR)**[72] 2997 3-9-5 0 ........ StevieDonohoe 9 — 88
(Sir Michael Stoute) *dwlt: sn trckd ldrs: rdn to chse ldr over 1f out: swtchd rt 1f out: kpt on but a hld* **11/8**[1]

3 **3** *9* **Island Of Life (USA)**[21] 4911 3-9-0 0 ........ MartinLane 7 — 63
(Saeed bin Suroor) *prom: rdn 3f out: wknd fnl f* **9/4**[2]

4 **4** *1 ½* **Mischief Managed (IRE)**[35] 4341 3-9-5 0 ........(e) DuranFentiman 5 — 64
(Tim Easterby) *midfield: rdn along 3f out: one pce and nvr threatened* **16/1**

**5** *shd* **Ludorum (IRE)** 3-9-5 0 ........ PaulHanagan 3 — 64
(Richard Fahey) *trckd ldrs: rdn along 3f out: wknd over 1f out* **7/1**

40 **6** *4 ½* **Excellent Story**[6] 5458 3-9-5 0 ........ SamJames 6 — 54
(John Davies) *hld up in midfield: nudged along over 2f out: nvr threatened* **50/1**

0 **7** *5* **Fikhaar**[36] 4309 3-9-0 0 ........ TomEaves 8 — 37
(Kevin Ryan) *trckd ldrs on outer: rdn over 2f out: wknd over 1f out* **22/1**

00 **8** *5* **Silken Moonlight**[24] 4764 3-9-0 0 ........ BenCurtis 1 — 26
(Scott Dixon) *a outpcd in rr* **66/1**

0 **9** *3 ½* **Callaloo**[6] 5458 3-9-0 0 ........ CamHardie 2 — 17
(Tony Coyle) *slowly away: a rr* **80/1**

1m 43.58s (3.48) **Going Correction** +0.35s/f (Good) — **9** Ran SP% **117.0**
Speed ratings (Par 105): **96,95,86,84,84 80,75,70,66**
CSF £12.31 TOTE £6.80: £1.80, £1.10, £1.40; EX 17.50 Trifecta £43.30.
**Owner** Sir Robert Ogden **Bred** Sir Robert Ogden **Trained** Upper Helmsley, N Yorks

**FOCUS**
Race distance increased by 20yds. A fair maiden and the winner made all at a sensible pace. The first two came well clear. The level is a bit fluid.

## 5671 BET TOTEEXACTA AT BETFRED.COM H'CAP — 6f
**5:40** (5:41) (Class 4) (0-85,87) 3-Y-O+ **£5,175** (£1,540; £769; £384) **Stalls** Centre

Form — RPR

1216 **1** **The Armed Man**[28] 4616 4-8-8 **73** ........ PaulaMuir(7) 2 — 82
(Chris Fairhurst) *stmbld sltly s but sn prom: pushed along to ld over 1f out: rdn and kpt on* **9/2**[3]

4030 **2** *nk* **Bogart**[8] 5379 8-9-7 **79** ........(tp) TomEaves 7 — 87
(Kevin Ryan) *led: rdn 2f out: hdd over 1f out: kpt on* **9/1**

0624 **3** *2 ¼* **Scofflaw**[17] 5018 3-9-8 **84** ........ PaulHanagan 9 — 84
(Richard Fahey) *chsd ldrs: rdn 2f out: kpt on same pce* **7/2**[1]

6-05 **4** *nk* **Singeur (IRE)**[91] 2409 10-9-12 **84** ........ DuranFentiman 10 — 84
(Rebecca Bastiman) *hld up in midfield: rdn 2f out: kpt on fnl f* **40/1**

2160 **5** *¾* **My Name Is Rio (IRE)**[26] 4686 7-9-10 **87** ........ CallumRodriguez(5) 6 — 84
(Michael Dods) *chsd ldrs: rdn 2f out: no ex fnl 75yds* **7/1**

0-10 **6** *2 ¼* **The Commendatore**[35] 4353 4-10-0 **86** ........ BenCurtis 8 — 76
(David Barron) *slowly away: hld up: rdn along over 2f out: nvr threatened* **9/1**

1331 **7** *¾* **Meshardal (GER)**[17] 5018 7-9-6 **78** ........(p) JamesSullivan 4 — 66
(Ruth Carr) *hld up: nvr threatened* **4/1**[2]

0500 **8** *2* **Ninjago**[35] 4353 7-9-11 **83** ........(v[1]) PaulMulrennan 5 — 64
(Paul Midgley) *hld up: pushed along over 2f out: rdn appr fnl f: nvr threatened* **5/1**

1046 **9** *20* **Zapper Cass (FR)**[10] 5288 4-9-8 **80** ........(h[1]) CamHardie 1
(Tony Coyle) *v.s.a: a bhd* **20/1**

1m 12.89s (0.19) **Going Correction** +0.025s/f (Good)
**WFA** 3 from 4yo+ 4lb — **9** Ran SP% **116.8**
Speed ratings (Par 105): **99,98,95,95,94 91,90,87,60**
CSF £44.96 CT £159.36 TOTE £4.70: £1.50, £3.00, £1.70; EX 59.90 Trifecta £351.60.
**Owner** Mrs C A Arnold **Bred** C W Fairhurst **Trained** Middleham, N Yorks

**FOCUS**
A fair handicap in which they came down the centre and the first two had the race to themselves from the front. The runner-up has been rated close to his best since last spring.
T/Plt: £56.20 to a £1 stake. Pool: £7,0887.08 - 919.55 winning units. T/Qpdt: £20.50 to a £1 stake. Pool: £3,337.43 - 120 winning units. **Andrew Sheret**

5672 - 5675a (Foreign Racing) - See Raceform Interactive

# KLAMPENBORG
Saturday, August 5

**OFFICIAL GOING: Turf: good**

## 5676a FIRM MANAGEMENT SCANDINAVIAN OPEN CHAMPIONSHIP (GROUP 3) (3YO+) (TURF) — 1m 4f
**2:30** 3-Y-O+ **£28,669** (£11,467; £5,733; £3,440; £2,293)

RPR

**1** **Giuseppe Piazzi (IRE)**[23] 4825 5-9-5 0 ........(p) OliverWilson 8 — 98
(Flemming Velin, Denmark) **77/20**[3]

**2** *4* **Eye In The Sky (IRE)**[23] 4825 6-9-3 0 ........ MarkLarsen 2 — 90
(Niels Petersen, Norway) **3/1**[2]

**3** *hd* **Jubilance (IRE)**[23] 4825 8-9-3 0 ........ ElioneChaves 5 — 89
(Bent Olsen, Denmark) **27/1**

**4** *1* **Hurricane Red (IRE)**[23] 4825 7-9-5 0 ........ JacobJohansen 7 — 90
(Lennart Reuterskiold Jr, Sweden) **12/5**[1]

**5** *½* **Suspicious Mind (DEN)**[91] 4-9-3 0 ........ Per-AndersGraberg 1 — 87
(Niels Petersen, Norway) **43/10**

**6** *5* **Falconet (DEN)**[62] 7-9-3 0 ........ NelsonDeSouza 4 — 79
(Bent Olsen, Denmark) **231/10**

**7** *4* **Fields Of Athenry (IRE)**[83] 2667 5-9-3 0 ........ Jan-ErikNeuroth 3 — 72
(Flemming Velin, Denmark) **22/5**

**8** *dist* **Berling (IRE)**[23] 10-9-3 0 ........ MrFredrikJanetzky 6
(Jessica Long, Sweden) **15/1**

2m 33.7s — **8** Ran SP% **126.4**

**Owner** Majken & Flemming Velin **Bred** Rockhart Trading Ltd **Trained** Denmark

5677 - 5678a (Foreign Racing) - See Raceform Interactive

# 5312 VICHY
Saturday, August 5

**OFFICIAL GOING: Turf: soft**

## 5679a PRIX DES JOUVENCEAUX ET DES JOUVENCELLES (LISTED RACE) (2YO) (TURF) — 7f
**5:00** 2-Y-O **£25,641** (£10,256; £7,692; £5,128; £2,564)

RPR

**1** **De Bruyne Horse**[13] 5195 2-9-2 0 ........(p) ChristopheSoumillon 2 — 96+
(Richard Hannon) **9/2**[2]

**2** *nk* **Red Line (FR)** 2-8-13 0 ........ CristianDemuro 9 — 92
(A De Watrigant, France) **48/10**[3]

**3** *1 ¼* **Fastidious (FR)**[30] 2-9-2 0 ........ ThibaultSpeicher 4 — 92
(Louis Baudron, France) **46/1**

**4** *1* **Patascoy (FR)**[25] 2-9-2 0 ........ EmilienRevolte 10 — 89
(X Thomas-Demeaulte, France) **9/1**

**5** *hd* **Sonjeu (FR)**[32] 2-8-13 0 ........ MaximeGuyon 3 — 86
(C Ferland, France) **7/2**[1]

**6** *¾* **Yayajonh (FR)**[43] 2-9-2 0 ........ MickaelBarzalona 8 — 87
(Jane Soubagne, France) **12/1**

**7** *1* **Dann (FR)**[22] 4876 2-9-2 0 ........ AlexandreGavilan 7 — 84
(D Guillemin, France) **7/1**

**8** *1* **Tax Exile (IRE)** 2-9-2 0 ........ AntoineHamelin 5 — 81
(Matthieu Palussiere, France) **44/5**

**9** *nse* **Kenshow (FR)** 2-8-13 0 ........ AnthonyCrastus 6 — 78
(P Sogorb, France) **12/1**

**10** *3* **Pimpinehorse (FR)**[56] 3611 2-9-2 0 ........ Pierre-CharlesBoudot 12 — 73
(R Chotard, France) **23/1**

**11** *hd* **Heads Together**[27] 2-8-13 0 ........ AlexisBadel 11 — 70
(S Kobayashi, France) **29/1**

**12** *4 ½* **Feroe D'Illiat (FR)** 2-9-2 0 ........(b) FranckBlondel 1 — 60
(P Decouz, France) **45/1**

1m 28.15s — **12** Ran SP% **117.5**
PARI-MUTUEL (all including 1 euro stake): WIN 5.50; PLACE 2.40, 2.00, 8.00; DF 17.40; SF 34.80.
**Owner** Middleham Park Racing Lxv & K Sohi **Bred** Frazer Hood **Trained** East Everleigh, Wilts

# 5398 CHESTER (L-H)
Sunday, August 6

**OFFICIAL GOING: Good to soft (6.6)**
Wind: breezy, across Weather: overcast, cool

## 5680 CALDWELL CONSTRUCTION/EBF NOVICE STKS (PLUS 10 RACE) — 7f 1y
**2:05** (2:05) (Class 4) 2-Y-O **£6,225** (£1,864; £932; £466; £233; £117) **Stalls** Low

Form — RPR

6 **1** **Zoffalee (FR)**[43] 4083 2-9-2 0 ........ RichardKingscote 1 — 81+
(Tom Dascombe) *trckd ldrs: hdwy into 2nd 2f out: rdn to ld 1f out: jnd by runner-up ins fnl f: hld on wl u.p last 150yds* **10/3**[2]

3 **2** *hd* **Porth Swtan (IRE)**[37] 4297 2-9-2 0 ........ PaulHanagan 6 — 80+
(Charles Hills) *hld up: gd hdwy on outer 2f out: drvn to chal 1f out: jnd wnr ins fnl f: rdn and r.o wl last 150yds: jst hld* **4/1**

04 **3** *5* **Snooker Jim**[22] 4880 2-9-2 0 RoystonFfrench 2 67
(Steph Hollinshead) *led: 1 l clr 2f out: rdn over 1f out: sn hdd: no ex ins fnl f* **7/1**

244 **4** *1* **Red Force One**[31] 4526 2-9-2 78 MartinHarley 5 64
(Tom Dascombe) *chsd ldr: pushed along 2f out: rdn over 1f out: one pce fnl f* **7/2**[3]

**5** *2* **Lineofintelligence** 2-9-2 0 PJMcDonald 8 59+
(Richard Fahey) *slowly away and sn detached fr rest of field: drvn along first 3f: last 2f out: r.o under hand riding fnl 2 fs* **16/1**

3 **6** *1 3/4* **Delph Crescent (IRE)**[30] 4577 2-9-2 0 TonyHamilton 3 55
(Richard Fahey) *trckd ldrs: pushed along 3f out: drvn and lost pl 2f out: wknd* **11/4**[1]

0 **7** *hd* **Surrender**[29] 4597 2-9-2 0 DavidAllan 4 54
(Tim Easterby) *hld up: drvn along 2f out: sn rdn and wknd* **28/1**

1m 29.61s (3.11) **Going Correction** +0.50s/f (Yiel) **7** Ran SP% **113.8**
Speed ratings (Par 96): **102,101,96,94,92 90,90**
CSF £16.87 TOTE £4.20: £3.10, £1.70; EX 18.50 Trifecta £90.40.
**Owner** D R Passant **Bred** Hugues Rousseau **Trained** Malpas, Cheshire
■ Stewards' Enquiry : Richard Kingscote caution: careless riding

**FOCUS**
Add 24yds to race distance. This looked a strong race of its type and it was run an an even gallop. The front two pulled clear.

## 5681 HORSERADISH HOSPITALITY AT SOUTHPORT FLOWER SHOW/EBF STALLIONS CONDITIONS STKS (PLUS 10 RACE) 6f 17y
**2:35** (2:35) (Class 2) 2-Y-O **£12,450** (£3,728; £1,864; £932; £466) **Stalls** Low

Form RPR

01 **1** **Prestbury Park (USA)**[16] 5099 2-9-1 0 FrannyNorton 5 90
(Mark Johnston) *mde all: drvn 2f out: rdn and 1 l clr 1f out: strly pressed ins fnl f: r.o gamely u.p: jst hld on* **10/1**

21 **2** *shd* **Regulator (IRE)**[13] 5202 2-8-12 0 PaulHanagan 3 87+
(Richard Fahey) *trckd ldrs: pushed along in 3rd 2f out: effrt on inner whn n.m.r over 1f out: sn bk in clr: rdn and hdwy ent fnl f: r.o wl to cl on wnr: jst failed* **9/4**[1]

41 **3** *1/2* **Ulshaw Bridge (IRE)**[22] 4919 2-9-3 0 DanielTudhope 4 90+
(James Bethell) *in rr and sn adrift of pack: 5 l bhd rest 2f out: rdn and hdwy wl over 1f out: rapid prog fnl f: tk 3rd nr fin* **7/2**[3]

3102 **4** *hd* **Dragons Tail (IRE)**[23] 4827 2-9-3 93 RichardKingscote 1 89
(Tom Dascombe) *trckd ldr: pushed along 2f out: ev ch and drvn over 1f out: rdn and one pce fnl f: lost 3rd nr fin* **5/2**[2]

3013 **5** *1 3/4* **Haddaf (IRE)**[17] 5090 2-9-3 99 MartinHarley 2 84
(James Tate) *trckd ldrs: relegated to 4th and drvn 2f out: rdn over 1f out: no ex* **9/2**

1m 16.33s (2.53) **Going Correction** +0.50s/f (Yiel) **5** Ran SP% **108.8**
Speed ratings (Par 100): **103,102,102,101,99**
CSF £31.76 TOTE £7.20: £3.40, £1.20; EX 13.40 Trifecta £46.60.
**Owner** Sheikh Hamdan bin Mohammed Al Maktoum **Bred** Godolphin **Trained** Middleham Moor, N Yorks
■ Stewards' Enquiry : Franny Norton two-day ban: excessive use of whip (Aug 20-21)

**FOCUS**
Add 24yds to race distance. A decent little conditions contest. The fourth has been rated to his nursery form.

## 5682 MBNA FESTIVAL OF FOOTBALL H'CAP 1m 6f 87y
**3:10** (3:11) (Class 2) 3-Y-O
**£31,125** (£9,320; £4,660; £2,330; £1,165; £585) **Stalls** Low

Form RPR

3312 **1** **Tor**[6] 5468 3-7-13 79 JamieGormley(7) 7 89
(Iain Jardine) *mde all: slowed pce 1/2-way: 1 l clr 2f out: pushed into 3 l ld 1f out: briefly kpt up to work and extended advantage ent fnl f: r.o strly: easily* **6/1**[3]

1314 **2** *3 3/4* **Here And Now**[22] 4891 3-9-0 87 PaulHanagan 1 92
(Ralph Beckett) *prom: drvn in 3rd 2f out: r.o ent fnl f: tk 2nd pl last 150yds: no ch w wnr* **7/1**

-211 **3** *1/2* **Zenon (IRE)**[29] 4612 3-9-7 94 RobertTart 4 98
(John Gosden) *trckd ldr: pushed along 2f out: rdn and losing tch w wnr over 1f out: one pce fnl f: lost 2nd pl last 150yds* **7/4**[1]

3512 **4** *5* **Amelia Dream**[15] 5153 3-7-9 73 oh1 DavidEgan(5) 3 70
(Mick Channon) *mid-div: drvn 2f out: rdn over 1f out: r.o one pce fnl f* **20/1**

152 **5** *nk* **Twenty Times (IRE)**[16] 5113 3-8-7 80 ShaneKelly 8 77
(Richard Hughes) *mid-div: hdwy on outer 3f out: sn ev ch: drvn 2f out: rdn over 1f out: wknd* **25/1**

1626 **6** *1 1/2* **Cray (IRE)**[29] 4612 3-8-1 74 (p) AndrewMullen 6 69
(James Bethell) *hld up: pushed along 3f out: drvn 2f out: sn rdn and no ex* **25/1**

2312 **7** *1/2* **Nadaitak**[10] 5328 3-8-12 85 (p[1]) RichardKingscote 2 79+
(Sir Michael Stoute) *hld up: effrt on outer 3f out: drvn 2f out: rdn and wknd over 1f out* **11/4**[2]

4002 **8** *3 3/4* **Mister Manduro (FR)**[9] 5351 3-9-5 92 FrannyNorton 5 81
(Mark Johnston) *a in rr: drvn and lost tch 2f out* **8/1**

3m 14.44s (7.44) **Going Correction** +0.50s/f (Yiel) **8** Ran SP% **113.4**
Speed ratings (Par 106): **98,95,95,92,92 91,91,89**
CSF £44.83 CT £102.20 TOTE £7.00: £1.90, £2.50, £1.20; EX 53.50 Trifecta £185.60.
**Owner** I Wilson **Bred** Iain Wilson **Trained** Carrutherstown, D'fries & G'way

**FOCUS**
Add 46yds to race distance. This looked a competitive heat on paper but it was run at a dawdle and the horse that was allowed to dictate on his own terms cleared away in the straight. The level is fluid.

## 5683 FLIP OUT MILE H'CAP 7f 127y
**3:40** (3:42) (Class 3) (0-95,91) 3-Y-O+
**£8,092** (£2,423; £1,211; £605; £302; £152) **Stalls** Low

Form RPR

-004 **1** **Breakable**[8] 5422 6-10-0 91 DavidAllan 4 96
(Tim Easterby) *trckd ldrs on inner: hdwy into 3rd 2f out: fnd gap and chal over 1f out: rdn ent fnl f: r.o wl to ld last 100yds: won gng away* **4/1**[2]

0003 **2** *3/4* **Gabrial The Tiger (IRE)**[37] 4294 5-8-12 78 AdamMcNamara(3) 7 81
(Richard Fahey) *narrow ld tl drvn 1 l clr 2f out: rdn over 1f out: r.o fnl f but hdd last 100yds: no ex* **11/1**

0050 **3** *1/2* **Gabrial's Kaka (IRE)**[9] 5382 7-9-3 80 (b[1]) TonyHamilton 8 82
(Richard Fahey) *hld up: hdwy on inner 2f out: rdn over 1f out: r.o strly ins fnl f: tk 3rd last 50yds:* **20/1**

5442 **4** *1* **Zlatan (IRE)**[11] 5276 4-9-1 78 (p) DanielTudhope 1 77
(Ed de Giles) *mid-div: pushed along and hdwy into 3rd 2f out: rdn and ev ch 1f out: no ex fnl f: lost 3rd last 50yds* **3/1**[1]

0213 **5** *1 3/4* **Calder Prince (IRE)**[9] 5382 4-9-8 90 PaddyPilley(5) 5 85
(Tom Dascombe) *prom: cl 2nd over 2f out: sn drvn and lost pl: no ex ent fnl f* **9/2**[3]

-242 **6** *1 1/2* **Chosen Character (IRE)**[17] 5062 9-8-9 79 (vt) ElishaWhittington(7) 3 70
(Tom Dascombe) *in rr: pushed along and struggling 2f out: reminders over 1f out: r.o one pce fnl f* **16/1**

0010 **7** *2 1/4* **Michele Strogoff**[7] 5457 4-9-9 89 (b) JoshDoyle(3) 2 75
(Tony Coyle) *prom: cl 3rd 3f out: pushed along and lost pl 2f out: rdn over 1f out: wknd* **11/2**

3124 **8** *5* **Navarone (IRE)**[13] 5213 3-8-8 78 PaulHanagan 6 50
(Richard Fahey) *hld up: drvn and effrt 2f out: rdn and wknd over 1f out* **11/2**

1m 36.17s (2.37) **Going Correction** +0.50s/f (Yiel)
**WFA** 3 from 4yo+ 7lb **8** Ran SP% **112.9**
Speed ratings (Par 107): **108,107,106,105,104 102,100,95**
CSF £45.21 CT £781.84 TOTE £6.00: £1.40, £3.60, £4.10; EX 51.80 Trifecta £343.50.
**Owner** Ryedale Partners No 9 **Bred** Habton Farms **Trained** Great Habton, N Yorks

**FOCUS**
Add 24yds to race distance. Not the strongest 0-95 given how many of these had a bit to prove. The winner has been rated close to last August's C&D win.

## 5684 TOTAL FITNESS QUEENSFERRY STKS (LISTED RACE) 6f 17y
**4:15** (4:15) (Class 1) 3-Y-O+ **£20,982** (£7,955; £3,981; £1,983; £995) **Stalls** Low

Form RPR

0330 **1** **Kimberella**[21] 4940 7-9-1 109 PaulHanagan 4 114
(Richard Fahey) *chsd ldr tl led after 1f: mde rest: pushed along and 2 l clr over 1f out: rdn ins fnl f: r.o wl to maintain advantage* **9/4**[2]

1114 **2** *1 3/4* **Judicial (IRE)**[22] 4920 5-9-1 107 (e) JoeDoyle 6 108
(Julie Camacho) *mid-div: hdwy on outer into 2nd 2f out: tried to cl on wnr ent fnl f: rdn and r.o but no imp* **3/1**[3]

-110 **3** *1 1/2* **Unabated (IRE)**[24] 4813 3-8-11 104 DanielMuscutt 5 103
(Marco Botti) *trckd ldrs: pushed along 2f out: rdn over 1f out: r.o one pce to take 3rd ent fnl f* **8/1**

0003 **4** *1* **Cotai Glory**[22] 4920 5-9-1 109 RichardKingscote 2 100
(Charles Hills) *led early: lugged off rail: hdd after 1f: remained prom: drvn 2f out: wknd and lost 3rd ent fnl f* **6/4**[1]

4216 **5** *1 1/4* **Avon Breeze**[7] 5457 8-8-10 89 LewisEdmunds 7 91
(Richard Whitaker) *hld up: pushed along and struggling 2f out: rdn over 1f out: no imp* **20/1**

1m 15.22s (1.42) **Going Correction** +0.50s/f (Yiel)
**WFA** 3 from 4yo+ 4lb **5** Ran SP% **111.6**
Speed ratings (Par 111): **110,107,105,104,102**
CSF £9.48 TOTE £3.30: £1.30, £1.60; EX 10.10 Trifecta £22.50.
**Owner** C Titcomb **Bred** P And Mrs A G Venner **Trained** Musley Bank, N Yorks

**FOCUS**
Add 24yds to race distance. This Listed race was decimated by four non-runners and two of the main protagonists are 5f horses, so this isn't strong Listed form, despite the fact that the winner won impressively. The winner has been rated to form.

## 5685 BRITVIC NURSERY H'CAP 6f 17y
**4:50** (4:53) (Class 4) 2-Y-O
**£6,225** (£1,864; £932; £466; £233; £117) **Stalls** Low

Form RPR

2521 **1** **Demons Rock (IRE)**[17] 5047 2-9-6 77 RichardKingscote 2 86+
(Tom Dascombe) *mde all: kicked 2 l clr 2f out: rdn over 1f out: sn extended advantage to 5 l: in n.d ins fnl f: eased nr fin: easily* **15/8**[1]

442 **2** *2 1/4* **Kimifive (IRE)**[17] 5048 2-9-6 77 JFEgan 6 76+
(Joseph Tuite) *hld up: hdwy 2f out: briefly checked over 1f out: sn in clr: rdn and hdwy ins fnl f: tk 2nd nr fin* **8/1**

542 **3** *1/2* **Angel Islington (IRE)**[25] 4749 2-9-5 76 OisinMurphy 4 73
(Andrew Balding) *trckd ldrs: 4th 3f out: rdn and wnt 2nd ent fnl f: r.o: lost 2nd nr fin* **4/1**[2]

4236 **4** *1* **Auntie Pam (IRE)**[6] 5479 2-8-7 69 (p) PaddyPilley(5) 10 63
(Tom Dascombe) *mid-div on outer: rdn 2f out: hdwy ent fnl f: styd on one pce* **33/1**

1320 **5** *hd* **Inviolable Spirit (IRE)**[15] 5150 2-9-7 78 PaulHanagan 8 72
(Richard Fahey) *in rr: hdwy over 1f out: r.o wl fnl f: nvr nrr* **14/1**

1034 **6** *hd* **Magnus (IRE)**[17] 5079 2-9-3 74 BenCurtis 3 67+
(Tom Dascombe) *mid-div: n.m.r on inner over 1f out: sme hdwy fnl f* **13/2**[3]

5000 **7** *nk* **Mabo**[9] 5373 2-8-7 67 SammyJoBell(3) 7 59
(Richard Fahey) *in rr: pushed along 2f out: no imp* **20/1**

000 **8** *2* **Admiral Spice (IRE)**[31] 4526 2-8-7 64 JoeFanning 1 50
(Tom Dascombe) *prom: 3rd 2f out: sn rdn and wknd* **10/1**

2412 **9** *1/2* **Our Man In Havana**[16] 5127 2-9-3 74 MartinHarley 5 58
(Tom Dascombe) *chsd wnr: lft bhd by wnr fr 2f out: rdn and stl 2nd ent fnl f: wknd qckly* **15/2**

1m 17.6s (3.80) **Going Correction** +0.50s/f (Yiel) **9** Ran SP% **114.5**
Speed ratings (Par 96): **94,91,90,89,88 88,88,85,84**
CSF £17.51 CT £54.29 TOTE £2.50: £1.40, £2.90, £1.60; EX 18.70 Trifecta £51.40.
**Owner** The Famous Five Partnership **Bred** James & Geoff Mulcahy **Trained** Malpas, Cheshire

**FOCUS**
Add 24yds to race distance. This race was taken apart from the front by a horse who looks ahead of his mark. The third and fourth have been rated close to their turf figures.

## 5686 MERSEYRAIL H'CAP 1m 2f 70y
**5:20** (5:20) (Class 4) (0-80,82) 3-Y-O+
**£6,225** (£1,864; £932; £466; £233; £117) **Stalls** High

Form RPR

3215 **1** **Alexander M (IRE)**[8] 5404 3-8-11 71 JoeFanning 6 84+
(Mark Johnston) *mde all: 1 l clr 2f out: pushed along and kicked 5 l clr over 1f out: kpt up to work ins fnl f tl heavily eased nr fin: easily* **5/1**[3]

-242 **2** *2 1/4* **Golden Wolf (IRE)**[20] 4981 3-9-1 75 ShaneKelly 4 82+
(Richard Hughes) *hld up: hdwy and pushed along 2f out: rdn ent fnl f: r.o wl to take clr 2nd last 150yds: no ch w easy wnr* **8/1**

0442 **3** *3* **Outback Blue**[15] 5135 4-9-7 73 (vt) JFEgan 8 73
(David Evans) *hld up: hdwy 1/2-way: 3rd 3f out: drvn into 2nd 2f out: rdn and chsd wnr ent fnl f: no imp: lost 2nd last 150yds* **12/1**

1446 **4** *2* **Energia Fox (BRZ)**[17] 5060 7-9-9 82 ConnorMurtagh(7) 7 78
(Richard Fahey) *mid-div: drvn 2f out: rdn over 1f out: r.o one pce fnl f* **12/1**

0152 **5** *1 ¼* **X Rated (IRE)**[6] 5475 3-9-4 **78**........................................ FrannyNorton 1 73
(Mark Johnston) *trckd ldrs on inner: pushed along and hdwy into 3rd 2f out: sn drvn: wknd over 1f out* **4/1**[2]

260 **6** *3 ½* **Melabi (IRE)**[52] 3740 4-8-9 **66**................................. CallumRodriguez(5) 2 53
(Richard Ford) *mid-div: pushed along 3f out: rdn wl over 1f out: no imp* **16/1**

-155 **7** *2* **Al Zaman (IRE)**[71] 3081 3-9-6 **80**.........................(tp) RichardKingscote 3 64
(Simon Crisford) *chsd ldr: pushed along 2f out and sn lost pl: wknd* **15/8**[1]

1-00 **8** *3* **Fort Jefferson**[31] 4522 4-9-7 **73**........................................ OisinMurphy 5 51
(Andrew Balding) *hld up: pushed along on outer 3f out: suffered minor interference 2f out: wknd qckly: eased* **8/1**

2m 15.1s (3.90) **Going Correction** +0.50s/f (Yiel)
**WFA** 3 from 4yo+ 8lb **8** Ran SP% **114.9**
Speed ratings (Par 105): **104,102,99,98,97 94,92,90**
CSF £44.32 CT £454.33 TOTE £5.50: £1.50, £2.70, £3.30; EX 39.80 Trifecta £304.10.
**Owner** Christinee Budden, M Budden, Matthew Budden **Bred** Christine E Budden & Partners **Trained** Middleham Moor, N Yorks

**FOCUS**
Add 26yds to race distance. Yet another emphatic winner from the front but, given his overall profile, this result takes some believing. The well-backed market leader bombed out completely.
T/Jkpt: Not won. T/Plt: £53.00 to a £1 stake. Pool: £88,115.00 - 1,659.42 winning units. T/Qpdt: £8.50 to a £1 stake. Pool: £6,773.00 - 788.82 winning units. **Keith McHugh**

5687 - (Foreign Racing) - See Raceform Interactive

# 5672 GALWAY (R-H)
Sunday, August 6

**OFFICIAL GOING: Jumps courses - soft; flat course - soft to heavy**

## 5688a IRISH STALLION FARMS EBF "AHONOORA" H'CAP (PREMIER HANDICAP) 7f
**3:55** (3:56) 3-Y-0+

**£50,427** (£16,239; £7,692; £3,418; £1,709; £854)

RPR

**1** **Dream Walker (FR)**[5] 5517 8-9-3 **90**..............................(t) ChrisHayes 14 98+
(Brian Ellison) *racd in rr: niggled along 1/2-way: prog 2f out: swtchd lft off home turn into 4th ent fnl f where edgd lft: styd on strly to ld cl home* **7/1**[3]

**2** *½* **Baraweez (IRE)**[5] 5517 7-9-7 **94**................................................ WJLee 4 101
(Brian Ellison) *chsd ldrs in 5th: rdn in 3rd ent fnl f: led ins fnl 50yds tl hdd cl home* **6/1**[2]

**3** *¾* **Be Kool (IRE)**[3] 5582 4-8-12 **85**.................................(v) BenRobinson(5) 6 95
(Brian Ellison) *chsd ldrs in 6th: rdn in 3rd appr fnl f and sn led: hdd fnl 50yds and dropped to 3rd cl home* **16/1**

**4** *hd* **Canary Row (IRE)**[62] 3419 7-8-10 **90**.......................(v) DylanHogan(7) 13 94+
(P J Prendergast, Ire) *hld up: prog whn short of room on inner under 3f out: wnt 9th 1f out: styd on strly into 4th cl home: nrst fin* **8/1**

**5** *hd* **Riven Light (IRE)**[5] 5517 5-9-12 **99** 7ex.................. DeclanMcDonogh 15 104+
(W P Mullins, Ire) *racd towards rr: swtchd rt to inner 3f out: chsd ldrs whn short of room 2f out and lost position: swtchd off rails over 1f out: kpt on strly clsng stages: nvr nrr* **9/4**[1]

**6** *1 ½* **Stenographer (USA)**[15] 5175 4-9-0 **87**......................... KevinManning 7 87
(J S Bolger, Ire) *racd in mid-div: clsr 2f out: wnt 5th ent fnl f: kpt on same pce* **25/1**

**7** *6* **Truffles (IRE)**[35] 4415 4-8-10 **83**........................................ RoryCleary 16 67
(Ms Sheila Lavery, Ire) *sn trckd ldrs in 3rd: rdn to briefly dispute over 1f out: sn hdd & wknd ins fnl f* **25/1**

**8** *nse* **Penwortham (IRE)**[38] 4264 4-9-1 **88**.........................(h) MichaelHussey 9 72
(Richard Fahey) *racd in rr of mid-div: prog on outer 2f out: no imp ent fnl f: kpt on same pce* **33/1**

**9** *¾* **Katiymann (IRE)**[36] 4384 5-9-1 **88**.................................(t[1]) ShaneFoley 3 69
(M Halford, Ire) *racd in mid-div: rdn towards rr over 2f out: kpt on ins fnl f: nvr on terms* **10/1**

**10** *1 ¼* **Not A Bad Oul Day (IRE)**[42] 4125 5-9-0 **87**.................... PatSmullen 12 70
(John James Feane, Ire) *sn trckd ldr in 2nd: rdn and nt qckn appr fnl f: on the retreat whn short of room on inner 1f out and eased* **12/1**

**11** *nk* **Tithonus (IRE)**[22] 4925 6-9-6 **96**..................................(bt) GaryHalpin(3) 1 73
(Denis Gerard Hogan, Ire) *led: strly pressed over 1f out and hdd: wknd* **7/1**[3]

**12** *4 ¾* **Ma Fee Heela (FR)**[22] 4925 3-8-4 **90**..........................(p) SeanDavis(7) 10 52
(M D O'Callaghan, Ire) *racd in mid-div: rdn and no imp under 2f out: sn one pce* **14/1**

**13** *4 ¼* **Geological (IRE)**[5] 5517 5-9-6 **98**......................... DonaghO'Connor(5) 2 51
(Damian Joseph English, Ire) *trckd ldrs in 4th tl under 2f out: sn wknd: eased ins fnl f* **33/1**

**14** *1 ¾* **Reckless Endeavour (IRE)**[70] 3114 4-9-8 **95**................ ColinKeane 11 43
(G M Lyons, Ire) *racd in mid-div: rdn and no imp under 2f out* **25/1**

**15** *8 ½* **Secret Wizard (IRE)**[5] 5517 4-9-3 **90**.......................... RonanWhelan 8 15
(Ms Sheila Lavery, Ire) *racd in mid-div: pushed along bef 1/2-way: dropped towards rr over 2f out: eased ins fnl f* **16/1**

**16** *nk* **Stipulate**[5] 5517 8-9-2 **89**.................................................. WayneLordan 5 14
(Brian Ellison) *racd in rr of mid-div: pushed along 3f out: detached in rr fr 2f out: eased fnl f* **20/1**

1m 33.92s (2.32)
**WFA** 3 from 4yo+ 6lb **16** Ran SP% **138.6**
CSF £51.36 CT £714.63 TOTE £9.50: £2.20, £1.90, £3.50, £2.70; DF 49.10 Trifecta £1593.30.
**Owner** Keith Brown **Bred** John Berry **Trained** Norton, N Yorks

**FOCUS**
A messy finish to this hugely competitive handicap but the real story of the race was the outstanding training performance by Brian Ellison. Not only did he record a 1-2-3 in the race but Dream Walker, last year's winner, extended the trainer's winning sequence to four. To win just one premier handicap at Galway is an achievement in itself but to win four on the trot is special. A fine training performance. The fourth and fifth help set the standard.

## 5689a JPK FENCING H'CAP 1m 5f 186y
**5:30** (5:30) (50-75,75) 3-Y-0+ **£8,423** (£2,611; £1,244; £560; £218)

RPR

**1** **Dara Tango (FR)**[59] 3513 10-8-13 **57**.............................(t) ColinKeane 9 62+
(A J Martin, Ire) *racd in mid-div: pushed along in 7th under 2f out: prog into 3rd 1f out: styd on wl to ld ins fnl 50yds* **11/4**[1]

**2** *½* **Highland Fling (IRE)**[4] 6173 5-9-7 **65**..........................(t) RoryCleary 6 69
(Gavin Cromwell, Ire) *chsd ldrs in 3rd: rdn to chse ldr in 2nd under 2f out: kpt on same pce and dropped to 3rd ins fnl f: squeezed for room cl home and rallied wl into 2nd on line* **11/2**[2]

**3** *nse* **Bottleofsmoke (IRE)**[3] 5584 4-9-8 **66**............................ ChrisHayes 10 70
(Gavin Cromwell, Ire) *trckd ldr in 2nd tl pressed ldr over 2f out and sn led: 2 l advantage ent fnl f: hdd ins fnl 50yds: dropped to 3rd on line* **12/1**

**4** *2 ¾* **Plain Talking (IRE)**[2] 7238 5-9-0 **58**............................ RonanWhelan 8 58
(Gavin Cromwell, Ire) *led: strly pressed and hdd 2f out: kpt on same pce in 4th fnl f* **8/1**

**5** *1 ¼* **Runyon Rattler (IRE)**[25] 4772 7-8-5 **56**..................... DannySheehy(7) 4 54
(P J Rothwell, Ire) *racd in rr: rdn and prog under 2f out: wnt 5th ent fnl f: kpt on same pce: nvr nrr* **25/1**

**6** *1 ½* **Face Value**[26] 4067 9-9-4 **67**...................................(p) DanielRedmond(5) 12 63
(Adrian McGuinness, Ire) *chsd ldrs in 4th: rdn and no imp over 1f out in 6th: kpt on one pce* **20/1**

**7** *4 ¾* **Royal Flag**[15] 5138 7-9-10 **68**............................................... WJLee 1 57
(Brian Ellison) *racd in mid-div: rdn in 6th over 2f out: no imp appr fnl f: wknd* **14/1**

**8** *hd* **Set To Fire (IRE)**[9] 5389 4-8-8 **59**.............................. SeanDavis(7) 14 47
(John James Feane, Ire) *racd towards rr: rdn and no imp 2f out: kpt on one pce for press fnl f: nvr on terms* **16/1**

**9** *hd* **Whats The Plot (IRE)**[13] 5226 5-9-2 **60**........................... PatSmullen 2 48
(A L T Moore, Ire) *hld up: pushed along towards rr over 2f out: kpt on one pce fnl f: nvr on terms* **7/1**[3]

**10** *¾* **Mr Adjudicator**[6] 5489 3-9-2 **75**................................ KillianLeonard(5) 18 65
(Joseph G Murphy, Ire) *chsd early ldrs: mid-div at 1/2-way: rdn and no imp under 2f out: sn no ex* **7/1**[3]

**11** *17* **Dawerann (IRE)**[21] 5346 8-9-6 **64**..........................(b) DeclanMcDonogh 11 25
(Gordon Elliott, Ire) *racd towards rr: clsr in mid-div 3f out: wknd qckly under 2f out: eased fnl f* **25/1**

**12** *15* **Ensign**[64] 3348 3-9-7 **75**.........................................(p[1]) DonnachaO'Brien 17 17
(A P O'Brien, Ire) *hld up: towards rr whn checked 4f out: sn rdn and detached 2f out: eased in st* **10/1**

**P** **Shamar (FR)**[3] 5584 9-9-6 **64**...................................(t) WayneLordan 13
(R K Watson, Ire) *racd in mid-div: keen and gd hdwy on outer to trck ldr in 2nd after 4f: sn rn wd and p.u* **16/1**

3m 18.85s (10.85)
**WFA** 3 from 4yo+ 11lb **13** Ran SP% **125.8**
CSF £17.32 CT £162.15 TOTE £3.60: £1.60, £2.50, £4.40; DF 21.10 Trifecta £205.20.
**Owner** A Shiels/Niall Reilly **Bred** Sarl Ecurie Haras De Quetieville **Trained** Summerhill, Co. Meath

**FOCUS**
A decent performance from the victor, who wasn't winning out of turn by any means. Gavin Cromwell saddled the second, third and fourth. It paid to be handily ridden in general here. Eight non-runners made life easier for those involved. The standard is set around the placed horses.

# 5626 DEAUVILLE (R-H)
Sunday, August 6

**OFFICIAL GOING: Turf: good; polytrack: standard**

## 5690a LARC PRIX MAURICE DE GHEEST (GROUP 1) (3YO+) (TURF) 6f 110y(S)
**2:45** 3-Y-0+ **£185,582** (£74,246; £37,123; £18,545; £9,288)

RPR

**1** **Brando**[22] 4907 5-9-3 **0**........................................................ TomEaves 12 120+
(Kevin Ryan) *w.w in midfield: shkn up and began to cl wl over 2f out: pressed ldr appr fnl f: drvn to ld last 150yds: edgd lft: rdn out* **9/1**[3]

**2** *½* **Aclaim (IRE)**[5] 5502 4-9-3 **0**............................................ OlivierPeslier 8 119
(Martyn Meade) *sn hld up towards rr: effrt 2f out: 9th and rdn appr fnl 1 1/2f: styd on wl ins fnl f: a looked hld by wnr* **28/1**

**3** *1 ¾* **Tupi (IRE)**[15] 5149 5-9-3 **0**................................................ SeanLevey 13 113
(Richard Hannon) *w.w in fnl trio: pushed along to take clsr order 2f out: rdn to chse ldrs 1f out: styd on u.p* **66/1**

**4** *2* **Magical Memory (IRE)**[15] 5149 5-9-3 **0**........................ AndreaAtzeni 9 108
(Charles Hills) *prom: cl 8th and rdn 1 1/2f out: styd on ins fnl f: nt pce to get on terms* **20/1**

**5** *nse* **Signs Of Blessing (IRE)**[47] 3926 6-9-3 **0**.............. StephanePasquier 4 108
(F Rohaut, France) *led: 2 l clr 1 1/2f out: hdd fnl 150yds: no ex* **5/1**[2]

**6** *hd* **Caravaggio (USA)**[22] 4907 3-8-13 **0**................................. RyanMoore 1 107
(A P O'Brien, Ire) *dwlt: settled towards rr on inner: drvn and no imp wl over 2f out: 3rd last and drvn along wl over 1 1/2f out: rdn and kpt on ins fnl f: sltly impeded 125yds out: nvr in contention* **8/11**[1]

**7** *1* **The Right Man**[43] 4071 5-9-3 **0**......................... Francois-XavierBertras 6 104
(D Guillemin, France) *chsd ldng pair: nt qckn whn rdn 2f out: kpt on at same pce* **28/1**

**8** *¾* **Zalamea (IRE)**[22] 4884 4-9-3 **0**....................................... AntoineCoutier 5 102
(Carina Fey, France) *w.w in midfield: no imp u.p ins fnl 2f: one pce* **100/1**

**9** *1* **Rosa Imperial (IRE)**[39] 4234 4-9-0 **0**......................... MickaelBarzalona 7 96
(A Fabre, France) *settled in fnl trio: drvn over 2f out: rdn and began to cl over 1f out: kpt on at same pce: nvr in contention* **9/1**[3]

**10** *snk* **Bound For Nowhere (USA)**[44] 4030 3-8-13 **0**........... FrankieDettori 11 99
(Wesley A Ward, U.S.A) *prom on outer: wnt 3rd bef 1/2-way: a little outpcd and drvn 3f out: sn rdn and rallied: grad dropped away fr 1f out* **9/1**[3]

**11** *2* **Black Max (FR)**[29] 4653 4-9-3 **0**............................ Pierre-CharlesBoudot 2 93
(H-A Pantall, France) *dwlt: racd in rr: drvn 2 1/2f out: n.d* **100/1**

**12** *nk* **Intelligence Cross (USA)**[22] 4907 3-8-13 **0**.........(b) SeamieHeffernan 3 92
(A P O'Brien, Ire) *chsd ldr: drvn sn after 1/2-way: rdn and no imp 2f out: wknd fnl f* **80/1**

**13** *12* **Fas (IRE)**[119] 1660 3-8-13 **0**............................................... MaximeGuyon 10 57
(Mme Pia Brandt, France) *prom between horses: lost pl over 2f out: wknd fnl f* **22/1**

1m 15.61s (-1.59)
**WFA** 3 from 4yo+ 4lb **13** Ran SP% **125.3**
PARI-MUTUEL (all including 1 euro stake): WIN 11.40; PLACE 3.60, 9.00, 20.40; DF 125.60; SF 312.40.
**Owner** Mrs Angie Bailey **Bred** Car Colston Hall Stud **Trained** Hambleton, N Yorks

**FOCUS**
A race that didn't go the way widely expected, with the two market leaders falling short. The British runners dominated. The runner-up has been rated in line with the best view of his Group 2 win, and the third close to his best.

## 5691a HARAS FIRMAMENTO PRIX DE POMONE (GROUP 2) (3YO+ FILLIES & MARES) (TURF) 1m 4f 110y

**3:23** 3-Y-0+ **£63,333** (£24,444; £11,666; £7,777; £3,888)

RPR

1 **Bateel (IRE)**[57] 3586 5-9-4 0 ..............................(h) Pierre-CharlesBoudot 2 110
(F-H Graffard, France) *racd keenly: hld up bhd ldr on inner: clsd on inner 2f out: sn rdn along and sustained run to ld 1f out: rdn to assert: in control whn eased fnl strides* **11/2**[3]

2 *nk* **Traffic Jam (IRE)**[19] 5014 4-9-4 0 .................................. OlivierPeslier 3 110
(N Clement, France) *led: drvn whn pressed 2f out: hdd 1f out: kpt on gamely fnl f: a hld by wnr* **25/1**

3 *1 1/2* **Abingdon (USA)**[29] 4613 4-9-4 0 ........................................ RyanMoore 4 107+
(Sir Michael Stoute) *w.w in tch bhd ldrs: dropped into fnl pair bef 1/2-way: drvn on outer 2 1/2f out: began to cl 1 1/2f out: styd on ins fnl f: nt pce to get on terms* **1/1**[1]

4 *1 1/4* **The Juliet Rose (FR)**[309] 6972 4-9-4 0 .................. StephanePasquier 5 105
(N Clement, France) *hld up in fnl pair: clsd on outer to press ldr 1/2-way: disputing 3rd whn scrubbed along wl over 2f out: kpt on at one pce* **11/2**[3]

5 *2* **Kitesurf**[49] 3881 3-8-8 0 ............................................. MickaelBarzalona 6 104
(A Fabre, France) *prom on outer: chsd ldr on outer after 2 1/2f: disputing 3rd and drvn along 2f out: no imp on ldrs: dropped away fnl f* **3/1**[2]

6 *1 1/4* **Thrones Game (FR)**[52] 4-9-4 0 .................................... GeraldMosse 1 100
(A De Royer-Dupre, France) *hld up in fnl pair: last appr 1/2-way: drvn and no imp 1 1/2f out: wl hld fnl f* **18/1**

2m 39.54s (-6.86)
**WFA** 3 from 4yo+ 10lb **6** Ran SP% **114.9**
PARI-MUTUEL (all including 1 euro stake): WIN 4.70; PLACE 2.50, 5.00; SF 36.20.
**Owner** Al Asayl Bloodstock Ltd **Bred** Sheikh Sultan Bin Khalifa Al Nayhan **Trained** France

**FOCUS**
A steadily run affair. The first and third help set the standard.

## 5692a HARAS DE LA POMME PRIX DE REUX (GROUP 3) (3YO+) (TURF) 1m 4f 110y

**4:01** 3-Y-0+ **£34,188** (£13,675; £10,256; £6,837; £3,418)

RPR

1 **Tiberian (FR)**[35] 4423 5-9-10 0 ........................................ OlivierPeslier 1 112
(Alain Couetil, France) *broke wl and led at stdy pce: hdd after 1f: led again on inner after 2f: drvn 2l clr 1 1/2f out: styd on gamely under sustained chal fnl f* **11/4**[2]

2 *shd* **Doha Dream (FR)**[35] 4423 4-9-5 0 ..................... Pierre-CharlesBoudot 7 107
(A Fabre, France) *dwlt sltly: led on outer after 1f: hdd after 2f: remained cl up: 2l 2nd and drvn 1 1/2f out: sn styd on: sustained chal fnl f: jst failed* **7/2**[3]

3 *1 1/2* **Tamelly**[29] 4-9-5 0 ....................................................... VincentCheminaud 2 104
(A Fabre, France) *w.w in fnl trio: last and scrubbed along 2 1/2f out: rdn and began to stay on over 1f out: sustained run fnl f: tk 3rd fnl strides: nt rch ldrs* **20/1**

4 *shd* **Berdibek (FR)**[21] 4941 3-8-9 0 ............................................ AlexisBadel 4 106
(M Delzangles, France) *racd keenly: hld up bhd ldrs on inner: 4th and drvn 2 1/2f out: kpt on u.p fnl f: nt pce to get on terms* **9/1**

5 *hd* **Parabellum (IRE)**[23] 4878 3-8-9 0 ......................... MickaelBarzalona 5 106
(A Fabre, France) *settled in fnl trio: tk clsr order on outer 3f out: 3rd and ev ch over 2f out: sn rdn along: styd on at same pce fnl f* **13/8**[1]

6 *3 1/2* **Savoir Vivre (IRE)**[278] 7759 4-9-5 0 .......................... MaximeGuyon 6 98
(Jean-Pierre Carvalho, Germany) *plld v hrd: restrained bhd ldrs on outer: lost pl 3f out: wl hld fr over 1f out* **11/2**

7 *3* **Black Night (IRE)**[14] 5-9-5 0 .......................................... EddyHardouin 3 94
(J Moon, Jersey) *w.w in rr: scrubbed along and effrt on outer 2/12f fr home: sn btn: bhd fnl f* **25/1**

2m 40.6s (-5.80)
**WFA** 3 from 4yo+ 10lb **7** Ran SP% **121.0**
PARI-MUTUEL (all including 1 euro stake): WIN 4.70; PLACE 2.20, 2.30; SF 17.40.
**Owner** Earl Haras Du Logis, Heiko Volz & Stefan Falk **Bred** H Volz , J Ince & S Falk **Trained** France

**FOCUS**
A steadily run race, and the winner dominated from the front.

# [3882]DUSSELDORF (R-H)

Sunday, August 6

**OFFICIAL GOING: Turf: soft**

## 5693a 159TH HENKEL-PREIS DER DIANA - GERMAN OAKS (GROUP 1) (3YO FILLIES) (TURF) 1m 3f

**2:55** 3-Y-0

**£256,410** (£85,470; £42,735; £23,076; £11,111; £8,547)

RPR

1 **Lacazar (GER)**[36] 4393 3-9-2 0 ................................... AndraschStarke 8 111+
(P Schiergen, Germany) *w.w in tch on inner: rdn and clsd 1 1/2f out: chal appr 1f out: led ent fnl f: styd on wl under hands and heels: a holding runner-up* **41/10**[2]

2 *3/4* **Megera (FR)**[36] 4393 3-9-2 0 .............................................. JimCrowley 3 110+
(A Wohler, Germany) *w.w towards rr of midfield: began to cl over 3f out: rdn and cl on ldng pair wl over 1f out: styd on fnl f: a hld by wnr* **28/1**

3 *4* **Wuheida**[23] 4857 3-9-2 0 ............................................... WilliamBuick 2 103
(Charlie Appleby) *a cl up: led early: sn hdd and trckd ldrs: shkn up and styd on to ld 1 1/2f out: rdn and edgd lft wl over 1f out: hdd ent fnl f: one pce u.p* **11/10**[1]

4 *2* **Tusked Wings (IRE)**[63] 3371 3-9-2 0 ................................ FilipMinarik 7 99
(Jean-Pierre Carvalho, Germany) *hld up in fnl trio: tk cl order 3f out: rdn to chse ldrs wl over 1 1/2f out: styd on at same pce fnl f* **124/10**

5 *1 1/4* **Ashiana (GER)**[28] 3-9-2 0 ............................................... FabriceVeron 5 97
(P Schiergen, Germany) *settled towards rr: hdwy u.p wl over 1 1/2f out: styd on fnl f: nrest at fin* **129/10**

6 *nk* **Diana Storm (GER)**[36] 4393 3-9-2 0 ................................. MarcLerner 16 96
(Waldemar Hickst, Germany) *w.w in fnl pair: tk clsr order over 2f out: kpt on u.p: nvr in contention* **157/10**

7 *shd* **Navaro Girl (IRE)**[36] 4393 3-9-2 0 ..................................... DaneO'Neill 4 96
(P Schiergen, Germany) *settled in midfield: rdn and effrt 2f out: kpt on fnl f: nvr trbld ldrs* **33/1**

8 *4* **Alicante (GER)**[36] 4393 3-9-2 0 ..................................... AdriedeVries 12 89
(Markus Klug, Germany) *w.w towards rr: rdn and no real imp fr 2f out: wl hld fnl f* **146/10**

9 *1 1/2* **Prima Violetta (IRE)**[28] 3-9-2 0 ............................. EduardoPedroza 13 86
(A Wohler, Germany) *racd promly: lost pl bef 1/2-way: rdn and brief effrt 2f out: sn btn* **17/2**[3]

10 *1/2* **Gondora (GER)**[36] 4393 3-9-2 0 ...................... BauyrzhanMurzabayev 10 85
(R Dzubasz, Germany) *racd towards rr on outer: last bef 1/2-way: rdn and began to cl 1 1/2f out: effrt sn petered out: bhd fnl f* **73/1**

11 *hd* **Sky Full Of Stars (GER)**[28] 3-9-2 0 ..................................... DarioVargiu 6 85
(Henk Grewe, Germany) *chsd ldr: led after 2 1/2f: kicked 3l clr 3f out: drvn 2f out: hdd 1 1/2f out: sn btn* **50/1**

12 *3* **Litaara (GER)**[63] 3371 3-9-2 0 ........................................... DanielePorcu 1 80
(P Schiergen, Germany) *racd keenly: sn led under restraint: hdd after 2 1/2f and styd cl up: sn rdn: wknd u.p over 1f out* **38/1**

13 *2 1/2* **Well Spoken (GER)**[36] 4393 3-9-2 0 .................................... MartinSeidl 15 75
(Markus Klug, Germany) *prom: racd alone on outside: dropped in to join rest bef 1/2-way: lost pl over 3 1/2f out: bhd fr over 1 1/2f out* **246/10**

14 *5* **Allegro Lady (GER)**[49] 3-9-2 0 ................................. MichaelCadeddu 9 66
(Dr A Bolte, Germany) *w.w in midfield: rdn and lost pl 2 1/2f out: wl hld fnl 1 1/2f* **31/1**

15 *3/4* **Shy Angel**[63] 3371 3-9-2 0 ................................................... JozefBojko 11 65
(A Wohler, Germany) *settled in midfield: rdn and btn ins fnl 2f* **269/10**

16 *5* **Pemina (GER)**[28] 3-9-2 0 .......................................... AlexanderPietsch 14 56
(J Hirschberger, Germany) *rushed up to chse ldrs after 1f: 2nd and drvn 3f out: no imp whn rdn over 2f out: wknd ins fnl 1 1/2f* **231/10**

2m 17.45s **16** Ran SP% **131.8**
PARI-MUTUEL (all including 10 euro stake): WIN 51 PLACE: 17, 49, 16; SF: 906.
**Owner** Gestut Haus Zoppenbroich **Bred** Frau Ina Emma Zimmermann **Trained** Germany

**FOCUS**
The fifth, seventh and tenth have been rated close to their marks.

5694a (Foreign Racing) - See Raceform Interactive

# [4833]CARLISLE (R-H)

Monday, August 7

**OFFICIAL GOING: Good to soft (good in places; 6.9)**
Wind: Breezy, half against in over 2f of home straight Weather: Cloudy, dry

## 5695 PLAY COSTABINGO.COM ON YOUR MOBILE H'CAP (PRO-AM LADY RIDERS' RACE) 5f

**5:30** (5:31) (Class 6) (0-65,65) 4-Y-0+ **£3,234** (£962; £481; £240) **Stalls** Low

Form RPR

0631 **1** **Our Place In Loule**[13] 5260 4-9-1 **50** ......................... MissKLAdams(5) 1 58
(Noel Wilson) *trckd ldrs: smooth hdwy to ld over 1f out: pushed out fnl f: comf* **5/1**[2]

0050 **2** *1 1/4* **Knockamany Bends (IRE)**[5] 5542 7-9-2 **46** ................(h[1]) HollieDoyle 2 50
(John Wainwright) *led at decent gallop: rdn and hdd over 1f out: rallied: kpt on same pce last 100yds* **13/2**

0020 **3** *3/4* **Insolenceofoffice (IRE)**[61] 3468 9-9-4 **48** ..................(p) MissCWalton 8 49+
(Richard Ford) *bhd and outpcd: rdn over 2f out: gd hdwy on outside fnl f: nrst fin* **25/1**

5214 **4** *1/2* **Perfect Words (IRE)**[7] 5472 7-10-1 **59** ................(p) MissBeckySmith 10 58
(Marjorie Fife) *bhd on outside: effrt over 2f out: kpt on fnl f: nvr able to chal* **9/2**[1]

5000 **5** *1/2* **Space War**[24] 4833 10-10-7 **65** ...........................(t) MissJoannaMason 12 64+
(Michael Easterby) *s.i.s: outpcd tl gd hdwy fnl f: kpt on: nrst fin* **20/1**

6055 **6** *shd* **Red Stripes (USA)**[17] 5098 5-10-3 **61** ...........................(v) JaneElliott 11 58
(Lisa Williamson) *chsd ldr: hung lft and lost grnd over 3f out: rallied over 1f out: kpt on same pce ins fnl f* **10/1**

6000 **7** *2* **Reflation**[3] 5620 5-9-4 **53** .........................................(p) MissAMcCain(5) 4 43
(Patrick Holmes) *hld up on ins: pushed along over 2f out: sme late hdwy: n.d* **66/1**

4300 **8** *nse* **Very First Blade**[34] 4478 8-9-2 **46** oh1 ...............(p) MissMMullineaux 3 35
(Michael Mullineaux) *towards rr: pushed along over 2f out: no imp fr over 1f out* **33/1**

00-2 **9** *hd* **Red Forever**[29] 4664 6-9-2 **46** ................................ MissHelenCuthbert 13 35
(Thomas Cuthbert) *t.k.h: in tch: checked over 3f out: rdn over 1f out: wknd fnl f* **8/1**

0004 **10** *2* **A J Cook (IRE)**[5] 5542 7-9-2 **46** oh1 ....................(p) RachelRichardson 6 28
(Ron Barr) *towards rr: pushed along over 2f out: shortlived effrt over 1f out: sn wknd* **11/2**[3]

5031 **11** *nk* **Toni's A Star**[18] 5052 5-9-13 **57** .........................................(b) AliceMills 7 37
(Tony Carroll) *cl up: disp 2nd pl over 3f out: rdn and wknd over 1f out* **6/1**

4300 **12** *1* **Tinsill**[9] 5419 6-9-2 **46** oh1 ............................................(p) ShelleyBirkett 9 23
(Nigel Tinkler) *dwlt: bhd and outpcd: hdwy whn nt clr run briefly over 1f out: sn no imp: btn whn n.m.r ins fnl f* **20/1**

1m 3.72s (2.92) **Going Correction** +0.325s/f (Good) **12** Ran SP% **115.9**
Speed ratings (Par 101): **89,87,85,85,84 84,80,80,80,77 76,75**
CSF £33.88 CT £750.30 TOTE £3.70: £1.60, £3.30, £6.60; EX 42.60 Trifecta £825.60.
**Owner** Paver & Marwood Racing Limited **Bred** John And Susan Davis **Trained** Marwood, Co Durham

**FOCUS**
There was reportedly a cross-headwind in the straight. All race distances were as advertised. The first two held those positions virtually throughout and seemed to get a jump on the field, who were closing gradually by the finish but never looked like getting there.

## 5696 300% FIRST DEPOSIT BONUS AT COSTABINGO.COM H'CAP (PRO-AM LADY RIDERS' RACE) 5f 193y

**6:00** (6:00) (Class 5) (0-75,75) 4-Y-0+ **£3,234** (£962; £481; £240) **Stalls** Low

Form RPR

0124 **1** **Cliff (IRE)**[10] 5379 7-9-6 **65** ................................ FayeMcManoman(5) 10 72
(Nigel Tinkler) *hld up: pushed along and hdwy on outside over 1f out: led ins fnl f: hld on wl cl home* **6/1**[3]

6023 **2** *nk* **Willsy**[11] 5318 4-9-8 **62** ...............................................(b) GemmaTutty 8 68
(Karen Tutty) *in tch: drvn along and outpcd over 2f out: rallied and edgd rt over 1f out: styd on wl fnl f to take 2nd nr fin* **14/1**

0653 **3** *nk* **Ticks The Boxes (IRE)**[3] 5620 5-9-13 **67** ....................(p) HollieDoyle 7 72
(John Wainwright) *hld up: pushed along over 2f out: swtchd sharply lft and hdwy over 1f out: kpt on strly fnl f: hld nr fin* **15/2**

6423 **4** *nk* **Kenny The Captain (IRE)**[23] 4897 6-10-5 **73** ............. MissEEasterby 2 77
(Tim Easterby) *w ldr: led over 1f out to ins fnl f: no ex and lost two pls towards fin* **2/1**[1]

3031 **5** 1 1/2 **Miningold**[35] 4433 4-10-0 **73**....................(p) MissCADods(5) 3 72
(Michael Dods) *trckd ldrs gng wl: shkn up appr fnl f: outpcd last 100yds* **20/1**

0053 **6** nse **B Fifty Two (IRE)**[10] 5379 8-10-5 **73**....................(bt) MissBeckySmith 1 72
(Marjorie Fife) *led: hdd and pushed along over 1f out: rallied: no ex ins fnl f* **9/2**[2]

4-30 **7** nk **General Alexander (IRE)**[10] 5379 4-10-5 **73**...........(p) MeganNicholls 9 71
(Brian Ellison) *bhd on outside: rdn along and hdwy on outside over 2f out: edgd rt and no imp fnl f* **20/1**

5442 **8** 2 3/4 **Buccaneers Vault (IRE)**[11] 5318 5-10-5 **73**..............(b) SammyJoBell 4 62
(Paul Midgley) *trckd ldrs on outside: pushed along over 1f out: wknd fnl f* **10/1**

4600 **9** 3/4 **Merdon Castle (IRE)**[12] 5288 5-10-2 **75**...........(e) MissEmilyBullock(5) 6 62
(Ruth Carr) *dwlt: sn wl bhd: nvr on terms* **11/1**

555- **10** 5 **Yair Hill (IRE)**[273] 7850 9-9-2 **56** oh9....................(p) MissHelenCuthbert 5 27
(Thomas Cuthbert) *hld up midfield on ins: pushed along over 2f out: wknd over 1f out* **80/1**

1m 15.8s (2.10) **Going Correction** +0.325s/f (Good) **10** Ran SP% **112.4**
Speed ratings (Par 103): **99,98,98,97,95 95,95,91,90,84**
CSF £80.12 CT £477.02 TOTE £7.20: £3.00, £3.40, £3.00; EX 65.80 Trifecta £589.20.
**Owner** W F Burton **Bred** John O'Connor **Trained** Langton, N Yorks

**FOCUS**
The leaders went hard and the result was a finish in which a pair of closers from deep were held off by one who had been played just that bit earlier. It could be that the reported headwind had an effect. This has been rated around the first two.

## 5697 COSTABINGO.COM BIG JACKPOTS H'CAP (PROFESSIONAL LADY RIDERS' RACE) 5f 193y
**6:30** (6:34) (Class 4) (0-80,81) 3-Y-O **£6,469** (£1,925; £962; £481) **Stalls** Low

Form RPR
1060 **1** **Suitcase 'N' Taxi**[43] 4122 3-9-2 **71**.................... RachelRichardson(3) 4 80
(Tim Easterby) *pressed ldr: led gng wl over 2f out: drvn along over 1f out: kpt on strly fnl f* **8/1**

-231 **2** 1 **Castle Hill Cassie (IRE)**[73] 3054 3-9-0 **71**.............. MeganNicholls(5) 5 77
(Ben Haslam) *prom: hdwy to chse wnr over 2f out: rdn wl over 1f out: kpt on same pce fnl f* **7/2**[2]

4051 **3** 1 1/4 **Redarna**[7] 5467 3-8-4 **61** 6ex.................................... JaneElliott(5) 6 63
(Dianne Sayer) *uns rdr and bolted bef s: hld up: hdwy on outside over 2f out: rdn and kpt on fnl f: nt rch first two* **3/1**[1]

1630 **4** 4 **Control Centre (IRE)**[29] 4663 3-9-4 **73**....................(p) HollieDoyle(3) 2 62
(Marjorie Fife) *prom: rdn along 1/2-way: rallied: outpcd fr over 1f out* **11/2**[3]

4450 **5** 1/2 **Night Law**[10] 5383 3-9-1 **70**.................................... SammyJoBell(3) 7 58
(Richard Fahey) *flj. and wnt lft s: bhd: hdwy on outside over 2f out: rdn: edgd rt and no imp fr over 1f out* **8/1**

1630 **6** 3 1/4 **Grinty (IRE)**[17] 5132 3-9-1 **70**.................................... ShelleyBirkett(3) 1 47
(Michael Dods) *hld up: shortlived effrt 2f out: btn fnl f* **11/2**[3]

-3 **7** 12 **Tan**[26] 4783 3-9-10 **81**.................................... LucyKBarry(5) 3 20
(Tony Coyle) *led to over 2f out: sn rdn and wknd* **7/1**

1m 15.31s (1.61) **Going Correction** +0.325s/f (Good) **7** Ran SP% **112.7**
Speed ratings (Par 102): **102,100,99,93,93 88,72**
CSF £34.92 TOTE £8.90: £3.10, £2.30; EX 39.70 Trifecta £202.10.
**Owner** Ontoawinner 10 & Partner 3 **Bred** Crossfields Bloodstock Ltd **Trained** Great Habton, N Yorks

**FOCUS**
In contrast to the first two races they came down the centre of the track, where a fast-finisher had ended race two. The first three came clear, the first two having been in those positions a long way out.

## 5698 EYES DOWN WITH SUNNY AT COSTABINGO.COM H'CAP (PRO-AM LADY RIDERS' RACE) 1m 1f
**7:00** (7:06) (Class 5) (0-75,74) 4-Y-O+ **£3,234** (£962; £481; £240) **Stalls** Low

Form RPR
3/00 **1** **Parole (IRE)**[16] 5166 5-9-10 **63**....................(t[1]) RachelRichardson 4 72
(Tim Easterby) *chsd ldng pair: hdwy to ld over 2f out: rdn over 1f out: kpt on wl fnl f* **16/1**

1223 **2** 1 1/2 **Sir Jack**[12] 5299 4-9-10 **63**.................................... HollieDoyle 6 69
(Tony Carroll) *hld up: hdwy over 2f out: effrt and chsd wnr over 1f out: edgd lft and kpt on ins fnl f: nt pce to chal* **2/1**[1]

0051 **3** 2 1/4 **Mr Sundowner (USA)**[15] 5181 5-9-5 **58**....................(t) SammyJoBell 1 59
(Wilf Storey) *hld up: stdy hdwy over 2f out: effrt and prom over 1f out: kpt on same pce ins fnl f* **8/1**

2605 **4** hd **Hanseatic**[37] 4339 8-10-7 **74**....................(t) MissJoannaMason 3 75
(Michael Easterby) *in tch: hdwy to chse wnr over 2f out to over 1f out: no ex ins fnl f* **7/2**[2]

0062 **5** 3/4 **Sikandar (IRE)**[9] 5417 5-9-6 **64**....................(tp) MissEllaMcCain(5) 8 63
(Brian Ellison) *dwlt: hld up: hdwy on outside over 2f out: rdn and kpt on fnl f: no imp* **12/1**

4241 **6** 7 **Kiwi Bay**[15] 5183 12-9-10 **68**.................................... MissSEDods(5) 5 53
(Michael Dods) *slowly away: bhd: stdy hdwy whn checked wl over 1f out: kpt on fnl f: nvr able to chal* **8/1**

2533 **7** 1 1/4 **Kingthistle**[23] 4899 4-10-5 **72**....................(tp) MissCWalton 7 54
(Rebecca Menzies) *in tch: drvn and outpcd over 2f out: n.d after* **15/2**[3]

552- **8** 1/2 **Weapon Of Choice (IRE)**[33] 4038 9-9-12 **65**.....(tp) MissEmmaSayer 11 46
(Dianne Sayer) *hld up: rdn over 2f out: no imp whn hung rt over 1f out: sn btn* **11/1**

300 **9** 3 1/4 **Royal Holiday (IRE)**[20] 5002 10-9-10 **63**.............(p) MissBeckySmith 10 37
(Marjorie Fife) *led at decent gallop: hdd over 2f out: wknd over 1f out* **25/1**

0200 **10** 9 **Muqarred (USA)**[39] 4260 5-9-13 **71**....................(p) MrsDebbieBoyes(5) 13 26
(Roger Fell) *pressed ldr to over 2f out: rdn and wknd over 1f out* **33/1**

6000 **11** 3 1/2 **Swiss Lait**[2] 5649 6-9-2 **55** oh6.................................... MissAWaugh 2 3
(Patrick Holmes) *s.s: bhd: shortlived effrt on wd outside over 2f out: sn wknd* **25/1**

2m 0.12s (2.52) **Going Correction** +0.325s/f (Good) **11** Ran SP% **122.1**
Speed ratings (Par 103): **101,99,97,97,96 90,89,89,86,78 75**
CSF £49.21 CT £302.70 TOTE £16.90: £4.40, £1.30, £2.60; EX 66.60 Trifecta £887.40.
**Owner** The Mount Fawcus Partnership **Bred** F Montauban **Trained** Great Habton, N Yorks
■ Stewards' Enquiry : Hollie Doyle caution: careless riding

**FOCUS**
The principals again came down the centre of the track and once more jockeyship was important, the winner proving better placed than the runner-up for all the pace was sound overall.

## 5699 PLAY AT COSTABINGO.COM WHATEVER THE WEATHER H'CAP (PRO-AM LADY RIDERS' RACE) 7f 173y
**7:30** (7:32) (Class 4) (0-85,82) 4-Y-O+ **£6,469** (£1,925; £962; £481) **Stalls** Low

Form RPR
4213 **1** **El Principe**[6] 5497 4-9-10 **71**....................(t) JaneElliott 9 80
(Les Eyre) *w ldr and sn clr of rest: led over 2f out: rdn over 1f out: hld on gamely ins fnl f* **11/2**[3]

3313 **2** 1/2 **Kenstone (FR)**[31] 4563 4-10-0 **75**....................(p) HollieDoyle 11 83
(Adrian Wintle) *t.k.h early: hld up: hdwy on outside over 2f out: rdn and ev ch ins fnl f: kpt on: jst hld* **5/1**[2]

3404 **3** 1 3/4 **Worlds His Oyster**[20] 5000 4-10-5 **80**.................... RachelRichardson 8 84
(John Quinn) *hld up: hdwy on outside over 2f out: effrt and ch ins fnl f: kpt on same pce last 50yds* **9/2**[1]

140 **4** 2 **Toboggan's Fire**[60] 3497 4-10-4 **79**.................... MissSBrotherton 5 78
(Ann Duffield) *in tch: effrt and pushed along over 2f out: kpt on same pce ins fnl f* **18/1**

5503 **5** 2 **Invermere**[23] 4901 4-10-0 **75**.................................... SammyJoBell 4 70
(Richard Fahey) *chsd clr ldng pair: effrt and wnt 2nd briefly over 1f out: rdn and outpcd ins fnl f* **8/1**

1-65 **6** 1 1/4 **Big Time Dancer (IRE)**[20] 5000 4-9-5 **66**.................... MeganNicholls 6 58
(Brian Ellison) *hld up: pushed along and hdwy 2f out: no imp fnl f* **6/1**

2400 **7** nk **Mustaqbal (IRE)**[24] 4833 5-9-3 **69**....................(p) MissSEDods(5) 1 60
(Michael Dods) *missed break: wl bhd tl sme late hdwy: nvr on terms* **16/1**

2142 **8** 1 3/4 **Inexes**[23] 4897 5-10-5 **80**....................(p) MissBeckySmith 3 67
(Marjorie Fife) *in tch: effrt and rdn over 1f out: wknd fnl f* **9/2**[1]

2054 **9** 5 **Forever A Lady (IRE)**[23] 4901 4-9-13 **74**.................... MrsCBartley 10 50
(Keith Dalgleish) *hld up: effrt and pushed along over 2f out: wknd over 1f out* **11/1**

6300 **10** 3 3/4 **Baltic Prince (IRE)**[32] 4529 7-9-5 **66**.................... AliceMills 2 33
(Tony Carroll) *led at decent gallop: hdd over 2f out: wknd wl over 1f out* **40/1**

1m 41.54s (1.54) **Going Correction** +0.325s/f (Good) **10** Ran SP% **115.7**
Speed ratings (Par 105): **105,104,102,100,98 97,97,95,90,86**
CSF £32.90 CT £122.60 TOTE £6.00: £1.90, £1.80, £2.00; EX 32.20 Trifecta £145.50.
**Owner** M Rozenbroek **Bred** Mrs Irene Clifford **Trained** Catwick, N Yorks
■ Stewards' Enquiry : Hollie Doyle two-day ban: excessive use of whip (Aug 21-22)

**FOCUS**
The winner soon went clear with one that finished tailed off and had to dig deep to hold off more patiently-ridden rivals.

## 5700 NEWS & STAR AMAZING LADY DARCIE SAFFILL H'CAP (PRO-AM LADY RIDERS' RACE) 2m 1f 47y
**8:00** (8:00) (Class 5) (0-70,72) 4-Y-O+ **£3,234** (£962; £481; £240) **Stalls** Low

Form RPR
/5-0 **1** **Tawseef (IRE)**[19] 5021 9-9-1 **55**.................... MissEllaMcCain(5) 6 63
(Donald McCain) *prom: led against far rail over 2f out: rdn and clr over 1f out: kpt on wl fnl f* **12/1**

0044 **2** 1 **Transpennine Star**[25] 4790 4-10-9 **72**....................(p[1]) ShelleyBirkett 3 79
(Michael Dods) *hld up bhd ldng gp: pushed along and outpcd over 3f out: rallied to chse (clr) wnr over 1f out: kpt on fnl f* **17/2**

16-6 **3** 2 1/4 **Almost Gemini (IRE)**[26] 4742 8-10-7 **70**....................(p) MissAWaugh 1 75
(Kenneth Slack) *prom: effrt over 2f out: edgd lft and kpt on same pce fnl f* **7/1**[3]

0050 **4** 1 3/4 **La Bacouetteuse (FR)**[9] 5413 12-9-11 **60**....................(b) SammyJoBell 5 63
(Iain Jardine) *hld up midfield: drvn and outpcd over 5f out: rallied over 1f out: kpt on fnl f: no imp* **14/1**

51-5 **5** 2 **Gold Chain (IRE)**[6] 1716 7-9-12 **61**....................(p) MissEmmaSayer 2 62+
(Dianne Sayer) *hld up: outpcd over 4f out: hdwy over 1f out: kpt on fnl f: nvr on terms* **7/2**[2]

4022 **6** nk **Stormin Tom (IRE)**[13] 5259 5-10-7 **70**.................... RachelRichardson 11 71
(Tim Easterby) *led: rdn and hdd over 2f out: rallied: btn fnl f* **7/2**[2]

5134 **7** 1 **Miss Tree**[19] 5021 6-9-6 **55**.................................... JaneElliott 7 55
(John Quinn) *pressed ldr: ev ch over 2f out: edgd rt and wknd fnl f* **10/3**[1]

3056 **8** 1 3/4 **Chelsea's Boy (IRE)**[37] 4346 4-10-3 **71**.................... MissAMcCain(5) 8 69
(Donald McCain) *hld up: outpcd over 4f out: btn fnl 2f* **22/1**

0654 **9** 2 1/2 **Buyer Beware (IRE)**[24] 4852 5-10-5 **68**.................... MissCWalton 9 63
(Patrick Holmes) *in tch: drvn and outpcd over 3f out: btn fnl 2f* **16/1**

3020 **10** 21 **Thackeray**[21] 4962 10-9-2 **51** oh6.................................... PaulaMuir 4 25
(Chris Fairhurst) *bhd: struggling over 5f out: sn lost tch: t.o* **50/1**

5-06 **11** 42 **Nashville (IRE)**[58] 3566 8-9-3 **52**.................................... HollieDoyle 10
(Andrew Crook) *bhd: struggling over 5f out: sn lost tch: t.o* **22/1**

3m 59.12s (6.12) **Going Correction** +0.325s/f (Good) **11** Ran SP% **121.4**
Speed ratings (Par 103): **98,97,96,95,94 94,94,93,92,82 62**
CSF £111.20 CT £783.80 TOTE £13.80: £3.30, £2.90, £2.70; EX 107.50 Trifecta £1205.10.
**Owner** D McCain Jnr **Bred** Shadwell Estate Company Limited **Trained** Cholmondeley, Cheshire

**FOCUS**
A leading group of six essentially had the race to themselves. The winner kept to the inside rail and the runner-up ended up across there, too, so maybe the track bias was not all it had been perceived to be.

## 5701 WATCH RACING UK ON THE GO H'CAP (PRO-AM LADY RIDERS' RACE) 1m 3f 39y
**8:30** (8:32) (Class 5) (0-70,70) 4-Y-O+ **£3,234** (£962; £481; £240) **Stalls** High

Form RPR
6513 **1** **Diamonds A Dancing**[20] 5002 7-9-9 **63**....................(h) MissAMcCain(5) 7 74
(Donald McCain) *chsd clr ldng trio: effrt and pushed along over 2f out: styd on wl fnl f to ld towards fin* **12/1**

4433 **2** nk **Omotesando**[7] 5483 7-9-13 **62**....................(p) MeganNicholls 13 72
(Oliver Greenall) *cl up: led 4f out: pushed along over 2f out: edgd lft ins fnl f: hdd and one pce towards fin* **10/1**

5 **3** 2 1/2 **Bal De Rio (FR)**[14] 5212 4-10-7 **70**.................................... MissLWilson 4 76
(Brian Ellison) *hld up midfield: hdwy 3f out: rdn and kpt on fnl f: nt rch first two* **9/1**

4212 **4** shd **Thorntoun Care**[8] 5454 6-10-1 **64**....................(p) SammyJoBell 16 70+
(Iain Jardine) *hld up: stdy hdwy over 3f out: pushed along and sltly outpcd 2f out: kpt on wl fnl f* **5/2**[1]

0043 **5** 2 3/4 **Sheriff Of Nawton (IRE)**[11] 5313 6-10-7 **70**........ MissJoannaMason 10 71
(Roger Fell) *hld up midfield: hdwy to chse ldr over 2f out to over 1f out: wknd ins fnl f* **8/1**[2]

0225 **6** 1 **Luv U Whatever**[11] 5320 7-10-5 **68**....................(t[1]) MissBeckySmith 5 67
(Marjorie Fife) *hld up: pushed along 4f out: hdwy 2f out: kpt on fnl f: no imp* **14/1**

0212 **7** 3¼ **Question Of Faith**[13] 5257 6-9-6 **55**......................... MissSBrotherton 12 49
(Martin Todhunter) *hld up: rdn over 3f out: kpt on fnl f: nvr able to chal* **17/2**[3]

-133 **8** 1¼ **Deep Resolve (IRE)**[91] 2471 6-10-6 **69**.......................... JaneElliott 3 61
(Sally Haynes) *bhd: pushed along over 4f out: no imp fr 2f out* **33/1**

1133 **9** ½ **Tonto's Spirit**[19] 5021 5-9-6 **60**..............................(h) MissAMSlack(5) 11 51
(Kenneth Slack) *led to 4f out: rdn and wknd over 1f out* **8/1**[2]

00-0 **10** 2¾ **Frightened Rabbit (USA)**[14] 1101 5-8-12 **52**...........(t) MissJCooley(5) 9 38
(Susan Corbett) *hld up towards rr: outpcd over 3f out: btn fnl 2f* **50/1**

6661 **11** 1 **Firestorm (GER)**[11] 5320 6-9-5 **54**.................................. MissCWalton 2 38
(Richard Ford) *hld up: outpcd over 4f out: sn btn* **12/1**

0/06 **12** 3½ **Sergeant Pink (IRE)**[16] 3193 11-9-3 **52**................ MissHelenCuthbert 14 30
(Dianne Sayer) *hld up midfield: outpcd over 3f out: sn wknd* **25/1**

0460 **13** nse **Sherman McCoy**[12] 5284 11-9-2 **51** oh2.......................... HollieDoyle 17 29
(Marjorie Fife) *s.i.s: hld up: hdwy into midfield 1/2-way: hung rt and wknd over 2f out* **33/1**

0262 **14** 4½ **King Of The Celts (IRE)**[6] 5499 9-10-1 **64**...............(p) MissEEasterby 8 35
(Tim Easterby) *chsd ldrs tl rdn and wknd over 2f out* **14/1**

06-0 **15** 19 **My Valentino (IRE)**[14] 1312 4-9-7 **55** ow1.............(p) MissEmmaSayer 6
(Dianne Sayer) *dwlt: hld up: outpcd over 4f out: nvr on terms* **40/1**

1-00 **16** 8 **Galilee Chapel (IRE)**[17] 5097 8-9-13 **67**................(b) RhonaPindar(5) 1
(Alistair Whillans) *in tch: outpcd over 3f out: sn wknd* **50/1**

2m 29.41s (6.31) **Going Correction** +0.325s/f (Good) **16** Ran SP% **125.2**
Speed ratings (Par 103): **90,89,87,87,85 85,82,81,81,79 78,76,76,72,59 53**
CSF £123.67 CT £1151.76 TOTE £14.20: £2.50, £2.60, £2.70, £1.30; EX 172.80 Trifecta £2948.30.
**Owner** Mrs Sian McCain **Bred** Lady Caffyn-Parsons **Trained** Cholmondeley, Cheshire
■ Stewards' Enquiry : Miss Joanna Mason caution: entered wrong stall

**FOCUS**
For all Omotesando was reeled in late by the winner, this was a race in which it paid to be close to the front, if not exactly on it. The third and fourth were probably given a bit too much to do. The winner has been rated to his best since he was a 4yo.
T/Plt: £2,286.40 to a £1 stake. Pool: £68,125.07 - 21.75 winning units. T/Qpdt: £81.70 to a £1 stake. Pool: £7,837.13 - 70.90 winning units. **Richard Young**

## 5161 RIPON (R-H)

Monday, August 7

**OFFICIAL GOING: Good to soft (good in places; 7.3)**
Wind: light breeze, behind in straight Weather: sunny intervals, mild

### 5702 BRITISH STALLION STUDS EBF FILLIES' NOVICE STKS (PLUS 10 RACE) 6f
**2:15** (2:17) (Class 4) 2-Y-O **£4,851** (£1,443; £721; £360) **Stalls** High

Form RPR

5 **1** **Elation (IRE)**[17] 5107 2-9-0 0...................................... SilvestreDeSousa 1 77+
(Roger Varian) *hld up: hdwy 1/2-way: led wl over 1f out: rdn ent fnl f: r.o wl* **7/4**[1]

4 **2** ½ **Perfect Thought**[38] 4312 2-9-0 0.......................................... JoeFanning 7 75
(William Haggas) *prom: led 2f out: sn rdn and hdd: kpt on wl fnl f* **15/2**

32 **3** 1 **Clubbable**[17] 5092 2-9-0 0................................................ PaulHanagan 10 75+
(Richard Fahey) *hld up: hdwy 2f out: rdn and r.o wl fnl f: nvr nrr* **4/1**[3]

4 **4** nk **Hippeia (IRE)**[18] 5058 2-9-0 0.................................... ConnorBeasley 4 71
(Jedd O'Keeffe) *disp ld tl hdd 2f out: sn rdn: no ex fnl f* **33/1**

5 **5** 3¾ **Sulafaat (IRE)**[62] 3429 2-9-0 0.................................... AndrewMullen 2 59
(Mark Johnston) *mid-div: pushed along 2f out: rdn over 1f out: one pce fnl f* **40/1**

5020 **6** ½ **Lady Anjorica (IRE)**[16] 5150 2-9-0 84.......................... PaulMulrennan 8 58
(Keith Dalgleish) *mid-div: rdn over 1f out: no imp* **11/4**[2]

64 **7** 2½ **Foxy Lady**[20] 4995 2-9-0 0.................................................. TomEaves 9 50+
(Kevin Ryan) *mid-div: drvn 2f out: one pce fnl f* **40/1**

03 **8** ½ **Alaskan Beauty (IRE)**[16] 5162 2-9-0 0............................. DavidAllan 11 49
(Tim Easterby) *disp ld tl hdd & wknd 2f out* **33/1**

**9** 2½ **Lady Willpower** 2-9-0 0........................................................ JasonHart 6 41
(John Quinn) *slowly away: drvn 2f out: sn rdn and no imp* **25/1**

5 **10** 1¼ **Claramara (IRE)**[10] 5356 2-9-0 0................................... PJMcDonald 3 38
(Mark Johnston) *in rr: pushed along 3f out drvn 2f out: no imp* **28/1**

**11** 4½ **Salire (IRE)** 2-9-0 0.............................................................. ShaneGray 5 24
(Ann Duffield) *a in rr: lost tch 1/2-way* **125/1**

1m 15.3s (2.30) **Going Correction** -0.10s/f (Good) **11** Ran SP% **113.6**
Speed ratings (Par 93): **80,79,78,77,72 71,68,67,64,62 56**
CSF £14.10 TOTE £2.60: £1.10, £2.30, £1.50; EX 17.50 Trifecta £53.20.
**Owner** Highclere T'Bred Racing - Hallowed Park **Bred** Lodge Park Stud **Trained** Newmarket, Suffolk

**FOCUS**
Rail on bend from back straight to home straight dolled out by 4yds, adding 8yds to races on the round course. This wasn't a bad fillies' novice event and the form looks sound. The riders afterwards generally reported the ground was more like soft.

### 5703 SIS TRADING SERVICES (S) H'CAP 5f
**2:45** (2:45) (Class 6) (0-65,61) 3-Y-O **£2,587** (£770; £384; £192) **Stalls** High

Form RPR

1640 **1** **Ebitda**[44] 4107 3-8-9 **49**.......................................................... PJMcDonald 6 59
(Scott Dixon) *prom: pushed along 2f out: rdn and led over 1f out: r.o wl fnl f* **7/1**[2]

5000 **2** 1½ **Mr Enthusiastic**[24] 4847 3-8-5 **45**................................. PatrickMathers 8 50
(Noel Wilson) *led: rdn and hdd over 1f out: kpt on u.p fnl f* **50/1**

0356 **3** 1¼ **Poet's Time**[9] 5418 3-8-6 **46**........................................... JamesSullivan 2 46
(Tim Easterby) *mid-div: pushed along 2f out: rdn over 1f out: r.o to take 3rd ins fnl f* **15/2**[3]

002 **4** 1 **Celerity (IRE)**[13] 5252 3-7-13 **46**.........................(b) GabrieleMalune(7) 5 43
(David Evans) *hld up: hdwy over 2f out: sn drvn and ev ch: rdn and wknd ent fnl f* **11/1**

6-06 **5** shd **Quiet Moment (IRE)**[10] 5375 3-9-2 **56**..........................(b) GrahamLee 7 52
(Ben Haslam) *trckd ldrs: pushed along 2f out: rdn over 1f out: no imp* **10/1**

3000 **6** ¾ **Three C's (IRE)**[9] 5418 3-8-7 **52**...............................(tp) BenRobinson(5) 1 45
(David Dennis) *mid-div: drvn along 1/2-way: rdn over 2f out: one pce fnl f* **12/1**

43 **7** ¾ **Bourbonisto**[38] 4302 3-9-7 **61**.................................... SilvestreDeSousa 3 52
(Ben Haslam) *slowly away: in rr: pushed along 1/2-way: hdwy and rdn over 2f out: no further prog* **11/10**[1]

0402 **8** 3¼ **Joysunny**[20] 4997 3-8-9 **49**................................................ CamHardie 4 28
(Jacqueline Coward) *prom: 3rd 1/2-way: pushed along 2f out: sn rdn and lost pl: fdd* **8/1**

1m 2.14s (2.14) **Going Correction** -0.10s/f (Good) **8** Ran SP% **110.1**
Speed ratings (Par 98): **78,75,73,72,71 70,69,64**
CSF £235.79 CT £2527.77 TOTE £6.80: £2.60, £6.80, £2.80; EX 308.30 Trifecta £1548.70.
**Owner** Chesterfield Estates **Bred** Selwood, Hoskins & Trickledown **Trained** Babworth, Notts

**FOCUS**
A weak 3yo seller, with the winner rated to a better view of her Redcar success.

### 5704 FOLLOW @RIPONRACES ON TWITTER H'CAP 1m 1f 170y
**3:15** (3:15) (Class 4) (0-85,86) 3-Y-O+ **£5,175** (£1,540; £769; £384) **Stalls** Low

Form RPR

2121 **1** **Komodo (IRE)**[29] 4658 3-9-9 **86**........................................ PJMcDonald 1 94+
(Jedd O'Keeffe) *slowly away: sn rcvrd to trck ldrs: hdwy on inner 3f out: pushed along and led over 2f out: 1 l ahd and rdn over 1f out: r.o wl ins fnl f* **11/8**[1]

5251 **2** 1¼ **Save The Bees**[5] 5540 9-9-7 **83** 6ex.................................... GerO'Neill(7) 3 86
(Declan Carroll) *led: pushed along 3f out: drvn and hdd over 2f out: sn rdn: kpt on wl fnl f* **5/1**[3]

010 **3** nse **Auspicion**[9] 5417 5-9-5 **74**.............................................. AndrewMullen 6 77
(Tom Tate) *slowly away: in rr: stl last 3f out: hdwy and drvn over 2f out: rdn over 1f out: r.o ins fnl f* **9/1**

0141 **4** 1¾ **Cornborough**[16] 5135 6-9-2 **76**..........................(p) CallumRodriguez(5) 2 75
(Mark Walford) *trckd ldrs: pushed along 3f out: rdn over 1f out: no imp* **7/2**[2]

4331 **5** 15 **Racemaker**[28] 4690 3-8-10 **73**............................................... NeilFarley 5 56
(Andrew Crook) *chsd ldr: pushed along 3f out: rdn 2f out: wknd and lost pl over 1f out: eased* **15/2**

056 **6** nk **Coillte Cailin (IRE)**[27] 4718 7-10-0 **83**.......................... DanielTudhope 4 57
(David O'Meara) *hld up: pushed along 3f out: lost tch 2f out: eased* **14/1**

2m 9.04s (3.64) **Going Correction** +0.40s/f (Good)
**WFA** 3 from 5yo+ 8lb **6** Ran SP% **109.4**
Speed ratings (Par 105): **101,100,99,98,86 86**
CSF £8.09 TOTE £1.70: £1.10, £2.20; EX 7.70 Trifecta £36.00.
**Owner** Geoff & Sandra Turnbull **Bred** Irish National Stud **Trained** Middleham Moor, N Yorks

**FOCUS**
Add 8yds. A fair handicap, run at an average pace. The runner-up gives it a sound look.

### 5705 ARMSTRONG MEMORIAL H'CAP 6f
**3:45** (3:47) (Class 3) (0-95,95) 3-Y-O+
**£12,450** (£3,728; £1,864; £932; £466; £234) **Stalls** High

Form RPR

2165 **1** **Avon Breeze**[1] 5684 8-9-3 **89**.................................. LewisEdmunds(3) 10 98
(Richard Whitaker) *slowly away: in rr: pushed along and hdwy 2f out: clsd on ldrs over 1f out: rdn fnl f: r.o wl to ld last 50yds* **12/1**

0231 **2** 1 **Bossipop**[8] 5457 4-9-5 **88** 6ex..........................................(b) DavidAllan 11 94
(Tim Easterby) *trckd ldrs: pushed along over 1f out: hdwy ins fnl f: sn rdn: r.o wl to take 2nd nr fin* **11/4**[1]

0420 **3** nse **Jaywalker (IRE)**[9] 5435 6-9-6 **89**.................................. DanielTudhope 5 95
(Rebecca Bastiman) *prom: led 2f out: 1 l clr ent fnl f: rdn and r.o: but hdd last 50yds: lost 2nd nr fin* **8/1**

0030 **4** 2¾ **Red Pike (IRE)**[17] 5094 9-9-6 **89**................................ ConnorBeasley 6 86
(Bryan Smart) *mid-div: drvn 2f out: rdn over 1f out: swtchd to outer 1f out: r.o to take 4th ins fnl f* **11/2**[3]

0214 **5** 1 **Sir Billy Wright (IRE)**[17] 5123 6-9-3 **86**................... SilvestreDeSousa 1 80
(David Evans) *prom: pushed along in 4th 2f out: sn rdn: no ex whn sltly hmpd ins fnl f* **13/2**

1646 **6** 1½ **Art Collection (FR)**[60] 3492 4-9-1 **84**.............................. JamesSullivan 7 73
(Ruth Carr) *hld up: rdn 2f out: no imp* **20/1**

3264 **7** ½ **Captain Dion**[114] 1794 4-9-7 **90**....................................(b[1]) TomEaves 3 77
(Kevin Ryan) *led: rdn and hdd 2f out: wknd over 1f out* **16/1**

1040 **8** 11 **Wentworth Falls**[33] 4505 5-9-12 **95**..........................(p[1]) PhillipMakin 8 47
(Geoffrey Harker) *hld up: pushed along in rr 2f out: sn lost tch: eased fnl f* **10/1**

2320 **R** **Snap Shots (IRE)**[9] 5435 5-9-10 **93**.........................(p[1]) BarryMcHugh 4
(Tony Coyle) *planted feet in stalls and ref to r* **4/1**[2]

1m 13.8s (0.80) **Going Correction** -0.10s/f (Good) **9** Ran SP% **113.9**
Speed ratings (Par 107): **90,88,88,84,83 81,80,66,**
CSF £44.54 CT £286.90 TOTE £16.20: £3.30, £1.50, £2.00; EX 62.00 Trifecta £617.50.
**Owner** Grange Park Racing II & Partner **Bred** Hellwood Stud Farm **Trained** Scarcroft, W Yorks

**FOCUS**
A good-quality sprint handicap and a pb from the winner.

### 5706 VISIT RIPON-RACES.CO.UK H'CAP 1m 4f 10y
**4:15** (4:15) (Class 5) (0-75,77) 3-Y-O+ **£3,234** (£962; £481; £240) **Stalls** Low

Form RPR

5243 **1** **Pete So High (GER)**[20] 4989 3-8-13 **70**..............(p) SilvestreDeSousa 2 78
(Richard Hannon) *trckd ldrs: hdwy to ld 3f out: sn pushed along and jnd by runner-up: rdn over 1f out: narrow ld ent fnl f: grad asserted u.p* **10/3**[2]

321 **2** ½ **Zack Mayo**[35] 4449 3-9-4 **75**................................................ PhillipMakin 6 82
(Philip McBride) *mid-div: hdwy 4f out: jnd wnr over 2f out: ev ch and rdn over 1f out: kpt on but hld by wnr ins fnl f* **5/1**

1655 **3** 4 **Mysterial**[8] 5454 7-9-2 **70**..................................................... GerO'Neill(7) 1 70
(Declan Carroll) *led: jnd briefly 4f out: drvn to regain advantage: rdn and hdd 3f out: kpt on one pce fnl 2 fs* **12/1**

5521 **4** 2¼ **Montanna**[38] 4307 3-9-6 **77**.................................................. JackGarritty 3 74
(Jedd O'Keeffe) *hld up: reminders 4f out: sn drvn: rdn 2f out: r.o to take 4th ins fnl f* **9/2**[3]

0123 **5** 1½ **Royal Reserve**[9] 5417 4-9-11 **72**.................................... DanielTudhope 4 66
(David O'Meara) *hld up: hdwy over 3f out: drvn 2f out: rdn over 1f out: no further prog* **11/4**[1]

665- **6** shd **Skiddaw Valleys**[273] 7847 5-9-7 **68**.................................. TonyHamilton 5 62
(Sally Haynes) *hld up: hdwy on inner 4f out: chsd ldrs 3f out: rdn 2f out: no ex* **50/1**

2503 **7** 16 **Albert Boy (IRE)**[18] 5080 4-9-0 **61**.................................... PJMcDonald 7 29
(Scott Dixon) *cl to pce: jnd ldr briefly 4f out: sn drvn and lost pl: wknd fnl 2 fs* **25/1**

2014 **8** 44 **Breakwater Bay (IRE)**[23] 4898 3-8-12 **69**........................... DavidAllan 8
(Tim Easterby) *chsd ldrs: pushed along 4f out: sn wknd and lost pl: eased wl over 2f out* **15/2**

2m 40.31s (3.61) **Going Correction** +0.40s/f (Good)
**WFA** 3 from 4yo+ 10lb **8** Ran SP% **109.9**
Speed ratings (Par 103): **103,102,100,98,97 97,86,57**
CSF £18.66 CT £160.72 TOTE £3.70: £1.10, £2.00, £3.60; EX 22.50 Trifecta £141.10.
**Owner** Middleham Park Racing VII & K Sohi **Bred** Stiftung Gestut Fahrhof **Trained** East Everleigh, Wilts

**FOCUS**
Add 8yds. The first pair came clear in this modest handicap.

## 5707 SIS STREAMING CONTENT GLOBALLY MAIDEN STKS — 1m 4f 10y
4:45 (4:47) (Class 5) 3-Y-0+ £3,234 (£962; £481; £240) Stalls Low

Form RPR
53 1 Tarte Tropezienne (IRE)[19] 5022 3-8-11 0........ JoeFanning 6 83+
(William Haggas) *racd in 2nd: hdwy gng wl to ld 3f out: pushed along 2f out: 1 l advantage over runner-up 1f out: drvn out and r.o wl fnl f* **11/8**[1]
4 2 1 ¼ State Sovereignty[33] 4497 5-9-7 0........ DougieCostello 2 80
(Michael Scudamore) *trckd ldrs: 3rd 3f out: tried to cl on wnr 2f out: rdn and 1 l down ent fnl f: kpt on but a hld* **16/1**
45 3 11 Munthany (USA)[25] 4808 3-9-2 0........ PaulHanagan 1 68
(Charles Hills) *led: pushed along and hdd 3f out: drvn and one pce fnl 2 fs* **5/2**[2]
0226 4 1 ¾ Sileel (USA)[17] 5124 3-8-11 77........ SilvestreDeSousa 3 61
(Ed Dunlop) *hld up: hdwy 3f out: rdn over 2f out: one pce fnl 2 fs* **7/2**[3]
2-22 5 1 ¾ American History (USA)[18] 5061 3-9-2 72........(b) PhillipMakin 5 63
(William Muir) *mid-div: drvn over 2f out and jinked rt: no ex* **9/1**
03 6 8 Love Candy (IRE)[43] 4117 3-8-11 0........ NeilFarley 4 45
(Sally Haynes) *hld up: pushed along 3f out: sn rdn: wknd* **66/1**

2m 40.55s (3.85) **Going Correction** +0.40s/f (Good)
**WFA** 3 from 5yo 10lb **6 Ran SP% 110.3**
Speed ratings (Par 103): **103,102,94,93,92 87**
CSF £23.29 TOTE £2.30: £1.30, £4.60; EX 21.20 Trifecta £42.10.
**Owner** Christopher Wright & Miss Emily Asprey **Bred** Stratford Place Stud **Trained** Newmarket, Suffolk

**FOCUS**
Add 8yds. A modest middle-distance maiden in which the runner-up is the key to the form.

## 5708 VISIT ATTHERACES.COM H'CAP — 5f
5:15 (5:15) (Class 4) (0-85,87) 3-Y-O £5,175 (£1,540; £769; £384) Stalls High

Form RPR
4541 1 Holmeswood[14] 5204 3-9-9 87........ PaulMulrennan 6 93+
(Michael Dods) *prom: pushed along 2f out: rdn and hdwy to ld ent fnl f: kpt up to work: r.o wl to get on top last 100yds* **10/11**[1]
1546 2 ½ Harome (IRE)[9] 5416 3-9-0 78........ TonyHamilton 7 82
(Roger Fell) *trckd ldr: hdwy alongside wnr ent fnl f: sn rdn: r.o but hld last 100yds* **16/1**
5240 3 1 ½ Full Intention[30] 4616 3-9-4 82........(p[1]) PJMcDonald 5 81
(Tom Dascombe) *in rr: drvn over 2f out: hdwy and rdn over 1f out: r.o to take 3rd ins fnl f* **6/1**[3]
3 4 nk Caesar's Comet (IRE)[19] 5020 3-8-3 67........ CamHardie 4 65
(Paul Midgley) *hld up: pushed along 2f out: rdn over 1f out: styd on to take 4th ins fnl f* **28/1**
2020 5 1 ¼ Merry Banter[24] 4867 3-9-7 85........ GrahamLee 2 78
(Paul Midgley) *early pce to grab stands' rail fr wd draw: led: drvn over 1f out: rdn and hdd ent fnl f: no ex* **9/1**
5606 6 3 ¾ Impart[10] 5383 3-9-7 85........ DanielTudhope 1 68
(David O'Meara) *prom: drvn 2f out: rdn over 1f out: no ex ins fnl f: eased* **5/1**[2]
-221 7 7 Liquid (IRE)[20] 5006 3-8-13 77........(b[1]) BenCurtis 8 31
(David Barron) *in rr: pushed along 2f out: sn lost tch* **8/1**

59.2s (-0.80) **Going Correction** -0.10s/f (Good) **7 Ran SP% 113.8**
Speed ratings (Par 102): **102,101,98,98,96 90,79**
CSF £17.82 CT £59.81 TOTE £1.60: £1.50, £8.00; EX 19.50 Trifecta £101.50.
**Owner** David W Armstrong **Bred** Highfield Farm Llp **Trained** Denton, Co Durham

**FOCUS**
A modest 3yo sprint handicap won by a progressive sort and rated around the runner-up.
T/Plt: £221.80 to a £1 stake. Pool: £78,053.85 - 256.88 winning units. T/Qpdt: £30.90 to a £1 stake. Pool: £6,022.99 - 143.85 winning units. **Keith McHugh**

# 5427 SALISBURY (R-H)
Monday, August 7

**OFFICIAL GOING: Good to soft (good in places; 7.1) changing to good (good to soft in places) after race 1 (2.00)**
Wind: light against Weather: cloudy

## 5709 M J CHURCH BRITISH EBF NOVICE STKS (PLUS 10 RACE) (DIV I) — 6f 213y
2:00 (2:00) (Class 4) 2-Y-O £4,690 (£1,395; £697; £348) Stalls Centre

Form RPR
4062 1 Move Over[13] 5246 2-9-2 72........(b) SeanLevey 6 80
(Richard Hannon) *mde all: kpt on wl fnl f: rdn out* **12/1**
2 2 1 Ode To Autumn[17] 5105 2-9-2 0........ WilliamBuick 4 77
(John Gosden) *trckd wnr: rdn over 2f out: kpt on same pce fnl f* **8/11**[1]
3 2 ¼ Adams Park 2-9-2 0........ AndreaAtzeni 1 71+
(Roger Varian) *in tch: pushed along whn swtchd lft jst over 2f out: sn rdn: r.o wl ins fnl f* **9/1**
4 ¾ Ateem (FR) 2-9-2 0........ JimCrowley 10 69+
(Richard Hannon) *trckd ldrs: rdn 2f out: kpt on but nt pce to chal* **7/1**[3]
6 5 1 ¼ Marble Bar[23] 4909 2-9-2 0........ DaneO'Neill 2 66
(Henry Candy) *trckd ldrs: rdn over 2f out: nt pce to get on terms: no ex fnl 75yds* **10/1**
0 6 3 ¾ Amaretto[31] 4583 2-9-2 0........ JackMitchell 8 56
(Jim Boyle) *hld up but in tch: rdn 2f out: little imp: fdd ins fnl f* **66/1**
7 ¾ Ghazan (IRE) 2-9-2 0........ AdamKirby 5 54
(Clive Cox) *in tch: rdn over 2f out: nvr threatened: wknd fnl f* **11/2**[2]
8 4 ½ Blackwood 2-9-2 0........ DavidProbert 3 43
(Michael Blanshard) *hld up: rdn over 2f out: wknd over 1f out* **66/1**
9 3 ¼ Deadly Accurate 2-9-2 0........ OisinMurphy 9 34
(Hughie Morrison) *hld up: rdn over 2f out: sn wknd* **28/1**

1m 29.18s (0.58) **Going Correction** -0.025s/f (Good) **9 Ran SP% 119.0**
Speed ratings (Par 96): **95,93,91,90,89 84,83,78,75**
CSF £21.84 TOTE £10.70: £3.00, £1.10, £2.30; EX 29.20 Trifecta £222.00.
**Owner** Middleham Park Racing LXXII **Bred** David Jamison Bloodstock **Trained** East Everleigh, Wilts

**FOCUS**
Drying conditions and following this opener the ground was changed to good, good to soft in places. The winner, who had shown just ordinary form in four starts, was allowed an uncontested lead against the rail and the runner-up raced in second pretty much throughout.

## 5710 M J CHURCH BRITISH EBF NOVICE STKS (PLUS 10 RACE) (DIV II) — 6f 213y
2:30 (2:31) (Class 4) 2-Y-O £4,690 (£1,395; £697; £348) Stalls Centre

Form RPR
3 1 Bullingdon[16] 5151 2-9-2 0........ SeanLevey 8 82
(Richard Hannon) *sn trcking ldr: rdn to chal 2f out: led ins fnl f: kpt on wl towards fin* **9/4**[1]
64 2 ½ Magnificent[24] 4860 2-9-2 0........ DaneO'Neill 7 81
(Richard Hannon) *led: rdn whn strly chal 2f out: hdd ins fnl f: kpt on but no ex nring fin* **9/2**[3]
3 ¾ Archie McKellar 2-9-2 0........ PatDobbs 1 79+
(Ralph Beckett) *hld up: hdwy over 2f out: chal for 3rd over 1f out: r.o wl fnl 120yds* **9/2**[3]
4 ½ Kitaabaat 2-9-2 0........ JimCrowley 3 78+
(Owen Burrows) *trckd ldrs: rdn to chse ldng pair over 2f out: kpt on fnl f but nt pce to get on terms* **4/1**[2]
5 3 ½ Connaught Ranger (IRE) 2-8-11 0........ PaddyPilley(5) 4 69
(Denis Coakley) *trckd ldrs: swtchd lft whn nt clrest of runs over 2f out: sn rdn: drifted lft over 1f out: one pce fnl f* **50/1**
6 ¾ Antagonist 2-9-2 0........ KieranShoemark 10 67+
(Roger Charlton) *dwlt: last pair: kpt on fnl f but nt pce to get involved* **8/1**
0 7 2 ½ Matewan (IRE)[31] 4583 2-9-2 0........ FranBerry 5 60
(Ian Williams) *in tch: rdn over 2f out: nt pce to threaten: fdd ins fnl f* **33/1**
8 nk Happy Ending (IRE) 2-8-11 0........ KieranO'Neill 2 54
(Seamus Mullins) *s.i.s: last pair: rdn 2f out: little imp* **66/1**
5 9 ½ Yorbelucky[42] 4151 2-9-2 0........ AdamKirby 9 58
(David Evans) *in tch: hdwy over 3f out: rdn over 2f out: wknd fnl f* **9/1**
10 1 Masters Apprentice (IRE) 2-8-11 0........ MitchGodwin(5) 6 56
(Sylvester Kirk) *s.i.s: sn in tch: rdn 3f out: wknd fnl f* **25/1**

1m 29.07s (0.47) **Going Correction** -0.025s/f (Good) **10 Ran SP% 118.5**
Speed ratings (Par 96): **96,95,94,94,90 89,86,85,85,84**
CSF £12.44 TOTE £3.20: £1.50, £1.80, £1.90; EX 11.20 Trifecta £57.70.
**Owner** Denford Stud **Bred** Denford Stud Ltd **Trained** East Everleigh, Wilts

**FOCUS**
A similar time to division one and again it proved hard to make ground, the one-two racing two-one for most of the way.

## 5711 PETER SYMONDS CATERING H'CAP — 6f
3:00 (3:01) (Class 5) (0-75,75) 3-Y-0+ £3,396 (£1,010; £505; £252) Stalls Low

Form RPR
0326 1 Field Of Vision (IRE)[10] 5379 4-9-10 73........ OisinMurphy 4 79
(Joseph Tuite) *trckd ldrs: rdn 2f out: led jst ins fnl f: r.o wl* **9/2**[2]
4524 2 ¾ Whitecrest[12] 5295 9-9-8 71........ WilliamCarson 1 74
(John Spearing) *mid-div: rdn and hdwy over 1f out: swtchd lft ent fnl f: kpt on to go 2nd towards fin but no threat to wnr* **12/1**
466 3 hd Otomo[41] 4178 3-9-4 71........(h) JamieSpencer 7 72
(Philip Hide) *trckd ldrs: rdn 2f out: kpt on to chse wnr ins fnl f but nt pce chal* **10/1**
251 4 ¾ Monteamiata (IRE)[12] 5295 3-9-8 75........ LiamKeniry 5 74
(Ed Walker) *mid-div: rdn 2f out: kpt on ins fnl f but nvr pce to get on terms* **5/2**[1]
063 5 1 ½ Miss Icon[40] 4198 3-9-1 68........ DavidProbert 9 62
(Patrick Chamings) *in tch: rdn over 2f out: sn one pce* **11/2**[3]
40-4 6 shd Hedging (IRE)[17] 5111 3-8-13 66........(p[1]) PatDobbs 3 59
(Eve Johnson Houghton) *hld up: rdn over 2f out: no imp tl kpt on ins fnl f* **6/1**
1-40 7 1 Wild Dancer[66] 3278 4-9-6 72........ HectorCrouch(3) 2 63
(Patrick Chamings) *hld up: hdwy 2f out: sn rdn: nt pce to threaten* **12/1**
-045 8 nse Evening Starlight[20] 4990 4-8-11 60........ KieranO'Neill 8 51
(Ron Hodges) *chsd ldr: rdn to take narrow advantage over 1f out: hdd jst ins fnl f: fdd* **20/1**
1565 9 1 ½ Bridge Builder[136] 1339 7-9-7 70........ KieranShoemark 10 56
(Peter Hedger) *led: rdn 2f out: hdd over 1f out: wknd ins fnl f* **33/1**
0020 10 3 ¾ Vincentti (IRE)[18] 5051 7-9-2 65........(p) AdamKirby 6 39
(Ronald Harris) *hld up: rdn over 2f out: no imp: wknd over 1f out* **14/1**

1m 14.18s (-0.62) **Going Correction** -0.025s/f (Good)
**WFA** 3 from 4yo+ 4lb **10 Ran SP% 115.3**
Speed ratings (Par 103): **103,102,101,100,98 98,97,97,95,90**
CSF £56.57 CT £526.53 TOTE £4.60: £1.70, £3.00, £3.20; EX 47.80 Trifecta £344.10.
**Owner** Shefford Valley Racing **Bred** Marathon Bloodstock **Trained** Lambourn, Berks

**FOCUS**
A fair sprint handicap and the winner has been rated to his best since last September.

## 5712 SORVIO INSURANCE MAIDEN FILLIES' STKS — 1m
3:30 (3:35) (Class 5) 3-Y-0+ £3,881 (£1,155; £577; £288) Stalls Low

Form RPR
-52 1 Keeper's Choice (IRE)[26] 4737 3-9-0 0........ OisinMurphy 12 76
(Denis Coakley) *trckd ldr: led jst over 2f out: sn rdn: strly chal ins fnl f: hld on v gamely: all out* **20/1**
65- 2 shd Ambrosia[282] 7696 3-9-0 0........ AndreaAtzeni 3 76
(Roger Varian) *trckd ldrs: rdn over 1f out: tight for room but str chal ins fnl f: kpt on* **10/3**[2]
2 3 shd Chalky (IRE)[19] 5038 3-9-0 0........ JackMitchell 6 75
(Martyn Meade) *trckd ldrs: rdn over 1f out: 4th ent fi nal f: r.o strly fnl 100yds: jst failed* **11/2**[3]
6-2 4 ¾ Awfaa (IRE)[17] 5118 3-9-0 0........ JimCrowley 13 73
(Sir Michael Stoute) *trckd ldrs: chal jst over 2f out: rdn and ev ch over 1f out: kpt on but no ex fnl 100yds* **10/11**[1]
45 5 4 ½ Gold Dust[36] 4409 3-8-11 0........ HectorCrouch(3) 7 63
(Clive Cox) *led: rdn and hdd jst over 2f out: kpt on same pce* **14/1**
220- 6 nk Lucky Esteem[22] 5840 3-9-0 67........(t[1]) JamieSpencer 10 62+
(Neil Mulholland) *hld up towards rr: midfield 2f out: sn rdn: styd on same pce fnl f* **25/1**
03 7 1 ½ Your Ladyship (IRE)[28] 4700 3-9-0 0........ PatDobbs 11 59
(Ralph Beckett) *mid-div: rdn 2f out: styd on same pce* **20/1**
0 8 ¾ Bubbles Arcade[9] 5428 5-9-7 0........ WilliamCarson 5 58
(Rod Millman) *a mid-div* **80/1**
0- 9 ½ Jazaalah (USA)[331] 6336 3-9-0 0........ DaneO'Neill 14 56
(Owen Burrows) *fly-leapt s: racd keenly in mid-div: rdn chsng ldrs 2f out: fdd ent fnl f* **20/1**

4033 **2** *hd* **Flowing Clarets**[12] 5295 4-9-1 **61**.................................. WilliamCarson 1 66
(John Bridger) *racd alone against nr side rail early then jnd others and on terms: rdn and nt qckn wl over 1f out: rallied ins fnl f: r.o to take 2nd last strides: jst hld* **3/1**[1]

0603 **3** *nse* **John Joiner**[9] 5429 5-8-10 **56**..................................... JosephineGordon 7 61
(Peter Hedger) *hld up in tch: prog 1/2-way: led jst over 1f out: drvn fnl f: hdd last 50yds* **7/2**[3]

2003 **4** *1 ½* **Zipedeedodah (IRE)**[21] 4965 5-9-11 **71**........................(t) OisinMurphy 2 70
(Joseph Tuite) *pressed ldrs: led wl over 1f out to jst over 1f out: nt qckn ins fnl f* **10/3**[2]

3455 **5** *1 ¼* **Mercers**[19] 5027 3-8-11 **60**...................................................... ShaneKelly 3 54
(Peter Crate) *chsd ldrs: rdn and struggling 2f out: tried to make prog over 1f out: one pce after* **8/1**

5006 **6** *2 ¼* **Torment**[2] 5657 4-8-4 **55**..................................................(b[1]) DavidEgan(5) 5 42
(Charlie Wallis) *pressed ldrs: nt qckn 2f out: lost pl over 1f out: fdd* **8/1**

0101 **7** *2 ½* **Red Invader (IRE)**[12] 5297 7-9-10 **70**................................. LiamKeniry 4 48
(John Butler) *hld up in last pair: rdn and no prog 2f out: wl btn after* **9/1**

1m 0.95s (0.65) **Going Correction** -0.075s/f (Good)
**WFA** 3 from 4yo+ 3lb **7** Ran SP% **112.5**
Speed ratings (Par 103): **91,90,90,88,86 82,78**
CSF £34.95 TOTE £10.30: £4.40, £2.00; EX 36.30 Trifecta £168.50.
**Owner** Muir Racing Partnership - Ayr **Bred** Cheveley Park Stud Ltd **Trained** Lambourn, Berks

**FOCUS**
Stalls on inner. A modest but competitive sprint handicap, run in driving rain, and it has been rated around the runner-up.
T/Plt: £17.70 to a £1 stake. Pool: £86,102.24 - 520.81 winning units. T/Qpdt: £11.40 to a £1 stake. Pool: £8,066.71 - 520.81 winning units. **Jonathan Neesom**

5724 - 5734a (Foreign Racing) - See Raceform Interactive

## [5277]CATTERICK (L-H)
Tuesday, August 8

**OFFICIAL GOING: Soft (7.8)**
Wind: light against Weather: Steady rain

### 5735 BRITISH STALLION STUDS EBF NOVICE STKS 7f 6y
**2:15** (2:15) (Class 5) 2-Y-O **£2,911** (£866; £432; £216) **Stalls** Low

Form RPR

53 **1** **Shrewd Approach (IRE)**[14] 5246 2-8-11 0....................... GrahamLee 3 66
(Simon Crisford) *trckd ldr: pushed along to ld over 1f out: rdn ins fnl f: strly pressed fnl 75yds: fnd ex* **15/8**[1]

**2** *hd* **Three Saints Bay (IRE)** 2-9-2 0...................................... PhillipMakin 6 70
(David O'Meara) *in tch: pushed along and hdwy over 1f out: rdn to chal strly fnl 75yds: jst hld* **4/1**[3]

40 **3** *2* **Burnieboozle (IRE)**[18] 5127 2-9-2 0.................................... JasonHart 7 65
(John Quinn) *trckd ldr: pushed along and bit outpcd over 1f out: rdn and styd on ins fnl f* **8/1**

06 **4** *1 ½* **Mountain Approach (IRE)**[22] 4956 2-9-2 0.................... JackGarritty 4 61
(Richard Fahey) *led: rdn whn hdd over 1f out: no ex ins fnl f* **9/1**

**5** *1* **Amazing Rock (SWI)** 2-9-2 0.......................................... JoeFanning 2 59
(Mark Johnston) *in tch: pushed along over 1f out: sn one pce and no prog* **5/2**[2]

**6** *1 ¾* **Lord Caprio (IRE)** 2-9-2 0.............................................. TomEaves 1 54
(Ben Haslam) *dwlt: hld up: pushed along over 2f out: nvr threatened* **20/1**

**7** *7* **Lady Isle** 2-8-11 0........................................................... JamesSullivan 8 31
(Grant Tuer) *dwlt: a towards rr* **40/1**

**8** *2 ½* **Cuppacoco** 2-8-11 0........................................................ ShaneGray 5 24
(Ann Duffield) *hld up: pushed along over 2f out: sn wknd* **40/1**

1m 31.21s (4.21) **Going Correction** +0.55s/f (Yiel) **8** Ran SP% **114.1**
Speed ratings (Par 94): **97,96,94,92,91 89,81,78**
CSF £9.52 TOTE £2.50: £1.20, £1.20, £2.30; EX 12.00 Trifecta £43.40.
**Owner** Ali Saeed **Bred** Rabbah Bloodstock Limited **Trained** Newmarket, Suffolk

**FOCUS**
It was dry overnight but the rain arrived in the morning, and following 3mm the going had eased to soft. The rail on the bend into the home straight was dolled out 2yds. Race distance increased by 6yds. As is usually the case on soft ground they came stands' side in the straight.

### 5736 LOVE PROPERTY/SMITH & GRAHAM H'CAP 5f
**2:45** (2:47) (Class 6) (0-60,62) 3-Y-O+ **£2,264** (£673; £336; £168) **Stalls** Low

Form RPR

2144 **1** **Perfect Words (IRE)**[1] 5695 7-8-13 **59**.................(p) HarrisonShaw(7) 11 68
(Marjorie Fife) *midfield: pushed along and hdwy to chse ldr appr fnl f: rdn and kpt on: led nr fin* **6/1**[3]

6062 **2** *nk* **Lady Joanna Vassa (IRE)**[5] 5567 4-8-7 **46**...........(v) ConnorBeasley 10 54
(Richard Guest) *led: 3 l clr 1/2-way: looked in command tl rdn and hung lft ins fnl f: pushed out w reduced advantage fnl 75yds: hdd towards fin* **3/1**[1]

3232 **3** *5* **Hadley**[10] 5419 4-8-13 **52**...................................................(p) BenCurtis 5 42
(Tracy Waggott) *chsd ldr: rdn 1/2-way: outpcd and hld in 3rd fr appr fnl f* **7/2**[2]

1660 **4** *¾* **Glyder**[17] 5134 3-9-4 **60**............................................. RoystonFfrench 3 46
(John Holt) *slowly away: hld up in rr: rdn 1/2-way: kpt on ins fnl f: nrst fin* **8/1**

3362 **5** *½* **Windforpower (IRE)**[7] 5495 7-9-0 **58**.......................(p) BenRobinson(5) 9 43
(Tracy Waggott) *midfield: rdn 1/2-way: wknd fnl f* **8/1**

6304 **6** *½* **Digital Revolution**[10] 5419 3-8-7 **49**.................................. CamHardie 7 32
(Antony Brittain) *hld up: rdn 1/2-way: nvr threatened* **20/1**

1500 **7** *¾* **Sir Geoffrey (IRE)**[13] 5282 11-8-7 **51** ow1.................(b) PaddyPilley(5) 8 32
(Scott Dixon) *chsd ldr: rdn 1/2-way: wknd ins fnl f* **10/1**

06/0 **8** *4 ½* **Time Continuum**[31] 4604 5-8-7 **46** oh1................................. NeilFarley 4 11
(Eric Alston) *dwlt: a rr* **66/1**

6332 **9** *shd* **See Vermont**[14] 5260 9-9-5 **58**.................................(b) DuranFentiman 12 22
(Rebecca Bastiman) *hld up: nvr threatened* **10/1**

5034 **10** *1* **Bond Bombshell**[14] 5260 4-9-2 **62**............................ PatrickVaughan(7) 1 23
(David O'Meara) *midfield: rdn 1/2-way: wknd fnl f* **16/1**

1m 1.45s (1.65) **Going Correction** +0.375s/f (Good)
**WFA** 3 from 4yo+ 3lb **10** Ran SP% **114.0**
Speed ratings (Par 101): **101,100,92,91,90 89,88,81,81,79**
CSF £23.74 CT £73.70 TOTE £7.00: £2.60, £1.30, £1.80; EX 29.90 Trifecta £157.40.
**Owner** Green Lane **Bred** Rathasker Stud **Trained** Stillington, N Yorks

**FOCUS**
Few got into this and the winner has been rated back to last year's best.

### 5737 CNG H'CAP (FOR THE ABF SOLDIER'S CHARITY PERPETUAL TROPHY) 1m 5f 192y
**3:15** (3:15) (Class 4) (0-85,86) 3-Y-O+
**£6,225** (£1,864; £932; £466; £233; £117) **Stalls** Low

Form RPR

1104 **1** **Pumblechook**[18] 5110 4-10-0 **83**........................................ JoeFanning 2 90
(Mark Johnston) *trckd ldrs: rdn 2f out: led ent fnl f: styd on* **11/4**[1]

0563 **2** *2 ½* **Ingleby Hollow**[16] 5186 5-8-13 **68**..................................(p) PhillipMakin 3 71
(David O'Meara) *trckd ldrs: rdn to join ldr wl over 2f out: led 2f out: hdd ent fnl f: no ex ins fnl f* **11/2**[2]

00-5 **3** *½* **Bulas Belle**[10] 5438 7-9-4 **73**.............................................. GrahamLee 5 75
(Grant Tuer) *prom: led over 7f out: jnd wl over 2f out: hdd 2f out: outpcd over 1f out: plugged on ins fnl f* **11/4**[1]

3-33 **4** *1 ¾* **Tenzing Norgay**[13] 5303 4-10-0 **83**..............................(b[1]) RyanPowell 6 83
(Sir Mark Prescott Bt) *hld up: clsr 4f out: rdn and in tch 2f out: no ex ins fnl f* **11/4**[1]

2465 **5** *15* **Itlaaq**[15] 5208 11-8-11 **73**.........................................(tp) HarrisonShaw(7) 1 52
(Michael Easterby) *hld up in tch: rdn 3f out: wknd* **16/1**

0014 **6** *9* **Be Perfect (USA)**[19] 5071 8-10-3 **86**.........................(p) JamesSullivan 4 52
(Ruth Carr) *led: hdd over 7f out: rdn 3f out and wknd* **12/1**[3]

3m 9.42s (5.82) **Going Correction** +0.55s/f (Yiel) **6** Ran SP% **109.0**
Speed ratings (Par 105): **105,103,103,102,93 88**
CSF £17.17 TOTE £4.50: £1.70, £2.10; EX 18.60 Trifecta £58.90.
**Owner** Christopher W T Johnston **Bred** Castlemartin Sky & Skymarc Farm **Trained** Middleham Moor, N Yorks

**FOCUS**
Race distance increased by 6yds. A fair handicap and the winner has been rated back to the level of his Newmarket success.

### 5738 SUPPORT ABF THE SOLDIERS' CHARITY H'CAP 5f 212y
**3:45** (3:46) (Class 6) (0-60,60) 3-Y-O+ **£2,911** (£866; £432; £216) **Stalls** Low

Form RPR

4022 **1** **Melaniemillie**[11] 5374 3-8-12 **52**...................................... JamesSullivan 5 58
(Ruth Carr) *trckd ldrs: pushed along to ld over 1f out: rdn and kpt on* **7/2**[1]

4022 **2** *½* **Deben**[13] 5283 4-8-9 **50**.................................................... PhilDennis(5) 7 56
(John Weymes) *trckd ldrs: pushed along over 1f out: rdn ins fnl f: kpt on* **11/2**[3]

3030 **3** *1 ¾* **Whipphound**[6] 5543 9-8-10 **46**....................................(b[1]) JackGarritty 10 46
(Ruth Carr) *hld up: hdwy into midfield 1/2-way: rdn to chse ldr over 1f out: one pce ins fnl f* **11/2**[3]

2650 **4** *1 ¾* **Misu Moneypenny**[13] 5283 4-9-0 **50**...........................(v[1]) DavidAllan 12 45
(Scott Dixon) *sn led: rdn whn hdd over 1f out: no ex ins fnl f* **20/1**

5651 **5** *1 ½* **Jazz Legend (USA)**[19] 5081 4-9-0 **53**........................(h) SammyJoBell(3) 2 44
(Mandy Rowland) *hld up in rr: pushed along over 1f out: kpt on ins fnl f: nvr threatened* **12/1**

-000 **6** *shd* **Robbian**[59] 3563 6-8-11 **52**.......................................... BenRobinson(5) 3 42
(Charles Smith) *chsd ldrs: rdn over 2f out: outpcd over 1f out: no threat after* **18/1**

5362 **7** *shd* **Rose Eclair**[6] 5542 4-9-6 **59**................................(p) RachelRichardson(3) 8 49
(Tim Easterby) *hld up towards outer: rdn over 1f out: nvr threatened* **4/1**[2]

000 **8** *1* **Sir Domino (FR)**[31] 4605 5-9-10 **60**...................................... GrahamLee 4 47
(Patrick Holmes) *hld up: nvr threatened* **25/1**

3402 **9** *2 ½* **Goadby**[13] 5282 6-8-11 **47**..........................................(v) RoystonFfrench 6 26
(John Holt) *prom: rdn over 2f out: wknd fnl f* **12/1**

3465 **10** *8* **Lucky Lodge**[12] 5318 7-9-10 **60**.......................................(v) CamHardie 1 15
(Antony Brittain) *dwlt: hld up: rdn over 2f out: wknd and bhd* **9/1**

04-0 **11** *43* **Good Boy Jasper**[92] 2455 3-9-4 **58**................................... DavidNolan 11
(James Moffatt) *dwlt: sn pushed along in rr and t.o after 2f* **33/1**

1m 17.66s (4.06) **Going Correction** +0.55s/f (Yiel)
**WFA** 3 from 4yo+ 4lb **11** Ran SP% **115.2**
Speed ratings (Par 101): **94,93,91,88,86 86,86,85,81,71 13**
CSF £21.56 CT £103.32 TOTE £3.50: £1.60, £2.00, £1.70; EX 20.60 Trifecta £152.20.
**Owner** John H Sissons **Bred** John H Sissons **Trained** Huby, N Yorks

**FOCUS**
Race distance increased by 6yds. Once again getting over to the stands' rail seemed a nice advantage.

### 5739 ROYAL DRAGOON GUARDS H'CAP 7f 6y
**4:15** (4:16) (Class 5) (0-75,76) 4-Y-O+ **£2,911** (£866; £432; £216) **Stalls** Low

Form RPR

3544 **1** **Tadaawol**[7] 5497 4-9-0 **68**........................................(p) ConnorBeasley 1 83
(Roger Fell) *mde all: rdn clr over 1f out: kpt on wl* **9/2**[2]

0311 **2** *7* **Mango Chutney**[34] 4506 4-9-3 **71**................................(p) PhillipMakin 4 68
(John Davies) *midfield: pushed along and hdwy 2f out: rdn to go 2nd jst ins fnl f: one pce* **2/1**[1]

3056 **3** *1 ¼* **Hitman**[17] 5165 4-9-3 **71**............................................. DuranFentiman 8 65
(Rebecca Bastiman) *hld up: rdn and hdwy over 1f out: plugged on* **12/1**

503 **4** *hd* **Short Work**[31] 4605 4-8-11 **68**.....................................(b) JoshDoyle(3) 6 61
(David O'Meara) *hld up: rdn over 3f out: plugged on fnl f: nvr threatened* **8/1**

-000 **5** *3 ¼* **Tadaany (IRE)**[13] 5288 5-9-7 **75**........................................ DavidNolan 5 60
(David O'Meara) *prom: rdn and outpcd over 1f out: wknd fnl f* **8/1**

6051 **6** *2 ¾* **Mywayistheonlyway (IRE)**[21] 4999 4-9-3 **76**................. PhilDennis(5) 9 53
(Grant Tuer) *hld up on outer: pushed along 2f out: nvr threatened* **7/1**[3]

-002 **7** *5* **Dyllan (IRE)**[13] 5280 4-9-2 **70**...................................(p[1]) JamesSullivan 2 34
(Ruth Carr) *chsd ldrs: rdn over 2f out: wknd over 1f out* **15/2**

0000 **8** *4 ½* **Shamaheart (IRE)**[42] 4168 7-9-6 **74**.................................(v) DavidAllan 3 27
(Geoffrey Harker) *hld up: nvr threatened* **25/1**

0200 **9** *7* **Like No Other**[32] 4556 4-9-5 **73**.....................................(p) JoeFanning 7 8
(Les Eyre) *chsd ldr over 2f out: wknd over 1f out* **22/1**

1m 30.53s (3.53) **Going Correction** +0.55s/f (Yiel) **9** Ran SP% **113.9**
Speed ratings (Par 103): **101,93,91,91,87 84,78,73,65**
CSF £13.67 CT £99.52 TOTE £5.30: £1.60, £1.20, £3.50; EX 16.60 Trifecta £198.50.
**Owner** Fell, Hamilton & Smeaton **Bred** Christopher & Annabelle Mason **Trained** Nawton, N Yorks

**FOCUS**
Race distance increased by 6yds. This proved one-way traffic from the turn in.

## 5740 CATTERICK GARRISON H'CAP — 1m 7f 189y
4:45 (4:46) (Class 6) (0-65,63) 3-Y-O+ £2,587 (£770; £384; £192) Stalls Low

| Form | | | | RPR |
|---|---|---|---|---|
| 34/4 | 1 | | **Attention Seaker**[39] 3311 7-9-11 60 ...(t1) DavidAllan 8 (Tim Easterby) *midfield: hdwy to ld over 4f out: rdn over 2f out: pressed over 1f out: styd on wl* **8/1** | 74 |
| -451 | 2 | 1 1/4 | **Bodacious Name (IRE)**[5] 5581 3-8-11 59 6ex... JasonHart 6 (John Quinn) *hld up in midfield: clsr over 4f out: pushed along to chse ldr over 2f out: rdn to chal over 1f out: kpt on: hld towards fin* **11/10**[1] | 72 |
| 0-02 | 3 | 17 | **Desktop**[14] 5244 5-9-6 55 ... CamHardie 9 (Antony Brittain) *hld up: sme hdwy 4f out: rdn over 2f out: plugged on to go remote 3rd towards fin* **14/1** | 47 |
| /1-2 | 4 | 3/4 | **Italian Riviera**[21] 5008 8-10-0 63 ...(h) JamesSullivan 2 (Kenneth Slack) *s.i.s: hld up in rr: pushed along over 5f out: rdn over 3f out: plugged on: nvr threatened* **11/4**[2] | 54 |
| 4-62 | 5 | 2 3/4 | **Angel In The Snow**[13] 5284 4-8-7 47 ... BenRobinson(5) 4 (Brian Ellison) *trckd ldrs: rdn over 2f out: wknd appr fnl f* **7/2**[3] | 35 |
| 6040 | 6 | 2 1/2 | **Jebulani**[30] 4660 7-8-3 45 ...(p) ConnorMurtagh(7) 1 (Barry Murtagh) *trckd ldrs: rdn over 3f out: sn outpcd and btn* **66/1** | 30 |
| 4305 | 7 | 14 | **Jan Smuts (IRE)**[14] 5259 9-9-5 57 ...(vt1) SammyJoBell(3) 3 (Wilf Storey) *dwlt: sn midfield: rdn over 3f out: sn wknd* **20/1** | 25 |
| 0600 | 8 | 50 | **Python**[10] 5413 5-8-10 45 ... NeilFarley 10 (Andrew Crook) *led: hdd over 4f out: sn rdn and wknd: eased and t.o fnl 2f* **66/1** | |

3m 45.01s (13.01) **Going Correction** +0.55s/f (Yiel)
**WFA** 3 from 4yo+ 13lb — 8 Ran SP% **122.0**
Speed ratings (Par 101): **89,88,79,79,78 76,69,44**
CSF £18.45 CT £131.92 TOTE £11.10: £2.50, £1.02, £2.90; EX 25.20 Trifecta £241.60.
**Owner** Ryedale Partners No 6 **Bred** Ryedale Partners No 6 **Trained** Great Habton, N Yorks

**FOCUS**
Race distance increased by 12yds. The first two pulled well clear in this staying contest, with the winner looking back to something like her best.

## 5741 18TH AUGUST IS LADIES' EVENING H'CAP — 7f 6y
5:15 (5:15) (Class 6) (0-65,64) 3-Y-O £2,264 (£673; £336; £168) Stalls Low

| Form | | | | RPR |
|---|---|---|---|---|
| 2606 | 1 | | **Stubytuesday**[29] 4694 3-8-13 63 ... HarrisonShaw(7) 5 (Michael Easterby) *hld up: sn pushed along: rdn and hdwy over 1f out: led 110yds out: kpt on wl* **10/1** | 71 |
| 0030 | 2 | 2 | **Redrosezorro**[16] 5182 3-8-11 54 ...(h) NeilFarley 1 (Eric Alston) *hld up: rdn and hdwy 2f out: wnt 2nd 110yds out: kpt on* **20/1** | 57 |
| 4421 | 3 | 1 1/2 | **Cupid's Arrow (IRE)**[13] 5282 3-9-7 64 ... JamesSullivan 2 (Ruth Carr) *racd keenly and sn trckd ldr: rdn 2f out: led appr fnl f: hdd 110yds out: wknd* **3/1**[2] | 63 |
| 452 | 4 | 3/4 | **Jack Blane**[8] 5467 3-8-11 54 ...(p) JoeFanning 10 (Keith Dalgleish) *midfield: checked and lost pl 5f out: bk in midfield over 3f out: pushed along to chse ldrs over 1f out: rdn and wknd ins fnl f* **11/8**[1] | 51 |
| -003 | 5 | nk | **Kulgri**[20] 5019 3-8-12 55 ... JoeDoyle 4 (Kevin Ryan) *chsd ldr: rdn and outpcd over 2f out: plugged on fnl f* **25/1** | 51 |
| 2000 | 6 | 3/4 | **Little Kingdom (IRE)**[29] 4694 3-8-11 54 ... BenCurtis 11 (Tracy Waggott) *hld up: rdn over 2f out: sn btn* **14/1** | 48 |
| 0002 | 7 | 1 1/2 | **Nellie's Dancer**[27] 4766 3-8-12 55 ... DavidAllan 8 (Scott Dixon) *in tch outer: rdn over 2f out: wknd over 1f out* **11/2**[3] | 46 |
| 0300 | 8 | 1 3/4 | **Tagur (IRE)**[17] 5167 3-9-6 63 ...(v1) TomEaves 7 (Kevin Ryan) *led: rdn over 2f out: hdd appr fnl f: wknd* **14/1** | 49 |

1m 32.62s (5.62) **Going Correction** +0.55s/f (Yiel) — 8 Ran SP% **113.5**
Speed ratings (Par 98): **89,86,85,84,83 82,81,79**
CSF £177.05 CT £744.21 TOTE £12.70: £3.40, £6.10, £1.70; EX 212.80 Trifecta £629.10.
**Owner** Stuart Daynes & Stittenham Racing **Bred** The National Stud **Trained** Sheriff Hutton, N Yorks

**FOCUS**
Race distance increased by 6yds. For once the winner didn't come home along the stands' rail, the ground possibly fresher up the centre by this stage of the day. The pace was good and three of the first four were in the last three places early on.
T/Jkpt: Not Won. T/Plt: £14.80 to a £1 stake. Pool: £76,201.84 - 3,740.67 winning units T/Qpdt: £6.80 to a £1 stake. Pool: £5,085.26 - 411.62 winning units **Andrew Sheret**

# 5239 CHELMSFORD (A.W) (L-H)
Tuesday, August 8

**OFFICIAL GOING: Polytrack: standard**
Wind: light, across Weather: overcast

## 5742 TOTEPLACEPOT NURSERY H'CAP — 7f (P)
5:50 (5:50) (Class 4) (0-85,83) 2-Y-O £7,115 (£2,117; £1,058; £529) Stalls Low

| Form | | | | RPR |
|---|---|---|---|---|
| 1034 | 1 | | **Joe's Spirit (IRE)**[11] 5366 2-9-2 78 ... SilvestreDeSousa 1 (Michael Bell) *sn led and mde rest: rdn and kicked clr over 1f out: in command and r.o wl ins fnl f: comf* **15/8**[1] | 83 |
| 2531 | 2 | 2 | **Kit Marlowe**[40] 4258 2-9-7 83 ... JamesDoyle 4 (Mark Johnston) *chsd wnr: drvn ent fnl 2f out: unable qck w wnr over 1f out: styd on same pce ins fnl f* **5/2**[2] | 83 |
| 623 | 3 | 3/4 | **Sardenya (IRE)**[39] 4296 2-8-10 72 ...(p1) KieranShoemark 3 (Roger Charlton) *trckd ldrs: swtchd rt and effrt wl over 1f out: unable qck and wnt rt u.p 1f out: kpt on fnl 100yds to snatch 3rd cl home: no ch w wnr* **7/2**[3] | 70 |
| 0133 | 4 | 1/2 | **Faradays Spark (IRE)**[13] 5279 2-8-0 62 ... PatrickMathers 2 (Richard Fahey) *rousted along early: trckd ldrs: effrt u.p on inner but unable qck over 1f out: styd on same pce ins fnl f: lost 3rd nr fin* **14/1** | 59 |
| 6225 | 5 | 7 | **The Love Doctor (IRE)**[12] 5322 2-8-9 71 ... AndrewMullen 5 (David Evans) *in tch in last pair: dropped to rr 5f out: sn pushed along: hung rt and outpcd 3f out: no ch fnl 2f out* **10/1** | 49 |
| 352 | 6 | 10 | **Coastal Drive**[24] 4910 2-8-11 73 ... KieranO'Neill 6 (Richard Hannon) *stdd s: hld up in last pair: rdn and outpcd over 2f out: wknd over 1f out: sn bhd* **9/1** | 25 |

1m 25.93s (-1.27) **Going Correction** -0.175s/f (Stan) — 6 Ran SP% **111.3**
Speed ratings (Par 96): **100,97,96,96,88 76**
CSF £6.67 TOTE £2.70: £1.20, £1.90; EX 6.90 Trifecta £16.30.
**Owner** Middleham Park Racing XCI & Partner **Bred** S Gorman **Trained** Newmarket, Suffolk

**FOCUS**
A fair and quite competitive nursery handicap but it went as the market suggested. The form looks sound enough for the grade, with the winner posting a pb.

## 5743 TOTEEXACTA NOVICE STKS (PLUS 10 RACE) — 1m (P)
6:20 (6:22) (Class 4) 2-Y-O £7,115 (£2,117; £1,058; £529) Stalls Low

| Form | | | | RPR |
|---|---|---|---|---|
| 61 | 1 | | **Aussie Wind**[10] 5412 2-9-5 0 ... JamesDoyle 1 (Hugo Palmer) *mde all: rdn 2f out: forged ahd u.p over 1f out: pressed wl ins fnl f: a holding on towards fin: rdn out* **6/4**[1] | 88+ |
| 52 | 2 | 1/2 | **Ibn Al Emarat (IRE)**[10] 5412 2-9-2 0 ... MartinHarley 2 (David Simcock) *chsd ldng pair: effrt and c centre wl over 1f out: hdwy and chsd wnr ent fnl f: styd on and grad clsng fnl 100yds: nvr quite getting to wnr* **9/4**[2] | 84+ |
| 01 | 3 | 7 | **Beringer**[24] 4909 2-9-1 0 ... FinleyMarsh(7) 6 (Alan King) *pressed ldr: rdn ent fnl 2f out: unable qck over 1f out: 3rd and btn 1f out: wknd ins fnl f* **4/1**[3] | 74 |
| 5 | 4 | 4 | **Mail Order**[14] 5246 2-8-11 0 ... JimCrowley 4 (Mark Johnston) *a in 4th: rdn and struggling 3f out: sn outpcd and wl btn 2f out* **10/1** | 54 |
| | 5 | 8 | **Ashington** 2-9-2 0 ... JamieSpencer 3 (Luca Cumani) *s.i.s: hld up in last pair: outpcd and pushed along over 2f out: sn wl btn* **8/1** | 40 |
| 04 | 6 | 23 | **Molly Mayhem (IRE)**[16] 5180 2-8-11 0 ... PatrickMathers 5 (Richard Fahey) *a last pair: rdn and hung rt 3f out: sn lost tch: t.o* **40/1** | |

1m 38.81s (-1.09) **Going Correction** -0.175s/f (Stan) — 6 Ran SP% **113.4**
Speed ratings (Par 96): **98,97,90,86,78 55**
CSF £5.23 TOTE £2.50: £1.50, £1.30; EX 5.90 Trifecta £10.20.
**Owner** Nick Bradley Racing 43 & Partner **Bred** Lady Juliet Tadgell **Trained** Newmarket, Suffolk

**FOCUS**
An interesting juvenile novice which only concerned the first three from halfway, and the first two are progressing.

## 5744 TOTEQUADPOT H'CAP — 1m (P)
6:50 (6:53) (Class 3) (0-95,95) 3-Y-O+ £16,172 (£4,812; £2,405; £1,202) Stalls Low

| Form | | | | RPR |
|---|---|---|---|---|
| 0-5 | 1 | | **Qassem (IRE)**[83] 2735 4-9-12 93 ... JamesDoyle 9 (Hugo Palmer) *chsd ldr: pushed rt over 4f out: rdn to chal over 1f out: led jst ins fnl f: r.o wl and in command fnl 100yds* **9/1** | 105 |
| 321 | 2 | 1 1/2 | **Mutarabby (IRE)**[32] 4563 3-9-6 94 ... JimCrowley 5 (Saeed bin Suroor) *dwlt: rcvrd and in wl in tch in midfield after 3f: effrt over 1f out: styd on ins fnl f: snatched 2nd last stride: nvr threatening wnr* **9/4**[1] | 102+ |
| 511 | 3 | shd | **La Rav (IRE)**[26] 4807 3-9-5 93 ... JamieSpencer 2 (Luca Cumani) *t.k.h: hld up in midfield: nt clr run and shuffled bk over 2f out: swtchd rt and hdwy over 1f out: styd on u.p to go 2nd towards fin: nvr getting to wnr and lost 2nd last stride* **9/2**[3] | 100 |
| 5112 | 4 | 3/4 | **Mukalal**[32] 4563 3-9-5 93 ... DaneO'Neill 8 (Marcus Tregoning) *led and set stdy gallop: ducked rt over 4f out: rdn wl over 1f out: hdd jst ins fnl f: no ex and outpcd fnl 100yds: lost 2 pls towards fin* **7/1** | 99 |
| 0100 | 5 | 3/4 | **Secret Art (IRE)**[17] 5157 7-9-11 92 ... MartinDwyer 11 (William Knight) *dwlt and rdn along in rr early: c wd and effrt wl over 1f out: hdwy u.p 1f out: styd on wl ins fnl f: nvr trbld ldrs* **50/1** | 97+ |
| 14 | 6 | 1 1/4 | **Casimiro (IRE)**[59] 3578 3-8-13 87 ... KieranShoemark 6 (Roger Charlton) *hld up in tch towards rr: effrt and swtchd rt over 1f out: hdwy 1f out: styd on wl fnl 100yds: nvr trbld ldrs* **10/1** | 88 |
| -100 | 7 | 3/4 | **Flashy Snapper**[83] 2739 3-8-10 87 ... EdwardGreatrex(3) 13 (Simon Crisford) *stdd s: t.k.h: hld up in tch in rr: effrt over 1f out: hdwy 1f out: styd on ins fnl f: nvr trbld ldrs* **50/1** | 86 |
| 6000 | 8 | 1 | **Tumbaga (USA)**[24] 4918 6-10-0 95 ...(h1) SilvestreDeSousa 1 (Saeed bin Suroor) *chsd ldrs: effrt over 1f out: unable qck u.p: btn 1f out: eased wl ins fnl f* **7/2**[2] | 93 |
| 440 | 9 | 1/2 | **Pactolus (IRE)**[31] 4636 6-9-11 95 ...(t) AaronJones(3) 12 (Stuart Williams) *hld up in tch towards rr: effrt on inner over 1f out: kpt on ins fnl f: nvr trbld ldrs* **25/1** | 92 |
| 0560 | 10 | 3/4 | **Gambit**[29] 4699 4-9-4 85 ... MartinHarley 3 (Tom Dascombe) *chsd ldrs: unable qck u.p over 1f out: wknd ins fnl f* **33/1** | 80 |
| 530 | 11 | shd | **Firmdecisions (IRE)**[53] 3792 7-9-7 91 ... JackDuern(3) 7 (Dean Ivory) *hld up in tch in midfield but stuck wd: rdn and unable qck over 1f out: wknd ins fnl f* **33/1** | 86 |
| 0065 | 12 | 2 1/4 | **Thomas Cranmer (USA)**[13] 5302 3-9-1 89 ... WilliamBuick 4 (Mark Johnston) *in tch in midfield: effrt over 2f out: unable qck over 1f out: wknd fnl f* **33/1** | 78 |
| 1-6 | 13 | 10 | **Kharbetation (IRE)**[11] 5382 4-9-12 93 ... DanielTudhope 10 (David O'Meara) *chsd ldrs: pushed rt over 4f out: lost pl and bhd over 1f out: sn wknd* **16/1** | 60 |

1m 38.04s (-1.86) **Going Correction** -0.175s/f (Stan)
**WFA** 3 from 4yo+ 7lb — 13 Ran SP% **125.2**
Speed ratings (Par 107): **102,100,100,99,98 97,96,95,95,94 94,92,82**
CSF £29.52 CT £113.16 TOTE £10.20: £2.40, £1.60, £2.20; EX 44.50 Trifecta £270.80.
**Owner** Al Shaqab Racing **Bred** S F Bloodstock LLC **Trained** Newmarket, Suffolk

**FOCUS**
One of the feature races and the decent prize money attracted a strong field, although weakened a little by the withdrawal of the three highest drawn runners. The time was 0.77secs faster than the preceding juvenile contest over the trip.

## 5745 TOTETRIFECTA FILLIES' H'CAP — 1m 2f (P)
7:20 (7:24) (Class 3) (0-90,89) 3-Y-O+ £16,172 (£4,812; £2,405; £1,202) Stalls Low

| Form | | | | RPR |
|---|---|---|---|---|
| -543 | 1 | | **Blushing Rose**[22] 4975 3-8-9 78 ... RyanMoore 2 (Sir Michael Stoute) *hld up in wl in tch in midfield: effrt to chse ldrs and nt clr run jst over 1f out: swtchd lft 1f out: styd on and str chal on inner 100yds out: r.o wl to ld towards fin* **11/4**[2] | 87 |
| 3164 | 2 | nk | **Vogueatti (USA)**[66] 3341 4-9-2 77 ... HarryBentley 1 (Marco Botti) *chsd ldr for 2f: styd trcking ldrs: effrt over 1f out: pressing wnr 1f out: drvn to ld ins fnl f: kpt on: hdd and no ex towards fin* **9/1** | 84 |
| -535 | 3 | 1 3/4 | **Blind Faith (IRE)**[31] 4621 4-9-4 79 ... JamieSpencer 5 (Luca Cumani) *stdd and squeezed for room leaving stalls: t.k.h: hld up in last trio: effrt over 1f out: styd on wl u.p ins fnl f: wnt 3rd last strides* **9/2**[3] | 83 |
| 1606 | 4 | hd | **Prosper**[24] 4915 3-9-2 85 ...(v1) SilvestreDeSousa 4 (Roger Varian) *hdwy to ld after 2f: t.k.h and set stdy gallop: rdn and fnd ex over 1f out: drvn and hdd ins fnl f: outpcd fnl 100yds: lost 3rd last strides* **5/1** | 89 |



The Form Book Flat, Raceform Ltd, Newbury, RG14 5SJ

4261 **5** ½ **Glittering Jewel (USA)**28 4729 3-9-5 **88** WilliamBuick 6 91
(Charlie Appleby) *led for 2f: styd pressing ldr: rdn and unable qck over 1f out: wknd ins fnl f* **5/2**1

123- **6** ½ **Mia Tesoro (IRE)**276 7816 4-9-4 **79** (h) StevieDonohoe 7 80
(Charlie Fellowes) *taken down early: t.k.h: hld up in tch in last trio: effrt and swtchd rt over 1f out: styd on ins fnl f: nt rch ldrs* **25/1**

0433 **7** 4½ **Sagely (IRE)**24 4915 4-9-11 **89** LewisEdmunds(3) 8 81
(Ed Dunlop) *chsd ldrs: effrt and clsd over 1f out: nt clrest of runs jst over 1f out: rdn 1f out: unable qck: wknd ins fnl f* **10/1**

4400 **8** 10 **Auntie Barber (IRE)**18 5113 4-9-0 **75** (t1) OisinMurphy 9 47
(Stuart Williams) *stdd and dropped in bhd sn after s: hld up in rr: pushed along over 1f out: sn wknd* **50/1**

5013 **9** 10 **Heartstone (IRE)**4 5591 4-8-11 **72** JFEgan 3 24
(David Evans) *awkward leaving stalls: hld up in tch in midfield: effrt over 1f out: sn btn and eased ins fnl f* **20/1**

2m 4.99s (-3.61) **Going Correction** -0.175s/f (Stan)
**WFA** 3 from 4yo 8lb 9 Ran SP% **119.7**
Speed ratings (Par 104): **107,106,105,105,104 104,100,92,84**
CSF £28.16 CT £111.19 TOTE £3.50: £1.30, £2.30, £2.10; EX 27.70 Trifecta £107.40.
**Owner** Sir Evelyn De Rothschild **Bred** Southcourt Stud **Trained** Newmarket, Suffolk

**FOCUS**
The other feature contest and a good fillies' handicap that had attracted runners from a number of major Newmarket stables. It produced a close finish. The winner built on earlier promise, rated around the 2nd/3rd/4th.

## 5746 TOTEPOOL FOLLOW US ON TWITTER MAIDEN STKS 1m 2f (P)
**7:50** (7:52) (Class 4) 3-Y-O+ **£8,086** (£2,406; £1,202; £601) **Stalls** Low

Form RPR
5-23 **1** **Karawaan (IRE)**88 2576 3-9-5 84 (t1) JimCrowley 2 85+
(Sir Michael Stoute) *mde all: rdn wl over 1f out: styd on and drew clr ins fnl f: comf* **8/11**1

**2** 4 **Military Parade** 3-9-5 0 JosephineGordon 1 78+
(Saeed bin Suroor) *sn chsng ldrs: pushed along at times: effrt on inner to chsd wnr over 1f out: no imp and eased wl ins fnl f* **7/4**2

3 **3** 4½ **Perfect Spy**46 4052 3-9-0 0 JamieSpencer 6 63+
(Luca Cumani) *chsd ldr: rdn ent fnl 2f: 3rd and btn 1f out: wknd ins fnl f* **6/1**3

**4** 2¾ **Grantchester (IRE)** 3-9-5 0 RyanTate 5 63
(James Eustace) *stdd s: hld up in rr: pushed along and hdwy on inner over 1f out: wnt 4th 1f out: kpt on but no threat to ldrs* **25/1**

60 **5** 1 **Royal Hall (FR)**10 5428 5-9-10 0 (p) HectorCrouch(3) 4 60
(Gary Moore) *hld up in tch in last trio: pushed along over 2f out: outpcd by ldrs and battling for 4th ent fnl f: plugged on same pce after* **33/1**

00 **6** 2 **The Iron Factor (USA)**11 5364 3-9-5 0 (t) DannyBrock 7 57
(Phil McEntee) *chsd ldng trio: effrt over 2f out: outpcd by ldrs and battling for modest 4th over 1f out: wknd ins fnl f* **100/1**

00 **7** nse **Alternate Route**14 5243 3-9-2 0 RosieJessop(3) 8 56
(Sir Mark Prescott Bt) *s.i.s: hld up in tch on outer: effrt in 4th 2f out: outpcd over 1f out: wknd ins fnl f* **66/1**

**8** 1½ **Kingdomforakitten (USA)** 3-9-5 0 StevieDonohoe 3 53
(David Lanigan) *dwlt: hld up in tch: effrt ent fnl 2f: outpcd by ldrs over 1f out and battling for 4th 1f out: wknd ins fnl f* **10/1**

2m 8.97s (0.37) **Going Correction** -0.175s/f (Stan)
**WFA** 3 from 5yo 8lb 8 Ran SP% **126.9**
Speed ratings (Par 105): **91,87,84,82,81 79,79,78**
CSF £2.60 TOTE £1.50: £1.10, £1.10, £1.60; EX 2.90 Trifecta £6.40.
**Owner** Hamdan Al Maktoum **Bred** D Phelan **Trained** Newmarket, Suffolk

**FOCUS**
Apart from the favourite, those with experience looked decidedly limited in this maiden and the betting suggested it was a match. The time was 3.98 secs slower than the preceding handicap after the early pace was very steady, so muddling form.

## 5747 TOTEPOOL LIKE US ON FACEBOOK H'CAP 1m 2f (P)
**8:20** (8:21) (Class 5) (0-75,77) 4-Y-O+ **£5,175** (£1,540; £769; £384) **Stalls** Low

Form RPR
1-03 **1** **Graceful James (IRE)**27 4751 4-9-7 **75** KieranO'Neill 4 85
(Jimmy Fox) *hld up in tch in midfield: effrt on inner over 1f out: rdn to ld 1f out: edgd rt but drew clr ins fnl f: r.o wl: comf* **5/1**3

5032 **2** 3 **Zorba The Greek**20 5024 5-9-2 **70** (p1) HarryBentley 5 74
(Ed Vaughan) *t.k.h: trckd ldrs: effrt and drvn over 1f out: outpcd by wnr and battling for 2nd ins fnl f: kpt on and wnt 2nd cl home* **11/4**1

051 **3** hd **Priors Brook**43 4147 6-9-4 **77** JoshuaBryan(5) 3 81
(Andrew Balding) *trckd ldrs: gap opened and effrt to chal over 1f out: outpcd by wnr and battling for 2nd ins fnl f: kpt on* **5/1**3

1-14 **4** 3½ **Estrella Eria (FR)**74 3036 4-9-3 **71** (h) AndrewMullen 1 68
(George Peckham) *t.k.h: led: rdn ent fnl 2f: hdd and no ex 1f out: wknd ins fnl f* **3/1**2

2-26 **5** 3¾ **San Quentin (IRE)**20 3817 6-9-5 **73** (b) StevieDonohoe 2 62
(Dr Richard Newland) *s.i.s: nvr travelling wl in rr: drvn 3f out: no ch after: swtchd rt over 1f out: plugged on ins fnl f* **12/1**

5533 **6** 2 **Foie Gras**48 3966 7-9-0 **68** SilvestreDeSousa 8 53
(Chris Dwyer) *stdd and dropped in bhd after s: hld up in tch: c wd and effrt over 1f out: sn btn: bhd and eased wl ins fnl f* **11/1**

5400 **7** ½ **Cape Banjo (USA)**24 4893 4-9-2 **75** PatrickO'Donnell(5) 7 59
(Ralph Beckett) *t.k.h: sn w ldr: rdn ent fnl 2f: lost pl and btn over 1f out: wknd ins fnl f* **6/1**

2m 5.66s (-2.94) **Going Correction** -0.175s/f (Stan) 7 Ran SP% **115.3**
Speed ratings (Par 103): **104,101,101,98,95 94,93**
CSF £19.49 CT £72.07 TOTE £6.60: £2.60, £2.00; EX 22.70 Trifecta £89.80.
**Owner** Abacus Employment Services Ltd **Bred** D Fuller **Trained** Collingbourne Ducis, Wilts

**FOCUS**
This older horse handicap was run 0.67 secs slower than the best of the two earlier races over the trip and proved less competitive than looked likely, but still another step forward from the winner.

## 5748 BOYZONE PLAYING HERE ON 2ND SEPTEMBER H'CAP 6f (P)
**8:50** (8:51) (Class 6) (0-65,67) 3-Y-O+ **£3,234** (£962; £481; £240) **Stalls** Centre

Form RPR
5004 **1** **Firesnake (IRE)**13 5282 4-8-8 **52** (v) CallumRodriguez(5) 4 64
(Lisa Williamson) *t.k.h: hld up in tch in midfield: clsd to chse ldrs and nt clr run ent fnl f: swtchd rt 1f out: drvn to chal ins fnl f: led wl ins fnl f: r.o wl* **8/1**

1045 **2** ¾ **See You Mush**36 4447 3-9-0 **57** (b) AdamBeschizza 3 65
(Mrs Ilka Gansera-Leveque) *trckd ldrs on inner: drvn over 1f out: chalng ent fnl f: hrd drvn to ld ins fnl f: hdd and styd on same pce wl ins fnl f* **9/4**1

-621 **3** ¾ **Wild Flower (IRE)**28 4710 5-9-0 **53** KieranO'Neill 12 60
(Jimmy Fox) *led: rdn over 1f out: hdd ins fnl f: styd on same pce fnl 100yds* **7/1**3

2544 **4** 4½ **Entertaining Ben**38 4352 4-9-4 **64** FinleyMarsh(7) 8 57
(Amy Murphy) *chsd ldrs: rdn over 1f out: unable qck 1f out: wknd ins fnl f* **10/1**

6600 **5** nk **Classic Flyer**3 5657 5-8-13 **52** (b) StevieDonohoe 1 44
(Christine Dunnett) *in tch in rr: effrt over 1f out: styd on u.p ins fnl f: nvr trbld ldrs* **25/1**

000 **6** hd **Singing Sands (IRE)**13 5275 3-9-7 **64** (p1) ShaneKelly 2 54
(Seamus Durack) *t.k.h: short of room on inner sn after s: sn trcking ldrs: effrt over 1f out: unable qck and wknd ins fnl f* **9/1**

6303 **7** 2¼ **Billyoakes (IRE)**13 5297 5-9-6 **64** (p) JoshuaBryan(5) 13 48
(Charlie Wallis) *chsd ldrs on outer: effrt ent fnl 2f: unable qck and lost pl over 1f out: wknd ins fnl f* **12/1**

6604 **8** nk **Ashwaq**11 5358 3-9-7 **67** (b) HollieDoyle(3) 6 49
(Richard Hannon) *squeezed for room and dropped to rr leaving stalls: sn rcvrd and t.k.h in midfield: effrt over 2f out: sn struggling: bhd over 1f out* **7/2**2

003 **9** ½ **Higgy's Heartbeat**83 2727 3-8-12 **58** JackDuern(3) 5 38
(Dean Ivory) *squeezed out and dropped to rr leaving stalls: in tch in rr: effrt over 1f out: no hdwy and wknd ins fnl f* **8/1**

1m 12.23s (-1.47) **Going Correction** -0.175s/f (Stan)
**WFA** 3 from 4yo+ 4lb 9 Ran SP% **118.3**
Speed ratings (Par 101): **102,101,100,94,93 93,90,89,89**
CSF £27.06 CT £137.79 TOTE £9.80: £2.30, £1.50, £2.10; EX 30.70 Trifecta £269.80.
**Owner** Pritchard & Woodward **Bred** Confey Stud **Trained** Saighton, Cheshire

**FOCUS**
The field for this low-grade sprint handicap was reduced by almost a third following withdrawals. The winner has been rated back to his C&D maiden success.
T/Plt: £17.30 to a £1 stake. Pool: £70,695.41 - 2,970.63 winning units T/Qpdt: £6.10 to a £1 stake. Pool: £6,961.49 - 842.77 winning units **Steve Payne**

# 5531 LEICESTER (R-H)
Tuesday, August 8

**OFFICIAL GOING: Soft (8.2)**
Wind: Light against Weather: Raining

## 5749 GLEBE NOVICE AUCTION STKS 7f
**2:00** (2:01) (Class 5) 2-Y-O **£3,881** (£1,155; £577; £288) **Stalls** High

Form RPR
**1** **Trumps Up** 2-8-10 0 JFEgan 3 65
(Mick Channon) *dwlt: hdwy over 5f out: shkn up to ld over 1f out: sn rdn and hung lft: styd on* **14/1**

0 **2** ¾ **Neverbeen To Paris (IRE)**48 3965 2-9-1 0 LouisSteward 2 68
(Michael Bell) *s.i.s: hld up: hdwy over 1f out: sn chsng wnr: styd on* **9/2**3

0 **3** shd **Tulane (IRE)**19 5047 2-9-1 0 TimmyMurphy 4 67
(Richard Phillips) *a.p: pushed along over 2f out: styd on* **50/1**

**4** 1¼ **Follow The Feeling (USA)** 2-8-3 0 DavidEgan(5) 10 57+
(Henry Spiller) *s.i.s: hld up: nt clr run over 2f out: r.o ins fnl f: nt rch ldrs* **14/1**

**5** 1 **Affluence (IRE)** 2-8-8 0 NoelGarbutt(3) 6 57
(Martin Smith) *s.i.s: hld up: r.o ins fnl f: nt trble ldrs* **33/1**

**6** 1 **Dashing Dusty (IRE)** 2-9-1 0 DougieCostello 1 59
(Jamie Osborne) *led to 1/2-way: rdn and ev ch over 1f out: wknd wl ins fnl f* **10/1**

5 **7** hd **Surfa Rosa**19 5048 2-9-1 0 TomMarquand 9 58
(Richard Hannon) *plld hrd: trckd ldr 2f: remained handy: rdn over 2f out: no ex fnl f* **4/1**2

522 **8** 1 **Iconic Sunset**31 4597 2-9-1 75 MartinHarley 8 56
(James Tate) *prom: chsd ldr 5f out: led 1/2-way: rdn and hdd over 1f out: wknd ins fnl f* **1/1**1

60 **9** 14 **Uncovered**13 5292 2-8-12 0 RichardKingscote 7 16
(Tom Dascombe) *s.i.s: hdwy 1/2-way: wknd 2f out* **25/1**

1m 31.38s (5.18) **Going Correction** +0.475s/f (Yiel) 9 Ran SP% **119.4**
Speed ratings (Par 94): **89,88,88,86,85 84,84,82,66**
CSF £77.24 TOTE £13.10: £3.40, £1.80, £12.50; EX 93.80 Trifecta £998.20.
**Owner** David Fitzgerald **Bred** Al Asayl Bloodstock Ltd **Trained** West Ilsley, Berks
■ Stewards' Enquiry : Dougie Costello one-day ban; no keeping straight from stalls (22ns Aug)

**FOCUS**
At least 23mm of rain overnight and on the day and little doubt the ground was testing. Bit of a turn up in this opening novice, with the favourite disappointing. The raced stands' side.

## 5750 CHARLES STREET H'CAP 6f
**2:30** (2:33) (Class 5) (0-70,71) 3-Y-O+ **£3,881** (£1,155; £577; £288) **Stalls** High

Form RPR
2060 **1** **Geoff Potts (IRE)**38 4379 4-9-8 **65** PaulHanagan 6 76
(Richard Fahey) *plld hrd: w ldrs: shkn up to ld over 1f out: rdn out* **5/2**1

60-0 **2** 1¼ **Operative**26 4810 4-9-11 **68** AdamKirby 5 75
(Ed de Giles) *hld up in tch: ev ch fr over 1f out: sn rdn: no ex wl ins fnl f* **9/2**2

2021 **3** 2¼ **Ambitious Icarus**10 5418 8-9-4 **61** (p1) LiamKeniry 7 61
(Richard Guest) *s.i.s: hld up: racd keenly: rdn over 1f out: styd on to go 3rd post: nt rch ldrs* **12/1**

045 **4** nse **Baron Run**13 5285 7-8-12 **55** JoeyHaynes 8 55
(K R Burke) *w ldrs: led 1/2-way: rdn and hdd over 1f out: styd on same pce ins fnl f* **5/1**3

3150 **5** 1 **East Coast Lady (IRE)**13 5295 5-9-9 **69** HollieDoyle(3) 12 65
(William Stone) *racd towards stands' side: up w the pce: hung rt 1/2-way: rdn 2f out: styd on same pce fnl f* **8/1**

4130 **6** 1 **Soaring Spirits (IRE)**20 5039 7-9-12 **69** (p) MartinHarley 13 62
(Dean Ivory) *racd towards stands' side: up w the pce tl lost grnd over 4f out: n.d after* **6/1**

0-40 **7** ¾ **Mallymkun**15 5205 5-8-12 **55** JosephineGordon 1 46
(David Loughnane) *prom: rdn and ev ch over 1f out: wknd wl ins fnl f* **8/1**

-200 **8** 2¼ **Harrison Stickle**40 4256 5-9-5 **62** FergusSweeney 2 46
(John Gallagher) *led to 1/2-way: rdn over 1f out: wknd ins fnl f* **8/1**

1m 15.16s (2.16) **Going Correction** +0.475s/f (Yiel)
**WFA** 3 from 4yo+ 4lb 8 Ran SP% **118.7**
Speed ratings (Par 103): **104,102,99,99,97 96,95,92**
CSF £14.42 CT £115.16 TOTE £3.60: £1.60, £1.50, £2.50; EX 15.70 Trifecta £90.30.
**Owner** Jamie Hart **Bred** Hyde Park Stud **Trained** Musley Bank, N Yorks

**FOCUS**
They raced centre-field in this moderate handicap. The winner has been rated close to his AW form.

## 5751 IRISH STALLION FARMS EBF FILLIES' NURSERY H'CAP — 6f
3:00 (3:02) (Class 4) (0-80,77) 2-Y-O — £6,469 (£1,925; £962; £481) Stalls High

Form — RPR

2561 **1** — **She Believes (IRE)**[19] 5048 2-9-4 74 — LiamKeniry 4 — 81
(Sylvester Kirk) *chsd ldr: led over 1f out: sn rdn and hung lft: styd on wl* — 4/1[3]

0661 **2** 1 ½ **Song Of Summer**[19] 5057 2-8-11 67 — JimmyQuinn 2 — 69
(Archie Watson) *hld up: hdwy over 1f out: rdn to chse wnr ins fnl f: no imp towards fin* — 7/2[2]

221U **3** 1 ¾ **Mraseel (IRE)**[27] 4739 2-9-7 77 — (p) MartinHarley 6 — 74
(James Tate) *unruly in stalls: chsd ldrs: rdn over 1f out: styd on same pce ins fnl f* — 5/1

2364 **4** nk **Auntie Pam (IRE)**[2] 5685 2-8-13 69 — (p) RichardKingscote 8 — 65
(Tom Dascombe) *led: rdn and hdd over 1f out: hmpd sn after: no ex ins fnl f* — 8/1

1216 **5** 3 ½ **Queen Of Kalahari**[25] 4827 2-9-0 73 — CallumShepherd(3) 5 — 58
(Charles Hills) *hld up: hdwy 1/2-way: rdn over 1f out: wknd fnl f* — 9/2

635 **6** 1 ½ **Peace Prevails**[39] 4296 2-8-10 66 — PaulHanagan 1 — 47
(Richard Fahey) *edgd rt s: chsd ldrs: hung rt almost thrght: rdn over 2f out: wknd over 1f out* — 3/1[1]

1m 15.45s (2.45) **Going Correction** +0.475s/f (Yiel) — **6** Ran SP% **113.2**
Speed ratings (Par 93): **102,100,97,97,92 90**
CSF £18.50 CT £69.67 TOTE £4.10: £2.10, £1.80; EX 18.10 Trifecta £101.30.
**Owner** Marchwood Recycling Ltd **Bred** Ringfort Stud **Trained** Upper Lambourn, Berks

**FOCUS**
The two last-time-out winners came to the fore in what was a modest nursery. They again raced down the centre.

## 5752 GALLOWGATE NURSERY H'CAP — 7f
3:30 (3:31) (Class 5) (0-70,70) 2-Y-O — £3,234 (£962; £481; £240) Stalls High

Form — RPR

053 **1** — **Shovel It On (IRE)**[13] 5277 2-8-10 59 — PJMcDonald 2 — 71
(David Evans) *chsd ldrs tl led over 1f out: rdn clr fnl f* — 5/1[3]

000 **2** 5 **Milan Reef (IRE)**[19] 5056 2-8-4 53 — JosephineGordon 9 — 52
(David Loughnane) *prom: rdn over 2f out: sn outpcd: rallied over 1f out: styd on to go 2nd wl ins fnl f* — 16/1

554 **3** 2 **Northern Law (IRE)**[25] 4848 2-9-2 70 — DavidEgan(5) 8 — 64
(John Quinn) *s.i.s and hmpd s: hdwy 5f out: rdn over 2f out: styd on same pce fr over 1f out* — 3/1[1]

4050 **4** ½ **Situation**[11] 5366 2-8-12 66 — KevinLundie(5) 4 — 59
(Richard Guest) *led: rdn and hdd over 1f out: hung rt and wknd ins fnl f* — 20/1

044 **5** 2 **Move To The Front (IRE)**[57] 3655 2-9-6 69 — (b) AdamKirby 7 — 56
(Clive Cox) *racd keenly in 2nd pl: ev ch over 2f out: sn rdn: wknd fnl f* — 5/1[3]

055 **6** 1 ¼ **Gabrial The Devil (IRE)**[22] 4956 2-9-5 68 — DanielTudhope 1 — 52
(David O'Meara) *hld up: plld hrd: hdwy over 2f out: rdn and wknd over 1f out* — 4/1[2]

004 **7** nk **Dark Blue (IRE)**[17] 5144 2-8-8 57 — JFEgan 5 — 40
(Mick Channon) *s.i.s: sn pushed along in rr: lost tch fnl 2f* — 6/1

000 **8** 1 **Progressive Jazz (IRE)**[31] 4597 2-8-5 54 — JoeyHaynes 6 — 35
(K R Burke) *prom: racd keenly: pushed along and lost pl 5f out: rdn over 2f out: sn wknd* — 33/1

403 **9** 2 ½ **Jo's Girl (IRE)**[28] 4709 2-9-7 70 — DougieCostello 3 — 44
(Jamie Osborne) *hld up: rdn over 2f out: wknd wl over 1f out* — 7/1

1m 28.96s (2.76) **Going Correction** +0.475s/f (Yiel) — **9** Ran SP% **118.7**
Speed ratings (Par 94): **103,97,95,94,92 90,90,89,86**
CSF £82.42 CT £284.70 TOTE £6.10: £2.30, £4.80, £1.50; EX 85.20 Trifecta £363.80.
**Owner** Power Geneva & Bruce Williams **Bred** Dylan Finucane **Trained** Pandy, Monmouths

**FOCUS**
Moderate nursery form, they raced centre-field and the winner won with loads in hand.

## 5753 NELSON H'CAP — 1m 3f 179y
4:00 (4:00) (Class 5) (0-70,72) 3-Y-O — £3,881 (£1,155; £577; £288) Stalls Low

Form — RPR

-334 **1** — **Bolder Bob (IRE)**[31] 4623 3-9-6 69 — FranBerry 1 — 86+
(David Barron) *trckd ldrs: led over 3f out: rdn clr fr over 1f out* — 5/1[3]

000- **2** 3 ¼ **Just In Time**[265] 7976 3-8-11 60 — FergusSweeney 6 — 71
(Alan King) *hld up: pushed along over 6f out: hdwy over 2f out: rdn to go 2nd over 1f out: styd on: no ch w wnr* — 10/1

1-24 **3** 7 **Crushed (IRE)**[29] 4691 3-9-7 70 — PaulHanagan 5 — 72
(William Haggas) *hld up in tch: chsd wnr over 2f out tl rdn over 1f out: wknd fnl f* — 2/1[1]

422 **4** 2 ¼ **Count Simon (IRE)**[18] 5128 3-9-2 72 — JasonWatson(7) 2 — 68
(Andrew Balding) *s.i.s: hld up: hdwy 4f out: rdn over 2f out: wknd over 1f out* — 9/2[2]

0633 **5** ½ **Challow (IRE)**[19] 5053 3-9-3 66 — LiamKeniry 7 — 61
(Sylvester Kirk) *led early: chsd ldr tl led 8f out: rdn and hdd over 3f out: wknd over 1f out* — 16/1

4433 **6** 75 **Second Page**[39] 4307 3-9-6 69 — TomMarquand 4
(Richard Hannon) *hld up: pushed along over 8f out: wknd over 3f out: eased* — 6/1

0250 **7** 17 **Powerful Love (IRE)**[22] 4959 3-9-4 67 — (b) PJMcDonald 8
(Mark Johnston) *s.i.s: sn prom: rdn over 4f out: wknd over 3f out: eased* — 14/1

4030 **8** 47 **Legato (IRE)**[31] 4623 3-9-1 64 — (p[1]) RichardKingscote 3
(Tom Dascombe) *sn led: hdd 8f out: chsd ldr tl rdn over 3f out: wknd and eased over 2f out* — 8/1

2m 40.32s (6.42) **Going Correction** +0.55s/f (Yiel) — **8** Ran SP% **115.2**
Speed ratings (Par 100): **100,97,93,91,91 41,30,**
CSF £53.45 CT £131.45 TOTE £6.80: £2.20, £2.80, £1.10; EX 37.50 Trifecta £294.70.
**Owner** S Chappell **Bred** Gerry And John Rowley **Trained** Maunby, N Yorks

**FOCUS**
No great gallop on early, but still a good test in the conditions. The front pair finished clear, with the winner building on earlier promise.

## 5754 ILLSTON-ON-THE-HILL H'CAP — 7f
4:30 (4:30) (Class 4) (0-80,80) 3-Y-O+ — £5,175 (£1,540; £769; £384) Stalls High

Form — RPR

4321 **1** — **Peach Melba**[11] 5358 3-9-2 76 — PJMcDonald 4 — 86
(Mark Johnston) *chsd ldr: rdn to ld wl ins fnl f: styd on wl* — 13/8[1]

6431 **2** 2 ½ **Childesplay**[12] 5326 6-9-6 79 — DavidEgan(5) 3 — 84
(Heather Main) *chsd ldrs: pushed along 1/2-way: rdn to ld over 1f out: hdd and no ex wl ins fnl f* — 9/4[2]

1002 **3** 3 ½ **Bahamian Bird**[19] 5078 4-9-10 78 — PaulHanagan 6 — 74
(Richard Fahey) *hld up: racd keenly: rdn over 1f out: no ex ins fnl f* — 4/1[3]

3124 **4** nk **Traveller (FR)**[26] 4807 3-9-4 78 — (t) DavidProbert 8 — 71
(Charles Hills) *hld up: rdn over 2f out: styd on same pce fr over 1f out* — 6/1

120 **5** 1 ¾ **Vroom (IRE)**[62] 3471 4-9-4 79 — (p) CameronNoble(7) 1 — 70
(Gay Kelleway) *sn led: rdn and hdd over 1f out: wknd ins fnl f* — 14/1

1m 28.58s (2.38) **Going Correction** +0.475s/f (Yiel)
**WFA** 3 from 4yo+ 6lb — **5** Ran SP% **109.8**
Speed ratings (Par 105): **105,102,98,97,95**
CSF £5.52 TOTE £1.90: £1.50, £1.20; EX 5.70 Trifecta £13.90.
**Owner** Lowther Racing & Partner **Bred** Lowther Racing **Trained** Middleham Moor, N Yorks

**FOCUS**
Racing a few widths off the stands' rail, they went steady early but the favourite got nicely on top late and is on the up.
T/Plt: £268.60 to a £1 stake. Pool: £71,872.86 - 195.32 winning units T/Qpdt: £12.30 to a £1 stake. Pool: £6,853.68 - 411.62 winning units **Colin Roberts**

# 5575 NOTTINGHAM (L-H)
Tuesday, August 8

**OFFICIAL GOING: Heavy (soft in places) changed to heavy after race 5 (7.05)**
Wind: light breeze Weather: very overcast following several hours of rain; 14 degrees; rain again from race three

## 5755 32RED ONLINE NOVICE MEDIAN AUCTION STKS — 6f 18y
5:05 (5:09) (Class 5) 2-Y-O — £3,234 (£962; £481; £240) Stalls High

Form — RPR

**1** — **Book Of Dreams (IRE)** 2-9-2 0 — FrannyNorton 3 — 77+
(Mark Johnston) *pressed ldr on outside: chal and hung lft 2f out: drvn and hung rt over 1f out: hung bdly lft again ins fnl f: ev ch fnl 100yds: led nr fin* — 4/1[2]

**2** shd **Qianlong** 2-9-2 0 — PaulMulrennan 1 — 77
(Roger Varian) *pressed ldrs: rdn and outpcd 3f out: styd on wl fnl f: jst failed* — 11/4[1]

**3** shd **Speak In Colours** 2-9-2 0 — DanielMuscutt 4 — 77
(Marco Botti) *t.k.h pressing ldrs: rdn to ld over 1f out: kpt on but ct fnl strides* — 4/1[2]

0 **4** ½ **Powerful Society (IRE)**[18] 5127 2-8-11 0 — BarryMcHugh 2 — 70
(Richard Fahey) *midfield: rdn and outpcd 3f out: str run ins fnl f: too much to do* — 6/1

33 **5** 3 **Diamond Dougal (IRE)**[3] 5654 2-9-2 0 — CharlesBishop 11 — 66
(Mick Channon) *led: drvn and hdd over 1f out: no ex ins fnl f* — 5/1[3]

**6** 8 **Cavalry Regiment** 2-9-2 0 — MartinLane 9 — 42
(John Quinn) *dwlt: rn green in rr and hanging lft and wandering arnd: btn over 2f out* — 16/1

00 **7** 1 ¾ **Crazy World**[16] 5179 2-9-2 0 — TonyHamilton 5 — 37
(Declan Carroll) *t.k.h in midfield: rdn and outpcd over 2f out* — 50/1

00 **8** shd **Dark Freedom (IRE)**[11] 5365 2-9-2 0 — SteveDrowne 6 — 36
(Charles Hills) *midfield: rdn 4f out: sn labouring: t.o* — 16/1

**9** 6 **Oliver's Betty** 2-8-11 0 — AlistairRawlinson 7 — 13
(Michael Appleby) *wnt rt and s.s: v green and wandering in last pl: t.o fr 1/2-way* — 20/1

1m 20.38s (5.68) **Going Correction** +0.825s/f (Soft) — **9** Ran SP% **116.1**
Speed ratings (Par 94): **95,94,94,94,90 79,77,76,68**
CSF £15.52 TOTE £4.60: £1.60, £1.50, £1.60; EX 16.40 Trifecta £47.30.
**Owner** The Passionate Partnership **Bred** Mrs Mary Rose Hayes **Trained** Middleham Moor, N Yorks

**FOCUS**
15mm of rain fell on the run up to this meeting, prompting a going change to heavy, soft in places. Rail movements meant that 18yds were added to all races on the round course. A fair event in which the gallop was reasonable and the first four finished in a bit of a heap but this race should throw up winners.

## 5756 32RED.COM NURSERY H'CAP (JOCKEY CLUB GRASSROOTS NURSERY QUALIFIER) — 1m 75y
5:35 (5:36) (Class 5) (0-70,72) 2-Y-O — £3,234 (£962; £481; £240) Stalls Centre

Form — RPR

060 **1** — **Hemingford (IRE)**[25] 4860 2-9-1 63 — RobertTart 4 — 68
(Charlie Fellowes) *t.k.h in midfield: rdn over 3f out: chsd ldr over 1f out: looked hld ins fnl f tl lunged late to ld on line* — 6/1[3]

002 **2** shd **Mr Carbonator**[13] 5277 2-8-5 53 — JimmyQuinn 11 — 57
(Philip Kirby) *plld hrd and cl up on outside: effrt 3f out: rdn to ld 2f out: looked wnr wl ins fnl fulrong: pipped on post* — 14/1

004 **3** 5 **Sixties Secret**[17] 5161 2-8-3 51 — ShaneGray 6 — 44
(Mick Channon) *2nd tl led after 2f: rdn and hdd 2f out: btn over 1f out* — 14/1

005 **4** 2 **Tony Soprano (IRE)**[63] 3437 2-9-0 62 — TonyHamilton 10 — 51
(Martyn Meade) *midfield: effrt 3f out: rdn and no imp fr 1f out* — 5/1[2]

006 **5** 2 ¼ **Font Vert (FR)**[19] 5063 2-9-3 65 — PatDobbs 7 — 49
(Ralph Beckett) *chsd ldrs: rdn and fdd over 2f out* — 8/1

030 **6** 1 **Gemologist (IRE)**[17] 5154 2-9-10 72 — FrannyNorton 8 — 54
(Mark Johnston) *bhd early: plugged past btn horses but nvr on terms* — 12/1

030 **7** 5 **Bezos (IRE)**[10] 5430 2-9-3 65 — SeanLevey 3 — 36
(Richard Hannon) *led: hdd after 2f: ev ch tl rdn and fdd 2f out* — 6/1[3]

002 **8** 2 ½ **Grimeford Lane (IRE)**[22] 4956 2-9-7 69 — PaulMulrennan 9 — 35
(Michael Dods) *t.k.h: cl up tl rdn and dropped out over 3f out* — 7/2[1]

053 **9** 8 **Far Dawn**[17] 5144 2-9-1 63 — SteveDrowne 5 — 12
(Simon Crisford) *last away: a bhd* — 7/1

006 **10** 4 ½ **Mountain Meadow**[26] 4786 2-8-7 55 — BarryMcHugh 1
(Richard Fahey) *t.k.h on ins: chsd ldrs: hrd rdn and wknd over 3f out: fnl 2f* — 12/1

000 **11** 1 ¼ **Harbour Rose**[38] 4340 2-8-5 53 — PaddyAspell 2
(Philip Kirby) *sn bhd: struggling 4f out: t.o fnl 2f* — 40/1

1m 55.73s (6.73) **Going Correction** +0.70s/f (Yiel) — **11** Ran SP% **122.2**
Speed ratings (Par 94): **94,93,88,86,84 83,78,76,68,63 62**
CSF £90.36 CT £1164.33 TOTE £7.40: £2.20, £4.40, £4.00; EX 115.10 Trifecta £2308.60 Not won..
**Owner** Never So Bold **Bred** Irish National Stud **Trained** Newmarket, Suffolk

**FOCUS**
Rail movements added 18yds onto the official distance of this race. A fair nursery run at a reasonable gallop and the first two pulled clear in the closing stages.

## 5757 £10 FREE AT 32RED.COM MAIDEN STKS — 1m 2f 50y
**6:05** (6:06) (Class 5) 3-Y-O+ — **£3,234** (£962; £481; £240) **Stalls** Low

Form — RPR

-222 **1** **Mafaaheem (IRE)**[45] 4097 3-9-6 **88** ............ PaulMulrennan 3 — 92
(Owen Burrows) *pressed ldrs travelling wl: led wl over 2f out: 10 l clr and in complete command 1f out* **4/6**[1]

00 **2** *11* **Raining Stars**[15] 5220 3-9-6 0 ............ TomQueally 1 — 71
(James Fanshawe) *towards rr: drvn and effrt 3f out: wnt remote 2nd 1f out* **25/1**

0- **3** *1 ¾* **Zeelander**[279] 7770 3-9-6 0 ............ PatDobbs 8 — 68
(Roger Varian) *w ldr: led 5f out: rdn and hdd wl over 2f out: no ch w wnr after and lost remote 2nd ins fnl f* **9/4**[2]

50 **4** *12* **The Groove**[15] 5220 4-10-0 0 ............ TrevorWhelan 9 — 45
(Fergal O'Brien) *settled in rr: effrt 4f out: rdn and no ch w ldrs fnl 2f: eased and t.o* **50/1**

**5** *½* **Casemates Square (IRE)**[106] 2049 3-9-6 0 ............ SeanLevey 4 — 46
(Ian Williams) *taken down early: pushed along in last pl: nvr gng wl: t.o fnl 2f* **25/1**

**6** *¾* **Lazarus (IRE)** 3-9-6 0 ............(t[1]) DanielMuscutt 7 — 44
(Amy Murphy) *led at stdy pce tl hdd after 3f: lft in ld again 6f out: only once taken to r on far rails in st and sn hdd and lost all ch: t.o fnl 2f* **14/1**

35 **7** *2 ¾* **Amazing Grazing (IRE)**[31] 4611 3-9-6 0 ............ FrannyNorton 5 — 39
(Brian Ellison) *midfield: rdn and fdd 3f out: t.o fnl 2f* **14/1**

2 **P** **Sketch Book Venue (IRE)**[120] 1676 3-9-6 0 ............ MartinLane 2
(Sally Haynes) *plld v hrd: led after 3f tl wnt wrong and p.u appr home turn: fatally injured* **8/1**[3]

2m 23.03s (8.73) **Going Correction** +0.70s/f (Yiel)
**WFA** 3 from 4yo 8lb — **8 Ran SP% 124.9**
Speed ratings (Par 103): **93,84,82,73,72 72,70,**
CSF £29.07 TOTE £1.50: £1.02, £6.80, £1.10; EX 17.20 Trifecta £52.10.
**Owner** Hamdan Al Maktoum **Bred** Shadwell Estate Company Limited **Trained** Lambourn, Berks

**FOCUS**
Rail movements meant 18yds were added to the official distance. An uncompetitive event.

## 5758 32REDSPORT.COM FILLIES' H'CAP — 6f 18y
**6:35** (6:38) (Class 4) (0-85,85) 3-Y-O+ — **£5,175** (£1,540; £769; £384) **Stalls** High

Form — RPR

-460 **1** **Guishan**[18] 5117 7-9-12 **85** ............(p) AlistairRawlinson 5 — 99
(Michael Appleby) *taken down early: 2nd tl led 1/2-way: rdn clr over 1f out: eased fnl 100yds: unchal* **10/1**

-014 **2** *6* **Magical Dreamer (IRE)**[39] 4317 3-9-4 **81** ............ DanielMuscutt 3 — 76
(James Fanshawe) *racd freely in ld tl hdd 1/2-way: drvn and lost tch w wnr over 1f out* **9/2**

0051 **3** *1 ½* **Jule In The Crown**[12] 5325 3-9-8 **85** ............ SeanLevey 1 — 76
(Richard Hannon) *chsd ldng pair: rdn over 2f out: kpt on same pce in wl hld 3rd after* **2/1**[1]

2215 **4** *8* **Dealer's Choice (IRE)**[26] 4788 3-8-13 **76** ............(v[1]) AndreaAtzeni 4 — 43
(Roger Varian) *outpcd in 4th pl: sn rdn: wl bhd 1/2-way* **7/2**[3]

6121 **5** *27* **Curious Fox**[17] 5156 4-9-11 **84** ............ DavidProbert 2
(Anthony Carson) *a outpcd: wl bhd after 2f: t.o and eased over 1f out* **3/1**[2]

1m 18.82s (4.12) **Going Correction** +0.825s/f (Soft)
**WFA** 3 from 4yo+ 4lb — **5 Ran SP% 107.8**
Speed ratings (Par 102): **105,97,95,84,48**
CSF £47.65 TOTE £7.30: £4.90, £2.40; EX 42.80 Trifecta £108.10.
**Owner** Brian D Cantle **Bred** B D Cantle **Trained** Oakham, Rutland
■ Tilly Trotter was withdrawn. Price at time of withdrawal 14/1. Rule 4 applies to all bets - deduction 5p in the pound.

**FOCUS**
A useful event on paper and a wide-margin winner who has been rated back to her best. The pace was sound and the field finished well strung out.

## 5759 32RED H'CAP — 6f 18y
**7:05** (7:06) (Class 5) (0-75,77) 3-Y-O — **£3,234** (£962; £481; £240) **Stalls** High

Form — RPR

-050 **1** **Lexington Sky (IRE)**[3] 5635 3-9-7 **69** ............ TonyHamilton 6 — 77
(Roger Fell) *hld up last tl effrt on outer 2f out: sn rdn: led 1f out: steadily forged clr: comf* **8/1**

0036 **2** *2 ½* **Stringybark Creek**[4] 5620 3-8-9 **57** ............ FrannyNorton 2 — 58
(Mick Channon) *led narrowly: rdn and hdd 1f out: sn no ch w wnr* **9/2**[2]

2214 **3** *2 ½* **Sheepscar Lad (IRE)**[11] 5383 3-10-0 **76** ............ PaulMulrennan 4 — 69
(Nigel Tinkler) *plld hrd: trckd ldrs: rdn and effrt 2f out: fdd 1f out* **5/2**[1]

30-0 **4** *3 ¾* **Lanjano**[102] 2122 3-10-0 **76** ............ KevinStott 1 — 58
(Kevin Ryan) *w ldr tl rdn and fdd 2f out* **5/2**[1]

1650 **5** *1 ½* **Savannah's Dream**[11] 5383 3-10-1 **77** ............(p[1]) AndreaAtzeni 5 — 54
(David O'Meara) *a towards rr: rdn and struggling 2f out* **7/1**

6301 **6** *shd* **Alfonso Manana (IRE)**[43] 4161 3-9-5 **67** ............(b) TomQueally 3 — 44
(James Given) *dwlt: sn rcvrd to press ldrs: rdn and wknd 2f out* **6/1**[3]

1m 20.74s (6.04) **Going Correction** +0.825s/f (Soft) — **6 Ran SP% 113.2**
Speed ratings (Par 100): **92,88,85,80,78 78**
CSF £43.34 TOTE £10.60: £5.30, £1.80; EX 42.00 Trifecta £163.00.
**Owner** Middleham Park Racing Cxiv & Partner **Bred** Stephanie Hanly **Trained** Nawton, N Yorks

**FOCUS**
A fair handicap on paper and a reasonable gallop but another race in which the winner was the only one that really handled the condtions in any satisfactory manner.

## 5760 32RED.COM H'CAP — 1m 75y
**7:35** (7:35) (Class 5) (0-75,76) 3-Y-O+ — **£3,234** (£962; £481; £240) **Stalls** Centre

Form — RPR

6231 **1** **Pacific Salt (IRE)**[18] 5126 4-9-4 **68** ............ CallumShepherd[(3)] 9 — 77
(Pam Sly) *racd enthusiastically and mde all: clr and gng best 3f out: c to stands' rails 2f out: pushed out and a in command* **7/4**[1]

0300 **2** *3 ¾* **Hijran (IRE)**[34] 4506 4-9-1 **62** ............(p) AlistairRawlinson 2 — 62
(Michael Appleby) *settled in 3rd pl: rdn 3f out: wnt 2nd 2f out: nvr making any imp on wnr* **6/1**

2050 **3** *2 ¼* **Ataman (IRE)**[26] 4804 5-9-7 **68** ............(t) TedDurcan 6 — 63
(Chris Wall) *settled towards rr: rdn and effrt 3f out: disp 2nd 2f out: struggling 1f out* **4/1**[3]

001 **4** *14* **Wasm**[12] 5315 3-9-7 **75** ............ TonyHamilton 7 — 37
(Roger Fell) *t.k.h in last pl: rdn and struggling over 3f out: t.o* **2/1**[2]

1-05 **5** *4* **Ace Master**[14] 5263 9-9-3 **69** ............ KevinLundie[(5)] 8 — 23
(Roy Bowring) *pressed wnr: drvn 3f out: lost 2nd 2f out and dropped out rapidly: t.o* **16/1**

4646 **6** *7* **White Tower (IRE)**[10] 5425 3-9-4 **72** ............ FrannyNorton 3 — 9
(Mark Johnston) *trckd ldng trio: rdn 4f out: sn struggling: t.o and eased 2f out* **12/1**

1m 58.19s (9.19) **Going Correction** +0.70s/f (Yiel)
**WFA** 3 from 4yo+ 7lb — **6 Ran SP% 117.6**
Speed ratings (Par 103): **82,78,76,62,58 51**
CSF £13.62 CT £37.83 TOTE £2.40: £1.40, £3.10; EX 18.10 Trifecta £138.70.
**Owner** D L Bayliss & G A Libson **Bred** Tally-Ho Stud **Trained** Thorney, Cambs

**FOCUS**
Rail movements meant 18yds were added onto the official distance. The ground was changed to heavy before this race. A modest and uncompetitive handicap in which the first three finished a long way clear.

## 5761 32RED ON THE APP STORE H'CAP — 1m 2f 50y
**8:05** (8:05) (Class 6) (0-60,62) 3-Y-O — **£2,587** (£770; £384; £192) **Stalls** Low

Form — RPR

0000 **1** **Bombero (IRE)**[24] 4914 3-9-4 **58** ............(p[1]) CallumShepherd[(3)] 4 — 68
(Ed de Giles) *settled in 3rd pl tl led gng wl over 3f out: immediately drew clr: rdn 2f out but nvr looked like being ct* **7/1**

0605 **2** *6* **Upended**[13] 5275 3-9-10 **61** ............ TedDurcan 6 — 60
(Chris Wall) *towards rr: rdn 5f out: wnt 3rd over 3f out: nt rch wnr after and chsd him vainly fnl f* **5/1**[2]

0025 **3** *1 ¼* **Ronni Layne**[14] 5266 3-9-0 **51** ............ RobertTart 5 — 48
(Conrad Allen) *trckd ldrs: wnt 2nd over 3f out but wnr already gng clr: rdn after: lost modest 2nd 1f out* **7/1**

-031 **4** *2 ¼* **Mr C (IRE)**[18] 5131 3-9-5 **56** ............ JoeDoyle 2 — 49
(Ollie Pears) *t.k.h in rr: effrt 3f out: sn no ch w wnr and plugged on same pce: wandering clsng stages* **5/2**[1]

0000 **5** *1 ¼* **Bridal March**[28] 4727 3-8-13 **50** ............ FrannyNorton 3 — 40
(John Mackie) *detached in last pl: rdn and outpcd 6f out: plugged on but nvr nr ldrs* **10/1**

6006 **6** *10* **Tranquil Tracy**[40] 4262 3-8-10 **47** ............ RoystonFfrench 1 — 19
(John Norton) *t.k.h in rr: rdn and struggling over 3f out: t.o fnl 2f* **14/1**

-032 **7** *8* **Medici Moon**[168] 848 3-8-10 **52** ............ PaddyPilley[(5)] 8 — 10
(Scott Dixon) *t.k.h: led tl rdn and hdd over 3f out: sn dropped out: t.o fnl 2f* **6/1**[3]

-503 **8** *50* **Masterfilly (IRE)**[22] 4967 3-9-3 **54** ............ LiamKeniry 9
(Ed Walker) *wnt 2nd 6f out: lost pl rapidly wl over 3f out: sn t.o and virtually p.u* **6/1**[3]

2m 31.16s (16.86) **Going Correction** +0.70s/f (Yiel) — **8 Ran SP% 114.6**
Speed ratings (Par 98): **60,55,54,52,51 43,37,**
CSF £41.81 CT £254.77 TOTE £7.30: £3.10, £1.80, £2.30; EX 45.50 Trifecta £996.50.
**Owner** Woodham Walter Partnership **Bred** Nesco II **Trained** Ledbury, H'fords

**FOCUS**
Rail movements added 18yds to the official distance. A moderate handicap in which Bombero coped with the ground better than anything else and won with plenty in hand.
T/Plt: £392.40 to a £1 stake. Pool: £51,964.40 - 96.65 winning units T/Qpdt: £37.90 to a £1 stake. Pool: £3,890.35 - 75.88 winning units **Iain Mackenzie**

5762 - 5765a (Foreign Racing) - See Raceform Interactive

# 3871 CORK (R-H)
## Tuesday, August 8
**OFFICIAL GOING: Good to yielding changed to soft after race 1 (5.30)**

## 5766a IRISH STALLION FARMS EBF GIVE THANKS STKS (GROUP 3) (F&M) — 1m 4f
**7:30** (7:31) 3-Y-O+
**£37,820** (£12,179; £5,769; £2,564; £1,282; £641)

RPR

**1** **Eziyra (IRE)**[24] 4928 3-8-12 107 ............(h) PatSmullen 6 — 105+
(D K Weld, Ire) *chsd ldrs: 4th 1/2-way: tk clsr order into st gng wl and disp ld nr side over 2f out: led narrowly gng best under 2f out: rdn clr ins fnl f where flashed tail: styd on wl: comf* **7/4**[1]

**2** *2 ½* **Bloomfield (IRE)**[41] 4229 3-8-12 95 ............ WJLee 2 — 101
(W McCreery, Ire) *mid-div: 6th 1/2-way: tk clsr order in 5th after 1/2-way and almost on terms into st: disp ld briefly nr side over 2f out: hdd under 2f out and no imp on easy wnr ins fnl f: kpt on same pce* **9/2**[3]

**3** *½* **Wild Irish Rose (IRE)**[5] 5569 3-8-12 93 ............ SeamieHeffernan 8 — 100+
(A P O'Brien, Ire) *hld up towards rr: 8th 1/2-way: hdwy nr side fr over 2f out to chse ldrs in 3rd ins fnl f: kpt on same pce clsng stages: nt trble easy wnr* **7/2**[2]

**4** *2* **Glamorous Approach (IRE)**[29] 4707 4-9-8 103 ............ KevinManning 9 — 96
(J S Bolger, Ire) *sn disp and led after 1f: 2 l clr at 1/2-way: rdn and strly pressed over 2f out: sn hdd and no imp on easy wnr u.p in 4th ins fnl f: kpt on same pce* **10/1**

**5** *5* **Key To My Heart (IRE)**[31] 4650 3-8-12 99 ow2..(b) DonnachaO'Brien 10 — 89
(A P O'Brien, Ire) *sn disp and led briefly tl settled bhd ldr after 1f: pushed along bhd ldrs into st: sn rdn and u.p far side over 2f out: no imp on ldrs over 1f out: one pce in 5th ins fnl f* **10/1**

**6** *3 ½* **Flying Fairies (IRE)**[29] 4707 4-9-8 105 ............ GaryCarroll 1 — 82
(John M Oxx, Ire) *broke wl to ld briefly tl sn hdd and settled bhd ldrs: 3rd 1/2-way: pushed along and swtchd rt bhd ldrs over 2f out where rdn: sn no imp on ldrs far side: one pce in 6th ins fnl f* **7/1**

**7** *¾* **Puppetshow (IRE)**[22] 4986 3-8-12 82 ............(t) WayneLordan 4 — 82
(A P O'Brien, Ire) *dwlt and settled in rr: last at 1/2-way: rdn over 2f out and sme modest hdwy: one pce in 7th ins fnl f* **25/1**

**8** *4 ¾* **Tilly's Chilli (IRE)**[19] 5088 3-8-12 88 ............ TomMadden 3 — 74
(Mrs John Harrington, Ire) *cl up early tl sn settled bhd ldrs: 5th 1/2-way: rdn far side under 3f out and sn no ex: one pce fnl 2f* **20/1**

**9** *26* **Dragon Fei (IRE)**[29] 4707 7-9-8 96 ............ ShaneFoley 7 — 32
(Dermot Anthony McLoughlin, Ire) *w.w in 7th for most: pushed along into st and wknd u.p to rr over 2f out: eased 1 1/2f out* **40/1**

2m 37.93s (-9.97)
**WFA** 3 from 4yo+ 10lb — **9 Ran SP% 118.5**
CSF £9.88 TOTE £2.40: £1.02, £2.10, £1.40; DF 11.10 Trifecta £46.00.
**Owner** H H Aga Khan **Bred** His Highness The Aga Khan's Studs S C **Trained** Curragh, Co Kildare

**FOCUS**
A test for the form of the Irish Oaks, in which the winner was third last time, and it was franked in good style by a filly who deserved to get off the mark for the season.

5767 - 5775a (Foreign Racing) - See Raceform Interactive

# 5690 DEAUVILLE (R-H)

Tuesday, August 8

**OFFICIAL GOING: Polytrack: fast; turf: good**

## 5776a PRIX DE L'ANE A THEME (PRIX DE CREVECOEUR) (MAIDEN) (UNRACED 2YO) (TURF) 7f 110y

1:20 (1:20) 2-Y-O **£11,538** (£4,615; £3,461; £2,307; £1,153)

RPR

1 **Olmedo (FR)** 2-9-2 0 ........ CristianDemuro 13 84
(J-C Rouget, France) **66/10[3]**

2 *4* **Alhadab (FR)** 2-9-2 0 ........ MaximeGuyon 12 75
(A Fabre, France) **69/10**

3 *1* **Giovanni Dal Ponte** 2-9-2 0 ........ JeffersonSmith 14 72
(J-C Rouget, France) **36/1**

4 *½* **Five Ice Cubes (FR)** 2-9-2 0 ........ StephanePasquier 5 71
(D Smaga, France) **208/10**

5 *½* **Lahdan (FR)** 2-9-2 0 ........ Francois-XavierBertras 2 70
(F Rohaut, France) **23/1**

6 *1* **Rannan (FR)** 2-9-2 0 ........ AlexisBadel 3 68
(H-F Devin, France) **224/10**

7 *nk* **King Of Camelot (FR)** 2-9-2 0 ........ Pierre-CharlesBoudot 9 67
(A Fabre, France) **57/10[2]**

8 *¾* **Khochenko (FR)** 2-9-2 0 ........ MickaelBarzalona 8 65
(Mme Pia Brandt, France) **178/10**

9 *snk* **Naturally High (FR)** 2-9-2 0 ........ GeraldMosse 10 65
(P Bary, France) **102/10**

10 *nk* **Mister Jo (IRE)** 2-9-2 0 ........ ChristopheSoumillon 4 64
(J-C Rouget, France) **81/10**

11 *nk* **Qatar Bolt** 2-9-2 0 ........ OlivierPeslier 6 63
(F Head, France) **4/1[1]**

12 *nk* **Busted Ice (IRE)** 2-9-2 0 ........ EduardoPedroza 15 63
(A Wohler, Germany) **225/10**

13 *4* **Smart Move (FR)** 2-9-2 0 ........ AurelienLemaitre 11 53
(F-H Graffard, France) **231/10**

14 *3* **Say About It** 2-9-2 0 ........ TonyPiccone 1 46
(J S Moore) *outpcd in fnl trio wl adrift of main pack: towards rr 2 1/2f out: sn rdn and no imp: nvr in contention* **34/1**

15 *8* **Tirage Au Sort (FR)** 2-9-2 0 ........ VincentCheminaud 7 27
(J-P Dubois, France) **42/1**

16 *2* **Refuseeveryoffer (FR)** 2-9-2 0 ........ TheoBachelot 16 23
(Andreas Suborics, Germany) **39/1**

1m 34.61s (6.21) **16 Ran SP% 117.8**
PARI-MUTUEL (all including 1 euro stake): WIN: 7.60; PLACE: 2.50, 2.90, 8.70; DF: 18.70; SF: 29.80.
**Owner** Ecurie Antonio Caro & Gerard Augustin-Normand **Bred** Dream With Me Stable **Trained** Pau, France

## 5777a PRIX JUSTWORLD INTERNATIONAL (PRIX DES CHAUMIERES) (CONDITIONS) (3YO) (TURF) 1m (R)

1:50 3-Y-O **£14,059** (£5,683; £4,188; £2,692; £1,645; £1,047)

RPR

1 **Enlighted (IRE)**[25] 3-8-9 0 ........ MaximeGuyon 7 89
(F Head, France) **54/10[3]**

2 *2 ½* **Buthela (FR)**[23] 3-8-13 0 ........ Pierre-CharlesBoudot 1 87
(A Fabre, France) **157/10**

3 *3* **Jazz Melodie (FR)**[108] 3-8-9 0 ........ FabienLefebvre 11 76
(P De Chevigny, France) **161/10**

4 *nk* **Vadsariya (FR)**[86] 3-8-9 0 ........ AlexisBadel 9 72
(A De Royer-Dupre, France) *fin 5th: plcd 4th* **13/1**

5 *snk* **Relief Quest (IRE)**[77] 3-8-9 0 ........ HugoJourniac 5 72
(J-C Rouget, France) *fin 6th: plcd 5th* **76/10**

6 *1 ¾* **Tresorier**[25] 3-8-13 0 ........ StephanePasquier 4 72
(Mme C Head-Maarek, France) *fin 7th: plcd 6th* **37/10[2]**

7 *1* **Parauari (FR)**[37] 4425 3-8-13 0 ........ MickaelBerto 3 70
(A De Royer-Dupre, France) *fin 8th: plcd 7th* **26/1**

8 *4 ½* **La Poutanesca (IRE)**[59] 3612 3-8-9 0 ........ MickaelBarzalona 10 55
(D Smaga, France) *fin 9th: plcd 8th* **68/10**

9 *snk* **Bay Of Biscaine (FR)**[48] 3-8-13 0 ........ AntoineHamelin 8 59
(Mario Hofer, Germany) *fin 10th: plcd 9th* **189/10**

10 *dist* **Island Brave (IRE)**[118] 1724 3-8-13 0 ........ TonyPiccone 6
(J S Moore) *racd in midfield: lost pl bef 1/2-way: wl adrift 2 1/2f out: t.o: fin 11th: plcd 10th* **43/1**

D *1 ½* **Ajjlan (FR)**[277] 3-8-13 0 ........ CristianDemuro 2 77
(J-C Rouget, France) *fin 4th: disqualified; caused interference* **27/10[1]**

1m 40.6s (-0.20) **11 Ran SP% 118.4**
PARI-MUTUEL (all including 1 euro stake): WIN: 6.40; PLACE: 2.30, 3.20, 4.80; DF: 30.40; SF: 50.40.
**Owner** Wertheimer & Frere **Bred** Wertheimer & Frere **Trained** France

# 5586 BATH (L-H)

Wednesday, August 9

**OFFICIAL GOING: Soft (6.2)**

Wind: moderate against Weather: cloudy, sunny periods

## 5778 LEXUS BRISTOL H'CAP (BATH SUMMER SPRINT SERIES QUALIFIER) 5f 10y

2:00 (2:00) (Class 6) (0-60,59) 3-Y-O+ **£2,264** (£673; £336; £168) **Stalls** Centre

Form RPR

1040 **1** **Jaganory (IRE)**[14] 5271 5-9-0 **57** ........(p) LuluStanford(5) 10 66
(Christopher Mason) *mde all: drifted lft fr over 1f out: kpt on wl: pushed out* **3/1[2]**

3106 **2** *¾* **Staffa (IRE)**[14] 5297 4-9-2 **54** ........ FranBerry 11 60
(Denis Coakley) *trckd ldrs: rdn over 1f out: kpt on ins fnl f but a being hld* **7/1**

5530 **3** *1 ¼* **David's Beauty (IRE)**[10] 5459 4-9-1 **53** ........ SamHitchcott 2 54
(Brian Baugh) *s.i.s: sn trcking ldrs: rdn over 2f out: chsd wnr over 1f out tl ins fnl f: no ex towards fin* **3/1[2]**

5012 **4** *1* **Lucky Clover**[20] 5052 6-9-7 **59** ........(p) DaneO'Neill 1 56
(Malcolm Saunders) *prom: rdn over 2f out: sn hld: kpt on same pce fnl f (b.b.v)* **7/4[1]**

4405 **5** *nk* **Tally's Song**[6] 5567 4-8-7 **45** ........(p) JimmyQuinn 4 41
(Grace Harris) *cl up: rdn over 2f out: kpt on same pce* **13/2[3]**

0-00 **6** *2* **Dramatic Voice**[140] 1305 4-8-4 **45** ........ HollieDoyle(3) 12 34
(Ken Cunningham-Brown) *hld up 6th: hdwy 2f out: sn rdn: wknd ent fnl f* **66/1**

1m 4.84s (2.34) **Going Correction** +0.325s/f (Good)
**WFA** 3 from 4yo+ 3lb **6 Ran SP% 113.7**
Speed ratings (Par 101): **94,92,90,89,88 85**
CSF £23.82 CT £66.91 TOTE £4.20: £2.20, £3.60; EX 26.60 Trifecta £91.60.
**Owner** Brian Hicks **Bred** Canice Farrell Jnr **Trained** Caewent, Monmouthshire

**FOCUS**
Distance as advertised. The ground was changed to soft before racing and looked pretty hard work. Half of the 12 declared runners defected in what was a moderate sprint. The winner has been rated close to his best, and a small pb from the runner-up.

## 5779 HOTEL INDIGO BATH OPENING 2018 MAIDEN AUCTION STKS 5f 10y

2:30 (2:30) (Class 5) 2-Y-O **£3,363** (£1,001; £500; £250) **Stalls** Centre

Form RPR

3 **1** **Sancerre (IRE)**[23] 4977 2-8-7 0 ........ SamHitchcott 6 70
(Sylvester Kirk) *mde all: pushed clr ent fnl f: comf* **9/4[1]**

0 **2** *3 ¾* **Zapateado**[16] 5216 2-8-7 0 ........ JohnFahy 2 57
(Richard Hughes) *trckd ldrs: trckd wnr over 2f out: rdn over 1f out: kpt on but nt pce to get on terms* **5/2[2]**

**3** *½* **Katie Lee (IRE)** 2-8-2 0 ........ GeorgiaCox(5) 7 55+
(Henry Candy) *outpcd in last: hdwy ent fnl f: wnt 3rd sn after: kpt on but no threat to wnr* **3/1[3]**

05 **4** *2* **Grand Acclaim (IRE)**[23] 4977 2-8-12 0 ........ DaneO'Neill 1 53
(Harry Dunlop) *trckd wnr tl rdn over 2f out: no ex ins fnl f* **11/1**

00 **5** *nk* **Compton Grace**[2] 5717 2-8-2 0 ........ DavidEgan(5) 8 46
(Mick Channon) *sn pushed along to chse ldng trio: nvr gng pce to get on terms* **9/2**

1m 4.34s (1.84) **Going Correction** +0.325s/f (Good) **5 Ran SP% 110.9**
Speed ratings (Par 94): **98,92,91,88,87**
CSF £8.26 TOTE £2.90: £1.90, £1.60; EX 6.60 Trifecta £22.10.
**Owner** Spiers & Hartwell & Partner **Bred** Thomas Downey **Trained** Upper Lambourn, Berks

**FOCUS**
A pretty weak maiden.

## 5780 ONE PM FINANCE H'CAP (BATH SUMMER STAYERS' SERIES QUALIFIER) 1m 6f

3:00 (3:00) (Class 6) (0-65,66) 3-Y-O **£2,911** (£866; £432; £216) **Stalls** Centre

Form RPR

060 **1** **Dukinta (IRE)**[21] 5022 3-9-7 **65** ........(v[1]) FranBerry 5 79+
(Hugo Palmer) *trckd ldr: chal 4f out: led 3f out: sn clr: styd on strly: comf* **11/1**

3050 **2** *8* **Percy Thrower (IRE)**[23] 4978 3-8-13 **57** ........ JimmyQuinn 1 60
(Charles Hills) *trckd ldrs: rdn to dispute 3rd 3f out: chsd wnr over 2f out: styd on same pce* **12/1**

0-00 **3** *1* **Franny Nisbet**[54] 3770 3-9-2 **60** ........ DougieCostello 10 62
(William Muir) *s.i.s: rousted along 1st f: towards rr: drvn over 3f out: hdwy over 2f out: styd on into 3rd ins fnl f: clsng on 2nd at fin* **16/1**

000 **4** *4* **Murchison River**[16] 5220 3-9-7 **65** ........ DaneO'Neill 9 61
(Henry Candy) *hld up towards rr: hdwy over 3f out: sn rdn: nvr threatened to get involved: styd on same pce fnl 2f* **5/1[2]**

-366 **5** *8* **Sheila's Fancy (IRE)**[27] 4809 3-9-8 **66** ........ LiamKeniry 4 51
(J S Moore) *s.i.s: towards rr: rdn 3f out: nvr any imp on ldrs but styd on past btn horses fnl f* **12/1**

0030 **6** *½* **Light Gunner (IRE)**[58] 3674 3-8-6 **50** ........(h[1]) JosephineGordon 7 34
(Henry Tett) *hld up towards rr: rdn 3f out: nvr any imp on ldrs* **8/1**

0024 **7** *3 ½* **High Wells**[25] 4914 3-9-3 **61** ........(b) FergusSweeney 3 40
(Seamus Durack) *hld up towards rr: hdwy 8f out: rdn to dispute 3rd wl over 2f out: wknd ent fnl f* **8/1**

3212 **8** *2 ¼* **Ingleby Mackenzie**[5] 5618 3-9-6 **64** ........ SamHitchcott 2 40
(Mick Channon) *led tl 3f out: sn rdn and hld: wknd ent fnl f* **3/1[1]**

0404 **9** *7* **Delannoy**[14] 5275 3-9-3 **61** ........(p) CharlesBishop 6 27
(Eve Johnson Houghton) *trckd ldrs tl rdn over 4f out: wknd over 2f out* **7/1[3]**

3030 **10** *58* **Nothing Compares**[6] 5581 3-8-6 **50** ........ JoeFanning 11
(Mark Johnston) *mid-div tl 5f out: sn wknd: eased fnl 2f: t.o* **10/1**

3m 9.84s (6.04) **Going Correction** +0.325s/f (Good) **10 Ran SP% 115.1**
Speed ratings (Par 98): **95,90,89,87,83 82,80,79,75,42**
CSF £133.14 CT £2096.71 TOTE £13.90: £4.10, £4.00, £5.50; EX 178.30 Trifecta £4112.60.
**Owner** Mrs Clodagh McStay & Mrs Cherry Faeste **Bred** Mrs Cherry Faeste & Mabaki Investments **Trained** Newmarket, Suffolk

**FOCUS**
Distance increased by 5yds. A modest staying handicap for 3yos but a clear-cut and improved winner.

## 5781 KELSTON CUP H'CAP 1m 2f 37y

3:30 (3:30) (Class 3) (0-90,92) 3-Y-O **£8,821** (£2,640; £1,320; £660; £329) **Stalls** Low

Form RPR

0421 **1** **Anythingtoday (IRE)**[11] 5421 3-9-6 **90** ........(p) JosephineGordon 7 101+
(Hugo Palmer) *trckd ldrs: shkn up over 2f out: chal over 1f out: led ins fnl f: pushed clr* **4/6[1]**

2505 **2** *2 ½* **Mikmak**[13] 5330 4-9-3 **79** ........(b) DougieCostello 9 84
(William Muir) *s.i.s: sn pressing ldr: led over 3f out: rdn over 1f out: sn jnd: hdd ins fnl f: no ex* **8/1**

-000 **3** *2 ½* **Cosmeapolitan**[32] 4614 4-10-0 **90** ........ FergusSweeney 4 90
(Alan King) *cl up: hdwy to chse ldr 3f out: sn rdn: styd on same pce* **5/1[3]**

40 **4** *2 ¾* **Storm Rock**[11] 5421 5-9-9 **85** ........ DaneO'Neill 2 80
(Harry Dunlop) *cl up: rdn over 2f out: nvr threatened to get on terms: styd on same pce* **4/1[2]**

0S/0 **5** *14* **White Nile (IRE)**[39] 4380 8-8-10 **75** ........(t) HollieDoyle(3) 1 42
(Laura Young) *stmbld leaving stalls: led tl over 3f out: sn wknd* **33/1**

2m 15.65s (4.65) **Going Correction** +0.325s/f (Good)
**WFA** 3 from 4yo+ 8lb **5 Ran SP% 110.7**
Speed ratings (Par 107): **94,92,90,87,76**
CSF £6.85 TOTE £1.50: £1.10, £4.00; EX 6.50 Trifecta £17.80.
**Owner** MPH Racing - II **Bred** T Whitehead **Trained** Newmarket, Suffolk

**FOCUS**
Add 5yds. A useful handicap, even with there being four non-runners, and it went to a progressive 3yo.

## 5782 DAVID LEIGHS 10YRS AT TRUE CLARITY FILLIES' H'CAP 1m 2f 37y
4:00 (4:00) (Class 5) (0-70,72) 3-Y-O+ £2,911 (£866; £432; £216) Stalls Low

Form RPR
0353 1 **Drumochter**[12] 5367 3-9-6 68 DaneO'Neill 3 78
(Charles Hills) *trckd ldrs: lft 2nd wl over 2f out: led ent fnl f: pushed clr: readily* **6/4**[2]
466 2 2 3/4 **Saint Helena (IRE)**[47] 4041 9-9-8 62 (b) FranBerry 9 65
(Mark Gillard) *trckd ldr: led 3f out: rdn and hdd ent fnl f: kpt on but sn hld by wnr* **10/1**[3]
3411 3 5 **Fanfair**[21] 5023 3-9-0 65 HollieDoyle(3) 2 59
(Richard Hannon) *trckd ldrs: pushed along over 4f out: rdn whn outpcd 3f out: nvr threatened to get on terms fnl 2f* **6/5**[1]
0600 4 99 **Coup De Vent**[4] 5653 6-8-9 49 oh4 FergusSweeney 6
(John O'Shea) *led: hung bdly lft and hdd 3f out: sn eased: virtually p.u fnl f* **16/1**
/6-0 P **Krafty One**[214] 121 5-8-11 51 SamHitchcott 8
(Michael Scudamore) *fly-leapt and stmbld bdly leaving stalls nrly unseating jockey: sn p.u* **10/1**[3]

2m 15.21s (4.21) **Going Correction** +0.325s/f (Good)
**WFA** 3 from 4yo+ 8lb 5 Ran SP% **109.5**
Speed ratings (Par 100): **96,93,89,10,**
CSF £15.22 TOTE £2.30: £1.30, £6.70; EX 10.40 Trifecta £15.50.
**Owner** Glorious 12th **Bred** Red House Stud **Trained** Lambourn, Berks

**FOCUS**
Distance increased by 5yds. Half of the those declared failed to take part and the race rather fell apart anyway.

## 5783 CB PROTECTION H'CAP 1m
4:30 (4:31) (Class 6) (0-65,67) 3-Y-O £2,264 (£673; £336; £168) Stalls Low

Form RPR
0032 1 **Accomplice**[15] 5266 3-9-3 61 DaneO'Neill 3 70
(Michael Blanshard) *trckd ldrs: led over 1f out: pushed clr: comf* **8/1**
50-2 2 3 1/4 **Captain Pugwash (IRE)**[21] 5031 3-9-8 66 LiamKeniry 10 68
(Henry Spiller) *racd keenly: stdd bk to last trio after 1f: hdwy over 4f out: rdn over 2f out: chsd wnr ent fnl f: kpt on but a being hld* **11/2**[3]
-442 3 2 **Heart Of Gold**[19] 5126 3-9-3 66 DavidEgan(5) 8 63
(William Muir) *led: rdn wl over 1f out: sn hdd: no ex ins fnl f* **13/8**[1]
0006 4 1 **Bois D'Ebene (IRE)**[36] 4468 3-9-7 65 TimmyMurphy 11 60
(John O'Shea) *s.i.s: in last pair tl hdwy over 4f out: rdn whn swtchd lft 2f out: styd on same pce* **33/1**
5150 5 7 **Viola Park**[23] 4968 3-9-0 58 (p) FranBerry 9 37
(Ronald Harris) *trckd ldr: rdn wl over 2f out: wknd jst over 1f out* **10/1**
3521 6 1 1/2 **Mordoree (IRE)**[15] 5266 3-9-2 60 (p) SamHitchcott 4 35
(Clive Cox) *mid-div tl pushed along over 5f out: in last pair and struggling 4f out: sme prog 2f out but nvr threatened to get involved* **7/2**[2]
0-44 7 3 1/4 **Sussex Girl**[74] 3075 3-9-3 66 GeorgiaCox(5) 2 34
(John Berry) *trckd ldrs: rdn over 2f out: wknd over 1f out* **22/1**
4060 8 3 1/4 **Striking For Gold**[32] 4633 3-8-3 50 (p) HollieDoyle(3) 5 10
(Sarah Hollinshead) *mid-div: rdn over 2f out: sn wknd* **66/1**
00-3 9 hd **Lady Gwhinnyvere (IRE)**[23] 4969 3-8-2 46 oh1 JimmyQuinn 1 6
(John Spearing) *mid-div tl 3f out: sn wknd* **12/1**
006 10 6 **Allofmelovesallofu**[33] 4562 3-9-9 67 SteveDrowne 6 13
(Ken Cunningham-Brown) *a towards rr* **20/1**

1m 43.78s (2.98) **Going Correction** +0.325s/f (Good) 10 Ran SP% **117.1**
Speed ratings (Par 98): **98,94,92,91,84 83,80,76,76,70**
CSF £49.59 CT £109.34 TOTE £8.00: £2.60, £1.40, £1.30; EX 50.30 Trifecta £169.30.
**Owner** The Reignmakers **Bred** Stowell Hill Ltd **Trained** Upper Lambourn, Berks

**FOCUS**
Distance increased by 5yds. Modest handicap form and they spread across the track.

## 5784 ROA/RACING POST OWNERS JACKPOT APPRENTICE H'CAP 5f 160y
5:00 (5:00) (Class 5) (0-70,70) 3-Y-O+ £3,234 (£962; £481; £240) Stalls Centre

Form RPR
221 1 **Our Lord**[11] 5429 5-9-11 69 DavidEgan 14 78
(Michael Attwater) *a.p: led wl over 1f out: kpt on wl: pushed out* **3/1**[1]
3445 2 1 **Indian Affair**[9] 5473 7-8-13 64 (bt) KerrieRaybould(7) 2 70
(Milton Bradley) *mid-div: rdn and hdwy over 2f out: chal for cl 2nd ent fnl f: kpt on* **12/1**
0514 3 1/2 **Secret Potion**[5] 5588 3-9-8 70 PatrickO'Donnell 10 73
(Ronald Harris) *prom: rdn and ev ch over 2f out: stl ev ch ent fnl f: kpt on but no ex towards fin* **4/1**[3]
0365 4 1 1/4 **Showmethewayavrilo**[6] 5564 4-9-11 69 GeorgiaCox 12 69
(Malcolm Saunders) *prom: led over 3f out: sn rdn: hdd wl over 1f out: kpt on but no ex ins fnl f* **7/1**
0065 5 nk **Essaka (IRE)**[14] 5271 5-8-5 54 AledBeech(5) 3 53
(Tony Carroll) *s.i.s: towards rr: hdwy over 2f out: sn rdn: kpt on same pce fnl f* **9/1**
0046 6 3/4 **Bushwise (IRE)**[4] 5651 4-8-4 51 oh5 (p) JordanUys(3) 6 48
(Milton Bradley) *hld up: rdn over 2f out: nt pce to get on terms* **16/1**
4203 7 1/2 **Langley Vale**[30] 4695 8-9-4 62 PaddyBradley 8 57
(Roger Teal) *hld up: effrt over 2f out: nt pce to get involved* **16/1**
0450 8 7 **Evening Starlight**[2] 5711 4-8-11 60 WilliamCox(5) 11 32
(Ron Hodges) *led for over 2f: rdn under 3f out: sn hld: wknd over 1f out* **18/1**
-323 9 3/4 **Liberatum**[12] 5377 3-8-13 66 SeamusCronin(5) 1 35
(Ruth Carr) *prom: rdn and ev ch over 2f out tl over 1f out: wknd fnl f* **7/2**[2]
000 10 7 **Allen's Folly**[7] 5535 4-8-0 51 oh6 SophieRalston(7) 13
(Peter Hiatt) *a towards rr: lost tch over 2f out* **40/1**

1m 12.62s (1.42) **Going Correction** +0.325s/f (Good)
**WFA** 3 from 4yo+ 4lb 10 Ran SP% **116.9**
Speed ratings (Par 103): **103,101,101,99,98 97,97,87,86,77**
CSF £40.46 CT £150.58 TOTE £3.20: £1.40, £2.60, £1.50; EX 28.50 Trifecta £101.40.
**Owner** Mrs M S Teversham **Bred** Mrs Monica Teversham **Trained** Epsom, Surrey

**FOCUS**
A pretty modest sprint and the runner-up looks the key to the form.
T/Plt: £191.00 to a £1 stake. Pool: £57,170.95 - 218.43 winning units T/Qpdt: £60.60 to a £1 stake. Pool: £5,280.63 - 64.38 winning units **Tim Mitchell**

# 4709 BRIGHTON (L-H)
Wednesday, August 9
**OFFICIAL GOING: Good to firm (firm in places; 9.1)**
Wind: light, behind Weather: mainly overcast, bright spells, light rain from race 3

## 5785 VISIT MARATHONBET.CO.UK NURSERY H'CAP 5f 60y
1:50 (1:50) (Class 5) (0-70,71) 2-Y-O £2,911 (£866; £432; £216) Stalls Low

Form RPR
5223 1 **Haveoneyerself (IRE)**[28] 4760 2-9-7 70 JFEgan 7 70
(John Butler) *dwlt: sn rcvrd to trck ldrs: effrt u.p to ld over 1f out: hld on wl ins fnl f* **9/4**[2]
5545 2 1/2 **Llamrei**[22] 4991 2-8-1 57 NicolaCurrie(7) 5 55
(Jo Hughes) *hld up in tch in last pair: effrt over 1f out: chsng ldrs whn nt clr run and swtchd lft ins fnl f: styd on wl u.p towards fin* **9/1**
635 3 shd **Sienna Says**[27] 4806 2-9-2 65 RobertWinston 2 63
(Tony Carroll) *t.k.h: pressed ldr: rdn and ev ch over 1f out: kpt on but a jst hld ins fnl f: lost 2nd last stride* **11/10**[1]
660 4 3/4 **Erastus**[20] 5063 2-8-9 58 ShaneKelly 6 53
(Mick Channon) *dwlt: hld up in tch in last pair: effrt over 1f out: rdn and sltly outpcd 1f out: rallied ins fnl f: kpt on towards fin* **14/1**
3525 5 3/4 **Terri Rules (IRE)**[9] 5479 2-8-10 59 AdamBeschizza 1 52
(Julia Feilden) *led: rdn and hdd over 1f out: styd pressing ldrs tl no ex 100yds out: wknd towards fin* **6/1**[3]

1m 2.27s (-0.03) **Going Correction** -0.15s/f (Firm) 5 Ran SP% **109.3**
Speed ratings (Par 94): **94,93,93,91,90**
CSF £20.05 TOTE £2.90: £1.40, £3.20; EX 19.10 Trifecta £43.50.
**Owner** M McKay & T Cassidy **Bred** Michael M Byrne **Trained** Newmarket, Suffolk

**FOCUS**
The going was good to firm (firm in places) ahead of the opener, after which John Egan said it was "good, quick ground". A small nursery and they finished close-up.

## 5786 BOMBARDIER EBF NOVICE STKS 6f 210y
2:20 (2:22) (Class 5) 2-Y-O £2,911 (£866; £432; £216) Stalls Low

Form RPR
0 1 **Al Ozzdi**[26] 4860 2-9-2 0 (t[1]) SilvestreDeSousa 7 72
(Simon Crisford) *hld up in tch in midfield: effrt ent fnl 2f: rdn and clsd to chal over 1f out: styd on u.p to ld wl ins fnl f: rdn out* **7/2**[2]
01 2 3/4 **Tadleel**[39] 4363 2-9-9 0 JimCrowley 4 77
(Ed Dunlop) *dwlt: hld up in tch in last pair: swtchd rt and effrt in centre 2f out: rdn and hdwy over 1f out: kpt on u.p ins fnl f: snatched 2nd last stride: nvr getting to wnr* **2/1**[1]
05 3 shd **Strategic (IRE)**[25] 4909 2-9-2 0 TomMarquand 9 70
(Richard Hannon) *pressed ldr after 1f: rdn and ev ch 2f out: stl chalng whn wandering on camber ins fnl f: hung lft and styd on same pce towards fin: lost 2nd last stride* **5/1**
65 4 1 1/2 **Reverberation**[13] 5321 2-9-2 0 MartinDwyer 8 68+
(Sylvester Kirk) *led after 1f: rdn over 1f out: kpt on wl u.p tl hdd wl ins fnl f: outpcd whn nt clr run towards fin and eased cl home* **25/1**
46 5 1/2 **Groveman**[11] 5420 2-9-2 0 HarryBentley 1 65
(Charles Hills) *hld up in tch in midfield: effrt to chse ldrs but nt clr run over 1f out: sn swtchd rt and rdn: kpt on same pce ins fnl f* **4/1**[3]
6 6 1 1/4 **General Marius (IRE)**[18] 5144 2-9-2 0 JackMitchell 2 61
(Roger Varian) *trckd ldrs: swtchd lft and effrt ent fnl 2f: rdn to chal over 1f out: no ex ins fnl f: wknd fnl 100yds* **11/1**
0 7 1 3/4 **Puramente**[71] 3187 2-9-2 0 JFEgan 3 57
(Jo Hughes) *hld up in tch in last pair: effrt 2f out: no imp u.p over 1f out: styd on same pce and no imp ins fnl f* **40/1**
05 8 4 1/2 **Couldn't Could She**[34] 4520 2-8-11 0 RoystonFfrench 5 40
(Adam West) *chsd ldrs tl rdn and lost pl over 1f out: wknd ins fnl f* **20/1**

1m 23.01s (-0.09) **Going Correction** -0.15s/f (Firm) 8 Ran SP% **111.6**
Speed ratings (Par 94): **94,93,93,91,90 89,87,82**
CSF £10.30 TOTE £3.80: £1.60, £1.20, £1.30; EX 10.60 Trifecta £38.80.
**Owner** Sultan Ali **Bred** Good Breeding **Trained** Newmarket, Suffolk
■ Fenagh was withdrawn not under orders. Rule 4 does not apply.

**FOCUS**
A moderate novice and not much of a pace. It paid to race prominently. The 2nd/3rd have been rated to form.

## 5787 WAINWRIGHT (S) H'CAP 1m 3f 198y
2:50 (2:52) (Class 6) (0-55,55) 3-Y-O+ £2,264 (£673; £336; £168) Stalls High

Form RPR
0000 1 **Tojosimbre**[46] 4087 3-8-5 46 oh1 (t[1]) MartinDwyer 5 53
(Richard Hughes) *stdd s: rdn and effrt over 2f out: hdwy to chse ldrs 1f out: wnt 2nd ins fnl f: styd on u.p to ld last stride* **8/1**[3]
6300 2 shd **Bizet (IRE)**[11] 5406 3-8-5 49 (b) GeorgeWood(3) 2 55
(John Ryan) *hld up in tch in midfield: swtchd rt and hdwy over 2f out: rdn to chal over 1f out: led 1f out: edgd rt and idling in front ins fnl f: hdd last stride* **20/1**
0542 3 2 3/4 **Eugenic**[28] 4734 6-9-6 51 SilvestreDeSousa 8 52
(Rod Millman) *in tch: effrt to chse ldrs whn hung lft ent fnl f: swtchd lft ins fnl f: styd on same pce: wnt 3rd last strides* **3/1**[1]
0000 4 nk **Seventii**[28] 4765 3-8-6 47 oh1 ow1 JFEgan 1 49
(Robert Eddery) *chsd ldrs: wnt 2nd over 3f out: rdn to ld over 1f out: hdd 1f out: wknd ins fnl f: lost 3rd last stride* **14/1**
3045 5 5 **Go On Gal (IRE)**[34] 4545 4-9-4 52 ShelleyBirkett(3) 7 45
(Julia Feilden) *hld up in tch in midfield: effrt and nt clr run over 2f out: effrt u.p but unable qck over 1f out: wl hld and kpt on same pce ins fnl f* **9/1**
0/5 6 3/4 **Flannery (IRE)**[12] 5362 6-9-1 51 (t) MitchGodwin(5) 4 42
(Tim Vaughan) *hld up in tch in last quartet: hdwy on inner to ld over 4f out: rdn and hdd over 1f out: wknd ins fnl f* **9/1**
0550 7 3/4 **Ring Eye (IRE)**[12] 5361 9-9-3 48 (v[1]) AdamKirby 9 38
(John O'Shea) *hld up in tch in midfield: hmpd 4f out: no imp u.p 2f out: wknd fnl f* **16/1**
3344 8 5 **Halling's Wish**[14] 5274 7-9-10 55 (b) ShaneKelly 10 37
(Gary Moore) *chsd ldrs: rdn over 2f out: drvn and lost pl over 1f out: wknd fnl f* **9/2**[2]
0006 9 3 1/4 **Le Tissier**[28] 4756 4-9-2 47 (p) AdamBeschizza 3 24
(Michael Attwater) *hld up in tch in last trio: effrt wl over 2f out: no prog: wl btn over 1f out* **12/1**
-060 10 6 **Bed Of Diamonds**[18] 5142 3-8-2 46 oh1 NoelGarbutt(3) 13 14
(Adam West) *t.k.h: hld up in tch in midfield: clsd to chse ldrs 5f out: hmpd 4f out and sn struggling: bhd 2f out* **33/1**

500 **11** *1 ¼* **Reel Leisure (GR)**[16] 5220 4-9-9 **54**............................(h) JimCrowley 14 19
(Amanda Perrett) *chsd ldr tl over 4f out: hmpd 4f out: losing pl whn bmpd over 2f out: sn wknd* **10/1**

6664 **P** **Par Three (IRE)**[28] 4756 6-9-6 **51**............................(p) GeorgeDowning 11
(Tony Carroll) *in rr and rousted along early: in tch: rdn and struggling over 3f out: wl bhd whn p.u and dismntd ins fnl f* **16/1**

00-0 **U** **Opera Buffa (IRE)**[36] 4461 4-8-12 **46**..............(tp) HectorCrouch(3) 12
(Steve Flook) *broke wl: led tl over 4f out: uns rdr 4f out* **50/1**

2m 32.96s (0.26) **Going Correction** -0.15s/f (Firm)
**WFA** 3 from 4yo+ 10lb **13** Ran SP% **119.2**
Speed ratings (Par 101): **93,92,91,90,87 87,86,83,81,77 76,,**
CSF £160.26 CT £592.83 TOTE £10.00: £3.20, £5.30, £1.50; EX 198.90 Trifecta £1460.70.There was no bid for the winner.
**Owner** Tojosimbre Racing Partnership **Bred** Rangefield Bloodstock **Trained** Upper Lambourn, Berks

**FOCUS**
A weak selling handicap and there was drama as Opera Buffa unseated Hector Crouch the bend when on the pace, leading to some trouble in behind. However, improved form from the winner.

## 5788 HOBGOBLIN BRIGHTON MILE CHALLENGE TROPHY H'CAP 7f 211y
**3:20** (3:23) (Class 4) (0-80,79) 3-Y-0+
**£12,450** (£3,728; £1,864; £932; £466; £234) **Stalls** Low

Form RPR

-621 **1** **Lord Clenaghcastle (IRE)**[20] 5067 3-9-5 **77**.................. ShaneKelly 10 85+
(Gary Moore) *trckd ldrs and travelled strly thrght: clsd to press ldr 3f out: rdn to ld wl over 1f out: in command and r.o wl ins fnl f* **5/1**[2]

1050 **2** *2* **Pendo**[33] 4563 6-9-12 **77**............................................ KierenFox 2 81
(John Best) *t.k.h: led: rdn ent fnl 2f: sn hdd: styd on same pce u.p ins fnl f* **11/1**

1213 **3** *nk* **Helfire**[25] 4883 4-9-7 **75**.................................... CharlieBennett(3) 8 78
(Hughie Morrison) *hld up in midfield: clsd to chse ldrs on inner and rdn over 1f out: kpt on same pce u.p ins fnl f* **9/2**[1]

0601 **4** *shd* **Cricklewood Green (USA)**[25] 4887 6-9-9 **79**.......... MitchGodwin(5) 14 82+
(Sylvester Kirk) *stdd after s: hld up off the pce in last quartet: hdwy and edging lft over 1f out: nt clr run and swtchd rt ins fnl f: styd on wl towards fin: no threat to wnr* **11/2**[3]

-006 **5** *1* **Zaeem**[20] 5059 8-9-11 **76**............................. SilvestreDeSousa 15 77
(Ivan Furtado) *styd wd early: chsd ldrs: effrt ent fnl 2f: unable qck over 1f out: kpt on same pce ins fnl f* **15/2**

6103 **6** *2* **Intensical (IRE)**[20] 5049 6-9-4 **76**.......................(p) ManuelFernandes(7) 1 72
(Ivan Furtado) *chsd ldr tl 3f: styd chsng ldrs: rdn ent fnl 2f: unable qck over 1f out: kpt on same pce ins fnl f* **16/1**

0615 **7** *hd* **Galinthias**[34] 4523 5-9-3 **68**...................................... HarryBentley 13 64
(Simon Dow) *hld up in tch in midfield: effrt u.p 2f out: unable qck and styd on same pce fr over 1f out* **14/1**

4141 **8** *½* **Exceeding Power**[25] 4912 6-9-10 **78**......................... GeorgeWood(3) 7 73
(Martin Bosley) *hld up off the pce in midfield: effrt ent fnl 2f: kpt on but nvr getting on terms w ldrs* **7/1**

2404 **9** *nk* **Squire**[34] 4523 6-9-9 **74**.........................................(t) AdamBeschizza 4 68
(Michael Attwater) *hld up off the pce in midfield: rdn over 2f out: no imp over 1f out: kpt on same pce: nvr trbld ldrs* **12/1**

1000 **10** *1 ½* **Mister Musicmaster**[14] 5276 8-9-3 **68**......................... KieranO'Neill 11 58
(Ron Hodges) *hld up off the pce in last quartet: effrt 2f out: no imp and wl hld whn swtchd rt 1f out: nvr trbld ldrs* **50/1**

66 **11** *3 ¼* **Pour La Victoire (IRE)**[27] 4803 7-9-2 **67**................(v[1]) GeorgeDowning 6 50
(Tony Carroll) *s.i.s: off the pce in last quartet: c centre and effrt over 2f out: no imp and wl hld whn hung lft over 1f out* **16/1**

4514 **12** *9* **Admirable Art (IRE)**[20] 5049 7-9-10 **75**............................. AdamKirby 3 37
(Tony Carroll) *hld up off the pce in last trio: effrt 2f out: no imp: n.d* **16/1**

1m 33.63s (-2.37) **Going Correction** -0.15s/f (Firm)
**WFA** 3 from 4yo+ 7lb **12** Ran SP% **116.8**
Speed ratings (Par 105): **105,103,102,102,101 99,99,98,98,97 93,84**
CSF £58.23 CT £270.88 TOTE £5.20: £2.00, £4.00, £1.90; EX 74.30 Trifecta £372.40.
**Owner** Michael Baldry **Bred** D McCarthy **Trained** Lower Beeding, W Sussex
■ Harlequin Striker was withdrawn not under orders. Rule 4 does not apply

**FOCUS**
The feature race was competitive enough, and they went a good clip, but it paid to race prominently.

## 5789 MARATHONBET FESTIVAL OF RACING/EBF FILLIES' H'CAP 6f 210y
**3:50** (3:50) (Class 4) (0-85,87) 3-Y-0+ **£5,828** (£1,744; £872; £436; £217) **Stalls** Low

Form RPR

4201 **1** **Bumptious**[15] 5247 4-9-5 **75**..........................................(p) JimCrowley 2 81
(Ismail Mohammed) *t.k.h: hld up wl in tch: effrt ent fnl 2f: clsd to chal u.p ent fnl f: edging lft but sustained chal to ld nr fin* **11/4**[2]

1064 **2** *shd* **Bint Dandy (IRE)**[12] 5369 6-9-12 **82**......................(p) SilvestreDeSousa 5 87
(Chris Dwyer) *trckd ldr: effrt over 2f out: drvn and ev ch over 1f out: led ins fnl f: kpt on wl u.p hdd nr fin* **4/1**[3]

2013 **3** *2 ¼* **Andalusite**[6] 5558 4-8-7 **63** oh1.................................(v) RoystonFfrench 3 62
(John Gallagher) *led: pushed along 2f out: rdn over 1f out: drvn and hdd ins fnl f: wknd towards fin* **5/1**

2311 **4** *4 ½* **Finale**[13] 5332 3-9-0 **76**............................................. AdamKirby 1 61
(Hughie Morrison) *trckd ldrs: effrt on inner and rdn to chal over 1f out: no ex ins fnl f: wknd fnl 100yds* **2/1**[1]

4035 **5** *2 ¼* **Fleeting Motion**[27] 4794 3-9-4 **80**.............................. TomMarquand 4 59
(Richard Hannon) *in tch in rr: pushed along 4f out: rdn 3f out: nvr looked like getting on terms after: wknd over 1f out* **11/2**

1m 21.12s (-1.98) **Going Correction** -0.15s/f (Firm)
**WFA** 3 from 4yo+ 6lb **5** Ran SP% **112.1**
Speed ratings (Par 102): **105,104,102,97,94**
CSF £14.00 TOTE £3.50: £1.80, £2.30; EX 14.50 Trifecta £48.20.
**Owner** Abdulla Al Mansoori **Bred** Swettenham Stud **Trained** Newmarket, Suffolk

**FOCUS**
A fair fillies' handicap and a tight finish. A small pb from the winner.

## 5790 SHIPYARD BREWERY H'CAP 1m 1f 207y
**4:20** (4:21) (Class 6) (0-55,56) 3-Y-0+ **£2,264** (£673; £336; £168) **Stalls** High

Form RPR

4000 **1** **Overhaugh Street**[14] 5271 4-9-7 **55**......................... SilvestreDeSousa 2 64
(Ed de Giles) *t.k.h: w ldr tl led 1/2-way: rdn ent fnl 2f: sustained duel w runner-up tl forged ahd ins fnl f: styd on wl: rdn out* **14/1**

0404 **2** *1 ¼* **Nouvelle Ere**[23] 4971 6-9-7 **55**..................................(t) GeorgeDowning 11 61
(Tony Carroll) *led tl 1/2-way: styd w wnr: rdn ent fnl 2f: sustained duel w wnr after tl no ex and outpcd ins fnl f* **16/1**

0-05 **3** *3 ¾* **Dragonite (IRE)**[50] 3939 3-8-3 **48** ow1..................... CharlieBennett(3) 13 48
(Daniel Mark Loughnane) *t.k.h: chsd ldrs: rdn ent fnl 2f: 3rd and outpcd by ldng pair over 1f out: kpt on same pce ins fnl f* **9/1**[3]

-036 **4** *2 ¼* **Henry Did It (IRE)**[28] 4754 3-8-9 **51**.............................. ShaneKelly 10 46
(Tony Carroll) *stdd s: t.k.h: hld up in tch in last quartet: effrt 2f out: hdwy u.p 1f out: styd on ins fnl f: no threat to ldrs* **14/1**

0400 **5** *hd* **Dawn Goddess**[11] 5410 3-8-1 **46** oh1............................ NoelGarbutt(3) 4 41
(Gary Moore) *stdd and awkward leaving stalls: t.k.h: hld up in tch in last quartet: effrt 2f out: styd on ins fnl f: nvr trbld ldrs* **33/1**

5-00 **6** *nse* **Midnight Mood**[13] 5336 4-9-5 **56**........................... CallumShepherd(3) 12 50
(Dominic Ffrench Davis) *chsd ldrs: effrt over 2f out: 4th and outpcd by ldng pair over 1f out: wknd ins fnl f* **16/1**

3524 **7** *1 ½* **Buzz Lightyere**[21] 5023 4-9-7 **55**........................................ JimCrowley 8 50+
(Philip Hide) *hld up in tch in last quartet: effrt to cl but stl plenty to do whn nt clr run and swtchd rt over 1f out: kpt on ins fnl f: no ch w ldrs* **6/4**[1]

0031 **8** *1 ¾* **Born To Please**[7] 5545 3-8-1 **50**.................................... NicolaCurrie(7) 6 38
(Mark Usher) *t.k.h: hld up in tch in midfield: effrt 2f out: hung lft and no imp fr over 1f out: wl hld whn rdr dropped whip ins fnl f: wknd* **9/2**[2]

5305 **9** *5* **Dukes Meadow**[28] 4765 6-8-5 **46** oh1............................ RhiainIngram(7) 1 27
(Roger Ingram) *t.k.h: hld up in tch in midfield: effrt on inner 2f out: no imp and wl hld whn hmpd ins fnl f* **25/1**

1060 **10** *6* **Master Of Heaven**[21] 5023 4-9-6 **54**...........................(p) TomMarquand 7 19
(Jim Boyle) *chsd ldrs: lost pl u.p over 1f out: sn wknd* **16/1**

5004 **11** *7* **Silver Alliance**[36] 4461 9-9-4 **55**............................(b) ShelleyBirkett(3) 9 6
(Julia Feilden) *in tch in midfield: rdn over 2f out: sn lost pl: bhd and wknd over 1f out* **10/1**

1556 **12** *dist* **Street Art (IRE)**[21] 5023 5-9-5 **53**..............................(bt) RobertWinston 5
(Mike Murphy) *s.i.s: nvr gng wl in rr: eased 3f out: t.o* **16/1**

2m 3.12s (-0.48) **Going Correction** -0.15s/f (Firm)
**WFA** 3 from 4yo+ 8lb **12** Ran SP% **120.9**
Speed ratings (Par 101): **95,94,91,89,89 89,87,86,82,77 72,**
CSF £223.67 CT £2136.68 TOTE £10.20: £3.20, £5.50, £3.40; EX 127.40 Trifecta £3636.10.
**Owner** Sharron & Robert Colvin **Bred** World Racing Network **Trained** Ledbury, H'fords
■ Stewards' Enquiry : Nicola Currie three-day ban: careless riding (Aug 26-28)

**FOCUS**
A moderate handicap in which the first two held those positions throughout. Several caught the eye trying to come from behind.

## 5791 RAZORBACK H'CAP (DIV I) 6f 210y
**4:50** (4:51) (Class 6) (0-52,54) 3-Y-0+ **£2,264** (£673; £336; £168) **Stalls** Low

Form RPR

5635 **1** **Whiteley (IRE)**[13] 5340 3-9-3 **54**.................................. SilvestreDeSousa 4 61
(Mick Channon) *chsd ldr: rdn to ld 2f out: drvn over 1f out: kpt on u.p and a holding chalrs towards fin* **7/2**[1]

4003 **2** *nk* **De Vegas Kid (IRE)**[23] 4970 3-8-13 **50**.....................(p) GeorgeDowning 2 56+
(Tony Carroll) *hld up in last trio: hdwy u.p on outer and edgd lft over 1f out: wnt 3rd and hung lft ins fnl f: styd on strly to go 2nd last strides: nvr quite getting to wnr* **5/1**[2]

5404 **3** *nk* **Limerick Lord (IRE)**[18] 5146 5-8-12 **46** oh1..........(p) ShelleyBirkett(3) 10 53
(Julia Feilden) *chsd ldrs: effrt ent fnl 2f: chsd wnr over 1f out: kpt on wl u.p but hld towards fin: lost 2nd last strides* **10/1**

606 **4** *4 ½* **African Quest**[44] 4152 3-8-6 **46** oh1.............................. GeorgeWood(3) 7 39
(Gary Moore) *midfield: rdn 4f out: styd on ins fnl f: no threat to ldng trio* **16/1**

0000 **5** *1 ¼* **Wilspa's Magic (IRE)**[20] 5052 4-9-1 **46** oh1................(b[1]) KieranO'Neill 5 37
(Ron Hodges) *led and sn clr: hdd 2f out: sn hung lft and outpcd: 3rd and btn 1f out: wknd ins fnl f* **66/1**

0400 **6** *1 ½* **Coachella (IRE)**[23] 4970 3-8-8 **48** oh1 ow2......(p[1]) CallumShepherd(3) 11 33
(Ed de Giles) *hld up in tch in midfield on outer: effrt 2f out: no imp and wl hld over 1f out* **14/1**

1050 **7** *¾* **Sadieroseclifford (IRE)**[21] 5040 3-9-1 **52**........................ RobertWinston 8 35
(Giles Bravery) *chsd ldng trio: unable qck u.p and no hdwy over 1f out: wknd ins fnl f* **16/1**

5006 **8** *1* **Majestic Girl (IRE)**[44] 4162 4-9-1 **46** oh1....................... TomMarquand 1 29
(Steve Flook) *s.i.s: hld up in last trio: effrt over 2f out: sme hdwy over 1f out: no threat to ldrs whn nt clr run ins fnl f* **10/1**

640- **9** *hd* **Yorkshire Star (IRE)**[17] 7571 3-8-4 **46** oh1.................. MitchGodwin(5) 3 26
(Bill Turner) *rrd as stalls opened: sn in last pair: struggling in last 1/2-way: n.d after and hung rt 2f out* **16/1**

0665 **10** *hd* **Doctor Bong**[23] 4970 5-9-9 **54**...........................................(b) ShaneKelly 6 36
(Grace Harris) *in tch in midfield: effrt 2f out: sn outpcd and btn: wknd fnl f* **8/1**

6043 **11** *7* **Cooperess**[12] 5357 4-9-4 **49**.................................................(v) JimCrowley 9 12
(John O'Shea) *in tch in midfield: effrt 2f out: no imp whn nt clr run: hmpd and lost pl over 1f out: wknd fnl f* **6/1**[3]

6030 **12** *3 ¼* **Noble Deed**[43] 4179 7-9-7 **52**.....................................(p) AdamBeschizza 12 6
(Michael Attwater) *taken down early: hld up in midfield: rdn over 2f out: sn struggling and lost pl: bhd over 1f out* **14/1**

1m 22.15s (-0.95) **Going Correction** -0.15s/f (Firm)
**WFA** 3 from 4yo+ 6lb **12** Ran SP% **114.9**
Speed ratings (Par 101): **99,98,98,93,91 90,89,88,87,87 79,75**
CSF £19.24 CT £160.28 TOTE £4.10: £1.70, £2.70, £3.40; EX 23.10 Trifecta £206.40.
**Owner** Peter Taplin & Susan Bunney **Bred** Yeomanstown Stud **Trained** West Ilsley, Berks

**FOCUS**
A weak handicap and it once again proved an advantage to race prominently. The first three came clear, with the winner back to something like her early season form.

## 5792 RAZORBACK H'CAP (DIV II) 6f 210y
**5:20** (5:20) (Class 6) (0-52,54) 3-Y-0+ **£2,264** (£673; £336; £168) **Stalls** Low

Form RPR

0461 **1** **The Special One (IRE)**[23] 4969 4-9-8 **53**.....................(t) TomMarquand 7 59
(Ali Stronge) *hld up in tch in midfield: effrt over 1f out: chsd ldr 1f out: styd on wl u.p to ld last strides* **8/1**

4050 **2** *nk* **Lady Morel (IRE)**[2] 5713 3-8-10 **54**........................ StephenCummins(7) 10 57
(Joseph Tuite) *hld up in tch in rr: clsd over 1f out: nt clr run and swtchd rt ins fnl f: r.o strly fnl 100yds: wnt 2nd last strides: nt quite rch wnr* **8/1**

4256 **3** *hd* **Lesanti**[7] 5545 3-8-12 **52**.......................................... CallumShepherd(3) 8 55
(Ed de Giles) *led: shkn up 2f out: sn rdn: hrd pressed ins fnl f: hdd and lost 2 pls last strides* **10/3**[1]

0420 **4** *2 ¾* **Spare Parts (IRE)**[20] 5050 3-9-0 **51**........................ SilvestreDeSousa 5 46
(Charles Hills) *chsd ldrs: wnt 2nd 4f out: effrt over 2f out: hung lft and lost 2nd 1f out: wknd ins fnl f* **7/2**[2]

-004 **5** *nk* **Suni Dancer**[12] 5357 6-9-5 **50**......................................... GeorgeDowning 3 46
(Tony Carroll) *dwlt: sn rcvrd and in tch in midfield: effrt over 1f out: kpt on ins fnl f: nvr trbld ldrs* **5/1**[3]

4663 **6** 1 1/4 **Stopdworldnletmeof**[60] 3569 3-8-6 **46** oh1 ................ GeorgeWood(3) 4 37
(David Flood) *t.k.h: led for 1f: chsd ldrs after: effrt over 1f out: no ex u.p 1f out: wknd ins fnl f* **7/1**

0-60 **7** 3/4 **Joshlee (IRE)**[11] 5410 3-9-0 **51** ................ (e1) ShaneKelly 11 40
(Richard Hughes) *hld up in tch in last trio: effrt but no imp u.p over 1f out: kpt on but no threat to ldrs ins fnl f* **14/1**

0244 **8** 1 3/4 **Black Truffle (FR)**[15] 5239 7-8-9 **47** ................ (v) NicolaCurrie(7) 6 33
(Mark Usher) *t.k.h: chsd ldng trio: effrt but unable qck over 1f out: wknd ins fnl f* **12/1**

0-66 **9** 2 3/4 **Silver Mist**[11] 5411 3-8-5 **47** oh1 ow1 ................ MitchGodwin(5) 12 24
(Sylvester Kirk) *hld up in tch in last trio on outer: effrt over 2f out: no imp and wandered over 1f out: wknd ins fnl f* **33/1**

1m 23.01s (-0.09) **Going Correction** -0.15s/f (Firm)
**WFA** 3 from 4yo+ 6lb **9** Ran SP% **114.0**
Speed ratings (Par 101): **94,93,93,90,89 88,87,85,82**
CSF £69.06 CT £254.80 TOTE £6.30: £2.50, £3.30, £1.50; EX 71.80 Trifecta £277.40.
**Owner** BGC Racing **Bred** Barouche Stud Ireland Ltd **Trained** Eastbury, Berks

**FOCUS**
A moderate handicap and the third set a steady tempo. This is the winner's best form since she was a 2yo.
T/Jkpt: Not Won. T/Plt: £565.70 to a £1 stake. Pool: £70,653.49 - 91.16 winning units T/Qpdt: £233.50 to a £1 stake. Pool: £4,922.86 - 15.60 winning units **Steve Payne**

# 4746 KEMPTON (A.W) (R-H)
Wednesday, August 9

**OFFICIAL GOING: Polytrack: standard to slow (watering)**
Wind: Quite Fresh, against Weather: Rain, uninterrupted

## 5793 TRISTAR WORLDWIDE CHAUFFEUR SERVICES H'CAP 1m (P)
**6:05** (6:07) (Class 6) (0-60,61) 3-Y-0+ **£2,587** (£770; £384; £192) **Stalls** Low

Form RPR

6652 **1** **Mutineer**[9] 5485 3-9-2 **60** ................ HarryBentley 5 69
(Daniel Kubler) *led 1f: trckd ldng pair after: led again jst over 2f out and sent for home: clr fnl f: rdn out* **10/3**[1]

4365 **2** 2 **Satchville Flyer**[15] 5248 6-9-4 **55** ................ KieranShoemark 6 60
(David Evans) *hld up in last pair: rdn and prog on outer 2f out: styd on wl to take 2nd last strides* **12/1**

0050 **3** 1/2 **Chetan**[13] 5339 5-8-13 **55** ................ (t) JoshuaBryan(5) 3 59
(Charlie Wallis) *chsd ldrs: rdn and prog over 2f out: chsd wnr wl over 1f out w hd to one side: no imp after: lost 2nd last strides* **14/1**

0045 **4** 1 1/2 **Dream Start**[18] 5158 3-9-2 **60** ................ (t) StevieDonohoe 7 60
(John Ryan) *chsd ldrs: urged along fr 1/2-way: styd in tch but flat out to hold pl fr over 2f out* **16/1**

40 **5** nk **Freddy With A Y (IRE)**[39] 4350 7-9-8 **59** ................ DavidProbert 8 59
(J R Jenkins) *hld up in midfield: rdn and prog over 2f out: disp 3rd over 1f out: one pce* **7/1**[3]

4344 **6** hd **Estibdaad (IRE)**[105] 2095 7-9-4 **58** ................ (t) EdwardGreatrex(3) 12 58
(Paddy Butler) *rousted along strly fr s and pressed ldr over 6f out: drvn over 2f out: stl disputing 3rd over 1f out: no ex* **16/1**

U101 **7** 1 1/4 **Misu Pete**[23] 4970 5-9-7 **58** ................ OisinMurphy 2 55
(Mark Usher) *hld up in midfield: effrt on inner jst over 2f out: sn rdn and no imp on ldrs over 1f out* **7/1**[3]

0635 **8** 1/2 **Casado (IRE)**[28] 4748 3-9-2 **60** ................ KierenFox 4 55
(John Best) *hld up in 9th: pushed along over 2f out: kpt on one pce after: no ch whn reminders ins fnl f* **4/1**[2]

4-36 **9** 1 1/4 **Barista (IRE)**[64] 3422 9-9-1 **59** ................ MillyNaseb(7) 13 52
(Brian Forsey) *lost grnd sn after s and detached in last: passed a few late on but nvr in it* **25/1**

036 **10** 4 1/2 **Sir Compton**[12] 5359 4-9-6 **57** ................ (b1) TedDurcan 1 39
(Stuart Kittow) *awkward s: hld up in last quartet: tried to make grnd on inner over 2f out: wknd over 1f out* **10/1**

5000 **11** 1 **Tifl**[19] 5111 4-9-7 **58** ................ (b1) JFEgan 10 38
(Heather Main) *led after 1f to jst over 2f out: wknd qckly* **12/1**

66-0 **12** 2 1/4 **Sandacres**[39] 4350 4-9-8 **59** ................ JohnFahy 14 34
(Laura Mongan) *racd wd in midfield: u.p 3f out: wknd 2f out* **25/1**

1m 39.72s (-0.08) **Going Correction** +0.175s/f (Slow)
**WFA** 3 from 4yo+ 7lb **12** Ran SP% **118.7**
Speed ratings (Par 101): **107,105,104,103,102 102,101,100,99,95 94,91**
CSF £44.52 CT £493.32 TOTE £4.60: £2.00, £3.90, £3.40; EX 49.70 Trifecta £906.90.
**Owner** Ontoawinner & Capture The Moment IV **Bred** Stourbank Stud **Trained** Lambourn, Berks

**FOCUS**
A low-grade handicap but run at a solid pace and the winner has been rated back to his best.

## 5794 32RED ON THE APP STORE MAIDEN STKS 1m (P)
**6:35** (6:37) (Class 4) 3-Y-0+ **£5,175** (£1,540; £769; £384) **Stalls** Low

Form RPR

02 **1** **Jus Pires (USA)**[37] 4444 3-9-5 0 ................ (t) JamesDoyle 7 83
(Jeremy Noseda) *pressed ldr: shkn up over 2f out: pressed new ldr over 1f out and sn chalng: impeded ins fnl f: drvn to ld last 75yds* **15/8**[1]

0 **2** hd **Zain Star (IRE)**[106] 2066 3-9-5 0 ................ JFEgan 12 82
(John Butler) *racd wd thrght: in tch: prog over 2f out to ld over 1f out: edgd rt u.p ins fnl f: hdd and jst hld last 75yds* **14/1**

03-2 **3** 1 1/2 **Harvest Wind (IRE)**[15] 5247 3-9-5 79 ................ AdamKirby 8 78
(Clive Cox) *trckd ldrs: shkn up over 2f out: prog to go 3rd ins fnl f: kpt on steadily but nvr able to chal* **9/2**[3]

63 **4** 1 1/4 **Ancient Foe**[15] 5243 3-9-5 0 ................ DavidProbert 1 75
(Andrew Balding) *mde most but pressed: rdn and hdd over 1f out: fdd ins fnl f* **3/1**[2]

345- **5** 2 1/4 **Caledonia Duchess**[249] 8205 4-9-2 65 ................ JoshuaBryan(5) 10 66
(Jo Hughes) *dwlt: wl in rr: nt clr run over 2f out and swtchd lft: urged along and prog over 1f out: kpt on same pce ins fnl f* **33/1**

**6** hd **Ashwass (USA)** 3-9-5 0 ................ JackMitchell 9 70
(Roger Varian) *hld up towards rr: pushed along and prog over 1f out: reminder and kpt on ins fnl f: no threat* **12/1**

06 **7** shd **Section D'Or**[15] 5243 3-9-5 0 ................ KieranShoemark 13 69
(David Menuisier) *mostly chsd ldng pair to over 2f out: wknd fnl f* **66/1**

2- **8** 5 **Shadow Beauty**[244] 8277 3-9-2 0 ................ MarcMonaghan(3) 2 57
(Marco Botti) *in tch: urged along wl over 2f out: wknd over 1f out* **9/1**

**9** 1/2 **Crystal Sunstone** 3-9-5 0 ................ CharlesBishop 3 56
(Eve Johnson Houghton) *s.s: a wl in rr: nvr a factor* **25/1**

**10** 1 1/4 **Bleu Et Noir**[54] 6-9-12 0 ................ (h) StevieDonohoe 6 54
(Tim Vaughan) *sed slowest of all: detached in last early: nvr a factor* **66/1**

**11** 3 3/4 **Captain Cockle** 4-9-9 0 ................ TimClark(3) 5 45
(Roger Teal) *slowly away: sn in midfield: rdn and wknd over 2f out* **100/1**

**12** 3/4 **Hawker Hurricane (IRE)** 3-9-5 0 ................ AntonioFresu 4 42
(Luke McJannet) *prom tl wknd over 2f out* **66/1**

1m 40.3s (0.50) **Going Correction** +0.175s/f (Slow)
**WFA** 3 from 4yo+ 7lb **12** Ran SP% **114.6**
Speed ratings (Par 105): **104,103,102,101,98 98,98,93,93,91 88,87**
CSF £28.51 TOTE £2.50: £1.40, £3.20, £1.70; EX 27.80 Trifecta £120.60.
**Owner** Nigel O'Sullivan **Bred** Adrian Regan & Fergus Galvin **Trained** Newmarket, Suffolk
■ Stewards' Enquiry : J F Egan caution: careless riding

**FOCUS**
A thrilling finish to the maiden with the favourite rallying gamely in the final 100 yards.

## 5795 BRITISH STALLION STUDS EBF FILLIES' NOVICE STKS (PLUS 10 RACE) 7f (P)
**7:05** (7:06) (Class 4) 2-Y-0 **£4,528** (£1,347; £673; £336) **Stalls** Low

Form RPR

**1** **Verandah** 2-9-0 0 ................ RobertTart 2 84+
(John Gosden) *dwlt: hld up in last pair: rapid prog on inner over 2f out to ld over 1f out: sn clr: eased last 75yds: impressive debut* **5/1**[2]

**2** 2 **Fille De Reve** 2-9-0 0 ................ JimCrowley 13 74+
(Ed Walker) *dwlt: hld up in midfield: stuck bhd rivals over 2f out to over 1f out: gd prog after: r.o fnl f to take 2nd last strides: no match for wnr but promising debut* **16/1**

**3** shd **West Palm Beach (IRE)** 2-9-0 0 ................ KieranShoemark 10 74+
(John Gosden) *dwlt: hld up in last: detached jst over 2f out: gd prog over 1f out: chsd wnr ins fnl f: no match for her but styd on: lost 2nd last strides: promising debut* **13/2**[3]

03 **4** 1 1/2 **Paint**[11] 5430 2-9-0 0 ................ DavidProbert 4 70
(Richard Hannon) *hld up in midfield: pushed along and prog 2f out: sn outpcd but kpt on* **14/1**

**5** 1 **Final Set (IRE)** 2-9-0 0 ................ TedDurcan 14 67+
(Sir Michael Stoute) *dwlt: flashed tail early: in rr: prog 2f out: tried to cl over 1f out but others gng much faster: kpt on same pce* **10/1**

**6** 1 1/4 **Najmah (IRE)** 2-9-0 0 ................ OisinMurphy 8 64
(Ismail Mohammed) *pressed ldr to 2f out: steadily fdd* **12/1**

5 **7** hd **Shaherezada (IRE)**[20] 5056 2-9-0 0 ................ AdamKirby 6 63
(Clive Cox) *racd lazily early and str reminder after 1f: effrt on inner over 2f out: no prog over 1f out* **5/1**[2]

43 **8** hd **Falcon's Vision**[34] 4528 2-9-0 0 ................ JamesDoyle 5 63
(David Simcock) *led: hung lft over 2f out: hdd and btn over 1f out: continued to hang lft and ended towards nr side rail* **7/2**[1]

04 **9** nse **Tell Me (IRE)**[12] 5372 2-9-0 0 ................ (v) HarryBentley 3 63
(Simon Crisford) *awkward s: sn chsd ldrs: urged along 3f out: wknd over 1f out* **10/1**

3 **10** 2 1/2 **Lady Of Petra**[13] 5321 2-9-0 0 ................ CharlesBishop 1 56
(Eve Johnson Houghton) *chsd ldng pair to 2f out: sn wknd* **14/1**

0 **11** 2 1/2 **Sunday Best**[41] 4253 2-8-7 0 ................ Pierre-LouisJamin(7) 7 49
(Jonathan Portman) *trapped out wd: chsd ldrs tl wknd jst over 2f out* **50/1**

1m 27.98s (1.98) **Going Correction** +0.175s/f (Slow) **11** Ran SP% **115.9**
Speed ratings (Par 93): **95,92,92,90,89 88,88,87,87,84 82**
CSF £80.75 TOTE £3.80: £1.60, £4.20, £3.10; EX 82.70 Trifecta £587.60.
**Owner** Cheveley Park Stud **Bred** Cheveley Park Stud Ltd **Trained** Newmarket, Suffolk
■ Stewards' Enquiry : Kieran Shoemark 10-day ban: failing to ride out

**FOCUS**
Some well-bred fillies in opposition and a striking winner. It will probably pay to take a positive view of the form.

## 5796 100% PROFIT BOOST AT 32REDSPORT.COM MAIDEN FILLIES' STKS 1m 3f 219y(P)
**7:35** (7:36) (Class 4) 3-Y-0+ **£5,175** (£1,540; £769; £384) **Stalls** Centre

Form RPR

0-64 **1** **Ouja**[12] 5364 3-9-0 72 ................ JimCrowley 4 78
(John Gosden) *trckd ldr: led over 2f out: pressed after but sn shkn up and drew clr over 1f out: comf* **9/4**[2]

05 **2** 3 **Lady Macha**[35] 4497 3-9-0 0 ................ HarryBentley 5 73
(Marco Botti) *hld up in last: wnt 3rd over 2f out and on terms w ldng pair: shkn up briefly and outpcd over 1f out: pushed along and styd on to take 2nd ins fnl f* **16/1**[3]

2 **3** 1 1/2 **Kohinur**[12] 5364 3-9-0 0 ................ JamesDoyle 3 71
(Hugo Palmer) *trckd ldng pair: shkn up to chse wnr over 2f out and sn chalng: nt qckn and outpcd over 1f out: wl hld after: lost 2nd ins fnl f* **4/9**[1]

60 **4** 16 **Dartmoor Girl (IRE)**[42] 4224 3-8-7 0 ................ (b1) JordanUys(7) 1 45
(Mark Gillard) *led at modest pce: hdd over 2f out: qckly lft bhd* **200/1**

2m 43.28s (8.78) **Going Correction** +0.175s/f (Slow)
**WFA** 3 from 4yo 10lb **4** Ran SP% **106.4**
Speed ratings (Par 102): **77,75,74,63**
CSF £23.18 TOTE £3.10; EX 11.20 Trifecta £19.50.
**Owner** Abdullah Saeed Al Naboodah **Bred** Stowell Park Stud **Trained** Newmarket, Suffolk

**FOCUS**
A steady pace for the maiden and the winner proved best equipped to deal with the sprint finish.

## 5797 32RED.COM CASINO H'CAP 7f (P)
**8:05** (8:06) (Class 5) (0-75,75) 3-Y-0 **£3,234** (£962; £481; £240) **Stalls** Low

Form RPR

-013 **1** **Sheikspear**[19] 5111 3-9-7 **75** ................ JFEgan 11 81
(Ed de Giles) *t.k.h: trckd ldng trio: wnt 2nd over 1f out: sn rdn and edgd rt: cajoled along fnl f to ld last 75yds: clung on as packed clsd qckly nr fin* **7/1**[3]

304- **2** nk **Tobrave (IRE)**[286] 7648 3-9-2 **75** ................ (h) DavidEgan(5) 8 80+
(Roger Varian) *s.i.s: hld up in rr: prog 2f out: rdn and r.o fnl f: tk 2nd last strides: nt rch wnr* **6/1**[2]

3-20 **3** shd **Narjes**[29] 4728 3-9-3 **71** ................ (h) TomQueally 12 76+
(James Fanshawe) *awkward s: hld up in last: prog on outer over 1f out: stl only 8th ins fnl f: fin best of all but too late* **14/1**

-544 **4** nse **Mudallel (IRE)**[39] 4332 3-9-2 **70** ................ JamesDoyle 1 75
(Ed Dunlop) *chsd ldrs: rdn and prog over 1f out: tk 3rd ins fnl f: clsd nr fin but passed by others last strides* **4/1**[1]

3331 **5** hd **Seprani**[21] 5028 3-9-0 **68** ................ (h) JosephineGordon 4 72
(Marco Botti) *trckd ldng pair: rdn to ld over 1f out: hdd last 75yds: lost pls fnl strides* **11/1**

4455 **6** shd **Diable D'Or (IRE)**[23] 4983 3-9-0 **71** ................ (v1) EdwardGreatrex(3) 10 75
(Eve Johnson Houghton) *hld up in rr: rdn over 2f out: prog on outer over 1f out: clsd on ldrs nr fin but nt as fast as others* **11/1**

006 **7** 2 **Red Gunner**[23] 4983 3-9-5 **73** ................ JimCrowley 2 72
(David O'Meara) *in tch in midfield: rdn and nt qckn 2f out: kpt on same pce after and no imp on ldrs* **8/1**

5050 **8** 1 3/4 **Milburn Jack**[21] 5031 3-9-1 **69**..........(v[1]) AdamKirby 3 63
(Clive Cox) *led to over 1f out: wknd fnl f* **7/1**[3]
0046 **9** 1/2 **Lonely The Brave (IRE)**[14] 5280 3-9-0 **68**.......... OisinMurphy 5 61
(Mark Johnston) *chsd ldrs: rdn over 2f out: no prog and fdd fnl f* **16/1**
0-02 **10** nk **Miss Anticipation (IRE)**[26] 4843 3-8-7 **66**.......... PaddyPilley(5) 6 58
(Roger Charlton) *t.k.h: trckd ldr to 2f out: sn wknd* **16/1**
0040 **11** nk **Know The Truth**[34] 4537 3-8-7 **68** ow1.......... MichaelColes(7) 7 59
(Andrew Balding) *dwlt: wl in rr: nt clr run briefly over 2f out: brief effrt on inner sn after: no prog over 1f out* **33/1**
420- **12** 2 3/4 **Desert Grey (IRE)**[230] 8486 3-9-5 **73**..........(t[1]) KieranShoemark 13 56
(Roger Charlton) *trapped out wd towards rr: no prog over 2f out: wknd over 1f out* **14/1**
1m 26.53s (0.53) **Going Correction** +0.175s/f (Slow) 12 Ran SP% **115.1**
Speed ratings (Par 100): **103,102,102,102,102 102,99,97,97,96 96,93**
CSF £47.16 CT £573.18 TOTE £8.00: £2.60, £2.80, £2.30; EX 55.20 Trifecta £154.40.
**Owner** Spear Family **Bred** Rosyground Stud **Trained** Ledbury, H'fords
**FOCUS**
A blanket finish for the 7f handicap, the winner doing well to overcome racing freely early.

## 5798 32RED H'CAP 1m 3f 219y(P)
**8:35** (8:36) (Class 4) (0-85,85) 3-Y-0+ **£5,175** (£1,540; £769; £384) **Stalls** Centre

Form RPR
1513 **1** **Arab Moon**[40] 4314 3-8-13 **80**.......... SilvestreDeSousa 11 92+
(William Knight) *hld up in last: stl plenty to do whn nt clr run jst over 2f out and swtchd lft: rapid prog on outer over 1f out: swept into the ld ins fnl f: sn clr: easily* **2/1**[1]
-262 **2** 2 1/2 **Whinging Willie (IRE)**[27] 4801 8-9-6 **82**..........(v) JoshuaBryan(5) 6 87
(Gary Moore) *hld up in midfield: prog over 2f out: chsd ldr briefly jst over 1f out: styd on to take 2nd again last 100yds but no match for wnr* **8/1**
3260 **3** 1 **Artful Rogue (IRE)**[13] 5330 6-9-9 **80**.......... PatDobbs 4 83
(Amanda Perrett) *trckd ldrs: wnt 2nd 3f out gng easily: led jst over 2f out: rdn over 1f out: hdd and outpcd ins fnl f* **14/1**
-556 **4** 1 3/4 **Banish (USA)**[33] 4585 4-10-0 **85**..........(vt[1]) JamesDoyle 1 86
(Hugo Palmer) *trckd ldrs: rdn and prog to chse ldr wl over 1f out to jst over 1f out: one pce* **7/2**[2]
0-44 **5** 7 **Rubensian**[58] 3658 4-9-10 **81**.......... JimCrowley 8 70
(David Simcock) *hld up in last trio: shkn up over 2f out: tk modest 5th fnl f: no ch* **8/1**
004 **6** 1/2 **Song Of Love (IRE)**[27] 4801 5-9-4 **78**.......... CharlieBennett(3) 2 67
(Shaun Harris) *c out of stall slowly: hld up in last trio: appeared to be hanging fnl 3f and no great prog: pushed along and nvr remotely involved* **50/1**
514 **7** 5 **Distant (USA)**[28] 4751 3-8-11 **78**..........(p[1]) KieranShoemark 7 60
(Roger Charlton) *sn led and clr: breather 1/2-way: stretched on again over 4f out: rdn and hdd jst over 2f out: wknd rapidly* **13/2**[3]
1356 **8** 3/4 **Voski (USA)**[37] 4450 3-8-10 **77**.......... OisinMurphy 5 57
(Mark Johnston) *trckd ldrs: urged along over 3f out: wknd over 2f out* **9/1**
2330 **9** 4 1/2 **Ardamir (FR)**[42] 4222 5-9-9 **80**.......... JohnFahy 3 52
(Laura Mongan) *blindfold late off and slowly away: urged along to chse ldr: lost 2nd 3f out: sn wknd* **33/1**
2m 34.72s (0.22) **Going Correction** +0.175s/f (Slow)
**WFA** 3 from 4yo+ 10lb 9 Ran SP% **112.7**
Speed ratings (Par 105): **106,104,103,102,97 97,94,93,90**
CSF £18.26 CT £172.61 TOTE £2.80: £1.30, £2.50, £3.30; EX 18.90 Trifecta £156.20.
**Owner** Angmering Park Thoroughbreds Iv **Bred** Genesis Green Stud Ltd **Trained** Patching, W Sussex
**FOCUS**
An impressive display from the winner, coming from well off the pace to win going away and he has been rated to form.

## 5799 32RED.COM H'CAP 1m 7f 218y(P)
**9:05** (9:06) (Class 4) (0-85,85) 3-Y-0+ **£5,175** (£1,540; £769; £384) **Stalls** Low

Form RPR
3314 **1** **Clowance One**[14] 5303 5-10-0 **85**..........(b) KieranShoemark 5 94
(Roger Charlton) *mde all and untrbld in front: stretched on over 3f out: clr whn hung rt briefly 1f out: pushed out: unchal* **7/2**[2]
1121 **2** 3 1/2 **Dominating (GER)**[26] 4852 3-8-12 **82**.......... JamesDoyle 3 88
(Mark Johnston) *hld up disputing 3rd: shkn up over 2f out: styd on to take 2nd jst over 1f out: no imp on wnr after* **2/1**[1]
2-63 **3** 1/2 **High Command (IRE)**[39] 4355 4-9-13 **84**.......... SilvestreDeSousa 4 88
(Roger Varian) *chsd wnr after 2f: rdn and no imp over 2f out: lost 2nd and one pce jst over 1f out* **4/1**[3]
422 **4** 1 1/2 **Normandie Attack (FR)**[18] 5141 3-8-7 **77**..........(v[1]) StevieDonohoe 7 79
(Charlie Fellowes) *chsd wnr 2f: disp 3rd after: rdn over 2f out and no imp: wknd fnl f* **8/1**
-212 **5** nk **King Calypso**[35] 4499 6-9-11 **82**.......... OisinMurphy 2 84
(Denis Coakley) *hld up disputing 5th: already outpcd whn rdn over 2f out: no ch after: kpt on fnl f* **15/2**
3305 **6** 3/4 **The Blues Master (IRE)**[22] 4998 3-8-0 **70**.......... FrannyNorton 8 71
(Mark Johnston) *dwlt: hld up disputing 5th: rdn over 2f out and already outpcd: no ch after: kpt on fnl f* **16/1**
1-03 **7** 2 1/2 **Going Up (IRE)**[74] 3086 4-10-0 **85**.......... DavidProbert 1 83
(Rae Guest) *hld up: a last: rdn and no prog over 2f out* **16/1**
3m 32.37s (2.27) **Going Correction** +0.175s/f (Slow)
**WFA** 3 from 4yo+ 13lb 7 Ran SP% **110.2**
Speed ratings (Par 105): **101,99,99,98,98 97,96**
CSF £10.09 CT £25.45 TOTE £4.00: £2.30, £1.70; EX 10.20 Trifecta £34.70.
**Owner** Seasons Holidays **Bred** Mrs S A J Kinsella-Hurley **Trained** Beckhampton, Wilts
**FOCUS**
A good-quality staying handicap that saw the winner receive a perfectly judged front-running ride.
T/Plt: £183.90 to a £1 stake. Pool: £71,626.40 - 284.32 winning units T/Qpdt: £67.60 to a £1 stake. Pool: £5,721.50 - 62.56 winning units **Jonathan Neesom**

# 5453 PONTEFRACT (L-H)
### Wednesday, August 9

**OFFICIAL GOING: Soft (7.3)**
Wind: Strong across Weather: Cloudy and blustery with sunny periods

## 5800 SAMANTHA KERLEY BIRTHDAY H'CAP (FOR GENTLEMAN AMATEUR RIDERS) 1m 2f 5y
**2:10** (2:10) (Class 5) (0-75,73) 3-Y-0+ **£3,119** (£967; £483; £242) **Stalls** Low

Form RPR
0021 **1** **See The Sea (IRE)**[14] 5275 3-10-3 **68**..........(p) MrBJames(5) 1 74
(Richard Hannon) *mde all: wd st to centre: rdn clr over 1f out: kpt on wl towards fin* **3/1**[3]
5312 **2** 1 1/4 **Hawridge Glory (IRE)**[11] 5427 3-10-3 **63**.......... MrPMillman 4 67+
(Rod Millman) *hld up and bhd: pushed along 2f out: wd to centre and rdn over 1f out: styd on wl fnl f* **11/4**[2]
2512 **3** nse **Bollin Ted**[16] 5215 3-9-11 **57**.......... MrWEasterby 3 60
(Tim Easterby) *trckd ldng pair: hdwy over 2f out: styd towards inner rail st and sn rdn: chsd wnr and drvn ins fnl f: no imp towards fin* **11/8**[1]
3500 **4** 1 1/2 **King Of Dreams**[74] 3095 4-11-0 **73**..........(p) MrMSJohnson(7) 5 72
(David Simcock) *trckd ldrs: pushed along 3f out: rdn over 2f out: wd to centre home st: sn drvn and kpt on same pce* **12/1**
0530 **5** 12 **Grey Diamond**[9] 5485 3-10-4 **64**.......... MrAlexFerguson 2 40
(Mark Johnston) *trckd wnr: wd st to stands' rail and sn rdn: wknd over 1f out* **12/1**
2m 19.51s (5.81) **Going Correction** +0.20s/f (Good)
**WFA** 3 from 4yo 8lb 5 Ran SP% **109.2**
Speed ratings (Par 103): **84,83,82,81,72**
CSF £11.32 TOTE £3.90: £1.90, £1.60; EX 11.30 Trifecta £18.70.
**Owner** Middleham Park Racing XXIX **Bred** James Doyle **Trained** East Everleigh, Wilts
**FOCUS**
26mm of rain since yesterday morning left the ground soft (7.3). They finished 10secs outside standard but seemed to go through it alright. Race distances as advertised. A modest contest for amateur riders with the winner given a good ride.

## 5801 JAYNE - ON COURSE LADY BOOKMAKER EBF NOVICE STKS (PLUS 10 RACE) 6f
**2:40** (2:41) (Class 4) 2-Y-O **£5,175** (£1,540; £769; £384) **Stalls** Low

Form RPR
2 **1** **Beatbox Rhythm (IRE)**[20] 5058 2-9-2 0.......... PJMcDonald 3 88
(K R Burke) *qckly away: mde all: clr and wd st towards stands' rail: rdn over 1f out: kpt on strly* **10/11**[1]
**2** 4 **Chief Justice** 2-9-2 0.......... PaulHanagan 10 76+
(Richard Fahey) *dwlt and in rr: hdwy and wd st to stands' rail: sn chsng ldrs: rdn to chse wnr over 1f out: kpt on fnl f* **4/1**[2]
55 **3** 2 3/4 **Tebay (IRE)**[17] 5179 2-9-2 0.......... PaulMulrennan 8 68
(Michael Dods) *trckd ldng pair: hdwy over 2f out: wd st and rdn to chse wnr wl over 1f out: sn drvn and kpt on same pce* **6/1**[3]
65 **4** 8 **Mecca's Spirit (IRE)**[26] 4834 2-8-11 0.......... ConnorBeasley 4 39
(Michael Dods) *trckd ldrs: hdwy 1/2-way: sn chsng wnr: wd st and rdn wl over 1f out: sn wknd* **8/1**
0 **5** 1 1/4 **Marconi**[12] 5370 2-9-2 0.......... PhillipMakin 1 40
(John Davies) *dwlt: sn chsng ldrs: rdn along over 2f out: sn wknd* **50/1**
**6** 7 **Dowitcher (USA)** 2-8-11 0.......... FrannyNorton 7 14
(Mark Johnston) *sn outpcd and a bhd* **8/1**
0 **7** 11 **Honey Gg**[16] 5210 2-8-6 0.......... PhilDennis(5) 11
(Declan Carroll) *chsd wnr to 1/2-way: rdn along over 2f out: sn wknd* **50/1**
1m 19.89s (2.99) **Going Correction** +0.20s/f (Good) 7 Ran SP% **112.8**
Speed ratings (Par 96): **88,82,79,68,66 57,42**
CSF £4.66 TOTE £1.80: £1.20, £2.10; EX 5.60 Trifecta £16.40.
**Owner** John Dance **Bred** Martyn J McEnery **Trained** Middleham Moor, N Yorks
**FOCUS**
Probably a reasonable novice contest for the track, the winner's experience told, but he won well.

## 5802 BET WITH JAYNE - YOUR LOCAL BOOKMAKER H'CAP (DIV I) 1m 6y
**3:10** (3:11) (Class 5) (0-70,71) 3-Y-0+ **£5,175** (£1,540; £769; £384) **Stalls** Low

Form RPR
-011 **1** **Im Dapper Too**[32] 4608 6-9-9 **65**.......... SamJames 1 74
(John Davies) *trckd ldrs: wd st to stands' rail: hdwy over 1f out: rdn to chal ins fnl f: led last 100yds* **9/4**[1]
0336 **2** 1/2 **Spinart**[22] 5002 4-9-10 **66**..........(p) GrahamLee 12 74
(Pam Sly) *trckd ldrs: hdwy and cl up 2f out: wd st towards stands' rail: rdn to ld over 1f out: jnd and drvn ins fnl f: hdd last 100yds: no ex* **7/1**
0300 **3** 2 1/2 **Orientelle**[4] 5666 3-8-3 **52**..........(b) AndrewMullen 14 53
(Richard Whitaker) *t.k.h: led and sn clr: wd st and rdn: hdd over 1f out: drvn and kpt on fnl f* **33/1**
0506 **4** 2 3/4 **Cadmium**[8] 5498 6-8-9 **51** oh2..........(p) TomEaves 8 47
(Micky Hammond) *trckd ldrs: wd st to stands' rail: rdn over 1f out: drvn and kpt on fnl f* **20/1**
2306 **5** shd **Break The Silence**[28] 4765 3-8-4 **53**.......... JamesSullivan 13 47
(Scott Dixon) *chsd ldr: wd st to centre and rdn wl over 1f out: drvn appr fnl f: kpt on same pce* **20/1**
0014 **6** 1/2 **Natajack**[15] 5265 3-9-8 **71**.......... PaulHanagan 6 64
(Richard Fahey) *trckd ldrs on inner: pushed along over 2f out: wd st and rdn wl over 1f out: sn no imp* **4/1**[3]
6420 **7** 1/2 **Grey Destiny**[8] 5497 7-9-4 **60**.......... CamHardie 10 53
(Antony Brittain) *hld up towards rr: wd st and sn rdn along: kpt on fnl f: n.d* **16/1**
5331 **8** nk **Arcane Dancer (IRE)**[16] 5214 4-9-7 **63**..........(p) DanielTudhope 7 55
(Lawrence Mullaney) *hld up in tch: styd alone nr inner rail and rdn wl over 1f out: kpt on same pce* **7/2**[2]
0065 **9** 1 1/4 **Bold Spirit**[14] 5283 6-8-5 **52**..........(t) PhilDennis(5) 9 42
(Declan Carroll) *dwlt: a in rr* **20/1**
60-3 **10** 3 1/4 **Calypso Delegator (IRE)**[89] 2591 4-8-9 **51** oh3..........(p) PJMcDonald 2 33
(Micky Hammond) *dwlt: a in rr* **20/1**
1m 47.75s (1.85) **Going Correction** +0.20s/f (Good)
**WFA** 3 from 4yo+ 7lb 10 Ran SP% **113.4**
Speed ratings (Par 103): **98,97,95,92,92 91,91,90,89,86**
CSF £15.94 CT £405.82 TOTE £3.20: £1.30, £1.70, £7.70; EX 18.20 Trifecta £443.30.
**Owner** Christopher Davies **Bred** Christopher T Dawson **Trained** Piercebridge, Durham
■ Stewards' Enquiry : James Sullivan two-day ban: careless riding (Aug 26-27)

**FOCUS**
A modest race but an improving winner.

## 5803 TIESPLANET.COM - LADIES LOVE GUYS IN TIES H'CAP 1m 4f 5y
3:40 (3:40) (Class 3) (0-95,95) 3-Y-O+ £9,337 (£2,796; £1,398; £699; £349) Stalls Low

Form RPR
1250 1 **Mutadaffeq (IRE)**[11] 5397 4-9-5 86 DanielTudhope 2 90
(David O'Meara) *sn led: clr over 7f out: wd st to stands' rail: rdn over 1f out: drvn ins fnl f: kpt on* **15/8**[1]
4330 2 hd **Sennockian Star**[12] 5353 7-9-5 86 FrannyNorton 3 89
(Mark Johnston) *trckd wnr: wd st and sn rdn: drvn and styd on wl fnl f: jst hld* **3/1**[2]
-605 3 6 **Azam**[30] 4701 3-8-5 82 AndrewMullen 4 76
(Michael Appleby) *trckd ldng pair: pushed along over 2f out: wd st and rdn wl over 1f out: kpt on same pce* **5/1**
1300 4 9 **Hot Beat (IRE)**[39] 4356 5-9-13 94 (h[1]) MartinHarley 6 73
(David Simcock) *hld up and bhd: hdwy over 3f out: in tch and rdn along 2f out: wd st: sn drvn and n.d* **15/2**
10-5 5 4 ½ **Icefall (IRE)**[30] 4692 4-9-4 85 JamesSullivan 5 57
(Tim Easterby) *hld up: pushed along 4f out: rdn along 3f out: sn outpcd and bhd* **7/2**[3]

2m 41.9s (1.10) **Going Correction** +0.20s/f (Good)
**WFA** 3 from 4yo+ 10lb 5 Ran SP% **110.4**
Speed ratings (Par 107): **104,103,99,93,90**
CSF £7.76 TOTE £2.30: £1.20, £1.80; EX 6.60 Trifecta £23.30.
**Owner** The Get Round The Back Syndicate **Bred** Shadwell Estate Company Limited **Trained** Upper Helmsley, N Yorks

**FOCUS**
They finished almost in the order they raced.

## 5804 CHAPLINS CLUB H'CAP 5f 3y
4:10 (4:11) (Class 5) (0-75,83) 3-Y-O+ £3,234 (£962; £481; £240) Stalls Low

Form RPR
0044 1 **Lexington Place**[15] 5263 7-9-6 71 JackGarritty 3 80
(Ruth Carr) *hld up in rr: gd hdwy over 2f out: wd st to centre and sn cl up: rdn ent fnl f: led last 100yds* **9/1**
611 2 ½ **Muatadel**[13] 5318 4-9-8 73 TonyHamilton 2 80+
(Roger Fell) *cl up: wd st to stands' rail: rdn over 1f out: styd on wl fnl f* **4/1**[2]
0226 3 ½ **Flash City (ITY)**[16] 5211 9-9-3 68 JamesSullivan 5 73
(Ruth Carr) *hld up in rr: gd hdwy on inner 2f out: sn chsng ldr nr inner rail: rdn and ev ch ins fnl f: kpt on* **16/1**
0222 4 hd **Seamster**[5] 5587 10-9-2 74 (t) LauraCoughlan[(7)] 1 78
(David Loughnane) *cl up: led 3f out: rdn clr wl over 1f out and styd towards inner rail: rdn ent fnl f: hdd and no ex last 100yds* **4/1**[2]
0101 5 1 **Tarboosh**[8] 5495 4-10-4 83 6ex CamHardie 7 84+
(Paul Midgley) *dwlt and towards rr: wd st to stands' rail and gd hdwy over 1f out: sn rdn and styd on fnl f* **7/2**[1]
5004 6 8 **Sandra's Secret (IRE)**[19] 5129 4-9-10 75 PJMcDonald 14 47
(Les Eyre) *slt ld on outer: hdd 3f out: cl up and wd st: sn rdn and wknd over 1f out* **11/1**
6453 7 ¾ **Compton River**[25] 4896 5-9-1 66 ConnorBeasley 4 35
(Bryan Smart) *chsd ldrs: rdn along 2f out: sn wknd* **12/1**
0401 8 3 **Crosse Fire**[10] 5459 5-9-4 69 6ex (v) TomEaves 11 27
(Scott Dixon) *dwlt: chsd ldrs on outer: rdn along 2f out: sn drvn and wknd* **14/1**
0000 9 3 **See The Sun**[12] 5379 6-9-1 69 (p) RachelRichardson[(3)] 13 17
(Tim Easterby) *cl up: rdn along and wd st: sn wknd* **7/1**[3]
2440 10 4 **Jack Luey**[10] 5459 10-9-5 70 (v) PaulMulrennan 9 3
(Lawrence Mullaney) *prom: rdn along over 2f out: wd st and sn wknd* **20/1**

1m 5.2s (1.90) **Going Correction** +0.20s/f (Good)
**WFA** 3 from 4yo+ 3lb 10 Ran SP% **118.1**
Speed ratings (Par 103): **92,91,90,90,88 75,74,69,64,58**
CSF £45.54 CT £578.92 TOTE £10.40: £2.80, £1.70, £4.80; EX 40.50 Trifecta £1113.90.
**Owner** Mrs Marion Chapman & Mrs Ruth A Carr **Bred** Christopher & Annabelle Mason **Trained** Huby, N Yorks

**FOCUS**
The winner has been rated back to his early season form, with the fourth looking the key.

## 5805 RIU HOTELS AND RESORTS LADIES DAY VETERANS H'CAP 1m 6y
4:40 (4:40) (Class 4) (0-80,82) 6-Y-O+ £5,175 (£1,540; £769; £384) Stalls Low

Form RPR
0013 1 **Echo Of Lightning**[5] 5601 7-8-13 77 (p) BenRobinson[(5)] 8 86
(Brian Ellison) *trckd ldr: hdwy and wd st: led wl over 1f out: sn rdn: clr: kpt on strly* **10/3**[3]
442 2 5 **Stanley (GER)**[16] 5221 6-9-2 75 GrahamLee 7 73
(Jonjo O'Neill) *trckd ldng pair: hdwy and wd st: rdn to chse wnr over 1f out: drvn and no imp fnl f* **6/5**[1]
3513 3 ½ **Chiswick Bey (IRE)**[19] 5091 9-8-11 70 PaulHanagan 3 66
(Richard Fahey) *led: pushed along over 2f out: wd st to stands' side: sn rdn and hdd wl over 1f out: wknd appr fnl f* **3/1**[2]
4000 4 64 **Dutch Art Dealer**[39] 4339 6-9-7 80 (p) DavidNolan 4
(Ivan Furtado) *v.s.i.s: a wl bhd* **6/1**

1m 46.33s (0.43) **Going Correction** +0.20s/f (Good) 4 Ran SP% **107.8**
Speed ratings: **105,100,99,35**
CSF £7.77 TOTE £4.40; EX 9.60 Trifecta £14.70.
**Owner** Victoria Greetham & Emily Beasley **Bred** Gracelands Stud **Trained** Norton, N Yorks

**FOCUS**
A field decimated by the rain and a race won from the front. This has been rated cautiously.

## 5806 KEITH HAMMILL MEMORIAL H'CAP 6f
5:10 (5:10) (Class 4) (0-80,82) 3-Y-O+ £5,175 (£1,540; £769; £384) Stalls Low

Form RPR
0022 1 **Cosmic Chatter**[15] 5264 7-9-6 73 (p) JamesSullivan 1 83
(Ruth Carr) *cl up on inner: led 2f out: rdn over 1f out: styd on strly and clr ins fnl f* **3/1**[2]
0220 2 4 ½ **Harwoods Volante (IRE)**[11] 5415 6-10-1 82 DanielTudhope 10 78
(David O'Meara) *trckd ldrs on outer: hdwy 2f out: sn chsng wnr and rdn over 1f out: drvn ins fnl f: sn no imp* **4/1**[3]
4211 3 ½ **Mr Orange (IRE)**[19] 5132 4-9-8 75 (p) TonyHamilton 2 69
(Paul Midgley) *hld up: hdwy on inner over 2f out: chsd ldng pair wl over 1f out: sn rdn: drvn and no imp fnl f* **9/4**[1]
-424 4 11 **Equiano Springs**[32] 4604 3-9-3 74 AndrewMullen 3 32
(Tom Tate) *chsd ldr: rdn along wl over 2f out: outpcd fr wl over 1f out* **9/1**
1423 5 7 **In Ken's Memory**[13] 5341 4-9-8 75 AlistairRawlinson 6 11
(Michael Appleby) *a in rr* **11/2**
-050 6 1 ¼ **Angel Meadow**[56] 3709 3-9-6 77 PJMcDonald 4 8
(Micky Hammond) *chsd ldrs: rdn along over 2f out: sn outpcd* **14/1**
400- 7 9 **Barkston Ash**[341] 6079 9-9-3 70 (p) JasonHart 7
(Eric Alston) *racd wd: led: rdn along and hdd 2f out: sn wknd* **25/1**

1m 17.44s (0.54) **Going Correction** +0.20s/f (Good)
**WFA** 3 from 4yo+ 4lb 7 Ran SP% **111.7**
Speed ratings (Par 105): **104,98,97,82,73 71,59**
CSF £14.63 CT £29.85 TOTE £3.70: £2.40, £2.00; EX 9.90 Trifecta £39.30.
**Owner** Grange Park Racing VII **Bred** Harrowgate Bloodstock Ltd **Trained** Huby, N Yorks

**FOCUS**
A decent Class 4 where the jockeys decided to stay up the far rail for the first time today. The race was once again dominated by a front-runner. The level is fluid.

## 5807 BET WITH JAYNE - YOUR LOCAL BOOKMAKER H'CAP (DIV II) 1m 6y
5:40 (5:40) (Class 5) (0-70,69) 3-Y-O+ £5,175 (£1,540; £769; £384) Stalls Low

Form RPR
5014 1 **Ventura Secret (IRE)**[12] 5376 3-8-10 61 RachelRichardson[(3)] 8 72
(Tim Easterby) *mde all: rdn wl over 1f out: jnd and drvn ins fnl f: hld on gamely towards fin* **2/1**[1]
6000 2 nk **Dandyleekie (IRE)**[13] 5318 5-10-0 69 DanielTudhope 5 80
(David O'Meara) *trckd ldrs: hdwy 2f out: chsd wnr over 1f out: sn rdn: drvn to chal ins fnl f: ev ch tl no ex towards fin* **4/1**[2]
4060 3 7 **Rockliffe**[20] 5074 4-8-9 50 oh1 (p[1]) PJMcDonald 4 45
(Micky Hammond) *hld up in tch: hdwy on inner 2f out: rdn over 1f out: kpt on u.p fnl f* **8/1**
5140 4 1 **Bit Of A Quirke**[7] 5540 4-9-11 66 JasonHart 13 59
(Mark Walford) *trckd ldrs: hdwy and cl up over 2f out: rdn along wl over 1f out: sn drvn and kpt on one pce* **7/1**
4545 5 3 ¼ **Sooqaan**[17] 5181 6-8-9 50 CamHardie 11 35
(Antony Brittain) *hld up: hdwy over 2f out: rdn along wl over 1f out: n.d* **17/2**
005 6 hd **Bertha Burnett (IRE)**[39] 4344 6-8-2 50 oh5 ConnorMurtagh[(7)] 7 35
(Brian Rothwell) *a towards rr* **25/1**
3-00 7 4 ½ **Buccaneers Cove (IRE)**[12] 5378 3-8-13 61 TonyHamilton 12 34
(Richard Fahey) *chsd wnr: rdn along over 2f out: sn wknd* **10/1**
0200 8 32 **Arithmetic (IRE)**[15] 5261 4-9-9 64 JamesSullivan 6
(Ruth Carr) *chsd ldrs on outer: rdn along over 3f out: sn wknd* **6/1**[3]

1m 47.94s (2.04) **Going Correction** +0.20s/f (Good)
**WFA** 3 from 4yo+ 7lb 8 Ran SP% **114.7**
Speed ratings (Par 103): **97,96,89,88,85 85,80,48**
CSF £9.97 CT £51.69 TOTE £2.70: £1.20, £1.30, £2.80; EX 9.80 Trifecta £67.70.
**Owner** Middleham Park Racing LXI & Partner **Bred** Audrey Frances Stynes **Trained** Great Habton, N Yorks

**FOCUS**
Division two was a modest enough affair but it produced a great finish between two very good jockeys.
T/Plt: £142.20 to a £1 stake. Pool: £63,271.23 - 324.66 winning units T/Qpdt: £46.50 to a £1 stake. Pool: £4,514.05 - 71.76 winning units **Joe Rowntree**

# 5507 YARMOUTH (L-H)
### Wednesday, August 9

**OFFICIAL GOING: Good to soft changing to soft after race 3 (6.15)**
Wind: Strong behind Weather: Showers

## 5808 BRITISH STALLION STUDS EBF "STALLION-RESTRICTED" NOVICE STKS (PLUS 10 RACE) 7f 3y
5:15 (5:18) (Class 4) 2-Y-O £6,469 (£1,925; £962; £481) Stalls Centre

Form RPR
42 1 **Barford (IRE)**[33] 4583 2-9-2 0 RobHornby 5 78
(Pam Sly) *mde virtually all: shkn up and qcknd over 2f out: styd on wl* **5/1**[3]
1 2 1 **The Last Emperor**[21] 5036 2-9-8 0 AndreaAtzeni 2 81
(Roger Varian) *hld up in tch: rdn to chse wnr over 1f out: r.o* **9/4**[2]
34 3 1 ¼ **Bartholomeu Dias**[46] 4068 2-9-2 0 WilliamBuick 7 72
(Charles Hills) *prom: chsd wnr over 2f out: sn rdn: lost 2nd over 1f out: styd on same pce ins fnl f* **4/5**[1]
0 4 1 **Taurean Dancer (IRE)**[26] 4860 2-9-2 0 JamieSpencer 1 69
(Michael Bell) *w wnr tl over 4f out: remained handy: rdn over 2f out: no ex ins fnl f* **25/1**
5 ½ **Losingmyreligion (FR)** 2-9-2 0 DanielMuscutt 3 68
(Marco Botti) *hld up: rdn over 1f out: nt trble ldrs* **20/1**

1m 25.04s (-1.56) **Going Correction** -0.275s/f (Firm) 5 Ran SP% **111.6**
Speed ratings (Par 96): **97,95,94,93,92**
CSF £16.79 TOTE £5.40: £2.50, £1.40; EX 18.00 Trifecta £24.20.
**Owner** G Libson & P M Sly **Bred** L Lynch & R Sherrard **Trained** Thorney, Cambs
■ Hidden Dream was withdrawn not under orders. Rule 4 does not apply.

**FOCUS**
A soggy day ensured the going downgraded to good to soft (from good to firm) prior to racing.

## 5809 BANHAM POULTRY H'CAP 1m 2f 23y
5:45 (5:46) (Class 6) (0-65,72) 4-Y-O+ £2,264 (£673; £336; £168) Stalls Low

Form RPR
0036 1 **Maestro Mac (IRE)**[41] 4257 4-9-9 66 AndreaAtzeni 9 72
(Tom Clover) *chsd ldrs: shkn up over 2f out: rdn to ld ins fnl f: jst hld on* **9/4**[1]
4120 2 shd **Tyrsal (IRE)**[11] 5421 6-9-0 64 (p) CameronNoble[(7)] 7 69
(Clifford Lines) *s.i.s: hld up: hdwy over 2f out: rdn: hung lft and ev ch ins fnl f: styd on* **4/1**[3]
061 3 2 ½ **Polar Forest**[8] 5498 7-9-12 72 6ex (e) CliffordLee[(3)] 6 72
(Richard Guest) *led: shkn up over 2f out: rdn over 1f out: hdd ins fnl f: styd on same pce* **5/2**[2]
-056 4 ¾ **Color Force (IRE)**[160] 988 4-7-13 47 (t) JaneElliott[(5)] 5 46
(Gay Kelleway) *chsd ldr: rdn over 2f out: ev ch over 1f out: no ex ins fnl f* **7/1**
-644 5 1 **Art Scholar (IRE)**[15] 5267 10-9-2 59 LouisSteward 2 56
(Michael Appleby) *hld up: pushed along and hdwy over 1f out: no ex ins fnl f* **9/2**

2m 11.47s (0.97) **Going Correction** +0.125s/f (Good) 5 Ran SP% **110.0**
Speed ratings (Par 101): **101,100,98,98,97**
CSF £11.37 TOTE £3.30: £1.50, £2.20; EX 10.40 Trifecta £19.70.
**Owner** B Keane & S Nugent **Bred** Tom McDonald **Trained** Newmarket, Suffolk
■ Thecornishbarron was withdrawn not under orders. Rule 4 does not apply

**FOCUS**
This moderate handicap was decimated by non-runners.

## 5810 CUSTOM KITCHENS H'CAP 1m 6f 17y
6:15 (6:15) (Class 5) (0-75,73) 3-Y-O+ £2,911 (£866; £432; £216) Stalls High

Form RPR
-526 1 **Veiled Secret (IRE)**[21] 5034 3-8-13 69 RyanPowell 1 79
(Sir Mark Prescott Bt) *mde all: qcknd 4f out: pushed clr fnl 2f: easily* 8/15[1]
6553 2 12 **Excellent Puck (IRE)**[13] 4095 7-9-9 68 JamieSpencer 4 61
(Shaun Lycett) *chsd wnr 12f out tl rdn over 2f out: sn outpcd: styd on to go 2nd post* 6/1[3]
043 3 hd **Orin Swift (IRE)**[69] 3248 3-9-3 73 MartinLane 6 69
(Jonathan Portman) *prom: chsd wnr after 1f tl 12f out: remained handy: rdn to chse wnr again over 2f out: wkng whn eased ins fnl f: shkn up nr fin: lost 2nd post* 9/2[2]
0-05 4 12 **Tayaar (IRE)**[15] 5244 4-8-11 56 DanielMuscutt 3 32
(John Ryan) *broke wl: sn stdd and lost pl: rdn over 4f out: wknd 3f out* 10/1
3m 9.04s (1.44) **Going Correction** +0.125s/f (Good)
**WFA** 3 from 4yo+ 11lb 4 Ran SP% **106.8**
Speed ratings (Par 103): **100,93,93,86**
CSF £3.99 TOTE £1.40; EX 4.00 Trifecta £6.50.
**Owner** Tim Bunting - Osborne House II **Bred** Mrs Olivia Hoare **Trained** Newmarket, Suffolk

**FOCUS**
Another handicap weakened by non-runners and there has to be a doubt over the beaten runners.

## 5811 MOULTON NURSERIES OF ACLE H'CAP 5f 42y
6:45 (6:45) (Class 4) (0-85,85) 3-Y-O+ £4,690 (£1,395; £697; £348) Stalls Centre

Form RPR
60-3 1 **Discreet Hero (IRE)**[28] 4732 4-9-7 82 (t) AndreaAtzeni 7 90+
(Simon Crisford) *prom: lost pl over 3f out: hdwy 2f out: shkn up to ld ins fnl f: rdn out* 3/1[2]
2142 2 ½ **Arzaak (IRE)**[22] 4992 3-9-7 85 (b) SaleemGolam 2 90
(Chris Dwyer) *chsd ldr: rdn and ev ch fr over 1f out: styd on* 3/1[2]
50 3 1¾ **Lydia's Place**[33] 4574 4-9-1 79 CliffordLee(3) 1 79
(Richard Guest) *led: rdn over 1f out: sn edgd rt: hdd ins fnl f: styd on same pce* 11/2
0000 4 2¾ **Exceed The Limit**[12] 5354 4-9-10 85 (p) JamieSpencer 5 75
(Robert Cowell) *trckd ldrs: shkn up 1/2-way: no ex fnl f* 11/4[1]
0601 5 ¾ **Just Us Two (IRE)**[27] 4795 5-9-3 78 (p) DanielMuscutt 8 66
(Robert Cowell) *hdwy over 3f out: rdn over 1f out: no ex* 9/2[3]
1m 2.01s (-0.69) **Going Correction** -0.275s/f (Firm)
**WFA** 3 from 4yo+ 3lb 5 Ran SP% **110.2**
Speed ratings (Par 105): **94,93,90,86,84**
CSF £12.24 TOTE £3.40: £2.20, £1.90; EX 9.90 Trifecta £38.30.
**Owner** Abdullah Saeed **Bred** Haras De Bernesq **Trained** Newmarket, Suffolk

**FOCUS**
The going was changed to soft after the preceding race. Despite three defections this was a fair little sprint handicap, with the winner on the up.

## 5812 USPGA GOLF AT 188BET H'CAP 5f 42y
7:15 (7:15) (Class 6) (0-60,61) 3-Y-O £2,264 (£673; £336; £168) Stalls Centre

Form RPR
5652 1 **Tea El Tee (IRE)**[14] 5289 3-8-8 52 (v) CameronNoble(7) 1 60
(Gay Kelleway) *led 4f out: rdn over 1f out: styd on* 8/1
325 2 1¾ **Agnethe (IRE)**[13] 5339 3-9-10 61 JoeyHaynes 4 63
(Paul D'Arcy) *chsd ldrs: chsd wnr 1/2-way: rdn over 1f out: kpt on* 9/4[1]
3500 3 2 **Atlanta Belle (IRE)**[29] 4723 3-9-6 57 AndreaAtzeni 3 52
(Chris Wall) *racd keenly: led 1f: chsd ldr to 1/2-way: sn rdn: no ex ins fnl f* 9/2
2351 4 nk **Wotadoll**[13] 5340 3-9-3 57 JackDuern(3) 9 51
(Dean Ivory) *prom: rdn over 1f out: edgd lft and styd on same pce fnl f* 3/1[3]
0214 5 7 **Cool Breeze (IRE)**[11] 5418 3-9-0 56 GeorgeBuckell(5) 8 25
(David Simcock) *broke wl: sn lost pl: nvr on terms after* 11/4[2]
1m 1.61s (-1.09) **Going Correction** -0.275s/f (Firm) 5 Ran SP% **111.7**
Speed ratings (Par 98): **97,94,91,90,79**
CSF £26.52 TOTE £9.70: £3.00, £1.60; EX 33.00 Trifecta £124.00.
**Owner** The Logistics Terminal LLP **Bred** Kilcarn Stud **Trained** Exning, Suffolk

**FOCUS**
An ordinary sprint handicap hit by defections.

## 5813 PREMIER LEAGUE FOOTBALL AT 188BET FILLIES' H'CAP 7f 3y
7:45 (7:45) (Class 5) (0-70,76) 3-Y-O+ £2,911 (£866; £432; £216) Stalls Centre

Form RPR
1011 1 **Whispered Kiss**[4] 5664 4-9-13 76 6ex GeorgeBuckell(5) 1 91
(Mike Murphy) *mde all: shkn up over 1f out: c readily clr fnl f* 4/7[1]
1202 2 5 **Patching**[8] 5510 3-9-3 67 (b) JamieSpencer 7 67
(Giles Bravery) *prom: chsd wnr over 5f out: rdn over 1f out: styd on same pce* 4/1[2]
6244 3 2¾ **Halinka (IRE)**[22] 5007 3-9-4 68 (p) PaoloSirigu 6 61
(Roger Varian) *sn chsng ldrs: rdn over 2f out: no ex fr over 1f out* 10/1[3]
4330 4 3¼ **Moi Aussie**[16] 5214 4-9-0 63 JaneElliott(5) 10 49
(Michael Appleby) *racd alone on stands' side: up w the pce 3f: rdn over 2f out: wknd over 1f out* 12/1
4-10 5 1¾ **Sea Tea Dea**[174] 763 3-9-3 67 RyanTate 8 47
(Anthony Carson) *s.i.s: sn pushed along in rr: sme hdwy over 2f out: wknd over 1f out* 14/1
5306 6 nse **Tigserin (IRE)**[33] 4561 4-8-13 57 DannyBrock 3 39
(Giles Bravery) *chsd wnr tl over 5f out: lost pl over 4f out: wknd over 2f out* 16/1
1m 24.02s (-2.58) **Going Correction** -0.275s/f (Firm)
**WFA** 3 from 4yo 6lb 6 Ran SP% **113.0**
Speed ratings (Par 100): **103,97,94,90,88 88**
CSF £3.22 CT £9.80 TOTE £1.50: £1.10, £2.30; EX 4.20 Trifecta £8.70.
**Owner** D Ellison, B Olkowicz, C Speller **Bred** T Ellison, B Olkowicz And C Speller **Trained** Westoning, Beds

**FOCUS**
Even before the non-runners this was all about the winner, who was well in following her latest Newmarket success.

## 5814 DAILY RACING SPECIALS AT 188BET H'CAP 6f 3y
8:15 (8:15) (Class 5) (0-75,75) 3-Y-O+ £2,911 (£866; £432) Stalls Centre

Form RPR
4150 1 **Summerghand (IRE)**[13] 5316 3-9-6 73 AndreaAtzeni 2 80
(David O'Meara) *disp 2nd pl tl shkn up to ld over 1f out: edgd rt ins fnl f: rdn out* 7/4[2]
0444 2 hd **Abiento (IRE)**[15] 5253 3-9-5 72 (h[1]) JamieSpencer 6 78
(Ed Walker) *disp 2nd: shkn up over 2f out: rdn over 1f out: ev ch ins fnl f: r.o* 5/4[1]
4165 3 3½ **Artscape**[12] 5369 5-9-9 75 JackDuern(3) 3 73
(Dean Ivory) *led: rdn and hdd over 1f out: no ex ins fnl f* 5/2[3]
1m 13.39s (-1.01) **Going Correction** -0.275s/f (Firm)
**WFA** 3 from 5yo+ 4lb 3 Ran SP% **109.4**
Speed ratings (Par 103): **95,94,90**
CSF £4.33 TOTE £2.80; EX 3.20 Trifecta £3.30.
**Owner** Hamad Rashed Bin Ghedayer **Bred** Airlie Stud **Trained** Upper Helmsley, N Yorks

**FOCUS**
This modest handicap was down to just a trio of sprinters.
T/Plt: £41.60 to a £1 stake. Pool: £49,667.67 - 870.38 winning units T/Qpdt: £11.10 to a £1 stake. Pool: £4,869.89 - 321.83 winning units **Colin Roberts**

# 5694 LA TESTE DE BUCH (R-H)
Wednesday, August 9
**OFFICIAL GOING: Turf: good**

## 5815a PRIX NOSTALGIE (MAIDEN) (2YO FILLIES) (TURF) 1m
4:10 2-Y-O £7,692 (£3,076; £2,307; £1,538; £769)

RPR
1 **Armoricaine** 2-9-2 0 MaximeGuyon 2 81+
(C Ferland, France) 6/4[1]
2 2 **La Houblonniere (FR)** 2-9-2 0 CristianDemuro 3 76
(J-C Rouget, France) 29/10[2]
3 1¾ **Romance Khaleesi (FR)** 2-8-8 0 DylanAlberca-Gavilan(8) 5 72
(X Thomas-Demeaulte, France) 15/2
4 2 **Carrouges (IRE)** 2-9-2 0 (p) Jean-BernardEyquem 7 68
(Simone Brogi, France) 61/10[3]
5 2 **Golden Escape (FR)** 2-8-11 0 MlleMarie-AnneBernadet(5) 10 63
(Mlle C Courtade, France) 46/1
6 ¾ **Lady Of The Court (IRE)**[11] 5448 2-9-2 0 (p) TonyPiccone 4 61
(J S Moore) *pushed along early: sn chsng ldrs on inner: led after 2f: hdd and drvn over 2 1/2f out: sn rdn and no imp: wknd appr 1f out* 61/10[3]
7 2 **Stop And Stare (FR)** 2-8-11 0 EmilienRevolte 8 52
(X Thomas-Demeaulte, France) 217/10
8 ½ **Valdaye (FR)** 2-8-11 0 FlavienGarnier 1 51
(C Gourdain, France) 61/1
9 3 **Saveurs British (IRE)** 2-8-11 0 (p) JulienAuge 6 44
(Y Durepaire, France) 241/10
10 8 **Erdiska (FR)** 2-9-2 0 Jean-BaptisteHamel 9 30
(F Seguin, France) 103/1

PARI-MUTUEL (all including 1 euro stake): WIN 2.50; PLACE 1.20, 1.20, 1.30; DF 2.80; SF 5.00.
**Owner** Wertheimer & Frere **Bred** Wertheimer & Frere **Trained** France

## 5816a PRIX ISABELLE DESMARAIS (CONDITIONS) (2YO) (TURF) 7f
4:40 2-Y-O £10,256 (£4,102; £3,076; £2,051; £1,025)

RPR
1 **Ballymount**[55] 2-9-0 0 (p) FabriceVeron 6 78
(E J O'Neill, France) 26/5[3]
2 ½ **Uther Pendragon (IRE)**[8] 5520 2-9-2 0 (p) TonyPiccone 3 79
(J S Moore) *sn led: drvn for home over 2f out: rdn whn pressed over 1f out: hdd ent fnl f: rallied gamely u.p* 13/10[1]
3 3½ **Aiyana Rose (FR)**[38] 2-9-1 0 AntoineHamelin 5 69
(Matthieu Palussiere, France) 54/10
4 nk **Danzig Spring (FR)** 2-8-7 0 HugoJourniac 7 60
(J-C Rouget, France) 19/10[2]
5 13 **Tolosane (FR)** 2-7-11 0 MlleAdelineMerou(10) 4 25
(B De Montzey, France) 205/10
6 14 **Samael (FR)** 2-8-6 0 DelphineSantiago(3) 1
(W Walton, France) 232/10
1m 30.96s 6 Ran SP% **118.5**
PARI-MUTUEL (all including 1 euro stake): WIN 6.20; PLACE 1.80, 1.40; SF 14.40.
**Owner** Mrs Melissa O'Neill **Bred** Mrs G P Booth And J Porteous **Trained** France

# 5785 BRIGHTON (L-H)
Thursday, August 10
**OFFICIAL GOING: Good to firm (firm in places 9.0)**
Wind: medium, behind Weather: sunny spells

## 5817 ROUTE MOBILE (S) H'CAP 6f 210y
2:00 (2:00) (Class 6) (0-60,59) 3-Y-O+ £2,264 (£673; £336; £168) Stalls Centre

Form RPR
0000 1 **Lutine Charlie (IRE)**[38] 4453 10-8-10 45 MartinDwyer 11 50
(Emma Owen) *t.k.h: led after 1f: mde rest: rdn 2f out: drvn and hrd pressed fr over 1f out: hld on wl ins fnl f: all out* 28/1
0005 2 nk **Corporal Maddox**[19] 5145 10-9-9 58 (p) DavidProbert 5 62
(Ronald Harris) *dwlt: sn rcvrd and hld up in tch in midfield: effrt over 1f out: hdwy u.p ins fnl f: styd on strly fnl 100yds: wnt 2nd last strides: nt quite rch wnr* 11/2
2222 3 nk **Tidal's Baby**[12] 5429 8-9-10 59 GeorgeDowning 4 62
(Tony Carroll) *hld up in tch in midfield: nudged lft jst over 2f out: hdwy u.p over 1f out: drvn and str chal 1f out: kpt on but a jst hld ins fnl f: lost 2nd last strides* 7/2[2]
0-02 4 nk **Time Medicean**[19] 5146 11-9-8 57 (t) JimCrowley 2 59
(Tony Carroll) *hld up in tch in midfield: effrt over 1f out: hdwy u.p 1f out: pressing ldrs wl ins fnl f: kpt on* 4/1[3]

0003 **5** 1 ½ **Princess Way (IRE)**[45] 4163 3-9-3 **58**....................................(v) JFEgan 8 54
(David Evans) *t.k.h early: chsd ldrs: effrt to press ldrs over 2f out: rdn 2f out: unable qck over 1f out: styd on same pce ins fnl f* **10/1**
5232 **6** ½ **Lawfilly**[21] 5050 3-9-1 **56**....................................................(p) ShaneKelly 10 51
(Richard Hughes) *t.k.h: hld up in midfield tl stdd bk to last pair after 2f out: sltly impeded jst over 2f out: effrt wd ent fnl f: styd on but no threat to ldrs* **11/4**[1]
6606 **7** nk **Fairy Mist (IRE)**[15] 5296 10-8-10 **45**............................(v) WilliamCarson 7 41
(John Bridger) *t.k.h: led for 1f out: chsd wnr after: effrt towards inner 2f out: unable qck and lost 2nd over 1f out: wknd ins fnl f* **11/1**
0060 **8** 2 ¼ **Majestic Girl (IRE)**[1] 5791 4-8-10 **45**................................ RyanTate 6 35
(Steve Flook) *s.i.s: hld up in tch in last pair: hdwy u.p on inner over 1f out: no imp 1f out: wknd ins fnl f* **16/1**
3000 **P** **Raise The Game (IRE)**[116] 1823 4-9-1 **55**.................. MitchGodwin(5) 9
(Bill Turner) *chsd ldng pair: cl up whn lost action over 2f out: p.u and dismntd 2f out (fatally injured)* **18/1**
1m 22.26s (-0.84) **Going Correction** -0.125s/f (Firm)
**WFA** 3 from 4yo+ 6lb 9 Ran SP% **116.3**
Speed ratings (Par 101): **99,98,98,97,96 95,95,92,**
CSF £175.98 CT £690.53 TOTE £28.00: £6.80, £1.70, £1.20; EX 187.90 Trifecta £1518.30.There were no bids for the winner
**Owner** Miss Emma L Owen **Bred** Patrice O'Connell **Trained** Nether Winchendon, Bucks
■ Stewards' Enquiry : Martin Dwyer two-day ban: used whip above permitted level (26th-27th Aug)
George Downing two-day ban: used whip above permitted level (26th-27th Aug)
**FOCUS**
Rail movements add 3 yards to all races. A modest selling handicap. They went a respectable gallop on ground officially described as good to firm, firm in places. Straightforward form.

## 5818 ROUTE MOBILE H'CAP 5f 60y
**2:30** (2:30) (Class 5) (0-75,76) 4-Y-0+ **£2,911** (£866; £432; £216) **Stalls** Centre

Form RPR
2060 **1** **Upavon**[16] 5241 7-9-7 **75**.........................................................(t) FranBerry 4 78
(Stuart Williams) *stdd s: trckd ldng pair: effrt over 1f out: chsd ldr u.p jst ins fnl f: styd on wl to ld last stride* **11/8**[1]
1420 **2** nse **Bronze Beau**[17] 5211 10-9-6 **74**.......................................(tp) JoeFanning 6 76
(Kristin Stubbs) *taken down early: led: rdn over 1f out: drvn and hrd pressed ins fnl f: battled on wl u.p: hdd on post* **11/2**
2266 **3** 2 ¼ **The Big Lad**[17] 5219 5-9-1 **76**.........................................(e) NicolaCurrie(7) 1 70
(Richard Hughes) *chsd ldr: effrt over 1f out: 3rd and no ex 150yds out: wknd ins fnl f* **2/1**[2]
34 **4** ½ **Sandfrankskipsgo**[44] 4178 8-9-7 **75**.................................. ShaneKelly 5 67
(Peter Crate) *stdd after s: t.k.h: hld up in tch in rr: swtchd rt wl over 1f out: sn rdn and no imp: kpt on same pce ins fnl f* **9/2**[3]
1m 1.67s (-0.63) **Going Correction** -0.125s/f (Firm) 4 Ran SP% **109.0**
Speed ratings (Par 103): **100,99,96,95**
CSF £8.74 TOTE £2.60; EX 11.30 Trifecta £28.30.
**Owner** Morley, Reynolds & Watkins **Bred** Major-Gen Guy Watkins **Trained** Newmarket, Suffolk
**FOCUS**
Race distance increased by 3 yards. A fair little sprint handicap which produced a thrilling photo-finish off an even pace. The runner-up has been rated to his best form over the past two years.

## 5819 RACEY MCRACE RACE MARATHONBET MAIDEN AUCTION STKS 7f 211y
**3:00** (3:00) (Class 5) 2-Y-0 **£2,911** (£866) **Stalls** Centre

Form RPR
02 **1** **Macaque**[22] 5030 2-9-2 0.................................................... DavidProbert 2 83
(Andrew Balding) *trckd ldr tl led on bit over 2f out: sn cruised clr: nt extended* **1/16**[1]
05 **2** 24 **Secratario (FR)**[15] 5292 2-9-1 0.......................................... ShaneKelly 3 35
(Richard Hughes) *bustled along to ld: rdn 3f out: hdd over 2f out: sn btn: eased ins fnl f* **8/1**[2]
1m 35.29s (-0.71) **Going Correction** -0.125s/f (Firm) 2 Ran SP% **105.2**
Speed ratings (Par 94): **98,74**
TOTE £1.10.
**Owner** Pink Hat Racing Partnership & Partner **Bred** Stilvi Compania Financiera Sa **Trained** Kingsclere, Hants
**FOCUS**
Race distance increased by 3 yards. A fair juvenile maiden match race. The runner-up tried to make a race of it from the front but couldn't get the long odds-on favourite off the bridle. The race has been given a token rating around the winner.

## 5820 MARATHONBET SPORTSBOOK BRIGHTON CHALLENGE CUP H'CAP 1m 3f 198y
**3:30** (3:31) (Class 4) (0-80,86) 3-Y-0+
**£12,450** (£3,728; £1,864; £932; £466; £234) **Stalls** High

Form RPR
-101 **1** **Curlew River**[8] 5533 3-9-10 **86** 6ex..................................... JoeFanning 9 97
(Mark Johnston) *mde all: travelling best over 2f out: shkn up and readily qcknd clr over 1f out: r.o wl: eased towards fin: easily* **4/1**[2]
2232 **2** 4 ½ **Sir Jack**[3] 5698 4-8-8 **63**...................................................... CliffordLee(3) 8 66
(Tony Carroll) *stdd after s: hld up in last pair: rdn and hdwy ent fnl 2f: chsd clr wnr and hung lft 1f out: kpt on but no ch w wnr* **6/1**[3]
0133 **3** ½ **Cotton Club (IRE)**[26] 4913 6-9-6 **72**............................ WilliamCarson 14 74
(Rod Millman) *stdd s: hld up in last pair: clsd whn nt clrest of runs and swtchd rt over 2f out: hdwy over 1f out: styd on to go 3rd 75yds out: no ch w wnr* **8/1**
3232 **4** 1 ¾ **Prendergast Hill (IRE)**[14] 5313 5-9-11 **80**........... CallumShepherd(3) 12 79
(Ed de Giles) *t.k.h: hld up in tch in midfield: hdwy to chse ldrs 6f out: wnt 2nd 3f out: sn rdn: outpcd over 1f out: lost 2nd and kpt on same pce fnl f* **7/2**[1]
1550 **5** 3 ¼ **Mullarkey**[27] 4865 3-8-10 **72**................................................. MartinDwyer 4 67
(John Best) *hld up in tch in midfield: effrt over 2f out: no imp u.p over 1f out: wknd ins fnl f* **13/2**
3130 **6** 5 **Star Of Lombardy (IRE)**[12] 5414 4-9-7 **73**......................... JFEgan 5 59
(Mark Johnston) *chsd wnr tl 8f out: rdn 3f out: lost pl and bhd 2f out: sn wknd* **14/1**
2221 **7** 1 **Therthaar**[42] 4260 4-9-11 **77**.................................................. JimCrowley 6 62
(Ismail Mohammed) *chsd ldrs: rdn over 2f out: sn struggling: wl btn over 1f out: wknd fnl f* **6/1**[3]
1240 **8** 8 **Start Seven**[14] 5330 5-9-12 **78**........................................ DougieCostello 13 50
(Jamie Osborne) *dwlt: sn rcvrd and in tch in midfield: lost 2nd 3f out and sn lost pl u.p: bhd fnl f* **33/1**
1010 **9** ½ **Spinners Ball (IRE)**[12] 5397 4-9-9 **80**.......................... MitchGodwin(5) 7 51
(Sylvester Kirk) *hld up in last trio: effrt 3f out: no imp and btn 2f out: sn wknd* **9/1**
2m 30.07s (-2.63) **Going Correction** -0.125s/f (Firm)
**WFA** 3 from 4yo+ 10lb 9 Ran SP% **114.8**
Speed ratings (Par 105): **103,100,99,98,96 93,92,87,86**
CSF £28.08 CT £182.37 TOTE £3.90: £1.70, £1.70, £2.50; EX 22.50 Trifecta £127.80.
**Owner** Sheikh Hamdan bin Mohammed Al Maktoum **Bred** Darley **Trained** Middleham Moor, N Yorks
**FOCUS**
Race distance increased by 3 yards. The feature contest was a decent middle-distance handicap. An improving filly thoroughly dominated in the quickest comparative time on the card so far. The second and third have been rated close to their recent form.

## 5821 SILK SERIES LADY RIDERS' H'CAP (FOR PRO-AM LADY RIDERS) 6f 210y
**4:00** (4:00) (Class 4) (0-80,82) 3-Y-0+ **£6,469** (£1,925; £962; £481) **Stalls** Centre

Form RPR
212 **1** **Honiara**[34] 4587 4-10-9 **82**...........................................(b) MeganNicholls 10 88
(Paul Cole) *t.k.h: w ldr: effrt over 1f out: rdn ins fnl f: edgd lft briefly ins fnl f: styd on to ld towards fin* **11/4**[2]
1411 **2** ½ **Believe It (IRE)**[57] 3718 5-10-2 **75**.................................(b) NicolaCurrie 5 80
(Richard Hughes) *t.k.h: sn led: rdn over 1f out: drvn 1f out: edgd lft wl ins fnl f: hdd and no ex towards fin* **5/2**[1]
0162 **3** 1 ¼ **Gold Hunter (IRE)**[27] 4844 7-10-4 **77**......................(p) MissSBrotherton 3 79
(Steve Flook) *trckd ldng pair: effrt on inner over 1f out: rdn 1f out: stl pressing ldrs but hld whn squeezed for room wl ins fnl f* **7/2**[3]
0206 **4** 5 **Palawan**[13] 5369 4-10-8 **81**...................................................... LucyKBarry 6 69
(Jamie Osborne) *hld up wl in tch in midfield: rdn 2f out: outpcd u.p over 1f out: wknd ins fnl f* **9/1**
3200 **5** ¾ **Athassel**[9] 5519 8-10-2 **80**........................................ MissEMacKenzie(5) 9 66
(David Evans) *racd in 5th: nvr on terms w ldrs: effrt over 2f out: no imp and wl hld over 1f out* **8/1**
2006 **6** ¾ **Spirit Of Sarwan (IRE)**[20] 5115 3-9-7 **72**..................(p) ShelleyBirkett 8 54
(Julia Feilden) *s.i.s: nvr travelling wl in rr: n.d* **7/1**
1m 21.64s (-1.46) **Going Correction** -0.125s/f (Firm)
**WFA** 3 from 4yo+ 6lb 6 Ran SP% **111.1**
Speed ratings (Par 105): **103,102,101,95,94 93**
CSF £9.82 CT £22.00 TOTE £3.40: £1.40, £1.80; EX 7.80 Trifecta £23.60.
**Owner** Meyrick Wright Asprey PJL Racing Wilcock **Bred** Scea Haras De Saint Pair **Trained** Whatcombe, Oxon
■ Stewards' Enquiry : Nicola Currie two-day ban: careless riding (Aug 29-30)
**FOCUS**
Race distance increased by 3 yards. A decent lady riders' handicap. They went a respectable gallop and it is sound form. The level is a bit fluid, but the winner has been rated in line with the better view of his turf form.

## 5822 MARATHONBET LIVE CASINO FILLIES' H'CAP 1m 1f 207y
**4:30** (4:31) (Class 4) (0-85,80) 3-Y-0+ **£4,690** (£1,395; £697; £348) **Stalls** High

Form RPR
6126 **1** **Impressive Day (IRE)**[47] 4089 4-9-9 **75**....................(p) TimmyMurphy 7 83
(Gary Moore) *hld up in last pair: shkn up over 2f out: rdn and clsd over 1f out: chsd wnr 1f out: styd on wl u.p to ld last stride* **12/1**
412 **2** shd **Marie Josephe**[31] 4699 3-9-4 **78**.......................................... ShaneKelly 2 86
(Richard Hughes) *led: rdn and fnd ex 2f out: drvn ent fnl f: kpt on ins fnl f: hdd last stride* **7/2**[3]
421 **3** 2 ¾ **Frosting**[20] 5124 3-9-6 **80**...................................................... JoeFanning 5 83
(William Haggas) *chsd ldng pair tl wnt 2nd 4f out: effrt over 2f out: unable qck u.p and lost 2nd 1f out: styd on same pce ins fnl f: eased nr fin* **10/3**[2]
0312 **4** 2 **Light Of Joy (USA)**[33] 4621 3-9-6 **80**................................ TomQueally 4 79
(David Lanigan) *stdd after s: hld up in last pair: effrt over 2f out: sme hdwy u.p over 1f out: no imp 1f out: styd on same pce ins fnl f* **9/4**[1]
045 **5** nse **Pernickety**[41] 4319 4-9-2 **68**.................................................(h) FranBerry 1 66
(Lucy Wadham) *hld up in tch in 4th: effrt over 2f out: no imp u.p: edgd lft and kpt on ins fnl f: no threat to ldrs* **7/1**
1640 **6** ¾ **Darkroom Angel**[9] 5506 3-9-0 **77**................................ HectorCrouch(3) 3 74
(Philip Hide) *chsd ldr tl 4f out: styd prom: rdn 3f out: unable qck over 1f out: wknd ins fnl f* **11/2**
2m 0.54s (-3.06) **Going Correction** -0.125s/f (Firm)
**WFA** 3 from 4yo+ 8lb 6 Ran SP% **111.6**
Speed ratings (Par 102): **107,106,104,103,103 102**
CSF £52.34 CT £171.07 TOTE £12.80: £5.20, £1.80; EX 72.00 Trifecta £196.00.
**Owner** Power Geneva Ltd **Bred** Darley **Trained** Lower Beeding, W Sussex
**FOCUS**
Race distance increased by 3 yards. A fairly decent fillies' handicap. They went a proper gallop and clocked marginally the quickest comparative winning time on the day. The winner has been rated back to her June form here.

## 5823 ROUTEMOBILE.COM H'CAP 7f 211y
**5:00** (5:00) (Class 6) (0-60,62) 3-Y-0+ **£2,911** (£866; £432; £216) **Stalls** Centre

Form RPR
5240 **1** **Buzz Lightyere**[1] 5790 4-9-7 **55**........................................ DavidProbert 5 64
(Philip Hide) *midfield tl hdwy to chse ldrs over 6f out: chsd ldr over 3f out: rdn and clsd to chal 1f out: led ins fnl f: r.o wl and holding chalr towards fin* **13/8**[1]
-554 **2** nk **Pick A Little**[27] 4846 9-9-9 **62**........................................ MitchGodwin(5) 10 70
(Michael Blake) *chsd ldr tl over 3f out: drvn and clsd over 1f out: chal ins fnl f: r.o wl and drew clr w wnr fnl 100yds: hld towards fin* **7/1**[3]
5632 **3** 2 ¾ **Live Dangerously**[12] 5410 7-9-11 **59**............................ WilliamCarson 13 61
(John Bridger) *led: rdn and fnd ex 2f out: drvn and hrd pressed 1f out: hdd ins fnl f: wknd towards fin* **5/1**[2]
0452 **4** 1 ½ **Rattle On**[5] 5651 4-9-7 **60**..........................................(p) PaddyBradley(5) 14 59
(Jim Boyle) *hld up in tch in midfield: effrt to chse ldng trio whn hung lft u.p 1f out: kpt on same pce ins fnl f* **5/1**[2]
6312 **5** 1 ½ **Aye Aye Skipper (IRE)**[43] 4203 7-9-5 **56**..............(b) HectorCrouch(3) 6 53+
(Ken Cunningham-Brown) *dwlt: hld up in last trio: nt clr run and swtchd rt wl over 1f out: hdwy 1f out: styd on ins fnl f: nvr trbld ldrs* **7/1**[3]
0000 **6** 4 **Jump Around**[24] 4968 3-8-5 **46** oh1..................................(t) JoeyHaynes 4 32
(Ali Stronge) *in tch in midfield: rdn over 2f out: unable qck u.p over 1f out: wknd ins fnl f* **25/1**
2456 **7** 2 ¾ **Hot Mustard**[43] 4203 7-9-13 **61**........................................... MartinDwyer 3 42
(William Muir) *t.k.h: hld up in tch in midfield: effrt u.p ent fnl 2f: sn drvn and no hdwy: wknd fnl f* **8/1**
-600 **8** 2 **Oddsocks (IRE)**[13] 5357 5-8-12 **46** oh1........................ GeorgeDowning 2 22
(Tony Carroll) *wl in tch in midfield: effrt ent fnl 2f: outpcd and btn over 1f out: wknd fnl f* **33/1**

000 **9** 2¼ **Hellarious**[16] 5250 4-8-12 **46** oh1 ........................................(t) RyanTate 8 17
(Geoffrey Deacon) *dwlt: hld up in last trio: no imp u.p wl over 1f out: n.d* **50/1**

-000 **10** *10* **Back To Love (CAN)**[79] 2916 4-8-7 **46** oh1 ................(h) GeorgiaCox(5) 9
(Mark Gillard) *a towards rr but in tch: rdn over 3f out: sn struggling and wknd 2f out: wl bhd ins fnl f* **50/1**

000- **11** *7* **Play The Blues (IRE)**[260] 8070 10-8-5 **46** oh1 .........(t) RhiainIngram(7) 1
(Roger Ingram) *taken down early: stdd s: plld hrd and hld up in rr: lost tch over 1f out: wl bhd ins fnl f* **50/1**

000- **P** **Katie Canford**[422] 3256 4-8-12 **46** oh1 ............................... ShaneKelly 11
(Mark Hoad) *chsd ldrs: rdn over 2f out: lost pl over 1f out: bhd whn eased ins fnl f: p.u and dismntd towards fin* **40/1**

1m 34.22s (-1.78) **Going Correction** -0.125s/f (Firm)
**WFA** 3 from 4yo+ 7lb **12** Ran SP% **122.6**
Speed ratings (Par 101): **103,102,99,98,96 92,90,88,85,75 68,**
CSF £13.57 CT £49.86 TOTE £2.60: £1.30, £2.10, £1.70; EX 13.90 Trifecta £59.40.
**Owner** Tara Moon Partnership **Bred** M H And Mrs G Tourle **Trained** Findon, W Sussex

**FOCUS**
Race distance increased by 3 yards. A modest handicap. They went a decent gallop and it is sound form. The winner has been rated a bit above his best, but might be worth a little more.
T/Plt: £81.90 to a £1 stake. Pool: £60,825.32 - 542.02 winning units. T/Qpdt: £10.40 to a £1 stake. Pool: £3,519.74 - 249.99 winning units. **Steve Payne**

## 5134 HAYDOCK (L-H)
### Thursday, August 10

**OFFICIAL GOING: Good to soft (soft in places) changing to good to soft after race 1 (1.50)**
Wind: Moderate, half against in straight of over 4f Weather: fine

## 5824 BETFRED "SUPPORTS JACK BERRY HOUSE" H'CAP (JOCKEY CLUB GRASSROOTS MIDDLE DISTANCE QUALIFIER) 1m 2f 42y
**1:50** (1:51) (Class 5) (0-70,72) 3-Y-0+ **£3,557** (£1,058; £529; £264) **Stalls** Centre

Form RPR

4-01 **1** **Punkawallah**[34] 4575 3-9-6 **67** ...............................(p) RichardKingscote 2 81
(Tom Dascombe) *mde all: rdn 2f out: pressed and jnd 1f out: kpt on gamely and fnd more fnl 50yds* **7/2**[2]

4312 **2** ½ **Indian Chief (IRE)**[5] 5648 7-10-5 **72** 6ex ...................... DanielTudhope 3 85
(Rebecca Bastiman) *s.s: racd keenly: hld up: hdwy 3f out: str chal and upsides 1f out: no ex and hld fnl 50yds* **6/4**[1]

6044 **3** 4½ **Daily Trader**[33] 4633 3-9-0 **61** ........................................ AndrewMullen 10 65
(David Evans) *racd keenly: prom: lost pl after 3f: rdn over 3f out: effrt to chal 2f out: unable qck over 1f out: styd on same pce ins fnl f* **7/1**

0032 **4** 3¼ **Strummer (IRE)**[17] 5212 4-9-11 **67** ........................(p) LewisEdmunds(3) 1 65
(Kevin Ryan) *midfield: hdwy 3f out: effrt and cl up on inner over 1f out: unable qck after: no ex fnl 100yds* **7/1**

150 **5** 3½ **Paddy's Rock (IRE)**[16] 5267 6-9-2 **55** ..........................(p) PaddyAspell 8 47
(Lynn Siddall) *hld up: struggling 3f out: kpt on whn no ch fnl f* **20/1**

304 **6** ½ **Bishop Of Bling (IRE)**[13] 5362 4-9-13 **66** ................... PaulHanagan 4 57
(Chris Wall) *racd keenly: prom tl rdn and wknd 2f out* **6/1**[3]

246 **7** 3¼ **Anton Chigurh**[28] 4802 8-9-12 **65** ................................ PhillipMakin 6 50
(Nikki Evans) *chsd ldrs tl rdn and wknd over 2f out* **66/1**

-303 **8** ¾ **Dream Free**[40] 4345 4-9-9 **62** ............................................(p) JasonHart 9 45
(Mark Walford) *hld up: struggling 4f out: nvr a threat* **10/1**

2m 12.79s (0.09) **Going Correction** +0.15s/f (Good)
**WFA** 3 from 4yo+ 8lb **8** Ran SP% **116.9**
Speed ratings (Par 103): **105,104,101,98,95 95,92,92**
CSF £9.38 CT £34.07 TOTE £4.00: £1.80, £1.10, £2.40; EX 10.00 Trifecta £51.70.
**Owner** Laurence Bellman & Chasemore Farm **Bred** Chasemore Farm **Trained** Malpas, Cheshire

**FOCUS**
All races run over the Inner home straight. Allowing for rail position on bends, race distances were: Race 1: 1m 2f 70yds Races 2, 3, 4 & 5: 6f Race 6: 7f 218yds Race 7: 1m 3f 161yds. After riding in the opener, Richard Kingscote called the 'ground good to soft', Danny Tudhope said it was 'soft' and Lewis Edmunds and Andrew Mullen both labelled it 'dead'.\n\x\x This modest handicap was fought out by the two market leaders. The runner-up has been rated to his best over the past two years.

## 5825 BETFRED TV BRITISH STALLION STUDS EBF NOVICE STKS (PLUS 10 RACE) 6f
**2:20** (2:22) (Class 4) 2-Y-O **£4,528** (£1,347; £673; £336) **Stalls** Centre

Form RPR

12 **1** **Staxton**[12] 5437 2-9-8 0 ........................................ JamesSullivan 7 94
(Tim Easterby) *in rr: hdwy over 2f out: led wl over 1f out: a pressed but r.o gamely ins fnl f: in control towards fin* **9/4**[2]

4 **2** ¾ **Humble Gratitude**[20] 5099 2-9-2 0 .................................. MartinHarley 6 86
(K R Burke) *racd keenly: hld up: hdwy 3f out: chalng fr wl over 1f out: hung lft ins fnl f: styd on: hld towards fin* **7/1**

3 **3** 4 **Cool Spirit**[61] 3556 2-9-2 0 .................................................. JoeDoyle 5 74
(James Given) *prom: effrt and ev ch 2f out: outpcd by front two fr over 1f out: no imp after* **2/1**[1]

06 **4** ½ **She's Different (IRE)**[21] 5058 2-8-11 0 ...................... AndrewMullen 4 67
(Nigel Tinkler) *in tch: lost pl over 2f out: kpt on fr over 1f out: no ch w front two: nt knocked abt* **66/1**

2 **5** 2½ **Diamond Set**[20] 5099 2-9-2 0 .............................. RichardKingscote 2 65
(Tom Dascombe) *led: rdn over 2f out: hdd wl over 1f out: sn wknd* **10/3**[3]

**6** 4½ **Bakht Khan (IRE)** 2-9-2 0 .................................................. TomEaves 1 51
(Kevin Ryan) *in tch: rdn and wknd ent fnl 2f* **8/1**

**7** 2 **Harrogate (IRE)** 2-9-2 0 .............................................. DanielTudhope 3 45
(James Bethell) *racd keenly: prom tl rdn and wknd over 2f out* **16/1**

1m 14.62s (0.82) **Going Correction** +0.15s/f (Good) **7** Ran SP% **118.2**
Speed ratings (Par 96): **100,99,93,93,89 83,81**
CSF £19.33 TOTE £3.00: £1.50, £3.40; EX 21.40 Trifecta £48.70.
**Owner** Ontoawinner 10 & Partner **Bred** B & B Equine Limited **Trained** Great Habton, N Yorks

**FOCUS**
A fair novice event. They went an average pace towards the far side. The third has been rated below his promising debut effort. The winner's latest effort could be rated as high as this, and this could be a bit better.

## 5826 BETFRED BINGO H'CAP (JOCKEY CLUB GRASSROOTS FLAT SPRINT SERIES QUALIFIER) 6f
**2:50** (2:50) (Class 5) (0-70,75) 3-Y-O **£3,557** (£1,058; £529; £264) **Stalls** Centre

Form RPR

5535 **1** **Haworth**[18] 5182 3-9-4 **66** ...........................................(b1) DanielTudhope 6 72
(James Bethell) *midfield: hdwy 2f out: led over 1f out: all out towards fin: jst hld on* **5/2**[1]

4541 **2** *nse* **Peachey Carnehan**[5] 5636 3-9-3 **70** 6ex ......................(v) PhilDennis(5) 5 76
(Michael Mullineaux) *prom: lost pl after 1f: racd in midfield: nt clr run over 1f out: impr after: r.o and str chal towards fin: jst failed* **14/1**

0501 **3** 1¼ **Lexington Sky (IRE)**[2] 5759 3-9-13 **75** 6ex ........................ BenCurtis 9 77
(Roger Fell) *hld up in rr: rdn and hdwy over 1f out: r.o ins fnl f: nt quite pce to mount serious chal: styd on* **13/2**

-002 **4** 1¾ **Twilight Spirit**[19] 5167 3-8-12 **60** ........................................ FrannyNorton 3 56
(Tony Carroll) *midfield: effrt wl over 1f out: kpt on ins fnl f: nt pce of ldrs* **3/1**[2]

4066 **5** ½ **Blue Rocks**[26] 4894 3-8-9 **57** .................................................. KevinStott 4 52
(Lisa Williamson) *hld up: rdn 2f out: styd on ins fnl f: nt rch ldrs* **20/1**

4000 **6** 1¼ **Lambrini Legacy**[26] 4892 3-8-7 **55** ..........................................(h) JoeDoyle 2 46
(Lisa Williamson) *racd keenly: prom: rdn and unable qck over 1f out: kpt on same pce ins fnl f* **25/1**

4062 **7** ½ **Mia Cara**[13] 5357 3-8-9 **64** ..................................(v) KatherineGlenister(7) 8 53
(David Evans) *prom: rdn to ld briefly wl over 1f out: wknd fnl 150yds* **7/1**

0004 **8** 4 **Allux Boy (IRE)**[20] 5122 3-8-12 **60** .......................................(t1) TomEaves 7 36
(Nigel Tinkler) *midfield: hdwy 3f out: rdn over 2f out: wknd over 1f out* **12/1**

3013 **9** ½ **Chickenfortea (IRE)**[15] 5291 3-9-4 **66** ..................................... JasonHart 1 41
(Eric Alston) *led: rdn and hdd wl over 1f out: wknd ins fnl f* **6/1**[3]

1m 14.69s (0.89) **Going Correction** +0.15s/f (Good) **9** Ran SP% **116.7**
Speed ratings (Par 100): **100,99,98,95,95 93,92,87,86**
CSF £39.46 CT £208.58 TOTE £3.50: £1.10, £3.30, £2.20; EX 40.90 Trifecta £223.40.
**Owner** Clarendon Thoroughbred Racing **Bred** R Kitching, H Mayer, M Pennell **Trained** Middleham Moor, N Yorks

**FOCUS**
Not a bad sprint handicap for the class. This time they went down the middle. The winner has been rated back to his best, with the third rated to her Nottingham form.

## 5827 BETFRED SUPER LEAGUE H'CAP 6f
**3:20** (3:21) (Class 5) (0-70,72) 4-Y-O+ **£3,557** (£1,058; £529; £264) **Stalls** Centre

Form RPR

0353 **1** **Specialv (IRE)**[10] 5471 4-9-3 **65** ..........................................(p) BenCurtis 8 74
(Brian Ellison) *midfield: hdwy over 1f out: led ins fnl f: kpt on wl towards fin* **9/2**[3]

5204 **2** 1 **Amood (IRE)**[12] 5415 6-9-7 **69** ......................................(p) AndrewMullen 5 75
(Simon West) *in rr:carried hd to one side: hdwy 2f out: rdn and hung lft fr over 1f out: impr to go 2nd ins fnl 100yds: styd on: nt quite rch wnr* **4/1**[2]

0061 **3** 1¼ **Danish Duke (IRE)**[6] 5620 6-9-3 **65** ...............................(p) JamesSullivan 9 67
(Ruth Carr) *chsd ldrs: led over 1f out: hdd ins fnl f: no ex towards fin* **11/4**[1]

3233 **4** 1¾ **Pushkin Museum (IRE)**[30] 4724 6-9-1 **68** ............ CallumRodriguez(5) 3 64
(Patrick Morris) *w ldr: led 2f out: hdd over 1f out: stl ev ch ins fnl f: kpt on same pce fnl 100yds* **10/1**

405 **5** ½ **Casterbridge**[7] 5580 5-9-10 **72** ..........................................(b1) PaulHanagan 7 67
(Eric Alston) *led: hdd 2f out: sn edgd rt: outpcd over 1f out: kpt on ins fnl f: edgd lft clsng stages* **17/2**

2450 **6** ¾ **Dodgy Bob**[12] 5396 4-8-7 **60** ..........................................(p) PhilDennis(5) 1 52
(Michael Mullineaux) *hld up: edgd rt and outpcd wl over 1f out: nvr able to trble ldrs* **20/1**

3114 **7** *nk* **Champagne Bob**[16] 5264 5-8-13 **64** .................................. HollieDoyle(3) 4 55
(Richard Price) *in tch: pushed along 1/2-way: one pce fnl f: nvr able to chal* **5/1**

6-00 **8** 2½ **Niqnaaqpaadiwaaq**[59] 3666 5-8-8 **56** .................................. NeilFarley 6 39
(Eric Alston) *chsd ldrs tl rdn and wknd over 1f out* **10/1**

0060 **9** *12* **Mr Conundrum**[10] 5482 4-8-2 **50** oh5 .................................. PaddyAspell 2
(Lynn Siddall) *midfield tl rdn and outpcd over 2f out* **66/1**

1m 14.6s (0.80) **Going Correction** +0.15s/f (Good) **9** Ran SP% **116.5**
Speed ratings (Par 103): **100,98,97,94,94 93,92,89,73**
CSF £23.10 CT £58.88 TOTE £5.60: £1.80, £1.50, £1.40; EX 27.00 Trifecta £97.60.
**Owner** D Gilbert, M Lawrence, A Bruce **Bred** Peter & Hugh McCutcheon **Trained** Norton, N Yorks

**FOCUS**
Again they came down the middle in this ordinary sprint handicap and it's straightforward form. The winner has been rated to her best bar her standout Ayr win.

## 5828 BRITISH STALLION STUDS EBF FILLIES' H'CAP 6f
**3:50** (3:51) (Class 2) (0-100,93) 3-Y-O+
**£18,675** (£5,592; £2,796; £1,398; £699; £351) **Stalls** Centre

Form RPR

-16 **1** **Sainted**[6] 5597 4-9-10 **91** ............................................... DanielTudhope 5 104+
(William Haggas) *hld up: hdwy gng wl 2f out: led wl over 1f out: r.o wl and in command ins fnl f* **4/7**[1]

-060 **2** 1½ **Clear Water (IRE)**[12] 5435 4-9-3 **84** ........................................ KevinStott 7 90
(Michael Wigham) *in rr: hdwy to take 2nd over 1f out: styd on ins fnl f: no imp on wnr* **50/1**

1425 **3** 1¼ **Southern Belle (IRE)**[26] 4889 4-9-12 **93** ........................... PhillipMakin 3 95
(Robert Cowell) *midfield: rdn and hdwy over 1f out: kpt on ins fnl f: one pce fnl 75yds* **8/1**

0-03 **4** 5 **Shamsaya (IRE)**[20] 5123 3-9-1 **86** ....................................... PaulHanagan 4 71
(Simon Crisford) *prom: rdn 2f out: one pce fnl f* **7/1**[3]

1064 **5** *hd* **Courier**[14] 5317 5-9-4 **85** ................................................ BarryMcHugh 9 70
(Marjorie Fife) *led: hdd 1/2-way: rdn and outpcd wl over 1f out: kpt on but n.d ins fnl f* **16/1**

6200 **6** 1 **Iseemist (IRE)**[39] 4411 6-9-6 **87** ...................................... FergusSweeney 2 69
(John Gallagher) *prom: led 1/2-way: rdn and hdd wl over 1f out: wknd ins fnl f* **18/1**

3406 **7** 2 **Futoon (IRE)**[12] 5435 4-9-6 **90** ...................................... LewisEdmunds(3) 1 66
(Kevin Ryan) *prom: rdn over 2f out: wknd over 1f out* **4/1**[2]

-040 **8** *hd* **Hope Solo (IRE)**[26] 4889 3-8-12 **83** JamesSullivan 6 57
(Tim Easterby) *a in rr: rdn 1/2-way: outpcd after* **16/1**

1m 14.3s (0.50) **Going Correction** +0.15s/f (Good)
**WFA** 3 from 4yo+ 4lb **8** Ran SP% **126.3**
Speed ratings (Par 96): **102,100,98,91,91 90,87,87**
CSF £48.18 CT £174.32 TOTE £1.50: £1.10, £6.20, £1.90; EX 50.60 Trifecta £338.80.
**Owner** Cheveley Park Stud **Bred** Cheveley Park Stud Ltd **Trained** Newmarket, Suffolk

**FOCUS**
This good-quality fillies' sprint handicap was all about the winner. The third has been rated close to form.

## 5829 BETFRED GOALS GALORE FILLIES' H'CAP 7f 212y
**4:20** (4:21) (Class 5) (0-75,74) 3-Y-O+ **£3,557** (£1,058; £529; £264) **Stalls** Low

Form RPR

2401 **1** **Always Thankful**[65] 3443 3-9-4 **71** DanielTudhope 6 78+
(Ismail Mohammed) *chsd ldrs: wnt 2nd over 4f out: led over 2f out: running on abt 2 l clr 1f out: hld on wl towards fin* **5/4**[1]

5103 **2** ½ **Lyric Harmony (IRE)**[10] 5478 3-9-7 **74** SamJames 2 78
(Giles Bravery) *racd keenly: sn led: hdd after 2f: handy: rdn and unable qck 2f out: rallied ins fnl f: tk 2nd fnl 150yds: r.o towards fin* **4/1**[2]

5353 **3** 2 **Bush Beauty (IRE)**[12] 5399 6-9-4 **64** NeilFarley 5 65
(Eric Alston) *chsd ldrs: lost pl over 3f out: renewing effrt whn n.m.r and lost momentum over 1f out: sn swtchd rt: styd on fnl 75yds: no imp on front two* **13/2**

2120 **4** 1 **Full Of Promise**[23] 4999 4-9-8 **68** PaulHanagan 8 66
(Richard Fahey) *broke wl: led early: sn stdd: hld up: hdwy over 3f out: wnt 2nd over 1f out: no imp on wnr: lost 2nd fnl 150yds: no ex* **9/2**[3]

00-4 **5** *shd* **Champagne Pink (FR)**[218] 48 3-8-8 **64** (h) JordanVaughan(3) 7 61
(K R Burke) *hld up: rdn and outpcd over 2f out: effrt over 1f out but no imp: one pce ins fnl f* **16/1**

-534 **6** 12 **Bella's Venture**[55] 3773 4-8-13 **59** FergusSweeney 9 29
(John Gallagher) *led after 2f: rdn and hdd over 2f out: wknd over 1f out* **9/1**

1m 43.45s (-0.25) **Going Correction** +0.15s/f (Good)
**WFA** 3 from 4yo+ 7lb **6** Ran SP% **111.8**
Speed ratings (Par 100): **107,106,104,103,103 91**
CSF £6.43 CT £21.46 TOTE £1.80: £1.30, £1.60; EX 4.60 Trifecta £22.30.
**Owner** Saeed H Al Tayer **Bred** T J Cooper **Trained** Newmarket, Suffolk

**FOCUS**
Add 6yds. A modest fillies' handicap. The runner-up has been rated to the better view of her maiden form.

## 5830 BETFRED FOLLOW US ON TWITTER H'CAP 1m 3f 140y
**4:50** (4:50) (Class 4) (0-80,80) 4-Y-O+ **£5,822** (£1,732; £865; £432) **Stalls** Centre

Form RPR

541 **1** **Indy (IRE)**[19] 5166 6-9-7 **80** RichardKingscote 2 87
(John Quinn) *broke wl: led early: sn chsd ldr: rdn over 2f out: led narrowly over 1f out: kpt on gamely and doing enough towards fin* **13/8**[1]

413 **2** *nk* **Starplex**[19] 5166 7-8-13 **77** RowanScott(5) 6 83
(Keith Dalgleish) *sn led: rdn over 2f out: hdd narrowly over 1f out: rallied wl ins fnl f: hld fnl strides* **10/3**[3]

3404 **3** ½ **Busy Street**[28] 4796 5-9-3 **76** BenCurtis 5 81
(Sally Haynes) *chsd ldrs: rdn and outpcd 2f out: rallied wl ins fnl f: fin wl* **5/1**

-332 **4** 2 **Azzir (IRE)**[7] 5579 5-9-1 **74** MartinHarley 3 76
(K R Burke) *hld up in tch: travelling wl over 2f out: rdn and chalng over 1f out: unable qck ins fnl f: no ex fnl 75yds* **5/1**

6021 **5** 1 **The New Pharaoh (IRE)**[14] 5313 6-9-3 **76** PaulHanagan 1 76
(Chris Wall) *hld up: rdn over 2f out: one pce fnl f: nvr able to chal* **3/1**[2]

5304 **6** 3 ¼ **Island Flame (IRE)**[12] 5417 4-8-6 **68** SammyJoBell(3) 4 63
(Richard Fahey) *in rr: rdn over 2f out: outpcd over 1f out: nvr a threat* **16/1**

2m 34.67s (1.67) **Going Correction** +0.15s/f (Good) **6** Ran SP% **113.5**
Speed ratings (Par 105): **100,99,99,98,97 95**
CSF £7.51 TOTE £2.40: £1.40, £2.40; EX 7.80 Trifecta £56.90.
**Owner** White Rose Racing **Bred** Maurice Burns **Trained** Settrington, N Yorks
■ Stewards' Enquiry : Rowan Scott two-day ban: used whip above permitted level (26th-27th Aug)

**FOCUS**
Add 21yds. It paid to be handy in this fair handicap. The third has been rated to the balance of this year's form.
T/Plt: £13.10 to a £1 stake. Pool: £68,969.93 - 3839.63 winning units. T/Qpdt: £4.00 to a £1 stake. Pool: £4,991.35 - 905.37 winning units. **Darren Owen**

# [5412]NEWCASTLE (A.W) (L-H)
Thursday, August 10

**OFFICIAL GOING: Tapeta: standard**
Wind: Breezy, half against in races on straight course and in over 3f of home straight on races on the rou Weather: Sunny

## 5831 GUTHRIE FINANCIAL PLANNING SERVICES LTD APPRENTICE H'CAP 1m 2f 42y (Tp)
**5:50** (5:52) (Class 6) (0-60,60) 3-Y-O+ **£2,264** (£673; £336; £168) **Stalls** High

Form RPR

00-0 **1** **Bigbadboy (IRE)**[42] 4262 4-8-12 **46** oh1 JoshQuinn 13 56
(Clive Mulhall) *in tch on outside: effrt and rdn over 2f out: led over 1f out: edgd lft ins fnl f: kpt on strly* **40/1**

2545 **2** 1 ¾ **Spirit Of The Vale (IRE)**[87] 2678 4-9-4 **55** (t) SeamusCronin(3) 10 61
(Oliver Greenall) *hld up in tch: stdy hdwy and prom over 2f out: effrt and rdn over 1f out: chsd wnr ins fnl f: kpt on same pce* **11/2**[3]

0645 **3** 2 ½ **Good Time Ahead (IRE)**[23] 5005 3-9-1 **60** RossTurner(3) 3 62
(Philip Kirby) *chsd ldrs: drvn and outpcd 4f out: rallied over 1f out: kpt on to take 3rd nr fin: nt rch first two* **4/1**[2]

5502 **4** 1 **Kerry Icon**[16] 5254 4-8-12 **51** (h) SebastianWoods(5) 5 50
(Iain Jardine) *t.k.h: pressed ldr: led over 5f out: rdn over 2f out: hdd over 1f out: lost 2nd and no ex ins fnl f* **8/1**

6316 **5** ½ **Sakhalin Star (IRE)**[9] 5499 6-9-8 **56** (e) KevinLundie 14 54
(Richard Guest) *t.k.h: prom: drvn along over 2f out: no ex fnl f* **14/1**

0060 **6** ½ **Shine Baby Shine**[14] 5319 3-8-6 **48** PaulaMuir 4 46
(Philip Kirby) *dwlt: hld up: rdn along over 3f out: hdwy whn n.m.r briefly over 1f out: kpt on ins fnl f* **40/1**

-060 **7** *nk* **Judicious**[17] 5215 10-9-4 **52** (p) PatrickVaughan 8 48
(Geoffrey Harker) *hld up midfield: hdwy and in tch over 3f out: drvn and outpcd over 1f out* **28/1**

5403 **8** 1 ¼ **Lozah**[18] 5181 4-9-7 **58** BenSanderson(3) 12 52
(Roger Fell) *dwlt: hld up: hdwy whn nt clr run over 3f out to over 2f out: rdn and no imp over 1f out* **10/3**[1]

260/ **9** *nk* **Ferngrove (USA)**[14] 6388 6-8-9 **48** (t) RobertDodsworth(5) 9 41
(Susan Corbett) *hld up: hdwy on outside over 3f: rdn and edgd lft 2f out: sn outpcd* **100/1**

40-0 **10** 2 **Snappydresser**[18] 5181 4-8-7 **46** oh1 TobyEley(5) 7 35
(Chris Grant) *hld up midfield: drvn and outpcd over 3f out: no imp fnl 2f* **100/1**

0050 **11** ¾ **Pindaric**[18] 5181 3-8-10 **52** (p[1]) ConnorMurtagh 6 41
(Alan Lockwood) *chsd ldrs: drvn along over 2f out: wknd over 1f out* **11/1**

4306 **12** 1 ½ **Mount Cheiron (USA)**[27] 4839 6-8-12 **46** oh1 GerO'Neill 2 31
(Richard Ford) *hld up: pushed along over 4f out: btn fnl 2f* **9/1**

6205 **13** 12 **Permanent**[24] 4971 3-9-3 **59** (p) JordanUys 11 21
(Daniel Kubler) *led to over 5f out: rdn and wknd over 2f out* **17/2**

00-0 **14** 61 **Ingleby Erin**[66] 3404 4-8-7 **46** oh1 TristanPrice(5) 1
(Colin Teague) *missed break: bhd: struggling over 5f out: lost tch fnl 3f* **150/1**

2m 11.63s (1.23) **Going Correction** +0.20s/f (Slow)
**WFA** 3 from 4yo+ 8lb **14** Ran SP% **116.1**
Speed ratings (Par 101): **103,101,99,98,98 98,97,96,96,94 94,93,83,34**
CSF £238.96 CT £1099.43 TOTE £47.40: £11.40, £1.80, £2.00; EX 522.30 Trifecta £3174.40.
**Owner** Ms Yvonne Featherstone & Carl Chapman **Bred** Pat McCarthy **Trained** Scarcroft, W Yorks
■ Stewards' Enquiry : Ger O'Neill five-day ban: used whip when out of contention (Aug 24th-28th)

**FOCUS**
A low-grade handicap run at a sound gallop and a surprise winner. The runner-up helps set the level.

## 5832 EXTRA PLACE RACES AT 188BET H'CAP 1m 4f 98y (Tp)
**6:20** (6:21) (Class 5) (0-70,70) 3-Y-O+ **£4,851** (£1,443; £721; £360) **Stalls** High

Form RPR

2 **1** **Chant (IRE)**[50] 3983 7-10-0 **70** ShaneGray 6 80
(Ann Duffield) *trckd ldrs: led over 2f out: rdn and edgd lft ins fnl f: jst hld on* **20/1**

6142 **2** *shd* **New Society (IRE)**[38] 4436 3-9-4 **70** PJMcDonald 8 79
(James Bethell) *hld up: hdwy over 2f out: effrt and chsd wnr over 1f out: angled rt ins fnl f: kpt on wl: jst hld* **9/4**[1]

2413 **3** 9 **Highway Robber**[12] 5413 4-8-11 **53** PaulMulrennan 3 48
(Wilf Storey) *led 2f: pressed ldr: led over 4f out to over 2f out: lost 2nd and outpcd by first two fr over 1f out* **10/1**

3025 **4** ¾ **Waiting For Richie**[28] 4791 4-10-0 **70** TomEaves 5 64
(Tom Tate) *pressed ldr: led after 2f: hdd over 4f out: drvn and outpcd over 2f out: rallied fnl f: no imp* **13/2**[3]

4440 **5** ¾ **Major Rowan**[47] 4102 6-9-12 **68** GrahamLee 9 61
(John Davies) *hld up: stdy hdwy on outside over 3f out: rdn 2f out: sn no imp* **9/1**

0543 **6** ¾ **Satish**[8] 5540 4-9-11 **67** (b) HarryBentley 7 59
(David O'Meara) *dwlt and swtchd lft s: hld up in tch: stdy hdwy over 2f out: sn rdn and edgd lft: wknd over 1f out* **11/4**[2]

-661 **7** ¾ **Hayward Field (IRE)**[23] 5005 4-9-11 **67** PatrickMathers 4 58
(Noel Wilson) *dwlt: hld up: rdn along over 3f out: no imp fr over 2f out* **7/1**

6122 **8** 7 **Cool Music (IRE)**[9] 5493 7-9-0 **56** (p) CamHardie 1 35
(Antony Brittain) *trckd ldrs: rdn over 4f out: wknd over 2f out* **28/1**

56-0 **9** 24 **Recognition (IRE)**[56] 2427 4-9-2 **65** (vt) ConnorMurtagh(7) 2 6
(Barry Murtagh) *hld up in tch: drvn along over 4f out: wknd over 2f out* **100/1**

2m 41.08s (-0.02) **Going Correction** +0.20s/f (Slow)
**WFA** 3 from 4yo+ 10lb **9** Ran SP% **111.6**
Speed ratings (Par 103): **108,107,101,101,100 100,99,95,79**
CSF £62.16 CT £483.28 TOTE £12.10: £3.60, £1.40, £2.50; EX 41.40 Trifecta £276.20.
**Owner** Mrs Ann Starkie & Mrs I Starkie **Bred** Roger K Lee **Trained** Constable Burton, N Yorks

**FOCUS**
An extended 1m4f handicap run at no more than a fair gallop in which the first two finished well clear. The winner has been rated to his best for now.

## 5833 PREMIER LEAGUE FOOTBALL AT 188BET FILLIES' NURSERY H'CAP 7f 14y (Tp)
**6:55** (6:55) (Class 4) (0-85,87) 2-Y-O **£6,469** (£1,925; £962) **Stalls** Centre

Form RPR

2105 **1** **Miss Bar Beach (IRE)**[21] 5057 2-10-5 **86** GrahamLee 1 88
(Keith Dalgleish) *trckd ldr: rdn to ld over 1f out: kpt on strly last 100yds* **6/4**[2]

0134 **2** 1 ¾ **Seaella (IRE)**[15] 5279 2-9-7 **74** JasonHart 4 71
(John Quinn) *t.k.h: led tl rdn and hdd over 1f out: rallied: kpt on same pce last 75yds* **4/5**[1]

404 **3** *hd* **Kylie Rules**[13] 5371 2-9-0 **67** ShaneGray 3 63
(Ann Duffield) *trckd ldrs: rdn and outpcd over 1f out: rallied ins fnl f: kpt on fin* **6/1**[3]

1m 29.77s (3.57) **Going Correction** +0.20s/f (Slow) **3** Ran SP% **109.8**
Speed ratings (Par 93): **87,85,84**
CSF £3.20 TOTE £2.30; EX 2.80 Trifecta £2.60.
**Owner** Middleham Park Racing Cxv **Bred** Tyrone Molloy **Trained** Carluke, S Lanarks

**FOCUS**
Just the three runners, not much of a gallop and probably not a race from which to draw too many firm conclusions as it developed into a bit of a sprint. It's been rated as straightforward form.

## 5834 IRISH STALLION FARMS EBF NOVICE MEDIAN AUCTION STKS 6f (Tp)
**7:25** (7:32) (Class 5) 2-Y-O **£4,528** (£1,347; £673; £336) **Stalls** Centre

Form RPR

**1** **Hikmaa (IRE)** 2-8-11 0 AdamBeschizza 7 80+
(Ed Vaughan) *prom: effrt and pushed along over 1f out: led ins fnl f: sn clr: comf* **14/1**

31 **2** 2 ½ **Ingenuity**[27] 4834 2-9-9 0 JackGarritty 10 84
(Jedd O'Keeffe) *cl up: led over 2f out: rdn and hdd ins fnl f: kpt on same pce* **3/1**[2]

64 **3** *shd* **Character Witness (IRE)**[13] 5365 2-9-2 0 HarryBentley 13 77
(Roger Varian) *cl up: ev ch over 2f out to 1f out: kpt on same pce last 100yds* **5/2**[1]

24 **4** 2 **Fabulous Red**[28] 4815 2-8-11 0 AntonioFresu 4 66
(Ed Dunlop) *hld up: rdn over 2f out: hdwy over 1f out: kpt on: nt pce to chal* **9/2**[3]

4 **5** 1 ¾ **Merkava**[14] 5334 2-9-2 0 PaulMulrennan 11 65
(Robyn Brisland) *hld up: shkn up and hdwy over 2f out: no imp fr over 1f out* **12/1**

4 **6** *1* **Awesometank**[24] 4972 2-8-11 0 KevinStott 2 57
(William Haggas) *reluctant to enter stalls: in tch: rdn over 2f out: hung lft and outpcd fr over 1f out* **8/1**

43 **7** *½* **Life For Rent**[20] 5127 2-8-13 0 RachelRichardson(3) 9 61
(Tim Easterby) *led to over 2f out: rdn and outpcd fr over 1f out* **20/1**

00 **8** *2* **North Road Revue**[8] 5537 2-8-11 0 JasonHart 14 50
(Tim Easterby) *hld up: rdn over 2f out: sme late hdwy: nvr on terms* **125/1**

00 **9** *hd* **El Bertie (IRE)**[12] 5412 2-9-2 0 DuranFentiman 3 54
(Tim Easterby) *in tch on far side of gp: rdn and outpcd 2f out: sn n.d* **125/1**

**10** *2¼* **Gorse (IRE)** 2-9-2 0 GrahamLee 1 48
(Ann Duffield) *hld up: rdn and outpcd over 2f out: sn btn* **40/1**

0 **11** *2* **The Auld Hoose (IRE)**[15] 5278 2-9-2 0 TonyHamilton 5 42
(Richard Fahey) *cl up: rdn over 2f out: wknd wl over 1f out* **25/1**

0 **12** *nk* **The Gingerbreadman**[47] 4101 2-8-9 0 PaulaMuir(7) 6 41
(Chris Fairhurst) *trckd ldrs tl rdn and wknd fr 2f out* **150/1**

0 **13** *5* **Lady Cashmere (IRE)**[17] 5202 2-8-11 0 PJMcDonald 12 21
(Alistair Whillans) *hld up: rdn and outpcd over 2f out: sn btn* **125/1**

**14** *shd* **True North (IRE)** 2-8-13 0 RosieJessop(3) 8 25
(Sir Mark Prescott Bt) *bhd and sn rdn along: detached over 3f out: nvr on terms* **25/1**

1m 15.53s (3.03) **Going Correction** +0.20s/f (Slow) **14** Ran SP% **115.2**
Speed ratings (Par 94): **87,83,83,80,78 77,76,73,73,70 67,67,60,60**
CSF £51.04 TOTE £14.20: £3.70, £1.70, £1.50; EX 72.00 Trifecta £332.40.
**Owner** Sheikh Hamed Dalmook Al Maktoum **Bred** L Wright **Trained** Newmarket, Suffolk

**FOCUS**
Quite an interesting juvenile event which was won in good style by a cheaply-bought filly making her debut.

## 5835 188BET H'CAP 7f 14y (Tp)
**8:00** (8:04) (Class 6) (0-65,65) 3-Y-0+ **£3,234** (£962; £481; £240) **Stalls** Centre

Form RPR

-444 **1** **Angel's Acclaim (IRE)**[31] 4688 3-9-2 **62** (p1) KevinStott 13 70
(Kevin Ryan) *hld up: gd hdwy on nr side of gp to ld over 1f out: edgd lft ins fnl f: rdn out* **7/2**[1]

160 **2** *1¼* **Rey Loopy (IRE)**[20] 5126 3-9-2 **62** PaulMulrennan 12 67
(Ben Haslam) *hld up: hdwy nr side of gp to dispute ld over 1f out to ins fnl f: one pce last 100yds* **7/1**

5-20 **3** *2¼* **Supreme Power (IRE)**[8] 5538 3-9-3 **63** JasonHart 9 62
(Tracy Waggott) *towards rr: drvn along over 3f out: rallied over 1f out: chsd clr ldng pair ins fnl f: r.o* **20/1**

1165 **4** *½* **Pass The Cristal (IRE)**[22] 5031 3-9-5 **65** PhillipMakin 11 63
(William Muir) *hld up: stdy hdwy over 2f out: effrt and rdn over 1f out: kpt on fnl f: nrst fin* **6/1**[2]

6410 **5** *1¼* **Iberica Road (USA)**[16] 5261 4-9-2 **63** PatrickVaughan(7) 4 60
(Grant Tuer) *cl up on far side of gp: rdn over 2f out: edgd lft and outpcd over 1f out* **16/1**

1630 **6** *1½* **Luath**[41] 4298 4-9-7 **61** TomEaves 2 54
(Suzzanne France) *hld up in tch: drvn along over 2f out: rallied: outpcd fr over 1f out* **20/1**

1010 **7** *½* **Symbolic Star (IRE)**[16] 5254 5-9-4 **65** (p) ConnorMurtagh(7) 1 56
(Barry Murtagh) *hld up: stdy hdwy over 2f out: sn rdn: no imp fr over 1f out* **9/1**

0254 **8** *3* **Faintly (USA)**[34] 4554 6-9-7 **61** (b) JamesSullivan 8 45
(Ruth Carr) *stdd in rr: hld up: hdwy over 2f out: drvn and no imp fr over 1f out* **13/2**[3]

4550 **9** *1½* **Beatbybeatbybeat**[18] 5185 4-9-9 **63** (p1) CamHardie 5 43
(Antony Brittain) *chsd ldrs: rdn 3f out: wknd wl over 1f out* **33/1**

-000 **10** *¾* **Heavenly Angel**[13] 5376 3-9-5 **65** JackGarritty 10 41
(Ruth Carr) *prom: hdwy over 2f out: effrt and ev ch briefly wl over 1f out: sn wknd* **33/1**

2041 **11** *1¾* **Destination Aim**[16] 5258 10-9-7 **61** GrahamLee 7 34
(Fred Watson) *midfield: rdn 3f out: wknd 2f out* **16/1**

2221 **12** *4* **Justice Pleasing**[154] 1106 4-9-0 **61** (p) BenSanderson(7) 6 24+
(Roger Fell) *led: rdn over 2f out: wknd over 1f out* **11/1**

060- **13** *½* **Truly**[367] 5223 6-9-6 **60** (h1) PaddyAspell 14 22
(Paul Collins) *hld up on nr side of gp: rdn over 3f out: btn fnl 2f* **22/1**

0003 **14** *9* **Nonno Giulio (IRE)**[8] 5544 6-9-2 **63** (p) SeamusCronin(7) 3 1
(Conor Dore) *prom on far side of gp: struggling over 2f out: sn btn* **25/1**

1m 27.4s (1.20) **Going Correction** +0.20s/f (Slow)
**WFA** 3 from 4yo+ 6lb **14** Ran SP% **116.0**
Speed ratings (Par 101): **101,99,97,96,95 93,92,89,87,86 84,80,79,69**
CSF £22.76 CT £420.31 TOTE £4.20: £1.30, £3.10, £6.20; EX 32.20 Trifecta £661.10.
**Owner** Hambleton Racing Ltd XLV **Bred** Miss Otis Partnership **Trained** Hambleton, N Yorks

**FOCUS**
A low-grade handicap but the pace was sound and it seemed an advantage to come from behind with the first four all being well back at halfway. The second and third help set a solid level.

## 5836 NEWCASTLE UNITED BETTING AT 188BET H'CAP 6f (Tp)
**8:30** (8:33) (Class 6) (0-65,65) 3-Y-0+ **£3,234** (£962; £481; £240) **Stalls** Centre

Form RPR

4650 **1** **Lucky Lodge**[2] 5738 7-9-7 **60** (v) CamHardie 10 68
(Antony Brittain) *prom on nr side of gp: hdwy to chse ldr over 1f out: led ins fnl f: rdn and r.o wl* **12/1**

6000 **2** *½* **Meandmyshadow**[13] 5379 9-9-3 **63** (b) CameronNoble(7) 12 69
(Alan Brown) *led and sn clr on nr side of gp: rdn 2f out: edgd lft and hdd ins fnl f: kpt on* **15/2**[3]

1503 **3** *½* **Epeius (IRE)**[41] 4310 4-9-11 **64** GrahamLee 13 69
(Ben Haslam) *dwlt: bhd: gd hdwy over 1f out: rdn and kpt on fnl f: nt rch first two* **9/2**[2]

26-0 **4** *1¾* **Dandy Bird (IRE)**[13] 5375 3-9-7 **64** JoeDoyle 9 62
(Julie Camacho) *hld up: rdn and hdwy over 2f out: sn rdn along: kpt on same pce ins fnl f* **33/1**

-500 **5** *2¾* **Caeser The Gaeser (IRE)**[6] 5620 5-9-12 **65** (p) PaulMulrennan 3 55
(Nigel Tinkler) *prom on far side of gp: rdn over 2f out: outpcd fr over 1f out* **8/1**

6062 **5** *dht* **Etienne Gerard**[8] 5543 5-9-4 **60** (p) LewisEdmunds(3) 7 50
(Nigel Tinkler) *t.k.h early: prom: rdn 2f out: kpt on same pce fnl f* **10/3**[1]

-006 **7** *1¾* **Bearag**[62] 3543 3-8-13 **56** DanielTudhope 8 40
(David O'Meara) *in tch: lost pl over 3f out: rallied and hung lft over 1f out: nvr able to chal* **10/1**

-206 **8** *hd* **Ad Vitam (IRE)**[33] 4625 9-9-10 **63** (bt) TomEaves 1 47
(Suzzanne France) *hld up: rdn over 2f out: kpt on fnl f: nrst fin* **25/1**

2200 **9** *½* **Portland Street (IRE)**[26] 4897 4-9-11 **64** (p) ConnorBeasley 2 47
(Bryan Smart) *hld up on far side of gp: drvn and outpcd 1/2-way: n.d after* **12/1**

0050 **10** *½* **Compton Park**[36] 4506 10-9-10 **63** (vt1) PJMcDonald 5 44
(Les Eyre) *hld up: rdn along over 2f out: no imp fr over 1f out* **14/1**

3005 **11** *1¾* **Indian Pursuit (IRE)**[15] 5281 4-9-10 **63** JasonHart 11 38
(John Quinn) *chsd clr ldr to over 2f out: rdn and wknd fnl f* **16/1**

0050 **12** *½* **Jacob Black**[8] 5540 6-9-9 **62** (t) JackGarritty 14 36
(Kenny Johnson) *hld up on nr side of gp: hld up on nr side of gp: struggling over 2f out: sn wknd* **66/1**

000- **13** *nse* **Sunnyside Bob (IRE)**[231] 8490 4-9-3 **63** FayeMcManoman(7) 4 37
(Neville Bycroft) *midfield on far side of gp: struggling over 2f out: sn btn* **66/1**

0000 **14** *1* **Slemy (IRE)**[17] 5205 6-9-7 **60** (p1) JamesSullivan 6 30
(Ruth Carr) *hld up in tch: struggling over 2f out: sn btn* **14/1**

1m 12.52s (0.02) **Going Correction** +0.20s/f (Slow)
**WFA** 3 from 4yo+ 4lb **14** Ran SP% **117.6**
Speed ratings (Par 101): **107,106,105,103,99 99,97,97,96,95 93,92,92,91**
CSF £94.81 CT £368.18 TOTE £11.10: £4.00, £2.90, £2.00; EX 129.50 Trifecta £824.60.
**Owner** Antony Brittain **Bred** Mel Brittain **Trained** Warthill, N Yorks
■ Stewards' Enquiry : Daniel Tudhope caution: careless riding

**FOCUS**
A low-grade handicap run at a fair gallop with no obvious pace bias though the first two raced handily. The form is unlikely to be anything special. The winner and third help set a solid enough level.

## 5837 RACING TICKET GIVEAWAY AT 188BET H'CAP 5f (Tp)
**9:00** (9:01) (Class 5) (0-75,76) 3-Y-0 **£4,851** (£1,443; £721; £360) **Stalls** Centre

Form RPR

21 **1** **Indian Raj**[15] 5289 3-9-8 **76** AdamBeschizza 4 82+
(Stuart Williams) *prom: effrt and hdwy over 1f out: led wl ins fnl f: kpt on strly* **5/2**[1]

3055 **2** *¾* **Suwaan (IRE)**[17] 5204 3-8-13 **67** JamesSullivan 7 70
(Ruth Carr) *led and racd away fr main centre gp: rdn: edgd lft and hdd wl ins fnl f: one pce* **5/2**[1]

2003 **3** *shd* **Little Miss Daisy**[23] 4990 3-9-0 **68** PhillipMakin 5 71
(William Muir) *chsd ldr: rdn and effrt over 1f out: kpt on ins fnl f* **16/1**

-000 **4** *1* **Desperados Destiny**[24] 4958 3-9-0 **68** (p) PaulMulrennan 6 67
(Michael Dods) *in tch: rdn along 2f out: kpt on ins fnl f* **8/1**[3]

2210 **5** *shd* **The Nazca Lines (IRE)**[17] 5211 3-9-7 **75** (v) JasonHart 2 74
(John Quinn) *hld up in tch: rdn and outpcd over 1f out: rallied ins fnl f: kpt on fin* **12/1**

0-42 **6** *½* **Maazel (IRE)**[30] 4715 3-9-8 **76** HarryBentley 3 73
(Roger Varian) *hld up: drvn along 1/2-way: rallied over 1f out: no imp ins fnl f* **4/1**[2]

2512 **7** *8* **Dundunah (USA)**[14] 5338 3-9-7 **75** (t) DanielTudhope 1 43
(David O'Meara) *cl up: rdn over 2f out: wknd appr fnl f* **9/1**

1m 0.54s (1.04) **Going Correction** +0.20s/f (Slow) **7** Ran SP% **111.8**
Speed ratings (Par 100): **99,97,97,96,95 95,82**
CSF £8.29 TOTE £2.70: £1.90, £2.00; EX 11.40 Trifecta £91.10.
**Owner** D A Shekells,J W Parry,Stuartc Williams **Bred** Old Mill Stud & S Williams & J Parry **Trained** Newmarket, Suffolk

**FOCUS**
A 5f handicap for three-year-olds and a blanket finish between six, though the winner is a lightly-raced sort who should progress further. The runner-up has been rated to his best since his reappearance C&D win.
T/Jkpt: Not won. T/Plt: £235.40 to a £1 stake. Pool: £63,620.32 - 197.21 winning units. T/Qpdt: £41.80 to a £1 stake. Pool: £4,325.06 - 76.50 winning units. **Richard Young**

# 5545 SANDOWN (R-H)
### Thursday, August 10

**OFFICIAL GOING: Round course - soft (heavy in places); sprint course - heavy**
Wind: Moderate, across Weather: Fine

## 5838 SLUG AND LETTUCE 2-4-1 COCKTAILS AMATEUR RIDERS' H'CAP 1m 1f 209y
**5:35** (5:35) (Class 4) (0-80,79) 3-Y-0+ **£4,991** (£1,548; £773; £387) **Stalls** Low

Form RPR

1326 **1** **Canberra Cliffs (IRE)**[24] 4975 3-10-8 **79** MrSWalker 7 89+
(Don Cantillon) *trckd ldrs: prog gng wl to ld over 1f out: shkn up and wl in command fnl f* **5/2**[1]

-132 **2** *2* **Dream Machine (IRE)**[28] 4798 3-9-13 **75** MrBJames(5) 2 80
(Michael Bell) *trckd ldr: led over 2f out to over 1f out: no ch w wnr after but kpt on to hold on for 2nd* **3/1**[3]

4025 **3** *nk* **England Expects**[37] 4473 3-9-1 **58** (h) MissPFuller 6 62
(K R Burke) *plld hrd: hld up: shkn up over 2f out: effrt to dispute 2nd fnl f: kpt on same pce after* **14/1**

10-0 **4** *1* **Unison (IRE)**[42] 4254 7-11-0 **77** MissEmmaSayer 4 78
(Jeremy Scott) *trckd ldrs: rdn over 2f out: effrt to press for 2nd pl fr over 1f out: no ex last 100yds* **7/1**

3124 **5** *4½* **Road To Dubai (IRE)**[40] 4365 3-10-7 **78** (p1) MrPMillman 1 71
(George Scott) *led: tk field to nr side in st: hdd over 2f out: steadily wknd* **11/4**[2]

550- **6** *3¾* **Top Diktat**[267] 7973 9-9-10 **66** MissBeckyButler(7) 5 51
(Gary Moore) *hld up in tch: shkn up and no prog over 2f out: sn btn* **14/1**

1510 **7** *4½* **Victor's Bet (SPA)**[62] 3547 8-10-3 **71** MissEllaSmith(5) 3 47
(Ralph J Smith) *s.s: detached in last: brief effrt and in tch 1/2-way: last and wkng 3f out* **25/1**

2m 17.96s (7.46) **Going Correction** +0.775s/f (Yiel)
**WFA** 3 from 7yo+ 8lb **7** Ran SP% **109.9**
Speed ratings (Par 105): **101,99,99,98,94 91,88**
CSF £9.43 TOTE £3.40: £1.90, £2.10; EX 11.90 Trifecta £67.40.
**Owner** Mrs Catherine Reed **Bred** Barry Davis **Trained** Newmarket, Suffolk

**FOCUS**
Races on the round course all 22 yards further than advertised due to dolling out of the rails.\n\x\x Testing ground to deal with and the field headed to the stands' side in the straight. The third has been rated to form.

## 5839 SLUG AND LETTUCE CHRISTMAS EBF NOVICE STKS 5f 10y
**6:10** (6:11) (Class 5) 2-Y-0 **£3,881** (£1,155; £577; £288) **Stalls** Low

Form RPR

**1** **Santorini Sun (IRE)** 2-8-11 0 CharlesBishop 7 73
(Mick Channon) *slowly away: last tl 1/2-way: prog to chse ldng pair over 1f out and cl up after: waiting for a gap tl squeezed through 100yds out: rdn and r.o to ld last stride* **9/1**

602 **2** *shd* **Time For Wine (IRE)**[10] 5476 2-8-11 0 JFEgan 3 73
(David Evans) *w ldr: led over 3f out but sn jnd: rdn to assert over 1f out: kpt on fnl f but hdd last stride* **3/1**[2]

5 **3** *4* **Sovereign State**[57] 3725 2-9-2 0 OisinMurphy 4 64
(Robert Cowell) *dwlt: t.k.h: in tch: trckd ldng pair after 2f to over 1f out: btn after but tk 3rd again last stride* **11/2**[3]

630 **4** *nse* **Billiebrookedit (IRE)**[20] 5099 2-9-2 71 RobertWinston 6 64
(Steph Hollinshead) *jnd wnr on outer after 2f: upsides tl over 1f out: wknd ins fnl f* **10/1**

652 **5** *25* **Highland Mary**[14] 5327 2-8-11 74 TomMarquand 1
(Richard Hannon) *led to over 3f out: sn dropped away and last by 1/2-way: t.o over 1f out* **1/1**[1]

1m 6.98s (5.38) **Going Correction** +0.95s/f (Soft) **5** Ran SP% **109.5**
Speed ratings (Par 94): **94,93,87,87,47**
CSF £34.78 TOTE £7.60: £2.40, £1.80; EX 37.80 Trifecta £89.80.
**Owner** Mrs T Burns **Bred** Rathasker Stud **Trained** West Ilsley, Berks

**FOCUS**
Heavy ground on the sprint course and a slow-motion finish with the eventual winner putting her head in front on the line. The runner-up has been rated just off her Windsor form.

## 5840 SLUG AND LETTUCE VALUE LUNCH EBF MAIDEN STKS 1m
**6:45** (6:45) (Class 5) 2-Y-O **£3,881** (£1,155; £577; £288) **Stalls** Low

Form RPR

4 **1** **Dubhe**[20] 5105 2-9-5 0 WilliamBuick 9 77+
(Charlie Appleby) *mde all: tk field to nr side in st: shkn up over 1f out: clr fnl f: readily* **8/11**[1]

**2** *2 ¼* **Nuits St Georges (IRE)** 2-9-5 0 KieranShoemark 7 72+
(David Menuisier) *dwlt: hld up in last trio: shkn up over 2f out where hanging and rn green: prog on outer over 1f out: kpt on to take 2nd nr fin* **33/1**

**3** *shd* **Cassini (IRE)** 2-9-5 0 (t[1]) AdamKirby 5 72+
(John Gosden) *slowly away: in tch in last trio: rdn over 2f out: prog to chse wnr over 1f out: no imp after: lost 2nd nr fin: kpt on* **9/2**[2]

**4** *hd* **Mt Augustus** 2-9-5 0 FranBerry 6 71+
(Henry Candy) *in tch: pushed along over 2f out: nvr able to mount a chal but kpt on steadily fr over 1f out* **16/1**

3 **5** *shd* **Ship Of The Fen**[22] 5036 2-9-5 0 JimCrowley 10 71
(Martyn Meade) *prom: shkn up and sltly outpcd 2f out: kpt on again fnl f to press for a pl nr fin* **5/1**[3]

**6** *1 ¾* **Berkshire Spirit** 2-9-5 0 RobHornby 11 67
(Andrew Balding) *in tch in last trio: shkn up over 2f out: no prog over 1f out: one pce after* **14/1**

05 **7** *4 ½* **Sotomayor**[15] 5301 2-9-5 0 TomMarquand 2 57
(Richard Hannon) *chsd wnr: rdn over 2f out: lost 2nd and wknd over 1f out* **20/1**

1m 50.57s (7.27) **Going Correction** +0.775s/f (Yiel) **7** Ran SP% **113.0**
Speed ratings (Par 94): **94,91,91,91,91 89,85**
CSF £29.46 TOTE £1.70: £1.20, £5.40; EX 27.60 Trifecta £93.60.
**Owner** Godolphin **Bred** Kincorth Investments Inc **Trained** Newmarket, Suffolk

**FOCUS**
Race distance 22 yards further than advertised.\n\x\x An interesting maiden despite testing conditions and while the winner did it well, there were some eyecatching performances in behind.

## 5841 FIZZ FRIDAYS AT SLUG AND LETTUCE H'CAP 1m 1f 209y
**7:15** (7:17) (Class 3) (0-90,90) 3-Y-O **£9,337** (£2,796; £1,398; £699) **Stalls** Low

Form RPR

11 **1** **Time Chaser**[55] 3786 3-9-3 **86** KieranShoemark 4 96+
(Roger Charlton) *trckd ldr: led over 2f out: rdn over 1f out: pressed 100yds out: pushed out and a holding rival* **6/5**[1]

4211 **2** *½* **Glenys The Menace (FR)**[12] 5404 3-8-13 **82** KierenFox 1 88
(John Best) *led at decent pce: hdd and shkn up over 2f out: rallied jst over 1f out: pressed wnr 100yds out: styd on but readily hld nr fin* **11/4**[2]

-640 **3** *3 ¾* **Star Of Rory (IRE)**[40] 4376 3-9-7 **90** AdamKirby 3 89
(Tom Dascombe) *trckd ldng pair: rdn and no imp over 2f out: one pce after* **11/2**

2410 **4** *¾* **Alwahsh (IRE)**[12] 5392 3-9-2 **85** JimCrowley 2 82
(William Haggas) *hld up in last: shkn up and no rspnse over 2f out: n.d after: kpt on fnl f* **7/2**[3]

2m 16.38s (5.88) **Going Correction** +0.775s/f (Yiel) **4** Ran SP% **109.7**
Speed ratings (Par 104): **107,106,103,103**
CSF £4.82 TOTE £2.10; EX 3.90 Trifecta £9.70.
**Owner** K Abdullah **Bred** Juddmonte Farms Ltd **Trained** Beckhampton, Wilts

**FOCUS**
Distance 22 yards further than advertised due to dolling out. A small field for this handicap but the front two emerge with plenty of credit. The runner-up has been rated to the better view of her Chester form.

## 5842 SLUG AND LETTUCE COCKTAIL SCHOOL H'CAP 7f
**7:45** (7:47) (Class 4) (0-85,90) 3-Y-O+ **£7,115** (£2,117; £1,058; £529) **Stalls** Low

Form RPR

1203 **1** **Black Bess**[15] 5294 4-9-9 **87** PaddyBradley[(5)] 4 97
(Jim Boyle) *led at gd pce: styd in centre st along w all but one of rivals: rdn and hdd 2f out: kpt on strly over 1f out: led last 100yds: won gng away* **12/1**

-513 **2** *1 ½* **Redgrave (IRE)**[21] 5059 3-9-2 **81** WilliamBuick 3 85+
(Charles Hills) *trckd ldng pair: only one to hd for nr side rail early in st and dashed into the ld 2f out: edgd rt u.p fr over 1f out: hdd and nt qckn last 100yds* **4/1**[3]

0211 **3** *2 ¼* **Frank Bridge**[8] 5548 4-10-3 **90** 6ex CharlesBishop 8 90
(Eve Johnson Houghton) *trckd ldng trio: styd centre st: rdn to go 3rd wl over 1f out: kpt on but nvr able to threaten* **5/2**[1]

2-21 **4** *4* **Easy Tiger**[33] 4622 5-9-12 **85** LiamKeniry 5 75
(Malcolm Saunders) *chsd wnr: styd centre st: lost 2nd jst over 2f out: steadily wknd* **9/2**

6-50 **5** *shd* **Tigerwolf (IRE)**[30] 4719 4-9-5 **78** JFEgan 9 68
(Mick Channon) *restless stalls: dwlt: hld up in last: styd centre st: shkn up over 2f out: nvr on terms but plugged on fnl f* **14/1**

3603 **6** *2 ¼* **Professor**[15] 5302 7-9-8 **81** (p) KierenFox 2 65
(Michael Attwater) *nvr really gng wl: rdn and struggling in rr over 2f out: no prog* **14/1**

-101 **7** *2 ¼* **Saluti (IRE)**[12] 5433 3-9-3 **82** JimCrowley 10 58
(Amanda Perrett) *hld up towards rr: shkn up and no prog over 2f out: sn btn* **3/1**[2]

1m 32.62s (3.12) **Going Correction** +0.775s/f (Yiel) **7** Ran SP% **112.8**
**WFA** 3 from 4yo+ 6lb
Speed ratings (Par 105): **113,111,108,104,104 101,98**
CSF £57.39 CT £159.86 TOTE £11.70: £4.60, £2.30; EX 76.50 Trifecta £280.60.
**Owner** The Clean Sweep Partnership **Bred** Paddock Space **Trained** Epsom, Surrey

**FOCUS**
Race distance 22 yards further than advertised due to dolling out.\n\x\x An eventful finish with the winner getting back up having looked in big trouble a furlong out. The third has been rated below his last week's win here.

## 5843 DEVINE HOMES H'CAP 1m
**8:20** (8:23) (Class 5) (0-75,79) 3-Y-O+ **£3,881** (£1,155; £577; £288) **Stalls** Low

Form RPR

3101 **1** **Wealth Tax**[7] 5578 4-9-13 **79** 6ex FinleyMarsh[(7)] 2 85
(Ed Dunlop) *trckd ldrs: clsd in centre over 2f out: rdn to ld jst over 1f out: kpt on gamely fnl f* **6/4**[1]

0013 **2** *1* **High Draw (FR)**[14] 5330 4-9-11 **73** CliffordLee[(3)] 6 77
(K R Burke) *led after 3f and sn clr: styd towards centre in st: rdn 2f out: hdd jst over 1f out: hld after but kpt on nr fin* **4/1**[2]

3634 **3** *hd* **Bridge Of Sighs**[54] 3817 5-9-7 **71** PaddyBradley[(5)] 7 75
(Lee Carter) *trckd ldrs gng wl: clsd w wnr in centre to chal over 1f out: sn rdn and nt qckn: hld ins fnl f and lost 2nd last strides* **9/1**

0255 **4** *1 ¾* **Malt Teaser (FR)**[28] 4798 3-8-13 **65** KierenFox 3 65
(John Best) *towards rr: struggling 1/2-way: no ch over 2f out but c to nr side rail after: styd on to take 4th ins fnl f: nrst fin* **12/1**

-126 **5** *¾* **Many Dreams (IRE)**[40] 4372 4-9-7 **69** HectorCrouch[(3)] 8 68
(Gary Moore) *hld up: urged along over 3f out: tk modest 4th over 1f out but hanging lft after and no imp: one pce fnl f* **7/1**

0501 **6** *4 ½* **Lyrica's Lion (IRE)**[26] 4914 3-8-3 **60** DavidEgan[(5)] 4 49
(Michael Attwater) *led 1f: prom tl wknd over 2f out* **11/2**[3]

6634 **7** *1 ½* **Ravenhoe (IRE)**[21] 5062 4-9-10 **69** OisinMurphy 1 56
(Mark Johnston) *led after 1f tl after 3f: prom tl wknd over 2f out* **14/1**

5-00 **8** *42* **Rock'n Gold**[125] 1598 4-9-11 **70** KieranShoemark 5
(Adrian Wintle) *reluctant to enter stalls: a in rr: rdn 1/2-way: sn bhd: t.o* **33/1**

1m 49.73s (6.43) **Going Correction** +0.775s/f (Yiel) **8** Ran SP% **115.2**
**WFA** 3 from 4yo+ 7lb
Speed ratings (Par 103): **98,97,96,95,94 89,88,46**
CSF £7.55 CT £39.28 TOTE £2.40: £1.10, £1.50, £2.60; EX 6.20 Trifecta £43.30.
**Owner** Mhs Partners & E Dunlop **Bred** Barry Walters **Trained** Newmarket, Suffolk

**FOCUS**
Race distance 22 yards further than advertised due to dolling out.\n\x\x Not the strongest race for the grade but the in-form winner was made to work quite hard for his success and the front three all have something to recommend them. The form has been rated cautiously.
T/Plt: £140.70 to a £1 stake. Pool: £54,114.19 - 280.59 winning units. T/Qpdt: £17.20 to a £1 stake. Pool: £4,497.29 - 193.05 winning units. **Jonathan Neesom**

# 5479 WOLVERHAMPTON (A.W) (L-H)
Thursday, August 10

**OFFICIAL GOING: Tapeta: standard**
Wind: light breeze Weather: sunny intervals, mild

## 5844 THE HUMAN LEAGUE AT WOLVERHAMPTON RACECOURSE NOVICE STKS 6f 20y (Tp)
**6:00** (6:01) (Class 5) 2-Y-O **£3,234** (£962; £481; £240) **Stalls** Low

Form RPR

5112 **1** **Amazing Alice**[16] 5240 2-9-2 81 (p) EdwardGreatrex[(3)] 2 79
(Archie Watson) *mde all: kicked 1 l clr over 1f out: rdn ent fnl f and extended advantage: r.o wl: comf* **5/2**[2]

120 **2** *1 ¾* **Way Of Wisdom**[20] 5109 2-9-9 86 JamesDoyle 6 78
(Charlie Appleby) *nt on even keel early: rcvrd to chse ldrs: 4th 2f out: hdwy into 2nd over 1f out: sn rdn: no imp on wnr ent fnl f: r.o one pce* **1/1**[1]

1636 **3** *nk* **Another Day Of Sun (IRE)**[13] 5366 2-9-6 70 PatDobbs 3 74
(Mick Channon) *trckd ldrs: pushed along in 4th wl over 1f out: rdn into 3rd and r.o fnl f* **18/1**

0 **4** *hd* **Expelled**[24] 4973 2-9-2 0 DanielMuscutt 11 69
(James Fanshawe) *hld up: drvn over 1f out: hdwy ent fnl f: r.o wl nr fin* **16/1**

04 **5** *¾* **Mutafarrid (IRE)**[34] 4560 2-9-2 0 DaneO'Neill 4 67
(Owen Burrows) *mid-div: drvn 2f out: rdn over 1f out: one pce* **15/2**[3]

6 **6** *3 ¼* **Dandiesque (IRE)**[8] 5534 2-8-11 0 KieranO'Neill 9 52
(Richard Hannon) *hld up: pushed along 2f out: drvn over 1f out: one pce* **20/1**

45 **7** *1* **Shootingthe Breeze**[21] 5058 2-9-2 0 FrannyNorton 10 54
(Tom Dascombe) *prom: pushed along 2f out: no ex fnl f* **16/1**

60 **8** *1 ¼* **Go Sandy**[12] 5398 2-8-11 0 SteveDrowne 7 46
(Lisa Williamson) *racd in cl 2nd: drvn and lost pl 2f out: rdn over 1f out: fdd* **200/1**

04 **9** *½* **Push N'Pull (IRE)**[12] 5437 2-9-2 0 DavidNolan 8 49
(Richard Fahey) *in rr: pushed along 1/2-way: drvn wl over 1f out: no imp* **40/1**

000 **10** *3 ¾* **Midnight Blue**[29] 4749 2-8-11 0 RyanPowell 5 33
(Sir Mark Prescott Bt) *racd in last: rdn 1/2-way: no imp* **150/1**

0 **11** *hd* **Redtedd**[21] 5048 2-8-11 0 PaddyPilley[(5)] 1 37+
(Tom Dascombe) *reluctant to load: mounted in stalls: hld up: rdn 2f out: no rspnse: eased ins fnl f* **66/1**

1m 14.58s (0.08) **Going Correction** -0.10s/f (Stan) **11** Ran SP% **117.2**
Speed ratings (Par 94): **95,92,92,92,91 86,85,83,83,78 77**
CSF £5.16 TOTE £3.70: £1.20, £1.10, £4.50; EX 7.40 Trifecta £27.90.
**Owner** C R Hirst **Bred** Home Farm **Trained** Upper Lambourn, W Berks

**FOCUS**
Bright, sunny conditions initially for this seven-race evening fixture and a fair novice sprint to begin with, though few were able to land a blow behind the tough all-the-way winner. The runner-up has again been rated below his earlier form.

## 5845 BETALYST.COM FOOTBALL BETTING ANALYST FILLIES' H'CAP 6f 20y (Tp)
**6:35** (6:36) (Class 5) (0-75,76) 3-Y-O+ **£3,234** (£962; £481; £240) **Stalls** Low

Form RPR

1126 **1** **Dusky Maid (IRE)**[28] 4797 3-9-4 **68** FrannyNorton 5 82+
(James Given) *disp ld to 1/2-way where settled into cl 2nd: hdwy to ld over 1f out: pushed along ent fnl f: briefly kpt up to work and qcknd clr: pushed out nr fin: easily* **15/8**[1]

4123 **2** *5* **Tooty Fruitti**[22] 5027 3-9-1 **65** JosephineGordon 3 63
(Jo Hughes) *trckd ldrs: wnt 2nd over 1f out: chsd wnr ent fnl f: sn rdn and r.o: no ch w wnr* **4/1**[2]

6165 **3** *2* **Magic Approach**[15] 5295 3-8-10 **60** (b[1]) KieranO'Neill 1 52
(David Simcock) *racd in last: wnt 5th 1/2-way: pushed along 2f out: 4th and drvn over 1f out: rdn fnl f: tk 3rd nr fin* **8/1**[3]

0-64 **4** *shd* **Loving**[14] 5338 3-9-12 **76** JamesDoyle 6 67
(William Haggas) *hld up: hdwy into 4th 3f out: pushed along 2f out: 3rd and drvn over 1f out: rdn fnl f: one pce: lost 3rd nr fin* **15/8**[1]

1000 **5** *3 ¼* **Krystallite**[10] 5481 4-9-4 **69**........ PaddyPilley(5) 4 51
(Scott Dixon) *disp ld to 1/2-way where tk narrow advantage: hdd and rdn over 1f out: wknd fnl f* **16/1**

-336 **P** **Sheila's Palace**[134] 1428 3-8-9 **59**........ JohnFahy 7
(J S Moore) *mid-div: racd wd: relegated to last 1/2-way: sn lost tch: p.u: lame* **20/1**

1m 13.82s (-0.68) **Going Correction** -0.10s/f (Stan)
**WFA** 3 from 4yo+ 4lb **6** Ran SP% **111.3**
Speed ratings (Par 100): **100,93,90,90,86**
CSF £9.63 TOTE £3.00: £1.90, £1.90; EX 8.80 Trifecta £29.40.
**Owner** The Cool Silk Partnership **Bred** L O'Donovan **Trained** Willoughton, Lincs

**FOCUS**
A routine fillies' handicap, but another generously run race in which few featured and a winning time 0.76 seconds faster than that of the preceding juvenile novice contest.

## 5846 VISIT ATTHERACES.COM H'CAP 1m 5f 219y (Tp)
**7:05** (7:17) (Class 6) (0-60,62) 3-Y-O **£2,749** (£818; £408; £204) **Stalls** Low

Form RPR

4212 **1** **Sheriff Garrett (IRE)**[6] 5617 3-9-9 **62**........(p) AndrewMullen 3 75+
(Tim Easterby) *hld up: hdwy 4f out: pushed along 3f out: 4th 2f out: trckd ldrs and drvn over 1f out: forced way between horses to ld ent fnl f: rdn and drew clr: readily* **11/8**[1]

0532 **2** *4 ½* **Easy Wind**[13] 5361 3-9-5 **58**........(p[1]) RyanPowell 11 63
(Sir Mark Prescott Bt) *prom: 3rd 4f out: drvn 3f out: hdwy to ld 2f out: rdn over 1f out: passed by wnr ent fnl f: one pce* **11/2**[3]

6006 **3** *¾* **Netley Abbey**[24] 4978 3-8-5 **47**........(p) EdwardGreatrex(3) 12 51
(Karen George) *chsd ldr: led 3f out: drvn and hdd 2f out: styd prom: rdn over 1f out: bmpd by wnr ent fnl f: no ex* **20/1**

000 **4** *1* **Volturnus**[19] 5141 3-8-7 **46** oh1........(b[1]) FrannyNorton 6 50
(Jamie Osborne) *mid-div: pushed along 3f out: drvn 2f out: sn rdn: r.o fnl f* **50/1**

4532 **5** *shd* **Padleyourowncanoe**[11] 4978 3-9-7 **60**........(b) DaneO'Neill 1 62
(Daniel Mark Loughnane) *hld up: gd hdwy 4f out: wnt 3rd 3f out: drvn 2f out: sn rdn: no ex ent fnl f* **8/1**

6640 **6** *13* **Haldaw**[12] 5406 3-9-4 **57**........ PatDobbs 7 41
(Mick Channon) *hld up: pushed along 3f out: drvn 2f out: no imp* **33/1**

000 **7** *1 ½* **Breton Belle (IRE)**[62] 3542 3-8-12 **54**........ HollieDoyle(3) 10 36
(David Simcock) *racd in last: pushed along 4f out: drvn 3f out: passed btn horses last 2 fs but nvr a factor* **33/1**

0-00 **8** *¾* **Shadow Of Hercules (IRE)**[183] 627 3-8-2 **46** oh1....(v) PhilDennis(5) 8 27
(Michael Mullineaux) *led: pushed along and hdd 3f out: sn drvn: wknd qckly* **150/1**

62-0 **9** *24* **Lulu The Rocket**[203] 305 3-9-4 **57**........ MartinHarley 4 5
(John Butler) *t.k.h in mid-div: lost pl 4f out: rdn 3f out: sn lost tch: eased* **5/1**[2]

-544 **10** *1* **Magic Beans**[22] 5034 3-9-3 **59**........ CharlieBennett(3) 5 5
(Hughie Morrison) *trckd ldrs: pushed along and lost pl 4f out: sn lost tch* **7/1**

3m 1.81s (-6.19) **Going Correction** -0.10s/f (Stan) **10** Ran SP% **111.0**
Speed ratings (Par 98): **113,110,110,109,109 101,101,100,86,86**
CSF £7.99 CT £94.54 TOTE £2.10: £1.10, £1.60, £5.60; EX 9.70 Trifecta £96.40.
**Owner** Ontoawinner 10 & Partner 4 **Bred** Eimear Mulhern **Trained** Great Habton, N Yorks

**FOCUS**
A moderate stayers' handicap, but a decent pace and another winner on the card continuing the improvement shown since cheekpieces were fitted.

## 5847 BETALYST.COM DAILY TIPS & PREVIEWS NOVICE AUCTION STKS 7f 36y (Tp)
**7:35** (7:43) (Class 6) 2-Y-O **£2,587** (£770; £384; £192) **Stalls** High

Form RPR

43 **1** **The Throstles**[12] 5437 2-9-2 0........ DavidNolan 7 70
(Kevin Frost) *chsd ldr: drvn in cl 2nd over 1f out: rdn fnl f: r.o wl to ld last two strides* **4/1**[3]

20 **2** *shd* **Oswald (IRE)**[15] 5292 2-9-2 0........ JamesDoyle 4 70
(Robyn Brisland) *led: narrow advantage and pushed along over 1f out: rdn ent fnl f: drifted rt u.p: r.o but hdd last two strides* **1/1**[1]

62 **3** *shd* **Tranquil Soul**[24] 4977 2-8-11 0........ StevieDonohoe 3 65
(David Lanigan) *chsd ldrs: pushed along and 2 l bhd over 1f out: hrd rdn and hdwy ent fnl f: r.o wl u.p: clsng qckly on front two nr fin* **5/2**[2]

00 **4** *6* **Wiltons (FR)**[19] 5144 2-8-13 0........(p[1]) HollieDoyle(3) 5 54
(Harry Dunlop) *a mid-div: pushed along and losing tch w front three 2f out: rdn over 1f out: one pce* **100/1**

**5** *1 ½* **Kalakchee** 2-9-2 0........(h[1]) LemosdeSouza 6 49
(Amy Murphy) *hld up: pushed along 2f out: rdn over 1f out: one pce fnl f* **25/1**

55 **6** *½* **Sauchiehall Street (IRE)**[24] 4963 2-9-2 0........ PatDobbs 2 48
(Sylvester Kirk) *hld up: pushed along 2f out: rdn over 1f out: no imp* **22/1**

0 **7** *13* **Rocus (IRE)**[15] 5292 2-9-2 0........ SteveDrowne 1 13
(Mark Usher) *racd in 5th tl relegated to last 4f out: drvn 3f out: sn lost tch* **66/1**

1m 29.03s (0.23) **Going Correction** -0.10s/f (Stan) **7** Ran SP% **109.2**
Speed ratings (Par 92): **94,93,93,86,85 84,69**
CSF £7.69 TOTE £4.50: £3.40, £1.20; EX 8.70 Trifecta £14.30.
**Owner** BGC Racing & Carl Hodgson **Bred** Aislabie Bloodstock Ltd **Trained** Market Drayton, Shropshire

**FOCUS**
Little strength in depth, but a thrilling finish between the three that mattered in the market. It's been rated around the first three's pre-race form.

## 5848 JOIN THE BLACK COUNTRY CHAMBER OF COMMERCE H'CAP 7f 36y (Tp)
**8:10** (8:11) (Class 6) (0-55,55) 3-Y-O+ **£2,587** (£770; £288; £288) **Stalls** High

Form RPR

0-60 **1** **La Isla Bonita**[120] 1727 3-8-8 **53**........ JennyPowell(5) 1 60
(Richard Spencer) *mde all: rdn over 1f out where 1 l ahd: extended advantage sltly ins fnl f: pushed out nr fin: comf* **16/1**

6042 **2** *1 ¼* **Danot (IRE)**[15] 5285 5-9-4 **55**........(p) AdamMcNamara(3) 2 61
(Jedd O'Keeffe) *a chsng wnr: rdn and 1 l bhd over 1f out: r.o fnl f but a hld* **9/2**[2]

3311 **3** *2* **Carlovian**[15] 5285 4-9-4 **52**........(p) DougieCostello 6 53
(Mark Walford) *chsd first and 2nd thrght: rdn over 1f out: one pce and jnd for 3rd on fining line* **3/1**[1]

45 **3** *dht* **State Residence (IRE)**[42] 4263 3-8-9 **52**........(t) JoshDoyle(3) 7 51+
(David O'Meara) *mid-div on inner: swtchd to centre: pushed along and hdwy over 1f out: rdn fnl f: r.o to secure share of 3rd on fining line* **5/1**[3]

0360 **5** *1 ½* **Major Muscari (IRE)**[71] 3201 9-9-4 **52**........(p) MartinHarley 11 49+
(Shaun Harris) *hld up: hdwy on outer 2f out: rdn fnl f: no ex* **18/1**

0112 **6** *1 ¼* **Tigerfish (IRE)**[9] 5512 3-8-12 **55**........(p) HollieDoyle(3) 8 46+
(William Stone) *in rr: drvn and brought wd wl over 1f out: sn rdn: sme late hdwy* **9/2**[2]

5000 **7** *1* **Fossa**[10] 5482 7-8-13 **50**........ CharlieBennett(3) 12 40
(Mark Brisbourne) *slowly away losing several l: sn rcvrd to latch on to pack: pushed along in rr 2f out: rdn over 1f out: r.o fnl f* **40/1**

0000 **8** *nse* **Divine Call**[15] 5271 10-8-12 **46**........(b) FrannyNorton 3 36
(Milton Bradley) *trckd ldrs: rdn in 4th 2f out: lost pl over 1f out: wknd* **20/1**

0400 **9** *½* **Hurricane Rock**[12] 5410 4-9-4 **52**........ JosephineGordon 5 41
(Simon Dow) *mid-div: pushed along 2f out: rdn over 1f out: wknd fnl f* **9/1**

0010 **10** *1 ½* **Poor Duke (IRE)**[33] 4625 7-8-12 **53**........(p) JamieGormley(7) 10 38
(Michael Mullineaux) *hld up: pushed along 2f out: briefly rdn ent fnl f: no imp* **22/1**

00 **11** *2 ½* **Twistsandturns (IRE)**[18] 5181 6-8-13 **52**........ PhilDennis(5) 9 30
(Declan Carroll) *racd wd: mid-div: pushed along 2f out: rdn and fdd over 1f out* **11/1**

1m 28.53s (-0.27) **Going Correction** -0.10s/f (Stan)
**WFA** 3 from 4yo+ 6lb **11** Ran SP% **119.1**
Speed ratings (Par 101): **97,95,93,93,91 90,89,88,88,86 83**
WIN: £22.20; PL: D £2.60, C £0.50, SR £1.40, LIB £5.10; EX: £154.00; CSF: £85.87; TC: LIB\D\C £141.69, LIB\D\SR £217.36; TF: LIB\D\C £681.60, LIB\D\SR £1018.10;.
**Owner** Rebel Racing (2) **Bred** Salisbury Bloodstock Ltd **Trained** Newmarket, Suffolk

**FOCUS**
A competitive-looking low-grade affair beforehand, but another in which few featured. The winning time was 0.5 seconds quicker than that of the juvenile novice event immediately beforehand. The runner-up helps pin the level.

## 5849 BETALYST.COM FREE FOOTBALL TIPS H'CAP 1m 142y (Tp)
**8:40** (8:41) (Class 4) (0-85,84) 3-Y-O+ **£5,175** (£1,540; £769; £384) **Stalls** Low

Form RPR

1 **1** **High End**[16] 5243 3-8-13 **80**........ EdwardGreatrex(3) 1 94+
(Saeed bin Suroor) *mde all: pushed along and 1 l ahd over 1f out: extended ld to 2 l ent fnl f: shkn up and r.o wl: comf* **5/4**[1]

1461 **2** *2 ¼* **Almoreb (IRE)**[15] 5300 3-9-6 **84**........ DaneO'Neill 6 92
(Richard Hannon) *t.k.h: chsd wnr thrght: pushed along 2f out: rdn and 1 l bhd over 1f out: 2 l down ent fnl f: r.o but a hld* **10/3**[2]

443 **3** *1 ¾* **Toga Tiger (IRE)**[10] 5484 10-9-8 **78**........ RichardKingscote 2 82
(Daniel Mark Loughnane) *trckd ldrs: rdn in 3rd over 1f out: r.o one pce fnl f* **20/1**

403 **4** *1 ½* **Ahlan Bil Zain (FR)**[36] 4491 3-9-1 **79**........ PatDobbs 7 80+
(David Simcock) *hld up: rdn and hdwy over 1f out: r.o wl to take 4th fnl f* **12/1**

2231 **5** *hd* **Cool Team (IRE)**[29] 4764 3-9-1 **79**........(tp) JosephineGordon 4 79
(Hugo Palmer) *hld up: drvn 2f out: 4th and rdn over 1f out: no ex fnl f* **7/1**[3]

100 **6** *1 ¼* **Weloof (FR)**[53] 3862 3-9-0 **78**........ MartinHarley 9 75
(Ed Dunlop) *hld up: effrt on outer over 1f out: sn rdn: styd on ins fnl f* **25/1**

6306 **7** *nk* **Berlusca (IRE)**[47] 4082 8-9-1 **71**........(h) SamJames 3 68
(David Loughnane) *hld up: pushed along over 1f out: rdn and one pce fnl f* **50/1**

2522 **8** *1* **Pumaflor (IRE)**[7] 5559 5-9-8 **81**........(p) JoshDoyle(3) 5 75
(David O'Meara) *mid-div: pushed along 2f out: drvn over 1f out: sn rdn and wknd* **20/1**

212- **9** *2* **Rebel Cause (IRE)**[424] 3187 4-9-11 **81**........ JamesDoyle 8 71
(Richard Spencer) *prom: 4th 2f out: rdn over 1f out: wknd fnl f* **8/1**

1m 48.49s (-1.61) **Going Correction** -0.10s/f (Stan)
**WFA** 3 from 4yo+ 8lb **9** Ran SP% **114.2**
Speed ratings (Par 105): **103,101,99,98,97 96,96,95,93**
CSF £4.88 CT £51.39 TOTE £2.00: £1.10, £1.40, £4.70; EX 5.60 Trifecta £31.40.
**Owner** Godolphin **Bred** Watership Down Stud **Trained** Newmarket, Suffolk

**FOCUS**
A fairly well-stocked feature, but the once-raced favourite took it apart. It's been rated around the well-placed third to his latest form.

## 5850 BETALYST.COM PRO TIPS H'CAP 1m 4f 51y (Tp)
**9:10** (9:11) (Class 6) (0-55,54) 3-Y-O+ **£2,587** (£770; £384; £192) **Stalls** Low

Form RPR

-552 **1** **Frozon**[24] 4980 4-9-5 **54**........(h) BenRobinson(5) 7 63
(Brian Ellison) *mid-div: hdwy 4f out: pushed along into 3rd 3f out: drvn over 2f out: hdwy to ld 1f out: rdn and r.o wl fnl f* **8/1**[3]

4505 **2** *1 ½* **The Juggler**[21] 5080 4-9-3 **47**........(v) MartinLane 10 53
(William Knight) *led: hdd over 3f out: sn drvn along: rallied in 3rd 1f out: rdn and regained 2nd pl wl ins fnl f* **8/1**[3]

4450 **3** *¾* **Flying Power**[21] 5080 9-9-2 **46**........(p) RoystonFfrench 5 51
(John Norton) *chsd ldr: led 3f out: pushed along over 1f out: sn rdn and hdd by wnr: no ex and lost 2nd pl wl ins fnl f* **14/1**

4/0- **4** *2 ¾* **Gold Class**[32] 5900 6-9-1 **45**........(bt) JamesDoyle 8 46
(Olly Murphy) *hld up: drvn 3f out: hdwy and rdn over 1f out: styd on wl to take 4th ins fnl f* **4/5**[1]

6344 **5** *½* **Elite Icon**[52] 3901 3-8-2 **49**........ JamieGormley(7) 2 50
(Iain Jardine) *hld up: pushed along and hdwy 2f out: rdn over 1f out: styd on fnl f* **7/1**[2]

460 **6** *¾* **Flowers Will Bloom (IRE)**[33] 4611 3-9-0 **54**........ MartinHarley 3 54
(David O'Meara) *mid-div: pushed along into 4th 2f out: sn drvn: rdn over 1f out: no ex ins fnl f* **9/1**

4-55 **7** *6* **Medieval Bishop (IRE)**[24] 4980 8-9-0 **51**........(p) WilliamCox(7) 11 40
(Tony Forbes) *slowly away: rcvrd qckly and sn trcking ldrs: pushed along 3f out: sn rdn: one pce fnl 2f* **25/1**

4445 **8** *5* **Touch The Clouds**[16] 5261 6-8-12 **45**........ HollieDoyle(3) 9 25
(William Stone) *slowly away and adrift of pack early: prog to join rest after 2 fs: drvn over 2f out: wknd* **16/1**

460- **9** *hd* **Black Iceman**[311] 3067 9-8-12 **45**........ SimonPearce(3) 12 25
(Lydia Pearce) *hld up: drvn 3f out: rdn over 1f out: no imp* **66/1**

06-0 **10** *6* **The Batham Boy (IRE)**[24] 4981 3-8-11 **51**........ SteveDrowne 4 22
(Daniel Mark Loughnane) *trckd ldrs: pushed along and lost pl 4f out: sn drvn and wknd* **50/1**

0050 **11** *2* **Barbary Prince**[16] 5267 5-9-1 **45**........ AndrewMullen 1 11
(Shaun Harris) *a in rr: drvn 3f out: no rspnse* **100/1**

0460 **12** *6* **Steady Major (IRE)**[32] 4158 5-8-12 **45**........(b) CharlieBennett(3) 6
(Mark Brisbourne) *trckd ldrs: drvn and lost pl 3f out: wknd fnl 2f* **50/1**

2m 39.18s (-1.62) **Going Correction** -0.10s/f (Stan)
**WFA** 3 from 4yo+ 10lb **12** Ran SP% **123.1**
Speed ratings (Par 101): **101,100,99,97,97 96,92,89,89,85 84,80**
CSF £71.41 CT £901.90 TOTE £9.10: £2.10, £2.50, £4.20; EX 77.30 Trifecta £556.50.
**Owner** A Barnes **Bred** Mrs Hugh Maitland-Jones **Trained** Norton, N Yorks

**FOCUS**
A mediocre middle-distance handicap run at a modest gallop, and the well-backed favourite disappointed. The winner and third help limit the form.

T/Plt: £8.40 to a £1 stake. Pool: £65,509.68 - 5627.36 winning units. T/Qpdt: £3.90 to a £1 stake. Pool: £5,126.08 - 952.14 winning units. **Keith McHugh**

## 5808 YARMOUTH (L-H)

Thursday, August 10

**OFFICIAL GOING: Good to soft (soft in places)**

Wind: Fresh behind Weather: Fine

### 5851 BRITISH STALLION STUDS EBF NOVICE STKS (PLUS 10 RACE) 6f 3y

2:10 (2:11) (Class 4) 2-Y-O £4,657 (£1,386; £692; £346) Stalls Centre

Form RPR

311 1 **Luis Fernandez (USA)**[28] 4805 2-9-3 83........................ DavidEgan(5) 7 83
(Kevin Ryan) *mde all: shkn up over 1f out: rdn and hung lft ins fnl f: styd on* **1/2**[1]

6 2 *hd* **Manthoor (IRE)**[56] 3754 2-9-2 0........................................ TedDurcan 4 76
(Owen Burrows) *chsd wnr: pushed along over 2f out: rdn over 1f out: ev ch whn carried lft ins fnl f: styd on* **2/1**[2]

3 *2 1/4* **Lalania** 2-8-8 0.............................................. AaronJones(3) 3 65+
(Stuart Williams) *dwlt: hld up: hdwy over 1f out: edgd lft ins fnl f: nt rch ldrs* **40/1**

00 4 *4 1/2* **Freebe Rocks (IRE)**[13] 5365 2-9-2 0............................. DannyBrock 2 56
(Michael Bell) *prom: racd keenly: rdn over 2f out: wkng whn edgd lft fnl f* **25/1**

56 5 *3 1/2* **Expediate**[35] 4539 2-9-2 0.............................................. LouisSteward 1 46
(Robert Cowell) *prom: rdn over 2f out: wknd over 1f out: hung lft ins fnl f* **20/1**[3]

1m 13.13s (-1.27) **Going Correction** -0.325s/f (Firm) 5 Ran SP% **111.0**

Speed ratings (Par 96): **95,94,91,85,81**

CSF £1.70 TOTE £1.30: £1.02, £1.30; EX 1.80 Trifecta £10.50.

**Owner** Mrs R G Hillen **Bred** Castleton Lyons & Kilboy Estate **Trained** Hambleton, N Yorks

■ Stewards' Enquiry : David Egan two-day ban: careless riding (Aug 26-27)

**FOCUS**

This novice looked a match and the big two duly dominated, with the favourite getting it done, helping his own cause by hanging left and carrying the runner-up with him. Another step forward from the winner, with the runner-up rated to his mark.

### 5852 USPGA GOLF AT 188BET (S) H'CAP 7f 3y

2:40 (2:40) (Class 6) (0-65,60) 3-Y-O £2,264 (£673; £336; £168) Stalls Centre

Form RPR

4642 1 **Shyarch**[14] 5339 3-8-12 56.............................................. JaneElliott(5) 2 62
(George Margarson) *s.i.s: sn pushed along in rr: swtchd rt and hdwy to chse ldr over 2f out: rdn over 1f out: edgd lft ins fnl f: styd on to ld post* **5/2**[1]

3256 2 *shd* **Ocean Temptress**[22] 5038 3-8-10 56........................(b[1]) JackOsborn(7) 1 62
(John Ryan) *led: clr 6f out tl rdn over 1f out: edgd rt ins fnl f: wnt lft towards fin: hdd post* **11/2**[3]

0335 3 *7* **Oakley Pride (IRE)**[15] 5280 3-8-13 57........................(vt) DavidEgan(5) 4 45
(Gay Kelleway) *chsd ldrs: rdn over 2f out: styd on same pce fr over 1f out* **7/2**[2]

3003 4 *shd* **Do You Know (IRE)**[21] 5076 3-9-4 60......................(t[1]) GeorgeWood(3) 5 48
(Marco Botti) *prom: chsd ldr who was clr over 4f out: rdn and lost 2nd over 2f out: styd on same pce fr over 1f out* **7/2**[2]

4000 5 *19* **Paquita Bailarina**[52] 3913 3-8-11 50.......................... SilvestreDeSousa 6
(James Given) *chsd ldr who wnt clr 6f out: lost 2nd over 4f out: pushed along 1/2-way: wknd and eased over 2f out* **7/2**[2]

1m 24.78s (-1.82) **Going Correction** -0.325s/f (Firm) 5 Ran SP% **110.6**

Speed ratings (Par 98): **97,96,88,88,67**

CSF £16.09 TOTE £2.50: £1.10, £2.90; EX 17.10 Trifecta £53.30.

**Owner** F Butler **Bred** F Butler **Trained** Newmarket, Suffolk

**FOCUS**

No hanging around here, with the runner-up charging off in the first-time blinkers. The runner-up has been rated in line with her best recent form.

### 5853 PREMIER LEAGUE FOOTBALL AT 188BET H'CAP 1m 2f 23y

3:10 (3:11) (Class 5) (0-70,72) 3-Y-O £2,911 (£866; £432; £216) Stalls Low

Form RPR

6302 1 **Entangling (IRE)**[14] 5319 3-9-9 72........................... SilvestreDeSousa 6 79+
(Chris Wall) *chsd ldrs: rdn 4f out: led over 1f out: styd on u.p* **4/5**[1]

33 2 *1/2* **Epitaph (IRE)**[12] 5404 3-9-5 68.............................................. DannyBrock 4 73
(Michael Appleby) *chsd ldrs: rdn over 2f out: hung lft over 1f out: styd on to go 2nd nr fin* **7/2**[2]

1410 3 *nk* **Chunkyfunkymonkey**[3] 5722 3-8-11 67........................ JackOsborn(7) 2 71
(John Ryan) *chsd ldr tl led over 3f out: rdn and hdd over 1f out: styd on: lost 2nd nr fin* **10/1**

-035 4 *2 1/4* **Starlight Circus (IRE)**[29] 4761 3-8-11 63..............(p[1]) GeorgeWood(3) 1 63
(Marco Botti) *led: hdd over 3f out: sn rdn: styd on same pce fnl f* **4/1**[3]

0500 5 *20* **Kyshoni (IRE)**[38] 4444 3-9-0 63.......................................... TedDurcan 8 23
(Mike Murphy) *s.i.s and wnt rt s: hld up: rdn and wknd over 2f out* **33/1**

2m 11.31s (0.81) **Going Correction** +0.075s/f (Good) 5 Ran SP% **109.8**

Speed ratings (Par 100): **99,98,98,96,80**

CSF £3.88 TOTE £1.60: £1.10, £2.60; EX 3.90 Trifecta £10.50.

**Owner** Ben CM Wong **Bred** Sweetmans Bloodstock **Trained** Newmarket, Suffolk

**FOCUS**

A modest 3yo handcap. The runner-up has been rated to his best.

### 5854 BEST ODDS GUARANTEED AT 188BET H'CAP 1m 1f 21y

3:40 (3:40) (Class 6) (0-65,67) 3-Y-O+ £2,264 (£673; £336; £168) Stalls Low

Form RPR

0-31 1 **Oh It's Saucepot**[13] 5367 3-9-7 66............................................ TedDurcan 4 76+
(Chris Wall) *a.p: chsd ldr 4f out: led over 2f out: sn rdn: styd on* **2/1**[1]

-342 2 *1 1/2* **Castle Talbot (IRE)**[16] 5261 5-9-11 65.....................(p) GeorgeWood(3) 1 70
(Tom Clover) *led: rdn and hdd over 2f out: styd on same pce wl ins fnl f* **11/4**[2]

4006 3 *1 1/4* **Ripper Street (IRE)**[14] 5336 3-7-12 48.............................. JaneElliott(5) 5 50
(Christine Dunnett) *hld up: racd keenly: hdwy over 4f out: rdn over 1f out: styd on same pce ins fnl f* **20/1**

3030 4 *4 1/2* **Harlequin Rock**[48] 4047 4-9-8 59.......................................... JamieSpencer 7 52
(Mick Quinn) *hld up: hdwy over 2f out: rdn over 1f out: wknd fnl f* **7/1**

-400 5 *2 3/4* **Thecornishbarron (IRE)**[122] 1687 5-9-9 67.................... JackOsborn(7) 6 54
(John Ryan) *chsd ldr 5f: rdn over 2f out: wknd over 1f out* **16/1**

6265 6 *1 1/4* **Fantasy Gladiator**[20] 5126 11-9-9 60......................(p) AlistairRawlinson 2 45
(Michael Appleby) *s.s: hld up: effrt over 3f out: wknd over 1f out* **5/1**[3]

0040 7 *18* **Arcanista (IRE)**[99] 2312 4-9-2 53.................................. SilvestreDeSousa 8
(Chris Dwyer) *prom: racd keenly: wknd and eased 2f out* **7/1**

1m 56.09s (0.29) **Going Correction** +0.075s/f (Good)

**WFA** 3 from 4yo+ 8lb 7 Ran SP% **112.3**

Speed ratings (Par 101): **101,99,98,94,92 91,75**

CSF £7.34 CT £77.36 TOTE £2.80: £1.40, £1.80; EX 7.20 Trifecta £114.90.

**Owner** The Eight Of Diamonds **Bred** Mrs C J Walker **Trained** Newmarket, Suffolk

**FOCUS**

Sound enough form for the level. The runner-up and third have been rated near their best.

### 5855 1/4 ODDS AT 188BET MAIDEN H'CAP 6f 3y

4:10 (4:12) (Class 6) (0-65,67) 3-Y-O+ £2,587 (£770; £384; £192) Stalls Centre

Form RPR

062 1 **Deciding Vote**[15] 5291 3-8-11 57.................................. GeorgeWood(3) 8 64+
(Chris Wall) *a.p: racd keenly: led over 1f out: rdn out* **7/2**[2]

0223 2 *1/2* **Flower Cup**[14] 5339 4-9-7 60........................................ SilvestreDeSousa 11 66
(Chris Dwyer) *w ldrs: rdn over 1f out: ev ch ins fnl f: styd on* **15/8**[1]

4043 3 *1* **Tawaafoq**[15] 5289 3-9-9 66................................................ TedDurcan 7 68
(Mick Quinn) *s.i.s: hld up: hdwy over 1f out: sn rdn: styd on same pce towards fin* **7/1**

0025 4 *1 1/4* **Gunmaker (IRE)**[14] 5326 3-9-5 67.............................. GeorgeBuckell(5) 12 65
(David Simcock) *hld up: hdwy over 1f out: r.o* **13/2**

40-6 5 *1 3/4* **Spinnaker Bay (IRE)**[219] 27 3-9-10 67.............................. LouisSteward 10 60
(William Jarvis) *w ldr tl led over 4f out: rdn and hdd over 1f out: no ex ins fnl f* **22/1**

3006 6 *1 1/2* **Inlawed**[22] 5031 3-9-7 64................................................. JamieSpencer 6 52
(Ed Walker) *s.i.s: hld up: hdwy u.p over 1f out: nt trble ldrs* **11/2**[3]

/526 7 *2* **Lily Ash (IRE)**[140] 1325 4-9-6 59.............................. AlistairRawlinson 13 42
(Mike Murphy) *in tch: pushed along over 3f out: wknd over 1f out* **25/1**

4565 8 *hd* **Cool Echo**[20] 5122 3-9-2 59.................................(p) DannyBrock 3 40
(J R Jenkins) *chsd ldrs: rdn over 2f out: wknd ins fnl f* **25/1**

0020 9 *4* **Proud Kate**[22] 5040 3-7-12 46 oh1...............................(h) JaneElliott(5) 9 15
(Christine Dunnett) *plld hrd: led: hdd over 4f out: remained handy: rdn and wknd over 1f out* **33/1**

506 10 *shd* **Verdi (IRE)**[30] 4710 3-7-12 48...............................(b[1]) JackOsborn(7) 5 17
(John Ryan) *free to post: hld up in tch: plld hrd: lost pl whn nt clr run over 2f out: hung lft and wknd over 1f out* **28/1**

1m 12.35s (-2.05) **Going Correction** -0.325s/f (Firm)

**WFA** 3 from 4yo 4lb 10 Ran SP% **116.7**

Speed ratings (Par 101): **100,99,98,96,94 92,89,89,83,83**

CSF £9.72 CT £42.84 TOTE £4.10: £1.40, £1.30, £1.90; EX 11.60 Trifecta £61.30.

**Owner** Mrs Barry Green & Partners **Bred** Jeremy Green And Sons **Trained** Newmarket, Suffolk

**FOCUS**

Moderate handicap form. Straightforward form in behind the winner.

### 5856 JOHN BATT 70TH BIRTHDAY FILLIES' H'CAP 1m 3y

4:40 (4:40) (Class 4) (0-85,85) 3-Y-O £4,690 (£1,395; £697; £348) Stalls Centre

Form RPR

-336 1 **Stellar Surprise**[6] 5591 3-8-12 79..............................(t) AaronJones(3) 8 86
(Stuart Williams) *trckd ldr: rdn and ev ch fr over 1f out: edgd lft ins fnl f: r.o to ld nr fin* **6/1**[2]

-254 2 *hd* **Panova**[28] 4794 3-9-5 83.......................................................... TedDurcan 6 89
(Sir Michael Stoute) *trckd ldrs: led over 1f out: rdn ins fnl f: hdd nr fin* **15/8**[1]

0552 3 *3* **Miss Pacific**[13] 5367 3-8-6 70.......................................... SilvestreDeSousa 3 71
(William Jarvis) *hld up: swtchd lft 1/2-way: hdwy over 2f out: sn rdn and ev ch: hung lft over 1f out: no ex and eased wl ins fnl f* **15/8**[1]

123- 4 *5* **Mistime (IRE)**[397] 4148 3-9-2 85.................................. RichardOliver(5) 5 73
(Mark Johnston) *led: rdn and hdd over 1f out: sn edgd rt and wknd* **6/1**[2]

2355 R **Shankara (IRE)**[22] 5038 3-8-3 70.................................. GeorgeWood(3) 7
(David Simcock) . **7/1**[3]

1m 37.54s (-3.06) **Going Correction** -0.325s/f (Firm) 5 Ran SP% **110.6**

Speed ratings (Par 99): **102,101,98,93,**

CSF £17.77 TOTE £7.70: £3.20, £1.40; EX 19.90 Trifecta £43.20.

**Owner** J W Parry & Robert Levitt **Bred** Southcourt Stud **Trained** Newmarket, Suffolk

**FOCUS**

A fair fillies' handicap, although it didn't take as much winning as had looked likely. A small pb from the runner-up, but in line with her better form.

### 5857 DAILY RACING SPECIALS AT 188BET APPRENTICE H'CAP 7f 3y

5:10 (5:10) (Class 5) (0-70,69) 4-Y-O+ £2,911 (£866; £432; £216) Stalls Centre

Form RPR

3505 1 **Flying Fantasy**[16] 5245 5-9-9 66..............................(p[1]) GabrieleMalune 7 73
(Michael Appleby) *chsd ldrs: rdn to ld 1f out: styd on wl* **4/1**[2]

4453 2 *1 1/4* **Caledonian Gold**[16] 5239 4-8-0 50..............................(b) OliverDaykin(7) 1 54
(Paul D'Arcy) *s.i.s: sn prom: chsd ldr over 5f out tl over 2f out: rdn over 1f out: styd on* **3/1**[1]

000 3 *hd* **The Firm (IRE)**[48] 4047 8-8-8 56..............................(b) GinaMangan(5) 6 59
(J R Jenkins) *led: clr 6f out tl c bk to the field over 2f out: rdn and hdd 1f out: edgd rt: styd on* **28/1**

5530 4 *1/2* **Intimately**[15] 5285 4-8-12 58.................................. Pierre-LouisJamin(3) 2 60
(Jonathan Portman) *s.i.s: hld up: hdwy u.p over 1f out: styd on* **9/1**[3]

-000 5 *nk* **Gabrielle**[13] 5369 4-9-2 62........................................(h) DarraghKeenan(3) 4 63
(Dr Jon Scargill) *hld up: hdwy on outer over 1f out: kpt on* **18/1**

0003 6 *1* **Ubla (IRE)**[13] 5363 4-9-2 59.............................................. StephenCummins 3 58
(Jane Chapple-Hyam) *chsd ldr tl over 5f out: remained handy: pushed along over 2f out: styd on same pce fnl f* **3/1**[1]

0012 7 *2* **Himalayan Queen**[10] 5482 4-9-1 65.................................. AarronMiller(7) 5 58
(William Jarvis) *in tch: chsd ldr over 2f out: sn rdn and edgd rt: lost 2nd over 1f out: wknd ins fnl f* **3/1**[1]

1m 25.39s (-1.21) **Going Correction** -0.325s/f (Firm) 7 Ran SP% **113.7**

Speed ratings (Par 103): **93,91,91,90,90 89,87**

CSF £16.22 CT £288.56 TOTE £4.80: £2.20, £2.20; EX 19.10 Trifecta £345.70.

**Owner** Infinity Racing & Craig Buckingham **Bred** Hascombe And Valiant Studs **Trained** Oakham, Rutland

**FOCUS**

Pretty weak form. The runner-up has been rated close to her AW latest.

T/Plt: £5.90 to a £1 stake. Pool: £52,959.43 - 6458.14 winning units. T/Qpdt: £2.80 to a £1 stake. Pool: £3,869.01 - 1002.61 winning units. **Colin Roberts**

5858 - 5861a (Foreign Racing) - See Raceform Interactive

# 5342 LEOPARDSTOWN (L-H)

Thursday, August 10

**OFFICIAL GOING: Good to firm changing to good after race 2 (5.45)**

## 5862a GRENKE FINANCE BALLYROAN STKS (GROUP 3) — 1m 4f

7:20 (7:21) 3-Y-0+

£31,769 (£10,230; £4,846; £2,153; £1,076; £538)

RPR

1 **Spanish Steps (IRE)**[27] 4878 3-8-12 100 .......... SeamieHeffernan 5 108+
(A P O'Brien, Ire) *trckd ldr tl led after 2f and mde rest: stl gng wl over 2 l clr over 3f out: extended advantage into st where c wd: rdn 1 1/2f out and pressed wl ins fnl f: kpt on wl clsng stages* 6/1[3]

2 ½ **Johannes Vermeer (IRE)**[39] 4417 4-9-11 112 .......... (t) RyanMoore 1 109+
(A P O'Brien, Ire) *chsd ldrs in 3rd: 4th fr 1/2-way: hdwy gng wl into st into 2nd 1 1/2f out: sn rdn and pressed wnr wl ins fnl f: kpt on wl clsng stages: nt match wnr* 4/5[1]

3 2½ **Stellar Mass (IRE)**[39] 4420 4-9-8 108 .......... KevinManning 7 102
(J S Bolger, Ire) *w.w: 5th 1/2-way: rdn in 5th over 2f out and clsd u.p into 4th ent fnl f: kpt on into 3rd wl ins fnl f: nvr trbld ldrs* 8/1

4 1½ **The Grey Gatsby (IRE)**[21] 5087 6-9-8 113 .......... (p) PatSmullen 2 100
(D K Weld, Ire) *hld up bhd ldrs in 4th: 3rd fr 1/2-way: impr into 2nd fr under 3f out: sn rdn and no imp on wnr 1 1/2f out where dropped to 3rd: one pce after and dropped to 4th wl ins fnl f* 5/1[2]

5 2½ **Santa Monica**[39] 4419 4-9-8 99 .......... DeclanMcDonogh 4 96+
(Charles O'Brien, Ire) *w.w in rr: last at 1/2-way: rdn appr st and sme hdwy u.p into 5th over 1f out: no imp on ldrs and one pce ins fnl f* 20/1

6 27 **Grandee (IRE)**[13] 5388 3-8-12 102 .......... ColmO'Donoghue 6 54
(Mrs John Harrington, Ire) *broke wl to ld tl hdd after 2f: 2nd 1/2-way: rdn in 2nd fr 3f out and sn no imp on wnr u.p in 3rd: wknd far side 1 1/2f out: eased in rr fnl f* 7/1

2m 37.87s (2.57) **Going Correction** +0.60s/f (Yiel)
**WFA** 3 from 4yo+ 10lb — 6 Ran SP% **114.9**
Speed ratings: **115,114,113,112,110 92**
CSF £11.71 TOTE £6.80: £2.50, £1.10; DF 32.20 Trifecta £124.70.
**Owner** Michael Tabor & Derrick Smith & Mrs John Magnier & **Bred** Stamar, Zaki Holdings & Meditsoi **Trained** Cashel, Co Tipperary

**FOCUS**
Aidan O'Brien saddled the first two, though not in the order generally expected. A pb from the winner, who was allowed to do his own thing in front.

5863 - 5864a (Foreign Racing) - See Raceform Interactive

# 5817 BRIGHTON (L-H)

Friday, August 11

**OFFICIAL GOING: Good to firm (8.8)**
Wind: medium, across Weather: sunny

## 5865 MARATHONBET EXTRAORDINARY/EBF NOVICE STKS — 5f 215y

2:10 (2:10) (Class 5) 2-Y-O — £2,911 (£866; £432; £216) Stalls Centre

Form — RPR

0 1 **Lake Volta (IRE)**[10] 5504 2-9-2 0 .......... SilvestreDeSousa 3 88+
(Mark Johnston) *mde all: readily wnt clr 2f out: rdn and r.o wl fr over 1f out: eased towards fin: unchal* 4/6[1]

0 2 4½ **Tiepolo (IRE)**[46] 4151 2-9-2 0 .......... TomQueally 7 74
(Gary Moore) *stdd s: hld up in rr: clsd and nt clrest of runs 2f out: swtchd lft over 1f out: rdn and hung lft but hdwy to chse clr wnr 1f out: styd on: no ch w wnr* 28/1

4323 3 3½ **Indian Warrior**[41] 4349 2-9-2 75 .......... DavidProbert 1 62
(Ed Dunlop) *dwlt: hld up in midfield: effrt ent fnl 2f: chsd clr wnr wl over 1f out: no imp: lost 2nd 1f out and wknd ins fnl f* 3/1[2]

16 4 2½ **Pranceabootthetoon (IRE)**[11] 5480 2-8-13 0 .......... JackOsborn(7) 2 58
(John Ryan) *chsd ldng pair: effrt ent fnl 2f out: carried lft and no imp jst over 1f out: wknd ins fnl f* 10/1

U205 5 3¾ **Rivas Rob Roy**[22] 5063 2-8-13 70 .......... HectorCrouch(3) 5 42
(John Gallagher) *hld up in tch in last pair: c wd 3f out: rdn over 2f out: sn struggling: wknd over 1f out* 17/2[3]

00 6 ¾ **Following Breeze (IRE)**[32] 4696 2-8-8 0 .......... CharlieBennett(3) 6 35
(Jim Boyle) *in tch in midfield: rdn ent fnl 2f: sn struggling and wknd over 1f out* 66/1

60 7 2 **Alaskan Star (IRE)**[69] 3328 2-9-2 0 .......... ShaneKelly 4 34
(Amanda Perrett) *chsd wnr tl wl over 1f out: sn lost pl u.p: bhd ins fnl f* 33/1

1m 9.81s (-0.39) **Going Correction** +0.20s/f (Good) — 7 Ran SP% **112.5**
Speed ratings (Par 94): **110,104,99,96,91 90,87**
CSF £25.26 TOTE £1.50: £1.10, £10.90; EX 20.30 Trifecta £61.50.
**Owner** Sheikh Hamdan bin Mohammed Al Maktoum **Bred** Godolphin **Trained** Middleham Moor, N Yorks

**FOCUS**
Add 5yds. Fast ground despite the watering. An ordinary novice but lots to like about the performance of the winner.

## 5866 CHECKATRADE.COM H'CAP — 1m 3f 198y

2:40 (2:40) (Class 6) (0-65,62) 3-Y-O+ — £2,264 (£673; £336; £168) Stalls High

Form — RPR

0003 1 **Ban Shoof**[20] 5142 4-9-11 62 .......... (b) HectorCrouch(3) 6 74
(Gary Moore) *stdd after s: hld up in 5th: clsd 5f out: trcking ldrs and travelling best over 2f out: rdn to ld over 1f out: sn clr: eased towards fin* 2/1[2]

/0-4 2 7 **Gold Class**[1] 5850 6-8-11 45 .......... (bt) SilvestreDeSousa 2 45
(Olly Murphy) *trckd ldr: clsd and upsides 4f out: rdn over 2f out: 3rd and outpcd over 1f out: no ch w wnr but plugged on into modest 2nd wl ins fnl f* 4/7[1]

5040 3 2½ **Montycristo**[13] 5405 4-9-1 49 .......... (b) ShaneKelly 1 45
(Philip Hide) *led: rdn and hdd over 1f out: sn hung lft and btn: wknd and lost 2nd wl ins fnl f* 16/1[3]

-005 4 8 **Fleetwood Poppy**[122] 1699 5-8-11 45 .......... TomMarquand 3 28
(Michael Attwater) *t.k.h: chsd ldrs: rdn over 2f out: sn outpcd and wl btn whn hung lft over 1f out* 25/1

00-5 5 ½ **Rod Of Iron**[13] 5405 4-8-11 45 .......... KieranO'Neill 4 27
(Michael Madgwick) *hld up in midfield: effrt u.p 3f out: sn struggling: wl btn whn hung lft over 1f out* 25/1

00-0 6 1½ **Selena Rose**[195] 457 4-8-11 45 .......... (h[1]) RyanPowell 7 25
(Ronald Harris) *s.i.s: hld up in detached last: nvr on terms: rdn and btn over 2f out: no ch whn hung lft 1f out* 50/1

2m 34.34s (1.64) **Going Correction** +0.20s/f (Good) — 6 Ran SP% **112.5**
Speed ratings (Par 101): **102,97,95,90,90 89**
CSF £3.44 TOTE £2.50: £1.30, £1.10; EX 4.30 Trifecta £13.20.
**Owner** Tommy Ware & Bob Pettett **Bred** Lady Legard **Trained** Lower Beeding, W Sussex

**FOCUS**
Add 5yds. A weak handicap that produced a clear winner. The winner has been rated back to his January form.

## 5867 CHECKAPROFESSIONAL.COM H'CAP — 1m 1f 207y

3:10 (3:12) (Class 6) (0-65,64) 3-Y-O — £2,264 (£673; £336; £168) Stalls High

Form — RPR

0316 1 **Av A Word**[37] 4494 3-9-6 63 .......... (p) SilvestreDeSousa 5 69
(Daniel Kubler) *trckd ldng pair: effrt 2f out: clsd u.p to ld ent fnl f: hld on wl ins fnl f: rdn out* 3/1[2]

000 2 ½ **Kings City (IRE)**[55] 3839 3-9-2 59 .......... (p[1]) PatCosgrave 4 64
(Luca Cumani) *t.k.h: chsd ldr: effrt jst over 2f out: clsd u.p to chal ent fnl f: kpt on wl u.p and sustained chal ins fnl f: hld towards fin* 10/3[3]

0001 3 hd **Free Forum (IRE)**[10] 5509 3-9-7 64 6ex .......... JamieSpencer 2 69+
(David Simcock) *t.k.h early: hld up in midfield: effrt over 2f out: hdwy u.p and edgd lft over 1f out: chsd clr ldng pair jst ins fnl f: styd on wl fnl 100yds: nt quite rch ldrs* 2/1[1]

-536 4 3¼ **Zoffanist (IRE)**[27] 4913 3-9-3 60 .......... (p[1]) ShaneKelly 8 58
(Amanda Perrett) *led: clr 4f out: rdn and wandered ent fnl 2f: edgd lft over 1f out: hdd and drvn ent fnl f: no ex and wknd ins fnl f* 9/1

600 5 1¾ **Celtik Secret**[44] 4224 3-9-1 61 .......... CharlieBennett(3) 6 56
(Hughie Morrison) *hld up in last pair: effrt ent fnl 2f: no imp whn swtchd rt 1f out: nvr enough pce to threaten ldrs* 16/1

4426 6 14 **Famous Dynasty (IRE)**[16] 5275 3-9-3 60 .......... DanielMuscutt 1 29
(Michael Blanshard) *hld up in midfield: clsd to chse ldrs 3f out: edgd lft u.p and wknd over 1f out: eased wl ins fnl f* 8/1

-00 7 7 **Lady Kaviar (IRE)**[42] 4320 3-9-2 59 .......... TomQueally 3 14
(George Margarson) *awkward leaving stalls: t.k.h: hld up in last pair: rdn 3f out: sn struggling and lost tch 2f out: eased wl ins fnl f* 25/1

2m 5.32s (1.72) **Going Correction** +0.20s/f (Good) — 7 Ran SP% **112.3**
Speed ratings (Par 98): **101,100,100,97,96 85,79**
CSF £12.91 CT £23.11 TOTE £3.30: £2.00, £2.10; EX 13.60 Trifecta £26.90.
**Owner** Peter Onslow & Kevin Nash **Bred** Peter Onslow **Trained** Lambourn, Berks

**FOCUS**
Add 5yds. Sound enough form for the level.

## 5868 MARATHONBET NON-LEAGUE CHALLENGE H'CAP — 1m 1f 207y

3:40 (3:42) (Class 4) (0-80,81) 3-Y-O+ — £5,175 (£1,540; £769; £384) Stalls High

Form — RPR

4614 1 **Bedouin (IRE)**[15] 5323 3-9-4 78 .......... (b) PatCosgrave 2 88
(Luca Cumani) *s.i.s and bustled along leaving stalls: in tch in 4th: swtchd rt and effrt over 2f out: hdwy u.p to ld over 1f out: drew ins fnl f: r.o strly* 5/2[2]

2-12 2 2¾ **Harbour Rock**[27] 4912 3-9-6 80 .......... JamieSpencer 3 84
(David Simcock) *stdd s: hld up in detached last: clsd to trck rivals and travelling strly over 2f out: effrt and drvn ent fnl f: nt match pce of wnr and hung lft ins fnl f: wnt 2nd fnl 75yds* 6/5[1]

3545 3 1½ **Berengaria (IRE)**[18] 5207 3-9-6 80 .......... SilvestreDeSousa 5 81
(Mark Johnston) *trckd ldr: effrt u.p and ev ch over 1f out: unable to match pce of wnr 1f out: outpcd and lost 2nd fnl 75yds* 3/1[3]

0200 4 1½ **Pink Ribbon (IRE)**[13] 5427 5-9-2 68 .......... (p) PatDobbs 4 65
(Sylvester Kirk) *led and set stdy gallop: rdn 2f out: hdd over 1f out: outpcd ins fnl f* 25/1

5053 5 1½ **Roy Rocket (FR)**[8] 5555 7-8-10 69 .......... NicolaCurrie(7) 1 63
(John Berry) *t.k.h: trckd ldrs: rdn and ev ch over 1f out: unable qck 1f out: outpcd ins fnl f* 16/1

2m 7.42s (3.82) **Going Correction** +0.20s/f (Good)
**WFA** 3 from 5yo+ 8lb — 5 Ran SP% **108.8**
Speed ratings (Par 105): **92,89,88,87,86**
CSF £5.76 TOTE £3.70: £1.50, £1.10; EX 5.90 Trifecta £11.30.
**Owner** Highclere T'Bred Racing-Edward Lear **Bred** Epona Bloodstock Ltd **Trained** Newmarket, Suffolk

**FOCUS**
Add 5yds. A fair handicap that the 3yos predictably dominated. They went a steady gallop. The runner-up has been rated to form.

## 5869 HARRY BLOOM MEMORIAL "BRIGHTON BULLET" H'CAP — 5f 215y

4:10 (4:11) (Class 4) (0-80,82) 3-Y-O+ — £7,561 (£2,263; £1,131; £566; £282) Stalls Centre

Form — RPR

-240 1 **Coronation Day**[17] 5245 4-10-0 82 .......... HarryBentley 3 94+
(James Tate) *chsd ldng trio: rdn and qcknd to ld over 1f out: in command fnl f: eased towards fin: easily* 15/2[3]

60 2 1½ **Pour La Victoire (IRE)**[2] 5788 7-8-13 67 .......... (v) GeorgeDowning 9 73
(Tony Carroll) *s.i.s: racd in last pair: c towards stands side over 2f out: swtchd rt and hdwy nrest stands rail over 1f out: chsd clr wnr and hung lft ins fnl f: styd on but no threat to wnr* 14/1

6525 3 1½ **One Big Surprise**[22] 5078 5-9-6 74 .......... (p) ShaneKelly 1 75
(Richard Hughes) *hld up in tch towards rr: swtchd lft and hdwy u.p over 1f out: chsd clr wnr 1f out: no imp and lost 2nd ins fnl f* 20/1

0601 4 1 **Upavon**[1] 5818 7-9-13 81 6ex .......... (t) PatCosgrave 7 79
(Stuart Williams) *hld up in midfield: effrt 2f out: styd on ins fnl f: no threat to wnr* 8/1

1000 5 nk **Zamjar**[7] 5612 3-9-9 81 .......... (v) DavidProbert 10 77
(Ed Dunlop) *hld up in tch: c towards stands side over 2f out: effrt and nt clr run over 1f out: swtchd rt 1f out: styd on ins fnl f: no ch w wnr* 8/1

4555 6 ½ **Mercers**[4] 5723 3-8-3 61 oh1 .......... KieranO'Neill 5 55
(Peter Crate) *hld up in tch towards rr: swtchd lft 1/2-way: effrt and sme hdwy over 1f out: keeping on but no threat to wnr whn swtchd lft again ins fnl f* 33/1

3642 7 ½ **Kamra (USA)**[11] 5481 3-8-13 74 .......... (tp) HectorCrouch(3) 12 67
(Michael Herrington) *in tch in midfield: c towards stands side over 2f out: unable qck u.p over 1f out: wknd ins fnl f* 5/1[2]

005 8 nse **Top Of The Bank**[22] 5070 4-9-0 68 .......... (p) TomQueally 6 61
(Kristin Stubbs) *led: rdn and hdd over 1f out: unable qck w wnr: wkng whn short of room ins fnl f* 25/1

1063 9 1½ **Jersey Breeze (IRE)**[7] 5587 4-9-12 80 .......... (v) PatDobbs 8 69
(Mick Channon) *chsd ldrs: c towards stands side over 2f out: drvn and lost pl over 1f out: wknd ins fnl f* 8/1

4012 **10** *4* **Under The Covers**[44] 4201 4-9-10 **78**............................ RyanPowell 14 54
(Ronald Harris) *taken down early and led to s: chsd ldrs but styd wd: racing towards stands side over 2f out: lost pl over 1f out: sn wknd* **15/2**[3]

561 **11** *2 ¾* **Highly Sprung (IRE)**[19] 5184 4-9-7 **75**.................... SilvestreDeSousa 4 42
(Mark Johnston) *sn dropped to rr: rdn 1/2-way: no imp u.p over 1f out: wl btn and eased wl ins fnl f* **3/1**[1]

1m 10.12s (-0.08) **Going Correction** +0.20s/f (Good)
**WFA** 3 from 4yo+ 4lb **11** Ran SP% **116.7**
Speed ratings (Par 105): **108,106,104,102,102 101,100,100,98,93 89**
CSF £103.33 CT £2040.81 TOTE £8.60: £2.60, £4.30, £4.50; EX 127.00 Trifecta £2972.90.
**Owner** James Tate Racing Limited **Bred** Whitsbury Manor Stud **Trained** Newmarket, Suffolk

**FOCUS**
Add 5yds. A reasonable handicap, plenty had their chance as they spread across the track. The third has been rated close to form.

## 5870 JMP HEATING LTD H'CAP 6f 210y
**4:40** (4:40) (Class 5) (0-75,75) 3-Y-0+ **£2,911** (£866; £432; £216) **Stalls** Centre

Form RPR

0420 **1** **Good Luck Charm**[21] 5119 8-9-6 **72**........................(v) HectorCrouch(3) 5 79
(Gary Moore) *trckd ldrs: effrt to chal over 1f out: drvn ins fnl f: led 100yds out: kpt on u.p: hld on cl home* **8/1**

202 **2** *shd* **Still Waiting**[15] 5341 3-8-10 **65**............................................ MartinLane 7 69
(William Jarvis) *hld up in tch in rr: effrt over 1f out: hdwy u.p and str chal 100yds out: styd on wl: jst hld* **6/1**

3441 **3** *½* **Easy Code**[11] 5482 4-9-7 **70** 6ex.......................................... PatCosgrave 1 75
(William Haggas) *stdd after s: hld up in tch in 4th: nt clr run and swtchd rt over 1f out: sn rdn and ev ch ins fnl f: kpt on: unable qck cl home* **9/4**[2]

0002 **4** *1* **Tailor's Row (USA)**[9] 5541 3-9-4 **73**................................ DavidProbert 6 73
(Mark Johnston) *led: rdn and hung lft over 1f out: stl hanging whn hdd and bmpd rival 100yds out: jst outpcd towards fin and short of room cl home* **7/2**[3]

04-2 **5** *nk* **Screaming Gemini (IRE)**[45] 4188 3-9-1 **70**.................(b) HarryBentley 2 69
(Roger Varian) *trckd ldr: effrt to chal over 1f out: stl ev ch whn bmpd 100yds out: jst outpcd towards fin* **2/1**[1]

1m 25.62s (2.52) **Going Correction** +0.20s/f (Good)
**WFA** 3 from 4yo+ 6lb **5** Ran SP% **111.7**
Speed ratings (Par 103): **93,92,92,91,90**
CSF £50.63 TOTE £7.30: £2.70, £3.40; EX 33.10 Trifecta £105.10.
**Owner** Heart Of The South Racing **Bred** John And Caroline Penny **Trained** Lower Beeding, W Sussex

**FOCUS**
Add 5yds. Modest handicap form, there was near enough five in a row at one stage and it went to the top weight. The winner has been rated back to last year's form with the second and third to their latest efforts.

## 5871 HELP HOPE HOUSE H'CAP 5f 60y
**5:15** (5:16) (Class 6) (0-60,60) 3-Y-0+ **£2,264** (£673; £336; £168) **Stalls** Centre

Form RPR

0421 **1** **Ask The Guru**[23] 5027 7-8-13 **52**..................................(b) HarryBentley 7 58
(Michael Attwater) *trckd ldrs tl led 2f out: rdn over 1f out: kpt on u.p ins fnl f: hrd pressed cl home: hld on* **13/2**

3234 **2** *shd* **Picansort**[16] 5297 10-8-12 **51**.............................................. ShaneKelly 12 57
(Peter Crate) *stdd after s: hld up in last pair: clsd over 1f out: swtchd rt and effrt nrest stands rail ent fnl f: gd hdwy u.p and str chal towards fin: hld cl home* **16/1**

0655 **3** *1 ½* **Essaka (IRE)**[2] 5784 5-8-10 **54**......................................... PaddyPilley(5) 6 54
(Tony Carroll) *hld up in tch: clsd and nt clr run over 1f out: gap opened and hdwy to press wnr ins fnl f: no ex and outpcd fnl 50yds* **4/1**[2]

5521 **4** *hd* **Defining Moment**[15] 5339 3-9-4 **60**................................ DavidProbert 11 59
(Rae Guest) *hld up in tch: clsd over 1f out: effrt 1f out: kpt on u.p ins fnl f: nvr getting to wnr* **7/4**[1]

10/0 **5** *2 ¾* **Satellite Express (IRE)**[55] 3811 6-8-10 **49**.............(bt) TomMarquand 10 39
(Tim Pinfield) *sn dropped to rr: pushed along over 2f out: hdwy 1f out: styd on to pass btn horses ins fnl f: nvr trbld ldrs* **66/1**

0400 **6** *hd* **General Gerrard**[38] 4458 3-8-1 **50**..........................(vt[1]) NicolaCurrie(7) 3 38
(Michael Madgwick) *t.k.h: hld up in tch in midfield: unable qck over 1f out: wknd ins fnl f* **40/1**

312 **7** *1 ¾* **Camino**[23] 5027 4-8-8 **47**.................................................. MartinLane 8 30
(Andi Brown) *t.k.h early: hld up in tch in midfield: effrt but unable qck over 1f out: wknd ins fnl f* **6/1**[3]

6240 **8** *1 ¼* **Hurricane Alert**[36] 4532 5-9-2 **55**...................................... KieranO'Neill 2 34
(Mark Hoad) *taken down early: nt that wl away: rcvrd to chse ldrs on inner after 1f: effrt 2f out: drvn over 1f out: no ex 1f out: wknd ins fnl f* **20/1**

24 **9** *2 ¾* **Miss Rosina (IRE)**[23] 5041 3-9-2 **58**................................. RyanPowell 5 26
(George Margarson) *led tl 2f out: sn rdn: lost 2nd and hung lft 1f out: sn wknd* **14/1**

0-52 **10** *1 ½* **Regal Miss**[16] 5297 5-9-1 **57**...................................... CharlieBennett(3) 9 21
(Patrick Chamings) *chsd ldr tl 2f out: sn rdn and lost pl: bhd ins fnl f* **14/1**

1m 2.91s (0.61) **Going Correction** +0.20s/f (Good)
**WFA** 3 from 4yo+ 3lb **10** Ran SP% **111.9**
Speed ratings (Par 101): **103,102,100,100,95 95,92,90,86,83**
CSF £97.06 CT £474.81 TOTE £6.70: £2.20, £3.50, £1.40; EX 87.80 Trifecta £761.80.
**Owner** Canisbay Bloodstock **Bred** Redmyre Bloodstock & Tweenhills Stud **Trained** Epsom, Surrey
■ Stewards' Enquiry : Harry Bentley two-day ban: used whip above permitted level (Aug 26-27)

**FOCUS**
Add 5yds. Lowly sprint form. The second and third help pin the opening level.
T/Plt: £230.60 to a £1 stake. Pool: £74,175.64 - 234.77 winning units. T/Qpdt: £101.70 to a £1 stake. Pool: £5,502.56 - 40.01 winning units. **Steve Payne**

# 5824 HAYDOCK (L-H)
Friday, August 11

**OFFICIAL GOING: Good to soft (7.7)**
Wind: light breeze, across Weather: overcast, mild

## 5872 BETFRED TV HAYDOCK PARK APPRENTICE H'CAP (PART OF THE RACING EXCELLENCE INITIATIVE) 1m 3f 140y
**5:40** (5:41) (Class 5) (0-70,70) 4-Y-0+ **£3,557** (£1,058; £529; £264) **Stalls** Centre

Form RPR

4332 **1** **Omotesando**[4] 5701 7-8-13 **62**..........................(p) MeganNicholls 2 71
(Oliver Greenall) *hld up: hdwy gng wl over 2f out: sn clsd on ldrs: hdwy to ld over 1f out: rdn: r.o wl to assert fnl f* **11/4**[2]

1121 **2** *1 ¼* **Donnachies Girl (IRE)**[13] 5414 4-9-1 **69**.................. SeamusCronin(5) 3 76
(Alistair Whillans) *trckd ldrs: hdwy over 2f out: sn chsd along in 2nd: led briefly wl over 1f out: sn hdd: rdn and tried to keep tabs on wnr ent fnl f: r.o but hld* **9/4**[1]

55 **3** *1 ¼* **Hurricane Hollow**[6] 5667 7-9-7 **70**.................................... JaneElliott 5 75
(David Barron) *hld up: rdn and effrt 2f out: hdwy wl over 1f out: r.o wl to take 3rd ins fnl f: nvr nrr* **15/2**[3]

010 **4** *6* **Invictus (GER)**[34] 4608 5-9-1 **67**............................(p) CameronNoble(3) 4 62
(David Loughnane) *cl 2nd: led over 3f out: rdn over 2f out: hdd wl over 1f out: no ex fnl f* **14/1**

2355 **5** *3* **Lady Natasha (IRE)**[17] 5267 4-8-10 **59**............................ CliffordLee 8 50
(K R Burke) *. trckd ldrs: pushed along over 3f out: hdwy over 2f out: sn drvn rdn wl over 1f out: one pce fnl f* **15/2**[3]

0105 **6** *hd* **Auxiliary**[15] 5313 4-9-4 **70**..........................................(p) PaulaMuir(3) 6 60
(Patrick Holmes) *slowly away: in rr: pushed along and detached by 4 l 4f out: rdn over 2f out: sme late hdwy to pass btn horses* **25/1**

10 **7** *4 ½* **Up Ten Down Two (IRE)**[57] 3740 8-9-1 **69**...............(t) RyanTimby(5) 9 52
(Michael Easterby) *mid-div: pushed along in 3rd 4f out: reminder over 3f out: drvn and n.m.r over 2f out: sn rdn and wknd* **25/1**

0-03 **8** *½* **Almutamarred (USA)**[16] 5284 5-8-0 **52**........................ KevinLundie(3) 7 34
(David Brown) *mid-div: pushed along 4f out: reminder over 3f out: drvn over 2f out: sn rdn and wknd* **8/1**

5012 **9** *¾* **Gold Merlion (IRE)**[8] 5555 4-9-2 **65**.............................. RichardOliver 1 46
(Mark Johnston) *led narrowly: pushed along and hdd over 3f out: rdn 2f out: wknd* **10/1**

2m 31.69s (-1.31) **Going Correction** 0.0s/f (Good) **9** Ran SP% **115.5**
Speed ratings (Par 103): **104,103,102,98,96 96,93,92,92**
CSF £9.36 CT £38.45 TOTE £3.50: £1.30, £1.30, £2.20; EX 10.80 Trifecta £56.90.
**Owner** Phil Evans **Bred** Darley **Trained** Oldcastle Heath, Cheshire

**FOCUS**
Rail movements increase advertised race distances as follows: Race 1 by 21 yards, Race 2 by 45 yards and Races 3, 4 and 5 by 6 yards. A modest middle-distance handicap for apprentice riders. They went a contested gallop on good to soft ground and it paid to be ridden patiently. The winner has been rated close to his old turf best, with the third rated to form.

## 5873 BETFRED SUPPORTS JACK BERRY HOUSE H'CAP 1m 6f
**6:15** (6:17) (Class 4) (0-80,82) 4-Y-0+ **£5,822** (£1,732; £865; £432) **Stalls** Low

Form RPR

2523 **1** **High On Light**[13] 5414 4-8-11 **73**........................ RachelRichardson(3) 1 82
(David Barron) *mde all: 2 l clr 4f out: 1 l ahd and gng wl 2f out: pushed along over 1f out: shkn up ent fnl f: kpt up to work: r.o wl to pull clr: comf* **7/2**[3]

2601 **2** *2 ¾* **Takbeer (IRE)**[29] 4809 5-9-1 **74**.............................(p) CharlesBishop 4 79
(Nikki Evans) *a chsng wnr: 2 l bhd 4f out: rdn and 1 l down 2f out: lft bhd ent fnl f: r.o to retain 2nd* **6/1**

0-64 **3** *2 ½* **Aramist (IRE)**[13] 5438 7-8-13 **72**..............................(p[1]) PJMcDonald 2 74
(Sally Haynes) *hld up: reminders 4f out: swtchd to centre and effrt over 2f out: rdn wl over 1f out: hdwy ent fnl f: r.o wl to take 3rd nr fin* **14/1**

/0-1 **4** *nk* **Kashmiri Sunset**[18] 5208 6-9-3 **76**.........................(tp) PaulHanagan 3 77
(Iain Jardine) *mid-div: wnt 3rd 5f out: urged along 4f out: drvn 3f out: rdn 2f out: one pce fnl f: lost 3rd nr fin* **11/4**[1]

05/0 **5** *1 ¼* **Mawaqeet (USA)**[27] 4921 8-9-2 **80**................................ JaneElliott(5) 8 79
(Michael Appleby) *hld up: pushed along 3f out: rdn over 2f out: r.o ins fnl f* **40/1**

/0-5 **6** *6* **Murgan**[65] 3458 5-9-9 **82**................................................ SteveDrowne 7 73
(Stuart Kittow) *mid-div: 4th and reminder 3f out: rdn over 2f out: no ex appr fnl f* **3/1**[2]

0640 **7** *nk* **Bertie Moon**[69] 3315 7-9-0 **76**...............................(p) CliffordLee(3) 5 67
(Lydia Pearce) *hld up: pushed along and hdwy on inner 4f out: rdn 3f out: losing grnd over 1f out: wknd fnl f* **14/1**

0430 **8** *11* **Torremar (FR)**[32] 4684 4-8-12 **71**..................................(p) JoeDoyle 6 46
(Kevin Ryan) *mid-div: pushed along 4f out: drvn 3f out: wknd over 1f out: lost tch ent fnl f* **10/1**

3m 6.39s **Going Correction** 0.0s/f (Good) **8** Ran SP% **113.0**
Speed ratings (Par 105): **87,85,84,83,83 79,79,73**
CSF £24.12 CT £256.78 TOTE £4.00: £1.50, £2.30, £3.00; EX 22.50 Trifecta £212.70.
**Owner** D G Pryde **Bred** Highclere Stud **Trained** Maunby, N Yorks
■ Stewards' Enquiry : P J McDonald caution: careless riding

**FOCUS**
Race distance increased by 45 yards. A fairly decent staying handicap. The winner made all at her own even tempo. The runner-up has been rated to form.

## 5874 BETFRED "FOLLOW US ON FACEBOOK" EBF NOVICE STKS (PLUS 10 RACE) 6f 212y
**6:45** (6:45) (Class 4) 2-Y-O **£4,592** (£1,366; £683; £341) **Stalls** Low

Form RPR

2 **1** **Exhort**[22] 5056 2-8-11 0.............................................. PaulHanagan 5 75+
(Richard Fahey) *chsd ldr: 1 l down 2f out: sn pushed along: rdn over 1f out: hdwy to ld ent fnl f: drvn out to assert last 100yds* **4/9**[1]

03 **2** *¾* **Kraka (IRE)**[39] 4452 2-9-2 0............................................. JimmyQuinn 7 78
(Tom Dascombe) *led: 1 l ahd 2f out: sn pushed along: rdn and hdd ent fnl f: tried to rally but hld last 100yds* **10/3**[2]

**3** *2 ½* **Skito Soldier** 2-9-2 0.................................................. PJMcDonald 6 72
(K R Burke) *hld up: hdwy into 4th 4f out: wnt 3rd 2f out: sn drvn: one pce and no imp on front two fnl f* **12/1**[3]

**4** *¾* **Cuddington (IRE)** 2-9-2 0............................................... ShaneGray 3 70+
(Tom Dascombe) *v.s.a and lost several l: rcvrd to join pack after 1f: in rr: last 4f out: hdwy 3f out: pushed along and repeatedly hung rt fr over 2f out: r.o ins fnl f: nvr nrr* **12/1**[3]

**5** *2 ¼* **Finnion Fox** 2-8-13 0.................................... RachelRichardson(3) 4 64
(Tim Easterby) *trckd ldrs: pushed along 3f out: drvn over 2f out: lost pl over 1f out: wknd* **20/1**

00 **6** *7* **Saxonroad Boy (USA)**[9] 5537 2-9-2 0................................ JoeDoyle 1 46
(Richard Fahey) *hld up: drvn and relegated to last 3f out: lost tch fnl 2 fs* **33/1**

1m 30.2s (-0.50) **Going Correction** 0.0s/f (Good) **6** Ran SP% **115.4**
Speed ratings (Par 96): **102,101,98,97,94 86**
CSF £2.39 TOTE £1.30: £1.10, £1.90; EX 2.50 Trifecta £9.20.
**Owner** Cheveley Park Stud **Bred** Cheveley Park Stud Ltd **Trained** Musley Bank, N Yorks

**FOCUS**
Race distance increased by 6 yards. A fairly decent juvenile novice contest. They went a respectable gallop and the two form horses came to the fore.

## 5875 JOHN FORSYTH COUNTRYWIDE FREIGHT NURSERY H'CAP (JOCKEY CLUB GRASSROOTS NURSERY QUALIFIER) 6f 212y
7:15 (7:16) (Class 4) (0-80,81) 2-Y-O £5,822 (£1,732; £865; £432) Stalls Low

| Form | | | | | RPR |
|---|---|---|---|---|---|
| 621 | 1 | | **Rhosneigr (IRE)**[17] 5246 2-9-6 **77** ... SteveDrowne 3 *(Charles Hills) mid-div: hdwy 3f out: rdn 2f out: clsd on ldrs over 1f out: led ent fnl f: immediately jnd by runner-up: responded wl u.p to repel chal* **9/2**[2] | | 81 |
| 110 | 2 | hd | **Veejay (IRE)**[8] 5572 2-9-10 **81** ... CharlesBishop 7 *(Mick Channon) hld up: hdwy on outer 3f out: pushed along 2f out: rdn and hdwy to join wnr ent fnl f: r.o: jst hld* **3/1**[1] | | 84 |
| 4002 | 3 | 1 ¼ | **Foxrush Take Time (FR)**[8] 5562 2-8-4 **61** ... JimmyQuinn 4 *(Richard Guest) hld up: pushed along and hdwy 2f out: reminders over 1f out: rdn and r.o to take 3rd wl ins fnl f* **12/1** | | 61 |
| 032 | 4 | ½ | **Queen's Sargent (FR)**[28] 4848 2-9-5 **76** ... ShaneGray 6 *(Kevin Ryan) chsd ldr: hdwy to ld 2f out: sn drvn into 1 l ld: clsd down by wnr over 1f out: hdd ent fnl f: rdn and no ex* **10/1** | | 75 |
| 0346 | 5 | 1 ½ | **Magnus (IRE)**[5] 5685 2-9-3 **74** ... RichardKingscote 5 *(Tom Dascombe) led: pushed along and narrow ld 3f out: rdn and hdd 2f out: one pce whn hmpd by 4th ins fnl f* **5/1**[3] | | 71 |
| 4514 | 6 | 2 ¾ | **Shazzab (IRE)**[28] 4836 2-9-1 **72** ... PaulHanagan 2 *(Richard Fahey) hld up: pushed along 3f out: rdn 2f out: sn lost pl: no ex* **8/1** | | 60 |
| 3416 | 7 | 3 | **Leeshaan (IRE)**[38] 4465 2-9-5 **76** ... PJMcDonald 1 *(James Tate) trckd ldrs: pushed along 3f out: rdn and wknd 2f out* **5/1**[3] | | 56 |
| 1503 | 8 | 27 | **Daddies Girl (IRE)**[28] 4841 2-9-2 **78** ... LuluStanford(5) 8 *(Rod Millman) in rr: struggling in last 1/2-way: drvn 3f out: lost tch 2f out: eased* **8/1** | | |

1m 28.29s (-2.41) **Going Correction** 0.0s/f (Good) 8 Ran SP% **115.5**
Speed ratings (Par 96): **113,112,111,110,109 105,102,71**
CSF £18.64 CT £151.77 TOTE £4.90: £1.70, £1.70, £2.80; EX 16.90 Trifecta £127.30.
**Owner** Julie Martin & David R Martin & Partner **Bred** Lismacue Mare Syndicate **Trained** Lambourn, Berks

**FOCUS**
Race distance increased by 6 yards. A fairly decent nursery handicap. The winner clocked the quickest comparative time on the card so far. The runner-up has been rated to his C&D mark.

## 5876 BETFRED SUPER LEAGUE NOVICE STKS (PLUS 10 RACE) 7f 212y
7:45 (7:45) (Class 4) 2-Y-O £4,528 (£1,347; £673; £336) Stalls Low

| Form | | | | RPR |
|---|---|---|---|---|
| | 1 | | **White Mocha (USA)** 2-9-2 0 ... JosephineGordon 6 *(Hugo Palmer) t.k.h: prom: chsng ldr 4f out: 1 l down 3f out: tk clsr order 2f out: rdn 1f out: drvn ins fnl f: responded wl to ld last few strides* **6/4**[1] | 79+ |
| | 2 | hd | **Rua Augusta (USA)** 2-9-2 0 ... KevinStott 3 *(Kevin Ryan) mid-div: pushed along 3f out: drvn 2f out: hdwy over 1f out: rdn and str run ins fnl f: clsng fast at fin: tk 2nd last stride* **7/2**[3] | 78+ |
| | 3 | shd | **Valdolobo (IRE)** 2-9-2 0 ... PJMcDonald 7 *(K R Burke) led: 1 l clr 3f out: narrow ld and pushed along 2f out: rdn over 1f out: narrow advantage ent fnl f: r.o wl but ct by wnr in last few strides: lost 2nd in shadow of post* **6/1** | 78 |
| | 4 | 1 ¼ | **Neeraan (USA)** 2-9-2 0 ... DaneO'Neill 1 *(Roger Varian) slowly away: sn rcvrd and racd in midfield: 4th 3f out: pushed along 2f out: reminders over 1f out: r.o ins fnl f* **3/1**[2] | 75 |
| | 5 | 7 | **Onefootinfront** 2-9-2 0 ... SteveDrowne 5 *(Daniel Mark Loughnane) hld up: pushed along and effrt 3f out: reminder over 2f out: one pce fnl 2 fs* **20/1** | 59 |
| 00 | 6 | ½ | **Duggary**[14] 5380 2-9-2 0 ... DavidNolan 4 *(Kevin Frost) trckd ldrs: pushed along and lost pl 2f out: no ex* **25/1** | 58 |
| | 7 | 2 ½ | **Breathable** 2-8-13 0 ... RachelRichardson(3) 2 *(Tim Easterby) mid-div: dropped to last over 4f out: drvn 2f out: no imp* **10/1** | 52 |

1m 45.46s (1.76) **Going Correction** 0.0s/f (Good) 7 Ran SP% **119.2**
Speed ratings (Par 96): **91,90,90,89,82 81,79**
CSF £7.59 TOTE £2.30: £1.40, £2.40; EX 7.90 Trifecta £32.00.
**Owner** Dr Ali Ridha **Bred** Woodford Thoroughbreds **Trained** Newmarket, Suffolk

**FOCUS**
Race distance increased by 6 yards. Another juvenile novice contest but very little form on show. They went a sensible gallop over the mile trip on testing ground. The level is fluid.

## 5877 BETFRED "GREAT VALUE EVERY DAY" FILLIES' H'CAP 5f
8:20 (8:20) (Class 5) (0-70,67) 3-Y-O+ £3,557 (£1,058; £529; £264) Stalls Centre

| Form | | | | RPR |
|---|---|---|---|---|
| 6031 | 1 | | **Teepee Time**[20] 5134 4-8-6 **54** ...(b) PhilDennis(5) 1 *(Michael Mullineaux) racd alone in centre of crse: a.p: 2nd and pushed along 1f out: drvn to ld last 150yds: r.o wl: gng away at fin* **10/1** | 64 |
| 2212 | 2 | ¾ | **Granny Roz**[6] 5636 3-9-4 **67** ... RachelRichardson(3) 7 *(David Barron) prom: drvn to ld over 1f out: wnt lft towards wnr ins fnl f: hdd last 150yds: wl hld by wnr nr finsh* **2/1**[1] | 73 |
| 0-45 | 3 | 1 ½ | **Lydiate Lady**[14] 5377 5-8-7 **50** ... FrannyNorton 4 *(Eric Alston) hld up: hdwy into 4th 1/2-way: in tch and chsng ldrs 2f out: drvn 1f out: swtchd rt and rdn ins fnl f: r.o to take 3rd last 50yds* **8/1** | 52 |
| 0-32 | 4 | 1 ½ | **Ayresome Angel**[8] 5580 4-9-8 **65** ... DavidNolan 6 *(John Mackie) led: rdn and hdd over 1f out: weakend ins fnl f: lost 3rd last 50yds* **9/4**[2] | 61 |
| 36 | 5 | 4 | **Spirit Of Rosanna**[6] 5635 5-9-5 **62** ...(t) AdamBeschizza 3 *(Steph Hollinshead) mid-div: relegated to last after 2f: sn drvn: no imp* **3/1**[3] | 44 |
| 001 | 6 | 1 ¼ | **Your Gifted (IRE)**[17] 5252 10-8-5 **48** ...(v) PaulHanagan 5 *(Lisa Williamson) slowly away: last tl wnt into 5th 3f out: drvn 2f out: rdn over 1f out: fdd* **20/1** | 25 |

1m 0.81s (0.01) **Going Correction** 0.0s/f (Good)
**WFA** 3 from 4yo+ 3lb 6 Ran SP% **114.1**
Speed ratings (Par 100): **99,97,95,93,86 84**
CSF £31.17 TOTE £13.60: £4.40, £1.70; EX 47.30 Trifecta £212.40.
**Owner** G Cornes **Bred** Brook Stud Bloodstock Ltd **Trained** Alpraham, Cheshire

**FOCUS**
A modest fillies' sprint handicap. They went a decent gallop spread right across the track with the winner heading in isolation towards the far rail. It's been rated at face value for now.
T/Plt: £14.30 to a £1 stake. Pool: £73,998.85 - winning units. T/Qpdt: £3.80 to a £1 stake. Pool: £5,570.31 - 1,083.53 winning units. **Keith McHugh**

# 5599 MUSSELBURGH (R-H)
Friday, August 11

**OFFICIAL GOING: Good to firm (7.2)**
Wind: Fresh, half behind in races on the sprint course and in over 3f of home straight in races on the rou Weather: Overcast, showers

## 5878 ISN'T IT WISER TO BET AT RACINGUK.COM NURSERY H'CAP 7f 33y
2:00 (2:01) (Class 6) (0-65,67) 2-Y-O £2,587 (£770; £384; £192) Stalls Low

| Form | | | | RPR |
|---|---|---|---|---|
| 026 | 1 | | **Kikini Bamalaam (IRE)**[7] 5603 2-8-12 **56** ... ConnorBeasley 8 *(Keith Dalgleish) t.k.h: hld up: rdn over 2f out: hdwy over 1f out: rdr dropped whip ins fnl f: led last 50yds: r.o wl* **7/1** | 58 |
| 033 | 2 | ¾ | **Sorority**[29] 4799 2-9-9 **67** ... JasonHart 2 *(Mark Johnston) sn led: rdn 2f out: edgd lft ins fnl f: hdd last 50yds: kpt on same pce* **3/1**[1] | 67 |
| 660 | 3 | ½ | **Panophobia**[20] 5162 2-9-7 **65** ... JackGarritty 9 *(Richard Fahey) hld up bhd ldng gp: effrt and hdwy on outside over 2f out: chsng ldrs whn hung rt 1f out: kpt on same pce towards fin* **5/1**[2] | 64 |
| 000 | 4 | 1 ¼ | **Ray Purchase**[27] 4895 2-8-5 **49** ... AndrewMullen 6 *(Keith Dalgleish) t.k.h: early ldr: pressed ldr: effrt and ev ch over 1f out: kpt on same pce fnl f* **12/1** | 44 |
| 0440 | 5 | ¾ | **Archie Perkins (IRE)**[14] 5373 2-9-4 **62** ... TomEaves 5 *(Nigel Tinkler) dwlt: t.k.h: hld up: rdn and outpcd over 2f out: rallied over 1f out: no imp fnl f* **12/1** | 56 |
| 600 | 6 | nse | **Plansina**[37] 4503 2-8-12 **56** ... DavidAllan 10 *(Tim Easterby) trckd ldrs: effrt and chsd ldr over 1f out to ins fnl f: sn no ex* **11/1** | 49 |
| 500 | 7 | 4 | **Ladycammyofclare (IRE)**[16] 5278 2-8-5 **49** ... JoeFanning 3 *(Mark Johnston) trckd ldrs: rdn over 2f out: effrt whn nt clr run briefly over 1f out: wknd fnl f* **11/1** | 32 |
| 050 | 8 | 1 ½ | **Lil Gem (IRE)**[23] 5015 2-8-3 **52** ... RowanScott(5) 7 *(Keith Dalgleish) sn pushed along in rr: drvn and struggling over 2f out: sn btn* **14/1** | 31 |
| 066 | 9 | 2 ½ | **Bad Dog**[56] 3789 2-9-2 **60** ... NathanEvans 4 *(Michael Easterby) t.k.h: hld up in tch: drvn and outpcd over 2f out: wknd over 1f out* **6/1**[3] | 33 |
| 650 | 10 | 11 | **Stopwatch**[14] 5370 2-8-12 **56** ...(p[1]) GrahamLee 11 *(Karen McLintock) s.i.s: sn wl bhd: no ch fr 1/2-way* **20/1** | |

1m 29.43s (0.43) **Going Correction** -0.125s/f (Firm) 10 Ran SP% **111.9**
Speed ratings (Par 92): **92,91,90,89,88 88,83,81,79,66**
CSF £27.05 CT £115.56 TOTE £5.90: £2.00, £1.20, £1.40; EX 21.60 Trifecta £72.10.
**Owner** Middleham Park Racing LXXXII **Bred** Vincent Hannon **Trained** Carluke, S Lanarks

**FOCUS**
Unlike much of the country, it had been relatively dry in the days preceding this afternoon meeting and a stiff, gusting cross-breeze had tightened up the ground. An overcast day with around 2mm of rainfall expected throughout the day and temperatures around 19C. A low-grade nursery to start, run at a decent pace and the winner came from some way off it. Fair form for the grade. The runner-up has been rated to her latest.

## 5879 BRITISH STALLION STUDS EBF STALLIONS CONDITIONS STKS (PLUS 10 RACE) 5f 1y
2:30 (2:31) (Class 3) 2-Y-O £8,086 (£2,406; £1,202; £601) Stalls High

| Form | | | | RPR |
|---|---|---|---|---|
| 20 | 1 | | **Falabelle (IRE)**[20] 5150 2-8-8 0 ... TomEaves 3 *(Kevin Ryan) mde virtually all: sn swtchd to r against stands' rail: rdn and jnd over 1f out: kpt on gamely cl home* **9/2**[2] | 76 |
| 412 | 2 | nse | **Rumshak (IRE)**[14] 5370 2-8-13 85 ... ConnorBeasley 1 *(Michael Dods) pressed ldr: effrt and disp ld over 1f out: rdn and kpt on wl fnl f: jst hld* **4/5**[1] | 81 |
| 4 | 3 | 1 | **Black Friday**[21] 5092 2-8-13 0 ... AndrewMullen 2 *(Karen McLintock) dwlt and n.m.r sn after s: sn in tch: effrt and rdn on outside 2f out: kpt on ins fnl f* **18/1** | 77 |
| 53 | 4 | 3 ¾ | **Mr Greenlight**[14] 5370 2-8-13 0 ... DavidAllan 4 *(Tim Easterby) trckd ldrs: rdn along wl over 1f out: wknd ins fnl f* **5/1**[3] | 64 |
| 00 | 5 | 7 | **Oriental Power**[18] 5202 2-8-13 0 ... NathanEvans 5 *(Jim Goldie) bhd and outpcd: no ch fr 1/2-way* **100/1** | 39 |
| 462 | 6 | ½ | **Global Academy (IRE)**[11] 5474 2-8-13 0 ...(b) GrahamLee 6 *(Gay Kelleway) t.k.h: trckd ldrs tl rdn and wknd fr 2f out* **8/1** | 37 |

59.18s (-1.22) **Going Correction** -0.125s/f (Firm) 6 Ran SP% **107.8**
Speed ratings (Par 98): **104,103,102,96,85 84**
CSF £7.84 TOTE £4.30: £1.80, £1.10; EX 8.40 Trifecta £39.80.
**Owner** K&J Bloodstock Ltd **Bred** D J Sweeney **Trained** Hambleton, N Yorks

**FOCUS**
A fair juvenile sprint and a tight finish, with the first three home drawing a little way clear of the remainder. This may well produce future winners. It's been rated at face value.

## 5880 WATERMANS H'CAP 1m 2y
3:00 (3:01) (Class 6) (0-65,67) 3-Y-O+ £2,587 (£770; £384; £192) Stalls Low

| Form | | | | RPR |
|---|---|---|---|---|
| 0032 | 1 | | **Relight My Fire**[10] 5497 7-9-10 **61** ...(p) DavidAllan 7 *(Tim Easterby) pressed ldr: led gng wl over 2f out: rdn and edgd rt over 1f out: kpt on wl fnl f* **9/2**[2] | 69 |
| 0400 | 2 | 1 ¾ | **Adventureman**[17] 5254 5-9-8 **59** ...(b) JamesSullivan 6 *(Ruth Carr) t.k.h early: led at ordinary gallop: rdn and hdd over 2f out: rallied: kpt on same pce ins fnl f* **7/1**[3] | 63 |
| 640 | 3 | 2 ¾ | **Let Right Be Done**[11] 5466 5-8-11 **48** ...(b) AndrewMullen 10 *(Linda Perratt) s.i.s: hld up: hdwy over 2f out: rdn and chsd clr ldng pair ins fnl f: kpt on: no imp* **16/1** | 45 |
| -245 | 4 | 1 ¾ | **Hellomoto**[31] 4721 3-9-1 **59** ...(p) TomEaves 9 *(Kevin Ryan) hld up in tch: rdn over 2f out: edgd rt and rallied over 1f out: kpt on ins fnl f: nt pce to chal* **9/1** | 51 |
| 1555 | 5 | nk | **Cliff Bay (IRE)**[11] 5466 3-9-9 **67** ...(h) JoeFanning 2 *(Keith Dalgleish) t.k.h: trckd ldrs: rdn over 2f out: outpcd fnl f* **4/1**[1] | 58 |
| 66 | 6 | ¾ | **Ralphy Boy (IRE)**[11] 5467 8-9-9 **65** ... RowanScott(5) 1 *(Alistair Whillans) cl up: drvn over 2f out: wknd fnl f* **9/2**[2] | 55 |
| -020 | 7 | 1 | **Twiggy**[7] 5604 3-9-2 **67** ...(h) JamieGormley(7) 8 *(Iain Jardine) t.k.h: in tch: effrt over 2f out: edgd lft and wknd fnl f* **10/1** | 54 |
| -046 | 8 | 2 | **Leopard (IRE)**[11] 5485 3-9-0 **61** ...(h) JoshDoyle(3) 5 *(Tony Coyle) hld up: rdn and outpcd over 2f out: nvr on terms* **25/1** | 43 |
| 3446 | 9 | 2 | **Joyful Star**[33] 4660 7-9-0 **51** ... GrahamLee 11 *(Fred Watson) bhd and sn pushed along: struggling over 2f out: nvr on terms* **12/1** | 29 |

3530 **10** *31* **Cabal**[24] 5007 10-9-10 **61**..........(b) SamJames 3
(Geoffrey Harker) *hld up towards rr: struggling 3f out: sn wknd: eased whn no ch fnl f* **12/1**

1m 39.19s (-2.01) **Going Correction** -0.125s/f (Firm)
**WFA** 3 from 5yo+ 7lb **10** Ran SP% **113.1**
Speed ratings (Par 101): **105,103,100,98,98 97,96,94,92,61**
CSF £34.85 CT £456.58 TOTE £4.20: £1.40, £2.20, £5.40; EX 38.00 Trifecta £447.70.
**Owner** Jonathan Gill **Bred** J Gill **Trained** Great Habton, N Yorks

**FOCUS**
A decent pace for this low-grade handicap which few got into. The runner-up has been rated within 3lb of his recent best.

## 5881 EBF SCOTTISH PREMIER SERIES FILLIES' H'CAP 7f 33y
**3:30** (3:31) (Class 4) (0-80,80) 3-Y-O+ **£8,086** (£2,406; £1,202; £601) **Stalls** Low

Form RPR
231 **1** **Whatsthemessage (IRE)**[6] 5666 3-9-3 **76** 6ex.......... GrahamLee 2 82
(Keith Dalgleish) *led at decent gallop 2f: pressed ldr and clr of rest: regained ld 2f out: rdn and r.o wl fnl f* **5/2**[1]

1524 **2** *1* **Alpine Dream (IRE)**[13] 5399 4-9-9 **76**..........(b) DavidAllan 1 81
(Tim Easterby) *chsd clr ldng pair: effrt and edgd rt over 1f out: chsd wnr ins fnl f: kpt on: nt pce to chal* **5/1**[3]

4610 **3** *2 1/4* **Maureb (IRE)**[18] 5211 5-9-0 **67**..........(p) BarryMcHugh 4 66
(Tony Coyle) *pressed ldr: led and maintained decent gallop after 2f: hdd over 2f out: rallied: lost 2nd and no ex ins fnl f* **12/1**

1440 **4** *nse* **Sea Of Green**[7] 5620 5-8-1 **61**..........(p) SeanMooney(7) 8 60+
(Jim Goldie) *s.i.s: hld up: rdn over 2f out: hdwy fnl f: nvr able to chal* **25/1**

0540 **5** *nk* **Forever A Lady (IRE)**[4] 5699 4-9-7 **74**.......... AndrewMullen 3 72
(Keith Dalgleish) *hld up in tch: rdn over 2f out: no imp fr over 1f out* **12/1**

4101 **6** *1* **The Stalking Moon (IRE)**[7] 5601 3-9-7 **80** 6ex.......... JasonHart 6 73
(John Quinn) *in tch: effrt on outside over 2f out: wknd appr fnl f* **3/1**[2]

001 **7** *hd* **Alexandrakollontai (IRE)**[19] 5185 7-7-7 **79**..........(b) RowanScott(5) 7 74
(Alistair Whillans) *s.i.s: hld up: drvn along over 2f out: sn no imp* **11/2**

0610 **8** *1* **Groupie**[14] 5376 3-9-5 **78**.......... JamesSullivan 5 68
(Tom Tate) *hld up in tch on ins: drvn along over 2f out: wknd over 1f out* **16/1**

1m 27.51s (-1.49) **Going Correction** -0.125s/f (Firm)
**WFA** 3 from 4yo+ 6lb **8** Ran SP% **110.7**
Speed ratings (Par 102): **103,101,99,99,98 97,97,96**
CSF £14.26 CT £115.76 TOTE £3.00: £1.10, £1.50, £3.60; EX 16.20 Trifecta £136.60.
**Owner** Ronnie Docherty **Bred** Lynn Lodge Stud **Trained** Carluke, S Lanarks

**FOCUS**
The pace again held up and the form looks viable. The runner-up has been rated to the better view of her form.

## 5882 ARCHERFIELD CUP H'CAP 1m 5f 216y
**4:00** (4:01) (Class 2) (0-100,98) 3-Y-O+ **£12,938** (£3,850; £1,924; £962) **Stalls** Low

Form RPR
1050 **1** **Yorkidding**[41] 4356 5-10-0 **98**.......... JoeFanning 2 104
(Mark Johnston) *pressed ldr: led over 2f out: rdn over 1f out: hld on wl fnl f* **11/4**[2]

6115 **2** *1 1/2* **Great Fighter**[27] 4921 7-8-10 **85**..........(v) PhilDennis(5) 1 89
(Jim Goldie) *dwlt: hld up in last pl but in tch: effrt on outside over 2f out: sn drvn: kpt on ins fnl f: nrst fin* **9/2**[3]

131 **3** *shd* **Sebastian's Wish (IRE)**[17] 5259 4-8-13 **83**.......... GrahamLee 6 87
(Keith Dalgleish) *led at ordinary gallop: rdn and hdd over 2f out: rallied: kpt on same pce ins fnl f* **5/2**[1]

03 **4** *1* **Codeshare**[13] 5438 5-9-0 **84**.......... DavidAllan 5 86
(Sally Haynes) *t.k.h early: trckd ldrs: effrt and rdn over 2f out: edgd rt over 1f out: one pce fnl f* **10/1**

1246 **5** *3/4* **Kensington Star**[20] 5164 4-9-3 **87**..........(p) JasonHart 3 88
(Keith Dalgleish) *trckd ldrs: drvn and outpcd over 2f out: no imp fr over 1f out* **5/2**[1]

3m 0.37s (-4.93) **Going Correction** -0.125s/f (Firm) **5** Ran SP% **111.1**
Speed ratings (Par 109): **109,108,108,107,107**
CSF £15.05 TOTE £3.60: £1.50, £2.10; EX 15.20 Trifecta £32.90.
**Owner** Paul Robert York **Bred** Bluehills Racing Limited **Trained** Middleham Moor, N Yorks

**FOCUS**
A decent gallop for this staying handicap. Solid form.

## 5883 EDGEN MURRAY H'CAP 1m 4f 104y
**4:30** (4:30) (Class 6) (0-65,67) 3-Y-O+ **£3,234** (£962; £481; £240) **Stalls** Low

Form RPR
2124 **1** **Thorntoun Care**[4] 5701 6-9-6 **64**..........(p) JamieGormley(7) 1 71
(Iain Jardine) *hld up in tch: smooth hdwy on outside over 2f out: led over 1f out: sn hrd pressed: rdn and hld on wl fnl f* **4/6**[1]

00-5 **2** *nse* **Mambo Dancer**[218] 65 3-9-4 **65**.......... JoeFanning 2 73+
(Mark Johnston) *led: j. winning line after 2f: rdn and hdd over 1f out: rallied: jst hld* **4/1**[2]

6402 **3** *1 1/2* **Schmooze (IRE)**[21] 5096 8-8-13 **50**.......... AndrewMullen 6 55
(Linda Perratt) *hld up in tch: pushed along over 4f out: rdn and outpcd over 2f out: rallied to chse ldng pair over 1f out: kpt on* **14/1**

30 **4** *10* **Steccando (IRE)**[12] 5454 4-9-10 **61**.......... DavidAllan 4 50
(Sally Haynes) *pressed ldr: rdn and ev ch over 2f out: rdn and wknd fnl f* **10/1**

035 **5** *2* **Falcon's Fire (IRE)**[7] 5599 4-10-2 **67**..........(t) GrahamLee 3 53
(Keith Dalgleish) *trckd ldrs: effrt and rdn over 2f out: wknd over 1f out* **13/2**[3]

2m 42.14s (0.14) **Going Correction** -0.125s/f (Firm)
**WFA** 3 from 4yo+ 10lb **5** Ran SP% **109.1**
Speed ratings (Par 101): **94,93,92,86,84**
CSF £3.53 TOTE £1.50: £1.10, £1.60; EX 4.10 Trifecta £13.90.
**Owner** Alba-Eire Syndicate **Bred** W M Johnstone **Trained** Carrutherstown, D'fries & G'way

**FOCUS**
Light rain arrived ahead of this penultimate contest. The pace was fair and another tight finish ensued. The form looks okay for the grade. The third has been rated near her better recent form.

## 5884 FISHER GROUP H'CAP 1m 7f 217y
**5:00** (5:01) (Class 6) (0-65,66) 4-Y-O+ **£3,234** (£962; £481; £240) **Stalls** High

Form RPR
044 **1** **Golden Jeffrey (SWI)**[24] 5003 4-9-4 **66**.......... JamieGormley(7) 4 74
(Iain Jardine) *mde all at modest gallop: shkn up 2f out: clr fnl f: eased nr fin: unchal* **7/4**[2]

0003 **2** *2 1/4* **Tectonic (IRE)**[17] 5257 8-9-7 **62**..........(v) JoeFanning 5 67
(Keith Dalgleish) *s.i.s: hld up in tch: stdy hdwy whn nt clr run over 1f out: swtchd and effrt ent fnl f: sn chsng (clr) wnr: no imp* **11/2**[3]

3061 **3** *2 1/4* **Jonny Delta**[17] 5257 10-9-4 **59**.......... DanielTudhope 1 62
(Jim Goldie) *trckd ldr to over 2f out: rallied: kpt on same pce fnl f* **11/10**[1]

00 **4** *2* **Maple Stirrup (IRE)**[19] 5186 5-8-12 **53**.......... ConnorBeasley 2 53
(Patrick Holmes) *trckd ldrs: wnt 2nd over 2f out to over 1f out: wknd ins fnl f* **12/1**

3m 32.79s (-0.71) **Going Correction** -0.125s/f (Firm) **4** Ran SP% **107.1**
Speed ratings (Par 101): **96,94,93,92**
CSF £10.31 TOTE £2.80; EX 11.30 Trifecta £10.60.
**Owner** Mrs Jo Tracey **Bred** Gestut La Irenita **Trained** Carrutherstown, D'fries & G'way

**FOCUS**
The sun was out again after the light shower. A modest staying handicap and the pace was fair.
T/Plt: £17.40 to a £1 stake. Pool: £60,658.74 - 2,538.19 winning units. T/Qpdt: £11.80 to a £1 stake. Pool: £3,731.82 - 233.81 winning units. **Richard Young**

# 5658 NEWMARKET (R-H)
Friday, August 11

**OFFICIAL GOING: Soft (6.4)**
Wind: Fresh across Weather: Overcast

## 5885 FLY LONDON SOUTHEND AIRPORT TO PERPIGNAN FILLIES' NOVICE STKS (PLUS 10 RACE) 6f
**5:30** (5:30) (Class 4) 2-Y-O **£4,528** (£1,347; £673; £336) **Stalls** High

Form RPR
**1** **Gavota** 2-9-0 0.......... JamesDoyle 4 83+
(Roger Charlton) *hld up in tch: pushed along to chse ldr 2f out: r.o to ld post* **13/8**[1]

4 **2** *shd* **Daybreak**[21] 5107 2-9-0 0.......... AdamKirby 7 83
(Hughie Morrison) *led at stdy pce: pushed along and qcknd clr over 1f out: rdn ins fnl f: hdd post* **2/1**[2]

**3** *3* **Goodnight Girl (IRE)** 2-8-11 0.......... GeorgeWood(3) 3 74
(Jonathan Portman) *hld up: rdn over 2f out: hdwy over 1f out: styd on: nt rch ldrs* **14/1**

**4** *5* **Priscilla's Dream** 2-9-0 0.......... LouisSteward 6 59
(Philip McBride) *s.i.s: hld up: rdn over 1f out: styd on to go 4th nr fin: nt trble ldrs* **28/1**

6 **5** *hd* **Roseau City**[14] 5365 2-8-9 0.......... DavidEgan(5) 5 58
(David Elsworth) *prom: rdn over 2f out: wknd over 1f out* **10/1**

0 **6** *3 1/4* **Lady Godiva (IRE)**[14] 5349 2-9-0 0.......... SeanLevey 1 48
(Richard Hannon) *prom: racd keenly: hung lft and wknd over 1f out* **7/1**[3]

0 **7** *2* **Pammi**[10] 5507 2-9-0 0.......... RyanTate 8 42
(Anthony Carson) *awkward leaving stalls: sn w ldr: rdn over 2f out: wknd over 1f out* **66/1**

**8** *shd* **Capesthorne (IRE)** 2-9-0 0.......... AndreaAtzeni 2 42+
(Sir Michael Stoute) *s.i.s: sn pushed along and rn green in rr: wknd 2f out* **9/1**

1m 14.29s (1.79) **Going Correction** +0.225s/f (Good) **8** Ran SP% **114.6**
Speed ratings (Par 93): **97,96,92,86,85 81,78,78**
CSF £5.05 TOTE £2.80: £1.40, £1.10, £3.70; EX 6.60 Trifecta £57.00.
**Owner** K Abdullah **Bred** Juddmonte Farms (east) Ltd **Trained** Beckhampton, Wilts

**FOCUS**
Stands' side course used. Stalls: far side, apart from 1m2f: centre. It was dry on Thursday and overnight, but the course had taken 33mm of rain on Wednesday and the going was still soft (GoingStick: 6.4). The re-positioning of the rail on the Beacon Course (8f-16f) increased the distance of the 1m2f race by 1.5yds. A fair fillies' novice. The runner-up has been rated as taking a nice step forward from her debut.

## 5886 FLY LONDON SOUTHEND AIRPORT TO MILAN (S) STKS 7f
**6:05** (6:05) (Class 5) 2-Y-O **£3,881** (£1,155; £577; £288) **Stalls** High

Form RPR
1540 **1** **Lexington Grace (IRE)**[20] 5150 2-8-13 68..........(p) SilvestreDeSousa 5 63
(Richard Hannon) *led 2f: chsd ldr: led again 2f out: rdn over 1f out: r.o* **4/5**[1]

660 **2** *2 1/4* **Red Snapper**[21] 5114 2-8-5 54.......... HollieDoyle(3) 4 52
(William Stone) *wnt rt s: trckd ldrs: racd keenly: nt clr run over 1f out: sn chsng wnr: rdn and hung lft ins fnl f: styd on same pce* **25/1**

**3** *1/2* **Little Poem** 2-8-8 0..........(h[1]) AntonioFresu 3 51
(Marco Botti) *s.i.s and hmpd s: hld up: hdwy over 2f out: nt clr run and swtchd rt over 1f out: styd on to go 3rd nr fin: nt trble ldrs* **5/1**[3]

2045 **4** *1/2* **Kheleyf's Girl**[28] 4836 2-8-9 63 ow1.......... KieranShoemark 2 51
(David Evans) *plld hrd: w ldr tl led 5f out: rdn: edgd rt and hdd 2f out: no ex fnl f* **9/2**[2]

00 **5** *10* **Rockwell Lloyd (IRE)**[6] 5655 2-8-13 0.......... BenCurtis 1 30
(Mick Channon) *hld up: pushed along 1/2-way: wknd 2f out* **8/1**

00 **6** *4 1/2* **Honey Blossom**[31] 4709 2-8-3 0.......... DavidEgan(5) 6 14
(Denis Quinn) *unruly to post and bhd stalls: s.s: a in rr: rdn and wknd over 2f out* **16/1**

1m 28.7s (3.00) **Going Correction** +0.225s/f (Good) **6** Ran SP% **111.2**
Speed ratings (Par 94): **91,88,87,87,75 70**
CSF £22.78 TOTE £1.60: £1.10, £4.20; EX 15.00 Trifecta £41.40.
**Owner** Middleham Park Racing XII & A E Denham **Bred** Tally-Ho Stud **Trained** East Everleigh, Wilts

**FOCUS**
A weak race for the track. It's been rated through the runner-up.

## 5887 FLY LONDON SOUTHEND AIRPORT TO LYON MAIDEN STKS (PLUS 10 RACE) 7f
**6:35** (6:41) (Class 4) 2-Y-O **£4,528** (£1,347; £673; £336) **Stalls** High

Form RPR
**1** **Vintager** 2-9-5 0.......... KieranShoemark 4 91+
(David Menuisier) *uns rdr to post: hld up in tch: led over 2f out: rdn over 1f out: r.o wl: comf* **33/1**

**2** *1 1/2* **Symbolization (IRE)** 2-9-5 0.......... WilliamBuick 13 87+
(Charlie Appleby) *hld up in tch: rdn to chse wnr over 1f out: edgd rt and no imp ins fnl f* **15/8**[1]

**3** *3 1/4* **Old Persian** 2-9-5 0.......... JamesDoyle 12 79
(Charlie Appleby) *disp ld over 4f: rdn over 1f out: no ex ins fnl f* **6/1**[3]

**4** *1/2* **Chilean** 2-9-5 0.......... FergusSweeney 6 78
(Martyn Meade) *prom: ev ch over 2f out: rdn over 1f out: no ex ins fnl f* **20/1**

**5** *3 1/4* **Rastrelli (FR)** 2-9-5 0.......... AdamKirby 10 70
(Charlie Appleby) *hld up: pushed along and hdwy over 2f out: wknd fnl f* **8/1**

**6** *nk* **Sergio Leone (IRE)** 2-9-5 0.......... SeanLevey 2 69
(Richard Hannon) *s.i.s: hld up: racd keenly: hdwy 2f out: rdn over 1f out: wknd fnl f* **8/1**

7 4 ½ **Enzemble (IRE)** 2-9-5 0 SilvestreDeSousa 5 58
(David Elsworth) *s.i.s: hld up: plld hrd: shkn up over 2f out: nvr on terms* **12/1**

8 ¾ **Blame Culture (USA)** 2-9-5 0 BenCurtis 9 56
(George Margarson) *s.i.s: hld up: plld hrd: shkn up and hung lft over 1f out: n.d* **66/1**

9 1 ¼ **The Emperor Within (FR)** 2-9-2 0 NoelGarbutt(3) 1 53
(Martin Smith) *plld hrd: disp ld over 4f: wknd over 1f out* **50/1**

10 ½ **Wafy (IRE)** 2-9-5 0 JimCrowley 11 52
(Charles Hills) *s.i.s: hld up: hdwy over 2f out: wknd over 1f out* **10/3²**

11 2 ¾ **Topapinion** 2-9-5 0 JoeyHaynes 7 45
(Mark H Tompkins) *hld up: plld hrd: hdwy over 2f out: rdn and wknd over 1f out* **100/1**

12 8 **Hidden Depths (IRE)** 2-9-5 0 AndreaAtzeni 8 25
(Sir Michael Stoute) *prom: pushed along 1/2-way: wknd over 2f out* **12/1**

1m 27.86s (2.16) **Going Correction** +0.225s/f (Good) **12 Ran SP% 121.9**
Speed ratings (Par 96): **96,94,90,90,86 85,80,79,78,77 74,65**
CSF £95.81 TOTE £46.20: £8.70, £1.30, £2.10; EX 237.80 Trifecta £1527.40.
**Owner** Gail Brown Racing (VIII) **Bred** Thurso Bloodstock Ltd **Trained** Pulborough, W Sussex
**FOCUS**
A good-looking maiden for unraced horses and it should throw up a number of future winners.

## 5888 FLY LONDON SOUTHEND AIRPORT TO PRAGUE H'CAP 1m 2f
**7:05** (7:09) (Class 5) (0-75,77) 3-Y-O+ **£3,881** (£1,155; £577; £288) **Stalls** Centre

Form RPR

3111 1 **Swilly Sunset**[28] 4846 4-10-4 **77** SilvestreDeSousa 4 83
(Anthony Carson) *chsd ldr 1f: remained handy: rdn over 2f out: styd on u.p to ld ins fnl f: drvn out* **9/4¹**

3320 2 ½ **Ghinia (IRE)**[34] 4621 6-9-13 **72** RobHornby 5 77
(Pam Sly) *chsd ldr over 8f out: led over 2f out: rdn over 1f out: hdd ins fnl f: styd on* **11/4²**

4423 3 nk **Outback Blue**[5] 5686 4-9-7 **73** (vt) KatherineGlenister(7) 6 77
(David Evans) *s.i.s: hld up: pushed along over 4f out: hdwy over 1f out: r.o* **11/2³**

0624 4 4 **The Gay Cavalier**[8] 5555 6-9-10 **69** (t) AdamKirby 2 65
(John Ryan) *s.i.s: hld up: rdn over 2f out: hdwy over 1f out: no ex ins fnl f* **12/1**

045 5 1 ¼ **Hard Toffee (IRE)**[30] 4755 6-9-10 **69** JimCrowley 7 63
(Conrad Allen) *led after 1f: rdn and hdd over 2f out: wknd ins fnl f* **8/1**

1230 6 4 ½ **Ourmullion**[17] 5242 3-9-6 **73** KierenFox 1 59
(John Best) *led 1f: chsd ldrs: rdn over 3f out: wknd over 1f out* **13/2**

5-42 7 nk **Broughtons Story**[183] 637 3-8-6 **62** GeorgeWood(3) 3 47
(Henry Spiller) *hld up: pushed along over 3f out: wknd over 1f out* **12/1**

2m 9.4s (3.90) **Going Correction** +0.225s/f (Good)
**WFA** 3 from 4yo+ 8lb **7 Ran SP% 112.6**
Speed ratings (Par 103): **93,92,92,89,88 84,84**
CSF £8.33 TOTE £2.90: £1.60, £2.20; EX 10.60 Trifecta £45.70.
**Owner** Alderson Carson Francis Hart **Bred** Aston House Stud **Trained** Newmarket, Suffolk
**FOCUS**
Race distance increased by 1.5yds. A fair handicap. Ordinary form, with the third rated to his recent form.

## 5889 FLY LONDON SOUTHEND AIRPORT TO BUDAPEST EBF STALLIONS FILLIES' H'CAP 1m
**7:35** (7:36) (Class 3) (0-95,94) 3-Y-O+ **£9,056** (£2,695; £1,346; £673) **Stalls** High

Form RPR

1152 1 **Titi Makfi**[9] 5529 3-9-6 **93** JamesDoyle 4 100
(Mark Johnston) *chsd ldr tl led 3f out: rdn over 1f out: styd on gamely* **5/4¹**

5266 2 nk **Prying Pandora (FR)**[20] 5163 4-8-9 **78** AdamMcNamara(3) 5 85
(Richard Fahey) *prom: outpcd over 1f out: rallied and edgd rt ins fnl f: r.o* **10/1**

2511 3 1 ¾ **Seduce Me**[8] 5559 3-9-4 **91** 6ex (p) JimCrowley 6 93
(K R Burke) *hld up: hdwy to chse wnr 2f out: rdn and ev ch over 1f out: no ex wl ins fnl f* **7/4²**

4 9 **Sunchisetagioo**[118] 3-9-2 **94** (h¹) DavidEgan(5) 1 75
(Marco Botti) *prom: pushed along over 3f out: rdn and wknd over 1f out* **14/1**

0130 5 3 ¾ **Flying North**[15] 5323 3-8-12 **85** TimmyMurphy 3 58
(Richard Hannon) *led 5f: wknd 2f out* **8/1³**

1m 40.22s (0.22) **Going Correction** +0.225s/f (Good)
**WFA** 3 from 4yo 7lb **5 Ran SP% 107.7**
Speed ratings (Par 104): **107,106,104,95,95**
CSF £13.01 TOTE £1.90: £1.20, £3.10; EX 11.60 Trifecta £20.90.
**Owner** Paul & Clare Rooney **Bred** Floors Farming **Trained** Middleham Moor, N Yorks
**FOCUS**
Not a bad fillies' handicap despite the small field. The runner-up has been rated to her best, with the third to her recent improved soft-ground form.

## 5890 FLY LONDON SOUTHEND AIRPORT TO VENICE H'CAP 6f
**8:10** (8:11) (Class 3) (0-95,93) 3-Y-O+ **£7,762** (£2,310; £1,154; £577) **Stalls** High

Form RPR

443 1 **Jordan Sport**[28] 4830 4-9-9 **91** (h) JamieSpencer 5 101
(David Simcock) *mde all: rdn over 1f out: edgd rt ins fnl f: r.o: comf* **7/4¹**

2032 2 2 ¾ **Major Pusey**[4] 5720 5-8-10 **83** GeorgeBuckell(5) 2 84
(John Gallagher) *prom: racd keenly: chsd wnr over 2f out: rdn over 1f out: styd on same pce ins fnl f* **7/4¹**

2102 3 3 ¼ **Tatlisu (IRE)**[11] 5471 7-9-0 **85** (p) AdamMcNamara(3) 4 76
(Richard Fahey) *s.i.s: hld up: rdn over 2f out: r.o ins fnl f: nt trble ldrs* **9/1**

104 4 ¾ **Reputation (IRE)**[36] 4521 4-9-9 **91** (v) SeanLevey 3 79
(John Quinn) *hmpd s: hld up: hdwy u.p over 1f out: wknd ins fnl f* **8/1³**

14-0 5 7 **Waqaas**[13] 5423 3-9-7 **93** JimCrowley 1 58
(Charles Hills) *chsd wnr over 3f: sn rdn: wknd over 1f out* **6/1²**

1m 12.26s (-0.24) **Going Correction** +0.225s/f (Good)
**WFA** 3 from 4yo+ 4lb **5 Ran SP% 108.1**
Speed ratings (Par 107): **110,106,102,101,91**
Pick Six: Part won. 33,431.30 - Pool: 47,759.10. Pool of 23,879.55 carried forward to Kilbeggan today. Tote Aggregate: 2017: 253,855.00 - 2016: 289,650.00 CSF £4.69 TOTE £2.40: £1.50, £1.30; EX 4.80 Trifecta £17.10.
**Owner** M Khan X2 Pip Walter Harry Wigan **Bred** Rabbah Bloodstock Limited **Trained** Newmarket, Suffolk
**FOCUS**
This proved straightforward for the winner once he bagged the early lead. The winner has been rated to the better view of his AW form.
T/Plt: £11.30 to a £1 stake. Pool: £60,083.44 - 3,848.42 winning units. T/Qpdt: £7.30 to a £1 stake. Pool: £4,931.21 - 497.57 winning units. **Colin Roberts**

# 5844 WOLVERHAMPTON (A.W) (L-H)
Friday, August 11

**OFFICIAL GOING: Tapeta: standard**
Wind: light behind Weather: overcast

## 5891 RENAULT CLIO NOVICE STKS 5f 21y (Tp)
**1:50** (1:50) (Class 5) 2-Y-O **£3,234** (£962; £481; £240) **Stalls** Low

Form RPR

1204 1 **Corinthia Knight (IRE)**[20] 5150 2-9-10 **88** OisinMurphy 4 97+
(Archie Watson) *pressed ldr: led over 2f out: qcknd clr over 1f out: rdn and kpt on: comf* **9/4²**

24 2 6 **Mokaatil**[52] 3929 2-9-2 0 DaneO'Neill 6 67
(Owen Burrows) *racd keenly: hld up in tch: pushed along and hdwy over 1f out: rdn to go 2nd jst ins fnl f: edgd lft: one pce and no ch w wnr* **4/5¹**

3 1 **Showmethedough** 2-9-2 0 DavidNolan 5 64
(Richard Fahey) *trckd ldrs: rdn 2f out: kpt on same pce* **50/1**

4 ½ **Swiss Chocolate (IRE)** 2-8-11 0 MartinHarley 7 57
(William Haggas) *slowly away: hld up: pushed along and hdwy over 1f out: kpt on fnl f* **16/1**

2100 5 ½ **Miss Dd (IRE)**[22] 5057 2-9-1 **73** (v¹) RichardKingscote 9 59
(Tom Dascombe) *trckd ldrs: rdn to chse clr ldr over 1f out: hung lft appr fnl f: no ex fnl 110yds* **25/1**

16 6 ½ **Moseeb (IRE)**[20] 5162 2-9-9 0 (h¹) JosephineGordon 10 65
(Saeed bin Suroor) *in tch on outside: rdn 2f out: edgd rt and no imp* **9/2³**

50 7 3 ¼ **Mouchee (IRE)**[13] 5430 2-9-2 0 JimmyQuinn 8 47
(David Evans) *dwlt: hld up: nvr threatened* **100/1**

0 8 5 **Sandie Gem**[23] 5015 2-8-11 0 TonyHamilton 2 24
(Richard Fahey) *led narrowly: pushed along whn hdd over 2f out: wknd* **80/1**

0 9 8 **Night Air**[9] 5534 2-8-5 0 ow1 (v¹) TobyEley(7) 3
(Derek Shaw) *hld up in tch: rdn over 2f out: wknd* **200/1**

1m 0.74s (-1.16) **Going Correction** -0.075s/f (Stan) **9 Ran SP% 118.9**
Speed ratings (Par 94): **106,96,94,94,93 92,87,79,66**
CSF £4.52 TOTE £3.10: £1.10, £1.02, £13.60; EX 5.10 Trifecta £63.10.
**Owner** Ontoawinner & Partner **Bred** Tally-Ho Stud **Trained** Upper Lambourn, W Berks
**FOCUS**
This looked quite a strong little race on paper but two of the three main protagonists proved disappointing and Corinthia Knight bolted up. The winner has been rated in line with his Kempton win.

## 5892 DACIA LOGAN SPORTS TOURER H'CAP 6f 20y (Tp)
**2:20** (2:21) (Class 6) (0-60,60) 3-Y-O+ **£2,587** (£770; £384; £192) **Stalls** Low

Form RPR

0210 1 **Bogsnog (IRE)**[11] 5482 7-9-7 **57** KevinStott 2 63
(Ruth Carr) *trckd ldrs: rdn 2f out: led 110yds out: kpt on* **3/1²**

0410 2 ½ **Burauq**[16] 5271 5-9-1 **51** (v) JosephineGordon 6 56
(Milton Bradley) *hld up in midfield on inner: rdn and hdwy over 1f out: kpt on: wnt 2nd 50yds out* **12/1**

00 3 ¾ **Wimboldsley**[55] 3812 6-8-12 **48** RichardKingscote 8 50
(Scott Dixon) *led: rdn 2f out: hdd 110yds out: no ex* **18/1**

-660 4 nk **Ambitious Boy**[147] 1247 8-8-10 **46** oh1 OisinMurphy 1 47
(John O'Shea) *dwlt: hld up in rr: rdn along over 2f out: bhd tl kpt on wl fnl f* **14/1**

5224 5 nse **Hungarian Rhapsody**[25] 4970 3-9-3 **57** DougieCostello 9 57
(Jamie Osborne) *dwlt: hld up: pushed along and hdwy on outside over 1f out: kpt on wl fnl f: nrst fin* **11/4¹**

6515 6 shd **Jazz Legend (USA)**[3] 5738 4-8-12 **53** (h) BenRobinson(5) 11 54
(Mandy Rowland) *sn trckd ldrs: rdn 2f out: kpt on same pce* **16/1**

6064 7 ½ **Rebel Heart**[22] 5052 3-8-13 **53** (v) JimmyQuinn 5 51
(Bill Turner) *s.i.s: sn in tch: rdn 2f out: kpt on same pce* **11/1**

0326 8 1 ¾ **Elusivity (IRE)**[22] 5081 9-9-9 **59** (p) MartinHarley 4 53
(Conor Dore) *prom: rdn 2f out: wknd ins fnl f* **14/1**

22-0 9 1 **La Fortuna**[190] 521 4-9-2 **55** (t¹) LewisEdmunds(3) 7 46
(Charlie Wallis) *midfield: rdn 2f out: keeping on whn hmpd 110yds out* **16/1**

3210 10 2 ½ **Strictly Carter**[21] 5119 4-9-5 **60** JoshuaBryan(5) 10 44
(Alan Bailey) *hld up in midfield: rdn 2f out: wknd fnl f* **5/1³**

3406 11 5 **Head Space (IRE)**[99] 2331 9-9-3 **60** JasonWatson(7) 3 29
(Brian Barr) *a rr* **66/1**

1m 14.14s (-0.36) **Going Correction** -0.075s/f (Stan)
**WFA** 3 from 4yo+ 4lb **11 Ran SP% 116.2**
Speed ratings (Par 101): **99,98,97,96,96 96,96,93,92,89 82**
CSF £38.70 CT £564.57 TOTE £3.50: £1.30, £3.70, £5.00; EX 47.50 Trifecta £513.80.
**Owner** Facts & Figures **Bred** J R Weston **Trained** Huby, N Yorks
**FOCUS**
A modest handicap run at what looked a decent gallop. The form looks solid enough for the grade. The first three set a straightforward level.

## 5893 RENAULT ALL NEW MEGANE FILLIES' (S) STKS 6f 20y (Tp)
**2:50** (2:50) (Class 6) 2-Y-O **£2,749** (£818; £408; £204) **Stalls** Low

Form RPR

0450 1 **Flo's Melody**[11] 5479 2-9-0 **63** TonyHamilton 5 57
(Richard Fahey) *mde all: rdn over 1f out: edgd rt: kpt on wl* **11/4²**

005 2 1 ¾ **Watch Tan**[13] 5408 2-9-0 **53** (h¹) JosephineGordon 6 52
(George Baker) *trckd ldrs: racd keenly: rdn 2f out: kpt on fnl f* **11/1**

6 3 shd **Formiga (IRE)**[35] 4595 2-9-0 0 OscarPereira 2 51
(Jose Santos) *trckd ldrs: rdn 2f out: kpt on* **20/1**

5656 4 nk **Felisa**[16] 5279 2-9-0 **65** (v¹) DaneO'Neill 4 51
(David Evans) *trckd ldrs: shuffled bk a bit and swtchd lft over 1f out: sn rdn: kpt on same pce* **8/13¹**

0 5 1 ¾ **Spix's Macaw**[39] 4440 2-8-11 0 EdwardGreatrex(3) 8 45
(Bill Turner) *prom: rdn 2f out: no ex fnl f* **28/1**

040 6 shd **Jean Paget (IRE)**[7] 5613 2-9-0 0 (v¹) FrannyNorton 1 49
(Mick Channon) *hld up: sme prog on inner whn short of room 1f out: no ch after* **8/1³**

0 7 8 **Ruby Sound**[22] 5047 2-9-0 0 RoystonFfrench 9 21
(Steph Hollinshead) *prom on outer: rdn over 2f out: wknd over 1f out* **100/1**

00 8 1 ½ **Lady Ensign**[13] 5398 2-9-0 0 FranBerry 3 17
(Mark Brisbourne) *hld up: rdn over 2f out: sn wknd* **100/1**

1m 16.12s (1.62) **Going Correction** -0.075s/f (Stan) **8 Ran SP% 118.2**
Speed ratings (Par 89): **86,83,83,83,80 80,70,68**
CSF £31.05 TOTE £3.80: £1.20, £3.00, £5.10; EX 32.50 Trifecta £198.10.
**Owner** Middleham Park Racing LXXXIX **Bred** Mrs Fiona Denniff **Trained** Musley Bank, N Yorks


The Form Book Flat, Raceform Ltd, Newbury, RG14 5SJ

**FOCUS**
A steadily run contest and the horse that controlled the tempo was not for catching in the straight. It's hard to think the form is much better than rated.

## 5894 RENAULT ALL NEW KOLEOS MAIDEN STKS — 1m 4f 51y (Tp)
**3:20** (3:21) (Class 5) 3-Y-O+ — **£3,234** (£962; £481; £240) **Stalls** Low

Form — RPR

62 **1** **Abjar**$^{69}$ 3342 3-9-2 0 ........ RichardKingscote 7 — 83+
(Sir Michael Stoute) *mde all: pushed along over 2f out: qcknd clr over 1f out: pushed out ins fnl f: bit in hand* **6/4**$^{2}$

2 **2** 1 ¾ **Impact Point (JPN)**$^{125}$ 1624 3-9-2 0 ........ OisinMurphy 4 — 78
(Andrew Balding) *prom: rdn and outpcd in 2nd over 1f out: edgd rt ins fnl f: styd on same pce* **8/11**$^{1}$

**3** 5 **Nelson's Touch**$^{149}$ 4-9-12 0 ........ FranBerry 6 — 69
(Denis Coakley) *trckd ldrs: rdn over 2f out: one pce in 3rd fr over 1f out* **7/1**$^{3}$

5 **4** 7 **Hazamar (IRE)**$^{45}$ 1190 4-9-7 70 ........(t) BenRobinson$^{(5)}$ 8 — 58+
(Sophie Leech) *awkward s and v.s.a away: hld up in rr: stl lot to do 2f out: rdn and kpt on over 1f out: wnt 4th post* **25/1**

06 **5** nk **The Last Melon**$^{8}$ 5563 5-9-7 0 ........ RachealKneller$^{(5)}$ 1 — 58
(James Bennett) *trckd ldrs: rdn over 2f out: wknd over 1f out* **150/1**

**6** 5 **Bumble Bay**$^{23}$ 7-9-12 0 ........(t) LiamKeniry 9 — 50
(Robert Stephens) *s.i.s: hld up: nvr threatened* **33/1**

5 **7** 2 ¾ **Casemates Square (IRE)**$^{3}$ 5757 3-9-2 0 ........ StevieDonohoe 10 — 46
(Ian Williams) *a towards rr* **33/1**

**8** 14 **Sundance Boy**$^{232}$ 8-9-12 0 ........ RoystonFfrench 3 — 23
(Giuseppe Fierro) *s.i.s: sn midfield: rdn over 3f out: wknd* **100/1**

2m 38.9s (-1.90) **Going Correction** -0.075s/f (Stan)
**WFA** 3 from 4yo+ 10lb — 8 Ran SP% **121.8**
Speed ratings (Par 103): **103,101,98,93,93 90,88,79**
CSF £3.10 TOTE £2.20: £1.10, £1.02, £1.70; EX 3.10 Trifecta £6.30.
**Owner** Al Shaqab Racing **Bred** Newsells Park Stud **Trained** Newmarket, Suffolk

**FOCUS**
No real depth to this maiden and the two that dominated the market came clear. The runner-up has been rated to his debut figure.

## 5895 RENAULT ALL NEW KADJAR H'CAP — 1m 1f 104y (Tp)
**3:50** (3:51) (Class 6) (0-65,65) 3-Y-O+ — **£2,587** (£770; £384; £192) **Stalls** Low

Form — RPR

0324 **1** **Alnasl (IRE)**$^{8}$ 5565 3-9-0 62 ........(h) EdwardGreatrex$^{(3)}$ 5 — 70
(Archie Watson) *led after 1f: mde rest: rdn 2f out: kpt on* **6/1**$^{3}$

0026 **2** 1 ¾ **Chelwood Gate (IRE)**$^{19}$ 5183 7-10-0 65 ........(v) JosephineGordon 9 — 70
(Conor Dore) *midfield on inner: rdn and hdwy over 1f out: kpt on fnl f: wnt 2nd fnl 50yds* **25/1**

0001 **3** 1 ¼ **Cat Royale (IRE)**$^{25}$ 4982 4-10-0 65 ........(p) DannyBrock 1 — 67
(John Butler) *led for 1f: prom: rdn over 2f out: no ex ins fnl f and lost 2nd fnl 50yds* **8/1**

0346 **4** ½ **Critical Thinking (IRE)**$^{13}$ 5404 3-8-8 60 ........ FinleyMarsh$^{(7)}$ 7 — 61
(Kevin Frost) *midfield: rdn and hdwy over 1f out: kpt on same pce* **3/1**$^{1}$

465 **5** 2 ½ **Aqua Libre**$^{23}$ 5039 4-10-0 65 ........ DavidNolan 2 — 62
(Jennie Candlish) *slowly away: hld up: kpt on fr over 1f out: nvr threatened* **6/1**$^{3}$

4361 **6** 1 ¼ **Outlaw Torn (IRE)**$^{15}$ 5336 8-9-4 55 ........(e) DougieCostello 4 — 49
(Richard Guest) *trckd ldrs: rdn over 2f out: grad wknd over 1f out* **16/1**

6500 **7** 1 ¾ **Masonic (IRE)**$^{80}$ 2931 3-9-0 64 ........ CallumRodriguez$^{(5)}$ 12 — 55
(Robyn Brisland) *slowly away: hld up: nvr threatened* **9/2**$^{2}$

2000 **8** ½ **Cockney Boy**$^{16}$ 5284 4-9-1 52 ........ AlistairRawlinson 6 — 42
(Michael Appleby) *midfield: rdn along 4f out: wknd over 1f out* **20/1**

133 **9** 3 ¼ **Shambra (IRE)**$^{23}$ 5017 3-9-5 64 ........ TonyHamilton 3 — 48
(Roger Fell) *trckd ldrs: rdn over 2f out: wknd over 1f out* **8/1**

0-05 **10** hd **Enchanted Moment**$^{16}$ 5290 5-9-2 53 ........(b$^{1}$) FranBerry 11 — 36
(Olly Murphy) *slowly away: a towards rr* **10/1**

000/ **11** 72 **Gifted Heir (IRE)**$^{1093}$ 5338 13-8-5 46 oh1 ow1 ........ BenRobinson$^{(5)}$ 10
(Ray Peacock) *trckd ldrs on outer: rdn along 4f out: wknd qckly and sn bhd: eased* **200/1**

1m 58.72s (-2.08) **Going Correction** -0.075s/f (Stan)
**WFA** 3 from 4yo+ 8lb — 11 Ran SP% **118.1**
Speed ratings (Par 101): **106,104,103,102,100 99,98,97,94,94 30**
CSF £147.73 CT £1212.09 TOTE £6.60: £1.80, £3.90, £2.40; EX 119.30 Trifecta £613.10.
**Owner** K Sohi **Bred** Shadwell Estate Company Limited **Trained** Upper Lambourn, W Berks

**FOCUS**
Run of the mill class 6 handicap form but the pace looked fairly even and the winner is totally unexposed on artificial surfaces.

## 5896 DACIA LOGAN STEPWAY H'CAP — 2m 120y (Tp)
**4:20** (4:20) (Class 5) (0-75,76) 4-Y-O+ — **£3,234** (£962; £481; £240) **Stalls** Low

Form — RPR

6100 **1** **Whitecliff Park (IRE)**$^{17}$ 5267 4-8-7 64 ........(p) BenRobinson$^{(5)}$ 8 — 72+
(Brian Ellison) *s.i.s: hld up: rdn and gd hdwy on outer over 1f out: led 1f out: styd on wl to draw clr* **13/2**$^{3}$

046 **2** 4 ½ **Lady Makfi (IRE)**$^{17}$ 5251 5-9-7 73 ........ StevieDonohoe 5 — 76
(Johnny Farrelly) *midfield: hdwy over 1f out: rdn to chal strly appr fnl f: rdn and edgd lft ins fnl f: one pce and sn no ch wnr* **7/1**

4030 **3** 1 ¼ **Cavalieri (IRE)**$^{24}$ 5008 7-9-0 66 ........(tp) KevinStott 6 — 68
(Philip Kirby) *prom: rdn to ld narrowly over 1f out: hdd 1f out: one pce and hld in 3rd whn short of room fnl 75yds* **13/2**$^{3}$

2204 **4** 1 ¼ **See And Be Seen**$^{23}$ 5025 7-8-6 63 ........(p) MitchGodwin$^{(5)}$ 10 — 63
(Sylvester Kirk) *trckd ldrs: rdn 2f out: no ex ins fnl f* **10/1**

214 **5** ½ **Wordiness**$^{20}$ 5138 9-9-4 70 ........ DaneO'Neill 4 — 69
(David Evans) *midfield: briefly short of room 2f out: rdn over 1f out: one pce* **9/2**$^{2}$

-420 **6** 1 ½ **Ruler Of The Nile**$^{59}$ 3685 5-9-5 71 ........ LiamKeniry 1 — 69
(Robert Stephens) *trckd ldrs: rdn over 2f out: wknd ins fnl f* **7/1**

00/ **7** 1 ¼ **Chevalgris**$^{62}$ 7250 7-8-13 65 ........(p$^{1}$) MartinHarley 7 — 61
(Dai Burchell) *hld up: rdn over 2f out: nvr threatened* **16/1**

0-0 **8** 7 **Lady Emma**$^{120}$ 1754 4-8-2 54 oh2 ........ RoystonFfrench 3 — 42
(Steph Hollinshead) *led: rdn 3f out: hdd over 1f out: wknd* **80/1**

3110 **9** 4 **Mr Globetrotter (USA)**$^{36}$ 3830 4-9-5 76 ........ CallumRodriguez$^{(5)}$ 9 — 59
(Iain Jardine) *trckd ldrs on outer: rdn along 4f out: sn outpcd and btn* **11/4**$^{1}$

604/ **10** ¾ **The Absent Mare**$^{10}$ 3579 9-7-13 54 oh5 ........(t) AaronJones$^{(3)}$ 2 — 36
(Sarah-Jayne Davies) *a towards rr* **80/1**

3m 41.39s (-2.31) **Going Correction** -0.075s/f (Stan) — 10 Ran SP% **114.0**
Speed ratings (Par 103): **102,99,99,98,98 97,97,93,92,91**
CSF £50.21 CT £305.50 TOTE £9.10: £2.70, £2.30, £2.80; EX 67.30 Trifecta £589.90.
**Owner** D Gilbert, M Lawrence, A Bruce **Bred** Rosetown Bloodstock Ltd **Trained** Norton, N Yorks

**FOCUS**
A wide open staying handicap on paper but it threw up a most impressive winner. The runner-up has been rated to this year's form.

## 5897 NEW RENAULT CAPTUR H'CAP (DIV I) — 1m 142y (Tp)
**4:50** (4:51) (Class 6) (0-60,62) 3-Y-O+ — **£2,587** (£770; £384; £192) **Stalls** Low

Form — RPR

0010 **1** **Beadlam (IRE)**$^{19}$ 5185 4-10-0 62 ........(p) TonyHamilton 3 — 67
(Roger Fell) *prom: rdn 2f out: led jst ins fnl f: edgd rt: kpt on* **13/2**$^{3}$

0560 **2** 1 ¼ **Pivotal Dream (IRE)**$^{25}$ 4982 4-8-12 46 oh1 ........ FranBerry 2 — 48
(Mark Brisbourne) *trckd ldrs: rdn over 2f out: kpt on: wnt 2nd post* **20/1**

6-04 **3** nse **Prince Jai**$^{11}$ 5482 4-9-4 52 ........(b$^{1}$) StevieDonohoe 1 — 54
(Ian Williams) *led: rdn 2f out: hdd jst ins fnl f: one pce: lost 2nd post* **14/1**

5000 **4** ¾ **Sir Lancelott**$^{132}$ 1484 5-9-6 59 ........(p) BenRobinson$^{(5)}$ 6 — 60
(Adrian Nicholls) *trckd ldrs: racd quite keenly: rdn 2f out: kpt on same pce* **5/1**$^{2}$

6300 **5** hd **False Id**$^{18}$ 5214 4-9-4 59 ........(t) FinleyMarsh$^{(7)}$ 10 — 59+
(Marjorie Fife) *hld up: pushed along and hdwy over 1f out: r.o ins fnl f: nrst fin* **4/1**$^{1}$

0000 **6** 1 **Molten Lava (IRE)**$^{31}$ 4727 5-8-12 53 ........(p) PatrickVaughan$^{(7)}$ 8 — 51
(Christian Williams) *racd keenly in midfield: rdn 2f out: one pce* **4/1**$^{1}$

6003 **7** ½ **Born To Reason (IRE)**$^{43}$ 4262 3-9-0 56 ........(h) DougieCostello 11 — 53
(Kevin Frost) *slowly away: hld up in rr: pushed along and hdwy over 1f out: rdn and one pce ins fnl f* **10/1**

6600 **8** 2 ¼ **Raashdy (IRE)**$^{57}$ 3761 4-9-4 55 ........ CallumShepherd$^{(3)}$ 7 — 47
(Peter Hiatt) *trckd ldrs towards outer: rdn over 2f out: wknd over 1f out* **12/1**

5035 **9** 2 ¾ **Binky Blue (IRE)**$^{38}$ 4459 5-9-10 58 ........(h) LiamKeniry 5 — 45
(Daniel Mark Loughnane) *dwlt: sn midfield on inner racing keenly: rdn over 2f out: wknd appr fnl f* **16/1**

3600 **10** 4 ½ **Royal Icon**$^{18}$ 5206 3-9-4 60 ........(p) KevinStott 4 — 37+
(Kevin Ryan) *in tch towards outer: rdn over 2f out: wknd over 1f out* **8/1**

0600 **11** 1 ¾ **Tawfeer**$^{25}$ 4982 3-8-8 50 ........ RoystonFfrench 9 — 24
(James Unett) *hld up on outer: rdn over 3f out: sn wknd* **66/1**

1m 51.21s (1.11) **Going Correction** -0.075s/f (Stan)
**WFA** 3 from 4yo+ 8lb — 11 Ran SP% **116.7**
Speed ratings (Par 101): **92,90,90,90,90 89,88,86,84,80 78**
CSF £126.73 CT £1185.26 TOTE £7.60: £2.30, £4.70, £3.60; EX 118.80 Trifecta £1740.30.
**Owner** Smarty Socks Racing **Bred** Pipe View Stud **Trained** Nawton, N Yorks

**FOCUS**
This looked to be run at a fairly even gallop but the pace held up and it proved difficult for anything to make an impact from off the pace.

## 5898 NEW RENAULT CAPTUR H'CAP (DIV II) — 1m 142y (Tp)
**5:25** (5:25) (Class 6) (0-60,66) 3-Y-O+ — **£2,587** (£770; £384; £192) **Stalls** Low

Form — RPR

6521 **1** **Mutineer**$^{2}$ 5793 3-9-7 66 6ex ........ EdwardGreatrex$^{(3)}$ 9 — 76+
(Daniel Kubler) *trckd ldrs: rdn to chse ldr 2f out: led 1f out: wandered but r.o wl to draw clr* **8/11**$^{1}$

03 **2** 5 **Top Offer**$^{39}$ 4453 8-9-10 58 ........(v) FranBerry 8 — 58
(Patrick Morris) *hld up: rdn over 2f out: styd on fr over 1f out: wnt 2nd 110yds out: no ch w wnr* **11/1**

4055 **3** 2 ½ **Rocket Ronnie (IRE)**$^{25}$ 4968 7-8-12 46 oh1 ........ StevieDonohoe 2 — 40
(Brian Barr) *slowly away: hld up in rr: swtchd to outer and hdwy over 1f out: kpt on to go 3rd fnl 75yds* **20/1**

2150 **4** 2 **Lord Murphy (IRE)**$^{46}$ 4165 4-9-12 60 ........ LiamKeniry 7 — 50
(Daniel Mark Loughnane) *midfield: rdn over 2f out: kpt on same pce* **8/1**$^{3}$

4004 **5** 1 ¾ **Russian Ranger (IRE)**$^{16}$ 5296 4-9-6 59 ........(b) MitchGodwin$^{(5)}$ 10 — 45
(Jonathan Portman) *prom: rdn to ld over 2f out: hdd 1f out: wknd* **12/1**

2304 **6** hd **The Dukkerer (IRE)**$^{19}$ 5181 6-9-7 58 ........ LewisEdmunds$^{(3)}$ 6 — 44
(James Given) *hld up: pushed along over 3f out: one pce and nvr threatened* **11/2**$^{2}$

6103 **7** 2 ¼ **Vivre La Reve**$^{104}$ 2166 5-9-7 55 ........(h) RoystonFfrench 4 — 36
(James Unett) *midfield: rdn over 2f out: wknd over 1f out* **25/1**

040 **8** 3 ¾ **Damo**$^{189}$ 545 3-9-1 57 ........ TonyHamilton 3 — 30
(Simon Dow) *trckd ldrs: racd keenly: rdn over 2f out: wknd over 1f out* **20/1**

000 **9** 1 ½ **Careyanne**$^{41}$ 4332 3-8-6 48 ........(p$^{1}$) PaddyAspell 5 — 18
(Brian Baugh) *led: rdn whn hdd over 2f out: wknd* **20/1**

1m 48.54s (-1.56) **Going Correction** -0.075s/f (Stan)
**WFA** 3 from 4yo+ 8lb — 9 Ran SP% **118.6**
Speed ratings (Par 101): **103,98,96,94,93 92,90,87,86**
CSF £9.45 CT £98.88 TOTE £2.10: £1.10, £2.70, £4.60; EX 10.80 Trifecta £102.50.
**Owner** Ontoawinner & Capture The Moment IV **Bred** Stourbank Stud **Trained** Lambourn, Berks

**FOCUS**
This looked all about Wednesday's Kempton winner Mutineer and he justified strong market support to run out a wide margin winner under a 6lb penalty.
T/Jkpt: £22,477.40 to a £1 stake. Pool: £494,503.25 - 22.00 winning units. T/Plt: £93.50 to a £1 stake. Pool: £75,094.04 - 586.10 winning units. T/Qpdt: £33.90 to a £1 stake. Pool: £5,636.69 - 122.75 winning units. **Andrew Sheret**

5899 - 5906a (Foreign Racing) - See Raceform Interactive

# 5731 CLAIREFONTAINE (R-H)
### Friday, August 11

**OFFICIAL GOING: Turf: soft**

## 5907a PRIX DES GARDENIAS (CLAIMER) (2YO) (YOUNG JOCKEYS & APPRENTICES) (TURF) — 7f
**12:40** 2-Y-O — **£9,829** (£3,931; £2,948; £1,965; £982)

RPR

**1** **Controversial Lady (IRE)**$^{8}$ 5585 2-8-6 0 ........ MathieuPelletan$^{(5)}$ 9 — 69
(J S Moore) *broke wl: sn settled bhd ldng trio on outer: drvn in 5th and chsd ldrs towards stands' rail 2f out: rdn and sustained chal wl over 1f out: led 110yds out: styd on wl* **6/1**

**2** 1 **Namar (IRE)**$^{26}$ 2-8-6 0 ........ KyllanBarbaud$^{(5)}$ 6 — 66
(C Laffon-Parias, France) **92/10**

**3** 2 ½ **Freddo Du Desert (FR)**$^{41}$ 4389 2-8-6 0 ........(p) ErwannLebreton$^{(5)}$ 11 — 59
(Louis Baudron, France) **118/10**

**4** nk **Vida Loca (FR)**$^{8}$ 5585 2-7-12 0 ........ MlleMickaelleMichel$^{(10)}$ 3 — 55
(M Boutin, France) **30/1**

**5** hd **You Make Me Smile (FR)**$^{66}$ 3444 2-7-12 0 ........ MlleLauraGrosso$^{(10)}$ 5 — 55
(N Clement, France) **19/1**

**6** snk **Please Be True (IRE)** 2-8-8 0 ........(b) ClementLecoeuvre$^{(3)}$ 1 — 57
(Matthieu Palussiere, France) **13/5**$^{1}$

7 *hd* **Shesgotthelot**[7] 5629 2-8-8 0................................ GabrielLeDevehat(3) 2 57
(J S Moore) *racd keenly: hld up bhd ldng between horses: drvn in 2nd and racd alone towards centre of trck 2f out: sltly outpcd and rdn wl over 1f out: kpt on at one pce fnl f* **11/2**[3]
8 *nse* **Jasmine A La Plage (FR)**[60] 3679 2-8-6 0 ow1. NicolasBarzalona(3) 10 55
(Matthieu Palussiere, France) **154/10**
9 *snk* **Valhala (FR)** 2-8-4 0................................ ClementGuitraud(7) 7 56
(Y Barberot, France) **17/5**[2]
10 *6* **Altavilla (IRE)**[18] 5232 2-8-4 0................................ JeromeMoutard(4) 4 37
(F Chappet, France) **149/10**
1m 25.6s **10** Ran SP% **118.4**
PARI-MUTUEL (all including 1 euro stake): WIN 7.00; PLACE 2.30, 3.40, 3.50; DF 29.10; SF 49.30.
**Owner** Mrs Wendy Jarrett & J S Moore **Bred** Edgeridge Ltd **Trained** Upper Lambourn, Berks

5908a (Foreign Racing) - See Raceform Interactive

## 5909a PRIX DES LOBELIAS (CLAIMER) (3YO COLTS & GELDINGS) (TURF) 1m
**3:10** 3-Y-O **£9,829** (£3,931; £2,948; £1,965; £982)

RPR
1 *hd* **Vieux Moulin (FR)**[25] 3-9-4 0................................(p) ChristopheSoumillon 3 70
(F Chappet, France) *fin 2nd: awrdd the r* **13/2**[3]
2 **Alliance Secrete (FR)**[10] 5521 3-8-9 0................(p) JeromeMoutard(6) 1 67
(T Castanheira, France) *fin 1st disqualified and plcd 2nd* **124/10**
3 *1 1/4* **Frosty Bay (FR)**[15] 3-8-10 0................................ KyllanBarbaud(8) 8 67
(N Caullery, France) **144/10**
4 *hd* **A Head Ahead (GER)**[26] 3-8-10 0................(b) AlexisPouchin(8) 11 67
(Y Gourraud, France) **33/1**
5 *1 1/2* **Power Becqua (FR)**[49] 3-8-6 0................................ GabrielBon(5) 2 56
(T Lemer, France) **66/10**
6 *shd* **Hold Me Tight (IRE)**[10] 5523 3-8-8 0................ ClementLecoeuvre(3) 6 56
(J S Moore) *w.w towards rr: drvn 2f out whn nt clr run: stuck bhd horses tl in clr and styd on last 75yds* **65/1**
7 *nse* **Gran Pierino (ITY)**[39] 3-9-4 0................ Pierre-CharlesBoudot 10 63
(Antonio Marcialis, Italy) **39/10**[2]
8 *2* **Tresor (IRE)**[41] 3-9-2 0................................ CristianDemuro 5 56
(Y Barberot, France) **13/2**[3]
9 *snk* **Spirit De Cerisy (FR)**[10] 5521 3-9-4 0................ AntoineHamelin 12 58
(Matthieu Palussiere, France) **248/10**
10 *snk* **Tap Tap Boom**[28] 3-9-10 0................................ TheoBachelot 4 64
(Mme P Butel, France) **27/10**[1]
11 *1 3/4* **Zaryio (FR)**[25] 3-8-11 0................................ MickaelBarzalona 9 47
(H-A Pantall, France) **112/10**
1m 37.3s **11** Ran SP% **117.7**
PARI-MUTUEL (all including 1 euro stake): WIN 7.50; PLACE 2.80, 3.60, 3.90; DF 55.80; SF 92.00.
**Owner** A Gilibert & B Van Dalfsen **Bred** B Van Dalfsen **Trained** France

## 5910a PRIX DES COLCHIQUES (CLAIMER) (3YO FILLIES) (TURF) 1m
**3:40** 3-Y-O **£9,829** (£3,931; £2,948; £1,965; £982)

RPR
1 **Dora Bruder (FR)** 3-8-11 0................................ HugoJourniac 3 67
(J-C Rouget, France) **51/10**
2 *1 1/2* **Ettu**[17] 5268 3-8-11 0................................(b) TheoBachelot 8 63
(S Wattel, France) **14/5**[1]
3 *shd* **La Fibrossi (FR)**[28] 3-9-5 0................ Pierre-CharlesBoudot 6 71
(H-A Pantall, France) **3/1**[2]
4 *1 1/2* **World Power (IRE)**[10] 5521 3-9-4 0................ StephanePasquier 2 67
(F Vermeulen, France) **73/10**
5 *3/4* **Esloobaha (IRE)**[66] 3-8-4 0................................ KyllanBarbaud(7) 5 58
(N Caullery, France) **68/1**
6 *hd* **Pacofilha**[85] 2754 3-9-1 0................................ ChristopheSoumillon 1 62
(Paul Cole) *hld up towards rr: clsd to dispute 4th on inner over 2f out: rdn to chse ldrs under 1 1/2f out: one pce fnl f* **7/2**[3]
7 *1 3/4* **Undiscovered Angel (FR)**[17] 5268 3-9-1 0................ TonyPiccone 4 58
(K R Burke) *chsd ldr on inner: cl 3rd and drvn 1 1/2f out: grad dropped away fnl f* **99/10**
8 *3 1/2* **Gog Elles (IRE)**[176] 766 3-8-11 0................................ FrankPanicucci 9 45
(J S Moore) *sn pressing ldr on outer: drvn over 2f out but no imp: lost pl 1 1/2f out: wl hld fnl f* **37/1**
9 *7* **Bellabel (FR)**[286] 3-8-8 0................................ ClementLecoeuvre(3) 7 29
(Stephane Chevalier, France) **29/1**
1m 37.3s **9** Ran SP% **118.6**
PARI-MUTUEL (all including 1 euro stake): WIN 6.10; PLACE 1.70, 1.60, 1.40; DF 11.20; SF 21.70.
**Owner** B Weill & D-Y Treves **Bred** M Daguzan-Garros **Trained** Pau, France

# 5391 ASCOT (R-H)
## Saturday, August 12

**OFFICIAL GOING: Good to soft (soft in places; str 6.9, rnd 6.4)**
Wind: Moderate, across Weather: Fine but cloudy

## 5911 DUBAI DUTY FREE SHERGAR CUP DASH (H'CAP) 5f
**1:05** (1:10) (Class 2) (0-105,105) 3-Y-O+
**£22,131** (£7,749; £3,541; £2,763; £2,434; £1,773) **Stalls** High

Form RPR
1260 1 **Stake Acclaim (IRE)**[7] 5640 5-9-6 **97**................................ JamieSpencer 12 106
(Dean Ivory) *hld up and last main gp: swtchd to outer and gd prog jst over 1f out: shkn up and r.o wl to ld last strides* **4/1**[1]
-160 2 *nk* **Sir Robert Cheval**[63] 3614 6-9-6 **100**................................ HollieDoyle(3) 6 108
(Robert Cowell) *hld up in rr: prog on outer over 2f out: rdn to ld over 1f out: styd on but hdd last strides* **10/1**
-224 3 *1* **Lexington Abbey**[28] 4881 6-9-6 **97**................................(b) KerrinMcEvoy 2 101
(Kevin Ryan) *chsd ldrs on outer: on terms over 1f out: styd on same pce fnl f* **4/1**[1]
1133 4 *1 1/2* **Pipers Note**[28] 4881 7-9-10 **101**................................ NeilCallan 3 100
(Ruth Carr) *sltly awkward s: sn chsd ldr: upsides wl over 1f out: chsd new ldr briefly after: one pce fnl f* **11/2**[2]
0060 5 *1 1/2* **Willytheconqueror (IRE)**[22] 5116 4-9-10 **101**.......... AlexanderPietsch 5 95
(William Muir) *n.m.r s: chsd ldrs: hrd rdn wl over 1f out: no imp but plugged on* **9/1**

000 6 *1/2* **Doc Sportello (IRE)**[43] 4306 5-9-9 **100**................................ AdriedeVries 1 92
(Tony Carroll) *heavily restrained s then swtchd sharply to r against nr side rail: wl detached in last: stl detached 1f out: r.o fnl 150yds: no ch of making an impact* **33/1**
1-03 7 *1/2* **Green Door (IRE)**[11] 5505 6-9-7 **98**................................(v) UmbertoRispoli 4 88
(Robert Cowell) *racd freely: led to over 1f out: wknd* **7/1**[3]
/604 8 *1 1/4* **Tropics (USA)**[22] 5116 9-9-9 **100**................................ Emma-JayneWilson 10 85
(Dean Ivory) *chsd ldrs: rdn over 1f out: sn wknd* **14/1**
0-52 9 *nk* **Mirza**[35] 4635 10-10-0 **105**................................(p) FranBerry 7 89
(Rae Guest) *chsd ldrs: rdn and wknd over 1f out* **11/2**[2]
-100 10 *hd* **Blaine**[41] 4411 7-9-6 **97**................................(b) KeitaTosaki 8 81
(Brian Barr) *wnt rt s: chsd ldrs: rdn 2f out: wknd fnl f* **20/1**
1m 1.29s (0.79) **Going Correction** +0.40s/f (Good) **10** Ran SP% **116.7**
Speed ratings (Par 109): **109,108,106,104,102 101,100,98,98,97**
CSF £45.20 CT £174.59 TOTE £5.20: £1.90, £3.80, £1.70; EX 50.50 Trifecta £362.60.
**Owner** M J Yarrow **Bred** G Devlin **Trained** Radlett, Herts
■ Stewards' Enquiry : Hollie Doyle two-day ban: excessive use of whip (Aug 26-27)

**FOCUS**
The running rail on the round course was positioned approximately 4yds out from its innermost position from the 1m4f start increasing to 9yds out at the bend entering the home straight. The rail then finished in a cutaway in the home straight. There was 0.5mm rain overnight to 6.30am Saturday. A competitive sprint handicap to start, and towards the middle of the track proved the place to be. The third has been rated to his C&D latest.

## 5912 DUBAI DUTY FREE SHERGAR CUP STAYERS (H'CAP) 1m 7f 209y
**1:40** (1:41) (Class 2) (0-100,97) 4-Y-O+
**£22,131** (£7,749; £3,541; £2,763; £2,434; £1,773) **Stalls** Low

Form RPR
3010 1 **Euchen Glen**[35] 4614 4-9-6 **89**................................ AdriedeVries 12 95+
(Jim Goldie) *hld up in last: gd prog and clr run on inner over 2f out: rdn to ld over 1f out: hrd pressed fnl f: kpt on wl* **7/1**
4022 2 *nk* **Byron Flyer**[28] 4921 6-9-9 **92**................................ AlexanderPietsch 3 97
(Ian Williams) *trckd ldng pair to 6f out: styd cl up: rdn to ld 2f out to over 1f out: kpt on fnl f: a jst hld* **7/1**
1242 3 *3/4* **Graceland (FR)**[42] 4355 5-9-8 **91**................................ KeitaTosaki 4 95
(Michael Bell) *t.k.h: hld up in midfield: prog 2f out: rdn to chal jst over 1f out: no ex last 100yds* **9/2**[2]
6222 4 *nk* **Fleeting Visit**[21] 5164 4-9-1 **84**................................(p) Emma-JayneWilson 8 88
(Eve Johnson Houghton) *wl in tch: effrt 2f out: rdn and ch jst over 1f out: one pce ins fnl f* **6/1**
0522 5 *nk* **Angel Gabrial (IRE)**[14] 5438 8-9-2 **85**................................ UmbertoRispoli 10 88
(Richard Fahey) *hld up in rr: prog on wd outside jst over 2f out: rdn and ch jst over 1f out: kpt on same pce* **8/1**
0606 6 *3 1/2* **Gavlar**[15] 5351 6-9-7 **90**................................(v) KerrinMcEvoy 7 89
(William Knight) *hld up in rr: rdn and no prog over 2f out: no ch after: kpt on ins fnl f* **20/1**
0-05 7 *shd* **Wolfcatcher (IRE)**[15] 5351 5-9-3 **86**................................(tp) HayleyTurner 5 85
(Ian Williams) *t.k.h: prom: trckd ldng pair 6f out tl rdn and lost pl jst over 2f out: steadily fdd* **12/1**
000 8 *shd* **Cosmelli (ITY)**[15] 5351 4-10-0 **97**................................(v[1]) AnthonyDelpech 11 96
(Gay Kelleway) *hld up towards rr: rdn and no prog over 2f out: no ch over 1f out* **33/1**
3301 9 *1/2* **Swashbuckle**[45] 4222 4-9-8 **91**................................ NeilCallan 9 89
(Andrew Balding) *trckd ldr to over 2f out: sn btn* **4/1**[1]
2211 10 *1/2* **Berrahri (IRE)**[14] 5403 6-9-2 **85**................................ JamieSpencer 6 83
(John Best) *led to 2f out: sn wknd* **11/2**[3]
3m 37.0s (8.00) **Going Correction** +0.55s/f (Yiel) **10** Ran SP% **119.4**
Speed ratings (Par 109): **102,101,101,101,101 99,99,99,99,98**
CSF £56.68 CT £248.89 TOTE £8.40: £2.60, £2.60, £1.60; EX 58.80 Trifecta £391.50.
**Owner** W M Johnstone **Bred** W M Johnstone **Trained** Uplawmoor, E Renfrews

**FOCUS**
Add 19yds. A well-contested staying handicap. The runner-up has been rated to form.

## 5913 DUBAI DUTY FREE SHERGAR CUP CHALLENGE (H'CAP) 1m 3f 211y
**2:15** (2:18) (Class 3) (0-95,95) 4-Y-O+
**£22,131** (£7,749; £3,541; £2,763; £2,434; £1,773) **Stalls** Low

Form RPR
0356 1 **Great Hall**[14] 5421 7-9-10 **92**................................ FranBerry 4 100
(Mick Quinn) *trckd ldrs in 6th: prog over 2f out: rdn to ld jst over 1f out: styd on wl* **12/1**
4301 2 *1 1/4* **Gawdawpalin (IRE)**[15] 5353 4-9-9 **91**................................ JamieSpencer 11 97
(Sylvester Kirk) *dropped in fr wd draw and hld up in 8th: rdn and prog jst over 2f out: styd on fnl f to take 2nd last strides* **2/1**[1]
3046 3 *hd* **Oasis Fantasy (IRE)**[11] 5500 6-9-10 **92**................................(p) AdriedeVries 9 97
(David Simcock) *trckd ldr: rdn to ld narrowly 2f out: hdd jst over 1f out: kpt on but lost 2nd last strides* **8/1**
3-52 4 *hd* **Niblawi (IRE)**[14] 5397 5-9-11 **93**................................ Emma-JayneWilson 12 98
(Neil Mulholland) *dropped in fr wd draw and hld up in 9th: rdn and prog 2f out: clsd on ldrs 1f out: styd on same pce ins fnl f* **7/2**[2]
2011 5 *hd* **Mukhayyam**[21] 5164 5-9-12 **94**................................(p) HayleyTurner 3 98
(Tim Easterby) *led: rdn and hdd 2f out: styd w ldr and stl upsides jst over 1f out: one pce ins fnl f* **7/1**[3]
2210 6 *1 3/4* **Kapstadt (FR)**[21] 4614 7-9-8 **93**................................ HollieDoyle(3) 7 94
(Ian Williams) *hld up in 7th: rdn over 2f out: kpt on fr over 1f out but nvr pce to threaten ldrs* **8/1**
1002 7 *2 3/4* **Petite Jack**[24] 5037 4-9-12 **94**................................(p[1]) AnthonyDelpech 1 91
(Archie Watson) *trckd ldng pair to 2f out: sn wknd* **16/1**
-200 8 *1/2* **Manjaam (IRE)**[50] 4033 4-9-13 **95**................................(p[1]) KerrinMcEvoy 5 91
(Ed Dunlop) *trckd ldrs to over 2f out: sn rdn and wknd* **12/1**
310- 9 *nk* **Kaatskill Nap (FR)**[309] 7117 4-9-10 **92**................ AlexanderPietsch 10 88
(Venetia Williams) *chsd ldrs: rdn over 2f out: steadily wknd* **40/1**
320 10 *6* **Jacob Cats**[42] 4370 8-9-11 **93**................................(v) KeitaTosaki 6 79
(William Knight) *s.s: a last: shkn up and no prog over 2f out: bhd after* **25/1**
2m 37.18s (4.68) **Going Correction** +0.55s/f (Yiel) **10** Ran SP% **117.8**
Speed ratings (Par 107): **106,105,105,104,104 103,101,101,101,97**
CSF £36.69 CT £213.70 TOTE £15.60: £3.70, £1.40, £2.20; EX 46.80 Trifecta £384.00.
**Owner** M Quinn **Bred** Aston House Stud **Trained** Newmarket, Suffolk

**FOCUS**
Add 16yds. Competitive stuff again. The fourth and fifth have been rated close to form.

## 5914 DUBAI DUTY FREE SHERGAR CUP MILE (H'CAP) 7f 213y(R)
**2:50** (2:55) (Class 2) (0-100,100) 4-Y-0+
**£22,131** (£7,749; £3,541; £2,763; £2,434; £1,773) **Stalls** Low

Form RPR

-P06 **1** **Raising Sand**$^{21}$ 5157 5-9-3 **92** AlexanderPietsch 12 102
(Jamie Osborne) *trapped out wd in midfield: smooth prog 2f out to ld over 1f out: shkn up and wl in command fnl f* **10/1**

1030 **2** 2 **Nicholas T**$^{14}$ 5393 5-9-2 **91** KerrinMcEvoy 10 96
(Jim Goldie) *hld up in midfield: clsd on ldrs fr 2f out: rdn to chse wnr fnl f: kpt on but no imp* **6/1$^{3}$**

65-0 **3** ½ **Leader Writer (FR)**$^{18}$ 5241 5-9-3 **92** (p$^{1}$) NeilCallan 8 96
(Henry Spiller) *t.k.h: trckd ldng trio: rdn whn n.m.r 2f out and lost pl: rallied fnl f: drvn to take 3rd last stride* **20/1**

5220 **4** nse **Brigliadoro (IRE)**$^{29}$ 4854 6-9-4 **93** AnthonyDelpech 4 97
(Philip McBride) *hld up in midfield: clsd on ldrs fr 2f out: tried to chal jst over 1f out: one pce after* **9/2$^{1}$**

0041 **5** shd **Breakable**$^{6}$ 5683 6-9-5 **94** 3ex UmbertoRispoli 1 98
(Tim Easterby) *chsd ldng pair: rdn and nt qckn over 1f out: one pce after* **5/1$^{2}$**

4100 **6** 1 ½ **Examiner (IRE)**$^{11}$ 5517 6-9-6 **95** (t) HayleyTurner 5 95
(Stuart Williams) *hld up in last trio: swtchd to inner and rdn 2f out: one pce after and no imp on ldrs* **10/1**

4-30 **7** 4 ½ **Knight Owl**$^{21}$ 5157 7-9-3 **92** FranBerry 9 82
(James Fanshawe) *hld up in last trio: rdn on outer over 2f out: no great prog* **6/1$^{3}$**

0-20 **8** 1 ¾ **Early Morning (IRE)**$^{52}$ 3963 6-9-8 **100** HollieDoyle$^{(3)}$ 11 86
(Harry Dunlop) *trckd ldr: led over 2f out to over 1f out: wknd qckly fnl f* **13/2**

2160 **9** 9 **Medburn Dream**$^{10}$ 5530 4-9-2 **91** Emma-JayneWilson 6 56
(Paul Henderson) *led to over 2f out: sn wknd* **16/1**

6646 **10** 4 **Basil Berry**$^{24}$ 5037 6-9-3 **92** (b) JamieSpencer 7 48
(Chris Dwyer) *hld up in last: shkn up and no prog over 2f out* **15/2**

1m 43.11s (2.41) **Going Correction** +0.55s/f (Yiel) **10 Ran SP% 117.3**
Speed ratings (Par 109): **109,107,106,106,106 104,100,98,89,85**
CSF £69.31 CT £1188.22 TOTE £10.10: £3.10, £2.00, £5.30; EX 67.10 Trifecta £997.00.
**Owner** Nick Bradley Racing 22 & Partner **Bred** Meon Valley Stud **Trained** Upper Lambourn, Berks

**FOCUS**
Add 11yds. Not many unexposed runners in this. The runner-up and fourth have been rated close to form.

## 5915 DUBAI DUTY FREE SHERGAR CUP CLASSIC (H'CAP) 1m 3f 211y
**3:25** (3:26) (Class 3) (0-95,95) 3-Y-O
**£22,131** (£7,749; £3,541; £2,763; £2,434; £1,773) **Stalls** Low

Form RPR

2112 **1** **Glenys The Menace (FR)**$^{2}$ 5841 3-9-1 **82** AnthonyDelpech 8 89
(John Best) *hld up in midfield: shkn up and prog on outer fr 2f out: clsd on ldrs fnl f: rdn to ld last 50yds* **8/1**

111 **2** ½ **Contango (IRE)**$^{21}$ 5160 3-9-11 **92** KerrinMcEvoy 10 98
(Andrew Balding) *trckd ldr: led over 2f out: sn hrd pressed: kpt on wl but hdd last 50yds* **2/1$^{1}$**

3000 **3** nk **Bear Valley (IRE)**$^{8}$ 5598 3-9-7 **88** FranBerry 5 93
(Mark Johnston) *hld up in midfield: prog on outer to trck ldng pair 4f out: rdn to chal jst over 2f out: sustained battle w ldr after but nt qckn and a jst hld: lost 2nd last 50yds* **9/1**

1351 **4** 2 ¼ **Rake's Progress**$^{16}$ 5323 3-9-0 **81** NeilCallan 4 83
(Heather Main) *t.k.h: trckd ldrs: hrd rdn fr 2f out: kpt on one pce after* **7/1$^{2}$**

-261 **5** 2 ¼ **Appointed**$^{14}$ 5439 3-9-11 **92** AlexanderPietsch 9 90
(Tim Easterby) *trckd ldng pair to 4f out: rdn over 2f out: steadily outpcd fr over 1f out* **10/1**

2121 **6** shd **Kasperenko**$^{30}$ 4796 3-10-0 **95** (b) AdriedeVries 6 93
(David Lanigan) *awkward s: hld up in 9th: rdn and no prog over 2f out: plugged on one pce after and no threat* **15/2$^{3}$**

1610 **7** 2 **Mister Blue Sky (IRE)**$^{28}$ 4886 3-8-9 **79** HollieDoyle$^{(3)}$ 3 74
(Sylvester Kirk) *hld up in detached last: tried to make prog on inner over 2f out but only limited hdwy: nvr in it* **16/1**

2135 **8** 2 ¼ **Hold Sway (IRE)**$^{9}$ 5568 3-9-6 **87** (b$^{1}$) HayleyTurner 2 78
(Charlie Appleby) *hld up in midfield: rdn and no prog over 2f out: sn wl btn* **7/1$^{2}$**

3352 **9** ½ **Italian Heiress**$^{10}$ 5533 3-9-0 **81** KeitaTosaki 1 71
(Clive Cox) *hld up in midfield: rdn and no prog over 2f out: fdd over 1f out* **20/1**

4100 **10** 13 **Reachforthestars (IRE)**$^{15}$ 5381 3-9-10 **91** UmbertoRispoli 11 60
(David O'Meara) *led to over 2f out: sn wknd and eased: t.o* **16/1**

2m 36.76s (4.26) **Going Correction** +0.55s/f (Yiel) **10 Ran SP% 116.8**
Speed ratings (Par 104): **107,106,106,104,103 103,102,100,100,91**
CSF £24.37 CT £151.30 TOTE £9.10: £2.70, £1.30, £2.70; EX 29.90 Trifecta £238.30.
**Owner** Curtis, Malt & Jenkins **Bred** Haras D'Etreham & Mr Georges Lugon **Trained** Oad Street, Kent

**FOCUS**
Add 16yds. A good 3yo handicap. The third helps set the standard.

## 5916 DUBAI DUTY FREE SHERGAR CUP SPRINT (H'CAP) 6f
**4:00** (4:02) (Class 2) (0-100,98) 3-Y-O
**£22,131** (£7,749; £3,541; £2,763; £2,434; £1,773) **Stalls** High

Form RPR

1140 **1** **Golden Apollo**$^{14}$ 5423 3-9-11 **95** FranBerry 3 103
(Tim Easterby) *hld up in last pair: stl there over 1f out: gd prog after: r.o to ld last 75yds: won gng away* **4/1$^{2}$**

3211 **2** 1 **Lualiwa**$^{29}$ 4868 3-9-9 **93** AnthonyDelpech 11 98
(Kevin Ryan) *t.k.h: w ldrs: led 2f out: rdn and kpt on fnl f but hdd last 75yds* **9/2$^{3}$**

1000 **3** nk **Megan Lily (IRE)**$^{9}$ 5574 3-9-4 **88** JamieSpencer 6 92
(Richard Fahey) *stdd and awkward s: hld up in last pair: stl there over 1f out: sltly checked whn effrt sn after: gd prog fnl f: tk 3rd last 50yds: nrst fin* **14/1**

2-34 **4** ¾ **Nobly Born**$^{14}$ 5423 3-9-13 **97** AdriedeVries 4 99
(John Gosden) *prom: rdn 2f out: pressed ldr jst over 1f out: kpt on same pce and lost 2 pls last 75yds* **5/2$^{1}$**

063- **5** ¾ **Belle Meade (IRE)**$^{329}$ 6555 3-9-8 **92** KeitaTosaki 10 91
(Andrew Balding) *wl in tch: rdn 2f out: no prog whn squeezed out 1f out: kpt on one pce after* **14/1**

500- **6** hd **Repton (IRE)**$^{315}$ 6954 3-9-11 **98** HollieDoyle$^{(3)}$ 9 97
(Richard Hannon) *hld up in midfield: rdn 2f out: tried to cl on ldrs over 1f out: nt qckn and one pce after* **25/1**

1100 **7** 2 ¼ **Goodwood Crusader (IRE)**$^{7}$ 5637 3-9-9 **93** NeilCallan 5 84
(Richard Hughes) *hld up in last trio: sme prog 2f out: wknd fnl f* **9/1**

0000 **8** ½ **Private Matter**$^{14}$ 5423 3-9-10 **94** (h$^{1}$) HayleyTurner 8 84
(Richard Fahey) *pressed ldr: led 1/2-way to 2f out: wknd jst over 1f out* **8/1**

300- **9** ½ **Bohemian Flame (IRE)**$^{338}$ 6260 3-9-8 **92** UmbertoRispoli 7 80
(Andrew Balding) *hld up in midfield: weaving arnd looking for a gap over 1f out: fdd fnl f* **11/1**

1000 **10** ¾ **Smokey Lane (IRE)**$^{14}$ 5423 3-10-0 **98** Emma-JayneWilson 12 84
(Christian Williams) *t.k.h: led to 1/2-way: wknd 2f out* **20/1**

1m 15.99s (1.49) **Going Correction** +0.40s/f (Good) **10 Ran SP% 118.1**
Speed ratings (Par 106): **106,104,104,103,102 102,99,98,97,96**
CSF £22.76 CT £236.52 TOTE £4.70: £1.60, £1.90, £3.30; EX 25.50 Trifecta £361.00.
**Owner** David Scott & Partner **Bred** Cheveley Park Stud Ltd **Trained** Great Habton, N Yorks

**FOCUS**
A good 3yo sprint handicap. It's been rated around the third.
T/Plt: £260.50 to a £1 stake. Pool: £171,271.62 - 479.83 winning units T/Qpdt: £60.30 to a £1 stake. Pool: £10,799.03 - 132.38 winning units **Jonathan Neesom**

# 5465 AYR (L-H)
Saturday, August 12

**OFFICIAL GOING: Good (good to firm in places; 7.5)**
Wind: Breezy, half against Weather: Overcast

## 5917 QTS WOMEN IN ENGINEERING LADY RIDERS' H'CAP (FOR PROFESSIONAL AND AMATEUR LADY RIDERS) 1m
**5:50** (5:51) (Class 6) (0-65,65) 4-Y-0+ **£2,587** (£770; £384; £192) **Stalls** Low

Form RPR

3632 **1** **Remember Rocky**$^{19}$ 5206 8-10-1 **59** (b) MissCWalton 14 66
(Lucy Normile) *pressed ldr: led over 2f out: sn hrd pressed: hld on gamely fnl f* **11/2$^{2}$**

403/ **2** ½ **Looking Good**$^{21}$ 5169 5-10-6 **64** (t$^{1}$) RachaelBlackmore 8 70
(S Curling, Ire) *prom: effrt and angled rt over 1f out: chsd wnr ins fnl f: r.o* **6/1$^{3}$**

1511 **3** 2 ¼ **Haymarket**$^{18}$ 5254 8-10-7 **65** MrsCBartley 13 66
(R Mike Smith) *led to over 2f out: sn rdn along: rallied fnl f: kpt on: nt rch first two* **6/1$^{3}$**

6403 **4** 2 **Let Right Be Done**$^{1}$ 5880 5-9-1 **48** (b) LeanneFerguson$^{(3)}$ 11 44
(Linda Perratt) *t.k.h: trckd ldrs: disp ld wl over 1f out: sn rdn and edgd lft: no ex ins fnl f* **10/1**

6340 **5** nse **Stardrifter**$^{12}$ 5467 5-9-9 **53** (p$^{1}$) SammyJoBell 9 49+
(Linda Perratt) *hld up: shkn up and hdwy over 2f out: kpt on ins fnl f: nt pce to chal* **16/1**

3002 **6** ½ **Rebel State (IRE)**$^{10}$ 5544 4-9-9 **56** (p) MissACawley$^{(3)}$ 10 51
(Jedd O'Keeffe) *prom: hdwy on outside over 2f out: rdn over 1f out: kpt on fnl f: nvr able to chal* **5/1$^{1}$**

4310 **7** ½ **Dark Confidant (IRE)**$^{17}$ 5285 4-9-11 **58** MissEllaMcCain$^{(3)}$ 4 52
(Donald McCain) *hld up towards rr: pushed along and hdwy over 2f out: kpt on fnl f: no imp* **10/1**

0064 **8** 1 ¼ **Argaki (IRE)**$^{19}$ 5206 7-10-1 **62** CharlotteMcFarland$^{(3)}$ 2 53
(Keith Dalgleish) *hld up: pushed along over 2f out: sme hdwy on ins over 1f out: sn no imp* **8/1**

3234 **9** nk **Jessie Allan (IRE)**$^{12}$ 5466 6-9-1 **48** MissRHill$^{(3)}$ 1 38
(Jim Goldie) *bhd: struggling over 2f out: sme late hdwy: nvr on terms* **9/1**

55-0 **10** ¾ **Yair Hill (IRE)**$^{5}$ 5696 9-9-3 **47** (p) MissHelenCuthbert 3 35
(Thomas Cuthbert) *midfield: shkn up over 2f out: outpcd fr over 1f out* **40/1**

566 **11** 2 ¼ **Danny Mc D**$^{13}$ 5458 4-10-0 **58** (p$^{1}$) MissAWaugh 7 41
(Iain Jardine) *hld up: stdy hdwy 2f out: sn no imp* **28/1**

0-00 **12** 3 ¼ **Wolf Heart (IRE)**$^{34}$ 4660 9-8-13 **46** oh1 RhonaPindar$^{(3)}$ 12 22
(Lucy Normile) *dwlt: sn midfield on outside: struggling over 2f out: sn btn* **66/1**

0560 **13** 1 ¼ **Fire Diamond**$^{18}$ 5258 4-10-6 **64** (p) MissADeniel 6 37
(Tom Dascombe) *t.k.h: hld up: struggling 3f out: sn btn* **22/1**

0040 **14** 6 **Schottische**$^{17}$ 5296 7-9-6 **53** (p) MissJCooley$^{(3)}$ 5 12
(Alan Bailey) *bhd: struggling over 3f out: sn btn* **20/1**

1m 41.88s (-1.92) **Going Correction** -0.20s/f (Firm) **14 Ran SP% 122.3**
Speed ratings (Par 101): **101,100,98,96,96 95,95,93,93,92 90,87,86,80**
CSF £36.86 CT £215.66 TOTE £7.10: £2.40, £3.10, £2.60; EX 52.90 Trifecta £218.30.
**Owner** Byrne Racing **Bred** Cherry Park Stud **Trained** Duncrievie, Perth & Kinross

**FOCUS**
Add 12yds. A 46-65 handicap for lady riders featuring plenty of hard-to-win-with sorts and unlikely to be strong form. The pace looked strong but the first and third were both raced close to the pace in a race in which few featured. Straightforward form, with the winner rated to his best over the past 12 months.

## 5918 QTS MISS SCOTLAND EBF NOVICE STKS 7f 50y
**6:20** (6:22) (Class 5) 2-Y-O **£4,528** (£1,347; £673; £336) **Stalls** High

Form RPR

**1** **Salazar (IRE)** 2-9-2 0 KevinStott 1 70+
(Kevin Ryan) *trckd ldrs: rdn over 2f out: hdwy to ld over 1f out: kpt on strly fnl f* **9/1**

2203 **2** ½ **Weellan**$^{11}$ 5492 2-9-2 72 JasonHart 2 69
(John Quinn) *t.k.h early: led: rdn and hdd over 1f out: rallied and regained 2nd pl ins fnl f: kpt on: hld nr fin* **5/4$^{1}$**

**3** nk **I'm Improving (IRE)** 2-9-2 0 GrahamLee 5 68+
(Keith Dalgleish) *dwlt: t.k.h in rr: shkn up over 2f out: hdwy over 1f out: kpt on fnl f: bttr for r* **7/1**

13 **4** nk **French Flyer (IRE)**$^{26}$ 4956 2-9-6 0 PaulMulrennan 3 72
(Michael Dods) *pressed ldr: rdn and led briefly over 1f out: kpt on same pce ins fnl f* **11/4$^{2}$**

00 **5** 2 ½ **Barney George**$^{26}$ 4956 2-8-13 0 LewisEdmunds$^{(3)}$ 6 61
(Iain Jardine) *hld up in tch: rdn over 2f out: rallied over 1f out: kpt on same pce fnl f* **50/1**

5 **6** 7 **Retirement Beckons**$^{22}$ 5092 2-9-2 0 ShaneGray 7 44
(Linda Perratt) *dwlt: hld up: rdn over 2f out: edgd lft and wknd over 1f out* **100/1**

**7** 6 **Dr Richard Kimble (IRE)** 2-9-2 0 JoeyHaynes 4 29
(Mark Johnston) *prom: drvn and outpcd over 2f out: sn btn* **6/1$^{3}$**

1m 32.09s (-1.31) **Going Correction** -0.20s/f (Firm) **7 Ran SP% 110.8**
Speed ratings (Par 94): **99,98,98,97,94 86,80**
CSF £19.52 TOTE £9.80: £4.00, £1.20; EX 21.40 Trifecta £97.00.

**Owner** Mrs Angie Bailey **Bred** Karis Bloodstock Ltd & Rathbarry Stud **Trained** Hambleton, N Yorks

**FOCUS**

Add 12yds. A bit of a bunch finish to this novice, but the runner-up has a mark of 72 and looks the key to the race. It's been rated at face value around the runner-up.

## 5919 QTS INVESTORS IN SPORT H'CAP 6f

6:50 (6:53) (Class 6) (0-65,65) 3-Y-O+ £3,234 (£962; £481; £240) Stalls Low

Form RPR

0615 **1** **Racquet**[19] 5203 4-9-11 **64**........ KevinStott 1 70
(Ruth Carr) *prom on far side of gp: shkn up to ld over 1f out: edgd rt ins fnl f: rdn out* **9/2**[1]

5030 **2** *nk* **Insurplus (IRE)**[12] 5467 4-8-9 **55**........ ConnorMurtagh(7) 8 60
(Jim Goldie) *in tch: rdn along on nr side of gp over 1f out: kpt on wl to take 2nd towards fin: jst hld* **9/2**[1]

3415 **3** *1 ¼* **Cheeni**[12] 5472 5-8-9 **48**........(p) PatrickMathers 6 49
(Jim Goldie) *dwlt: hld up: rdn and hdwy over 1f out: kpt on fnl f: nvr able to chal* **7/1**

3432 **4** *hd* **Hamidans Girl (IRE)**[7] 5645 3-9-6 **63**........ GrahamLee 9 63
(Keith Dalgleish) *tk t.k.h: cl up: effrt and ev ch over 1f out: no ex ins fnl f* **5/1**[2]

3530 **5** *¾* **Ss Vega**[12] 5466 4-8-0 **46**........(b[1]) SeanMooney(7) 10 44
(Jim Goldie) *dwlt: bhd: shkn up and hdwy on nr side of gp over 1f out: kpt on fnl f: no imp* **12/1**

3635 **6** *¾* **Eltanin (IRE)**[44] 4265 3-9-8 **65**........(v[1]) JasonHart 4 60
(John Quinn) *t.k.h: hld up: effrt and rdn on far side of gp 2f out: no imp fnl f* **6/1**[3]

-115 **7** *1 ¾* **Termsnconditions (IRE)**[83] 2853 3-8-13 **59**........ LewisEdmunds(3) 5 49
(Tim Vaughan) *bhd: rdn over 2f out: kpt on fnl f: nvr rchd ldrs* **10/1**

0605 **8** *1* **Roman Times (IRE)**[14] 5418 4-8-0 **46**........(p) JamieGormley(7) 2 36
(Colin Teague) *led to 1/2-way: rdn and wknd over 1f out: eased whn btn ins fnl f* **28/1**

6426 **9** *1 ¾* **Goninodaethat**[12] 5472 9-9-7 **60**........ PaulMulrennan 7 45
(Jim Goldie) *t.k.h towards rr: rdn and no imp whn nt clr run over 1f out: sn btn* **14/1**

3264 **10** *3 ½* **Dapper Man (IRE)**[15] 5377 3-8-13 **63**........(b) BenSanderson(7) 11 34
(Roger Fell) *cl up on nr side of gp: led 1/2-way to over 1f out: sn wknd* **17/2**

460- **11** *2 ¾* **Jebel Tara**[225] 8589 12-8-7 **51**........(bt) RowanScott(5) 3 15
(Alistair Whillans) *prom: drvn and outpcd over 2f out: sn btn* **33/1**

1m 12.86s (0.46) **Going Correction** +0.05s/f (Good)
**WFA** 3 from 4yo+ 4lb **11 Ran SP% 120.2**
Speed ratings (Par 101): **98,97,95,95,94 93,91,90,87,83 79**
CSF £25.01 CT £145.43 TOTE £5.40: £1.80, £2.10, £2.40; EX 29.70 Trifecta £290.80.
**Owner** Reach For The Moon & Mrs R Carr **Bred** P M Cunningham **Trained** Huby, N Yorks

**FOCUS**

A run-of-the-mill and open-looking sprint with most thoroughly exposed. The early gallop was only fair. Straightforward form.

## 5920 QTS LADIES' NIGHT GRAND SPECTACULAR H'CAP 5f

7:20 (7:21) (Class 4) (0-85,85) 3-Y-O+ £6,469 (£1,925; £962; £481) Stalls Low

Form RPR

00 **1** **Rosina**[29] 4867 4-9-1 **76**........(p[1]) ShaneGray 4 86
(Ann Duffield) *dwlt: hld up: hdwy on far side of gp over 1f out: rdn to ld ins fnl f: qcknd clr: readily* **18/1**

1062 **2** *2 ¼* **Desert Ace (IRE)**[19] 5204 6-8-7 **75**........(p) JamieGormley(7) 9 77+
(Iain Jardine) *led on nr side of gp: rdn whn carried rt by loose horse over 1f out: hdd ins fnl f: nt pce of wnr* **6/1**[3]

0332 **3** *½* **Pomme De Terre (IRE)**[15] 5379 5-9-7 **82**........(b) PaulMulrennan 2 82
(Michael Dods) *cl up on far side of gp: effrt and ch over 1f out: kpt on same pce ins fnl f* **6/4**[1]

5366 **4** *1 ½* **Economic Crisis (IRE)**[8] 5602 8-8-10 **71**........ PatrickMathers 3 66
(Colin Teague) *prom: pushed along whn checked and lost pl over 1f out: rallied ins fnl f: no imp* **20/1**

00 **5** *½* **Memories Galore (IRE)**[42] 4379 5-9-5 **80**........(p[1]) JasonHart 8 73
(Roger Fell) *hld up in tch on nr side of gp: effrt whn carried rt over 1f out: rdn and one pce fnl f* **16/1**

1153 **6** *nk* **Foxy Boy**[11] 5495 3-8-3 **74**........ ConnorMurtagh(7) 5 65
(Michael Dods) *prom: rdn and lost pl over 1f out: n.d after* **7/1**

6030 **7** *1 ¼* **Gamesome (FR)**[14] 5402 6-9-10 **85**........ GrahamLee 6 72
(Paul Midgley) *dwlt: hld up: rdn along over 2f out: no imp over 1f out* **7/2**[2]

-066 **8** *6* **Fast Act (IRE)**[19] 5204 5-9-6 **81**........ KevinStott 7 47
(Kevin Ryan) *t.k.h: disp ld: checked over 1f out: sn wknd* **14/1**

1313 **U** **Gnaad (IRE)**[109] 2065 3-7-11 **66**........ RichardOliver(5) 1
(Alan Bailey) *rrd and uns rdr leaving stalls* **22/1**

58.74s (-0.66) **Going Correction** +0.05s/f (Good)
**WFA** 3 from 4yo+ 3lb **9 Ran SP% 115.9**
Speed ratings (Par 105): **107,103,102,100,99 98,96,87,**
CSF £122.23 CT £265.26 TOTE £18.50: £4.70, £2.30, £1.10; EX 154.20 Trifecta £546.60.
**Owner** Ms J Bianco **Bred** Charley Knoll Partnership **Trained** Constable Burton, N Yorks

**FOCUS**

A strongly-run sprint in which a loose horse caused a few problems and the winner, who hails from a yard coming back to form, came from last to first. The winner has been rated to last year's form.

## 5921 QTS TRAINING H'CAP 1m 2f

7:50 (7:51) (Class 5) (0-75,73) 3-Y-O+ £4,528 (£1,347; £673; £336) Stalls Low

Form RPR

2161 **1** **Maulesden May (IRE)**[19] 5207 4-10-0 **73**........ GrahamLee 7 80
(Keith Dalgleish) *chsd ldr 1f: prom: smooth hdwy on outside to ld over 2f out: rdn over 1f out: kpt on strly fnl f* **6/1**[3]

0035 **2** *1 ½* **Beauden Barrett**[7] 5650 4-9-11 **70**........(t) JasonHart 2 74
(John Quinn) *trckd ldrs: n.m.r over 2f out: effrt over 1f out: chsd wnr ins fnl f: r.o* **15/2**

3253 **3** *nk* **Somnambulist**[23] 5073 3-9-3 **70**........ PaulMulrennan 6 73
(Keith Dalgleish) *chsd ldr after 1f: led briefly wl over 2f out: chsd wnr to ins fnl f: kpt on same pce* **4/1**[2]

5051 **4** *1* **Akamanto (IRE)**[10] 5532 3-9-0 **70**........ LewisEdmunds(3) 9 71
(R Mike Smith) *hld up in tch on outside: effrt and pushed along 2f out: edgd lft ins fnl f: kpt on* **6/1**[3]

2521 **5** *¾* **Archipeligo**[14] 5417 6-9-7 **73**........(p) JamieGormley(7) 4 73
(Iain Jardine) *hld up: shkn up over 2f out: effrt whn n.m.r briefly appr fnl f: sn no imp* **4/1**[2]

5036 **6** *3* **Red Star Dancer (IRE)**[23] 5073 3-8-3 **56**........ ShaneGray 8 50
(Linda Perratt) *hld up: drvn and outpcd over 2f out: n.d after* **25/1**

3231 **7** *½* **Snookered (IRE)**[19] 5212 3-9-2 **69**........ PatrickMathers 3 62
(Richard Fahey) *t.k.h: led to over 2f out: rdn and wknd over 1f out* **5/2**[1]

2m 10.94s (-1.06) **Going Correction** -0.20s/f (Firm)
**WFA** 3 from 4yo+ 8lb **7 Ran SP% 112.8**
Speed ratings (Par 103): **96,94,94,93,93 90,90**
CSF £47.54 CT £199.65 TOTE £6.00: £2.50, £3.70; EX 47.60 Trifecta £239.70.
**Owner** The County Set (Two) **Bred** Yeomanstown Stud **Trained** Carluke, S Lanarks

**FOCUS**

Add 12yds. A moderate gallop to this 1m2f handicap with the progressive winner was always close to the pace. The third has been rated to his better maiden form.

## 5922 GAS SURE & JAMES FREW H'CAP 7f 50y

8:20 (8:21) (Class 5) (0-70,73) 3-Y-O+ £3,234 (£962; £481; £240) Stalls High

Form RPR

3003 **1** **Inglorious**[8] 5604 3-8-7 **62**........(p) RowanScott(5) 8 71
(Keith Dalgleish) *pressed ldr: led gng wl over 2f out: rdn and clr over 1f out: kpt on wl fnl f* **8/1**

4345 **2** *1 ½* **Lady In Question (IRE)**[14] 5400 3-8-12 **69**........ ConnorMurtagh(7) 9 73
(Richard Fahey) *hld up in tch on outside: effrt and chsd (clr) wnr over 1f out: kpt on fnl f: nt pce to chal* **4/1**[2]

0050 **3** *1* **Chaplin Bay (IRE)**[19] 5213 5-9-12 **70**........(p) KevinStott 10 73
(Ruth Carr) *hld up: pushed along and hdwy over 1f out: kpt on fnl f: no imp* **9/2**[3]

6543 **4** *½* **Royal Duchess**[34] 4663 7-9-3 **68**........ JamieGormley(7) 7 70
(Lucy Normile) *dwlt: bhd: rdn and hdwy on outside over 1f out: kpt on fnl f: no imp* **7/2**[1]

4005 **5** *2 ¾* **Lotara**[7] 5635 5-8-9 **53**........ PatrickMathers 4 48
(Jim Goldie) *trckd ldrs: rdn over 2f out: hung lft and wknd over 1f out* **18/1**

0536 **6** *1 ¾* **Coral Princess (IRE)**[8] 5604 3-8-3 **53** oh5 ow2........ ShaneGray 3 41
(Keith Dalgleish) *hld up in tch: stdy hdwy over 2f out: rdn and wknd over 1f out* **20/1**

4545 **7** *nk* **Flinty Fell (IRE)**[18] 5258 4-9-7 **65**........ GrahamLee 5 55
(Keith Dalgleish) *t.k.h early: led to over 2f out: rdn and wknd over 1f out* **10/1**

3502 **8** *2 ¼* **Dark Crystal**[7] 5650 6-9-12 **73**........ LewisEdmunds(3) 1 57
(Linda Perratt) *rrd as stalls opened: hld up: rdn and outpcd over 2f out: n.d after* **8/1**

0206 **9** *5* **Chipping (IRE)**[20] 5182 3-9-6 **70**........(p) PaulMulrennan 2 39
(Michael Dods) *trckd ldrs: drvn along over 2f out: wknd wl over 1f out* **11/2**

1m 30.29s (-3.11) **Going Correction** -0.20s/f (Firm)
**WFA** 3 from 4yo+ 6lb **9 Ran SP% 117.1**
Speed ratings (Par 103): **109,107,106,105,102 100,100,97,91**
CSF £40.64 CT £148.93 TOTE £8.90: £2.90, £1.90, £2.20; EX 42.40 Trifecta £373.30.
**Owner** Weldspec Glasgow Limited **Bred** Kassala Limited **Trained** Carluke, S Lanarks

**FOCUS**

Add 12yds. An ordinary handicap run at a sound pace in which the winner fared best of the prominent racers with the other three in the frame all coming from further back. The runner-up has been rated in line with the better view of this year's form.

## 5923 NESELECTRICAL.COM H'CAP 1m 7f

8:50 (8:50) (Class 6) (0-65,72) 4-Y-O+ £2,587 (£770; £384; £192) Stalls Low

Form RPR

3-06 **1** **Chebsey Beau**[21] 3315 7-9-7 **65**........ JasonHart 10 72
(John Quinn) *in tch: drvn and outpcd 4f ou: rallied over 2f out: rdn and led ins fnl f: sn hrd pressed: styd on wl* **7/1**[3]

2120 **2** *hd* **Question Of Faith**[5] 5701 6-8-11 **55**........ PaulMulrennan 7 62
(Martin Todhunter) *hld up: stdy hdwy over 2f out: drvn and ev ch ins fnl f: kpt on: hld nr fin* **7/2**[2]

0032 **3** *2* **Tectonic (IRE)**[1] 5884 8-9-4 **62**........(v) GrahamLee 3 66
(Keith Dalgleish) *hld up: stdy hdwy and prom over 1f out: swtchd lft and effrt ins fnl f: kpt on same pce towards fin* **7/1**[3]

0441 **4** *1 ¾* **Golden Jeffrey (SWI)**[1] 5884 4-9-7 **72** 6ex........ JamieGormley(7) 8 74
(Iain Jardine) *chsd ldrs: hdwy to ld over 2f out: rdn over 1f out: hdd ins fnl f: sn outpcd* **2/1**[1]

0446 **5** *5* **Celtic Power**[14] 5413 5-8-0 **48** ow3........(b) ConnorMurtagh(7) 2 44
(Jim Goldie) *pressed ldr: led 1/2-way to over 2f out: rdn and wknd over 1f out* **16/1**

4023 **6** *1* **Schmooze (IRE)**[1] 5883 8-8-6 **50**........ ShaneGray 4 45
(Linda Perratt) *hld up: hdwy on outside 3f out: rdn and wknd over 1f out* **7/2**[2]

6500 **7** *8* **Nuova Scuola**[18] 5257 4-8-2 **46** oh1........(v) PatrickMathers 5 31
(Jim Goldie) *hld up in tch: drvn and outpcd over 3f out: sn struggling: n.d after* **40/1**

5532 **8** *3 ¼* **Esspeegee**[21] 5142 4-7-11 **46**........(p) RichardOliver(5) 1 28
(Alan Bailey) *led 2f: cl up: regained ld 1/2-way: rdn and hdd over 2f out: wknd over 1f out* **12/1**

3m 19.22s (-1.18) **Going Correction** -0.20s/f (Firm) **8 Ran SP% 118.8**
Speed ratings (Par 101): **95,94,93,92,90 89,85,83**
CSF £33.05 CT £182.25 TOTE £6.70: £1.80, £1.70, £2.40; EX 41.90 Trifecta £184.70.
**Owner** Kent, Greaves, Dawson **Bred** Mickley Stud & M A Greaves **Trained** Settrington, N Yorks

**FOCUS**

Add 33 yards to this staying handicap which ended up a strongly-run race with none of the pacesetters getting home. The winner has been rated just shy of last year's level, with the third to his recent best.

T/Plt: £159.60 to a £1 stake. Pool: £72,175.75 - 329.95 winning units T/Qpdt: £48.00 to a £1 stake. Pool: £4,729.49 - 72.90 winning units **Richard Young**

# 5872 HAYDOCK (L-H)

Saturday, August 12

**OFFICIAL GOING: Good to soft (7.3) changing to soft after race 4 (3.35)**

Wind: light breeze, against in straight Weather: cloudy, sunny intervals

## 5924 BETFRED HAYDOCK PARK LADIES' TROPHY H'CAP (PRO-AM LADY RIDERS' RACE) 1m 3f 175y

1:55 (1:55) (Class 3) (0-90,92) 3-Y-O+ £12,938 (£3,850; £1,924; £962) Stalls Centre

Form RPR

1326 **1** **Azari**[29] 4863 5-10-10 **92**........(p[1]) JennyPowell 8 101
(Tom Dascombe) *hld up: hdwy 2f out: rdn and ev ch over 1f out: jnd runner-up ins fnl f: sustained duel: r.o wl to ld last stride* **12/1**

12 **2** *nse* **Zubayr (IRE)**[38] 4498 5-10-1 **83**........ MeganNicholls 11 92
(Paul Nicholls) *hld up: hdwy 3f out: pushed along to ld over 1f out: rdn ent fnl f: sustained duel w wnr: r.o but hdd last stride* **11/4**[1]



The Form Book Flat, Raceform Ltd, Newbury, RG14 5SJ

0453 **3** 2 **William Hunter**[17] 5287 5-10-2 84 MissSBrotherton 6 90
(Alan King) trckd ldrs: tk clsr order 2f out: pushed along over 1f out: rdn 1f out: r.o to take 3rd last 100yds 9/2[2]

0105 **4** 3/4 **Swaheen**[17] 5287 5-9-9 80 (p[1]) MissAMcCain(3) 9 85
(Julie Camacho) mid-div: hdwy 3f out: rdn to ld 2f out: hdd over 1f out: no ex fnl f: lost 3rd last 100yds 11/1

1606 **5** 3 **Caponova (IRE)**[16] 5330 4-9-12 80 MissAnnaHesketh 3 80
(Tom Dascombe) in rr: pushed along 3f out: swtchd to outer over 2f out: sn rdn: styd on fnl f 25/1

3611 **6** 1 1/4 **Tapis Libre**[30] 4801 9-9-13 81 MissJoannaMason 4 79
(Jacqueline Coward) trckd ldrs: drvn 2f out: rdn and wknd over 1f out 7/1[3]

3054 **7** 3/4 **Gabrial's King (IRE)**[28] 4921 8-10-5 87 SammyJoBell 2 84
(Richard Fahey) mid-div: effrt on inner 3f out: n.m.r 2f out: swtchd to centre over 1f out: rdn and one pce fnl f 20/1

4341 **8** 1 **Dance King**[45] 4206 7-10-5 87 (tp) RachelRichardson 12 82
(Tim Easterby) mid-div: hdwy to trck ldrs 4f out: ev ch 2f out: rdn and wknd over 1f out 8/1

3102 **9** 7 **Jacbequick**[21] 5163 6-10-4 86 (p) ShelleyBirkett 5 70
(David O'Meara) mid-div: rdn over 2f out: one pce 11/1

6465 **10** 3/4 **Lord Franklin**[13] 5455 8-9-2 70 GemmaTutty 1 53
(Eric Alston) led tl hdd after 1f: remained prom: ev ch 3f out: rdn and wknd over 2f out 25/1

4000 **11** 9 **Intense Tango**[63] 3594 6-10-7 89 LucyKBarry 10 57
(K R Burke) led after 1f: drvn and hdd 3f out: sn rdn and wknd 25/1

0606 **12** 3 3/4 **Shamrokh (IRE)**[14] 5397 3-9-1 79 MissBeckySmith 7 42
(Michael Appleby) prom: wnt 2nd 4f out: led 3f out: hdd and drvn 2f out: wknd quicky: eased 16/1

2m 36.15s (2.35) **Going Correction** +0.275s/f (Good)
**WFA** 3 from 4yo+ 10lb 12 Ran SP% **115.0**
Speed ratings (Par 107): **103,102,101,101,99 98,97,97,92,91 85,83**
CSF £41.40 CT £173.02 TOTE £14.00: £3.20, £1.50, £1.90; EX 57.00 Trifecta £667.30.
**Owner** D Ward & Partner **Bred** Yeguada De Milagro Sa **Trained** Malpas, Cheshire

**FOCUS**
Add 20yds. A showery day and the potential of further softening of the ground, which was described as good to soft before the first of seven races. A good renewal of this lady riders' handicap. The third helps set the standard, while the fourth has been rated close to form.

## 5925 BETFRED ROSE OF LANCASTER STKS (GROUP 3) 1m 2f 100y
**2:30** (2:31) (Class 1) 3-Y-O+

**£35,727** (£13,545; £6,778; £3,376; £1,694; £850) **Stalls** Centre

Form RPR

4042 **1** **Frankuus (IRE)**[22] 5095 3-8-9 105 (b) JoeFanning 8 112
(Mark Johnston) mde all: 2 l ld 3f out: cajoled along over 2f out: rdn over 1f out where 3 l ahd: advantage reduced by runner-up ins fnl f: kpt on gamely last 100yds 8/1

3-33 **2** 3/4 **Mount Logan (IRE)**[42] 4360 6-9-3 106 AndreaAtzeni 3 110
(Roger Varian) trckd ldrs: pushed along to go 2nd over 2f out: rdn over 1f out: clsd on wnr ins f: no ex and hld cl home 6/1[2]

111 **3** 5 **Laraaib (IRE)**[28] 4882 3-8-9 103 JimCrowley 12 101
(Owen Burrows) mid-div: hdwy and ev ch 3f out: 2nd 2f out: rdn over 1f out: one pce fnl f 2/1[1]

0-21 **4** hd **Euginio (IRE)**[36] 4585 3-8-9 102 TomMarquand 5 101
(Richard Hannon) mid-div: pushed along 3f out: n.m.r 2f out: rdn and hdwy over 1f out: r.o to take 4th ins fnl f 14/1

2443 **5** 1 1/4 **Gabrial (IRE)**[13] 5456 8-9-3 110 PaulHanagan 11 97
(Richard Fahey) hld up: drvn and hdwy 2f out: rdn over 1f out: r.o fnl f 25/1

-602 **6** 1 **Arthenus**[21] 5148 5-9-3 105 (p) DanielTudhope 7 95
(James Fanshawe) hld up: drvn in rr over 2f out: sme late hdwy 14/1

1-61 **7** 2 1/4 **Autocratic**[79] 3012 4-9-6 114 TedDurcan 6 94
(Sir Michael Stoute) mid-div: pushed along 3f out: rdn 2f out: no imp 17/2

611- **8** nk **Francis Of Assisi (IRE)**[280] 7826 7-9-3 111 AdamKirby 9 91
(Charlie Appleby) prom: 3rd 4f out: pushed along 3f out: rdn over 2f out: wknd 15/2[3]

6-55 **9** shd **Ayrad (IRE)**[36] 4584 6-9-3 108 (p) RichardKingscote 1 90
(Roger Charlton) chsd ldr: 2nd and rdn 3f out: fdd 11/1

3505 **10** 3 1/2 **Restorer**[21] 5148 5-9-3 100 DougieCostello 2 84
(William Muir) mid-div: pushed along on inner 3f out: rdn over 1f out: wknd 50/1

5024 **11** 2 **Larchmont Lad (IRE)**[30] 4817 3-8-9 107 DavidProbert 13 81
(Richard Hannon) hld up: rdn in rr 2f out: no rspnse 14/1

2m 14.46s (-1.04) **Going Correction** +0.275s/f (Good)
**WFA** 3 from 4yo+ 8lb 11 Ran SP% **115.2**
Speed ratings (Par 113): **115,114,110,110,109 108,106,106,106,103 101**
CSF £54.23 TOTE £6.90: £2.40, £2.00, £1.30; EX 46.40 Trifecta £245.80.
**Owner** Hussain Lootah & Ahmad Al Shaikh **Bred** Ballylinch Stud **Trained** Middleham Moor, N Yorks

**FOCUS**
There was a heavy rain shower after the opening race but the going description was kept as good to soft. This Group 3 feature attracted a bigger field than usual and looked competitive on paper. Frankuus ensured a decent early pace and held on for a game success. It was third win in a row for 3yos in the extended 1m2f contest. The form is possibly better than rated.

## 5926 BETFRED DUKE OF LANCASTER'S OWN YEOMANRY H'CAP (LONDON MILE SERIES QUALIFIER) 1m 37y
**3:00** (3:01) (Class 3) (0-95,94) 3-Y-O+ **£9,703** (£2,887; £1,443; £721) **Stalls** Low

Form RPR

3512 **1** **El Cap (USA)**[11] 5496 3-9-3 90 TedDurcan 4 105+
(Sir Michael Stoute) mid-div: effrt over 2f out: briefly n.m.r: rdn and hdwy over 1f out: qcknd ent fnl f: led last 150 yds: sn plld clr: easily 4/1[3]

2135 **2** 3 1/2 **Calder Prince (IRE)**[6] 5683 4-9-10 90 RichardKingscote 6 96
(Tom Dascombe) led: 1 l clr 3f out: drvn 2f out: rdn over 1f out where 2 l ld: qckly clsd down by ldr ins fnl f: hdd last 150yds: no ex 7/2[2]

0104 **3** 1 1/4 **Two For Two (IRE)**[7] 5668 9-9-10 90 (p) JoeFanning 1 93
(Roger Fell) hld up in last: pushed along and effrt 3f out: drvn 2f out: swtchd to outer over 1f out: r.o wl to take 3rd ins fnl f 14/1

0005 **4** 2 **Briyouni (FR)**[45] 4207 4-9-1 81 (p) TomEaves 7 80
(Kevin Ryan) hld up: hdwy over 3f out: sn pushed along: drvn 2f out: chsng ldrs whn rdn over 1f out: one pce fnl f 25/1

0146 **5** hd **Just Hiss**[7] 5634 4-9-8 91 (p) RachelRichardson(3) 3 90+
(Tim Easterby) trckd ldrs: pushed along on inner 2f out: briefly n.m.r: one pce fnl f 15/2

600 **6** hd **Dark Devil (IRE)**[45] 4207 4-9-3 83 PaulHanagan 8 81
(Richard Fahey) prom: hdwy into 3rd 3f out: sn drvn: rdn 2f out: no ex ent fnl f 10/1

1002 **7** 5 **Fingal's Cave (IRE)**[14] 5434 5-9-12 92 DanielTudhope 9 78
(Philip Kirby) mid-div: hdwy over 3f out: drvn 2f out: rdn over 1f out: one pce 8/1

2520 **8** 8 **Mustarrid (IRE)**[14] 5392 3-9-7 94 JimCrowley 5 61
(Richard Hannon) prom: 2nd 4f out: pushed along 3f out: rdn 2f out: wknd and lost pl: eased fnl f 11/4[1]

0445 **9** 1 **Little Lady Katie (IRE)**[16] 5317 5-8-9 78 JordanVaughan(3) 2 43
(K R Burke) mid-div: drvn and lost pl 4f out: lft bhd fr 2f out: eased 18/1

1m 45.24s (0.54) **Going Correction** +0.275s/f (Good)
**WFA** 3 from 4yo+ 7lb 9 Ran SP% **116.6**
Speed ratings (Par 107): **108,104,103,101,101 100,95,87,86**
CSF £18.64 CT £180.03 TOTE £5.00: £1.70, £1.80, £3.30; EX 20.50 Trifecta £78.60.
**Owner** Flaxman Stables Ireland Ltd **Bred** Flaxman Holdings Limited **Trained** Newmarket, Suffolk

**FOCUS**
This was run at a good pace in the soft conditions and represents solid handicap form. It's been rated around the runner-up, with the third close to form.

## 5927 BETFRED TV/EBF STALLIONS DICK HERN STKS (LISTED RACE) (F&M) 1m 37y
**3:35** (3:36) (Class 1) 3-Y-O+

**£26,653** (£10,105; £5,057; £2,519; £1,264; £634) **Stalls** Low

Form RPR

-524 **1** **Sea Of Grace (IRE)**[29] 4857 3-8-9 109 AndreaAtzeni 8 110+
(William Haggas) confidently rdn: hld up in last: plenty to do 3f out: hdwy 2f out: nudged along to take clsr order over 1f out: pushed out ins fnl f: led last 150yds: sn drew clr: easily 8/11[1]

4122 **2** 4 1/2 **Lincoln Rocks**[11] 5506 4-9-5 100 DanielTudhope 4 104
(David O'Meara) fast s: led: pushed along 2f out: rdn and narrow advantage over 1f out: r.o ins fnl f: hdd by easy wnr 150 yds out: sn lft bhd 15/2[3]

6503 **3** 2 1/4 **Dancing Breeze (IRE)**[35] 4637 3-8-9 91 JoeFanning 5 94
(John Gosden) hld up: hdwy on to heels of ldrs 2f out: sn swtchd to inner: drvn and cl 2nd over 1f out: rdn ent fnl f: one pce 10/1

10-0 **4** 2 **Conselice**[70] 3334 4-9-2 100 CliffordLee 3 91
(K R Burke) cl up: 2nd and ev ch 3f out: pushed along 2f out: sn rdn and lost pl: one pce ent fnl f 50/1

2060 **5** 3 1/4 **Materialistic**[15] 5352 4-9-2 96 (p) AdamKirby 1 83
(Luca Cumani) prom: cl 3rd and ev ch 3f out: rdn 2f out: wknd over 1f out 16/1

3115 **6** 9 **Mittens**[15] 5352 3-8-9 99 PatSmullen 6 62
(Sir Michael Stoute) mid-div: pushed along 2f out: sn rdn: lost grnd qckly: eased 11/4[2]

1m 45.72s (1.02) **Going Correction** +0.275s/f (Good)
**WFA** 3 from 4yo 7lb 6 Ran SP% **113.3**
Speed ratings (Par 111): **105,100,98,96,93 84**
CSF £7.34 TOTE £1.50: £1.10, £3.40; EX 6.80 Trifecta £21.80.
**Owner** Sunderland Holding Inc **Bred** Robert Norton **Trained** Newmarket, Suffolk

**FOCUS**
This Listed event revolved around the odds-on favourite, who was upwards of 9lb clear on ratings. The runner-up has been rated to form, with the third close to her Sandown latest.

## 5928 BETFRED RACING "LIKE US ON FACEBOOK" H'CAP 1m 37y
**4:05** (4:06) (Class 4) (0-85,84) 3-Y-O **£5,822** (£1,732; £865; £432) **Stalls** Low

Form RPR

4153 **1** **Fire Brigade**[14] 5392 3-9-7 84 DanielTudhope 2 95+
(Michael Bell) hld up last: hdwy gng wl 2f out: cruised alongside ldrs over 1f out: pushed out to ld ent fnl f: sn clr and in command: easily 10/11[1]

034 **2** 1 3/4 **Glorious Forever**[50] 4035 3-9-7 84 (v[1]) AdamKirby 7 88
(Ed Walker) prom: cl 2nd 3f out: rdn 2f out: led over 1f out: hdd ent fnl f: kpt on but no ch w wnr 9/2[2]

0 **3** 3 **Pecheurs De Perles (IRE)**[15] 5376 3-9-5 82 PaulHanagan 1 79
(Iain Jardine) led: narrow ld 3f out: drvn 2f out: hdd over 1f out: no ex fnl f 14/1

5026 **4** 3 1/2 **Mutawakked (IRE)**[29] 4831 3-9-5 82 JimCrowley 5 71
(Brian Meehan) mid-div: relegated to 5th 3f out: rdn 2f out: wnt 4th over 1f out: one pce fnl f 9/2[2]

2161 **5** 3 **Wigan Warrior**[21] 5139 3-9-0 77 TomEaves 3 59
(David Brown) hld up: hdwy into 4th on inner 3f out: pushed along over 2f out: sn rdn and struggling: fdd ent fnl f 8/1[3]

5243 **6** 1/2 **Sterling Silva (IRE)**[10] 5548 3-9-3 80 (b[1]) TomMarquand 6 61
(Richard Hannon) prom: pushed along in 3rd 3f out: sn rdn and dropped to last 20/1

1m 45.79s (1.09) **Going Correction** +0.275s/f (Good) 6 Ran SP% **111.3**
Speed ratings (Par 102): **105,103,100,96,93 93**
CSF £5.22 TOTE £1.80: £1.10, £2.20; EX 4.80 Trifecta £34.40.
**Owner** The Fitzrovians **Bred** Stowell Hill Ltd **Trained** Newmarket, Suffolk

**FOCUS**
The official going was changed to soft all round from good to soft prior to the running of this handicap. This wasn't the strongest of races for the level but was won with real authority by the heavily punted favourite. Not the deepest form.

## 5929 BETFRED SUPPORTS JACK BERRY HOUSE H'CAP 6f
**4:35** (4:38) (Class 4) (0-85,86) 3-Y-O+ **£6,469** (£1,925; £962; £481) **Stalls** Centre

Form RPR

2004 **1** **Russian Realm**[13] 5457 7-9-8 81 DougieCostello 7 87
(Paul Midgley) mid-div: pushed along 2f out: hdwy and squeezed through gap over 1f out: rdn to ld ent fnl f: chal on both sides but hld on wl nr fin 10/1

1504 **2** 1/2 **Captain Lars (SAF)**[8] 5612 8-9-2 78 (v) AaronJones(3) 12 82
(Derek Shaw) prom: 2nd 3f out: rdn over 1f out and bmpd by 4th home: rallied u.p ins fnl f: tk 2nd nr fin 25/1

2521 **3** nse **Lexington Times (IRE)**[15] 5379 5-9-12 85 (p) JackGarritty 3 89
(Ruth Carr) trckd ldrs: hdwy 2f out: drvn over 1f out: rdn in cl 2nd ent fnl f: r.o: lost 2nd nr fin 9/2[1]

626 **4** 3/4 **Signore Piccolo**[14] 5402 6-9-5 85 (h) CameronNoble(7) 11 86
(David Loughnane) prom: led 3f out: pushed along 2f out: rdn over 1f out and jinked rt: sn stened: hdd ent fnl f: no ex 12/1

0042 **5** 1/2 **Clear Spring (IRE)**[8] 5612 9-9-12 85 DavidProbert 6 87+
(John Spearing) reluctant to load: rrd leaving stalls: in rr: hdwy over 1f out: ch ent fnl f: n.m.r and briefly lost momentum: r.o again nr fin 11/2[2]

0460 **6** shd **Toofi (FR)**[21] 5159 6-9-13 86 (p[1]) RobertWinston 9 86
(John Butler) mid-div: pushed along 2f out: drvn over 1f out: one pce 8/1

0344 **7** hd **Lathom**[8] 5602 4-9-8 81 (b[1]) DanielTudhope 8 80
(David O'Meara) hld up: hdwy 1/2-way: rdn over 1f out: one pce fnl f 7/1[3]

033 **8** *¾* **Letmestopyouthere (IRE)**[22] 5100 3-9-7 **84**.................... JimCrowley 1 79
(David Evans) *mid-div: effrt and pushed along 2f out: rdn over 1f out: no imp* **18/1**

0330 **9** *3* **Monks Stand (USA)**[28] 4892 3-8-8 **74**..............(p) RachelRichardson(3) 4 60
(Tim Easterby) *prom: pushed along 2f out: rdn and wknd wl over 1f out* **40/1**

0032 **10** *3 ½* **Gabrial The Tiger (IRE)**[6] 5683 5-9-5 **78**.................... PaulHanagan 10 54
(Richard Fahey) *led: hdd 3f out: pushed along over 2f out: sn wknd* **11/2**[2]

-504 **11** *5* **Somewhere Secret**[16] 5316 3-8-7 **75**.........................(h) PhilDennis(5) 2 34
(Michael Mullineaux) *mid-div: losing tch and pushed along 1/2-way: wnt lft and sn no ch: eased* **25/1**

2050 **12** *2 ¾* **Lucky Beggar (IRE)**[7] 5637 7-9-13 **86**................................ DavidAllan 5 37
(David C Griffiths) *prom: pushed along 1/2-way: drvn over 2f out: sn lost pl: fdd* **8/1**

1m 16.05s (2.25) **Going Correction** +0.45s/f (Yiel)
**WFA** 3 from 4yo+ 4lb **12** Ran SP% **115.9**
Speed ratings (Par 105): **103,102,102,101,100 100,100,99,95,90 83,80**
CSF £235.22 CT £1300.53 TOTE £11.40: £3.40, £6.70, £1.90; EX 326.80 Trifecta £2212.40.
**Owner** The Guys & Dolls & Partner **Bred** Cheveley Park Stud Ltd **Trained** Westow, N Yorks

**FOCUS**
A competitive sprint handicap, though it got messy late on with Clear Spring badly inconvenienced and certainly better than his finishing position. Straightforward form.

## 5930 BETFRED MOBILE H'CAP 5f
**5:05** (5:07) (Class 5) (0-70,73) 3-Y-0+ **£4,528** (£1,347; £673; £336) **Stalls** Centre

Form RPR

4131 **1** **Show Palace**[9] 5580 4-10-1 **73**............................................ JoeFanning 1 84
(Jennie Candlish) *hld up: hdwy 1/2-way: gd prog to draw alongside ldrs 1f out: shkn up to ld last 150yds: kpt up to work and sn wl on top: comf* **4/1**[2]

0556 **2** *1 ½* **Red Stripes (USA)**[5] 5695 5-9-3 **61**..............................(b) DavidProbert 9 66
(Lisa Williamson) *chsd ldr: pushed along and led over 1f out: rdn ent fnl f: hdd last 150yds: kpt on* **16/1**

0454 **3** *¾* **Hamish McGonagain**[38] 4495 4-9-5 **63**........................ DanielTudhope 8 65
(David O'Meara) *mid-div: pushed along on heels of ldrs over 1f out: swtchd rt and rdn to take 3rd ent fnl f: one pce* **3/1**[1]

-000 **4** *1 ¼* **Imperial Legend (IRE)**[15] 5377 8-9-1 **62**.......... RachelRichardson(3) 13 60
(Alan Brown) *hld up: hdwy and pushed along over 1f out: rdn and r.o to take 4th ins fnl f* **40/1**

-050 **5** *1 ¼* **The Hooded Claw (IRE)**[35] 4605 6-9-8 **66**........................ TomEaves 4 59
(Patrick Morris) *prom early: settled into mid-div 1/2-way: drvn 2f out: r.o ins fnl f* **25/1**

0522 **6** *shd* **Pearl Acclaim (IRE)**[18] 5256 7-9-10 **68**................................ DavidAllan 6 61
(David C Griffiths) *led: pushed along and hdd over 1f out: no ex* **5/1**[3]

0600 **7** *nk* **Big Amigo (IRE)**[8] 5587 4-9-0 **65**....................................... TobyEley(7) 3 57
(Daniel Mark Loughnane) *in rr: last 1/2-way: pushed along 2f out: passed btn horses last f* **40/1**

0302 **8** *hd* **Savannah Beau**[15] 5355 5-9-8 **69**.................................(v) AaronJones(3) 5 60
(Derek Shaw) *slowly away: t.k.h and sn on heels of ldrs: drvn over 1f out: sn rdn: no ex* **12/1**

6630 **9** *½* **One Boy (IRE)**[13] 5459 6-9-9 **67**.......................................... PaulHanagan 10 56
(Paul Midgley) *mid-div: pushed along 2f out: rdn over 1f out: wknd* **14/1**

6443 **10** *¾* **Oriental Splendour (IRE)**[13] 5459 5-9-13 **71**...................... JackGarritty 11 57
(Ruth Carr) *hld up: pushed along 2f out: rdn over 1f out: no imp* **8/1**

465 **11** *3 ¼* **First Bombardment**[19] 5211 4-10-0 **72**.............................. JimCrowley 12 47
(David O'Meara) *slowly away: sn rcvrd to go prom: pushed along 2f out: rdn and wknd over 1f out: eased* **7/1**

1m 2.4s (1.60) **Going Correction** +0.45s/f (Yiel) **11** Ran SP% **114.2**
Speed ratings (Par 103): **105,102,101,99,97 97,96,96,95,94 89**
CSF £62.65 CT £219.25 TOTE £4.80: £1.70, £4.10, £1.50; EX 75.20 Trifecta £368.90.
**Owner** P and Mrs G A Clarke **Bred** M C Humby **Trained** Basford Green, Staffs

**FOCUS**
A hotly contested sprint handicap and a stylish win from the progressive Show Palace. The level is a bit fluid.
T/Jkpt: Not Won. T/Plt: £17.80 to a £1 stake. Pool: £128,744.42 - 5,257.13 winning units T/Qpdt: £6.90 to a £1 stake. Pool: £5,841.28 - 625.90 winning units **Keith McHugh**

# 5651 LINGFIELD (L-H)
Saturday, August 12

**OFFICIAL GOING: Good to soft (good in places; 5.1)**
Wind: half against Weather: Fine

## 5931 USPGA GOLF AT 188BET MEDIAN AUCTION MAIDEN STKS 1m 2f
**5:10** (5:11) (Class 6) 3-4-Y-0 **£2,587** (£770; £384; £192) **Stalls** Low

Form RPR

2422 **1** **Golden Wolf (IRE)**[6] 5686 3-9-6 75................................ ShaneKelly 6 81+
(Richard Hughes) *settled bhd ldrs on rail: traveling sweetly over 2f out: nursed along and smooth prog between horses over 1f out: full of running and hld together ins fnl f: pushed along and qcknd up to ld fnl 75yds: snug* **11/10**[1]

00 **2** *¾* **Rainbow Rising (FR)**[22] 5124 3-9-1 0.............................. DidierGengoul 4 71
(David Menuisier) *chsd ldrs on outer: nt handle bnd into st: rdn along wl over 1f out: kpt on wl ins fnl f to snatch 2nd fnl strides: no match for wnr* **20/1**

3 **3** *1* **Hats Off To Larry**[19] 5220 3-9-6 0.................................. CharlesBishop 3 74
(Mick Channon) *chsd ldr: shkn up and led over 2f out gng wl: sn rdn: kpt on tl hdd fnl 75yds: lost 2nd sn after* **7/4**[2]

3-0 **4** *2 ½* **Staff College (FR)**[135] 1460 3-9-6 80............................ StevieDonohoe 8 69
(Henry Spiller) *chsd ldr: rdn over 2f out: ev ch over 1f out: sltly squeezed up ent fnl f: kpt on one pce* **14/1**

**5** *1 ¼* **Star Guide** 3-8-10 0........................................... MitchGodwin(5) 2 61
(Sylvester Kirk) *bdly missed break: in rr-div: niggled along at 1/2-way: rdn over 3f out: one pce after* **20/1**

50 **6** *5* **Outofthequestion**[19] 5220 3-9-6 0.............................. WilliamCarson 10 56
(Alan King) *in last on outer: shkn up over 3f out: rdn 3f out: no imp* **20/1**

30 **7** *1* **Abel Tasman**[19] 5220 3-9-6 0......................................... ThomasBrown 9 54
(Ed Walker) *hld up in rr: rdn along over 3f out: no qcknd fr 2f out* **9/1**[3]

**8** *2* **Kingwilliamstown**[20] 5189 3-9-6 40................................ OscarPereira 7 50
(Jose Santos) *sn led: shkn up over 3f out: hdd wl over 2f out: sn no ex and wknd fr over 1f out* **50/1**

2m 9.87s (-0.63) **Going Correction** 0.0s/f (Good) **8** Ran SP% **116.9**
Speed ratings (Par 101): **102,101,100,98,97 93,92,91**
CSF £29.83 TOTE £1.90: £1.10, £4.80, £1.10; EX 21.70 Trifecta £48.90.
**Owner** Aristotle's Elements **Bred** Eugene McDermott **Trained** Upper Lambourn, Berks

**FOCUS**
The going was given as good to soft, soft in places (GoingStick: 5.1). An ordinary maiden. The winner has been rated in line with his good Chester run.

## 5932 PREMIER LEAGUE FOOTBALL AT 188BET H'CAP 1m 3f 133y
**5:40** (5:40) (Class 5) (0-75,77) 3-Y-0 **£2,911** (£866; £432; £216) **Stalls** High

Form RPR

3015 **1** **Star Maker**[21] 5153 3-8-13 **74**........................................ MitchGodwin(5) 3 81
(Sylvester Kirk) *in rr on outer: c wd off home bnd: shkn up and gd prog out wd fr over 3f out: cl up wl over 1f out: led ent fnl f: edgd lft and kpt on wl* **9/2**[3]

160 **2** *¾* **Falcon Cliffs (IRE)**[66] 3457 3-9-4 **74**.................................. RobHornby 5 79
(William Muir) *cl up in rr: rdn over 2f out where swtchd to outer: kpt on wl fr over 1f out: gaining on wnr ins fnl f: no ex nr fin* **8/1**

5124 **3** *1 ¼* **Amelia Dream**[6] 5682 3-9-2 **72**.................................... CharlesBishop 6 75
(Mick Channon) *mid-div on outer: tk clsr order after 6f and narrowly led on outer: rdn wl over 2f out: hdd ent fnl f: lost 2nd 1f out: one pce* **11/4**[2]

0-05 **4** *2 ½* **First Quest (USA)**[17] 5298 3-9-4 **74**................................ ShaneKelly 2 73
(Ed Dunlop) *chsd ldrs on rail: rdn over 2f out: one pce fr over 1f out* **8/1**

124 **5** *4* **Ocean Drive (IRE)**[58] 3759 3-9-7 **77**............................ PatCosgrave 4 69
(William Haggas) *led after 2f: hdd 6f out: remained pressing ldr on inner: rdn along wl over 2f out: wknd qckly after* **15/8**[1]

14 **6** *14* **Conkering Hero (IRE)**[43] 4307 3-9-5 **75**......................... LiamKeniry 1 44
(Joseph Tuite) *led tl hdd after 2f and settled bhd ldrs: rdn wl over 2f out: no ex and eased fnl f* **10/1**

2m 31.99s (0.49) **Going Correction** 0.0s/f (Good) **6** Ran SP% **110.9**
Speed ratings (Par 100): **98,97,96,95,92 83**
CSF £36.92 TOTE £5.90: £2.50, £3.60; EX 32.40 Trifecta £149.30.
**Owner** J C Smith **Bred** Littleton Stud **Trained** Upper Lambourn, Berks

**FOCUS**
A fair handicap. Not entirely convincing form.

## 5933 188BET NURSERY H'CAP 6f
**6:10** (6:11) (Class 6) (0-60,60) 2-Y-0 **£2,587** (£770; £384; £192) **Stalls** Centre

Form RPR

355 **1** **Princess Lyla (IRE)**[70] 3328 2-9-6 **59**................................ ShaneKelly 6 64
(Richard Hughes) *t.k.h in mid-div: shkn up wl over 2f out and gd prog: rdn and led over 1f out: kpt on: rdn out ins fnl f: edgd lft nr fin: kpt on wl* **12/1**

5354 **2** *¾* **Global Exceed**[22] 5121 2-9-7 **60**...........................................(b[1]) FranBerry 1 63
(Ed Dunlop) *wnt lft s: in rr on wd outside: prog over 2f out: rdn wl over 1f out: kpt on wl ins fnl f: no ex nr fin* **5/1**[3]

0502 **3** *½* **Rock On Bertie (IRE)**[22] 5121 2-9-2 **55**...........................(p) JimmyQuinn 3 56
(Nigel Tinkler) *cl up on outer: rdn wl over 1f out: keeping on one pce ins fnl f: sltly hmpd nr fin* **9/2**[2]

0021 **4** *1* **Atalanta Queen**[17] 5293 2-9-0 **60**...................(b) ManuelFernandes(7) 10 58
(Michael Appleby) *pressed ldrs on rail: led over 3f out: sn rdn: hdd over 1f out: one pce after* **7/2**[1]

040 **5** *1 ¼* **Fusion Central (IRE)**[19] 5216 2-8-11 **53**......................... HollieDoyle(3) 4 48
(Richard Hannon) *chsd ldrs: rdn wl over 1f out: kpt on one pce fnl 110yds* **10/1**

4456 **6** *1 ¾* **Data Protection**[31] 4758 2-9-4 **57**...................................(b) RobHornby 2 46
(William Muir) *in rr-div: rdn along over 2f out: kpt on one pce fr over 1f out* **14/1**

0053 **7** *1* **Hope And Glory (IRE)**[21] 5143 2-9-2 **55**.............(p[1]) AlistairRawlinson 7 41
(Tom Dascombe) *marginal ldr: hdd over 3f out and remained prom: rdn over 2f out: no ex sn after* **8/1**

060 **8** *2 ¾* **Spot Lite**[14] 5430 2-9-3 **56**............................................ WilliamCarson 12 34
(Rod Millman) *chsd ldrs on rail: rdn over 2f out: sn no ex* **10/1**

6604 **9** *5* **Erastus**[3] 5785 2-9-5 **58**.................................................. CharlesBishop 9 21+
(Mick Channon) *s.s: a in rr* **8/1**

4062 **10** *15* **Cranworth Phoenix**[17] 5293 2-8-11 **53**................... EdwardGreatrex(3) 8
(Brian Barr) *bhd ldr: rdn over 2f out: sn no ex fr wl over 1f out: t.o* **25/1**

005 **11** *3 ½* **Manco Inca (IRE)**[21] 5151 2-9-3 **56**...............................(b[1]) LiamKeniry 5
(Joseph Tuite) *pressed ldr on outer: rdn over 2f out: sn wknd: t.o* **20/1**

1m 11.97s (0.77) **Going Correction** 0.0s/f (Good) **11** Ran SP% **120.4**
Speed ratings (Par 92): **94,93,92,91,89 87,85,82,75,55 50**
CSF £72.79 CT £324.66 TOTE £10.40: £3.10, £1.70, £2.00; EX 93.10 Trifecta £1119.00.
**Owner** Ourselves Alone **Bred** F Prendergast & L Elvidge **Trained** Upper Lambourn, Berks
■ Stewards' Enquiry : Shane Kelly caution: careless riding

**FOCUS**
A moderate nursery.

## 5934 INTERPRO PEOPLE EBF NOVICE STKS 7f 135y
**6:40** (6:44) (Class 5) 2-Y-0 **£2,911** (£866; £432; £216) **Stalls** Centre

Form RPR

033 **1** **Yaafour**[15] 5365 2-9-2 84........................................... SeanLevey 4 84
(Richard Hannon) *mde all: shkn up and travelling best 2f out: sn rdn: kpt on while being pressed by runner-up ent fnl f: asserted fnl 110yds* **11/10**[1]

**2** *½* **Blanchefleur (IRE)** 2-8-8 0.......................................... HollieDoyle(3) 5 78+
(Richard Hannon) *bhd ldrs on outer: shkn up over 2f out and prog to press wnr 2f out: sn rdn and kpt chalng: no ex fnl 110yds* **14/1**

4 **3** *2* **Harmonica**[9] 5575 2-8-11 0.............................................. RyanPowell 6 73+
(Sir Mark Prescott Bt) *chsd ldrs on inner: rdn over 2f out: nt gng pce to chal and hands and heels ins fnl f: can do bttr* **6/1**[2]

0 **4** *6* **Raven's Song (IRE)**[28] 4909 2-8-11 0........................... WilliamCarson 7 59
(Harry Dunlop) *settled bhd ldr: shkn up over 3f out: rdn over 2f out: sn lft bhd* **33/1**

6 **5** *hd* **Global Wonder (IRE)**[24] 5036 2-9-2 0.................................. FranBerry 1 64
(Ed Dunlop) *s.s: in rr: rdn over 2f out sme prog tl no ex fr over 1f out* **8/1**

0 **6** *4 ½* **Berkshire Royal**[45] 4218 2-9-2 0...................................... RobHornby 2 53
(Andrew Balding) *bolted for 2f gng to s: chsd ldr: rdn 3f out: struggling fr 2f out: sn no ex* **7/1**[3]

1m 32.56s (0.26) **Going Correction** 0.0s/f (Good) **6** Ran SP% **95.1**
Speed ratings (Par 94): **98,97,95,89,89 84**
CSF £11.68 TOTE £1.60: £1.10, £4.70; EX 8.60 Trifecta £20.90.
**Owner** Khalifa Mohammed Al Attiyah **Bred** Moyns Park Estate And Stud Ltd **Trained** East Everleigh, Wilts
■ Pacific Fleet was withdrawn. Price at time of withdrawal 4/1. Rule 4 applies to all bets - deduction 20p in the pound.

**FOCUS**
A one-two for Richard Hannon. The winner set a fair standard and the one to take from the race is the runner-up.

## 5935 ASTON GROUP H'CAP 7f 135y
**7:10** (7:13) (Class 6) (0-60,60) 3-Y-O **£2,587** (£770; £384; £192) **Stalls** Centre

Form RPR
4050 1 **Royal Melody**[23] 5050 3-8-8 **50**...(p) GeorgeWood(3) 9 58
(Heather Main) *hld up in mid-div on rail: rdn over 2f out: kpt on wl w clr run up rail fr over 1f out: led ent fnl f: kpt on wl* **15/2**

055 2 1 1/4 **Rocksette**[119] 1787 3-8-7 **46** oh1... AntonioFresu 3 51
(Philip Hide) *chsd ldr on outer: rdn over 2f out: kpt on wl fr over 1f out: ev ch ent fnl f: no ex nr fin* **20/1**

-564 3 3 1/4 **Queens Royale**[18] 5266 3-9-4 **57**... PatCosgrave 8 54
(Michael Appleby) *settled in mid-div: rdn over 2f out: kpt on and edgd lft fr over 1f out: one pce fnl f* **9/4**[1]

6636 4 2 3/4 **Stopdworldnletmeof**[3] 5792 3-8-4 **46** oh1...(v) HollieDoyle(3) 4 37
(David Flood) *sn led and set str pce: rdn over 2f out: stuck on tl hdd ent fnl f: no ex after* **5/1**[2]

004 5 1 3/4 **D'Waterside**[18] 5247 3-9-4 **60**... EdwardGreatrex(3) 10 47
(David Loughnane) *led early: sn taken bk and chsd ldr: shkn up 3f out: sn rdn: kpt on one pce fr over 1f out* **10/1**

5U50 6 nk **Belgravian (FR)**[47] 4150 3-9-6 **59**...(tp) OisinMurphy 7 45
(Archie Watson) *chsd ldr on outer: rdn along 3f out: wknd over 1f out* **6/1**[3]

4000 7 1 3/4 **Velvet Charm**[18] 5266 3-9-2 **55**...(h) SeanLevey 2 37
(Rae Guest) *s.s: a towards rr* **10/1**

0400 8 1 1/4 **Greyjoy (IRE)**[26] 4982 3-8-0 **46** oh1... ShariqMohd(7) 5 25
(Sylvester Kirk) *in rr-div: rdn over 3f out: nt qckn and sn no ex* **14/1**

660 9 14 **Harbour Force (FR)**[60] 3691 3-9-7 **60**...(b[1]) FranBerry 1 6
(William Muir) *s.s: a in rr: rdn over 2f out: no imp and eased fnl 150yds* **7/1**

0-00 10 1 1/4 **Sea My Diamond (IRE)**[24] 5027 3-8-7 **46** oh1... KieranO'Neill 6
(Mark Hoad) *a in rr: rdn over 3f out: eased ins fnl f* **66/1**

1m 32.15s (-0.15) **Going Correction** 0.0s/f (Good) **10** Ran SP% **117.1**
Speed ratings (Par 98): **100,98,95,92,91 90,88,87,73,72**
CSF £144.98 CT £455.19 TOTE £8.20: £2.60, £4.50, £1.30; EX 132.90 Trifecta £705.50.
**Owner** Mr & Mrs D R Guest **Bred** Clarendon Farm **Trained** Kingston Lisle, Oxon
■ Stewards' Enquiry : Hollie Doyle caution: careless riding

**FOCUS**
This was run at a good gallop. The winner has been rated back to her figures from her two previous attempts here.

## 5936 PLAY ROULETTE AT 188BET H'CAP 6f
**7:40** (7:42) (Class 5) (0-75,79) 3-Y-O+ **£2,911** (£866; £432; £216) **Stalls** Centre

Form RPR
2224 1 **Seamster**[3] 5804 10-9-4 **74**...(t) LauraCoughlan(7) 2 81
(David Loughnane) *s.s: sn mde up grnd and led after 2f: clr ldr in centre and shkn up 3f out: rdn 2f out and began to drift to far side rail over 1f out: on rail 1f out: rdn out ins fnl f: ld reducing but kpt on wl* **6/1**

5242 2 1 **Whitecrest**[5] 5711 9-9-8 **71**... WilliamCarson 8 74
(John Spearing) *chsd ldrs: niggled along to go pce over 2f out: rdn wl over 1f out: kpt on wl ins fnl f and tk 2nd nr fin* **11/2**[3]

5033 3 3/4 **Dream Farr (IRE)**[16] 5326 4-9-8 **71**...(t) ThomasBrown 5 72
(Ed Walker) *chsd ldr and t.k.h: rdn over 2f out: kpt on wl ent fnl f: styd on for 3rd* **7/2**[2]

0-31 4 shd **Glenamoy Lad**[8] 5606 3-9-12 **79**...(t) SilvestreDeSousa 6 78+
(Michael Wigham) *hld up in mid-div: rdn over 2f out: tk 2nd over 1f out: kpt on chsng wnr tl wknd nr fin and lost two pls* **5/4**[1]

0060 5 2 3/4 **Posh Bounty**[15] 5357 6-9-1 **64**... JimmyQuinn 3 55
(Paul Burgoyne) *got warm at s: t.k.h chsng ldrs: rdn over 2f out: no ex over 1f out* **33/1**

0003 6 1 1/4 **Consulting**[21] 5156 4-9-4 **67**...(vt) OisinMurphy 7 54
(Stuart Williams) *led for 2f: hdd and chsd ldrs on rail: rdn over 2f out: no imp fr over 1f out* **8/1**

0105 7 3/4 **Perfect Pastime**[42] 4373 9-9-0 **63**... PatCosgrave 1 48
(Jim Boyle) *t.k.h on outside in rr: rdn over 2f out: no imp after* **28/1**

1m 11.43s (0.23) **Going Correction** 0.0s/f (Good)
**WFA** 3 from 4yo+ 4lb **7** Ran SP% **113.8**
Speed ratings (Par 103): **98,96,95,95,91 90,89**
CSF £37.96 CT £132.33 TOTE £6.20: £2.90, £2.70; EX 31.50 Trifecta £133.00.
**Owner** Miss Sarah Hoyland **Bred** D G Hardisty Bloodstock **Trained** Market Drayton, Shropshire

**FOCUS**
The early gallop wasn't strong and several were pulling for their heads. The runner-up has been rated to her latest, with the third rated to his turf mark.

## 5937 TICKET GIVEAWAYS AT 188BET MAIDEN STKS 6f
**8:10** (8:12) (Class 5) 3-Y-O+ **£2,911** (£866; £432; £216) **Stalls** Centre

Form RPR
2222 1 **Buxted Dream (USA)**[21] 5158 3-8-10 79... PatCosgrave 1 83
(Luca Cumani) *broke wl and mde all: pressed whn rdn on rail wl over 1f out: kpt on strly ins fnl f: pushed out fnl strides* **2/1**[2]

23 2 1 3/4 **Ptarmigan Ridge**[42] 4341 3-8-7 0... GeorgeWood(3) 5 76
(James Fanshawe) *racd in 3rd on rail: rdn bhd ldrs over 2f out: no imp tl kpt on strly wl ins fnl f: tk 2nd nr fin* **6/4**[1]

3 1/2 **Perfect Sense** 3-8-10 0... OisinMurphy 4 75
(Saeed bin Suroor) *chsd ldr on outer: shkn up over 2f out: rdn 2f out: ev ch over 1f out: no ex whn rdr lost 2nd* **11/4**[3]

25 4 2 3/4 **Charleston Belle**[16] 5335 3-8-2 0... HollieDoyle(3) 2 61
(Giles Bravery) *racd in 4th: rdn wl over 2f out: gd prog to sit prom on outer over 1f out: no ex whn rdr lost whip 150yds out: pushed out after* **14/1**

5 10 **Fortune And Glory (USA)** 4-9-0 0... FranBerry 3 35
(Joseph Tuite) *s.s and in rr: swtchd wd and prog fr over 3f out: rdn 2f out and fnd nil: eased fnl f* **16/1**

1m 11.83s (0.63) **Going Correction** 0.0s/f (Good)
**WFA** 3 from 4yo 4lb **5** Ran SP% **112.5**
Speed ratings (Par 103): **95,92,92,88,75**
CSF £5.57 TOTE £2.70: £1.30, £1.20; EX 5.20 Trifecta £7.50.
**Owner** Buxted Partnership **Bred** SF Bloodstock LLC **Trained** Newmarket, Suffolk

**FOCUS**
Fair maiden form. It's been rated at face value around the first two.
T/Plt: £155.50 to a £1 stake. Pool: £62,427.52 - 293.02 winning units T/Qpdt: £24.30 to a £1 stake. Pool: £4,264.87 - 129.74 winning units **Cathal Gahan**

# 5885 NEWMARKET (R-H)
Saturday, August 12

**OFFICIAL GOING: Good to soft (7.0)**
Wind: Light behind Weather: Cloudy with sunny spells

## 5938 BBAG PREMIER YEARLING SALES MAIDEN FILLIES' STKS (PLUS 10 RACE) 7f
**2:00** (2:03) (Class 4) 2-Y-O **£4,528** (£1,347; £673; £336) **Stalls** Low

Form RPR
1 **Peace Trail** 2-9-0 0... JamesDoyle 10 83+
(Charlie Appleby) *mde all: rdn and edgd rt over 1f out: edgd lft ins fnl f: styd on: eased nr fin* **6/4**[1]

2 1/2 **Altyn Orda (IRE)** 2-9-0 0... HarryBentley 3 82+
(Roger Varian) *chsd ldrs: pushed along over 2f out: hung lft and outpcd over 1f out: r.o ins fnl f* **25/1**

3 nse **Vitamin (IRE)** 2-9-0 0... SeanLevey 8 82+
(Richard Hannon) *s.i.s: sn rcvrd to chse wnr: rdn and ev ch fr over 1f out: edgd lft ins fnl f: styd on* **14/1**

4 1/2 **Clairette (IRE)** 2-9-0 0... KieranShoemark 2 80+
(Roger Charlton) *chsd ldrs: rdn over 2f out: hung lft fr over 1f out: r.o* **20/1**

5 2 **Juliet Foxtrot** 2-9-0 0... PJMcDonald 4 75+
(Charles Hills) *s.s: hld up: hdwy over 1f out: styd on same pce wl ins fnl f: hung lft towards fin* **16/1**

6 6 **Gilded Heaven** 2-9-0 0... JackMitchell 5 59
(Roger Varian) *s.i.s: hld up: pushed along and hdwy over 1f out: wknd ins fnl f* **33/1**

7 3/4 **Late Change** 2-9-0 0... StevieDonohoe 1 58
(David Simcock) *hld up: pushed along 1/2-way: wknd over 1f out* **40/1**

8 7 **Simple Thought (IRE)** 2-9-0 0... SilvestreDeSousa 6 39
(Simon Crisford) *hld up: plld hrd: shkn up and hdwy over 2f out: hung rt and wknd over 1f out* **15/2**[3]

9 8 **Nawassi** 2-9-0 0... DaneO'Neill 11 19
(John Gosden) *hld up: pushed along 1/2-way: rdn and wknd 2f out: eased fnl f* **7/4**[2]

1m 27.12s (1.42) **Going Correction** +0.125s/f (Good) **9** Ran SP% **114.7**
Speed ratings (Par 93): **96,95,95,94,92 85,84,76,67**
CSF £46.16 TOTE £2.10: £1.10, £5.60, £3.70; EX 41.10 Trifecta £549.00.
**Owner** Godolphin **Bred** Mrs R D Peacock **Trained** Newmarket, Suffolk

**FOCUS**
Rail movements increase certain advertised race distances as follows: Races 3 and 7 by 1.5 yards. A fillies' maiden made up entirely by debutantes from notable stables and won last year by the subsequent Group 1 Prix Marcel Boussac winner Wuheida. They went a modest gallop on officially good to soft ground which is reportedly riding nearer to good on a drying day.

## 5939 ROYAL BRITISH LEGION NURSERY H'CAP 7f
**2:35** (2:35) (Class 3) (0-95,92) 2-Y-O **£7,762** (£2,310; £1,154; £577) **Stalls** Low

Form RPR
5503 1 **Gold Town**[29] 4858 2-9-6 **91**...(p) JamesDoyle 3 99
(Charlie Appleby) *mde all: qcknd over 2f out: rdn over 1f out: edgd rt: styd on wl: eased nr fin* **5/6**[1]

1024 2 3 3/4 **Dragons Tail (IRE)**[6] 5681 2-9-7 **92**... MartinHarley 1 90
(Tom Dascombe) *chsd wnr: rdn over 2f out: edgd lft over 1f out: no ex ins fnl f* **4/1**[2]

653 3 1 **Fleeting Freedom**[15] 5372 2-8-6 **77**... JimmyQuinn 4 72
(Alan Bailey) *wnt lft s: chsd ldrs: rdn over 2f out: no ex ins fnl f* **6/1**[3]

11 4 6 **Mutanaaseq (IRE)**[98] 2382 2-9-1 **86**... DaneO'Neill 2 66
(Richard Hannon) *s.i.s: hld up: racd keenly: rdn over 2f out: wknd and eased over 1f out* **4/1**[2]

1m 26.73s (1.03) **Going Correction** +0.125s/f (Good) **4** Ran SP% **108.8**
Speed ratings (Par 98): **99,94,93,86**
CSF £4.47 TOTE £1.40; EX 4.00 Trifecta £13.60.
**Owner** Godolphin **Bred** Godolphin **Trained** Newmarket, Suffolk

**FOCUS**
A decent little nursery handicap. The favourite kept pouring on the pressure from front and his opponents were left in his wake. It's been rated as straightforward form around the runner-up.

## 5940 GERMAN YOUNG OWNERS AND BREEDERS H'CAP 1m 2f
**3:05** (3:06) (Class 2) (0-100,99) 3-Y-O+ **£12,938** (£3,850; £1,924; £962) **Stalls** Centre

Form RPR
0331 1 **Thundering Blue (USA)**[23] 5066 4-8-12 **83**... KieranShoemark 4 93
(David Menuisier) *hld up: hdwy and swtchd lft over 1f out: rdn to ld ins fnl f: sn hung lft towards fin: r.o: comf* **11/2**

13 2 1 **Atkinson Grimshaw (FR)**[29] 4856 3-8-4 **83**... JimmyQuinn 3 92
(Andrew Balding) *led: rdn over 1f out: hdd ins fnl f: styd on* **7/2**[2]

4211 3 1/2 **Anythingtoday (IRE)**[3] 5781 3-9-4 **97** 6ex...(p) JosephineGordon 6 105
(Hugo Palmer) *hld up: swtchd lft 2f out: hdwy over 1f out: sn rdn: nt clr run wl ins fnl f: styd on same pce towards fin* **11/4**[1]

2060 4 1 1/4 **Eddystone Rock (IRE)**[11] 5500 5-9-12 **97**...(h) SilvestreDeSousa 5 103+
(John Best) *hld up: hdwy over 2f out: rdn and hung rt over 1f out: ev ch whn hmpd ins fnl f: styd on same pce* **7/2**[2]

2465 5 8 **Ay Ay (IRE)**[14] 5421 3-8-4 **88**... DavidEgan(5) 7 77
(David Elsworth) *hld up: racd keenly: hdwy over 5f out: rdn over 2f out: wknd over 1f out* **5/1**[3]

5-50 6 3/4 **Dolphin Vista (IRE)**[98] 2396 4-9-13 **98**... OisinMurphy 1 85
(Martyn Meade) *chsd ldrs: rdn over 2f out: wknd over 1f out* **14/1**

1060 7 10 **In The Red (IRE)**[7] 5643 4-8-6 **80**... NoelGarbutt(3) 2 47
(Martin Smith) *chsd ldr: pushed along over 3f out: wknd over 1f out* **33/1**

2m 5.11s (-0.39) **Going Correction** +0.125s/f (Good)
**WFA** 3 from 4yo+ 8lb **7** Ran SP% **112.8**
Speed ratings (Par 109): **106,105,104,103,97 96,88**
CSF £24.26 CT £63.13 TOTE £7.30: £2.70, £2.10; EX 26.80 Trifecta £60.90.
**Owner** Mrs Gay Jarvis **Bred** Dr Tom Castoldi **Trained** Pulborough, W Sussex
■ Stewards' Enquiry : Kieran Shoemark three-day ban: careless riding (Sep 2-4)

**FOCUS**
Race distance increased by 1.5 yards. A good handicap. They went a respectable gallop and it is sound form. The fourth has been rated close to this year's form.

## 5941 GERMAN-THOROUGHBRED.COM SWEET SOLERA STKS (GROUP 3) (FILLIES) 7f
3:40 (3:41) (Class 1) 2-Y-O
£22,684 (£8,600; £4,304; £2,144; £1,076; £540) Stalls Low

| Form | | | | RPR |
|---|---|---|---|---|
| 161 | 1 | | **Tajaanus (IRE)**[16] 5329 2-9-0 97 DaneO'Neill 2 (Richard Hannon) *racd stands' side: mde all: rdn and hung lft fr over 1f out: r.o: 1st of 2 that side* **10/1** | 102 |
| 0431 | 2 | 1 | **Juliet Capulet (IRE)**[15] 5372 2-9-0 83 (p) RobertTart 5 (John Gosden) *led centre: rdn and ev ch over 1f out: r.o: 1st of 7 in gp* **20/1** | 99 |
| 11 | 3 | 1 | **Capla Temptress (IRE)**[21] 5154 2-9-0 87 HarryBentley 3 (Marco Botti) *racd stands' side tl swtchd centre over 4f out: chsd ldrs: rdn over 1f out: r.o: 2nd of 7 in gp* **5/1**[3] | 97 |
| 210 | 4 | hd | **Ertiyad**[50] 4028 2-9-0 87 PatCosgrave 7 (William Haggas) *racd centre: chsd ldr over 2f: remained handy: rdn over 2f out: outpcd over 1f out: rallied ins fnl f: r.o: 3rd of 7 in gp* **16/1** | 96 |
| 1 | 5 | nk | **Poetic Charm**[28] 4902 2-9-0 0 JamesDoyle 8 (Charlie Appleby) *racd centre: hld up: hdwy over 2f out: rdn and ev ch ins fnl f: no ex towards fin: 4th of 7 in gp* **11/4**[1] | 96 |
| 1 | 6 | 1 ¾ | **Mayyasah (USA)**[22] 5107 2-9-0 0 SeanLevey 4 (Richard Hannon) *racd centre: hld up: plld hrd: shkn up over 1f out: styng on whn nt clr run wl ins fnl f: nt rch ldrs: 5th of 7 in gp* **12/1** | 91 |
| 5033 | 7 | nk | **Mamba Noire (FR)**[29] 4855 2-9-0 0 ColmO'Donoghue 1 (K J Condon, Ire) *trckd wnr on stands' side: swtchd lft 2f out: rdn and edgd lft over 1f out: wknd ins fnl f: last of 2 that side* **7/1** | 92 |
| 1112 | 8 | ½ | **Dance Diva**[14] 5391 2-9-0 100 SilvestreDeSousa 9 (Richard Fahey) *racd centre: hld up: hdwy over 2f out: rdn and ev ch ins fnl f: sn edgd lft and wknd: 6th of 7 in gp* **3/1**[2] | 90 |
| 41 | 9 | 2 ½ | **Jousi**[15] 5349 2-9-0 0 JosephineGordon 6 (Hugo Palmer) *racd centre: plld hrd and prom: wnt 2nd over 4f out tl rdn 2f out: wknd over 1f out: last of 7 in gp* **16/1** | 82 |

1m 26.35s (0.65) **Going Correction** +0.125s/f (Good) 9 Ran SP% **114.1**
Speed ratings (Par 101): **101,99,98,98,98 96,95,95,92**
CSF £183.46 TOTE £10.20: £2.80, £4.60, £1.80; EX 141.50 Trifecta £1123.60.
**Owner** Hamdan Al Maktoum **Bred** Shadwell Estate Company Limited **Trained** East Everleigh, Wilts

**FOCUS**
A competitive renewal of this Group 3 juvenile fillies' contest, won by the high-class Rainbow View in 2008. In the previous two 7f juvenile races on this card the near rail was shunned, but the winner made all up the stands' side from stall two. The winner has been rated as improving slightly.

## 5942 BBAG-SALES.DE H'CAP 7f
4:15 (4:15) (Class 2) (0-105,99) 3-Y-O+ £12,938 (£3,850; £1,924; £962) Stalls Low

| Form | | | | RPR |
|---|---|---|---|---|
| -500 | 1 | | **Accession (IRE)**[44] 4264 8-9-9 94 MartinLane 6 (Charlie Fellowes) *chsd ldrs: pushed along over 2f out: rdn to ld ins fnl f: r.o* **10/1** | 104 |
| 5453 | 2 | 2 ¼ | **War Glory (IRE)**[10] 5530 4-9-4 89 SeanLevey 3 (Richard Hannon) *chsd ldr tl led wl over 1f out: rdn: edgd lft and hdd ins fnl f: styd on same pce* **5/2**[1] | 93 |
| 6000 | 3 | ¾ | **Suzi's Connoisseur**[29] 4854 6-9-6 91 (t) OisinMurphy 8 (Stuart Williams) *hld up: hdwy over 1f out: sn rdn: styd on* **11/1** | 93 |
| 2500 | 4 | nse | **The Warrior (IRE)**[10] 5530 5-9-2 87 KieranShoemark 2 (Amanda Perrett) *hld up: hdwy u.p over 1f out: styd on* **12/1** | 89 |
| 6533 | 5 | 2 ½ | **That Is The Spirit**[8] 5616 6-10-0 99 HarryBentley 4 (David O'Meara) *led: rdn and hdd wl over 1f out: wknd ins fnl f* **8/1**[3] | 95 |
| 1251 | 6 | nk | **Khamaary (IRE)**[17] 5294 3-9-5 96 DaneO'Neill 9 (Mark Johnston) *w ldr: rdn and ev ch over 1f out: wknd ins fnl f* **5/2**[1] | 89 |
| 0402 | 7 | 10 | **Gulliver**[11] 5513 3-8-13 90 (vt) JamesDoyle 7 (Hugo Palmer) *broke wl: sn lost pl: effrt over 2f out: wknd over 1f out* **4/1**[2] | 68 |

1m 25.97s (0.27) **Going Correction** +0.125s/f (Good)
**WFA** 3 from 4yo+ 6lb 7 Ran SP% **113.4**
Speed ratings (Par 109): **103,100,99,99,96 96,84**
CSF £34.68 CT £283.51 TOTE £12.50: £4.40, £1.70; EX 31.50 Trifecta £485.50.
**Owner** Lady De Ramsey **Bred** Corduff Stud Ltd **Trained** Newmarket, Suffolk

**FOCUS**
A good handicap. They went a respectable gallop. There was a difference of opinion whether to race near side or more centrally. On this occasion, the horse racing centrally won well suggesting there isn't a lot in it. The runner-up has been rated close to his turf form.

## 5943 ROYAL BRITISH LEGION H'CAP 1m
4:50 (4:50) (Class 2) (0-100,92) 3-Y-O £12,938 (£3,850; £1,924; £962) Stalls Low

| Form | | | | RPR |
|---|---|---|---|---|
| 100 | 1 | | **Naval Warfare (IRE)**[14] 5392 3-9-6 92 OisinMurphy 6 (Andrew Balding) *mde all: swtchd rt 2f out: sn rdn: styd on wl* **5/1**[3] | 101 |
| 154 | 2 | 2 ½ | **Night Circus (IRE)**[38] 4507 3-9-5 91 JamesDoyle 5 (Charlie Appleby) *trckd ldrs: racd keenly: rdn over 2f out: chsd wnr over 1f out: styd on same pce ins fnl f* **4/1**[2] | 94 |
| -561 | 3 | 2 | **Plutonian (IRE)**[47] 4152 3-9-6 92 SilvestreDeSousa 2 (Charles Hills) *chsd ldr: rdn over 2f out: nt clr run over 1f out: no ex ins fnl f* **4/1**[2] | 91 |
| -400 | 4 | ½ | **Colibri (IRE)**[29] 4856 3-9-5 91 JosephineGordon 1 (Hugo Palmer) *prom: pushed along over 3f out: nt clr run and swtchd lft over 1f out: sn rdn: no ex ins fnl f* **4/1**[2] | 89 |
| 0040 | 5 | 1 ¼ | **Executive Force**[14] 5392 3-8-11 88 GeorgiaCox(5) 3 (William Haggas) *s.i.s: hld up: hdwy over 1f out: sn rdn: wknd ins fnl f* **8/1** | 83 |
| 5351 | 6 | 1 ¼ | **Tafaakhor (IRE)**[22] 5115 3-9-2 88 (b) DaneO'Neill 4 (Richard Hannon) *hld up: racd keenly: hdwy over 1f out: sn rdn: wknd ins fnl f* **10/3**[1] | 80 |

1m 39.33s (-0.67) **Going Correction** +0.125s/f (Good) 6 Ran SP% **110.9**
Speed ratings (Par 106): **108,105,103,103,101 100**
CSF £24.22 TOTE £5.70: £2.40, £2.20; EX 26.20 Trifecta £107.50.
**Owner** Qatar Racing Limited **Bred** Rathasker Stud **Trained** Kingsclere, Hants

**FOCUS**
A decent 3yo handicap. The winner clocked comparatively the second best time on the card after gradually coming over and making all up the near rail. The winner has been rated close to his Leicester win.

## 5944 ASPALL CYDER H'CAP 2m
5:20 (5:23) (Class 3) (0-90,88) 3-Y-O+ £7,762 (£2,310; £1,154; £577) Stalls Centre

| Form | | | | RPR |
|---|---|---|---|---|
| 11 | 1 | | **Rolling Maul (IRE)**[9] 5566 9-9-0 79 JoshuaBryan(5) 6 (Peter Bowen) *hld up: hdwy over 3f out: chsd ldr over 2f out: rdn to ld over 1f out: styd on gamely: all out* **8/1** | 91 |
| 421P | 2 | hd | **Addicted To You (IRE)**[12] 5468 3-8-7 80 SilvestreDeSousa 5 (Mark Johnston) *hld up: hdwy over 4f out: led 3f out: rdn: edgd lft and hdd over 1f out: styd on gamely* **5/2**[2] | 91 |
| 5232 | 3 | 2 ¼ | **Look My Way**[28] 4891 3-8-4 77 JosephineGordon 3 (Andrew Balding) *chsd ldrs: lost pl over 5f out: swtchd lft over 4f out: hdwy over 3f out: rdn over 2f out: styd on* **15/8**[1] | 85 |
| 1643 | 4 | 20 | **Grumeti**[25] 4998 9-9-6 80 (p) FergusSweeney 8 (Alan King) *hld up: hdwy over 4f out: rdn over 2f out: wknd over 1f out* **14/1** | 64 |
| 000- | 5 | 3 | **Wind Place And Sho**[197] 7150 5-10-0 88 RyanTate 1 (James Eustace) *chsd ldrs: rdn over 4f out: wknd over 2f out* **33/1** | 68 |
| 10-2 | 6 | 1 ¾ | **Slunovrat (FR)**[17] 5303 6-9-12 86 KieranShoemark 9 (David Menuisier) *chsd ldr after 1f: rdn and ev ch 3f out: wknd wl over 1f out: eased nr fin* **5/1**[3] | 64 |
| 1503 | 7 | 8 | **Mark Hopkins**[15] 5351 5-9-8 87 DavidEgan(5) 4 (David Elsworth) *led: edgd lft over 4f out: hdd 3f out: hung lft and wknd 2f out* **13/2** | 56 |
| 5025 | 8 | 36 | **Lanceur (FR)**[38] 4499 8-9-5 79 AdamBeschizza 7 (William Stone) *hld up: hdwy over 6f out: rdn and wknd over 3f out* **40/1** | 5 |

3m 25.14s (-1.86) **Going Correction** +0.125s/f (Good)
**WFA** 3 from 5yo+ 13lb 8 Ran SP% **116.5**
Speed ratings (Par 107): **109,108,107,97,96 95,91,73**
CSF £28.96 CT £54.02 TOTE £8.40: £2.30, £1.40, £1.10; EX 31.00 Trifecta £98.40.
**Owner** Roddy Owen & Paul Fullagar **Bred** Rathmore Stud **Trained** Little Newcastle, Pembrokes

**FOCUS**
Race distance increased by 1.5 yards. A decent staying handicap. A stirring battle produced an even quicker comparative winning time than the previous race. The winner was a 140-rated hurdler at his best and has been rated in line with that.
T/Plt: £682.60 to a £1 stake. Pool: £76,134.18 - 81.41 winning units T/Qpdt: £134.20 to a £1 stake. Pool: £4,366.29 - 24.06 winning units **Colin Roberts**

# 5537 REDCAR (L-H)
Saturday, August 12

**OFFICIAL GOING: Good to soft (7.6)**
Wind: light against Weather: showery

## 5945 BET AT RACINGUK.COM (S) STKS 5f 217y
1:30 (1:33) (Class 6) 2-Y-O £2,911 (£866; £432; £216) Stalls Centre

| Form | | | | RPR |
|---|---|---|---|---|
| 643P | 1 | | **Society's Dream (IRE)**[17] 5277 2-8-6 50 RoystonFfrench 1 (K R Burke) *w ldr: led 3f out: rdn over 1f out: edgd rt: kpt on* **5/1**[2] | 50 |
| 00 | 2 | 1 ½ | **Little Monkey**[31] 4740 2-8-6 0 CamHardie 3 (Antony Brittain) *in tch: rdn over 2f out: chsd ldr jst ins fnl f: kpt on* **40/1** | 45 |
| 004 | 3 | nse | **Angie B (IRE)**[8] 5613 2-8-6 48 JamesSullivan 7 (John Wainwright) *hld up in tch: rdn along over 3f out: swtchd lft over 1f out: kpt on ins fnl f* **20/1** | 45 |
| 2 | 4 | 1 ¾ | **Silverlight (IRE)**[8] 5613 2-8-6 0 PaddyAspell 4 (Philip Kirby) *s.i.s: sn trckd ldrs: rdn over 1f out: no ex ins fnl f* **2/1**[1] | 40 |
| 60 | 5 | 4 | **Jaimie's Joy**[25] 4996 2-8-11 0 BarryMcHugh 2 (Tony Coyle) *led narrowly: hdd 3f out: sn rdn: wknd over 1f out* **5/1**[2] | 33 |
| 0 | 6 | 1 ¾ | **Racing Radio (IRE)**[11] 5494 2-8-11 0 BenCurtis 8 (David Barron) *w ldr: rdn over 2f out: wknd over 1f out* **22/1** | 28 |
| 0565 | 7 | 6 | **Sausage Fingers**[17] 5293 2-8-11 61 (p) FrannyNorton 6 (Tom Dascombe) *w ldr: pushed along and lost pl over 2f out: sn wknd* **7/1**[3] | 10 |

1m 14.92s (3.12) **Going Correction** +0.275s/f (Good) 7 Ran SP% **90.7**
Speed ratings (Par 92): **90,88,87,85,80 77,69**
CSF £106.40 TOTE £4.10: £2.00, £6.20; EX 56.40 Trifecta £363.10.There was no bid for the winner.
**Owner** Hambleton Racing Ltd XXXV & E Burke **Bred** Helen Smith & Sally Mullen **Trained** Middleham Moor, N Yorks
■ Sam James was withdrawn. Price at time of withdrawal 7/2. Rule 4 applies to all bets - deduction 20p in the pound.

**FOCUS**
The going had started to tighten up as the track had been largely bereft of rainfall in the previous four days. Less than 1mm fell in the preceding 24 hours, although there was a sharp downpour 50 minutes before this first race. There was a possibility of more light rain throughout the meeting. The temperature was cool for the time of year at around 16C. A very modest race, even for this grade, and it was a slowly-run affair.

## 5946 CELEBRATE THE LIFE OF JOE NEWTON MEDIAN AUCTION MAIDEN STKS 7f
2:05 (2:07) (Class 5) 3-4-Y-O £3,234 (£962; £481; £240) Stalls Centre

| Form | | | | RPR |
|---|---|---|---|---|
| -222 | 1 | | **Bassmah**[42] 4351 3-9-0 78 BenCurtis 7 (Ismail Mohammed) *hld up: smooth hdwy over 2f out: led over 1f out: kpt on pushed out fnl f* **1/3**[1] | 63+ |
| 000 | 2 | 1 ¾ | **Starboard Watch**[67] 3435 3-9-0 46 JamesSullivan 5 (James Given) *hld up: pushed along and hdwy over 1f out: rdn to go 2nd ins fnl f: kpt on* **50/1** | 58 |
| -6 | 3 | ½ | **Chosen World**[16] 5315 3-9-5 0 JoeDoyle 4 (Julie Camacho) *in tch: rdn over 1f out: kpt on* **4/1**[2] | 62 |
| 44 | 4 | 2 ¼ | **Mischief Managed (IRE)**[7] 5670 3-9-5 0 (e) DuranFentiman 6 (Tim Easterby) *prom: racd keenly: led over 2f out: rdn whn hdd over 1f out: no ex ins fnl f* **5/1**[3] | 56 |
| 6 | 5 | 2 ¼ | **Betty Grable (IRE)**[10] 5538 3-9-0 0 NathanEvans 9 (Wilf Storey) *midfield: rdn and hdwy over 2f out: ev ch over 1f out: wknd ins fnl f* **10/1** | 45 |
| 04 | 6 | ½ | **Spike's Princess (IRE)**[183] 656 3-9-0 0 BarryMcHugh 1 (Adrian Nicholls) *trckd ldrs: rdn along and outpcd over 2f out: plugged on fnl f* **33/1** | 44 |

7 3 ¼ **Spring Beauty** 3-9-0 0 ConnorBeasley 2 35
(John Weymes) *led: hdd over 3f out: sn pushed along: wknd over 1f out* 25/1

00 8 10 **Monsieur Mel**[24] 5019 3-9-5 0 CamHardie 10 13
(Antony Brittain) *dwlt: sn trckd ldrs: rdn over 2f out: wknd over 1f out* 33/1

-000 9 8 **Zarkavon**[20] 5182 3-9-0 23 (p[1]) PaddyAspell 8
(John Wainwright) *in tch: rdn and lost pl over 3f out: sn weakend and bhd* 150/1

0/ 10 13 **Encoded (IRE)**[690] 6613 4-8-13 0 RyanTimby[(7)] 3
(Lynn Siddall) *s.i.s: hld up: hdwy to ld over 3f out: hdd over 2f out: wknd qckly and eased* 66/1

1m 27.13s (2.63) **Going Correction** +0.275s/f (Good)
**WFA** 3 from 4yo 6lb 10 Ran SP% **134.6**
Speed ratings (Par 103): **95,93,92,89,87 86,83,71,62,47**
CSF £52.73 TOTE £1.20: £1.02, £7.90, £1.10; EX 27.40 Trifecta £137.80.
**Owner** Abdulla Al Mansoori **Bred** Hants And Herts **Trained** Newmarket, Suffolk

**FOCUS**
A weak maiden for the class and the odds-on favourite took this with little fuss from a 46-rated filly, which says plenty about the strength of the race. It's been rated around the third and fourth.

## 5947 ALL NEW RACINGUK.COM H'CAP 5f 217y
**2:40** (2:41) (Class 4) (0-85,84) 3-Y-O+ **£6,469** (£1,925; £962; £481) **Stalls** Centre

Form RPR
2635 1 **Magical Effect (IRE)**[13] 5457 5-9-7 79 JamesSullivan 10 90
(Ruth Carr) *dwlt: hld up: pushed along and hdwy over 1f out: rdn to ld ins fnl f: kpt on wl* 7/2[2]

0204 2 2 **Tricky Dicky**[21] 5156 4-9-1 73 SamJames 6 78
(Olly Williams) *prom: rdn 2f out: led appr fnl f: hdd ins fnl f: one pce* 12/1

3551 3 ¾ **Questo**[38] 4509 5-8-8 66 RoystonFfrench 11 69
(Tracy Waggott) *chsd ldrs: rdn and ev ch over 1f out: one pce ins fnl f* 10/1

5030 4 1 **Duke Cosimo**[13] 5457 7-9-1 73 JoeDoyle 8 72
(Michael Herrington) *hld up: rdn 2f out: kpt on fnl f: nrst fin* 25/1

5000 5 ¾ **Ninjago**[7] 5671 7-9-9 81 CamHardie 3 78
(Paul Midgley) *midfield: rdn 2f out: kpt on same pce and nvr threatened* 16/1

0353 6 hd **Jessinamillion**[16] 5316 3-8-11 73 NathanEvans 4 68
(James Bethell) *hld up: rdn and hdwy over 1f out: one pce ins fnl f* 11/1

4234 7 ½ **Kenny The Captain (IRE)**[5] 5696 6-8-8 73 (p) RobertDodsworth[(7)] 2 68
(Tim Easterby) *prom: rdn over 2f out: wknd ins fnl f* 11/2[3]

6-10 8 ½ **Adam's Ale**[58] 3741 8-9-11 83 (p) BarryMcHugh 7 76
(Marjorie Fife) *midfield: rdn 2f out: nvr threatened* 18/1

3025 9 ½ **Aprovado (IRE)**[12] 5471 5-9-7 84 (b) CallumRodriguez[(5)] 12 76
(Michael Dods) *led: rdn over 2f out: hdd appr fnl f: wknd* 22/1

5032 10 8 **Tommy G**[7] 5637 4-9-6 78 PhillipMakin 5 44
(Jim Goldie) *midfield: pushed along 3f out: rdn 2f out: sn btn* 2/1[1]

1m 12.06s (0.26) **Going Correction** +0.275s/f (Good)
**WFA** 3 from 4yo+ 4lb 10 Ran SP% **115.4**
Speed ratings (Par 105): **109,106,105,104,103 102,102,101,100,90**
CSF £44.61 CT £384.32 TOTE £6.10: £1.60, £3.50, £2.60; EX 54.00 Trifecta £198.30.
**Owner** Miss Vanessa Church **Bred** W Maxwell Ervine **Trained** Huby, N Yorks
■ Majdool was withdrawn. Price at time of withdrawal 66/1. Rule 4 does not apply.

**FOCUS**
Relatively competitive for the grade and the pace was solid enough for the conditions. The winner came from off the pace. The runner-up has been rated close to form.

## 5948 MARKET CROSS JEWELLERS H'CAP 7f
**3:15** (3:25) (Class 4) (0-80,82) 3-Y-O+ **£6,469** (£1,925; £962; £481) **Stalls** Centre

Form RPR
4143 1 **Hajjam**[17] 5288 3-9-4 75 (h) PhillipMakin 3 81
(David O'Meara) *dwlt: hld up: rdn and hdwy over 1f out: led narrowly 110yds out: kpt on* 3/1[1]

4500 2 nk **Fieldsman (USA)**[15] 5379 5-9-9 77 JoshDoyle[(3)] 10 84
(David O'Meara) *trckd ldrs: rdn 2f out: chal jst ins fnl f: kpt on* 11/1

3615 3 hd **Favourite Treat (USA)**[12] 5481 7-9-4 69 (e) JamesSullivan 8 75
(Ruth Carr) *dwlt: hld up: rdn and hdwy over 1f out: ev ch fnl 110yds: kpt on* 16/1

0064 4 1 **Roll On Rory**[22] 5125 4-9-13 78 (p) DavidNolan 7 81
(Jason Ward) *prom: rdn along 3f out: kpt on* 10/1

3125 5 nk **Raselasad (IRE)**[10] 5541 3-9-11 82 RoystonFfrench 11 82
(Tracy Waggott) *led: pushed along 2f out: rdn and hung repeatedly lft fr appr fnl f: hdd 110yds out: no ex* 7/1[3]

2224 6 1 ½ **Kirkham**[17] 5288 4-9-3 68 (p) JoeDoyle 5 66
(Julie Camacho) *trckd ldrs: rdn over 1f out: one pce* 5/1[2]

1410 7 nk **Our Charlie Brown**[14] 5400 3-9-3 74 CamHardie 12 70
(Tim Easterby) *hld up: rdn 2f out: kpt on ins fnl f: nvr threatened* 16/1

2253 8 nse **Right Action**[15] 5376 3-9-5 76 TonyHamilton 13 71
(Richard Fahey) *in tch: rdn 2f out: hung repeatedly lft and one pce* 8/1

0265 9 3 **Florencio**[14] 5415 4-9-8 73 (p) ConnorBeasley 6 62
(Roger Fell) *trckd ldrs: rdn 2f out: wknd fnl f* 11/1

0556 10 3 ¼ **Maldonado (FR)**[10] 5541 3-8-8 72 HarrisonShaw[(7)] 2 51
(Michael Easterby) *prom: rdn over 2f out: sn wknd* 25/1

210 11 shd **Parys Mountain (IRE)**[28] 4892 3-9-8 79 (h) BenCurtis 4 57
(David Brown) *prom: racd keenly: rdn over 2f out: wknd* 10/1

1m 24.04s (-0.46) **Going Correction** +0.275s/f (Good)
**WFA** 3 from 4yo+ 6lb 11 Ran SP% **115.7**
Speed ratings (Par 105): **113,112,112,111,110 109,108,108,105,101 101**
CSF £36.54 CT £461.82 TOTE £3.30: £1.60, £3.50, £4.40; EX 46.50 Trifecta £397.30.Curzon Line was withdrawn. Price at time of withdrawal 16/1. Rule 4 does not apply.
**Owner** Sheikh Abdullah Almalek Alsabah **Bred** Mrs Janis Macpherson **Trained** Upper Helmsley, N Yorks

**FOCUS**
A modest pace for this competitive handicap, although the form looks solid. Straightforward form, with the second, third and fourth rated close to this year's form.

## 5949 RACING UK STRAIGHT-MILE SERIES H'CAP (RACING UK STRAIGHT MILE SERIES QUALIFIER) 7f 219y
**3:50** (3:52) (Class 4) (0-85,86) 3-Y-O+ **£6,469** (£1,925; £962; £240; £240) **Stalls** Centre

Form RPR
0115 1 **Zodiakos (IRE)**[7] 5668 4-9-8 82 (p) AdamMcNamara[(3)] 5 89
(Roger Fell) *dwlt: sn in tch: pushed along and hdwy over 1f out: rdn to ld 1f out: edgd lft: kpt on wl* 7/2[2]

0630 2 1 ½ **Rashford's Double (IRE)**[14] 5392 3-9-3 81 (p) TonyHamilton 6 84
(Richard Fahey) *hld up: pushed along and hdwy over 1f out: rdn to chse ldr ins fnl f: kpt on* 11/1

11 3 3 ¼ **Bouclier (IRE)**[110] 2026 7-10-0 85 NathanEvans 9 82
(Michael Easterby) *hld up: rdn and sme hdwy over 1f out: one pce fnl f* 12/1

2201 4 ½ **Strong Steps**[12] 5469 5-10-1 86 PhillipMakin 7 81
(Jim Goldie) *in tch: rdn over 2f out: one pce* 9/2[3]

-656 4 dht **Pullman Brown (USA)**[95] 2497 5-9-3 74 PaddyAspell 3 69
(Philip Kirby) *led: rdn 2f out: hdd 1f out: no ex* 16/1

2000 6 ½ **Intense Style (IRE)**[13] 5457 5-9-11 82 (v[1]) ConnorBeasley 4 76
(Les Eyre) *trckd ldrs: rdn over 2f out: bit outpcd over 1f out: one pce fnl f* 9/1

0141 7 ¾ **Ventura Secret (IRE)**[3] 5807 3-8-3 67 6ex DuranFentiman 1 59
(Tim Easterby) *prom: rdn over 2f out: wknd ins fnl f* 11/4[1]

4646 8 5 **Town Charter (USA)**[14] 5415 3-9-1 79 FrannyNorton 2 59
(Mark Johnston) *hld up in tch: rdn over 2f out: sn wknd* 6/1

1m 38.56s (1.96) **Going Correction** +0.275s/f (Good)
**WFA** 3 from 4yo+ 7lb 8 Ran SP% **113.3**
Speed ratings (Par 105): **101,99,96,95,95 95,94,89**
CSF £40.09 CT £411.41 TOTE £4.10: £1.50, £3.10, £3.20; EX 35.40 Trifecta £228.00.
**Owner** C Varley & R G Fell **Bred** Brian Walsh **Trained** Nawton, N Yorks

**FOCUS**
A handicap qualifier for the Straight-Mile Series and the first two came from off the pace and drew a little way clear of the remainder. The form looks viable. The runner-up has been rated to the better view of his form.

## 5950 WISE BETTING AT RACINGUK.COM H'CAP 1m 2f 1y
**4:25** (4:26) (Class 5) (0-70,72) 3-Y-O+ **£3,234** (£962; £481; £240) **Stalls** Low

Form RPR
1553 1 **Diamond Runner (IRE)**[13] 5454 5-8-11 55 (b) AdamMcNamara[(3)] 4 63
(Lawrence Mullaney) *hld up in midfield: stdy hdwy fr 3f out: rdn to ld 1f out: strly pressed fnl 110yds: hld on wl* 9/2[1]

2504 2 shd **Yensir**[17] 5284 4-9-3 65 PatrickVaughan[(7)] 12 73
(Grant Tuer) *dwlt and swtchd lft s: hld up in rr: n.m.r over 2f out: swtchd rt wl over 1f out: pushed along and sn gd hdwy: rdn to chal strly fnl 110yds: kpt on: jst failed* 8/1

224 3 2 **Lucy's Law (IRE)**[50] 4056 3-9-6 69 JamesSullivan 8 73
(Tom Tate) *hld up: rdn and hdwy on outer over 2f out: kpt on fnl f* 6/1[2]

6006 4 1 **Rock Island Line**[65] 3499 3-8-13 62 (p[1]) NathanEvans 2 64
(Mark Walford) *midfield: rdn and hdwy 2f out: ev ch ent fnl f: one pce* 17/2

2222 5 nk **Bling King**[10] 5539 8-9-6 61 (p) SamJames 11 62
(Geoffrey Harker) *prom: pushed along to ld 2f out: sn rdn: hdd 1f out: one pce* 10/1

65 6 nk **La Havrese (FR)**[36] 4575 6-9-4 59 PaddyAspell 1 60
(Lynn Siddall) *midfield on inner: pushed along 2f out: angled rt over 1f out: rdn and r.o fnl f* 18/1

0642 7 1 **Akkadian Empire**[22] 5131 3-9-8 71 (h) DavidNolan 6 70
(Iain Jardine) *trckd ldrs: racd keenly: rdn over 2f out: one pce* 9/2[1]

0125 8 ½ **Graceful Act**[11] 5499 9-8-7 53 (p) CallumRodriguez[(5)] 10 54
(Ron Barr) *trckd ldrs: pushed along 2f out: persistently short of room towards inner fr appr fnl f tl fnl 75yds: nvr able to chal* 16/1

2340 9 1 ¾ **Spiritofhayton (IRE)**[7] 5650 3-9-7 70 BenCurtis 7 64
(David Barron) *hld up: rdn over 2f out: plugged on fnl f: nvr threatened* 7/1[3]

3212 10 2 **Hernando Torres**[15] 5359 9-9-7 69 (tp) RyanTimby[(7)] 9 59
(Michael Easterby) *midfield on outer: rdn over 2f out: wknd fnl f* 14/1

0-00 11 nk **Arizona Sunrise**[10] 5540 4-9-0 55 JoeDoyle 5 45
(Tina Jackson) *led: rdn whn hdd 2f out: wknd fnl f* 66/1

3304 12 2 **Hussar Ballad (USA)**[11] 5498 8-9-6 61 CamHardie 15 47
(Antony Brittain) *swtchd lft s: hld up: nvr threatened* 25/1

30-0 13 13 **Highfield Lass**[64] 3529 6-8-9 50 oh4 RoystonFfrench 13 10
(Tracy Waggott) *trckd ldrs: racd keenly: rdn over 2f out: wknd over 1f out* 50/1

2m 9.56s (2.46) **Going Correction** +0.30s/f (Good)
**WFA** 3 from 4yo+ 8lb 13 Ran SP% **119.0**
Speed ratings (Par 103): **102,101,100,99,99 99,98,97,96,94 94,93,82**
CSF £39.61 CT £221.10 TOTE £5.70: £1.90, £3.00, £2.10; EX 53.50 Trifecta £643.90.
**Owner** Bawtry Racing Club **Bred** Edmond Kent **Trained** Great Habton, N Yorks

**FOCUS**
The first three home came from off the pace in a competitive handicap for the grade and the pace was fair for the conditions. The runner-up has been rated to this year's form.

## 5951 LADIES' & GENTS' EVENING 26TH AUGUST H'CAP 1m 5f 218y
**5:00** (5:01) (Class 6) (0-65,72) 3-Y-O+ **£2,911** (£866; £432; £216) **Stalls** Low

Form RPR
0304 1 **Stanarley Pic**[14] 5413 6-9-5 56 NeilFarley 2 64
(Sally Haynes) *led: rdn over 3f out: hdd narrowly wl over 1f out: rallied to ld again 110yds out: styd on wl* 18/1

4641 2 ½ **Vindicator (IRE)**[8] 5617 3-9-7 72 (p) AdamMcNamara[(3)] 8 81
(Michael Dods) *midfield: pushed along and gd hdwy over 3f out: rdn to ld narrowly wl over 1f out: drvn whn hdd 110yds out: one pce towards fin* 1/1[1]

3-00 3 6 **Calliope**[70] 3343 4-9-11 62 JamesSullivan 5 61
(Kenneth Slack) *hld up: rdn over 2f out: hdwy over 1f out: styd on fnl f: wnt 3rd fnl 75yds* 14/1

-543 4 1 ¾ **Mister Bob (GER)**[144] 1291 8-9-13 64 (p) PhillipMakin 6 60
(James Bethell) *hld up in midfield: pushed along and hdwy whn involved in barging match over 1f out: rdn and one pce fnl f* 16/1

/46- 5 1 **Oliver's Gold**[19] 4239 9-8-7 49 ow1 CallumRodriguez[(5)] 3 44
(Mark Walford) *trckd ldrs: pushed along over 2f out: bit short of room over 1f out: rdn and one pce fnl f* 5/1[2]

-001 6 ¾ **Adherence**[67] 3436 4-9-7 58 BarryMcHugh 4 52
(Tony Coyle) *midfield: rdn over 2f out: one pce and nvr threatened* 14/1

4424 7 ¾ **Jan De Heem**[13] 5454 7-9-4 60 BenRobinson[(5)] 12 53
(Tina Jackson) *hld up: rdn and hdd over 2f out: no ex fnl f* 12/1

5630 8 nk **Yasir (USA)**[12] 5483 9-9-5 56 DavidNolan 9 48
(Conor Dore) *hld up in midfield on inner: pushed along over 2f out: swtchd rt over 1f out: nvr threatened* 25/1

050- 9 3 ¼ **Slipper Satin (IRE)**[340] 6219 7-9-4 55 (t) FrannyNorton 10 43
(Simon West) *prom: rdn over 2f out: wknd fnl f* 40/1

5213 10 1 ¾ **Midnight Warrior**[8] 5599 7-9-7 58 (t) JoeDoyle 7 48
(Ron Barr) *trckd ldrs: rdn along over 2f out: losing pl whn hmpd over 1f out: eased* 8/1[3]

2400 11 nse **Percy Verence**[25] 5008 4-9-0 51 RoystonFfrench 1 36
(Tracy Waggott) *trckd ldrs: rdn over 3f out: wknd over 1f out* 20/1

00/5 12 19 **Rock A Doodle Doo (IRE)**221 30 10-9-10 61......... NathanEvans 11 20
(Sean Regan) *a rr* **66/1**

3m 8.26s (3.56) **Going Correction** +0.30s/f (Good)
**WFA** 3 from 4yo+ 11lb 12 Ran SP% **122.5**
Speed ratings (Par 101): **101,100,97,96,95 95,94,94,92,91 91,80**
CSF £36.58 CT £299.12 TOTE £25.20: £5.70, £1.10, £3.50; EX 64.50 Trifecta £699.20.
**Owner** The Twopin Partnership **Bred** J L Dunlop **Trained** Melsonby, N Yorks

**FOCUS**
A low-grade staying handicap run a modest pace and the winner made all, with the first two drawing clear. It's been rated with feet on the ground.
T/Plt: £347.10 to a £1 stake. Pool: £56,896.73 - 119.64 winning units T/Qpdt: £58.80 to a £1 stake. Pool: £4,242.91 - 53.36 winning units **Andrew Sheret**

## 5988 DEAUVILLE (R-H)
Saturday, August 12
**OFFICIAL GOING: Turf: very soft; polytrack: fast**

### 5952a PRIX DE VAL SEVRY (MAIDEN) (UNRACED 2YO COLTS & GELDINGS) (POLYTRACK) 6f 110y
4:15 2-Y-O £11,538 (£4,615; £3,461; £2,307; £1,153)

RPR

1 **Fakir Bere (FR)** 2-9-2 0.................................... CristianDemuro 10 82
(Y Barberot, France) **118/10**
2 snk **Matar (FR)** 2-9-2 0.................................... MickaelBarzalona 3 82
(F-H Graffard, France) **141/10**
3 2 ½ **Wilderness Now (IRE)** 2-9-2 0.................................... GeraldMosse 13 75
(F Chappet, France) **132/10**
4 shd **Epic Adventure (FR)** 2-9-2 0....................(p) TheoBachelot 8 74
(S Cerulis, France) **204/10**
5 ¾ **Crystal Deauville (FR)** 2-9-2 0.................................... JulienAuge 7 72
(Gay Kelleway) **41/1**
6 1 ¾ **Spirit Mission (USA)** 2-9-2 0.................... ChristopheSoumillon 12 67
(J-C Rouget, France) **17/5**2
7 ½ **Ne Jamais Renoncer (IRE)** 2-9-2 0.................... HugoJourniac 11 66
(J-C Rouget, France) **154/10**
8 ¾ **Forban Du Large (FR)** 2-9-2 0.................................... AntoineHamelin 1 64
(J-P Perruchot, France) **32/1**
9 1 ¼ **Arriviste (FR)** 2-8-10 0.................................... JeromeMoutard(6) 5 60
(J-M Lefebvre, France) **60/1**
10 ½ **Cabotin (FR)** 2-9-2 0.................................... Pierre-CharlesBoudot 6 59
(A Fabre, France) **11/5**1
11 hd **Easyrider (FR)** 2-8-13 0.................................... ClementLecoeuvre(3) 9 58
(J-M Lefebvre, France) **49/1**
12 12 **Honorable Spirit (FR)** 2-9-2 0....................(b1) TonyPiccone 14 25
(F Chappet, France) **134/10**
13 1 ½ **Ruby Flash (FR)** 2-8-11 0.................................... MlleChloeHue(5) 2 21
(A Lamotte D'Argy, France) **63/1**
D nk **The Gates Of Dawn (FR)** 2-9-2 0....................(b1) AurelienLemaitre 4 74
(F Head, France) **61/10**3

1m 18.82s 14 Ran SP% **117.9**
PARI-MUTUEL (all including 1 euro stake): WIN 12.80; PLACE 3.70, 4.50, 4.30; DF 61.90; SF 132.50.
**Owner** Gerard Augustin-Normand **Bred** Snc Regnier **Trained** France

## ARLINGTON PARK (L-H)
Saturday, August 12
**OFFICIAL GOING: Dirt: fast, turf: firm**

### 5953a SECRETARIAT STKS (GRADE 1) (3YO) (TURF) 1m 2f
9:50 3-Y-O
£195,121 (£65,040; £32,520; £16,260; £9,756; £6,504)

RPR

1 **Oscar Performance (USA)**35 4652 3-9-0 0.................... JoseLOrtiz 4 117+
(Brian A Lynch, Canada) **6/4**1
2 2 ¼ **The Taj Mahal (IRE)**35 4638 3-8-7 0....................(b) RyanMoore 6 106+
(A P O'Brien, Ire) **79/10**
3 1 ½ **Afandem (FR)**27 4941 3-8-7 0.................... FrankieDettori 1 103
(J-C Rouget, France) **16/5**3
4 ¾ **Sonic Boom (USA)**35 3-8-7 0.................... JulienRLeparoux 2 101
(Ian Wilkes, U.S.A) **113/10**
5 3 ¾ **Gorgeous Kitten (USA)**35 3-8-7 0....................(b) FlorentGeroux 5 94
(Michael J Maker, U.S.A) **143/10**
6 3 ½ **Permian (IRE)**29 4878 3-9-0 0.................... WilliamBuick 3 94
(Mark Johnston) **2/1**2

2m 1.79s (0.15) 6 Ran SP% **123.0**
PARI-MUTUEL (all including 2 usd stake): WIN 5.00; PLACE (1-2) 3.40, 6.00; SHOW (1-2-3) 2.40, 4.00, 3.20; SF 37.00.
**Owner** Amerman Racing Stables LLC **Bred** Mrs Jerry Amerman **Trained** Canada

### 5954a BEVERLY D. STKS (GRADE 1) (3YO+ FILLIES & MARES) (TURF) 1m 1f 110y
11:35 3-Y-O+
£280,975 (£70,243; £70,243; £23,414; £14,048; £9,365)

RPR

1 **Dacita (CHI)**64 3552 6-8-11 0....................(b) IradOrtizJr 1 110
(Chad C Brown, U.S.A) *hld up towards rr of midfield: stdy hdwy on outer fr 3f out: rdn 1 1/2f out: drvn 1f out: led 75yds out: kpt on wl* **69/10**
2 ½ **Dona Bruja (ARG)**35 5-8-11 0.................... DeclanCannon 4 109
(Ignacio Correas IV, U.S.A) *hld up towards rr of midfield: stdy hdwy to trck ldrs 2 1/2f out: rdn to ld 1f out: hdd 75yds out: kpt on* **23/10**1
2 dht **Grand Jete**29 4-8-11 0.................... JoelRosario 5 109+
(Chad C Brown, U.S.A) *midfield: hdwy on inner fr 1 1/2f out: nt clr run 1f out: rdn 150yds out: styd on: nt rch wnr* **33/10**2
4 1 ¼ **Rainha Da Bateria (USA)**41 5-8-11 0....................(b) JoseLOrtiz 7 106+
(Chad C Brown, U.S.A) *hld up in rr: rdn 1 1/2f out: styd on ins fnl f: nrst fin* **107/10**
5 nse **Kitten's Roar (USA)**64 3552 5-8-11 0.................... FlorentGeroux 3 106+
(Michael J Maker, U.S.A) *midfield: dropped towards rr under 2f out: rdn 1f out: styd on fnl f* **175/10**
6 ¾ **Sarandia (GER)**34 4-8-11 0.................... AndraschStarke 8 105
(P Schiergen, Germany) *hld up towards rr: rdn and kpt on fr under 2f out: n.d* **215/10**
7 ¾ **Hawksmoor (IRE)**64 3552 4-8-11 0....................(b) JulienRLeparoux 9 103
(Arnaud Delacour, U.S.A) *chsd ldr: led 2f out: rdn 1 1/2f out: hdd 1f out: wknd ins fnl f* **53/10**3
8 1 ½ **Rain Goddess (IRE)**28 4928 3-8-6 0 ow1.................... RyanMoore 10 104
(A P O'Brien, Ire) *trckd ldrs: rdn 1 1/2f out: lost pl and bmpd over 1f out: sn btn* **59/10**
9 nk **Zipessa (USA)**35 5-8-11 0.................... FrankieDettori 6 100
(Michael Stidham, U.S.A) *led: hdd 2f out: rdn over 1f out: wknd ins fnl f* **191/10**
10 nse **Prado's Sweet Ride (USA)**35 5-8-11 0.................... CarlosHMarquezJr 2 99
(Chris Block, U.S.A) *in tch: rdn and outpcd over 1f out: sn btn* **55/1**

1m 55.49s (0.02)
**WFA** 3 from 4yo+ 8lb 10 Ran SP% **121.7**
PARI-MUTUEL (all including 2 usd stake): WIN 15.80; PLACE (1-2) 5.20, 2.40 (Dona Bruja), 3.00 (Grand Jete); SHOW (1-2-3) 4.40, 2.80, 3.80; SF 27.40 (with Dona Bruja), 35.60 (with Grand Jete).
**Owner** Sheep Pond Partners & Bradley Thoroughbreds **Bred** Haras Paso Nevado **Trained** USA

**FOCUS**
It's been rated around the balance of the third to the sixth.

5955a (Foreign Racing) - See Raceform Interactive

## 5749 LEICESTER (R-H)
Sunday, August 13
**OFFICIAL GOING: Good to soft**
Wind: Light across Weather: Cloudy with sunny spells

### 5956 SRI LANKA THE WONDER OF ASIA H'CAP 6f
2:10 (2:10) (Class 5) (0-70,68) 3-Y-O £4,528 (£1,347; £673; £336) Stalls High

Form RPR

5412 1 **Peachey Carnehan**3 5826 3-9-0 66....................(v) PhilDennis(5) 2 72
(Michael Mullineaux) *pushed along early in rr: hdwy over 2f out: led and edgd lft fr over 1f out: rdn out* **5/4**1
2533 2 1 **Lightoller (IRE)**9 5588 3-9-7 68....................(v) SilvestreDeSousa 3 70
(Mick Channon) *broke wl: sn stdd and lost pl: pushed along over 3f out: swtchd rt over 2f out: hdwy u.p and n.m.r over 1f out: styd on* **11/4**2
0665 3 nk **Blue Rocks**3 5826 3-8-10 57.................... BenCurtis 6 58
(Lisa Williamson) *sn chsng ldrs: rdn over 2f out: edgd lft ins fnl f: styd on* **6/1**3
6400 4 5 **Who Told Jo Jo (IRE)**15 5429 3-9-2 63....................(b1) OisinMurphy 5 48
(Joseph Tuite) *led: hdd over 4f out: chsd ldr: led again wl over 1f out: sn rdn and hdd: wknd ins fnl f* **16/1**
6650 5 1 ½ **Hisar (IRE)**19 5247 3-9-4 65....................(b1) ShaneKelly 4 45
(Ronald Harris) *w ldr tl led over 4f out: rdn over 2f out: hung rt and hdd wl over 1f out: no ex fnl f* **16/1**
0003 6 1 **Naralsaif (IRE)**8 5635 3-8-1 51....................(v) AaronJones(3) 1 28
(Derek Shaw) *sn chsng ldrs: rdn over 2f out: wknd fnl f* **7/1**

1m 13.41s (0.41) **Going Correction** -0.05s/f (Good) 6 Ran SP% **109.7**
Speed ratings (Par 100): **95,93,93,86,84 83**
CSF £4.56 TOTE £1.80: £1.10, £1.70; EX 4.90 Trifecta £14.70.
**Owner** Keith Jones **Bred** J M Duggan & The Late T Duggan **Trained** Alpraham, Cheshire

**FOCUS**
The going was good to soft, soft in places. (GoingStick: 7.7). Stalls were on the stands' side on the straight course, and inside on the round course. Ben Curtis said: "It's lovely, good ground," Aaron Jones described it as "on the easy side of good," and Oisin Murphy: "I'd say it's dried out a fair bit." An ordinary sprint handicap, but an improving winner. The second and third have been rated to form.

### 5957 SRI LANKA PARADISE ISLAND FILLIES' H'CAP 1m 3f 179y
2:40 (2:40) (Class 4) (0-85,83) 3-Y-O+ £6,301 (£1,886; £943; £472) Stalls Low

Form RPR

1 **Satisfy (IRE)**34 4705 3-8-5 70.................... RoystonFfrench 1 79
(K R Burke) *a.p: racd keenly: shkn up to chse ldr over 3f out: led wl over 1f out: sn rdn: styd on wl* **6/1**3
1-14 2 2 ½ **Vuela**57 3840 4-10-0 83.................... KieranShoemark 5 88
(Luca Cumani) *led at stdy pce after 1f: qcknd over 3f out: rdn over 2f out: hdd wl over 1f out: no ex ins fnl f* **9/4**2
32-5 3 1 ¼ **Bybrook**15 5414 4-9-4 73.................... OisinMurphy 2 75
(David Simcock) *led 1f: chsd ldr tl pushed along over 3f out: outpcd 2f out: styd on towards fin* **2/1**1
4166 4 4 **Perfect In Pink**37 4571 3-8-13 78.................... SilvestreDeSousa 4 76
(Mick Channon) *hld up: racd keenly early: rdn over 2f out: eased whn no ch ins fnl f* **9/4**2

2m 33.62s (-0.28) **Going Correction** +0.075s/f (Good)
**WFA** 3 from 4yo 10lb 4 Ran SP% **109.2**
Speed ratings (Par 102): **103,101,100,97**
CSF £19.14 TOTE £5.30; EX 7.60 Trifecta £24.10.
**Owner** Ms J J Murphy **Bred** J Hanly, T Stewart & A Stroud **Trained** Middleham Moor, N Yorks

**FOCUS**
Only four runners, but a fair fillies' handicap and a nice handicap prospect in the convincing winner. The runner-up has been rated close to form.

### 5958 HEINEKEN (S) STKS 7f
3:10 (3:12) (Class 5) 3-4-Y-O £3,234 (£962; £481; £240) Stalls High

Form RPR

5045 1 **African Blessing**18 5288 4-9-7 70.................... BenCurtis 5 71
(David Barron) *mde all: rdn over 2f out: styd on wl to draw clr towards fin* **2/1**2
0006 2 3 **Queen Beatrice**19 5250 3-8-5 55.................... SilvestreDeSousa 1 51
(William Muir) *prom: chsd wnr 1/2-way: rdn over 1f out: no ex wl ins fnl f* **8/1**
0006 3 1 ¼ **Luduamf (IRE)**15 5410 3-8-10 49.................... SeanLevey 3 53
(Richard Hannon) *s.i.s and hmpd s: hld up: pushed along over 2f out: styd on fr over 1f out: nt trble ldrs* **16/1**
5041 4 hd **Major Cornwallis (IRE)**24 5076 3-8-8 65.................... ConnorMurtagh(7) 7 57
(Richard Fahey) *chsd ldrs: lost pl over 4f out: pushed along over 2f out: hdwy and hung rt over 1f out: kpt on* **9/2**3
006 5 hd **Hi Milady (IRE)**6 5713 3-8-6 55 ow1....................(b) RobHornby 2 48
(Dominic Ffrench Davis) *s.i.s: hld up: rdn over 2f out: sme hdwy over 1f out: nt trble ldrs* **10/1**

15-5 **6** *5* **Red Trooper (FR)**$^{193}$ 506 4-9-7 **77** ... PatCosgrave 4 46
(George Baker) *trckd ldrs: plld hrd: rdn over 1f out: wknd ins fnl f* **7/4**$^{1}$

0-5 **7** *12* **Coral Caye**$^{83}$ 2895 3-8-5 0 ...(h) RoystonFfrench 6 3
(Steph Hollinshead) *s.i.s: a in rr: pushed along over 4f out: wknd over 2f out* **33/1**

0-00 **8** *15* **Here I Go Again (IRE)**$^{24}$ 5075 3-8-7 0 ...(h) AaronJones$^{(3)}$ 8
(Christine Dunnett) *s.i.s: hdwy to chse wnr over 5f out: rdn and lost 2nd 1/2-way: sn rdn and wknd* **150/1**

1m 25.42s (-0.78) **Going Correction** -0.05s/f (Good)
**WFA** 3 from 4yo 6lb **8** Ran SP% **117.6**
Speed ratings (Par 103): **102,98,97,96,96 90,77,60**
CSF £19.25 TOTE £3.00: £1.10, £2.10, £3.70; EX 21.10 Trifecta £170.90.
**Owner** M Rozenbroek & Harrowgate Bloodstock Ltd **Bred** Michael Turner **Trained** Maunby, N Yorks

**FOCUS**
Not a bad race for the grade. The winner looks capable of mixing it in better company. The second and third have been rated close to form.

## 5959 VISIT SRI LANKA H'CAP 6f
**3:45** (3:48) (Class 3) (0-90,85) 3-Y-O **£12,602** (£3,772; £1,886; £944; £470) **Stalls** High

Form RPR

1-51 **1** **Dark Power (IRE)**$^{19}$ 5264 3-9-7 **85** ...(t) AdamKirby 5 94+
(Clive Cox) *racd keenly in disp 2nd: rdn to ld over 1f out: hung lft ins fnl f: r.o: readily* **2/1**$^{1}$

4510 **2** *1* **Stanhope**$^{22}$ 5156 3-9-4 **82** ... FranBerry 7 88
(Mick Quinn) *disp 2nd tl rdn and hung rt over 1f out: sn hung lft: r.o* **16/1**

1-15 **3** *nk* **Pennsylvania Dutch**$^{30}$ 4868 3-9-6 **84** ... PatCosgrave 6 89
(William Haggas) *hld up: hdwy and nt clr run over 1f out: rdn ins fnl f: r.o* **11/4**$^{2}$

6243 **4** *nk* **Scofflaw**$^{8}$ 5671 3-8-11 **82** ... ConnorMurtagh$^{(7)}$ 3 86
(Richard Fahey) *chsd ldrs: rdn over 1f out: r.o* **5/1**

3611 **5** *1/2* **Gaval**$^{11}$ 5535 3-8-11 **75** ... BenCurtis 8 77
(David Barron) *sn led: rdn and hdd over 1f out: no ex wl ins fnl f* **7/2**$^{3}$

1031 **6** *3 1/4* **Stoneyford Lane (IRE)**$^{9}$ 5588 3-9-2 **80** ...(p) RoystonFfrench 2 72
(Steph Hollinshead) *hld up: pushed along over 2f out: wknd ins fnl f* **18/1**

1m 11.48s (-1.52) **Going Correction** -0.05s/f (Good) **6** Ran SP% **110.0**
Speed ratings (Par 104): **108,106,106,105,105 100**
CSF £31.19 CT £81.35 TOTE £2.50: £1.60, £4.60; EX 25.40 Trifecta £93.60.
**Owner** Alan G Craddock **Bred** Guy O'Callaghan **Trained** Lambourn, Berks

**FOCUS**
Not many runners for the money, but this looked a good sprint contested by some progressive handicappers. The winner could be very useful. The third and fourth have been rated close to form.

## 5960 BRITISH STALLION STUDS EBF NOVICE STKS (PLUS 10 RACE) 7f
**4:20** (4:21) (Class 4) 2-Y-O **£6,469** (£1,925; £962; £481) **Stalls** High

Form RPR

26 **1** **Algam (IRE)**$^{12}$ 5504 2-9-2 0 ... SeanLevey 4 80
(Richard Hannon) *a.p: racd keenly: chsd ldr 1/2-way: rdn to ld and hung lft ins fnl f: r.o* **11/8**$^{1}$

0 **2** *3/4* **Dark Spec**$^{25}$ 5036 2-9-2 0 ... RobHornby 5 78
(Pam Sly) *led 6f out: rdn over 1f out: hdd and edgd lft ins fnl f: styd on* **20/1**

02 **3** *3 1/2* **Cuban Heel**$^{29}$ 4885 2-9-2 0 ... AdamKirby 3 69+
(Clive Cox) *hld up in tch: rdn over 1f out: hung lft and no ex ins fnl f* **3/1**$^{2}$

0 **4** *1 1/4* **Verstappen (IRE)**$^{25}$ 5036 2-9-2 0 ... SilvestreDeSousa 6 66
(Marco Botti) *prom: rdn and hung rt over 1f out: styd on same pce* **5/1**

**5** *shd* **Comrade In Arms (USA)** 2-9-2 0 ... TedDurcan 7 65+
(Sir Michael Stoute) *s.s: rn green and pushed along in rr: nt trble ldrs* **4/1**$^{3}$

**6** *1* **Blacklooks (IRE)** 2-9-2 0 ... DavidNolan 1 63
(Ivan Furtado) *s.s: in rr: styd on fnl f: nvr on terms* **33/1**

65 **7** *11* **The Fettler (IRE)**$^{17}$ 5314 2-9-2 0 ... DougieCostello 2 34
(Kevin Frost) *led 1f: chsd ldr to 1/2-way: rdn and wknd over 1f out* **66/1**

1m 25.53s (-0.67) **Going Correction** -0.05s/f (Good) **7** Ran SP% **113.0**
Speed ratings (Par 96): **101,100,96,94,94 93,80**
CSF £30.31 TOTE £2.20: £2.10, £5.80; EX 23.30 Trifecta £84.10.
**Owner** Al Shaqab Racing **Bred** The Evangeline Syndicate **Trained** East Everleigh, Wilts

**FOCUS**
Some nicely-bred juveniles were on show and the winner did it well in the end.

## 5961 AMAZING SRI LANKA H'CAP 1m 53y
**4:50** (4:51) (Class 5) (0-75,81) 3-Y-O **£3,881** (£1,155; £577; £288) **Stalls** Low

Form RPR

5205 **1** **Duchess Of Fife**$^{13}$ 5478 3-8-10 **64** ow1 ...(v) MartinLane 2 69
(William Knight) *sn pushed along and prom: jnd ldr over 6f out: pushed along over 3f out: rdn over 1f out: styd on to ld towards fin* **16/1**

351 **2** *shd* **Fastar (IRE)**$^{13}$ 5478 3-9-9 **77** ... OisinMurphy 1 81
(Brian Meehan) *s.i.s: hdwy 6f out: rdn over 2f out: led ins fnl f: hdd towards fin* **9/2**$^{3}$

1653 **3** *3/4* **Keepup Kevin**$^{26}$ 4999 3-9-3 **71** ... RobHornby 6 73
(Pam Sly) *w ldr tl over 6f out: remained handy: led over 2f out: rdn and edgd lft fr over 1f out: hdd ins fnl f: unable qck towards fin* **13/8**$^{1}$

2143 **4** *5* **Alemaratalyoum (IRE)**$^{17}$ 5333 3-9-7 **75** ... SilvestreDeSousa 3 66
(Ed Dunlop) *racd keenly: prom: hmpd and lost pl over 6f out: hdwy over 2f out: rdn over 1f out: wknd wl ins fnl f* **11/4**$^{2}$

-021 **5** *5* **Vibes (IRE)**$^{8}$ 5656 3-9-13 **81** ... DougieCostello 4 60
(Jamie Osborne) *led: rdn and hdd over 2f out: wknd over 1f out* **9/1**

1634 **6** *3/4* **Zebulon (IRE)**$^{13}$ 5478 3-9-6 **74** ... SeanLevey 5 51
(Richard Hannon) *hld up: racd keenly: pushed along over 3f out: rdn and wknd over 1f out* **8/1**

1m 45.15s (0.05) **Going Correction** +0.075s/f (Good) **6** Ran SP% **109.9**
Speed ratings (Par 100): **102,101,101,96,91 90**
CSF £80.52 TOTE £13.30: £4.20, £2.30; EX 101.70 Trifecta £283.60.
**Owner** Mrs Melba Bryce **Bred** Laundry Cottage Stud Farm **Trained** Patching, W Sussex

**FOCUS**
An ordinary handicap which produced a thrilling finish. The winner showed a marked improvement on previous efforts.

## 5962 SRI LANKA SOMETHING FOR EVERYONE H'CAP 5f
**5:20** (5:21) (Class 6) (0-65,65) 3-Y-O+ **£3,234** (£962; £481; £240) **Stalls** High

Form RPR

4663 **1** **Kings Academy**$^{43}$ 4368 3-9-5 **63** ...(t) SilvestreDeSousa 4 72
(Paul Cole) *hld up: plld hrd: hdwy 2f out: rdn to ld and hung lft ins fnl f: r.o* **15/8**$^{1}$

3043 **2** *1* **Angel Palanas**$^{8}$ 5636 3-8-8 **59** ...(p) RussellHarris$^{(7)}$ 5 64
(K R Burke) *w ldr: led over 3f out: rdn over 1f out: hdd ins fnl f: styd on same pce towards fin* **11/2**

0306 **3** *1 1/2* **Classic Pursuit**$^{14}$ 5459 6-9-9 **64** ...(b) RoystonFfrench 1 65
(Michael Appleby) *broke wl: sn stdd and lost pl: pushed along 1/2-way: r.o ins fnl f: nt rch ldrs* **9/2**$^{3}$

4052 **4** *1 1/4* **Racing Angel (IRE)**$^{12}$ 5514 5-9-9 **64** ... TedDurcan 7 61
(Mick Quinn) *trckd ldrs: rdn and edgd rt over 1f out: styd on same pce ins fnl f* **5/2**$^{2}$

6350 **5** *nk* **Corridor Kid (IRE)**$^{52}$ 4005 4-9-3 **65** ...(v) TobyEley$^{(7)}$ 3 60
(Derek Shaw) *chsd ldrs: rdn over 1f out: no ex ins fnl f* **16/1**

3030 **6** *shd* **Billyoakes (IRE)**$^{5}$ 5748 5-9-9 **64** ...(p) BenCurtis 6 59
(Charlie Wallis) *led: hdd over 3f out: rdn 1/2-way: no ex ins fnl f* **12/1**

1m 0.48s (0.48) **Going Correction** -0.05s/f (Good)
**WFA** 3 from 4yo+ 3lb **6** Ran SP% **110.5**
Speed ratings (Par 101): **94,92,90,88,87 87**
CSF £12.16 TOTE £2.20: £1.80, £2.30; EX 11.30 Trifecta £30.90.
**Owner** P F I Cole Ltd **Bred** Bearstone Stud Ltd **Trained** Whatcombe, Oxon

**FOCUS**
A low-grade sprint handicap dominated by the two 3yos. The winner was having his first start since being gelded.
T/Jkpt: £6,666.60 to a £1 stake. Pool: £10,000.00 - 1.50 winning units T/Plt: £473.70 to a £1 stake. Pool: £73,553.60 - 113.34 winning units T/Qpdt: £76.00 to a £1 stake. Pool: £4,699.07 - 45.75 winning units **Colin Roberts**

# 5717 WINDSOR (R-H)
Sunday, August 13

**OFFICIAL GOING: Good (7.5)**
Wind: light behind Weather: mainly sunny

## 5963 GO JUMP IN FILLIES' NOVICE AUCTION STKS (PLUS 10 RACE) 6f 12y
**2:25** (2:25) (Class 5) 2-Y-O **£2,911** (£866; £432; £216) **Stalls** Low

Form RPR

0 **1** **Boreagh Lass (IRE)**$^{69}$ 3390 2-8-8 0 ... HarryBentley 6 71+
(Henry Candy) *hld up in tch in last pair: effrt and hdwy to chse ldr over 1f out: shkn up to ld 1f out: sn clr and styd on wl: pushed out: comf* **1/1**$^{1}$

462 **2** *1 1/2* **Polly's Gold (IRE)**$^{16}$ 5356 2-8-7 0 ... FinleyMarsh$^{(7)}$ 5 72
(Richard Hughes) *stdd after s: trckd ldrs: nt clr run 2f out: gap opened and hdwy jst over 1f out: chsd wnr jst ins fnl f: kpt on wl for clr 2nd but nvr threatening wnr* **5/2**$^{2}$

**3** *2 1/2* **Storm Jazz (IRE)** 2-9-0 0 ... JimmyQuinn 3 63
(Ed Dunlop) *s.i.s: hld up in tch in last pair: effrt ent fnl 2f: rn green and hung lft over 1f out: hdwy to go 3rd 100yds out: no threat ldng pair and eased nr fin* **14/1**

3310 **4** *2 3/4* **Firenze Rosa (IRE)**$^{11}$ 5526 2-8-10 **78** ... DavidEgan$^{(5)}$ 7 55
(John Bridger) *w ldr tl rdn to ld over 2f out: drvn and hdd 1f out: sn btn and wknd ins fnl f* **4/1**$^{3}$

0 **5** *3/4* **Amarone Red (IRE)**$^{31}$ 4806 2-8-13 0 ... LiamKeniry 4 51
(Tom Dascombe) *mde most tl rdn and hdd over 1f out: lost pl and swtchd lft jst over 1f out: edgd lft and wknd ins fnl f* **20/1**

1m 12.35s (-0.65) **Going Correction** 0.0s/f (Good) **5** Ran SP% **110.0**
Speed ratings (Par 91): **104,102,98,95,94**
CSF £3.73 TOTE £2.10: £1.40, £1.10; EX 3.50 Trifecta £17.10.
**Owner** North Yorkshire Bloodstock Racing **Bred** Austin Curran **Trained** Kingston Warren, Oxon

**FOCUS**
The going had dried out to good (GoingStick: 7.5). Jimmy Quinn said the ground was on the slow side, while Harry Bentley called it good. The rail was dolled out by 12yds in the straight. An ordinary fillies' race.

## 5964 CHILDREN'S TRUST CHARITY NOVICE AUCTION STKS 1m 31y
**2:55** (2:55) (Class 5) 2-Y-O **£2,911** (£866; £432; £216) **Stalls** Low

Form RPR

**1** **Yabass (IRE)** 2-8-13 0 ... EdwardGreatrex$^{(3)}$ 5 76+
(Archie Watson) *t.k.h: hld up in tch in last pair: effrt and rdn over 2f out: hdwy to press ldng pair 1f out: r.o wl to ld towards fin* **5/2**$^{3}$

**2** *nk* **Soldier To Follow** 2-9-1 0 ... DavidProbert 1 75+
(Andrew Balding) *trckd ldr for 2f: styd trcking ldrs: nt clr run 2f out: sn swtchd sharply lft: rdn and hdwy to chal 1f out: led ins fnl f: hdd and no ex towards fin* **9/4**$^{2}$

1 **3** *1* **Regimented (IRE)**$^{18}$ 5292 2-9-8 0 ... KieranO'Neill 6 79
(Richard Hannon) *dwlt: trckd ldrs after 1f: wnt 2nd 5f out: gng best and upsides ldr over 2f out: rdn to ld over 1f out: flashed tail u.p and hdd ins fnl f: outpcd fnl 100yds* **6/4**$^{1}$

0 **4** *4* **Boniface (IRE)**$^{30}$ 4859 2-8-8 0 ... DavidEgan$^{(5)}$ 3 61
(Robert Eddery) *led: rdn jst over 2f out: hdd over 1f out: no ex and outpcd 1f out: wknd ins fnl f* **12/1**

5 **5** *4* **Kingfast (IRE)**$^{55}$ 3908 2-9-2 0 ... DaneO'Neill 2 55
(David Dennis) *stdd s: t.k.h: hld up in tch in last pair: effrt over 2f out: outpcd and btn over 1f out: wknd fnl f* **25/1**

1m 46.9s (2.20) **Going Correction** 0.0s/f (Good) **5** Ran SP% **110.9**
Speed ratings (Par 94): **89,88,87,83,79**
CSF £8.60 TOTE £2.80: £1.40, £1.40; EX 7.00 Trifecta £17.40.
**Owner** The Ride The Lightning Partnership **Bred** Grangecon Stud **Trained** Upper Lambourn, W Berks

**FOCUS**
A decent little contest.

## 5965 OSSIE & HUTCH MEMORIAL FILLIES' H'CAP 6f 12y
**3:25** (3:25) (Class 4) (0-85,83) 3-Y-O+ **£4,690** (£1,395; £697; £348) **Stalls** Low

Form RPR

5226 **1** **Pepita (IRE)**$^{29}$ 4892 3-9-4 **80** ... TomMarquand 3 86
(Richard Hannon) *pressed ldr: upsides and rdn over 1f out: drvn to ld ent fnl f: edgd rt jst ins fnl f: hld on wl u.p fnl 100yds* **3/1**$^{2}$

1240 **2** *nk* **Angel Of Darkness**$^{23}$ 5117 3-9-4 **83** ... CallumShepherd$^{(3)}$ 2 88
(Charles Hills) *trckd ldng pair: effrt over 1f out: hdwy u.p and str chal ins fnl f: styd on wl but a jst hld* **5/2**$^{1}$

5501 **3** *2* **Chupalla**$^{37}$ 4556 3-9-6 **82** ... DaneO'Neill 4 81
(David Evans) *hld up wl in tch in midfield: effrt and swtchd lft over 1f out: kpt on to chse ldng pair 100yds out: no imp after and eased cl home* **6/1**

4-01 **4** *1 3/4* **Paradwys (IRE)**$^{27}$ 4964 3-8-7 **72** ...(p) EdwardGreatrex$^{(3)}$ 6 65
(Archie Watson) *led: rdn ent fnl 2f: hdd ent fnl f: jst getting outpcd whn squeezed for room and hmpd jst ins fnl f: wknd fnl 100yds* **7/2**$^{3}$

15 **5** *3/4* **In The Spotlight (IRE)**$^{46}$ 4198 3-8-6 **75** ... CameronNoble$^{(7)}$ 5 66
(Henry Spiller) *stdd after s: hld up in tch in last pair: effrt over 1f out: no imp and styd on same pce ins fnl f* **10/1**

5603 **6** 2 ½ **Pretty Bubbles**[17] 5325 8-9-6 **78**..............................(v) FergusSweeney 1 62
(J R Jenkins) *hld up in tch in last pair: effrt over 1f out: no imp and wknd ins fnl f* **7/1**

1m 12.92s (-0.08) **Going Correction** 0.0s/f (Good)
**WFA** 3 from 8yo 4lb **6** Ran SP% **111.7**
Speed ratings (Par 102): **100,99,96,94,93 90**
CSF £10.80 TOTE £3.30: £1.70, £2.10; EX 11.70 Trifecta £50.90.
**Owner** Rockcliffe Stud **Bred** R O'Callaghan And D Veitch **Trained** East Everleigh, Wilts

**FOCUS**
A tight little sprint, but the early pace wasn't that strong and it was an advantage to race handily. The winner has been rated to the better view of her form, with the runner-up to a small pb and the third close to her latest Beverley 7f win.

## 5966 BOYZONE HERE ON 26TH AUGUST H'CAP — 1m 31y
**4:00** (4:00) (Class 3) (0-90,92) 3-Y-O+ **£7,246** (£2,168; £1,084; £542; £270) **Stalls** Low

Form RPR
6013 **1** **Angel Down**[23] 5115 3-8-12 **81**.............................................. DaneO'Neill 3 90+
(Henry Candy) *stdd after s: hld up in tch: clsd to press ldr 2f out: shkn up to ld 1f out: r.o wl and in command ins fnl f: comf* **5/2**[2]

6006 **2** 2 **Repercussion**[29] 4882 4-9-13 **89**.............................................. StevieDonohoe 2 94
(Charlie Fellowes) *sn led: t.k.h and awkward hd carriage: rdn ent fnl 2f: hdd 1f out: styd on same pce after* **3/1**[3]

1005 **3** *nk* **Secret Art (IRE)**[5] 5744 7-10-2 **92**.............................................. HarryBentley 1 96+
(William Knight) *broke wl: sn stdd to trck ldng pair: nt clr run on inner 2f out: effrt and drvn ent fnl f: kpt on u.p to press for 2nd towards fin: no threat to wnr* **2/1**[1]

0-31 **4** 1 ¾ **Afonso De Sousa (USA)**[183] 683 7-10-0 **90**.......... AlistairRawlinson 5 90
(Michael Appleby) *dwlt: hld up wl in tch in rr: effrt over 1f out: wnt 4th and kpt on ins fnl f: nvr trbld ldrs* **14/1**

4460 **5** 1 ½ **Highland Colori (IRE)**[22] 5157 9-10-1 **91**...................(b) DavidProbert 4 88
(Andrew Balding) *chsd ldr: rdn over 2f out: outpcd u.p and btn 4th 1f out: wknd ins fnl f* **6/1**

1m 42.77s (-1.93) **Going Correction** 0.0s/f (Good)
**WFA** 3 from 4yo+ 7lb **5** Ran SP% **107.9**
Speed ratings (Par 107): **109,107,106,104,103**
CSF £9.83 TOTE £2.90: £1.60, £2.00; EX 9.50 Trifecta £24.10.
**Owner** Thurloe Thoroughbreds XX **Bred** Kirtlington Stud & Mr C Budgett **Trained** Kingston Warren, Oxon

**FOCUS**
A comfortable winner, but the favourite might have given him more to do with a clear run. The runner-up has been rated close to his British form.

## 5967 ROYAL WINDSOR RACECOURSE FIREWORKS ON 4TH NOVEMBER H'CAP — 5f 21y
**4:35** (4:35) (Class 5) (0-75,75) 3-Y-O+ **£2,911** (£866; £432; £216) **Stalls** Low

Form RPR
0214 **1** **Vimy Ridge**[25] 5035 5-9-0 **74**........................................(t) JoshuaBryan(5) 4 83
(Alan Bailey) *hld up off the pce in 4th: clsd to trck ldrs 2f out: rdn and ev ch over 1f out: led ins fnl f: r.o wl: rdn out* **11/4**[3]

1413 **2** 1 ¼ **Major Valentine**[10] 5580 5-9-1 **75**.............................................. BenRobinson(5) 3 80
(John O'Shea) *bustled along early: chsd ldrs: effrt to chal over 1f out: kpt on same pce u.p ins fnl f: wnt 2nd last strides* **2/1**[1]

-032 **3** *nk* **Wiley Post**[20] 5219 4-8-11 **71**........................................(b) DavidEgan(5) 2 74
(Tony Carroll) *w ldr tl rdn to ld over 1f out: sn hrd pressed: hdd ins fnl f: styd on same pce after: lost 2nd last strides* **9/4**[2]

0034 **4** 2 ¼ **Zipedeedodah (IRE)**[6] 5723 5-8-9 **71**...............(t) StephenCummins(7) 1 66
(Joseph Tuite) *awkward leaving stalls: off the pce in rr: rdn and hdwy over 1f out: kpt on ins fnl f: nvr trbld ldrs* **5/1**

130- **5** 14 **Pucon**[357] 5669 8-9-2 **71**.............................................. LiamKeniry 5 16
(Simon Dow) *led tl rdn and hdd over 1f out: sn lost pl and wknd fnl f* **25/1**

59.22s (-1.08) **Going Correction** 0.0s/f (Good) **5** Ran SP% **111.3**
Speed ratings (Par 103): **108,106,105,101,79**
CSF £8.78 TOTE £3.70: £1.70, £1.10; EX 10.20 Trifecta £19.90.
**Owner** Dr S P Hargreaves **Bred** Mrs Sheila Oakes **Trained** Newmarket, Suffolk

**FOCUS**
This was run at a good gallop.

## 5968 ROYAL WINDSOR AMATEUR RIDERS' H'CAP — 1m 3f 99y
**5:05** (5:07) (Class 5) (0-70,70) 4-Y-O+ **£2,807** (£870; £435; £217) **Stalls** Centre

Form RPR
4433 **1** **Take Two**[17] 5320 8-10-3 **66**.............................................. MrJBrace(7) 8 74
(Alex Hales) *stdd s: hld up in tch towards rr: effrt and hdwy over 1f out: led 1f out: r.o wl ins fnl f: rdn out* **9/2**[2]

1500 **2** 1 **Powered (IRE)**[13] 5483 4-9-10 **57**.............................................. MrJFlook(5) 1 63
(David Evans) *hld up in last pair: clsd and nt clr run jst over 2f out: sn swtchd lft and hdwy u.p over 1f out: chsd wnr ins fnl f: styd on but a hld* **12/1**

3-23 **3** 1 ¾ **Thahab Ifraj (IRE)**[54] 286 4-10-7 **68**..............................(p) MrBJames(5) 6 71
(Alexandra Dunn) *chsd ldrs tl wnt 2nd 6f out: rdn and ev ch over 2f out tl unable qck 1f out: styd on same pce ins fnl f* **10/1**

4322 **4** 1 ¾ **Maroc**[13] 5477 4-11-0 **70**..............................................(p) MrSWalker 7 70
(Nikki Evans) *led: rdn over 2f out: hung lft and hdd 1f out: no ex and sn outpcd: wknd ins fnl f* **5/2**[1]

1401 **5** 1 ¼ **Grams And Ounces**[16] 5362 10-9-12 **61**................(tp) MissCMBerry(7) 3 59
(Grace Harris) *dwlt: hld up in tch in midfield: hdwy to chse ldrs on inner 3f out: rdn and ev ch over 2f out tl no ex ent fnl f: wknd ins fnl f* **10/1**

3224 **6** *hd* **Strictly Art (IRE)**[12] 5508 4-9-13 **60**.............................................. MissJCooley(5) 4 58
(Alan Bailey) *chsd ldr tl 6f out: styd chsng ldrs: n.m.r over 2f out: sn swtchd rt and unable qck u.p over 1f out: wknd ins fnl f* **9/2**[2]

4-40 **7** *hd* **Jersey Jewel (FR)**[17] 5320 5-10-7 **68**..............(t[1]) MissCAGreenway(5) 9 66
(Tom Dascombe) *hld up in tch in midfield tl dropped to rr 5f out: swtchd lft and effrt over 2f out: kpt on same pce fr over 1f out* **8/1**[3]

6-10 **8** *nse* **City Ground (USA)**[41] 4439 10-10-10 **66**.................... MissSBrotherton 5 63
(Michael Appleby) *stdd s: t.k.h: hld up in tch in last pair: effrt 2f out: swtchd lft ins fnl f: kpt on but nvr trbld ldrs* **16/1**

40-4 **9** 5 **Royal Etiquette (IRE)**[28] 4181 10-9-9 **51** oh4...................(tp) MrHHunt 2 40
(Lawney Hill) *hld up wl in tch in midfield: effrt over 2f out: lost pl u.p over 1f out: wknd ins fnl f: eased towards fin* **33/1**

-505 **10** 1 ¼ **Gannicus**[10] 5555 6-10-1 **64**..............................(tp) MissMStratton(7) 10 51
(Brendan Powell) *wl in tch in midfield: rdn and losing pl whn impeded 2f out: bhd ins fnl f* **25/1**

2m 29.43s (-0.07) **Going Correction** 0.0s/f (Good) **10** Ran SP% **114.6**
Speed ratings (Par 103): **100,99,98,96,95 95,95,95,91,90**
CSF £56.21 CT £511.25 TOTE £4.70: £2.10, £4.00, £2.30; EX 64.40 Trifecta £897.60.
**Owner** Edging Ahead **Bred** Steven & Petra Wallace **Trained** Edgcote, Northamptonshire

**FOCUS**
An ordinary affair run at a sound pace. The runner-up helps set the standard.

## 5969 OVERTONES LIVE ON 26TH AUGUST MAIDEN FILLIES' STKS — 6f 12y
**5:35** (5:35) (Class 5) 3-Y-O+ **£2,911** (£866; £432; £216) **Stalls** Low

Form RPR
3250 **1** **Angel's Quest (FR)**[12] 5506 3-9-0 74.............................................. ShaneKelly 1 66+
(Richard Hughes) *w ldr tl led 1/2-way: rdn and forged ahd over 1f out: drvn ins fnl f: a jst doing enough towards fin* **1/2**[1]

6 **2** *nk* **Charlie's Dreamer**[37] 4568 3-9-0 0.............................................. AlistairRawlinson 7 65
(Michael Appleby) *chsd ldng pair: rdn and outpcd 1/2-way: rallied u.p over 1f out: chsd wnr ins fnl f: kpt on wl: hld towards fin* **18/1**

5 **3** 1 **Cherished (IRE)**[41] 4445 3-9-0 0.............................................. TimmyMurphy 6 63
(Geoffrey Deacon) *s.i.s: sn rdn along and rn green in rr: hdwy over 1f out: swtchd rt and chsd ldrs ins fnl f: short of room cl home* **8/1**[3]

5 **4** 1 ¼ **Mooroverthebridge**[19] 5247 3-8-9 0.............................................. JennyPowell(5) 3 58
(Grace Harris) *s.i.s: off the pce in last pair: clsd and shifting lft over 1f out: chsng ldrs whn rn green and wandered ins fnl f: no imp fnl 100yds* **40/1**

3 **5** 3 ¼ **Razzmatazz**[92] 2620 3-9-0 0.............................................. SamHitchcott 2 48
(Clive Cox) *led tl 1/2-way: rdn and unable to match pce of wnr over 1f out: lost 2nd and wknd ins fnl f* **3/1**[2]

0-4 **6** 3 **Assertor**[27] 4964 3-9-0 0.............................................. GeorgeDowning 4 38
(Tony Carroll) *taken down early: outpcd in midfield: rdn over 2f out: nvr getting on terms* **40/1**

**7** 3 ¼ **Dollywaggon Pike** 3-8-7 0.............................................. GinaMangan(7) 5 28
(J R Jenkins) *outpcd in midfield: rdn and hung lft over 2f out: no imp over 1f out: bhd ins fnl f* **66/1**

1m 12.71s (-0.29) **Going Correction** 0.0s/f (Good) **7** Ran SP% **114.4**
Speed ratings (Par 100): **101,100,99,97,93 89,84**
CSF £12.42 TOTE £1.40: £1.10, £5.80; EX 13.60 Trifecta £44.20.
**Owner** HP Racing Angel's Quest **Bred** Ecurie Haras De Beauvoir **Trained** Upper Lambourn, Berks

**FOCUS**
A modest maiden, and the winner was unimpressive, but that was largely a consequence of the way the race was run.
T/Plt: £59.90 to a £1 stake. Pool: £83,650.07 - 1,018.83 winning units T/Qpdt: £18.10 to a £1 stake. Pool: £5,578.17 - 226.84 winning units **Steve Payne**

5970 - 5972a (Foreign Racing) - See Raceform Interactive

# [5724] CURRAGH (R-H)
Sunday, August 13

**OFFICIAL GOING: Good to firm (watered)**

## 5973a KEENELAND PHOENIX STKS (GROUP 1) (ENTIRE COLTS & FILLIES) — 6f
**3:35** (3:36) 2-Y-O
**£121,794** (£40,598; £19,230; £8,547; £4,273; £2,136)

RPR
**1** **Sioux Nation (USA)**[52] 3993 2-9-3 106.............................................. RyanMoore 3 115
(A P O'Brien, Ire) *dwlt sltly: hld up in tch: 5th 1/2-way: prog fr under 2f out to chal far side 1f out: led ins fnl f and rdn out clsng stages where pressed: hld on wl* **2/1**[2]

**2** ½ **Beckford**[43] 4386 2-9-3 113.............................................. DeclanMcDonogh 6 113
(Gordon Elliott, Ire) *chsd ldrs: 4th 1/2-way: rdn bhd ldrs nr side over 1f out and clsd u.p into 2nd wl ins fnl f: kpt on wl wout matching wnr clsng stages* **15/8**[1]

**3** 1 ½ **Actress (IRE)**[29] 4926 2-9-0 105.............................................. SeamieHeffernan 2 106
(A P O'Brien, Ire) *cl up bhd ldr: rdn almost on terms ins fnl f and no imp on ldrs u.p in 3rd wl ins fnl f: kpt on same pce* **5/1**[3]

**4** ½ **U S Navy Flag (USA)**[31] 4812 2-9-3 105..............(bt) DonnachaO'Brien 1 107
(A P O'Brien, Ire) *led: narrow advantage at 1/2-way: rdn over 1f out and sn edgd sltly lft u.p: hdd ins fnl f and no ex clsng stages where dropped to 4th: jst hld 4th* **11/1**

**5** *hd* **Frozen Angel (IRE)**[21] 5195 2-9-3 108.............................................. RichardKingscote 8 106
(Tom Dascombe) *hld up towards rr: 6th 1/2-way: rdn nr side ins fnl f and r.o u.p clsng stages: jst failed for 4th: nvr trbld ldrs* **16/1**

**6** ½ **Romanised (IRE)**[54] 3925 2-9-3 0........................................(t) PatSmullen 4 105
(K J Condon, Ire) *on toes befhand: dwlt sltly: w.w towards rr: last at 1/2-way: tk clsr order far side over 2f out: sn rdn and no imp on ldrs u.p in 5th ins fnl f: denied 5th cl home* **8/1**

**7** *shd* **Declarationofpeace (USA)**[54] 3929 2-9-3 0..............(t) WayneLordan 7 105
(A P O'Brien, Ire) *w.w: 7th 1/2-way: rdn ins fnl f and no imp on ldrs: kpt on same pce* **16/1**

**8** 1 ¾ **Helvetian**[9] 5586 2-9-3 0.............................................. RonanWhelan 5 99
(Mick Channon) *on toes befhand: chsd ldrs and racd keenly early: 3rd 1/2-way: rdn bhd ldrs under 2f out and dropped to rr 1f out: one pce after* **66/1**

1m 11.72s (-3.78) **8** Ran SP% **117.5**
CSF £6.38 CT £15.63 TOTE £2.80: £1.30, £1.02, £1.80; DF 6.60 Trifecta £20.20.
**Owner** Michael Tabor & Derrick Smith & Mrs John Magnier **Bred** Fethard Bloodstock **Trained** Cashel, Co Tipperary

**FOCUS**
What looked a weak enough renewal of this race may prove to be somewhat better than that.

## 5974a AT THE RACES PHOENIX SPRINT STKS (GROUP 3) — 6f
**4:10** (4:10) 3-Y-O+
**£31,769** (£10,230; £4,846; £2,153; £1,076; £538)

RPR
**1** **Washington DC (IRE)**[9] 5595 4-9-7 110..............................(bt) RyanMoore 5 114
(A P O'Brien, Ire) *dwlt sltly: sn settled in rr: clsr in 9th fr 1/2-way: hdwy gng wl 2f out: swtchd lft disputing 6th over 1f out where sltly bmpd rival: r.o wl ins fnl f to ld cl home: readily* **11/4**[1]

**2** ½ **Cougar Mountain (IRE)**[28] 4935 6-9-7 111..........(tp) DonnachaO'Brien 2 112
(A P O'Brien, Ire) *in tch: 5th 1/2-way: hdwy gng wl far side under 2f out: rdn to ld narrowly ins fnl f: all out wl ins fnl f and hdd cl home* **9/1**

**3** ½ **Gordon Lord Byron (IRE)**[28] 4935 9-9-12 111.................... WayneLordan 6 116
(T Hogan, Ire) *cl up bhd ldrs: cl 3rd at 1/2-way: effrt over 1f out: ev ch u.p in cl 2nd ins fnl f: no imp on wnr in 3rd cl home* **20/1**

**4** ½ **Moviesta (USA)**[32] 4771 7-9-7 104..............................(p) RobbieDowney 3 109
(Edward Lynam, Ire) *in tch: 6th 1/2-way: rdn and bmpd sltly over 1f out: kpt on wl u.p in 4th wl ins fnl f: nt trble wnr* **22/1**

**5** ½ **Mr Lupton (IRE)**[8] 5633 4-9-7 109.............................................. WJLee 10 108
(Richard Fahey) *dwlt sltly: hld up towards rr: 8th 1/2-way: rdn nr side over 1f out: r.o wl u.p wl ins fnl f into nvr threatening 5th on line* **8/1**

6 *shd* **Intelligence Cross (USA)**[7] 5690 3-9-3 112........(bt) SeamieHeffernan 8 106
(A P O'Brien, Ire) *cl up bhd ldrs: cl 4th at 1/2-way: almost on terms over 1f out: no ex u.p wl ins fnl f and wknd into 5th clsng stages: denied 5th on line* **6/1[3]**

7 *¾* **Koropick (IRE)**[22] 5149 3-9-6 109............................ JosephineGordon 4 107
(Hugo Palmer) *in tch: 7th 1/2-way: pushed along 2f out and no imp on ldrs ins fnl f where n.m.r and swtchd rt: kpt on clsng stages* **8/1**

8 *hd* **Kimberella**[7] 5684 7-9-7 109.................................... DeclanMcDonogh 7 104
(Richard Fahey) *sn disp and led narrowly after 1f: narrow advantage at 1/2-way: rdn and strly pressed over 1f out: sn hdd and no ex: wknd clsng stages* **4/1[2]**

9 *2 ¼* **Mr Scarlet**[51] 4030 3-9-3 105............................................ PatSmullen 1 96
(Ms Sheila Lavery, Ire) *wnt sltly rt s: sn disp ld briefly tl settled bhd ldr after 1f: cl 2nd at 1/2-way: rdn 2f out and no ex bhd ldrs over 1f out: wknd and eased fnl f* **12/1**

10 *¾* **Khukri (IRE)**[84] 2863 3-9-3 106.......................................... ColinKeane 9 94
(Mrs John Harrington, Ire) *hld up towards rr: last at 1/2-way: rdn over 2f out and no imp over 1f out: wknd and eased ins fnl f* **10/1**

1m 11.77s (-3.73)
**WFA** 3 from 4yo+ 4lb **10** Ran SP% **119.1**
CSF £29.16 TOTE £3.00: £1.50, £2.60, £4.60; DF 27.30 Trifecta £226.90.
**Owner** Mrs John Magnier & Michael Tabor & Derrick Smith **Bred** P Hyland & C & J McHale **Trained** Cashel, Co Tipperary

**FOCUS**
Not much between a lot of these on ratings but the winner had marginally the strongest overall form on offer, though he did disappoint on soft ground last time. He would have been an unlucky loser had he not got up, and this was a deserved first Group success. The winner, second and fifth set the standard, rated to their recent form.

5975 - 5976a (Foreign Racing) - See Raceform Interactive

## 5953 ARLINGTON PARK (L-H)
Sunday, August 13

**OFFICIAL GOING: Turf: firm**

### 5977a ARLINGTON MILLION XXXV STKS (GRADE 1) (3YO+) (TURF) 1m 2f
**12:19** (12:39) 3-Y-0+
**£458,536** (£152,845; £76,422; £38,211; £22,926; £15,284)

RPR

1 **Beach Patrol (USA)**[43] 4396 4-9-0 0............................(b) JoelRosario 9 114
(Chad C Brown, U.S.A) *t.k.h: w ldr: rdn to ld narrowly 1 1/2f out: hdd over 1f out: drvn 1f out: rallied to ld 100yds out: drvn out* **49/10[2]**

2 *½* **Fanciful Angel (IRE)**[37] 4584 5-9-0 0........................... DanielMuscutt 6 113
(Marco Botti) *midfield: rdn under 2f out: drvn and styd on fnl f: no imp on wnr clsng stages* **73/1**

3 *nk* **Deauville (IRE)**[24] 5087 4-9-0 0......................................(p) RyanMoore 5 112
(A P O'Brien, Ire) *trckd ldrs: hdwy on inner fr under 2f out: rdn to ld over 1f out: drvn ins fnl f: hdd 100yds out: wknd clsng stages* **9/5[1]**

4 *hd* **Enterprising (USA)**[56] 6-9-0 0..................................(b) CoreyJLanerie 3 112+
(Michael J Maker, U.S.A) *towards rr: rdn and styd on fr 1 1/2f out: nrst fin* **80/1**

5 *½* **Ascend (USA)**[15] 5-9-0 0................................................(b) JoseLOrtiz 11 111
(H Graham Motion, U.S.A) *dwlt: towards rr: rdn and kpt on wl fr 2f out: nrst fin* **96/10**

6 *1* **Oak Brook (USA)**[36] 5-9-0 0.........................................(b) SantoSanjur 1 109
(Brian Williamson, U.S.A) *led: hdd 1 1/2f out: sn rdn: wknd ins fnl f* **57/1**

7 *nk* **Divisidero (USA)**[64] 3609 5-9-0 0............................ JulienRLeparoux 10 108
(William Bradley, U.S.A) *towards rr: rdn and kpt on steadily on outer fr 1 1/2f out: n.d* **89/10**

8 *hd* **Oscar Nominated (USA)**[43] 4396 4-9-0 0..................(b) FlorentGeroux 2 108
(Michael J Maker, U.S.A) *in tch: rdn 2f out: wknd steadily fnl f* **163/10**

9 *½* **Kasaqui (ARG)**[36] 7-9-0 0........................................... JamesGraham 8 107
(Ignacio Correas IV, U.S.A) *midfield: rdn and outpcd 2f out: sn no imp* **7/1**

10 *½* **Mekhtaal**[53] 3962 4-9-0 0................................................ FrankieDettori 12 106
(J-C Rouget, France) *dwlt: towards rr: rdn and kpt on steadily fr 1 1/2f out: n.d* **59/10[3]**

11 *½* **Ghost Hunter (USA)**[36] 7-9-0 0.................................. EdwinGonzalez 4 105
(Jamie Ness, U.S.A) *trckd ldrs: rdn 2 1/2f out: lost pl 1 1/2f out: sn btn* **196/10**

12 *1 ¾* **The Pizza Man (USA)**[36] 8-9-0 0..................................... IradOrtizJr 7 102
(Roger Brueggemann, U.S.A) *midfield on outer: lost pl under 2f out: sn btn* **117/10**

2m 2.39s (0.75) **12** Ran SP% **122.0**
PARI-MUTUEL (all including 2 usd stake): WIN 11.80; PLACE (1-2) 6.00, 51.40; SHOW (1-2-3) 4.00, 10.40, 2.80; SF 995.00.
**Owner** James Covello, Sheep Pond Partners & Head Of Plain **Bred** Nancy C Shuford **Trained** USA

**FOCUS**
The winner has been rated to his best.

## 5952 DEAUVILLE (R-H)
Sunday, August 13

**OFFICIAL GOING: Polytrack: fast; turf: soft**

### 5978a PRIX FRANCOIS BOUTIN (LISTED RACE) (2YO) (STRAIGHT) (TURF) 7f
**1:55** 2-Y-0 **£25,641** (£10,256; £7,692; £5,128; £2,564)

RPR

1 **Mythical Magic (IRE)**[16] 5350 2-9-2 0......................... JamieSpencer 7 100+
(Charlie Appleby) *mde all: led gp of four in centre of trck and overall ldr: drvn appr fnl f: r.o u.p fnl f: readily* **43/10[2]**

2 *¾* **Cascadian**[35] 2-9-2 0........................................... MickaelBarzalona 2 98+
(A Fabre, France) *settled in 3rd in centre gp: drvn to cl 2f out: 1 l 2nd and rdn appr fnl f: styd on fnl f: a hld by wnr* **4/5[1]**

3 *3* **Salt Lake City (FR)**[88] 2-9-2 0........................ Pierre-CharlesBoudot 6 91
(Robert Collet, France) *hld up in rr of centre gp: drvn to cl over 1 1/2f out: 3 l 3rd appr fnl f: kpt on at same pce* **198/10**

4 *3 ½* **Dice Roll (FR)**[28] 2-9-2 0.............................................. CristianDemuro 3 82
(F Chappet, France) *w.w last of three on stands' side: angled out and pushed along to cl 2f out: rdn and btn wl over 1f out: one pce* **48/10[3]**

5 *1 ½* **Audacious Girl (FR)**[28] 2-8-13 0.................................... TonyPiccone 5 75
(E Lellouche, France) *chsd ldr in centre: lost pl and drvn fr 1 1/2f out: wl hld fnl f* **113/10**

6 *5* **Debutante's Ball (IRE)**[14] 5461 2-8-13 0.................(p) AntoineHamelin 1 63
(J S Moore) *chsd ldr stands' side gp: outpcd and drvn in last under 2f out: bhd fnl f* **118/10**

7 *1* **Get Even**[15] 5448 2-8-13 0................................................. OlivierPeslier 4 60
(Jo Hughes) *led stands' side gp disputing 2nd overall: outpcd and lost pl 1 1/2f out: wknd over 1f out* **183/10**

1m 24.41s (-3.89) **7** Ran SP% **117.6**
PARI-MUTUEL (all including 1 euro stake): WIN: 1.30 (coupled with Cascadian); PLACE: 1.60, 1.20; SF 6.20.
**Owner** Godolphin **Bred** Peter Kelly And Ms Wendy Daly **Trained** Newmarket, Suffolk

**FOCUS**
The field split into two groups initially, and the first three came from the four who raced up the centre of the track.

### 5979a GRAND H'CAP DE DEAUVILLE (3YO+) (STRAIGHT) (TURF) 1m (R)
**2:30** 3-Y-0+
**£40,170** (£16,239; £11,965; £7,692; £4,700; £2,991)

RPR

1 **Blessed Silence (FR)**[71] 3354 4-8-13 **0**................(h) MickaelBarzalona 1 94
(J-M Beguigne, France) **104/10**

2 *1 ¼* **Sant'Amanza (FR)**[91] 6-8-11 **0** ow1................... ChristopheSoumillon 17 89
(R Le Dren Doleuze, France) **47/10[1]**

3 *1* **Iron Spirit (FR)**[42] 7-8-11 **0**...................................... AntoineHamelin 2 87
(Mme M Bollack-Badel, France) **197/10**

4 *1* **Aprilios (FR)**[42] 5-8-9 **0**.................................................. EddyHardouin 5 82
(J-M Lefebvre, France) **196/10**

5 *snk* **Zarose (FR)**[105] 4-9-0 **0**............................................... TheoBachelot 10 87
(H-A Pantall, France) **199/10**

6 *¾* **Geonpi (IRE)**[12] 6-8-5 **0**............................................... JeromeMoutard 7 76
(N Bellanger, France) **27/1**

7 *snk* **London Protocol (FR)**[19] 5269 4-9-2 **0**.........................(p) TonyPiccone 8 87
(K R Burke) **178/10**

8 *¾* **Ross Castle (IRE)**[46] 4-8-9 **0**....................................... AntoineCoutier 3 78
(Matthieu Palussiere, France) **60/1**

9 *1* **Skiperia (FR)**[42] 6-9-0 **0**...........................................(b) MaximeGuyon 14 81
(Y Barberot, France) **11/1**

10 *¾* **Kay Kay Boy (IRE)**[58] 4-9-2 **0**...................................... OlivierPeslier 6 81
(G E Mikhalides, France) **30/1**

11 *1 ¼* **Nice To See You (FR)**[14] 4-8-11 **0**.................(p) VincentCheminaud 13 73
(Robert Collet, France) **97/10[3]**

12 *½* **Gaetano Donizetti (IRE)**[42] 4-8-6 **0**............................ ThierryThulliez 4 67
(D Smaga, France) **153/10**

13 *½* **Snaad**[105] 5-9-6 **0**............................................... Pierre-CharlesBoudot 9 80
(F-H Graffard, France) **56/10[2]**

14 *2 ½* **Vilaro (FR)**[74] 4-9-1 **0**........................................... StephanePasquier 11 69
(D Smaga, France) **185/10**

15 *1 ¼* **Dylan Dancing (IRE)**[13] 5490 4-8-8 **0**............................ RonanThomas 16 59
(C Le Veel, France) **209/10**

16 *1* **Flag Fen**[14] 4-8-10 **0**..........................................(b) AurelienLemaitre 12 59
(N Caullery, France) **32/1**

17 *4* **Diwan Senora (FR)**[41] 4454 4-8-7 **0** ow1....................(p) JeromeCabre 15 47
(Y Barberot, France) **173/10**

18 *3 ½* **Eternal Army (FR)**[83] 4-8-9 **0**.................................... CristianDemuro 18 41
(H-A Pantall, France) **164/10**

1m 36.54s (-4.26) **18** Ran SP% **117.4**
PARI-MUTUEL (all including 1 euro stake): WIN: 11.40; PLACE: 3.70, 2.30, 5.30; DF: 26.70; SF: 53.20.
**Owner** Ecurie Noel Forgeard & P Bonnier **Bred** Earl Haras Du Taillis **Trained** France

### 5980a PRIX DU HARAS DE FRESNAY-LE-BUFFARD - JACQUES LE MAROIS (GROUP 1) (3YO+ NO GELDINGS) (STR) (TURF) 1m (R)
**3:15** 3-Y-0+ **£341,863** (£136,769; £68,384; £34,162; £17,111)

RPR

1 **Al Wukair (IRE)**[28] 4942 3-8-13 0.................................... FrankieDettori 6 120
(A Fabre, France) *trckd ldrs: rdn over 2f out: drvn and styd on last 100yds: led last stride* **4/1**

2 *shd* **Inns Of Court (IRE)**[43] 4390 3-8-13 0....................... MickaelBarzalona 3 120
(A Fabre, France) *hld up in rr: rdn and hdwy fr 2f out: drvn ins fnl f: styd on wl to ld clsng stages: hdd last stride* **151/10**

3 *snk* **Thunder Snow (IRE)**[35] 4666 3-8-13 0...........(p) ChristopheSoumillon 4 119
(Saeed bin Suroor) *led: rdn under 2f out: wknd and hdd clsng stages* **17/10[1]**

4 *1 ¼* **Trais Fluors**[35] 4666 3-8-13 0................................... VincentCheminaud 5 117
(A Fabre, France) *midfield: rdn 2f out: nt clr run ent fnl f: kpt on same pce* **18/5[3]**

5 *1* **Taareef (USA)**[28] 4942 4-9-5 0.............................. Jean-BernardEyquem 2 114+
(J-C Rouget, France) *t.k.h: chsd ldr: rdn over 2f out: drvn 1 1/2f out: wknd steadily fr over 1f out* **29/10[2]**

6 *1 ¼* **Gold Luck (FR)**[35] 4666 3-8-9 0......................................... MaximeGuyon 1 107
(F Head, France) *midfield: rdn and outpcd over 2f out: kpt on same pce* **124/10**

1m 38.51s (-2.29)
**WFA** 3 from 4yo 7lb **6** Ran SP% **118.1**
PARI-MUTUEL (all including 1 euro stake): WIN: 5.00; PLACE :2.50, 4.30; SF: 29.40.
**Owner** Al Shaqab Racing **Bred** Ballylinch Stud **Trained** Chantilly, France

**FOCUS**
A small field and only one Group 1 winner lined up, but it contained both proven class and potential. They came as one group down the middle of the track, not going quick early, and it produced a very tight finish. The standard is set around the winner, third and fourth.

### 5981a PRIX MINERVE (GROUP 3) (3YO FILLIES) (TURF) 1m 4f 110y
**3:55** 3-Y-0 **£34,188** (£13,675; £10,256; £6,837; £3,418)

RPR

1 **God Given**[22] 5155 3-8-11 0............................................. JamieSpencer 3 105
(Luca Cumani) *mde all: rdn 2 1/2f out: pressed appr fnl f: drvn and fnd ex to assert ins fnl f* **47/10[3]**

2 *1 ¾* **Calayana (FR)**[24] 3-8-11 0........................................... MickaelBerto 7 102
(A De Royer-Dupre, France) *hld up towards rr: rdn and hdwy fr 2 1/2f out: drvn and styd on wl fr 1 1/2f out: wnt 2nd clsng stages: nt rch wnr* **26/1**

3 *nk* **Lady Montdore (USA)**[30] 4877 3-8-11 0............... Pierre-CharlesBoudot 10 102
(A Fabre, France) *hld up in rr: rdn 2 1/2f out: drvn and kpt on fr 1 1/2f out* **15/2**

4 *hd* **Elas Ruby**[42] 4424 3-8-11 0 ............ FrankieDettori 2 101
(John Gosden) *trckd ldrs: chsd ldr under 3f out: rdn over 2f out: pressed ldr and ev ch appr fnl f: no ex last 150yds* **29/10**[1]

5 *1 3/4* **Lady Paname (FR)**[70] 3366 3-8-11 0 ............ TonyPiccone 9 99+
(E Lellouche, France) *towards rr of midfield: rdn and sltly outpcd over 2f out: kpt on fr over 1f out* **36/5**

6 *1* **Standing Rock (IRE)**[29] 4915 3-8-11 0 ............ AndreaAtzeni 8 97
(John Gosden) *in tch in midfield: rdn under 3f out: drvn over 1f out: kpt on same pce* **19/1**

7 *2* **Saxon Rose**[44] 3-8-11 0 ............ MickaelBarzalona 6 94
(A Fabre, France) *hld up towards rr of midfield: rdn and effrt under 2f out: wknd last 100yds* **74/10**

8 *snk* **Sirrin (IRE)**[58] 3804 3-8-11 0 ............ ChristopheSoumillon 1 94
(J-C Rouget, France) *midfield: rdn 1 1/2f out: wknd ent fnl f* **39/10**[2]

9 *1/2* **Mademoiselle Marie (FR)**[56] 3881 3-8-11 0 ............ OlivierPeslier 5 93
(K Borgel, France) *in tch in midfield: rdn and outpcd over 2f out: sn no imp* **106/10**

10 *7* **Nacida (GER)**[42] 3-8-11 0 ............ MickaelForest 4 82
(Yasmin Almenrader, Germany) *chsd ldr: rdn 2 1/2f out: lost pl over 2f out: sn btn: eased ins fnl f* **67/1**

2m 43.67s (-2.73) **10** Ran SP% **118.3**
PARI-MUTUEL (all including 1 euro stake): WIN: 5.70; PLACE: 2.90, 6.60, 3.30; DF: 61.80; SF: 75.40.
**Owner** St Albans Bloodstock Limited **Bred** St Albans Bloodstock Llp **Trained** Newmarket, Suffolk

## 5982a PRIX MICHEL HOUYVET (LISTED RACE) (3YO) (TURF) 1m 7f
**4:35** 3-Y-O **£23,504** (£9,401; £7,051; £4,700; £2,350)

RPR

1 **Darbuzan (FR)**[59] 3-9-0 0 ............ ChristopheSoumillon 5 106+
(M Delzangles, France) **13/10**[1]

2 *3* **Canndera (FR)**[59] 3-8-10 0 ............ MickaelBerto 1 96+
(A De Royer-Dupre, France) **30/1**

3 *nse* **Galipad**[56] 3879 3-9-0 0 ............ MaximeGuyon 6 100
(A Fabre, France) **6/1**[3]

4 *nk* **Light Pillar (IRE)**[37] 3-9-0 0 ............ StephanePasquier 9 100
(A Fabre, France) **67/10**

5 *1/2* **Agathonia (USA)**[30] 4877 3-8-10 0 ............ MickaelBarzalona 10 95
(H-A Pantall, France) **26/1**

6 *6* **Galikeo**[58] 3804 3-9-0 0 ............(b) AurelienLemaitre 8 91
(F Head, France) **125/10**

7 *nk* **Royal Associate**[15] 5397 3-9-0 0 ............ JamieSpencer 3 91
(Charlie Appleby) **47/10**[2]

8 *3/4* **Tansholpan**[95] 2523 3-8-10 0 ............ AndreaAtzeni 7 86
(Roger Varian) **105/10**

9 *20* **Pesk Ebrel (FR)**[36] 3-9-0 0 ............ OlivierPeslier 2 64
(Y Gourraud, France) **26/1**

10 *12* **No Joy (USA)**[23] 5133 3-9-0 0 ............(b) JulienAuge 4 48
(C Ferland, France) **25/1**

3m 11.7s (-7.40) **10** Ran SP% **118.9**
PARI-MUTUEL (all including 1 euro stake): WIN: 2.30; PLACE: 1.50, 4.00, 2.00; DF: 32.70; SF: 40.10.
**Owner** Princess Zahra Aga Khan **Bred** Princess Zahra Aga Khan **Trained** France

# 3371 HOPPEGARTEN (R-H)
Sunday, August 13
**OFFICIAL GOING: Turf: good**

## 5983a 127TH LONGINES GROSSER PREIS VON BERLIN (GROUP 1) (3YO+) (TURF) 1m 4f
**4:05** 3-Y-O+ **£94,017** (£34,188; £12,820; £8,547)

RPR

1 **Dschingis Secret (GER)**[43] 4392 4-9-6 0 ............ AdriedeVries 3 118+
(Markus Klug, Germany) *trckd ldrs: rdn over 2f out: drvn to ld 1f out: styd on wl fnl f: readily* **14/5**[2]

2 *1* **Hawkbill (USA)**[31] 4814 4-9-6 0 ............(p) JamesDoyle 5 116
(Charlie Appleby) *led: rdn 1 1/2f out: hdd 1f out: kpt on wl fnl f: nt pce of wnr* **7/5**[1]

3 *3 1/2* **Racing History (IRE)**[285] 7759 5-9-6 0 ............(p) GeraldMosse 4 111
(Saeed bin Suroor) *chsd ldr: rdn 2 1/2f out: outpcd by front pair fnl f: kpt on* **4/1**[3]

4 *nk* **Colomano**[42] 4422 3-8-10 0 ............ AndreasHelfenbein 2 111
(Markus Klug, Germany) *midfield: rdn and effrt 2f out: outpcd by front pair fnl f: kpt on* **23/5**

5 *3/4* **Instigator (GER)**[56] 3-8-10 0 ............(p) FilipMinarik 1 110
(Jean-Pierre Carvalho, Germany) *missed break and lost abt 5l: racd in last pair: rdn and kpt on steadily fr over 2f out: n.d* **141/10**

6 *3 1/2* **Sirius (GER)**[30] 4879 6-9-6 0 ............ MarcLerner 6 104
(Andreas Suborics, Germany) *midfield: rdn over 2f out: wknd ins fnl f: coasted last 100yds* **112/10**

7 *9* **Shanjo (GER)**[42] 4422 3-8-10 0 ............ MartinSeidl 7 90
(Markus Klug, Germany) *hld up in last pair: stmbld 3f out: rdn over 2f out: hung lft 1 1/2f out: eased whn btn fnl f* **115/10**

2m 32.89s (3.59)
**WFA** 3 from 4yo+ 10lb **7** Ran SP% **128.7**
PARI-MUTUEL (all including 10 euro stake): WIN 38 PLACE: 18, 17; SF: 59.
**Owner** Horst Pudwill **Bred** Gestut Park Wiedingen **Trained** Germany

# 5200 LES LANDES
Sunday, August 13
**OFFICIAL GOING: Turf : good**

## 5984a LADBROKES LIVE IN PLAY H'CAP 7f
**3:05** (3:05) 3-Y-O+ **£1,780** (£640; £380)

RPR

1 **Chapeau Bleu (IRE)**[21] 5201 5-9-3 0 ............ AliceMills 50
(Mrs C Gilbert, Jersey) *hld up: hdwy fr 2f out: led ins fnl f: pushed out* **3/1**[3]

2 *2* **National Service (USA)**[21] 5200 6-9-6 0 ............(tp) PaddyPilley 48
(Clare Ellam) *led: set fast pce: drvn and wandered u.p fr over 1f out: hdd ins fnl f: no ex* **4/1**

3 *1/2* **Purley Queen (IRE)**[21] 5200 8-9-7 0 ............ PhilipPrince 47
(Mrs C Gilbert, Jersey) *hld up: rdn but stl last into st: styd on fr over 1f out* **6/1**

4 *2 1/2* **Order Of Service**[21] 5201 7-10-12 0 ............ PaddyAspell 60
(K Kukk, Jersey) *rdn away fr s but nvr travelling in rr: c wd st: nt rch ldrs* **13/8**[1]

5 *5* **Princess Kodia (IRE)**[21] 5200 4-9-12 0 ............ MrFTett 32
(Mrs A Malzard, Jersey) *chsd ldrs to 2f out: sn wknd* **13/2**

6 *4* **Pas D'Action**[21] 5201 9-9-6 0 ............(p) JemmaMarshall 15
(Mrs A Malzard, Jersey) *taken bk s: rapid hdwy to chse ldrs after 1f: wknd fr wl over 1f out* **5/2**[2]

7 *6* **Country Blue (FR)**[21] 5200 8-10-4 0 ............ MattieBatchelor 11
(Mrs A Malzard, Jersey) *t.k.h: pressed ldr in clr 2nd: wknd fr over 1f out: eased* **6/1**

**Owner** Saltire Racing **Bred** Woodleigh Stables **Trained** Jersey

## 5985a COUTTS FEATURE H'CAP MILE 1m 100y
**3:40** (3:40) 3-Y-O+ **£2,380** (£860; £510)

RPR

1 **Lucifers Shadow (IRE)**[63] 3958 8-9-12 0 ............(v) AliceMills 42
(Mrs C Gilbert, Jersey) *trckd ldrs: smooth hdwy to chal fr over 1f out: shkn up to ld cl home* **6/4**[1]

2 *hd* **Hawaiian Freeze**[21] 8-10-1 0 ............ PhilipPrince 45
(J Moon, Jersey) *disp ld: hdd 6f out: led again over 4f out: sn drvn: hdd cl home: no ex* **3/1**[2]

3 *4* **George Baker (IRE)**[33] 4713 10-10-12 0 ............ MarcGoldstein 47
(George Baker) *disp ld tl tk clr ld 6f out: hdd over 4f out: kpt on one pce* **3/1**[2]

4 *2* **First Cat**[21] 5201 10-9-7 0 ............ PaddyAspell 24
(K Kukk, Jersey) *trckd ldrs: rdn and ch over 1f out: hung lft u.p* **4/1**[3]

5 *hd* **Larch (IRE)**[21] 5201 5-8-9 0 ow1 ............(h) JemmaMarshall 11
(Mrs A Malzard, Jersey) *hld up: mod late hdwy but nvr able to chal ldrs* **22/1**

6 *hd* **Ron's Ballad**[21] 5200 4-9-8 0 ............ PaddyPilley 24
(K Kukk, Jersey) *hld up: c wd st: nvr able to chal ldrs* **12/1**

7 *hd* **Mendacious Harpy (IRE)**[21] 5201 6-10-8 0 ............(p) MattieBatchelor 37
(Mrs A Malzard, Jersey) *trckd ldrs: wnt 3rd over 4f out: wknd fnl f* **3/1**[2]

**Owner** Capricorn Racing **Bred** J & M & E Doyle **Trained** Jersey

## 5986a LADBROKES LADIES DAY H'CAP 1m 2f
**4:15** (4:15) 3-Y-O+ **£1,780** (£640; £380)

RPR

1 **Brown Velvet**[21] 5201 5-8-9 0 ............ AliceMills 36
(Mrs C Gilbert, Jersey) *trckd ldrs: smooth hdwy to ld over 1f out: pushed out* **13/8**[1]

2 *2* **Benoordenhout (IRE)**[21] 6-10-3 0 ............(p) JemmaMarshall 54
(T Le Brocq, Jersey) *hld up: hdwy fr 3f out: ev ch fr over 1f out: no ex* **5/2**[2]

3 *5* **Cecilator**[14] 4914 3-8-11 0 ............(p) MissMHooper 33
(Noel Williams) *trckd ldrs: wnt cl 2nd over 5f out: led 3f out: hdd and no ex fr over 1f out* **8/1**

4 *1/2* **Flutterbee**[21] 5-10-12 0 ............(p) MattieBatchelor 52
(Mrs A Malzard, Jersey) *trckd ldrs: rdn fr 3f out: ch fr 2f out: one pce* **7/2**

5 *2* **Gabster (IRE)**[21] 4-9-8 0 ............ PaddyPilley 30
(K Kukk, Jersey) *trckd ldrs: rdn and one pce fr 3f out* **8/1**

6 *nk* **Darling Baie (FR)** 4-9-9 0 ............ MrFTett 30
(Mrs A Malzard, Jersey) *led tl hdd 3f out: sn wknd* **20/1**

7 *4* **Hard To Handel**[21] 5201 5-10-7 0 ............(b) PaddyAspell 34
(Mrs A Malzard, Jersey) *hld up: rdn and btn fr 3f out* **3/1**[3]

P **Blue Sea Of Ibrox (IRE)**[21] 9-8-7 0 oh14 ow2 ............(b) PhilipPrince
(Mrs A Corson, Jersey) *dwlt: rdn to sn press ldr: wknd rapidly fr 6f out: p.u over 2f out* **25/1**

**Owner** La Vallette Ltd **Bred** D R Botterill **Trained** Jersey

## 5987a LADBROKES BEST ODDS GUARANTEED H'CAP 1m 4f
**4:50** (4:50) 3-Y-O+ **£1,780** (£640; £380)

RPR

1 **Barwick**[15] 5397 9-10-12 0 ............ MattieBatchelor 83
(George Baker) *mde all: 4 l clr into st: rdn out fnl f* **1/2**[1]

2 *3* **Aussie Lyrics (FR)**[21] 7-10-1 0 ............ AliceMills 67
(Mrs C Gilbert, Jersey) *trckd wnr in 2nd: 4 l bhd into st: no imp* **13/8**[2]

3 *7* **Ocean Crystal**[21] 5-8-5 0 oh21 ............(b) PaddyAspell 32
(Mrs A Malzard, Jersey) *trckd ldrs in 3rd: unable to chal fr over 2f out* **8/1**

4 *3* **Grey Gem (IRE)**[21] 6-8-8 0 oh17 ow3 ............ PaddyPilley 30
(K Kukk, Jersey) *hld up in last: unable to chal fr 3f out* **15/2**[3]

**Owner** Michael H Watt **Bred** Dullingham Park **Trained** Manton, Wilts

# 5776 DEAUVILLE (R-H)
Thursday, August 10
**OFFICIAL GOING: Polytrack: fast; turf: good to soft changing to soft after race 3 (12.25)**

## 5988a PRIX DE FALAISE (MAIDEN) (2YO FILLIES) (TURF) 7f
**2:40** 2-Y-O **£11,538** (£4,615; £3,461; £2,307; £1,153)

RPR

1 **Hello Princess (FR)**[50] 2-9-2 0 ............ OlivierPeslier 3 80
(Louis Baudron, France) **76/10**

2 *3/4* **Red Duma (FR)**[23] 2-9-2 0 ............ Pierre-CharlesBoudot 9 78
(H-A Pantall, France) **6/4**[1]

3 ¾ **Snowflake (FR)**[32] 2-9-2 0........................................ WilliamsSaraiva 1 76
(M Nigge, France) **73/10**[3]

4 2 **Rachael's Rocket (IRE)**[6] 5629 2-9-2 0........................ TonyPiccone 12 71
(J S Moore) **17/2**

5 hd **Ballet De La Reine (USA)**[32] 2-9-2 0.................. ChristopheSoumillon 2 70
(J-C Rouget, France) **3/1**[2]

6 shd **Perle Et Or (FR)**[50] 2-9-2 0..................................... MickaelBarzalona 6 70
(D & P Prod'Homme, France) **29/1**

7 3 **Star Of Vendome (FR)**[49] 4007 2-9-2 0........................ TheoBachelot 4 62
(Harry Dunlop) **50/1**

8 ¾ **Dance Colony**[39] 2-9-2 0........................................... CristianDemuro 13 60
(F Vermeulen, France) **17/1**

9 nk **Soizie (FR)** 2-9-2 0........................................................ AntoineHamelin 8 59
(N Bellanger, France) **88/1**

10 snk **Tosen Hardi**[32] 2-9-2 0.............................................. AurelienLemaitre 5 58
(S Kobayashi, France) **42/1**

11 1 **J'Adore (FR)**[39] 2-9-2 0.................................................... GeraldMosse 10 56
(J-P Dubois, France) **60/1**

12 2 ½ **Rich Girl (FR)**[58] 2-9-2 0................................................(p) DavidBreux 7 49
(Edouard Thueux, France) **23/1**

1m 27.84s (-0.46) **12** Ran SP% **119.3**
PARI-MUTUEL (all including 1 euro stake): WIN 8.60; PLACE 1.90, 1.30, 2.10; DF 10.00; SF 30.50.
**Owner** Jean-Philippe Dubois **Bred** J-P Dubois **Trained** France

## 5989a PRIX DE TOUR-EN-BESSIN (MAIDEN) (2YO COLTS & GELDINGS) (TURF) 7f

**3:10** 2-Y-O **£11,538** (£4,615; £3,461; £2,307; £1,153)

RPR

1 **Zyzzyva (FR)**[24] 4973 2-9-2 0.................................. MickaelBarzalona 10 80
(Robyn Brisland) *hld up in tch: angled out and rdn early in st: drifted rt u.p but r.o and chal fnl f: led towards fin* **69/10**

2 ½ **Baillolet (FR)**[32] 2-9-2 0............................................. CristianDemuro 9 79
(Mme Pia Brandt, France) **9/5**[1]

3 1 ½ **Senoville (IRE)**[36] 4678 2-9-2 0...................................... JulienAuge 6 75
(C Ferland, France) **73/10**

4 3 **Loup Des Steppes (FR)** 2-9-2 0..................................... JeffersonSmith 7 67
(J-C Rouget, France) **31/1**

5 1 **Tadeem (IRE)**[29] 4782 2-9-2 0........................................ GeraldMosse 2 64
(J E Hammond, France) **6/1**[3]

6 1 ½ **Barag (IRE)**[74] 2-9-2 0......................................... ChristopheSoumillon 4 60
(J-C Rouget, France) **63/10**

7 3 **Ace Of Aces (FR)** 2-9-2 0.............................................. AurelienLemaitre 1 52
(J-P Gallorini, France) **71/1**

8 20 **Energy Chop (FR)**[39] 2-9-2 0.......................................... AntoineHamelin 8
(Matthieu Palussiere, France) **10/1**

9 snk **Marsh Harbour (FR)**[25] 2-9-2 0........................................ MaximeGuyon 3
(Mario Hofer, Germany) **9/2**[2]

1m 28.13s (-0.17) **9** Ran SP% **120.2**
PARI-MUTUEL (all including 1 euro stake): WIN 7.90; PLACE 2.10, 1.50, 1.60; DF 10.80; SF 29.60.
**Owner** Paul Hancock **Bred** Scpa Fertilia **Trained** Newmarket, Suffolk

# 5917 AYR (L-H)

## Monday, August 14

**OFFICIAL GOING: Good changing to good to soft after race 2 (2:15)**
Wind: quite windy Weather: overcast, showers, mild

## 5990 BRITISH STALLION STUDS EBF FILLIES' NOVICE STKS (PLUS 10 RACE) 7f 50y

**1:45** (1:47) (Class 4) 2-Y-O **£5,175** (£1,540; £769; £384) **Stalls** High

Form RPR

41 1 **Affina (IRE)**[17] 5371 2-9-6 0........................................... GrahamLee 7 83+
(Simon Crisford) *trckd ldrs: hdwy 3f out: led over 2f out: pushed along over 1f out: reminder and kpt up to work fnl f: r.o wl: sn clr: readily* **3/1**[2]

032 2 2 **Kirbec (IRE)**[46] 4245 2-9-0 71.......................................... PaulMulrennan 11 71
(Keith Dalgleish) *prom: hdwy to ld over 2f out: sn hdd: rdn and swtchd over 1f out: r.o ins fnl f* **17/2**

450 3 ¾ **Che Bella (IRE)**[87] 2801 2-9-0 0........................................ JoeFanning 4 69
(Keith Dalgleish) *led: hdd over 2f out: pushed along 2f out: reminders over 1f out: kpt on fnl f* **25/1**

4 hd **Chrisellaine (IRE)** 2-9-0 0.............................................. BenCurtis 1 69+
(Charles Hills) *t.k.h: trckd ldrs: pushed along 2f out: reminders over 1f out: hmpd by 2nd over 1f out: r.o ins fnl f* **13/2**

0 5 ¾ **Ventura Royal (IRE)**[17] 5372 2-9-0 0.................................... SamJames 3 67+
(David O'Meara) *in rr: hdwy on inner 2f out: pushed along over 1f out: r.o fnl f* **25/1**

5 6 ½ **Island Affair (IRE)**[9] 5673 2-9-0 0.................................(h) RonanWhelan 5 66
(Adrian McGuinness, Ire) *hld up: effrt 2f out: drvn and hdwy over 1f: one pce fnl f* **8/1**

41 7 1 **Double Reflection**[17] 5356 2-9-0 0.................................... CliffordLee[(3)] 9 66
(K R Burke) *trckd ldrs: pushed along on outer 3f out: drvn 2f out: rdn over 1f out: no imp* **5/1**[3]

3 8 ½ **Frolic**[9] 5660 2-9-0 0........................................................ RyanPowell 8 62
(Sir Mark Prescott Bt) *mid-div: hdwy to go 3rd 3f out: drvn 2f out: wknd over 1f out* **9/4**[1]

9 nk **Flamin Audi (GER)** 2-9-0 0............................................. JamesSullivan 6 61
(Lee Smyth, Ire) *in rr: pushed along 3f out: drvn 2f out: one pce* **66/1**

10 1 ½ **Endless Tangent (IRE)** 2-9-0 0........................................ PJMcDonald 2 57
(Tom Dascombe) *hld up: pushed along 3f out: drvn 2f out: no rspnse* **22/1**

1m 33.54s (0.14) **Going Correction** +0.025s/f (Good) **10** Ran SP% **120.9**
Speed ratings (Par 93): **100,97,96,96,95 95,94,93,93,91**
CSF £28.55 TOTE £4.10: £1.40, £2.40, £6.60; EX 29.80 Trifecta £307.40.
**Owner** Sheikh Juma Dalmook Al Maktoum **Bred** Max Morris **Trained** Newmarket, Suffolk

**FOCUS**
Rail movements increased certain advertised race distances as follows: Races 1,2,3 and 4 by 12 yards; Races 7 and 8 by 33 yards. A fair juvenile fillies' novice contest. They went a respectable gallop, at best, on officially good ground following overnight rain. The top of the surface was loose and it paid to race prominently. The runner-up helps the level.

## 5991 WILLIAM HILL JOIN PLUS IN SHOP TODAY H'CAP (DIV I) 7f 50y

**2:15** (2:15) (Class 6) (0-60,60) 3-Y-O+ **£2,587** (£770; £384; £192) **Stalls** High

Form RPR

5343 1 **Size Matters**[9] 5666 3-9-0 56............................................ JasonHart 1 62
(Mark Walford) *trckd ldr: led 3f out: drvn over 2f out: rdn over 1f out: narrow ld ent fnl f: drvn along and extended advantage last 150yds: rdn out* **7/2**[3]

2340 2 1 **Jessie Allan (IRE)**[2] 5917 6-8-5 48........................ SeanMooney[(7)] 11 54
(Jim Goldie) *hld up: hdwy and swtchd to outer over 2f out: pushed along to take clsr order 1f out: drvn into 2nd ent fnl f: kpt on but hld* **12/1**

2311 3 shd **Yes You (IRE)**[12] 5543 3-8-11 60...................................... JamieGormley[(7)] 3 63
(Iain Jardine) *trckd ldrs: pushed along on inner 2f out: reminders ent fnl f: r.o wl* **3/1**[2]

1322 4 1 ¾ **Magic Journey (IRE)**[14] 5466 3-8-11 60.............................. JoshQuinn[(7)] 7 59
(John Quinn) *mid-div: trckd ldrs gng wl 2f out: plld out to chal and drvn over 1f out: sn rdn: once pce* **11/4**[1]

0530 5 3 ½ **Free To Roam (IRE)**[3] 5905 4-8-12 48.............................. RonanWhelan 9 40
(Adrian McGuinness, Ire) *chsd ldrs: hdwy into 2nd 3f out: sn alongside wnr: rdn over 1f out: wknd and lost pl fnl f* **9/2**

6060 6 2 ¼ **Lady Molly (IRE)**[41] 4478 3-8-6 48...................................... JoeFanning 10 33
(Keith Dalgleish) *mid-div: hdwy 3f out: pushed along 2f out: one pce fnl f* **28/1**

0400 7 3 ½ **New Decade**[14] 5467 8-8-10 46 oh1...............................(p) PJMcDonald 8 24
(Jim Goldie) *hld up: hdwy into mid-div over 2f out: rdn ent fnl f: no ex* **50/1**

440 8 5 **Kensington Palace (IRE)**[30] 4900 4-9-5 55...........(t[1]) JamesSullivan 12 20
(Marjorie Fife) *in rr: last 3f out: effrt and rdn on outer over 2f out: no imp* **14/1**

600 9 2 ½ **Kafoo**[41] 4459 4-9-8 58...................................................... AndrewMullen 4 17
(Michael Appleby) *in rr: drvn 2f out: briefly n.m.r over 1f out: sn rdn: no imp* **20/1**

50- 10 11 **Spirit Be With You (IRE)**[51] 4110 4-9-2 52.............(b[1]) PaulMulrennan 2
(Lee Smyth, Ire) *led: hdd 3f out: sn rdn: wknd qckly* **40/1**

1m 31.89s (-1.51) **Going Correction** +0.025s/f (Good)
**WFA** 3 from 4yo+ 6lb **10** Ran SP% **119.0**
Speed ratings (Par 101): **109,107,107,105,101 99,95,89,86,74**
CSF £43.48 CT £145.77 TOTE £4.30: £1.60, £3.30, £1.30; EX 42.20 Trifecta £208.50.
**Owner** R Kent & M D Eddery **Bred** Mickley Stud **Trained** Sherriff Hutton, N Yorks

**FOCUS**
Race distance increased 12 yards. The first division of a moderate handicap. They went a decent gallop and the winning time suggests there was a bit of cut in the ground. The official going description was changed to good to soft after this race. The winner took a minor step forward.

## 5992 WILLIAM HILL JOIN PLUS IN SHOP TODAY H'CAP (DIV II) 7f 50y

**2:45** (2:45) (Class 6) (0-60,58) 3-Y-O+ **£2,587** (£770; £384; £192) **Stalls** High

Form RPR

603/ 1 **Harry Speed (IRE)**[3] 5905 4-9-4 55..........................(t) LewisEdmunds[(3)] 9 67
(Garvan Donnelly, Ire) *mde all: 2 l clr 2f out: rdn over 1f out: in command ent fnl f: pushed along and r.o wl: comf* **3/1**[1]

524 2 1 ¾ **Jack Blane**[6] 5741 3-9-3 57............................................(p) GrahamLee 7 63
(Keith Dalgleish) *trckd ldrs: rdn and hdwy into 2nd over 1f out: chsd wnr ent fnl f: r.o* **7/2**[2]

0060 3 1 ¼ **Rioja Day (IRE)**[21] 5206 7-9-4 52...................................(b) NathanEvans 12 57
(Jim Goldie) *trckd ldr: drvn 2f out: rdn and lost pl over 1f out: rallied ent fnl f: tk 3rd nr fin* **18/1**

0213 4 ½ **Harbour Patrol (IRE)**[14] 5467 5-9-7 55.........................(b) DuranFentiman 8 59
(Rebecca Bastiman) *mid-div: hdwy and drvn 2f out: rdn in 3rd over 1f out: no ex fnl f: lost 3rd nr fin* **7/1**[3]

340- 5 1 ¾ **Cheers Buddy (IRE)**[241] 8414 9-8-4 45.......................... DannySheehy[(7)] 1 44
(Lee Smyth, Ire) *mid-div: effrt to trck ldrs 2f out: sn drvn: rdn over 1f out: one pce* **20/1**

0620 6 shd **Irvine Lady (IRE)**[21] 5205 4-8-11 45...............................(p) PJMcDonald 11 44
(R Mike Smith) *chsd wnr: drvn 2f out: sn rdn and lost pl* **25/1**

6052 7 hd **Darvie**[22] 5182 3-9-4 58.................................................. SamJames 6 55
(David Barron) *hld up: pushed along 2f out: rdn 1f out: one pce fnl f* **7/2**[2]

-004 8 1 ½ **Pipe Dreamer**[14] 5467 3-8-5 45............................................(p) ShaneGray 4 38
(Kevin Ryan) *hld up: drvn 2f out: rdn over 1f out: no imp* **8/1**

4034 9 hd **Let Right Be Done**[2] 5917 5-9-0 48...............................(b) AndrewMullen 5 42
(Linda Perratt) *in rr: effrt and drvn 2f out: rdn over 1f out: no imp* **9/1**

0653 10 4 **Red Shadow**[14] 5466 8-8-7 46.........................................(v) RowanScott[(5)] 2 30
(Alistair Whillans) *slowly away: a in rr* **22/1**

1m 33.34s (-0.06) **Going Correction** +0.025s/f (Good)
**WFA** 3 from 4yo+ 6lb **10** Ran SP% **121.3**
Speed ratings (Par 101): **101,99,97,97,95 94,94,92,92,88**
CSF £13.77 CT £165.69 TOTE £4.50: £2.00, £1.70, £4.40; EX 16.90 Trifecta £260.10.
**Owner** G P Clarke **Bred** M C Bloodstock Ltd & Cbs Bloodstock **Trained** Garristown, Co Dublin

**FOCUS**
Race distance increased 12 yards. The second division of a moderate handicap. The heavily backed winner controlled his own tempo from the front and the winning time was notably slower. The winner is rated back towards his best 2016 figure.

## 5993 WILLIAM HILL THIS IS MORE H'CAP 1m

**3:15** (3:15) (Class 5) (0-75,77) 3-Y-O+ **£3,557** (£1,058; £529; £264) **Stalls** Low

Form RPR

5440 1 **Chinese Spirit (IRE)**[14] 5466 3-8-12 65.................................. JoeFanning 8 72
(R Mike Smith) *chsd ldr: pushed along to ld over 1f out: sn drvn: 1 l ld ent fnl f: r.o wl: comf* **10/1**

3604 2 1 **Jay Kay**[18] 5333 8-9-6 66...........................................(h) JoeyHaynes 9 72
(K R Burke) *led: 2 l clr 3f out: drvn 2f out: rdn and hdd over 1f out: kpt on fnl f* **7/1**

3325 3 1 **Abushamah (IRE)**[14] 5469 6-9-13 73............................(p) JamesSullivan 4 77
(Ruth Carr) *t.k.h: mid-div: trckd ldrs gng wl over 2f out: hdwy and rdn over 1f out: wnt 3rd ent fnl f: r.o* **5/1**

0512 4 1 ½ **Crazy Tornado (IRE)**[14] 5469 4-9-11 71..........................(h) GrahamLee 6 71
(Keith Dalgleish) *mid-div: hdwy into 3rd 3f out: pushed along 2f out: rdn over 1f out: lost 3rd ent fnl f: one pce* **9/2**[3]

0003 5 ¾ **Gun Case**[21] 5206 5-9-1 66.........................................(p) RowanScott[(5)] 10 65
(Alistair Whillans) *in rr: reminder 4f out: hdwy 3f out: tk clsr order and rdn over 2f out: one pce fnl f* **14/1**

-024 **6** ½ **Scottish Summit (IRE)**[23] 5135 4-9-10 **70**........................ SamJames 1 67
(Geoffrey Harker) *mid-div: pushed along 3f out: drvn over 1f out: one pce fnl f* **25/1**

2212 **7** ¾ **Breanski**[17] 5378 3-9-7 **74**................................................ RonanWhelan 7 69
(David O'Meara) *hld up: pushed along 3f out: rdn 2f out: lugged rt and n.m.r over 1f out: no ex fnl f* **11/4**[1]

6321 **8** 4 **Remember Rocky**[2] 5917 8-8-12 **65** 6ex..............(b) ConnorMurtagh(7) 3 51
(Lucy Normile) *trckd ldrs: drvn and lost pl over 2f out: sn rdn: wknd and eased* **4/1**[2]

2-60 **9** 7 **Dark Alliance (IRE)**[16] 5396 6-9-10 **77**...................... DannySheehy(7) 5 47
(Adrian Paul Keatley, Ire) *in rr: hdwy 3f out: rdn 2f out: sn dropped bk to last* **20/1**

1m 43.25s (-0.55) **Going Correction** +0.025s/f (Good)
**WFA** 3 from 4yo+ 7lb **9** Ran SP% **118.4**
Speed ratings (Par 103): **103,102,101,99,98 98,97,93,86**
CSF £79.80 CT £400.67 TOTE £8.50: £2.40, £2.00, £1.90; EX 86.60 Trifecta £466.30.
**Owner** Y C Luk **Bred** J Murphy **Trained** Galston, E Ayrshire

**FOCUS**
Race distance increased 12 yards. A fair handicap. Once again they went a sensible gallop on the easy surface and it paid to race prominently. Improvement from the winner.

## 5994 WILLIAM HILL GET THE APP ON GOOGLE PLAY H'CAP 6f
**3:45** (3:46) (Class 5) (0-75,75) 3-Y-0+ **£3,557** (£1,058; £529; £264) **Stalls** Low

Form RPR

-166 **1** **Alfie's Angel (IRE)**[24] 5132 3-9-4 **71**........................ GrahamLee 1 79
(Bryan Smart) *mid-div: reminders over 2f out: hdwy over 1f out: rdn appr fnl f: led last 150yds: sn clr: won gng away* **8/1**

2601 **2** 1 ½ **Jacob's Pillow**[9] 5646 6-9-7 **75**..................................(p) RowanScott(5) 3 79
(Rebecca Bastiman) *led: rdn 2f out: narrow ld ent fnl f: hdd last 150yds: kpt on* **12/1**

-102 **3** nk **Duncan Of Scotland (IRE)**[17] 5385 4-9-1 **64**...........(b) PaulMulrennan 4 67
(Lee Smyth, Ire) *a.p: cl 2nd over 1f out: rdn and no ex ent fnl f* **7/1**

4260 **4** hd **Goninodaethat**[2] 5919 9-8-11 **60**.................................... NathanEvans 7 62
(Jim Goldie) *chsd ldrs: pushed along 2f out: rdn and hdwy over 1f out: one pce fnl f* **20/1**

3102 **5** 1 ¾ **Benjamin Thomas (IRE)**[11] 5560 3-9-1 **75**..........(v) ConnorMurtagh(7) 2 71
(John Quinn) *mid-div: rdn over 1f out: no ex fnl f* **7/4**[1]

20-0 **6** shd **Rosenborg Rider (IRE)**[7] 5729 4-9-2 **65**.................(p) RonanWhelan 10 61
(Adrian McGuinness, Ire) *in rr: effrt 1/2-way: rdn over 1f out: mod prog fnl f* **11/2**[3]

-020 **7** 1 **Sahreej (IRE)**[3] 5902 4-9-5 **75**.................................... DannySheehy(7) 9 68
(Adrian Paul Keatley, Ire) *chsd ldrs: pushed along 2f out: rdn over 1f out: wknd fnl f* **4/1**[2]

0000 **8** 4 **Bapak Asmara (IRE)**[21] 5211 5-9-9 **72**...........................(p) TomEaves 6 52
(Kevin Ryan) *prom: drvn and lost pl over 1f out: fdd* **22/1**

-005 **9** 6 **Funding Deficit (IRE)**[22] 5184 7-9-7 **70**......................(h) PJMcDonald 8 31
(Jim Goldie) *hld up: pushed along 1/2-way: rdn over 2f out: no rspnse* **20/1**

1m 13.56s (1.16) **Going Correction** +0.225s/f (Good)
**WFA** 3 from 4yo+ 4lb **9** Ran SP% **116.9**
Speed ratings (Par 103): **101,99,98,98,96 95,94,89,81**
CSF £95.05 CT £708.67 TOTE £9.30: £2.50, £2.60, £2.20; EX 78.90 Trifecta £255.80.
**Owner** Ms Dawn Aldridge **Bred** Penolva Partnership **Trained** Hambleton, N Yorks

**FOCUS**
A fair sprint handicap. They went a decent gallop centrally in gradually worsening conditions. A length+ pb from the winner.

## 5995 WILLIAM HILL BEST ODDS GUARANTEED H'CAP 5f
**4:15** (4:15) (Class 6) (0-65,66) 3-Y-0+ **£2,587** (£770; £384; £192) **Stalls** Low

Form RPR

0663 **1** **Star Cracker (IRE)**[14] 5472 5-9-2 **55**...........................(p) PJMcDonald 12 64
(Jim Goldie) *hld up: hdwy 1/2-way: drvn 1f out: rdn and str run ins fnl f: led last 50yds: on top nr fin* **5/1**

/026 **2** ¾ **Pillar**[17] 5385 4-9-5 **58**................................................ RonanWhelan 4 64
(Adrian McGuinness, Ire) *disp ld tl led on own over 2f out: rdn over 1f out: narrow ld ent fnl f: r.o u.p: hdd last 50yds* **3/1**[2]

0622 **3** ½ **Lady Joanna Vassa (IRE)**[6] 5736 4-8-9 **48**..................(v) JoeFanning 2 53
(Richard Guest) *disp ld tl relegated to cl 2nd over 2f out: reminders over 1f out: kpt on fnl f* **9/4**[1]

020- **4** ½ **Catwilldo (IRE)**[31] 4874 7-9-1 **54**...............................(b) BenCurtis 7 57
(Garvan Donnelly, Ire) *prom: pushed along 2f out: rdn and ev ch 1f out: no ex fnl f* **7/2**[3]

6 **5** 1 ¾ **Olaudah**[7] 5728 3-7-13 **48**....................................... DannySheehy(7) 3 44
(Adrian Paul Keatley, Ire) *slowly away: hdwy 2f out: drvn over 1f out: reminders and one pce fnl f* **8/1**

0440 **6** 2 ½ **Dawoodi**[14] 5471 3-9-6 **62**...................................(h) AndrewMullen 10 48
(Linda Perratt) *hld up: pushed along 2f out: rdn over 1f out: no imp* **25/1**

0036 **7** ¾ **Brendan (IRE)**[10] 5605 4-8-6 **45**................................ NathanEvans 6 30
(Jim Goldie) *trckd ldrs: drvn 1/2-way: rdn over 2f out: wknd* **20/1**

1m 0.21s (0.81) **Going Correction** +0.225s/f (Good)
**WFA** 3 from 4yo+ 3lb **7** Ran SP% **114.4**
Speed ratings (Par 101): **102,100,100,99,96 92,91**
CSF £20.38 CT £42.36 TOTE £5.50: £2.60, £2.20; EX 27.00 Trifecta £61.70.
**Owner** The Vital Sparks **Bred** James Mc Claren **Trained** Uplawmoor, E Renfrews
■ Stewards' Enquiry : Ronan Whelan caution: careless riding

**FOCUS**
A modest sprint handicap. They went a contested gallop and it is sound form for the grade. The winner's latest form is working form ok.

## 5996 WILLIAM HILL PROUD TO SUPPORT SCOTTISH SPORT H'CAP 1m 2f
**4:45** (4:46) (Class 3) (0-90,92) 3-Y-0+ **£7,762** (£2,310; £1,154; £577) **Stalls** Low

Form RPR

3P62 **1** **Weekend Offender (FR)**[14] 5470 4-10-0 **92**...................... TomEaves 4 102
(Kevin Ryan) *mid-div: hdwy gng wl over 2f out: sn pushed into ld: rdn over 1f out: 1 l ahd whn wnt lft towards runner-up ins fnl f: sn stened: asserted last 100yds* **7/4**[1]

1333 **2** 1 ¾ **Royal Regent**[21] 5207 5-9-1 **82**.................................. SammyJoBell(3) 9 89
(Lucy Normile) *hdwy 2f out: cl 2nd whn rdn over 1f out: 1 l down and keeping on ins fnl f whn briefly n.m.r on rail: no ex last 100yds* **9/2**[2]

6316 **3** 5 **Royal Shaheen (FR)**[14] 5469 4-9-2 **80**......................(v) PaulMulrennan 3 76
(Alistair Whillans) *prom: led 3f out: pushed along and hdd 2f out: sn rdn: one pce and lft bhd by first two over 1 f out* **8/1**

1623 **4** 2 ½ **Gworn**[14] 5470 7-8-10 **81**.......................................... ConnorMurtagh(7) 2 72
(R Mike Smith) *hld up: pushed along and hdwy over 2f out: sn rdn: r.o to take 4th ent fnl f* **17/2**

5000 **5** 1 ¾ **Corton Lad**[23] 5164 7-9-6 **89**.......................................(vt[1]) RowanScott(5) 5 77
(Keith Dalgleish) *prom tl led after 1f: drvn and hdd 3f out: no ex* **22/1**

640 **6** ¾ **Testa Rossa (IRE)**[16] 5417 7-8-10 **81**......................(b) SeanMooney(7) 8 67
(Jim Goldie) *in rr: pushed along 3f out: one pce but passed btn horses fnl 2f* **16/1**

0043 **7** 2 **Bahama Moon (IRE)**[13] 5496 5-8-12 **81**....................... BenRobinson(5) 6 63
(David Barron) *led tl hdd after 1f: remained prom: chsd along 3f out: rdn 2f out: wknd* **11/2**[3]

0 **8** 2 **Mutamaded (IRE)**[93] 2610 4-9-12 **90**............................ JamesSullivan 7 68
(Ruth Carr) *prom: pushed along 3f out: fdd fnl 2f* **20/1**

4361 **9** 99 **Desert Way (IRE)**[25] 5060 4-9-5 **83**................................ PJMcDonald 10
(Rebecca Menzies) *hld up: pushed along 1/2-way: sn lost tch: detached 4f out: heavily eased* **13/2**

2m 11.7s (-0.30) **Going Correction** +0.025s/f (Good) **9** Ran SP% **119.9**
Speed ratings (Par 107): **102,100,96,94,93 92,91,89,10**
CSF £10.00 CT £51.68 TOTE £2.80: £1.10, £2.10, £2.20; EX 10.70 Trifecta £62.20.
**Owner** Matt & Lauren Morgan **Bred** Mathieu Daguzan-Garros Et Al **Trained** Hambleton, N Yorks

**FOCUS**
Race distance increased 33 yards. The feature contest was a decent handicap. They went quite hard up front in the worsening conditions and it paid to be ridden more patiently. The winner's awarded a length pb in pulling clear of the rest.

## 5997 BOOK FOR THE WILLIAM HILL AYR GOLD CUP H'CAP 1m 2f
**5:15** (5:17) (Class 6) (0-65,65) 3-Y-0+ **£2,587** (£770; £384; £192) **Stalls** Low

Form RPR

6603 **1** **Sepal (USA)**[9] 5648 4-9-11 **62**........................................... JoeFanning 12 74+
(Iain Jardine) *prom: smooth hdwy to ld over 2f out: qckly drew clr: 5 l ahd 1f out: extended advantage tl rdr eased rt down last 150yds: v easily* **7/2**[1]

6456 **2** 6 **New Abbey Angel (IRE)**[20] 5254 4-8-12 **54**.............. RowanScott(5) 14 54
(Keith Dalgleish) *chsd ldrs: hdwy into 4th 4f out: pushed along in pursuit of wnr 2f out: rdn and drifted lft to far rail over 1f out: kpt on for clr 2nd pl ins fnl f* **8/1**[2]

6-60 **3** 2 ½ **Lenoire**[10] 5591 3-8-9 **57**..........................................(p[1]) LewisEdmunds(3) 8 54
(Michael Appleby) *hld up: hdwy 3f out: drvn 2f out: rdn wl over 1f out: r.o to take 3rd ins fnl f* **8/1**[2]

3405 **4** 1 **Stardrifter**[2] 5917 5-9-2 **53**...........................................(p) PaulMulrennan 6 47
(Linda Perratt) *hld up: hdwy 3f out: n.m.r and hmpd over 1f out: rdn and r.o to take 4th ins fnl f* **10/1**

4230 **5** 1 ½ **Rosemay (FR)**[9] 5648 3-9-1 **65**..................................... BenRobinson(5) 2 57
(Iain Jardine) *hld up: drvn 3f out: swtchd over 1f out: r.o ins fnl f* **9/1**[3]

04-4 **6** 1 ½ **Clarabel**[46] 4247 4-9-10 **61**............................................ AndrewMullen 7 49
(John Weymes) *trckd ldrs: rdn 2f out: wknd fnl f* **20/1**

/60- **7** 2 ¾ **Granite City Doc**[312] 7096 4-8-2 **46** oh1..................... ConnorMurtagh(7) 4 29
(Lucy Normile) *trckd ldrs: pushed along 2f out: wknd and lost pl over 1f out* **33/1**

0400 **8** ½ **Penelope Pitstop**[36] 4660 5-8-6 **46** oh1.................. SammyJoBell(3) 13 28
(Lee Smyth, Ire) *prom: led 1/2-way: pushed along and hdd over 2f out: rdn and wknd over 1f out* **11/1**

5113 **9** 1 ¾ **Haymarket**[2] 5917 8-10-0 **65**.......................................... PJMcDonald 10 44
(R Mike Smith) *led: hdd 1/2-way: styd prom: drvn and wknd 3f out* **7/2**[1]

0632 **10** 7 **John Caesar (IRE)**[13] 5498 6-9-4 **55**......................(tp) DuranFentiman 5 22
(Rebecca Bastiman) *mid-div: drvn 3f out: rdn over 2f out: fdd* **10/1**

5 **11** nk **Quiet Company**[4] 5861 3-7-10 **48**............................(p[1]) DannySheehy(7) 3 15
(Adrian Paul Keatley, Ire) *hld up: hdwy on outer 3f out: drvn 2f out: fdd* **12/1**

5660 **12** ½ **Danny Mc D**[2] 5917 4-9-0 **58**.................................(p) JamieGormley(7) 11 23
(Iain Jardine) *a in rr: pushed along 3f out: no imp* **22/1**

0366 **13** 6 **Red Star Dancer (IRE)**[2] 5921 3-8-11 **56**........................ ShaneGray 1 11
(Linda Perratt) *a in rr: drvn 3f out: no rspnse* **25/1**

2m 13.26s (1.26) **Going Correction** +0.025s/f (Good)
**WFA** 3 from 4yo+ 8lb **13** Ran SP% **126.8**
Speed ratings (Par 101): **95,90,88,87,86 85,82,82,81,75 75,74,69**
CSF £32.34 CT £221.36 TOTE £4.80: £1.90, £2.70, £2.90; EX 39.20 Trifecta £249.50.
**Owner** I J Jardine **Bred** Juddmonte Farms Inc **Trained** Carrutherstown, D'fries & G'way

**FOCUS**
Race distance increased 33 yards. A modest handicap which took place in the heaviest rain of the day. The winner was value for extra.
T/Jkpt: Not Won. T/Plt: £310.50 to a £1 stake. Pool: £83,659.62 - 196.63 winning units T/Qpdt: £65.30 to a £1 stake. Pool: 7,459.65 - 84.5 winning units **Keith McHugh**

# 5702 RIPON (R-H)
Monday, August 14

**OFFICIAL GOING: Good (good to soft in places; 7.7)**
Wind: light half behind Weather: fine

## 5998 SIS.TV FILLIES' NOVICE AUCTION STKS (PLUS 10 RACE) 6f
**2:00** (2:01) (Class 5) 2-Y-O **£3,234** (£962; £481; £240) **Stalls** High

Form RPR

45 **1** **Dorcas**[18] 5334 2-8-10 0........................................ SilvestreDeSousa 5 68
(James Given) *in tch on outer: sn pushed along: rdn and hdwy to chal over 1f out: kpt on: led towards fin* **7/1**

5 **2** ½ **Dangerous Lady**[9] 5665 2-8-12 0.................................. DavidAllan 2 69
(Tim Easterby) *led: pushed along 2f out: rdn and pressed over 1f out: edgd slly lft 1f: one pce and hdd towards fin* **13/2**[3]

4 **3** 1 ¼ **Bungee Jump (IRE)**[16] 5412 2-9-0 0................................. KevinStott 8 70
(Kevin Ryan) *trckd ldrs: bit short of room over 2f out: rdn 2f out: attempting to chal whn short of room on rail 1f out: swtchd rt 110yds out: kpt on same pce* **15/8**[2]

0 **4** 5 **Sitsi**[21] 5210 2-8-10 0............................................ ConnorBeasley 6 48
(Bryan Smart) *in tch: rdn over 2f out: chsd ldrs over 1f out: wknd ins fnl f* **20/1**

6 **5** 7 **Out Last**[10] 5600 2-8-10 0........................................ BarryMcHugh 9 27
(Keith Dalgleish) *prom: rdn over 2f out: wknd over 1f out* **28/1**

**6** 9 **Champarisi** 2-8-10 0............................................... JackGarritty 4
(Grant Tuer) *s.i.s: a towards rr* **50/1**

2643 **7** 4 **Take Shelter**[18] 5334 2-9-0 75.................................... DanielTudhope 7
(James Tate) *trckd ldrs: rdn over 2f out: sn wknd and eased* **7/4**[1]

**8** 5 **Baileys Rockstar** 2-9-0 0.......................................... JoeDoyle 10
(James Given) *s.i.s: a outpcd in rr* **16/1**

**9** 8 **Laharna (IRE)** 2-8-12 0........................................ PatrickMathers 1
(Noel Wilson) *dwlt: a in rr* **33/1**

1m 13.58s (0.58) **Going Correction** -0.05s/f (Good) **9** Ran SP% **116.0**
Speed ratings (Par 91): **94,93,91,85,75 63,58,51,41**
CSF £49.28 TOTE £6.50: £2.90, £2.30, £1.10; EX 38.40 Trifecta £198.60.
**Owner** Stephanie Oliver **Bred** Bearstone Stud Ltd **Trained** Willoughton, Lincs

**FOCUS**
After the first David Allan called the ground "just on the easy side of good", which fits with the official description. Just a fair race of its type, in which they finished quite spread out. The time was 3.18sec slower than standard. The first two showed progress.

## 5999 SIS CELEBRATING 30 YEARS IN HORSE RACING FILLIES' NOVICE AUCTION STKS (PLUS 10 RACE) 1m
**2:30** (2:30) (Class 4) 2-Y-O **£5,175** (£1,540; £769; £384) **Stalls** Low

Form RPR
3 **1** **Voicemail**[17] 5371 2-9-0 0 DanielTudhope 1 75+
(James Tate) *trckd ldrs: racd keenly: pushed along over 3f out: rdn to chal over 2f out: drvn to ld over 1f out: styd on to draw clr ins fnl f* **1/4**[1]
0040 **2** 3 **Show Of Force**[23] 5154 2-9-0 64 JackGarritty 6 66
(Jonathan Portman) *led: rdn over 2f out: hdd over 1f out: no ex fnl f* **18/1**
6 **3** 1 **Rayna's World (IRE)**[25] 5056 2-9-0 0 PaddyAspell 5 64+
(Philip Kirby) *dwlt: hld up: pushed along over 2f out: styd on fr over 1f out: nrst fin* **7/1**[2]
45 **4** 2 3/4 **Ryedale Encore**[17] 5371 2-9-0 0 DavidAllan 2 57
(Tim Easterby) *trckd ldr: rdn to chal 2f out: wknd ins fnl f* **10/1**[3]
60 **5** 10 **American Ruby (USA)**[10] 5600 2-9-0 0 SilvestreDeSousa 4 34
(Mark Johnston) *midfield: pushed along and in tch over 3f out: wknd over 1f out* **20/1**
50 **6** 3 **Princess Jessica (FR)**[25] 5056 2-9-0 0 TonyHamilton 7 27
(Richard Fahey) *dwlt: hld up: nvr threatened* **50/1**
00 **7** 13 **Gift Of Loulins**[17] 5371 2-9-0 0 BarryMcHugh 3
(Tony Coyle) *dwlt: sn midfield: rdn over 3f out: sn wknd* **125/1**

1m 42.52s (1.12) **Going Correction** -0.025s/f (Good) 7 Ran SP% **114.4**
Speed ratings (Par 93): **93,90,89,86,76 73,60**
CSF £6.95 TOTE £1.10: £1.02, £6.10; EX 6.70 Trifecta £20.80.
**Owner** Saeed Manana **Bred** Whatton Manor Stud **Trained** Newmarket, Suffolk

**FOCUS**
The rail on the home bend was dolled out by 4 yards, adding 8 yards to the distance of this race. Ordinary form but the winner has more to offer.

## 6000 FOLLOW @RIPONRACES ON TWITTER H'CAP 1m 6f
**3:00** (3:00) (Class 4) (0-85,87) 4-Y-O+ **£5,175** (£1,540; £769; £384) **Stalls** High

Form RPR
0226 **1** **Stormin Tom (IRE)**[7] 5700 5-8-4 70 RachelRichardson(3) 4 77
(Tim Easterby) *mde all: rdn along over 2f out: strly pressed thrght fnl 2f: hld on gamely* **8/1**
0150 **2** nk **Renfrew Street**[24] 5108 4-9-1 78 SilvestreDeSousa 5 84
(Mark Johnston) *midfield: trckd ldr 8f out: rdn to chal strly 2f out: kpt on but a jst hld* **7/1**
1542 **3** 2 1/2 **On Fire**[23] 5138 4-8-12 75 (p) PhillipMakin 3 78
(James Bethell) *trckd ldrs: rdn over 2f out: kpt on same pce* **7/2**[2]
6324 **4** 4 **Chancery (USA)**[19] 5287 9-9-7 84 (p) DanielTudhope 1 81
(David O'Meara) *hld up: rdn over 3f out: no imp: wnt modest 4th over 1f out* **9/2**[3]
4151 **5** 11 **West Drive (IRE)**[19] 5303 4-9-10 87 (p) AndreaAtzeni 7 69
(Roger Varian) *hld up: pushed along over 4f out: drvn over 3f out: wknd over 1f out* **11/8**[1]
3-06 **6** 2 1/2 **Highland Castle**[27] 4998 9-9-5 82 (t) NeilFarley 2 60
(Lucinda Egerton) *hld up: rdn over 3f out: wknd over 1f out* **150/1**
1305 **P** **Gaelic Tiger**[16] 5397 4-9-7 87 (p) JoshDoyle(3) 6
(David O'Meara) *trckd ldr: wnt wrong and p.u and dismntd over 9f out* **14/1**

3m 2.42s 7 Ran SP% **113.4**
CSF £60.14 TOTE £10.40: £3.50, £3.30; EX 62.70 Trifecta £236.30.
**Owner** Three Jolly Farmers **Bred** Mill House, Donald, Fowlston & McStay **Trained** Great Habton, N Yorks

**FOCUS**
Only the second 1m6f race run at Ripon, this was run over an additional 8 yards due to rail movements. The winner dictated the gallop and is rated in line with this year's form.

## 6001 RIPON ANNUAL BADGEHOLDERS H'CAP 1m
**3:30** (3:30) (Class 3) (0-95,95) 3-Y-O **£7,561** (£2,263; £1,131; £566; £282) **Stalls** Low

Form RPR
0560 **1** **Cullingworth (IRE)**[16] 5392 3-8-8 82 BarryMcHugh 6 95
(Richard Fahey) *mde all: pushed along over 2f out: qcknd clr over 1f out: kpt on wl: easily* **2/1**[1]
1036 **2** 7 **Fujaira Bridge (IRE)**[40] 4491 3-8-7 81 AndreaAtzeni 4 78
(Roger Varian) *in tch: rdn over 2f out: kpt on to go 2nd ins fnl f: no threat wnr* **9/4**[2]
1315 **3** 1 1/4 **Brother McGonagall**[17] 5378 3-8-2 76 CamHardie 1 70
(Tim Easterby) *trckd ldrs: rdn and outpcd over 2f out: plugged on* **7/1**
5114 **4** 1 **Helovaplan (IRE)**[45] 4299 3-8-9 83 ConnorBeasley 5 75
(Bryan Smart) *dwlt: sn in tch: trckd ldr 4f out: rdn over 2f out: outpcd over 1f out: no ex ins fnl f* **5/1**
1150 **5** 11 **La Casa Tarifa (IRE)**[12] 5529 3-8-9 83 SilvestreDeSousa 3 65
(Mark Johnston) *s.i.s: hld up in tch: rdn over 2f out: wknd over 1f out and eased* **9/2**[3]

1m 40.76s (-0.64) **Going Correction** -0.025s/f (Good) 5 Ran SP% **111.5**
Speed ratings (Par 104): **102,95,93,92,81**
CSF £6.92 TOTE £2.90: £1.30, £1.50; EX 7.10 Trifecta £23.40.
**Owner** Tiffin Sandwiches Limited & Partner **Bred** John Foley **Trained** Musley Bank, N Yorks

**FOCUS**
Race run over an additional 8 yards. The winner blew them away from the front. The time was modest and it's hard to know how much he improved.

## 6002 SIS TRUSTED PARTNER TO THE RACING INDUSTRY H'CAP 1m 4f 10y
**4:00** (4:00) (Class 5) (0-70,72) 3-Y-O **£3,234** (£962; £481; £240) **Stalls** Centre

Form RPR
5353 **1** **Fire Leopard**[10] 5617 3-9-6 66 (h) DanielTudhope 1 79+
(David O'Meara) *hld up: smooth hdwy over 4f out: pushed along to ld 2f out: edgd rt: kpt on wl to draw clr* **5/2**[1]
0223 **2** 6 **Theglasgowwarrior**[26] 5024 3-9-5 65 (p[1]) LouisSteward 3 67
(Michael Bell) *chsd clr ldng pair: tk clsr order 4f out: rdn to ld 3f out: hdd 2f out: one pce and sn no ch w wnr* **3/1**[2]
3341 **3** 3 **Bonnie Arlene (IRE)**[12] 5549 3-9-12 72 SilvestreDeSousa 2 71
(Mark Johnston) *hld up: rdn along 4f out: plugged on to go poor 3rd ins fnl f: nvr threatened* **3/1**[2]
0631 **4** 4 1/2 **Tewafeedj**[10] 5618 3-9-2 62 KevinStott 4 52
(Kevin Ryan) *led narrowly: clr w one other tl 4f out: rdn whn hdd 3f out: wknd fnl 2f* **4/1**[3]
6515 **5** 55 **American Craftsman (IRE)**[67] 3489 3-9-3 63 JackGarritty 5
(Jedd O'Keeffe) *pressed ldr: clr of remainder tl 4f out: rdn over 3f out: wknd* **13/2**

2m 35.6s (-1.10) **Going Correction** -0.025s/f (Good) 5 Ran SP% **111.9**
Speed ratings (Par 100): **102,98,96,93,56**
CSF £10.43 TOTE £2.80: £1.70, £1.90; EX 9.60 Trifecta £18.00.
**Owner** Chris Napthine **Bred** Carwell Equities Ltd **Trained** Upper Helmsley, N Yorks

**FOCUS**
This modest handicap was run over an extra 8 yards. The fourth and fifth went clear and cut each other's throats. The winner improved again.

## 6003 VISIT RIPON-RACES.CO.UK APPRENTICE H'CAP 1m
**4:30** (4:30) (Class 6) (0-60,68) 4-Y-O+ **£2,587** (£770; £384; £192) **Stalls** Low

Form RPR
5-05 **1** **Euro Mac**[21] 5215 5-8-10 49 GemmaTutty 7 56
(Neville Bycroft) *chsd ldng pair: tk clsr order over 3f out: pushed along and briefly outpcd 2f out: styd on fnl f: led 25yds out* **8/1**
003 **2** 1 **Green Howard**[9] 5649 9-9-4 57 (p) GeorgeBuckell 8 62
(Rebecca Bastiman) *midfield: pushed along and hdwy over 2f out: led appr fnl f: sn rdn 2 l clr: idled and hdd 25yds out* **9/2**[2]
0101 **3** 2 1/2 **Beadlam (IRE)**[3] 5897 4-9-12 68 6ex (p) CameronNoble(3) 1 67
(Roger Fell) *in tch: tk clsr order over 2f out whn rdn: ev ch appr fnl f: one pce ins fnl f* **6/1**[3]
0-00 **4** 1 3/4 **Cosmic Dust**[22] 5181 4-8-7 46 oh1 CallumRodriguez 2 41
(Richard Whitaker) *led at gd pce: clr w one other tl over 2f out: rdn over 2f out: hdd appr fnl f: no ex* **20/1**
3230 **5** 3/4 **Tom's Anna (IRE)**[24] 5126 7-8-7 46 RichardOliver 6 39
(Sean Regan) *chsd ldr: clr of remainder tl over 2f out whn rdn: no ex over 1f out* **7/1**
0405 **6** nk **Leonard Thomas**[33] 4744 7-8-11 50 (p) PhilDennis 3 43
(Philip Kirby) *s.i.s: hld up: rdn along over 2f out: plugged on fnl f: nvr threatened* **9/1**
5220 **7** hd **Billy Bond**[13] 5497 5-8-6 55 SebastianWoods(10) 4 47
(Richard Fahey) *midfield: rdn along 3f out: no imp* **4/1**[1]
0020 **8** 4 **Monsieur Jimmy**[14] 5466 5-8-11 56 GerO'Neill(6) 9 39
(Declan Carroll) *hld up: nvr threatened* **14/1**
4030 **9** 1/2 **Lozah**[4] 5831 4-8-11 58 BenSanderson(8) 11 40
(Roger Fell) *a towards rr* **13/2**
0603 **10** 7 **Ivors Involvement (IRE)**[13] 5499 5-8-4 46 oh1 (h[1]) PaulaMuir(3) 10 12
(Tina Jackson) *s.i.s: hld up: rdn over 3f out: wknd fnl 2f* **14/1**

1m 40.72s (-0.68) **Going Correction** -0.025s/f (Good) 10 Ran SP% **117.5**
Speed ratings (Par 101): **102,101,98,96,96 95,95,91,91,84**
CSF £44.28 CT £240.57 TOTE £9.50: £3.00, £2.00, £2.10; EX 53.10 Trifecta £458.80.
**Owner** P Burrow & N Bycroft **Bred** Limestone And Tara Studs **Trained** Norton, N Yorks

**FOCUS**
This was run over an extra 8 yards. A moderate handicap for apprentices which was run at a decent clip. Straightforward form.
T/Plt: £66.60 to a £1 stake. Pool: £69,238.61 - 758.4 winning units T/Qpdt: £44.50 to a £1 stake. Pool: £4,865.55 - 80.91 winning units **Andrew Sheret**

# 5963 WINDSOR (R-H)
### Monday, August 14

**OFFICIAL GOING: Good to firm (good in places; 7.9)**
Wind: Light, behind Weather: Cloudy, warm

## 6004 BOYZONE HERE ON 26TH AUGUST APPRENTICE H'CAP 6f 12y
**5:40** (5:41) (Class 6) (0-60,61) 3-Y-O+ **£2,264** (£673; £336; £168) **Stalls** Low

Form RPR
6213 **1** **Wild Flower (IRE)**[6] 5748 5-9-5 53 MeganNicholls 2 63
(Jimmy Fox) *pressed ldr: led 2f out: sn pressed and rdn: edgd lft into centre of crse but styd on wl to draw clr ins fnl f* **7/4**[1]
3230 **2** 2 1/4 **Captain Ryan**[16] 5429 6-9-13 61 PaddyPilley 10 64
(Geoffrey Deacon) *trckd ldng pair: rdn to go 2nd over 1f out: sn chalng and only threat to wnr: fdd last 100yds* **7/1**[3]
5401 **3** 1/2 **Cee Jay**[41] 4458 4-9-7 58 FinleyMarsh(3) 13 60
(Patrick Chamings) *pressed ldrs: rdn and cl up 2f out: one pce over 1f out and wl hld in 3rd fnl f* **9/2**[2]
0045 **4** 3/4 **Kath's Boy (IRE)**[28] 4969 3-8-4 45 AledBeech(3) 11 44
(Tony Carroll) *in tch on outer: rdn 2f out: kpt on fnl f but nvr able to chal* **20/1**
240 **5** 1/2 **Double Spin**[33] 4731 3-9-1 58 JonathanFisher(5) 9 55
(Robert Cowell) *t.k.h: hld up in midfield: rdn 2f out and no prog: styd on ins fnl f* **20/1**
0504 **5** dht **Monarch Maid**[25] 5081 6-9-10 61 RhiainIngram(3) 5 59
(Peter Hiatt) *led: rdn and hdd 2f out: nt qckn over 1f out: one pce after* **10/1**
0003 **7** nk **Royal Normandy**[20] 5252 5-8-11 45 (b) PatrickO'Donnell 1 42
(Grace Harris) *hld up in midfield: rdn and no prog 2f out: swtchd lft ins fnl f: kpt on nr fin but n.d* **16/1**
6000 **8** 1/2 **Parisian Chic (IRE)**[47] 4211 3-9-4 56 (p) PaddyBradley 14 51
(Lee Carter) *s.i.s: mostly in last trio: rdn over 2f out: kpt on fnl f: nrst fin* **33/1**
00 **9** 3/4 **Leith Bridge**[16] 5410 5-8-11 45 (p) LuluStanford 12 38
(Mark Usher) *in tch on wd outside: rdn 2f out: kpt on same pce fr over 1f out: nvr a threat* **33/1**
0024 **10** 1/2 **Celerity (IRE)**[7] 5703 3-8-5 46 (v) KatherineGlenister(3) 3 37
(David Evans) *chsd ldrs: styd against rail fr 2f out and steadily wknd* **14/1**
0000 **11** 3/4 **Tisa River (IRE)**[42] 4447 3-8-6 47 WilliamCox(3) 8 36
(Milton Bradley) *v s.i.s: a in last trio and off the pce: nvr a factor* **16/1**
1650 **12** 4 **Everkyllachy (IRE)**[25] 5050 3-8-12 55 (b) GeorgiaDobie(5) 6 32
(J S Moore) *s.i.s: a in last trio: styd against rail fr over 2f out and sn wknd* **14/1**

1m 12.32s (-0.68) **Going Correction** -0.05s/f (Good)
**WFA** 3 from 4yo+ 4lb 12 Ran SP% **116.6**
Speed ratings (Par 101): **102,99,98,97,96 96,96,95,94,93 92,87**
CSF £12.68 CT £47.50 TOTE £2.30: £1.20, £2.10, £2.10; EX 16.90 Trifecta £33.20.
**Owner** Mrs Sarah-Jane Fox **Bred** Peter Harms **Trained** Collingbourne Ducis, Wilts

**FOCUS**
The ground had dried out appreciably since the previous day's meeting. The rail was once again dolled out by 12 yards in the straight. A moderate apprentice race.

## 6005 EBF NOVICE STKS 6f 12y
**6:10** (6:12) (Class 5) 2-Y-O **£2,911** (£866; £432; £216) **Stalls** Low

Form RPR

1 **Lansky (IRE)** 2-9-2 0 GeraldMosse 6 80+
(Jeremy Noseda) *s.i.s: sn rcvrd to chse ldrs: wnt 2nd jst over 2f out: rdn to chal over 1f out: led ins fnl f: pushed out nr fin and a in command* **15/8**[1]

42 2 *nk* **Jupiter**[23] 5144 2-9-2 0 DaneO'Neill 2 79
(Henry Candy) *led and styd against rail: rdn 2f out: hdd ins fnl f: kpt on wl but a safely hld by wnr* **4/1**[2]

0 3 *5* **Ojala (IRE)**[62] 3690 2-8-11 0 PaddyBradley(5) 5 64
(Simon Dow) *chsd ldr to jst over 2f out: sltly outpcd over 1f out: edgd rt but styd on again to take 3rd last 100yds* **28/1**

4 *1 1/4* **Queens Gallery** 2-9-2 0 SeanLevey 9 60+
(Richard Hannon) *towards rr: pushed along over 2f out to rch midfield: nvr a threat but kpt on fnl f to take 4th nr fin* **8/1**[3]

5 *hd* **Crack On Crack On** 2-9-2 0 SamHitchcott 3 60
(Clive Cox) *free to post: t.k.h: hld up in midfield: effrt 2f out: hanging lft over 1f out: keeping on whn hmpd fnl 100yds* **8/1**[3]

6 *1/2* **Avon Green** 2-8-8 0 EdwardGreatrex(3) 8 53
(Joseph Tuite) *sn chsd ldrs on outer: disp 2nd briefly over 2f out: fading whn edgd rt ins fnl f* **50/1**

3 7 *nk* **Immortal Romance (IRE)**[69] 3437 2-9-2 0 LukeMorris 4 57
(Michael Bell) *chsd ldng pair 2f: pushed along bef 1/2-way: styd cl up tl fdd over 1f out* **4/1**[2]

0 8 *1 1/2* **Smooth Sailing**[42] 4440 2-8-11 0 KieranShoemark 1 48
(Charles Hills) *hld up in tch: pushed along over 2f out: one pce whn reminder over 1f out* **20/1**

00 9 *7* **Cherubic**[86] 2832 2-8-11 0 JimmyQuinn 11 27+
(Charles Hills) *s.v.s: mostly in last: nudged along and passed two rivals over 1f out: wknd fnl f* **33/1**

00 10 *3/4* **Maveway (IRE)**[34] 4725 2-8-11 0 SaleemGolam 10 25
(David Evans) *sn in rr and racd on outer: no prog 2f out: wknd over 1f out* **100/1**

54 11 *3 3/4* **Blazing Beryl (IRE)**[16] 5430 2-8-11 0 MartinLane 7 13
(Brian Meehan) *chsd ldrs on outer: lost pl 1/2-way: wknd 2f out* **14/1**

1m 12.14s (-0.86) **Going Correction** -0.05s/f (Good) **11 Ran SP% 117.8**
Speed ratings (Par 94): **103,102,95,94,94 93,92,90,81,80 75**
CSF £8.75 TOTE £2.70: £1.40, £1.70, £6.60; EX 11.70 Trifecta £169.00.
**Owner** Phoenix Thoroughbred Limited **Bred** Mrs S M Rogers & Sir Thomas Pilkington **Trained** Newmarket, Suffolk
■ Stewards' Enquiry : Paddy Bradley two-day ban: careless riding (Aug 28-29)

**FOCUS**
No previous winners took their chance in this fair novice. The first two pulled clear and it will be no surprise if the winner proves a good deal better than this.

## 6006 PAUL BURCH RED WINE & MOTORBIKE RETIREMENT H'CAP 1m 2f
**6:40** (6:41) (Class 5) (0-70,72) 3-Y-O **£2,911** (£866; £432; £216) **Stalls** Centre

Form RPR

5301 1 **Medalla De Oro**[7] 5722 3-9-10 72 6ex (h) JackMitchell 6 80
(Peter Chapple-Hyam) *mde all: shkn up 3f out: pressed over 2f out: drvn and asserted ins fnl f* **5/6**[1]

4113 2 *2* **Fanfair**[5] 5782 3-9-3 65 SeanLevey 4 69
(Richard Hannon) *in tch: prog to chse wnr wl over 3f out: rdn to chal over 2f out: nt qckn ins fnl f* **4/1**[2]

0055 3 *1* **Broad Appeal**[11] 5565 3-8-8 61 (h) MitchGodwin(5) 5 63
(Jonathan Portman) *hld up off the pce in 6th: prog 4f out: rdn and clsd on ldrs to take 3rd fnl f: one pce after* **10/1**

4640 4 *2 1/4* **Becuna (USA)**[18] 5331 3-8-9 64 TristanPrice(7) 9 62
(Michael Bell) *in tch: prog to dispute 2nd pl wl over 3f out to over 2f out: rdn and fdd over 1f out* **20/1**

0045 5 *3* **Fire Palace**[16] 5439 3-9-0 69 DarraghKeenan(7) 2 61+
(Robert Eddery) *s.v.s and lost abt 10 l: t.k.h and ct up at bk of field after 3f: lft bhd by ldrs fr 1/2-way: rdn and kpt on to take 5th over 1f out: nrst fin but nvr any ch* **7/1**[3]

-406 6 *7* **Presence Process**[33] 4747 3-8-11 59 FergusSweeney 1 37
(Pat Phelan) *hld up in 7th: shkn up and no real prog 3f out: nvr a factor* **16/1**

060 7 *5* **Lady Prima**[11] 5577 3-8-3 51 KieranO'Neill 3 19
(Mike Murphy) *t.k.h: chsd wnr to wl over 3f out: wknd qckly* **33/1**

0365 8 *5* **Crystal Secret**[7] 5718 3-7-13 50 oh4 (b[1]) HollieDoyle(3) 7 8
(John Bridger) *disp 2nd pl to 1/2-way: sn wknd u.p: bhd 2f out* **9/1**

2m 8.39s (-0.31) **Going Correction** -0.05s/f (Good) **8 Ran SP% 119.7**
Speed ratings (Par 100): **99,97,96,94,92 86,82,78**
CSF £4.71 CT £20.71 TOTE £1.80: £1.02, £1.60, £3.10; EX 5.40 Trifecta £40.60.
**Owner** The Rogues Gallery Two **Bred** Hascombe And Valiant Studs **Trained** Newmarket, Suffolk

**FOCUS**
A modest handicap which provided a good opportunity for the favourite to follow up.

## 6007 MPM FLOORING H'CAP 1m 2f
**7:10** (7:10) (Class 3) (0-90,91) 3-Y-O+ **£7,246** (£2,168; £1,084; £542; £270) **Stalls** Centre

Form RPR

12 1 **Don't Give Up**[16] 5425 3-9-8 91 MartinLane 6 100+
(Saeed bin Suroor) *sn dropped to midfield: shkn up over 2f out: prog wl over 1f out: drvn ahd ins fnl f: hld on nr fin* **5/4**[1]

15-3 2 *hd* **New Agenda**[26] 1598 5-9-7 82 (h) DaneO'Neill 7 90
(Paul Webber) *trckd ldr: shkn up to ld 2f out: hdd ins fnl f: rallied last 75yds: jst hld* **25/1**

0-05 3 *hd* **Seniority**[40] 4491 3-8-13 82 PatCosgrave 8 90+
(William Haggas) *stdd s: hld up in last: prog and squeezed through rivals to take 2nd 1f out: rdn and clsd on ldng pair last 100yds: jst too late* **7/1**

2113 4 *2* **Chiefofchiefs**[9] 5668 4-9-13 88 (p) StevieDonohoe 4 92
(Charlie Fellowes) *hld up in 7th: rdn on outer over 2f out: kpt on to take 4th fnl f: nvr pce to chal* **4/1**[2]

1104 5 *1 1/2* **Toulson**[16] 5421 4-10-0 89 (p[1]) CharlesBishop 3 90
(Eve Johnson Houghton) *trckd ldrs: rdn over 2f out: stl cl up and ch jst over 1f out: fdd fnl f* **5/1**[3]

2/24 6 *1 1/4* **Breden (IRE)**[77] 3160 7-10-0 89 (h) KieranShoemark 2 87
(Linda Jewell) *trckd ldrs: rdn over 2f out: nt qckn over 1f out: fdd ins fnl f* **25/1**

2505 7 *3* **Tomahawk Kid**[31] 4832 4-9-5 80 GeorgeDowning 1 72
(Ian Williams) *t.k.h: hld up in midfield: rdn over 2f out: no rspnse and wknd over 1f out* **25/1**

2101 8 *2 1/4* **Celebration Day (IRE)**[28] 4976 4-9-11 89 EdwardGreatrex(3) 5 77
(Simon Crisford) *led at mod pce: tried to stretched on 3f out: hdd 2f out: wknd tamely* **10/1**

2m 8.76s (0.06) **Going Correction** -0.05s/f (Good)
**WFA** 3 from 4yo+ 8lb **8 Ran SP% 114.2**
Speed ratings (Par 107): **97,96,96,95,93 92,90,88**
CSF £41.05 CT £160.51 TOTE £2.00: £1.10, £4.40, £1.80; EX 32.40 Trifecta £204.50.
**Owner** Godolphin **Bred** Darley **Trained** Newmarket, Suffolk

**FOCUS**
A few potentially progressive sorts in this above-average handicap.

## 6008 THAMES NURSERY H'CAP 1m 31y
**7:40** (7:40) (Class 4) (0-85,78) 2-Y-O **£4,690** (£1,395; £697; £348) **Stalls** Low

Form RPR

11 1 **Codicil**[13] 5492 2-9-5 76 LukeMorris 4 79
(Sir Mark Prescott Bt) *trckd ldng pair: first one rdn 3f out: tk 2nd 2f out and sn hrd drvn to chal: narrow ld ins fnl f: hld on* **10/11**[1]

6622 2 *hd* **Ferik (IRE)**[25] 5079 2-9-7 78 StevieDonohoe 3 81
(David Evans) *trckd ldr: led jst over 2f out: sn drvn and pressed: hdd ins fnl f: kpt on wl nr fin: jst hld* **10/3**[2]

600 3 *2 1/2* **Puchita (IRE)**[12] 5528 2-8-10 67 SeanLevey 2 66
(Richard Hannon) *hld up in last: pushed along and waiting for a gap wl over 2f out: swtchd rt and barged rival over 1f out: rdn and nt qckn bhd ldng pair after* **9/2**[3]

5220 4 *19* **Barbarianatthegate**[11] 5572 2-9-6 77 (b) MartinLane 1 60
(Brian Meehan) *led: rdn and hdd jst over 2f out: wkng whn bdly hmpd over 1f out: eased* **7/1**

1m 44.58s (-0.12) **Going Correction** -0.05s/f (Good) **4 Ran SP% 106.1**
Speed ratings (Par 96): **98,97,95,76**
CSF £3.99 TOTE £1.40; EX 3.00 Trifecta £9.40.
**Owner** Cheveley Park Stud **Bred** Cheveley Park Stud Ltd **Trained** Newmarket, Suffolk

**FOCUS**
A disappointing turnout for the nursery with only one previous winner in the line up - it's probably still fair form though. This year's Dante and King Edward VII winner Permian took this in 2016.

## 6009 27 FIXTURES APRIL TO OCTOBER 2018 MAIDEN STKS 5f 21y
**8:10** (8:12) (Class 5) 3-4-Y-O **£2,911** (£866; £432; £216) **Stalls** Low

Form RPR

0 1 **Look Surprised**[42] 4445 4-8-12 0 MitchGodwin(5) 10 70
(Roger Teal) *trckd ldr after 2f: led 2f out: sn clr: comf* **28/1**

4- 2 *2 3/4* **Silently**[282] 7815 4-9-3 0 GeorgeDowning 4 60
(Daniel Kubler) *chsd ldrs: rdn 2f out: tk 2nd 1f out: kpt on but no ch w wnr* **7/1**

344 3 *1* **Harlequin Storm (IRE)**[154] 1179 3-9-2 64 JackDuern(3) 6 60
(Dean Ivory) *slowly away: rcvrd to chse ldrs on outer: rdn 2f out: disp 2nd 1f out: one pce* **5/1**[2]

0 4 *3/4* **Emilysbutterscotch**[54] 3970 3-9-0 0 AdamBeschizza 8 52
(Rae Guest) *in tch in midfield: rdn sn after 1/2-way: kpt on to take 4th nr fin: n.d* **11/1**

2600 5 *nk* **Deer Song**[35] 4695 4-9-5 52 HollieDoyle(3) 3 57
(John Bridger) *fast away: led to 2f out: lost 2nd 1f out: wknd* **6/1**[3]

0 6 *1/2* **Spitfire Limited**[16] 5431 3-9-0 0 (h[1]) FergusSweeney 1 49
(George Baker) *hld up in last trio: pushed along 2f out: reminder and kpt on fnl f: nvr nrr* **20/1**

3 7 *1* **Golden Easter (USA)**[91] 2674 3-9-0 71 LukeMorris 2 46
(Robert Cowell) *reluctant to enter stalls: chsd ldrs: steadily lost pl and struggling sn after 1/2-way: wl btn over 1f out* **5/4**[1]

5 8 *1 3/4* **Fortune And Glory (USA)**[2] 5937 4-9-5 0 EdwardGreatrex(3) 9 46
(Joseph Tuite) *mostly in last trio and off the pce: pushed along and plugged on fnl f* **20/1**

6000 9 *3/4* **Shamonix (IRE)**[12] 5545 3-9-0 38 KieranO'Neill 7 37
(Mark Usher) *trckd ldr 2f: wknd sn after 1/2-way* **66/1**

10 *14* **Val's Magic Touch** 3-9-0 0 TimmyMurphy 5
(John O'Shea) *s.s: a bhd: t.o* **14/1**

59.87s (-0.43) **Going Correction** -0.05s/f (Good)
**WFA** 3 from 4yo 3lb **10 Ran SP% 117.4**
Speed ratings (Par 103): **101,96,95,93,93 92,90,88,86,64**
CSF £206.07 TOTE £29.30: £5.90, £2.20, £1.70; EX 273.60 Trifecta £3743.40.
**Owner** Withyslade **Bred** Withyslade **Trained** Great Shefford, Berks

**FOCUS**
This didn't take much winning.
T/Plt: £27.20 to a £1 stake. Pool: £94,201.46 - 2527.31 winning units T/Qpdt: £15.30 to a £1 stake. Pool: £6,669.76 - 321.02 winning units **Jonathan Neesom**

# 5891 WOLVERHAMPTON (A.W) (L-H)
### Monday, August 14

**OFFICIAL GOING: Tapeta: standard**
Wind: Light across Weather: Overcast

## 6010 FCLGF.COM EBF FILLIES' NOVICE STKS (PLUS 10 RACE) 6f 20y (Tp)
**5:20** (5:22) (Class 5) 2-Y-O **£3,234** (£962; £481; £240) **Stalls** Low

Form RPR

333 1 **Shania Says (IRE)**[12] 5546 2-8-7 66 ManuelFernandes(7) 6 69
(Tony Carroll) *sn led: shkn up over 1f out: rdn out* **12/1**

5 2 *hd* **Forever In Love**[26] 5026 2-9-0 0 RyanMoore 1 68
(Sir Michael Stoute) *trckd ldrs: wnt 2nd over 1f out: rdn and ev ch ins fnl f: r.o* **1/1**[1]

3 *hd* **Odyssa (IRE)** 2-9-0 0 ShaneKelly 7 68
(Richard Hughes) *hld up in tch: plld hrd: nt clr run over 1f out tl ins fnl f: rdn and r.o wl towards fin* **25/1**

24 4 *1/2* **Indicia**[17] 5349 2-9-0 0 DavidProbert 3 66
(Charles Hills) *pushed along leaving stalls: hld up: hdwy and nt clr run fr over 1f out tl swtchd lft ins fnl f: unable qck nr fin* **7/4**[2]

5 *2 3/4* **Long Embrace** 2-9-0 0 OisinMurphy 2 58+
(Simon Crisford) *dwlt: hld up: hdwy and nt clr run over 1f out: nt trble ldrs* **5/1**[3]

40 6 *nk* **Prezzie**[58] 3821 2-9-0 0 DougieCostello 8 57
(William Muir) *chsd wnr: pushed along 1/2-way: lost 2nd over 1f out: rdn: edgd rt and no ex ins fnl f* **50/1**

7 *3* **Displaying Amber** 2-9-0 0 FranBerry 5 48
(Ben Haslam) *hld up: shkn up over 1f out: nvr on terms* **50/1**

8 7 **Calling Rio (IRE)** 2-9-0 0 JosephineGordon 4 45+
(David Loughnane) *s.s: outpcd* **50/1**
1m 14.88s (0.38) **Going Correction** -0.175s/f (Stan) 8 Ran SP% **120.5**
Speed ratings (Par 91): **90,89,89,88,85 84,80,79**
CSF £25.90 TOTE £14.80: £2.70, £1.10, £5.30; EX 44.30 Trifecta £535.10.
**Owner** Randolph & Mortimer Racing **Bred** Cecil And Martin McCracken **Trained** Cropthorne, Worcs

**FOCUS**
Standard ahead of the opener, a moderate novice sprint in which the winner made all. She showed improved form.

## 6011 FCL GLOBAL FORWARDING - MAKING LOGISTICS PERSONAL CLAIMING STKS 5f 21y (Tp)

**5:50** (5:50) (Class 6) 2-Y-O £2,587 (£770; £384) **Stalls** Low

Form RPR
6630 **1** **Funkadelic**[31] 4866 2-9-6 68 FranBerry 3 59
(Ben Haslam) *mde all: plld hrd: rdn over 1f out: edgd rt ins fnl f: jst hld on* **5/6**[1]
042 **2** *shd* **Christmas Night**[37] 4620 2-9-6 64 RoystonFfrench 1 59
(Ollie Pears) *pushed along and prom: chsd wnr over 1f out: r.o* **15/8**[2]
0603 **3** *nk* **Sandama (IRE)**[10] 5613 2-8-9 55 TonyHamilton 2 47
(Richard Fahey) *chsd wnr tl rdn and hung lft over 1f out: sn hung rt: wnt lft again ins fnl f: r.o* **9/2**[3]
1m 3.64s (1.74) **Going Correction** -0.175s/f (Stan) 3 Ran SP% **107.5**
Speed ratings (Par 92): **79,78,78**
CSF £2.67 TOTE £1.70; EX 2.70 Trifecta £3.10.Funkadelic was the subject of a friendly claim
**Owner** Mrs C Barclay & Partners **Bred** Cheveley Park Stud Ltd **Trained** Middleham Moor, N Yorks

**FOCUS**
A weak claimer and the winning favourite made all. Not form to place much faith in.

## 6012 FCL GLOBAL FORWARDING - MAKING LOGISTICS PERSONAL NOVICE AUCTION STKS 5f 21y (Tp)

**6:20** (6:20) (Class 6) 2-Y-O £2,587 (£770; £384; £192) **Stalls** Low

Form RPR
6220 **1** **Hello Girl**[23] 5150 2-8-11 70 FrannyNorton 4 70+
(Dean Ivory) *mde all: shkn up and c readily clr fnl f: easily* **8/13**[1]
04 **2** 3 ¾ **Lucky Lucky Man (IRE)**[14] 5480 2-9-2 0 DavidNolan 1 62
(Richard Fahey) *chsd ldrs: lost pl over 3f out: hdwy 1/2-way: rdn to chse wnr over 1f out: styd on same pce fnl f* **7/2**[2]
05 **3** *nk* **Leaderofthepack**[27] 4996 2-8-13 0 AdamMcNamara(3) 6 60
(Bryan Smart) *outpcd: r.o ins fnl f: nvr nrr* **20/1**
02 **4** 2 **Zapateado**[5] 5779 2-8-11 0 ShaneKelly 3 48
(Richard Hughes) *plld hrd and prom: rdn over 1f out: hung lft and styd on same pce* **10/1**[3]
5012 **5** 3 ½ **Dreamboat Annie**[27] 4991 2-9-4 69 SteveDrowne 5 43
(Mark Usher) *prom: ct wd and edgd rt 1/2-way: sn wknd* **12/1**
63 **6** 2 ¾ **Mocead Cappall**[94] 2583 2-8-11 0 (h[1]) RoystonFfrench 2 26
(John Holt) *w wnr tl settled into 2nd over 3f out: rdn and lost pl over 1f out: wknd fnl f* **25/1**
1m 1.25s (-0.65) **Going Correction** -0.175s/f (Stan) 6 Ran SP% **109.5**
Speed ratings (Par 92): **98,92,91,88,82 78**
CSF £2.79 TOTE £1.40: £1.10, £1.70; EX 3.40 Trifecta £15.70.
**Owner** A Chapman **Bred** Max Weston **Trained** Radlett, Herts

**FOCUS**
A moderate novice and another winner from the front. The time was 2.39s faster than the previous juvenile race.The winner just replicated her pre-race form.

## 6013 FCL GLOBAL FORWARDING FILLIES' H'CAP 1m 4f 51y (Tp)

**6:50** (6:50) (Class 5) (0-75,77) 3-Y-O+ £3,234 (£962; £481; £240) **Stalls** Low

Form RPR
5225 **1** **Tomorrow Mystery**[18] 5331 3-9-2 72 DougieCostello 5 85
(Jamie Osborne) *mde all: pushed clr over 2f out: rdn over 1f out: eased wl ins fnl f* **11/1**
1123 **2** 6 **La Vie En Rose**[55] 3933 3-9-4 74 FrannyNorton 4 77
(Mark Johnston) *pushed along in rr early: swtchd rt and hdwy over 2f out: rdn to go 2nd over 1f out: no ch w wnr* **5/1**[2]
215 **3** 2 ½ **Stepney**[34] 4730 3-9-0 70 DavidProbert 6 69
(Robyn Brisland) *hld up: hdwy on outer and hung rt over 2f out: styd on u.p to go 3rd wl ins fnl f* **8/1**
3323 **4** *nk* **African Beat (IRE)**[28] 4966 3-9-4 74 ShaneKelly 7 73
(Richard Hughes) *hdwy to go prom 10f out: chsd wnr over 2f out: sn rdn: lost 2nd over 1f out: wknd ins fnl f* **7/2**[1]
2343 **5** 4 ½ **Monaco Rose**[16] 5403 4-9-11 74 (h) AdamMcNamara(3) 3 64
(Richard Fahey) *chsd ldrs: pushed along over 9f out: lost pl over 6f out: nt clr run over 2f out: hung lft over 1f out: n.d after* **6/1**[3]
414 **6** 7 **Sure To Explore (IRE)**[19] 5273 3-9-2 77 DavidEgan(5) 1 57
(William Muir) *hld up: hdwy over 6f out: sn pushed along: wknd over 2f out* **5/1**[2]
-226 **7** 3 **Plage Depampelonne**[56] 3909 3-8-10 66 TedDurcan 2 46
(James Bethell) *chsd wnr 1f: remained handy: rdn to go 2nd again over 3f out tl over 2f out: sn wknd: eased over 1f out* **13/2**
6224 **8** 3 ¼ **Inke (IRE)**[18] 5330 5-10-0 77 CharlieBennett(3) 8 46
(Jim Boyle) *chsd wnr after 1f tl rdn over 3f out: wknd over 2f out* **10/1**
2m 35.72s (-5.08) **Going Correction** -0.175s/f (Stan)
**WFA** 3 from 4yo+ 10lb 8 Ran SP% **111.7**
Speed ratings (Par 100): **109,105,103,103,100 95,93,91**
CSF £61.84 CT £461.05 TOTE £12.10: £2.90, £1.60, £2.40; EX 82.80 Trifecta £606.60.
**Owner** Mehmet Kurt **Bred** Mehmet Kurt **Trained** Upper Lambourn, Berks
■ Stewards' Enquiry : Franny Norton caution: careless riding

**FOCUS**
A surprise winner, and a fourth consecutive winning front-runner on the card. The time was decent and the form was taken at something like face value.

## 6014 FCL GLOBAL FORWARDING - MAKING LOGISTICS PERSONAL H'CAP 1m 142y (Tp)

**7:20** (7:22) (Class 4) (0-85,85) 3-Y-O+ £5,175 (£1,540; £769; £384) **Stalls** Low

Form RPR
-165 **1** **Pensax Boy**[9] 5634 5-9-12 83 SteveDrowne 10 92
(Daniel Mark Loughnane) *hld up: hdwy over 3f out: rdn and r.o wl to ld nr fin* **14/1**
0000 **2** ¾ **Ibazz**[35] 4699 4-8-5 69 ManuelFernandes(7) 3 76
(Ian Williams) *chsd ldrs: pushed along over 2f out: rdn and ev ch wl ins fnl f: r.o* **15/2**[3]
1114 **3** ½ **Commodity (IRE)**[65] 3589 4-9-12 83 RyanMoore 4 89
(Sir Michael Stoute) *racd keenly: ld after 1f: hdd over 3f out: remained handy: rdn and ev ch wl ins fnl f: styd on* **2/1**[2]
-212 **4** *nse* **Big Tour (IRE)**[18] 5323 3-9-1 85 DavidEgan(5) 6 91+
(Saeed bin Suroor) *plld hrd and prom: hung rt almost thrght: wnt 2nd over 6f out: led over 3f out: rdn ins fnl f: hdd nr fin* **5/4**[1]
0503 **5** 5 **Gabrial's Kaka (IRE)**[8] 5683 7-9-6 80 (b) AdamMcNamara(3) 11 74
(Richard Fahey) *s.i.s: hld up: pushed along over 2f out: styd on ins fnl f: nvr nrr* **11/1**
10-0 **6** 1 **Arlecchino's Leap**[111] 2054 5-9-12 83 (p) LiamKeniry 7 75
(Mark Usher) *hld up: hdwy u.p over 1f out: nt trble ldrs* **50/1**
3203 **7** 1 **Caledonia Laird**[26] 5039 6-8-9 66 oh3 (b) TomMarquand 13 56
(Jo Hughes) *hld up: effrt on outer over 2f out: nvr on terms* **40/1**
043 **8** ½ **Captain Revelation**[39] 4529 5-9-11 82 RichardKingscote 1 70
(Tom Dascombe) *led 1f: chsd ldrs: rdn over 2f out: wknd fnl f* **28/1**
003 **9** 2 **Wind In My Sails**[60] 3750 5-9-13 84 (h) DougieCostello 9 68
(Ed de Giles) *s.i.s: hld up: pushed along over 2f out: a in rr* **18/1**
4206 **10** 2 **Lord Commander**[72] 3336 3-8-10 75 TonyHamilton 8 54
(Richard Fahey) *prom: rdn over 2f out: wknd over 1f out* **33/1**
0100 **11** *nk* **Idol Deputy (FR)**[14] 5484 11-8-10 72 (p) RachealKneller(5) 2 51
(James Bennett) *prom tl pushed along and wknd over 2f out* **66/1**
0000 **12** 3 ½ **Pivotman**[58] 3845 9-8-11 75 (bt) HarrisonShaw(7) 12 46
(Michael Easterby) *hld up: pushed along over 2f out: a in rr* **50/1**
1m 47.46s (-2.64) **Going Correction** -0.175s/f (Stan)
**WFA** 3 from 4yo+ 8lb 12 Ran SP% **124.0**
Speed ratings (Par 105): **104,103,102,102,98 97,96,96,94,92 92,89**
CSF £114.57 CT £312.50 TOTE £16.00: £3.40, £3.70, £1.10; EX 348.40 Trifecta £1238.00.
**Owner** S & A Mares **Bred** C A Cyzer **Trained** Rock, Worcs

**FOCUS**
A fair handicap, but they didn't go much of a gallop. The first four came well clear in a race with no real depth.

## 6015 FCL GLOBAL FORWARDING - MAKING LOGISTICS PERSONAL FILLIES' H'CAP 7f 36y (Tp)

**7:50** (7:50) (Class 5) (0-75,76) 3-Y-O+ £3,881 (£1,155; £577; £288) **Stalls** High

Form RPR
0213 **1** **Flourishing**[22] 5185 3-9-6 75 OisinMurphy 9 84
(Sir Michael Stoute) *chsd ldrs: pushed along over 2f out: chsd ldr and edgd lft over 1f out: rdn to ld ins fnl f: styd on* **5/2**[2]
1261 **2** ½ **Dusky Maid (IRE)**[4] 5845 3-9-5 74 6ex FrannyNorton 2 82
(James Given) *hld up: swtchd rt and hdwy over 1f out: rdn and r.o wl ins fnl f* **2/1**[1]
5000 **3** 1 ¾ **Jumping Around (IRE)**[33] 4741 3-8-5 67 ManuelFernandes(7) 4 70
(Ian Williams) *chsd ldrs: nt clr run over 2f out: nt clr run and swtchd lft over 1f out: styd on* **10/1**
2011 **4** 1 ¼ **Clear As A Bell (IRE)**[22] 5182 3-8-9 64 DavidAllan 10 64
(Tim Easterby) *led: rdn over 1f out: hdd and no ex ins fnl f* **11/1**
3320 **5** 2 ½ **Alouja (IRE)**[30] 4903 3-9-7 76 JosephineGordon 1 69
(Hugo Palmer) *hld up: rdn over 2f out: hdwy over 1f out: styd on same pce ins fnl f* **10/1**
3-54 **6** 1 **Many A Tale**[20] 5248 3-9-2 71 TomMarquand 8 62
(Ismail Mohammed) *prom: lost pl over 5f out: rdn over 1f out: hung lft and no imp ins fnl f* **15/2**[3]
6-35 **7** 2 ¼ **Welsh Rose**[52] 4043 4-9-4 67 LiamKeniry 3 53
(Ed de Giles) *hld up: plld hrd: nt clr run over 1f out: nvr on terms* **28/1**
006 **8** *shd* **Langham**[14] 5482 4-8-11 60 AlistairRawlinson 5 46
(Michael Appleby) *chsd ldr: rdn over 2f out: lost 2nd over 1f out: wknd ins fnl f* **33/1**
0323 **9** 2 **Loveatfirstsight**[14] 5482 4-8-8 57 RoystonFfrench 7 38
(Michael Attwater) *s.i.s: hld up: effrt on outer over 2f out: sn lost pl* **14/1**
60 **10** 1 ¾ **Little Miss Kodi (IRE)**[30] 4887 4-9-5 75 TobyEley(7) 6 51
(Daniel Mark Loughnane) *s.i.s: hdwy over 5f out: rdn: hung rt and wknd over 1f out* **25/1**
1m 27.2s (-1.60) **Going Correction** -0.175s/f (Stan)
**WFA** 3 from 4yo 6lb 10 Ran SP% **117.1**
Speed ratings (Par 100): **102,101,99,98,95 94,91,91,89,87**
CSF £7.75 CT £41.84 TOTE £3.70: £1.80, £1.10, £2.90; EX 9.60 Trifecta £105.00.
**Owner** Qatar Racing Limited **Bred** Aston House Stud **Trained** Newmarket, Suffolk

**FOCUS**
An interesting handicap in which they went a fair pace and the form looks solid with a progressive pair coming to the fore. The winner looked on a good mark and improved on her maiden win.

## 6016 FCL GLOBAL FORWARDING APPRENTICE H'CAP 7f 36y (Tp)

**8:20** (8:21) (Class 6) (0-65,69) 3-Y-O £2,587 (£770; £384; £192) **Stalls** High

Form RPR
0311 **1** **Anna Medici**[13] 5511 3-9-2 59 ManuelFernandes(5) 11 64+
(Sir Mark Prescott Bt) *s.i.s: hdwy over 4f out: rdn to ld and edgd lft wl ins fnl f: jst hld on* **7/2**[2]
0-05 **2** *shd* **Outfox**[26] 5019 3-9-8 60 AdamMcNamara 2 66
(Bryan Smart) *prom: lost pl over 3f out: hdwy and nt clr run fr over 1f out tl wl ins fnl f: fin wl* **22/1**
-601 **3** 1 **La Isla Bonita**[4] 5848 3-9-4 59 6ex JennyPowell(3) 3 63
(Richard Spencer) *chsd ldr tl rdn over 2f out: nt clr run over 1f out: swtchd rt: nt clr run ins fnl f: r.o* **11/4**[1]
0320 **4** *hd* **Joys Delight**[14] 5485 3-9-3 62 TobyEley(7) 9 64
(Daniel Mark Loughnane) *s.i.s: hld up: hdwy on outer over 2f out: rdn over 1f out: r.o* **25/1**
6061 **5** *nse* **Stubytuesday**[6] 5741 3-9-12 69 6ex HarrisonShaw(5) 7 72
(Michael Easterby) *prom: pushed along 1/2-way: nt clr run fr over 1f out: r.o* **13/2**
1103 **6** ½ **A Sure Welcome**[44] 4350 3-9-11 63 (p) CallumShepherd 6 63
(John Spearing) *trckd ldrs: plld hrd: led on bit over 2f out: hrd rdn fr over 1f out: hdd and no ex wl ins fnl f* **4/1**[3]
6604 **7** 1 ½ **Lovely Acclamation (IRE)**[12] 5536 3-9-11 63 HectorCrouch 8 60
(Ismail Mohammed) *led: rdn and hdd over 2f out: no ex wl ins fnl f* **14/1**
0504 **8** *nk* **Captain Hawk**[18] 5326 3-9-5 64 (p) LukeCatton(7) 5 60
(Ian Williams) *hld up: hdwy 1/2-way: rdn: nt clr run and hung lft over 1f out: nt trble ldrs* **18/1**
56 **9** 1 ¼ **My Girl Maisie (IRE)**[18] 5339 3-8-12 55 KevinLundie(5) 1 48
(Richard Guest) *hld up: nt clr run over 1f out: nvr on terms* **7/1**
2530 **10** 2 ½ **Circulate**[27] 5007 3-9-4 61 (b[1]) MillyNaseb(5) 4 48
(Tom Clover) *hld up: nvr on terms* **33/1**
1m 28.61s (-0.19) **Going Correction** -0.175s/f (Stan) 10 Ran SP% **117.8**
Speed ratings (Par 98): **94,93,92,92,92 91,90,89,88,85**
CSF £80.69 CT £249.22 TOTE £3.60: £2.00, £5.80, £1.60; EX 86.90 Trifecta £523.40.
**Owner** Neil Greig **Bred** W N Greig **Trained** Newmarket, Suffolk
■ Stewards' Enquiry : Jenny Powell caution: careless riding

**FOCUS**
A moderate handicap in which they finished in a heap, and there were a few hard-luck stories. The placed horses help pin the level.
T/Plt: £44.50 to a £1 stake. Pool: £60,217.10 - 985.97 winning units T/Qpdt: £12.70 to a £1 stake. Pool: £6,712.65 - 389.49 winning units **Colin Roberts**

## 5907 CLAIREFONTAINE (R-H)
Monday, August 14

**OFFICIAL GOING: Turf: good**

### 6017a PRIX LE BOUGNAT DEAUVILLE / DIVES-SUR-MER (PRIX MATAHAWK) (CONDITIONS) (2YO) (TURF) 7f
11:40 2-Y-O £11,111 (£4,444; £3,333; £2,222; £1,111)

RPR
1 **African Sky**[43] 2-8-10 0 ........ Pierre-CharlesBoudot 3 78+
(A Fabre, France) **2/5**[1]
2 1 **Uther Pendragon (IRE)**[5] 5816 2-9-0 0 ........(p) TonyPiccone 2 79
(J S Moore) *wnt a little lft s: racd keenly: hld up wl in tch on outer: drvn to ld wl over 1f out: hdd ins fnl f: kpt on to hold 2nd* **27/10**[2]
3 hd **Bombetta (FR)**[10] 5629 2-8-4 0 ........(p) KyllanBarbaud(6) 5 75
(N Caullery, France) **117/10**
4 7 **Autumn Lodge**[10] 5627 2-8-10 0 ........ AntoineHamelin 4 56
(J S Moore) *led: drvn ins fnl 2f: hdd wl over 1f out: wknd fnl f* **83/10**[3]
5 5 **Dancing Master (FR)**[40] 4678 2-8-10 0 ........(p) FabriceVeron 1 42
(E J O'Neill, France) **23/1**

1m 24.8s 5 Ran SP% **121.2**
PARI-MUTUEL (all including 1 euro stake): WIN 1.40; PLACE 1.10, 1.10; SF 2.20.
**Owner** Ballymore Thoroughbred Ltd **Bred** Dayton Investments Ltd **Trained** Chantilly, France

### 6018a PRIX VILLE DE SAINT-GATIEN-DES-BOIS (PRIX DES IRIS) (CLAIMER) (4YO+) (TURF) 1m 3f
1:50 4-Y-O+ £6,837 (£2,735; £2,051; £1,367; £683)

RPR
1 **East India**[32] 4802 5-8-7 0 ........ MlleCoraliePacaut(4) 2 53
(George Baker) *a cl up: 4th and pushed along more than 2f out: styd on ins fnl f: led 75yds fr home: drvn out* **31/10**[1]
2 1 1/4 **Warrigal (IRE)**[210] 7-8-11 0 ........ FrankPanicucci 11 51
(Leo Braem, Belgium) **103/10**[3]
3 snk **Zappeuse (FR)**[13] 4-9-2 0 ........ ThierryThulliez 3 55
(Y Barberot, France) **31/10**[1]
4 1 1/4 **Mavilla**[75] 4-9-1 0 ........ ThomasHuet 4 52
(E Lyon, France) **111/10**
5 hd **Mer Et Jardin**[21] 5229 5-8-11 0 ........ MlleLauraGrosso(5) 12 53
(M Le Forestier, France) **4/1**[2]
6 1 3/4 **Lustre (FR)**[73] 9-8-7 0 ........(p) MlleAlisonMassin(4) 5 44
(H De Nicolay, France) **135/10**
7 1 **All Dynamite (FR)**[82] 8-8-7 0 ........(b) MlleMickaelleMichel(4) 7 43
(Leo Braem, Belgium) **69/1**
8 snk **Miracle Ninetynine (IRE)**[209] 277 5-9-5 0 ........ WilliamsSaraiva 1 50
(Joeri Goossens, Belgium) **109/10**
9 5 **Paulaim (FR)**[77] 4-8-10 0 ........(p) MlleLauraPoggionovo(5) 9 37
(E Lellouche, France) **226/10**
10 nse **Al Udeid (IRE)**[670] 7-8-10 0 ........ MlleCharleneMannier(5) 6 37
(R Le Gal, France) **27/1**
11 1 1/4 **Zimri (FR)**[31] 13-8-11 0 ........ NicolasLarenaudie 10 31
(Mme M Bollack-Badel, France) **142/10**
12 9 **Kafeine La Grange (FR)** 5-8-8 0 ........ AlexisAchard 8 12
(Caroline Auvray, France) **77/1**

2m 23.8s 12 Ran SP% **118.3**
PARI-MUTUEL (all including 1 euro stake): WIN 4.10; PLACE 1.70, 2.50, 1.80; DF 21.30; SF 32.20.
**Owner** M A Sherwood **Bred** Grundy Bloodstock Srl **Trained** Manton, Wilts

6019 & 6020a VOID

## 5742 CHELMSFORD (A.W) (L-H)
Tuesday, August 15

**OFFICIAL GOING: Polytrack: standard**
Wind: virtually nil Weather: sunny and bright

### 6021 BVS VETS NURSERY H'CAP 5f (P)
5:40 (5:40) (Class 5) (0-75,77) 2-Y-O £4,528 (£1,347; £673; £168; £168) Stalls Low

Form RPR
5116 1 **Milton Road**[13] 5546 2-9-2 72 ........ CallumShepherd(3) 9 75
(Mick Channon) *off the pce in last trio: effrt on inner over 1f out: hdwy u.p 1f out: swtchd rt ins fnl f: styd on wl to ld towards fin* **16/1**
5342 2 1/2 **Gold Filigree (IRE)**[13] 5546 2-9-5 72 ........ PatDobbs 6 73
(Richard Hughes) *chsd ldng pair: effrt over 1f out: ev ch fnl f: kpt on u.p* **5/1**[3]
2043 3 nk **Big Time Maybe (IRE)**[17] 5398 2-9-7 74 ........(v1) RichardKingscote 4 74
(Tom Dascombe) *led: rdn over 1f out: drvn 1f out: hdd and no ex wl ins fnl f: lost 2nd last strides* **10/1**
2315 4 1/2 **Jive Lady (IRE)**[17] 5440 2-9-10 77 ........ FrannyNorton 3 75
(Mark Johnston) *chsd ldr: ev ch and rdn over 1f out: edgd rt 1f out: styd on same pce fnl 100yds* **9/2**[2]
3620 4 dht **Kodiac Express (IRE)**[25] 5107 2-9-2 69 ........ AntonioFresu 1 68
(Mike Murphy) *in tch in midfield: effrt over 1f out: keeping on whn squeezed for room ins fnl f: kpt on same pce fnl 100yds* **5/1**[3]
2302 6 1 3/4 **Zalshah**[10] 5654 2-9-6 76 ........ HollieDoyle(3) 7 68
(Richard Hannon) *in rr: effrt and hdwy on outer 2f out: no imp u.p 1f out: sn edgd lft and no imp ins fnl f* **10/3**[1]
050 7 1/2 **Wiff Waff**[33] 4792 2-8-9 65 ........ AaronJones(3) 2 55
(Stuart Williams) *dwlt: hld up in tch in midfield: effrt over 1f out: unable qck and kpt on same pce ins fnl f* **5/1**[3]
0003 8 3 **Ivy Leaguer**[28] 4991 2-9-3 70 ........ JamesDoyle 8 49
(Brian Meehan) *a towards rr: clsd and nt clr run over 1f out: sn rdn and no imp: bhd ins fnl f* **8/1**

59.36s (-0.84) **Going Correction** -0.125s/f (Stan) 8 Ran SP% **117.3**
Speed ratings (Par 94): **101,100,99,98,98 96,95,90**
CSF £95.91 CT £863.03 TOTE £11.30: £4.10, £1.60, £3.10; EX 77.60 Trifecta £601.70.
**Owner** M Channon **Bred** M P Bishop **Trained** West Ilsley, Berks
■ Stewards' Enquiry : Pat Dobbs two-day ban: used whip above permitted level (Aug 29-30)
Callum Shepherd three-day ban: careless riding (Aug 29-31)

**FOCUS**
They went a strong pace in this nursery and the winner swooped late to snatch the prize. He's rated back to his pre-race high.

### 6022 PRB ESTATES LTD NURSERY H'CAP 1m (P)
6:10 (6:12) (Class 6) (0-60,62) 2-Y-O £3,234 (£962; £481; £240) Stalls Low

Form RPR
0044 1 **Four Fifty Three**[14] 5507 2-9-2 55 ........ JoeyHaynes 4 57
(Mark H Tompkins) *hld up in rr of main gp: pushed along and nt clrest of runs over 2f out: swtchd rt and hdwy over 1f out: clsng and edgd lft 1f out: styd on wl to ld towards fin* **10/1**
064 2 1/2 **Bombshell Bay**[12] 5557 2-9-9 62 ........ SeanLevey 6 63
(Richard Hannon) *sn led: rdn ent fnl 2f: drvn over 1f out: pricking ears but kpt on press: hdd and no ex towards fin* **7/2**[1]
0043 3 1 1/4 **Sixties Secret**[7] 5756 2-8-9 51 ........ CallumShepherd(3) 2 49
(Mick Channon) *chsd ldrs: rdn and lft chsng ldr again 2f out: kpt on u.p and ev ch 1f out: no ex and one pce fnl 100yds* **9/2**[3]
500 4 1 **Le Gros Serpant (IRE)**[10] 5665 2-8-10 54 ........ RowanScott(5) 1 50
(Keith Dalgleish) *in tch in midfield: reminder over 4f out: hdwy u.p on inner over 1f out: chsd ldrs ins fnl f: keeping on whn nt clr run towards fin* **7/1**
600 5 2 1/4 **Headline Act**[20] 5292 2-8-9 51 ........(p1) EdwardGreatrex(3) 9 42
(Archie Watson) *bustled along leaving stalls: chsd ldr for 2f: 4th and drvn 3f out: unable qck over 1f out: wl hld and kpt on same pce ins fnl f* **5/1**
0055 6 3 1/2 **Heavenly Pulse (IRE)**[11] 5613 2-8-7 46 ........ FrannyNorton 10 28
(Ann Duffield) *t.k.h: hld up in tch in midfield: effrt whn bmpd over 1f out: no imp and wknd ins fnl f* **28/1**
006 7 2 **Daffrah**[35] 4709 2-9-7 60 ........ MartinHarley 8 38
(James Tate) *dwlt: rcvrd to join ldrs after 2f: wnt 2nd 5f out: rdn and hung rt bnd 2f out: unable qck u.p over 1f out: wknd ins fnl f* **4/1**[2]
0660 8 10 **Bad Dog**[4] 5878 2-9-7 60 ........ JimCrowley 3 15
(Michael Easterby) *chsd ldr early: sn stdd bk into midfield: reminder 4f out: sn rdn: lost pl and wl btn over 1f out: bhd and eased ins fnl f* **8/1**
0064 9 2 **Miss Mazzie**[20] 5277 2-8-8 47 ........ CamHardie 5
(Michael Easterby) *s.i.s: nvr gng wl in rr and sn rdn along: lost tch over 1f out: wl bhd and eased ins fnl f* **16/1**

1m 41.31s (1.41) **Going Correction** -0.125s/f (Stan) 9 Ran SP% **119.1**
Speed ratings (Par 92): **87,86,85,84,82 78,76,66,64**
CSF £46.48 CT £186.19 TOTE £10.10: £2.60, £2.00, £1.50; EX 40.60 Trifecta £187.30.
**Owner** Sarabex **Bred** R E Crutchley **Trained** Newmarket, Suffolk
■ Stewards' Enquiry : Joey Haynes caution: careless riding

**FOCUS**
A modest nursery but the winner produced a powerful finishing burst to beat two of the market leaders.

### 6023 ROSSDALES VETERINARY SURGEONS H'CAP 2m (P)
6:40 (6:44) (Class 5) (0-70,70) 3-Y-O £5,175 (£1,540; £769; £384) Stalls Low

Form RPR
0-00 1 **Noble Behest**[80] 3087 3-8-6 58 ........(p1) GeorgeWood(3) 1 69
(Marcus Tregoning) *chsd ldrs: rdn over 3f out: clsd to squeeze between rivals and chal 2f out: wnt clr w ldr and sustained duel fr over 1f out: led wl ins fnl f: forged ahd towards fin* **7/1**[3]
4335 2 1/2 **Oxford Blu**[12] 5581 3-8-10 62 ........(p) RosieJessop(3) 4 72
(Sir Mark Prescott Bt) *chsd ldr:nt clr run over 2f out: effrt and swtchd rt ent fnl 2f: led and wnt clr w wnr fr over 1f out: sustained duel u.p after: hdd and no ex wl ins fnl f* **11/4**[1]
3246 3 9 **Chaparrachik (IRE)**[20] 5298 3-9-7 70 ........(h1) JimCrowley 2 69
(Amanda Perrett) *in tch in midfield: effrt to press ldrs 2f out: outpcd u.p and btn over 1f out: plugged on into modest 3rd ins fnl f* **11/4**[1]
4000 4 1 3/4 **Inspector (IRE)**[22] 5209 3-9-2 65 ........(vt1) JamesDoyle 7 62
(Hugo Palmer) *led: increased pce 4f out: rdn and hdd over 1f out: sn btn: wknd fnl f* **12/1**
3002 5 8 **Bizet (IRE)**[6] 5787 3-7-13 51 oh2 ........ HollieDoyle(3) 6 39
(John Ryan) *s.i.s: in tch in rr: rdn 4f out: sn struggling: no ch w ldrs fnl 2f* **7/1**[3]
2553 6 20 **Gee Sixty Six**[27] 5034 3-9-2 65 ........ JoeyHaynes 5 29
(Mark H Tompkins) *t.k.h: hld up in tch in last trio: rdn 4f out: sn struggling and lost tch w ldrs over 2f out: wl bhd and eased ins fnl f: t.o* **9/2**[2]
0050 7 49 **Justice Frederick (IRE)**[19] 5336 3-8-5 57 ........(t) EdwardGreatrex(3) 3
(Paul D'Arcy) *in tch in last trio: niggled along 1/2-way: rdn 4f out: sn bhd: lost tch over 2f out: t.o* **9/1**

3m 31.25s (1.25) **Going Correction** -0.125s/f (Stan) 7 Ran SP% **114.2**
Speed ratings (Par 100): **91,90,86,85,81 71,46**
CSF £26.50 TOTE £8.60: £4.40, £2.20; EX 31.30 Trifecta £173.30.
**Owner** The FOPS **Bred** Mr & Mrs A E Pakenham **Trained** Whitsbury, Hants
■ Stewards' Enquiry : George Wood regarding the apparent improvement in form, trainer said gelding was wearing cheek pieces for the first time and appreciated the step up in trip from 1 mile 4 furlongs to 2 miles

**FOCUS**
The first two pulled a long way clear in this steadily run staying handicap. Not the most convincing/progressive field.

### 6024 MOULSHAM MILE H'CAP 1m (P)
7:10 (7:14) (Class 2) (0-105,105) £32,346 (£9,625; £4,810; £1,202; £1,202) Stalls Low

Form RPR
24-0 1 **Mustashry**[11] 5594 4-9-10 105 ........ JimCrowley 11 113+
(Sir Michael Stoute) *hld up in last pair: swtchd rt and stl plenty to do over 1f out: hdwy on outer jst over 1f out: str run ins fnl f to ld towards fin* **5/1**[2]
2556 2 1/2 **Masham Star (IRE)**[11] 5594 3-8-10 98 ........ FrannyNorton 3 104
(Mark Johnston) *chsd ldr tl led over 1f out: edgd lft u.p jst ins fnl f: kpt on u.p tl hdd and no ex towards fin* **5/1**[2]
5 3 1 3/4 **Manson**[38] 4636 4-8-13 94 ........(p1) PaulMulrennan 12 97
(Dominic Ffrench Davis) *hld up in tch in midfield: effrt over 1f out: hdwy 1f out: styd on to go 3rd wl ins fnl f: nvr getting on terms w ldng pair* **14/1**
4400 4 1 **Pactolus (IRE)**[7] 5744 6-8-11 95 ........(tp) AaronJones(3) 5 96
(Stuart Williams) *in tch in midfield: effrt over 1f out: kpt on u.p ins fnl f: no threat to ldrs* **20/1**
0040 4 dht **Sutter County**[31] 4905 3-9-3 105 ........ JamesDoyle 4 105
(Mark Johnston) *t.k.h: hld up in tch in midfield: carried lft after 1f: rdn and unable qck whn n.m.r over 1f out: rallied ins fnl f: kpt on wl fnl 100yds: nvr getting on terms w ldrs* **14/1**
0401 6 hd **Swift Approval (IRE)**[10] 5662 5-9-0 95 ........(t) AndreaAtzeni 1 95
(Stuart Williams) *led: rdn and hdd over 1f out: drvn and swtchd rt jst ins fnl f: no ex and lost 2nd 100yds out: wknd towards fin* **10/1**



The Form Book Flat, Raceform Ltd, Newbury, RG14 5SJ

5003 **7** *nk* **Muntazah**[38] 4636 4-9-8 **103** DaneO'Neill 9 103
(Owen Burrows) *dwlt: hld up in tch towards rr: effrt and swtchd rt 2f out: hdwy 1f out: styd on ins fnl f: nvr trbld ldrs* **6/1**[3]

0400 **8** *shd* **Mr Scaramanga**[45] 4334 3-9-2 **104** HarryBentley 8 102
(Simon Dow) *chsd ldrs: rdn over 1f out: drvn and unable qck 1f out: kpt on same pce ins fnl f* **20/1**

1454 **9** *1 ¼* **Leshlaa (USA)**[32] 4856 3-8-12 **103** EdwardGreatrex(3) 15 98+
(Saeed bin Suroor) *dwlt: hld up in rr: effrt and hdwy over 1f out: clsng whn nt clr run 1f out: squeezed for room and hmpd jst ins fnl f: unable to make any imp after* **9/2**[1]

-010 **10** *nk* **Murad Khan (FR)**[14] 5500 4-9-8 **103** JosephineGordon 2 99
(Hugo Palmer) *in tch in midfield: effrt on inner over 1f out: unable qck and swtchd rt jst ins fnl f: no imp after* **5/1**[2]

0240 **11** *½* **Supersta**[17] 5396 6-9-4 **102** (p) GeorgeWood(3) 6 97
(Michael Appleby) *dwlt: hld up in tch towards rr: effrt on inner and sme hdwy 1f out: nt clrest of runs and no imp ins fnl f: nvr trbld ldrs* **33/1**

4310 **12** *4* **War Department (IRE)**[25] 5094 4-8-12 **93** (v) ConnorBeasley 10 78
(Keith Dalgleish) *in tch in midfield: rdn and unable qck over 1f out: sn lost pl: wknd fnl f* **20/1**

0-05 **13** *5* **Battle Of Marathon (USA)**[16] 5456 5-9-8 **103** MartinHarley 7 77
(John Ryan) *hld up in tch towards rr: effrt on outer over 2f out: struggling whn wandered rt over 1f out: sn btn and bhd ins fnl f* **50/1**

1m 36.8s (-3.10) **Going Correction** -0.125s/f (Stan)
**WFA** 3 from 4yo+ 7lb **13** Ran SP% **124.1**
Speed ratings (Par 109): **110,109,107,106,106 106,106,106,104,104 104,100,95**
CSF £29.23 CT £349.98 TOTE £5.70: £2.40, £2.40, £5.10; EX 35.70 Trifecta £322.70.
**Owner** Hamdan Al Maktoum **Bred** Shadwell Estate Company Limited **Trained** Newmarket, Suffolk

**FOCUS**
The pace was not strong in this valuable handicap and the winner did really well to snatch the prize out wide from a long way back. Smart form from the winner, with the form rated around the runner-up.

## 6025 ESSEX SPRINT H'CAP 5f (P)
**7:40** (7:44) (Class 2) (0-105,105) 3-Y-O+ **£32,345** (£9,625; £4,810; £2,405) **Stalls** Low

Form RPR

2010 **1** **Doctor Sardonicus**[31] 4881 6-9-4 **99** MartinHarley 9 110
(David Simcock) *chsd ldr tl rdn to chal over 1f out: led ins fnl f: r.o wl and drew away fnl 75yds: comf* **12/1**

0001 **2** *1 ¾* **El Astronaute (IRE)**[14] 5505 4-9-0 **95** JasonHart 3 100
(John Quinn) *led: rdn and hrd pressed over 1f out: kpt on u.p: hdd ins fnl f: no ex and outpcd wl ins fnl f* **8/1**

0261 **3** *¾* **Mazzini**[21] 5241 4-9-2 **100** (p) GeorgeWood(3) 7 102+
(James Fanshawe) *midfield: rdn 1/2-way: no imp tl styd on ins fnl f: wnt 3rd cl home: nvr enough pce to threaten ldng pair* **5/2**[1]

3600 **4** *hd* **Verne Castle**[18] 5354 4-9-4 **99** (h) DavidProbert 12 101
(Andrew Balding) *chsd ldrs: rdn and edgd rt over 1f out: styd on same pce ins fnl f* **33/1**

0020 **5** *½* **Royal Birth**[31] 4881 6-9-6 **104** (t) AaronJones(3) 2 104+
(Stuart Williams) *bmpd leaving stalls: hld up in midfield: effrt on inner over 1f out: rdn 1f out: styd on ins fnl f: no threat to wnr* **6/1**[3]

0502 **6** *nk* **Sign Of The Kodiac (IRE)**[21] 5241 4-8-13 **94** PaulMulrennan 4 93
(James Given) *chsd ldrs: rdn over 1f out: unable qck over 1f out: kpt on same pce ins fnl f* **12/1**

0103 **7** *½* **Encore D'Or**[17] 5450 5-9-10 **105** RyanMoore 10 102+
(Robert Cowell) *hld up in last trio and stuck wd: effrt over 1f out: hdwy ins fnl f: styd on towards fin: nvr trbld ldrs* **6/1**[3]

1050 **8** *2 ½* **Equimou**[32] 4864 3-9-0 **98** AndreaAtzeni 8 85
(Robert Eddery) *hld up in last trio: effrt over 1f out: kpt on ins fnl f: nvr trbld ldrs* **25/1**

0600 **9** *¾* **Boom The Groom (IRE)**[14] 5505 6-9-5 **100** RobertWinston 11 85
(Tony Carroll) *taken down early: hld up in last pair: effrt over 1f out: no imp: nvr trbld ldrs* **20/1**

0 **10** *nk* **Yalta (IRE)**[53] 4030 3-9-4 **102** JamesDoyle 1 85
(Mark Johnston) *wnt rt s: in tch in midfield: hmpd wl over 3f out: rdn 2f out: no imp over 1f out: wknd ins fnl f* **9/2**[2]

2-00 **11** *2* **Gravity Flow (IRE)**[32] 4864 4-9-0 **95** PatCosgrave 6 72
(William Haggas) *hld up in tch in midfield: rdn 2f out: no imp over 1f out: nvr trbld ldrs* **12/1**

1266 **12** *2 ¼* **Zac Brown (IRE)**[17] 5426 6-8-12 **98** (t) JoshuaBryan(5) 5 67
(Charlie Wallis) *hld up in tch in midfield: rdn and unable qck over 1f out: sn lost pl and wknd ins fnl f* **33/1**

58.16s (-2.04) **Going Correction** -0.125s/f (Stan)
**WFA** 3 from 4yo+ 3lb **12** Ran SP% **124.0**
Speed ratings (Par 109): **111,108,107,106,105 105,104,100,99,98 95,92**
CSF £104.94 CT £327.82 TOTE £15.70: £4.10, £2.60, £1.60; EX 157.20 Trifecta £970.70.
**Owner** Charles Wentworth **Bred** D M James **Trained** Newmarket, Suffolk

**FOCUS**
Two prominent runners dominated this hot handicap and the hold-up performers couldn't get involved. A clear best from the winner.

## 6026 MONAGHAN CIVIL ENGINEERING LTD H'CAP 7f (P)
**8:10** (8:13) (Class 3) (0-90,92) 3-Y-O **£16,172** (£4,812; £2,405; £1,202) **Stalls** Low

Form RPR

014 **1** **Important Mission (USA)**[21] 5242 3-8-13 **81** RyanMoore 12 95+
(William Haggas) *stdd s: sn swtchd lft and hld up in rr on inner: hdwy into midfield 2f out: rdn and qcknd to ld jst over 1f out: sn drew clr: v readily* **7/1**

1015 **2** *3 ½* **Aventinus (IRE)**[10] 5642 3-9-6 **88** JackMitchell 1 93
(Hugo Palmer) *trckd ldrs: wnt 2nd wl over 1f out: rdn to ld over 1f out: sn hdd and nt match pce of wnr 1f out: kpt on same pce ins fnl f* **6/1**

5006 **3** *nk* **Via Serendipity**[39] 4563 3-9-4 **86** (t) DanielTudhope 4 90
(Stuart Williams) *broke wl: sn stdd and hld up in tch in midfield: swtchd rt and effrt wl over 1f out: kpt on u.p ins fnl f: no ch w wnr but pressing for 2nd nr fin* **5/1**[3]

15 **4** *½* **Moolazim**[46] 4299 3-9-4 **86** AndreaAtzeni 2 89
(Marco Botti) *hld up in tch in midfield: swtchd rt and effrt over 1f out: nt match pce of wnr 1f out: styd on same pce ins fnl f* **4/1**[2]

3221 **5** *½* **Open Wide (USA)**[28] 4992 3-9-5 **87** (b) JimCrowley 3 88
(Amanda Perrett) *t.k.h: hld up in tch towards rr: swtchd lft and hdwy u.p over 1f out: kpt on ins fnl f: no ch w wnr* **10/1**

11 **6** *nk* **Golden Goal (IRE)**[21] 5245 3-9-2 **84** MartinLane 5 84+
(Saeed bin Suroor) *hld up in midfield: effrt and rdn ent fnl 2f: nt clr run over 1f out: swtchd rt and u.p 1f out: styd on fnl 100yds: no ch w wnr* **9/4**[1]

6066 **7** *3 ¾* **Majeste**[10] 5661 3-9-4 **86** SeanLevey 8 76
(Richard Hannon) *stdd after s: hld up in tch in last trio: effrt over 1f out: no imp: nvr trbld ldrs* **25/1**

41-0 **8** *nk* **Mississippi Miss**[46] 4313 3-8-3 **74** GeorgeWood(3) 11 64
(Dr Jon Scargill) *hld up in tch towards rr: effrt wl over 1f out: no imp u.p: wl hld and kpt on same pce ins fnl f* **50/1**

0650 **9** *hd* **Aardwolf (USA)**[17] 5434 3-9-7 **89** JamesDoyle 9 78
(Mark Johnston) *chsd ldr tl ld 5f out: drvn and hdd over 1f out: sn outpcd and wknd ins fnl f* **33/1**

6045 **10** *shd* **Volatile**[27] 5032 3-9-10 **92** (p[1]) MartinHarley 6 81
(James Tate) *racd keenly: led for 2f: chsd ldr tl drifted rt bnd 2f out: sn lost pl: wknd fnl f* **20/1**

221 **11** *5* **Jalela**[89] 2753 3-9-4 **86** DaneO'Neill 7 61
(Richard Hannon) *hld up in midfield on outer: rdn and lost pl whn wd bnd 2f out: bhd and eased wl ins fnl f* **20/1**

6126 **12** *3 ¾* **Miss Sheridan (IRE)**[19] 5317 3-8-7 **75** CamHardie 10 40
(Michael Easterby) *chsd ldrs: rdn 3f out: lost pl over 1f out: bhd and eased wl ins fnl f* **66/1**

1m 24.47s (-2.73) **Going Correction** -0.125s/f (Stan) **12** Ran SP% **123.1**
Speed ratings (Par 104): **110,106,105,105,104 104,99,99,99,99 93,89**
CSF £46.65 CT £239.17 TOTE £5.90: £1.60, £2.20, £2.00; EX 61.20 Trifecta £347.50.
**Owner** Sheikh Juma Dalmook Al Maktoum **Bred** Brian Kahn & More Than Ready Syndicate **Trained** Newmarket, Suffolk

**FOCUS**
The winner powered clear from some way back in this good handicap. The form is taken at face value.

## 6027 BROOKE ACTION FOR WORKING EQUINES MAIDEN FILLIES' STKS 1m 2f (P)
**8:40** (8:41) (Class 5) 3-Y-O+ **£5,175** (£1,540; £769; £384) **Stalls** Low

Form RPR

0222 **1** **Superioritycomplex (IRE)**[8] 5721 3-9-0 79 RyanMoore 4 77+
(Sir Michael Stoute) *hld up in 3rd: effrt ent fnl 2f: styd on to chal and hung lft 1f out: led ins fnl f: styd on: bit slipped through mouth* **4/11**[1]

05 **2** *1 ½* **Line Of Beauty**[25] 5124 3-9-0 0 JimCrowley 1 74
(Simon Crisford) *led: rdn and fnd ex 2f out: drvn and hdd ins fnl f: kpt on same pce after* **5/1**[2]

30 **3** *2 ¼* **Sugardrop**[46] 4300 3-9-0 0 (t[1]) PatDobbs 2 70
(Amanda Perrett) *hld up in tch in 4th: swtchd rt and effrt to chse ldr wl over 1f out tl 3rd and no ex u.p 1f out: kpt on same ins fnl f* **5/1**[2]

34 **4** *12* **Relevant (IRE)**[67] 3542 3-9-0 0 DanielTudhope 3 46
(K R Burke) *t.k.h: chsd ldr: rdn over 2f out: lost pl and dropped to rr over 2f out: bhd and eased ins fnl f* **16/1**[3]

2m 7.54s (-1.06) **Going Correction** -0.125s/f (Stan) **4** Ran SP% **112.5**
Speed ratings (Par 100): **99,97,96,86**
CSF £2.90 TOTE £1.20; EX 3.00 Trifecta £6.50.
**Owner** Ballymacoll Stud **Bred** Ballymacoll Stud Farm Ltd **Trained** Newmarket, Suffolk

**FOCUS**
The hot favourite had to work to overhaul the leader but she landed the odds with some authority in the end. The form is rated around the second and third.
T/Jkpt: Not Won. T/Plt: £236.70 to a £1 stake. Pool: £81,126.44 - 250.18 winning units T/Qpdt: £37.00 to a £1 stake. Pool: £10,018.72 - 200.20 winning units **Steve Payne**

# 5561 FFOS LAS (L-H)
### Tuesday, August 15

**OFFICIAL GOING: Heavy (soft in places; 5.4)**
Wind: fresh breeze, mainly across Weather: sunny

## 6028 BET TOTEPLACEPOT AT BETFRED.COM FILLIES' H'CAP 6f
**2:15** (2:17) (Class 5) (0-70,71) 3-Y-O+ **£3,234** (£962; £481; £240) **Stalls** Centre

Form RPR

5205 **1** **Incentive**[17] 5429 3-8-13 **61** (p) LiamKeniry 3 67
(Stuart Kittow) *racd in centre: mde virtually all: drvn over 1f out: sn edgd rt: kpt on wl to assert fnl 100yds* **11/2**[3]

3252 **2** *2 ¼* **Fastnet Spin (IRE)**[18] 5358 3-9-9 **71** (bt) SteveDrowne 6 71
(David Evans) *racd keenly: hld up in centre: clsd 1/2-way: rdn 2f out: sn chsng wnr: trying to chal whn carried rt ins fnl f: nt qckn fnl 100yds* **2/1**[1]

0440 **3** *5* **Kingstreet Lady**[29] 4969 4-8-7 **51** KieranO'Neill 5 37
(Richard Price) *trckd wnr in centre: rdn and ev ch 2f out: sn lost 2nd and one pce: wknd fnl f* **6/1**

5060 **4** *1 ¼* **Diminutive (IRE)**[12] 5567 5-8-7 **51** oh6 (b) LukeMorris 7 34
(Grace Harris) *s.i.s: sn led one other on stands' side and cl up overall: drvn and lost pl 2f out: kpt on ins fnl f* **18/1**

133 **5** *1* **Zambezi Queen (IRE)**[32] 4843 3-9-0 **67** (p[1]) MeganNicholls(5) 8 46
(Paul Cole) *wnt to post early: trckd one other on stands' side: clsd 1/2-way: rdn over 2f out: disp hld 3rd 1f out: grad wknd* **5/2**[2]

3 **6** *2 ¼* **Evies Wish (IRE)**[47] 4280 3-9-2 **69** (p[1]) PaddyBradley(5) 4 41
(John C McConnell, Ire) *trckd ldrs in centre: rdn and ch 2f out: wknd appr fnl f* **6/1**

1m 15.68s (5.68) **Going Correction** +0.875s/f (Soft)
**WFA** 3 from 4yo+ 4lb **6** Ran SP% **111.1**
Speed ratings (Par 100): **97,94,87,85,84 81**
CSF £16.61 CT £64.50 TOTE £5.80: £2.60, £1.40; EX 18.10 Trifecta £52.40.
**Owner** The Incentive Partnership **Bred** The Hon Mrs R Pease **Trained** Blackborough, Devon

**FOCUS**
There was 22mm of rain on Monday; testing ground. Only two of these really seemed to handle the conditions. The winner is rated to form, with the race rated cautiously.

## 6029 BET TOTEEXACTA AT BETFRED.COM NOVICE STKS 7f 80y(R)
**2:45** (2:46) (Class 5) 2-Y-O **£3,881** (£1,155; £577; £288) **Stalls** Low

Form RPR

02 **1** **Livingstones Quest (IRE)**[17] 5430 2-9-2 0 WilliamCarson 5 71+
(Rod Millman) *mde all: pressed and rdn 2f out: drvn and styd on wl fnl f* **2/1**[2]

2121 **2** *2 ¼* **Indomeneo**[24] 5144 2-9-6 81 ConnorMurtagh(7) 1 76
(Richard Fahey) *s.i.s: trckd ldrs: wnt 2nd 3f out: rdn and ch 2f out: one pce whn hung lft 1f out* **8/11**[1]

0024 **3** *3 ¼* **Coal Stock (IRE)**[21] 5246 2-9-2 74 SteveDrowne 3 57
(David Evans) *last and niggled along: hung sltly rt bnd over 4f out: drvn 3f out: wnt 3rd 2f out: one pce and no real imp* **9/2**[3]

00 **4** *10* **Lucky's Dream**[25] 5106 2-9-2 0 CharlesBishop 2 32
(David Evans) *trckd wnr over 4f: rdn 2f out: qckly outpcd in last: wknd fnl f* **25/1**

1m 39.3s (5.70) **Going Correction** +0.875s/f (Soft) **4** Ran SP% **113.3**
Speed ratings (Par 94): **102,99,95,84**
CSF £4.10 TOTE £2.80; EX 4.30 Trifecta £5.30.
**Owner** Five Horses Ltd **Bred** Five Horses Ltd **Trained** Kentisbeare, Devon

**FOCUS**
Just fair-looking form, rated around the front pair to their marks.

## 6030 BET TOTEQUADPOT AT BETFRED.COM NURSERY H'CAP 7f 80y(R)
3:15 (3:17) (Class 5) (0-75,75) 2-Y-O £3,881 (£1,155; £577) Stalls Low

Form RPR
3165 1 **Ventura Dragon (IRE)**[26] 5079 2-8-12 **73**............... ConnorMurtagh(7) 4 78
(Richard Fahey) *trckd ldr: rdn: hung lft and led over 1f out: drvn and styd on strly to draw clr fnl f* **6/4**[2]
531 2 7 **Liva (IRE)**[29] 4963 2-9-7 **75**............................................ SteveDrowne 2 63
(David Evans) *chsd other pair: drvn over 2f out: one pce and no imp: styd on to go modest 2nd fnl 110 yds* **5/4**[1]
0226 3 4 **Airshow**[29] 4972 2-9-3 **71**............................................(h) WilliamCarson 1 49
(Rod Millman) *t.k.h: led: rdn wl over 1f out: sn hdd and sltly hmpd: wknd fnl f: lost 2nd fnl 110 yds* **11/4**[3]
1m 39.41s (5.81) **Going Correction** +0.875s/f (Soft) **3** Ran SP% **111.1**
Speed ratings (Par 94): **101,93,88**
CSF £3.85 TOTE £2.50; EX 4.50 Trifecta £4.70.
**Owner** Middleham Park Racing XLII & Partner **Bred** Laurence & Carla Sheedy **Trained** Musley Bank, N Yorks
**FOCUS**
This race looked to fall apart and the form is treated with caution.

## 6031 BET TOTETRIFECTA AT BETFRED.COM MAIDEN STKS 1m 3f 209y(R)
3:45 (3:48) (Class 5) 3-Y-O+ £3,234 (£962; £481; £240) Stalls Low

Form RPR
3-23 1 **Hawridge Flyer**[70] 3426 3-9-4 79........................................ LukeMorris 1 66
(Stuart Kittow) *mde all: set slow pce tl increased tempo 3f out: rdn and edgd lft 2f out: hung lft ins fnl f: styd on* **2/5**[1]
P0 2 1 ½ **War Brigade (FR)**[10] 5632 3-9-4 0.................................... KieranO'Neill 8 64
(David Simcock) *t.k.h: hld up: gd hdwy on inner to chse wnr over 2f out: hmpd 2f out: sn rdn: looked hld whn nt clr run on rail and swtchd rt 110 yds out: one pce* **12/1**[3]
0 3 2 ¼ **Sky Eagle (IRE)**[22] 5220 3-9-4 0........................................ LiamKeniry 7 60
(Ed Walker) *trckd ldrs: rdn and sltly outpcd in 4th over 2f out: styd on to go 3rd towards fin* **16/1**
56 4 ¾ **Monar Lad (IRE)**[17] 5428 5-10-0 0................................ CharlesBishop 9 58
(Dai Burchell) *t.k.h towards rr: hdwy to chse ldng pair over 2f out: kpt on same pce: lost 3rd towards fin* **33/1**
5 10 **Freedom Fighter (IRE)**[1869] 3741 7-10-0 0..............(t[1]) TimmyMurphy 4 42
(Tim Pinfield) *trckd wnr tl lost 2nd over 2f out: nudged along and grad wknd* **25/1**
6 1 **Still Believing (IRE)**[16] 9-9-9 0....................................... SamHitchcott 10 35
(Evan Williams) *s.i.s: pushed along and sn chsng ldrs: rdn over 3f out: wknd 2f out* **7/2**[2]
05/ 7 35 **I'mwaitingforyou**[1041] 7067 8-9-9 0............................. GeorgeDowning 6
(Peter Bowen) *s.s: hld up: hdwy on outer 3f out: rdn 2f out: sn wknd: t.o* **40/1**
2m 49.42s (12.02) **Going Correction** +0.875s/f (Soft)
**WFA** 3 from 5yo+ 10lb **7** Ran SP% **116.5**
Speed ratings (Par 103): **94,93,91,91,84 83,60**
CSF £7.06 TOTE £1.30: £1.10, £4.80; EX 6.00 Trifecta £32.80.
**Owner** Eric Gadsden **Bred** Meon Valley Stud **Trained** Blackborough, Devon
**FOCUS**
Not a deep race. The winner was unimpressive and the form is shaky.

## 6032 TOTEPOOL RACECOURSE DEBIT CARD BETTING AVAILABLE H'CAP 1m 3f 209y(R)
4:15 (4:19) (Class 6) (0-60,60) 3-Y-O £2,587 (£770; £384; £192) Stalls Low

Form RPR
003 1 **Bianca Minola (FR)**[21] 5249 3-9-5 **58**.....................(p) KieranShoemark 5 77+
(David Menuisier) *mde all: drvn 3f out: styd on strly to draw clr fnl 2f: rdn out* **2/1**[1]
2 14 **Stander (IRE)**[115] 1986 3-8-11 **50**................................ GeorgeDowning 4 48
(John C McConnell, Ire) *hdwy to trck wnr after 2f: rdn and lost 2nd 3f out: no ch after: styd on u.p to go mod 2nd towards fin* **5/1**
0-65 3 nk **Katabatika**[21] 5250 3-9-4 **60**.......................................... CharlieBennett(3) 3 58
(Hughie Morrison) *hld up in last: rdn over 2f out: hung lft and one pce: styd on to dispute mod 2nd towards fin* **5/2**[2]
500S 4 ¾ **Penny Red**[17] 5401 3-9-7 **60**........................................... CharlesBishop 1 57
(Nikki Evans) *chsd ldrs: wnt 2nd 3f out: sn rdn: outpcd by easy wnr fnl 2f: lost 2 pls towards fin* **22/1**
0503 5 6 **Trautmann (IRE)**[26] 5061 3-9-3 **56**.................................... LukeMorris 6 44
(Daniel Mark Loughnane) *trckd wnr 2f: chsd ldrs after: drvn 3f out: wknd 2f out* **4/1**[3]
4000 6 1 ¾ **Russian Regard (IRE)**[29] 4971 3-8-13 **55**..................... HectorCrouch(3) 2 40
(Jonathan Portman) *hld up: drvn on inner 3f out: wknd 2f out* **8/1**
2m 46.06s (8.66) **Going Correction** +0.875s/f (Soft) **6** Ran SP% **114.0**
Speed ratings (Par 98): **106,96,96,95,91 90**
CSF £12.76 TOTE £2.60: £1.40, £3.30; EX 12.50 Trifecta £39.60.
**Owner** Clive Washbourn **Bred** Patrick Burel **Trained** Pulborough, W Sussex
**FOCUS**
The winner proved much better than her lowly rating, hammering these in a time more than 3sec faster than the preceding maiden. The form is taken at face value but there are obvious doubts about the winner repeating this.

## 6033 TOTEPOOL BETTING ON ALL UK RACING H'CAP 1m 6f (R)
4:45 (4:46) (Class 4) (0-85,85) 3-Y-O+ £5,175 (£1,540; £769; £384) Stalls Low

Form RPR
1323 1 **Sternrubin (GER)**[39] 4586 6-9-13 **84**........................... KieranShoemark 8 99
(Philip Hobbs) *trckd ldr: chal 4f out: rdn to ld over 2f out: styd on strly to draw clr fnl f* **7/2**[2]
51 2 9 **Moabit (GER)**[17] 5432 5-9-2 **78**...............................(t) MeganNicholls(5) 7 82
(Paul Nicholls) *hld up in last: hdwy 3f out: drvn in 4th 2f out: no real imp: styng on whn nt clr run ins fnl f: tk modest 2nd post* **7/2**[2]
5261 3 nse **Veiled Secret (IRE)**[6] 5810 3-8-7 **75** 6ex............................ LukeMorris 2 77
(Sir Mark Prescott Bt) *s.i.s: sn trcking ldrs: drvn in 3rd 3f out: one pce after: wnt modest 2nd wl ins fnl f tl post* **11/8**[1]
401 4 1 ½ **Thistimenextyear**[24] 5141 3-8-7 **80**................................. JennyPowell(5) 3 80
(Richard Spencer) *reluctant to enter stalls: led: jnd 4f out: rdn 3f out: sn hdd: wknd and no ch w wnr fnl f: lost 2 pls towards fin* **6/1**[3]
1 5 3 ¼ **Catcher On The Go (IRE)**[12] 5563 7-9-10 **81**................ SamHitchcott 4 77
(Evan Williams) *hld up in 5th: rdn 5f out: kpt on same pce and no real hdwy* **8/1**
1/ 6 35 **Souriyan (FR)**[115] 2575 6-9-11 **85**................................. HectorCrouch(3) 9 35
(Peter Bowen) *hld up: rdn 5f out: wknd over 2f out: t.o* **33/1**
140- 7 13 **Mayasa (IRE)**[298] 7512 4-9-8 **79**.......................................(b) LiamKeniry 5 12
(John Flint) *chsd ldrs: rdn over 3f out: wknd qckly: t.o* **50/1**
3m 15.36s (11.56) **Going Correction** +0.875s/f (Soft)
**WFA** 3 from 4yo+ 11lb **7** Ran SP% **116.8**
Speed ratings (Par 105): **101,95,95,94,93 73,65**
CSF £16.80 CT £24.13 TOTE £4.60: £1.90, £2.00; EX 18.10 Trifecta £40.20.
**Owner** Terry Warner **Bred** Gestut Karlshof **Trained** Withycombe, Somerset
**FOCUS**
A useful staying handicap but nothing could live with the winner. The winner is rated in line with his jumps mark.

## 6034 COLLECT TOTEPOOL WINNINGS AT BETFRED SHOPS H'CAP 1m (R)
5:15 (5:15) (Class 5) (0-70,72) 3-Y-O+ £3,234 (£962; £481; £240) Stalls Low

Form RPR
P63 1 **Ejayteekay**[20] 5290 4-9-12 **71**.......................................... CharlieBennett(3) 1 75
(Hughie Morrison) *trckd ldr: rdn to chal 2f out: drvn fnl f: led nr fin* **9/4**[2]
2322 2 hd **Lucky Louie**[19] 5326 4-9-10 **69**..................................(p) HectorCrouch(3) 8 72
(Roger Teal) *awkward s: hld up in last: swtchd rt over 2f out: chsd ldrs over 1f out: ev ch ins fnl f: nt qckn and jst hld* **15/8**[1]
2020 3 hd **Spirit Of Belle**[24] 5139 3-9-9 **72**....................................... SteveDrowne 2 74
(David Evans) *led: rdn and pressed 2f out: kpt on: hdd nr fin* **9/2**
2/ 4 2 **Prussian Eagle (IRE)**[15] 1512 6-10-0 **70**........................ SamHitchcott 4 68
(Evan Williams) *s.i.s: chsd ldrs: rdn over 2f out: lost 3rd over 1f out: styd on same pce* **7/2**[3]
5-00 5 11 **Aqshion Stations**[38] 4633 3-8-2 **51** oh1.......................... KieranO'Neill 5 23
(Richard Price) *t.k.h: chsd ldrs: drvn over 2f out: wknd over 1f out* **20/1**
1m 52.18s (11.18) **Going Correction** +0.875s/f (Soft)
**WFA** 3 from 4yo+ 7lb **5** Ran SP% **110.7**
Speed ratings (Par 103): **79,78,78,76,65**
CSF £6.94 TOTE £3.00: £1.40, £2.20; EX 6.70 Trifecta £13.90.
**Owner** Miss Magdalena Gut **Bred** Pinehurst Stud **Trained** East Ilsley, Berks
**FOCUS**
A modest but competitive handicap. It was slowly run and is rated cautiously given the conditions.
T/Plt: £124.20 to a £1 stake. Pool: £62,760.14 - 368.63 winning units T/Qpdt: £23.00 to a £1 stake. Pool: £3,726.40 - 119.84 winning units **Richard Lowther**

# 5755 NOTTINGHAM (L-H)
Tuesday, August 15

**OFFICIAL GOING: Good (good to soft in places; 7.2)**
Wind: Light against Weather: Fine

## 6035 MAJESTIC BINGO.COM & APOLLO MANSFIELD APPRENTICE H'CAP 1m 2f 50y
4:55 (4:56) (Class 6) (0-60,62) 4-Y-O+ £2,587 (£770; £384; £192) Stalls Low

Form RPR
000 1 **Nazzaa (IRE)**[76] 3209 4-9-10 **60**........................................ JoshuaBryan 1 71+
(Steve Flook) *mde all: clr over 3f out: shkn up over 1f out: styd on wl: comf* **16/1**
0441 2 3 ¼ **Druid's Diamond**[22] 5215 4-9-3 **53**...............................(p[1]) FinleyMarsh 5 57
(Mark Walford) *prom: racd keenly: hmpd and lost pl after 1f: hdwy over 3f out: chsd wnr over 2f out: sn rdn: styd on same pce fnl f* **5/1**[2]
0-01 3 nk **Champagne Rules**[21] 5261 6-8-13 **52**............................ RossTurner(3) 4 54
(Sharon Watt) *hld up: swtchd rt over 2f out: hdwy over 1f out: r.o: nrst fin* **4/1**[1]
560- 4 3 ¾ **Chilli Jam**[420] 3482 4-9-1 **54**..................................... StephenCummins(3) 9 49
(Ed de Giles) *pushed along early towards rr: hdwy over 2f out: sn rdn: styd on same pce fr over 1f out* **8/1**
00-5 5 3 ½ **Navajo Storm (IRE)**[19] 5336 4-9-1 **54**.................... GabrieleMalune(3) 15 43
(Michael Appleby) *chsd ldrs: rdn over 2f out: wknd fnl f* **14/1**
0001 6 1 ¾ **Breakheart (IRE)**[20] 5299 10-8-12 **53**...............(v) KayleighStephens(5) 10 38
(Andrew Balding) *s.i.s: hld up: bhd 1/2-way: nt clr run over 2f out: nvr on terms* **14/1**
2255 7 3 ½ **Stoneboat Bill**[28] 5008 5-9-12 **62**.................................. GerO'Neill 8 41
(Declan Carroll) *slowl into stride: hld up: rdn and edgd rt over 2f out: n.d* **5/1**[2]
6600 8 4 ½ **Patent**[14] 5499 4-8-10 **51**......................................(p) SebastianWoods(5) 12 21
(Peter Niven) *hld up: wknd 3f out* **25/1**
0133 9 1 ¾ **Mamnoon (IRE)**[34] 4734 4-9-9 **59**............................(b) JamieGormley 13 26
(Roy Brotherton) *chsd wnr after 1f tl rdn over 2f out: wknd over 1f out* **10/1**
4032 10 shd **Weardiditallgorong**[21] 5250 5-9-6 **59**.........................(b) WilliamCox(3) 7 26
(Des Donovan, Ire) *hld up: rdn and wknd over 2f out* **11/2**[3]
0650 11 1 ½ **Port Lairge**[14] 5499 7-8-9 **50**.................................(b) JacobMitchell(5) 6 14
(Michael Chapman) *s.i.s: in rr: pushed along and rn wd ent st: wknd over 3f out* **50/1**
-400 12 nk **Champagne Freddie**[185] 684 4-9-2 **57**...................... DarraghKeenan(5) 14 20
(John O'Shea) *prom tl rdn and wknd over 2f out* **33/1**
0000 13 7 **Thou Swell (IRE)**[62] 3726 5-8-13 **49**.......................(b) ManuelFernandes 3
(Shaun Harris) *prom: rdn over 3f out: wknd over 2f out* **25/1**
2m 10.47s (-3.83) **Going Correction** -0.675s/f (Hard) **13** Ran SP% **120.7**
Speed ratings (Par 101): **88,85,85,82,79 77,75,71,70,70 68,68,63**
CSF £92.20 CT £393.93 TOTE £20.40: £4.80, £2.10, £2.50; EX 134.20 Trifecta £1274.40.
**Owner** Glyn Byard **Bred** Pier House Stud **Trained** Leominster, Herefordshire
**FOCUS**
Outer track used and all race distances as advertised. A dry day and the ground was officially good, good to soft in places. \n\x\x A low-grade handicap to open but the winner, who is bred to be a very smart performer, looked one to keep on the right side of. Straightfoward bare form.

## 6036 RATEDBOOKIES.COM NURSERY H'CAP (JOCKEY CLUB GRASSROOTS NURSERY QUALIFIER) 6f 18y
5:25 (5:27) (Class 5) (0-75,75) 2-Y-O £3,234 (£962; £481; £240) Stalls Centre

Form RPR
531 1 **Shovel It On (IRE)**[7] 5752 2-8-11 **65** 6ex............................. RobertTart 4 69
(David Evans) *s.i.s: sn pushed along in rr: swtchd rt over 3f out: hdwy over 1f out: hung lft and r.o to ld towards fin* **5/2**[1]
3454 2 1 **Ce De Nullis (IRE)**[17] 5440 2-9-0 **68**............................... RobHornby 6 69
(Paul Midgley) *hld up in tch: racd keenly: rdn to ld 1f out: hdd towards fin* **16/1**
0546 3 ¾ **Contribute**[31] 4922 2-8-12 **66**..................................... FergusSweeney 5 65
(Martyn Meade) *sn led: rdn over 2f out: hdd 1f out: styd on same pce* **8/1**[3]
405 4 nk **Hard Graft**[45] 4359 2-9-7 **75**............................................ FranBerry 1 73
(David Brown) *hld up: hdwy over 1f out: sn rdn: styd on* **16/1**

034 **5** *nk* **Hermana Santa (IRE)**[18] 5370 2-9-0 **68**............................ SamJames 9 65
(David Barron) *w ldrs: rdn and ev ch over 1f out: styd on same pce ins fnl f* **16/1**

3433 **6** *shd* **Story Minister (IRE)**[19] 5322 2-9-3 **71**........................(p[1]) PJMcDonald 3 68
(Tom Dascombe) *prom: rdn and ev ch over 1f out: styd on same pce ins fnl f* **8/1**[3]

064 **7** *1* **Polar Light**[25] 5114 2-9-0 **73**............................................ DavidEgan(5) 11 67
(David Elsworth) *s.i.s: hld up: rdn over 1f out: edgd lft and styd on ins fnl f: nt trble ldrs* **16/1**

104 **8** *shd* **Blessed To Empress (IRE)**[75] 3230 2-9-0 **68**.................. AdamKirby 2 61
(Amy Murphy) *chsd ldrs: rdn over 2f out: ev ch over 1f out: no ex wl ins fnl f* **25/1**

166 **9** *4 ½* **Our Kid (IRE)**[13] 5537 2-8-12 **66**..................................... TonyHamilton 7 46
(Richard Fahey) *s.i.s: hld up: pushed along and hdwy over 2f out: rdn over 1f out: sn wknd* **16/1**

5534 **10** *½* **Moonlit Sands (IRE)**[26] 5057 2-8-7 **66**...................... BenRobinson(5) 8 44
(Brian Ellison) *chsd ldrs: rdn over 1f out: wknd fnl f* **8/1**[3]

1342 **11** *¾* **Alaska (IRE)**[19] 5322 2-9-2 **75**...................... MitchGodwin(5) 10 51
(Sylvester Kirk) *prom: rdn over 2f out: hung lft fr over 1f out: wknd fnl f* **9/2**[2]

1m 15.13s (0.43) **Going Correction** -0.15s/f (Firm) **11** Ran SP% **113.3**
Speed ratings (Par 94): **91,89,88,88,87 87,86,86,80,79 78**
CSF £44.07 CT £278.50 TOTE £2.90: £1.30, £4.30, £2.60; EX 39.10 Trifecta £274.80.
**Owner** Power Geneva & Bruce Williams **Bred** Dylan Finucane **Trained** Pandy, Monmouths

**FOCUS**
A competitive nursery saw the field race down the centre of the track, with no obvious track bias on this occasion. The form is rated around the second, third and fourth.

## 6037 BETTINGGODS.COM EBF FILLIES' NOVICE STKS (PLUS 10 RACE) 1m 75y
5:55 (5:56) (Class 5) 2-Y-O £3,234 (£962; £481; £240) **Stalls** Centre

Form RPR

**1** **Perfect Clarity** 2-9-0 0........................................................ AdamKirby 5 79+
(Clive Cox) *hld up in tch: shkn up over 2f out: r.o to ld wl ins fnl f: comf* **3/1**[2]

0205 **2** *1 ¼* **Cosmopolitan Queen**[12] 5572 2-8-9 78......................... DavidEgan(5) 8 76
(David Elsworth) *led: shkn up over 2f out: rdn: hdd and unable qck wl ins fnl f* **5/4**[1]

**3** *1 ¾* **Ceramist** 2-9-0 0................................................................ RobertTart 2 72+
(John Gosden) *dwlt: hld up: swtchd rt over 2f out: shkn up over 1f out: edgd lft and r.o ins fnl f to go 3rd nr fin: nt rch ldrs* **4/1**[3]

36 **4** *¾* **Dark Liberty (IRE)**[25] 5114 2-9-0 0................................ DanielMuscutt 3 71
(Simon Crisford) *prom: chsd ldr over 5f out: rdn and ev ch over 1f out: no ex ins fnl f* **6/1**

**5** *1* **Giving Glances** 2-9-0 0.............................................. FergusSweeney 6 68
(Alan King) *s.i.s: hld up: shkn up: hdwy and hung lft fr over 1f out: nt trble ldrs* **33/1**

50 **6** *1 ½* **Gigi (IRE)**[59] 3815 2-9-0 0................................................ PJMcDonald 1 65
(Charles Hills) *hld up in tch: rdn over 1f out: no ex fnl f* **33/1**

**7** *3* **Railport Dolly** 2-9-0 0.................................................. AdamBeschizza 4 59
(Steph Hollinshead) *chsd ldr tl over 5f out: rdn over 2f out: wknd over 1f out* **100/1**

1m 46.47s (-2.53) **Going Correction** -0.675s/f (Hard) **7** Ran SP% **110.6**
Speed ratings (Par 91): **85,83,82,81,80 78,75**
CSF £6.64 TOTE £3.70: £1.80, £1.20; EX 6.80 Trifecta £19.50.
**Owner** Dr Bridget Drew & David J Keast **Bred** Bluehills Racing Limited **Trained** Lambourn, Berks

**FOCUS**
Some well-bred newcomers taking on a filly who had already shown a useful level of ability. The pace, set by the runner-up, looked stop-start. The second also sets the level of the form.

## 6038 BETTINGGODS.COM FREE RACING TIPS H'CAP 1m 6f
6:25 (6:26) (Class 5) (0-75,75) 3-Y-O+
£3,112 (£932; £466; £233; £116; £58) **Stalls** Low

Form RPR

4343 **1** **Melinoe**[25] 5108 3-9-1 **73**........................................................ AdamKirby 4 83+
(Sir Mark Prescott Bt) *hld up in tch: shkn up to ld over 2f out: sn rdn and hung lft: drvn out* **13/8**[1]

4042 **2** *1 ¾* **Master Archer (IRE)**[13] 5550 3-9-3 **75**......................(p) DanielMuscutt 9 81
(James Fanshawe) *hld up: hdwy over 2f out: rdn to chse wnr over 1f out: styd on same pce ins fnl f* **2/1**[2]

-006 **3** *2* **The Twisler**[24] 5166 5-10-0 **75**......................................(p[1]) TonyHamilton 8 78
(Neil Mulholland) *trckd ldrs: racd keenly: shkn up and ev ch whn hmpd 2f out: sn rdn: styd on same pce fnl f* **7/1**[3]

6462 **4** *5* **Goldslinger (FR)**[18] 5362 5-9-4 **65**............................ RoystonFfrench 3 61
(Dean Ivory) *led: clr after 2f: c bk to the field over 8f out: rdn and hdd over 2f out: hmpd sn after: styd on same pce* **12/1**

0-05 **5** *3* **Cousin Khee**[25] 5110 10-10-0 **75**..................................(b[1]) PJMcDonald 5 67
(Hughie Morrison) *hld up: pushed along over 3f out: rdn: hung lft and wknd over 1f out* **16/1**

221 **6** *4* **Deinonychus**[12] 5579 6-9-4 **70**.............................. BenRobinson(5) 1 56
(Michael Appleby) *plld hrd in 2nd pl: ldr wnt clr after 2f: tk clsr order over 8f out: rdn and ev ch over 2f out: wknd over 1f out* **7/1**[3]

4000 **7** *1 ¾* **Benissimo (IRE)**[38] 4630 7-8-2 **56** oh2........................(p[1]) WilliamCox(7) 7 40
(Tony Forbes) *hld up: hdwy over 4f out: rdn and wknd over 2f out* **66/1**

**8** *½* **Polkarenix (FR)**[44] 5-10-0 **75**.......................................(t) FranBerry 6 58
(Brendan Powell) *hld up: hdwy over 6f out: rdn and wknd over 2f out* **50/1**

3m 1.26s (-5.74) **Going Correction** -0.675s/f (Hard)
**WFA** 3 from 4yo+ 11lb **8** Ran SP% **113.5**
Speed ratings (Par 103): **89,88,86,84,82 80,79,78**
CSF £4.94 CT £15.50 TOTE £2.30: £1.10, £1.70, £2.80; EX 5.90 Trifecta £29.20.
**Owner** Fergus Anstock **Bred** Litex Commerce **Trained** Newmarket, Suffolk
■ Stewards' Enquiry : Adam Kirby four-day ban: careless riding (Aug 29th-31st & Sep 1st)

**FOCUS**
A finish fought out by the two 3yos in the line up, the winner another typical Sir Mark Prescott improver. The runner-up is rated to form.

## 6039 BRITISH STALLION STUDS EBF CONDITIONS STKS 5f 8y
6:55 (6:57) (Class 3) 3-Y-O+
£9,960 (£2,982; £1,491; £745; £372; £187) **Stalls** Centre

Form RPR

6051 **1** **Ornate**[25] 5116 4-9-0 107...................................................(h) PJMcDonald 4 112
(Robert Cowell) *mde all: rdn over 1f out: edgd lft ins fnl f: r.o* **5/2**[1]

206 **2** *¾* **Kyllang Rock (IRE)**[11] 5595 3-8-11 107........................ TonyHamilton 5 108
(James Tate) *hld up: hdwy on bit over 1f out: sn chsng wnr: rdn and edgd lft ins fnl f: styd on same pce* **3/1**[2]

-030 **3** *3 ¼* **Green Door (IRE)**[3] 5911 6-9-0 98......................................(v) FranBerry 3 98
(Robert Cowell) *trckd ldrs: rdn over 1f out: hung lft and no ex ins fnl f* **8/1**

-320 **4** *2 ¼* **Bounce**[31] 4920 4-8-9 95.................................................. FergusSweeney 7 85
(Henry Candy) *s.i.s: hld up: hdwy on outer 2f out: rdn over 1f out: wknd ins fnl f* **3/1**[2]

5020 **5** *nk* **Monsieur Joe (IRE)**[18] 5354 10-9-0 94................................ SamJames 6 88
(Paul Midgley) *chsd ldrs: pushed along and edgd lft 1/2-way: wknd fnl f* **33/1**

2000 **6** *2 ¼* **Gracious John (IRE)**[38] 4635 4-9-4 103............................ AdamKirby 2 84
(David Evans) *chsd wnr tl rdn over 1f out: wknd fnl f* **11/2**[3]

59.6s (-1.90) **Going Correction** -0.15s/f (Firm)
**WFA** 3 from 4yo+ 3lb **6** Ran SP% **108.0**
Speed ratings (Par 107): **109,107,102,99,98 94**
CSF £9.41 TOTE £2.30: £1.30, £1.70; EX 6.90 Trifecta £36.60.
**Owner** Cheveley Park Stud **Bred** Cheveley Park Stud Ltd **Trained** Six Mile Bottom, Cambs

**FOCUS**
The field came stands' side in the feature event with the winner providing Robert Cowell with another success in this contest. The first two are rated to form.

## 6040 BETTINGGODS.COM H'CAP 5f 8y
7:25 (7:27) (Class 5) (0-70,72) 3-Y-O+ £3,234 (£962; £481; £240) **Stalls** Centre

Form RPR

3063 **1** **Classic Pursuit**[2] 5962 6-9-5 **64**..................................(b) RoystonFfrench 3 77
(Michael Appleby) *chsd ldrs: rdn 1/2-way: r.o u.p to ld nr fin* **6/1**[3]

0-02 **2** *½* **Operative**[7] 5750 4-9-9 **68**................................................ AdamKirby 5 79
(Ed de Giles) *hld up: hdwy 1/2-way: shkn up to ld: carried hd high and hung rt over 1f out: rdn and nt run on wl ins fnl f: hdd nr fin* **3/1**[2]

0213 **3** *2 ¼* **Ambitious Icarus**[7] 5750 8-9-2 **61**................................(b[1]) RobHornby 2 64
(Richard Guest) *dwlt: hld up: rdn and r.o ins fnl f: nt rch ldrs* **17/2**

3514 **4** *¾* **Nag's Wag (IRE)**[14] 5514 4-9-10 **69**................................. FranBerry 7 69
(Conor Dore) *hld up: shkn up and hdwy over 1f out: rdn ins fnl f: styd on same pce* **20/1**

0111 **5** *½* **Culloden**[11] 5605 5-9-0 **66**..................................(v) ManuelFernandes(7) 4 65
(Shaun Harris) *disp ld over 3f: styd on same pce fnl f* **7/1**

5131 **6** *2 ½* **Sitar**[21] 5263 3-9-10 **72**.........................................................(h) DanielMuscutt 6 61
(James Fanshawe) *hld up in tch: pushed along and outpcd 1/2-way: n.d after* **6/4**[1]

0306 **7** *½* **Roy's Legacy**[12] 5580 8-8-7 **59**........................................... TobyEley(7) 1 47
(Shaun Harris) *disp ld over 3f: wknd ins fnl f* **40/1**

1m 0.09s (-1.41) **Going Correction** -0.15s/f (Firm)
**WFA** 3 from 4yo+ 3lb **7** Ran SP% **109.5**
Speed ratings (Par 103): **105,104,100,99,98 94,93**
CSF £22.21 TOTE £6.20: £2.70, £1.90; EX 23.10 Trifecta £160.20.
**Owner** From The Front Racing **Bred** B & B Equine Limited **Trained** Oakham, Rutland

**FOCUS**
A modest sprint handicap in which the field stayed in the middle of the track. The winner is rated back to his early-season C&D form.

## 6041 FREE RACING TIPS FROM BETTINGGODS.COM H'CAP 6f 18y
7:55 (7:56) (Class 6) (0-60,60) 3-Y-O+ £2,587 (£770; £384; £192) **Stalls** Centre

Form RPR

0300 **1** **Kaaber (USA)**[50] 4149 6-8-8 **49**.................................... MitchGodwin(5) 8 56
(Michael Blake) *hld up: hdwy over 2f out: rdn and r.o to ld nr fin* **6/1**[3]

003 **2** *½* **Fantasy Justifier (IRE)**[10] 5657 6-9-9 **59**........................(p[1]) FranBerry 1 65
(Ronald Harris) *trckd ldrs: led over 1f out: sn rdn: hdd nr fin* **5/1**[2]

0006 **3** *¾* **Robbian**[7] 5738 6-8-11 **52**........................................... BenRobinson(5) 4 55
(Charles Smith) *w ldrs: rdn and ev ch fr over 1f out tl no ex wl ins fnl f* **12/1**

0030 **4** *3* **Multi Quest**[19] 5339 5-8-10 **46**........................................(b) PaddyAspell 2 40
(John E Long) *led: rdn and hdd over 1f out: no ex ins fnl f* **16/1**

0060 **5** *1* **Morello (IRE)**[24] 5145 3-8-8 **53**.................................... GeorgiaCox(5) 6 43
(Henry Candy) *s.i.s: hdwy over 2f out: rdn over 1f out: wknd ins fnl f* **6/1**[3]

4006 **6** *1 ¼* **Coachella (IRE)**[6] 5791 3-8-1 **46** oh1............................ DavidEgan(5) 9 33
(Ed de Giles) *mid-div: pushed along and lost pl over 3f out: n.d after* **7/1**

00 **7** *½* **Secret Asset (IRE)**[21] 5252 12-8-11 **52**......................(p) JaneElliott(5) 12 38
(Lisa Williamson) *chsd ldrs tl rdn and wknd over 1f out* **33/1**

0453 **8** *1* **Tango Sky (IRE)**[13] 5542 8-9-6 **56**................................(v) AdamKirby 10 39
(Paul Midgley) *s.i.s: nvr on terms* **9/2**[1]

0563 **9** *2 ¼* **Captain Scooby**[12] 5567 11-8-5 **46** oh1........................(b[1]) KevinLundie(5) 3 22
(Richard Guest) *s.s: n.d* **10/1**

6443 **10** *9* **Manipura**[13] 5535 4-8-13 **49**.............................................(p) RyanPowell 11
(Derek Shaw) *s.i.s: wknd over 2f out* **8/1**

0-00 **11** *5* **Ciaras Cookie (IRE)**[35] 4726 5-8-10 **46** oh1..................(t) JimmyQuinn 5
(Mandy Rowland) *w ldrs to 1/2-way: wknd over 2f out* **100/1**

1m 14.28s (-0.42) **Going Correction** -0.15s/f (Firm)
**WFA** 3 from 4yo+ 4lb **11** Ran SP% **113.6**
Speed ratings (Par 101): **96,95,94,90,89 87,86,85,82,70 63**
CSF £34.75 CT £352.98 TOTE £6.00: £2.90, £2.10, £3.40; EX 41.50 Trifecta £501.80.
**Owner** Jeremy Holt **Bred** Shadwell Farm LLC **Trained** Trowbridge, Wilts

**FOCUS**
A low-grade finale but an exciting finish, the winner landing the race for the second year in succession. He and the third set a straightforward level.
T/Plt: £28.60 to a £1 stake. Pool: £47,274.04 - 1,203.50 winning units T/Qpdt: £6.40 to a £1 stake. Pool: £5,979.36 - 681.85 winning units **Colin Roberts**

# 5665 THIRSK (L-H)
## Tuesday, August 15

**OFFICIAL GOING: Good (8.0)**
Wind: Strong behind Weather: Cloudy with sunny periods

## 6042 "STAR WARS FAMILY DAY" HERE TODAY NOVICE AUCTION STKS 7f
2:00 (2:01) (Class 6) 2-Y-O £2,587 (£770; £384; £192) **Stalls** Low

Form RPR

234 **1** **Wahoo**[25] 5127 2-9-2 77............................................... PaulMulrennan 1 71
(Michael Dods) *led: hung rt home turn and sn narrowly hdd: led again wl over 2f out: rdn over 1f out: kpt on wl towards fin* **13/8**[1]

50 **2** *½* **Claramara (IRE)**[8] 5702 2-8-11 0..................................... JoeFanning 8 64
(Mark Johnston) *trckd ldrs: hdwy over 2f out: rdn wl over 1f out: kpt on wl u.p fnl f* **10/1**

00 **3** *shd* **Urban Soul (IRE)**[18] 5380 2-9-2 0..................................... PJMcDonald 5 68
(James Bethell) *trckd ldng pair: hdwy on inner to take slt advantage home turn: pushed along 3f out: sn rdn and hdd wl over 2f out: cl up and ev ch over 1f out: drvn and kpt on fnl f* **7/1**[3]

| | 4 | hd | **Vera Drake (FR)** 2-8-11 0 TonyHamilton 4 | 63+ |
|---|---|---|---|---|
| | | | (Richard Fahey) dwlt and green towards rr: hdwy 1/2-way: chsd ldrs 2f out: swtchd rt and rdn over 1f out: kpt on wl fnl f 15/2 | |
| 0 | 5 | 6 | **Bertie Wallace (IRE)**88 2771 2-9-2 0 GrahamLee 2 | 52 |
| | | | (Keith Dalgleish) trckd ldrs: hdwy 3f out: rdn along 2f out: sn drvn and kpt on same pce 14/1 | |
| 3 | 6 | ½ | **Harbour Vision**14 5507 2-9-2 0 SeanLevey 3 | 51 |
| | | | (David Brown) cl up: pushed along wl over 2f out: rdn wl over 1f out: sn outpcd 11/4² | |
| 00 | 7 | 1 | **Surrender**9 5680 2-9-2 0 DuranFentiman 6 | 48 |
| | | | (Tim Easterby) wnt rt s: towards rr: pushed along 3f out: sn rdn and n.d 40/1 | |
| 0 | 8 | ½ | **Troop**14 5492 2-9-2 0 ShaneGray 9 | 47 |
| | | | (Ann Duffield) a rr 50/1 | |
| | 9 | 1 | **Shef Wedsneigh (IRE)** 2-8-11 0 ConnorBeasley 7 | 40+ |
| | | | (Roger Fell) sltly hmpd s: green and a rr 25/1 | |

1m 31.44s (4.24) **Going Correction** +0.425s/f (Yiel) **9 Ran SP% 113.0**
Speed ratings (Par 92): **92,91,91,91,84 83,82,81,80**
CSF £18.48 TOTE £2.50: £1.10, £2.90, £2.60; EX 20.50 Trifecta £107.40.
**Owner** J Blackburn & A Turton **Bred** Llety Farms **Trained** Denton, Co Durham

**FOCUS**
Just 0.5mm of rain overnight and the going had dried out to good (GoingStick: 8.0). After riding in the opener Connor Beasley, Duran Fentiman, Sean Levey and Shane Gray all called the ground good, while Joe Fanning reckoned: "It's just on the slow side." The rail on the home bend was dolled out by about 9 metres and the away bend was dolled out by about 3 metres. Race distance increased by 30yds. A steadily run novice. The winner is rated a bit below his debut level.

## 6043 JW 4X4 NORTHALLERTON NURSERY H'CAP 6f
**2:30** (2:31) (Class 6) (0-65,67) 2-Y-O £2,587 (£770; £384; £192) **Stalls** Centre

| Form | | | | RPR |
|---|---|---|---|---|
| 6425 | 1 | | **Brockey Rise (IRE)**12 5562 2-9-5 63 (v1) PJMcDonald 13 | 69+ |
| | | | (David Evans) in tch towards stands side: pushed along wl over 2f out: rdn and hdwy wl over 1f out: led ent fnl f: kpt on strly 12/1 | |
| 004 | 2 | 2¾ | **Excellent Times**22 5210 2-9-2 60 DavidAllan 7 | 58 |
| | | | (Tim Easterby) prom: pushed along 2f out: sn rdn: kpt on u.p fnl f 15/2³ | |
| 0311 | 3 | ¾ | **Placebo Effect (IRE)**20 5277 2-9-4 62 AndrewMullen 2 | 58 |
| | | | (Ollie Pears) trckd ldrs centre: hdwy over 2f out: led wl over 1f out: rdn and hdd ent fnl f: kpt on same pce 9/2¹ | |
| 00 | 4 | 2¼ | **Go Bananas**27 5030 2-9-3 61 HarryBentley 14 | 50 |
| | | | (Brian Meehan) racd towards stands side: cl up: led wl over 2f out: rdn along and hdd wl over 1f out: sn drvn and kpt on same pce 6/1² | |
| 454 | 5 | ¾ | **Just For Fun**21 5262 2-9-1 62 AdamMcNamara(3) 15 | 49 |
| | | | (Richard Fahey) towards rr: hdwy over 2f out: rdn wl over 1f out: kpt on fnl f 8/1 | |
| 3050 | 6 | 1¼ | **Aristodemus (IRE)**20 5279 2-8-13 57 (b1) JamesSullivan 9 | 40 |
| | | | (Tim Easterby) towards rr: hdwy over 2f out: sn rdn and kpt on fnl f 20/1 | |
| 6355 | 7 | 4 | **Monkey Magic**18 5373 2-8-12 56 TomEaves 5 | 27 |
| | | | (Nigel Tinkler) racd centre: led: hdd over 3f out: chsd ldrs: rdn along 2f out: sn wknd 18/1 | |
| 5506 | 8 | 1½ | **Highland Bobby**56 3930 2-9-7 65 PhillipMakin 4 | 31 |
| | | | (David O'Meara) awkward s: a towards rr 16/1 | |
| 660 | 9 | 1¾ | **Where's Jeff**32 4862 2-9-2 60 NathanEvans 11 | 21 |
| | | | (Michael Easterby) a towards rr 14/1 | |
| 6005 | 10 | ½ | **Mount Hellvelyn**71 3398 2-9-4 62 DavidNolan 1 | 22 |
| | | | (Clive Mulhall) nvr bttr than midfield 20/1 | |
| 0003 | 11 | 6 | **Westfield Wonder**16 5453 2-9-7 65 JimmyQuinn 3 | 7 |
| | | | (Ronald Thompson) racd centre: in tch: rdn along wl over 2f out: sn wknd 50/1 | |
| 004 | 12 | 1 | **Lady Lintera (IRE)**24 5162 2-9-3 61 GrahamLee 12 | |
| | | | (Ann Duffield) prom: led over 3f out: hdd wl over 2f out: sn rdn and wknd 33/1 | |
| 554 | 13 | 1¾ | **Plundered (IRE)**55 3973 2-9-4 62 (p1) SeanLevey 8 | |
| | | | (David Brown) a rr 17/2 | |

1m 12.58s (-0.12) **Going Correction** -0.15s/f (Firm) **13 Ran SP% 105.8**
Speed ratings (Par 92): **94,90,89,86,85 83,78,76,74,73 65,64,61**
CSF £79.41 CT £401.62 TOTE £10.80: £3.00, £2.20, £1.80; EX 88.60 Trifecta £330.50.
**Owner** Power Geneva Ltd & John Abbey **Bred** P O'Rourke **Trained** Pandy, Monmouths
■ Moremoneymoreparty was withdrawn. Price at time of withdrawal 11/1. Rule 4 applies to all bets - deduction 5p in the pound.

**FOCUS**
A modest nursery in which the winner showed a bit of improvement.

## 6044 "CREATURES FAMILY DAY" - MONDAY 21ST AUGUST MAIDEN FILLIES' STKS 1m 4f 8y
**3:00** (3:02) (Class 5) 3-Y-O+ £3,881 (£1,155; £577; £288) **Stalls** High

| Form | | | | RPR |
|---|---|---|---|---|
| 452 | 1 | | **Nathalie**27 5022 3-9-0 76 DanielMuscutt 3 | 80+ |
| | | | (James Fanshawe) trckd ldng pair: hdwy 3f out: led wl over 1f out: pushed out: readily 1/2¹ | |
| 054 | 2 | 1¾ | **Saniyaat**25 5124 3-9-0 75 (v) HarryBentley 7 | 75 |
| | | | (George Peckham) sn led: hdd over 7 out: cl up and led again 1/2-way: jnd and rdn along wl over 2f out: hdd wl over 1f out: sn drvn and kpt on fnl f 9/4² | |
| | 3 | ½ | **Misscarlett (IRE)** 3-9-0 0 BenCurtis 6 | 73 |
| | | | (Sally Haynes) dwlt and towards rr: hdwy over 4f out: chsd ldng pair 3f out: rdn along over 2f out: kpt on wl fnl f 16/1 | |
| 0 | 4 | 11 | **Poppyinthepark**38 4611 4-9-5 0 CallumRodriguez(5) 5 | 55? |
| | | | (Richard Ford) chsd ldrs: rdn along over 4f out: sn outpcd 33/1 | |
| | 5 | 8 | **Biba** 3-9-0 0 GrahamLee 8 | 43 |
| | | | (Keith Dalgleish) a rr 15/2³ | |
| | 6 | 13 | **Newgate Duchess** 3-9-0 0 BarryMcHugh 1 | 22 |
| | | | (Tony Coyle) in tch: pushed along 1/2-way: outpcd and bhd fnl 3f 33/1 | |
| 0 | 7 | 28 | **Stellekaya (IRE)**71 3408 3-9-0 0 JoeFanning 2 | |
| | | | (Mark H Tompkins) a rr: outpcd and bhd fnl 3f 40/1 | |
| -6 | 8 | 3¾ | **Anna's Legacy**37 4657 4-9-10 0 JamesSullivan 4 | |
| | | | (Jim Goldie) plld hrd: chsd ldr: led over 7f out: hdd over 6f out: rdn along 4f out: sn lost pl and bhd 33/1 | |

2m 40.66s (4.46) **Going Correction** +0.425s/f (Yiel)
**WFA** 3 from 4yo 10lb **8 Ran SP% 126.3**
Speed ratings (Par 100): **102,100,100,93,87 79,60,58**
CSF £2.17 TOTE £1.40: £1.10, £1.10, £3.60; EX 2.10 Trifecta £7.80.
**Owner** Normandie Stud Ltd **Bred** Normandie Stud Ltd **Trained** Newmarket, Suffolk

**FOCUS**
Race distance increased by 40yds. A two-horse race on paper, but the winner proved a cut above. She's been rated a bit better than the bare form.

## 6045 ANDERSON BARROWCLIFF H'CAP (DIV I) 6f
**3:30** (3:31) (Class 6) (0-60,65) 4-Y-O+ £2,587 (£770; £384; £192) **Stalls** Centre

| Form | | | | RPR |
|---|---|---|---|---|
| 2323 | 1 | | **Hadley**7 5736 4-9-0 52 (p) BenCurtis 6 | 65 |
| | | | (Tracy Waggott) qckly away: mde all: rdn clr over 1f out: kpt on strly 3/1¹ | |
| 0000 | 2 | 5 | **Spirit Of Zebedee (IRE)**28 4997 4-9-7 59 (v) JackGarritty 12 | 57 |
| | | | (John Quinn) t.k.h: trckd ldrs: hdwy and cl up 1/2-way: rdn wl over 1f out: drvn and kpt on same pce fnl f 10/1 | |
| 410 | 3 | hd | **Ypres**25 5132 8-9-9 61 (p) KevinStott 10 | 58 |
| | | | (Jason Ward) dwlt and bhd: hdwy over 2f out: rdn wl over 1f out: styd on strly fnl f 17/2 | |
| 0036 | 4 | nk | **Mitchum**13 5543 8-9-1 56 (p) PhilDennis(3) 5 | 53 |
| | | | (Ron Barr) trckd ldrs: hdwy over 2f out: rdn over 1f out: drvn and kpt on same pce fnl f 16/1 | |
| 1441 | 5 | ¾ | **Perfect Words (IRE)**7 5736 7-9-6 65 6ex (p) HarrisonShaw(7) 11 | 60 |
| | | | (Marjorie Fife) trckd ldrs: hdwy 1/2-way: rdn and n.m.r over 1f out: sn swtchd rt: drvn and kpt on same pce fnl f 8/1³ | |
| 5065 | 6 | nk | **Nellie Deen (IRE)**11 5620 4-8-4 49 (b) BenSanderson(7) 2 | 42 |
| | | | (Roger Fell) chsd ldrs on outer: rdn along and edgd lft wl over 1f out: sn drvn and kpt on same pce 9/1 | |
| 0303 | 7 | 1 | **Whipphound**7 5738 9-8-7 45 (b) JamesSullivan 8 | 40 |
| | | | (Ruth Carr) towards rr: hdwy 2f out: rdn and styng on whn hmpd 1f out: one pce after 7/2² | |
| 4406 | 8 | 4 | **Diamond Indulgence**13 5535 4-8-6 47 (h) LewisEdmunds(3) 1 | 25 |
| | | | (Derek Shaw) wnt lft s: chsd ldrs on outer: rdn along over 2f out: sn drvn and wknd 25/1 | |
| 0566 | 9 | 3¾ | **Six Of The Best**28 4997 5-8-7 45 NathanEvans 7 | 12 |
| | | | (Bryan Smart) prom: rdn along wl over 2f out: drvn wl over 1f out: grad wknd 14/1 | |
| 6-20 | 10 | 4 | **Vecheka (IRE)**17 5419 6-9-2 54 (tp) AndrewMullen 3 | 9 |
| | | | (Kenny Johnson) prom: rdn along 2f out: sn wknd 28/1 | |
| 0600 | 11 | 5 | **Whispering Wolf**28 4997 4-8-7 45 RoystonFfrench 4 | |
| | | | (Suzzanne France) chsd ldrs: rdn wl over 2f out: sn wknd 66/1 | |
| 6030 | 12 | 2½ | **Jess**13 5543 4-8-13 51 (p) TomEaves 9 | |
| | | | (Kevin Ryan) a rr 18/1 | |

1m 11.76s (-0.94) **Going Correction** -0.15s/f (Firm) **12 Ran SP% 114.5**
Speed ratings (Par 101): **100,93,93,92,91 91,89,84,79,74 67,64**
CSF £31.76 CT £233.39 TOTE £3.50: £1.50, £3.60, £2.40; EX 34.80 Trifecta £164.50.
**Owner** David Tate **Bred** G A E & J Smith Bloodstock Ltd **Trained** Spennymoor, Co Durham
■ Stewards' Enquiry : Harrison Shaw two-day ban: careless riding (Aug 29th-30th)

**FOCUS**
Moderate sprinting form, but a welcome win for Hadley, who deserved this following a string of placed efforts. The form is possibly worth 6lb more but it's not hard to have reservations.

## 6046 ANDERSON BARROWCLIFF H'CAP (DIV II) 6f
**4:00** (4:00) (Class 6) (0-60,62) 4-Y-O+ £2,587 (£770; £384; £192) **Stalls** Centre

| Form | | | | RPR |
|---|---|---|---|---|
| 0340 | 1 | | **Le Manege Enchante (IRE)**11 5620 4-9-1 54 (v1) PhillipMakin 10 | 60 |
| | | | (Derek Shaw) dwlt and rr: hdwy 1/2-way: rdn to chse ldng pair ent fnl f: sn drvn and kpt on wl to ld last 50 yds 6/1³ | |
| 0604 | 2 | ½ | **Mighty Bond**13 5543 5-8-7 46 oh1 (p) RoystonFfrench 11 | 51 |
| | | | (Tracy Waggott) cl up: slt ld 2f out: rdn over 1f out: drvn and edgd lft ins fnl f: hdd last 50 yds: no ex 14/1 | |
| 3620 | 3 | ½ | **Rose Eclair**7 5738 4-9-7 60 (p) DavidAllan 7 | 63 |
| | | | (Tim Easterby) led: pushed along 1/2-way: hdd 2f out and sn rdn: drvn and cl up ent fnl f: kpt on same pce 10/3¹ | |
| 5641 | 4 | 1 | **Gaelic Wizard (IRE)**13 5542 9-8-11 55 (b) GemmaTutty(5) 1 | 55 |
| | | | (Karen Tutty) dwlt and sn outpcd in rr: rdn 2f out: swtchd rt wl over 1f: styd on strly fnl f 4/1² | |
| 3006 | 5 | shd | **Bingo George (IRE)**13 5542 4-8-9 48 GrahamLee 6 | 48 |
| | | | (Mark Rimell) dwlt and rr: hdwy over 2f out: rdn to chse ldrs whn edgd lft ins fnl f: kpt on same pce 16/1 | |
| 0-64 | 6 | 1¼ | **Excellent World (IRE)**99 2472 4-8-13 52 BarryMcHugh 2 | 48 |
| | | | (Tony Coyle) chsd ldng pair: rdn along wl over 1f out: sn drvn and wknd 18/1 | |
| 0625 | 7 | 1¼ | **Etienne Gerard**5 5836 5-9-6 62 (p) LewisEdmunds(3) 5 | 54 |
| | | | (Nigel Tinkler) a towards rr 4/1² | |
| 0041 | 8 | ½ | **Firesnake (IRE)**7 5748 4-9-0 58 6ex (v) CallumRodriguez(5) 9 | 49 |
| | | | (Lisa Williamson) trckd ldrs: hdwy over 2f out: sn chsng ldng pair: rdn over 1f out: and sn wknd 8/1 | |
| 0050 | 9 | 9 | **George Bailey (IRE)**28 4997 5-8-7 46 oh1 NathanEvans 8 | 10 |
| | | | (Suzzanne France) chsd ldrs: rdn along over 2f out: sn wknd 20/1 | |
| 5000 | 10 | 6 | **Nefetari**17 5418 4-8-7 46 oh1 BenCurtis 4 | |
| | | | (Alan Brown) chsd ldrs: rdn along wl over 2f out: sn wknd 40/1 | |

1m 12.36s (-0.34) **Going Correction** -0.15s/f (Firm) **10 Ran SP% 113.5**
Speed ratings (Par 101): **96,95,94,93,93 91,89,89,77,69**
CSF £83.71 CT £323.93 TOTE £6.60: £2.10, £4.40, £1.60; EX 76.20 Trifecta £497.20.
**Owner** Nigel Franklin **Bred** Tally-Ho Stud **Trained** Sproxton, Leics

**FOCUS**
The slower of the two divisions by 0.60sec. Straightforward, modest form.

## 6047 ROA/RACING POST OWNERS JACKPOT FILLIES' H'CAP 7f 218y
**4:30** (4:32) (Class 5) (0-70,72) 3-Y-O+ £3,881 (£1,155; £577; £288) **Stalls** Low

| Form | | | | RPR |
|---|---|---|---|---|
| 61 | 1 | | **Miss Goldsmith (IRE)**15 5466 4-9-6 61 GrahamLee 7 | 69 |
| | | | (Rebecca Menzies) trckd ldrs: hdwy over 2f out: disp ld over 1f out: sn rdn: kpt on to ld nr fin 8/1 | |
| 2232 | 2 | hd | **Totally Magic (IRE)**23 5185 5-9-6 64 LewisEdmunds(3) 6 | 71 |
| | | | (Richard Whitaker) trckd ldrs: hdwy over 2f out: rdn to take slt ld over 1f out: drvn ins fnl f: hdd and no ex towards fin 4/1¹ | |
| 0444 | 3 | 1¾ | **Dominannie (IRE)**12 5578 4-9-3 58 BenCurtis 9 | 61 |
| | | | (Sally Haynes) hld up: hdwy over 3f out: rdn to chse ldrs over 1f out: drvn and kpt on fnl f 11/1 | |
| 000 | 4 | ½ | **Lil Sophella (IRE)**23 5185 8-10-0 69 JackGarritty 13 | 71 |
| | | | (Patrick Holmes) hld up towards rr: hdwy 3f out: rdn wl over 1f out: kpt on wl fnl f 22/1 | |
| -304 | 5 | shd | **Dellaguista (IRE)**43 4437 3-9-10 72 DavidAllan 10 | 73 |
| | | | (Tim Easterby) led: rdn along wl over 2f out: drvn wl over 1f out: hdd appr fnl f: kpt on 15/2³ | |
| 0546 | 6 | 2¼ | **Yorkshire Pudding**10 5666 3-8-11 59 (p1) JamesSullivan 8 | 54 |
| | | | (Tim Easterby) prom: rdn along over 2f out: drvn wl over 1f out: grad wknd fnl f 14/1 | |

3310 **7** *2* **Arcane Dancer (IRE)**[6] 5802 4-9-4 **62**................(p) AdamMcNamara(3) 5 54
(Lawrence Mullaney) *bhd: hdwy over 2f out: sn rdn and kpt on fnl f* **9/1**

0-50 **8** *3/4* **Al Hawraa**[100] 2430 4-9-5 **60**................................................ ShaneGray 11 50
(Kevin Ryan) *dwlt: a towards rr* **25/1**

2402 **9** *6* **Mama Africa (IRE)**[10] 5666 3-9-1 **68**............................(p) JaneElliott(5) 1 43
(David Barron) *cl up: rdn along over 2f out: sn drvn and wknd over 1f out* **8/1**

2520 **10** *9* **Wedding Breakfast (IRE)**[105] 2274 3-9-0 **67**....... CallumRodriguez(5) 2 22
(Richard Ford) *chsd ldrs on inner: rdn along over 2f out: sn wknd* **50/1**

0010 **11** *23* **Cline**[26] 5074 4-9-5 **60**...................................................(p) KevinStott 12
(Kevin Ryan) *midfield: effrt 3f out and sn rdn along and wknd 2f out* **10/1**

2211 **12** *3 1/2* **Rosy Ryan (IRE)**[14] 5497 7-9-7 **62**........................................ JoeDoyle 4
(Tina Jackson) *dwlt: a bhd* **9/2**[2]

5-0 **13** *1 1/4* **Lilly Ballerina (IRE)**[102] 2362 3-8-2 **50** oh5.............(t[1]) DuranFentiman 3
(Lee James) *wnt rt s: midfield: rdn along 1/2-way: sn lost pl and bhd* **150/1**

1m 42.61s (2.51) **Going Correction** +0.425s/f (Yiel)
**WFA** 3 from 4yo+ 7lb **13** Ran SP% **117.1**
Speed ratings (Par 100): **104,103,102,101,101 99,97,96,90,81 58,54,53**
CSF £38.03 CT £358.38 TOTE £7.50: £2.70, £1.40, £3.40; EX 43.20 Trifecta £641.60.
**Owner** West Coast Racing & Partner **Bred** G Devlin **Trained** Mordon, Durham

**FOCUS**
Race distance increased by 30yds. The first two raced alongside each other much of the way and had a good scrap up the straight. Ordinary fillies' form, rated around the runner-up.

## 6048 "PIRATES FAMILY DAY" - FRIDAY 1ST SEPTEMBER H'CAP 1m 4f 8y
**5:00** (5:00) (Class 6) (0-60,62) 3-Y-O £3,234 (£962; £481; £240) **Stalls** High

Form RPR

3523 **1** **Clenymistra (IRE)**[11] 5618 3-9-11 **62**........................................ PhillipMakin 9 69
(David O'Meara) *hld up: hdwy on wd outside 3f out: chsd ldrs 2f out: rdn over 1f out and sn chal: led ins fnl f: drvn out* **15/2**[3]

00-4 **2** *nk* **Eyreborn (IRE)**[10] 5648 3-9-8 **62**..................................(h) CliffordLee(3) 6 68
(Keith Dalgleish) *hld up: hdwy 3f out: chsd ldrs 2f out: rdn over 1f out: kpt on wl fnl f* **12/1**

0633 **3** *3/4* **Arcadian Sea (IRE)**[17] 5406 3-9-2 **53**................................ JoeFanning 8 58
(William Jarvis) *trckd ldr: hdwy to ld 21/2f out: rdn wl over 1f out: drvn and hdd ins fnl f: kpt on same pce* **5/1**[2]

-023 **4** *1/2* **Broughtons Admiral**[19] 5336 3-9-7 **58**..................(v[1]) StevieDonohoe 12 63
(Henry Spiller) *dwlt and towards rr: hdwy into midfield after 4f: effrt to trck ldrs whn hmpd over 2f out: chsd ldrs and hmpd again over 1f out: sn swtchd rt and rdn: styd on wl fnl f* **17/2**

4544 **5** *1 1/4* **Princess Nearco (IRE)**[11] 5618 3-9-10 **61**................(p[1]) JackGarritty 10 63
(Patrick Holmes) *dwlt and rr: hdwy on wd outside over 2f out: rdn to chse ;ldrs and edgd lft over 1f out and ins fnl f: kpt on wl towards fin* **14/1**

5123 **6** *1 3/4* **Bollin Ted**[6] 5800 3-9-6 **57**..................................................... DavidAllan 7 56
(Tim Easterby) *trckd ldrs.: hdwy 3f out: hung lft over 2f out: rdn and hung lft again over 1f out: sn drvn and btn* **9/4**[1]

0000 **7** *2 1/4* **Neptune Star**[22] 5215 3-8-8 **45**......................................... NathanEvans 11 41
(Michael Easterby) *hld up and bhd: hdwy 3f out: rdn over 2f out: styd on appr fnl f* **16/1**

0-02 **8** *4* **Velvet Voice**[10] 5653 3-9-10 **61**................................................ BenCurtis 4 51
(Mark H Tompkins) *chsd ldrs: hdwy over 3f out: rdn along over 2f out: sn drvn and wknd* **12/1**

0-00 **9** *3 1/4* **Hot Gossip (IRE)**[135] 1514 3-8-8 **45**.................................. JamesSullivan 3 30
(Dianne Sayer) *towards rr whn hmpd after 31/2f: a bhd* **50/1**

5050 **10** *3 1/2* **Spirit Of Rome (IRE)**[29] 4978 3-9-2 **53**.............................(p) KevinStott 2 32
(James Bethell) *trckd ldng pair on inner: rdn along over 3f out: sn wknd* **25/1**

0000 **11** *1* **Thornton Mary**[11] 5617 3-8-8 **45**.............................................. JoeDoyle 5 23
(Brian Rothwell) *chsd ldng pair: hung rt home turn over 3f out: sn rdn along and wknd* **100/1**

-334 **12** *1 1/4* **Siyahamba (IRE)**[11] 5617 3-9-2 **53**........................................ GrahamLee 13 29
(Bryan Smart) *in tch: pushed along over 4f out: rdn 3f out: sn wknd* **14/1**

0434 **13** *8* **Conistone**[38] 4603 3-9-1 **55**..................................(p[1]) AdamMcNamara(3) 1 18
(James Bethell) *led: rdn along 3f out: hdd 21/2f out: sn wknd* **14/1**

2m 40.39s (4.19) **Going Correction** +0.425s/f (Yiel) **13** Ran SP% **117.8**
Speed ratings (Par 98): **103,102,102,101,101 99,98,95,93,91 90,89,84**
CSF £92.00 CT £497.19 TOTE £8.70: £2.80, £2.50, £2.30; EX 51.20 Trifecta £632.70.
**Owner** Hambleton Racing Ltd XXVII **Bred** Mrs E Fitzsimons **Trained** Upper Helmsley, N Yorks

**FOCUS**
Race distance increased by 40yds. The two at the top of the weights came to the fore. Modest, straightforward form.

## 6049 BETFAIR "NOVICE" FLAT AMATEUR RIDERS' H'CAP 7f
**5:30** (5:30) (Class 5) (0-75,75) 4-Y-0+ £3,743 (£1,161; £580; £290) **Stalls** Low

Form RPR

3100 **1** **Dark Confidant (IRE)**[3] 5917 4-9-11 **58**.................... MissEllaMcCain 4 67
(Donald McCain) *mde all: rdn along 2f out: kpt on wl fnl f* **6/1**[3]

6533 **2** *1* **Ticks The Boxes (IRE)**[8] 5696 5-10-6 **67**..................(p) MissAMcCain 3 72
(John Wainwright) *t.k.h: trckd ldng pair: hdwy 1/2-way and sn chsng wnr: rdn 2f out: kpt on u.p fnl f* **9/2**[2]

4000 **3** *1 3/4* **Mustaqbal (IRE)**[8] 5699 5-10-5 **69**...........................(p) MissCADods(3) 6 69
(Michael Dods) *hld up: hdwy on wd outside 3f out: rdn and hung lft wl over 1f out: kpt on fnl f* **10/1**

0056 **4** *3/4* **Sunnua (IRE)**[21] 5258 4-10-1 **62**..................................(p[1]) MrBillyGarritty 8 60
(Richard Fahey) *wnt rt s: towards rr: hdwy over 2f out: rdn wl over 1f out: kpt on fnl f* **6/1**[3]

1055 **5** *nk* **Mr Cool Cash**[14] 5497 5-10-7 **68**.............................. MrTGreenwood 5 65
(Richard Guest) *trckd ldrs: hdwy wl over 2f out: rdn wl over 1f out: edgd lft appr fnl f: kpt on same pce* **4/1**[1]

1006 **6** *shd* **Tanawar (IRE)**[15] 5466 7-10-2 **63**...........................(b) MissEmilyBullock 7 60
(Ruth Carr) *hld up in rr: hdwy wl over 2f out: rdn wl over 1f out: kpt on same pce fnl f* **9/1**

0-06 **7** *1/2* **Woody Bay**[38] 4609 7-11-0 **75**............................................... MrWJMilburn 2 71
(Mark Walford) *t.k.h: chsd ldrs on inner: swtchd rt to outer and hdwy 3f out: rdn along 2f out: sn drvn and one pce* **15/2**

2664 **8** *3/4* **Make On Madam (IRE)**[14] 5496 5-10-9 **70**...........(h) PoppyBridgwater 9 64
(Les Eyre) *dwlt: a rr* **15/2**

2110 **9** *19* **Prince Of Time**[69] 3454 5-10-5 **69**.................... MrJordanSwarbrick(3) 1 11
(Richard Ford) *t.k.h: chsd wnr: rdn along wl over 2f out: wknd wl over 1f out: bhd and eased fnl f* **33/1**

1m 29.8s (2.60) **Going Correction** +0.425s/f (Yiel) **9** Ran SP% **112.3**
Speed ratings (Par 103): **102,100,98,98,97 97,96,96,74**
CSF £31.97 CT £262.54 TOTE £9.00: £2.70, £1.50, £4.10; EX 40.70 Trifecta £497.20.
**Owner** D McCain Jnr **Bred** Rabbah Bloodstock Limited **Trained** Cholmondeley, Cheshire

**FOCUS**
Race distance increased by 30yds. A modest contest dominated from the front by the winner, who's rated back to his best.
T/Plt: £35.60 to a £1 stake. Pool: £80,968.79 - 1,657.89 winning units T/Qpdt: £11.80 to a £1 stake. Pool: £6,200.25 - 385.65 winning units **Joe Rowntree**

# 5978 DEAUVILLE (R-H)
Tuesday, August 15

**OFFICIAL GOING: Polytrack: fast; turf: good**

## 6050a PRIX DU PORT DE DEAUVILLE (CLAIMER) (2YO) (ROUND) (TURF) 1m (R)
**12:35** (12:35) 2-Y-0 **£11,538** (£4,615; £3,461; £2,307; £1,153)

RPR

**1** **Controversial Lady (IRE)**[4] 5907 2-8-3 0........... MathieuPelletan(5) 12 73
(J S Moore) *broke wl: led narrowly on outer: 1 1/2l clr bef 1/2-way: drvn clr 1 1/2f out: pushed out fnl f: comf* **48/10**[3]

**2** *3 1/2* **Tremont (FR)** 2-9-1 0.................................................... CristianDemuro 7 72
(S Wattel, France) **12/5**[1]

**3** *snk* **Uchronique (FR)**[19] 2-8-8 0............................................... AlexisBadel 2 65
(M Boutin, France) **111/10**

**4** *nk* **Jugeotte (FR)**[12] 5585 2-8-11 0.............................(b) StephanePasquier 8 67
(Y Gourraud, France) **91/10**

**5** *3 1/2* **Palya (FR)**[12] 5585 2-8-8 0.........................................(b) AntoineHamelin 4 56
(Matthieu Palussiere, France) **7/2**[2]

**6** *snk* **Occhiobello (FR)**[11] 5629 2-8-8 0......................... VincentCheminaud 9 56
(Robert Collet, France) **234/10**

**7** *snk* **Story Begins (FR)** 2-8-5 0......................... MmeAlexiaCeccarello(10) 11 62
(A Spanu, France) **89/1**

**8** *1 3/4* **Alifax**[12] 5572 2-9-4 0............................................................ DougieCostello 5 61
(Jamie Osborne) *broke wl: pressed ldr on inner: angled out and drvn 2 1/2f out: rdn and no imp 1 1/2f out: lost 2nd ent fnl f and wknd* **51/10**

**9** *1 1/2* **First Pond (FR)**[12] 5585 2-8-0 0.................................... AlexisPouchin(8) 10 48
(Y Gourraud, France) **87/1**

**10** *7* **Say About It**[7] 5776 2-9-1 0.................................................... TonyPiccone 3 39
(J S Moore) *dwlt: rapid hdwy to chse ldrs on inner: scrubbed along to hold share of 4th over 2 1/2f out: wknd u.p fnl 1 1/2f* **27/1**

**11** *3/4* **Wise Wishes (FR)** 2-9-4 0......................................... RonanThomas 6 40
(Robert Collet, France) **202/10**

1m 43.57s (2.77) **11** Ran SP% **118.1**
PARI-MUTUEL (all including 1 euro stake): WIN 5.80; PLACE 2.00, 1.50, 2.60; DF 8.20; SF 20.50.
**Owner** Mrs Wendy Jarrett & J S Moore **Bred** Edgeridge Ltd **Trained** Upper Lambourn, Berks

## 6051a PRIX DE LA VALLEE D'AUGE - ETALON KENDARGENT (LISTED RACE) (2YO) (TURF) 5f
**1:05** (1:05) 2-Y-0 **£25,641** (£10,256; £7,692; £5,128; £2,564)

RPR

**1** **Pursuing The Dream (IRE)**[24] 5150 2-8-13 0............ DougieCostello 9 100
(Jamie Osborne) *w.w towards rr on outer: n.m.r but travelling wl whn shkn up appr fnl f: r.o u.p to ld last 25yds* **201/10**

**2** *nk* **Coeur De Beaute (FR)**[22] 5230 2-8-13 0................ StephanePasquier 6 99
(M Delcher Sanchez, France) **19/5**[2]

**3** *1 1/4* **Ken Colt (IRE)**[39] 4595 2-9-2 0......................................... CristianDemuro 7 98
(F Chappet, France) **144/10**

**4** *2* **Denaar (IRE)**[13] 5526 2-9-2 0............................................. FrankieDettori 4 90
(Richard Hannon) *a cl up: 4th and drvn over 2f out: outpcd by ldrs 1 1/2f out: kpt on at same pce* **22/5**[3]

**5** *1/2* **Reflect Alexander (IRE)**[27] 5015 2-8-13 0.................. MaximeGuyon 5 86
(David Evans) *racd in fnl trio but wl in tch: drvn and nt clr run wl over 1 1/2f out: kpt on at one pce fnl f: nvr on terms* **106/10**

**6** *1/2* **Sagres**[34] 2-8-13 0...................................................(b) MickaelBarzalona 2 84
(F-H Graffard, France) **93/10**

**7** *2 1/2* **Mister Five Euros (FR)**[26] 5090 2-9-2 0.................(b[1]) TonyPiccone 10 78
(F Chappet, France) **33/1**

**8** *nk* **Sestilio Jet (FR)**[51] 4131 2-9-2 0......................... ChristopheSoumillon 3 77
(Antonio Marcialis, Italy) **44/5**

**9** *1/2* **Teckwin (FR)**[112] 2-9-2 0........................................................ OlivierPeslier 1 75
(J-V Toux, France) **194/10**

**10** *1 1/4* **Rimini (FR)**[26] 5090 2-9-2 0................................................ JulienAuge 8 70
(C Ferland, France) **11/5**[1]

58.17s (0.67) **10** Ran SP% **118.2**
PARI-MUTUEL (all including 1 euro stake): WIN 21.10; PLACE 5.30, 2.30, 4.20; DF 64.80; SF 149.20.
**Owner** S Short, I Barratt, A Signy & B Spiers **Bred** Kildaragh Stud **Trained** Upper Lambourn, Berks

**FOCUS**
The form makes sense,

## 6052a PRIX GONTAUT-BIRON HONG KONG JOCKEY CLUB (GROUP 3) (4YO+) (TURF) 1m 2f
**3:00** (3:00) 4-Y-0+
**£34,188** (£13,675; £10,256; £6,837; £1,709; £1,709)

RPR

**1** **First Sitting**[59] 3856 6-9-0 0.................................................... GeraldMosse 6 115
(Chris Wall) *chsd ldr: rdn to ld 2f out: hung rt 1f out: began to weaken 75yds out: hld on wl* **68/10**

**2** *3/4* **Garlingari (FR)**[27] 5046 6-9-0 0.......................................(p) RonanThomas 1 114+
(Mme C Barande-Barbe, France) *trckd ldrs: rdn and kpt on wl fr 2f out: nt able to chal* **11/2**[3]

**3** *2* **Zafiro (FR)**[18] 5-8-11 0................................................ Jean-BernardEyquem 2 107
(J-C Rouget, France) *led: rdn and hdd 2f out: no ex fr over 1f out* **28/1**

**4** *nse* **Subway Dancer (IRE)**[27] 5046 5-8-11 0.................. VincentCheminaud 4 106+
(Z Koplik, Czech Republic) *hld up in rr: rdn over 2f out: kpt on fnl f: nrst fin* **28/1**

**5** *3/4* **Alignement**[18] 4-8-11 0..................................................... MaximeGuyon 3 105
(C Laffon-Parias, France) *hld up in 4th: rdn and no imp fr 2 1/2f out* **9/2**[2]

**5** *dht* **Almanzor (FR)**[304] 7353 4-8-11 0......................... ChristopheSoumillon 5 105
(J-C Rouget, France) *dwlt: hld up in 5th: rdn and unable qck under 2f out: wknd last 100yds* **1/2**[1]

2m 6.11s (-4.09) **6** Ran SP% **120.0**
PARI-MUTUEL (all including 1 euro stake): WIN 7.80; PLACE 5.50, 4.20; SF 41.40.
**Owner** Bringloe & Clarke **Bred** Juddmonte Farms Ltd **Trained** Newmarket, Suffolk

**FOCUS**
This looked a gilt-edged opportunity for Almanzor to make a winning return following a long absence, but he proved to be way below expectations. The pace seemed fairly decent throughout.

## 6053a PRIX GUILLAUME D'ORNANO HARAS DU LOGIS SAINT-GERMAIN (GROUP 2) (3YO) (TURF) 1m 2f
**3:45** (3:45) 3-Y-O **£194,871** (£75,213; £35,897; £23,931; £11,965)

RPR
1 **Eminent (IRE)**[38] 4638 3-9-2 0 ........ RyanMoore 4 117
(Martyn Meade) *mde all: rdn and kpt on wl fr 2f out: unchal* **17/5**[3]
2 3 **Salouen (IRE)**[38] 4638 3-9-2 0 ........ MaximeGuyon 3 111
(Sylvester Kirk) *chsd ldr: rdn and kpt on fr 2f out: no imp on wnr fnl f* **25/1**
3 1 3/4 **Avilius**[30] 4941 3-9-2 0 ........ MickaelBarzalona 6 107+
(A Fabre, France) *in tch in 4th: rdn and kpt on fr 2f out* **15/1**
4 2 1/2 **Last Kingdom (USA)**[48] 4235 3-9-2 0 ........ SilvestreDeSousa 5 102+
(A Fabre, France) *towards rr of midfield: rdn and kpt on steadily fr 2f out: n.d* **44/5**
5 2 1/2 **Brametot (IRE)**[72] 3368 3-9-2 0 ........ CristianDemuro 8 97+
(J-C Rouget, France) *missed break and s.i.s: in rr: rdn and kpt on steadily fr over 2f out: nvr in contention* **13/10**[1]
6 2 1/2 **Mask Of Time (IRE)**[14] 5522 3-9-2 0 ........ VincentCheminaud 7 92+
(A Fabre, France) *a towards rr* **57/1**
7 snk **Recoletos (FR)**[72] 3368 3-9-2 0 ........ OlivierPeslier 1 92+
(C Laffon-Parias, France) *midfield: rdn 2f out: wknd fnl f* **3/1**[2]
8 3 **Soleil Marin (IRE)**[72] 3368 3-9-2 0 ........ Pierre-CharlesBoudot 2 86+
(A Fabre, France) *trckd ldrs: rdn 2f out: wknd 1 1/2f out: eased ins fnl f* **22/1**

2m 2.26s (-7.94) **8 Ran SP% 117.6**
PARI-MUTUEL (all including 1 euro stake): WIN 4.40; PLACE 3.00, 6.80, 5.40; DF 43.60; SF 72.50.
**Owner** Sir Peter Vela **Bred** Premier Bloodstock **Trained** Newmarket, Suffolk
**FOCUS**
This looked a Group 1 contest in disguise considering the calibre of the horse running, but it was blown apart by the winner, who adopted new tactics.

## 6054a PRIX DE LIEUREY (GROUP 3) (3YO FILLIES) (ROUND) (TURF) 1m (R)
**4:30** (4:30) 3-Y-O **£34,188** (£13,675; £10,256; £6,837; £3,418)

RPR
1 **Lady Frankel**[66] 3612 3-8-11 0 ........ Pierre-CharlesBoudot 8 105+
(A Fabre, France) *hld up towards rr: rdn and hdwy fr 2f out: nt clr run 1 1/2f out: forced to wait for gap and stmbld sltly appr fnl f: swtchd to outer ins fnl f: sn drvn: styd on wl to ld cl home* **23/5**[3]
2 snk **Tisbutadream (IRE)**[18] 5352 3-8-11 0 ........ RyanMoore 6 105
(David Elsworth) *chsd ldr: rdn 2f out: led narrowly 1 1/2f out: hdd appr fnl f: drvn and rallied to ld again ins fnl f: kpt on: hdd cl home* **7/1**
3 3/4 **Limited Edition (FR)**[23] 5196 3-8-11 0 ........ TonyPiccone 5 103
(E Lellouche, France) *led: rdn under 2f out: hdd narrowly 1 1/2f out: led again appr fnl f: drvn and hdd ins fnl f: no ex clsng stages* **22/1**
4 snk **Esquisse**[23] 5196 3-8-11 0 ........ MaximeGuyon 3 103
(A Fabre, France) *midfield: rdn 2f out: gd hdwy appr fnl f: ev ch 1f out: no ex last 75yds* **6/4**[1]
5 nk **Enlighted (IRE)**[7] 5777 3-8-11 0 ........ AurelienLemaitre 4 102
(F Head, France) *towards rr of midfield: hdwy fr 2f out: rdn 1 1/2f out: drvn and ev ch 1f out: no ex last 75yds* **10/1**
6 1 1/4 **Monroe Bay (IRE)**[37] 4665 3-8-11 0 ........(b) ChristopheSoumillon 1 99
(P Bary, France) *trckd ldrs: rdn 2f out: nt clr run 1 1/2f out: wknd steadily fr under 1f out* **7/2**[2]
7 4 **Silver Storm (FR)**[43] 4456 3-8-11 0 ........ OlivierPeslier 7 90
(C Ferland, France) *a towards rr* **12/1**
8 8 **Charm Appeal (FR)**[94] 2644 3-8-11 0 ........ AlexisBadel 2 71
(H-F Devin, France) *in tch: rdn over 2f out: lost pl 1 1/2f out: sn btn* **12/1**

1m 41.02s (0.22) **8 Ran SP% 121.4**
PARI-MUTUEL (all including 1 euro stake): WIN 5.60; PLACE 2.30, 3.00, 4.60; DF 19.60; SF 40.00.
**Owner** Gestut Ammerland **Bred** Ammerland Verwaltung Gmbh & Co Kg **Trained** Chantilly, France

# 5492 BEVERLEY (R-H)
Wednesday, August 16

**OFFICIAL GOING: Good to firm (good in places; 7.7)**
Wind: Blustery across Weather: Fine and dry

## 6055 WELCOME TO FLEMINGATE LADIES DAY NOVICE AUCTION STKS (DIV I) 5f
**2:10** (2:11) (Class 5) 2-Y-O **£3,881** (£1,155; £577; £288) **Stalls Low**

Form RPR
0221 1 **Arcavallo (IRE)**[15] 5494 2-9-9 76 ........ PaulMulrennan 2 80
(Michael Dods) *trckd ldrs: led 3f out: rdn over 1f out: edgd lft ins fnl f: kpt on* **6/4**[1]
5 2 1 1/2 **Biddy Brady (USA)**[15] 5494 2-8-11 0 ........ DavidAllan 10 62
(Tim Easterby) *wnt lft s: sn led: hdd 3f out: cl up: rdn and ev ch over 1f out: kpt on same pce fnl f* **10/1**
3120 3 1 1/2 **Undercover Brother**[18] 5440 2-9-9 73 ........ DanielTudhope 3 69
(David O'Meara) *prom: rdn along wl over 1f out: kpt on same pce fnl f* **7/2**[3]
4 3/4 **Bonanza Bowls** 2-9-2 0 ........ ConnorBeasley 8 59
(Bryan Smart) *prom: rdn along over 2f out: kpt on same pce fnl f* **16/1**
00 5 2 1/4 **Navarra Princess (IRE)**[11] 5665 2-8-11 0 ........ TomEaves 4 46
(Don Cantillon) *in rr: rdn along 2f out: kpt on fnl f* **22/1**
0 6 1/2 **Stark Reality (IRE)**[27] 5058 2-8-11 0 ........ AndrewMullen 1 44
(Nigel Tinkler) *dwlt and in rr: rdn along 2f out: kpt on fnl f* **33/1**
7 1 1/4 **Barney Bullet (IRE)** 2-9-2 0 ........ PatrickMathers 6 45
(Noel Wilson) *dwlt and wnt rt s: a towards rr* **25/1**
62 8 1/2 **Dandy's Beano (IRE)**[13] 5575 2-8-11 0 ........ KevinStott 9 38+
(Kevin Ryan) *t.k.h: chsd ldrs on outer: hdwy 2f out: rdn and hung persistently rt fr over 1f out: wknd fnl f* **2/1**[2]

1m 4.26s (0.76) **Going Correction** 0.0s/f (Good) **8 Ran SP% 121.7**
Speed ratings (Par 94): **93,90,88,87,83 82,80,79**
CSF £18.92 TOTE £2.50: £1.02, £2.90, £1.40; EX 21.50 Trifecta £67.70.
**Owner** P Appleton & Mrs Anne Elliott **Bred** Nicola And Eleanor Kent **Trained** Denton, Co Durham

**FOCUS**
The going was good to firm, good in places. After riding in the opener Tom Eaves and Kevin Stott called the ground good while Andrew Mullen and Paul Mulrennan said it was just on the quick side. An interesting contest run at an honest pace. A step forward from the winner.

## 6056 WELCOME TO FLEMINGATE LADIES DAY NOVICE AUCTION STKS (DIV II) 5f
**2:40** (2:42) (Class 5) 2-Y-O **£3,881** (£1,155; £577; £288) **Stalls Low**

Form RPR
1 **Equitant** 2-9-2 0 ........ TonyHamilton 1 77+
(Richard Fahey) *cl up on inner: led 2f out: rdn clr appr fnl f: kpt on strly* **8/1**
6 2 2 3/4 **Kyllachy Dragon (IRE)**[19] 5370 2-9-2 0 ........ DavidNolan 3 68
(Iain Jardine) *trckd ldrs: swtchd rt to inner and effrt 2f out: n.m.r and swtchd lft over 1f out: sn rdn to chse wnr ent fnl f: sn no imp* **3/1**[2]
521 3 1 1/2 **Wensley**[17] 5453 2-9-9 85 ........ DanielTudhope 7 69
(James Bethell) *led: hdd 2f out and sn rdn along: drvn and kpt on same pce fnl f* **5/2**[1]
30 4 shd **Weeton (IRE)**[39] 4606 2-9-2 0 ........ JoeDoyle 4 62
(Julie Camacho) *t.k.h early: trckd ldrs: effrt 2f out: sn rdn and n.m.r over 1f out: drvn and kpt on fnl f* **5/1**[3]
4 5 1/2 **Ghost**[11] 5665 2-8-11 0 ........ JasonHart 9 55
(John Quinn) *wnt lft s: t.k.h and sn chsng ldrs on outer: rdn along wl over 1f out: kpt on fnl f* **6/1**
6 3/4 **Sir Derrick (IRE)** 2-9-2 0 ........ DavidAllan 5 57+
(Tim Easterby) *dwlt and green in rr: bhd 1/2-way: hdwy over 1f out: kpt on wl fnl f* **20/1**
7 11 **Carpet Time (IRE)** 2-9-2 0 ........ BenCurtis 8 18
(David Barron) *chsd ldrs: rdn along 1/2-way: sn outpcd* **25/1**
33 8 nk **Me Before You (IRE)**[23] 5210 2-8-11 0 ........ PhillipMakin 2 12
(David O'Meara) *cl up: rdn along and ev ch wl over 1f out: wknd appr fnl f* **8/1**
9 8 **Pavarella Shoes** 2-8-11 0 ........ PatrickMathers 6
(Noel Wilson) *chsd ldrs: rdn along 1/2-way: sn outpcd and bhd* **40/1**

1m 4.16s (0.66) **Going Correction** 0.0s/f (Good) **9 Ran SP% 117.8**
Speed ratings (Par 94): **94,89,87,87,86 85,67,66,54**
CSF £32.28 TOTE £9.50: £2.60, £1.50, £1.40; EX 40.70 Trifecta £156.50.
**Owner** Bearstone Stud Ltd & J Stimpson **Bred** Bearstone Stud Ltd **Trained** Musley Bank, N Yorks
**FOCUS**
A truly run contest with a nice start from the winner.

## 6057 GUEST AND PHILIPS AT FLEMINGATE EBF NOVICE STKS 7f 96y
**3:10** (3:12) (Class 5) 2-Y-O **£3,881** (£1,155; £577; £288) **Stalls Low**

Form RPR
3 1 **Baileys Excelerate (FR)**[12] 5600 2-9-2 0 ........ JoeFanning 8 76
(Mark Johnston) *mde most: rdn wl over 1f out: drvn and edgd lft ins fnl f: kpt on wl towards fin* **3/1**[2]
14 2 nk **International Man**[15] 5492 2-9-9 0 ........ JackGarritty 2 82
(Richard Fahey) *in tch: hdwy on outer over 2f out: rdn over 1f out: drvn and styd on strly to chal wl ins fnl f: kpt on* **7/2**[3]
6 3 1 3/4 **Global Conqueror**[33] 4859 2-9-2 0 ........ AndreaAtzeni 12 74+
(Simon Crisford) *in tch: hdwy on wd outside whn bmpd over 2f out: rdn along wl over 1f out: kpt on wl fnl f* **5/2**[1]
46 4 1/2 **Poppy Walton (IRE)**[37] 4689 2-8-11 0 ........ AndrewMullen 7 64
(Ollie Pears) *t.k.h early: chsd ldng pair on inner: pushed along 2f out: rdn over 1f out: drvn and kpt on same pce fnl f* **40/1**
5 2 1/2 **Real Gent** 2-9-2 0 ........ TomEaves 11 63+
(Kevin Ryan) *in tch: hdwy on outer whn hmpd over 2f out: sn swtchd rt and rdn over 1f out: no imp* **11/2**
6 1 **A Bit Of A Touch (IRE)** 2-9-2 0 ........ TonyHamilton 9 61
(Richard Fahey) *towards rr: pushed along and hdwy over 2f out: rdn over 1f out: kpt on wl fnl f: nrst fin* **14/1**
3342 7 3/4 **Miss Mo Brown Bear (IRE)**[14] 5537 2-8-6 70 ......(p) BenRobinson(5) 10 54
(Richard Hannon) *cl up: chal over 2f out: sn rdn and ev ch: drvn and wknd ent fnl f* **10/1**
0 8 3 3/4 **Carlini (IRE)**[26] 5105 2-9-2 0 ........ JasonHart 3 50
(Brian Meehan) *chsd ldrs: rdn along over 2f out: drvn and wknd over 1f out* **11/1**
05 9 13 **Cum Spiro Spero (IRE)**[15] 5492 2-8-11 0 ........ BarryMcHugh 5 13
(Tony Coyle) *a in rr* **50/1**
5 10 1/2 **Nunnery Lane**[24] 5180 2-9-2 0 ........ NathanEvans 4 17
(Michael Easterby) *in tch: rdn along wl over 2f out: sn wknd* **50/1**
0 11 1/2 **Lady Isle**[8] 5735 2-8-11 0 ........ JamesSullivan 1 11
(Grant Tuer) *dwlt: a in rr* **66/1**
0 12 39 **Arabellas Fortune**[21] 5278 2-8-11 0 ........ PaulMulrennan 6
(James Ewart) *a in rr* **80/1**

1m 34.34s (0.54) **Going Correction** 0.0s/f (Good) **12 Ran SP% 124.4**
Speed ratings (Par 94): **96,95,93,93,90 89,88,83,69,68 67,23**
CSF £14.58 TOTE £3.60: £1.60, £1.50, £1.40; EX 15.10 Trifecta £46.00.
**Owner** G R Bailey Ltd (Baileys Horse Feeds) **Bred** Baileys Horse Feeds **Trained** Middleham Moor, N Yorks
**FOCUS**
Race run over an additional 7yds. The pace was sound for this open contest. Straightforward form rated around the first four.

## 6058 DEBENHAMS AT FLEMINGATE CLASSIFIED CLAIMING STKS 7f 96y
**3:40** (3:40) (Class 6) 3-Y-O+ **£2,587** (£770; £384; £192) **Stalls Low**

Form RPR
1140 1 **Talent Scout (IRE)**[23] 5213 11-8-8 75 ........(p) GemmaTutty(5) 6 51+
(Karen Tutty) *sn led: rdn over 1f out: drvn ins fnl f: hld on gamely* **9/4**[2]
5133 2 nk **Chiswick Bey (IRE)**[7] 5805 9-8-9 70 ........ AdamMcNamara(3) 1 50+
(Richard Fahey) *trckd ldrs on inner: hdwy 2f out: swtchd rt and rdn whn n.m.r over 1f out: drvn ent fnl f: kpt on wl towards fin* **6/4**[1]
0650 3 1/2 **Bold Spirit**[7] 5802 6-9-0 52 ........(t) DanielTudhope 8 51+
(Declan Carroll) *hld up in rr: hdwy and swtchd lft to outer 1 1/2f out: sn rdn: drvn and styd on wl fnl f* **12/1**
0305 4 2 1/4 **Palindrome (USA)**[11] 5649 4-8-13 44 ........(b) LewisEdmunds(3) 3 47
(Ronald Thompson) *t.k.h: cl up: chal over 2f out: rdn along wl over 1f out: drvn ent fnl f: kpt on same pce* **20/1**
6000 5 1/2 **Merdon Castle (IRE)**[9] 5696 5-9-6 75 ........(e) JamesSullivan 9 50+
(Ruth Carr) *trckd ldrs: hdwy over 2f out: rdn over 1f out: drvn and kpt on same pce fnl f* **5/1**[3]
5455 6 3/4 **Dream Team**[34] 4785 3-9-5 67 ........(p) PaulMulrennan 5 50+
(Michael Dods) *hld up in rr: hdwy on inner over 1f out: sn rdn and n.m.r ins fnl f: no imp* **17/2**

0053 7 12 **Zebedee Star**[19] 5374 3-8-7 45 CamHardie 4 9
(Karen Tutty) *chsd ldng pair on outer: pushed along over 2f out: rdn wl over 1f out: wknd appr fnl f: sn eased* **20/1**

1m 34.52s (0.72) **Going Correction** 0.0s/f (Good)
**WFA** 3 from 4yo+ 5lb 7 Ran SP% **115.2**
Speed ratings (Par 101): **95,94,94,91,90 90,76**
CSF £6.12 TOTE £3.00: £1.70, £1.40; EX 6.50 Trifecta £37.80.Merdon Castle was claimed by Mrs Jane Chapple-Hyam £8,000. Palindrome was claimed by Mrs Marjorie Fife for £6,000.
**Owner** Thoroughbred Homes Ltd **Bred** Johnston King **Trained** Osmotherley, N Yorks

**FOCUS**
Race run over an additional 7yds. Not a bad race for the grade with the winner following up his success in this 12 months earlier. It was very slowly run and the third and fourth govern the bare merit.

## 6059 JILL WILLOWS H'CAP 1m 1f 207y
**4:10** (4:11) (Class 4) (0-85,84) 3-Y-O+ **£6,301** (£1,886; £943; £472; £235) **Stalls** Low

Form RPR
2512 1 **Save The Bees**[9] 5704 9-9-3 80 GerO'Neill(7) 5 86
(Declan Carroll) *cl up: led after 1 1/2f: rdn along 3f out: hdd wl over 1f out and sn drvn: cl up ent fnl f: rallied gamely to ld again towards fin* **6/1**

32 2 hd **Hollywood Road (IRE)**[30] 4976 4-10-0 84 (b) TomEaves 4 89
(Don Cantillon) *hld up in rr: swtchd to outer and hdwy over 1f out: rdn ent fnl f: fin strly* **4/1**[3]

2151 3 nk **Alexander M (IRE)**[10] 5686 3-9-0 77 6ex JoeFanning 1 81
(Mark Johnston) *cl up: slt ld wl over 1f: rdn ent fnl f: sn drvn: hdd and no ex towards fin* **6/5**[1]

0013 4 2 1/2 **Sunglider (IRE)**[37] 4692 4-9-9 79 (vt) DanielTudhope 6 78
(David O'Meara) *trckd ldrs: hdwy 2f out: rdn over 1f out: drvn fnl f and no imp* **3/1**[2]

06 5 1 3/4 **Maraakib (IRE)**[17] 5455 5-9-5 75 (p) DavidNolan 3 71
(David O'Meara) *led 1 1/2f: trckd ldng pair: pushed along 3f out: rdn wl over 1f out: sn drvn and one pce fnl f* **10/1**

2m 5.18s (-1.82) **Going Correction** 0.0s/f (Good)
**WFA** 3 from 4yo+ 7lb 5 Ran SP% **113.8**
Speed ratings (Par 105): **107,106,106,104,103**
CSF £29.72 TOTE £5.60: £2.40, £2.10; EX 25.60 Trifecta £33.70.
**Owner** Steve Ryan **Bred** S P Ryan **Trained** Malton, N Yorks

**FOCUS**
Race run over an additional 7yds. A decent handicap despite the small field. It was run at a sound pace and produced a thrilling finish. The first three are rated close to form.

## 6060 FLEMINGATE BEVERLEY H'CAP 1m 1f 207y
**4:40** (4:42) (Class 5) (0-70,69) 3-Y-O+ **£3,780** (£1,131; £565; £283; £141) **Stalls** Low

Form RPR
2226 1 **Liquid Gold (IRE)**[17] 5454 3-9-4 67 TonyHamilton 2 76+
(Richard Fahey) *hld up in rr: hdwy 2f out: chsd ldrs and n.m.r over 1f out: swtchd rt to inner and rdn ins fnl f: styd on wl to ld nr fin* **5/2**[1]

5042 2 nk **Yensir**[4] 5950 4-9-2 65 PatrickVaughan(7) 7 72
(Grant Tuer) *trckd ldrs: hdwy 2f out: chsd ldr over 1f out: rdn to chal ent fnl f: drvn to ld last 100yds: hdd and no ex nr fin* **7/2**[3]

6511 3 1 **Inflexiball**[21] 5290 5-9-5 61 FrannyNorton 4 66
(John Mackie) *trckd ldrs: hdwy over 2f out: rdn and n.m.r jst over 1f out: drvn and kpt on fnl f* **8/1**

4206 4 nk **Perceived**[23] 5212 5-9-11 67 CamHardie 5 71
(Antony Brittain) *hld up towards rr: hdwy on outer 2f out: rdn to chse ldrs over 1f out: drvn ins fnl f: kpt on same pce* **20/1**

2331 5 1 **Beverley Bullet**[17] 5455 4-9-7 63 (p) DanielTudhope 6 65
(Lawrence Mullaney) *racd wd: prom: led over 6f out: pushed clr 2f out: rdn over 1f out: drvn ent fnl f: hdd & wknd last 100yds* **11/4**[2]

6553 6 3 1/4 **Mysterial**[9] 5706 7-9-6 69 GerO'Neill(7) 3 65
(Declan Carroll) *led: hdd over 6f out: chsd ldr: rdn along wl over 1f out: drvn appr fnl f: sn wknd* **7/1**

22-6 7 3 3/4 **Miss Danby (IRE)**[114] 2035 3-9-2 65 JoeFanning 1 54
(Mark Johnston) *trckd ldng pair on inner: rdn along wl over 1f out: wknd appr fnl f* **8/1**

506 8 3/4 **Arrowzone**[27] 5053 6-9-4 60 RyanPowell 8 47
(Kevin Frost) *a in rr* **33/1**

2m 7.11s (0.11) **Going Correction** 0.0s/f (Good)
**WFA** 3 from 4yo+ 7lb 8 Ran SP% **119.9**
Speed ratings (Par 103): **99,98,97,97,96 94,91,90**
CSF £12.31 CT £62.21 TOTE £3.10: £1.30, £1.50, £2.50; EX 13.20 Trifecta £78.00.
**Owner** Mrs H Steel **Bred** C Beale, C Kavanagh, J & D Cantillon **Trained** Musley Bank, N Yorks

**FOCUS**
Race run over an additional 7yds. This was competitive enough for the grade and the form is rated around the second and third.

## 6061 SECRET GARDEN GIN BAR H'CAP 1m 4f 23y
**5:15** (5:15) (Class 5) (0-75,76) 3-Y-O+ **£3,780** (£1,131; £565; £283; £141) **Stalls** Low

Form RPR
5224 1 **Maori Bob (IRE)**[13] 5581 3-8-4 65 LuluStanford(5) 3 74
(Michael Bell) *trckd ldrs: hdwy on inner over 2f out: sn chal: rdn to ld over 1f out: kpt on wl* **5/2**[2]

0306 2 2 3/4 **Alphabetical Order**[20] 5313 9-10-0 75 DanielTudhope 10 79
(David O'Meara) *hld up towards rr: hdwy 3f out: swtchd rt to inner and effrt wl over 1f out: sn rdn: styd on fnl f* **14/1**

5345 3 1 1/2 **Peterhouse (USA)**[25] 5138 5-9-12 73 (v) KevinStott 2 74
(Jason Ward) *trckd ldrs: hdwy and cl up 1/2-way: chal 3f out: sn rdn and led: hdd and drvn over 1f out: kpt on same pce* **7/2**[3]

1306 4 1 1/2 **Star Of Lombardy (IRE)**[6] 5820 4-9-12 73 JoeFanning 7 72
(Mark Johnston) *hld up in rr: pushed along over 3f out: rdn 2f out: drvn over 1f out: kpt on: n.d* **8/1**

1111 5 3/4 **Regal Mirage (IRE)**[17] 5454 3-8-12 68 DavidAllan 5 67
(Tim Easterby) *led: hdd after 4f: prom: pushed along 3f out: rdn over 2f out: drvn and btn over 1f out* **6/4**[1]

3-00 6 37 **The Resdev Way**[18] 5417 4-10-1 76 DavidNolan 4 14
(David O'Meara) *trckd ldr: led after 4f: rdn along over 3f out: hdd wl over 2f out: sn drvn and wknd wl over 1f out: eased* **28/1**

2m 37.44s (-2.36) **Going Correction** 0.0s/f (Good)
**WFA** 3 from 4yo+ 9lb 6 Ran SP% **112.0**
Speed ratings (Par 103): **107,105,104,103,102 78**
CSF £33.47 CT £120.59 TOTE £3.10: £1.50, £4.70; EX 40.60 Trifecta £157.30.
**Owner** P Philipps, C Philipps, T Redman **Bred** Peter Molony **Trained** Newmarket, Suffolk

**FOCUS**
Race run over an additional 7yds. They went a sound pace for this fair handicap. The winner was on a fair mark based on his two Newmarket runs.

## 6062 RACING AGAIN TOMORROW H'CAP 5f
**5:45** (5:46) (Class 5) (0-75,77) 3-Y-O+ **£5,040** (£1,508; £754; £377; £188) **Stalls** Low

Form RPR
6112 1 **Muatadel**[7] 5804 4-9-8 73 TonyHamilton 4 84+
(Roger Fell) *hld up: pushed along and nt clr run 2f out: sn swtchd markedly lft to outer and rdn over 1f out: hdwy ent fnl f: sn drvn and r.o strly to ld nr line* **15/8**[1]

1034 2 hd **Fujin**[100] 2462 6-9-2 70 CharlieBennett(3) 2 80
(Shaun Harris) *trckd ldrs on inner: hdwy 1/2-way: sn chsng ldr: led over 1f out and sn rdn: drvn ins fnl f: hdd and no ex nr line* **17/2**[3]

5600 3 1 1/2 **Ballesteros**[18] 5402 8-9-1 73 ConnorMurtagh(7) 1 78+
(Richard Fahey) *hld up: hdwy on inner wl over 1f out: swtchd lft and rdn ent fnl f: sn chsng ldr and drvn: kpt on* **12/1**

0264 4 3 1/2 **Foxtrot Knight**[13] 5580 5-9-11 76 JamesSullivan 7 68
(Ruth Carr) *prom: rdn along whn n.m.r 2f out: drvn over 1f out: kpt on same pce* **6/1**[2]

0045 5 1 **Pea Shooter**[28] 5018 8-9-2 72 BenRobinson(5) 5 61
(Brian Ellison) *chsd ldrs: rdn along over 1f out: kpt on same pce* **6/1**[2]

5-25 6 2 1/4 **Canford Bay (IRE)**[12] 5619 3-8-6 59 AndrewMullen 3 40+
(Antony Brittain) *dwlt and in rr: hdwy wl over 1f out: sn rdn and nt clr run ins fnl f: no ch after* **14/1**

000 7 1 1/4 **Bosham**[39] 4600 7-9-12 77 (b) NathanEvans 6 53
(Michael Easterby) *qckly away and led: rdn along wl over 1f out: drvn and hdd jst over 1f out: sn wknd* **10/1**

4010 8 4 1/2 **Crosse Fire**[7] 5804 5-9-6 71 (v) DavidAllan 8 31
(Scott Dixon) *wnt lft s: prom: rdn along and n.m.r 2f out: sn drvn and wknd* **11/1**

343- 9 9 **Another Angel (IRE)**[438] 2913 3-9-8 75 PhillipMakin 10
(Antony Brittain) *dwlt: a in rr* **25/1**

050 10 8 **Kibaar**[19] 5379 5-9-8 73 (v[1]) KevinStott 9
(Kevin Ryan) *bmpd s: sn chsng ldrs on outer: rdn along over 2f out: sn drvn and wknd* **9/1**

1m 2.74s (-0.76) **Going Correction** 0.0s/f (Good)
**WFA** 3 from 4yo+ 2lb 10 Ran SP% **119.5**
Speed ratings (Par 103): **106,105,103,97,96 92,90,83,68,56**
CSF £19.15 CT £146.37 TOTE £2.40: £1.10, £2.10, £3.60; EX 14.50 Trifecta £162.20.
**Owner** R G Fell **Bred** Lofts Hall Stud & B Sangster **Trained** Nawton, N Yorks

**FOCUS**
The pace was strong for this fair handicap. A clear turf best from the winner.
T/Plt: £20.30 to a £1 stake. Pool: £64,064.49 - 2,300.90 winning units. T/Qpdt: £7.60 to a £1 stake. Pool: £4,186.54 - 403.42 winning units. **Joe Rowntree**

# 5793 KEMPTON (A.W) (R-H)
### Wednesday, August 16

**OFFICIAL GOING: Polytrack: standard to slow**
Wind: light, across Weather: sunny

## 6063 TAMDOWN NURSERY H'CAP (JOCKEY CLUB GRASSROOTS NURSERY QUALIFIER) 7f (P)
**6:10** (6:15) (Class 6) (0-60,61) 2-Y-O **£2,587** (£770; £384; £192) **Stalls** Low

Form RPR
000 1 **Mountain Peak**[19] 5365 2-9-4 57 LiamKeniry 1 62
(Ed Walker) *trckd ldrs: effrt 2f out: chsd ldr ins fnl f: r.o wl to ld towards fin* **8/1**[2]

000 2 1/2 **Shoyd**[26] 5107 2-9-6 59 SeanLevey 12 63
(Richard Hannon) *chsd ldr tl rdn to ld over 1f out: drvn ins fnl f: hdd and no ex towards fin* **12/1**

200 3 1 1/2 **Super Florence (IRE)**[65] 3655 2-9-5 61 EdwardGreatrex(3) 11 61
(Eve Johnson Houghton) *hld up in midfield: rdn over 2f out: hdwy into 5th over 1f out: styd on strly u.p ins fnl f: nvr getting on terms w ldrs* **18/1**

4056 4 1 **Inuk (IRE)**[27] 5079 2-9-3 56 ShaneKelly 4 53
(Richard Hughes) *hld up in tch in midfield: rdn 3f out: hdwy u.p over 1f out: swtchd lft kpt on ins fnl f: nvr enough pce to get on terms w ldrs* **10/1**[3]

666 5 3/4 **Catch The Pigeon**[19] 5356 2-9-1 57 CallumShepherd(3) 7 52
(Ed de Giles) *led: rdn 2f out: hdd over 1f out: no ex and lost 2nd ins fnl f: wknd fnl 100yds* **8/1**[2]

3542 6 2 1/4 **Global Exceed**[4] 5933 2-9-7 60 (b) FranBerry 5 49
(Ed Dunlop) *t.k.h early: chsd ldrs: unable qck u.p over 1f out: wknd ins fnl f* **6/4**[1]

060 7 3/4 **My Guy (IRE)**[36] 4725 2-8-11 50 (p[1]) JohnFahy 6 37
(J S Moore) *hld up in midfield: effrt on inner 2f out: drvn and no imp over 1f out: kpt on same pce ins fnl f* **33/1**

0243 8 3 **Roses In June (IRE)**[21] 5293 2-8-7 49 HollieDoyle(3) 3 28
(J S Moore) *hld up in rr: effrt and plenty to do jst over 2f out: plugged on ins fnl f: nvr trbld ldrs* **12/1**

006 9 1 **Bullseye Bullet**[30] 4977 2-9-4 57 SteveDrowne 2 33
(Mark Usher) *hld up towards rr: rdn over 2f out: no imp: wl hld and plugged on same pce fr over 1f out* **20/1**

550 10 2 1/4 **Lyford (IRE)**[43] 4465 2-9-0 58 MitchGodwin(5) 8 28
(Sylvester Kirk) *chsd ldrs: rdn 3f out: lost pl qckly 2f out: sn wknd* **12/1**

0556 11 1 1/2 **Heavenly Pulse (IRE)**[1] 6022 2-8-7 46 SilvestreDeSousa 9 12
(Ann Duffield) *awkward leaving stalls and s.i.s: hld up towards rr: hdwy into midfield 1/2-way: effrt u.p over 1f out: sme hdwy but struggling to get on terms whn hung rt over 1f out: eased fnl f* **8/1**[2]

050 12 3 3/4 **Afterthisone**[114] 2029 2-8-6 45 RobHornby 10
(Robin Dickin) *awkward and wnt lft leaving stalls: a in rr: swtchd rt and no hdwy whn rdn over 2f out: n.d* **66/1**

054 13 nse **Istanbul Pasha (IRE)**[16] 5474 2-9-1 54 SaleemGolam 13 10
(David Evans) *hld up towards rr on outer: dropped to rr and rdn over 2f out: no rspnse and wl btn 2f out* **22/1**

1m 28.11s (2.11) **Going Correction** +0.025s/f (Slow) 13 Ran SP% **124.3**
Speed ratings (Par 92): **88,87,85,84,83 81,80,76,75,73 71,67,67**
CSF £100.32 CT £1752.22 TOTE £11.40: £2.90, £3.60, £4.70; EX 142.20 Trifecta £1382.10.
**Owner** Ebury Racing **Bred** Mrs Hugh Maitland-Jones **Trained** Upper Lambourn, Berks

**FOCUS**
They went quite steady early and few got into it. The winner improved for the move into handicaps.

## 6064 O' HALLORAN & O'BRIEN/BRITISH STALLION STUDS EBF FILLIES' NOVICE STKS (PLUS 10 RACE) 7f (P)
**6:40** (6:47) (Class 5) 2-Y-O **£3,234** (£962; £481; £240) **Stalls** Low

Form RPR
0 1 **Quargent (USA)**[32] 4902 2-9-0 0 JamieSpencer 2 81+
(Jeremy Noseda) *trckd ldr: rdn to chal over 1f out: drvn and styd on to ld wl ins fnl f: steadily gng away at fin* **8/11**[1]
03 2 1 3/4 **Amandine**[14] 5531 2-9-0 0 FranBerry 1 76
(David Elsworth) *t.k.h early: trckd ldrs: effrt on inner 2f out: led ent fnl f: drvn ins fnl f: hdd and no ex wl ins fnl f* **7/1**[3]
510 3 1 1/4 **Royal Parks**[20] 5329 2-9-7 86 MartinHarley 7 80
(James Tate) *led: rdn 2f out: hrd pressed over 1f out: hdd ent fnl f: no ex and styd on same pce fnl 150yds* **5/1**[2]
4 1 3/4 **Cavatina** 2-9-0 0 PatCosgrave 9 68+
(William Haggas) *hld up in tch in midfield: effrt ent fnl 2f: hdwy over 1f out: styd on ins fnl f wout threatening ldrs* **14/1**
5 shd **Rasima** 2-9-0 0 HarryBentley 14 68+
(Roger Varian) *s.i.s: swtchd rt after s and hld up in last trio: effrt over 2f out: hdwy over 1f out: nt clr run and swtchd lft 1f out: styd on wl fnl 100yds: no threat to ldrs* **18/1**
6 nse **Sharp Reminder** 2-9-0 0 LukeMorris 6 68
(James Tate) *hld up wl in tch in midfield: rdn over 2f out: outpcd by ldng trio 2f out: kpt on same pce fr over 1f out* **25/1**
7 3/4 **Sarasota (IRE)** 2-9-0 0 TimmyMurphy 5 66
(Jamie Osborne) *hld up in tch in midfield: effrt 2f out: rdn and sn outpcd by ldng trio: kpt on same pce fr over 1f out* **50/1**
8 3 **Obrigada** 2-9-0 0 JimCrowley 3 58
(Tom Clover) *s.i.s: outpcd in rr early: clsd in tch 1/2-way: pushed along over 2f out: unable qck: wl hld and kpt on same pce fnl 2f* **33/1**
43 9 2 1/4 **Golden Footsteps (IRE)**[41] 4533 2-9-0 0 (h[1]) LiamKeniry 10 52
(Ed Walker) *hld up in tch in midfield: effrt 2f out: sn rdn and no rspnse: wl hld whn sltly impeded ent fnl f: sn wknd* **8/1**
0 10 1/2 **Lucky Reset**[27] 5056 2-9-0 0 SteveDrowne 11 50
(David Evans) *s.i.s: a in rr: rdn over 2f out: sn struggling and no ch fnl 2f* **100/1**
04 11 2 1/2 **Fenagh (IRE)**[27] 5048 2-8-11 0 EdwardGreatrex(3) 4 44
(David Loughnane) *racd wd: in tch in midfield: rdn over 3f out: hung lft and v wd bnd 3f out: lost pl u.p over 2f out: bhd ins fnl f* **22/1**

1m 26.53s (0.53) **Going Correction** +0.025s/f (Slow) 11 Ran SP% **124.2**
Speed ratings (Par 91): **97,95,93,91,91 91,90,87,84,83 81**
CSF £6.65 TOTE £1.80: £1.10, £2.30, £1.40; EX 9.30 Trifecta £22.50.
**Owner** Marc Keller **Bred** Orpendale/Chelston/Wynatt **Trained** Newmarket, Suffolk
■ Copilot was withdrawn not under orders. Price at time of withdrawal 66-1. Rule 4 does not apply.

**FOCUS**
Another race in which the pace held up, the first three racing in those positions throughout. It's doubtful if the third is the best guide.

## 6065 CAREY GROUP NURSERY H'CAP (JOCKEY CLUB GRASSROOTS NURSERY QUALIFIER) 6f (P)
**7:10** (7:10) (Class 4) (0-85,83) 2-Y-O **£4,528** (£1,347; £673; £336) **Stalls** Low

Form RPR
3150 1 **Elizabeth Bennet (IRE)**[20] 5329 2-9-7 **83** JamesDoyle 6 87
(Charles Hills) *trckd ldrs on outer: effrt ent fnl 2f: drvn over 1f out: clsd to chal and edgd rt ins fnl f: led 75yds out: r.o wl* **6/4**[1]
350 2 1 **George (IRE)**[15] 5504 2-9-4 **80** PatDobbs 2 82
(Sylvester Kirk) *led for over 1f out: trckd ldrs after: nt clr run 2f out tl swtchd lft jst ins fnl f: barging w rival and squeezed through ins fnl f: r.o wl towards fin to snatch 2nd cl home* **17/5**[3]
313 3 1/2 **Shaheen (IRE)**[27] 5079 2-8-12 **74** (t) PatCosgrave 5 74
(John Quinn) *t.k.h: chsd ldrs tl led over 4f out: rdn 2f out: edgd rt u.p 1f out: hdd and styd on same pce fnl 75yds: lost 2nd cl home* **10/3**[2]
010 4 nse **Cameo Star (IRE)**[19] 5370 2-8-10 **75** SammyJoBell(3) 1 75
(Richard Fahey) *hld up in tch in rr: shkn up and clsd over 1f out: nt clrest of runs 1f out: swtchd lft styd on wl towards fin* **14/1**
5431 5 1 1/2 **Ragstone View (IRE)**[18] 5408 2-9-0 **76** ShaneKelly 4 72
(Richard Hughes) *short of room after s: sn swtchd lft: t.k.h and hdwy to join ldr over 4f out: rdn 2f out: stl pressing ldrs but struggling to qckn whn c off worse in barging match w rival and btn ins fnl f* **8/1**
1020 6 9 **Silca Mistress**[19] 5373 2-8-9 **71** SilvestreDeSousa 3 39+
(Mick Channon) *t.k.h: hld up in tch: dropped to rr and rdn 2f out: sn outpcd: bhd and eased ins fnl f* **9/1**

1m 14.01s (0.91) **Going Correction** +0.025s/f (Slow) 6 Ran SP% **113.6**
Speed ratings (Par 96): **94,92,92,91,89 77**
CSF £7.00 TOTE £2.20: £1.30, £1.90; EX 7.40 Trifecta £23.30.
**Owner** Mr & Mrs T O'Donohoe **Bred** Awbeg Stud **Trained** Lambourn, Berks

**FOCUS**
This was steadily run and turned into a dash in the straight. The third is rated to his mark and the form's not the most solid.

## 6066 CAPPAGH GROUP/BREEDERS BACKING RACING EBF MAIDEN FILLIES' STKS 7f (P)
**7:40** (7:41) (Class 5) 3-Y-O+ **£4,204** (£1,251; £625; £312) **Stalls** Low

Form RPR
42-0 1 **First Dance (IRE)**[119] 1885 3-9-0 81 MartinHarley 3 84
(James Tate) *trckd ldng pair: swtchd rt and effrt on inner over 1f out: qcknd to ld ent fnl f: sn clr and r.o wl: comf* **1/1**[1]
2 3 **Natheer (USA)** 3-9-0 0 JimCrowley 5 75
(Roger Varian) *pressed ldr: rdn to chal and rn green 2f out: chsd wnr 1f out: no ch w wnr but kpt on ins fnl f* **7/2**[3]
4 3 1 1/2 **Counter Spirit (IRE)**[20] 5335 3-9-0 0 SilvestreDeSousa 2 71
(Ismail Mohammed) *racd keenly: led: rdn 2f out: hdd and outpcd by wnr ent fnl f: 3rd and styd on same pce fnl f* **3/1**[2]
0-2 4 8 **Amenta (IRE)**[67] 3571 3-9-0 0 KieranShoemark 4 49
(Roger Charlton) *stdd leaving stalls: t.k.h: hld up in tch in 4th: rdn 2f out: sn outpcd and hung rt over 1f out: wl btn 4th fnl f* **6/1**
4U0- 5 3/4 **Sovrano Dolce (IRE)**[266] 8075 4-9-0 64 GeorgeBuckell(5) 1 49
(Mike Murphy) *hld up in tch in last pair: effrt 2f out: sn outpcd and wl btn over 1f out* **20/1**
6 4 1/2 **Musical Fire** 3-9-0 0 CharlesBishop 6 35
(Peter Hedger) *s.i.s: rn green in last pair: rdn jst over 2f out: sn outpcd and wl btn over 1f out* **50/1**

1m 27.23s (1.23) **Going Correction** +0.025s/f (Slow)
**WFA** 3 from 4yo 5lb 6 Ran SP% **118.2**
Speed ratings (Par 100): **93,89,87,78,77 72**
CSF £5.36 TOTE £2.00: £1.10, £2.30; EX 6.10 Trifecta £13.00.
**Owner** Saif Ali **Bred** Mount Coote Stud **Trained** Newmarket, Suffolk

**FOCUS**
This proved an easy enough task for the favourite, who set a good standard.

## 6067 GALLAGHER GROUP H'CAP (LONDON MILE SERIES QUALIFIER) 1m (P)
**8:10** (8:11) (Class 5) (0-70,72) 3-Y-O **£3,234** (£962; £481; £240) **Stalls** Low

Form RPR
5444 1 **Mudallel (IRE)**[7] 5797 3-9-7 **70** JamesDoyle 11 81
(Ed Dunlop) *hld up in last pair: nt clr run ent fnl 2f: swtchd lft and hdwy on outer over 1f out: edging rt but qcknd to ld 1f out: sn wl clr: eased towards fin: easily* **10/3**[1]
0-03 2 3 3/4 **Precious Angel (IRE)**[90] 2760 3-9-6 **69** SeanLevey 3 72+
(Richard Hannon) *dwlt: sn bustled along and rcvrd to r in tch in midfield: clsd to chse ldrs and nt clr run over 1f out: swtchd lft 1f out: r.o strly ins fnl f to snatch 2nd last strides: no ch w wnr* **16/1**
1361 3 nse **Dangerous Ends**[35] 4747 3-9-6 **69** (p[1]) JackMitchell 5 72+
(Brett Johnson) *hld up in last trio: nt clr run over 2f out: swtchd lft 1f out: r.o strly ins fnl f: snatched 3rd last stride: no ch w wnr* **6/1**[3]
0-05 4 shd **Scoones**[22] 5243 3-9-2 **65** DanielMuscutt 8 66
(James Fanshawe) *trckd ldrs: swtchd lft and clsd to join ldrs 2f out: sn rdn and ev ch tl nt match pce of wnr 1f out: chsd clr wnr ins fnl f: kpt on same pce and lost 2 pls last strides* **11/2**[2]
50-0 5 1/2 **Mach One**[85] 2931 3-8-11 **63** EdwardGreatrex(3) 4 63
(Archie Watson) *chsd ldr: rdn and ev ch 2f out: drvn to ld ent fnl f: sn hdd and outpcd by wnr: kpt on same pce ins fnl f: lost 2 pls nr fin* **15/2**
-005 6 3 1/4 **Iftitah (IRE)**[46] 4350 3-9-2 **65** (bt[1]) SamHitchcott 10 58
(George Peckham) *stdd after s: hld up in rr: clsd and swtchd rt 2f out: no imp u.p over 1f out: wknd ins fnl f* **50/1**
5420 7 1 **Nibras Again**[26] 5132 3-9-9 **72** TomMarquand 1 62
(Ismail Mohammed) *chsd ldrs: rdn and ev ch 2f out tl unable qck jst over 1f out: wknd ins fnl f* **8/1**
-400 8 2 1/4 **Eternal Dream**[28] 5031 3-8-11 **60** MartinLane 2 45
(William Knight) *taken down early: led whn rdn and hrd pressed 2f out: hdd ent fnl f: sn btn and wknd ins fnl f* **25/1**
4242 9 1 3/4 **Music Lesson**[22] 5242 3-9-9 **72** (b) StevieDonohoe 7 53
(Hughie Morrison) *in tch in midfield: shuffled bk towards rr and rdn 2f out: sn outpcd and wknd fnl f* **6/1**[3]
-060 10 1/2 **Marilyn**[35] 4761 3-9-3 **66** TedDurcan 9 46
(Chris Wall) *chsd ldrs on outer: rdn over 2f out: struggling and lost pl over 1f out: wknd fnl f* **10/1**
3560 11 1 1/4 **George Reme (IRE)**[11] 5666 3-9-7 **70** (b[1]) FranBerry 6 47
(John Quinn) *dwlt: sn in tch in midfield: effrt over 2f out: sn hung rt and no imp: bhd ins fnl f* **7/1**

1m 38.7s (-1.10) **Going Correction** +0.025s/f (Slow) 11 Ran SP% **123.2**
Speed ratings (Par 100): **106,102,102,102,101 98,97,95,93,92 91**
CSF £64.85 CT £325.93 TOTE £4.70: £1.40, £4.60, £2.10; EX 65.70 Trifecta £206.10.
**Owner** Abdullah Saeed Al Naboodah **Bred** Tullpark Ltd **Trained** Newmarket, Suffolk

**FOCUS**
There was a good gallop on here and it set up for the closers. The winner is rated back to his debut form.

## 6068 BYRNE GROUP H'CAP 7f (P)
**8:40** (8:41) (Class 4) (0-85,87) 3-Y-O+ **£5,175** (£1,540; £769; £384) **Stalls** Low

Form RPR
5434 1 **Mazyoun**[11] 5642 3-9-8 **86** (b) JamesDoyle 12 93+
(Hugo Palmer) *stdd and dropped in bhd after s: hld up in last trio: rdn jst over 2f out: hdwy over 1f out: pressing ldrs and hung rt 1f out: stened and led ins fnl f: r.o wl* **10/3**[1]
0403 2 3/4 **Ower Fly**[19] 5369 4-9-11 **87** (b) HollieDoyle(3) 7 94
(Richard Hannon) *led: rdn 2f out: hrd pressed and drvn over 1f out: hdd ins fnl f: styd on same pce after* **9/1**
2424 3 nk **Envisaging (IRE)**[42] 4508 3-9-0 **78** (t[1]) SilvestreDeSousa 13 82
(James Fanshawe) *hld up in tch towards rr: swtchd rt and effrt on inner 2f out: hdwy u.p over 1f out: drvn and ev ch ins fnl f: styd on same pce fnl 100yds* **7/1**[3]
2666 4 1 **Sea Shack**[47] 4313 3-8-12 **76** JimCrowley 2 77
(William Knight) *taken down early: trckd ldng pair: effrt on inner 2f out: drvn and ev ch over 1f out: no ex and styd on same pce ins fnl f* **7/2**[2]
5023 5 nse **Plant Pot Power (IRE)**[18] 5400 3-9-7 **85** SeanLevey 4 86
(Richard Hannon) *hld up in tch in midfield: effrt 2f out: hdwy and clsng whn squeezed for room and impeded 1f out: rallied and styd on wl fnl 100yds* **7/1**[3]
353 6 shd **Baron Bolt**[47] 4321 4-9-9 **87** (p) DavidEgan(5) 11 90+
(Paul Cole) *wl in tch in midfield: clsd and rdn to chal 2f out tl unable qck jst ins fnl f: no ex and outpcd fnl 100yds* **8/1**
0-60 7 nse **Queensbrydge**[15] 5506 3-9-2 **80** LukeMorris 6 81
(Robyn Brisland) *hld up in tch towards rr: effrt 2f out: hdwy and swtchd rt 1f out: styd on u.p ins fnl f: nvr trbld ldrs* **20/1**
-220 8 1 3/4 **Falbon**[63] 3715 3-8-12 **79** (p) MarcMonaghan(3) 9 75
(Marco Botti) *t.k.h: trckd ldng trio: effrt 2f out: stl pressing ldrs but struggling to qckn whn squeezed for room and hmpd 1f out: nt rcvr* **16/1**
0006 9 1 1/4 **Lacan (IRE)**[13] 5555 6-9-2 **75** JackMitchell 5 70
(Brett Johnson) *short of room leaving stalls: plld hrd and hld up in rr: effrt ent fnl f: styd on ins fnl f: nvr trbld ldrs* **40/1**
0605 10 nse **Dutiful Son (IRE)**[22] 5241 7-9-3 **76** JamieSpencer 3 71
(Simon Dow) *t.k.h: hld up in tch in midfield: effrt 2f out: sn drvn and no imp over 1f out: kpt on same pce after* **16/1**
160 11 3/4 **Zefferino**[39] 4634 3-9-2 **80** KieranShoemark 8 71
(Roger Charlton) *hld up in last trio: effrt over 2f out: no imp tl styd on ins fnl f: nvr trbld ldrs* **7/1**[3]
4400 12 1/2 **Varsovian**[16] 5481 7-8-12 **71** RobertWinston 10 64
(Dean Ivory) *chsd ldrs: rdn and ev ch ent fnl 2f: squeezed for room and dropped away over 1f out: short of room again and wknd ins fnl f* **33/1**

1m 24.93s (-1.07) **Going Correction** +0.025s/f (Slow)
**WFA** 3 from 4yo+ 5lb 12 Ran SP% **125.8**
Speed ratings (Par 105): **107,106,105,104,104 104,104,102,101,100 100,99**
CSF £35.62 CT £210.84 TOTE £3.80: £1.60, £2.80, £3.80; EX 20.80 Trifecta £110.40.
**Owner** Al Shaqab Racing **Bred** Cheveley Park Stud Ltd **Trained** Newmarket, Suffolk
■ Awesome Allan was withdrawn not under orders. Price at time of withdrawal 66-1. Rule 4 does not apply.


The Form Book Flat, Raceform Ltd, Newbury, RG14 5SJ

**FOCUS**
Not a bad handicap, and it was well run. It's rated around the second.

## 6069 THAMES MATERIALS H'CAP 1m 3f 219y(P)
9:10 (9:11) (Class 6) (0-60,61) 3-Y-0+ £2,587 (£770; £384; £192) Stalls Low

Form RPR
000 1 **Wolfcatcherjack (IRE)**[62] 3755 3-9-0 **57**.......... LukeMorris 5 69+
(Sir Mark Prescott Bt) *hld up in midfield: rdn over 3f out: gd hdwy and swtchd rt over 1f out: led ins fnl f: styd on strly and gng away at fin* **9/4**[1]
020 2 1 ½ **Rianna Star**[43] 4461 4-9-3 **54**.......... HectorCrouch(3) 11 58
(Gary Moore) *taken down early: led for over 1f out: chsd ldr tl rdn to ld again 3f out: edgd lft u.p ent fnl f: hdd and kpt on same pce ins fnl f* **20/1**
5002 3 shd **Powered (IRE)**[3] 5968 4-9-4 **57**.......... DavidEgan(5) 6 61
(David Evans) *s.i.s: hld up towards rr: rdn and gd hdwy ent fnl 2f: chsd ldrs and styd on wl ins fnl f* **7/1**[3]
552 4 nk **Tuolumne Meadows**[46] 4346 4-9-12 **60**.......... JamesDoyle 12 63
(Tony Newcombe) *wl in tch in midfield: rdn 3f out: styd on to chse ldrs and swtchd rt 1f out: kpt on u.p ins fnl f* **6/1**[2]
5314 5 2 **Lady Of York**[23] 5215 3-8-7 **50**.......... JoeyHaynes 9 51
(Alan Bailey) *t.k.h: chsd ldrs: rdn to chse ldr over 2f out tl unable qck over 1f out: outpcd ins fnl f* **9/1**
4300 6 2 **Zamadance**[20] 5336 3-9-1 **58**.......... SilvestreDeSousa 13 56
(Ed Dunlop) *stdd and swtchd rt after s: t.k.h: hld up in midfield: swtchd rt 2f out and hdwy u.p over 1f out: no imp 1f out: btn and eased wl ins fnl f* **6/1**[2]
1/00 7 3 ¼ **Storming Harry**[19] 5361 5-9-2 **50**.......... LiamKeniry 1 42
(Robin Dickin) *hld up in rr: effrt but hanging rt over 2f out: styd on ins fnl f: nvr trbld ldrs* **50/1**
6-01 8 nk **Howardian Hills (IRE)**[30] 4980 4-9-11 **59**..........(p) KieranShoemark 14 50
(Victor Dartnall) *styd wd early: led over 10f out tl rdn and hdd 3f out: styd pressing ldrs tl no ex and btn over 1f out: wknd ins fnl f* **7/1**[3]
0/36 9 3 **Whipcrackaway (IRE)**[9] 5722 8-9-3 **51**..........(b) JohnFahy 4 37
(Peter Hedger) *stdd s: hld up towards rr: effrt over 2f out: no imp and wl btn over 1f out* **33/1**
0504 10 ¾ **Never Folding (IRE)**[35] 4754 3-9-0 **57**..........(h[1]) RobertWinston 3 43
(Seamus Durack) *taken down early: t.k.h: chsd ldrs: rdn ent fnl 2f: lost pl and btn over 1f out: wknd fnl f* **16/1**
0645 11 1 ¾ **Feel The Vibes**[16] 5485 3-9-2 **59**..........(p[1]) RobHornby 10 42
(Michael Blanshard) *hld up in midfield: rdn 3f out: wknd over 1f out* **14/1**
500 12 2 ¼ **Callaghan (GER)**[39] 4627 4-9-7 **55**..........(t) FranBerry 7 34
(Tom Gretton) *stdd s: hld up in rr: effrt over 2f out: sn btn and bhd over 1f out* **25/1**
5000 13 23 **Karam Albaari (IRE)**[22] 5261 9-9-13 **61**..........(v) JamieSpencer 2 3
(J R Jenkins) *stdd s: hld up towards rr: short lived effrt on outer 3f out: bhd and eased fnl f: t.o* **25/1**
060 14 100 **Xylophone**[36] 4729 3-8-11 **57**..........(t[1]) EdwardGreatrex(3) 8
(Archie Watson) *midfield: rdn and lost pl over 2f out: virtually p.u over 1f out: t.o* **20/1**

2m 34.07s (-0.43) **Going Correction** +0.025s/f (Slow)
**WFA** 3 from 4yo+ 9lb 14 Ran SP% **129.0**
Speed ratings (Par 101): **102,101,100,100,99 98,95,95,93,93 92,90,75,**
CSF £60.75 CT £300.90 TOTE £2.90: £1.60, £5.60, £2.30; EX 52.50 Trifecta £290.20.
**Owner** Ne'Er Do Wells V **Bred** Mrs S M Rogers & Miss K Rausing **Trained** Newmarket, Suffolk

**FOCUS**
A moderate affair won by a handicap debutant who has the potential to add to this success. Straightforward form behind him.
T/Plt: £82.70 to a £1 stake. Pool: £64,466.67 - 568.57 winning units. T/Qpdt: £6.30 to a £1 stake. Pool: £6,528.02 - 762.50 winning units. **Steve Payne**

# 5709 SALISBURY (R-H)
Wednesday, August 16

**OFFICIAL GOING: Good to firm (good in places; 8.0)**
Wind: Almost nil Weather: Fine

## 6070 BRITISH EBF MOLSON COORS NOVICE STKS (PLUS 10 RACE) (DIV I) 6f
1:50 (1:50) (Class 4) 2-Y-O £4,690 (£1,395; £697; £348) Stalls Low

Form RPR
2 1 **Exceedingly Diva**[51] 4151 2-8-11 0.......... KieranShoemark 1 79
(Marcus Tregoning) *mde all: shkn up 2f out: at least 2 l up whn hit rail 1f out: rdn out* **4/1**[2]
16 2 1 **Kick On Kick On**[83] 3002 2-9-5 0.......... HectorCrouch(3) 10 87
(Clive Cox) *prom: rdn to chse wnr 2f out: kpt on but a wl hld fnl f* **7/1**[3]
0 3 2 ¼ **Foxtrot Lady**[14] 5528 2-8-11 0.......... DavidProbert 4 69
(Andrew Balding) *chsd wnr to 2f out: racd awkwardly whn rdn after: one pce fnl f* **20/1**
4 4 4 **Strategist (IRE)**[19] 5350 2-9-2 0.......... RyanMoore 3 63
(William Haggas) *cl up: drvn and no rspnse jst over 2f out: wl hld after: wknd ins fnl f* **4/6**[1]
5 1 **Ornamental** 2-9-2 0.......... HarryBentley 2 59+
(Henry Candy) *s.s: wl off the pce in last trio: shkn up over 2f out: styd on fnl f: nvr nrr* **9/1**
0 6 hd **Quick Breath**[26] 5105 2-9-2 0.......... LukeMorris 7 59
(Jonathan Portman) *dwlt: chsd ldrs: rdn and outpcd over 2f out: n.d after* **100/1**
5 7 ½ **Chillala (IRE)**[41] 4533 2-8-11 0..........(h) StevieDonohoe 5 52
(Harry Dunlop) *dwlt: in tch whn j. path over 3f out: sn outpcd and btn* **14/1**
0 8 2 ¼ **Good Impression**[75] 3305 2-9-2 0..........(b[1]) PatDobbs 6 50
(Amanda Perrett) *dwlt: nvr beyond midfield: outpcd fr 1/2-way* **50/1**
65 9 5 **Solid Man (JPN)**[78] 3165 2-9-2 0.......... FranBerry 9 35
(David Simcock) *slowly away: a wl bhd* **33/1**
10 2 ½ **Caviar Royale** 2-9-2 0.......... JimCrowley 8 28
(Brian Meehan) *c out of stalls slowly: a wl bhd* **33/1**

1m 13.37s (-1.43) **Going Correction** -0.175s/f (Firm) 10 Ran SP% **122.7**
Speed ratings (Par 96): **102,100,97,92,91 90,90,87,80,77**
CSF £32.09 TOTE £5.30: £2.10, £2.80, £6.70; EX 41.60 Trifecta £346.40.
**Owner** FTP Equine Holdings Ltd **Bred** Shadwell Estate Company Limited **Trained** Whitsbury, Hants

**FOCUS**
A rail was erected on the straight course up to 16ft off the permanent far-side rail. Drying conditions, and after the opener Hector Crouch said the ground was "lovely and good to firm". David Probert felt it was "good ground". This was run just 1.07sec outside standard, and 1.6sec quicker than the second division. The winner made all and the next three were always prominent too. The winner took a minor step forward.

## 6071 BRITISH EBF MOLSON COORS NOVICE STKS (PLUS 10 RACE) (DIV II) 6f
2:20 (2:20) (Class 4) 2-Y-O £4,690 (£1,395; £697; £348) Stalls Low

Form RPR
444 1 **Rogue**[11] 5641 2-9-2 79.......... RyanMoore 6 77
(Richard Hannon) *mde all: hrd pressed over 2f out: edgd lft after: drvn and kpt on fnl f* **5/2**[1]
2 ½ **Ragstone Road (IRE)** 2-9-2 0.......... ShaneKelly 3 76+
(Richard Hughes) *t.k.h early: in tch: rdn over 2f out: prog over 1f out: styd on to take 2nd nr fin and clsd on wnr* **15/2**
0 3 hd **The Great Dandini (IRE)**[15] 5504 2-9-2 0.......... DaneO'Neill 9 75
(Seamus Durack) *chsd ldrs: rdn over 2f out: prog over 1f out: chsd wnr ins fnl f: kpt on wl but lost 2nd nr fin* **16/1**
4 ¾ **Buffer Zone** 2-9-2 0.......... KieranShoemark 1 73+
(Roger Charlton) *dwlt: mostly in last pair: pushed along over 2f out: prog fnl f and shkn up 100yds out: gng on wl at fin* **3/1**[2]
6 5 ¾ **Lord Vetinari**[19] 5350 2-9-2 0.......... DavidProbert 7 70
(Andrew Balding) *dwlt and awkward s: mostly in last trio: rdn sn after 1/2-way: kpt on fr over 1f out: nrst fin* **3/1**[2]
0 6 hd **Insurgence**[33] 4859 2-8-13 0.......... GeorgeWood(3) 8 70
(James Fanshawe) *chsd wnr: chal fr 1/2-way: edgd lft fr 2f out: nt qckn over 1f out: lost 2nd ins fnl f: fdd* **25/1**
0 7 1 ¾ **Makambe (IRE)**[15] 5504 2-9-2 0.......... FranBerry 4 65
(Charles Hills) *chsd ldrs: shkn up over 2f out: wknd jst over 1f out* **40/1**
8 3 ¾ **Laubali** 2-9-2 0.......... JimCrowley 5 53
(Owen Burrows) *dwlt: in tch: taken to outer and shkn up over 2f out: wknd over 1f out* **6/1**[3]
9 nse **Dance Emperor (IRE)** 2-9-2 0.......... LiamKeniry 10 53
(Ed Walker) *s.s: rn green and a in last pair* **25/1**

1m 14.97s (0.17) **Going Correction** -0.175s/f (Firm) 9 Ran SP% **120.6**
Speed ratings (Par 96): **91,90,90,89,88 87,85,80,80**
CSF £22.85 TOTE £2.50: £1.30, £2.00, £3.30; EX 20.70 Trifecta £433.20.
**Owner** Michael Daniels & Norman Woodcock **Bred** Maywood Stud **Trained** East Everleigh, Wilts

**FOCUS**
Fillies were first and third in the other division, but there were none involved this time. It was slower by 1.6sec, and again the winner did it from the front. It's hard to start higher at this stage given compressed nature of this.

## 6072 S H JONES WINES H'CAP 5f
2:50 (2:51) (Class 4) (0-80,81) 3-Y-O+ £5,175 (£1,540; £769; £384) Stalls Low

Form RPR
6640 1 **Waseem Faris (IRE)**[12] 5587 8-9-6 **76**.......... PatDobbs 4 83
(Ken Cunningham-Brown) *hld up in rr: gng strly bhd ldrs and waiting for a gap over 1f out: burst through ins fnl f to ld last stride* **14/1**
3123 2 hd **Trick Of The Light (IRE)**[18] 5416 3-9-3 **80**.......... DavidEgan(5) 7 86
(Roger Varian) *wl in tch: rdn over 1f out: prog fnl f: drvn ahd fnl 50yds: hdd last stride* **11/4**[1]
03 3 1 **Lydia's Place**[7] 5811 4-9-9 **79**.......... RobHornby 5 81
(Richard Guest) *pressed ldr: rdn to ld 2f out: kpt on but hdd and outpcd last 50yds* **12/1**
5314 4 1 **Justice Lady (IRE)**[19] 5355 4-9-11 **81**.......... ShaneKelly 3 80
(David Elsworth) *t.k.h: hld up in last pair: smooth prog to trck ldrs 1/2-way: rdn and nt qckn over 1f out: one pce after* **3/1**[2]
5011 5 1 ¾ **Dandy Flame (IRE)**[16] 5473 3-9-2 **81**.......... FinleyMarsh(7) 6 74
(Richard Hughes) *taken down early: racd wd: chsd ldrs: drvn 2f out: nt on terms over 1f out: one pce after* **11/2**[3]
332 6 nk **Flowing Clarets**[9] 5723 4-8-5 **61**.......... KieranO'Neill 8 52
(John Bridger) *trapped out wd: in tch: rdn sn after 1/2-way: nt on terms over 1f out: one pce after* **9/1**
2241 7 hd **Seamster**[4] 5936 10-9-3 **80** 6ex..........(t) LauraCoughlan(7) 2 71+
(David Loughnane) *in tch: pushed along and cl up against rail over 1f out: nowhere to go after: lost pl and all ch ins fnl f* **7/1**
4114 8 ¾ **Fethiye Boy**[35] 4732 3-9-7 **79**.......... LukeMorris 1 67
(Ronald Harris) *led to 2f out: wknd fnl f* **8/1**

1m 0.07s (-0.93) **Going Correction** -0.175s/f (Firm)
**WFA** 3 from 4yo+ 2lb 8 Ran SP% **115.0**
Speed ratings (Par 105): **100,99,98,96,93 93,92,91**
CSF £52.94 CT £488.35 TOTE £17.60: £3.80, £1.30, £3.30; EX 70.80 Trifecta £716.70.
**Owner** Danebury Racing Stables **Bred** Rabbah Bloodstock Limited **Trained** Danebury, Hants

**FOCUS**
A competitive handicap which was fast and furious. Things got rather tight on the inside rail and the winner took advantage of a good mark.

## 6073 BRUNTON PUBLICATIONS PEMBROKE CUP H'CAP 1m
3:20 (3:20) (Class 4) (0-85,87) 3-Y-O £6,469 (£1,925; £962; £481) Stalls Low

Form RPR
-113 1 **Surrey Hope (USA)**[48] 4271 3-9-9 **87**.......... RyanMoore 6 97
(Joseph Tuite) *pressed ldr: led over 3f out: hrd rdn over 1f out: hld on nr fin* **11/4**[2]
31 2 nk **Kryptos**[32] 4894 3-9-6 **84**.......... FranBerry 8 93
(John Berry) *hld up in last pair: pushed along and prog on outer wl over 1f out: rdn to chse wnr ins fnl f: clsd nr fin but too late* **6/1**
5114 3 ¾ **Rigoletto (SWI)**[26] 5115 3-9-7 **85**.......... JamieSpencer 3 92
(Luca Cumani) *hld up in last pair: shkn up over 2f out: swtchd lft jst over 1f out: drvn and r.o to take 3rd last strides: nrst fin* **5/2**[1]
3660 4 ¾ **Whip Nae Nae (IRE)**[74] 3317 3-9-2 **80**.......... TomMarquand 5 86
(Richard Hannon) *cl up: chsd wnr over 2f out: no imp u.p over 1f out: lost 2nd and one pce ins fnl f* **10/1**
2650 5 3 ¼ **Glory Of Paris (IRE)**[34] 4810 3-8-12 **76**.......... WilliamCarson 1 74
(Rod Millman) *trckd ldrs: rdn and no prog over 2f out: fdd fnl f* **22/1**
2323 6 4 **Black Trilby (IRE)**[42] 4490 3-9-6 **84**..........(h) SamHitchcott 2 73
(Clive Cox) *taken down early: led to over 3f out: sn shoved along: wknd over 1f out* **12/1**
1-35 7 shd **Baashiq (IRE)**[20] 5323 3-9-5 **83**.......... JimCrowley 7 72
(Roger Varian) *trckd ldrs: rdn over 2f out: wknd over 1f out* **7/2**[3]

1m 40.24s (-3.26) **Going Correction** -0.175s/f (Firm) 7 Ran SP% **112.9**
Speed ratings (Par 102): **109,108,107,107,103 99,99**
CSF £18.95 CT £44.71 TOTE £4.40: £2.10, £2.60; EX 19.90 Trifecta £44.20.
**Owner** Surrey Racing (sh) **Bred** Nancy Mazzoni **Trained** Lambourn, Berks
■ Itsakindamagic was withdrawn not under orders. Rule 4 does not apply.

**FOCUS**
A decent little 3yo handicap, the first three all looking progressive sorts. The fourth looks the best guide.

## 6074 BRITISH STALLION STUDS EBF UPAVON FILLIES' STKS (LISTED RACE) 1m 1f 201y
3:50 (3:50) (Class 1) 3-Y-0+

£28,355 (£10,750; £5,380; £2,680; £1,345; £675) Stalls Low

Form RPR
2121 1 **Billesdon Bess**[14] 5529 3-8-9 91 ................ HollieDoyle 2 102+
(Richard Hannon) *trckd ldng pair: n.m.r and lost pl sltly 2f out: prog over 1f out: cajoled along to ld jst ins fnl f: pushed out* **6/1**[3]
-210 2 1 **High Hopes**[25] 5155 4-9-2 94 ................ JimCrowley 1 99
(David Simcock) *hld up in 7th: rdn and prog on outer over 1f out: r.o to take 2nd nr fin: no ch to chal* **6/1**[3]
3-45 3 ½ **Rosental**[19] 5381 5-9-2 100 ................ JamieSpencer 9 98
(Luca Cumani) *trckd ldng trio: prog to ld wl over 1f out: drvn and hdd jst ins fnl f: one pce and lost 2nd nr fin* **8/1**
-120 4 1 **Coconut Creme**[55] 3995 3-8-9 97 ................ PatCosgrave 3 96
(William Haggas) *trckd ldng trio: urged along 3f out: kpt on u.p fr over 1f out but nt pce to chal* **9/2**[2]
1300 5 1 **Serenada**[25] 5155 3-8-9 98 ................ SilvestreDeSousa 6 94
(Roger Varian) *dwlt: t.k.h: hld up in last and wl off the pce: reminders and fnd nil wl over 2f out: stl adrift over 1f out: wandered after but fnlly styd on last 150yds* **8/1**
-103 6 ½ **Playful Sound**[19] 5381 4-9-2 100 ................ RyanMoore 7 93
(Sir Michael Stoute) *hld up in 6th: rdn and prog over 2f out: chal over 1f out: sn nt qckn and lost pl fnl f* **5/2**[1]
0/04 7 1 **Uele River**[32] 4915 5-9-2 88 ................ DaneO'Neill 8 91
(Henry Candy) *led at decent pce: hdd and steadily wknd wl over 1f out* **25/1**
-065 8 hd **Skiffle**[14] 5529 4-9-2 100 ................(p) JamesDoyle 10 91
(Charlie Appleby) *hld up in last trio: rdn on outer over 2f out: one pce and no real prog* **6/1**[3]
3344 9 nk **Indian Blessing**[30] 4988 3-8-9 96 ................ LiamKeniry 4 90
(Ed Walker) *trckd ldr to 2f out: steadily wknd* **12/1**

2m 5.8s (-4.10) **Going Correction** -0.175s/f (Firm)
**WFA** 3 from 4yo+ 7lb 9 Ran SP% **123.4**
Speed ratings (Par 108): **109,108,107,107,106 105,105,104,104**
CSF £44.85 TOTE £6.30: £2.00, £2.20, £1.80; EX 47.30 Trifecta £318.90.
**Owner** Pall Mall Partners & Partners **Bred** Stowell Hill Partners **Trained** East Everleigh, Wilts

**FOCUS**
This Listed race has been won by the likes of Chorist, Promising Lead and Journey, and this edition looked up to scratch if lacking an obvious star. For the seventh time in the last 11 years it went to a 3yo. The time was exactly on standard and the winner took another step forward. The fourth and fifth were close to their Ribblesdale form.

## 6075 CHAMPAGNE JOSEPH PERRIER H'CAP (FOR HORSES THAT HAVE NOT WON A FLAT RACE THIS YEAR) 1m 1f 201y
4:20 (4:20) (Class 5) (0-75,76) 3-Y-0+ £3,396 (£1,010; £505; £252) Stalls Low

Form RPR
405 1 **Viking Hoard (IRE)**[43] 4468 3-9-4 72 ................(b[1]) JimCrowley 11 79
(Harry Dunlop) *hld up in last: prog on inner 2f out: rdn and styd on to ld last 130yds: in command after* **5/1**[3]
-322 2 ¾ **Know Your Limit (IRE)**[16] 5478 3-9-8 76 ................ JamieSpencer 8 81
(Ed Walker) *hld up in midfield: smooth prog to trck ldr 3f out: sn shkn up to chal: mde heavy weather of getting past but eventually tk narrow ld fnl f: sn hdd and outpcd* **5/2**[1]
332 3 ¾ **Funky Footsteps (IRE)**[9] 5718 3-9-2 70 ................(p) CharlesBishop 7 74
(Eve Johnson Houghton) *led: rdn and pressed over 2f out: kpt on u.p: narrowly hdd fnl f: outpcd last 100yds* **4/1**[2]
-324 4 ¾ **Biotic**[44] 4443 6-10-0 75 ................ WilliamCarson 4 76
(Rod Millman) *hld up in last pair: prog on outer wl over 2f out: rdn and fnd nil wl over 1f out: one pce after* **4/1**[2]
4350 5 ½ **Pack It In (IRE)**[21] 5299 4-9-8 69 ................(p[1]) DaneO'Neill 6 69
(Brian Meehan) *hld up in midfield: rdn and no prog over 2f out: n.d after: kpt on last 100yds* **10/1**
3644 6 ¾ **Helf (IRE)**[11] 5652 3-9-1 69 ................ TomMarquand 1 69
(Richard Hannon) *pressed ldng pair to 3f out: sn rdn: one pce over 1f out* **8/1**
3633 7 3½ **Josh The Plod (IRE)**[14] 5532 3-8-6 67 ................ JasonWatson[(7)] 12 60
(Andrew Balding) *hld up in last trio: gng wl 4f out: rdn on outer wl over 2f out: fnd nil and sn btn* **12/1**
215- 8 16 **Tower Power**[564] 399 6-10-0 75 ................ LukeMorris 13 35
(Phil McEntee) *mostly chsd ldr to 3f out: wknd qckly 2f out* **50/1**

2m 8.54s (-1.36) **Going Correction** -0.175s/f (Firm)
**WFA** 3 from 4yo+ 7lb 8 Ran SP% **115.1**
Speed ratings (Par 103): **98,97,96,96,95 95,92,79**
CSF £18.07 CT £54.49 TOTE £7.20: £2.00, £1.40, £1.80; EX 22.10 Trifecta £122.30.
**Owner** Be Hopeful Partnership **Bred** P Monahan **Trained** Lambourn, Berks

**FOCUS**
A modest handicap with unusual conditions, as highlighted in the race title. There was a compressed finish and 3yos filled the places. The winner was back to form in the blinkers.

## 6076 SHADWELL STUD RACING EXCELLENCE APPRENTICE H'CAP (WHIPS SHALL BE CARRIED BUT NOT USED) 6f 213y
4:50 (4:51) (Class 5) (0-70,71) 3-Y-0+ £4,528 (£1,347; £673; £336) Stalls Centre

Form RPR
3-42 1 **Bengal Lancer**[20] 5333 3-9-11 71 ................ ManuelFernandes 9 85
(Ian Williams) *trckd ldr: led over 2f out: racd awkwardly in front tl drew clr fnl f* **5/2**[1]
4022 2 3½ **Fine Example**[22] 5258 4-9-11 69 ................(b) SeamusCronin[(3)] 8 76
(Kevin Ryan) *led to over 2f out: pressed wnr to over 1f out: outpcd fnl f but clr of rest* **7/2**[2]
1064 3 3½ **Moonshine Dancer**[28] 5031 3-9-1 64 ................(h) GabrieleMalune[(3)] 2 60
(Christian Williams) *hld up in midfield: outpcd but prog fr 2f out: styd on fnl f to take 3rd last strides* **12/1**
5236 4 hd **Characterized**[19] 5357 3-9-8 68 ................ JoshuaBryan 4 63
(Geoffrey Deacon) *chsd ldng pair: outpcd fr 2f out: no imp after: lost 3rd last strides* **7/1**[3]
2550 5 1¾ **Ceyhan**[33] 4840 5-9-5 67 ................ EmmaTaff[(7)] 10 59
(Jamie Osborne) *wl in rr: stdy prog fr 2f out: nvr in it but kpt on to take 5th last strides* **33/1**
00 6 nk **Topology**[23] 5221 4-9-10 68 ................(v[1]) StephenCummins[(3)] 3 59
(Joseph Tuite) *trckd ldrs: urged along and outpcd over 2f out: sn no ch* **14/1**
000 7 1¼ **Mr Andros**[22] 5248 4-9-2 60 ................(t[1]) NicolaCurrie[(3)] 13 48
(Brendan Powell) *hld up in midfield: outpcd over 2f out: no ch after: kpt on* **50/1**
2664 8 2 **Welsh Inlet (IRE)**[11] 5651 9-8-10 56 ................ SophieRalston[(5)] 12 39
(John Bridger) *wl in tch: outpcd over 2f out: sn no ch* **16/1**
0405 9 hd **Born To Finish (IRE)**[33] 4851 4-9-10 68 ................(t) WilliamCox[(3)] 11 50
(Jamie Osborne) *s.i.s: wl in rr: no ch over 1f out: hanging but kpt on fnl f* **8/1**
4000 10 2¾ **Greyjoy (IRE)**[4] 5935 3-7-11 50 oh5 ................ ShariqMohd[(7)] 7 23
(Sylvester Kirk) *t.k.h: wl in tch tl wknd 2f out* **66/1**
2005 11 nk **Virile (IRE)**[83] 3008 6-9-1 56 ................ FinleyMarsh 5 30
(Sylvester Kirk) *a wl in rr: no ch fnl 2f* **20/1**
5304 12 ¾ **Intimately**[6] 5857 4-8-12 58 ................ Pierre-LouisJamin[(5)] 1 30
(Jonathan Portman) *rel to r and lft 10 l: t.k.h and ct up after 2f: wknd 2f out* **9/1**
1630 13 nk **Altiko Tommy (IRE)**[35] 4748 3-9-2 67 ................ JasonWatson[(5)] 6 36
(George Baker) *stmbld bdly s: a wl in rr* **14/1**

1m 26.44s (-2.16) **Going Correction** -0.175s/f (Firm)
**WFA** 3 from 4yo+ 5lb 13 Ran SP% **122.5**
Speed ratings (Par 103): **105,101,97,96,94 94,93,90,90,87 87,86,85**
CSF £10.66 CT £94.76 TOTE £3.00: £1.30, £1.80, £4.70; EX 13.90 Trifecta £95.80.
**Owner** G S Tuck **Bred** G S Tuck **Trained** Portway, Worcs

**FOCUS**
The first two dominated this modest event for apprentices. A clear pb from the winner.
T/Jkpt: Not Won T/Plt: £266.80 to a £1 stake. Pool: £71,439.85 - 195.45 winning units. T/Qpdt: £35.40 to a £1 stake. Pool: £6,371.29 - 132.96 winning units. **Jonathan Neesom**

6077 - 6079a (Foreign Racing) - See Raceform Interactive

# 5168 GOWRAN PARK (R-H)
Wednesday, August 16

**OFFICIAL GOING: Soft (yielding in places)**

## 6080a IRISH STALLION FARMS EBF HURRY HARRIET STKS (LISTED RACE) 1m 1f 100y
6:30 (6:31) 3-Y-0+

£27,735 (£8,931; £4,230; £1,880; £940; £470)

RPR
1 **Alluringly (USA)**[32] 4928 3-9-0 105 ................ SeamieHeffernan 12 105+
(A P O'Brien, Ire) *racd towards rr: clsr in mid-div 3f out: c wd into st: gd hdwy to chse ldrs over 1f out in 5th: kpt on strly to ld cl home* **7/4**[1]
2 nk **Making Light (IRE)**[69] 3510 3-9-0 101 ................ PatSmullen 9 104+
(D K Weld, Ire) *racd in mid-div: t.k.h: 6th at 1/2-way: clsr to press ldrs 1f out and led fnl 100yds: kpt on wl: hdd cl home* **7/2**[2]
3 1¼ **Elegant Pose (IRE)**[43] 4483 3-9-0 93 ................ ColinKeane 3 102
(G M Lyons, Ire) *racd towards rr: prog on inner 3f out: chsd ldrs appr fnl f and sn disp: hdd fnl 100yds: kpt on same pce in 3rd* **8/1**
4 ¾ **Glamorous Approach (IRE)**[8] 5766 4-9-10 101 ........ KevinManning 10 103+
(J S Bolger, Ire) *hld up: clsr in mid-div 3f out: c wd in st: kpt on wl ins fnl f into 4th fnl 100yds: nvr nrr* **10/1**
5 2½ **Pocketfullofdreams (FR)**[31] 4934 3-9-0 97 ........ DonnachaO'Brien 13 95
(A P O'Brien, Ire) *chsd ldrs on outer tl led after 2f: hdd appr fnl f: kpt on one pce* **12/1**
6 nk **Black Ruby (IRE)**[24] 5193 3-9-0 88 ................ ChrisHayes 4 95
(Mrs John Harrington, Ire) *chsd ldrs on inner: 7th 3f out: brought to centre of trck in st: rdn and no imp appr fnl f: kpt on again clsng stages: nvr nrr* **33/1**
7 nk **I'm So Fancy (IRE)**[13] 5583 3-9-0 92 ................ NGMcCullagh 2 94
(Mrs John Harrington, Ire) *led for 2f: keen and trckd ldr in 2nd tl briefly on terms under 2f out: hdd appr fnl f: wknd fnl 100yds* **25/1**
8 1¼ **Flirt (IRE)**[13] 5583 4-9-7 90 ................(v[1]) RoryCleary 5 91
(J P Murtagh, Ire) *trckd ldr in 2nd: sn 3rd: rdn and nt qckn appr fnl f: sn one pce* **66/1**
9 2½ **Aurora Butterfly (IRE)**[32] 4928 3-9-0 101 ................ WJLee 6 86
(W McCreery, Ire) *chsd ldrs: 5th at 1/2-way: rdn and nt qckn over 1f out: nt hrd rdn ins fnl f* **7/1**[3]
10 ½ **Pavlenko (JPN)**[8] 5765 3-9-0 93 ................(p) WayneLordan 7 85
(A P O'Brien, Ire) *racd in mid-div: nt qckn under 2f out: kpt on one pce fnl f* **20/1**
11 5½ **Sea Swift (IRE)**[31] 4934 4-9-7 98 ................(h) LeighRoche 14 74
(D K Weld, Ire) *racd in rr: rdn and sme hdwy under 2f out: sn no imp* **16/1**
12 2¾ **Valentana (IRE)**[13] 5583 5-9-7 87 ................(t) GaryCarroll 1 68
(W McCreery, Ire) *trckd ldrs in 3rd: sn 4th: pushed along 3f out on inner: nt qckn 2f out: sn no ex* **50/1**
13 1¾ **Kamili (IRE)**[31] 4938 3-9-0 84 ................ PBBeggy 8 65
(Joseph Patrick O'Brien, Ire) *racd in rr of mid-div: clsr 3f out: rdn and no imp over 2f out* **50/1**
14 1½ **Dragon Fei (IRE)**[8] 5766 7-9-7 94 ................(p[1]) ConnorKing 11 62
(Dermot Anthony McLoughlin, Ire) *hld up: towards rr at 1/2-way: rdn and no imp over 2f out* **50/1**

2m 7.79s (0.79)
**WFA** 3 from 4yo+ 7lb 14 Ran SP% **123.8**
CSF £7.09 TOTE £2.80: £1.40, £1.50, £2.20; DF 10.00 Trifecta £61.30.
**Owner** Derrick Smith & Mrs John Magnier & Michael Tabor **Bred** All For Glory Syndicate **Trained** Cashel, Co Tipperary

**FOCUS**
This represented nothing more than a confidence booster for \bAlluringly\p.

6081 - 6083a (Foreign Racing) - See Raceform Interactive

# 6017 CLAIREFONTAINE (R-H)
Wednesday, August 16

**OFFICIAL GOING: Turf: good to firm**

## 6084a PRIX AUBEPINES (CLAIMER) (3YO) (TURF) 1m 1f
5:10 3-Y-0 £8,119 (£3,247; £2,435; £1,623; £811)

RPR
1 **Gnily (IRE)**[24] 3-9-1 0 ................ ChristopheSoumillon 5 73
(C Lerner, France) **68/10**[3]

2 2 1/2 **Manipur (GER)**[107] 2246 3-9-4 0 MaximPecheur 10 70
(Markus Klug, Germany) 11/1
3 snk **Mybee Davis (IRE)**[100] 3-9-1 0 AlexandreChesneau(7) 11 74
(G Botti, France) 19/1
4 hd **Certaldo (FR)**[27] 3-8-11 0 (b) JulienAuge 12 63
(C Ferland, France) 15/2
5 2 **A Head Ahead (GER)**[5] 5909 3-8-10 0 (b) AlexisPouchin(8) 6 65
(Y Gourraud, France) 8/1
6 3 **Cropus (FR)**[31] 4943 3-8-10 0 DelphineSantiago(5) 8 56
(R Le Gal, France) 16/1
7 5 **Jeu Celebre (IRE)**[20] 3-9-1 0 (b) HugoJourniac 7 46
(J-C Rouget, France) 6/1[2]
8 snk **April Angel (FR)**[44] 4455 3-8-6 0 (p) MathieuPelletan(5) 9 41
(P Demercastel, France) 75/1
9 nk **Spunky Heart (IRE)**[162] 3-8-7 0 MlleAlisonMassin(4) 4 41
(Mlle L Kneip, France) 147/1
10 2 **Hold Me Tight (IRE)**[5] 5909 3-8-8 0 ClementLecoeuvre(3) 14 36
(J S Moore) 15/1
11 5 **Princesse Hartwood (FR)**[48] 3-8-9 0 ow1 FabienLefebvre 18 24
(H De Nicolay, France) 79/1
12 3/4 **Mounirchop (FR)**[78] 3-9-1 0 (b) AntoineHamelin 16 28
(S Smrczek, Germany) 42/1
13 3/4 **Tresor (IRE)**[5] 5909 3-9-2 0 (p) CristianDemuro 3 28
(Y Barberot, France) 9/1
14 3 1/2 **Simply Genius (FR)**[9] 5732 3-9-4 0 (b[1]) Pierre-CharlesBoudot 15 22
(F Chappet, France) 53/10[1]
15 4 1/2 **Husani (IRE)**[20] 3-8-8 0 (b) TristanBaron(3) 2 6
(C Lerner, France) 77/1
16 hd **Satica** 3-8-11 0 MickaelBarzalona 17 6
(P Schiergen, Germany) 11/1
17 10 **Members Only (FR)** 3-8-11 0 StephanePasquier 1
(H-A Pantall, France) 53/1

PARI-MUTUEL (all including 1 euro stake): WIN 7.80; PLACE 2.50, 4.10, 5.60; DF 61.30; SF 90.50.
**Owner** Ecurie Carre Magique Sas **Bred** John & Anne-Marie O'Connor **Trained** France

## 6055 BEVERLEY (R-H)

Thursday, August 17

**OFFICIAL GOING: Good (good to soft in places; 7.1)**
Wind: Moderate against Weather: Sunny periods

### 6085 NIGEL'S 60TH BIRTHDAY EBF FILLIES' NOVICE STKS (PLUS 10 RACE) (DIV I) 5f
2:10 (2:10) (Class 5) 2-Y-O £3,881 (£1,155; £577; £288) Stalls Low

Form RPR
0 1 **Elnadim Star (IRE)**[41] 4555 2-9-0 0 TomEaves 7 71+
(Kevin Ryan) *trckd ldrs: hdwy 2f out: chal over 1f out: rdn to ld ent fnl f: kpt on wl* 11/4[3]
2 1 1/4 **Zip Along (IRE)** 2-9-0 0 TonyHamilton 1 67+
(Richard Fahey) *slt ld on inner: rdn along over wl over 1f out: hdd ent fnl f: kpt on u.p* 9/4[1]
3235 3 1/2 **Our Little Pony**[18] 5453 2-9-0 68 JoeFanning 5 65
(Lawrence Mullaney) *trckd ldrs: n.m.r on inner over 1f out: sn swtchd lft and rdn: kpt on* 5/2[2]
4 2 **Miss Wolverine** 2-9-0 0 NathanEvans 2 58
(Michael Easterby) *dwlt: green and outpcd in rr: hdwy on inner over 1f out: kpt on wl fnl f* 33/1
60 5 1/2 **Eller Brook**[20] 5370 2-9-0 0 PaulMulrennan 9 56
(Michael Dods) *wnt lft s: t.k.h: trckd ldrs: hdwy 2f out: rdn over 1f out: kpt on same pce* 9/1
64 6 3/4 **Rema Al Kuwait (IRE)**[29] 5015 2-9-0 0 PhillipMakin 6 53
(David O'Meara) *trckd ldrs: pushed along on inner and outpcd 2f out: n.m.r wl over 1f out: swtchd lft and kpt on u.p fnl f* 14/1
04 7 1/2 **Optimickstickhill**[22] 5278 2-9-0 0 DavidAllan 3 52
(Scott Dixon) *cl up: disp ld 1/2-way: rdn along wl over 1f out: grad wknd appr fnl f* 12/1

1m 5.5s (2.00) **Going Correction** +0.325s/f (Good) 7 Ran SP% 113.3
Speed ratings (Par 91): **97,95,94,91,90 89,88**
CSF £9.20 TOTE £3.80: £1.90, £1.50; EX 10.40 Trifecta £33.40.
**Owner** Jaber Abdullah **Bred** Mrs M Marnane **Trained** Hambleton, N Yorks

**FOCUS**
After 8mm of rain overnight the going was changed to good, good to soft in places. The pace was not strong in this opening novice, but the three market leaders filled the first three places. Paul Mulrennan said it was "beautiful ground", while Joe Fanning said "softer than yesterday, but not bad." Ordinary form.

### 6086 NIGEL'S 60TH BIRTHDAY EBF FILLIES' NOVICE STKS (PLUS 10 RACE) (DIV II) 5f
2:40 (2:42) (Class 5) 2-Y-O £3,881 (£1,155; £577; £288) Stalls Low

Form RPR
2 1 **Gold Stone**[24] 5210 2-9-0 0 TomEaves 8 73+
(Kevin Ryan) *trckd ldrs: smooth hdwy to take slt ld over 3f out: rdn over 1f out: clr ins fnl f: kpt on* 10/11[1]
2 1 1/4 **Debawtry (IRE)** 2-9-0 0 DavidNolan 2 69
(David O'Meara) *hld up towards rr on inner: n.m.r and swtchd lft wl over 1f out: hdwy and sn rdn: chsd wnr ins fnl f: kpt on wl* 14/1
5 3 2 1/4 **La Belle Mayson**[57] 3980 2-9-0 0 TonyHamilton 3 60
(Richard Fahey) *wnt lft s: trckd ldrs: hdwy to chse wnr wl over 1f out: sn rdn: drvn and kpt on same pce fnl f* 5/1[3]
4 4 3/4 **Call Dawn**[71] 3460 2-8-7 0 HarrisonShaw(7) 4 58
(Michael Easterby) *hmpd s: in tch: hdwy 2f out: rdn over 1f out: kpt on fnl f* 11/1
5 shd **Bee Ina Bonnet** 2-9-0 0 DavidAllan 5 57+
(Tim Easterby) *hmpd s: green and rr: rdn along on outer wl over 1f out: kpt on wl fnl f* 12/1
6 4 1/2 **Cat Ballou** 2-9-0 0 PhillipMakin 1 41
(David O'Meara) *trckd ldrs on inner: pushed along over 2f out: sn rdn and wknd wl over 1f out* 4/1[2]
0 7 1/2 **Siena Flyer (IRE)**[24] 5210 2-9-0 0 JackGarritty 6 39
(Jedd O'Keeffe) *qckly away and led: hdd over 3f out: cl up: rdn along 2f out: grad wknd* 50/1

6 8 6 **Sabellum (IRE)**[18] 5453 2-8-11 0 SammyJoBell(3) 9 18+
(Richard Fahey) *wnt bdly lft s and rr: hdwy on outer to chse ldrs 4f out: rdn along over 2f out: sn wknd* 16/1

1m 5.76s (2.26) **Going Correction** +0.325s/f (Good) 8 Ran SP% 119.6
Speed ratings (Par 91): **94,92,88,87,87 79,79,69**
CSF £17.62 TOTE £1.70: £1.10, £3.90, £2.20; EX 20.60 Trifecta £78.60.
**Owner** Jaber Abdullah **Bred** Fittocks Stud **Trained** Hambleton, N Yorks

**FOCUS**
The clear form pick landed the odds with some authority in this novice. The bare form has only an ordinary feel.

### 6087 CONSTANT SECURITY NURSERY H'CAP 7f 96y
3:10 (3:11) (Class 5) (0-75,73) 2-Y-O £3,780 (£1,131; £565; £283; £141) Stalls Low

Form RPR
0241 1 **Go Now Go Now (IRE)**[22] 5279 2-9-2 68 PJMcDonald 8 74
(Mark Johnston) *mde all: rdn clr over 1f out: drvn ins fnl f: hld on wl* 6/1[2]
3032 2 nk **Crownthorpe**[22] 5279 2-9-4 70 TonyHamilton 12 76
(Richard Fahey) *hld up towards rr: stdy hdwy 2f out: chsd ldrs and rdn over 1f out: keeping on whn n.m.r jst ins fnl f: sn drvn and fin strly: jst hld* 8/1
0022 3 hd **Mr Carbonator**[9] 5756 2-8-1 53 JimmyQuinn 10 58
(Philip Kirby) *in tch: effrt on outer and hdwy over 2f out: rdn wl over 1f out: swtchd rt and drvn ins fnl f: sn edgd rt: styd on wl towards fin* 6/1[2]
2320 4 1 1/4 **Arabian Jazz (IRE)**[34] 4858 2-9-1 67 LouisSteward 3 69
(Michael Bell) *trckd ldrs: hdwy on wd outside over 2f out: rdn to chse wnr and ev ch over 1f out: drvn and kpt on same pce fnl f* 11/2[1]
0136 5 3 **Poet's Dawn**[16] 5492 2-9-7 73 DavidAllan 6 68
(Tim Easterby) *dwlt and rr: swtchd lft towards outer and hdwy 2f out: rdn over 1f out: styd on wl fnl f* 7/1[3]
0542 6 shd **Reinbeau Prince**[20] 5373 2-9-4 70 DavidNolan 2 64
(Richard Fahey) *midfield on inner whn hmpd after 1 1/2f: sn in tch: hdwy over 2f out: rdn along wl over 1f out: drvn and no imp fnl f* 10/1
0403 7 1/2 **Admiral Rooke (IRE)**[20] 5373 2-9-2 68 PaulMulrennan 7 61
(Michael Dods) *prom: trckd ldr after 2f: rdn along on inner over 2f out: drvn wl over 1f out: grad wknd* 7/1[3]
016 8 4 **Jackontherocks**[34] 4834 2-9-2 73 CallumRodriguez(5) 9 56
(Michael Dods) *a towards rr* 9/1
5543 9 1/2 **Northern Law (IRE)**[9] 5752 2-9-4 70 JasonHart 4 52
(John Quinn) *midfield: effrt and sme hdwy 3f out: rdn along over 2f out: sn wknd* 8/1
344 10 1 1/2 **Here In The Dark**[23] 5255 2-9-2 68 GrahamLee 11 46
(Keith Dalgleish) *dwlt: a rr* 16/1
6460 11 5 **Ventura Crest (IRE)**[42] 4527 2-8-6 58 JamesSullivan 5 24
(Tim Easterby) *prom: rdn along wl over 2f out: sn wknd* 40/1

1m 36.85s (3.05) **Going Correction** +0.325s/f (Good) 11 Ran SP% 118.6
Speed ratings (Par 94): **95,94,94,93,89 89,88,84,83,82 76**
CSF £53.91 CT £304.44 TOTE £5.70: £2.50, £3.20, £1.70; EX 28.20 Trifecta £119.20.
**Owner** Paul & Clare Rooney **Bred** Gerry Ross **Trained** Middleham Moor, N Yorks

**FOCUS**
Race run over an extra 7yds. The winner made all in this nursery and the first four were clear of the rest. The first two took a small step forward from their Catterick form.

### 6088 SUNDAY HOP NEXT ON 27TH AUGUST (S) H'CAP (BEVERLEY MIDDLE DISTANCE SERIES) 1m 4f 23y
3:40 (3:40) (Class 6) (0-60,60) 3-Y-O+ £2,587 (£770; £384; £192) Stalls Low

Form RPR
3165 1 **Sakhalin Star (IRE)**[7] 5831 6-9-8 56 (p[1]) ConnorBeasley 5 62
(Richard Guest) *hld up and bhd: stdy hdwy 3f out: chsd ldrs over 1f out: rdn to take narrow ld jst ins fnl f: sn drvn kpt on wl* 8/1
0354 2 3/4 **Knightsbridge Liam (IRE)**[30] 5001 3-8-4 54 HarrisonShaw(7) 3 60
(Michael Easterby) *hld up: hdwy on inner 3f out: rdn to ld wl over 1f out: drvn and hdd jst ins fnl f: rallied gamely and ev ch tl no ex towards fin* 5/1[2]
1220 3 3 **Cool Music (IRE)**[7] 5832 7-9-7 55 (p) CamHardie 10 55
(Antony Brittain) *hld up: hdwy on outer over 3f out: chsd ldrs over 2f out: sn rdn and ev ch over 1f out: drvn and kpt on same pce fnl f* 7/1[3]
4100 4 5 **Lean On Pete (IRE)**[17] 5483 8-9-12 60 AndrewMullen 1 52
(Ollie Pears) *led 1f: trckd ldng pair: effrt 3f out: rdn along 2f out: drvn over 1f out: kpt on one pce fnl f*
4000 5 1 3/4 **Percy Verence**[5] 5951 4-9-3 51 (vt[1]) BenCurtis 7 40
(Tracy Waggott) *midfield: hdwy over 3f out: chsd ldrs over 2f out and sn rdn: drvn over 1f out: sn one pce* 7/1[3]
0500 6 2 **Barbary Prince**[7] 5850 5-8-12 46 oh1 JoeDoyle 2 32+
(Shaun Harris) *prom: chsd ldr after 2f: cl up over 3f out: led wl over 2f out: rdn and hdd wl over 1f out: grad wknd* 66/1
0632 7 3 1/4 **Chauvelin**[34] 4839 6-9-4 52 (b) TomEaves 9 33
(Nigel Tinkler) *hld up in rr: sme hdwy over 2f out: sn rdn along and n.d* 7/1[3]
0042 8 1 1/2 **Sevilla**[22] 5296 4-9-9 57 (p[1]) PJMcDonald 11 35
(Olly Murphy) *trckd ldrs: rdn along over 3f out: sn wknd* 2/1[1]
6000 9 2 3/4 **Python**[9] 5740 5-8-5 46 oh1 RussellHarris(7) 6 20
(Andrew Crook) *a rr* 50/1
0000 10 7 **Scruffy McGuffy**[69] 3529 4-9-9 57 ShaneGray 4 20
(Ann Duffield) *chsd ldrs: rdn along over 3f out: sn wknd* 25/1
000 11 17 **Tin Pan Alley**[41] 4558 9-9-6 54 (p) DavidAllan 8 +
(David C Griffiths) *prom: led after 1f: rdn along over 3f out: hdd wl over 2f out: sn wknd* 14/1

2m 43.23s (3.43) **Going Correction** +0.325s/f (Good)
**WFA** 3 from 4yo+ 9lb 11 Ran SP% 120.3
Speed ratings (Par 101): **101,100,98,95,94 92,90,89,87,83 71**
CSF £48.42 CT £301.17 TOTE £8.80: £2.50, £1.80, £2.30; EX 60.70 Trifecta £474.30.
**Owner** Bamboozelem **Bred** Sig Massimo Parri **Trained** Ingmanthorpe, W Yorks

**FOCUS**
Race run over an extra 7yds. They went a fair pace and the first two came from some way back. The winner found a bit more on this year's form.

### 6089 BRIDGE MCFARLAND H'CAP 5f
4:10 (4:14) (Class 5) (0-70,72) 3-Y-O+ £3,881 (£1,155; £577; £288) Stalls Low

Form RPR
53 1 **Noah Amor (IRE)**[16] 5514 4-9-7 67 DavidNolan 6 75
(David O'Meara) *cl up: led wl over 1f out: rdn ent fnl f: kpt on wl towards fin* 7/1
0022 2 1 1/4 **Astrophysics**[18] 5459 5-9-9 69 PaddyAspell 11 73
(Lynn Siddall) *towards rr: hdwy over 2f out: rdn to chse ldrs over 1f out and sn edgd rt: drvn and edgd rt ins fnl f: kpt on wl towards fin* 11/2[3]

3531 **3** 3/4 **Roaring Rory**[30] 4997 4-8-12 **65**....................(p) SeamusCronin(7) 1 68
(Ollie Pears) *chsd ldrs on inner: pushed along and outpcd 1/2-way: swtchd lft and hdwy whn hmpd over 1f out: rdn and n.m.r ent fnl f: sn swtchd lft and styd on wl u.p towards fin* **4/1**[1]

0362 **4** 1 **You're Cool**[35] 4795 5-9-5 **68**.................... LewisEdmunds(3) 7 65
(John Balding) *prom: cl up 2f out: sn rdn: drvn and kpt on same pce fnl f* **4/1**[1]

0340 **5** 1 **Bond Bombshell**[9] 5736 4-8-13 **62**....................(p) JoshDoyle(3) 5 56
(David O'Meara) *prom: rdn along wl over 1f out: drvn and hung rt ins fnl f: kpt on same pce* **10/1**

3625 **6** 1 3/4 **Windforpower (IRE)**[9] 5736 7-8-12 **58**....................(p) BenCurtis 9 45
(Tracy Waggott) *in tch on outer: rdn along wl over 1f out: sn drvn and no imp fnl f* **14/1**

0335 **7** 1 1/4 **Pearl Noir**[35] 4795 7-9-1 **61**....................(b) PJMcDonald 4 46
(Scott Dixon) *sn led: rdn along and hdd wl over 1f out: drvn and wknd ent* **5/1**[2]

3000 **8** 1/2 **Tinsill**[10] 5695 6-8-5 **51** oh6.................... JoeDoyle 3 32
(Nigel Tinkler) *rr: hdwy on inner wl over 1f out: chsd ldrs and rdn whn nt clr run and hmpd over 1f out: no ch after* **33/1**

-025 **9** 2 **Whigwham**[84] 2989 3-8-4 **52**.................... CamHardie 2 26
(Gary Sanderson) *a towards rr* **25/1**

650 **10** 3/4 **First Bombardment**[5] 5930 4-9-5 **72**....................(v) PatrickVaughan(7) 8 43
(David O'Meara) *dwlt and swtchd rt s: t.k.h and sn chsng ldrs: rdn along 2f out: sn wknd* **7/1**

1m 5.49s (1.99) **Going Correction** +0.325s/f (Good)
**WFA** 3 from 4yo+ 2lb **10** Ran SP% **119.6**
Speed ratings (Par 103): **97,95,93,92,90 87,85,85,81,80**
CSF £46.55 CT £182.16 TOTE £8.90: £2.80, £2.20, £1.60; EX 45.10 Trifecta £276.10.
**Owner** Gallop Racing & N Bradley **Bred** Mrs Claire Doyle **Trained** Upper Helmsley, N Yorks
■ Stewards' Enquiry : Josh Doyle 3 day ban - guilty of careless riding in that he allowed his mount to drift right under a left-handed whip drive (31 Aug-2 Sep)

**FOCUS**
The winner was always prominent in this minor sprint handicap. The runner-up is the best guide.

## 6090 BARBARA'S SPECIAL BIRTHDAY YEAR H'CAP 2m 32y
**4:40** (4:41) (Class 4) (0-85,85) 3-Y-O+
**£6,225** (£1,864; £932; £466; £233; £117) **Stalls Low**

Form RPR

4/41 **1** **Attention Seaker**[9] 5740 7-8-9 **66** 6ex....................(t) DavidAllan 8 75
(Tim Easterby) *trckd ldrs: hdwy over 3f out: chal wl over 1f out and sn rdn: led ent fnl f: drvn out* **3/1**[2]

5022 **2** 2 1/2 **Taper Tantrum (IRE)**[61] 3840 5-9-8 **79**....................(p) LouisSteward 4 84
(Michael Bell) *trckd ldng pair on inner: hdwy 3f out: cl up 2f out: sn rdn and ev ch: drvn and sltly outpcd over 1f out: n.m.r ins fnl f: sn swtchd lft and kpt on towards fin* **13/2**

5330 **3** 1/2 **Royal Flag**[11] 5689 7-8-11 **68**.................... TomEaves 1 72
(Brian Ellison) *hld up in tch: hdwy 3f out: rdn along 2f out: drvn over 1f out: styd on fnl f* **14/1**

-210 **4** nk **Maghfoor**[84] 3005 3-9-2 **85**.................... JimmyQuinn 6 89+
(Saeed bin Suroor) *trckd ldrs: hdwy 5f out: cl up 3f out: led 2f out: sn jnd and rdn: drvn and hdd ent fnl f: sn hung rt: wknd last 100yds* **9/4**[1]

6266 **5** 12 **Cray (IRE)**[11] 5682 3-8-5 **74**....................(p) PJMcDonald 3 64
(James Bethell) *sn trcking ldr: cl up 1/2-way: led 3f out: sn rdn along and hdd 2f out: sn drvn and wknd* **7/2**[3]

0-53 **6** 12 **Bulas Belle**[9] 5737 7-9-2 **73**.................... GrahamLee 9 48
(Grant Tuer) *led: pushed along over 4f out: rdn and hdd 3f out: sn wknd* **7/1**

0020 **7** 3 **Saved By The Bell (IRE)**[19] 5438 7-9-4 **75**....................(v) DavidNolan 2 47
(David O'Meara) *a bhd* **16/1**

3m 42.36s (2.56) **Going Correction** +0.325s/f (Good)
**WFA** 3 from 5yo+ 12lb **7** Ran SP% **116.4**
Speed ratings (Par 105): **106,104,104,104,98 92,90**
CSF £23.34 CT £236.74 TOTE £4.00: £1.70, £2.80; EX 22.60 Trifecta £138.80.
**Owner** Ryedale Partners No 6 **Bred** Ryedale Partners No 6 **Trained** Great Habton, N Yorks

**FOCUS**
Race run over an extra 7yds. The winner showed plenty of stamina to complete a double, while the favourite didn't find much after travelling best of all. The winner is rated back to her old best.

## 6091 MICHAEL JAGGER 70TH BIRTHDAY H'CAP 1m 100y
**5:10** (5:12) (Class 5) (0-70,72) 3-Y-O **£3,780** (£1,131; £565; £283; £141) **Stalls Low**

Form RPR

-201 **1** **Pantera Negra (IRE)**[13] 5604 3-9-5 **68**.................... NathanEvans 7 75+
(David Barron) *hld up: hdwy 3f out: rdn along to chse ldrs wl over 1f out: drvn ins fnl f: styd on wl to ld nr fin* **6/1**[3]

4360 **2** 3/4 **Tesko Fella (IRE)**[12] 5666 3-8-12 **61**.................... JamesSullivan 6 66
(Ruth Carr) *prom: chsd clr ldr 5f out: hdwy over 2f out: rdn to chal 2f out: led over 1f out: drvn ins fnl f: hdd and no ex nr fin* **16/1**

2322 **3** 1 1/2 **Golconda Prince (IRE)**[13] 5604 3-9-2 **65**.................... TonyHamilton 5 67
(Richard Fahey) *hld up and towards rr: hdwy wl over 2f out: rdn wl over 1f out: kpt on strly fnl f* **5/1**[2]

4040 **4** 2 **Armagnac (IRE)**[15] 5545 3-9-2 **65**.................... LouisSteward 2 62
(Michael Bell) *led and sn clr: pushed along and jnd 2f out: sn rdn: hdd over 1f out: kpt on same pce* **11/1**

331 **5** 2 **Dreamofdiscovery (IRE)**[22] 5286 3-8-13 **62**....................(p) JoeDoyle 3 55
(Julie Camacho) *chsd ldrs on inner: hdwy 3f out: rdn along 2f out: drvn over 1f out and sn no imp* **8/1**

630 **6** 1 1/2 **Four Wishes**[21] 5319 3-9-1 **64**.................... DavidAllan 1 53
(Tim Easterby) *hld up: hdwy wl over 2f out: rdn wl over 1f out: plugged on: n.d* **7/1**

5-33 **7** 2 1/4 **Portledge (IRE)**[15] 5541 3-9-9 **72**.................... PJMcDonald 8 56
(James Bethell) *hld up and bhd: sme late hdwy* **5/1**[2]

424- **8** 1 1/4 **Nepeta (USA)**[296] 7598 3-9-7 **70**.................... JoeFanning 10 51
(Mark Johnston) *chsd ldrs: rdn along wl over 2f out: sn wknd* **12/1**

-500 **9** nse **Seebring (IRE)**[30] 5001 3-8-6 **55**....................(p) ShaneGray 9 36
(Brian Ellison) *chsd ldrs: rdn along wl over 2f out: sn wknd* **25/1**

041 **10** 6 **Mont Royal (FR)**[30] 5000 3-9-7 **70**.................... AndrewMullen 12 37
(Ollie Pears) *hld up: a rr* **9/2**[1]

4500 **11** 7 **Zone In**[37] 4723 3-8-4 **53**.................... CamHardie 4 4
(David C Griffiths) *chsd ldng pair: pushed along 1/2-way: rdn 3f out: sn wknd* **33/1**

-264 **12** 1 3/4 **Moonlight Blue (IRE)**[34] 4838 3-9-1 **64**....................(p) PaulMulrennan 11 11
(Michael Dods) *a bhd* **33/1**

1m 49.92s (2.32) **Going Correction** +0.325s/f (Good) **12** Ran SP% **121.0**
Speed ratings (Par 100): **101,100,98,96,94 93,91,89,89,83 76,74**
CSF £97.87 CT £519.36 TOTE £5.60: £1.80, £4.90, £1.90; EX 119.00 Trifecta £887.60.
**Owner** D G Pryde **Bred** Lynch Bages & Camas Park Stud **Trained** Maunby, N Yorks
■ Stewards' Enquiry : James Sullivan 2 day ban - used his whip above the permitted level (31 Aug/1 Sep)

**FOCUS**
Race run over an extra 7yds. They went a good pace and the winner pounced late to complete a double. The second looks the best guide.

## 6092 WHITE ROSE SADDLERY AMATEUR RIDERS' H'CAP 1m 100y
**5:40** (5:41) (Class 6) (0-65,66) 4-Y-O+ **£2,495** (£774; £386; £193) **Stalls Low**

Form RPR

0-01 **1** **Bigbadboy (IRE)**[7] 5831 4-9-4 **45**.................... MissAMcCain(5) 3 60
(Clive Mulhall) *trckd ldrs: smooth hdwy over 2f out: led wl over 1f out: rdn clr ent fnl f: styd on strly* **15/2**[2]

1250 **2** 6 **Graceful Act**[5] 5950 9-10-3 **53**....................(p) MissMMullineaux 10 55
(Ron Barr) *trckd ldrs: hdwy over 3f out: rdn along 2f out: drvn over 1f out: kpt on u.p fnl f* **33/1**

0321 **3** 1/2 **Relight My Fire**[6] 5880 7-10-13 **66** 6ex....................(p) MissEEasterby(3) 2 67
(Tim Easterby) *midfield: hdwy 3f out: rdn along on inner to chse ldrs wl over 1f out: drvn to chse wnr ins fnl f: kpt on same pce* **4/1**[1]

0026 **4** 1/2 **Rebel State (IRE)**[5] 5917 4-9-13 **56**....................(p) MissACawley(5) 16 56
(Jedd O'Keeffe) *towards rr: hdwy wl over 2f out: rdn wl over 1f out: n.m.r and swtchd lft 1f out: styd on: nrst fin* **10/1**

-000 **5** 1/2 **Fledermaus (IRE)**[15] 5544 7-9-3 **46** ow1....................(t) MissBJohnson(7) 4 45
(Tina Jackson) *bhd: wd st: rdn along over 2f out: styd on wl nr stands rail fnl f: nrst fin* **80/1**

340 **6** 1 **I'm Super Too (IRE)**[24] 5214 10-9-11 **54**....................(b) MissACollier(7) 12 51
(Karen Tutty) *dwlt and bhd: hdwy 3f out: rdn along over 2f out: styd on on inner fr over 1f out: nrst fin* **20/1**

6030 **7** nk **Ivors Involvement (IRE)**[3] 6003 5-9-9 **45**.................... MissPFuller 11 41
(Tina Jackson) *sn led: clr over 3f out: rdn along over 2f out: hdd wl over 1f out: sn drvn and kpt on same pce* **20/1**

0501 **8** 3 **Ellaal**[15] 5544 8-10-9 **64**....................(p) MissEmilyBullock(5) 15 54
(Ruth Carr) *trckd ldr: hdwy 3f out: rdn along over 2f out: drvn wl over 1f out: grad wknd* **9/1**

-045 **9** 1 1/2 **Ingleby Spring (IRE)**[15] 5544 5-10-3 **58**.................... MrBillyGarritty(5) 13 45
(Richard Fahey) *midfield: hdwy over 3f out: in tch and rdn over 2f out: drvn and hung rt wl over 1f out: n.d* **11/1**

0222 **10** 3/4 **Catastrophe**[12] 5649 4-10-8 **58**....................(p) MrSWalker 1 43
(John Quinn) *chsd ldrs: rdn along 3f out: wknd fnl 2f* **4/1**[1]

0323 **11** 2 1/2 **Zephyros (GER)**[26] 5140 6-10-9 **64**.................... PoppyBridgwater(5) 6 44
(David Bridgwater) *a rr* **8/1**[3]

3060 **12** 2 1/4 **Mount Cheiron (USA)**[7] 5831 6-9-9 **45**....................(p) MissBeckySmith 5 20
(Richard Ford) *a rr* **33/1**

5455 **13** 1/2 **Sooqaan**[8] 5807 6-10-0 **50**.................... MissSBrotherton 9 24
(Antony Brittain) *chsd ldrs: rdn along wl over 2f out: grad wknd* **8/1**[3]

355 **14** 1 3/4 **Rupert Boy (IRE)**[133] 1587 4-9-9 **45**.................... MrJordanWilliams 8 15
(Scott Dixon) *in tch on inner: rdn along over 3f out: sn wknd* **40/1**

5-00 **15** 1/2 **Yair Hill (IRE)**[5] 5917 9-9-8 **47**....................(p) MissHelenCuthbert(3) 7 16
(Thomas Cuthbert) *a rr* **50/1**

-000 **16** 9 **Stanlow**[40] 4626 7-9-7 **48** ow3....................(v) MrLewisStones(5) 14
(Michael Mullineaux) *a rr* **50/1**

1m 51.33s (3.73) **Going Correction** +0.325s/f (Good) **16** Ran SP% **124.4**
Speed ratings (Par 101): **94,88,87,87,86 85,85,82,80,79 77,75,74,72,72 63**
CSF £247.64 CT £1188.00 TOTE £8.70: £2.30, £5.70, £1.30, £2.80; EX 192.10 Trifecta £981.90.
**Owner** Ms Yvonne Featherstone & Carl Chapman **Bred** Pat McCarthy **Trained** Scarcroft, W Yorks

**FOCUS**
Race run over an extra 7yds. The pace was strong and there was an emphatic winner in this amateur riders' event. The second and third help offer perspective.
T/Plt: £112.50 to a £1 stake. Pool: £69,915.94 - 454.74 winning units. T/Qpdt: £41.90 to a £1 stake. Pool: 4,353.64 - 76.80 winning units. **Joe Rowntree**

# 5356 CHEPSTOW (L-H)
### Thursday, August 17

**OFFICIAL GOING: Good to soft (6.9)**
Wind: Fresh half-against Weather: Fine

## 6093 CRICKET BETTING AT 188BET NOVICE AUCTION STKS (PLUS 10 RACE) 7f 16y
**5:15** (5:17) (Class 4) 2-Y-O **£4,528** (£1,347; £673; £336) **Stalls Centre**

Form RPR

4 **1** **Shepherd Market (IRE)**[26] 5154 2-8-11 0.................... DavidProbert 5 80+
(Clive Cox) *mde all: racd keenly: qcknd over 2f out: pushed clr fr over 1f out: easily* **10/11**[1]

6 **2** 4 1/2 **Great Vizier**[29] 5030 2-8-13 0.................... EdwardGreatrex(3) 2 70
(Eve Johnson Houghton) *w wnr tl settled into 2nd over 5f out: rdn and edgd lft over 2f out: styd on same pce fr over 1f out* **11/4**[2]

02 **3** 1/2 **Neverbeen To Paris (IRE)**[9] 5749 2-9-2 0.................... LukeMorris 3 69
(Michael Bell) *chsd ldrs: pushed along 1/2-way: rdn over 1f out: styd on same pce* **5/1**[3]

**4** 6 **Poucor** 2-9-2 0.................... FrannyNorton 7 54
(Mick Channon) *s.i.s and edgd rt s: hld up: pushed along 1/2-way: rdn and wknd over 1f out* **14/1**

0 **5** 1/2 **Changing (IRE)**[49] 4252 2-8-11 0.................... GeorgeDowning 1 48
(Daniel Kubler) *prom: rdn over 2f out: wknd over 1f out* **100/1**

**6** 1 1/4 **Appenzeller (USA)** 2-9-2 0.................... FranBerry 6 50+
(Richard Hughes) *hld up: plld hrd: shkn up over 2f out: wknd over 1f out* **16/1**

**7** 5 **My Rock (IRE)** 2-8-11 0.................... BenRobinson(5) 4 37
(David Dennis) *s.i.s: hld up: rdn and wknd over 1f out* **33/1**

1m 26.1s (2.90) **Going Correction** +0.325s/f (Good) **7** Ran SP% **112.2**
Speed ratings (Par 96): **96,90,90,83,82 81,75**
CSF £3.40 TOTE £1.80: £1.10, £2.00; EX 5.00 Trifecta £9.80.
**Owner** Windmill Racing **Bred** Rabbah Bloodstock Limited **Trained** Lambourn, Berks

**FOCUS**
The ground had eased a little from the overnight Good, good to soft in places and the opener was 5.4sec slower than standard. Easy for the winner, who took a nice step forward in this ordinary event.

## 6094 PREMIER LEAGUE FOOTBALL AT 188BET H'CAP 1m 2f
**5:45** (5:45) (Class 4) (0-80,81) 3-Y-O **£5,175** (£1,540; £769; £384) **Stalls Low**

Form RPR

4450 **1** **Blushing Red (FR)**[30] 5005 3-9-0 **73**.................... FrannyNorton 2 80
(Ed Dunlop) *chsd ldrs: nt clr run and lost pl over 3f out: rallied and swtchd rt over 1f out: shkn up to ld and edgd lft wl ins fnl f: r.o* **6/1**[3]



The Form Book Flat, Raceform Ltd, Newbury, RG14 5SJ

0242 **2** 1 1/4 **Native Prospect**[35] 4800 3-9-8 **81** DavidProbert 5 85
(Andrew Balding) *led: rdn over 1f out: hdd wl ins fnl f: styd on same pce* **4/5**[1]

51 **3** 1 1/2 **Fools And Kings**[31] 4981 3-9-5 **78** LukeMorris 4 79
(Robyn Brisland) *hld up: hdwy over 3f out: chsd ldr over 2f out: sn ev ch: rdn over 1f out: styng on same pce whn nt clr run wl ins fnl f* **8/1**

2141 **4** 1 1/4 **Pondering**[21] 5331 3-8-9 **71** (v) EdwardGreatrex(3) 1 70
(Eve Johnson Houghton) *s.i.s and pushed along early in rr: rdn over 3f out: hdwy 2f out: edgd lft and no ex ins fnl f* **3/1**[2]

60-6 **5** 14 **Poet's Charm (IRE)**[216] 210 3-8-3 **62** (h[1]) KieranO'Neill 6 33
(Martin Hill) *racd keenly in 2nd tl rdn over 2f out: wknd over 1f out* **18/1**

2m 12.49s (1.89) **Going Correction** +0.225s/f (Good) 5 Ran SP% **111.2**
Speed ratings (Par 102): **101,100,98,97,86**
CSF £11.60 TOTE £6.90: £2.60, £1.10; EX 13.70 Trifecta £47.20.
**Owner** The Hon R J Arculli **Bred** Robert Brard & Jean Dupont Cariot **Trained** Newmarket, Suffolk

**FOCUS**
The runner-up set a decent gallop in what looked an ordinary race for the grade. The second is the best guide.

## 6095 DAILY RACING SPECIALS AT 188BET H'CAP 1m 4f
**6:15** (6:20) (Class 5) (0-70,72) 3-Y-0+ **£3,234** (£962; £481; £240) **Stalls** Low

Form RPR

6233 **1** **Becca Campbell (IRE)**[14] 5556 4-9-9 **69** (p) EdwardGreatrex(3) 9 76
(Eve Johnson Houghton) *prom: lost pl over 9f out: nt clr run and swtchd rt over 2f out: rdn over 1f out: r.o to ld wl ins fnl f* **7/2**[1]

011 **2** 2 1/4 **The Detainee**[16] 5508 4-9-5 **62** (p) FranBerry 8 65
(Neil Mulholland) *a.p: chsd ldr over 2f out: rdn to ld over 1f out: sn hdd: edgd lft and styng on same pce whn lft 2nd wl ins fnl f* **4/1**[2]

6214 **3** 3 1/4 **Rahmah (IRE)**[19] 5432 5-9-12 **69** KieranO'Neill 2 67
(Geoffrey Deacon) *dwlt: hdwy over 9f out: nt clr run over 3f out: nt clr run and swtchd rt over 1f out: sn rdn: styng on same pce whn lft 3rd wl ins fnl f* **9/2**[3]

-542 **4** 3 **What A Scorcher**[25] 4840 6-9-13 **70** LukeMorris 4 63
(Nikki Evans) *chsd ldr tl led over 2f out: rdn and hdd over 1f out: wknd ins fnl f* **8/1**

-654 **5** 7 **Kaisan**[14] 5566 4-9-5 **62** (bt[1]) DavidProbert 3 44
(Bernard Llewellyn) *prom: lost pl over 9f out: rdn over 3f out: wknd over 2f out* **33/1**

-466 **6** 1 **Eastern Lady (IND)**[13] 5607 4-8-10 **60** (t) JonathanFisher(7) 1 40
(Richard Price) *hld up: hdwy 3f out: rdn and wknd 2f out* **33/1**

-042 **7** 1 3/4 **Mr Frankie**[69] 3519 6-8-11 **59** MitchGodwin(5) 10 36
(John Spearing) *led: rdn and hdd over 2f out: wknd over 1f out* **4/1**[2]

0511 **U** **Tobougaloo**[28] 5054 6-9-5 **69** WilliamCox(7) 6 79+
(Stuart Kittow) *hld up: hdwy over 3f out: nt clr run and swtchd rt over 2f out: breast girth broke and sddle slipped over 1f out: sn led: edgd lft and rdr unable to do much whn hdd and uns rdr wl ins fnl f* **5/1**

2m 40.78s (1.78) **Going Correction** +0.225s/f (Good) 8 Ran SP% **114.1**
Speed ratings (Par 103): **103,101,99,97,92 92,90,**
CSF £17.60 CT £61.79 TOTE £4.50: £1.60, £1.70, £1.70; EX 22.50 Trifecta £103.70.
**Owner** Eden Racing Club **Bred** Lynn Lodge Stud **Trained** Blewbury, Oxon
■ Stewards' Enquiry : Fran Berry £140 fine - failed to arrive in time to weigh out

**FOCUS**
Late drama in what looked like a fair race for the grade. The winner was fortunate and is rated to her best, with the unseater rated a 2l winner.

## 6096 GET 1/4 ODDS AT 188BET H'CAP 2m
**6:45** (6:49) (Class 4) (0-85,83) 4-Y-0+ **£6,469** (£1,925; £962; £481) **Stalls** Low

Form RPR

0/04 **1** **Taws**[15] 5524 6-9-2 **83** (p) DavidEgan(5) 2 91
(Rod Millman) *chsd ldrs: rdn 3f out: styd on u.p to ld wl ins fnl f* **10/3**[2]

10-2 **2** 1 **Project Bluebook (FR)**[14] 4742 4-9-4 **80** FranBerry 6 87
(John Quinn) *a.p: pushed along to chse ldr over 3f out: led over 2f out: sn rdn: hdd and unable qck wl ins fnl f* **2/1**[1]

304- **3** 1 3/4 **Arty Campbell (IRE)**[25] 6919 7-9-1 **82** (p) MitchGodwin(5) 5 87
(Bernard Llewellyn) *s.i.s: hld up: hdwy over 3f out: jnd ldr over 2f out: sn hung lft and rdn: no ex wl ins fnl f* **25/1**

4220 **4** 1 **Medburn Cutler**[54] 4073 7-9-2 **78** (p) FrannyNorton 7 82
(Paul Henderson) *chsd ldr tl led over 3f out: rdn and hdd over 2f out: no ex ins fnl f* **5/1**[3]

151/ **5** 2 3/4 **Sleep Easy**[17] 6704 5-9-6 **82** (tp) RobertWinston 3 83
(Neil Mulholland) *hld up: shkn up over 2f out: nt trble ldrs* **16/1**

-010 **6** nk **Sir Pass I Am**[85] 2966 4-8-8 **70** DavidProbert 8 70
(Andrew Balding) *hld up: hdwy 3f out: rdn over 1f out: edgd lft and styd on same pce* **6/1**

5-22 **7** 4 1/2 **All For The Best (IRE)**[43] 3663 5-8-13 **75** (tp) LukeMorris 4 70
(Robert Stephens) *hld up in tch: rdn over 2f out: sn wknd* **7/1**

20-3 **8** 15 **Norab (GER)**[23] 5251 6-9-0 **76** (b) LiamKeniry 1 53
(Bernard Llewellyn) *led: rdn and hdd over 3f out: wknd over 2f out* **20/1**

3m 39.11s (0.21) **Going Correction** +0.225s/f (Good) 8 Ran SP% **114.4**
Speed ratings (Par 105): **108,107,106,106,104 104,102,94**
CSF £10.42 CT £136.65 TOTE £4.50: £1.30, £1.20, £6.00; EX 13.40 Trifecta £136.30.
**Owner** R K & Mrs J M R Arrowsmith **Bred** Harts Farm Stud **Trained** Kentisbeare, Devon

**FOCUS**
A competitive staying handicap, run at what looked an ordinary gallop. Straightforward form rated around the third.

## 6097 READ SILVESTRE DE SOUSA AT 188BET H'CAP 5f 16y
**7:15** (7:19) (Class 6) (0-65,67) 3-Y-0+ **£3,234** (£962; £481; £240) **Stalls** Centre

Form RPR

6500 **1** **Everkyllachy (IRE)**[3] 6004 3-8-10 **55** (b) HollieDoyle(3) 7 65
(J S Moore) *sn pushed along in rr: hdwy over 1f out: rdn and r.o to ld post* **6/1**

4506 **2** shd **Dodgy Bob**[7] 5827 4-9-3 **60** (v[1]) PhilDennis(3) 6 70
(Michael Mullineaux) *chsd ldrs: hmpd over 3f out: rdn to ld 1f out: hdd post* **7/1**

3152 **3** 1 3/4 **Zavikon**[12] 5657 3-9-11 **67** FranBerry 3 70
(Richard Hughes) *chsd ldrs: rdn and ev ch 1f out: no ex wl ins fnl f* **6/4**[1]

-040 **4** nk **Wahaab (IRE)**[17] 5482 6-9-10 **64** DavidProbert 8 66
(Sophie Leech) *racd alone on stands' side tl over 3f out: prom: lost pl over 3f out: hdwy over 1f out: styd on* **16/1**

4006 **5** 2 1/4 **Swendab (IRE)**[20] 5360 9-9-5 **64** (b) BenRobinson(5) 2 58
(John O'Shea) *chsd ldrs: led 3f out: rdn and hdd 1f out: no ex ins fnl f* **16/1**

3316 **6** 3/4 **Coronation Cottage**[13] 5588 3-9-8 **67** CharlieBennett(3) 4 58
(Malcolm Saunders) *chsd ldr: led 4f out: swtchd rt to stands' side over 3f out: hdd 3f out: chsd ldr again: rdn and ev ch 1f out: wknd wl ins fnl f* **11/2**[3]

0362 **7** 5 **Stringybark Creek**[9] 5759 3-8-8 **55** DavidEgan(5) 1 28+
(Mick Channon) *s.s: outpcd* **9/2**[2]

6400 **8** 14 **Rockalater**[149] 1297 3-8-3 **45** LukeMorris 5
(John Spearing) *led 1f: sn pushed along: wknd 1/2-way* **33/1**

1m 0.73s (1.43) **Going Correction** +0.325s/f (Good)
**WFA** 3 from 4yo+ 2lb 8 Ran SP% **115.1**
Speed ratings (Par 101): **101,100,98,97,93 92,84,62**
CSF £47.39 CT £94.60 TOTE £7.70: £1.80, £2.00, £1.60; EX 54.70 Trifecta £150.40.
**Owner** Ever Equine & J S Moore **Bred** Mrs T Mahon **Trained** Upper Lambourn, Berks

**FOCUS**
Modest sprint form. The winner is rated back to her best.

## 6098 PLAY CASINO AT 188BET H'CAP 5f 16y
**7:45** (7:45) (Class 4) (0-80,78) 3-Y-0+ **£4,851** (£1,443; £721; £360) **Stalls** Centre

Form RPR

5622 **1** **Bellevarde (IRE)**[13] 5606 3-8-8 **64** JosephineGordon 5 70
(Richard Price) *w ldr tl rdn to ld and hung lft fr over 1f out: jst hld on* **4/1**[3]

6114 **2** hd **Kinglami**[12] 5646 8-9-10 **78** (p) LukeMorris 4 83
(John O'Shea) *pushed along in rr: rdn over 1f out: hung lft and r.o ins fnl f: nt quite get there* **9/1**

4132 **3** 3/4 **Major Valentine**[4] 5967 5-9-2 **75** BenRobinson(5) 1 78
(John O'Shea) *led: rdn and hdd over 1f out: styd on* **5/2**[2]

0212 **4** 1 1/4 **Glacier Point**[23] 5263 3-9-5 **75** (b[1]) DavidProbert 3 73
(Clive Cox) *sn w ldr tl pushed along over 3f out: remained handy: rdn 1/2-way: styd on same pce ins fnl f* **6/4**[1]

310 **5** 2 1/2 **Think Fashion (IRE)**[21] 5325 3-9-5 **75** FranBerry 2 64
(Brian Meehan) *trckd ldrs: pushed along 1/2-way: hung lft and wknd ins fnl f* **7/1**

1m 0.2s (0.90) **Going Correction** +0.325s/f (Good)
**WFA** 3 from 5yo+ 2lb 5 Ran SP% **111.1**
Speed ratings (Par 105): **105,104,103,101,97**
CSF £34.55 TOTE £5.40: £2.20, £3.00; EX 46.20 Trifecta £29.30.
**Owner** Barry Veasey **Bred** Tally-Ho Stud **Trained** Ullingswick, H'fords

**FOCUS**
This was half a second quicker than the preceding Class 6 handicap. Stall 5 beat stall 4 and the market 1-2 both disappointed.

## 6099 FOLLOW US ON TWITTER AT 188BET H'CAP 6f 16y
**8:15** (8:18) (Class 5) (0-75,77) 3-Y-0+ **£5,175** (£1,540; £769; £384) **Stalls** Centre

Form RPR

0411 **1** **Pastfact**[50] 4198 3-8-13 **67** LiamKeniry 1 74+
(Malcolm Saunders) *hld up: hdwy 1/2-way: rdn over 1f out: r.o to ld wl ins fnl f* **8/1**

0532 **2** 1 **Jacksonfire**[15] 5535 5-8-2 **56** oh10 (p) PhilDennis(3) 3 59
(Michael Mullineaux) *chsd ldrs: rdn over 2f out: led over 1f out: hdd ins fnl f: styd on* **10/1**

5143 **3** shd **Secret Potion**[8] 5784 3-9-2 **70** LukeMorris 2 73
(Ronald Harris) *led 1f: chsd ldrs: rdn over 1f out: led ins fnl f: sn hdd: no ex nr fin* **6/1**

1600 **4** nk **Air Of York (IRE)**[13] 5587 5-8-7 **63** (p) MitchGodwin(5) 6 65
(John Flint) *hld up: rdn over 1f out: r.o ins fnl f: nt rch ldrs* **22/1**

5543 **5** shd **Bonjour Steve**[14] 5564 6-8-11 **62** (p) DavidProbert 4 64
(Richard Price) *hld up: hdwy 1/2-way: rdn over 1f out: styd on same pce ins fnl f* **4/1**[2]

413 **6** 1 1/4 **Oeil De Tigre (FR)**[27] 5112 6-9-3 **68** GeorgeDowning 5 66
(Tony Carroll) *chsd ldrs: rdn over 2f out: hung lft over 1f out: styd on same pce fnl f* **8/1**

4055 **7** 1 **Tally's Song**[8] 5778 4-8-5 **56** oh11 (p) FrannyNorton 9 51?
(Grace Harris) *hld up: rdn over 1f out: nvr trbld ldrs* **50/1**

2342 **8** nk **Del Parco**[23] 5253 3-9-7 **75** (bt[1]) FranBerry 7 69
(Clive Cox) *s.i.s and hmpd s: rcvrd to ld 5f out: rdn and hdd over 1f out: edgd lft and no ex ins fnl f* **5/2**[1]

06-0 **9** nk **Polkadot Princess (IRE)**[36] 4735 3-7-11 **56** oh4 DavidEgan(5) 10 49
(Nikki Evans) *chsd ldrs: outpcd over 3f out: n.d after* **50/1**

4063 **10** 4 **Picket Line**[22] 5271 5-9-6 **71** (p) JosephineGordon 11 51
(Geoffrey Deacon) *prom: lost pl over 3f out: n.d after: eased ins fnl f* **11/2**[3]

1m 13.1s (1.10) **Going Correction** +0.325s/f (Good)
**WFA** 3 from 4yo+ 3lb 10 Ran SP% **117.8**
Speed ratings (Par 103): **105,103,103,103,103 101,100,99,99,93**
CSF £84.22 CT £397.68 TOTE £8.30: £2.30, £3.30, £1.80; EX 69.80 Trifecta £416.20.
**Owner** Premier Conservatory Roofs **Bred** M S Saunders & D Collier **Trained** Green Ore, Somerset

**FOCUS**
Moderate sprint form, held down by the runner-up. Low draws dominated, with the principals coming down the centre. The winner picked up his early-season progress.
T/Plt: £36.60 to a £1 stake. Pool: £57,924.24 - 1152.42 winning units. T/Qpdt: £17.00 to a £1 stake. Pool: £5,379.84 - 233.29 winning units. **Colin Roberts**

# 6070 SALISBURY (R-H)
Thursday, August 17

**OFFICIAL GOING: Good (good to firm in places: 7.4)**
Wind: mild breeze across Weather: sunny

## 6100 BET TOTEPLACEPOT AT BETFRED.COM MAIDEN AUCTION FILLIES' STKS (PLUS 10 RACE) 6f 213y
**1:50** (1:51) (Class 5) 2-Y-0 **£4,043** (£1,203; £601; £300) **Stalls** Low

Form RPR

22 **1** **Autumn Leaves**[35] 4806 2-8-9 0 RyanMoore 5 77
(Clive Cox) *led: rdn over 1f out: hdd ent fnl f: drvn to regain ld fnl 120yds: drifted lft: kpt on gamely* **4/9**[1]

44 **2** nk **Escape The City**[24] 5216 2-8-4 0 CharlieBennett(3) 2 74
(Hughie Morrison) *trckd wnr: rdn to take narrow advantage ent fnl f: hdd fnl 120yds: kpt on* **11/4**[2]

**3** 1 3/4 **Golden Image** 2-8-7 0 RobHornby 6 69+
(Jonathan Portman) *cmpt: s.i.s: mid-div after 1f: hdwy over 2f out: rdn to chse ldng pair wl over 1f out: kpt on but nt pce to get on terms* **33/1**

05 **4** 6 **Titchy Digits**[14] 5573 2-8-2 0 DavidEgan(5) 4 53
(Michael Attwater) *swtg: mid-div: rdn 3f out: kpt on same pce fnl 2f* **10/1**[3]

**5** 2 3/4 **Viktoriya Taraban (IRE)** 2-8-4 0 EdwardGreatrex(3) 12 46
(Joseph Tuite) *leggy: sn swtchd rt fr wd draw: last trio: pushed along over 3f out: sme late prog: nvr trbld ldrs* **33/1**

0 6 2 ½ **Chickpea**[15] 5534 2-8-11 0 ................ HayleyTurner 11 43
(Michael Bell) *w'like: q tall: last trio of main gp: rdn over 2f out: little imp* **20/1**

0 7 1 **Courteous Crown**[13] 5586 2-8-7 0 ................ TomMarquand 8 36
(Richard Hannon) *q str: trckd ldrs: chal over 3f out: rdn over 2f out: wkng whn hung rt over 1f out* **28/1**

6 8 2 ¾ **Mirror Magic**[22] 5292 2-8-9 0 ................ JosephineGordon 7 31
(Geoffrey Deacon) *w'like: warm: mid-div early: pushed along in last trio over 3f out: nvr gng pce to get bk on terms* **20/1**

00 9 2 ¾ **Royal Wave**[15] 5528 2-9-0 0 ................ HarryBentley 3 29
(William Knight) *trckd ldrs: rdn wl over 2f out: sn wknd* **50/1**

05 10 35 **Lady Maldiva (IRE)**[14] 5557 2-8-7 0 ................(t[1]) OscarPereira 1
(Jose Santos) *w'like: dwlt: veered bdly lft sn after s: v green: a wl bhd* **100/1**

1m 29.3s (0.70) **Going Correction** +0.025s/f (Good) **10** Ran SP% **126.8**
Speed ratings (Par 91): **97,96,94,87,84 81,80,77,74,34**
CSF £1.99 TOTE £1.30: £1.02, £1.10, £8.60; EX 2.40 Trifecta £29.20.
**Owner** J T & K M Thomas **Bred** Miss K J Keir **Trained** Lambourn, Berks

**FOCUS**
There was 6mm of rain overnight and the going was given as good, good to firm in places (GoingStick: 7.4). The result was as the market predicted, albeit after a scare for favourite backers. The form is rated around the winner.

## 6101 BET TOTEEXACTA AT BETFRED.COM H'CAP (DIV I) 1m
**2:20** (2:23) (Class 6) (0-65,75) 3-Y-O+ **£3,234** (£962; £481; £240) **Stalls** Low

Form RPR

-360 1 **Barista (IRE)**[8] 5793 9-9-3 **59** ................ HollieDoyle(3) 8 67
(Brian Forsey) *mid-div: hdwy 3f out: led wl over 1f out: strly pressed but kpt on gamely fnl f: rdn out* **16/1**

4400 2 ½ **Jack Of Diamonds (IRE)**[22] 5299 8-9-11 **64** ................ RobertWinston 10 71
(Roger Teal) *s.i.s: towards rr: hdwy in centre 3f out: rdn 2f out: str chal ent fnl f: kpt on: hld nring fin* **11/1**

-650 3 1 ¾ **Beatisa**[23] 5249 3-9-0 **59** ................ RichardKingscote 5 61
(Ed Walker) *mid-div: rdn and hdwy fr 2f out: kpt on ins fnl f: wnt 3rd fnl 120yds* **16/1**

5003 4 nse **McDelta**[19] 5427 7-9-3 **56** ................ JosephineGordon 3 59
(Geoffrey Deacon) *trckd ldrs: rdn 2f out: nt quite pce to chal but kpt on ins fnl f* **7/1**[3]

4232 5 shd **Masquerade Bling (IRE)**[16] 5511 3-8-12 **57** ................ RobHornby 6 58
(Daniel Mark Loughnane) *mid-div: rdn and hdwy fr 2f out: kpt on ins fnl f: wnt 5th ins fnl 120yds* **8/1**

0553 6 1 ¾ **Rocket Ronnie (IRE)**[6] 5898 7-8-7 **46** oh1 ................ LukeMorris 13 44
(Brian Barr) *lw: hld up towards rr: rdn over 2f out: hdwy wl over 1f out: kpt on but nt pce to get on terms* **16/1**

5542 7 4 ½ **Pick A Little**[7] 5823 9-9-4 **62** ................ MitchGodwin(5) 11 50
(Michael Blake) *broke wl: prom: led over 3f out tl rdn wl over 1f out: wknd fnl f* **6/1**[2]

4204 8 ½ **Spare Parts (IRE)**[8] 5792 3-8-6 **51** ................ JFEgan 12 37
(Charles Hills) *trckd ldrs: rdn to chal over 2f out: ev ch over 1f out: wknd fnl 120yds* **16/1**

3/00 9 1 ¾ **Rolling Dice**[32] 2909 6-9-11 **64** ................(h) LiamKeniry 4 47
(Dominic Ffrench Davis) *hld up towards rr: hdwy on far rails 2f out: sn rdn: wknd ent fnl f* **50/1**

2P 10 4 ½ **Spiritual Star (IRE)**[64] 3718 8-9-6 **62** ................ CharlieBennett(3) 14 35
(Lee Carter) *hld up towards rr: rdn and sme prog over 2f out: nvr threatened: wknd fnl f* **22/1**

2355 11 ½ **Betsalottie**[12] 5653 4-9-1 **54** ................(b[1]) WilliamCarson 9 25
(John Bridger) *in tch: effrt 3f out: wknd 2f out* **7/1**[3]

-340 12 1 **Kassandra (IRE)**[129] 1686 3-9-6 **65** ................(p[1]) HarryBentley 2 33
(Amy Murphy) *lw: s.i.s: sn trcking ldrs: rdn 3f out: wknd 2f out* **20/1**

5211 13 nk **Mutineer**[6] 5898 3-9-13 **75** 12ex ................ EdwardGreatrex(3) 1 42
(Daniel Kubler) *led tl over 3f out: wknd tamely 2f out* **11/4**[1]

1000 P **Olympic Duel (IRE)**[26] 5145 4-9-2 **55** ................ TomMarquand 7
(Peter Hiatt) *towards rr of midfield for 2f: struggling in rr 3f out: nvr threatened: lost action whn p.u cl home* **50/1**

1m 43.24s (-0.26) **Going Correction** +0.025s/f (Good)
**WFA** 3 from 4yo+ 6lb **14** Ran SP% **122.0**
Speed ratings (Par 101): **102,101,99,99,99 97,93,92,91,86 86,85,84,**
CSF £177.68 CT £2865.68 TOTE £19.30: £4.70, £3.60, £6.00; EX 214.70 Trifecta £2545.80.
**Owner** Three Oaks Racing & Mrs P Bosley **Bred** Rathasker Stud **Trained** Ash Priors, Somerset

**FOCUS**
It paid to be held up here. The winner is rated close to last season's best.

## 6102 BET TOTEEXACTA AT BETFRED.COM H'CAP (DIV II) 1m
**2:50** (2:57) (Class 6) (0-65,67) 3-Y-O+ **£3,234** (£962; £481; £240) **Stalls** Low

Form RPR

4635 1 **Masarzain (IRE)**[12] 5651 4-9-9 **62** ................ LukeMorris 3 70+
(Archie Watson) *lw: trckd ldrs: gng wl but nt clr run jst over 2f out: led wl over 1f out: kpt on: rdn out* **9/2**[1]

-030 2 ¾ **Bradfield Magic (IRE)**[20] 5357 3-8-12 **57** ................ JimCrowley 6 62
(Charles Hills) *hld up towards rr: rdn and hdwy fr over 2f out: swtchd lft ent fnl f: r.o wl to go 2nd cl home* **8/1**

0011 3 ¾ **Suitsus**[50] 4203 6-9-10 **63** ................(t) JosephineGordon 9 68
(Geoffrey Deacon) *s.i.s: towards rr: rdn 2f out: hdwy jst over 1f out: r.o ins fnl f: wnt 3rd nring fin* **11/2**[3]

1500 4 hd **Passing Star**[17] 5481 6-10-0 **67** ................(tp) GeorgeDowning 8 71
(Daniel Kubler) *mid-div: hdwy 3f out: chal 2f out: sn rdn: ev ch ent fnl f: no ex fnl 100yds* **9/1**

4510 5 3 **Miss Osier**[23] 5268 3-9-6 **65** ................(p) DavidProbert 7 61
(Rae Guest) *trckd ldrs: chal 2f out: sn rdn: ev ch jst over 1f out: no ex ins fnl f* **5/1**[2]

6140 6 hd **Moonstone Rock**[28] 5067 3-8-11 **59** ................(b) CharlieBennett(3) 2 54
(Jim Boyle) *s.i.s: towards rr: rdn over 2f out: kpt on ins fnl f but nvr gng pce to get involved* **25/1**

3231 7 nse **Fair Selene**[20] 5359 3-9-8 **67** ................ TomMarquand 12 62
(Heather Main) *lw: prom: rdn and ev ch over 2f out tl jst over 1f out: no ex fnl f* **6/1**

3125 8 1 ½ **Aye Aye Skipper (IRE)**[7] 5823 7-9-3 **56** ................(b) PatDobbs 1 49
(Ken Cunningham-Brown) *mid-div: hdwy whn nt clr run on far rails over 2f out: rdn over 1f out: wknd ins fnl f* **10/1**

-001 9 2 **Red Dragon (IRE)**[10] 5713 7-9-4 **57** 6ex ................ RobHornby 10 45
(Michael Blanshard) *mid-div: rdn over 3f out: wknd over 1f out* **12/1**

5220 10 6 **Carcharias (IRE)**[28] 5049 4-9-8 **64** ................ CallumShepherd(3) 11 38
(Ed de Giles) *led: rdn and hdd wl over 1f out: wknd ins fnl f* **10/1**

5405 11 6 **Machiavelian Storm (IRE)**[55] 4040 5-8-2 **46** oh1 ....... LuluStanford(5) 5 7
(Richard Mitchell) *a towards rr* **66/1**

0000 12 1 ¼ **A Definite Diamond**[31] 4968 4-8-4 **46** oh1 .......(p[1]) EdwardGreatrex(3) 13 4
(Grace Harris) *s.i.s: a towards rr* **200/1**

1m 44.49s (0.99) **Going Correction** +0.025s/f (Good)
**WFA** 3 from 4yo+ 6lb **12** Ran SP% **117.3**
Speed ratings (Par 101): **96,95,94,94,91 91,91,89,87,81 75,74**
CSF £39.81 CT £207.15 TOTE £4.50: £1.80, £2.50, £2.70; EX 42.80 Trifecta £410.10.
**Owner** Masarzain Partnership **Bred** Mrs Josephine Hughes **Trained** Upper Lambourn, W Berks

**FOCUS**
The slower of the two divisions by 1.25sec. The second and third look the best guides.

## 6103 BET TOTEQUADPOT AT BETFRED.COM MAIDEN STKS 6f 213y
**3:20** (3:27) (Class 5) 3-4-Y-O **£3,881** (£1,155; £577; £288) **Stalls** Low

Form RPR

22 1 **Killay**[19] 5431 3-9-0 0 ................ CharlesBishop 5 80
(Eve Johnson Houghton) *trckd ldrs: led 2f out: r.o strly: rdn out* **4/1**[3]

3 2 3 **Majboor (IRE)**[19] 5431 3-9-5 0 ................ LiamKeniry 1 76
(Dominic Ffrench Davis) *w'like: trckd ldrs: rdn over 2f out: edgd lft briefly over 1f out: kpt on to go 2nd fnl 120yds but nt pce of wnr* **33/1**

2222 3 2 ½ **Spinnaka (IRE)**[30] 5003 3-9-0 77 ................(p[1]) RyanMoore 12 64
(Luca Cumani) *hld up: pushed along and stdy prog fr 3f out: r.o to chse wnr u.p ent fnl f: no ex fnl 120yds* **9/4**[1]

24 4 2 ½ **Subhaan**[23] 5243 3-9-5 0 ................ JimCrowley 3 62
(Roger Varian) *cmpt: led: rdn and hdd 2f out: sn no ex* **3/1**[2]

5 1 **Psychotic** 4-9-7 0 ................ DidierGengoul(3) 10 62
(David Menuisier) *q str: s.i.s: towards rr: prog u.p over 2f out: styd on ins fnl f:* **20/1**

5 6 1 **Circuit Judge**[24] 5220 3-9-5 0 ................ PatDobbs 4 57
(William Knight) *cmpt: mid-div: rdn over 2f out: kpt on but nvr gng pce to get involved* **16/1**

23 7 1 ¼ **Raawy**[21] 5315 3-9-5 0 ................ HarryBentley 7 54
(Simon Crisford) *cmpt: trckd ldrs: rdn over 2f out: wknd over 1f out* **6/1**

2-2 8 1 ¾ **Waqt (IRE)**[31] 4964 3-9-5 0 ................ KieranShoemark 9 49
(Marcus Tregoning) *sn prom: rdn wl over 2f out: wknd over 1f out* **14/1**

5 9 1 ¾ **Suit Of Lights (IRE)**[19] 5431 3-9-5 0 ................ KierenFox 11 44
(Henry Tett) *mid-div for 2f: sn outpcd towards rr: nvr bk on terms* **100/1**

10 2 ½ **Treacherous** 3-9-2 0 ................ CallumShepherd(3) 6 37
(Ed de Giles) *q str: mid-div: effrt over 2f out: wknd ent fnl f* **50/1**

00 11 10 **Bamo Mc**[14] 5577 3-9-5 0 ................ RobertWinston 2 10
(Mike Murphy) *w'like: s.i.s: a in rr* **100/1**

12 8 **Sky Marshal (IRE)** 3-9-5 0 ................ RichardKingscote 8
(Ed Walker) *q str: mid-div: pushed along over 4f out: wknd 2f out* **25/1**

1m 27.72s (-0.88) **Going Correction** +0.025s/f (Good)
**WFA** 3 from 4yo 5lb **12** Ran SP% **118.1**
Speed ratings (Par 103): **106,102,99,96,95 94,93,91,89,86 74,65**
CSF £138.74 TOTE £4.70: £1.50, £6.30, £1.20; EX 128.90 Trifecta £607.90.
**Owner** D J Deer **Bred** D J And Mrs Deer **Trained** Blewbury, Oxon

**FOCUS**
A fair maiden. The first two both improved on their 6f form here.

## 6104 EBF BREEDERS' SERIES FILLIES' H'CAP 1m 4f 5y
**3:50** (3:54) (Class 2) (0-100,97) 3-Y-O+
**£18,675** (£5,592; £2,796; £1,398; £699; £351) **Stalls** Low

Form RPR

1110 1 **Cribbs Causeway (IRE)**[40] 4612 3-8-3 **81** ................ JosephineGordon 2 91
(Roger Charlton) *trckd ldr: led 2f out: kpt on strly: rdn out* **3/1**[2]

332 2 1 ½ **Notice (IRE)**[27] 5108 4-8-12 **81** ................ JimCrowley 5 88
(David Simcock) *lw: hld up in tch: rdn and hdwy over 2f out: chsd wnr jst over 1f out: kpt on but a being hld* **9/4**[1]

1411 3 3 ½ **Pacharana**[22] 5273 4-9-10 **93** ................ RyanMoore 8 94
(Luca Cumani) *lw: trckd ldr: rdn 3f out: kpt on fnl 2f but nt quite pce to chal* **4/1**[3]

-212 4 nk **Jive Talking (IRE)**[24] 5217 3-8-1 **79** ................ HayleyTurner 4 81
(Michael Bell) *hld up in tch: hdwy over 2f out: rdn over 1f out: kpt on same pce fnl f* **6/1**

2653 5 3 ¼ **Jelly Monger (IRE)**[10] 5715 5-8-13 **87** ................(p) JoshuaBryan(5) 1 83
(Dominic Ffrench Davis) *led: rdn and hdd 2f out: kpt on tl no ex ent fnl f* **10/1**

4260 6 2 ¼ **Lucy The Painter (IRE)**[14] 5569 5-9-7 **93** ................ CallumShepherd(3) 7 85
(Ed de Giles) *hld up last but in tch: effrt 3f out: nt pce to get on terms* **10/1**

0-25 7 4 **Elysian Fields (GR)**[57] 3968 6-10-0 **97** ................ KieranShoemark 6 83
(Amanda Perrett) *hld up in tch: rdn 3f out: sn one pce* **16/1**

2m 36.27s (-1.73) **Going Correction** -0.025s/f (Good)
**WFA** 3 from 4yo+ 9lb **7** Ran SP% **114.1**
Speed ratings (Par 96): **104,103,100,100,98 96,94**
CSF £10.16 CT £25.95 TOTE £3.70: £2.00, £1.80; EX 10.70 Trifecta £51.60.
**Owner** Nick Bradley Racing 13 **Bred** N Bradley **Trained** Beckhampton, Wilts

**FOCUS**
A pretty decent fillies' handicap, rated around the runner-up.

## 6105 TOTEPOOL SOVEREIGN STKS (GROUP 3) (C&G) 1m
**4:20** (4:23) (Class 1) 3-Y-O+
**£42,532** (£16,125; £8,070; £4,020; £2,017; £1,012) **Stalls** Low

Form RPR

5641 1 **Ballet Concerto**[33] 4918 4-9-0 105 ................ RyanMoore 2 114
(Sir Michael Stoute) *lw: trckd ldrs: pushed along wl over 2f out: led narrowly jst ins fnl f: kpt on wl: rdn out* **5/2**[2]

2150 2 nk **Tabarrak (IRE)**[33] 4905 4-9-0 110 ................ JimCrowley 1 113
(Richard Hannon) *trckd ldrs: rdn to dispute ld wl over 1f out: narrowly hdd jst ins fnl f: kpt on* **2/1**[1]

622- 3 shd **Carry On Deryck**[313] 7152 5-9-0 109 ................ WilliamCarson 5 113
(Saeed bin Suroor) *trckd ldr: led 2f out: sn rdn and jnd: narrowly hdd jst ins fnl f: kpt on* **6/1**

5021 4 1 ¼ **Master The World (IRE)**[13] 5594 6-9-0 108 ................(p) PatDobbs 4 110+
(David Elsworth) *hld up bhd ldrs: gng wl enough but nt clr run over 1f out: swtchd lft but hemmed in by rival ent fnl f: swtchd bk rt but bhd wall of horses and unable to mount chal* **9/2**[3]

2565 5 hd **Firmament**[19] 5393 5-9-0 109 ................ RichardKingscote 7 109
(David O'Meara) *lw: little slowly away: last pair wl in tch: effrt over 2f out: nt quite pce to chal but kpt on fnl f* **11/2**

16-0 6 5 **Isomer (USA)**[41] 4584 3-8-8 99 ................ LiamKeniry 6 96
(Andrew Balding) *led: rdn 2f out: kpt on tl no ex ins fnl f* **33/1**

1m 42.49s (-1.01) **Going Correction** +0.025s/f (Good)
**WFA** 3 from 4yo+ 6lb **6** Ran SP% **112.7**
Speed ratings (Par 113): **106,105,105,104,104 99**
CSF £8.01 TOTE £3.00: £1.80, £1.30; EX 8.20 Trifecta £22.50.
**Owner** Saeed Suhail **Bred** Meon Valley Stud **Trained** Newmarket, Suffolk

**FOCUS**
This threatened to be tactical, and indeed there was a muddling pace and they finished in a bit of heap. Ballet Concerto improved again, with the next two close to form.

## 6106 BILL GARNETT MEMORIAL FILLIES' H'CAP — 6f
4:50 (4:53) (Class 5) (0-70,71) 3-Y-O+ — **£3,396** (£1,010; £505; £252) **Stalls** Low

Form — RPR

5003 **1** **Chica De La Noche**[37] 4711 3-9-4 **67** .......... JimCrowley 11 — 74
(Simon Dow) *pressed ldr: disp ld 2f out: sn rdn: kpt on wl to edge ahd towards fin* **16/1**

532 **2** *nk* **Island Cloud**[30] 4990 3-9-3 **66** .......... RichardKingscote 8 — 72
(Heather Main) *led: rdn whn jnd 2f out: kpt on but no ex whn narrowly hdd towards fin* **7/2**[2]

2311 **3** *½* **Sweet Pursuit**[12] 5657 3-9-1 **64** .......... CharlesBishop 5 — 68+
(Rod Millman) *lw: little slowly away: mid-div: swtchd lft and hdwy fr 2f out: rdn to chse ldng pair over 1f out: kpt on wl fnl 100yds* **3/1**[1]

550 **4** *2* **Vixen (IRE)**[63] 3748 3-8-1 **55** ..........(h[1]) GeorgiaCox(5) 4 — 53
(Eve Johnson Houghton) *lw: trckd ldrs: rdn over 2f out: nt pce to chal but kpt on fnl 120yds* **10/1**

6522 **5** *1 ¼* **Baby Gal**[22] 5295 3-8-7 **59** .......... CharlieBennett(3) 13 — 53
(Jim Boyle) *hld up towards rr: hdwy over 2f out: sn rdn: kpt on same pce fnl f* **9/1**

0565 **6** *2* **Flying Sakhee**[12] 5657 4-8-5 **51** oh3 ..........(b[1]) RyanTate 10 — 39
(John Bridger) *mid-div: rdn 2f out: sn one pce* **33/1**

4510 **7** *1 ½* **Chicago Star**[34] 4846 3-9-6 **69** .......... JFEgan 2 — 52
(Mick Channon) *mid-div: rdn over 2f out: nvr any imp* **10/1**

65-4 **8** *½* **Grand Myla (IRE)**[30] 4990 3-9-4 **67** ..........(p) RyanMoore 6 — 48
(Gary Moore) *rdn over 2f out: nvr bttr than mid-div* **10/1**

000- **9** *nse* **Miss Geronimo**[290] 7727 5-8-2 **51** oh6 .......... HollieDoyle(3) 14 — 32
(Ken Cunningham-Brown) *t.k.h in rr: rdn over 2f out: little imp* **33/1**

1460 **10** *2 ¼* **Fleeting Glimpse**[56] 4011 4-8-13 **59** .......... RobHornby 3 — 33
(Patrick Chamings) *trckd ldrs: rdn over 2f out: wknd ent fnl f* **25/1**

4-44 **11** *1 ½* **South Sea Belle (IRE)**[41] 4568 3-9-7 **70** ..........(t[1]) KieranShoemark 12 — 39
(David Menuisier) *lw: awkwardly away: a towards rr* **5/1**[3]

0605 **12** *16* **Posh Bounty**[5] 5936 6-9-4 **64** .......... PatDobbs 7
(Paul Burgoyne) *trckd ldrs: rdn over 2f out: wknd over 1f out* **25/1**

1m 14.39s (-0.41) **Going Correction** +0.025s/f (Good)
**WFA** 3 from 4yo+ 3lb — 12 Ran SP% **120.6**
Speed ratings (Par 100): **103,102,101,99,97 94,92,92,92,89 87,65**
CSF £70.17 CT £223.99 TOTE £13.80: £4.20, £1.70, £1.60; EX 87.30 Trifecta £234.90.
**Owner** Robert Moss **Bred** Horizon Bloodstock Limited **Trained** Ashtead, Surrey

**FOCUS**
They didn't go that quick early and the pace held up. The winner took advantage of a good mark.

## 6107 KEVIN HALL & PAT BOAKES MEMORIAL H'CAP — 1m 6f 44y
5:25 (5:26) (Class 4) (0-85,83) 3-Y-O — **£5,175** (£1,540; £769; £384) **Stalls** Far side

Form — RPR

3643 **1** **Orsino (IRE)**[21] 5328 3-8-9 **71** .......... RobHornby 2 — 76
(Andrew Balding) *lw: led for over 2f: trckd ldr: rdn for str chal over 2f out: led fnl 120yds: styd on* **2/1**[1]

-023 **2** *nk* **Phoenix Dawn**[25] 4016 3-8-6 **68** .......... JFEgan 3 — 72
(Brendan Powell) *prom for 3f: trckd ldrs: rdn wl over 2f out: styd on wl fnl 120yds: snatched 2nd cl home* **12/1**

-243 **3** *nk* **Sable Island (IRE)**[20] 5368 3-9-0 **76** .......... RyanMoore 8 — 80
(Sir Michael Stoute) *lw: hld up: tk clsr order into 5th over 6f out: rdn over 2f out: cl 3rd and ch ent fnl f: styd on* **7/2**[3]

5225 **4** *nk* **Duke's Girl**[19] 5406 3-8-5 **67** .......... HayleyTurner 1 — 70
(Michael Bell) *racd keenly: led after 2f: rdn whn strly chal over 2f out: stuck to task gamely tl hdd fnl 120yds: no ex* **14/1**

0213 **5** *¾* **Key Bid**[12] 5630 3-9-5 **81** ..........(p) JimCrowley 6 — 83
(Charlie Appleby) *hld up bhd ldrs: rdn over 2f out: styd on ins fnl f but nvr quite threatened to get on terms* **9/4**[2]

0213 **6** *5* **Padrinho (IRE)**[15] 5550 3-8-11 **73** .......... KierenFox 7 — 68
(John Best) *trckd ldrs: rdn wl over 2f out: wknd ent fnl f* **7/1**

3m 5.06s (-2.34) **Going Correction** -0.025s/f (Good) — 6 Ran SP% **113.2**
Speed ratings (Par 102): **105,104,104,104,104 101**
CSF £25.66 CT £78.92 TOTE £2.70: £1.60, £5.30; EX 23.30 Trifecta £60.00.
**Owner** David Brownlow **Bred** Ecurie Des Monceaux **Trained** Kingsclere, Hants

**FOCUS**
They didn't go a great gallop early, and there was a bunched finish to this staying handicap. The runner-up was not an obvious improver.
T/Plt: £77.60 to a £1 stake. Pool: £69,310.59 - 651.44 winning units. T/Qpdt: £5.90 to a £1 stake. Pool: £5,269.35 - 653.72 winning units. **Tim Mitchell**

# 5851 YARMOUTH (L-H)
### Thursday, August 17

**OFFICIAL GOING: Good to firm (good in places 7.4)**
Wind: medium, across Weather: bright, spells

## 6108 BET TOTEPLACEPOT AT BETFRED.COM / EBF NOVICE STKS (PLUS 10 RACE) — 7f 3y
4:55 (4:57) (Class 4) 2-Y-O — **£4,528** (£1,347; £673; £336) **Stalls** Centre

Form — RPR

**1** **Il Primo Sole** 2-9-2 0 .......... RobertTart 15 — 87+
(John Gosden) *mde all: shkn up and readily qcknd clr over 1f out: in n.d and easing up ins fnl f: unchal: impressive* **3/1**[2]

**2** *4 ½* **Tanseeq** 2-9-2 0 .......... DaneO'Neill 12 — 67
(William Haggas) *chsd ldrs: effrt to chse wnr 2f out: outpcd by wnr over 1f out: battled on to hold 2nd ins fnl f* **5/2**[1]

**3** *shd* **Jurz (IRE)** 2-9-2 0 .......... JackMitchell 7 — 67+
(Roger Varian) *stdd s: t.k.h in midfield: nt clrest of runs 2f out: rdn and hdwy over 1f out: battling for 2nd ins fnl f: kpt on: no ch w wnr* **20/1**

**4** *1* **Cracker Factory** 2-9-2 0 .......... PatCosgrave 1 — 64+
(William Haggas) *s.i.s: hld up in tch in rr: stl in rr whn nt clr run wl over 1f out: hdwy ent fnl f: styd on steadily: no ch w wnr* **8/1**[3]

**5** *¾* **Turquoise Bay (USA)** 2-9-2 0 .......... SilvestreDeSousa 5 — 62
(Chris Dwyer) *t.k.h: chsd wnr tl 2f out: sn rdn and outpcd by wnr over 1f out:: kpt on same pce ins fnl f* **11/1**

**6** *shd* **Gembari** 2-8-9 0 .......... ManuelFernandes(7) 6 — 62
(Ivan Furtado) *s.i.s: hld up in tch in last quartet: swtchd lft and hdwy 1/2-way: rdn over 2f out: outpcd by wnr but battling for placings over 1f out: kpt on same pce ins fnl f* **100/1**

**7** *hd* **Maverick Officer** 2-9-2 0 .......... MartinLane 9 — 61
(David Simcock) *hld up in tch in last quartet: effrt 2f out: rdn and outpcd by wnr over 1f out: no ch w wnr and kpt on same pce ins fnl f* **16/1**

**8** *hd* **Braemar** 2-9-2 0 .......... DanielMuscutt 14 — 61
(Sir Michael Stoute) *hld up in tch in midfield: effrt 2f out: rdn and outpcd by wnr over 1f out: kpt on ins fnl f: no ch w wnr* **14/1**

**9** *nk* **Whitehall** 2-9-2 0 .......... TedDurcan 13 — 60
(Sir Michael Stoute) *trckd ldrs: rdn: rn green and hung lft 2f out: sn outpcd by wnr: wl hld and kpt on same pce ins fnl f* **12/1**

**10** *¾* **Compliance (IRE)** 2-9-2 0 .......... MartinHarley 11 — 58
(James Tate) *wl in tch in midfield: rdn and losing pl whn short of room 2f out: no ch w wnr and kpt on same pce after* **14/1**

0 **11** *shd* **Thunder North (IRE)**[55] 4049 2-9-2 0 .......... StevieDonohoe 4 — 58
(David Lanigan) *hld up in tch in midfield: effrt 2f out: sn rdn and outpcd by wnr: wl hld and plugged on ins fnl f* **40/1**

**12** *½* **To Arms (USA)** 2-9-2 0 .......... SteveDrowne 2 — 56
(John Gosden) *hld up in tch in midfield: pushed along wl over 1f out: sn outpcd by wnr and wl hld 1f out: wknd ins fnl f* **10/1**

**13** *3 ¼* **Sa'ada (USA)** 2-8-11 0 .......... AdamBeschizza 10 — 42
(George Peckham) *t.k.h: chsd ldrs: rdn 2f out: sn outpcd by wnr and lost pl over 1f out: wknd fnl f* **100/1**

**14** *4 ½* **Best Company (IRE)** 2-8-13 0 .......... JackDuern(3) 3 — 35
(Dean Ivory) *dwlt: hld up in tch in last quartet: rdn 3f out: struggling and lost pl 2f out: bhd ins fnl f* **100/1**

1m 26.95s (0.35) **Going Correction** -0.175s/f (Firm) — 14 Ran SP% **119.2**
Speed ratings (Par 96): **91,85,85,84,83 83,83,83,82,81 81,81,77,72**
CSF £10.45 TOTE £3.90: £1.70, £1.70, £5.10; EX 16.60 Trifecta £184.00.
**Owner** Mr & Mrs Leoni Sceti **Bred** Biddestone Stud Ltd **Trained** Newmarket, Suffolk

**FOCUS**
Parade ring bend dolled off by 2m from after the crossing. A juvenile novice contest with barely any form on show but some well-bred newcomers from leading stables in the field. They went a respectable gallop, at best, on loose-topped ground officially described as good to firm, good in places. The winner impressed but the bare form is not up to much.

## 6109 BET TOTEJACKPOT AT BETFRED.COM H'CAP — 1m 3f 104y
5:30 (5:30) (Class 6) (0-65,65) 4-Y-O+ — **£2,264** (£673; £336; £168) **Stalls** Low

Form — RPR

1232 **1** **Hope Is High**[16] 5508 4-9-1 **59** .......... SilvestreDeSousa 10 — 71
(John Berry) *chsd ldr tl led 3f out: rdn and wnt clr 2f out: styd on wl and in n.d after: easily* **11/10**[1]

4043 **2** *7* **Best Example (USA)**[16] 5508 5-9-7 **65** .......... AdamBeschizza 8 — 65
(Julia Feilden) *hld up in tch in midfield: effrt to chse wnr 2f out: no imp and wl hld over 1f out: kpt on same pce to hold 2nd ins fnl f* **13/2**[3]

5030 **3** *1* **Albert Boy (IRE)**[10] 5706 4-8-12 **61** .......... GeorgeBuckell(5) 9 — 60
(Scott Dixon) *led tl 3f out: rdn and outpcd by wnr 2f out: wl hld 3rd whn swtchd rt jst over 1f out: kpt on same pce ins fnl f* **16/1**

434 **4** *1 ¾* **Angelical (IRE)**[22] 5290 4-9-1 **59** .......... MartinHarley 3 — 55
(Daniel Mark Loughnane) *chsd ldng trio: rdn 3f out: unable qck u.p 2f out: wl hld 4th and plugged on same pce after* **6/1**[2]

5003 **5** *2* **Galuppi**[19] 5405 6-8-3 **47** ..........(v) DannyBrock 4 — 40
(J R Jenkins) *hld up in tch in midfield: effrt over 2f out: drvn 2f out: wl hld 5th and plugged on same pce fr over 1f out* **40/1**

6445 **6** *1 ½* **Art Scholar (IRE)**[8] 5809 10-9-1 **59** .......... JamieSpencer 5 — 49
(Michael Appleby) *hld up in rr: clsd whn nt clr run and swtchd rt 2f out: stl nt clr run and lost any ch tl gap opened 1f out: styd on to pass btn rivals ins fnl f: n.d* **16/1**

4640 **7** *1 ½* **Attain**[13] 5599 8-9-1 **64** .......... JennyPowell(5) 2 — 52
(Archie Watson) *chsd ldrs: rdn over 2f out: sn lost pl u.p: wl btn over 1f out* **12/1**

1202 **8** *shd* **Tyrsal (IRE)**[8] 5809 6-8-13 **64** ..........(p) CameronNoble(7) 1 — 51
(Clifford Lines) *stdd s: t.k.h: hld up in last pair: clsd over 3f out: rdn and no hdwy over 2f out: wknd over 1f out* **13/2**[3]

6500 **9** *1 ¾* **Astrosecret**[13] 5080 4-8-6 **50** ..........(p[1]) JoeyHaynes 7 — 35
(Mark H Tompkins) *stdd s: hld up in last trio: sme hdwy over 3f out: rdn and no imp over 2f out: wl btn over 1f out* **66/1**

2m 26.72s (-1.98) **Going Correction** -0.175s/f (Firm) — 9 Ran SP% **112.0**
Speed ratings (Par 101): **100,94,94,92,91 90,89,89,87**
CSF £8.13 CT £70.02 TOTE £1.70: £1.02, £2.00, £4.00; EX 7.50 Trifecta £61.20.
**Owner** Mrs Emma Berry & John Berry **Bred** Miss K Rausing **Trained** Newmarket, Suffolk

**FOCUS**
A modest middle-distance handicap. They went a decent gallop and the favourite fairly routed this field. This form may underplay the winner.

## 6110 BET TOTEQUADPOT AT BETFRED.COM H'CAP — 1m 1f 21y
6:00 (6:00) (Class 4) (0-80,80) 3-Y-O+ — **£5,336** (£1,588; £793; £396) **Stalls** Low

Form — RPR

0255 **1** **Hajaj (IRE)**[33] 4904 3-9-7 **80** .......... StevieDonohoe 1 — 87
(Charlie Fellowes) *chsd ldrs: effrt on inner 2f out: nt clr run and swtchd rt over 1f out: hdwy u.p to chal ins fnl f: r.o wl to ld nr fin* **5/2**[1]

5016 **2** *nk* **Voi**[21] 5331 3-8-11 **70** ..........(t) RobertTart 5 — 76
(Conrad Allen) *in tch in midfield: effrt 2f out: drvn and styd on to ld over 1f out: kpt on wl u.p tl hdd and no ex nr fin* **11/1**

2043 **3** *1 ¼* **War At Sea (IRE)**[28] 5066 3-9-4 **77** ..........(h) JamieSpencer 4 — 80
(David Simcock) *dwlt: hld up in tch in rr: effrt on inner 2f out: forced to swtchd rt arnd ldrs ins fnl f: styd on wl fnl 100yds to go 3rd towards fin* **7/2**[3]

313 **4** *1* **Whosyourhousemate**[12] 5664 3-9-7 **80** .......... AdamBeschizza 6 — 81
(Ed Vaughan) *chsd ldr: rdn 2f out: drvn and ev ch over 1f out tl no ex ins fnl f: wknd towards fin* **11/4**[2]

0-10 **5** *hd* **Lord Reason**[30] 5000 5-9-9 **78** .......... TimClark(3) 3 — 79
(John Butler) *led: rdn ent fnl 2f: drvn and hdd over 1f out: no ex ins fnl f: wknd towards fin* **20/1**

3100 **6** *¾* **Valley Of Rocks (IRE)**[16] 5496 3-8-11 **70** .......... DaneO'Neill 2 — 69
(Mark Johnston) *in tch in midfield: effrt ent fnl 2f: drvn and styd on same pce fr over 1f out* **14/1**

0405 **7** *4* **Oasis Spear**[12] 5664 5-9-8 **77** .......... GeorgeWood(3) 8 — 68
(Chris Wall) *t.k.h: hld up in last pair and styd wd early: effrt ent fnl 2f: no imp and wknd fnl f* **5/1**

1m 54.22s (-1.58) **Going Correction** -0.175s/f (Firm)
**WFA** 3 from 5yo 7lb — 7 Ran SP% **113.9**
Speed ratings (Par 105): **100,99,98,97,97 96,93**
CSF £29.72 CT £95.68 TOTE £3.40: £1.50, £4.60; EX 25.50 Trifecta £142.40.
**Owner** Khalifa Bin Hamad Al Attiyah **Bred** Lismacue Mare Syndicate **Trained** Newmarket, Suffolk

**FOCUS**
The feature contest was a fair handicap. They went a modest gallop and the favourite did well to get up close home. He posted a length pb.

## 6111 BET TOTEEXACTA AT BETFRED.COM H'CAP 7f 3y
**6:30** (6:30) (Class 5) (0-75,77) 3-Y-O+ **£2,911** (£866; £432; £216) **Stalls** Centre

Form RPR

4-23 **1** **Multicultural (IRE)**[41] 4579 3-9-4 **73**.............................(b[1]) MartinHarley 7 84+
(James Tate) *hld up in tch: clsd to trck ldrs on bit 2f out: shkn up to chal ins f: sn rdn and qckndl to ld: sn in command: comf* **8/1**[3]

-124 **2** *2* **Call Me Grumpy (IRE)**[34] 4837 3-9-8 **77**................. SilvestreDeSousa 5 83
(Roger Varian) *trckd ldrs: clsd to join ldr ent fnl 2f: ev ch and edgd lft u.p over 1f out: outpcd by wnr fnl 100yds: kpt on* **2/1**[1]

0230 **3** *1* **Shyron**[13] 5610 6-9-4 **73**...................................................... JaneElliott[(5)] 2 78
(George Margarson) *sn led: hdd over 5f out but styd upsides ldr tl led again jst over 2f out: hrd pressed and rdn over 1f out: hdd ins fnl f: sn outpcd by wnr and kpt on same pce after* **14/1**

5-40 **4** *2¾* **Rouge Nuage (IRE)**[23] 5245 7-9-3 **74**...................... DarraghKeenan[(7)] 10 72
(Conrad Allen) *t.k.h: hld up in tch in midfield: effrt 2f out: wnt 4th and hung lft 1f out: styd on same pce and no imp ins fnl f* **33/1**

3232 **5** *¾* **Stosur (IRE)**[13] 5591 6-9-2 **73**.................................(b) CameronNoble[(7)] 1 69
(Gay Kelleway) *hld up in tch in midfield: effrt over 2f out: unable qck u.p over 1f out: wknd ins fnl f* **16/1**

3503 **6** *1* **Buckland Beau**[16] 5510 6-9-8 **72**................................ StevieDonohoe 3 65
(Charlie Fellowes) *hld up in tch towards rr: effrt jst over 2f out: no imp over 1f out: wl hld and kpt on same pce ins fnl f* **16/1**

6144 **7** *¾* **North Creek**[23] 5245 4-9-9 **76**.......................................... GeorgeWood[(3)] 6 67
(Chris Wall) *broke wl: sn restrained and t.k.h in midfield: rdn 1/2-way: lost pl and hmpd 2f out: sn swtchd rt: kpt on ins fnl f: nvr trbld ldrs* **9/2**[2]

0645 **8** *½* **Poetic Force (IRE)**[34] 4831 3-9-3 **72**..............................(t) DaneO'Neill 11 59
(Tony Carroll) *stdd and swtchd lft leaving stalls: hld up in tch in rr: effrt ent fnl 2f: no imp over 1f out: wl hld and plugged on same pce ins fnl f* **12/1**

0065 **9** *½* **Zaeem**[8] 5788 8-9-5 **76**.............................................. ManuelFernandes[(7)] 8 64
(Ivan Furtado) *trckd ldrs: rdn and ev ch jst over 2f out: lost pl over 1f out: wknd ins fnl f* **8/1**[3]

5051 **10** *1¼* **Flying Fantasy**[7] 5857 5-9-2 **66**.......................................(p) DannyBrock 4 51
(Michael Appleby) *hdwy to ld over 5f out: hdd and rdn jst over 2f out: sn struggling and lost pl over 1f out: wknd fnl f* **8/1**[3]

560 **11** *3½* **Dot Green (IRE)**[30] 4999 4-9-5 **69**.......................................... JoeyHaynes 9 44
(Mark H Tompkins) *hld up in tch: effrt 2f out: sn rdn and no hdwy: wknd jst over 1f out* **25/1**

1m 24.8s (-1.80) **Going Correction** -0.175s/f (Firm)
**WFA** 3 from 4yo+ 5lb **11** Ran SP% **117.8**
Speed ratings (Par 103): **103,100,99,96,95 94,93,93,92,91 87**
CSF £24.29 CT £233.73 TOTE £7.70: £2.60, £1.30, £4.20; EX 30.80 Trifecta £148.40.
**Owner** Saeed Manana **Bred** Clarecastle Farm Limited **Trained** Newmarket, Suffolk

**FOCUS**
A fair handicap. They went an increasing tempo and the favourite couldn't cope with an unexposed filly off a clearly lenient opening mark. The form is rated around the second.

## 6112 BET TOTETRIFECTA AT BETFRED.COM H'CAP 7f 3y
**7:00** (7:02) (Class 6) (0-55,55) 3-Y-O+ **£2,264** (£673; £336; £168) **Stalls** Centre

Form RPR

640 **1** **Slow To Hand**[13] 5611 3-9-2 **55**...............................(b[1]) JamieSpencer 14 67+
(William Jarvis) *stdd after s: hld up in rr: clsd and trckd runner up through 2f out: rdn to chse wnr ins fnl f styd on u.p to ld wl ins fnl f: gng away at fin* **14/1**

0020 **2** *1¼* **Tallulah's Quest (IRE)**[19] 5410 3-9-2 **55**................... AdamBeschizza 11 64
(Julia Feilden) *hld up in tch in last quartet: smooth hdwy over 2f out: rdn to ld ent fnl f: sn hung lft: hdd and one pced wl ins fnl f* **18/1**

0020 **3** *6* **Nellie's Dancer**[9] 5741 3-8-11 **55**............................(p) GeorgeBuckell[(5)] 1 48
(Scott Dixon) *chsd ldr: rdn and ev ch ent fnl 2f: led wl over 1f out tl hdd ent fnl f: sn outpcd and wknd fnl 150yds* **16/1**

4532 **4** *nk* **Caledonian Gold**[7] 5857 4-8-9 **50**.........................(b) CameronNoble[(7)] 7 44
(Paul D'Arcy) *taken down down early: stdd s: t.k.h: hld up in midfield: hdwy over 2f out: rdn and ev ch wl over 1f out tl ent fnl f: wknd fnl 150yds* **6/1**[2]

040 **5** *1* **Swiftee (IRE)**[24] 5206 4-9-4 **52**...........................................(b) MartinHarley 4 43
(Ivan Furtado) *led: rdn over 1f out: hdd wl over 1f out: no ex u.p and wknd fnl f* **28/1**

0503 **6** *1½* **Chetan**[8] 5793 5-9-4 **55**.........................................(t) GeorgeWood[(3)] 13 42
(Charlie Wallis) *taken down early: hld up in tch in midfield: effrt u.p to chse ldrs 2f out: outpcd over 1f out: wknd fnl f* **15/2**

0400 **7** *shd* **Caribbean Spring (IRE)**[31] 4971 4-9-0 **53**...................... JaneElliott[(5)] 9 40
(George Margarson) *hld up in tch in midfield: effrt 2f out: no imp over 1f out: wl hld and plugged on same pce fnl f* **25/1**

6446 **8** *2* **Tommy's Secret**[22] 5285 7-9-0 **53**.............................(p) PaddyBradley[(5)] 6 35
(Jane Chapple-Hyam) *hld up in tch in midfield: effrt and hdwy over 2f out: no imp u.p over 1f out: sn wknd* **13/2**[3]

000 **9** *1¾* **Babette (IRE)**[82] 3085 3-9-2 **55**.......................................... SteveDrowne 2 30
(Tony Newcombe) *wl in tch in midfield: effrt u.p over 2f out: drvn and no hdwy wl over 1f out: sn wknd* **5/1**[1]

5-60 **10** *3¼* **Solitary Sister (IRE)**[41] 4565 3-9-2 **55**.....................(bt[1]) StevieDonohoe 3 21
(Richard Spencer) *flashing tail leaving stalls: chsd ldrs tl ent fnl 2f: sn lost pl and wknd over 1f out* **33/1**

4400 **11** *3½* **Little Indian**[37] 4727 7-9-1 **49**.......................................... AlistairRawlinson 10 8
(J R Jenkins) *stdd after s: hld up towards rr: effrt 2f out: sn rdn and btn: wknd over 1f out* **33/1**

1-10 **12** *1½* **Great Colaci**[36] 4744 4-9-4 **55**.......................................... CliffordLee[(3)] 12 10
(Gillian Boanas) *wl in tch in midfield: rdn over 2f out: unable qck and sn struggling: wknd over 1f out* **6/1**[2]

-05 **13** *1¾* **Roman Legion (IRE)**[37] 4714 3-8-13 **55**.............................. JackDuern[(3)] 16
(Dean Ivory) *chsd ldrs: rdn over 2f out: sn struggling and lost pl: wknd over 1f out* **20/1**

4332 **14** *1* **Wedgewood Estates**[36] 4735 6-9-7 **55**.............................. DaneO'Neill 15
(Tony Carroll) *hld up in rr: n.d: bhd and eased wl ins fnl f* **16/1**

05R/ **15** *nk* **Dylan's Centenary**[630] 7995 6-9-2 **50**................................... DannyBrock 8
(Phil McEntee) *in tch in midfield: rdn over 2f out: sn lost pl: bhd and eased wl ins fnl f* **50/1**

0033 **16** *8* **Sakhee's Jem**[21] 5340 4-9-7 **55**....................................... SilvestreDeSousa 5
(Gay Kelleway) *t.k.h: chsd ldrs tl over 2f out: sn lost pl: bhd and eased ins fnl f* **8/1**

1m 24.24s (-2.36) **Going Correction** -0.175s/f (Firm)
**WFA** 3 from 4yo+ 5lb **16** Ran SP% **125.0**
Speed ratings (Par 101): **106,104,97,97,96 94,94,92,90,86 82,80,78,77,77 68**
CSF £231.88 CT £4205.28 TOTE £15.10: £3.00, £4.20, £3.40, £1.90; EX 303.40 Trifecta £3095.60.
**Owner** William Jarvis **Bred** R J Cornelius **Trained** Newmarket, Suffolk

**FOCUS**
A moderate handicap. They went a decent gallop and Jamie Spencer timed his winning run to perfection on board the winner. The winner was a notable improver.

## 6113 BET TOTEWIN AT BETFRED.COM H'CAP 6f 3y
**7:30** (7:33) (Class 5) (0-75,75) 3-Y-O+ **£2,911** (£866; £432; £216) **Stalls** Centre

Form RPR

155 **1** **In The Spotlight (IRE)**[4] 5965 3-9-7 **75**........................(p[1]) TedDurcan 2 86
(Henry Spiller) *hld up in tch in midfield: clsd 2f out: rdn and qcknd to ld over 1f out: clr and r.o wl ins fnl f: comf* **8/1**

4125 **2** *2¾* **Mulzim**[20] 5376 3-9-7 **75**.......................................................... DaneO'Neill 8 77
(Ed Dunlop) *hld up wl in tch in midfield: clsd to press ldrs 2f out: rdn and ev ch over 1f out: sn outpcd by wnr: 2nd and kpt on same pce ins fnl f* **5/2**[1]

6455 **3** *1½* **Commanche**[16] 5511 8-8-7 **58**...................................(b) SilvestreDeSousa 4 55
(Chris Dwyer) *led for 2f: styd w ldr: rdn over 2f out: kpt on u.p tl unable to match pce of wnr over 1f out: 3rd and kpt on same pce fnl f* **6/1**[3]

6000 **4** *1¼* **Plucky Dip**[13] 5610 6-8-13 **71**....................................(p) JackOsborn[(7)] 10 64
(John Ryan) *hld up in rr: rdn over 2f out: sme hdwy whn nt clr run and swtchd rt over 1f out: styd on u.p ins fnl f: snatched 4th last strides: no threat to ldrs* **14/1**

5001 **5** *nk* **Cat Silver**[38] 4695 4-9-2 **70**.....................................(p) GeorgeWood[(3)] 6 62
(Charlie Wallis) *stdd after s: t.k.h: hld up in tch in midfield: clsd to trck ldrs 2f out: rdn and unable qck over 1f out: edgd lft and wknd ins fnl f* **7/1**

5054 **6** *2½* **Big Lachie**[22] 5272 3-9-7 **75**.......................................................... MartinLane 1 59
(Daniel Mark Loughnane) *t.k.h: midfield tl hdwy to ld after 2f: rdn 2f out: hdd over 1f out and sn outpcd: wknd ins fnl f* **12/1**

0562 **7** *¾* **Musical Comedy**[17] 5473 6-9-9 **74**.......................................... AntonioFresu 7 56
(Mike Murphy) *hld up in tch in last trio: shkn up 2f out: no hdwy over 1f out: wknd ins fnl f* **5/1**[2]

0-00 **8** *½* **Fever Few**[29] 5039 8-8-9 **60**.......................................................... AdamBeschizza 5 40
(Chris Wall) *taken down early: broke fast but awkwardly: stdd and t.k.h in midfield: effrt ent fnl 2f: sn struggling and lost pl: wknd fnl f* **14/1**

0100 **9** *shd* **Picture Dealer**[17] 5481 8-9-5 **73**.......................................... SimonPearce[(3)] 9 53
(Lydia Pearce) *hld up in tch in rr: urged along 2f out: no hdwy: n.d* **11/1**

1m 12.51s (-1.89) **Going Correction** -0.175s/f (Firm)
**WFA** 3 from 4yo+ 3lb **9** Ran SP% **112.5**
Speed ratings (Par 103): **105,101,99,97,97 93,92,92,92**
CSF £27.43 CT £129.33 TOTE £8.80: £2.30, £1.50, £2.10; EX 32.30 Trifecta £176.70.
**Owner** Dethrone Racing **Bred** Ms Patricia Walsh **Trained** Newmarket, Suffolk

**FOCUS**
A fair sprint handicap. They went a muddling gallop and it paid to race relatively prominently. This was a bit out of line with the winner's profile.

## 6114 BET TOTEPLACE AT BETFRED.COM H'CAP 5f 42y
**8:00** (8:04) (Class 6) (0-55,57) 3-Y-O+ **£2,264** (£673; £336; £168) **Stalls** Centre

Form RPR

6401 **1** **Ebitda**[10] 5703 3-9-0 **55** 6ex.......................................... GeorgeBuckell[(5)] 11 68
(Scott Dixon) *hld up in tch in midfield: clsd to trck ldrs 2f out: sn rdn to ld: r.o strly and clr ins fnl f: readily* **9/1**

120 **2** *2¾* **Camino**[6] 5871 4-8-13 **47**.......................................................... MartinLane 3 50
(Andi Brown) *stdd after s: hld up in last pair: hdwy on far side 2f out: rdn to chse wnr ent fnl f: kpt on same pce and no imp ins fnl f* **6/1**[3]

132 **3** *1* **Justice Rock**[37] 4710 4-9-2 **50**...................................(t) SilvestreDeSousa 6 50
(Phil McEntee) *hld up in tch towards rr: clsd over 2f out: effrt 2f out: 3rd and kpt on ins fnl f: no threat to wnr* **7/2**[1]

46 **4** *1½* **Shelneverwalkalone**[14] 5567 3-9-7 **57**.......................................... MartinHarley 1 51
(Ivan Furtado) *led: rdn and hdd over 1f out: sn outpcd by wnr: wknd ins fnl f* **10/1**

0043 **5** *hd* **African Girl**[29] 5040 3-8-9 **48**.......................................... SimonPearce[(3)] 16 41
(Lydia Pearce) *stdd after s: hld up in tch towards rr: effrt over 1f out: styd on wl ins fnl f: nvr trbld ldrs* **11/2**[2]

6530 **6** *nk* **Hot Stuff**[28] 5052 4-8-12 **53**...................................(p) ManuelFernandes[(7)] 13 45
(Tony Carroll) *hld up in tch in midfield: effrt over 1f out: rdn 1f out: kpt on ins fnl f: no threat to wnr* **12/1**

0000 **7** *1* **Men United (FR)**[15] 5543 4-8-7 **46** oh1.......................... KevinLundie[(5)] 8 35
(Roy Bowring) *hld up in tch in midfield: effrt 2f out: no imp u.p over 1f out: styd on same pce ins fnl f* **12/1**

0500 **8** *1* **Only Ten Per Cent (IRE)**[114] 2069 9-9-7 **55**.......(v) AlistairRawlinson 10 40
(J R Jenkins) *hld up in tch in midfield: effrt whn nt clr run and swtchd rt over 1f out: no imp and wl hld ins fnl f* **33/1**

03 **9** *shd* **Lizzy's Dream**[13] 5605 9-8-12 **46** oh1.......................... AdamBeschizza 15 31
(Rebecca Bastiman) *stdd after s: hld up in tch towards rr: effrt 2f out: sme hdwy ins fnl f: kpt on: nvr trbld ldrs* **9/1**

000 **10** *1½* **Frangarry (IRE)**[26] 5146 5-9-0 **55**.......................... KatherineGlenister[(7)] 5 34
(Alan Bailey) *dwlt: sn rcvrd and wl in tch in midfield: unable qck u.p over 1f out: wknd ins fnl f* **9/1**

060 **11** *1½* **Verdi (IRE)**[7] 5855 3-8-5 **48**.......................................(b) JackOsborn[(7)] 2 22
(John Ryan) *dwlt: sn rcvrd and in tch in midfield: rdn 2f out: sn struggling and lost pl: wknd fnl f* **33/1**

0405 **12** *¾* **Percy Toplis**[21] 5338 3-8-7 **46**.......................................(b) GeorgeWood[(3)] 7 17
(Christine Dunnett) *w ldr tl over 2f out: sn struggling and losing pl whn short of room over 1f out: wknd fnl f* **22/1**

00-0 **13** *3* **Burnt Cream**[190] 622 10-8-12 **46** oh1..............................(t) StevieDonohoe 9
(Martin Bosley) *restless in stalls: s.i.s: hld up in rr: effrt over 1f out: no hdwy: n.d* **66/1**

0006 **14** *1½* **Willow Spring**[42] 4543 5-8-9 **46** oh1.......................................... TimClark[(3)] 14
(Denis Quinn) *in tch in midfield: rdn 2f out: sn struggling and lost pl: bhd ins fnl f* **25/1**

1m 1.89s (-0.81) **Going Correction** -0.175s/f (Firm)
**WFA** 3 from 4yo+ 2lb **14** Ran SP% **121.9**
Speed ratings (Par 101): **99,94,93,90,90 89,88,86,86,84 81,80,75,73**
CSF £59.84 CT £236.24 TOTE £11.50: £3.70, £3.20, £1.50; EX 59.10 Trifecta £208.70.
**Owner** Chesterfield Estates **Bred** Selwood, Hoskins & Trickledown **Trained** Babworth, Notts

**FOCUS**
A moderate sprint handicap. They went a respectable gallop and it is sound form for the grade. The winner took another step forward.

T/Jkpt: Not won. T/Plt: £53.90 to a £1 stake. Pool: £61,980.12 - 838.46 winning units. T/Qpdt: £27.10 to a £1 stake. Pool: £5,631.30 - 153.74 winning units. **Steve Payne**

6115 - 6118a (Foreign Racing) - See Raceform Interactive

## 5858 LEOPARDSTOWN (L-H)

Thursday, August 17

**OFFICIAL GOING: Good (good to yielding in places)**

### 6119a INVESCO PENSION CONSULTANTS DESMOND STKS (GROUP 3) 1m

**7:10** (7:11) 3-Y-0+

**£31,769** (£10,230; £4,846; £2,153; £1,076; £538)

RPR

1 **Alexios Komnenos (IRE)**47 4383 3-9-1 106 ChrisHayes 2 111
(J A Stack, Ire) *chsd ldrs: 3rd 1/2-way: gng wl into st where n.m.r briefly: swtchd rt in 2nd 1 1/2f out: rdn to ld ins fnl f and kpt on wl clsng stages* **6/1**2

2 1 ½ **Music Box (IRE)**14 5583 3-8-12 96 SeamieHeffernan 5 105+
(A P O'Brien, Ire) *s.i.s and in rr early tl sn tk clsr order in mid-div: 5th 1/2-way: gng wl into st and wnt 4th under 2f out where nt clr run: sn swtchd rt and r.o wl into nvr threatening 2nd fnl strides* **10/1**

3 shd **Custom Cut (IRE)**18 5456 8-9-10 107 DanielTudhope 1 112
(David O'Meara) *attempted to make all: over 1 l clr at 1/2-way: pushed along into st: rdn 1 1/2f out and hdd u.p ins fnl f: no imp on wnr clsng stages and denied 2nd fnl strides* **12/1**

4 ¾ **Morando (FR)**47 4371 4-9-7 113 AndreaAtzeni 6 107+
(Roger Varian) *hld up bhd ldrs in 5th early: 6th bef 1/2-way: pushed along appr st and no imp on ldrs disputing 6th between horses u.p over 1f out: r.o into nvr nrr 4th clsng stages* **6/4**1

5 nk **Intricately (IRE)**33 4928 3-8-12 108 WayneLordan 9 102
(Joseph Patrick O'Brien, Ire) *settled bhd ldr: 2nd 1/2-way: rdn under 2f out and u.p in 3rd ent fnl f: no ex wl ins fnl f and wknd clsng stages* **7/1**

6 1 **Diamond Fields (IRE)**108 2241 4-9-7 106 WJLee 4 104+
(J A Stack, Ire) *hld up towards rr: 7th 1/2-way: pushed along under 2f out and no imp on ldrs u.p in 6th ins fnl f: kpt on same pce: jst hld 6th* **25/1**

7 hd **Flight Risk (IRE)**32 4935 6-9-10 112 KevinManning 8 107+
(J S Bolger, Ire) *sn settled in rr: checked sltly at 1/2-way: stl gng wl in rr over 1f out where nt clr run and swtchd wl rt: r.o wl clsng stages: jst failed for 6th: nrst fin* **16/1**

8 ¾ **Sea Wolf (IRE)**47 4383 5-9-7 108 ColinKeane 7 102+
(G M Lyons, Ire) *w.w towards rr: 8th 1/2-way: tk clsr order on outer briefly fr 3f out: rdn and no ex over 1f out: one pce after* **13/2**3

9 1 ¼ **True Valour (IRE)**47 4383 3-9-1 108 PatSmullen 3 98
(J P Murtagh, Ire) *chsd ldrs: racd keenly early: 4th 1/2-way: rdn under 2f out and no imp on ldrs u.p in 5th over 1f out: wknd and eased ins fnl f* **8/1**

1m 43.98s (2.78) **Going Correction** +0.55s/f (Yiel)
**WFA** 3 from 4yo+ 6lb 9 Ran SP% **117.7**
Speed ratings: **108,106,106,105,105 104,104,103,102**
CSF £65.27 TOTE £6.80: £1.90, £2.30, £2.70; DF 69.40 Trifecta £811.40.
**Owner** Werrett Bloodstock PTY Ltd & Ms G Britton & D S Mc **Bred** P Motherway **Trained** Golden, Co. Tipperary

**FOCUS**
An intriguing renewal of this Group 3 Desmond Stakes with three of the first four in the market renewing rivalry after clashing in the Celebration Stakes 47 days earlier. The winner has improved with every start.

6120 - 6122a (Foreign Racing) - See Raceform Interactive

## 6050 DEAUVILLE (R-H)

Thursday, August 17

**OFFICIAL GOING: Polytrack: fast; turf: soft**

### 6123a PRIX DE SAINT-ETIENNE LA THILLAYE - CATEGORIE PERSONNEL DE HARAS (CONDITIONS) (4YO+) (TURF) 1m 5f 110y

**12:10** 4-Y-0+ **£14,102** (£5,641; £4,230; £2,820; £1,410)

RPR

1 **Matauri Jewel (IRE)**25 5198 4-8-10 0 VincentCheminaud 7 90
(M Delzangles, France) **12/5**1

2 6 **Echauffour (FR)**58 4-9-0 0 CristianDemuro 4 85
(J-C Rouget, France) **27/10**2

3 nk **Notte D'Oro (IRE)**26 5-8-10 0 MickaelBarzalona 8 81
(Mme Pia Brandt, France) **41/5**

4 1 ¾ **Dagobert Duke**52 7-8-8 0 JeromeMoutard(6) 6 82
(P Sobry, France) **36/5**

5 1 ½ **Pearl Dragon (FR)**26 6-9-0 0 (b) ChristopheSoumillon 2 80
(M Delzangles, France) **39/10**3

6 3 ½ **Swordshire (GER)**55 6-9-0 0 TheoBachelot 1 75
(Werner Glanz, Germany) **144/10**

7 3 **Cosmelli (ITY)**5 5912 4-9-0 0 (b) Pierre-CharlesBoudot 3 70
(Gay Kelleway) **19/1**

8 4 **Satanicjim (IRE)**30 5014 8-8-9 0 MlleMarylineEon(6) 5 65
(Alain Couetil, France) **136/10**

3m 3.34s (183.34) 8 Ran SP% **118.3**
PARI-MUTUEL (all including 1 euro stake): WIN 3.40; PLACE 1.50, 1.60, 2.30; DF 6.20; SF 13.70.
**Owner** Dieter Burkle **Bred** Mr & Mrs Dieter Buerkle **Trained** France

### 6124a PRIX DE VILLERVILLE - CATEGORIE JEUNE ESPOIR (CLAIMER) (3YO) (POLYTRACK) 1m 1f 110y

**1:50** 3-Y-0 **£11,538** (£4,615; £3,461; £2,307; £1,153)

RPR

1 **Fullmoon In Paris (FR)**20 3-8-11 0 ChristopheSoumillon 5 79
(J-C Rouget, France) **7/5**1

2 snk **Pando (IRE)**47 3-8-8 0 KyllanBarbaud(8) 10 84
(N Caullery, France) **43/10**2

3 nk **Song Of Life**46 3-8-11 0 (h) AlexisBadel 7 78
(Mme M Bollack-Badel, France) **96/10**

4 3 **Lodi (FR)**7 3-8-11 0 ClementLecoeuvre(4) 1 76
(N Caullery, France) **10/1**

5 ½ **Silver Casina (IRE)**151 3-8-11 0 CristianDemuro 2 71
(G Botti, France) **84/10**

6 1 ¾ **Island Brave (IRE)**9 5777 3-8-11 0 (b1) TonyPiccone 11 67
(J S Moore) **30/1**

7 nk **Saint Rhuys (FR)**43 3-8-11 0 EddyHardouin 3 67
(C Lotoux, France) **40/1**

8 1 ¼ **Mon Tresor (FR)**43 3-9-2 0 (b) MickaelBarzalona 9 69
(G Botti, France) **51/10**3

9 2 ½ **Lindsar**108 2247 3-9-4 0 FilipMinarik 8 66
(M G Mintchev, Germany) **61/1**

10 2 ½ **Silver Ring (FR)**66 3-9-4 0 AurelienLemaitre 4 61
(Mme C Head-Maarek, France) **41/1**

11 18 **Windsun Laujac (FR)** 3-9-1 0 AntoineCoutier 6 21
(J Parize, France) **50/1**

PARI-MUTUEL (all including 1 euro stake): WIN 2.40; PLACE 1.30, 1.80, 2.20; DF 5.40; SF 9.50.
**Owner** Sarl Ecurie J L Tepper **Bred** Mme G Forien & Sarl Ecurie J-L Tepper **Trained** Pau, France

### 6125a PRIX DE VALOGNES - CATEGORIE PERSONNEL ADMINISTRATIF (H'CAP) (4YO) (POLYTRACK) 1m 1f 110y

**3:25** 4-Y-0 **£8,119** (£3,247; £2,435; £1,623; £811)

RPR

1 **Gallarate (FR)**19 4-9-2 0 AurelienLemaitre 16 65
(N Caullery, France) **103/10**

2 3 **Capital Gearing**164 1070 4-8-9 0 (b) DelphineSantiago(6) 6 58
(Leo Braem, Belgium) **172/10**

3 hd **Tour**103 4-9-5 0 JeromeCabre 3 61
(M Nigge, France) **193/10**

4 ½ **Love Cape (USA)**55 4-9-3 0 MarcNobili 10 58
(D Windrif, France) **182/10**

5 snk **Enki Girl (FR)**19 4-9-2 0 (p) ChristopheSoumillon 1 57
(P Leblanc, France) **17/2**

6 2 ½ **Carbutt's Ridge (IRE)**55 4-9-5 0 (b) MickaelBarzalona 8 55
(N Caullery, France) **17/5**1

7 snk **My Hollow (FR)**109 4-9-1 0 FilipMinarik 5 51
(Frau Hella Sauer, Germany) **61/10**2

8 snk **Heart Angel (FR)**59 4-9-2 0 (b) AlexisBadel 14 51
(C Scandella, France) **151/10**

9 ½ **Vodka Double (FR)**244 4-9-3 0 FabriceVeron 7 51
(C Lotoux, France) **15/2**3

10 nk **Phenix Bay (FR)**61 4-9-2 0 FabienLefebvre 13 50
(Mlle A Voraz, France) **224/10**

11 1 ¾ **Ayguemorte (FR)**19 4-9-4 0 AnthonyCaramanolis 11 48
(P-L Guerin, France) **39/1**

12 4 **Franko Folie (FR)**298 4-9-2 0 Pierre-CharlesBoudot 12 38
(Gay Kelleway) **10/1**

13 ½ **Excellor (FR)**19 4-9-2 0 (p) CristianDemuro 2 37
(Charley Rossi, France) **32/1**

14 8 **Elevaz (IRE)**55 4-9-0 0 (p) EmmanuelEtienne 9 19
(C Le Veel, France) **80/1**

15 nse **Private School (IRE)**19 4-8-10 0 MlleMickaelleMichel(8) 4 22
(D Smaga, France) **155/10**

16 hd **Alyce (IRE)**37 4955 4-9-4 0 TheoBachelot 15 22
(N Branchu, France) **62/1**

PARI-MUTUEL (all including 1 euro stake): WIN 3.10 (coupled with Carbutt's Ridge); PLACE 2.70, 6.00, 6.10; DF 51.60; SF 92.00.
**Owner** Julien Caullery **Bred** G Laboureau **Trained** France

## 5735 CATTERICK (L-H)

Friday, August 18

**OFFICIAL GOING: Good (8.2)**

Wind: fresh 1/2 behind Weather: fine and sunny, breezy

### 6126 LADIES' EVENING AMATEUR RIDERS' H'CAP 1m 4f 13y

**5:30** (5:30) (Class 5) (0-70,76) 3-Y-0+ **£3,119** (£967; £483; £242) **Stalls** Centre

Form RPR

1 **All For Nothing (IRE)**25 5222 4-9-7 56 (vt) MrJordanWilliams 5 65
(John C McConnell, Ire) *mid-div: hdwy on outer over 2f out: led 1f out: edgd lft: drvn out* **16/1**

3335 2 1 ¾ **Sellingallthetime (IRE)**29 5060 6-10-8 71 (p) MissSBrotherton 9 77
(Michael Appleby) *sn chsng ldrs: edgd rt and kpt on same pce fnl f* **5/1**2

2431 3 1 ¾ **Pete So High (GER)**11 5706 3-10-4 76 6ex (p) MrAlexFerguson 6 79
(Richard Hannon) *hld up in mid-div: hdwy 4f out: chsng ldrs over 1f out: kpt on same pce* **7/2**1

2130 4 hd **Midnight Warrior**6 5951 7-9-9 58 (t) MissBeckySmith 1 61
(Ron Barr) *led early: chsd ldr: led 2f out: edgd rt and hdd 1f out: kpt on one pce* **33/1**

0230 5 1 ¼ **Wotabreeze (IRE)**20 5403 4-10-7 70 MrSWalker 10 71
(John Quinn) *mid-div: hdwy over 6f out: chsng ldrs 3f out: one pce whn n.m.r 1f out* **6/1**

3550 6 shd **Duke Of Yorkshire**20 5417 7-9-13 65 (p) MissEEasterby(3) 2 66
(Tim Easterby) *trckd ldrs: effrt over 2f out: one pce* **14/1**

3210 7 1 ¾ **Swansway**23 5284 4-10-5 68 MissJoannaMason 4 66
(Michael Easterby) *chsd ldrs: drvn over 3f out: one pce fnl 2f* **8/1**

1330 8 5 **Tonto's Spirit**11 5701 5-9-11 60 (h) MissEmmaSayer 11 50
(Kenneth Slack) *sn led: hdd 2f out: sn wknd* **11/2**3

200 9 1 ½ **Serenity Now (IRE)**26 5186 9-10-0 70 ow1 MrMWBrown(7) 7 58
(Brian Ellison) *hld up in rr: outpcd and bhd over 4f out: brief effrt over 2f out: nvr on terms* **50/1**

2/40 10 9 **Tropical Bachelor (IRE)**35 4853 11-8-11 51 oh3 MissEmilyBullock(5) 8 24
(Ruth Carr) *hld up in rr: outpcd over 4f out: sn bhd* **20/1**

-520 11 28 **Nordic Combined (IRE)**36 4809 3-9-7 68 MissLWilson(3) 3
(Brian Ellison) *rrd s: in last whn slipped bnd after 2f and rdr briefly lost irons: sn bhd: t.o 4f out* **6/1**

2m 38.47s (-0.43) **Going Correction** -0.075s/f (Good)
**WFA** 3 from 4yo+ 9lb 11 Ran SP% **116.2**
Speed ratings (Par 103): **98,96,95,95,94 94,93,90,89,83 64**
CSF £91.49 CT £350.74 TOTE £13.10: £3.40, £2.00, £1.80; EX 83.40 Trifecta £118.40.
**Owner** Sean F Gallagher **Bred** Nanallac Stud **Trained** Stamullen, Co Meath

**FOCUS**
A handicap for amateur riders in which they set off pretty fast, but the pace steadied down the far side. The winner came off the pace in a race run 12 yards further than advertised. The winner is rated back to his best.

## 6127 OOPS A DAISY FLORISTS (S) STKS — 7f 6y
**6:00** (6:01) (Class 6) 2-Y-O — £2,587 (£770) **Stalls** Low

Form — RPR
1334 **1** **Faradays Spark (IRE)**[10] 5742 2-9-0 62 ........ PatrickMathers 5 61
(Richard Fahey) *trckd ldr: effrt and chal ocver 2f out: rdn ocver 1f out: kpt on to ld last 100yds* **Evs**[2]
6564 **2** *nk* **Felisa**[7] 5893 2-8-9 65 ........ JoeFanning 3 55
(David Evans) *led: shkn up 4f out: rdn over 1f out: hdd last 100yds: no ex* **10/11**[1]
1m 29.03s (2.03) **Going Correction** -0.075s/f (Good) — **2** Ran SP% **102.4**
Speed ratings (Par 92): **85,84**
TOTE £1.30.There was no bid for the winner
**Owner** Nick Bradley Racing 35 & Partner **Bred** Roundhill Stud **Trained** Musley Bank, N Yorks
■ Miss Mazzie was withdrawn. Price at time of withdrawal 14-1. Rule 4 applies to all bets - deduction 5p in the pound.

**FOCUS**
Race run over an extra 12yds. Just two of the six declared runners remained in this 7f seller and it was an uninformative affair. The form is rated through the winner.

## 6128 RAYDALE PRESERVES NURSERY H'CAP — 5f 212y
**6:30** (6:30) (Class 4) (0-85,83) 2-Y-O — £5,175 (£1,540; £769; £384) **Stalls** Low

Form — RPR
5211 **1** **Demons Rock (IRE)**[12] 5685 2-9-8 83 6ex ........ PaddyPilley(5) 5 95+
(Tom Dascombe) *sn led: drvn clr over 2f out: eased clsng stages* **15/8**[1]
3440 **2** *3 ¾* **Central City (IRE)**[15] 5572 2-9-6 76 ........ BenCurtis 2 73
(Hugo Palmer) *led early: chsd ldrs: drvn 3f out: kpt on to take modest 2nd clsng stages* **10/3**[2]
2642 **3** *nse* **Seen The Lyte (IRE)**[14] 5603 2-8-12 68 ........ JasonHart 4 65
(John Quinn) *trckd ldrs: drvn over 2f out: kpt on same pce* **17/2**
602 **4** *nk* **Super Major (IRE)**[44] 4503 2-8-13 74 ........ CallumRodriguez(5) 3 70
(Michael Dods) *sn prom: effrt over 2f out: kpt on same pce over 1f out* **15/2**
3166 **5** *3* **Quayside**[14] 5596 2-9-6 76 ........ PatrickMathers 1 62
(Richard Fahey) *prom: drvn over 3f out: sn outpcd: sme hdwy over 2f out: wknd fnl f: eased clsng stages* **6/1**
0332 **6** *9* **Sorority**[7] 5878 2-8-11 67 ........ JoeFanning 6 25
(Mark Johnston) *sn trcking ldrs: effrt ocver 2f out: wknd and eased last 150yds* **5/1**[3]
1m 12.79s (-0.81) **Going Correction** -0.075s/f (Good) — **6** Ran SP% **111.1**
Speed ratings (Par 96): **102,97,96,96,92 80**
CSF £8.08 TOTE £2.30: £1.90, £1.70; EX 10.00 Trifecta £48.00.
**Owner** The Famous Five Partnership **Bred** James & Geoff Mulcahy **Trained** Malpas, Cheshire

**FOCUS**
Race run over an extra 12yds. Probably not the strongest of nurseries but the winner continues in fine form and the way he is going suggests he could hold his own in better-class events. He's value for extra.

## 6129 BLACK BULL INN MOULTON MAIDEN STKS — 1m 4f 13y
**7:05** (7:05) (Class 5) 3-Y-O+ — £3,234 (£962; £481; £240) **Stalls** Centre

Form — RPR
42 **1** **State Sovereignty**[11] 5707 5-9-9 0 ........ DougieCostello 7 81+
(Michael Scudamore) *trckd ldr: led over 2f out: sn wnt wl clr: heavily eased last 100yds* **13/8**[2]
6 **2** *19* **Bumble Bay**[7] 5894 7-9-9 0 ........ (t) CallumRodriguez(5) 3 53
(Robert Stephens) *chsd ldrs: outpcd and drvn over 3f out: hdwy over 2f out: kpt on to take modest 2nd last 100yds* **20/1**
60/0 **3** *2 ¼* **Ferngrove (USA)**[8] 5831 6-10-0 48 ........ (t) PaddyAspell 9 49
(Susan Corbett) *chsd ldrs: drvn over 3f out: one pce fnl 2f* **100/1**
0 **4** *½* **Pantera**[19] 5458 3-9-0 0 ........ SamJames 4 44
(David O'Meara) *hld up in mid-div: t.k.h: hdwy over 3f out: one pce fnl 2f* **9/1**[3]
2 **5** *¾* **Itsalonglongroad**[40] 4657 3-9-5 0 ........ (t) JoeFanning 5 48
(John C McConnell, Ire) *led: hdd over 2f out: wknd last 150yds* **4/5**[1]
**6** *66* **The Foozler** 4-9-11 0 ........ AdamMcNamara(3) 8
(Peter Niven) *s.s: reluctant in rr: hung rt and sn bhd: t.o 4f out: eventually completed* **33/1**
**7** *30* **My Distant Murphy** 3-9-5 0 ........ NathanEvans 2
(Jacqueline Coward) *in rr: reminders after 3f: drvn 6f out: sn wl bhd: t.o 4f out: eventually completed* **80/1**
2m 36.92s (-1.98) **Going Correction** -0.075s/f (Good)
**WFA** 3 from 4yo+ 9lb — **7** Ran SP% **113.6**
Speed ratings (Par 103): **103,90,88,88,88 44,24**
CSF £29.60 TOTE £2.60: £1.10, £12.00; EX 33.40 Trifecta £170.70.
**Owner** J C G Chua **Bred** Rabbah Bloodstock Limited **Trained** Bromsash, H'fords

**FOCUS**
Race run over an extra 12yds. With the well-supported favourite running well below form this took little winning, but it still produced a wide-margin winner.

## 6130 BERBER LEATHER H'CAP — 5f
**7:40** (7:40) (Class 6) (0-60,65) 3-Y-O+ — £2,587 (£770; £384; £192) **Stalls** Low

Form — RPR
4415 **1** **Perfect Words (IRE)**[3] 6045 7-9-6 65 6ex ........ (p) HarrisonShaw(7) 6 71
(Marjorie Fife) *mid-div: hdwy over 2f out: kpt on wl fnl f: led towards fin* **5/1**[3]
5000 **2** *nk* **Sir Geoffrey (IRE)**[10] 5736 11-8-8 51 ow1 ........ (b) PaddyPilley(5) 3 56
(Scott Dixon) *chsd ldrs: edgd rt appr fnl f: kpt on to take 2nd fnl strides* **16/1**
6223 **3** *½* **Lady Joanna Vassa (IRE)**[4] 5995 4-8-10 48 ........ (p[1]) ConnorBeasley 5 51
(Richard Guest) *wore earplugs: led: hdd and no ex clsng stages* **11/4**[1]
0002 **4** *1 ¼* **Mr Enthusiastic**[11] 5703 3-8-5 45 ........ PatrickMathers 8 44
(Noel Wilson) *chsd ldrs: kpt on same pce last 100yds* **40/1**
6256 **5** *nk* **Windforpower (IRE)**[1] 6089 7-9-6 58 ........ (v) BenCurtis 7 56
(Tracy Waggott) *mid-div: hdwy over 2f out: kpt on same pce fnl f* **8/1**
02 **6** *nse* **Sarabi**[42] 4559 4-9-10 62 ........ (p) DavidAllan 4 59
(Scott Dixon) *chsd ldrs: drvn and outpcd 2f out: kpt on fnl f* **6/1**
3000 **7** *½* **Very First Blade**[11] 5695 8-8-4 45 ........ (p) PhilDennis(3) 9 41
(Michael Mullineaux) *sn outpcd and detached in last: hdwy and edgd lft over 1f out: nvr a factor* **20/1**
0422 **8** *¾* **Nuala Tagula (IRE)**[14] 5605 4-9-6 58 ........ (t) JasonHart 2 51
(John Quinn) *dwlt: in rr: sme hdwy 2f out: nvr a threat* **9/2**[2]
1614 **9** *nk* **Kodimoor (IRE)**[14] 5605 4-9-9 61 ........ (bt) JoeFanning 1 53
(Christopher Kellett) *mid-div: drvn over 2f out: nvr a factor* **13/2**
59.69s (-0.11) **Going Correction** +0.05s/f (Good)
**WFA** 3 from 4yo+ 2lb — **9** Ran SP% **113.3**
Speed ratings (Par 101): **102,101,100,98,98 98,97,96,95**
CSF £78.53 CT £261.12 TOTE £6.30: £2.00, £4.00, £1.10; EX 87.90 Trifecta £515.90.
**Owner** Green Lane **Bred** Rathasker Stud **Trained** Stillington, N Yorks

**FOCUS**
Exposed sorts in this 5f handicap which was run at a strong gallop. The form's rated around the front pair.

## 6131 30TH AUGUST IS FAMILY DAY H'CAP — 7f 6y
**8:10** (8:11) (Class 6) (0-60,60) 3-Y-O+ — £2,587 (£770; £384; £192) **Stalls** Low

Form — RPR
6300 **1** **Prazeres**[27] 5167 3-9-3 58 ........ JoeFanning 5 63
(Les Eyre) *mde all: rdn over 1f out: hld on clsng stages* **33/1**
0422 **2** *½* **Danot (IRE)**[8] 5848 5-9-3 56 ........ (p) AdamMcNamara(3) 10 62
(Jedd O'Keeffe) *chsd wnr: kpt on unsder press fnl f: no ex nr fin* **6/1**[2]
4364 **3** *¾* **Someone Exciting**[26] 5185 4-9-4 54 ........ PatrickMathers 12 58
(David Thompson) *s.i.s: in rr: hdwy outside over 2f out: tk 3rd last 100yds: kpt on* **10/1**
2440 **4** *1 ½* **Cool Strutter (IRE)**[16] 5544 5-9-5 55 ........ SamJames 6 55
(Karen Tutty) *mid-div: hdwy over 2f out: kpt on same pce to take 4th clsng stages* **15/2**
3113 **5** *1 ¾* **Carlovian**[8] 5848 4-9-3 53 ........ (p) DougieCostello 3 48
(Mark Walford) *mid-div: hdwy over 2f out: kpt on same pce to take 5th nr fin* **7/2**[1]
6606 **6** *nk* **Peny Arcade**[39] 4688 3-8-11 52 ........ CamHardie 1 44
(Alistair Whillans) *in rr: hdwy over 2f out: kpt on fnl f* **33/1**
3000 **7** *1 ½* **Broughtons Fancy**[42] 4561 4-9-4 59 ........ GemmaTutty(5) 9 49
(Karen Tutty) *mid-div: hdwy over 2f out: kpt on one pce over 1f out* **14/1**
222 **8** *nk* **Deben**[10] 5738 4-8-11 50 ........ PhilDennis(3) 13 39
(John Weymes) *chsd ldrs: one pce fnl 2f* **7/1**
0600 **9** *1 ½* **Win Lose Draw (IRE)**[53] 4163 5-9-7 57 ........ AlistairRawlinson 15 42
(Michael Appleby) *s.i.s: in rr: effrt outer over 2f out: nvr a factor* **33/1**
-660 **10** *1* **Whip Up A Frenzy (IRE)**[176] 880 5-8-11 50 ........ JoshDoyle(3) 4 32
(David O'Meara) *chsd ldrs: drvn over 3f out: one pce fnl 2f* **13/2**[3]
60-0 **11** *shd* **Truly**[8] 5835 6-9-10 60 ........ (h) PaddyAspell 7 42
(Paul Collins) *in tch: effrt over 2f out: fdd over 1f out* **50/1**
0000 **12** *3 ¼* **Bad Girl Caoimhe (IRE)**[25] 5215 4-9-3 53 ........ BarryMcHugh 8 26
(Marjorie Fife) *s.i.s: in rr: effrt over 2f out: nvr on terms* **25/1**
6303 **13** *6* **Bo Selecta (IRE)**[17] 5512 3-9-5 60 ........ (p[1]) GrahamLee 2 15
(Richard Spencer) *chsd ldrs: wknd over 1f out* **15/2**
4-00 **14** *2* **Good Boy Jasper**[10] 5738 3-9-3 58 ........ NathanEvans 11
(James Moffatt) *in rr: brief effrt over 2f out: sn wknd* **100/1**
400- **15** *6* **Chookie Valentine**[417] 3710 4-8-12 48 ........ (p[1]) JasonHart 14
(Keith Dalgleish) *a towards rr: bhd whn eased clsng stages* **40/1**
1m 26.29s (-0.71) **Going Correction** -0.075s/f (Good)
**WFA** 3 from 4yo+ 5lb — **15** Ran SP% **119.7**
Speed ratings (Par 101): **101,100,99,97,95 95,93,93,91,90 90,86,79,77,70**
CSF £212.14 CT £2208.75 TOTE £31.60: £9.10, £2.50, £3.30; EX 265.90 Trifecta £986.80.
**Owner** J N Blackburn **Bred** Saleh Al Homaizi & Imad Al Sagar **Trained** Catwick, N Yorks

**FOCUS**
Race run over an extra 12yds. A low-grade handicap with mainly exposed sorts most of whom are hard to win with. The pace was strong but the winner made all. He did not quite need to reproduce the best of this year's form.
T/Plt: £146.50 to a £1 stake. Pool: £47,767.06 - 237.99 winning units. T/Qpdt: £31.60 to a £1 stake. Pool: £4,510.87 - 105.42 winning units. **Walter Glynn**

# 5320 NEWBURY (L-H)
Friday, August 18

**OFFICIAL GOING: Good (good to soft in places) changing to soft after race 2 (2.10)**
Wind: quite strong at times, against Weather: showers/thunderstorms

## 6132 DON DEADMAN MEMORIAL EBF MAIDEN STKS (PLUS 10 RACE) (DIV I) — 7f (S)
**1:40** (1:40) (Class 4) 2-Y-O — £4,528 (£1,347; £673; £336) **Stalls** Centre

Form — RPR
**1** **Purser (USA)** 2-9-5 0 ........ RyanMoore 8 85+
(John Gosden) *mid-div: hdwy fr 2f out: chal ent fnl f: kpt on under hands and heels to ld fnl stride* **2/1**[2]
3 **2** *hd* **Merlin Magic**[21] 5350 2-9-5 0 ........ SilvestreDeSousa 5 82
(David Elsworth) *mid-div: hdwy over 2f out: led over 1f out: rdn ins fnl f: kpt on: hdd fnl stride* **15/8**[1]
4 **3** *1 ½* **Ateem (FR)**[11] 5709 2-9-5 0 ........ FrankieDettori 6 78
(Richard Hannon) *trckd ldrs: ev ch whn rn green u.p jst over 1f out: kpt on but no ex ins fnl f* **13/2**[3]
3 **4** *1* **Blue Laureate**[23] 5301 2-9-5 0 ........ AdamKirby 3 76
(Clive Cox) *mid-div: hdwy over 2f out: sn rdn: ev ch over 1f out: kpt on same pce fnl f* **8/1**
0 **5** *hd* **Deadly Accurate**[11] 5709 2-9-5 0 ........ RobertWinston 1 75
(Hughie Morrison) *trckd ldr: rdn to ld briefly wl over 1f out: kpt on same pce fnl f* **100/1**
5 **6** *2 ¼* **Robinson Crusoe (IRE)**[56] 4049 2-9-5 0 ........ SeanLevey 2 69
(Richard Hannon) *s.i.s: sn mid-div: hdwy over 2f out but hanging lft: sn rdn: fdd ins fnl f* **14/1**
**7** *nk* **Arthenia (IRE)** 2-9-0 0 ........ JimmyFortune 10 63
(Charles Hills) *s.i.s: towards rr: styd on fnl f: nvr trbld ldrs* **33/1**
0 **8** *3* **Universal Command**[28] 5106 2-9-5 0 ........ KieranShoemark 12 61
(Roger Charlton) *a towards rr* **100/1**
**9** *3 ½* **Island Sound** 2-9-5 0 ........ RichardKingscote 11 51
(Heather Main) *a towards rr* **40/1**
**10** *½* **Tansheet (IRE)** 2-9-5 0 ........ DaneO'Neill 13 50
(William Haggas) *mid-div: rdn over 2f out: nvr any imp: wknd ins fnl f* **16/1**
**11** *3* **Foxangel** 2-9-0 0 ........ (h[1]) OscarPereira 4 37
(Jose Santos) *led: rdn and hdd wl over 1f out: sn wknd* **125/1**
0 **12** *6* **Surrey Blaze (IRE)**[16] 5547 2-9-5 0 ........ JFEgan 9 27
(Joseph Tuite) *mid-div: rdn over 3f out: sn wknd* **66/1**
1m 29.3s (3.60) **Going Correction** +0.325s/f (Good) — **12** Ran SP% **114.8**
Speed ratings (Par 96): **92,91,90,88,88 86,85,82,78,77 74,67**
CSF £5.74 TOTE £2.80: £1.10, £1.10, £2.30; EX 6.90 Trifecta £27.80.
**Owner** K Abdullah **Bred** Juddmonte Farms Inc **Trained** Newmarket, Suffolk

**FOCUS**
The time for the opener was 7.2sec outside standard, confirming that the ground was indeed riding on the soft side of good, with the jockeys agreeing. Elm Park, who went on to land the Racing Post Trophy, was the best recent winner of this maiden. They raced down the centre and the principals were among those positioned towards the far side of the group. Some of these will progress significantly from the bare form.

## 6133 DON DEADMAN MEMORIAL EBF MAIDEN STKS (PLUS 10 RACE) (DIV II) 7f (S)
**2:10** (2:25) (Class 4) 2-Y-O **£4,528** (£1,347; £673; £336) **Stalls** Centre

Form RPR
2 **1** **Qaroun**[22] 5314 2-9-5 0 FrankieDettori 12 81+
(Sir Michael Stoute) *trckd ldr: led ent fnl f: sn shkn up: kpt on wl* **11/8**[1]

3 **2** *1* **He's Amazing (IRE)**[28] 5106 2-9-5 0 AdamKirby 3 78
(Clive Cox) *mid-div: hdwy over 2f out: sn rdn: chsd ldrs over 1f out: kpt on ins fnl f: snatched 2nd cl home* **4/1**[2]

3 **3** *nse* **Jawwaal**[20] 5420 2-9-5 0 DaneO'Neill 2 78
(John Gosden) *trckd ldrs: hung lft whn rdn over 1f out: kpt on ins fnl f* **9/2**[3]

0 **4** *hd* **Rum Runner**[36] 4805 2-9-5 0 SeanLevey 5 77
(Richard Hannon) *prom: led 3f out: rdn and hdd ent fnl f: kpt on but no ex fnl 100yds* **40/1**

**5** *1 1/4* **Istanbul Sultan (IRE)** 2-9-5 0 RyanMoore 7 74+
(William Haggas) *s.i.s: towards rr: hdwy fr 2f out: styd on nicely fnl f but nvr threatened to get on terms* **8/1**

**6** *3/4* **Soldiers Bay (IRE)** 2-9-5 0 JimmyFortune 4 72+
(Brian Meehan) *s.i.s: towards rr: hdwy fr 2f out: kpt on nicely fnl f but nt pce to get involved* **16/1**

**7** *2* **Apex Predator (IRE)** 2-9-5 0 RobertWinston 6 67
(Seamus Durack) *mid-div: hdwy over 2f out: sn rdn to chse ldrs: one pce fnl f* **50/1**

**8** *6* **Bodie And Doyle** 2-9-5 0 DavidProbert 11 51
(Andrew Balding) *s.i.s: towards rr: sme minor late prog: nvr trbld ldrs* **28/1**

0 **9** *nk* **Swift Fox**[63] 3782 2-9-2 0 HectorCrouch(3) 8 51
(Gary Moore) *mid-div: rdn over 2f out: nvr threatened: fdd fnl f* **100/1**

50 **10** *nk* **Rustang (FR)**[13] 5641 2-9-5 0 RyanTate 1 50
(Richard Hughes) *racd keenly: in tch: hdwy 3f out: effrt 2f out: sn wknd* **66/1**

00 **11** *5* **Ritha**[21] 5349 2-9-0 0 FranBerry 10 32
(Richard Hannon) *mid-div tl wknd 2f out* **100/1**

44 **12** *3 1/4* **Metatrons Cube (IRE)**[28] 5106 2-9-5 0 RichardKingscote 9 28
(Charles Hills) *led tl 3f out: sn rdn: wknd 2f out* **16/1**

1m 29.87s (4.17) **Going Correction** +0.325s/f (Good) **12** Ran SP% **114.5**
Speed ratings (Par 96): **89,87,87,87,86 85,83,76,75,75 69,66**
CSF £6.13 TOTE £2.10: £1.10, £1.60, £1.20; EX 7.90 Trifecta £16.80.
**Owner** Al Shaqab Racing **Bred** Eminent Kind Ltd **Trained** Newmarket, Suffolk

**FOCUS**
This was delayed due to thunder and lightning. It looked a little weaker than the first division and the time was around half a second slower, but a decent race nonetheless. This time they congregated on the stands' side.

## 6134 CHRISTOPHER SMITH ASSOCIATES H'CAP 1m (S)
**2:40** (2:56) (Class 4) (0-80,80) 3-Y-O+ **£4,690** (£1,395; £697; £348) **Stalls** Centre

Form RPR
0161 **1** **Set In Stone (IRE)**[13] 5650 3-8-13 **78** RowanScott(5) 11 88+
(John Patrick Shanahan, Ire) *trckd ldrs: led over 1f out: drifted lft: r.o strly: rdn out* **9/1**

6014 **2** *2 1/4* **Cricklewood Green (USA)**[9] 5788 6-9-4 **77** MitchGodwin(5) 4 82
(Sylvester Kirk) *hld up towards rr: hdwy fr 2f out: r.o wl fnl f: wnt 2nd fnl 100yds but no ch w wnr* **7/1**

060 **3** *1/2* **Grand Inquisitor**[49] 4294 5-9-12 **80** (p) FranBerry 2 83
(Ian Williams) *in tch: nt clr run 2f out: sn swtchd lft and rdn: kpt on to go 3rd ins fnl f but nvr any threat to wnr* **12/1**

1410 **4** *hd* **Exceeding Power**[9] 5788 6-9-10 **78** DaneO'Neill 15 81
(Martin Bosley) *racd stands' side tl swtchd to main gp in centre ins first f: mid-div: rdn over 2f out: no imp tl r.o wl fnl f: wnt 4th cl home* **25/1**

152 **5** *hd* **Jumira Prince (IRE)**[27] 5139 3-9-2 **76** (v[1]) SilvestreDeSousa 13 78
(Roger Varian) *s.i.s: sn mid-div: hdwy 2f out: sn rdn: chsd wnr ent fnl f: kpt on same pce* **6/1**[3]

-025 **6** *nk* **Cadeaux Boxer**[28] 5111 4-9-4 **72** (h) JohnFahy 9 74
(Martin Smith) *led: rdn and hdd over 1f out: kpt on same pce ins fnl f* **33/1**

0350 **7** *nk* **Archie (IRE)**[35] 4832 5-9-12 **80** PatCosgrave 1 81
(Tom Clover) *mid-div: nt best of runs over 1f out: swtchd lft: sn rdn: r.o but nt pce to get on terms ins fnl f* **20/1**

4-60 **8** *1* **Vanity Queen**[92] 2761 3-9-2 **76** KieranShoemark 5 74
(Luca Cumani) *mid-div: hdwy 2f out: sn rdn: fdd ins fnl f* **11/1**

1111 **9** *1 3/4* **Pursuing Steed**[23] 5288 3-9-2 **79** CharlieBennett(3) 7 73
(Hughie Morrison) *nvr bttr than mid-div* **9/2**[1]

344 **10** *1/2* **Harlequin Striker (IRE)**[23] 5300 5-9-10 **78** RobertWinston 12 72
(Dean Ivory) *prom: rdn and ev ch over 1f out: wknd ent fnl f* **20/1**

0-50 **11** *2 1/4* **Titan Goddess**[21] 5369 5-9-1 **69** AntonioFresu 8 58
(Mike Murphy) *dwlt: a towards rr* **25/1**

3224 **12** *3/4* **Mr Tyrrell (IRE)**[15] 5559 3-9-4 **78** (b[1]) RyanMoore 10 64
(Richard Hannon) *trckd ldrs: effrt 2f out: wknd ent fnl f* **16/1**

131 **13** *nk* **Dragons Voice**[25] 5221 3-9-4 **78** RichardKingscote 6 63
(Philip Hide) *trckd ldrs: rdn wl over 2f out: wknd ent fnl f* **11/2**[2]

2205 **14** *2 1/4* **Directorship**[35] 4861 11-9-8 **79** HectorCrouch(3) 14 60
(Patrick Chamings) *towards rr of midfield: pushed along over 4f out: rdn wl over 2f out: wknd over 1f out* **50/1**

0332 **15** *4 1/2* **Kingston Kurrajong**[23] 5300 4-9-10 **78** (p) KierenFox 16 49
(Michael Attwater) *racd stands' side tl swtchd to main gp after 1f: prom: rdn 3f out: sn wknd* **16/1**

0530 **16** *8* **Young John (IRE)**[14] 5610 4-9-7 **80** GeorgeBuckell(5) 3 32
(Mike Murphy) *slowly away: a towards rr* **50/1**

1m 40.43s (0.73) **Going Correction** +0.325s/f (Good)
**WFA** 3 from 4yo+ 6lb **16** Ran SP% **122.2**
Speed ratings (Par 105): **109,106,106,106,105 105,105,104,102,102 99,99,98,96,91 83**
CSF £65.03 CT £802.45 TOTE £11.60: £2.80, £2.10, £3.00, £5.20; EX 99.70 Trifecta £1227.30.
**Owner** Thistle Bloodstock Limited **Bred** Thistle Bloodstock Limited **Trained** Kells, Co Kilkenny

**FOCUS**
The ground was officially soft by now. A competitive handicap on paper. They formed one group down the centre, two initially trapped on the stands' side soon tacking over. They finished in a bunch behind the improving winner and the form is ordinary.

## 6135 BERRY BROS. & RUDD CELLAR PLAN H'CAP 1m 5f 61y
**3:10** (3:23) (Class 3) (0-90,90) 3-Y-O+ **£7,762** (£2,310; £1,154; £577) **Stalls** Centre

Form RPR
13 **1** **Great Sound (IRE)**[51] 4221 3-9-2 **87** FrankieDettori 6 96+
(John Gosden) *mid-div: hdwy whn briefly squeezed up 6f out: pushed along fr over 5f out: hdwy to ld 2f out: rdn clr: styd on wl: readily* **6/4**[1]

155 **2** *1/2* **Comrade Conrad (IRE)**[74] 3392 3-8-8 **79** KieranShoemark 8 85
(Roger Charlton) *trckd ldrs: hanging lft whn rdn wl over 1f out: styd on ins fnl f: wnt 2nd fnl 150yds but a being hld by wnr* **5/1**[3]

350 **3** *1/2* **Paris Protocol**[55] 4073 4-9-10 **86** (p) SeanLevey 5 91
(Richard Hannon) *led tl 6f out: trckd ldr: rdn and ev ch 2f out: styd on but no ex ins fnl f* **20/1**

1-12 **4** *1/2* **Machine Learner**[42] 4586 4-9-12 **88** (v) RyanMoore 9 92
(Joseph Tuite) *hld up: hdwy 2f out: sn hung lft: shkn up and styd on same pce fnl f* **4/1**[2]

5226 **5** *nse* **New World Power (JPN)**[23] 5287 4-9-6 **82** SilvestreDeSousa 4 86+
(David Simcock) *hld up: swtchd rt and rdn over 1f out: styd on fnl f but nt pce to get on terms* **5/1**[3]

/30- **6** *nk* **Cool Macavity (IRE)**[371] 5358 9-9-10 **86** DaneO'Neill 2 89
(Nicky Henderson) *slowly away: mid-div: rdn 2f out: sn swtchd lft: styd on fnl 120yds but nvr any threat* **50/1**

3254 **7** *1 3/4* **Rydan (IRE)**[13] 5663 6-9-4 **83** (v) HectorCrouch(3) 3 84
(Gary Moore) *mid-div: rdn 2f out: nt pce to get involved* **10/1**

340- **8** *1/2* **Poyle Thomas**[366] 5559 8-10-0 **90** FranBerry 1 90
(Michael Madgwick) *trckd ldrs: rdn over 2f out: outpcd over 1f out* **50/1**

626 **9** *2 3/4* **Clovelly Bay (IRE)**[47] 4413 6-8-7 **76** ow1 TylerSaunders(7) 7 72
(Marcus Tregoning) *racd keenly: mid-div: hdwy to ld over 5f out: rdn and hdd 2f out: wknd ins fnl f* **33/1**

3m 0.04s (8.04) **Going Correction** +0.325s/f (Good)
**WFA** 3 from 4yo+ 9lb **9** Ran SP% **114.0**
Speed ratings (Par 107): **88,87,87,87,87 86,85,85,83**
CSF £8.78 CT £100.14 TOTE £2.30: £1.10, £1.90, £4.60; EX 9.40 Trifecta £94.50.
**Owner** Bermuda Thoroughbred Racing Limited **Bred** Churchtown House Stud **Trained** Newmarket, Suffolk

**FOCUS**
A steady pace only increased turning in, the time was slow, and the form is worth taking with a pinch of salt. The first three raced prominently and the field raced down the stands' side in the home straight. It's rated around the third and fourth.

## 6136 BATHWICK TYRES ST HUGH'S STKS (LISTED RACE) (FILLIES) 5f 34y
**3:45** (3:55) (Class 1) 2-Y-O
**£14,461** (£5,482; £2,743; £1,366; £685; £344) **Stalls** Centre

Form RPR
312 **1** **Eirene**[15] 5576 2-9-0 78 RobertWinston 2 99
(Dean Ivory) *hld up far side: swtchd to centre and gd hdwy fr 2f out: led jst over 1f out: edgd rt: r.o strly* **10/1**

**2** *1 3/4* **Sankari Royale (IRE)**[21] 5384 2-9-0 85 NGMcCullagh 7 93
(J P Murtagh, Ire) *racd stands' side: hld up: hdwy 2f out: sn rdn: gd ch whn edgd lft over 1f out: nt pce of wnr fnl f* **8/1**[3]

101 **3** *1 3/4* **Mrs Gallagher**[41] 4628 2-9-0 88 SilvestreDeSousa 16 87
(William Jarvis) *led stands' side gp: overall ldr tl rdn 2f out: edgd lft: kpt on gamely but nt pce of front pair ent fnl f* **9/1**

011 **4** *hd* **Yogi's Girl (IRE)**[100] 2522 2-9-0 82 JFEgan 4 86
(David Evans) *led far side gp: prom overall: rdn to dispute 2f out: hdd over 1f out: kpt on but no ex fnl f* **33/1**

210 **5** *shd* **Looks A Million**[28] 5109 2-9-0 77 KieranShoemark 6 86
(Joseph Tuite) *trckd ldr on far side: rdn and ev ch 2f out: kpt on same pce fnl f* **66/1**

01 **6** *3/4* **Sarshampla (IRE)**[13] 5654 2-9-0 0 SeanLevey 8 83
(David Simcock) *racd centre: mid-div: hdwy over 2f out: gd ch whn rdn over 1f out: kpt on same pce fnl f* **12/1**

3135 **7** *1 3/4* **Out Of The Flames**[35] 4855 2-9-0 98 RyanMoore 5 77
(Richard Hannon) *hld up far side: hdwy 2f out: trckd ldrs over 1f out: rdn ent fnl f: nt qckn* **11/4**[1]

021 **8** *1 1/4* **Misty Spirit**[16] 5534 2-9-0 76 DaneO'Neill 11 72
(David Elsworth) *led centre gp: prom overall: rdn 2f out: sn outpcd* **25/1**

2616 **9** *1/2* **Listen Alexander (IRE)**[28] 5109 2-9-0 81 CharlesBishop 9 70
(David Evans) *prom in centre: rdn and ev ch 2f out: wknd over 1f out* **50/1**

121 **10** *1 1/2* **One Minute (IRE)**[35] 4862 2-9-0 87 PatCosgrave 12 65
(William Haggas) *racd centre: mid-div: rdn 2f out: drifted bdly lft: nvr any imp* **9/2**[2]

3122 **11** *hd* **Validator**[20] 5440 2-9-0 83 FrankieDettori 1 70
(William Haggas) *racd far side: travelled strly in mid-div: smooth hdwy 2f out: effrt over 1f out: qckly btn and eased* **9/1**

6104 **12** *hd* **Wings Of The Rock (IRE)**[16] 5526 2-9-0 86 (h) DavidProbert 3 63
(Scott Dixon) *racd far side: chsd ldr: rdn 2f out: sn wknd* **22/1**

4315 **13** *2* **Reflect Alexander (IRE)**[3] 6051 2-9-0 82 JimmyFortune 13 56
(David Evans) *racd stands' side: hld up: hdwy over 2f out: sn rdn: wknd over 1f out* **50/1**

**14** *4* **Boragh Steps (IRE)**[11] 5726 2-9-0 85 FranBerry 10 42
(Joseph Patrick O'Brien, Ire) *squeezed up s: a towards rr of centre gp* **12/1**

61 **15** *1* **Wirral Girl (IRE)**[42] 4555 2-9-0 0 JackGarritty 14 38
(Richard Fahey) *racd stands' side: in tch: effrt 2f out: sn wknd* **50/1**

1m 3.31s (1.91) **Going Correction** +0.325s/f (Good) **15** Ran SP% **118.9**
Speed ratings (Par 99): **97,94,91,91,90 89,86,84,84,81 81,81,77,71,69**
CSF £81.43 TOTE £12.40: £3.80, £2.80, £2.80; EX 90.80 Trifecta £1162.00.
**Owner** M J Yarrow **Bred** Scuderia Archi Romani **Trained** Radlett, Herts

**FOCUS**
A bigger than usual field for this Listed sprint. Rosdhu Queen added the Cheveley Park to this in 2012, while last season's winner Mrs Danvers took the Cornwallis next time. They spread across the track, the winner coming from a group of six who raced towards the far side.

## 6137 BIG GROUP INSIGHT H'CAP 5f 34y
**4:20** (4:22) (Class 4) (0-85,87) 3-Y-O+ **£5,175** (£1,540; £769; £384) **Stalls** Centre

Form RPR
0120 **1** **Under The Covers**[7] 5869 4-9-3 **78** SamHitchcott 8 86
(Ronald Harris) *led: rdn and narrowly hdd jst over 1f out: rallied wl fnl f: edgd lft cl home: led fnl stride* **20/1**

4021 **2** *shd* **Erissimus Maximus (FR)**[22] 5338 3-9-5 **82**..................(b) RyanMoore 1 90
(Chris Dwyer) *prom: tended to hang lft: rdn for str chal over 1f out: tk v narrow advantage ins fnl f: kpt on: hdd fnl stride* **11/2**

1-1 **3** *nk* **Storm Over (IRE)**[81] 3152 3-9-9 **86**.................................. AdamKirby 6 93
(Robert Cowell) *trckd ldr: rdn to take narrow advantage jst over 1f out: v narrowly hdd ins fnl f: kpt on w ev ch: hld cl home* **13/8**[1]

0140 **4** *3 1/4* **Union Rose**[17] 5505 5-9-12 **87**........................................ FranBerry 4 82
(Ronald Harris) *cl up: rdn 2f out: nt pce to chal* **5/1**[3]

0-20 **5** *1/2* **Ladweb**[68] 3617 7-9-3 **83**........................................ GeorgeBuckell(5) 3 76
(John Gallagher) *cl up: rdn 2f out: nt pce to chal* **9/1**

-110 **6** *5* **Madame Bounty (IRE)**[37] 4752 3-8-9 **77**..................... JennyPowell(5) 7 53
(Ed Walker) *awkwardly away: sn chsng ldrs: rdn 2f out: nt pce to chal: fdd fnl f* **3/1**[2]

1m 3.22s (1.82) **Going Correction** +0.325s/f (Good)
**WFA** 3 from 4yo+ 2lb **6** Ran SP% **109.9**
Speed ratings (Par 105): **98,97,97,92,91 83**
CSF £115.66 CT £264.38 TOTE £24.50: £9.40, £2.00; EX 84.10 Trifecta £423.90.
**Owner** Ridge House Stables Ltd **Bred** Llety Farms **Trained** Earlswood, Monmouths

**FOCUS**
A tight three-way finish to this ordinary sprint handicap. A small pb from the winner.

## 6138 HIGHCLERE THOROUGHBRED RACING EBF FILLIES' NOVICE STKS (PLUS 10 RACE) 6f
4:50 (4:53) (Class 4) 2-Y-O £5,822 (£1,732; £865; £432) **Stalls** Centre

Form RPR

00 **1** **The Mums**[34] 4902 2-9-0 0........................................ FrankieDettori 3 76+
(John Gosden) *trckd ldrs: led jst over 1f out: edgd rt: strly chal thrght fnl f: hld on* **11/4**[2]

**2** *nse* **Beshaayir** 2-9-0 0........................................ PatCosgrave 10 76+
(William Haggas) *trckd ldrs: rdn for str chal thrght fnl f: kpt on wl: jst hld* **6/4**[1]

**3** *1 1/2* **Aim Of Artemis (IRE)** 2-9-0 0........................................ RyanMoore 1 71+
(Sir Michael Stoute) *mid-div: hdwy over 1f out: kpt on ins fnl f but nt pce to threaten front pair* **10/1**

**4** *1 1/2* **Hula Girl** 2-9-0 0........................................ DavidProbert 6 67
(Charles Hills) *mid-div: hdwy over 1f out: kpt on ins fnl f but nt pce to get on terms* **14/1**

**5** *1 1/4* **Two Weeks** 2-9-0 0........................................ AdamKirby 13 63
(Clive Cox) *prom: led after 1f: rdn and hdd jst over 1f out: fdd ins fnl f* **9/2**[3]

**6** *shd* **Still Got It** 2-9-0 0........................................ JFEgan 9 63
(Mick Channon) *hld up: rdn over 2f out: styd on fnl f but nvr any threat* **33/1**

**7** *3/4* **Hurricane Lil (IRE)** 2-9-0 0........................................ FranBerry 4 61
(George Baker) *s.i.s: last trio: rdn over 2f out: styd on fnl f but nvr any threat* **66/1**

**8** *1/2* **Kodina** 2-9-0 0........................................ RichardKingscote 7 60
(Charles Hills) *led for 1f: prom: stl upsides u.p whn squeezed out ent fnl f: wknd* **33/1**

**9** *1 1/4* **Daddys Poppit (USA)** 2-9-0 0........................................ RobertWinston 11 55
(William Haggas) *slowly away: towards rr: sme prog 2f out: wknd fnl f* **16/1**

0 **10** *5* **Pollyissimo**[37] 4749 2-9-0 0........................................ JimmyFortune 5 40
(Richard Hughes) *a towards rr* **50/1**

1m 16.66s (3.66) **Going Correction** +0.325s/f (Good) **10** Ran SP% **115.8**
Speed ratings (Par 93): **88,87,85,83,82 82,81,80,78,72**
CSF £7.02 TOTE £3.50: £1.30, £1.20, £2.90; EX 9.20 Trifecta £46.50.
**Owner** Marian Lyons & Patricia Zanelli **Bred** Glebe Farm Stud **Trained** Newmarket, Suffolk

**FOCUS**
They were racing into a quite a breeze at this stage. Fairly useful fillies' form.

## 6139 MOBILE PIMM'S BARS APPRENTICE H'CAP 1m 1f
5:25 (5:26) (Class 5) (0-75,75) 3-Y-O+ £3,234 (£962; £481; £240) **Stalls** Centre

Form RPR

1246 **1** **Fivehundredmiles (IRE)**[13] 5650 4-9-12 **73**........................ RowanScott 2 84
(John Patrick Shanahan, Ire) *hld up off fast pce: stmbld on bnd after 2f: stdy hdwy fr 3f out: led over 1f out: kpt on wl to assert fnl 100yds* **5/1**[3]

0443 **2** *1/2* **Daily Trader**[8] 5824 3-8-4 **61**........................ KatherineGlenister(3) 5 71
(David Evans) *prom: stdd bk off str pce after 2f: rdn and ev ch fr over 2f out: kpt on: no ex fnl 100yds* **11/4**[2]

3135 **3** *8* **Ashazuri**[16] 5545 3-8-7 **66**..............................(h) Pierre-LouisJamin(5) 10 59
(Jonathan Portman) *set str pce: hdd 6f out: chsd ldr: rdn over 2f out: chsd ldng pair but hld sn after: styd on same pce* **9/1**

504 **4** *2 1/4* **Queen Moon (IRE)**[55] 4086 3-8-3 **62**........................ JasonWatson(5) 6 50
(Andrew Balding) *hld up: rdn wl over 2f out: sn swtchd to centre: styd on fr over 1f out but no threat to ldrs* **16/1**

2314 **5** *2 3/4* **Glens Wobbly**[27] 5140 9-9-8 **74**........................ WilliamCox(5) 8 57
(Jonathan Geake) *mid-div: rdn wl over 2f out: nvr any imp* **20/1**

0650 **6** *1* **Udogo**[18] 5477 6-9-8 **69**........................ JennyPowell 4 50
(Brendan Powell) *outpcd in last: n.d* **33/1**

-250 **7** *2 1/4* **Beyond Recall**[22] 5331 3-8-13 **72**........................(v[1]) GabrieleMalune(5) 9 48
(Luca Cumani) *chsd ldrs: chal over 3f out: rdn over 2f out: sn hld: wknd over 1f out* **16/1**

1306 **8** *3/4* **Rita's Man (IRE)**[30] 5033 3-9-0 **73**........................ TinaSmith(5) 7 47
(Richard Hannon) *chsd ldrs: rdn wl over 2f out: sn hld: wknd over 1f out* **10/1**

-413 **9** *1/2* **Paradise Cove**[22] 5331 3-9-6 **74**........................ GeorgiaCox 11 47+
(William Haggas) *s.i.s: towards rr: hdwy on outer to ld on bnd over 6f out: continued str pce: rdn and hdd over 2f out: sn wknd* **7/4**[1]

1m 57.37s (1.87) **Going Correction** +0.325s/f (Good)
**WFA** 3 from 4yo+ 7lb **9** Ran SP% **118.3**
Speed ratings (Par 103): **104,103,96,94,92 91,89,88,88**
CSF £19.67 CT £122.77 TOTE £6.10: £2.10, £1.40, £3.20; EX 26.80 Trifecta £130.00.
**Owner** Thistle Bloodstock Limited **Bred** Thistle Bloodstock Ltd **Trained** Kells, Co Kilkenny

**FOCUS**
Two finished well clear in this apprentice handicap, which was run at far too strong an early gallop. Nothing else ran their races. The winner was back to his best Hamilton form.
T/Jkpt: Not won. T/Plt: £167.90 to a £1 stake. Pool: £86,085.74 - 374.25 winning units. T/Qpdt: £92.10 to a £1 stake. Pool: £6,240.11 - 50.10 winning units. **Tim Mitchell**

# 5938 NEWMARKET (R-H)
Friday, August 18

**OFFICIAL GOING: Good changing to good to soft after race 2 (5.50)**
Wind: light, behind Weather: overcast, thunder storm between race 1 and 2

## 6140 FLY LONDON SOUTHEND AIRPORT TO PERPIGNAN NOVICE AUCTION STKS (PLUS 10 RACE) 7f
5:20 (5:21) (Class 4) 2-Y-O £3,946 (£1,174; £586; £293) **Stalls** High

Form RPR

203 **1** **Highlight Reel (IRE)**[20] 5412 2-9-1 78........................(h[1]) JamieSpencer 4 80
(Michael Bell) *stdd and short of room leaving stalls: hld up in rr: smooth hdwy to trck ldrs over and nt clr run over 1f out: gap opened and rdn to ld whn edgd lft 1f out: styd on: drvn out* **7/2**[2]

**2** *1/2* **Alternative Fact** 2-9-2 0........................................ JamesDoyle 8 80
(Ed Dunlop) *hld up in tch in midfield: nt clr run and hmpd jst over 2f out: sn swtchd lft and rallied u.p over 1f out: chsd wnr ins fnl f: kpt on wl* **16/1**

510 **3** *1/2* **Finsbury Park**[17] 5501 2-9-4 76........................................ ShaneKelly 6 80
(Robyn Brisland) *wnt rt leaving stalls: t.k.h: w ldr for 2f: styd prom tl led again 2f out: edgd rt u.p over 1f out: hdd 1f out: kpt on same pce u.p ins fnl f* **8/1**[3]

2 **4** *1 1/2* **La Diva**[27] 5154 2-8-10 0........................................ HarryBentley 5 69
(Roger Varian) *hld up in tch in midfield: clsd to trck ldrs: 2f out: effrt to press ldr and carried rt over 1f out: sn rdn and fnd little for press: styd on same pce u.p ins fnl f* **8/11**[1]

04 **5** *9* **Ruby's Gem**[28] 5114 2-8-7 0........................................ SilvestreDeSousa 10 42
(Philip McBride) *t.k.h: trckd ldrs: effrt 2f out: unable qck u.p over 1f out: wknd fnl f* **8/1**[3]

60 **6** *1* **Letsbe Avenue (IRE)**[28] 5105 2-9-2 0........................ TomMarquand 7 49
(Richard Hannon) *hld up in tch in midfield: nt clr run jst over 2f out: sn rdn and struggling: lost pl and btn over 1f out: wknd fnl f* **20/1**

0 **7** *1/2* **Petra's Pony (IRE)**[23] 5301 2-9-1 0........................ MartinLane 9 46
(Brian Meehan) *racd keenly: led tl 2f: sn rdn and lost pl over 1f out: wknd fnl f* **33/1**

**8** *3* **Mandarin Princess** 2-8-7 0........................................ DannyBrock 2 30
(Philip McBride) *chsd ldrs: clsd to join ldr after 2f tl rdn over 2f out: sn rn green and wandered rt: lost pl and bhd over 1f out: bhd ins fnl f* **33/1**

50 **9** *6* **Tarnemah (IRE)**[13] 5660 2-8-7 0........................ AaronJones(3) 1 18
(George Peckham) *t.k.h: hld up in tch in midfield: rdn 2f out: sn dropped to rr: bhd fnl f* **100/1**

30 **10** *4* **Casey Banter**[17] 5507 2-8-7 0........................................ JoeyHaynes 3
(Julia Feilden) *stdd s: hld up in last pair: rdn over 2f out: sn struggling: bhd fnl f* **66/1**

1m 27.27s (1.57) **Going Correction** +0.225s/f (Good) **10** Ran SP% **121.4**
Speed ratings (Par 96): **100,99,98,97,86 85,85,81,74,70**
CSF £54.39 TOTE £4.30: £1.30, £3.70, £2.10; EX 56.30 Trifecta £394.20.
**Owner** The Deflators & Partner **Bred** Skymarc Farm **Trained** Newmarket, Suffolk

**FOCUS**
Race distance increased by 20yds for race five. The going was good ahead of the opener, after which Jamie Spencer said it was "good to soft". A fair novice in which they went an even pace. They raced centre to far side and the first four came clear.

## 6141 FLY LONDON SOUTHEND AIRPORT TO MILAN H'CAP 6f
5:50 (5:55) (Class 4) (0-85,86) 3-Y-O+ £5,175 (£1,540; £769; £384) **Stalls** High

Form RPR

0001 **1** **Related**[41] 4629 7-9-8 **81**..............................(b) MartinLane 9 90
(Paul Midgley) *bustled along leaving stalls and sn w ldr: led after 2f: drvn over 1f out: styd on wl u.p ins fnl f: rdn out* **16/1**

2120 **2** *1 1/4* **Patchwork**[35] 4830 3-9-5 **81**........................................ ShaneKelly 6 86
(Richard Hughes) *stdd s: hld up in tch in midfield: clsd over 2f out: effrt to chse ldrs 1f out: 3rd and swtchd rt ins fnl f: styd on wl to go 2nd nr fin* **11/1**

0250 **3** *nk* **Interlink (USA)**[21] 5379 4-8-8 **67**........................ TomMarquand 10 71
(Michael Appleby) *led for 2f: chsd ldr: rdn 2f out: drvn over 1f out: kpt on same pce u.p ins fnl f: lost 2nd nr fin* **25/1**

1-02 **4** *1 1/4* **Cold Snap (IRE)**[55] 4099 4-9-8 **81**........................ JamesDoyle 7 81
(William Jarvis) *broke wl: sn restrained to chse ldrs but t.k.h: effrt 2f out: rdn and unable qck over 1f out: kpt on same pce ins fnl f* **9/4**[1]

2110 **5** *2* **Hart Stopper**[20] 5423 3-9-8 **84**........................ JamieSpencer 2 78
(Michael Bell) *stdd s: hld up in tch in last pair: clsd 2f out: effrt over 1f out: 5th and edging rt ins fnl f: kpt on but nvr getting on terms w ldrs* **9/2**[2]

0221 **6** *2 1/2* **Cosmic Chatter**[9] 5806 7-9-6 **79** 6ex........................(p) JamesSullivan 3 65
(Ruth Carr) *bustled along leaving stalls: in tch in midfield: rdn ent fnl 2f out: unable qck over 1f out: wl hld and styd on same pce fnl f* **7/1**

120 **7** *2 1/4* **Samarmadi**[22] 5326 3-9-1 **77**........................ HarryBentley 11 55
(Hugo Palmer) *hld up in tch in midfield: rdn over 2f out: sn struggling and outpcd: wl hld over 1f out* **8/1**

1052 **8** *1 1/2* **Diamond Lady**[20] 5426 6-9-11 **84**........................(p[1]) AdamBeschizza 5 58
(William Stone) *t.k.h: chsd ldrs: rdn over 2f out: sn struggling and outpcd over 1f out: wknd* **14/1**

5200 **9** *3 1/4* **Red Tycoon (IRE)**[48] 4343 5-9-6 **82**........................ CallumShepherd(3) 1 45
(Ken Cunningham-Brown) *hld up in tch in last trio: effrt ent fnl 2f: sn btn and wknd over 1f out* **25/1**

640 **10** *6* **Russian Soul (IRE)**[24] 5241 9-9-13 **86**........................(p) SilvestreDeSousa 4 30
(Jamie Osborne) *s.i.s: hld up in rr: effrt 2f out: sn btn and wl bhd 1f out* **11/2**[3]

0500 **11** *13* **Sadierosclifford (IRE)**[9] 5791 3-7-11 **66** oh14........... JackOsborn(7) 8
(Giles Bravery) *in tch in midfield: rdn 3f out: bhd and lost tch over 1f out: t.o ins fnl f* **100/1**

1m 12.93s (0.43) **Going Correction** +0.225s/f (Good)
**WFA** 3 from 4yo+ 3lb **11** Ran SP% **117.5**
Speed ratings (Par 105): **106,104,103,102,99 96,93,91,86,78 61**
CSF £177.18 CT £4333.54 TOTE £17.60: £4.40, £3.30, £6.00; EX 194.00 Trifecta £2809.70.
**Owner** Taylor's Bloodstock Ltd **Bred** Laundry Cottage Stud Farm **Trained** Westow, N Yorks


The Form Book Flat, Raceform Ltd, Newbury, RG14 5SJ

**FOCUS**
An average sprint handicap and it paid to race prominently. There was a heavy shower beforehand. The winner was still on a good mark re last year's form.

## 6142 FLY LONDON SOUTHEND AIRPORT TO LYON EBF NOVICE STKS (PLUS 10 RACE) 1m
**6:20** (6:25) (Class 4) 2-Y-O **£4,528** (£1,347; £673; £336) **Stalls** High

Form RPR
1 **Roaring Lion (USA)** 2-9-2 0 HarryBentley 6 82+
(John Gosden) *hld up in tch in midfield: clsd to trck ldrs 2f out: edgd out rt and wnt 2nd over 1f out: rdn to ld 1f out: sn asserted and rn wl ins fnl f: quite comf* **7/2**[3]

0 2 1 ¾ **Abandon Ship (IRE)**[55] 4068 2-9-2 0 MartinLane 3 78
(Paul Cole) *led and set stdy gallop: rdn and qcknd 2f out: hdd 1f out: nt match pce of wnr but kpt on for clr 2nd ins fnl f* **25/1**

3 1 ¾ **Ghostwatch (IRE)** 2-9-2 0 JamieSpencer 1 74+
(Charlie Appleby) *chsd ldrs tl wnt 2nd 2f out: sn rdn and struggling to qckn: clr 3rd and styd on same pce ins fnl f* **3/1**[2]

4 4 1 ½ **Homerton**[42] 4583 2-9-2 0 ShaneKelly 5 71
(Robyn Brisland) *chsd ldr tl 2f out: sn u.p and outpcd: no threat to ldng trio but kpt on again ins fnl f* **16/1**

5 ½ **Kind Act (USA)** 2-9-2 0 JamesDoyle 4 70
(Charlie Appleby) *hld up in tch in midfield: rdn over 2f out: unable qck over 1f out: wl hld and kpt on same pce ins fnl f* **9/4**[1]

6 hd **Crossed Baton** 2-9-2 0 TedDurcan 9 69+
(John Gosden) *stdd s: hld up in tch in midfield: pushed along and sme hdwy 2f out: kpt on over 1f out and kpt on same pce ins fnl f* **8/1**

7 1 **Knightly Spirit** 2-9-2 0 AndreaAtzeni 7 67
(Roger Varian) *dwlt: rn green and hld up in last trio: clsd and nt clrest of runs over 2f out: sn rdn and outpcd over 1f out: wl hld and kpt on same pce fnl f* **10/1**

8 1 **Global Style (IRE)** 2-9-2 0 SilvestreDeSousa 2 65
(Ed Dunlop) *stdd s: hld up in tch in last pair: swtchd rt and effrt over 2f out: no hdwy u.p 2f out: wl hld and plugged on same pce fnl f* **12/1**

0 9 7 **Sackeb**[38] 4709 2-9-2 0 (t[1]) LouisSteward 8 50
(Hugo Palmer) *chsd ldng trio: rdn over 2f out: sn lost pl: bhd over 1f out* **50/1**

00 10 11 **Glacier (IRE)**[28] 5106 2-9-2 0 TomMarquand 10 25
(Richard Hannon) *hld up in rr: swtchd rt and rdn 3f out: hung lft and lost tch 2f out: wl bhd ins fnl f* **66/1**

1m 43.37s (3.37) **Going Correction** +0.225s/f (Good) **10** Ran SP% **119.1**
Speed ratings (Par 96): **92,90,88,87,86 86,85,84,77,66**
CSF £88.83 TOTE £4.60: £1.50, £4.50, £1.60; EX 91.70 Trifecta £789.90.
**Owner** Qatar Racing Limited **Bred** Ranjan Racing Inc **Trained** Newmarket, Suffolk

**FOCUS**
The going was changed to good to soft. An interesting novice featuring plenty of well-bred newcomers. They went steady until the pace quickened after halfway.

## 6143 FLY LONDON SOUTHEND AIRPORT TO PRAGUE H'CAP 1m
**6:50** (6:52) (Class 5) (0-75,77) 3-Y-O+ **£3,881** (£1,155; £577; £288) **Stalls** High

Form RPR
5041 1 **Salt Whistle Bay (IRE)**[20] 5411 3-9-4 70 SilvestreDeSousa 4 78
(Rae Guest) *trckd ldr tl led jst over 2f out: sn jnd and rdn: forged ahd u.p jst ins fnl f: styd on* **4/1**[2]

3-24 2 1 **Kitty Boo**[49] 4300 3-9-7 73 (h) JamieSpencer 9 79
(Luca Cumani) *stdd and dropped into last trio sn after s: hld up: effrt and hdwy u.p over 1f out: swtchd lft and chse wnr ins fnl f: styd on but nvr getting to wnr* **9/4**[1]

2311 3 1 ¾ **Pacific Salt (IRE)**[10] 5760 4-9-11 74 6ex CallumShepherd(3) 1 77
(Pam Sly) *chsd ldng pair tl clsd to join ldr ent fnl 2f: sn rdn: drvn over 1f out: no ex and btn whn lost 2nd ins fnl f: wknd towards* **5/1**[3]

-266 4 1 ¾ **Fashaak (IRE)**[42] 4587 4-10-3 77 AdamBeschizza 8 76
(John Butler) *taken down early: hld up in tch in midfield: swtchd to r alone towards far rail 1/2-way: rdn 2f out: no imp u.p 1f out: styd on same pce ins fnl f* **12/1**

5-15 5 ½ **Tan Arabiq**[43] 4541 4-9-10 70 TomMarquand 3 68
(Michael Appleby) *dwlt and niggled along leaving stalls: in tch in last trio: effrt 2f out: no imp whn sltly impeded over 1f out: styd on ins fnl f: nvr trbld ldrs* **20/1**

0505 6 1 ½ **Candesta (USA)**[31] 5002 7-8-6 55 oh1 (p) AaronJones(3) 5 50
(Julia Feilden) *dwlt and bustled along early: in tch in last trio: effrt over 2f out: edgd rt u.p over 1f out: no imp and kpt on same pce ins fnl f* **33/1**

206 7 1 ¼ **Rock Warbler (IRE)**[43] 4529 4-9-11 71 (t) KevinStott 6 63
(Oliver Greenall) *stdd s: t.k.h: hld up in tch in midfield: effrt to chse ldng pair over 1f out: no imp u.p: wknd ins fnl f* **11/1**

4002 8 1 ¾ **Adventureman**[7] 5880 5-8-13 59 (b) JamesSullivan 2 47
(Ruth Carr) *led tl jst over 2f out: sn rdn and lost pl over 1f out: wknd ins fnl f* **10/1**

015 9 8 **Rubens Dream**[53] 4153 3-9-11 77 JamesDoyle 7 47
(Charles Hills) *chsd ldrs: rdn over 2f out: sn struggling and lost pl: bhd and eased ins fnl f* **11/2**

1m 40.41s (0.41) **Going Correction** +0.225s/f (Good)
**WFA** 3 from 4yo+ 6lb **9** Ran SP% **115.6**
Speed ratings (Par 103): **106,105,103,101,101 99,98,96,88**
CSF £13.43 CT £45.45 TOTE £4.00: £1.50, £1.20, £2.00; EX 12.50 Trifecta £45.20.
**Owner** The Hightailers & Rae Guest **Bred** Shortgrove Manor Stud **Trained** Newmarket, Suffolk

**FOCUS**
A fair handicap and an even gallop. The form is rated through the third.

## 6144 FLY LONDON SOUTHEND AIRPORT TO BUDAPEST H'CAP 1m 2f
**7:25** (7:26) (Class 5) (0-70,71) 3-Y-O+ **£3,881** (£1,155; £577; £288) **Stalls** Centre

Form RPR
-123 1 **Seven Clans (IRE)**[17] 5509 5-9-9 65 (b) JamieSpencer 9 72+
(Neil Mulholland) *dwlt: dropped in bhd and hld up in rr: clsd to chse ldrs 2f out: swtchd lft and effrt over 1f out: drvn and str chal 1f out: led towards fin: all out* **6/1**[2]

6-56 2 shd **Duchy**[16] 5549 4-9-13 69 DannyBrock 7 75
(Michael Bell) *chsd ldr over 9f out: rdn and ev ch over 1f out: sustained effrt u.p to ld jst ins fnl f: hdd towards fin: kpt on gamely: jst hld* **18/1**

5453 3 ¾ **Time To Sea (IRE)**[16] 5536 3-9-1 64 SilvestreDeSousa 3 69
(John Butler) *t.k.h: chsd ldrs: rdn to chal over 2f out: drvn over 1f out: no ex and one pced wl ins fnl f* **2/1**[1]

455 4 hd **Hard Toffee (IRE)**[7] 5888 6-9-13 69 RobertTart 8 73
(Conrad Allen) *t.k.h: hld up in midfield: hdwy to ld after 1f and settled in front: rdn and pressed 2f out: hdd jst ins fnl f: no ex and one pced fnl 100yds* **9/1**

2153 5 3 ½ **Stepney**[4] 6013 3-9-7 70 TomMarquand 2 68
(Robyn Brisland) *hld up in tch in last trio: rdn 3f out: no imp tl styd on ins fnl f: no threat to ldrs* **8/1**

1262 6 2 ½ **Bartholomew J (IRE)**[49] 4320 3-9-2 68 SimonPearce(3) 4 61
(Lydia Pearce) *in tch in midfield: rdn over 2f out: no imp and outpcd over 1f out: rallied ins fnl f: kpt on but no threat to ldrs* **9/1**

-144 7 1 ¾ **Estrella Eria (FR)**[10] 5747 4-9-10 71 (h) JoshuaBryan(5) 6 60
(George Peckham) *hld up in tch in midfield: rdn over 2f out: chsng ldrs but no ex u.p over 1f out: wknd ins fnl f* **8/1**

-155 8 10 **London Master**[29] 5061 3-8-7 63 SebastianWoods(7) 5 33
(Chris Wall) *awkward leaving stalls: plld hrd and hld up in midfield: dropped to rr and rdn over 2f out: sn struggling and lost tch over 1f out* **10/1**

0001 9 ½ **Bombero (IRE)**[10] 5761 3-8-12 64 6ex (p) CallumShepherd(3) 1 33
(Ed de Giles) *led for 1f: chsd ldrs tl lost pl u.p over 2f out: bhd over 1f out* **7/1**[3]

2m 10.0s (4.50) **Going Correction** +0.225s/f (Good)
**WFA** 3 from 4yo+ 7lb **9** Ran SP% **116.7**
Speed ratings (Par 103): **91,90,90,90,87 85,83,75,75**
CSF £106.17 CT £291.23 TOTE £5.80: £2.00, £4.80, £1.20; EX 109.20 Trifecta £611.70.
**Owner** The Affordable (2) Partnership **Bred** Darley **Trained** Limpley Stoke, Wilts

**FOCUS**
Race distance increased by 20yds. A tight handicap and an even tighter finish. The second and third seem the best guides.

## 6145 FLY LONDON SOUTHEND AIRPORT TO DUBROVNIK H'CAP 1m
**7:55** (7:55) (Class 3) (0-95,91) 3-Y-O+ **£7,762** (£2,310; £1,154; £577) **Stalls** High

Form RPR
405 1 **Zymyran**[63] 3778 3-8-9 79 (h[1]) HarryBentley 7 88+
(David Simcock) *hld up in tch in rr: swtchd rt 2f out: str run u.p 1f out: led ins fnl f: sn clr and r.o wl* **5/1**[3]

-621 2 2 ¼ **Dowayla (IRE)**[37] 4736 3-9-7 91 MartinLane 2 94
(Saeed bin Suroor) *trckd ldrs tl clsd to press ldr 2f out: rdn to ld over 1f out: drvn and hdd ins fnl f: nt match pce of wnr and kpt on same pce ins fnl f* **11/4**[1]

1631 3 hd **Florenza**[13] 5668 4-9-12 90 JamieSpencer 4 94
(Chris Fairhurst) *led: rdn and hdd over 1f out: kpt on u.p and ev ch tl outpcd by wnr 100yds out: kpt on same pce after* **7/1**

102 4 shd **Red Tea**[28] 5130 4-9-8 91 LuluStanford(5) 5 95
(Peter Hiatt) *stdd s: hld up in tch: effrt to chse ldrs oer 1f out: styd on same pce ins fnl f* **7/1**

0001 5 1 **Lawmaking**[21] 5363 4-9-2 80 JamesDoyle 1 81
(Henry Spiller) *stdd s: hld up in tch towards rr: effrt and hdwy over 1f out: no imp 1f out: kpt on same pce ins fnl f* **4/1**[2]

0642 6 2 ½ **Bint Dandy (IRE)**[9] 5789 6-9-4 82 (p) SilvestreDeSousa 8 78
(Chris Dwyer) *w ldr tl ent fnl 2f: sn u.p: outpcd 1f out: wknd ins fnl f* **7/1**

0125 7 ½ **Derek Duval (USA)**[13] 5661 3-8-7 80 (t) AaronJones(3) 6 74
(Stuart Williams) *trckd ldrs: effrt ent fnl 2f: outpcd and dropped to rr over 1f out: wknd ins fnl f* **11/2**

1m 40.23s (0.23) **Going Correction** +0.225s/f (Good)
**WFA** 3 from 4yo+ 6lb **7** Ran SP% **116.2**
Speed ratings (Par 107): **107,104,104,104,103 100,100**
CSF £19.76 CT £96.67 TOTE £6.00: £3.00, £2.20; EX 24.90 Trifecta £169.00.
**Owner** The Khat Partnership **Bred** Hesmonds Stud Ltd **Trained** Newmarket, Suffolk

**FOCUS**
A nice handicap and plenty of good recent form on show, though they didn't go much of a gallop. The third and fourth set the standard.
T/Plt: £590.00 to a £1 stake. Pool: £73,013.92 - 90.33 winning units. T/Qpdt: £7.50 to a £1 stake. Pool: £8,251.99 - 806.07 winning units. **Steve Payne**

# 6035 NOTTINGHAM (L-H)
Friday, August 18

**OFFICIAL GOING: Good to soft (good in places; 7.0)**
Wind: Moderate against Weather: Cloudy with sunny periods

## 6146 PAWSON TRANSPORT EBF MAIDEN STKS (DIV I) 6f 18y
**1:30** (1:31) (Class 5) 2-Y-O **£3,234** (£962; £481; £240) **Stalls** Centre

Form RPR
1 **Eqtidaar (IRE)** 2-9-5 0 JimCrowley 6 91+
(Sir Michael Stoute) *prom: cl up 1/2-way: led wl over 1f out: pushed clr ins fnl f: readily* **6/4**[1]

2 2 ½ **Mountain Guard (IRE)** 2-9-5 0 AndreaAtzeni 2 81
(Roger Varian) *trckd ldrs: hdwy and cl up 2f out: rdn to chse wnr jst over 1f out: kpt on fnl f* **3/1**[2]

2 3 3 ½ **Barig Al Thumama**[28] 5120 2-9-2 0 MarcMonaghan(3) 9 70
(Marco Botti) *racd nr stands rail: led: jnd over 2f out: pushed along and hdd wl over 1f out: sn rdn and kpt on same pce* **7/2**[3]

0 4 1 ¼ **Lady Willpower**[11] 5702 2-9-0 0 JasonHart 3 61
(John Quinn) *t.k.h: trckd ldrs on outer: green and pushed along 2f out: kpt on same pce fnl f* **28/1**

5 ½ **Battle Commence (IRE)** 2-9-5 0 DanielTudhope 7 65
(David O'Meara) *trckd ldrs: pushed along 2f out: rdn over 1f out: kpt on same pce* **10/1**

0 6 ½ **Charles Fox**[15] 5576 2-9-5 0 DanielMuscutt 4 63
(James Fanshawe) *trckd ldrs: effrt 2f out: sn rdn and kpt on same pce* **16/1**

00 7 1 **Two Seas**[41] 4598 2-9-5 0 AndrewMullen 5 60
(George Peckham) *rr: rdn along 2f out: sn one pce* **20/1**

0 8 10 **Partry Flyer (IRE)**[64] 3742 2-9-5 0 KevinStott 1 30
(Oliver Greenall) *rr: rdn along 2f out: sn wknd* **100/1**

1m 16.63s (1.93) **Going Correction** +0.05s/f (Good) **8** Ran SP% **111.4**
Speed ratings (Par 94): **89,85,81,79,78 78,76,63**
CSF £5.67 TOTE £3.00: £1.50, £1.10, £1.20; EX 6.00 Trifecta £18.50.
**Owner** Hamdan Al Maktoum **Bred** Shadwell Estate Company Limited **Trained** Newmarket, Suffolk

**FOCUS**
Outer track used and race distances as advertised. The first division of a fair juvenile maiden. They went a respectable gallop, at best, on drying loose-topped ground officially described as good to soft, good in places.

## 6147 PAWSON TRANSPORT EBF MAIDEN STKS (DIV II) 6f 18y
**2:00** (2:00) (Class 5) 2-Y-O **£3,234** (£962; £481; £240) **Stalls** Centre

Form RPR
2 1 **Northern Angel (IRE)**[23] 5278 2-9-0 0 JasonHart 4 69
(John Quinn) *mde all: pushed along 2f out: rdn over 1f out: drvn and edgd lft ins fnl f: hld on gamely* **3/1**[3]

2 shd **Bowler Hat** 2-9-5 0........................ JosephineGordon 3 74+
(Hugo Palmer) *trckd ldrs: hdwy 2f out: sltly hmpd on outer over 1f out: chal ent fnl f: sn rdn and ev ch: edgd lft and no ex nr line* **11/4**[2]

66 3 2 ¼ **Dandiesque (IRE)**[8] 5844 2-9-0 0........................ KieranO'Neill 5 62
(Richard Hannon) *trckd ldrs: swtchd lft over 1f out: sn rdn and kpt on same pce* **25/1**

05 4 ¾ **Stormy Sand (IRE)**[21] 5365 2-9-2 0........................ MarcMonaghan(3) 6 65
(Marco Botti) *in tch: hdwy 2f out: rdn over 1f out: styd on fnl f* **15/2**

66 5 ½ **General Marius (IRE)**[9] 5786 2-9-5 0........................ JackMitchell 7 64
(Roger Varian) *trckd ldrs: cl up 2f out: sn rdn and kpt on same pce appr fnl f* **10/1**

0 6 2 ¾ **Wotamadam**[37] 4749 2-9-0 0........................ GrahamLee 8 50
(Dean Ivory) *in rr tl styd on fr over 1f out* **100/1**

22 7 ¾ **Global Passion (FR)**[37] 4782 2-9-5 0........................ SteveDrowne 9 53
(Charles Hills) *cl up: chal 2f out: sn rdn and ev ch: drvn appr fnl f: wknd* **5/2**[1]

24 8 12 **Bomad**[24] 5240 2-9-5 0........................(h[1]) FrannyNorton 1 17
(Derek Shaw) *wnt lft s: a outpcd in rr* **14/1**

9 2 ¾ **Ms Tilly** 2-9-0 0........................ AndrewMullen 2 4
(David Brown) *chsd ldrs on outer: rdn along wl over 2f out: sn wknd* **50/1**

1m 16.68s (1.98) **Going Correction** +0.05s/f (Good) **9** Ran SP% **114.6**
Speed ratings (Par 94): **88,87,84,83,83 79,78,62,58**
CSF £11.47 TOTE £3.00: £1.10, £1.10, £6.70; EX 13.80 Trifecta £221.30.
**Owner** D Ward **Bred** Yeomanstown Stud **Trained** Settrington, N Yorks

**FOCUS**
The second division of a fair juvenile maiden. The winning time was virtually identical but the first race winner was clearly the best juvenile on show on this card.

## 6148 BURTON H'CAP 5f 8y
**2:30** (2:32) (Class 6) (0-65,69) 3-Y-O+ **£2,587** (£770; £384; £192) **Stalls** Centre

Form RPR

4543 1 **Hamish McGonagain**[6] 5930 4-9-8 **63**........................(p) DanielTudhope 2 69
(David O'Meara) *racd centre: trckd ldrs: pushed along and hdwy 2f out: rdn over 1f out: chal ent fnl f: sn drvn and kpt on wl to ld nr fin* **13/8**[1]

6662 2 nk **Boogie Babe**[18] 5472 3-8-9 **52**........................ TonyHamilton 3 57
(Richard Fahey) *in tch: pushed along on outer 1/2-way: hdwy 2f out: rdn to chse ldrs over 1f out: drvn and edgd lft ins fnl f: kpt on wl towards fin* **6/1**[2]

5015 3 ½ **The Big Short**[48] 4352 3-9-5 **62**........................ JimCrowley 10 65
(Charles Hills) *racd alone nr stands rail: led: rdn wl over 1f out: drvn and edgd lft ins fnl f: hdd and no ex towards fin* **8/1**[3]

2133 4 2 **Ambitious Icarus**[3] 6040 8-9-6 **61**........................(p) DougieCostello 9 57
(Richard Guest) *rrd s and bhd: hdwy 2f out: rdn over 1f out: kpt on strly fnl f* **8/1**[3]

2046 5 1 ½ **Malcolm The Pug (IRE)**[23] 5271 3-9-10 **67**........................ KieranO'Neill 7 58
(Richard Hannon) *racd centre: trckd ldrs: hdwy 2f out: rdn over 1f out: kpt on same pce* **6/1**[2]

3505 6 2 ½ **Corridor Kid (IRE)**[5] 5962 4-9-10 **65**........................(v) FrannyNorton 6 47
(Derek Shaw) *dwlt and in rr: pushed along and sme hdwy whn nt clr run and swtchd rt over 1f out: kpt on fnl f* **16/1**

5630 7 hd **Captain Scooby**[3] 6041 11-8-5 **46** oh1........................(b) JimmyQuinn 5 27
(Richard Guest) *hld up: pushed along over 2f out: rdn over 1f out: n.d* **11/1**

2640 8 2 ¾ **Dapper Man (IRE)**[6] 5919 3-9-6 **63**........................(b) JasonHart 8 34
(Roger Fell) *racd towards centre: chsd ldr: rdn along 2f out: wknd over 1f out* **10/1**

-000 9 4 ½ **Bilash**[118] 1965 10-8-3 **47**........................ JackDuern(3) 4 2
(Sarah Hollinshead) *prom centre: rdn along 2f out: sn wknd* **50/1**

1m 1.3s (-0.20) **Going Correction** +0.05s/f (Good)
**WFA** 3 from 4yo+ 2lb **9** Ran SP% **114.2**
Speed ratings (Par 101): **103,102,101,98,96 92,91,87,80**
CSF £11.29 CT £59.90 TOTE £2.30: £1.20, £2.20, £2.40; EX 11.10 Trifecta £48.10.
**Owner** The Lawton Bamforth Partnership **Bred** Llety Farms **Trained** Upper Helmsley, N Yorks

**FOCUS**
A modest sprint handicap. There was a difference of opinion whether to race centrally or far side but a close three-way finish proved there wasn't a lot in it.

## 6149 HALL FILLIES' H'CAP (A JOCKEY CLUB GRASSROOTS SPRINT SERIES QUALIFIER) 6f 18y
**3:00** (3:01) (Class 4) (0-80,79) 3-Y-O+ **£5,175** (£1,540; £769; £384) **Stalls** Centre

Form RPR

3341 1 **Thafeera (USA)**[22] 5335 3-9-7 **79**........................ JimCrowley 5 96+
(Charles Hills) *racd centre: cl up: led over 2f out: rdn jst over 1f out: kpt on strly* **11/4**[1]

11 2 1 ¼ **Maid In India (IRE)**[13] 5635 3-8-13 **71**........................ NeilFarley 2 84+
(Eric Alston) *trckd ldrs on outer: hdwy 1/2-way: rdn: green and edgd lft 11/2f out: chsd wnr ent fnl f: sn drvn and no imp towards fin* **3/1**[2]

1063 3 3 **Fortitude (IRE)**[18] 5473 3-9-3 **75**........................ JosephineGordon 8 78
(Hugo Palmer) *trckd ldr nr stands rail: effrt 2f out: swtchd lft and rdn over 1f out: chsd ldng pair ins fnl f: kpt in same pce* **8/1**

2312 4 1 ½ **Castle Hill Cassie (IRE)**[11] 5697 3-8-13 **71**........................ GrahamLee 7 70
(Ben Haslam) *racd nr stands rail: led : pushed along 1/2-way: sn hdd and rdn: wknd over 1f out* **8/1**

5013 5 1 ½ **Lexington Sky (IRE)**[8] 5826 3-9-1 **73** 6ex........................ TonyHamilton 3 67
(Roger Fell) *chsd ldrs centre: rdn along over 2f out: sn wknd* **12/1**

3531 6 1 ½ **Specialv (IRE)**[8] 5827 4-9-2 **71** 6ex........................(p) BenCurtis 1 60
(Brian Ellison) *hld up in rr: sme hdwy 2f out: rdn over 1f out: n.d* **7/1**

1222 7 1 ½ **Marseille (IRE)**[22] 5316 3-9-2 **74**........................ JoeDoyle 6 58
(Julie Camacho) *prom centre: pushed along wl over 2f out: sn rdn and wknd wl over 1f out* **9/2**[3]

1m 14.77s (0.07) **Going Correction** +0.05s/f (Good)
**WFA** 3 from 4yo 3lb **7** Ran SP% **112.3**
Speed ratings (Par 102): **101,99,95,93,91 89,87**
CSF £10.80 CT £55.55 TOTE £2.60: £1.80, £1.60; EX 7.50 Trifecta £76.30.
**Owner** Hamdan Al Maktoum **Bred** Shadwell Farm LLC **Trained** Lambourn, Berks

**FOCUS**
A fair fillies' sprint handicap and interesting form. They went a respectable gallop and the favourite beat the second favourite in good style.

## 6150 CHALKLEY MAIDEN STKS 1m 75y
**3:35** (3:35) (Class 5) 3-Y-O+ **£3,234** (£962; £481; £240) **Stalls** Centre

Form RPR

32 1 **Sharja Bridge**[19] 5458 3-9-6 0........................ AndreaAtzeni 2 97+
(Roger Varian) *trckd ldrs. smooth hdwy to ld over 2f out: sn qcknd clr: v easily* **4/6**[1]

5-0 2 4 **Rising (IRE)**[120] 1906 3-9-6 0........................ GrahamLee 5 81
(Brian Meehan) *t.k.h: trckd ldrs: hdwy over 2f out: rdn wl over 1f out: drvn ins fnl f: kpt on to take 2nd nr line* **5/1**[3]

502 3 nse **Dawaaleeb (USA)**[14] 5611 3-9-6 83........................ JimCrowley 13 81
(Charles Hills) *cl up: effrt over 2f out: sn rdn: drvn to chse wnr over 1f out: kpt on same pce fnl f: lost 2nd nr line* **5/2**[2]

63 4 2 **Powderhouse (IRE)**[74] 3394 3-9-6 0........................(t[1]) PhillipMakin 6 76
(Charlie Appleby) *in tch on inner: hdwy 3f out: chsd ldrs 2f out: sn rdn and no imp fnl f* **7/1**

00 5 5 **Afterburner**[15] 5577 3-9-6 0........................ JosephineGordon 12 65
(Hugo Palmer) *led: rdn along 3f out: hdd over 2f out: sn drvn and grad wknd* **25/1**

0 6 2 ¼ **Bleu Et Noir**[9] 5794 6-9-12 0........................(h) KieranO'Neill 1 61+
(Tim Vaughan) *dwlt and bhd: stdy hdwy 1/2-way: n.m.r and swtchd rt over 2f out: swtchd lft wl over 1f out: sn nt clr run: swtchd rt appr fnl f: kpt on fnl f* **100/1**

00 7 nk **Fikhaar**[13] 5670 3-9-1 0........................ JoeDoyle 3 54
(Kevin Ryan) *in tch on inner: pushed along 3f out: rdn over 2f out: sn one pce* **66/1**

00 8 1 **Bubbles Arcade**[11] 5712 5-9-7 0........................ WilliamCarson 11 53
(Rod Millman) *dwlt: a in rr* **50/1**

00 9 3 ½ **Poet's Quest**[37] 4764 3-9-1 0........................ FrannyNorton 10 44
(Dean Ivory) *dwlt: a in rr* **66/1**

50 10 1 ½ **Stolen Angel (IRE)**[16] 5538 3-9-6 0........................ AndrewMullen 9 45
(Antony Brittain) *plld hrd: racd wd: chsd ldrs tl wknd 3f out* **50/1**

00 11 3 ¼ **Desi Daru (IRE)**[27] 5141 5-9-12 0........................ SaleemGolam 7 39
(Conrad Allen) *t.k.h: in tch: chsd ldrs on outer over 4f out: rdn along 3f out: sn wknd* **100/1**

1m 45.81s (-3.19) **Going Correction** -0.20s/f (Firm)
**WFA** 3 from 4yo+ 6lb **11** Ran SP% **130.5**
Speed ratings (Par 103): **107,103,102,100,95 93,93,92,88,87 84**
CSF £5.64 TOTE £1.40: £1.02, £1.40, £1.50; EX 5.20 Trifecta £10.40.
**Owner** Sheikh Mohammed Obaid Al Maktoum **Bred** Stiftung Gestut Fahrhof **Trained** Newmarket, Suffolk

**FOCUS**
A decent maiden. They went a proper gallop and the odds-on favourite cruised clear to win well in a promising time. The second and third set the level.

## 6151 CLOSE BROTHERS COLWICK CUP H'CAP 1m 6f
**4:10** (4:11) (Class 3) (0-95,95) 3-Y-O+ **£22,641** (£6,737; £3,367; £1,683) **Stalls** Low

Form RPR

14-1 1 **Dubawi Fifty**[18] 5468 4-9-4 **85**........................ GrahamLee 5 93+
(Karen McLintock) *hld up towards rr: hdwy 3f out: effrt on wd outside 2f out: chsd ldrs and rdn over 1f out: styd on strly fnl f to ld nr fin* **5/1**[3]

-111 2 nk **Quloob**[34] 4908 3-9-3 **94**........................ JimCrowley 7 101
(Owen Burrows) *hld up towards rr: hdwy over 3f out: chsd ldrs wl over 1f out and sn rdn: drvn to chse ldr ins fnl f: kpt on wl towards fin* **5/2**[1]

4034 3 nk **Ravenous**[20] 5397 6-8-9 **76**........................ KieranO'Neill 9 83
(Luke Dace) *led: rdn clr 3f out: drvn ent fnl f: wandered and wknd last 100 yds: hdd nr fin* **20/1**

0031 4 1 ½ **Precision**[16] 5550 3-8-2 **79**........................ JimmyQuinn 11 84
(Sir Michael Stoute) *prom: effrt 3f out: chsd clr ldr 2f out: sn rdn: drvn and hung lft ins fnl f: kpt on* **4/1**[2]

3303 5 2 ¼ **Champagne Champ**[28] 5110 5-9-9 **90**........................ DanielTudhope 1 92
(Rod Millman) *trckd ldrs on inner: hdwy 3f out: rdn along 2f out: kpt on same pce u.p appr fnl f* **10/1**

3302 6 ¾ **Sennockian Star**[9] 5803 7-9-5 **86**........................ FrannyNorton 6 87
(Mark Johnston) *trckd ldrs: hdwy over 3f out: rdn to chse ldrs over 2f out: drvn wl over 1f out: kpt on same pce* **25/1**

2014 7 1 ½ **Marmajuke Bay**[35] 4828 4-9-7 **88**........................(p) SteveDrowne 4 88
(Mark Usher) *prom: hdwy 3f out: rdn along on inner over 2f out: sn drvn and grad wknd* **25/1**

6004 8 1 ¼ **Saunter (FR)**[21] 5353 4-9-10 **94**........................ DidierGengoul(3) 2 91
(David Menuisier) *hld up in rr: hdwy over 3f out: swtchd rt wl over 2f out: sn rdn and no imp* **7/1**

0044 9 7 **Desert God (IND)**[21] 5351 5-10-0 **95**........................ JosephineGordon 13 82
(Richard Hughes) *trckd ldr: hdwy and cl up 4f out: rdn along wl over 2f out: drvn and wknd wl over 1f out* **18/1**

4404 10 ½ **Gabrial's Star**[18] 5468 8-9-0 **81**........................(v) DavidNolan 3 67
(Richard Fahey) *a towards rr* **66/1**

2456 11 6 **Sam Missile (IRE)**[48] 4356 4-9-8 **89**........................(v[1]) DanielMuscutt 12 67
(James Fanshawe) *stdd and swtchd lft s: hld up towards rr: effrt 4f out: rdn along 3f out: sn btn* **16/1**

-212 12 2 ¼ **Stamford Raffles**[13] 5663 4-9-0 **86**........................ PaddyBradley(5) 10 61
(Jane Chapple-Hyam) *trckd ldrs: hdwy over 4f out: rdn along over 3f out: sn drvn and wknd* **12/1**

3m 1.08s (-5.92) **Going Correction** -0.20s/f (Firm)
**WFA** 3 from 4yo+ 10lb **12** Ran SP% **119.6**
Speed ratings (Par 107): **108,107,107,106,105 105,104,103,99,99 95,94**
CSF £17.24 CT £235.81 TOTE £6.50: £2.00, £1.50, £6.80; EX 23.40 Trifecta £645.60.
**Owner** Paul & Clare Rooney **Bred** Hesmonds Stud Ltd **Trained** Ingoe, Northumberland

**FOCUS**
The feature contest was a good staying handicap and it is strong form, producing the best winning time on the day. The winner, second and fourth are progressive, with the third the key.

## 6152 EBF MALTSTERS FILLIES' H'CAP 1m 2f 50y
**4:40** (4:41) (Class 3) (0-95,93) 3-Y-O+ **£9,703** (£2,887; £1,443; £721) **Stalls** Low

Form RPR

-534 1 **Empress Ali (IRE)**[20] 5439 6-9-9 **88**........................ AndrewMullen 4 94
(Tom Tate) *trckd ldr: hdwy to ld wl over 2f out: rdn wl over 1f out: drvn and kpt on wl fnl f* **17/2**

1-13 2 1 ¼ **Indulged**[16] 5529 4-9-11 **93**........................ GeorgeWood(3) 3 99+
(James Fanshawe) *trckd ldng pair: pushed along on inner 3f out: nt clr run and hmpd wl over 1f out: sn swtchd rt and rdn: styd on wl fnl f: tk 2nd nr line* **5/4**[1]

4-01 3 nk **Neshmeya**[61] 3866 3-8-9 **81**........................ JimCrowley 2 84
(Charles Hills) *s.i.s and bhd: tk clsr order 1/2-way: trckd ldrs 3f out: effrt whn nt clr and hmpd wl over 1f out: swtchd rt and rdn to chse wnr ent fnl f: sn drvn and kpt on same pce: lost 2nd nr line* **7/2**[2]

42 4 1 **Fengate**[20] 5439 4-9-2 **81**........................ TrevorWhelan 6 82
(Roger Charlton) *trckd ldrs: hdwy on outer 3f out: cl up 2f out: sn rdn and hung lft: drvn and one pce appr fnl f* **5/1**

33-1 **5** 2 ½ **Al Mayda (USA)**[25] 5220 3-8-7 **79**..........................(t) JosephineGordon 5 76
(Hugo Palmer) *t.k.h: led and sn clr: jnd and pushed along over 3f out: hdd wl over 2f out: hld whn n.m.r on inner wl over 1f out: wknd after* **9/2**[3]

2m 11.17s (-3.13) **Going Correction** -0.20s/f (Firm)
**WFA** 3 from 4yo+ 7lb **5** Ran SP% **112.0**
Speed ratings (Par 104): **104,103,102,101,99**
CSF £20.22 TOTE £10.60: £3.60, £1.30; EX 20.90 Trifecta £75.00.
**Owner** T T Racing **Bred** Denis McDonnell **Trained** Tadcaster, N Yorks
■ Stewards' Enquiry : Trevor Whelan four-day ban; careless riding (1st-4th Sept)

**FOCUS**
A good little fillies' handicap. They went a muddling gallop in a messy race. The favourite, who finished second, should have won. The winner's rated to form.

## 6153 BETFAIR NOVICE FLAT AMATEUR RIDERS' H'CAP 1m 2f 50y
**5:10** (5:14) (Class 6) (0-65,69) 3-Y-O+ £2,495 (£774; £386; £193) Stalls Low

Form RPR
3040 **1** **Tingo In The Tale (IRE)**[24] 5267 8-10-0 **51**.....................(p) MrMEnnis 1 61
(Tony Forbes) *trckd ldrs: hdwy over 4f out: cl up 3f out: chal 2f out: rdn over 1f out: led last 100yds: drvn out* **10/1**[3]

5131 **2** ½ **Diamonds A Dancing**[11] 5701 7-11-4 **69** 6ex...........(h) MissAMcCain 11 78
(Donald McCain) *led: pushed along 3f out: rdn over 2f out: drvn over 1f out: hdd last 100yds* **7/2**[2]

014 **3** 6 **Snowy Winter (USA)**[14] 5604 3-10-3 **61**..........................(t) MrBJames 6 60
(Archie Watson) *towards rr: hdwy over 4f out: rdn along over 2f out: chsd ldrs over 1f out: drvn and no imp fnl f* **7/2**[2]

4001 **4** 2 **Pretty Jewel**[20] 5427 4-10-9 **60**...................................... DrMVoikhansky 7 58
(Kevin Frost) *s.i.s and bhd: wd st: hdwy over 3f out: chsd ldrs and rdn whn hung lft wl over 1f out: kpt on u.p fnl f* **14/1**

2-60 **5** shd **Bob's Boy**[30] 5021 4-10-5 **59**..................................(bt) MrHMyddelton(3) 8 57
(Oliver Greenall) *trckd ldrs on inner: pushed along and hdwy 3f out: rdn 2f out: sn no imp* **33/1**

4412 **6** 1 ¼ **Druid's Diamond**[3] 6035 4-10-2 **53**..............................(p) MrWJMilburn 4 49
(Mark Walford) *dwlt and towards rr: hdwy and in tch after 3f: effrt to chse ldrs over 3f out: rdn 2f out: sn drvn and grad wknd* **9/4**[1]

02-0 **7** nk **Buskin River (IRE)**[108] 2259 3-10-8 **66**........................ MrJamesSmith 3 62
(James Eustace) *t.k.h: cl up: rdn along 3f out: wknd 2f out* **14/1**

0334 **8** 2 ¼ **Saga Sprint (IRE)**[43] 4545 4-10-7 **58**........................ PoppyBridgwater 2 49
(J R Jenkins) *dwlt: a in rr* **16/1**

0262 **9** 2 ¼ **Chelwood Gate (IRE)**[7] 5895 7-11-0 **65**......................(v) MissJCooley 5 52
(Conor Dore) *towards rr: sme hdwy 4f out: rdn along 3f out: n.d* **16/1**

000- **10** 17 **Designamento (IRE)**[310] 7283 3-9-2 **46** oh1........................ MissRHill 10 4
(Ed de Giles) *t.k.h: cl up: rdn along over 3f out: sn wknd* **33/1**

0606 **R** **Balmont Belle (IRE)**[35] 4840 7-9-6 **46** oh1................. MrCAJones(3) 12
(Barry Leavy) *ref to r tk no part* **50/1**

2m 12.86s (-1.44) **Going Correction** -0.20s/f (Firm)
**WFA** 3 from 4yo+ 7lb **11** Ran SP% **117.2**
Speed ratings (Par 101): **97,96,91,90,90 89,88,87,85,71**
CSF £44.32 CT £150.53 TOTE £11.00: £4.00, £1.50, £1.70; EX 46.50 Trifecta £222.60.
**Owner** Tony Forbes **Bred** Brian Williamson **Trained** Stramshall, Staffs

**FOCUS**
A modest handicap for novice Flat amateur riders. They went an increasing tempo and the front two pulled clear.
T/Plt: £10.80 to a £1 stake. Pool: £53,794.37 - 3,635.21 winning units. T/Qpdt: £3.60 to a £1 stake. Pool: £3,941.85 - 800.59 winning units. **Joe Rowntree**

# 6010 WOLVERHAMPTON (A.W) (L-H)
### Friday, August 18

**OFFICIAL GOING: Tapeta: standard**
Wind: Fresh behind Weather: Cloudy with sunny spells and a shower prior to and during race 4

## 6154 QATAR AIRWAYS NURSERY H'CAP 5f 21y (Tp)
**1:20** (1:20) (Class 6) (0-60,65) 2-Y-O £2,587 (£770; £384; £192) Stalls Low

Form RPR
3551 **1** **Princess Lyla (IRE)**[6] 5933 2-9-6 **65** 6ex...................... FinleyMarsh(7) 1 65
(Richard Hughes) *a.p: chsd ldr over 1f out: rdn to ld ins fnl f: styd on* **5/4**[1]

054 **2** nk **Hypnotic Dancer (IRE)**[105] 2373 2-9-1 **53**..............(t[1]) ConnorBeasley 2 52
(Keith Dalgleish) *sn led: rdn and hung lft over 1f out: hdd ins fnl f: styd on* **12/1**

5255 **3** ½ **Terri Rules (IRE)**[9] 5785 2-9-6 **58**.............................. AdamBeschizza 9 55
(Julia Feilden) *s.s: hdwy 2f out: rdn over 1f out: r.o* **8/1**[3]

5452 **4** ¾ **Llamrei**[9] 5785 2-8-12 **57**........................................ NicolaCurrie(7) 5 51
(Jo Hughes) *prom: hmpd and lost pl sn after s: hdwy over 1f out: r.o* **10/1**

035 **5** ½ **Cherry Oak (IRE)**[15] 5575 2-9-6 **58**.............................. PaulMulrennan 8 51
(Ben Haslam) *chsd ldr tl rdn over 1f out: styd on same pce ins fnl f* **16/1**

045 **6** hd **Roman Spinner**[17] 5507 2-9-0 **52**.................................(t) LukeMorris 3 44
(Rae Guest) *chsd ldrs: pushed along over 3f out: rdn and swtchd rt over 1f out: hung lft and styd on ins fnl f* **11/1**

6040 **7** 2 ½ **Erastus**[6] 5933 2-9-3 **58**........................................ CallumShepherd(3) 4 41
(Mick Channon) *prom: sn lost pl: hdwy over 1f out: nt trble ldrs* **12/1**

5050 **8** 4 ½ **I Am Dandy (IRE)**[43] 4527 2-9-4 **56**.............................. TomEaves 11 23
(James Ewart) *s.i.s: nvr on terms* **50/1**

055 **9** hd **Savannah's Show**[24] 5262 2-8-13 **58**........................ CameronNoble(7) 6 24
(Richard Guest) *hld up: racd keenly: effrt on outer over 2f out: sn hung rt and wknd* **13/2**[2]

5120 **10** 2 ¾ **Popsi**[69] 3557 2-9-2 **54**........................................ BarryMcHugh 10 10
(Marjorie Fife) *plld hrd and prom: rdn and wknd over 1f out* **25/1**

1m 2.05s (0.15) **Going Correction** -0.10s/f (Stan) **10** Ran SP% **113.4**
Speed ratings (Par 92): **94,93,92,91,90 90,86,79,78,74**
CSF £17.15 CT £88.47 TOTE £2.00: £1.10, £4.50, £3.30; EX 17.80 Trifecta £144.10.
**Owner** Ourselves Alone **Bred** F Prendergast & L Elvidge **Trained** Upper Lambourn, Berks

**FOCUS**
A modest nursery.

## 6155 QATAR AIRWAYS - GOING PLACES TOGETHER H'CAP 5f 21y (Tp)
**1:50** (1:51) (Class 5) (0-70,70) 3-Y-O £3,881 (£1,155; £577; £288) Stalls Low

Form RPR
3542 **1** **Midnightly**[30] 5041 3-9-7 **70**..........................................(t) MartinHarley 1 78
(Rae Guest) *broke wl: mde all: rdn and edgd lft over 1f out: edgd rt ins fnl f: sn wnt lft again: styd on u.p* **10/3**[2]

4333 **2** ½ **Wild Approach (IRE)**[22] 5338 3-9-6 **69**......................(h) LukeMorris 8 75
(Robert Cowell) *chsd wnr: rdn over 1f out: styd on* **9/2**[3]

0552 **3** nk **Suwaan (IRE)**[8] 5837 3-9-4 **67**..................................(e[1]) TomEaves 6 72
(Ruth Carr) *hld up: plld hrd: hdwy 1/2-way: hrd rdn ins fnl f: nt run on* **9/4**[1]

5-10 **4** 1 ½ **Flying Foxy**[30] 5041 3-9-5 **68**........................................ RobertTart 5 68
(Michael Wigham) *chsd ldrs: shkn up over 1f out: styd on same pce ins fnl f* **10/1**

5660 **5** 4 **Rapid Rise (IRE)**[87] 2931 3-9-1 **67**........................ EdwardGreatrex(3) 2 52
(Milton Bradley) *sn pushed along in rr: sme hdwy 2f out: wknd fnl f* **20/1**

23-2 **6** hd **Jeany (IRE)**[41] 4604 3-9-1 **67**.................................... AdamMcNamara(3) 4 51
(Bryan Smart) *s.i.s: pushed along early in rr then plld hrd: rdn over 1f out: nvr on terms* **10/1**

3600 **7** 1 **Reedanjas (IRE)**[21] 5355 3-8-13 **69**..................(p) CameronNoble(7) 7 50
(Gay Kelleway) *sn bhd: rdn 1/2-way: n.d* **12/1**

1056 **8** 1 ½ **Secret Strategy (IRE)**[30] 5041 3-9-4 **67**.................(p[1]) AdamBeschizza 9 42
(Julia Feilden) *prom: rdn 1/2-way: wknd over 1f out* **10/1**

1m 0.75s (-1.15) **Going Correction** -0.10s/f (Stan) **8** Ran SP% **111.8**
Speed ratings (Par 100): **105,104,103,101,94 94,93,90**
CSF £17.83 CT £38.91 TOTE £3.80: £1.40, £1.20, £1.40; EX 18.60 Trifecta £35.30.
**Owner** Bradmill Ltd **Bred** C J Mills **Trained** Newmarket, Suffolk

**FOCUS**
A modest handicap and an all-the-way winner, who confirmed Yarmouth form with the runner-up.

## 6156 BIRMINGHAM TO DOHA AND BEYOND H'CAP (DIV I) 6f 20y (Tp)
**2:20** (2:20) (Class 6) (0-65,67) 3-Y-O+ £2,587 (£770; £384; £192) Stalls Low

Form RPR
6600 **1** **Newstead Abbey**[41] 4616 7-9-8 **62**..................................(p) TomEaves 10 69
(Michael Herrington) *a.p: rdn to ld over 1f out: hung lft ins fnl f: styd on u.p: all out* **9/2**[3]

4452 **2** hd **Indian Affair**[9] 5784 7-9-9 **63**......................................(bt) LukeMorris 7 69
(Milton Bradley) *hld up: hdwy and hung lft fr over 1f out: r.o wl* **3/1**[2]

4660 **3** 2 ½ **Gold Club**[18] 5481 6-9-13 **67**......................................(t) StevieDonohoe 1 66
(Tom Clover) *chsd ldrs: nt clr run and swtchd rt over 1f out: styd on same pce ins fnl f* **11/4**[1]

5562 **4** ½ **Red Stripes (USA)**[6] 5930 5-9-2 **61**..........................(b) JaneElliott(5) 9 58
(Lisa Williamson) *led: rdn and hdd over 1f out: no ex ins fnl f* **9/2**[3]

4600 **5** 1 **Fleeting Glimpse**[1] 6106 4-9-2 **59**........................ EdwardGreatrex(3) 6 53
(Patrick Chamings) *dwlt: in rr tl hdwy 1f out: no ex wl ins fnl f* **20/1**

000 **6** 5 **Noble Act**[24] 5239 4-9-1 **58**........................................ TimClark(3) 2 37
(Phil McEntee) *s.i.s: pushed along in rr: nvr on terms* **50/1**

4040 **7** 1 ¼ **Spike (IRE)**[23] 5282 4-8-2 **49**.............................(b) ConnorMurtagh(7) 3 25
(Donald McCain) *sn w ldr tl over 4f out: rdn over 1f out: wknd fnl f* **8/1**

1400 **8** 9 **Endeavour (IRE)**[49] 4303 3-9-7 **64**................................ BarryMcHugh 4 13
(Marjorie Fife) *w ldrs 2f: remained handy: rdn over 2f out: hung rt and wknd wl over 1f out* **12/1**

1m 13.77s (-0.73) **Going Correction** -0.10s/f (Stan)
**WFA** 3 from 4yo+ 3lb **8** Ran SP% **113.6**
Speed ratings (Par 101): **100,99,96,95,94 87,86,74**
CSF £18.14 CT £43.12 TOTE £7.00: £2.00, £1.20, £1.20; EX 20.90 Trifecta £56.20.
**Owner** Tony Culhane Racing Club **Bred** Grasshopper 2000 Ltd **Trained** Cold Kirby, N Yorks

**FOCUS**
A modest sprint handicap.

## 6157 BIRMINGHAM TO DOHA AND BEYOND H'CAP (DIV II) 6f 20y (Tp)
**2:50** (2:50) (Class 6) (0-65,66) 3-Y-O+ £2,587 (£770; £384; £192) Stalls Low

Form RPR
5155 **1** **Magic Moments**[43] 4529 4-9-5 **59**................................ MartinHarley 7 68
(Alan King) *mde all: qcknd over 2f out: pushed out* **10/3**[2]

3-35 **2** 2 ¾ **Triple Dream**[38] 4710 12-8-12 **59**........................ KerrieRaybould(7) 6 60
(Milton Bradley) *chsd wnr: wnt upsides 3f out tl 2f out: sn pushed along and edgd lft: styd on same pce ins fnl f* **50/1**

403 **3** ½ **Chatoyer (FR)**[36] 4793 3-9-6 **66**............................(h) HollieDoyle(3) 10 65+
(Richard Hannon) *s.s: bhd: rdn: edgd lft and r.o to go 3rd wl ins fnl f: nrst fin* **5/2**[1]

-354 **4** 1 ¼ **Rapid Ranger**[14] 5619 3-9-4 **64**................................ JoshDoyle(3) 2 60
(David O'Meara) *plld hrd and hdwy over 4f out: rdn over 2f out: no ex ins fnl f* **8/1**

3065 **5** ½ **Fleckerl (IRE)**[16] 5535 7-9-10 **64**..............................(p) PaulMulrennan 8 58
(Conor Dore) *hld up: r.o ins fnl f: nvr nrr* **13/2**

5444 **5** dht **Entertaining Ben**[10] 5748 4-9-3 **64**........................ FinleyMarsh(7) 4 58
(Amy Murphy) *hld up in tch: rdn over 1f out: styd on same pce fnl f* **15/2**

3465 **7** 1 ½ **Quite A Story**[18] 5482 5-9-4 **61**........................ EdwardGreatrex(3) 9 51
(Patrick Chamings) *hld up: hdwy over 1f out: btn whn hmpd wl ins fnl f* **11/2**[3]

1060 **8** ½ **Compton Prince**[37] 4735 8-9-8 **62**..............................(b) LukeMorris 5 50
(Milton Bradley) *chsd ldrs: rdn over 1f out: wknd fnl f* **22/1**

3000 **9** 7 **Rat Catcher (IRE)**[29] 5069 7-8-0 **45**........................(b) JaneElliott(5) 1 12
(Lisa Williamson) *s.i.s: hld up: racd keenly: wknd over 1f out* **80/1**

1m 14.17s (-0.33) **Going Correction** -0.10s/f (Stan)
**WFA** 3 from 4yo+ 3lb **9** Ran SP% **110.8**
Speed ratings (Par 101): **98,94,93,92,91 91,89,88,79**
CSF £148.45 CT £460.51 TOTE £3.00: £1.20, £9.90, £1.30; EX 92.70 Trifecta £641.40.
**Owner** Ray Bailey **Bred** Peter & Tony Hockenhull **Trained** Barbury Castle, Wilts

**FOCUS**
The second division of a modest handicap and the time was slightly slower than the first leg.

## 6158 SILKS LADY RIDERS' H'CAP 1m 142y (Tp)
**3:25** (3:27) (Class 4) (0-85,82) 3-Y-O+ £6,469 (£1,925; £962; £481) Stalls Low

Form RPR
5526 **1** **Fayez (IRE)**[13] 5669 3-10-1 **80**................................ ShelleyBirkett 5 85
(David O'Meara) *hld up: shkn up over 1f out: hung lft and r.o to ld wl ins fnl f* **7/1**

2236 **2** ½ **Character Onesie (IRE)**[17] 5496 5-10-0 **72**................... SammyJoBell 2 76
(Richard Fahey) *hld up: hdwy 2f out: nt clr run over 1f out: edgd lft ins fnl f: r.o* **6/1**[3]

3040 **3** nk **Devil's Bridge (IRE)**[16] 5541 3-10-3 **82**...........................(p) HollieDoyle 6 85
(Richard Hannon) *sn chsng ldr who wnt clr 7f out: tk clsr order over 2f out: led over 1f out: rdn and hdd wl ins fnl f: styd on* **11/4**[2]

3033 **4** ¾ **Madroos**[28] 5125 4-10-7 **79**........................................ MeganNicholls 3 81
(Michael Easterby) *prom: pushed along over 2f out: hmpd ins fnl f: styd on same pce* **15/8**[1]

0156 **5** 2 ½ **Know Your Name**[16] 5544 6-9-3 **66**........................ MissEllaMcCain(5) 7 62
(Donald McCain) *sn led: clr 7f out tl c bk to the field over 2f out: hdd over 1f out: no ex ins fnl f* **6/1**[3]

1363 **6** nse **Mr Red Clubs (IRE)**[70] 3546 8-10-3 **75**.....................(p) JaneElliott 1 71
(Henry Tett) *hld up: rdn over 1f out: nt trble ldrs* **16/1**

1000 7 4 **Idol Deputy (FR)**[4] 6014 11-10-0 72..........(p) RachealKneller 4 59
(James Bennett) *chsd ldrs: shkn up over 1f out: wknd fnl f* **33/1**
1m 48.87s (-1.23) **Going Correction** -0.10s/f (Stan)
**WFA** 3 from 4yo+ 7lb **7 Ran SP% 111.3**
Speed ratings (Par 105): **101,100,100,99,97 97,93**
CSF £45.09 TOTE £6.00: £2.70, £3.50; EX 42.00 Trifecta £189.40.
**Owner** Northern Lads & Nawton Racing **Bred** Miss Siobhan Ryan **Trained** Upper Helmsley, N Yorks

**FOCUS**
A fair handicap run at a good pace, albeit not the strongest for the level. The winner is rated to a better view of his previous form.

## 6159 BIRMINGHAM TO THE WORLD MAIDEN STKS (STALLION-RESTRICTED RACE) 1m 142y (Tp)
**4:00** (4:01) (Class 5) 2-Y-0 **£3,881** (£1,155; £577; £288) **Stalls** Low

Form RPR
5 1 **Deja (FR)**[35] 4859 2-9-5 0.......... GeraldMosse 1 76+
(Jeremy Noseda) *mde all: rdn and edgd rt over 1f out: styd on wl towards fin* **1/5**[1]
2 2 3/4 **Miss Mumtaz (IRE)** 2-8-7 0.......... ManuelFernandes(7) 4 65+
(Tony Carroll) *dwlt: plld hrd and sn prom: nt clr run and chsd wnr over 2f out: shkn up and ev ch whn edgd rt over 1f out: hung lft and no ex wl ins fnl f* **7/1**[3]
3 1/2 **Eyecatcher (IRE)** 2-9-5 0.......... RyanPowell 2 69+
(Simon Crisford) *s.i.s: rn green in r: hdwy 2f out: nt clr run over 1f out swtchd lft ins fnl f: nt clr run and swtchd rt towards fin: r.o* **13/2**[2]
4 1/2 **Iconic Code** 2-9-0 0.......... PaulMulrennan 8 63
(Mick Channon) *hld up: hdwy over 1f out: shkn up and edgd lft ins fnl f: r.o* **25/1**
5 5 3 1/2 **Onefootinfront**[7] 5876 2-9-5 0.......... LukeMorris 7 61
(Daniel Mark Loughnane) *prom: rdn over 2f out: wknd over 1f out* **28/1**
0 6 1 **Normandy Blue**[13] 5631 2-9-2 0.......... SammyJoBell(3) 3 58
(Richard Fahey) *chsd wnr tl rdn over 2f out: wknd fnl f* **33/1**
1m 51.13s (1.03) **Going Correction** -0.10s/f (Stan) **6 Ran SP% 119.4**
Speed ratings (Par 94): **91,88,88,87,84 83**
CSF £2.74 TOTE £1.10: £1.02, £3.20; EX 3.50 Trifecta £7.50.
**Owner** Phoenix Thoroughbred Limited **Bred** Laurent Dulong & Yannick Dulong **Trained** Newmarket, Suffolk

**FOCUS**
An uncompetitive maiden, the short-priced favourite asserting late on.

## 6160 QATAR - SKYTRAX AIRLINE OF THE YEAR H'CAP 1m 1f 104y (Tp)
**4:30** (4:32) (Class 5) (0-75,77) 3-Y-0 **£3,881** (£1,155; £577; £288) **Stalls** Low

Form RPR
1054 1 **Ice Dancing (IRE)**[41] 4632 3-9-7 74..........(h) ConnorBeasley 5 82
(Michael Bell) *chsd ldrs: rdn to ld over 1f out: r.o* **8/1**
-650 2 1 1/4 **My Brother Mike (IRE)**[14] 5617 3-8-6 59.......... RyanPowell 11 64
(Kevin Frost) *hld up: hdwy to chse ldr over 6f out: led over 2f out: rdn and hdd over 1f out: edgd lft: styd on same pce ins fnl f* **66/1**
6225 3 1 **Sir Gnet (IRE)**[28] 5131 3-8-13 66..........(h) TomEaves 8 69+
(Ed Dunlop) *hld up: hdwy over 1f out: r.o: nt rch ldrs* **8/1**
0650 4 1 1/2 **Northdown**[16] 5536 3-9-5 72..........(p) PaulMulrennan 2 72
(David Lanigan) *prom: nt clr run and lost pl over 5f out: hdwy over 1f out: sn rdn: styd on same pce ins fnl f* **33/1**
14 5 hd **African**[41] 4640 3-9-7 74.......... StevieDonohoe 10 73
(Charlie Fellowes) *hld up: rdn over 2f out: r.o ins fnl f: nt rch ldrs* **5/2**[1]
515 6 1 1/4 **Dreaming Time**[160] 1142 3-9-6 73.......... MartinHarley 1 70
(James Tate) *chsd ldr 3f: remained handy: rdn over 2f out: wknd wl ins fnl f* **14/1**
3464 7 1 **Critical Thinking (IRE)**[7] 5895 3-8-0 60.......... ManuelFernandes(7) 9 55
(Kevin Frost) *hld up in tch: rdn over 1f out: wknd ins fnl f* **8/1**
5045 8 hd **Plead**[42] 4580 3-9-7 77.......... EdwardGreatrex(3) 4 71
(Archie Watson) *s.s and wnt rt s: shkn up over 1f out: nvr on terms* **7/1**
0350 9 1 **Quinteo (IRE)**[17] 5523 3-9-5 72..........(b) GeraldMosse 6 64
(Jo Hughes) *led: rdn and hdd over 2f out: wknd fnl f* **11/2**[2]
4516 10 8 **Scala Regia (FR)**[24] 5242 3-9-1 68.......... LukeMorris 7 43
(Sir Mark Prescott Bt) *hld up: pushed along over 4f out: rdn over 2f out: sn wknd* **13/2**[3]
1m 58.29s (-2.51) **Going Correction** -0.10s/f (Stan) **10 Ran SP% 114.2**
Speed ratings (Par 100): **107,105,105,103,103 102,101,101,100,93**
CSF £384.72 CT £4274.20 TOTE £9.00: £2.50, £12.40, £2.70; EX 552.40 Trifecta £4926.30.
**Owner** Sheikh Marwan Al Maktoum **Bred** Darley **Trained** Newmarket, Suffolk

**FOCUS**
A fair handicap run at an even pace. The 1-2 were always well placed.

## 6161 BIRMINGHAM TO DOHA AND SYDNEY MAIDEN FILLIES' STKS 1m 1f 104y (Tp)
**5:00** (5:00) (Class 5) 3-Y-0+ **£3,234** (£962; £481; £240) **Stalls** Low

Form RPR
3-53 1 **Great Court (IRE)**[16] 5549 3-9-0 75.......... JackMitchell 1 80+
(Roger Varian) *chsd ldrs: led over 1f out: rdn out* **4/1**[3]
24 2 1 1/4 **Pretty Passe**[30] 5038 3-9-0 0.......... MartinHarley 6 77
(William Haggas) *hld up: swtchd rt over 2f out: hdwy over 1f out: rdn and edgd lft ins fnl f: r.o* **7/2**[2]
2-23 3 3/4 **Sea Tide**[11] 5721 3-9-0 80..........(t[1]) LukeMorris 5 75
(Hugo Palmer) *chsd ldr: rdn and hung rt over 1f out: sn ev ch: hmpd ins fnl f: styd on same pce* **4/6**[1]
42 4 2 **Alfa Queen (IRE)**[38] 4729 3-9-0 0.......... TomEaves 3 71
(Iain Jardine) *stmbld sn after s: hld up: hdwy over 1f out: styd on same pce ins fnl f* **25/1**
5 9 **Cagliari** 3-9-0 0..........(h[1]) RyanPowell 4 52
(Simon Crisford) *sn pushed along to ld: rdn and hdd over 1f out: wknd fnl f* **33/1**
2m 0.32s (-0.48) **Going Correction** -0.10s/f (Stan) **5 Ran SP% 109.0**
Speed ratings (Par 100): **98,96,96,94,86**
CSF £17.46 TOTE £4.20: £1.70, £2.50; EX 21.10 Trifecta £24.40.
**Owner** J Shack & G Barnard **Bred** James Waldron **Trained** Newmarket, Suffolk

**FOCUS**
A fair maiden but a bit of a dash from the home turn. The winner improved a bit on her second start for the yard.
T/Plt: £20.20 to a £1 stake. Pool: £60,450.78 - 2,181.03 winning units. T/Qpdt: £12.60 to a £1 stake. Pool: £4,602.01 - 269.22 winning units. **Colin Roberts**

6162 - 6169a (Foreign Racing) - See Raceform Interactive

# 6084 CLAIREFONTAINE (R-H)
Friday, August 18

**OFFICIAL GOING: Turf: good**

## 6170a PRIX D'AUBERVILLE - ETALON LE HAVRE (MAIDEN) (2YO COLTS & GELDINGS) (TURF) 7f
**12:40** (12:40) 2-Y-0 **£11,538** (£4,615; £3,461; £2,307; £1,153)

RPR
1 **Forza Capitano (FR)** 2-9-2 0.......... Pierre-CharlesBoudot 8 80
(H-A Pantall, France) **177/10**
2 hd **Day Of Rest (FR)**[17] 5520 2-9-2 0.......... MaximeGuyon 5 79
(George Baker) *racd keenly: pressed ldr under restraint: led after 1f: drvn whn pressed 2f out: kicked for home 1 1/2f out: styd on wl u.p: hdd fnl strides* **31/10**[2]
3 1 **Pier Cesar (FR)**[48] 2-9-2 0.......... MickaelBarzalona 1 76
(Antonio Marcialis, Italy) **113/10**
4 1 1/4 **Saint Roch (FR)**[62] 2-9-2 0.......... CristianDemuro 6 73
(Mme Pia Brandt, France) **9/10**[1]
5 snk **Fun To Mas (FR)** 2-9-2 0.......... RonanThomas 4 73
(C Lerner, France) **91/10**
6 3 **Al Mashrab**[20] 2-9-2 0.......... ChristopheSoumillon 2 64
(J-C Rouget, France) **58/10**[3]
7 1 3/4 **Chalco (FR)**[63] 2-9-2 0.......... RaphaelMarchelli 7 60
(A Bonin, France) **42/1**
8 8 **Dr Shepherd (FR)** 2-9-2 0.......... AlexisBadel 3 38
(C Scandella, France) **61/1**
1m 25.6s **8 Ran SP% 119.0**
PARI-MUTUEL (all including 1 euro stake): WIN 18.70; PLACE 3.80, 1.80, 3.20; DF 28.40; SF 49.60.
**Owner** Georg Kern **Bred** G Kern **Trained** France

## 6171a PRIX DE TOLLEVILLE (MAIDEN) (2YO FILLIES) (TURF) 7f
**1:10** (1:10) 2-Y-0 **£11,538** (£4,615; £3,461; £2,307; £1,153)

RPR
1 **Crown Vallary (FR)**[21] 5372 2-9-2 0.......... TonyPiccone 4 75
(K R Burke) **32/5**
2 hd **Infinite Cheers (FR)**[19] 2-9-2 0.......... ChristopheSoumillon 6 74
(J-C Rouget, France) **12/5**[1]
3 snk **La Canche (FR)**[91] 2881 2-9-2 0.......... EddyHardouin 10 74
(T Clout, France) **41/10**[2]
4 hd **Roksaneh (FR)** 2-9-2 0.......... Pierre-CharlesBoudot 2 74
(A Fabre, France) **47/10**[3]
5 3 1/2 **Briateke (FR)**[48] 2-9-2 0.......... CristianDemuro 3 64
(Antonio Marcialis, Italy) **49/10**
6 snk **Gossipe (FR)** 2-8-10 0.......... MathieuPelletan(6) 12 64
(Y Gourraud, France) **86/1**
7 2 **Digha (FR)**[33] 2-8-10 0.......... JeromeMoutard(6) 1 58
(P Demercastel, France) **46/1**
8 1 1/2 **Lilac Fairy (FR)** 2-8-11 0.......... MickaelBarzalona 9 49
(F-H Graffard, France) **97/10**
9 1 3/4 **Beywin (FR)**[33] 2-8-10 0.......... TristanBaron(6) 8 49
(H-A Pantall, France) **51/1**
10 1 **Maine D'Ange (IRE)** 2-8-8 0.......... ClementLecoeuvre(3) 11 42
(P Sogorb, France) **229/10**
11 1 1/4 **La Cataleya (FR)** 2-8-4 0.......... IvanLoutte(7) 7 38
(R Le Dren Doleuze, France) **42/1**
1m 26.5s **11 Ran SP% 118.1**
PARI-MUTUEL (all including 1 euro stake): WIN 7.40; PLACE 1.90, 1.50, 1.60; DF 13.10; SF 24.70.
**Owner** Ontoawinner, R Mckeown & E Burke **Bred** Gerard Rollain **Trained** Middleham Moor, N Yorks

## 6172a PRIX PELLEAS (LISTED RACE) (3YO COLTS & GELDINGS) (TURF) 1m 1f
**1:40** (1:40) 3-Y-0 **£23,504** (£9,401; £7,051; £4,700; £2,350)

RPR
1 **Bay Of Poets (IRE)**[17] 5522 3-9-0 0.......... CristianDemuro 1 109+
(Charlie Appleby) **23/5**[3]
2 1 3/4 **Born To Be Alive (IRE)**[13] 5643 3-9-0 0.......... TonyPiccone 3 105
(K R Burke) **54/10**
3 1 1/2 **Volfango (IRE)**[33] 4941 3-9-0 0.......... AurelienLemaitre 4 102
(F Head, France) **11/10**[1]
4 hd **Glen Shiel**[17] 5522 3-9-0 0.......... MickaelBarzalona 5 101
(A Fabre, France) **63/10**
5 1 3/4 **Neguev (IRE)**[51] 4235 3-9-0 0.......... ChristopheSoumillon 2 98
(J-C Rouget, France) **31/10**[2]
1m 49.7s **5 Ran SP% 119.2**
PARI-MUTUEL (all including 1 euro stake): WIN 3.20 (coupled with Glen Shiel); PLACE 2.70, 3.40; SF 31.10.
**Owner** Godolphin **Bred** Ammerland Verwaltung Gmbh & Co Kg **Trained** Newmarket, Suffolk

## 6173a PRIX DU DEFI DU GALOP (CONDITIONS) (4YO+) (TURF) 1m 1f
**2:10** 4-Y-0+ **£19,230** (£7,692; £5,769; £3,846; £1,923)

RPR
1 **Smart Whip (FR)**[31] 5014 6-9-5 0.......... EddyHardouin 5 111
(C Lotoux, France) **19/5**[3]
2 1 **Boomshackerlacker (IRE)**[14] 5594 7-8-13 0..........(p) MaximeGuyon 4 103
(George Baker) **8/1**
3 1 **Shutterbug (FR)**[33] 4942 5-8-13 0..........(b) AntoineHamelin 6 101
(M Figge, Germany) **6/4**[1]
4 2 **Cafe Royal (GER)**[21] 6-8-13 0.......... StephanePasquier 1 97
(A Schutz, France) **74/10**
5 3 1/2 **Cashman (FR)**[34] 4931 4-9-5 0.......... JozefBojko 7 95
(A Wohler, Germany) **8/1**
6 3/4 **Djiguite (FR)**[76] 3354 5-9-2 0.......... ChristopheSoumillon 3 91
(D Smaga, France) **17/5**[2]

PARI-MUTUEL (all including 1 euro stake): WIN 4.80; PLACE 2.70, 3.80; SF 33.20.
**Owner** Mme Ernest Le Clezio **Bred** Ronchalon Racing (uk) Ltd **Trained** France


The Form Book Flat, Raceform Ltd, Newbury, RG14 5SJ

# [5778]BATH (L-H)

Saturday, August 19

**OFFICIAL GOING: Good to soft (soft in places) changing to good to soft after race 2 (5:40)**

Wind: Fresh half against Weather: Fine

## 6174 NOVIA HIGH FLYER H'CAP 5f 160y

**5:10** (5:11) (Class 6) (0-55,57) 3-Y-O+ **£2,264** (£673; £336; £168) **Stalls** Centre

Form RPR

6040 **1** **Cryptonite (IRE)**[17] 5542 3-9-0 **55**.................................. JaneElliott(5) 16 60
(Michael Appleby) *hld up: hdwy over 1f out: rdn and hung lft ins fnl f: r.o to ld nr fin* **8/1**

3120 **2** *hd* **Frank Cool**[40] 4695 4-9-8 **55**.................................. GeorgeDowning 5 59
(Tony Carroll) *hld up in tch: led over 1f out: sn rdn and hung lft: hdd nr fin* **10/1**

4102 **3** *2 ½* **Burauq**[8] 5892 5-9-0 **52**..........................................(v) LuluStanford(5) 9 48
(Milton Bradley) *w ldrs: rdn and ev ch over 1f out: edgd lft and no ex wl ins fnl f* **7/1[3]**

3620 **4** *nk* **Stringybark Creek**[2] 6097 3-9-7 **57**.............................. MartinLane 15 52
(Mick Channon) *chsd ldrs: rdn over 1f out: edgd lft ins fnl f: styd on same pce* **14/1**

6553 **5** *½* **Essaka (IRE)**[8] 5871 5-9-1 **53**.................................. MitchGodwin(5) 17 46
(Tony Carroll) *hld up: hdwy 1/2-way: rdn over 1f out: styd on* **7/1[3]**

000 **6** *nk* **Leith Bridge**[5] 6004 5-8-6 **46** oh1..................................(v) NicolaCurrie(7) 4 38
(Mark Usher) *s.i.s: hld up: hdwy over 1f out: nt clr run and no ex wl ins fnl f* **20/1**

0466 **7** *nse* **Bushwise (IRE)**[10] 5784 4-8-13 **46** oh1..........................(b) RyanPowell 10 38
(Milton Bradley) *s.i.s: sn pushed along in rr: rdn and hung lft over 1f out: r.o towards fin* **16/1**

6521 **8** *½* **Tea El Tee (IRE)**[10] 5812 3-9-0 **57**..........................(v) CameronNoble(7) 6 48
(Gay Kelleway) *s.i.s: hld up: hdwy over 1f out: nt trble ldrs* **4/1[2]**

06-6 **9** *2 ½* **Amberine**[127] 1761 3-9-0 **53**.................................. CharlieBennett(3) 12 35
(Malcolm Saunders) *led: hdd over 3f out: rdn over 1f out: wknd fnl f* **25/1**

1062 **10** *nk* **Staffa (IRE)**[10] 5778 4-9-7 **54**.................................. LukeMorris 13 35
(Denis Coakley) *s.i.s: hld up: effrt over 1f out: wknd fnl f* **10/1**

-400 **11** *nk* **Charlie Victor**[16] 5567 3-8-8 **51**.............................. KatherineGlenister(7) 7 31
(Malcolm Saunders) *w ldrs: led over 3f out: rdn and hdd over 1f out: sn edgd lft: wknd fnl f* **25/1**

-022 **12** *1 ½* **Harlequin Rose (IRE)**[46] 4458 3-9-2 **55**..........................(v) HectorCrouch(3) 3 30
(Patrick Chamings) *prom: rdn over 2f out: wkng whn hmpd over 1f out* **7/2[1]**

0024 **13** *17* **Monsieur Paddy**[25] 5252 4-9-7 **54**.................................. JoeyHaynes 1
(Tony Carroll) *prom: rdn over 2f out: wknd and eased over 1f out* **12/1**

1m 13.82s (2.62) **Going Correction** +0.30s/f (Good)
**WFA** 3 from 4yo+ 3lb **13** Ran SP% **129.2**
Speed ratings (Par 101): **94,93,90,90,89 88,88,88,84,84 84,82,59**
CSF £90.65 CT £620.30 TOTE £10.70: £3.50, £1.80, £2.80; EX 105.30 Trifecta £1417.60 Part Won..
**Owner** C L Bacon **Bred** Yeomanstown Stud **Trained** Oakham, Rutland

**FOCUS**

Significant rain had softened the ground from good, good to firm in places two days previously, but racing itself took place in bright and breezy conditions. Rail movements added 5yds to races 2, 3 and 7, and the stalls were in the centre for this moderate opening sprint.

## 6175 OMEGA RESOURCE GROUP VETERANS' H'CAP 1m 2f 37y

**5:40** (5:42) (Class 5) (0-70,70) 6-Y-O+ **£2,911** (£866; £432; £216) **Stalls** Low

Form RPR

3043 **1** **Camakasi (IRE)**[19] 5477 6-9-4 **70**.................................. GeorgeWood(3) 4 81
(Ali Stronge) *hld up: hdwy over 2f out: led over 1f out: sn edgd lft and pushed clr: easily* **11/2[3]**

-055 **2** *8* **Silver Dixie (USA)**[31] 5024 7-9-0 **63**..........................(p) CharlesBishop 2 58
(Peter Hedger) *hld up: hdwy 2f out: sn rdn: styd on to go 2nd nr fin* **8/1**

3321 **3** *shd* **Omotesando**[8] 5872 7-9-1 **67**..........................(p) CharlieBennett(3) 8 62
(Oliver Greenall) *hld up: hdwy over 3f out: rdn to ld wl over 1f out: sn hdd: hung lft and outpcd* **15/8[1]**

4331 **4** *nse* **Avocadeau (IRE)**[30] 5053 6-8-9 **58**..........................(tp) MartinLane 1 53
(Stuart Kittow) *awkward s: hdwy to ld over 8f out: rdn and hdd wl over 1f out: sn outpcd* **11/2[3]**

522- **5** *½* **Mrs Burbidge**[236] 7262 7-8-3 **52**..........................(tp) LukeMorris 6 46
(Neil Mulholland) *chsd ldrs: rdn over 2f out: styd on same pce* **3/1[2]**

30-0 **6** *2 ¼* **Heezararity**[19] 5477 9-8-11 **63**.................................. HectorCrouch(3) 7 52
(Jonathan Geake) *prom: rdn over 3f out: sn lost pl* **16/1**

4042 **7** *hd* **Nouvelle Ere**[10] 5790 6-8-8 **57**..........................(t) GeorgeDowning 3 46
(Tony Carroll) *led: hdd over 8f out: chsd ldr: rdn and ev ch over 2f out: no ex fr over 1f out* **12/1**

2m 13.57s (2.57) **Going Correction** +0.30s/f (Good) **7** Ran SP% **115.2**
Speed ratings: **101,94,94,94,94 92,92**
CSF £48.11 CT £112.19 TOTE £6.30: £2.60, £3.20; EX 47.50 Trifecta £229.50.
**Owner** Shaw Racing 2 & Friends Of Castle Piece **Bred** Mrs Emily Henry **Trained** Eastbury, Berks

**FOCUS**

Add 5yds to race distance. Stalls on inner. This was taken apart by a runner previously winless on turf. It's hard to rate the wide-margin winner at face value.

## 6176 SILK SERIES LADY RIDERS' H'CAP 1m 2f 37y

**6:10** (6:12) (Class 4) (0-85,84) 3-Y-O+ **£6,469** (£1,925; £962; £481) **Stalls** Low

Form RPR

3261 **1** **Canberra Cliffs (IRE)**[9] 5838 3-10-4 **84**.......................... MeganNicholls 3 93+
(Don Cantillon) *hld up in tch: chsd ldr over 1f out: led ins fnl f: styd on wl* **9/4[2]**

3505 **2** *1 ¼* **Pack It In (IRE)**[3] 6075 4-9-10 **69**..........................(b) LuluStanford 7 74
(Brian Meehan) *chsd ldr tl wnt upsides over 3f out: led over 2f out: rdn: hung lft and hdd ins fnl f: styd on same pce* **13/2**

1500 **3** *½* **Sean O'Casey (IRE)**[52] 4216 4-10-5 **78**.......................... JaneElliott 2 82
(Michael Appleby) *led: rdn and hdd over 2f out: styd on* **11/1**

6431 **4** *6* **In First Place**[22] 5378 3-10-1 **81**.................................. SammyJoBell 4 74
(Richard Fahey) *hld up: rdn over 2f out: hdwy over 1f out: nt trble ldrs* **7/4[1]**

1561 **5** *½* **Earthly (USA)**[81] 3178 3-9-10 **76**.................................. HayleyTurner 8 68
(Bernard Llewellyn) *prom: lost pl over 8f out: rdn over 3f out: no imp fr over 1f out* **7/1**

16R0 **6** *2* **Retrieve (AUS)**[14] 5643 10-10-6 **79**..........................(t) AliceMills 5 66
(Carroll Gray) *chsd ldrs: rdn over 2f out: wknd over 1f out* **50/1**

2461 **7** *¾* **Plymouth Sound**[56] 4089 5-10-7 **80**..........................(v) MissSBrotherton 1 66
(Bernard Llewellyn) *s.s: hdwy over 6f out: rdn over 2f out: sn btn* **6/1[3]**

2m 12.27s (1.27) **Going Correction** +0.30s/f (Good)
**WFA** 3 from 4yo+ 7lb **7** Ran SP% **117.5**
Speed ratings (Par 105): **106,105,104,99,99 97,97**
CSF £18.09 CT £134.86 TOTE £3.20: £1.60, £3.50; EX 17.80 Trifecta £131.80.
**Owner** Mrs Catherine Reed **Bred** Barry Davis **Trained** Newmarket, Suffolk

**FOCUS**

Add 5yds. Stalls on inner. The ground was changed to good to soft all over ahead of this fair contest for lady riders. The form is rated around the second and third.

## 6177 BE WISER INSURANCE H'CAP 5f 10y

**6:40** (6:40) (Class 3) (0-90,91) 3-Y-O+ **£7,439** (£2,213; £1,106; £553) **Stalls** Centre

Form RPR

2201 **1** **Compas Scoobie**[21] 5426 4-9-0 **87**..........................(v) CameronNoble(7) 8 101
(Roger Varian) *hld up: hdwy 2f out: shkn up to ld over 1f out: edgd lft: rdn and r.o wl* **9/4[1]**

2410 **2** *4 ½* **Seamster**[3] 6072 10-8-4 **77**..........................(t) LauraCoughlan(7) 4 75
(David Loughnane) *chsd ldrs: led 3f out: rdn: hung lft and hdd over 1f out: no ex ins fnl f* **5/1**

-230 **3** *hd* **Orvar (IRE)**[37] 4816 4-9-11 **91**.................................. LukeMorris 5 88
(Robert Cowell) *chsd ldrs: rdn 1/2-way: styd on same pce fnl f* **4/1[2]**

4615 **4** *shd* **Blitz**[31] 5029 3-8-12 **83**.................................. HectorCrouch(3) 6 80
(Clive Cox) *led 2f: rdn 1/2-way: styd on same pce fnl f* **9/2[3]**

0030 **5** *2 ¼* **Majestic Hero (IRE)**[26] 5219 5-9-8 **88**.................................. FranBerry 3 77
(Ronald Harris) *hld up: swtchd rt over 1f out: nvr trbld ldrs* **8/1**

1511 **6** *hd* **Ocelot**[31] 5029 3-9-0 **82**.................................. HayleyTurner 1 70
(Robert Cowell) *plld hrd and prom: rdn 1/2-way: no ex fr over 1f out* **4/1[2]**

1m 2.92s (0.42) **Going Correction** +0.30s/f (Good)
**WFA** 3 from 4yo+ 2lb **6** Ran SP% **116.7**
Speed ratings (Par 107): **108,100,100,100,96 96**
CSF £14.62 CT £42.62 TOTE £2.90: £1.80, £2.60; EX 11.90 Trifecta £60.00.
**Owner** Michael Hill **Bred** Aston Mullins Stud **Trained** Newmarket, Suffolk

**FOCUS**

Stalls in centre. A decent feature event, but another race on the evening won very easily. The pace was strong.

## 6178 CANCER RESEARCH UK EBF MAIDEN STKS 5f 10y

**7:10** (7:10) (Class 5) 2-Y-O **£2,911** (£866; £432; £216) **Stalls** Centre

Form RPR

**1** **Equilateral** 2-9-5 0.................................. SteveDrowne 4 92+
(Charles Hills) *hld up: hdwy 1/2-way: led on bit over 1f out: shkn up and sn clr: easily* **7/2[3]**

52 **2** *3 ½* **Swing Out Sister (IRE)**[15] 5586 2-9-0 0.......................... SamHitchcott 7 72
(Clive Cox) *chsd ldr tl led 2f out: sn rdn and hdd: styd on same pce* **1/1[1]**

**3** *4* **Bbob Alula** 2-9-5 0..........................(t[1]) LukeMorris 6 63
(Bill Turner) *disp 2nd tl pushed along 3f out: sn outpcd: kpt on to go 3rd nr fin* **28/1**

03 **4** *hd* **Choosey (IRE)**[18] 5494 2-9-5 0.................................. FranBerry 8 62
(Henry Candy) *hld up: plld hrd: hdwy 1/2-way: shkn up over 1f out: hung lft and wknd ins fnl f* **11/4[2]**

6525 **5** *3 ½* **Highland Mary**[9] 5839 2-9-0 74.................................. KieranO'Neill 2 44
(Richard Hannon) *led 3f: sn rdn: wknd fnl f* **12/1**

04 **6** *14* **Comselle**[23] 5327 2-9-0 0.................................. MartinLane 1
(Stuart Kittow) *prom: racd keenly: wknd 2f out* **25/1**

**7** *47* **Maddi** 2-8-7 0.................................. WilliamCox(7) 5
(Luke Dace) *s.s: outpcd* **25/1**

1m 4.03s (1.53) **Going Correction** +0.30s/f (Good) **7** Ran SP% **117.7**
Speed ratings (Par 94): **99,93,87,86,81 58,**
CSF £7.63 TOTE £3.70: £1.70, £1.10; EX 12.00 Trifecta £124.10.
**Owner** K Abdullah **Bred** Juddmonte Farms Ltd **Trained** Lambourn, Berks

**FOCUS**

Stalls in centre. Probably not that much strength in depth, but an impressive debutant winner. The winning time was 1.11 seconds slower than that of the 87-rated scorer in the preceding contest.

## 6179 NOVIA FINANCIAL H'CAP (BATH SUMMER SPRINT SERIES QUALIFIER) 5f 10y

**7:40** (7:40) (Class 6) (0-60,61) 4-Y-O+ **£2,264** (£673; £336; £168) **Stalls** Centre

Form RPR

0401 **1** **Jaganory (IRE)**[10] 5778 5-9-3 **61**..........................(p) LuluStanford(5) 11 66
(Christopher Mason) *chsd ldr tl wnt upsides over 3f out: rdn to ld over 1f out: jst hld on* **7/2[3]**

5303 **2** *hd* **David's Beauty (IRE)**[10] 5778 4-8-13 **52**..........................(b[1]) LukeMorris 3 56
(Brian Baugh) *led: rdn and hdd over 1f out: styd on u.p* **9/2**

634 **3** *1 ¼* **Prominna**[16] 5567 7-9-6 **59**.................................. GeorgeDowning 5 59
(Tony Carroll) *hld up: plld hrd: rdn over 1f out: hung lft and r.o to go 3rd wl ins fnl f: nt rch ldrs* **3/1[2]**

4500 **4** *½* **Evening Starlight**[10] 5784 4-9-3 **56**.................................. KieranO'Neill 4 54
(Ron Hodges) *plld hrd and prom: rdn over 1f out: styd on same pce ins fnl f* **11/1**

0032 **5** *½* **Fantasy Justifier (IRE)**[4] 6041 6-9-6 **59**..........................(b[1]) FranBerry 6 55
(Ronald Harris) *hld up: plld hrd: hdwy 1/2-way: rdn and hung rt over 1f out: styng on same pce whn hmpd nr fin* **6/4[1]**

1m 3.81s (1.31) **Going Correction** +0.30s/f (Good) **5** Ran SP% **113.7**
Speed ratings (Par 101): **101,100,98,97,97**
CSF £19.33 TOTE £4.50: £2.20, £1.40; EX 16.10 Trifecta £27.50.
**Owner** Brian Hicks **Bred** Canice Farrell Jnr **Trained** Caewent, Monmouthshire

**FOCUS**

Stalls in centre. A low-grade sprint absolutely decimated by non-runners, and a winning time 0.89 seconds slower than that of the feature sprint

## 6180 LEXUS BRISTOL H'CAP (BATH SUMMER STAYERS' SERIES QUALIFIER) 1m 6f

**8:10** (8:10) (Class 6) (0-55,57) 3-Y-O **£2,911** (£866; £432; £216) **Stalls** Centre

Form RPR

0104 **1** **Affair**[37] 4804 3-8-8 **49**.................................. TheodoreLadd(7) 11 58
(Hughie Morrison) *chsd ldr tl over 8f out: wnt 2nd again over 6f out: led over 2f out: sn rdn: clr over 1f out: styd on wl* **14/1**

1224 **2** *3 ¼* **The Secrets Out**[21] 5406 3-9-8 **56**..........................(h) KieranO'Neill 10 61
(Luke Dace) *led: rdn and hdd over 2f out: styd on same pce fnl f* **5/2[1]**

0502 **3** *1 ¼* **Percy Thrower (IRE)**[10] 5780 3-9-6 **57**.................. CallumShepherd(3) 1 60
(Charles Hills) *chsd ldrs: wnt 2nd over 8f out tl over 6f out: remained handy: rdn over 2f out: styd on same pce fr over 1f out* **4/1[3]**

0305 **4** *1* **Curtsy (IRE)**[22] 5361 3-9-9 **57**.................................. FranBerry 5 59
(Hughie Morrison) *hld up: hdwy over 6f out: rdn over 2f out: styd on same pce fr over 1f out* **7/2[2]**

066 **5** 1 ¼ **Artic Nel**[39] 4729 3-9-7 **55** GeorgeDowning 9 55
(Ian Williams) *hld up: hdwy over 2f out: rdn over 1f out: styd on same pce* **16/1**

166 **6** 1 ½ **Crucial Moment**[20] 3024 3-9-8 **56** LukeMorris 8 54
(Bill Turner) *hld up: hdwy over 2f out: sn rdn: no ex fnl f* **7/1**

0001 **7** 1 ¼ **Tojosimbre**[10] 5787 3-9-2 **50** (t) RyanTate 2 47
(Richard Hughes) *hld up in tch: rdn over 2f out: wknd fnl f* **6/1**

6-00 **8** ¾ **The Batham Boy (IRE)**[9] 5850 3-9-0 **48** (p[1]) MartinLane 6 44
(Daniel Mark Loughnane) *hld up: rdn over 2f out: nvr on terms* **33/1**

0004 **9** 4 **Volturnus**[9] 5846 3-8-13 **47** oh1 ow1 (b) DougieCostello 3 37
(Jamie Osborne) *chsd ldrs: rdn over 3f out: wknd over 1f out* **12/1**

44-0 **10** 8 **Hoover Fever**[12] 5713 3-8-6 **47** (p[1]) WilliamCox(7) 12 27
(Carroll Gray) *hld up: rdn over 2f out: sn wknd* **66/1**

3m 10.18s (6.38) **Going Correction** +0.30s/f (Good) **10** Ran SP% **122.3**
Speed ratings (Par 98): **93,91,90,89,89 88,87,87,84,80**
CSF £51.56 CT £176.55 TOTE £11.80: £3.10, £1.20, £2.10; EX 57.10 Trifecta £521.40.
**Owner** H Morrison **Bred** H Morrison **Trained** East Ilsley, Berks
■ Street Jester was withdrawn. Price at time of withdrawal 28/1. Rule 4 does not apply

**FOCUS**
Add 5yds. Stalls in centre. A moderate stayers' event, run at a steady gallop.
T/Plt: £281.20 to a £1 stake. Pool: £48,000.87 - 124.57 winning units T/Qpdt: £21.70 to a £1 stake. Pool: £5,859.76 - 199.75 winning units **Colin Roberts**

# 5630 DONCASTER (L-H)
## Saturday, August 19

**OFFICIAL GOING: Good (good to firm in places; 7.9) changing to good after race 3 (2:30)**
Wind: Strong against Weather: Sunny periods & showers

## 6181 SUN BETS DOWNLOAD THE APP H'CAP (DIV I) 7f 6y
**1:25** (1:25) (Class 5) (0-70,72) 3-Y-O+ **£3,234** (£962; £481; £240) **Stalls** Centre

Form RPR

404 **1** **Deansgate (IRE)**[44] 4529 4-9-10 **68** JoeDoyle 9 78
(Julie Camacho) *trckd ldrs: smooth hdwy 2f out: led over 1f out: rdn ins fnl f: kpt on strly* **9/2**[2]

2420 **2** 1 **Athollblair Boy (IRE)**[23] 5318 4-9-5 **66** LewisEdmunds(3) 7 73
(Nigel Tinkler) *in tch: hdwy over 2f out: rdn and n.m.r over 1f out: swtchd rt ent fnl f: sn drvn and kpt on* **15/2**

4540 **3** 1 ¼ **Haraz (IRE)**[22] 5379 4-9-9 **70** (v) JoshDoyle(3) 10 74
(David O'Meara) *hld up: stdy hdwy over 2f out: sn trcking ldrs: effrt over 1f out: rdn to chse wnr ent fnl f: kpt on same pce* **11/2**[3]

0232 **4** 4 **Willsy**[12] 5696 4-9-0 **63** (b) GemmaTutty(5) 2 56
(Karen Tutty) *prom: led 2f out: rdn and hdd over 1f out: sn drvn and wknd fnl f* **4/1**[1]

1500 **5** hd **Jet Setter (IRE)**[24] 5288 3-8-7 **63** ManuelFernandes(7) 12 53
(Tony Carroll) *hld up in rr: hdwy on outer wl over 2f out: rdn to chse ldrs over 1f out: kpt on fnl f: nrst fin* **9/1**

2-63 **6** ½ **Let's Twist**[107] 2346 5-10-0 **72** ShaneGray 5 63
(Kristin Stubbs) *cl up: effrt 2f out: sn rdn and ev ch: drvn ent fnl f: grad wknd* **8/1**

5200 **7** 1 ¼ **Magical Molly Joe**[22] 5375 3-8-7 **61** BenRobinson(5) 1 47
(David Barron) *dwlt: sn in tch on inner: hdwy to chse ldrs 3f out: rdn along 2f out: drvn over 1f out: grad wknd* **20/1**

0640 **8** ½ **Hamriyah**[17] 5543 3-8-6 **55** (p[1]) AndrewMullen 6 39
(Tim Easterby) *chsd ldrs: rdn along over 2f out: hld whn n.m.r wl over 1f out* **25/1**

0520 **9** 4 ½ **Sophisticated Heir (IRE)**[24] 5288 7-9-11 **69** TrevorWhelan 11 43
(Kevin Frost) *chsd ldrs: rdn along wl over 2f out: sn wknd* **22/1**

0600 **10** 3 ½ **Mr Conundrum**[9] 5827 4-8-7 **51** oh6 PaddyAspell 14 16
(Lynn Siddall) *towards rr: sme hdwy 1/2-way: rdn along wl over 2f out: sn wknd* **100/1**

0563 **11** 3 ¼ **Hitman**[11] 5739 4-9-11 **69** DuranFentiman 4 25
(Rebecca Bastiman) *dwlt and towards rr: sme hdwy 1/2-way: rdn along wl over 2f out: sn wknd* **13/2**

26-0 **12** 12 **Roger Thorpe**[42] 4626 8-8-8 **55** ow2 PaddyPilley(5) 8
(John Balding) *led: rdn along 3f out: hdd jst over 2f out and sn wknd* **16/1**

1m 27.66s (1.36) **Going Correction** +0.275s/f (Good)
**WFA** 3 from 4yo+ 5lb **12** Ran SP% **119.6**
Speed ratings (Par 103): **103,101,100,95,95 95,93,93,87,83 80,66**
CSF £36.92 CT £193.02 TOTE £5.70: £2.10, £2.30, £2.10; EX 41.70 Trifecta £192.70.
**Owner** Axom LXIII **Bred** Paul McEnery **Trained** Norton, N Yorks

**FOCUS**
The round course was railed out 6yds from 1m2f to where it joins the straight, adding about 18yds to races 7 and 8. The official going was good, good to firm in places. A fair handicap run at an ordinary pace. The winner is rated to his best.

## 6182 SUN BETS DOWNLOAD THE APP H'CAP (DIV II) 7f 6y
**1:55** (1:56) (Class 5) (0-70,70) 3-Y-O+ **£3,234** (£962; £481; £240) **Stalls** Centre

Form RPR

0063 **1** **Habbad (FR)**[16] 5560 3-9-4 **67** (p) TomMarquand 4 75
(Richard Hannon) *in tch: hdwy on outer over 2f out: rdn to ld jst over 1f out: drvn ins fnl f: hld on wl towards fin* **15/2**

-000 **2** hd **Acrux**[42] 4629 4-9-12 **70** (h) PhillipMakin 12 79+
(David O'Meara) *hld up in rr: swtchd rt to outer and smooth hdwy 2f out: effrt ent fnl f: sn jinked rt: rdn dropped whip: rdn and styd on wl towards fin: jst failed* **16/1**

0302 **3** nk **Insurplus (IRE)**[7] 5919 4-8-6 **57** SeanMooney(7) 9 65
(Jim Goldie) *trckd ldrs: hdwy over 2f out: sn cl up: rdn and ev ch ent fnl f: sn drvn and kpt on* **6/1**[3]

0520 **4** 4 **Darvie**[5] 5992 3-8-4 **58** BenRobinson(5) 10 53
(David Barron) *dwlt and rr: swtchd lft: rdn and hdwy wl over 1f out: styd on wl fnl f: nrst fin* **9/2**[2]

4060 **5** hd **Thornaby Nash**[17] 5544 6-9-0 **58** (p) SamJames 11 55
(Karen Tutty) *prom: cl up 1/2-way: chal 2f out: rdn to ld briefly jst over 1f out: sn hdd: drvn and wknd fnl f* **8/1**

0-06 **6** ½ **Discovered (IRE)**[15] 5611 3-9-6 **69** TrevorWhelan 7 62
(Roger Charlton) *dwlt: hld up in tch: hdwy to chse ldrs 2f out: rdn over 1f out: sn drvn and kpt on same pce* **6/1**[3]

4 **7** 3 **Donnelly's Rainbow (IRE)**[45] 4506 4-9-4 **67** RowanScott(5) 1 54
(Rebecca Bastiman) *trckd ldrs: rdn along over 2f out: grad wknd* **3/1**[1]

0366 **8** hd **Marbooh (IRE)**[39] 4728 4-9-12 **70** (t) PaulMulrennan 8 57
(Denis Quinn) *trckd ldrs: rdn along 2f out: sn wknd* **14/1**

0000 **9** 2 ½ **Slemy (IRE)**[9] 5836 6-8-12 **56** (p) AndrewMullen 3 36
(Ruth Carr) *led: rdn along 2f out: hdd over 1f out: sn wknd* **20/1**

6/50 **10** 17 **Media World (IRE)**[26] 5214 4-8-11 **55** JoeDoyle 2
(Julie Camacho) *t.k.h: prom: rdn along over 2f out: sn wknd* **25/1**

1m 26.93s (0.63) **Going Correction** +0.275s/f (Good)
**WFA** 3 from 4yo+ 5lb **10** Ran SP% **115.8**
Speed ratings (Par 103): **107,106,106,101,101 101,97,97,94,75**
CSF £118.61 CT £784.63 TOTE £8.20: £2.20, £4.10, £2.00; EX 74.30 Trifecta £1180.70.
**Owner** Salem Fahad S A Ghorab **Bred** Stilvi Compania Financiera **Trained** East Everleigh, Wilts

**FOCUS**
The second division was run 0.73sec quicker than the first leg. The form is rated around the third.

## 6183 FOLLOW SUN BETS ON INSTAGRAM EBF MAIDEN FILLIES' STKS (PLUS 10 RACE) 1m (S)
**2:30** (2:31) (Class 5) 2-Y-O **£3,234** (£962; £481; £240) **Stalls** Centre

Form RPR

5 **1** **Dark Rose Angel (IRE)**[14] 5660 2-9-0 0 PaulMulrennan 5 92+
(Simon Crisford) *.mde all: rdn and qcknd clr wl over 1f out: readily* **7/2**[2]

**2** 4 **Lubinka (IRE)** 2-9-0 0 JackMitchell 1 80
(Peter Chapple-Hyam) *trckd ldrs: hdwy over 2f out: chsd wnr wl over 1f out: sn rdn and kpt on: no ch w wnr* **14/1**

4 **3** 2 **Amazing Michele (FR)**[14] 5631 2-9-0 0 DavidNolan 6 76
(Richard Fahey) *trckd ldng pair: pushed along over 2f out: rdn wl over 1f out: kpt on same pce* **8/1**

0 **4** ½ **Stream Song**[22] 5349 2-9-0 0 RobertTart 7 75
(John Gosden) *dwlt: sn in tch: chsd ldrs over 2f out: sn rdn: kpt on u.p fnl f* **10/11**[1]

00 **5** 1 ¾ **Toomer**[17] 5528 2-9-0 0 TomMarquand 3 71
(Richard Hannon) *trckd wnr: rdn along wl over 2f out: sn wknd* **20/1**

56 **6** 5 **Zoffinia (IRE)**[22] 5371 2-9-0 0 AndrewMullen 2 60
(Richard Fahey) *towards rr: pushed along 3f out: rdn over 2f out: nvr a factor* **40/1**

0 **7** 5 **Bessie Warfield**[35] 4902 2-9-0 0 StevieDonohoe 4 49
(Luca Cumani) *hld up in rr: pushed along 3f out: sn rdn and no hdwy* **13/2**[3]

1m 41.14s (1.84) **Going Correction** +0.275s/f (Good) **7** Ran SP% **112.9**
Speed ratings (Par 91): **101,97,95,94,92 87,82**
CSF £47.18 TOTE £4.30: £1.70, £4.70; EX 47.50 Trifecta £175.60.
**Owner** Hussain Alabbas Lootah **Bred** Skymarc Farm **Trained** Newmarket, Suffolk

**FOCUS**
A fair maiden and the winner was impressive.

## 6184 BET & WATCH AT SUNBETS.CO.UK MAIDEN STKS 6f 2y
**3:05** (3:06) (Class 5) 3-Y-O+ **£3,234** (£962; £481; £240) **Stalls** Centre

Form RPR

3 **1** **Equitation**[14] 5645 3-9-5 0 JackMitchell 13 77+
(Roger Varian) *trckd ldrs: hdwy over 2f out: led 11/2f out: rdn ent fnl f: kpt on wl* **7/1**

44 **2** 1 **Mohsen**[28] 5158 3-9-5 0 LouisSteward 8 74
(Marcus Tregoning) *in tch: hdwy to trck ldrs 1/2-way: effrt on inner 2f out and sn cl up: rdn over 1f out: drvn and kpt on fnl f* **17/2**

**3** ½ **One Master** 3-9-0 0 TomMarquand 12 67+
(William Haggas) *hld up in rr whn hmpd after 2f: hdwy 2f out: rdn over 1f out: styd on strly fnl f* **7/2**[2]

04 **4** nk **Katheefa (USA)**[37] 4793 3-9-2 0 CallumShepherd(3) 7 71
(Charles Hills) *in tch: hdwy to chse ldrs over 2f out: rdn along wl over 1f out: kpt on fnl f* **13/2**[3]

02 **5** ¾ **Blazed (IRE)**[67] 3691 3-9-0 0 (t[1]) PaddyPilley(5) 5 69
(Roger Charlton) *hld up: hdwy to trck ldrs 1/2-way: sn slt ld: rdn wl over 1f out: sn hdd and drvn: kpt on same pce* **11/4**[1]

65 **6** 1 ½ **Betty Grable (IRE)**[7] 5946 3-9-0 0 PaulMulrennan 4 59
(Wilf Storey) *in rr: hdwy wl over 2f out: rdn along wl over 1f out: kpt on fnl f: nrst fin* **33/1**

2 **7** nk **Nuns Walk**[15] 5619 3-9-0 0 DuranFentiman 9 58
(Tim Easterby) *chsd ldrs: rdn along wl over 1f out: sn no imp* **12/1**

**8** 1 **Lady Of The Lamp (IRE)** 3-9-0 0 StevieDonohoe 10 55
(Rae Guest) *towards rr: pushed along 1/2-way: rdn along 2f out: kpt on fnl f* **16/1**

00 **9** 4 **Fintry Flyer**[15] 5619 3-9-0 0 JoeDoyle 3 42
(Jim Goldie) *dwlt: a towards rr* **200/1**

**10** 5 **Coviglia (IRE)**[88] 2939 3-9-5 0 DavidNolan 14 31
(David O'Meara) *chsd ldrs: rdn along wl over 2f out: sn wknd* **15/2**

00- **11** 1 ¼ **Suraat (IRE)**[341] 6413 3-9-0 0 PhillipMakin 2 22
(Robert Cowell) *cl up: rdn along over 2f out: sn wknd* **33/1**

4/-0 **12** 2 ¼ **Pound Note**[23] 5315 5-9-5 0 PhilDennis(3) 15 20
(Michael Mullineaux) *a towards rr* **100/1**

4 **13** ½ **Swing Time (IRE)**[24] 5289 3-9-2 0 LewisEdmunds(3) 11 18
(Eric Alston) *t.k.h: chsd ldrs: losing pl whn hung rt after 2f: sn bhd* **40/1**

0 **14** 19 **Redeeming**[15] 5619 3-9-5 0 NeilFarley 1
(Eric Alston) *.racd centre: led: hung bdly rt to stands rails 1/2-way: sn hdd & wknd* **50/1**

1m 13.65s (0.05) **Going Correction** +0.275s/f (Good)
**WFA** 3 from 5yo 3lb **14** Ran SP% **122.4**
Speed ratings (Par 103): **110,108,108,107,106 104,104,102,97,90 89,86,85,60**
CSF £64.52 TOTE £9.00: £2.70, £3.10, £1.50; EX 71.40 Trifecta £509.80.
**Owner** The Equitation Partnership **Bred** Newsells Park Stud **Trained** Newmarket, Suffolk

**FOCUS**
An ordinary maiden run at an even pace. The favourite didn't set a great standard. The winner was a big improvement from his debut.

## 6185 LIKE SUN BETS ON FACEBOOK H'CAP 5f 3y
**3:40** (3:40) (Class 3) (0-95,95) 3-Y-O+ **£7,762** (£2,310; £1,154; £577) **Stalls** Centre

Form RPR

0005 **1** **Desert Law (IRE)**[15] 5602 9-9-2 **87** PaulMulrennan 9 98
(Paul Midgley) *trckd ldrs stands side: cl up 2f out: rdn to ld ent fnl f: sn drvn and kpt on wl* **14/1**

6120 **2** 1 **Vibrant Chords**[18] 5505 4-9-10 **95** JackMitchell 7 103
(Henry Candy) *trckd ldrs stands side: hdwy and cl up 2f out: rdn to dispuite ld over 1f out: ev ch ent fnl f: sn drvn and kpt on* **4/1**[1]

2643 **3** 2 ¼ **Soie D'Leau**[22] 5354 5-9-7 **92** JoeDoyle 10 93
(Kristin Stubbs) *led stands side gp: rdn along and jnd 2f out: drvn and hdd ent fnl f: kpt on same pce* **9/2**[2]

4314 **4** nse **Royal Brave (IRE)**[14] 5637 6-8-10 **86** RowanScott(5) 11 87
(Rebecca Bastiman) *in tch stands side: effrt wl over 1f out: sn rdn and kpt on fnl f* **13/2**[3]

5042 **5** 1 ½ **Captain Lars (SAF)**[7] 5929 8-8-5 **79** (v) AaronJones(3) 12 75
(Derek Shaw) *hld up towards rr stands side: hdwy wl over 1f out: sn rdn: kpt on fnl f* **16/1**



The Form Book Flat, Raceform Ltd, Newbury, RG14 5SJ

-000 **6** ½ **Venturous (IRE)**84 3092 4-9-0 **85** SamJames 14 79
(David Barron) *cl up stands side: rdn along wl over 1f out: wknd ent fnl f* **18/1**

-110 **7** *nk* **Rich Again (IRE)**173 957 8-8-8 **84** (b) CallumRodriguez(5) 6 77
(James Bethell) *dwlt and rr stands side: hdwy 2f out: rdn over 1f out: kpt on fnl f* **28/1**

264 **8** 1¾ **Signore Piccolo**7 5929 6-9-0 **85** (h) StevieDonohoe 2 73
(David Loughnane) *chsd ldr far side: rdn along 2f out: sn edgd rt towards main gp and wknd* **11/1**

5144 **9** ½ **Orient Class**21 5402 6-9-3 **88** PhillipMakin 8 74
(Paul Midgley) *prom stands side: rdn along 2f out: sn wknd* **12/1**

0100 **10** ¾ **Tylery Wonder (IRE)**15 5602 7-8-11 **82** (v) NeilFarley 1 66
(Paul Midgley) *overall ldr far side: rdn along over 2f out: sn hdd and edgd rt towards main gp: wknd over 1f out* **20/1**

3333 **11** 1¼ **Bashiba (IRE)**36 4867 6-8-11 **85** (t) LewisEdmunds(3) 3 65
(Nigel Tinkler) *racd far side: trckd ldng pair: pushed along over 2f out: sn rdn and wknd* **9/2**2

06 **12** 1¾ **Computable**36 4835 3-8-6 **79** (t1) AndrewMullen 13 53
(Tim Easterby) *a towards rr stands side* **25/1**

2015 **13** 9 **Highland Acclaim (IRE)**18 5513 6-9-3 **88** (h) DavidNolan 4 33
(David O'Meara) *racd far side: in tch: rdn along over 2f out: sn wknd* **20/1**

59.24s (-1.26) **Going Correction** -0.05s/f (Good)
**WFA** 3 from 4yo+ 2lb **13** Ran SP% **120.4**
Speed ratings (Par 107): **108,106,102,102,100 99,99,96,95,94 92,89,75**
CSF £66.25 CT £302.97 TOTE £17.80: £4.60, £1.90, £2.20; EX 115.90 Trifecta £591.70.
**Owner** Taylor's Bloodstock Ltd **Bred** Littleton Stud **Trained** Westow, N Yorks

**FOCUS**
A competitive, good-quality sprint. They split into two groups before merging after halfway, the four runners on the far side making no impact, and the two principals pulled a little way clear of the rest. Sound form, the winner rated to his best in the past year.

## 6186 SUNBETS.CO.UK YOUBETCHA H'CAP 7f 6y
**4:10** (4:11) (Class 2) (0-105,101) 3-Y-0+
**£12,450** (£3,728; £1,864; £932; £466; £234) **Stalls** Centre

Form RPR

5520 **1** **Bertiewhittle**14 5669 9-8-11 **91** RowanScott(5) 1 98
(David Barron) *hld up: hdwy wl over 1f out: n.m.r and rdn appr fnl f: styd on wl to ld nr fin* **12/1**

1344 **2** *nk* **Qeyaadah (IRE)**15 5610 4-8-10 **85** RyanTate 10 91
(Michael Appleby) *trckd ldrs: hdwy over 2f out: led wl over 1f out: rdn ent fnl f: sn drvn: hdd and no ex nr fin* **8/1**

-230 **3** *shd* **Six Strings**14 5637 3-8-7 **87** AndrewMullen 9 91
(Richard Fahey) *trckd ldrs: hdwy 2f out: rdn to chal and edgd lft jst over 1f out: drvn and ev ch ins fnl f: kpt on* **9/2**3

0451 **4** 1¾ **Get Knotted (IRE)**21 5434 5-9-10 **99** (p) PaulMulrennan 5 100
(Michael Dods) *hld up in tch: smooth hdwy to trck ldrs 2f out: effrt over 1f out: ev ch ent fnl f: sn drvn and kpt on one pce* **3/1**2

1005 **5** ½ **Normandy Barriere (IRE)**14 5662 5-9-4 **96** LewisEdmunds(3) 12 96
(Nigel Tinkler) *hld up in rr: hdwy wl over 1f out: sn rdn and kpt on fnl f* **8/1**

5253 **6** ½ **Johnny Cavagin**20 5457 8-8-4 **82** oh1 (t) AaronJones(3) 3 80
(Ronald Thompson) *hld up: hdwy 2f out: chsd ldrs over 1f out: rdn and ch ent fnl f: sn drvn and one pce* **16/1**

5562 **7** 3 **Masham Star (IRE)**4 6024 3-9-4 **98** RoystonFfrench 8 86
(Mark Johnston) *led: pushed along over 2f out: rdn and hdd wl over 1f out: sn wknd* **11/4**1

000- **8** *nk* **Barracuda Boy (IRE)**296 7651 7-9-6 **95** PhillipMakin 6 84
(Marjorie Fife) *chsd ldrs: rdn along wl over 2f out: sn wknd* **33/1**

340 **9** 8 **Belgian Bill**59 3963 9-9-10 **99** (b) TrevorWhelan 11 67
(George Baker) *dwlt and towards rr: sme hdwy on outer 1/2-way: rdn along over 2f out: sn btn* **12/1**

5-42 **10** 6 **Fort Bastion (IRE)**219 199 8-8-11 **91** BenRobinson(5) 4 43
(Brian Ellison) *dwlt: sn chsng ldrs: cl up after 2f: rdn along wl over 2f out: sn wknd* **33/1**

1m 26.52s (0.22) **Going Correction** +0.275s/f (Good)
**WFA** 3 from 4yo+ 5lb **10** Ran SP% **119.2**
Speed ratings (Par 109): **109,108,108,106,105 105,101,101,92,85**
CSF £106.64 CT £514.69 TOTE £14.10: £3.20, £2.40, £1.80; EX 143.80 Trifecta £1484.50.
**Owner** Jkb Racing & Partners 2 **Bred** E Dafydd **Trained** Maunby, N Yorks

**FOCUS**
Not the strongest handicap for the grade, with the topweights rated 6lb below the ceiling, but it was competitive and they went a good pace. The winner is rated back to form.

## 6187 SUNBETS.CO.UK H'CAP 1m 2f 43y
**4:45** (4:45) (Class 4) (0-85,85) 3-Y-0 **£5,175** (£1,540; £769; £384) **Stalls** Low

Form RPR

-124 **1** **Alfarris (FR)**35 4886 3-9-6 **84** (p1) TomMarquand 8 93
(William Haggas) *trckd ldr: cl up 4f out: led over 2f out: sn rdn and edgd lft 1f out: sn drvn and hld on wl towards fin* **4/1**2

311 **2** *shd* **Barwell (IRE)**65 3745 3-9-1 **79** PaulMulrennan 5 87
(Michael Dods) *trckd ldrs: hdwy wl over 1f out: rdn to chse wnr ins fnl f: sn drvn and kpt on: jst failed* **7/2**1

3106 **3** ¾ **The Statesman**35 4904 3-8-8 **79** ManuelFernandes(7) 7 85
(Ian Williams) *hld up in rr: hdwy 3f out: rdn to chse ldrs over 1f out: drvn and kpt on fnl f* **9/2**3

0-16 **4** 2¼ **Redicean**52 4221 3-9-7 **85** PhillipMakin 6 86
(David O'Meara) *hld up: hdwy 2f out: rdn over 1f out: styd on u.p fnl f* **10/1**

-414 **5** ½ **Solar Cross**50 4314 3-8-11 **80** PaddyPilley(5) 2 80
(Roger Charlton) *led: rdn along and jnd 4f out: hdd and drvn 2f out: hld whn n.m.r 1f out: wknd* **4/1**2

1424 **6** 5 **True Romance (IRE)**17 5540 3-8-10 **74** JoeDoyle 1 64
(James Given) *in tch: hdwy 4f out: rdn along 3f out: sn drvn and outpcd fnl 2f* **9/1**

4200 **7** 1½ **Society Red**16 5568 3-9-1 **79** DavidNolan 4 83
(Richard Fahey) *trckd ldng pair: hdwy on inner over 2f out: rdn and clsng whn n.m.r and hmpd 1f out: wknd* **11/2**

2m 13.47s (4.07) **Going Correction** +0.50s/f (Yiel) **7** Ran SP% **114.9**
Speed ratings (Par 102): **103,102,102,100,100 96,94**
CSF £18.55 CT £64.63 TOTE £4.90: £2.60, £2.40; EX 18.80 Trifecta £67.00.
**Owner** Hamdan Al Maktoum **Bred** Ecurie Des Monceaux **Trained** Newmarket, Suffolk
■ Stewards' Enquiry : Paul Mulrennan two-day ban: used whip above permitted level (Sep 2-3)

**FOCUS**
Race distance increased by 18yds. A competitive 3yo handicap and solid form for the grade. The winner has improved with each run.

## 6188 FOLLOW SUN BETS ON TWITTER APPRENTICE H'CAP 1m 2f 43y
**5:20** (5:20) (Class 5) (0-75,75) 4-Y-0+ **£3,234** (£962; £481; £240) **Stalls** Low

Form RPR

062 **1** **Ski Blast**23 5337 6-9-3 **66** RichardOliver 5 75
(Ivan Furtado) *trckd ldrs: hdwy to ld over 2f out: rdn over 1f out: drvn and kpt on wl fnl f* **12/1**

1235 **2** 1 **Royal Reserve**12 5706 4-9-6 **72** PatrickVaughan(3) 8 79+
(David O'Meara) *hld up: hdwy 3f out: chsd ldrs over 1f out: rdn ent fnl f: sn swtchd rt and styd on wl towards fin* **8/1**

5531 **3** 3½ **Diamond Runner (IRE)**7 5950 5-8-7 **59** (b) JamieGormley(3) 6 59
(Lawrence Mullaney) *trckd ldrs: hdwy on inner: 2f out: chsd wnr ent fnl f: sn drvn and kpt on same pce* **5/1**3

0345 **4** 1¼ **Footlight**19 5470 4-9-2 **70** SebastianWoods(5) 4 68
(Richard Fahey) *trckd ldng pair on inner: hdwy and cl up 4f out: disp ld 3f out: rdn along over 2f out: drvn over 1f out: kpt on same pce* **14/1**

2322 **5** 1¼ **Sir Jack**9 5820 4-9-1 **64** PaddyPilley 11 59
(Tony Carroll) *hld up in rr: hdwy on outer over 3f out: rdn to chse ldrs over 1f out: drvn and kpt on* **4/1**2

3421 **6** *shd* **Monsieur Glory**44 4538 4-9-9 **75** (v) FinleyMarsh(3) 1 70
(Tom Clover) *led: rdn along 3f out: hdd over 2f out: drvn along wl over 1f out: grad wknd* **3/1**1

0004 **7** 1½ **Buonarroti (IRE)**23 5313 6-9-7 **73** (t) GerO'Neill(3) 10 65
(Declan Carroll) *hld up: hdwy on outer to trck ldrs 1/2-way: rdn along 3f out: wknd fnl 2f* **6/1**

56 **8** 2¾ **La Havrese (FR)**7 5950 6-8-9 **58** CallumRodriguez 7 44
(Lynn Siddall) *trckd ldr: cl up 4f out: rdn along 3f out: sn wknd* **9/1**

2012 **9** 18 **Hannington**27 5183 6-8-11 **60** (t) BenRobinson 9 10
(Michael Appleby) *a in rr* **12/1**

2m 15.25s (5.85) **Going Correction** +0.50s/f (Yiel) **9** Ran SP% **119.1**
Speed ratings (Par 103): **96,95,92,91,90 90,89,86,72**
CSF £106.88 CT £551.73 TOTE £15.90: £3.60, £2.30, £2.00; EX 146.00 Trifecta £1652.00 Part Won..
**Owner** The Giggle Factor Partnership **Bred** Juddmonte Farms Ltd **Trained** Wiseton, Nottinghamshire

**FOCUS**
Race distance increased by 18yds. A fair handicap, in which they went an ordinary pace, and it developed into two-furlong sprint. The winner is rated to the balance of his form.
T/Plt: £1,357.50 to a £1 stake Pool: £66,020.04 - 35.50 winning units T/Qpdt: £150.00 to a £1 stake. Pool: £4,496.89 - 22.17 winning units **Joe Rowntree**

# 6132 NEWBURY (L-H)
### Saturday, August 19

**OFFICIAL GOING: Soft (good to soft in places; 6.0)**
Wind: light breeze against Weather: cloudy periods

## 6189 BETFRED "SUPPORTS JACK BERRY HOUSE" H'CAP (DIV I) 1m 2f
**1:20** (1:22) (Class 4) (0-85,84) 3-Y-0+ **£5,175** (£1,540; £769; £384) **Stalls** Centre

Form RPR

3021 **1** **Nathan**15 5589 3-9-7 **84** FergusSweeney 6 94+
(Alan King) *lw: hld up last pair: hdwy over 3f out: shkn up and drifted lft over 1f out: rdn to ld jst over 1f out: drifted rt: styd on strly: readily* **9/4**1

6301 **2** 1½ **Doctor Bartolo (IRE)**51 4254 3-9-4 **81** JimCrowley 8 87
(Charles Hills) *lw: mid-div: hdwy 3f out: rdn to chse ldrs 2f out: styd on fnl f: wnt 2nd towards fin* **4/1**2

4213 **3** *nk* **Fast And Hot (IRE)**19 5475 4-9-2 **79** (b) TinaSmith(7) 4 84
(Richard Hannon) *travelled strly: trckd ldr: led 4f out: rdn and hdd jst over 1f out: styd on tl no ex fnl 75yds* **10/1**

0453 **4** 5 **Reaver (IRE)**35 4882 4-9-13 **83** CharlesBishop 5 78
(Eve Johnson Houghton) *mid-div: hdwy over 3f out: rdn to chse ldr 2f out tl over 1f out: no ex ins fnl f* **10/1**

40-2 **5** 3 **See The Rock (IRE)**79 3249 7-9-13 **83** (h) FranBerry 9 72
(Jonjo O'Neill) *hld up last: rdn over 3f out: styd on fnl 2f but nt pce to get on terms* **33/1**

2353 **6** 6 **Warp Factor (IRE)**30 5071 4-9-9 **79** TadhgO'Shea 7 56
(John Patrick Shanahan, Ire) *trckd ldrs: rdn over 2f out: wknd over 1f out* **16/1**

661 **7** 10 **Lightly Squeeze**23 5319 3-9-1 **78** (p) DavidProbert 2 36
(Philip Hide) *led tl 4f out: sn rdn: wknd over 1f out* **15/2**

5052 **8** 1¼ **Mikmak**10 5781 4-9-9 **79** (b) SilvestreDeSousa 1 34
(William Muir) *lw: racd keenly: trckd ldrs: rdn over 2f out: wknd over 1f out* **7/1**3

4126 **9** 7 **Ray's The Money (IRE)**16 5568 3-8-13 **83** (v) TristanPrice(7) 3 25
(Michael Bell) *mid-div: hdwy over 3f out: effrt over 2f out: wknd qckly* **7/1**3

2m 9.29s (0.49) **Going Correction** +0.275s/f (Good)
**WFA** 3 from 4yo+ 7lb **9** Ran SP% **114.5**
Speed ratings (Par 105): **109,107,107,103,101 96,88,87,81**
CSF £10.89 CT £72.77 TOTE £3.00: £1.30, £1.70, £2.20; EX 12.60 Trifecta £64.40.
**Owner** Normandie Stud Ltd **Bred** Normandie Stud Ltd **Trained** Barbury Castle, Wilts
■ Stewards' Enquiry : Fergus Sweeney caution: careless riding

**FOCUS**
After the first Fran Berry said: "It's gluey and tacky ground, and drying out after the rain yesterday." David Probert said: "It's certainly slow" and Charles Bishop said: It's drying out but fairly dead." There was headwind in the straight. The rail was moved overnight, putting it 4yds from the inside line at the 8f and 5f bends. The effect on round course distances was to add 14.5yds. An improving winner of this ordinary handicap, in which they raced down the centre in the straight. The form looks the best guide.

## 6190 DENFORD STKS (LISTED RACE) (FORMERLY THE WASHINGTON SINGER STAKES) 7f (S)
**1:50** (1:53) (Class 1) 2-Y-0
**£14,461** (£5,482; £2,743; £1,366; £685; £344) **Stalls** Centre

Form RPR

0101 **1** **Hey Gaman**21 5424 2-9-1 **103** MartinHarley 1 102
(James Tate) *lw: mde all: rdn ins fnl f: fnd enough whn strly chal fnl 120yds: drifted lft: hld on* **10/3**3

1 **2** *shd* **Red Mist**24 5301 2-9-1 **0** SilvestreDeSousa 3 102
(Simon Crisford) *q str: lw: hld up 4th: rdn and hdwy over 1f out: str chal fnl 120yds: drifted lft: kpt on* **9/4**1

0132 **3** 1 ¾ **Another Batt (IRE)**[21] 5395 2-9-1 101 .......................... RobertWinston 4 97
(George Scott) *trckd wnr: rdn and ev ch over 1f out: kpt on tl no ex fnl 120yds* **9/2**

31 **4** *nk* **Learn By Heart**[50] 4297 2-9-1 0 .......................... AndreaAtzeni 2 97
(William Haggas) *neat: trckd ldrs: rdn 2f out: kpt on fnl f but nt pce to chal* **5/2[2]**

3 **5** *3* **Ann Without An E**[16] 5573 2-8-10 0 .......................... TedDurcan 5 84
(Mick Channon) *s.i.s: last pair: effrt 2f out: sn one pce* **20/1**

2 **6** *hd* **Ripley (IRE)**[16] 5573 2-8-10 0 .......................... FranBerry 6 84
(Charles Hills) *hld up: rdn over 1f out: nt pce to get involved* **16/1**

1m 28.79s (3.09) **Going Correction** +0.275s/f (Good) **6** Ran SP% **111.2**
Speed ratings (Par 102): **93,92,90,90,87 86**
CSF £11.05 TOTE £3.90: £2.00, £1.70; EX 11.00 Trifecta £24.80.
**Owner** Sultan Ali **Bred** Rabbah Bloodstock Limited **Trained** Newmarket, Suffolk
■ Master Of Wine was withdrawn. Price at time of withdrawal 16-1. Rule 4 \n\x\x does not apply

**FOCUS**
A fine finish to the Listed race, which has been won in recent seasons by later Group 1 winners Just The Judge, Belardo and Somewhat (when renamed It's Somewhat in Australia). They initially raced in Indian file down the centre, moved more towards the stands' rail from halfway then the first two veered over to the far side.

## 6191 BETFRED GEOFFREY FREER STKS (GROUP 3) 1m 5f 61y
**2:25** (2:26) (Class 1) 3-Y-O+
**£34,026** (£12,900; £6,456; £3,216; £1,614; £810) **Stalls** Centre

Form RPR

-111 **1** **Defoe (IRE)**[29] 5095 3-8-10 110 .......................... AndreaAtzeni 4 116+
(Roger Varian) *hld up: smooth hdwy to ld wl over 1f out: shkn up ins fnl f: a doing enough: shade cosily* **13/8[1]**

6240 **2** ¾ **Wall Of Fire (IRE)**[71] 3553 4-9-5 107 ..........(b) JosephineGordon 9 114
(Hugo Palmer) *lw: hld up: rdn and hdwy over 1f out: cl 2nd whn short of room on rails and snatched up ent fnl f: swtchd lft then drifted lft: kpt on fnl 120yds but a being hld* **14/1**

122 **3** 3 ½ **Frontiersman**[37] 4814 4-9-5 117 ..........(p) JimCrowley 8 109
(Charlie Appleby) *in tch: tk clsr order 4f out: led briefly 2f out: sn rdn: lost 2nd ent fnl f: no ex fnl 120yds* **15/8[2]**

1-40 **4** 2 ½ **Crimean Tatar (TUR)**[92] 2803 4-9-5 109 ..........(b[1]) MartinHarley 5 105
(Hugo Palmer) *in tch: rdn over 2f out: wnt 4th over 1f out: styd on same pce* **25/1**

30-0 **5** 2 ¾ **Harlequeen**[16] 5569 4-9-2 107 .......................... SilvestreDeSousa 3 98
(Mick Channon) *trckd ldrs effrt over 2f out: sn hld* **25/1**

0/4- **6** ¾ **Agent Murphy**[539] 757 6-9-5 109 .......................... JimmyFortune 6 100
(Brian Meehan) *trckd ldr: rdn and ev ch briefly 2f out:* **16/1**

-315 **7** 2 ¾ **The Tartan Spartan (IRE)**[22] 5388 4-9-5 102 .......... TadhgO'Shea 1 96
(John Patrick Shanahan, Ire) *in tch: rdn 3f out: nt pce to threaten: wknd jst over 1f out* **16/1**

12-1 **8** *hd* **To Eternity**[14] 5658 4-9-2 103 .......................... FranBerry 7 92
(John Gosden) *lw: led: rdn and hdd 2f out: wknd jst over 1f out* **9/2[3]**

2m 51.5s (-0.50) **Going Correction** +0.275s/f (Good)
**WFA** 3 from 4yo+ 9lb **8** Ran SP% **117.2**
Speed ratings (Par 113): **112,111,109,107,106 105,104,103**
CSF £26.76 TOTE £2.50: £1.10, £3.50, £1.20; EX 25.30 Trifecta £71.60.
**Owner** Sheikh Mohammed Obaid Al Maktoum **Bred** Darley **Trained** Newmarket, Suffolk
■ Stewards' Enquiry : Fran Berry trainer's rep said filly was not suited by the soft, good to soft in places going, which was in his opinion holding
Andrea Atzeni caution: careless riding

**FOCUS**
Race run over an additional 14.5yds. A fair edition of this Group 3 event. They gradually tacked over to the stands' side in the straight, and it seemed an advantage to be nearer the rail than wider out. The winner and second were both held up. Defoe is not far off the St Leger principals on form now. The runner-up seems the key.

## 6192 BETFRED TV LADIES DAY H'CAP 7f (S)
**3:00** (3:01) (Class 3) (0-95,95) 3-Y-O+
**£12,450** (£3,728; £1,864; £932; £466; £234) **Stalls** Centre

Form RPR

0000 **1** **Squats (IRE)**[21] 5393 5-9-7 **95** .......................... GeorgiaCox[(5)] 11 106
(William Haggas) *lw: hld up last trio: travelling wl on heels of ldrs whn nt clr run over 1f out: qckd up sharply to ld ent fnl f: r.o: readily* **7/1[2]**

6205 **2** ¾ **Graphite Storm**[24] 5294 3-8-13 **87** .......................... JimCrowley 16 95+
(Clive Cox) *hld up: hdwy whn nt clr run over 1f out: r.o strly whn clr ent fnl f: clsng on wnr fnl 75yds but a being hld* **8/1[3]**

5000 **3** 2 ¼ **Sir Roderic (IRE)**[15] 5594 4-9-7 **90** ..........(t) DavidProbert 5 93
(Rod Millman) *mid-div: hdwy 2f out: rdn and ev ch briefly ent fnl f: kpt on but nt pce of front pair* **10/1**

3223 **4** ¾ **Ionization (IRE)**[46] 4475 4-9-10 **93** .......................... TadhgO'Shea 10 94
(John Patrick Shanahan, Ire) *slowly away: last pair: rdn and hdwy whn swtchd lft over 1f out: kpt on ins fnl f but nt pce to threaten* **8/1[3]**

4061 **5** *hd* **Theodorico (IRE)**[14] 5669 4-9-7 **90** .......................... JosephineGordon 9 91
(David Loughnane) *trckd ldr: rdn to ld over 1f out: hdd ent fnl f: no ex* **8/1[3]**

1352 **6** *nk* **Noble Peace**[17] 5530 4-9-4 **87** .......................... MartinHarley 1 87
(Henry Candy) *lw: mid-div: rdn 2f out: hdwy whn nt clr run ent fnl f: kpt on but hld after* **4/1[1]**

0621 **7** *1* **Mountain Rescue (IRE)**[15] 5610 5-9-8 **91** .......................... TedDurcan 3 88
(Chris Wall) *trckd ldrs: rdn and ev ch over 1f out: wknd ent fnl f* **4/1[1]**

20-2 **8** 1 ¼ **Francisco**[24] 5304 5-8-11 **80** .......................... CharlesBishop 12 74
(Tony Carroll) *lw: led: rdn whn strly chal 2f out: hdd over 1f out: fdd fnl f* **25/1**

4000 **9** *nk* **Mullionheir**[35] 4887 5-8-10 **79** .......................... KierenFox 6 72
(John Best) *trckd ldrs: rdn and ev ch jst over 1f out: wknd fnl 150yds* **8/1[3]**

165- **10** *6* **Fighting Temeraire (IRE)**[315] 7153 4-9-10 **93** .......... RobertWinston 13 71
(Dean Ivory) *mid-div: rdn 2f out: sn wknd* **10/1**

1m 28.06s (2.36) **Going Correction** +0.275s/f (Good)
**WFA** 3 from 4yo+ 5lb **10** Ran SP% **119.0**
Speed ratings (Par 107): **97,96,93,92,92 92,91,89,89,82**
CSF £63.18 CT £578.83 TOTE £7.40: £2.20, £2.60, £3.20; EX 68.10 Trifecta £679.90.
**Owner** Sheikh Rashid Dalmook Al Maktoum **Bred** Paul McEnery **Trained** Newmarket, Suffolk

**FOCUS**
A decent handicap, but half a dozen non-runners weakened it. Again the field converged on the stands' side in the latter stages. The winner is rated back to form.

## 6193 BETFRED HUNGERFORD STKS (GROUP 2) 7f (S)
**3:35** (3:36) (Class 1) 3-Y-O+
**£85,065** (£32,250; £16,140; £8,040; £4,035; £2,025) **Stalls** Centre

Form RPR

200- **1** **Massaat (IRE)**[373] 5329 4-9-6 116 .......................... JimCrowley 4 118
(Owen Burrows) *lw: trckd ldrs: led over 1f out: rdn clr: kpt on wl* **12/1**

6-40 **2** 1 ¾ **Librisa Breeze**[18] 5502 5-9-6 112 .......................... RobertWinston 5 113
(Dean Ivory) *hld up: hdwy 2f out: w.w bhd ldrs: nt best of runs whn pushed through ent fnl f: r.o to chse wnr fnl 140yds but a being hld* **13/8[1]**

03-6 **3** ½ **Nathra (IRE)**[22] 5352 4-9-3 108 .......................... FranBerry 7 109
(John Gosden) *trckd ldrs: shkn up 2f out: rdn ent fnl f: edgd lft but r.o wl fnl 140yds* **6/1[3]**

3531 **4** 1 ½ **Breton Rock (IRE)**[18] 5502 7-9-9 113 .......................... AndreaAtzeni 11 111+
(David Simcock) *hld up: nudged along bhd ldrs whn nt clr run ent fnl f: r.o wl but no ch fnl 140yds* **11/2[2]**

6020 **5** *hd* **Sir Dancealot (IRE)**[14] 5640 3-9-1 110 .......................... DanielMuscutt 10 106
(David Elsworth) *lw: trckd ldrs: led 2f out: rdn: hung lft: and hdd over 1f out: no ex fnl f* **14/1**

0-42 **6** *2* **Ibn Malik (IRE)**[28] 5137 4-9-6 107 .......................... SilvestreDeSousa 1 103
(Charles Hills) *led: rdn and hdd 2f out: disputing cl 3rd but hld whn bmpd ent fnl f: fdd* **8/1**

5252 **7** *hd* **Kaspersky (IRE)**[35] 4884 6-9-6 113 .......................... MartinHarley 2 102
(Jane Chapple-Hyam) *trckd ldrs: rdn w ch over 1f out: wknd ins fnl f* **11/2[2]**

-304 **8** *11* **Poet's Vanity**[84] 3078 3-8-12 103 .......................... DavidProbert 3 68
(Andrew Balding) *racd alone nrest stands' side: in tch: rdn over 2f out: sn btn* **16/1**

1m 25.84s (0.14) **Going Correction** +0.275s/f (Good)
**WFA** 3 from 4yo+ 5lb **8** Ran SP% **114.5**
Speed ratings (Par 115): **110,108,107,105,105 103,102,90**
CSF £32.09 TOTE £13.00: £3.30, £1.20, £1.70; EX 38.70 Trifecta £194.90.
**Owner** Hamdan Al Maktoum **Bred** Shadwell Estate Company Limited **Trained** Lambourn, Berks

**FOCUS**
A reasonable renewal of this Group 2 contest, run 3.74sec outside standard. The field raced in a cluster down the middle, with the exception of the filly in last. Massaat is rated back to his Guineas form.

## 6194 BETFRED PROUD TO WORK WITH SIMPSON GROUP EBF MAIDEN STKS (PLUS 10 RACE) 1m 4f
**4:05** (4:06) (Class 3) 3-Y-O **£9,703** (£2,887; £1,443; £721) **Stalls** Centre

Form RPR

3 **1** **Gold Star**[22] 5364 3-9-2 0 .......................... EdwardGreatrex[(3)] 11 90+
(Saeed bin Suroor) *str: trckd ldrs: shkn up to ld jst over 1f out: styd on strly: comf* **2/1[1]**

0-22 **2** *3* **Reverend Jacobs**[21] 5404 3-9-5 78 .......................... SilvestreDeSousa 2 83
(William Haggas) *led: rdn 2f out: hdd jst over 1f out: styd on but nt pce of wnr* **11/4[2]**

**3** 1 ¼ **Erdogan** 3-9-5 0 .......................... JimmyFortune 12 81+
(John Gosden) *str: bit bkwd: mid-div: rdn into 4th 2f out: styd on to go 3rd ins fnl f but no threat to front pair* **7/2[3]**

5 **4** 3 ¾ **Ancient Longing**[21] 5428 3-9-0 0 .......................... JimCrowley 10 70
(Roger Charlton) *unf: trckd ldr tl rdn 2f out: sn hld: styd on same pce fnl f* **7/1**

0-3 **5** 2 ¼ **Zeelander**[11] 5757 3-9-5 0 .......................... AndreaAtzeni 5 71
(Roger Varian) *q str: mid-div: rdn over 2f out: styd on same pce* **12/1**

0252 **6** ½ **Footman (GER)**[24] 5298 3-9-5 81 .......................... FranBerry 9 71
(Richard Hughes) *trckd ldrs: rdn over 2f out: nt pce to chal: fdd ins fnl f* **16/1**

0 **7** 1 ¼ **Kirkland Forever**[31] 5022 3-9-0 0 .......................... TedDurcan 7 64
(Brendan Powell) *leggy: mid-div: rdn over 2f out: nvr any imp* **100/1**

40 **8** *nk* **Seinfeld**[26] 5220 3-9-5 0 .......................... FergusSweeney 8 68
(David Simcock) *w'like: hld up towards rr: rdn over 1f out: styd on but nvr pce ins fnl f: nvr threatened* **66/1**

**9** 1 ¼ **Towie (IRE)** 3-9-5 0 .......................... RobertWinston 1 66
(Hughie Morrison) *q tall: lengthy: s.i.s: towards rr: rdn and sme prog jst over 1f out: no further imp fnl f* **20/1**

**10** *1* **Dock Of The Bay** 3-9-5 0 .......................... CharlesBishop 3 65
(Mick Channon) *w'like: s.i.s: towards rr: sme prog u.p over 1f out: wknd ins fnl f* **25/1**

6 **11** ½ **Golden Set**[14] 5632 3-9-0 0 .......................... DanielMuscutt 4 59
(James Fanshawe) *q lengthy: mid-div: rdn over 2f out: wknd fnl f* **40/1**

**12** *42* **Farage (IRE)** 3-9-0 0 .......................... TadhgO'Shea 6
(John Patrick Shanahan, Ire) *w'like: bit on the leg: s.i.s: a towards rr: lost tch 2f out* **25/1**

2m 37.89s (2.39) **Going Correction** +0.275s/f (Good) **12** Ran SP% **125.7**
Speed ratings (Par 104): **103,101,100,97,96 95,95,94,93,93 92,64**
CSF £7.55 TOTE £3.00: £1.30, £1.30, £1.80; EX 8.60 Trifecta £27.10.
**Owner** Godolphin **Bred** Darley **Trained** Newmarket, Suffolk

**FOCUS**
Race run over an additional 14.5yds. Some backward types in this maiden, but a nice effort from the winner, who, like the second and fourth, is by Nathaniel. They came down the middle again. The form looks sound amongst the principals.

## 6195 BETFRED "SUPPORTS JACK BERRY HOUSE" H'CAP (DIV II) 1m 2f
**4:40** (4:40) (Class 4) (0-85,83) 3-Y-O+ **£5,175** (£1,540; £769; £384) **Stalls** Centre

Form RPR

-202 **1** **Capton**[22] 5363 4-9-10 **79** .......................... FergusSweeney 7 85
(Henry Candy) *mde all: jnd 2f out: sn rdn: styd on wl fnl f* **9/2[2]**

2310 **2** ½ **Fast Dancer (IRE)**[14] 5643 5-9-11 **83** .......................... EdwardGreatrex[(3)] 8 88
(Joseph Tuite) *hld up last pair: hdwy whn swtchd rt 2f out: sn rdn: styd on wl ins fnl f: wnt 2nd fnl 120yds: clsng on wnr at fin* **4/1[1]**

5020 **3** 1 ¼ **Parish Boy**[23] 5313 5-9-9 **78** .......................... SilvestreDeSousa 1 81
(David Loughnane) *hld up: hdwy over 4f out: rdn in cl 3rd 2f out: styd on same pce fnl f* **8/1**

6001 **4** ½ **Native Soldier (IRE)**[44] 4537 3-9-2 **78** .......................... DanielMuscutt 6 80
(John Flint) *mid-div: hdwy fr 2f out: rdn for str chal 2f out: no ex ins fnl f: lost 2 pls fnl 120yds* **11/1**

4420 **5** *6* **Tamayef (IRE)**[21] 5404 3-9-1 **77** .......................... JosephineGordon 5 67
(Hugo Palmer) *trckd ldr tl rdn 2f out: wknd fnl f* **15/2**

0003 **6** 1 ¼ **Top Beak (IRE)**[45] 4498 4-9-12 **81** ..........(t) KierenFox 2 68
(Michael Attwater) *trckd ldrs: rdn over 2f out: wknd ent fnl f* **8/1**



The Form Book Flat, Raceform Ltd, Newbury, RG14 5SJ

42-0 **7** *shd* **So Celebre (GER)**[65] 3744 4-9-7 **76** FranBerry 3 63
(Ian Williams) *lw: trckd ldrs: rdn over 2f out: wknd over 1f out* **6/1**[3]

01- **8** *43* **Black Bolt (IRE)**[291] 7733 3-9-6 **82** AndreaAtzeni 4
(Richard Hannon) *stmbld leaving stalls: towards rr: struggling 4f out: wknd over 2f out: sn eased* **4/1**[1]

2m 10.03s (1.23) **Going Correction** +0.275s/f (Good)
**WFA** 3 from 4yo+ 7lb **8** Ran SP% **114.8**
Speed ratings (Par 105): **106,105,104,104,99 98,98,63**
CSF £22.95 CT £138.95 TOTE £5.10: £1.80, £1.70, £2.40; EX 22.50 Trifecta £132.40.
**Owner** W P Wyatt **Bred** Dunchurch Lodge Stud Company **Trained** Kingston Warren, Oxon

**FOCUS**
Add 14.5yds to race distance. A fair handicap and once more they came down the centre. This was slower division by 0.74sec. The form is rated around the runner-up.

## 6196 BETFRED LADIES DERBY H'CAP (FOR LADY AMATEUR RIDERS) 1m 4f
**5:15** (5:15) (Class 4) (0-80,82) 3-Y-0+ **£5,615** (£1,741; £870; £435) **Stalls** Centre

Form RPR

151 **1** **Mam'Selle (IRE)**[31] 5024 3-10-0 **80** MrsCBartley 2 89+
(William Haggas) *swtg: trckd ldrs: pressed ldr over 3f out: led 2f out: sn rdn and jnd: styd on wl to assert ins fnl f* **11/8**[1]

0331 **2** *1 ¾* **With Pleasure**[15] 5590 4-9-7 **69** MissIsabelWilliams(5) 9 75
(John Flint) *hld up last pair: hdwy fr 4f out: rdn to dispute ld wl over 1f out tl jst ins fnl f: no ex* **9/1**

4224 **3** *1* **Count Simon (IRE)**[11] 5753 3-9-1 **72** PoppyBridgwater(5) 4 76
(Andrew Balding) *in tch: hdwy over 3f out: rdn in cl 3rd 2f out: styd on same pce fnl f* **5/1**[3]

4134 **4** *3 ¼* **Wefait (IRE)**[14] 5630 3-10-0 **80** MissJoannaMason 5 79
(Richard Hannon) *trckd ldrs: rdn 3f out: styd on same pce fnl 2f* **6/1**

130 **5** *¾* **What Wonders Weave (IRE)**[21] 5432 3-9-7 **73** MsLO'Neill 7 71
(John Patrick Shanahan, Ire) *trckd ldr: led over 3f out tl rdn 2f out: styd on same pce* **8/1**

2622 **6** *nse* **Whinging Willie (IRE)**[10] 5798 8-10-8 **82** (v) MissHayleyMoore(3) 8 80
(Gary Moore) *hld up last pair: hdwy 4f out: rdn to chse ldrs over 2f out: styd on same pce fnl f* **9/2**[2]

3160 **7** *22* **Belabour**[21] 5403 4-10-4 **78** MissBeckyBrisbourne(3) 3 40
(Mark Brisbourne) *swtg: in tch: rdn 3f out: wknd 2f out* **25/1**

2-00 **8** *13* **Threediamondrings**[114] 2111 4-9-1 **63** (t) MissEMacKenzie(5) 1 5
(Mark Usher) *led tl over 3f out: wknd over 2f out* **20/1**

2m 39.57s (4.07) **Going Correction** +0.275s/f (Good)
**WFA** 3 from 4yo+ 9lb **8** Ran SP% **121.0**
Speed ratings (Par 105): **97,95,95,93,92 92,77,69**
CSF £16.48 CT £52.87 TOTE £2.20: £1.20, £2.30, £1.60; EX 17.50 Trifecta £62.00.
**Owner** Highclere Thoroughbred Racing - TS Eliot **Bred** Roundhill Stud & C & M Murphy **Trained** Newmarket, Suffolk

**FOCUS**
Race run over an additional 14.5yds. A modest event run at rather a stop-start gallop. This time the runners remained on the far side in the straight. The second and third are the best guides.
T/Jkpt: Not won. T/Plt: £19.70 to a £1 stake. Pool: £146,926.09 - 5,430.71 winning units. T/Qpdt: £7.40 to a £1 stake. Pool: £10,413.24 - 1,028.84 winning units. **Tim Mitchell**

# 6140 NEWMARKET (R-H)
## Saturday, August 19

**OFFICIAL GOING: Soft (6.2)**
Wind: medium, behind Weather: cloud and brighter spells

## 6197 RANDOX HEALTH GREY HORSE H'CAP 6f
**2:10** (2:11) (Class 4) (0-85,91) 3-Y-0+
**£12,450** (£3,728; £1,864; £932; £466; £234) **Stalls** Low

Form RPR

5422 **1** **Case Key**[31] 5035 4-9-1 **73** (p) BenCurtis 9 78
(Michael Appleby) *chsd ldr: rdn and ev ch 2f out: sustained chal u.p to ld 100yds: hld on gamely towards fin: all out* **8/1**[3]

6346 **2** *nse* **Zebulon (IRE)**[6] 5961 3-8-13 **74** SeanLevey 7 79
(Richard Hannon) *led: rdn 2f out: drvn and maintained narrow advantage over 1f out tl hdd 100yds out: battled bk gamely u.p towards fin: jst hld* **25/1**

-663 **3** *nk* **Vincenzo Coccotti (USA)**[51] 4256 5-8-5 **66** HollieDoyle(3) 10 70
(Ken Cunningham-Brown) *hld up in tch in midfield: effrt and hdwy over 1f out: str chal ins fnl f: styd on wl u.p towards fin* **8/1**[3]

4420 **4** *hd* **Buccaneers Vault (IRE)**[12] 5696 5-9-1 **73** PatDobbs 6 76
(Paul Midgley) *stdd s: t.k.h: chsd ldrs: clsd to join ldrs 1/2-way: drvn and ev ch over 1f out: sustained chal fnl f: unable qck cl home* **10/1**

0066 **5** *¾* **Syrian Pearl**[18] 5513 6-9-7 **79** HarryBentley 5 80+
(Chris Wall) *stdd s: hld up in tch in last quartet: clsd and nt clr run over 1f out: tl swtchd rt jst ins fnl f: styd on wl fnl 100yds: wnt 4th last strides* **11/2**[2]

3401 **6** *nk* **Le Manege Enchante (IRE)**[4] 6046 4-8-2 **60** 6ex.. (v) PatrickMathers 11 61
(Derek Shaw) *hld up wl in tch in midfield: effrt to chse ldrs over 1f out: stl pressing ldrs and keeping on whn squeezed for room and hmpd ins fnl f: kpt on same pce towards fin* **14/1**

0-00 **7** *nk* **He's My Boy (IRE)**[44] 4542 6-8-6 **67** (v) GeorgeWood(3) 4 66
(James Fanshawe) *stdd s: hld up in tch in last quartet: effrt and switching lft over 1f out: drvn to chse ldrs ins fnl f: kpt on same pce towards fin* **20/1**

-511 **8** *½* **Dark Power (IRE)**[6] 5959 3-10-2 **91** 6ex (t) AdamKirby 13 88
(Clive Cox) *t.k.h: hld up wl in tch in midfield: clsd to press ldrs 1/2-way: drvn over 1f out: no ex u.p ins fnl f: wknd fnl 75yds* **7/4**[1]

1140 **9** *½* **Champagne Bob**[9] 5827 5-7-12 **63** GabrieleMalune(7) 8 59
(Richard Price) *t.k.h: chsd ldrs: rdn over 1f out: unable qck and sltly outpcd 1f out: kpt on same pce ins fnl f* **14/1**

-024 **10** *1 ¼* **Time Medicean**[9] 5817 11-7-7 **58** oh2 (t) SophieRalston(7) 3 50
(Tony Carroll) *hld up in tch in rr: struggling and outpcd 2f out: styd on ins fnl f: no threat to ldrs* **25/1**

-505 **11** *1* **Fareeq**[15] 5606 3-9-0 **75** (t) TomEaves 12 64
(Charlie Wallis) *sn stdd bk and hld up in last trio: rdn 2f out: sn outpcd: wl hld and kpt on same pce fnl ins fnl f* **50/1**

0630 **12** *2 ¼* **Jersey Breeze (IRE)**[8] 5869 4-9-6 **78** JFEgan 1 59
(Mick Channon) *in tch in midfield: lost pl and rdn 2f out: sn struggling: bhd ins fnl f* **16/1**

1m 13.54s (1.04) **Going Correction** +0.15s/f (Good)
**WFA** 3 from 4yo+ 3lb **12** Ran SP% **116.7**
Speed ratings (Par 105): **99,98,98,98,97 96,96,95,95,93 92,89**
CSF £195.98 CT £1648.82 TOTE £5.80: £2.10, £5.80, £2.50; EX 164.60 Trifecta £2862.60.
**Owner** Terry Pryke **Bred** Lady Cobham **Trained** Oakham, Rutland

**FOCUS**
Race distances increased 20yds for races 5 & 6. The going was soft ahead of the opener, after which Harry Bentley called it "a bit dead, but not soft", while Pat Dobbs described it as being "on the soft side of good". A competitive sprint handicap for grey horses in which the last two winners followed up in valuable events. They didn't go fast and ended up in a heap down the centre, the first two holding prominent positions throughout. A bunch finish and ordinary form.

## 6198 RANDOX HEALTH H'CAP 6f
**2:45** (2:45) (Class 2) (0-105,105) 3-Y-0
**£28,012** (£8,388; £4,194; £2,097; £1,048; £526) **Stalls** Low

Form RPR

3053 **1** **Bacchus**[21] 5423 3-9-2 **100** AdamKirby 7 109
(Brian Meehan) *racd nr side: hld up in tch: swtchd lft and effrt over 1f out: drvn to chal 1f out: led 100yds out: styd on u.p: won on the nod: 1st of 5 in gp* **9/2**[2]

121 **2** *shd* **Dakota Gold**[22] 5383 3-8-9 **93** ConnorBeasley 5 102
(Michael Dods) *racd nr side: plld hrd: sn chsng ldrs: rdn and ev ch whn drifted lft u.p over 1f out: sustained chal u.p ins fnl f: jst btn on the nod: 2nd of 5 in gp* **4/1**[1]

1121 **3** *1 ½* **Merlin**[29] 5100 3-8-11 **95** SeanLevey 8 99
(Michael Bell) *racd nr side: led gp and chsd overall ldrs tl led overall over 3f out: rdn over 1f out: hdd and no ex 100yds out: outpcd towards fin: 3rd of 5 in gp* **11/2**[3]

-116 **4** *1 ¼* **Silent Echo**[36] 4868 3-8-7 **91** (h[1]) KieranShoemark 1 91
(Roger Charlton) *racd nr side: chsd gp ldr and chsd ldrs overall: rdn and unable qck over 1f out: outpcd ins fnl f: 4th of 5 in gp* **12/1**

1000 **5** *1 ¼* **Danielsflyer (IRE)**[21] 5423 3-9-0 **98** BenCurtis 2 94
(David Barron) *racd nr side: hld up in tch towards rr: effrt and switching lft over 1f out: no imp and styd on same pce ins fnl f: 5th of 5 in gp* **14/1**

005 **6** *nk* **Poet's Society**[16] 5574 3-8-3 **87** JoeFanning 10 82
(Mark Johnston) *racd in centre: chsd overall ldr tl over 3f out: led gp briefly 2f out but outpcd by nr side gp: wl hld and kpt on same pce ins fnl f: 1st of 4 in gp* **12/1**

-320 **7** *½* **Tommy Taylor (USA)**[21] 5423 3-9-2 **100** TomEaves 11 94
(Kevin Ryan) *racd in centre: swtchd lft after s: hld up in midfield: effrt 2f out: led gp wl over 1f out but nvr threatening nr side gp: wl hld and kpt on same pce ins fnl f: 2nd of 4 in gp* **4/1**[1]

015 **8** *3 ¼* **Eqtiraan (IRE)**[21] 5423 3-9-7 **105** DaneO'Neill 6 88
(Richard Hannon) *racd in centre: swtchd lft after s: hld up towards rr: effrt to press for gp ld but outpcd by nr side gp wl over 1f out: wknd 1f out: bhd and eased wl ins fnl f: 3rd of 4 in gp* **10/1**

1323 **9** *15* **Farleigh Mac**[24] 5272 3-8-0 **84** oh4 JimmyQuinn 9 19
(Andrew Balding) *taken down early: racd in centre: overall ldr for over 2f: rdn and dropped out qckly 2f out: bhd and eased ins fnl f: 4th of 4 in gp* **10/1**

1m 12.22s (-0.28) **Going Correction** +0.15s/f (Good) **9** Ran SP% **113.8**
Speed ratings (Par 106): **107,106,104,103,101 101,100,96,76**
CSF £22.49 CT £99.77 TOTE £5.30: £1.90, £1.60, £1.80; EX 21.60 Trifecta £111.30.
**Owner** G P M Morland,D J Erwin,John G S Woodman **Bred** D J Erwin Bloodstock **Trained** Manton, Wilts

**FOCUS**
A quality sprint handicap which served as a useful stepping stone for future Group/Listed sprinters such as King's Apostle, Eastern Impact, Hamza and Bounty Box, while last year's winner, Summer Chorus, took a valuable sprint handicap back at Newmarket. They split into two groups, and the stands' side group came out best. They didn't go flat out. The form is rated around the race averages.

## 6199 RANDOX HEALTH EBF NOVICE STKS (PLUS 10 RACE) 6f
**3:20** (3:20) (Class 4) 2-Y-0 **£4,528** (£1,347; £673; £336) **Stalls** Low

Form RPR

3 **1** **Shabaaby**[62] 3868 2-9-2 0 DaneO'Neill 7 88+
(Owen Burrows) *trckd ldng pair tl wnt 2nd ent fnl 2f: rdn to ld over 1f out: edgd rt but styd on strly to draw clr ins fnl f: readily* **9/4**[2]

31 **2** *3 ¾* **Travelcard (USA)**[31] 5026 2-9-3 0 JoeFanning 3 78
(Mark Johnston) *led: rdn and hdd over 1f out: outpcd whn swtchd lft 1f out: wl hld in clr 2nd and kpt on same pce ins fnl f* **7/1**[3]

422 **3** *3* **Rebel Streak**[18] 5504 2-9-2 82 RobHornby 2 68
(Andrew Balding) *trckd ldr tl ent fnl 2f: sn swtchd lft and rdn: drifted lft and no hdwy over 1f out: wknd fnl f* **10/11**[1]

**4** *3 ¾* **Tullyallen (IRE)** 2-9-2 0 SeanLevey 5 57
(Richard Hannon) *stdd s: hld up in tch in rr: wnt 4th 2f out: sn rdn and btn: wknd over 1f out* **8/1**

6 **5** *4 ½* **Agent Of Fortune**[23] 5334 2-8-11 0 (h[1]) SaleemGolam 1 38
(Christine Dunnett) *in tch in 4th: dropped to rr and rdn 2f out: sn bhd and wknd* **50/1**

1m 14.79s (2.29) **Going Correction** +0.15s/f (Good) **5** Ran SP% **108.7**
Speed ratings (Par 96): **90,85,81,76,70**
CSF £16.54 TOTE £2.90: £1.10, £2.10; EX 14.80 Trifecta £16.70.
**Owner** Hamdan Al Maktoum **Bred** Bearstone Stud Ltd **Trained** Lambourn, Berks

**FOCUS**
A small novice event, but an impressive winner. They didn't go flat out up the stands' rail.

## 6200 RANDOX.COM FILLIES' NURSERY H'CAP 7f
**3:55** (3:56) (Class 2) 2-Y-0 **£9,056** (£2,695; £1,346; £673) **Stalls** Low

Form RPR

041 **1** **Dathanna (IRE)**[14] 5660 2-9-3 **79** (h) AdamKirby 1 85
(Charlie Appleby) *taken down early: hld up in tch in rr: clsd and rdn to chal 2f out: led and hung lft over 1f out: styd on u.p ins fnl f: drvn out* **5/2**[1]

402 **2** *shd* **Amourice (IRE)**[14] 5660 2-8-8 **75** (h) PaddyBradley(5) 7 81
(Jane Chapple-Hyam) *racd keenly: led: rdn 2f out: hdd over 1f out: kpt on wl u.p ins fnl f: a jst hld* **12/1**

1504 **3** *2* **Elysium Dream**[14] 5659 2-9-7 **83** SeanLevey 8 84
(Richard Hannon) *chsd ldrs: effrt 2f out: 3rd and styd on same pce ins fnl f* **9/1**

101 **4** *1 ¼* **Electric Landlady (IRE)**[37] 4806 2-9-6 **82** JFEgan 2 80
(Denis Coakley) *in tch: effrt over 2f out: chsd ldrs but unable qck over 1f out: outpcd ins fnl f* **9/2**[2]

5051 **5** *4 ½* **That's My Girl (IRE)**[23] 5322 2-8-1 **66** HollieDoyle(3) 6 52
(Richard Hannon) *sn dropped to rr: nvr travelling and sn bustled along: rdn and struggling whn edgd lft 2f out: styd on to pass btn horses ins fnl f: nvr trbld ldrs* **17/2**

531 **6** *hd* **Shrewd Approach (IRE)**[11] 5735 2-8-6 **68** JoeFanning 3 56
(Simon Crisford) *awkward leaving stalls: sn rcvrd to chse ldrs: jnd ldr wl over 2f out tl unable qck whn carried lft and hmpd over 1f out: sn swtchd rt: wknd ins fnl f* **8/1**[3]

423 **7** *2* **Sultanaa**[30] 5056 2-9-1 **77** ........ BenCurtis 11 58
(Ismail Mohammed) *chsd ldr tl wl over 2f out: sn rdn: lost pl over 1f out: wknd fnl f* **8/1**[3]

453 **8** *7* **Collateral Beauty**[17] 5534 2-8-5 **67** ........ PatrickMathers 9 30
(Richard Fahey) *wnt lft: sn rcvrd and in tch in midfield: rdn over 2f out: sn struggling and bhd over 1f out: wknd* **10/1**

0410 **9** *hd* **One For June (IRE)**[28] 5150 2-8-10 **72** ........ PatCosgrave 4 35
(William Haggas) *chsd ldrs: rdn 3f out: lost pl and bhd over 1f out: wknd fnl f* **12/1**

1m 26.56s (0.86) **Going Correction** +0.15s/f (Good) **9** Ran SP% **114.0**
Speed ratings (Par 97): **101,100,98,97,92 91,89,81,81**
CSF £33.71 CT £233.29 TOTE £3.10: £1.50, £3.80, £2.30; EX 35.30 Trifecta £267.70.
**Owner** Godolphin **Bred** Godolphin **Trained** Newmarket, Suffolk

**FOCUS**
While only one of the last six winners of this nursery won again that season, it looked a good renewal with the majority making their handicap debuts. The pace looked decent.

## 6201 RANDOXHEALTH.COM H'CAP 1m 4f
**4:30** (4:30) (Class 2) (0-110,108) 3-Y-O+ **£16,172** (£4,812; £2,405; £1,202) **Stalls** Centre

Form RPR

123- **1** **Danehill Kodiac (IRE)**[316] 7117 4-9-1 **97** ........ SeanLevey 7 106
(Richard Hannon) *trckd ldr: effrt 3f out: rdn to ld 2f out: edgd rt and asserting 1f out: styd on and drew clr ins fnl f* **3/1**[2]

1030 **2** *3 ½* **Sofia's Rock (FR)**[17] 5525 3-8-9 **100** ........ JoeFanning 5 103
(Mark Johnston) *led: rdn and hdd 2f out: no ex over 1f out: swtchd lft ins fnl f: outpcd fnl 150yds: eased nr fin* **1/1**[1]

3200 **3** *3 ¾* **Jacob Cats**[7] 5913 8-9-0 **96** ........(v) HarryBentley 6 93
(William Knight) *hld up in last pair: effrt in 3rd over 2f out: drvn and no imp over 1f out: wknd ins fnl f* **20/1**

04-0 **4** *6* **Eye Of The Storm (IRE)**[18] 5500 7-9-4 **100** ........ PatDobbs 3 87
(Amanda Perrett) *dwlt: sn rcvrd to trck ldng pair: rdn over 2f out: 4th and wknd over 1f out* **8/1**

240- **5** *9* **Second Wave (IRE)**[301] 7552 5-9-12 **108** ........(h) AdamKirby 2 81
(Charlie Appleby) *hld up in last pair: pushed along briefly 4f out: rdn 3f out: sn hung lft and btn: no ch over 1f out: eased ins fnl f* **4/1**[3]

2m 33.4s (0.50) **Going Correction** +0.15s/f (Good)
**WFA** 3 from 4yo+ 9lb **5** Ran SP% **110.9**
Speed ratings (Par 109): **104,101,99,95,89**
CSF £6.51 TOTE £4.30: £1.60, £1.20; EX 7.40 Trifecta £48.00.
**Owner** Davies, Smith, Carr, Brown, Govier **Bred** Rathbarry Stud **Trained** East Everleigh, Wilts

**FOCUS**
Race distances increased 20yds. Not the most competitive of 0-110 handicaps, and they didn't go much of a pace before finishing fairly strung out. an improved effort from the winner.

## 6202 RANDOX H'CAP 1m 4f
**5:05** (5:07) (Class 4) (0-85,86) 3-Y-O+ **£5,175** (£1,540; £769; £384) **Stalls** Centre

Form RPR

2143 **1** *nk* **Okool (FR)**[31] 5033 3-9-1 **80** ........ DaneO'Neill 9 89
(Owen Burrows) *sn led: rdn and hdd wl over 1f out: stl pressing wnr and carried lft ins fnl f: rallied wl ins fnl f: nt quite getting to wnr: fin 2nd: promoted to 1st after a Stewards Inquiry* **3/1**[2]

61-0 **2** **Star Of The East (IRE)**[15] 5598 3-9-0 **79** ........ JoeFanning 5 89
(Mark Johnston) *chsd ldr tl 9f out: styd chsng ldrs: rdn to ld wl over 1f out: hung lft u.p ins fnl f: hld on cl home: all out: fin 1st: disqualified and plcd 2nd after a Stewards Inquiry* **8/1**[3]

2-10 **3** *3 ½* **Opinionate**[15] 5598 3-9-1 **80** ........ PatDobbs 4 83
(Amanda Perrett) *in tch in midfield: effrt ent fnl 2f: 3rd and no imp 1f out: wl hld and kpt on same pce ins fnl f* **3/1**[2]

566- **4** *4 ½* **Knight Music**[351] 6074 5-9-11 **81** ........ HarryBentley 3 76
(Michael Attwater) *hld up in tch: effrt over 2f out: 4th and no imp u.p over 1f out: wknd ins fnl f* **20/1**

3006 **5** *6* **Farquhar (IRE)**[15] 5609 6-10-0 **84** ........ AdamKirby 6 69
(Michael Appleby) *taken down early: t.k.h: chsd ldrs: wnt 2nd 9f out and c centre st: rdn over 2f out: lost pl qckly and btn over 1f out: wknd* **9/1**

-122 **6** *hd* **Stone The Crows**[52] 4221 3-9-7 **86** ........(p[1]) KieranShoemark 11 72
(Roger Charlton) *hld up in tch: c centre st: effrt over 2f out: sn drvn and btn over 1f out: fdd ins fnl f* **9/4**[1]

00 **7** *6* **Dolphin Village (IRE)**[49] 4357 7-9-9 **79** ........(h) TomEaves 10 54
(Shaun Harris) *hld up in rr of main gp: effrt 3f out: sn btn and bhd 2f out:* **33/1**

3100 **8** *13* **Investigation**[73] 3457 3-8-10 **75** ........(h[1]) RobHornby 8 30
(Andrew Balding) *v.s.a: t.k.h in rr: clsd and in tch after 4f: rdn 3f out: sn lost tch and bhd: t.o* **16/1**

2m 36.18s (3.28) **Going Correction** +0.15s/f (Good)
**WFA** 3 from 5yo+ 9lb **8** Ran SP% **115.5**
Speed ratings (Par 105): **94,95,92,89,85 85,81,72**
CSF £27.42 CT £77.52 TOTE £3.90: £1.30, £2.00, £1.40; EX 24.50 Trifecta £82.10.
**Owner** Hamdan Al Maktoum **Bred** Madame Maja Sundstrom **Trained** Lambourn, Berks
■ Stewards' Enquiry : Joe Fanning caution: careless riding

**FOCUS**
Race distance increased 20yds. A fair handicap in which the first two pulled away from the third, who was clear of the rest. The result was reversed by the stewards. The time was modest but the principals were unexposed.

## 6203 RANDOX FOOD H'CAP 7f
**5:40** (5:46) (Class 4) (0-80,82) 3-Y-O **£5,175** (£1,540; £769; £384) **Stalls** Low

Form RPR

31 **1** **Kynren (IRE)**[37] 4784 3-9-6 **79** ........ BenCurtis 4 90+
(David Barron) *pressed ldr: rdn and ev ch 2f out: led over 1f out and sn wnt clr w chalr: asserted 100yds out: styd on: rdn out* **9/2**[2]

0240 **2** *1 ¼* **Inner Circle (IRE)**[35] 4887 3-9-4 **77** ........ SeanLevey 10 85
(Richard Hannon) *bmpd s: chsd ldrs: clsd to join ldrs over 2f out: rdn wl over 1f out: forged ahd w wnr ent fnl f: no ex and btn 100yds out* **7/1**[3]

044 **3** *6* **Saaheq**[67] 3691 3-9-1 **74** ........ DaneO'Neill 3 66
(Brian Meehan) *sn led: rdn and hdd over 1f out: sn outpcd and swtchd lft 1f out: wknd ins fnl f* **9/1**

0140 **4** *1 ½* **Cyrus Dallin**[25] 5242 3-9-7 **80** ........ HarryBentley 7 69
(William Muir) *hld up in tch in midfield: rdn over 2f out: sn outpcd: wnt modest 4th over 1f out: no ch w ldng pair but plugged on ins fnl f* **9/2**[2]

2022 **5** *4 ½* **Patching**[10] 5813 3-8-10 **69** ........(b) JoeFanning 11 46
(Giles Bravery) *wnt rt s: hld up in last pair: clsd 1/2-way: rdn over 2f out: sn outpcd: wl btn whn swtchd lft over 1f out* **8/1**

552 **6** *1 ½* **Ember's Glow**[17] 5538 3-9-2 **75** ........ TomEaves 6 48
(Jason Ward) *chsd ldrs tl rdn and lost pl over 2f out: wknd over 1f out* **16/1**

5132 **7** *hd* **Redgrave (IRE)**[9] 5842 3-9-9 **82** ........ KieranShoemark 9 54
(Charles Hills) *short of room leaving stalls: hld up in last pair: clsd 1/2-way: rdn over 2f out: sn btn and bhd over 1f out* **9/4**[1]

1100 **8** *11* **Dark Destroyer (IRE)**[69] 3621 3-9-1 **74** ........ JFEgan 8 18
(Joseph Tuite) *hld up in last trio: effrt over 2f out: sn btn: bhd and eased ins fnl f* **9/1**

1m 25.64s (-0.06) **Going Correction** +0.15s/f (Good) **8** Ran SP% **116.6**
Speed ratings (Par 102): **106,104,97,96,90 89,88,76**
CSF £36.49 CT £275.27 TOTE £5.20: £1.70, £2.10, £2.70; EX 32.30 Trifecta £384.00.
**Owner** Elliott Brothers & Peacock & Partner **Bred** Rathasker Stud **Trained** Maunby, N Yorks

**FOCUS**
A fair handicap in which one of the least exposed runners impressed. The first two came clear but there are doubts over the depth of this.
T/Plt: £180.90 to a £1 stake. Pool: £83,115.39 - 335.29 winning units T/Qpdt: £15.50 to a £1 stake. Pool: £4,827.00 - 229.58 winning units **Steve Payne**

# 5998 RIPON (R-H)
### Saturday, August 19

**OFFICIAL GOING: Good (7.9)**
Wind: Light, half behind in straight of nearly 5f Weather: Cloudy

## 6204 CHS VEHICLES NOVICE AUCTION STKS 1m
**2:05** (2:06) (Class 5) 2-Y-O **£4,528** (£1,347; £673; £336) **Stalls** Low

Form RPR

**1** **Austrian School (IRE)** 2-8-12 0 ........ FrannyNorton 1 73+
(Mark Johnston) *rn green thrght: in rr: swtchd lft over 2f out: hdwy over 1f out: rn to ld fnl 75yds: in command after* **7/4**[2]

522 **2** *¾* **Cosa Nostra (IRE)**[19] 5465 2-9-2 79 ........ TonyHamilton 3 74
(Richard Fahey) *chsd ldrs: effrt over 2f out: sn wnt 2nd: led over 1f out: hdd fnl 75yds: hld after* **5/6**[1]

0 **3** *1 ¾* **Breathable**[8] 5876 2-8-10 0 ........ DavidAllan 6 63
(Tim Easterby) *chsd ldr: rdn 3f out: lost 2nd 2f out: unable qck over 1f out: kpt on u.p but hld ins fnl f* **15/2**[3]

000 **4** *¾* **Foxy's Spirit**[50] 4291 2-8-3 41 ........ JamesSullivan 4 54
(Tim Easterby) *led: rdn 2f out: hdd over 1f out: kpt on same pce ins fnl f* **40/1**

0 **5** *1* **Airplane (IRE)**[14] 5631 2-8-5 0 ........ RachelRichardson(3) 2 57
(Tim Easterby) *hld up: rdn over 2f out: kpt on same pce ins fnl f: nvr able to chal* **16/1**

1m 43.07s (1.67) **Going Correction** -0.025s/f (Good) **5** Ran SP% **111.0**
Speed ratings (Par 94): **90,89,87,86,85**
CSF £3.59 TOTE £2.40: £1.10, £1.10; EX 4.00 Trifecta £7.30.
**Owner** Dr J Walker **Bred** G O'Brien **Trained** Middleham Moor, N Yorks

**FOCUS**
Good ground (GoingStick 7.9) for Ripon's big day of the year. There wasn't much depth to this novice event and they finished in a bit of a heap in a slow time, but the winner defied obvious greenness to make a winning debut and he looks likely to prove a good deal better than these rivals in time. There are questions over the true worth of the bare form.

## 6205 WILLIAM HILL SILVER TROPHY H'CAP (CONSOLATION RACE FOR THE WILLIAM HILL GREAT ST WILFRID STKS) 6f
**2:40** (2:43) (Class 2) 3-Y-O+
**£12,450** (£3,728; £1,864; £932; £466; £234) **Stalls** High

Form RPR

0-04 **1** **Teruntum Star (FR)**[21] 5435 5-9-9 **91** ........(p) KevinStott 20 104
(Kevin Ryan) *racd stands' side: a.p: led overall over 2f out: rdn and hung rt fr over 1f out: pressed ins fnl f: fnd ex towards fin: 1st of 13 in gp* **12/1**

0304 **2** *nk* **Red Pike (IRE)**[12] 5705 6-9-2 **87** ........ AdamMcNamara(3) 17 99
(Bryan Smart) *racd stands' side: midfield: hdwy over 2f out: r.o and str chal ins fnl f: hld towards fin: 2nd of 13 in gp* **11/1**

6351 **3** *3 ½* **Magical Effect (IRE)**[7] 5947 5-9-4 **86** ........ JamesSullivan 14 87
(Ruth Carr) *racd stands' side: towards rr: sn outpcd: swtchd rt and hdwy over 1f out: r.o ins fnl f: nt trble front two: 3rd of 13 in gp* **9/2**[1]

4601 **4** *shd* **Guishan**[11] 5758 7-9-9 **91** ........(p) AlistairRawlinson 9 91
(Michael Appleby) *racd stands' side: chsd ldrs: rdn over 2f out: hung rt over 1f out: styd on ins fnl f: nt pce of front two: 4th of 13 in gp* **25/1**

054 **5** *½* **Singeur (IRE)**[14] 5671 10-9-0 **82** ........ DanielTudhope 4 81
(Rebecca Bastiman) *racd far side: a.p: rdn 3f out: led gp over 2f out: styd on ins fnl f: no imp on overall ldrs: 1st of 7 in gp* **20/1**

0030 **6** *hd* **King Robert**[29] 5094 4-9-6 **88** ........ GrahamLee 3 86
(Bryan Smart) *racd far side: chsd ldrs: effrt 2f out: chalng gp ldr ins fnl f: styd on: no imp on overall ldrs: 2nd of 7 in gp* **10/1**[3]

2161 **7** *nk* **The Armed Man**[14] 5671 4-8-3 **78** ........ PaulaMuir(7) 19 75
(Chris Fairhurst) *racd stands' side: chsd ldrs: rdn over 2f out: unable qck over 1f out: kpt on ins fnl f: no imp: 5th of 13 in gp* **12/1**

1510 **8** *1* **Art Obsession (IRE)**[20] 5457 6-9-0 **82** ........ BarryMcHugh 15 76
(Paul Midgley) *racd stands' side: s.i.s: in rr: outpcd 4f out: hdwy u.p 2f out: styd on ins fnl f: nt pce of ldrs: no ex fnl 100yds: 6th of 13 in gp* **25/1**

1156 **9** *½* **Hee Haw (IRE)**[14] 5646 3-8-9 **80** ........ FrannyNorton 10 72
(Paul Midgley) *racd stands' side: midfield: rdn and outpcd over 2f out: styd on u.p ins fnl f: nt clr run fnl 100yds: nt rch ldrs: 7th of 13 in gp* **40/1**

3140 **10** *shd* **Stanghow**[25] 5241 5-9-5 **87** ........ CamHardie 12 79
(Antony Brittain) *racd stands' side: chsd ldrs: rdn to chal 2f out: unable qck over 1f out: styng on same pce ins fnl f tl no ex fnl 75yds: 8th of 13 in gp* **33/1**

044 **11** *½* **Reputation (IRE)**[8] 5890 4-9-8 **90** ........(v) JasonHart 2 81
(John Quinn) *racd far side: trckd ldrs: rdn wl over 1f out: no ex fnl 75yds: 3rd of 7 in gp* **22/1**

0-00 **12** *½* **Start Time (IRE)**[14] 5669 4-9-1 **83** ........ TomQueally 5 72
(Paul Midgley) *prom: swtchd lft to r in stands' side gp after 1f: sn dropped to midfield: effrt over 1f out: looked ill at ease on trck: no imp fnl f: 9th of 13 in gp* **50/1**

0030 **13** *2* **Rasheeq (IRE)**[14] 5637 4-9-2 **87** ........ RachelRichardson(3) 1 70
(Tim Easterby) *racd far side: led gp tl over 2f out: stl there 1f out: fdd fnl 100yds: 4th of 7 in gp* **12/1**

0U05 **14** *1 ½* **Paddy Power (IRE)**[25] 5256 4-8-11 **79** ........ TonyHamilton 18 57
(Richard Fahey) *racd stands' side: midfield: rdn 2f out: wknd wl over 1f out: 10th of 13 in gp* **33/1**

5213 **15** *hd* **Lexington Times (IRE)**[7] 5929 5-9-4 **86** ........(p) JackGarritty 6 63
(Ruth Carr) *racd far side: towards rr: rdn and outpcd wl over 1f out: nvr a threat: 5th of 7 in gp* **10/1**[3]

2312 **16** ¾ **Bossipop**[12] 5705 4-9-6 **88**......(b) DavidAllan 11 63
(Tim Easterby) *racd stands' side: led overall: rdn and hdd over 2f out: wknd over 1f out: 11th of 13 in gp* **6/1**[2]

0011 **17** ½ **Related**[1] 6141 7-9-3 **85** 4ex......(b) RichardKingscote 13 58
(Paul Midgley) *racd stands' side: prom tl rdn and wknd over 2f out: 12th of 13 in gp* **12/1**

330- **18** 13 **Fendale**[302] 7497 5-9-2 **89**...... GeorgeBuckell(5) 16 21
(Antony Brittain) *racd stands' side: bhd: hung rt u.p over 2f out: nvr a threat: 13th of 13 in gp* **28/1**

2202 **19** 5 **Harwoods Volante (IRE)**[10] 5806 6-9-0 **82**......(p) JamieSpencer 8
(David O'Meara) *racd far side: hld up in rr: struggling over 2f out: eased whn btn over 1f out: 6th of 7 in gp* **18/1**

5410 **P** **Jack Dexter**[21] 5393 8-9-10 **92**...... WilliamCarson 7
(Jim Goldie) *racd far side: chsd ldrs tl wnt bdly wrong and p.u over 3f out: fatally injured* **14/1**

1m 9.96s (-3.04) **Going Correction** -0.15s/f (Firm)
**WFA** 3 from 4yo+ 3lb **20** Ran SP% **132.2**
Speed ratings (Par 109): **114,113,108,108,108 107,107,106,105,105 104,104,101,99,99 98,97,80,73,**
CSF £129.89 CT £707.67 TOTE £14.20: £3.30, £3.10, £2.00, £5.80; EX 130.40 Trifecta £1151.70.

**Owner** T A Rahman **Bred** Petra Bloodstock Agency **Trained** Hambleton, N Yorks

**FOCUS**
A competitive handicap and they predictably split into two groups but the bigger group that stayed stands' side were always holding sway and the far side runners never really looked like getting involved. Teruntum Star posted a time 1.74sec quicker than the winner of the following Great St Wilfrid. The winner built on his latest effort.

## 6206 WILLIAM HILL GREAT ST WILFRID H'CAP 6f
**3:15** (3:17) (Class 2) 3-Y-O+
**£46,687** (£13,980; £6,990; £3,495; £1,747; £877) **Stalls** High

Form RPR

00-4 **1** **Mattmu**[14] 5633 5-9-1 **100**......(p) DavidAllan 10 110
(Tim Easterby) *racd far side: mde all: rdn over 1f out: pressed and edgd lft ins fnl f: r.o gamely: 1st of 8 in gp* **25/1**

1334 **2** ¾ **Pipers Note**[7] 5911 7-9-0 **99**...... JamesSullivan 3 106
(Ruth Carr) *racd far side: trckd ldrs: rdn to take 2nd over 1f out: chalng ins fnl f: hld nr fin: 2nd of 8 in gp* **8/1**[2]

1-05 **3** nse **Shanghai Glory (IRE)**[14] 5640 4-9-2 **101**...... JamieSpencer 15 108+
(Charles Hills) *racd stands' side: hld up: hdwy 2f out: rdn to chse ldrs over 1f out: r.o ins fnl f: nt quite get to front two: 1st of 11 in gp* **8/1**[2]

320R **4** 1 **Snap Shots (IRE)**[12] 5705 5-8-8 **93**...... BarryMcHugh 5 97
(Tony Coyle) *racd far side: hld up: rdn and hdwy over 1f out: edgd lft ins fnl f: r.o: nt quite get to ldrs: 3rd of 8 in gp* **25/1**

6101 **5** ¾ **Flying Pursuit**[21] 5435 4-8-8 **96**......(p) RachelRichardson(3) 13 97
(Tim Easterby) *racd stands' side: led gp: rdn 2f out: hdd fnl 150yds: kpt on u.p but nt pce of ldrs: 2nd of 11 in gp* **10/1**[3]

1006 **6** nk **George Bowen (IRE)**[14] 5637 5-8-8 **93**......(p) TonyHamilton 19 93
(Richard Fahey) *racd stands' side: hld up: hdwy and edgd rt over 1f out: chalng gp ldr ins fnl f: no ex towards fin: 3rd of 11 in gp* **18/1**

5566 **7** 1¼ **Right Touch**[21] 5434 7-8-10 **95**...... FrannyNorton 7 91
(Richard Fahey) *racd far side: prom: rdn 2f out: unable qck 1f out: styd on same pce fnl 100yds: 4th of 8 in gp* **20/1**

-300 **8** hd **Maarek**[35] 4925 10-8-6 **96**...... KillianHennessy(5) 2 92
(Miss Evanna McCutcheon, Ire) *racd far side: in rr: rdn 2f out: hdwy over 1f out: edgd rt ins fnl f: styd on: nt trble ldrs: 5th of 8 in gp* **33/1**

0U64 **9** ½ **Growl**[14] 5640 5-9-7 **109**......(p) AdamMcNamara(3) 18 103
(Richard Fahey) *racd stands' side: in rr: rdn over 1f out: hdwy after: edgd rt ins fnl f: styd on: nvr able to trble ldrs: 4th of 11 in gp* **5/1**[1]

0020 **10** hd **Al Qahwa (IRE)**[14] 5640 4-8-13 **98**......(p[1]) GrahamLee 20 91
(David O'Meara) *racd stands' side: towards rr: pushed along over 3f out: rdn 2f out: hdwy over 1f out: edgd rt ent fnl f: kpt on: nvr trbld ldrs: 5th of 11 in gp* **14/1**

1150 **11** 1 **Classic Seniority**[14] 5640 5-8-10 **95**......(p) WilliamCarson 6 85
(Marjorie Fife) *racd far side: s.i.s: midfield: effrt to chse ldrs 2f out: edgd lft and wknd 1f out: 6th of 8 in gp* **25/1**

0-0 **12** nk **Hoofalong**[21] 5435 7-8-9 **94**......(h) NathanEvans 4 83
(Michael Easterby) *racd far side: hld up: u.p 2f out: nvr a threat: 7th of 8 in gp* **40/1**

3200 **13** nse **Eastern Impact (IRE)**[14] 5640 6-9-3 **102**......(p) JackGarritty 8 91
(Richard Fahey) *racd far side: prom: rdn 2f out: wknd 1f out: 8th of 8 in gp* **14/1**

2060 **14** 1 **Muntadab (IRE)**[21] 5435 5-8-10 **95**...... JasonHart 14 81
(Roger Fell) *racd stands' side: w gp ldr: carried hd high: rdn over 2f out: wknd over 1f out: 6th of 11 in gp* **14/1**

410 **15** 1 **Out Do**[35] 4920 8-9-5 **104**......(v) DanielTudhope 17 87
(David O'Meara) *racd stands' side: midfield: rdn over 1f out: one pce ins fnl f: eased fnl 100yds: 7th of 11 in gp* **12/1**

1515 **16** 6 **Robero**[35] 4905 5-8-11 **96**...... TomQueally 11 59
(Michael Easterby) *racd stands' side: chsd ldrs: rdn 2f out: wknd over 1f out: 8th of 11 in gp* **10/1**[3]

-500 **17** ½ **George Dryden (IRE)**[15] 5616 5-8-10 **95**......(p[1]) ShaneGray 16 57
(Ann Duffield) *racd stands' side: chsd ldrs: rdn 2f out: wknd over 1f out: 9th of 11 in gp* **14/1**

5000 **18** 2¾ **Naadirr (IRE)**[35] 4881 6-8-13 **98**......(v) KevinStott 9 51
(Kevin Ryan) *racd stands' side: hld up: u.p over 2f out: nvr a threat: 10th of 11 in gp* **16/1**

5000 **19** ½ **Nameitwhatyoulike**[21] 5435 8-8-8 **97** ow1...... GeorgeBuckell(5) 12 49
(Bryan Smart) *racd stands' side: chsd ldrs: rdn 2f out: wknd over 1f out: 11th of 11 in gp* **16/1**

1m 11.72s (-1.28) **Going Correction** -0.15s/f (Firm) **19** Ran SP% **130.1**
Speed ratings (Par 109): **102,101,100,99,98 98,96,96,95,95 94,93,93,92,90 82,82,78,77**
CSF £210.03 CT £1831.54 TOTE £32.60: £4.90, £2.60, £2.30, £5.30; EX 253.30 Trifecta £3179.20.

**Owner** James Bowers **Bred** J Bowers **Trained** Great Habton, N Yorks

**FOCUS**
A very strong renewal of this historic handicap with five horses rated 100 or higher and a topweight that brought Group One form to the table. High numbers dominated the consolation race 35 minutes earlier but, significantly, the rider of Mattmu elected to go far side from his middle stall and he made all of the running up that rail. The winner posted a time 1.74sec slower than the winner of the consolation race 35 minutes earlier. The winner is rated close to his old best.

## 6207 WILLIAM HILL RIPON HORN BLOWER CONDITIONS STKS (PLUS 10 RACE) 6f
**3:50** (3:50) (Class 3) 2-Y-O **£9,451** (£2,829; £1,414) **Stalls** High

Form RPR

01 **1** **Lake Volta (IRE)**[8] 5865 2-9-2 0...... FrannyNorton 1 98+
(Mark Johnston) *mde all: rdn over 1f out: effrtlessly wnt clr fnl 150yds: easily* **8/11**[1]

3024 **2** 5 **Simmy's Copshop**[29] 5109 2-9-2 92...... TonyHamilton 2 82
(Richard Fahey) *hld up in rr: effrt to take 2nd over 1f out: no ch w wnr fnl 150yds* **7/2**[3]

31 **3** 2 **Alkhalifa (IRE)**[28] 5151 2-9-2 0...... DanielTudhope 3 76
(Brian Meehan) *w wnr: rdn over 2f out: lost 2nd over 1f out: one pce after* **11/4**[2]

1m 13.2s (0.20) **Going Correction** -0.15s/f (Firm) **3** Ran SP% **106.8**
Speed ratings (Par 98): **92,85,82**
CSF £3.38 TOTE £1.10; EX 1.70 Trifecta £2.30.

**Owner** Sheikh Hamdan bin Mohammed Al Maktoum **Bred** Godolphin **Trained** Middleham Moor, N Yorks

**FOCUS**
A small but select field but the physically impressive Lake Volta proved a class apart and looks a Group horse in the making.

## 6208 BRITISH STALLION STUDS EBF FILLIES' H'CAP 1m 1f 170y
**4:25** (4:25) (Class 4) (0-80,79) 3-Y-O+ **£6,931** (£2,074; £1,037; £519; £258) **Stalls** Low

Form RPR

1034 **1** **Katebird (IRE)**[16] 5579 3-8-12 **70**...... FrannyNorton 4 79
(Mark Johnston) *mde all: rdn clr 1f out: styd on strly: comf* **7/1**

253 **2** 3 **Duck Egg Blue (IRE)**[23] 5319 3-8-5 **70**......(p) PaulaMuir(7) 2 73
(Patrick Holmes) *chsd ldrs: pushed along over 3f out: rdn over 2f out: kpt on to take 2nd fnl 120yds: no ch w wnr* **20/1**

243 **3** ¾ **Lucy's Law (IRE)**[7] 5950 3-8-11 **69**...... JamesSullivan 3 70
(Tom Tate) *chsd ldrs: pushed along over 3f out: rdn to take 2nd over 2f out: unable to go w wnr over 1f out: lost 2nd fnl 120yds: kpt on same pce* **4/1**[2]

4225 **4** 2¼ **Henpecked**[14] 5648 7-9-6 **71**......(p) TomQueally 6 67
(Alistair Whillans) *hld up: rdn over 2f out: sme hdwy: kpt on fnl f: nvr able to trble ldrs* **12/1**

2124 **5** ¾ **Livella Fella (IRE)**[50] 4292 4-9-12 **77**...... GrahamLee 7 71
(Keith Dalgleish) *chsd wnr: pushed along over 4f out: lost 2nd over 2f out: one pce over 1f out* **6/1**[3]

010 **6** 9 **Alexandrakollontai (IRE)**[8] 5881 7-10-0 **79**......(b) BarryMcHugh 5 55
(Alistair Whillans) *midfield: rdn 3f out: wknd 2f out* **20/1**

5353 **7** 7 **Blind Faith (IRE)**[11] 5745 4-9-13 **78**......(h[1]) JamieSpencer 1 40
(Luca Cumani) *hld up in rr: rdn 3f out: no imp: eased whn wl btn ins fnl f* **1/1**[1]

2m 4.68s (-0.72) **Going Correction** -0.025s/f (Good)
**WFA** 3 from 4yo+ 7lb **7** Ran SP% **114.0**
Speed ratings (Par 102): **101,98,98,96,95 88,82**
CSF £120.78 TOTE £8.20: £2.80, £5.40; EX 96.00 Trifecta £278.60.

**Owner** J David Abell **Bred** Peter Grimes & The Late Jackie Grimes **Trained** Middleham Moor, N Yorks

**FOCUS**
An ordinary 0-80 fillies' handicap on paper but it was dictated by the front runner who never saw another rival and ran out an easy winner. The runner-up is rated to her British form.

## 6209 ATTHERACES.COM H'CAP 1m
**5:00** (5:03) (Class 3) (0-90,91) 3-Y-O+ **£9,451** (£2,829; £1,414; £708; £352) **Stalls** Low

Form RPR

5024 **1** **Brilliant Vanguard (IRE)**[21] 5425 4-9-2 **78**......(p) KevinStott 6 91
(Kevin Ryan) *in tch: led 2f out: edgd rt over 1f out: r.o strly ins fnl f: eased fnl strides* **6/1**[3]

4150 **2** 2 **Sands Chorus**[18] 5517 5-10-0 **90**...... JamesSullivan 8 97
(James Given) *led: rdn and hdd 2f out: unable to go w wnr over 1f out: no imp after* **12/1**

0036 **3** 2 **Rousayan (IRE)**[14] 5668 6-9-4 **80**......(h) DanielTudhope 12 83
(David O'Meara) *midfield: rdn and hdwy to chse ldrs over 1f out: kpt on ins fnl f: no real imp* **7/1**

5214 **4** 1¾ **Mulligatawny (IRE)**[19] 5470 4-10-1 **91**......(p) TonyHamilton 5 90
(Roger Fell) *chsd ldrs: rdn over 1f out: kpt on same pce fnl f* **8/1**

0343 **5** 2 **Boots And Spurs**[14] 5643 8-9-1 **82**......(v) GeorgeBuckell(5) 11 76
(Scott Dixon) *chsd ldrs: rdn over 2f out: sn lost pl: one pce after* **14/1**

0-00 **6** 2 **Father Bertie**[112] 2155 5-9-13 **89**......(tp) DavidAllan 9 79
(Tim Easterby) *hld up: pushed along over 2f out: plugged on ins fnl f: nvr able to trble ldrs:* **11/1**

6013 **7** 1¾ **Shouranour (IRE)**[14] 5669 7-9-7 **86**......(b) JoshDoyle(3) 10 72
(Alan Brown) *chsd ldr to 3f out: rdn and wknd over 1f out* **16/1**

1043 **8** 9 **Two For Two (IRE)**[7] 5926 9-10-0 **90**......(p) JamieSpencer 2 66
(Roger Fell) *in rr: wnt sltly lft wl over 2f out: sn pushed along: eased whn wl btn over 1f out* **13/2**

0006 **9** 1½ **Intense Style (IRE)**[7] 5949 5-9-4 **80**......(b) JasonHart 4 55
(Les Eyre) *midfield: pushed along 3f out: hmpd wl over 2f out: wknd over 1f out* **22/1**

1465 **B** **Just Hiss**[7] 5926 4-9-11 **90**......(p) RachelRichardson(3) 1
(Tim Easterby) *hld up: b.d wl over 2f out* **5/1**[2]

-563 **F** **Mount Rock**[22] 5378 3-8-3 **71**...... NathanEvans 3
(Michael Easterby) *midfield: pushed along whn fell wl over 2f out: fatally injured* **9/2**[1]

1m 39.61s (-1.79) **Going Correction** -0.025s/f (Good)
**WFA** 3 from 4yo+ 6lb **11** Ran SP% **119.0**
Speed ratings (Par 107): **107,105,103,101,99 97,95,86,85,**
CSF £76.80 CT £530.10 TOTE £8.60: £1.50, £3.60, £2.20; EX 67.40 Trifecta £644.40.

**Owner** J C G Chua & C K Ong **Bred** Frank Moynihan **Trained** Hambleton, N Yorks

**FOCUS**
A wide open handicap on paper but the race was marred by a horrible-looking incident up the inside rail where the strongly-fancied Mount Rock came down, bringing down Just Hiss who was directly behind him. The winner improved on his recent form.

## 6210 WILLIAM HILL JOIN PLUS IN SHOP TODAY H'CAP — 1m 4f 10y
5:35 (5:41) (Class 5) (0-75,75) 3-Y-O — £4,528 (£1,347; £673; £336) Stalls Centre

Form — RPR

-214 1 **Solo Mission**[35] 4913 3-9-7 74 ......(p) TomQueally 7 — 83
(William Haggas) *chsd ldr: led over 3f out: styd on ins fnl f: in command fnl 100yds* — 13/2[3]

025 2 2 1/2 **Chocolate Box (IRE)**[37] 4809 3-9-5 72 ......(p) JamieSpencer 4 — 77
(Luca Cumani) *chsd ldrs: rdn over 4f out: rdn over 3f out: edgd lft u.p whn ev ch over 2f out: unable qck over 1f out: kpt on ins fnl f but no imp on wnr* — 10/3[2]

3056 3 1 3/4 **The Blues Master (IRE)**[10] 5799 3-9-1 68 ...... FrannyNorton 1 — 70
(Mark Johnston) *in tch: rdn over 2f out: kpt on ins fnl f: nvr able to mount serious chal* — 8/1

-216 4 nse **King's Coinage (IRE)**[14] 5667 3-9-6 73 ......(h) JamesSullivan 5 — 75
(Ruth Carr) *in rr: rdn and hdwy over 2f out: edgd rt over 1f out: sn nt clr run briefly: kpt on ins fnl f: nvr able to chal* — 22/1

2533 5 4 1/2 **Somnambulist**[7] 5921 3-9-3 70 ...... JasonHart 8 — 65
(Keith Dalgleish) *led: rdn and hdd over 3f out: rallied 2f out: wknd ins fnl f* — 16/1

332 6 1 3/4 **Epitaph (IRE)**[9] 5853 3-9-1 68 ...... TonyHamilton 3 — 60
(Michael Appleby) *racd keenly: in tch: rdn over 2f out: wknd over 1f out* — 9/1

3531 7 4 **Fire Leopard**[5] 6002 3-9-8 75 6ex ......(h) DanielTudhope 6 — 61
(David O'Meara) *hld up: rdn over 3f out: no imp: bhd fnl f* — 11/8[1]

3615 8 1 1/4 **Aelius**[28] 5163 3-9-2 69 ...... DavidAllan 2 — 53
(Michael Easterby) *hld up: rdn 6f out: nvr a threat: bhd fnl f* — 16/1

2m 36.83s (0.13) **Going Correction** -0.025s/f (Good) — **8** Ran SP% **115.7**
Speed ratings (Par 100): **98,96,95,95,92 90,88,87**
CSF £28.84 CT £177.28 TOTE £5.80: £1.90, £1.20, £1.90; EX 28.80 Trifecta £241.40.
**Owner** Mohamed Obaida **Bred** Rabbah Bloodstock Limited **Trained** Newmarket, Suffolk

**FOCUS**
Reasonably competitive for the grade but it looked hard work for some of these 3yo's up the straight. The form is rated around the second and fourth's Newbury form.
T/Plt: £578.00 to a £1 stake. Pool: £75,481.14 - 95.32 winning units T/Qpdt: £239.30 to a £1 stake. Pool: £3,428.63 - 10.60 winning units **Darren Owen**

6211 - 6213a (Foreign Racing) - See Raceform Interactive

# 5970 CURRAGH (R-H)
Saturday, August 19

**OFFICIAL GOING: Straight course - yielding to soft; round course - yielding**

## 6214a COMER GROUP INTERNATIONAL IRISH ST LEGER TRIAL STKS (GROUP 3) — 1m 6f
3:30 (3:30) 3-Y-O+
£31,769 (£10,230; £4,846; £2,153; £1,076; £538)

RPR

1 **Order Of St George (IRE)**[58] 3996 5-9-8 120 ...... RyanMoore 5 — 119+
(A P O'Brien, Ire) *pushed along briefly early: chsd ldrs: 3rd 1/2-way: impr into 2nd gng wl 3f out: led fr 2f out and drvn clr over 1f out where edgd rt: styd on under hands and heels: easily* — 1/2[1]

2 4 3/4 **Rekindling**[48] 4420 3-9-3 109 ...... DonnachaO'Brien 2 — 118
(Joseph Patrick O'Brien, Ire) *w.w towards rr: pushed along in 5th 3f out and impr between horses over 2f out: rdn into 2nd over 1f out and no imp on easy wnr ins fnl f: kpt on same pce* — 13/2[3]

3 2 1/2 **Twilight Payment (IRE)**[22] 5388 4-9-8 106 ......(tp) KevinManning 6 — 108
(J S Bolger, Ire) *cl up bhd ldr tl disp and led after 3f: pushed along 3f out: sn pressed clly u.p and hdd fr 2f out: no imp on easy wnr disputing 3rd 1f out: kpt on same pce in 3rd wl ins fnl f* — 20/1

4 1/2 **Wicklow Brave**[18] 5503 8-9-8 115 ...... ChrisHayes 1 — 107
(W P Mullins, Ire) *hld up bhd ldrs in 4th: tk clsr order in 3rd under 3f out: rdn to chal in 2nd under 2f out: sn no imp on easy wnr and lost pl over 1f out: kpt on same pce in 4th wl ins fnl f* — 8/1

5 6 **Renneti (FR)**[15] 5625 8-9-8 110 ...... PatSmullen 4 — 98
(W P Mullins, Ire) *led narrowly tl jnd and hdd after 3f: 2nd 1/2-way: pushed along in 2nd over 3f out and sn wknd into 5th* — 6/1[2]

6 9 1/2 **Aussie Reigns (IRE)**[14] 7115 7-9-8 102 ...... WJLee 3 — 85
(W P Mullins, Ire) *in rr thrght: rdn over 3f out and sn wknd* — 50/1

3m 5.44s (-3.96) **Going Correction** +0.15s/f (Good)
**WFA** 3 from 4yo+ 10lb — **6** Ran SP% **112.1**
Speed ratings: **117,114,112,112,109 103**
CSF £4.38 TOTE £1.30: £1.02, £2.40; DF 4.10 Trifecta £17.50.
**Owner** M Tabor/D Smith/Mrs Magnier/L J Williams **Bred** Paget Bloodstock **Trained** Cashel, Co Tipperary

**FOCUS**
With the previous two Irish St Leger winners on show plus an up and coming Group 2 winner, this was a strong race for the grade. However, on his day, this winner is a formidable opponent and this was impressive. He's rated to form.

6215 - 6224a (Foreign Racing) - See Raceform Interactive

# 6123 DEAUVILLE (R-H)
Saturday, August 19

**OFFICIAL GOING: Polytrack: fast; turf: good to soft**

## 6225a PRIX DE L'ORBIQUET (CLAIMER) (3YO) (TURF) — 1m 7f
1:05 3-Y-O — £9,829 (£3,931; £2,948; £1,965; £982)

RPR

1 **Micolys (FR)**[18] 5523 3-8-6 0 ......(p) JeromeMoutard(5) 9 — 68
(J-M Lefebvre, France) — 219/10

2 hd **Appalachian Spring (IRE)**[15] 3-9-1 0 ......(b) MickaelBarzalona 4 — 72
(H-A Pantall, France) — 14/5[1]

3 snk **Sermando (FR)**[26] 5235 3-9-1 0 ...... FabriceVeron 5 — 72
(F Monnier, France) — 53/10[3]

4 2 1/2 **Maison D'Or (IRE)**[18] 5523 3-9-1 0 ......(b) ChristopheSoumillon 10 — 69
(Robert Collet, France) — 61/10

5 snk **Azamix (FR)**[15] 3-9-4 0 ......(b) MaximeGuyon 11 — 72
(R Le Gal, France) — 39/10[2]

6 1/2 **Smentana (GER)**[113] 3-8-8 0 ...... CristianDemuro 1 — 61
(Waldemar Hickst, Germany) — 54/10

7 2 **Augustini (FR)**[18] 5523 3-8-11 0 ...... EmmanuelEtienne 2 — 62
(H De Nicolay, France) — 35/1

8 3/4 **Riviere Argentee (FR)**[14] 5630 3-8-11 0 ......(p) PJMcDonald 3 — 61
(K R Burke) *hld up towards rr of midfield: rdn and kpt on same pce fr 2 1/2f out: n.d* — 16/1

9 9 **Gog Elles (IRE)**[8] 5910 3-8-3 0 ...... MathieuPelletan(5) 6 — 47
(J S Moore) *t.k.h: in tch: dropped towards rr of main gp 3f out: rdn and outpcd fr over 2f out: eased ins fnl f* — 56/1

10 3 **Lady Kathleen (FR)** 3-8-8 0 ...... AurelienLemaitre 8 — 44
(N Caullery, France) — 216/10

11 dist **Alessa (GER)** 3-8-5 0 ...... ClementLecoeuvre(3) 7
(Henk Grewe, Germany) — 137/10

3m 18.5s (-0.60) — **11** Ran SP% **118.3**
PARI-MUTUEL (all including 1 euro stake): WIN 22.90; PLACE 4.10, 1.70, 2.00; DF 37.70; SF 99.60.
**Owner** Michel Ghys **Bred** S C E A Haras Du Grand Lys Et Al **Trained** France

## 6226a PRIX ETALON MUKHADRAM (CONDITIONS) (4YO+) (POLYTRACK) — 7f 110y
1:35 4-Y-O+ — £11,965 (£4,786; £3,589; £2,393; £1,196)

RPR

1 **Shadad (IRE)**[406] 4157 4-9-0 0 ...... AnthonyCrastus 5 — 75
(P Sogorb, France) — 12/5[1]

2 nk **Le Juge (IRE)**[25] 5269 4-8-9 0 ...... MllePaulineDominois(5) 3 — 74
(A Fabre, France) — 17/5[2]

3 2 **Kool And The Gang (IRE)**[7] 7-9-0 0 ...... CyrilleStefan 8 — 69
(J Albrecht, Czech Republic) — 242/10

4 nk **Sky Ship**[316] 7108 4-9-6 0 ......(p) PanagiotisDimitsanis 9 — 74
(Christos Kouvaras, France) — 28/1

5 3/4 **I Am Charlie (FR)**[20] 4-8-10 0 ...... Pierre-CharlesBoudot 2 — 62
(J-P Gauvin, France) — 77/10

6 1/2 **Atlantik Cup (GER)**[25] 5269 4-9-0 0 ...... StephanePasquier 7 — 65
(A Kleinkorres, Germany) — 197/10

7 1 1/4 **Asterina**[56] 4115 4-8-10 0 ...... GeraldMosse 6 — 58
(A De Royer-Dupre, France) — 11/2[3]

8 nse **Yeah Baby Yeah (IRE)**[15] 5628 4-8-10 0 ...... MaximeGuyon 1 — 58
(Gay Kelleway) *hld up in midfield on inner: trapped in pocket travelling okay fr 2f out: dropped towards rr appr fnl f: sltly hmpd under 1f out: rdn and styd on last 50yds but r already over* — 13/2

9 3 **Kahouanne (FR)**[119] 5-9-3 0 ...... ChristopheSoumillon 4 — 57
(G Botti, France) — 13/2

PARI-MUTUEL (all including 1 euro stake): WIN 3.40; PLACE 1.80, 1.80, 4.40; DF 7.70; SF 11.90.
**Owner** H H Sheikh Mohammed Bin Khalifa Al Thani **Bred** Barronstown Stud **Trained** France

## 6227a SHADWELL PRIX DE LA NONETTE (GROUP 2) (3YO FILLIES) (TURF) — 1m 2f
2:50 3-Y-O — £63,333 (£24,444; £11,666; £7,777; £3,888)

RPR

1 **Sobetsu**[16] 5571 3-9-0 0 ...... JamesDoyle 6 — 113+
(Charlie Appleby) *led: hdd after 1 1/2f: trckd ldrs: rdn to ld under 2f out: drvn and kpt on strly ins fnl f* — 2/1[1]

2 2 1/2 **Onthemoonagain (FR)**[21] 5449 3-9-0 0 ...... ChristopheSoumillon 4 — 108
(J-C Rouget, France) *hld up towards rr of midfield: rdn and kpt on fr under 2f out: wnt 2nd 100yds out: no ch w wnr* — 66/10[3]

3 3/4 **Senga (USA)**[62] 3881 3-9-0 0 ...... StephanePasquier 9 — 107
(P Bary, France) *hld up in midfield: gd hdwy to press ldrs under 2f out: sn rdn: outpcd by wnr ins fnl f: no ex last 100yds* — 11/5[2]

4 hd **Strathspey**[48] 4424 3-9-0 0 ...... MickaelBarzalona 8 — 106+
(A Fabre, France) *hld up towards rr: stdy hdwy fr 2f out: chsd ldrs 1f out: drvn and kpt on same pce fnl f* — 87/10

5 3 **Araaja (IRE)**[33] 4988 3-9-0 0 ...... AurelienLemaitre 3 — 100
(A De Watrigant, France) *hld up towards rr: rdn and kpt on steadily fr under 2f out: n.d* — 99/10

6 1 3/4 **Penny Lane (GER)**[41] 4665 3-9-0 0 ...... Pierre-CharlesBoudot 1 — 97
(F-H Graffard, France) *in tch: rdn 2 1/2f out: nt clr run 2f out: drvn and outpcd appr fnl f: sn btn* — 191/10

7 4 **Vue Fantastique (FR)**[21] 5449 3-9-0 0 ...... OlivierPeslier 5 — 89
(F Chappet, France) *led after 1 1/2f: hdd after 3f: chsd ldr: rdn and unable qck under 2f out: wknd qckly* — 169/10

8 1 **Ibiza (FR)**[41] 4665 3-9-0 0 ...... CristianDemuro 2 — 87
(N Clement, France) *hld up towards rr: rdn and outpcd under 2f out: sn wl btn* — 133/10

9 3 1/2 **Body Sculpt (FR)**[97] 2665 3-9-0 0 ...... AlexisBadel 7 — 80
(S Kobayashi, France) *in tch tl led after 3f: rdn and hdd under 2f out: wknd qckly* — 37/1

2m 5.94s (-4.26) — **9** Ran SP% **117.4**
PARI-MUTUEL (all including 1 euro stake): WIN 2.20 (coupled with Strathspey); PLACE 1.30, 1.90, 1.40; DF 11.60; SF 19.40.
**Owner** Godolphin **Bred** Darley **Trained** Newmarket, Suffolk

## 6228a SHADWELL PRIX DU CALVADOS (GROUP 3) (2YO FILLIES) (STRAIGHT) (TURF) — 7f
3:25 2-Y-O — £34,188 (£13,675; £10,256; £6,837; £3,418)

RPR

1 **Polydream (IRE)**[20] 2-8-11 0 ...... MaximeGuyon 10 — 109+
(F Head, France) *racd in far side gp: hld up towards rr: stdy hdwy fr 3f out: chsd ldrs 1 1/2f out: rdn to ld over 1f out: in command fr under 1f out: comf* — 8/5[1]

2 1 3/4 **Laurens (FR)**[30] 5056 2-8-11 0 ...... PJMcDonald 7 — 104
(K R Burke) *racd in far side gp: trckd ldrs: rdn 2 1/2f out: drvn and edgd lft under 2f out: led 1 1/2f out: hdd over 1f out: sn outpcd by wnr: kpt on* — 74/10

3 2 1/2 **Bonita Fransisca (FR)**[55] 4131 2-8-11 0 ...... CristianDemuro 5 — 98
(Antonio Marcialis, Italy) *racd in far side gp: in rr: rdn and hdwy fr 2 1/2f out: drvn and wnt 3rd 1f out: kpt on same pce fnl f* — 39/1

4 2 1/2 **Capomento (IRE)**[23] 5329 2-8-11 0 ...... GeraldMosse 9 — 91
(Tom Dascombe) *racd in far side gp: midfield: rdn and kpt on same pce fr 2 1/2f out* — 94/10

5 nk **Spring Cosmos (IRE)**[21] 5391 2-8-11 0 ........................ JamesDoyle 6 91
(Charlie Appleby) *racd in far side gp: overall ldr: rdn over 2f out: hdd 1 1/2f out: wknd fnl f* **66/10**[3]

6 shd **Musical Art (IRE)**[21] 5391 2-8-11 0 .................. ChristopheSoumillon 3 90+
(Paul Cole) *led gp of four in stands' side gp: rdn over 2f out: outpcd over 1f out: sn no imp* **56/10**[2]

7 3 **Fou Rire (IRE)**[20] 2-8-11 0 .............................. Pierre-CharlesBoudot 8 83
(F Chappet, France) *racd in far side gp: chsd ldr: rdn 2f out: outpcd over 1f out: wknd ins fnl f* **134/10**

8 5 **Model (FR)**[21] 5448 2-8-11 0 ............................... MickaelBarzalona 11 70
(Richard Hannon) *racd in far side gp: midfield: tk clsr order under 3f out: rdn 2 1/2f out: wknd 1 1/2f out: eased ins fnl f* **71/10**

9 2 **Ellthea (IRE)**[23] 5329 2-8-11 0 ...............................(b[1]) TonyPiccone 1 64
(K R Burke) *racd in stands' side gp: in tch: rdn and outpcd fr 2 1/2f out: eased whn wl btn ins fnl f* **43/1**

10 4 **Debutante's Ball (IRE)**[6] 5978 2-8-11 0 ..........................(p) AlexisBadel 2 54
(J S Moore) *racd in stands' side gp: in tch: rdn 2 1/2f out: sn lost pl and wl btn* **36/1**

11 3 1/2 **Lili Du Sud (FR)**[15] 5629 2-8-11 0 ............................ MathieuPelletan 4 45
(Y Gourraud, France) *racd in stands' side gp: in tch: rdn and outpcd over 2f out: sn btn: eased over 1f out* **31/1**

1m 23.21s (-5.09) **11** Ran SP% **118.2**
PARI-MUTUEL (all including 1 euro stake): WIN 2.60; PLACE 1.70, 3.00, 7.20; DF 12.30; SF 19.20.
**Owner** Wertheimer & Frere **Bred** Wertheimer Et Frere **Trained** France

**FOCUS**
A strong renewal.

## 6229a CRITERIUM DU FONDS EUROPEEN DE L'ELEVAGE (LISTED RESTRICTED RACE) (2YO) (ROUND) (TURF) 1m (R)
**4:00** 2-Y-O **£52,136** (£20,854; £15,641; £10,427; £5,213)

RPR

1 **Francesco Bere (FR)**[27] 2-9-0 0 ............................ AlexandreGavilan 2 100
(D Guillemin, France) **14/1**

2 shd **Stage Magic (IRE)**[29] 5106 2-9-0 0 ............................... JamesDoyle 1 100
(Charlie Appleby) *hld up towards rr of midfield: stdy hdwy fr 4f out: trckd ldrs 2 1/2f out: rdn to ld 1 1/2f out: drvn ins fnl f: kpt on wl tl no ex clsng stages: hdd last stride* **8/5**[1]

3 2 1/2 **Sully (FR)**[21] 5448 2-8-10 0 ................................ CristianDemuro 4 90
(Rod Collet, France) **172/10**

4 1 **Alounak (FR)** 2-9-0 0 .......................................... AntoineHamelin 6 92
(Jean-Pierre Carvalho, Germany) **13/1**

5 1 **Masterpiece (FR)**[18] 5520 2-9-0 0 .......................... VincentCheminaud 7 90
(A Fabre, France) **12/5**[2]

6 hd **Uther Pendragon (IRE)**[5] 6017 2-9-0 0 ......................(p) TonyPiccone 5 89
(J S Moore) *hld up towards rr: rdn and hdwy 2f out: wknd ins fnl f* **77/10**

7 1/2 **Myboyhenry (IRE)**[15] 5600 2-9-0 0 ................................ PJMcDonald 3 88
(K R Burke) *led: rdn under 2f out: hdd 1 1/2f out: wknd fnl f* **236/10**

8 1 1/4 **Kenshow (FR)**[14] 5679 2-8-10 0 ............................... AnthonyCrastus 9 81
(P Sogorb, France) **29/1**

P **Aussie Wind**[11] 5743 2-9-0 0 ............................... ChristopheSoumillon 8
(Hugo Palmer) *chsd ldr tl broke down and p.u sharply 2 1/2f out* **69/10**[3]

1m 44.3s (3.50) **9** Ran SP% **118.7**
PARI-MUTUEL (all including 1 euro stake): WIN 15.00; PLACE 3.30, 1.70, 3.30; DF 17.00; SF 45.20.
**Owner** Mme Gerard Lesur **Bred** Snc Regnier, F Regnier & T Regnier **Trained** France

6230 - (Foreign Racing) - See Raceform Interactive

# [5800] PONTEFRACT (L-H)
Sunday, August 20

**OFFICIAL GOING: Good (good to firm in places; 8.2)**
Wind: light half behind Weather: fine

## 6231 TREVOR WOODS MEMORIAL EBF NOVICE STKS (PLUS 10 RACE) 5f 3y
**2:15** (2:16) (Class 4) 2-Y-O **£5,175** (£1,540; £769; £384) **Stalls** Low

Form RPR

10 1 **Viscount Loftus (IRE)**[59] 3993 2-9-8 0 ..................... SilvestreDeSousa 1 86
(Mark Johnston) *trckd ldrs: rdn to ld over 1f out: kpt on wl: edgd rt towards fin* **6/4**[1]

3 2 1 1/2 **Showmethedough**[9] 5891 2-9-2 0 ............................... TonyHamilton 7 75
(Richard Fahey) *trckd ldrs: pushed along and bit outpcd over 2f out: kpt on fr over 1f out: wnt 2nd fnl 110yds* **16/1**

22 3 1 1/2 **Ginbar (IRE)**[26] 5262 2-9-2 0 ................................ RichardKingscote 3 69
(Tom Dascombe) *prom: rdn over 2f out: bit outpcd appr fnl f: kpt on same pce ins fnl f: wnt 3rd towards fin* **2/1**[2]

14 4 1/2 **Awsaaf**[71] 3576 2-9-8 0 ............................................ DaneO'Neill 2 73
(Simon Crisford) *racd keenly: led: rdn whn hdd over 1f out: no ex and lost 2 pls fnl 110yds* **4/1**[3]

5 2 1/4 **Loulin** 2-9-2 0 ..................................................... DanielTudhope 5 59
(David O'Meara) *in tch: rdn 2f out: no ex ins fnl f* **12/1**

00 6 1 3/4 **Magic Ship (IRE)**[15] 5665 2-9-2 0 ..............................(h[1]) MartinHarley 4 53
(Ollie Pears) *hld up: pushed along over 2f out: nvr threatened* **50/1**

7 1 3/4 **Feebs** 2-8-9 0 ................................................ HarrisonShaw(7) 6 47
(Michael Easterby) *slowly away: sn pushed along: hung rt and a rr* **40/1**

1m 3.25s (-0.05) **Going Correction** -0.10s/f (Good) **7** Ran SP% **111.3**
Speed ratings (Par 96): **96,93,91,90,86 84,81**
CSF £25.33 TOTE £2.60: £1.30, £5.30; EX 21.60 Trifecta £42.90.
**Owner** Mrs Christine E Budden & Partners **Bred** Mrs C E Budden & Partners **Trained** Middleham Moor, N Yorks

**FOCUS**
The ground had dried out during the morning and racing got under way on good, good to firm in places (GoingStick: 8.2). The stalls were placed on the inside for all races. A fair juvenile contest which saw the winner return to form after a two-month break.

## 6232 TOTEPOOL BETTING AT BETFRED.COM H'CAP 1m 4f 5y
**2:50** (2:50) (Class 3) (0-90,92) 3-Y-0+ **£8,409** (£2,502; £1,250; £625) **Stalls** Low

Form RPR

2044 1 **Croquembouche (IRE)**[69] 3671 8-9-3 **82** .........(p[1]) CallumShepherd(3) 3 88
(Ed de Giles) *mde all: rdn over 2f out: drvn over 1f out: 1 1/2 l up 110yds out: reduced advantage towards fin: all out* **25/1**

1326 2 nse **Melting Dew**[36] 4886 3-9-0 **85** .............................. TedDurcan 5 91
(Sir Michael Stoute) *dwlt and pushed along early: hld up in tch: rdn over 2f out: hdwy over 1f out: sn chsd wnr: styd on: jst failed* **11/4**[2]

010 3 hd **Airton**[22] 5403 4-9-3 **79** ........................................ JosephineGordon 2 84
(James Bethell) *hld up in tch: rdn over 2f out: sme hdwy appr fnl f: styd on wl fnl 100yds* **14/1**

1120 4 3/4 **Amlad (IRE)**[18] 5525 3-9-1 **86** ................................ PaulMulrennan 7 90
(Ed Dunlop) *hld up: rdn over 2f out: sme hdwy appr fnl f: styd on same pce* **9/2**[3]

1025 5 6 **Theos Lolly (IRE)**[22] 5403 4-9-4 **80** ............................ TonyHamilton 1 74
(Richard Fahey) *trckd ldr: rdn over 2f out: wknd ins fnl f* **8/1**

2501 6 13 **Mutadaffeq (IRE)**[11] 5803 4-10-2 **92** .......................... DanielTudhope 4 66
(David O'Meara) *trckd ldr: rdn over 2f out: wknd appr fnl f* **6/1**

0003 7 40 **Bear Valley (IRE)**[8] 5915 3-9-3 **88** ........................ SilvestreDeSousa 6
(Mark Johnston) *trckd ldr on outer: rdn over 2f out: wknd qckly and eased* **9/4**[1]

2m 36.99s (-3.81) **Going Correction** -0.10s/f (Good)
**WFA** 3 from 4yo+ 9lb **7** Ran SP% **111.5**
Speed ratings (Par 107): **108,107,107,107,103 94,68**
CSF £88.39 TOTE £22.90: £6.60, £1.70; EX 119.90 Trifecta £984.30.
**Owner** John Manser **Bred** Ballymacoll Stud Farm Ltd **Trained** Ledbury, H'fords

**FOCUS**
A competitive middle-distance handicap which produced a thrilling finish. The winner proved game in first-time cheekpieces.

## 6233 MOOR TOP FARM SHOP HEMSWORTH H'CAP 2m 1f 27y
**3:25** (3:25) (Class 5) (0-70,70) 3-Y-O+ **£3,234** (£962; £481; £240) **Stalls** Low

Form RPR

2145 1 **Wordiness**[9] 5896 9-9-12 **68** .............................. SilvestreDeSousa 4 75
(David Evans) *midfield: rdn and hdwy on outer over 1f out: styd on: led towards fin* **7/2**[2]

6-63 2 nk **Almost Gemini (IRE)**[13] 5700 8-10-0 **70** ..................(p) JamesSullivan 2 76
(Kenneth Slack) *in tch: rdn and hdwy over 1f out: led narrowly 1f out: styd on: hdd towards fin* **5/1**

-536 3 1 1/2 **Mcvicar**[22] 5403 8-9-0 **56** ..........................................(p) SamJames 1 60
(John Davies) *trckd ldr: rdn over 2f out: ev ch 1f out: one pce fnl 75yds* **7/1**

5200 4 nk **Madam Lilibet (IRE)**[78] 3340 8-9-0 **56** ............................ JoeyHaynes 6 60
(Sharon Watt) *hld up: rdn over 2f out: styd on wl fnl f: nrst fin* **25/1**

3326 5 1 1/4 **Hallstatt (IRE)**[43] 4630 11-9-3 **62** ......................(t) LewisEdmunds(3) 10 65
(John Mackie) *s.i.s: sn in tch: rdn over 2f out: ev ch appr fnl f: no ex fnl 110yds* **16/1**

1324 6 3 **La Fritillaire**[33] 4998 5-9-9 **65** .................................. AndrewMullen 5 64
(James Given) *trckd ldr: rdn to chal over 2f out: wknd fnl 110yds* **9/2**[3]

5632 7 1 **Ingleby Hollow**[12] 5737 5-9-12 **68** ..........................(p) DanielTudhope 3 66
(David O'Meara) *led: rdn and pressed over 2f out: hdd 1f out: sn wknd* **3/1**[1]

2105 8 1/2 **Tuscan Gold**[27] 4120 10-9-7 **63** ..........................(p) PaulMulrennan 8 61
(Micky Hammond) *s.i.s: hld up in midfield: rdn over 2f out: nvr threatened* **14/1**

0060 9 3 3/4 **Ice Galley (IRE)**[24] 5313 4-9-8 **64** ................................ PhillipMakin 9 58
(Philip Kirby) *a rr* **16/1**

3m 49.18s (4.58) **Going Correction** -0.10s/f (Good) **9** Ran SP% **116.8**
Speed ratings (Par 103): **85,84,84,84,83 82,81,81,79**
CSF £21.73 CT £116.66 TOTE £4.30: £1.40, £1.80, £2.30; EX 22.20 Trifecta £121.20.
**Owner** Mrs E Evans **Bred** Juddmonte Farms Ltd **Trained** Pandy, Monmouths

**FOCUS**
An ordinary stayers' handicap which saw the winner prevail under a strong ride.

## 6234 EBF STALLIONS HIGHFIELD FARM FLYING FILLIES' STKS (LISTED RACE) 6f
**4:00** (4:02) (Class 1) 3-Y-O+
**£31,190** (£11,825; £4,433; £4,433; £1,479; £742) **Stalls** Low

Form RPR

5032 1 **Queen Kindly**[37] 4864 3-8-13 103 .................................. TomEaves 2 100
(Richard Fahey) *mde all: pushed along over 1f out: drvn ent fnl f: kpt on: all out* **7/4**[1]

-013 2 hd **Eartha Kitt**[37] 4864 3-8-13 92 ..........................(p) RichardKingscote 6 99+
(Tom Dascombe) *dwlt: hld up inner: pushed along and hdwy over 1f out: rdn fnl f: r.o strly fnl 110yds: gaining at fin* **9/1**

-145 3 1/2 **Classical Times**[60] 3964 3-8-13 96 .............................. JackMitchell 9 97
(Peter Chapple-Hyam) *prom: rdn over 2f out: one pce fnl 50yds* **12/1**

5311 3 dht **Raven's Lady**[30] 5117 3-8-13 95 .................................. GeorgeWood 3 97
(Marco Botti) *trckd ldrs: rdn over 2f out: kpt on* **5/1**[2]

-565 5 2 1/2 **Peticoatgovernment (IRE)**[25] 5308 4-9-2 95 ............. DanielTudhope 5 89
(W McCreery, Ire) *midfield: rdn over 2f out: kpt on same pce and nvr threatened* **11/1**

0116 6 shd **Excellent Sounds**[22] 5422 4-9-2 84 ............................ CharlieBennett 1 89
(Hughie Morrison) *prom: rdn over 2f out: wknd ins fnl f* **33/1**

0153 7 hd **Savannah Slew**[24] 5317 3-8-13 87 ..........................(b) PaulMulrennan 4 88
(James Given) *dwlt: hld up: rdn 2f out: kpt on fnl f: nvr threatened* **50/1**

0-00 8 4 1/2 **Show Stealer**[37] 4864 4-9-2 89 ..............................(p[1]) MartinHarley 7 74
(Rae Guest) *midfield: rdn 1/2-way: wknd fnl f* **33/1**

5104 9 3/4 **Buying Trouble (USA)**[37] 4864 4-9-2 97 .................. AndrewMullen 8 71
(David Evans) *chsd ldrs: rdn 1/2-way: wknd fnl f* **16/1**

0115 10 1 3/4 **Staintondale Lass (IRE)**[30] 5117 4-9-2 92 ................. HarryBentley 14 66
(Ed Vaughan) *dwlt: a towards rr* **33/1**

10- 11 nk **Spain Burg (FR)**[48] 4456 3-8-13 107 ..................... JosephineGordon 11 65
(N Clement, France) *dwlt: hld up: rdn over 2f out: nvr threatened* **8/1**[3]

0210 12 2 **The Wagon Wheel (IRE)**[15] 5637 3-8-13 98 ............(b) TonyHamilton 12 58
(Richard Fahey) *midfield on outside: rdn over 2f out: wknd over 1f out* **16/1**

2-10 13 18 **Tundra**[16] 5597 3-8-13 87 ...................................... SilvestreDeSousa 15
(Roger Varian) *prom on outer: bmpd after 1f and racd keenly: rdn over 2f out: wknd over 1f out: eased* **20/1**

0111 P **Glenrowan Rose (IRE)**[15] 5647 4-9-2 99 ...................... ConnorBeasley 10
(Keith Dalgleish) *bmpd s: lost action and p.u and dismntd* **16/1**

1m 15.31s (-1.59) **Going Correction** -0.10s/f (Good)
**WFA** 3 from 4yo 3lb **14** Ran SP% **123.4**
Speed ratings (Par 108): **106,105,105,105,101 101,101,95,94,92 91,88,64,**
WIN: £2.60; PL: QK £1.40, EK £3.20, CT £1.90, RL £1.10; EX: £22.30; CSF: £17.33; TF: QK/EK/CT £106.80, QK/EK/RL £43.30;.
**Owner** Jaber Abdullah **Bred** Rabbah Bloodstock Limited **Trained** Musley Bank, N Yorks
■ Stewards' Enquiry : Tom Eaves two-day ban; used whip above the permitted level (3rd-4th Sept)

**FOCUS**
An excellent renewal of this Listed sprint which produced a thrilling finish and a talented winner who was returning to her smart juvenile form.

## 6235 ERNIE'S H'CAP 1m 6y
**4:35** (4:35) (Class 3) (0-95,95) 3-Y-O **£8,409** (£2,502; £1,250; £625) **Stalls Low**

Form RPR
4-1 **1** **Isabella (IRE)**[15] 5670 3-8-6 80 JoeFanning 1 88+
(David O'Meara) *mde all: pushed along 2f out: kpt on wl pushed out* 85/40[1]
5-10 **2** 1 ½ **Eagle Creek (IRE)**[106] 2402 3-9-7 95 HarryBentley 2 98
(Simon Crisford) *trckd ldr: pushed along 2f out: drvn ent fnl f: kpt on same pce and a hld* 9/4[2]
-330 **3** ¾ **Portledge (IRE)**[3] 6091 3-8-2 76 oh4 (b[1]) JamesSullivan 3 77
(James Bethell) *hld up in tch: racd keenly: rdn 2f out: kpt on fnl f* 12/1
14-1 **4** nk **Lomu (IRE)**[57] 4075 3-8-12 86 PaulMulrennan 6 86
(Keith Dalgleish) *in tch on inner: pushed along over 2f out: rdn over 1f out: no ex towards fin* 11/2
6302 **5** 11 **Rashford's Double (IRE)**[8] 5949 3-8-8 82 (p) BarryMcHugh 5 57
(Richard Fahey) *hld up: rdn over 2f out: sn wknd* 8/1
3600 **6** 17 **Morning Suit (USA)**[15] 5643 3-8-12 86 SilvestreDeSousa 4 54
(Mark Johnston) *trckd ldr on outer: rdn over 2f out: wknd and eased* 5/1[3]

1m 43.68s (-2.22) **Going Correction** -0.10s/f (Good) 6 Ran SP% 113.6
Speed ratings (Par 104): **107,105,104,104,93 76**
CSF £7.41 TOTE £2.70: £2.00, £1.60; EX 9.00 Trifecta £51.10.
**Owner** Sir Robert Ogden **Bred** Sir Robert Ogden **Trained** Upper Helmsley, N Yorks

**FOCUS**
A decent 3yo handicap which produced a decisive winner. The form should stand up.

## 6236 COLLECT TOTEPOOL WINNINGS AT BETFRED SHOPS MAIDEN STKS 1m 6y
**5:10** (5:10) (Class 4) 3-Y-O+ **£5,175** (£1,540; £769; £384) **Stalls Low**

Form RPR
-33 **1** **Glassy Waters (USA)**[88] 2963 3-9-5 0 JosephineGordon 2 87+
(Saeed bin Suroor) *mde all: pushed clr over 2f out: carried hd bit awkwardly: reduced advantage towards fin but nvr in danger* 1/1[1]
3 **2** 1 ½ **Caravela (IRE)**[79] 3309 3-9-0 0 CharlesBishop 9 75+
(Mick Channon) *dwlt: midfield: pushed along and hdwy over 2f out: rdn to chse clr ldr appr fnl f: kpt on* 6/1[3]
**3** 1 **Morning Chimes (IRE)** 3-9-0 0 SilvestreDeSousa 5 73+
(Mark Johnston) *dwlt: midfield: pushed along and outpcd over 2f out: rdn and hung lft over 1f out: r.o strly ins fnl f* 9/1
5 **4** 1 ¾ **Ludorum (IRE)**[15] 5670 3-9-5 0 TonyHamilton 1 74
(Richard Fahey) *trckd ldrs: rdn over 2f out: one pce* 20/1
5 **5** hd **Teomaria**[18] 5538 3-8-11 0 CliffordLee(3) 3 68
(K R Burke) *racd keenly: prom: rdn and outpcd by ldr over 2f out: no ex ins fnl f* 14/1
0 **6** 11 **Mr Slicker (FR)**[18] 5538 3-9-5 0 RichardKingscote 10 48
(Tom Dascombe) *hld up: nvr threatened* 40/1
36 **7** 1 ¾ **True Colors**[17] 5577 3-9-5 0 JackGarritty 8 44
(Richard Fahey) *hld up: nvr threatened* 25/1
63- **8** 2 **Never A Word (USA)**[282] 7906 3-9-5 0 (t) KevinStott 7 39
(Oliver Greenall) *.trckd ldrs: rdn along 3f out: wknd over 1f out* 40/1
4 **9** nk **Little Jo**[21] 5458 3-9-5 0 GrahamLee 6 39
(Chris Grant) *midfield towards outer: pushed along over 2f out: wknd over 1f out* 33/1
-043 **10** 32 **Ascot Week (USA)**[63] 3862 3-9-5 80 JasonHart 4
(John Quinn) *trckd ldrs: rdn over 2f out: wknd qckly and eased* 7/2[2]

1m 43.86s (-2.04) **Going Correction** -0.10s/f (Good) 10 Ran SP% 119.6
Speed ratings (Par 105): **106,104,103,101,101 90,88,86,86,54**
CSF £7.21 TOTE £1.70: £1.10, £1.90, £2.30; EX 8.80 Trifecta £37.60.
**Owner** Godolphin **Bred** Darley **Trained** Newmarket, Suffolk

**FOCUS**
An ordinary maiden, but quite a decisive winner who should progress as he gains experience.

## 6237 NOVA DISPLAY H'CAP (DIV I) 6f
**5:40** (5:42) (Class 5) (0-75,75) 3-Y-O+ **£3,234** (£962; £481; £240) **Stalls Low**

Form RPR
0046 **1** **Sandra's Secret (IRE)**[11] 5804 4-9-8 73 JosephineGordon 1 81
(Les Eyre) *mde all: rdn over 1f out: kpt on wl* 7/2[1]
0233 **2** 1 ¼ **The Amber Fort (USA)**[34] 4983 3-9-2 70 DanielTudhope 10 74
(David O'Meara) *trckd ldr: rdn 2f out: kpt on but a hld* 9/2[2]
324 **3** nk **Major Crispies**[26] 5258 6-9-6 71 (vt) PhillipMakin 9 74+
(David O'Meara) *hld up in midfield: sltly hmpd over 2f out: pushed along and hdwy appr fnl f: swtchd rt ins fnl f: rdn and kpt on* 8/1
00 **4** 1 **Avenue Of Stars**[51] 4310 4-9-1 66 (p) AndrewMullen 2 66
(Karen McLintock) *chsd ldr: rdn over 2f out: one pce* 8/1
0020 **5** ½ **Dyllan (IRE)**[12] 5739 4-9-5 70 (p) JamesSullivan 6 68
(Ruth Carr) *midfield: rdn over 2f out: one pce* 14/1
1241 **6** nk **Cliff (IRE)**[13] 5696 7-8-9 67 FayeMcManoman(7) 8 64
(Nigel Tinkler) *slowly away: hld up on outer: rdn and sme hdwy over 1f out: one pce ins fnl f* 7/1
0024 **7** hd **Rose Marmara**[29] 5134 4-9-7 72 (t) BarryMcHugh 5 69
(Brian Rothwell) *midfield: rdn over 2f out: one pce* 16/1
610 **8** 11 **Highly Sprung (IRE)**[9] 5869 4-9-10 75 SilvestreDeSousa 7 36
(Mark Johnston) *dwlt: hld up: rdn over 2f out: wknd* 5/1[3]
1/2- **9** 6 **Dream Bounty**[485] 1600 5-8-9 60 PatrickMathers 4 2
(Steph Hollinshead) *hld up: sn pushed along: wknd 2f out and bhd* 14/1
-030 **10** 11 **Kommander Kirkup**[24] 5318 6-9-3 68 TomEaves 3
(Michael Herrington) *midfield: hmpd on rail over 2f out: dropped to rr and no ch after* 16/1

1m 15.93s (-0.97) **Going Correction** -0.10s/f (Good)
**WFA** 3 from 4yo+ 3lb 10 Ran SP% 116.9
Speed ratings (Par 103): **102,100,99,98,97 97,97,82,74,59**
CSF £18.97 CT £120.22 TOTE £2.40: £1.90, £1.80, £2.90; EX 22.10 Trifecta £114.60.
**Owner** Sunpak Potatoes **Bred** Tally-Ho Stud **Trained** Catwick, N Yorks

**FOCUS**
A low-grade handicap which saw the winner cash in on a falling handicap mark.

## 6238 NOVA DISPLAY H'CAP (DIV II) 6f
**6:10** (6:10) (Class 5) (0-75,75) 3-Y-O+ **£3,234** (£962; £481; £240) **Stalls Low**

Form RPR
034 **1** **Short Work**[12] 5739 4-9-1 66 (b) DanielTudhope 9 80
(David O'Meara) *mde all: rdn over 2f out: kpt on: hld on towards fin* 5/1[3]
-020 **2** ½ **Penny Pot Lane**[15] 5635 4-8-13 67 LewisEdmunds(3) 1 79
(Richard Whitaker) *hld up: sn pushed along: hdwy to chse ldr wl over 1f out: rdn and kpt on* 4/1[2]
4244 **3** 3 **Equiano Springs**[11] 5806 3-9-4 72 DavidNolan 6 74
(Tom Tate) *hld up: rdn over 2f out: wnt modest 3rd over 1f out: kpt on same pce: nvr threatened* 12/1
2200 **4** shd **Mishaal (IRE)**[21] 5457 7-9-7 72 PaulMulrennan 8 74
(Michael Herrington) *dwlt: hld up: rdn 1/2-way: kpt on fnl f: nvr threatened* 7/1
2113 **5** 15 **Mr Orange (IRE)**[11] 5806 4-9-10 75 (p) TonyHamilton 2 29
(Paul Midgley) *chsd ldr: rdn and outpcd over 2f out: wknd over 1f out* 7/4[1]
3206 **6** 9 **Swanton Blue (IRE)**[36] 4910 4-9-3 71 CallumShepherd(3) 7
(Ed de Giles) *prom: rdn over 2f out: wknd over 1f out and eased* 9/1
0015 **7** nk **Be Bold**[18] 5542 5-8-12 63 (b) ConnorBeasley 5
(Rebecca Bastiman) *chsd ldrs on outer: rdn over 2f out: sn wknd and bhd* 10/1

1m 16.1s (-0.80) **Going Correction** -0.10s/f (Good)
**WFA** 3 from 4yo+ 3lb 7 Ran SP% 112.3
Speed ratings (Par 103): **101,100,96,96,76 64,63**
CSF £24.23 CT £223.53 TOTE £5.70: £2.90, £2.50; EX 23.90 Trifecta £325.90.
**Owner** N D Crummack Ltd & Arthur Rhodes **Bred** Downfield Cottage Stud **Trained** Upper Helmsley, N Yorks

**FOCUS**
A weak sprint handicap in which the favourite flopped. The winner showed a good attitude.
T/Jkpt: Not won. T/Plt: £85.50 to a £1 stake. Pool: £94,612.90 - 807.75 winning units T/Qpdt: £7.50 to a £1 stake. Pool: £8,431.27 - 821.62 winning units **Andrew Sheret**

6239a (Foreign Racing) - See Raceform Interactive

# 6211 CURRAGH (R-H)
Sunday, August 20

**OFFICIAL GOING: Yielding to soft changing to soft on the straight course after race 2 (2.10)**

## 6240a GALILEO IRISH EBF FUTURITY STKS (GROUP 2) 7f
**2:10** (2:11) 2-Y-O **£65,555** (£21,111; £10,000; £4,444; £2,222)

RPR
**1** **Rostropovich (IRE)**[43] 4644 2-9-3 94 (t[1]) RyanMoore 4 106
(A P O'Brien, Ire) *chsd ldrs: pushed along in 3rd fr 1/2-way and impr to dispute ld briefly under 2f out: r.o wl u.p in 2nd ins fnl f to ld fnl strides: all out* 11/8[1]
**2** shd **Coat Of Arms (IRE)**[24] 5343 2-9-3 0 DonnachaO'Brien 2 106
(A P O'Brien, Ire) *w.w: 4th 1/2-way: hdwy between horses under 2f out and rdn to ld over 1f out: all out wl ins fnl f and hdd fnl strides* 7/1
**3** 1 ¾ **Berkeley Square (IRE)**[24] 5345 2-9-3 97 SeamieHeffernan 5 101
(A P O'Brien, Ire) *w.w: last at 1/2-way: rdn nr side under 2f and no imp on ldrs 1f out: r.o wl u.p clsng stages into nvr nrr 3rd fnl stride* 4/1[3]
**4** hd **Camelback (USA)**[43] 4644 2-9-3 97 ColinKeane 6 101
(G M Lyons, Ire) *prom tl sn settled bhd ldr: effrt between horses fr 2f out where disp ld briefly: sn hdd and no ex u.p in 3rd wl ins fnl f: denied 3rd fnl stride* 5/2[2]
**5** 2 ¼ **Swiss Cottage**[7] 5971 2-9-3 0 GaryCarroll 1 95
(Joseph G Murphy, Ire) *sn led: rdn over 2f out and sn hdd: no ex over 1f out: wknd* 11/1

1m 29.29s (-1.51) **Going Correction** -0.05s/f (Good) 5 Ran SP% 111.5
Speed ratings: **106,105,103,103,101**
CSF £11.51 TOTE £2.00: £1.10, £2.30; DF 10.00 Trifecta £29.60.
**Owner** Michael Tabor & Derrick Smith & Mrs John Magnier & **Bred** Epona Bloodstock Ltd **Trained** Cashel, Co Tipperary

**FOCUS**
Hard work on softening ground here and how good any of these are is hard to quantify.

## 6241a QATAR RACING AND EQUESTRIAN CLUB CURRAGH STKS (GROUP 3) 5f
**2:45** (2:46) 2-Y-O

**£30,256** (£9,743; £4,615; £2,051; £1,025; £512) **Stalls Centre**

RPR
**1** **Treasuring**[9] 5901 2-9-0 96 ColinKeane 4 101
(G M Lyons, Ire) *led and disp: led narrowly gng wl after 1/2-way: extended advantage over 1f out: sn rdn and pressed u.p wl ins fnl f where flashed tail: hld on wl* 3/1[2]
**2** ½ **Goodthingstaketime (IRE)**[22] 5442 2-9-0 0 ChrisHayes 7 99
(J A Stack, Ire) *w.w: last at 1/2-way: gng wl but sltly hmpd over 1f out and clsd u.p nr side into 3rd wl ins fnl f: wnt 2nd cl home: a hld* 9/4[1]
**3** ½ **Sirici (IRE)**[45] 4680 2-9-0 97 PatSmullen 6 97
(J A Stack, Ire) *cl up bhd ldr tl sn disp ld: rdn in cl 2nd after 1/2-way and no ex cl home where dropped to 3rd* 9/2
**4** 2 ½ **Raramauri (IRE)**[9] 5900 2-9-0 0 WJLee 8 88
(W McCreery, Ire) *in rr early tl tk clsr order in 3rd bef 1/2-way: rdn under 2f out and no imp on ldrs u.p in 4th ins fnl f: one pce clsng stages* 11/1
**5** 1 ½ **Emadee (IRE)**[25] 5305 2-9-0 0 DeclanMcDonogh 5 83
(Andrew Slattery, Ire) *chsd ldrs: 5th 1/2-way: rdn 1 1/2f out and sn no ex: one pce in 5th ins fnl f* 4/1[3]
**6** 6 **Wolfofbaggotstreet (IRE)**[45] 4680 2-9-3 97 ConnorKing 3 64
(J P Murtagh, Ire) *hooded to load: chsd ldrs: 4th 1/2-way: rdn 2f out and sn wknd* 10/1

1m 2.35s (-0.55) **Going Correction** 0.0s/f (Good) 6 Ran SP% 111.4
Speed ratings: **104,103,102,98,96 86**
CSF £10.01 TOTE £2.60: £1.30, £1.40; DF 10.00 Trifecta £33.50.
**Owner** Qatar Racing Limited **Bred** The Pocock Family **Trained** Dunsany, Co Meath

**FOCUS**
A competitive contest, the winner probably wasn't at home on the ground but she tried hard and got it done

## 6242a BREAST CANCER RESEARCH DEBUTANTE STKS (GROUP 2) (FILLIES) 7f
**3:20** (3:21) 2-Y-O

**£57,991** (£18,675; £8,846; £3,931; £1,965; £982)

RPR
**1** **Magical (IRE)**[12] 5762 2-9-0 0 DonnachaO'Brien 3 110
(A P O'Brien, Ire) *mde all: over 1 l clr at 1/2-way: stl gng wl 2f out: pushed out over 1f out and kpt on wl under hands and heels: comf* 11/1[3]



The Form Book Flat, Raceform Ltd, Newbury, RG14 5SJ

2 1 1/4 **Happily (IRE)**[24] 5344 2-9-0 109.........................(t) RyanMoore 8 107
(A P O'Brien, Ire) *trckd ldr: pushed along fr over 2f out and no imp on wnr under hands and heels ins fnl f: kpt on same pce* **6/4**[2]

3 1 1/4 **Mary Tudor (IRE)**[12] 5762 2-9-0 0.............................. WJLee 1 104
(W McCreery, Ire) *hld up towards rr: gng wl over 2f out: hdwy 1 1/2f out and rdn into 3rd ins fnl f where no imp on wnr: kpt on same pce* **12/1**

4 3/4 **September (IRE)**[57] 4068 2-9-0 0.......................... SeamieHeffernan 7 102
(A P O'Brien, Ire) *chsd ldrs: disp 3rd at 1/2-way: rdn under 2f out and no imp on wnr ent fnl f: kpt on same pce in 4th wl ins fnl f* **11/10**[1]

5 2 1/2 **Shekiba (IRE)**[19] 5515 2-9-0 0.......................... GaryCarroll 5 95
(Joseph G Murphy, Ire) *hld up: 7th after 1/2-way: rdn 1 1/2f out and clsd u.p into 5th wl ins fnl f where no imp on ldrs* **28/1**

6 1 3/4 **Black Sails**[58] 4028 2-9-0 0.......................... ColinKeane 4 91
(G M Lyons, Ire) *dwlt: sn chsd ldrs and racd keenly: 5th 1/2-way: rdn under 2f out and no ex u.p in 5th ent fnl f: one pce after and dropped to 6th wl ins fnl f* **12/1**

7 4 1/2 **Dawn Delivers**[24] 5344 2-9-0 94.......................... KevinManning 2 79
(J S Bolger, Ire) *chsd ldrs: disp 3rd at 1/2-way: pushed along fr 2f out where n.m.r on inner and sn lost tch: wknd over 1f out* **25/1**

8 nk **Feisty Katerina (IRE)**[28] 5187 2-9-0 0.......................... RonanWhelan 6 78
(Brendan W Duke, Ire) *w.w in rr: clsr in 6th fr 1/2-way: pushed along under 2f out and sn wknd* **66/1**

1m 29.64s (-1.16) **Going Correction** -0.05s/f (Good) **8** Ran SP% **120.1**
Speed ratings: **104,102,101,100,97 95,90,89**
CSF £29.27 TOTE £12.70: £2.40, £1.02, £3.30; DF 29.90 Trifecta £222.10.
**Owner** Derrick Smith & Mrs John Magnier & Michael Tabor **Bred** Orpendale, Chelston & Wynatt **Trained** Cashel, Co Tipperary

**FOCUS**
A race run at a steady pace and whether this form would be replicated in a good ground Moyglare would be quite doubtful, but it was certainly Magical's day

## 6243a QATAR AIRWAYS ROYAL WHIP STKS (GROUP 3) 1m 2f
**3:55** (3:55) 3-Y-0+ **£32,777** (£10,555; £5,000; £2,222; £1,111)

RPR

1 **Shamreen (IRE)**[49] 4417 4-9-3 107.........................(b[1]) PatSmullen 4 106+
(D K Weld, Ire) *settled bhd ldr: clsr in 2nd fr 1/2-way: led travelling wl under 3f out: drvn clr over 1f out and sn in command: easily* **11/4**[2]

2 3 1/4 **Massif Central (IRE)**[22] 5447 3-8-13 86.......................... ShaneFoley 2 102
(John Joseph Murphy, Ire) *led: narrow advantage appr st and hdd under 3f out: rdn in 2nd under 2f out and no imp on easy wnr ent fnl f: kpt on same pce* **33/1**

3 1 1/4 **Central Square (IRE)**[22] 5436 5-9-6 107.........................(p[1]) ColinKeane 1 98
(Roger Varian) *chsd ldrs in 3rd: pushed along over 3f out: rdn over 2f out and no imp on easy wnr u.p in 4th ent fnl f: kpt on same pce in 3rd wl ins fnl f* **6/4**[1]

4 nk **Qatari Hunter (IRE)**[324] 6932 4-9-6 107.......................... KevinManning 5 97
(J S Bolger, Ire) *w.w in rr: prog on outer fr 2f out: rdn and hung sltly rt 1 1/2f out: no imp on easy wnr u.p in 3rd ent fnl f: kpt on same pce in 4th wl ins fnl f* **5/1**

5 15 **Reckless Gold (IRE)**[70] 3633 4-9-6 101...............(p[1]) DonnachaO'Brien 3 73
(Joseph Patrick O'Brien, Ire) *chsd ldrs in 4th: tk clsr order on outer under 4f out: disp 3rd appr st: rdn over 2f out and no ex over 1f out: sn wknd and eased* **3/1**[3]

2m 11.44s (2.14) **Going Correction** +0.30s/f (Good)
**WFA** 3 from 4yo+ 7lb **5** Ran SP% **111.3**
Speed ratings: **103,100,99,99,87**
CSF £54.18 TOTE £3.70: £1.60, £4.40; DF 42.70 Trifecta £124.50.
**Owner** H H Aga Khan **Bred** His Highness The Aga Khan's Studs S C **Trained** Curragh, Co Kildare

**FOCUS**
The winner proved a different proposition on this ground and may have booked her place in next month's Blandford Stakes.

6244 - 6246a (Foreign Racing) - See Raceform Interactive

# 6225 DEAUVILLE (R-H)
Sunday, August 20

**OFFICIAL GOING: Polytrack: standard; turf: good**

## 6247a PRIX IRISH RIVER (MAIDEN) (2YO COLTS & GELDINGS) (TURF) 6f
**1:05** 2-Y-0 **£11,538** (£4,615; £3,461; £2,307; £1,153)

RPR

1 **A Quiet Man (IRE)**[22] 2-9-2 0.......................... TonyPiccone 5 92
(F Chappet, France) **8/5**[2]

2 1 **French Pegasus (FR)**[22] 2-9-2 0.......................... Pierre-CharlesBoudot 3 89
(Y Barberot, France) **7/5**[1]

3 12 **Hoquilebo (FR)**[35] 2-8-10 0.......................... JeromeMoutard(6) 1 53
(T Castanheira, France) **204/10**

4 snk **Autumn Lodge**[6] 6017 2-8-10 0.......................... MathieuPelletan(6) 2 53
(J S Moore) **57/10**

5 3 1/2 **Caliste** 2-9-2 0.......................... MickaelBarzalona 4 42
(H-A Pantall, France) **43/10**[3]

1m 9.95s (-1.05) **5** Ran SP% **118.6**
PARI-MUTUEL (all including 1 euro stake): WIN 2.60; PLACE 1.30, 1.30; SF 2.70.
**Owner** A Gilibert & B Chalmel **Bred** Ecurie Haras Du Cadran & M Parrish **Trained** France

## 6248a DARLEY PRIX JEAN ROMANET (GROUP 1) (4YO+ FILLIES & MARES) (TURF) 1m 2f
**2:45** 4-Y-0+ **£122,094** (£48,846; £24,423; £12,200; £6,111)

RPR

1 **Ajman Princess (IRE)**[23] 5381 4-9-0 0.........................(p) AndreaAtzeni 8 113
(Roger Varian) *mde all: drvn 2 1/2f out: rdn appr fnl f: styd on wl under driving: gamely* **144/10**

2 1 1/4 **Siyoushake (IRE)**[21] 5460 5-9-0 0.......................... AurelienLemaitre 4 111
(F Head, France) *racd in midfield: drvn to chse ldr over 1 1/2f out: styd on fnl f but nt match wnr: jst hld on for 2nd* **54/10**[3]

3 shd **Left Hand**[49] 4423 4-9-0 0.........................(p) MaximeGuyon 7 110+
(C Laffon-Parias, France) *settled in midfield: drvn to cl 1 1/2f out: styd on fnl f: nvr on terms: jst missed 2nd* **37/10**[2]

4 shd **Smart Call (SAF)**[49] 4419 6-9-0 0.......................... JimCrowley 5 110+
(Sir Michael Stoute) *hld up in fnl trio: last and drvn appr 1 1/2f out: sn rdn and styd on fnl f: nvr nrr* **111/10**

5 2 1/2 **So Mi Dar**[17] 5571 4-9-0 0.......................... FrankieDettori 3 105
(John Gosden) *racd a little freely early: hld up in midfield: tk clsr order on inner 2f out: 3rd whn rdn and nt qckn wl over 1f out: one pce fnl f* **6/4**[1]

6 3 1/2 **That Which Is Not (USA)**[64] 3856 4-9-0 0........(h) StephanePasquier 10 98
(F-H Graffard, France) *racd keenly: hld up in fnl pair: rdn to cl 2f out: kpt on at same pce: nvr in contention* **144/10**

7 snk **Haggle**[89] 2946 4-9-0 0.......................... AlexisBadel 2 98
(H-F Devin, France) *chsd ldr between horses: rdn and lost pl over 1 1/2f out: one pce fnl f* **116/10**

8 2 **Syrita (FR)**[21] 4-9-0 0.........................(p) VincentCheminaud 6 94
(M Nigge, France) *sltly outpcd early: in rr: sing to cl whn sltly impeded 1 1/2f out: sn drvn and no further imp: wl hld fnl f* **55/1**

9 3/4 **Furia Cruzada (CHI)**[21] 5460 6-9-0 0.......................... GregoryBenoist 1 92
(S Kobayashi, France) *cl up on inner: rdn and lost pl under 2f out: wl hld whn eased ins fnl f* **37/1**

10 1 1/4 **Wilamina (IRE)**[35] 4934 4-9-0 0.......................... JamesDoyle 9 90
(Martyn Meade) *cl up on outer: pushed along 3f out: rdn and lost pl ins fnl 2f: bhd whn eased ins fnl f* **119/10**

2m 4.13s (-6.07) **Going Correction** -0.25s/f (Firm) **10** Ran SP% **118.3**
Speed ratings: **114,113,112,112,110 108,107,106,105,104**
PARI-MUTUEL (all including 1 euro stake): WIN 15.40; PLACE 3.50, 2.00, 2.10; DF 43.20; SF 90.70.
**Owner** Sheikh Mohammed Obaid Al Maktoum **Bred** Darley **Trained** Newmarket, Suffolk

**FOCUS**
Just three previous Group 1 winners in this field, with only \bLeft Hand\p winning one in the Northern hemisphere, so perhaps not the strongest edition. They went a steady early gallop which was set by the winner, who gradually wound things up from the front. She recorded a personal best.

## 6249a DARLEY PRIX MORNY (GROUP 1) (2YO COLTS & FILLIES) (TURF) 6f
**3:30** 2-Y-0 **£170,931** (£68,384; £34,192; £17,081; £8,555)

RPR

1 **Unfortunately (IRE)**[28] 5195 2-9-0 0.........................(b) TonyPiccone 7 115
(K R Burke) **57/10**

2 1 1/4 **Havana Grey**[18] 5526 2-9-0 0.......................... PJMcDonald 6 111
(K R Burke) **31/5**

3 shd **Different League (FR)**[58] 4028 2-8-10 0.......................... AntoineHamelin 2 107
(Matthieu Palussiere, France) **4/1**[2]

4 snk **Zonza (FR)**[50] 4391 2-8-10 0.......................... CristianDemuro 8 107
(D Guillemin, France) **77/10**

5 2 **High Dream Milena (FR)**[28] 5195 2-8-10 0....... Pierre-CharlesBoudot 1 101
(Mme C Head-Maarek, France) **79/10**

6 hd **Nyaleti (IRE)**[22] 5391 2-8-10 0.......................... JamesDoyle 5 100
(Mark Johnston) **53/10**[3]

7 1 3/4 **Tantheem**[21] 5461 2-8-10 0.......................... AurelienLemaitre 3 95
(F Head, France) **13/5**[1]

8 5 **Dameron (FR)**[22] 2-9-0 0.......................... JulienAuge 4 84
(C Ferland, France) **37/1**

1m 8.92s (-2.08) **Going Correction** -0.125s/f (Firm) **8** Ran SP% **117.8**
Speed ratings: **108,106,106,106,103 103,100,94**
PARI-MUTUEL (all including 1 euro stake): WIN 6.70; PLACE 2.10, 2.10, 2.00; DF 16.30; SF 32.20.
**Owner** J Laughton & Mrs E Burke **Bred** Tally-Ho Stud **Trained** Middleham Moor, N Yorks

**FOCUS**
Probably not a strong renewal. The pace was sound thanks to \bHavana Grey\p although he ultimately had to give second best to his stablemate who was completing the Prix Robert Papin / Prix Morny double. Improved efforts from the Burke pair with the third to her Albany form.

## 6250a DARLEY PRIX KERGORLAY (GROUP 2) (3YO+) (TURF) 1m 7f
**4:10** 3-Y-0+ **£63,333** (£24,444; £11,666; £7,777; £3,888)

RPR

1 **Marmelo**[37] 4879 4-9-4 0.......................... ChristopheSoumillon 5 115
(Hughie Morrison) **14/5**[2]

2 1 1/4 **Desert Skyline (IRE)**[19] 5503 3-8-7 0.........................(p) DavidProbert 9 114+
(David Elsworth) **31/5**

3 1 **Holdthasigreen (FR)**[33] 5014 5-9-4 0.........................(p) TonyPiccone 1 112
(C Le Lay, France) **12/1**

4 1/2 **Nearly Caught (IRE)**[43] 4639 7-9-4 0.......................... MaximeGuyon 10 112
(Hughie Morrison) **5/2**[1]

5 3 1/2 **Red Cardinal (IRE)**[72] 3553 5-9-6 0.......................... EduardoPedroza 6 110+
(A Wohler, Germany) **37/10**[3]

6 1 1/4 **Pallasator**[19] 5503 8-9-4 0.......................... LukeMorris 3 106
(Sir Mark Prescott Bt) **143/10**

7 nk **Way To Paris**[63] 3884 4-9-4 0.........................(b[1]) CristianDemuro 4 106
(Antonio Marcialis, Italy) **16/1**

8 4 **Moonshiner (GER)**[37] 4879 4-9-4 0.......................... Pierre-CharlesBoudot 2 103
(Jean-Pierre Carvalho, Germany) **113/10**

3m 9.56s (-9.54) **Going Correction** -0.25s/f (Firm)
**WFA** 3 from 4yo+ 11lb **8** Ran SP% **118.3**
Speed ratings: **115,114,113,113,111 111,110,108**
PARI-MUTUEL (all including 1 euro stake): WIN 3.80; PLACE 1.70, 2.20, 2.90; DF 12.20; SF 21.80.
**Owner** The Fairy Story Partnership **Bred** Deepwood Farm Stud **Trained** East Ilsley, Berks

**FOCUS**
This became something of a sprint.

## 6251a PRIX D'AVRANCHES (MAIDEN) (2YO FILLIES) (TURF) 6f
**4:50** 2-Y-0 **£11,538** (£4,615; £3,461; £2,307; £1,153)

RPR

1 **River Cannes (FR)** 2-8-11 0.......................... MaximeGuyon 9 82
(T Castanheira, France) **188/10**

2 hd **Arabica**[16] 2-9-2 0.......................... ChristopheSoumillon 7 86
(Simone Brogi, France) **17/5**[2]

3 1 1/4 **Marvellous Night (FR)**[14] 2-8-13 0.......................... ClementLecoeuvre(3) 6 82
(H De Nicolay, France) **78/10**

4 1 3/4 **Evertogether (IRE)**[27] 5230 2-9-2 0.......................... AntoineHamelin 12 77
(H-F Devin, France) **81/10**

5 hd **Miss Sienna**[21] 2-9-2 0.......................... AlexisBadel 5 76
(H-F Devin, France) **27/10**[1]

6 1 1/2 **Easy Break (FR)**[39] 2-9-2 0.......................... Pierre-CharlesBoudot 2 72
(F Chappet, France) **153/10**

7 4 1/2 **Star Of Vendome (FR)**[10] 5988 2-9-2 0.......................... TheoBachelot 4 58
(Harry Dunlop) **45/1**

8 2 1/2 **Malalaika (FR)**[42] 2-9-2 0.......................... AurelienLemaitre 8 51
(Mlle B Renk, France) **73/1**

9 hd **Colleville (FR)** 2-8-11 0.......................... CristianDemuro 1 45
(N Caullery, France) **115/10**

10 *snk* **Rachael's Rocket (IRE)**[10] 5988 2-9-2 0........................ TonyPiccone 3 50
(J S Moore) **13/1**
11 *1 1/4* **Vlatka (IRE)**[21] 2-9-2 0........................ MickaelBarzalona 10 46
(Mme Pia Brandt, France) **6/1**[3]
12 *15* **Rue De Lille (FR)**[44] 4595 2-9-2 0........................ AnthonyCrastus 11 1
(I Endaltsev, Czech Republic) **59/1**

1m 9.94s (-1.06) **12 Ran SP% 117.9**
PARI-MUTUEL (all including 1 euro stake): WIN 19.80; PLACE 5.60, 2.10, 2.60; DF 45.90; SF 98.20.
**Owner** Mme Stephanie Castanheira **Bred** M Pehu **Trained** France

# 5733 DEL MAR (L-H)
Sunday, August 20

**OFFICIAL GOING: Dirt: fast; turf: firm**

## 6252a $1 MILLION TVG PACIFIC CLASSIC STKS (GRADE 1) (3YO+) (DIRT) 1m 2f
**1:30** 3-Y-O+
**£487,804** (£162,601; £97,560; £48,780; £16,260; £280)

RPR

1 **Collected (USA)**[57] 4-8-12 0........................ MartinGarcia 2 126
(Bob Baffert, U.S.A) *mde all: kicked clr fr 2f out: styd on gamely u.p fnl f* **3/1**[2]
2 *1/2* **Arrogate (USA)**[28] 5194 4-8-12 0........................ MikeESmith 7 125+
(Bob Baffert, U.S.A) *chsd ldrs on outer: a little outpcd and drvn 3f out: 3l 3rd and rdn 1 1/2f out: r.o fnl f: nvr quite on terms* **7/10**[1]
3 *3 3/4* **Accelerate (USA)**[28] 5194 4-8-12 0........................(b) VictorEspinoza 3 117
(John W Sadler, U.S.A) *pressed ldr: rdn and nt qcknd ins last 2f: kpt on at same pce* **16/5**[3]
4 *6 1/2* **Curlin Road (USA)**[24] 4-8-12 0........................ FlavienPrat 6 104
(Doug O'Neill, U.S.A) *racd in fnl pair: rdn and lost grnd on ldrs fr 2f out: plugged on to pass btn horses* **30/1**
5 *1/2* **Hard Aces (USA)**[24] 7-8-12 0........................(b) SantiagoGonzalez 4 103
(John W Sadler, U.S.A) *settled in rr: rdn and no imp 2f out: nvr in contention* **30/1**
6 *21* **Royal Albert Hall**[27] 5-8-12 0........................ CoreySNakatani 1 103
(Kristin Mulhall, U.S.A) *racd in midfield: rdn and lost pl 2 1/2f out: t.o* **86/1**
7 *2 3/4* **Donworth (USA)**[28] 5194 5-8-12 0........................ MarioGutierrez 5 98
(Doug O'Neill, U.S.A) *chsd ldrs: outpcd and rdn over 2f: sn wknd: t.o* **208/10**

PARI-MUTUEL (all including 2 usd stake): WIN 8.00; PLACE (1-2) 2.80, 2.60; SHOW (1-2-3) 2.20, 2.10, 2.20; DF 6.20; SF 19.20.
**Owner** Speedway Stable, LLC **Bred** Runnymede Farm Inc & Peter J Callahan **Trained** USA

6253 - (Foreign Racing) - See Raceform Interactive

# 5693 DUSSELDORF (R-H)
Sunday, August 20

**OFFICIAL GOING: Turf: soft**

## 6254a 31ST GROSSER SPARKASSENPREIS - PREIS DER STADTSPARKASSE DUSSELDORF (LISTED RACE) 7f
**4:30** 3-Y-O+
**£14,957** (£5,982; £4,273; £2,564; £1,282; £854)

RPR

1 **Pirouette**[23] 5352 4-9-4 0........................(b) RobertWinston 3 106
(Hughie Morrison) *mde all: led on ins rail: qcknd clr 1 1/2f out: styd on strly fnl f: unchal* **9/5**[1]
2 *5* **Wild Approach (GER)**[16] 5597 4-9-4 0........................ WladimirPanov 8 93
(D Moser, Germany) **22/5**[3]
3 *3/4* **Middle East (IRE)**[37] 3-8-11 0........................ HugoJourniac 6 86+
(J-C Rouget, France) **23/5**
4 *nk* **Silver Cloud (GER)**[294] 3-8-11 0........................ AndreBest 5 86
(S Smrczek, Germany) **135/10**
5 *nse* **Liwa Palace**[46] 4679 4-9-2 0........................ FranckBlondel 11 88
(Rod Collet, France) **183/10**
6 *1/2* **Dalila (GER)**[112] 3-8-11 0........................ FilipMinarik 9 84
(P Schiergen, Germany) **166/10**
7 *hd* **Fons Salera (IRE)** 3-8-11 0........................ MaximPecheur 2 84
(A Wohler, Germany) **188/10**
8 *shd* **Scapina (GER)**[301] 7563 3-8-11 0........................ MarcoCasamento 4 83
(Henk Grewe, Germany) **134/10**
9 *3 1/2* **Arazza (GER)**[28] 5196 3-9-0 0........................ AlexanderPietsch 1 77
(J Hirschberger, Germany) **19/5**[2]
10 *1 1/2* **Intendantin (GER)**[48] 4518 4-9-2 0........................ MartinSeidl 7 72
(Ferdinand J Leve, Germany) **25/1**
11 *3/4* **Viva La Flora (GER)**[63] 3882 3-8-11 0........................ DanielePorcu 10 68
(P Schiergen, Germany) **156/10**

1m 27.88s
**WFA** 3 from 4yo 5lb **11 Ran SP% 132.5**
PARI-MUTUEL (all including 10 euro stake): WIN 28 PLACE: 13, 14, 16; SF: 1906.
**Owner** The End-R-Ways Partnership & Partners **Bred** The Lavington Stud **Trained** East Ilsley, Berks

# HANOVER (L-H)
Sunday, August 20

**OFFICIAL GOING: Turf: good**

## 6255a GROSSER PREIS DES AUDI-ZENTRUMS HANNOVER (FURSTENBERG-RENNEN) (GROUP 3) (3YO) (TURF) 1m 2f
**3:35** 3-Y-O
**£27,350** (£10,256; £5,128; £2,564; £1,709)

RPR

1 **Real Value (FR)**[23] 3-9-2 0........................ FabriceVeron 1 103+
(Mario Hofer, Germany) **47/10**[3]
2 *1 1/2* **Ming Jung (FR)**[49] 4422 3-9-0 0........................ AdriedeVries 2 98
(Markus Klug, Germany) **59/10**
3 *2* **Amigo (GER)**[36] 4931 3-9-2 0........................ BauyrzhanMurzabayev 3 96
(Eva Fabianova, Germany) **31/10**[2]
4 *1/2* **Enjoy Vijay (GER)**[21] 5464 3-9-2 0........................ AndraschStarke 5 95
(P Schiergen, Germany) **1/2**[1]
5 *3/4* **Kick And Rush (GER)**[184] 799 3-9-0 0........................ StephenHellyn 4 93
(Mario Hofer, Germany) **103/10**

PARI-MUTUEL (all including 10 euro stake): WIN 57 PLACE: 31, 30; SF: 254.
**Owner** Eckhard Sauren **Bred** B Van Dalfsen **Trained** Germany

# LE TOUQUET (L-H)
Sunday, August 20

**OFFICIAL GOING: Turf: good**

## 6256a PRIX DU RESTAURANT "LE SAINT JEAN" LE TOUQUET (MAIDEN) (3YO COLTS & GELDINGS) (TURF) 1m 2f 110y
**4:00** 3-Y-O
**£5,128** (£2,051; £1,538; £1,025; £512)

RPR

1 **Daynawar (FR)**[83] 3-8-11 0........................ MlleAlisonMassin(5) 4 71
(Andrew Hollinshead, France) **101/10**[1]
2 *4 1/2* **So Pleasing (FR)**[139] 3-8-10 0........................ NicolasLarenaudie(6) 10 66
(G Collet, France)
3 *3/4* **Hernandes (FR)**[27] 5218 3-9-2 0........................ FabienLefebvre 1 65
(Ian Williams)
4 *1/2* **Valdelino (FR)**[78] 3-8-10 0........................ TristanBaron(6) 14 64
(H-A Pantall, France)
5 *3* **Mowafrost (FR)**[93] 3-9-2 0........................(p) MickaelBerto 12 58
(Mme P Butel, France)
6 *3/4* **Imprudent (IRE)** 3-8-6 0........................ JeremyMoisan(5) 13 52
(J-M Beguigne, France)
7 *4 1/2* **Ken Party (FR)**[131] 3-8-8 0........................ AdrienMoreau(3) 8 43
(B Delariviere, France)
8 *2* **Jelmood (FR)** 3-8-11 0........................ StephaneBreux 6 39
(Mme J Hendriks, Holland)
9 *1 1/4* **Gaillon (FR)** 3-8-11 0........................ LoidBekaert 3 37
(T de Vlaminck, Belgium)
10 *3/4* **Saint Ferdinand (IRE)**[39] 4783 3-8-13 0........................ ValentinGambart(3) 5 40
(P Favereaux, France)
11 *1/2* **Keef D'Ouilly (FR)**[54] 3-8-6 0........................(p) FlorentMalbran(5) 7
(F Lenglart, France)
12 *5 1/2* **First America (FR)** 3-8-7 0........................ MlleChloeHue(4) 11
(A Lamotte D'Argy, France)
13 *dist* **Furous (FR)**[12] 3-9-2 0........................ CyrilleStefan 2
(J Albrecht, Czech Republic)
14 *dist* **Airpearl (FR)** 3-8-11 0........................ StephaneLaurent 9
(X Richard, France)

PARI-MUTUEL (all including 1 euro stake): WIN 11.10; PLACE 2.40, 2.30, 2.30; DF 40.00.
**Owner** N Chapman & P Shaw **Bred** S.A. Aga Khan **Trained** France

# 5931 LINGFIELD (L-H)
Monday, August 21

**OFFICIAL GOING: Good to soft (7.4)**
Wind: virtually nil Weather: overcast

## 6257 SIGN UP TO 188BET AFFILIATES H'CAP 1m 2f
**2:00** (2:03) (Class 6) (0-60,62) 3-Y-O+ **£2,264** (£673; £336; £168) **Stalls** Low

Form RPR

0416 1 **Take A Turn (IRE)**[17] 5618 3-9-8 **62**........................ TomQueally 2 69+
(David Lanigan) *hld up in tch in midfield and travelled strly thrght: clsd to trck ldrs 2f out: led over 1f out: sn rdn: styd on: rdn out* **8/1**
0043 2 *1/2* **Rock N Roll Global (IRE)**[40] 4748 3-9-8 **62**........................(b) JamieSpencer 6 68
(Richard Hughes) *hld up in tch in midfield: effrt over 2f out: chsd wnr u.p over 1f out: styd on but a hld ins fnl f* **5/2**[1]
0103 3 *1 3/4* **Venetian Proposal (IRE)**[16] 5653 3-9-2 **56**........................(p) KieranO'Neill 11 59
(Zoe Davison) *hld up in tch in rr of main gp: pushed along briefly 7f out: rdn and hdwy whn nt clr run and swtchd rt wl over 1f out: drifting lft u.p and chsd ldrs 1f out: kpt on but nvr threatening ldng pair* **7/1**[3]
0552 4 *1* **Rocksette**[9] 5935 3-8-8 **48**........................ AntonioFresu 13 49
(Philip Hide) *t.k.h: hld up in tch in midfield: clsd and nt clr run 2f out tl hdwy and edging lft 1f out: styd on wl ins fnl f: nvr threatening ldng pair* **5/1**[2]
0626 5 *3 1/4* **California Cliffs (IRE)**[19] 5532 3-9-1 **55**........................ DavidProbert 5 50
(Rae Guest) *hld up in tch in midfield: effrt and rdn to chse ldrs 2f out: no imp u.p 1f out: wknd ins fnl f* **14/1**
6044 6 *1 1/4* **Solent Meads (IRE)**[14] 5722 3-9-4 **58**........................(b) GeorgeDowning 1 51
(Daniel Kubler) *chsd ldrs: rdn and pressing ldrs 2f out: no ex u.p over 1f out: wknd ins fnl f* **7/1**[3]
0-60 7 *nk* **Mistress Viz (IRE)**[111] 2269 3-9-5 **59**........................ LukeMorris 4 51+
(Daniel Mark Loughnane) *chsd ldr tl 7f out: styd chsng ldrs: rdn over 3f out: no ex and btn over 1f out: wknd fnl f* **12/1**
2050 8 *4 1/2* **Permanent**[11] 5831 3-9-3 **57**........................(b[1]) RobHornby 3 41+
(Daniel Kubler) *led tl rdn and hdd over 1f out: sn btn and wknd fnl f* **16/1**
5305 9 *shd* **Grey Diamond**[12] 5800 3-9-7 **61**........................(b[1]) JoeFanning 10 45
(Mark Johnston) *dwlt: steadily rcvrd to chse ldr 7f out: rdn over 2f out: btn and lost pl qckly over 1f out: wknd fnl f* **16/1**
6350 10 *2 1/4* **Casado (IRE)**[12] 5793 3-9-5 **59**........................ KierenFox 9 39
(John Best) *hld up in tch in rr of main gp: swtchd lft and effrt on inner over 2f out: no imp and btn over 1f out: eased ins fnl f* **12/1**
006- 11 *3 3/4* **Desidero (SPA)**[315] 7208 3-8-1 **48**........................(p[1]) SophieRalston(7) 8 21
(Pat Phelan) *uns rdr and galloped bk to paddock on the wat to s: dwlt and swtchd lft after s: a rr and nvr travelling wl: lost tch 4f out* **66/1**

2m 11.2s (0.70) **Going Correction** +0.25s/f (Good) **11 Ran SP% 116.7**
Speed ratings (Par 101): **107,106,105,104,101 100,100,96,96,95 92**
CSF £27.98 CT £150.37 TOTE £8.80: £2.40, £1.50, £2.60; EX 31.80 Trifecta £118.00.
**Owner** 21st Century Farms Ltd **Bred** 21st Century Farms Ltd **Trained** Newmarket, Suffolk



The Form Book Flat, Raceform Ltd, Newbury, RG14 5SJ

**FOCUS**
The going was updated twice earlier in the day, ultimately changing from Good to Good to Soft. Tom Queally said "It's testing enough for the time of year - quite tacky", Jamie Spencer said "(it's worse) than good to soft", while Kieran O'Neill said "there's no good in it". The two previous winners came to the fore finishing first and third.

## 6258 188BET.CO.UK H'CAP 1m 3f 133y
**2:30** (2:32) (Class 5) (0-75,75) 3-Y-O+ **£2,911** (£866; £432; £216) **Stalls** High

Form RPR
4313 **1** **Pete So High (GER)**[3] 6126 3-9-4 **74**....................(p) SilvestreDeSousa 3 80
(Richard Hannon) *trckd ldrs tl pushed along and outpcd in 4th on downhill run 4f out: rallied and hdwy to chal 2f out: led and edging lft u.p over 1f out: styd on and forged clr wl ins fnl f* **1/1**[1]

3123 **2** 2 ½ **Light Of Air (FR)**[46] 4519 4-9-13 **74**.................................. RyanMoore 1 76
(Gary Moore) *hld up wl in tch: 5th and outpcd on downhill run 4f out: rallied and hdwy on inner 2f out: pressing ldrs u.p 1f out: chsd wnr ins fnl f: no imp and outpcd towards fin* **4/1**[2]

2325 **3** 1 **Prerogative (IRE)**[37] 4913 3-9-5 **75**.........................(p) TomMarquand 4 75
(Richard Hannon) *led tl 6f out: styd pressing ldr tl led again 3f out: rdn and hdd over 1f out: no ex and lost 2nd ins f: wknd towards fin* **13/2**[3]

-604 **4** 1 **Archimento**[26] 5299 4-9-9 **70**..........................................(t) DavidProbert 7 68
(Philip Hide) *chsd ldrs tl wnt 2nd over 9f out: led 6f out tl hdd 3f out: stl pressing ldrs but struggling to qckn u.p whn squeezed for room and hmpd over 1f out: kpt on same pce ins fnl f* **15/2**

421- **5** 1 **Fearless Lad (IRE)**[345] 6335 7-8-12 **59**................................ KierenFox 2 56
(John Best) *sn dropped to rr and nvr travelling: lost tch on downhill run 4f out: rdn 3f out: styd on and clsd over 1f out: swtchd lft 1f out: kpt on clsng but nvr getting on terms w ldrs* **14/1**

350 **6** 2 ¾ **Tinker Tailor (IRE)**[16] 5658 4-9-6 **72**............................(t) DavidEgan(5) 6 64
(Denis Quinn) *dwlt: rcvrd to press ldrs 9f out: rdn and ev ch 3f out: struggling whn sltly impeded 2f out: wknd over 1f out* **10/1**

2m 36.15s (4.65) **Going Correction** +0.25s/f (Good)
**WFA** 3 from 4yo+ 9lb **6 Ran SP% 110.9**
Speed ratings (Par 103): **94,92,91,91,90 88**
CSF £5.06 CT £14.71 TOTE £1.90: £1.30, £1.80; EX 5.60 Trifecta £17.00.
**Owner** Middleham Park Racing VII & K Sohi **Bred** Stiftung Gestut Fahrhof **Trained** East Everleigh, Wilts

**FOCUS**
A moderate small-field event but they seemed to go a decent gallop, the winner showcased Silvestre de Sousa's skills. The winner rates a small pb.

## 6259 PLAY CASINO AT 188BET H'CAP 2m 68y
**3:00** (3:00) (Class 5) (0-70,72) 3-Y-O+ **£2,911** (£866; £432; £216) **Stalls** High

Form RPR
0-31 **1** **Piedita (IRE)**[28] 5209 3-9-5 **72**........................................... LukeMorris 8 82+
(Sir Mark Prescott Bt) *in tch in midfield tl wnt 3rd 7f out: trckd ldr and travelling strly 3f out: led 2f out: sn urged along and readily wnt clr: easily* **4/6**[1]

3226 **2** 4 ½ **Fitzwilly**[17] 5590 7-9-11 **66**.......................................... SilvestreDeSousa 2 69
(Mick Channon) *stdd and dropped in bhd after s: hld up in rr: swtchd lft and effrt 3f out: chsd clr wnr u.p over 1f out: kpt on but no imp ins fnl f* **11/2**[2]

0-10 **3** ½ **Avenue Des Champs**[22] 5454 5-9-6 **66**...............(p) PaddyBradley(5) 10 68
(Jane Chapple-Hyam) *t.k.h early: hld up in midfield: effrt 3f out: 3rd and no imp on wnr 1f out: kpt on same pce ins fnl f* **16/1**

/5-6 **4** 1 ¼ **Linguine (FR)**[33] 5025 7-10-3 **72**.................................(b) JamieSpencer 6 73
(Seamus Durack) *led for over 1f: chsd ldr tl led again over 3f out: drvn and hdd 2f out: sn brushed aside by wnr: lost 2nd and kpt on same pce fr over 3f out* **33/1**

0012 **5** 1 ½ **Ablaze**[23] 5405 3-8-3 **59** ow2.............................. EdwardGreatrex(3) 7 58
(Laura Mongan) *trckd ldng pair tl 7f: styd chsng ldrs: rdn over 2f out: unable qck u.p over 1f out: wknd ins fnl f* **6/1**[3]

2044 **6** 13 **Bamako Du Chatelet (FR)**[33] 5024 6-10-0 **69**........ JosephineGordon 5 53
(Ian Williams) *bustled along early: in tch in midfield: rdn over 2f out: sn btn* **6/1**[3]

0253 **7** 13 **Topalova**[27] 5244 4-8-9 **50** oh2............................................ JoeyHaynes 4 18
(Mark H Tompkins) *hld up in last pair: effrt 3f out: sn btn: wl bhd and eased ins fnl f* **20/1**

0403 **8** 21 **Montycristo**[10] 5866 4-8-9 **50** oh5.................................(b) DavidProbert 3
(Philip Hide) *t.k.h: led over 14f out tl hdd over 3f out: sn dropped out: t.o and eased fnl f* **28/1**

3m 40.65s (5.85) **Going Correction** +0.25s/f (Good)
**WFA** 3 from 4yo+ 12lb **8 Ran SP% 121.0**
Speed ratings (Par 103): **95,92,92,91,91 84,78,67**
CSF £5.19 CT £34.99 TOTE £1.60: £1.02, £2.00, £3.50; EX 6.70 Trifecta £45.50.
**Owner** Mrs Carmen Frubeck & Denford Stud **Bred** D J & Mrs Brown **Trained** Newmarket, Suffolk

**FOCUS**
An odds-on winner ahead of her mark in this staying handicap. The runner-up is rated close to form.

## 6260 INJURED JOCKEYS FUND EBF NOVICE STKS 7f
**3:30** (3:34) (Class 5) 2-Y-O **£2,911** (£866; £432; £216) **Stalls** Centre

Form RPR
2 **1** **Radio Source (IRE)**[33] 5036 2-9-2 0.................................. RyanMoore 8 84+
(Sir Michael Stoute) *chsd ldrs: pushed along jst over 2f out: chsd ldr wl over 1f out: rdn and qcknd to ld 1f out: r.o strly: readily* **1/1**[1]

**2** 5 **Staunch (USA)** 2-9-2 0............................................ JamieSpencer 12 72+
(Jeremy Noseda) *s.i.s: off the pce in last trio: rdn and hdwy 2f out: styd on wl ins fnl f to snatch 2nd last strides: nvr trbld ldrs* **6/1**[3]

05 **3** ½ **Adulate**[21] 5476 2-9-2 0.....................................(b[1]) JosephineGordon 5 69
(Hugo Palmer) *racd freely: led and qckly crossed to r against stands rail: rdn and hung lft over 1f out: hdd 1f out: sn outpcd: wknd and lost 2nd last strides* **25/1**

4 **4** 1 ¾ **Poets Dream (IRE)**[52] 4318 2-9-2 0.................................. TomQueally 4 64+
(Mohamed Moubarak) *hld up in tch in midfield: pushed along 2f out: edgd rt u.p wl over 1f out: pushed along and kpt on ins fnl f: no ch w wnr* **40/1**

2 **5** nk **Ambient (IRE)**[16] 5655 2-9-2 0............................. SilvestreDeSousa 9 64
(Roger Varian) *chsd ldrs: hmpd after 1f: wnt 2nd 1/2-way tl wl over 1f out: sn rdn and btn 3rd 1f out: wknd ins fnl f* **5/2**[2]

35 **6** 1 ½ **He's Our Star (IRE)**[17] 5586 2-9-2 0............................. TomMarquand 7 60
(Ali Stronge) *hld up in tch in midfield: effrt 2f out: no imp and btn over 1f out: no ch w wnr and kpt on same pce ins fnl f* **20/1**

0 **7** 3 ¼ **Sunstorm**[45] 4567 2-9-2 0............................................ RobertWinston 6 51
(David Brown) *s.i.s: off the pce in rr: rdn and sme hdwy over 1f out: pushed along and no imp ins fnl f: nvr trbld ldrs* **66/1**

0 **8** 2 ½ **Elsaakb (USA)**[31] 5106 2-9-2 0............................................ DaneO'Neill 1 45
(John Gosden) *chsd ldrs: rdn over 2f out: sn carried rt and outpcd: wknd fnl f* **10/1**

**9** ½ **Compass Point** 2-9-2 0............................................ JohnFahy 3 44
(Laura Mongan) *s.i.s: sn swtchd rt: rn green and wl off the pce in rr: passed sme btn rivals but no ch whn nt clr run and swtchd rt over 1f out: nvr trbld ldrs* **66/1**

00 **10** ¾ **Surrey Blaze (IRE)**[3] 6132 2-8-13 0..................... EdwardGreatrex(3) 11 42+
(Joseph Tuite) *chsd ldrs: losing pl whn swtchd lft over 2f out: wl btn 2f out: wknd over 1f out* **66/1**

0 **11** 6 **Filly Mignon**[53] 4253 2-8-11 0............................................ MartinDwyer 13 21
(Brendan Powell) *chsd ldr: sltly impeded after 1f: lost 2nd 1/2-way and sn struggling: bhd and eased ins fnl f* **100/1**

**12** 2 ¾ **Valerie's Memory** 2-8-11 0............................................ DavidProbert 2 14
(Philip Hide) *midfield but nvr on terms w ldrs: rdn and struggling whn carried lft over 2f out: bhd and eased ins fnl f* **66/1**

0 **13** 49 **Usher**[21] 5476 2-9-2 0............................................ KieranShoemark 10
(Roger Charlton) *a towards rr: dropped to last and no rspnse to press 1/2-way: eased 2f out: t.o* **33/1**

1m 26.07s (2.77) **Going Correction** +0.25s/f (Good) **13 Ran SP% 122.9**
Speed ratings (Par 94): **94,88,87,85,85 83,79,77,76,75 68,65,9**
CSF £7.49 TOTE £1.90: £1.10, £2.20, £4.90; EX 9.40 Trifecta £112.10.
**Owner** Robert Ng **Bred** Rathregan Stud **Trained** Newmarket, Suffolk
■ Stewards' Enquiry : Josephine Gordon three-day ban: careless riding (Sep 4-6)

**FOCUS**
Quite an interesting novice event with some decent RPRs on show and a good display from the winner.

## 6261 EBF "BREEDERS' SERIES" FILLIES' H'CAP 7f 135y
**4:00** (4:01) (Class 3) (0-95,90) 3-Y-O+ **£12,450** (£3,728; £1,864; £932; £466) **Stalls** Centre

Form RPR
3211 **1** **Peach Melba**[13] 5754 3-8-13 **82**.......................................... JoeFanning 4 94
(Mark Johnston) *trckd ldr tl shkn up hung lft and led over 1f out: sn rdn and readily wnt clr: r.o wl: easily* **2/1**[2]

3111 **2** 4 ½ **Harba (IRE)**[25] 5341 3-9-0 **83**.......................................... RyanMoore 2 84
(William Haggas) *led tl rdn and hdd over 1f out: clr 2nd but no ch w wnr and kpt on same pce ins fnl f* **6/4**[1]

6426 **3** 1 ¾ **Bint Dandy (IRE)**[3] 6145 6-9-6 **83**.........................(b) SilvestreDeSousa 5 81
(Chris Dwyer) *trckd ldrs: effrt 2f out: sn drvn and unable qck: wl hld 3rd and kpt on same pce ins fnl f* **13/2**

1240 **4** 2 ¾ **Rebel Surge (IRE)**[24] 5352 4-9-13 **90**..........................(p) JamieSpencer 3 81
(Richard Spencer) *stdd s: hld up in tch in rr: swtchd lft and effrt wl over 1f out: no imp and wl hld fnl f* **9/2**[3]

4 **5** ½ **Sunchisetagioo**[10] 5889 3-9-2 **90**..................................(h) DavidEgan(5) 1 79
(Marco Botti) *t.k.h: trckd ldrs: effrt over 2f out: sn rdn: no imp and no ch w wnr over 1f out: plugged on same pce ins fnl f* **20/1**

1m 32.58s (0.28) **Going Correction** +0.25s/f (Good)
**WFA** 3 from 4yo+ 6lb **5 Ran SP% 109.6**
Speed ratings (Par 104): **108,103,101,99,98**
CSF £5.35 TOTE £2.70: £1.20, £1.40; EX 4.90 Trifecta £17.90.
**Owner** Lowther Racing & Partner **Bred** Lowther Racing **Trained** Middleham Moor, N Yorks

**FOCUS**
The feature had only a small field but an impressive winner who is clearly thriving. She took a clear step forward here.

## 6262 READ SILVESTRE DE SOUSA AT 188BET NOVICE AUCTION STKS 6f
**4:30** (4:31) (Class 6) 2-Y-O **£2,264** (£673; £336; £168) **Stalls** Centre

Form RPR
0 **1** **Sing Out Loud (IRE)**[16] 5641 2-9-0 0................................ RyanMoore 1 78+
(Gary Moore) *trckd ldrs: effrt 2f out: rdn to ld ent fnl f: asserted and edgd rt ins fnl f: styd on wl: rdn out* **3/1**[2]

0 **2** 2 ½ **Havana Heart**[47] 4503 2-8-9 0.............................. SilvestreDeSousa 6 66
(Ismail Mohammed) *chsd ldr tl rdn to ld 2f out: drvn and hdd ent fnl f: clr 2nd and styd on same pce ins fnl f* **13/2**[3]

44 **3** 5 **Fortunate Vision**[20] 5494 2-8-10 0.............................. KieranShoemark 2 52
(David Brown) *sn dropped to rr: pushed along 1/2-way: nvr on terms w ldrs after: modest hdwy to go 3rd ins fnl f: no ch w ldng pair* **15/2**

6 **4** 2 ¼ **Dashing Dusty (IRE)**[13] 5749 2-9-1 0.............................. DougieCostello 4 50
(Jamie Osborne) *dwlt: hld up in last pair: pushed along 1/2-way: drifted lft and outpcd 2f out: wl hld and plugged on same pce fnl f* **11/1**

**5** nse **Harbour Storm** 2-9-0 0............................................ JohnFahy 5 49
(Laura Mongan) *dwlt and rdn along early: chsd ldrs tl 1/2-way: sn rdn and outpcd: no ch w ldrs whn swtchd lft and kpt on same pce ins fnl f* **50/1**

2201 **6** ½ **Hello Girl**[7] 6012 2-8-13 70.............................. RobertWinston 3 46+
(Dean Ivory) *led and grad crossed over to r nr stands rail: hdd and rdn 2f out: sn struggling and outpcd: wl hld 3rd 1f out: wknd ins fnl f* **1/1**[1]

1m 13.37s (2.17) **Going Correction** +0.25s/f (Good) **6 Ran SP% 110.4**
Speed ratings (Par 92): **95,91,85,82,81 81**
CSF £21.25 TOTE £3.80: £1.70, £2.80; EX 17.60 Trifecta £105.40.
**Owner** Mrs Susan Neville & Mike George **Bred** J S Bolger **Trained** Lower Beeding, W Sussex

**FOCUS**
The last-time-out winning favourite found little for pressure as two juveniles improved on their second starts.

## 6263 188BET TRAINING SERIES APPRENTICE H'CAP (PART OF THE RACING EXCELLENCE INITIATIVE) 7f 135y
**5:05** (5:07) (Class 5) (0-70,71) 4-Y-O+ **£2,911** (£866; £432; £216) **Stalls** Centre

Form RPR
4111 **1** **Arctic Flower (IRE)**[16] 5651 4-8-12 **56**.............................. JoshuaBryan 6 66+
(John Bridger) *broke fast: mde all: pushed along and readily asserted over 1f out: in command and r.o wl ins fnl f: unchal* **1/1**[1]

5-20 **2** 3 ¾ **World Record (IRE)**[40] 4765 7-8-9 **58**.............................. DarraghKeenan(5) 5 58
(Mick Quinn) *trckd wnr: rdn ent fnl 2f: outpcd by wnr and btn over 1f out: clr 2nd and kpt on same pce ins fnl f* **7/1**[3]

5433 **3** 2 ¾ **Cyflymder (IRE)**[23] 5410 11-8-4 **51** oh3.............................. NicolaCurrie(3) 4 44
(David C Griffiths) *hld up in tch: pushed along ent fnl 2f: rdn over 1f out: no ch w wnr but kpt on to go 3rd ins fnl f* **5/1**[2]

6340 **4** ¾ **Ravenhoe (IRE)**[11] 5843 4-9-10 **68**.............................. FinleyMarsh 7 60
(Mark Johnston) *in tch in rr: pushed along 1/2-way: rdn to go 3rd over 1f out: nvr threatening ldrs: kpt on same pce after and lost 3rd ins fnl f* **5/1**[2]

130- **5** 2 ¾ **German Whip**[233] 8590 4-9-8 **71**.............................. JasonWatson(5) 2 56
(Gary Moore) *swtchd rt sn after s: chsd ldrs: rdn over 2f out: lost pl and swtchd lft wl over 1f out: no ch and plugged on same pce after* **14/1**

3660 **6** *7* **Marbooh (IRE)**[2] 6182 4-9-12 **70**....................(t) CameronNoble 3 38
(Denis Quinn) *hld up wl in tch in midfield: effrt over 2f out: sn struggling and lost pl over 1f out: bhd and wknd fnl f* **12/1**

1m 33.61s (1.31) **Going Correction** +0.25s/f (Good) **6** Ran SP% **110.2**
Speed ratings (Par 103): **103,99,96,95,93 86**
CSF £8.24 TOTE £1.70: £1.10, £2.70; EX 10.20 Trifecta £24.90.
**Owner** Mr & Mrs K Finch **Bred** B Kennedy **Trained** Liphook, Hants

**FOCUS**
An apprentice race to end things and a four-timer brought up in tremendous fashion. The winner recorded a clear pb, but this was a weak race.
T/Plt: £13.90 to a £1 stake. Pool: £75,149.61 - 3,925.76 winning units T/Qpdt: £10.50 to a £1 stake. Pool: £4,288.88 - 302.24 winning units **Steve Payne**

# 6042 THIRSK (L-H)
## Monday, August 21

**OFFICIAL GOING: Good (7.9)**
Wind: light across Weather: Fine

## 6264 BRITISH STALLION STUDS EBF - RACINGUK.COM/HD NOVICE STKS (PLUS 10 RACE) 6f
**2:15** (2:16) (Class 4) 2-Y-O **£4,528** (£1,347; £673; £336) **Stalls** Centre

Form RPR

2 **1** **No I'm Easy (IRE)**[24] 5350 2-9-2 0.................... RichardKingscote 6 77+
(Tom Dascombe) *trckd ldrs: pushed along and angled rt over 1f out: rdn and r.o wl fnl f: led towards fin* **15/8**[2]

0 **2** *nk* **Harrogate (IRE)**[11] 5825 2-9-2 0.................... PJMcDonald 7 76
(James Bethell) *trckd ldrs: rdn to ld ins fnl f: kpt on but hdd towards fin* **28/1**

6 **3** *1* **Champarisi**[7] 5998 2-8-11 0.................... JackGarritty 8 68
(Grant Tuer) *prom: pushed along to ld over 1f out: hdd ins fnl f: one pce* **100/1**

**4** *hd* **Soldier's Minute** 2-8-11 0.................... RowanScott(5) 9 73
(Keith Dalgleish) *hld up in midfield: rdn along 2f out: kpt on wl fnl f* **20/1**

5 **5** *1* **Saisons D'Or (IRE)**[31] 5099 2-9-2 0.................... GrahamLee 3 70
(Jedd O'Keeffe) *trckd ldrs: rdn 2f out: one pce* **16/1**

**6** *1 ½* **Al Mustashar (IRE)** 2-9-2 0.................... MartinLane 10 65
(Saeed bin Suroor) *dwlt: hld up: hdwy into midfield 1/2-way: rdn over 1f out: sn one pce and no prog* **10/11**[1]

1 **7** *1* **That's A Surprise (IRE)**[44] 4599 2-9-8 0.................... BarryMcHugh 2 68
(Tony Coyle) *led: rdn whn hdd over 1f out: wknd ins fnl f* **7/1**[3]

00 **8** *2 ¼* **Aliento**[47] 4502 2-8-11 0.................... AndrewMullen 12 50
(Ollie Pears) *dwlt: hld up: pushed along over 2f out: kpt on steadily* **200/1**

05 **9** *½* **Marconi**[12] 5801 2-9-2 0.................... PhillipMakin 11 54
(John Davies) *hld up in midfield: pushed along over 2f out: nvr threatened* **150/1**

00 **10** *4* **Albarino**[91] 2882 2-9-2 0.................... TomEaves 13 42
(Kevin Ryan) *hld up in rr: pushed along 2f out: nvr threatened* **80/1**

**11** *2 ¼* **Chef United** 2-8-11 0.................... TonyHamilton 5 30
(Roger Fell) *dwlt: hld up in midfield: pushed along over 2f out: wknd over 1f out* **100/1**

**12** *3* **Sentimental Gent (FR)** 2-9-2 0.................... KevinStott 4 26
(Kevin Ryan) *dwlt: hld up: nvr threatened* **33/1**

**13** *6* **Eeh Bah Gum (IRE)** 2-9-2 0.................... DanielTudhope 1 8
(David O'Meara) *trckd ldrs: rdn over 2f out: wknd over 1f out* **20/1**

1m 13.68s (0.98) **Going Correction** -0.175s/f (Firm) **13** Ran SP% **125.8**
Speed ratings (Par 96): **86,85,84,84,82 80,79,76,75,70 67,63,55**
CSF £63.67 TOTE £2.80: £1.02, £6.40, £27.30; EX 53.30 Trifecta £7938.80.
**Owner** The Groundhog Day Partnership **Bred** D Phelan **Trained** Malpas, Cheshire

**FOCUS**
Race distances increased 30yds for races 2, 3 & 5, and 40yds for races 6 & 7. The going had dried out to Good ahead of the opener, an uncompetitive novice in which they came down the middle. The protagonists finished in a heap and it looks ordinary form.

## 6265 JAMES HERRIOT "ALL CREATURES" FAMILY DAY TODAY H'CAP 7f
**2:45** (2:46) (Class 5) (0-75,77) 3-Y-O **£3,881** (£1,155; £577; £288) **Stalls** Low

Form RPR

0430 **1** **Proud Archi (IRE)**[24] 5376 3-9-4 **77**.................... CallumRodriguez(5) 12 83
(Michael Dods) *dwlt: hld up: pushed along and hdwy over 2f out: rdn to chse ldr over 1f out: led 110yds out: kpt on* **5/1**[1]

3452 **2** *nk* **Lady In Question (IRE)**[9] 5922 3-8-13 **70**.......... AdamMcNamara(3) 10 75
(Richard Fahey) *midfield on outside: rdn and hdwy over 2f out: led over 1f out: hdd 110yds out: kpt on* **5/1**[1]

634- **3** *1* **Heaven's Rock (IRE)**[248] 8405 3-9-1 **69**.................... RichardKingscote 6 71
(Tom Dascombe) *trckd ldr: rdn over 2f out: kpt on same pce* **33/1**

5643 **4** *nk* **Queens Royale**[9] 5935 3-7-11 **56**.................... JaneElliott(5) 1 57
(Michael Appleby) *trckd ldr: rdn to chal over 2f out: one pce fnl f* **25/1**

0031 **5** *1 ½* **Inglorious**[9] 5922 3-8-8 **67**....................(p) RowanScott(5) 2 64
(Keith Dalgleish) *hld up: pushed along over 3f out: kpt on ins fnl f: nrst fin* **8/1**[3]

6306 **6** *1* **Grinty (IRE)**[14] 5697 3-8-13 **67**.................... PaulMulrennan 7 61
(Michael Dods) *trckd ldrs: rdn over 2f out: no ex fnl f* **25/1**

1004 **7** *½* **Oud Metha Bridge (IRE)**[24] 5363 3-9-5 **73**.................... TomEaves 5 66
(Ed Dunlop) *midfield on inner: rdn over 2f out: one pce and nvr threatened* **18/1**

0114 **8** *1 ½* **Clear As A Bell (IRE)**[7] 6015 3-8-10 **64**.................... DavidAllan 3 53
(Tim Easterby) *led: rdn over 2f out: hdd over 1f out: wknd ins fnl f* **11/2**[2]

0-03 **9** *1 ¾* **Ghaseedah**[45] 4568 3-9-3 **71**....................(h) GrahamLee 9 55
(Simon Crisford) *dwlt: midfield: pushed along over 2f out: wknd ins fnl f* **14/1**

4213 **10** *2 ¼* **Cupid's Arrow (IRE)**[13] 5741 3-8-10 **64**.................... JamesSullivan 11 42
(Ruth Carr) *hld up in midfield on wd outside: sltly hmpd and dropped towards rr 5f out: pushed along and sme hdwy over 2f out: wknd over 1f out* **8/1**[3]

-032 **11** *¾* **Perfect Symphony (IRE)**[31] 5132 3-9-7 **75**....................(p) KevinStott 8 51
(Kevin Ryan) *trckd ldrs: racd keenly: rdn 3f out: wknd over 1f out* **11/2**[2]

4-25 **12** *2 ½* **Screaming Gemini (IRE)**[10] 5870 3-9-1 **69**....................(p[1]) JackMitchell 4 38
(Roger Varian) *hld up: rdn over 2f out: sn btn* **11/1**

1m 28.87s (1.67) **Going Correction** +0.35s/f (Good) **12** Ran SP% **117.2**
Speed ratings (Par 100): **104,103,102,102,100 99,98,97,95,92 91,88**
CSF £28.40 CT £757.95 TOTE £6.30: £1.90, £2.20, £7.30; EX 32.20 Trifecta £705.70.
**Owner** Eagle Racing **Bred** Robert Allcock **Trained** Denton, Co Durham

**FOCUS**
Race distance increased 30yds. A competitive handicap in which two of the last three winners of the race won next time out, and they went a fair pace. The winner is back to his reappearance form off this mark.

## 6266 WORLD OF JAMES HERRIOT H'CAP 7f 218y
**3:15** (3:16) (Class 4) (0-80,81) 3-Y-O+ **£5,822** (£1,732; £865; £432) **Stalls** Low

Form RPR

4333 **1** **Mon Beau Visage (IRE)**[34] 5000 4-10-0 **80**..........(p) DanielTudhope 11 91
(David O'Meara) *hld up in midfield: smooth hdwy on outer over 2f out: pushed along to ld 1f out: rdn and kpt on* **9/2**[1]

0054 **2** *1 ¾* **Briyouni (FR)**[9] 5926 4-9-13 **79**....................(p) TomEaves 12 86
(Kevin Ryan) *s.i.s: hld up in rr: rdn and hdwy on outer 2f out: kpt on wl fnl f: wnt 2nd towards fin* **15/2**

-241 **3** *nk* **Whitkirk**[63] 3906 4-9-3 **69**.................... JackGarritty 2 75
(Jedd O'Keeffe) *trckd ldrs: rdn over 2f out: led over 1f out: hdd 1f out: one pce: lost 2nd towards fin* **8/1**

06 **4** *½* **Celtic Artisan (IRE)**[20] 5510 6-8-13 **65**....................(bt) PJMcDonald 4 70
(Rebecca Menzies) *midfield on inner: swtchd rt 2f out: sn rdn and hdwy: kpt on wl fnl f* **40/1**

4150 **5** *1* **Vaulted**[16] 5666 3-8-10 **68**.................... TonyHamilton 3 70
(Richard Fahey) *dwlt: sn in tch: smooth hdwy 2f out: rdn over 1f out: edgd lft ins fnl f: no ex* **16/1**

5005 **6** *1 ¼* **Off Art**[20] 5496 7-9-4 **70**....................(p) DavidAllan 8 70
(Tim Easterby) *midfield: rdn over 2f out: one pce and nvr threatened* **6/1**[2]

2530 **7** *2* **Sovereign Bounty**[16] 5668 5-9-13 **79**.................... GrahamLee 1 74+
(Jedd O'Keeffe) *trckd ldrs on inner: pushed along whn bit short of room and lost pl 2f out: short of room again ins fnl f: no ch after* **8/1**

1045 **8** *1 ½* **Sidewinder (IRE)**[52] 4290 3-9-7 **79**.................... RichardKingscote 7 70
(Tom Dascombe) *in tch: rdn over 2f out: wknd fnl f* **7/1**[3]

2414 **9** *hd* **Destroyer**[31] 5130 4-10-1 **81**.................... JamesSullivan 6 72
(Tom Tate) *prom: led 6f out: rdn whn hdd over 1f out: wknd* **8/1**

4043 **10** *1 ¼* **Worlds His Oyster**[14] 5699 4-10-0 **80**.................... JasonHart 9 69
(John Quinn) *hld up: rdn over 2f out: nvr threatened* **6/1**[2]

0200 **11** *½* **Shearian**[20] 5497 7-8-9 **61**....................(b[1]) KevinStott 10 48
(Declan Carroll) *led: hdd 6f out: remained cl up: rdn over 2f out: sn wknd* **40/1**

3-40 **12** *5* **Different Journey**[91] 2887 4-9-7 **73**.................... CamHardie 5 49
(Michael Easterby) *dwlt: a towards rr* **66/1**

1m 41.8s (1.70) **Going Correction** +0.35s/f (Good)
**WFA** 3 from 4yo+ 6lb **12** Ran SP% **116.6**
Speed ratings (Par 105): **105,103,102,102,101 100,98,96,96,95 94,89**
CSF £36.99 CT £267.34 TOTE £5.40: £1.90, £2.70, £2.70; EX 40.50 Trifecta £331.70.
**Owner** The Pink Pot Partnership LLP **Bred** Stephanie Hanly **Trained** Upper Helmsley, N Yorks

**FOCUS**
Race distance increased 30yds. An average handicap in which they went a good pace, and there were several eyecatching efforts as a couple got blocked on the inside rail behind the weakening front-runner. A clear step forward from the winner.

## 6267 RACING UK CLUB DAY HERE TODAY H'CAP 5f
**3:45** (3:46) (Class 4) (0-80,81) 4-Y-O+ **£6,469** (£1,925; £962; £481) **Stalls** Centre

Form RPR

05 **1** **Memories Galore (IRE)**[9] 5920 5-9-6 **78**..........(p) TonyHamilton 14 89
(Roger Fell) *trckd ldr towards stands' side: pushed along to ld ins fnl f: kpt on wl* **33/1**

0302 **2** *¾* **Bogart**[16] 5671 8-9-9 **81**....................(tp) TomEaves 18 90
(Kevin Ryan) *trckd ldr towards stands' side: rdn to ld over 1f out: hdd ins fnl f: kpt on wl but a hld* **15/2**[3]

4-1 **3** *4* **African Friend (IRE)**[51] 4368 4-9-5 **77**.................... BenCurtis 19 74
(Henry Candy) *dwlt: midfield towards stands' side: rdn 2f out: kpt on fnl f: wnt 3rd fnsl 50yds* **3/1**[1]

020 **4** *¾* **Alsvinder**[17] 5602 4-9-6 **78**.................... DanielTudhope 11 73
(David O'Meara) *racd stands' side: led: rdn whn hdd over 1f out: no ex ins fnl f* **18/1**

3546 **5** *½* **Invincible Ridge (IRE)**[42] 4686 9-9-4 **76**.................... NeilFarley 8 69+
(Eric Alston) *dwlt: hld up centre: rdn and sme hdwy over 1f out: kpt on fnl f: nrst fin* **25/1**

3500 **6** *nk* **Grandad's World (IRE)**[70] 3653 5-9-4 **76**.................... JackGarritty 5 68
(Richard Fahey) *chsd ldrs centre: rdn 2f out: one pce fnl f* **20/1**

003 **7** *shd* **Elysian Flyer (IRE)**[16] 5647 5-9-9 **81**.................... CamHardie 15 73
(Paul Midgley) *hld up stands' side: rdn and edgd lft to centre over 1f out: kpt on fnl f* **16/1**

0222 **8** *2* **Point Of Woods**[17] 5620 4-8-6 **64**....................(p) JoeDoyle 12 50
(Tina Jackson) *midfield towards stands' side: rdn 1/2-way: wknd ins fnl f* **20/1**

6432 **9** *shd* **Landing Night (IRE)**[26] 5281 5-9-0 **72**....................(tp) PJMcDonald 16 58
(Rebecca Menzies) *in tch stands' side: rdn over 2f out: wknd ins fnl f* **12/1**

644 **10** *½* **Olivia Fallow (IRE)**[26] 5281 5-9-7 **79**.................... GrahamLee 9 63
(Paul Midgley) *dwlt: hld up centre: pushed along 2f out: kpt on fnl f: nvr threatened* **14/1**

2263 **11** *½* **Flash City (ITY)**[12] 5804 9-8-10 **68**.................... JamesSullivan 17 51
(Ruth Carr) *slowly away: hld up stands' side and nvr threatened* **20/1**

4202 **12** *½* **Bronze Beau**[11] 5818 10-9-3 **75**....................(tp) ShaneGray 7 56
(Kristin Stubbs) *racd centre: w ldr: rdn 1/2-way: wknd over 1f out* **33/1**

4 **13** *shd* **Eternalist**[46] 4531 4-8-3 **61**....................(h) PatrickMathers 3 42
(Jim Goldie) *prom towards centre: rdn 1/2-way: wknd over 1f out* **18/1**

3625 **14** *½* **Fruit Salad**[39] 4787 4-8-12 **75**....................(p) CallumRodriguez(5) 13 54
(James Bethell) *hld up stands' side: nvr threatened* **14/1**

0536 **15** *¾* **B Fifty Two (IRE)**[14] 5696 8-9-0 **72**....................(t[1]) BarryMcHugh 1 49
(Marjorie Fife) *chsd ldrs towards centre: rdn 1/2-way: wknd over 1f out* **10/1**

0455 **16** *nk* **Pea Shooter**[5] 6062 8-8-9 **72**....................(t) BenRobinson(5) 6 48
(Brian Ellison) *chsd ldrs towards centre: rdn 1/2-way: wknd over 1f out* **25/1**

2503 **17** *¾* **Interlink (USA)**[3] 6141 4-8-9 **67**.................... KevinStott 10 41
(Michael Appleby) *rrd s: a towards rr* **6/1**[2]

31-0 **18** *2* **Mysterious Glance**[35] 4965 4-8-12 **70**.................... RoystonFfrench 2 38
(Sarah Hollinshead) *hld up centre: rdn 1/2-way: sn wknd* **66/1**

50-5 **19** *4* **L C Saloon**[139] 1542 4-9-3 **75**.................... DavidAllan 4 31
(David C Griffiths) *midfield centre: rdn 1/2-way: sn wknd* **33/1**

58.05s (-1.55) **Going Correction** -0.175s/f (Firm) **19** Ran SP% **129.9**
Speed ratings (Par 105): **105,103,97,96,95 94,94,91,91,90 89,89,88,88,86 86,85,81,75**
CSF £250.91 CT £782.83 TOTE £36.70: £6.00, £2.20, £1.60, £4.10; EX 402.90 Trifecta £1596.90.
**Owner** High Hopes 2017 **Bred** Windflower Overseas Holdings Inc **Trained** Nawton, N Yorks


The Form Book Flat, Raceform Ltd, Newbury, RG14 5SJ

**FOCUS**
Competitive stuff despite the short-priced favourite. It was very much a draw race, with the first four home coming up the stands' rail from double-figure stalls. The winner was back to his turf best.

## 6268 BREEDERS BACKING RACING EBF - RACINGUK.COM/DAYPASS MAIDEN STKS 7f
4:15 (4:17) (Class 4) 3-Y-0+ £5,822 (£1,732; £865; £432) Stalls Low

Form RPR
062 1 **Dance Teacher (IRE)**[31] 5111 3-9-0 69........................ DanielTudhope 9 80+
(Ralph Beckett) *mde all: slipped clr over 3f out: pushed along over 2f out: rdn over 1f out: eased towards fin* **15/8**[2]
2 *5* **Sacred Way** 3-9-5 0...................................................... TomEaves 10 69
(Kevin Ryan) *midfield: rdn and sme hdwy over 2f out: kpt on but no ch w easy wnr* **14/1**
5 3 *shd* **Naaeebb (USA)**[68] 3714 3-9-5 0......................................(p[1]) KevinStott 11 68+
(Saeed bin Suroor) *hld up: stl lot to do over 3f out: rdn and hdwy over 2f out: kpt on* **5/4**[1]
33 4 *2* **Glenn Coco**[18] 5577 3-9-5 0.............................................. PJMcDonald 7 63
(Stuart Williams) *midfield: pushed along and hdwy 2f out: rdn to chse clr ldr appr fnl f: no ex fnl 110yds* **16/1**
-63 5 *4 1/2* **Chosen World**[9] 5946 3-9-5 0.............................................. JoeDoyle 3 51+
(Julie Camacho) *midfield: pushed along over 2f out: nvr threatened* **16/1**
62 6 *nk* **Charlie's Dreamer**[8] 5969 3-8-9 0................................ JaneElliott(5) 13 45
(Michael Appleby) *chsd clr ldr: rdn 3f out: wknd fnl f* **16/1**
6 7 *2* **Boogey Wonderland**[49] 4445 3-9-0 0................................ DavidAllan 5 39
(Scott Dixon) *hld up: pushed along over 4f out: nvr threatened* **40/1**
50 8 *hd* **My Angel**[19] 5538 3-9-0 0................................................ AndrewMullen 2 39
(Ollie Pears) *in tch: rdn over 2f out: wknd over 1f out* **100/1**
00 9 *1/2* **Precious Rock (IRE)**[19] 5538 3-9-5 0...............................(h[1]) JackGarritty 4 43
(Jedd O'Keeffe) *chsd clr ldr: rdn along over 3f out: wknd over 1f out* **100/1**
3632 10 *5* **Arnarson**[39] 4784 3-9-5 77............................................(t[1]) PaulMulrennan 8 29
(Ed Dunlop) *trckd ldrs: rdn to chse clr clr 2f out: wknd over 1f out* **8/1**[3]
0000 11 *3 3/4* **Zarkavon**[9] 5946 3-9-0 23............................................(h[1]) JamesSullivan 1 14
(John Wainwright) *hld up: nvr threatened* **200/1**
12 *3/4* **Major Minus** 3-9-2 0........................................... RachelRichardson(3) 6 17
(Tim Easterby) *slowly away: a rr* **66/1**
05-0 13 *12* **Kirkby's Phantom**[19] 5538 3-9-0 40.............................. PatrickMathers 12
(Colin Teague) *dwlt: a towards rr* **200/1**

1m 28.96s (1.76) **Going Correction** +0.35s/f (Good) 13 Ran SP% **122.0**
Speed ratings (Par 105): **103,97,97,94,89 89,87,86,86,80 76,75,61**
CSF £29.42 TOTE £3.00: £1.50, £4.20, £1.10; EX 33.90 Trifecta £74.10.
**Owner** Clipper Logistics **Bred** Oakhill Stud **Trained** Kimpton, Hants

**FOCUS**
Race distance increased 30yds. A moderate maiden and an easy winner who made all. The time comes out 10lb slower than the earlier handicap.

## 6269 @THIRSKRACES "PIRATES FAMILY DAY" FRIDAY 1ST SEPTEMBER H'CAP (DIV I) 1m 4f 8y
4:45 (4:45) (Class 6) (0-65,68) 3-Y-0+ £3,234 (£962; £481; £240) Stalls High

Form RPR
6031 1 **Sepal (USA)**[7] 5997 4-10-1 68 6ex........................... CallumRodriguez(5) 8 80+
(Iain Jardine) *midfield: hdwy over 3f out: rdn over 2f out: led over 1f out: styd on wl to draw clr* **1/1**[1]
304 2 *7* **Steccando (IRE)**[10] 5883 4-9-11 59.................................... BenCurtis 4 57
(Sally Haynes) *hld up: rdn and hdwy over 2f out: styd on but no threat wnr* **18/1**
0300 3 *shd* **Ivors Involvement (IRE)**[4] 6092 5-8-11 45............................ TomEaves 6 43
(Tina Jackson) *led: rdn over 2f out: hdd over 1f out: sn no ch w wnr: plugged on* **33/1**
0622 4 *5* **Correggio**[22] 5455 7-10-0 62.............................................. PJMcDonald 9 52
(Micky Hammond) *midfield: rdn 3f out: plugged on* **6/1**[3]
0403 5 *1 3/4* **Decima (IRE)**[20] 5498 3-9-4 61.........................................(t[1]) CamHardie 3 49
(Michael Easterby) *hld up: rdn along and outpcd in rr over 3f out: plugged on fnl f: nvr threatened* **12/1**
2000 6 *1* **Arithmetic (IRE)**[12] 5807 4-10-0 62.................................. JamesSullivan 1 48
(Ruth Carr) *hld up in midfield: rdn 3f out: sn no prog: wknd fnl f* **22/1**
2256 7 *2* **Luv U Whatever**[14] 5701 7-10-4 66..............................(t) BarryMcHugh 5 48
(Marjorie Fife) *trckd ldrs: rdn over 3f out: wknd over 1f out* **5/1**[2]
5002 8 *11* **In Focus (IRE)**[17] 5599 6-9-6 54...................................(h) PaulMulrennan 7 19
(Dianne Sayer) *trckd ldr: rdn over 3f out: wknd fnl 2f* **7/1**

2m 37.56s (1.36) **Going Correction** +0.35s/f (Good)
**WFA** 3 from 4yo+ 9lb 8 Ran SP% **113.7**
Speed ratings (Par 101): **109,104,104,100,99 99,97,90**
CSF £22.24 CT £371.62 TOTE £1.90: £1.10, £3.90, £6.90; EX 19.80 Trifecta £301.10.
**Owner** I J Jardine **Bred** Juddmonte Farms Inc **Trained** Carrutherstown, D'fries & G'way

**FOCUS**
Race distance increased 40yds. An uncompetitive handicap in which the short-priced favourite won easily.

## 6270 @THIRSKRACES "PIRATES FAMILY DAY" FRIDAY 1ST SEPTEMBER H'CAP (DIV II) 1m 4f 8y
5:15 (5:15) (Class 6) (0-65,67) 3-Y-0+ £3,234 (£962; £481; £240) Stalls High

Form RPR
1310 1 **Percys Princess**[26] 5290 6-9-11 67............................... JaneElliott(5) 8 74
(Michael Appleby) *mde all: rdn over 2f out: kpt on* **8/1**
6453 2 *3/4* **Good Time Ahead (IRE)**[11] 5831 3-9-0 60.......................... KevinStott 4 67
(Philip Kirby) *midfield: rdn and hdwy over 2f out: chsd ldr over 1f out: kpt on* **7/2**[1]
3030 3 *2 1/2* **Dream Free**[11] 5824 4-9-9 60.......................................(p) JasonHart 5 62
(Mark Walford) *chsd ldr: racd quite keenly: rdn over 2f out: one pce fnl f* **8/1**
0046 4 *1/2* **Silver Gleam (IRE)**[17] 5617 3-8-2 48............................ DuranFentiman 9 50
(Chris Fairhurst) *hld up: rdn and sme hdwy over 2f out: kpt on same pce* **8/1**
003 5 *2 1/4* **Calliope**[9] 5951 4-9-4 62...............................(h[1]) JamieGormley(7) 2 59
(Kenneth Slack) *hld up: rdn over 2f out: kpt on ins fnl f: nvr threatened* **9/2**[2]
-660 6 *hd* **Pennerley**[33] 5017 4-9-1 52............................................. PJMcDonald 7 49
(Micky Hammond) *midfield: rdn over 2f out: no imp* **33/1**
4106 7 *1/2* **Infiniti (IRE)**[41] 4730 4-9-6 57........................................ GrahamLee 6 53
(Barry Leavy) *in tch: rdn over 2f out: wknd over 1f out* **13/2**[3]
4364 8 *3/4* **Surround Sound**[17] 5599 7-9-5 59..................(tp) RachelRichardson(3) 1 54
(Tim Easterby) *dwlt: hld up: nvr threatened* **10/1**
606 9 *1* **Melabi (IRE)**[15] 5686 4-9-9 65................................ CallumRodriguez(5) 3 58
(Richard Ford) *hld up in midfield: rdn over 2f out: wknd fnl f* **13/2**[3]

2m 39.8s (3.60) **Going Correction** +0.35s/f (Good)
**WFA** 3 from 4yo+ 9lb 9 Ran SP% **112.4**
Speed ratings (Par 101): **102,101,99,99,98 97,97,97,96**
CSF £34.98 CT £230.92 TOTE £5.60: £2.30, £1.50, £2.90; EX 34.10 Trifecta £203.00.
**Owner** C A Blyth **Bred** Norman A Blyth **Trained** Oakham, Rutland

**FOCUS**
Race distance increased 40yds. The second division looked weaker and there was another all-the-way winner on the card.

## 6271 @THIRSKRACES LADIES' DAY SATURDAY 9TH SEPTEMBER H'CAP (FOR LADY AMATEUR RIDERS) 6f
5:45 (5:47) (Class 6) (0-60,60) 3-Y-0+ £2,495 (£774; £386; £193) Stalls Centre

Form RPR
3030 1 **Whipphound**[6] 6045 9-9-2 46 oh1.......................(b) MissEmilyBullock(5) 13 56
(Ruth Carr) *chsd ldrs: rdn 2f out: led 1f out: kpt on wl* **6/1**[2]
0006 2 *3* **Bop It**[83] 3186 8-10-7 60.............................................(t) MissJoannaMason 10 61
(Michael Easterby) *prom: rdn to ld 2f out: hdd 1f out: one pce* **16/1**
0040 3 *1 3/4* **A J Cook (IRE)**[14] 5695 7-9-4 46 oh1............................ MissLWilson(3) 6 42
(Ron Barr) *midfield: rdn over 2f out: kpt on fr over 1f out* **28/1**
510 4 *1/2* **Searanger (USA)**[19] 5543 4-10-4 57.......................... MissEmmaSayer 12 51
(Rebecca Menzies) *hld up: rdn 2f out: kpt on fnl f: nrst fin* **8/1**[3]
0364 5 *nse* **Mitchum**[6] 6045 8-10-2 55.........................................(p) MissSBrotherton 5 49
(Ron Barr) *chsd ldrs towards outer: rdn over 2f out: no ex ins fnl f* **8/1**[3]
6203 6 *1 1/4* **Rose Eclair**[6] 6046 4-10-4 60...................................(p) MissEEasterby(3) 14 50
(Tim Easterby) *led: rdn whn hdd 2f out: wknd ins fnl f* **7/2**[1]
6414 7 *1/2* **Gaelic Wizard (IRE)**[6] 6046 9-9-11 55..........................(b) MissJCooley(5) 8 44
(Karen Tutty) *chsd ldrs: rdn 2f out: wknd ins fnl f* **7/2**[1]
0000 8 *2* **Very First Blade**[3] 6130 8-9-7 46 oh1......................(p) MissMMullineaux 11 29
(Michael Mullineaux) *hld up: nvr threatened* **28/1**
5305 9 *2 1/4* **Ss Vega**[9] 5919 4-9-2 46 oh1.........................................(b) MissRHill(5) 1 22
(Jim Goldie) *sn outpcd in rr: minor late hdwy* **22/1**
605 10 *1 1/4* **Major Muscari (IRE)**[11] 5848 9-9-10 49...........................(p) MrsCBartley 4 21
(Shaun Harris) *dwlt: hld up: hdwy on outer over 2f out: wknd fnl f* **16/1**
0006 11 *nk* **Three C's (IRE)**[14] 5703 3-9-7 49...................................(tp) MissPFuller 15 20
(David Dennis) *in tch: rdn over 2f out: wknd over 1f out* **33/1**
0000 12 *1/2* **Hitchcock**[29] 5182 3-9-8 57.........................................(p[1]) MissHTLees(7) 2 27
(Kevin Ryan) *dwlt: a rr* **9/1**

1m 12.77s (0.07) **Going Correction** -0.175s/f (Firm)
**WFA** 3 from 4yo+ 3lb 12 Ran SP% **116.9**
Speed ratings (Par 101): **92,88,85,85,84 83,82,79,76,75 74,74**
CSF £91.13 CT £2510.18 TOTE £6.30: £2.10, £4.80, £7.40; EX 104.50 Trifecta £3935.20.
**Owner** Grange Park Racing IX & Ruth Carr **Bred** Mrs B Skinner **Trained** Huby, N Yorks

**FOCUS**
A moderate sprint handicap for lady amateurs and the draw was again a factor as those near the stands' rail were favoured.
T/Jkpt: Not Won. T/Plt: £41.10 to a £1 stake. Pool: £77,646.89 - 1,376.38 winning units T/Qpdt: £4.70 to a £1 stake. Pool: £6,868.54 - 1,059.67 winning units **Andrew Sheret**

# 6004 WINDSOR (R-H)
Monday, August 21

**OFFICIAL GOING: Good to soft (6.3)**
Wind: Light, against Weather: Overcast, quite humid

## 6272 SKY BET BRITISH STALLION STUDS EBF NOVICE STKS (PLUS 10 RACE) 6f 12y
5:20 (5:21) (Class 4) 2-Y-0 £4,592 (£1,366; £683; £341) Stalls Low

Form RPR
1 1 **Snazzy Jazzy (IRE)**[80] 3305 2-9-8 0................................ AdamKirby 6 90
(Clive Cox) *led or disp thrght: tk field towards far side 1/2-way: jnd by runner-up 2f out and pair sn clr: drvn to assert last 75yds* **11/4**[2]
2 *1/2* **Society Power (IRE)** 2-9-2 0.......................................... PatCosgrave 10 83+
(William Haggas) *s.s: sn rcvrd into midfield: prog to join wnr 2f out: rn green against far rail over 1f out: urged along and no ex last 75yds* **7/2**[3]
2 3 *5* **Qianlong**[13] 5755 2-9-2 0............................................... AndreaAtzeni 4 68
(Roger Varian) *trckd ldrs: outpcd and rdn 2f out: tk 3rd over 1f out: no threat to ldng pair* **13/8**[1]
6 4 *1/2* **Pastamakesufaster**[48] 4466 2-8-11 0................................ RobertTart 12 61
(David Evans) *trckd ldrs: outpcd over 2f out: disp 3rd over 1f out: kpt on* **33/1**
56 5 *2* **Graffitista (IRE)**[33] 5026 2-8-11 0.................................. HarryBentley 2 55
(George Scott) *hld up towards rr: outpcd over 2f out: pushed along and sme hdwy over 1f out: reminders fnl f and kpt on* **20/1**
6 *3/4* **Heidi** 2-8-11 0........................................................... SeanLevey 8 53
(Richard Hannon) *t.k.h: hld up in midfield: shkn up and outpcd over 2f out: one pce after* **17/2**
7 *1 1/4* **Kath's Lustre** 2-8-11 0................................................ RobHornby 1 49
(Ben De Haan) *in tch: shkn up and outpcd over 2f out: no ch after* **100/1**
60 8 *1/2* **Swissal (IRE)**[32] 5048 2-9-2 0...................................... LukeMorris 9 53
(David Dennis) *wl in rr: pushed along in last 1/2-way: rdn and prog 2f out: disp 3rd briefly over 1f out: wknd qckly fnl f* **66/1**
9 *1/2* **Count Otto (IRE)** 2-9-2 0............................................... PatDobbs 7 51
(Amanda Perrett) *chsd ldrs: outpcd over 2f out: fdd over 1f out* **20/1**
5 10 *2 1/4* **Hollie's Dream**[91] 2904 2-8-11 0................................. StevieDonohoe 11 39
(David Evans) *w wnr to 1/2-way: lost 2nd and wknd rapidly wl over 1f out* **66/1**

1m 16.29s (3.29) **Going Correction** +0.425s/f (Yiel) 10 Ran SP% **114.0**
Speed ratings (Par 96): **95,94,87,87,84 83,81,81,80,77**
CSF £11.60 TOTE £3.60: £1.70, £1.60, £1.10; EX 14.80 Trifecta £26.30.
**Owner** Mrs Olive Shaw **Bred** Bluegate Stud **Trained** Lambourn, Berks

**FOCUS**
Cloudy but dry conditions, following 8mm of rain overnight. The stands' rail was dolled out 12yds in the straight but no changes to distances were advised. The stalls were on the inner for this fair sprint novice event, in which the whole field shifted to the far rail over 2f out.

## 6273 SKY BET SUPPORTING GIVE A DUCK H'CAP 1m 2f
5:50 (5:50) (Class 4) (0-80,82) 4-Y-0+ £4,690 (£1,395; £697; £348) Stalls Centre

Form RPR
6000 1 **Essenaitch (IRE)**[20] 5518 4-8-9 67........................................ JFEgan 6 74
(David Evans) *trckd ldrs: clsd to take 2nd over 2f out: rdn to ld over 1f out: hrd pressed ins fnl f: hld on wl* **8/1**

5051 **2** *nk* **Michael's Mount**[30] 5140 4-9-7 **79**......(b) LukeMorris 8 85
(Ed Dunlop) *hld up in tch: stdy prog over 2f out: rdn to take 2nd jst over 1f out: hrd drvn to chal fnl f: hanging and nt qckn last 75yds* **8/1**

126 **3** *2* **Eskendash (USA)**[91] 2893 4-9-6 **78**...... AdamKirby 9 80
(Pam Sly) *trckd ldr: led after 3f: drvn over 2f out: hdd and one pce over 1f out* **5/2**[1]

4233 **4** *½* **Outback Blue**[10] 5888 4-9-1 **73**......(vt) JamesDoyle 7 74
(David Evans) *s.s: hld up in last: rdn and prog jst over 2f out: rchd 4th over 1f out* **6/1**[3]

1200 **5** *nk* **Boycie**[32] 5060 4-9-7 **79**...... SeanLevey 3 79
(Richard Hannon) *trckd ldrs: rdn and nt qckn over 2f out: nt on terms after: kpt on ins fnl f* **9/1**

3026 **6** *¾* **Glorious Poet**[28] 5221 4-8-7 **72**...... ManuelFernandes(7) 4 71
(John Spearing) *taken down early: t.k.h: hld up in rr: rdn over 2f out: hanging rt and no prog over 1f out: kpt on last 100yds* **8/1**

0053 **7** *2¾* **Carnival King (IRE)**[14] 5719 5-9-4 **81**......(b) DavidEgan(5) 5 74
(Amy Murphy) *led 3f: chsd ldr to over 2f out: steadily wknd* **25/1**

0605 **8** *5* **Captain Peacock**[26] 5303 4-9-10 **82**......(v) AndreaAtzeni 2 65
(William Knight) *in tch in rr: urged along over 3f out: little rspnse and wknd 2f out* **14/1**

4333 **9** *2* **Lexington Law (IRE)**[18] 5579 4-9-9 **81**......(v[1]) TomMarquand 10 60
(Alan King) *in tch: rdn over 2f out: sn wknd* **5/1**[2]

2m 13.08s (4.38) **Going Correction** +0.425s/f (Yiel) **9** Ran SP% **113.4**
Speed ratings (Par 105): **99,98,97,96,96 95,93,89,88**
CSF £68.67 CT £205.46 TOTE £10.70: £2.80, £2.30, £1.40; EX 58.40 Trifecta £583.80.
**Owner** Spiers & Hartwell Ltd & Mrs E Evans **Bred** Charel Park Stud **Trained** Pandy, Monmouths

**FOCUS**
Stalls in centre. Just a fair event for the grade, and the initial good pace slackened as the leader stacked them up at the bottom bend. The runners chose the centre and far sides down the straight. The winner is rated back to his spring form.

## 6274 SKY BET BEST ODDS GUARANTEED FILLIES' H'CAP 1m 31y
**6:20** (6:21) (Class 4) (0-80,78) 3-Y-0+ **£4,690** (£1,395; £697; £348) **Stalls** Low

Form RPR

1612 **1** **Kyllachys Tale (IRE)**[25] 5332 3-9-2 **74**...... JamesDoyle 7 87
(Roger Teal) *taken down early: mde all: kicked clr 3f out and taken to far rail: in n.d after: pushed out fnl f* **6/1**

301 **2** *5* **UAE Queen**[33] 5038 3-9-5 **77**...... AndreaAtzeni 3 78
(Roger Varian) *chsd ldrs: rdn wl over 2f out: tk 2nd 2f out but no ch w wnr fr then on: plugged on* **3/1**[1]

2522 **3** *½* **Fastnet Spin (IRE)**[6] 6028 3-9-0 **72**......(vt) JFEgan 9 71
(David Evans) *sn last and nt gng wl: rdn and prog 2f out: chal for 2nd fnl f: kpt on but no ch w wnr* **8/1**

1024 **4** *nk* **Snow Squaw**[28] 5221 3-8-10 **73**...... DavidEgan(5) 1 72
(David Elsworth) *t.k.h: hld up in midfield: styd towards nr side in st: rdn and pressed for a pl fr 2f out: kpt on* **11/2**[3]

1145 **5** *¾* **La Celebs Ville (IRE)**[30] 5135 4-9-6 **77**......(p) PaddyPilley(5) 6 75
(Tom Dascombe) *trckd ldrs: drvn and outpcd over 2f out: one pce after* **20/1**

1-42 **6** *1½* **Medicean Ballet (IRE)**[25] 5324 3-9-4 **76**...... DaneO'Neill 2 69
(Henry Candy) *slowly away: mostly in last trio: rdn and no prog over 2f out* **5/1**[2]

0321 **7** *1½* **Accomplice**[12] 5783 3-8-9 **67**...... RobHornby 4 57
(Michael Blanshard) *hld up in last trio: pushed along and lft bhd fr 3f out: no ch after* **9/1**

1642 **8** *½* **Carducci**[19] 5549 3-9-6 **78**...... SeanLevey 8 67
(Richard Hannon) *mostly chsd wnr to 2f out: wknd* **5/1**[2]

1m 47.29s (2.59) **Going Correction** +0.425s/f (Yiel)
**WFA** 3 from 4yo 6lb **8** Ran SP% **113.9**
Speed ratings (Par 102): **104,99,98,98,97 95,94,93**
CSF £24.15 CT £144.94 TOTE £7.00: £2.30, £1.50, £2.50; EX 21.10 Trifecta £152.90.
**Owner** Barry Kitcherside **Bred** Old Carhue Stud **Trained** Great Shefford, Berks

**FOCUS**
Stalls on inner. A fair fillies' handicap, won for the ninth time in eleven seasons by a three-year-old and on this occasion courtesy of an enterprising piece of front-running. This confirms the winner to be on the upgrade, but there was little depth behind.

## 6275 SKY BET WINDSOR SPRINT SERIES FINALE H'CAP 6f 12y
**6:50** (6:51) (Class 2) 3-Y-0+
**£46,687** (£13,980; £6,990; £3,495; £1,747; £877) **Stalls** Low

Form RPR

3401 **1** **Ice Age (IRE)**[14] 5720 4-8-11 **91**...... EdwardGreatrex(3) 11 101
(Eve Johnson Houghton) *mde virtually all: rdn over 1f out: kpt on wl fnl f and a holding rivals* **7/1**[3]

0213 **2** *1* **Upstaging**[16] 5640 5-9-4 **100**......(p) DavidEgan(5) 6 107
(Paul Cole) *prom: rdn to chse wnr wl over 1f out: kpt on u.p but no imp ins fnl f* **6/1**[2]

2601 **3** *hd* **Stake Acclaim (IRE)**[9] 5911 5-9-10 **101**...... RobertWinston 1 107
(Dean Ivory) *racd alone against nr side rail and rt on terms w ldrs: rdn over 1f out: styd on* **8/1**

4206 **4** *nse* **Englishman**[31] 5123 7-8-5 **82**...... LukeMorris 16 88
(Milton Bradley) *chsd ldrs: r against far rail fr 1/2-way: hrd rdn over 2f out: tried to cl over 1f out: styd on but nvr able to chal* **25/1**

3402 **5** *nse* **Spring Loaded (IRE)**[35] 4974 5-9-1 **92**...... AdamKirby 4 98+
(Paul D'Arcy) *hld up and sn towards rr: rdn 2f out: prog in centre jst over 1f out: fin wl but jst too late to be plcd* **7/1**[3]

4020 **6** *½* **Gulliver**[9] 5942 3-8-9 **89**......(t) HarryBentley 3 93
(Hugo Palmer) *nt travelling in rr and urged along: styd on fr over 1f out in centre: nrst fin* **25/1**

0322 **7** *hd* **Major Pusey**[10] 5890 5-8-7 **84** ow1...... FergusSweeney 9 88
(John Gallagher) *pressed wnr: rdn 2f out: styd in ldng trio tl no ex and lost pls last 75yds* **12/1**

2065 **8** *½* **Dougan**[23] 5435 5-9-1 **92**...... RobertTart 10 94
(David Evans) *chsd ldrs: rdn over 2f out: tried to cl over 1f out: kpt on but no imp last 150yds* **12/1**

3260 **9** *1¼* **Pettochside**[16] 5637 8-8-7 **84**...... JosephineGordon 5 82
(John Bridger) *nvr beyond midfield: rdn 2f out in centre: one pce* **25/1**

2510 **10** *1¼* **Lightning Charlie**[16] 5637 5-8-13 **90**...... SteveDrowne 13 84
(Amanda Perrett) *wl in rr: rdn and sme prog 2f out: no hdwy fr over 1f out* **33/1**

1050 **11** *1¼* **Goring (GER)**[16] 5637 5-8-8 **85** ow1...... JohnFahy 2 75
(Eve Johnson Houghton) *racd towards nr side to 1/2-way then jnd main gp: on terms to over 2f out: fdd* **16/1**

0214 **12** *½* **Parnassian (IRE)**[44] 4610 3-8-9 **89**...... KieranShoemark 12 77
(Amanda Perrett) *dwlt sltly: a wl in rr: struggling bdly in last 1/2-way* **25/1**

3515 **13** *nk* **Atletico (IRE)**[20] 5505 5-9-1 **92**...... AndreaAtzeni 14 79
(Roger Varian) *dwlt sltly: wl in rr: rdn over 2f out: no significant prog* **4/1**[1]

0/05 **14** *4½* **Secondo (FR)**[28] 5219 7-8-8 **85**...... JFEgan 8 58
(Joseph Tuite) *a in rr: rdn and no prog over 2f out: wknd over 1f out* **33/1**

0445 **15** *5* **Tomily (IRE)**[34] 4992 3-8-13 **93**...... SeanLevey 7 50
(Richard Hannon) *pressed wnr to over 2f out: wknd rapidly* **22/1**

1m 13.85s (0.85) **Going Correction** +0.425s/f (Yiel)
**WFA** 3 from 4yo+ 3lb **15** Ran SP% **117.3**
Speed ratings (Par 109): **111,109,109,109,109 108,108,107,106,104 102,102,101,95,88**
CSF £42.36 CT £350.43 TOTE £7.30: £2.50, £2.40, £3.30; EX 44.70 Trifecta £186.60.
**Owner** Eden Racing III **Bred** Piercetown Stud **Trained** Blewbury, Oxon

**FOCUS**
Stalls on inner. The second running of this series final and a cracking contest, notably stronger than last year's inaugural event. Five of the nine series winners lined up, and the first three home possessed official ratings of 91, 100 and 101, so this looks like strong sprint form. The form makes sense among the principals.

## 6276 GIVE A DUCK SPREADING HUGGABLE HOPE H'CAP 5f 21y
**7:20** (7:20) (Class 4) (0-80,79) 3-Y-0+ **£4,690** (£1,395; £697; £348) **Stalls** Low

Form RPR

3230 **1** **Liberatum**[12] 5784 3-8-4 **66**...... DavidEgan(5) 3 74
(Ruth Carr) *trckd ldr after 2f: taken to far rail and led 2f out: rdn over 1f out: styd on wl* **7/1**

033 **2** *1¼* **Lydia's Place**[5] 6072 4-9-9 **78**...... RobHornby 8 81
(Richard Guest) *led: styd off far rail and hdd 2f out: rdn wl over 1f out: kpt on same pce after* **9/2**[3]

3216 **3** *1½* **Beck And Call**[25] 5325 3-9-1 **77**...... GeorgiaCox(5) 10 75
(Henry Candy) *trckd ldrs: shkn up over 2f out: nt qckn wl over 1f out: kpt on one pce fnl f* **9/4**[1]

344 **4** *½* **Sandfrankskipsgo**[11] 5818 8-9-4 **73**...... FergusSweeney 9 69
(Peter Crate) *trckd ldr 2f: rdn 2f out: one pce fr over 1f out* **12/1**

0005 **5** *2* **Awesome Allan (IRE)**[27] 5253 3-9-4 **75**...... JFEgan 5 64
(David Evans) *t.k.h: hld up in tch: effrt 1/2-way: shkn up and nt qckn wl over 1f out: fdd fnl f* **11/2**

-426 **6** *3¾* **Maazel (IRE)**[11] 5837 3-9-5 **76**......(b[1]) AndreaAtzeni 1 51
(Roger Varian) *missed break and urged along: in tch but nvr really gng wl: wknd over 1f out* **4/1**[2]

0-36 **7** *1¼* **Shackled N Drawn (USA)**[40] 4732 5-9-4 **73**...... TomMarquand 7 44
(Peter Hedger) *missed break: in rr: effrt and sme prog 1/2-way: wknd over 1f out: eased* **16/1**

1m 2.18s (1.88) **Going Correction** +0.425s/f (Yiel)
**WFA** 3 from 4yo+ 2lb **7** Ran SP% **110.4**
Speed ratings (Par 105): **101,99,96,95,92 86,84**
CSF £35.47 CT £87.71 TOTE £7.60: £3.60, £2.30; EX 34.00 Trifecta £197.20.
**Owner** Rhd **Bred** The Pocock Family **Trained** Huby, N Yorks

**FOCUS**
Stalls on inner. Still not too bad a sprint handicap despite the absentees, but the first four had it between them throughout. The form is not entirely convincing.

## 6277 SKY BET RACING CASH OUT MAIDEN STKS 1m 2f
**7:50** (7:51) (Class 5) 3-4-Y-O **£2,911** (£866; £432; £216) **Stalls** Centre

Form RPR

4246 **1** **Turnpike Trip**[24] 5364 3-9-5 78...... DaneO'Neill 1 83
(Henry Candy) *trckd ldr 4f: styd prom: rdn to chal 2f out: drvn ahd ins fnl f: styd on and drew clr* **5/2**[2]

**2** *2¾* **Ennjaaz (IRE)** 3-9-5 0...... PatCosgrave 5 78+
(Saeed bin Suroor) *dwlt: rcvrd to trck ldrs: shkn up and prog to ld jst over 2f out: rdn and hdd ins fnl f: one pce* **1/1**[1]

3 **3** *1¾* **Fearsome**[213] 328 3-9-5 0...... PatDobbs 9 74
(Ralph Beckett) *dwlt: rcvrd to trck ldr after 4f: chal against far rail fr 2f out: stl on terms 1f out: fdd* **5/1**

24 **4** *1¾* **Lewinsky (IRE)**[35] 4981 3-9-0 0...... JamesDoyle 10 66
(Hugo Palmer) *led: shkn up and hdd jst over 2f out: one pce in 4th pl fr over 1f out* **9/2**[3]

60 **5** *6* **Hajaam (IRE)**[166] 1083 3-9-5 0...... StevieDonohoe 6 59
(Charlie Fellowes) *hld up: outpcd fr 3f out: pushed along to take modest 5th 2f out: nvr a factor* **16/1**

00 **6** *2* **Sampaquita (FR)**[69] 3682 3-8-11 0...... HectorCrouch(3) 4 50
(Gary Moore) *nvr beyond midfield: outpcd fr 3f out: no ch after* **50/1**

65 **7** *nk* **My Name Is Jeff**[32] 5075 3-9-2 0...... AaronJones(3) 11 54
(Julia Feilden) *a in rr: lft bhd fr 3f out: no ch after* **33/1**

0/ **8** *8* **Arrucian**[706] 6404 4-9-7 0...... AntonioFresu 7 32
(Ms N M Hugo) *chsd ldrs: rdn and wknd over 3f out* **125/1**

00 **9** *7* **Breeze Up**[23] 5428 3-9-2 0...... CallumShepherd(3) 8 24
(Ed de Giles) *a in last pair: wd bnd 5f out: sn bhd* **66/1**

0 **10** *shd* **What A Welcome**[23] 5428 3-9-5 0...... JoeyHaynes 3 24
(Eric Wheeler) *a in rr: bhd fnl 2f* **150/1**

2m 15.16s (6.46) **Going Correction** +0.425s/f (Yiel)
**WFA** 3 from 4yo 7lb **10** Ran SP% **127.2**
Speed ratings (Par 103): **91,88,87,86,81 79,79,72,67,67**
CSF £5.95 TOTE £3.60: £1.30, £1.10, £1.80; EX 6.90 Trifecta £22.10.
**Owner** Mrs David Blackburn **Bred** Mrs M J Blackburn **Trained** Kingston Warren, Oxon

**FOCUS**
Stalls in centre. A pretty ordinary-looking maiden, and a winning time 2.08 seconds slower than that of the 67-rated winner of the earlier C&D handicap. The winner is rated in line with a better view of his form.

T/Plt: £44.00 to a £1 stake. Pool: £89,728.81 - 1,487.0 winning units T/Qpdt: £15.80 to a £1 stake. Pool: £7,942.72 - 370.38 winning units **Jonathan Neesom**

# 5865 BRIGHTON (L-H)
Tuesday, August 22

**OFFICIAL GOING: Good to soft (good in places; 7.2)**
Wind: light, against Weather: light cloud

## 6278 GOOD PEOPLE RECRUITMENT H'CAP 5f 60y
**2:00** (2:00) (Class 5) (0-75,77) 3-Y-0+ **£2,911** (£866; £432; £216) **Stalls** Centre

Form RPR

0560 **1** **Secret Strategy (IRE)**[4] 6155 3-8-13 **67**...... HollieDoyle(3) 5 74
(Julia Feilden) *sn outpcd in last and pushed along: rdn and clsd over 1f out: styd on to ld wl ins fnl f: pricked ears in front but sn in command* **13/8**[1]

0030 **2** *1* **Monumental Man**[40] 4803 8-9-9 **77**......(p) PaddyBradley(5) 1 81
(Michael Attwater) *w ldr and sn clr: rdn to ld over 1f out: drvn 1f out: hdd and styd on same pce wl ins fnl f* **5/1**[3]

0013 **3** 2 **Quantum Dot (IRE)**[39] 4842 6-8-11 **63**................(b) CallumShepherd(3) 2 60
(Ed de Giles) *led and sn clr w rival: rdn and hdd over 1f out: drvn and no ex u.p 1f out: wknd fnl 100yds and eased towards fin* **5/1**[3]

1256 **4** 7 **Taajub (IRE)**[47] 4521 10-9-7 **70**.................................... FergusSweeney 4 42
(Peter Crate) *taken down early and led to post: hld up in 3rd bhd clr ldrs: swtchd lft to far rail and effrt 2f out: clsd to chse ldrs but hung lft and no further imp 1f out: heavily eased wl ins fnl f* **7/4**[2]

1m 3.25s (0.95) **Going Correction** +0.125s/f (Good)
**WFA** 3 from 6yo+ 2lb **4** Ran SP% **107.8**
Speed ratings (Par 103): **97,95,92,81**
CSF £9.24 TOTE £3.40; EX 13.00 Trifecta £27.10.
**Owner** The Strategists **Bred** Tom And Hazel Russell **Trained** Exning, Suffolk

**FOCUS**
Race distance increased by 6yds. A weak four-runner sprint, they went fast and the race set up nicely for the well-backed winner. The winner is rated to a better view of his maiden form.

## 6279 CALL STAR SPORTS ON 08000 521 321 NOVICE STKS 7f 211y
**2:30** (2:30) (Class 5) 2-Y-O **£2,911** (£866; £432; £216) **Stalls** High

Form RPR
0 **1** **Enzo (IRE)**[20] 5531 2-9-2 0................................................(t[1]) LiamKeniry 5 69+
(Ed Walker) *stdd and dropped in bhd after s: hld up in tch in rr: nt clrest of runs over 1f out: swtchd rt 1f out: rn green and edging lft ins fnl f but qcknd to ld towards fin* **16/1**

30 **2** ½ **Trogon (IRE)**[17] 5641 2-9-2 0.................................................. PatDobbs 4 68
(Mick Channon) *w ldr: rdn 2f out: forged into narrow ld 1f out: kpt on u.p tl hdd and no ex towards fin* **11/4**[3]

**3** ½ **King Of The Sand (IRE)** 2-8-13 0........................... HectorCrouch(3) 1 67
(Gary Moore) *hld up and trckd ldrs: effrt ent fnl 2f: ev ch over 1f out tl rn green and edgd lft 100yds out: no ex and jst outpcd wl ins fnl f* **11/2**

01 **4** 1 **Al Ozzdi**[13] 5786 2-9-9 0...................................................(t) JoeFanning 3 72
(Simon Crisford) *trckd ldrs: effrt to chal u.p over 1f out tl no ex ins fnl f: styd on same pce fnl 100yds* **2/1**[1]

45 **5** ¾ **Tiny Tempest (IRE)**[20] 5534 2-8-11 0........................... CharlesBishop 2 61
(Eve Johnson Houghton) *led: rdn ent fnl 2f: hdd 1f out: jst getting outpcd whn squeezed for room: btn wl ins fnl f* **9/4**[2]

1m 37.2s (1.20) **Going Correction** +0.125s/f (Good) **5** Ran SP% **112.0**
Speed ratings (Par 94): **99,98,98,97,96**
CSF £59.32 TOTE £17.80: £5.50, £1.40; EX 67.20 Trifecta £88.30.
**Owner** P K Siu **Bred** Rabbah Bloodstock Limited **Trained** Upper Lambourn, Berks
■ Stewards' Enquiry : Hector Crouch caution: careless riding

**FOCUS**
Race distance increased by 6yds. A modest novice that went to the complete outsider.

## 6280 SOLDIERSCHARITY.ORG H'CAP 1m 3f 198y
**3:00** (3:00) (Class 6) (0-60,60) 4-Y-0+ **£2,264** (£673; £336; £168) **Stalls** High

Form RPR
5660 **1** **Kilim**[25] 5362 4-8-1 **47**....................................................(t) NicolaCurrie(7) 4 54
(John Berry) *t.k.h: hld up in tch in midfield: c to stands' rail and effrt over 2f out: ev ch over 1f out: styd on wl to ld wl ins fnl f* **16/1**

0202 **2** ½ **Rianna Star**[6] 6069 4-8-12 **54**.......................................... HectorCrouch(3) 6 60
(Gary Moore) *taken down early: chsd ldng pair: swtchd rt and effrt ent fnl 2f: ev ch u.p over 1f out: led ins fnl f: hdd and one pce wl ins fnl f* **2/1**[1]

0001 **3** ½ **Overhaugh Street**[13] 5790 4-9-7 **60**.................................... LiamKeniry 7 65
(Ed de Giles) *led: rdn 2f out: hrd pressed and hung lft over 1f out: hdd and kpt on same pce ins fnl f* **9/2**

0420 **4** 3 ½ **Sevilla**[5] 6088 4-8-11 **57**...........................................(b[1]) DarraghKeenan(7) 2 57
(Olly Murphy) *hld up in tch in rr: effrt ent fnl 2f: 4th and no imp whn hung lft over 1f out: kpt on same pce fnl f* **4/1**[3]

13 **5** 10 **Hallingham**[48] 4494 7-9-7 **60**................................................(p) PatDobbs 5 44
(Ken Cunningham-Brown) *hld up tch in last pair: rdn 3f out: no imp: wknd fnl f* **7/2**[2]

0420 **6** 1 **Nouvelle Ere**[3] 6175 6-9-4 **57**.......................................... WilliamCarson 3 39
(Tony Carroll) *chsd ldr: rdn over 2f out: lost pl and wl btn over 1f out: wknd fnl f* **6/1**

2m 35.04s (2.34) **Going Correction** +0.125s/f (Good) **6** Ran SP% **113.9**
Speed ratings (Par 101): **97,96,96,94,87 86**
CSF £49.42 TOTE £10.00: £3.60, £1.60; EX 55.60 Trifecta £98.10.
**Owner** John Berry **Bred** Fittocks Stud **Trained** Newmarket, Suffolk
■ Gunner Moyne was withdrawn not under orders. Rule 4 does not \n\x\x apply

**FOCUS**
Race distance increased by 6yds. The two at the bottom of the weights came to the fore, with the winner racing stands' side late on. Moderate, straightforward form.

## 6281 NICOLA O'LEARY'S TEAM - SAGA MAIDEN H'CAP 1m 1f 207y
**3:30** (3:30) (Class 5) (0-70,70) 3-Y-0+ **£2,911** (£866; £432; £216) **Stalls** High

Form RPR
-225 **1** **American History (USA)**[15] 5707 3-9-4 **70**...........(p) HectorCrouch(3) 2 76
(William Muir) *led: rdn jst over 2f out: hdd over 1f out: stl ev ch and battled on wl u.p ins fnl f: led again on post* **10/1**

4232 **2** nse **Prosecution**[19] 5578 3-9-2 **68**...................................... CharlieBennett(3) 1 74
(Hughie Morrison) *trckd ldrs: effrt to chal: rdn to ld narrowly over 1f out: kpt on wl u.p ins fnl f: hdd on post* **6/4**[1]

-436 **3** 1 ¾ **Pacofilha**[11] 5910 3-9-6 **69**.................................................. RaulDaSilva 5 71
(Paul Cole) *t.k.h early: hld up in tch in midfield: effrt 2f out: drvn over 1f out: kpt on ins fnl f: nvr quite enough pce to threaten ldrs* **9/2**[3]

0002 **4** ¾ **Kings City (IRE)**[11] 5867 3-8-13 **62**...............................(p) PatCosgrave 8 63
(Luca Cumani) *trckd ldr: rdn ent fnl 2f out: unable qck jst over 1f out: styd on same pce and lost 3rd ins fnl f* **2/1**[2]

0025 **5** 3 ¼ **Bizet (IRE)**[7] 6023 3-8-4 **52** ow1..........................................(v) RyanTate 7 47
(John Ryan) *s.i.s: sn rcvrd and in tch in midfield: effrt 2f out: drifting and no imp over 1f out: kpt on same pce ins fnl f* **16/1**

4005 **6** 1 **Dawn Goddess**[13] 5790 3-7-13 **51** oh6.......................... NoelGarbutt(3) 4 43
(Gary Moore) *s.i.s: t.k.h: hld up in tch in rr: effrt ent fnl 2f: no imp and kpt on same pce fr over 1f out* **25/1**

05-0 **7** 3 ¼ **Nargiza (USA)**[22] 5485 3-8-13 **62**................................... FergusSweeney 3 48
(Chris Wall) *hld up in tch in last pair: effrt over 2f out: no imp and dropped to last over 1f out: wknd fnl f* **50/1**

2m 4.97s (1.37) **Going Correction** +0.125s/f (Good) **7** Ran SP% **112.3**
Speed ratings (Par 103): **99,98,97,96,94 93,90**
CSF £24.64 CT £78.22 TOTE £10.00: £4.00, £1.10; EX 31.00 Trifecta £72.40.
**Owner** Byrne, Devlin, Edginton, Jeffery **Bred** Woodford Thoroughbreds **Trained** Lambourn, Berks

**FOCUS**
Race distance increased by 6yds. Little got into this modest handicap, the main action unfolding more stands' side late on. The winner is rated in line with a better view of his form.

## 6282 ROA/RACING POST OWNERS JACKPOT H'CAP 5f 215y
**4:00** (4:00) (Class 4) (0-80,79) 3-Y-0+ **£4,690** (£1,395; £697; £348) **Stalls** Centre

Form RPR
2221 **1** **Buxted Dream (USA)**[10] 5937 3-9-7 **79**........................... PatCosgrave 1 86+
(Luca Cumani) *broke wl: sn restrained to trck ldr and t.k.h: c towards stands' side over 2f out: effrt to chal over 1f out: rdn to ld ins fnl f: drifting lft but a holding runner-up after* **5/6**[1]

2601 **2** nk **Bahamian Sunrise**[27] 5304 5-9-7 **79**.......................(b) HectorCrouch(3) 2 85
(John Gallagher) *sn led: shkn up 2f out: rdn over 1f out: hdd ins fnl f: kpt on but a jst hld after* **5/1**[3]

0005 **3** 3 ¼ **Zamjar**[11] 5869 3-9-7 **79**........................................................(b) PatDobbs 5 75
(Ed Dunlop) *t.k.h: hld up in 3rd: sltly hmpd over 2f out: rdn 2f out: unable qck over 1f out: wl hld and kpt on same pce fnl f* **5/1**[3]

4663 **4** 19 **Otomo**[15] 5711 3-8-13 **71**....................................................(h) LiamKeniry 4 6
(Philip Hide) *stdd and sltly impeded leaving stalls: t.k.h: hld up in rr: effrt jst over 2f out: sn struggling and btn over 1f out: eased ins fnl f* **4/1**[2]

1m 10.11s (-0.09) **Going Correction** +0.125s/f (Good)
**WFA** 3 from 5yo+ 3lb **4** Ran SP% **107.9**
Speed ratings (Par 105): **105,104,100,74**
CSF £5.22 TOTE £1.60; EX 3.90 Trifecta £6.20.
**Owner** Buxted Partnership **Bred** SF Bloodstock LLC **Trained** Newmarket, Suffolk

**FOCUS**
Race distance increased by 6yds. A fair little sprint despite there being just the four runners. The form is rated around the runner-up.

## 6283 FOLLOW US ON TWITTER @STARSPORTS_BET MEDIAN AUCTION MAIDEN STKS 6f 210y
**4:30** (4:31) (Class 6) 3-5-Y-O **£2,264** (£673; £336; £168) **Stalls** Centre

Form RPR
2562 **1** **Ocean Temptress**[12] 5852 3-8-12 57...............................(v[1]) PatDobbs 5 69
(John Ryan) *mde all: rdn over 1f out: styd on and in command fnl f: unchal* **3/1**[2]

5346 **2** 3 ¾ **Bella's Venture**[12] 5829 4-9-3 56.............................. FergusSweeney 10 61
(John Gallagher) *t.k.h: chsd ldrs: wnt 2nd over 2f out: effrt u.p but no imp over 1f out: wknd ins fnl f* **8/1**

-42 **3** ¾ **The Bear Can Fly**[24] 5409 3-8-9 0.......................... CallumShepherd(3) 3 57
(David Menuisier) *chsd ldng trio: effrt in 3rd over 1f out: no imp and kpt on same pce ins fnl f* **5/2**[1]

0502 **4** 3 ½ **Lady Morel (IRE)**[13] 5792 3-8-9 55......................... EdwardGreatrex(3) 2 47
(Joseph Tuite) *hld up in tch in rr of main gp: sme hdwy u.p over 1f out: 4th and no imp ins fnl f* **15/2**

**5** 2 ½ **I'm A Believer** 3-8-12 0................................................. CharlesBishop 8 41
(Mick Channon) *dwlt: hld up in tch in midfield: effrt ent fnl 2f: 5th and no imp whn rn green over 1f out* **4/1**[3]

6000 **6** 3 ½ **Oddsocks (IRE)**[12] 5823 5-9-3 36................................ WilliamCarson 7 33
(Tony Carroll) *wl in tch in midfield: rdn over 2f out: sn struggling u.p: wknd over 1f out* **100/1**

0- **7** hd **Kath's Legend**[328] 6867 3-8-12 0...........................................(h[1]) RyanTate 1 31
(Ben De Haan) *t.k.h: hld up in tch in rr of main gp: effrt over 2f out: no imp and wandered over 1f out: wknd fnl f* **20/1**

040 **8** 3 **Kalani Rose**[50] 4444 3-8-12 54........................................(p[1]) JoeFanning 6 23
(Ben De Haan) *t.k.h: chsd wnr tl over 2f out: lost pl over 1f out: wknd fnl f* **14/1**

**9** 8 **Mini Moruga** 3-8-9 0.............................................. HectorCrouch(3) 9
(Gary Moore) *v.s.a: nvr on terms* **12/1**

**10** 22 **No Damage (IRE)** 3-8-12 0.......................................... KierenFox 4
(Michael Attwater) *taken down early: stdd s: t.k.h: hld up in tch: lost pl 3f out: eased 2f out: t.o* **50/1**

1m 22.56s (-0.54) **Going Correction** +0.125s/f (Good)
**WFA** 3 from 4yo+ 5lb **10** Ran SP% **118.5**
Speed ratings (Par 101): **108,103,102,98,96 92,91,88,79,54**
CSF £27.51 TOTE £4.10: £1.50, £2.50, £1.50; EX 27.60 Trifecta £71.60.
**Owner** The Temptations **Bred** Old Mill Stud Ltd And Oomswell Ltd **Trained** Newmarket, Suffolk

**FOCUS**
Race distance increased by 6yds. Weak maiden form, the ready winner being an exposed 57-rated performer.

## 6284 STARSPORTSBET.CO.UK APPRENTICE H'CAP (PART OF THE RACING EXCELLENCE TRAINING SERIES) 7f 211y
**5:00** (5:00) (Class 6) (0-65,67) 4-Y-0+ **£2,264** (£673; £336; £168) **Stalls** High

Form RPR
050- **1** **Rock Icon**[262] 8207 4-9-1 **56**..................................................(h[1]) JoshQuinn 3 63
(Jo Hughes) *t.k.h: w ldr tl led 6f out: mde rest: edgd lft but hld on wl ins fnl f* **11/2**[3]

2401 **2** nk **Buzz Lightyere**[12] 5823 4-9-1 **59**............................ SebastianWoods(3) 7 65
(Philip Hide) *t.k.h: led for 2f: styd pressing wnr: ev ch and rdn over 1f out: kpt on but hld towards fin* **8/11**[1]

1130 **3** 4 ½ **Papou Tony**[40] 4810 4-9-7 **65**......................................... JasonWatson(3) 2 61
(George Baker) *stdd s: hld up in rr: effrt and hung lft over 1f out: 3rd and no imp ins fnl f: nvr trbld ldrs* **9/2**[2]

3220 **4** 7 **With Approval (IRE)**[56] 4176 5-8-11 **57**.............................(p) OllieJago(5) 1 37
(Laura Mongan) *rdr lost irons leaving stalls: chsd ldrs tl dropped to 4th after 2f: effrt to chse clr ldng pair 2f out: no imp: lost 3rd and wknd fnl f* **6/1**

00-0 **5** 18 **Play The Blues (IRE)**[12] 5823 10-8-5 **46** oh1...............(t) RhiainIngram 5
(Roger Ingram) *taken down early: stdd s: t.k.h: chsd ldrs after 2f tl 2f out: sn dropped out: bhd and eased ins fnl f* **50/1**

1m 35.98s (-0.02) **Going Correction** +0.125s/f (Good) **5** Ran SP% **107.7**
Speed ratings (Par 101): **105,104,100,93,75**
CSF £9.67 TOTE £6.70: £3.30, £1.10; EX 10.20 Trifecta £26.00.
**Owner** D G Bird **Bred** Maurice Black **Trained** Lambourn. Berks

**FOCUS**
Race distance increased by 6yds. Two came clear in this moderate handicap. The winner was well treated on form from a year ago and did not need to replicate that.
T/Plt: £150.20 to a £1 stake. Pool: £70,453.52 - 342.35 winning units. T/Qpdt: £9.10 to a £1 stake. Pool: £6,606.90 - 536.54 winning units. **Steve Payne**

6063 **KEMPTON (A.W)** (R-H)

Tuesday, August 22

**OFFICIAL GOING: Polytrack: standard to slow (watered)**

Wind: Moderate, half behind Weather: Cloudy, warm

## 6285 WINNERS WELCOME AT MATCHBOOK EXCHANGE NURSERY H'CAP (JOCKEY CLUB GRASSROOTS NURSERY QUALIFIER) 6f (P)

2:15 (2:19) (Class 6) (0-65,65) 2-Y-O £2,587 (£770; £384; £192) Stalls Low

Form RPR

455 1 **W G Grace (IRE)**[38] 4888 2-9-3 **61** FrannyNorton 4 64
(Mark Johnston) *w ldrs on inner: led after 2f: rdn and edgd lft over 1f out: sn jnd: drvn and fnd more to assert ins fnl f* **2/1**[1]

0506 2 *nk* **Laura Knight (IRE)**[35] 4991 2-9-4 **62** AdamKirby 6 64
(Gary Moore) *trckd ldrs: wnt 2nd 2f out: rdn to chal and w wnr over 1f out: kpt on but nt qckn ins fnl f* **5/1**[2]

50 3 *¾* **Vegas Boy (IRE)**[52] 4367 2-8-12 **56** (t) DougieCostello 9 56
(Jamie Osborne) *chsd ldrs: rdn over 2f out: prog to chse ldng pair fnl f: styd on but nvr able to chal* **8/1**

506 4 *1 ¼* **Silver Bullet (IRE)**[50] 4440 2-9-2 **60** (v[1]) RichardKingscote 11 56
(Tom Dascombe) *hld up in last pair fr wd draw: prog on inner 2f out: rdn and kpt on fr over 1f out: nrst fin* **8/1**

404 5 *nse* **Jan's Joy**[34] 5026 2-9-2 **63** (t) AaronJones(3) 2 59
(Stuart Williams) *in tch: rdn and sme prog 2f out: disp 3rd briefly 1f out: kpt on same pce after* **12/1**

336 6 *1 ¾* **Raven's Raft (IRE)**[19] 5576 2-9-7 **65** LukeMorris 8 56
(Michael Appleby) *led 2f: chsd wnr to over 2f out: wknd fnl f* **6/1**[3]

004 7 *2 ¾* **Red For Danger**[56] 4175 2-8-2 **51** GeorgiaCox(5) 3 33
(Eve Johnson Houghton) *t.k.h: pressed ldrs on outer: wnt 2nd briefly over 2f out: wknd over 1f out* **20/1**

0406 8 *2* **Jean Paget (IRE)**[11] 5893 2-9-1 **59** (v) JFEgan 1 35
(Mick Channon) *t.k.h: hld up in midfield: shkn up and no prog over 2f out: fdd* **25/1**

004 9 *3 ¼* **Gold Eagle**[20] 5534 2-9-5 **63** DavidProbert 7 30+
(Philip McBride) *t.k.h: hld up in rr: shkn up and no prog over 2f out: eased whn no ch fnl f* **8/1**

000 10 *1 ½* **Rue Cambon (IRE)**[45] 4599 2-8-6 **50** AndrewMullen 5 12
(George Peckham) *reluctant to enter stall: slowly away: a in rr: no prog u.p 1/2-way* **40/1**

3000 11 *4* **Dark Hedges**[34] 5015 2-8-8 **52** ow3 RobHornby 10 2
(Olly Williams) *chsd ldrs on outer: wknd rapidly over 2f out* **100/1**

1m 12.98s (-0.12) **Going Correction** -0.075s/f (Stan) 11 Ran SP% **117.3**
Speed ratings (Par 92): **97,96,95,93,93 91,87,85,80,78 73**
CSF £11.12 CT £67.68 TOTE £2.80: £1.30, £1.60, £2.80; EX 12.80 Trifecta £78.90.
**Owner** Sheikh Hamdan bin Mohammed Al Maktoum **Bred** Godolphin **Trained** Middleham Moor, N Yorks

■ Grand Acclaim was withdrawn not under orders. Price at time of withdrawal 25-1. Rule 4 does not apply.

**FOCUS**
The surface, which had been watered, was described as standard to slow. A modest nursery in which it proved hard to make up significant ground.

## 6286 HAPPY BIRTHDAY LAURA MACMILLAN NOVICE AUCTION STKS 1m (P)

2:45 (2:46) (Class 5) 2-Y-O £3,234 (£962; £481; £240) Stalls Low

Form RPR

303 1 **We Are The World**[36] 4963 2-9-2 79 (p[1]) LukeMorris 3 75
(Archie Watson) *led after 100yds and dictated ordinary pce: shkn up over 2f out: drvn out fnl f but nvr seriously threatened* **4/11**[1]

2 *1 ¾* **Great Shot Sam (USA)** 2-8-11 0 DavidProbert 6 66
(Andrew Balding) *trckd ldrs: moved up over 2f out: rdn and nt qckn wl over 1f out: tk 2nd fnl f: no imp on wnr* **6/1**[2]

50 3 *1* **Queen Adelaide**[38] 4902 2-8-11 0 FranBerry 5 64
(John Ryan) *led 100yds then stdd into 3rd: effrt to chse wnr over 2f out: no imp over 1f out: lost 2nd and one pce fnl f* **15/2**[3]

4 *3* **Sicario (IRE)** 2-9-2 0 (b[1]) DougieCostello 1 62+
(Jamie Osborne) *s.i.s: rn green and urged along thrght: detached in last over 2f out: styd on fnl f* **14/1**

5 *nk* **Hidden Dream (IRE)** 2-8-8 0 AaronJones(3) 2 56
(Christine Dunnett) *hld up in 5th: outpcd and shkn up briefly over 2f out: nvr on terms after* **200/1**

5 6 *5* **Kalakchee**[12] 5847 2-9-2 0 (h) LemosdeSouza 4 50
(Amy Murphy) *tk fierce hold and pressed wnr after 1f to over 2f out: wknd rapidly* **33/1**

1m 42.0s (2.20) **Going Correction** -0.075s/f (Stan) 6 Ran SP% **109.5**
Speed ratings (Par 94): **86,84,83,80,79 74**
CSF £2.84 TOTE £1.20: £1.02, £3.00; EX 3.00 Trifecta £6.90.
**Owner** C R Hirst **Bred** Lady Juliet Tadgell **Trained** Upper Lambourn, W Berks

**FOCUS**
A weak novice race.

## 6287 MATCHBOOK BETTING EXCHANGE MAIDEN FILLIES' STKS 1m (P)

3:15 (3:16) (Class 5) 3-Y-O+ £3,234 (£962; £481; £240) Stalls Low

Form RPR

6- 1 **Influent (IRE)**[247] 8443 3-9-0 0 MartinHarley 6 81+
(James Tate) *trckd ldng pair: clsd over 2f out: drvn to ld jst over 1f out: styd on and won gng away* **11/2**[2]

65-2 2 *2* **Ambrosia**[15] 5712 3-9-0 73 AndreaAtzeni 9 75
(Roger Varian) *trckd ldr: led over 2f out: drvn and hdd jst over 1f out: nt qckn and sn hld: hld: nr fin* **4/5**[1]

0-0 3 *1* **Jazaalah (USA)**[15] 5712 3-9-0 0 (h[1]) JimCrowley 11 73
(Owen Burrows) *led at decent pce: hdd over 2f out: styd in tch w ldng pair tl one pce fnl f* **20/1**

4 *1 ½* **Isstoora (IRE)** 3-9-0 0 DanielMuscutt 1 69+
(Marco Botti) *slowly away: sn in tch in midfield: shkn up over 2f out: kpt on steadily fr over 1f out to take 4th ins fnl f* **14/1**

0-30 5 *¾* **Zafaranah (USA)**[15] 5721 3-9-0 71 RobHornby 4 68
(Pam Sly) *chsd ldng quartet: rdn over 2f out: kpt on same pce after and nvr able to cl* **12/1**

40 6 *2 ¾* **Pequeninha**[24] 5428 3-9-0 0 JackMitchell 10 61+
(David Simcock) *sn restrained into last: stl there 3f out and long way off the pce: pushed along and stylish prog fr over 2f out: tk 6th nr fin: likely improver* **25/1**

7 *1 ¼* **Tennessee Belle** 3-9-0 0 RichardKingscote 2 58
(James Tate) *in tch in midfield: outpcd over 2f out: n.d after* **16/1**

30 8 *3 ¾* **Scribbler**[18] 5611 3-9-0 0 DavidProbert 12 50
(Rae Guest) *racd on outer in rr: wl off the pce 3f out: no real prog after: plugged on* **25/1**

35 9 *shd* **Western Safari (IRE)**[115] 2144 3-9-0 0 SeanLevey 3 49
(Richard Hannon) *chsd ldng pair: shkn up over 2f out: wknd qckly over 1f out* **10/1**[3]

10 *7* **Maid Of Rock (IRE)** 3-9-0 0 AntonioFresu 7 33
(Mike Murphy) *t.k.h: hld up: wknd 3f out: bhd after* **100/1**

50- 11 *6* **Send Up (IRE)**[337] 6624 3-9-0 0 LukeMorris 5 20
(Sir Mark Prescott Bt) *s.i.s: a wl in rr: bhd 3f out* **50/1**

0 12 *30* **Steady (IRE)**[19] 5577 3-9-0 0 TrevorWhelan 8
(Dan Skelton) *in tch in midfield tl wknd rapidly 3f out: t.o* **100/1**

1m 38.55s (-1.25) **Going Correction** -0.075s/f (Stan) 12 Ran SP% **116.7**
Speed ratings (Par 100): **103,101,100,98,97 95,93,90,89,82 76,46**
CSF £9.47 TOTE £6.30: £2.00, £1.10, £5.20; EX 12.00 Trifecta £138.80.
**Owner** Saeed Manana **Bred** Rabbah Bloodstock Limited **Trained** Newmarket, Suffolk

**FOCUS**
Just a fair-looking maiden and not much got involved from off the pace.The form is rated around the runner-up with the winner a nice improver.

## 6288 SMARTER BETS WITH MATCHBOOK BETTING EXCHANGE H'CAP 1m (P)

3:45 (3:46) (Class 5) (0-70,69) 3-Y-O+ £3,234 (£962; £481; £240) Stalls Low

Form RPR

4200 1 **Bluff Crag**[26] 5313 4-9-6 **69** FinleyMarsh(7) 11 77
(Richard Hughes) *trckd ldr: rdn over 2f out: clsd to ld jst over 1f out: kpt on and in command fnl f* **25/1**

3613 2 *1 ½* **Dangerous Ends**[6] 6067 3-9-7 **69** (p) JackMitchell 3 73+
(Brett Johnson) *hld up in midfield: swtchd lft and shkn up 2f out: prog over 1f out: r.o to take 2nd last 75yds: too late to threaten wnr* **7/2**[2]

0400 3 *1 ¼* **Mezmaar**[42] 4728 8-9-11 **67** DougieCostello 5 69
(Mark Usher) *led at gd pce: rdn over 2f out: hdd jst over 1f out: fdd but hld on for 3rd* **25/1**

3111 4 *nk* **Anna Medici**[8] 6016 3-8-11 **59** LukeMorris 7 59+
(Sir Mark Prescott Bt) *sn urged along in rr: nvr really gng but fnlly mde prog fr 2f out: styd on fnl f and nrly snatched 3rd* **3/1**[1]

0002 5 *nk* **Ibazz**[8] 6014 4-9-6 **69** ManuelFernandes(7) 4 70
(Ian Williams) *trckd ldng trio: rdn 2f out: kpt on same pce and nvr able to chal* **9/2**[3]

3362 6 *nk* **Spinart**[13] 5802 4-9-13 **69** (p) RobHornby 2 69
(Pam Sly) *trckd ldrs: rdn over 2f out: tried to cl over 1f out: one pce after* **7/1**

0036 7 *1* **Ubla (IRE)**[12] 5857 4-9-10 **66** (p) DanielMuscutt 12 64
(Jane Chapple-Hyam) *trckd ldng pair: rdn and tried to chal fr 2f out: wknd ins fnl f* **20/1**

3652 8 *1 ½* **Satchville Flyer**[13] 5793 6-9-0 **56** KieranShoemark 9 50+
(David Evans) *towards rr: rdn over 2f out: plugged on fr over 1f out but no ch* **16/1**

122 9 *¾* **Makhfar (IRE)**[41] 4747 6-9-9 **65** (p) SteveDrowne 10 57+
(Mark Usher) *hld up wl in rr: urged along 3f out: modest late hdwy* **20/1**

0203 10 *nse* **Jack Nevison**[41] 4765 4-9-7 **63** TomMarquand 8 55
(Michael Appleby) *a in rr: no prog u.p 3f out* **25/1**

166 11 *1 ½* **Duke Of North (IRE)**[26] 5333 5-9-8 **69** PaddyBradley(5) 14 58
(Jim Boyle) *dropped in fr wdst draw and sn hld up in last: pushed along and modest prog 2f out: no hdwy whn reminder fnl f* **66/1**

5600 12 *1* **Fire Diamond**[10] 5917 4-9-12 **68** (p) RichardKingscote 6 55
(Tom Dascombe) *dwlt: a wl in rr: shkn up and no prog wl over 2f out* **25/1**

0-40 13 *1 ¼* **Girl Squad**[18] 5611 3-9-2 **64** DavidProbert 1 47
(William Jarvis) *dwlt: rcvrd into midfield: drvn on inner over 2f out: no prog wl over 1f out: sn wknd* **33/1**

0000 14 *15* **Multitask**[27] 5300 7-9-13 **69** AdamKirby 13 18
(Gary Moore) *racd wd in midfield: wknd rapidly over 2f out: t.o* **25/1**

1m 38.38s (-1.42) **Going Correction** -0.075s/f (Stan)
**WFA** 3 from 4yo+ 6lb 14 Ran SP% **117.0**
Speed ratings (Par 103): **104,102,101,100,100 100,99,97,97,97 95,94,93,78**
CSF £96.55 CT £2325.13 TOTE £36.50: £8.10, £1.40, £9.00; EX 158.70 Trifecta £6999.10.
**Owner** Michael Williams & Partner **Bred** Mrs Fiona Denniff **Trained** Upper Lambourn, Berks

**FOCUS**
Another race where few got involved, with the winner and third, both 25-1, racing two-one for most of the way. It was the pick of the three C&D times and the form seems sound, the winner rated back to his best.

## 6289 MATCHBOOK TRADERS CONFERENCE H'CAP 7f (P)

4:15 (4:16) (Class 3) (0-90,91) 3-Y-O+

£7,470 (£2,236; £1,118; £559; £279; £140) Stalls Low

Form RPR

2312 1 **Manton Grange**[64] 3920 4-9-6 **83** (p[1]) TrevorWhelan 8 95
(George Baker) *hld up in last: gd prog on outer fr 2f out: rdn to ld last 150yds: r.o and sn clr* **16/1**

2500 2 *3* **Intransigent**[102] 2568 8-9-7 **91** (h) WilliamCox(7) 4 95
(Andrew Balding) *hld up in midfield: rdn jst over 2f out: prog over 1f out: r.o to take 2nd nr fin: no ch w wnr* **14/1**

300 3 *½* **Firmdecisions (IRE)**[14] 5744 7-9-9 **89** JackDuern(3) 5 92
(Dean Ivory) *trckd ldrs: wnt 2nd over 2f out: hanging and racd awkwardly but clsd to ld over 1f out: hdd and fdd last 150yds* **14/1**

2005 4 *½* **Athassel**[12] 5821 8-8-13 **83** KatherineGlenister(7) 6 84
(David Evans) *hld up in last pair: prog on inner fr 2f out: styd on but nvr any real threat* **25/1**

-530 5 *nk* **Ernststavroblofeld (USA)**[102] 2567 3-9-3 **85** TomMarquand 2 84
(Martyn Meade) *pushed along early: wl in rr: rdn in last pair wl over 1f out: styd on fnl f: n.d* **4/1**[2]

0024 6 *nk* **Tailor's Row (USA)**[11] 5870 3-8-7 **75** FrannyNorton 1 73
(Mark Johnston) *in tch in midfield: rdn and tried to make prog fr 2f out: one pce fnl f* **20/1**

0-50 7 *hd* **Claim The Roses (USA)**[46] 4570 6-10-0 **91** LukeMorris 9 90
(Ed Vaughan) *hld up in rr: rdn in last 2f out: styd on fnl f: no ch* **8/1**

111- 8 *2 ¼* **Finelcity (GER)**[307] 7462 4-9-11 **88** (b) JimCrowley 7 81
(Harry Dunlop) *chsd ldrs: urged along over 2f out: no prog over 1f out: lost pl and wknd fnl f* **7/1**

6514 9 *½* **Human Nature (IRE)**[33] 5064 4-8-13 **83** (t) MillyNaseb(7) 10 75
(Stuart Williams) *led at str pce: hdd & wknd over 1f out* **14/1**

00-3 10 *3 ½* **Cape Icon**[45] 4631 6-9-7 **84** (v[1]) AdamKirby 3 67
(Clive Cox) *t.k.h: pressed ldng pair to over 2f out: wknd qckly over 1f out* **6/1**[3]

-112 **11** 3/4 **Sir Titan**[17] 5642 3-9-6 **88** SteveDrowne 11 67
(Marcus Tregoning) *gd spd fr wdst draw to press ldr: lost 2nd over 2f out and immediately wknd* **7/2**[1]

1m 24.37s (-1.63) **Going Correction** -0.075s/f (Stan)
**WFA** 3 from 4yo+ 5lb **11** Ran SP% **114.6**
Speed ratings (Par 107): **106,102,102,101,101 100,100,97,97,93 92**
CSF £215.96 CT £3182.32 TOTE £14.60: £3.50, £4.60, £3.50; EX 111.40 Trifecta £1790.30.
**Owner** Goltz, Finegold & McGeever **Bred** Follow The Flag Partnership **Trained** Manton, Wilts

**FOCUS**
The leaders looked to overdo it. The winner progressed again after a break.

## 6290 MATCHBOOK BETTING PODCAST H'CAP 6f (P)
**4:45** (4:45) (Class 4) (0-85,84) 3-Y-0+ **£5,175** (£1,540; £769; £384) **Stalls** Low

Form RPR
613 **1** **Maakaasib**[19] 5574 3-9-7 **84** (e) AdamKirby 1 92+
(Simon Crisford) *sltly awkward s: trckd ldng pair: wnt 2nd over 2f out: rdn to chal fnl f: drvn ahd narrowly last 50yds* **6/4**[1]

2133 **2** *nk* **Dark Side Dream**[28] 5245 5-8-9 **76** MillyNaseb(7) 4 83
(Chris Dwyer) *led: tried to go for home over 2f out: urged along over 1f out: worn down last 50yds* **5/1**[3]

312 **3** 1 3/4 **Hackney Road**[41] 4752 4-9-0 **79** JoshuaBryan(5) 2 80+
(John Butler) *t.k.h: hld up in 4th: pushed along to take 3rd over 1f out: nt qckn and no imp after* **5/2**[2]

2266 **4** *1* **Storm Cry**[28] 5264 3-9-3 **80** FrannyNorton 3 78
(Mark Johnston) *pressed ldr to over 2f out: one pce fr over 1f out* **11/1**

0004 **5** 2 1/2 **Plucky Dip**[5] 6113 6-9-5 **79** JimCrowley 5 69
(John Ryan) *hld up in last: cajoled along and no prog over 2f out: wl hld after* **6/1**

1m 12.95s (-0.15) **Going Correction** -0.075s/f (Stan)
**WFA** 3 from 4yo+ 3lb **5** Ran SP% **107.9**
Speed ratings (Par 105): **98,97,95,93,90**
CSF £8.85 TOTE £2.50: £1.10, £3.00; EX 7.00 Trifecta £12.70.
**Owner** Abdulla Al Mansoori **Bred** Newsells Park Stud **Trained** Newmarket, Suffolk

**FOCUS**
They didn't look to go that quick for a sprint. The form is rated around the runner-up, who dictated in a muddling pace.

## 6291 BETTER ODDS WITH MATCHBOOK BETTING EXCHANGE H'CAP 1m 3f 219y(P)
**5:15** (5:16) (Class 5) (0-70,78) 3-Y-0 **£3,234** (£962; £481; £240) **Stalls** Low

Form RPR
0001 **1** **Wolfcatcherjack (IRE)**[6] 6069 3-9-0 **63** 6ex LukeMorris 1 77+
(Sir Mark Prescott Bt) *trckd ldrs: wnt 2nd 4f out: pushed along to cl over 2f out: led over 1f out: rdn out* **5/6**[1]

2251 **2** 2 1/4 **Tomorrow Mystery**[8] 6013 3-10-1 **78** 6ex DougieCostello 4 88+
(Jamie Osborne) *led: sent for home 4f out: drvn over 2f out: hdd over 1f out: kpt on but no ch w wnr after* **4/1**[2]

50 **3** 1 3/4 **Casemates Square (IRE)**[11] 5894 3-8-2 **51** oh6 AndrewMullen 8 58
(Ian Williams) *pushed along in rr early: prog into 4th wl over 3f out but sn rdn: styd on fr 2f out to take 3rd fnl f* **33/1**

0055 **4** 2 1/2 **Sputnik Planum (USA)**[33] 5065 3-9-8 **71** (t[1]) JimCrowley 7 74
(David Lanigan) *dwlt: hld up in last pair: prog on inner fr 3f out: tk 3rd briefly over 1f out: one pce after* **14/1**

5306 **5** *3* **Fields Of Fortune**[67] 3779 3-9-1 **67** HollieDoyle(3) 9 65
(Alan King) *hld up in last pair: prog over 2f out but ldrs already gone: rdn and kpt on to take 5th ins fnl f: no ch* **6/1**[3]

4402 **6** 1 1/4 **It's How We Roll (IRE)**[19] 5565 3-9-1 **64** (b) TomMarquand 6 60
(John Spearing) *chsd ldrs: tk 3rd 4f out but sn drvn: wknd over 1f out* **20/1**

2120 **7** 3 3/4 **Ingleby Mackenzie**[13] 5780 3-9-2 **65** JFEgan 3 55
(Mick Channon) *chsd ldrs: rdn and outpcd over 3f out: no hdwy after* **14/1**

6345 **8** *5* **Lemon Drop**[17] 5652 3-8-2 **51** oh3 (b) FrannyNorton 2 33
(Jim Boyle) *dwlt: chsd ldrs: wknd over 3f out* **100/1**

5364 **9** *25* **Zoffanist (IRE)**[11] 5867 3-8-9 **58** (p) KieranShoemark 5
(Amanda Perrett) *pressed ldr to 4f out: wknd rapidly: t.o* **16/1**

0405 **10** *37* **Titan**[31] 5142 3-8-11 **60** FranBerry 10
(Ed Dunlop) *prom early: struggling in midfield sn after 1/2-way: t.o 4f out* **33/1**

2m 32.01s (-2.49) **Going Correction** -0.075s/f (Stan) **10** Ran SP% **119.7**
Speed ratings (Par 100): **105,103,102,100,98 97,95,92,75,50**
CSF £4.23 CT £63.96 TOTE £1.80: £1.02, £2.00, £10.70; EX 5.50 Trifecta £186.90.
**Owner** Ne'Er Do Wells V **Bred** Mrs S M Rogers & Miss K Rausing **Trained** Newmarket, Suffolk

**FOCUS**
A couple of progressive types filled the first two places. The winner progressed again and can do better.
T/Jkpt: Not Won. T/Plt: £96.60 to a £1 stake. Pool: £66,994.86 - 506.23 winning units. T/Qpdt: £28.70 to a £1 stake. Pool: £4,507.49 - 115.90 winning units. **Jonathan Neesom**

# 6108 YARMOUTH (L-H)
Tuesday, August 22

**OFFICIAL GOING: Good to firm (watered; 8.0)**
Wind: light breeze Weather: hot and very sunny; 23 degrees

## 6292 TOTEPOOL RACECOURSE CASHBACK AVAILABLE FILLIES' NOVICE STKS (PLUS 10 RACE) 1m 3y
**4:40** (4:40) (Class 5) 2-Y-0 **£3,622** (£1,078; £538; £269) **Stalls** Centre

Form RPR
**1** **Wild Illusion** 2-9-0 0 JamesDoyle 3 91+
(Charlie Appleby) *mde all: rdn over 2f out: drvn over 1f out: gng best after and styd on wl: comf* **15/8**[1]

2 **2** 2 1/2 **Give And Take**[25] 5349 2-9-0 0 JosephineGordon 5 83
(William Haggas) *3rd tl wnt 2nd over 2f out: sn rdn: no match for wnr fnl f* **9/4**[2]

**3** 3 1/2 **Momentarily** 2-9-0 0 RyanMoore 7 75+
(Hugo Palmer) *awkward s and v green for 2f: t.k.h: stdy prog 1/2-way: rdn and disp 2nd over 1f out: no ex ins fnl f and nt given a hrd time* **7/2**[3]

**4** 2 1/4 **Orchid Lily** 2-9-0 0 TedDurcan 1 70+
(John Gosden) *stdd s: chsd ldrs: rdn and outpcd 2f out: edgd rt ins fnl f* **9/1**

**5** 2 1/2 **Come With Me** 2-9-0 0 MartinLane 6 64
(John Gosden) *t.k.h in last early: rdn and struggling over 2f out* **10/1**

**6** *1* **Sigrid Nansen** 2-9-0 0 StevieDonohoe 2 62
(George Scott) *a towards rr: drvn and btn over 3f out* **28/1**

**7** *9* **Grasmere (IRE)** 2-9-0 0 RobertWinston 4 41
(Alan Bailey) *chsd wnr tl rdn and wknd over 2f out: eased fnl f: t.o* **80/1**

1m 38.34s (-2.26) **Going Correction** -0.225s/f (Firm) **7** Ran SP% **111.5**
Speed ratings (Par 91): **102,99,96,93,91 90,81**
CSF £5.99 TOTE £2.50: £1.20, £1.60; EX 5.60 Trifecta £12.30.
**Owner** Godolphin **Bred** Godolphin **Trained** Newmarket, Suffolk

**FOCUS**
A dry run up to a meeting staged on fast ground. This looked an above-average maiden in which the field finished well strung out and it unearthed a potentially smart sort in Wild Illusion, who is very much the type to hold her own in stronger company.

## 6293 FOLLOW @TOTEPOOLRACING ON TWITTER MAIDEN H'CAP 1m 3f 104y
**5:10** (5:12) (Class 5) (0-70,71) 3-Y-0+ **£3,622** (£1,078; £538; £269) **Stalls** Low

Form RPR
0-22 **1** **Astute Boy (IRE)**[17] 5652 3-9-6 **69** MartinLane 12 78
(Ed Vaughan) *prom on outer bk st: rdn 3f out: chse ldr over 3f out: chal 2f out: led w high hd carriage over 1f out: drvn and all out* **6/1**[2]

0-52 **2** 1 1/2 **Mambo Dancer**[11] 5883 3-9-5 **68** SilvestreDeSousa 9 75
(Mark Johnston) *3rd or 4th pl tl led 4f out: sn drvn: jnd 2f out where clr of rest: hdd over 1f out: nt qckn and hld fnl 100yds* **5/2**[1]

03-0 **3** 1 3/4 **Glassalt**[89] 2997 3-9-0 **63** JamesDoyle 11 67
(Michael Bell) *chsd ldrs: rdn and outpcd 3f out: rallied over 1f out: styd on wl to go 3rd clsng stages* **22/1**

0665 **4** *1* **Broughtons Knight**[18] 5618 3-9-0 **63** StevieDonohoe 5 65
(Henry Spiller) *bhd: prog towards outer 3f out: sn rdn: one pce 3rd wl over 1f out tl cl to home* **8/1**[3]

423 **5** *2* **Perla Blanca (USA)**[27] 5298 3-8-10 **62** GeorgeWood(3) 2 61+
(Marcus Tregoning) *midfield: effrt on outer and rdn 3f out: one pce and nvr looked like landing a blow* **5/2**[1]

0433 **6** 1 3/4 **Orin Swift (IRE)**[13] 5810 3-9-3 **71** MitchGodwin(5) 1 67
(Jonathan Portman) *pressed ldrs: rdn and outpcd by ldng pair 2f out: plugged on same pce* **20/1**

000 **7** 3/4 **Mr Davies**[21] 5509 3-8-12 **61** JosephineGordon 7 56
(David Brown) *disp 3rd pl: rdn and outpcd by ldng pair 2f out: grad fdd* **66/1**

0046 **8** *3* **Two Dollars (IRE)**[24] 5406 3-8-13 **62** (t[1]) RobertWinston 3 52
(William Jarvis) *t.k.h in midfield: rdn and btn 4f out* **10/1**

0054 **9** *2* **Sakurajima (IRE)**[46] 4575 3-9-1 **64** (t) TomQueally 6 51
(Charles Hills) *t.k.h on outside in midfield: rdn over 4f out: sn btn* **14/1**

000 **10** 1/2 **Alternate Route**[14] 5746 3-8-9 **58** RyanPowell 4 44
(Sir Mark Prescott Bt) *slowly away and rdn: nvr gng wl: no ch fnl 4f* **14/1**

-054 **11** *5* **Tayaar (IRE)**[13] 5810 4-8-12 **53** (p[1]) DannyBrock 10 30
(John Ryan) *led: rdn and hdd 4f out: wknd over 2f out: eased ins fnl f* **66/1**

2-65 **12** *6* **The Salmon Man**[47] 4519 5-9-12 **67** TedDurcan 8 34
(Brendan Powell) *stdd s: a wl bhd: no ch fnl 4f: t.o and eased* **28/1**

2m 25.94s (-2.76) **Going Correction** -0.225s/f (Firm)
**WFA** 3 from 4yo+ 8lb **12** Ran SP% **120.5**
Speed ratings (Par 103): **101,99,98,97,96 95,94,92,91,90 87,82**
CSF £20.62 CT £316.94 TOTE £6.70: £2.20, £1.40, £5.00; EX 24.60 Trifecta £325.70.
**Owner** The Vamp Collective **Bred** Successori del Marchese G Guglielmi **Trained** Newmarket, Suffolk

**FOCUS**
A modest event in which the leaders ddin't come back in the straight but this race should throw up its share of winners. The winner and second are progressing.

## 6294 TOTEPOOL RACECOURSE DEBIT CARD BETTING H'CAP 1m 1f 21y
**5:40** (5:45) (Class 5) (0-75,75) 4-Y-0+ **£3,105** (£924; £461; £230) **Stalls** Low

Form RPR
-566 **1** **Blaze Of Hearts (IRE)**[29] 5218 4-9-4 **72** RobertWinston 3 80
(Dean Ivory) *wnt 2nd after 3f: led wl over 2f out: sn rdn: idling in front and making it look v hrd work whn holding chalr fnl f* **11/2**[3]

2325 **2** 1 1/2 **Stosur (IRE)**[5] 6111 6-9-0 **73** (b) DavidEgan(5) 6 77
(Gay Kelleway) *sn drvn to ld: rdn and hdd wl over 2f out: plodded on and hld by idling wnr thrght fnl f* **5/1**[2]

4005 **3** 1/2 **Thecornishbarron (IRE)**[12] 5854 5-8-11 **65** StevieDonohoe 7 68
(John Ryan) *settled in last pair: rdn 3f out: kpt on wout threatening ins fnl f* **16/1**

0-55 **4** 3/4 **Navajo Storm (IRE)**[7] 6035 4-7-11 **56** oh2 JaneElliott(5) 1 57
(Michael Appleby) *2nd for 3f: pressed ldng pair: rdn 3f out: outpcd over 1f out* **8/1**

4523 **5** 2 1/2 **Life Of Luxury**[22] 5485 4-8-4 **58** KieranO'Neill 4 54
(Mark Brisbourne) *last trio: shkn up over 4f out: drvn and outpcd over 2f out: edgd rt ins fnl f* **9/1**

-445 **6** *5* **Rubensian**[13] 5798 4-9-7 **75** SilvestreDeSousa 2 67
(David Simcock) *lost 5 l s: nvr really travelling: rdn over 2f out: swtchd rt but no imp over 1f out: eased ins fnl f* **2/1**[1]

1m 52.71s (-3.09) **Going Correction** -0.225s/f (Firm) **6** Ran SP% **92.4**
Speed ratings (Par 103): **104,102,102,101,99 94**
CSF £21.04 TOTE £5.70: £2.40, £2.30; EX 22.10 Trifecta £178.60.
**Owner** Miss N Yarrow **Bred** Camogue Stud Ltd **Trained** Radlett, Herts
■ Issue was withdrawn not under orders. Price at time of withdrawal was 4-1. Rule 4 applies to all bets. Deduction - 20p in the pound.

**FOCUS**
Mainly exposed sorts in a fair handicap but the modest gallop suited those closest to the pace. It's rated around the runner-up.

## 6295 @ TOTEPOOLRACING WIN RACING TICKETS ON TWITTER MEDIAN AUCTION MAIDEN STKS 6f 3y
**6:10** (6:12) (Class 6) 3-4-Y-0 **£2,975** (£885; £442; £221) **Stalls** Centre

Form RPR
2 **1** **Miami Sunset**[195] 615 3-9-0 0 SilvestreDeSousa 6 70
(Philip McBride) *stdd s: bhd: swtchd lft and trckd ldrs on outer 3f out: led 2f out: sn rdn and in command: edgd rt ins fnl f* **8/1**

-022 **2** 2 3/4 **Seyasah (IRE)**[17] 5635 3-9-0 69 TedDurcan 8 61
(Chris Wall) *chsd ldrs: rdn and effrt over 2f out: sn chsng wnr but a hld* **1/1**[1]

-026 **3** *nk* **Canadian Royal**[27] 5291 3-9-5 60 (t) StevieDonohoe 5 65
(Stuart Williams) *t.k.h: midfield: rdn and outpcd after n.m.r over 2f out: styd on ins fnl f: no ch w wnr but catching runner-up* **13/2**[3]

253 **4** 1/2 **Nuncio**[24] 5409 3-9-5 70 JosephineGordon 2 63
(Daniel Kubler) *pressed ldr: led over 3f out: rdn and hdd 2f out: no ex fnl f* **3/1**[2]

4-2 **5** *2* **Silently**[8] 6009 4-9-3 0 GeorgeDowning 4 52
(Daniel Kubler) *towards rr: rdn over 2f out: nvr trbld ldrs* **10/1**

0 **6** 2¾ **Dollywaggon Pike**[9] 5969 3-9-0 0........................ AlistairRawlinson 7 43
(J R Jenkins) *plld hrd: led tl over 3f out: sn rdn: wknd over 1f out* **100/1**

**7** 6 **Danica Ashton** 3-8-11 0........................ RosieJessop(3) 3 24
(Miss Joey Ellis) *s.s: immediately rdn and toiling* **66/1**

05 **8** nk **Elemento**[161] 1183 3-9-5 32........................ DannyBrock 1 28
(Phil McEntee) *midfield: rdn and btn over 2f out: fin weakly* **150/1**

6 **9** 23 **Waitomo**[110] 2344 3-9-0 0........................ TomQueally 9
(Charles Hills) *racd freely: prom: rdn 1/2-way: lost pl over 2f out: heavily eased 1f out: t.o after* **20/1**

1m 12.55s (-1.85) **Going Correction** -0.225s/f (Firm)
**WFA** 3 from 4yo 3lb **9** Ran SP% **116.4**
Speed ratings (Par 101): **103,99,98,98,95 91,83,83,52**
CSF £16.54 TOTE £7.20: £2.00, £1.10, £2.00; EX 20.20 Trifecta £75.40.
**Owner** Mrs Jacqui Barrs & P J McBride **Bred** Clive Dennett **Trained** Newmarket, Suffolk

**FOCUS**
Little strength in depth in this ordinary event but an improved effort from the winner on this turf debut. The form is rated around the third with the winner a big improver.

## 6296 TOTEPOOLLIVEINFO.COM H'CAP 1m 3y
**6:40** (6:40) (Class 6) (0-55,57) 4-Y-0+ **£2,264** (£673; £336; £168) **Stalls** Centre

Form RPR

0-36 **1** **Appease**[21] 5509 8-8-9 46 oh1........................ ShelleyBirkett(3) 4 52
(Julia Feilden) *towards rr: hdwy over 2f out: pushed along to chal 1f out: led sn ins fnl f and kidded home* **6/1**[2]

46R- **2** ¾ **Honey Badger**[359] 5929 6-9-3 54........................(p) GeorgeWood(3) 5 58
(Michael Herrington) *trckd ldrs: effrt 2f out: rdn to ld 1f out: sn hdd: nt qckn fnl 100yds* **9/1**

6-65 **3** ¾ **Indiana Dawn**[25] 5357 4-8-12 51........................(p[1]) MitchGodwin(5) 8 54
(Robert Stephens) *taken down early: towards rr: travelled wl tl shkn up to improve over 2f out: styd on ins fnl f: nt quite rch ldrs* **8/1**

5602 **4** 3 **Pivotal Dream (IRE)**[11] 5897 4-8-12 46........................ KieranO'Neill 10 42
(Mark Brisbourne) *chsd ldrs: drvn 1/2-way: clsd on sufferance to ld briefly over 1f out: sn edgd lft: plodded on whn btn 120yds out* **12/1**

0004 **5** 2½ **Dor's Law**[26] 5336 4-9-7 55........................ RobertWinston 1 45+
(Dean Ivory) *prom: led over 2f out: hdd over 1f out: fdd ins fnl f* **4/1**[1]

003 **6** 2 **The Firm (IRE)**[12] 5857 8-9-1 56........................(b) GinaMangan(7) 11 41
(J R Jenkins) *sn prom: rdn and lost pl over 2f out* **33/1**

6035 **7** 2¼ **Moving Robe (IRE)**[53] 4323 4-8-7 46 oh1........................(t) DavidEgan(5) 6 26
(Conrad Allen) *bhd and sn pushed along: nvr on terms* **15/2**[3]

0304 **8** 3½ **Harlequin Rock**[12] 5854 4-9-9 57........................ TomQueally 12 29
(Mick Quinn) *nvr bttr than midfield: rdn and struggling over 2f out: rdr's whip broke 2f out* **6/1**[2]

0060 **9** 1¾ **Langham**[8] 6015 4-9-9 57........................(p) AlistairRawlinson 3 25
(Michael Appleby) *t.k.h: cl up tl rdn and lost pl over 2f out* **25/1**

4306 **10** 2¼ **Rosie Crowe (IRE)**[21] 5512 5-8-13 47........................(v) JosephineGordon 2 10
(Shaun Harris) *led: rdn and hdd over 2f out: sn lost pl* **15/2**[3]

0066 **11** 8 **Torment**[15] 5723 4-9-3 51........................(t[1]) SilvestreDeSousa 7
(Charlie Wallis) *last away: rn in snatches and nvr looking keen: rdn and btn 1/2-way: eased 2f out: t.o* **11/1**

1m 38.45s (-2.15) **Going Correction** -0.225s/f (Firm) **11** Ran SP% **116.0**
Speed ratings (Par 101): **101,100,99,96,94 92,89,86,84,82 74**
CSF £58.25 CT £436.03 TOTE £9.60: £3.10, £3.60, £3.20; EX 95.50 Trifecta £796.40.
**Owner** T Healy **Bred** Juddmonte Farms Ltd **Trained** Exning, Suffolk

**FOCUS**
A low-grade handicap in which the decent gallop suited those ridden with a bit of patience.

## 6297 TOTEPOOL LIVE INFO DOWNLOAD THE APP H'CAP 7f 3y
**7:10** (7:11) (Class 4) (0-80,80) 3-Y-0+ **£4,787** (£1,424; £711; £355) **Stalls** Centre

Form RPR

4010 **1** **Warsaw Road (IRE)**[27] 5288 3-8-13 75........................ GeorgeWood(3) 4 82
(Luca Cumani) *cl up: rdn over 2f out: pressed ldr wl over 1f out: edgd in front 150yds out: in command cl to home* **9/1**[3]

5002 **2** ¾ **Fieldsman (USA)**[10] 5948 5-9-11 79........................ SilvestreDeSousa 3 86
(David O'Meara) *trckd ldrs: led 2f out: rdn and hrd pressed 1f out: hdd and nt qckn fnl 150yds* **5/2**[2]

-231 **3** 2½ **Multicultural (IRE)**[5] 6111 3-9-6 79 6ex........................(b) MartinHarley 5 77
(James Tate) *stdd in last pl and racing keenly: rdn and effrt over 1f out: n.g.t: hung rt but tk wl hld 3rd nr fin* **11/10**[1]

0036 **4** nk **Dubai's Secret**[27] 5300 4-9-12 80........................(v[1]) JosephineGordon 1 79
(David Brown) *led: shkn up 3f out: hdd 2f out: fnd nil after: lost 3rd cl home* **12/1**

0052 **5** 1 **Roaring Forties (IRE)**[18] 5601 4-9-10 78........................ ConnorBeasley 2 75
(Rebecca Bastiman) *t.k.h towards rr: rdn 2f out: sn btn* **14/1**

0006 **6** nk **Outer Space**[28] 5245 6-9-7 80........................ MitchGodwin(5) 7 76
(Jamie Osborne) *pressed ldr tl 1/2-way: sn rdn: btn 2f out* **12/1**

0053 **7** 3¼ **Anfaass (IRE)**[18] 5606 3-9-5 78........................ TomQueally 6 63
(George Margarson) *bhd: rdn 1/2-way: sn labouring* **33/1**

1m 25.26s (-1.34) **Going Correction** -0.225s/f (Firm)
**WFA** 3 from 4yo+ 5lb **7** Ran SP% **111.2**
Speed ratings (Par 105): **98,97,94,93,92 92,88**
CSF £30.05 TOTE £9.30: £5.20, £1.90; EX 33.70 Trifecta £98.40.
**Owner** Mrs A Silver & Partner **Bred** Tally-Ho Stud **Trained** Newmarket, Suffolk

**FOCUS**
A fair handicap in which the first two finished clear but a modest gallop means this bare form isn't entirely reliable. It's rated around the runner-up.

## 6298 COLLECT TOTEPOOL WINNINGS AT BETFRED SHOPS H'CAP 5f 42y
**7:40** (7:40) (Class 6) (0-60,68) 3-Y-0+ **£2,264** (£673; £336; £168) **Stalls** Centre

Form RPR

5214 **1** **Defining Moment**[11] 5871 3-9-5 60........................ MartinHarley 8 73+
(Rae Guest) *stdd and last early: smooth prog over 1f out to ld 1f out: sn clr: easily* **9/2**[3]

40 **2** 2 **Miss Rosina (IRE)**[11] 5871 3-8-10 56........................(p[1]) JaneElliott(5) 4 59
(George Margarson) *led: pushed along and hdd 1f out: immediately outpcd: jst clung on to 2nd pl* **14/1**

323 **3** hd **Justice Rock**[5] 6114 4-8-11 50........................(t) SilvestreDeSousa 3 52
(Phil McEntee) *prom: rdden 2f out: ev ch 1f out: sn no ch w wnr* **6/1**

252 **4** nk **Agnethe (IRE)**[13] 5812 3-9-1 61........................ DavidEgan(5) 2 62
(Paul D'Arcy) *cl up: pushed along and ev ch 1f out but wnr sn dashed clr* **2/1**[1]

5431 **5** 1 **Hamish McGonagain**[4] 6148 4-9-8 68 6ex..........(p) PatrickVaughan(7) 9 66
(David O'Meara) *midfield: rdn 2f out: btn 1f out* **3/1**[2]

40 **6** 2¼ **Maggi May (IRE)**[24] 5419 3-8-9 50........................ JosephineGordon 7 40
(David Brown) *pressed ldrs: drvn over 1f out: weaekned ins fnl f* **20/1**

3320 **7** nk **See Vermont**[14] 5736 9-9-5 58........................(b) ConnorBeasley 5 46
(Rebecca Bastiman) *midfield: drvn 1/2-way: sn btn* **12/1**

0000 **8** ¾ **Rat Catcher (IRE)**[4] 6157 7-8-2 46 oh1........................(b) KevinLundie(5) 6 32
(Lisa Williamson) *taken down early: pushed along and nvr gng pce in rr* **66/1**

0330 **9** 7 **Sakhee's Jem**[5] 6112 4-8-9 55........................ CameronNoble(7) 1 16
(Gay Kelleway) *cl up: fdd 2f out: wnt rt fnl f and eased* **20/1**

1m 1.8s (-0.90) **Going Correction** -0.225s/f (Firm)
**WFA** 3 from 4yo+ 2lb **9** Ran SP% **116.2**
Speed ratings (Par 101): **98,94,94,94,92 88,88,87,75**
CSF £62.48 CT £383.39 TOTE £5.50: £2.00, £3.50, £1.90; EX 59.10 Trifecta £328.80.
**Owner** Derek J Willis **Bred** Derek J Willis **Trained** Newmarket, Suffolk

**FOCUS**
An open handicap on paper but one turned into a procession by the very easy winner, who is a sprinter to follow in the short term.
T/Plt: £197.70 to a £1 stake. Pool: £56,137.83 - 207.24 winning units. T/Qpdt: £67.40 to a £1 stake. Pool: £5,111.93 - 56.08 winning units. **Iain Mackenzie**

6299a (Foreign Racing) - See Raceform Interactive

# 6247 DEAUVILLE (R-H)
Tuesday, August 22

**OFFICIAL GOING: Turf: good; polytrack: standard**

## 6300a PRIX BEACHCOMBER VICTORIA (PRIX DE BOULLEVILLE) (CLAIMER) (5YO+) (POLYTRACK) 7f 110y
**12:10** 5-Y-0+ **£8,119** (£3,247; £2,435; £1,623; £811)

RPR

**1** **Longray (FR)**[92] 5-8-10 0........................ AlexandreChesneau(8) 7 84
(G Botti, France) **87/10**

**2** hd **Wink Oliver**[66] 3808 5-9-4 0........................(p) MickaelBarzalona 10 84
(Jo Hughes) *settled in rr trio: impr to trck ldrs over 2f out: hdwy to chal 1f out: drvn ins fnl f: jst failed* **124/10**

**3** 1¼ **Yume (FR)**[10] 6-8-8 0........................(b) ClementLecoeuvre(3) 4 73
(C Lerner, France) **9/2**[2]

**4** snk **Diamant De Vati (FR)**[16] 6-9-1 0........................ TheoBachelot 1 77
(S Wattel, France) **22/5**[1]

**5** snk **Asulaman (GER)**[16] 10-8-11 0........................(b) AurelienLemaitre 9 73
(S Cerulis, France) **93/10**

**6** 2 **Lotus Garden (FR)**[22] 5490 6-9-3 0........................ JeromeMoutard(5) 6 79
(F Chappet, France) **32/5**

**7** nk **Louvain (FR)**[81] 8-9-2 0........................(b) ChristopheSoumillon 2 72
(G Nicot, France) **49/10**[3]

**8** 4 **Blacksou (FR)**[147] 7-8-11 0........................ AntoineHamelin 8 57
(F Vermeulen, France) **108/10**

**9** 1 **Don Mimi (ITY)**[81] 5-9-2 0........................ VincentCheminaud 11 59
(Gianluca Bietolini, Italy) **132/10**

**10** 1¼ **Fawley (IRE)**[9] 5-9-5 0........................ EddyHardouin 5 59
(M Boutin, France) **181/10**

**11** 10 **Coup Fatale (FR)**[658] 5-9-0 0........................ MlleSanneDeCeulaer(4) 3 33
(Ecurie Avant-Garde, Belgium) **40/1**

PARI-MUTUEL (all including 1 euro stake): WIN 9.70; PLACE 3.10, 3.80, 2.10; DF 57.40; SF 118.00.
**Owner** C Pellegatti, L Biffi & G Botti **Bred** Franklin Finance S.A. **Trained** France

6201a (Foreign Racing) - See Raceform Interactive

## 6302a PRIX BEACHCOMBER CANONNIER (PRIX DE BEUZEVILLE) (CLAIMER) (4YO) (POLYTRACK) 7f 110y
**3:30** 4-Y-0 **£8,119** (£3,247; £2,435; £1,623; £811)

RPR

**1** **Ali Spirit (IRE)**[14] 4-9-1 0........................ ChristopheSoumillon 3 78
(F Vermeulen, France) **19/10**[1]

**2** ½ **Alberobello (FR)**[14] 4-9-4 0........................ StephanePasquier 10 80
(M Delcher Sanchez, France) **51/10**[2]

**3** 1¾ **Bat Aloufat (FR)**[41] 4-9-2 0........................ FranckBlondel 7 73
(M Pimbonnet, France) **106/10**

**4** 1¼ **Blue Moon Rising (IRE)**[10] 4-8-8 0........................(b) PanagiotisDimitsanis 9 62
(Christos Kouvaras, France) **56/10**[3]

**5** nk **Little Ghetto Boy**[103] 4-9-1 0........................ AlbertoSanna 8 69
(Tamara Richter, Austria) **218/10**

**6** 3½ **Rougeoyant (FR)**[51] 4-9-1 0........................(b) EddyHardouin 4 60
(Gerard Martin, Austria) **42/1**

**7** hd **Verti Chop (FR)**[14] 4-9-1 0........................ TomLefranc(7) 2 66
(C Boutin, France) **98/10**

**8** 6 **Vroom (IRE)**[14] 5754 4-9-1 0........................(p) Pierre-CharlesBoudot 6 44
(Gay Kelleway) *wl into stride: led: rdn and hdd 2f out: sn no ex: wknd fnl f* **94/10**

**9** nk **Enduring Power (IRE)**[22] 5490 4-9-4 0..............(b[1]) MickaelBarzalona 5 47
(Jo Hughes) *settled bhd ldr: pushed along over 2f out: rdn and limited rspnse over 1f out: eased fnl f* **118/10**

**10** 5 **Normandy Kitten (USA)**[10] 4-8-11 0........................(p) VincentCheminaud 1 27
(Gianluca Bietolini, Italy) **44/5**

PARI-MUTUEL (all including 1 euro stake): WIN 2.90; PLACE 1.60, 2.00, 2.40; DF 8.10; SF 13.80.
**Owner** Sydney Saadia **Bred** Zalim Bifov **Trained** France

# 6174 BATH (L-H)
Wednesday, August 23

**OFFICIAL GOING: Good (good to soft in places; 7.5)**
Wind: quite strong against Weather: cloudy

## 6303 DRIBUILD GROUP APPRENTICE H'CAP (PART OF THE RACING EXCELLENCE INITIATIVE) (SPRINT SERIES QUAL.) 5f 160y
**1:45** (1:46) (Class 5) (0-75,77) 3-Y-0+ **£2,911** (£866; £432; £216) **Stalls** Centre

Form RPR

2211 **1** **Our Lord**[14] 5784 5-9-10 73........................ DavidEgan 1 87
(Michael Attwater) *mde all: kpt on strly: readily* **2/1**[1]

3261 **2** 3¼ **Field Of Vision (IRE)**[16] 5711 4-9-12 75........................ FinleyMarsh 3 78
(Joseph Tuite) *chsd ldrs: wnt 2nd over 1f out: sn rdn: kpt on but nt pce to get on terms w wnr* **10/3**[2]

3654 **3** 2¾ **Showmethewayavrilo**[14] 5784 4-9-5 68........................ CameronNoble 2 62
(Malcolm Saunders) *s.i.s: in last trio: hdwy 2f out: sn rdn: kpt on but nt gng pce to get on terms fnl f* **8/1**



The Form Book Flat, Raceform Ltd, Newbury, RG14 5SJ

623 **4** *1 ½* **Gold Hunter (IRE)**[13] 5821 7-10-0 **77**..........................(p) JoshuaBryan 5 66
(Steve Flook) *last trio: rdn whn swtchd to centre and hdwy 2f out: kpt on ins fnl f* **11/2**

4102 **5** *2 ½* **Seamster**[4] 6177 10-9-9 **77**..........................(t) LauraCoughlan(5) 4 58
(David Loughnane) *pressed wnr: rdn over 2f out: fdd over 1f out* **5/1**[3]

5006 **6** *2 ¼* **Silverrica (IRE)**[19] 5587 7-9-3 **69**.......................... NicolaCurrie(3) 7 42
(Malcolm Saunders) *chsd ldrs tl wknd over 1f out* **9/1**

5030 **7** *2* **Kyllukey**[23] 5481 4-8-11 **67**..........................(t[1]) KerrieRaybould(7) 8 33
(Milton Bradley) *chsd ldrs: rdn over 2f out: drifted lft: wknd over 1f out* **22/1**

6-00 **8** *2* **Sandacres**[14] 5793 4-8-5 **61** oh6.......................... OllieJago(7) 6 21
(Laura Mongan) *sn pushed along in last trio: nvr threatened: wknd over 1f out* **80/1**

1m 11.65s (0.45) **Going Correction** +0.175s/f (Good) 8 Ran SP% **115.2**
Speed ratings (Par 103): **104,99,96,94,90 87,85,82**
CSF £8.81 CT £42.40 TOTE £2.40: £1.10, £1.40, £2.30; EX 10.00 Trifecta £49.80.
**Owner** Mrs M S Teversham **Bred** Mrs Monica Teversham **Trained** Epsom, Surrey

**FOCUS**
Rail moved out between the 4f and 3f markers, adding 5 yards to Race 3, 4, 5, 7 and 8's advertised distances. A fair sprint handicap for apprentice riders. They went a decent gallop on loose-topped, drying ground officially described as good, good to soft in places. Not the most robust field, with the second and third rated a bit below their recent form.

## 6304 FRIARY VINTNERS EUROPEAN BREEDERS FUND NOVICE STKS 5f 160y
**2:15** (2:16) (Class 5) 2-Y-O **£3,234** (£962; £481; £240) **Stalls** Centre

Form RPR

422 **1** **Yafta**[21] 5531 2-9-2 80.......................... DaneO'Neill 3 83+
(Richard Hannon) *prom: led over 3f out: shkn up to draw clr ent fnl f: comf* **4/5**[1]

543 **2** *3* **Expecting**[37] 4972 2-9-2 76.......................... SteveDrowne 7 73
(Charles Hills) *trckd ldrs: rdn to chse wnr over 2f out: kpt on but nt pce to get on terms* **4/1**[2]

**3** *2* **Go Roo** 2-8-13 0.......................... HectorCrouch(3) 5 66+
(Clive Cox) *in tch: pushed along over 3f out: rdn 2f out: kpt on ins fnl f but nt pce to threaten* **9/2**[3]

0 **4** *nk* **City Gent**[32] 5151 2-9-2 0.......................... PatDobbs 4 65
(Ralph Beckett) *s.i.s (hood removed sltly late): towards rr: hdwy 2f out: kpt on same pce fnl f* **11/1**

00 **5** *nk* **Madame Jo Jo**[34] 5056 2-8-6 0.......................... JaneElliott(5) 9 59
(Sarah Hollinshead) *chsd ldrs: rdn over 2f out: no ex fnl 120yds* **66/1**

0 **6** *1 ½* **Dizzy G (IRE)**[21] 5528 2-8-11 0.......................... RoystonFfrench 1 54
(K R Burke) *sn trcking ldrs: rdn over 2f out: wknd ent fnl f* **6/1**

00 **7** *1* **Puramente**[14] 5786 2-9-2 0.......................... DougieCostello 8 56
(Jo Hughes) *little slowly away: sn outpcd in rr: nvr any imp* **50/1**

00 **8** *24* **Redtedd**[13] 5844 2-9-2 0.......................... LiamKeniry 2
(Tom Dascombe) *led tl over 3f out: wknd qckly wl over 2f out: t.o* **66/1**

1m 12.65s (1.45) **Going Correction** +0.175s/f (Good) 8 Ran SP% **121.3**
Speed ratings (Par 94): **97,93,90,89,89 87,86,54**
CSF £4.83 TOTE £1.50: £1.02, £1.50, £2.10; EX 4.20 Trifecta £10.40.
**Owner** Hamdan Al Maktoum **Bred** Lordship Stud **Trained** East Everleigh, Wilts

**FOCUS**
A fair juvenile novice sprint. The odds-on favourite made virtually all in a respectable time, but there are doubts over the form.

## 6305 GRAHAM PLUMBERS MERCHANT H'CAP (DIV I) 1m 2f 37y
**2:50** (2:50) (Class 6) (0-55,62) 4-Y-O+ **£2,264** (£673; £336; £168) **Stalls** Low

Form RPR

0260 **1** **Altaira**[16] 5713 6-9-1 **49**..........................(b[1]) WilliamCarson 10 54
(Tony Carroll) *chsd ldng pair clr of remainder: drvn to chse ldr 3f out: led over 1f out: styd on wl* **11/1**

1651 **2** *2 ¼* **Sakhalin Star (IRE)**[6] 6088 6-9-11 **62** 6ex..........(p) CallumShepherd(3) 8 63
(Richard Guest) *racd keenly in midfield: rdn wl over 2f out: hdwy over 1f out: styd o to go 2nd ins fnl f: no threat to wnr* **4/1**[3]

5225 **3** *2 ½* **Eben Dubai (IRE)**[42] 4734 5-9-3 **51**.......................... CharlesBishop 4 47
(Tracey Barfoot-Saunt) *led: 10 l clr 3f out: sn rdn: hdd over 1f out: no ex* **5/2**[2]

0-06 **4** *2* **Selena Rose**[12] 5866 4-8-7 **46** oh1..........................(h) DavidEgan(5) 9 39
(Ronald Harris) *mid-div: rdn over 3f out: styd on fnl 2f but nt pce to get on terms* **66/1**

000 **5** *3 ¼* **Callaghan (GER)**[7] 6069 4-9-7 **55**..........................(t) StevieDonohoe 5 42
(Tom Gretton) *s.i.s: towards rr: rdn over 3f out: styd on fnl f but nvr any threat* **28/1**

-066 **6** *nk* **Fire Empress**[37] 4981 4-8-12 **46** oh1..........................(h) SamHitchcott 1 32
(James Unett) *mid-divsion of chsng gp: rdn over 3f out: nvr threatened to get involved (b.b.vs)* **40/1**

5423 **7** *2 ¼* **Eugenic**[14] 5787 6-9-3 **51**.......................... SilvestreDeSousa 3 33
(Rod Millman) *prom in chsng gp: rdn into 4th 3f out: nvr threatened to get on terms: wknd fnl f* **7/4**[1]

4300 **8** *1* **Jazri**[89] 3028 6-8-9 **50** ow3..........................(p) KerrieRaybould(7) 2 31
(Milton Bradley) *hld up: hdwy into midfield 3f out: sn rdn: nvr threatened: wknd fnl f* **18/1**

4600 **9** *7* **Steady Major (IRE)**[13] 5850 5-8-9 **46** oh1.......................... CharlieBennett(3) 6 14
(Mark Brisbourne) *chsd ldr tl over 3f out: wknd over 2f out* **50/1**

000 **10** *½* **Koubba (IRE)**[16] 5712 4-8-12 **46**..........................(t) FranBerry 7 13
(Neil Mulholland) *stdd s: rdn over 3f out: a towards rr* **14/1**

0-0U **11** *24* **Opera Buffa (IRE)**[14] 5787 4-8-7 **46**..........................(tp) PaddyPilley(5) 12
(Steve Flook) *chsd ldng trio tl over 3f out: wknd over 2f out* **40/1**

2m 12.62s (1.62) **Going Correction** +0.175s/f (Good) 11 Ran SP% **117.0**
Speed ratings (Par 101): **100,98,96,94,92 91,89,89,83,83 63**
CSF £52.86 CT £147.73 TOTE £12.30: £3.20, £1.70, £1.40; EX 76.40 Trifecta £251.20.
**Owner** Mrs Susan Keable **Bred** Skymarc Farm Inc **Trained** Cropthorne, Worcs

**FOCUS**
Race distance increased 5 yards. The first division of a moderate handicap. The second favourite, who finished a tired third, couldn't sustain his strong gallop. The winner is rated back near his 2016 turf high.

## 6306 GRAHAM PLUMBERS MERCHANT H'CAP (DIV II) 1m 2f 37y
**3:25** (3:26) (Class 6) (0-55,56) 4-Y-O+ **£2,264** (£673; £336; £168) **Stalls** Low

Form RPR

0464 **1** **Windsorlot (IRE)**[16] 5714 4-9-2 **50**.......................... GeorgeDowning 12 61
(Tony Carroll) *mid-div: hdwy over 2f out: sn rdn: led ent fnl f: styd on wl: rdn out* **11/1**

0653 **2** *¾* **Edge (IRE)**[16] 5713 6-8-9 **48**..........................(b) JoshuaBryan(5) 7 58
(Bernard Llewellyn) *hld up towards rr: hdwy over 2f out: sn rdn: str chal ins fnl f: styd on* **9/2**[2]

60-4 **3** *3* **Chilli Jam**[8] 6035 4-9-3 **54**.......................... CallumShepherd(3) 2 58
(Ed de Giles) *chsd ldrs: led wl over 2f out: sn rdn: hdd ent fnl f: no ex* **4/1**[1]

0504 **4** *1 ¼* **Just Fred (IRE)**[42] 4734 4-8-12 **46** oh1..........................(t) FranBerry 6 48
(Neil Mulholland) *mid-div: rdn over 2f out: styd on fr over 1f out: wnt 4th ins fnl f* **7/1**

452 **5** *5* **Spirit Of The Vale (IRE)**[13] 5831 4-9-8 **56**..........................(t) KevinStott 1 49
(Oliver Greenall) *towards rr of mid-div: hdwy to trck ldrs after 2f: chsd ldrs over 1f out: edgd lft and fdd fnl f* **6/1**[3]

0-45 **6** *1 ¼* **Nightswift**[16] 5714 5-8-13 **47**.......................... DougieCostello 11 38
(James Evans) *rn freely to post: hld up towards rr: midfield 3f out: sn rdn: styd on same pce fnl 2f* **7/1**

616 **7** *¾* **Outlaw Torn (IRE)**[12] 5895 8-9-7 **55**..........................(e) RobHornby 5 44
(Richard Guest) *chsd ldrs: rdn 3f out: wknd ent fnl f* **7/1**

-005 **8** *7* **Solid Justice (IRE)**[28] 5296 6-8-12 **46** oh1.......................... DanielMuscutt 3 23
(Mark Pattinson) *chsd ldrs: hung rt fnl 4f: rdn wl over 2f out: wknd ent fnl f* **12/1**

6-0P **9** *5* **Krafty One**[14] 5782 5-9-0 **51**.......................... EdwardGreatrex(3) 10 19
(Michael Scudamore) *s.i.s: towards rr: drvn 3f out: no imp* **25/1**

0564 **10** *nse* **Color Force (IRE)**[14] 5809 4-8-7 **46**..........................(bt[1]) JaneElliott(5) 9 14
(Gay Kelleway) *led: sn clr: rdn and hdd wl over 2f out: wknd over 1f out* **12/1**

00-0 **11** *11* **Nordenfelt (IRE)**[44] 4700 4-8-12 **46** oh1.......................... SteveDrowne 8
(Natalie Lloyd-Beavis) *mid-div tl 6f out: wknd over 3f out* **66/1**

0300 **12** *32* **Mr Standfast**[29] 5267 4-8-12 **46** oh1..........................(t[1]) StevieDonohoe 4
(Alan Phillips) *mid-div tl 6f out: wknd over 3f out* **50/1**

2m 12.79s (1.79) **Going Correction** +0.175s/f (Good) 12 Ran SP% **121.0**
Speed ratings (Par 101): **99,98,96,95,91 90,89,83,79,79 70,45**
CSF £60.63 CT £239.71 TOTE £11.90: £3.40, £1.80, £2.00; EX 76.50 Trifecta £339.60.
**Owner** Sf Racing Club **Bred** John Irish **Trained** Cropthorne, Worcs

**FOCUS**
Race distance increased 5 yards. The second division of a moderate handicap. The winning time was only marginally slower. The winner was near last year's Irish form.

## 6307 UNIVERSITY AND LITERARY CLUB EBF FILLIES' H'CAP 1m 3f 137y
**4:00** (4:00) (Class 4) (0-80,81) 3-Y-O+ **£6,301** (£1,886; £943; £472; £235) **Stalls** Low

Form RPR

-416 **1** **Camerone (IRE)**[40] 4829 3-9-6 **81**.......................... PatDobbs 5 93
(Ralph Beckett) *trckd ldrs: pushed along and hdwy over 2f out: led ent fnl f: kpt on wl to assert cl home* **9/1**

531 **2** *1* **Tarte Tropezienne (IRE)**[16] 5707 3-9-4 **79**.......................... PatCosgrave 8 89
(William Haggas) *prom: led jst over 2f out: rdn and narrowly hdd ent fnl f: kpt on: hld cl home* **5/6**[1]

56 **3** *7* **Green Or Black (IRE)**[144] 609 5-9-9 **75**.......................... SilvestreDeSousa 6 72
(Neil Mulholland) *led: rdn and hdd jst over 2f out: styd on same pce* **13/2**[3]

3124 **4** *8* **Light Of Joy (USA)**[13] 5822 3-9-5 **80**.......................... StevieDonohoe 1 65
(David Lanigan) *hld up: hdwy over 2f out: rdn over 1f out: nvr threatened ldrs: fdd ins fnl f* **10/1**

1 **5** *4* **Satisfy (IRE)**[10] 5957 3-9-1 **76** 6ex.......................... RoystonFfrench 4 55
(K R Burke) *trckd ldrs: rdn 3f out: wknd over 1f out* **11/2**[2]

-512 **6** *nk* **Rowlestonerendezvu**[19] 5607 4-8-2 **61** oh2.......................... AledBeech(7) 2 38
(Tony Carroll) *hld up: rdn and hdwy over 2f out: nvr threatened: wknd ent fnl f* **14/1**

04-0 **7** *5* **Miss Minuty**[39] 4915 5-9-0 **73**.......................... FinleyMarsh(7) 7 42
(Jeremy Scott) *hld up: rdn wl over 1f out: no imp and wknd ent fnl f* **20/1**

2m 30.88s (0.28) **Going Correction** +0.175s/f (Good)
**WFA** 3 from 4yo+ 9lb 7 Ran SP% **113.8**
Speed ratings (Par 102): **106,105,100,95,92 92,89**
CSF £16.89 CT £54.27 TOTE £7.60: £4.20, £1.20; EX 23.30 Trifecta £100.00.
**Owner** H H Sheikh Mohammed Bin Khalifa Al Thani **Bred** Al Shahania Stud **Trained** Kimpton, Hants

**FOCUS**
Race distance increased 5 yards. The feature contest was a fairly decent middle-distance fillies' handicap. They went a respectable gallop and it is sound form with the first two clear. Hard form to gauge.

## 6308 PARKER TRANSPORT SW H'CAP 5f 10y
**4:35** (4:35) (Class 5) (0-75,79) 3-Y-O **£2,911** (£866; £432; £216) **Stalls** Centre

Form RPR

331 **1** **Delagate This Lord**[55] 4256 3-8-12 **70**.......................... DavidEgan(5) 4 79
(Michael Attwater) *chsd ldrs: led wl over 1f out: kpt on wl: pushed out* **13/8**[1]

1433 **2** *1 ¼* **Secret Potion**[6] 6099 3-9-3 **70**.......................... SamHitchcott 1 74
(Ronald Harris) *sn led: rdn whn strly chal over 2f out: hdd wl over 1f out: kpt on tl no ex fnl 120yds* **9/2**[3]

2105 **3** *2* **The Nazca Lines (IRE)**[13] 5837 3-9-7 **74**..........(v) SilvestreDeSousa 6 71
(John Quinn) *broke wl: prom: rdn for str chal over 2f out tl ent fnl f: sn edgd lft: no ex* **9/4**[2]

2225 **4** *4 ½* **Secret Agent**[19] 5588 3-8-13 **69**..........................(b[1]) GeorgeWood(3) 3 50
(William Muir) *trckd ldrs: rdn over 2f out: wknd ent fnl f* **6/1**

4121 **5** *2* **Peachey Carnehan**[10] 5956 3-9-9 **79** 6ex..........(v) PhilDennis(3) 2 52
(Michael Mullineaux) *trckd ldrs: rdn over 2f out: drifted rt and wknd over 1f out* **9/1**

1m 3.49s (0.99) **Going Correction** +0.175s/f (Good) 5 Ran SP% **111.3**
Speed ratings (Par 100): **99,97,93,86,83**
CSF £9.37 TOTE £2.00: £1.40, £2.10; EX 7.00 Trifecta £19.50.
**Owner** Mrs M S Teversham **Bred** Mrs Monica Teversham **Trained** Epsom, Surrey

**FOCUS**
A fair 3yo sprint handicap. The favourite justified the strong support down in trip and is improving. The form is rated around the runner-up.

## 6309 EY AND GUESTS H'CAP (BATH SUMMER STAYERS' SERIES QUALIFIER) 1m 5f 11y
**5:10** (5:10) (Class 6) (0-60,65) 4-Y-O+ **£2,264** (£673; £336; £168) **Stalls** High

Form RPR

2321 **1** **Hope Is High**[6] 6109 4-9-12 **65** 6ex.......................... SilvestreDeSousa 13 71
(John Berry) *hld up towards rr: hmpd 1st bnd and snatched up: hdwy over 2f out: rdn over 1f out: swtchd rt ins fnl f: drifting lft but fin strly: led cl home* **8/11**[1]

315 **2** *¾* **Wassail**[42] 4733 4-8-7 **49**.......................... CallumShepherd(3) 3 54
(Ed de Giles) *trckd ldrs: led 2f out: sn rdn: drifting lft and strly pressed ent fnl f: styd on: hdd cl home* **14/1**

0023 **3** *½* **Powered (IRE)**[7] 6069 4-9-4 **57**.......................... TimmyMurphy 6 61
(David Evans) *mid-div: hdwy in centre wl over 2f out: swtchd lft over 1f out: rdn and edgd to far rails ent fnl f: ev ch fnl f: no ex towards fin* **10/1**[3]

0653 **4** *½* **Penny Poet (IRE)**[158] 1256 4-8-12 **51**.......................... LiamKeniry 9 55
(Neil Mulholland) *mid-div tl lost pl fnl bnd: hdwy in centre fr over 2f out: rdn over 1f out: sn edgd lft: styd on ins fnl f: wnt 4th cl home* **8/1**[2]

/034 **5** *nk* **Vexillum (IRE)**[45] 4040 8-8-4 **46** oh1..........................(p) HollieDoyle(3) 11 49
(Neil Mulholland) *hld up towards rr: plld way through to ld over 6f out: rdn and hdd 2f out: stl ev ch ent fnl f: no ex towards fin* **25/1**

4003 **6** *3 ¾* **Briac (FR)**[16] 5716 6-8-12 **51**.......................................... DanielMuscutt 1 49
(Mark Pattinson) *in tch: rdn 3f out: nvr threatened: styd on same pce fnl 2f* **20/1**

-543 **7** *1 ½* **Captain George (IRE)**[28] 5274 6-9-7 **60**.................... SteveDrowne 12 56
(Michael Blake) *mid-div: rdn wl over 2f out: little imp* **8/1**[2]

0-20 **8** *3 ½* **Sir Dylan**[16] 5716 8-8-12 **51**..........................................(h) SamHitchcott 10 41
(Polly Gundry) *hld up towards rr: hmpd 1st bnd: hdwy onto midfield 5f out: rdn over 2f out:* **25/1**

5540 **9** *½* **Ivanhoe**[25] 5432 7-9-7 **60**..................................................(b) RobHornby 7 50
(Michael Blanshard) *mid-div: rdn 3f out: wknd over 1f out* **16/1**

5010 **10** *½* **Quay Point (IRE)**[16] 5716 4-9-3 **56**...................................... JohnFahy 8 45
(Laura Mongan) *led for 1f: trckd ldr: rdn 3f out: wknd over 1f out* **12/1**

0-06 **11** *4 ½* **Ayla's Emperor**[26] 5361 8-9-2 **58**..............................(p) GeorgeWood(3) 5 40
(John Flint) *hmpd 1st bnd: a towards rr* **22/1**

25/6 **12** *¾* **Shot In The Dark (IRE)**[28] 5274 8-8-4 **46** oh1.........(p) NoelGarbutt(3) 14 27
(Jonathan Geake) *racd keenly: led after 1f: hdd over 6f out: rdn over 3f out: wknd over 1f out* **50/1**

0054 **13** *4* **Fleetwood Poppy**[12] 5866 5-8-4 **46** oh1.............. EdwardGreatrex(3) 4 22
(Michael Attwater) *trckd ldrs: rdn wl over 2f out: wknd over 1f out* **50/1**

2m 58.97s (6.97) **Going Correction** +0.175s/f (Good) **13** Ran SP% **130.2**
Speed ratings (Par 101): **85,84,84,83,83 81,80,78,78,77 74,74,72**
CSF £13.37 CT £77.58 TOTE £1.60: £1.10, £4.30, £2.40; EX 19.70 Trifecta £129.30.
**Owner** Mrs Emma Berry & John Berry **Bred** Miss K Rausing **Trained** Newmarket, Suffolk

**FOCUS**
Race distance increased by 5 yards. A modest handicap. They went a muddling gallop until some pace was injected over 6f out.

## 6310 HAPPY WEDDING ANNIVERSARY ALEX AND LIZ H'CAP 1m
**5:40** (5:40) (Class 5) (0-75,74) 3-Y-O+ **£2,911** (£866; £432; £216) **Stalls** Low

Form RPR

0000 **1** **Mister Musicmaster**[14] 5788 8-9-4 **66**........................ SteveDrowne 9 76
(Ron Hodges) *hld up: hdwy 2f out: led jst ins fnl f: r.o wl: readily* **25/1**

424 **2** *2 ½* **Rinaria (IRE)**[26] 5378 3-9-2 **70**............................................(h) JoeyHaynes 2 73
(K R Burke) *trckd ldrs: rdn over 2f out: led over 1f out: hdd jst ins fnl f: nt pce of wnr* **6/1**

-105 **3** *2* **Masterofdiscovery**[68] 3780 3-9-6 **74**.......................................(b) JohnFahy 7 72
(Clive Cox) *mid-div: hdwy in centre over 2f out: sn rdn: styd on to go 3rd wl ins fnl f* **3/1**[1]

0-00 **4** *¾* **My Fantasea (IRE)**[25] 5403 4-9-5 **67**............................ TimmyMurphy 6 65
(David Evans) *in tch: rdn over 2f out: styd on but nt pce to get involved fnl f* **25/1**

4560 **5** *nk* **Hot Mustard**[13] 5823 7-8-11 **59**...........................................(h[1]) MartinDwyer 8 56
(William Muir) *trckd ldr: rdn and ev ch over 2f out: fdd ins fnl f* **14/1**

4556 **6** *1* **Diable D'Or (IRE)**[14] 5797 3-9-1 **72**............................(v) EdwardGreatrex(3) 5 66
(Eve Johnson Houghton) *hld up: hdwy over 2f out: rdn to chse ldrs wl over 1f out: fdd ins fnl f* **9/2**[3]

2654 **7** *¾* **British Embassy (IRE)**[28] 5276 5-9-4 **73**........................(p) AledBeech(7) 4 66
(Bill Turner) *led: rdn over 2f out: hdd over 1f out: fdd ins fnl f* **12/1**

**8** *5* **Nutini (IRE)**[92] 2937 4-9-3 **65**............................................ LiamKeniry 1 46
(Malcolm Saunders) *s.i.s: a towards rr* **9/2**[3]

0236 **9** *4 ½* **Unit Of Assessment (IRE)**[19] 5589 3-9-5 **73**......(v[1]) SilvestreDeSousa 3 43
(William Knight) *in tch: rdn 3f out: wknd 2f out: sn eased* **4/1**[2]

1m 41.95s (1.15) **Going Correction** +0.175s/f (Good)
**WFA** 3 from 4yo+ 6lb **9** Ran SP% **117.7**
Speed ratings (Par 103): **101,98,96,95,95 94,93,88,84**
CSF £170.68 CT £592.71 TOTE £17.20: £3.80, £1.80, £1.60; EX 158.30 Trifecta £875.80.
**Owner** Mrs L Sharpe & Mrs S G Clapp **Bred** Mrs J Fuller And S Dutfield **Trained** Charlton Mackrell, Somerset

**FOCUS**
Race distance increased by 5 yards. A fair handicap. They went a respectable gallop. A C&D specialist came to the fore, running his best race since early last year.
T/Plt: £15.70 to a £1 stake. Pool: £54,946.49 - 2,554.76 winning units. T/Qpdt: £13.80 to a £1 stake. Pool: £3,175.65 - 170.15 winning units. **Tim Mitchell**

# 5695 CARLISLE (R-H)
Wednesday, August 23

**OFFICIAL GOING: Good to soft changing to good to soft (soft in places) after race 3 (2.40)**
Wind: Light, half against in over 2f of home straight Weather: Cloudy, bright

## 6311 EBF STALLIONS MAIDEN STKS (DIV I) 5f 193y
**1:35** (1:35) (Class 5) 2-Y-O **£3,396** (£1,010; £505; £252) **Stalls** Low

Form RPR

**1** **Highest Rank (IRE)** 2-9-2 0.......................................... CliffordLee(3) 7 69
(K R Burke) *cl up on outside: rdn 2f out: led ent fnl f: hld on wl towards fin* **3/1**[1]

04 **2** *nk* **Geesala Brave (IRE)**[21] 5537 2-9-5 0................................ JackGarritty 6 68
(John Quinn) *pressed ldr: rdn 2f out: chal ent fnl f: kpt on: hld nr fin* **4/1**[2]

**3** *nse* **Poet's Pride** 2-9-5 0.................................................................. BenCurtis 10 68+
(David Barron) *wnt lft s and s.i.s: bhd and green: last and plenty to do over 2f out: gd hdwy fnl f: fin strly: improve* **3/1**[1]

5 **4** *1 ¼* **Finnion Fox**[12] 5874 2-9-2 0.................................. RachelRichardson(3) 3 64
(Tim Easterby) *prom: drvn and outpcd over 2f out: rallied over 1f out: kpt on same pce ins fnl f* **8/1**[3]

6 **5** *2 ½* **Barefoot Baby (IRE)**[25] 5437 2-9-0 0............................ TonyHamilton 9 51
(Richard Fahey) *s.i.s: hld up: rdn over 2f out: drifted rt and hdwy over 1f out: no imp fnl f* **8/1**[3]

**6** *3* **Final Go** 2-9-5 0...................................................................... NeilFarley 2 47
(Sally Haynes) *t.k.h: prom tl rdn: wandered and wknd fnl f* **11/1**

**7** *2 ½* **Twelve A** 2-9-5 0.................................................................. SamJames 1 39
(David O'Meara) *led: rdn and edgd lft over 1f out: hdd ent fnl f: sn wknd* **10/1**

6 **8** *4* **Lord Caprio (IRE)**[15] 5735 2-9-5 0..................................... TomEaves 4 27
(Ben Haslam) *s.i.s: hld up on ins: outpcd over 2f out: btn over 1f out* **33/1**

**9** *8* **Borders Dream** 2-9-5 0.................................................. ConnorBeasley 8 2
(Donald Whillans) *t.k.h: in tch: hung lft thrght: lost pl over 4f out: sn struggling* **25/1**

1m 17.44s (3.74) **Going Correction** +0.475s/f (Yiel) **9** Ran SP% **116.4**
Speed ratings (Par 94): **94,93,93,91,88 84,81,75,65**
CSF £15.16 TOTE £3.90: £1.70, £1.50, £1.30; EX 15.00 Trifecta £41.20.
**Owner** Ontoawinner 14 & Mrs E Burke **Bred** Michael Fennessy **Trained** Middleham Moor, N Yorks

**FOCUS**
Bend into home straight moved out by 2yds. They went a fair pace in this 2yo maiden and it saw a tight four-way finish. Quite ordinary form.

## 6312 EBF STALLIONS MAIDEN STKS (DIV II) 5f 193y
**2:05** (2:05) (Class 5) 2-Y-O **£3,396** (£1,010; £505; £252) **Stalls** Low

Form RPR

6 **1** **Canford's Joy (IRE)**[22] 5494 2-9-5 0.............................. JamesSullivan 1 75
(Ann Duffield) *in tch: hdwy over 2f out: rdn to ld ins fnl f: hld on wl cl home* **16/1**

**2** *½* **Ormesher** 2-9-5 0........................................................................ DavidNolan 7 73
(Donald McCain) *hld up towards rr: rdn and rn green fr over 2f out: hdwy over 1f out: hung rt and chsd wnr wl ins fnl f: kpt on: hld cl home* **40/1**

3 **3** *1* **Captain Jameson (IRE)**[20] 5576 2-9-5 0.......................... JackGarritty 3 70
(John Quinn) *dwlt: hld up bhd ldng gp: hdwy 1/2-way: effrt and rdn over 1f out: kpt on same pce ins fnl f* **7/1**[3]

44 **4** *hd* **Picture No Sound (IRE)**[33] 5120 2-9-5 0...................... TonyHamilton 5 70
(Richard Fahey) *led: rdn and hdd over 1f out: rallied: kpt on same pce ins fnl f* **5/4**[1]

42 **5** *½* **Albert Street (IRE)**[34] 5068 2-9-5 0.............................. ConnorBeasley 4 68
(Michael Dods) *t.k.h: w ldr: led over 1f out to ins fnl f: sn no ex* **7/4**[2]

**6** *2* **Handsome Bob (IRE)** 2-9-5 0............................................ GrahamLee 8 62
(Keith Dalgleish) *dwlt: bhd and green: hdwy and edgd rt over 1f out: kpt on fnl f: no imp* **8/1**

05 **7** *1 ¾* **Hic Bibi**[32] 5136 2-9-0 0............................................................ TomEaves 6 52
(David Brown) *chsd ldng pair to 1/2-way: rdn and wknd wl over 1f out* **66/1**

00 **8** *1* **Graphite Girl (IRE)**[18] 5665 2-8-11 0................... RachelRichardson(3) 9 48
(Tim Easterby) *hld up in tch: drvn and struggling wl over 2f out: sn btn* **50/1**

1m 16.78s (3.08) **Going Correction** +0.475s/f (Yiel) **8** Ran SP% **116.2**
Speed ratings (Par 94): **98,97,96,95,95 92,90,88**
CSF £438.00 TOTE £18.30: £4.40, £9.70, £2.50; EX 388.80 Trifecta £5834.90.
**Owner** J R Dwyer **Bred** Dr D Harron **Trained** Constable Burton, N Yorks

**FOCUS**
The second division of the 2yo maiden was run in a time 0.66secs quicker than the first. An improved effort from the winner and the form could be rated higher.

## 6313 TOMMY JOHNSTONE 65TH BIRTHDAY H'CAP (JOCKEY CLUB GRASSROOTS FLAT SPRINT SERIES QUALIFIER) 5f 193y
**2:40** (2:44) (Class 5) (0-70,71) 3-Y-O **£3,396** (£1,010; £505; £252) **Stalls** Low

Form RPR

3113 **1** **Yes You (IRE)**[9] 5991 3-8-4 **60**................................. JamieGormley(7) 7 67+
(Iain Jardine) *trckd ldrs: rdn along 2f out: led ins fnl f: hld on wl* **9/4**[1]

1305 **2** *nk* **Kody Ridge (IRE)**[22] 5495 3-9-8 **71**..............................(h) TonyHamilton 6 77
(Roger Fell) *led: rdn along 2f out: hdd ins fnl f: kpt on: hld cl home* **14/1**

0100 **3** *½* **Uncle Charlie (IRE)**[54] 4303 3-9-2 **65**................................ TomEaves 1 69
(Ann Duffield) *hld up: hdwy on nr side of gp 2f out: rdn and kpt on ins fnl f: hld nr fin* **18/1**

5320 **4** *nk* **Roys Dream**[31] 5182 3-9-5 **68**.......................................... JamesSullivan 10 71
(Paul Collins) *prom: effrt and drvn along wl over 1f out: kpt on same pce ins fnl f* **9/1**

4134 **5** *1 ¾* **Metisian**[24] 5459 3-9-5 **68**.................................................... DavidNolan 9 66
(Jedd O'Keeffe) *hld up bhd ldng gp: hdwy and prom over 1f out: sn rdn: no ex ins fnl f* **7/2**[2]

4543 **6** *7* **Melrose Girl**[21] 5543 3-8-10 **59**.................................... ConnorBeasley 5 34
(Bryan Smart) *t.k.h: prom: rdn over 2f out: wknd over 1f out* **11/1**

5351 **7** *1 ¼* **Haworth**[13] 5826 3-9-2 **70**........................................(b) CallumRodriguez(5) 2 41
(James Bethell) *hld up: stdy hdwy over 2f out: rdn over 1f out: sn wknd* **9/2**[3]

0225 **8** *4* **Majestic Stone (IRE)**[28] 5291 3-8-6 **55**...............................(v) JoeDoyle 4 14
(Julie Camacho) *dwlt: hld up: rdn and outpcd over 2f out: btn over 1f out* **9/1**

-230 **9** *2 ¾* **Sulafah (IRE)**[145] 1471 3-9-3 **66**..........................................(p) NeilFarley 3 16
(Simon West) *cl up: rdn over 2f out: hung rt and wknd wl over 1f out* **66/1**

1m 16.01s (2.31) **Going Correction** +0.475s/f (Yiel) **9** Ran SP% **112.9**
Speed ratings (Par 100): **103,102,101,101,99 89,88,82,79**
CSF £35.24 CT £451.91 TOTE £2.80: £1.40, £2.80, £4.00; EX 27.00 Trifecta £285.80.
**Owner** Taco Partners **Bred** Tower Place Bloodstock **Trained** Carrutherstown, D'fries & G'way

**FOCUS**
An ordinary 3yo sprint handicap in which again the middle of the home straight was favoured. The winner continues to progress, with the runner-up rated to his best.

## 6314 WATCH RACING UK ON SKY 432 H'CAP 5f
**3:15** (3:15) (Class 4) (0-85,87) 3-Y-O+ **£5,498** (£1,636; £817; £408) **Stalls** Low

Form RPR

1015 **1** **Tarboosh**[14] 5804 4-9-10 **84**.................................................. CamHardie 2 91
(Paul Midgley) *trckd ldrs: effrt and rdn over 1f out: disp ld last 100yds: led cl home* **8/1**

0622 **2** *nse* **Desert Ace (IRE)**[11] 5920 6-8-9 **76**..........................(p) JamieGormley(7) 3 83
(Iain Jardine) *led: hrd pressed and rdn over 1f out: kpt on fnl f: hdd cl home* **8/1**

0010 **3** *¾* **Confessional**[22] 5505 10-9-10 **87**..............................(e) LewisEdmunds(3) 5 91
(Tim Easterby) *hld up bhd ldng gp: effrt and rdn 2f out: kpt on ins fnl f* **13/2**

3033 **4** *shd* **Twizzell**[26] 5383 3-8-13 **78**............................................ CliffordLee(3) 7 82
(K R Burke) *pressed ldr: effrt and ev ch over 1f out to ins fnl f: no ex towards fin* **11/2**[2]

0601 **5** *1 ½* **Geoff Potts (IRE)**[15] 5750 4-8-10 **70**.......................... TonyHamilton 8 69
(Richard Fahey) *prom: effrt and edgd lft over 1f out: kpt on same pce ins fnl f* **6/1**[3]

0441 **6** *2 ¾* **Lexington Place**[14] 5804 7-9-0 **74**.............................. JamesSullivan 9 63
(Ruth Carr) *hld up: rdn and effrt over 2f out: no imp fr over 1f out* **14/1**

1311 **7** *½* **Show Palace**[11] 5930 4-9-5 **79**............................................ GrahamLee 10 66
(Jennie Candlish) *t.k.h: hld up in tch: effrt and rdn wl over 1f out: sn no imp* **5/1**[1]

1605 **8** *2 ¾* **My Name Is Rio (IRE)**[18] 5671 7-9-12 **86**.................... ConnorBeasley 1 63
(Michael Dods) *hld up: rdn over 2f out: wknd wl over 1f out* **10/1**

3323 **9** *1* **Pomme De Terre (IRE)**[11] 5920 5-9-3 **82**..........(b) CallumRodriguez(5) 6 55
(Michael Dods) *hld up: drvn and outpcd over 2f out: sn btn* **5/1**[1]

1m 2.32s (1.52) **Going Correction** +0.475s/f (Yiel)
**WFA** 3 from 4yo+ 2lb **9** Ran SP% **114.3**
Speed ratings (Par 105): **106,105,104,104,102 97,96,92,90**
CSF £69.27 CT £441.07 TOTE £9.90: £3.20, £3.10, £2.30; EX 99.90 Trifecta £632.00.
**Owner** The Guys & Dolls & Sandfield Racing **Bred** Landmark Racing Limited **Trained** Westow, N Yorks

**FOCUS**
A fair sprint handicap in which it paid to be handy. The form is rated around the front-running second.

## 6315 WATCH RACING UK ON THE GO H'CAP 7f 173y
3:50 (3:51) (Class 5) (0-75,76) 3-Y-O £3,396 (£1,010; £505; £252) Stalls Low

Form RPR

3350 1 **Born To Boom (IRE)**[61] 4036 3-9-0 71 ........ CliffordLee(3) 6 78
(K R Burke) *pressed ldr: effrt and rdn 2f out: led wl ins fnl f: hld on wl* 12/1

1324 2 hd **Heir Of Excitement (IRE)**[21] 5541 3-9-1 76 ........(p[1]) SeamusCronin(7) 4 82
(Kevin Ryan) *led: rdn over 2f out: hdd wl ins fnl f: r.o* 11/4[1]

0513 3 shd **Redarna**[16] 5697 3-8-6 60 ........ JamesSullivan 5 66+
(Dianne Sayer) *stdd s: hld up: rdn and outpcd 3f out: rallied over 1f out: kpt on strly fnl f: nrst fin* 5/1[2]

3430 4 2 **Champion Harbour (IRE)**[23] 5467 3-8-3 57 ........ PatrickMathers 8 58
(Richard Fahey) *t.k.h: hld up in tch: effrt and chsd ldrs over 1f out: edgd rt: one pce ins fnl f* 20/1

3153 5 ¾ **Brother McGonagall**[9] 6001 3-9-5 76 ........ RachelRichardson(3) 1 76
(Tim Easterby) *t.k.h early: prom: rdn along over 2f out: edgd rt over 1f out: sn outpcd* 11/2[3]

-203 6 hd **Supreme Power (IRE)**[13] 5835 3-8-7 61 ........ BarryMcHugh 7 60
(Tracy Waggott) *hld up towards rr: rdn and hdwy over 2f out: outpcd fnl f* 12/1

3315 7 3 ¼ **Racemaker**[16] 5704 3-9-5 73 ........ NeilFarley 9 65
(Andrew Crook) *hld up: drvn along and outpcd wl over 2f out: n.d after* 20/1

0315 8 ¾ **Inglorious**[2] 6265 3-8-8 67 ........(p) RowanScott(5) 2 57
(Keith Dalgleish) *t.k.h: in tch: drvn over 2f out: wknd over 1f out* 5/1[2]

304 9 11 **Mellor Brook (IRE)**[70] 3714 3-9-7 75 ........ ConnorBeasley 3 40
(Michael Dods) *s.i.s: hld up: struggling 3f out: sn wknd* 8/1

1m 42.36s (2.36) **Going Correction** +0.475s/f (Yiel) 9 Ran SP% **111.4**
Speed ratings (Par 100): **107,106,106,104,103 103,100,99,88**
CSF £42.91 CT £185.23 TOTE £13.20: £3.40, £1.40, £1.20; EX 45.20 Trifecta £391.10.
**Owner** The Albatross Club & Mrs E Burke **Bred** Newlands House Stud **Trained** Middleham Moor, N Yorks

**FOCUS**
Race distance increased by 6yds. Not a bad 3yo handicap. It was yet another race where it helped to be handy. The form is rated around the runner-up.

## 6316 WATCH RACING UK ON VIRGIN 536 H'CAP (JOCKEY CLUB GRASSROOTS FLAT MIDDLE DISTANCE QUALIFIER) 1m 1f
4:25 (4:25) (Class 5) (0-70,72) 3-Y-O+ £3,396 (£1,010; £505; £252) Stalls Low

Form RPR

2340 1 **Savannah Moon (IRE)**[18] 5648 3-8-13 62 ........ TomEaves 3 68+
(Kevin Ryan) *hld up: smooth hdwy over 2f out: rdn to ld ins fnl f: kpt on wl* 7/1

0111 2 nk **Im Dapper Too**[14] 5802 6-10-0 70 ........ SamJames 8 75
(John Davies) *trckd ldrs: effrt and swtchd lft wl over 1f out: rdn and disp ld ins fnl f: kpt on: hld nr fin* 2/1[1]

2532 3 nse **Duck Egg Blue (IRE)**[4] 6208 3-9-0 70 ........(p) PaulaMuir(7) 12 75
(Patrick Holmes) *led: rdn over 2f out: edgd rt over 1f out: hdd ins fnl f: kpt on: hld nr fin* 13/2[3]

0302 4 ½ **Quoteline Direct**[21] 5540 4-9-5 61 ........(h) AndrewMullen 2 65
(Micky Hammond) *hld up towards rr: hdwy and prom 3f out: rdn 2f out: kpt on wl fnl f: nt pce to chal* 12/1

4605 5 1 ¼ **Warfare**[22] 5498 8-9-8 64 ........(p) BarryMcHugh 9 65
(Tim Fitzgerald) *in tch: smooth hdwy over 2f out: rdn wl over 1f out: one pce ins fnl f* 14/1

0 6 2 ½ **Zihaam**[24] 5458 3-9-2 65 ........ BenCurtis 7 61
(Roger Fell) *midfield on ins: drvn and outpcd over 2f out: rallied over 1f out: sn no imp* 13/2[3]

6503 7 3 ¼ **Archie's Advice**[18] 5650 6-10-2 72 ........ GrahamLee 5 61
(Keith Dalgleish) *dwlt: hld up: rdn along and hdwy over 2f out: no imp fr over 1f out* 4/1[2]

0005 8 5 **Indian Giver**[29] 5254 9-8-2 51 oh6 ........ JamieGormley(7) 10 30
(John David Riches) *prom: drvn and outpcd over 2f out: btn over 1f out* 40/1

0064 9 2 ¾ **Lukoutoldmakezebak**[21] 5539 4-8-9 51 oh6 ........ PatrickMathers 11 24
(David Thompson) *t.k.h: pressed ldr to 3f out: sn wknd* 80/1

0006 10 3 ¾ **Glance My Way (IRE)**[65] 3910 4-9-6 65 ........(b) RachelRichardson(3) 1 30
(Tim Easterby) *hld up: rdn over 4f out: wknd fr 3f out* 20/1

2m 2.85s (5.25) **Going Correction** +0.475s/f (Yiel)
**WFA** 3 from 4yo+ 7lb 10 Ran SP% **115.3**
Speed ratings (Par 103): **95,94,94,94,93 90,88,83,81,77**
CSF £20.82 CT £99.64 TOTE £9.00: £2.30, £1.30, £2.10; EX 25.70 Trifecta £114.20.
**Owner** Hambleton Racing Ltd XXXVI **Bred** Mrs Renata Coleman **Trained** Hambleton, N Yorks

**FOCUS**
Race distance increased by 6yds. There was a solid pace on in this ordinary handicap. The third and fourth fit with the form.

## 6317 WATCH RACING UK ON TALK TALK TV H'CAP 1m 6f 32y
4:55 (4:56) (Class 4) (0-85,82) 3-Y-O+ £5,498 (£1,636; £817; £408) Stalls Low

Form RPR

1502 1 **Renfrew Street**[9] 6000 4-9-9 78 ........ AndrewMullen 5 88+
(Mark Johnston) *mde all: qcknd clr over 2f out: kpt on strly fnl f* 7/2[2]

0-14 2 2 ½ **Kashmiri Sunset**[12] 5873 6-9-0 76 ........(tp) JamieGormley(7) 6 82
(Iain Jardine) *hld up in last pl: pushed along over 3f out: hdwy on outside to chse (clr) wnr over 1f out: kpt on fnl f: nt pce to chal* 3/1[1]

6116 3 6 **Tapis Libre**[11] 5924 9-9-7 81 ........ MeganNicholls(5) 1 79
(Jacqueline Coward) *prom: rdn and outpcd over 3f out: rallied over 2f out: kpt on same pce fr over 1f out* 6/1

030- 4 ½ **Always Resolute**[319] 7150 6-9-9 78 ........ BenCurtis 9 75
(Brian Ellison) *chsd wnr 2f: cl up: regained 2nd over 3f out: rdn over 2f out: no ex fr over 1f out* 9/2[3]

0033 5 6 **Wor Lass**[23] 5468 9-9-3 75 ........ RachelRichardson(3) 7 64
(Donald Whillans) *hld up in tch: stdy hdwy over 3f out: rdn and wknd wl over 1f out* 5/1

034/ 6 2 ½ **Bourne**[84] 6569 11-9-3 72 ........(b) GrahamLee 4 57
(Donald McCain) *in tch: hdwy to chse wnr after 2f: rdn and lost pl over 3f out: sn btn* 12/1

-643 7 ¾ **Aramist (IRE)**[12] 5873 7-9-2 71 ........(p) TomEaves 8 55
(Sally Haynes) *hld up: rdn and outpcd over 3f out: btn fnl 2f* 10/1

3m 13.77s (6.27) **Going Correction** +0.475s/f (Yiel) 7 Ran SP% **113.1**
Speed ratings (Par 105): **101,99,96,95,92 91,90**
CSF £14.11 CT £58.98 TOTE £4.30: £1.40, £2.60; EX 11.40 Trifecta £58.50.
**Owner** Douglas Livingston/Mark Johnston Racing Ltd **Bred** D Curran **Trained** Middleham Moor, N Yorks

**FOCUS**
Race distance increased by 6yds. A modest staying handicap. They were fairly strung out early and the winner wasn't for catching. She's rated back to her best.

## 6318 BETFAIR AMATEUR RIDERS' H'CAP (FOR NOVICE AMATEUR RIDERS) 5f 193y
5:25 (5:27) (Class 6) (0-65,67) 4-Y-O+ £2,807 (£870; £435; £217) Stalls Low

Form RPR

5062 1 **Dodgy Bob**[6] 6097 4-10-13 57 ........(v) MrLewisStones 4 69
(Michael Mullineaux) *in tch: hdwy to ld over 1f out: drifted rt ins fnl f: kpt on strly* 4/1[2]

0400 2 1 ¾ **Arcanista (IRE)**[13] 5854 4-10-3 50 ........(p) MrMSHarris(3) 6 58
(Chris Dwyer) *hld up: hdwy over 2f out: effrt whn nt clr run over 1f out: sn swtchd rt: chsd wnr wl ins fnl f: r.o* 20/1

6151 3 1 **Racquet**[11] 5919 4-11-9 67 ........ MissEmilyBullock 8 70
(Ruth Carr) *prom: effrt and ev ch over 1f out: sn chsng wnr: lost 2nd and no ex wl ins fnl f* 9/2[3]

3320 4 nk **Picks Pinta**[23] 5467 6-11-5 63 ........ MissAMcCain 1 66
(John David Riches) *in tch: effrt on outside over 2f out: rdn and one pce fnl f* 15/2

6311 5 2 **Our Place In Loule**[16] 5695 4-10-11 55 ........ MissKLAdams 5 51
(Noel Wilson) *hld up: rdn and hdwy on outside over 2f out: wknd over 1f out* 13/2

2604 6 hd **Goninodaethat**[9] 5994 9-11-0 58 ........ MissRHill 3 54
(Jim Goldie) *led tl rdn and hdd over 1f out: wknd ins fnl f* 16/1

5033 7 3 ½ **Epeius (IRE)**[13] 5836 4-11-7 65 ........ MrBJames 7 50
(Ben Haslam) *blindfold slow to remove and s.v.s: wl bhd: hdwy 2f out: kpt on fnl f: no imp* 7/2[1]

1001 8 ½ **Dark Confidant (IRE)**[8] 6049 4-11-5 63 6ex ........ MissEllaMcCain 9 46
(Donald McCain) *in tch: outpcd over 2f out: edgd rt and wknd wl over 1f out* 5/1

1m 18.76s (5.06) **Going Correction** +0.475s/f (Yiel) 8 Ran SP% **112.8**
Speed ratings (Par 101): **85,82,81,80,78 78,73,72**
CSF £74.13 CT £372.37 TOTE £4.10: £1.60, £4.70, £1.60; EX 45.40 Trifecta £471.10.
**Owner** J P Daly And S & M Ashbrooke **Bred** Whatton Manor Stud & Robert Cornelius **Trained** Alpraham, Cheshire

**FOCUS**
A moderate sprint handicap, confined to amateur riders. Fair enough form, with the winner well in.
T/Plt: £545.60 to a £1 stake. Pool: £47,808.61 - 63.96 winning units. T/Qpdt: £33.60 to a £1 stake. Pool: £4,588.21 - 100.87 winning units. **Richard Young**

# 6285 KEMPTON (A.W) (R-H)
### Wednesday, August 23

**OFFICIAL GOING: Polytrack: standard to slow**
Wind: Moderate, across (away from stands) Weather: Cloudy, warm

## 6319 32RED CASINO NOVICE AUCTION STKS (PLUS 10 RACE) 7f (P)
6:15 (6:15) (Class 4) 2-Y-O £3,946 (£1,174; £586; £293) Stalls Low

Form RPR

5220 1 **Iconic Sunset**[15] 5749 2-9-1 73 ........ MartinHarley 4 74
(James Tate) *trckd ldr: shkn up to ld 2f out: wandered both ways u.p after: drvn rt out* 13/8[2]

2 ½ **Jack Crow** 2-9-1 0 ........ CharlesBishop 2 73
(Eve Johnson Houghton) *dwlt: hld up in last: shkn up 2f out: prog to chse wnr jst over 1f out: clsd 100yds out: no imp nr fin* 8/1[3]

2 3 2 ¾ **Azezati (IRE)**[22] 5507 2-8-9 0 ........ SeanLevey 1 59
(David Simcock) *t.k.h: trckd ldng pair: shkn up over 2f out: nt qckn and btn over 1f out* 5/6[1]

4 nk **Cristal Pallas Cat (IRE)** 2-8-6 0 ........ RhiainIngram(7) 3 62
(Roger Ingram) *led: pushed along and hdd 2f out: lost 2nd jst over 1f out: fdd* 33/1

1m 27.07s (1.07) **Going Correction** +0.025s/f (Slow) 4 Ran SP% **106.7**
Speed ratings (Par 96): **94,93,90,89**
CSF £12.17 TOTE £2.30; EX 7.70 Trifecta £10.70.
**Owner** Saeed Manana **Bred** Rabbah Bloodstock Limited **Trained** Newmarket, Suffolk

**FOCUS**
An ordinary novice race rated around the winner.

## 6320 100% PROFIT BOOST AT 32REDSPORT.COM MEDIAN AUCTION MAIDEN FILLIES' STKS 1m 3f 219y(P)
6:45 (6:47) (Class 4) 3-5-Y-O £4,690 (£1,395; £697; £348) Stalls Low

Form RPR

3246 1 **Munstead Star**[25] 5401 3-9-0 73 ........ OisinMurphy 6 77
(Andrew Balding) *trckd ldrs: clsd to ld wl over 1f out: pushed clr and styd on wl: comf* 1/1[1]

5 2 3 ½ **Star Guide**[11] 5931 3-8-9 0 ........ MitchGodwin(5) 1 71
(Sylvester Kirk) *hld up in 5th: pushed along over 2f out: prog to chse wnr over 1f out: styd on but readily outpcd* 8/1[3]

3 3 ¾ **Tiar Na Nog (IRE)**[204] 5-9-9 0 ........ PatCosgrave 3 64
(Denis Coakley) *trckd ldrs: nt clr run briefly over 2f out: tk 3rd over 1f out but sn easily outpcd* 14/1

444 4 4 **Luna Magic**[18] 5632 3-8-11 70 ........(h) SimonPearce(3) 2 59
(Lydia Pearce) *awkward s: hld up in last pair: shkn up over 2f out: kpt on same pce after and no ch w ldrs* 8/1[3]

052 5 ¾ **Lady Macha**[14] 5796 3-9-0 71 ........ MartinHarley 5 58
(Marco Botti) *trckd ldr: led over 2f out: hdd and fnd nil wl over 1f out: qckly btn* 5/2[2]

3650 6 5 **Crystal Secret**[9] 6006 3-8-11 46 ........ HectorCrouch(3) 4 50
(John Bridger) *led to over 2f out: wknd* 100/1

7 33 **Theatre Royale**[183] 5-9-9 0 ........ StevieDonohoe 7
(Brian Barr) *a in last pair: wknd 4f out: sn t.o* 100/1

2m 35.36s (0.86) **Going Correction** +0.025s/f (Slow)
**WFA** 3 from 5yo 9lb 7 Ran SP% **109.4**
Speed ratings (Par 102): **98,95,93,90,90 86,64**
CSF £9.15 TOTE £1.70: £1.10, £3.10; EX 9.40 Trifecta £57.20.
**Owner** Lady Gillian Brunton **Bred** Sir Gordon Brunton **Trained** Kingsclere, Hants
■ The Lady Rules was withdrawn. Price at time of withdrawal 20-1. Rule 4 does not apply.

**FOCUS**
Not a strong maiden, and it provided a straightforward opportunity for the favourite. She's rated to form.

## 6321 32RED ON THE APP STORE FILLIES' H'CAP 7f (P)
7:15 (7:16) (Class 4) (0-85,85) 3-Y-0+ £5,175 (£1,540; £769; £384) Stalls Low

Form RPR

-242 **1** **Peak Princess (IRE)**[27] 5317 3-9-7 **85**..........................(b[1]) SeanLevey 5 92
(Richard Hannon) *hld up in last pair: rdn over 2f out: sme prog over 1f out but stl looked to have little ch: str run fnl f and burst between rivals to ld last five strides: won gng away* **8/1**

1032 **2** *1* **Nostalgie**[37] 4983 3-9-3 **81**.......................................... MartinHarley 3 85
(James Tate) *hld up in midfield: prog jst over 2f out to press ldr over 1f out: rdn to take narrow ld jst ins fnl f: hdd and outpcd last strides* **6/1**

-051 **3** *shd* **Phalaborwa**[37] 4983 3-9-6 **84**.......................... AdamBeschizza 10 88
(Ed Vaughan) *spd fr wdst draw to ld after 2f: rdn 2f out: hdd jst ins fnl f: kpt on wl but outpcd last strides* **7/2**[1]

15-4 **4** *½* **Dubai Elegance**[23] 5484 3-9-2 **80**..........................(p[1]) OisinMurphy 7 83
(Saeed bin Suroor) *prom: trckd ldr after 3f: rdn and tried to chal 2f out: nt qckn over 1f out: styd on ins fnl f but a hld* **4/1**[2]

361 **5** *nk* **Simply Me**[75] 3548 4-9-3 **81**..........................(p) PaddyPilley(5) 8 85
(Tom Dascombe) *trckd ldrs on outer: shkn up and sltly outpcd 2f out: kpt on fnl f: nvr quite pce to chal* **16/1**

6132 **6** *¾* **Dragon Dream (IRE)**[21] 5545 3-7-9 **66** oh2.......... RhiainIngram(7) 6 66
(Roger Ingram) *led 2f: trckd ldrs after: rdn to chal 2f out: fdd wl ins fnl f* **20/1**

-434 **7** *½* **Parlance (IRE)**[34] 5078 3-9-5 **83**.......................... TedDurcan 4 84+
(Sir Michael Stoute) *trckd ldrs: darted to inner and effrt 2f out: nt qckn over 1f out then briefly short of room: kpt on same pce after* **9/2**[3]

5013 **8** *2 ¼* **Chupalla**[10] 5965 3-9-4 **82**..........................(v[1]) DaneO'Neill 1 74
(David Evans) *hld up in rr: shkn up in last pair over 2f out: no significant prog* **16/1**

040- **9** *¾* **Cliffhanger**[389] 4881 4-8-9 **68**.......................................... JFEgan 9 60
(Paul Cole) *hld up fr wd draw: shkn up over 2f out: no prog over 1f out: short of room briefly fnl f and eased* **66/1**

522 **10** *10* **Nightingale Valley**[20] 5558 4-9-6 **79**.......................... TomQueally 2 44
(Stuart Kittow) *nvr beyond midfield: rdn over 2f out: sn lost pl and bhd* **12/1**

1m 25.57s (-0.43) **Going Correction** +0.025s/f (Slow)
**WFA** 3 from 4yo 5lb 10 Ran SP% **111.5**
Speed ratings (Par 102): **103,101,101,101,100 99,99,96,95,84**
CSF £52.83 CT £198.66 TOTE £9.20: £2.90, £1.80, £2.00; EX 59.10 Trifecta £287.70.
**Owner** Rockcliffe Stud **Bred** Roland H Alder **Trained** East Everleigh, Wilts
■ Stewards' Enquiry : Rhiain Ingram caution: careless riding

**FOCUS**
A fair fillies' handicap, and an eyecatching performance from the winner, who came from last to first inside the final 2f. The second and third were closely matched on Wolverhampton form.

## 6322 32RED H'CAP (LONDON MILE SERIES QUALIFIER) 1m (P)
7:45 (7:45) (Class 3) (0-90,92) 3-Y-0+
£7,470 (£2,236; £1,118; £559; £279; £140) Stalls Low

Form RPR

5430 **1** **Timeless Art (IRE)**[18] 5664 4-9-3 **80**..........................(e) MartinHarley 10 92
(K R Burke) *nt that wl away but swift move to ld over 6f out and sn clr: nvr threatened after: stl 5 l ahd whn rdn over 1f out: unchal* **16/1**

2620 **2** *2 ½* **Golden Wedding (IRE)**[40] 4832 5-9-5 **82**.......................... CharlesBishop 5 87
(Eve Johnson Houghton) *led at mod pce to over 6f out: chsd clr wnr after: rdn and no imp fr 2f out: kpt on to hold on for 2nd* **15/2**

034 **3** *nk* **Ahlan Bil Zain (FR)**[13] 5849 3-8-10 **79**.......................... SeanLevey 11 83
(David Simcock) *trckd ldng trio: rdn 2f out: pressed runner-up thrght fnl f but no ch w wnr* **6/1**[2]

5004 **4** *1* **The Warrior (IRE)**[11] 5942 5-9-8 **85**.......................... TomMarquand 7 87
(Amanda Perrett) *towards rr: urged along fr 1/2-way: no prog tl styd on fr over 1f out to take 4th nr fin* **8/1**

4341 **5** *nk* **Mazyoun**[7] 6068 3-9-4 **92** 6ex..........................(b) DavidEgan(5) 1 93
(Hugo Palmer) *t.k.h: trckd ldng pair: shkn up and nt qckn 2f out: nvr a threat to wnr and fdd ins fnl f* **2/1**[1]

3301 **6** *½* **Georgian Bay (IRE)**[25] 5396 7-9-9 **89**..........................(v) JordanVaughan(3) 4 89
(K R Burke) *hld up in midfield: shkn up and no prog 2f out: nvr a threat but kpt on ins fnl f* **13/2**[3]

04-0 **7** *2* **Run To The Hills (USA)**[95] 2838 4-9-8 **85**.......................... StevieDonohoe 2 81
(George Peckham) *nvr bttr than midfield: rdn and no prog over 2f out* **12/1**

0450 **8** *¾* **Presumido (IRE)**[156] 1288 7-9-7 **84**.......................... JFEgan 3 78
(Simon Dow) *chsd ldrs in 5th: shkn up and no prog over 2f out: fdd fnl f* **25/1**

0505 **9** *3 ½* **Eltezam (IRE)**[47] 4570 4-9-10 **87**.......................... PatDobbs 6 73
(Amanda Perrett) *stdd s: hld up in last trio: pushed along over 2f out: no prog and nvr involved* **11/1**

6006 **10** *nk* **Dutch Uncle**[28] 5302 5-9-11 **88**.......................... OisinMurphy 8 73
(Robert Cowell) *stdd s: hld up in last trio: pushed along over 2f out: no prog and nvr involved* **20/1**

-351 **11** *1* **War Of Succession**[57] 4173 3-9-3 **86**.......................... RobertWinston 9 68
(Tony Newcombe) *stdd after s: hld up in last trio: pushed along over 2f out: no prog and nvr involved* **50/1**

1m 38.64s (-1.16) **Going Correction** +0.025s/f (Slow)
**WFA** 3 from 4yo+ 6lb 11 Ran SP% **116.3**
Speed ratings (Par 107): **106,103,103,102,101 101,99,98,95,94 93**
CSF £126.91 CT £825.94 TOTE £16.70: £4.80, £2.20, £2.70; EX 115.70 Trifecta £590.80.
**Owner** Owners For Owners: Timeless Art **Bred** Sarl Elevage Du Haras De Bourgeauville **Trained** Middleham Moor, N Yorks

**FOCUS**
This proved a one-horse race, the winner stealing it from the front. He's rated back to his best.

## 6323 32RED.COM H'CAP 1m 7f 218y(P)
8:15 (8:15) (Class 4) (0-85,86) 4-Y-0+ £5,175 (£1,540; £769; £384) Stalls Low

Form RPR

4200 **1** **Velvet Revolution**[53] 4355 4-9-3 **81**.......................... MartinHarley 5 90+
(Marco Botti) *stdd s: hld up wl off the pce in last gp: stdy prog fr 4f out: clsd on ldrs 2f out: shkn up to ld jst over 1f out: idled briefly but sn asserted* **9/1**

1315 **2** *2 ¼* **Denmead**[21] 5524 4-9-1 **79**.......................... RobertWinston 7 83
(John Butler) *prom: led after 5f: kicked for home over 4f out: rdn and hdd 2f out and sn dropped to 3rd: kpt on to take 2nd again nr fin* **11/2**[3]

2224 **3** *nk* **Fleeting Visit**[11] 5912 4-9-6 **84**..........................(p) CharlesBishop 10 88
(Eve Johnson Houghton) *trckd ldrs: rdn to ld 2f out: hdd and one pce jst over 1f out: lost 2nd nr fin* **4/1**[1]

1001 **4** *1* **Whitecliff Park (IRE)**[12] 5896 4-8-4 **73** ow2..........(p) BenRobinson(5) 9 76
(Brian Ellison) *s.s: hld up wl off the pce in last gp: urged along over 4f out: prog over 2f out: styd on after to take 4th nr fin* **16/1**

30 **5** *1 ½* **Percy Veer**[189] 746 5-9-3 **81**..........................(p) OisinMurphy 4 82
(Sylvester Kirk) *chsd ldr 4f: styd prom: urged along over 4f out: nvr pl to cl after: one pce u.p fnl 2f* **16/1**

4221 **6** *½* **Corpus Chorister (FR)**[36] 4998 4-9-7 **85**.......................... KevinStott 1 85
(David Menuisier) *led at mod pce for 5f: trckd ldr after: urged along over 4f out: lost pl over 2f out: fdd over 1f out* **9/2**[2]

030 **7** *1* **Age Of Wisdom (IRE)**[25] 5432 4-8-6 **73**.......................... NoelGarbutt(3) 6 72
(Gary Moore) *chsd ldrs: urged along over 4f out: steadily fdd u.p fnl 2f* **25/1**

3000 **8** *1* **October Storm**[21] 5524 4-8-11 **75**.......................... JFEgan 12 73
(Mick Channon) *hld up wl off the pce in last gp: urged along over 4f out: no great prog and nvr in it: kpt on fnl f* **8/1**

00-5 **9** *3 ¼* **Wind Place And Sho**[11] 5944 5-9-8 **86**..........................(b[1]) RyanTate 3 80
(James Eustace) *slowly away: hld up wl off the pce in last gp: rdn and no prog over 4f out: no ch fnl 2f* **25/1**

-633 **10** *3 ¼* **High Command (IRE)**[14] 5799 4-9-6 **84**.......................... SilvestreDeSousa 8 74
(Roger Varian) *racd in 6th and last of ldng gp: rdn 3f out: no prog and sn btn: wknd over 1f out* **4/1**[1]

2-0 **11** *11* **Sporty Yankee (USA)**[29] 5251 4-8-10 **74**..........................(t[1]) TomQueally 2 51
(Martin Keighley) *racd in 7th and sme way off ldrs: rdn and wknd 4f out: t.o* **66/1**

-665 **12** *4* **Mighty Lady**[32] 5140 4-8-5 **74**.......................... DavidEgan(5) 11 46
(Robyn Brisland) *dwlt and stdd s: tk fierce hold in last and wl off the pce: no prog 4f out: sn t.o* **25/1**

3m 27.08s (-3.02) **Going Correction** +0.025s/f (Slow) 12 Ran SP% **119.5**
Speed ratings (Par 105): **108,106,106,106,105 105,104,104,102,100 95,93**
CSF £56.25 CT £234.32 TOTE £10.90: £3.40, £1.50, £1.60; EX 68.80 Trifecta £346.20.
**Owner** Heart of the South Racing & Partner **Bred** Newsells Park Stud **Trained** Newmarket, Suffolk

**FOCUS**
A fair staying handicap run in an ordinary time. The level is set around the second and third.

## 6324 RACING UK IN HD H'CAP 6f (P)
8:45 (8:48) (Class 6) (0-60,58) 3-Y-0 £2,587 (£770; £384; £192) Stalls Low

Form RPR

5003 **1** **Atlanta Belle (IRE)**[14] 5812 3-9-3 **54**.......................... TedDurcan 6 61
(Chris Wall) *mde all: stl gng wl 2f out: shkn up and 2 l clr over 1f out: a in command after* **6/1**[3]

0605 **2** *¾* **Morello (IRE)**[8] 6041 3-9-2 **53**.......................... DaneO'Neill 4 57
(Henry Candy) *hld up in rr: prog on inner over 2f out: rdn to chse wnr jst over 1f out: styd on and clsd nr fin but nvr able to chal* **5/1**[2]

0650 **3** *¾* **Socrates**[16] 5714 3-9-0 **51**..........................(b[1]) GeorgeDowning 10 53
(Daniel Kubler) *had to be dismntd and led to s: s.s: hld up in last pair: prog on inner over 2f out: rdn to dispute 2nd jst over 1f out: styd on* **20/1**

000 **4** *1 ½* **Innstigator**[27] 5339 3-8-10 **52**.......................... PaddyBradley(5) 11 50
(Ralph J Smith) *dropped in fr wd draw and sn in last: detached over 2f out: rdn and gd prog on wd outside over 1f out: styd on wl to take 4th last strides: too late to threaten* **20/1**

2563 **5** *½* **Lesanti**[14] 5792 3-9-1 **52**.......................... SilvestreDeSousa 1 48
(Ed de Giles) *trckd ldrs: rdn to go 2nd 2f out to jst over 1f out: one pce* **9/4**[1]

0035 **6** *nk* **Princess Way (IRE)**[13] 5817 3-8-12 **54**..........................(v) DavidEgan(5) 7 49
(David Evans) *towards rr: rdn over 2f out: sme prog over 1f out but nvr a threat* **20/1**

0500 **7** *½* **Silver Penny**[28] 5295 3-9-0 **51**..........................(p) PatCosgrave 8 45
(Jim Boyle) *chsd wnr: rdn and fnd nil over 2f out: sn lost 2nd and btn* **25/1**

405 **8** *nk* **Double Spin**[9] 6004 3-9-7 **58**..........................(p[1]) MartinHarley 9 51
(Robert Cowell) *chsd ldrs: rdn over 2f out: steadily lost pl over 1f out* **12/1**

5405 **9** *2* **Cherry Leyf**[35] 5041 3-8-13 **50**..........................(t) OisinMurphy 2 37
(Stuart Williams) *n.m.r after 1f: nvr beyond midfield: shkn up and lost pl fr 2f out* **10/1**

600 **10** *½* **Banta Bay**[62] 4006 3-8-11 **48**.......................... KierenFox 3 33
(John Best) *tried to r promly but n.m.r and forced to chse ldrs: rdn over 2f out: sn lost pl* **8/1**

000- **11** *4* **Highland Clearance (FR)**[259] 8243 3-9-1 **52**.......................... KevinStott 12 25
(Giles Bravery) *a wl in rr: bhd over 1f out* **50/1**

0056 **12** *3* **Mahna Mahna (IRE)**[67] 3810 3-8-12 **49**.......................... WilliamCarson 5 13
(David W Drinkwater) *prom to over 2f out: wkng whn hmpd jst over 1f out: eased* **10/1**

1m 12.78s (-0.32) **Going Correction** +0.025s/f (Slow) 12 Ran SP% **118.8**
Speed ratings (Par 98): **103,102,101,99,98 97,97,96,94,93 88,84**
CSF £33.24 CT £579.44 TOTE £7.60: £2.10, £1.90, £6.30; EX 44.40 Trifecta £620.70.
**Owner** The Leap Year Partnership **Bred** Prof C Green **Trained** Newmarket, Suffolk
■ Stewards' Enquiry : David Egan three-day ban: careless riding (Aug 6-8)

**FOCUS**
A moderate sprint, but a nice front-running performance from the winner, who has the potential to rate higher. She's rated near this year's best.
T/Plt: £361.10 to a £1 stake. Pool: £61,711.20 - 124.75 winning units. T/Qpdt: £39.90 to a £1 stake. Pool: £7,305.54 - 135.40 winning units. **Jonathan Neesom**

# 5434 YORK (L-H)
Wednesday, August 23

**OFFICIAL GOING: Good to soft (soft in places; 6.6)**
Wind: Light across freshening after 3.00 race Weather: Cloudy

## 6325 SYMPHONY GROUP H'CAP 5f 89y
1:55 (1:56) (Class 2) (0-105,104) 3-Y-0+
£43,575 (£13,048; £6,524; £3,262; £1,631; £819) Stalls Centre

Form RPR

0051 **1** **Desert Law (IRE)**[4] 6185 9-8-13 **93** 6ex.......................... LukeMorris 8 103
(Paul Midgley) *racd centre: trckd ldr: smooth hdwy over 1f out: rdn to ld ins fnl f: kpt on strly* **14/1**

5600 **2** *1 ¼* **Edward Lewis**[18] 5640 4-9-5 **99**.......................... DanielTudhope 5 105
(David O'Meara) *dwlt: sn midfield: hdwy over 2f out: rdn over 1f out: chsd ldng pair ins fnl f: kpt on* **6/1**[1]

-003 **3** *nk* **Thesme**[64] 3932 5-9-6 **100**.......................... FrankieDettori 2 105
(Nigel Tinkler) *qckly away: led and racd centre: rdn along over 1f out: hdd ins fnl f: kpt on same pce* **12/1**

4332 **4** *nk* **A Momentofmadness**[22] 5505 4-9-1 **95**..........................(h) HarryBentley 9 99
(Charles Hills) *blind removed late: sn trcking ldrs: hdwy 2f out: rdn over 1f out: drvn and kpt on same pce fnl f* **7/1**[2]

0110 **5** *shd* **Tithonus (IRE)**[17] 5688 6-8-13 **96**..............................(bt) GaryHalpin(3) 16 99
(Denis Gerard Hogan, Ire) *racd wd: towards rr: hdwy 1/2-way: rdn along wl over 1f out: kpt on fnl f* **14/1**

3-06 **6** *hd* **Hoof It**[18] 5640 10-9-4 **98**.............................................. PaulMulrennan 11 100+
(Michael Easterby) *towards rr centre: hdwy wl over 1f out: kpt on fnl f* **12/1**

00 **7** *1 1/4* **Hoofalong**[4] 6206 7-8-7 **94**..............................(b) HarrisonShaw(7) 15 92+
(Michael Easterby) *blind removed late and dwlt: racd towards stands' side: towards rr: rdn along 2f out: hdwy over 1f out: kpt on u.p fnl f* **28/1**

6433 **8** *1/2* **Soie D'Leau**[4] 6185 5-8-12 **92**.............................................. JoeFanning 10 88
(Kristin Stubbs) *chsd ldrs centre: rdn along wl over 1f out: drvn and kpt on same pce appr fnl f* **8/1[3]**

0050 **9** *1/2* **Move In Time**[25] 5435 9-8-12 **92**..............................(v) JamesDoyle 17 87
(David O'Meara) *racd towards stands' side: towards rr: rdn along and hdwy wl over 1f out: sn drvn and n.d* **14/1**

0316 **10** *1* **Shamshon (IRE)**[26] 5354 6-8-10 **90**..............................(t) JimCrowley 6 81
(Stuart Williams) *midfield centre: swtchd lft 1/2-way: rdn along 2f out: n.d* **10/1**

0006 **11** *2 1/2* **Gracious John (IRE)**[8] 6039 4-9-2 **103**............ KatherineGlenister(7) 19 85
(David Evans) *racd towards stands' side: midfield: rdn along wl over 1f out: drvn and no imp fnl f* **25/1**

6500 **12** *nk* **Robot Boy (IRE)**[26] 5354 7-8-13 **93**.............................. JamieSpencer 4 74
(David Barron) *dwlt: racd towards inner and sn trcking ldrs: rdn along over 2f out: sn wknd* **12/1**

5604 **13** *1/2* **Moviesta (USA)**[10] 5974 7-9-7 **104**......................(p) RobbieDowney(3) 12 84
(Edward Lynam, Ire) *a towards rr centre* **10/1**

346 **14** *2 1/4* **Watchable**[63] 3969 7-9-0 **94**..............................(v) AdamKirby 20 66
(David O'Meara) *racd towards stands' side: towards rr: rdn along over 2f out: n.d* **20/1**

4035 **15** *nk* **Orion's Bow**[39] 4881 6-9-9 **103**.............................................. DavidAllan 13 74
(Tim Easterby) *racd centre: chsd ldrs: rdn along 2f out: sn wknd* **8/1[3]**

0000 **16** *4* **Afandem (IRE)**[26] 5354 3-8-13 **95**............................ JosephineGordon 18 52
(Hugo Palmer) *a towards rr stands side* **25/1**

1m 4.2s (0.10) **Going Correction** +0.275s/f (Good)
**WFA** 3 from 4yo+ 2lb **16** Ran SP% **126.2**
Speed ratings (Par 109): **110,108,107,107,106 106,104,103,102,101 97,96,96,92,92 85**
CSF £94.42 CT £729.51 TOTE £19.30: £3.70, £2.10, £2.80, £1.90; EX 159.30 Trifecta £2164.70.

**Owner** Taylor's Bloodstock Ltd **Bred** Littleton Stud **Trained** Westow, N Yorks

**FOCUS**
The Ebor meeting started with a fiendishly difficult sprint handicap, a race that virtually nothing could be ruled out of with any certainty. To make things even more confusing, due to 15mm of rain falling in the morning, the official going was changed from good to firm (good in places) to good to soft (soft in places) before they charged down the straight in the first. Desert Law is rated to last year's best in a race in which pace held up.

## 6326 TATTERSALLS ACOMB STKS (GROUP 3) 7f
**2:25** (2:26) (Class 1) 2-Y-O
**£51,039** (£19,350; £9,684; £4,824; £2,421; £1,215) **Stalls** Low

Form RPR

1 **1** **Wells Farhh Go (IRE)**[26] 5380 2-9-1 0.............................................. DavidAllan 8 110
(Tim Easterby) *hld up towards rr: stdy hdwy on outer 3f out: rdn along over 1f out: drvn to chal and edgd lft ins fnl f: kpt on wl to ld on line* **10/1**

3314 **2** *nse* **James Garfield (IRE)**[22] 5501 2-9-1 104.......................... FrankieDettori 6 110
(George Scott) *hld up towards rr: hdwy 3f out: trckd ldrs over 2f out: rdn to ld appr fnl f: drvn and edgd rt wl ins fnl f: hdd on line* **10/1**

1 **3** *3 3/4* **Lansky (IRE)**[9] 6005 2-9-1 0.............................................. GeraldMosse 11 100
(Jeremy Noseda) *hld up in rr: hdwy on wd outside 2f out: rdn over 1f out: edgd lft ins fnl f: kpt on* **8/1[3]**

25 **4** *1/2* **Zaaki**[39] 4906 2-9-1 0.............................................. JimCrowley 5 99
(Mohamed Moubarak) *hld up in rr: hdwy over 2f out: rdn over 1f out: kpt on wl u.p fnl f* **20/1**

631 **5** *1* **Danzan (IRE)**[33] 5127 2-9-1 91.............................................. DavidProbert 7 96+
(Andrew Balding) *cl up on inner: led 1/2-way: rdn wl over 1f out: hdd and drvn appr fnl f: grad wknd* **25/1**

1 **6** *2 1/4* **Dee Ex Bee**[18] 5641 2-9-1 0.............................................. JamesDoyle 1 90
(Mark Johnston) *trckd ldrs on inner: pushed along 3f out: rdn over 2f out: sn drvn and btn* **6/5[1]**

21 **7** *3 1/2* **Beatbox Rhythm (IRE)**[14] 5801 2-9-1 0.......................... PJMcDonald 9 81
(K R Burke) *trckd ldrs: effrt and cl up over 2f out: rdn wl over 1f out: sn drvn and wknd* **25/1**

31 **8** *1/2* **Jazeel (IRE)**[18] 5655 2-9-1 0.............................................. AndreaAtzeni 3 80
(Mick Channon) *a towards rr* **50/1**

**9** *2 3/4* **Fleet Review (USA)**[16] 5726 2-9-1 0..............................(t) RyanMoore 10 73
(A P O'Brien, Ire) *slt ld to 1/2-way: cl up: rdn along 2f out: sn wknd* **9/2[2]**

413 **10** *5* **Ulshaw Bridge (IRE)**[17] 5681 2-9-1 92.......................... DanielTudhope 4 60
(James Bethell) *trckd ldrs: swtchd rt and hdwy over 3f out: rdn along over 2f out: sn wknd* **14/1**

2 **R** **Chief Justice**[14] 5801 2-9-1 0.............................................. PaulHanagan 2
(Richard Fahey) *ref to r and uns rdr s* **33/1**

1m 26.32s (1.02) **Going Correction** +0.275s/f (Good) **11** Ran SP% **117.0**
Speed ratings (Par 104): **105,104,100,100,98 96,92,91,88,82**
CSF £96.89 TOTE £9.10: £2.50, £2.80, £2.60; EX 102.10 Trifecta £552.40.
**Owner** S A Heley & Partner **Bred** Ms Maria Marron **Trained** Great Habton, N Yorks
■ Stewards' Enquiry : David Allan 7 day ban - used his whip above the permitted level (6-12 Sep)

**FOCUS**
Distance as advertised. Run at a good gallop, the closers came to the fore late on and the form looks sound for the level, even if the two market leaders disappointed. It's par form for the race.

## 6327 BETWAY GREAT VOLTIGEUR STKS (GROUP 2) (C&G) 1m 3f 188y
**3:00** (3:00) (Class 1) 3-Y-O
**£96,407** (£36,550; £18,292; £9,112; £4,573; £2,295) **Stalls** Centre

Form RPR

-132 **1** **Cracksman**[53] 4387 3-9-0 117.............................................. FrankieDettori 3 123+
(John Gosden) *trckd ldrs: hdwy ld 3f out: sn pushed clr: rdn along ins fnl f: kpt on strly* **4/6[1]**

103 **2** *6* **Venice Beach (IRE)**[40] 4878 3-9-0 113..........................(tp) RyanMoore 5 113
(A P O'Brien, Ire) *trckd ldrs: hdwy and cl up 3f out: sn chsng wnr: rdn along wl over 1f out: kpt on: no imp* **9/2[2]**

1-43 **3** *6* **Mirage Dancer**[62] 3994 3-9-0 111.............................................. AndreaAtzeni 2 104
(Sir Michael Stoute) *hld up in rr: hdwy over 3f out: rdn to chse ldng pair 2f out: drvn and kpt on same pce fr over 1f out* **5/1[3]**

2105 **4** *1/2* **Douglas Macarthur (IRE)**[53] 4387 3-9-0 114...........(h[1]) WayneLordan 6 103
(A P O'Brien, Ire) *hld up in rr: hdwy over 3f out: rdn along 2f out: drvn and kpt on same pce fnl f* **14/1**

01 **5** *16* **Spanish Steps (IRE)**[13] 5862 3-9-0 110.......................... SeamieHeffernan 7 77
(A P O'Brien, Ire) *cl up: led 5f out: rdn along and hdd 3f out: sn wknd* **16/1**

1210 **6** *22* **Atty Persse (IRE)**[41] 4811 3-9-0 102..............................(p) JamesDoyle 4 42
(Roger Charlton) *led: hdd 5f out and sn pushed along: rdn over 3f out: sn outpcd and bhd whn eased fnl 2f* **25/1**

2m 34.65s (1.45) **Going Correction** +0.40s/f (Good) **6** Ran SP% **111.2**
Speed ratings (Par 112): **111,107,103,102,92 77**
CSF £3.93 TOTE £1.40: £1.10, £1.60; EX 4.60 Trifecta £8.60.
**Owner** A E Oppenheimer **Bred** Hascombe And Valiant Studs **Trained** Newmarket, Suffolk

**FOCUS**
The rail was moved out from the inside line on the back straight and home bend, adding 32yds to this one to make it exactly 1m4f. This looked a really good renewal of a well-established race and, after two came out, it saw three sons of Frankel take on three runners by Galileo. The gallop appeared to be decent. Cracksman has improved from his Derby runs and is rated up there with the better race winners.

## 6328 JUDDMONTE INTERNATIONAL STKS (BRITISH CHAMPIONS SERIES) (GROUP 1) 1m 2f 56y
**3:35** (3:35) (Class 1) 3-Y-O+
**£567,100** (£215,000; £107,600; £53,600; £26,900; £13,500) **Stalls** Low

Form RPR

1312 **1** **Ulysses (IRE)**[25] 5394 4-9-6 121.............................................. JimCrowley 3 127
(Sir Michael Stoute) *trckd ldrs: smooth hdwy 3f out: cl up 2f out: led jst ins fnl f: sn rdn and kpt on strly* **4/1[3]**

-114 **2** *2* **Churchill (IRE)**[64] 3927 3-8-13 123.............................................. RyanMoore 5 124
(A P O'Brien, Ire) *trckd ldng pair: hdwy 4f out: cl up 3f out: chal over 2f out: rdn wl over 1f out: ev ch: drvn ent fnl f: kpt on same pce* **5/2[1]**

1212 **3** *nk* **Barney Roy**[46] 4638 3-8-13 120.............................................. JamesDoyle 7 123
(Richard Hannon) *trckd ldr: cl up over 3f out: tk slt ld over 2f out: rdn wl over 1f out: hdd ent fnl f: sn drvn and kpt on same pce* **11/4[2]**

124 **4** *4 1/2* **Cliffs Of Moher (IRE)**[46] 4638 3-8-13 118..............(t) SeamieHeffernan 2 114
(A P O'Brien, Ire) *led: pushed along 4f out: rdn and hdd over 2f out: drvn wl over 1f out: kpt on one pce* **9/2**

6126 **5** *1 3/4* **Decorated Knight**[46] 4638 5-9-6 119.............................. AndreaAtzeni 1 110
(Roger Charlton) *trckd ldrs on inner: pushed along 4f out: rdn 3f out: drvn and one pce fnl 2f* **16/1**

114 **6** *4 1/2* **Shutter Speed**[66] 3881 3-8-10 109..............................(t[1]) FrankieDettori 6 99
(John Gosden) *hld up in rr: effrt and sme hdwy over 3f out: rdn along wl over 2f out: sn outpcd* **9/1**

3240 **7** *1* **My Dream Boat (IRE)**[25] 5394 5-9-6 113..........................(v[1]) AdamKirby 4 99
(Clive Cox) *t.k.h early: hld up in rr: sme hdwy over 4f out: rdn along over 3f out: sn outpcd* **28/1**

2m 12.11s (-0.39) **Going Correction** +0.40s/f (Good)
**WFA** 3 from 4yo+ 7lb **7** Ran SP% **112.8**
Speed ratings (Par 117): **117,115,115,111,110 106,105**
CSF £14.01 TOTE £4.60: £2.00, £2.00; EX 17.40 Trifecta £37.20.
**Owner** Flaxman Stables Ireland Ltd **Bred** Flaxman Stables Ireland Ltd **Trained** Newmarket, Suffolk

**FOCUS**
Rail movements meant this was run over 1m2f 88yds. A top event run at a good gallop and it produced an impressive winner. Strong form, Ulysses improving again with the next two close to form.

## 6329 FINE EQUINITY H'CAP 2m 56y
**4:15** (4:15) (Class 2) (0-105,105) 4-Y-O+
**£43,575** (£13,048; £6,524; £3,262; £1,631; £819) **Stalls** Low

Form RPR

-550 **1** **Magic Circle (IRE)**[64] 3928 5-9-2 **97**.............................. HarryBentley 13 106+
(Ralph Beckett) *trckd ldrs: hdwy over 2f out: chal over 1f out: rdn to ld jst ins fnl f: kpt on wl* **7/2[1]**

0154 **2** *1* **My Reward**[18] 5638 5-9-0 **95**.............................................. DavidAllan 7 101
(Tim Easterby) *led: pushed along 3f out: rdn over 2f out: jnd and drvn over 1f out: hdd jst ins fnl f: kpt on* **11/1**

0101 **3** *1 1/4* **Euchen Glen**[11] 5912 4-8-10 **91**.............................. PaulMulrennan 8 95+
(Jim Goldie) *hld up in rr: hdwy wl over 2f out: rdn over 1f out: styd on strly fnl f: nrst fin* **8/1**

10-0 **4** *hd* **Penglai Pavilion (USA)**[123] 1994 7-9-5 **100**.................. JamesDoyle 15 104
(Charlie Appleby) *trckd ldr: cl up 3f out: rdn along 2f out: ev ch over 1f out: sn drvn and kpt on same pce fnl f* **7/1[2]**

-546 **5** *1/2* **Platitude**[18] 5638 4-9-9 **104**.............................................. RyanMoore 6 107
(Sir Michael Stoute) *in tch: hdwy to trck ldrs 4f out: effrt over 2f out and sn cl up: rdn over 1f out: kpt on same pce* **9/1**

210 **6** *1/2* **Saigon City**[18] 5638 7-9-3 **98**.............................................. DanielTudhope 9 101
(Declan Carroll) *trckd ldrs: pushed along wl over 2f out: rdn wl over 1f out: sn drvn and edgd lft: kpt on same pce after* **15/2[3]**

5520 **7** *hd* **Oceane (FR)**[64] 3928 5-8-13 **94**..............................(v[1]) FergusSweeney 16 97
(Alan King) *hld up: hdwy 3f out: rdn along 2f out: styd on fnl f* **20/1**

0501 **8** *3/4* **Yorkidding**[12] 5882 5-9-5 **100**.............................................. PJMcDonald 14 102
(Mark Johnston) *towards rr: pushed along over 3f out: rdn over 2f out: kpt on fnl f* **14/1**

0-00 **9** *nk* **Shrewd**[20] 3928 7-8-10 **98**.............................. ConnorMurtagh(7) 11 99
(Iain Jardine) *midfield: effrt and sme hdwy over 3f out: rdn along 2f out: sn drvn and n.d* **16/1**

5150 **10** *1 1/2* **Oriental Fox (GER)**[22] 5503 9-9-10 **105**.............................. JoeFanning 1 105
(Mark Johnston) *in tch: hdwy on inner over 2f out: sn chsng ldrs: rdn wl over 1f out: wknd* **33/1**

60/3 **11** *1 1/2* **Edge Of Sanity (IRE)**[39] 4921 8-8-12 **93**..............................(t) PaulHanagan 3 91
(Iain Jardine) *trckd ldng pair: pushed along 3f out: rdn over 2f out: grad wknd* **10/1**

2500 **12** *14* **Suegioo (FR)**[21] 5524 8-9-2 **97**..............................(p) JamieSpencer 2 78
(Richard Fahey) *hld up in rr: hdwy 3f out: rdn over 2f out: sn drvn and nvr a factor* **12/1**

0500 **13** *3 1/4* **Isharah (USA)**[26] 5351 4-8-10 **91**.............................................. FrannyNorton 4 68
(Mark Johnston) *hld up: a in rr* **66/1**

-660 **14** *4* **Star Rider**[21] 5524 5-8-11 **92**..............................(p) OisinMurphy 5 64
(Hughie Morrison) *trckd ldrs on inner: pushed along over 4f out: sn rdn and wknd over 3f out* **12/1**

3m 46.29s (11.79) **Going Correction** +0.40s/f (Good) **14** Ran SP% **122.2**
Speed ratings (Par 109): **86,85,84,84,84 84,84,83,83,82 82,75,73,71**
CSF £42.69 CT £297.77 TOTE £4.10: £1.90, £3.50, £2.80; EX 45.10 Trifecta £287.10.
**Owner** Mr and Mrs David Aykroyd **Bred** Mr & Mrs David Aykroyd **Trained** Kimpton, Hants

**FOCUS**
Rail adjustments meant this was run over 2m 88yds. The gallop for this staying contest was pretty ordinary early and they finished quite bunched, so the form may not be reliable, although the winner was entitled to take the prize. The form is rated around the second.

## 6330 BETWAY NURSERY H'CAP 6f
4:50 (4:53) (Class 2) 2-Y-O

**£43,575** (£13,048; £6,524; £3,262; £1,631; £819) **Stalls** Low

Form RPR
2111 1 **Demons Rock (IRE)**[5] 6128 2-9-2 **92** 6ex................ RichardKingscote 5 100
(Tom Dascombe) *racd centre: mde all: rdn and qckng wl over 1f out: drvn and edgd rt ins fnl f: hld on wl* **8/1**[3]
0324 2 *hd* **Queen's Sargent (FR)**[12] 5875 2-8-0 **76**...................... JimmyQuinn 19 83
(Kevin Ryan) *racd towards stands side: hld up towards rr: hdwy whn nt clr run and hmpd 2f out: sn rdn to chse ldrs: styd on strly fnl f* **12/1**
3501 3 1 ¾ **Areen Faisal (IRE)**[43] 4716 2-8-4 **80**............................ PaulHanagan 18 82
(Richard Fahey) *trckd ldrs towards stands side: hdwy 2f out: rdn to chse wnr ent fnl: sn swtchd lft and drvn: kpt on same pce towards fin* **10/1**
1121 4 2 ¾ **John Kirkup**[19] 5615 2-9-2 **92**............................ PaulMulrennan 16 88
(Michael Dods) *dwlt and sltly hmpd s: in rr towards stands side: hdwy whn n.m.r 2f out: swtchd lft and rdn wl over 1f out: styd on wl fnl f* **20/1**
1001 5 ½ **Red Roman**[19] 5596 2-9-0 **90**............................ HarryBentley 4 82
(Charles Hills) *racd centre: trckd ldrs: hdwy to chse wnr 2f out: rdn over 1f out: wknd fnl f* **8/1**[3]
134 6 ¾ **Zap**[51] 4434 2-8-11 **90**.................... AdamMcNamara(3) 15 80
(Richard Fahey) *swtchd lft to r centre: midfield: hdwy 2f out: sn rdn and kpt on fnl f* **14/1**
531 7 *nk* **Savalas (IRE)**[26] 5370 2-8-5 **81**............................ ShaneGray 8 70
(Kevin Ryan) *racd centre: chsd wnr: rdn along 2f out: grad wknd* **6/1**[2]
1161 8 *nse* **Milton Road**[5] 6021 2-8-2 **78** 6ex........................ KieranO'Neill 20 67
(Mick Channon) *racd towards stands side: towards rr: hdwy 1/2-way: rdn and edgd lft 2f out: sn drvn and kpt on fnl f* **50/1**
312 9 2 ¾ **Kalagia (IRE)**[24] 5453 2-8-1 **77**............................ JoeFanning 2 58
(Mark Johnston) *dwlt and towards rr on inner: rdn along over 2f out: kpt on u.p fnl f* **16/1**
144 10 ½ **Ghayadh**[21] 5531 2-8-6 **82**............................ JosephineGordon 10 61
(Hugo Palmer) *racd centre: in tch: rdn along over 2f out: sn wknd* **28/1**
014 11 1 **Brandy Station (IRE)**[81] 3333 2-8-3 **79**.................... DuranFentiman 12 55
(Tony Coyle) *racd centre: cl up: rdn along 2f out: wknd over 1f out* **66/1**
0412 12 ¾ **Faithful Promise**[18] 5659 2-8-4 **80**............................ PJMcDonald 14 54
(Mark Johnston) *racd towards stands side: chsd ldrs: rdn along over 2f out: sn wknd* **33/1**
2013 13 ¾ **Gift In Time (IRE)**[19] 5596 2-8-6 **82**............................ LukeMorris 13 54
(James Given) *a towards rr* **20/1**
144 14 *nk* **Falmouth Light (FR)**[31] 5179 2-8-4 **80**............................ FrannyNorton 9 51
(Mark Johnston) *dwlt: a in rr* **33/1**
031 15 2 ¼ **Tathmeen (IRE)**[27] 5321 2-8-9 **85**............................ JimCrowley 11 49
(Richard Hannon) *racd centre: chsd ldrs: rdn 2f out: sn wknd* **5/1**[1]
0104 16 8 **Etefaaq (IRE)**[20] 5570 2-9-7 **97**............................ FrankieDettori 6 37
(Richard Hannon) *in tch on inner: rdn along over 2f out: sn wknd* **16/1**
131 17 16 **Green Fortune**[29] 5240 2-8-11 **87**............................(p) AndreaAtzeni 7
(William Haggas) *a in rr: rdn along after 1 1/2f: sn outpcd and bhd fr 1/2-way* **5/1**[1]

1m 12.99s (1.09) **Going Correction** +0.275s/f (Good) **17 Ran SP% 127.4**
Speed ratings (Par 100): **103,102,100,96,96 95,94,94,90,90 88,87,86,86,83 72,51**
CSF £97.12 CT £1026.04 TOTE £9.50: £2.30, £3.60, £3.00, £4.20; EX 147.80 Trifecta £1981.80.

**Owner** The Famous Five Partnership **Bred** James & Geoff Mulcahy **Trained** Malpas, Cheshire
**FOCUS**
A deep field for Britain's most valuable nursery and a highly progressive winner, although not that many got into it. The winner is going from strength to strength.
T/Jkpt: Not won. T/Plt: £198.30 to a £1 stake. Pool: £299,082.84 - 1,100.51 winning units. T/Qpdt: £19.10 to a £1 stake. Pool: £18,568.87 - 719.06 winning units. **Joe Rowntree**

6331-6333a (Foreign Racing) - See Raceform Interactive

# 5082 KILLARNEY (L-H)
Wednesday, August 23

**OFFICIAL GOING: Soft**

## 6334a VINCENT O'BRIEN RUBY STKS (LISTED) 1m 50y
4:45 (4:47) 3-Y-O+

**£22,692** (£7,307; £3,461; £1,538; £769; £384)

RPR
1 **Canary Row (IRE)**[4] 6215 7-9-9 90..............................(v) RonanWhelan 9 101+
(P J Prendergast, Ire) *chsd ldrs in 3rd: rdn to cl over 1f out: 2nd ent fnl f: styd on wl to ld ins fnl 100yds* **15/2**[3]
2 1 **Bumbasina (IRE)**[38] 4936 3-8-12 93.......................................... WJLee 6 93
(W McCreery, Ire) *hld up: 7th at 1/2-way: prog on outer under 2f out: wnt 4th ent fnl f: 3rd fnl 100yds: kpt on wl into 2nd cl home: nt rch wnr* **4/1**[2]
3 *hd* **Duchess Of France (IRE)**[20] 5583 4-9-4 90...............(t) LeighRoche 11 94
(Adrian Paul Keatley, Ire) *led: rdn 2f out: kpt on wl for press fnl f tl hdd ins fnl 100yds: dropped to 3rd cl home* **12/1**
4 *hd* **Psychedelic Funk**[28] 5311 3-9-3 107................................ ColinKeane 1 97
(G M Lyons, Ire) *hld up: 6th at 1/2-way: rdn over 2f out: clsr to chse ldrs in 3rd ent fnl f: bit short of room fnl 100yds and swtchd lft to rails: no ex and dropped to 4th fnl 50yds* **5/4**[1]
5 2 ½ **Groundfrost (IRE)**[20] 5583 3-8-12 83................................ GaryCarroll 2 86
(John James Feane, Ire) *racd in mid-div: rdn whn short of room under 2f out: wnt 5th ent fnl f: kpt on same pce* **25/1**
6 1 ½ **Ceol Na Nog (IRE)**[41] 4822 4-9-4 91.............................. KevinManning 3 84
(J S Bolger, Ire) *racd in rr for most: swtchd lft to inner ins fnl f and kpt on clsng stages: nvr on terms* **8/1**
7 ½ **Pocketfullofdreams (FR)**[7] 6080 3-8-12 97............(h) MichaelHussey 5 82
(A P O'Brien, Ire) *chsd ldr in 2nd: rdn over 2f out: nt qckn over 1f out: sn no ex* **8/1**
8 2 ¾ **St Gallen (IRE)**[10] 5976 4-9-9 85......................................(p) ShaneFoley 7 81
(John Joseph Murphy, Ire) *racd in mid-div: rdn and nt qckn 2f out: no imp appr fnl f: eased and dropped to rr cl home* **25/1**

1m 46.64s (-0.46)
**WFA** 3 from 4yo+ 6lb **8 Ran SP% 113.8**
CSF £37.16 TOTE £9.10: £2.30, £1.60, £3.10; DF 37.30 Trifecta £350.70.
**Owner** Richard Barnes **Bred** Grangecon Stud **Trained** Melitta Lodge, Co Kildare
■ Casla was withdrawn. Price at time of withdrawal 33-1. Rule 4 does not apply.

**FOCUS**
An average race for the grade. Everything fell right for the winner but it would be hard to begrudge him a win at this level.

6335 - 6337a (Foreign Racing) - See Raceform Interactive

# 6093 CHEPSTOW (L-H)
Thursday, August 24

**OFFICIAL GOING: Good to soft (good in places; 7.1)**
Wind: slight across Weather: sunny spells

## 6338 YORK EBOR BETTING AT 188BET/EBF NOVICE STKS 5f 16y
2:05 (2:05) (Class 5) 2-Y-O **£3,234** (£962; £481; £240) **Stalls** Centre

Form RPR
2305 1 **Spoof**[22] 5546 2-8-13 70..................................(h) CallumShepherd(3) 4 78
(Charles Hills) *chsd ldrs: nt clr run fr 2f out tl swtchd rt over 1f out: rdn to nose ahd 110yds out: won on nod* **25/1**
022 2 *shd* **Time For Wine (IRE)**[14] 5839 2-8-11 72.................. SilvestreDeSousa 7 73
(David Evans) *mounted on trck: cl up: rdn 1/2-way: chal over 1f out: sn led: jst hdd 110yds out: kpt on: lost on nod* **11/8**[1]
4333 3 2 ½ **Qaaraat**[24] 5480 2-9-2 77..........................................(b[1]) DaneO'Neill 6 69
(Ed Dunlop) *led: rdn over 1f out: hung lft and hdd appr fnl f: unable qck* **6/1**[3]
03 4 1 **Maygold**[21] 5575 2-8-11 0.......................................... LiamKeniry 2 60
(Ed Walker) *plld hrd: hld up: clsd 1/2-way: effrt 2f out: sn one pce: flashed tail ent fnl f* **10/1**
1400 5 1 ½ **Campion**[28] 5329 2-9-4 79...................................... TomMarquand 1 62
(Richard Hannon) *prom: rdn and hung lft 1/2-way: outpcd by ldrs over 1f out* **9/1**
3205 6 *hd* **Bath And Tennis (IRE)**[47] 4598 2-8-11 75.......................... LukeMorris 3 54
(Sir Mark Prescott Bt) *slipped leaving stalls: sn chsng ldrs: drvn 2f out: outpcd over 1f out* **5/2**[2]
6 7 5 **Avon Green**[10] 6005 2-8-8 0.................................. EdwardGreatrex(3) 5 36
(Joseph Tuite) *hld up: rdn 1/2-way: wknd over 1f out* **12/1**

1m 1.2s (1.90) **Going Correction** +0.30s/f (Good) **7 Ran SP% 115.6**
Speed ratings (Par 94): **96,95,91,90,87 87,79**
CSF £61.62 TOTE £21.40: £9.20, £1.40; EX 62.20 Trifecta £274.20.
**Owner** Gary And Linnet Woodward **Bred** Scuderia Blueberry SRL **Trained** Lambourn, Berks
**FOCUS**
Probably just a modest start to the day. The winner's spring form is in keeping with this.

## 6339 MAYWEATHER V MCGREGOR H'CAP 5f 16y
2:35 (2:36) (Class 6) (0-60,62) 3-Y-O **£3,234** (£962; £481; £240) **Stalls** Centre

Form RPR
1 **Passionatta (IRE)**[50] 4510 3-8-7 46 oh1....................(v[1]) DavidProbert 10 54
(J P Murtagh, Ire) *mde virtually all: drvn over 1f out: hung lft fnl f: r.o* **7/1**
3653 2 1 ¼ **Exquisite Ruby**[68] 3806 3-9-7 60.................................. SteveDrowne 11 63
(Charles Hills) *wnt to post early: trckd ldrs: drvn 2f out: r.o fnl f: wnt 2nd towards fin* **14/1**
6351 3 *hd* **Whiteley (IRE)**[15] 5791 3-9-3 56.............................. SilvestreDeSousa 6 58
(Mick Channon) *towards rr: rdn and hdwy over 1f out: r.o wl u.p fnl f* **5/2**[1]
6604 4 1 ¼ **Glyder**[16] 5736 3-9-6 59.......................................... RoystonFfrench 3 58
(John Holt) *chsd ldrs: clsd and edgd rt 2f out: chal gng wl over 1f out: sn rdn: jst hld whn sltly hmpd by wnr ins fnl f: no ex and lost 2 pls towards fin* **6/1**[3]
0240 5 2 ½ **Celerity (IRE)**[10] 6004 3-8-0 46 oh1....................(v) GabrieleMalune(7) 2 35
(David Evans) *hld up: hdwy after 2f: rdn 2f out: kpt on same pce* **18/1**
0340 6 ¾ **Billy's Boots**[26] 5419 3-8-10 49....................................(p[1]) KierenFox 5 35
(J R Jenkins) *prom: drvn 1/2-way: one pce appr fnl f* **16/1**
6653 7 1 ¾ **Blue Rocks**[11] 5956 3-9-3 56.......................................... FrannyNorton 4 36
(Lisa Williamson) *chsd ldrs: rdn and lost pl 1/2-way: styd on fnl f* **4/1**[2]
-610 8 1 ¼ **Snoozy Sioux (IRE)**[136] 1688 3-9-6 62.......................... NoelGarbutt(3) 7 37
(Martin Smith) *w ldr tl rdn 1/2-way: wknd appr fnl f* **33/1**
6364 9 *hd* **Stopdworldnletmeof**[12] 5935 3-8-4 46 oh1..........(b[1]) GeorgeWood(3) 12 21
(David Flood) *midfield on stands' side: rdn 1/2-way: wknd over 1f out* **7/1**
506 10 2 ¾ **Kodiac Pearl (IRE)**[37] 5006 3-8-10 49..............................(h[1]) LukeMorris 8 14
(Robert Cowell) *midfield: rdn over 3f out: wknd over 1f out* **16/1**
36-0 11 1 ¾ **Sweet Sienna**[36] 5040 3-8-4 46...................................... JackDuern(3) 9 4
(Dean Ivory) *towards rr: rdn 1/2-way: wknd 2f out* **16/1**
00-0 12 17 **Bills Delight**[30] 5252 3-8-4 46 oh1..........................(b[1]) EdwardGreatrex(3) 1
(Bill Turner) *broke wl: prom: rdn after 2f: sn lost pl: bhd and eased fnl f* **66/1**

1m 0.83s (1.53) **Going Correction** +0.30s/f (Good) **12 Ran SP% 121.9**
Speed ratings (Par 98): **99,97,96,94,90 89,86,84,84,79 77,49**
CSF £103.92 CT £321.60 TOTE £7.40: £2.60, £3.60, £1.30; EX 79.00 Trifecta £267.90.
**Owner** JP Murtagh Racing **Bred** Andy Collins & Intense Focus Syndicate **Trained** Coolaghknock Glebe,Co Kildare
**FOCUS**
A moderate contest that featured plenty of runners in first-time headgear. The form is rated around the second and third.

## 6340 CHALLENGE CUP FINAL BETTING AT 188BET FILLIES' H'CAP 1m 14y
3:10 (3:11) (Class 5) (0-75,76) 3-Y-O+ **£3,234** (£962; £481; £240) **Stalls** Centre

Form RPR
1455 1 **Pattie**[20] 5591 3-9-7 **76**.......................................... SilvestreDeSousa 8 82
(Mick Channon) *hld up: rdn 2f out: hdwy to ld over 1f out: edgd rt ins fnl f: r.o wl* **5/2**[1]
201 2 ¾ **Here's Two**[27] 5357 4-9-7 **70**.......................................... KieranO'Neill 5 75
(Ron Hodges) *trckd ldr: rdn over 2f out: ev ch over 1f out: r.o fnl f* **9/2**
0620 3 ½ **Mia Cara**[14] 5826 3-8-9 **64**..................................................(v) SteveDrowne 3 67
(David Evans) *t.k.h in midfield: rdn over 2f out: nt clr run over 1f out: swtchd lft ins fnl f: r.o* **20/1**
0302 4 ¾ **Bradfield Magic (IRE)**[7] 6102 3-8-2 **57**.......................... FrannyNorton 6 58
(Charles Hills) *trckd ldrs: rdn over 2f out: kpt on same pce fnl f* **4/1**[3]
5131 5 2 ¾ **Fantasy Queen**[35] 5049 4-9-6 **69**.......................................... CharlesBishop 4 65
(Eve Johnson Houghton) *hld up: pushed along and hdwy 3f out: drvn 2f out: nvr able to chal* **7/2**[2]
0620 6 6 **Delirium (IRE)**[17] 5713 3-7-10 **56** oh2..............................(p) JaneElliott(5) 7 37
(Ed de Giles) *in rr: rdn 1/2-way: wknd 2f out* **12/1**
6330 7 *hd* **Canterbury Quad (FR)**[54] 4365 3-9-1 **75**................(v[1]) JennyPowell(5) 2 56
(Henry Spiller) *t.k.h: led: rdn 2f out: nt run on: hdd over 1f out: wknd fnl f* **16/1**

5223 **8** 2½ **Getna (USA)**[19] 5656 3-9-1 **70** (b[1]) TomMarquand 1 45
(Richard Hannon) *sn trcking ldrs: rdn 3f out: wknd over 1f out* **11/1**

1m 37.69s (1.49) **Going Correction** +0.30s/f (Good)
**WFA** 3 from 4yo 6lb **8** Ran SP% **115.6**
Speed ratings (Par 100): **104,103,102,102,99 93,93,90**
CSF £14.21 CT £182.96 TOTE £2.90: £1.30, £1.80, £5.50; EX 15.90 Trifecta £138.60.
**Owner** M Channon **Bred** Mike Channon Bloodstock Ltd **Trained** West Ilsley, Berks

**FOCUS**
A competitive handicap confined to fillies. Straightforward form.

## 6341 188BET H'CAP (DIV I) 1m 14y
3:40 (3:43) (Class 6) (0-55,56) 3-Y-O+ £2,587 (£770; £384; £192) **Stalls** Centre

Form RPR

3444 **1** **Topmeup**[17] 5713 3-8-13 **52** (v) SilvestreDeSousa 9 62
(David Evans) *s.i.s: hld up: hdwy 3f out: drvn 2f out: led jst ins fnl f: edgd rt: r.o wl* **5/2**[1]

0 **2** 2¼ **Imbucato**[16] 5772 3-8-13 **52** (v) DavidProbert 3 57
(J P Murtagh, Ire) *midfield: rdn over 3f out: edgd rt and led over 1f out: hdd jst ins fnl f: kpt on: no ex towards fin* **11/4**[2]

5340 **3** hd **Zaria**[17] 5713 6-8-11 **51** (p) GabrieleMalune(7) 2 56
(Richard Price) *chsd ldrs: rdn over 3f out: ev ch 2f out: r.o fnl f* **8/1**

5062 **4** 1¾ **Pitch High (IRE)**[22] 5536 3-9-0 **53** AdamBeschizza 11 53
(Julia Feilden) *led one other on stands' side tl field merged 1/2-way: prom overall: led narrowly over 3f out: hdd over 1f out: one pce fnl f* **6/1**[3]

4046 **5** 1¼ **Tally's Son**[17] 5714 3-8-11 **50** LukeMorris 12 47
(Grace Harris) *trckd one other on stands' side tl field merged 1/2-way: midfield overall: hdwy 3f out: rdn over 2f out: one pce fnl f* **12/1**

0100 **6** 10 **Poor Duke (IRE)**[14] 5848 7-9-6 **56** (v) PhilDennis(3) 6 31
(Michael Mullineaux) *midfield: rdn 3f out: wknd over 1f out* **16/1**

0564 **7** 2 **Caius College Girl (IRE)**[102] 2672 5-9-2 **54** (p) JoshuaBryan(5) 7 25
(Adrian Wintle) *t.k.h: chsd ldrs: clsd 3f out: sn rdn: wknd over 1f out* **10/1**

454 **8** 2½ **Kath's Boy (IRE)**[10] 6004 3-8-6 **45** FrannyNorton 10 9
(Tony Carroll) *midfield: shkn up over 2f out: sn wknd* **8/1**

0006 **9** 1 **Toolatetodelegate**[38] 4970 3-8-8 **47** RaulDaSilva 8 9
(Brian Barr) *t.k.h: trckd wnr: drvn over 2f out: wknd over 1f out* **40/1**

-660 **10** nk **Silver Mist**[15] 5792 3-8-6 **45** (b[1]) MartinDwyer 5 6
(Sylvester Kirk) *s.s: rdn over 4f out: a in rr* **50/1**

20 **11** 12 **Take A Drop (IRE)**[17] 5714 4-9-1 **48** (h) KieranO'Neill 4
(Seamus Mullins) *led tl hdd over 3f out: wknd qckly: t.o* **33/1**

1m 37.91s (1.71) **Going Correction** +0.30s/f (Good)
**WFA** 3 from 4yo+ 6lb **11** Ran SP% **121.8**
Speed ratings (Par 101): **103,100,100,98,97 87,85,83,82,81 69**
CSF £9.73 CT £50.02 TOTE £3.40: £1.50, £1.20, £2.70; EX 12.30 Trifecta £52.10.
**Owner** M W Lawrence **Bred** Whitwell Bloodstock **Trained** Pandy, Monmouths

**FOCUS**
Nothing more that a moderate race. The form makes sense.

## 6342 188BET H'CAP (DIV II) 1m 14y
4:10 (4:16) (Class 6) (0-55,55) 3-Y-O+ £2,587 (£770; £384; £192) **Stalls** Centre

Form RPR

6650 **1** **Doctor Bong**[15] 5791 5-9-3 **51** (b) LukeMorris 4 59
(Grace Harris) *prom: led 1/2-way: shkn up over 1f out: 3 l up and drvn ins fnl f: idled but a doing enough* **12/1**

0501 **2** 1½ **Royal Melody**[12] 5935 3-8-12 **55** (p) GeorgeWood(3) 9 59
(Heather Main) *midfield: rdn 3f out: sn chsng ldrs: wnt 2nd ins fnl f: styd on and clsng on idling wnr towards fin* **3/1**[1]

0360 **3** 2¼ **Imperial Link**[17] 5713 5-8-9 **46** oh1 (v) EdwardGreatrex(3) 8 45
(John O'Shea) *led to 1/2-way: rdn and outpcd by ldrs 3f out: styd on u.p fnl f: wnt 3rd post* **7/1**

065- **4** shd **Jock Talk (IRE)**[13] 5904 3-8-12 **52** (t[1]) DavidProbert 1 50
(Seamus Fahey, Ire) *hld up in midfield: clsd 1/2-way: rdn over 2f out: briefly in 2nd ent fnl f: wknd: lost 3rd post* **4/1**[2]

0063 **5** nk **Luduamf (IRE)**[11] 5958 3-8-2 **49** TinaSmith(7) 7 46
(Richard Hannon) *hld up towards rr: rdn 3f out: styd on fnl 2f: nrst fin* **6/1**[3]

40-0 **6** ¾ **Yorkshire Star (IRE)**[15] 5791 3-8-3 **46** oh1 (b) PhilDennis(3) 5 42
(Bill Turner) *s.s: towards rr: drvn over 3f out: no hdwy tl swtchd rt over 1f out: styd on fnl f* **33/1**

0066 **7** 2¼ **Coachella (IRE)**[9] 6041 3-8-6 **46** oh1 SilvestreDeSousa 3 37
(Ed de Giles) *prom: chsd wnr 1/2-way: rdn 3f out: lost 2nd ent fnl f: no ex* **6/1**[3]

2400 **8** 9 **Greyfriarschorista**[38] 4970 10-8-6 **47** (bt) KatherineGlenister(7) 6 18
(David Evans) *t.k.h: chsd ldrs: rdn 3f out: wknd over 2f out* **14/1**

0050 **9** 7 **Go On Mayson**[30] 5249 3-8-7 **54** (b[1]) PatrickVaughan(7) 10 8
(Christian Williams) *trckd ldrs: rdn over 3f out: wknd 2f out* **12/1**

6000 **10** 4 **Raashdy (IRE)**[13] 5897 4-9-4 **52** (b) LiamKeniry 11
(Peter Hiatt) *rdn over 3f out: a towards rr* **16/1**

0000 **11** 7 **Secret Look**[19] 5653 7-9-7 **55** (p) TimmyMurphy 12
(Richard Phillips) *racd alone stands' side: drvn over 2f out: a in rr overall* **25/1**

1m 38.4s (2.20) **Going Correction** +0.30s/f (Good)
**WFA** 3 from 4yo+ 6lb **11** Ran SP% **120.8**
Speed ratings (Par 101): **101,99,97,97,96 96,93,84,77,73 66**
CSF £49.30 CT £288.57 TOTE £12.30: £3.80, £1.40, £2.20; EX 51.40 Trifecta £521.80.
**Owner** Ronald Davies & Mrs Candida Davies **Bred** Aiden Murphy **Trained** Shirenewton, Monmouthshire

**FOCUS**
The second division of a moderate handicap. The runner-up helps the opening level.

## 6343 188BET.CO.UK H'CAP 2m 2f
4:40 (4:42) (Class 6) (0-65,65) 3-Y-O+ £2,587 (£770; £384; £192) **Stalls** Low

Form RPR

3352 **1** **Oxford Blu**[9] 6023 3-8-9 **62** (p) RosieJessop(3) 10 75+
(Sir Mark Prescott Bt) *chsd ldr who wnt clr: 14 l down 7f out but himself clr of others: clsd 5f out: led over 2f out: drvn and styd on wl* **11/8**[1]

4003 **2** ¾ **Riptide**[27] 5361 11-9-6 **57** TomMarquand 9 63
(Michael Scudamore) *towards rr: rdn along after 5f: hdwy 5f out: wnt 3rd over 3f out: drvn and styd on to go 2nd over 1f out: clsng wl ins fnl f* **16/1**

**3** 3¾ **Balkinstown (IRE)**[4] 4281 7-8-12 **49** (vt) LiamKeniry 1 51
(Robert Stephens) *dwlt: hld up in last: drvn over 4f out: hdwy 3f out: wnt 3rd over 1f out: styd on tl no ex wl ins fnl f* **9/1**

4624 **4** 10 **Goldslinger (FR)**[9] 6038 5-9-11 **65** JackDuern(3) 3 55
(Dean Ivory) *led: clr after 5f: over 14 l up 7f out: stl 8 l up whn rdn 4f out: hdd over 2f out: grad wknd* **8/1**

2533 **5** ¾ **Macksville (IRE)**[30] 5267 4-9-10 **61** (p) RyanTate 13 50
(James Eustace) *chsd ldrs: rdn 4f out: one pce* **13/2**[3]

00/0 **6** 10 **Chevalgris**[13] 5896 7-9-11 **62** CharlesBishop 2 39
(Dai Burchell) *midfield: drvn over 3f out: wknd 2f out* **25/1**

2044 **7** 1½ **See And Be Seen**[13] 5896 7-9-6 **62** (p) MitchGodwin(5) 8 37
(Sylvester Kirk) *chsd ldng pair who wnt clr: rdn and lost 3rd over 3f out: wknd over 1f out* **14/1**

0-52 **8** 4 **Hermarna (IRE)**[43] 4756 4-9-1 **57** GeorgiaCox(5) 11 27
(Neil King) *hld up: rdn over 5f out: sn wknd* **6/1**[2]

-130 **9** 6 **Danglydontask**[51] 4471 6-9-13 **64** (b) LukeMorris 5 27
(David Arbuthnot) *s.i.s: sn chsng ldrs who were clr: rdn 5f out: wknd 3f out* **10/1**

1/60 **10** 13 **Rocky Elsom (USA)**[97] 2781 10-9-3 **59** (t) JoshuaBryan(5) 4 6
(Adrian Wintle) *towards rr: wknd 6f out: t.o* **25/1**

4m 6.12s (2.52) **Going Correction** +0.30s/f (Good)
**WFA** 3 from 4yo+ 13lb **10** Ran SP% **120.2**
Speed ratings (Par 101): **106,105,104,99,99 94,94,92,89,83**
CSF £28.35 CT £151.26 TOTE £2.30: £1.40, £3.40, £2.60; EX 25.20 Trifecta £204.50.
**Owner** Mrs Olivia Hoare & J M Castle **Bred** Mrs Olivia Hoare **Trained** Newmarket, Suffolk

**FOCUS**
A marathon contest run at a good gallop. The first three finished well clear and the form could be rated 3lb better.

## 6344 READ SILVESTRE DE SOUSA AT 188BET H'CAP 1m 4f
5:15 (5:15) (Class 4) (0-85,85) 3-Y-O+ £5,175 (£1,540; £769; £384) **Stalls** Low

Form RPR

-222 **1** **Seafarer (IRE)**[20] 5589 3-9-4 **84** HayleyTurner 1 96
(Marcus Tregoning) *chsd ldrs: rdn 3f out: drvn to ld over 1f out: r.o strly* **10/3**[2]

1-01 **2** 2¼ **Star Of The East (IRE)**[5] 6202 3-8-13 **79** FrannyNorton 8 87
(Mark Johnston) *a.p: chsd ldr 3f out: sn rdn: ev ch over 1f out: unable qck and outpcd by wnr fnl f* **7/4**[1]

510 **3** 7 **Sparte Quercus (IRE)**[26] 5403 4-9-2 **73** SilvestreDeSousa 9 71
(Ed Dunlop) *chsd ldrs: hdwy into 2nd 7f out: rdn to ld over 3f out: hdd over 1f out: wknd but hld modest 3rd* **6/1**[3]

5- **4** 2½ **Full Court Press (IRE)**[16] 5774 4-9-10 **81** DavidProbert 2 73
(J P Murtagh, Ire) *t.k.h towards rr: rdn and hdwy on inner 3f out: one pce and no imp on ldrs fnl 2f* **8/1**

025 **5** hd **Our Boy (IRE)**[19] 5630 3-8-9 **75** SteveDrowne 6 67
(David Evans) *squeezed out s: hld up in last: rdn 4f out: nt clr run over 2f out: styd on fnl f* **25/1**

265 **6** 1¾ **Panko (IRE)**[40] 4908 4-9-7 **81** CallumShepherd(3) 5 70
(Ed de Giles) *led 4f: styd prom: rdn 3f out: qckly outpcd by ldrs: wknd fnl f* **7/1**

-046 **7** 14 **Ghayyar (IRE)**[77] 3505 3-9-2 **82** TomMarquand 3 49
(Richard Hannon) *midfield: rdn 4f out: wknd 2f out* **12/1**

535 **8** 5 **Entihaa**[30] 5251 9-8-9 **66** oh2 (p) CharlesBishop 4 24
(Dai Burchell) *s.i.s: chsd along early in midfield: hdwy to ld after 4f: drvn 4f out: sn hdd: wknd qckly* **33/1**

**9** 7 **Canyon City**[311] 4-10-0 **85** TrevorWhelan 7 32
(Neil King) *hld up: brief effrt on outer 3f out: sn wknd* **20/1**

2m 41.63s (2.63) **Going Correction** +0.30s/f (Good)
**WFA** 3 from 4yo+ 9lb **9** Ran SP% **116.6**
Speed ratings (Par 105): **103,101,96,95,95 93,84,81,76**
CSF £9.42 CT £32.79 TOTE £4.80: £1.20, £1.30, £1.80; EX 14.00 Trifecta £52.10.
**Owner** Green, Hoare, Raw & Tregoning **Bred** Airlie Stud **Trained** Whitsbury, Hants
■ Stewards' Enquiry : David Probert 2 day ban - used his whip down the shoulder in the forehand position (7/8 Sep)

**FOCUS**
This looked one of the more competitive and classy events on the whole card. Three horses dominated the final stages. A good step up from the winner to beat the well treated runner-up.

## 6345 US OPEN TENNIS AT 188BET H'CAP 7f 16y
5:45 (5:48) (Class 6) (0-65,66) 3-Y-O+ £2,587 (£770; £384; £192) **Stalls** Centre

Form RPR

0-46 **1** **Hedging (IRE)**[17] 5711 3-9-6 **64** (p) CharlesBishop 8 70
(Eve Johnson Houghton) *midfield: rdn and clsd 3f out: pressed ldr 1f out: r.o gamely to ld towards fin* **11/2**[3]

3604 **2** nse **Tulip Dress**[27] 5367 4-9-7 **60** SilvestreDeSousa 3 68
(Anthony Carson) *hld up: rdn and hdwy over 2f out: r.o to ld narrowly 1f out: hdd towards fin* **6/1**

**3** 2 **Camiyra (IRE)**[16] 5772 3-9-8 **66** (t) DavidProbert 6 67
(J P Murtagh, Ire) *towards rr: rdn 1/2-way: hdwy 2f out: n.m.r over 1f out: wnt 3rd ins fnl f: r.o* **5/1**[2]

0356 **4** 1¾ **Princess Way (IRE)**[1] 6324 3-8-11 **55** (v) SteveDrowne 2 51
(David Evans) *chsd ldrs: rdn over 2f out: unable qck fnl f* **33/1**

0202 **5** ½ **Tallulah's Quest (IRE)**[7] 6112 3-8-11 **55** AdamBeschizza 7 50
(Julia Feilden) *towards rr: stdy hdwy 1/2-way: rdn over 1f out: styd on fnl f* **4/1**[1]

3000 **6** 1¾ **Baltic Prince (IRE)**[17] 5699 7-9-9 **62** GeorgeDowning 10 54
(Tony Carroll) *prom: drvn 1/2-way: wknd fnl f* **20/1**

5322 **7** ¾ **Jacksonfire**[7] 6099 5-8-4 **46** (p) PhilDennis(3) 1 36
(Michael Mullineaux) *chsd ldrs: wnt 2nd 1/2-way: drvn to ld 2f out: hdd 1f out: grad wknd* **5/1**[2]

0052 **8** 1½ **Corporal Maddox**[14] 5817 10-9-5 **58** (p) LukeMorris 4 44
(Ronald Harris) *towards rr: hdwy to chse ldrs 1/2-way: wknd fnl f* **16/1**

0064 **9** 2 **Bois D'Ebene (IRE)**[15] 5783 3-9-6 **64** TimmyMurphy 12 43
(John O'Shea) *hld up: rdn and hung lft over 3f out: kpt on fnl 2f but no real imp* **20/1**

3030 **10** 7 **Gala Celebration (IRE)**[55] 4290 3-9-8 **66** FergusSweeney 11 27
(John Gallagher) *wnt to post early: chsd ldr to 1/2-way: rdn 3f out: wknd over 1f out* **8/1**

4- **11** 1 **Fox Mint**[260] 3-7-11 **48** (p) RhiainIngram(7) 15 6
(Karen George) *midfield: rdn 1/2-way: wknd 2f out* **50/1**

5060 **12** 1½ **Big Chill (IRE)**[34] 5111 5-9-12 **65** TrevorWhelan 9 22
(Patrick Chamings) *chsd ldrs tl rdn and lost pl 1/2-way: wknd 2f out* **14/1**

0030 **13** 2 **Royal Normandy**[10] 6004 5-8-4 **46** oh1 (b) EdwardGreatrex(3) 5
(Grace Harris) *led: rdn 3f out: hdd 2f out: wknd qckly* **25/1**

-400 **14** ½ **Mallymkun**[16] 5750 5-8-13 **52** TomMarquand 13 2
(David Loughnane) *led to post: midfield: rdn and wknd over 2f out* **25/1**

00/0 **15** 30 **Gifted Heir (IRE)**[13] 5895 13-8-7 **46** (p) KieranO'Neill 14
(Ray Peacock) *in tch 2f: sn rdn and bhd: t.o* **125/1**

1m 25.47s (2.27) **Going Correction** +0.30s/f (Good)
**WFA** 3 from 4yo+ 5lb **15** Ran SP% **129.6**
Speed ratings (Par 101): **99,98,96,94,94 92,91,89,87,79 78,76,74,73,39**
CSF £38.43 CT £185.35 TOTE £7.00: £2.20, £2.50, £2.20; EX 46.40 Trifecta £202.30.
**Owner** The Picnic Partnership **Bred** Old Carhue & Graeng Bloodstock **Trained** Blewbury, Oxon

**FOCUS**
The final race on the card looked pretty strong for the level, with plenty appearing fancied in the market to some extent. The form is rated around the runner-up.
T/Plt: £28.10 to a £1 stake. Pool: £54,744.50 - 1,422.0 winning units T/Qpdt: £9.40 to a £1 stake. Pool: £4,932.47 - 387.45 winning units **Richard Lowther**

## 5644 HAMILTON (R-H)

Thursday, August 24

**OFFICIAL GOING: Good to soft (good in places; 5.8) changing to soft after race 5 (7.10)**
Wind: Light, half behind Weather: Overcast, showers from race 2

### 6346 MOET & CHANDON #MOETMOMENT "HANDS AND HEELS" APPRENTICE H'CAP (RACING EXCELLENCE INITIATIVE) 1m 68y
5:10 (5:10) (Class 6) (0-60,61) 4-Y-0+ £3,234 (£962; £481; £240) Stalls Low

Form RPR
0603 **1** **Rioja Day (IRE)**[10] 5992 7-8-13 52..........(b) SeanMooney(3) 4 59
(Jim Goldie) *dwlt: hdwy to ld after 1f: sn clr: rdn and hrd pressed fr over 2f out: edgd lft over 1f out: rdn and kpt on wl fnl f* **12/1**
0640 **2** 1 1/2 **Argaki (IRE)**[12] 5917 7-9-7 60.......... TobyEley(3) 2 64
(Keith Dalgleish) *hld up in tch: effrt and rdn over 2f out: chsd wnr ins fnl f: r.o* **8/1**
3450 **3** 2 1/4 **Colour Contrast (IRE)**[19] 5649 4-9-3 56..........(p) JamieGormley(3) 12 55
(Iain Jardine) *hld up in tch: smooth hdwy and ev ch over 2f out: rdn over 1f out: kpt on same pce fnl f* **7/1**[3]
6530 **4** nse **Red Shadow**[10] 5992 8-8-2 46..........(v) RhonaPindar(8) 14 45
(Alistair Whillans) *hld up midfield: hdwy on outside over 2f out: effrt and rdn over 1f out: one pce fnl f* **50/1**
-004 **5** 3/4 **Little Pippin**[19] 5649 4-8-10 46 oh1.......... SeamusCronin 9 43
(Tony Coyle) *hld up: rdn and hdwy over 2f out: no imp over 1f out* **15/2**
-011 **6** 3 1/4 **Bigbadboy (IRE)**[7] 6092 4-9-6 56 6ex.......... ConnorMurtagh 3 46
(Clive Mulhall) *t.k.h: chsd clr ldr after 1f: ev ch and rdn over 1f out: checked and outpcd over 1f out* **9/4**[1]
0340 **7** 3 1/2 **Let Right Be Done**[10] 5992 5-8-5 47..........(b) LeanneFerguson(6) 1 29
(Linda Perratt) *s.i.s: plld hrd in rr: rdn and effrt over 2f out: sn no imp* **10/1**
0000 **8** 1 3/4 **Swiss Lait**[17] 5698 6-8-7 46.......... PaulaMuir(3) 8 24
(Patrick Holmes) *s.i.s: hld up: rdn and effrt over 2f out: sn n.d* **33/1**
3005 **9** 1 1/2 **False Id**[13] 5897 4-9-9 59..........(t) HarrisonShaw 6 34
(Marjorie Fife) *chsd ldrs: rdn 3f out: wknd over 1f out* **5/1**[2]
050 **10** 4 **Intiwin (IRE)**[46] 4661 5-9-8 61.......... SebastianWoods(3) 5 27
(Linda Perratt) *hld up: rdn over 3f out: btn fnl 2f* **16/1**
5064 **11** 4 **Cadmium**[15] 5802 6-8-3 47..........(p) LaurenSteade(8) 7 4
(Micky Hammond) *dwlt: hld up: stdy hdwy on outside 3f out: wknd wl over 1f out* **20/1**
00-0 **12** 13 **Dark Illustrator**[76] 3550 4-8-9 48.......... RyanTimby(3) 13
(Lynn Siddall) *dwlt: hld up: struggling over 3f out: sn btn* **66/1**
1m 52.44s (4.04) **Going Correction** +0.25s/f (Good) 12 Ran SP% 116.6
Speed ratings (Par 101): **89,87,85,85,84 81,77,75,74,70 66,53**
CSF £99.89 CT £740.07 TOTE £10.70: £3.50, £2.70, £2.20; EX 65.60 Trifecta £523.80.
**Owner** Ayrshire Racing & Partner **Bred** Mrs Eleanor Commins **Trained** Uplawmoor, E Renfrews
**FOCUS**
After a dry day the official going was changed to good to soft, good in places. Races 1,4,5 & 7 increased by 13yds. The opener was a just modest apprentice handicap. It's rate around the winner to the best of this year's form.

### 6347 BILL AND DAVID MCHARG EBF MAIDEN STKS (PLUS 10 RACE) 6f 6y
5:40 (5:41) (Class 4) 2-Y-0 £5,175 (£1,540; £769; £384) Stalls High

Form RPR
0233 **1** **Queen Penn**[19] 5659 2-8-11 74.......... SammyJoBell(3) 2 78+
(Richard Fahey) *prom on outside: hdwy to ld over 1f out: sn rdn and drifted lft: drew clr ins fnl f* **3/1**[1]
**2** 3 1/2 **Grise Lightning (FR)** 2-9-0 0.......... JackGarritty 8 68
(Richard Fahey) *in tch: hdwy to chse wnr over 1f out: checked and swtchd rt ins fnl f: edgd rt: no ch w wnr* **6/1**[3]
0322 **3** 2 **Kirbec (IRE)**[10] 5990 2-9-0 71.......... PaulMulrennan 5 62
(Keith Dalgleish) *w ldr: rdn whn checked over 1f out: kpt on same pce fnl f* **3/1**[1]
55 **4** 1 3/4 **Sulafaat (IRE)**[17] 5702 2-9-0 0.......... JoeFanning 1 56
(Mark Johnston) *bhd and outpcd: hdwy on outside 2f out: rdn and no imp fnl f* **14/1**
**5** 3/4 **Gabrials Centurion (IRE)** 2-9-5 0.......... DavidNolan 3 59
(David O'Meara) *in tch: rdn and outpcd wl over 1f out: r.o ins fnl f: no imp* **7/1**
**6** 2 1/4 **Jonboy** 2-9-2 0.......... CliffordLee(3) 7 52
(David Barron) *slt ld to over 1f out: rdn and wknd fnl f* **9/2**[2]
56 **7** 2 1/2 **Retirement Beckons**[12] 5918 2-9-5 0.......... ShaneGray 6 45
(Linda Perratt) *dwlt: bhd and outpcd: struggling whn hung rt over 2f out: nvr on terms* **100/1**
2 **8** 1 1/4 **Eva Docc (IRE)**[84] 3237 2-9-0 0.......... JasonHart 9 36
(Keith Dalgleish) *w ldrs against stands' rail: rdn over 2f out: wknd over 1f out* **17/2**
1m 14.71s (2.51) **Going Correction** +0.40s/f (Good) 8 Ran SP% 113.2
Speed ratings (Par 96): **99,94,91,89,88 85,82,80**
CSF £21.03 TOTE £3.70: £1.40, £2.10, £1.20; EX 25.80 Trifecta £61.00.
**Owner** Nick Bradley Racing 36 & Partner **Bred** Lyndsey Shaw & Mr Brian Johnson **Trained** Musley Bank, N Yorks
**FOCUS**
A fair maiden and a decisive winner. The form is rated with feet on the ground.

### 6348 BETFREEBETS.UK WILLIAM THE LION H'CAP 6f 6y
6:10 (6:10) (Class 4) (0-85,86) 3-Y-0+ £6,469 (£1,925; £962; £481) Stalls High

Form RPR
2210 **1** **Manshood (IRE)**[19] 5637 4-9-9 81..........(b) PaulMulrennan 7 90+
(Paul Midgley) *prom: effrt whn nt clr run over 1f out to ins fnl f: sn swtchd rt: styd on wl to ld last stride* **5/1**[2]
2030 **2** nse **Distant Past**[55] 4306 6-9-7 86..........(p) SeamusCronin(7) 2 94
(Kevin Ryan) *prom on outside: hdwy to ld appr fnl f: kpt on: hdd last stride* **11/1**
2231 **3** 1 1/4 **Dirchill (IRE)**[19] 5645 3-9-0 75.......... JoeFanning 8 79
(David Barron) *cl up: effrt and ev ch over 1f out to ins fnl f: one pce towards fin* **9/4**[1]
1420 **4** 2 1/4 **Inexes**[17] 5699 5-9-8 80..........(p) BarryMcHugh 4 77
(Marjorie Fife) *dwlt: bhd and outpcd: hdwy over 1f out: kpt on fnl f: nvr able to chal* **8/1**
2020 **5** 1 **Harwoods Volante (IRE)**[5] 6205 6-9-10 82.......... SamJames 6 76
(David O'Meara) *led against stands' rail: rdn and hdd appr fnl f: sn outpcd* **6/1**[3]
1661 **6** 2 1/4 **Alfie's Angel (IRE)**[10] 5994 3-8-13 77 6ex.......... AdamMcNamara(3) 1 63
(Bryan Smart) *bhd on outside: rdn along 1/2-way: no imp over 1f out* **8/1**
0320 **7** 7 **Tommy G**[12] 5947 4-8-13 78.......... SeanMooney(7) 3 42
(Jim Goldie) *bhd and sn outpcd: sme hdwy over 2f out: sn no imp* **8/1**
002 **8** 3 1/4 **Dark Forest**[35] 5070 4-8-11 69..........(p) CamHardie 5 23
(Marjorie Fife) *chsd ldrs: drvn and outpcd over 2f out: sn btn* **10/1**
1m 13.67s (1.47) **Going Correction** +0.40s/f (Good)
**WFA** 3 from 4yo+ 3lb 8 Ran SP% 112.5
Speed ratings (Par 105): **106,105,104,101,99 96,87,83**
CSF £55.45 CT £155.94 TOTE £5.40: £1.40, £2.50, £1.50; EX 39.70 Trifecta £233.90.
**Owner** Taylor's Bloodstock Ltd **Bred** John McEnery **Trained** Westow, N Yorks
**FOCUS**
A decent handicap and a thrilling finish. The winner is rated a shade better than the bare form.

### 6349 SODEXO SCOTTISH TROPHY H'CAP 1m 1f 35y
6:40 (6:40) (Class 3) (0-90,91) 3-Y-0+
£15,562 (£4,660; £2,330; £1,165; £582; £292) Stalls Low

Form RPR
2311 **1** **Whatsthemessage (IRE)**[13] 5881 3-8-10 79.......... JoeFanning 1 94
(Keith Dalgleish) *chsd clr ldng pair: smooth hdwy to ld over 1f out: sn rdn: edgd lft ins fnl f: kpt on wl* **7/1**[3]
2123 **2** hd **To Dibba**[26] 5425 3-9-3 86.......... HarryBentley 12 100
(Roger Varian) *hld up midfield: pushed along and hdwy over 3f out: effrt and ev ch over 1f out: kpt on fnl f: hld cl home* **9/4**[1]
3116 **3** 4 1/2 **Company Asset (IRE)**[26] 5439 4-9-10 89.......... LewisEdmunds(3) 14 94
(Kevin Ryan) *s.i.s: hld up: rdn over 3f out: hdwy wl over 1f out: chsd clr ldng pair ins fnl f: r.o: nt pce to chal* **13/2**[2]
310 **4** 1 3/4 **Carnageo (FR)**[19] 5668 4-9-6 85..........(v[1]) AdamMcNamara(3) 3 86
(Richard Fahey) *in tch: effrt and drvn along 3f out: no imp fr over 1f out* **11/1**
040 **5** 2 **Candelisa (IRE)**[61] 4077 4-10-1 91.......... JackGarritty 5 88
(Jedd O'Keeffe) *hld up in tch: hdwy to chse ldrs over 2f out: wknd ins fnl f* **11/1**
1011 **6** 2 1/4 **Wealth Tax**[14] 5843 4-9-7 83.......... PaulMulrennan 8 75
(Ed Dunlop) *midfield: drvn and outpcd 4f out: rallied over 1f out: sn no imp* **9/1**
3601 **7** hd **Apres Midi (IRE)**[24] 5475 4-8-12 77.......... CliffordLee(3) 9 69
(K R Burke) *pressed ldr and clr of remainder after 2f: led over 3f out: rdn and hdd over 1f out: wknd ins fnl f* **10/1**
5030 **8** 1 3/4 **Archie's Advice**[1] 6316 6-8-5 72.......... RowanScott(5) 4 60
(Keith Dalgleish) *dwlt: hld up: drvn along over 3f out: hdwy over 1f out: sn no imp* **33/1**
0103 **9** 1 1/4 **Auspicion**[17] 5704 5-8-12 74.......... AndrewMullen 2 60
(Tom Tate) *midfield: drvn along and outpcd over 2f out: n.d after* **14/1**
404 **10** 3 3/4 **Toboggan's Fire**[17] 5699 4-9-1 77.......... ShaneGray 6 55
(Ann Duffield) *s.i.s: hld up: rdn and outpcd over 2f out: sn btn* **20/1**
2014 **11** 3 **Strong Steps**[12] 5949 5-9-10 86.......... PatrickMathers 15 58
(Jim Goldie) *hld up: drvn and struggling over 3f out: nvr on terms* **33/1**
1020 **12** 1 1/4 **Jacbequick**[12] 5924 6-9-7 86..........(p) JoshDoyle(3) 11 55
(David O'Meara) *hld up midfield: rdn and outpcd over 2f out: sn btn* **33/1**
1010 **13** 4 1/2 **Amy Blair**[19] 5650 4-8-10 72..........(h) JasonHart 7 31
(Keith Dalgleish) *led: clr w one other after 2f: hdd over 3f out: wknd fnl 2f* **20/1**
2m 0.26s (0.56) **Going Correction** +0.25s/f (Good)
**WFA** 3 from 4yo+ 7lb 13 Ran SP% 117.4
Speed ratings (Par 107): **107,106,102,101,99 97,97,95,94,91 88,87,83**
CSF £20.99 CT £106.28 TOTE £7.60: £2.20, £2.00, £2.10; EX 33.50 Trifecta £159.00.
**Owner** Ronnie Docherty **Bred** Lynn Lodge Stud **Trained** Carluke, S Lanarks
**FOCUS**
Race distance increased by 13yds. A useful handicap and the only three-year-olds in the field fought out a close finish, clear of the rest. The winner has improved plenty in recent starts.

### 6350 SODEXO MAIDEN STKS 1m 1f 35y
7:10 (7:10) (Class 5) 3-Y-0+ £3,881 (£1,155; £577; £288) Stalls Low

Form RPR
23 **1** **White Rosa (IRE)**[54] 4378 3-9-0 0..........(h[1]) PaulMulrennan 2 71
(Hugo Palmer) *t.k.h early: trckd ldr: led and edgd rt wl over 1f out: pushed out fnl f: comf* **2/5**[1]
**2** 3 **Haroon (IRE)**[68] 3850 3-9-2 72..........(t) JoshDoyle(3) 5 70
(Tony Coyle) *led at modest gallop: rdn and hdd wl over 1f out: sn one pce* **5/1**[2]
5436 **3** 4 **Satish**[14] 5832 4-9-12 66..........(b) DavidNolan 3 62
(David O'Meara) *hld up in tch: stdy hdwy 3f out: rdn and outpcd by first two wl over 1f out* **5/1**[2]
5 **4** 8 **Biba**[9] 6044 3-8-9 0..........(p[1]) RowanScott(5) 1 40
(Keith Dalgleish) *t.k.h: trckd ldrs: drvn and outpcd over 3f out: n.d after* **25/1**[3]
-60 **5** 11 **Anna's Legacy**[9] 6044 4-9-0 0.......... SeanMooney(7) 6 17
(Jim Goldie) *t.k.h: trckd ldrs: drvn and wknd over 2f out* **100/1**
2m 6.05s (6.35) **Going Correction** +0.25s/f (Good)
**WFA** 3 from 4yo 7lb 5 Ran SP% 109.6
Speed ratings (Par 103): **81,78,74,67,57**
CSF £2.84 TOTE £1.20: £1.10, £2.10; EX 2.90 Trifecta £4.30.
**Owner** Highbank Stud **Bred** Highbank Stud Llp **Trained** Newmarket, Suffolk
**FOCUS**
Race distance increased by 13yds. An ordinary maiden, run at a steady pace, and the short-priced favourite made no mistake. She didn't have to improve.

### 6351 OVERTON FARM H'CAP 5f 7y
7:40 (7:40) (Class 5) (0-70,70) 3-Y-0+ £3,881 (£1,155; £577; £288) Stalls Centre

Form RPR
6300 **1** **One Boy (IRE)**[12] 5930 6-9-4 64.......... PaulMulrennan 1 75
(Paul Midgley) *swtchd lft sn after s: mde all: pushed clr fr over 1f out: comf* **4/1**[3]
0133 **2** 2 3/4 **Camanche Grey (IRE)**[26] 5418 6-8-9 55.......... CamHardie 6 56
(Ben Haslam) *bhd and outpcd: rdn and hdwy over 1f out: chsd (clr) wnr last 50yds: kpt on* **11/2**
4530 **3** 1 **Compton River**[15] 5804 5-9-2 65.......... AdamMcNamara(3) 3 63
(Bryan Smart) *fly-jmpd s: pressed wnr: rdn over 1f out: no ex and lost 2nd last 50yds* **7/1**

4324 **4** *shd* **Hamidans Girl (IRE)**[12] 5919 3-9-0 **62**......................(p[1]) AndrewMullen 4 59
(Keith Dalgleish) *bhd on outside: rdn and hdwy over 2f out: effrt and disp 2nd pl over 1f out: no ex ins fnl f* **5/2**[1]

3664 **5** *¾* **Economic Crisis (IRE)**[12] 5920 8-9-10 **70**.................. PatrickMathers 2 64
(Colin Teague) *taken early to post: cl up tl rdn and outpcd over 1f out: btn fnl f* **15/2**

6631 **6** *shd* **Star Cracker (IRE)**[10] 5995 5-8-8 **61** 6ex................(p) JamieGormley(7) 5 55
(Jim Goldie) *chsd ldng gp: effrt whn nt clr run briefly wl over 1f out: edgd rt and sn wknd* **7/2**[2]

1m 1.71s (1.71) **Going Correction** +0.40s/f (Good)
**WFA** 3 from 5yo+ 2lb **6 Ran SP% 110.4**
Speed ratings (Par 103): **102,97,96,95,94 94**
CSF £24.59 TOTE £5.10: £2.10, £3.30; EX 18.70 Trifecta £131.30.
**Owner** R Wardlaw & Partner **Bred** Tom Radley **Trained** Westow, N Yorks

**FOCUS**
The going was changed to soft before the sixth race. Not the strongest handicap for the grade. The winner bounced back to form.

## 6352 RACING UK PROFITS RETURNED TO RACING H'CAP 1m 4f 15y

**8:10** (8:10) (Class 6) (0-55,55) 3-Y-O+ **£3,234** (£962; £481; £240) **Stalls** Low

Form RPR

06 **1** **Mick The Poser (IRE)**[25] 4611 3-8-6 **46** oh1...............(p[1]) JoeFanning 12 52
(Jennie Candlish) *chsd ldrs: effrt and rdn over 2f out: led ins fnl f: hld on wl* **5/1**[3]

1505 **2** *hd* **Paddy's Rock (IRE)**[14] 5824 6-9-6 **54**.........................(p) JoshDoyle(3) 4 59
(Lynn Siddall) *hld up: rdn and hdwy over 2f out: chsd wnr ins fnl f: r.o fin* **11/1**

64 **3** *1* **Tambour**[73] 3650 4-9-10 **55**...........................................(t) AndrewMullen 7 58
(Keith Dalgleish) *dwlt: hld up: hdwy on outside 3f out: led over 1f out to ins fnl f: no ex* **12/1**

3445 **4** *2 ½* **Elite Icon**[14] 5850 3-7-13 **46**........................................... JamieGormley(7) 9 46
(Iain Jardine) *midfield on outside: effrt and drvn along over 2f out: one pce fr over 1f out* **11/4**[1]

4133 **5** *2* **Highway Robber**[14] 5832 4-9-8 **53**............................... PaulMulrennan 6 49
(Wilf Storey) *chsd ldr: smooth hdwy to ld over 2f out: rdn and hdd over 1f out: wknd ins fnl f* **9/2**[2]

**6** *3 ¼* **Miller And Cook (IRE)**[58] 4193 6-8-13 **47**............ AdamMcNamara(3) 2 38
(Mark Michael McNiff, Ire) *dwlt: sn midfield on ins: drvn along 3f out: outpcd fnl 2f* **14/1**

4562 **7** *3* **New Abbey Angel (IRE)**[10] 5997 4-9-4 **54**................ RowanScott(5) 11 40
(Keith Dalgleish) *led to over 2f out: sn rdn and wknd* **17/2**

0236 **8** *2 ¼* **Schmooze (IRE)**[12] 5923 8-9-2 **50**........................ SammyJoBell(3) 10 32
(Linda Perratt) *hld up: drvn along and outpcd over 3f out: sn btn* **16/1**

0306 **9** *1* **Hellavashock**[19] 5649 4-9-4 **49**.......................................... BarryMcHugh 8 30
(Alistair Whillans) *hld up towards rr: drvn and outpcd over 2f out: sn btn* **16/1**

4054 **10** *3 ½* **Stardrifter**[10] 5997 5-9-7 **52**..............................................(p) DavidNolan 5 27
(Linda Perratt) *bhd: struggling over 3f out: nvr on terms* **14/1**

0255 **11** *15* **Moon Over Rio (IRE)**[23] 5493 6-9-7 **52**.........................(p[1]) CamHardie 3 3
(Ben Haslam) *midfield: drvn and outpcd over 3f out: btn fnl 2f* **16/1**

2m 45.73s (7.13) **Going Correction** +0.25s/f (Good)
**WFA** 3 from 4yo+ 9lb **11 Ran SP% 119.0**
Speed ratings (Par 101): **86,85,85,83,82 80,78,76,75,73 63**
CSF £59.84 CT £634.18 TOTE £5.50: £1.90, £3.30, £3.50; EX 67.50 Trifecta £1601.50.
**Owner** Alan Baxter & Matt Barrett **Bred** Mrs E Thompson **Trained** Basford Green, Staffs

**FOCUS**
Race distance increased by 13yds. A low-grade handicap and another close finish. Straightforward, modest form.
T/Plt: £26.40 to a £1 stake. Pool: £49,682.25 - 1,372.16 winning units T/Qpdt: £6.00 to a £1 stake. Pool: £5,520.83 - 674.06 winning units **Richard Young**

# 6325 YORK (L-H)

Thursday, August 24

**OFFICIAL GOING: Good to soft (good in places; overall 6.7, home straight: far side 6.8, centre 6.8, stands' side 6.7)**
Wind: Moderate across Weather: Cloudy with showers

## 6353 GOFFS PREMIER YEARLING STKS 6f

**1:55** (1:56) (Class 2) 2-Y-O

**£184,350** (£55,350; £27,510; £13,680; £6,840; £3,600) **Stalls** Low

Form RPR

241 **1** **Tangled (IRE)**[41] 4858 2-8-11 **88**........................................... SeanLevey 3 102
(Richard Hannon) *trckd ldrs towards far side: hdwy over 1f out: rdn to ld ent fnl f: drvn out* **15/2**

13 **2** *nk* **Great Prospector (IRE)**[40] 4906 2-8-11 **0**...................... PaulHanagan 4 101
(Richard Fahey) *trckd ldrs towards far side: hdwy over 1f out: rdn to chal ent fnl f: sn drvn and ev ch: kpt on. 2nd of 11 in gp* **9/2**[2]

21 **3** *½* **Hey Jonesy (IRE)**[26] 5437 2-9-0 **0**...................................... KevinStott 18 103+
(Kevin Ryan) *led stands side gp: cl up: rdn and ev ch over 1f out: drvn ins fnl f: kpt on: 1st of 8 in gp* **3/1**[1]

6153 **4** *1 ½* **Alba Power (IRE)**[26] 5395 2-8-11 **97**............................... JamesDoyle 5 95
(Hugo Palmer) *hld up towards far side: hdwy wl over 1f out: sn swtchd lft to far rail and rdn: kpt on wl fnl f. 3rd of 11 in gp* **7/1**[3]

1002 **5** *3* **Darkanna (IRE)**[25] 5461 2-8-6 **97**.............................. BarryMcHugh 17 81
(Richard Fahey) *prom stands side: rdn along and outpcd over 1f out: drvn and edgd lft ins fnl f: kpt on wl towards fin. 2nd of 8 in gp* **11/1**

1212 **6** *¾* **Silver Starlight**[20] 5614 2-8-6 **80**..................................... DavidAllan 2 79
(Tim Easterby) *racd towards far side: overall ldr: rdn along wl over 1f out: drvn and hdd ent fnl f: grad wknd 4th of 11 in gp* **25/1**

2324 **7** *1* **Charnock Richard**[20] 5603 2-8-11 **74**.............................. TomEaves 6 81
(David Brown) *cl up towards far side: rdn to dispute ld wl over 1f out: drvn and wknd ent fnl f. 5th of 11 in gp* **100/1**

2601 **8** *nk* **Marnie James**[41] 4866 2-8-11 **82**..................................(t) OisinMurphy 10 80
(Iain Jardine) *midfield centre: rdn along wl over 1f out: kpt on fnl f. 6th of 11 in gp* **33/1**

3205 **9** *1 ½* **Inviolable Spirit (IRE)**[18] 5685 2-8-11 **76**................... JamieSpencer 12 75
(Richard Fahey) *.awkward s: sn swtchd towards far side: towards rr tl rdn along and kpt on fr over 1f out. 7th of 11 in gp* **33/1**

2410 **10** *¾* **Rufus King**[20] 5596 2-9-2 **102**.......................................... PJMcDonald 1 78
(Mark Johnston) *chsd ldrs far side: rdn along over 2f out: sn drvn and wknd. 8th of 11 in gp* **20/1**

115 **11** *½* **Guzman (IRE)**[41] 4858 2-8-11 **79**..................................(h[1]) FrankieDettori 19 72+
(Richard Fahey) *a towards rr stands side. 3rd of 8 in gp* **25/1**

534 **12** *hd* **Mr Greenlight**[13] 5879 2-8-11 **72**..................................... JamesSullivan 8 71
(Tim Easterby) *a towards rr far side. 9th of 11 in gp* **100/1**

44 **13** *1 ¼* **Gossip Column (IRE)**[20] 5608 2-8-11 **0**................................ FranBerry 7 67
(Charles Hills) *a towards rr far side. 9th of 11 in gp* **66/1**

1413 **14** *1 ¼* **Chatburn (IRE)**[26] 5440 2-8-11 **83**....................................... GrahamLee 9 64
(David O'Meara) *chsd ldrs towards far side: rdn along 2f out: sn wknd 10th of 11 in gp* **33/1**

0230 **15** *1 ½* **Angel Of The South (IRE)**[56] 4253 2-8-6 **74**......... JosephineGordon 13 54+
(Dean Ivory) *dwlt and rr stands side: rdn along and sme hdwy over 2f out n.d. 4th of 8 in gp* **50/1**

035 **16** *2 ¼* **Levante Player (IRE)**[54] 4335 2-8-11 **73**...........(p[1]) RichardKingscote 14 52+
(Tom Dascombe) *a towards rr stands side 5th of 8 in gp* **66/1**

1651 **17** *1 ¾* **Ventura Dragon (IRE)**[9] 6030 2-8-11 **73**...................... AndreaAtzeni 15 47+
(Richard Fahey) *chsd ldrs stands side: rdn along over 2f out: sn wknd 6th of 8 in gp* **33/1**

0461 **18** *8* **De Bruyne Horse**[19] 5679 2-9-2 **101**............................(b[1]) RyanMoore 16 28+
(Richard Hannon) *rr stands side whn j. path after 1f: sme hdwy over 2f out: rdn along wl over 1f out: bhd and eased fnl f 7th of 8 in gp* **7/1**[3]

243 **19** *¾* **Prince Ahwahnee**[41] 4826 2-8-11 **79**............................ SamHitchcott 20 21+
(Clive Cox) *a towards rr stands side 8th of 8 in gp* **50/1**

1m 12.23s (0.33) **Going Correction** +0.25s/f (Good) **19 Ran SP% 121.4**
Speed ratings (Par 100): **107,106,105,103,99 98,97,97,95,94 93,93,91,89,87 84,82,71,70**
CSF £35.66 TOTE £7.80: £2.50, £1.90, £1.50; EX 41.60 Trifecta £138.70.
**Owner** Martin Hughes & Nick Robinson **Bred** Tally-Ho Stud **Trained** East Everleigh, Wilts

**FOCUS**
The going was given as good to soft, good in places (GoingStick: 6.7. Home straight readings - far side 6.8; centre 6.8; stands' side 6.7). Wind: westerly 12mph, gusting 20mph, moderate crosswind). The rail was out 3 metres from the 1m1f point to the entrance to the home straight. They split into two groups and, as is often the case here, the far side had it. Hey Jonesy deserves plenty of credit for being involved in the finish given he drew clear on the stands' side. A step forward from Tangled, whose nursery win couldn't be working out better.

## 6354 SKY BET LOWTHER STKS (GROUP 2) (FILLIES) 6f

**2:25** (2:27) (Class 1) 2-Y-O

**£142,058** (£53,857; £26,953; £13,426; £6,738; £3,381) **Stalls** Low

Form RPR

1 **1** **Threading (IRE)**[22] 5528 2-9-0 **0**......................................... JamesDoyle 7 110
(Mark Johnston) *trckd ldrs: hdwy 2f out: chal over 1f out: rdn to ld ent fnl f: kpt on strly* **9/2**[3]

5151 **2** *1 ¾* **Madeline (IRE)**[34] 5109 2-9-0 **102**.................................. AndreaAtzeni 9 105
(Roger Varian) *trckd ldrs: hdwy 2f out: rdn over 1f out: chsd wnr ins fnl f: sn drvn and no imp towards fin* **7/2**[2]

0330 **3** *¾* **Mamba Noire (FR)**[12] 5941 2-9-0 **0**..............................(v[1]) ShaneFoley 4 102
(K J Condon, Ire) *towards rr: pushed along over 2f out: rdn and hdwy over 1f out: kpt on wl fnl f* **25/1**

1364 **4** *¾* **So Hi Society (IRE)**[28] 5329 2-9-0 **93**...................... RichardKingscote 3 100
(Archie Watson) *prom: rdn along and sltly outpcd wl over 1f out: kpt on u.p fnl f* **16/1**

11 **5** *nse* **Special Purpose (IRE)**[31] 5210 2-9-0 **88**........................... OisinMurphy 5 100
(William Haggas) *hld up in tch: hdwy on outer 2f out: sn chsng ldrs: rdn over 1f out: kpt on same pce fnl f* **6/1**

2 **6** *½* **Happy Like A Fool (USA)**[64] 3960 2-9-0 **0**...............(bt) FrankieDettori 6 99
(Wesley A Ward, U.S.A) *sn led: jnd and rdn over 1f out: hdd ent fnl f: wknd* **11/2**

102 **7** *3 ½* **Natural (IRE)**[34] 5109 2-9-0 **96**..................................... JamieSpencer 8 88
(Richard Hannon) *dwlt and rr: hdwy and swtchd lft to inner 2f out: sn chsng ldrs: wknd over 1f out* **12/1**

2566 **8** *½* **Neola**[19] 5659 2-9-0 **91**....................................................... GrahamLee 2 87
(Mick Channon) *trckd ldrs: pushed along over 2f out: sn rdn and wknd* **50/1**

2613 **9** *12* **Actress (IRE)**[11] 5973 2-9-0 **0**........................................... RyanMoore 1 51
(A P O'Brien, Ire) *prom: cl up over 3f out: rdn along over 2f out: sn wknd* **10/3**[1]

1m 12.48s (0.58) **Going Correction** +0.25s/f (Good) **9 Ran SP% 112.5**
Speed ratings (Par 103): **106,103,102,101,101 100,96,95,79**
CSF £19.96 TOTE £5.00: £1.90, £1.40, £5.60; EX 18.60 Trifecta £295.70.
**Owner** Sheikh Hamdan bin Mohammed Al Maktoum **Bred** Darley **Trained** Middleham Moor, N Yorks

**FOCUS**
Run at a good gallop, this is smart form and the ready winner is a top-class prospect. The runner-up's Newbury form could be rated this high.

## 6355 CLIPPER LOGISTICS H'CAP 7f 192y

**3:00** (3:02) (Class 2) 3-Y-O+

**£52,912** (£15,844; £7,922; £3,961; £1,980; £994) **Stalls** Low

Form RPR

1-10 **1** **Flaming Spear (IRE)**[26] 5393 5-9-2 **101**.......................... RobertWinston 4 112+
(Kevin Ryan) *trckd ldrs: smooth hdwy over 2f out: rdn to ld ent fnl f: kpt on strly* **10/1**[3]

0-51 **2** *1 ¾* **Qassem (IRE)**[16] 5744 4-8-13 **98**.......................... JosephineGordon 5 105
(Hugo Palmer) *trckd ldng pair: hdwy and cl up over 2f out: led wl over 1f out: sn jnd and rdn: hdd ent fnl f: kpt on* **10/1**[3]

5655 **3** *nk* **Firmament**[7] 6105 5-9-10 **109**..................................... DanielTudhope 6 115
(David O'Meara) *in tch: hdwy 3f out: rdn to chse ldrs over 1f out: drvn and kpt on same pce fnl f* **12/1**

0062 **4** *1 ¾* **Baraweez (IRE)**[18] 5688 7-8-10 **95**......................................... FranBerry 8 97
(Brian Ellison) *midfield: hdwy wl over 2f out: rdn wl over 1f out: styd on wl fnl f* **20/1**

6201 **5** *nse* **El Hayem (IRE)**[47] 4636 4-8-11 **96**.............................. FrankieDettori 13 98+
(Sir Michael Stoute) *dwlt and rr: gd hdwy on wd outside 3f out: chsd ldrs 2f out: rdn over 1f out: kpt on same pce fnl f* **10/1**[3]

0050 **6** *1* **Big Baz (IRE)**[64] 3963 7-8-13 **98**..................................... DougieCostello 18 98
(William Muir) *dwlt and rr: hdwy on outer over 2f out: rdn wl over 1f out: styd on strly fnl f* **40/1**

0000 **7** *hd* **Bravery (IRE)**[23] 5500 4-9-0 **99**................................... RichardKingscote 1 98
(David O'Meara) *trckd ldrs on inner: hdwy 3f out: rdn along over 2f out: drvn over 1f out: grad wknd* **20/1**

-304 **8** *1 ¼* **Victory Bond**[26] 5436 4-9-8 **107**..................................... PatCosgrave 15 104
(William Haggas) *trckd ldrs: hdwy over 2f out: n.m.r and rdn along wl over 1f out: sn no imp* **8/1**[2]

-P23 **9** *½* **Chelsea Lad (IRE)**[53] 4410 4-8-13 **98**.............................. AndreaAtzeni 2 93
(Martyn Meade) *in tch on inner: hdwy whn n.m.r and hmpd 2f out: swtchd rt and rdn over 1f out: no imp* **6/1**[1]

000 **10** *nk* **Mythical Madness**[20] 5594 6-9-1 **100**..........................(v) PhillipMakin 17 95
(David O'Meara) *hld up towards rr: hdwy over 2f out: sn rdn: kpt on fnl f* **33/1**

1100 **11** *nk* **G K Chesterton (IRE)**[20] 5594 4-9-0 **99**..........................(p) MartinLane 3 93
(Charlie Appleby) *trckd ldr: cl up 3f out: rdn along to dispute ld 2f out: sn drvn and wknd over 1f out* **25/1**

4021 **12** *1/2* **Northgate Lad (IRE)**[26] 5415 5-8-5 **95**.......................... BenRobinson(5) 11 88
(Brian Ellison) *led: rdn along over 2f out: drvn and hdd wl over 1f out: sn wknd* **50/1**

451 **13** *1 1/4* **Quixote (GER)**[117] 2141 7-8-10 **95**.......................... JimCrowley 10 85
(Michael Easterby) *towards rr: hdwy on outer 3f out: rdn along to chse ldrs 2f out: sn wknd* **25/1**

-126 **14** *1/2* **Ronald R (IRE)**[42] 4817 3-8-13 **104**.......................... RyanMoore 7 92
(Michael Bell) *midfield: sme hdwy on inner 3f out: rdn along 2f out: n.d* **6/1**[1]

0405 **15** *3/4* **One Word More (IRE)**[20] 5594 7-8-7 **92**..........................(h) DavidAllan 16 79
(Tim Easterby) *dwlt: a in rr* **10/1**[3]

2-20 **16** *5* **Blair House (IRE)**[20] 5594 4-9-3 **102**..........................(p[1]) JamesDoyle 19 78
(Charlie Appleby) *hld up: a towards rr* **12/1**

010 **17** *3 3/4* **El Vip (IRE)**[64] 3963 4-9-0 **99**.......................... JamieSpencer 12 66
(Luca Cumani) *midfield: pushed along 3f out: rdn over 2f out: sn wknd* **10/1**[3]

1m 41.27s (2.27) **Going Correction** +0.575s/f (Yiel)
**WFA** 3 from 4yo+ 6lb **17** Ran SP% **125.1**
Speed ratings (Par 109): **111,109,108,107,107 106,105,104,104,103 103,103,101,101,100 95,91**
CSF £99.57 CT £799.25 TOTE £12.40: £3.00, £2.70, £3.30, £4.70; EX 137.10 Trifecta £1490.60.

**Owner** Tony Bloom **Bred** Gerry Flannery Developments **Trained** Hambleton, N Yorks
■ Stewards' Enquiry : Robert Winston 3 day ban - failed to weigh in with all the equipment with which he weighed out (7/8/10 Sep)

**FOCUS**
Race distance increased by 36.5yds. A competitive handicap on paper, but not that many got into it, and the winner finished well on top. Solid form, Flaming Spear stepping up on his AW win.

## 6356 DARLEY YORKSHIRE OAKS (GROUP 1) (BRITISH CHAMPIONS SERIES) (F&M) 1m 3f 188y
**3:35** (3:36) (Class 1) 3-Y-O+

**£198,485** (£75,250; £37,660; £18,760; £9,415; £4,725) **Stalls** Centre

Form RPR

1111 **1** **Enable**[26] 5394 3-8-12 126.......................... FrankieDettori 1 124+
(John Gosden) *mde all: pushed along and qcknd 3f out: rdn clr wl over 1f out: kpt on strly: v readily* **1/4**[1]

3514 **2** *5* **Coronet**[40] 4928 3-8-12 108.......................... OlivierPeslier 6 115
(John Gosden) *trckd ldng pair: hdwy over 2f out: rdn along wl over 1f out: kpt on fnl f: tk 2nd towards fin* **16/1**

-446 **3** *3/4* **Queen's Trust**[21] 5571 4-9-7 118.......................... JimCrowley 2 114
(Sir Michael Stoute) *trckd wnr: effrt 3f out: rdn along 2f out: drvn over 1f out: kpt on same pce fnl f: lost 2nd towards fin* **12/1**[3]

11 **4** *hd* **Nezwaah**[53] 4419 4-9-7 116.......................... AndreaAtzeni 4 113
(Roger Varian) *hld up: hdwy wl over 2f out: rdn wl over 1f out: drvn and kpt on fnl f* **7/1**[2]

3661 **5** *9* **Alluringly (USA)**[8] 6080 3-8-12 105.......................... RyanMoore 5 99
(A P O'Brien, Ire) *.hld up in rr: effrt over 3f out: sn rdn along and n.d* **16/1**

-123 **6** *13* **Abingdon (USA)**[18] 5691 4-9-7 108.......................... RichardKingscote 3 78
(Sir Michael Stoute) *trckd ldrs: pushed along 4f out: rdn over 3f out: outpcd and bhd fnl 2f* **33/1**

2m 35.79s (2.59) **Going Correction** +0.575s/f (Yiel)
**WFA** 3 from 4yo 9lb **6** Ran SP% **114.9**
Speed ratings (Par 117): **114,110,110,110,104 95**
CSF £6.66 TOTE £1.20: £1.10, £4.60; EX 5.20 Trifecta £27.00.
**Owner** K Abdullah **Bred** Juddmonte Farms Ltd **Trained** Newmarket, Suffolk

**FOCUS**
Race distance increased by 43yds. This looked a straightforward opportunity for Enable and the brilliant filly duly won as she liked. She's rated below her best, with stablemate Coronet the best guide to the standard.

## 6357 BRITISH EBF & SIR HENRY CECIL GALTRES STKS (LISTED RACE) (F&M) 1m 3f 188y
**4:15** (4:17) (Class 1) 3-Y-O+

**£39,697** (£15,050; £7,532; £3,752; £1,883; £945) **Stalls** Centre

Form RPR

-103 **1** **Fleur Forsyte**[19] 5658 3-8-12 94..........................(h) DanielMuscutt 6 105+
(James Fanshawe) *hld up towards rr: stdy hdwy 4f out: chsd ldrs 3f out: led over 2f out: jnd and rdn wl over 1f out: drvn and kpt on wl fnl f* **12/1**

0-13 **2** *2 1/4* **More Mischief**[33] 5155 5-9-11 102.......................... JoeyHaynes 9 105
(Jedd O'Keeffe) *trckd ldrs: hdwy on outer 4f out: effrt over 2f out and sn cl up: rdn to chal wl over 1f out: drvn and kpt on same pce fnl f* **9/1**

1-3 **3** *1* **Aljezeera**[96] 2827 3-8-12 88.......................... FrankieDettori 8 99
(Luca Cumani) *in tch: pushed along over 5f out: rdn along and lost pl over 4f out: sn in rr: hdwy wl over 1f out: kpt on u.p fnl f* **6/1**[2]

-641 **4** *1 3/4* **Ouja**[15] 5796 3-8-12 77.......................... JimCrowley 5 97
(John Gosden) *hld up in rr: hdwy on outer 3f out: rdn along 2f out: kpt on u.p fnl f* **20/1**

3005 **5** *nse* **Serenada**[8] 6074 3-8-12 98.......................... AndreaAtzeni 3 97
(Roger Varian) *trckd ldrs: hdwy 3f out: rdn along 2f out: swtchd lft and drvn ent fnl f: kpt on* **20/1**

3541 **6** *1 3/4* **Euro Nightmare (IRE)**[24] 5470 3-8-12 91.......................... GrahamLee 10 94
(Keith Dalgleish) *hld up in rr: hdwy 3f out: rdn along to chse ldrs wl over 1f out: sn drvn and no imp fnl f* **20/1**

5112 **7** *3/4* **Mori**[63] 3995 3-9-2 106.......................... RyanMoore 7 97
(Sir Michael Stoute) *trckd ldr: cl up 4f out: rdn along 3f out: drvn wl over 1f out: sn btn* **10/11**[1]

1011 **8** *3/4* **Curlew River**[14] 5820 3-8-12 95.......................... JamesDoyle 4 91
(Mark Johnston) *led: pushed along 4f out: rdn over 3f out: hdd over 2f out: sn wknd* **7/1**[3]

352 **9** *7* **Shearling**[26] 5401 4-9-7 0.......................... BenCurtis 1 79
(Brian Ellison) *trckd ldng pair on inner: pushed along 4f out: rdn over 3f out: wknd over 2f out* **50/1**

1210 **10** *8* **Zain Arion (IRE)**[75] 3586 4-9-7 85.......................... JFEgan 2 66
(John Butler) *in tch: hdwy over 4f out: rdn along over 3f out: sn outpcd and bhd fnl 2f* **50/1**

2m 37.12s (3.92) **Going Correction** +0.575s/f (Yiel)
**WFA** 3 from 4yo+ 9lb **10** Ran SP% **115.1**
Speed ratings (Par 111): **109,107,106,105,105 104,103,103,98,93**
CSF £102.82 TOTE £14.20: £3.00, £2.50, £2.30; EX 65.20 Trifecta £1416.90.

**Owner** Normandie Stud Ltd **Bred** Normandie Stud Ltd **Trained** Newmarket, Suffolk

**FOCUS**
Race distance increased by 43yds. The runner-up is a reliable performer at this level and helps set the standard, as does the fifth.

## 6358 BRITISH STALLION STUDS EBF FILLIES' H'CAP 7f
**4:50** (4:51) (Class 2) (0-105,100) 3-Y-O+

**£43,575** (£13,048; £6,524; £3,262; £1,631; £819) **Stalls** Low

Form RPR

1222 **1** **Lincoln Rocks**[12] 5927 4-9-10 **100**.......................... DanielTudhope 10 110
(David O'Meara) *racd wd: cl up: led over 2f out: rdn over 1f out: drvn and kpt on wl fnl f* **8/1**[3]

0415 **2** *1 1/4* **Breakable**[12] 5914 6-9-4 **94**.......................... DavidAllan 2 100
(Tim Easterby) *in tch: hdwy to trck ldrs 3f out: rdn to chse wnr over 1f out: drvn and kpt on fnl f* **10/1**

2402 **3** *3/4* **Angel Of Darkness**[11] 5965 3-8-2 **83**.......................... PaulHanagan 16 85
(Charles Hills) *stdd and swtchd lft s: in rr: hdwy 3f out: rdn wl over 1f out: kpt on wl u.p fnl f* **25/1**

4131 **4** *1* **Bint Arcano (FR)**[28] 5317 4-9-0 **90**.......................... JoeDoyle 9 91
(Julie Camacho) *in tch: hdwy to trck ldrs 1/2-way: chsd ldrs wl over 1f out: sn rdn: drvn and kpt on same pce fnl f* **16/1**

441 **5** *3/4* **Caridade (USA)**[22] 5538 3-8-2 **83**.......................... JimmyQuinn 13 80
(Kevin Ryan) *swtchd lft s and towards rr: hdwy over 3f out: rdn to chse ldrs 2f out: drvn and kpt on same pce appr fnl f* **14/1**

2-45 **6** *nk* **Gheedaa (USA)**[41] 4864 3-8-11 **92**.......................... JimCrowley 8 88
(William Haggas) *trckd ldrs: hdwy over 2f out: rdn wl over 1f out: drvn and kpt on same pce fnl f* **5/1**[2]

052 **7** *nk* **Lavetta**[20] 5616 5-8-8 **84**.......................... BenCurtis 12 82
(Sally Haynes) *racd wd: prom: rdn along 3f out: grad wknd fnl 2f* **20/1**

1-05 **8** *1/2* **Cristal Fizz (IRE)**[67] 3882 3-9-4 **99**..........................(p[1]) RyanMoore 4 93
(William Haggas) *dwlt and rr: hdwy over 2f out: sn rdn: kpt on fnl f* **4/1**[1]

0111 **9** *3 3/4* **Whispered Kiss**[15] 5813 4-8-9 **85**.......................... GrahamLee 7 71
(Mike Murphy) *t.k.h: cl up: rdn along wl over 2f out: sn wknd* **8/1**[3]

06 **10** *nk* **Cheval Blanche (USA)**[40] 4903 3-7-13 **85**.......................... DavidEgan(5) 5 68
(Michael Bell) *dwlt and rr: hdwy wl over 2f out: swtchd lft and rdn wl over 1f out: sn ev ch: drvn and wknd fnl f* **16/1**

0602 **11** *2 1/4* **Clear Water (IRE)**[14] 5828 4-8-11 **87**.......................... KevinStott 15 66
(Michael Wigham) *stdd and swtchd lft s: a in rr* **12/1**

3521 **12** *1 1/2* **Acadian Angel (IRE)**[42] 4797 3-8-0 **81** oh4.......................... JamesSullivan 3 54
(John Quinn) *midfield: hdwy and in tch 1/2-way: rdn along wl over 2f out: sn wknd* **28/1**

0200 **13** *4 1/2* **Poet's Princess**[34] 5117 3-8-5 **86**.......................... PJMcDonald 6 47
(Hughie Morrison) *led: rdn along over 3f out: hdd over 2f out: sn drvn and wknd* **20/1**

1214 **14** *8* **Ghadaayer (IRE)**[23] 5506 3-8-4 **85**.......................... AntonioFresu 1 24
(Sir Michael Stoute) *chasded ldrs: rdn along wl over 2f out: sn wknd* **10/1**

1m 26.51s (1.21) **Going Correction** +0.40s/f (Good)
**WFA** 3 from 4yo+ 5lb **14** Ran SP% **120.0**
Speed ratings (Par 96): **109,107,106,105,104 104,104,103,99,98 96,94,89,80**
CSF £80.68 CT £1975.34 TOTE £8.40: £2.40, £2.90, £4.90; EX 84.00 Trifecta £2960.90.
**Owner** Peter Smith P C Coaches Limited **Bred** James Ortega Bloodstock **Trained** Upper Helmsley, N Yorks

**FOCUS**
Run at a good gallop, two of the older performers came to the fore and the form looks useful. A smart effort from Lincoln Rocks under top weight.
T/Jkpt: Not Won. T/Plt: £667.60 to a £1 stake. Pool: £304,134.02 - 332.53 winning units T/Qpdt: £136.50 to a £1 stake. Pool: £15,510.23 - 84.06 winning units **Joe Rowntree**

6359 - 6364a (Foreign Racing) - See Raceform Interactive

# 6170 CLAIREFONTAINE (R-H)
Thursday, August 24

**OFFICIAL GOING: Turf: good**

## 6365a PRIX DE L'EPINE (H'CAP) (4YO) (TURF) 1m 4f
**2:35** 4-Y-O **£8,119** (£3,247; £2,435; £1,623; £811)

RPR

**1** **Dostoyevsky (IRE)**[87] 4-9-5 **0**.......................... DavidBreux 11 59
(N Caullery, France) **131/10**

**2** *3/4* **Swing Glaz (FR)**[108] 4-9-4 **0**..........................(b) MaximeGuyon 6 57
(C Lotoux, France) **23/5**[1]

**3** *2* **Scottish Sun (FR)**[87] 4-8-5 **0**.......................... AurelienLemaitre 4 41
(C Boutin, France) **89/10**

**4** *1/2* **Franko Folie (FR)**[7] 6125 4-9-2 **0**.......................... JulienAuge 3 51
(Gay Kelleway) *settled midfield: racd w gp wd on crse: pushed along 3f out: rdn 2f out: styd on one pce fnl f* **185/10**

**5** *nse* **Calajani (FR)**[87] 4-8-9 **0**.......................... MlleAlisonMassin(5) 7 49
(Andrew Hollinshead, France) **44/5**

**6** *1 1/4* **Gaea (FR)**[85] 4-8-13 **0**..........................(b) AntoineHamelin 8 46
(S Jesus, France) **49/10**[2]

**7** *3/4* **Ernestine (FR)**[87] 4-8-10 **0**.......................... JeromeMoutard(4) 5 46
(J-M Lefebvre, France) **61/10**

**8** *1* **Parti Pris**[70] 4-8-13 **0**..........................(b) StephaneLaurent 12 43
(Mlle S Verrier, France) **218/10**

**9** *hd* **Debt Of Honour (FR)**[93] 4-9-2 **0**.......................... StephanePasquier 2 46
(C Boutin, France) **17/2**

**10** *6* **Kil Al Jamal (FR)**[25] 4-8-13 **0**.......................... MllePaulineDominois(4) 9 37
(J Albrecht, Czech Republic) **38/1**

**11** *1 1/4* **Waldenon (FR)**[87] 4-8-11 **0**.......................... TonyPiccone 1 29
(S Jesus, France) **244/10**

**12** *nk* **Miss Fuisse (FR)**[62] 4-9-6 **0**..........................(b) TheoBachelot 10 38
(P Monfort, France) **56/10**[3]

2m 34.5s (-3.40) **12** Ran SP% **118.0**
PARI-MUTUEL (all including 1 euro stake): WIN 14.10; PLACE 4.00, 2.50, 2.80; DF 39.30; SF 85.60.
**Owner** Julien Caullery **Bred** Bjorn Nielsen **Trained** France

## 6028 FFOS LAS (L-H)

Friday, August 25

**OFFICIAL GOING: Good to soft (soft in places; 6.3)**

Wind: moderate breeze, partly against them in the home straight Weather: sunny spells

### 6366 PERSIMMON HOMES NURSERY H'CAP 7f 80y(R)

**2:15** (2:16) (Class 6) (0-65,67) 2-Y-O **£2,587** (£770; £384; £192) **Stalls** Low

Form RPR

4566 1 **Data Protection**[13] 5933 2-8-8 **54** LewisEdmunds(3) 5 59
*(William Muir) hld up: rdn and clsd over 2f out: led over 1f out: r.o wl* **5/1**[3]

5321 2 2 1/4 **Give Em A Clump (IRE)**[51] 4504 2-9-3 **60** (v) TimmyMurphy 6 60
*(David Evans) t.k.h: trckd ldr: upsides gng wl 3f out: led narrowly 2f out: sn hdd and rdn: kpt on* **11/1**

0023 3 3 **Foxrush Take Time (FR)**[14] 5875 2-9-5 **62** LiamKeniry 7 54
*(Richard Guest) hld up: effrt over 2f out: drvn and chsd ldrs over 1f out: styd on same pce fnl f* **1/1**[1]

0300 4 4 **Bezos (IRE)**[17] 5756 2-9-1 **63** BenRobinson(5) 9 46
*(Richard Hannon) trckd ldrs: rdn over 2f out: sn ev ch: wknd appr fnl f: fin lame* **6/1**

623 5 3 1/2 **Tranquil Soul**[15] 5847 2-9-10 **67** ShaneKelly 1 41
*(David Lanigan) trckd ldrs: drvn over 2f out: wknd over 1f out* **4/1**[2]

433 6 13 **Sixties Secret**[10] 6022 2-8-6 **53** ow1 CallumShepherd(3) 3
*(Mick Channon) led: jnd 3f out: sn shkn up: fnd little and hdd 2f out: wknd and sn eased* **7/1**

1m 38.03s (4.43) **Going Correction** +0.725s/f (Yiel) 6 Ran SP% **121.8**

Speed ratings (Par 92): **103,100,97,92,88 73**

CSF £57.63 CT £98.76 TOTE £6.80: £3.20, £4.30; EX 70.20 Trifecta £289.50.

**Owner** Muir Racing Partnership - Santa Anita **Bred** Mr & Mrs J Laws **Trained** Lambourn, Berks

**FOCUS**

The going was good to soft, soft in places and there was quite a strong headwind up the straight. The stalls were in the centre for the sprint races and on the inside for the other events. The pace was not strong in this opening nursery but the winner scored in good style from the clear second. The time was 8.43 seconds slower than standard. The winner has been rated back to something like his debut effort, with the runner-up close to his recent form.

### 6367 HEATFORCE/EBF NOVICE STKS 7f 80y(R)

**2:50** (2:52) (Class 5) 2-Y-O **£4,528** (£1,347; £673; £336) **Stalls** Low

Form RPR

0621 1 **Move Over**[18] 5709 2-9-4 78 (b) BenRobinson(5) 2 79
*(Richard Hannon) led: racd keenly: rdn 2f out: hdd narrowly 1f out: rallied gamely u.p to ld again nr fin* **5/4**[1]

163 2 nk **Tunes Of Glory**[31] 5240 2-9-9 80 RyanPowell 4 78
*(Sir Mark Prescott Bt) trckd wnr: rdn over 2f out: sn hung lft: led narrowly 1f out: pushed along fnl f: hdd nr fin* **7/1**

50 3 1 1/4 **Yorbelucky**[18] 5710 2-9-2 0 TimmyMurphy 8 68
*(David Evans) broke wl: chsd ldrs: rdn: wnt 3rd and hung lft over 1f out: r.o towards fin* **14/1**

4 4 3 1/2 **Bajan Gold (IRE)**[37] 5036 2-9-2 0 AdamBeschizza 1 60
*(Stuart Williams) trckd ldng pair: rdn over 2f out: sn lost 3rd and sltly outpcd: styd on ins fnl f* **9/2**[3]

0 5 1/2 **Maverick Officer**[8] 6108 2-9-2 0 DanielMuscutt 6 59
*(David Simcock) midfield: rdn to dispute 3rd over 1f out: fdd fnl f: fin lame* **4/1**[2]

6 3/4 **Global Excel** 2-9-2 0 LiamKeniry 7 57
*(Ed Walker) s.i.s: hld up: rdn over 2f out: no real imp but kpt on steadily* **6/1**

7 7 **The Night King** 2-8-13 0 CallumShepherd(3) 5 40
*(Mick Channon) s.i.s: in tch in rr: rdn over 2f out: wknd over 1f out* **12/1**

8 15 **Masons Belle** 2-9-2 0 ShaneKelly 9 4
*(Ronald Harris) s.s: in rr: rdn 3f out: qckly lost tch* **25/1**

1m 38.78s (5.18) **Going Correction** +0.725s/f (Yiel) 8 Ran SP% **127.6**

Speed ratings (Par 94): **99,98,97,93,92 91,83,66**

CSF £12.93 TOTE £2.10: £1.10, £2.50, £5.30; EX 10.70 Trifecta £87.40.

**Owner** Middleham Park Racing LXXII **Bred** David Jamison Bloodstock **Trained** East Everleigh, Wilts

**FOCUS**

The two previous winners dominated this novice event.

### 6368 FINNING UK LTD MAIDEN STKS 1m (R)

**3:25** (3:25) (Class 5) 3-Y-O+ **£3,234** (£962; £481; £240) **Stalls** Low

Form RPR

03 1 **Casement (IRE)**[21] 5611 3-9-5 0 ShaneKelly 5 79+
*(Roger Charlton) mde all: shkn up ins fnl f: easily* **1/4**[1]

6- 2 2 1/2 **Spanish History (USA)**[317] 7291 3-9-5 0 TimmyMurphy 4 68
*(Seamus Durack) hld up in last: gd hdwy over 2f out: wnt 2nd over 1f out: shkn up ins fnl f: a hld by easy wnr* **9/1**[3]

0-46 3 5 **Assertor**[12] 5969 3-8-11 0 (h[1]) GeorgeWood(3) 9 51
*(Tony Carroll) t.k.h on outer: trckd ldrs: rdn: hung rt and lost pl over 2f out: r.o fnl f: wnt 3rd towards fin* **50/1**

43 4 1 1/4 **Astone Man (FR)**[31] 5247 3-9-5 0 GeorgeDowning 6 53
*(Tony Carroll) midfield: rdn to chse ldrs over 2f out: drvn and one pce fnl f: lost 3rd towards fin* **10/1**

500- 5 nk **Warofindependence (USA)**[389] 4940 5-9-6 67 BenRobinson(5) 1 53
*(John O'Shea) t.k.h in midfield: clsd on inner to chse wnr 3f out: drvn 2f out: lost 2nd over 1f out: fdd fnl f* **25/1**

6 nse **Manners Maketh Man (IRE)** 3-9-0 0 PatrickO'Donnell(5) 10 52
*(Ralph Beckett) s.i.s: hld up: rdn and sme prog 3f out: nudged along and styd on fnl f* **4/1**[2]

60 7 hd **Big Bad Lol (IRE)**[22] 5577 3-9-5 0 LiamKeniry 3 52
*(Ed Walker) hld up: rdn 3f out: no imp tl styd on fnl f* **20/1**

0 8 3 1/4 **Treacherous**[8] 6103 3-9-2 0 CallumShepherd(3) 8 44
*(Ed de Giles) s.i.s: hld up: sme hdwy 3f out: shkn up 2f out: grad fdd* **50/1**

9 1/2 **Jumbo's Boy** 3-9-0 0 JoshuaBryan(5) 7 43
*(Peter Bowen) trckd wnr: shkn up and lost 2nd 3f out: drvn, edgd lft and wknd over 1f out* **14/1**

05/0 10 12 **I'mwaitingforyou**[10] 6031 8-9-6 0 DanielMuscutt 2 12
*(Peter Bowen) chsd ldrs: rdn over 2f out: wknd over 1f out* **25/1**

1m 48.28s (7.28) **Going Correction** +0.725s/f (Yiel)

**WFA** 3 from 5yo+ 6lb 10 Ran SP% **142.1**

Speed ratings (Par 103): **92,89,84,83,82 82,82,79,78,66**

CSF £5.79 TOTE £1.30: £1.02, £2.30, £11.10; EX 8.10 Trifecta £162.10.

**Owner** Beckhampton Racing **Bred** Mrs Clodagh McStay **Trained** Beckhampton, Wilts

**FOCUS**

The hot favourite scored with plenty in hand in this maiden. It's been rated loosely around the third to her previous form.

### 6369 BRITISH STALLION STUDS EBF FILLIES' H'CAP 1m 2f (R)

**3:55** (3:56) (Class 3) (0-95,87) 3-Y-0+ **£9,703** (£2,887; £1,443; £721) **Stalls** Low

Form RPR

25 1 **Twenty Times (IRE)**[19] 5682 3-8-13 **79** (p[1]) ShaneKelly 4 91
*(Richard Hughes) chsd ldrs: effrt on outer over 2f out: sn hung lft: drvn to chse ldr over 1f out: led 110yds out: in command whn hung lft nr fin* **3/1**[1]

-405 2 1 1/4 **Brief Visit**[23] 5533 4-9-5 **78** LiamKeniry 6 86
*(Andrew Balding) led: drvn and styd on over 1f out: hdd 110yds out: hld nr fin* **10/1**

0103 3 4 1/2 **Hadeeqa (IRE)**[24] 5506 3-9-3 **83** (h) DanielMuscutt 1 83
*(Simon Crisford) hld up: hdwy whn nt clr run and swtchd lft over 2f out: sn drvn and one pce* **7/2**[2]

4263 4 nk **Cotinga**[23] 5533 3-8-3 **74** PatrickO'Donnell(5) 3 73
*(Ralph Beckett) dwlt: hld up: hdwy on inner to go 2nd 3f out: rdn 2f out: sn lost 2nd: one pce fnl f* **3/1**[1]

4213 5 nk **Frosting**[15] 5822 3-8-11 **80** GeorgeWood(3) 2 79
*(William Haggas) trckd ldrs: rdn over 2f out: no ex fnl f* **3/1**[1]

4655 6 1 1/4 **Aqua Libre**[14] 5895 4-8-6 **68** oh4 CallumShepherd(3) 5 63
*(Jennie Candlish) s.s: t.k.h in rr: drvn over 2f out: hung lft over 1f out: no real imp* **16/1**

1032 7 3 3/4 **Lyric Harmony (IRE)**[15] 5829 3-8-4 **75** BenRobinson(5) 8 64
*(Giles Bravery) trckd ldrs: rdn and lost 2nd 3f out: wknd over 1f out* **9/2**[3]

2m 15.93s (6.53) **Going Correction** +0.725s/f (Yiel)

**WFA** 3 from 4yo 7lb 7 Ran SP% **130.4**

Speed ratings (Par 104): **102,101,97,97,96 95,92**

CSF £38.89 CT £118.14 TOTE £4.00: £1.60, £4.10; EX 37.20 Trifecta £184.90.

**Owner** True Reds **Bred** Kildaragh Stud **Trained** Upper Lambourn, Berks

**FOCUS**

This looked competitive but the first two pulled well clear. The runner-up has been rated close to her 3yo best.

### 6370 HONEYWELL H'CAP 1m 6f (R)

**4:30** (4:32) (Class 6) (0-65,67) 3-Y-0+ **£2,587** (£770; £384; £192) **Stalls** Low

Form RPR

1020 1 **Incus**[18] 5716 4-9-3 **59** JaneElliott(5) 3 66+
*(Ed de Giles) mde all: racd keenly: sn several l clr: shkn up over 2f out: drvn over 1f out: styd on: unchal* **5/1**[3]

060 2 3 3/4 **Tyrolean**[27] 5432 4-10-0 **65** TimmyMurphy 5 67
*(Seamus Durack) bmpd leaving stalls: chsd ldrs: wnt 2nd gng wl over 2f out: rdn over 1f out: styd on but nvr able to chal wnr* **12/1**

4341 3 1 1/4 **Ocean Gale**[18] 5716 4-8-11 **51** GeorgeWood(3) 1 52
*(Richard Price) chsd ldrs: rdn over 3f out: styd on one pce fnl 2f* **9/4**[2]

-052 4 3/4 **Leapt**[27] 5406 3-9-6 **67** ShaneKelly 7 69
*(Richard Hughes) hld up: rdn 3f out: sn hung lft: styd on same pce* **6/4**[1]

436/ 5 1/2 **Red Riverman**[19] 5801 9-9-9 **60** (p) LiamKeniry 2 59
*(Nigel Twiston-Davies) hld up: rdn 3f out: sn swtchd rt: styd on fnl f* **7/1**

541 6 7 **Frantical**[31] 5249 5-9-9 **60** GeorgeDowning 6 50
*(Tony Carroll) hld up in last: drvn 4f out: no hdwy* **7/1**

0040 7 1/2 **Nigh Or Never (IRE)**[71] 3745 3-8-11 **58** (t[1]) DanielMuscutt 4 49
*(Rebecca Curtis) wnt rt leaving stalls: chsd wnr tl rdn and lost 2nd over 2f out: grad wknd* **11/1**

3m 13.98s (10.18) **Going Correction** +0.725s/f (Yiel)

**WFA** 3 from 4yo+ 10lb 7 Ran SP% **128.5**

Speed ratings (Par 101): **99,96,96,95,95 91,91**

CSF £67.89 TOTE £6.60: £2.90, £5.50; EX 92.50 Trifecta £682.40.

**Owner** Mange Tout II **Bred** Lilly Hall Farm **Trained** Ledbury, H'fords

**FOCUS**

There was an emphatic all-the-way winner in this staying handicap. A minor pb at least from the winner.

### 6371 PLUMBASE H'CAP 6f

**5:00** (5:02) (Class 3) (0-95,96) 3-Y-0+ **£7,561** (£2,263; £1,131; £566; £282) **Stalls** Centre

Form RPR

1201 1 **Under The Covers**[7] 6137 4-8-13 **84** 6ex ShaneKelly 4 96
*(Ronald Harris) mde all: drvn 2f out: r.o strly to draw clr fnl 110yds* **3/1**[2]

3600 2 3 **Go Far**[20] 5640 7-9-5 **95** (v) JoshuaBryan(5) 1 97
*(Alan Bailey) in 2nd virtually thrght: rdn over 2f out: kpt on: outpcd by wnr fnl 110yds* **3/1**[2]

2145 3 1/2 **Sir Billy Wright (IRE)**[18] 5705 6-8-7 **85** KatherineGlenister(7) 7 85
*(David Evans) chsd ldrs: rdn 2f out: edgd sltly lft and r.o fnl f* **5/2**[1]

0000 4 1 **Smokey Lane (IRE)**[13] 5916 3-9-8 **96** TimmyMurphy 3 93
*(Christian Williams) trckd ldrs: rdn over 1f out: unable qck fnl f* **8/1**

6520 5 1/2 **Satchville Flyer**[3] 6288 6-7-12 **76** oh2 GabrieleMalune(7) 5 72
*(David Evans) taken steadily to post: t.k.h in rr: rdn: hdwy and hung lft 2f out: one pce fnl f* **6/1**

1142 6 1 **Kinglami**[8] 6098 8-8-2 **78** (p) BenRobinson(5) 6 70
*(John O'Shea) towards rr: pushed along after 2f: drvn over 2f out: no hdwy* **4/1**[3]

0-50 7 3/4 **Leontes**[76] 3579 3-8-12 **86** LiamKeniry 2 76
*(Andrew Balding) awkward s: towards rr: drvn 2f out: wknd over 1f out* **7/1**

1m 11.84s (1.84) **Going Correction** +0.50s/f (Yiel)

**WFA** 3 from 4yo+ 3lb 7 Ran SP% **136.5**

Speed ratings (Par 107): **107,103,102,101,100 99,98**

CSF £15.59 TOTE £4.70: £3.00, £1.80; EX 20.10 Trifecta £77.00.

**Owner** Ridge House Stables Ltd **Bred** Llety Farms **Trained** Earlswood, Monmouths

**FOCUS**

The winner completed a double in good style under another positive ride.

### 6372 VIESSMAN H'CAP 5f

**5:35** (5:36) (Class 6) (0-65,66) 3-Y-0+ **£2,587** (£770; £384; £192) **Stalls** Centre

Form RPR

313U 1 **Gnaad (IRE)**[13] 5920 3-9-5 **66** JoshuaBryan(5) 3 77
*(Alan Bailey) trckd ldng pair: smooth prog to ld wl over 1f out: drvn and r.o strly fnl f* **9/2**

0033 2 3 1/4 **Little Miss Daisy**[15] 5837 3-9-5 **64** LewisEdmunds(3) 1 63
*(William Muir) hld up wl in tch in last pair: rdn and clsd 2f out: duelled for 2nd fnl f but no ch w wnr* **2/1**[2]

4403 3 shd **Kingstreet Lady**[10] 6028 4-8-8 **51** GeorgeWood(3) 5 50
*(Richard Price) hld up wl in tch in last pair: rdn 1/2-way: r.o to dispute 2nd ins fnl f but no ch w wnr* **4/1**[3]

2233 4 7 **Lady Joanna Vassa (IRE)**[7] 6130 4-8-9 **49** (h[1]) LiamKeniry 7 23
*(Richard Guest) w ldr tl drvn 1/2-way: wknd fnl f* **1/1**[1]

0065 **5** 2 1/4 **Swendab (IRE)**[8] 6097 9-9-5 64..............................(v) BenRobinson(5) 2 30
(John O'Shea) *led tl rdn and hdd wl over 1f out: sn wknd* **10/1**
1m 0.75s (2.45) **Going Correction** +0.50s/f (Yiel)
**WFA** 3 from 4yo+ 2lb **5** Ran SP% **130.6**
Speed ratings (Par 101): **100,94,94,83,79**
CSF £16.66 TOTE £6.60: £2.70, £1.70; EX 19.90 Trifecta £97.60.
**Owner** AB Racing Limited **Bred** Rabbah Bloodstock Limited **Trained** Newmarket, Suffolk
**FOCUS**
There were not may runners and the favourite didn't fire but the winner scored in good style and has raised his form to a new level. The winner has been rated to his Southwell win in April.
T/Plt: £1,628.70 to a £1 stake. Pool: £59,906.27 - 26.85 winning units T/Qpdt: £144.70 to a £1 stake. Pool: £3,876.49 - 19.82 winning units **Richard Lowther**

## 5637 GOODWOOD (R-H)

Friday, August 25

**OFFICIAL GOING: Good (good to soft in places on straight course; 7.0)**
Wind: Almost nil Weather: Sunny, warm

## 6373 THAMES MATERIALS LTD APPRENTICE H'CAP 6f

**5:10** (5:10) (Class 5) (0-70,71) 3-Y-O+ **£3,234** (£962; £481; £240) **Stalls** High

Form RPR
322 **1** **Island Cloud**[8] 6106 3-9-6 66..............................DavidEgan 6 74
(Heather Main) *trckd ldng pair: wnt 2nd sn after 1/2-way: shkn up to ld over 1f out: styd on wl: readily* **7/4**[1]
3422 **2** 1 1/2 **Jashma (IRE)**[21] 5588 3-9-6 69..............................FinleyMarsh(3) 10 72
(Richard Hughes) *trckd ldrs: waiting for a gap fr 2f out tl in the clr jst over 1f out: drvn and styd on fnl f: tk 2nd nr fin* **13/2**
5656 **3** 1/2 **Flying Sakhee**[8] 6106 4-8-7 50 oh2..............................(b) MitchGodwin 4 51
(John Bridger) *trckd ldrs in 5th: prog on outer wl over 1f out then edgd rt: rdn to chse wnr 100yds out: no imp: lost 2nd nr fin* **20/1**
1044 **4** nk **Qatari Riyals (IRE)**[20] 5636 3-9-4 71..............................TinaSmith(7) 8 71
(Richard Hannon) *pressed ldr: led 1/2-way: rdn and hdd over 1f out: one pce* **12/1**
2422 **5** shd **Whitecrest**[13] 5936 9-9-9 71..............................StephenCummins(5) 3 71
(John Spearing) *t.k.h: hld up in 6th: pushed along over 2f out: sme prog against nr side rail over 1f out: kpt on but nvr able to chal* **9/1**
2131 **6** 1 1/4 **Wild Flower (IRE)**[11] 6004 5-9-2 59 6ex..............................MeganNicholls 9 55
(Jimmy Fox) *led to 1/2-way: sn pushed along: lost pl steadily fr 2f out* **6/1**[3]
602 **7** 1/2 **Pour La Victoire (IRE)**[14] 5869 7-9-11 68..............................(v) GeorgiaCox 2 63
(Tony Carroll) *slowly away: in tch in last trio: prog on outer 1/2-way: pressed ldrs 2f out: fdd fnl f* **9/2**[2]
0-20 **8** 1 1/2 **Lucky Di**[60] 4162 7-8-13 56..............................GeorgeBuckell 7 46
(Peter Hedger) *hld up in last trio: shkn up over 2f out: no prog* **16/1**
6005 **9** hd **Deer Song**[11] 6009 4-8-4 52..............................NicolaCurrie(5) 5 41
(John Bridger) *rrd s and slowly away: hld up in last trio: shkn up and no prog 2f out* **20/1**
1m 12.36s (0.16) **Going Correction** +0.125s/f (Good)
**WFA** 3 from 4yo+ 3lb **9** Ran SP% **115.3**
Speed ratings (Par 103): **103,101,100,99,99 98,97,95,95**
CSF £13.40 CT £163.77 TOTE £2.20: £1.10, £1.90, £5.30; EX 14.70 Trifecta £194.60.
**Owner** Donald M Kerr **Bred** Mr & Mrs James Main **Trained** Kingston Lisle, Oxon
**FOCUS**
Race distance increased by 10yds for races 3, 5 & 6, and 7yds for race 4. The going was good (good to soft in places) ahead of the opener, an average sprint handicap. The runner-up has been rated close to form.

## 6374 EBF MAIDEN STKS (PLUS 10 RACE) 1m

**5:45** (5:48) (Class 4) 2-Y-O **£6,469** (£1,925; £962; £481) **Stalls** Low

Form RPR
**1** **Bon Scotte (IRE)** 2-9-2 0..............................HollieDoyle(3) 1 82
(Richard Hannon) *led: pushed along and hdd 2f out: rallied over 1f out: led ins fnl f: edgd lft after but hld on wl* **16/1**
4 **2** 1/2 **Kitaabaat**[18] 5710 2-9-5 0..............................DaneO'Neill 5 81
(Owen Burrows) *pressed ldr: shkn up to ld 2f out: sn pressed: hdd ins fnl f: carried lft after but a hld* **6/4**[1]
3 **3** 3/4 **Adams Park**[18] 5709 2-9-0 0..............................DavidEgan(5) 2 79
(Roger Varian) *dwlt: rcvrd to trck ldng pair: rdn over 2f out dropped to 4th sn after: styd on to go 3rd again ins fnl f: clsd nr fin* **2/1**[2]
5 **4** 2 **Rastrelli (FR)**[14] 5887 2-9-2 0..............................HectorCrouch(3) 7 75
(Charlie Appleby) *hld up in tch: prog on outer 3f out: shkn up to chse ldng pair 2f out: no imp over 1f out: lost 3rd and one pce ins fnl f* **7/1**
**5** 1 **Bowditch (IRE)** 2-9-5 0..............................SaleemGolam 9 72
(John Gosden) *dropped in fr wd draw and hld up in last: pushed along over 2f out: nvr on terms but kpt on steadily* **6/1**[3]
**6** 2 1/4 **Danceteria (FR)** 2-9-5 0..............................WilliamCarson 6 67
(David Menuisier) *hld up in tch: shkn up over 2f out: steadily outpcd* **12/1**
50 **7** 3 1/4 **Sukhovey (USA)**[41] 4902 2-9-0 0..............................(t[1]) KierenFox 3 55
(Michael Attwater) *hld up in tch: pushed along over 3f out: no prog 2f out: wknd over 1f out* **66/1**
**8** 10 **Atomic Jack** 2-9-5 0..............................FergusSweeney 4 37
(George Baker) *t.k.h: trckd ldrs: lost pl over 2f out: wknd and bhd fnl f* **25/1**
1m 41.3s (1.40) **Going Correction** +0.075s/f (Good) **8** Ran SP% **119.0**
Speed ratings (Par 96): **96,95,94,92,91 89,86,76**
CSF £42.33 TOTE £13.80: £3.90, £1.10, £1.50; EX 66.10 Trifecta £180.60.
**Owner** Sullivan Bloodstock Ltd & Chris Giles **Bred** Limetree Stud **Trained** East Everleigh, Wilts
■ Larksborough was withdrawn. Price at time of withdrawal 10-1. Rule 4 applies to board prices prior to withdrawal but not to SP bets. Deduction - 5p in the pound. New market formed.
■ Stewards' Enquiry : Hollie Doyle four-day ban: careless riding (Sept 8-12)
**FOCUS**
Race run over an extra 10yds. The going was changed to good before this. A fair maiden in which two of the last four winners triumphed again next time out, before adding a Listed success the following year. They didn't go flat out and the first two came clear.

## 6375 CHICHESTER OBSERVER NURSERY H'CAP 7f

**6:15** (6:18) (Class 4) (0-80,80) 2-Y-O **£6,469** (£1,925; £962; £481) **Stalls** Low

Form RPR
611 **1** **She Believes (IRE)**[17] 5751 2-9-1 79..............................DavidEgan(5) 3 95
(Sylvester Kirk) *hld up disputing 4th: prog to chse clr ldr over 2f out and sn clsd: shkn up to ld over 1f out: drew rt away fnl f* **3/1**[2]
613 **2** 6 **Simply Breathless**[37] 5030 2-8-11 70..............................SamHitchcott 7 70
(Clive Cox) *led: clr after 3f: rdn and hdd over 1f out: no ch w wnr but kpt on wl enough for 2nd* **8/1**
5240 **3** 1 1/4 **Tig Tog (IRE)**[20] 5659 2-9-3 76..............................DaneO'Neill 2 73
(Richard Hannon) *hld up disputing 4th: pushed along wl over 2f out and no prog: kpt on fr over 1f out to take 3rd last strides* **6/1**
2140 **4** nk **Royal Household**[22] 5572 2-9-2 78..............................HollieDoyle(3) 4 74
(Richard Hannon) *chsd clr ldr to over 2f out: rdn and one pce after* **5/2**[1]
5300 **5** 2 **Chai Chai (IRE)**[22] 5572 2-8-13 72..............................DavidProbert 5 62
(Andrew Balding) *trckd ldng pair to over 2f out: nt qckn sn after: hanging and racd awkwardly over 1f out whn pressing for a pl: fdd last 100yds* **7/2**[3]
013 **6** 5 **Beringer**[17] 5743 2-9-5 78..............................FergusSweeney 9 55
(Alan King) *stdd at s: t.k.h and hld up in last trio: sme inroads jst over 2f out: shkn up and no prog over 1f out: fdd fnl f: eased last 75yds* **14/1**
335 **7** shd **Diamond Dougal (IRE)**[17] 5755 2-8-9 68..............................JFEgan 6 45
(Mick Channon) *t.k.h: hld up in last trio: shkn up and no prog over 2f out: wl btn after* **16/1**
302 **8** 1/2 **Ghepardo**[25] 5480 2-8-10 69..............................KieranO'Neill 8 44
(Richard Hannon) *stdd s: t.k.h and trapped out wd: shkn up no prog over 2f out: wl btn after* **33/1**
1m 27.37s (0.37) **Going Correction** +0.075s/f (Good) **8** Ran SP% **116.7**
Speed ratings (Par 96): **100,93,91,91,89 83,83,82**
CSF £27.77 CT £137.82 TOTE £4.10: £1.50, £2.10, £2.00; EX 20.50 Trifecta £84.00.
**Owner** Marchwood Recycling Ltd **Bred** Ringfort Stud **Trained** Upper Lambourn, Berks
**FOCUS**
Race distance increased 10yds. An average nursery in which they went a good gallop.

## 6376 BUTLINS H'CAP 2m

**6:45** (6:45) (Class 5) (0-75,77) 3-Y-O **£3,234** (£962; £481; £240) **Stalls** Low

Form RPR
-211 **1** **Imphal**[38] 4994 3-9-0 72..............................(p) TylerSaunders(7) 1 80+
(Marcus Tregoning) *t.k.h: hld up: detached in last over 3f out: prog on outer over 2f out: clsd on ldng pair over 1f out: rdn and styd on fnl f to ld last stride* **2/1**[1]
04-5 **2** shd **Kozier (GER)**[39] 4978 3-8-2 56..............................HollieDoyle(3) 2 63
(Alan King) *stdd s: hld up in last then tended to run in snatches: prog over 4f out: rdn to chse ldr 2f out: narrow ld over 1f out: kpt on but hdd last stride* **4/1**
0321 **3** 2 1/4 **Sussex Ranger (USA)**[27] 5406 3-9-8 76..............................(p[1]) HectorCrouch(3) 3 80
(Gary Moore) *prom: chsd ldr 5f out: rdn to ld over 2f out: narrowly hdd over 1f out: no ex last 150yds* **3/1**[2]
6452 **4** 3 1/2 **General Allenby**[22] 5581 3-8-2 53 oh3..............................(be) KieranO'Neill 4 53
(Henry Tett) *chsd ldr to 6f out: sn rdn and in trble: trying to rally whn nt clr run over 2f out and swtchd lft: outpcd over 1f out* **12/1**
-003 **5** 1 1/4 **Franny Nisbet**[16] 5780 3-8-9 60..............................SamHitchcott 5 59
(William Muir) *prom: chsd ldr 6f out to 5f out: sn drvn: steadily fdd fr over 2f out* **16/1**
2613 **6** 1/2 **Veiled Secret (IRE)**[10] 6033 3-9-12 77..............................DavidProbert 6 75
(Sir Mark Prescott Bt) *led at gd pce: breather after 6f: had most rivals at work 4f out: hdd over 2f out and shkn up: fnd nil and sn btn* **7/2**[3]
3m 30.7s (1.70) **Going Correction** +0.075s/f (Good) **6** Ran SP% **114.1**
Speed ratings (Par 100): **98,97,96,95,94 94**
CSF £10.66 TOTE £3.00: £1.90, £2.40; EX 10.70 Trifecta £34.10.
**Owner** Mrs M E Slade **Bred** G S Bishop **Trained** Whitsbury, Hants
**FOCUS**
Race distance increased by 7yds. A tight little handicap in which a good pace was set, suiting those coming from behind.

## 6377 THAMES MATERIALS LTD EBF FILLIES' H'CAP 1m

**7:15** (7:18) (Class 3) (0-95,91) 3-Y-O+ **£9,703** (£2,887; £1,443; £721) **Stalls** Low

Form RPR
-324 **1** **Dubara**[44] 4763 3-9-1 86..............................DavidProbert 6 95
(Luca Cumani) *t.k.h: hld up in rr: prog over 2f out to chal over 1f out: rdn to ld last 75yds: kpt on wl* **9/2**[3]
2542 **2** nk **Panova**[15] 5856 3-8-10 86..............................DavidEgan(5) 5 94
(Sir Michael Stoute) *hld up in tch: prog to chse ldr jst over 2f out: rdn to ld over 1f out: kpt on wl but hdd and hld last 75yds* **10/3**[2]
2031 **3** 2 1/4 **Black Bess**[15] 5842 4-9-7 91..............................PaddyBradley(5) 4 95
(Jim Boyle) *led at gd pce: rdn and hdd over 1f out: sn in 3rd and one pce after but clr of rest* **10/1**
1305 **4** 5 **Flying North**[14] 5889 3-8-9 83..............................HollieDoyle(3) 1 75
(Richard Hannon) *trckd ldr to jst over 2f out: steadily wknd* **15/2**
-104 **5** 3 1/4 **Bahamadam**[30] 5294 3-8-12 88..............................GeorgiaCox(5) 2 72
(Eve Johnson Houghton) *hld up in rr: rousted along to make and effrt on inner over 3f out: wknd 2f out* **9/1**
2122 **6** hd **Shaaqaaf (IRE)**[27] 5399 3-9-5 90..............................DaneO'Neill 3 74
(John Gosden) *trckd ldng pair to over 2f out: sn wknd* **2/1**[1]
-300 **7** 10 **Soldier's Girl (IRE)**[25] 5484 3-8-11 82..............................(b[1]) KieranO'Neill 7 43
(Richard Hannon) *wnt lft s: plld hrd and hld up: wknd over 2f out: sn bhd* **16/1**
1m 38.98s (-0.92) **Going Correction** +0.075s/f (Good)
**WFA** 3 from 4yo 6lb **7** Ran SP% **111.3**
Speed ratings (Par 104): **107,106,104,99,96 96,86**
CSF £18.75 CT £135.54 TOTE £5.90: £2.20, £2.10; EX 11.50 Trifecta £148.20.
**Owner** Fittocks Stud **Bred** Fittocks Stud **Trained** Newmarket, Suffolk
**FOCUS**
Race distance increased 10yds. A fair handicap won by a subsequent Listed winner 12 months ago, and the first three came clear. A pb from the second, with the winner rated in line with the better view of her form.

## 6378 THAMES MATERIALS LTD H'CAP 7f

**7:45** (7:47) (Class 5) (0-75,76) 3-Y-O+ **£3,234** (£962; £481; £240) **Stalls** Low

Form RPR
4034 **1** **Wannabe Friends**[29] 5315 4-9-3 73..............................FinleyMarsh(7) 3 85
(Richard Hughes) *hld up in midfield: prog 2f out: tending to hang over 1f out but clsd on ldrs: led jst ins fnl f: rdn clr* **3/1**[1]
0131 **2** 2 1/4 **Sheikspear**[16] 5797 3-9-3 76..............................DavidEgan(5) 4 80
(Ed de Giles) *trckd ldng pair: clsd to chal 2f out: led jst over 1f out to jst ins fnl f: sn outpcd by wnr* **3/1**[1]
4041 **3** 1 1/4 **Another Boy**[29] 5333 4-9-6 74..............................(p) GeorgiaCox(5) 7 77
(Ralph Beckett) *chsd clr ldr: clsd 2f out but sn lost 2nd: nt qckn over 1f out: one pce fnl f* **9/1**
4455 **4** nk **Mister Music**[30] 5300 8-9-12 75..............................(p) DavidProbert 1 77
(Tony Carroll) *hld up in last pair: rdn and nt qckn over 2f out: styd on fr over 1f out: nrly snatched 3rd but too late to threaten* **9/2**[2]
4201 **5** 1/2 **Good Luck Charm**[14] 5870 8-9-7 73..............................(v) HectorCrouch(3) 2 73
(Gary Moore) *hld up in last pair: shkn up and no prog over 2f out: styd on fnl f: nrst fin* **9/1**

505 **6** *nk* **Tigerwolf (IRE)**[15] 5842 4-9-12 **75**............................................ JFEgan 8 75
(Mick Channon) *pushed up to ld and sn clr: 6 l up 1/2-way: hdd & wknd jst over 1f out* **7/1**[3]

200 **7** *2 ¼* **Highway One (USA)**[31] 5248 3-9-7 **75**..................(b[1]) FergusSweeney 5 67
(George Baker) *stdd s: hld up in last pair: effrt on outer 2f out: wknd over 1f out* **33/1**

6323 **8** *11* **Live Dangerously**[15] 5823 7-8-10 **59**............................ WilliamCarson 6 23
(John Bridger) *t.k.h: disp 3rd pl to 1/2-way: sn wknd* **9/1**

1m 28.34s (1.34) **Going Correction** +0.075s/f (Good)
**WFA** 3 from 4yo+ 5lb **8** Ran SP% **113.6**
Speed ratings (Par 103): **95,92,91,90,90 89,87,74**
CSF £11.64 CT £70.38 TOTE £3.70: £1.40, £1.40, £2.70; EX 11.60 Trifecta £72.10.
**Owner** Normandie Stud Ltd **Bred** Normandie Stud Ltd **Trained** Upper Lambourn, Berks

**FOCUS**
Race distance increased 10yds. A competitive handicap featuring three recent winners and, with a strong pace, the form looks solid. A small pb from the winner, with the runner-up a bit below his AW latest.
T/Plt: £27.90 to a £1 stake. Pool: £57,627.22 - 1,503.37 winning units. T/Qpdt: £12.70 to a £1 stake. Pool: £4,920.94 - 286.24 winning units. **Jonathan Neesom**

# 6346 HAMILTON (R-H)
## Friday, August 25

**OFFICIAL GOING: Soft (5.3)**
Wind: Breezy, half behind Weather: Overcast

## 6379 LADBROKES NURSERY H'CAP — 6f 6y
5:30 (5:33) (Class 5) (0-75,75) 2-Y-O **£3,881** (£1,155; £577; £288) **Stalls** High

Form RPR

064 **1** **She's Different (IRE)**[15] 5825 2-8-9 **63**......................... AndrewMullen 8 68
(Nigel Tinkler) *in tch: hdwy against stands' rail and led over 1f out: rdn and kpt on strly fnl f* **5/1**[3]

133 **2** *1 ½* **Havana Star (IRE)**[23] 5537 2-9-7 **75**.................................... TomEaves 5 76
(Kevin Ryan) *trckd ldrs: effrt and ev ch over 1f out: sn chsng wnr: kpt on ins fnl f* **7/2**[2]

616 **3** *1* **Byron's Choice**[27] 5412 2-9-6 **74**.................................. ConnorBeasley 2 72
(Michael Dods) *hld up bhd ldng gp: effrt on outside over 2f out: rdn and kpt on fnl f: nt pce to chal* **11/4**[1]

3644 **4** *2* **Auntie Pam (IRE)**[17] 5751 2-8-12 **66**......................(p) AlistairRawlinson 6 58
(Tom Dascombe) *w ldr to over 1f out: drvn and outpcd fnl f* **8/1**

430 **5** *nk* **Corton Lass**[41] 4895 2-8-7 **66**......................................... RowanScott(5) 7 57
(Keith Dalgleish) *t.k.h: trckd ldrs: rdn and outpcd wl over 1f out: edgd rt: kpt on ins fnl f: no imp* **14/1**

2544 **6** *2 ¾* **Villa Tora**[21] 5615 2-9-5 **73**.................................................. JoeFanning 3 55
(Mark Johnston) *t.k.h: slt ld to over 1f out: wknd ins fnl f* **7/1**

0000 **7** *½* **Mabo**[19] 5685 2-8-11 **65**............................................... JackGarritty 4 46
(Richard Fahey) *s.i.s: bhd and sn outpcd: n.d fr 1/2-way* **9/1**

6505 **8** *3 ½* **Lord Of The Glen**[21] 5603 2-8-2 **56**...........................(p) PatrickMathers 1 26
(Jim Goldie) *s.i.s: bhd and outpcd: struggling over 2f out: sn btn* **22/1**

1m 15.32s (3.12) **Going Correction** +0.425s/f (Yiel) **8** Ran SP% **110.2**
Speed ratings (Par 94): **96,94,92,90,89 85,85,80**
CSF £21.12 CT £53.41 TOTE £5.90: £1.70, £1.50, £1.40; EX 23.70 Trifecta £81.20.
**Owner** A Killoran **Bred** Patrick Cassidy **Trained** Langton, N Yorks

**FOCUS**
Rain throughout the week and on race day left the going as soft (GoingStick: 5.3). Rails: Straight reduced to 14m wide (far side rail moved in 2m). Loop rail out 5yds adding approximately 13yds to races 2, 3 & 5\n\x\x Stalls: 5f - centre; 6f & 1m4f - stands' side; 1m - Inside. A fair nursery with three previous winners taking on some unexposed types. The winner is improving and can find another race of this type. A minor pb from the winner.

## 6380 WHYSETTLE IT NOVICE STKS — 1m 68y
6:05 (6:06) (Class 5) 2-Y-O **£3,881** (£1,155; £577; £288) **Stalls** Low

Form RPR

**1** **Lisheen Castle (IRE)** 2-9-2 0............................................ JasonHart 3 84+
(John Quinn) *trckd ldrs: wnt 2nd 3f out: effrt and edgd lft over 1f out: led last 50yds: styd on strly* **8/1**

**2** *1 ¼* **Ayutthaya (IRE)** 2-9-2 0...................................................... TomEaves 1 82+
(Kevin Ryan) *led at ordinary gallop: rdn and qcknd over 2f out: hdd last 50yds: one pce* **5/2**[2]

3 **3** *3* **I'm Improving (IRE)**[13] 5918 2-9-2 0............................. AndrewMullen 8 75
(Keith Dalgleish) *t.k.h early: prom: effrt and pushed along 3f out: hung rt over 1f out: sn one pce* **13/8**[1]

**4** *3 ¾* **Unwritten** 2-9-2 0.................................................................. BenCurtis 5 67
(K R Burke) *s.i.s: hld up: effrt and rdn 3f out: no imp fr 2f out* **12/1**

**5** *¾* **Buckstopper Kit (USA)** 2-9-2 0......................................... DavidNolan 7 65
(Richard Fahey) *s.i.s: hld up: effrt and drvn along over 3f out: no imp fr over 2f out* **7/1**[3]

**6** *11* **French Resistance (IRE)** 2-9-2 0............................. ConnorBeasley 2 41
(Roger Fell) *s.i.s: sn in tch: outpcd 3f out: sn btn* **33/1**

0 **7** *1 ¼* **Dr Richard Kimble (IRE)**[13] 5918 2-9-2 0........................ JoeFanning 6 38
(Mark Johnston) *chsd ldr to 3f out: rdn and wknd fr 2f out* **15/2**

00 **8** *11* **Lady Cashmere (IRE)**[15] 5834 2-8-6 0........................... RowanScott(5) 4 9
(Alistair Whillans) *towards rr: pushed along after 2f: rdn and struggling over 3f out: sn wknd* **66/1**

1m 52.02s (3.62) **Going Correction** +0.65s/f (Yiel) **8** Ran SP% **114.2**
Speed ratings (Par 94): **107,105,102,99,98 87,86,75**
CSF £28.28 TOTE £8.80: £2.70, £1.10, £1.10; EX 29.70 Trifecta £75.30.
**Owner** Ross Harmon & Partner **Bred** Aidan Sexton **Trained** Settrington, N Yorks

**FOCUS**
Add 13yds. A decent-looking juvenile contest containing some quite costly and well-bred types. The first two look promising. The runner-up is perhaps the key to the level.

## 6381 CALA HOMES (WEST) JUST ASK CALA H'CAP — 1m 68y
6:35 (6:36) (Class 6) (0-65,66) 3-Y-O **£3,234** (£962; £481; £240) **Stalls** Low

Form RPR

605 **1** **Fleetfoot Jack (IRE)**[20] 5666 3-9-2 **60**...........................(p) DavidNolan 9 72
(David O'Meara) *hld up in tch: rdn 3f out: rallied over 1f out: led ins fnl f: sn clr* **9/2**[3]

3602 **2** *3 ¼* **Tesko Fella (IRE)**[8] 6091 3-9-3 **61**...................................... JackGarritty 5 66
(Ruth Carr) *pressed ldr: led over 2f out: rdn and hdd ins fnl f: one pce* **6/4**[1]

0035 **3** *1* **Kulgri**[17] 5741 3-8-8 **52**.....................................................(p[1]) JoeDoyle 4 55
(Kevin Ryan) *led to over 2f out: rallied over 1f out: one pce ins fnl f* **9/1**

5555 **4** *½* **Cliff Bay (IRE)**[14] 5880 3-9-8 **66**..................................... ConnorBeasley 1 68
(Keith Dalgleish) *t.k.h: prom: effrt and rdn over 2f out: kpt on same pce fnl f* **7/2**[2]

3000 **5** *1 ½* **Cool Run Girl (IRE)**[23] 5542 3-8-2 **46** oh1.....................(t[1]) JoeFanning 2 44
(Iain Jardine) *in tch: rdn over 2f out: edgd rt: no imp fr over 1f out* **17/2**

0066 **6** *1 ¾* **Tranquil Tracy**[17] 5761 3-8-3 **47**........................................ PaddyAspell 7 42
(John Norton) *missed break: bhd: drvn and outpcd over 3f out: no imp fr 2f out* **33/1**

6400 **7** *10* **Hamriyah**[6] 6181 3-8-8 **55**..................................(p) RachelRichardson(3) 8 28
(Tim Easterby) *dwlt: hld up: drvn and outpcd over 2f out: sn wknd* **11/1**

1m 54.18s (5.78) **Going Correction** +0.65s/f (Yiel) **7** Ran SP% **112.2**
Speed ratings (Par 98): **97,93,92,92,90 89,79**
CSF £11.23 CT £55.47 TOTE £5.50: £2.20, £1.50; EX 13.00 Trifecta £62.70.
**Owner** F Gillespie **Bred** Marston Stud **Trained** Upper Helmsley, N Yorks
■ Stewards' Enquiry : David Nolan two-day ban: used whip above the permitted level (8-10 Sept)

**FOCUS**
Add 13yds. A moderate handicap which produced a decisive winner. The runner-up has been rated a bit below his latest effort.

## 6382 EBF STALLIONS SCOTTISH PREMIER SERIES FILLIES' H'CAP — 6f 6y
7:05 (7:07) (Class 3) (0-90,89) 3-Y-O+
**£11,205** (£3,355; £1,677; £838; £419; £210) **Stalls** High

Form RPR

12 **1** **Clon Coulis (IRE)**[35] 5117 3-9-7 **89**...................................... BenCurtis 9 101+
(David Barron) *hld up: rdn along over 2f out: hdwy over 1f out: led ins fnl f: sn clr* **11/10**[1]

1431 **2** *2 ½* **Rutherford (IRE)**[27] 5399 3-8-13 **81**.................................... ShaneGray 5 85
(Kevin Ryan) *cl up: led over 1f out: hdd ins fnl f: kpt on same pce* **7/1**[3]

0645 **3** *1 ¾* **Courier**[15] 5828 5-9-4 **83**.................................................... BarryMcHugh 4 81
(Marjorie Fife) *led: rdn and hdd over 1f out: rallied: kpt on same pce fnl f* **16/1**

5405 **4** *2 ¾* **Forever A Lady (IRE)**[14] 5881 4-8-6 **71**......................... AndrewMullen 1 60
(Keith Dalgleish) *hld up in tch on outside: rdn and effrt over 2f out: no imp fr over 1f out* **33/1**

2400 **5** *1 ½* **Honeysuckle Lil (IRE)**[20] 5635 5-8-2 **70** oh2..(p) RachelRichardson(3) 8 54
(Tim Easterby) *racd against stands' rail: w ldr: rdn and hung rt over 1f out: sn outpcd* **10/1**

0135 **6** *½* **Lexington Sky (IRE)**[7] 6149 3-8-7 **75**.......................... ConnorBeasley 2 58
(Roger Fell) *hld up: rdn over 2f out: no imp over 1f out* **20/1**

0003 **7** *shd* **Megan Lily (IRE)**[13] 5916 3-9-0 **89**........................ ConnorMurtagh(7) 3 71+
(Richard Fahey) *hld up in tch: effrt whn nt clr run over 2f out to over 1f out: sn wknd* **9/1**

23-4 **8** *¾* **Mistime (IRE)**[15] 5856 3-9-3 **85**.......................................... JoeFanning 6 65
(Mark Johnston) *chsd ldrs: rdn over 2f out: wknd over 1f out* **20/1**

-043 **9** *14* **Marie Of Lyon**[27] 5422 3-8-12 **83**........................... AdamMcNamara(3) 7 18
(Richard Fahey) *hld up in tch: rdn over 2f out: wknd wl over 1f out: eased whn btn ins fnl f* **11/2**[2]

1m 13.7s (1.50) **Going Correction** +0.425s/f (Yiel)
**WFA** 3 from 4yo+ 3lb **9** Ran SP% **112.9**
Speed ratings (Par 104): **107,103,101,97,95 95,94,93,75**
CSF £8.51 CT £77.68 TOTE £1.80: £1.30, £1.80, £3.80; EX 10.60 Trifecta £62.50.
**Owner** Ms Colette Twomey **Bred** Collette Twomey **Trained** Maunby, N Yorks

**FOCUS**
A competitive fillies' handicap which saw the winner cut through the pack to score impressively. She could go quite a long way in the sprint division. It's been rated around the runner-up.

## 6383 LADBROKES LANARK SILVER BELL H'CAP — 1m 4f 15y
7:35 (7:38) (Class 3) (0-90,90) 3-Y-O+
**£16,185** (£4,846; £2,423; £1,211; £605; £304) **Stalls** Low

Form RPR

0311 **1** **Sepal (USA)**[4] 6269 4-8-1 **74** 12ex............................ JamieGormley(7) 5 87
(Iain Jardine) *in tch: lost pl over 4f out: gd hdwy on outside over 2f out: led over 1f out: drew clr ins fnl f* **7/2**[2]

1410 **2** *3 ½* **Brimham Rocks**[23] 5525 3-9-0 **89**........................................ BenCurtis 3 96
(Ralph Beckett) *hld up on ins: rdn and effrt over 3f out: chsd wnr ins fnl f: kpt on: nt pce to chal* **7/2**[2]

1212 **3** *1 ½* **Donnachies Girl (IRE)**[14] 5872 4-8-5 **71**...................... BarryMcHugh 11 76
(Alistair Whillans) *in tch: hdwy to ld over 2f out: rdn and hdd over 1f out: kpt on same pce ins fnl f* **10/1**

1121 **4** *hd* **Archi's Affaire**[41] 4899 3-9-0 **89**.................................. AndrewMullen 1 93+
(Michael Dods) *hld up: rdn and outpcd over 3f out: rallied and in tch whn nt clr run over 1f out: styd on ins fnl f* **10/3**[1]

0005 **5** *6* **Corton Lad**[11] 5996 7-9-4 **89**........................................(tp) RowanScott(5) 4 84
(Keith Dalgleish) *t.k.h: trckd ldrs: rdn along over 3f out: wknd over 1f out* **50/1**

411 **6** *1 ¼* **Indy (IRE)**[15] 5830 6-9-3 **83**................................................... JasonHart 10 76
(John Quinn) *hld up in tch: effrt and drvn along 3f out: no imp fr over 1f out* **10/1**

2465 **7** *½* **Kensington Star**[14] 5882 4-9-6 **86**............................(b[1]) ConnorBeasley 9 78
(Keith Dalgleish) *dwlt: hld up towards rr: drvn along over 3f out: no imp fnl 2f* **10/1**

1041 **8** *nk* **Pumblechook**[17] 5737 4-9-8 **88**........................................... JoeFanning 7 79
(Mark Johnston) *hld up: hdwy and cl up over 2f out: rdn and wknd over 1f out* **7/1**[3]

0146 **9** *2 ½* **Be Perfect (USA)**[17] 5737 8-9-5 **85**..........................(b) JamesSullivan 6 72
(Ruth Carr) *led to over 2f out: rdn and wknd over 1f out* **50/1**

3026 **10** *13* **Sennockian Star**[7] 6151 7-9-10 **90**...................................... TomEaves 8 57
(Mark Johnston) *trckd ldr tl rdn and wknd fr 3f out* **22/1**

6234 **11** *13* **Gworn**[11] 5996 7-8-10 **81**.......................................... CallumRodriguez(5) 12 27
(R Mike Smith) *hld up on outside: rdn over 3f out: wknd over 2f out* **28/1**

2m 44.24s (5.64) **Going Correction** +0.65s/f (Yiel)
**WFA** 3 from 4yo+ 9lb **11** Ran SP% **119.0**
Speed ratings (Par 107): **107,104,103,103,99 98,98,98,96,87 79**
CSF £15.87 CT £111.90 TOTE £4.30: £1.70, £1.90, £2.20; EX 19.30 Trifecta £136.40.
**Owner** I J Jardine **Bred** Juddmonte Farms Inc **Trained** Carrutherstown, D'fries & G'way

**FOCUS**
Add 13yds. A really good renewal of this race ended in one-way traffic for the winner, who completed her hat-trick in emphatic style. The runner-up has been rated similar to his penultimate C&D form.

## 6384 DOWNLOAD THE LADBROKES APP H'CAP 5f 7y
**8:05** (8:06) (Class 6) (0-65,69) 3-Y-0+ **£3,234** (£962; £481; £240) **Stalls** Centre

Form RPR
0502 **1** **Knockamany Bends (IRE)**[18] 5695 7-8-5 **46**..........(h) JamesSullivan 11 52
(John Wainwright) *prom against stands' rail: rdn and effrt over 1f out: kpt on wl fnl f to ld towards fin* **5/1**[3]
0501 **2** *nse* **Hot Hannah**[25] 5472 3-9-2 **64**.............................. CallumRodriguez[(5)] 3 70
(Michael Dods) *led: rdn over 1f out: kpt on fnl f: hdd towards fin* **5/2**[1]
4151 **3** *¾* **Perfect Words (IRE)**[7] 6130 7-9-7 **69** 6ex...............(p) HarrisonShaw[(7)] 4 72
(Marjorie Fife) *trckd ldrs: effrt and ev ch over 1f out: kpt on ins fnl f* **8/1**
4153 **4** *¾* **Cheeni**[13] 5919 5-8-7 **48**.......................................(p) PatrickMathers 5 48
(Jim Goldie) *in tch: effrt and drvn along 2f out: kpt on ins fnl f* **13/2**
0004 **5** *½* **Imperial Legend (IRE)**[13] 5930 8-9-2 **60**............ RachelRichardson[(3)] 1 59
(Alan Brown) *hld up: hdwy on outside 2f out: rdn and kpt on same pce ins fnl f* **14/1**
000 **6** *1* **Sir Domino (FR)**[17] 5738 5-9-0 **55**.................................(v[1]) JackGarritty 2 50
(Patrick Holmes) *cl up: rdn and ev ch wl over 1f out: rdn and outpcd fnl f* **14/1**
1210 **7** *1 ¾* **Dutch Dream**[25] 5472 4-8-13 **54**.................................... AndrewMullen 8 43
(Linda Perratt) *dwlt and swtchd lft s: bhd: rdn over 2f out: kpt on fnl f: nvr on terms* **9/2**[2]
0000 **8** *¾* **Reflation**[18] 5695 5-8-8 **49**.......................................(p) ConnorBeasley 7 35
(Patrick Holmes) *bhd: drvn and outpcd over 2f out: nvr on terms* **22/1**
0000 **9** *shd* **Tinsill**[8] 6089 6-8-5 **46** oh1..................................... JoeDoyle 9 32
(Nigel Tinkler) *trckd ldrs: rdn over 2f out: wknd over 1f out* **9/1**

1m 3.0s (3.00) **Going Correction** +0.425s/f (Yiel)
**WFA** 3 from 4yo+ 2lb **9** Ran SP% **115.5**
Speed ratings (Par 101): **93,92,91,90,89 88,85,84,83**
CSF £17.91 CT £98.83 TOTE £6.50: £2.10, £1.40, £2.70; EX 26.70 Trifecta £179.10.
**Owner** D R & E E Brown **Bred** Mike Hyde **Trained** Kennythorpe, N Yorks

**FOCUS**
An ordinary sprint handicap which produced a thrilling finish and a winner who repeated his success of a year ago. The second and third have been rated to their recent marks.
T/Plt: £9.50 to a £1 stake. Pool: £52,833.84 - 4,059.01 winning units. T/Qpdt: £7.20 to a £1 stake. Pool: £4,491.17 - 456.82 winning units. **Richard Young**

# 6197 NEWMARKET (R-H)
Friday, August 25
**OFFICIAL GOING: Good (good to firm in places; 7.7)**
Wind: Light behind Weather: Fine

## 6385 TRM EXCELLENCE IN EQUINE NUTRITION EBF FILLIES' NOVICE STKS (PLUS 10 RACE) (DIV I) 7f
**1:35** (1:39) (Class 4) 2-Y-O **£4,528** (£1,347; £673; £336) **Stalls** Low

Form RPR
3 **1** **Expressiy (FR)**[28] 5349 2-9-0 0..............................(h) ColmO'Donoghue 7 87
(Charlie Appleby) *sn led: shkn up over 1f out: rdn clr fnl f* **11/4**[2]
4 **2** *4* **Tivoli (IRE)**[20] 5660 2-9-0 0..................................... RobertTart 4 76
(John Gosden) *dwlt: hld up: pushed along over 2f out: hdwy and edgd rt over 1f out: stdy on to go 2nd wl ins fnl f: no ch w wnr* **5/6**[1]
2 **3** *½* **Blanchefleur (IRE)**[13] 5934 2-9-0 0........................... TomMarquand 2 75
(Richard Hannon) *prom: chsd wnr over 2f out: rdn over 1f out: no ex ins fnl f* **8/1**[3]
**4** *5* **Going Native** 2-8-9 0........................................... JennyPowell[(5)] 6 61
(Ed Walker) *hld up: pushed along and hdwy over 2f out: wknd ins fnl f* **66/1**
**5** *½* **Girls Talk (IRE)** 2-9-0 0........................................ LouisSteward 5 60
(Michael Bell) *hld up: shkn up and hung lft over 1f out: nvr trbld ldrs* **40/1**
**6** *3 ½* **Light Relief** 2-9-0 0............................................. GeraldMosse 10 51
(James Tate) *chsd wnr after 1f tl rdn over 2f out: wknd fnl f* **20/1**
**7** *1 ¾* **Admired** 2-9-0 0................................................... OisinMurphy 1 46
(Sir Michael Stoute) *hld up: shkn up 1/2-way: wknd over 1f out* **14/1**
**8** *3 ¼* **Faay (IRE)** 2-9-0 0.............................................. AntonioFresu 3 37
(Ed Dunlop) *chsd ldrs: flashed tail: pushed along 3f out: wknd over 1f out* **20/1**
**9** *½* **Kazeera** 2-9-0 0.................................................. TrevorWhelan 8 36
(Roger Charlton) *s.i.s: hld up: pushed along over 2f out: hung lft and wknd over 1f out* **33/1**
**10** *shd* **Narodowa** 2-9-0 0............................................... RobertWinston 9 35
(David Lanigan) *plld hrd and prom: stdd and lost pl after 1f: wknd 2f out* **50/1**

1m 25.59s (-0.11) **Going Correction** -0.075s/f (Good) **10** Ran SP% **117.4**
Speed ratings (Par 93): **97,92,91,86,85 81,79,75,75,75**
CSF £5.04 TOTE £3.60: £1.40, £1.02, £1.70; EX 6.60 Trifecta £19.10.
**Owner** Godolphin **Bred** Elevage De La Croix De Place **Trained** Newmarket, Suffolk

**FOCUS**
Rail movements increased advertised distances for Races 5 and 7 by 2 yards. The first division of a fairly decent juvenile fillies' novice contest. They went a respectable gallop on loose-topped ground officially described as good, good to firm in places. The third has been rated 5lb below her debut effort.

## 6386 TRM EXCELLENCE IN EQUINE NUTRITION EBF FILLIES' NOVICE STKS (PLUS 10 RACE) (DIV II) 7f
**2:05** (2:05) (Class 4) 2-Y-O **£4,528** (£1,347; £673; £336) **Stalls** Low

Form RPR
3 **1** **Vitamin (IRE)**[13] 5938 2-9-0 0..................................... TomMarquand 5 84
(Richard Hannon) *chsd ldr tl led over 1f out: rdn out* **5/2**[2]
**2** *2* **Soliloquy** 2-9-0 0................................................. ColmO'Donoghue 6 79+
(Charlie Appleby) *chsd ldrs: shkn up to chse wnr over 1f out: rdn and hung lft ins fnl f: styd on same pce* **11/8**[1]
36 **3** *½* **Ziarah (IRE)**[105] 2563 2-9-0 0.....................................(h) GeraldMosse 8 77
(James Tate) *hld up: pushed along and hdwy over 2f out: rdn over 1f out: styd on* **8/1**
5 **4** *3 ¼* **Diva Star**[71] 3747 2-9-0 0............................................. MartinDwyer 4 68
(Marcus Tregoning) *hld up: shkn up over 2f out: nt clr run sn after: hdwy over 1f out: no ex ins fnl f* **11/2**[3]
**5** *6* **Takiah** 2-9-0 0....................................................... JimmyFortune 3 52
(Brian Meehan) *chsd ldrs: rdn over 2f out: wknd over 1f out* **20/1**
00 **6** *¾* **Forest Dragon**[28] 5371 2-9-0 0.............................. JosephineGordon 1 50
(Hugo Palmer) *led: hung lft over 2f out: rdn and hdd over 1f out: wknd fnl f* **66/1**
**7** *3 ¾* **More Than More (USA)** 2-9-0 0.................................. HarryBentley 2 40
(George Peckham) *hld up: pushed along 1/2-way: hung lft and wknd over 1f out* **50/1**
**8** *2 ½* **Sister Celine (IRE)** 2-9-0 0...................................... TrevorWhelan 7 33
(Roger Charlton) *s.i.s: rn green: hung lft and a in rr* **33/1**
**9** *23* **Briscola** 2-9-0 0.................................................... RobertTart 9
(John Gosden) *dwlt: rn green: hung lft and a in rr* **12/1**

1m 25.0s (-0.70) **Going Correction** -0.075s/f (Good) **9** Ran SP% **116.0**
Speed ratings (Par 93): **101,98,98,94,87 86,82,79,53**
CSF £6.14 TOTE £2.90: £1.10, £1.10, £2.30; EX 7.80 Trifecta £37.70.
**Owner** Hussain Alabbas Lootah **Bred** B V Sangster **Trained** East Everleigh, Wilts

**FOCUS**
The second division of a fairly decent juvenile fillies' novice contest. The winning time was over half-a-second quicker than the first. It's been rated as straightforward form around the winner and third.

## 6387 TRMSUPPLEMENTS.CO.UK H'CAP 1m
**2:40** (2:41) (Class 4) (0-80,80) 3-Y-O **£5,175** (£1,540; £769; £384) **Stalls** Low

Form RPR
6604 **1** **Whip Nae Nae (IRE)**[9] 6073 3-9-7 **80**.......................... TomMarquand 8 84
(Richard Hannon) *a.p: rdn to ld 1f out: styd on* **6/1**[3]
6401 **2** *1 ¼* **Slow To Hand**[8] 6112 3-8-2 **61** 6ex.........................(b) JosephineGordon 2 62+
(William Jarvis) *hld up: pushed along 3f out: rdn over 1f out: r.o wl ins fnl f to go 2nd nr fin: nt rch wnr* **6/1**[3]
1020 **3** *hd* **Rumpole**[22] 5568 3-9-7 **80**........................................ RobertWinston 7 81
(Hughie Morrison) *led: rdn and hdd 1f out: edgd rt ins fnl f: styd on same pce* **9/2**[2]
0324 **4** *½* **Abatement**[42] 4831 3-9-5 **78**.................................... HarryBentley 5 78
(Roger Charlton) *s.i.s: sn prom: rdn over 1f out: nt clr run ins fnl f: kpt on* **5/2**[1]
-321 **5** *shd* **Working Class**[27] 5409 3-9-5 **78**.................................. OisinMurphy 4 78
(Peter Chapple-Hyam) *chsd ldr: rdn over 2f out: lost 2nd over 1f out: styd on* **8/1**
512 **6** *hd* **Fastar (IRE)**[12] 5961 3-9-4 **77**................................... JimmyFortune 9 76
(Brian Meehan) *chsd ldrs: rdn and ev ch over 1f out: no ex wl ins fnl f* **8/1**
6044 **7** *2 ¼* **Kreb's Cycle (IRE)**[20] 5664 3-9-2 **75**............................(t[1]) MartinDwyer 3 69
(Ian Williams) *hld up: rdn and edgd lft over 1f out: nt trble ldrs* **12/1**
0-22 **8** *1* **Captain Pugwash (IRE)**[16] 5783 3-8-7 **66**..................... JoeyHaynes 1 58
(Henry Spiller) *edgd rt s: hld up: rdn over 2f out: sme hdwy 1f out: sn hung lft: wknd wl ins fnl f* **16/1**
006 **9** *1 ¾* **Weloof (FR)**[15] 5849 3-9-3 **76**.................................(b[1]) GeraldMosse 6 64
(Ed Dunlop) *hld up in tch: rdn over 1f out: wknd ins fnl f* **33/1**

1m 39.3s (-0.70) **Going Correction** -0.075s/f (Good) **9** Ran SP% **114.1**
Speed ratings (Par 102): **100,98,98,98,97 97,95,94,92**
CSF £41.22 CT £177.75 TOTE £7.50: £1.90, £1.90, £1.80; EX 44.90 Trifecta £283.20.
**Owner** Sullivan Bloodstock Limited/Mr R Hannon **Bred** Paul Starr **Trained** East Everleigh, Wilts

**FOCUS**
A fairly decent 3yo handicap. They went an, at best, respectable gallop centrally despite the first two winners coming up the near rail. The runner-up and third help set the standard, with the fourth to his turf form.

## 6388 FARM & STABLE TRM DISTRIBUTION EBF NOVICE STKS (PLUS 10 RACE) 7f
**3:15** (3:19) (Class 4) 2-Y-O **£4,528** (£1,347; £673; £336) **Stalls** Low

Form RPR
14 **1** **Fortune's Pearl (IRE)**[28] 5380 2-9-3 0............................ OisinMurphy 2 91
(Andrew Balding) *chsd ldr tl led 2f out: rdn and hung lft ins fnl f: jst hld on* **12/1**[3]
**2** *hd* **Thrave** 2-9-0 0...................................................... HarryBentley 11 87+
(Henry Candy) *hld up in tch: shkn up over 1f out: chsd wnr ins fnl f: r.o* **25/1**
6 **3** *3 ¼* **Power Of Darkness**[20] 5641 2-9-0 0.............................. MartinDwyer 10 79
(Marcus Tregoning) *trckd ldrs: rdn and hung lft over 1f out: nt clr run ins fnl f: styd on same pce* **18/1**
2 **4** *¾* **Al Hajar (IRE)**[27] 5420 2-9-0 0.................................. ColmO'Donoghue 7 77
(Charlie Appleby) *s.i.s: sn rcvrd into mid-div: hdwy over 4f out: rdn and ev ch over 1f out: hmpd and no ex ins fnl f* **4/6**[1]
**5** *¾* **Deyaarna (USA)** 2-9-0 0........................................... MartinLane 12 75+
(Saeed bin Suroor) *s.i.s: rn green in rr: r.o ins fnl f: nrst fin* **16/1**
22 **6** *shd* **Ode To Autumn**[18] 5709 2-9-0 0.................................(p[1]) RobertTart 1 74
(John Gosden) *led 5f: no ex ins fnl f* **6/1**[2]
**7** *½* **Agar's Plough** 2-9-0 0............................................. JimmyQuinn 14 73
(Ed Dunlop) *hld up: pushed along over 2f out: r.o ins fnl f: nvr nrr* **100/1**
21 **8** *¾* **Al Barg (IRE)**[25] 5476 2-9-6 0.................................... TomMarquand 5 77
(Richard Hannon) *chsd ldrs: rdn and hung lft over 1f out: wknd ins fnl f* **6/1**[2]
45 **9** *4* **Fiery Breath**[27] 5437 2-9-0 0.......................................(t[1]) PaoloSirigu 6 60
(Robert Eddery) *hld up: plld hrd: wknd over 1f out* **100/1**
**10** *10* **Revolutionary Man (IRE)** 2-9-0 0.............................. GeraldMosse 8 33
(Simon Crisford) *s.i.s: hdwy 1/2-way: wknd over 1f out* **33/1**
**11** *5* **Prince Consort (IRE)** 2-9-0 0.................................... JimmyFortune 13 20
(Brian Meehan) *mid-div: rdn over 2f out: wknd over 1f out* **100/1**
**12** *15* **Banjo's Voice** 2-8-11 0......................................... CharlieBennett[(3)] 9
(Jane Chapple-Hyam) *a in rr: wknd 3f out* **100/1**
**13** *1 ¾* **Tommy Boy** 2-9-0 0................................................ RobertWinston 4
(Tony Carroll) *s.i.s: a in rr: wknd 3f out* **66/1**

1m 24.96s (-0.74) **Going Correction** -0.075s/f (Good) **13** Ran SP% **119.6**
Speed ratings (Par 96): **101,100,97,96,95 95,94,93,89,77 72,54,52**
CSF £272.53 TOTE £13.80: £2.90, £7.70, £4.90; EX 389.90 Trifecta £8680.20 Part Won..
**Owner** Qatar Racing Limited **Bred** Miss Joann Lyons **Trained** Kingsclere, Hants
■ Airglow was withdrawn. Price at time of withdrawal 40/1. Rule 4 does not apply

**FOCUS**
A decent juvenile novice contest. The wayward winner produced the quickest comparative time on the card thus far, racing mainly up the near rail.

## 6389 EQUINE SUPPLEMENTS YOU CAN TRUST H'CAP 1m 2f
**3:45** (3:47) (Class 4) (0-80,82) 3-Y-O **£5,175** (£1,540; £769; £384) **Stalls** Centre

Form RPR
231 **1** **Torcello (IRE)**[27] 5428 3-9-9 **81**.................................... OisinMurphy 5 91+
(Andrew Balding) *sn led: hdd over 6f out: chsd ldr: led again wl over 1f out: sn rdn and hdd: rallied to ld and n.m.r wl ins fnl f: r.o wl* **7/4**[1]

4206 **2** 1 1/4 **Lunar Jet**[49] 4580 3-8-12 **70** JimmyQuinn 3 77
(John Mackie) *plld hrd and prom: lost pl over 5f out: hdwy and nt clr run over 2f out: rdn to ld over 1f out: hung rt and hdd wl ins fnl f* **20/1**

2505 **3** nk **Ply**[79] 3457 3-9-3 **75** HarryBentley 1 81+
(Roger Charlton) *hld up: nt clr run over 2f out: hdwy u.p over 1f out: edgd lft ins fnl f: r.o* **4/1**[3]

4150 **4** hd **Near Kettering**[26] 5455 3-9-7 **79** GeraldMosse 2 85
(Luca Cumani) *chsd ldrs: nt clr run over 2f out: rdn over 1f out: r.o* **14/1**

322 **5** 6 **Balashakh (USA)**[41] 4913 3-9-2 **74** (h) JoeyHaynes 6 68
(David Simcock) *hld up: pushed along 3f out: hdwy u.p and nt clr much room over 1f out: wknd ins fnl f* **8/1**

5150 **6** 12 **Desert Dream**[27] 5404 3-9-6 **78** JosephineGordon 7 48
(Sir Michael Stoute) *hld up: hdwy over 2f out: rdn and wknd over 1f out* **18/1**

2251 **7** hd **Maratha (IRE)**[48] 4631 3-9-10 **82** JimmyFortune 8 52
(Stuart Williams) *chsd ldr over 8f out: led over 6f out: rdn and hdd wl over 1f out: wknd fnl f: eased towards fin* **7/2**[2]

3531 **8** 8 **Drumochter**[16] 5782 3-9-2 **74** RobertWinston 4 28
(Charles Hills) *hld up in tch: rdn over 2f out: wknd and eased over 1f out* **11/1**

2m 5.46s (-0.04) **Going Correction** -0.075s/f (Good) 8 Ran SP% **114.7**
Speed ratings (Par 102): **97,96,95,95,90 81,81,74**
CSF £40.88 CT £126.48 TOTE £2.60: £1.20, £4.80, £1.50; EX 42.50 Trifecta £152.50.
**Owner** Mick and Janice Mariscotti **Bred** Rathasker Stud **Trained** Kingsclere, Hants
■ Stewards' Enquiry : Jimmy Quinn caution: careless riding

**FOCUS**
A fairly decent 3yo handicap. They went a muddling gallop but the heavily supported favourite justified the market confidence. It's been rated around the runner-up, with the third in line with the better view of his form.

## 6390 HORSE REQUISITES NEWMARKET STOCKIST OF TRM MAIDEN STKS 1m
**4:20** (4:23) (Class 5) 3-Y-O+ **£3,881** (£1,155; £577; £288) **Stalls** Low

Form RPR

3- **1** **Dynamic**[307] 7548 3-9-0 0 OisinMurphy 1 86
(William Haggas) *trckd ldr tl shkn up to ld and edgd rt over 1f out: r.o wl: comf* **8/11**[1]

**2** 3 3/4 **Stage Name** 3-9-0 0 JosephineGordon 3 77
(Hugo Palmer) *s.i.s: racd keenly and sn prom: shkn up and edgd rt over 1f out: styd on same pce ins fnl f* **6/1**[3]

3-34 **3** 2 1/4 **Red Royalist**[102] 2682 3-9-5 80 (p[1]) MartinDwyer 6 77
(Marcus Tregoning) *led at stdy pce tl qcknd over 2f out: rdn and hdd over 1f out: no ex ins fnl f* **9/4**[2]

**4** 3/4 **Dash Of Spice** 3-9-5 0 TomMarquand 5 75
(David Elsworth) *s.i.s: hld up: pushed along over 2f out: sn outpcd: r.o towards fin* **10/1**

1m 41.77s (1.77) **Going Correction** -0.075s/f (Good) 4 Ran SP% **112.0**
Speed ratings (Par 103): **88,84,82,81**
CSF £5.81 TOTE £1.50; EX 4.60 Trifecta £5.10.
**Owner** Michael & Mrs Michelle Morris **Bred** W And R Barnett Ltd **Trained** Newmarket, Suffolk

**FOCUS**
A fairly decent small-field maiden. They went a modest gallop but the odds-on favourite won with plenty in hand. The level is a bit fluid.

## 6391 TBA CENTENARY FILLIES' H'CAP 1m 6f
**4:55** (4:57) (Class 3) (0-95,95) 3-Y-O+ **£16,172** (£4,812; £2,405; £1,202) **Stalls** Centre

Form RPR

1340 **1** **Fire Jet (IRE)**[35] 5108 4-9-3 **84** JimmyQuinn 2 91
(John Mackie) *a.p: shkn up 3f out: rdn to ld ins fnl f: styd on* **14/1**

3431 **2** nk **Melinoe**[10] 6038 3-8-2 **79** 6ex MartinDwyer 6 86
(Sir Mark Prescott Bt) *chsd ldr 1f: remained handy: led wl over 2f out: rdn and edgd rt over 1f out: hdd ins fnl f: styd on* **15/8**[2]

/2-5 **3** 1/2 **Groovejet**[20] 5658 6-9-9 **95** JennyPowell[(5)] 4 101
(Richard Spencer) *hld up: hdwy over 3f out: rdn: edgd rt and ev ch fr over 1f out: styd on* **14/1**

322 **4** 1 1/4 **Notice (IRE)**[8] 6104 4-9-0 **81** HarryBentley 3 86
(David Simcock) *hld up: hdwy u.p over 1f out: styd on same pce towards fin* **5/4**[1]

0000 **5** 1 **Intense Tango**[13] 5924 6-9-1 **85** (t) CliffordLee[(3)] 1 88
(K R Burke) *led: rdn and hdd wl over 2f out: styd on same pce wl ins fnl f* **20/1**

5040 **6** 4 1/2 **Moorside**[20] 5658 4-9-7 **88** OisinMurphy 5 85
(Charles Hills) *pushed along to chse ldr after 1f: wnt upsides over 4f out: rdn and ev ch over 2f out: wknd fnl f* **6/1**[3]

2m 57.9s (0.20) **Going Correction** -0.075s/f (Good)
**WFA** 3 from 4yo+ 10lb 6 Ran SP% **111.6**
Speed ratings (Par 104): **96,95,95,94,94 91**
CSF £40.29 TOTE £11.60: £4.30, £1.50; EX 25.50 Trifecta £128.00.
**Owner** Ladas **Bred** Ladas **Trained** Church Broughton , Derbys
■ Stewards' Enquiry : Jimmy Quinn two-day ban: used whip above the permitted level (Sept 8-10)

**FOCUS**
The feature contest was a good staying fillies' handicap. The stands' rail bias had been the feature of the day and was well to the fore in this race. The third has been rated close to form.

## 6392 INVEST IN CALPHORMIN H'CAP 6f
**5:25** (5:28) (Class 3) (0-90,90) 3-Y-O **£7,762** (£2,310; £1,154; £577) **Stalls** Low

Form RPR

2625 **1** **Rely On Me (IRE)**[27] 5433 3-8-11 **80** (p[1]) OisinMurphy 1 89
(Andrew Balding) *w ldr tl rdn to ld over 1f out: styd on u.p* **4/1**[1]

5102 **2** 3/4 **Stanhope**[12] 5959 3-8-13 **82** TomMarquand 4 88
(Mick Quinn) *chsd ldrs: rdn and ev ch over 1f out: styd on* **7/1**

2215 **3** 3 **Open Wide (USA)**[10] 6026 3-9-4 **87** (b) MartinDwyer 7 83
(Amanda Perrett) *prom: lost pl over 3f out: hdwy u.p over 1f out: styd on same pce ins fnl f* **9/2**[2]

162 **4** nse **Muscika**[33] 5184 3-9-1 **84** MartinLane 6 80
(David O'Meara) *hld up: hdwy over 2f out: rdn over 1f out: styd on same pce ins fnl f* **4/1**[1]

4-60 **5** hd **Kodiline (IRE)**[69] 3844 3-9-7 **90** (v[1]) GeraldMosse 3 86
(Clive Cox) *s.i.s: racd keenly and sn trcking ldrs: rdn over 1f out: styd on same pce* **6/1**

1551 **6** 3 1/4 **In The Spotlight (IRE)**[8] 6113 3-8-12 **81** 6ex (p) LouisSteward 5 66
(Henry Spiller) *hld up: effrt and nt clr run over 1f out: wknd fnl f* **10/1**

2226 **7** 1 1/2 **Love Oasis**[21] 5612 3-8-10 **79** HarryBentley 8 59
(Mark Johnston) *led: rdn and hdd over 1f out: wknd ins fnl f* **5/1**[3]

1m 11.55s (-0.95) **Going Correction** -0.075s/f (Good) 7 Ran SP% **110.7**
Speed ratings (Par 104): **103,102,98,97,97 93,91**
CSF £29.66 CT £123.01 TOTE £4.30: £2.00, £4.10; EX 29.20 Trifecta £128.00.
**Owner** Sheikh Juma Dalmook Al Maktoum **Bred** Old Carhue Stud **Trained** Kingsclere, Hants

**FOCUS**
Race distance increased by 2 yards. A decent 3yo handicap. The stands' rail bias struck again, with the winner, emerging from stall 1, recording the quickest comparative time on the day. The runner-up has been rated to form.
T/Plt: £125.80 to a £1 stake. Pool: £57,085.75 - 331.18 winning units T/Qpdt: £214.90 to a £1 stake. Pool: £3,137.13 - 10.80 winning units **Colin Roberts**

# 6100 SALISBURY (R-H)
Friday, August 25

**OFFICIAL GOING: Good (good to firm in places) changing to good after race 2 (5.50)**
Wind: almost nil Weather: warm

## 6393 SHIPSEYS MARQUEES AMATEUR RIDERS' H'CAP 1m
**5:15** (5:16) (Class 5) (0-70,68) 3-Y-O+ **£3,275** (£1,015; £507; £254) **Stalls** Low

Form RPR

3122 **1** **Hawridge Glory (IRE)**[16] 5800 3-10-3 **63** MrPMillman 14 76
(Rod Millman) *hld up: hdwy over 2f out: led ent fnl f: r.o wl: readily* **3/1**[2]

6351 **2** 3 **Masarzain (IRE)**[8] 6102 4-11-0 **68** 6ex MrSWalker 9 75
(Archie Watson) *trckd ldrs: led over 2f out: sn rdn: hdd ent fnl f: kpt on same pce* **7/4**[1]

0034 **3** 2 1/2 **McDelta**[8] 6101 7-10-2 **56** MissSBrotherton 1 57
(Geoffrey Deacon) *chsd ldrs: rdn over 2f out: kpt on to go 3rd over 1f out but nt pce to get on terms* **4/1**[3]

5030 **4** 5 **Smart Mover (IRE)**[18] 5714 4-9-4 **51** MrsDScott[(7)] 8 41
(Nikki Evans) *trckd ldrs tl squeezed up after 3f: in tch and sn pushed along: styd on to go 4th ins fnl f but nvr gng pce to get bk involved* **50/1**

24-4 **5** 1 1/4 **Swot**[188] 811 5-10-5 **59** (p) MrsCBartley 3 46
(Roger Teal) *prom: rdn and ev ch over 2f out tl over 1f out: fdd fnl f* **10/1**

-606 **6** nk **Wordismybond**[27] 5427 8-10-5 **64** (p) MrJamiePerrett[(5)] 12 50
(Brendan Powell) *trckd ldrs: rdn over 2f out: sn one pce* **25/1**

205 **7** 11 **Living Leader**[58] 4203 8-9-6 **53** MissCMBerry[(7)] 2 14
(Grace Harris) *led tl rdn over 2f out: wknd over 1f out* **16/1**

0643 **8** 13 **Moonshine Dancer**[9] 6076 3-9-13 **64** (h) MissIsabelWilliams[(5)] 13
(Christian Williams) *s.i.s: a in rr* **8/1**

00-0 **9** 16 **Zebs Lad (IRE)**[25] 5473 5-9-12 **55** (p) MissJodieHughes[(3)] 5
(Nikki Evans) *chsd ldrs tl wknd over 3f out* **50/1**

1m 44.2s (0.70) **Going Correction** -0.125s/f (Firm)
**WFA** 3 from 4yo+ 6lb 9 Ran SP% **115.2**
Speed ratings (Par 103): **91,88,85,80,79 78,67,54,38**
CSF £8.50 CT £19.76 TOTE £3.70: £1.30, £1.30, £1.10; EX 10.60 Trifecta £29.40.
**Owner** Eric Gadsden **Bred** Alan O'Flynn **Trained** Kentisbeare, Devon
■ Stewards' Enquiry : Miss C M Berry 14-day ban: used whip above the permitted level and when her horse was showing no response

**FOCUS**
Competitive enough for the grade and the two in-form horses finished first and second, so the form looks solid enough for the level. The runner-up has been rated as finding a bit on his latest C&D win.

## 6394 BATHWICK TYRES NOVICE AUCTION STKS (PLUS 10 RACE) 6f
**5:50** (5:51) (Class 4) 2-Y-O **£4,043** (£1,203; £601; £300) **Stalls** Low

Form RPR

13 **1** **Bambino Lola**[34] 5154 2-8-10 0 RoystonFfrench 8 85+
(Adam West) *trckd ldrs: shkn up to ld wl over 1f out: r.o wl: comf* **9/4**[1]

23 **2** 3 1/2 **Bombastic (IRE)**[24] 5504 2-9-2 0 DougieCostello 4 81
(Ed de Giles) *led: rdn and hdd wl over 1f out: kpt on but nt pce of wnr* **11/4**[2]

0 **3** 2 **Blackheath**[41] 4909 2-9-2 0 RyanTate 2 75
(Ed Walker) *s.i.s: sn trcking ldrs: rdn 2f out: kpt on same pce* **5/1**[3]

**4** 2 1/4 **Scenery** 2-8-11 0 CharlesBishop 1 63
(Eve Johnson Houghton) *trckd ldrs: rdn 2f out: kpt on but nt pce to get on terms* **6/1**

50 **5** 3 1/4 **Surfa Rosa**[17] 5749 2-8-13 0 SeanLevey 3 55
(Richard Hannon) *prom: rdn 2f out: wknd ent fnl f* **8/1**

**6** 6 **Claudine (IRE)** 2-8-1 0 RosieJessop[(3)] 5 28
(Henry Candy) *sn outpcd in rr: nvr on terms* **20/1**

4 **7** shd **Achianna (USA)**[29] 5321 2-8-11 0 SteveDrowne 6 35
(Rod Millman) *chsd ldrs: rdn over 2f out: wknd over 1f out* **33/1**

**8** 1 **Beyond Equal** 2-8-8 0 EdwardGreatrex[(3)] 7 32
(Stuart Kittow) *s.i.s: a in last pair* **14/1**

1m 13.66s (-1.14) **Going Correction** -0.125s/f (Firm) 8 Ran SP% **113.9**
Speed ratings (Par 96): **102,97,94,91,87 79,79,77**
CSF £8.48 TOTE £3.40: £1.40, £1.10, £1.50; EX 6.40 Trifecta £30.40.
**Owner** Maharaj Freeze **Bred** M E Broughton **Trained** Epsom, Surrey

**FOCUS**
This didn't look a bad little race on paper, but the winner has looked no superstar in two previous runs and was still able to beat the boys with something to spare under a penalty, so the colts in here might not be up to much. The runner-up has been rated to his Goodwood mark.

## 6395 BATHWICK CAR & VAN HIRE NURSERY H'CAP 1m
**6:20** (6:20) (Class 5) (0-75,77) 2-Y-O **£3,396** (£1,010; £505; £252) **Stalls** Low

Form RPR

005 **1** **El Borracho (IRE)**[45] 4709 2-8-11 **65** CharlesBishop 8 69
(Simon Dow) *fly-leapt s: hld up: hdwy 3f out: led 2f out: sn rdn: hld on wl fnl f: all out* **6/1**

003 **2** nk **Motabassim (IRE)**[22] 5557 2-9-3 **71** (b[1]) RyanTate 1 74
(Brian Meehan) *prom: rdn and ev ch fr over 2f out: kpt on ins fnl f: jst hld* **9/1**

6345 **3** 3/4 **Deadly Reel (IRE)**[43] 4786 2-8-12 **69** EdwardGreatrex[(3)] 2 71
(Archie Watson) *hld up in last pair: rdn 2f out: r.o wl fnl f: snatched 3rd cl to home* **13/2**

5030 **4** 1 **Daddies Girl (IRE)**[14] 5875 2-9-7 **75** SteveDrowne 4 74
(Rod Millman) *chsd ldrs: pushed along to hold pl over 3f out: hdwy over 1f out to chse front pair: kpt on same pce fnl f: lost 3rd cl home* **10/1**

2444 **5** 6 **Red Force One**[19] 5680 2-9-9 **77** (t[1]) RoystonFfrench 10 62
(Tom Dascombe) *led: rdn and hdd 2f out: fdd fnl f* **9/1**

565 **6** 2 3/4 **Galactic (IRE)**[23] 5547 2-9-0 **68** SeanLevey 3 47
(Richard Hannon) *in tch: rdn wl over 2f out: wknd over 1f out* **11/2**[3]

053 **7** nk **Strategic (IRE)**[16] 5786 2-9-3 **71** (b[1]) PatDobbs 9 49
(Richard Hannon) *hld up in last pair: rdn 3f out: nvr threatened* **5/1**[2]

6233 **8** hd **Sardenya (IRE)**[17] 5742 2-8-12 **71** (b[1]) PaddyPilley[(5)] 6 49
(Roger Charlton) *trckd ldrs: chal 3f out: sn rdn: wknd over 1f out* **10/3**[1]

0630 **9** *25* **General Zoff**[28] 5366 2-9-3 **71**........................................ DougieCostello 5
(William Muir) *prom for over 3f* **16/1**

1m 42.74s (-0.76) **Going Correction** -0.125s/f (Firm) 9 Ran SP% **117.7**
Speed ratings (Par 94): **98,97,96,95,89 87,86,86,61**
CSF £59.72 CT £367.59 TOTE £9.90: £3.10, £2.40, £1.90; EX 76.00 Trifecta £480.70.
**Owner** Robert Moss **Bred** Christopher Maye **Trained** Ashtead, Surrey
■ Stewards' Enquiry : Charles Bishop four-day ban: used whip above the permitted level (Sept 8-12)

**FOCUS**
A wide open nursery on paper and the front four came clear. It's been rated around the balance of the first four.

## 6396 BRITISH STALLION STUDS EBF STONEHENGE STKS (LISTED RACE) 1m
**6:55** (6:55) (Class 1) 2-Y-O
**£17,013** (£6,450; £3,228; £1,608; £807; £405) **Stalls** Low

Form RPR
113 **1** **Mildenberger**[24] 5501 2-9-1 104........................................ FrannyNorton 2 101
(Mark Johnston) *trckd ldr: edgd rt whn sltly outpcd jst over 2f out: r.o wl fnl 120yds: led fnl stride* **11/10[1]**
12 **2** *nse* **Albishr (IRE)**[35] 5106 2-9-1 0........................................ DougieCostello 1 101
(Richard Hannon) *led: qcknd 2 l clr jst over 2f out: sn rdn: kpt on fnl f: hdd fnl stride* **28/1**
14 **3** *¾* **Tigre Du Terre (FR)**[27] 5395 2-9-1 0........................................ SeanLevey 6 99
(Richard Hannon) *hld up: making hdwy whn swtchd lft over 2f out: rdn to chse ldr ent fnl f: kpt on but no ex fnl 70yds* **7/2[2]**
21 **4** *8* **Time Change**[57] 4253 2-8-10 0........................................ PatDobbs 4 76
(Ralph Beckett) *trckd ldrs: rdn over 2f out: wknd ins fnl f* **8/1**
12 **5** *3* **The Last Emperor**[16] 5808 2-9-1 0........................................ AndreaAtzeni 7 74
(Roger Varian) *hld up: effrt wl over 2f out: nt pce to get on terms: fdd fnl f* **6/1[3]**
115 **6** *1 ¼* **Ghost Serge (IRE)**[27] 5395 2-9-1 99........................................ LukeMorris 3 71
(Archie Watson) *wnt lft s: trckd ldrs: rdn over 2f out: wknd ent fnl f* **8/1**
41 **7** *6* **Watheer**[49] 4560 2-9-1 0........................................ SteveDrowne 5 57
(Marcus Tregoning) *racd keenly: sn trcking ldrs: rdn over 2f out: sn hung rt: wknd over 1f out* **18/1**

1m 42.15s (-1.35) **Going Correction** -0.125s/f (Firm) 7 Ran SP% **115.1**
Speed ratings (Par 102): **101,100,100,92,89 87,81**
CSF £37.06 TOTE £1.80: £1.30, £10.50; EX 27.80 Trifecta £120.90.
**Owner** Sheikh Hamdan bin Mohammed Al Maktoum **Bred** Godolphin **Trained** Middleham Moor, N Yorks

**FOCUS**
A decent Listed race that produced a thrilling finish as the 'form' horse pulled the race out of the fire having looked cooked two furlongs out.

## 6397 EDWARDS FORD FORAY MOTOR GROUP H'CAP 6f 213y
**7:25** (7:26) (Class 4) (0-85,86) 3-Y-O **£5,175** (£1,540; £769; £384) **Stalls** Centre

Form RPR
-421 **1** **Bengal Lancer**[9] 6076 3-8-1 71........................................ ManuelFernandes(7) 4 92
(Ian Williams) *trckd clr ldr: led 2f out: drifted rt but sn qcknd clr: easily* **10/11[1]**
0553 **2** *8* **Rebel De Lope**[44] 4736 3-9-7 84........................................ SteveDrowne 3 84
(Charles Hills) *in tch: hdwy fr 3f out: swtchd rt 2f out: sn rdn to chse wnr: kpt on but readily outpcd sn after* **10/1**
0213 **3** *3 ¾* **Limelite (IRE)**[36] 5078 3-8-9 72........................................(h[1]) SeanLevey 1 62
(Richard Hannon) *s.i.s: in last pair: hung bdly lft over 2f out: hdwy u.p on stands' side rails over 1f out: kpt on fnl f but nt pce to get involved* **8/1[3]**
113 **4** *hd* **Family Fortunes**[113] 2334 3-9-9 86........................................ PatDobbs 7 76
(Sylvester Kirk) *in tch: chal for 3rd wl over 1f out: sn rdn: kpt on same pce fnl f* **9/2[2]**
4600 **5** *hd* **Jackhammer (IRE)**[29] 5323 3-9-2 79........................................ LukeMorris 6 68
(William Knight) *chsd clr ldr: clsd whn rdn over 2f out: kpt on same pce* **20/1**
4300 **6** *3 ¼* **Arc Royal**[27] 5400 3-8-12 75........................................(v[1]) RoystonFfrench 5 56
(Tom Dascombe) *set str gallop: hdd 2f out: wknd* **14/1**
-046 **7** *7* **Warrior's Spirit (IRE)**[76] 3588 3-9-1 78........................................ DougieCostello 2 41
(Richard Hannon) *awkwardly away: a in last pair: wknd over 1f out* **10/1**

1m 26.43s (-2.17) **Going Correction** -0.125s/f (Firm) 7 Ran SP% **111.3**
Speed ratings (Par 102): **107,97,93,93,93 89,81**
CSF £10.45 TOTE £1.70: £1.50, £4.60; EX 10.40 Trifecta £40.70.
**Owner** G S Tuck **Bred** G S Tuck **Trained** Portway, Worcs

**FOCUS**
This race was taken apart by a horse a long way ahead of the assessor. The runner-up has been rated close to this year's form.

## 6398 PAM BRUFORD MEMORIAL H'CAP 1m 6f 44y
**7:55** (7:55) (Class 5) (0-75,76) 3-Y-O+ **£3,396** (£1,010; £505; £252) **Stalls** Far side

Form RPR
6001 **1** **Brandon Castle**[25] 5483 5-9-4 68........................................(t) EdwardGreatrex(3) 2 78
(Archie Watson) *plld hrd: led after 2f: sn drew wl clr: rdn and hung lft over 1f out: a in command: unchal* **4/1[3]**
4423 **2** *2* **Really Super**[30] 5273 3-9-4 75........................................(b) PatDobbs 7 81
(Ralph Beckett) *hld up in tch: hdwy fr 4f out: rdn to chse wnr over 2f out: styd on but nvr threatened to get on terms* **9/2**
0063 **3** *3 ¼* **The Twisler**[10] 6038 5-10-0 75........................................(p) TrevorWhelan 8 77
(Neil Mulholland) *hld up in tch: hdwy 3f out: rdn to chal for 2nd over 2f out: styd on same pce fnl f* **3/1[2]**
6034 **4** *5* **Pioneertown (IRE)**[30] 5298 3-9-2 73........................................ LukeMorris 3 68
(Sir Mark Prescott Bt) *trckd ldrs: rdn over 3f out: nvr threatened: one pce fnl 2f* **2/1[1]**
0000 **5** *½* **Calvinist**[27] 5397 4-9-7 75........................................(t[1]) ManuelFernandes(7) 5 70
(Ian Williams) *hld up: rdn 3f out: nvr threatened to get involved* **9/1**
2400 **6** *5* **Start Seven**[15] 5820 5-10-1 76........................................ DougieCostello 6 64
(Jamie Osborne) *slowly away and hmpd s: sn trcking ldrs: rdn 3f out: sn wknd* **25/1**
502/ **7** *44* **Beat Route**[1477] 5231 10-8-9 56........................................ KierenFox 4
(Michael Attwater) *hld up: rdn over 3f out: sn wknd* **40/1**
1340 **8** *dist* **Iona Island**[58] 4217 4-9-2 63........................................ JohnFahy 1
(Peter Hiatt) *led for 2f: chsd ldr tl lost pl over 6f out: struggling and detached over 5f out: t.o* **40/1**

3m 8.17s (0.77) **Going Correction** -0.125s/f (Firm)
**WFA** 3 from 4yo+ 10lb 8 Ran SP% **115.2**
Speed ratings (Par 103): **92,90,89,86,85 83,57,**
CSF £22.09 CT £59.86 TOTE £5.10: £1.60, £1.60, £1.40; EX 21.20 Trifecta £82.50.
**Owner** C R Hirst **Bred** Barry Walters **Trained** Upper Lambourn, W Berks

**FOCUS**
The winner stole this from the front and it looks unreliable form. The runner-up has been rated to form.
T/Plt: £15.20 to a £1 stake. Pool: £47,165.65 - 2,257.61 winning units. T/Qpdt: £7.00 to a £1 stake. Pool: £3,125.64 - 329.99 winning units. **Tim Mitchell**

# 6353 YORK (L-H)
Friday, August 25

**OFFICIAL GOING: Good (good to soft in places; overall 7.0; home straight: far side 6.9, centre 7.0, stands side' 6.8)**
Wind: Light across Weather: Cloudy with sunny periods

## 6399 SKY BET FIRST RACE SPECIAL H'CAP 1m 3f 188y
**1:55** (1:57) (Class 2) (0-105,104) 3-Y-O+
**£43,575** (£13,048; £6,524; £3,262; £1,631; £819) **Stalls** Centre

Form RPR
-100 **1** **Fidaawy**[28] 5353 4-9-4 98........................................ JimCrowley 11 108
(Sir Michael Stoute) *trckd ldr: smooth hdwy to ld over 2f out: jnd and rdn over 1f out: drvn and kpt on wl fnl f* **11/1**
3002 **2** *½* **Red Galileo**[28] 5353 6-9-8 102........................................ DanielTudhope 10 111
(Saeed bin Suroor) *trckd ldng pair: hdwy over 2f out: chal over 1f out and sn rdn: drvn and ev ch ins fnl f: kpt on same pce towards fin* **7/1[3]**
6001 **3** *2 ¾* **Erik The Red (FR)**[20] 5634 5-9-6 100........................................(p) KevinStott 14 105
(Kevin Ryan) *hld up towards rr: hdwy 3f out: chsd ldrs over 1f out: sn rdn: styd on to chse ldng pair ins fnl f: drvn and no imp towards fin* **6/1[1]**
4-26 **4** *1 ¾* **Al Neksh**[56] 4316 4-8-11 91........................................ FrankieDettori 6 93+
(William Haggas) *t.k.h early: trckd ldrs: hdwy over 2f out: rdn wl over 1f out: drvn and kpt on same pce fnl f* **9/1**
2312 **5** *½* **Londinium**[21] 5598 3-8-5 94........................................ PJMcDonald 3 96
(Mark Johnston) *trckd ldrs on inner: hdwy over 3f out: rdn along 2f out: kpt on same pce u.p fnl f* **6/1[1]**
3410 **6** *¾* **Dance King**[13] 5924 7-8-7 87........................................(tp) JamesSullivan 5 87
(Tim Easterby) *hld up in midfield: hdwy wl over 2f out: rdn along wl over 1f out: sn drvn and kpt on same pce* **25/1**
1260 **7** *½* **Speedo Boy (FR)**[42] 4856 3-8-11 100........................................ SilvestreDeSousa 7 100
(Ian Williams) *t.k.h early: hld up towards rr: hdwy over 2f out: rdn along and swtchd lft to inner 1 1/2f out: sn drvn and kpt on fnl f* **13/2[2]**
-125 **8** *1* **Appeared**[28] 5353 5-9-10 104........................................ AndreaAtzeni 16 101
(Roger Varian) *trckd ldrs: hdwy over 3f out: pushed along to chse ldng pair over 2f out: rdn wl over 1f out: sn one pce* **6/1[1]**
3601 **9** *hd* **Amazing Red (IRE)**[20] 5663 4-8-10 90........................................ PaulMulrennan 8 87
(Ed Dunlop) *hld up towards rr: hdwy 3f out: rdn along 2f out: sn no imp* **12/1**
0- **10** *3 ¼* **Landsman (IRE)**[33] 5192 4-8-8 88........................................(t) PaulHanagan 9 80
(A J Martin, Ire) *nvr bttr than midfield* **14/1**
00-0 **11** *¾* **Moonmeister (IRE)**[21] 5622 6-8-10 90........................................(t) FranBerry 2 81
(A J Martin, Ire) *led early: in tch on inner: hdwy over 2f out: rdn to chse ldrs 1 1/2f out: sn drvn and wknd* **20/1**
0115 **12** *1 ½* **Mukhayyam**[13] 5913 5-9-0 94........................................(p) DavidAllan 13 82
(Tim Easterby) *rdn along s and sn led: pushed along over 3f out: rdn and hdd over 2f out: sn wknd* **14/1**
206- **13** *11* **Master Of Finance (IRE)**[111] 3666 6-9-1 95........................................ GrahamLee 15 66
(Malcolm Jefferson) *a in rr: lost tch and bhd fr over 3f out* **50/1**
046 **14** *26* **Song Of Love (IRE)**[16] 5798 5-7-10 81 oh10 ow1...(p) RichardOliver(5) 1 10
(Shaun Harris) *a towards rr: rdn along wl over 3f out: sn outpcd and bhd* **100/1**

2m 30.13s (-3.07) **Going Correction** 0.0s/f (Good)
**WFA** 3 from 4yo+ 9lb 14 Ran SP% **119.6**
Speed ratings (Par 109): **110,109,107,106,106 105,105,104,104,102 102,101,93,76**
CSF £82.94 CT £515.16 TOTE £14.20: £4.70, £2.30, £2.60; EX 101.50 Trifecta £533.60.
**Owner** Hamdan Al Maktoum **Bred** Shadwell Estate Company Limited **Trained** Newmarket, Suffolk

**FOCUS**
The rail had been moved out to provide fresh ground and the course had dried out overnight leading to a description of good, good to soft in places. After the opener winning jockey Jim Crowley agreed that it was "generally good", Paul Hanagan stated it was, "on the slow side of good but drying all the time", but Graham Lee called it, "a bit dead." They went 15yds further than the advertised distance in this good handicap. There was a bit of an uneven gallop and it proved hard to come from off the pace.

## 6400 WEATHERBYS HAMILTON LONSDALE CUP STKS (GROUP 2) (BRITISH CHAMPIONS SERIES) 2m 56y
**2:25** (2:29) (Class 1) 3-Y-O+
**£113,420** (£43,000; £21,520; £10,720; £5,380; £2,700) **Stalls** Low

Form RPR
0-12 **1** **Montaly**[48] 4639 6-9-3 105........................................ PJMcDonald 4 114
(Andrew Balding) *hld up in rr: hdwy over 3f out: chsd ldrs on outer 2f out: rdn over 1f out: carried rt ins fnl f: drvn and styd on gamely to ld on line* **16/1**
2-14 **2** *nse* **Dartmouth**[62] 4070 5-9-6 115........................................ RyanMoore 8 117
(Sir Michael Stoute) *trckd ldrs: hdwy over 3f out: chal 2f out: rdn to take narrow advantage over 1f out: sn drvn and edgd persistently rt ins fnl f: hdd on line* **11/4[1]**
0-22 **3** *½* **St Michel**[77] 3553 4-9-3 112........................................(b) LukeMorris 7 113+
(Sir Mark Prescott Bt) *hld up in rr: smooth hdwy on outer over 2f out: trckd ldrs over 1f out: chal ent fnl f: sn rdn and ev ch whn carried rt ins fnl f: drvn and no ex towards fin* **14/1**
3360 **4** *2* **Sheikhzayedroad**[24] 5503 8-9-3 115........................................(h) MartinHarley 1 111
(David Simcock) *trckd ldrs: hdwy wl over 2f out: rdn to chse ldrs over 1f out: drvn and kpt on same pce fnl f* **15/2**
/350 **5** *1* **High Jinx (IRE)**[24] 5503 9-9-3 109........................................ DavidAllan 9 110
(Tim Easterby) *led and set sound gallop: pushed along over 3f out: rdn and hdd over 2f out: drvn over 1f out: kpt on fnl f* **33/1**
-616 **6** *shd* **Dal Harraild**[62] 4070 4-9-3 111........................................ PatCosgrave 3 110
(William Haggas) *hld up towards rr: hdwy 3f out: trckd ldrs whn n.m.r 2f out: rdn and n.m.r over 1f out: chsd ldrs ent fnl f: sn drvn and no imp* **7/2[2]**
1/12 **7** *1 ¼* **Thomas Hobson**[62] 4073 7-9-3 110........................................ JimCrowley 6 108
(W P Mullins, Ire) *trckd ldng pair: hdwy to trck ldr 3f out: led over 2f out: rdn wl over 1f out: hdd and drvn appr fnl f: grad wknd* **4/1[3]**
5200 **8** *12* **Prince Of Arran**[24] 5503 4-9-3 107........................................(p) StevieDonohoe 5 94
(Charlie Fellowes) *trckd ldng pair: pushed along over 4f out: rdn and wknd over 3f out* **25/1**

2210 **9** 2 ½ **Higher Power**[24] 5503 5-9-3 110........................ JamesDoyle 2 91
(James Fanshawe) *sn chsng ldr: pushed along over 4f out: rdn along 3f out: sn wknd* **7/1**

3m 31.06s (-3.44) **Going Correction** 0.0s/f (Good) 9 Ran SP% **112.5**
Speed ratings (Par 115): **108,107,107,106,106 106,105,99,98**
CSF £58.19 TOTE £18.50: £4.00, £1.40, £3.10; EX 79.40 Trifecta £799.00.
**Owner** Farleigh Racing **Bred** Farleigh Court Racing Partnership **Trained** Kingsclere, Hants

**FOCUS**
Distance increased by 15yds. A really competitive edition of this, it was run at a good gallop and several had their chance. The second and third help with the standard.

## 6401 SKY BET CITY OF YORK STKS (GROUP 3) 7f

**3:00** (3:03) (Class 1) 3-Y-0+

**£99,242** (£37,625; £18,830; £9,380; £4,707; £2,362) **Stalls** Low

Form RPR

1-40 **1** **Talaayeb**[71] 3749 3-8-6 109........................ ChrisHayes 8 111
(Owen Burrows) *midfield: pushed along hdwy over 2f out: rdn to ld narrowly over 1f out: kpt on* **9/1**

5005 **2** *nk* **Toscanini (IRE)**[23] 5527 5-9-0 110........................ PaulHanagan 15 115
(Richard Fahey) *chsd ldrs: rdn over 2f out: kpt on wl fnl 110yds: wnt 2nd nr fin* **20/1**

0303 **3** *shd* **Suedois (FR)**[24] 5502 6-9-0 112........................ DanielTudhope 18 115
(David O'Meara) *prom: rdn and ev ch 2f out: one pce fnl 50yds: lost 2nd nr fin* **13/2**[2]

2030 **4** *1* **Jallota**[24] 5502 6-9-0 109........................ JamieSpencer 14 112
(Charles Hills) *hld up in midfield: bit short of room over 2f out: angled rt wl over 1f out: sn rdn and hdwy: kpt on fnl f* **14/1**

3425 **5** *hd* **So Beloved**[24] 5502 7-9-0 111........................(h) AdamKirby 6 111
(David O'Meara) *s.i.s: hld up: pushed along over 2f out: swtchd lft over 1f out: sn hdwy: rdn and kpt on fnl f* **10/1**

2210 **6** *hd* **Jungle Cat (IRE)**[24] 5502 5-9-0 113........................(b) JamesDoyle 7 111
(Charlie Appleby) *in tch: rdn to chse ldr 2f out: one pce fnl 110yds* **8/1**[3]

1443 **7** *1 ½* **Gordon Lord Byron (IRE)**[12] 5974 9-9-5 111........................ WJLee 3 112
(T Hogan, Ire) *trckd ldrs: rdn over 2f out: no ex ins fnl f* **33/1**

4410 **8** *hd* **Above The Rest (IRE)**[27] 5393 6-9-0 107...........(h) SilvestreDeSousa 16 106
(David Barron) *in tch towards outer: rdn over 2f out: kpt on same pce* **33/1**

5-20 **9** *¾* **Don't Touch**[55] 4354 5-9-0 109........................ PhillipMakin 2 104
(Richard Fahey) *in tch: rdn over 2f out: one pce fnl f* **16/1**

5613 **10** *3 ½* **Love Dreams (IRE)**[20] 5662 3-8-9 100........................ PJMcDonald 19 93
(Mark Johnston) *midfield towards outer: rdn over 2f out: no imp* **40/1**

3330 **11** *hd* **Mubtasim (IRE)**[40] 4935 3-8-9 107........................(p) DavidAllan 4 92
(William Haggas) *led: rdn over 2f out: hdd over 1f out: edgd lft and wknd* **12/1**

110 **12** *¾* **Mix And Mingle (IRE)**[65] 3961 4-9-0 113........................ TedDurcan 11 92
(Chris Wall) *midfield: rdn over 2f out: no imp* **16/1**

511- **13** *4 ½* **Spangled**[350] 6281 5-8-11 107........................ AndreaAtzeni 1 77
(Roger Varian) *hld up in midfield: rdn over 2f out: sn wknd* **12/1**

6242 **14** *1* **Aeolus**[20] 5640 6-9-0 103........................(p) PatCosgrave 9 77
(Ed Walker) *hld up: nvr threatened* **25/1**

-205 **15** *1* **Escobar (IRE)**[21] 5593 3-8-9 105........................(p) FranBerry 5 73
(Hugo Palmer) *hld up: racd keenly: rdn over 2f out: sn wknd* **40/1**

1001 **16** *4* **Rusumaat (IRE)**[34] 5147 3-8-9 109........................ JimCrowley 13 62
(Mark Johnston) *prom: rdn over 2f out: sn wknd* **12/1**

1050 **17** *23* **Perfect Pasture**[20] 5640 7-9-0 106........................(v) PaulMulrennan 10 2
(Michael Easterby) *a in rr* **66/1**

136 **P** **Daban (IRE)**[65] 3959 3-8-9 111........................ FrankieDettori 12
(John Gosden) *hld up: p.u and dismntd after 1f* **4/1**[1]

1m 24.08s (-1.22) **Going Correction** +0.175s/f (Good)
**WFA** 3 from 4yo+ 5lb 18 Ran SP% **125.9**
Speed ratings (Par 113): **113,112,112,111,111 110,109,109,108,104 103,103,97,96,95 91,64,**
CSF £187.08 TOTE £10.40: £4.00, £6.30, £2.60; EX 265.70 Trifecta £2802.20.
**Owner** Hamdan Al Maktoum **Bred** Shadwell Estate Company Limited **Trained** Lambourn, Berks
■ Stewards' Enquiry : W J Lee four-day ban: used whip above the permitted level (Sept 8-12)

**FOCUS**
The second year of this race being run as a Group 3 and, despite coming just six days after the Group 2 Hungerford over the same distance, there was a good, high-class turnout. 13lb covered the whole field on official ratings and it was a shame that the well-backed favourite was pulled up soon after the start. For the third year in a row it went to a 3yo filly.

## 6402 COOLMORE NUNTHORPE STKS (GROUP 1) (BRITISH CHAMPIONS SERIES) 5f

**3:35** (3:37) (Class 1) 2-Y-0+

**£198,485** (£75,250; £37,660; £18,760; £9,415; £4,725) **Stalls** Low

Form RPR

1323 **1** **Marsha (IRE)**[21] 5595 4-9-8 114........................ LukeMorris 8 122
(Sir Mark Prescott Bt) *racd towards stands' side: trckd ldrs: n.m.r wl over 1f out: sn chsng ldng pair: rdn to chse ldr ent fnl f: sn drvn: edgd lft and kpt on wl towards fin: led on line* **8/1**[3]

3-11 **2** *nse* **Lady Aurelia (USA)**[66] 3926 3-9-6 122........................ FrankieDettori 3 122+
(Wesley A Ward, U.S.A) *ponied to s: qckly away and led towards centre: rdn and qcknd ent fnl f: drvn and edgd lft ins fnl f: hdd on line* **10/11**[1]

0034 **3** *3 ¾* **Cotai Glory**[19] 5684 5-9-11 108........................ SilvestreDeSousa 4 111
(Charles Hills) *in rr centre: rdn along over 2f out: hdwy over 1f out: styd on fnl f* **50/1**

-111 **4** *1 ½* **Battaash (IRE)**[21] 5595 3-9-9 122........................ JimCrowley 9 106
(Charles Hills) *racd towards stands' side: prom: chsd ldr 2f out: rdn over 1f out: drvn and kpt on same pce fnl f* **11/4**[2]

5100 **5** *shd* **Priceless**[21] 5595 4-9-8 108........................ AdamKirby 2 102
(Clive Cox) *racd centre: chsd ldrs: rdn along 2f out: sn drvn and kpt on fnl f* **33/1**

-222 **6** *½* **Profitable (IRE)**[21] 5595 5-9-11 116........................ JamesDoyle 1 103
(Clive Cox) *racd towards far side: towards rr: rdn along over 2f out: kpt on fnl f* **8/1**[3]

0520 **7** *1* **Final Venture**[21] 5595 5-9-11 111........................ PaulMulrennan 12 100
(Paul Midgley) *racd towards stands' side: prom: rdn along 2f out: sn drvn and wknd over 1f out* **40/1**

3602 **8** *shd* **Alpha Delphini**[20] 5647 6-9-11 109........................(p) GrahamLee 5 99
(Bryan Smart) *racd centre: chsd ldrs: rdn along 2f out: drvn and wknd over 1f out* **50/1**

0363 **9** *nk* **Goldream**[35] 5116 8-9-11 107........................(v[1]) MartinHarley 10 98
(Robert Cowell) *racd towards stands' side: a towards rr* **66/1**

6051 **10** *3* **Washington DC (IRE)**[12] 5974 4-9-11 110........................(bt) RyanMoore 7 88
(A P O'Brien, Ire) *hmpd s: a bhd* **20/1**

0514 **11** *nse* **Take Cover**[21] 5595 10-9-11 111........................ DavidAllan 6 87
(David C Griffiths) *chsd ldr centre: rdn along over 2f out: wknd over 1f out* **25/1**

57.97s (-1.33) **Going Correction** +0.175s/f (Good)
**WFA** 3 from 4yo+ 2lb 11 Ran SP% **120.7**
Speed ratings: **117,116,110,108,108 107,105,105,105,100 100**
CSF £15.43 CT £381.30 TOTE £8.90: £2.30, £1.02, £11.60; EX 19.80 Trifecta £725.00.
**Owner** Elite Racing Club **Bred** Elite Racing Club **Trained** Newmarket, Suffolk

**FOCUS**
A cracking edition of the race and, although it very much looked a match on paper, that's not how it worked out. Top-class sprinting form. Marsha reversed recent form with the market 1-2, with Cotai Glory rated close to his form in this race last year.

## 6403 BRITISH STALLION STUDS EBF CONVIVIAL MAIDEN STKS (PLUS 10 RACE) 7f

**4:15** (4:21) (Class 2) 2-Y-0

**£43,575** (£13,048; £6,524; £3,262; £1,631; £819) **Stalls** Low

Form RPR

**1** **Dream Today (IRE)** 2-9-5 0........................ PJMcDonald 11 95+
(Mark Johnston) *prom: led 3f out: pushed along over 2f out: rdn over 1f out: wandered lft and rt ins fnl f: kpt on* **14/1**

2 **2** *1 ½* **Gabr**[21] 5608 2-9-5 0........................ JimCrowley 4 91+
(Sir Michael Stoute) *trckd ldrs: rdn over 2f out: chsd ldr over 1f out: kpt on but a hld* **3/1**[1]

32 **3** *3* **Laugh A Minute**[28] 5380 2-9-5 0........................ AndreaAtzeni 18 83
(Roger Varian) *trckd ldrs on outer: rdn to chse ldr over 1f out: one pce ins fnl f* **7/1**[3]

5 **4** *1 ¾* **Dubai Empire (FR)**[28] 5380 2-9-5 0........................ AdamKirby 12 79
(John Quinn) *hld up in midfield: rdn over 2f out: styd on fr over 1f out: wnt 4th nr fin* **16/1**

**5** *nk* **Corrosive (USA)** 2-9-5 0........................ JamesDoyle 8 78+
(Hugo Palmer) *dwlt: sn midfield on inner: rdn over 2f out: kpt on same pce* **33/1**

**6** *2* **Sha La La La Lee** 2-9-5 0........................ RichardKingscote 14 73
(Tom Dascombe) *hld up: pushed along 3f out: stl towards rr 2f out: styd on wl fnl f* **50/1**

3 **7** *nse* **Capital Flight (IRE)**[20] 5641 2-9-5 0........................ JamieSpencer 9 73
(Paul Cole) *sn led: hdd 3f out: sn rdn: wknd over 1f out* **11/2**[2]

44 **8** *½* **Arrogant (IRE)**[36] 5063 2-9-5 0........................ SilvestreDeSousa 15 71
(Jose Santos) *midfield: t.k.h early: rdn over 2f out: no imp* **50/1**

**9** *½* **Commander Han (FR)** 2-9-5 0........................ KevinStott 13 70+
(Kevin Ryan) *slowly away: rdn over 2f out: styd on fr over 1f out* **9/1**

2 **10** *nk* **Miss Mumtaz (IRE)**[7] 6159 2-9-0 0........................ DavidAllan 2 64
(Tony Carroll) *in tch: rdn over 2f out: wknd ins fnl f* **33/1**

32 **11** *1 ¾* **Porth Swtan (IRE)**[19] 5680 2-9-5 0........................ PaulHanagan 7 65
(Charles Hills) *trckd ldrs: rdn over 2f out: wknd over 1f out* **12/1**

**12** *nk* **Broken Force (USA)** 2-9-5 0........................ MartinHarley 5 64
(K R Burke) *dwlt: sn midfield: rdn over 2f out: sn wknd* **66/1**

2 **13** *1 ¼* **Kannapolis (IRE)**[81] 3399 2-9-5 0........................ CamHardie 6 61
(Michael Easterby) *prom: rdn over 2f out: wknd over 1f out* **66/1**

4 **14** *14* **Zilara (IRE)**[22] 5573 2-9-0 0........................ GrahamLee 16 19
(Ralph Beckett) *midfield: sn pushed along: wknd over 3f out* **33/1**

4 **15** *2* **Safrani (IRE)**[74] 3648 2-9-5 0........................ PhillipMakin 1 19
(David O'Meara) *trckd ldrs: rdn over 2f out: sn wknd* **66/1**

**16** *2 ¾* **Newborough** 2-9-5 0........................ LukeMorris 20 12
(Charles Hills) *dwlt: a towards rr* **40/1**

5 **17** *12* **Ganton Par**[42] 4862 2-9-5 0........................ PaulMulrennan 17
(Michael Easterby) *a towards rr* **100/1**

1m 26.4s (1.10) **Going Correction** +0.175s/f (Good) 17 Ran SP% **103.8**
Speed ratings (Par 100): **100,98,94,92,92 90,90,89,89,88 86,86,84,68,66 63,49**
CSF £36.36 TOTE £14.20: £4.00, £1.50, £2.20; EX 55.10 Trifecta £424.00.
**Owner** The Passionate Partnership **Bred** Ballylinch Stud **Trained** Middleham Moor, N Yorks
■ Doswell was withdrawn. Price at time of withdrawal 7/2. Rule 4 applies to all bets - deduction 20p in the pound.

**FOCUS**
Britain's richest maiden and it's no surprise that this looked very strong on paper. They took an age to load, some were in the gates for a long time and Doswell was withdrawn after getting fractious in the stalls. Subsequent Champagne Stakes & Racing Post Trophy winner Rivet took the race 12 months ago and the winner this time holds an entry in the former race.

## 6404 NATIONWIDE ACCIDENT REPAIR SERVICES H'CAP 7f 192y

**4:50** (4:53) (Class 2) (0-105,102) 3-Y-0

**£43,575** (£13,048; £6,524; £3,262; £1,631; £819) **Stalls** Low

Form RPR

3311 **1** **Mojito (IRE)**[20] 5661 3-9-0 **95**........................ JimCrowley 5 107+
(William Haggas) *t.k.h early: trckd ldrs: smooth hdwy to ld wl over 1f out: rdn ent fnl f: drvn and kpt on wl towards fin* **3/1**[1]

1351 **2** *2 ¼* **Battered**[20] 5642 3-9-1 **96**........................(b) SilvestreDeSousa 11 102
(William Haggas) *hld up in rr: hdwy on wd outside over 2f out: rdn to chse ldrs over 1f out: drvn and hung lft ins fnl f: kpt on* **8/1**

0030 **3** *1* **Kings Gift (IRE)**[22] 5568 3-9-5 **100**........................ PaulMulrennan 2 104
(Michael Dods) *cl up: led over 5f out: rdn over 2f out: hdd wl over 1f out: drvn and keeping on same pce whn sltly hmpd ins fnl f* **12/1**

2013 **4** *½* **Medahim (IRE)**[20] 5642 3-9-5 **100**........................ FrankieDettori 9 103
(Richard Hannon) *hld up: hdwy on inner 3f out: chsd ldrs 2f out: rdn over 1f out: kpt on same pce fnl f* **17/2**

1100 **5** *¾* **City Of Joy**[41] 4904 3-8-13 **94**........................ RyanMoore 14 95
(Sir Michael Stoute) *s.i.s and bhd: hdwy wl over 1f out: sn swtchd rt to outer and rdn: styd on wl fnl f* **16/1**

051 **6** *½* **Zymyran**[7] 6145 3-8-1 **85** 6ex........................(h) AaronJones[(3)] 1 85
(David Simcock) *dwlt and hld up in rr: hdwy on inner over 2f out: rdn along over 1f out: kpt on fnl f* **20/1**

-200 **7** *1* **Syphax (USA)**[43] 4817 3-9-5 **100**........................ JamesDoyle 10 98
(Kevin Ryan) *racd wd early: led: hdd over 5f out: cl up: rdn along over 2f out: drvn wl over 1f out: grad wknd* **6/1**[2]

3622 **8** *½* **Areen Heart (FR)**[34] 5165 3-8-7 **88**........................(h) PaulHanagan 15 85
(Richard Fahey) *trckd ldrs on outer: hdwy 1/2-way: cl up over 3f out: rdn along over 2f out: drvn wl over 1f out: grad wknd* **20/1**

2200 **9** *shd* **Wahash (IRE)**[55] 4334 3-9-1 **96**........................ RichardKingscote 12 92
(Richard Hannon) *nvr bttr than midfield* **33/1**

5113 **10** *½* **La Rav (IRE)**[17] 5744 3-8-13 **94**........................ JamieSpencer 4 93+
(Luca Cumani) *t.k.h: towards rr: hdwy over 2f out: rdn along wl over 1f out: keeping on but hld whn tk wrong step and eased ins fnl f* **13/2**[3]

3120 **11** ½ **Starlight Romance (IRE)**[27] 5434 3-8-6 **90**.............. SammyJoBell(3) 7 84
(Richard Fahey) *in tch: hdwy 3f out: rdn along over 2f out: sn drvn and wknd* **25/1**

2615 **12** ¾ **Appointed**[13] 5915 3-8-11 **92**........................................ DavidAllan 8 84
(Tim Easterby) *hld up towards rr: hdwy towards outer 3f out: rdn along and in tch over 2f out: sn drvn and wknd* **14/1**

601 **13** 2 **Balestra**[51] 4490 3-8-3 **84**........................................ CamHardie 3 72
(Charles Hills) *in tch on inner: hdwy over 4f out: rdn along 3f out: wknd 2f out* **33/1**

1402 **14** 1¼ **Horroob**[27] 5415 3-8-12 **93**........................................ JackMitchell 6 78
(Roger Varian) *in tch: hdwy to chse ldrs 1/2-way: rdn along 3f out: n.m.r and swtchd rt 2f out: sn drvn and wknd* **14/1**

64-0 **15** 6 **Montataire (IRE)**[129] 1861 3-9-7 **102**.............................. PJMcDonald 13 73
(Mark Johnston) *prom: rdn along 3f out: wknd over 2f out* **28/1**

1m 36.47s (-2.53) **Going Correction** 0.0s/f (Good) **15** Ran SP% **123.9**
Speed ratings (Par 106): **109,106,105,105,104 104,103,102,102,101 101,100,98,97,91**
CSF £24.25 CT £265.46 TOTE £3.50: £1.70, £2.70, £3.90; EX 20.60 Trifecta £320.70.
**Owner** Fiona and Ian Carmichael-Jennings **Bred** Earl Ecurie Du Grand Chene **Trained** Newmarket, Suffolk

**FOCUS**
Distance increased by 11yds. Strong 3yo handicap form and a one-two for William Haggas. The pace was good and the first four came from the rear. Mojito continues to progress.
T/Jkpt: Not Won. T/Plt: £149.00 to a £1 stake. Pool: £339,523.03 - 1663.43 winning units T/Qpdt: £18.30 to a £1 stake. Pool: £2,2576.92 - 912.66 winning units **Andrew Sheret & Joe Rowntree**

6405 - 6408a (Foreign Racing) - See Raceform Interactive

## 4943 SAINT-MALO (L-H)
Friday, August 25

**OFFICIAL GOING: Turf: good**

## 6409a PRIX ABBATIALE (CLAIMER) (2YO) (TURF) 5f 110y
**12:22** (12:22) 2-Y-O **£5,555** (£2,222; £1,666; £1,111; £555)

RPR

**1** **Good To Talk**[59] 4196 2-9-4 0............................(b) ClementLecoeuvre(3) 6 80
(Matthieu Palussiere, France) **3/1**[2]

**2** 5 **Dragon's Teeth (IRE)**[21] 5626 2-9-4 0.......................(b) TheoBachelot 8 60
(Jo Hughes) *sn led: hdd 1/2-way: sn drvn to chse ldr: kpt on fnl f: no match for wnr* **8/5**[1]

**3** 1¾ **Autumn Lodge**[5] 6247 2-9-4 0.......................................... TonyPiccone 7 54
(J S Moore) *chsd ldrs: drvn to chse ldng pair 1 1/2f out: kpt on same pce fnl f* **17/5**[3]

**4** 4½ **Cidjle Dangles (FR)** 2-8-8 0................................(b) LudovicBoisseau 9 29
(C Plisson, France) **53/1**

**5** 3 **Altavilla (IRE)**[14] 5907 2-9-1 0............................................ SylvainRuis 1 26
(F Chappet, France) **209/10**

**6** 1 **Lastyouni (FR)**[80] 3444 2-8-8 0...................................(p) EddyHardouin 2 16
(Matthieu Palussiere, France) **113/10**

**7** 1¼ **Full Sentimentale (FR)** 2-8-11 0..........................(p) AnthonyBernard 5 15
(C Plisson, France) **40/1**

**8** nk **Meran (FR)**[51] 4678 2-8-11 0.........................................(b1) HugoJourniac 4 14
(M Nigge, France) **106/10**

**9** 16 **Vanturi (IRE)**[103] 2664 2-9-1 0........................................ FabriceVeron 10
(J-V Toux, France) **237/10**

**10** 5 **Anapa (FR)** 2-9-1 0................................................(b) MorganDelalande 3
(W Delalande, France) **60/1**

PARI-MUTUEL (all including 1 euro stake): WIN 4.00; PLACE 1.20, 1.10, 1.30; DF 3.40; SF 7.00.
**Owner** Mrs Theresa Marnane **Bred** O Costello & R Morehead **Trained** France

## 5680 CHESTER (L-H)
Saturday, August 26

**OFFICIAL GOING: Good (6.8)**
Wind: light breeze Weather: sunny intervals, warm

## 6410 CHESTERBET NOVICE AUCTION STKS (PLUS 10 RACE) 7f 1y
**1:50** (1:55) (Class 4) 2-Y-O

**£6,225** (£1,864; £932; £466; £233; £117) **Stalls** Low

Form RPR

2204 **1** **Barbarianatthegate**[12] 6008 2-9-2 74..........................(b) PaulMulrennan 8 74
(Brian Meehan) *rushed out to ld fr wd draw: mde all: 5 l clr after 1f: 3 l clr 2f out: pushed along over 1f out: kpt up to work to maintain advantage ins fnl f: kpt on strly* **3/1**[3]

06 **2** 2¾ **Normandy Blue**[8] 6159 2-9-2 0.............................................. DavidNolan 7 67
(Richard Fahey) *mid-div: pushed along briefly after 2 fs: hdwy into 4th 3f out: pushed along and wnt 3rd 2f out: drvn into 2nd 1f out: chsd ldr ent fnl f: reminders and r.o wl: no ch w wnr* **8/1**

**3** 6 **Coast Guard** 2-8-11 0.......................................................... BenCurtis 5 45+
(Tom Dascombe) *chsd ldrs on outer: wnt 3rd 1/2-way: pushed along 3f out: drvn and briefly relegated to 4th 2f out: reminders over 1f out: r.o to take 3rd ins fnl f* **11/4**[2]

0 **4** 2 **Mariah's Melody (IRE)**[28] 5398 2-8-11 0.........................(h) SteveDrowne 4 40
(Lisa Williamson) *mid-div: pushed along 2f out: drvn over 1f out: r.o fnl f: tk 4th cl home* **50/1**

**5** ½ **Allnite (IRE)** 2-8-11 0............................................ PaddyPilley(5) 2 44
(Tom Dascombe) *trckd ldrs: hdwy into 2nd 1/2-way: pushed along 3f out: drvn 2f out: lost 2nd over 1f out: wknd fnl f* **9/4**[1]

05 **6** 4½ **Amarone Red (IRE)**[13] 5963 2-8-11 0.................................. LiamKeniry 3 26
(Tom Dascombe) *hld up: pushed along 1/2-way: one pce fnl 2 fs* **5/1**

00 **7** 1½ **Partry Flyer (IRE)**[8] 6146 2-8-11 0.......................... MeganNicholls(5) 1 27
(Oliver Greenall) *hld up: pushed along 2f out: rdn over 1f out: no impression* **40/1**

0 **8** 69 **Mydadsared**[34] 5180 2-9-2 0.............................................(t1) DuranFentiman 6
(Tony Coyle) *a in rr: wl bhd fr 1/2-way* **25/1**

1m 29.27s (2.77) **Going Correction** +0.275s/f (Good) **8** Ran SP% **118.5**
Speed ratings (Par 96): **95,91,85,82,82 77,75,**
CSF £27.45 TOTE £2.90: £1.20, £2.20, £1.40; EX 18.70 Trifecta £63.10.
**Owner** D McLean-Reid & Partner **Bred** Alan & Robin Craddock **Trained** Manton, Wilts

**FOCUS**
Drying ground that was officially good. After the first Paul Mulrennan called it "Nice, good ground," and David Nolan said it was "Good to soft." Rail movements meant the actual distance of the opener was 7f 14yds. This novice auction event had no depth to it.

## 6411 #MBNATEAM H'CAP 5f 15y
**2:30** (2:33) (Class 4) (0-80,80) 3-Y-O+

**£6,225** (£1,864; £932; £466; £233; £117) **Stalls** Low

Form RPR

0310 **1** **Normal Equilibrium**[28] 5402 7-9-7 **77**............................ DavidProbert 3 86
(Ivan Furtado) *mde all: 1 l clr over 1f out: rdn ent fnl f: r.o strly: readily* **5/1**[3]

6003 **2** 1½ **Ballesteros**[10] 6062 8-9-3 **73**................................................ DavidNolan 1 77
(Richard Fahey) *trckd ldrs: hdwy on inner 2f out: wnt 2nd over 1f out: rdn over 1f out: r.o fnl f: but no imp on wnr* **3/1**[1]

-004 **3** 3 **Quick Look**[98] 2837 4-9-0 **77**........................................ RyanTimby(7) 2 70+
(Michael Easterby) *hld up: effrt on inner 2f out: pushed along and hdwy into 3rd ent fnl f: r.o* **11/1**

342 **4** 1 **Fujin**[10] 6062 6-9-1 **74**.................................................(v) CharlieBennett(3) 7 63
(Shaun Harris) *trckd ldrs: pushed along over 2f out: drvn over 1f out: r.o to take 4th ins fnl f* **8/1**

0013 **5** hd **Silvanus (IRE)**[32] 5256 12-9-10 **80**................................ PaulMulrennan 10 68
(Paul Midgley) *cl up: 3rd and ev ch 2f out: sn pushed along: drvn over 1f out: one pce* **16/1**

-026 **6** 1¼ **Royal Mezyan (IRE)**[52] 4489 6-9-5 **80**.......................... JennyPowell(5) 6 64
(Henry Spiller) *hld up in last: plenty to to over 1f out: stdy hdwy on inner ins fnl f* **14/1**

6112 **7** 1 **Come On Dave (IRE)**[53] 4464 8-9-7 **77**............................(v) LiamKeniry 4 57
(John Butler) *chsd wnr: pushed along 2f out: rdn and lost pl ent fnl f* **7/2**[2]

5465 **8** hd **Invincible Ridge (IRE)**[5] 6267 9-9-6 **76**................................ NeilFarley 5 56+
(Eric Alston) *mid-div: pushed along 1/2-way: effrt and n.m.r 2f out: denied clr run ent fnl f: no ch after* **5/1**[3]

2535 **9** ¾ **Monte Cinq (IRE)**[29] 5383 3-9-3 **75**................................(h) BenCurtis 11 52
(Jason Ward) *mid-div on outer: hdwy 1/2-way: drvn 2f out: rdn and no ex fr over 1f out* **33/1**

151- **10** 1½ **Four Dragons**[316] 7313 3-8-12 **75**................................ PaddyPilley(5) 9 47
(Tom Dascombe) *hld up: pushed along over 2f out: drvn over 1f out: no imp* **20/1**

5646 **11** 6 **Brother Tiger**[32] 5241 8-9-2 **72**........................................ SteveDrowne 8 22
(David C Griffiths) *in rr: drvn 2f out: wknd* **25/1**

1m 1.13s (0.13) **Going Correction** +0.275s/f (Good)
**WFA** 3 from 4yo+ 2lb **11** Ran SP% **124.1**
Speed ratings (Par 105): **109,106,101,100,99 97,96,95,94,92 82**
CSF £21.13 CT £150.28 TOTE £6.70: £1.70, £1.60, £3.20; EX 26.00 Trifecta £255.40.
**Owner** John L Marriott & Albert L Marriott **Bred** D R Tucker **Trained** Wiseton, Nottinghamshire

**FOCUS**
Actual race distance 5f 25yds. The draw played a significant role in this with the first three coming out of stalls 3, 1 and 2. The winner has been rated up a length on his penultimate C&D win.

## 6412 LIVERPOOL GIN H'CAP 5f 110y
**3:05** (3:06) (Class 3) (0-95,94) 3-Y-O+

**£12,450** (£3,728; £1,864; £932; £466; £234) **Stalls** Low

Form RPR

6014 **1** **Guishan**[7] 6205 7-9-4 **91**..........................................(p) AlistairRawlinson 11 99
(Michael Appleby) *pushed along fr outside draw to take early position in mid-div: sn chsng ldrs: hdwy into 4th 2f out: rdn over 1f out: str run ent fnl f: led last 100yds: rdn out* **25/1**

3120 **2** nk **Bossipop**[7] 6205 4-9-1 **88**.................................................(b) DavidNolan 7 95
(Tim Easterby) *trckd ldrs: 3rd 2f out: drvn over 1f out: rdn and ev ch ins fnl f: almost alongside wnr last 100yds: r.o wl: but jst hld cl home* **12/1**

0103 **3** 1¼ **Confessional**[3] 6314 10-9-0 **87**............................................(e) JasonHart 5 91
(Tim Easterby) *mid-div: effrt and n.m.r on inner 2f out: pushed along over 1f out: rdn and r.o wl fnl f: tk 3rd nr fin* **8/1**

-233 **4** shd **Fumbo Jumbo (IRE)**[22] 5602 4-8-11 **84**........................ PaulMulrennan 4 86+
(Michael Dods) *led: 1 l clr and pushed along over 1f out: sn rdn: hdd by first two last 100yds: no ex: lost 3rd nr fin* **5/1**[2]

1400 **5** nk **Stanghow**[7] 6205 5-8-13 **86**................................................ CamHardie 12 87
(Antony Brittain) *mid-div: pushed along 2f out: swtchd to outer over 1f out: rdn and r.o wl: nvr nrr* **50/1**

5026 **6** ¾ **Sign Of The Kodiac (IRE)**[11] 6025 4-8-5 **85**............... FinleyMarsh(7) 3 84
(James Given) *trckd ldrs: 4th on inner 2f out: drvn over 1f out: one pce fnl f* **7/1**[3]

6220 **7** ¾ **Powerallied (IRE)**[28] 5402 4-8-10 **83**................................ LiamKeniry 8 79
(Richard Fahey) *hld up: pushed along over 1f out: rdn fnl f: r.o* **20/1**

0500 **8** ½ **Lucky Beggar (IRE)**[14] 5929 7-8-11 **84**.......................... SteveDrowne 2 79
(David C Griffiths) *hld up: pushed along over 2f out: n.m.r ent fnl f: one pce* **10/1**

0305 **9** ¾ **Stellarta**[21] 5637 6-9-3 **90**................................................ DavidProbert 10 82
(Michael Blanshard) *slowly away: in rr: rdn over 1f out: one pce* **14/1**

112 **10** 5 **Longroom**[43] 4850 5-8-10 **83**................................................ BenCurtis 6 58
(Noel Wilson) *prom: 2nd and ev ch 2f out: drvn and lost pl over 1f out: wknd* **8/1**

6013 **11** 3½ **Reflektor (IRE)**[28] 5402 4-9-2 **94**.................................. PaddyPilley(5) 1 87
(Tom Dascombe) *hld up: pushed along over 2f out: rdn and nt clr run over 1f out: eased* **11/4**[1]

4330 **12** ½ **Soie D'Leau**[3] 6325 5-9-4 **91**............................................... ShaneGray 9 52
(Kristin Stubbs) *in rr: drvn over 2f out: no imp* **10/1**

1m 6.74s (0.54) **Going Correction** +0.275s/f (Good) **12** Ran SP% **121.2**
Speed ratings (Par 107): **107,106,104,104,104 103,102,101,100,94 89,88**
CSF £299.78 CT £2662.87 TOTE £34.40: £6.80, £3.40, £2.20; EX 384.40 Trifecta £2602.60.
**Owner** Brian D Cantle **Bred** B D Cantle **Trained** Oakham, Rutland

**FOCUS**
Actual race distance 5f 121yds. This decent handicap was fast and furious. The second has been rated to form, and the third close to form.

## 6413 FLAVOUR OF THE SEASON 1539 RESTAURANT MAIDEN STKS 1m 4f 63y
**3:40** (3:44) (Class 4) 3-Y-O+

**£6,225** (£1,864; £932; £466; £233; £117) **Stalls** Low

Form RPR

2433 **1** **Sable Island (IRE)**[9] 6107 3-9-2 76................................ DavidProbert 5 77+
(Sir Michael Stoute) *mid-div: cl 4th 2f out: briefly drvn over 1f out: hdwy to chal 1f out: led ent fnl f: reminder and qckly drew clr: comf* **6/4**[1]

**2** 2 **Clemency**[29] 6-9-6 0.......................................................... PaulMulrennan 6 68
(Donald McCain) *prom: pushed along 3f out: rdn over 1f out: r.o to secure 2nd ins fnl f but wl hld by wnr* **16/1**

33 **3** *3 ½* **Hats Off To Larry**[14] 5931 3-9-2 0 ........ LiamKeniry 1 69
(Mick Channon) *led: 1 l clr 2f out: sn pushed along: rdn over 1f out: hdd ent fnl f: no ex* **5/2**[3]

6-0 **4** *2 ¼* **Struck By The Moon**[19] 5721 3-8-11 0 ........ SteveDrowne 2 60
(Charles Hills) *trckd ldrs: pushed along in 3rd 3f out: drvn 2f out: rdn in 4th over 1f out: no ex* **20/1**

04 **5** *5* **Poppyinthepark**[11] 6044 4-9-6 0 ........ CamHardie 4 51
(Richard Ford) *hld up: pushed along in 5th 3f out: drvn 2f out: no imp* **20/1**

**6** *8* **Scottsdale**[41] 4-9-11 0 ........ BenCurtis 3 43
(Brian Ellison) *hld up: drvn 4f out: lost tch over 2f out* **9/4**[2]

6000 **7** *39* **Just Heather (IRE)**[21] 5632 3-8-11 37 ........(p) NeilFarley 7
(John Wainwright) *in rr: drvn and reminders 4f out: sn lft wl bhd* **100/1**

2m 42.02s (3.52) **Going Correction** +0.275s/f (Good)
**WFA** 3 from 4yo+ 9lb 7 Ran SP% **115.7**
Speed ratings (Par 105): **99,97,95,93,90 85,59**
CSF £26.29 TOTE £2.10: £1.20, £6.50; EX 27.50 Trifecta £61.70.

**Owner** Niarchos Family **Bred** Niarchos Family **Trained** Newmarket, Suffolk

**FOCUS**
Actual race distance 1m 4f 83yds. An ordinary maiden. They went a decent initial pace before it slowed up. The level is determined by the fourth and fifth.

## 6414 BOODLES ROODEE CHALLENGE CUP POLO SEPTEMBER H'CAP 7f 127y
**4:15** (4:18) (Class 3) (0-90,90) 4-Y-0+

**£12,450** (£3,728; £1,864; £932; £466; £234) **Stalls** Low

Form RPR

3132 **1** **Kenstone (FR)**[19] 5699 4-8-2 78 ow1 ........(p) FinleyMarsh(7) 3 93
(Adrian Wintle) *trckd ldrs: wnt 2nd gng wl 2f out: pushed along to chal over 1f out: sn led: rdn ins fnl f: sn clr: comf* **15/2**

1-22 **2** *3 ½* **Sun Lover**[50] 4570 4-9-6 89 ........ JackMitchell 8 96+
(Roger Varian) *hld up: pushed along and hdwy 2f out: swtchd to outer over 1f out: rdn and r.o wl fnl f: snatched 2nd nr fin* **3/1**[1]

6006 **3** *hd* **Dark Devil (IRE)**[14] 5926 4-8-8 80 ........ SammyJoBell(3) 9 86
(Richard Fahey) *hld up: pushed along and hdwy on outer 3f out: drvn 2f out: rdn into 2nd ins fnl f: r.o: lost 2nd nr fin* **10/1**

1352 **4** *1 ½* **Calder Prince (IRE)**[14] 5926 4-9-2 90 ........ PaddyPilley(5) 1 92
(Tom Dascombe) *led: pushed along and 1 l clr 2f out: rdn wl over 1f out: sn hdd: no ex ins fnl f* **4/1**[2]

2000 **5** *nk* **Penwortham (IRE)**[20] 5688 4-9-2 85 ........(h) DavidNolan 2 87
(Richard Fahey) *trckd ldrs: hdwy into 3rd on inner 2f out: rdn ent fnl f: one pce* **9/2**[3]

2040 **6** *nk* **Twin Appeal (IRE)**[21] 5668 6-9-6 89 ........(b) BenCurtis 5 90
(David Barron) *mid-div: drvn in 5th over 1f out: no ex fnl f* **9/1**

5035 **7** *3 ¼* **Gabrial's Kaka (IRE)**[12] 6014 7-8-10 79 ........(b) LiamKeniry 4 72
(Richard Fahey) *hld up: pushed along 2f out: rdn 1f out: one pce* **16/1**

0131 **8** *2 ¼* **Echo Of Lightning**[17] 5805 7-9-0 83 ........(p) PaulMulrennan 6 70
(Brian Ellison) *trckd ldrs: pushed along 3f out: rdn and lost pl over 1f out: no ex* **12/1**

0240 **9** *1 ¾* **Heir To A Throne (FR)**[21] 5668 4-8-13 82 ........(p[1]) ShaneGray 11 65
(Kevin Ryan) *mid-div on outer: pushed along 2f out: wknd over 1f out* **20/1**

2100 **10** *1* **Explain**[21] 5669 5-9-4 87 ........(p) DavidProbert 7 67
(Ruth Carr) *hld up: pushed along in rr 2f out: rdn over 1f out: no imp* **20/1**

113 **11** *3 ¼* **Bouclier (IRE)**[14] 5949 7-9-2 85 ........ CamHardie 10 57
(Michael Easterby) *hld up: pushed along 2f out: rdn over 1f out: no rspnse* **33/1**

1120 **12** *15* **Call Out Loud**[108] 2528 5-8-9 78 ........(vt) AlistairRawlinson 12 13
(Michael Appleby) *chsd ldr: drvn and lost pl 2f out: wknd qckly* **40/1**

1m 32.92s (-0.88) **Going Correction** +0.275s/f (Good) 12 Ran SP% **122.5**
Speed ratings (Par 107): **115,111,111,109,109 109,105,103,101,100 97,82**
CSF £29.95 CT £239.79 TOTE £7.00: £2.20, £1.50, £3.20; EX 33.80 Trifecta £293.20.

**Owner** Glyn Byard **Bred** Guy Pariente Holding Sprl **Trained** Westbury-On-Severn, Gloucs

**FOCUS**
Actual race distance 7f 140yds. A competitive handicap. The third has been rated to this year's form.

## 6415 A GUARANTEED WINNER THE WHITE HORSE H'CAP 1m 5f 84y
**4:45** (4:47) (Class 4) (0-85,84) 3-Y-0

**£6,225** (£1,864; £932; £466; £233; £117) **Stalls** Low

Form RPR

2135 **1** **Key Bid**[9] 6107 3-9-4 81 ........(b[1]) JackMitchell 4 91
(Charlie Appleby) *trckd ldr: led 5f out: 3 l clr gng wl 2f out: drvn into 5 l ld wl over 1f out: rdn 1f out: in command fnl f: easily* **4/1**[3]

3130 **2** *3 ½* **Galactic Prince**[24] 5525 3-9-3 80 ........ DavidProbert 2 85+
(Andrew Balding) *hld up: hdwy 4f out: pushed along 3f out: drvn into 3rd over 2f out: rdn over 1f out: r.o fnl f: grabbed 2nd nr fin* **2/1**[1]

1243 **3** *shd* **Amelia Dream**[14] 5932 3-8-9 72 ........ BenCurtis 5 77
(Mick Channon) *chsd ldrs: wnt 2nd 5f out: pushed along 3f out: rdn over 2f out: sn lft trailing by wnr: kpt on ins fnl f: lost 2nd nr fin* **12/1**

3103 **4** *6* **See Of Rome**[22] 5598 3-9-0 84 ........ FinleyMarsh(7) 3 80
(Richard Hughes) *3rd early: shuffled bk to rr 1/2-way: hdwy on outer over 3f out: pushed along over 2f out: drvn and hmpd 5th horse home over 1f out: one pce* **5/2**[2]

2121 **5** *nk* **Sheriff Garrett (IRE)**[16] 5846 3-8-8 71 ........(p) CamHardie 1 68
(Tim Easterby) *hld up: pushed along and hdwy 4f out: drvn and outpcd 3f out: rdn 2f out: hmpd by 4th horse home and snatched up over 1f out: one pce* **8/1**

-216 **6** *99* **Beach Break**[44] 4796 3-9-2 79 ........(b) PaulMulrennan 7
(Ralph Beckett) *led: hdd 5f out: sn drvn and wknd qckly into remote last: eased* **7/1**

2m 56.21s (3.51) **Going Correction** +0.275s/f (Good) 6 Ran SP% **113.2**
Speed ratings (Par 102): **100,97,97,94,93 32**
CSF £12.67 TOTE £4.40: £2.10, £1.90; EX 16.90 Trifecta £70.00.

**Owner** Godolphin **Bred** Aldridge Racing Partnership **Trained** Newmarket, Suffolk

■ Stewards' Enquiry : Finley Marsh caution: careless riding

**FOCUS**
Actual race distance 1m 5f 107yds. This handicap was run at a fair clip. The third has been rated to form.

## 6416 HORSERADISH CATERING AND EVENT CREATIVES APPRENTICE H'CAP 1m 2f 70y
**5:20** (5:20) (Class 4) (0-85,79) 3-Y-0+

**£6,225** (£1,864; £932; £466; £233; £117) **Stalls** Centre

Form RPR

1513 **1** **Alexander M (IRE)**[10] 6059 3-9-6 79 ........ ManuelFernandes 4 92
(Mark Johnston) *mde all: 1 l ld 2f out: pushed into 3 l ld over 1f out: reminders to extend advantage ins fnl f: sn in total command: easily* **6/4**[1]

3060 **2** *6* **Berlusca (IRE)**[16] 5849 8-9-2 68 ........(h) CameronNoble 5 70
(David Loughnane) *hld up: gd hdwy on outer 3f out: chsd wnr 2f out: rdn over 1f out: nt go w wnr but kpt on fnl f* **25/1**

163 **3** *1* **Royal Shaheen (FR)**[12] 5996 4-9-13 79 ........(v) PatrickVaughan 8 79
(Alistair Whillans) *mid-div on outer: drvn in 4th 2f out: sn rdn: r.o to take 3rd ins fnl f* **8/1**

0341 **4** *¾* **Katebird (IRE)**[7] 6208 3-9-3 76 ........ JoshQuinn 7 74
(Mark Johnston) *prom: pushed along in 2nd 3f out: relegated to 3rd 2f out: rdn over 1f out: one pce* **13/2**[3]

00 **5** *1* **Modernism**[28] 5403 8-9-8 74 ........(v[1]) FinleyMarsh 2 70
(Ian Williams) *mid-div: pushed along 3f out: drvn 2f out: rdn and no ex fnl f* **8/1**

0430 **6** *¾* **Bahama Moon (IRE)**[12] 5996 5-9-10 79 ........ BenSanderson(3) 6 74
(David Barron) *mid-div: drvn over 2f out: sn rdn and one pce* **8/1**

2334 **7** *¾* **Outback Blue**[5] 6273 4-9-4 73 ........(vt) KatherineGlenister(3) 1 67
(David Evans) *hld up: pushed along 3f out: drvn 2f out: rdn over 1f out: no imp* **9/2**[2]

-062 **8** *18* **Inniscastle Lad**[133] 1788 5-9-8 79 ........(v) SebastianWoods(5) 3 38
(Donald McCain) *trckd ldr: lost pl qckly 3f out: sn drvn and wknd* **12/1**

2m 13.11s (1.91) **Going Correction** +0.275s/f (Good)
**WFA** 3 from 4yo+ 7lb 8 Ran SP% **116.4**
Speed ratings (Par 105): **103,98,97,96,96 95,94,80**
CSF £45.86 CT £239.13 TOTE £1.90: £1.10, £7.90, £1.10; EX 48.30 Trifecta £379.90.
**Owner** Christinee Budden, M Budden, Matthew Budden **Bred** Christine E Budden & Partners **Trained** Middleham Moor, N Yorks

**FOCUS**
Actual race distance 1m 2f 84yds. An ordinary handicap for apprentices. The level is fluid.
T/Plt: £245.90 to a £1 stake. Pool: £57,583.98 - 170.93 winning units T/Qpdt: £62.50 to a £1 stake. Pool: £2,883.76 - 34.11 winning units **Keith McHugh**

# 6373 GOODWOOD (R-H)
Saturday, August 26

**OFFICIAL GOING: Good (7.5)**
Wind: Nil Weather: Sunny, warm

## 6417 ABSOLUTE AESTHETICS FILLIES' NOVICE AUCTION STKS (PLUS 10 RACE) 6f
**1:35** (1:35) (Class 4) 2-Y-0 **£6,469** (£1,925; £962; £481) **Stalls** High

Form RPR

00 **1** **Tricksy Spirit**[35] 5154 2-9-0 0 ........ JFEgan 1 77+
(Mick Channon) *hld up in last trio: prog on outer 2f out: shkn up and clsd to ld 150yds out: sn in command: readily* **14/1**

**2** *1 ½* **Tarnhelm** 2-9-0 0 ........ PJMcDonald 10 73
(Mark Johnston) *led and racd against rail: rdn over 1f out: hdd and outpcd last 150yds: kpt on* **10/1**

4622 **3** *1 ¾* **Polly's Gold (IRE)**[13] 5963 2-9-0 70 ........ ShaneKelly 2 67
(Richard Hughes) *hld up in tch on outer: prog over 2f out: rdn to chse ldr over 1f out: lost 2nd and one pce ins fnl f* **4/1**[2]

233 **4** *nk* **Kareva**[29] 5356 2-9-0 78 ........ AndreaAtzeni 3 68
(Charles Hills) *dwlt sltly: chsd ldrs but nvr that much room: rdn 2f out: kpt on fnl f but nvr a real threat* **10/11**[1]

**5** *2* **Chizz De Biz (IRE)** 2-9-0 0 ........ RoystonFfrench 11 60
(Daniel Kubler) *slowly away: outpcd in last and pushed along in last: no prog tl swtchd out wd and styd on fr over 1f out: nvr nrr* **25/1**

0 **6** *nk* **Hurricane Lil (IRE)**[8] 6138 2-9-0 0 ........ TrevorWhelan 7 59
(George Baker) *chsd ldrs: rdn whn short of room 2f out and sn outpcd: kpt on again fnl f* **14/1**

032 **7** *1 ¼* **Bhindi**[19] 5717 2-9-0 70 ........ CharlesBishop 9 56
(Eve Johnson Houghton) *chsd ldrs: rdn 2f out: no prog over 1f out: fdd* **7/1**[3]

0 **8** *3* **Hold Your Breath**[44] 4806 2-9-0 0 ........ SeanLevey 6 47
(Tony Carroll) *t.k.h: disp 2nd pl tl wknd qckly over 1f out* **66/1**

**9** *½* **Sugar Plum Fairy** 2-9-0 0 ........ OisinMurphy 12 45
(Tony Carroll) *in tch in rr 4f: sn wknd* **25/1**

5000 **10** *5* **Butterfly Spirit**[26] 5479 2-9-0 49 ........ WilliamCarson 5 30
(Michael Attwater) *disp 2nd pl to 2f out: wknd rapidly* **66/1**

1m 12.4s (0.20) **Going Correction** -0.05s/f (Good) 10 Ran SP% **118.0**
Speed ratings (Par 93): **96,94,91,91,88 88,86,82,81,75**
CSF £141.25 TOTE £16.00: £3.00, £2.70, £1.50; EX 126.70 Trifecta £386.60.
**Owner** J Mitchell **Bred** Jeremy Green And Sons **Trained** West Ilsley, Berks
■ Stewards' Enquiry : Andrea Atzeni two-day ban: careless riding (Sep 10-11)

**FOCUS**
The top bend was dolled out 3yds increasing race distances. Fresh ground lower bend. It was dry overnight, and a warm day. A fair fillies' novice race. It's feasible that the race could be rated a few lengths better around those close up behind the winner.

## 6418 GROSVENOR SPORT PRESTIGE STKS (GROUP 3) (FILLIES) 7f
**2:10** (2:11) (Class 1) 2-Y-0

**£22,684** (£8,600; £4,304; £2,144; £1,076; £540) **Stalls** Low

Form RPR

2131 **1** **Billesdon Brook**[23] 5572 2-9-0 96 ........ SeanLevey 8 101
(Richard Hannon) *hld up in midfield: prog on outer over 2f out: clsd on ldrs 1f: rdn to ld last 100yds: styd on wl* **4/1**[2]

05 **2** *¾* **Whitefountainfairy (IRE)**[30] 5329 2-9-0 92 ........ OisinMurphy 1 99
(Andrew Balding) *in tch in midfield: prog over 2f out to chse ldr over 1f out: rdn to ld jst ins fnl f: hdd and outpcd last 100yds* **10/1**

1051 **3** *¾* **Miss Bar Beach (IRE)**[16] 5833 2-9-0 89 ........ ShaneKelly 7 97
(Keith Dalgleish) *hld up in midfield: shkn up 2f out: styd on fr over 1f out to take 3rd last strides* **33/1**

11 **4** ½ **Quivery (USA)**[36] 5114 2-9-0 88 JamieSpencer 5 96
(Jeremy Noseda) *hld up in last trio: shkn up 2f out: styd on fr over 1f out despite hanging sltly: pressed for 3rd nr fin* **11/2**

1 **5** *nk* **Verandah**[17] 5795 2-9-0 0 AndreaAtzeni 6 95
(John Gosden) *dwlt sltly: hld up in last trio: shkn up over 2f out: styd on fr over 1f out on outer to press for a pl nr fin but no threat* **3/1**[1]

2104 **6** *shd* **Ertiyad**[14] 5941 2-9-0 96 PatCosgrave 4 95
(William Haggas) *wl plcd: effrt on outer 2f out: rdn over 1f out: edgd rt and nt qckn: one pce fnl f* **15/2**

1131 **7** *hd* **Izzy Bizu (IRE)**[28] 5448 2-9-0 97 PJMcDonald 3 94
(Mark Johnston) *led: drvn over 1f out: hdd jst ins fnl f: no ex and lost pls nr fin* **5/1**[3]

1 **8** 4½ **Santorini Sun (IRE)**[16] 5839 2-9-0 0 JFEgan 9 82
(Mick Channon) *dropped in fr wd draw and hld up in last: shkn up over 2f out: no prog and nvr a factor* **25/1**

22 **9** ¾ **Your Choice**[24] 5528 2-9-0 0 JohnFahy 2 80
(Laura Mongan) *chsd ldng pair to 2f out: sn wknd* **25/1**

1 **10** ½ **Peace Trail**[14] 5938 2-9-0 0 AdamKirby 10 78
(Charlie Appleby) *chsd ldr to over 1f out: losing pl whn nudged by rival sn after: eased* **12/1**

1m 26.55s (-0.45) **Going Correction** +0.125s/f (Good) **10** Ran SP% **116.2**
Speed ratings (Par 101): **107,106,105,104,104 104,104,98,98,97**
CSF £42.29 TOTE £4.60: £1.60, £2.70, £8.80; EX 42.30 Trifecta £610.40.
**Owner** Pall Mall Partners & Late R J McCreery **Bred** Stowell Hill Partners **Trained** East Everleigh, Wilts

**FOCUS**
This did not look a strong running of the Prestige Stakes. The second and third might help govern the merit of the form in time.

## 6419 GROSVENOR SPORT H'CAP 7f
2:45 (2:48) (Class 2) 3-Y-O+
**£62,250** (£18,640; £9,320; £4,660; £2,330; £1,170) **Stalls** Low

Form RPR

0434 **1** **Johnny Barnes (IRE)**[28] 5393 5-9-3 **101** RobertTart 2 111
(John Gosden) *hld up towards rr: prog on inner and dream run through fr over 2f out: rdn to ld jst ins fnl f: r.o wl* **13/2**[2]

602 **2** 1 **Burnt Sugar (IRE)**[21] 5669 5-8-6 **90** ow1 JFEgan 6 97
(Roger Fell) *hld up in midfield: effrt 2f out: prog over 1f out: r.o to take 2nd last 100yds and clsd nr fin but wnr already gone* **14/1**

4305 **3** 2 **Straight Right (FR)**[35] 5147 3-9-0 **103** OisinMurphy 11 103
(Andrew Balding) *hld up wl in rr: prog on inner 2f out: styd on wl fnl f to take 3rd last strides* **16/1**

1124 **4** ¾ **Mukalal**[18] 5744 3-8-4 **93** MartinDwyer 9 91+
(Marcus Tregoning) *taken down early: led: rdn and hung lft over 1f out: hdd and outpcd jst ins fnl f* **9/1**

5620 **5** ¾ **Masham Star (IRE)**[7] 6186 3-8-11 **100** PJMcDonald 10 96
(Mark Johnston) *trckd ldrs: rdn and on terms 2f out: nt qckn over 1f out: one pce after* **14/1**

2661 **6** *nse* **Fox Trotter (IRE)**[31] 5302 5-8-4 **88** LiamJones 3 85
(Brian Meehan) *hld up in midfield: effrt 2f out: no imp on ldrs over 1f out: styd on ins fnl f: nvr nrr* **20/1**

3221 **7** *hd* **Truth Or Dare**[24] 5530 6-8-7 **91** WilliamCarson 4 88
(James Bethell) *trckd ldrs: rdn 2f out: disp 2nd and chalng jst over 1f out: fdd* **15/2**[3]

214 **8** 1 **Easy Tiger**[16] 5842 5-7-11 **84** NoelGarbutt(3) 13 78
(Malcolm Saunders) *pressed ldrs: drvn over 2f out: steadily fdd fnl f* **28/1**

33 **9** *nk* **Ultimate Avenue (IRE)**[44] 4813 3-8-11 **100** (t) JamieSpencer 5 91
(Ed Walker) *t.k.h: hld up in midfield: hanging bdly whn asked for an effrt over 2f out: nvr able to threaten* **5/1**[1]

0400 **10** *hd* **Shady McCoy (USA)**[28] 5393 7-8-3 **87** RyanPowell 16 80+
(Ian Williams) *dwlt and impeded s: wl in rr: stl in last pair 2f out: prog 1f out: weaved through and running on: no ch whn rn out of room last 50yds* **25/1**

4040 **11** *nk* **Raucous**[21] 5640 4-9-4 **102** (tp) AdamKirby 8 94
(William Haggas) *hld up towards rr: shkn up over 2f out: hanging and no prog: no ch whn short of room briefly fnl f* **9/1**

5201 **12** *hd* **Bertiewhittle**[7] 6186 9-8-4 **93** RowanScott(5) 19 84
(David Barron) *hld up wl in rr: shkn up over 2f out: no great prog tl kpt on ins fnl f* **33/1**

4016 **13** 1¼ **Swift Approval (IRE)**[11] 6024 5-8-11 **95** (t) PatCosgrave 7 83
(Stuart Williams) *prom: chsd ldr 2f out to jst over 1f out: wknd qckly* **22/1**

4-40 **14** ¾ **Certificate**[63] 4072 6-9-10 **108** (p[1]) AndreaAtzeni 12 94
(Roger Varian) *hld up in midfield: shkn up on outer over 2f out: no prog and sn btn* **14/1**

2113 **15** ¾ **Frank Bridge**[16] 5842 4-8-9 **93** CharlesBishop 1 77
(Eve Johnson Houghton) *chsd ldrs: rdn 2f out: no imp over 1f out: losing pl whn impeded ins fnl f* **12/1**

0003 **16** *hd* **Suzi's Connoisseur**[14] 5942 6-8-5 **89** (t) AdamBeschizza 17 73
(Stuart Williams) *slowly away: a wl in rr: rdn and no prog over 2f out* **25/1**

00-6 **17** 1½ **Repton (IRE)**[14] 5916 3-8-7 **96** JohnFahy 20 73
(Richard Hannon) *slowly away: a wl in rr: nvr a factor* **66/1**

0404 **18** 9 **Sutter County**[11] 6024 3-9-0 **103** (b[1]) JoeFanning 14 56
(Mark Johnston) *awkward s but spd fr wd draw to chse ldr: lost 2nd 2f out: wknd rapidly over 1f out: eased* **22/1**

204 **P** **Mount Tahan (IRE)**[22] 5616 5-8-9 **93** ShaneKelly 15
(Kevin Ryan) *v awkward s: nvr rcvrd and sn eased in last pl: p.u ins fnl f* **33/1**

1m 25.66s (-1.34) **Going Correction** +0.125s/f (Good)
**WFA** 3 from 4yo+ 5lb **19** Ran SP% **127.3**
Speed ratings (Par 109): **112,110,108,107,106 106,106,105,105,104 104,104,102,102,101 100,99,88,**
CSF £84.02 CT £1464.91 TOTE £7.10: £1.80, £3.60, £4.10, £2.70; EX 104.60 Trifecta £1009.80.

**Owner** Bermuda Thoroughbred Racing Limited **Bred** Citadel Stud **Trained** Newmarket, Suffolk

**FOCUS**
A good, competitive handicap run at a decent pace. The winner has been rated back to his best, with the runner-up in line with this year's form.

## 6420 GROSVENOR SPORT CELEBRATION MILE STKS (GROUP 2) 1m
3:20 (3:22) (Class 1) 3-Y-O+
**£62,040** (£23,521; £11,771; £5,863; £2,942; £1,476) **Stalls** Low

Form RPR

2003 **1** **Lightning Spear**[24] 5527 6-9-4 117 OisinMurphy 3 117
(David Simcock) *hld up in 4th: chsd ldng pair over 1f out but plenty to do: drvn and r.o wl last 150yds: led fnl stride* **1/1**[1]

012- **2** *nse* **Zonderland**[364] 5873 4-9-4 112 AdamKirby 1 116
(Clive Cox) *t.k.h: trckd ldng pair: wnt 2nd over 1f out: drvn to cl on ldrs: led last 75yds: edgd lft and hdd post* **9/2**[2]

0-33 **3** ¾ **Hathal (USA)**[28] 5436 5-9-4 112 (p) PatCosgrave 5 114
(William Haggas) *led: sent for home 2f out and sn 2 l up: drvn fnl f: styd on but hdd last 75yds* **11/2**[3]

1300 **4** 4 **Oh This Is Us (IRE)**[25] 5502 4-9-4 108 SeanLevey 2 105
(Richard Hannon) *hld up in 5th: rdn 2f out: kpt on one pce to take 4th ins fnl f: no ch* **8/1**

56-0 **5** 2 **Richard Pankhurst**[56] 4362 5-9-4 114 AndreaAtzeni 4 100
(John Gosden) *hld up in last: pushed along and no prog 3f out: nvr a factor* **7/1**

4200 **6** 2 **Opal Tiara (IRE)**[43] 4857 4-9-4 107 JFEgan 6 96
(Mick Channon) *chsd ldr: rdn 3f out: lost 2nd and wknd over 1f out* **28/1**

1m 38.89s (-1.01) **Going Correction** +0.125s/f (Good) **6** Ran SP% **110.6**
Speed ratings (Par 115): **110,109,109,105,103 101**
CSF £5.60 TOTE £1.70: £1.10, £2.50; EX 5.40 Trifecta £14.80.
**Owner** Qatar Racing Limited **Bred** Newsells Park Stud **Trained** Newmarket, Suffolk

**FOCUS**
The same one-two as the previous year, but there wasn't much depth to this. The third has been rated close to form.

## 6421 GOODWOOD REVIVAL MARCH STKS (LISTED RACE) 1m 6f
3:55 (3:57) (Class 1) 3-Y-O **£28,355** (£10,750; £5,380; £2,680; £1,345) **Stalls** Low

Form RPR

1363 **1** **Call To Mind**[36] 5095 3-9-2 107 PatCosgrave 2 109
(William Haggas) *t.k.h early: awkward bnd after 2f but then trckd ldr: chal fr over 3f out: drvn to ld over 1f out: styd on* **11/4**[2]

-152 **2** 1¼ **Count Octave**[64] 4032 3-9-2 103 OisinMurphy 4 107
(Andrew Balding) *hld up in 4th: effrt over 3f out: drvn wl over 1f out: chsd wnr fnl f: styd on but no imp* **2/1**[1]

2111 **3** 3 **UAE King**[29] 5351 3-9-2 99 AndreaAtzeni 5 103
(Roger Varian) *t.k.h early: led after 1f: pressed 4f out but then sent for home: drvn and edgd lft 2f out: hdd and one pce over 1f out* **7/2**[3]

11 **4** ½ **Walton Street**[22] 5598 3-9-2 94 AdamKirby 1 102
(Charlie Appleby) *hld up in last: swift move to press ldng pair 4f out: nt qckn 3f out: nt on terms after: kpt on nr fin* **4/1**

2113 **5** 27 **Zenon (IRE)**[20] 5682 3-9-2 94 (p[1]) RobertTart 3 76
(John Gosden) *t.k.h early: led 1f: trckd ldrs tl dropped to last 4f out: sn wknd: t.o* **8/1**

3m 5.23s (1.63) **Going Correction** +0.125s/f (Good) **5** Ran SP% **113.3**
Speed ratings (Par 108): **100,99,97,97,81**
CSF £8.98 TOTE £3.30: £1.60, £1.70; EX 9.90 Trifecta £15.10.
**Owner** The Queen **Bred** The Queen **Trained** Newmarket, Suffolk

**FOCUS**
Add 7yds. A decent Listed race. It's now confined to 3yos again, as it was until 1999. The third and fourth have been rated close to their wins in good handicaps last time.

## 6422 WHITELEY CLINIC H'CAP 1m 1f 11y
4:30 (4:35) (Class 3) (0-90,92) 3-Y-O+
**£9,337** (£2,796; £1,398; £699; £349; £175) **Stalls** Low

Form RPR

1 **1** **Mountain Hunter (USA)**[22] 5611 3-9-4 **87** WilliamCarson 13 101+
(Saeed bin Suroor) *trckd ldng trio: shkn up to ld wl over 1f out: sn rdn clr: readily* **9/2**[1]

0015 **2** 2¾ **Lawmaking**[8] 6145 4-9-4 **80** (h[1]) JFEgan 12 86
(Henry Spiller) *hld up towards rr: pushed along over 2f out: prog over 1f out: rdn to take 2nd last 100yds: styd on but no ch w wnr* **25/1**

4324 **3** ¾ **Dr Julius No**[22] 5609 3-9-7 **90** ShaneKelly 4 94
(Richard Hughes) *trckd ldrs: chal on inner 2f out but nt qckn and lost pl sn after: renewed effrt and nt clr run briefly 1f out: drvn and styd on to take 3rd last 100y* **9/1**[3]

1413 **4** ½ **Captain Courageous (IRE)**[38] 5032 4-9-13 **89** PatCosgrave 1 92
(Ed Walker) *trckd ldng pair: on terms 2f: hrd rdn and one pce fr over 1f out* **16/1**

4112 **5** *shd* **See The Master (IRE)**[24] 5548 3-9-0 **83** AdamKirby 10 86
(Clive Cox) *trckd ldr: led jst over 2f out to wl over 1f out: one pce u.p after* **9/2**[1]

4523 **6** *hd* **Itsakindamagic**[31] 5300 3-9-3 **86** (t) OisinMurphy 7 88+
(Andrew Balding) *stdd s: plld hrd and hld up in last: stl keen 4f out: effrt whn nt clr run over 1f out: racd awkwardly but styd on fnl f: nvr nrr* **6/1**[2]

0-10 **7** ¾ **Nayel (IRE)**[42] 4882 5-10-0 **90** (p) SeanLevey 9 91
(Richard Hannon) *led to jst over 2f out: kpt on to chse wnr over 1f out to last 100yds: wknd* **25/1**

4534 **8** ½ **Reaver (IRE)**[7] 6189 4-9-6 **82** PJMcDonald 8 82
(Eve Johnson Houghton) *trckd ldrs: shkn up over 2f out: nt qckn over 1f out: one pce after and nvr any imp* **6/1**[2]

5201 **9** 1¾ **Mohab**[37] 5072 4-9-10 **86** (p) TimmyMurphy 6 82
(Kevin Ryan) *t.k.h: hld up in rr: shkn up and no prog over 2f out: no ch after* **11/1**

0030 **10** *hd* **Balmoral Castle**[21] 5643 8-9-2 **85** Pierre-LouisJamin(7) 2 81
(Jonathan Portman) *trckd ldrs: shkn up over 2f out: lost pl over 1f out: wl btn after* **18/1**

030 **11** ½ **Wind In My Sails**[12] 6014 5-9-4 **83** (h) CliffordLee(3) 3 78
(Ed de Giles) *t.k.h: hld up in rr: effrt on outer over 2f out: sn no prog* **10/1**

10-6 **12** 2½ **Argenterie**[108] 2523 3-9-9 **92** MartinDwyer 5 81
(Marcus Tregoning) *a in rr: pushed along 3f out: struggling fnl 2f* **12/1**

1m 55.63s (-0.67) **Going Correction** +0.125s/f (Good)
**WFA** 3 from 4yo+ 7lb **12** Ran SP% **118.9**
Speed ratings (Par 107): **107,104,103,103,103 103,102,102,100,100 99,97**
CSF £124.12 CT £969.54 TOTE £4.40: £1.90, £6.30, £3.00; EX 124.40 Trifecta £2230.60.
**Owner** Godolphin **Bred** Darley **Trained** Newmarket, Suffolk
■ Stewards' Enquiry : Shane Kelly two-day ban: careless riding (Sep 10-11)

**FOCUS**
Nothing could live with the winner, a smart prospect. The placed horses set the standard.

## 6423 GOLF ACADEMY AT GOODWOOD H'CAP 1m 3f 218y
5:05 (5:09) (Class 4) (0-80,81) 3-Y-O **£6,469** (£1,925; £962; £481) **Stalls** High

Form RPR

00-2 **1** **Just In Time**[18] 5753 3-8-3 **60** MartinDwyer 1 68+
(Alan King) *hld up in 6th: swift move on inner to ld over 2f out: rdn and edgd lft then rt fr over 1f out: hrd pressed ins fnl f: hld on wl* **5/2**[1]

1550 **2** *nk* **Al Zaman (IRE)**[20] 5686 3-9-7 **78** (tp) TimmyMurphy 7 85
(Simon Crisford) *hld up in last: stl there over 2f out: swtchd to inner and prog wl over 1f out: chsd wnr ins fnl f and sn chalng: hld whn edgd lft nr fin* **16/1**

3511 **3** 1 1/4 **Koeman**31 5298 3-9-10 **81** ................ JFEgan 2 86
(Mick Channon) *trckd ldrs: rdn and prog to chse wnr wl over 1f out: nt qckn u.p and lost 2nd ins fnl f: kpt on* **7/1**

1245 **4** 3 1/2 **Road To Dubai (IRE)**16 5838 3-9-7 **78** ................ PatCosgrave 4 77
(George Scott) *t.k.h: led 2f then stdd and sn in 4th: effrt whn nt clr run 3f out: rdn on outer 2f out: kpt on but nvr pce to chal* **6/1**3

1 **5** nk **White Desert (IRE)**44 4808 3-9-6 **77** ................ AdamKirby 5 76
(Charlie Appleby) *hld up in last pair: pushed along over 3f out: no real prog tl kpt on fnl f: n.d* **11/4**2

2463 **6** 1 **Chaparrachik (IRE)**11 6023 3-8-11 **68** ................(h) ShaneKelly 8 65
(Amanda Perrett) *led after 2f: mde most to over 2f out: wknd over 1f out* **25/1**

6241 **7** 2 1/4 **Mancini**36 5128 3-9-2 **73** ................ SeanLevey 6 67
(Jonathan Portman) *trckd ldr after 3f: chal and upsides fr 4f out to over 2f out: wknd over 1f out* **7/1**

0151 **8** 1 **Star Maker**14 5932 3-9-1 **77** ................ MitchGodwin(5) 3 69
(Sylvester Kirk) *trckd ldrs: chal and upsides fr 4f out to over 2f out: wknd* **11/1**

2m 38.9s (0.50) **Going Correction** +0.125s/f (Good) 8 Ran SP% **112.6**
Speed ratings (Par 102): **103,102,101,99,99 98,97,96**
CSF £41.10 CT £246.30 TOTE £3.40: £1.30, £4.50, £2.20; EX 41.20 Trifecta £275.10.
**Owner** HP Racing Just In Time **Bred** Overbury Stallions Ltd And D Boocock **Trained** Barbury Castle, Wilts

**FOCUS**
Add 7yds. A fair handicap. The fourth could back this race being rated a bit higher on his course form.
T/Plt: £240.40 to a £1 stake. Pool: £87,285.27 - 265.02 winning units T/Qpdt: £20.30 to a £1 stake. Pool: £7,279.56 - 265.22 winning units **Jonathan Neesom**

## 6385 NEWMARKET (R-H)

Saturday, August 26

**OFFICIAL GOING: Good to firm (firm in places; 8.1)**
Wind: Light half behind Weather: Cloudy with sunny spells

## 6424 HEATH COURT HOTEL EBF NOVICE STKS (PLUS 10 RACE) 6f

**2:05** (2:07) (Class 4) 2-Y-O **£4,528** (£1,347; £673; £336) **Stalls** Low

Form RPR

**1** **Betty F** 2-8-11 0 ................ GeraldMosse 2 81+
(Jeremy Noseda) *trckd ldrs: swtchd lft over 1f out: rdn ins fnl f: r.o to ld nr fin: comf* **5/2**1

41 **2** 3/4 **Rockies Spirit**52 4503 2-9-5 0 ................ SilvestreDeSousa 8 85
(Denis Quinn) *racd alone in centre: overall ldr: rdn over 1f out: hdd nr fin* **4/1**3

**3** 2 1/4 **Moqarrar (USA)** 2-9-2 0 ................ PatSmullen 5 75
(Sir Michael Stoute) *chsd ldr tl led main gp over 1f out: sn rdn: hdd ins fnl f: styd on same pce* **12/1**

**4** 2 **Balletomane** 2-9-2 0 ................ TomMarquand 4 68
(Richard Hannon) *prom: rdn over 2f out: hmpd and outpcd over 1f out: styd on ins fnl f* **10/1**

4 **5** nk **It's Not Unusual**52 4496 2-8-11 0 ................ TedDurcan 1 62
(Roger Charlton) *led main gp over 4f: sn edgd lft: no ex fnl f* **7/2**2

0 **6** 1/2 **Mashaheer**91 3093 2-9-2 0 ................ DaneO'Neill 9 66
(William Haggas) *s.i.s: sn prom: rdn over 2f out: no ex fnl f* **9/2**

**7** 3/4 **Blooriedotcom (IRE)** 2-9-2 0 ................ DanielMuscutt 7 63
(Peter Chapple-Hyam) *s.i.s: sn pushed along in rr: rdn over 1f out: no imp* **33/1**

**8** 4 1/2 **Global Spirit** 2-9-2 0 ................ FranBerry 6 49
(Ed Dunlop) *hld up: racd keenly: rdn over 2f out: wknd over 1f out* **25/1**

**9** 2 3/4 **Philamundo (IRE)** 2-9-2 0 ................ StevieDonohoe 3 40
(Richard Spencer) *hld up: rdn and wknd over 1f out* **25/1**

1m 12.62s (0.12) **Going Correction** -0.075s/f (Good) 9 Ran SP% **116.4**
Speed ratings (Par 96): **96,95,92,89,88 88,87,81,77**
CSF £12.46 TOTE £3.00: £1.20, £1.70, £2.60; EX 13.50 Trifecta £108.50.
**Owner** C Fox & B Wilson **Bred** Charles Fox **Trained** Newmarket, Suffolk

**FOCUS**
Stands' side course. Stalls on stands' side except 1m6f: centre. Not a bad novice event. The centre proved the place to be. The level is fluid.

## 6425 SAEED SUHAIL SAEED HEATH COURT HOTEL NURSERY H'CAP 7f

**2:40** (2:42) (Class 3) (0-95,83) 2-Y-O **£6,469** (£1,925; £962; £481) **Stalls** Low

Form RPR

510 **1** **Maksab (IRE)**42 4906 2-9-7 **83** ................ SilvestreDeSousa 7 86
(Mick Channon) *a.p: rdn and ev ch fr over 1f out: r.o u.p to ld post* **10/3**2

012 **2** nse **Tadleel**17 5786 2-9-4 **80** ................ DaneO'Neill 5 83
(Ed Dunlop) *s.i.s: hld up: hdwy wl over 1f out: rdn to ld 1f out: r.o: hdd post* **9/1**

5103 **3** nk **Finsbury Park**8 6140 2-9-2 **78** ................ FranBerry 6 80
(Robyn Brisland) *chsd ldr: rdn and ev ch fr over 1f out: r.o* **3/1**1

411 **4** 1/2 **Affina (IRE)**12 5990 2-9-6 **82** ................ DanielMuscutt 4 83
(Simon Crisford) *led: qcknd 3f out: rdn: hung lft and hdd 1f out: styd on same pce towards fin* **4/1**3

435 **5** 1 1/4 **El Chapo**28 5412 2-8-6 **68** ................ AndrewMullen 3 65
(Richard Fahey) *s.i.s: hld up: rdn over 1f out: r.o towards fin: nt rch ldrs* **14/1**

321 **6** 1 1/4 **Midnight Wilde**25 5507 2-9-3 **79** ................ GeraldMosse 1 73
(John Ryan) *trckd ldrs: nt clr run 2f out: sn rdn: swtchd rt over 1f out: no ex wl ins fnl f* **4/1**3

4325 **7** 1 **Dontgiveuponbob**32 5255 2-8-6 **75** ................ ConnorMurtagh(7) 2 66
(Richard Fahey) *hld up in tch: rdn and nt clr run over 1f out: hung lft and no ex ins fnl f* **12/1**

1m 26.78s (1.08) **Going Correction** -0.075s/f (Good) 7 Ran SP% **112.4**
Speed ratings (Par 98): **90,89,89,89,87 86,85**
CSF £31.25 TOTE £4.10: £2.10, £4.30; EX 34.00 Trifecta £113.90.
**Owner** M Al-Qatami & K M Al-Mudhaf **Bred** D J And Mrs Deer **Trained** West Ilsley, Berks

**FOCUS**
A fair nursery. They went stands' side but the main action late was again down the centre.

## 6426 ASPALL CYDER H'CAP 7f

**3:15** (3:16) (Class 3) (0-90,89) 3-Y-O **£7,762** (£2,310; £1,154; £577) **Stalls** Low

Form RPR

-263 **1** **Musawaat**21 5661 3-9-4 **86** ................ DaneO'Neill 6 93
(Charles Hills) *chsd ldr: rdn over 1f out: led wl ins fnl f: r.o* **7/2**2

0235 **2** 1 1/4 **Plant Pot Power (IRE)**10 6068 3-9-1 **83** ................ SilvestreDeSousa 2 87
(Richard Hannon) *led: edgd lft after s: qcknd over 2f out: rdn and edgd lft over 1f out: hdd wl ins fnl f: styd on same pce* **2/1**1

6-45 **3** hd **Ariena (IRE)**49 4634 3-8-11 **79** ................ SamHitchcott 3 82
(Clive Cox) *hmpd after s: trckd ldrs: shkn up over 2f out: rdn and hung lft fr over 1f out: r.o* **11/2**3

5000 **4** 1 3/4 **Miss Infinity (IRE)**42 4903 3-9-5 **87** ................ FrannyNorton 4 85
(Mark Johnston) *hld up in tch: rdn over 1f out: styd on* **11/1**

13 **5** 2 1/2 **Bernardo O'Reilly**28 5433 3-9-1 **83** ................ TedDurcan 5 75
(Richard Spencer) *s.i.s: hld up: hdwy over 2f out: rdn and hung lft over 1f out: no ex ins fnl f* **7/1**

0650 **6** 3 3/4 **Thomas Cranmer (USA)**18 5744 3-9-3 **85** ................ AndrewMullen 8 66
(Mark Johnston) *chsd ldrs: rdn over 2f out: wknd over 1f out* **14/1**

00-0 **7** 8 **Bohemian Flame (IRE)**14 5916 3-9-2 **89** ................ JoshuaBryan(5) 7 49
(Andrew Balding) *prom: rdn over 2f out: wknd over 1f out* **10/1**

01-0 **8** 11 **Black Bolt (IRE)**7 6195 3-9-0 **82** ................ FranBerry 1 12
(Richard Hannon) *s.i.s: hld up: shkn up and wknd over 2f out* **16/1**

1m 23.89s (-1.81) **Going Correction** -0.075s/f (Good) 8 Ran SP% **113.4**
Speed ratings (Par 104): **107,105,105,103,100 96,87,74**
CSF £10.72 CT £36.20 TOTE £3.80: £1.30, £1.30, £1.80; EX 10.40 Trifecta £63.10.
**Owner** Hamdan Al Maktoum **Bred** Lark Copse Ltd **Trained** Lambourn, Berks

**FOCUS**
This fair 3yo handicap saw the field merge down the middle from the off this time. It's been rated around the runner-up.

## 6427 CJ MURFITT LTD H'CAP 1m 6f

**3:50** (3:54) (Class 2) (0-105,97) 3-Y-O+

**£28,012** (£8,388; £4,194; £2,097; £1,048; £526) **Stalls** Centre

Form RPR

1126 **1** **Hochfeld (IRE)**24 5525 3-8-9 **92** ................ FrannyNorton 7 106
(Mark Johnston) *mde all: pushed clr and edgd lft fr over 1f out: easily* **9/4**1

0222 **2** 6 **Kajaki (IRE)**28 5403 4-8-6 **79** ................(p) AndrewMullen 6 84
(Kevin Ryan) *prom: chsd wnr over 2f out: rdn over 1f out: sn outpcd* **10/1**

1055 **3** 4 **Jaameh (IRE)**21 5638 4-9-10 **97** ................ DaneO'Neill 8 96
(Mark Johnston) *hld up: hdwy over 3f out: rdn over 2f out: styd on same pce fr over 1f out* **8/1**3

0442 **4** 1 1/4 **Blakeney Point**21 5638 4-9-10 **97** ................ TedDurcan 3 95
(Roger Charlton) *hld up: hdwy over 3f out: rdn and hung lft over 1f out: wknd fnl f* **11/2**2

4111 **5** 3/4 **Theydon Grey**42 4921 4-9-0 **92** ................ GeorgiaCox(5) 1 89
(William Haggas) *trckd wnr: racd keenly: rdn and lost 2nd over 2f out: hung lft over 1f out: sn wknd* **11/2**2

4163 **6** 1 1/2 **Sporting Times**42 4908 3-8-0 **83** oh1 ................ JoeyHaynes 2 80
(Ed Dunlop) *hld up: hdwy over 2f out: rdn and wknd over 1f out* **11/2**2

6 **7** 8 **Reshoun (FR)**22 5598 3-8-2 **85** ................ RoryCleary 9 70
(Ian Williams) *hld up: hdwy over 3f out: rdn and wknd over 1f out* **9/1**

4-06 **8** 9 **Goldmember**49 4639 4-9-8 **95** ................ DanielMuscutt 5 66
(David Simcock) *hld up: rdn over 2f out: sn wknd* **20/1**

034 **9** 32 **Codeshare**15 5882 5-8-10 **83** ................ SilvestreDeSousa 10 9
(Sally Haynes) *trckd ldrs: racd keenly: rdn over 2f out: wknd and eased over 1f out* **20/1**

2m 54.1s (-3.60) **Going Correction** -0.075s/f (Good)
**WFA** 3 from 4yo+ 10lb 9 Ran SP% **116.6**
Speed ratings (Par 109): **107,103,101,100,100 99,94,89,71**
CSF £26.79 CT £150.24 TOTE £3.00: £1.50, £2.70, £2.60; EX 22.30 Trifecta £135.70.
**Owner** Sheikh Hamdan bin Mohammed Al Maktoum **Bred** Kenilworth House Stud **Trained** Middleham Moor, N Yorks

**FOCUS**
Race run over an extra 2yds. A decent staying handicap, run at a solid gallop. The runner-up is a reliable guide. It's been rated around the runner-up.

## 6428 PLAY COSTABINGO.COM ON YOUR MOBILE HOPEFUL STKS (LISTED RACE) 6f

**4:25** (4:27) (Class 1) 3-Y-O+

**£20,982** (£7,955; £3,981; £1,983; £995; £499) **Stalls** Low

Form RPR

4001 **1** **Gifted Master (IRE)**21 5633 4-9-1 109 ................(b) PatSmullen 1 113
(Hugo Palmer) *chsd ldr tl led 1/2-way: rdn and hdd over 1f out: rallied ins fnl f: r.o to ld post* **11/4**1

4423 **2** shd **Steady Pace**42 4905 4-9-1 107 ................ GeorgeDowning 14 113
(Saeed bin Suroor) *prom: rdn to ld and edgd lft over 1f out: r.o: hdd post* **4/1**2

2060 **3** hd **Intisaab**21 5640 6-9-1 107 ................(p) AntonioFresu 9 112
(David O'Meara) *hld up in tch: rdn and swtchd lft 1f out: r.o* **20/1**

0511 **4** 1 3/4 **Ornate**11 6039 4-9-1 108 ................(h) AndrewMullen 6 106
(Robert Cowell) *led to 1/2-way: remained handy: rdn and hung lft over 1f out: styd on same pce ins fnl f* **16/1**

1-40 **5** 1 1/2 **Kassia (IRE)**63 4071 4-8-10 98 ................ FrannyNorton 2 97
(Mick Channon) *prom: shkn up and edgd lft over 1f out: styd on same pce ins fnl f* **33/1**

0/40 **6** hd **Glass Office**22 5595 7-9-1 103 ................ DaneO'Neill 10 101+
(David Simcock) *s.i.s: hld up: rdn and hung lft over 1f out: r.o ins fnl f: nt rch ldrs* **16/1**

2512 **7** shd **Mythmaker**69 3867 5-9-1 104 ................ FranBerry 12 101
(Bryan Smart) *chsd ldrs: rdn over 1f out: no ex ins fnl f* **14/1**

0342 **8** 1 **Polybius**42 4881 6-9-1 106 ................ DanielMuscutt 11 97
(David Simcock) *hld up: hdwy over 2f out: rdn over 1f out: no ex ins fnl f* **6/1**3

603 **9** 2 1/2 **Tupi (IRE)**20 5690 5-9-4 109 ................ SilvestreDeSousa 15 92
(Richard Hannon) *hld up: rdn over 2f out: sme hdwy over 1f out: eased wl ins fnl f* **4/1**2

22-2 **10** 2 3/4 **Dream Of Dreams (IRE)**111 2425 3-8-12 105 ................ TedDurcan 5 81
(Sir Michael Stoute) *s.i.s: hld up: pushed along 1/2-way: wknd fnl f* **14/1**

-30 **11** 11 **Windfast (IRE)**63 4071 6-9-1 107 ................(p1) RyanTate 4 45
(Brian Meehan) *hld up: pushed along over 3f out: wknd over 1f out* **20/1**

1m 9.68s (-2.82) **Going Correction** -0.075s/f (Good)
**WFA** 3 from 4yo+ 3lb 11 Ran SP% **118.5**
Speed ratings (Par 111): **115,114,114,112,110 110,109,108,105,101 86**
CSF £13.11 TOTE £3.50: £1.80, £1.90, £5.10; EX 17.80 Trifecta £165.00.
**Owner** Dr Ali Ridha **Bred** Tally-Ho Stud **Trained** Newmarket, Suffolk

**FOCUS**
A highly competitive feature. The winner has been rated close to his best.

## 6429 SAEED SUHAIL SAEED HEATH COURT H'CAP (JOCKEY CLUB GRASSROOTS SPRINT SERIES QUALIFIER) 6f
5:00 (5:02) (Class 4) (0-85,85) 3-Y-O+ £5,175 (£1,540; £769; £384) Stalls Low

Form RPR
0005 1 **Ninjago**14 5947 7-9-3 78 PatSmullen 7 85
(Paul Midgley) *trckd ldrs: rdn over 1f out: r.o to ld nr fin* 6/1[3]
300 2 nk **General Alexander (IRE)**19 5696 4-8-10 71 SilvestreDeSousa 10 77
(Brian Ellison) *hld up: hdwy over 2f out: rdn to ld ins fnl f: hdd nr fin* 8/1
0513 3 nk **Jule In The Crown**18 5758 3-9-7 85 DaneO'Neill 5 90
(Richard Hannon) *hld up: rdn over 1f out: edgd lft and r.o wl ins fnl f* 13/2
0665 4 nse **Syrian Pearl**7 6197 6-9-4 79 FranBerry 9 85+
(Chris Wall) *hld up: nt clr run fr over 1f out tl wl ins fnl f: r.o wl: nvr able to chal* 9/2[1]
1013 5 ½ **Bahamian Dollar**19 5720 4-9-7 82 AndrewMullen 3 85
(David Evans) *led: rdn and hdd over 1f out: r.o* 6/1[3]
5352 6 ½ **Cool Bahamian (IRE)**35 5156 6-9-4 79 (v) RobertWinston 8 81
(Eve Johnson Houghton) *chsd ldrs: led over 1f out: rdn and hdd ins fnl f: styd on same pce towards fin* 5/1[2]
1215 7 1¼ **Curious Fox**18 5758 4-9-9 84 RyanTate 1 82
(Anthony Carson) *s.i.s: hld up: swtchd lft and hdwy over 1f out: no ex wl ins fnl f* 12/1
3310 8 ½ **Meshardal (GER)**21 5671 7-8-10 78 (p) ConnorMurtagh(7) 2 74
(Ruth Carr) *hld up: hdwy over 2f out: ev ch over 1f out: sn rdn: no ex ins fnl f* 10/1
-106 9 1½ **The Commendatore**21 5671 4-9-10 85 FrannyNorton 4 76
(David Barron) *w ldr: shkn up and ev ch wl over 1f out: no ex fnl f* 8/1

1m 11.4s (-1.10) **Going Correction** -0.075s/f (Good)
**WFA** 3 from 4yo+ 3lb 9 Ran SP% 115.8
Speed ratings (Par 105): **104,103,103,103,102 101,100,99,97**
CSF £53.14 CT £324.79 TOTE £7.20: £2.30, £2.90, £2.60; EX 67.60 Trifecta £676.40.
**Owner** Taylor's Bloodstock Ltd **Bred** Newsells Park Stud **Trained** Westow, N Yorks
■ Stewards' Enquiry : Silvestre De Sousa two-day ban: used whip above the permitted level (Sep 10-11)

**FOCUS**
A wide-open looking sprint handicap and a bunched finish. The runner-up has been rated to this year's form for now, with the third to form.

## 6430 HEATH COURT HOTEL LONG SERVICE AWARDS H'CAP 5f
5:35 (5:36) (Class 4) (0-85,86) 3-Y-O+ £5,175 (£1,540; £769; £384) Stalls Low

Form RPR
351 1 **Foxy Forever (IRE)**36 5098 7-9-10 85 (t) FrannyNorton 2 91+
(Michael Wigham) *hld up: shkn up and qcknd ins fnl f: r.o to ld post* 4/1[1]
0520 2 shd **Diamond Lady**8 6141 6-9-4 84 JoshuaBryan(5) 4 89
(William Stone) *chsd ldrs: swtchd lft over 1f out: rdn to ld wl ins fnl f: eased and hdd last stride* 17/2
1055 3 nk **Tallinski (IRE)**28 5416 3-9-0 77 SilvestreDeSousa 11 81
(Brian Ellison) *led: hdd over 3f out: remained handy: rdn to ld again 1f out: hdd wl ins fnl f* 9/2[2]
2210 4 ½ **Liquid (IRE)**19 5708 3-8-10 73 RobHornby 8 75
(David Barron) *w ldrs: rdn and ev ch over 1f out: hung lft ins fnl f: styd on same pce towards fin* 16/1
0614 5 ¾ **Musharrif**25 5495 5-9-6 81 AntonioFresu 9 81
(Declan Carroll) *chsd ldrs: rdn over 1f out: styd on same pce wl ins fnl f* 9/1
6015 6 ¾ **Just Us Two (IRE)**17 5811 5-9-3 78 (p) SamHitchcott 10 75
(Robert Cowell) *w ldrs: led over 3f out: rdn and hdd 1f out: no ex wl ins fnl f* 14/1
0245 7 nk **Excellent George**22 5587 5-8-9 77 (t) MillyNaseb(7) 5 73
(Stuart Williams) *hld up: rdn and hung lft over 1f out: nt trble ldrs* 8/1
5065 8 ½ **Oh So Sassy**28 5426 7-9-11 86 FranBerry 7 80
(Chris Wall) *hld up: hdwy over 1f out: no ex ins fnl f* 5/1[3]
13 9 2¾ **Always Amazing**63 4098 3-9-6 83 AndrewMullen 1 67
(Robert Cowell) *s.s: sn drvn along and a in rr* 5/1[3]

58.63s (-0.47) **Going Correction** -0.075s/f (Good)
**WFA** 3 from 4yo+ 2lb 9 Ran SP% 115.7
Speed ratings (Par 105): **100,99,99,98,97 96,95,94,90**
CSF £38.31 CT £159.81 TOTE £4.50: £1.80, £2.70, £1.80; EX 40.50 Trifecta £201.50.
**Owner** D Hassan, J Cullinan **Bred** Tally-Ho Stud **Trained** Newmarket, Suffolk

**FOCUS**
This was run at a furious pace and there was another blanket finish. It's been rated as ordinary form.
T/Plt: £110.70 to a £1 stake. Pool: £73,462.10 - 484.21 winning units T/Qpdt: £25.20 to a £1 stake. Pool: £3,853.15 - 113.04 winning units **Colin Roberts**

# 5945 REDCAR (L-H)
Saturday, August 26

**OFFICIAL GOING: Good to firm (good in places; watered; 8.5)**
Wind: virtually nil Weather: fine

## 6431 BET AT RACINGUK.COM H'CAP (FOR LADY AMATEUR RIDERS ) 1m 2f 1y
4:50 (4:51) (Class 5) (0-75,75) 3-Y-O+ £3,431 (£1,064; £531; £266) Stalls Low

Form RPR
233- 1 **Time To Blossom**313 7410 4-10-7 75 MissSBrotherton 8 86+
(Simon Crisford) *midfield: pushed along and hdwy over 3f out: led over 2f out: edgd rt ins fnl f: kpt on and a doing enough* 4/1[2]
624 2 1 **Broadway Dreams**46 4720 3-9-12 73 MissBeckySmith 9 79
(Marjorie Fife) *hld up: pushed along in rr 4f out: gd hdwy over 2f out: wnt 2nd jst ins fnl f: kpt on but a hld* 7/1[3]
1130 3 2 **Haymarket**12 5997 8-9-9 63 MissCWalton 2 65
(R Mike Smith) *sn prom: rdn along 3f out: plugged on* 16/1
1330 4 2 **Miningrocks (FR)**21 5667 5-10-3 74 MissLWilson(3) 6 72
(Declan Carroll) *led: rdn whn hdd over 2f out: no ex fnl 110yds* 10/1
2502 5 4½ **Graceful Act**9 6092 9-9-2 56 oh5 (p) MissJoannaMason 7 45
(Ron Barr) *trckd ldrs: rdn over 2f out: wknd ins fnl f* 16/1
4240 6 2½ **Jan De Heem**14 5951 7-9-5 59 MissAWaugh 4 43
(Tina Jackson) *dwlt: hld up in midfield: rdn along 3f out: nvr threatened* 14/1
5215 7 nse **Archipeligo**14 5921 6-10-5 73 (p) MrsCBartley 5 57
(Iain Jardine) *hld up: nvr threatened* 17/2
3223 8 ¾ **Golconda Prince (IRE)**9 6091 3-8-13 65 MissEllaMcCain(5) 1 48
(Richard Fahey) *trckd ldrs: rdn 3f out: wknd over 1f out* 7/4[1]
0352 9 24 **Beauden Barrett**14 5921 4-10-3 71 (t) MissEmmaSayer 3 5
(John Quinn) *trckd ldrs: rdn along over 3f out: sn wknd and bhd* 12/1

2m 5.75s (-1.35) **Going Correction** -0.10s/f (Good)
**WFA** 3 from 4yo+ 7lb 9 Ran SP% 114.6
Speed ratings (Par 103): **101,100,98,97,93 91,91,90,71**
CSF £31.83 CT £401.53 TOTE £4.60: £1.70, £2.00, £4.10; EX 28.50 Trifecta £430.00.
**Owner** Sultan Ali **Bred** W And R Barnett Ltd **Trained** Newmarket, Suffolk

**FOCUS**
A fair lady amateur riders' handicap. They went a strong gallop and it paid to be delivered patiently on watered ground officially described as good to firm, good in places. The runner-up has been rated in line with the better view of his maiden form.

## 6432 BAKERS TAILORING AND FORMAL HIRE NOVICE AUCTION STKS 5f 217y
5:25 (5:26) (Class 5) 2-Y-O £3,557 (£1,058; £529; £264) Stalls Centre

Form RPR
22 1 **Fyre Cay (IRE)**30 5334 2-9-7 0 KevinStott 5 77
(Kevin Ryan) *w ldr: pushed along over 1f out: rdn fnl f: kpt on to ld towards fin* 7/2[2]
3440 2 hd **Mistress Of Venice**28 5391 2-8-11 99 LukeMorris 9 66
(James Given) *prom: led narrowly over 4f out: rdn 2f out: drvn ins fnl f: kpt on but hdd towards fin* 1/1[1]
64 3 nk **Fink Hill (USA)**52 4502 2-9-0 0 ConnorBeasley 6 68
(Richard Guest) *trckd ldrs: racd keenly: rdn appr fnl f: edgd lft but kpt on wl* 8/1[3]
03 4 2¼ **Emerald Rocket (IRE)**82 3398 2-8-7 0 PatrickO'Hanlon(7) 7 61+
(K R Burke) *midfield: pushed along over 2f out: hdwy over 1f out: kpt on fnl f* 22/1
0 5 ½ **Gorse (IRE)**16 5834 2-9-0 0 JackGarritty 12 59
(Ann Duffield) *led : hdd over 4f out: remained cl up: rdn over 2f out: no ex fnl f* 80/1
3413 6 1 **Benadalid**58 4258 2-8-10 79 PaulaMuir(7) 11 59
(Chris Fairhurst) *chsd ldrs: rdn 3f out: no ex fnl f* 9/1
5 7 ¾ **Arctic Treasure (IRE)**24 5537 2-8-12 0 DougieCostello 4 52
(Richard Fahey) *hld up: pushed along over 2f out: kpt on fnl f: nrst fin* 9/1
0 8 1 **Barney Bullet (IRE)**10 6055 2-9-0 0 PatrickMathers 8 50
(Noel Wilson) *s.i.s: sn chsd ldrs: rdn over 2f out: wknd ins fnl f* 100/1
60 9 1 **Viking Way (IRE)**21 5631 2-9-0 0 SamJames 1 47
(Olly Williams) *hld up in midfield: rdn along over 2f out: kpt on fnl f: nvr threatened* 100/1
6 10 hd **By Royal Approval (IRE)**31 5278 2-8-12 0 DannyBrock 10 45
(Michael Appleby) *chsd ldrs: rdn along 3f out: wknd over 1f out* 50/1
11 1½ **Little Red Berry (IRE)** 2-8-5 0 JoeDoyle 3 33
(James Given) *bdly outpcd in rr tl sme late hdwy* 50/1
6 12 2 **Sir Derrick (IRE)**10 6056 2-8-9 0 RachelRichardson(3) 14 33
(Tim Easterby) *midfield: rdn along over 2f out: wknd over 1f out* 20/1
60 13 7 **Makofitwhatyouwill**52 4503 2-8-12 0 BarryMcHugh 2 11
(Nigel Tinkler) *s.i.s: a rr* 100/1
06 14 1 **Stark Reality (IRE)**10 6055 2-8-0 0 FayeMcManoman(7) 15 3
(Nigel Tinkler) *sn outpcd and towards rr* 100/1
15 5 **Bayelsa Boy (IRE)** 2-9-2 0 DuranFentiman 13
(Tim Easterby) *midfield: rdn 3f out: sn wknd and bhd* 33/1

1m 11.02s (-0.78) **Going Correction** -0.10s/f (Good) 15 Ran SP% 124.5
Speed ratings (Par 94): **101,100,100,97,96 95,94,93,91,91 89,86,77,76,69**
CSF £7.11 TOTE £5.60: £1.60, £1.02, £3.10; EX 8.90 Trifecta £44.20.
**Owner** Fyre Partners **Bred** L Wright **Trained** Hambleton, N Yorks

**FOCUS**
A good juvenile novice contest. They went a decent gallop and the leaders drifted right from past halfway to race up the near rail. It's been rated around the winner, the third and those down the field.

## 6433 MARKET CROSS JEWELLERS FILLIES' NOVICE AUCTION STKS (PLUS 10 RACE) 7f
5:55 (5:58) (Class 5) 2-Y-O £3,557 (£1,058; £529; £264) Stalls Centre

Form RPR
442 1 **Escape The City**9 6100 2-8-11 75 CharlieBennett(3) 9 74
(Hughie Morrison) *hld up in tch: pushed along whn bit short of room and angled lft appr fnl f: styd on wl: led towards fin* 4/5[1]
2 ½ **Rotherhithe** 2-9-0 0 JoeDoyle 1 72
(Robyn Brisland) *dwlt: hld up: hdwy to trck ldrs over 3f out: pushed along to ld over 1f out: wandered lft and rt u.p ins fnl f: hdd towards fin* 12/1
23 3 3¾ **Elysee Star**52 4502 2-9-0 0 KevinStott 10 62
(Ben Haslam) *chsd ldrs: rdn over 2f out: ev ch over 1f out: one pce ins fnl f* 13/2
40 4 ½ **Show Princess**33 5210 2-9-0 0 DougieCostello 3 60
(Michael Appleby) *hld up: rdn along over 2f out: hdwy over 1f out: kpt on ins fnl f* 66/1
4 5 1 **Follow The Feeling (USA)**18 5749 2-9-0 0 DanielTudhope 2 57
(Henry Spiller) *trckd ldrs: pushed along to chal over 1f out: rdn whn sltly hmpd jst ins fnl f: one pce* 5/1[2]
6 1 **The Cliff Horse (IRE)** 2-9-0 0 JackGarritty 8 55
(Donald McCain) *prom: rdn and outpcd over 1f out: kpt on again towards fin* 20/1
451 7 ½ **Dorcas**12 5998 2-9-7 71 LukeMorris 4 60
(James Given) *led: rdn whn hdd over 1f out: wknd ins fnl f* 6/1[3]
0 8 3¾ **Shef Wedsneigh (IRE)**11 6042 2-9-0 0 ConnorBeasley 5 43
(Roger Fell) *a towards rr* 66/1
00 U **La Plusbelle**28 5412 2-9-0 0 BarryMcHugh 7
(Richard Fahey) *trckd ldrs: lost pl qckly over 3f out: wnt wrong and eased: rdr uns whn attempting to pull up* 66/1

1m 24.49s (-0.01) **Going Correction** -0.10s/f (Good) 9 Ran SP% 116.8
Speed ratings (Par 91): **96,95,91,90,89 88,87,83,**
CSF £12.23 TOTE £1.40: £1.02, £3.50, £1.90; EX 12.20 Trifecta £61.20.
**Owner** MNC Racing **Bred** Melksham Craic **Trained** East Ilsley, Berks

**FOCUS**
A fair juvenile fillies' novice contest. They went a decent gallop and the strong favourite came through late to get off the mark. It's been rated around the winner and those down the field.

## 6434 RACING UK STRAIGHT MILE SERIES H'CAP (RACING UK STRAIGHT MILE SERIES QUALIFIER) 7f 219y
6:25 (6:25) (Class 4) (0-85,86) 3-Y-O+ £6,469 (£1,925; £962; £481) Stalls Centre

Form RPR
3331 1 **Mon Beau Visage (IRE)**5 6266 4-10-4 86 6ex (p) DanielTudhope 2 92
(David O'Meara) *hld up in midfield: pushed along and hdwy over 1f out: chsd ldr appr fnl f: rdn and kpt on: led nr fin* 3/1[1]


The Form Book Flat, Raceform Ltd, Newbury, RG14 5SJ

6406 **2** *shd* **Testa Rossa (IRE)**[12] 5996 7-9-4 **79**.........................(b) SeanMooney(7) 3 85
(Jim Goldie) *hld up towards outer: rdn over 2f out: r.o strly fnl f: edgd lft towards fin: jst failed* **25/1**

0056 **3** *nk* **Off Art**[5] 6266 7-8-13 **70**.....................................(p) RachelRichardson(3) 11 75
(Tim Easterby) *prom: rdn to ld 2f out: kpt on: hdd nr fin: lost 2nd post* **11/1**

0-05 **4** *¾* **Bamber Bridge (IRE)**[21] 5669 3-9-12 **86**.......................... PhillipMakin 7 89
(Michael Dods) *midfield: rdn over 2f out: kpt on fnl f: hmpd nr line* **5/1**[3]

060 **5** *nse* **Palmerston**[26] 5484 4-9-12 **80**.................................. DougieCostello 4 83
(Michael Appleby) *chsd ldrs: rdn along 3f out: edgd lft towards far rial over 1f out: kpt on same pce fnl f* **12/1**

1003 **6** *nse* **Zeshov (IRE)**[26] 5469 6-9-8 **76**......................................... ConnorBeasley 8 79
(Rebecca Bastiman) *dwlt: hld up: hdwy and gng wl in bhd horses over 1f out: rdn ent fnl f: kpt on same pce* **12/1**

3253 **7** *½* **Abushamah (IRE)**[12] 5993 6-9-4 **72**.............................. JackGarritty 1 74
(Ruth Carr) *hld up: pushed along over 2f out: rdn over 1f out: kpt on same pce fnl f* **9/2**[2]

-656 **8** *3 ½* **Big Time Dancer (IRE)**[19] 5699 4-8-10 **64**.......................(p) JoeDoyle 6 58
(Brian Ellison) *prom: rdn over 2f out: wknd fnl f* **9/1**

1-12 **9** *nk* **Big Storm Coming**[43] 4837 7-9-12 **80**.............................. LukeMorris 9 73
(David Brown) *chsd ldrs: rdn over 2f out: wknd fnl f* **14/1**

2200 **10** *hd* **Throckley**[21] 5668 6-10-0 **82**.........................................(t) SamJames 10 75
(John Davies) *hld up: rdn over 2f out: nvr threatened* **9/1**

0050 **11** *3 ½* **Funding Deficit (IRE)**[12] 5994 7-8-9 **63**...................(h) PatrickMathers 5 48
(Jim Goldie) *led: rdn whn hdd 2f out: wknd fnl f* **50/1**

1m 35.86s (-0.74) **Going Correction** -0.10s/f (Good)
**WFA** 3 from 4yo+ 6lb **11** Ran SP% **116.0**
Speed ratings (Par 105): **99,98,98,97,97 97,97,93,93,93 89**
CSF £83.93 CT £745.95 TOTE £4.00: £1.40, £5.90, £3.60; EX 75.40 Trifecta £2005.50.
**Owner** The Pink Pot Partnership LLP **Bred** Stephanie Hanly **Trained** Upper Helmsley, N Yorks
■ Stewards' Enquiry : Sean Mooney three-day ban: careless riding (Sep 10-12)

**FOCUS**
The feature contest was a decent handicap. The went a good gallop and the favourite narrowly prevailed in a bunched finish. The runner-up has been rated to his turf best, and the third to this year's form.

## 6435 ALL NEW RACINGUK.COM H'CAP 7f
**6:55** (6:56) (Class 6) (0-65,65) 3-Y-O+ **£2,911** (£866; £432; £216) **Stalls** Centre

Form RPR

3023 **1** **Insurplus (IRE)**[7] 6182 4-9-5 **58**..................................... DanielTudhope 4 66
(Jim Goldie) *hld up in midfield: pushed along and hdwy over 1f out: rdn to ld ins fnl f: kpt on* **9/2**[1]

2640 **2** *½* **Old China**[33] 5214 4-9-9 **62**............................................... SamJames 1 69
(John Davies) *hld up in rr: pushed along and hdwy over 1f out: rdn and kpt on wl fnl f* **14/1**

6003 **3** *nse* **Showdance Kid**[51] 4540 3-9-4 **62**.................................. DougieCostello 2 67
(Neville Bycroft) *chsd ldrs: rdn to ld appr fnl f: hdd ins fnl f: kpt on* **14/1**

0035 **4** *3* **Gun Case**[12] 5993 5-9-11 **64**...........................................(p) PhillipMakin 12 62
(Alistair Whillans) *hld up: hdwy 2f out: rdn to chse ldr appr fnl f: no ex ins fnl f* **6/1**[2]

4222 **5** *¾* **Danot (IRE)**[8] 6131 5-9-4 **57**.........................................(p) JackGarritty 6 53
(Jedd O'Keeffe) *chsd ldrs: rdn over 2f out: no ex fnl f* **7/1**[3]

3054 **6** *1 ¼* **Broctune Papa Gio**[24] 5544 10-9-2 **55**..................(b) PatrickMathers 15 48
(Gillian Boanas) *chsd ldrs: rdn and ev ch over 1f out: wknd ins fnl f* **20/1**

2060 **7** *2 ¾* **Ad Vitam (IRE)**[16] 5836 9-9-5 **61**.....................(bt) JordanVaughan(3) 11 47
(Suzzanne France) *s.i.s: hld up: sme late hdwy: nvr threatened* **50/1**

1056 **8** *¾* **Blue Jacket (USA)**[47] 4687 6-9-5 **61**................. RachelRichardson(3) 13 45
(Dianne Sayer) *trckd ldrs: rdn over 2f out: wknd fnl f* **16/1**

6000 **9** *¾* **Royal Icon**[15] 5897 3-9-0 **58**.........................................(p) KevinStott 17 38
(Kevin Ryan) *hld up: rdn and hdwy to chse ldrs over 1f out: wknd fnl f* **20/1**

0002 **10** *shd* **Meandmyshadow**[16] 5836 9-9-12 **65**......................(b) DuranFentiman 16 46
(Alan Brown) *led narrowly: rdn over 2f out: hdd appr fnl f: wknd* **20/1**

5005 **11** *1 ¾* **Caeser The Gaeser (IRE)**[16] 5836 5-9-11 **64**..............(p) TomEaves 10 41
(Nigel Tinkler) *midfield: rdn 2f out: no imp* **22/1**

2324 **12** *nk* **Willsy**[7] 6181 4-9-5 **63**...........................................(b) GemmaTutty(5) 18 39
(Karen Tutty) *hld up: rdn over 2f out: nvr threatened* **12/1**

0002 **13** *shd* **Starboard Watch**[14] 5946 3-9-6 **64**.......................................... JoeDoyle 3 37
(James Given) *prom: rdn over 2f out: wknd over 1f out* **20/1**

2540 **14** *1 ½* **Faintly (USA)**[16] 5835 6-9-6 **59**....................................... JamesSullivan 20 30
(Ruth Carr) *hld up: nvr threatened* **14/1**

430 **14** *dht* **Bourbonisto**[19] 5703 3-9-2 **60**............................................. LukeMorris 14 29
(Ben Haslam) *midfield: rdn over 12f out: wknd over 1f out* **33/1**

005R **16** *nk* **Tellovoi (IRE)**[24] 5544 9-9-6 **64**................................(p) KevinLundie(5) 19 35
(Richard Guest) *s.i.s: hld up: rdn and hdwy into midfield over 2f out: wknd over 1f out* **20/1**

/23- **17** *1 ½* **Oregon Gift**[274] 8100 5-9-10 **63**............................................ ConnorKing 5 30
(Brian Ellison) *s.i.s: hld up: rdn over 2f out: nvr threatened* **25/1**

5560 **18** *3* **Fidelma Moon (IRE)**[21] 5650 5-9-1 **54**.................................. JasonHart 8 12
(Tracy Waggott) *prom: rdn and lost pl 2f out: sn wknd* **16/1**

-052 **19** *6* **Outfox**[12] 6016 3-9-5 **63**................................................ ConnorBeasley 9
(Bryan Smart) *trckd ldrs: lost pl over 2f out: wknd and eased* **14/1**

1m 23.38s (-1.12) **Going Correction** -0.10s/f (Good)
**WFA** 3 from 4yo+ 5lb **19** Ran SP% **128.0**
Speed ratings (Par 101): **102,101,101,97,97 95,92,91,90,90 88,88,88,86,86 86,84,81,74**
CSF £58.11 CT £594.81 TOTE £4.80: £1.10, £4.70, £5.60, £2.30; EX 77.90 Trifecta £2138.80.
**Owner** Mr & Mrs G Grant & Partner **Bred** Patrick J Monahan **Trained** Uplawmoor, E Renfrews

**FOCUS**
A modest handicap. Not surprisingly there was a decent pace in such a big field, initially right across the track. The action later developed middle to far side. It's been rated a shade positively.

## 6436 WISE BETTING AT RACINGUK.COM H'CAP 1m 5f 218y
**7:25** (7:25) (Class 6) (0-65,65) 3-Y-O **£2,911** (£866; £432; £216) **Stalls** Low

Form RPR

2260 **1** **Plage Depampelonne**[12] 6013 3-9-6 **64**.......................(p[1]) KevinStott 1 71
(James Bethell) *trckd ldrs: rdn over 2f out: styd on: led 75yds out* **6/1**

5231 **2** *½* **Clenymistra (IRE)**[11] 6048 3-9-7 **65**............................ DanielTudhope 10 71
(David O'Meara) *hld up in midfield: pushed along and hdwy over 2f out: rdn to ld over 1f out: edgd lft ins fnl f: hdd 75yds out: one pce* **5/2**[2]

0354 **3** *3* **Starlight Circus (IRE)**[16] 5853 3-9-3 **61**.....................(p) LukeMorris 4 63
(Marco Botti) *trckd ldrs: rdn over 2f out: hmpd between wnr and 2nd ins fnl f: no ch after but styd on: wnt 3rd nr fin* **11/2**[3]

5440 **4** *nk* **Magic Beans**[16] 5846 3-8-10 **57**.................................... CharlieBennett(3) 6 59
(Hughie Morrison) *prom: racd keenly: pushed along to ld over 2f out: rdn over 1f out: hdd 1f out: edgd lft and no ex: lost 3rd nr fin* **10/1**

0-42 **5** *2 ½* **Eyreborn (IRE)**[11] 6048 3-9-6 **64**.................................(h) ConnorBeasley 3 62
(Keith Dalgleish) *in tch: pushed along over 3f out: rdn and outpcd 2f out: plugged on fnl f* **9/4**[1]

0500 **6** *1 ¼* **Sambuca Nera**[33] 5209 3-8-4 **48**........................................ JoeDoyle 8 44
(James Given) *led: rdn whn hdd over 2f out: wknd ins fnl f* **66/1**

030 **7** *¾* **Grey Mist**[21] 5632 3-9-4 **65**..............................(p[1]) RachelRichardson(3) 7 60
(Tim Easterby) *hld up: rdn over 2f out: nvr threatened* **22/1**

3465 **8** *hd* **Archibelle**[28] 5401 3-9-4 **62**............................................. JamesSullivan 9 57
(R Mike Smith) *midfield: rdn over 2f out: hung persistently lft and sn btn* **16/1**

2640 **9** *1 ¼* **Moonlight Blue (IRE)**[9] 6091 3-9-4 **62**................................(p) TomEaves 2 55
(Michael Dods) *s.i.s: hld up in rr: pushed along over 2f out: sme hdwy over 1f out: wknd ins fnl f* **33/1**

3m 11.43s (6.73) **Going Correction** -0.10s/f (Good) **9** Ran SP% **112.8**
Speed ratings (Par 98): **76,75,74,73,72 71,71,71,70**
CSF £20.53 CT £86.20 TOTE £6.60: £2.50, £1.10, £2.10; EX 19.60 Trifecta £88.40.
**Owner** Chris Wright & The Hon Mrs J M Corbett **Bred** Denford Stud Ltd **Trained** Middleham Moor, N Yorks

**FOCUS**
A modest 3yo staying handicap. They went a sedate gallop and three of the first four home raced relatively prominently.

## 6437 WATCH RACE REPLAYS AT RACINGUK.COM H'CAP 5f 217y
**7:55** (8:00) (Class 6) (0-55,59) 3-Y-O+ **£3,067** (£905; £453) **Stalls** Centre

Form RPR

53 **1** **State Residence (IRE)**[16] 5848 3-9-0 **51**.................(vt) DanielTudhope 1 60
(David O'Meara) *mde all: rdn over 2f out: edgd rt appr fnl f: drvn and kpt on* **6/1**[2]

60 **2** *1 ½* **My Girl Maisie (IRE)**[12] 6016 3-9-3 **54**....................... ConnorBeasley 14 58
(Richard Guest) *chsd ldrs: rdn over 2f out: chsd wnr appr fnl f: kpt on but a hld* **8/1**[3]

3643 **3** *nk* **Someone Exciting**[8] 6131 4-9-5 **53**.............................. PatrickMathers 7 56
(David Thompson) *midfield: rdn over 2f out: hdwy over 1f out: kpt on* **9/2**[1]

550 **4** *hd* **Thorntoun Lady (USA)**[193] 732 7-9-6 **54**....................... JamesSullivan 12 58
(Jim Goldie) *dwlt: hld up: pushed along whn n.m.r wl over 1f out: hdwy and swtchd lft appr fnl f: kpt on wl: nrst fin* **40/1**

343 **5** *1 ¾* **Regal Decree**[34] 5182 3-9-4 **55**................................(b[1]) JackGarritty 19 52
(Jedd O'Keeffe) *chsd ldrs: rdn over 2f out: no ex ins fnl f* **6/1**[2]

0401 **6** *¾* **Cryptonite (IRE)**[7] 6174 3-9-8 **59**....................................... LukeMorris 20 54
(Michael Appleby) *midfield: rdn over 2f out: one pce and nvr threatened* **12/1**

000 **7** *shd* **Twistsandturns (IRE)**[16] 5848 6-8-13 **50**..................(b[1]) PhilDennis(3) 13 44
(Declan Carroll) *wnt lft s: sn chsd ldrs: rdn over 2f out: no ex fnl f* **25/1**

4140 **8** *shd* **Gaelic Wizard (IRE)**[5] 6271 9-9-2 **55**.......................(b) GemmaTutty(5) 17 49
(Karen Tutty) *s.i.s and sn pushed along in rr: kpt on fnl f: nvr threatened* **20/1**

6450 **9** *1* **Atrafan (IRE)**[34] 5182 3-9-0 **54**........................................ JoshDoyle(3) 18 45
(Alan Brown) *hld up in midfield: rdn over 2f out: sme hdwy over 1f out: nvr threatened* **33/1**

0065 **10** *¾* **Bingo George (IRE)**[11] 6046 4-8-12 **46**................................. KevinStott 2 34
(Mark Rimell) *prom: rdn over 2f out: wknd ins fnl f* **10/1**

0656 **11** *½* **Nellie Deen (IRE)**[11] 6045 4-8-12 **46**.............................(b) SamJames 6 33
(Roger Fell) *chsd ldrs: rdn over 2f out: wknd over 1f out* **14/1**

0006 **12** *½* **Little Kingdom (IRE)**[18] 5741 3-8-13 **50**....................... DougieCostello 9 35
(Tracy Waggott) *chsd ldrs: rdn along 3f out: wknd over 1f out* **33/1**

-044 **13** *¾* **She's Zoff (IRE)**[29] 5374 3-8-10 **47**.................................... JasonHart 11 30
(John Quinn) *midfield: pushed along whn bit short of room over 2f out: nvr threatened* **16/1**

2134 **14** *3 ¼* **Harbour Patrol (IRE)**[12] 5992 5-9-6 **54**..................(b) DuranFentiman 16 26
(Rebecca Bastiman) *midfield: rdn over 2f out: wknd over 1f out* **20/1**

0340 **15** *¾* **Vaux (IRE)**[28] 5419 3-8-10 **47**............................................. TomEaves 10 17
(Ben Haslam) *hld up: nvr threatened* **50/1**

2250 **16** *nk* **Majestic Stone (IRE)**[3] 6313 3-9-4 **55**..............................(b[1]) JoeDoyle 3 24
(Julie Camacho) *dwlt: hld up: nvr threatened* **14/1**

6042 **17** *1 ¼* **Mighty Bond**[11] 6046 5-8-9 **48**................................(p) BenRobinson(5) 5 13
(Tracy Waggott) *dwlt: sn prom: rdn over 2f out: wknd over 1f out* **14/1**

000 **18** *13* **Monsieur Mel**[14] 5946 3-8-13 **53**........................... RachelRichardson(3) 4
(Antony Brittain) *a towards rr* **66/1**

1m 10.78s (-1.02) **Going Correction** -0.10s/f (Good)
**WFA** 3 from 4yo+ 3lb **18** Ran SP% **125.7**
Speed ratings (Par 101): **102,100,99,99,97 96,95,95,94,93 92,92,91,86,85 85,83,66**
CSF £49.35 CT £251.10 TOTE £7.20: £2.40, £3.70, £1.60, £6.30; EX 71.70 Trifecta £345.00.
**Owner** Dr Marwan Koukash **Bred** Grangecon Holdings Ltd **Trained** Upper Helmsley, N Yorks
■ Goadby was withdrawn. Price at time of withdrawal 25/1. Rule 4 does not apply

**FOCUS**
A moderate sprint handicap. The winner made all at a decent tempo middle to far side from a low draw. The winner has been rated back to near his best.
T/Plt: £54.60 to a £1 stake. Pool: £35,971.14 - 480.76 winning units T/Qpdt: £18.70 to a £1 stake. Pool: £5,150.67 - 202.97 winning units **Andrew Sheret**

# [6272]WINDSOR (R-H)
Saturday, August 26

**OFFICIAL GOING: Good to firm (good in places; watered; 8.3)**
Wind: light, behind Weather: sunny, warm

## 6438 FENWICK BRACKNELL AT THE LEXICON OPENING SEPTEMBER NOVICE STKS 6f 12y
**5:10** (5:11) (Class 5) 2-Y-O **£2,911** (£866; £432; £216) **Stalls** Low

Form RPR

6 **1** **Lamya (GER)**[44] 4815 2-8-11 0........................................ TomMarquand 3 77+
(Richard Hannon) *mde all: pushed along and fnd ex over 1f out: in command and r.o wl ins fnl f: comf* **6/4**[1]

**2** *2 ¼* **Angel's Whisper (IRE)** 2-8-11 0........................................ GeraldMosse 7 70
(Jeremy Noseda) *chsd wnr: rdn ent fnl 2f: unable to match pce of wnr over 1f out: kpt on same pce ins fnl f* **13/2**

02 **3** *¾* **Tiepolo (IRE)**[15] 5865 2-8-13 0.................................. HectorCrouch(3) 5 72
(Gary Moore) *hld up in tch in midfield: swtchd lft and bmpd rival ent fnl 2f: chsd ldng pair over 1f out: kpt on same pce ins fnl f* **5/1**[3]

00 **4** *3 ½* **Makambe (IRE)**[10] 6071 2-8-13 0............................. CallumShepherd(3) 2 61
(Charles Hills) *stdd s: hld up in tch in rr of main gp: rdn and hdwy over 1f out: styd on to go 4th ins fnl f: nvr trbld ldrs* **25/1**

**5** *1* **Bint Huwaar (USA)** 2-8-11 0 StevieDonohoe 6 53
(George Peckham) *chsd ldrs early: in tch in midfield mainly: pushed along and lost pl over 2f out: rn green and awkward hd carriage over 1f out: wl hld and kpt on same pce ins fnl f* **10/1**

4625 **6** *2 ½* **Collateral (IRE)**[22] 5600 2-9-2 78 (b[1]) JoeFanning 8 53
(James Tate) *wnt sharply lft leaving stalls: sn rcvrd to chse ldrs: rdn over 2f out: unable qck and btn over 1f out: wknd fnl f* **7/2**[2]

**7** *hd* **Prince Maurice (USA)** 2-9-2 0 JamieSpencer 10 49
(Jeremy Noseda) *carried lft leaving stalls: sn rcvrd and in tch in midfield: effrt over 2f out: sn struggling and outpcd whn drifted rt over 1f out: wknd ins fnl f* **14/1**

**8** *5* **Goodbye Lulu (IRE)** 2-8-11 0 TrevorWhelan 9 28
(George Baker) *impeded leaving stalls: in tch: effrt and drifting lft 2f out: sn struggling and btn over 1f out: wknd fnl f* **28/1**

**9** *17* **Rock Chic** 2-8-11 0 FergusSweeney 4
(Rod Millman) *squeezed for room leaving stalls: sn bhd and a struggling: rdn 1/2-way: lost tch 1/2-way* **40/1**

1m 11.95s (-1.05) **Going Correction** -0.15s/f (Firm) **9** Ran SP% **117.7**
Speed ratings (Par 94): **101,98,97,92,91 87,87,80,58**
CSF £12.00 TOTE £2.20: £1.20, £1.60, £2.00; EX 14.00 Trifecta £45.30.
**Owner** Hussain Alabbas Lootah **Bred** Gestut Graditz **Trained** East Everleigh, Wilts

**FOCUS**
A fair novices' sprint although very few got into it and the winner made virtually all. The first three drew a little way clear and the form should hold fast. The third has been rated to his mark for now.

## 6439 SPORT OF KINGS WATCHES FILLIES' H'CAP 1m 31y
**5:40** (5:41) (Class 5) (0-75,74) 3-Y-0+ **£2,911** (£866; £432; £216) **Stalls** Low

Form RPR

0224 **1** **Sandy Shores**[24] 5545 3-8-10 **64** (b) TomMarquand 3 72
(Brian Meehan) *in tch in midfield: effrt and rdn to chal 2f out: led u.p 1f out: styd on strly and drew clr ins fnl f* **9/2**[2]

0054 **2** *2 ¾* **Conqueress (IRE)**[35] 5139 3-8-8 **67** (p) JaneElliott(5) 1 69
(Tom Dascombe) *t.k.h: led: rdn 2f out: hdd 1f out: no ex and outpcd by wnr ins fnl f: hld on for 2nd towards fin* **5/1**[3]

120 **3** *nse* **Himalayan Queen**[16] 5857 4-9-3 **65** GeraldMosse 4 68
(William Jarvis) *stdd after s: hld up in rr: clsd to chse ldrs and swtchd rt over 1f out: pressing ldrs 1f out: no ex and outpcd by wnr ins fnl f: battling for 2nd after: kpt on* **6/1**

0050 **4** *2* **Doodle Dandy (IRE)**[82] 3397 4-8-7 **55** oh2 (p[1]) RyanPowell 6 53
(David Bridgwater) *chsd clr ldng pair: clsd 1/2-way: rdn to chse ldr over 2f out tl over 1f out: no ex and wknd ins fnl f* **25/1**

6443 **5** *14* **First Experience**[65] 4010 6-9-7 **74** (p) PaddyBradley(5) 8 40
(Lee Carter) *hld up in tch in last trio: effrt on outer over 2f out: no imp and btn over 1f out: sn wknd* **14/1**

1111 **6** *3 ½* **Arctic Flower (IRE)**[5] 6263 4-8-6 **57** ow1 HectorCrouch(3) 5 15
(John Bridger) *t.k.h: w ldr tl chsd ldr after 2f: rdn and lost 2nd over 2f out: wknd over 1f out* **13/8**[1]

0-65 **7** *6* **Love Me Again**[23] 5577 3-8-11 **65** StevieDonohoe 7 8
(Charlie Fellowes) *dwlt and rousted along leaving stalls: in tch in midfield: rdn over 2f out: sn lost pl: wl btn over 1f out* **10/1**

060 **8** *45* **Coya**[128] 1905 3-8-8 **65** (h) CallumShepherd(3) 2
(Charles Hills) *bustled along early: hld up in last trio: rdn and dropped to rr over 2f out: sn bhd and eased fr over 1f out: t.o* **20/1**

1m 41.17s (-3.53) **Going Correction** -0.15s/f (Firm)
**WFA** 3 from 4yo+ 6lb **8** Ran SP% **111.6**
Speed ratings (Par 100): **111,108,108,106,92 88,82,37**
CSF £25.81 CT £131.49 TOTE £5.30: £1.70, £1.70, £2.00; EX 27.70 Trifecta £196.60.
**Owner** J H Widdows **Bred** J H Widdows **Trained** Manton, Wilts

**FOCUS**
The early gallop was generous for this modest fillies' handicap and it suited those coming from off the pace. The winner has been rated in line with her Epsom form, with the third to her turf form.

## 6440 SRI LANKA AUGUST STKS (LISTED RACE) 1m 3f 99y
**6:10** (6:11) (Class 1) 3-Y-0+
**£20,982** (£7,955; £3,981; £1,983; £995; £499) **Stalls** Centre

Form RPR

3122 **1** **Second Step (IRE)**[22] 5592 6-9-6 110 JamieSpencer 4 112+
(Roger Charlton) *pressed ldr for 2f: upsides and travelling strly over 2f out: led 2f out: wnt rt u.p over 1f out: in command and r.o wl ins fnl f: quite comf* **6/4**[1]

4044 **2** *2 ½* **Law And Order (IRE)**[38] 5037 3-8-12 100 JoeFanning 5 109
(James Tate) *s.i.s: hld up in tch in last pair: rdn and effrt 2f out: hdwy over 1f out: chsd wnr ins fnl f: styd on but no threat to wnr* **12/1**

0013 **3** *1 ¼* **King Bolete (IRE)**[29] 5353 5-9-3 102 (p) AndreaAtzeni 3 103
(Roger Varian) *led: jnd and rdn over 2f out: hdd 2f out: stl pressing wnr but struggling to qckn whn carried rt and impeded over 1f out: kpt on same pce and lost 2nd ins fnl f* **7/2**[2]

/040 **4** *¾* **Uele River**[10] 6074 5-8-12 88 TomMarquand 1 97
(Henry Candy) *hld up in tch in midfield: effrt over 2f out: swtchd lft 2f out and hdwy u.p to chse ldrs over 1f out: kpt on same pce and no imp ins fnl f* **66/1**

0-05 **5** *1 ¼* **Harlequeen**[7] 6191 4-8-12 104 (v[1]) CharlesBishop 8 95
(Mick Channon) *taken down early and led to post: t.k.h: chsd ldr for 2f: styd prom: rdn and struggling to qckn whn hmpd over 1f out: no threat to wnr after* **12/1**

/4-6 **6** *½* **Agent Murphy**[7] 6191 6-9-3 105 JimmyFortune 2 99
(Brian Meehan) *chsd ldrs: effrt over 2f out: no hdwy u.p over 1f out: wknd ins fnl f* **8/1**[3]

0105 **7** *nk* **Carbon Dating (IRE)**[92] 3057 5-9-3 107 RowanScott 6 98
(John Patrick Shanahan, Ire) *hld up in tch in midfield: clsd to chse ldrs 4f out: rdn over 2f out: no ex and outpcd over 1f out: wknd ins fnl f* **25/1**

3-50 **8** *1 ½* **Across The Stars (IRE)**[63] 4070 4-9-3 113 (h[1]) TedDurcan 7 96
(Sir Michael Stoute) *stdd s: hld up in tch in rr: hdwy on inner over 4f out: nt clr run and nvr looked like getting a run fr 2f out: bhd ins fnl f* **7/2**[2]

2m 26.44s (-3.06) **Going Correction** -0.15s/f (Firm)
**WFA** 3 from 4yo+ 8lb **8** Ran SP% **116.3**
Speed ratings (Par 111): **105,103,102,101,100 100,100,99**
CSF £22.61 TOTE £2.10: £1.10, £3.10, £1.30; EX 17.40 Trifecta £41.80.
**Owner** Merry Fox Stud Limited **Bred** Merry Fox Stud Limited **Trained** Beckhampton, Wilts
■ Stewards' Enquiry : Jamie Spencer four-day ban: careless riding (Sep 10-13)

**FOCUS**
This Listed race has been won in the past by the likes of Berkshire, Spanish Moon and Cameron Highland, and this edition looked up to scratch. While a 3yo or 4yo had won eight of the previous 10 renewals, this time victory went to a 6yo. The early pace was weak and there were a couple of hard-luck stories in behind, but the winner is a class act. Muddling form, with the runner-up the key.

## 6441 BET & WATCH AT SUNBETS.CO.UK WINTER HILL STKS (GROUP 3) 1m 2f
**6:40** (6:40) (Class 1) 3-Y-O+
**£34,026** (£12,900; £6,456; £3,216; £1,614; £810) **Stalls** Centre

Form RPR

4462 **1** **Fabricate**[25] 5500 5-9-1 106 (p) GeraldMosse 7 115
(Michael Bell) *hld up in tch: effrt over 2f out: rdn and hdwy to chse ldr over 1f out: led 1f out: styd on wl and in command fnl 75yds* **11/2**

251 **2** *1 ¼* **Spark Plug (IRE)**[50] 4584 6-9-1 110 (p) JimmyFortune 8 112
(Brian Meehan) *stdd after s and hld up in rr: effrt and clsd 3f out: hdwy u.p to chse ldrs over 1f out: styd on to go 2nd 75yds out: nvr threatening wnr* **7/2**[3]

1-62 **3** *1 ¼* **Chain Of Daisies**[57] 4308 5-8-12 107 FergusSweeney 1 106
(Henry Candy) *w ldr tl led after 1f: rdn over 1f out: drvn and hdd 1f out: no ex: lost 2nd 75yds out and wknd towards fin* **10/3**[2]

1-03 **4** *3* **Best Of Days**[35] 5148 3-8-8 110 (t) OisinMurphy 6 104
(Hugo Palmer) *s.i.s: in tch in last pair: rdn and dropped to rr over 2f out: trying to rally whn nt clr run and swtchd lft 1f out: kpt on to pass btn rivals ins fnl f: no threat to ldrs* **6/1**

0421 **5** *2 ½* **Frankuus (IRE)**[14] 5925 3-8-11 112 (b) JoeFanning 5 102
(Mark Johnston) *t.k.h: led for 1f: chsd ldr tl lost pl u.p over 1f out: 4th and btn 1f out: wknd fnl f* **3/1**[1]

-610 **6** *2* **Autocratic**[14] 5925 4-9-4 112 TedDurcan 3 99
(Sir Michael Stoute) *trckd ldrs: rdn ent fnl 2f: lost pl and btn ent fnl f: bhd and eased towards fin* **6/1**

2m 4.25s (-4.45) **Going Correction** -0.15s/f (Firm)
**WFA** 3 from 4yo+ 7lb **6** Ran SP% **114.3**
Speed ratings (Par 113): **111,110,109,106,104 103**
CSF £25.39 TOTE £5.90: £2.80, £2.00; EX 30.00 Trifecta £136.40.
**Owner** The Queen **Bred** The Queen **Trained** Newmarket, Suffolk

**FOCUS**
The 23rd running of this long-established contest as a Group 3, won in the past by the likes of Stotsfold, Campanologist and Prince Siegfried, was another well-contested affair. Run at a fair pace, it was won for the third time in 10 years by a 5yo. The runner-up has been rated close to his conditions race best.

## 6442 FOLLOW SUN BETS ON TWITTER H'CAP 6f 12y
**7:10** (7:12) (Class 4) (0-80,80) 3-Y-O+ **£4,690** (£1,395; £697; £348) **Stalls** Low

Form RPR

4442 **1** **Abiento (IRE)**[17] 5814 3-8-13 **72** JamieSpencer 8 79
(Ed Walker) *mde all: shkn up ent fnl f: styd on wl ins fnl f: rdn out* **5/1**[3]

3-00 **2** *1 ¼* **Himself**[76] 3621 3-9-1 **74** TomMarquand 9 77
(Richard Hannon) *hld up in tch in midfield: effrt over 2f out: hdwy u.p ent fnl f: styd on to snatch 2nd last strides: nvr getting on terms w wnr* **14/1**

2612 **3** *hd* **Field Of Vision (IRE)**[3] 6303 4-9-5 **75** OisinMurphy 3 77
(Joseph Tuite) *in tch in midfield: effrt 2f out: hdwy u.p jst over 1f out: chsd wnr ins fnl f: edgd rt and no imp after: lost 2nd last strides* **7/2**[2]

1-35 **4** *nk* **Fivetwoeight**[35] 5156 3-9-5 **78** AndreaAtzeni 1 81+
(Peter Chapple-Hyam) *trckd ldng trio: stl travelling wl whn nt clr run over 1f out: swtchd lft ins fnl f: hdwy and styd on towards fin: no threat to wnr* **3/1**[1]

0015 **5** *1 ½* **Cat Silver**[9] 6113 4-9-0 **70** (p) WilliamCarson 4 67
(Charlie Wallis) *chsd wnr tl over 2f out: styd prom: drvn over 1f out: no ex and wknd ins fnl f* **28/1**

1653 **6** *1* **Artscape**[17] 5814 5-9-4 **74** CharlesBishop 2 67
(Dean Ivory) *t.k.h: chsd ldrs: wnt 2nd over 2f out: unable qck u.p over 1f out: lost 2nd and wknd ins fnl f* **14/1**

541 **7** *2* **Cappananty Con**[26] 5481 3-9-6 **79** RobertWinston 7 66
(Dean Ivory) *stdd s: swtchd rt and hld up in midfield on stands rail: nt clr run wl over 1f out: gap nvr c and nvr able to cl: eased wl ins fnl f* **7/1**

-300 **8** *3 ¾* **War Whisper (IRE)**[72] 3757 4-9-10 **80** JimmyFortune 5 55
(Richard Hannon) *s.i.s: a towards rr: effrt over 1f out: no hdwy and wl btn whn eased towards fin* **7/1**

0600 **9** *2 ½* **In The Red (IRE)**[14] 5940 4-9-5 **78** NoelGarbutt(3) 6 45
(Martin Smith) *midfield: rdn and dropped towards rr 1/2-way: n.d after* **20/1**

0105 **10** *2 ½* **Souls In The Wind (IRE)**[21] 5646 3-8-7 **71** (b[1]) RowanScott(5) 10 30
(John Patrick Shanahan, Ire) *s.i.s and stmbld leaving stalls: nvr travelling and sn rdn: nvr on terms* **25/1**

1m 11.43s (-1.57) **Going Correction** -0.15s/f (Firm)
**WFA** 3 from 4yo+ 3lb **10** Ran SP% **114.3**
Speed ratings (Par 105): **104,102,102,101,99 98,95,90,87,84**
CSF £68.18 CT £280.89 TOTE £5.40: £1.80, £4.30, £1.50; EX 68.90 Trifecta £286.20.
**Owner** David Kilburn / John Nicholls Trading **Bred** Colman O'Flynn **Trained** Upper Lambourn, Berks

**FOCUS**
Fairly competitive for the grade and as is so often here, the stands' rail was the place to be, with the winner making all. The runner-up has been rated to his 2yo form.

## 6443 MASERATI MARANELLO EGHAM CORSE DI CAVALLI H'CAP 1m 3f 99y
**7:40** (7:44) (Class 5) (0-70,72) 3-Y-O+ **£2,911** (£866; £432; £216) **Stalls** Centre

Form RPR

3550 **1** **Unite The Clans (IRE)**[53] 4474 3-9-5 **72** RowanScott(5) 2 77
(John Patrick Shanahan, Ire) *t.k.h: chsd ldr 8f out: rdn to chal over 2f out: led 1f out: hld on wl u.p ins fnl f: all out* **10/1**

022 **2** *hd* **Love Conquers (JPN)**[44] 4808 3-9-9 **71** OisinMurphy 5 75
(Ralph Beckett) *t.k.h: chsd ldrs tl stdd bk into midfield after 3f: rdn over 2f out: unable qck and no imp tl rallied and swtchd lft ins fnl f: styd on strly to go 2nd last strides: nt quite rch wnr* **5/4**[1]

300 **3** *hd* **Abel Tasman**[14] 5931 3-9-2 **64** JamieSpencer 4 67
(Ed Walker) *hld up in tch: effrt over 2f out: hdwy to chal over 1f out: sustained chal: no ex towards fin: lost 2nd last strides* **11/2**[3]

2242 **4** *2 ¼* **The Secrets Out**[7] 6180 3-8-8 **56** (h) TedDurcan 7 56
(Luke Dace) *led: rdn over 2f out: hdd 1f out: no ex and wknd ins fnl f* **9/4**[2]

-360 **5** *½* **Avantgardist (GER)**[38] 5034 3-8-10 **63** (b) PaddyBradley(5) 8 62
(Pat Phelan) *chsd ldr tl 8f out: styd chsng ldrs: rdn and ev ch over 2f tl unable qck over 1f out: hld and kpt on same pce ins fnl f* **33/1**

6-52 **6** ½ **Rock On Dandy (FR)**[40] 4971 3-8-9 **64**........................(b) WilliamCox[(7)] 3 62
(Harry Dunlop) *hld up in tch in midfield: effrt over 2f out: no imp and styd on same pce fnl f* **12/1**

1504 **7** 1 **Lord Murphy (IRE)**[15] 5898 4-9-5 **59**............................ RobertWinston 6 54
(Daniel Mark Loughnane) *hld up in tch in rr: effrt jst over 2f out: kpt on same pce and nvr able to get on terms* **20/1**

2m 30.39s (0.89) **Going Correction** -0.15s/f (Firm)
**WFA** 3 from 4yo+ 8lb **7** Ran SP% **115.1**
Speed ratings (Par 103): **90,89,89,88,87 87,86**
CSF £23.40 CT £79.23 TOTE £11.40: £4.20, £1.30; EX 29.70 Trifecta £133.20.
**Owner** Thistle Bloodstock Limited **Bred** Thistle Bloodstock Ltd **Trained** Kells, Co Kilkenny

**FOCUS**
A modest staying handicap and the first three, all making their respective handicap debuts, finished in a heap. Muddling form. The fourth has been rated close to form.
T/Plt: £38.80 to a £1 stake. Pool: £68,892.04 - 1,295.40 winning units T/Qpdt: £9.00 to a £1 stake. Pool: £7,106.64 - 580.91 winning units **Steve Payne**

## 6399 YORK (L-H)
### Saturday, August 26

**OFFICIAL GOING: Good (overall 7.1; home straight: far side 7.1, centre 7.1 stands' side 7.0)**
Wind: Light across Weather: Cloudy with sunny periods

### 6444 BETFRED MOBILE STRENSALL STKS (GROUP 3) 1m 177y
**1:55** (1:55) (Class 1) 3-Y-O+
**£51,039** (£19,350; £9,684; £4,824; £2,421; £1,215) **Stalls** Low

Form RPR

4-01 **1** **Mustashry**[11] 6024 4-9-5 110.............................................. JimCrowley 1 114
(Sir Michael Stoute) *trckd ldrs: hdwy over 2f out: swtchd lft and rdn to chal over 1f out: led jst ins fnl f: drvn out* **5/2**[1]

6523 **2** ¾ **Forest Ranger (IRE)**[22] 5593 3-8-12 106.......................... JackGarritty 3 112
(Richard Fahey) *led: pushed along over 2f out: rdn over 1f out: hdd jst ins fnl f: drvn and kpt on wl u.p* **13/2**

1115 **3** 1½ **Sovereign Debt (IRE)**[42] 4884 8-9-10 116.................. JamesSullivan 4 114
(Ruth Carr) *.trckd ldng pair: hdwy over 2f out: rdn and edgd lft over 1f out: drvn and kpt on same pce fnl f* **6/1**[3]

0214 **4** 2 **Master The World (IRE)**[9] 6105 6-9-5 108.......................(p) PatDobbs 2 104
(David Elsworth) *hld up in tch: hdwy over 2f out: rdn along wl over 1f out: kpt on fnl f* **8/1**

4435 **5** ½ **Gabrial (IRE)**[14] 5925 8-9-5 108.......................................... GrahamLee 7 103
(Richard Fahey) *t.k.h in rr: hdwy on outer 3f out: rdn along wl over 1f out: kpt on same pce* **20/1**

6462 **6** 2 **Mondialiste (IRE)**[28] 5436 7-9-5 113............................. DanielTudhope 6 99
(David O'Meara) *hld up in rr: hdwy on inner wl over 2f out: rdn wl over 1f out: wknd appr fnl f* **4/1**[2]

-012 **7** 1¼ **Make Time (IRE)**[22] 5593 3-8-12 107............................... PaulHanagan 5 96
(David Menuisier) *trckd ldr: hdwy 3f out: rdn along over 2f out: wknd over 1f out* **4/1**[2]

1m 47.85s (-4.15) **Going Correction** -0.175s/f (Firm)
**WFA** 3 from 4yo+ 7lb **7** Ran SP% **112.1**
Speed ratings (Par 113): **111,110,109,107,106 105,103**
CSF £18.40 TOTE £2.90: £1.80, £3.20; EX 16.90 Trifecta £96.50.
**Owner** Hamdan Al Maktoum **Bred** Shadwell Estate Company Limited **Trained** Newmarket, Suffolk

**FOCUS**
All race distances as advertised. Solid form for the level and a winner very much on the up. The runner-up has been rated in line with the better view of his form.

### 6445 BETFRED MELROSE H'CAP (HERITAGE HANDICAP) 1m 5f 188y
**2:25** (2:27) (Class 2) (0-105,101) 3-Y-O
**£65,362** (£19,572; £9,786; £4,893; £2,446; £1,228) **Stalls** Low

Form RPR

2235 **1** **Secret Advisor (FR)**[24] 5525 3-9-2 **96**............................ JamesDoyle 13 106+
(Charlie Appleby) *.hld up in rr: hdwy over 2f out: rdn along and swtchd lft to inner 2f out: drvn ent fnl f: kpt on wl to ld nr fin* **5/1**[1]

3401 **2** nk **Bin Battuta**[42] 4886 3-9-4 **98**...............................................(p) MartinLane 4 107+
(Saeed bin Suroor) *hld up in rr: hdwy 4f out: trckd ldrs over 2f out: led wl over 1f out and sn rdn: drvn ins fnl f: hdd and no ex nr fin* **8/1**[2]

3142 **3** nk **Here And Now**[20] 5682 3-8-7 **87**...................................... PaulHanagan 14 96
(Ralph Beckett) *hld up: hdwy 3f out: chsd ldrs 2f out: sn rdn and hung bdly lft jst over 1f out: drvn to chal ent fnl f: ev ch: sn edgd lft and no ex last 50 yds yds* **16/1**

2132 **4** 1½ **On To Victory**[24] 5525 3-9-4 **101**..........................(h) EdwardGreatrex[(3)] 16 108
(Eve Johnson Houghton) *hld up in rr: hdwy towards inner 3f out: rdn along 2f out: chsd ldrs and drvn over 1f out: kpt on fnl f* **10/1**

1641 **5** 1 **The Grand Visir**[29] 5368 3-8-11 **91**..............................(p) DanielTudhope 3 97+
(William Haggas) *prom: hdwy and cl up over 3f out: led wl over 2f out: rdn and hdd wl over 1f out: sn drvn and kpt on same pce fnl f* **9/1**[3]

3313 **6** ¾ **Winston C (IRE)**[24] 5525 3-8-3 **88**..................................... DavidEgan[(5)] 8 92
(Michael Bell) *hld up towards rr: hdwy over 3f out: chsd ldrs 2f out: rdn and n.m.r over 1f out: kpt on fnl f* **11/1**

3213 **7** 2½ **Dark Pearl (IRE)**[28] 5397 3-8-3 **83**.................................... LukeMorris 9 84
(Ed Walker) *hld up towards rr: hdwy over 4f out: effrt on wd outside over 3f out: rdn along and chsd ldrs wl over 1f out: drvn and kpt on fnl f* **16/1**

3132 **8** 1 **Northwest Frontier (IRE)**[21] 5667 3-8-1 **81**.............. PatrickMathers 18 81
(Richard Fahey) *trckd ldng pair: hdwy and cl up 4f out: rdn to dispute ld 3f out: drvn along wl over 1f out: sn n.m.r and grad wknd* **16/1**

2323 **9** ¾ **Look My Way**[14] 5944 3-8-0 **80** oh1.................................. JimmyQuinn 7 79
(Andrew Balding) *towards rr: hdwy into midfield 3f out: n.m.r and swtchd lft towards inner wl over 1f out: n.d* **20/1**

1212 **10** 1½ **Dominating (GER)**[17] 5799 3-7-12 **83**........................ RichardOliver[(5)] 20 79
(Mark Johnston) *chsd ldrs on outer: hdwy 4f out: and sn cl up:. rdn to dispute ld 3f out: drvn over 2f out: grad wknd* **33/1**

-164 **11** 2¼ **Redicean**[7] 6187 3-8-0 **83**........................................... ShelleyBirkett[(3)] 2 76
(David O'Meara) *hld up: midfield and effrt whn n.m.r 3f out: rdn along to chse ldrs and n.m.r 2f out: sn drvn and wknd* **33/1**

1121 **12** ½ **Glenys The Menace (FR)**[14] 5915 3-8-5 **85**...................... KierenFox 15 78
(John Best) *towards rr: hdwy whn n.m.r and hmpd 3f out: sn rdn along and n.d* **16/1**

3121 **13** 3¼ **Tor**[20] 5682 3-7-12 **85**................................................... JamieGormley[(7)] 11 73
(Iain Jardine) *led: rdn along 4f out: hdd 3f out: sn wknd* **14/1**

00 **14** 2½ **Night Of Glory**[43] 4863 3-9-2 **96**...................................... PhillipMakin 12 81
(Andrew Balding) *hld up towards rr: hdwy over 3f out: rdn along over 2f out: sn drvn and wknd* **25/1**

6021 **15** 1¼ **Qaviy Cash**[54] 4430 3-8-2 **85**..........................................(t) HollieDoyle[(3)] 17 68
(Dan Skelton) *hld up in rr: effrt and sme hdwy on inner over 3f out: rdn along over 2f out: sn btn* **11/1**

-310 **16** 3½ **Master Singer (USA)**[65] 3998 3-9-2 **96**........................... GrahamLee 19 74
(John Gosden) *hld up towards rr: hdwy over 4f out: rdn along 3f out: sn drvn and wknd* **20/1**

401 **17** 6 **Bush House (IRE)**[45] 4751 3-8-6 **86**.......................(b) JosephineGordon 5 55
(Hugo Palmer) *in tch: hdwy over 3f out: chsd ldrs and rdn wl over 2f out: sn wknd* **33/1**

0302 **18** 6 **Sofia's Rock (FR)**[7] 6201 3-9-6 **100**................................. JimCrowley 1 61
(Mark Johnston) *t.k.h: trckd ldrs on inner: rdn along over 3f out: sn drvn and wknd* **16/1**

611 **19** 11 **Intellect (IRE)**[35] 5153 3-8-12 **92**............................. RichardKingscote 10 38
(Sir Michael Stoute) *trckd ldr: pushed along 4f out: rdn alonver 3f out: sn wknd and bhd fnl 2f* **8/1**[2]

2m 57.27s (-2.93) **Going Correction** -0.175s/f (Firm) **19** Ran SP% **132.9**
Speed ratings (Par 106): **101,100,100,99,99 98,97,96,96,95 94,93,92,90,89 87,84,81,74**
CSF £41.18 CT £621.36 TOTE £5.50: £1.90, £2.80, £4.50, £3.20; EX 45.90 Trifecta £612.50.
**Owner** Godolphin **Bred** S C E A Haras De Saint Pair **Trained** Newmarket, Suffolk
■ Stewards' Enquiry : Martin Lane seven-day ban: used whip above the permitted level (Sep 9-15)
Edward Greatrex two-day ban: used whip above the permitted level (Sep 10-11)

**FOCUS**
Like the Ebor later on the card, this looked impossible to unravel before the off considering how many of the runners could be given an obvious chance. The pace seemed solid without being manic but, interestingly, the first two were in rear early. It's been rated on the positive side, with the runner-up posting a pb and the third continuing to progress.

### 6446 AL BASTI EQUIWORLD GIMCRACK STKS (GROUP 2) (C&G) 6f
**3:00** (3:01) (Class 1) 2-Y-O
**£127,597** (£48,375; £18,135; £18,135; £6,052; £3,037) **Stalls** Low

Form RPR

01 **1** **Sands Of Mali (FR)**[23] 5576 2-9-0 0................................ PaulHanagan 4 115
(Richard Fahey) *mde all: pressed tl over 2f out: rdn 2f out: kpt on wl* **14/1**

2142 **2** 2¾ **Invincible Army (IRE)**[24] 5526 2-9-0 103....................... MartinHarley 10 107
(James Tate) *hld up: hdwy over 2f out: rdn 2f out: chsd ldr appr fnl f: kpt on but a hld* **9/2**[1]

1313 **3** 1 **Cardsharp**[23] 5570 2-9-3 110............................................ JamesDoyle 6 107
(Mark Johnston) *chsd ldrs: rdn over 2f out: one pce ins fnl f* **5/1**[2]

126 **3** dht **Headway**[23] 5570 2-9-0 107.............................................. HarryBentley 7 104
(William Haggas) *midfield: pushed along over 3f out: rdn over 2f out: kpt on same pce* **9/2**[1]

121 **5** 1 **Staxton**[16] 5825 2-9-0 88.................................................... DavidAllan 12 101
(Tim Easterby) *dwlt: hld up: pushed along and hdwy over 2f out: rdn over 1f out: kpt on same pce* **10/1**

1022 **6** 1½ **Nebo (IRE)**[23] 5570 2-9-0 109............................................ JimCrowley 9 97
(Charles Hills) *midfield: rdn over 2f out: no ex ins fnl f* **9/2**[1]

31 **7** nk **Stormbringer**[24] 5537 2-9-0 0............................................. TomEaves 3 96
(Kevin Ryan) *dwlt: sn pressed ldr: rdn and outpcd over 2f out: no threat after* **16/1**

2425 **8** ¾ **Frozen Angel (IRE)**[13] 5973 2-9-0 108................... RichardKingscote 11 93
(Tom Dascombe) *chsd ldrs: rdn over 2f out: wknd over 1f out* **6/1**[3]

10 **9** 7 **That's A Surprise (IRE)**[5] 6264 2-9-0 0.......................... BarryMcHugh 1 72
(Tony Coyle) *hld up: rdn over 2f out: sn wknd* **100/1**

21 **10** 3¼ **Nobleman's Nest**[29] 5365 2-9-0 0..................................... DanielTudhope 8 63
(Simon Crisford) *hld up: racd keenly: rdn over 2f out: wknd over 1f out* **10/1**

1m 11.16s (-0.74) **Going Correction** +0.125s/f (Good) **10** Ran SP% **117.2**
Speed ratings (Par 106): **109,105,104,104,102 100,100,99,89,85**
WIN: 16.20 Sands Of Mali; PL: .90 Cardsharp, 4.40 Sands Of Mali, .90 Headway, 1.80 Invincible Army; EX: 88.30; CSF: 76.43; TC: ; TF: 284.60, 450.80;.
**Owner** The Cool Silk Partnership **Bred** Simon Urizzi **Trained** Musley Bank, N Yorks

**FOCUS**
Not a particularly strong edition of this race but hard to knock the clear-cut winner. It's been rated in line with the race averages.

### 6447 BETFRED EBOR H'CAP (HERITAGE HANDICAP) 1m 5f 188y
**3:35** (3:36) (Class 2) 3-Y-O+
**£177,412** (£53,124; £26,562; £13,281; £6,640; £3,334) **Stalls** Low

Form RPR

-024 **1** **Nakeeta**[77] 3594 6-9-0 **103**.....................................(h) CallumRodriguez[(5)] 18 113
(Iain Jardine) *hld up towards rr early: hdwy over 4f out: trckd ldrs over 2f out: rdn and squeezed though jst over 1f out: sn rdn to chal: drvn ins fnl f: kpt on wl to ld nr fin: rdr lost rein nr line* **12/1**

1-13 **2** hd **Flymetothestars**[56] 4356 4-9-4 **102**................................. LukeMorris 21 111
(Sir Mark Prescott Bt) *hld up in rr: pushed along and hdwy towards inner 3f out: trckd ldrs 2f out: rdn to ld jst over 1f out: jnd and drvn ins fnl f: hdd and no ex towards fin* **7/1**[1]

1624 **3** 2 **Natural Scenery**[23] 5569 4-9-4 **105**.......................(p) EdwardGreatrex[(3)] 6 111+
(Saeed bin Suroor) *hld up: hdwy 3f out: effrt to chse ldrs and n.m.r 11/2f out: sn swtchd rt and rdn: styd on wl fnl f* **14/1**

001- **4** 1¼ **Arch Villain (IRE)**[385] 5144 8-9-6 **104**............................... PatDobbs 12 108
(Amanda Perrett) *trckd ldrs:: hdwy 3f out: rdn to ld jst over 2f out: drvn and hdd jst over 1f out: kpt on same pce* **50/1**

5501 **5** 2 **Magic Circle (IRE)**[3] 6329 5-9-3 **101** 4ex......................... HarryBentley 5 103
(Ralph Beckett) *hld up in midfield: hdwy towards inner over 3f out: trckd ldrs 2f out: sn rdn and ev ch: drvn appr fnl f: kpt on same pce* **15/2**[2]

6003 **6** hd **Clever Cookie**[42] 4917 9-9-8 **106**....................................(p) GrahamLee 17 107
(Peter Niven) *hld up towards rr: stdy hdwy over 3f out: hmpd 2f out: sn swtchd rt and rdn: styd on wl fnl f* **20/1**

2150 **7** ½ **Winning Story**[63] 4073 4-9-10 **108**.................................(v[1]) MartinLane 16 109
(Saeed bin Suroor) *chsd ldrs: rdn along over 2f out: drvn wl over 1f out: kpt on same pce fnl f* **33/1**

45-6 **8** 1 **Battersea**[115] 2288 6-9-2 **105**........................................... DavidEgan[(5)] 15 104
(Roger Varian) *hld up towards rr: pushed along 4f out: hdwy over 2f out: sn rdn: kpt on fnl f* **11/1**

2165 **9** ½ **Wild Hacked (USA)**[69] 3884 4-9-4 **102**........................... PaulHanagan 14 101
(Marco Botti) *trckd ldrs: hdwy and cl up 3f out: chal 2f out: sn rdn and ev ch: drvn appr fnl f and kpt on same pce* **16/1**

2-30 **10** hd **Seamour (IRE)**[56] 4356 6-8-13 **102**............................. BenRobinson[(5)] 22 100
(Brian Ellison) *midfield: hdwy to trck ldrs 3f out: cl up 2f out: sn rdn and edgd lft: ev ch: drvn and wknd appr fnl f* **20/1**

6202 **11** shd **Dubka**[23] 5569 4-9-4 **102**.......................................... JosephineGordon 19 100
(Sir Michael Stoute) *trckd ldrs: hdwy whn n.m.r 2f out: sn rdn and hmpd over 1f out: kpt on same pce* **12/1**

-603 **12** 2 ¾ **Scarlet Dragon**[22] 5592 4-9-7 **108**..............................(h) HollieDoyle(3) 9 102
(Eve Johnson Houghton) *hld up in rr: hdwy on inner wl over 2f out: rdn along wl over 1f out: n.d* **15/2**[2]

0231 **13** 2 **Soldier In Action (FR)**[21] 5638 4-9-12 **110** 4ex....... RichardKingscote 4 102
(Mark Johnston) *trckd ldrs: hdwy 4f out: rdn along and cl up 3f out: drvn whn hmpd 2f out: sn wknd* **20/1**

-214 **14** 11 **Top Tug (IRE)**[64] 4033 6-9-7 **105**.............................. MartinHarley 2 81
(Alan King) *hld up in midfield: hdwy 3f out: rdn along over 2f out: sn drvn and n.d* **12/1**

5/0- **15** 3 ½ **Ivan Grozny (FR)**[23] 4851 7-9-7 **105**..............................(h) JimCrowley 11 76
(W P Mullins, Ire) *racd wd early: cl up: rdn along 3f out: drvn over 2f out: grad wknd* **12/1**

-163 **16** 3 ¾ **Elidor**[55] 4420 7-9-10 **108**.............................. RonanWhelan 7 74
(Mick Channon) *hld up: a towards rr* **33/1**

-115 **17** 4 ½ **Lord Yeats**[22] 5592 4-9-10 **108**.............................. DanielTudhope 8 68
(Jedd O'Keeffe) *led: rdn along 3f out: hdd and edgd lft 2f out: sn wknd* **12/1**

36P4 **18** 32 **Maleficent Queen**[43] 4849 5-9-3 **101**..............................(p[1]) PhillipMakin 3 16
(Keith Dalgleish) *in tch: pushed along over 4f out: lost pl qckly over 3f out: sn wl bhd and eased* **40/1**

4-23 **P** **Star Storm (IRE)**[64] 4033 5-9-6 **104**.............................. JamesDoyle 20
(James Fanshawe) *hld up: hdwy on inner over 3f out: rdn to chal wl over 1f out: ev ch tl lost action and wknd qckly ins fnl f: p.u* **10/1**[3]

2m 56.54s (-3.66) **Going Correction** -0.175s/f (Firm) **19** Ran SP% **129.0**
Speed ratings (Par 109): **103,102,101,101,99 99,99,98,98,98 98,96,95,89,87 85,82,64,**
CSF £89.46 CT £1229.65 TOTE £12.90: £2.80, £2.50, £3.80, £9.30; EX 130.80 Trifecta £1675.80.

**Owner** Alex and Janet Card **Bred** Mike Channon Bloodstock Ltd **Trained** Carrutherstown, D'fries & G'way

**FOCUS**
A classy field contested this competitive handicap as one would expect for the money on offer and, much like the Melrose Handicap earlier on the card, the first two home were among the last four turning in. A pb from the winner and a small pb from the third.

## 6448 JULIA GRAVES ROSES STKS (LISTED RACE) 5f
**4:10** (4:11) (Class 1) 2-Y-O

**£39,697** (£15,050; £7,532; £3,752; £1,883; £945) **Stalls** Low

Form RPR

1410 **1** **Sound And Silence**[44] 4812 2-9-3 103..............................(t[1]) JamesDoyle 9 105
(Charlie Appleby) *hld up: pushed along and hdwy over 1f out: rdn and r.o strly fnl f: led towards fin* **9/2**[3]

121 **2** ½ **Abel Handy (IRE)**[21] 5665 2-9-0 88.............................. TomEaves 11 100
(Declan Carroll) *led for 1f: remained cl up: rdn 2f out: led again 1f out: kpt on but hdd towards fin* **10/1**

1350 **3** nk **Out Of The Flames**[8] 6136 2-8-9 98.............................. MartinLane 8 94
(Richard Hannon) *dwlt: hld up: rdn and hdwy towards far side appr fnl f: ev ch fnl 110yds: kpt on* **9/1**

1221 **4** shd **Bengali Boys (IRE)**[35] 5150 2-9-0 105.............................. PaulHanagan 1 99
(Richard Fahey) *midfield: rdn and hdwy over 1f out: ev ch ins fnl f: kpt on* **3/1**[1]

6412 **5** 2 **Angel Force (IRE)**[22] 5615 2-8-9 70..............................(h) DavidAllan 14 87
(David C Griffiths) *w ldrs: rdn 2f out: no ex ins fnl f* **66/1**

1233 **6** ¾ **To Wafij (IRE)**[24] 5526 2-9-0 103.............................. HarryBentley 6 89
(Roger Varian) *chsd ldrs: rdn 2f out: one pce* **7/2**[2]

62 **7** ½ **Elizabeth Darcy (IRE)**[56] 4391 2-8-9 0..............................(b) DavidEgan 13 82
(Wesley A Ward, U.S.A) *led after 1f: pushed along 2f out: rdn whn hdd 1f out: wknd fnl 110yds* **6/1**

201 **8** ½ **Falabelle (IRE)**[15] 5879 2-8-9 79.............................. GrahamLee 12 80
(Kevin Ryan) *dwlt: sn chsd ldrs: rdn 1/2-way: grad wknd fnl f* **33/1**

2105 **9** nk **Looks A Million**[8] 6136 2-8-9 90.............................. JimmyQuinn 15 79
(Joseph Tuite) *chsd ldrs: rdn 1/2-way: wknd over 1f out* **40/1**

0135 **10** ¾ **Haddaf (IRE)**[20] 5681 2-9-0 97.............................. MartinHarley 4 81
(James Tate) *hld up: rdn along 1/2-way: sn no imp* **16/1**

0130 **11** 1 ¼ **Encrypted**[24] 5526 2-9-0 84.............................. JosephineGordon 3 77
(Hugo Palmer) *dwlt: sn chsd ldrs: rdn 1/2-way: wknd over 1f out* **20/1**

3102 **12** 2 ¼ **Declarationoflove (IRE)**[35] 5150 2-9-0 89.............................. KieranO'Neill 2 69
(Tom Clover) *a outpcd towards rr* **20/1**

59.19s (-0.11) **Going Correction** +0.125s/f (Good) **12** Ran SP% **121.1**
Speed ratings (Par 102): **105,104,103,103,100 99,98,97,97,95 93,90**
CSF £46.84 TOTE £5.80: £2.00, £3.20, £3.40; EX 57.10 Trifecta £526.50.

**Owner** Godolphin **Bred** Godolphin **Trained** Newmarket, Suffolk

■ Stewards' Enquiry : Paul Hanagan two-day ban: used whip above permitted level (Sep 10-11)
Martin Lane two-day ban: used whip above the permitted level (Sep 17-18)

**FOCUS**
Solid Listed form, with the right horses coming to the fore. The third has been rated close to her pre-race mark, with the fourth to his Super Sprint win.

## 6449 BETFRED SUPPORTS JACK BERRY HOUSE H'CAP 1m 2f 56y
**4:40** (4:44) (Class 2) (0-105,105) 3-Y-O+

**£43,575** (£13,048; £6,524; £3,262; £1,631; £819) **Stalls** Low

Form RPR

0604 **1** **Eddystone Rock (IRE)**[14] 5940 5-9-2 **97**.............................. PatDobbs 6 106
(John Best) *hld up: hdwy towards outer over 3f out: trckd ldrs 2f out: rdn to chse ldr ent fnl f: styd on wl to ld nr fin* **20/1**

1521 **2** shd **Titi Makfi**[15] 5889 3-8-9 **97**.............................. RichardKingscote 12 107
(Mark Johnston) *in tch: hdwy over 3f out: c wd towards stands' rail: led wl over 1f out: rdn ent fnl f: drvn last 100yds: hdd nr fin* **8/1**[3]

4031 **3** 1 ¾ **Dark Red (IRE)**[25] 5500 5-9-1 **96**.............................. PhillipMakin 3 101
(Ed Dunlop) *trckd ldrs: hdwy over 2f out: rdn wl over 1f out: kpt on fnl f* **12/1**

5032 **4** ¾ **Brorocco**[22] 5609 4-8-8 **89**..............................(h) JimmyQuinn 15 93
(Andrew Balding) *dwlt and in rr: hdwy over 2f out: rdn wl over 1f out: sn n.m.r. styd on wl fnl f* **12/1**

0150 **5** hd **Speed Company (IRE)**[25] 5500 4-9-1 **99**.........(h) AdamMcNamara(3) 19 103
(John Quinn) *hld up towards rr: hdwy 3f out: rdn along over 2f out: styng on to chse ldrs whn nt clr run and swtchd rt 1f out: drvn and kpt on towards fin* **50/1**

0/20 **6** ¾ **First Flight (IRE)**[38] 5037 6-8-11 **97**.............................. DavidEgan(5) 14 99
(Heather Main) *hld up in rr: hdwy over 2f out: swtchd rt towards stands' rail: rdn wl over 1f out: kpt on u.p fnl f* **25/1**

0000 **7** 3 **Bravery (IRE)**[2] 6355 4-9-4 **99**.............................. MartinHarley 7 96
(David O'Meara) *trckd ldrs: hdwy on wd outside 3f out: cl up over 2f out: sn rdn and ev ch: drvn: edgd lft and one pce appr fnl f* **25/1**

-400 **8** 2 **Awake My Soul (IRE)**[28] 5421 8-8-7 **88**.............................. JamesSullivan 9 81
(Tom Tate) *cl up: chal wl over 2f out: sn rdn and ev ch: drvn over 1f out: grad wknd* **25/1**

0302 **9** ½ **Nicholas T**[14] 5914 5-8-6 **92**.............................. CallumRodriguez(5) 4 84
(Jim Goldie) *midfield: hdwy on inner 3f out: rdn along to chse ldrs 2f out: drvn and ch over 1f out: wknd fnl f* **25/1**

5121 **10** ¾ **Save The Bees**[10] 6059 9-7-13 **83**.............................. AaronJones(3) 5 73
(Declan Carroll) *led: rdn along 2f out: hdd wl over 1f out: sn drvn and wknd* **33/1**

6430 **11** 1 **Spring Offensive (IRE)**[21] 5643 5-8-7 **88**.............................. PaulHanagan 20 76
(Richard Fahey) *hld up in rr: sme hdwy over 2f out: rdn along and plugged on appr fnl f: n.d* **33/1**

1544 **12** 1 ¼ **UAE Prince (IRE)**[25] 5500 4-9-2 **97**.............................. HarryBentley 1 83
(Roger Varian) *trckd ldrs on inner: hdwy 3f out: effrt and cl up 2f out: sn rdn and wknd* **7/2**[1]

4425 **13** nse **Beardwood**[43] 4863 5-8-2 **88**..............................(p) RichardOliver(5) 16 74
(Mark Johnston) *dwlt and in rr: hdwy on inner 3f out: rdn along 2f out: sn drvn and wknd* **50/1**

0011 **14** shd **Storm King**[21] 5643 8-8-8 **92**.............................. EdwardGreatrex(3) 18 78
(David C Griffiths) *chsd ldrs on outer: rn wd bnd after 3f out: sn bhd* **33/1**

5052 **15** 2 ½ **Kentuckyconnection (USA)**[58] 4261 4-8-11 **92**.............. GrahamLee 10 73
(Bryan Smart) *chsd ldrs: rdn along over 2f out: grad wknd* **50/1**

0104 **16** shd **Snoano**[22] 5592 5-9-9 **104**.............................. DavidAllan 11 85
(Tim Easterby) *a towards rr* **20/1**

-103 **17** ½ **Khairaat (IRE)**[25] 5500 4-9-10 **105**.............................. JimCrowley 13 85
(Sir Michael Stoute) *hld up towards rr: hdwy and swtchd wd towards stands' rail 3f: rdn to chse ldrs 2f out: sn drvn and wknd* **4/1**[2]

0000 **18** 11 **Baydar**[25] 5500 4-9-5 **100**..............................(p[1]) JamesDoyle 17 59
(Hugo Palmer) *hld up in rr: sme hdwy on inner 3f out: rdn along over 2f out: n.d* **10/1**

1140 **19** 6 **Gulf Of Poets**[29] 5382 5-8-2 **90**.............................. HarrisonShaw(7) 2 38
(Michael Easterby) *trckd ldr on inner: pushed along over 3f out: sn rdn and wknd* **50/1**

P621 **20** 24 **Weekend Offender (FR)**[12] 5996 4-9-3 **98**.............................. TomEaves 8
(Kevin Ryan) *in tch on inner: rdn along wl over 2f out: sn wknd* **8/1**[3]

2m 7.28s (-5.22) **Going Correction** -0.175s/f (Firm)
**WFA** 3 from 4yo+ 7lb **20** Ran SP% **130.5**
Speed ratings (Par 109): **113,112,111,110,110 110,107,106,105,105 104,103,103,103,101 101,100,91,87,67**
CSF £160.72 CT £2040.84 TOTE £28.30: £5.10, £2.30, £2.60, £3.20; EX 290.60 Trifecta £5082.50 Part won..

**Owner** Curtis, Malt & Williams **Bred** Ballygallon Stud Limited **Trained** Oad Street, Kent

**FOCUS**
Another really difficult race to work out and the finish involved those coming down the stands' side this time. It's likely to be strong form for the remainder of the turf season. The winner has been rated to the better view of his form, while the third helps set the standard.

## 6450 BETFRED APPRENTICE H'CAP 5f
**5:15** (5:18) (Class 2) (0-105,100) 3-Y-O

**£28,311** (£28,311; £6,524; £3,262; £1,631; £819) **Stalls** Centre

Form RPR

5411 **1** **Holmeswood**[19] 5708 3-8-10 **92**.............................. CallumRodriguez(3) 8 103+
(Michael Dods) *racd centre: hld up: hdwy 2f out: chsd ldrs over 1f out: rdn to chal ins fnl f: drvn and kpt on wl towards fin* **9/2**[1]

1214 **1** dht **Intense Romance (IRE)**[23] 5574 3-8-4 **86**.............................. BenRobinson(3) 3 97
(Michael Dods) *racd towards far side: chsd ldrs: hdwy over 1f out: rdn ins fnl f: led last 75 yds: jnd nr line* **14/1**

215 **3** 1 ¼ **Evergate**[69] 3861 3-8-5 **91**.............................. JonathanFisher(7) 6 97
(Robert Cowell) *in tch towards far side: hdwy 2f out: rdn to chal ins fnl f: sn ev ch:. drvn and nt qckn last 50 yds* **10/1**

3100 **4** shd **Justanotherbottle (IRE)**[28] 5402 3-8-13 **92**.............................. PhilDennis 4 98+
(Declan Carroll) *racd towards far side: cl up: rdn and slt ld over 1f out: drvn ins fnl f: hdd and no ex last 75 yds* **14/1**

4002 **5** 3 ¼ **Mayleaf Shine (IRE)**[22] 5602 3-8-9 **88**..............................(h) RobbieDowney 19 82
(Iain Jardine) *racd towards stands side: hld up towards rr: swtchd lft and hdwy over 1f out: sn rdn and kpt on wl fnl f* **25/1**

1304 **6** shd **Copper Knight (IRE)**[29] 5354 3-9-7 **100**..............................(t[1]) AdamMcNamara 1 94
(Tim Easterby) *racd far side: led: rdn along and hdd over 1f out: wknd fnl f* **5/1**[2]

6066 **7** ½ **Impart**[19] 5708 3-8-4 **83**.............................. ShelleyBirkett 18 75
(David O'Meara) *racd wd towards stands side: in tch: hdwy to chse ldrs 12f out: rdn over 1f out: kpt on fnl f* **40/1**

0500 **8** ¾ **Equimou**[11] 6025 3-8-9 **95**..............................(p[1]) DarraghKeenan(7) 15 84
(Robert Eddery) *racd towards stands side: towards rr: swtchd rt and hdwy wl over 1f out: sn rdn and kpt on fnl f* **40/1**

1232 **9** 1 **Major Jumbo**[55] 4412 3-8-12 **91**.............................. LewisEdmunds 14 76
(Kevin Ryan) *racd centre: chsd ldrs: rdn and cl up 11/2f out: drvn and wknd fnl f* **9/1**

-153 **10** ½ **Pennsylvania Dutch**[13] 5959 3-8-5 **84**.............................. GeorgeWood 7 68
(William Haggas) *racd towards far side: towards rr: rdn along 2f out: n.d* **13/2**[3]

1520 **11** ½ **Coolfitch (IRE)**[29] 5354 3-9-0 **93**.............................. JoshDoyle 5 75
(David O'Meara) *racd towards far side: a towards rr* **20/1**

314 **12** nk **Tahoo (IRE)**[38] 5029 3-8-5 **84**.............................. JackDuern 9 65
(K R Burke) *racd centre: chsd ldrs: rdn along 11/2f out: drvn ent fnl f: sn wknd* **25/1**

16-0 **13** 2 ½ **Rozy Boys**[22] 5602 3-8-5 **84**.............................. HollieDoyle 10 56
(David Barron) *dwlt: a towards rr far side* **33/1**

1100 **14** 2 ¾ **Carlton Frankie**[23] 5574 3-8-3 **89**.............................. HarrisonShaw(7) 11 51
(Michael Easterby) *racd centre: cl up: rdn along wl over 1f out: sn wknd* **20/1**

1232 **15** nk **Trick Of The Light (IRE)**[10] 6072 3-8-0 **82**..............................(b[1]) DavidEgan(3) 12 43
(Roger Varian) *chsd ldrs centre: rdn along wl over 1f out: sn wknd* **11/1**

3616 **16** nk **Yorkshiredebut (IRE)**[23] 5574 3-8-0 **79** oh1..............................(p) AaronJones 16 39
(Paul Midgley) .*racd wd towards stands side: chsd ldrs: rdn along 2f out: sn wknd* **25/1**

1620 **17** 1 ½ **Black Isle Boy (IRE)**[29] 5383 3-8-6 **85**.............................. EdwardGreatrex 2 39
(David O'Meara) *racd far side: a towards rr* **33/1**

5412 **18** ¾ **Batten The Hatches**[29] 5383 3-8-10 **89**..............................(b) LouisSteward 17 41
(David Barron) *racd alone nr stands rail: a towards rr* **9/1**

5500 **19** 4 ½ **Queen In Waiting (IRE)**[22] 5602 3-8-8 **90**.............................. RichardOliver(3) 13 25
(Mark Johnston) *dwlt and hmpd s: a rr* **28/1**

58.77s (-0.53) **Going Correction** +0.125s/f (Good) **19** Ran SP% **134.2**
Speed ratings (Par 106): **109,109,107,106,101 101,100,99,97,97 96,95,91,87,86 86,84,82,75**
WIN: 10.90 Intense Romance, 2.70 Holmeswood; PL: 3.20 Justanotherbottle, 4.10 Intense Romance, 2.80 Evergate, 1.90 Holmeswood; EX: 55.30, 80.10; CSF: 32.27, 36.38; TC: 316.40, 348.37; TF: 1246.50, 1071.20;.

**Owner** David W Armstrong **Bred** Highfield Farm Llp **Trained** Denton, Co Durham
**Owner** Hugh Malcolm Linsley **Bred** John O'Connor **Trained** Denton, Co Durham
■ Stewards' Enquiry : Callum Rodriguez two-day bay: used whip above the permitted level (Sep 10-11)

**FOCUS**
A very useful 3yo sprint, with it looking a wide-open race, and a dead-heat between the two Dods runners was the outcome. The third has been rated to form.
T/Jkpt: Not Won. T/Plt: £938.50 to a £1 stake. Pool: £303,770.16 - 236.28 winning units T/Qpdt: £137.90 to a £1 stake. Pool: £18,251.90 - 97.94 winning units **Joe Rowntree**

# 3115 BADEN-BADEN (L-H)
Saturday, August 26

**OFFICIAL GOING: Turf: good**

## 6451a 62ND PREIS DER SPARKASSEN FINANZGRUPPE (EX SPRETI-RENNEN) (GROUP 3) (4YO+) (TURF) 1m 2f
3:25 (3:25) 4-Y-0+ **£27,350** (£10,256; £5,128; £2,564; £1,709)

RPR
1 **Palace Prince (GER)**27 5464 5-9-4 0.....(p) FilipMinarik 8 113+
(Jean-Pierre Carvalho, Germany) *settled midfield: hdwy 2f out: pushed along to ld over 1f out: rdn to go clr fnl f* **97/10**
2 2 **Devastar (GER)**42 4931 5-8-11 0..... AdriedeVries 3 102
(Markus Klug, Germany) *led first f: hdd after 1f and trckd ldr: rdn to chse ldr 2f out: kpt on fnl 2f but nt pce of wnr: jst hld 2nd* **78/10**
3 nse **Potemkin (GER)**27 5464 6-9-0 0..... EduardoPedroza 5 105
(A Wohler, Germany) *rr of midfield: hdwy to chse ldr 2f out: rdn along and kpt on wl fnl 2f: nt pce of wnr fnl f* **7/10**1
4 1 **Space Cowboy (GER)**56 4392 5-8-11 0..... DanielePorcu 1 100
(Markus Klug, Germany) *racd in 3rd: pushed along and lost position 3f out: rdn and kpt on fnl 2f: rdn out* **143/10**
5 shd **El Loco (GER)**13 4-8-11 0..... MartinSeidl 2 100
(Markus Klug, Germany) *led after 1f: 3 l clr at 1/2-way: pressed fr 2f out: hdd over 1f out: wknd fnl f* **96/10**
6 2 **Matchwinner (GER)**53 4487 6-9-2 0..... StephenHellyn 7 101
(A Kleinkorres, Germany) *racd in rr: sme late hdwy but nvr on terms* **53/10**2
7 5 **Tikiouine (FR)**34 5197 5-8-10 0..... MickaelForest 6 85
(Carmen Bocskai, Germany) *a towards rr* **66/10**3
8 7 **Felician (GER)**13 9-8-11 0..... MichaelCadeddu 4 72
(Ferdinand J Leve, Germany) *a towards rr* **223/10**

2m 1.77s (-3.22) 8 Ran SP% **128.8**

**Owner** Gestut Hony-Hof **Bred** Gestut Hony-Hof **Trained** Germany

# 6299 DEAUVILLE (R-H)
Saturday, August 26

**OFFICIAL GOING: Polytrack: standard; turf: good**

## 6452a PRIX DU MONT CANISY (CLAIMER) (2YO) (POLYTRACK) 6f 110y
1:05 2-Y-0 **£11,538** (£4,615; £3,461; £2,307; £1,153)

RPR
1 **Denaar (IRE)**11 6051 2-9-5 0..... Pierre-CharlesBoudot 8 88
(J Phelippon, France) **8/5**1
2 3 **Lamchope (FR)**20 2-9-2 0.....(p) TheoBachelot 1 77
(Y Barberot, France) **61/10**3
3 3 1/2 **Pimpinehorse (FR)**21 5679 2-9-4 0.....(p) ChristopheSoumillon 5 69
(R Chotard, France) **32/5**
4 nk **Controversial Lady (IRE)**11 6050 2-8-7 0..... MathieuPelletan(6) 6 63
(J S Moore) **19/5**2
5 1/2 **Rachael's Rocket (IRE)**6 6251 2-8-9 0 ow1..... TonyPiccone 9 58
(J S Moore) **153/10**
6 1 **Bombetta (FR)**12 6017 2-8-7 0.....(b) KyllanBarbaud(8) 2 61
(N Caullery, France) **7/1**
7 3/4 **Viento Sur (IRE)**25 5694 2-9-2 0.....(p) Roberto-CarlosMontenegro 7 60
(J A Remolina Diez, France) **121/10**
8 12 **Timeless Gift (IRE)**45 2-8-8 0..... AntoineHamelin 4 18
(Matthieu Palussiere, France) **35/1**
9 5 **Beaute Absolue (FR)**48 2-8-11 0.....(p) ClementLecoeuvre(4) 3 11
(F Vermeulen, France) **53/1**

PARI-MUTUEL (all including 1 euro stake): WIN 2.60; PLACE 1.50, 1.90, 1.80; DF 8.80; SF 12.70.
**Owner** Al Shaqab Racing **Bred** Gerry Burke **Trained** East Everleigh, Wilts

## 6453a PRIX DE COLLEVILLE (CONDITIONS) (2YO) (POLYTRACK) 6f 110y
1:35 2-Y-0 **£11,111** (£4,444; £3,333; £2,222; £1,111)

RPR
1 **Epic Adventure (FR)**14 5952 2-8-10 0.....(p) TheoBachelot 5 90
(S Cerulis, France) **97/10**
2 4 **Cabotin (FR)**14 5952 2-8-10 0..... Pierre-CharlesBoudot 3 79
(A Fabre, France) **31/10**2
3 1/2 **Mon Amie Chop (FR)**33 5232 2-8-11 0 ow1..... ChristopheSoumillon 6 78
(J-P Gauvin, France) **13/5**1
4 3/4 **Fatou (FR)**20 2-8-10 0..... EddyHardouin 2 75
(F Chappet, France) **41/10**3
5 snk **Uther Pendragon (IRE)**7 6229 2-9-0 0..... TonyPiccone 1 79
(J S Moore) **13/5**1
6 3/4 **Crystal Deauville (FR)**14 5952 2-8-10 0..... JulienAuge 4 56
(Gay Kelleway) **245/10**
D 6 **La Glorieuse (FR)**30 2-7-11 0.....(p) MlleCoraliePacaut(10) 7 55
(T Castanheira, France) **183/10**

PARI-MUTUEL (all including 1 euro stake): WIN 10.70; PLACE 4.20, 2.10; SF 38.10.
**Owner** David Bond **Bred** Mat Daguzan-Garros & F Daguzan-Garros **Trained** France

## 6454a PRIX DE LA VALLEE (CONDITIONS) (4YO+) (POLYTRACK) 7f 110y
3:30 4-Y-0+ **£14,102** (£5,641; £4,230; £2,820; £1,410)

RPR
1 **Dylaban (IRE)**20 5-9-0 0..... OlivierPeslier 3 85
(Alain Couetil, France) **47/10**3
2 3/4 **Hello My Love (FR)**329 6975 6-9-0 0..... EddyHardouin 5 83
(Carina Fey, France) **21/10**1
3 1 1/4 **Sky Ship**7 6226 4-9-0 0.....(p) PanagiotisDimitsanis 6 80
(Christos Kouvaras, France) **21/1**
4 snk **Yeah Baby Yeah (IRE)**7 6226 4-8-11 0 ow1..(p) ChristopheSoumillon 1 77
(Gay Kelleway) **57/10**
5 1 3/4 **Kool And The Gang (IRE)**7 6226 7-9-0 0..... CyrilleStefan 4 75
(J Albrecht, Czech Republic) **29/1**
6 1 3/4 **Alfieri (FR)**18 4-9-0 0..... MaximeGuyon 2 71
(T Castanheira, France) **59/10**
7 3 1/2 **Metropol (IRE)**13 6-9-0 0.....(b) Pierre-CharlesBoudot 8 62
(F Vermeulen, France) **19/5**2
8 1 1/2 **Dancing Hawk (GER)** 4-9-3 0.....(p) ClementLecoeuvre(3) 7 64
(Andreas Suborics, Germany) **87/10**

PARI-MUTUEL (all including 1 euro stake): WIN 5.70; PLACE 1.90, 1.50, 3.90; DF 8.00; SF 17.70.
**Owner** Sc La Haute Perriere **Bred** Indivision La Bastoche **Trained** France

## 6455a PRIX DE BELLEME (CLAIMER) (3YO) (POLYTRACK) 6f 110y
4:45 3-Y-0 **£9,829** (£3,931; £2,948; £1,965; £982)

RPR
1 **Galinka (FR)**14 3-8-8 0..... HugoJourniac 13 78
(J-C Rouget, France) **154/10**
2 1 **Mangaia (FR)**13 3-8-11 0..... TheoBachelot 4 78
(S Wattel, France) **41/5**
3 shd **Fongani (FR)**25 5521 3-9-3 0.....(b) ClementLecoeuvre(3) 16 87
(Simone Brogi, France) **125/10**
4 2 **Sivinsk (FR)**13 3-8-11 0..... ChristopheSoumillon 12 72
(Simone Brogi, France) **58/10**2
5 snk **Finalize (FR)**172 3-8-11 0..... AntoineWerle 9 71
(T Lemer, France) **166/10**
6 hd **Fils De L'Air (FR)**29 3-8-11 0.....(b) GregoryBenoist 7 71
(S Cerulis, France) **105/10**
7 2 1/2 **Cry Baby (IRE)**9 3-9-5 0.....(b) MaximeGuyon 15 72
(Y Barberot, France) **59/10**3
8 nk **Lord Cooper**28 5416 3-9-1 0.....(p) MickaelBarzalona 1 67
(Jose Santos) **89/10**
9 3/4 **Silk Of Rio (FR)**22 3-8-11 0.....(b) EddyHardouin 10 61
(P Van De Poele, France) **31/1**
10 1 3/4 **Ucel (IRE)**13 3-9-0 0.....(b) JeromeMoutard(5) 8 64
(F Chappet, France) **19/1**
11 3/4 **Swanning Around (IRE)**14 3-8-8 0..... AntoineHamelin 6 50
(Matthieu Palussiere, France) **33/1**
12 hd **Bajazzo (GER)**30 3-9-1 0.....(b) OlivierPeslier 14 57
(H-A Pantall, France) **243/10**
13 5 **Ecrin Des Bieffes (FR)**9 3-9-5 0.....(b) Roberto-CarlosMontenegro 3 46
(J A Remolina Diez, France) **4/1**1
14 5 **Island Brave (IRE)**9 6124 3-8-6 0.....(b) MathieuPelletan(5) 2 24
(J S Moore) **26/1**
15 7 **Amazigh World (FR)**375 3-8-11 0.....(p) AntoineCoutier 5
(P Monfort, France) **92/1**

PARI-MUTUEL (all including 1 euro stake): WIN 7.40; PLACE 4.90, 2.90, 4.90; DF 49.40; SF 77.90.
**Owner** Alain Jathiere **Bred** Plersch Breeding Sarl **Trained** Pau, France

## 6456a PRIX DE LA CROIX D'HEULAND (CLAIMER) (2YO) (POLYTRACK) 7f 110y
5:15 2-Y-0 **£8,119** (£3,247; £2,435; £1,623; £811)

RPR
1 **Valhala (FR)**15 5907 2-9-1 0..... ChristopheSoumillon 8 69
(Y Barberot, France) **5/2**1
2 1 3/4 **Formiga (IRE)**15 5893 2-8-11 0..... MickaelBarzalona 3 61
(Jose Santos) **68/10**
3 1 3/4 **Peterhof (FR)** 2-9-1 0..... ClementLecoeuvre(3) 9 64
(C Boutin, France) **37/10**3
4 3/4 **Vida Loca (FR)**15 5907 2-8-2 0..... MlleMickaelleMichel(9) 7 55
(M Boutin, France) **10/1**
5 3/4 **Shesgotthelot**15 5907 2-9-1 0..... TonyPiccone 10 57
(J S Moore) **7/2**2
6 1/2 **Belle Vendome (FR)** 2-9-1 0.....(p) Pierre-CharlesBoudot 1 56
(M Pimbonnet, France) **157/10**
7 1 1/4 **Say About It**11 6050 2-8-13 0..... MathieuPelletan(5) 6 56
(J S Moore) **27/1**
8 3/4 **Maine D'Ange (IRE)**8 6171 2-7-12 0..... MlleCamilleFlechon(10) 2 44
(P Sogorb, France) **26/1**
9 nk **Reggae Traou Land (FR)** 2-8-9 0.....(b) ErwannLebreton(6) 11 51
(G Derat, France) **38/1**
10 3 **Cherry Lips (ITY)** 2-8-3 0..... TomLefranc(5) 5 37
(A Giorgi, Italy) **11/1**

PARI-MUTUEL (all including 1 euro stake): WIN 3.50; PLACE 1.60, 2.00, 1.60; DF 11.80; SF 20.20.
**Owner** Passion Racing Club **Bred** Ecurie La Vallee Martigny Earl, T Pien & R Grosset **Trained** France

6257-6460a (Foreign Racing) - See Raceform Interactive

# 6230 SARATOGA (R-H)

Saturday, August 26

**OFFICIAL GOING: Dirt: fast; turf: firm**

## 6461a SWORD DANCER STKS (GRADE 1) (3YO+) (TURF) 1m 4f

9:49 3-Y-O+

£434,959 (£150,406; £81,300; £52,845; £32,520; £24,390)

RPR

1 **Sadler's Joy (USA)**[28] 4-8-8 0 .................................. JulienRLeparoux 3 113
(Thomas Albertrani, U.S.A) *s.i.s: confidently rdn in last pl: rdn and gd hdwy on outside over 1f out: kpt on wl to ld towards fin: comf* **7/1**

2 ½ **Money Multiplier (USA)**[27] 5-8-8 0 .......................... JavierCastellano 5 112
(Chad C Brown, U.S.A) *hld up in tch: niggled along over 2f out: effrt and hdwy over 1f out: disp ld thrght fnl f: kpt on: hld towards fin* **23/10[2]**

3 nse **Bigger Picture (USA)**[28] 6-8-12 0 ..................................(b) JoseLOrtiz 2 116
(Michael J Maker, U.S.A) *trckd ldrs: pushed along over 2f out: hdwy to ld appr fnl f: sn hrd pressed: hdd and no ex towards fin* **78/10**

4 ¾ **Hunter O'Riley (USA)**[28] 4-8-8 0 ...............................(b) FlorentGeroux 4 111
(James J Toner, U.S.A) *s.i.s: hld up in tch: rdn and outpcd over 2f out: rallied over 1f out: kpt on ins fnl f: nvr able to chal* **142/10**

5 2½ **Erupt (IRE)**[55] 4423 5-8-10 0 ..................................(p) StephanePasquier 6 109
(F-H Graffard, France) *trckd ldrs: rdn along 2f out: wknd last 100yds* **11/2[3]**

6 nk **Idaho (IRE)**[28] 5394 4-8-10 0 .............................................. RyanMoore 7 108
(A P O'Brien, Ire) *w ldr: drvn along and outpcd over 1f out: btn ins fnl f* **29/20[1]**

7 1 **Frank Conversation (USA)**[28] 4-8-8 0 ......................... MarioGutierrez 1 105
(Doug O'Neill, U.S.A) *led at ordinary gallop: rdn and hdd appr fnl f: wknd last 150yds* **31/1**

PARI-MUTUEL (all including 2 usd stake): WIN 16.00; PLACE (1-2) 5.50, 3.90; SHOW (1-2-3) 3.80, 2.90, 3.60; SF 58.00.
**Owner** Woodslane Farm **Bred** Woodslane Farm Llc **Trained** USA

6462 - 6463a (Foreign Racing) - See Raceform Interactive

# 6085 BEVERLEY (R-H)

Sunday, August 27

**OFFICIAL GOING: Good to firm (watered; 7.9)**
Wind: Virtually nil Weather: Sunny

## 6464 JOHN JENKINS MEMORIAL CLAIMING STKS 7f 96y

1:55 (1:56) (Class 5) 3-Y-O+ £3,780 (£1,131; £565; £283; £141) Stalls Low

Form RPR

0363 1 **Rousayan (IRE)**[8] 6209 6-9-10 79 ..............................(h) DanielTudhope 3 86
(David O'Meara) *trckd ldrs: smooth hdwy over 2f out: swtchd lft and chal on bit over 1f out: shkn up to ld ent fnl f: sn rdn and kpt on* **2/1[1]**

0050 2 1½ **Al Khan (IRE)**[29] 5434 8-9-7 84 ..............................(p) LewisEdmunds(3) 2 82
(Kevin Ryan) *hld up towards rr: hdwy over 2f out: rdn over 1f out: chsd wnr ins fnl f: kpt on* **5/1[2]**

1332 3 1½ **Chiswick Bey (IRE)**[11] 6058 9-8-13 68 .......................... PaulHanagan 1 67
(Richard Fahey) *in tch on inner: hdwy 2f out: swtchd lft and rdn over 1f out: kpt on fnl f* **12/1**

2004 4 ½ **Mishaal (IRE)**[7] 6238 7-9-5 72 ..................................... PaulMulrennan 6 72
(Michael Herrington) *led: rdn along 2f out: drvn and hdd jst over 1f out: kpt on u.p fnl f* **12/1**

6153 5 nk **Favourite Treat (USA)**[15] 5948 7-9-3 70 .......................(e) JackGarritty 5 69
(Ruth Carr) *trckd ldr: hdwy and cl up 2f out: rdn to take slt ld jst over 1f out: hdd ent fnl f: sn drvn and kpt on same pce* **11/1**

1023 6 nk **Tatlisu (IRE)**[16] 5890 7-9-3 85 .................................. ConnorMurtagh(7) 4 75
(Richard Fahey) *hld up: hdwy on outer over 2f out: rdn along over 1f out: kpt on fnl f* **13/2**

5300 7 nse **Sovereign Bounty**[6] 6266 5-9-10 79 ................................... GrahamLee 8 75
(Jedd O'Keeffe) *trckd ldrs: hdwy 2f out: rdn along over 1f out: kpt on u.p fnl f* **11/2[3]**

6503 8 2¾ **Bold Spirit**[11] 6058 6-8-13 52 ..........................................(t) PhilDennis(3) 7 60
(Declan Carroll) *stdd s: hld up: a towards rr* **50/1**

1401 9 1¼ **Talent Scout (IRE)**[11] 6058 11-8-9 75 ..........................(p) GemmaTutty(5) 9 55
(Karen Tutty) *prom: rdn along over 2f out: sn drvn and wknd* **14/1**

3000 10 4 **Shah Of Armaan (IRE)**[27] 5469 4-9-5 67 ............................(p) TomEaves 10 49
(Kevin Ryan) *a in rr* **40/1**

1m 31.13s (-2.67) **Going Correction** -0.275s/f (Firm) 10 Ran SP% 113.5
Speed ratings (Par 103): **104,102,100,100,99 99,99,96,94,90**
CSF £11.20 TOTE £2.40: £1.10, £2.00, £3.00; EX 12.90 Trifecta £100.30.
**Owner** The Roses Partnership **Bred** Haras De Son Altesse L'Aga Khan Scea **Trained** Upper Helmsley, N Yorks

**FOCUS**
All rails in original wide position. Race distances as advertised. Not a bad claimer, run at a strong pace.

## 6465 SILK MILL BAR RIPPONDEN WELCOMES YOU NOVICE AUCTION STKS 7f 96y

2:30 (2:31) (Class 5) 2-Y-O £3,881 (£1,155; £577; £288) Stalls Low

Form RPR

513 1 **Alfa McGuire (IRE)**[31] 5314 2-9-9 81 ..................................... GrahamLee 5 86
(Bryan Smart) *trckd ldng pair: hdwy 3f out: led 2f out: rdn: green and hung lft jst over 1f out: sn clr and kpt on strly* **2/1[2]**

1 2 5 **Book Of Dreams (IRE)**[19] 5755 2-9-9 0 ............................ FrannyNorton 4 74+
(Mark Johnston) *cl up: rdn along to dispute ld over 2f out: drvn wl over 1f out: edgd rt and kpt on same pce fnl f* **7/4[1]**

3 3 4 **Skito Soldier**[16] 5874 2-8-13 0 ...................................... CliffordLee(3) 3 57+
(K R Burke) *towards rr: green and pushed along bef 1/2-way: hdwy wl over 2f out: rdn to chse ldrs and edgd rt over 1f out: kpt on fnl f* **11/4[3]**

464 4 ¾ **Poppy Walton (IRE)**[11] 6057 2-8-11 65 ........................... AndrewMullen 2 51+
(Ollie Pears) *slt ld: pushed along 3f out: rdn and hdd 2f out: cl up on inner and drvn over 1f out: grad wknd* **8/1**

00 5 1¼ **Echo (IRE)**[26] 5492 2-9-2 0 ............................................. JackGarritty 6 53
(Jedd O'Keeffe) *wnt lft s: green and outpcd in rr: hdwy 3f out: rdn along wl over 1f out: swtchd rt to inner ent fnl f: kpt on: nrst fin* **33/1**

00 6 ½ **Troop**[12] 6042 2-9-2 0 .............................................................. ShaneGray 1 51
(Ann Duffield) *chsd ldrs: rdn along wl over 2f out: sn one pce* **66/1**

1m 32.61s (-1.19) **Going Correction** -0.275s/f (Firm) 6 Ran SP% 111.9
Speed ratings (Par 94): **95,89,84,83,82 81**
CSF £5.86 TOTE £2.90: £1.50, £1.30; EX 6.50 Trifecta £11.10.
**Owner** Alfa Site Services Ltd **Bred** O Costello & R Moorhead **Trained** Hambleton, N Yorks

**FOCUS**
Useful 2yo form. It's been rated cautiously.

## 6466 EDUCARE OF BEVERLEY NURSERY H'CAP 5f

3:05 (3:06) (Class 3) (0-95,83) 2-Y-O £6,301 (£1,886; £943; £472; £235) Stalls Low

Form RPR

133 1 **Shaheen (IRE)**[11] 6065 2-8-11 73 ..........................................(t) JasonHart 2 77
(John Quinn) *trckd ldrs on inner: swtchd lft and hdwy over 1f out: rdn to chal fnl f: led last 75yds: drvn and hld on wl towards fin* **9/2[3]**

2006 2 hd **Requinto Dawn (IRE)**[29] 5440 2-9-4 80 ............................ PaulHanagan 4 83
(Richard Fahey) *trckd ldrs: hdwy 2f out: rdn to ld ent fnl f: sn jnd: drvn and hdd last 75yds: kpt on wl* **11/1**

021 3 1¾ **Roundhay Park**[40] 4996 2-8-12 74 ....................................... TomEaves 3 73
(Nigel Tinkler) *trckd ldrs: hdwy 2f out: effrt and nt clr run over 1f out: rdn to chse ldng pair ins fnl f: kpt on* **10/1**

0225 4 3½ **Gangland**[37] 5121 2-8-4 69 ................................................(h) SammyJoBell(3) 6 53
(Richard Fahey) *blind removed late and bhd: rdn along and outpcd bef 1/2-way: hdwy over 1f out: styd on wl u.p fnl f* **11/1**

2353 5 nk **Our Little Pony**[10] 6085 2-7-13 68 .............................. JamieGormley(7) 7 51
(Lawrence Mullaney) *chsd ldrs on outer: rdn along wl over 1f out: grad wknd* **16/1**

3154 6 ½ **Jive Lady (IRE)**[12] 6021 2-9-0 76 .................................... FrannyNorton 1 57
(Mark Johnston) *led: rdn along 2f out: drvn over 1f out: hdd ent fnl f: sn wknd* **4/1[2]**

4122 7 ½ **Rumshak (IRE)**[16] 5879 2-9-7 83 .................................... PaulMulrennan 5 62
(Michael Dods) *t.k.h early: hld up in tch: effrt 2f out: rdn over 1f out: sn btn* **15/8[1]**

513 8 ½ **Bow Belles**[22] 5665 2-8-13 75 ............................................ DavidAllan 8 53
(Tim Easterby) *cl up: rdn along 2f out: drvn over 1f out: sn wknd* **8/1**

1m 2.38s (-1.12) **Going Correction** -0.125s/f (Firm) 8 Ran SP% 115.7
Speed ratings (Par 98): **103,102,99,94,93 93,92,91**
CSF £52.58 CT £470.82 TOTE £5.10: £1.80, £3.00, £2.70; EX 50.80 Trifecta £459.60.
**Owner** Al Shaqab Racing **Bred** Tally-Ho Stud **Trained** Settrington, N Yorks

**FOCUS**
A modest nursery in which the first pair came clear. The runner-up has been rated to his early season form.

## 6467 BEVERLEY MIDDLE DISTANCE SERIES FINAL ROUND H'CAP 1m 4f 23y

3:40 (3:40) (Class 5) (0-75,77) 3-Y-O+ £5,040 (£1,508; £754; £377; £188) Stalls Low

Form RPR

2241 1 **Maori Bob (IRE)**[11] 6061 3-8-10 71 ................................. LuluStanford(5) 3 81
(Michael Bell) *t.k.h: prom: trckd ldr over 7f out: led over 2f out: rdn clr appr fnl f: kpt on wl* **6/4[1]**

2352 2 1¾ **Royal Reserve**[8] 6188 4-10-2 77 .................................... DanielTudhope 2 83
(David O'Meara) *hld up in rr: hdwy over 3f out: trckd ldrs 2f out: effrt and nt clr run 1 1/2f out: rdn to chse wnr jst ins fnl f: sn swtchd rt and drvn: no imp* **3/1[2]**

1414 3 1 **Cornborough**[20] 5704 6-10-1 76 ...................................(p) DougieCostello 9 80
(Mark Walford) *hld up in rr: hdwy over 2f out: rdn along wl over 1f out: styd on fnl f* **11/1**

3062 4 2 **Alphabetical Order**[11] 6061 9-9-13 74 ..............................(h[1]) SamJames 4 75
(David O'Meara) *trckd ldrs: pushed along and sltly outpcd 3f out: hdwy 2f out: sn rdn and kpt on fnl f* **8/1[3]**

3046 5 2¼ **Island Flame (IRE)**[17] 5830 4-9-4 65 ............................... PaulHanagan 5 63
(Richard Fahey) *trckd ldrs: hdwy 3f out: rdn along 2f out: drvn over 1f out: sn one pce* **14/1**

6610 6 1 **Hayward Field (IRE)**[17] 5832 4-9-6 67 ........................ PatrickMathers 10 63
(Noel Wilson) *trckd ldrs: hdwy over 3f out: rdn along over 2f out: drvn and wknd over 1f out* **20/1**

5536 7 2¾ **Mysterial**[11] 6060 7-9-2 66 .............................................. PhilDennis(3) 11 58
(Declan Carroll) *led: pushed along over 3f out: rdn and hdd over 2f out: sn drvn and wknd* **14/1**

1000 8 3 **Samtu (IRE)**[63] 4120 6-10-0 75 ........................................ BarryMcHugh 8 62
(Marjorie Fife) *midfield: hdwy 4f out: rdn along wl over 2f out: sn wknd* **40/1**

2305 9 nk **Wotabreeze (IRE)**[9] 6126 4-9-7 68 ....................................(v[1]) JasonHart 1 54
(John Quinn) *chsd ldr over 4f: prom: rdn along over 2f out: sn wknd* **9/1**

2m 35.68s (-4.12) **Going Correction** -0.275s/f (Firm)
**WFA** 3 from 4yo+ 9lb 9 Ran SP% 115.0
Speed ratings (Par 103): **102,100,100,98,97 96,94,92,92**
CSF £5.81 CT £34.01 TOTE £2.00: £1.10, £1.40, £2.80; EX 5.90 Trifecta £34.30.
**Owner** P Philipps, C Philipps, T Redman **Bred** Peter Molony **Trained** Newmarket, Suffolk

**FOCUS**
This was dominated by the two market leaders.

## 6468 PAT AND GRAHAM ROBERTS SAPPHIRE WEDDING ANNIVERSARY H'CAP 1m 100y

4:15 (4:17) (Class 4) (0-80,82) 3-Y-O £5,040 (£1,508; £754; £377; £188) Stalls Low

Form RPR

242 1 **Rinaria (IRE)**[4] 6310 3-9-2 70 ............................................(h) JoeyHaynes 4 76
(K R Burke) *trckd ldr: led over 2f out: rdn over 1f out: drvn and kpt on wl fnl f* **5/1**

2343 2 2 **Election Day**[60] 4215 3-9-13 81 ....................................... FrannyNorton 2 82
(Mark Johnston) *trckd ldr on inner: effrt over 2f out: rdn along over 1f out: chsd wnr ins fnl f: no imp towards fin* **3/1[2]**

-210 3 ½ **Everything For You (IRE)**[57] 4376 3-9-13 81 ..................(p[1]) TomEaves 6 81
(Kevin Ryan) *wnt lft s and sn pushed along in rr: rdn along and outpcd 3f out: hdwy wl over 1f out: styd on strly u.p fnl f* **13/2**

4-21 4 1¾ **Asaas (USA)**[55] 4444 3-9-13 81 ..................................... PaulMulrennan 1 77
(Roger Varian) *hld up in tch: hdwy on inner to trck ldrs over 3f out: pushed along over 2f out: rdn wl over 1f out: kpt on same pce* **7/2[3]**

1226 5 1½ **Lamloom (IRE)**[22] 5664 3-9-13 81 .................................. DanielTudhope 3 74
(David O'Meara) *led: rdn along 3f out: hdd over 2f out: sn drvn and wknd over 1f out* **11/4[1]**

0260 6 2¼ **Muirsheen Durkin**[22] 5669 3-10-0 82 ..........................(p) DougieCostello 5 70
(Neville Bycroft) *trckd ldrs: hdwy over 2f out: rdn along wl over 1f out: sn drvn and btn* **16/1**

1m 44.65s (-2.95) **Going Correction** -0.275s/f (Firm) 6 Ran SP% 109.8
Speed ratings (Par 102): **103,101,100,98,97 95**
CSF £19.32 TOTE £5.10: £2.80, £1.60; EX 20.40 Trifecta £129.90.



The Form Book Flat, Raceform Ltd, Newbury, RG14 5SJ

**Owner** The Mount Racing Club & A Kavanagh **Bred** Rathdown Stud Ltd **Trained** Middleham Moor, N Yorks
**FOCUS**
A fair 3yo handicap in which it paid to be handy.

## 6469 BEVERLEY LIONS H'CAP 5f
**4:50** (4:52) (Class 6) (0-60,62) 3-Y-O **£2,587** (£770; £384; £192) **Stalls** Low

Form RPR
3244 **1** **Hamidans Girl (IRE)**[3] 6351 3-9-9 **62**.............................. GrahamLee 5 70+
(Keith Dalgleish) *towards rr: pushed along and hdwy 2f out: n.m.r and hmpd on inner wl over 1f out: swtchd lft jst over 1f out: nt clr run and swtchd rt to inner jst ins fnl f: rdn and qcknd wl to ld last 50yds* **7/2**[1]
0-56 **2** *1 1/2* **The Night Before**[22] 5636 3-9-3 **56**.............................. BenCurtis 12 56+
(Robert Cowell) *qckly away and slt ld: rdn over 1f out: drvn ins fnl f: hdd and no ex last 50yds* **14/1**
5005 **3** *hd* **La Haule Lady**[40] 4997 3-8-8 **47**.............................. PaulHanagan 2 46
(Paul Midgley) *in tch: hdwy to trck ldrs 2f out: rdn to chal ent fnl f: sn drvn and ev ch: kpt on same pce towards fin* **5/1**[3]
445 **4** *1* **Bay Station**[36] 5134 3-9-7 **60**..............................(p) DanielTudhope 6 58
(Jason Ward) *trckd ldrs: hdwy 2f out: ev ch whn nt clr run and swtchd lft ent fnl f: sn rdn and kpt on same pce* **7/2**[1]
3046 **5** *1 3/4* **Digital Revolution**[19] 5736 3-8-8 **47**.............................. CamHardie 3 38
(Antony Brittain) *trckd ldrs: hdwy 2f out: nt clr run over 1f out: swtchd lft and rdn ent fnl f: kpt on* **20/1**
6400 **6** *2 1/4* **Dapper Man (IRE)**[9] 6148 3-9-7 **60**..............................(b) ConnorBeasley 1 41
(Roger Fell) *cl up: rdn along 2f out: drvn and ev ch over 1f out: grad wknd fnl f* **9/2**[2]
-256 **7** *3/4* **Canford Bay (IRE)**[11] 6062 3-9-3 **56**.............................. DavidAllan 11 35
(Antony Brittain) *chsd ldrs: rdn along wl over 1f out: sn drvn and wknd* **8/1**
0506 **8** *1/2* **Tess Graham**[46] 4731 3-8-4 **46** oh1..............................(p) SammyJoBell(3) 7 23
(Sarah Hollinshead) *dwlt and bhd tl sme late hdwy* **33/1**
0600 **9** *3/4* **Newgate Sioux**[64] 4107 3-8-11 **50**..............................(t[1]) BarryMcHugh 13 24
(Tony Coyle) *in tch: rdn along and edgd rt wl over 1f out: sn drvn and wknd* **33/1**
4020 **10** *4 1/2* **Joysunny**[20] 5703 3-8-2 **48**.............................. HarrisonShaw(7) 8 6
(Jacqueline Coward) *prom: rdn along 2f out: sn drvn and wknd* **20/1**
00-0 **11** *1/2* **Equipe**[98] 2853 3-8-7 **46** oh1.............................. AndrewMullen 4 24+
(Richard Whitaker) *towards rr: hdwy 1/2-way: chsd ldrs whn hmpd over 1f out: nt rcvr* **50/1**
5350 **12** *1 1/2* **Henrietta's Dream**[22] 5636 3-8-7 **46** oh1..............................(b) FrannyNorton 10
(John Wainwright) *a outpcd in rr* **40/1**

1m 3.7s (0.20) **Going Correction** -0.125s/f (Firm) 12 Ran SP% **116.9**
Speed ratings (Par 98): **93,90,90,88,85 82,81,80,79,71 71,68**
CSF £48.74 CT £250.65 TOTE £4.10: £1.80, £4.00, £1.80; EX 55.50 Trifecta £316.10.
**Owner** Middleham Park Racing LXVII **Bred** Patrick Byrnes **Trained** Carluke, S Lanarks
**FOCUS**
They went a fair pace in this moderate 3yo handicap. The second and third pin the level.

## 6470 RACING AGAIN NEXT SATURDAY H'CAP (DIV I) 1m 1f 207y
**5:25** (5:27) (Class 6) (0-65,67) 3-Y-O+ **£2,587** (£770; £384; £192) **Stalls** Low

Form RPR
1236 **1** **Bollin Ted**[12] 6048 3-8-13 **57**.............................. DavidAllan 9 63
(Tim Easterby) *sn trcking ldr: cl up 3f out: led over 2f out: rdn over 1f out: drvn ins fnl f: kpt on* **15/8**[1]
525 **2** *1/2* **Spirit Of The Vale (IRE)**[4] 6306 4-9-5 **56**..............................(t) KevinStott 5 60
(Oliver Greenall) *v unruly in paddock and rdr led to s: dwlt and hld up in rr: hdwy on inner over 1f out: nt clr run: swtchd lft and rdn ent fnl f: fin strly* **11/1**
5330 **3** *1* **Lord Kitten (USA)**[27] 5485 3-9-6 **64**..............................(t[1]) PaulMulrennan 6 67
(David Lanigan) *prom: hdwy over 2f out: rdn to chal over 1f out: ev ch ent fnl f: sn drvn and kpt on same pce* **17/2**[3]
0000 **4** *nse* **Neptune Star**[12] 6048 3-8-2 **46** oh1.............................. AndrewMullen 3 49
(Michael Easterby) *trckd ldrs on inner: effrt and nt clr run over 1f out: sn swtchd lft and rdn: kpt on same pce* **20/1**
1404 **5** *1* **Bit Of A Quirke**[18] 5807 4-9-13 **64**.............................. DougieCostello 1 64
(Mark Walford) *led: pushed along 3f out: rdn and hdd over 2f out: drvn over 1f out: wknd ins fnl f* **4/1**[2]
4056 **6** *3 1/4* **Leonard Thomas**[13] 6003 7-8-11 **48**..............................(p) PaddyAspell 7 42
(Philip Kirby) *hld up towards rr: hdwy over 3f out: rdn along and chsd ldrs whn n.m.r appr fnl f: sn drvn and no imp* **20/1**
440 **7** *1/2* **Lopito De Vega (IRE)**[36] 5135 5-9-10 **61**.............................. FrannyNorton 4 54
(David C Griffiths) *hld up in rr: hdwy wl over 2f out: rdn wl over 1f: sn no imp* **12/1**
2064 **8** *hd* **Perceived**[11] 6060 5-10-2 **67**.............................. CamHardie 2 60
(Antony Brittain) *hld up in rr: hdwy 3f out: in tch and rdn along over 2f out: sn drvn and n.d* **14/1**
200 **9** *2 3/4* **Twiggy**[16] 5880 3-9-0 **65**..............................(h) JamieGormley(7) 10 53
(Iain Jardine) *t.k.h: in tch: effrt over 2f out: sn rdn along and wknd over 1f out* **10/1**
406 **10** *3 1/2* **I'm Super Too (IRE)**[10] 6092 10-8-10 **52**..............................(b) GemmaTutty(5) 11 33
(Karen Tutty) *in tch: hdwy on outer to chse ldrs over 3f out: rdn along 2f out: sn wknd* **14/1**
1160 **11** *1 1/2* **Ching Ching Lor (IRE)**[22] 5666 3-9-4 **62**..............................(b[1]) TomEaves 8 42
(Declan Carroll) *chsd ldrs: rdn along 3f out: drvn 2f out: sn wknd* **20/1**

2m 5.12s (-1.88) **Going Correction** -0.275s/f (Firm)
**WFA** 3 from 4yo+ 7lb 11 Ran SP% **118.0**
Speed ratings (Par 101): **96,95,94,94,93 91,90,90,88,85 84**
CSF £23.21 CT £138.92 TOTE £2.40: £1.50, £2.40, £2.10; EX 22.60 Trifecta £113.60.
**Owner** Neil Arton & Partner **Bred** Habton Farms **Trained** Great Habton, N Yorks
■ Stewards' Enquiry : Kevin Stott caution: guilty of careless riding
**FOCUS**
A weak handicap. Modest form, with the second, third and fourth looking quite exposed.

## 6471 RACING AGAIN NEXT SATURDAY H'CAP (DIV II) 1m 1f 207y
**5:55** (5:55) (Class 6) (0-65,66) 3-Y-O+ **£2,587** (£770; £384; £192) **Stalls** Low

Form RPR
4620 **1** **Pioneering (IRE)**[22] 5666 3-9-6 **64**.............................. DanielTudhope 6 69+
(David O'Meara) *led: hdd 1/2-way: cl up: led again 3f out: rdn over 1f out: drvn out* **11/2**[3]
0300 **2** *3/4* **Lozah**[13] 6003 4-9-5 **56**.............................. JasonHart 7 59
(Roger Fell) *hld up in tch: hdwy on outer 2f out: rdn over 1f out: drvn ent fnl f: kpt on wl towards fin* **16/1**
160 **3** *3/4* **Outlaw Torn (IRE)**[4] 6306 8-9-4 **55**..............................(e) ConnorBeasley 8 57
(Richard Guest) *prom: effrt over 2f out: rdn to chse wnr over 1f out: drvn ent fnl f: kpt on same pce* **8/1**
0060 **4** *1 1/4* **Pontecarlo Boy**[58] 4302 3-8-2 **46** oh1..............................(p) CamHardie 2 46
(Richard Whitaker) *trckd ldrs on inner: pushed along and hdwy over 2f out: rdn wl over 1f out: drvn and kpt on same pce fnl f* **40/1**
6320 **5** *hd* **Chauvelin**[10] 6088 6-9-1 **52**..............................(b) TomEaves 1 51
(Nigel Tinkler) *hld up in midfield: hdwy over 2f out: rdn wl over 1f out: kpt on u.p fnl f* **22/1**
2553 **6** *1/2* **Trinity Star (IRE)**[55] 4438 6-9-10 **66**..............................(p) CallumRodriguez(5) 5 64
(Michael Dods) *hld up in rr: hdwy on wd outside 2f out: rdn over 1f out: drvn and kpt on fnl f* **7/2**[1]
0314 **7** *3* **Mr C (IRE)**[19] 5761 3-8-12 **56**.............................. JoeDoyle 4 49
(Ollie Pears) *trckd ldrs: pushed along wl over 2f out: rdn wl over 1f out: swtchd rt and drvn appr fnl f: sn wknd* **6/1**
3100 **8** *1 3/4* **Arcane Dancer (IRE)**[12] 6047 4-9-10 **61**..............................(p) DavidAllan 9 50
(Lawrence Mullaney) *trckd ldrs on outer: hdwy to ld 1/2-way: rdn along and hdd 3f out: drvn along wl over 1f out: grad wknd* **11/2**[3]
1200 **9** *1 1/4* **Bromance**[34] 5212 4-9-9 **60**..............................(p) GrahamLee 3 46
(Peter Niven) *hld up: a towards rr* **14/1**
0062 **10** *6* **Getgo**[26] 5509 3-9-7 **65**..............................(b) PaulMulrennan 10 41
(David Lanigan) *a in rr: rdn along 3f out: nvr a factor* **4/1**[2]

2m 6.25s (-0.75) **Going Correction** -0.275s/f (Firm)
**WFA** 3 from 4yo+ 7lb 10 Ran SP% **117.7**
Speed ratings (Par 101): **92,91,90,89,89 89,86,85,84,79**
CSF £89.86 CT £706.22 TOTE £6.60: £2.40, £4.90, £2.20; EX 105.70 Trifecta £500.40.
**Owner** Ebor Racing Club Vi **Bred** Miss Joan Murphy **Trained** Upper Helmsley, N Yorks
**FOCUS**
They went an average pace in this second division of the weak handicap. It's been rated around the balance of the first four.
T/Jkpt: £6,283.30 to a £1 stake. Pool: £78,542.08 - 12.50 winning units. T/Plt: £29.60 to a £1 stake. Pool: £79,759.36 - 1,964.22 winning units. T/Qpdt: £14.80 to a £1 stake. Pool: £4,377.01 - 218.36 winning units. **Joe Rowntree**

# 6417 GOODWOOD (R-H)
Sunday, August 27

**OFFICIAL GOING: Good (good to firm in places; 7.8)**
Wind: Nil Weather: Fine, warm

## 6472 BUTLINS NOVICE AUCTION STKS 1m
**2:10** (2:10) (Class 5) 2-Y-O **£4,528** (£1,347; £673; £336) **Stalls** Low

Form RPR
522 **1** **Ibn Al Emarat (IRE)**[19] 5743 2-9-2 81.............................. OisinMurphy 3 84
(David Simcock) *trckd clr ldng pair: clsd over 2f out: rdn over 1f out: led ins fnl f: styd on* **13/8**[2]
021 **2** *1/2* **Macaque**[17] 5819 2-9-4 79.............................. JoshuaBryan(5) 2 90
(Andrew Balding) *t.k.h: trckd clr ldr: clsd over 2f out: rdn to ld over 1f out: hdd ins fnl f: styd on but hld after* **11/8**[1]
635 **3** *5* **Lucifugous (IRE)**[36] 5154 2-8-7 64.............................. SilvestreDeSousa 6 62
(Stuart Williams) *racd freely: sn led and clr: c bk to rivals over 2f out: hdd over 1f out: hanging lft after and wknd ins fnl f* **9/2**[3]
5 **4** *2 1/4* **Affluence (IRE)**[19] 5749 2-8-8 0.............................. NoelGarbutt(3) 1 61
(Martin Smith) *hld up in tch: pushed along and no imp on clr ldrs over 2f out: one pce after* **16/1**
0 **5** *9* **Masters Apprentice (IRE)**[20] 5710 2-8-8 0.............................. MitchGodwin(5) 5 42
(Sylvester Kirk) *in tch: shkn up sn after 1/2-way: sn wl btn* **25/1**
0 **6** *8* **Free Talkin**[22] 5655 2-8-8 0.............................. KierenFox 4 19
(Michael Attwater) *t.k.h: hld up: pushed along 3f out: sn wknd and bhd* **40/1**
**7** *24* **Zappa** 2-8-11 0.............................. CharlesBishop 8
(Mick Channon) *rn green in last pair: lost tch over 3f out: t.o* **12/1**
005 **8** *1 1/2* **Rockwell Lloyd (IRE)**[16] 5886 2-8-12 54..............................(v[1]) RobHornby 7
(Mick Channon) *a last: t.o sn after 1/2-way* **33/1**

1m 39.42s (-0.48) **Going Correction** +0.025s/f (Good) 8 Ran SP% **121.2**
Speed ratings (Par 94): **103,102,97,95,86 78,54,52**
CSF £4.48 TOTE £2.30: £1.10, £1.10, £1.50; EX 4.10 Trifecta £6.70.
**Owner** Ahmad Abdulla Al Shaikh **Bred** Haras Du Logis St Germain **Trained** Newmarket, Suffolk
**FOCUS**
It was dry overnight and a warm day; fresh ground top bend. Not much depth to this but the first two, fair sorts at least, pulled clear. The winner has been rated to his latest form.

## 6473 CHICHESTER CITY (S) STKS 1m 3f 44y
**2:45** (2:46) (Class 4) 3-Y-O **£6,469** (£1,925; £962; £481) **Stalls** High

Form RPR
040 **1** **Delannoy**[18] 5780 3-9-0 58..............................(v[1]) JimCrowley 4 63
(Eve Johnson Houghton) *racd wd early: trckd ldr after 3f: led 4f out: shkn up whn pressed over 2f out: steadily drew clr: rdn out* **3/1**[2]
0255 **2** *6* **Bizet (IRE)**[5] 6281 3-9-0 52..............................(v) JosephineGordon 7 53
(John Ryan) *slowly away and urged along in last early: prog 4f out: sn rdn: kpt on after to take 2nd nr fin: no ch w wnr* **12/1**
3640 **3** *1/2* **Zoffanist (IRE)**[5] 6291 3-9-0 58.............................. PatDobbs 6 52
(Amanda Perrett) *t.k.h early: cl up: rdn 3f out: chsd wnr wl over 1f out: no imp and lost 2nd nr fin* **13/2**[3]
5-43 **4** *7* **Iconic Belle**[65] 4042 3-8-9 71.............................. CharlesBishop 3 35
(Mick Channon) *trckd ldr 3f: styd cl up: chsd wnr over 3f out: rdn to chal over 2f out but fnd nil and sn btn: wknd over 1f out* **10/11**[1]
5 **5** *8* **Cagliari**[9] 6161 3-8-9 0..............................(h) RyanPowell 2 21
(Simon Crisford) *hld up: pushed along over 3f out: steadily dropped away* **16/1**
6506 **6** *18* **Crystal Secret**[4] 6320 3-8-5 46 ow1.............................. MitchGodwin(5) 5
(John Bridger) *led to 4f out: sn wknd: t.o* **25/1**
0006 **7** *5* **Russian Regard (IRE)**[12] 6032 3-9-0 50.............................. RobHornby 1
(Jonathan Portman) *cl up to 1/2-way: urged along over 4f out: sn wknd: t.o* **16/1**

2m 26.93s (0.43) **Going Correction** +0.025s/f (Good) 7 Ran SP% **114.0**
Speed ratings (Par 102): **99,94,94,89,83 70,66**
CSF £36.86 TOTE £3.80: £1.80, £4.10; EX 28.80 Trifecta £78.20.The winner was sold to Andy Smith for £10,000.
**Owner** The Picnic Partnership **Bred** Newsells Park Stud **Trained** Blewbury, Oxon

**FOCUS**
A weak seller.

## 6474 GOODWOOD "FAMOUS FOR FOOD" H'CAP — 1m 1f 197y
3:20 (3:21) (Class 2) (0-100,97) 3-Y-O
£31,125 (£9,320; £4,660; £2,330; £1,165; £585) Stalls Low

Form RPR
0061 1 **Novoman (IRE)**[44] 4865 3-8-13 **94** GeorgiaCox(5) 1 104+
(William Haggas) *t.k.h: mostly trckd ldng pair: led on inner over 2f out: sn pushed clr: 4 l ahd fnl f: ld dwindled nr fin but nvr in any danger* **9/1**
2113 2 1 **Anythingtoday (IRE)**[15] 5940 3-9-7 **97** (p) JosephineGordon 9 104+
(Hugo Palmer) *hld up in last trio: pushed along and prog on outer 2f out: tk 3rd 1f out: styd on and snatched 2nd last strides: no ch w wnr* **10/1**
1230 3 shd **Emenem**[24] 5568 3-8-13 **89** TomMarquand 7 96
(Simon Dow) *mostly chsd ldng trio: rdn 3f out: prog to chse clr wnr jst over 1f out: styd on and clsd gap but no ch and lost 2nd last strides* **16/1**
1312 4 1 1/2 **Eynhallow**[31] 5330 3-9-2 **92** PatDobbs 5 96
(Roger Charlton) *hld up in last trio: prog 2f out: rdn to go 4th jst ins fnl f: no imp or hdwy after* **7/2**[2]
405 5 3 3/4 **Twin Star (IRE)**[37] 5095 3-9-7 **97** (t[1]) OisinMurphy 3 93
(Andrew Balding) *dwlt: sn in tch: shkn up over 2f out: sn lft bhd* **14/1**
-231 6 nse **Karawaan (IRE)**[19] 5746 3-8-8 **84** (t) JimCrowley 4 80
(Sir Michael Stoute) *wl in tch: shkn up over 2f out: nt qckn and no hdwy over 1f out: fdd* **7/1**[3]
-132 7 hd **Frontispiece**[24] 5568 3-8-12 **88** SilvestreDeSousa 6 84
(Sir Michael Stoute) *sn restrained into last: pushed along and detached 4f out: struggling after: modest late hdwy* **2/1**[1]
231 8 5 **Tribal Conquest (IRE)**[22] 5632 3-8-13 **89** MartinLane 8 75
(Charlie Appleby) *led or disp tl def advantage 1/2-way: hdd over 2f out: lost 2nd and wknd qckly jst over 1f out* **8/1**
1000 9 6 **Never Surrender (IRE)**[25] 5525 3-8-6 **85** (p) CallumShepherd(3) 2 59
(Charles Hills) *dwlt: rapid rcvry to dispute ld to 1/2-way: rdn 3f out: wknd qckly wl over 1f out* **20/1**
2m 4.64s (-3.46) **Going Correction** +0.025s/f (Good) **9** Ran SP% **115.6**
Speed ratings (Par 106): **114,113,113,111,108 108,108,104,99**
CSF £94.54 CT £1416.86 TOTE £8.90: £2.80, £2.50, £4.50; EX 101.10 Trifecta £2449.60.
**Owner** Sheikh Ahmed Al Maktoum **Bred** Gerard Mullins **Trained** Newmarket, Suffolk

**FOCUS**
A decent 3yo handicap.

## 6475 GOODWOOD AMATEUR RIDERS' H'CAP — 1m 1f 11y
3:55 (3:56) (Class 5) (0-75,77) 4-Y-O+ £4,991 (£1,548; £773; £387) Stalls Low

Form RPR
3636 1 **Mr Red Clubs (IRE)**[9] 6158 8-11-6 **73** (p) MrFTett 1 82
(Henry Tett) *hld up off the pce in midfield: rdn and prog on outer over 2f out: led over 1f out: kpt on and clr fnl f* **25/1**
-100 2 2 **City Ground (USA)**[14] 5968 10-10-11 **64** MissSBrotherton 6 69
(Michael Appleby) *chsd clr ldrs: pushed along over 3f out: lost pl sltly over 2f out: rdn and prog over 1f out: styd on to take 2nd last 75yds* **8/1**
422 3 1 1/4 **Stanley (GER)**[18] 5805 6-11-7 **74** (p[1]) MrJamesKing 5 76
(Jonjo O'Neill) *chsd clr ldng pair: rdn wl over 2f out: chsd ldr sn after to over 1f out: kpt on u.p* **5/1**[3]
0460 4 nk **Knight Of The Air**[51] 4561 5-9-9 **55** (t[1]) MrsCPownall(7) 11 57
(Joseph Tuite) *led at furious pce: 6 l clr 1/2-way: hdd and no ex over 1f out: lost 2 pls ins fnl f* **40/1**
6244 5 2 3/4 **The Gay Cavalier**[16] 5888 6-10-10 **68** (t) MissHVKnowles(5) 2 64
(John Ryan) *dwlt: hld up in last trio and way off the pce: nudged along and stdy prog over 3f out: chsd ldrs over 1f out: kpt on same pce after* **9/1**
3244 6 shd **Biotic**[11] 6075 6-11-7 **74** (p[1]) MrPMillman 4 70
(Rod Millman) *prog to chse clr ldng trio 1/2-way: rdn 3f out: fdd fr 2f out* **7/2**[2]
5100 7 nse **Victor's Bet (SPA)**[17] 5838 8-10-11 **69** MissEllaSmith(5) 8 65
(Ralph J Smith) *hld up in last trio and way off the pce: rdn and plugged on fr over 2f out: nrst fin but no ch* **16/1**
033- 8 6 **Ritasun (FR)**[21] 8379 4-11-1 **73** MrBJames(5) 3 56
(Harry Whittington) *chsd clr ldrs rdn 3f out: wknd 2f out* **10/1**
50-6 9 3/4 **Top Diktat**[17] 5838 9-10-4 **64** MissBeckyButler(7) 9 45
(Gary Moore) *hld up off the pce in midfield: rdn 3f out: no real prog* **16/1**
112 10 15 **Believe It (IRE)**[17] 5821 5-11-10 **77** (b) MrHHunt 7 27
(Richard Hughes) *chsd clr ldr to over 2f out: wknd qckly over 1f out: t.o* **10/3**[1]
0016 11 6 **Breakheart (IRE)**[12] 6035 10-9-9 **55** oh2 (v) MrCallumMcBride(7) 12
(Andrew Balding) *s.i.s: hld up in last trio and a wl bhd: t.o 3f out* **20/1**
1m 57.54s (1.24) **Going Correction** +0.025s/f (Good) **11** Ran SP% **115.0**
Speed ratings (Par 103): **95,93,92,91,89 89,89,83,83,69 64**
CSF £205.00 CT £1174.72 TOTE £27.40: £6.70, £1.90, £2.00; EX 358.50 Trifecta £2268.40.
**Owner** Mrs Victoria Tett **Bred** Tally-Ho Stud **Trained** Lambourn, Berks

**FOCUS**
They were soon strung out, with the fourth-placed finisher opening up a clear lead.

## 6476 WEATHERBYS RACING BANK SUPREME STKS (GROUP 3) — 7f
4:30 (4:30) (Class 1) 3-Y-O+
£34,026 (£12,900; £6,456; £3,216; £1,614; £810) Stalls Low

Form RPR
0-66 1 **Dutch Connection**[42] 4935 5-9-0 112 JimCrowley 9 115
(Charles Hills) *chsd clr ldr: clsd fr over 2f out: rdn to ld 1f out: drew away last 100yds* **13/8**[1]
4352 2 2 **Salateen**[22] 5662 5-9-0 107 PhillipMakin 1 110
(David O'Meara) *led at str pce and spreadeagled rivals: rdn 2f out: hdd 1f out: no ex last 100yds* **9/4**[2]
6110 3 1 **Viscount Barfield**[29] 5393 4-9-0 105 (h) RobHornby 4 107
(Andrew Balding) *chsd clr ldng pair: shkn up to cl over 2f out: kpt on fr over 1f out: nvr pce to chal* **7/1**
4 4 3 1/2 **Orangey Red (IRE)**[24] 5583 4-8-11 94 FranBerry 5 94
(W T Farrell, Ire) *chsd clr ldng trio: shkn up jst over 2f out: no imp after* **25/1**
1351 5 2 **Bless Him (IRE)**[66] 3997 3-8-9 100 (h) OisinMurphy 6 90
(David Simcock) *stdd s: hld up in last and wl off the pce: nvr able to make any impact: tk modest 5th over 1f out* **7/2**[3]
211- 6 4 **Phijee**[379] 5416 3-8-9 96 SamHitchcott 2 79
(William Muir) *awkward s: racd wl off the pce in 5th and sn struggling: nvr a factor: wknd fnl f* **20/1**
1m 24.21s (-2.79) **Going Correction** +0.025s/f (Good)
**WFA** 3 from 4yo+ 5lb **6** Ran SP% **112.2**
Speed ratings (Par 113): **116,113,112,108,106 101**
CSF £5.53 TOTE £2.00: £1.20, £1.70; EX 5.90 Trifecta £16.80.
**Owner** Godolphin **Bred** Mrs S M Roy **Trained** Lambourn, Berks

**FOCUS**
An ordinary Group 3 that only really concerned the first two, with the runners (in the order in which they finished) racing 2-1-3-4-6-5.

## 6477 LEVIN DOWN FILLIES' H'CAP — 1m 3f 218y
5:05 (5:05) (Class 3) (0-90,85) 3-Y-O+ £12,450 (£3,728; £1,864; £932; £466) Stalls High

Form RPR
0113 1 **Lady Bergamot (FR)**[29] 5439 3-8-9 **78** GeorgeWood(3) 6 85
(James Fanshawe) *mde all: shkn up over 2f out: hrd pressed fr over 1f out: drvn and hld on wl fnl f* **9/4**[2]
1124 2 hd **White Chocolate (IRE)**[25] 5529 3-9-5 **85** JimCrowley 5 92
(David Simcock) *trckd ldng pair: rdn to take 2nd 2f out and sn chalng: pressed wnr hrd thrght fnl f: jst hld* **13/8**[1]
4116 3 1 3/4 **Three Duchesses**[25] 5529 3-9-5 **85** SilvestreDeSousa 4 89
(Michael Bell) *hld up in last pair: rdn over 2f out: styd on to take 3rd 1f out: no imp on ldng pair fnl 100yds* **8/1**
2332 4 2 1/4 **Nathania**[20] 5715 3-9-4 **84** ShaneKelly 1 85
(Richard Hughes) *c out of stall slowly: hld up in last pair: clsd on ldrs over 2f out: rdn and nt qckn wl over 1f out: fdd ins fnl f* **9/2**[3]
1602 5 1 3/4 **Falcon Cliffs (IRE)**[15] 5932 3-8-9 **75** RobHornby 3 73
(William Muir) *chsd wnr: rdn and lost 2nd 2f out: stl cl up jst over 1f out: wknd fnl f* **9/1**
2m 40.09s (1.69) **Going Correction** +0.025s/f (Good) **5** Ran SP% **108.2**
Speed ratings (Par 104): **95,94,93,92,91**
CSF £6.07 TOTE £2.60: £2.40, £1.40; EX 5.60 Trifecta £17.80.
**Owner** Andrew & Julia Turner **Bred** Sarl Elevage Du Haras De Bourgeauville **Trained** Newmarket, Suffolk

**FOCUS**
A fair fillies' handicap, although the winner was allowed the run of the race.

## 6478 MOLECOMB BLUE H'CAP — 5f
5:40 (5:41) (Class 5) (0-70,74) 3-Y-O+ £4,528 (£1,347; £673; £336) Stalls High

Form RPR
-022 1 **Operative**[12] 6040 4-9-10 **70** SilvestreDeSousa 2 79
(Ed de Giles) *slowly away: chsd other pair in centre: clsd 2f out: drvn to chal fnl f: led cl home* **15/8**[1]
0153 2 nk **The Big Short**[9] 6148 3-9-1 **63** JimCrowley 4 71
(Charles Hills) *racd centre and on terms: drvn and overall ldr 1f out: kpt on wl but hdd cl home* **9/2**[2]
425- 3 1 1/2 **Her Terms**[251] 8453 3-9-2 **67** HectorCrouch(3) 6 70
(Clive Cox) *w ldrs: overall ldr on outer of nr side gp 2f out to 1f out: one pce* **8/1**[3]
1140 4 1 **Roundabout Magic (IRE)**[118] 2235 3-8-13 **66** PaddyBradley(5) 7 65
(Simon Dow) *w ldrs towards nr side: overall ldr 3f out to 2f out: one pce over 1f out* **25/1**
0344 5 shd **Zipedeedodah (IRE)**[14] 5967 5-9-9 **69** (t) OisinMurphy 8 68
(Joseph Tuite) *hld up towards nr side: trckd ldrs 2f out: rdn and nt qckn over 1f out: one pce after* **10/1**
6343 6 1 1/4 **Prominna**[8] 6179 7-8-12 **58** TomMarquand 10 52
(Tony Carroll) *hld up: effrt and cl up bhd ldrs 2f out: nt qckn over 1f out: fdd* **16/1**
2302 7 nse **Captain Ryan**[13] 6004 6-9-1 **61** TimmyMurphy 11 55
(Geoffrey Deacon) *hld up towards nr side: effrt wl over 1f out: sn rdn and no prog* **9/1**
50 8 nk **Archimedes (IRE)**[23] 5587 4-9-6 **66** (tp) FranBerry 15 59
(David C Griffiths) *w ldr towards nr side: nt qckn 2f out: fdd over 1f out* **20/1**
211 9 1 **Ask The Guru**[16] 5871 7-8-9 **55** (b) KierenFox 3 44
(Michael Attwater) *w ldr in centre tl wknd u.p over 1f out* **12/1**
2000 10 3/4 **Harrison Stickle**[19] 5750 5-8-13 **59** ShaneKelly 16 46
(John Gallagher) *dwlt: hld up towards nr side: rdn 2f out: no prog* **25/1**
020 11 2 1/4 **Pour La Victoire (IRE)**[2] 6373 7-9-3 **68** (v) GeorgiaCox(5) 5 46
(Tony Carroll) *slowly away: outpcd and a bhd* **11/1**
0050 12 3 1/4 **Deer Song**[2] 6373 4-8-5 **56** ow2 MitchGodwin(5) 13 23
(John Bridger) *overall ldr towards nr side 2f: hrd rdn over 2f out: sn btn* **33/1**
006 13 21 **Molly Jones**[65] 4043 8-8-5 **51** oh2 RyanPowell 12
(Matthew Salaman) *rdr lost both irons sn after s: allowed to coast home in own time* **40/1**
57.32s (-2.88) **Going Correction** -0.50s/f (Hard)
**WFA** 3 from 4yo+ 2lb **13** Ran SP% **122.9**
Speed ratings (Par 103): **103,102,100,98,98 96,96,95,94,93 89,84,50**
CSF £9.06 CT £58.06 TOTE £2.60: £1.60, £2.30, £2.80; EX 12.80 Trifecta £88.60.
**Owner** Gwyn & Samantha Powell & Partner **Bred** Whitsbury Manor Stud **Trained** Ledbury, H'fords

**FOCUS**
The middle of the track was the place to be, with low-drawn runners dominating.
T/Plt: £158.00 to a £1 stake. Pool: £96,375.57 - 445.20 winning units. T/Qpdt: £35.40 to a £1 stake. Pool: £6,218.89 - 129.89 winning units. **Jonathan Neesom**

# 6292 YARMOUTH (L-H)
Sunday, August 27

**OFFICIAL GOING: Good to firm (watered; 7.8)**
Wind: light, behind Weather: sunny and warm

## 6479 BET TOTEPLACEPOT AT BETFRED.COM APPRENTICE H'CAP — 1m 2f 23y
2:20 (2:20) (Class 5) (0-70,71) 4-Y-O+ £4,528 (£1,347; £673; £336) Stalls Low

Form RPR
0120 1 **Hannington**[8] 6188 6-8-13 **60** (t) GabrieleMalune(3) 5 65
(Michael Appleby) *trckd ldrs: rdn to ld over 2f out: sustained duel w runner-up after: kpt on wl u.p ins fnl f: jst prevailed on the nod* **9/1**
554 2 shd **Hard Toffee (IRE)**[9] 6144 6-9-11 **69** FinleyMarsh 2 73
(Conrad Allen) *led tl over 2f out: sn rdn and sustained duel w wnr fnl 2f: kpt on wl u.p ins fnl f: jst btn on the nod* **3/1**[2]

5004 **3** 2 **King Of Dreams**$^{18}$ 5800 4-9-6 **71** ................................ GeorgeBass$^{(7)}$ 3 71
(David Simcock) *stdd s: hld up in tch in last pair: swtchd rt and hdwy over 3f out: rdn to chse ldng pair 2f out: kpt on ins fnl f: nvr quite enough pce to rch ldng pair* **4/1$^{3}$**

5640 **4** 5 **Color Force (IRE)**$^{4}$ 6306 4-8-7 **51** oh5............................(p) MillyNaseb 4 41
(Gay Kelleway) *stdd and awkward leaving stalls: hld up in tch in rr: effrt to go 4th 2f out: no imp after: plugged on same pce* **22/1**

6520 **5** 6 **Sunshineandbubbles**$^{31}$ 5336 4-8-6 **55**.........................(p) TobyEley$^{(5)}$ 6 33
(Daniel Mark Loughnane) *trckd ldrs: rdn over 3f out: lost pl and bhd ent fnl 2f: wknd over 1f out* **12/1**

0322 **6** 2 **Zorba The Greek**$^{19}$ 5747 5-9-12 **70**.........................(b$^{1}$) CameronNoble 1 44
(Ed Vaughan) *t.k.h: chsd ldr: clsd to join ldr over 3f out: rdn over 2f out: sn btn and lost pl: wknd over 1f out* **11/8$^{1}$**

2m 8.49s (-2.01) **Going Correction** -0.50s/f (Hard) 6 Ran SP% **109.1**
Speed ratings (Par 103): **88,87,86,82,77 75**
CSF £33.90 TOTE £10.70: £3.20, £1.80; EX 29.00 Trifecta £161.80.
**Owner** From The Front Racing **Bred** Bearstone Stud Ltd **Trained** Oakham, Rutland

**FOCUS**
A warm sunny day and ground on the quick side for this seven-race card. There was a slight tailwind up the straight. A modest little handicap to kick things off and the form is weakened further by the warm favourite running no sort of race.

## 6480 BET TOTEJACKPOT AT BETFRED.COM EBF FILLIES' NOVICE STKS (PLUS 10 RACE) 6f 3y
**2:55** (2:57) (Class 4) 2-Y-O **£5,175** (£1,540; £769; £384) **Stalls** Centre

Form RPR

**1** **Zain Hana** 2-9-0 0........................................................................ JFEgan 5 80+
(Jeremy Noseda) *in tch in midfield: clsd to chse ldrs over 3f out: rdn wl over 1f out: styd on to chal over 1f out: led 1f out: kpt on wl and a holding runner-up ins fnl f* **7/1**

03 **2** nk **Foxtrot Lady**$^{11}$ 6070 2-9-0 0.............................................. DavidProbert 4 80
(Andrew Balding) *led: rdn 2f out: jnd and rdn over 1f out: kpt on wl u.p but a jst hld by wnr* **7/1**

42 **3** 1 1/2 **Perfect Thought**$^{20}$ 5702 2-9-0 0.................................. RobertWinston 15 75
(William Haggas) *taken down early: chsd ldrs tl wnt 2nd ent fnl 2f: 3rd and unable qck over 1f out: kpt on same pce ins fnl f* **9/2$^{2}$**

**4** 2 1/4 **Ganayem (IRE)** 2-9-0 0........................................................ DaneO'Neill 2 68+
(Owen Burrows) *stdd after s: t.k.h: rn green and hld up in tch towards rr: rdn and hdwy over 1f out: styd on steadily to go 4th ins fnl f: kpt on: no threat to ldrs* **3/1$^{1}$**

04 **5** nk **Hollywood Dream**$^{25}$ 5528 2-9-0 0.......................... RichardKingscote 12 67
(William Muir) *t.k.h: hld up in tch in midfield: effrt and hdwy to chse ldrs over 1f out: sn rdn and kpt on same pce ins fnl f* **6/1$^{3}$**

**6** 1 **Club Tropicana** 2-9-0 0................................................ StevieDonohoe 8 64+
(Richard Spencer) *hld up in tch towards rr: rdn over 2f out: hdwy into midfield over 1f out: swtchd lft ins fnl f: kpt on wl fnl 100yds: nvr trbld ldrs* **16/1**

**7** 1/2 **Image** 2-9-0 0.......................................................................... MartinHarley 6 63
(Philip McBride) *hld up in tch in midfield: rdn and unable qck over 1f out: no threat to ldrs but kpt on steadily ins fnl f* **50/1**

**8** hd **Shesaidyes (IRE)** 2-9-0 0............................................ DanielMuscutt 13 62
(Henry Spiller) *dwlt: hld up in tch towards rr: pushed along ent fnl 2f: swtchd rt hdwy ent fnl f: rdn and styd on ins fnl f: nvr trbld ldrs* **33/1**

0 **9** 1 1/4 **Wild Impala (FR)**$^{45}$ 4815 2-9-0 0.............................................. TedDurcan 3 59
(John Gosden) *in tch in midfield: pushed along over 2f out: unable qck and no imp tl kpt on ins fnl f: nvr trbld ldrs* **9/2$^{2}$**

**10** 1 **Miss Minding (IRE)** 2-9-0 0............................................. LiamKeniry 16 56
(Ed Dunlop) *stdd after s: t.k.h: hld up in tch towards rr: shkn up wl over 1f out: no real imp whn sltly squeezed for room 1f out: nvr trbld ldrs* **50/1**

05 **11** 3/4 **Elusive Bird**$^{52}$ 4539 2-9-0 0.............................................. PatCosgrave 9 53
(Giles Bravery) *hld up in tch towards rr: clsd to chse ldrs over 3f out: rdn jst over 2f out: sn struggling and outpcd whn edgd lft over 1f out: wknd fnl f* **150/1**

25 **12** 1/2 **Princess Keira (IRE)**$^{31}$ 5327 2-9-0 0.......................... JamieSpencer 1 52
(Mick Quinn) *in tch in midfield: effrt and hdwy over 2f out: rdn and no imp over 1f out: wknd ins fnl f* **14/1**

0 **13** 7 **Chloellie**$^{25}$ 5534 2-8-7 0.............................................. GinaMangan$^{(7)}$ 10 31
(J R Jenkins) *chsd ldr tl ent fnl 2f: pushed along and lost pl qckly over 1f out: bhd ins fnl f* **150/1**

5 **14** 7 **Ferrier**$^{24}$ 5576 2-9-0 0...............................................(h) LukeMorris 7 10
(Sir Mark Prescott Bt) *chsd ldrs tl 1/2-way: sn rdn and steadily lost pl: bhd over 1f out: eased wl ins fnl f* **50/1**

00 **15** 3 3/4 **Raise A Little Joy**$^{25}$ 5534 2-9-0 0.......................... AlistairRawlinson 11
(J R Jenkins) *chsd ldrs tl rdn and lost pl over 2f out: bhd over 1f out: eased wl ins fnl f* **100/1**

0 **16** 9 **Koin**$^{82}$ 3437 2-8-9 0................................................ GeorgeBuckell$^{(5)}$ 14
(Mark H Tompkins) *sn outpcd in detached last: t.o fnl 2f* **150/1**

1m 10.69s (-3.71) **Going Correction** -0.50s/f (Hard) 16 Ran SP% **125.0**
Speed ratings (Par 93): **104,103,101,98,98 96,96,95,94,92 91,91,81,72,67 55**
CSF £56.15 TOTE £9.40: £3.10, £2.40, £1.90; EX 66.90 Trifecta £354.60.
**Owner** Asaad Al Banwan **Bred** Al-Baha Bloodstock **Trained** Newmarket, Suffolk

**FOCUS**
This looked a warm event with those that have run setting a reasonable standard and several of the newcomers were interesting on paper, not least Ganayem. This ought to throw up winners. The level is fluid. The third and fifth help set the opening level.

## 6481 TOTEQUADPOT AT BETFRED.COM NURSERY H'CAP 6f 3y
**3:30** (3:31) (Class 4) (0-80,79) 2-Y-O **£5,040** (£1,508; £754; £377; £188) **Stalls** Centre

Form RPR

1313 **1** **Tulip Fever**$^{23}$ 5614 2-9-6 **78**............................................. PatCosgrave 2 81
(William Haggas) *t.k.h: sn trcking ldrs: rdn 2f out: sn ev ch: led 1f out and forged ahd ins fnl f: styd on: rdn out* **7/2$^{2}$**

21U3 **2** 1/2 **Mraseel (IRE)**$^{19}$ 5751 2-9-4 **76**.....................................(p) MartinHarley 7 77
(James Tate) *t.k.h: hld up in tch: effrt 2f out: nt clr run and swtchd rt over 1f out: hdwy u.p 1f out: edgd lft but styd on wl to go 2nd towards fin* **4/1$^{3}$**

0234 **3** 1/2 **Austin Powers (IRE)**$^{22}$ 5644 2-9-0 **72**.............................. DaneO'Neill 1 72
(Mark Johnston) *led: rdn ent fnl 2f: hdd 1f out: styd on but unable qck fnl 100yds: lost 2nd towards fin* **8/1**

1614 **4** 3/4 **Holy Tiber (IRE)**$^{23}$ 5596 2-9-7 **79**.................................. JamieSpencer 5 76
(George Scott) *stdd and awkward leaving stalls: hld up in tch in rr: rdn and hdwy ent fnl 2f: pressed ldrs over 1f out: kpt on same pce ins fnl f: edgd lft towards fin* **3/1$^{1}$**

2010 **5** 3/4 **First Drive**$^{22}$ 5659 2-9-2 **74**............................................. LouisSteward 6 69
(Michael Bell) *hld up in tch in last pair: swtchd lft and hdwy u.p over 1f out: hung lft ins fnl f: no imp fnl 100yds* **11/2**

3051 **6** 1 3/4 **City Guest (IRE)**$^{27}$ 5474 2-8-12 **75**.................................. JaneElliott$^{(5)}$ 3 64
(George Margarson) *trckd ldrs: rdn 2f out: unable qck over 1f out: wknd ins fnl f* **14/1**

0060 **7** 1 1/2 **Devil's Cowboy (IRE)**$^{24}$ 5572 2-8-10 **68**......................... DavidProbert 4 53
(Charles Hills) *t.k.h: pressed ldr tl rdn and ev ch 2f out: unable qck and lost pl ent fnl f: wknd ins fnl f* **15/2**

1m 11.48s (-2.92) **Going Correction** -0.50s/f (Hard) 7 Ran SP% **112.1**
Speed ratings (Par 96): **99,98,97,96,95 93,91**
CSF £17.12 TOTE £3.70: £1.40, £2.90; EX 20.00 Trifecta £51.50.
**Owner** Mrs Deborah June James **Bred** Mrs D J James **Trained** Newmarket, Suffolk

**FOCUS**
A competitive little event for the grade and a few were still in with a chance entering the final furlong. The runner-up and third help set a straightforward looking level.

## 6482 BET TOTEEXACTA AT BETFRED.COM H'CAP 1m 2f 23y
**4:05** (4:05) (Class 2) (0-100,91) 3-Y-O+
**£14,317** (£4,287; £2,143; £1,071; £535; £269) **Stalls** Low

Form RPR

4011 **1** **Teodoro (IRE)**$^{51}$ 4580 3-9-3 **88**...........................(h) RichardKingscote 7 99
(Tom Dascombe) *mde all: rdn ent fnl 2f: styd on strly u.p and in command ins fnl f: rdn out* **8/1**

2221 **2** 2 1/2 **Mafaaheem (IRE)**$^{19}$ 5757 3-9-6 **91**.................................... DaneO'Neill 1 97
(Owen Burrows) *chsd ldng pair: effrt to chse wnr ent fnl 2f: drvn and unable qck over 1f out: clr 2nd and styd on same pce ins fnl f* **11/4$^{2}$**

2312 **3** 2 **Another Eclipse (IRE)**$^{22}$ 5634 3-9-2 **87**....................... JamieSpencer 4 89
(David Simcock) *chsd ldng trio: effrt to chse ldrs 2f out: 3rd and unable qck over 1f out: kpt on same pce ins fnl f* **2/1$^{1}$**

204- **4** 2 **Shabbah (IRE)**$^{339}$ 6715 4-9-12 **90**........................................ TedDurcan 6 87
(Sir Michael Stoute) *hld up in tch in midfield: swtchd rt and effrt over 2f out: kpt on same pce and no imp fr over 1f out: wnt 4th wl ins fnl f* **16/1**

21- **5** 1/2 **Laqab (IRE)**$^{315}$ 7384 4-9-5 **83**......................................... DanielMuscutt 2 79
(Roger Varian) *chsd wnr tl rdn and dropped to 4th ent fnl 2f: unable qck and plugged on same pce u.p after: lost 4th wl ins fnl f* **9/2$^{3}$**

6120 **6** 1/2 **Daawy (IRE)**$^{44}$ 4856 3-9-3 **88**......................................(p$^{1}$) PatCosgrave 3 84
(William Haggas) *s.i.s and bmpd leaving stalls: rousted along early: in tch in rr: rdn 4f out: no imp tl kpt on ins fnl f: nvr trbld ldrs* **11/2**

4000 **7** 1/2 **Vettori Rules**$^{32}$ 5287 4-9-4 **82**........................................... LukeMorris 8 76
(Gay Kelleway) *in tch in midfield: rdn and lost pl over 2f out: keeping on same pce and wl hld whn nt clrest of runs ins fnl f* **50/1**

-314 **8** 2 **Afonso De Sousa (USA)**$^{14}$ 5966 7-9-12 **90**........... AlistairRawlinson 5 80
(Michael Appleby) *hld up in last pair: shkn up ent fnl 2f: sn rdn and no hdwy: nvr trbld ldrs* **33/1**

2m 3.66s (-6.84) **Going Correction** -0.50s/f (Hard)
**WFA** 3 from 4yo+ 7lb 8 Ran SP% **115.5**
Speed ratings (Par 109): **107,105,103,101,101 101,100,99**
CSF £30.66 CT £61.56 TOTE £9.20: £2.30, £1.10, £1.40; EX 33.80 Trifecta £70.60.
**Owner** Laurence Bellman & Caroline Ingram **Bred** John Connaughton **Trained** Malpas, Cheshire

**FOCUS**
The feature event on the card but this wouldn't be a strong 0-100 handicap given the highest rated horse was racing off a mark 9lb below the ceiling for the grade, which is a notable gap. The gallop looked fairly steady and the winner made all the running.

## 6483 BET TOTETRIFECTA AT BETFRED.COM H'CAP 1m 3y
**4:40** (4:41) (Class 3) (0-95,93) 3-Y-O-**£9,451** (£2,829; £1,414; £708; £352) **Stalls** Centre

Form RPR

2204 **1** **Brigliadoro (IRE)**$^{15}$ 5914 6-10-0 **93**................................ DavidProbert 5 99
(Philip McBride) *hld up in tch in last pair: clsd 3f out: rdn and ev ch over 1f out: kpt on u.p to ld ins fnl f: hld on wl* **4/1$^{2}$**

2120 **2** nk **Mountain Angel (IRE)**$^{43}$ 4904 3-8-13 **84**....................... PatCosgrave 7 88
(Roger Varian) *s.i.s: hld up in tch in last pair: rdn over 2f out: hdwy to chal over 1f out: kpt on u.p: unable qck cl home* **5/2$^{1}$**

0302 **3** nse **Glory Awaits (IRE)**$^{32}$ 5294 7-9-10 **89**........................(b) JamieSpencer 3 94
(David Simcock) *led: wnt to r alone towards far side after 1f: rdn 2f out: drvn and hrd pressed over 1f out: hdd ins fnl f: unable qck cl home* **8/1**

0062 **4** 4 **Repercussion**$^{14}$ 5966 4-9-10 **89**................................... StevieDonohoe 4 85
(Charlie Fellowes) *chsd ldrs: wnt 2nd and rdn to press wnr jst over 2f out tl outpcd over 1f out: 4th btn whn sltly impeded 1f out: wknd ins fnl f* **9/2$^{3}$**

154 **5** 9 **Takatul (USA)**$^{51}$ 4570 4-9-8 **87**...............................(b) DaneO'Neill 2 62
(Charles Hills) *s.i.s: rousted along and sn rcvrd to chse ldr: rdn and lost 2nd jst over 2f out: 5th and btn over 1f out: no ch whn eased ins fnl f* **4/1$^{2}$**

024 **6** 3/4 **Red Tea**$^{9}$ 6145 4-9-12 **91**.............................................. LukeMorris 6 65
(Peter Hiatt) *in tch in midfield: rdn over 3f out: sn struggling: bhd over 1f out* **7/1**

1m 35.1s (-5.50) **Going Correction** -0.50s/f (Hard)
**WFA** 3 from 4yo+ 6lb 6 Ran SP% **110.4**
Speed ratings (Par 107): **107,106,106,102,93 92**
CSF £13.89 TOTE £5.00: £2.60, £1.70; EX 15.00 Trifecta £113.10.
**Owner** Serafinoagodino,C M Budgett,P J McBride **Bred** D Naughton, Zubieta & Javier Salmean **Trained** Newmarket, Suffolk

**FOCUS**
A competitive little heat in which the front three came clear, with the fourth well clear of the rest. The 'right' horses fought out the finish and the form looks sound enough for the grade.

## 6484 BET TOTEWIN AT BETFRED.COM H'CAP 7f 3y
**5:15** (5:15) (Class 3) (0-95,94) 3-Y-O-**£9,451** (£2,829; £1,414; £708; £352) **Stalls** Centre

Form RPR

-300 **1** **Hyde Park**$^{45}$ 4813 3-9-7 **94**.............................................(t$^{1}$) TedDurcan 8 104
(John Gosden) *hld up in tch in midfield: clsd to trck ldrs 1/2-way: rdn to ld 2f out: kpt on wl ins fnl f: rdn out* **8/1**

0315 **2** 1 1/4 **Firefright (IRE)**$^{23}$ 5612 3-9-2 **89**.................................... JamieSpencer 1 96
(Jeremy Noseda) *hld up in tch in midfield: effrt over 1f out: rdn to chse wnr 1f out: pressing wnr but unable qck u.p ins fnl f: one pce wl ins fnl f* **9/4$^{1}$**

2134 **3** 1 1/4 **Horsted Keynes (FR)**$^{22}$ 5662 7-9-5 **92**..................... GeorgeBuckell$^{(5)}$ 3 98
(David Simcock) *hld up in tch in rr: clsd ent fnl 2f: rdn to press ldng pair 1f out: no ex and outpcd ins fnl f* **7/2$^{2}$**

65-0 **4** 4 1/2 **Fighting Temeraire (IRE)**$^{8}$ 6192 4-9-11 **93**................ RobertWinston 9 86
(Dean Ivory) *t.k.h: chsd ldr tl ent fnl 2f: chsng wnr and drvn over 1f out: lost 2nd and btn 1f out: hung lft and wknd ins fnl f* **12/1**

500 **5** 1 **Gothic Empire (IRE)**$^{29}$ 5415 5-9-3 **85**......................... DanielMuscutt 5 76
(James Fanshawe) *stdd s: hld up in tch in rr: effrt 2f out: struggling to qckn whn nt clrest of runs over 1f out: no prog and wl hld ins fnl f* **6/1**

0022 **6** 4 1/2 **Sultan Baybars**$^{32}$ 5302 3-9-7 **94**................................(v$^{1}$) PatCosgrave 4 71
(Roger Varian) *led: rdn and hdd 2f out: sn dropped out and bhd 1f out* **4/1$^{3}$**

00-0 **7** *1¾* **Barracuda Boy (IRE)**[8] 6186 7-9-9 **91**........................ RichardKingscote 7 65
(Marjorie Fife) *taken down early and ponied to s: chsd ldrs: rdn and lost pl jst over 2f out: bhd 1f out* **18/1**

1m 22.45s (-4.15) **Going Correction** -0.50s/f (Hard)
**WFA** 3 from 4yo+ 5lb **7** Ran SP% **111.3**
Speed ratings (Par 107): **103,101,100,95,93 88,86**
CSF £25.00 CT £72.62 TOTE £8.30: £2.60, £1.80; EX 31.60 Trifecta £155.80.
**Owner** K Abdullah **Bred** Juddmonte Farms Ltd **Trained** Newmarket, Suffolk

**FOCUS**
A competitive heat and the front three came away in the final furlong.

## 6485 BET TOTEPLACE AT BETFRED.COM H'CAP — 7f 3y
**5:50** (5:50) (Class 5) (0-70,72) 3-Y-0+ **£4,410** (£1,320; £660; £330; £164) **Stalls** Centre

Form RPR

034 **1** **Noble Masterpiece**[29] 5431 3-9-11 **72**.................. StevieDonohoe 1 81+
(Sir Michael Stoute) *taken down early: stdd s: hld up in tch in last trio: clsd and travelling strly whn nt clr run 2f out: gap opened 1f out: rdn and qcknd to ld ins fnl f: sn in command: comf* **9/2**[1]

0115 **2** *2* **Golden Guest**[24] 5560 3-9-3 **69**........................................ JaneElliott(5) 8 72
(George Margarson) *hld up in tch in last trio: effrt 2f out: hdwy and rdn to chal over 1f out: kpt on u.p but nt match pce of wnr fnl 100yds* **11/2**[3]

0225 **3** *nse* **Patching**[8] 6203 3-9-6 **67**...............................................(b) JFEgan 9 69
(Giles Bravery) *t.k.h: chsd ldr for 2f: styd prom: rdn to ld 2f out: kpt on u.p tl hdd and nt match pce of wnr ins fnl f* **5/1**[2]

-014 **4** *¾* **Paradwys (IRE)**[14] 5965 3-9-7 **71**............................(p) EdwardGreatrex(3) 6 71
(Archie Watson) *taken down early: chsd ldrs: effrt to press ldrs ent fnl 2f: ev ch u.p over 1f out: no ex and outpcd fnl 100yds* **8/1**

0451 **5** *4* **African Blessing**[14] 5958 4-10-0 **70**.................................. LukeMorris 7 62
(Charlie Wallis) *hld up wl in tch in midfield: effrt to chal 2f out: drvn and outpcd over 1f out: wknd fnl f* **10/1**

022 **6** *2¾* **Still Waiting**[16] 5870 3-9-4 **65**........................................ DavidProbert 3 47
(William Jarvis) *s.i.s: hld up in tch in rr: clsd over 2f out: nt clr run wl over 1f out: no hdwy u.p jst over 1f out: wl hld fnl f* **9/2**[1]

5045 **7** *2½* **Monarch Maid**[13] 6004 6-8-11 **60**.................................. WilliamCox(7) 4 37
(Peter Hiatt) *led tl rdn and hdd 2f out: sn lost pl: bhd 1f out* **20/1**

1654 **8** *2* **Pass The Cristal (IRE)**[17] 5835 3-9-2 **63**.................. RichardKingscote 5 33
(William Muir) *t.k.h: chsd ldrs tl wnt 2nd after 2f: rdn and lost pl ent fnl 2f: bhd 1f out* **9/2**[1]

1m 23.13s (-3.47) **Going Correction** -0.50s/f (Hard)
**WFA** 3 from 4yo+ 5lb **8** Ran SP% **111.6**
Speed ratings (Par 103): **99,96,96,95,91 88,85,82**
CSF £27.74 CT £125.01 TOTE £3.90: £1.30, £2.30, £2.10; EX 30.80 Trifecta £172.80.
**Owner** Saeed Suhail **Bred** Cheveley Park Stud Ltd **Trained** Newmarket, Suffolk

**FOCUS**
A run-of-the-mill Class 5 handicap but it threw up a lightly-raced winner who looks some way ahead of his opening mark.
T/Plt: £46.10 to a £1 stake. Pool: £78,693.86 - 1,245.36 winning units. T/Qpdt: £9.00 to a £1 stake. Pool: £6,155.08 - 502.44 winning units. **Steve Payne**

6486 - (Foreign Racing) - See Raceform Interactive

# 6239 CURRAGH (R-H)
Sunday, August 27

**OFFICIAL GOING: Straight course - yielding (good in places) ; round course - good**

## 6487a FLAME OF TARA IRISH EBF STKS (GROUP 3) (FILLIES) — 1m
**2:00** (2:00) 2-Y-0
**£40,341** (£12,991; £6,153; £2,735; £1,367; £683)

RPR

**1** **Liquid Amber (USA)**[8] 6211 2-9-0 **0**........................................ WJLee 3 107+
(W McCreery, Ire) *chsd ldrs in 4th: pushed along over 2f out and gd prog to chal in 2nd ent fnl f: led 200yds out and sn rdn clr: impressive* **10/1**[3]

**2** *5* **Ballet Shoes (IRE)**[16] 5903 2-9-0 **104**.................................. RyanMoore 7 96
(A P O'Brien, Ire) *chsd ldrs in 3rd: rdn over 2f out and prog to ld under 2f out: sn pressed for ld and hdd 200yds out: no ex u.p and one pce* **2/7**[1]

**3** *2* **Sometimesadiamond (IRE)**[56] 4418 2-9-0 **0**.............. KevinManning 1 92
(J S Bolger, Ire) *towards rr in 6th: rdn over 2f out and kpt on steadily u.p to go 3rd over 1f out: kpt on but nvr a threat* **14/1**

**4** *2* **Bye Bye Baby (IRE)**[14] 5972 2-9-0 **0**.................. SeamieHeffernan 2 87
(A P O'Brien, Ire) *bit slowly away: towards rr in 5th: rdn 3f out and sme prog u.p to go 4th 1f out but nvr nr to chal* **12/1**

**5** *7* **Beach Wedding (IRE)**[19] 5769 2-9-0 **0**............................ RoryCleary 4 72
(J P Murtagh, Ire) *trckd ldr in 2nd: rdn over 2f out and sn nt qckn w principals: no ex and one pce* **33/1**

**6** *1¼* **Black Sails**[7] 6242 2-9-0 **0**................................................ ColinKeane 6 69
(G M Lyons, Ire) *sn led: set str pce: stl 3 l clr over 2f out and rdn: sn reduced advantage and hdd under 2f out: no ex u.p and wknd* **7/1**[2]

**7** *12* **Quite Subunctious (IRE)**[9] 6163 2-9-0 **0**...................... RossCoakley 5 43
(Keith Henry Clarke, Ire) *a in rr of strung out field: detached over 2f out: nvr in contention* **100/1**

1m 39.17s (-6.83) **Going Correction** -0.65s/f (Hard) **7** Ran SP% **117.6**
Speed ratings: **108,103,101,99,92 90,78**
CSF £13.98 TOTE £10.80: £5.50, £1.02; DF 18.10 Trifecta £52.00.
**Owner** Niarchos Family **Bred** Flaxman Holdings Limited **Trained** Rathbride, Co Kildare

**FOCUS**
A race run at a good gallop produced a surprise, with the long odds-on favourite proving no match for a filly who was making a quick reappearance after a debut second. The runner-up has been rated a bit below her Tipperary win.

## 6488a PLUSVITAL ROUND TOWER STKS (GROUP 3) — 6f
**2:35** (2:35) 2-Y-0
**£31,769** (£10,230; £4,846; £2,153; £1,076; £538) **Stalls** Centre

RPR

**1** **U S Navy Flag (USA)**[14] 5973 2-9-3 **108**..........................(bt) RyanMoore 5 114
(A P O'Brien, Ire) *mde all: pushed along 2f out: rdn clr 1f out: kpt on strly ins fnl f* **5/4**[1]

**2** *6* **Landshark**[17] 5858 2-9-3 **0**........................................ ColmO'Donoghue 7 96
(Mrs John Harrington, Ire) *chsd ldrs in 3rd: rdn over 2f out and kpt on wl u.p but no imp on wnr fr over 1f out: wnt 2nd cl home* **7/2**[2]

**3** *nk* **Ball Girl (IRE)**[19] 5769 2-9-0 **0**................................................ ColinKeane 1 92
(G M Lyons, Ire) *racd alone in centre of crse: sn 2nd: rdn over 2f out: kpt on wl u.p but nt qckn w wnr ent fnl f and one pce: dropped to 3rd cl home* **9/2**[3]



**4** *hd* **Sankari Royale (IRE)**[9] 6136 2-9-0 **0**.................................. NGMcCullagh 3 91
(J P Murtagh, Ire) *hld up in 6th: rdn over 2f out: keeping on whn short of room between horses ent fnl f and swtchd lft: r.o wl to go 4th cl home* **8/1**

**5** *1* **Golden Spell**[8] 6213 2-9-0 **93**........................................ ShaneFoley 8 88
(J P Murtagh, Ire) *chsd ldrs in 5th: rdn over 2f out: shifted to rt u.p under 2f out: sn no ex and one pce* **14/1**

**6** *4¾* **Gasta (IRE)**[56] 4418 2-9-0 **93**........................................ KevinManning 6 74
(J S Bolger, Ire) *s.i.s and sn in rr: rdn over 2f out but no ex and kpt on same pce u.p* **22/1**

**7** *1¾* **Youareiffraaj (IRE)** 2-9-3 **0**................................................ GaryHalpin 4 72
(John James Feane, Ire) *bit s.i.s and pushed along early: hld up in 7th: pushed along on outer after 1/2-way but sn no imp: nvr in contention* **100/1**

**8** *nk* **Betsey Trotter (IRE)**[14] 5970 2-9-0 **0**.................................. PatSmullen 2 77+
(D K Weld, Ire) *chsd ldrs in 4th: rdn over 2f out and no ex u.p: sn hung rt: eased ins fnl f* **12/1**

1m 12.73s (-2.77) **Going Correction** -0.375s/f (Firm) **8** Ran SP% **115.7**
Speed ratings: **103,95,94,94,93 86,84,83**
CSF £5.79 TOTE £1.60: £1.02, £1.70, £2.00; DF 6.10 Trifecta £20.10.
**Owner** Derrick Smith & Mrs John Magnier & Michael Tabor **Bred** Misty For Me Syndicate **Trained** Cashel, Co Tipperary

**FOCUS**
The favourite stood out on paper and duly won in decisive fashion. He appeals as a horse who can compete effectively at a high level.

## 6490a SNOW FAIRY FILLIES STKS (GROUP 3) — 1m 1f
**3:45** (3:47) 3-Y-0+
**£32,777** (£10,555; £5,000; £2,222; £1,111; £555)

RPR

**1** **Rain Goddess (IRE)**[15] 5954 3-9-0 **110**............................(t) RyanMoore 7 103+
(A P O'Brien, Ire) *sn trckd ldr in 2nd: rdn to cl 2f out and kpt on wl u.p to ld 100yds out: styd on strly but reduced advantage cl home* **11/4**[1]

**2** *½* **Intimation**[113] 2392 5-9-7 **104**........................................ ColinKeane 1 102+
(Sir Michael Stoute) *mid-div: 8th 1/2-way: gng wl 2f out but short of room bhd horses and sn taken to outer: r.o wl u.p to go 2nd cl home: nrst fin* **11/4**[1]

**3** *½* **Dawn Of Hope (IRE)**[47] 4718 4-9-7 **105**........................ AndreaAtzeni 13 101+
(Roger Varian) *chsd ldrs: 6th 1/2-way: rdn over 2f out and prog u.p to go 4th 2f out: wnt 3rd ins fnl f: kpt on wl but no ex cl home* **8/1**[3]

**4** *shd* **Key To My Heart (IRE)**[19] 5766 3-9-0 **99**..............(b) SeamieHeffernan 6 101
(A P O'Brien, Ire) *attempted to make all: 4 l clr 3f out: sn rdn and reduced advantage ent fnl f: hdd 100yds out and no ex: dropped to 4th cl home* **20/1**

**5** *nk* **Beautiful Morning**[106] 2637 4-9-7 **102**.................................. ShaneFoley 5 100
(Mrs John Harrington, Ire) *chsd ldrs: 5th 1/2-way: rdn over 2f out and kpt on wl u.p but no ex ins fnl f and one pce cl home* **16/1**

**6** *¾* **Glamorous Approach (IRE)**[11] 6080 4-9-7 **100**......(p[1]) KevinManning 2 99+
(J S Bolger, Ire) *in rr of mid-div: rdn 3f out and sme prog u.p: kpt on wl ins fnl f: nrst fin* **14/1**

**7** *1* **Making Light (IRE)**[11] 6080 3-9-0 **101**.................................. PatSmullen 3 96
(D K Weld, Ire) *chsd ldrs: 4th 1/2-way: rdn over 2f out and kpt on wl u.p but no ex ent fnl f and grad wknd* **9/2**[2]

**8** *2¼* **Flying Fairies (IRE)**[19] 5766 4-9-7 **103**.................................. GaryCarroll 8 92
(John M Oxx, Ire) *mid-div: rdn over 2f out and sme prog u.p but one pce ent fnl f* **33/1**

**9** *¾* **Aurora Butterfly (IRE)**[11] 6080 3-9-0 **101**................................(h) WJLee 4 90
(W McCreery, Ire) *mid-div: 7th 1/2-way: rdn over 2f out but no imp* **25/1**

**10** *nk* **Dilmun (USA)**[41] 4986 3-9-0 **86**..............................(t) DonnachaO'Brien 12 90
(Joseph Patrick O'Brien, Ire) *chsd ldrs: 3rd 1/2-way: rdn over 2f out and no imp: wknd* **40/1**

**11** *1½* **Puppetshow (IRE)**[19] 5766 3-9-0 **85**.......................................(t) PBBeggy 9 86
(A P O'Brien, Ire) *slowly away: in rr: rdn 3f out and sme prog on far side but no ex ent fnl f and wknd* **66/1**

**12** *nk* **Aim To Please (FR)**[30] 5381 4-9-7 **106**........................(h[1]) PJMcDonald 14 86
(K R Burke) *in rr: rdn over 2f out and sme prog but nvr a factor* **16/1**

**13** *1½* **Kamili (IRE)**[11] 6080 3-9-0 **83**........................................ NGMcCullagh 10 83
(Joseph Patrick O'Brien, Ire) *mid-div: rdn over 2f out but no imp: wknd* **100/1**

**14** *nk* **Signe (IRE)**[63] 4119 4-9-7 **85**........................................ ColmO'Donoghue 15 82
(Mrs John Harrington, Ire) *bit slowly away: sn in rr: rdn over 2f out and sme prog on far side: sn no ex and one pce* **40/1**

**15** *¾* **Pavlenko (JPN)**[11] 6080 3-9-0 **93**......................................(p) WayneLordan 11 80
(A P O'Brien, Ire) *towards rr: rdn 3f out but no imp* **50/1**

1m 53.45s (-1.45) **Going Correction** -0.10s/f (Good)
**WFA** 3 from 4yo+ 7lb **15** Ran SP% **121.9**
Speed ratings: **102,101,101,101,100 100,99,97,96,96 94,94,93,93,92**
CSF £8.85 TOTE £3.20: £1.30, £1.50, £2.50; DF 11.20 Trifecta £51.50.
**Owner** Mrs John Magnier & Michael Tabor & Derrick Smith **Bred** Where Syndicate **Trained** Cashel, Co Tipperary

**FOCUS**
A decent field for this Group 3 event. Ballydoyle got the tactics right, with the pacemaker setting it up nicely for the Irish Oaks runner-up Rain Goddess, who was the class-act of the race. The standard is set around the fourth, fifth, sixth, tenth, 11th and 13th.

## 6491a TOTE IRISH CAMBRIDGESHIRE (PREMIER H'CAP) — 1m
**4:20** (4:21) 3-Y-0+
**£50,427** (£16,239; £7,692; £3,418; £1,709; £854)

RPR

**1** **Elusive Time (IRE)**[29] 5444 9-8-9 **85**....................(p) RossCoakley(3) 27 99+
(Takashi Kodama, Ire) *hld up towards rr: pushed along over 2f out and gd prog on nr side to go 2nd 1f out: kpt on wl to ld 100yds out* **25/1**

**2** *2* **Surrounding (IRE)**[19] 5764 4-8-11 **84**................................ ConorHoban 6 93
(M Halford, Ire) *cl-up: gng wl under 2f out and sn pushed along to ld 1f out: kpt on wl u.p but hdd 100yds out and no ex cl home* **14/1**

**3** *1¾* **Sinfonietta (FR)**[25] 5530 5-9-3 **90**............................ SeamieHeffernan 21 95
(David Menuisier) *mid-div: tk clsr order 3f out and sn rdn: kpt on wl u.p to go 3rd cl home but hld by front pair* **10/1**[3]

**4** *shd* **So You Thought (USA)**[25] 5552 3-8-6 **85**..................(b[1]) LeighRoche 18 89
(D K Weld, Ire) *mid-div: rdn over 2f out and gd hdwy u.p to go 4th cl home but hld* **7/1**[1]

**5** *¾* **Katiymann (IRE)**[21] 5688 5-9-0 **87**.....................................(t) ShaneFoley 14 90
(M Halford, Ire) *in rr: rdn over 2f out sn short of room bhd horses: swtchd lft ent fnl f and str burst between horses to get up for 5th cl home: nrst fin* **12/1**

6 *hd* **Gold Spinner (IRE)**[26] 5517 3-9-4 **97**....(b[1]) ColinKeane 25 99
(G M Lyons, Ire) *towards rr: pushed along and stl lot to do 2f out: short of room briefly but sn qcknd and r.o wl between horses fr over 1f out: nrst fin* **14/1**

7 *hd* **Breathe Easy (IRE)**[43] 4929 7-8-9 **89**.... DannySheehy[(7)] 9 92
(Gavin Cromwell, Ire) *cl-up: trckd ldr in 2nd: prog to ld 3f out: sn rdn and kpt on strly u.p: hdd 1f out and no ex wl ins fnl f* **12/1**

8 *shd* **Another Story (IRE)**[118] 2241 4-9-8 **95**.... RonanWhelan 15 97
(Ms Sheila Lavery, Ire) *towards rr: rdn over 2f out but short of room bhd horses ent fnl f and swtchd lft: r.o wl again ins fnl f* **33/1**

9 *½* **Stenographer (USA)**[21] 5688 4-8-12 **85**.... KevinManning 26 86
(J S Bolger, Ire) *mid-div: rdn 2f out: kpt on same pce u.p but nvr able to chal* **16/1**

10 *hd* **Hibou**[26] 5517 4-9-11 **98**....(b) DavidNolan 11 99
(Iain Jardine) *mid-div: rdn over 2f out and r.o wl u.p but no ex ins fnl f and styd on same pce* **8/1[2]**

11 *½* **Dream Walker (FR)**[21] 5688 8-9-9 **96**....(t) ChrisHayes 1 96
(Brian Ellison) *towards rr: rdn over 2f out and gd prog ent fnl f: kpt on wl u.p but no ex* **14/1**

12 *nk* **Turbine (IRE)**[26] 5517 4-8-11 **89**....(tp) KillianHennessy[(5)] 22 88
(Denis Gerard Hogan, Ire) *chsd ldrs: 4th 3f out: sn rdn and kpt on wl but no ex fr over 1f out and one pce* **20/1**

12 *dht* **Dinkum Diamond (IRE)**[14] 5976 9-8-5 **83**.... KillianLeonard[(5)] 17 82
(Andrew Slattery, Ire) *in rr of mid-div: rdn and sme prog fr over 2f out but no ex and one pce ins fnl f* **20/1**

14 *hd* **Hasselnott**[10] 6120 4-8-4 **77** oh2.... SeanKirrane[(7)] 23 82
(J F Levins, Ire) *mid-div: rdn over 2f out and hdwy on nr side: no ex ins fnl f but kpt on same pce* **14/1**

15 *nse* **Auckland (IRE)**[14] 5976 3-8-7 **86**....(bt[1]) MichaelHussey 13 83
(A P O'Brien, Ire) *mid-div: rdn over 2f out and sme prog ent fnl f but sn no ex u.p and wknd* **20/1**

16 *¾* **Johann Bach (IRE)**[205] 557 8-9-2 **92**.... GaryHalpin[(3)] 4 89
(Patrick G Harney, Ire) *sn cl-up: wnt cl 2nd 3f out: sn rdn and no ex: wknd* **33/1**

17 *1 ½* **Red Avenger (USA)**[26] 5517 7-8-12 **90**.... DonaghO'Connor[(5)] 24 83
(Damian Joseph English, Ire) *towards rr: rdn over 2f out on nr side but sn no imp u.p and one pce* **66/1**

18 *nk* **Mizaah (IRE)**[26] 5517 4-9-2 **96**....(t) DylanHogan[(7)] 10 88
(Kevin Prendergast, Ire) *in rr of mid-div: rdn 3f out and sme prog but no ex ent fnl f and wknd* **16/1**

19 *nk* **Elusive Beauty (IRE)**[24] 5583 3-9-0 **93**.... NGMcCullagh 5 84
(K J Condon, Ire) *mid-div: rdn over 2f out: sn no imp and wknd* **50/1**

20 *hd* **Onlyhuman (IRE)**[19] 5774 4-8-12 **85**.... WayneLordan 8 76
(Edward Lynam, Ire) *chsd ldrs: rdn 3f out and no ex: wknd* **14/1**

21 *nk* **Tribal Path (IRE)**[10] 6116 7-8-9 **82**....(t) RoryCleary 16 73
(Damian Joseph English, Ire) *sn led: hdd 3f out and sn rdn: no ex and wknd* **25/1**

22 *½* **Stormy Belle (IRE)**[19] 5764 3-8-13 **92**.... DeclanMcDonogh 7 80
(P A Fahy, Ire) *sn chsd ldrs: rdn 2f out and no ex: wknd* **20/1**

23 *1* **Pandagreen (IRE)**[25] 5552 3-8-4 **83** oh2....(tp) AndrewBreslin[(7)] 2 76
(Gavin Cromwell, Ire) *mid-div: rdn 3f out and sme prog but no ex ent fnl f and wknd* **33/1**

24 *1 ¾* **Remarkable Lady (IRE)**[19] 5774 4-9-7 **94**....(tp) WJLee 20 77
(H Rogers, Ire) *in rr of mid-div: rdn under 3f out and sn no ex u.p: wknd* **25/1**

25 *11* **Secret Wizard (IRE)**[21] 5688 4-8-10 **88**.... OisinOrr[(5)] 3 46
(Ms Sheila Lavery, Ire) *mid-div: rdn over 3f out and no ex: sn wknd and eased* **40/1**

26 *9* **Foxtrot Charlie (USA)**[57] 4383 4-9-12 **99**....(t) PatSmullen 19 36
(D K Weld, Ire) *chsd ldrs: rdn 1/2-way and sn no imp: wknd and sn eased* **20/1**

27 *½* **Windsor Beach (IRE)**[14] 5976 5-9-2 **94**.... DenisLinehan[(5)] 12 30
(J P Murtagh, Ire) *in rr of mid-div: rdn over 2f out and sme prog but short of room bhd horses under 2f out and sn no ch: eased ent fnl f* **14/1**

1m 39.37s (-6.63) **Going Correction** -0.65s/f (Hard)
**WFA** 3 from 4yo+ 6lb 27 Ran SP% **149.9**
Speed ratings: **107,105,103,103,102 102,102,101,101,101 100,100,100,100,100 99,97,97,97,97 96,96,95,93,82 73,**
CSF £341.42 CT £3819.84 TOTE £38.20: £9.60, £4.20, £2.80, £3.00; DF 1528.70 Trifecta £21641.90.
**Owner** Elusive Time Syndicate **Bred** Oghill House Stud **Trained** Kildare, Co Kildare

**FOCUS**
This looked a lottery on paper and it duly produced a long-priced winner in the shape of an old horse who has returned to form this season. The runner-up was always placed, but plenty came too late on the scene to threaten. The winner has been rated close to his old figures, with a pb from the runner-up.

6492 - 6493a (Foreign Racing) - See Raceform Interactive

## 6451 BADEN-BADEN (L-H)
Sunday, August 27

**OFFICIAL GOING: Turf: good**

### 6494a PREIS DES CASINO BADEN-BADEN (BBAG AUKTIONSRENNEN) (CONDITIONS) (2YO FILLIES) (TURF) 6f
**1:40** 2-Y-O
**£42,735** (£17,094; £10,683; £8,547; £4,273; £2,136)

RPR

1 **Cabarita (GER)** 2-8-11 0.... FilipMinarik 6 93
(H-J Groschel, Germany) **56/10[3]**

2 *shd* **Binti Al Nar (GER)** 2-8-11 0.... AndraschStarke 7 92
(P Schiergen, Germany) **67/10**

3 *1 ¾* **American Oxygen**[27] 2-8-11 0.... JackMitchell 9 87
(C Von Der Recke, Germany) **59/10**

4 *2 ½* **Schesaplana (GER)** 2-9-2 0.... MartinSeidl 10 84
(C Von Der Recke, Germany) **184/10**

5 *shd* **Whaling Story (GER)**[56] 2-8-11 0.... DanielePorcu 5 79
(M Rulec, Germany) **23/5[2]**

6 *nk* **La Magique (GER)** 2-8-11 0.... MarcoCasamento 11 78
(Henk Grewe, Germany) **269/10**

7 *1 ¾* **Emilia James**[67] 3960 2-9-2 0.... JoeFanning 3 78
(Mark Johnston) *chsd ldrs: drvn wl outpcd by ldrs appr 2f out: kpt on under driving fnl f: nt pce to get bk on terms* **2/1[1]**

8 *1 ¼* **Cherina Dynamite (SPA)**[56] 2-8-11 0.... BauyrzhanMurzabayev 8 69
(V Luka Jr, Czech Republic) **54/1**

9 *1 ¾* **Folklore (GER)** 2-8-11 0.... AdamBeschizza 2 64
(Mrs Ilka Gansera-Leveque) *outpcd towards rr: rowed along to cl over 3f out: sn chsng ldng gp:lost pl 2f out: kpt on at one pce fnl 1 1/2f* **109/10**

10 *4* **Anna Jammeela** 2-8-11 0.... JozefBojko 4 52
(A Wohler, Germany) **155/10**

11 *7* **Shilo (IRE)** 2-8-11 0.... AlexanderPietsch 13 31
(C Von Der Recke, Germany) **245/10**

12 *1 ¼* **Wonderful Gorl (GER)** 2-8-11 0.... RenePiechulek 12 27
(Gerald Geisler, Germany) **231/10**

13 *4 ¼* **Sorina (GER)**[61] 4196 2-8-11 0.... MichaelCadeddu 1 15
(Henk Grewe, Germany) **41/1**

1m 9.19s (-1.10) 13 Ran SP% **129.3**
PARI-MUTUEL (all including 10 euro stake): WIN: 66; PLACE: 18, 25, 22; SF: 379.
**Owner** Carsten Biedermann **Bred** Gestut Evershorst **Trained** Germany

### 6495a 147TH SPORT-WELT GOLDENE PEITSCHE (GROUP 2) (3YO+) (TURF) 6f
**2:55** 3-Y-O+
**£34,188** (£13,247; £6,837; £3,418; £2,136)

RPR

1 **Son Cesio (FR)**[29] 5450 6-9-4 0.... AdriedeVries 5 111
(H-A Pantall, France) *chsd ldr: led stands' side gp of 11 under 2f out: rdn and styd on strly fnl f: led cl home* **11/5[1]**

2 *hd* **Daring Match (GER)**[14] 6-9-4 0.... JackMitchell 13 110
(J Hirschberger, Germany) *a cl up: racd alone on ins: drvn to ld 2f out: styd on gamely on own fnl f: hdd cl home* **144/10**

3 *1 ½* **Millowitsch (GER)**[42] 4939 4-9-4 0.... AndreasHelfenbein 3 105
(Markus Klug, Germany) *a.p: rdn to chse ldrs 1 1/2f out: styd on fnl f: nt pce to chal* **33/10[2]**

4 *nse* **Shining Emerald**[20] 6-9-4 0.... EduardoPedroza 2 105
(A Wohler, Germany) *w.w in tch towards stands' side: styd on u.p fnl f: nvr rchd ldrs* **6/1**

5 *½* **Making Trouble (GER)**[20] 5-9-4 0.... WladimirPanov 9 103
(D Moser, Germany) *w.w bhd front rnk: drvn and nt qckn 2f out: styd on at same pce* **28/1**

6 *½* **Alwina (GER)**[32] 3-8-11 0.... DarioVargiu 12 98
(Henk Grewe, Germany) *prom: rdn but no imp 2f out: kpt on at same pce* **269/10**

7 *shd* **Hargeisa (USA)**[14] 3-8-11 0.... AndraschStarke 8 98
(Mario Hofer, Germany) *settled towards rr: hdwy 1 1/2f out: kpt on fnl f: nvr in contention* **125/10**

8 *½* **Mc Queen (FR)**[53] 4517 5-9-4 0.... StephenHellyn 7 100
(Yasmin Almenrader, Germany) *towards rr: rdn and styd on fr over 1f out: nvr trbld ldrs* **199/10**

9 *2 ½* **Westfalica (GER)**[14] 3-8-11 0.... MichaelCadeddu 10 88
(Jean-Pierre Carvalho, Germany) *led in centre: rdn and hdd 2f out: wknd fnl f* **194/10**

10 *½* **Schang (GER)**[29] 5450 4-9-4 0.... JozefBojko 4 90
(P Vovcenko, Germany) *drvn towards rr: last and rdn under 2f out: nvr got involved* **171/10**

11 *hd* **Donnerschlag**[92] 3105 7-9-4 0....(b) FilipMinarik 11 90
(Jean-Pierre Carvalho, Germany) *racd in midfield: rdn and no imp 2f out: wl hld fnl f* **22/5[3]**

12 *1 ¼* **Forgino (GER)**[53] 4517 6-9-4 0.... MarcoCasamento 1 86
(T Potters, Germany) *outpcd in rr early: towards rr bef 1/2-way: no imp whn rdn 1 1/2f out: wl hld fnl f* **171/10**

1m 7.76s (-2.53)
**WFA** 3 from 4yo+ 3lb 12 Ran SP% **129.0**
PARI-MUTUEL (all including 10 euro stake): WIN: 32; PLACE: 13, 20, 13, 14; SF: 438.
**Owner** Yves Borotra **Bred** Yves Borotra **Trained** France

## 6452 DEAUVILLE (R-H)
Sunday, August 27

**OFFICIAL GOING: Turf: good; polytrack: standard**

### 6496a PRIX CASINO BARRIERE TROUVILLE (CLAIMER) (3YO) (POLYTRACK) 1m 4f 110y
**1:35** 3-Y-O
**£9,829** (£3,931; £2,948; £1,965; £982)

RPR

1 **Somewhere In Time (FR)**[37] 5133 3-9-1 0....(p) Pierre-CharlesBoudot 2 71
(M Pimbonnet, France) **22/5[3]**

2 *1 ¼* **Marcoussis**[51] 3-9-1 0.... JeromeCabre 9 69
(Y Barberot, France) **21/10[1]**

3 *shd* **Noir Intense (FR)**[233] 3-8-11 0....(p) GabrieleCongiu 10 65
(J-P Gauvin, France) **8/1**

4 *shd* **El Cat Bere (FR)**[51] 3-9-1 0.... TheoBachelot 3 69
(M Rolland, France) **4/1[2]**

5 *snk* **Tryst (GER)** 3-9-2 0....(p) AntoineHamelin 6 69
(Henk Grewe, Germany) **13/2**

6 *2 ½* **Flash Of Dreams (IRE)**[138] 3-8-8 0.... MickaelBarzalona 7 57
(Jean-Pierre Carvalho, Germany) **61/10**

7 *3 ½* **Sister Vic (FR)**[31] 3-8-5 0.... KyllanBarbaud[(8)] 8 57
(N Caullery, France) **29/1**

8 *¾* **Midnight Express (FR)**[12] 3-8-3 0.... MathieuPelletan[(5)] 4 51
(G E Mikhalides, France) **29/1**

9 *4* **Gog Elles (IRE)**[8] 6225 3-8-9 0 ow1.... TonyPiccone 5 45
(J S Moore) **37/1**

PARI-MUTUEL (all including 1 euro stake): WIN 5.40; PLACE 1.90, 1.50, 2.10; DF 7.60; SF 17.10.
**Owner** Fabrice Petit **Bred** Sca Elevage De Tourgeville & Mme H Erculiani **Trained** France

### 6497a PRIX DE MEAUTRY BARRIERE (GROUP 3) (3YO+) (TURF) 6f
**2:45** 3-Y-O+
**£34,188** (£13,675; £10,256; £6,837; £3,418)

RPR

1 **Signs Of Blessing (IRE)**[21] 5690 6-9-4 0.... StephanePasquier 6 118+
(F Rohaut, France) *mde all: broke wl and led towards centre of crse: drvn over 1f out on strly: readily* **1/1[1]**

2 *2* **Finsbury Square (IRE)**[64] 4071 5-9-2 0....(b) ChristopheSoumillon 7 110
(F Chappet, France) *trckd ldr towards centre of crse: chsd ldr into fnl f: styd on but no match for wnr* **42/10[2]**

**3** 3/4 **Spiritfix**[29] 5450 4-8-13 0........................................ MaximeGuyon 4 105
(A Fabre, France) *racd keenly: ctsd ldrs stands' side gp: moved towards centre 2 1/2f out and last of that gp of 5: drvn to cl 1 1/2f out: styd on fnl f: nt pce to get on terms* **164/10**

**4** 1 3/4 **Stunning Spirit**[71] 3855 3-8-13 0........................................ GeraldMosse 2 102
(F Head, France) *in rr stands' side gp: jnd gp towards centre 2 1/2f out and chsd ldng trio: 3rd and rdn 1 1/2f out: kpt on at same pce fnl f* **93/10**

**5** 7 **Lahore (USA)**[56] 4407 3-8-13 0........................................ OlivierPeslier 1 80
(Roger Varian) *w.w in fnl pair stands' side: lft 2nd in stands' side pair 2 1/2f out but last overall: rdn and effrt 1 1/2f out: sn btn: wl hld fnl f* **87/10**

**6** 3 1/2 **Aiming For Rio (FR)**[55] 4456 3-8-9 0........................................ MickaelBarzalona 3 64
(A Fabre, France) *cl up stands' side gp: lft in front of stands' side pair 2 1/2f out but in fnl trio overall: rdn and nt qckn wl over 1 1/2f out: wknd fnl f and eased* **71/10**

**7** 3 **Fas (IRE)**[21] 5690 3-9-1 0........................................(b[1]) Pierre-CharlesBoudot 5 61
(Mme Pia Brandt, France) *led stands' side gp of five: jnd centre gp 2 1/2f out and chsd ldr: rdn and lost pl wl over 1 1/2f out: btn whn eased fnl f* **7/1[3]**

1m 8.96s (-2.04)
**WFA** 3 from 4yo+ 3lb **7** Ran SP% **119.8**
PARI-MUTUEL (all including 1 euro stake): WIN 2.00; PLACE 1.40, 1.80; SF 5.40.
**Owner** Mme Isabelle Corbani **Bred** S Boucheron **Trained** Sauvagnon, France

## 6498a PRIX QUINCEY BARRIERE (GROUP 3) (3YO+) (STRAIGHT) (TURF) 1m (R)
**3:25** 3-Y-0+ **£34,188** (£13,675; £10,256; £6,837; £3,418)

RPR

**1** **Attendu (FR)**[42] 4942 4-9-2 0........................................ MaximeGuyon 1 111
(C Laffon-Parias, France) *led: hdd after 1f: trckd ldr: drvn to regain ld 1 1/2f out: rdn ent fnl fnl f: r.o u.p* **11/10[1]**

**2** nk **Wireless (FR)**[42] 4942 6-9-0 0........................................ TheoBachelot 2 108+
(V Luka Jr, Czech Republic) *w.w in rr: clsd over 1 1/2f out: 3rd and drvn 1f out: r.o fnl f: nvr quite on terms w wnr* **56/10**

**3** 3/4 **Dicton**[91] 3118 4-9-2 0........................................ OlivierPeslier 4 108
(Gianluca Bietolini, Italy) *trckd ldr: led after 1f: hdd 1 1/2f out: remained cl up: 2nd whn rdn between horses 1f out: styd on fnl f: a looked hld* **3/1[2]**

**4** 2 **Nordic Dream (IRE)**[70] 3880 4-9-0 0........................................ VincentCheminaud 3 102
(A Fabre, France) *hld up in fnl pair: drvn over 1 1/2f out but no imp: rdn appr fnl f: kpt on fr over 1f out: nt pce to get involved* **129/10**

**5** snk **Graphite (FR)**[140] 1658 3-9-1 0........................................ MickaelBarzalona 5 107
(A Fabre, France) *chsd ldng pair: drvn and nt qckn 2f out: kpt on at same pce fnl f* **33/10[3]**

1m 40.01s (-0.79)
**WFA** 3 from 4yo+ 6lb **5** Ran SP% **118.2**
PARI-MUTUEL (all including 1 euro stake): WIN 2.10; PLACE 1.20, 2.10; SF 6.70.
**Owner** Wertheimer & Frere **Bred** Wertheimer & Frere **Trained** Chantilly, France

## 6499a LUCIEN BARRIERE GRAND PRIX DE DEAUVILLE (GROUP 2) (3YO+) (TURF) 1m 4f 110y
**4:05** 3-Y-0+ **£97,435** (£37,606; £17,948; £11,965; £5,982)

RPR

**1** **Tiberian (FR)**[21] 5692 5-9-6 0........................................ OlivierPeslier 5 115+
(Alain Couetil, France) *w.w towards rr: tk clsr order 1/2-way: 3rd and pushed along 1 1/2f out: rdn to chal 1f out: led fnl 130yds: styd on but edgd rt: a holding runner-up* **9/2[3]**

**2** snk **Doha Dream (FR)**[21] 5692 4-9-6 0........................................ GregoryBenoist 3 114
(A Fabre, France) *chsd ldr: 2nd and pushed along 2 1/2f out: led appr 2f out: rdn whn chal 1f out: hdd fnl 130yds: rallied u.p and carried rt: a hld* **16/5[2]**

**3** 1 **Travelling Man**[35] 5198 4-9-3 0........................................ MickaelBarzalona 2 109+
(F Head, France) *settled in share of 3rd: dropped towards rr 1/2-way: drvn 2 1/2f out: styd on wl u.str.p fnl f: nt rch front two* **53/10**

**4** 3/4 **Savoir Vivre (IRE)**[21] 5692 4-9-3 0........................................ MaximeGuyon 4 108
(Jean-Pierre Carvalho, Germany) *settled in share of 3rd: 3rd and pushed along 2 1/2f out: styd on fnl f: nt pce to chal* **106/10**

**5** 1 **Garlingari (FR)**[12] 6052 6-9-3 0........................................(p) RonanThomas 7 107
(Mme C Barande-Barbe, France) *w.w in rr: rdn and effrt over 1 1/2f out: kpt on fnl f: could nvr muster pce to get on terms* **119/10**

**6** 3/4 **Frontiersman**[8] 6191 4-9-3 0........................................(p) JamesDoyle 6 105
(Charlie Appleby) *settled in fnl pair: last and drvn 3f out: kpt on fnl f: nvr trbld ldrs* **17/10[1]**

**7** 5 **Mille Et Mille**[44] 4879 7-9-3 0........................................ ChristopheSoumillon 1 97
(C Lerner, France) *led: scrubbed along 2 1/2f out: hdd appr 2f out: sn wknd* **134/10**

2m 44.68s (-1.72) **7** Ran SP% **118.2**
PARI-MUTUEL (all including 1 euro stake): WIN 5.50; PLACE 2.60, 2.20; SF 14.10.
**Owner** Earl Haras Du Logis, Heiko Volz & Stefan Falk **Bred** H Volz , J Ince & S Falk **Trained** France

**FOCUS**
The runner-up has been rated to his best.

# 4825 OVREVOLL (R-H)
## Sunday, August 27

**OFFICIAL GOING: Turf: good**

## 6500a ALTIA POLAR CUP (GROUP 3) (3YO+) (TURF) 6f 187y
**2:00** 3-Y-0+ **£28,195** (£14,097; £6,766; £4,511; £2,819)

RPR

**1** **Tinnitus (IRE)**[42] 4940 4-9-4 0........................................ Per-AndersGraberg 4 100
(Niels Petersen, Norway) *hld up in fnl trio: prog to go 8l 3rd sn after 1/2-way: rdn to cl 1 1/2f out: sustained run to ld fnl 100yds: drvn out* **69/10**

**2** nse **Captain America (SWE)**[69] 7-9-4 0........................................(b) CarlosLopez 3 100
(Annike Bye Hansen, Norway) *racd in fnl pair: last and plenty to do wl over 2 1/2f out: rdn to take clsr order 1 1/2f out: str run fnl f: nvr on terms* **19/10[2]**

**3** 2 3/4 **Hoku (IRE)**[29] 6-9-1 0........................................ Jan-ErikNeuroth 2 90
(Bent Olsen, Denmark) *led: rdn whn pressed 1 1/2f out: hdd fnl 100yds: no ex* **11/2[3]**

**4** 1 1/4 **Guerre (USA)**[25] 6-9-4 0........................................ OliverWilson 7 89
(Flemming Velin, Denmark) *chsd ldr on outer: rdn to chal 1 1/2f out: one pce fnl f* **11/10[1]**

**5** 3/4 **Saving Kenny (IRE)**[42] 4940 7-9-4 0........................................ MrFredrikJanetzky 6 87
(Roy Arne Kvisla, Sweden) *scrubbed along to go early pce: in rr: hdwy u.p 1 1/2f out: kpt on fnl f: nvr nrr* **141/10**

**6** nse **Breakdancer (FR)**[96] 2943 4-9-4 0........................................(b) ElioneChaves 5 87
(Fredrik Reuterskiold, Sweden) *chsd ldng pair: lost pl sn after 1/2-way: kpt on at one pce* **44/5**

**Owner** E Nagell-Erichsen Family **Bred** Awbeg Stud **Trained** Norway

## 6501a MARIT SVEAAS MINNELOP (GROUP 3) (3YO+) (TURF) 1m 1f
**2:50** 3-Y-0+ **£75,187** (£24,436; £11,278; £6,766; £4,511)

RPR

**1** **Trouble Of Course (FR)**[25] 3-8-11 0........................................ Per-AndersGraberg 3 97
(Niels Petersen, Norway) *hld up in fnl trio: hdwy 2 1/2f out: styng-on 3rd and drvn 2f out: sustained run to ld 50yds out: hld on gamely* **9/2[3]**

**2** nk **Jubilance (IRE)**[22] 5676 8-9-4 0........................................ ElioneChaves 5 96
(Bent Olsen, Denmark) *sn led: hdd after 1 1/2f: remained cl up: drvn to ld 2f out: styd on u.p: hdd fnl 50yds: rallied gamely* **34/1**

**3** 1/2 **Brownie (FR)**[45] 5-9-4 0........................................ OliverWilson 6 95
(Bent Olsen, Denmark) *chsd ldrs: c stands' side over 2f out: styd on fnl f: nvr quite on terms* **19/10[1]**

**4** nk **Hurricane Red (IRE)**[22] 5676 7-9-6 0........................................ JacobJohansen 2 96
(Lennart Reuterskiold Jr, Sweden) *racd keenly: hld up in midfield on inner: rdn and styd on towards stands' side fr 1 1/2f out: nt pce to chal* **27/10[2]**

**5** 1/2 **Pas De Secrets (IRE)**[69] 3923 4-9-4 0........................................ Jan-ErikNeuroth 9 93
(Wido Neuroth, Norway) *w.w in rr: last of main gp bef 1/2-way: prog 2f out: styd on fnl f: nvr trbld ldrs* **14/1**

**6** 1/2 **Bokan (FR)**[45] 4825 5-9-4 0........................................ NelsonDeSouza 8 92
(Wido Neuroth, Norway) *settled midfield on outer: rdn and nt qckn 2f out: styd on fnl f: n.d* **135/10**

**7** 2 1/4 **Ruler Of Course (IRE)**[25] 4-9-4 0........................................ CarlosLopez 7 87
(Niels Petersen, Norway) *pressed ldr on outer: led after 1 1/2f: hdd after 2 1/2f and chsd ldr: rdn and nt qckn 2f out: one pce fnl f* **207/10**

**8** 3 3/4 **Berling (IRE)**[22] 5676 10-9-4 0........................................ DinaDanekilde 4 80
(Jessica Long, Sweden) *w.w in fnl pair: lost pl and wl adrift in last bef 1/2-way: hdwy 1 1/2f out: styd on fnl f: nrest at fin* **98/10**

**9** 2 **Coprah**[25] 9-9-4 0........................................ RafaeldeOliveira 1 75
(Cathrine Erichsen, Norway) *cl up: led after 2 1/2f: rousted along and hdd 2f out: wknd fnl f* **51/10**

1m 49.3s (-0.60)
**WFA** 3 from 4yo+ 7lb **9** Ran SP% **126.4**

**Owner** E Nagell-Erichsen Family **Bred** Ian Fair **Trained** Norway

# 6338 CHEPSTOW (L-H)
## Monday, August 28

**OFFICIAL GOING: Good (8.1)**
Wind: almost nil Weather: sunny/warm

## 6502 ST PIERRE BIG SUMMER SHAPE UP H'CAP (DIV I) 7f 16y
**12:45** (12:46) (Class 6) (0-65,67) 3-Y-0+ **£3,234** (£962; £481; £240) **Stalls** Centre

Form RPR

033 **1** **Chatoyer (FR)**[10] 6157 3-9-8 **66**........................................(h) SeanLevey 7 72
(Richard Hannon) *racd keenly: trckd ldrs: led over 2f out: sn rdn: kpt on fnl f: rdn out* **3/1[1]**

526 **2** 1/2 **Bounty Pursuit**[38] 5111 5-9-8 **66**........................................ MitchGodwin(5) 4 73
(Michael Blake) *mid-div: hdwy 3f out: rdn to chse ldr 2f out: kpt on but a being hld ins fnl f* **9/2[3]**

0404 **3** 1 1/2 **Wahaab (IRE)**[11] 6097 6-9-10 **63**........................................ TimmyMurphy 12 66
(Sophie Leech) *hld up bhd: pushed along 3f out: rdn and hdwy ent fnl f: r.o wl to go 3rd fnl 70yds* **16/1**

0030 **4** nk **Higgy's Heartbeat**[20] 5748 3-8-11 **58**........................................ JackDuern(3) 10 58
(Dean Ivory) *mid-div: hdwy over 2f out: sn rdn: wnt 3rd over 1f out: edgd lft: kpt on same pce fnl f* **20/1**

0350 **5** 1/2 **Binky Blue (IRE)**[17] 5897 5-9-2 **55**........................................ SteveDrowne 2 56
(Daniel Mark Loughnane) *mid-div: rdn and hdwy 2f out: kpt on fnl f but nt pce to threaten* **16/1**

5004 **6** 1/2 **Passing Star**[11] 6102 6-10-0 **67**........................................(tp) RobHornby 5 66
(Daniel Kubler) *trckd ldrs: rdn over 2f out: sn one pce* **7/2[2]**

3000 **7** 1 **Beepeecee**[30] 5411 3-9-4 **62**........................................(b[1]) ShaneKelly 11 57
(Richard Hughes) *a mid-div* **20/1**

0000 **8** 1/2 **Herm (IRE)**[45] 4843 3-8-13 **57**........................................ JFEgan 3 50
(David Evans) *mid-div: rdn over 2f out: little imp whn nt clr run ent fnl f* **9/1**

6004 **9** 2 3/4 **Air Of York (IRE)**[11] 6099 5-9-4 **62**........................................(p) DavidEgan(5) 1 50
(John Flint) *prom: rdn wl over 2f out: wknd over 1f out* **13/2**

0550 **10** 1 3/4 **Tally's Song**[11] 6099 4-8-10 **49**........................................(p) MartinDwyer 9 32
(Grace Harris) *prom: led after 2f: rdn and hdd over 2f out: kpt chsng ldrs tl wknd ent fnl f* **20/1**

0060 **11** 4 **Allofmelovesallofu**[19] 5783 3-9-7 **65**........................................ FranBerry 8 35
(Ken Cunningham-Brown) *prom for 4f: sn wknd* **25/1**

-005 **12** 14 **Aqshion Stations**[13] 6034 3-8-2 **46**........................................(h[1]) KieranO'Neill 6
(Richard Price) *led for over 2f: wknd 2f out* **66/1**

1m 23.87s (0.67) **Going Correction** -0.05s/f (Good)
**WFA** 3 from 4yo+ 5lb **12** Ran SP% **120.1**
Speed ratings (Par 101): **94,93,91,91,90 90,89,88,85,83 78,62**
CSF £15.35 CT £192.52 TOTE £3.30: £1.40, £2.10, £3.80; EX 20.50 Trifecta £116.60.
**Owner** J Cullinan & R Marley **Bred** Stilvi Compania Financiera **Trained** East Everleigh, Wilts
■ Stewards' Enquiry : Mitch Godwin two-day ban: used whip above permitted level (Sep 11-12)

**FOCUS**
The going was good ahead of the opener, after which Sean Levey reported it was "lovely summer ground - just on the quick side". A moderate handicap in which they went a fair gallop, and the winner came down the centre. The second and third limit the form.

## 6503 ST PIERRE BIG SUMMER SHAPE UP H'CAP (DIV II) 7f 16y
**1:15** (1:18) (Class 6) (0-65,66) 3-Y-0+ **£3,234** (£962; £481; £240) **Stalls** Centre

Form RPR

0520 **1** **Corporal Maddox**[4] 6345 10-9-5 **58**........................................(p) SamHitchcott 10 67
(Ronald Harris) *a.p: led over 2f out: kpt on wl* **10/1**

2200 **2** *2* **Carcharias (IRE)**$^{11}$ 6102 4-9-7 **63** .......................... CallumShepherd$^{(3)}$ 4 67
(Ed de Giles) *prom: led after 2f: rdn over 3f out: hdd over 2f out: kpt on but a being hld fnl f* **6/1**$^{3}$

3601 **3** *1½* **Barista (IRE)**$^{11}$ 6101 9-9-5 **61** .......................... HollieDoyle$^{(3)}$ 6 61
(Brian Forsey) *mid-div: pushed along 3f out: hdwy 2f out: kpt on same pce ins fnl f* **2/1**$^{1}$

105- **4** *1½* **Al's Memory (IRE)**$^{454}$ 2769 8-9-9 **62** .......................... JFEgan 1 58
(David Evans) *chsd ldrs: rdn over 2f out: kpt on same pce* **16/1**

5365 **5** *nse* **Captain Marmalade (IRE)**$^{21}$ 5713 5-8-11 **50** .......................... KieranO'Neill 8 45
(Jimmy Fox) *hmpd s: in last pair: hdwy fr 2f out: kpt on ins fnl f but nt gng pce to get involved* **5/1**$^{2}$

4050 **6** *3* **Born To Finish (IRE)**$^{12}$ 6076 4-9-13 **66** ..........(bt) TimmyMurphy 9 53
(Jamie Osborne) *v awkwardly away and reminders: midfield and hrd drvn 3f out: nvr threatened* **5/1**$^{2}$

1250 **7** *1¾* **Aye Aye Skipper (IRE)**$^{11}$ 6102 7-9-2 **55** ..........(b) FranBerry 11 38
(Ken Cunningham-Brown) *mid-div: rdn whn outpcd 3f out: n.d* **9/1**

4000 **8** *1* **Champagne Freddie**$^{13}$ 6035 4-9-1 **54** .......................... FergusSweeney 3 34
(John O'Shea) *mid-div: hung lft over 2f out u.p: wknd ent fnl f* **25/1**

0460 **9** *½* **Rising Sunshine (IRE)**$^{42}$ 4982 4-8-7 **46** oh1 ..........(p$^{1}$) MartinDwyer 5 24
(Milton Bradley) *prom tl rdn over 2f out: wknd ent fnl f* **20/1**

0-65 **10** *16* **Poet's Charm (IRE)**$^{11}$ 6094 3-9-0 **58** ..........(h) RobHornby 7
(Martin Hill) *led for over 2f: chsd ldrs tl wknd 2f out* **25/1**

1m 23.06s (-0.14) **Going Correction** -0.05s/f (Good)
**WFA** 3 from 4yo+ 5lb **10** Ran SP% **118.4**
Speed ratings (Par 101): **98,95,94,92,92 88,86,85,85,66**
CSF £68.02 CT £173.68 TOTE £11.00: £2.50, £2.30, £1.50; EX 79.10 Trifecta £607.40.
**Owner** Ridge House Stables Ltd **Bred** Theobalds Stud **Trained** Earlswood, Monmouths

**FOCUS**
The second division and run in a 0.81sec faster time. The winner came more towards the stands' side. The runner-up helps set the level.

## 6504 ALAN BUSHELL RACING FILLIES' NOVICE AUCTION STKS (PLUS 10 RACE) 1m 14y

**1:45** (1:47) (Class 5) 2-Y-O **£3,881** (£1,155; £577; £288) **Stalls** Centre

Form RPR

0402 **1** **Show Of Force**$^{14}$ 5999 2-9-0 67 .......................... RobHornby 7 66
(Jonathan Portman) *led stands' side quartet: drifted lft 2f out: sn rdn to mount str chal: kpt on wl to ld fnl 100yds* **11/4**$^{2}$

0405 **2** *nk* **Fusion Central (IRE)**$^{16}$ 5933 2-9-0 51 .......................... SeanLevey 2 65
(Richard Hannon) *overall ldr in center: rdn whn strly chal 2f out: kpt on but no ex whn hdd fnl 100yds* **9/1**

410 **3** *½* **Double Reflection**$^{14}$ 5990 2-9-4 72 .......................... CliffordLee$^{(3)}$ 8 71
(K R Burke) *trckd ldr on stands' side: rdn 2f out: sn drifted lft: kpt on ins fnl f but nt pce to mount chal* **6/4**$^{1}$

**4** *6* **Sassie (IRE)** 2-9-0 0 .......................... MartinDwyer 6 50+
(Sylvester Kirk) *dwlt: last pair on stands' side: kpt on steadily fnl 2f wout ever gng pce to get involved: wnt 4th ins fnl f* **20/1**

**5** *¾* **Ainne** 2-8-9 0 .......................... MitchGodwin$^{(5)}$ 4 48
(Sylvester Kirk) *trckd ldr in center: rdn 2f out: hung lft and wknd ent fnl f* **12/1**

5 **6** *5* **Viktoriya Taraban (IRE)**$^{11}$ 6100 2-8-9 0 .......................... DavidEgan$^{(5)}$ 3 36
(Joseph Tuite) *chsd ldrs in center: rdn 3f out: sn outpcd* **8/1**$^{3}$

**7** *6* **So Near So Farhh** 2-9-0 0 .......................... ShaneKelly 5 21
(Mick Channon) *dwlt: last pair on stands' side: nvr gng pce pce to get on terms* **8/1**$^{3}$

0 **8** *21* **Western Dynamisme (FR)**$^{24}$ 5586 2-9-0 0 .......................... MartinLane 1
(Harry Dunlop) *trckd ldrs in center: rdn over 2f out: sn wknd: t.o* **50/1**

1m 35.86s (-0.34) **Going Correction** -0.05s/f (Good) **8** Ran SP% **113.3**
Speed ratings (Par 91): **99,98,98,92,91 86,80,59**
CSF £27.00 TOTE £3.00: £1.20, £2.80, £1.10; EX 24.10 Trifecta £64.30.
**Owner** The Sawgrass Survivors **Bred** Whatton Manor Stud **Trained** Upper Lambourn, Berks

**FOCUS**
A weak novice in which they initially split into two groups, before the protagonists merged on the far side. The level is a bit fluid.

## 6505 DOROTHY MORT MEMORIAL/EBF NOVICE STKS (PLUS 10 RACE) (C&G) 1m 14y

**2:15** (2:15) (Class 4) 2-Y-O **£5,175** (£1,540; £769; £384) **Stalls** Centre

Form RPR

13 **1** **Regimented (IRE)**$^{15}$ 5964 2-9-0 0 .......................... HollieDoyle$^{(3)}$ 1 84
(Richard Hannon) *trckd ldrs: shkn up to chal over 1f out: led jst ins fnl f: kpt on wl: pushed out* **11/8**$^{1}$

610 **2** *nk* **Sallab (IRE)**$^{27}$ 5501 2-9-3 0 .......................... SeanLevey 2 82
(Richard Hannon) *racd keenly: led: rdn whn strly chal 2f out: hdd jst ins fnl f: kpt on wl* **5/2**$^{3}$

34 **3** *hd* **Blue Laureate**$^{10}$ 6132 2-9-0 0 .......................... SamHitchcott 6 79
(Clive Cox) *pressed ldr: rdn w ev ch over 1f out: tended to edge lft: kpt on wl clsng stages* **9/4**$^{2}$

0 **4** *4½* **Island Sound**$^{10}$ 6132 2-8-11 0 .......................... GeorgeWood$^{(3)}$ 4 68
(Heather Main) *slowly away: last but sn in tch: hdwy 2f out: kpt on but nt pce to get on terms* **16/1**

0 **5** *¾* **The Night King**$^{5}$ 6367 2-9-0 0 .......................... ShaneKelly 3 66
(Mick Channon) *trckd ldrs: effrt 2f out: sn one pce* **20/1**

00 **6** *35* **Bunch Of Thyme (IRE)**$^{23}$ 5655 2-8-9 0 .......................... MitchGodwin$^{(5)}$ 5
(Bill Turner) *prom for over 2f: sn struggling in last pair: wknd over 2f out: eased* **50/1**

1m 37.18s (0.98) **Going Correction** -0.05s/f (Good) **6** Ran SP% **114.1**
Speed ratings (Par 96): **93,92,92,88,87 52**
CSF £5.30 TOTE £2.50: £1.70, £1.40; EX 7.30 Trifecta £9.50.
**Owner** Mason Brown Partnership **Bred** J P Keappock **Trained** East Everleigh, Wilts

**FOCUS**
An average novice and the first three came well clear. The level is a bit muddling but it's been rated around the winner and third to their pre-race form for now.

## 6506 RISE HELICOPTERS H'CAP 6f 16y

**2:50** (2:51) (Class 4) (0-85,85) 3-Y-O+ **£5,175** (£1,540; £769; £384) **Stalls** Centre

Form RPR

536 **1** **Baron Bolt**$^{12}$ 6068 4-9-5 **85** ..........(p) DavidEgan$^{(5)}$ 8 94
(Paul Cole) *hld up in last pair: hdwy 2f out: led ent fnl f: kpt on wl: pushed out* **3/1**$^{2}$

1323 **2** *1¾* **Major Valentine**$^{11}$ 6098 5-8-9 **75** .......................... BenRobinson$^{(5)}$ 5 78
(John O'Shea) *prom: rdn over 2f out: kpt on wl fnl 70yds: regained 2nd cl home* **12/1**

330 **3** *hd* **Letmestopyouthere (IRE)**$^{16}$ 5929 3-9-5 **83** .......................... JFEgan 2 86
(David Evans) *chsd ldrs: swtchd lft to chal ent fnl f: sn rdn: no ex towards fin* **8/1**

0300 **4** *½* **Moonraker**$^{24}$ 5612 5-9-8 **83** .......................... ShaneKelly 1 84
(Mick Channon) *hld up in last pair: rdn over 2f out: no imp tl rna on fnl f: snatched 4th fnl strides* **8/1**

0135 **5** *nk* **Bahamian Dollar**$^{2}$ 6429 4-9-4 **82** .......................... CliffordLee$^{(3)}$ 7 82
(David Evans) *trckd ldrs: rdn over 2f out: no ex ins fnl f: lost 4th fnl strides: bled fr nose* **5/2**$^{1}$

0-23 **6** *3¼* **Tanasoq (IRE)**$^{86}$ 3330 4-9-2 **77** ..........(b$^{1}$) DaneO'Neill 3 67
(Owen Burrows) *led: rdn and edgd lft over 1f out: hdd ent fnl f: wknd* **7/2**$^{3}$

410 **7** *17* **Mamillius**$^{45}$ 4832 4-9-10 **85** ..........(p$^{1}$) FranBerry 6 20
(George Baker) *chsd ldrs: rdn over 2f out: wknd over 1f out: bled fr nose* **9/1**

1m 10.49s (-1.51) **Going Correction** -0.05s/f (Good)
**WFA** 3 from 4yo+ 3lb **7** Ran SP% **115.7**
Speed ratings (Par 105): **108,105,105,104,104 100,77**
CSF £38.02 CT £262.98 TOTE £4.30: £2.10, £3.80; EX 39.00 Trifecta £234.20.
**Owner** Asprey Wright Meyrick PJL Racing Wilcock **Bred** J A And M A Knox **Trained** Whatcombe, Oxon

**FOCUS**
A small sprint handicap, but they went a good clip.

## 6507 ORCHARD MEDIA APPRENTICE (S) STKS 6f 16y

**3:25** (3:26) (Class 6) 3-5-Y-O **£2,587** (£770; £384; £192) **Stalls** Centre

Form RPR

0000 **1** **Tifl**$^{19}$ 5793 4-8-12 55 ..........(bt) DavidEgan 1 56
(Heather Main) *mid-div: hdwy 2f out: rdn for str chal ent fnl f: kpt on wl: won on nod* **14/1**

0333 **2** *nse* **Dream Farr (IRE)**$^{16}$ 5936 4-9-8 70 ..........(t) JennyPowell 7 65
(Ed Walker) *trckd ldr: led over 1f out: sn rdn and strly pressed: kpt on wl: lost on nod* **1/1**$^{1}$

00 **3** *1¾* **Blackadder**$^{30}$ 5431 5-8-12 40 ..........(h) MeganNicholls 5 50
(Mark Gillard) *hld up bhd: hdwy u.p over 2f out: chsd ldng pair over 1f out: kpt on same pce fnl f* **80/1**

6505 **4** *2¾* **Hisar (IRE)**$^{15}$ 5956 3-8-9 61 .......................... MitchGodwin 3 42
(Ronald Harris) *mid-div: little hdwy u.p whn nt clr run over 1f out: sn swtchd lft: kpt on but no ch fnl f* **6/1**$^{3}$

0005 **5** *nk* **Wilspa's Magic (IRE)**$^{19}$ 5791 4-8-2 40 ..........(b) WilliamCox$^{(5)}$ 8 36
(Ron Hodges) *led: rdn and hdd over 1f out: no ex ins fnl f* **25/1**

024 **6** *shd* **Go Amber Go**$^{41}$ 4993 5-9-13 65 .......................... LuluStanford 2 56
(Rod Millman) *chsd ldr: rdn and ev ch 2f out: one pce fnl f* **11/4**$^{2}$

0604 **7** *1¼* **Diminutive (IRE)**$^{13}$ 6028 5-8-12 44 ..........(b) BenRobinson 4 37
(Grace Harris) *chsd ldrs: rdn 2f out: fdd ins fnl f* **20/1**

0300 **8** *1½* **Royal Normandy**$^{4}$ 6345 5-8-12 41 ..........(b) JoshuaBryan 10 32
(Grace Harris) *racd alone on stands' side for 3f: prom: rdn wl over 2f out: wknd fnl f* **20/1**

0-50 **9** *½* **Coral Caye**$^{15}$ 5958 3-8-2 42 ow3 .......................... TristanPrice$^{(5)}$ 6 26
(Steph Hollinshead) *s.i.s: a towards rr* **33/1**

0600 **10** *1* **Striking For Gold**$^{19}$ 5783 3-8-9 48 ..........(v$^{1}$) JaneElliott 9 28
(Sarah Hollinshead) *mid-div tl outpcd over 2f out* **33/1**

1m 11.43s (-0.57) **Going Correction** -0.05s/f (Good)
**WFA** 3 from 4yo+ 3lb **10** Ran SP% **118.1**
Speed ratings (Par 101): **101,100,98,94,94 94,92,90,90,88**
CSF £27.36 TOTE £16.00: £3.10, £1.10, £11.10; EX 53.00 Trifecta £2888.50.
**Owner** Mrs Helen Adams & Mark Telfer **Bred** R F And S D Knipe **Trained** Kingston Lisle, Oxon

**FOCUS**
A weak seller in which they went a good pace. The third and fifth limit the form.

## 6508 SIR GORDON RICHARDS H'CAP (SPONSORED BY OAKGROVE STUD) 2m

**4:00** (4:00) (Class 3) (0-90,86) 3-Y-O+
**£12,450** (£3,728; £1,864; £932; £466; £234) **Stalls** Low

Form RPR

/041 **1** **Taws**$^{11}$ 6096 6-9-9 **86** ..........(p) DavidEgan$^{(5)}$ 1 95
(Rod Millman) *chsd ldrs: pushed along in 6th 1/2-way: hdwy 3f out: sn rdn: chsd ldr over 1f out: str chal ins fnl f: led fnl stride: game* **2/1**$^{1}$

2204 **2** *hd* **Medburn Cutler**$^{11}$ 6096 7-9-4 **76** ..........(p) SteveDrowne 12 84
(Paul Henderson) *trckd ldrs: led 3f out: rdn 2f out: jnd ins fnl f: styd on: hdd fnl stride* **9/1**

04-3 **3** *3¾* **Arty Campbell (IRE)**$^{11}$ 6096 7-9-10 **82** ..........(p) MartinLane 6 85
(Bernard Llewellyn) *s.i.s: in last pair: hdwy fr 3f out: rdn whn swtchd rt over 1f out: styd on wl fnl f* **7/1**$^{3}$

0-30 **4** *2¼* **Norab (GER)**$^{11}$ 6096 6-8-11 **74** ..........(b) JoshuaBryan$^{(5)}$ 9 74
(Bernard Llewellyn) *mid-div: hdwy to join ldr 1/2-way: led over 3f out: rdn and hdd sn after: styd on same pce fnl 2f* **20/1**

1451 **5** *2½* **Wordiness**$^{8}$ 6233 9-9-2 **74** 6ex .......................... JFEgan 4 71
(David Evans) *mid-div: hdwy 3f out: sn rdn: styd on same pce fnl 2f* **14/1**

0-56 **6** *4* **Murgan**$^{17}$ 5873 5-9-8 **80** .......................... DaneO'Neill 7 73
(Stuart Kittow) *sn led: jnd 1/2-way: hdd over 3f out: rdn and hld whn short of room over 2f out: no threat after* **11/1**

5023 **7** *½* **Silver Quay (IRE)**$^{28}$ 4801 5-9-0 **77** .......................... MeganNicholls$^{(5)}$ 11 69
(Jimmy Frost) *hld up towards rr: sme late prog: n.d* **20/1**

33-2 **8** *8* **Yes Daddy (IRE)**$^{8}$ 4852 9-8-13 **71** ..........(bt) DanielMuscutt 5 53
(Robert Stephens) *sn trcking ldrs: rdn 3f out: wknd over 1f out* **10/1**

-050 **9** *3½* **Wolfcatcher (IRE)**$^{16}$ 5912 5-9-12 **84** ..........(bt$^{1}$) FranBerry 3 62
(Ian Williams) *prom: trckd ldrs 1/2-way: rdn 3f out: wknd 2f out* **9/2**$^{2}$

6412 **10** *7* **Nabhan**$^{12}$ 5251 5-9-6 **78** ..........(tp) TimmyMurphy 13 48
(Bernard Llewellyn) *hld up towards rr: rdn 3f out: nvr threatened* **8/1**

3m 30.1s (-8.80) **Going Correction** -0.375s/f (Firm) **10** Ran SP% **118.7**
Speed ratings (Par 107): **107,106,105,103,102 100,100,96,94,91**
CSF £21.50 CT £105.22 TOTE £2.50: £1.30, £2.50, £2.70; EX 23.20 Trifecta £57.70.
**Owner** R K & Mrs J M R Arrowsmith **Bred** Harts Farm Stud **Trained** Kentisbeare, Devon

**FOCUS**
The feature race was a fair staying handicap and they went a sensible pace.

## 6509 OAKGROVE STUD SUPPORTS BREAST CANCER CARE CYMRU H'CAP 1m 4f

**4:35** (4:35) (Class 6) (0-65,63) 3-Y-O+ **£3,234** (£962; £481; £240) **Stalls** Low

Form RPR

0004 **1** **Murchison River**$^{19}$ 5780 3-9-5 **63** .......................... DaneO'Neill 2 71+
(Henry Candy) *trckd ldrs: rdn over 2f out: chal ent fnl f: led fnl 100yds: asserting nr fin* **7/2**$^{2}$

63-6 **2** *nk* **Casaclare (IRE)**$^{83}$ 3431 3-9-0 **58** ..........(t$^{1}$) FranBerry 10 66
(Jonjo O'Neill) *racd keenly: led for 4f: trckd ldr: led over 2f out: sn rdn: styd on: hdd cl home* **12/1**

5102 **3** 1 ½ **Incredible Dream (IRE)**[21] 5722 4-9-9 **61**..................(p) JackDuern(3) 6 65
(Dean Ivory) *hld up towards rr: gd hdwy 3f out: sn rdn: wnt 3rd ent fnl f: styd on but nt pce to get on terms* **3/1**[1]

004 **4** 2 ¼ **Iley Boy**[26] 5532 3-8-9 **53**.................................. FergusSweeney 1 55
(John Gallagher) *trckd ldrs: rdn over 2f out: styd on but nt quite pce to mount chal* **20/1**

0233 **5** ½ **Powered (IRE)**[5] 6309 4-9-5 **59**.............................. DavidEgan(5) 13 59
(David Evans) *hld up towards rr: hdwy over 3f out: sn rdn: styd on same pce fnl 2f* **7/2**[2]

4015 **6** 4 **Grams And Ounces**[15] 5968 10-9-11 **60**..................(tp) TimmyMurphy 8 53
(Grace Harris) *in tch: hdwy to ld 8f out: rdn and hdd over 2f out: wknd fnl f* **7/1**[3]

-530 **7** ¾ **Everlasting Sea**[31] 5362 3-9-2 **60**.............................. MartinLane 12 53
(Stuart Kittow) *hld up towards rr: hdwy and in tch whn rdn over 2f out: wknd ent fnl f* **25/1**

2425 **8** 2 ¾ **St Andrews (IRE)**[21] 5722 4-9-3 **52**...................(tp) ShaneKelly 3 40
(Ian Williams) *trckd ldrs tl dropped to midfield 6f out: rdn wl over 2f out: wknd wl over 1f out* **7/1**[3]

0/56 **9** 1 **Flannery (IRE)**[19] 5787 6-8-8 **48**...............................(t[1]) MitchGodwin(5) 7 34
(Tim Vaughan) *mid-div: hdwy 5f out: effrt over 3f out: wknd 2f out* **16/1**

-064 **10** 17 **Selena Rose**[5] 6305 4-8-10 **45**.......................................(h) SamHitchcott 5
(Ronald Harris) *slowly away: towards rr: racd keenly: rdn over 3f out: sn wknd* **33/1**

2m 39.89s (0.89) **Going Correction** -0.375s/f (Firm)
**WFA** 3 from 4yo+ 9lb **10** Ran SP% **119.6**
Speed ratings (Par 101): **82,81,80,79,78 76,75,73,73,61**
CSF £44.89 CT £142.78 TOTE £3.80: £1.20, £3.80, £1.80; EX 65.10 Trifecta £398.10.
**Owner** The Earl Cadogan **Bred** The Earl Cadogan **Trained** Kingston Warren, Oxon

**FOCUS**
There were some unexposed types in this moderate handicap, and several made the frame. They didn't go flat out and it proved difficult coming from behind. The third, fourth and fifth set a base level.
T/Plt: £23.80 to a £1 stake. Pool: £59,627.30 - 1,824.83 winning units. T/Qpdt: £6.50 to a £1 stake. Pool: £3,808.86 - 428.48 winning units. **Tim Mitchell**

## 5555 EPSOM (L-H)
### Monday, August 28

**OFFICIAL GOING: Good (good to firm in places; rnd 7.1, spr 7.5)**
Wind: Light, across Weather: Sunny, very warm

### 6510 POUNDLAND'S SUPERHERO NOVICE AUCTION STKS — 7f 3y
**2:05** (2:05) (Class 5) 2-Y-O **£4,528** (£1,347; £673; £336) **Stalls** Low

Form RPR

05 **1** **Deadly Accurate**[10] 6132 2-9-2 0................................ RobertWinston 5 75
(Hughie Morrison) *mde all but pressed by runner-up thrght: shkn up over 1f out: a doing jst enough to maintain narrow ld fnl f* **9/2**[3]

26 **2** ½ **Hateya (IRE)**[77] 3655 2-8-11 0.................................... LiamKeniry 8 69
(Jim Boyle) *w wnr: rdn wl over 1f out: stl chalng fnl f: styd on but hld nr fin* **14/1**

04 **3** 2 ¼ **Powerful Society (IRE)**[20] 5755 2-8-10 0 ow2..... AdamMcNamara(3) 4 65
(Richard Fahey) *dwlt: rcvrd into 5th: shkn up over 2f out: tk 3rd wl over 1f out: rdn and kpt on but no real imp on ldng pair* **9/2**[3]

**4** 1 **Voice Of The North** 2-9-2 0................................... JoeFanning 2 67+
(Mark Johnston) *rn green and sn towards rr: 6th st: shkn up over 2f out: no prog tl styd on fnl f to take 4th last strides* **9/4**[1]

012 **5** ½ **Make Good (IRE)**[23] 5631 2-9-9 81............................ RyanMoore 7 71
(David Brown) *chsd ldng pair: rdn and nt qckn 2f out: sn lost 3rd and one pce after* **5/2**[2]

**6** 2 ¾ **King Athelstan (IRE)** 2-9-2 0.......................... JosephineGordon 3 56
(John Best) *chsd ldng trio: pushed along fr 1/2-way: stl cl up 2f out: fdd jst over 1f out* **14/1**

06 **7** 8 **Chickpea**[11] 6100 2-8-11 0......................................... OisinMurphy 6 30
(Michael Bell) *a in last pair: shkn up and lft bhd over 2f out* **25/1**

00 **8** 1 **The Naughty Step (IRE)**[33] 5292 2-9-2 0.................... JackMitchell 1 32
(Jim Boyle) *hld up in last pair: keen and awkward downhill: shkn up and lft bhd 2f out: eased ins fnl f* **33/1**

1m 24.58s (1.28) **Going Correction** -0.125s/f (Firm) **8** Ran SP% **115.8**
Speed ratings (Par 94): **87,86,83,82,82 79,69,68**
CSF £64.31 TOTE £6.00: £1.70, £2.80, £1.60; EX 81.80 Trifecta £265.90.
**Owner** Simon Malcolm & Partners **Bred** Kirtlington Stud Ltd **Trained** East Ilsley, Berks

**FOCUS**
The rail out 3-4yds from 1m to the winning post; add 7yds to this race distance. It was dry overnight and a hot day. A muddling race, with the first two in the top two spots throughout. The level is a bit fluid but the winner has been rated to his Newbury form for now.

### 6511 ALL NEW FIESTA AT TRUST FORD H'CAP (JOCKEY CLUB GRASSROOTS FLAT SPRINT SERIES QUALIFIER) — 6f 3y
**2:40** (2:41) (Class 5) (0-75,75) 3-Y-O **£4,528** (£1,347; £673; £336) **Stalls** High

Form RPR

3315 **1** **Seprani**[19] 5797 3-9-1 **69**................................(h) JosephineGordon 8 78+
(Marco Botti) *chsd ldng trio: clsd on outer fr 2f out: shkn up to ld 150yds out: pushed out after* **7/1**

1501 **2** ¾ **Summerghand (IRE)**[19] 5814 3-9-6 **74**......................... AndreaAtzeni 4 80
(David O'Meara) *chsd ldng pair: rdn to chal between them 1f out but wnr sn wnt past: styd on same pce after* **3/1**[2]

4111 **3** nse **Pastfact**[11] 6099 3-9-3 **71**............................................ LiamKeniry 6 76
(Malcolm Saunders) *chsd ldr: clsd to chal w others jst over 1f out: styd on same pce ins fnl f* **5/1**[3]

10 **4** 2 ¼ **Peace Dreamer (IRE)**[24] 5606 3-9-0 **75**.................. JonathanFisher(7) 5 73
(Robert Cowell) *s.s and rousted along early: in tch in last pair: shkn up 2f out: nt pce to threaten ldrs but kpt on fnl f* **12/1**

-644 **5** ¾ **Loving**[18] 5845 3-9-5 **73**..............................................(p[1]) RyanMoore 3 69
(William Haggas) *t.k.h: led: shkn up over 1f out: hdd & wknd qckly last 150yds* **13/2**

5225 **6** 6 **Baby Gal**[11] 6106 3-7-12 **59**...................................... IsobelFrancis(7) 2 36
(Jim Boyle) *in tch to over 2f out: sn bhd* **12/1**

0031 **U** **Chica De La Noche**[11] 6106 3-9-2 **70**...................(p[1]) HarryBentley 7
(Simon Dow) *stmbld bdly s and uns rdr* **9/4**[1]

1m 10.16s (0.76) **Going Correction** -0.125s/f (Firm) **7** Ran SP% **113.7**
Speed ratings (Par 100): **89,88,87,84,83 75,**
CSF £27.90 CT £114.46 TOTE £7.40: £3.50, £1.90; EX 34.50 Trifecta £155.20.
**Owner** Book 3 Partnership **Bred** Rabbah Bloodstock Limited **Trained** Newmarket, Suffolk
■ Stewards' Enquiry : Isobel Francis 5 day ban: used her whip when out of contention (11-15 Sep)

**FOCUS**
Add 6yds. A modest sprint handicap.

### 6512 CASPIAN PRINCE H'CAP — 5f
**3:15** (3:16) (Class 2) (0-100,97) 3-Y-O+
**£12,450** (£3,728; £1,864; £932; £466; £234) **Stalls** High

Form RPR

2023 **1** **Midnight Malibu (IRE)**[31] 5355 4-8-9 **82**........................... JoeFanning 3 90
(Tim Easterby) *mde all and grabbed nr side rail: edgd lft fr over 1f out but a in command: rdn out* **7/2**[2]

0010 **2** 1 **Love On The Rocks (IRE)**[27] 5505 4-9-3 **90**...........(h) WilliamCarson 8 94
(Charles Hills) *in tch: chsd ldng pair 2f out: styd on against nr side rail to take 2nd ins fnl f: nvr able to chal* **13/2**

0305 **3** 1 **Majestic Hero (IRE)**[9] 6177 5-8-13 **86**.......................... OisinMurphy 2 87
(Ronald Harris) *chsd wnr: shkn up and no imp 1f out: sn lost 2nd and one pce after* **10/1**

0-31 **4** shd **Discreet Hero (IRE)**[19] 5811 4-8-12 **85**.....................(t) AndreaAtzeni 5 85+
(Simon Crisford) *in tch in last pair: pushed along and no prog 2f out: styd on fnl f and nrly snatched 3rd* **4/1**[3]

2011 **5** ¾ **Compas Scoobie**[9] 6177 4-9-3 **95**.........................(v) CameronNoble(5) 1 93+
(Roger Varian) *dwlt: racd wd: nvr quite on terms w ldrs: one pce fnl f* **9/2**

-30 **6** 1 ½ **Tan**[21] 5697 3-8-3 **78** oh1...................................(t[1]) JosephineGordon 6 70
(Tony Coyle) *chsd ldng pair to 2f out: steadily wknd* **20/1**

6000 **U** **Boom The Groom (IRE)**[13] 6025 6-9-10 **97**................ RobertWinston 7
(Tony Carroll) *stmbld and uns rdr s* **11/4**[1]

55.26s (-0.44) **Going Correction** +0.125s/f (Good)
**WFA** 3 from 4yo+ 2lb **7** Ran SP% **114.3**
Speed ratings (Par 109): **108,106,104,104,103 101,**
CSF £26.05 CT £205.84 TOTE £4.30: £2.10, £3.60; EX 28.30 Trifecta £201.10.
**Owner** D A West & Partner **Bred** Kabansk Ltd & Rathbarry Stud **Trained** Great Habton, N Yorks

**FOCUS**
Aleef was withdrawn after getting loose beforehand, and Boom The Groom unseated his jockey after stumbling badly out of the stalls, and the winner got her own way up front, so not as competitive a race as it might have been.

### 6513 POUNDLAND SAVES THE DAY AMATEURS' DERBY H'CAP (FOR GENTLEMAN AMATEUR RIDERS) — 1m 4f 6y
**3:50** (3:56) (Class 4) (0-85,85) 4-Y-O+ **£6,239** (£1,935; £967; £484) **Stalls** Centre

Form RPR

6113 **1** **C'Est No Mour (GER)**[23] 5663 4-11-0 **78**........................ MrSWalker 4 86
(Peter Hedger) *dwlt and stdd s: hld up in last: stdy prog on wd outside over 2f out: rdn to ld last 150yds: r.o wl* **5/2**[1]

6012 **2** 1 ¼ **Thames Knight**[78] 3616 5-10-12 **82**...................... MrGTregoning(6) 10 88
(Marcus Tregoning) *wl in tch: stdy prog on outer fr 2f out: shkn up to ld jst ins fnl f: sn hdd and outpcd* **7/2**[3]

322 **3** ½ **Hollywood Road (IRE)**[12] 6059 4-11-7 **85**..........(b) MrDerekO'Connor 9 90
(Don Cantillon) *dwlt and stdd s: hld up in last trio: prog over 3f out: rdn to join ldrs 2f out: led and hung lft jst over 1f out: hdd jst ins fnl f and kpt on same pce* **10/3**[2]

2234 **4** 2 ¼ **Safira Menina**[25] 5556 5-10-6 **74**................................ MrBJames(4) 8 75
(Martin Smith) *reluctant to enter stalls: chsd ldrs: cl 4th st: rdn to ld 2f out: hdd and fdd jst over 1f out* **12/1**

0535 **5** nk **Roy Rocket (FR)**[17] 5868 7-10-3 **67**................................ MrRBirkett 1 68
(John Berry) *trckd ldr 4f: cl up in 3rd st: nt clr run and swtchd rt 2f out: outpcd after* **33/1**

1333 **6** 2 ½ **Cotton Club (IRE)**[18] 5820 6-10-8 **72**............................ MrPMillman 3 69
(Rod Millman) *hld up in tch: dropped to last st: nvr on terms after but plugged on fnl f* **8/1**

6226 **7** shd **Whinging Willie (IRE)**[9] 6196 8-10-12 **80**................(v) MrLWilliams(4) 7 77
(Gary Moore) *t.k.h: trckd ldr after 4f: rdn to ld briefly over 2f out: wknd wl over 1f out* **9/2**

3064 **8** 5 **Star Of Lombardy (IRE)**[12] 6061 4-10-8 **72**.............. MrAlexFerguson 6 61
(Mark Johnston) *led at stdy pce: hdd & wknd over 2f out* **14/1**

2m 47.17s (8.27) **Going Correction** -0.125s/f (Firm) **8** Ran SP% **120.5**
Speed ratings (Par 105): **67,66,65,64,64 62,62,59**
CSF £12.22 CT £30.11 TOTE £3.10: £1.50, £1.50, £1.40; EX 12.60 Trifecta £34.80.
**Owner** D Wilbrey **Bred** Graf U Grafin V Stauffenberg **Trained** Hook, Hampshire

**FOCUS**
Add 14yds. A fair running of the Amateurs' Derby.

### 6514 POUNDLAND FAMILY FAVOURITE CONDITIONS STKS — 1m 2f 17y
**4:20** (4:23) (Class 3) 3-Y-O+ **£9,337** (£2,796; £1,398; £699; £349) **Stalls** Low

Form RPR

536 **1** **Midterm**[58] 4360 4-9-2 108............................................. RyanMoore 6 114+
(Sir Michael Stoute) *hld up in last: shkn up wl over 2f out: clsd on ldrs after: swept into the ld 150yds out: sn clr* **7/4**[2]

-332 **2** 2 ½ **Mount Logan (IRE)**[16] 5925 6-9-2 110.....................(p[1]) AndreaAtzeni 4 109
(Roger Varian) *chsd clr ldr: clsd to ld on inner wl over 2f out but pressed: drvn over 1f out: hdd and no ex last 150yds* **11/10**[1]

5206 **3** 5 **Fierce Impact (JPN)**[38] 5095 3-8-9 95......................(p[1]) OisinMurphy 3 99
(David Simcock) *hld up in 4th: effrt to chse ldng pair over 2f out to over 1f out: wl btn after but tk 3rd again nr fin* **16/1**

-550 **4** 1 ¼ **Ayrad (IRE)**[16] 5925 6-9-2 106...........................(b[1]) RichardKingscote 5 97
(Roger Charlton) *racd in 3rd: chal on outer wl over 2f out and pressed ldr: btn over 1f out: sn lost 2nd and wknd* **9/2**[3]

0/2- **5** 26 **Fanoulpifer**[119] 6-9-2 0....................................................(p) JoeFanning 1 45
(Michael Attwater) *tore off in front and sn 12 l clr: wknd and hdd wl over 2f out: t.o* **50/1**

2m 5.15s (-4.55) **Going Correction** -0.125s/f (Firm)
**WFA** 3 from 4yo+ 7lb **5** Ran SP% **110.0**
Speed ratings (Par 107): **113,111,107,106,85**
CSF £4.03 TOTE £2.70: £1.80, £1.10; EX 3.90 Trifecta £15.90.
**Owner** K Abdullah **Bred** Juddmonte Farms Ltd **Trained** Newmarket, Suffolk

**FOCUS**
Add 14yds. Some frustrating but talented sorts, and the pace looked good despite the small field.

### 6515 STANLEY WOOTTON H'CAP — 1m 2f 17y
**4:55** (4:55) (Class 3) (0-90,90) 3-Y-O+
**£9,337** (£2,796; £1,398; £699; £349; £175) **Stalls** Low

Form RPR

11 **1** **High End**[18] 5849 3-9-3 **89**............................ EdwardGreatrex(3) 6 103+
(Saeed bin Suroor) *wl in tch: 4th st: clsd on outer over 2f out: shkn up to ld over 1f out: in command after: readily* **11/8**[1]

332 **2** 2 1/4 **Lorelina**79 3582 4-9-2 78 OisinMurphy 8 87
(Andrew Balding) *hld up in rr: 6th st: prog on outer over 2f out: rdn to chse wnr fnl f: styd on but no imp* **8/1**
5635 **3** 2 3/4 **Count Calabash (IRE)**24 5598 3-9-4 87 RyanMoore 4 90
(Eve Johnson Houghton) *trckd ldr after 3f: shkn up to chal over 2f out tl wnr shor past over 1f out: kpt on same pce after* **3/1**2
6245 **4** 1 1/4 **Innocent Touch (IRE)**31 5382 6-9-11 90 AdamMcNamara(3) 3 91
(Richard Fahey) *trckd ldr 3f: cl 3rd st: led on inner over 2f out: hdd and fdd over 1f out* **5/1**3
0045 **5** 1/2 **Grapevine (IRE)**24 5609 4-9-9 85 AndreaAtzeni 1 85
(Charles Hills) *stdd s: hld up: 7th st: tried to make prog over 2f out ubt hanging lft: nvr able to threaten but kpt on fnl f* **16/1**
0/6- **6** 5 **East Indies**133 1636 4-9-0 79 HectorCrouch(3) 2 69
(Gary Moore) *hld up: last st: pushed along and lost tch fr 3f out* **50/1**
0100 **7** 1 **Michele Strogoff**22 5683 4-9-11 87 (p) JosephineGordon 7 75
(Tony Coyle) *led at decent pce: hdd over 2f out: wknd qckly over 1f out* **33/1**
0264 **8** 4 1/2 **Sound Bar**30 5404 3-8-10 79 (b) PatDobbs 5 59
(Ralph Beckett) *trckd ldrs: 5th st: sn lost pl tamely and wl btn* **10/1**

2m 6.46s (-3.24) **Going Correction** -0.125s/f (Firm)
**WFA** 3 from 4yo+ 7lb **8 Ran SP% 114.8**
Speed ratings (Par 107): **107,105,103,102,101 97,96,93**
CSF £13.65 CT £29.03 TOTE £1.90: £1.10, £2.70, £1.40; EX 12.50 Trifecta £25.50.
**Owner** Godolphin **Bred** Watership Down Stud **Trained** Newmarket, Suffolk

**FOCUS**
Add 14yds. A useful handicap.

## 6516 MUSTANG HORSEPOWER AT TRUST FORD H'CAP — 1m 113y
**5:25** (5:25) (Class 4) (0-80,82) 3-Y-0+ **£6,469** (£1,925; £962; £481) **Stalls** Low

Form RPR
0362 **1** **Fujaira Bridge (IRE)**14 6001 3-9-6 81 AndreaAtzeni 2 90+
(Roger Varian) *trckd ldrs: wnt 2nd st: rdn to ld 2f out: drvn clr jst over 1f out: in n.d after* **11/2**3
6211 **2** 1 1/2 **Lord Clenaghcastle (IRE)**19 5788 3-9-7 82 RyanMoore 1 85
(Gary Moore) *trckd ldrs: shkn up and nt qckn 2f out: n.m.r briefly sn after: kpt on fnl f to win battle for 2nd but no threat to wnr* **5/4**1
1425 **3** nse **Shifting Star (IRE)**35 5221 12-9-2 70 (vt) JosephineGordon 3 72
(John Bridger) *led at gd pce: rdn and hdd 2f out: kpt trying and only jst pipped for 2nd last stride* **22/1**
0364 **4** 1/2 **Dubai's Secret**6 6297 4-9-9 80 (h1) HectorCrouch(3) 6 81
(David Brown) *hld up in last pair: shkn up and no prog over 2f out: styd on ins fnl f: nrst fin but no threat* **16/1**
4560 **5** 3/4 **Groor**32 5313 5-9-7 75 PatDobbs 8 75+
(Mohamed Moubarak) *dwlt: hld up in tch: effrt whn n.m.r 2f out: trying to cl whn repeatedly had nowhere to go fnl f: might have been plcd* **33/1**
2362 **6** 3/4 **Character Onesie (IRE)**10 6158 5-9-0 71 (b) AdamMcNamara(3) 5 69
(Richard Fahey) *trckd ldrs: rdn and cl up 2f out: sing to fade whn bmpd by rival 1f out* **15/2**
1151 **7** 29 **Sir Plato (IRE)**21 5719 3-9-7 82 OisinMurphy 7 13
(Rod Millman) *tried to ld but unable to: chsd ldr: lost 2nd st and sn wknd: eased and t.o* **5/1**2
5220 **P** **Pumaflor (IRE)**18 5849 5-9-13 81 (p) HarryBentley 4
(David O'Meara) *p.u after 1f and dismntd* **6/1**

1m 44.84s (-1.26) **Going Correction** -0.125s/f (Firm)
**WFA** 3 from 4yo+ 7lb **8 Ran SP% 115.7**
Speed ratings (Par 105): **100,98,98,98,97 96,71,**
CSF £12.96 CT £140.81 TOTE £5.80: £1.70, £1.10, £4.50; EX 14.10 Trifecta £139.90.
**Owner** Sheikh Mohammed Obaid Al Maktoum **Bred** Aston Mullins Stud **Trained** Newmarket, Suffolk

**FOCUS**
Add 14yds. A fair handicap.
T/Plt: £121.20 to a £1 stake. Pool: £90,213.67 - 543.10 winning units. T/Qpdt: £6.60 to a £1 stake. Pool: £6,326.23 - 699.32 winning units. **Jonathan Neesom**

# 6204 RIPON (R-H)
Monday, August 28

**OFFICIAL GOING: Good (8.0)**
Wind: virtually nil Weather: fine, sunny spells

## 6517 SALLIE LINDLEY MEMORIAL (S) STKS — 6f
**2:10** (2:12) (Class 5) 2-Y-0 **£3,234** (£962; £481; £240) **Stalls** High

Form RPR
4501 **1** **Flo's Melody**17 5893 2-9-2 60 PaulHanagan 5 64
(Richard Fahey) *sn prom: pushed along to ld wl over 1f out: rdn and kpt on* **11/4**2
5642 **2** 1 1/4 **Felisa**10 6127 2-8-11 62 PJMcDonald 10 55
(David Evans) *chsd ldrs: pushed along over 2f out: angled rt towards outer 2f out: sn chsd ldr: edgd further rt: kpt on but a hld* **9/4**1
6006 **3** 2 **Plansina**17 5878 2-8-11 54 (p1) DavidAllan 6 49
(Tim Easterby) *led: rdn whn hdd wl over 2f out: one pce ins fnl f* **6/1**3
06 **4** hd **Racing Radio (IRE)**16 5945 2-9-2 0 BenCurtis 8 54
(David Barron) *hld up: pushed along 3f out: rdn 2f out: kpt on fnl f: nrst fin* **33/1**
0040 **5** 1/2 **Lady Lintera (IRE)**13 6043 2-8-11 57 (h1) ShaneGray 2 47
(Ann Duffield) *midfield: rdn over 2f out: kpt on fnl f* **22/1**
24 **6** 9 **Silverlight (IRE)**16 5945 2-8-11 0 KevinStott 9 20
(Philip Kirby) *trckd ldrs: rdn 2f out: wknd fnl f* **8/1**
05 **7** 1 1/2 **Changing (IRE)**11 6093 2-8-11 0 TomMarquand 7 16
(Daniel Kubler) *hld up: nvr threatened* **33/1**
4060 **8** 2 1/2 **Jean Paget (IRE)**6 6285 2-8-11 59 SilvestreDeSousa 1 17
(Mick Channon) *in tch towards outer: rdn along over 2f out: wknd over 1f out* **9/1**
0406 **9** 3/4 **Sam James (IRE)**45 4836 2-8-9 62 JamieGormley(7) 3 11
(Iain Jardine) *a towards rr* **9/1**
605 **10** 1 **Jaimie's Joy**16 5945 2-9-2 53 (p1) BarryMcHugh 4 8
(Tony Coyle) *slowly away: a rr* **25/1**

1m 13.66s (0.66) **Going Correction** -0.15s/f (Firm) **10 Ran SP% 116.9**
Speed ratings (Par 94): **89,87,84,84,83 71,69,66,65,64**
CSF £8.94 TOTE £3.30: £1.20, £1.40, £1.90; EX 11.10 Trifecta £51.90.winner bought in for £5,500
**Owner** Middleham Park Racing LXXXIX **Bred** Mrs Fiona Denniff **Trained** Musley Bank, N Yorks
■ Stewards' Enquiry : Jamie Gormley two-day ban: careless riding (Sep 11-12)

**FOCUS**
The market leaders dominated the finish of this weak 2yo seller. Afterwards Paul Hanagan and Kevin Stott agreed with the official going description. The winner has been rated to her best, with the second and third near their recent marks.

## 6518 YORKSHIRE AIR AMBULANCE H'CAP — 1m 1f 170y
**2:45** (2:49) (Class 5) (0-75,75) 3-Y-0 **£3,881** (£1,155; £577; £288) **Stalls** Low

Form RPR
606- **1** **Bahkit (IRE)**389 5058 3-8-4 58 JoeDoyle 6 70
(Sally Haynes) *mde all: rdn over 2f out: edgd lft ins fnl f: kpt on* **66/1**
0-03 **2** 1 3/4 **Oden**23 5632 3-9-6 74 (p) SilvestreDeSousa 3 82
(Roger Varian) *prom: rdn over 2f out: kpt on but a hld* **3/1**1
1322 **3** 1 3/4 **Dream Machine (IRE)**18 5838 3-9-7 75 LouisSteward 11 80
(Michael Bell) *in tch: hdwy over 3f out: rdn to chse ldrs over 2f out: one pce* **4/1**3
2120 **4** 2 **Breanski**14 5993 3-9-6 74 DanielTudhope 10 75
(David O'Meara) *hld up in midfield: rdn along 4f out: one pce in modest 4th fr over 1f out* **7/2**2
4131 **5** 3 **Alfred Richardson**69 3934 3-9-7 75 PhillipMakin 9 70
(John Davies) *hld up: pushed along over 4f out: sme late hdwy: nvr threatened* **5/1**
10 **6** 1/2 **Mont Royal (FR)**11 6091 3-9-2 70 MartinHarley 7 64
(Ollie Pears) *slowly away: hld up in rr: rdn and sme hdwy over 2f out: no further imp* **12/1**
-460 **7** hd **Mister Moosah (IRE)**24 5617 3-8-7 61 PJMcDonald 1 54
(Micky Hammond) *in tch: rdn 3f out: wknd over 1f out* **28/1**
-420 **8** 3/4 **Broughtons Story**17 5888 3-8-2 56 PaulHanagan 4 48
(Henry Spiller) *trckd ldrs: rdn over 3f out: wknd fnl 2f* **16/1**
2-60 **9** 16 **Miss Danby (IRE)**12 6060 3-8-8 62 FrannyNorton 5 21
(Mark Johnston) *hld up: nvr threatened* **22/1**
2036 **10** 36 **Tread Lightly**44 4891 3-8-12 66 DavidAllan 8
(Tim Easterby) *prom: rdn over 3f out: wknd qckly: eased* **15/2**

2m 3.25s (-2.15) **Going Correction** -0.30s/f (Firm) **10 Ran SP% 118.5**
Speed ratings (Par 100): **96,94,93,91,89 88,88,88,75,46**
CSF £258.74 CT £1023.57 TOTE £68.20: £15.60, £1.80, £1.50; EX 368.10 Trifecta £1404.50.
**Owner** Mrs J Porter **Bred** Miss Elaine Marie Smith **Trained** Melsonby, N Yorks

**FOCUS**
A fair and competitive 3yo handicap. It suited those racing handily.

## 6519 BILLY NEVETT MEMORIAL H'CAP — 6f
**3:20** (3:22) (Class 4) (0-80,80) 3-Y-0 **£5,175** (£1,540; £769; £384) **Stalls** High

Form RPR
1560 **1** **Hee Haw (IRE)**9 6205 3-9-6 79 DanielTudhope 4 87
(Paul Midgley) *trckd ldrs: stl on bit appr fnl f: pushed along to ld jst ins fnl f: kpt on* **9/2**2
-663 **2** 1 **Sfumato**54 4489 3-9-5 78 DavidNolan 6 83
(Iain Jardine) *hld up: pushed along and hdwy over 1f out: rdn and kpt on* **11/2**3
5462 **3** nk **Harome (IRE)**21 5708 3-9-7 80 PJMcDonald 3 84
(Roger Fell) *prom: rdn to ld over 1f out: hdd jst ins fnl f: kpt on same pce* **6/1**
1111 **4** 4 1/2 **Kaeso**32 5316 3-9-3 76 TomEaves 8 65
(Nigel Tinkler) *trckd ldrs: rdn and outpcd over 3f out: plugged on fnl f* **3/1**1
3300 **5** 1 **Monks Stand (USA)**16 5929 3-8-12 71 (p) DavidAllan 7 57
(Tim Easterby) *hld up: rdn over 2f out: nvr threatened* **16/1**
2100 **6** 3 **Parys Mountain (IRE)**16 5948 3-9-6 79 (h) JimCrowley 1 56
(David Brown) *s.i.s: hld up: nvr threatened* **11/1**
0601 **7** 2 **Suitcase 'N' Taxi**21 5697 3-9-0 76 RachelRichardson(3) 5 46
(Tim Easterby) *led: rdn whn hdd over 1f out: wknd* **8/1**
0-04 **8** 1 1/2 **Lanjano**20 5759 3-9-1 74 KevinStott 9 39
(Kevin Ryan) *chsd ldrs: rdn 3f out: wknd over 1f out* **11/2**3

1m 11.58s (-1.42) **Going Correction** -0.15s/f (Firm) **8 Ran SP% 113.6**
Speed ratings (Par 102): **103,101,101,95,93 89,87,85**
CSF £28.91 CT £147.99 TOTE £5.50: £2.10, £2.00, £1.60; EX 36.30 Trifecta £188.30.
**Owner** Taylor's Bloodstock Ltd **Bred** Ballinvana House Stud **Trained** Westow, N Yorks
■ Stewards' Enquiry : Rachel Richardson one-day ban: not keep str from stalls (Sep 11)

**FOCUS**
The principals came clear in this fair 3yo sprint handicap.

## 6520 RIPON ROWELS H'CAP — 1m
**3:55** (3:55) (Class 2) (0-100,98) 3-Y-0+
**£12,450** (£3,728; £1,864; £932; £466; £234) **Stalls** Low

Form RPR
0241 **1** **Brilliant Vanguard (IRE)**9 6209 4-8-12 84 (p) KevinStott 1 96+
(Kevin Ryan) *trckd ldrs: squeezed through gap to ld over 1f out: rdn and kpt on wl* **11/4**1
6042 **2** 2 **Home Cummins (IRE)**31 5382 5-9-6 92 (p) PaulHanagan 8 98
(Richard Fahey) *midfield: rdn over 2f out: hdwy wl over 1f out: chsd ldr appr fnl f: kpt on* **9/1**
1-12 **3** 2 3/4 **Laidback Romeo (IRE)**72 3837 5-9-12 98 MartinHarley 6 98
(Clive Cox) *midfield inner: angled lft 2f out: sn pushed along to chse ldr: rdn appr fnl f: no ex fnl 110yds* **5/1**3
-420 **4** 2 1/4 **Fort Bastion (IRE)**9 6186 8-9-0 86 BenCurtis 4 80
(Brian Ellison) *slowly away: hld up: rdn and hdwy on inner over 1f out: kpt on fnl f: nrst fin* **33/1**
4050 **5** 1 **One Word More (IRE)**4 6355 7-9-3 92 (h) RachelRichardson(3) 7 84
(Tim Easterby) *hld up in rr: rdn over 2f out: hdwy over 1f out: kpt on fnl f: nrst fin* **8/1**
1130 **6** 3 1/2 **Gurkha Friend**72 3842 5-9-8 94 SilvestreDeSousa 2 79
(Karen McLintock) *led narrowly: rdn 3f out: hdd over 1f out: wknd* **7/2**2
0430 **7** 3 1/4 **Two For Two (IRE)**9 6209 9-9-3 89 (p) PJMcDonald 9 65
(Roger Fell) *hld up: nvr threatened* **20/1**
-006 **8** 3 1/2 **Father Bertie**9 6209 5-9-2 88 (tp) DavidAllan 3 55
(Tim Easterby) *w ldr: rdn 3f out: wknd over 1f out* **14/1**
6313 **9** 2 1/2 **Florenza**10 6145 4-9-4 90 TomEaves 10 51
(Chris Fairhurst) *w ldr on outer: rdn over 3f out: wknd fnl 2f* **20/1**
60 **10** 3 **Kharbetation (IRE)**20 5744 4-9-4 90 DanielTudhope 5 44
(David O'Meara) *in tch: rdn over 3f out: wknd over 2f out* **9/1**

1m 37.16s (-4.24) **Going Correction** -0.30s/f (Firm) **10 Ran SP% 115.8**
Speed ratings (Par 109): **109,107,104,102,101 95,91,88,85,82**
CSF £27.24 CT £121.13 TOTE £5.50: £2.90, £2.50, £3.70; EX 35.90 Trifecta £154.00.
**Owner** J C G Chua & C K Ong **Bred** Frank Moynihan **Trained** Hambleton, N Yorks

**FOCUS**
A good-quality handicap that served up a decent test. Solid form.

## 6521 LONGINES IRISH CHAMPIONS WEEKEND EBF RIPON CHAMPION TWO YRS OLD TROPHY, 2017 STKS (LISTED RACE) 6f
**4:30** (4:31) (Class 1) 2-Y-O

**£17,013** (£6,450; £3,228; £1,608; £807; £405) **Stalls** High

Form RPR
016 **1** **Enjazaat**[46] 4812 2-9-3 96 JimCrowley 4 101+
(Owen Burrows) *hld up in tch: smooth hdwy 2f out: sn chsd ldr: rdn to ld 1f out: kpt on wl pushed out* **7/2**[2]
13 **2** *2* **Tip Two Win**[28] 5476 2-9-3 0 TomMarquand 7 94
(Roger Teal) *hld up in tch: pushed along over 2f out: angled rt to outer over 1f out: sn rdn and hdwy: kpt on: wnt 2nd fnl 50yds: no ch w wnr* **16/1**
011 **3** *3/4* **Lake Volta (IRE)**[9] 6207 2-9-3 100 FrannyNorton 6 92
(Mark Johnston) *led: pushed along 2f out: rdn whn hdd 1f out: sn no ex: lost 2nd fnl 50yds* **5/4**[1]
010 **4** *2* **Helvetian**[15] 5973 2-9-3 102 SilvestreDeSousa 3 86
(Mick Channon) *prom: rdn over 2f out: outpcd over 1f out: plugged on fnl f* **9/1**
212 **5** *1 3/4* **Regulator (IRE)**[22] 5681 2-9-3 88 PaulHanagan 8 81
(Richard Fahey) *trckd ldrs: rdn over 2f out: outpcd over 1f out: no threat after* **5/1**[3]
0125 **6** *5* **Green Power**[25] 5570 2-9-3 97 BenCurtis 1 66
(John Gallagher) *wnt rt s: sn trckd ldrs on outer: rdn over 2f out: wknd over 1f out* **10/1**
10 **7** *13* **Chookie Dunedin**[69] 3925 2-9-3 0 DougieCostello 5 27
(Keith Dalgleish) *prom: rdn over 2f out: wknd over 1f out and bhd* **12/1**

1m 11.79s (-1.21) **Going Correction** -0.15s/f (Firm) 7 Ran SP% **116.0**
Speed ratings (Par 102): **102,99,98,95,93 86,69**
CSF £55.36 TOTE £3.90: £1.80, £6.40; EX 38.60 Trifecta £197.00.
**Owner** Hamdan Al Maktoum **Bred** C J Mills **Trained** Lambourn, Berks

**FOCUS**
The feature Listed event was run at a sound pace. The level is fluid, with the third rated a few lengths below his recent win here.

## 6522 FOLLOW @RIPONRACES ON TWITTER MAIDEN STKS 1m
**5:05** (5:05) (Class 5) 3-4-Y-O **£3,234** (£962; £481; £240) **Stalls** Low

Form RPR
234 **1** **Musical Terms**[83] 3438 3-9-5 78 JimCrowley 2 75+
(William Haggas) *prom: rdn to ld over 1f out: edgd lft: kpt on* **4/6**[1]
**2** *1 3/4* **Bombay (IRE)** 3-9-5 0 DanielTudhope 5 71
(David O'Meara) *hld up in tch: pushed along and hdwy over 1f out: rdn to chse ldr ent fnl f: kpt on* **9/2**[3]
6 **3** *1 3/4* **Global Roar**[83] 3435 4-9-8 0 PhilDennis(3) 1 68
(John Weymes) *led: rdn over 2f out: hdd over 1f out: no ex ins fnl f* **40/1**
**4** *3 1/2* **Kaylen's Mischief** 4-9-11 0 KevinStott 3 59
(Philip Kirby) *trckd ldrs: pushed along over 4f out: rdn over 2f out: wknd ins fnl f* **33/1**
3 **5** *2 1/2* **Perfect Sense**[16] 5937 3-9-5 0 TomMarquand 4 52
(Saeed bin Suroor) *trckd ldrs: rdn over 2f out: wknd fnl f* **11/4**[2]
0 **6** *12* **Major Minus**[7] 6268 3-9-2 0 RachelRichardson(3) 6 24
(Tim Easterby) *dwlt: hld up: pushed along over 4f out: sn wknd* **40/1**

1m 40.43s (-0.97) **Going Correction** -0.30s/f (Firm)
**WFA** 3 from 4yo 6lb 6 Ran SP% **112.7**
Speed ratings (Par 103): **92,90,88,85,82 70**
CSF £4.19 TOTE £1.60: £1.10, £1.50; EX 4.00 Trifecta £54.60.
**Owner** The Queen **Bred** Darley **Trained** Newmarket, Suffolk

**FOCUS**
A modest maiden.

## 6523 BETFAIR NOVICE FLAT AMATEUR RIDERS' H'CAP 1m 2f 190y
**5:35** (5:36) (Class 6) (0-60,62) 4-Y-O+ **£3,119** (£967; £483; £242) **Stalls** Low

Form RPR
2246 **1** **Strictly Art (IRE)**[15] 5968 4-11-7 59 MissJCooley 6 67
(Alan Bailey) *prom: led over 3f out: rdn 2f out: kpt on* **9/2**[3]
1 **2** *1 1/4* **All For Nothing (IRE)**[10] 6126 4-11-10 62 (vt) MrThomasReiley 5 68
(John C McConnell, Ire) *hld up: hdwy 3f out: rdn 2f out: edgd rt appr fnl f but sn 2nd: kpt on but nvr getting to wnr* **11/8**[1]
5024 **3** *4 1/2* **Kerry Icon**[18] 5831 4-10-11 49 (h) MissAMcCain 4 47
(Iain Jardine) *led: hdd over 3f out: rdn over 2f out: wknd ins fnl f* **11/4**[2]
0020 **4** *1 1/4* **Adventureman**[10] 6143 5-11-7 59 MissEmilyBullock 8 54
(Ruth Carr) *trckd ldrs: racd keenly: rdn 3f out: sn one pce: hld in poor 4th over 1f out* **15/2**
0600 **5** *4 1/2* **Mount Cheiron (USA)**[11] 6092 6-10-2 45 (b) MrJordanSwarbrick(5) 2 32
(Richard Ford) *hld up: rdn over 2f out: wknd over 1f out* **25/1**
0005 **6** *10* **Fledermaus (IRE)**[11] 6092 7-10-2 45 (t) MissBJohnson(5) 1 14
(Tina Jackson) *a towards rr* **20/1**
343- **7** *7* **Barnaby Brook (CAN)**[319] 7310 7-10-11 54 MrHMyddelton(5) 9 11
(Tom Dascombe) *trckd ldrs: racd keenly: rdn over 3f out: sn wknd* **9/1**

2m 22.0s (142.00) 7 Ran SP% **117.3**
CSF £11.62 CT £20.12 TOTE £5.60: £2.70, £2.20; EX 13.50 Trifecta £36.40.
**Owner** AB Racing Limited **Bred** Lismacue Mare Syndicate **Trained** Newmarket, Suffolk

**FOCUS**
An ordinary handicap, confirmed to amateur riders. The winner has been rated to this year's course form.
T/Plt: £71.70 to a £1 stake. Pool: £78,087.47 - 794.08 winning units. T/Qpdt: £23.00 to a £1 stake. Pool: £4,408.15 - 141.80 winning units. **Andrew Sheret**

# 2466 SOUTHWELL (L-H)
Monday, August 28

**OFFICIAL GOING: Fibresand: standard**
Wind: Light across Weather: Fine

## 6524 NOTTINGHAM POST H'CAP 1m 4f 14y(F)
**12:30** (12:31) (Class 6) (0-60,60) 3-Y-O+ **£2,587** (£770; £384; £192) **Stalls** Low

Form RPR
0455 **1** **Go On Gal (IRE)**[19] 5787 4-9-1 50 ShelleyBirkett(3) 1 61
(Julia Feilden) *mid-div: hdwy over 5f out: chsd ldr over 3f out: led over 2f out: edgd rt and pushed clr fr over 1f out* **16/1**
1004 **2** *4 1/2* **Lean On Pete (IRE)**[11] 6088 8-9-13 59 AndrewMullen 14 63
(Ollie Pears) *chsd ldrs: hmpd over 10f out: led 8f out: hdd over 6f out: chsd ldr tl rdn over 3f out: swtchd rt over 1f out: styd on to go 2nd wl ins fnl f* **12/1**
0640 **3** *2* **Mungo Madness**[26] 5532 3-8-2 50 MillyNaseb(7) 11 52
(Julia Feilden) *prom: swtchd rt over 7f out: pushed along over 3f out: no ex ins fnl f* **33/1**
6406 **4** *nk* **Star Ascending (IRE)**[28] 5483 5-9-7 53 (p) CamHardie 9 53
(Jennie Candlish) *s.i.s: pushed along early in rr: hdwy u.p over 3f out: styd on same pce fr over 1f out* **10/1**
6255 **5** *3/4* **Moojaned (IRE)**[21] 5716 6-9-1 54 RossaRyan(7) 6 53+
(John Flint) *hld up in tch: hmpd and lost pl over 10f out: hdwy to chse ldr over 7f out: led over 6f out: rdn and hdd over 2f out: no ex fnl f* **7/1**[3]
6333 **6** *6* **Arcadian Sea (IRE)**[13] 6048 3-8-13 54 RoystonFfrench 2 44
(William Jarvis) *edgd rt s: sn pushed along in rr: rdn over 3f out: nvr on terms* **4/1**[1]
0000 **7** *1/2* **Cockney Boy**[17] 5895 4-9-4 50 (p[1]) AlistairRawlinson 4 39
(Michael Appleby) *wnt prom whn hmpd over 10f out: wknd over 2f out: b.b.v* **22/1**
0600 **8** *8* **Fast Play (IRE)**[28] 5483 5-10-0 60 (b) GrahamLee 3 36
(Conor Dore) *s.i.s and hmpd s: outpcd* **66/1**
0303 **9** *32* **Albert Boy (IRE)**[11] 6109 4-8-12 49 GeorgeBuckell(5) 5
(Scott Dixon) *prom tl rdn and wknd 5f out: b.b.v* **11/1**
0000 **10** *7* **Thou Swell (IRE)**[13] 6035 5-9-8 54 (b) StevieDonohoe 7
(Shaun Harris) *s.i.s: outpcd* **50/1**
3040 **11** *42* **Les Pecheurs (IRE)**[23] 5649 3-8-13 54 (h) DougieCostello 13
(James Ewart) *sn led: edgd rt over 10f out: hdd over 7f out: wknd over 4f out* **50/1**
03 **12** *10* **Gunner Moyne**[33] 5296 5-9-10 59 (b) HectorCrouch(3) 10
(Gary Moore) *mid-div: rdn and lost pl over 7f out: wknd 1/2-way* **13/2**[2]
606 **P** **Beach Party**[34] 5247 3-8-10 54 CharlieBennett(3) 8
(Hughie Morrison) *mid-div: rdn and lost pl over 7f out: bhd fr 1/2-way: p.u and dismntd over 3f out* **10/1**
5325 **U** **Padleyourowncanoe**[18] 5846 3-9-4 59 (b) LukeMorris 12 +
(Daniel Mark Loughnane) *prom: hmpd and uns rdr over 10f out* **4/1**[1]

2m 42.89s (1.89) **Going Correction** +0.20s/f (Slow)
**WFA** 3 from 4yo+ 9lb 14 Ran SP% **118.6**
Speed ratings (Par 101): **101,98,96,96,95 91,91,86,64,60 32,25, ,**
CSF £185.65 CT £6126.38 TOTE £15.50: £4.60, £3.60, £7.40; EX 220.40.
**Owner** Go On Gal Partnership **Bred** Mrs Eleanor Commins **Trained** Exning, Suffolk

**FOCUS**
A modest middle-distance handicap. They went an initially contested gallop into the first turn in a rough race on standard Fibresand. The winner has been rated to this year's course form.

## 6525 NOTTINGHAMPOST.COM NOVICE STKS 4f 214y(F)
**1:00** (1:05) (Class 5) 2-Y-O **£3,234** (£962; £481; £240) **Stalls** Centre

Form RPR
50 **1** **Royal Diplomat (IRE)**[24] 5596 2-9-2 76 JackGarritty 7 85+
(Richard Fahey) *disp ld tl wnt on 1/2-way: pushed clr fnl f: eased towards fin* **7/2**[3]
4520 **2** *6* **Jim Rockford**[44] 4922 2-9-2 72 GrahamLee 1 62
(Ralph Beckett) *disp ld to 1/2-way: rdn over 1f out: sn outpcd* **13/8**[1]
65 **3** *2* **Skyva**[80] 3538 2-9-2 0 (h[1]) CamHardie 3 54
(Brian Ellison) *in tch: outpcd over 3f out: hdwy u.p over 1f out: nt trble ldrs* **9/1**
306 **4** *1 3/4* **Medici Oro**[41] 4995 2-9-2 66 AndrewMullen 6 48
(David Brown) *prom: rdn 1/2-way: edgd rt over 1f out: sn wknd* **14/1**
05 **5** *nk* **Fab (IRE)**[56] 4440 2-8-13 77 ow2 DougieCostello 2 44
(Jamie Osborne) *prom: rdn over 1f out: wknd fnl f* **5/2**[2]
636 **6** *3 3/4* **Mocead Cappall**[14] 6012 2-8-11 63 (h) RoystonFfrench 8 28
(John Holt) *prom: rdn 1/2-way: wknd over 1f out* **25/1**
0 **7** *2 3/4* **True North (IRE)**[18] 5834 2-9-2 0 StevieDonohoe 4 23
(Sir Mark Prescott Bt) *sn outpcd* **33/1**
**8** *8* **Magic Buddy** 2-8-8 0 ShelleyBirkett(3) 5
(J R Jenkins) *s.i.s: outpcd* **100/1**

59.7s **Going Correction** +0.15s/f (Slow) 8 Ran SP% **113.3**
Speed ratings (Par 94): **106,96,93,90,89 83,79,66**
CSF £9.39 TOTE £4.70: £1.60, £1.02, £2.30; EX 11.60 Trifecta £53.10.
**Owner** Alan Harte **Bred** Woodtown House Stud **Trained** Musley Bank, N Yorks

**FOCUS**
A fair juvenile novice sprint. They went a strong gallop and the third in the betting saw off the favourite from over 1f out. The winner could be rated 5lb higher but it's always worth being cautious with wide-margin winners here.

## 6526 EXCLUSIVE MAGAZINE MAIDEN STKS 4f 214y(F)
**1:30** (1:34) (Class 5) 3-Y-O+ **£2,911** (£866; £432; £216) **Stalls** Centre

Form RPR
03 **1** **Jabbarockie**[24] 5619 4-9-7 65 NeilFarley 4 74+
(Eric Alston) *mde virtually all: rdn clr fnl f: eased nr fin* **3/1**[2]
50 **2** *1 3/4* **Fortune And Glory (USA)**[14] 6009 4-9-7 0 JimmyQuinn 10 66+
(Joseph Tuite) *s.i.s: bhd: hdwy over 1f out: r.o to go 2nd wl ins fnl f: nvr nr to chal* **16/1**
600 **3** *1 1/2* **Bithynia (IRE)**[25] 5580 3-9-0 62 (t) PatrickMathers 11 55
(Christopher Kellett) *prom: rdn to chse wnr over 1f out: sn edgd lft: no ex ins fnl f* **25/1**
6400 **4** *7* **Ejabah (IRE)**[99] 2853 3-9-0 48 JoeyHaynes 3 29
(Charles Smith) *prom: rdn over 3f out: wknd over 1f out* **50/1**
351- **5** *1/2* **Sky Gypsy**[379] 5433 3-9-0 0 AndrewMullen 5 27
(David Brown) *chsd ldrs: rdn 1/2-way: sn hung lft: wknd over 1f out* **7/1**
0200 **6** *hd* **Proud Kate**[18] 5855 3-9-0 42 (p[1]) StevieDonohoe 6 26
(Christine Dunnett) *outpcd: nvr nrr* **100/1**
30 **7** *hd* **Golden Easter (USA)**[14] 6009 3-8-11 67 (p[1]) LewisEdmunds(3) 2 26
(Robert Cowell) *sn prom: rdn 1/2-way: wknd over 1f out* **5/1**[3]
0 **8** *2 1/2* **Be Be King (IRE)**[124] 2090 3-9-5 0 CharlesBishop 8 31
(Eve Johnson Houghton) *w wnr tl rdn 1/2-way: lost 2nd over 1f out: wknd and eased fnl f* **11/8**[1]
04- **9** *shd* **Faulkwood**[401] 4663 3-9-5 0 RoystonFfrench 7 21
(K R Burke) *sn outpcd* **12/1**
06 **10** *5* **Dollywaggon Pike**[6] 6295 3-9-0 0 AlistairRawlinson 1
(J R Jenkins) *s.i.s: sn prom: rdn 1/2-way: wknd 2f out* **66/1**

1m 0.03s (0.33) **Going Correction** +0.15s/f (Slow)
**WFA** 3 from 4yo+ 2lb 10 Ran SP% **118.1**
Speed ratings (Par 103): **103,100,97,86,85 85,85,81,81,73**
CSF £48.55 TOTE £3.80: £1.40, £5.20, £6.80; EX 55.30 Trifecta £784.20.
**Owner** M Balmer, K Sheedy, P Copple, C Dingwall **Bred** Paul Green **Trained** Longton, Lancs
■ Skadi was withdrawn not under orders. Price at time of withdrawal 33-1. Rule 4 does not apply.

**FOCUS**
An ordinary maiden sprint. The second favourite dominated from a traditionally favourable draw.

## 6527 @NOTTINGHAM_POST ON TWITTER H'CAP 6f 16y(F)
2:00 (2:01) (Class 5) (0-75,75) 3-Y-0+ £3,234 (£962; £481; £240) Stalls Low

Form RPR

2042 **1** **Tricky Dicky**[16] 5947 4-9-9 **74** SamJames 9 85
(Olly Williams) *mde all: rdn over 1f out: styd on* **6/4**[1]

5030 **2** 1¾ **Interlink (USA)**[7] 6267 4-9-6 **71** AlistairRawlinson 2 76
(Michael Appleby) *hld up: hdwy over 2f out: rdn to chse wnr over 1f out: styd on same pce wl ins fnl f* **11/2**[3]

1000 **3** 1½ **Treaty Of Rome (USA)**[58] 4343 5-9-7 **75** (v) LewisEdmunds(3) 3 76
(Derek Shaw) *hld up: swtchd rt and hdwy over 1f out: r.o: nt rch ldrs* **9/2**[2]

0613 **4** 2¾ **Danish Duke (IRE)**[18] 5827 6-9-5 **70** (p) JackGarritty 4 62
(Ruth Carr) *chsd ldrs: rdn over 2f out: no ex fnl f* **14/1**

26 **5** 4 **Sarabi**[10] 6130 4-8-3 **61** (b[1]) RPWalsh(7) 10 40
(Scott Dixon) *plld hrd and sn prom: wnt 2nd over 4f out tl 3f out: sn rdn: edgd lft over 1f out: sn wknd* **25/1**

0005 **6** 1 **Krystallite**[18] 5845 4-8-11 **67** GeorgeBuckell(5) 6 43
(Scott Dixon) *n.m.r after s: sn outpcd* **66/1**

2663 **7** ¾ **The Big Lad**[18] 5818 5-9-2 **74** (b) FinleyMarsh(7) 5 47
(Richard Hughes) *hld up in tch: shkn up over 2f out: sn wknd* **6/1**

1356 **8** 1½ **Lexington Sky (IRE)**[3] 6382 3-9-7 **75** ConnorBeasley 8 44
(Roger Fell) *s.i.s: in rr: rdn over 2f out: no ch whn hung lft over 1f out* **11/1**

030 **9** 4½ **Just Surprise Me (IRE)**[24] 5611 4-9-8 **73** (t) GrahamLee 7 27
(Mohamed Moubarak) *hld up: hdwy on outer over 3f out: rdn and wknd over 2f out* **20/1**

5144 **10** 1¾ **Nag's Wag (IRE)**[13] 6040 4-9-2 **67** AndrewMullen 1 16
(Conor Dore) *chsd ldrs: wnt 2nd briefly 1/2-way: rdn and wknd over 1f out* **33/1**

1m 17.29s (0.79) **Going Correction** +0.20s/f (Slow)
**WFA** 3 from 4yo+ 3lb **10** Ran SP% **115.9**
Speed ratings (Par 103): **102,99,97,94,88 87,86,84,78,76**
CSF £9.34 CT £31.17 TOTE £2.30: £1.40, £1.50, £1.90; EX 11.50 Trifecta £49.90.
**Owner** Eight Gents and a Lady **Bred** Onslow, Stratton & Parry **Trained** Market Rasen, Lincs

**FOCUS**
A fair handicap. The favourite got on the lead from a wide draw and the outcome was in little doubt thereafter.

## 6528 NOTTINGHAM POST ON FACEBOOK H'CAP (DIV I) 7f 14y(F)
2:35 (2:36) (Class 6) (0-60,61) 3-Y-0+ £2,587 (£770; £384; £192) Stalls Low

Form RPR

0200 **1** **Monsieur Jimmy**[14] 6003 5-9-4 **54** StevieDonohoe 11 69
(Declan Carroll) *s.i.s: hld up: hdwy over 2f out: rdn to ld over 1f out: sn clr: eased towards fin* **5/1**[1]

6002 **2** 6 **Breaking Free**[34] 5239 3-8-7 **48** JasonHart 3 45
(John Quinn) *prom: rdn over 4f out: edgd lft and ev ch over 1f out: styd on same pce fnl f* **15/2**[2]

0000 **3** ½ **Fossa**[18] 5848 7-8-9 **48** (h) CharlieBennett(3) 14 45
(Mark Brisbourne) *trckd ldrs: rdn to chse ldr over 1f out: no ex ins fnl f* **16/1**

6306 **4** ¾ **Luath**[18] 5835 4-9-8 **61** SammyJoBell(3) 6 56
(Suzzanne France) *prom: sn lost pl: last over 3f out: hdwy over 1f out: nt rch ldrs* **5/1**[1]

6560 **5** ¾ **Nellie Deen (IRE)**[2] 6437 4-8-10 **46** (b) ConnorBeasley 12 39
(Roger Fell) *chsd ldrs: led over 5f out: clr 3f out: sn rdn: hdd over 1f out: wknd ins fnl f* **12/1**

00 **6** 3½ **Geordie George (IRE)**[27] 5497 5-9-10 **60** (t) GrahamLee 7 44
(Rebecca Menzies) *prom: lost pl after 1f: nvr on terms after* **5/1**[1]

000 **7** 2 **Mr Andros**[12] 6076 4-9-5 **55** (tp) JimmyQuinn 8 34
(Brendan Powell) *mid-div: rdn over 4f out: outpcd fr 1/2-way* **33/1**

6-00 **8** 1¾ **Roger Thorpe**[9] 6181 8-9-0 **53** LewisEdmunds(3) 1 27
(John Balding) *chsd ldrs: rdn over 2f out: wknd over 1f out* **9/1**

0060 **9** nk **Rock Of Monaco**[35] 5215 4-8-10 **46** oh1 (b) CamHardie 13 19
(Antony Brittain) *dwlt: nvr on terms* **25/1**

0000 **10** ½ **Broughtons Fancy**[10] 6131 4-8-12 **53** GemmaTutty(5) 5 25
(Karen Tutty) *sn pushed along in rr: nvr on terms* **22/1**

405 **11** 2¼ **Freddy With A Y (IRE)**[19] 5793 7-9-7 **57** (p) KierenFox 10 23
(J R Jenkins) *sn pushed along in rr: n.d* **8/1**[3]

-000 **12** nk **Jungle George**[42] 4970 3-8-5 **46** oh1 RoystonFfrench 2 9
(Scott Dixon) *sn pushed along and a in rr* **66/1**

0402 **13** 1½ **Canford Belle**[134] 1823 4-9-1 **51** AndrewMullen 9 12
(Grant Tuer) *prom: rdn over 2f out: sn wknd* **10/1**

6/00 **14** 1¾ **Time Continuum**[20] 5736 5-8-10 **46** oh1 NeilFarley 4
(Eric Alston) *led: hdd over 5f out: chsd ldr: rdn over 2f out: sn wknd* **100/1**

1m 31.05s (0.75) **Going Correction** +0.20s/f (Slow)
**WFA** 3 from 4yo+ 5lb **14** Ran SP% **119.2**
Speed ratings (Par 101): **103,96,95,94,93 89,87,85,85,84 82,81,80,78**
CSF £39.60 CT £582.36 TOTE £6.10: £2.20, £2.90, £5.80; EX 56.10 Trifecta £924.70.
**Owner** Ray Flegg & John Bousfield **Bred** J Repard & M Stokes **Trained** Malton, N Yorks

**FOCUS**
The first division of a modest handicap. They went a respectable gallop and it is sound form.

## 6529 NOTTINGHAM POST ON FACEBOOK H'CAP (DIV II) 7f 14y(F)
3:10 (3:11) (Class 6) (0-60,60) 3-Y-0+ £2,587 (£770; £384; £192) Stalls Low

Form RPR

0-00 **1** **Noble Ballad**[26] 5545 3-9-2 **57** (b[1]) GrahamLee 13 63
(Ralph Beckett) *s.i.s: hdwy over 4f out: led over 2f out: rdn out* **10/1**

3030 **2** ½ **Bo Selecta (IRE)**[10] 6131 3-9-3 **58** (p) CharlesBishop 10 63
(Richard Spencer) *prom: lost pl over 5f out: hdwy u.p over 2f out: r.o* **14/1**

3065 **3** ¾ **Break The Silence**[19] 5802 3-8-3 **51** RPWalsh(7) 12 54
(Scott Dixon) *chsd ldrs: rdn over 3f out: ev ch over 2f out: styd on same pce wl ins fnl f* **8/1**[3]

3400 **4** 1½ **Jennies Gem**[35] 5215 4-8-11 **47** AndrewMullen 14 48
(Ollie Pears) *hld up: hdwy over 2f out: rdn over 1f out: no ex towards fin* **50/1**

3431 **5** 2¼ **Size Matters**[14] 5991 3-9-4 **59** JasonHart 4 52
(Mark Walford) *sn led: rdn and hdd over 2f out: wknd ins fnl f* **2/1**[1]

4200 **6** ½ **Grey Destiny**[19] 5802 7-9-9 **59** CamHardie 9 52
(Antony Brittain) *s.i.s: sn pushed along in rr: hung lft over 1f out: styd on ins fnl f: nvr nrr* **10/1**

00-6 **7** 2 **Unonothinjonsnow**[26] 5536 3-8-5 **46** oh1 RoystonFfrench 1 32
(Richard Guest) *hld up: rdn 1/2-way: nt trble ldrs* **14/1**

0425 **8** shd **Trust Me Boy**[132] 1868 9-9-0 **53** SimonPearce(3) 5 40
(John E Long) *led early: chsd ldrs: pushed along over 4f out: wknd over 1f out* **20/1**

3446 **9** 8 **Treagus**[49] 4697 3-9-0 **55** (p) StevieDonohoe 8 19
(Charlie Fellowes) *in tch: lost pl over 5f out: n.d after* **6/1**[2]

000 **10** 6 **Royal Holiday (IRE)**[21] 5698 10-9-10 **60** (p) JackGarritty 6 10
(Marjorie Fife) *sn pushed along in rr: swtchd rt 6f out: rdn and hung lft over 2f out: nvr on terms* **8/1**[3]

3260 **11** ¾ **Elusivity (IRE)**[17] 5892 9-9-2 **57** (p) CallumRodriguez(5) 11 5
(Conor Dore) *sn w ldr: rdn and ev ch over 2f out: wknd over 1f out* **14/1**

0006 **12** 8 **Leith Bridge**[9] 6174 5-8-4 **47** oh1 ow1 (p) FinleyMarsh(7) 7
(Mark Usher) *sn pushed along and a in rr* **33/1**

0530 **13** 4 **Zebedee Star**[12] 6058 3-8-5 **46** oh1 JimmyQuinn 2
(Karen Tutty) *chsd ldrs tl rdn and wknd over 2f out* **66/1**

1m 33.3s (3.00) **Going Correction** +0.20s/f (Slow)
**WFA** 3 from 4yo+ 5lb **13** Ran SP% **119.2**
Speed ratings (Par 101): **90,89,88,86,84 83,81,81,72,65 64,55,50**
CSF £137.30 CT £807.32 TOTE £11.40: £4.20, £4.20, £2.20; EX 188.00 Trifecta £1703.10.
**Owner** Melody Racing **Bred** Melody Bloodstock **Trained** Kimpton, Hants

**FOCUS**
The second division of a modest handicap. The winning time was over two seconds slower and the favourite may have done too much too soon in a bunched finish. It's been rated around the runner-up to his pre-race mark.

## 6530 NOTTS COUNTY NEWS ON NOTTINGHAMPOST.COM H'CAP 2m 102y(F)
3:45 (3:48) (Class 6) (0-55,55) 3-Y-0+ £2,264 (£673; £336; £168) Stalls Low

Form RPR

0606 **1** **Shine Baby Shine**[18] 5831 3-8-4 **47** PatrickMathers 3 60+
(Philip Kirby) *s.i.s: hld up: hdwy over 5f out: chsd ldr over 3f out: led over 2f out: rdn clr fr over 1f out* **8/1**

0-60 **2** 11 **Tynecastle Park**[122] 508 4-9-9 **54** PaoloSirigu 9 52
(Robert Eddery) *hld up: hdwy over 4f out: outpcd: nt clr run and swtchd rt over 3f out: sn rdn: styd on to go 2nd wl ins fnl f* **9/1**

5320 **3** 1¼ **Esspeegee**[16] 5923 4-9-1 **46** oh1 (p) JimmyQuinn 14 43
(Alan Bailey) *prom: chsd ldr over 5f out: led over 4f out: rdn and hdd over 2f out: wknd fnl f* **13/2**[2]

2 **4** 26 **Stander (IRE)**[13] 6032 3-8-7 **50** JasonHart 1 17
(John C McConnell, Ire) *chsd ldrs: rdn over 3f out: wknd over 2f out* **11/2**[1]

0650 **5** 1¾ **Rob's Legacy**[34] 5267 4-8-12 **46** oh1 CharlieBennett(3) 10 9
(Shaun Harris) *sn led: hdd over 4f out: rdn and wknd wl over 2f out* **25/1**

6300 **6** 3½ **Yasir (USA)**[16] 5951 9-9-9 **54** AndrewMullen 13 13
(Conor Dore) *slowly in to stride: hdwy over 8f out: rdn over 3f out: sn wknd* **7/1**[3]

002/ **7** 9 **Pahente**[999] 8010 9-8-8 **46** oh1 AledBeech(7) 11
(Tony Carroll) *hld up: rdn and wknd over 4f out* **50/1**

-023 **8** 16 **Desktop**[20] 5740 5-9-10 **55** CamHardie 7
(Antony Brittain) *hld up: rdn over 6f out: wknd over 4f out* **8/1**

P-00 **9** 29 **Oracle Boy**[67] 4018 6-9-2 **47** (p) GrahamLee 12
(Michael Chapman) *chsd ldr tl rdn over 5f out: wknd over 4f out* **200/1**

00-6 **10** 13 **Legalized**[35] 5209 3-8-8 **51** ow1 ConnorBeasley 6
(James Given) *prom: pushed along and lost pl over 11f out: wknd over 8f out* **7/1**[3]

5455 **11** 1½ **Toast Of London**[30] 5413 4-9-3 **48** RoystonFfrench 4
(Antony Brittain) *chsd ldrs: rdn over 8f out: wknd over 7f out* **20/1**

0002 **12** 1¼ **Astroshadow**[35] 5209 3-8-5 **48** JoeyHaynes 5
(Mark H Tompkins) *hld up: hdwy over 8f out: wknd over 6f out* **8/1**

-002 **13** 99 **Toptempo**[30] 5407 8-9-5 **50** JackGarritty 8
(Ralph J Smith) *s.i.s: sn pushed along in rr: rdn over 10f out: bhd fr 1/2-way* **16/1**

0006 **P** **Jeremy's Jet (IRE)**[53] 4545 6-9-4 **49** (t) GeorgeDowning 2
(Tony Carroll) *prom: pushed along 8f out: wknd over 4rf out: bhd whn p.u and dismntd over 3f out* **20/1**

3m 48.22s (2.72) **Going Correction** +0.20s/f (Slow)
**WFA** 3 from 4yo+ 12lb **14** Ran SP% **118.8**
Speed ratings (Par 101): **101,95,94,81,81 79,74,66,52,45 45,44, ,**
CSF £72.75 CT £502.02 TOTE £10.80: £3.10, £3.80, £2.70; EX 108.00 Trifecta £853.00.
**Owner** David Gray & P Kirby **Bred** Horizon Bloodstock Limited **Trained** East Appleton, N Yorks
■ Stewards' Enquiry : Patrick Mathers caution: guilty of careless riding in that he allowed his mount to drift left when insufficiently clear

**FOCUS**
A moderate staying handicap and an unexposed 3yo filly in receipt of 12lb weight-for-age routed the opposition. The winner has been rated a big improver up in trip.

## 6531 NOTTINGHAM FOREST NEWS ON NOTTINGHAMPOST.COM H'CAP 4f 214y(F)
4:15 (4:20) (Class 6) (0-60,61) 4-Y-0+ £2,587 (£770; £384; £192) Stalls Centre

Form RPR

-453 **1** **Lydiate Lady**[17] 5877 5-8-9 **48** NeilFarley 3 56
(Eric Alston) *led: hdd over 3f out: remained handy: rdn over 1f out: styd on to ld nr fin* **8/1**

0000 **2** nk **Men United (FR)**[11] 6114 4-8-2 **46** oh1 (b) KevinLundie(5) 2 53
(Roy Bowring) *sn chsng ldr: led over 3f out: rdn over 1f out: hdd nr fin* **5/1**[1]

3350 **3** 1¾ **Pearl Noir**[11] 6089 7-8-10 **54** (b) GeorgeBuckell(5) 10 55
(Scott Dixon) *chsd ldrs: rdn 1/2-way: styd on same pce ins fnl f* **8/1**

6504 **4** ½ **Misu Moneypenny**[20] 5738 4-8-8 **47** (v) ConnorBeasley 4 46
(Scott Dixon) *sn pushed along towards rr: hdwy over 1f out: nt rch ldrs* **6/1**[2]

6140 **5** 1 **Kodimoor (IRE)**[10] 6130 4-9-7 **60** PatrickMathers 9 55
(Christopher Kellett) *sn pushed along towards rr: r.o ins fnl f: nvr nrr* **12/1**

003 **6** ¾ **Wimboldsley**[17] 5892 6-8-1 **47** RPWalsh(7) 11 39
(Scott Dixon) *s.i.s: hdwy 1/2-way: rdn and hung lft over 1f out: styd on same pce ins fnl f* **12/1**

6005 **7** hd **Classic Flyer**[20] 5748 5-8-8 **47** (b[1]) JimmyQuinn 5 38
(Christine Dunnett) *s.i.s: outpcd: nvr nrr* **20/1**

0002 **8** hd **Sir Geoffrey (IRE)**[10] 6130 11-8-11 **55** (b) PaddyPilley(5) 6 46
(Scott Dixon) *chsd ldrs: rdn 1/2-way: no ex fnl f* **7/1**[3]

0/05 **9** 2¼ **Satellite Express (IRE)**[17] 5871 6-8-7 **46** (bt) RoystonFfrench 7 28
(Tim Pinfield) *sn pushed along towards rr: rdn 1/2-way: wknd over 1f out* **25/1**

6105 **10** ½ **Fortinbrass (IRE)**[74] 3758 7-9-5 **61** LewisEdmunds(3) 8 42
(John Balding) *chsd ldrs: lost pl 1/2-way: wknd over 1f out* **6/1**[2]

3060 **11** nk **Roy's Legacy**[13] 6040 8-9-0 **56** CharlieBennett(3) 1 35
(Shaun Harris) *chsd ldrs: rdn 1/2-way: wknd wl over 1f out* **7/1**[3]

1m 0.46s (0.76) **Going Correction** +0.15s/f (Slow) **11** Ran SP% **116.5**
Speed ratings (Par 101): **99,98,95,94,93 92,91,91,87,87 86**
CSF £47.27 CT £339.34 TOTE £7.70: £2.30, £2.60, £2.30; EX 63.10 Trifecta £767.00.

**Owner** The Scotch Piper Racing **Bred** Catridge Farm Stud **Trained** Longton, Lancs
■ Stewards' Enquiry : Kevin Lundie 3 day ban: weighed in at 8st 4lb, weighed out at 8st 2lb (11-13 Sep)

**FOCUS**
A modest sprint handicap and the favourite couldn't quite finish off his opposition. Straightforward form rated around the second, third and fourth to their course form.
T/Jkpt: Not Won. T/Plt: £3,558.70 to a £1 stake. Pool: £61,182.02 - 12.55 winning units. T/Qpdt: £156.90 to a £1 stake. Pool: £5,514.28 - 26.0 winning units. **Colin Roberts**

6532 - 6539a (Foreign Racing) - See Raceform Interactive

## 6496 DEAUVILLE (R-H)
Monday, August 28
**OFFICIAL GOING: Polytrack: fast; turf: good**

### 6540a PRIX DES ROUGES (CONDITIONS) (4YO+) (POLYTRACK) 6f 110y
11:55 4-Y-0+ £14,102 (£5,641; £4,230; £2,820; £1,410)

RPR
1 **Miracle Of Medinah**[45] 4854 6-9-1 0 ow1 ... TheoBachelot 8 92
(Mark Usher) *dwlt: hld up towards rr: pushed along over 2f out: drvn to cl over 1f out: r.o u.p fnl f to ld cl home* **145/10**
2 ½ **Absalon (USA)**[22] 6-9-4 0 ow1 ... MaximeGuyon 7 93
(F Head, France) **2/5**[1]
3 1½ **For Ever (FR)**[22] 6-9-4 0 ow1 ... (b) AntoineCoutier 1 89
(Carina Fey, France) **98/10**[3]
4 1 **Walec**[24] 5628 5-9-1 0 ow1 ... Pierre-CharlesBoudot 2 83
(P Sogorb, France) **59/10**[2]
5 hd **Mesmerism (USA)**[869] 1362 5-9-1 0 ow1 ... PanagiotisDimitsanis 4 83
(Christos Kouvaras, France) **192/10**
6 nse **Mylenajonh (FR)**[20] 4-8-11 0 ow1 ... HugoJourniac 6 78
(Jane Soubagne, France) **243/10**
7 1¾ **Rocking Lady (IRE)**[387] 4-8-6 0 ow1 ... JeromeMoutard(5) 5 73
(J-M Lefebvre, France) **34/1**
8 ½ **Jonh Jonh (FR)**[132] 6-9-1 0 ow1 ... MickaelBarzalona 3 76
(Jane Soubagne, France) **125/10**

1m 15.96s **8 Ran SP% 120.8**
PARI-MUTUEL (all including 1 euro stake): WIN 15.50; PLACE 1.10, 1.10, 1.10; DF 8.80; SF 32.40.
**Owner** The High Jinks Partnership **Bred** A C M Spalding **Trained** Upper Lambourn, Berks

### 6541a PRIX DU GUE (CLAIMER) (4YO+) (POLYTRACK) 7f 110y
12:25 4-Y-0+ £6,837 (£2,735; £2,051; £1,367; £683)

RPR
1 **See You Soon (FR)**[30] 6-9-3 0 ow1 ... ThierryThulliez 8 73
(P Sobry, France) **54/10**[3]
2 nk **Xarco (IRE)**[8] 4-9-1 0 ow1 ... MlleAlisonMassin(4) 4 74
(Christos Kouvaras, France) **121/10**
3 hd **Malaspina (ITY)**[14] 5-9-0 0 ow1 ... (b) MlleJessicaMarcialis(4) 7 72
(Antonio Marcialis, Italy) **17/5**[1]
4 1¼ **Well Fleeced**[16] 5-9-5 0 ow1 ... WilliamsSaraiva 14 70
(Carina Fey, France) **47/10**[2]
5 1¼ **Stormbound (IRE)**[61] 4203 8-9-1 0 ow1 ... (b) MlleCoraliePacaut(4) 10 67
(Paul Cole) *in rr early: effrt over 2f out: rdn and styd on one pce fnl f* **68/10**
6 hd **Beruska (FR)**[72] 4-9-2 0 ow1 ... PaulineProd'homme(4) 5 68
(Carina Fey, France) **96/10**
7 2½ **Rebel Lightning (IRE)**[167] 1189 4-9-1 0 ow1 .. (b) MlleLauraGrosso(4) 11 60
(P Monfort, France) **184/10**
8 ½ **Its My Story (FR)**[98] 5-9-3 0 ow1 ... BrunoPanicucci 9 57
(J Reynier, France) **102/10**
9 ½ **Mustaqqil (IRE)**[11] 5-8-11 0 ow1 ... (p) MlleMickaelleMichel(5) 13 55
(Christos Kouvaras, France) **269/10**
10 2 **Peut Etre Ici (IRE)**[131] 4-9-2 0 ow1 ... (p) JimmyTastayre 3 50
(G Botti, France) **198/10**
11 ½ **Xedra**[186] 5-9-0 0 ow1 ... (p) StephaneLaurent 2 47
(H De Nicolay, France) **72/1**
12 3 **Daring Storm (GER)**[11] 7-9-2 0 ow1 ... (b) ErwannLebreton 1 41
(F Cheyer, France) **232/10**
13 ¾ **Vroom (IRE)**[6] 6302 4-9-2 0 ow1 ... (p) KyllanBarbaud 6 39
(Gay Kelleway) *disp ld early: dropped in bhd ldr after 1f: rdn over 2f out: sn no rspnse and eased ins fnl f* **36/1**
14 1¾ **Sanam (USA)**[11] 5-8-13 0 ow2 ... (p) JordanDelaunay 12 32
(Louis Baudron, France) **65/1**

PARI-MUTUEL (all including 1 euro stake): WIN 6.40; PLACE 2.40, 4.10, 1.90; DF 34.60; SF 46.70.
**Owner** Antoine Boucher **Bred** Mme A Tamagni **Trained** France

### 6542a PRIX TANIT (MAIDEN) (2YO FILLIES) (ROUND) (TURF) 1m (R)
1:05 2-Y-0 £11,538 (£4,615; £3,461; £2,307; £1,153)

RPR
1 **Marie De Medicis**[20] 2-9-3 0 ow1 ... ChristopheSoumillon 1 82
(J-C Rouget, France) **5/2**[1]
2 1¼ **Zomara (FR)** 2-8-13 0 ow2 ... MaximeGuyon 5 75
(F Head, France) **53/10**[3]
3 2½ **Star Of Vendome (FR)**[8] 6251 2-9-3 0 ow1 ... EddyHardouin 8 73
(Harry Dunlop) *wl into stride: sn led: rdn over 1f out: hdd ins fnl f: styd on one pce* **43/1**
4 hd **Love And Peace (FR)**[24] 2-9-3 0 ow1 ... MickaelBarzalona 9 73
(Mme Pia Brandt, France) **27/10**[2]
5 ¾ **Samphire (FR)**[24] 2-9-3 0 ow1 ... AlexisBadel 13 71
(H-F Devin, France) **127/10**
6 1¼ **Lypharty Ka (FR)**[16] 2-9-3 0 ow1 ... StephanePasquier 2 68
(Y Gourraud, France) **236/10**
7 1 **Perle Et Or (FR)**[18] 5988 2-9-3 0 ow1 ... TheoBachelot 12 66
(D & P Prod'Homme, France) **188/10**
8 ¾ **Zoraya (FR)**[61] 4212 2-9-3 0 ow1 ... TonyPiccone 6 64
(Paul Cole) *hld up in midfield: pushed along over 2f out: effrt over 1f out: styd on same pce fnl f* **17/2**
9 shd **Envy (IRE)**[43] 2-9-3 0 ow1 ... RonanThomas 10 64
(Robert Collet, France) **78/1**
10 2 **Trust In You (FR)** 2-9-3 0 ow1 ... OlivierPeslier 11 59
(Alex Fracas, France) **29/1**
11 1¼ **Tosen Hardi**[18] 5988 2-9-3 0 ow1 ... GregoryBenoist 3 56
(S Kobayashi, France) **73/1**
12 3 **Signature Piece (USA)**[20] 2-9-3 0 ow1 ... VincentCheminaud 7 49
(D Smaga, France) **77/10**

1m 45.18s (4.38) **12 Ran SP% 118.1**
PARI-MUTUEL (all including 1 euro stake): WIN 3.50; PLACE 1.50, 2.50, 8.00; DF 8.30; SF 15.10.
**Owner** Claudio Marzocco **Bred** Minster Stud **Trained** Pau, France

## OSTEND (R-H)
Monday, August 28
**OFFICIAL GOING: Turf: good**

### 6543a PRIJS S. KERVYN D'OUD MOOREGHEM (H'CAP) (4YO+) (LADY AMATEUR RIDERS) (TURF) 1m 2f 110y
5:55 4-Y-0+ £3,418 (£1,025; £512; £341; £170)

RPR
1 **Flers (GER)**[114] 8-10-10 0 ... MlleSaraVermeersch 8 55
(Ecurie Fievez, Belgium) **8/5**[1]
2 5 **Greeleys Love (USA)**[276] 7-10-8 0 ... MissBethanyBaumgardner 7 43
(Ecurie Fievez, Belgium) **31/1**
3 1¾ **Boccaccina (FR)** 6-9-7 0 ow1 ... MmeAnneEngels 3 25
(Mme A Engels, Belgium) **183/10**
4 snk **Shendini (IRE)**[72] 5-9-11 0 ... (b) FrauLarissaBiess 2 29
(F Caenepeel-Legrand, Belgium) **92/10**
5 10 **Alcatraz (IRE)**[30] 5397 5-12-6 0 ... (p) MmeMelissaBoisgontier 4 46
(George Baker) *slow into stride: sn rcvrd to r midfield: tk clsr order 4f out: pushed along over 2f out: rdn but limited rspnse over 1f out: no ex fnl f* **27/10**[2]
6 5 **Amoretti (FR)**[2279] 13-9-2 0 ... (b) MlleAliceBertiaux 9
(M Creveau, France) **28/1**
7 4½ **Pandana (FR)**[1181] 7-9-2 0 ... (p) MlleNoraHagelund-Holm 6
(M Rosseel, France) **59/1**
8 15 **Capital Gearing**[11] 6125 4-10-3 0 ... (b) FrauCelinaWeber 5
(Leo Braem, Belgium) **16/5**[3]
9 16 **Hail Caesar (IRE)**[2223] 653 11-9-2 0 ... MlleElisabettaMarcialis 1
(Bram Bruneel, Belgium) **137/10**

PARI-MUTUEL (all including 1 euro stake): WIN 2.40; PLACE 1.40, 1.90, 2.50; DF 10.40; SF 12.10.
**Owner** Ecurie Fievez **Bred** Graf & Grafin von Stauffenberg **Trained** Belgium

## 5984 LES LANDES
Monday, August 28
**OFFICIAL GOING: Turf: firm**

### 6544a EUROPEAN & MEDITERRANEAN HORSE RACING FEDERATION H'CAP SPRINT (TURF) 5f 100y
3:05 (3:07) 3-Y-0+ £1,780 (£640; £380)

RPR
1 **National Service (USA)**[15] 5984 6-10-3 0 ... (tp) PaddyAspell 51
(Clare Ellam) *pressed ldr: led 2f out: all out* **10/11**[1]
2 ½ **Country Blue (FR)**[15] 5984 8-10-12 0 ... (p) MattieBatchelor 58
(Mrs A Malzard, Jersey) *narrow ld to 2f out: kpt on same pce* **9/4**[2]
3 1½ **Ron's Ballad**[15] 5985 4-8-11 0 ... (b) PhilipPrince 24
(K Kukk, Jersey) *chsd ldrs: wnt 3rd 3f out: kpt on one pce* **15/2**
4 3½ **Purley Queen (IRE)**[15] 5984 8-10-2 0 ... (v) AliceMills 32
(Mrs C Gilbert, Jersey) *s.s: outpcd: nvr a factor* **5/2**[3]
5 16 **Princess Kodia (IRE)**[15] 5984 4-10-4 0 ... (b) MissMHooper
(Mrs A Malzard, Jersey) *chsd ldrs: wknd 3f out* **8/1**

**Owner** Matt Watkinson **Bred** Three Chimneys Farm Llc **Trained** Market Drayton, Shropshire

## 6311 CARLISLE (R-H)
Tuesday, August 29
**OFFICIAL GOING: Good to soft (7.3)**
Wind: Breezy, half against in over 2f of home straight Weather: Overcast

### 6545 ARMSTRONG WATSON NOVICE AUCTION STKS 5f 193y
4:45 (4:46) (Class 5) 2-Y-0 £3,234 (£962; £481; £240) Stalls High

Form RPR
0 1 **Fake News**[55] 4503 2-9-2 0 ... BenCurtis 4 75+
(David Barron) *pressed ldr: rdn to ld over 1f out: pushed out ins fnl f: comf* **25/1**
042 2 1¾ **Lucky Lucky Man (IRE)**[15] 6012 2-9-2 72 ... TonyHamilton 9 70
(Richard Fahey) *hld up in tch: rdn over 2f out: hung rt and hdwy to chse wnr ins fnl f: kpt on: nt pce to chal* **9/2**[2]
0 3 ¾ **Havana Mariposa**[32] 5370 2-8-11 0 ... JoeyHaynes 5 63
(K R Burke) *chsd ldrs: drvn along over 2f out: rallied and disp 2nd pl briefly ins fnl f: kpt on same pce* **11/2**[3]
31 4 2½ **Han Solo Berger (IRE)**[39] 5092 2-9-9 0 ... PaulMulrennan 8 67
(Keith Dalgleish) *dwlt and wnt lft s: hld up: effrt whn nt clr run briefly wl over 1f out: kpt on ins fnl f: nrst fin* **4/5**[1]
5 nk **Se You** 2-8-13 0 ... RachelRichardson(3) 1 59
(Tim Easterby) *prom: drvn over 2f out: edgd rt over 1f out: sn one pce* **18/1**
4 6 1 **Bonanza Bowls**[13] 6055 2-9-2 0 ... ConnorBeasley 2 56
(Bryan Smart) *led: rdn and hdd over 1f out: wknd ins fnl f* **10/1**
65 7 2 **Out Last**[15] 5998 2-8-6 0 ... RowanScott(5) 7 45
(Keith Dalgleish) *hld up bhd ldng gp: drvn along over 2f out: no imp fr over 1f out* **40/1**

8 5 **North Angel (IRE)** 2-8-11 0 TomEaves 6 30
(David Brown) *dwlt: hld up: effrt on wd outside over 2f out: wknd wl over 1f out* **16/1**

1m 14.84s (1.14) **Going Correction** +0.20s/f (Good) 8 Ran SP% **115.6**
Speed ratings (Par 94): **100,97,96,93,92 91,88,82**
CSF £134.92 TOTE £22.80: £4.90, £1.40, £2.10; EX 136.20 Trifecta £1930.20.
**Owner** Miss N J Barron **Bred** Andrew Parrish **Trained** Maunby, N Yorks

**FOCUS**
The bend into the home straight was moved out 4yds. Races 4 & 7 increased by 12 yds and races 5 & 6 increased by 6yds. The going had eased overnight and the official description was good to soft. A fair maiden run at an ordinary pace. The runner-up has been rated to his best.

## 6546 KINGMOOR PARK PROPERTIES H'CAP 5f 193y
**5:15** (5:18) (Class 5) (0-70,72) 3-Y-0+ **£3,234** (£962; £481; £240) **Stalls** High

Form RPR
0443 **1** **Manatee Bay**[41] 5016 7-9-3 **68** (v) NatalieHambling(7) 8 75
(Noel Wilson) *t.k.h: trckd ldrs: effrt and plld out over 1f out: edgd rt and led ins fnl f: kpt on wl* **20/1**

2416 **2** 3/4 **Cliff (IRE)**[9] 6237 7-9-2 **67** FayeMcManoman(7) 6 71
(Nigel Tinkler) *hld up: effrt and hdwy over 1f out: led briefly ins fnl f: kpt on* **6/1**[2]

2624 **3** nse **Semana Santa**[24] 5635 4-9-7 **65** BenCurtis 7 69
(David Barron) *pressed ldr: led 2f out to ins fnl f: kpt on fin* **10/1**

103 **4** shd **Ypres**[14] 6045 8-9-3 **61** (p) KevinStott 14 66+
(Jason Ward) *stdd s: hdwy over 1f out: rdn and kpt on fnl f: nrst fin* **11/1**

1131 **5** nk **Yes You (IRE)**[6] 6313 3-8-12 **66** 6ex JamieGormley(7) 9 69
(Iain Jardine) *trckd ldrs: rdn to chal 2f out: edgd rt ins fnl f: no ex last 100yds* **11/4**[1]

444 **6** 1 **Mischief Managed (IRE)**[17] 5946 3-9-3 **64** (e) DuranFentiman 2 63
(Tim Easterby) *midfield on ins: drvn along over 2f out: rallied appr fnl f: kpt on: no imp* **16/1**

053 **7** nse **Market Choice (IRE)**[24] 5646 4-9-4 **67** CallumRodriguez(5) 1 66
(Tracy Waggott) *missed break: hld up: effrt whn nt clr run briefly over 1f out: kpt on ins fnl f: no imp* **7/1**[3]

0055 **8** nk **Lotara**[17] 5922 5-8-1 **52** (p[1]) SeanMooney(7) 5 50
(Jim Goldie) *walked to s: hld up in midfield: drvn along and outpcd over 2f out: rallied fnl f: nt pce to chal* **16/1**

00 **9** 1 1/2 **Keene's Pointe**[29] 5482 7-8-6 **50** (p) RoystonFfrench 3 43
(Steph Hollinshead) *prom: rdn over 2f out: wknd ins fnl f* **50/1**

2500 **10** 1/2 **Extrasolar**[29] 5481 7-9-9 **67** (t) PhillipMakin 10 59
(Geoffrey Harker) *stdd s: hld up: short-lived effrt on outside over 2f out: n.d fr over 1f out* **25/1**

3240 **11** hd **Willsy**[3] 6435 4-9-0 **63** (b) GemmaTutty(5) 12 54
(Karen Tutty) *prom: drvn along over 2f out: wknd over 1f out* **11/1**

1561 **12** 1 1/4 **Ki Ki**[32] 5375 5-9-8 **66** ConnorBeasley 13 53
(Bryan Smart) *dwlt: bhd: rdn and effrt wl over 1f out: wknd fnl f* **9/1**

00-0 **13** 5 **Barkston Ash**[20] 5806 9-9-9 **67** (p) NeilFarley 4 38
(Eric Alston) *led to 2f out: sn rdn and wknd* **33/1**

1m 14.44s (0.74) **Going Correction** +0.20s/f (Good)
**WFA** 3 from 4yo+ 3lb 13 Ran SP% **114.5**
Speed ratings (Par 103): **103,102,101,101,101 100,100,99,97,96 96,95,88**
CSF £126.52 CT £1284.73 TOTE £19.90: £5.00, £2.20, £2.40; EX 157.90 Trifecta £1170.40.
**Owner** Mrs Alex Nicholls **Bred** Miss A J Rawding & P M Crane **Trained** Marwood, Co Durham

**FOCUS**
A modest handicap and they finished in a bit of a heap.

## 6547 BAINES WILSON LLP NURSERY H'CAP (QUALIFIER FOR THE JOCKEY CLUB GRASSROOTS NURSERY SERIES) 5f
**5:45** (5:46) (Class 5) (0-75,76) 2-Y-0 **£3,881** (£1,155; £577; £288) **Stalls** High

Form RPR
2302 **1** **Porchy Party (IRE)**[29] 5479 2-9-6 **72** (p) RichardKingscote 8 75
(Tom Dascombe) *mde all: rdn and over 2 l clr over 1f out: hld on wl fnl f* **15/2**

0345 **2** 1/2 **Hermana Santa (IRE)**[14] 6036 2-9-0 **66** BenCurtis 11 67
(David Barron) *bhd: rdn and outpcd 1/2-way: effrt and drifted to stands' rail over 1f out: gd hdwy to chse wnr wl ins fnl f: kpt on wl: jst hld* **12/1**

432 **3** 1/2 **Lina's Star (IRE)**[28] 5494 2-8-12 **64** PhillipMakin 5 63
(Richard Fahey) *hld up bhd ldng gp: effrt whn nt clr run over 2f out to over 1f out: kpt on ins fnl f* **8/1**

532 **4** hd **Rossall**[24] 5665 2-9-10 **76** PaulMulrennan 7 75
(Michael Dods) *trckd ldrs: effrt and chsd wnr over 1f out to wl ins fnl f: kpt on same pce* **3/1**[2]

430 **5** 3/4 **Life For Rent**[19] 5834 2-8-10 **65** RachelRichardson(3) 9 61
(Tim Easterby) *hld up: effrt and drvn along on outside 2f out: kpt on same pce ins fnl f* **16/1**

336 **6** 4 **Magic Mark**[45] 4919 2-9-3 **72** CliffordLee(3) 4 54
(K R Burke) *t.k.h: trckd ldrs tl rdn and wknd appr fnl f* **85/40**[1]

4251 **7** 1 1/4 **Brockey Rise (IRE)**[14] 6043 2-8-13 **70** (v) BenRobinson(5) 6 47
(David Evans) *chsd wnr to over 1f out: sn rdn and wknd* **7/1**[3]

630 **8** 3/4 **Rocket Man Dan (IRE)**[73] 3826 2-9-1 **67** GrahamLee 1 41
(Keith Dalgleish) *prom: effrt and drvn along 2f out: wknd fnl f* **20/1**

304 **9** 6 **Billiebrookedit (IRE)**[19] 5839 2-9-2 **68** (h[1]) RoystonFfrench 3 21
(Steph Hollinshead) *cl up tl rdn: edgd rt and wknd over 1f out* **25/1**

1m 2.55s (1.75) **Going Correction** +0.20s/f (Good) 9 Ran SP% **114.6**
Speed ratings (Par 94): **94,93,92,92,90 84,82,81,71**
CSF £91.64 CT £743.91 TOTE £6.90: £2.30, £2.90, £2.30; EX 84.30 Trifecta £535.00.
**Owner** R F H Partnership 1 **Bred** Seamus O'Neill **Trained** Malpas, Cheshire

**FOCUS**
A fair nursery and an all-the-way winner.

## 6548 CARLISLE YOUTH ZONE MAIDEN STKS 1m 1f
**6:15** (6:16) (Class 5) 3-4-Y-0 **£3,234** (£962; £481; £240) **Stalls** Low

Form RPR
-233 **1** **Sea Tide**[11] 6161 3-9-0 81 (tp) BenCurtis 4 67
(Hugo Palmer) *t.k.h: chsd ldr: effrt and rdn over 1f out: led ins fnl f: pushed out towards fin* **8/15**[1]

2 **2** 1/2 **Haroon (IRE)**[5] 6350 3-9-5 72 (t) BarryMcHugh 6 71
(Tony Coyle) *led: rdn over 2f out: edgd rt over 1f out: hdd ins fnl f: rallied: hld nr fin* **3/1**[2]

40 **3** 11 **Little Jo**[9] 6236 3-9-5 0 GrahamLee 3 49
(Chris Grant) *dwlt: hld up in last pl: hdwy to chse ldng pair 3f out: rdn: edgd rt and outpcd fr 2f out* **33/1**

**4** 2 1/2 **Kai Tak And Back** 3-9-5 0 PhillipMakin 2 44
(William Muir) *dwlt: sn prom: rdn and outpcd 3f out: btn fnl 2f* **5/1**[3]

54 **5** 1 **Biba**[5] 6350 3-8-9 0 (p) RowanScott(5) 1 37
(Keith Dalgleish) *in tch: drvn and outpcd over 3f out: sn wknd* **33/1**

1m 58.54s (0.94) **Going Correction** +0.20s/f (Good) 5 Ran SP% **112.8**
Speed ratings (Par 103): **103,102,92,90,89**
CSF £2.57 TOTE £1.50: £1.10, £1.60; EX 2.50 Trifecta £12.90.
**Owner** K Abdullah **Bred** Millsec Limited **Trained** Newmarket, Suffolk

**FOCUS**
Race distance increased by 12yds. An uncompetitive maiden and the two market leaders pulled clear of the rest.

## 6549 CARR'S GROUP PLC H'CAP 7f 173y
**6:45** (6:45) (Class 6) (0-65,67) 3-Y-0+ **£2,911** (£866; £432; £216) **Stalls** Low

Form RPR
0605 **1** **Thornaby Nash**[10] 6182 6-8-13 **55** (p) GemmaTutty(5) 8 61
(Karen Tutty) *t.k.h: early ldr trckd ldrs: rdn over 2f out: led wl ins fnl f: kpt on* **9/1**

0014 **2** shd **Pretty Jewel**[11] 6153 4-9-9 **60** TomEaves 15 66
(Kevin Frost) *dwlt: hld up: rdn and hdwy over 1f out: ev ch ins fnl f: kpt on: hld cl home* **12/1**

6042 **3** hd **Jay Kay**[15] 5993 8-10-1 **66** (h) JoeyHaynes 3 72
(K R Burke) *stmbld leaving stalls: sn led: qcknd clr over 2f out: edgd rt 1f out: hdd wl ins fnl f: r.o* **5/1**[2]

2036 **4** nk **Supreme Power (IRE)**[6] 6315 3-9-4 **61** RoystonFfrench 10 65
(Tracy Waggott) *t.k.h: prom: rdn over 2f out: rallied fnl f: kpt on fin* **14/1**

555 **5** shd **Mr Cool Cash**[14] 6049 5-10-2 **67** ConnorBeasley 6 72
(Richard Guest) *t.k.h: in tch: rdn over 2f out: kpt on fnl f: nt pce to chal* **9/1**

3002 **6** 3/4 **Lozah**[2] 6471 4-9-5 **56** TonyHamilton 17 59
(Roger Fell) *dwlt: hld up and swtchd rt s: hdwy over 1f out: rdn and kpt on ins fnl f: nrst fin* **9/1**

-051 **7** 3/4 **Euro Mac**[15] 6003 5-8-8 **52** JamieGormley(7) 9 55
(Neville Bycroft) *t.k.h in midfield: rdn over 2f out: one pce whn nt clr run over 1f out and ins fnl f: no ex* **9/2**[1]

0302 **8** 1 **Redrosezorro**[21] 5741 3-8-11 **54** (h) NeilFarley 5 52
(Eric Alston) *t.k.h early: in tch: rdn along over 2f out: wknd ins fnl f* **16/1**

0460 **9** 3/4 **Leopard (IRE)**[18] 5880 3-9-1 **58** BarryMcHugh 11 55
(Tony Coyle) *hld up: rdn over 2f out: edgd rt and no imp over 1f out* **28/1**

0066 **10** 1 1/4 **Tanawar (IRE)**[14] 6049 7-9-12 **63** (v) JamesSullivan 12 58
(Ruth Carr) *hld up towards rr: drvn over 2f out: wknd over 1f out* **25/1**

1204 **11** nk **Full Of Promise**[19] 5829 4-9-9 **67** SebastianWoods(7) 1 61
(Richard Fahey) *chsd ldr: rdn over 1f out: wknd fnl f* **8/1**

2220 **12** 3/4 **Catastrophe**[12] 6092 4-9-6 **57** DanielTudhope 13 50
(John Quinn) *t.k.h: hld up: rdn over 2f out: btn over 1f out* **6/1**[3]

3000 **13** 13 **Port Master**[56] 4479 3-8-8 **51** ShaneGray 16 14
(Ann Duffield) *bhd: drvn and struggling over 2f out: sn btn* **100/1**

1m 41.97s (1.97) **Going Correction** +0.20s/f (Good)
**WFA** 3 from 4yo+ 6lb 13 Ran SP% **118.8**
Speed ratings (Par 101): **98,97,97,97,97 96,95,94,94,92 92,91,78**
CSF £110.15 CT £625.88 TOTE £10.40: £3.50, £4.30, £1.60; EX 169.10 Trifecta £1919.20.
**Owner** Dave Scott **Bred** Dave Scott **Trained** Osmotherley, N Yorks

**FOCUS**
Race distance increased by 6yds. A modest handicap, run at a good pace, and several had a chance inside the final furlong. Straightforward form rated around those involved.

## 6550 HALSTON APARTHOTEL H'CAP 6f 195y
**7:15** (7:17) (Class 5) (0-70,71) 3-Y-0+ **£3,234** (£962; £481; £240) **Stalls** Low

Form RPR
4522 **1** **Lady In Question (IRE)**[8] 6265 3-9-7 **70** TonyHamilton 1 76
(Richard Fahey) *t.k.h: hld up in midfield: shkn up and hdwy wl over 1f out: rdn to ld ins fnl f: kpt on* **2/1**[1]

1050 **2** nk **Reinforced**[29] 5466 4-9-1 **64** (tp) CallumRodriguez(5) 9 71
(Michael Dods) *racd wd: pressed ldr: led wl over 2f out: drvn and hdd over 1f out: rallied and ev ch ins fnl f: hld cl home* **4/1**[3]

0202 **3** 2 1/2 **Penny Pot Lane**[9] 6238 4-9-6 **67** LewisEdmunds(3) 5 68
(Richard Whitaker) *prom: rdn and hdwy to ld over 1f out: hdd ins fnl f: kpt on same pce* **11/4**[2]

3533 **4** 3 1/4 **Bush Beauty (IRE)**[19] 5829 6-9-5 **63** NeilFarley 11 55
(Eric Alston) *dwlt: hld up: rdn over 2f out: hdwy to chse clr ldng trio over 1f out: no imp fnl f* **15/2**

0636 **5** nse **Circuitous**[36] 5203 9-9-0 **58** (v) TomEaves 8 50
(Keith Dalgleish) *trckd ldrs: drvn over 2f out: outpcd wl over 1f out: n.d after* **25/1**

6000 **6** 1 3/4 **Mr Conundrum**[10] 6181 4-8-7 **51** oh6 (p[1]) JamesSullivan 2 39
(Lynn Siddall) *t.k.h: hld up: rdn over 2f out: no imp fr over 1f out* **66/1**

-636 **7** 7 **Let's Twist**[10] 6181 5-9-12 **70** (b) ShaneGray 6 39
(Kristin Stubbs) *led to over 2f out: rallied: wknd over 1f out* **17/2**

460 **8** 3 1/4 **Fortuities (IRE)**[29] 5467 3-9-1 **64** (h[1]) JackGarritty 12 23
(Jedd O'Keeffe) *dwlt: hld up in tch: struggling over 2f out: sn btn* **18/1**

1m 27.91s (0.81) **Going Correction** +0.20s/f (Good)
**WFA** 3 from 4yo+ 5lb 8 Ran SP% **112.9**
Speed ratings (Par 103): **103,102,99,96,96 94,86,82**
CSF £10.01 CT £21.02 TOTE £2.90: £1.60, £1.30, £1.20; EX 9.80 Trifecta £25.80.
**Owner** Amie Canham I **Bred** M Phelan **Trained** Musley Bank, N Yorks

**FOCUS**
Race distance increased by 6yds. A fair handicap and solid form for the grade. The runner-up has been rated to this year's mark.

## 6551 WYG H'CAP 1m 3f 39y
**7:45** (7:46) (Class 5) (0-70,69) 3-Y-0+ **£3,234** (£962; £481; £240) **Stalls** High

Form RPR
0435 **1** **Sheriff Of Nawton (IRE)**[22] 5701 6-10-0 **69** TonyHamilton 3 75
(Roger Fell) *hld up in tch: hdwy to ld over 1f out: rdn and r.o wl fnl f* **7/2**[2]

1241 **2** 1/2 **Thorntoun Care**[18] 5883 6-9-6 **68** (p) JamieGormley(7) 8 72
(Iain Jardine) *hld up: hdwy over 2f out: effrt and ev ch over 1f out: kpt on ins fnl f: hld nr fin* **7/4**[1]

5445 **3** 1/2 **Princess Nearco (IRE)**[14] 6048 3-8-11 **60** (p) JackGarritty 2 63
(Patrick Holmes) *dwlt: t.k.h and sn chsng ldrs: effrt and drvn over 2f out: kpt on ins fnl f* **4/1**[3]

24-0 **4** 1 **Nepeta (USA)**[12] 6091 3-9-6 **69** PJMcDonald 7 71
(Mark Johnston) *led: rdn and hdd over 1f out: one pce fnl f* **13/2**

520- **5** 1 **Ghostly Arc (IRE)**[142] 7251 5-9-7 **62** PatrickMathers 5 62
(Noel Wilson) *t.k.h: pressed ldr: ev ch over 2f out to over 1f out: no ex fnl f* **28/1**

3 **6** 1 1/4 **Polar Forest**[20] 5809 7-10-0 **69** (e[1]) ConnorBeasley 1 67
(Richard Guest) *t.k.h: hld up: rdn over 2f out: hung lft over 1f out: sn btn* **11/1**

0560 **7** 1 ¼ **Chelsea's Boy (IRE)**[22] 5700 4-10-0 **69**.................... GrahamLee 4 65
(Donald McCain) *t.k.h: prom: rdn over 2f out: wknd wl over 1f out* **11/1**

2m 31.31s (8.21) **Going Correction** +0.20s/f (Good)
**WFA** 3 from 4yo+ 8lb **7** Ran SP% **112.0**
Speed ratings (Par 103): **78,77,77,76,75 74,74**
CSF £9.62 CT £23.66 TOTE £4.20: £2.20, £1.50; EX 11.10 Trifecta £36.10.
**Owner** R G Fell **Bred** Lawman Syndicate & Pipe View Stud **Trained** Nawton, N Yorks

**FOCUS**
Race distance increased by 12yds. Just a modest finale.
T/Jkpt: Not Won. T/Plt: £293.90 to a £1 stake. Pool: £56,482.40 - 140.28 winning units T/Qpdt: £15.60 to a £1 stake. Pool: £7,020.53 - 332.13 winning units **Richard Young**

# 6510 EPSOM (L-H)
Tuesday, August 29

**OFFICIAL GOING: Good to firm (7.3)**
Wind: virtually nil Weather: fine, warm

## 6552 JRA NURSERY H'CAP (JOCKEY CLUB GRASSROOTS NURSERY QUALIFIER) 7f 3y
**2:00** (2:01) (Class 5) (0-75,74) 2-Y-0 **£4,528** (£1,347; £673; £336) **Stalls** Low

Form RPR

5401 **1** **Lexington Grace (IRE)**[18] 5886 2-9-1 **68**....................(p) TomMarquand 9 75
(Richard Hannon) *trckd ldng pair: effrt to chal over 1f out: rdn to ld jst ins fnl f: edgd lft but styd on strly to draw clr fnl 100yds* **11/2**

1342 **2** 2 ¼ **Seaella (IRE)**[19] 5833 2-9-6 **73**.................... JasonHart 2 74
(John Quinn) *pressed ldr tl rdn to ld 2f out: drvn over 1f out: hdd jst ins fnl f: no ex and outpcd fnl 100yds* **7/2**[1]

035 **3** nk **Viceroy Mac**[27] 5531 2-9-4 **71**.................... JosephineGordon 8 71+
(David Loughnane) *sn dropped to rr and nt handle early downhill run: rdn and detached last 4f out: stl last but rallying and clsng 1f out: styd on wl ins fnl f to go 3rd last strides: nvr trbld ldrs* **4/1**[2]

340 **4** nk **Rainbow Jazz (IRE)**[34] 5292 2-9-3 **70**....................(p[1]) SteveDrowne 3 69
(Mark Usher) *led: hdd and rdn 2f out: styd pressing ldr tl no ex jst ins fnl f: styd on same pce after* **8/1**

436 **5** ½ **Ruysch (IRE)**[24] 5660 2-9-5 **72**.................... DavidProbert 4 70+
(Ed Dunlop) *s.i.s: in tch in rr: effrt 3f out: no imp tl drvn and styd on 1f out: nt clrest of runs and swtchd rt ins fnl f: gng on at fin: no threat to ldrs* **11/2**

6603 **6** shd **Panophobia**[18] 5878 2-8-9 **65**.................... AdamMcNamara(3) 6 63
(Richard Fahey) *in tch in midfield: effrt to chse ldrs 2f out: rdn and nvr clr enough run fr over 1f out: styd on same pce ins fnl f* **9/2**[3]

5040 **7** 1 ½ **Diamond Pursuit**[25] 5629 2-9-2 **69**.................... JFEgan 7 63
(Jo Hughes) *in tch in midfield: effrt over 2f out: no imp over 1f out: wknd ins fnl f* **11/1**

1m 22.61s (-0.69) **Going Correction** -0.10s/f (Good) **7** Ran SP% **110.6**
Speed ratings (Par 94): **99,96,96,95,95 95,93**
CSF £23.30 CT £80.05 TOTE £4.70: £2.70, £2.20; EX 20.60 Trifecta £74.20.
**Owner** Middleham Park Racing XII & A E Denham **Bred** Tally-Ho Stud **Trained** East Everleigh, Wilts

**FOCUS**
The going was good to firm (GoingStick: 7.3). The rail was on its inner configuration and all distances were as advertised. A fair nursery which could well throw up a winner or two at a similar level. It's been rated around the balance of the principals.

## 6553 BRITISH STALLION STUDS EBF MAIDEN STKS 1m 113y
**2:35** (2:36) (Class 5) 2-Y-0 **£3,881** (£1,155; £577; £288) **Stalls** Low

Form RPR

**1** **Lynwood Gold (IRE)** 2-9-5 0.................... JoeFanning 1 84+
(Mark Johnston) *rousted along leaving stalls: hdwy to ld after 1f: mde rest: travelling best over 2f out: urged along and readily wnt clr wl over 1f out: r.o strly: unchal* **4/1**[3]

5 **2** 5 **I'm A Star (IRE)**[31] 5420 2-9-5 0.................... MartinHarley 3 73
(Stuart Williams) *led for 1f: chsd wnr: rdn over 2f out: nt match pce of wnr and lost 2nd over 1f out: bmpd and pushed rt ins fnl f: battled bk to regain 2nd wl ins fnl f: no ch w wnr* **6/1**

0 **3** ½ **Global Style (IRE)**[11] 6142 2-9-5 0.................... SilvestreDeSousa 2 72
(Ed Dunlop) *chsd ldng pair: effrt over 2f out: chsd clr wnr over 1f out: no imp and wl hld whn wnt rt and bmpd rival ins fnl f: kpt on same pce and lost 2nd wl ins fnl f* **10/3**[1]

4 **4** 4 ½ **Iconic Code**[11] 6159 2-9-0 0.................... CharlesBishop 8 57
(Mick Channon) *hld up in tch in last trio: swtchd rt over 3f out: outpcd and rdn over 2f out: wl btn over 1f out* **9/1**

6 **5** 1 **Berkshire Spirit**[19] 5840 2-9-5 0.................... RobHornby 7 60
(Andrew Balding) *dwlt and rousted along leaving stalls: hdwy to chse ldng trio over 6f out: rdn over 2f out: sn struggling and outpcd: wl btn over 1f out* **7/2**[2]

**6** 2 ¼ **We Know (IRE)** 2-9-5 0....................(t[1]) OisinMurphy 6 55
(Simon Crisford) *rn green: s.i.s: in tch in last trio: effrt over 2f out: sn struggling and outpcd ent fnl f: no ch over 1f out* **5/1**

04 **7** 6 **Raven's Song (IRE)**[17] 5934 2-9-0 0.................... WilliamCarson 5 37
(Harry Dunlop) *hld up in tch in rr: shkn up 3f out: sn struggling: hung lft and outpcd: bhd over 1f out* **50/1**

050 **8** 2 ¼ **Colorado Dream**[45] 4880 2-9-5 0....................(p) PatCosgrave 4 38
(George Baker) *t.k.h: hld up wl in tch in midfield: rdn and lost pl over 2f out: bhd over 1f out* **33/1**

1m 44.57s (-1.53) **Going Correction** -0.10s/f (Good) **8** Ran SP% **111.2**
Speed ratings (Par 94): **102,97,97,93,92 90,84,82**
CSF £26.44 TOTE £4.40: £1.50, £1.80, £1.50; EX 28.60 Trifecta £97.50.
**Owner** J Barson **Bred** Epona Bloodstock Ltd **Trained** Middleham Moor, N Yorks

**FOCUS**
A useful performance from the winner. It's been rated around the runner-up to his debut figure for now.

## 6554 TERRY MILLS & JOHN AKEHURST H'CAP 6f 3y
**3:10** (3:10) (Class 3) (0-90,89) 3-Y-0+
**£9,337** (£2,796; £1,398; £699; £349; £175) **Stalls** High

Form RPR

0150 **1** **Highland Acclaim (IRE)**[10] 6185 6-9-8 **87**....................(h) HarryBentley 7 95
(David O'Meara) *trckd ldrs and travelled strly: nudged along and clsd to chal over 1f out: rdn to ld 1f out: forged ahd ins fnl f: r.o* **11/2**

6125 **2** ¾ **Handytalk (IRE)**[22] 5720 4-9-6 **85**.................... OisinMurphy 5 90
(Rod Millman) *pressed ldr: rdn and ev ch 2f out: drvn 1f out: kpt on same pce ins fnl f* **4/1**[1]

0056 **3** ½ **Poet's Society**[10] 6198 3-9-5 **87**.................... JoeFanning 3 90
(Mark Johnston) *led: rdn 2f out: hdd 1f out: no ex and kpt on same pce after* **8/1**

2401 **4** ¾ **Coronation Day**[18] 5869 4-9-10 **89**.................... MartinHarley 4 90
(James Tate) *trckd ldrs: stl travelling strly whn nt clr run 2f out: swtchd rt over 1f out: kpt on ins fnl f* **9/2**[2]

6023 **5** hd **Huntsmans Close**[28] 5513 7-9-9 **88**....................(h) RobertWinston 1 88
(Robert Cowell) *stdd s: hld up off the pce in last trio: effrt over 1f out: hdwy ins fnl f: styd on* **8/1**

2434 **6** shd **Scofflaw**[16] 5959 3-8-10 **81**.................... AdamMcNamara(3) 6 81
(Richard Fahey) *s.i.s: sn pushed along and off the pce in last pair: rdn 3f out: clsd but hung lft over 1f out: stuck bhd horses but kpt on ins fnl f* **9/2**[2]

0440 **7** 2 **Reputation (IRE)**[10] 6205 4-9-9 **88**....................(v) JasonHart 2 81
(John Quinn) *s.i.s: pushed along early: in rr: hdwy on inner 2f out: sn rdn and no imp: eased towards fin* **5/1**[3]

1m 8.52s (-0.88) **Going Correction** -0.10s/f (Good)
**WFA** 3 from 4yo+ 3lb **7** Ran SP% **110.6**
Speed ratings (Par 107): **101,99,99,98,97 97,94**
CSF £25.75 TOTE £6.80: £4.00, £2.10; EX 27.20 Trifecta £173.90.
**Owner** Evan M Sutherland **Bred** Rathbarry Stud **Trained** Upper Helmsley, N Yorks

**FOCUS**
The three who were held up could never quite get close enough, albeit it was a bit of a bunched finish.

## 6555 ROA/RACING POST OWNERS JACKPOT H'CAP 7f 3y
**3:45** (3:45) (Class 4) (0-80,82) 3-Y-0+ **£7,115** (£2,117; £1,058; £529) **Stalls** Low

Form RPR

4100 **1** **Favourite Royal (IRE)**[35] 5242 3-9-4 **77**....................(p) MartinDwyer 2 83
(Eve Johnson Houghton) *midfield: squeezed for room and dropped to rr sn after s: struggling to handle downhill run and outpcd: hdwy ent fnl 2f: hanging lft and swtchd rt over 1f out: str run ins fnl f to ld nr fin* **9/1**

2000 **2** ½ **Red Tycoon (IRE)**[11] 6141 5-9-6 **79**.................... FinleyMarsh(5) 10 85
(Ken Cunningham-Brown) *hld up in midfield: hdwy and swtchd rt 2f out: rdn to ld and edgd lft 1f out: stl edging lft but wnt clr ins fnl f: kpt on: hdd nr fin* **20/1**

5465 **3** 1 ¾ **Munfallet (IRE)**[40] 5051 6-9-9 **80**.................... HectorCrouch(3) 3 81
(David Brown) *sn led: rdn wl over 1f out: hdd 1f out: no ex and styd on same pce ins fnl f* **15/2**[3]

056 **4** 1 **Tigerwolf (IRE)**[4] 6378 4-9-7 **75**.................... JFEgan 4 73
(Mick Channon) *awkward leaving stalls: bustled along leaving stalls: hdwy to chse ldr after 1f: rdn and hung lft ent fnl 2f: styd pressing ldr tl no ex 1f out: wknd ins fnl f* **5/1**[2]

410 **5** hd **Swiss Cross**[25] 5612 10-9-1 **69**....................(tp) JosephineGordon 6 67
(Phil McEntee) *in tch in midfield: effrt over 2f out: styd on same pce u.p ins fnl f* **25/1**

6150 **6** 1 ¼ **Thaqaffa (IRE)**[25] 5610 4-9-12 **80**.................... SilvestreDeSousa 8 74
(Amy Murphy) *mounted on crse and taken down early: hld up towards rr: swtchd rt and effrt over 2f out: hdwy 1f out: kpt on ins fnl f: nvr trbld ldrs* **9/1**

3262 **7** nk **Flyboy (IRE)**[34] 5288 4-9-7 **78**....................(b) AdamMcNamara(3) 1 72
(Richard Fahey) *chsd ldrs: clsd to trck ldrs but nt clr run on inner over 2f out: gap opened and rdn over 1f out: little rspnse and btn 1f out: wknd ins fnl f* **10/3**[1]

1651 **8** 1 ¾ **Coral Sea**[26] 5558 3-9-9 **82**....................(h) HarryBentley 9 69
(Charles Hills) *taken down early: hld up in rr: effrt and hung lft ent fnl 2f: no imp: nvr trbld ldrs* **5/1**[2]

0133 **9** 12 **Andalusite**[20] 5789 4-8-8 **62**....................(v) FergusSweeney 5 18
(John Gallagher) *chsd ldr for 1f: styd chsng ldrs tl lost pl 2f: bhd and eased ins fnl f* **10/1**

3150 **10** 7 **Carpe Diem Lady (IRE)**[45] 4910 4-9-8 **76**....................(v) OisinMurphy 7 13
(Ralph Beckett) *chsd ldrs early: steadily lost pl: dropping out whn squeezed for room over 1f out: bhd and eased ins fnl f* **8/1**

1m 21.58s (-1.72) **Going Correction** -0.10s/f (Good)
**WFA** 3 from 4yo+ 5lb **10** Ran SP% **117.0**
Speed ratings (Par 105): **105,104,102,101,101 99,99,97,83,75**
CSF £171.98 CT £1444.05 TOTE £9.10: £2.10, £5.90, £2.80; EX 185.40 Trifecta £2070.10.
**Owner** J Cross,M Duckham,L Godfrey,P Wollaston **Bred** Emma Capon Bloodstock **Trained** Blewbury, Oxon

**FOCUS**
The leaders went off a bit too fast and this was set up for a closer.

## 6556 CHARLOTTE LAJOIE FOREVER IN OUR HEARTS H'CAP (JOCKEY CLUB GRASSROOTS FLAT MIDDLE DISTANCE SERIES) 1m 4f 6y
**4:20** (4:20) (Class 5) (0-70,69) 3-Y-0+ **£3,881** (£1,155; £577; £288) **Stalls** Centre

Form RPR

5354 **1** **Cordite (IRE)**[29] 5477 6-10-0 **69**....................(h) PatCosgrave 1 77
(Jim Boyle) *taken down early: chsd ldrs: sltly hmpd 9f out: effrt to chse ldr and swtchd rt over 2f out: rdn and clsd to ld 1f out: styd on and clr ins fnl f: rdn out* **9/2**[3]

6233 **2** 1 ½ **Ode To Glory**[22] 5718 3-8-13 **63**.................... DavidProbert 6 69
(Rae Guest) *dwlt and bustled along leaving stalls: hld up in rr: effrt and hdwy ent fnl 2f: nt clr run: swtchd rt and jostling w rival over 1f out: hdwy 1f out: styd on wl to go 2nd wl ins fnl f: nvr getting to wnr* **6/1**

6335 **3** 1 ¼ **Challow (IRE)**[21] 5753 3-9-1 **65**.................... LiamKeniry 4 69
(Sylvester Kirk) *led: rdn ent fnl 2f: hdd 1f out: no ex and lost 2nd wl ins fnl f* **11/2**

0232 **4** 8 **Hepplewhite**[26] 5556 4-9-13 **68**....................(p) MartinDwyer 5 58
(William Muir) *hld up in tch: effrt over 1f out: jostling w rival over 1f out: no imp and wl hld 1f out: wnt modest 4th ins fnl f* **11/4**[1]

2123 **5** 1 ½ **Let's Be Happy (IRE)**[22] 5722 3-8-13 **63**....................(p) ShaneKelly 7 51
(Richard Hughes) *chsd ldr tl over 2f out: unable qck u.p and btn over 1f out: wknd ins fnl f* **7/2**[2]

0-06 **6** ¾ **Spin Point (IRE)**[120] 1839 5-9-12 **67**....................(p) StevieDonohoe 3 53
(Ian Williams) *in tch: effrt 3f out: sn struggling and outpcd: bhd over 1f out* **14/1**

0120 **7** 16 **Gold Merlion (IRE)**[18] 5872 4-9-11 **66**.................... JoeFanning 2 27
(Mark Johnston) *midfield tl dropped to rr over 2f out: bhd and eased fnl f* **10/1**

2m 37.52s (-1.38) **Going Correction** -0.10s/f (Good)
**WFA** 3 from 4yo+ 9lb **7** Ran SP% **112.5**
Speed ratings (Par 103): **100,99,98,92,91 91,80**
CSF £30.06 TOTE £5.10: £2.20, £3.20; EX 28.40 Trifecta £150.40.
**Owner** Duncan Buckell **Bred** Raymond Sutton **Trained** Epsom, Surrey

**FOCUS**
Few got involved here, the pace holding up pretty well.

## 6557 MOLSON COORS H'CAP 1m 2f 17y
4:50 (4:53) (Class 5) (0-70,72) 3-Y-0+ £3,881 (£1,155; £577; £288) Stalls Low

Form RPR
3161 1 **Av A Word**[18] 5867 3-9-4 **67**......(p) SilvestreDeSousa 7 73+
(Daniel Kubler) *hld up in last trio: effrt over 2f out: hdwy u.p ent fnl f: str run ins fnl f to ld 75yds out: sn in command and eased clsd home* **11/4**[1]
065 2 1 1/4 **Maraakib (IRE)**[13] 6059 5-10-1 **71**......(p) HarryBentley 1 73
(David O'Meara) *led: pushed along and qcknd 2f out: clr and rdn over 1f out: kpt on tl hdd and nt match pce of wnr fnl 75yds* **4/1**[2]
2445 3 nk **The Gay Cavalier**[2] 6475 6-9-5 **68**......(t) JackOsborn[(7)] 6 69
(John Ryan) *awkward leaving stalls and slowly away: hld up in tch in rr: hdwy on inner over 2f: rdn to chse ldrs over 1f out: wnt 2nd 1f out tl ins fnl f: kpt on same pce after* **9/1**
2004 4 1/2 **Pink Ribbon (IRE)**[18] 5868 5-9-5 **66**......(p) MitchGodwin[(5)] 9 66
(Sylvester Kirk) *hld up in tch in midfield: effrt whn nt clr run and swtchd lft 2f out: hdwy and drvn to chse ldrs 1f out: kpt on same pce ins fnl f* **10/1**
1536 5 1 **Bayston Hill**[22] 5718 3-9-4 **67**...... DanielMuscutt 2 66
(Mark Usher) *chsd ldrs: rdn to chse ldr 2f out: lost 2nd 1f out and kpt on same pce ins fnl f* **8/1**
4040 6 1 **Squire**[20] 5788 6-10-2 **72**......(t) AdamBeschizza 3 68
(Michael Attwater) *t.k.h: chsd ldrs: effrt ent fnl 2f: edgd lft u.p over 1f out: no imp and kpt on same pce ins fnl f* **8/1**
6210 7 3 3/4 **Epsom Secret**[34] 5298 3-8-10 **59**...... JFEgan 10 49
(Pat Phelan) *hld up in tch in midfield: effrt over 2f out: no imp whn nt clr run and hmpd over 1f out: sn swtchd lft: no imp and wl hld after* **13/2**[3]
6150 8 1/2 **Galinthias**[20] 5788 5-9-11 **67**...... TomMarquand 5 55
(Simon Dow) *chsd ldr tl 2f out: losing pl u.p whn squeezed for room and hmpd over 1f out: wl btn after* **10/1**
605 9 19 **Royal Hall (FR)**[21] 5746 5-9-3 **62**......(p) HectorCrouch[(3)] 4 12
(Gary Moore) *t.k.h: stdd after s: hld up in tch in rr: struggling 4f out: bhd 2f out: wknd and eased wl ins fnl f* **25/1**

2m 10.04s (0.34) **Going Correction** -0.10s/f (Good)
**WFA** 3 from 5yo+ 7lb 9 Ran SP% **114.3**
Speed ratings (Par 103): **94,93,92,92,91 90,87,87,72**
CSF £13.33 CT £85.00 TOTE £3.50: £1.40, £1.80, £2.80; EX 15.50 Trifecta £77.90.
**Owner** Peter Onslow & Kevin Nash **Bred** Peter Onslow **Trained** Lambourn, Berks

**FOCUS**
A modest affair.

## 6558 BET AT RACINGUK.COM H'CAP 7f 3y
5:20 (5:23) (Class 5) (0-75,76) 3-Y-0 £4,528 (£1,347; £673; £336) Stalls Low

Form RPR
5-51 1 **Dourado (IRE)**[26] 5560 3-9-8 **76**...... DavidProbert 2 82+
(Patrick Chamings) *hld up in last pair: clsd to trck ldrs over 2f out: rdn to chal over 1f out: led ins fnl f: hld on wl u.p* **6/4**[1]
2530 2 hd **Right Action**[17] 5948 3-9-4 **75**...... AdamMcNamara[(3)] 4 79
(Richard Fahey) *trckd ldng pair: effrt to chal over 1f out: drvn and ev ch fnl f: kpt on wl: jst hld cl home* **9/2**[3]
1244 3 nse **Traveller (FR)**[21] 5754 3-9-6 **74**......(t) HarryBentley 6 78
(Charles Hills) *dwlt: bustled along and rcvrd to chse ldr after 1f: rdn to chal over 1f out: led 1f out: sn hdd: kpt on wl: jst hld cl home* **7/2**[2]
5332 4 1 1/4 **Lightoller (IRE)**[16] 5956 3-9-0 **68**......(b) SilvestreDeSousa 1 69
(Mick Channon) *stdd bk to rr sn after s and t.k.h: effrt in 5th over 2f out: drvn over 1f out: styd on ins fnl f: nvr getting to ldrs* **8/1**
3001 5 2 1/2 **Prazeres**[11] 6131 3-8-6 **60**...... JoeFanning 5 54
(Les Eyre) *broke fast and led: rdn and hrd pressed over 1f out: hdd 1f out: wknd ins fnl f* **8/1**
1326 6 11 **Dragon Dream (IRE)**[6] 6321 3-8-3 **64**...... RhiainIngram[(7)] 3 29
(Roger Ingram) *chsd ldr for 1f: steadily lost pl and bhd 2f out: sn wknd* **9/1**

1m 22.59s (-0.71) **Going Correction** -0.10s/f (Good) 6 Ran SP% **112.6**
Speed ratings (Par 100): **100,99,99,98,95 82**
CSF £8.64 TOTE £2.50: £1.70, £2.10; EX 9.60 Trifecta £31.60.
**Owner** Mrs Alexandra J Chandris **Bred** Canice M Farrell Jnr **Trained** Baughurst, Hants

**FOCUS**
A tight finish to this handicap.
T/Plt: £412.40 to a £1 stake. Pool: £69,154.24 - 122.39 winning units T/Qpdt: £68.40 to a £1 stake. Pool: £5,344.43 - 57.77 winning units **Steve Payne**

# 6517 RIPON (R-H)
Tuesday, August 29

**OFFICIAL GOING: Good (8.1)**
Wind: Light across Weather: Overcast

## 6559 DOWNLOAD THE FREE AT THE RACES APP FILLIES' NOVICE STKS (PLUS 10 RACE) 5f
2:15 (2:17) (Class 5) 2-Y-0 £3,557 (£1,058; £529; £264) Stalls High

Form RPR
5 1 **Revived**[27] 5528 2-9-0 **0**......(h[1]) DanielTudhope 4 73+
(Michael Bell) *trckd ldrs on outer: pushed along to chse ldr over 1f out: led ins fnl f: kpt on pushed out* **6/5**[1]
01 2 1 1/4 **Deviate (IRE)**[29] 5480 2-9-2 **0**...... PaddyPilley[(5)] 11 75
(Tom Dascombe) *led: rdn 2f out: hdd ins fnl f: edgd rt and no ex* **20/1**
3 shd **Machree (IRE)** 2-9-0 **0**...... TomEaves 9 70+
(Declan Carroll) *dwlt: sn midfield: hdwy whn bit short of room over 1f out: sltly hmpd ins fnl f: rdn and kpt on wl fnl 110yds* **50/1**
4 shd **Rastacap** 2-9-0 **0**...... FrannyNorton 2 67+
(Mark Johnston) *hld up: sn pushed along: kpt on wl fnl f: nrst fin* **20/1**
5 1 **Enrolment** 2-9-0 **0**...... PaulHanagan 7 64
(Richard Fahey) *trckd ldrs: rdn 2f out: kpt on same pce* **8/1**
6 3/4 **Kaaba Stone (IRE)** 2-9-0 **0**...... JamieSpencer 1 61
(David Simcock) *dwlt: hld up in rr: pushed along and hdwy on outside over 1f out: kpt on: eased towards fin* **12/1**
22 7 hd **Tonkolili (IRE)**[59] 4369 2-9-0 **0**...... PhillipMakin 8 60
(William Muir) *prom: rdn 2f out: no ex ins fnl f* **13/2**[3]
52 8 1 1/2 **Dangerous Lady**[15] 5998 2-9-0 **0**...... DavidAllan 6 55
(Tim Easterby) *prom: rdn 2f out: hung lft ins fnl f: wknd fnl 110yds* **11/2**[2]
5 9 1 1/2 **Bee Ina Bonnet**[12] 6086 2-9-0 **0**...... PaulMulrennan 5 49
(Tim Easterby) *hld up: pushed along 2f out: nvr threatened* **28/1**
0 10 1/2 **Alaskan Bay (IRE)**[43] 4972 2-9-0 **0**...... LukeMorris 10 48
(Rae Guest) *chsd ldrs: rdn 1/2-way: wknd over 1f out* **28/1**
00 11 3 3/4 **Sandie Gem**[18] 5891 2-9-0 **0**...... JackGarritty 3 34
(Richard Fahey) *a towards rr* **100/1**

1m 0.32s (0.32) **Going Correction** -0.025s/f (Good) 11 Ran SP% **112.3**
Speed ratings (Par 91): **96,94,93,93,92 90,90,88,85,84 78**
CSF £33.32 TOTE £2.00: £1.10, £4.20, £10.30; EX 26.10 Trifecta £3102.50.
**Owner** Clipper Logistics **Bred** Brightwalton Bloodstock Ltd **Trained** Newmarket, Suffolk

**FOCUS**
An ordinary fillies' novice but a useful winner. It's been rated as modest form, but a few showed promise.

## 6560 FREE TIPS DAILY ON ATTHERACES.COM (S) STKS 1m 1f 170y
2:50 (2:50) (Class 6) 3-4-Y-0 £2,587 (£770; £384; £192) Stalls Low

Form RPR
0-30 1 **Calypso Delegator (IRE)**[20] 5802 4-9-2 **47**......(v[1]) AndrewMullen 2 56
(Micky Hammond) *hld up: rdn and hdwy over 1f out: swtchd lft over 1f out: led jst ins fnl f: kpt on to draw clr* **25/1**
0603 2 6 **Rockliffe**[20] 5807 4-9-2 **48**......(p) PJMcDonald 3 45
(Micky Hammond) *chsd ldr: rdn over 3f out: led over 1f out: hdd jst ins fnl f: wknd* **8/1**
0050 3 3/4 **False Id**[5] 6346 4-9-2 **59**......(t[1]) BarryMcHugh 1 43
(Marjorie Fife) *led: clr over 3f out: rdn and reduced advantage 2f out: hdd over 1f out: wknd ins fnl f* **6/4**[1]
6265 4 12 **California Cliffs (IRE)**[8] 6257 3-8-4 **55**...... LukeMorris 6 16
(Rae Guest) *hld up in tch: rdn over 3f out: wknd over 1f out* **9/4**[2]
0005 5 16 **Percy Verence**[12] 6088 4-9-2 **49**......(p) FrannyNorton 4
(Tracy Waggott) *trckd ldr: lost pl qckly over 3f out: wknd and bhd* **5/1**[3]
0500 6 31 **Permanent**[8] 6257 3-8-9 **57**......(b) GeorgeDowning 5
(Daniel Kubler) *racd keenly: trckd ldr on outer: wknd qckly 4f out: sn t.o* **8/1**

2m 5.51s (0.11) **Going Correction** -0.025s/f (Good)
**WFA** 3 from 4yo 7lb 6 Ran SP% **113.5**
Speed ratings (Par 101): **98,93,92,83,70 45**
CSF £198.40 TOTE £20.60: £6.10, £3.10; EX 84.70 Trifecta £806.90.No bid for the winner
**Owner** Ms Sherene Ure & Partner **Bred** Jim McCormack **Trained** Middleham, N Yorks

**FOCUS**
A weak seller, with the complete outsider, who is rated just 47, running out a clear winner. A pb from the winner, but no depth to the race, and it's been rated negatively around the runner-up to his recent level.

## 6561 21 ENGINEER REGIMENT SAPPER NURSERY H'CAP 1m
3:25 (3:25) (Class 4) (0-85,84) 2-Y-0 £4,851 (£1,443; £721; £360) Stalls Low

Form RPR
1102 1 **Veejay (IRE)**[18] 5875 2-9-7 **84**...... GrahamLee 1 88+
(Mick Channon) *mde all: racd keenly: pushed along over 2f out: strly pressed over 1f out: kpt on: a doing enough* **11/8**[1]
1365 2 nk **Poet's Dawn**[12] 6087 2-8-9 **72**...... DavidAllan 3 75
(Tim Easterby) *trckd ldrs: rdn over 2f out: kpt on fnl f* **15/2**
3325 3 1 3/4 **Paramount Love**[24] 5659 2-8-11 **74**...... PaulHanagan 4 73
(Richard Fahey) *trckd ldrs: pushed along over 2f out: rdn to chal strly over 1f out: no ex ins fnl f* **4/1**[3]
044 4 2 1/2 **Bibbidibobbidiboo (IRE)**[25] 5600 2-8-0 **63**...... LukeMorris 6 56
(Ann Duffield) *hld up: rdn and hdwy over 2f out: one pce ins fnl f* **17/2**
6341 5 2 3/4 **Noble Manners (IRE)**[32] 5366 2-9-0 **77**...... FrannyNorton 5 64
(Mark Johnston) *s.i.s: hld up: rdn along 3f out: one pce and nvr threatened* **7/2**[2]
640 6 19 **Fastalong (IRE)**[32] 5372 2-8-0 **63** oh3...... CamHardie 2 6
(Tim Easterby) *pressed ldr: rdn over 2f out: wknd qckly and bhd* **25/1**

1m 41.8s (0.40) **Going Correction** -0.025s/f (Good) 6 Ran SP% **110.5**
Speed ratings (Par 96): **97,96,94,92,89 70**
CSF £12.02 TOTE £2.00: £1.30, £2.80; EX 11.30 Trifecta £38.20.
**Owner** John & Zoe Webster **Bred** Messrs Billy McEnery & Paul McEnery **Trained** West Ilsley, Berks

**FOCUS**
None of these wanted to lead and as a result the pace was steady one, with the winning favourite getting the run of the race. The runner-up has been rated just above his pre-race best.

## 6562 FOLLOW @ATTHERACES ON TWITTER CONDITIONS STKS (PLUS 10 RACE) 1m
4:00 (4:00) (Class 3) 3-Y-0 £7,561 (£2,263; £1,131; £566) Stalls Low

Form RPR
-250 1 **Rodaini (USA)**[68] 3994 3-8-12 **100**......(b) FrannyNorton 3 95+
(Simon Crisford) *mde all: pushed along over 2f out: rdn and strly pressed over 1f out: kpt on and in command ins fnl f* **9/4**[2]
1341 2 1 3/4 **Hugin (IRE)**[27] 5541 3-8-12 **89**...... JamieSpencer 2 90+
(David Simcock) *trckd ldr: pushed along over 2f out: rdn to chal strly over 1f out: one pce and sn hld in 2nd ins fnl f* **2/5**[1]
6600 3 2 **Mitigate**[76] 3722 3-8-4 **70**...... HollieDoyle[(3)] 1 80?
(Jane Chapple-Hyam) *hld up: racd keenly: pushed along over 2f out: rdn 2f out: kpt on ins fnl f but no threat to ldng pair* **33/1**[3]
063 4 10 **Used To Be**[32] 5358 3-8-12 **66**...... PJMcDonald 4 62
(K R Burke) *hld up: rdn over 2f out: wknd over 1f out* **50/1**

1m 39.68s (-1.72) **Going Correction** -0.025s/f (Good) 4 Ran SP% **107.1**
Speed ratings (Par 104): **107,105,103,93**
CSF £3.51 TOTE £3.00; EX 3.00 Trifecta £6.30.
**Owner** Abdullah Saeed Al Naboodah **Bred** Greenwood Lodge Farm **Trained** Newmarket, Suffolk

**FOCUS**
This looked a match and the highest-rated runner triumphed, despite the market not speaking in his favour.

## 6563 VISIT ATTHERACES.COM CITY OF RIPON H'CAP 1m 1f 170y
4:30 (4:30) (Class 3) (0-90,91) 3-Y-0 -£7,561 (£2,263; £1,131; £566; £282) Stalls Low

Form RPR
00 1 **Mutamaded (IRE)**[15] 5996 4-9-9 **85**...... JamesSullivan 3 91
(Ruth Carr) *in tch: rdn to chse ldr over 1f out: chal ins fnl f: kpt on to ld fnl 50yds* **50/1**
2144 2 1/2 **Mulligatawny (IRE)**[10] 6209 4-9-7 **90**......(p) BenSanderson[(7)] 2 95
(Roger Fell) *trckd ldr: angled lft to outer over 2f out: sn rdn: led 1f out: edgd rt: hdd 50yds out: one pce* **5/1**[2]
0200 3 1 1/2 **Jacbequick**[5] 6349 6-9-6 **85**......(p) JoshDoyle[(3)] 4 87
(David O'Meara) *in tch: rdn over 2f out: wnt 3rd ins fnl f: kpt on same pce* **14/1**
5131 4 1 1/4 **Alexander M (IRE)**[3] 6416 3-8-10 **79**...... PJMcDonald 7 79
(Mark Johnston) *trckd ldr: pushed along to ld over 2f out: rdn over 1f out: hdd 1f out: wknd ins fnl f* **11/10**[1]
1260 5 1 **Ray's The Money (IRE)**[10] 6189 3-8-13 **82**......(v) LouisSteward 1 80
(Michael Bell) *hld up: rdn over 2f out: kpt on ins fnl f: nvr threatened* **8/1**

1502 **6** *hd* **Sands Chorus**10 6209 5-10-1 **91** LukeMorris 6 88
(James Given) *led: rdn whn hdd over 2f out: wknd fnl f* **6/1**3

2200 **7** *5* **Monticello (IRE)**26 5568 3-9-4 **87** FrannyNorton 5 75
(Mark Johnston) *in tch on outside: rdn 3f out: wknd over 1f out* **13/2**

2m 3.25s (-2.15) **Going Correction** -0.025s/f (Good)
**WFA** 3 from 4yo+ 7lb **7** Ran SP% **111.6**
Speed ratings (Par 107): **107,106,105,104,103 103,99**
CSF £266.52 TOTE £20.00: £5.70, £2.80; EX 231.00 Trifecta £1933.90.

**Owner** The Bottom Liners & Mrs R Carr **Bred** Shadwell Estate Company Limited **Trained** Huby, N Yorks

**FOCUS**
A useful handicap even if it went to the complete outsider.

## 6564 DOWNLOAD THE AT THE RACES APP FOR IPAD H'CAP 1m
**5:00** (5:02) (Class 5) (0-75,74) 3-Y-O+ **£3,557** (£1,058; £529; £264) **Stalls** Low

Form RPR

2110 **1** **Rosy Ryan (IRE)**14 6047 7-9-2 **64** JoeDoyle 9 72
(Tina Jackson) *midfield: hdwy to trck ldrs whn briefly short of room over 2f out: rdn 2f out: led 1f out: kpt on* **16/1**

2120 **2** *1* **Hernando Torres**17 5950 9-9-0 **69** (tp) RyanTimby(7) 8 75+
(Michael Easterby) *hld up: briefly short of room over 2f out: angled lft and hdwy over 1f out: kpt on wl fnl f: wnt 2nd towards fin* **33/1**

1410 **3** *½* **Ventura Secret (IRE)**17 5949 3-8-13 **67** DavidAllan 1 71
(Tim Easterby) *led narrowly: rdn over 2f out: sn edgd lft: hdd 1f out: one pce: lost 2nd towards fin* **3/1**1

3150 **4** *2¼* **Racemaker**6 6315 3-9-2 **73** PhilDennis(3) 4 71
(Andrew Crook) *chsd ldrs towards outer: rdn over 2f out: ev ch appr fnl f: one pce ins fnl f* **14/1**

2413 **5** *1¼* **Whitkirk**8 6266 4-9-7 **69** JackGarritty 3 66
(Jedd O'Keeffe) *trckd ldrs: rdn over 2f out: one pce* **3/1**1

4443 **6** *¾* **Dominannie (IRE)**14 6047 4-8-9 **57** CamHardie 7 52
(Sally Haynes) *hld up: rdn and hdd on outer over 2f out: no ex fnl f* **11/1**

2322 **7** *1* **Totally Magic (IRE)**14 6047 5-9-2 **67** LewisEdmunds(3) 11 59
(Richard Whitaker) *hld up towards outer: rdn 3f out: sn no imp* **5/1**2

430 **8** *nk* **Captain Revelation**15 6014 5-9-3 **70** PaddyPilley(5) 2 62
(Tom Dascombe) *prom: rdn and losing pl whn n.m.r over 2f out: grad wknd over 1f out* **12/1**

0002 **9** *6* **Dandyleekie (IRE)**20 5807 5-9-12 **74** DavidNolan 6 52
(David O'Meara) *midfield: rdn 3f out: sn wknd* **8/1**3

0-60 **10** *1½* **Indian Vision (IRE)**33 5319 3-8-1 **55** oh2 AndrewMullen 10 29
(Micky Hammond) *s.i.s: a towards rr* **40/1**

-550 **11** *23* **Venutius**50 4699 10-9-8 **70** PaulHanagan 5
(Charles Hills) *pressed ldr on outside: wkng whn short of room over 2f out: sn dropped to rr and eased* **20/1**

1m 40.68s (-0.72) **Going Correction** -0.025s/f (Good)
**WFA** 3 from 4yo+ 6lb **11** Ran SP% **116.5**
Speed ratings (Par 103): **102,101,100,98,97 96,95,94,88,87 64**
CSF £455.19 CT £2043.71 TOTE £14.40: £3.50, £8.50, £1.50; EX 155.30 Trifecta £1350.80.

**Owner** H L Thompson **Bred** Roger A Ryan **Trained** Liverton, Cleveland

■ Stewards' Enquiry : Paddy Pilley caution: careless riding

**FOCUS**
Modest handicap form.

## 6565 FOLLOW AT THE RACES ON INSTAGRAM STAYERS H'CAP 2m
**5:30** (5:31) (Class 6) (0-65,66) 3-Y-O+ **£3,234** (£962; £481; £240) **Stalls** Low

Form RPR

2262 **1** **Fitzwilly**8 6259 7-9-10 **66** DavidEgan(5) 6 73
(Mick Channon) *midfield: rdn and hdwy to chse ldr over 2f out: led over 1f out: styd on wl* **9/2**2

3050 **2** *3* **Jan Smuts (IRE)**21 5740 9-8-11 **55** (tp) ConnorMurtagh(7) 4 58
(Wilf Storey) *hld up in midfield: pushed along and hdwy over 3f out: rdn over 2f out: styd on: wnt 2nd fnl 110yds* **16/1**

3246 **3** *2* **La Fritillaire**9 6233 5-10-0 **65** AndrewMullen 11 66
(James Given) *prom: led 7f out: briefly rdn 3 l clr over 3f out: hdd over 1f out: wknd ins fnl f* **7/1**

04 **4** *1½* **Maple Stirrup (IRE)**18 5884 5-8-6 **50** PaulaMuir(7) 7 49
(Patrick Holmes) *hld up in midfield: rdn along over 4f out: plugged on into poor 4th over 1f out* **25/1**

0000 **5** *5* **Thomas Crown (IRE)**25 5618 3-8-0 **49** (p) CamHardie 5 44
(Roger Fell) *trckd ldrs: rdn 3f out: wknd over 1f out* **25/1**

0605 **6** *12* **Russian Royale**41 5017 7-9-6 **57** PaulHanagan 9 36
(Micky Hammond) *midfield: rdn over 3f out: sn wknd* **22/1**

0464 **7** *2¾* **Silver Gleam (IRE)**8 6270 3-8-0 **49** oh1 JimmyQuinn 3 27
(Chris Fairhurst) *hld up: rdn along 4f out: sn no hdwy: eased fr over 1f out* **6/1**3

0220 **8** *6* **Crakehall Lad (IRE)**66 4102 6-8-6 **46** (b) PhilDennis(3) 1 14
(Andrew Crook) *hld up: rdn over 5f out: sn btn* **25/1**

2232 **9** *12* **Theglasgowwarrior**15 6002 3-9-1 **64** (p) LouisSteward 12 20
(Michael Bell) *trckd ldrs: rdn to briefly chse ldr 3f out: wknd over 2f out: eased* **5/4**1

-000 **10** *7* **Rajapur**112 2501 4-8-9 **46** oh1 (b) PaddyAspell 2
(Philip Kirby) *led: hdd 7f out: remained prom tl wknd over 3f out* **40/1**

000 **11** *59* **Strikemaster (IRE)**28 5493 11-8-2 **46** oh1 (bt) ManuelFernandes(7) 8
(Lee James) *hld up: rdn over 7f out: sn wknd: t.o fnl 5f* **66/1**

3m 31.2s (-0.60) **Going Correction** -0.025s/f (Good)
**WFA** 3 from 4yo+ 12lb **11** Ran SP% **115.1**
Speed ratings (Par 101): **100,98,97,96,94 88,86,83,77,74 44**
CSF £61.76 CT £497.21 TOTE £4.90: £1.70, £3.20, £1.80; EX 60.10 Trifecta £223.20.

**Owner** Peter Taplin & M Channon **Bred** Imperial & Mike Channon Bloodstock Ltd **Trained** West Ilsley, Berks

**FOCUS**
A pretty moderate staying event and the form isn't up to much with two of the fancied 3yos failing to run any sort of race.

T/Plt: £3,511.40 to a £1 stake. Pool: £59,262.38 - 12.32 winning units T/Qpdt: £198.80 to a £1 stake. Pool: £4,888.72 - 18.19 winning units **Andrew Sheret**

# 6364 CLAIREFONTAINE (R-H)
Tuesday, August 29

**OFFICIAL GOING: Good**

## 6566a PRIX RADIO BRUNET (PRIX DE LA PETITE FERME) (MAIDEN) (3YO FILLIES) (TURF) 1m 4f
**2:55** 3-Y-O **£10,683** (£4,273; £3,205; £2,136; £1,068)

RPR

**1** **Lady Valdean**41 5022 3-9-3 0 ow1 MickaelBarzalona 11 70
(Jose Santos) *wl into stride: disp ld early: led after 1f: pushed along over 2f out: rdn to maintain advantage over 1f out: u.p and styd on strly ins fnl f* **41/5**

**2** *1* **Deccan Queen**78 3-9-3 0 ow1 VincentCheminaud 10 68
(D Smaga, France) **9/5**1

**3** *2½* **Groovy Filly (FR)**26 3-9-3 0 ow1 StephanePasquier 7 64
(Y Gourraud, France) **15/2**3

**4** *3½* **Pangania (GER)** 3-9-3 0 ow1 ChristopheSoumillon 13 59
(P Vovcenko, Germany) **128/10**

**5** *snk* **Asara (GER)** 3-9-3 0 ow1 AlexisBadel 5 59
(H-F Devin, France) **11/1**

**6** *½* **Tayara**26 3-9-3 0 ow1 CristianDemuro 8 58
(Rod Collet, France) **6/1**2

**7** *nk* **Laem Sing (FR)** 3-9-3 0 ow1 OlivierPeslier 12 57
(Alain Couetil, France) **79/10**

**8** *¾* **Ocean Fairy (IRE)** 3-9-3 0 ow1 EddyHardouin 6 56
(Carina Fey, France) **141/10**

**9** *3* **Loca Furiosa (IRE)**60 3-9-3 0 ow1 RonanThomas 1 51
(C Lerner, France) **168/10**

**10** *2½* **Milly May (FR)**144 3-9-3 0 ow1 SebastienMaillot 2 47
(L Rovisse, France) **247/10**

**11** *5* **Decidement (FR)**26 3-8-11 0 ow1 ClementLecoeuvre(6) 9 39
(E Lellouche, France) **50/1**

**12** *7* **Eurvad Pembo (FR)**26 3-8-9 0 ow1 AlexisPouchin(8) 3 28
(Y Gourraud, France) **101/1**

2m 32.0s (-5.90) **12** Ran SP% **118.5**
PARI-MUTUEL (all including 1 euro stake): WIN 9.20; PLACE 2.30, 1.40, 1.90; DF 10.10; SF 19.90.

**Owner** R Cooper Racing Ltd **Bred** Bearstone Stud Ltd **Trained** Upper Lambourn, Berks

# 6126 CATTERICK (L-H)
Wednesday, August 30

**OFFICIAL GOING: Good (good to firm in places; watered; 8.3)**
Wind: Virtually nil Weather: Cloudy

## 6567 BET TOTEPLACEPOT AT BETFRED.COM NOVICE MEDIAN AUCTION STKS 5f
**1:50** (1:52) (Class 5) 2-Y-O **£2,911** (£866; £432; £216) **Stalls** Low

Form RPR

33 **1** **Cool Spirit**20 5825 2-9-2 0 JoeDoyle 6 75
(James Given) *mde all: rdn jst over 1f out: drvn ins fnl f: sn hung rt: kpt on wl towards fin* **1/2**1

**2** *½* **Paco Escostar** 2-8-11 0 CamHardie 2 68+
(Paul Midgley) *dwlt and rr: hdwy 1/2-way: rdn to chse ldrs over 1f out: chal ins fnl f and ev ch tl drvn and no ex towards fin* **40/1**

0 **3** *2¼* **Feebs**10 6231 2-8-9 0 RyanTimby(7) 8 65
(Michael Easterby) *trckd ldrs: hdwy on outer over 2f out: chsd wnr over 1f out: sn rdn and kpt on same pce* **50/1**

0 **4** *2* **Cool Baby**42 5015 2-8-4 0 JonathanFisher(7) 7 53
(Robert Cowell) *dwlt: sn trcking ldrs: hdwy 1/2-way: cl up 2f out: rdn over 1f out: wknd appr fnl f* **25/1**

00 **5** *1¼* **The Auld Hoose (IRE)**20 5834 2-9-2 0 PaulHanagan 1 53
(Richard Fahey) *prom on inner: pushed along 1/2-way: rdn along 2f out: sn one pce* **14/1**

000 **6** *¾* **French Silk**28 5537 2-8-4 36 PaulaMuir(7) 4 46
(Chris Fairhurst) *towards rr: hdwy wl over 1f out: kpt on fnl f* **250/1**

45 **7** *½* **Ghost**14 6056 2-8-11 0 JasonHart 3 44
(John Quinn) *chsd ldrs: rdn along 1/2-way: sn wknd* **9/2**2

006 **8** *shd* **Furni Factors**84 3460 2-9-2 59 GrahamLee 10 49
(Ronald Thompson) *a in rr* **40/1**

05 **9** *½* **Lady Sandy (IRE)**37 5210 2-8-11 0 BenCurtis 5 42
(David Barron) *a in rr* **7/1**3

6 **10** *2* **Cat Ballou**13 6086 2-8-11 0 SamJames 9 35
(David O'Meara) *cl up: rdn along 2f out: sn drvn and wknd over 1f out* **16/1**

1m 0.31s (0.51) **Going Correction** -0.025s/f (Good) **10** Ran SP% **121.0**
Speed ratings (Par 94): **94,93,89,86,84 83,82,82,81,78**
CSF £42.82 TOTE £1.30: £1.02, £8.20, £11.00; EX 35.30 Trifecta £1860.50.
**Owner** The Cool Silk Partnership **Bred** John Hanson **Trained** Willoughton, Lincs
**FOCUS**
Bend into home straight dolled out 4yds and parade ring bend dolled out 6yds. This was an ordinary novice race yet it should produce future sprint winners. The winner has been rated just off his latest effort, with nothing reliable or convincing in behind.

## 6568 BET TOTEJACKPOT AT BETFRED.COM MAIDEN FILLIES' STKS 7f 6y
**2:20** (2:22) (Class 5) 3-Y-O+ **£2,911** (£866; £432; £216) **Stalls** Low

Form RPR

**1** **La Sioux (IRE)** 3-9-0 0 JackGarritty 4 69+
(Richard Fahey) *dwlt and green: sn outpcd and detached in rr: rdn along over 4f out: tk cl order 3f out: cl up 2f out: chal u.p over 1f out: kpt on gamely fnl f to ld on line* **7/2**3

20 **2** *nse* **Nuns Walk**11 6184 3-9-0 0 DavidAllan 3 68
(Tim Easterby) *sn trcking ldr: cl up 3f out: led 2f out: rdn over 1f out: drvn ins fnl f: hdd on line* **9/4**1

5246 **3** *2* **Eponina (IRE)**61 4303 3-9-0 62 GrahamLee 2 62
(Ben Haslam) *trckd ldng pair: swtchd rt and hdwy 2f out: sn cl up: rdn to chal and ev ch ent fnl f: drvn and hld whn n.m.r nr fin* **11/4**2

2-60 **4** *16* **Fairy Lights**[110] 2585 3-9-0 71 AndreaAtzeni 5 19
(Roger Varian) *led: jnd 3f out and sn pushed along: hdd 2f out: sn rdn and wknd* **11/4**[2]

1m 26.52s (-0.48) **Going Correction** -0.025s/f (Good)
**WFA** 3 from 5yo 5lb 4 Ran SP% **106.3**
Speed ratings (Par 100): **101,100,98,80**
CSF £11.08 TOTE £4.70; EX 8.70 Trifecta £24.20.
**Owner** Mrs Una Towell **Bred** P J Towell **Trained** Musley Bank, N Yorks

**FOCUS**
Race distance increased 12yds. This moderate fillies' maiden proved eventful. It's rated around the third.

## 6569 BET TOTEQUADPOT AT BETFRED.COM H'CAP 1m 7f 189y
**2:50** (2:52) (Class 5) (0-70,72) 3-Y-0+ **£2,911** (£866; £432; £216) **Stalls** Low

Form RPR
1202 **1** **Question Of Faith**[18] 5923 6-9-3 **57** PaulHanagan 3 67+
(Martin Todhunter) *dwlt and rr: hdwy 6f out: cl up on outer over 4f out: chsd ldr over 2f out: rdn to ld wl over 1f out: sn edgd lft to inner rail: drvn and kpt on wl fnl f* **5/2**[1]

1-24 **2** *2 1/2* **Italian Riviera**[22] 5740 8-9-8 **62** (h) AndrewMullen 6 68
(Kenneth Slack) *trckd ldr 6f: cl up: pushed along 4f out and sn outpcd: rdn along 3f out: drvn and styd on to chse ent fnl f: sn drvn and no imp towards fin* **11/4**[2]

-536 **3** *5* **Bulas Belle**[13] 6090 7-10-4 **72** GrahamLee 4 72
(Grant Tuer) *trckd ldrs: hdwy to chse ldr after 6f: pushed along over 4f out: rdn wl over 2f out: drvn wl over 1f out: sn wknd* **9/2**

6320 **4** *10* **Ingleby Hollow**[10] 6233 5-10-0 **68** (p) DanielTudhope 5 61
(David O'Meara) *led: pushed along 4f out: rdn 3f out: hdd wl over 1f out: sn wknd* **10/3**[3]

0303 **5** *3* **Cavalieri (IRE)**[19] 5896 7-9-5 **59** (tp) KevinStott 2 43
(Philip Kirby) *in tch: pushed along over 4f out: rdn 3f out: sn outpcd* **9/1**

6606 **6** *20* **Pennerley**[9] 6270 4-8-12 **52** PJMcDonald 1 12
(Micky Hammond) *prom: pushed along over 5f out: rdn wl over 3f out: sn outpcd and bhd* **25/1**

3m 30.6s (-1.40) **Going Correction** -0.025s/f (Good) 6 Ran SP% **110.3**
Speed ratings (Par 103): **102,100,98,93,91 81**
CSF £9.32 TOTE £3.30: £1.60, £1.50; EX 10.70 Trifecta £32.10.
**Owner** K Fitzsimons & G Fell **Bred** Sir Robert Ogden **Trained** Orton, Cumbria

**FOCUS**
There was a fair gallop on in this run-of-the-mill staying handicap. Race distance increased 30yds.

## 6570 BET TOTEEXACTA AT BETFRED.COM H'CAP 7f 6y
**3:20** (3:24) (Class 4) (0-85,87) 3-Y-0+ **£5,822** (£1,732; £865; £432) **Stalls** Low

Form RPR
0540 **1** **Sakhee's Return**[25] 5669 5-9-2 **75** (t) DavidAllan 8 83+
(Tim Easterby) *dwlt and bhd:. hdwy on inner 3f out: swtchd rt over 2f out: n.m.r and swtchd to outer wl over 1f out: rdn to chse ldrs over 1f out: styd on ins fnl f to ld nr fin* **8/1**

3606 **2** *nk* **Lagenda**[26] 5610 4-9-6 **79** (b[1]) KevinStott 5 85
(Kevin Ryan) *prom: hdwy and cl up over 2f out: rdn to ld wl over 1f out: drvn ins fnl f: hdd and no ex nr fin* **9/2**[2]

3513 **3** *nk* **Magical Effect (IRE)**[11] 6205 5-9-13 **86** JamesSullivan 2 92+
(Ruth Carr) *hld up in tch on inner: swtchd rt and effrt whn nt clr run and hmpd 11/2f out: swtchd lft and rdn ent fnl f: styd on. n.m.r nr line* **11/4**[1]

5441 **4** *1/2* **Tadaawol**[22] 5739 4-9-5 **78** (p) TonyHamilton 11 82
(Roger Fell) *led: rdn along and hdd wl over 1f out: drvn and rallied ins fnl f: ev ch tl no ex towards fin* **10/1**

2536 **5** *nse* **Johnny Cavagin**[11] 6186 8-9-6 **79** (t) GrahamLee 3 83
(Ronald Thompson) *hld up towards rr: hdwy on outer over 2f out: rdn to chse ldrs and hung lft 11/2f out: sn drvn and ch: kpt on same pce towards fin* **11/1**

100 **6** *3 1/4* **Adam's Ale**[18] 5947 8-9-9 **82** (e[1]) BarryMcHugh 1 77
(Marjorie Fife) *trckd ldrs on inner: hdwy 3f out: rdn along 2f out: drvn wl over 1f out: grad wknd* **33/1**

0130 **7** *2 1/4* **Shouranour (IRE)**[11] 6209 7-9-9 **85** (b) JoshDoyle[(3)] 6 74
(Alan Brown) *.in tch: hdwy to chse ldrs over 2f out: rdn whn n.m.r and hmpd 11/2f out: sn btn* **12/1**

0023 **8** *3 1/4* **Bahamian Bird**[22] 5754 4-9-4 **77** PaulHanagan 4 57+
(Richard Fahey) *trckd ldrs: hdwy wl over 2f out: rdn whn n.m.r and hmpd 11/2f out: sn wknd* **17/2**

0002 **9** *4* **Acrux**[11] 6182 4-9-1 **74** (h) DanielTudhope 12 43
(David O'Meara) *hld up: a in rr* **11/2**[3]

6103 **10** *1 3/4* **Maureb (IRE)**[19] 5881 5-8-7 **66** (p) DuranFentiman 7 31
(Tony Coyle) *chsd ldrs on outer: cl up 1/2-way: rdn along over 2f out: sn wknd* **66/1**

415- **11** *27* **Jacquard (IRE)**[357] 6228 3-9-9 **87** PJMcDonald 9
(Mark Johnston) *chsd ldrs on outer: rdn along and lost pl 1/2-way: sn bhd* **25/1**

1m 25.73s (-1.27) **Going Correction** -0.025s/f (Good)
**WFA** 3 from 4yo+ 5lb 11 Ran SP% **115.3**
Speed ratings (Par 105): **106,105,105,104,104 100,98,94,90,88 57**
CSF £42.38 CT £127.15 TOTE £9.40: £2.70, £1.50, £2.10; EX 60.20 Trifecta £238.00.
**Owner** Ontoawinner, M Hulin & Partner **Bred** W Brackstone & S J Whitear **Trained** Great Habton, N Yorks

**FOCUS**
Race distance increased 12yds. This feature was run to suit the closers and it saw a messy finish.

## 6571 BET TOTETRIFECTA AT BETFRED.COM H'CAP (DIV I) 5f 212y
**3:50** (3:51) (Class 6) (0-60,62) 3-Y-0+ **£2,264** (£673; £336; £168) **Stalls** Low

Form RPR
0050 **1** **Indian Pursuit (IRE)**[20] 5836 4-9-11 **61** JasonHart 8 69
(John Quinn) *trckd ldr: hdwy to chal wl over 1f out: sn rdn: drvn to ld ins fnl f: kpt on* **8/1**

0221 **2** *1 1/4* **Melaniemillie**[22] 5738 3-9-1 **54** JamesSullivan 2 58
(Ruth Carr) *led: rdn along and jnd wl over 1f out: drvn ent fnl f: sn hdd: kpt on same pce* **2/1**[1]

5104 **3** *3/4* **Searanger (USA)**[9] 6271 4-9-7 **57** PJMcDonald 4 59
(Rebecca Menzies) *trckd ldrs: hdwy over 2f out: rdn wl over 1f out: drvn and kpt on same pce fnl f* **9/4**[2]

6-00 **4** *1* **Ginger Love**[70] 3984 3-9-2 **55** DuranFentiman 1 53+
(Bryan Smart) *hld up in rr: hdwy on inner over 2f out: rdn to chse ldrs over 1f out: kpt on fnl f* **50/1**

2565 **5** *shd* **Windforpower (IRE)**[12] 6130 7-9-6 **56** (p) BenCurtis 3 54
(Tracy Waggott) *trckd ldrs on inner: rdn along over 2f out: drvn wl over 1f out: grad wknd* **11/1**

2220 **6** *1* **Deben**[12] 6131 4-8-11 **50** PhilDennis[(3)] 9 45
(John Weymes) *in tch: hdwy on outer 1/2-way: chsd ldrs over 2f out: sn rdn: drvn and one pce fnl f* **5/1**[3]

0640 **7** *1 1/2* **Lukoutoldmakezebak**[7] 6316 4-8-9 **45** PaddyAspell 7 35
(David Thompson) *a towards rr* **66/1**

6600 **8** *hd* **Salvatore Fury (IRE)**[46] 4896 7-9-12 **62** (p) GrahamLee 6 51
(Keith Dalgleish) *a towards rr* **12/1**

-500 **9** *6* **Nifty Niece (IRE)**[82] 3525 3-8-6 **45** (p) PaulHanagan 5 15
(Ann Duffield) *plld hrd: cl up: effrt over 2f out: sn rdn: wknd wl over 1f out* **50/1**

1m 14.08s (0.48) **Going Correction** -0.025s/f (Good)
**WFA** 3 from 4yo+ 3lb 9 Ran SP% **113.3**
Speed ratings (Par 101): **95,93,92,91,90 89,87,87,79**
CSF £23.86 CT £48.41 TOTE £8.80: £2.20, £1.50, £1.30; EX 29.80 Trifecta £104.20.
**Owner** Malcolm Walker **Bred** Sean Gorman **Trained** Settrington, N Yorks

**FOCUS**
It paid to be handy in this moderate sprint handicap. Sound form for the class. Race distance increased 12yds. Straightforward form, with the winner rated near this year's best and the runner-up to her latest effort.

## 6572 BET TOTETRIFECTA AT BETFRED.COM H'CAP (DIV II) 5f 212y
**4:20** (4:21) (Class 6) (0-60,62) 3-Y-0+ **£2,264** (£673; £336; £168) **Stalls** Low

Form RPR
0002 **1** **Spirit Of Zebedee (IRE)**[15] 6045 4-9-4 **57** (p) JasonHart 5 67
(John Quinn) *mde all: rdn and qcknd clr over 1f out: kpt on strly* **9/2**[2]

5030 **2** *1* **Bold Spirit**[3] 6464 6-8-10 **52** (t) PhilDennis[(3)] 2 60
(Declan Carroll) *hld up in rr: hdwy on inner wl over 2f out: chsd ldrs whn nt clr run and swtchd lft over 1f out: sn rdn and chsd wnr ent fnl f: kpt on* **9/2**[2]

3450 **3** *3 1/4* **Willbeme**[34] 5318 9-9-6 **62** (t[1]) CliffordLee[(3)] 8 56
(Simon West) *chsd ldrs: effrt on outer over 2f out: rdn over 1f out: drvn and one pce fnl f* **13/2**[3]

-000 **4** *3/4* **Le Laitier (FR)**[28] 5542 6-8-11 **50** (v[1]) DavidAllan 7 42
(Scott Dixon) *trckd wnr: cl up 1/2-way: rdn over 2f out: drvn wl over 1f out: sn one pce* **20/1**

531 **5** *3 1/4* **State Residence (IRE)**[4] 6437 3-9-1 **57** 6ex (vt) DanielTudhope 9 39+
(David O'Meara) *cl up on outer: pushed along over 2f out: rdn and edgd lft over 1f out: sn drvn and on wknd appr fnl f* **6/4**[1]

3563 **6** *2 1/2* **Poet's Time**[23] 5703 3-8-4 **46** oh1 AndrewMullen 6 20
(Tim Easterby) *dwlt and rr: hdwy on outer wl over 2f out: sn rdn along and wknd* **14/1**

5660 **7** *4* **Six Of The Best**[15] 6045 5-8-7 **46** oh1 PaulHanagan 4 7
(Bryan Smart) *chsd ldrs: rdn along over 2f out: sn wknd* **28/1**

0062 **8** *3/4* **Bop It**[9] 6271 8-9-7 **60** (bt) CamHardie 1 18
(Michael Easterby) *chsd ldrs on inner: rdn along over 2f out: sn drvn and wknd* **10/1**

1m 13.6s **Going Correction** -0.025s/f (Good)
**WFA** 3 from 4yo+ 3lb 8 Ran SP% **113.7**
Speed ratings (Par 101): **99,97,93,92,88 84,79,78**
CSF £24.70 CT £130.43 TOTE £5.60: £1.40, £1.50, £1.50; EX 24.50 Trifecta £107.40.
**Owner** Malcolm Walker **Bred** N Hartery **Trained** Settrington, N Yorks

**FOCUS**
This ordinary sprint handicap was run at a solid tempo. Race distance increased 18yds. The winner has been rated back to his best.

## 6573 BET TOTEWIN AT BETFRED.COM H'CAP (A QUALIFIER FOR THE 2017 CATTERICK TWELVE FURLONG SERIES FINAL) 1m 4f 13y
**4:50** (4:50) (Class 4) (0-85,77) 3-Y-0 **£6,469** (£1,925; £962; £481) **Stalls** Centre

Form RPR
3205 **1** **Je Suis Charlie**[26] 5589 3-9-7 **77** LouisSteward 6 87
(Michael Bell) *t.k.h early: hld up in tch: hdwy over 3f out: cl up over 2f out: rdn to ld wl over 1f out: clr ent fnl f: kpt on strly* **4/1**[3]

5310 **2** *5* **Fire Leopard**[11] 6210 3-9-5 **75** (h) DanielTudhope 5 77
(David O'Meara) *dwlt and hld up in rr: hdwy over 3f out: chsd ldrs 2f out: rdn to chse wnr over 1f out: drvn ins fnl f: sn no imp* **7/2**[2]

-522 **3** *2 1/2* **Mambo Dancer**[8] 6293 3-8-12 **68** PJMcDonald 1 66
(Mark Johnston) *pushed along early and sn trcking ldrs: pushed along on inner and hdwy 4f out: rdn along over 2f out: sn drvn and kpt on one pce* **11/8**[1]

06 **4** *hd* **Zihaam**[7] 6316 3-8-9 **65** (p[1]) BenCurtis 3 63
(Roger Fell) *trckd ldr: cl up over 5f out: led over 3f out: jnd and rdn over 2f out: hdd wl over 1f out: sn drvn and grad wknd* **12/1**

3560 **5** *8* **Voski (USA)**[21] 5798 3-9-5 **75** JasonHart 4 60
(Mark Johnston) *trckd ldrs: pushed along over 3f out: sn rdn: drvn 2f out: sn wknd* **12/1**

0140 **6** *18* **Breakwater Bay (IRE)**[23] 5706 3-8-13 **69** DavidAllan 2 43
(Tim Easterby) *led: rdn along 4f out: hdd 3f out: sn wknd* **10/1**

2m 37.99s (-0.91) **Going Correction** -0.025s/f (Good) 6 Ran SP% **108.8**
Speed ratings (Par 102): **102,98,97,96,91 79**
CSF £17.04 TOTE £3.20: £1.50, £1.50; EX 17.10 Trifecta £48.10.
**Owner** Mrs G Rowland-Clark & C M Budgett **Bred** Kirtlington Stud Ltd **Trained** Newmarket, Suffolk

**FOCUS**
A modest 3yo handicap with the top weight 8lb off the race ceiling.

## 6574 BET TOTEPLACE AT BETFRED.COM H'CAP 5f
**5:20** (5:20) (Class 5) (0-75,77) 3-Y-0+ **£2,911** (£866; £432; £108; £108) **Stalls** Low

Form RPR
1444 **1** **Penny Dreadful**[44] 4965 5-8-8 **66** (p) RPWalsh[(7)] 1 78
(Scott Dixon) *midfield on inner: swtchd rt and hdwy after 2f: sn chsng ldr: led 2f out: rdn clr ent fnl f: kpt on strly* **12/1**

4320 **2** *3 1/4* **Landing Night (IRE)**[9] 6267 5-9-7 **72** (tp) PJMcDonald 12 72+
(Rebecca Menzies) *in tch on outer: sltly hmpd 1/2-way: hdwy 2f out: rdn over 1f out: drvn and kpt on fnl f* **5/1**[2]

0315 **3** *nse* **Mininggold**[23] 5696 4-9-8 **73** (p) AndrewMullen 3 73
(Michael Dods) *chsd ldrs: rdn along and sltly outpcd over 2f out: drvn over 1f out: chsd wnr ins fnl f: kpt on* **8/1**

2644 **4** *2* **Foxtrot Knight**[14] 6062 5-9-9 **74** JamesSullivan 7 67
(Ruth Carr) *trckd ldrs: pushed along and sltly outpcd over 2f out: rdn wl over 1f out: kpt on fnl f* **6/1**[3]

100 **4** *dht* **Crosse Fire**[14] 6062 5-9-5 **70** (v) DavidAllan 2 63
(Scott Dixon) *cl up on inner: led after 1f: rdn along 1/2-way: hdd wl over 1f out: sn drvn and kpt on same pce* **18/1**

4011 **6** *1* **Ebitda**[13] 6114 3-8-9 **65** ow1 CliffordLee[(3)] 6 54
(Scott Dixon) *chsd ldrs: hdwy over 2f out: rdn wl over 1f out: drvn and wknd appr fnl f* **10/1**

4430 **7** ½ **Oriental Splendour (IRE)**[18] [5930] 5-9-5 **70**.................. JackGarritty 10 58
(Ruth Carr) *chsd ldrs: hdwy over 2f out: rdn along wl over 1f out: sn no imp* **12/1**

0000 **8** ½ **Bapak Asmara (IRE)**[16] [5994] 5-9-3 **68**.............................(b¹) KevinStott 8 54
(Kevin Ryan) *a in rr* **6/1**³

2020 **9** 1¾ **Bronze Beau**[9] [6267] 10-9-10 **75**.................................(tp) TonyHamilton 9 54
(Kristin Stubbs) *led 1f: prom: rdn along 2f out: sn drvn and wknd* **40/1**

-306 **10** 3¼ **Tan**[2] [6512] 3-9-10 **77**.......................................................(t¹) BenCurtis 5 45
(Tony Coyle) *stmbld bdly s: a bhd* **16/1**

3332 **U** **Wild Approach (IRE)**[12] [6155] 3-9-3 **70**..................(h) DanielTudhope 11
(Robert Cowell) *prom whn lost action and uns rdr 1/2-way: fatally injured* **4/1**¹

59.5s (-0.30) **Going Correction** +0.075s/f (Good)
**WFA** 3 from 4yo+ 2lb **11** Ran SP% **114.4**
Speed ratings (Par 103): **105,99,99,96,96 94,94,93,90,85**
CSF £69.07 CT £524.27 TOTE £11.60: £4.10, £3.40, £2.90; EX 68.30 Trifecta £823.40.
**Owner** Sexy Six Partnership **Bred** B A McGarrigle **Trained** Babworth, Notts
■ Stewards' Enquiry : Clifford Lee one-day ban: weighed in 2lb over (Sep 13)

**FOCUS**
They went hard early on on this modest sprint handicap. Fair form.
T/Plt: £77.20 to a £1 stake. Pool: £56,374.54 - 532.94 winning units T/Qpdt: £11.60 to a £1 stake. Pool: £3,696.65 - 234.56 winning units **Joe Rowntree**

## [6319] KEMPTON (A.W) (R-H)
Wednesday, August 30

**OFFICIAL GOING: Polytrack: standard to slow changing to standard after race 2 (6.25)**
Wind: Nil Weather: Cloudy

### 6575 BRITISH STALLION STUDS EBF FILLIES' NOVICE STKS (PLUS 10 RACE) 1m (P)
**5:55** (5:56) (Class 5) 2-Y-O **£3,234** (£962; £481; £240) **Stalls** Low

Form RPR

05 **1** **Mahaarat**[33] [5349] 2-9-0 0.............................................. JimCrowley 6 82+
(Sir Michael Stoute) *settled bhd ldrs on inner: swtchd off rail over 2f out and shkn up: 2 l down whn drvn over 1f out: gd prog and led ent fnl f: kpt up to work fnl 150yds: easily* **3/1**²

43 **2** 4 **Harmonica**[18] [5934] 2-9-0 0.............................................. LukeMorris 9 73
(Sir Mark Prescott Bt) *racd in mid-div: shkn up 3f out: angled wdst and rdn over 2f out: no imp chsng ldrs tl wl over 1f out: qcknd up ent fnl f: tk 2nd 150yds out but no ch w wnr* **8/1**

31 **3** 1¾ **Voicemail**[16] [5999] 2-9-4 0.............................................. MartinHarley 8 73
(James Tate) *sn led: rdn 2f out: hdd over 1f out: kpt on one pce ins fnl f* **4/1**³

2052 **4** ¾ **Cosmopolitan Queen**[15] [6037] 2-9-0 78............................ DaneO'Neill 2 67
(David Elsworth) *cl up w ldr on inner: upsides ldr and rdn 2f: led over 1f out: hdd ent fnl f: wknd fnl 110yds* **2/1**¹

**5** nk **Imminent Approach** 2-9-0 0.............................................. OisinMurphy 5 67+
(James Tate) *missed break and pushed along in rr to keep in tch for 2f: shuffled along fr over 3f out: no imp tl gd prog fr 2f out: kpt on wl fr over 1f out past btn horses: nvr nrr: rn green* **16/1**

0 **6** 3 **Casima**[25] [5660] 2-9-0 0.....................................................(h) SamHitchcott 4 60
(Clive Cox) *racd in rr-div: niggled along fr 1/2-way: rdn over 3f out: kpt on one pce fr over 1f out* **16/1**

**7** 3 **Gattaia (USA)** 2-9-0 0.............................................. SeanLevey 11 53
(Ralph Beckett) *cl up on outer: shkn up 2f out and almost upsides ldrs: sn rdn and fnd nil: one pce after* **12/1**

**8** hd **Speed Craft** 2-9-0 0.....................................................(p¹) RyanTate 7 52
(James Eustace) *in rr-div on inner: rdn over 2f out: one pce fr over 1f out* **66/1**

**9** ¾ **Dependable (GER)** 2-9-0 0.............................................. DavidProbert 3 51
(Charles Hills) *settled in mid-div on inner: rdn ent 2f out: hld fr over 1f out* **33/1**

00 **10** 3½ **Lucky Reset**[14] [6064] 2-9-0 0.............................................. RobertTart 1 43
(David Evans) *a in rr: rdn over 3f out: no imp fr over 1f out* **100/1**

00 **11** 12 **Filly Mignon**[9] [6260] 2-9-0 0.............................................. FranBerry 10 15
(Brendan Powell) *in rr: rdn over 3f out: no ex fr over 1f out* **150/1**

1m 37.94s (-1.86) **Going Correction** -0.175s/f (Stan) **11** Ran SP% **115.0**
Speed ratings (Par 91): **102,98,96,95,95 92,89,89,88,84 72**
CSF £26.42 TOTE £4.00: £1.30, £2.10, £1.30; EX 23.30 Trifecta £95.60.
**Owner** Hamdan Al Maktoum **Bred** Shadwell Estate Company Limited **Trained** Newmarket, Suffolk

**FOCUS**
A fair juvenile fillies' novice contest. They went a decent gallop on watered, standard to slow Polytrack. The second, third and fourth give the form substance.

### 6576 32RED.COM H'CAP (LONDON MILE SERIES QUALIFIER) 1m (P)
**6:25** (6:25) (Class 4) (0-80,82) 3-Y-O **£5,175** (£1,540; £769; £384) **Stalls** Low

Form RPR

4441 **1** **Mudallel (IRE)**[14] [6067] 3-9-4 **78**.............................................. JamesDoyle 5 89+
(Ed Dunlop) *hld up in rr: stl in rr 2f out: hld together bhd horses tl swtchd to outer over 1f out: rdn and qcknd up wl to ld nr fin* **2/1**¹

2064 **2** ½ **Ventura Blues (IRE)**[26] [5591] 3-8-10 **77**..............................(p) RossaRyan⁽⁷⁾ 3 86
(Richard Hannon) *covered up between horses chsng ldrs: rdn over 1f out: kpt on wl and led 150yds out: hdd nr fin* **8/1**

011- **3** 1 **Under Control (IRE)**[335] [6898] 3-9-2 **76**.............................. PatCosgrave 1 83+
(William Haggas) *in mid-div on inner and t.k.h: rdn over 1f out and nt qckn for a few strides: gd prog ins fnl f: nt get to front pair* **13/2**

-600 **4** ¾ **Queensbrydge**[14] [6068] 3-9-4 **78**.............................................. LukeMorris 6 83
(Robyn Brisland) *chsd ldrs: upsides ldr fr 2f out: rdn wl over 1f out and sn led: hdd fnl 110yds: wknd and lost two pls cl home* **12/1**

0424 **5** 1¼ **Esprit De Corps**[25] [5661] 3-9-6 **80**.............................................. JamieSpencer 9 82
(Roger Charlton) *hld up in rr: shkn up over 1f out and smooth prog: rdn ent fnl f: nt qckn and kpt on one pce* **11/2**²

0213 **6** 1 **Badenscoth**[27] [5578] 3-9-4 **81**.............................................. JackDuern⁽³⁾ 8 81
(Dean Ivory) *in rr: c wdst 2f out: rdn over 1f out: no imp and shuffled along ins fnl f* **6/1**³

2436 **7** 6 **Sterling Silva (IRE)**[18] [5928] 3-9-3 **77**..............................(p¹) SeanLevey 4 63
(Richard Hannon) *led: shkn up and hdd wl over 1f out: no ex and fdd sn after* **20/1**

1010 **8** shd **Saluti (IRE)**[20] [5842] 3-9-8 **82**.............................................. JimCrowley 7 68
(Amanda Perrett) *chsd ldrs on outer: rdn wl over 1f out: no ex and one pce ent fnl f* **9/1**

02 **9** 4½ **High On Love (IRE)**[44] [4975] 3-9-4 **78**.............................. StevieDonohoe 2 53
(Charlie Fellowes) *chsd ldrs on rail: rdn 2f out: wknd qckly ent fnl f* **20/1**

1m 37.78s (-2.02) **Going Correction** -0.175s/f (Stan) **9** Ran SP% **114.7**
Speed ratings (Par 102): **103,102,101,100,99 98,92,92,87**
CSF £18.52 CT £86.36 TOTE £2.50: £1.40, £2.50, £2.20; EX 21.00 Trifecta £136.40.
**Owner** Abdullah Saeed Al Naboodah **Bred** Tullpark Ltd **Trained** Newmarket, Suffolk

**FOCUS**
A fairly decent 3yo handicap. They went a proper gallop and the favourite came through from well off the pace to oblige. The official going description was changed to plain standard after this race following a drop in temperature and rain before racing.

### 6577 32RED CASINO MAIDEN FILLIES' STKS 7f (P)
**6:55** (6:58) (Class 5) 3-Y-O+ **£3,234** (£962; £481; £240) **Stalls** Low

Form RPR

2524 **1** **Euqranian (USA)**[26] [5611] 3-9-0 78..................................(h) JamieSpencer 1 74+
(Jeremy Noseda) *racd in 3rd on inner: shkn up and prog into 2nd 2f out: sn drvn and upsides ldr fr over 1f out: led fnl 110yds: comf on top nr fin* **11/8**¹

36 **2** 1¼ **Deleyla**[76] [3748] 3-9-0 0.............................................. HarryBentley 3 71
(Roger Varian) *led on rail: rdn wl over 1f out: pressed by wnr sn after but kpt on wl: hdd fnl 110yds: no ex nr fin* **7/2**²

54 **3** 4½ **Mooroverthebridge**[17] [5969] 3-9-0 0.............................................. LukeMorris 4 58
(Grace Harris) *pressed ldr on outer: rdn over 2f out briefly looked to get involved: sn outpcd: kpt on one pce fnl f* **33/1**

**4** 7 **Wasted Sunsets (FR)** 3-9-0 0.......................................(t¹) MartinHarley 5 40
(John Berry) *racd in 5th: rdn over 2f out: no imp after* **20/1**³

000 **5** 7 **Our Ruth**[23] [5712] 4-8-12 32.............................................. RossaRyan⁽⁷⁾ 8 23
(Jimmy Fox) *t.k.h early: hld up in rr: rdn over 2f out: wknd sn after* **100/1**

00 **6** 6 **Steady (IRE)**[8] [6287] 3-9-0 0.............................................. TrevorWhelan 6 4
(Dan Skelton) *racd in 4th on outer: sn btn and pushed out fr over 1f out* **66/1**

1m 26.49s (0.49) **Going Correction** -0.175s/f (Stan)
**WFA** 3 from 4yo 5lb **6** Ran SP% **74.5**
Speed ratings (Par 100): **90,88,83,75,67 60**
CSF £2.07 TOTE £1.50: £1.10, £1.10; EX 2.40 Trifecta £7.90.
**Owner** Marc Keller **Bred** Forging Oaks Farm Llc **Trained** Newmarket, Suffolk
■ Diagnostic was withdrawn. Price at time of withdrawal 6/4. Rule 4 applies to all bets - deduction 40p in the pound.

**FOCUS**
An ordinary fillies' maiden. They went a modest gallop but the favourite still outstayed her only serious rival on form beforehand.

### 6578 100% PROFIT BOOST AT 32REDSPORT.COM FILLIES' H'CAP 1m 3f 219y(P)
**7:25** (7:26) (Class 5) (0-70,72) 3-Y-O+ **£3,234** (£962; £481; £240) **Stalls** Low

Form RPR

650 **1** **Moonlight Silver**[27] [5565] 3-8-7 **58**.............................................. MartinDwyer 8 65
(William Muir) *mid-div on outer: shkn up over 2f out and prog to ld 2f out: sn rdn and kpt on wl ins fnl f: nudged out nr fin* **16/1**

002 **2** nk **Rainbow Rising (FR)**[18] [5931] 3-9-1 **69**.................... DidierGengoul⁽³⁾ 4 75
(David Menuisier) *in rr: swtchd to inner and rdn 2f out: chal between horses over 1f out: ev ch 1f out: kpt on wl nr fin but nt getting to wnr* **10/1**

0-51 **3** 1¼ **Kerrera**[26] [5607] 4-9-12 **68**.............................................. FranBerry 3 71
(Paul Webber) *in rr-div: shkn up and angled to outer ent 2f out: one pce tl picked up wl 1f out and tk 3rd: nvr nrr* **10/3**²

4363 **4** 2 **Pacofilha**[8] [6281] 3-9-4 **69**.............................................. LukeMorris 2 69
(Paul Cole) *chsd ldrs on inner: rdn over 1f out and ev ch: nt qckn ent fnl f and wknd out of contention* **4/1**³

505/ **5** ¾ **Island Authority**[736] [5717] 5-9-0 **59**.............................................. AaronJones⁽³⁾ 1 57
(Eugene Stanford) *in rr-div on inner: rdn on rail 2f out: ev ch ent fnl f: no ex sn after* **50/1**

4000 **6** nk **Auntie Barber (IRE)**[22] [5745] 4-10-2 **72**..............................(t) OisinMurphy 7 70
(Stuart Williams) *in rr: rdn in last over 2f out: one pce after* **16/1**

2403 **7** 1 **Tapdanceallthewa**y[26] [5607] 3-9-2 **67**.............................................. SteveDrowne 5 64
(Amanda Perrett) *led fr 4f: chsd clr ldr after: rdn 3f out: no ex 2f out: sn wknd* **8/1**

0533 **8** 2½ **Miss Liguria**[32] [5401] 3-9-5 **70**.............................................. JamieSpencer 6 63
(Ed Walker) *chsd ldrs tl mde sweeping move to ld after 4f: 3 l ldr at 1/2-way: slowed pce in bk st: rdn 3f out: hdd 2f out: one pce after: wknd wl ins fnl f* **7/4**¹

2m 33.37s (-1.13) **Going Correction** -0.175s/f (Stan)
**WFA** 3 from 4yo+ 9lb **8** Ran SP% **113.4**
Speed ratings (Par 100): **96,95,94,93,93 92,92,90**
CSF £159.23 CT £665.14 TOTE £14.90: £4.30, £2.50, £1.50; EX 103.20 Trifecta £1149.10.
**Owner** Foursome Thoroughbreds **Bred** Foursome Thoroughbreds **Trained** Lambourn, Berks

**FOCUS**
A modest middle-distance fillies' handicap. The tempo picked up down the back when the favourite went on but she couldn't sustain her effort after racing a tad keenly.

### 6579 32RED ON THE APP STORE H'CAP (LONDON MIDDLE DISTANCE SERIES QUALIFIER) 1m 2f 219y(P)
**7:55** (7:57) (Class 4) (0-85,84) 3-Y-O **£5,175** (£1,540; £769; £384) **Stalls** Low

Form RPR

-004 **1** **Pivoine (IRE)**[26] [5589] 3-9-3 **80**.......................................(v¹) TedDurcan 5 92+
(Sir Michael Stoute) *hld up bhd clr ldrs on rail: mid-div at 1/2-way: gng wl whn kpt to inner over 2f out: rdn 2f out: kpt on and led ent fnl f: styd on wl* **7/2**²

-410 **2** 2½ **Tuff Rock (USA)**[26] [5598] 3-9-6 **83**.............................................. JamieSpencer 2 90
(Ed Walker) *racd in 4th on outer: plld hrd particularly on bnds: clsr on outer over 3f out: sn shkn up: rdn 2f out and ev ch: kpt on fr over 1f out and tk 2nd nr fin* **7/1**³

132 **3** ½ **Atkinson Grimshaw (FR)**[18] [5940] 3-9-7 **84**.................... DavidProbert 4 90
(Andrew Balding) *pressed ldr tl led 7f out: rdn 2f out: plugged on tl hdd ent fnl f: kpt on one pce tl wknd fnl 100yds and lost 2nd nr fin* **13/8**¹

1102 **4** nk **Arctic Sea**[49] [4736] 3-9-0 **77**.............................................. LukeMorris 7 82
(Paul Cole) *missed break: in rr: plld hrd most of way: rdn over 2f out wd: kpt on wl fr over 1f out: one pce ins fnl f: can do bttr* **11/1**

1 **5** 2½ **Eyes On Asha (IRE)**[180] [1003] 3-9-1 **78**.............................................. JamesDoyle 3 79
(Kevin Ryan) *in rr: rdn out wd over 2f out: kpt on one pce fr over 1f out* **7/1**³

255 **6** 1¾ **Our Boy (IRE)**[6] [6344] 3-8-12 **75**.............................................. SilvestreDeSousa 6 73
(David Evans) *racd in 4th: rdn over 2f out: no imp fr over 1f out* **8/1**

-130 **7** 6 **Outcrop (IRE)**[37] [5218] 3-8-12 **75**.............................................. OisinMurphy 1 62
(Hughie Morrison) *sn led and set str pce: hdd 7f out: rdn over 2f out: lost pl 2f out and wknd over 1f out* **16/1**

2m 19.65s (-2.25) **Going Correction** -0.175s/f (Stan) **7** Ran SP% **110.6**
Speed ratings (Par 102): **101,99,98,98,96 95,91**
CSF £25.81 TOTE £4.30: £2.00, £3.60; EX 33.40 Trifecta £87.80.

**Owner** Ballymacoll Stud **Bred** Ballymacoll Stud Farm Ltd **Trained** Newmarket, Suffolk
**FOCUS**
A decent middle-distance 3yo handicap. They went a stop-start gallop but a well-supported gelding ran out a convincing winner.

## 6580 32RED H'CAP — 1m 7f 218y(P)
**8:25** (8:25) (Class 4) (0-85,85) 3-Y-O — **£5,175** (£1,540; £769; £384) **Stalls** Low

Form — RPR

1-3 **1** **Percy's Word**[123] 2149 3-9-6 **84** .......... SilvestreDeSousa 5 93+
(Simon Crisford) *chsd ldr tl led after 3f: shkn up over 3f out: gng wl 2f out: sn rdn: kpt on wl ins fnl f* **3/1**[2]

3120 **2** *1 3/4* **Nadaitak**[24] 5682 3-9-7 **85** .......... (p) JimCrowley 3 90
(Sir Michael Stoute) *wnt lft s: sn chsd ldrs: rdn over 3f out: dropped to rr 3f out: kpt on again fr over 1f out: styd on wl to take 2nd ent fnl f: nt get to wnr* **6/5**[1]

-605 **3** *2 1/2* **Lethal Impact (JPN)**[77] 3711 3-8-12 **76** .......... (p[1]) OisinMurphy 2 78
(David Simcock) *racd in 4th on inner: rdn over 3f out: chsd wnr over 1f out: lost 2nd ent fnl f: no ex* **10/1**

3065 **4** *8* **Fields Of Fortune**[8] 6291 3-8-0 **67** .......... HollieDoyle(3) 4 59
(Alan King) *sltly hmpd s: in rr: shkn up over 3f out: rdn 2f out: in 3rd wl over 1f out: sn wknd* **7/1**

5322 **5** *11* **Waterville Dancer (IRE)**[27] 5563 3-9-1 **79** .......... ShaneKelly 1 67
(Richard Hughes) *led for 3f: chsd ldr after: rdn over 3f out: wknd fr over 1f out* **5/1**[3]

3m 23.88s (-6.22) **Going Correction** -0.175s/f (Stan) **5** Ran SP% **108.7**
Speed ratings (Par 102): **108,107,105,101,96**
CSF £6.86 TOTE £2.90: £1.90, £1.10; EX 7.20 Trifecta £25.40.
**Owner** Saeed H Al Tayer **Bred** Mr & Mrs A E Pakenham **Trained** Newmarket, Suffolk
**FOCUS**
A decent 3yo staying handicap. The second favourite got into a wonderful, galloping rhythm on the lead and, kicked on 2f out, won this in the best comparative time on the card.

## 6581 WATCH RACING UK ON BT TV H'CAP — 6f (P)
**8:55** (8:55) (Class 6) (0-65,65) 3-Y-O — **£2,587** (£770; £384; £192) **Stalls** Low

Form — RPR

0066 **1** **Inlawed**[20] 5855 3-9-4 **62** .......... JamieSpencer 6 68
(Ed Walker) *immediately rdn leaving stalls to ld: narrowly hdd 2f out: sn shkn up and led again: drifted lft over 1f out: hrd rdn ins fnl f: kpt on wl* **5/1**[3]

0452 **2** *1* **See You Mush**[22] 5748 3-9-1 **59** .......... (b) AdamBeschizza 9 62
(Mrs Ilka Gansera-Leveque) *chsd ldrs: rdn over 1f out and angle to nrside rail: kpt on wl ins fnl f and tk 2nd nr fin* **3/1**[1]

06-0 **3** *nk* **Vote**[25] 5635 3-9-7 **65** .......... RyanTate 5 67
(James Eustace) *settled in rr-div: rdn over 1f out on inner: kpt on strly ins fnl fnl f to take 2nd nr fin: lost 2nd post* **8/1**

5365 **4** *hd* **Zilza (IRE)**[27] 5558 3-9-6 **64** .......... (bt[1]) MartinDwyer 12 66
(Conrad Allen) *chsd wnr: pressed wnr and briefly led 2f out: sn rdn and stl upsides: carried lft tl 1f out: one pce after and lost two pls nr fin* **12/1**

4004 **5** *3/4* **Who Told Jo Jo (IRE)**[17] 5956 3-9-4 **62** .......... OisinMurphy 2 61
(Joseph Tuite) *hld up in rr-div on rail: rdn over 1f out and sme prog: kpt on one pce ins fnl f* **16/1**

5000 **6** *1/2* **Silver Penny**[7] 6324 3-8-4 **51** .......... (p) CharlieBennett(3) 10 49
(Jim Boyle) *chsd ldrs: rdn bhd ldrs 2f out: swtchd to inner: ev ch ent fnl f: no ex and fdd ins fnl f* **25/1**

5-40 **7** *1 1/2* **Grand Myla (IRE)**[13] 6106 3-9-3 **64** .......... (b[1]) HectorCrouch(3) 7 57
(Gary Moore) *in rr: swtchd to wd outside over 2f out: rdn 2f out: keeping on one pce whn rival hung slt across her ent fnl f: sn pushed out* **14/1**

0263 **8** *3/4* **Canadian Royal**[8] 6295 3-9-2 **60** .......... (t) MartinHarley 8 51
(Stuart Williams) *chsd ldrs between horses: tk a fierce hold tl settled bttr at 1/2-way: rdn 2f out and prog: ev ch over 1f out: sn no ex and wknd qckly ent fnl f* **9/2**[2]

4600 **9** *1* **Brother In Arms (IRE)**[35] 5291 3-9-3 **61** .......... JimCrowley 3 49
(Tony Carroll) *chsd ldr on inner: rdn over 1f out: wknd ins fnl f* **5/1**[3]

6605 **10** *nse* **Rapid Rise (IRE)**[12] 6155 3-9-6 **64** .......... LukeMorris 11 52
(Milton Bradley) *in rr: rdn and c wd 2f out: plugged on one pce ins fnl f* **25/1**

1m 12.22s (-0.88) **Going Correction** -0.175s/f (Stan) **10** Ran SP% **115.6**
Speed ratings (Par 98): **98,96,96,96,95 94,92,91,90,89**
CSF £20.16 CT £115.42 TOTE £5.80: £2.00, £2.00, £3.00; EX 21.30 Trifecta £132.10.
**Owner** Laurence Bellman **Bred** Snailwell Stud Co Ltd **Trained** Upper Lambourn, Berks
**FOCUS**
A modest 3yo sprint handicap. They went a respectable gallop and there is little reason to doubt the form. The third and fourth have been rated close to their pre-race marks.
T/Plt: £52.00 to a £1 stake. Pool: £76,261.58 - 1,070.20 winning units T/Qpdt: £17.30 to a £1 stake. Pool: £5,824.96 - 247.86 winning units **Cathal Gahan**

# 6257 LINGFIELD (L-H)
Wednesday, August 30

**OFFICIAL GOING: Good to firm (good in places) changing to good after race 1 (1.40) changing to good to soft after race 4 (3.10)**
Wind: light, against Weather: rain

## 6582 US OPEN TENNIS AT 188BET (S) STKS — 6f
**1:40** (1:40) (Class 6) 3-Y-O+ — **£2,264** (£673; £336; £168) **Stalls** Centre

Form — RPR

0465 **1** **Malcolm The Pug (IRE)**[12] 6148 3-8-12 64 .......... HollieDoyle(3) 5 71
(Richard Hannon) *t.k.h early: chsd clr ldr: clsd and pushed into ld over 1f out: sn clr and r.o strly: easily* **8/11**[1]

5-56 **2** *8* **Red Trooper (FR)**[17] 5958 4-9-9 74 .......... (h[1]) PatCosgrave 8 50
(George Baker) *chsd ldng pair: effrt wl over 1f out: chsd clr wnr 1f out: no imp* **6/4**[2]

4060 **3** *2 1/2* **Head Space (IRE)**[19] 5892 9-9-2 55 .......... JasonWatson(7) 3 42
(Brian Barr) *hld up in last pair: effrt over 1f out: wnt 3rd 150yds out: no ch w wnr* **33/1**

0000 **4** *3 3/4* **Divine Call**[20] 5848 10-9-9 44 .......... (p) LukeMorris 2 30
(Milton Bradley) *racd in last pair: rdn 1/2-way: no imp: wl btn over 1f out* **16/1**[3]

600 **5** *3 1/2* **Verdi (IRE)**[13] 6114 3-8-8 44 .......... (b) JackOsborn(7) 1 14
(John Ryan) *sn led and clr: rdn ent fnl 2f: hdd over 1f out: sn btn: lost 2nd 1f out: fdd fnl f* **33/1**

1m 12.57s (1.37) **Going Correction** +0.40s/f (Good)
**WFA** 3 from 4yo+ 3lb **5** Ran SP% **109.7**
Speed ratings (Par 101): **106,95,92,87,82**
CSF £2.01 TOTE £1.50: £1.10, £1.20; EX 2.20 Trifecta £7.60.The winner was bought by Mr David Brown for 7,600 guineas.

**Owner** J Palmer-Brown & Partner **Bred** Stall Perlen **Trained** East Everleigh, Wilts
**FOCUS**
A race that concerned only two and the strongly backed winner bolted up. The winner has been rated back to this year's best.

## 6583 INJURED JOCKEYS FUND EBF FILLIES' NOVICE MEDIAN AUCTION STKS (PLUS 10 RACE) (DIV I) — 7f
**2:10** (2:11) (Class 5) 2-Y-O — **£3,881** (£1,155; £577; £288) **Stalls** Centre

Form — RPR

1 **1** **Gavota**[19] 5885 2-9-5 0 .......... JamesDoyle 8 95+
(Roger Charlton) *hld up in tch: clsd to trck ldrs 2f out: pushed and qcknd to ld over 1f out: readily drew clr fnl f: v easily* **30/100**[1]

**2** *6* **Unchaining Melody** 2-8-9 0 .......... MarcMonaghan(3) 7 68+
(Marco Botti) *s.i.s: hld up in tch: swtchd lft and effrt in 4th over 1f out: styd on steadily ins fnl f: wnt 2nd cl home: no ch w wnr* **14/1**

**3** *1/2* **Qafilah (IRE)** 2-8-12 0 .......... JimCrowley 4 67
(Charles Hills) *s.i.s: hld up in tch: clsd to chse ldrs 1/2-way: sn pushed along to chse wnr over 1f out: sn brushed aside by wnr: kpt on same pce and lost 2nd cl home* **5/1**[2]

66 **4** *2 1/2* **Lady Marigold (IRE)**[41] 5048 2-8-12 0 .......... CharlesBishop 11 60
(Eve Johnson Houghton) *t.k.h: mde most tl rdn and hdd over 1f out: 3rd and btn 1f out: wknd ins fnl f* **14/1**

6 **5** *3/4* **Still Got It**[12] 6138 2-8-12 0 .......... RobHornby 3 58
(Mick Channon) *hld up in tch in last pair: swtchd lft and pushed along wl over 1f out: rdn and hdwy ent fnl f: kpt on steadily: no ch w wnr* **10/1**

50 **6** *2 3/4* **Hollie's Dream**[9] 6272 2-8-12 0 .......... RobertTart 2 51
(David Evans) *hld up in tch in midfield: rdn jst over 2f out: no imp and outpcd over 1f out: wknd ins fnl f* **50/1**

**7** *3/4* **Peggie Sue** 2-8-12 0 .......... RoystonFfrench 6 49
(Adam West) *t.k.h: chsd ldr for 2f: styd chsng ldrs tl lost pl 2f out: pushed along and wl hld fr over 1f out* **50/1**

05 **8** *4* **Spix's Macaw**[19] 5893 2-8-12 0 .......... LukeMorris 1 38
(Bill Turner) *chsd ldrs tl jnd ldr after 2f: rdn and struggling ent fnl 2f: lost pl qckly wl over 1f out: bhd ins fnl f* **100/1**

**9** *5* **Cypria Charis (IRE)** 2-8-12 0 .......... TedDurcan 5 24
(Sir Michael Stoute) *a rr: rdn over 2f out: lost tch over 1f out* **7/1**[3]

1m 25.67s (2.37) **Going Correction** +0.40s/f (Good) **9** Ran SP% **133.4**
Speed ratings (Par 91): **102,95,94,91,90 87,86,82,76**
CSF £9.77 TOTE £1.20: £1.02, £5.20, £1.30; EX 12.50 Trifecta £41.30.
**Owner** K Abdullah **Bred** Juddmonte Farms (east) Ltd **Trained** Beckhampton, Wilts
**FOCUS**
The stronger of the two divisions and a taking winner. The fourth helps set the level.

## 6584 INJURED JOCKEYS FUND EBF FILLIES' NOVICE MEDIAN AUCTION STKS (PLUS 10 RACE) (DIV II) — 7f
**2:40** (2:42) (Class 5) 2-Y-O — **£3,881** (£1,155; £577; £288) **Stalls** Centre

Form — RPR

**1** **Teppal (FR)** 2-8-12 0 .......... JamieSpencer 11 85+
(David Simcock) *hld up in tch in midfield: clsd to trck ldrs over 1f out: sn swtchd lft and cruised upsides ldr jst ins fnl f: nudged into ld wl ins fnl f: cleverly* **11/4**[1]

46 **2** *nk* **Awesometank**[20] 5834 2-8-12 0 .......... PatCosgrave 2 80
(William Haggas) *t.k.h: hld up in tch in midfield: effrt ent fnl 2f: rdn to ld over 1f out: jnd by cantering wnr ins fnl f: hdd and styd on same pce ins fnl f* **7/2**[2]

**3** *4* **Hollydaze (IRE)** 2-8-12 0 .......... ShaneKelly 9 69+
(Richard Hughes) *stdd after s: rn green and hld up in tch towards rr: pushed along and sme hdwy whn rn green and swtchd rt over 1f out: kpt on to go 3rd wl ins fnl f: no threat to ldng pair* **25/1**

3 **4** *1 1/4* **Storm Jazz (IRE)**[17] 5963 2-8-12 0 .......... JimmyQuinn 7 66
(Ed Dunlop) *led and set stdy gallop tl qcknd 1/2-way: rdn and hdd over 1f out: 3rd and btn 1f out: wknd ins fnl f* **5/1**[3]

30 **5** *4* **Lady Of Petra**[21] 5795 2-8-12 0 .......... CharlesBishop 6 55
(Eve Johnson Houghton) *t.k.h: pressed ldrs: rdn and ev ch 2f out tl no ex jst over 1f out: wknd ins fnl f* **14/1**

64 **6** *1 1/2* **Pastamakesufaster**[9] 6272 2-8-12 0 .......... RobertTart 4 51
(David Evans) *plld hrd: hld up in tch: pushed along ent fnl 2f: sn outpcd and wl btn 1f out* **14/1**

0 **7** *1 1/2* **Rozanne (IRE)**[25] 5660 2-8-7 0 .......... DavidEgan(5) 3 47
(Jeremy Noseda) *plld hrd: pressed ldr: rdn ent fnl 2f: outpcd and btn over 1f out: sn wknd* **11/4**[1]

**8** *4* **Elegance (IRE)** 2-8-9 0 .......... NoelGarbutt(3) 1 36
(Martin Smith) *t.k.h: hld up in tch: rdn and struggling over 2f out: sn wknd* **66/1**

**9** *2 3/4* **Miss Recycled** 2-8-12 0 .......... KieranO'Neill 8 29
(Michael Madgwick) *s.i.s: in tch in rr and rn green: rdn over 2f out: sn struggling: bhd over 1f out* **100/1**

**10** *11* **Night Myth (IRE)** 2-8-12 0 .......... SeanLevey 5
(Richard Hannon) *rn green: in tch in last pair: pushed along 1/2-way: lost tch 2f out* **8/1**

1m 26.08s (2.78) **Going Correction** +0.40s/f (Good) **10** Ran SP% **123.0**
Speed ratings (Par 91): **100,99,95,93,89 87,85,81,77,65**
CSF £13.27 TOTE £3.60: £1.30, £1.40, £7.10; EX 16.20 Trifecta £318.80.
**Owner** Never Say Die Partnership **Bred** Gestut Zur Kuste Ag **Trained** Newmarket, Suffolk
**FOCUS**
The rain appeared to have started getting into the ground by this stage. Racing centre-field this time, two came clear and the winner scored with more in hand than the result suggests. The form could be a bit better than rated.

## 6585 HANSON REGAN 11TH BIRTHDAY NURSERY H'CAP — 7f
**3:10** (3:14) (Class 6) (0-60,62) 2-Y-O — **£2,587** (£770; £384; £192) **Stalls** Centre

Form — RPR

000 **1** **Dream Of Delphi (IRE)**[66] 4116 2-8-9 **48** .......... (b[1]) JosephineGordon 2 62+
(William Haggas) *hld up in tch towards rr: effrt ent fnl 2f: hdwy to chal ent fnl f: led jst ins fnl f: styd on strly and drew clr fnl 100yds: readily* **16/1**

500 **2** *3 1/2* **Mouchee (IRE)**[19] 5891 2-9-4 **57** .......... SilvestreDeSousa 5 61
(David Evans) *hld up in tch in midfield: effrt over 2f out: hdwy u.p to ld over 1f out: sn jnd and wnt clr w wnr 1f out: hdd jst ins fnl f: sn outpcd but kpt on for clr 2nd* **7/1**[2]

5023 **3** *6* **Rock On Bertie (IRE)**[18] 5933 2-9-2 **55** .......... (p) TomMarquand 3 43
(Nigel Tinkler) *hld up in tch in midfield: effrt ent fnl 2f out: no imp u.p over 1f out: no ch w ldng pair 1f out: plugged on to go 3rd towards fin* **5/1**[1]

2003 **4** *1/2* **Super Florence (IRE)**[14] 6063 2-9-8 **61** .......... CharlesBishop 11 48
(Eve Johnson Houghton) *t.k.h: hld up towards rr: hdwy to ld 5f out: rdn and hdd over 1f out: sn outpcd: wknd ins fnl f: lost 3rd towards fin* **8/1**[3]

004 **5** *nk* **Freebe Rocks (IRE)**[20] 5851 2-9-7 **60**.................. DannyBrock 7 46
(Michael Bell) *hld up in tch towards rr: switching rt and effrt wl over 1f out: sn u.p and outpcd by ldng pair: wl hld and plugged on same pce ins fnl f* **10/1**

503 **6** *3* **Vegas Boy (IRE)**[8] 6285 2-9-3 **56**..................(t) TimmyMurphy 13 34
(Jamie Osborne) *trckd ldrs: effrt ent fnl 2f: sn rdn and outpcd over 1f out: wknd ins fnl f* **5/1**[1]

500 **7** *2 1/4* **Tarnemah (IRE)**[12] 6140 2-8-13 **52**.................. HarryBentley 1 24
(George Peckham) *hld up in tch: effrt 3f out: no imp u.p over 1f out: wknd fnl f* **20/1**

0002 **8** *3 1/4* **Shoyd**[14] 6063 2-9-2 **62**.................. RossaRyan(7) 12 25
(Richard Hannon) *in tch towards rr: rdn and struggling in rr: no ch but plugged on to pass btn rivals ins fnl f* **8/1**[3]

0004 **9** *1 1/2* **Rio Santos**[27] 5562 2-8-12 **51**.................. WilliamCarson 6 10
(Rod Millman) *in tch in midfield: rdn ent fnl 2f: sn struggling and wknd over 1f out* **16/1**

0055 **10** *3/4* **Deauville Society (IRE)**[23] 5717 2-9-4 **57**.................. LukeMorris 14 14
(Sir Mark Prescott Bt) *midfield: rdn and struggling 3f out: sn lost pl: no ch fnl 2f* **7/1**[2]

6200 **11** *1/2* **Storm Doris (IRE)**[44] 4977 2-8-13 **52**..................(v[1]) SamHitchcott 9 7
(James Unett) *chsd ldr for 2f: rdn and lost pl 1/2-way: bhd over 1f out* **33/1**

0400 **12** *3 1/2* **Erastus**[12] 6154 2-8-10 **54**.................. DavidEgan(5) 4
(Mick Channon) *stdd and swtchd rt s: hld up in rr: effrt ent fnl 2f: sn btn and bhd over 1f out* **25/1**

6665 **13** *11* **Catch The Pigeon**[14] 6063 2-9-2 **55**.................. LiamKeniry 8
(Ed de Giles) *stdd s: in tch in midfield: lost pl 1/2-way: bhd fnl 2f* **14/1**

6602 **14** *7* **Red Snapper**[19] 5886 2-8-13 **55**.................. HollieDoyle(3) 15
(William Stone) *chsd ldrs: j. path 5f out: lost pl over 2f out: wl bhd over 1f out* **14/1**

000 **15** *1 1/4* **Maveway (IRE)**[16] 6005 2-8-6 **45**.................. JimmyQuinn 10
(David Evans) *led for 2f: steadily lost pl: bhd over 1f out* **66/1**

1m 25.14s (1.84) **Going Correction** +0.40s/f (Good) **15** Ran SP% **127.8**
Speed ratings (Par 92): **105,101,94,93,93 89,87,83,81,80 80,76,63,55,54**
CSF £126.53 CT £498.63 TOTE £18.30: £4.80, £2.20, £2.20; EX 189.10 Trifecta £1209.80.
**Owner** T Bridge **Bred** Ballyphilip Stud **Trained** Newmarket, Suffolk

**FOCUS**
Racing centre-to-stands' side for this moderate nursery, the front pair came clear down the middle of the track.

## 6586 T20 FINALS BETTING AT 188BET H'CAP 6f
**3:40** (3:41) (Class 4) (0-80,86) 3-Y-O+ **£4,690** (£1,395; £697; £348) **Stalls** Centre

Form RPR

5621 **1** **Ocean Temptress**[8] 6283 3-7-11 **63** 6ex..................(v) JackOsborn(7) 6 70
(John Ryan) *mde all: rdn over 1f out: hld on wl ins fnl f: rdn out* **7/2**[2]

4225 **2** *3/4* **Whitecrest**[5] 6373 9-9-1 **71**.................. LukeMorris 3 75
(John Spearing) *trckd wnr: effrt over 1f out: drvn and styd on to press wnr 1f out: kpt on but a hld ins fnl f* **5/1**[3]

3232 **3** *1* **Major Valentine**[2] 6506 5-9-5 **75**.................. TomMarquand 4 75
(John O'Shea) *hld up in tch in last pair: effrt 2f out: kpt on same pce u.p ins fnl f* **11/8**[1]

0005 **4** *3/4* **Fairway To Heaven (IRE)**[34] 5333 8-8-6 **65**.................. CharlieBennett(3) 1 63
(Lee Carter) *in tch in last pair: effrt 2f out: drvn and styd on to press ldrs 1f out: no ex ins fnl f: wknd towards fin* **8/1**

6300 **5** *4 1/2* **Jersey Breeze (IRE)**[11] 6197 4-9-2 **77**.................. DavidEgan(5) 5 61
(Mick Channon) *t.k.h: trckd ldrs: effrt and swtchd rt 2f out: sn u.p and no hdwy: wknd ins fnl f* **5/1**[3]

1m 12.97s (1.77) **Going Correction** +0.40s/f (Good)
**WFA** 3 from 4yo+ 3lb **5** Ran SP% **108.8**
Speed ratings (Par 105): **104,103,101,100,94**
CSF £19.61 TOTE £4.30: £2.30, £1.10; EX 14.60 Trifecta £28.90.
**Owner** The Temptations **Bred** Old Mill Stud Ltd And Oomswell Ltd **Trained** Newmarket, Suffolk

**FOCUS**
A modest sprint and the 3yo made all.

## 6587 WORLD CUP QUALIFIERS AT 188BET CLAIMING STKS 1m 1f
**4:10** (4:10) (Class 6) 3-Y-O **£2,264** (£673; £336; £168) **Stalls** Low

Form RPR

4340 **1** **Conistone**[15] 6048 3-8-2 52..................(p) JosephineGordon 4 50
(James Bethell) *mde all: rdn ent fnl 2f: styd on to forge ahd ins fnl f: gng away at fin* **7/2**[1]

0635 **2** *1 3/4* **Luduamf (IRE)**[6] 6342 3-8-13 53.................. SeanLevey 6 58
(Richard Hannon) *chsd wnr: rdn 3f out: pressing wnr over 1f out: styd on same pce u.p ins fnl f* **6/1**

6403 **3** *3/4* **Zoffanist (IRE)**[3] 6473 3-8-13 58..................(be[1]) PatDobbs 7 56
(Amanda Perrett) *hld up in tch in midfield: effrt ent fnl 2f: nt clr run over 1f out: shifting lft u.p and hdwy 1f out: wnt 3rd ins fnl f: kpt on* **5/1**[3]

2-0 **4** *3/4* **Shadow Beauty**[21] 5794 3-9-4 0.................. MarcMonaghan(3) 2 63
(Marco Botti) *hld up wl in tch in midfield: effrt over 2f out: chsng ldrs but awkward hd carriage and hung lft over 1f out: kpt on same pce ins fnl f* **10/1**

0032 **5** *2 3/4* **De Vegas Kid (IRE)**[21] 5791 3-8-9 51..................(p) GeorgeDowning 8 45
(Tony Carroll) *t.k.h: hld up in tch in last pair: effrt ent fnl 2f: edgd lft u.p and no imp 1f out: kpt on same pce fnl f* **5/1**[3]

2552 **6** *1/2* **Bizet (IRE)**[3] 6473 3-8-4 52..................(v) HollieDoyle(3) 5 42
(John Ryan) *s.i.s: a in rr: rdn over 2f out: no imp: nvr trbld ldrs* **9/2**[2]

4103 **7** *3 3/4* **Chunkyfunkymonkey**[20] 5853 3-9-0 67.................. JackOsborn(7) 1 49
(John Ryan) *trckd ldrs: effrt on inner and pressed ldrs u.p 2f out: no ex and btn over 1f out: wknd ins fnl f* **9/2**[2]

1m 59.58s (2.98) **Going Correction** +0.15s/f (Good) **7** Ran SP% **115.3**
Speed ratings (Par 98): **92,90,89,89,86 86,82**
CSF £25.10 TOTE £4.50: £2.20, £3.30; EX 27.50 Trifecta £163.80.Conistone was the subject of a friendly claim by Mr J. D. Bethell for £5,000.
**Owner** Clarendon Thoroughbred Racing **Bred** Whitwell Bloodstock **Trained** Middleham Moor, N Yorks

**FOCUS**
A competitive if rather weak claimer. The form might not even be as good as rated.

## 6588 PLAY CASINO AT 188BET H'CAP 1m 2f
**4:40** (4:42) (Class 6) (0-65,66) 4-Y-O+ **£2,264** (£673; £336; £168) **Stalls** Low

Form RPR

6423 **1** **Transmitting**[36] 5261 4-9-5 **63**..................(e[1]) HarryBentley 1 69
(Ed Vaughan) *hld up in tch: clsd to chse ldr 4f out: edgd lft u.p but styd on to press ldr over 1f out: led ins fnl f: styd on* **7/4**[1]

0552 **2** *1 3/4* **Silver Dixie (USA)**[11] 6175 7-9-3 **61**..................(p) CharlesBishop 5 64
(Peter Hedger) *hld up in tch in rr of main gp: effrt 2f out: chsd ldng pair over 1f out: styd on u.p ins fnl f: wnt 2nd last strides* **8/1**

50-1 **3** *nk* **Rock Icon**[8] 6284 4-8-5 **56**..................(h) JoshQuinn(7) 2 58
(Jo Hughes) *t.k.h: pressed ldr tl led 1/2-way: rdn over 1f out: hdd and no ex ins fnl f: lost 2nd last strides* **9/4**[2]

0031 **4** *4 1/2* **Ban Shoof**[19] 5866 4-9-4 **65**..................(b) HectorCrouch(3) 3 59
(Gary Moore) *hld up wl in tch: swtchd rt and effrt in centre over 2f out: 4th and no imp u.p over 1f out: wl hld after* **3/1**[3]

0050 **5** *7* **Elusive Cowboy (USA)**[34] 5320 4-9-6 **64**..................(p) JosephineGordon 4 46
(Chris Gordon) *led tl 1/2-way: lost pl bnd over 3f out: sn rdn: wknd 2f out* **20/1**

0604 **6** *2* **Pivotal Flame (IRE)**[120] 2254 4-9-3 **66**.................. PaddyBradley(5) 8 44
(Pat Phelan) *trckd ldrs: wnt 3rd over 3f out: rdn and little rspnse 2f out: sn btn and wknd* **25/1**

-000 **7** *20* **Threediamondrings**[11] 6196 4-9-0 **58**..................(t) LiamKeniry 9
(Mark Usher) *v.s.a: a detached in last* **33/1**

2m 11.09s (0.59) **Going Correction** +0.15s/f (Good) **7** Ran SP% **114.8**
Speed ratings (Par 101): **103,101,101,97,92 90,74**
CSF £16.22 CT £32.23 TOTE £2.90: £1.50, £2.50; EX 15.70 Trifecta £40.20.
**Owner** A M Pickering **Bred** Juddmonte Farms Ltd **Trained** Newmarket, Suffolk

**FOCUS**
Three came clear in this modest handicap. The winner has been rated near his best.

## 6589 188BET H'CAP 1m 3f 133y
**5:10** (5:13) (Class 6) (0-55,55) 4-Y-O+ **£2,587** (£770; £384; £192) **Stalls** High

Form RPR

60-1 **1** **Hermosa Vaquera (IRE)**[13] 5405 7-9-4 **55**..................(p) HectorCrouch(3) 7 62
(Gary Moore) *trckd ldrs: rdn to ld over 2f out: drvn 1f out: kpt on but reduced advantage fnl 100yds: jst lasted home* **2/1**[1]

6-03 **2** *hd* **Ravenswood**[25] 5652 4-9-4 **52**.................. RobHornby 10 60
(Patrick Chamings) *hld up in tch in midfield: swtchd lft and hdwy 2f out: chsd wnr but n.m.r on inner 1f out: gap opened and styd on u.p fnl 100yds: nt quite rch wnr* **11/4**[2]

3440 **3** *5* **Halling's Wish**[21] 5787 7-9-4 **52**..................(b) TomQueally 5 51
(Gary Moore) *stdd after s: hld up in tch in last pair: hdwy to go 2nd 5f out: rdn and unable qck over 1f out: 3rd and wknd ins fnl f* **7/2**[3]

0-55 **4** *shd* **Rod Of Iron**[19] 5866 4-8-12 **46** oh1..................(v[1]) KieranO'Neill 6 45
(Michael Madgwick) *led tl rdn and hdd over 2f out: 4th and outpcd whn swtchd rt over 1f out: plugged on same pce ins fnl f* **33/1**

-000 **5** *hd* **Tatawu (IRE)**[30] 5477 5-9-5 **53**..................(b[1]) WilliamCarson 4 52
(Peter Hiatt) *stmbld leaving stalls and s.i.s: bhd: effrt 3f out: hdwy over 1f out: styd on ins fnl f and pressing for 3rd nr fin: nvr trbld ldrs* **8/1**

-200 **6** *2* **Sir Dylan**[7] 6309 8-9-3 **51**..................(h) LiamKeniry 2 46
(Polly Gundry) *hld up in tch in last trio: effrt 3f out: no imp: nvr trbld ldrs* **12/1**

5006 **7** *shd* **Barbary Prince**[13] 6088 5-8-5 **46** oh1.................. ManuelFernandes(7) 3 41
(Shaun Harris) *chsd ldr tl 5f out: lost pl and rdn over 3f out: wl hld and plugged on same pce fnl 2f* **12/1**

033- **8** *7* **Ocean Bentley (IRE)**[309] 6030 5-8-12 **46** oh1.................. GeorgeDowning 1 30
(Tony Carroll) *hld up in tch in midfield: lost pl and effrt 3f out: no imp and wknd over 1f out: bhd ins fnl f* **25/1**

2m 37.27s (5.77) **Going Correction** +0.15s/f (Good) **8** Ran SP% **115.5**
Speed ratings (Par 101): **86,85,82,82,82 81,80,76**
CSF £7.72 CT £17.31 TOTE £3.00: £1.30, £1.20, £1.80; EX 9.70 Trifecta £21.30.
**Owner** Michael Baldry **Bred** James Burns And A Moynan **Trained** Lower Beeding, W Sussex

**FOCUS**
The right horses came to the fore in this moderate handicap, although the outcome may have been different had the runner-up got a run when needed. The winner's latest effort could be rated nearly as good as this.
T/Plt: £48.50 to a £1 stake. Pool: £63,698.55 - 957.73 winning units T/Qpdt: £56.10 to a £1 stake. Pool: £4,397.83 - 57.95 winning units **Steve Payne**

# 5878 MUSSELBURGH (R-H)
### Wednesday, August 30

**OFFICIAL GOING: Good to firm (good in places in places; 7.0)**
Wind: Light, half against Weather: Cloudy, dry

## 6590 BRITISH STALLION STUDS EBF NOVICE STKS 7f 33y
**2:00** (2:01) (Class 5) 2-Y-O **£3,234** (£962; £481; £240) **Stalls** Low

Form RPR

4 **1** **Soldier's Minute**[9] 6264 2-9-2 0.................. ConnorBeasley 3 80+
(Keith Dalgleish) *t.k.h: trckd ldrs: effrt whn nt clr run over 2f out to over 1f out: swtchd lft and rdn to ld ins fnl f: qcknd clr last 100yds: readily* **9/2**[3]

55 **2** *2 1/2* **Mi Capricho (IRE)**[30] 5465 2-8-11 0.................. RowanScott(5) 8 72
(Keith Dalgleish) *hld up in tch: rdn and outpcd over 2f out: rallied and edgd lft over 1f out: chsd (clr) wnr wl ins fnl f: r.o* **50/1**

56 **3** *1 1/2* **Vj Day (USA)**[55] 4526 2-9-2 0.................. TomEaves 5 68
(Kevin Ryan) *s.i.s: hld up: hdwy and angled lft over 2f out: led and rdn over 1f out: hdd ins fnl f: one pce last 100yds* **3/1**[2]

2 **4** *1 1/4* **Three Saints Bay (IRE)**[22] 5735 2-9-2 0.................. PhillipMakin 6 65
(David O'Meara) *trckd ldrs: smooth hdwy to ld over 2f out: rdn and hdd over 1f out: edgd rt and sn one pce* **5/2**[1]

44 **5** *2 1/2* **Hippeia (IRE)**[23] 5702 2-8-11 0.................. PaulMulrennan 2 53
(Jedd O'Keeffe) *t.k.h: led 1f: cl up: rdn and ev ch over 2f out: edgd rt over 1f out: wknd fnl f* **7/1**

5 **6** *3 3/4* **Amazing Rock (SWI)**[22] 5735 2-9-2 0.................. JoeFanning 1 49
(Mark Johnston) *s.i.s: hdwy to ld after 1f: rn wd first bnd after 2f: rdn and hdd over 2f out: wknd over 1f out* **11/2**

66 **7** *1 1/2* **Crown Of Cortez**[79] 3648 2-8-13 0.................. AdamMcNamara(3) 7 45
(Richard Fahey) *s.i.s: sn drvn along in rr: outpcd over 2f out: n.d after* **12/1**

**8** *hd* **Party Fears Too (IRE)** 2-9-2 0.................. ShaneGray 4 44
(Jim Goldie) *s.i.s: hld up: pushed along and outpcd over 2f out: sn btn* **33/1**

1m 28.86s (-0.14) **Going Correction** -0.175s/f (Firm) **8** Ran SP% **112.2**
Speed ratings (Par 94): **93,90,88,87,84 79,78,77**
CSF £164.49 TOTE £5.50: £1.70, £8.70, £1.20; EX 214.60 Trifecta £711.60.
**Owner** Weldspec Glasgow Limited **Bred** Rabbah Bloodstock Limited **Trained** Carluke, S Lanarks

**FOCUS**
The going was good, good to firm in places. The pace was sound for this fair contest. The third helps set the opening level.

## 6591 ISN'T IT WISER TO BET AT RACINGUK.COM H'CAP 1m 2y
**2:30** (2:31) (Class 5) (0-70,72) 4-Y-0+ £3,234 (£962; £481; £240) Stalls Low

Form RPR

3512 **1** **Masarzain (IRE)**[5] 6393 4-9-3 **66** EdwardGreatrex(3) 6 80
(Archie Watson) *hld up towards rr: rdn along over 2f out: gd hdwy and led 1f out: pushed clr: comf* **15/8**[1]

5010 **2** 4 ½ **Ellaal**[13] 6092 8-9-3 **63** (p) PaulMulrennan 7 67
(Ruth Carr) *led 2f: pressed ldr: rdn over 2f out: kpt on fnl f to take 2nd nr fin: no ch w wnr* **10/1**

3213 **3** *nk* **Relight My Fire**[13] 6092 7-9-2 **65** (p) RachelRichardson(3) 9 68
(Tim Easterby) *t.k.h: cl up on outside: led after 2f: rdn over 2f out: hdd 1f out: sn one pce: lost 2nd nr fin* **10/1**

004 **4** 2 ¼ **Lil Sophella (IRE)**[15] 6047 8-9-7 **67** NeilFarley 10 65
(Patrick Holmes) *s.i.s: hld up: drvn along over 2f out: hdwy over 1f out: kpt on: no imp* **10/1**

5124 **5** ¾ **Crazy Tornado (IRE)**[16] 5993 4-9-6 **71** (h) RowanScott(5) 5 67
(Keith Dalgleish) *hld up: rdn over 3f out: hdwy over 1f out: nt pce to chal* **7/1**[3]

3210 **6** 2 ½ **Remember Rocky**[16] 5993 8-8-10 **63** (b) ConnorMurtagh(7) 1 54
(Lucy Normile) *midfield on ins: drvn and outpcd over 2f out: sme late hdwy: nvr able to chal* **14/1**

4333 **7** 1 **Cyflymder (IRE)**[9] 6263 11-8-2 **48** JoeyHaynes 8 36
(David C Griffiths) *hld up: rdn and edgd rt over 2f out: sn no imp: btn over 1f out* **25/1**

03 **8** 1 ¾ **Billy Roberts (IRE)**[34] 5337 4-9-12 **72** ConnorBeasley 11 56
(Richard Guest) *trckd ldrs: drvn along over 2f out: wknd fnl f* **7/1**[3]

0060 **9** 3 ¼ **Foresight (FR)**[55] 4529 4-9-2 **62** (t[1]) TomEaves 3 39
(Kevin Ryan) *hld up: drvn and struggling wl over 2f out: sn btn* **25/1**

6600 **10** 8 **Danny Mc D**[16] 5997 4-8-2 **55** (p) JamieGormley(7) 4 13
(Iain Jardine) *s.i.s: bhd: struggling 3f out: nvr on terms* **50/1**

5450 **11** 54 **Flinty Fell (IRE)**[18] 5922 4-9-3 **63** JoeFanning 2
(Keith Dalgleish) *t.k.h: in tch: rdn over 2f out: wknd over 1f out: btn whn virtually p.u fnl f* **6/1**[2]

1m 38.35s (-2.85) **Going Correction** -0.175s/f (Firm) 11 Ran SP% **117.7**
Speed ratings (Par 103): **107,102,102,99,99 96,95,93,90,82 28**
CSF £21.39 CT £153.59 TOTE £2.40: £1.20, £2.60, £3.00; EX 28.40 Trifecta £179.30.
**Owner** Masarzain Partnership **Bred** Mrs Josephine Hughes **Trained** Upper Lambourn, W Berks

**FOCUS**
A strongly run handicap.

## 6592 RAY HAWTHORNE MEMORIAL H'CAP 1m 4f 104y
**3:00** (3:00) (Class 6) (0-60,59) 4-Y-0+ £3,234 (£962; £481; £240) Stalls Low

Form RPR

0513 **1** **Mr Sundowner (USA)**[23] 5698 5-9-1 **56** (t) SammyJoBell(3) 6 62
(Wilf Storey) *hld up: hdwy and prom 4f out: led over 2f out: sn pushed along: hld on wl fnl f* **5/1**

0613 **2** ½ **Jonny Delta**[19] 5884 10-9-0 **59** SeanMooney(7) 5 64
(Jim Goldie) *prom: hdwy to press ldr after 3f: chal 1/2-way to over 2f out: rallied and sn chsng wnr: kpt on fnl f* **9/2**[3]

643 **3** 1 ¼ **Tambour**[6] 6352 4-8-12 **55** (t) RowanScott(5) 8 58
(Keith Dalgleish) *chsd ldr 3f: cl up: pushed along over 2f out: effrt and disp 2nd pl over 1f out: edgd rt and one pce ins fnl f* **2/1**[1]

3003 **4** 2 ¼ **Ivors Involvement (IRE)**[9] 6269 5-8-0 **45** ConnorMurtagh(7) 3 45
(Tina Jackson) *led: jnd 1/2-way: rdn and hdd over 2f out: outpcd fr over 1f out* **11/2**

6512 **5** 1 ¼ **Sakhalin Star (IRE)**[7] 6305 6-9-7 **59** (p) ConnorBeasley 4 57
(Richard Guest) *hld up: pushed along and outpcd over 4f out: rallied over 2f out: edgd rt and no imp fr over 1f out* **4/1**[2]

-000 **6** 14 **Wolf Heart (IRE)**[18] 5917 9-8-0 **45** RhonaPindar(7) 2 20
(Lucy Normile) *hld up in tch: drvn and struggling over 5f out: sn btn* **50/1**

045 **7** ¾ **Wee Bogus**[28] 5539 4-9-5 **57** PaulMulrennan 1 31
(Alistair Whillans) *t.k.h early: chsd ldrs 3f: in tch: struggling over 5f out: sn btn* **22/1**

2m 41.42s (-0.58) **Going Correction** -0.175s/f (Firm) 7 Ran SP% **109.9**
Speed ratings (Par 101): **94,93,92,91,90 81,80**
CSF £25.30 CT £54.14 TOTE £5.80: £2.10, £2.90; EX 32.50 Trifecta £100.60.
**Owner** W Storey **Bred** Hunter Valley Farm Et Al **Trained** Muggleswick, Co Durham

**FOCUS**
A modest handicap run at a solid pace. Straightforward form rated around the winner to his best over the past two years and the runner-up to his recent best.

## 6593 HAWTHORNE GIRLS H'CAP 5f 1y
**3:30** (3:31) (Class 4) (0-85,87) 3-Y-0+ £5,175 (£1,540; £769; £384) Stalls High

Form RPR

1034 **1** **Kinloch Pride**[47] 4850 5-8-6 **66** (p) PatrickMathers 4 73
(Noel Wilson) *prom on outside: effrt and drvn over 1f out: led ins fnl f: hld on wl cl home* **20/1**

3144 **2** *shd* **Royal Brave (IRE)**[11] 6185 6-9-7 **86** RowanScott(5) 8 93
(Rebecca Bastiman) *prom: effrt and rdn over 1f out: ev ch ins fnl f: kpt on: hld cl home* **11/2**[3]

1440 **3** *hd* **Orient Class**[11] 6185 6-9-6 **87** ConnorMurtagh(7) 3 93
(Paul Midgley) *hld up on outside: hdwy and pushed along wl over 1f out: ev ch ins fnl f: kpt on: hld cl home* **6/1**

2334 **4** 1 ¼ **Fumbo Jumbo (IRE)**[4] 6412 4-9-5 **84** CallumRodriguez(5) 5 85
(Michael Dods) *dwlt: bhd and outpcd: hdwy over 1f out: kpt on fnl f: nrst fin* **11/4**[1]

0300 **5** 2 ¼ **Gamesome (FR)**[18] 5920 6-9-8 **82** PaulMulrennan 1 75
(Paul Midgley) *hld up: shkn up wl over 1f out: kpt on fnl f: nt pce to chal* **8/1**

3022 **6** *nse* **Bogart**[9] 6267 8-9-7 **81** (tp) TomEaves 9 74
(Kevin Ryan) *cl up: drvn along 2f out: wknd ins fnl f* **10/3**[2]

6645 **7** ½ **Economic Crisis (IRE)**[6] 6351 8-8-7 **70** LewisEdmunds(3) 6 61
(Colin Teague) *hld up in tch: effrt and rdn over 1f out: no imp whn n.m.r ins fnl f* **25/1**

332 **8** *hd* **Lydia's Place**[9] 6276 4-9-4 **78** ConnorBeasley 10 69
(Richard Guest) *led at decent gallop: rdn over 1f out: edgd rt and hdd ins fnl f: sn btn* **14/1**

5226 **9** 2 ¾ **Pearl Acclaim (IRE)**[18] 5930 7-8-4 **67** EdwardGreatrex(3) 7 48
(David C Griffiths) *cl up: rdn over 2f out: edgd rt and wknd over 1f out* **16/1**

01 **10** 1 ¾ **Rosina**[18] 5920 4-9-8 **82** (p) ShaneGray 2 56
(Ann Duffield) *bhd and sn bdly outpcd: no ch fr 1/2-way* **20/1**

59.08s (-1.32) **Going Correction** -0.075s/f (Good) 10 Ran SP% **116.4**
Speed ratings (Par 105): **107,106,106,104,100 100,100,99,95,92**
CSF £123.23 CT £774.41 TOTE £20.30: £5.40, £1.80, £2.20; EX 247.80 Trifecta £1818.60.
**Owner** G J Paver **Bred** Mrs C K Paver **Trained** Marwood, Co Durham
■ Stewards' Enquiry : Rowan Scott two-day ban: used whip above permitted level (Sep 13-14)

**FOCUS**
The pace was sound for the competitive handicap, with the action unfolding towards the centre.

## 6594 AIUA INSURANCE H'CAP 1m 208y
**4:00** (4:01) (Class 6) (0-65,68) 3-Y-O £2,587 (£770; £384; £192) Stalls Low

Form RPR

3241 **1** **Alnasl (IRE)**[19] 5895 3-9-7 **67** (h) EdwardGreatrex(3) 1 76+
(Archie Watson) *t.k.h: trckd ldr 3f: smooth hdwy to ld over 2f out: pushed clr fr over 1f out: comf* **7/2**[2]

2305 **2** 2 ¼ **Rosemay (FR)**[16] 5997 3-9-2 **64** BenRobinson(5) 8 68
(Iain Jardine) *hld up in tch: effrt and rdn over 2f out: hdwy to chse (clr) wnr ins fnl f: kpt on: nt pce to chal* **11/2**[3]

0041 **3** 1 ¾ **Prancing Oscar (IRE)**[30] 5485 3-9-0 **62** CallumRodriguez(5) 7 62
(Ben Haslam) *led at ordinary gallop: rdn and hdd over 2f out: chsd wnr to ins fnl f: no ex* **7/2**[2]

4161 **4** 2 ¾ **Take A Turn (IRE)**[9] 6257 3-9-11 **68** 6ex PaulMulrennan 4 63
(David Lanigan) *hld up: pushed along over 2f out: hdwy and edgd rt over 1f out: sn no imp* **11/4**[1]

2454 **5** 1 ¾ **Hellomoto**[19] 5880 3-9-0 **57** (p) TomEaves 3 48
(Kevin Ryan) *trckd ldrs: wnt 2nd after 3f to 3f out: rdn and wknd over 1f out* **11/1**

0-06 **6** *hd* **Hazy Manor (IRE)**[77] 3708 3-8-0 **50** JamieGormley(7) 2 40
(Julia Brooke) *in tch: effrt and drvn along over 2f out: wknd over 1f out* **50/1**

6420 **7** 2 **Devil's Guard (IRE)**[25] 5649 3-8-5 **53** (v) RowanScott(5) 6 39
(Keith Dalgleish) *s.i.s: hld up: drvn and struggling over 3f out: btn fnl 2f* **8/1**

0606 **8** 4 ½ **Lady Molly (IRE)**[16] 5991 3-8-3 **46** JoeFanning 5 23
(Keith Dalgleish) *t.k.h: hld up: drvn and outpcd wl over 2f out: sn btn* **20/1**

1m 51.59s (-2.31) **Going Correction** -0.175s/f (Firm) 8 Ran SP% **112.7**
Speed ratings (Par 98): **103,101,99,97,95 95,93,89**
CSF £22.32 CT £70.97 TOTE £4.50: £1.40, £2.00, £1.60; EX 24.90 Trifecta £96.60.
**Owner** K Sohi **Bred** Shadwell Estate Company Limited **Trained** Upper Lambourn, W Berks

**FOCUS**
A fair handicap run at an even tempo. The runner-up has been rated near his best.

## 6595 CATHERINE ROACHE H'CAP 1m 7f 217y
**4:30** (4:30) (Class 6) (0-65,62) 3-Y-0+ £3,234 (£962; £481) Stalls High

Form RPR

3164 **1** **Adrakhan (FR)**[38] 5186 6-8-11 **48** SammyJoBell(3) 1 53
(Wilf Storey) *trckd ldr: led gng wl over 2f: rdn and hdd over 1f out: rallied and regained ld last 25yds: kpt on* **11/4**[3]

0323 **2** ½ **Tectonic (IRE)**[18] 5923 8-10-0 **62** (p) JoeFanning 5 66
(Keith Dalgleish) *trckd ldrs: plld out over 2f out: shkn up to ld over 1f out: rdn: carried hd high and edgd lft ins fnl f: fnd little and hdd last 25yds* **11/8**[1]

0504 **3** 20 **La Bacouetteuse (FR)**[23] 5700 12-9-5 **58** (b) CallumRodriguez(5) 4 36
(Iain Jardine) *led: stdd 1/2-way: rdn and hdd over 2f out: wknd over 1f out: eased whn no ch fnl f* **13/8**[2]

3m 31.23s (-2.27) **Going Correction** -0.175s/f (Firm)
**WFA** 3 from 6yo+ 12lb 3 Ran SP% **106.9**
Speed ratings (Par 101): **98,97,87**
CSF £6.56 TOTE £3.80; EX 5.30 Trifecta £6.70.
**Owner** W Storey **Bred** E A R L Haras Du Camp Benard **Trained** Muggleswick, Co Durham

**FOCUS**
A small field but they went an honest pace and it produced an exciting finish. The winner has been rated up a bit on this year's form.

## 6596 ALL NEW RACINGUK.COM H'CAP 5f 1y
**5:00** (5:01) (Class 6) (0-65,67) 3-Y-O £2,587 (£770; £384; £192) Stalls High

Form RPR

5523 **1** **Suwaan (IRE)**[12] 6155 3-9-9 **67** TomEaves 2 75
(Ruth Carr) *mde all: gng wl over 1f out: rdn whn carried hd high and edgd rt ins fnl f: kpt on wl towards fin* **5/2**[1]

3-26 **2** 1 ½ **Jeany (IRE)**[12] 6155 3-9-7 **65** ConnorBeasley 7 67
(Bryan Smart) *chsd ldrs: wnt 2nd and drvn along 1/2-way: kpt on ins fnl f: nt rch wnr* **7/2**[2]

3544 **3** 1 ½ **Rapid Ranger**[12] 6157 3-9-4 **62** (h[1]) PhillipMakin 5 59
(David O'Meara) *trckd ldrs: effrt and drvn along over 1f out: kpt on same pce ins fnl f* **7/2**[2]

0501 **4** 1 ½ **Pavers Pride**[26] 5619 3-9-5 **66** AdamMcNamara(3) 4 58
(Noel Wilson) *dwlt: hld up: hdwy 1/2-way: effrt and rdn over 1f out: no ex ins fnl f* **8/1**[3]

0-50 **5** 2 **Whiteandgold**[37] 5211 3-9-6 **64** (b[1]) PaulMulrennan 6 48
(Bryan Smart) *chsd wnr to 1/2-way: rdn and wknd over 1f out* **9/1**

2305 **6** 4 ½ **Luv U Always**[26] 5605 3-7-13 **50** (p) JamieGormley(7) 1 18
(Iain Jardine) *hld up on outside: effrt and pushed along whn hung rt over 1f out: sn btn* **10/1**

0024 **7** 4 ½ **Mr Enthusiastic**[12] 6130 3-8-2 **46** oh1 PatrickMathers 3
(Noel Wilson) *trckd ldrs: drvn along over 2f out: wknd wl over 1f out: eased whn no ch ins fnl f* **14/1**

000 **8** 2 ½ **Fintry Flyer**[11] 6184 3-8-6 **50** ShaneGray 8
(Jim Goldie) *s.i.s: bhd and outpcd: no ch fr 1/2-way: eased whn btn ins fnl f* **33/1**

59.65s (-0.75) **Going Correction** -0.075s/f (Good) 8 Ran SP% **112.8**
Speed ratings (Par 98): **103,100,98,95,92 85,78,74**
CSF £10.96 CT £29.35 TOTE £2.80: £1.40, £1.40, £1.30; EX 12.20 Trifecta £39.50.
**Owner** J A Swinburne & Mrs Ruth A Carr **Bred** Shadwell Estate Company Limited **Trained** Huby, N Yorks

**FOCUS**
Not a great race for the grade. They went a decent pace and the winner did it well. The winner has been rated as improving a little on his latest effort.
T/Jkpt: Not Won. T/Plt: £135.20 to a £1 stake. Pool: £63,811.60 - 344.43 winning units T/Qpdt: £45.30 to a £1 stake. Pool: £3,871.83 - 63.23 winning units **Richard Young**

6597 - 6604a (Foreign Racing) - See Raceform Interactive

## [6494] BADEN-BADEN (L-H)
### Wednesday, August 30

**OFFICIAL GOING: Turf: good**

## 6605a COOLMORE STUD BADEN-BADEN CUP (LISTED RACE) (3YO+ FILLIES & MARES) (TURF) 7f
5:40 3-Y-O+ £11,965 (£5,555; £2,564; £1,282)

RPR
1 **Celebrity (GER)**[73] 3882 3-8-10 0 ow1 AdriedeVries 8 94
(D Moser, Germany) 13/2
2 *hd* **Sunny Belle (IRE)**[58] 4518 3-8-9 0 AndraschStarke 3 92
(P Schiergen, Germany) 66/10
3 *1 1/4* **Sante (IRE)**[67] 4085 4-9-0 0 MichaelCadeddu 5 91
(Jean-Pierre Carvalho, Germany) 17/2
4 *3/4* **Shy Witch (GER)**[58] 4518 4-9-4 0 EduardoPedroza 2 93
(H-J Groschel, Germany) 17/5[2]
5 *3/4* **Sugar Free (GER)**[17] 4-9-0 0 WladimirPanov 4 87
(D Moser, Germany) 171/10
6 *2* **Hells Babe**[88] 3334 4-9-0 0 AlistairRawlinson 1 81
(Michael Appleby) *led: hdd after 1f: chsd ldrs: 3rd and drvn 2f out: rdn and no imp appr 1f out: grad dropped away fnl f* 13/10[1]
7 *1 3/4* **Sailana (GER)**[302] 7757 3-8-9 0 MaximPecheur 6 74
(Christina Bucher, Switzerland) 11/2[3]
8 *2* **Scapina (GER)**[10] 6254 3-8-9 0 MarcoCasamento 7 69
(Henk Grewe, Germany) 18/1

1m 22.97s (-0.93)
**WFA** 3 from 4yo 5lb 8 Ran SP% **129.4**
PARI-MUTUEL (all including 10 euro stake): WIN 75 PLACE: 24, 23, 23; SF: 324.
**Owner** Gestut Brummerhof **Bred** Gestut Brummerhof **Trained** Germany

6606 - 6607a (Foreign Racing) - See Raceform Interactive

## [6540] DEAUVILLE (R-H)
### Wednesday, August 30

**OFFICIAL GOING: Polytrack: fast; turf: soft changing to very soft after race 4 (1.50)**

## 6608a PRIX DE LA BANCHE (CLAIMER) (2YO) (TURF) 6f
2:55 (2:55) 2-Y-O £9,829 (£3,931; £2,948; £1,965; £982)

RPR
1 **Good To Talk**[5] 6409 2-8-11 0 (b) AntoineHamelin 5 80
(Matthieu Palussiere, France) 12/5[1]
2 *4* **Stromboli (FR)** 2-8-11 0 EddyHardouin 8 68
(T Lemer, France) 11/2
3 *1/2* **Pour La Famille (IRE)** 2-8-11 0 PanagiotisDimitsanis 4 67
(Christos Kouvaras, France) 135/10
4 *3/4* **Oona (FR)**[26] 5629 2-8-11 0 AnthonyCrastus 6 64
(P Sogorb, France) 3/1[2]
5 *3* **See You In Paris (IRE)**[64] 4196 2-8-8 0 MaximeGuyon 3 52
(Gianluca Bietolini, Italy) 32/5
6 *4* **Shesgotthelot**[4] 6456 2-8-3 0 MathieuPelletan(5) 7 40
(J S Moore) *wl into stride: disp ld early: pushed along over 2f out: sn rdn w limited rspnse: no ex and eased ins fnl f* 147/10
7 *3/4* **Illadore (FR)** 2-8-13 0 ow2 ChristopheSoumillon 2 43
(D Guillemin, France) 43/10[3]
8 *10* **Tekedici (FR)**[102] 2-8-11 0 (b[1]) CristianDemuro 1 11
(Antonio Marcialis, Italy) 35/1

1m 13.48s (2.48) 8 Ran SP% **118.2**
PARI-MUTUEL (all including 1 euro stake): WIN 3.40; PLACE 1.70, 1.90, 3.30; DF 9.20; SF 14.00.
**Owner** Mrs Theresa Marnane **Bred** O Costello & R Morehead **Trained** France

## [6303] BATH (L-H)
### Thursday, August 31

**OFFICIAL GOING: Good to firm (8.8)**
Wind: mild breeze, against Weather: sunny

## 6609 FLEET ALLIANCE NURSERY H'CAP 5f 10y
1:40 (1:41) (Class 6) (0-65,65) 2-Y-O £2,264 (£673; £336; £168) **Stalls** Centre

Form RPR
303 1 **Zain Smarts (IRE)**[31] 5479 2-8-13 **62** DavidEgan(5) 9 70
(David Evans) *mde all: kpt on wl: rdn out* 6/1[3]
006 2 *2 1/4* **Following Breeze (IRE)**[20] 5865 2-7-12 **45** HollieDoyle(3) 2 45+
(Jim Boyle) *hld up towards rr: hdwy 2f out: nt clr run and swtchd rt ent fnl f: r.o strly: snatched 2nd fnl strides* 16/1
430 3 *nk* **Jonnysimpson (IRE)**[75] 3821 2-8-12 **61** JennyPowell(5) 5 60
(Brendan Powell) *trckd wnr: rdn over 1f out: nt quite pce pce to mount chal: lost 2nd fnl strides* 14/1
060 4 *1* **Cent Flying**[73] 3917 2-8-13 **57** MartinDwyer 12 52
(William Muir) *mid-div: hdwy over 2f out: chalng for 2nd whn rdn and edgd lft ent fnl f: kpt on same pce* 6/1[3]
0040 5 *shd* **Red For Danger**[9] 6285 2-8-4 **51** (h[1]) EdwardGreatrex(3) 3 49
(Eve Johnson Houghton) *racd keenly: hld up towards rr: hdwy but nt clr run over 1f out: r.o ins fnl f: fin wl* 20/1
643 6 *1/2* **Dream Prospect**[31] 5474 2-9-7 **65** DaneO'Neill 1 58
(Roger Charlton) *in tch: rdn to chse ldrs wl over 1f out: no ex fnl f* 6/1[3]
600 7 *1 1/4* **Alaskan Star (IRE)**[20] 5865 2-9-5 **63** (p[1]) SteveDrowne 10 53
(Amanda Perrett) *mid-div: rdn whn shot of room jst over 1f out: nt pce to get on terms* 33/1
4066 8 *1/2* **Nobrassnolass (IRE)**[92] 3215 2-9-4 **62** (p[1]) RichardKingscote 4 49
(Tom Dascombe) *trckd wnr: rdn 2f out: fdd ins fnl f* 12/1
04 9 *nk* **Go Bananas**[16] 6043 2-9-1 **59** (p[1]) JimmyFortune 11 45
(Brian Meehan) *hld up towards rr: hdwy in center 2f out: sn rdn: nvr threatened: edgd lft and one pce fnl f* 11/2[2]
600 10 *nk* **Go Sandy**[21] 5844 2-8-7 **51** RobHornby 8 36
(Lisa Williamson) *chsd ldrs: rdn 2f out: wknd ins fnl f* 33/1
005 11 *1 1/4* **Navarra Princess (IRE)**[15] 6055 2-8-10 **54** JohnFahy 7 34
(Don Cantillon) *s.i.s: sn outpcd: a in rr* 9/1
5401 12 *2 3/4* **Just For The Craic (IRE)**[50] 4740 2-9-4 **62** RobertWinston 6 46
(Neil Mulholland) *mid-div: pushed along whn short of room 2f out and lost pl: nt clr run over 1f out: no ch after and eased* 9/2[1]

1m 2.8s (0.30) **Going Correction** -0.075s/f (Good) **12** Ran SP% **117.3**
Speed ratings (Par 92): **94,90,89,88,88 87,85,84,84,83 81,77**
CSF £94.35 CT £1296.66 TOTE £6.30: £1.50, £4.70, £4.20; EX 120.20 Trifecta £2744.00.
**Owner** Asaad Al Banwan **Bred** C Marnane **Trained** Pandy, Monmouths

**FOCUS**
A moderate nursery and little got involved from off the pace. Those in behind the winner suggest the form has been rated high enough.

## 6610 MOLSON GROUP H'CAP 1m 3f 137y
2:10 (2:11) (Class 5) (0-75,75) 4-Y-O+ £2,911 (£866; £432; £216) **Stalls** Low

Form RPR
4216 1 **Monsieur Glory**[12] 6188 4-9-7 **75** PatCosgrave 5 82+
(Tom Clover) *trckd ldrs: rdn 2f out: edgd lft ent fnl f: sn led: styd on wl: comf* 11/4[2]
3534 2 *1 1/2* **Pastoral Music**[27] 5590 4-9-2 **70** (p) RobertWinston 2 74
(Hughie Morrison) *led: rdn 2f out: hdd jst ins fnl f: styd on but sn no ex* 7/2[3]
511U 3 *4 1/2* **Tobougaloo**[14] 6095 6-8-8 **69** WilliamCox(7) 1 65
(Stuart Kittow) *s.i.s: last: tk clsr order 7f out: rdn over 2f out: sn hung lft: wnt 3rd jst ins fnl f: styd on but nt pce to get on terms* 7/2[3]
2324 4 *3 1/4* **Hepplewhite**[2] 6556 4-9-0 **68** (p) MartinDwyer 4 59
(William Muir) *trckd wnr: rdn over 2f out: hld over 1f out: snatched up whn briefly hmpd jst ins fnl f: fdd* 2/1[1]
650 5 *3 1/2* **The Salmon Man**[9] 6293 5-8-10 **67** (v[1]) EdwardGreatrex(3) 3 53
(Brendan Powell) *trckd ldrs: nt quite pce to chal: rdn over 2f out: wknd ins fnl f* 16/1
40-0 6 *18* **Mayasa (IRE)**[16] 6033 4-9-7 **75** (b) DanielMuscutt 6 32
(John Flint) *chsd ldrs tl dropped to last but stl wl in tch 7f out: pushed along over 3f out: wknd over 1f out* 33/1

2m 29.12s (-1.48) **Going Correction** -0.075s/f (Good) 6 Ran SP% **113.3**
Speed ratings (Par 103): **101,100,97,94,92 80**
CSF £12.97 TOTE £3.00: £1.60, £1.70; EX 12.90 Trifecta £44.00.
**Owner** J Collins & C Fahy **Bred** Crossfields Bloodstock Ltd **Trained** Newmarket, Suffolk

**FOCUS**
Modest handicap form, although the first two came clear.

## 6611 OCTAGON CONSULTANCY H'CAP 1m 3f 137y
2:40 (2:43) (Class 6) (0-60,61) 3-Y-O £2,911 (£866; £432; £216) **Stalls** Low

Form RPR
0240 1 **High Wells**[22] 5780 3-9-7 **60** (b) RobertWinston 6 69+
(Seamus Durack) *hld up: pushed along and hdwy fr over 2f out: led ent fnl f: sn clr: comf* 7/1[3]
0143 2 *4* **Snowy Winter (USA)**[13] 6153 3-9-5 **61** (t) EdwardGreatrex(3) 3 61
(Archie Watson) *hld up: rdn and hdwy fr wl over 2f out: styd on to go 2nd ins fnl f: no ch w wnr* 4/1[1]
1041 3 *1 1/4* **Affair**[12] 6180 3-8-8 **54** TheodoreLadd(7) 8 52
(Hughie Morrison) *led: rdn and hdd ent fnl f: sn no ex* 6/1[2]
5035 4 *3/4* **Trautmann (IRE)**[16] 6032 3-8-11 **55** DavidEgan(5) 7 51
(Daniel Mark Loughnane) *trckd ldrs: rdn wl over 2f out: styd on same pce* 10/1
6502 5 *5* **My Brother Mike (IRE)**[13] 6160 3-9-1 **61** ManuelFernandes(7) 9 49
(Kevin Frost) *pressed ldr for 3f: trckd ldr: rdn wl over 2f out: wknd ins fnl f* 7/1[3]
0364 6 *17* **Henry Did It (IRE)**[22] 5790 3-8-10 **49** SteveDrowne 5 10
(Tony Carroll) *hld up: rdn wl over 2f out: nvr threatened and sn wknd* 18/1
0-00 7 *17* **Street Jester**[215] 464 3-8-7 **46** oh1 RobHornby 1
(Robert Stephens) *trckd ldrs: pushed along in tch 5f out: rdn wl over 2f out: sn wknd* 50/1
5030 8 *4* **Masterfilly (IRE)**[23] 5761 3-9-1 **54** PatCosgrave 2
(Ed Walker) *trckd ldr tl rdn 3f out: wknd 2f out (fin lame)* 20/1

2m 28.64s (-1.96) **Going Correction** -0.075s/f (Good) 8 Ran SP% **80.4**
Speed ratings (Par 98): **103,100,99,99,95 84,73,70**
CSF £17.09 CT £54.23 TOTE £5.60: £1.60, £1.90, £1.20; EX 21.20 Trifecta £95.10.
**Owner** Ownaracehorse & Stephen Tucker **Bred** Moran & Billington **Trained** Upper Lambourn, Berkshire

■ Casemates Square was withdrawn. Price at time of withdrawal 15-8f. Rule 4 applies to all bets - deduction of 30p in the pound.

**FOCUS**
There was a key non-runner with Casements Square failing to enter the stalls. The pace was a steady one but still there was a clear-cut winner. A step forward from the winner, with the third rated to her previous 1m4f fast ground form.

## 6612 M J CHURCH H'CAP (BATH SUMMER SPRINT QUALIFIER) 5f 10y
3:10 (3:11) (Class 5) (0-70,71) 3-Y-O+ £4,140 (£1,232; £615; £307) **Stalls** Centre

Form RPR
3166 1 **Coronation Cottage**[14] 6097 3-9-3 **67** CharlieBennett(3) 8 76
(Malcolm Saunders) *chsd ldrs: rdn to ld ent fnl f: edgd sltly lft: r.o wl* 6/1
3131 2 *1 3/4* **Dandilion (IRE)**[55] 4559 4-9-4 **63** (t) PatCosgrave 3 66
(Alex Hales) *s.i.s: last: hdwy on outer over 2f out: sn rdn: r.o to go 2nd ins fnl f but no threat to wnr* 9/4[1]
0655 3 *1 3/4* **Swendab (IRE)**[6] 6372 9-8-12 **62** (b) DavidEgan(5) 5 58
(John O'Shea) *prom: rdn 2f out: ev ch over 1f out: kpt on same pce fnl f* 9/1
01 4 *nk* **Look Surprised**[17] 6009 4-9-4 **68** MitchGodwin(5) 4 63
(Roger Teal) *prom: led wl over 1f out: rdn and hdd ent fnl f: kpt on same pce* 5/1[2]
00 5 *1 1/2* **Archimedes (IRE)**[4] 6478 4-9-7 **66** (tp) SteveDrowne 2 56
(David C Griffiths) *sn pushed along in tch: rdn 2f out: kpt on but nvr gng pce to get on terms* 5/1[2]
0000 6 *2 3/4* **Candelaria**[26] 5657 4-8-9 **54** (p) FergusSweeney 1 34
(Jonjo O'Neill) *in tch: effrt over 2f out: nt pce to threaten: wknd ins fnl f* 16/1
640 7 *1* **Broadhaven Honey (IRE)**[55] 4574 3-9-7 **68** (h[1]) SamHitchcott 7 44
(Ronald Harris) *led: rdn and hdd wl over 1f out: wknd ins fnl f* 25/1
204 8 *nse* **Powerful Dream (IRE)**[27] 5587 4-9-12 **71** (p) JosephineGordon 6 47
(Ronald Harris) *nvr travelling: sn pushed along in tch: no threat fr 2f out* 11/2[3]

1m 1.46s (-1.04) **Going Correction** -0.075s/f (Good)
**WFA** 3 from 4yo+ 2lb 8 Ran SP% **113.5**
Speed ratings (Par 103): **105,102,99,98,96 92,90,90**
CSF £19.61 CT £120.74 TOTE £6.80: £2.20, £1.10, £3.10; EX 23.80 Trifecta £121.30.
**Owner** Pat Hancock & Eric Jones **Bred** Eric Jones, Pat Hancock **Trained** Green Ore, Somerset

**FOCUS**
A pretty moderate sprint and it went to one of the 3yos.

## 6613 JMK GROUP UK NURSERY H'CAP 1m
3:40 (3:40) (Class 5) (0-70,70) 2-Y-O £2,975 (£885; £442; £221) Stalls Low

Form RPR
034 1 **Paint**[22] 5795 2-9-3 **69** HollieDoyle(3) 10 74+
(Richard Hannon) *mid-div: hdwy over 2f out: kpt on wl to ld ins fnl f: pushed out* 5/2[1]
0040 2 3/4 **Dark Blue (IRE)**[23] 5752 2-8-5 **54** RaulDaSilva 5 56
(Mick Channon) *mid-div: hdwy over 2f out: rdn to chal over 1f out: led narrowly ent fnl f: sn hdd: kpt on but no ex* 16/1
0530 3 shd **Far Dawn**[23] 5756 2-8-11 **60** SteveDrowne 4 62
(Simon Crisford) *led: rdn over 2f out: hdd narrowly ent fnl f: kpt on* 14/1
0065 4 1 1/2 **Font Vert (FR)**[23] 5756 2-8-9 **63** PatrickO'Donnell(5) 9 62
(Ralph Beckett) *hld up: hdwy on outer over 2f out: rdn over 1f out: sn hung lft: kpt on same pce fnl f* 7/1
3212 5 1 1/4 **Give Em A Clump (IRE)**[6] 6366 2-8-11 **60** CharlesBishop 2 56
(David Evans) *trckd ldrs: rdn 2f out: keeping on but nt clr run on rails ent fnl f: kpt on same pce fnl 120yds* 11/2[3]
003 6 1/2 **Mr Large (IRE)**[26] 5655 2-9-6 **69** TimmyMurphy 6 66
(Jamie Osborne) *s.i.s: last pair: nt clrest of runs fr 2f out: kpt on but nt pce to get on terms fnl f* 7/1
053 7 2 1/2 **Giovanni Medici**[36] 5292 2-9-3 **66** RobertWinston 7 55
(Seamus Durack) *hld up last trio: hdwy over 2f out: sn rdn: nvr threatened: wknd ins fnl f* 9/2[2]
0002 8 3/4 **Milan Reef (IRE)**[23] 5752 2-7-13 **53** DavidEgan(5) 3 40
(David Loughnane) *trckd ldrs: rdn 3f out: sn hung rt: wknd over 1f out* 13/2
0545 9 1/2 **Captain Kissinger**[27] 5627 2-8-8 **57** (b) FergusSweeney 8 43
(Jo Hughes) *w ldr: rdn wl over 2f out: wknd ent fnl f* 33/1

1m 41.3s (0.50) **Going Correction** -0.075s/f (Good) 9 Ran SP% **116.0**
Speed ratings (Par 94): **94,93,93,91,90 89,87,86,86**
CSF £46.32 CT £474.52 TOTE £3.30: £1.60, £4.50, £3.50; EX 47.60 Trifecta £421.50.
**Owner** Lady Rothschild **Bred** Kincorth Investments Inc **Trained** East Everleigh, Wilts

**FOCUS**
Ordinary nursery form, but it's a race that should produce winners at a similar level. A small step forward from the winner, with the second, third and fourth all rated close to their pre-race marks.

## 6614 CDL RECRUITMENT / EBF MAIDEN FILLIES' STKS 1m
4:10 (4:10) (Class 5) 3-Y-O+ £3,105 (£924; £461; £230) Stalls Low

Form RPR
1 **Good Way Off (USA)**[389] 4-9-6 0 JimmyFortune 6 79+
(Luca Cumani) *hld up bhd ldrs: pushed along and hdwy over 2f out: ldng whn drifted lft ent fnl f: kpt on wl: readily* 11/4[3]
23 2 1 3/4 **Chalky (IRE)**[24] 5712 3-9-0 0 FergusSweeney 4 72
(Martyn Meade) *little slowly away: sn trcking ldrs: rdn 2f out: ev ch ent fnl f: kpt on but nt pce of wnr* 5/2[2]
3 3/4 **Holiday Girl (IRE)**[141] 1739 3-9-0 85 CharlesBishop 3 70
(Eve Johnson Houghton) *trckd ldr: rdn 2f out: ev ch whn squeezed up ent fnl f: hld after but kpt on* 7/1
4 1 **Eastern (IRE)** 3-9-0 0 RobHornby 1 68+
(Andrew Balding) *trckd ldrs: rdn over 2f out: kpt on but nt ace to get on terms* 12/1
6-24 5 nk **Awfaa (IRE)**[24] 5712 3-9-0 80 DaneO'Neill 2 67
(Sir Michael Stoute) *led: rdn whn strly pressed 2f out: hdd ent fnl f: no ex* 15/8[1]
6 2 3/4 **Triple First** 3-9-0 0 SteveDrowne 5 60
(Seamus Mullins) *s.i.s: last but in tch: rdn over 2f out: nt pce to threaten* 66/1

1m 40.31s (-0.49) **Going Correction** -0.075s/f (Good)
**WFA** 3 from 4yo 6lb 6 Ran SP% **111.7**
Speed ratings (Par 100): **99,97,96,95,95 92**
CSF £9.95 TOTE £3.50: £1.80, £1.30; EX 9.70 Trifecta £40.30.
**Owner** P Stokes & S Krase **Bred** Juddmonte Farms Inc **Trained** Newmarket, Suffolk

**FOCUS**
An ordinary maiden but a likeable British debut from the winner.

## 6615 CRAPPER & SONS "HANDS AND HEELS" APPRENTICE H'CAP (PART OF THE RACING EXCELLENCE INITIATIVE) 5f 160y
4:40 (4:40) (Class 5) (0-70,71) 4-Y-O+ £4,690 (£1,395; £697; £348) Stalls Centre

Form RPR
136 1 **Oeil De Tigre (FR)**[14] 6099 6-9-6 **67** SophieRalston(3) 9 72
(Tony Carroll) *chsd ldrs: r.o wl ins fnl f: led fnl stride* 13/2
6543 2 hd **Showmethewayavrilo**[8] 6303 4-9-10 **68** KatherineGlenister 7 72
(Malcolm Saunders) *prom: led jst ins fnl f: looked to be idling w ears pricked whn ct fnl stride* 11/4[1]
1023 3 3/4 **Burauq**[12] 6174 5-8-10 **54** oh3 (v) ManuelFernandes 8 56
(Milton Bradley) *chsd ldrs: rdn over 2f out: kpt on wl fnl 120yds: snatched 3rd fnl stride* 8/1
4011 4 shd **Jaganory (IRE)**[12] 6179 5-9-5 **63** (p) DavidEgan 3 65
(Christopher Mason) *prom: led over 2f out: hdd jst fnl f: no ex and lost 2 pls cl home* 4/1[2]
4445 5 3/4 **Entertaining Ben**[13] 6157 4-9-0 **61** (t[1]) DarraghKeenan(3) 5 60
(Amy Murphy) *chsd ldrs: rdn 2f out: no ex ins fnl f* 8/1
2066 6 1/2 **Swanton Blue (IRE)**[11] 6238 4-9-13 **71** FinleyMarsh 2 68
(Ed de Giles) *led tl over 2f out: sn rdn: one pce fnl f* 9/2[3]
5500 7 4 **Tally's Song**[3] 6502 4-8-10 **54** oh5 (p) WilliamCox 4 38
(Grace Harris) *hld up bhd ldrs: rdn over 2f out: little imp: wknd ins fnl f* 25/1
5535 8 1 **Essaka (IRE)**[12] 6174 5-8-10 **54** oh2 AledBeech 1 35
(Tony Carroll) *hld up bhd ldrs: rdn over 2f out: nt pce to get on terms: wknd fnl f* 14/1
6604 9 11 **Ambitious Boy**[20] 5892 8-8-10 **54** oh9 GabrieleMalune 6
(John O'Shea) *dwlt bdly: a bhd* 16/1

1m 11.38s (0.18) **Going Correction** -0.075s/f (Good) 9 Ran SP% **116.8**
Speed ratings (Par 103): **95,94,93,93,92 91,86,85,70**
CSF £25.04 CT £135.84 TOTE £8.10: £2.20, £2.40, £2.30; EX 31.40 Trifecta £299.60.
**Owner** A W Carroll **Bred** Jedburgh Stud & Madame Clody Norton **Trained** Cropthorne, Worcs

**FOCUS**
Reasonable enough form for the level.
T/Plt: £105.80 to a £1 stake. Pool: £63,443.78. 437.35 winning units. T/Qpdt: £7.50 to a £1 stake. Pool: £5,720.29. 562.96 winning units. **Tim Mitchell**

# 6021 CHELMSFORD (A.W) (L-H)
Thursday, August 31

**OFFICIAL GOING: Polytrack: standard**
Wind: virtually nil Weather: mostly fine, shower between races 5 and 6

## 6616 EAST COAST IPA NOVICE STKS (PLUS 10 RACE) 1m (P)
1:20 (1:23) (Class 3) 2-Y-O £12,291 (£3,657; £1,827; £913) Stalls Low

Form RPR
4 1 **Chilean**[20] 5887 2-9-2 0 OisinMurphy 1 83
(Martyn Meade) *trckd ldrs: swtchd lft and effrt on inner over 1f out: squeezed through ins fnl f to ld 100yds out: styd on wl to draw away towards fin: rdn out* 11/4[2]
5 2 1 1/4 **Kind Act (USA)**[13] 6142 2-9-2 0 JamesDoyle 2 80
(Charlie Appleby) *led: pushed along ent fnl 2f: rdn wl over 1f out: drvn 1f out: hdd 100yds out: no ex and kpt on same pce after* 5/2[1]
2 3 1 1/4 **Rua Augusta (USA)**[20] 5876 2-9-2 0 KevinStott 4 77
(Kevin Ryan) *t.k.h: pressed ldr: pushed along ent fnl 2f: ev ch and rdn wl over 1f out tl no ex ins fnl f: outpcd fnl 100yds* 5/2[1]
0 4 3 1/4 **To Arms (USA)**[14] 6108 2-9-2 0 RyanMoore 5 70
(John Gosden) *wl in tch in midfield: rdn over 3f out: outpcd u.p over 2f out: no threat to ldng trio and kpt on same pce fr over 1f out* 7/1[3]
1 5 hd **Austrian School (IRE)**[12] 6204 2-9-7 0 FrannyNorton 6 74
(Mark Johnston) *niggled along leaving stalls: in tch in last pair: effrt on outer wl over 2f out: sn outpcd and drvn: wl hld and kpt on same pce fr over 1f out* 7/1[3]
5 6 7 **Ashington**[23] 5743 2-9-2 0 LukeMorris 3 53
(Luca Cumani) *sn stdd to rr: in tch: rdn ent fnl 2f: sn struggling and outpcd: wknd fnl f* 33/1

1m 38.4s (-1.50) **Going Correction** -0.05s/f (Stan) 6 Ran SP% **111.8**
Speed ratings (Par 98): **105,103,102,99,99 92**
CSF £9.96 TOTE £3.50: £1.70, £1.40; EX 11.50 Trifecta £24.40.
**Owner** Sefton Lodge (Thoroughbred Racing) **Bred** Ed's Stud Ltd **Trained** Newmarket, Suffolk

**FOCUS**
A good battle between the first three in this fair maiden. The third has been rated a bit below his debut effort.

## 6617 OLD SPECKLED HEN H'CAP 1m (P)
1:50 (1:51) (Class 4) (0-85,87) 3-Y-O+ £5,246 (£5,246; £1,202; £601) Stalls Low

Form RPR
4612 1 **Almoreb (IRE)**[21] 5849 3-9-8 **87** JimCrowley 5 98
(Richard Hannon) *hld up in tch in midfield: nt clr run 2f out tl swtchd sharply lft 1f out: hdwy to chse wnr ins fnl f: r.o strly to join ldr on post* 7/2[3]
116 1 dht **Golden Goal (IRE)**[16] 6026 3-9-0 **84** PaddyBradley(5) 8 95
(Saeed bin Suroor) *hld up in tch: effrt and bmpd over 1f out: hdwy u.p to ld ent fnl f: kpt on but jnd on post* 10/3[2]
1-55 3 2 1/4 **Omeros**[50] 4763 3-9-3 **82** JamesDoyle 1 88
(Hugo Palmer) *chsd ldrs: effrt wl over 1f out: hdwy to chse wnr and drvn ent fnl f: lost 2nd and styd on same pce wl ins fnl f* 2/1[1]
5261 4 1 **Fayez (IRE)**[13] 6158 3-9-3 **82** DavidProbert 7 86
(David O'Meara) *hld up in tch in last trio: effrt on outer over 1f out: hdwy 1f out: kpt on ins fnl f wout threatening ldrs* 12/1
1000 5 2 3/4 **Flashy Snapper**[23] 5744 3-9-5 **84** RyanPowell 4 84+
(Simon Crisford) *hld up in tch in last trio: effrt on inner and sme hdwy whn bdly hmpd and snatched up 1f out: rallied and styd on ins fnl f: no threat to ldrs* 12/1
0502 6 1 **Pendo**[22] 5788 6-9-7 **80** KierenFox 9 76
(John Best) *taken down early: in tch in last trio: pushed along over 3f out: drvn and swtchd rt over 1f out: kpt on but no threat to ldrs ins fnl f* 20/1
6210 7 1 3/4 **Armandihan (IRE)**[33] 5400 3-9-2 **81** (p) KevinStott 6 72
(Kevin Ryan) *bustled along leaving stalls: sn pressing ldr tl rdn to ld 2f out: drvn and hdd ent fnl f: sn btn and wknd ins fnl f* 16/1
5600 8 nse **Gambit**[23] 5744 4-9-7 **80** (v[1]) MartinHarley 2 72
(Tom Dascombe) *bustled along leaving stalls: hld up in tch in midfield: rdn over 1f out: sn struggling and losing pl u.p 1f out: wknd ins fnl f* 20/1
6621 9 4 1/2 **London (FR)**[154] 1450 4-9-7 **80** DannyBrock 3 61
(Phil McEntee) *led: hdd and rdn 2f out: struggling whn squeezed for room jst over 1f out: sn wknd* 20/1
121 10 19 **Honiara**[21] 5821 4-9-13 **86** (b) LukeMorris 10 24
(Paul Cole) *chsd ldng pair: rdn over 2f out: edgd rt and bmpd rival over 1f out: sn btn: bhd and eased ins fnl f* 14/1

1m 37.91s (-1.99) **Going Correction** -0.05s/f (Stan)
**WFA** 3 from 4yo+ 6lb 10 Ran SP% **120.9**
Speed ratings (Par 105): **107,107,104,103,101 100,98,98,93,74**
WIN: GG 2.10, A 2.20; PL: GG 1.80, A 1.30, O 1.30; EX: GG-A 7.50, A-GG 8.20; CSF: GG-A 7.79; A-GG 7.87; TC: GG-A-O 14.14, A-GG-O 14.28; TF: GG-A-O 24.00; A-GG-O 24.30.
**Owner** Godolphin **Bred** Yeomanstown Stud **Trained** Newmarket, Suffolk
**Owner** Hamdan Al Maktoum **Bred** Stowell Park Stud **Trained** East Everleigh, Wilts
■ Stewards' Enquiry : Jim Crowley 2 day ban: guilty of careless riding in that he switched left-handed when not sufficiently clear (14/15 Sep)

**FOCUS**
The dead-heaters both had things go against them but finished clear of the rest and look progressive. The race set up for those ridden with some patience.

## 6618 ABBOT ALE H'CAP 2m (P)
2:20 (2:22) (Class 5) (0-75,78) 3-Y-O+ £5,175 (£1,540; £769; £384) Stalls Low

Form RPR
5434 1 **Mister Bob (GER)**[19] 5951 8-9-13 **74** (p) TedDurcan 5 82
(James Bethell) *stdd s: hld up in tch in last pair: clsd and travelling wl over 2f out: swtchd rt and effrt over 1f out: rdn to chal 1f out: led ins fnl f: styd on wl* 16/1
-311 2 nk **Piedita (IRE)**[10] 6259 3-9-5 **78** 6ex LukeMorris 7 86
(Sir Mark Prescott Bt) *wl in tch in midfield: rdn over 3f out: hdwy to press ldr ent fnl 2f: rdn to ld over 1f out: sn hrd pressed: drvn: hdd and kpt on same pce ins fnl f* 11/10[1]
0222 3 5 **Taper Tantrum (IRE)**[14] 6090 5-10-0 **75** (p) RyanMoore 2 76
(Michael Bell) *trckd ldrs: n.m.r over 2f out: gap opened and effrt on inner to chse ldrs over 1f out: little rspnse to press and btn 1f out: wknd ins fnl f* 3/1[2]
146 4 2 **Conkering Hero (IRE)**[19] 5932 3-9-0 **73** OisinMurphy 6 72
(Joseph Tuite) *chsd ldr: rdn 4f out: lost 2nd and struggling to qckn over 2f out: outpcd and btn over 1f out: wknd ins fnl f* 14/1[3]

2145 **5** 3/4 **Bracken Brae**[50] 4762 5-9-13 **74** JoeyHaynes 8 71
(Mark H Tompkins) *stdd and dropped in bhd after s: hld up in tch in last pair: clsd over 2f out: swtchd rt and effrt u.p over 1f out: no imp and sn outpcd* **25/1**

0601 **6** 3 3/4 **Dukinta (IRE)**[22] 5780 3-9-3 **76** (v) FranBerry 4 71
(Hugo Palmer) *led: rdn ent fnl 2f out: hdd and outpcd over 1f out: wknd fnl f* **3/1**[2]

3m 30.16s (0.16) **Going Correction** -0.05s/f (Stan)
**WFA** 3 from 5yo+ 12lb **6** Ran SP% **114.0**
Speed ratings (Par 103): **97,96,94,93,92 91**
CSF £35.38 CT £71.87 TOTE £11.70: £3.60, £1.20; EX 46.70 Trifecta £111.00.
**Owner** Robert Gibbons Partnership **Bred** Newsells Park Stud Ltd **Trained** Middleham Moor, N Yorks

**FOCUS**
A tight staying handicap where the action unfolded late and and two pulled clear up the middle.

## 6619 GREENE KING IPA CHARLOTTE FILLIES' CONDITIONS STKS 7f (P)
2:50 (2:53) (Class 2) 3-Y-O+
£28,012 (£8,388; £4,194; £2,097; £1,048; £526) Stalls Low

Form RPR

2-42 **1** **Aljuljalah (USA)**[54] 4617 4-9-5 **98** AndreaAtzeni 8 90+
(Roger Varian) *stdd s: hld up in tch in rr: shkn up ent fnl 2f: swtchd rt and rdn over 1f out: hdwy 1f out: str run ins fnl f to ld towards fin* **10/3**[2]

2011 **2** 3/4 **Bumptious**[22] 5789 4-9-5 **77** (p) SeanLevey 6 88
(Ismail Mohammed) *chsd ldr over 5f out: rdn to chal over 1f out: led and edgd lft u.p ins fnl f: hdd and no ex towards fin* **25/1**

3054 **3** 1 1/4 **Zest (IRE)**[40] 5152 4-9-5 **96** (v) GeorgeWood 1 85
(James Fanshawe) *t.k.h: chsd ldr for over 1f: styd chsng ldrs: shkn up over 1f out: sn drvn and kpt on same pce ins fnl f* **8/1**

3113 **4** nse **Raven's Lady**[11] 6234 3-9-0 **95** RyanMoore 2 82
(Marco Botti) *t.k.h: hld up wl in tch in 4th: effrt over 1f out: sn drvn: kpt on same pce ins fnl f* **10/11**[1]

2612 **5** 1/2 **Dusky Maid (IRE)**[17] 6015 3-9-0 **78** FrannyNorton 7 81
(James Given) *sn led and grad crossed to inner rail: set stdy gallop: rdn wl over 1f out: hdd and jostled ins fnl f: no ex and wknd wl ins fnl f* **25/1**

4-64 **6** 1 **Castleacre**[94] 3159 3-9-0 **91** (h[1]) MartinHarley 5 78
(James Tate) *stdd s: t.k.h: hld up in tch in last trio: effrt over 1f out: sn drvn and kpt on same pce ins fnl f: nvr trbld ldrs* **7/1**[3]

63-5 **7** nk **Belle Meade (IRE)**[19] 5916 3-9-0 **91** DavidProbert 3 78
(Andrew Balding) *hld up in tch towards rr: effrt and swtchd rt over 1f out: drvn ent fnl f: styd on same pce: nvr trbld ldrs* **10/1**

1m 26.0s (-1.20) **Going Correction** -0.05s/f (Stan)
**WFA** 3 from 4yo 5lb **7** Ran SP% **115.9**
Speed ratings (Par 96): **104,103,101,101,101 99,99**
CSF £74.50 TOTE £4.10: £1.80, £6.90; EX 50.20 Trifecta £224.90.
**Owner** Salem Rashid **Bred** Audley Farm Equine **Trained** Newmarket, Suffolk

**FOCUS**
This was steadily run and several failed to settle.

## 6620 OLD GOLDEN HEN H'CAP 7f (P)
3:20 (3:24) (Class 5) (0-70,72) 3-Y-O+ £5,175 (£1,540; £769; £384) Stalls Low

Form RPR

1243 **1** **Siege Of Boston (IRE)**[72] 3949 4-10-2 **71** (t) JFEgan 3 79
(John Butler) *t.k.h: hld up in tch in midfield: swtchd rt over 1f out: hdwy u.p 1f out: styd on strly to ld on post* **9/2**[2]

2116 **2** nse **Cainhoe Star**[34] 5363 4-10-0 **69** LukeMorris 6 77
(Anthony Carson) *wl in tch in midfield: effrt over 1f out: drvn to chse ldr 1f out: styd on u.p to ld last strides: hdd on post* **9/2**[2]

1162 **3** hd **Murdanova (IRE)**[108] 2676 4-10-2 **71** DannyBrock 1 78+
(Denis Quinn) *trckd ldr tl over 2f out: wnt 2nd again and shkn up wl over 1f out: rdn to ld over 1f out: drvn 1f out: kpt on u.p tl hdd and lost 2 pls last strides* **33/1**

4406 **4** 2 **Widnes**[43] 5039 3-9-2 **67** (b) JoshuaBryan[(5)] 11 67
(Alan Bailey) *s.i.s: in tch in rr: swtchd rt and hdwy over 1f out: hdwy ins fnl f: styd on strly fnl 100yds: nt rch ldrs* **16/1**

60-2 **5** hd **Sentinel**[229] 245 3-9-1 **61** StevieDonohoe 8 61+
(Charlie Fellowes) *hld up in tch in midfield: nt clr run and shuffled bk wl over 1f out: rdn and hdwy ent fnl f: styd on wl fnl 100yds: nvr trbld ldrs* **8/1**

11-3 **6** 3/4 **Medicean El Diablo**[49] 4810 4-9-12 **67** KieranO'Neill 4 66
(Jimmy Fox) *hld up in tch in midfield: effrt u.p over 1f out: unable qck 1f out: styd on same pce ins fnl f* **4/1**[1]

6000 **7** 1 **Choral Clan (IRE)**[24] 5718 6-10-2 **71** OisinMurphy 10 68+
(Brendan Powell) *hld up in last pair: swtchd lft and effrt 1f out: hdwy ins fnl f: styd on wl fnl 100yds: nvr trbld ldrs* **33/1**

243 **8** nk **Major Crispies**[11] 6237 6-10-2 **71** (bt) JamesDoyle 9 67
(David O'Meara) *hld up in tch towards rr: swtchd rt and effrt over 1f out: rdn and kpt on ins fnl f: nvr trbld ldrs* **7/1**[3]

2054 **9** hd **Toy Theatre**[33] 5400 3-9-12 **72** TomQueally 13 65
(Michael Appleby) *chsd ldrs on outer: wnt 2nd over 2f out tl rdn and unable qck wl over 1f out: wknd ins fnl f* **12/1**

2210 **10** 1/2 **Isntshesomething**[94] 3139 5-9-2 **57** (v) FrannyNorton 12 51
(Richard Guest) *led: rdn and hdd over 1f out: wknd ins fnl f* **20/1**

3060 **11** 1 1/4 **Rita's Man (IRE)**[13] 6139 3-9-12 **72** SeanLevey 7 61
(Richard Hannon) *hld up in tch in midfield: effrt over 1f out: unable qck and styd on same pce ins fnl f* **16/1**

0400 **12** nk **Porto Ferro (IRE)**[28] 5558 3-9-0 **60** (b[1]) MartinLane 5 48
(Dr Jon Scargill) *s.i.s: in tch towards rr: rdn 3f out: no imp u.p over 1f out: wknd ins fnl f* **25/1**

3016 **13** shd **Alfonso Manana (IRE)**[23] 5759 3-9-7 **67** (b) FranBerry 2 55
(James Given) *t.k.h: hld up in tch in midfield: rdn over 1f out: keeping on same pce and hld whn nt clr run ins fnl f: eased wl ins fnl f* **20/1**

060 **14** 11 **Red Gunner**[22] 5797 3-9-11 **71** MartinHarley 14 29
(David O'Meara) *chsd ldrs on outer: rdn over 2f out: lost pl and bhd 1f out: eased wl ins fnl f* **10/1**

1m 26.46s (-0.74) **Going Correction** -0.05s/f (Stan)
**WFA** 3 from 4yo+ 5lb **14** Ran SP% **127.8**
Speed ratings (Par 103): **102,101,101,99,99 98,97,96,96,96 94,94,94,81**
CSF £24.88 CT £621.08 TOTE £5.30: £1.90, £2.20, £5.90; EX 30.10 Trifecta £564.30.
**Owner** Mark McKay **Bred** Willie McKay **Trained** Newmarket, Suffolk
■ Stewards' Enquiry : Danny Brock 2 day ban: used his whip with his arm above shoulder height (15/17 Sep)

**FOCUS**
A competitive handicap.

## 6621 LONDON GLORY H'CAP (DIV I) 1m 2f (P)
3:50 (3:57) (Class 6) (0-55,57) 3-Y-O+ £3,234 (£962; £481; £240) Stalls Low

Form RPR

5052 **1** **The Juggler**[21] 5850 4-8-13 **47** (v) MartinLane 4 60
(William Knight) *taken down early: led for 2f: trckd ldr tl rdn to ld again over 1f out: sn in command and drew wl clr ins fnl f: easily* **7/4**[1]

0103 **2** 7 **Just Fab (IRE)**[24] 5714 4-9-0 **53** (b) PaddyBradley[(5)] 1 53
(Lee Carter) *hld up in tch in midfield: effrt over 2f out: 4th 2f out: no ch w wnr: kpt on same pce ins fnl f to go 2nd towards fin* **6/1**[2]

0600 **3** 1 **Master Of Heaven**[22] 5790 4-9-5 **53** (p) DavidProbert 9 51
(Jim Boyle) *midfield tl hdwy to ld after 2f: rdn ent fnl 2f: hdd over 1f out: sn outpcd: wknd ins fnl f: lost 2nd towards fin* **8/1**

-004 **4** 1 1/4 **Understory (USA)**[161] 1322 10-8-12 **46** oh1 LukeMorris 2 41
(Tim McCarthy) *trckd ldrs: shkn up 2f out: sn rdn and outpcd: no ch w wnr and kpt on same pce ins fnl f* **20/1**

3046 **5** 1 1/2 **The Dukkerer (IRE)**[20] 5898 6-9-9 **57** TomQueally 8 50
(James Given) *chsd ldrs: rdn 3f out: drvn and outpcd over 1f out: no ch w wnr and kpt on same pce ins fnl f* **10/1**

-000 **6** 1 **Lady Nahema (IRE)**[35] 5336 4-9-0 **51** GeorgeWood[(3)] 5 42
(Martin Bosley) *in tch in midfield: rdn over 2f out: unable qck and no hdwy over 1f out: no ch fnl f* **7/1**[3]

2-00 **7** shd **Lulu The Rocket**[21] 5846 3-8-11 **55** (h[1]) TimClark[(3)] 3 46
(John Butler) *hld up towards rr: effrt and sme hdwy whn drifted lft over 1f out: kpt on ins fnl f: nvr trbld ldrs* **10/1**

0006 **8** 3/4 **Jump Around**[21] 5823 3-8-5 **46** oh1 (t) KieranO'Neill 7 36
(Ali Stronge) *wnt rt leaving stalls and bustled along early: swtchd lft and hdwy into midfield after 1f: rdn and unable qck over 2f out: wknd over 1f out* **14/1**

00-0 **9** 3 1/4 **Charlie Chaplin (GER)**[30] 5511 3-8-12 **53** (t[1]) PaoloSirigu 6 37
(Robert Eddery) *a in last trio: struggling u.p over 2f out: sn wl btn* **16/1**

5005 **10** shd **Kyshoni (IRE)**[21] 5853 3-9-2 **57** AntonioFresu 11 41
(Mike Murphy) *wnt sharply lft sn after s: in tch in last trio: effrt wl over 1f out: sn btn and wknd* **50/1**

0000 **11** 3 1/4 **Cookie Ring (IRE)**[37] 5239 6-8-5 **46** oh1 PaulaMuir[(7)] 12 23
(Patrick Holmes) *s.i.s: t.k.h: hld up in tch in rr: effrt wl over 1f out: no hdwy and sn wknd* **25/1**

0063 **12** 1 3/4 **Ripper Street (IRE)**[21] 5854 3-8-1 **47** JaneElliott[(5)] 10 21
(Christine Dunnett) *hld up in tch in midfield :hung rt: lost pl and rdn 2f out: sn dropped to rr: bhd fnl f* **8/1**

2m 6.89s (-1.71) **Going Correction** -0.05s/f (Stan)
**WFA** 3 from 4yo+ 7lb **12** Ran SP% **126.7**
Speed ratings (Par 101): **104,98,97,96,95 94,94,93,91,91 88,87**
CSF £12.75 CT £74.11 TOTE £2.50: £1.10, £2.50, £3.20; EX 14.30 Trifecta £82.40.
**Owner** Mrs Susie Hartley **Bred** Miss K Rausing **Trained** Patching, W Sussex

**FOCUS**
The market got it spot on, with the well-backed winner running away with the race having always been prominent and very little getting into it from behind. The winner has been rated back near his best, and the fourth near his better recent form.

## 6622 LONDON GLORY H'CAP (DIV II) 1m 2f (P)
4:20 (4:26) (Class 6) (0-55,58) 3-Y-O+ £3,234 (£962; £481; £240) Stalls Low

Form RPR

0-43 **1** **Chilli Jam**[8] 6306 4-9-5 **53** (p) LiamKeniry 13 61
(Ed de Giles) *midfield: effrt 4f out: chsd clr ldng trio over 2f out: styd on steadily to chse clr but tiring ldr 150yds out: kpt on to ld wl ins fnl f: sn clr* **4/1**[2]

4460 **2** 2 3/4 **Tommy's Secret**[14] 6112 7-9-2 **50** (p) MartinHarley 6 53
(Jane Chapple-Hyam) *sn bhd: swtchd to outer and last 1/2-way: hdwy over 2f out but stl plenty to do: styd on wl ins fnl f: wnt 2nd nr fin: nvr getting to wnr* **7/2**[1]

400 **3** 1/2 **Avocet (USA)**[45] 4967 4-8-5 **46** MillyNaseb[(7)] 14 49
(Julia Feilden) *bustled along and swtchd lft after s: hld up off the pce in last quintet: effrt and nt clr run over 1f out: hdwy jst over 1f out: styd on ins fnl f: wnt 3rd cl home: nvr getting to wnr* **33/1**

3050 **4** 1 **Dukes Meadow**[22] 5790 6-8-9 **50** RhiainIngram[(7)] 4 50+
(Roger Ingram) *chsd ldr: wnt clr w ldr 5f out: pushed into ld 2f out: rdn over 1f out: tired and hdd wl ins fnl f: wknd and lost 2 pls nr fin* **16/1**

5524 **5** 4 1/2 **Rocksette**[10] 6257 3-8-7 **48** DavidProbert 2 40
(Philip Hide) *chsd ldrs: 3rd and clr of field 5f out: effrt u.p jst over 2f out: no imp and btn over 1f out: wknd ins fnl f* **9/2**[3]

0045 **6** 1 1/4 **Dor's Law**[9] 6296 4-9-4 **55** JackDuern[(3)] 1 44+
(Dean Ivory) *led: wnt clr w rival 1/2-way: hdd 2f out: sn u.p and outpcd: lost 2nd and wknd fnl 150yds* **10/1**

0605 **7** 1 3/4 **First Summer**[43] 3221 5-9-3 **54** (p) GeorgeWood[(3)] 3 40
(Shaun Harris) *midfield: rdn 4f out: nvr on terms w ldrs after: wl btn over 1f out* **13/2**

055- **8** 3 1/4 **Master Of Song**[245] 8567 10-8-8 **47** (p) KevinLundie[(5)] 9 27
(Roy Bowring) *hld up off the pce in last quintet: n.d* **33/1**

0004 **9** 2 3/4 **Seventii**[22] 5787 3-8-5 **46** PaoloSirigu 10 21
(Robert Eddery) *chsd ldrs tl lost pl 1/2-way: sn drvn and outpcd by ldrs: no ch after: wknd 2f out* **10/1**

5560 **10** 1 1/4 **Street Art (IRE)**[22] 5790 5-9-5 **53** (bt) ShaneKelly 5 25
(Mike Murphy) *awkward leaving stalls and s.i.s: hld up off the pce in last quintet: effrt on outer bnd 2f out: n.d* **20/1**

0-06 **11** 5 **Yorkshire Star (IRE)**[7] 6342 3-8-2 **46** oh1 (p[1]) NoelGarbutt[(3)] 8 9
(Bill Turner) *midfield tl rdn and dropped to last quintet over 7f out: nvr travelling wl and n.d after: wl bhd and eased ins fnl f* **25/1**

6400 **12** 4 1/2 **Stragar**[92] 3220 3-8-12 **53** LukeMorris 12 8
(Michael Appleby) *midfield: rdn over 4f out: wnt prom in main gp but no ch w ldrs over 3f out: lost pl and bhd over 1f out: eased ins fnl f* **20/1**

2005 **13** 25 **Cahar Fad (IRE)**[91] 3264 5-9-1 **49** (bt) OisinMurphy 11
(Steph Hollinshead) *rousted along leaving stalls: chsd ldrs after 1f out tl outpcd u.p over 4f out: bhd and eased over 1f out: t.o* **14/1**

2m 7.65s (-0.95) **Going Correction** -0.05s/f (Stan)
**WFA** 3 from 4yo+ 7lb **13** Ran SP% **123.7**
Speed ratings (Par 101): **101,98,98,97,94 93,91,89,86,85 81,78,58**
CSF £17.69 CT £414.53 TOTE £4.80: £1.80, £1.80, £5.80; EX 17.40 Trifecta £521.60.
**Owner** Moukey Ltd & Partner **Bred** G S Bishop **Trained** Ledbury, H'fords

**FOCUS**
They went a strong gallop here and the race played into the hands of the closers. It was the slower of the two divisions by 0.76sec. The winner has been rated as building slightly on his Bath form.

## 6623 OKTOBERFEST HERE ON 13TH OCTOBER MAIDEN STKS 1m 5f 66y(P)
**4:50** (4:52) (Class 5) 3-Y-O+ **£5,175** (£1,540; £769; £384) **Stalls** Low

Form RPR

1 **Mobbhij** 3-9-5 0 ... OisinMurphy 7 85+
(Saeed bin Suroor) *rn green: s.i.s: hld up in rr: wnt lft after 1f: nt clr run 3f out: hdwy into 3rd but plenty to do over 1f out: chsd clr ldr ins fnl f: rn green and hung lft u.p: str run to ld nr fin* **11/8**[1]

2264 2 ½ **Sileel (USA)**[24] 5707 3-9-0 74 ... (v) JamesDoyle 3 74
(Ed Dunlop) *led: rdn and qcknd clr w rival over 2f out: clr over 1f out: kpt on steadily u.p: hdd and no ex nr fin* **9/2**[3]

032- 3 2 ¼ **Stanley**[303] 7753 4-10-0 77 ... ShaneKelly 6 76
(Richard Hughes) *hld up in last trio: nt clr run 2f out: hdwy into 4th and jst bhd wnr but stl plenty to do over 1f out: styd on steadily ins fnl f: wnt 3rd towards fin* **7/2**[2]

3 4 ½ **Nelson's Touch**[20] 5894 4-10-0 0 ... FranBerry 5 75
(Denis Coakley) *sn chsng ldr: clsd to join ldr and rdn clr 3f out: sn drvn: outpcd and btn over 1f out: lost 2nd and kpt on same pce ins fnl f* **6/1**

00- 5 8 **Fortia**[294] 7885 3-9-0 0 ... FrannyNorton 2 59
(Dean Ivory) *chsd ldrs: rdn and outpcd 3f out: lost 3rd and wl btn over 1f out: wknd fnl f* **50/1**

4336 6 6 **Second Page**[23] 5753 3-8-12 75 ... (p) RossaRyan(7) 8 56
(Richard Hannon) *t.k.h: hld up in tch in midfield: rdn 3f out: sn struggling and bhd 2f out* **8/1**

62 7 nk **Bumble Bay**[13] 6129 7-10-0 0 ... (t) LiamKeniry 4 55
(Robert Stephens) *hld up in last pair: sme hdwy on inner over 3f out: no hdwy u.p over 2f out: wknd over 1f out* **50/1**

04-6 8 20 **Caracas**[223] 328 3-9-5 71 ... LukeMorris 1 27
(Harry Dunlop) *in tch in midfield: rdn over 3f out: sn struggling: dropped to rr and lost tch over 1f out: eased ins fnl f* **25/1**

2m 53.04s (-0.56) **Going Correction** -0.05s/f (Stan)
**WFA** 3 from 4yo+ 9lb 8 Ran SP% **115.7**
Speed ratings (Par 103): **99,98,97,97,92 88,88,75**
CSF £7.94 TOTE £2.00: £1.10, £1.40, £1.80; EX 8.00 Trifecta £23.00.
**Owner** Godolphin **Bred** Darley **Trained** Newmarket, Suffolk

**FOCUS**
A fair maiden.
T/Jkpt: Not won. T/Plt: £64.40 to a £1 stake. Pool: £57,946.14. 656.41 winning units. T/Qpdt: £18.80 to a £1 stake. Pool: £5,041.66. 197.90 winning units. **Steve Payne**

# 6590 MUSSELBURGH (R-H)
Thursday, August 31

**OFFICIAL GOING: Good to firm (7.1)**
Wind: Slight, half behind in over 3f of home straight Weather: Cloudy, dry

## 6624 WITHERBYS NOVICE AUCTION STKS 5f 1y
**1:30** (1:30) (Class 6) 2-Y-O **£2,587** (£770; £384; £192) **Stalls** High

Form RPR

2 1 **Debawtry (IRE)**[14] 6086 2-8-12 0 ow1 ... PhillipMakin 6 68+
(David O'Meara) *in tch: effrt and chsng ldr whn nt clr run over 1f out: rallied and led ins fnl f: r.o wl* **4/7**[1]

0140 2 nk **Brandy Station (IRE)**[8] 6330 2-9-9 79 ... BarryMcHugh 3 76
(Tony Coyle) *t.k.h: led and sn crossed to stands' rail: hung rt 1/2-way: sn corrected: rdn over 1f out: hdd ins fnl f: kpt on* **5/2**[2]

0 3 2 ¾ **Pavarella Shoes**[15] 6056 2-8-11 0 ... PatrickMathers 2 54
(Noel Wilson) *dwlt: sn chsng ldrs: effrt and drvn along 2f out: kpt on same pce fnl f* **50/1**

04 4 3 ½ **Sitsi**[17] 5998 2-8-11 0 ... PaulMulrennan 4 42
(Bryan Smart) *t.k.h: carried lft sn after s: chsd wnr to over 1f out: wknd fnl f* **6/1**[3]

59.8s (-0.60) **Going Correction** -0.20s/f (Firm) 4 Ran SP% **108.5**
Speed ratings (Par 92): **96,95,91,85**
CSF £2.28 TOTE £1.30; EX 2.00 Trifecta £7.80.
**Owner** P Sutherland **Bred** Hugh O'Brien & Michael McCallan **Trained** Upper Helmsley, N Yorks
■ Stewards' Enquiry : Barry McHugh caution: guilty of careless riding

**FOCUS**
All distances as advertised. An ordinary little juvenile novice sprint. They went a decent gallop on good to firm ground. The runner-up has been rated roughly to his pre-race mark.

## 6625 ADDLESHAW GODDARD LLP NURSERY H'CAP (DIV I) 7f 33y
**2:00** (2:01) (Class 6) (0-65,66) 2-Y-O **£2,587** (£770; £384; £192) **Stalls** Low

Form RPR

3113 1 **Placebo Effect (IRE)**[16] 6043 2-9-5 63 ... AndrewMullen 10 67
(Ollie Pears) *hld up midfield: effrt and rdn over 1f out: chsng ldrs whn nt clr run over 1f out: swtchd rt and led ins fnl f: r.o wl* **4/1**[1]

0004 2 1 ¼ **Ray Purchase**[20] 5878 2-8-4 48 ... JoeDoyle 11 49
(Keith Dalgleish) *t.k.h: w ldr: led over 3f out: rdn and hrd pressed over 2f out: hdd ins fnl f: kpt on same pce* **7/1**[3]

403 3 1 ¼ **Burnieboozle (IRE)**[23] 5735 2-9-8 66 ... JasonHart 4 64
(John Quinn) *prom: effrt and rdn over 2f out: kpt on same pce ins fnl f* **4/1**[1]

5000 4 ¾ **Ladycammyofclare (IRE)**[20] 5878 2-8-3 47 ... JoeFanning 2 43
(Mark Johnston) *chsd ldrs: effrt and ev ch over 2f out: edgd rt over 1f out: sn no ex* **25/1**

43P1 5 ½ **Society's Dream (IRE)**[19] 5945 2-8-9 53 ... RoystonFfrench 8 50
(K R Burke) *hld up: rdn and hdwy over 2f out: no imp over 1f out* **12/1**

4405 6 5 **Archie Perkins (IRE)**[20] 5878 2-9-2 60 ... TomEaves 6 41
(Nigel Tinkler) *hld up: rdn over 2f out: wknd wl over 1f out* **14/1**

043 7 ½ **Cuillin Hills**[31] 5465 2-9-2 65 ... RowanScott(5) 5 45
(Keith Dalgleish) *s.i.s: hld up: rdn over 2f out: sn btn* **10/1**

064 8 2 ¾ **Mountain Approach (IRE)**[23] 5735 2-9-4 62 ... (b[1]) PaulHanagan 3 35
(Richard Fahey) *t.k.h: hld up in tch: drvn and outpcd over 2f out: sn btn* **9/2**[2]

504 9 2 ¾ **Situation**[23] 5752 2-9-6 64 ... ConnorBeasley 9 30
(Richard Guest) *led to over 3f out: rallied: wknd over 1f out* **10/1**

003 10 13 **Hamba Moyo (IRE)**[39] 5180 2-9-0 58 ... (b) DavidAllan 1
(Tim Easterby) *s.i.s: hld up: drvn and struggling over 3f out: sn wknd* **20/1**

1m 28.16s (-0.84) **Going Correction** -0.20s/f (Firm) 10 Ran SP% **111.8**
Speed ratings (Par 92): **96,94,93,92,91 86,85,82,79,64**
CSF £30.59 CT £118.44 TOTE £3.60: £1.30, £2.50, £1.70; EX 25.30 Trifecta £104.30.
**Owner** Timothy O'Gram, Keith West & Ollie Pears **Bred** Hawaiian Dream Partnership **Trained** Norton, N Yorks

**FOCUS**
The first division of a modest nursery handicap. They went a contested gallop and the two joint-favourites finished first and third. The form could possibly be a fraction better than rated.

## 6626 ADDLESHAW GODDARD LLP NURSERY H'CAP (DIV II) 7f 33y
**2:30** (2:31) (Class 6) (0-65,66) 2-Y-O **£2,587** (£770; £384; £192) **Stalls** Low

Form RPR

0261 1 **Kikini Bamalaam (IRE)**[20] 5878 2-9-2 60 ... ConnorBeasley 2 63
(Keith Dalgleish) *s.i.s: hld up: hdwy over 2f out: rdn and led ins fnl f: styd on wl* **10/3**[1]

6654 2 ¾ **Ventura Gold (IRE)**[40] 5143 2-9-5 66 ... AdamMcNamara(3) 10 67
(Richard Fahey) *trckd ldrs: effrt and drvn over 2f out: led over 1f out to ins fnl f: kpt on: hld nr fin* **10/1**

3440 3 2 **Here In The Dark**[14] 6087 2-9-7 65 ... (p[1]) GrahamLee 5 61
(Keith Dalgleish) *t.k.h: cl up: disp ld after 2f to over 1f out: rdn and kpt on same pce fnl f* **15/2**

640 4 1 ½ **Foxy Lady**[24] 5702 2-9-2 60 ... TomEaves 3 53+
(Kevin Ryan) *trckd ldrs: drvn and edgd lft over 1f out: rallied ins fnl f: nt pce to chal* **5/1**[3]

0500 5 1 ½ **I Am Dandy (IRE)**[13] 6154 2-8-1 52 ... JamieGormley(7) 6 40
(James Ewart) *hld up: drvn along over 2f out: kpt on fnl f: nvr able to chal* **28/1**

454 6 ½ **Ryedale Encore**[17] 5999 2-9-5 63 ... DavidAllan 9 50
(Tim Easterby) *led tl rdn and hdd over 1f out: wknd ins fnl f* **6/1**

502 7 shd **Claramara (IRE)**[16] 6042 2-9-7 65 ... JoeFanning 8 51
(Mark Johnston) *in tch on outside: rdn and effrt over 2f out: wknd fnl f* **7/2**[2]

006 8 2 **Saxonroad Boy (USA)**[20] 5874 2-8-9 53 ... PaulHanagan 1 34
(Richard Fahey) *sn pushed along in rr: struggling over 3f out: nvr on terms* **11/1**

005 9 28 **Oriental Power**[20] 5879 2-8-3 47 ... JoeDoyle 7
(Jim Goldie) *in tch: rdn along and outpcd over 2f out: sn btn: t.o* **33/1**

1m 29.1s (0.10) **Going Correction** -0.20s/f (Firm) 9 Ran SP% **111.8**
Speed ratings (Par 92): **91,90,87,86,84 83,83,81,49**
CSF £35.25 CT £228.66 TOTE £3.50: £1.50, £2.90, £2.30; EX 42.10 Trifecta £510.00.
**Owner** Middleham Park Racing LXXXII **Bred** Vincent Hannon **Trained** Carluke, S Lanarks

**FOCUS**
The second division of a modest nursery handicap. The winning time was nearly a second slower off a respectable gallop. The first two have been rated as progressing.

## 6627 BROWN SHIPLEY H'CAP 7f 33y
**3:00** (3:00) (Class 4) (0-80,81) 3-Y-O **£6,469** (£1,925; £962; £481) **Stalls** Low

Form RPR

1255 1 **Raselasad (IRE)**[19] 5948 3-9-10 81 ... RoystonFfrench 2 92
(Tracy Waggott) *mde all: hrd pressed over 2f out: rdn and styd on strly fnl f* **6/4**[1]

4100 2 1 ¾ **Our Charlie Brown**[19] 5948 3-9-3 74 ... DavidAllan 5 80
(Tim Easterby) *pressed ldr: chal over 2f out: rdn over 1f out: sn one pce* **7/4**[2]

3150 3 2 ¾ **Inglorious**[8] 6315 3-8-5 67 ... (p) RowanScott(5) 1 66
(Keith Dalgleish) *s.i.s: sn pushed along in last pl: effrt on outside over 2f out: no imp fr over 1f out: eased whn hld towards fin* **13/2**

1016 4 3 ½ **The Stalking Moon (IRE)**[20] 5881 3-9-7 78 ... JasonHart 4 68
(John Quinn) *trckd ldrs: drvn along over 2f out: wknd over 1f out* **9/2**[3]

1m 26.68s (-2.32) **Going Correction** -0.20s/f (Firm) 4 Ran SP% **107.9**
Speed ratings (Par 102): **105,103,99,95**
CSF £4.41 TOTE £2.50; EX 4.40 Trifecta £7.80.
**Owner** David Tate **Bred** Shadwell Estate Company Limited **Trained** Spennymoor, Co Durham

**FOCUS**
A fairly decent little 3yo handicap. The favourite made all from the second favourite in a time only marginally above standard.

## 6628 DAM WEALTH MANAGEMENT FILLIES' H'CAP 1m 4f 104y
**3:30** (3:30) (Class 5) (0-75,77) 3-Y-O+ **£3,234** (£962; £481; £240) **Stalls** Low

Form RPR

3413 1 **Bonnie Arlene (IRE)**[17] 6002 3-9-2 72 ... JoeFanning 4 78
(Mark Johnston) *trckd ldr: led gng wl over 2f out: pushed along over 2f out: styd on strly fnl f* **2/1**[2]

0335 2 ¾ **Wor Lass**[8] 6317 9-9-9 75 ... RowanScott(5) 6 78
(Donald Whillans) *hld up in tch: hdwy to chse wnr over 2f out: rdn and edgd rt over 1f out: kpt on ins fnl f* **12/1**

1-55 3 3 ½ **Gold Chain (IRE)**[5] 5700 7-8-11 61 ... (p) PhilDennis(3) 3 58
(Dianne Sayer) *s.i.s: hld up: effrt and rdn over 2f out: no imp over 1f out* **14/1**

6-10 4 7 **Erinyes (IRE)**[26] 5658 3-9-7 77 ... (p[1]) PaulMulrennan 1 64
(Archie Watson) *t.k.h: cl up: rdn whn n.m.r over 2f out: edgd lft and wknd over 1f out* **1/1**[1]

1245 5 5 **Livella Fella (IRE)**[12] 6208 4-10-0 75 ... GrahamLee 5 53
(Keith Dalgleish) *led: rdn and reminder bnd after 3f: hdd over 2f out: sn wknd* **8/1**[3]

2m 41.37s (-0.63) **Going Correction** -0.20s/f (Firm)
**WFA** 3 from 4yo+ 9lb 5 Ran SP% **108.8**
Speed ratings (Par 100): **94,93,91,86,83**
CSF £21.92 TOTE £3.60: £2.30, £3.80; EX 18.70 Trifecta £73.90.
**Owner** Paul Dean **Bred** Tinnakill Bloodstock **Trained** Middleham Moor, N Yorks

**FOCUS**
A fair middle-distance fillies' handicap. The strongly-supported second favourite won well in a decent time.

## 6629 EBF STALLIONS BREEDING WINNERS FILLIES' H'CAP 7f 33y
**4:00** (4:01) (Class 3) (0-90,92) 3-Y-O+ **£9,703** (£2,887; £1,443; £721) **Stalls** Low

Form RPR

3124 1 **Tirania**[47] 4883 3-9-2 86 ... PaulMulrennan 5 92+
(William Haggas) *stdd in last pl: hdwy whn nt clr run and swtchd lft over 1f out: sn rdn: kpt on wl fnl f to ld towards fin* **15/8**[2]

2111 2 ¾ **Peach Melba**[10] 6261 3-9-4 88 6ex ... JoeFanning 1 92
(Mark Johnston) *t.k.h: led: hrd pressed and rdn over 1f out: edgd lft: kpt on fnl f: hdd and no ex towards fin* **13/8**[1]

-336 3 shd **Rajar**[189] 889 3-9-8 92 ... (h) PaulHanagan 2 95
(Richard Fahey) *t.k.h: trckd ldr: effrt and disp ld over 1f out: kpt on fnl f: hld towards fin* **15/2**

4054 4 4 ½ **Forever A Lady (IRE)**[6] 6382 4-8-7 72 oh1 ... AndrewMullen 4 65
(Keith Dalgleish) *hld up in tch: effrt and rdn over 2f out: wknd over 1f out* **14/1**

5242 **5** 1¾ **Alpine Dream (IRE)**[20] 5881 4-8-11 **76**............................(b) DavidAllan 3 64
(Tim Easterby) *t.k.h: trckd ldrs tl ridden and wknd appr 2f out* 9/2[3]
1m 27.27s (-1.73) **Going Correction** -0.20s/f (Firm)
**WFA** 3 from 4yo+ 5lb **5** Ran SP% **109.5**
Speed ratings (Par 104): **101,100,100,94,92**
CSF £5.25 TOTE £3.60: £1.10, £1.60; EX 5.10 Trifecta £16.30.
**Owner** Miss Yvonne Jacques **Bred** Mill House Stud & Cheveley Park Stud Ltd **Trained** Newmarket, Suffolk

**FOCUS**
The feature contest was a good fillies' handicap. They went a decent gallop and the well-supported second favourite got on top of the favourite in a thrilling three-way go.

## 6630 TUV-SUD H'CAP 7f 33y
4:35 (4:37) (Class 6) (0-60,59) 3-Y-O £2,587 (£770; £384; £192) Stalls Low

Form RPR
602 **1** **My Girl Maisie (IRE)**[5] 6437 3-9-2 **54**............................ ConnorBeasley 4 64+
(Richard Guest) *t.k.h: cl up: rdn to ld over 1f out: edgd rt: styd on strly fnl f* 5/2[1]
3000 **2** 1¾ **Tagur (IRE)**[23] 5741 3-9-7 **59**............................ TomEaves 3 64
(Kevin Ryan) *led at modest gallop: rdn and hdd over 1f out: kpt on same pce fnl f* 7/1[3]
242 **3** 2 **Jack Blane**[17] 5992 3-9-5 **57**............................(p) GrahamLee 7 57
(Keith Dalgleish) *in tch: effrt and rdn over 2f out: one pce fr over 1f out* 3/1[2]
0066 **4** ½ **Trick Of The Lyte (IRE)**[36] 5282 3-8-12 **50**............................ JasonHart 1 49+
(John Quinn) *plld hrd: cl up: drvn along over 2f out: outpcd fr over 1f out* 10/1
6061 **5** 1¼ **Cosmic Sky**[34] 5374 3-9-1 **53**............................(h) DavidAllan 5 48+
(Tim Easterby) *t.k.h: hld up: rdn over 2f out: sn no imp* 3/1[2]
-065 **6** 5 **Quiet Moment (IRE)**[24] 5703 3-9-1 **53**............................(h[1]) PaulMulrennan 8 35+
(Keith Dalgleish) *hld up: drvn and outpcd over 2f out: sn btn* 10/1
-006 **7** ½ **I Dare To Dream**[34] 5374 3-8-7 **45**............................(p) JoeDoyle 2 26+
(Lisa Williamson) *s.i.s: hld up in tch: struggling 3f out: sn btn* 66/1
1m 28.62s (-0.38) **Going Correction** -0.20s/f (Firm) **7** Ran SP% **110.7**
Speed ratings (Par 98): **94,92,89,89,87 82,81**
CSF £19.12 CT £50.54 TOTE £2.80: £1.50, £3.00; EX 18.70 Trifecta £55.70.
**Owner** Alfa Site Services Ltd/Mrs Alison Guest **Bred** Patrick M Ryan **Trained** Ingmanthorpe, W Yorks

**FOCUS**
A moderate 3yo handicap. The favourite won well off an, at best, respectable gallop.

## 6631 SCOTT COPPOLA ELECTRICAL DISTRIBUTORS H'CAP 5f 1y
5:10 (5:11) (Class 6) (0-60,60) 4-Y-O+ £2,587 (£770; £384; £192) Stalls High

Form RPR
3200 **1** **See Vermont**[9] 6298 9-9-5 **58**............................(b) DuranFentiman 3 62
(Rebecca Bastiman) *prom on outside: effrt and drvn along over 1f out: disp ld ins fnl f: led cl home* 14/1
3231 **2** *nse* **Hadley**[16] 6045 4-9-2 **60**............................(p) BenRobinson[(5)] 4 64
(Tracy Waggott) *unruly bef s: led: rdn 2f out: kpt on wl fnl f: hdd cl home* 2/1[1]
0-20 **3** *shd* **Red Forever**[24] 5695 6-8-4 **46**............................ RachelRichardson[(3)] 1 49
(Thomas Cuthbert) *bhd and outpcd: hdwy over 1f out: ev ch wl ins fnl f: jst hld* 12/1
0655 **4** *nk* **Groundworker (IRE)**[47] 4896 6-9-1 **54**............................(t) PaulMulrennan 5 56
(Paul Midgley) *prom: effrt and rdn over 1f out: kpt on fnl f: hld nr fin* 4/1[2]
0360 **5** ¾ **Brendan (IRE)**[17] 5995 4-8-7 **46** oh1............................(h) JoeDoyle 10 48
(Jim Goldie) *dwlt: bhd and outpcd: hdwy fnl f: kpt on: nt pce to chal* 28/1
6046 **6** *hd* **Goninodaethat**[8] 6318 9-8-12 **58**............................ SeanMooney[(7)] 2 57
(Jim Goldie) *bhd on outside: rdn and hdwy over 1f out: kpt on same pce wl ins fnl f* 12/1
2334 **7** *nk* **Lady Joanna Vassa (IRE)**[6] 6372 4-8-9 **48**............................(p) ConnorBeasley 8 46
(Richard Guest) *cl up: drvn along 2f out: outpcd ins fnl f* 6/1[3]
00-0 **8** *nk* **Sunnyside Bob (IRE)**[21] 5836 4-9-5 **58**............................(p[1]) BarryMcHugh 7 55
(Neville Bycroft) *hld up bhd ldng gp: drvn along over 2f out: no imp fnl f* 16/1
040 **9** 2½ **Thornaby Princess**[55] 4559 6-8-7 **46**............................(p) RoystonFfrench 6 34
(Colin Teague) *in tch: rdn over 2f out: wknd over 1f out* 20/1
1500 **10** ½ **Lackaday**[36] 5282 5-8-12 **58**............................(p) NatalieHambling[(7)] 9 44
(Noel Wilson) *hld up: rdn over 2f out: edgd rt and wknd over 1f out* 7/1
59.1s (-1.30) **Going Correction** -0.20s/f (Firm) **10** Ran SP% **116.3**
Speed ratings (Par 101): **102,101,101,101,100 99,99,98,94,94**
CSF £42.15 CT £321.26 TOTE £15.90: £4.10, £1.40, £3.50; EX 51.20 Trifecta £688.30.
**Owner** John Smith & Mrs P Bastiman **Bred** Oakhill Stud **Trained** Cowthorpe, N Yorks
■ Stewards' Enquiry : Duran Fentiman 2 day ban: used his whip above the permitted level (14/15 Sep)

**FOCUS**
A moderate sprint handicap. They went a decent gallop and it produced a thrilling three-way photo finish. Ordinary form, with the runner-up pretty much replicating the level of his Thirsk win.
T/Plt: £55.70 to a £1 stake. Pool: £42,387.69. 555.03 winning units. T/Qpdt: £19.00 to a £1 stake. Pool: £2,761.52. 107.04 winning units. **Richard Young**

# 6154 WOLVERHAMPTON (A.W) (L-H)
### Thursday, August 31

**OFFICIAL GOING: Tapeta: standard**
Wind: Light, across Weather: Cloudy with sunny spells

## 6632 INVEST CITY OF WOLVERHAMPTON AMATEUR RIDERS' H'CAP 1m 4f 51y (Tp)
5:40 (5:43) (Class 5) (0-70,68) 3-Y-O+ £2,807 (£870; £435; £217) Stalls Low

Form RPR
0011 **1** **Wolfcatcherjack (IRE)**[9] 6291 3-10-5 **68** 6ex............ MissSBrotherton 7 82+
(Sir Mark Prescott Bt) *trckd ldrs: racd keenly: led over 3f out: shkn up over 1f out: styd on* 30/100[1]
0432 **2** 1¾ **Best Example (USA)**[14] 6109 5-10-11 **65**............................ MrRBirkett 2 72
(Julia Feilden) *hld up: hdwy over 2f out: chsd wnr over 1f out: sn rdn: styd on* 5/1[2]
3205 **3** 8 **Gabrial The Terror (IRE)**[43] 5021 7-11-0 **68**............................ MrSWalker 5 62
(Patrick Morris) *s.s: hld up: hdwy over 2f out: rdn and hung lft fr over 1f out: nt run on* 11/1[3]
3600 **4** ½ **Gabrial The Duke (IRE)**[33] 5403 7-10-2 **59**............(p) MissAMcCain[(3)] 4 52
(Patrick Morris) *s.i.s: hld up: effrt over 1f out: n.d* 25/1
/00- **5** 3¼ **Madrasa (IRE)**[420] 4045 9-9-2 **49**............................(t) MissLKHammond[(7)] 6 37
(Ken Wingrove) *hld up: plld hrd: hdwy to go 2nd over 8f out: led 5f out: hdd over 3f out: sn rdn: wknd fnl f* 250/1
3446 **6** 4½ **Estibdaad (IRE)**[22] 5793 7-10-0 **59** ow3............................(t) MissMBryant[(5)] 3 40
(Paddy Butler) *led at stdy pce 7f: remained handy tl wknd over 1f out* 28/1
000/ **7** 8 **Yorkshire Monarch (IRE)**[1202] 2354 6-9-7 **52**............................ MissJCooley[(5)] 1 20
(Sarah Hollinshead) *chsd ldr over 3f: remained handy: nt clr run and lost pl over 3f out: sn rdn and wknd* 150/1
2m 44.23s (3.43) **Going Correction** -0.125s/f (Stan)
**WFA** 3 from 5yo+ 9lb **7** Ran SP% **110.3**
Speed ratings (Par 103): **83,81,76,76,74 71,65**
CSF £1.88 TOTE £1.10: £1.02, £2.20; EX 2.50 Trifecta £5.40.
**Owner** Ne'Er Do Wells V **Bred** Mrs S M Rogers & Miss K Rausing **Trained** Newmarket, Suffolk

**FOCUS**
The track had been harrowed to a depth of 3.5" and reinstated with a Gallop Master finish. A slowly run and uncompetitive amateurs' handicap.

## 6633 HELLERMANNTYTON CABLE MANAGEMENT SOLUTIONS MAIDEN STKS 1m 1f 104y (Tp)
6:10 (6:10) (Class 5) 3-Y-O+ £3,072 (£914; £456; £228) Stalls Low

Form RPR
**1** **Power Surge (IRE)** 3-9-5 0............................ PatDobbs 7 81+
(Ralph Beckett) *chsd ldrs: led over 1f out: rdn out* 12/1
5 **2** 2¾ **Mesbaar**[87] 3394 3-9-5 0............................ SilvestreDeSousa 11 75
(Roger Varian) *plld hrd: jnd ldrs after 1f: led over 6f out: rdn and hdd over 1f out: no ex ins fnl f* 9/4[2]
2 **3** ½ **Military Parade**[23] 5746 3-9-5 0............................ JosephineGordon 3 74
(Saeed bin Suroor) *s.i.s: sn rcvrd to ld: shkn up 1/2-way: rdn over 2f out: styd on same pce fnl f* 8/13[1]
33 **4** 1½ **Perfect Spy**[23] 5746 3-9-0 0............................ HarryBentley 8 66
(Luca Cumani) *chsd ldrs: rdn over 2f out: hung lft and no ex ins fnl f* 8/1[3]
**5** 1 **Fintech (IRE)** 3-9-5 0............................(t[1]) AdamBeschizza 10 69
(Mrs Ilka Gansera-Leveque) *s.i.s: hld up: hdwy over 1f out: sn rdn: no ex ins fnl f* 40/1
40 **6** ½ **Waiting A Lot (IRE)**[58] 4474 3-9-0 0............................ DavidNolan 6 63
(David O'Meara) *hld up: hdwy 2f out: shkn up over 1f out: wknd wl ins fnl f* 50/1
-5 **7** ½ **In Dreams**[28] 5563 3-9-5 0............................(p[1]) TomMarquand 5 67
(Brian Meehan) *hld up: hdwy over 3f out: rdn over 2f out: wknd ins fnl f* 33/1
0 **8** 3¾ **Crystal Sunstone**[22] 5794 3-9-2 0............................ EdwardGreatrex[(3)] 9 59
(Eve Johnson Houghton) *plld hrd: sn w ldr tl over 6f out: outpcd over 3f out: sn rdn: wknd over 1f out* 40/1
0 **9** 5 **Cable Car**[28] 5563 6-9-12 0............................(p[1]) DanielMuscutt 4 49
(John Flint) *s.i.s: hld up: pushed along over 2f out: sn wknd* 100/1
**10** 28 **Shanghai Shane (IRE)** 3-9-0 0............................ CallumRodriguez[(5)] 2
(Brian Barr) *s.i.s: outpcd: lost tch fr over 3f out* 150/1
2m 0.52s (-0.28) **Going Correction** -0.125s/f (Stan)
**WFA** 3 from 6yo 7lb **10** Ran SP% **122.9**
Speed ratings (Par 103): **96,93,93,91,90 90,90,86,82,57**
CSF £41.02 TOTE £15.90: £3.90, £1.10, £1.02; EX 57.90 Trifecta £88.10.
**Owner** The Outlaws **Bred** Silver Skates Syndicate **Trained** Kimpton, Hants
■ Stewards' Enquiry : Adam Beschizza 2 day ban: used his whip above shoulder height (14/15 Sep)

**FOCUS**
Not a bad maiden for the time of year. It has a decent race average but the time was slow and this one might not be quite up to the same level.

## 6634 INVEST CITY OF WOLVERHAMPTON - CITY OF OPPORTUNITY NURSERY H'CAP 6f 20y (Tp)
6:40 (6:42) (Class 6) (0-65,65) 2-Y-O £2,425 (£721; £360; £180) Stalls Low

Form RPR
4545 **1** **Just For Fun**[16] 6043 2-9-1 **59**............................(b[1]) TonyHamilton 3 63
(Richard Fahey) *mid-div: hdwy: nt clr run and swtchd rt over 1f out: shkn up and r.o to ld wl ins fnl f* 9/1
5062 **2** ½ **Laura Knight (IRE)**[9] 6285 2-9-4 **62**............................(p[1]) SilvestreDeSousa 10 64
(Gary Moore) *hld up: hdwy over 1f out: rdn ins fnl f: r.o* 3/1[1]
0530 **3** 1 **Hope And Glory (IRE)**[19] 5933 2-8-10 **54**............................ AlistairRawlinson 8 53
(Tom Dascombe) *led: rdn and hung lft over 1f out: hdd and unable qck wl ins fnl f* 14/1
5060 **4** 1 **Highland Bobby**[16] 6043 2-9-4 **62**............................ DavidNolan 4 58
(David O'Meara) *a.p: rdn over 1f out: styd on same pce ins fnl f* 20/1
640 **5** ½ **Revenge**[101] 2890 2-8-12 **56**............................(b[1]) JackGarritty 1 51
(Tim Easterby) *s.i.s: hld up: hdwy over 1f out: sn rdn: nt clr run and swtchd rt ins fnl f: r.o: nt rch ldrs* 25/1
6353 **6** ¾ **Sienna Says**[22] 5785 2-9-7 **65**............................ RobertWinston 6 57
(Tony Carroll) *w ldr: rdn and ev ch over 1f out: no ex ins fnl f* 11/2[2]
4524 **7** *hd* **Llamrei**[13] 6154 2-8-12 **56**............................ BenCurtis 2 48
(Jo Hughes) *chsd ldrs: pushed along over 3f out: no ex ins fnl f* 9/1
5064 **8** *nk* **Silver Bullet (IRE)**[9] 6285 2-9-2 **60**............................(v) RichardKingscote 11 51
(Tom Dascombe) *s.i.s: hld up: hdwy and nt clr run over 1f out: nt trble ldrs* 8/1[3]
0422 **9** *hd* **Christmas Night**[17] 6011 2-9-2 **65**............................ CallumRodriguez[(5)] 12 55
(Ollie Pears) *prom: lost pl 5f out: rdn on outer over 2f out: nt rch ldrs* 14/1
0060 **10** ½ **Bullseye Bullet**[15] 6063 2-8-4 **55**............................(p[1]) NicolaCurrie[(7)] 13 44
(Mark Usher) *hld up: rdn over 2f out: nvr on terms* 80/1
350 **11** 1¾ **Marsh Storm (IRE)**[34] 5371 2-9-4 **62**............................ PJMcDonald 5 45
(K R Burke) *hld up: rdn over 1f out: n.d* 8/1[3]
646 **12** 4½ **Owen The Law**[41] 5121 2-8-10 **54**............................ TomMarquand 7 24
(David Evans) *mid-div: rdn 1/2-way: wknd over 1f out* 22/1
2553 **13** 12 **Terri Rules (IRE)**[13] 6154 2-9-0 **58**............................ AdamBeschizza 9
(Julia Feilden) *trckd ldrs: shkn up whn nt clr run over 1f out: eased* 11/1
1m 13.8s (-0.70) **Going Correction** -0.125s/f (Stan) **13** Ran SP% **118.5**
Speed ratings (Par 92): **99,98,97,95,95 94,93,93,93,92 90,84,68**
CSF £34.24 CT £398.73 TOTE £9.60: £2.70, £1.60, £5.00; EX 32.80 Trifecta £916.10.
**Owner** M P Coleman **Bred** Mrs J Kersey **Trained** Musley Bank, N Yorks

**FOCUS**
There was a compressed finish to this very modest nursery, in which the pace only collapsed late on. The second and third help set the level.

## 6635 HELLERMANNTYTON.CO.UK H'CAP 6f 20y (Tp)
7:10 (7:11) (Class 6) (0-65,66) 3-Y-O+ £2,425 (£721; £360; £180) Stalls Low

Form RPR
4000 **1** **Hurricane Rock**[21] 5848 4-8-8 **47**............................ HarryBentley 3 56
(Simon Dow) *hld up: hdwy over 1f out: rdn and r.o to ld post* 8/1
6001 **2** *nse* **Newstead Abbey**[13] 6156 7-9-12 **65**............................(p) PJMcDonald 12 74+
(Michael Herrington) *chsd ldrs: rdn to ld and hung lft ins fnl f: hdd post* 9/2[1]


The Form Book Flat, Raceform Ltd, Newbury, RG14 5SJ

050 **3** 2 1/4 **Top Of The Bank**[20] 5869 4-9-12 **65**............................(p) TonyHamilton 1 67
(Kristin Stubbs) *led: rdn and edgd rt over 1f out: hdd ins fnl f: styd on same pce* **9/2**[1]

2101 **4** 1 1/2 **Bogsnog (IRE)**[20] 5892 7-9-7 **60**........................................ JackGarritty 10 58
(Ruth Carr) *w ldr: rdn and ev ch over 2f out: nt clr run and swtchd lft over 1f out: styd on same pce ins fnl f* **9/1**

1232 **5** 1/2 **Tooty Fruitti**[21] 5845 3-9-9 **65**........................................ DougieCostello 7 61
(Jo Hughes) *prom: rdn over 1f out: styd on same pce ins fnl f* **12/1**

4553 **6** 1 **Commanche**[14] 6113 8-9-13 **66**...............................(b) SilvestreDeSousa 5 62
(Chris Dwyer) *prom: nt clr run and lost pl over 5f out: rdn 1/2-way: r.o ins fnl f: nt trble ldrs* **11/2**[3]

-352 **7** 3/4 **Triple Dream**[13] 6157 12-8-13 **59**............................... KerrieRaybould(7) 4 50
(Milton Bradley) *chsd ldrs: rdn over 1f out: wknd ins fnl f* **25/1**

1064 **8** 2 1/2 **Mad Endeavour**[29] 5535 6-9-10 **63**....................................(b) BenCurtis 9 46
(Stuart Kittow) *s.i.s: hld up: rdn over 2f out: nvr trbld ldrs* **8/1**

4522 **9** 5 **Indian Affair**[13] 6156 7-9-12 **65**........................................(bt) MartinDwyer 6 33
(Milton Bradley) *hld up: pushed along 1/2-way: nvr on terms* **5/1**[2]

0006 **10** 3 3/4 **Oddsocks (IRE)**[9] 6283 5-8-7 **46** oh1............................... JimmyQuinn 13 3
(Tony Carroll) *hld up: hung rt 4f out: wknd over 2f out* **125/1**

-006 **11** 26 **Dramatic Voice**[22] 5778 4-8-7 **46** oh1............................... LiamJones 2
(Ken Cunningham-Brown) *stmbld sn after s: hdwy over 3f out: sn rdn: wknd over 2f out* **150/1**

0-00 **P** **Gambino (IRE)**[134] 1893 7-8-13 **59**.......................... ConnorMurtagh(7) 8
(John David Riches) *s.i.s: hld up: wnt wrong and p.u over 2f out; fatally injured* **66/1**

1m 13.4s (-1.10) **Going Correction** -0.125s/f (Stan)
**WFA** 3 from 4yo+ 3lb **12** Ran SP% **115.1**
Speed ratings (Par 101): **102,101,98,96,96 94,93,90,83,78 44,**
CSF £42.19 CT £185.92 TOTE £8.70: £2.30, £1.90, £2.10; EX 53.00 Trifecta £221.70.
**Owner** Malcolm & Alicia Aldis **Bred** Kempsons Stud **Trained** Ashtead, Surrey

**FOCUS**
A tight finish to this low-grade sprint. The winner has been rated near his best, while the fourth helps set the level.

## 6636 INVEST WOLVERHAMPTON - CITY OF OPPORTUNITY NOVICE AUCTION STKS 7f 36y (Tp)
**7:40** (7:43) (Class 6) 2-Y-O £2,425 (£721; £360; £180) **Stalls** High

Form RPR

03 **1** **Eesha Beauty (IRE)**[24] 5717 2-8-11 0.............................. HarryBentley 8 67+
(Marco Botti) *hld up: hdwy over 1f out: rdn to ld ins fnl f: r.o* **11/2**[2]

45 **2** 1 1/4 **Merkava**[21] 5834 2-9-2 0.................................................. TomMarquand 4 69
(Robyn Brisland) *led: hdd over 5f out: chsd ldrs: rdn and ev ch ins fnl f: edgd lft and styd on same pce* **8/1**

2213 **3** nk **Star Of Zaam (IRE)**[26] 5644 2-9-6 71.........................(p) CliffordLee(3) 11 75
(K R Burke) *chsd ldrs: rdn over 1f out: styd on same pce ins fnl f* **6/1**[3]

**4** 1/2 **Gripper** 2-9-2 0........................................................................ PatDobbs 9 67+
(Ralph Beckett) *s.i.s: hld up: hdwy over 1f out: rdn ins fnl f: styng on whn nt clr run wl ins fnl f* **10/1**

6363 **5** nse **Another Day Of Sun (IRE)**[21] 5844 2-9-9 74.......... SilvestreDeSousa 7 74
(Mick Channon) *prom: led over 5f out: rdn over 1f out: hdd ins fnl f: no ex towards fin* **7/2**[1]

03 **6** hd **Ojala (IRE)**[17] 6005 2-8-11 0........................................ PaddyBradley(5) 3 66+
(Simon Dow) *plld hrd and prom: shkn up and nt clr run over 1f out: styd on* **11/2**[2]

**7** 2 **Laytown (IRE)** 2-8-12 0 ow1........................................ DougieCostello 2 57+
(Jamie Osborne) *s.i.s: hld up: hdwy over 1f out: no ex wl ins fnl f* **25/1**

3 **8** 2 1/2 **Moxy Mares**[26] 5631 2-9-2 0.............................................. SteveDrowne 6 55
(Daniel Mark Loughnane) *s.i.s: hld up: pushed along 1/2-way: bhd whn hung rt over 1f out* **11/2**[2]

5 **9** 1 **Tommy Shelby (FR)**[80] 3648 2-9-2 0................................ TonyHamilton 10 53
(Richard Fahey) *s.i.s: hld up: rdn 1/2-way: a in rr* **16/1**

0 **10** 7 **Calvin's Gal (IRE)**[45] 4972 2-8-11 0.................................. DannyBrock 1 31
(Luke McJannet) *plld hrd and prom: wnt 2nd 4f out tl rdn over 1f out: wknd fnl f* **125/1**

**P** **Tipi** 2-9-2 0.................................................................................... AdamBeschizza 12
(Charlie Wallis) *s.s: bhd whn p.u over 5f out* **100/1**

1m 29.25s (0.45) **Going Correction** -0.125s/f (Stan) **11** Ran SP% **114.4**
Speed ratings (Par 92): **92,90,90,89,89 89,87,84,83,75**
CSF £47.23 TOTE £5.70: £1.70, £2.70, £2.10; EX 58.10 Trifecta £375.80.
**Owner** Equity Racing **Bred** John O'Kelly Bloodstock Services **Trained** Newmarket, Suffolk

**FOCUS**
They went no pace early in this ordinary race. The fifth dictates the level.

## 6637 VISIT HELLERMANNTYTON ACADEMY - ACADEMY@HELLERMANNTYTON.CO.UK H'CAP 7f 36y (Tp)
**8:10** (8:14) (Class 4) (0-80,80) 3-Y-O+ £4,851 (£1,443; £721; £360) **Stalls** High

Form RPR

-404 **1** **Rouge Nuage (IRE)**[14] 6111 7-9-3 **74**.............................. JimmyQuinn 1 80
(Conrad Allen) *a.p: shkn up and edgd lft over 2f out: rdn and r.o to ld post* **12/1**

3-02 **2** shd **Energia Flavio (BRZ)**[51] 4728 7-8-13 **75**.............. CallumRodriguez(5) 2 81
(Patrick Morris) *hld up: hmpd over 2f out: hdwy over 1f out: rdn to ld ins fnl f: hdd post* **9/1**

2650 **3** shd **Florencio**[19] 5948 4-9-9 **80**..............................................(p) TonyHamilton 9 85+
(Roger Fell) *hld up: hdwy over 1f out: r.o: n.m.r nr fin* **9/1**

4243 **4** shd **Envisaging (IRE)**[15] 6068 3-9-2 **78**..........................(t) SilvestreDeSousa 8 81
(James Fanshawe) *prom: rdn and hung lft 1f out: sn ev ch: r.o* **7/4**[1]

63 **5** 3/4 **Miracle Garden**[31] 5481 5-8-9 **73**..............................(p) ManuelFernandes(7) 3 76
(Ian Williams) *hld up: hdwy over 1f out: r.o: nt rch ldrs* **8/1**[3]

5240 **6** 2 1/2 **Red Touch (USA)**[86] 3433 5-9-4 **75**.............................. AlistairRawlinson 6 71
(Michael Appleby) *hld up: rdn: edgd lft and r.o ins fnl f: nvr nrr* **14/1**

4000 **7** 1 1/2 **Alkashaaf (USA)**[50] 4736 3-9-1 **80**..........................(tp) EdwardGreatrex(3) 7 70
(Archie Watson) *hld up: rdn over 2f out: styd on same pce fr over 1f out* **16/1**

0460 **8** 3/4 **Zapper Cass (FR)**[26] 5671 4-9-7 **78**.................................... BenCurtis 12 68
(Tony Coyle) *sn led: rdn and edgd rt over 1f out: hdd & wknd ins fnl f* **22/1**

-213 **9** 1 1/4 **Mehdi (IRE)**[201] 685 8-9-5 **76**.............................................. LiamKeniry 11 63
(Patrick Morris) *prom: chsd ldr over 5f out: rdn and ev ch whn hmpd 1f out: wknd ins fnl f* **28/1**

0000 **10** nk **Accurate**[33] 5396 4-9-2 **73**........................................ JosephineGordon 10 59
(Ian Williams) *hld up: rdn over 2f out: wknd over 1f out* **20/1**

5200 **11** nk **Sophisticated Heir (IRE)**[12] 6181 7-9-2 **73**................ DougieCostello 4 58
(Kevin Frost) *hld up: shkn up over 1f out: nvr on terms* **33/1**

3002 **12** 2 3/4 **Kingsley Klarion (IRE)**[50] 4746 4-9-6 **77**..................... RobertWinston 5 55
(John Butler) *led early: chsd ldrs: rdn over 1f out: wknd ins fnl f* **6/1**[2]

1m 26.76s (-2.04) **Going Correction** -0.125s/f (Stan)
**WFA** 3 from 4yo+ 5lb **12** Ran SP% **117.5**
Speed ratings (Par 105): **106,105,105,105,104 101,100,99,97,97 97,94**
CSF £108.90 CT £1045.43 TOTE £14.60: £3.30, £2.70, £2.90; EX 131.80 Trifecta £2522.90.
**Owner** sportsdays.co.uk **Bred** Dermot Farrington **Trained** Newmarket, Suffolk

**FOCUS**
A desperate finish to this ordinary handicap. Stall 1 beat stall 2.

## 6638 SUSAN BOX MEMORIAL H'CAP 7f 36y (Tp)
**8:40** (8:44) (Class 6) (0-65,65) 3-Y-O+ £2,425 (£721; £360; £180) **Stalls** High

Form RPR

0056 **1** **Iftitah (IRE)**[15] 6067 3-9-2 **62**..........................................(bt) HarryBentley 2 69+
(George Peckham) *hld up: hdwy 2f out: nt clr run and swtchd rt 1f out: r.o to ld wl ins fnl f* **7/1**[2]

213 **2** 1 3/4 **Robbie Roo Roo**[41] 5119 4-9-5 **60**..............................(vt) AdamBeschizza 9 65
(Mrs Ilka Gansera-Leveque) *chsd ldr: rdn to ld over 1f out: hdd wl ins fnl f* **7/1**[2]

316 **3** nk **Bell Heather (IRE)**[33] 5399 4-9-1 **61**..................... CallumRodriguez(5) 3 65
(Patrick Morris) *chsd ldrs: rdn over 1f out: styd on u.p* **15/2**[3]

3204 **4** 3/4 **Joys Delight**[17] 6016 3-9-2 **62**........................................ SteveDrowne 12 62+
(Daniel Mark Loughnane) *s.s: hld up: rdn and r.o ins fnl f: nt rch ldrs* **40/1**

1013 **5** hd **Beadlam (IRE)**[17] 6003 4-9-10 **65**...................................(p) TonyHamilton 1 67
(Roger Fell) *led: rdn and hdd over 1f out: no ex wl ins fnl f* **7/1**[2]

0330 **6** nse **Art's Desire (IRE)**[31] 5485 3-9-5 **65**.................................... LiamKeniry 10 65
(Ed Walker) *hld up: hdwy 2f out: sn rdn: styd on: nt trble ldrs* **11/1**

5040 **7** 1 1/2 **Captain Hawk**[17] 6016 3-9-2 **62**..............................(p) JosephineGordon 5 58
(Ian Williams) *hld up: sme hdwy over 1f out: no ex ins fnl f* **9/1**

2232 **8** 1 1/2 **Flower Cup**[21] 5855 4-9-8 **63**....................................(b) SilvestreDeSousa 8 57
(Chris Dwyer) *hld up in tch: plld hrd: rdn over 1f out: wknd ins fnl f* **7/2**[1]

2030 **9** hd **Caledonia Laird**[17] 6014 6-8-13 **61**...............................(b) JoshQuinn(7) 6 55
(Jo Hughes) *hld up: plld hrd: nt trble ldrs* **10/1**

1565 **10** 2 1/2 **Know Your Name**[13] 6158 6-9-10 **65**................................ DavidNolan 11 53
(Donald McCain) *chsd ldrs: rdn over 1f out: wknd fnl f* **14/1**

1036 **11** nse **A Sure Welcome**[17] 6016 3-9-3 **63**............................(p) TomMarquand 7 48
(John Spearing) *hld up in tch: plld hrd: rdn over 1f out: wknd fnl f* **9/1**

1m 26.72s (-2.08) **Going Correction** -0.125s/f (Stan)
**WFA** 3 from 4yo+ 5lb **11** Ran SP% **118.0**
Speed ratings (Par 101): **106,104,103,102,102 102,100,99,98,96 95**
CSF £55.59 CT £390.15 TOTE £7.50: £2.30, £2.10, £2.70; EX 56.60 Trifecta £493.80.
**Owner** Fawzi Abdulla Nass **Bred** Palmerston Bloodstock Ltd **Trained** Newmarket, Suffolk

**FOCUS**
This was run very slightly quicker than the earlier Class 4 handicap. The runner-up has been rated near her recent best.
T/Plt: £71.00 to a £1 stake. Pool: £73,588.19. 756.25 winning units. T/Qpdt: £70.90 to a £1 stake. Pool: £7,141.30. 74.52 winning units. **Colin Roberts**

6639 - (Foreign Racing) - See Raceform Interactive

# 5899 TIPPERARY (L-H)
Thursday, August 31

**OFFICIAL GOING: Soft**

## 6640a KILFRUSH STUD ABERGWAUN STKS (LISTED RACE) 5f
**4:55** (5:27) 3-Y-O+
£27,735 (£8,931; £4,230; £1,880; £940; £470)

RPR

**1** **Gorane (IRE)**[74] 3873 3-9-0 99................................ DeclanMcDonogh 9 104
(Henry De Bromhead, Ire) *hmpd s: sn disp and led narrowly: rdn ent fnl f where pressed clly: kpt on wl clsng stages: all out* **14/1**

**2** 1/2 **Snowstar (IRE)**[18] 5975 3-9-0 83.............................................. WJLee 4 102
(W McCreery, Ire) *disp early tl sn settled bhd ldrs: 5th 1/2-way: gd hdwy to chal ent fnl f: rdn into 2nd wl ins fnl f and kpt on wl wout matching wnr* **16/1**

**3** 1/2 **Ardhoomey (IRE)**[47] 4927 5-9-7 110..............................(t) ColinKeane 5 105
(G M Lyons, Ire) *hooded to load: wnt rt s and bmpd rival: towards rr: swtchd lft in 8th fr 1/2-way and sme hdwy on outer over 1f out: rdn in 4th ins fnl f and kpt on to snatch 3rd on line: nt trble wnr* **3/1**[2]

**4** shd **Green Door (IRE)**[16] 6039 6-9-7 97..................................(v) PatSmullen 2 105
(Robert Cowell) *cl up far side: disp 2nd at 1/2-way: rdn almost on terms 1 1/2f out and ev ch ins fnl f: no ex in 3rd cl home: denied 3rd on line* **14/1**

**5** 1 3/4 **Son Of Rest**[82] 3601 3-9-5 112........................................ ChrisHayes 6 99
(J A Stack, Ire) *bmpd s: in tch: 7th at 1/2-way: rdn under 2f out and sme hdwy u.p into 5th ins fnl f: no ex clsng stages* **11/8**[1]

**6** 2 1/4 **Magic Bear (IRE)**[20] 5902 4-9-2 93....................................... OisinOrr 7 86
(Edward Lynam, Ire) *hmpd between horses s: in rr: swtchd lft fr 1/2-way and sme hdwy on outer to chse ldrs: no ex u.p in 6th ins fnl f and one pce clsng stages* **7/1**[3]

**7** 1 **Ostatnia (IRE)**[20] 5902 5-9-2 90........................................(v) WayneLordan 1 82
(W McCreery, Ire) *chsd ldrs far side: 4th 1/2-way: rdn 2f out and no ex over 1f out: wknd* **25/1**

**8** 4 1/4 **Sahreej (IRE)**[17] 5994 4-9-7 75..........................................(b) GaryCarroll 3 72
(Adrian Paul Keatley, Ire) *chsd ldrs far side: 6th 1/2-way: rdn and no ex 1 1/2f out: wknd* **66/1**

**9** 12 **Alphabet**[28] 5583 3-9-0 94............................................(t) SeamieHeffernan 8 24
(A P O'Brien, Ire) *cl up nr side: disp 2nd at 1/2-way: lost pl after 1/2-way: rdn bhd ldrs 2f out and sn wknd: eased ins fnl f* **7/1**[3]

58.65s (-0.35)
**WFA** 3 from 4yo+ 2lb **9** Ran SP% **116.7**
CSF £202.92 TOTE £18.50: £3.60, £2.00, £1.20; DF 236.70 Trifecta £1885.80.
**Owner** Clipper Logistics Group Ltd **Bred** Michael O'Mahony **Trained** Knockeen, Co Waterford
■ Spirit Quartz was withdrawn. Price at time of withdrawal 10-1. Rule 4 applies to all bets - deduction of 5p in the pound.

**FOCUS**
A game performance from the winner under a terrific drive from the former champion. The third and fourth help set the standard, with the winner rated in line with the best view of her form.

6641a (Foreign Racing) - See Raceform Interactive

## 6642a COOLMORE STUD FAIRY BRIDGE STKS (GROUP 3) (F&M) 7f 100y
5:55 (6:19) 3-Y-0+

£32,777 (£10,555; £5,000; £2,222; £1,111; £555)

RPR

1 **Realtra (IRE)**32 5460 5-9-8 105 ColinKeane 12 109+
(Roger Varian) *broke wl to ld briefly tl sn settled bhd ldrs: brought to nr side gng wl into st: rdn 1 1/2f out and r.o strly ins fnl f to ld ins fnl 50yds: won gng away: comf* **4/1**2

2 1 3/4 **Drumfad Bay (IRE)**28 5583 3-9-0 96 ColmO'Donoghue 8 99
(Mrs John Harrington, Ire) *chsd ldrs: 4th bef 1/2-way: hdwy to chal into st and led far side 1 1/2f out: all out wl ins fnl f where strly pressed and hdd ins fnl 50yds: no ch w wnr* **6/1**3

3 1 **Music Box (IRE)**14 6119 3-9-0 101 SeamieHeffernan 10 96+
(A P O'Brien, Ire) *chsd ldrs: 5th bef 1/2-way: brought to nr side into st: rdn under 2f out and sme hdwy ent fnl f: kpt on wl into 3rd cl home: nt trble wnr* **9/4**1

4 1/2 **I'm So Fancy (IRE)**15 6080 3-9-0 92 NGMcCullagh 2 95
(Mrs John Harrington, Ire) *chsd ldrs: 3rd bef 1/2-way: tk clsr order into st: sn rdn in 2nd and pressed ldr far side over 1f out: no ex ins fnl f and one pce clsng stages where dropped to 4th* **20/1**

5 1/2 **Smoulder**28 5583 3-9-0 88 (h) DonnachaO'Brien 9 94+
(A P O'Brien, Ire) *w.w towards rr: brought to nr side into st: swtchd lft under 2f out and sme hdwy over 1f out where rdn: kpt on same pce in 5th wl ins fnl f: nvr trbld ldrs* **33/1**

6 3 **Tempera**306 7703 3-9-0 97 LeighRoche 5 86
(D K Weld, Ire) *hld up: disp 9th gng wl at 1/2-way: rdn under 2f out and sme hdwy over 1f out: kpt on one pce in 6th wl ins fnl f* **16/1**

7 1 1/4 **Elusive Beauty (IRE)**4 6491 3-9-0 93 (v1) ShaneFoley 3 83
(K J Condon, Ire) *s.i.s and detached in rr early: pushed along in 11th bef st and sme hdwy far side u.p over 1f out: kpt on one pce in 7th wl ins fnl f* **25/1**

8 1 3/4 **Another Story (IRE)**4 6491 4-9-5 95 RonanWhelan 4 81
(Ms Sheila Lavery, Ire) *hld up: pushed along in 10th fr bef 1/2-way: rdn into st and no imp: one pce fnl 2f* **14/1**

9 hd **Duchess Of France (IRE)**8 6334 4-9-5 90 (t) GaryCarroll 6 80
(Adrian Paul Keatley, Ire) *sn led: 2 l clr bef 1/2-way: reduced advantage appr st: rdn 2f out and sn hdd: wknd over 1f out* **14/1**

10 1 1/2 **Ionization (IRE)**12 6192 4-9-5 92 WJLee 11 76
(John Patrick Shanahan, Ire) *hld up: 9th bef 1/2-way: brought to nr side into st: sn rdn and no ex under 2f out: one pce after* **12/1**

11 12 **Raymonda (USA)**28 5583 4-9-5 102 (v) PatSmullen 7 46
(D K Weld, Ire) *settled bhd ldr: rdn in 2nd over 2f out and sn wknd: eased ins fnl f* **10/1**

12 7 1/2 **Same Jurisdiction (SAF)**27 5597 6-9-5 99 KevinManning 1 28
(Ed Dunlop) *chsd ldrs: 6th bef 1/2-way: rdn over 2f out and sn wknd: eased ins fnl f: clinically abnormal* **14/1**

1m 36.95s
**WFA** 3 from 4yo+ 5lb 12 Ran SP% **119.3**
CSF £27.79 TOTE £4.40: £1.70, £2.50, £1.10; DF 28.10 Trifecta £100.50.
**Owner** Yasushi Kubota **Bred** Tom & Geraldine Molan **Trained** Newmarket, Suffolk

**FOCUS**
For the second time in recent months an Irish Group 3 proved within the range of a five-year-old mare who is having a fine season. The second and third have clashed three times in a row now and continue to be closely matched. It's been rated around the balance of the first two and fourth to the seventh.

6643 - 6646a (Foreign Racing) - See Raceform Interactive

# 6605 BADEN-BADEN (L-H)
Thursday, August 31

**OFFICIAL GOING: Turf: good**

## 6647a 84TH DARLEY OETTINGEN-RENNEN (GROUP 2) (3YO+) (TURF) 1m
5:55 3-Y-0+ £34,188 (£13,247; £6,837; £3,418; £2,136)

RPR

1 **Pas De Deux (GER)**46 4939 7-9-0 0 StephenHellyn 1 112
(Yasmin Almenrader, Germany) *mde all: rdn into st: kpt on and a doing enough* **19/10**1

2 3/4 **Palace Prince (GER)**5 6451 5-9-3 0 (p) FilipMinarik 2 113
(Jean-Pierre Carvalho, Germany) *cl up: rdn for effrt st: kpt on but a hld by wnr* **19/10**1

3 1 1/4 **Poetic Dream (IRE)**46 4939 3-8-11 0 EduardoPedroza 4 109
(A Wohler, Germany) *hld up in tch: rdn into st: kpt on but nt quite pce to chal* **3/1**2

4 7 1/2 **A Raving Beauty (GER)**18 4-8-10 0 (b) DarioVargiu 6 86
(Andreas Suborics, Germany) *trckd wnr: rdn and outpcd in st: wknd* **73/10**

5 1 1/2 **Vive Marie (GER)**18 3-8-5 0 AndreasHelfenbein 3 83
(J Hirschberger, Germany) *hld up in rr: toiling u.p appr st: plugged on but wl btn and nvr threatened* **113/10**

6 11 **Degas (GER)**18 4-9-0 0 AdriedeVries 5 61
(Markus Klug, Germany) *hld up in tch: rdn and outpcd in st: wknd and dropped to last: eased whn btn* **51/10**3

1m 40.39s (1.28)
**WFA** 3 from 4yo+ 6lb 6 Ran SP% **130.5**
PARI-MUTUEL (all including 10 euro stake): WIN: 29; PLACE: 18, 15; SF: 54.
**Owner** Dirk Von Mitzlaff **Bred** Dirk Von Mitzlaff **Trained** Germany

# 4876 SAINT-CLOUD (L-H)
Thursday, August 31

**OFFICIAL GOING: Turf: good to soft**

## 6648a PRIX TEDDY (H'CAP) (4YO+) (TURF) 1m
12:47 4-Y-0+

£20,888 (£8,444; £6,222; £3,222; £3,222; £1,555)

RPR

1 **Saint Pois (FR)**30 6-8-7 0 MaximeGuyon 11 79
(J-P Sauvage, France) **44/5**3

2 1/2 **Arvios**19 5-9-1 0 StephanePasquier 5 86
(F-X Belvisi, France) **103/10**

3 1/2 **Iron Spirit (FR)**18 5979 7-9-5 0 (p) AlexisBadel 12 89
(Mme M Bollack-Badel, France) **13/2**1

4 1/2 **London Protocol (FR)**18 5979 4-9-8 0 TonyPiccone 16 91
(K R Burke) *wl into stride: settled bhd ldrs: pushed along over 2f out: drvn to dispute ld over 1f out: hdd ins fnl f and styd on one pce* **126/10**

4 dht **Xotic (FR)**19 8-8-5 0 AurelienLemaitre 1 74
(D & P Prod'Homme, France) **175/10**

6 3/4 **Babel's Book (FR)**19 4-8-5 0 (b) RonanThomas 13 72
(F-H Graffard, France) **15/2**2

7 1 **Matken (FR)**19 5-8-3 0 FabriceVeron 2 68
(D & P Prod'Homme, France) **106/10**

8 snk **Yume (FR)**9 6300 6-8-7 0 ow1 (b) AntoineHamelin 14 71
(S Cerulis, France) **163/10**

9 nse **Rominou (FR)**32 4-8-11 0 CristianDemuro 6 75
(C Lerner, France) **174/10**

10 hd **Lyavenita (FR)**53 5-8-3 0 LudovicBoisseau 4 67
(J-V Toux, France) **37/1**

11 1 **Shanawest (FR)**86 5-8-0 0 DavidBreux 7 61
(N Caullery, France) **189/10**

12 2 **Nice To See You (FR)**18 5979 4-9-5 0 (b) VincentCheminaud 8 76
(Robert Collet, France) **92/10**

13 snk **Aprilios (FR)**18 5979 5-9-3 0 EddyHardouin 10 74
(J-M Lefebvre, France) **111/10**

14 3/4 **Prince Apache**19 4-8-9 0 GeraldMosse 3 64
(Andreas Suborics, Germany) **187/10**

15 4 **Diamant De Vati (FR)**9 6300 6-8-7 0 TheoBachelot 9 53
(S Wattel, France) **29/1**

16 3 1/2 **Geonpi (IRE)**18 5979 6-8-11 0 MickaelBarzalona 15 49
(N Bellanger, France) **139/10**

1m 40.05s (-7.45) 16 Ran SP% **117.6**
PARI-MUTUEL (all including 1 euro stake): WIN 9.80; PLACE 3.40, 4.20, 2.50; DF 45.00; SF 107.20.
**Owner** Philippe Sauvage **Bred** S A Franklin Finance **Trained** France

## 6649a PRIX D'ELANCOURT (CLAIMER) (3YO) (TURF) 1m 6f
1:50 3-Y-0 £8,119 (£3,247; £2,435; £1,623; £811)

RPR

1 **Sowgay (FR)**35 3-9-1 0 (b) RonanThomas 2 65
(C Plisson, France) **126/10**

2 1/2 **Mr Maximum (USA)**38 5235 3-8-11 0 (b) HayleyTurner(5) 8 61
(F-H Graffard, France) **8/5**1

3 hd **Sister Vic (FR)**4 6496 3-8-5 0 KyllanBarbaud(8) 7 62
(N Caullery, France) **152/10**

4 2 **Chiquit Indian (FR)**41 5133 3-8-11 0 EddyHardouin 3 57
(E Caroux, France) **68/10**

5 3/4 **Poudreuse (FR)**147 3-8-11 0 (p) Pierre-CharlesBoudot 5 56
(J-P Gauvin, France) **9/2**2

6 1 **Mowafrost (FR)**11 6256 3-9-1 0 (p) TheoBachelot 6 58
(Mme P Butel, France) **5/1**3

7 5 **National Velvet (FR)**35 3-8-10 0 (p) JeromeMoutard(6) 1 52
(S Dehez, France) **134/10**

8 7 **Riviere Argentee (FR)**12 6225 3-9-1 0 (p) ChristopheSoumillon 9 42
(K R Burke) *wl away: settled bhd ldr: rowed along over 2f out: sn rdn and limited rspnse: eased ins fnl f* **76/10**

3m 5.63s (-6.57) 8 Ran SP% **118.2**
PARI-MUTUEL (all including 1 euro stake): WIN 13.60; PLACE 3.00, 1.50, 3.30; DF 13.30; SF 38.00.
**Owner** Christophe Plisson **Bred** M Melin & M Melin **Trained** France

## 6650a PRIX DE MONTMAGNY (CLAIMER) (3YO) (TURF) 1m
2:55 3-Y-0 £9,829 (£3,931; £2,948; £1,965; £982)

RPR

1 **La Michodiere (IRE)**14 3-8-7 0 JeromeMoutard(6) 6 83
(J-C Rouget, France) **101/10**

2 1 3/4 **Premiere Gachette (IRE)**435 3-8-13 0 HugoJourniac 9 79
(J-C Rouget, France) **47/10**1

3 3/4 **Angel Baby (FR)**63 4289 3-8-8 0 ClementLecoeuvre(3) 15 75
(Alex Fracas, France) **94/10**

4 3/4 **Rebecca (FR)**35 3-9-3 0 ChristopheSoumillon 14 80
(C Lerner, France) **51/10**2

5 snk **Alliance Secrete (FR)**20 5909 3-9-1 0 (p) MaximeGuyon 1 77
(T Castanheira, France) **6/1**3

6 3/4 **Streets Of Rio (FR)**25 3-9-3 0 TristanBaron(5) 7 82
(H-A Pantall, France) **108/10**

7 2 **Dora Bruder (FR)**20 5910 3-9-2 0 Pierre-CharlesBoudot 3 72
(D Cottin, France) **104/10**

8 nk **Power Becqua (FR)**20 5909 3-9-1 0 AntoineHamelin 9 70
(P Van De Poele, France) **128/10**

9 3 1/2 **Tap Tap Boom**20 5909 3-9-10 0 TheoBachelot 12 71
(Mme P Butel, France) **43/5**

10 1/2 **A Head Ahead (GER)**15 6084 3-8-7 0 (b) AlexisPouchin(8) 2 61
(Y Gourraud, France) **195/10**

11 shd **World Power (IRE)**20 5910 3-9-1 0 DavidBreux 4 61
(F Vermeulen, France) **179/10**

12 3 **Dear Django (FR)**59 3-8-11 0 AurelienLemaitre 11 50
(D & P Prod'Homme, France) **58/1**

13 1 3/4 **Norwegian Highness (FR)**[27] 5606 3-8-11 0.................... JulienAuge 5 46
(Kevin Ryan) *wl into stride: keen early: racd bhd ldrs: shkn up and rdn 2f out: sn lost pl and eased ins fnl f* **22/1**

1m 42.52s (-4.98) **13** Ran SP% **118.0**
PARI-MUTUEL (all including 1 euro stake): WIN 7.00; PLACE 2.70, 2.20, 3.20; DF 26.10; SF 27.20.
**Owner** Stephan Hoffmeister **Bred** Edgeridge Ltd & Glenvale Stud **Trained** Pau, France

## 5838 SANDOWN (R-H)

### Friday, September 1

**OFFICIAL GOING: Round course - good to soft (good in places, 6.9); sprint course - good (good to soft in places, 7.0)**
Wind: Mostly light, behind race 1, half against after Weather: Fine, warm

## 6651 WATCH RACING UK ON SKY 432 NURSERY H'CAP (JOCKEY CLUB GRASSROOTS NURSERY QUALIFIER) 5f 10y

**1:40** (1:42) (Class 5) (0-75,76) 2-Y-O **£4,528** (£1,347; £673; £336) **Stalls** Low

Form RPR

3051 **1** **Spoof**[8] 6338 2-9-5 **76** 6ex........................................(h) CallumShepherd(3) 6 79
(Charles Hills) *lw: taken down early: pressed ldrs: wnt 2nd 1/2-way: led wl over 1f out: cajoled along and looked in command ins fnl f: jst hld on* **8/1**

6204 **2** *nk* **Kodiac Express (IRE)**[17] 6021 2-9-1 **69**........................ AntonioFresu 11 71
(Mike Murphy) *racd wdst of all in last trio: prog over 1f out: drvn and r.o to take 2nd nr fin: clsd qckly on wnr after* **11/1**

0030 **3** *3/4* **Ivy Leaguer**[17] 6021 2-9-0 **68**........................................ JimmyFortune 9 67
(Brian Meehan) *racd on outer: in tch: rdn and prog 1/2-way: pressed wnr jst over 1f out: hld ins fnl f: lost 2nd nr fin* **25/1**

0125 **4** *nk* **Dreamboat Annie**[18] 6012 2-9-1 **69**............................ SteveDrowne 7 67
(Mark Usher) *hld up in last trio: prog fr 2f out: rdn and styd on to dispute 2nd nr fin: no ex last strides* **25/1**

2146 **5** *2* **Aquadabra (IRE)**[28] 5614 2-9-3 **71**.......................... SilvestreDeSousa 5 62
(Mick Channon) *t.k.h: hld up in tch: effrt to chse ldrs over 1f out: fdd ins fnl f* **7/1**

3200 **6** *1* **Onefootinparadise**[27] 5659 2-9-2 **70**............................... DavidProbert 4 58
(Philip McBride) *cl up on rail: short of room briefly over 1f out: wknd ins fnl f* **9/2**[3]

046 **7** *1* **Comselle**[13] 6178 2-8-10 **64**........................................ OisinMurphy 10 48+
(Stuart Kittow) *dropped in fr wd draw and hld up in last: nudged along over 1f out: passed a few late on: nvr involved* **33/1**

4531 **8** *1/2* **The Golden Cue**[30] 5546 2-9-4 **72**.............................. AdamBeschizza 2 54
(Steph Hollinshead) *t.k.h: led against rail: hdd wl over 1f out: wknd qckly fnl f* **7/2**[1]

3026 **9** *3/4* **Zalshah**[17] 6021 2-9-6 **74**................................................ TomMarquand 3 53
(Richard Hannon) *chsd ldr after 1f to 1/2-way: wknd jst over 1f out* **4/1**[2]

3104 **10** *7* **Firenze Rosa (IRE)**[19] 5963 2-9-7 **75**........................ JosephineGordon 1 29
(John Bridger) *chsd ldr 1f: sn lost pl and struggling: wl btn sn after 1/2-way* **10/1**

1m 1.54s (-0.06) **Going Correction** -0.125s/f (Firm) **10** Ran SP% **112.1**
Speed ratings (Par 95): **95,94,93,92,89 88,86,85,84,73**
CSF £85.97 CT £2071.50 TOTE £7.30: £2.50, £3.00, £8.20; EX 97.30 Trifecta £3482.10.
**Owner** Gary And Linnet Woodward **Bred** Scuderia Blueberry SRL **Trained** Lambourn, Berks

**FOCUS**
A modest but competitive nursery. Plenty had their chance and there was little between first first four at the line, with the winner replicating his Chepstow win. He may not be the easiest, but looks the type to run better in a better race.

## 6652 VISIT RACINGUK.COM H'CAP 5f 10y

**2:10** (2:11) (Class 5) (0-75,77) 3-Y-O+ **£3,881** (£1,155; £577; £288) **Stalls** Low

Form RPR

13U1 **1** **Gnaad (IRE)**[7] 6372 3-9-1 **72** 6ex.................................. JoshuaBryan(5) 6 80
(Alan Bailey) *hld up in 7th: swtchd to wd outside and prog jst over 2f out: drvn to ld ins fnl f: hung lft but styd on wl* **7/1**

6033 **2** *1* **John Joiner**[25] 5723 5-8-5 **56**........................................ FrannyNorton 10 60
(Peter Hedger) *t.k.h: hld up in tch: prog on outer over 1f out: chal fnl f: one pce last 100yds* **12/1**

16 **3** *shd* **Red Alert**[67] 4159 3-9-7 **73**.......................................... SilvestreDeSousa 1 77
(William Muir) *led and racd towards far rail: drvn and hrd pressed fr over 1f out: hdd ins fnl f: kpt on* **6/1**[3]

2111 **4** *1* **Our Lord**[9] 6303 5-9-8 **73**.................................................. RobHornby 2 73
(Michael Attwater) *trckd ldrs against rail: rdn over 1f out: kpt on same pce and nvr able to chal* **11/8**[1]

0034 **5** *1* **Very Honest (IRE)**[29] 5558 4-9-9 **74**............................... JackMitchell 8 71
(Brett Johnson) *lw: prom: tk 2nd 2f out and sn pressed ldr: upsides 1f out: lost pl rather qckly last 150yds* **14/1**

0331 **6** *hd* **Babyfact**[37] 5271 6-9-7 **77**............................................. GeorgiaCox(5) 4 73
(Malcolm Saunders) *chsd ldrs: pushed along and dropped to rr 1/2-way: n.d after: kpt on nr fin* **11/2**[2]

0005 **7** *3/4* **Merdon Castle (IRE)**[16] 6058 5-9-5 **70**........................... MartinHarley 3 63
(Jane Chapple-Hyam) *n.m.r sn after s then faltered: mostly in last: drvn over 1f out: kpt on fnl f but no ch to threaten* **8/1**

00 **8** *3/4* **Secret Asset (IRE)**[17] 6041 12-8-5 **56** oh8....................(p) KieranO'Neill 7 47
(Lisa Williamson) *pressed ldr to 2f out: sn lost pl and btn* **50/1**

1m 0.72s (-0.88) **Going Correction** -0.125s/f (Firm)
**WFA** 3 from 4yo+ 1lb **8** Ran SP% **111.7**
Speed ratings (Par 103): **102,100,100,98,97 96,95,94**
CSF £81.10 CT £529.37 TOTE £7.60: £2.30, £2.90, £2.10; EX 65.70 Trifecta £483.90.
**Owner** AB Racing Limited **Bred** Rabbah Bloodstock Limited **Trained** Newmarket, Suffolk

**FOCUS**
A modest sprint with the short-priced favourite disappointing. The runner-up has been rated to this year's form.

## 6653 BRITISH STALLION STUDS EBF MAIDEN STKS (DIV I) 7f

**2:45** (2:48) (Class 5) 2-Y-O **£3,881** (£1,155; £577; £288) **Stalls** Low

Form RPR

04 **1** **Rum Runner**[14] 6133 2-9-5 0................................................ SeanLevey 6 84
(Richard Hannon) *w'like: trckd ldng pair: clsd fr 2f out: rdn to ld 1f out: styd on wl* **11/1**

0 **2** *1 1/4* **Enzemble (IRE)**[21] 5887 2-9-5 0.................................. SilvestreDeSousa 10 81
(David Elsworth) *tall: trckd ldng trio: shkn up to cl fr 2f out: chsd wnr jst ins fnl f: styd on but nvr really a threat* **5/1**[3]

**3** *1 3/4* **History Writer (IRE)** 2-9-5 0.................................. RichardKingscote 14 77+
(David Menuisier) *athletic: lw: slowly away fr wd draw: stdy prog fr rr over 3f out: shkn up over 1f out: styd on to take 3rd ins fnl f: encouraging debut* **20/1**

**4** *3/4* **Emaraaty** 2-9-5 0.................................................................. JimCrowley 15 75+
(John Gosden) *str: bit bkwd: slowest away fr wd draw: mostly in last trio: steered sharply rt 3f out: stylish prog through rivals over 2f out: pushed along briefly over 1f out: styd on to take 4th nr fin: v encouraging debut* **3/1**[1]

0 **5** *1 1/2* **Masked Defender (USA)**[99] 3002 2-9-5 0.......................... JackMitchell 12 71
(Amanda Perrett) *bit bkwd: trckd ldr: led 2f out gng strly: rdn and hdd 1f out: wknd* **66/1**

02 **6** *hd* **Dark Spec**[19] 5960 2-9-5 0................................................ RobHornby 2 70
(Pam Sly) *led to 2f out: wknd fnl f* **8/1**

**7** *2* **Sam Gold (IRE)** 2-9-5 0.................................................. AndreaAtzeni 13 65+
(Roger Varian) *athletic: pushed along in midfield bef 1/2-way: rdn 2f out: kpt on fr over 1f out: n.d* **7/2**[2]

**8** *1 1/4* **Delsheer (FR)** 2-9-5 0........................................................ JamesDoyle 3 62
(Hugo Palmer) *leggy: athletic: nvr beyond midfield: pushed along and no imp ldrs fr 2f out* **12/1**

**9** *1/2* **Westbrook Bertie** 2-9-5 0.............................................. CharlesBishop 16 61
(Mick Channon) *unf: slowly away fr wd draw: wl in rr: effrt on outer over 2f out: no real prog over 1f out* **50/1**

6 **10** *1/2* **Technological**[50] 4792 2-9-5 0............................................ TomQueally 5 60
(George Margarson) *leggy: chsd ldrs: shkn up and no prog 2f out: fdd* **100/1**

**11** *1/2* **Beachwalk** 2-9-5 0................................................................ RyanMoore 4 59+
(Sir Michael Stoute) *tall: athletic: a towards rr: pushed along and no prog over 2f out* **10/1**

04 **12** *1 1/2* **Taurean Dancer (IRE)**[23] 5808 2-9-5 0............................ JamieSpencer 8 55
(Michael Bell) *str: a in rr: pushed along and no prog over 2f out* **33/1**

6 **13** *5* **Blacklooks (IRE)**[19] 5960 2-9-5 0.................................... FrannyNorton 11 42
(Ivan Furtado) *cl-cpld: t.k.h: hld up in last trio: no prog fr 3f out* **40/1**

**14** *1 1/2* **Night Spark (GER)** 2-9-5 0.................................................. PatDobbs 1 39
(Ralph Beckett) *cmpt: bit bkwd: chsd ldrs tl wknd over 2f out* **40/1**

0 **15** *hd* **Lady Jayne (IRE)**[79] 3712 2-9-0 0.................................. GeorgeDowning 9 33
(Ian Williams) *leggy: a in rr: sltly impeded 3f out: no prog 2f out* **100/1**

6 **16** *49* **Becky Sharp**[27] 5655 2-9-0 0.............................................. PatCosgrave 7
(Jim Boyle) *tall: rrd s: t.k.h early: pushed along in rr whn bdly hmpd 3f out: eased and t.o* **66/1**

1m 30.43s (0.93) **Going Correction** +0.15s/f (Good) **16** Ran SP% **119.6**
Speed ratings (Par 95): **100,98,96,95,94 93,91,90,89,88 88,86,80,79,78 22**
CSF £60.51 TOTE £12.30: £3.60, £2.10, £6.10; EX 86.50 Trifecta £1425.30.
**Owner** Michael Geoghegan **Bred** Biddestone Stud **Trained** East Everleigh, Wilts

**FOCUS**
Race distance increased by 12yds. A decent maiden that should produce its share of winners and those with experience came to the fore. It paid to race handily.

## 6654 BRITISH STALLION STUDS EBF MAIDEN STKS (DIV II) 7f

**3:20** (3:24) (Class 5) 2-Y-O **£3,881** (£1,155; £577; £288) **Stalls** Low

Form RPR

522 **1** **Bathsheba Bay (IRE)**[27] 5641 2-9-5 87.............................. RyanMoore 4 85+
(Richard Hannon) *lw: trckd ldng pair: shkn up to ld 2f out: clr and rdn out fnl f* **10/11**[1]

0 **2** *2 1/4* **Breath Caught**[59] 4465 2-9-5 0............................................ PatDobbs 8 79
(Ralph Beckett) *lengthy: lw: trckd ldr: upsides fr 3f out tl wnr wnt past 2f out: chsng after: kpt on but no imp* **14/1**

**3** *3/4* **Zaajer** 2-9-5 0........................................................................ JimCrowley 5 78+
(Owen Burrows) *cmpt: lw: hld up in rr: stdy prog over 2f out: shkn up over 1f out: tk 3rd ins fnl f: styd on* **4/1**[2]

**4** *1/2* **Graffiti Master** 2-9-5 0...................................................... JamesDoyle 1 76+
(John Gosden) *cmpt: lw: hld up in last trio: stdy prog over 2f out: pushed along and styd on to take 4th nr fin: encouraging debut* **9/2**[3]

**5** *nk* **Pompey Chimes (IRE)** 2-9-2 0.................................. HectorCrouch(3) 3 76+
(Gary Moore) *lengthy: v difficult to load into stall: in tch: prog and cl up 2f out: one pce fr over 1f out* **40/1**

**6** *1 1/4* **Port Of Call** 2-9-5 0........................................................ JackMitchell 13 72+
(Amanda Perrett) *lengthy: s.s: rn green and detached in last: gd prog on inner over 2f out: chsd ldrs over 1f out: no hdwy fnl f but nt disgracd* **33/1**

**7** *1 1/4* **Echo Cove (IRE)** 2-9-5 0.................................................. MartinHarley 7 69
(Jane Chapple-Hyam) *unf: chsd ldrs: shkn up over 2f out: wknd over 1f out* **16/1**

0 **8** *1/2* **Ocean Side**[57] 4534 2-9-5 0.............................................. SeanLevey 12 68
(Richard Hannon) *leggy: in tch: outpcd fr 2f out: nvr on terms after* **40/1**

6 **9** *2 1/2* **Gembari**[15] 6108 2-9-5 0................................................... FrannyNorton 2 62
(Ivan Furtado) *w'like: chsd ldrs: cl up 2f out: sn wknd* **50/1**

0 **10** *hd* **Caviar Royale**[16] 6070 2-9-5 0.......................................... JimmyFortune 14 61
(Brian Meehan) *mde most to 2f out: wknd* **66/1**

**11** *9* **Isle Of Man** 2-9-5 0........................................................... SamHitchcott 11 39
(Clive Cox) *str: sltly impeded early: wl in rr: pushed along 1/2-way: sn lost tch: t.o* **20/1**

6 **12** *1 1/4* **Quick Recovery**[50] 4799 2-9-0 0......................................... PatCosgrave 10 31
(Jim Boyle) *plld hrd: hld up but sn in midfield: wknd over 2f out: eased and t.o* **66/1**

1m 31.73s (2.23) **Going Correction** +0.15s/f (Good) **12** Ran SP% **120.6**
Speed ratings (Par 95): **93,90,89,89,88 87,85,85,82,82 71,70**
CSF £16.17 TOTE £1.80: £1.10, £3.20, £1.70; EX 14.10 Trifecta £30.60.
**Owner** Michael Geoghegan **Bred** Danny Coogan **Trained** East Everleigh, Wilts

**FOCUS**
Race distance increased by 12yds. Similar to division one in that it paid to race prominently and the experienced runners held the advantage over the promising newcomers. Again, it's a race that should produce winners.

## 6655 ALL NEW FIESTA AT TRUST FORD H'CAP 1m

**3:55** (3:55) (Class 3) (0-90,91) 3-Y-O
**£8,092** (£2,423; £1,211; £605; £302; £152) **Stalls** Low

Form RPR

1210 **1** **Archetype (FR)**[29] 5568 3-9-9 **91**...................................... OisinMurphy 7 102
(Simon Crisford) *trckd ldr: pushed into ld 2f out: rdn clr over 1f out: kpt on wl* **13/2**

1-20 **2** *2 1/2* **Icespire**[99] 3006 3-9-3 **85**.................................................(h) AndreaAtzeni 5 89
(John Gosden) *hld up in last pair: sltly impeded after 150yds: cajoled along and no prog over 2f out: styd on fr over 1f out to take 2nd last stride* **7/2**[1]

3334 **3** *nse* **High Acclaim (USA)**[61] 4407 3-9-5 **87**.................(p) SilvestreDeSousa 2 91
(Roger Teal) *chsd ldng pair: shkn up over 2f out: drvn to chse wnr ins fnl f: no imp and lost 2nd last stride* **16/1**

1-05 **4** *1* **Elucidation (IRE)**[114] 2520 3-9-5 **87**.................................... RyanMoore 4 89
(Sir Michael Stoute) *lw: hld up in last pair: sltly impeded after 150yds: shkn up over 2f out and no prog: kpt on fr over 1f out but nvr a real threat* **9/2**[3]

2121 **5** *¾* **Pillar Of Society (IRE)**[34] 5425 3-9-7 **89**.......................... SeanLevey 6 89
(Richard Hannon) *led at str pce: hdd 2f out: wknd fnl f* **4/1**[2]

1 **6** *1 ¼* **Robin Weathers (USA)**[48] 4911 3-9-2 **84**...................... PatCosgrave 3 81
(William Haggas) *str: lw: hld up in 5th: shkn up over 2f out: nvr able to make significant hdwy* **11/2**

3-23 **7** *3* **Harvest Wind (IRE)**[23] 5794 3-8-11 **79**.......................... SamHitchcott 8 69
(Clive Cox) *chsd ldng trio: rdn over 2f out: sn lost pl: steadily wknd* **20/1**

5111 **U** **Madeleine Bond**[28] 5591 3-8-10 **83**............................ GeorgiaCox(5) 1
(Henry Candy) *stmbld and uns rdr after 150yds* **7/1**

1m 43.46s (0.16) **Going Correction** +0.15s/f (Good) **8** Ran SP% **112.3**
Speed ratings (Par 105): **105,102,102,101,100 99,96,**
CSF £28.39 CT £348.63 TOTE £6.90: £2.20, £1.40, £3.40; EX 31.70 Trifecta £268.60.
**Owner** Highclere Thoroughbred Racing-Wordsworth **Bred** E A R L Ecurie Du Grand Chene Haras **Trained** Newmarket, Suffolk

**FOCUS**
Race distance increased by 12yds. A useful handicap, but it ended up being a little messy with two of the fancied runners hampered early after Madeleine Bond unseated. The runner-up has been rated close to form with the third rated to handicap best.

## 6656 HAPPY 10TH BIRTHDAY AMETHYST LETTINGS FILLIES' H'CAP — 7f
**4:25** (4:28) (Class 5) (0-75,75) 3-Y-O+ **£3,881** (£1,155; £577; £288) **Stalls** Low

Form RPR

012 **1** **Here's Two**[8] 6340 4-9-7 **70**........................................ KieranO'Neill 2 79
(Ron Hodges) *chsd ldng pair but often pushed along: rdn to cl 2f out: led over 1f out: drvn and kpt on wl whn pressed fnl 100yds* **7/2**[1]

2133 **2** *¾* **Helfire**[23] 5788 4-9-9 **75**............................................. CharlieBennett(3) 9 82
(Hughie Morrison) *walked to post by jockey: hld up off the pce in last trio: gd prog on inner 2f out: chsd wnr jst ins fnl f: threatened 100yds out: styd on but no imp nr fin* **4/1**[2]

5105 **3** *3* **Miss Osier**[15] 6102 3-8-11 **64**..........................(p) SilvestreDeSousa 6 61
(Rae Guest) *lw: chsd ldng pair: rdn 2f out: disp 2nd briefly 1f out: one pce after* **4/1**[2]

0024 **4** *1* **Twilight Spirit**[22] 5826 3-8-6 **59**...................................... FrannyNorton 3 53
(Tony Carroll) *lw: hld up disputing 5th: rdn and prog over 2f out: disp 2nd briefly 1f out: fdd nr fin* **7/1**

4434 **5** *1 ¼* **Anastazia**[36] 5337 5-9-5 **68**............................................ JoeyHaynes 1 61
(Paul D'Arcy) *lw: hld up in midfield: pushed along over 2f out: no real hdwy and nvr involved* **9/1**

024 **6** *1* **Violet's Lads (IRE)**[34] 5409 3-8-12 **65**................................ JackMitchell 7 53
(Brett Johnson) *hld up off the pce in last trio: prog on outer over 2f out: drvn and no hdwy over 1f out* **33/1**

2142 **7** *2* **Emily Goldfinch**[42] 5119 4-8-11 **60**.................................. DannyBrock 5 45
(Phil McEntee) *lw: disp ld at str pce tl led over over 2f out: hdd over 1f out: wknd qckly* **6/1**[3]

3043 **8** *5* **Sarangoo**[43] 5064 9-9-5 **73**............................................ GeorgiaCox(5) 10 44
(Malcolm Saunders) *disp ld at str pce to over 2f out: wknd qckly over 1f out* **10/1**

30-0 **9** *1 ¼* **Poyle Emily**[25] 5712 4-8-13 **62**........................................ FranBerry 8 30
(Michael Madgwick) *hld up off the pce in last trio: shkn up over 2f out: hanging and no prog: eased* **33/1**

1m 30.66s (1.16) **Going Correction** +0.15s/f (Good)
**WFA** 3 from 4yo+ 4lb **9** Ran SP% **114.0**
Speed ratings (Par 100): **99,98,94,93,92 91,88,83,81**
CSF £17.27 CT £56.50 TOTE £4.40: £1.80, £1.50, £1.70; EX 14.60 Trifecta £59.70.
**Owner** K Corcoran, C E Weare, R J Hodges **Bred** D R Tucker **Trained** Charlton Mackrell, Somerset

**FOCUS**
Race distance increased by 12yds. The right horses came to the fore in this fillies' handicap, which was run at a good gallop, and so the form looks sound for the level. The winner has been rated to her better 3yo form and a personal best for the runner-up.

## 6657 BISHOPSGATE PAY H'CAP — 1m 1f 209y
**5:00** (5:00) (Class 4) (0-80,80) 3-Y-O **£5,822** (£1,732; £865; £432) **Stalls** Low

Form RPR

6100 **1** **Mister Blue Sky (IRE)**[20] 5915 3-9-1 **79**...................... MitchGodwin(5) 4 88
(Sylvester Kirk) *prog to trck ldr after 4f: led over 2f out and struck for home: drvn over 1f out: kpt on wl fnl f* **15/2**

3222 **2** *1 ¼* **Know Your Limit (IRE)**[16] 6075 3-9-5 **78**.............. JamieSpencer 10 84
(Ed Walker) *hld up in last pair: cajoled along and prog jst over 2f out: rdn to chse wnr jst ins fnl f: nt qckn and no imp last 100yds* **11/2**

4221 **3** *¾* **Golden Wolf (IRE)**[20] 5931 3-9-6 **79**............................ ShaneKelly 8 83
(Richard Hughes) *swtg: hld up but prog into midfield after 4f: hdwy to chse wnr 2f out: drvn and no imp after: lost 2nd jst ins fnl f: kpt on* **5/1**[3]

5-02 **4** *3 ½* **Rising (IRE)**[14] 6150 3-9-7 **80**........................................ JamesDoyle 9 77
(Brian Meehan) *lw: trckd ldr 8f out to 6f out: rdn and nt qckn over 2f out: lost 3rd over 1f out: fdd* **4/1**[1]

-032 **5** *nk* **Precious Angel (IRE)**[16] 6067 3-8-10 **69**.................... SeanLevey 1 65
(Richard Hannon) *in tch towards rr: rdn over 2f out: one pce and nvr able to threaten* **7/1**

-521 **6** *2 ¼* **Keeper's Choice (IRE)**[25] 5712 3-9-1 **74**...................... TomQueally 7 66
(Denis Coakley) *hld up towards rr: rdn and prog on outer over 2f out: no hdwy over 1f out: wknd* **16/1**

3561 **7** *2 ¼* **Eolian**[29] 5565 3-8-13 **72**................................................(p) OisinMurphy 6 59
(Andrew Balding) *led after 1f: rdn and hdd over 2f out: sn wknd* **9/2**[2]

-040 **8** *6* **See The City (IRE)**[79] 3727 3-9-0 **73**................................ RyanTate 3 48
(James Eustace) *led 1f: sn in midfield: rdn and wknd over 2f out* **16/1**

1-20 **9** *1 ½* **Peace And Plenty**[142] 1736 3-8-11 **70**............................ MartinDwyer 2 42
(William Muir) *chsd ldrs: rdn and wknd qckly over 2f out* **25/1**

051 **10** *1 ¾* **Viking Hoard (IRE)**[16] 6075 3-9-4 **77**............................(b) JimCrowley 5 46
(Harry Dunlop) *t.k.h early: hld up in last pair: rdn and no prog over 2f out: no ch after* **14/1**

2m 10.85s (0.35) **Going Correction** +0.15s/f (Good) **10** Ran SP% **116.8**
Speed ratings (Par 103): **104,103,102,99,99 97,95,90,89,88**
CSF £48.53 CT £228.61 TOTE £8.60: £2.30, £1.90, £1.90; EX 47.80 Trifecta £240.60.
**Owner** Deauville Daze Partnership 1 **Bred** Shadwell Estate Company Limited **Trained** Upper Lambourn, Berks

**FOCUS**
Race distance increased by 12yds. Fair handicap form with another personal best for the runner-up.
T/Jkpt: Not won. T/Plt: £853.40 to a £1 stake. Pool: £100,460.62 - 85.93 winning units T/Qpdt: £21.90 to a £1 stake. Pool: £10,091.61 - 339.50 winning units **Jonathan Neesom**

# [6264] THIRSK (L-H)
Friday, September 1

**OFFICIAL GOING: Good to firm (good in places; 8.5)**
Wind: light across Weather: overcast

## 6658 TODAY IS "PIRATES FAMILY DAY" @THIRSKRACES NOVICE AUCTION STKS — 7f 218y
**1:50** (1:51) (Class 6) 2-Y-O **£2,587** (£770; £384; £192) **Stalls** Low

Form RPR

1 **1** **Trumps Up**[24] 5749 2-9-9 0...................................................... JFEgan 5 76
(Mick Channon) *prom: rdn to ld narrowly 2f out: kpt on* **9/2**[3]

134 **2** *¾* **French Flyer (IRE)**[20] 5918 2-9-9 75.............................. PaulMulrennan 1 74
(Michael Dods) *led: pushed along 3f out: rdn whn hdd 2f out: kpt on but a hld* **13/8**[1]

03 **3** *1 ¼* **Breathable**[13] 6204 2-9-2 0.................................................. DavidAllan 3 64
(Tim Easterby) *trckd ldrs: rdn over 2f out: kpt on* **10/1**

**4** *2 ¼* **Golden Guide** 2-8-11 0.................................................... PJMcDonald 7 54+
(K R Burke) *midfield on outside: pushed along and lost pl 5f out: sme hdwy over 1f out: kpt on fnl f* **7/2**[2]

05 **5** *nse* **Airplane (IRE)**[13] 6204 2-8-13 0........................... RachelRichardson(3) 6 59
(Tim Easterby) *in tch towards outer: keen early: rdn over 2f out: one pce* **50/1**

**6** *¾* **Sincerely Resdev** 2-9-2 0.................................................. DavidNolan 10 57+
(David O'Meara) *hld up in rr: pushed along over 2f out: kpt on fnl f* **13/2**

**7** *1* **Gabriel's Oboe (IRE)** 2-9-2 0........................................... DougieCostello 9 55+
(Mark Walford) *s.i.s: hld up in midfield: pushed along over 2f out: n.m.r fnl 110yds: nvr threatened* **66/1**

**8** *nse* **The Knot Is Tied (IRE)** 2-9-2 0.................................... JamesSullivan 2 55+
(Tim Easterby) *s.i.s: sn midfield: rdn along over 2f out: grad wknd fnl f* **25/1**

**9** *¾* **Weinberg** 2-9-2 0.............................................................. GrahamLee 8 54+
(Donald McCain) *hld up: nvr threatened* **22/1**

1m 41.06s (0.96) **Going Correction** -0.05s/f (Good) **9** Ran SP% **112.6**
Speed ratings (Par 93): **93,92,91,88,88 87,86,86,86**
CSF £11.52 TOTE £5.80: £1.80, £1.10, £2.50; EX 14.30 Trifecta £35.80.
**Owner** David Fitzgerald **Bred** Al Asayl Bloodstock Ltd **Trained** West Ilsley, Berks

**FOCUS**
It was dry overnight and the going was good to firm, good in places (GoingStick: 8.5). The rail on the home bend was dolled out circa 3m from the inside line, increasing distances of races on the round course by 10yds. Few got into this ordinary novice, the market leaders dominating throughout and having a good battle up the straight. The runner-up sets the opening level.

## 6659 BRITISH STALLION STUDS EBF FILLIES' NOVICE STKS (PLUS 10 RACE) — 7f 218y
**2:20** (2:21) (Class 4) 2-Y-O **£4,269** (£1,270; £634; £317) **Stalls** Low

Form RPR

21 **1** **Exhort**[21] 5874 2-9-6 0......................................................... PaulHanagan 3 79
(Richard Fahey) *trckd ldr: rdn to ld narrowly over 1f out: kpt on* **5/6**[1]

50 **2** *nk* **Gamesters Icon**[35] 5371 2-9-0 0.............................................. GrahamLee 1 72
(Bryan Smart) *led: rdn over 2f out: hdd over 1f out: kpt on but a jst hld* **66/1**

05 **3** *2 ¼* **Ventura Royal (IRE)**[18] 5990 2-9-0 0.............................. PhillipMakin 2 67
(David O'Meara) *dwlt: sn trckd ldr: rdn over 2f out: no ex ins fnl f* **8/1**[3]

**4** *hd* **Sempre Presto (IRE)** 2-9-0 0............................................. TonyHamilton 7 67+
(Richard Fahey) *hld up: pushed along over 2f out: sme hdwy over 1f out: kpt on ins fnl f* **10/1**

**5** *3 ¼* **Bollin Joan** 2-9-0 0.............................................................. DavidAllan 4 59
(Tim Easterby) *in tch: pushed along over 3f out: wknd ins fnl f* **66/1**

35 **6** *hd* **Ann Without An E**[13] 6190 2-9-0 0.............................................. JFEgan 8 59
(Mick Channon) *dwlt: hld up: rdn along over 3f out: sme hdwy over 2f out: wknd ins fnl f* **2/1**[2]

1m 40.58s (0.48) **Going Correction** -0.05s/f (Good) **6** Ran SP% **111.1**
Speed ratings (Par 94): **95,94,92,92,89 88**
CSF £48.91 TOTE £1.70: £1.10, £16.00; EX 33.60 Trifecta £132.50.
**Owner** Cheveley Park Stud **Bred** Cheveley Park Stud Ltd **Trained** Musley Bank, N Yorks

**FOCUS**
Race distance increased by 10yds. Question marks about this with the second favourite miles below form and winner tentatively allowed her mark.

## 6660 CAPTAIN JACK SPARROW IS HERE TODAY (S) H'CAP — 5f
**2:55** (2:55) (Class 6) (0-65,64) 3-5-Y-O **£2,726** (£805; £402) **Stalls** Centre

Form RPR

2 **1** **Mr Strutter (IRE)**[53] 4694 3-9-6 **64**.................................(h) JasonHart 3 68
(John Quinn) *prom: rdn to ld over 2f out: hdd over 1f out: led again 1f out: edgd rt: pressed fnl 110yds: kpt on* **6/4**[1]

4006 **2** *nk* **Dapper Man (IRE)**[5] 6469 3-9-2 **60**.............................. TonyHamilton 7 63
(Roger Fell) *trckd ldrs: pushed along to chal 1f out: drvn fnl 110yds: kpt on same pce* **5/1**[3]

0300 **3** *2* **Twentysvnthlancers**[50] 4795 4-9-3 **60**.........................(b[1]) GrahamLee 1 56
(Paul Midgley) *chsd ldrs: rdn to ld over 1f out: hdd 1f out: one pce* **7/1**

0150 **4** *¾* **Be Bold**[12] 6238 5-9-1 **63**.............................................(v) RowanScott(5) 2 56
(Rebecca Bastiman) *dwlt: hld up: rdn over 2f out: kpt on same pce and nvr threatened* **11/2**

6204 **5** *½* **Stringybark Creek**[13] 6174 3-8-8 **55**............................ DavidEgan(3) 4 46
(Mick Channon) *prom: rdn over 2f out: no ex fnl f* **9/2**[2]

0400 **6** *4* **Spike (IRE)**[14] 6156 4-8-1 **51** oh5 ow1.....................(bt) ConnorMurtagh(7) 6 28
(Donald McCain) *sn led: rdn whn hdd 2f out: sn wknd* **14/1**

0-00 **7** *nse* **Precious Skye (IRE)**[108] 2699 3-8-6 **50** oh4.......................... PaddyAspell 5 27
(Ronald Thompson) *slowly away: a rr* **100/1**

58.74s (-0.86) **Going Correction** -0.15s/f (Firm)
**WFA** 3 from 4yo+ 1lb **7** Ran SP% **110.4**
Speed ratings (Par 101): **100,99,96,95,94 87,87**
CSF £8.60 CT £35.65 TOTE £2.10: £1.40, £3.10; EX 9.50 Trifecta £41.70.The winner was sold for £6,800 to Ron Thompson.
**Owner** JJ Quinn Racing Ltd **Bred** Wardstown Stud Ltd **Trained** Settrington, N Yorks



The Form Book Flat, Raceform Ltd, Newbury, RG14 5SJ

**FOCUS**
A moderate contest rated around front pair.

## 6661 A FOR AGENCY H'CAP 2m 13y
**3:30** (3:30) (Class 4) (0-80,75) 3-Y-O+ **£4,851** (£1,443; £721; £360) **Stalls** Centre

Form RPR
-001 **1** **Noble Behest**17 6023 3-8-3 **64**.................................(p) GeorgeWood(3) 3 72+
(Marcus Tregoning) *in tch: rdn to ld narrowly over 2f out: styd on pushed out fnl f: asserted fnl 110yds* **15/8**2
5423 **2** 1 1/2 **On Fire**18 6000 4-10-0 **75**.................................................. PaulHanagan 5 81
(James Bethell) *hld up: clsr 6f out: rdn to chal strly over 2f out: one pce fnl 110yds* **6/4**1
2261 **3** 1 1/2 **Stormin Tom (IRE)**18 6000 5-9-9 **73**.................. RachelRichardson(3) 2 76
(Tim Easterby) *led: rdn whn hdd over 2f out: no ex fnl f* **9/2**3
2525 **4** 3 **Braes Of Lochalsh**32 5468 6-9-8 **69**................................ PJMcDonald 1 69
(Jim Goldie) *trckd ldr: rdn 3f out: wknd fnl f* **6/1**
3m 29.72s (1.42) **Going Correction** -0.05s/f (Good)
**WFA** 3 from 4yo+ 11lb 4 Ran SP% **107.3**
Speed ratings (Par 105): **94,93,92,91**
CSF £5.00 TOTE £2.00; EX 5.50 Trifecta £5.90.
**Owner** The FOPS **Bred** Mr & Mrs A E Pakenham **Trained** Whitsbury, Hants

**FOCUS**
Race distance increased by 10yds. A triumph of youth over experience. The unexposed winner took another step forward with the runner-up rated to form.

## 6662 THEAKSTON LIGHTFOOT H'CAP 6f
**4:05** (4:06) (Class 3) (0-95,93) 3-Y-O+ **£7,439** (£2,213; £1,106; £553) **Stalls** Centre

Form RPR
321 **1** **El Hombre**50 4787 3-9-0 **90**............................................ RowanScott(5) 2 98
(Keith Dalgleish) *chsd ldrs: rdn over 2f out: led 110yds out: edgd rt: kpt on* **6/1**2
1500 **2** 3/4 **Classic Seniority**13 6206 5-9-10 **93**.........................(p) BarryMcHugh 3 99
(Marjorie Fife) *midfield: rdn along over 2f out: hdwy appr fnl f: kpt on: wnt 2nd nr fin* **8/1**
3042 **3** nse **Red Pike (IRE)**13 6205 6-9-7 **93**............................ AdamMcNamara(3) 6 99
(Bryan Smart) *prom: pushed along to ld over 2f out: rdn over 1fout: edgd lft ins fnl f: hdd 110yds out: one pce* **5/1**1
1105 **4** 1 **Hart Stopper**14 6141 3-8-13 **84**...................................... LouisSteward 4 87+
(Michael Bell) *dwlt: hld up: pushed along over 2f out: stl plenty to do over 1f out: hdwy appr fnl f: kpt on* **10/1**
2130 **5** 1/2 **Lexington Times (IRE)**13 6205 5-9-2 **85**.................(p) JamesSullivan 11 86
(Ruth Carr) *dwlt: hld up in midfield: rdn over 2f out: kpt on fnl f* **11/1**
6466 **6** 1/2 **Art Collection (FR)**25 5705 4-8-12 **81**................................ JackGarritty 7 80
(Ruth Carr) *trckd ldrs: rdn 2f out: one pce* **16/1**
0110 **7** 1/2 **Related**13 6205 7-9-3 **86**...................................................(b) MartinLane 5 84
(Paul Midgley) *led: rdn whn hdd over 2f out: no ex fnl f* **14/1**
1610 **8** 1 1/4 **The Armed Man**13 6205 4-8-2 **78**...................................... PaulaMuir(7) 9 72
(Chris Fairhurst) *stmbld sltly s: sn prom: rdn over 2f out: wknd fnl f* **13/2**3
0600 **9** 1 **Muntadab (IRE)**13 6206 5-9-9 **92**.................................. TonyHamilton 12 83
(Roger Fell) *hld up: pushed along over 2f out: rdn over 1f out: wknd ins fnl f* **15/2**
2403 **10** shd **Full Intention**25 5708 3-8-10 **81**..............................(p) PJMcDonald 10 71
(Tom Dascombe) *midfield: rdn over 2f out: wknd fnl f* **12/1**
2640 **11** 3 1/2 **Captain Dion**25 5705 4-9-6 **89**.......................................(p) KevinStott 8 68
(Kevin Ryan) *stdd s: a towards rr* **10/1**
300- **12** 8 **Mujassam**349 6556 5-9-6 **89**............................................... PhillipMakin 1 43
(David O'Meara) *prom: rdn and lost pl 1/2-way: wknd over 1f out* **33/1**
1m 10.64s (-2.06) **Going Correction** -0.15s/f (Firm)
**WFA** 3 from 4yo+ 2lb 12 Ran SP% **116.9**
Speed ratings (Par 107): **107,106,105,104,103 103,102,100,99,99 94,84**
CSF £52.65 CT £259.43 TOTE £6.30: £1.80, £2.50, £2.50; EX 64.40 Trifecta £248.40.
**Owner** Weldspec Glasgow Limited **Bred** Mrs J McMahon **Trained** Carluke, S Lanarks

**FOCUS**
A good sprint handicap, the action developing centre to far side. The form looks straightforward and has been rated through the placed horses.

## 6663 NICK QUINN 50 NOT OUT H'CAP 7f
**4:40** (4:43) (Class 4) (0-80,80) 3-Y-O+ **£4,851** (£1,443; £721; £360) **Stalls** Low

Form RPR
2246 **1** **Kirkham**20 5948 4-8-12 **66**.........................................(p) JoeDoyle 12 74
(Julie Camacho) *trckd ldrs: rdn over 2f out: led appr fnl f: kpt on* **9/1**
0050 **2** 1/2 **God Willing**27 5669 6-9-1 **76**.......................................(b) GerO'Neill(7) 11 82
(Declan Carroll) *racd keenly: sn pressed ldr towards outer: rdn to ld over 2f out: hdd appr fnl f: kpt on* **8/1**
0022 **3** hd **Fieldsman (USA)**10 6297 5-9-11 **79**................................ DavidNolan 4 84
(David O'Meara) *trckd ldrs: rdn to chal strly appr fnl f: one pce towards fin* **4/1**1
1535 **4** 3/4 **Favourite Treat (USA)**5 6464 7-9-2 **70**.........................(e) JackGarritty 6 73
(Ruth Carr) *midfield: pushed along and hdwy to chse ldrs whn short of room briefly over 1f out: short of room again ent fnl f: swtchd rt ins fnl f: kpt on* **12/1**
2130 **5** hd **Round The Island**55 4616 4-8-11 **68**........................ LewisEdmunds(3) 3 71
(Richard Whitaker) *trckd ldrs: rdn over 2f out: one pce fnl 110yds* **22/1**
0050 **6** 1 3/4 **Zylan (IRE)**32 5471 5-9-12 **80**...................................... TonyHamilton 1 78
(Roger Fell) *hld up: pushed along over 2f out: hdwy whn hmpd ins fnl f: kpt on* **50/1**
6633 **7** hd **Vincenzo Coccotti (USA)**13 6197 5-8-9 **66**.................... HollieDoyle(3) 9 63
(Ken Cunningham-Brown) *hld up: rdn over 2f out: kpt on ins fnl f: nvr threatened* **9/1**
3112 **8** shd **Mango Chutney**24 5739 4-9-3 **71**...............................(p) PhillipMakin 10 68
(John Davies) *led narrowly: rdn whn hdd over 2f out: wknd ins fnl f* **7/1**3
4204 **9** 1/2 **Inexes**8 6348 5-9-12 **80**............................................(p) BarryMcHugh 7 76
(Marjorie Fife) *hld up in rr: rdn over 2f out: sme late hdwy: nvr threatened* **12/1**
5320 **10** 1 1/4 **My Dad Syd (USA)**28 5610 5-9-0 **75**..................(v) ManuelFernandes(7) 2 67
(Ian Williams) *midfield: rdn over 2f out: wknd fnl f* **6/1**2
0503 **11** 3/4 **Chaplin Bay (IRE)**20 5922 5-9-1 **69**.........................(p) JamesSullivan 5 59
(Ruth Carr) *hld up in rr: rdn over 2f out: no imp whn hmpd ins fnl f* **9/1**
1025 **12** 5 **Benjamin Thomas (IRE)**18 5994 3-9-3 **75**.....................(v) JasonHart 8 50
(John Quinn) *dwlt: midfield on outside: rdn over 2f out: wknd and bhd* **14/1**
1m 25.94s (-1.26) **Going Correction** -0.05s/f (Good)
**WFA** 3 from 4yo+ 4lb 12 Ran SP% **116.3**
Speed ratings (Par 105): **105,104,104,103,103 101,100,100,100,98 97,92**
CSF £77.63 CT £340.46 TOTE £12.00: £3.60, £3.60, £1.70; EX 113.00 Trifecta £1560.10.
**Owner** The Kirkham Partnership **Bred** Highfield Farm Llp **Trained** Norton, N Yorks
■ Stewards' Enquiry : Jack Garritty 2 day ban: guilty of careless riding (15/17 Sep)

**FOCUS**
Race distance increased by 10yds. A messy race run at a steady early gallop and they finished in a heap. It paid to race handily and the winner has been rated to his best.

## 6664 LADIES' DAY NEXT @THIRSKRACES SATURDAY 9TH SEPTEMBER APPRENTICE H'CAP 7f 218y
**5:10** (5:11) (Class 5) (0-70,71) 3-Y-O **£3,234** (£962; £481; £240) **Stalls** Low

Form RPR
0404 **1** **Armagnac (IRE)**15 6091 3-8-10 **64**............................ TristanPrice(10) 9 68
(Michael Bell) *trckd ldrs: swtchd rt wl over 1f out: sn rdn: edgd lft ins fnl f: r.o to ld towards fin* **8/1**
2443 **2** nk **Halinka (IRE)**23 5813 3-9-7 **68**........................................ DavidEgan(3) 3 71
(Roger Varian) *trckd ldrs: rdn to ld wl over 1f out: one pce and hdd towards fin* **4/1**2
5156 **3** nk **Dreaming Time**14 6160 3-9-3 **71**.................................. PaulHainey(10) 7 73
(James Tate) *dwlt: hld up in rr: pushed along and hdwy on inner 2f out: rdn and kpt on fnl f* **11/1**
3304 **4** 1 1/2 **Kilbaha Lady (IRE)**27 5666 3-9-0 **61**.........................(t) RowanScott(3) 11 60
(Nigel Tinkler) *dwlt: hld up: rdn and hdwy on outer over 1f out: one pce fnl f* **13/2**3
0615 **5** nse **Stubytuesday**18 6016 3-9-1 **69**................................ HarrisonShaw(10) 5 68
(Michael Easterby) *midfield: rdn over 2f out: kpt on ins fnl f* **7/1**
-440 **6** hd **Sussex Girl**23 5783 3-8-11 **62**...................................... NicolaCurrie(7) 2 60
(John Berry) *midfield: rdn over 2f out: kpt on ins fnl f: nvr threatened* **28/1**
0533 **7** 1 **Lady Volante (IRE)**120 2338 3-9-2 **60**.............................. HollieDoyle 6 56
(Rebecca Menzies) *prom: racd keenly: rdn over 2f out: wknd ins fnl f* **16/1**
1152 **8** 1 1/4 **Golden Guest**5 6485 3-9-5 **69**...................................... JaneElliott(6) 10 62
(George Margarson) *trckd ldrs towards outer: rdn over 2f out: wknd ins fnl f* **9/4**1
-036 **9** 2 1/4 **Our Greta (IRE)**35 5378 3-9-4 **65**........................ AlistairRawlinson(3) 4 53
(Michael Appleby) *led: rdn whn hdd wl over 1f out: wknd fnl f* **12/1**
1m 38.85s (-1.25) **Going Correction** -0.05s/f (Good) 9 Ran SP% **113.1**
Speed ratings (Par 101): **104,103,103,101,101 101,100,99,97**
CSF £39.15 CT £354.10 TOTE £10.10: £2.80, £1.50, £3.20; EX 47.50 Trifecta £434.30.
**Owner** The Fitzrovians **Bred** Lismacue Mare Syndicate **Trained** Newmarket, Suffolk
■ Stewards' Enquiry : Rowan Scott caution: guilty of careless riding

**FOCUS**
Race distance increased by 10yds. Modest form rated around the first two.
T/Plt: £25.30 to a £1 stake. Pool: £61,360.38 - 1,767.20 winning units T/Qpdt: £18.50 to a £1 stake. Pool: £4,132.75 - 165.09 winning units **Andrew Sheret**

# 3274 FONTAINEBLEAU
Friday, September 1

**OFFICIAL GOING: Turf: good**

## 6665a GRAND PRIX DE FONTAINEBLEAU (LISTED RACE) (4YO+ FILLIES & MARES) (TURF) 1m 2f
**12:55** 4-Y-O+ **£20,512** (£8,205; £6,153; £4,102; £2,051)

RPR
**1** **Meliora (IRE)**21 5908 5-8-13 0................................ StephanePasquier 4 101
(N Clement, France) **49/10**3
**2** 2 1/2 **Thank You Bye Bye (FR)**21 5908 5-8-13 0...... Pierre-CharlesBoudot 1 96
(J-P Gauvin, France) **13/5**1
**3** 1/2 **Cozy Girl (FR)**21 5908 5-8-13 0...................................... EddyHardouin 5 95
(F Vermeulen, France) **32/5**
**4** 3/4 **Avenue Dargent (FR)**40 5197 4-8-13 0......................... MaximeGuyon 3 94
(J-M Osorio, Spain) **7/2**2
**5** nse **Westadora (IRE)**39 5229 4-8-13 0........................... VincentCheminaud 6 93
(J Reynier, France) **22/1**
**6** 1/2 **Capricious Cantor (IRE)**27 5658 4-8-13 0.................... TonyPiccone 2 92
(Ed Dunlop) *broke wl and led: drvn 3f out: hdd 2 1/2f out: kpt on at same pce and grad lft bhd fnl f* **41/5**
**7** 1/2 **Tikiouine (FR)**6 6451 5-8-13 0....................................... MickaelForest 8 91
(Carmen Bocskai, Germany) **83/10**
**8** 2 1/2 **Rosvana (FR)**132 4-8-13 0................................... ChristopheSoumillon 7 86
(A De Royer-Dupre, France) **76/10**
2m 2.3s 8 Ran SP% **118.1**
PARI-MUTUEL (all including 1 euro stake): WIN 5.90; PLACE 1.70, 1.20, 1.80; DF 10.60; SF 23.10.
**Owner** Robert G Schaedle III **Bred** Litex Commerce **Trained** Chantilly, France

# 6464 BEVERLEY (R-H)
Saturday, September 2

**OFFICIAL GOING: Good to firm (good in places; 7.8)**
Wind: Light across Weather: Cloudy with sunny periods

## 6666 HULL CARTRIDGE ANNIVERSARY IRISH EBF FILLIES' NOVICE STKS (PLUS 10 RACE) 7f 96y
**2:05** (2:06) (Class 4) 2-Y-O **£5,175** (£1,540; £769; £384) **Stalls** Low

Form RPR
22 **1** **Akvavera**36 5371 2-9-0 0...................................................... GrahamLee 3 78
(Ralph Beckett) *mde all: rdn over 1f out: drvn out* **5/6**1
30 **2** 1 1/2 **Frolic**19 5990 2-9-0 0...................................................... LukeMorris 4 74
(Sir Mark Prescott Bt) *trckd ldrs: hdwy 3f out: rdn along over 1f out: drvn to chse wnr and edgd rt ins fnl f: sn no imp* **7/2**2
54 **3** 2 1/4 **Mail Order**25 5743 2-9-0 0................................................ JoeFanning 2 69
(Mark Johnston) *trckd wnr: pushed along 3f out: rdn over 2f out: drvn over 1f out: kpt on same pce* **7/1**
6 **4** 1 1/4 **Sigrid Nansen**11 6292 2-9-0 0.......................................... CamHardie 1 66
(George Scott) *in tch: pushed along and sltly outpcd 3f out: sn rdn: styd on u.p fr over 1f out* **33/1**
0 **5** hd **Calling Rio (IRE)**19 6010 2-9-0 0.................................... SamJames 5 66
(David Loughnane) *chsd ldrs: rdn along 3f out: drvn wl over 1f out: one pce* **80/1**
43 **6** hd **Bungee Jump (IRE)**19 5998 2-9-0 0................................ TomEaves 8 65
(Kevin Ryan) *s.i.s and bhd: hdwy 4f out: chsd ldrs on outer wl over 2f out: rdn along wl over 1f out: grad wknd* **5/1**3

0 **7** *6* **Stripey**[36] 5372 2-9-0 0 ........ PaulHanagan 7 51
(Richard Fahey) *towards rr: green and hung lft bnd 4f out: sn rdn along and outpcd fnl 3f* **25/1**

1m 34.02s (0.22) **Going Correction** 0.0s/f (Good) 7 Ran SP% **114.0**
Speed ratings (Par 94): **98,96,93,92,92 91,84**
CSF £3.97 TOTE £1.60: £1.20, £1.60; EX 4.00 Trifecta £14.20.
**Owner** Miss K Rausing **Bred** Miss K Rausing **Trained** Kimpton, Hants

**FOCUS**
The rail was in its original wide position and all distances as advertised. The ground was officially good to firm, good in places and clerk of the course Sally Iggulden said: "It is on the easy side of good to firm. After riding in the opener Graham Lee and Luke Morris called the ground good, while Joe Fanning and Cam Hardie both reckoned it was on the easy side. A fair maiden with the winner running to her pre-race mark.

## 6667 BET TOTESCOOP6 AT BETFRED.COM MAIDEN STKS 7f 96y
**2:40** (2:40) (Class 4) 3-Y-O+ **£5,040** (£1,508; £754; £377; £188) **Stalls** Low

Form RPR

2443 **1** **Equiano Springs**[13] 6238 3-9-5 70 ........ TomEaves 1 74
(Tom Tate) *mde all: rdn along 2f out: drvn and kpt on wl fnl f* **5/4**[1]

2 **2** *2* **Van Velde (IRE)**[218] 442 3-9-5 0 ........ (p[1]) GrahamLee 3 68
(John Quinn) *trckd ldng pair: hdwy to trck wnr over 4f out: pushed along 3f out: rdn 2f out: drvn appr fnl f: no imp* **5/2**[2]

5526 **3** *2 ½* **Ember's Glow**[14] 6203 3-9-5 72 ........ CamHardie 6 62
(Jason Ward) *trckd ldrs: hdwy 3f out: rdn along on outer and chsd ldng pair wl over 1f out: drvn and kpt on same pce fnl f* **3/1**[3]

0 **4** *7* **Coviglia (IRE)**[14] 6184 3-9-5 70 ........ DavidNolan 2 43
(David O'Meara) *trckd wnr on inner: pushed along over 3f out: rdn over 2f out: sn drvn and wknd* **7/1**

0/U- **5** *11* **Knotty Jack (IRE)**[368] 6003 5-9-9 0 ........ JackGarritty 4 17
(Chris Grant) *hld up in rr: rdn along and outpcd fnl 3f* **33/1**

1m 33.35s (-0.45) **Going Correction** 0.0s/f (Good)
**WFA** 3 from 5yo+ 4lb 5 Ran SP% **113.5**
Speed ratings (Par 105): **102,99,96,88,76**
CSF £4.89 TOTE £2.00: £1.40, £1.20; EX 5.20 Trifecta £9.80.
**Owner** T T Racing **Bred** Paddock Space **Trained** Tadcaster, N Yorks

**FOCUS**
A second all-the-way winner on card. An ordinary maiden with the winner the form pick and rated close to form up in trip.

## 6668 TOTESCOOP6 BEVERLEY BULLET SPRINT STKS (LISTED RACE) 5f
**3:15** (3:18) (Class 1) 3-Y-O+
**£28,355** (£10,750; £5,380; £2,680; £1,345; £675) **Stalls** Low

Form RPR

5140 **1** **Take Cover**[8] 6402 10-9-3 110 ........ TomQueally 2 113
(David C Griffiths) *mde all: rdn over 1f out: drvn ins fnl f: kpt on strly towards fin* **3/1**[1]

5200 **2** *1* **Final Venture**[8] 6402 5-9-3 110 ........ LukeMorris 7 109
(Paul Midgley) *prom: rdn along over 1f out: drvn ins fnl f: kpt on wl* **9/2**[3]

2100 **3** *hd* **The Wagon Wheel (IRE)**[13] 6234 3-8-8 96 ........ (b) CamHardie 3 101
(Richard Fahey) *in rr: outpcd and bhd 1/2-way: sn rdn: hdwy ent fnl f: styd on strly on inner rail last 100yds* **22/1**

3010 **4** *nk* **Kimberella**[20] 5974 7-9-3 111 ........ PaulHanagan 4 108
(Richard Fahey) *trckd ldrs: rdn along over 1f out: drvn and kpt on fnl f* **7/2**[2]

520 **5** *shd* **Mirza**[21] 5911 10-9-0 105 ........ (p) JoeFanning 1 104
(Rae Guest) *dwlt: sn chsng ldrs on inner: rdn along and hdwy over 1f out: drvn ent fnl f: kpt on* **8/1**

0511 **6** *nk* **Desert Law (IRE)**[10] 6325 9-9-0 98 ........ PaulMulrennan 6 103
(Paul Midgley) *cl up: rdn over 1f out: drvn ent fnl f: one pce last 75yds* **14/1**

6020 **7** *hd* **Alpha Delphini**[8] 6402 6-9-0 108 ........ (p) GrahamLee 11 102
(Bryan Smart) *chsd ldrs: hdwy 2f out: rdn over 1f out: drvn and kpt on same pce fnl f* **8/1**

1100 **8** *1 ¼* **Line Of Reason (IRE)**[32] 5505 7-9-0 103 ........ MartinLane 5 98
(Paul Midgley) *midfield: hdwy over 1f out: sn rdn: no imp fnl f* **9/1**

3342 **9** *1 ¼* **Pipers Note**[14] 6206 7-9-0 101 ........ JamesSullivan 8 93
(Ruth Carr) *chsd ldrs: rdn along over 1f out: sn drvn and wknd* **11/1**

10-0 **10** *¾* **Go On Go On Go On**[98] 3080 4-8-9 95 ........ TomEaves 9 86
(Clive Cox) *dwlt: a towards rr* **40/1**

1m 2.58s (-0.92) **Going Correction** +0.075s/f (Good)
**WFA** 3 from 4yo+ 1lb 10 Ran SP% **119.4**
Speed ratings (Par 111): **110,108,108,107,107 106,106,104,102,101**
CSF £17.08 TOTE £3.60: £1.70, £2.10, £5.10; EX 18.90 Trifecta £495.10.
**Owner** Norcroft Park Stud **Bred** Norcroft Park Stud **Trained** Bawtry, S Yorks

**FOCUS**
A good-quality and competitive Listed event which had been won by a horse drawn four or lower in each of the last five years, and that sequence continued with the winner making all from stall two. Three of the first four home were carrying a penalty with the veteran winner the form pick, seeing this out well from good draw and rated close to form.

## 6669 TOTEPOOLLIVEINFO.COM H'CAP (DIV I) 5f
**3:50** (3:56) (Class 5) (0-75,77) 3-Y-O+ **£5,040** (£1,508; £754; £377; £188) **Stalls** Low

Form RPR

3153 **1** **Miningggold**[3] 6574 4-9-8 73 ........ (p) PaulMulrennan 2 82
(Michael Dods) *trckd ldrs: hdwy 2f out: rdn to chse ldr ent fnl f: led last 75 yds: kpt on* **7/2**[2]

0461 **2** *1 ¼* **Sandra's Secret (IRE)**[13] 6237 4-9-7 77 ........ JaneElliott[(5)] 4 81
(Les Eyre) *cl up: led 3f out: rdn and edgd lft jst ins fnl f: hdd and no ex last 75 yds* **3/1**[1]

2220 **3** *½* **Point Of Woods**[12] 6267 4-8-12 63 ........ (p) JamesSullivan 1 65
(Tina Jackson) *in tch: hdwy wl over 1f out: sn rdn: chsng ldng pair whn swtchd lft over 1f out: kpt on wl towards fin* **8/1**

5006 **4** *3* **Grandad's World (IRE)**[12] 6267 5-9-9 74 ........ PaulHanagan 8 65
(Richard Fahey) *towards rr: rdn along 1/2-way: hdwy wl over 1f out: kpt on wl u.p fnl f* **12/1**[3]

5400 **5** *1* **Hilary J**[34] 5457 4-9-11 76 ........ JoeFanning 10 64
(Ann Duffield) *prom: cl up 2f out: rdn over 1f out: drvn and wknd fnl f* **7/2**[2]

154 **6** *nk* **Spirit Of Wedza (IRE)**[33] 5481 5-9-4 69 ........ JoeDoyle 11 56
(Julie Camacho) *chsd ldrs: rdn along wl over 1f out: grad wknd* **12/1**

5120 **7** *3 ¾* **Dundunah (USA)**[23] 5837 3-9-9 75 ........ (t) DavidNolan 6 48
(David O'Meara) *in tch: rdn along wl over 1f out: sn btn* **20/1**

-055 **8** *¾* **Ace Master**[25] 5760 9-8-11 67 ........ (b) KevinLundie[(5)] 9 38
(Roy Bowring) *a outpcd in rr* **40/1**

0300 **9** *2 ¾* **Kommander Kirkup**[13] 6237 6-9-0 65 ........ (p) TomEaves 3 26
(Michael Herrington) *sn outpcd in rr: bhd fr 1/2-way* **25/1**

000 **10** *10* **Bosham**[17] 6062 7-9-3 75 ........ (bt) HarrisonShaw[(7)] 7
(Michael Easterby) *led 2f: cl up: rdn along 2f out: sn wknd* **20/1**

1m 3.44s (-0.06) **Going Correction** +0.075s/f (Good)
**WFA** 3 from 4yo+ 1lb 10 Ran SP% **117.4**
Speed ratings (Par 103): **103,101,100,95,93 93,87,86,81,65**
CSF £13.76 CT £77.31 TOTE £3.90: £1.40, £1.50, £2.70; EX 16.40 Trifecta £92.60.
**Owner** Mrs C E Dods **Bred** Mrs G S Rees **Trained** Denton, Co Durham
■ L C Saloon was withdrawn. Price at time of withdrawal 33/1. Rule 4 does not apply.

**FOCUS**
The first division of a competitive handicap and solid form for the grade. Not many got into it and the first two home were up there throughout. A small personal best from the winner.

## 6670 TOTEPOOLLIVEINFO.COM H'CAP (DIV II) 5f
**4:25** (4:31) (Class 5) (0-75,77) 3-Y-O+ **£5,040** (£1,508; £754; £377; £188) **Stalls** Low

Form RPR

2143 **1** **Sheepscar Lad (IRE)**[25] 5759 3-9-9 75 ........ TomEaves 2 83
(Nigel Tinkler) *trckd ldrs on inner: hdwy over 1f out: rdn to chal ins fnl f: drvn and kpt on strly to ld nr fin* **10/1**

31 **2** *hd* **Noah Amor (IRE)**[16] 6089 4-9-6 71 ........ DavidNolan 7 78
(David O'Meara) *qckly away and led: rdn ent fnl f: drvn last 100 yds: hdd and no ex nr fin* **7/1**

0553 **3** *1 ¼* **Tallinski (IRE)**[7] 6430 3-9-6 77 ........ BenRobinson[(5)] 1 80
(Brian Ellison) *trckd ldng pair: effrt wl over 1f out and sn rdn: drvn ent fnl f: kpt on same pce* **7/2**[1]

3260 **4** *1* **Burtonwood**[29] 5620 5-8-10 64 ........ (p) LewisEdmunds[(3)] 10 63
(Julie Camacho) *t.k.h early: hld up in tch: hdwy 2f out: rdn to chse ldrs over 1f out: drvn and no imp fnl f* **16/1**

1053 **5** *1 ½* **The Nazca Lines (IRE)**[10] 6308 3-9-7 73 ........ (v) JackGarritty 4 67
(John Quinn) *chsd ldrs: rdn along wl over 1f out: sn drvn and one pce* **9/1**

0222 **6** *½* **Astrophysics**[16] 6089 5-9-4 69 ........ GrahamLee 6 61
(Lynn Siddall) *midfield: hdwy wl over 1f out: sn rdn and no imp fnl f* **4/1**[2]

0631 **7** *hd* **Classic Pursuit**[18] 6040 6-9-3 68 ........ (b) TomQueally 5 59
(Michael Appleby) *dwlt: a towards rr* **14/1**

5313 **8** *2* **Roaring Rory**[16] 6089 4-8-9 65 ........ (p) MeganNicholls[(5)] 8 49
(Ollie Pears) *dwlt: a towards rr* **20/1**

0406 **9** *1 ¼* **Oriental Relation (IRE)**[43] 5129 6-9-9 74 ........ (b) JoeDoyle 11 53
(James Given) *cl up: rdn along 2f out: sn drvn and wknd* **16/1**

3405 **10** *3 ¾* **Bond Bombshell**[16] 6089 4-8-6 60 ........ (p) ShelleyBirkett[(3)] 9 26
(David O'Meara) *chsd ldrs on outer: rdn along 2f out: sn wknd* **22/1**

-040 **11** *4 ½* **Apricot Sky**[29] 5602 7-9-12 77 ........ PaulMulrennan 3 27
(Michael Dods) *chsd ldrs: rdn along wl over 1f out: sn drvn and wknd* **9/2**[3]

1m 3.11s (-0.39) **Going Correction** +0.075s/f (Good)
**WFA** 3 from 4yo+ 1lb 11 Ran SP% **119.5**
Speed ratings (Par 103): **106,105,103,102,99 98,98,95,93,87 80**
CSF £79.66 CT £304.99 TOTE £10.10: £3.30, £2.50, £1.70; EX 76.30 Trifecta £541.00.
**Owner** Leeds Plywood And Doors Ltd **Bred** Stockvale Bloodstock Ltd **Trained** Langton, N Yorks

**FOCUS**
Like the first leg, a competitive and open-looking handicap for the grade and once again it paid to race prominently. A small personal best from the winner and the runner-up has also improved having got his act together in handicaps recently.

## 6671 TOTEPOOLLIVEINFO DOWNLOAD THE APP H'CAP 1m 1f 207y
**5:00** (5:02) (Class 2) (0-105,98) 3-Y-O
**£28,012** (£8,388; £4,194; £2,097; £1,048; £526) **Stalls** Low

Form RPR

2000 **1** **Society Red**[14] 6187 3-8-2 79 ........ JamesSullivan 3 87
(Richard Fahey) *mde all: pushed along over 2f out: jnd and rdn over 1f out: drvn ins fnl f: hld on wl towards fin* **7/1**[2]

1063 **2** *nk* **The Statesman**[14] 6187 3-8-2 79 ........ JoeDoyle 5 86+
(Ian Williams) *hld up in tch: hdwy on outer over 2f out: rdn to chse ldng pair and edgd rt jst ins fnl f: sn drvn and styd on strly towards fin* **7/1**[2]

6150 **3** *1 ¼* **Appointed**[8] 6404 3-8-11 91 ........ RachelRichardson[(3)] 9 96
(Tim Easterby) *trckd wnr: hdwy 3f out: cl up 2f out: sn rdn to chal: ev ch tl drvn ent fnl f and kpt on same pce* **9/1**

4-00 **4** *1 ¼* **Montataire (IRE)**[8] 6404 3-9-7 98 ........ PaulMulrennan 4 100
(Mark Johnston) *in tch on inner: hdwy over 2f out: rdn to chse ldrs over 1f out: drvn and kpt on same pce fnl f* **14/1**

4104 **5** *nk* **Alwahsh (IRE)**[23] 5841 3-8-6 83 ........ LiamJones 8 86+
(William Haggas) *bhd: hdwy over 2f: nt clr run and hmpd 1 1/2f out: swtchd lft and rdn: styd on wl fnl f* **15/2**[3]

5416 **6** *hd* **Euro Nightmare (IRE)**[9] 6357 3-9-1 92 ........ GrahamLee 6 93
(Keith Dalgleish) *trckd ldrs: pushed along 3f out: rdn over 2f out: drvn wl over 1f out: sn wknd* **8/1**

4666 **7** *nk* **Sea Fox (IRE)**[29] 5616 3-9-3 94 ........ (t) TomEaves 1 95
(David Evans) *rr: hdwy 2f out: rdn over 1f out: kpt on u.p fnl f* **33/1**

0030 **8** *1 ½* **Bear Valley (IRE)**[13] 6232 3-8-11 88 ........ JoeFanning 2 86
(Mark Johnston) *trckd ldng pair on inner: pushed along over 2f out: rdn wl over 1f out: sn drvn and wknd* **7/1**[2]

411 **9** *17* **Mudaarab (USA)**[78] 3778 3-8-13 90 ........ PaulHanagan 7 54
(Sir Michael Stoute) *trckd ldrs: hdwy 3f out: rdn along over 2f out: drvn wl over 1f out: sn wknd* **13/8**[1]

2m 5.53s (-1.47) **Going Correction** 0.0s/f (Good) 9 Ran SP% **118.1**
Speed ratings (Par 107): **105,104,103,102,102 102,102,100,87**
CSF £56.36 CT £450.25 TOTE £9.20: £2.50, £2.10, £2.80; EX 57.30 Trifecta £489.80.
**Owner** M J Macleod **Bred** Select Bloodstock **Trained** Musley Bank, N Yorks

**FOCUS**
A high-class 3yo handicap, albeit not the strongest for the grade with the topweight rated 7lb below the ceiling, and once again the winner was never headed. A small personal best from him, in line with his better form.

## 6672 COLLECT TOTEPOOL WINNINGS AT BETFRED SHOPS H'CAP 7f 96y
**5:35** (5:35) (Class 4) (0-85,85) 3-Y-O+
**£7,470** (£2,236; £1,118; £559; £279; £140) **Stalls** Low

Form RPR

3631 **1** **Rousayan (IRE)**[6] 6464 6-9-5 85 6ex ........ (h) PatrickVaughan[(7)] 6 93
(David O'Meara) *trckd ldng pair on inner: swtchd lft and effrt 1 1/2f out: rdn to chal ent fnl f: sn drvn out* **11/2**[3]

0430 **2** *½* **Worlds His Oyster**[12] 6266 4-9-6 79 ........ (v) JoeFanning 2 85
(John Quinn) *trckd ldrs on inner: effrt and nt clr run 1 1/2f out: swtchd lft and rdn ent fnl f: styd on wl towards fin* **5/1**[2]

0644 **3** *1* **Roll On Rory**[21] 5948 4-9-4 77 ........ (p) DavidNolan 9 80
(Jason Ward) *prom: cl up 5f out: chal wl over 2f out: rdn to take slt advantage over 1f out: drvn and hdd jst ins fnl f: kpt on same pce* **7/1**

1636 **4** ¾ **Luis Vaz De Torres (IRE)**[31] 5530 5-9-11 **84**..............(h) PaulHanagan 8 85
(Richard Fahey) *hld up and bhd: hdwy over 2f out: rdn over 1f out: n.m.r ins fnl f: kpt on wl towards fin* **12/1**

0405 **5** shd **Executive Force**[21] 5943 3-9-7 **84**.................................. LiamJones 1 83
(William Haggas) *hld up towards rr: hdwy 3f out: rdn along to chse ldrs and n.m.r over 1f out: kpt on same pce fnl f* **4/1**[1]

3101 **6** 1 ½ **Dark Profit (IRE)**[50] 4837 5-9-10 **83**..................(p) GrahamLee 4 80
(Keith Dalgleish) *trckd ldrs: hdwy 3f out: rdn along 2f out: prom and drvn over 1f out: grad wknd* **7/1**

0320 **7** nk **Gabrial The Tiger (IRE)**[21] 5929 5-9-5 **78**...................... JackGarritty 5 74
(Richard Fahey) *led: pushed along wl over 2f out: rdn wl over 1f out: sn drvn and hdd: grad wknd* **14/1**

0054 **8** 2 ¼ **Athassel**[11] 6289 8-8-11 **77**................................ KatherineGlenister(7) 10 67
(David Evans) *in tch: pushed along 3f out: rdn over 2f out: sn wknd* **33/1**

4301 **9** ¾ **Proud Archi (IRE)**[12] 6265 3-9-3 **80**.............................. PaulMulrennan 7 66
(Michael Dods) *hld up in rr: hdwy on outer wl over 2f out: rdn to chse ldrs 1 1/2f: sn edgd rt and wknd* **5/1**[2]

002 **10** 12 **General Alexander (IRE)**[7] 6429 4-8-8 **72**..............(p) BenRobinson(5) 3 29
(Brian Ellison) *in tch: rdn along 3f out: sn wknd* **12/1**

1m 32.6s (-1.20) **Going Correction** 0.0s/f (Good)
**WFA** 3 from 4yo+ 4lb **10** Ran SP% **118.7**
Speed ratings (Par 105): **106,105,104,103,103 101,101,98,97,84**
CSF £33.84 CT £202.33 TOTE £6.20: £2.10, £1.80, £2.80; EX 35.50 Trifecta £269.30.
**Owner** The Roses Partnership **Bred** Haras De Son Altesse L'Aga Khan Scea **Trained** Upper Helmsley, N Yorks

**FOCUS**
A useful handicap and the winner maintained his revival. He was well placed tracking the good pace and has been rated back to his best.

## 6673 READER'S 60 NOT OUT APPRENTICE H'CAP 1m 1f 207y
**6:05** (6:06) (Class 6) (0-65,66) 4-Y-0+ **£3,234** (£962; £481; £240) **Stalls** Low

Form RPR

0034 **1** **Ivors Involvement (IRE)**[3] 6592 5-8-3 **45**..............(p[1]) RhiainIngram(5) 9 52
(Tina Jackson) *mde all: rdn along 2f out: drvn ins fnl f: kpt on wl towards fin* **10/1**

603 **2** 2 **Outlaw Torn (IRE)**[6] 6471 8-8-10 **54**.....................(e) BenSanderson(7) 11 57
(Richard Guest) *t.k.h early: trckd wnr: cl up 3f out: rdn along wl over 1f out: drvn ent fnl f: kpt on same pce* **7/1**[3]

560 **3** hd **La Havrese (FR)**[14] 6188 6-9-5 **56**............................... LewisEdmunds 2 59+
(Lynn Siddall) *hld up in midfield: hdwy wl over 2f out: rdn to chse ldrs over 1f out: drvn and kpt on fnl f* **9/2**[1]

6-00 **4** 2 ¾ **Bergholt (IRE)**[78] 3773 4-9-6 **60**................................... MitchGodwin(3) 1 57
(Tim Vaughan) *trckd ldrs: rdn along 2 1/2f out: drvn over 1f out: kpt on same pce ent fnl f* **8/1**

200 **5** 1 ¾ **So It's War (FR)**[40] 5214 6-9-9 **63**..........................(p) MeganNicholls(3) 4 59+
(Keith Dalgleish) *hld up and bhd: hdwy 3f out: rdn wl over 1f out: sn n.m.r: drvn and kpt on fnl f* **7/1**[3]

060 **6** ½ **I'm Super Too (IRE)**[6] 6470 10-8-12 **52**...................... GemmaTutty(3) 3 45
(Karen Tutty) *towards rr: hdwy over 3f out: rdn along and chsd ldrs on inner over 1f: sn drvn and no imp* **12/1**

2000 **7** 3 ¾ **Shearian**[12] 6266 7-9-2 **58**........................................ GerO'Neill(5) 8 44
(Declan Carroll) *a towards rr* **11/1**

1201 **8** 2 **Hannington**[6] 6479 6-9-8 **66** 6ex..........................(t) GabrieleMalune(7) 13 48
(Michael Appleby) *in tch: hdwy on outer over 3f out: rdn along to chse ldrs 2f out: sn drvn and wknd* **8/1**

4220 **9** 6 **Little Choosey**[83] 3628 7-9-6 **62**..............................(bt) KevinLundie(5) 10 33
(Roy Bowring) *a in rr* **20/1**

0006 **10** 5 **Arithmetic (IRE)**[12] 6269 4-9-5 **59**.................................(p) JaneElliott(3) 6 20
(Ruth Carr) *in tch: hdwy to chse ldrs 3f out: rdn along over 2f out: sn drvn and wknd* **13/2**[2]

0600 **11** 4 **Judicious**[23] 5831 10-8-7 **49**...............................(p) PatrickVaughan(5) 12 3
(Geoffrey Harker) *prom: rdn along 2f out: drvn and wknd over 1f out* **16/1**

2340 **12** 12 **Ingleby Angel (IRE)**[30] 5578 8-9-8 **62**........................... BenRobinson(3) 7
(Colin Teague) *a in rr* **14/1**

00-6 **13** 99 **Shudbeme**[95] 3185 4-8-5 **45**.......................................(p) LuluStanford(3) 5
(Neville Bycroft) *a in rr: bhd whn virtually p.u over 2f out* **25/1**

2m 6.86s (-0.14) **Going Correction** 0.0s/f (Good) **13** Ran SP% **125.0**
Speed ratings (Par 101): **100,98,98,96,94 94,91,89,84,80 77,68,**
CSF £82.12 CT £370.70 TOTE £12.10: £3.10, £2.60, £2.10; EX 125.40 Trifecta £1059.30.
**Owner** H L Thompson **Bred** Irish National Stud **Trained** Liverton, Cleveland

**FOCUS**
A modest apprentice handicap and once again the pace held up, the winner making all.
T/Plt: £53.90 to a £1 stake. Pool: £73,779.42 - 998.32 winning units. T/Qpdt: £29.20 to a £1 stake. Pool: £4,742.97 - 132.47 winning units. **Joe Rowntree**

# 6410 CHESTER (L-H)
Saturday, September 2

**OFFICIAL GOING: Good (7.0)**
Wind: Almost nil Weather: Fine

## 6674 BRITISH STALLION STUDS EBF NOVICE STKS (PLUS 10 RACE) 7f 1y
**1:40** (1:47) (Class 4) 2-Y-O **£6,225** (£1,864; £932; £466; £233; £117) **Stalls** Low

Form RPR

223 **1** **Mutakatif (IRE)**[57] 4567 2-9-2 85........................................ DaneO'Neill 1 83
(Charles Hills) *racd keenly: mde all: qcknd 2f out: rdn abt 3 l clr over 1f out: kpt on ins fnl f: advantage reduced bef eased cl home* **13/8**[1]

**2** nk **Spud (IRE)** 2-9-2 0.............................................. RichardKingscote 8 83+
(Tom Dascombe) *wnt rt s: rn green early and racd off the pce: hdwy whn nt clr run over 1f out: plld off ins rail ent fnl f: r.o to take 2nd fnl 75yds: clsd on wnr nr fin: promising* **12/1**

5222 **3** 1 ¾ **Cosa Nostra (IRE)**[14] 6204 2-9-2 80............................. FrannyNorton 4 76
(Richard Fahey) *trckd ldrs: rdn 2f out: wnt 2nd wl over 1f out: kpt on u.p ins fnl f: no real imp on wnr: eased whn hld nr fin* **5/1**[3]

43 **4** 3 ¼ **Ateem (FR)**[15] 6132 2-9-2 0...................................... TomMarquand 7 68
(Richard Hannon) *trckd ldrs: rdn over 2f out: hung lft and disorganised over 1f out: one pce fnl f* **6/1**

5 **5** ½ **Gabrials Centurion (IRE)**[9] 6347 2-9-2 0.......................... DavidAllan 6 66
(David O'Meara) *racd off the pce: rdn 2f out: nvr a threat* **25/1**

6 **6** nse **Manor Park**[31] 5547 2-9-2 0........................................ MartinDwyer 5 66
(Alan King) *s.i.s: in rr: pushed along 3f out: kpt on ins fnl f: nvr able to trble ldrs* **25/1**

6235 **7** hd **Carouse (IRE)**[29] 5596 2-9-2 84...................................... DavidProbert 3 66
(Andrew Balding) *w wnr: rdn and unable qck 2f out: lost 2nd wl over 1f out: wknd ins fnl f* **5/2**[2]

1m 26.45s (-0.05) **Going Correction** +0.10s/f (Good) **7** Ran SP% **113.0**
Speed ratings (Par 97): **104,103,101,97,97 97,97**
CSF £21.94 TOTE £1.80: £1.10, £5.30; EX 20.70 Trifecta £99.20.
**Owner** Hamdan Al Maktoum **Bred** T Molan **Trained** Lambourn, Berks

■ Isabella Ruby was withdrawn. Price at time of withdrawal 100-1. Rule 4 does not apply.

**FOCUS**
All distances as advertised. The going was good. A fair contest run at an even pace, but just a bit of doubt to depth with field compressed.

## 6675 CORBETTSPORTS.COM CHESTER STKS (H'CAP) (LISTED RACE) 1m 5f 84y
**2:10** (2:15) (Class 1) (0-110,102) 3-Y-O+ **£20,982** (£7,955; £3,981; £1,983; £995; £499) **Stalls** Low

Form RPR

1542 **1** **My Reward**[10] 6329 5-9-5 **96**.................................................. DavidAllan 2 102
(Tim Easterby) *mde all setting stdy pce: rdn over 1f out: kpt on ins fnl f: doing enough towards fin: gd ride* **11/2**[3]

4112 **2** ¾ **Cape Coast**[49] 4886 3-8-5 **90**........................................ FrannyNorton 11 95+
(Mark Johnston) *chsd ldrs: unable qck over 2f out: styd on to take 2nd fnl 150yds: clsd on wnr towards fin* **3/1**[1]

-055 **3** 1 ¼ **Harlequeen**[7] 6440 4-9-10 **101**..........................................(v) JFEgan 6 104
(Mick Channon) *racd keenly: trckd ldrs: rdn to take 2nd wl over 1f out: no imp on wnr: lost 2nd fnl 150yds: styd on* **25/1**

1546 **4** ¾ **Apphia (IRE)**[28] 5658 3-8-13 **98**..............................(p[1]) JosephineGordon 7 100
(Hugo Palmer) *w wnr: lost 2nd after 5f: remained handy: rdn 5f out: kpt on ins fnl f: nt pce of ldrs* **16/1**

0110 **5** ¾ **Curlew River**[9] 6357 3-8-10 **95**................................ RichardKingscote 9 96
(Mark Johnston) *midfield: effrt on outer over 2f out: kpt on ins fnl f: nvr able to chal* **8/1**

4-04 **6** shd **Eye Of The Storm (IRE)**[14] 6201 7-9-4 **95**..................... MartinDwyer 1 96
(Amanda Perrett) *sed awkwardly: hld up: swtchd rt over 1f out: hdwy ins fnl f: kpt on: nvr able to trble ldrs* **18/1**

3150 **7** nse **The Tartan Spartan (IRE)**[14] 6191 4-9-11 **102**........... RoystonFfrench 4 105+
(John Patrick Shanahan, Ire) *in tch: lost pl over 2f out: rdn and hdwy over 1f out: styng on whn nt clr run and snatched up fnl 75yds: eased after* **12/1**

6520 **8** 1 ½ **Cliff Face (IRE)**[28] 5658 4-9-2 **93**..............................(p[1]) RyanPowell 3 93
(Sir Mark Prescott Bt) *dwlt: n.m.r whn bustled along jst after s: hld up in rr: effrt whn nt clr run ins fnl f: sn swtchd lft: nvr able to trble ldrs* **25/1**

2423 **9** hd **Graceland (FR)**[21] 5912 5-9-0 **91**.................................... LouisSteward 5 89
(Michael Bell) *dwlt: hld up in rr: rdn on outer over 1f out: no imp* **6/1**

5-43 **10** 2 ¾ **Who Dares Wins (IRE)**[74] 3928 5-9-2 **93**.................(p) TomMarquand 8 87
(Alan King) *hld up: rdn 3f out: sn outpcd* **5/1**[2]

-430 **11** ½ **Shraaoh (IRE)**[28] 5638 4-9-2 **93**...................................... TedDurcan 10 86
(Sir Michael Stoute) *midfield on outer: hdwy to go prom 2nd after 5f: rdn and lost 2nd wl over 1f out: wknd ins fnl f* **10/1**

2m 54.02s (1.32) **Going Correction** +0.10s/f (Good)
**WFA** 3 from 4yo+ 8lb **11** Ran SP% **118.1**
Speed ratings (Par 111): **99,98,97,97,96 96,96,95,95,94 93**
CSF £22.40 CT £377.64 TOTE £6.40: £2.00, £1.70, £6.70; EX 29.30 Trifecta £1013.90.
**Owner** M J Macleod **Bred** Millsec Limited **Trained** Great Habton, N Yorks

**FOCUS**
A decent contest initially run at a steady pace, before the tempo quickened down the far side. The race has been rated around the third.

## 6676 RAYMOND & KATHLEEN CORBETT MEMORIAL H'CAP 7f 127y
**2:45** (2:47) (Class 2) 3-Y-0+ **£28,012** (£8,388; £4,194; £2,097; £1,048; £526) **Stalls** Low

Form RPR

0005 **1** **Penwortham (IRE)**[7] 6414 4-8-0 **83** oh1....................(h) PatrickMathers 6 92
(Richard Fahey) *racd keenly in midfield: hdwy whn nt clr run and snatched up over 2f out: nt clr run over 1f out: sn swtchd rt: led jst over 1f out: r.o ins fnl f whn pressed: in command nr fin* **8/1**

4532 **2** ½ **War Glory (IRE)**[21] 5942 4-8-6 **89**.................................. TomMarquand 5 97
(Richard Hannon) *trckd ldrs: waited for run over 1f out: str chal 1f out and thrght fnl f: hld nr fin* **5/1**[2]

4152 **3** 3 ½ **Breakable**[9] 6358 6-9-0 **97**.......................................... DavidAllan 2 97
(Tim Easterby) *led: hdd over 4f out: remained prom: chalng 1f out: unable to go w front two fnl 150yds: styd on same pce after* **4/1**[1]

2516 **4** 1 ¼ **Khamaary (IRE)**[21] 5942 3-8-8 **96**.................................... DaneO'Neill 9 92
(Mark Johnston) *bmpd s: hld up in midfield: rdn 2f out: prog ins fnl f: styd on towards fin: nvr able to trble ldrs* **10/1**

1062 **5** nse **Wink Oliver**[11] 6300 5-8-2 **85**..............................(p) JosephineGordon 1 82
(Jo Hughes) *in tch: unable qck over 1f out: kpt on towards fin* **20/1**

6130 **6** nk **Love Dreams (IRE)**[8] 6401 3-8-12 **100**........................ FrannyNorton 8 95
(Mark Johnston) *w ldr: led over 4f out: rdn over 1f out: sn hdd: styd on same ins fnl 150yds* **8/1**

0020 **7** ¾ **Fingal's Cave (IRE)**[21] 5926 5-8-2 **92**...................... JamieGormley(7) 11 87
(Philip Kirby) *trckd ldrs: rdn over 1f out: no ex fnl 100yds* **28/1**

0003 **8** 1 ¼ **Sir Roderic (IRE)**[14] 6192 4-8-5 **88**..................................(t) JFEgan 10 80
(Rod Millman) *midfield: lost pl 3f out: rdn over 1f out: one pce fnl f* **16/1**

5410 **9** 1 ½ **Sharp Defence (USA)**[15] 6164 3-8-6 **94**..................... RoystonFfrench 7 81
(John Patrick Shanahan, Ire) *fly-jmpd s and missed break: hld up: pushed along over 2f out: no imp* **8/1**

5002 **10** nk **Intransigent**[11] 6289 8-8-8 **91**........................................ DavidProbert 3 79
(Andrew Balding) *midfield: rdn over 1f out: no imp: wl btn ins fnl f* **10/1**

4355 **11** 3 **Gabrial (IRE)**[7] 6444 8-9-7 **107**............................ AdamMcNamara(3) 4 88
(Richard Fahey) *missed break: hld up: rdn 2f out: nvr a threat* **7/1**[3]

1005 **12** 6 **Sound Advice**[29] 5616 8-9-3 **100**..............................(t[1]) DougieCostello 12 67
(Keith Dalgleish) *hld up: rdn on outer wl over 1f out: no imp: eased whn wl btn ins fnl f* **33/1**

1m 32.68s (-1.12) **Going Correction** +0.10s/f (Good)
**WFA** 3 from 4yo+ 5lb **12** Ran SP% **117.7**
Speed ratings (Par 109): **109,108,105,103,103 103,102,101,99,99 96,90**
CSF £46.31 CT £186.69 TOTE £10.50: £3.10, £1.80, £1.70; EX 59.40 Trifecta £334.00.
**Owner** Richard Fahey Ebor Racing Club Ltd **Bred** Kilfeacle Stud **Trained** Musley Bank, N Yorks

**FOCUS**
A strong renewal of this decent handicap which was run at a sound pace.

## 6677 #THEMBNATEAM H'CAP 5f 110y
**3:20** (3:23) (Class 2) (0-100,98) 3-Y-O+

**£11,827** (£3,541; £1,770; £885; £442; £222) **Stalls** Low

Form RPR

2200 **1** **Powerallied (IRE)**[7] 6412 4-8-7 **81**.............................. PatrickMathers 4 90
(Richard Fahey) *dwlt: midfield: hdwy over 1f out: r.o to ld fnl 100yds: won a shade comf* **5/1**[2]

0012 **2** 1 ¼ **El Astronaute (IRE)**[18] 6025 4-9-7 **95**.............................. JasonHart 10 100
(John Quinn) *displayed plenty of spd to ld: rdn abt 3 l clr over 1f out: hdd fnl 100yds: no ex nr fin* **9/1**

4025 **3** nk **Spring Loaded (IRE)**[12] 6275 5-9-4 **92**.............................. JoeyHaynes 9 96+
(Paul D'Arcy) *hld up: rdn 2f out: hdwy ins fnl f: r.o: gng on at fin* **10/1**

4006 **4** hd **East Street Revue**[50] 4867 4-9-2 **90**..........................(b) DuranFentiman 2 93
(Tim Easterby) *chsd ldrs: rdn 2f out: wnt 2nd over 1f out: lost 2nd ins fnl f: kpt on u.p: nt quite pce of ldrs towards fin* **6/1**[3]

0064 **5** nk **Taexali (IRE)**[28] 5647 4-9-4 **92**..........................(b) RoystonFfrench 8 94
(John Patrick Shanahan, Ire) *in rr: sn pushed along: hdwy u.p over 1f out: styd on ins fnl f: gng on at fin* **25/1**

0060 **6** ¾ **Gracious John (IRE)**[10] 6325 4-9-9 **97**.............................. JFEgan 3 97
(David Evans) *racd keenly: chsd ldrs: rdn over 1f out: kpt on u.p ins fnl f: hld whn n.m.r and hmpd towards fin* **6/1**[3]

1033 **7** ¾ **Confessional**[7] 6412 10-8-13 **87**..........................(e) DavidAllan 6 88+
(Tim Easterby) *in tch: sn dropped to midfield: effrt whn nt clr run 1f out and continually denied a run ins fnl f: eased: shkn up nr fin* **8/1**

0563 **8** 2 **Poet's Society**[4] 6554 3-8-11 **87**.............................. FrannyNorton 1 77
(Mark Johnston) *midfield: pushed along over 3f out: rdn over 2f out: one pce and no imp ins fnl f* **7/2**[1]

5000 **9** ¾ **Lucky Beggar (IRE)**[7] 6412 7-8-9 **83**.............................. SteveDrowne 12 70
(David C Griffiths) *dwlt: in rr: u.p over 2f out: nvr a threat* **33/1**

6004 **10** ½ **Verne Castle**[18] 6025 4-9-5 **93**..........................(h) DavidProbert 5 79
(Andrew Balding) *in tch: rdn 2f out: outpcd over 1f out: n.m.r whn u.p ins fnl f: sn dropped away* **14/1**

0605 **11** nk **Willytheconqueror (IRE)**[21] 5911 4-9-10 **98**.............................. MartinDwyer 7 83
(William Muir) *towards rr: pushed along 3f out: nvr a threat* **16/1**

0002 **12** 4 **Blithe Spirit**[35] 5402 6-8-8 **82**.............................. NeilFarley 11 53
(Eric Alston) *w ldr: rdn and lost 2nd over 1f out: wknd ins fnl f* **33/1**

1m 6.82s (0.62) **Going Correction** +0.10s/f (Good)
**WFA** 3 from 4yo+ 1lb **12** Ran SP% **119.9**
Speed ratings (Par 109): **99,97,96,96,96 95,94,91,90,89 89,84**
CSF £49.27 CT £441.15 TOTE £5.10: £1.70, £2.80, £3.30; EX 63.90 Trifecta £704.00.
**Owner** Dr Marwan Koukash **Bred** John R Jeffers **Trained** Musley Bank, N Yorks
■ Stewards' Enquiry : Joey Haynes caution: guilty of careless riding in that he had allowed his mount to drift left without sufficient correction

**FOCUS**
With plenty of prominent runners in the field this was always going to be run at a strong pace. The first two have been rated to form.

## 6678 KINDERTONS/EBF FILLIES' CONDITIONS STKS (PLUS 10 RACE) 6f 17y
**3:55** (3:57) (Class 2) 2-Y-O

**£12,450** (£3,728; £1,864; £932; £466; £234) **Stalls** Low

Form RPR

51 **1** **Peggy's Angel**[54] 4696 2-8-12 0.............................. DougieCostello 2 83
(Jo Hughes) *trckd ldrs: waited for run over 1f out: sn plld out: chalng ins fnl f: r.o to ld fnl 75yds* **8/1**

16 **2** ½ **Mayyasah (USA)**[21] 5941 2-9-1 0.............................. TomMarquand 7 85
(Richard Hannon) *hld up: hdwy on outer wl over 1f out: led ins fnl f: hdd fnl 75yds: hld nr fin* **6/4**[1]

0114 **3** ¾ **Yogi's Girl (IRE)**[15] 6136 2-9-5 90.............................. JFEgan 1 86
(David Evans) *led: rdn over 1f out: hdd ins fnl f: stl ev ch tl no ex towards fin* **3/1**[2]

3150 **4** 3 **Reflect Alexander (IRE)**[15] 6136 2-8-12 82.............................. DaneO'Neill 6 72
(David Evans) *in tch: nt clr run 2f out: effrt whn bmpd over 1f out: kpt on ins fnl f: no imp on ldrs* **7/1**[3]

04 **5** 6 **Mariah's Melody (IRE)**[7] 6410 2-8-12 0.............................. SteveDrowne 8 52
(Lisa Williamson) *towards rr: pushed along and outpcd over 2f out: nvr a threat* **100/1**

012 **6** nk **Deviate (IRE)**[4] 6559 2-8-12 0.............................. AlistairRawlinson 3 51
(Tom Dascombe) *racd keenly: w wnr tl rdn over 1f out: wknd ins fnl f* **8/1**

610 **7** nk **Wirral Girl (IRE)**[15] 6136 2-9-1 77.............................. AdamMcNamara 4 53
(Richard Fahey) *trckd ldrs: u.p and losing pl whn bmpd over 1f out: n.d after* **12/1**

40 **8** 14 **Supersymmetry (IRE)**[31] 5528 2-8-12 0.............................. DavidProbert 5
(Tom Dascombe) *a bhd and outpcd: nvr a threat* **20/1**

1m 15.26s (1.46) **Going Correction** +0.10s/f (Good) **8** Ran SP% **113.2**
Speed ratings (Par 98): **94,93,92,88,80 79,79,60**
CSF £20.03 TOTE £11.60: £2.20, £1.10, £1.70; EX 23.60 Trifecta £88.80.
**Owner** Dalwhinnie Bloodstock Limited **Bred** Dalwhinnie Bloodstock **Trained** Lambourn, Berks

**FOCUS**
A decent contest run at a fair pace.

## 6679 STELLA ARTOIS H'CAP 5f 15y
**4:30** (4:34) (Class 4) (0-85,83) 3-Y-O

**£6,225** (£1,864; £932; £466; £233; £117) **Stalls** Low

Form RPR

2212 **1** **Boundsy (IRE)**[35] 5416 3-9-3 **82**.............................. AdamMcNamara(3) 4 91+
(Richard Fahey) *midfield: hdwy over 1f out and plld out: str run ins fnl f: led nr fin* **3/1**[1]

2301 **2** nk **Liberatum**[12] 6276 3-8-1 **70**.............................. JamieGormley(7) 2 78
(Ruth Carr) *led: rdn over 1f out: all out ins fnl f: hdd nr fin* **9/2**[3]

6420 **3** 1 **Kamra (USA)**[22] 5869 3-9-1 **77**..........................(tp) FrannyNorton 1 81
(Michael Herrington) *trckd ldrs: rdn whn tk 2nd jst over 1f out: lost 2nd wl ins fnl f: styd on but nt pce of front two* **4/1**[2]

6160 **4** 3 **Yorkshiredebut (IRE)**[7] 6450 3-9-1 **77**..........................(p) NeilFarley 7 70
(Paul Midgley) *midfield: rdn and hdwy over 1f out: styd on ins fnl f: nt rch ldrs* **20/1**

0660 **5** ½ **Impart**[7] 6450 3-9-5 **81**.............................. DavidAllan 3 72
(David O'Meara) *trckd ldrs: rdn 2f out: one pce ins fnl f* **3/1**[1]

6154 **6** 1 ½ **Blitz**[14] 6177 3-9-6 **82**..........................(t[1]) DavidProbert 5 68
(Clive Cox) *towards rr: pushed along 3f out: nvr able to trble ldrs* **9/1**

1215 **7** shd **Peachey Carnehan**[10] 6308 3-8-7 **72**..........................(v) PhilDennis(3) 10 58
(Michael Mullineaux) *bhd: effrt over 3f out: no real prog* **33/1**

0130 **8** 1 ¼ **Chickenfortea (IRE)**[23] 5826 3-8-4 **66**.............................. DuranFentiman 11 47
(Eric Alston) *w ldr tl rdn over 1f out: wknd ins fnl f* **33/1**

6530 **9** 1 **Blue Rocks**[9] 6339 3-8-2 **64** oh9..........................(b[1]) RoystonFfrench 6 42
(Lisa Williamson) *bhd: pushed along over 3f out: outpcd over 2f out: nvr a threat* **50/1**

0205 **10** ½ **Merry Banter**[26] 5708 3-9-0 **83**.............................. ConnorMurtagh(7) 12 59
(Paul Midgley) *chsd ldrs: rdn 3f out: wknd wl over 1f out* **14/1**

1m 1.55s (0.55) **Going Correction** +0.10s/f (Good) **10** Ran SP% **117.5**
Speed ratings (Par 103): **99,98,96,92,91 88,88,86,85,84**
CSF £16.22 CT £54.74 TOTE £3.20: £1.50, £2.00, £1.30; EX 16.40 Trifecta £45.70.
**Owner** Kevin Mercer & Partner **Bred** Glenview House Stud **Trained** Musley Bank, N Yorks

**FOCUS**
A strongly run handicap with plenty of prominent runners in the field. The winner progressed again and could do better.

## 6680 THYME PEOPLE STAFFING AND EVENTS H'CAP 1m 7f 196y
**5:05** (5:08) (Class 4) (0-85,87) 3-Y-O+

**£6,225** (£1,864; £932; £466; £233; £117) **Stalls** Low

Form RPR

1062 **1** **St Mary's**[30] 5566 4-9-2 **80**.............................. WilliamCox(7) 4 88
(Andrew Balding) *midfield: hdwy 3f out: rdn over 2f out: styd on ins fnl f: led nr fin* **7/1**

4303 **2** nk **Arthur Mc Bride (IRE)**[31] 5524 8-9-12 **83**..........................(t) LiamKeniry 10 90
(Nigel Twiston-Davies) *led: rdn over 2f out: strly pressed ins fnl f: hdd nr fin* **7/1**

5225 **3** 2 ¼ **Angel Gabrial (IRE)**[21] 5912 8-9-11 **85**.............................. AdamMcNamara(3) 1 89
(Richard Fahey) *chsd ldrs: wnt 2nd 3f out: rdn over 2f out: tried to chal ins fnl f: no ex fnl 75yds* **9/2**[2]

1232 **4** 8 **La Vie En Rose**[19] 6013 3-8-6 **74**.............................. FrannyNorton 8 71
(Mark Johnston) *chsd ldrs: rdn and lost pl 4f out: outpcd 3f out: kpt on ins fnl f: no imp* **5/1**[3]

3164 **5** 1 ¾ **Zenafire**[35] 5403 8-8-12 **72**..........................(p) SammyJoBell(3) 6 65
(Sarah Hollinshead) *midfield: pushed along and lost pl 4f out: plugged on fr over 1f out: nvr able to trble ldrs* **11/1**

4040 **6** 1 ½ **Gabrial's Star**[15] 6151 8-9-7 **78**..........................(v) PatrickMathers 2 69
(Richard Fahey) *hld up: u.p 3f out: nvr a threat* **14/1**

4111 **7** 5 **Ya Jammeel**[30] 5556 4-9-9 **80**.............................. SamHitchcott 5 65
(Mick Channon) *chsd ldr to 3f out: sn rdn: wknd over 1f out* **4/1**[1]

3536 **8** nk **Warp Factor (IRE)**[14] 6189 4-9-7 **78**.............................. RoystonFfrench 7 62
(John Patrick Shanahan, Ire) *in rr: sme hdwy 6f out: pushed along 3f out: wknd over 2f out* **10/1**

0540 **9** 16 **Gabrial's King (IRE)**[21] 5924 8-8-9 **86**.............................. ConnorMurtagh(7) 9 51
(Richard Fahey) *hld up in midfield: hdwy 6f out: rdn whn chsng ldrs 3f out: wknd over 2f out* **14/1**

/32- **10** 10 **Rite To Reign**[449] 3117 6-10-2 **87**.............................. DavidProbert 3 40
(Philip McBride) *hld up: u.p 3f out: wl bhd over 1f out* **14/1**

3m 32.92s (4.92) **Going Correction** +0.10s/f (Good)
**WFA** 3 from 4yo+ 11lb **10** Ran SP% **117.3**
Speed ratings (Par 105): **91,90,89,85,84 84,81,81,73,68**
CSF £55.63 CT £247.21 TOTE £8.80: £2.80, £2.80, £1.50; EX 73.60 Trifecta £444.80.
**Owner** Kingsclere Racing Club **Bred** Kingsclere Stud **Trained** Kingsclere, Hants

**FOCUS**
A competitive race for the grade run at a steady pace. The race has been rated around the second.
T/Plt: £27.10 to a £1 stake. Pool: £110,025.14 - 2953.17 winning units. T/Qpdt: £6.10 to a £1 stake. Pool: £6,659.17 - 798.89 winning units. **Darren Owen**

# 6616 CHELMSFORD (A.W) (L-H)
Saturday, September 2

**OFFICIAL GOING: Polytrack: standard**
Wind: virtually nil Weather: fine

## 6681 GATES FORD APPRENTICE H'CAP 7f (P)
**5:50** (5:51) (Class 6) (0-65,69) 3-Y-O+ **£3,234** (£962; £481; £240) **Stalls** Low

Form RPR

6253 **1** **King Of Swing**[28] 5651 4-9-5 **63**..........................(h) FinleyMarsh(3) 7 75
(Richard Hughes) *hld up in midfield: clsd and travelling wl over 2f out: trcking ldrs whn nt clr run and swtchd rt ent fnl f: rdn and qcknd to ld 150yds out: sn clr and r.o wl: readily* **7/2**[2]

0003 **2** 5 **Jumping Around (IRE)**[19] 6015 3-9-7 **66**..........................(p[1]) RichardOliver 8 63
(Ian Williams) *chsd ldr: rdn to ld over 1f out: hdd 150yds: totally outpcd by wnr but kpt on to hold 2nd fnl 100yds* **6/1**

2364 **3** nk **Characterized**[17] 6076 3-9-6 **65**.............................. GeorgiaCox 6 61
(Geoffrey Deacon) *chsd ldng trio: effrt ent fnl 2f: styd on same pce and no ch w wnr ins fnl f: pressing for 2nd towards fin* **7/1**

0030 **4** ½ **Nonno Giulio (IRE)**[23] 5835 6-9-1 **61**..........................(b[1]) NicolaCurrie(5) 1 57
(Conor Dore) *chsd ldng pair: effrt wl over 1f out: no ch w wnr and kpt on same pce ins fnl f* **25/1**

4363 **5** 2 **Miss Mirabeau**[60] 4463 3-8-13 **61**..........................(b) ManuelFernandes(3) 5 50
(Sir Mark Prescott Bt) *rousted along early: nvr travelling wl in enough in rr: rdn and swtchd rt over 1f out: hdwy and styd on ins fnl f: nvr trbld ldrs* **11/4**[1]

0503 **6** ½ **False Id**[4] 6560 4-8-13 **57**..........................(b[1]) CameronNoble(3) 2 47
(Marjorie Fife) *chsd ldrs early: sn stdd bk into midfield and midfield on outer: rdn over 1f out: unable qck: wknd ins fnl f* **5/1**[3]

6211 **7** ½ **Ocean Temptress**[3] 6586 3-9-3 **69** 6ex..........................(v) JackOsborn(7) 9 55+
(John Ryan) *led: rdn and hdd over 1f out: sn outpcd and btn: wknd ins fnl f* **8/1**

524 **8** 3 **The Happy Hammer (IRE)**[32] 5512 11-9-7 **62**.............................. JoshuaBryan 3 42
(Eugene Stanford) *hld up in last trio: effrt over 1f out: no imp: wknd ins fnl f* **20/1**

0626 **9** 6 **Auric Goldfinger (IRE)**[68] 4144 3-9-1 **65**..........................(b) RossaRyan(5) 4 27
(Richard Hannon) *s.i.s: a in last trio: effrt 2f out: no prog: bhd and wknd fnl f* **10/1**

1m 26.99s (-0.21) **Going Correction** -0.075s/f (Stan)
**WFA** 3 from 4yo+ 4lb **9** Ran SP% **121.2**
Speed ratings (Par 101): **98,92,91,91,89 88,87,84,77**
CSF £26.31 CT £143.69 TOTE £4.30: £1.60, £2.40, £2.10; EX 28.10 Trifecta £508.70.
**Owner** Gallagher Bloodstock Limited **Bred** Petra Bloodstock Agency Ltd **Trained** Upper Lambourn, Berks



The Form Book Flat, Raceform Ltd, Newbury, RG14 5SJ

**FOCUS**
This was run at a good gallop. The winner won well and this could rate 2-6lb higher.

## 6682 DONE BROTHERS NOVICE STKS (PLUS 10 RACE) 5f (P)
6:20 (6:20) (Class 4) 2-Y-O £7,115 (£2,117; £1,058; £529) Stalls Low

Form RPR
220 1 **Global Passion (FR)**[15] 6147 2-9-2 0 RyanMoore 1 78
(Charles Hills) *mde all: veered rt over 4f out: rdn over 1f out: edgd rt 1f out: styd on wl ins fnl f: rdn out* 4/1[3]
1013 2 1 ¼ **Billy Dylan (IRE)**[35] 5424 2-9-7 87 RossaRyan(7) 3 85
(Richard Hannon) *wnt lft and cannoned into rival s: t.k.h: trckd ldng pair: effrt on inner over 1f out: chsd wnr ins fnl f: kpt on but no imp* 15/8[2]
450 3 1 **Gaelic Spirit (IRE)**[84] 3611 2-8-11 0 ShaneKelly 4 64
(Joseph Tuite) *chsd wnr: rdn wl over 1f out: unable qck and lost 2nd ins fnl f: kpt on same pce after* 16/1
2 4 nk **Tarnhelm**[7] 6417 2-8-11 0 PJMcDonald 2 63
(Mark Johnston) *cannoned into leaving stalls and slowly away: a last but wl in tch: effrt and swtchd rt wl over 1f out: kpt on fnl 100yds: nvr enough pce to threaten wnr* 11/10[1]

1m 2.06s (1.86) **Going Correction** -0.075s/f (Stan) 4 Ran SP% **108.3**
Speed ratings (Par 97): **82,80,78,77**
CSF £11.67 TOTE £3.50; EX 9.50 Trifecta £31.30.
**Owner** Dr Johnny Hon **Bred** Zied Ben M'Rad & Samy Torgeman **Trained** Lambourn, Berks

**FOCUS**
Just a small field, and Ryan Moore had the run of things out in front on the winner. The race has been rated around the runner-up.

## 6683 BETSI GOLDEN MILE NOVICE STKS (PLUS 10 RACE) 1m (P)
6:50 (6:52) (Class 4) 2-Y-O £7,439 (£2,213; £1,106; £553) Stalls Low

Form RPR
3 1 **Old Persian**[22] 5887 2-9-2 0 JamesDoyle 6 90+
(Charlie Appleby) *hld up in tch in last pair: swtchd rt and hdwy on outer 3f out: rdn and ev ch ent fnl 2f: led over 1f out: styd on strly and drew clr ins fnl f: readily* 10/11[1]
261 2 3 ¼ **Algam (IRE)**[20] 5960 2-9-8 81 FrankieDettori 4 85
(Richard Hannon) *taken down early: mde most: jnd over 3f out: rdn wl over 1f out: sn hdd: outpcd by wnr and kpt on same pce ins fnl f* 4/1[2]
5312 3 1 ¼ **Kit Marlowe**[25] 5742 2-9-5 83 PJMcDonald 1 79
(Mark Johnston) *w ldr tl over 3f out: styd chsng ldrs: rdn and ev ch 2f out: outpcd and swtchd rt ent fnl f: kpt on same pce and no ch w wnr ins fnl f* 9/2[3]
4 4 ½ **Gododdin** 2-9-2 0 RyanMoore 2 65+
(Hugo Palmer) *dwlt: sn rcvrd and wl in tch in midfield: rdn over 3f out: swtchd rt over 1f out: no imp and btn: wknd ins fnl f* 5/1
0 5 ¾ **Real Estate (IRE)**[70] 4094 2-9-2 0 MartinHarley 3 63
(James Tate) *trckd ldrs tl hdwy to join ldr over 3f out: rdn and ev ch 2f out tl outpcd and lost pl qckly over 1f out: bhd ins fnl f* 16/1
0 6 ½ **Topapinion**[22] 5887 2-9-2 0 ShaneKelly 7 62
(Mark H Tompkins) *stdd s and sn swtchd lft: t.k.h: hld up in last pair: swtchd rt and effrt over 1f out: sn outpcd and bhd ins fnl f* 100/1

1m 39.45s (-0.45) **Going Correction** -0.075s/f (Stan) 6 Ran SP% **114.1**
Speed ratings (Par 97): **99,95,94,90,89 88**
CSF £5.12 TOTE £1.60: £1.50, £2.00; EX 4.90 Trifecta £11.20.
**Owner** Godolphin **Bred** Godolphin **Trained** Newmarket, Suffolk

**FOCUS**
Not a bad novice race with the runner-up setting the standard.

## 6684 BETFRED 50TH ANNIVERSARY CONDITIONS STKS (PLUS 10 RACE) 7f (P)
7:20 (7:21) (Class 2) 2-Y-O £32,345 (£9,625; £4,810; £2,405) Stalls Low

Form RPR
110 1 **Cape Bunting (IRE)**[37] 5329 2-9-3 86 JamesDoyle 6 89
(Mark Johnston) *pressed ldr for 2f: styd chsng ldrs: effrt to press ldrs ent fnl 2f: rdn and ev ch over 1f out: led ins fnl f: r.o strly* 2/1[1]
2102 2 ¾ **Westerland**[31] 5547 2-9-5 86 (p[1]) FrankieDettori 5 89
(John Gosden) *hld up in tch in last pair: hdwy on outer to chse ldr after 2f: rdn and ev ch over 1f out: kpt on wl but nt quite match pce on wnr fnl 100yds: eased cl home* 9/4[2]
1121 3 3 **Amazing Alice**[23] 5844 2-9-3 81 (p) LukeMorris 3 79
(Archie Watson) *broke fast: t.k.h: led and set stdy gallop: rdn and qckd over 1f out: hdd and edgd lft ins fnl f: wknd fnl 100yds* 7/1
1610 4 1 ½ **Milton Road**[10] 6330 2-9-8 75 AndreaAtzeni 2 80
(Mick Channon) *stdd s: hld up in tch in rr: clsd to chse ldrs and swtchd lft 1f out: nt clr run: sltly hmpd and swtchd rt ins fnl f: no ch after* 20/1
1110 5 1 ½ **Ventura Knight (IRE)**[35] 5395 2-9-8 93 SilvestreDeSousa 4 76
(Mark Johnston) *trckd ldrs on outer: effrt ent fnl 2f out: unable qck over 1f out: outpcd and hung lft 1f out: wknd ins fnl f* 4/1[3]
3216 6 nk **Midnight Wilde**[7] 6425 2-9-5 77 JimCrowley 1 72
(John Ryan) *hld up in tch: effrt over 1f out: unable qck and carried lft 1f out: sn swtchd rt and wknd ins fnl f* 8/1

1m 26.71s (-0.49) **Going Correction** -0.075s/f (Stan) 6 Ran SP% **112.5**
Speed ratings (Par 101): **99,98,94,93,91 90**
CSF £6.83 TOTE £3.00: £1.90, £1.40; EX 7.80 Trifecta £27.60.
**Owner** Sheikh Hamdan bin Mohammed Al Maktoum **Bred** Godolphin **Trained** Middleham Moor, N Yorks

**FOCUS**
A good performance from the winner, who showed her running last time to be all wrong. The first two showed slight progress as rated.

## 6685 BETFRED CHELMSFORD CITY CUP H'CAP 7f (P)
7:50 (7:53) (Class 2) (0-105,105) 3-Y-O£51,752 (£15,400; £7,696; £3,848) Stalls Low

Form RPR
6205 1 **Masham Star (IRE)**[7] 6419 3-9-3 100 PJMcDonald 8 107
(Mark Johnston) *wl in tch in midfield: hdwy u.p to chse ldrs over 1f out: styd on strly ins fnl f to ld last strides* 8/1[3]
4040 2 hd **Sutter County**[7] 6419 3-9-4 101 JamesDoyle 1 107
(Mark Johnston) *mostly chsd ldr: rdn to ld over 1f out: kpt on wl u.p ins fnl f: hdd last strides* 9/1
2613 3 ½ **Mazzini**[18] 6025 4-9-4 100 (p) GeorgeWood(3) 5 107
(James Fanshawe) *taken down early: chsd ldrs: effrt over 1f out: chsd ldr 1f out: kpt on wl u.p ins fnl f* 6/1[2]
0624 4 nk **Baraweez (IRE)**[9] 6355 7-9-0 93 FranBerry 4 99
(Brian Ellison) *hld up in tch in midfield: effrt over 1f out: hdwy ins fnl f: styd on wl fnl 100yds: nt rch ldrs* 10/1
2210 5 1 **Constantino (IRE)**[49] 4916 4-9-1 94 (b) ShaneKelly 7 97
(Richard Fahey) *hld up in midfield: effrt u.p wl over 1f out: hdwy ins fnl f: styd on wl fnl 100yds: nt rch ldrs* 14/1
0205 6 nk **Royal Birth**[18] 6025 6-9-7 103 (t) AaronJones(3) 2 105
(Stuart Williams) *hld up in tch in midfield: effrt on inner to chse ldrs and edgd lft u.p 1f out: outpcd fnl 100yds* 25/1
0030 7 ¾ **Suzi's Connoisseur**[7] 6419 6-9-3 96 (vt) OisinMurphy 6 96
(Stuart Williams) *hld up in tch in midfield: effrt on inner over 1f out: nt clr run and swtchd rt 1f out: kpt on same pce ins fnl f* 25/1
0001 8 ½ **Squats (IRE)**[14] 6192 5-9-2 100 GeorgiaCox(5) 12 106+
(William Haggas) *taken down early: hld up in last quartet: rdn and hdwy towards inner over 1f out: swtchd lft 1f out: nvr got a clr run after and no imp* 12/1
5335 9 hd **That Is The Spirit**[21] 5942 6-9-6 99 MartinHarley 13 97
(David O'Meara) *broke fast to ld: rdn and hdd over 1f out: no ex and lost 2nd 1f out: wknd ins fnl f* 25/1
0160 10 1 ¾ **Swift Approval (IRE)**[7] 6419 5-9-2 95 (t[1]) LukeMorris 15 89
(Stuart Williams) *hld up in tch in midfield: effrt over 1f out: nt clr run and swtchd sharply rt 1f out: kpt on same pce after* 33/1
1100 11 1 ¾ **Fastnet Tempest (IRE)**[35] 5393 4-9-5 98 (p) RyanMoore 11 98+
(William Haggas) *s.i.s and rdn along in rr: nvr travelling wl enough: sme hdwy into midfield whn hmpd 1f out: nt given a hrd time and no imp after* 4/1[1]
-426 12 nse **Ibn Malik (IRE)**[14] 6193 4-9-12 105 JimCrowley 14 94
(Charles Hills) *chsd ldrs on outer: rdn and struggling ent fnl 2f: lost pl over 1f out: wknd ins fnl f* 8/1[3]
20 13 shd **Mr Bossy Boots (IRE)**[29] 5610 6-9-3 96 (t) JosephineGordon 3 85
(Amanda Perrett) *rrd as stalls opened and slowly away: sn outpcd and rdn along in last trio: nvr trbld ldrs* 14/1
2400 14 1 ¼ **Supersta**[18] 6024 6-9-7 100 (p) SilvestreDeSousa 10 85
(Michael Appleby) *s.i.s: a in rr: pushed along over 1f out: no imp and swtchd rt 1f out: n.d* 20/1
1600 15 ½ **Omran**[42] 5147 3-9-0 97 AndreaAtzeni 9 79
(Marco Botti) *hld up in midfield: effrt on inner but no imp over 1f out: bhd ins fnl f* 6/1[2]

1m 24.76s (-2.44) **Going Correction** -0.075s/f (Stan)
**WFA** 3 from 4yo+ 4lb 15 Ran SP% **130.2**
Speed ratings (Par 109): **110,109,109,108,107 107,106,105,105,103 101,101,101,100,99**
CSF £78.66 CT £490.91 TOTE £10.80: £3.20, £3.40, £2.90; EX 114.00 Trifecta £1015.00.
**Owner** 3 Batterhams and A Reay **Bred** Petra Bloodstock Agency Ltd **Trained** Middleham Moor, N Yorks
■ Stewards' Enquiry : Luke Morris 2 day ban: guilty of careless riding in that he manoeuvered right when insufficiently clear (17/18 Sep)

**FOCUS**
Surprisingly few got into this, the first three racing close up throughout. The race has been rated around the first two.

## 6686 TOTEPOOL H'CAP 7f (P)
8:20 (8:21) (Class 4) (0-85,89) 3-Y-O+ £8,086 (£2,406; £1,202; £601) Stalls Low

Form RPR
2124 1 **Big Tour (IRE)**[19] 6014 3-9-9 86 PatCosgrave 2 93+
(Saeed bin Suroor) *trckd ldrs: effrt and rdn to chal over 1f out: led ins fnl f: styd on wl u.p: rdn out* 7/4[1]
0032 2 ½ **Summer Chorus**[29] 5610 4-9-13 86 OisinMurphy 1 93
(Andrew Balding) *hld up in tch in midfield: clsd to trck ldrs and nt clr run jst over 1f out: gap opened and rdn to press ldrs jst ins fnl f: kpt on: wnt 2nd towards fin* 4/1[2]
1332 3 ¾ **Dark Side Dream**[11] 6290 5-9-4 77 SilvestreDeSousa 7 82
(Chris Dwyer) *t.k.h: w ldr tl rdn t o ld over 1f out: sn drvn and hdd ins fnl f: styd on same pce after: lost 2nd towards fin* 8/1
3136 4 1 ½ **Boy In The Bar**[50] 4830 6-9-8 81 (p[1]) JosephineGordon 9 82
(Ian Williams) *t.k.h: hld up in tch in last trio: effrt wl over 1f out: hdwy whn nt clrest of runs ent fnl f: chsd ldng trio ins fnl f: kpt on but nvr threatening ldrs* 12/1
2421 5 ½ **Peak Princess (IRE)**[10] 6321 3-9-12 89 (b) RyanMoore 3 87
(Richard Hannon) *hld up in tch in rr of main gp: clsd jst over 1f out: rdn and kpt on same pce ins fnl f: nvr trbld ldrs* 5/1[3]
506 6 3 ¼ **Saleh (IRE)**[44] 5064 4-9-3 76 DanielMuscutt 8 67
(Lee Carter) *t.k.h early: hld up in tch in midfield: effrt and hdwy over 1f out: 4th and no imp 1f out: wknd ins fnl f* 33/1
1502 7 1 ¼ **Sans Souci Bay**[35] 5433 3-9-3 83 (b) HollieDoyle(3) 6 68
(Richard Hannon) *v.s.a: grad rcvrd and tagged onto bk of field 1/2-way: rdn and sme hdwy whn nt clr run and swtchd rt 1f out: switching bk lft and no imp ins fnl f* 25/1
132 8 1 **Fantasy Keeper**[43] 5122 3-8-9 72 LukeMorris 5 55
(Michael Appleby) *chsd ldrs on outer: rdn over 2f out: lost pl over 1f out: wknd fnl f* 16/1
-610 9 7 **Etikaal**[39] 5245 3-9-8 85 (p) JimCrowley 4 49
(Simon Crisford) *led tl rdn and hdd wl over 1f out: sn dropped out and bhd 1f out: wknd and eased ins fnl f* 7/1

1m 25.05s (-2.15) **Going Correction** -0.075s/f (Stan)
**WFA** 3 from 4yo+ 4lb 9 Ran SP% **117.0**
Speed ratings (Par 105): **109,108,107,105,105 101,100,99,91**
CSF £8.76 CT £44.43 TOTE £2.30: £1.10, £1.80, £2.20; EX 9.80 Trifecta £47.60.
**Owner** Godolphin **Bred** Rabbah Bloodstock Limited **Trained** Newmarket, Suffolk

**FOCUS**
The early pace wasn't that strong, but the winner is on the upgrade and can improve again..

## 6687 JOE SCANLON BIRTHDAY CELEBRATION FILLIES' H'CAP 1m 2f (P)
8:50 (8:52) (Class 3) (0-95,97) 3-Y-O+ £19,407 (£5,775; £2,886; £1,443) Stalls Low

Form RPR
5431 1 **Blushing Rose**[25] 5745 3-8-12 82 RyanMoore 5 94+
(Sir Michael Stoute) *trckd ldrs: effrt to chal towards inner over 1f out: led 1f out: r.o strly and drew clr ins fnl f* 9/4[2]
013 2 2 ½ **Ickymasho**[59] 4679 5-10-5 97 LukeMorris 7 103
(Jonathan Portman) *t.k.h: stdd into midfield after 2f: swtchd rt and effrt over 1f out: styd on ins fnl f to go 2nd towards fin: nvr matching pce of wnr* 6/1[3]
6212 3 ½ **Dowayla (IRE)**[15] 6145 3-9-7 91 JimCrowley 3 96
(Saeed bin Suroor) *led and set stdy gallop: rdn and qcknd over 1f out: edgd rt and hdd 1f out: sn outpcd and lost 2nd towards fin* 6/4[1]
1642 4 2 ¾ **Vogueatti (USA)**[25] 5745 4-9-1 79 DanielMuscutt 6 79
(Marco Botti) *pressed ldr: rdn ent fnl 2f: keeping on same pce whn sltly impeded and swtchd rt 1f out: wknd ins fnl f* 8/1

6064 **5** 1 ¾ **Prosper**[25] 5745 3-9-0 **84**..........(v) AndreaAtzeni 4 80
*(Roger Varian) hld up in tch in last pair: effrt over 2f out: no imp u.p over 1f out: wknd ins fnl f* **7/1**

566 **6** 6 **Coillte Cailin (IRE)**[26] 5704 7-10-0 **92**.......... MartinHarley 1 76
*(David O'Meara) hld up in tch in last pair: effrt over 1f out: sn rdn and outpcd: bhd ins fnl f* **25/1**

1505 **R** **La Casa Tarifa (IRE)**[19] 6001 3-8-10 **80**.......... PJMcDonald 2
*(Mark Johnston) ref to r* **25/1**

2m 6.6s (-2.00) **Going Correction** -0.075s/f (Stan)
**WFA** 3 from 4yo+ 6lb 7 Ran SP% **116.4**
Speed ratings (Par 104): **105,103,102,100,99 94,**
CSF £16.75 TOTE £3.10: £1.60, £2.60; EX 18.60 Trifecta £39.50.
**Owner** Sir Evelyn De Rothschild **Bred** Southcourt Stud **Trained** Newmarket, Suffolk
**FOCUS**
This was steadily run, but the winner looks a progressive filly to keep onside.
T/Plt: £65.40 to a £1 stake. Pool: £75,311.68 - 839.84 winning units. T/Qpdt: £7.10 to a £1 stake. Pool: £8,521.55 - 883.15 winning units. **Steve Payne**

## 6379 HAMILTON (R-H)

### Saturday, September 2

**OFFICIAL GOING: Good to soft (good in places; 7.0)**
Wind: Breezy, half behind in sprints and in over 4f of home straight of races on the round course Weather: Overcast

## 6688 BET TOTEPLACEPOT AT BETFRED.COM AMATEUR RIDERS' H'CAP 6f 6y
4:15 (4:16) (Class 6) (0-65,61) 4-Y-O+ **£3,119** (£967; £483; £242) **Stalls** High

Form RPR

242/ **1** **Breezolini**[22] 5904 9-10-3 **57**.......... MissEChaston(7) 1 67
*(Adrian Brendan Joyce, Ire) hld up on outside: hdwy over 2f out: led and drifted lft over 1f out: rdn and r.o strly fnl f* **13/2**

5021 **2** 2 **Knockamany Bends (IRE)**[8] 6384 7-10-2 **49**..........(h) MissCWalton 9 53
*(John Wainwright) led against stands' rail: rdn and hdd over 1f out: rallied ins fnl f: nt pce of wnr* **10/1**

60-0 **3** hd **Jebel Tara**[21] 5919 12-9-10 **46** ow1..........(bt) MrBLynn(3) 4 49
*(Alistair Whillans) cl up: rdn over 2f out: ev ch briefly over 1f out: sn checked: kpt on same pce ins fnl f* **40/1**

0301 **4** nk **Whipphound**[12] 6271 9-10-1 **53**..........(b) MissEmilyBullock(5) 10 56
*(Ruth Carr) dwlt: t.k.h: hld up: hdwy and prom whn nt clr run briefly over 1f out: kpt on same pce fnl f* **4/1**[2]

3645 **5** ½ **Mitchum**[12] 6271 8-10-3 **50**.......... MissSBrotherton 8 51
*(Ron Barr) prom: rdn over 2f out: rallied over 1f out: no imp fnl f* **6/1**[3]

0454 **6** hd **Baron Run**[25] 5750 7-9-13 **53**.......... MrJCummins(7) 12 53
*(K R Burke) dwlt: bhd and outpcd: drifted bdly rt 1/2-way: effrt 2f out: no imp fnl f* **3/1**[1]

3204 **7** ¾ **Picks Pinta**[10] 6318 6-10-11 **61**..........(b) MissAMcCain(3) 5 59
*(John David Riches) hld up: pushed along and effrt wl over 1f out: edgd rt and sn no imp* **9/1**

0203 **8** hd **Insolenceofoffice (IRE)**[26] 5695 9-10-1 **48**..........(p) MissBeckySmith 7 46
*(Richard Ford) chsd ldrs: rdn over 2f out: wknd over 1f out* **14/1**

0403 **9** 1 **A J Cook (IRE)**[12] 6271 7-9-9 **45**.......... MissLWilson(3) 11 40
*(Ron Barr) hld up: pushed along over 2f out: sn no imp* **12/1**

3400 **10** 4 **Let Right Be Done**[9] 6346 5-9-12 **45**..........(b) MrsCBartley 2 28
*(Linda Perratt) s.i.s: bhd and sn struggling: no ch fr 1/2-way* **18/1**

0000 **11** 4 ½ **Reflation**[8] 6384 5-9-8 **46**..........(p) MissEllaMcCain(5) 6 15
*(Patrick Holmes) chaed ldrs: rdn and outpcd over 2f out: wknd wl over 1f out* **33/1**

1m 14.28s (2.08) **Going Correction** +0.275s/f (Good) 11 Ran SP% **116.7**
Speed ratings (Par 101): **97,94,94,93,93 92,91,91,90,84 78**
CSF £69.35 CT £2431.13 TOTE £7.70: £2.30, £3.30, £12.90; EX 79.10 Trifecta £1273.10.
**Owner** Mrs Christina Joyce **Bred** Hellwood Stud Farm **Trained** Athlone, Co Roscommon
■ Stewards' Enquiry : Miss E Chaston two-day ban: careless riding (Sep 26-Oct 9)
**FOCUS**
This was a low-grade sprint handicap for amateur riders in which the winner came from the least favourable draw. The form stacks up around those nearest the winner.

## 6689 BET TOTEEXACTA AT BETFRED.COM NOVICE STKS (PLUS 10 RACE) 6f 6y
4:50 (4:50) (Class 4) 2-Y-O **£5,175** (£1,540; £769; £384) **Stalls** High

Form RPR

42 **1** **Humble Gratitude**[23] 5825 2-8-13 **0**.......... CliffordLee(3) 2 84+
*(K R Burke) t.k.h: trckd ldr: shkn up to ld over 1f out: rdn and hd high ins fnl f: kpt on wl* **8/11**[1]

24 **2** 1 ¾ **Up Sticks And Go**[60] 4472 2-9-2 **0**.......... ConnorBeasley 3 79
*(Keith Dalgleish) led against stands' rail: rdn and hdd over 1f out: kpt on same pce ins fnl f* **17/2**

1 **3** 4 ½ **Equitant**[17] 6056 2-9-5 **0**.......... TonyHamilton 4 68
*(Richard Fahey) dwlt: t.k.h in tch: effrt and chsd ldng pair over 1f out: sn outpcd* **7/2**[2]

3 **4** 1 ½ **Poet's Pride**[10] 6311 2-9-2 **0**.......... BenCurtis 1 61
*(David Barron) t.k.h: trckd ldrs tl rdn and wknd wl over 1f out* **9/2**[3]

1m 13.26s (1.06) **Going Correction** +0.275s/f (Good) 4 Ran SP% **108.8**
Speed ratings (Par 97): **103,100,94,92**
CSF £7.18 TOTE £1.40; EX 7.00 Trifecta £37.20.
**Owner** H Strecker & Mrs E Burke **Bred** Whitsbury Manor Stud **Trained** Middleham Moor, N Yorks
**FOCUS**
A decent little juvenile novice despite the small field. The time was 1.02sec faster than the opening handicap and the form could prove decent.

## 6690 BET TOTEQUADPOT AT BETFRED.COM H'CAP 1m 1f 35y
5:25 (5:27) (Class 6) (0-60,56) 4-Y-O+ **£3,234** (£962; £481; £240) **Stalls** Low

Form RPR

-500 **1** **Al Hawraa**[18] 6047 4-9-6 **55**.......... KevinStott 2 63+
*(Kevin Ryan) hld up midfield on ins: effrt and rdn over 2f out: led over 1f out: kpt on strly fnl f* **4/1**[2]

60-0 **2** 2 ¼ **Granite City Doc**[19] 5997 4-8-3 **45**.......... PaulaMuir(7) 5 49
*(Lucy Normile) sn disputing ld: led over 2f out: rdn: hung lft and hdd over 1f out: stened and kpt on same pce fnl f* **20/1**

5620 **3** 2 ½ **New Abbey Angel (IRE)**[9] 6352 4-9-0 **54**.......... RowanScott(5) 13 53
*(Keith Dalgleish) hld up on outside: stdy hdwy and in tch over 2f out: sn rdn: kpt on same pce fnl f* **8/1**

4503 **4** 1 ¾ **Colour Contrast (IRE)**[9] 6346 4-9-0 **54**..........(p) CallumRodriguez(5) 11 49
*(Iain Jardine) midfield: drvn and outpcd over 3f out: rallied wl over 1f out: kpt on fnl f: nvr able to chal* **3/1**[1]

0540 **5** 1 **Stardrifter**[9] 6352 5-9-0 **49**..........(p) AndrewMullen 9 42
*(Linda Perratt) s.i.s: hld up: rdn over 2f out: styd on fr 2f out: nvr able to chal* **16/1**

5304 **6** ¾ **Red Shadow**[9] 6346 8-8-3 **45**..........(v) RhonaPindar(7) 8 37
*(Alistair Whillans) hld up: stdy hdwy on outside over 3f out: rdn over 2f out: wknd over 1f out* **22/1**

0450 **7** nk **Ingleby Spring (IRE)**[16] 6092 5-9-7 **56**.......... TonyHamilton 4 47
*(Richard Fahey) trckd ldrs: shkn up and ev ch whn carried lft over 1f out: sn rdn and outpcd: btn ins fnl f* **7/1**[3]

0-00 **8** ¾ **Dark Illustrator**[9] 6346 4-8-13 **48**.......... BarryMcHugh 12 37
*(Lynn Siddall) s.i.s: hld up: pushed along and outpcd over 3f out: styd on fnl f: nvr on terms* **66/1**

00-0 **9** ½ **Chookie Valentine**[15] 6131 4-8-10 **45**..........(p) ConnorBeasley 1 33
*(Keith Dalgleish) trckd ldrs: drvn and outpcd over 3f out: no imp fr 2f out* **33/1**

0050 **10** 6 **Indian Giver**[10] 6316 9-8-10 **45**..........(p) ShaneGray 7 21
*(John David Riches) hld up towards rr: drvn and struggling 4f out: nvr on terms* **28/1**

0001 **11** shd **Riponian**[28] 5649 7-9-6 **55**..........(t) PaddyAspell 6 31
*(Susan Corbett) mde most to over 2f out: sn hung rt: wknd over 1f out* **8/1**

6031 **12** 1 **Rioja Day (IRE)**[9] 6346 7-8-13 **55**..........(b) SeanMooney(7) 10 29
*(Jim Goldie) prom: drvn and outpcd over 3f out: btn fnl 2f* **8/1**

6206 **13** 16 **Irvine Lady (IRE)**[19] 5992 4-8-10 **45**..........(p) BenCurtis 3
*(R Mike Smith) t.k.h: hld up on ins: struggling 4f out: sn btn* **14/1**

1m 59.99s (0.29) **Going Correction** +0.075s/f (Good) 13 Ran SP% **120.4**
Speed ratings (Par 101): **101,99,96,95,94 93,93,92,92,86 86,85,71**
CSF £89.28 CT £624.24 TOTE £4.70: £1.70, £6.60, £2.60; EX 119.90 Trifecta £1260.90.
**Owner** Allan Kerr & Peter McGivney **Bred** Shadwell Estate Company Limited **Trained** Hambleton, N Yorks
**FOCUS**
Rail movements added 8 yards to the race distance. Quite a large field for this very moderate handicap and it got rather rough in the closing stages. The placed horses pin the level.

## 6691 BET TOTETRIFECTA AT BETFRED.COM EBF FILLIES' H'CAP (AN EBF SCOTTISH PREMIER SERIES RACE) 1m 68y
6:00 (6:00) (Class 4) (0-80,85) 3-Y-O+ **£7,762** (£2,310; £1,154; £577) **Stalls** Low

Form RPR

3111 **1** **Whatsthemessage (IRE)**[9] 6349 3-9-12 **85**.......... AndrewMullen 3 94
*(Keith Dalgleish) trckd ldrs: wnt 2nd over 2f out: sn drvn along: kpt on wl fnl f to ld nr fin* **2/1**[1]

4-11 **2** nk **Isabella (IRE)**[13] 6235 3-9-12 **85**.......... PhillipMakin 6 93
*(David O'Meara) led at stdy gallop: rdn and qcknd over 2 l clr over 1f out: edgd lft: kpt on wl fnl f: hdd nr fin* **2/1**[1]

2011 **3** 2 ¾ **Pantera Negra (IRE)**[16] 6091 3-9-0 **73**.......... BenCurtis 1 75
*(David Barron) hld up in last pl: effrt and plld to outside over 2f out: hdwy and edgd rt over 1f out: kpt on fnl f: nt rch first two* **4/1**[2]

5035 **4** nk **Invermere**[26] 5699 4-9-5 **73**.......... TonyHamilton 2 75
*(Richard Fahey) t.k.h: hld up in tch: effrt over 2f out: n.m.r briefly wl over 1f out: sn rdn and no imp* **14/1**

4450 **5** 3 **Little Lady Katie (IRE)**[21] 5926 5-9-4 **75**..........(v[1]) CliffordLee(3) 4 70
*(K R Burke) trckd ldr to over 2f out: rdn and wknd over 1f out* **12/1**

1505 **6** 1 ½ **Vaulted**[12] 6266 3-8-8 **67**..........(p) BarryMcHugh 5 58
*(Richard Fahey) in tch: effrt on outside over 2f out: rdn and wknd over 1f out: eased whn btn ins fnl f* **17/2**[3]

1m 48.69s (0.29) **Going Correction** +0.075s/f (Good)
**WFA** 3 from 4yo+ 5lb 6 Ran SP% **111.6**
Speed ratings (Par 102): **101,100,97,97,94 93**
CSF £5.96 TOTE £2.40: £1.30, £2.10; EX 7.60 Trifecta £12.50.
**Owner** Ronnie Docherty **Bred** Lynn Lodge Stud **Trained** Carluke, S Lanarks
**FOCUS**
Rail movements added 8 yards to the race distance. The decent prize produced a fair fillies' handicap and it produced a terrific finish between the market leaders. The form looks sound with the winner rated to form.

## 6692 BET TOTEWIN AT BETFRED.COM H'CAP 1m 3f 15y
6:35 (6:35) (Class 5) (0-75,76) 3-Y-O **£3,881** (£1,155; £577; £288) **Stalls** Low

Form RPR

0051 **1** **Taxmeifyoucan (IRE)**[12] 5648 3-9-7 **75**..........(v) ConnorBeasley 2 86
*(Keith Dalgleish) hld up in tch: stdy hdwy 3f out: rdn and led over 1f out: drew clr ins fnl f: comf* **15/8**[1]

-425 **2** 4 ½ **Eyreborn (IRE)**[7] 6436 3-8-5 **64**.......... RowanScott(5) 5 68
*(Keith Dalgleish) chsd ldr: rdn over 2f out: led briefly over 1f out: kpt on fnl f: no ch w wnr* **9/2**[3]

5323 **3** 1 **Duck Egg Blue (IRE)**[10] 6316 3-8-10 **71**.......... PaulaMuir(7) 1 73
*(Patrick Holmes) prom: effrt and rdn over 2f out: kpt on ins fnl f: nt pce to chal* **9/1**

4401 **4** 2 ¾ **Chinese Spirit (IRE)**[19] 5993 3-9-0 **68**.......... TonyHamilton 3 65
*(R Mike Smith) hld up in last pl: stdy hdwy on outside over 3f out: rdn and outpcd whn hung rt 2f out: n.d after* **7/2**[2]

3414 **5** 1 **Katebird (IRE)**[7] 6416 3-9-8 **76**.......... AndrewMullen 4 72
*(Mark Johnston) led: qcknd 1/2-way: rdn and hdd over 1f out: wknd ins fnl f* **6/1**

3400 **6** 12 **Spiritofhayton (IRE)**[21] 5950 3-8-12 **66**.......... BenCurtis 6 41
*(David Barron) dwlt: sn chsng ldrs: rdn and outpcd over 3f out: lost tch 2f out: eased* **8/1**

2m 25.81s (0.21) **Going Correction** +0.075s/f (Good) 6 Ran SP% **110.6**
Speed ratings (Par 101): **102,98,98,96,95 86**
CSF £10.22 TOTE £2.70: £1.90, £2.00; EX 10.70 Trifecta £61.30.
**Owner** Straightline Bloodstock **Bred** E Lonergan **Trained** Carluke, S Lanarks
**FOCUS**
Rail movements added 8 yards to the race distance. This tight little 3yo handicap was run at a steady pace early and they finished fairly strung out. The race has been rated around the second.

## 6693 BB FOODSERVICE 2-Y-O SERIES FINAL (A NURSERY H'CAP) 6f 6y
7:05 (7:06) (Class 2) 2-Y-O
**£12,450** (£3,728; £1,864; £932; £466; £234) **Stalls** High

Form RPR

0521 **1** **Magic Jazz (IRE)**[28] 5644 2-8-11 **74**.......... KevinStott 10 82
*(Kevin Ryan) mde virtually all against stands' rail: shkn up over 1f out: kpt on strly fnl f* **7/2**[2]

323 **2** 1 1/4 **Clubbable**[26] 5702 2-8-10 **73** TonyHamilton 6 77
(Richard Fahey) *in tch: effrt and chsd wnr over 1f out: kpt on fnl f: nt pce to chal* **4/1**[3]
5211 **3** 1 3/4 **Camacho Chief (IRE)**[29] 5603 2-9-2 **84** CallumRodriguez(5) 7 83
(Michael Dods) *n.m.r and blkd sn after s: hld up on stands' rail: hdwy over 1f out: checked ent fnl f: kpt on: no imp* **9/4**[1]
5213 **4** 3 1/4 **Wensley**[17] 6056 2-9-1 **81** CliffordLee(3) 4 70
(James Bethell) *in tch on outside: effrt and rdn over 2f out: kpt on fnl f: no imp* **20/1**
3552 **5** shd **Sinaloa (IRE)**[28] 5644 2-8-10 **73** BarryMcHugh 2 62
(Richard Fahey) *bhd and sn pushed along: rdn over 2f out: hdwy over 1f out: no imp* **14/1**
1665 **6** 2 **Quayside**[15] 6128 2-8-11 **74** (b1) ConnorBeasley 5 57
(Richard Fahey) *w ldrs to over 1f out: rdn and wknd ins fnl f* **12/1**
4305 **7** 1 1/2 **Corton Lass**[8] 6379 2-8-0 **63** AndrewMullen 9 41+
(Keith Dalgleish) *t.k.h: in tch: rdn and outpcd 2f out: n.d after* **18/1**
110 **8** 1/2 **Poetic Steps (FR)**[30] 5572 2-9-5 **82** BenCurtis 8 59
(Mark Johnston) *w ldrs to over 2f out: wknd over 1f out* **9/1**
2210 **9** 1 **Poet's Prince**[30] 5572 2-9-1 **78** PhillipMakin 3 52
(Mark Johnston) *t.k.h: prom on outside: rdn and lost pl wl over 1f out: sn struggling* **10/1**

1m 13.05s (0.85) **Going Correction** +0.275s/f (Good) **9** Ran SP% **116.5**
Speed ratings (Par 101): **105,103,101,96,96 93,91,91,89**
CSF £18.14 CT £38.03 TOTE £4.20: £1.40, £1.60, £1.50; EX 21.20 Trifecta £64.50.
**Owner** Hambleton Racing Xxxi & Partner **Bred** Golden Vale Stud **Trained** Hambleton, N Yorks

**FOCUS**
The feature race and a competitive contest for this nursery series final. The time was 0.21 secs faster than the earlier juvenile race over the trip. The first three came clear and the form looks sound.

## 6694 BET TOTEPLACE AT BETFRED.COM MAIDEN STKS 6f 6y
**7:35** (7:35) (Class 5) 3-Y-O+ **£3,881** (£1,155; £577; £288) **Stalls High**

Form RPR
3536 **1** **Jessinamillion**[21] 5947 3-9-5 73 KevinStott 4 71+
(James Bethell) *chsd ldrs: outpcd over 3f out: rallied: bk on bridle and led over 1f out: edgd lft and pushed clr fnl f: comf* **2/7**[1]
0220 **2** 3 1/4 **Vintage Dream (IRE)**[34] 5459 3-9-5 59 BenCurtis 1 60
(Noel Wilson) *led: rdn: hung rt and hdd over 1f out: no ch w wnr* **7/2**[2]
406 **3** 2 1/4 **Dawoodi**[19] 5995 3-9-5 58 (h) AndrewMullen 3 53
(Linda Perratt) *dwlt: plld hrd and sn cl up: rdn and ev ch over 1f out: wknd ins fnl f* **14/1**[3]
3500 **4** 1 3/4 **Henrietta's Dream**[6] 6469 3-8-9 45 (b) CallumRodriguez(5) 2 42
(John Wainwright) *dwlt: in tch: rdn over 2f out: wknd over 1f out* **25/1**

1m 14.66s (2.46) **Going Correction** +0.275s/f (Good) **4** Ran SP% **110.5**
Speed ratings (Par 103): **94,89,86,84**
CSF £1.70 TOTE £1.10; EX 1.80 Trifecta £2.50.
**Owner** Culture Club **Bred** Mrs James Bethell **Trained** Middleham Moor, N Yorks

**FOCUS**
With one exception in the small field they looked a moderate bunch in this maiden. The time was the slowest of the four races over the trip on the night.
T/Plt: £114.70 to a £1 stake. Pool: £40,995.93 - 260.88 winning units. T/Qpdt: £8.80 to a £1 stake. Pool: £4,582.68 - 384.59 winning units. **Richard Young**

# 6651 SANDOWN (R-H)
Saturday, September 2

**OFFICIAL GOING: Good (good to soft in places on round course) changing to good after race 4 (3.35)**
Wind: Almost nil Weather: Fine, warm

## 6695 BETFINDER BY BETBRIGHT H'CAP 5f 10y
**1:50** (1:52) (Class 3) (0-95,92) 3-Y-O+
**£9,337** (£2,796; £1,398; £699; £349; £175) **Stalls Low**

Form RPR
3144 **1** **Justice Lady (IRE)**[17] 6072 4-8-12 **80** ShaneKelly 7 89
(David Elsworth) *lw: hld up in last: gd prog on wd outside over 1f out: produced to ld last 100yds: sn clr* **8/1**
115 **2** 1 1/4 **Super Julius**[47] 4974 3-9-1 **84** (p) CharlesBishop 6 88
(Eve Johnson Houghton) *hld up in rr: prog on outer over 1f out: rdn to join ldr ins fnl f: sn hdd and outpcd* **12/1**
6012 **3** nk **Bahamian Sunrise**[11] 6282 5-8-11 **79** (b) SilvestreDeSousa 5 82
(John Gallagher) *prom: rdn to chsd ldr over 1f out: drvn to ld briefly ins fnl f: outpcd last 75yds* **5/1**[1]
3160 **4** 1 **Shamshon (IRE)**[10] 6325 6-9-7 **89** (t) JimCrowley 4 89+
(Stuart Williams) *lw: trckd ldrs: rdn over 1f out: styd on same pce fnl f* **5/1**[1]
5020 **5** 1 **Kasbah (IRE)**[32] 5505 5-9-6 **88** JackMitchell 1 86+
(Amanda Perrett) *hld up in midfield on inner: pushed along to trck ldrs over 1f out: gap nvr appeared and lost all ch fnl f* **13/2**[3]
3320 **6** hd **Lydia's Place**[3] 6593 4-8-7 **78** DavidEgan(3) 3 73
(Richard Guest) *taken down early: led against far rail: rdn over 1f out: hdd & wknd ins fnl f* **8/1**
3230 **7** 3/4 **Farleigh Mac**[14] 6198 3-8-11 **80** (b1) OisinMurphy 9 72
(Andrew Balding) *taken down early: trckd ldrs on outer: cl enough over 1f out: sn rdn and wknd* **12/1**
-000 **8** 1/2 **Show Stealer**[13] 6234 4-9-4 **86** (p) MartinHarley 2 77+
(Rae Guest) *hld up in last trio: effrt on inner whn nt clr run over 1f out: nvr able to become competitive after* **11/2**[2]
0205 **9** 2 3/4 **Monsieur Joe (IRE)**[18] 6039 10-9-10 **92** AdamKirby 8 73
(Paul Midgley) *lost prom pl after 1f and sn shoved along: toiling in rr 2f out* **14/1**
3053 **10** 2 3/4 **Majestic Hero (IRE)**[5] 6512 5-9-4 **86** JamieSpencer 10 57
(Ronald Harris) *lw: chsd ldr: rdn 2f out: sn lost 2nd: wkng whn hmpd jst ins fnl f* **11/1**

1m 0.46s (-1.14) **Going Correction** -0.05s/f (Good)
**WFA** 3 from 4yo+ 1lb **10** Ran SP% **114.7**
Speed ratings (Par 107): **107,105,104,102,101 101,99,99,94,90**
CSF £97.66 CT £528.89 TOTE £7.50: £2.30, £3.90, £2.00; EX 120.80 Trifecta £420.70.
**Owner** Robert Ng **Bred** Miss Audrey F Thompson **Trained** Newmarket, Suffolk

**FOCUS**
Drying conditions on a warmish day and with no rail movements, all distances as advertised. The pace looked overly strong, with the first two finishers closing from out the back and, unlike some, avoiding trouble on the outside. The runner-up sets the level.

## 6696 BETBRIGHT SOLARIO STKS (GROUP 3) 7f
**2:25** (2:26) (Class 1) 2-Y-O
**£25,519** (£9,675; £4,842; £2,412; £1,210; £607) **Stalls Low**

Form RPR
13 **1** **Masar (IRE)**[70] 4068 2-9-1 0 JamesDoyle 2 107
(Charlie Appleby) *lw: trckd ldng pair: rdn to ld over 1f out: styd on strly ins fnl f: readily* **11/8**[1]
06 **2** 2 **Romanised (IRE)**[20] 5973 2-9-1 107 (t) ShaneFoley 3 102
(K J Condon, Ire) *hld up in tch: prog 2f out: rdn to chse wnr over 1f out: styd on but readily outpcd last 100yds* **7/1**
221 **3** 1 1/4 **Arbalet (IRE)**[41] 5179 2-9-1 86 RyanMoore 5 99
(Hugo Palmer) *str: hld up in last pair: pushed along over 2f out: prog and rdn over 1f out: styd on to take 3rd ins fnl f: n.d* **14/1**
1 **4** 1/2 **Purser (USA)**[15] 6132 2-9-1 0 FrankieDettori 1 98
(John Gosden) *athletic: swtg: trckd ldrs on inner: nt clr run fr jst over 2f out to fnl f: pushed along and effrt to dispute 3rd 150yds out: no hdwy after* **9/2**[2]
1 **5** 3/4 **Vintager**[22] 5887 2-9-1 0 JimCrowley 6 95
(David Menuisier) *w'like: hld up in last pair: effrt on outer over 2f out: nt qckn over 1f out and wl hld after* **11/2**[3]
41 **6** 7 **Connect**[31] 5547 2-9-1 0 AdamKirby 4 76
(Clive Cox) *sn led at str pce: jnd over 2f out: hdd & wknd qckly over 1f out* **8/1**
4610 **7** 1/2 **De Bruyne Horse**[9] 6353 2-9-1 101 (p) SilvestreDeSousa 7 75
(Richard Hannon) *sn trckd ldr: chal and upsides over 2f out to over 1f out: wknd: eased last 100yds* **20/1**

1m 27.89s (-1.61) **Going Correction** -0.05s/f (Good) **7** Ran SP% **110.7**
Speed ratings (Par 105): **107,104,103,102,101 93,93**
CSF £10.79 TOTE £1.90: £1.30, £2.90; EX 9.20 Trifecta £65.40.
**Owner** Godolphin **Bred** Godolphin **Trained** Newmarket, Suffolk

**FOCUS**
Raven's Pass (2007) and Kingman (2013), both top class, were the best winners of this in the last decade. The bare form of this latest running doesn't look anything special, but still smart with only one renewal better than a rating of 107 in the last decade.

## 6697 BETBRIGHT CASINO ATALANTA STKS (GROUP 3) (F&M) 1m
**3:00** (3:00) (Class 1) 3-Y-O+
**£36,861** (£13,975; £6,994; £3,484; £1,748; £877) **Stalls Low**

Form RPR
-152 **1** **Aljazzi**[73] 3961 4-9-1 112 (h) AndreaAtzeni 3 114
(Marco Botti) *dwlt: hld up in last pair: pushed along wl over 2f out: gd prog on outer sn after: rdn to ld over 1f out: drew clr fnl f: convincingly* **9/2**[3]
3-63 **2** 3 **Nathra (IRE)**[14] 6193 4-9-1 108 FrankieDettori 6 107
(John Gosden) *lw: dwlt: trapped out wd in midfield early: prog over 2f out: rdn to chal over 1f out but wnr sn shot by: chsng after and no imp* **3/1**[2]
0132 **3** 1 1/2 **Tisbutadream (IRE)**[18] 6054 3-8-10 102 SilvestreDeSousa 4 103
(David Elsworth) *trckd ldrs: rdn and nt qckn jst over 2f out: drvn and styd on fr jst over 1f out to take 3rd nr fin* **7/1**
2006 **4** 3/4 **Opal Tiara (IRE)**[7] 6420 4-9-1 104 OisinMurphy 5 102
(Mick Channon) *trckd ldng pair: shkn up over 2f out: cl enough over 1f out: kpt on same pce after* **33/1**
1-22 **5** hd **Intimation**[6] 6490 5-9-1 104 RyanMoore 9 101
(Sir Michael Stoute) *swtg: hld up in rr: prog over 2f out: rdn to cl on ldrs over 1f out: one pce after* **11/4**[1]
5033 **6** nk **Dancing Breeze (IRE)**[21] 5927 3-8-10 93 JimCrowley 13 100
(John Gosden) *trckd ldr: led 2f out: rdn and hdd over 1f out: wknd ins fnl f* **20/1**
2- **7** 3 1/4 **Lbretha (FR)**[38] 5312 4-9-1 100 GregoryBenoist 2 93
(F-H Graffard, France) *cmpt: hld up in last pair: shkn up on outer over 2f out: brief prog sn after: no hdwy over 1f out* **16/1**
2004 **8** 3/4 **Urban Fox**[36] 5352 3-8-10 100 (b) MartinHarley 10 91
(James Tate) *lw: trckd ldrs: shkn up over 2f out: wknd over 1f out* **25/1**
2221 **9** 4 1/2 **Lincoln Rocks**[9] 6358 4-9-1 106 AdamKirby 12 81
(David O'Meara) *led to 2f out: sn wknd* **12/1**
06 **10** 7 **Greta G (ARG)**[50] 4857 4-9-1 105 (t1) JamesDoyle 7 65
(John Gosden) *sn towards rr: no prog over 2f out: eased whn no ch fnl f* **16/1**
4011 **11** 1 **Always Thankful**[23] 5829 3-8-10 75 (p1) SeanLevey 1 62
(Ismail Mohammed) *in tch to over 2f out: wknd u.p* **100/1**

1m 40.64s (-2.66) **Going Correction** -0.05s/f (Good)
**WFA** 3 from 4yo+ 5lb **11** Ran SP% **114.3**
Speed ratings (Par 113): **111,108,106,105,105 105,102,101,96,89 88**
CSF £17.11 TOTE £4.00: £1.60, £1.50, £2.20; EX 18.10 Trifecta £78.20.
**Owner** Saleh Al Homaizi & Imad Al Sagar **Bred** Saleh Al Homaizi & Imad Al Sagar **Trained** Newmarket, Suffolk

**FOCUS**
A decent Group 3. The winner set the standard on her improved Royal Ascot run. She showed that did not flatter her and has been rated to form.

## 6698 BETBRIGHT RECALL H'CAP 1m 1f 209y
**3:35** (3:35) (Class 2) 3-Y-O+
**£31,125** (£9,320; £4,660; £2,330; £1,165; £585) **Stalls Low**

Form RPR
3311 **1** **Thundering Blue (USA)**[21] 5940 4-8-8 **87** JimCrowley 8 96+
(David Menuisier) *hld up in last: gd prog on wd outside fr 2f out: stormed into the ld 100yds out: jinked lft sn after but drew clr* **11/2**[2]
-144 **2** 1 1/2 **Monarchs Glen**[99] 3032 3-9-1 **100** RobertTart 11 107
(John Gosden) *trapped out wd in midfield: prog over 2f out: hrd rdn to chse ldr jst over 1f out: chalng whn wnr shot past 100yds out: outpcd after* **9/1**
1216 **3** shd **Rotherwick (IRE)**[28] 5643 5-8-9 **88** (t) PJMcDonald 4 94
(Paul Cole) *hld up in last trio: prog on inner and clr passage fr over 2f out: rdn and styd on wl fnl f: nrly snatched 2nd* **20/1**
2111 **4** 1/2 **Silver Ghost (IRE)**[37] 5330 4-9-0 **93** CharlesBishop 2 98
(Eve Johnson Houghton) *trckd ldr: led over 2f out and drvn for home: edgd lft 1f out: hdd and no ex last 100yds* **13/2**

-214 **5** 1 **Euginio (IRE)**21 5925 3-9-3 **102** AndreaAtzeni 6 106+
(Richard Hannon) *sn restrained into midfield: dropped to rr 3f out: rdn and prog 2f out: styng on but nt gng to win whn hmpd ins fnl f: tk 5th nr fin* **6/1**3

-215 **6** ½ **Across Dubai**28 5639 3-8-10 **95** PatCosgrave 5 97
(William Haggas) *lw: hld up in 8th: prog over 2f out: drvn and cl enough jst over 1f out: one pce fnl f* **4/1**1

0052 **7** 1¼ **Pacify**35 5421 5-9-4 **97** PatDobbs 13 97
(Ralph Beckett) *in tch in midfield: lost pl over 2f out: in last pair over 1f out: styd on again ins fnl f* **16/1**

04-4 **8** hd **Shabbah (IRE)**6 6482 4-8-11 **90** RyanMoore 3 89
(Sir Michael Stoute) *lw: trckd ldrs: rdn over 2f out: stl cl up over 1f out: wknd ins fnl f* **12/1**

0463 **9** 1 **Oasis Fantasy (IRE)**21 5913 6-8-13 **92**(b) JamieSpencer 7 89
(David Simcock) *hld up in last pair: shkn up over 2f out: no real prog* **16/1**

2305 **10** ½ **Noble Gift**32 5500 7-9-2 **98** CallumShepherd(3) 10 94
(William Knight) *led to over 2f out: wknd over 1f out* **50/1**

0330 **11** nk **Mutarakez (IRE)**49 4882 5-8-8 **87** SilvestreDeSousa 1 85
(Brian Meehan) *dwlt: t.k.h and sn in midfield: effrt 2f out: in tch but no great prog whn nt clr run briefly 1f out: fdd* **14/1**

0100 **12** 2¼ **Master Carpenter (IRE)**49 4918 6-9-7 **103** DavidEgan(3) 9 94
(Rod Millman) *trckd ldrs: steadily wknd fr 2f out* **16/1**

-460 **13** ¾ **Abdon**32 5500 4-9-9 **102** FrankieDettori 12 92
(Sir Michael Stoute) *trckd ldng pair: rdn over 2f out: wknd over 1f out: eased* **16/1**

2m 7.37s (-3.13) **Going Correction** -0.05s/f (Good)
**WFA** 3 from 4yo+ 6lb **13** Ran SP% **117.6**
Speed ratings (Par 109): **110,108,108,108,107 107,106,105,105,104 104,102,102**
CSF £53.54 CT £926.61 TOTE £6.60: £2.50, £2.90, £5.70; EX 65.70 Trifecta £1337.30.
**Owner** Mrs Gay Jarvis **Bred** Dr Tom Castoldi **Trained** Pulborough, W Sussex

**FOCUS**
The going was changed to good all over following this race. A decent handicap rated around the third.

## 6699 BETBRIGHT NURSERY H'CAP (JOCKEY CLUB GRASSROOTS NURSERY QUALIFIER) 7f
**4:10** (4:12) (Class 4) (0-85,83) 2-Y-O **£5,822** (£1,732; £865; £432) **Stalls Low**

Form RPR

0322 **1** **Crownthorpe**16 6087 2-8-11 **73** SilvestreDeSousa 6 81
(Richard Fahey) *lengthy: lw: hld up in last pair: taken to outer and set alight 2f out: rapid prog and swept into the ld over 1f out: edgd rt but drvn clr* **4/1**2

6003 **2** 3 **Puchita (IRE)**19 6008 2-8-1 **66** HollieDoyle(3) 2 66
(Richard Hannon) *t.k.h early: trckd ldng trio: effrt 2f out: sltly impeded over 1f out: styd on fnl f to take 2nd last 75yds* **14/1**

0352 **3** ½ **Cheeky Rascal (IRE)**30 5572 2-8-13 **75** RyanMoore 8 74
(Richard Hannon) *lw: trckd ldr: rdn to ld wl over 1f out: sn hdd and outpcd by wnr: one pce and lost 2nd last 75yds* **3/1**1

031 **4** shd **Lethal Lunch**50 4826 2-9-7 **83** AdamKirby 7 81
(Clive Cox) *lw: hld up in last pair: shkn up over 2f out: styd on fr over 1f out to press for a pl nr fin* **11/2**

421 **5** ¾ **Barford (IRE)**24 5808 2-9-6 **82** RobHornby 1 78
(Pam Sly) *trckd ldng pair: squeezed through to try to mount chal over 1f out: one pce fnl f* **5/1**3

1154 **6** 1¾ **Jedi Master (IRE)**30 5572 2-9-7 **83** JamieSpencer 3 77
(Richard Fahey) *hld up in 6th: shkn up and dropped to last wl over 1f out: renewed effrt fnl f: nt rch ldrs and eased last 50yds* **15/2**

313 **7** 2 **Alkhalifa (IRE)**14 6207 2-9-7 **83** JimCrowley 5 69
(Brian Meehan) *str: wl in tch: shkn up on outer 2f out: wknd over 1f out* **12/1**

021 **8** 3 **Livingstones Quest (IRE)**18 6029 2-8-13 **75** OisinMurphy 4 60
(Rod Millman) *led: rdn and hdd wl over 1f out: hmpd on inner sn after and no ch after* **8/1**

1m 29.89s (0.39) **Going Correction** -0.05s/f (Good) **8** Ran SP% **114.3**
Speed ratings (Par 97): **95,91,91,90,90 88,85,82**
CSF £56.70 CT £190.65 TOTE £4.50: £1.70, £4.10, £1.40; EX 64.50 Trifecta £271.40.
**Owner** Richard Fahey Ebor Racing Club Ltd **Bred** Mrs Sheila Oakes **Trained** Musley Bank, N Yorks
■ Stewards' Enquiry : Rob Hornby 2 day ban: guilty of careless riding in that he had maneuvered right-handed for a gap when there was insufficient room (17/18 Sep)

**FOCUS**
This looked an ordinary race of its type with the placed horses running near their marks.

## 6700 BETBRIGHT CASINO H'CAP 1m
**4:45** (4:47) (Class 4) (0-80,82) 3-Y-O+ **£5,822** (£1,732; £865; £432) **Stalls Low**

Form RPR

1410 **1** **Al Nafoorah**32 5506 3-9-5 **79** AndreaAtzeni 5 86
(Ed Dunlop) *dwlt: hld up in last: gd prog on wd outside 2f out: drvn to ld 1f out: kpt on u.p after* **8/1**2

4104 **2** ¾ **Exceeding Power**15 6134 6-9-6 **78** GeorgeWood(3) 9 84
(Martin Bosley) *hld up in midfield: urged along and prog over 2f out: clsd to ld for a few strides jst over 1f out: pressed wnr fnl f: hld nr fin* **11/1**

603 **3** nk **Grand Inquisitor**15 6134 5-9-11 **80**(p) FranBerry 10 85
(Ian Williams) *lw: hld up in last trio: rdn and prog over 2f out: styd on fnl f to take 3rd last strides: nvr quite able to chal* **8/1**2

6202 **4** ½ **Golden Wedding (IRE)**10 6322 5-9-13 **82** CharlesBishop 6 86
(Eve Johnson Houghton) *trckd ldng pair: wnt 2nd over 2f out: drvn to ld wl over 1f out: hdd jst over 1f out: kpt on same pce after* **10/1**3

320 **5** 1 **Kingston Kurrajong**15 6134 4-9-9 **78**(p) AdamBeschizza 12 80
(Michael Attwater) *hld up in last pair: prog and weaved through rivals fr 2f out: styd on and nrst fin but nt pce to chal* **25/1**

2050 **6** nk **Directorship**15 6134 11-9-7 **76** AdamKirby 7 77
(Patrick Chamings) *towards rr: dropped to last and struggling 2f out: styd on again fnl f: gng on at fin* **33/1**

031 **7** ½ **Najashee (IRE)**70 4086 3-9-4 **78** JimCrowley 1 77
(Owen Burrows) *angular: trckd ldrs: effrt on inner over 2f out: rdn and one pce fr over 1f out* **2/1**1

310 **8** 2¾ **Dragons Voice**15 6134 3-9-2 **76** JamieSpencer 11 69
(Philip Hide) *trapped out wd 1st 2f: in tch: rdn and nt qckn 2f out: fdd over 1f out* **12/1**

0660 **9** ½ **Majeste**18 6026 3-9-5 **82** HollieDoyle(3) 4 74
(Richard Hannon) *nvr bttr than midfield: no great prog on inner fr 2f out* **12/1**

110 **10** 1¼ **Fire Tree (IRE)**28 5643 4-9-12 **81** StevieDonohoe 2 71
(Charlie Fellowes) *hld up in midfield: shkn up over 2f out: losing pl whn hmpd over 1f out: kpt on again last 150yds* **11/1**

2-00 **11** 3 **Lady Perignon**31 5529 4-9-10 **79** OisinMurphy 3 62
(Andrew Balding) *led to wl over 1f out: wknd* **14/1**

0132 **12** 11 **High Draw (FR)**23 5843 4-9-5 **74** MartinHarley 8 31
(K R Burke) *racd wd 1st 2f: chsd ldr to over 2f out: sn wknd: eased fnl f: t.o* **16/1**

1m 43.18s (-0.12) **Going Correction** -0.05s/f (Good)
**WFA** 3 from 4yo+ 5lb **12** Ran SP% **116.0**
Speed ratings (Par 105): **98,97,96,96,95 95,94,91,91,90 87,76**
CSF £90.94 CT £738.29 TOTE £9.40: £2.90, £3.50, £2.80; EX 86.60 Trifecta £833.70.
**Owner** Mohammed Jaber **Bred** Aston Mullins Stud **Trained** Newmarket, Suffolk

**FOCUS**
A useful handicap. The runner-up sets the standard.

## 6701 BETBRIGHT H'CAP 1m 1f 209y
**5:20** (5:23) (Class 4) (0-85,86) 3-Y-O+ **£5,822** (£1,732; £865; £432) **Stalls Low**

Form RPR

342 **1** **Glorious Forever**21 5928 3-9-6 **84**(v) PatCosgrave 6 96+
(Ed Walker) *trckd ldr: led jst over 2f out gng wl: idled in front and rdn over 1f out: edgd lft but kpt on wl whn hrd pressed fnl f* **4/1**1

1111 **2** hd **Swilly Sunset**22 5888 4-9-8 **80** SilvestreDeSousa 11 91
(Anthony Carson) *lw: hld up in midfield: rdn and prog over 2f out: chsd wnr over 1f out: str chal fnl f: styd on but jst hld* **13/2**3

5-32 **3** 4½ **New Agenda**19 6007 5-9-13 **85**(h) AdamKirby 1 87
(Paul Webber) *led to jst over 2f out: readily lft bhd by ldng pair fnl f but clung on for 3rd* **9/1**

3102 **4** ¾ **Fast Dancer (IRE)**14 6195 5-9-10 **85** DavidEgan(3) 10 86
(Joseph Tuite) *hld up in rr: rdn and prog over 2f out: kpt on to press for 3rd nr fin* **10/1**

-020 **5** ½ **Zambeasy**35 5397 6-9-8 **80** FranBerry 12 80
(Philip Hide) *racd on outer: trckd ldrs: rdn and nt qckn over 2f out: kpt on same pce after* **20/1**

6141 **6** ¾ **Bedouin (IRE)**22 5868 3-9-6 **84**(b) JamieSpencer 9 83
(Luca Cumani) *swtg: dropped to last pair sn after s and urged along: tended to run in snatches: effrt on outer over 2f out: kpt on fnl f but n.d* **6/1**2

2110 **7** ¾ **Vernatti**44 5060 4-9-8 **80** RobHornby 3 77
(Pam Sly) *trckd ldrs: fnd nil whn rdn over 2f out and dropped to rr: kpt on again ins fnl f* **16/1**

0520 **8** 1½ **Mikmak**14 6189 4-9-2 **77**(p) GeorgeWood(3) 5 71
(William Muir) *in tch in midfield: effrt over 2f out: wknd over 1f out* **25/1**

0203 **9** 1½ **Parish Boy**14 6195 5-9-3 **78** HollieDoyle(3) 14 69
(David Loughnane) *slowly away: tk no interest and sn t.o: latched on to bk of field 1/2-way: nvr threatened to play a part but passed a few late on* **16/1**

4501 **10** nk **Blushing Red (FR)**16 6094 3-8-12 **76** AndreaAtzeni 7 67
(Ed Dunlop) *hld up wl in rr: hanging and fnd nil whn rdn over 2f out: no prog* **8/1**

0036 **11** nk **Top Beak (IRE)**14 6195 4-9-4 **79**(t) CharlieBennett(3) 2 68
(Michael Attwater) *cl up on inner: rdn over 2f out: steadily wknd over 1f out* **33/1**

0-04 **12** ½ **Unison (IRE)**23 5838 7-9-4 **76** RyanTate 4 64
(Jeremy Scott) *pressed ldrs: rdn over 2f out: steadily wknd over 1f out* **20/1**

-046 **P** **Rosarno (IRE)**58 4535 3-8-11 **78**(bt) CallumShepherd(3) 8
(Charles Hills) *wl in tch tl p.u 3f out: dismntd* **9/1**

2m 8.1s (-2.40) **Going Correction** -0.05s/f (Good)
**WFA** 3 from 4yo+ 6lb **13** Ran SP% **115.9**
Speed ratings (Par 105): **107,106,103,102,102 101,101,99,98,98 98,97,**
CSF £26.14 CT £220.87 TOTE £4.40: £1.70, £2.40, £2.70; EX 27.50 Trifecta £166.40.
**Owner** Kangyu International Racing (HK) Limited **Bred** Miss K Rausing **Trained** Upper Lambourn, Berks

**FOCUS**
Another useful handicap. The first two finished clear and have improved.
T/Jkpt: Not won. T/Plt: £258.40 to a £1 stake. Pool: £158,571.86 - 447.96 winning units. T/Qpdt: £50.60 to a £1 stake. Pool: £11,327.78 - 165.52 winning units. **Jonathan Neesom**

6702 - 6709a (Foreign Racing) - See Raceform Interactive

# 6647 BADEN-BADEN (L-H)
Saturday, September 2

**OFFICIAL GOING: Turf: good**

## 6710a T VON ZASTROW STUTENPREIS (GROUP 2) (3YO+ FILLIES & MARES) (TURF) 1m 4f
**3:25** 3-Y-O+ **£34,188** (£13,247; £6,837; £3,418; £2,136)

RPR

**1** **Ashiana (GER)**27 5693 3-8-11 0 AndraschStarke 6 104
(P Schiergen, Germany) *midfield: outpcd and dropped towards rr 2 1/2f out: rdn and gd hdwy 1 1/2f out: led 1f out: rdn out* **43/10**3

**2** ½ **Diana Storm (GER)**27 5693 3-8-11 0 MarcLerner 7 103
(Waldemar Hickst, Germany) *midfield: pushed along and hdwy turning in: chal 1f out: a hld fnl f: all out* **51/10**

**3** 1¼ **Erica (GER)**100 4-9-5 0 StephenHellyn 9 100
(Lennart Hammer-Hansen, Germany) *trckd ldr: jnd ldr turning in: sn rdn to chal: led briefly over 1f out: qckly hdd: nt pce of front two fnl f* **33/1**

**4** nk **Tusked Wings (IRE)**27 5693 3-8-11 0 FilipMinarik 5 101+
(Jean-Pierre Carvalho, Germany) *settled towards rr: pushed along to make hdwy turning in: kpt on fnl 2f but nt the pce to chal* **37/10**2

**5** shd **Navaro Girl (IRE)**27 5693 3-8-11 0 DennisSchiergen 3 100
(P Schiergen, Germany) *rr of midfield: pushed along to chse ldrs 2f out: kpt on wl but nt pce to chal* **166/10**

**6** ½ **Son Macia (GER)**27 4-9-5 0(b) AlexanderPietsch 8 99
(Andreas Suborics, Germany) *led: pushed along turning in: u.p and hdd over 1f out: no ex fnl f* **142/10**

**7** 2¼ **Fosun (GER)**18 4-9-5 0 MartinSeidl 10 95
(Markus Klug, Germany) *racd in rr: hdwy ins 2f out bef wkng fnl f* **151/10**

**8** ½ **Megera (FR)**27 5693 3-8-11 0 EduardoPedroza 1 95
(A Wohler, Germany) *chsd ldrs: outpcd 1 1/2f out: kpt on tl eased fnl 1/2f* **13/5**1

**9** ¾ **Distain**18 5-9-5 0(p) MickaelBerto 2 93
(Frau S Steinberg, Germany) *settled midfield on inner: outpcd fnl 2f: nvr a danger* **38/1**

**10** 1½ **Litaara (GER)**27 5693 3-8-11 0 DanielePorcu 4 92
(P Schiergen, Germany) *a towards rr* **245/10**



The Form Book Flat, Raceform Ltd, Newbury, RG14 5SJ

11 3 ¾ **Near England (IRE)**[27] 4-9-5 0........................................ AdriedeVries 11 85
(Markus Klug, Germany) *midfield early: tk clsr order 1/2-way: pushed along and outpcd 2f out: eased fnl f* **49/10**

2m 35.11s (1.65)
**WFA** 3 from 4yo+ 8lb **11** Ran SP% **129.2**
PARI-MUTUEL (all including 10 euro stake): WIN 53; PLACE: 23, 23; 69; SF: 373.
**Owner** Eckhard Sauren **Bred** H Wirth **Trained** Germany

6711 - 6713a (Foreign Racing) - See Raceform Interactive

## [1994]RANDWICK (L-H)
Saturday, September 2
**OFFICIAL GOING: Turf: good**

### 6714a TATTERSALLS CLUB CHELMSFORD STKS (GROUP 2) (3YO+) (TURF) 1m
**6:50** 3-Y-0+
**£84,356** (£27,485; £13,377; £6,505; £3,581; £1,827)

RPR

1 **Winx (AUS)**[14] 6-9-0 0........................................ HughBowman 3 111+
(Chris Waller, Australia) **1/11**[1]

2 1 **Red Excitement (AUS)**[14] 8-9-4 0........................................(t) JoshuaParr 5 112
(Gerald Ryan, Australia) **25/1**[2]

3 3 ¾ **Chocante (NZ)**[84] 5-9-4 0........................................ RoryHutchings 9 103
(Stephen Marsh, New Zealand) **80/1**

4 1 ½ **Antonio Giuseppe (NZ)**[14] 5-9-4 0........................................(p) TyeAngland 10 100
(Chris Waller, Australia) **40/1**

5 1 ¾ **Life Less Ordinary (IRE)**[14] 5-9-4 0........................................ KerrinMcEvoy 11 96
(Chris Waller, Australia) **25/1**[2]

6 ¾ **Libran (IRE)**[133] 1994 6-9-4 0........................................(t) GlynSchofield 8 94
(Chris Waller, Australia) **200/1**

7 shd **Harper's Choice (AUS)**[14] 4-9-3 0........................................ BrentonAvdulla 6 93
(Gerald Ryan, Australia) **80/1**

8 1 ½ **Sense Of Occasion (AUS)**[105] 7-9-4 0........................................ CoreyBrown 2 91
(Kris Lees, Australia) **30/1**[3]

9 shd **Who Shot Thebarman (NZ)**[133] 1994 9-9-4 0........................................(t) ChristianReith 1 90
(Chris Waller, Australia) **100/1**

10 shd **Allergic (AUS)**[14] 6-9-4 0........................................(b) TimothyClark 12 90
(James Cummings, Australia) **200/1**

11 ¾ **Sarrasin**[21] 5-9-4 0........................................ MichaelWalker 4 88
(Chris Waller, Australia) **50/1**

12 2 ¾ **Lasqueti Spirit (AUS)**[9] 4-8-13 0........................................(b) JayFord 7 77
(Lee Curtis, Australia) **100/1**

**Owner** Magic Bloodstock Racing, R G Treweeke & Mrs D N Ke **Bred** Fairway Thoroughbreds **Trained** Australia

6715 - 6716a (Foreign Racing) - See Raceform Interactive

## VELIEFENDI
Saturday, September 2
**OFFICIAL GOING: Polytrack: standard; turf: good to soft**

### 6717a INTERNATIONAL FRANCE GALOP FRBC ANATOLIA TROPHY (LOCAL GROUP 2) (3YO+) (POLYTRACK) 1m 2f (P)
**5:30** 3-Y-0+ **£98,290** (£39,316; £19,658; £9,829)

RPR

1 **Leshlaa (USA)**[18] 6024 3-9-1 0........................................ JimmyQuinn 5 107+
(Saeed bin Suroor) *little slowly away: sn moved into midfield: pushed along to chse ldrs turning in: swtchd out for a run and rdn 2f out: hdwy to chal fnl f: led 110yds out: wnt clr* **57/20**[2]

2 1 ½ **Cerastes (TUR)**[48] 3-9-1 0........................................(t) SadettinBoyraz 9 104
(Ibrahim Bekirogullari, Turkey) *sn led: pushed along to go 2 l clr turning in: rdn 2f out: kpt on wl u.p: hdd 110yds out: no ex* **16/5**

3 1 **Absolute Blast (IRE)**[48] 4934 5-9-2 0........................................ EdwardGreatrex 4 96
(Archie Watson) *settled 3rd early: wnt 2nd by 1/2-way: pushed along to chse ldr turning in: chal 2f out: a jst hld: nt pce of front two late on* **7/2**

4 2 ½ **Qurbaan (USA)**[45] 5046 4-9-6 0........................................ Francois-XavierBertras 2 95
(F Rohaut, France) *midfield: rdn 2f out: nt the pce to cl on ldrs: styd on fnl f but nvr a danger* **7/20**[1]

5 1 ½ **Belgian Bill**[14] 6186 9-9-6 0........................................ HectorCrouch 1 92
(George Baker) *away wl and trckd ldr: rdn along to chal 1 1/2f out: wknd fnl f* **61/20**[3]

6 1 **Sinyor Samil (TUR)**[24] 3-9-1 0........................................(b) HalisKaratas 7 92
(Ibrahim Cak, Turkey) *a towards rr* **7/1**

7 7 ½ **My Billionaire (TUR)**[20] 4-9-6 0........................................(b) GokhanKocakaya 8 75
(S Mutlu, Turkey) *a towards rr* **29/4**

8 42 **Oglum Beratim (TUR)**[27] 3-9-1 0........................................(bt) UgurPolat 6
(Mulayim Anat, Turkey) *settled midfield early: outpcd and dropped to last turning in: sn detached* **145/10**

2m 4.56s (-0.44)
**WFA** 3 from 4yo+ 6lb **8** Ran SP% **201.8**

**Owner** Godolphin **Bred** Darley **Trained** Newmarket, Suffolk
**FOCUS**
They only went steady early which makes the winner's performance all the more commendable.

### 6718a INTERNATIONAL ISTANBUL TROPHY (GROUP 3) (3YO+ FILLIES & MARES) (TURF) 1m
**6:30** 3-Y-0+ **£98,290** (£39,316; £19,658; £9,829)

RPR

1 **Arabian Hope (USA)**[34] 5460 3-9-2 0........................................(h) GeraldMosse 3 104+
(Saeed bin Suroor) *racd in 3rd on inner: travelling wl but boxed in 2f out: pushed through narrow opening 1f out: sn chal: led 110yds out: pushed out* **1/20**[1]

2 1 ½ **Cheri Cheri Lady (TUR)**[17] 5-9-6 0........................................(bt) SadettinBoyraz 2 101
(Ibrahim Bekirogullari, Turkey) *led: pushed along 2f out to maintain 1 l ld: hrd pressed ins fnl f: hdd 110yds out: jst hld 2nd* **5/2**[3]

3 nse **Willpower (TUR)**[17] 7-9-6 0........................................(t) HalisKaratas 4 101
(Ibrahim Bekirogullari, Turkey) *settled 4th: shkn up 2f out: clsd fnl f: jst failed to take 2nd* **19/20**[2]

4 nk **Tatvan Incisi (TUR)**[38] 5-9-6 0........................................(t) SelimKaya 5 100
(Ibrahim Bekirogullari, Turkey) *trckd ldr: attempted to get on terms w ldr ins 2f out but a hld: lost pl fnl f* **19/20**[2]

5 1 **Iskra**[69] 4-9-6 0........................................ AhmetCelik 1 98
(D Ergin, Turkey) *a in tch in last: kpt on wl cl home but nvr a danger* **66/10**

1m 35.4s (0.07)
**WFA** 3 from 4yo+ 5lb **5** Ran SP% **239.5**

**Owner** Godolphin **Bred** Hill 'N' Dale Equine Holdings Inc Et Al **Trained** Newmarket, Suffolk
**FOCUS**
Something of a no-contest. The favourite had a few anxious moments, but in the end won with a bit to spare.

## [6278]BRIGHTON (L-H)
Sunday, September 3
**OFFICIAL GOING: Good to firm (good in places; 8.5)**
Wind: medium, across Weather: light rain, blustery

### 6719 HERTZ BRIGHTON MAIDEN AUCTION STKS 5f 60y
**2:00** (2:01) (Class 6) 2-Y-O **£2,264** (£673; £336; £168) **Stalls** Low

Form RPR

3020 1 **Ghepardo**[9] 6375 2-8-10 66........................................ TomMarquand 4 73
(Richard Hannon) *sn led and mde rest: rdn and fnd ex to assert over 1f out: clr and in command ins fnl f: eased towards fin: comf* **13/2**

4 2 2 ¼ **Episcia (IRE)**[27] 5717 2-8-10 0........................................ AdamBeschizza 5 64
(Stuart Williams) *hld up in tch in last pair: effrt and swtchd rt over 1f out: hdwy u.p 1f out: styd on to chse clr wnr ins fnl f: kpt on but no threat to wnr* **5/1**[3]

2060 3 1 ¼ **Mother Of Dragons (IRE)**[31] 5575 2-8-6 77........................................ LukeMorris 7 56
(Joseph Tuite) *in tch: hdwy into midfield 4f out: effrt in 3rd over 1f out: unable qck and kpt on same pce ins fnl f* **9/4**[1]

06 4 nk **Three Little Birds**[31] 5575 2-8-5 71........................................ MitchGodwin[(5)] 6 59
(Sylvester Kirk) *broke fast: w wnr: rdn 2f out: unable qck w wnr over 1f out: lost 2nd ins fnl f: wknd towards fin* **5/2**[2]

5 ½ **Pretty Risky** 2-8-4 0 ow1........................................ CharlieBennett[(3)] 2 54
(Patrick Chamings) *chsd ldng pair: rdn and unable qck over 1f out: 4th and btn 1f out: wknd ins fnl f* **25/1**

6 1 **Section Onesixsix (IRE)** 2-8-13 0........................................ SilvestreDeSousa 1 56
(Mick Channon) *dwlt: rn green and sn pushed along in rr: rdn over 1f out: kpt on ins fnl f: nvr trbld ldrs* **11/2**

0 7 3 **Equilibrium**[46] 5026 2-8-8 0........................................(b[1]) DavidProbert 3 41
(Robert Eddery) *t.k.h: hld up in tch in midfield: rdn 2f out: unable qck and sn outpcd: wknd ins fnl f* **33/1**

1m 3.29s (0.99) **Going Correction** +0.05s/f (Good) **7** Ran SP% **111.5**
Speed ratings (Par 93): **94,90,88,87,87 85,80**
CSF £36.51 TOTE £8.20: £3.10, £2.00; EX 38.90 Trifecta £116.00.
**Owner** Miss I Keogh & Partner **Bred** D Redvers & G Middlebrook **Trained** East Everleigh, Wilts
**FOCUS**
All distances as advertised. The ground had been watered and they were kicking the top off. A modest 2yo maiden rated through the first two.

### 6720 MARATHONBET SPORTSBOOK H'CAP 5f 215y
**2:30** (2:34) (Class 4) (0-85,86) 3-Y-O+ **£5,175** (£1,540; £769) **Stalls** Low

Form RPR

24 1 **Fujin**[8] 6411 6-8-11 74........................................(v) CharlieBennett[(3)] 2 81
(Shaun Harris) *mde all: rdn wl over 1f out: sustained duel w chalr after: kpt on gamely and forged ahd wl ins fnl f* **7/1**[3]

2006 2 nk **Iseemist (IRE)**[24] 5828 6-9-5 84........................................ MitchGodwin[(5)] 3 90
(John Gallagher) *pressed wnr: rdn over 2f out: sustained duel w wnr fr wl over 1f out: kpt on wl but hld wl ins fnl f* **10/3**[1]

6014 3 5 **Upavon**[23] 5869 7-9-3 77........................................(t) FranBerry 5 67
(Stuart Williams) *restless in stalls: a rr: effrt over 2f out: no imp and hung lft over 1f out: wl btn ins fnl f: eased towards fin* **9/2**[2]

1m 9.35s (-0.85) **Going Correction** +0.05s/f (Good)
**WFA** 3 from 6yo+ 2lb **3** Ran SP% **53.8**
Speed ratings (Par 105): **107,106,99**
CSF £6.64 TOTE £3.20; EX 5.20 Trifecta £6.40.
**Owner** Mrs S L Robinson **Bred** Juddmonte Farms Ltd **Trained** Carburton, Notts
■ Buxted Dream was withdrawn. Price at time of withdawal 5-6f. Rule 4 applies to all bets - deduction 50p in the pound.
■ Stewards' Enquiry : Mitch Godwin two-day ban; used whip above the permitted level (17th-18th Sept)
**FOCUS**
Buxted Dream was withdrawn at the start (broken bridle), and Upavon was not on a going day, so this only seriously concerned two horses.

### 6721 ROUTE MOBILE NOVICE STKS (PLUS 10 RACE) 6f 210y
**3:00** (3:01) (Class 4) 2-Y-O **£3,946** (£1,174; £586; £293) **Stalls** Low

Form RPR

0 1 **Wilson (IRE)**[36] 5420 2-9-2 0........................................ DavidProbert 7 82+
(Luca Cumani) *stdd after s: hld up in tch in last pair: effrt and hdwy on outer over 1f out: chsd ldr ent fnl f: led 150yds out: r.o strly and drew clr after: readily* **6/1**

5110 2 3 ½ **Myboyhenry (IRE)**[15] 6229 2-9-8 88........................................ CliffordLee[(3)] 10 82
(K R Burke) *led: rdn ent fnl 2f: hdd 150yds out: sn outpcd by wnr and kpt on same pce after* **6/4**[1]

023 3 1 ¾ **Tiepolo (IRE)**[8] 6438 2-9-2 74........................................ AdamKirby 3 68
(Gary Moore) *hld up in tch in last pair: rdn and hdwy to chse ldrs whn nt clr run and swtchd rt over 1f out: chsd ldr briefly jst over 1f out: 3rd and kpt on same pce ins fnl f* **5/2**[2]

00 4 1 ¾ **Counterfeit**[38] 5327 2-8-11 0........................................(bt[1]) ShaneKelly 4 59
(Richard Hughes) *stdd after s: t.k.h: hld up in tch in midfield: effrt to press ldrs ent fnl 2f: unable qck and hung lft over 1f out: wl hld 4th and kpt on same pce ins fnl f* **33/1**

4 5 2 ½ **Queens Gallery**[20] 6005 2-9-2 0........................................ TomMarquand 9 57
(Richard Hannon) *sn chsng ldr: rdn and lost pl jst over 2f out: wl hld and in last whn swtchd rt 1f out: kpt on same pce ins fnl f* **7/2**[3]

0 **6** 2 1/2 **Prince Consort (IRE)**[9] 6388 2-9-2 0 ........................ RyanTate 2 50
(Brian Meehan) *chsd ldrs: effrt on inner ent fnl 2f: outpcd and btn over 1f out: wknd ins fnl f* **33/1**

1m 23.31s (0.21) **Going Correction** +0.05s/f (Good) **6** Ran SP% **111.0**
Speed ratings (Par 97): **100,96,94,92,89 86**
CSF £15.16 TOTE £6.30: £2.20, £1.40; EX 14.60 Trifecta £38.00.
**Owner** Stilvi, Boorer, Booth, Bengough **Bred** Castlefarm Stud **Trained** Newmarket, Suffolk

**FOCUS**
An ordinary-looking novice race rated through the places horses.

## 6722 BRITISH STALLIONS STUDS EBF FILLIES' H'CAP 1m 1f 207y
**3:30** (3:30) (Class 4) (0-85,85) 3-Y-0+ **£6,458** (£1,933; £966; £483; £240) **Stalls** High

Form RPR

261 **1** **Impressive Day (IRE)**[24] 5822 4-9-6 **79** ..................(p) AdamKirby 4 87
(Gary Moore) *stdd bk into midfield after s: swtchd rt and effrt in centre ent fnl 2f: hdwy to chal and hung lft 1f out: led ins fnl f: hld on wl fnl 75yds* **8/1**

-531 **2** *nk* **Great Court (IRE)**[16] 6161 3-8-10 **78** ..................... DavidEgan(3) 2 85
(Roger Varian) *hld up in tch in midfield: rdn and hdwy towards inner to ld 2f out: hdd and drvn ins fnl f: kpt on wl but a jst hld after* **12/1**

-345 **3** 1 1/2 **Kath's Legacy**[32] 5549 4-8-8 **72** ..................... FinleyMarsh(5) 5 76
(Ben De Haan) *led after 1f: rdn and hdd 2f out: stl pressing ldrs but struggling to qckn whn sltly impeded jst ins fnl f: kpt on same pce after* **25/1**

1242 **4** 1/2 **White Chocolate (IRE)**[7] 6477 3-9-1 **85** .............. GeorgeBuckell(5) 1 89
(David Simcock) *hld up in last trio: effrt ent fnl 2f: hdwy to chse ldrs towards inner ent fnl f: no ex whn sltly short of room ins fnl f: styd on same pce after* **3/1**[1]

3314 **5** 2 1/4 **Millie's Kiss**[27] 5718 3-8-4 **69** ..................... SilvestreDeSousa 6 68
(Philip McBride) *jnd ldr after 1f tl 5f out: effrt ent fnl 2f: stl pressing ldrs but struggling to qckn whn squeezed for room jst ins fnl f: no threat to ldrs after* **11/1**

23-6 **6** 1 1/2 **Mia Tesoro (IRE)**[26] 5745 4-9-6 **79** ..................(h) StevieDonohoe 9 75
(Charlie Fellowes) *taken down early: t.k.h: hld up in tch in last trio: rdn and hdwy over 1f out: sltly impeded and swtchd rt 1f out: styd on same pce ins fnl f* **13/2**[3]

122 **7** 2 **Marie Josephe**[24] 5822 3-9-2 **81** ..................... ShaneKelly 7 74
(Richard Hughes) *stmbld leaving stalls: chsd ldrs: clsd to join ldr 1/2-way: rdn and ev ch ent fnl 2f: sn struggling and lost pl over 1f out: wl hld ins fnl f* **9/2**[2]

-242 **8** *hd* **Kitty Boo**[16] 6143 3-8-12 **77** ..................(h) LukeMorris 3 69
(Luca Cumani) *hld up in rr: effrt jst over 2f out: hung lft and no imp over 1f out: nvr trbld ldrs* **9/2**[2]

2124 **9** 2 1/4 **Jive Talking (IRE)**[17] 6104 3-9-0 **79** ..................... LouisSteward 8 67
(Michael Bell) *plld hrd early: led for 1f: stdd bk to chse ldrs: effrt towards inner to press ldrs u.p over 1f out: no ex 1f out: wknd ins fnl f* **8/1**

2m 3.15s (-0.45) **Going Correction** +0.05s/f (Good)
**WFA** 3 from 4yo 6lb **9** Ran SP% **116.8**
Speed ratings (Par 102): **103,102,101,101,99 98,96,96,94**
CSF £99.39 CT £2284.59 TOTE £9.10: £2.50, £3.40, £6.70; EX 123.00 Trifecta £5122.60.
**Owner** Power Geneva Ltd **Bred** Darley **Trained** Lower Beeding, W Sussex
■ Stewards' Enquiry : Adam Kirby three-day ban; allowed his mount to drift left-handed (17th-19th Sept)

**FOCUS**
A fair fillies' handicap with the winner improving again.

## 6723 TOTEPOOL.COM H'CAP 1m 3f 198y
**4:00** (4:00) (Class 5) (0-75,78) 3-Y-0+ **£2,911** (£866; £432; £216) **Stalls** High

Form RPR

3131 **1** **Pete So High (GER)**[13] 6258 3-9-9 **78** ..................(p) SilvestreDeSousa 1 83
(Richard Hannon) *chsd ldr tl led after 2f: mde rest: rdn ent fnl 2f: drvn and edgd lft over 1f out: styd on and a doing enough ins fnl f* **5/6**[1]

2333 **2** 1 1/4 **Inconceivable (IRE)**[36] 5432 3-9-6 **75** ..................... PatDobbs 3 78
(Ralph Beckett) *stdd s: hld up wl in tch in rr: effrt and pressed ldrs over 2f out: chsd wnr ins fnl f: kpt on same pce and no imp after* **7/4**[2]

5016 **3** 1 **Lyrica's Lion (IRE)**[24] 5843 3-8-1 **59** ..................... DavidEgan(3) 4 60
(Michael Attwater) *stdd after s: chsd ldrs tl trckd wnr 8f out: effrt over 2f out: kpt on but nvr quite getting on terms w wnr: lost 2nd and kpt on same pce ins fnl f* **8/1**[3]

6060 **4** 13 **Melabi (IRE)**[13] 6270 4-8-11 **63** ..................(v[1]) CallumRodriguez(5) 2 43
(Richard Ford) *t.k.h: led for 2f: chsd ldr tl 8f out: styd handy: rdn over 2f out: outpcd and btn over 1f out: eased ins fnl f* **14/1**

2m 34.85s (2.15) **Going Correction** +0.05s/f (Good)
**WFA** 3 from 4yo+ 8lb **4** Ran SP% **108.7**
Speed ratings (Par 103): **94,93,92,83**
CSF £2.56 TOTE £1.20; EX 2.40 Trifecta £4.20.
**Owner** Middleham Park Racing VII & K Sohi **Bred** Stiftung Gestut Fahrhof **Trained** East Everleigh, Wilts

**FOCUS**
A weak race.

## 6724 ROUTE MOBILE H'CAP 5f 60y
**4:30** (4:30) (Class 6) (0-65,67) 3-Y-0 **£2,264** (£673; £336; £168) **Stalls** Low

Form RPR

25-3 **1** **Her Terms**[7] 6478 3-10-1 **67** ..................(p) AdamKirby 4 72
(Clive Cox) *broke fast: mde all: styd far side over 2f out: rdn and hung rt fr over 1f out: hld on wl ins fnl f: all out* **11/4**[1]

5556 **2** *shd* **Mercers**[23] 5869 3-9-6 **58** ..................... ShaneKelly 8 63
(Peter Crate) *hld up tch in midfield: c centre over 2f out: rdn to chal 2f out: kpt on u.p: a jst hld ins fnl f* **8/1**

5001 **3** 3/4 **Everkyllachy (IRE)**[17] 6097 3-9-4 **59** ..................(b) HollieDoyle(3) 2 61
(J S Moore) *sn dropped to last pair: styd towards inner over 2f out: hdwy u.p over 1f out: styd on ins fnl f: wnt 3rd towards fin* **10/1**

3513 **4** 3/4 **Whiteley (IRE)**[10] 6339 3-9-4 **56** ..................... SilvestreDeSousa 1 55
(Mick Channon) *chsd ldrs: styd towards far side over 2f out: pressing wnr and drvn over 1f out: no ex and styd on same pce ins fnl f* **3/1**[2]

0433 **5** 2 1/4 **Tawaafoq**[24] 5855 3-10-0 **66** ..................... FranBerry 3 58+
(Mick Quinn) *s.i.s: hld up in rr: c towards stands side over 2f out: effrt u.p over 1f out: kpt on same pce ins fnl f: nvr trbld ldrs* **9/2**[3]

4006 **6** 1 **General Gerrard**[23] 5871 3-8-8 **46** ..................(v) KieranO'Neill 7 34+
(Michael Madgwick) *chse ldrs: c towards stands side over 2f out: lost pl u.p over 1f out: wl hld and kpt on same pce ins fnl f* **40/1**

0006 **7** 1/2 **Lambrini Legacy**[24] 5826 3-9-0 **52** ..................(h) DavidProbert 9 38
(Lisa Williamson) *taken down early: hld up in tch in midfield: c centre over 2f out: rdn and no hdwy over 1f out: kpt on same pce ins fnl f* **12/1**

0126 **8** 1 **Iron Lady (IRE)**[46] 5040 3-9-3 **55** ..................... MartinDwyer 5 38+
(William Muir) *in tch in midfield: c centre over 2f out: no imp u.p over 1f out: wknd ins fnl f* **7/1**

4050 **9** 3 **Cherry Leyf**[11] 6324 3-8-11 **49** ..................(t) LukeMorris 6 21+
(Stuart Williams) *chsd wnr tl c towards stands side over 2f out: lost pl over 1f out: bhd ins fnl f* **25/1**

1m 2.78s (0.48) **Going Correction** +0.05s/f (Good) **9** Ran SP% **116.5**
Speed ratings (Par 99): **98,97,96,95,91 90,89,87,83**
CSF £25.70 CT £194.56 TOTE £3.50: £1.10, £2.00, £2.70; EX 25.20 Trifecta £146.20.
**Owner** Apple Tree Stud **Bred** W And R Barnett Ltd **Trained** Lambourn, Berks

**FOCUS**
The runners were spread all over the place in the closing stages, but the winner, third and fourth were the only three to stay towards the far side throughout.

## 6725 ROUTE MOBILE APPRENTICE H'CAP 7f 211y
**5:00** (5:00) (Class 5) (0-75,77) 4-Y-0+ **£2,911** (£866; £432; £216) **Stalls** Low

Form RPR

4012 **1** **Buzz Lightyere**[12] 6284 4-8-13 **60** ..................... SebastianWoods(5) 1 67
(Philip Hide) *chsd ldng pair: effrt and hdwy over 1f out: led 1f out: styd on wl ins fnl f* **9/4**[1]

2426 **2** 1 1/4 **Chosen Character (IRE)**[28] 5683 9-9-11 **77**..(vt) ElishaWhittington(10) 2 80
(Tom Dascombe) *chsd ldr tl led 4f out: rdn and hdd 1f out: styd on same pce ins fnl f* **4/1**

-500 **3** 3 1/2 **Titan Goddess**[16] 6134 5-9-11 **67** ..................... KevinLundie 4 62
(Mike Murphy) *s.i.s: sn rcvrd and hld up in tch in last pair: swtchd rt and rdn 3f out: nvr getting on terms w ldrs: wnt 3rd ins fnl f: eased towards fin* **3/1**[2]

2002 **4** 5 **Carcharias (IRE)**[6] 6503 4-9-4 **63** ..................(p) WilliamCox(3) 5 46
(Ed de Giles) *t.k.h: led tl 4f out: rdn and ev ch 2f out tl 3rd and outpcd ent fnl f: sn wknd* **10/3**[3]

032 **5** 2 1/4 **Top Offer**[23] 5898 8-8-13 **55** ..................(v) FinleyMarsh 3 33
(Patrick Morris) *hld up in tch in last pair: effrt 2f out: sn rdn and btn: bhd ins fnl f* **7/1**

1m 35.82s (-0.18) **Going Correction** +0.05s/f (Good) **5** Ran SP% **111.3**
Speed ratings (Par 103): **102,100,97,92,90**
CSF £11.56 TOTE £2.50: £1.50, £1.90; EX 9.80 Trifecta £23.40.
**Owner** Tara Moon Partnership **Bred** M H And Mrs G Tourle **Trained** Findon, W Sussex
■ Stewards' Enquiry : Elisha Whittington four-day ban; used whip above the permitted level (17th-20th Sept)

**FOCUS**
An uncompetitive race.
T/Jkpt: £30,394.30 to a £1 stake. Pool: £30,394.33 - 1 winning unit. T/Plt: £2,450.90 to a £1 stake. Pool: £121,639.82 - 36.23 winning units. T/Qpdt: £35.70 to a £1 stake. Pool: £9,653.50 - 199.67 winning units. **Steve Payne**

# 6710 BADEN-BADEN (L-H)
Sunday, September 3

**OFFICIAL GOING: Turf: good**

## 6726a 144TH STEINHOFF ZUKUNFTSRENNEN (GROUP 3) (2YO) (TURF) 7f
**2:05** 2-Y-0 **£27,350** (£10,256; £5,128; £2,564; £1,709)

RPR

**1** **Narella (IRE)**[56] 2-8-13 0 ..................... AdriedeVries 7 103
(Markus Klug, Germany) *settled towards rr: travelling wl and hdwy ins 2f out: pushed along to chal 1f out: led 150yds out: pushed out* **7/2**[2]

**2** 2 **Auenperle (GER)**[32] 2-8-13 0 ..................... NicolasGuilbert 1 97
(Christina Bucher, Switzerland) *led early: hdd after 1f and racd 3rd: rdn along to ld 1 1/2f out: hdd 110yds out: no ex* **114/10**

**3** 4 **Julio (GER)**[34] 2-9-2 0 ..................... StephenHellyn 2 90
(Mario Hofer, Germany) *midfield: t.k.h early: chsd ldrs 2f out: no ch w front two fnl f* **17/10**[1]

**4** 4 1/2 **Tax Exile (IRE)**[29] 5679 2-9-2 0 ..................(p) ClementLecoeuvre 8 77
(Matthieu Palussiere, France) *led after 1f: pushed along in front 2f out: sn pressed and hdd 1 1/2f out: kpt on* **104/10**

**5** 1/2 **Domberg (GER)** 2-9-2 0 ..................... MarcLerner 3 76
(C Zschache, Germany) *midfield: early: sn dropped bk to r in fnl trio: last turning in: pushed along and hdwy over 2f out: unable to get on terms: no ex fnl f* **79/10**

**6** 3/4 **Starlight Mystery (IRE)**[31] 5572 2-8-13 0 ..................... MartinLane 9 71
(Mark Johnston) *racd cl 2nd: rdn along and lost position ins 2f out: grad dropped away* **99/10**

**7** *shd* **South Coast (GER)** 2-8-13 0 ..................... MarcoCasamento 6 71
(Henk Grewe, Germany) *towards rr: pushed along turning in: sn rdn but unable to get on terms* **132/10**

**8** *hd* **Dusky Dance (IRE)** 2-9-2 0 ..................... AndraschStarke 4 73
(P Schiergen, Germany) *midfield: dropped towards rr 2f out: unable to get bk on terms* **7/1**

**9** 1 1/2 **Kabir (GER)** 2-9-2 0 ..................... EduardoPedroza 5 69
(A Wohler, Germany) *towards rr early: sn moved up to settle midfield: outpcd fr 2f out* **67/10**[3]

1m 25.57s (1.67) **9** Ran SP% **129.0**
PARI-MUTUEL (all including 10 euro stake): WIN 45 PLACE: 17, 20, 14; SF: 680.
**Owner** Gestut Rottgen **Bred** Gestut Rottgen **Trained** Germany

## 6727a 145TH LONGINES GROSSER PREIS VON BADEN (GROUP 1) (3YO+) (TURF) 1m 4f
**3:20** 3-Y-0+ **£128,205** (£51,282; £21,367; £12,820)

RPR

**1** **Guignol (GER)**[64] 4392 5-9-6 0 ..................... FilipMinarik 6 115
(Jean-Pierre Carvalho, Germany) *led: increased pce 3f out: 2 l clr and rdn 1 1/2f out: kpt on wl under hands and heels fnl f* **19/5**[3]

**2** 2 1/2 **Iquitos (GER)**[35] 5464 5-9-6 0 ..................... AndraschStarke 2 111+
(H-J Groschel, Germany) *settled last: pushed along and hdwy turning in: chsd ldr on far rail ins fnl 2f: a wl hld* **6/5**[1]

**3** *shd* **Colomano**[21] 5983 3-8-13 0 ..................... EduardoPedroza 1 113
(Markus Klug, Germany) *racd in 5th: tk clsr order and rdn along 2f out: chsd ldr fnl 2f: wl hld* **15/2**

**4** 1 **Windstoss (GER)**[63] 4422 3-8-13 0 ..................... AdriedeVries 4 111
(Markus Klug, Germany) *racd 3rd: outpcd 2f out: kpt on again fnl f but no ch w wnr* **14/5**[2]



The Form Book Flat, Raceform Ltd, Newbury, RG14 5SJ

5 2 1/4 **Best Solution (IRE)**[35] 5464 3-8-13 0............................ WilliamCarson 5 108
(Saeed bin Suroor) *settled 4th: pushed along and dropped to last turning in: short of spce ins 2f out: kpt on but n.d* **51/10**

6 7 **Prize Money**[35] 5464 4-9-6 0............................................(p) MartinLane 7 95
(Saeed bin Suroor) *wnt rt s: trckd ldr: pushed along in 2nd 3f out: rdn and lost position 2f out: wknd fnl f* **93/10**

2m 32.55s (-0.91)
**WFA** 3 from 4yo+ 8lb **6** Ran SP% **130.5**
PARI-MUTUEL (all including 10 euro stake): WIN 48 PLACE: 19, 13; SF: 90.
**Owner** Stall Ullmann **Bred** Stall Ullmann **Trained** Germany

## 5229 CHANTILLY (R-H)

Sunday, September 3

**OFFICIAL GOING: Turf: soft; polytrack: standard**

### 6728a PRIX D'ARENBERG (GROUP 3) (2YO) (TURF) 5f
3:10 2-Y-O £34,188 (£13,675; £10,256; £6,837; £3,418)

RPR

1 **Rimini (FR)**[19] 6051 2-9-0 0.................................................. JulienAuge 7 106
(C Ferland, France) *racd promly on outer: pushed along and led jst ins 2f out: edgd lft bef styng on wl fnl f* **109/10**

2 1/2 **Sound And Silence**[8] 6448 2-9-0 0..............................(p) JamesDoyle 4 104
(Charlie Appleby) *trckd ldr in midfield: pushed along in bhd horses over 2f out: swtchd out and rdn 1f out: kpt on wl: clst fin* **4/5**[1]

3 hd **Over Reacted (FR)**[35] 5461 2-8-10 0.............................. TonyPiccone 5 99
(F Chappet, France) *led: pressed and pushed along 2f out: hdd jst ins 2f out: rdn fnl f: lost 2nd cl home* **91/10**

4 nk **Rioticism (FR)**[45] 5090 2-8-10 0.............................. AntoineHamelin 3 98
(Matthieu Palussiere, France) *wnt lft s: t.k.h in midfield: pushed along and hdwy 1 1/2f out: rdn fnl f: nt the pce to chal* **41/5**

5 2 1/2 **Arecibo (FR)**[33] 5694 2-9-0 0.............................................. MaximeGuyon 2 93
(C Laffon-Parias, France) *bmpd s: racd promly: pushed along to chal 2f out: sn rdn and lost position: wknd fnl f* **76/10**[3]

6 snk **Mister Picnic (FR)**[35] 5461 2-9-0 0.................... Pierre-CharlesBoudot 6 93
(D Guillemin, France) *a towards rr: outpcd fnl 2f* **23/5**[2]

7 3/4 **Formidable Kitt**[58] 4582 2-8-10 0.............................. MickaelBarzalona 1 86
(Tom Dascombe) *a towards rr* **215/10**

58.26s (-0.04) **Going Correction** +0.05s/f (Good) 7 Ran SP% **118.7**
Speed ratings: **102,101,100,100,96 96,94**
PARI-MUTUEL (all including 1 euro stake): WIN 11.90; PLACE 2.90, 1.40; SF 35.60.
**Owner** LG Bloodstock **Bred** Mlle J Rusu **Trained** France

### 6729a PRIX DU PIN (GROUP 3) (3YO+) (TURF) 7f
4:25 3-Y-O+ £34,188 (£13,675; £10,256; £6,837; £3,418)

RPR

1 **Karar**[20] 5-9-2 0.............................................................. GregoryBenoist 5 115+
(F-H Graffard, France) *led after 1/2f: 2 l clr and pushed along 2f out: rdn out fnl f* **48/10**[3]

2 1 1/2 **Empire Of The Star (FR)**[33] 5522 3-8-13 0........ ChristopheSoumillon 2 109
(A Wohler, Germany) *led first 1/2f: hdd and settled in 3rd on inner: wnt 2nd and chsd ldr over 1f out: a wl hld fnl f* **115/10**

3 1 **Dame Du Roi (IRE)**[35] 5460 3-8-9 0........................ MickaelBarzalona 6 102+
(F Head, France) *settled in rr: pushed along in bhd horses 2f out: rdn along and gd hdwy fnl f: nvr on terms w ldrs* **5/1**

4 snk **Zalamea (IRE)**[28] 5690 4-9-2 0.......................................... EddyHardouin 4 107+
(Carina Fey, France) *towards rr: travelling wl in bhd horses 2f out: c w a gd run fnl f but nvr a danger* **38/1**

5 1 1/2 **Jallota**[9] 6401 6-9-2 0.................................................. JamieSpencer 3 103
(Charles Hills) *settled 2nd: pushed along to chse ldr over 2f out: sn rdn: lost position fnl f* **29/10**[2]

6 3 1/2 **African Ride**[64] 4390 3-8-13 0.......................................... MaximeGuyon 9 92
(C Laffon-Parias, France) *racd towards rr early: midfield 3f out: pushed along but nt qckn 2f out: eased fnl f* **13/5**[1]

7 3/4 **Blue Soave (FR)**[25] 9-9-2 0.............................................. TonyPiccone 7 91
(F Chappet, France) *midfield on outer: pushed along as pce qcknd 2f out: lost position over 1f out: eased* **181/10**

8 nk **Royal Julius (IRE)**[57] 4653 4-9-2 0.................................... TheoBachelot 8 91
(J Reynier, France) *midfield early: sn dropped towards rr: pushed along in last 2f out: eased fnl f* **79/10**

R **Black Max (FR)**[28] 5690 4-9-2 0........................ Pierre-CharlesBoudot 1
(H-A Pantall, France) *ref to r* **236/10**

1m 24.05s (-2.05) **Going Correction** +0.05s/f (Good)
**WFA** 3 from 4yo+ 4lb 9 Ran SP% **118.4**
Speed ratings: **113,111,110,109,108 104,103,103,**
PARI-MUTUEL (all including 1 euro stake): WIN 5.80; PLACE 2.30, 2.80, 2.20; DF 35.80; SF 40.50.
**Owner** Al Shaqab Racing **Bred** James Wigan **Trained** France

### 6730a PRIX DES CHENES (GROUP 3) (2YO COLTS & GELDINGS) (TURF) 1m
5:40 2-Y-O £34,188 (£13,675; £10,256; £6,837; £3,418)

RPR

1 **Stage Magic (IRE)**[15] 6229 2-9-2 0.................................... JamesDoyle 3 106
(Charlie Appleby) *led: increased pce 2 1/2f out: sn pressed and rdn: battled on wl: jst hld off fast finer* **14/5**[2]

2 shd **Olmedo (FR)**[26] 5776 2-9-2 0.......................................... CristianDemuro 5 106
(J-C Rouget, France) *settled in 4th early: pushed along to chse ldng pair 2f out: styd on strly fnl f: jst failed* **3/5**[1]

3 nk **Zyzzyva (FR)**[24] 5989 2-9-2 0...................................... MickaelBarzalona 4 105
(Robyn Brisland) *racd in 2nd: pushed along and pressed ldr 2f out: rdn fnl f: a jst hld: lost 2nd late on* **113/10**

4 6 **Diamond Vendome (FR)**[30] 5626 2-9-2 0.............................. JulienAuge 2 92
(C Ferland, France) *last: detached and rdn along 2f out: passed one fnl f but nvr involved* **108/10**

5 3 **Contortioniste**[35] 5461 2-9-2 0.......................................... MaximeGuyon 1 85
(C Laffon-Parias, France) *settled 3rd on inner: chsd ldrs 2f out: sn btn: eased fnl f* **32/5**[3]

1m 38.77s (0.77) **Going Correction** +0.05s/f (Good) 5 Ran SP% **118.9**
Speed ratings: **98,97,97,91,88**
PARI-MUTUEL (all including 1 euro stake): WIN 3.80; PLACE 1.10, 1.10, SF 6.30.
**Owner** Godolphin **Bred** Paul & Billy McEnery **Trained** Newmarket, Suffolk

**FOCUS**
A tight finish between the front three.

### 6731a PRIX D'AUMALE (GROUP 3) (2YO FILLIES) (TURF) 1m
6:10 2-Y-O £34,188 (£13,675; £10,256; £6,837; £3,418)

RPR

1 **Soustraction (IRE)**[26] 2-9-0 0.......................................... MaximeGuyon 2 104+
(C Laffon-Parias, France) *settled 3rd: pushed along and hdwy to ld 2f out: pressed fnl f but a in control* **58/10**

2 1 **Efaadah (IRE)**[26] 2-9-0 0.................................................. OlivierPeslier 4 102
(F Head, France) *last: c w a str run fr 2f out: wnt 2nd 75yds out: nt pce to rch wnr* **9/10**[1]

3 hd **Wild Illusion**[12] 6292 2-9-0 0............................................ JamesDoyle 3 101
(Charlie Appleby) *settled 4th: nudged along fr 3f out: rdn and hdwy ins 2f out: chsd ldr but a hld fnl f: lost 2nd 75yds out* **7/2**[2]

4 8 **Chipolata (FR)**[52] 2-9-0 0................................................ TheoBachelot 1 84
(J Reynier, France) *led: pressed over 2f out: pushed along and hdd 2f out: sn rdn: wknd* **8/1**

5 4 1/2 **Expressiy (FR)**[9] 6385 2-9-0 0.................................. MickaelBarzalona 5 74
(Charlie Appleby) *racd in 2nd: keen early: rdn and lost position 2f out: sn btn and eased fnl f* **49/10**[3]

1m 37.88s (-0.12) **Going Correction** +0.05s/f (Good) 5 Ran SP% **117.6**
Speed ratings: **102,101,100,92,88**
PARI-MUTUEL (all including 1 euro stake): WIN 6.80; PLACE 2.10, 1.40, SF 15.80.
**Owner** Wertheimer & Frere **Bred** Wertheimer Et Frere **Trained** Chantilly, France

### 6732a PRIX DE LIANCOURT (LISTED RACE) (3YO FILLIES) (TURF) 1m 2f 110y
6:40 3-Y-O £23,504 (£9,401; £7,051; £4,700; £2,350)

RPR

1 **Golden Legend (FR)**[48] 4988 3-8-11 0.............................. AlexisBadel 2 100
(H-F Devin, France) **19/5**[2]

2 1 1/4 **Baltic Duchess (IRE)**[48] 4988 3-8-11 0............. Pierre-CharlesBoudot 9 98
(A Fabre, France) **29/1**

3 nk **Normandel (FR)**[36] 5449 3-9-2 0.................................. CristianDemuro 8 102
(Mme Pia Brandt, France) **101/10**

4 1 1/4 **Val De Marne**[24] 3-8-11 0...................................... MickaelBarzalona 5 95
(A Fabre, France) *settled towards rr: impr to take clsr order over 2f out: rdn over 1f out: styd on one pce fnl f* **36/5**

5 nk **Diablesse**[51] 4877 3-8-11 0.............................................. MaximeGuyon 3 94
(F Head, France) **49/10**[3]

6 1 1/2 **Shemda (IRE)**[22] 3-8-11 0.................................. ChristopheSoumillon 7 91
(A De Royer-Dupre, France) **76/10**

7 7 **La Gommeuse (IRE)**[98] 3121 3-9-2 0.......................... StephanePasquier 1 83
(Mme C Head-Maarek, France) **171/10**

8 1/2 **Panthelia (FR)**[77] 3881 3-8-11 0...................................... GregoryBenoist 4 77
(P Sogorb, France) **18/5**[1]

9 4 **Melesina (IRE)**[168] 1270 3-9-2 0.......................................... TonyPiccone 6 74
(Richard Fahey) *wl into stride: led early: disp ld after 1f: pushed along whn chal 2f out: rdn w limited rspnse over 1f out: eased ins fnl f* **49/10**[3]

2m 11.87s (3.07) **Going Correction** +0.05s/f (Good) 9 Ran SP% **118.2**
Speed ratings: **90,89,88,87,87 86,81,81,78**
PARI-MUTUEL (all including 1 euro stake): WIN 4.80; PLACE 2.10, 6.80, 4.10; DF 49.40; SF 62.00.
**Owner** Mme Henri Devin **Bred** Mme H Devin **Trained** France

6733 - 6743a (Foreign Racing) - See Raceform Interactive

## 6717 VELIEFENDI

Sunday, September 3

**OFFICIAL GOING: Turf: good to soft**

### 6744a INTERNATIONAL BOSPHORUS CUP (GROUP 2) (3YO+) (TURF) 1m 4f
2:00 3-Y-O+ £153,846 (£61,538; £30,769; £15,384)

RPR

1 **Secret Number**[295] 7948 7-9-6 0........................................ GeraldMosse 7 110+
(Saeed bin Suroor) *midfield: pushed along to ld ins 2f out: drew clr under hands and heels fnl f* **7/20**[1]

2 2 **Elbereth**[36] 5436 6-9-2 0.................................................. OisinMurphy 2 103
(Andrew Balding) *trckd ldr: hdwy to chal top of st: led briefly 2f out: sn hdd: nt pce of wnr fnl f* **19/10**[3]

3 nk **Victory Is Ours (TUR)**[23] 4-9-6 0..............................(bt) HalisKaratas 5 107
(Aydin Kucukaksoy, Turkey) *in fnl pair: pushed along 2f out but unable to get on terms: gd hdwy fnl f to take 3rd* **11/5**

4 1/2 **Crimean Tatar (TUR)**[15] 6191 4-9-6 0..........................(b) JackMitchell 1 106
(Hugo Palmer) *midfield: gd hdwy on inner to chal 2f out: dropped away fnl f* **5/4**[2]

5 1 1/2 **Blaze To Win (TUR)**[21] 6-9-6 0..............................(t) GokhanKocakaya 4 103
(Aydin Kucukaksoy, Turkey) *led: set stdy pce: increased tempo turning in: sn u.p and hdd 2f out: grad dropped away* **11/5**

6 10 **Oglum Berat (TUR)**[23] 5-9-6 0..........................................(b) UgurPolat 6 87
(Mulayim Anat, Turkey) *a towards rr: detached fnl 2f* **19/4**

2m 32.41s (3.61) 6 Ran SP% **232.9**

**Owner** Godolphin **Bred** Darley **Trained** Newmarket, Suffolk

**FOCUS**
Another prize for Godolphin at the meeting with the winner making a successful return from a long absence.

### 6745a INTERNATIONAL TRAKYA (THRACE) TROPHY (LOCAL GROUP 3) (2YO) (TURF) 6f
2:30 2-Y-O £98,290 (£39,316; £19,658; £9,829)

RPR

1 **Another Batt (IRE)**[15] 6190 2-9-0 0.................................... OisinMurphy 6 99
(George Scott) *sn racing cl 2nd: pushed along to chse ldr 1 1/2f out: gd hdwy to ld 1f out: rdn out fnl f* **7/5**[2]

2 1 1/2 **Armondo (TUR)**[7] 2-9-0 0..........................................(tp) OzcanYildirim 5 95
(T Turkmen, Turkey) *midfield: pushed along 2f out: sn rdn and hdwy to chse ldr: a hld fnl f* **67/20**

3 5 **Yele (TUR)**[9] 2-9-0 0 ow5.................................................. SelimKaya 2 80
(Fehmi Dizdaroglu, Turkey) *racd in 3rd: rdn along to chse ldr 2f out: kpt on wl but outpcd by front two fnl f* **101/20**

4 1 **Bayezid (IRE)**[35] 2-9-0 0 ........ GokhanKocakaya 8 77
(S Tasbek, Turkey) *midfield: pushed along 2f out: kpt on same pce: nvr a danger* **87/10**

5 1 **Has (TUR)**[7] 2-9-0 0 ........ (b) MehmetKaya 1 74
(Fehmi Dizdaroglu, Turkey) *settled in rr: sme late hdwy* **177/10**

5 dht **Rufus King**[10] 6353 2-9-0 0 ........ RichardKingscote 4 74
(Mark Johnston) *towards rr: kpt on fnl f but nvr on terms* **57/20**

7 1 **Timetosaygoodbye (TUR)**[25] 2-8-10 0 ow1 ........ JackMitchell 7 67
(S Bilgic, Turkey) *led: rdn along 2 l clr 2f out: sn u.p and hdd 1f out: wknd fnl f* **13/5**[3]

8 7 ½ **Chess Move (IRE)**[52] 4799 2-9-0 0 ........ HectorCrouch 3 48
(George Baker) *a towards rr: eased fnl f* **19/20**[1]

1m 10.74s 8 Ran SP% **201.9**

**Owner** Excel Racing (Another Batt) **Bred** J W Nicholson **Trained** Newmarket, Suffolk

**FOCUS**

A game winner and a first Group success for his trainer.

## 6746a INTERNATIONAL TOPKAPI TROPHY (GROUP 2) (3YO+) (TURF) 1m
3:30 3-Y-0+ £230,769 (£92,307; £46,153; £23,076)

RPR

1 **Wonnemond (GER)**[49] 4939 4-9-6 0 ........ DanielePorcu 2 112+
(S Smrczek, Germany) *settled in last: pushed along turning in: sn rdn: gd hdwy fnl 1 1/2f: c w str run to ld 50yds out* **193/10**

2 1 **Dream Castle**[33] 5502 3-9-3 0 ow1 ........ GeraldMosse 9 111
(Saeed bin Suroor) *racd midfield: pushed along 2f out: gd hdwy to ld 1f out: hld of chalrs tl hdd 50yds out* **1/20**[1]

3 2 **Yildirimbey (TUR)**[21] 6-9-6 0 ........ (h) OzcanYildirim 10 105
(Adil Yilmaz, Turkey) *settled towards rr: rdn 2f out: stdy hdwy but nt pce to chal: tk 3rd fnl strides* **147/10**

4 nse **Touch The Wolf (TUR)**[21] 4-9-6 0 ........ (h) HalisKaratas 4 105
(A Sivgin, Turkey) *settled towards rr: pushed along 2f out: hdwy to press ldr ins fnl f: nt pce of front two fnl 110yds* **167/20**[3]

5 2 **Carry On Deryck**[17] 6105 5-9-6 0 ........ OisinMurphy 8 101
(Saeed bin Suroor) *midfield: pushed along but nt qckn 2f out: kpt on again fnl f: nvr threatened* **1/20**[1]

6 1 ½ **Mr Scaramanga**[19] 6024 3-9-2 0 ........ JFEgan 5 97
(Simon Dow) *trckd ldr in 3rd: pushed along to chse ldr 2f out: rdn and lost position 1f out: no ex* **166/10**

7 1 ½ **Copperfield (TUR)**[21] 3-9-2 0 ........ GokhanKocakaya 6 94
(S Tasbek, Turkey) *led: pushed along 2f out: chal and hdd 1f out: wknd* **604/100**[2]

8 hd **Arcanada (IRE)**[50] 4916 4-9-6 0 ........ RichardKingscote 7 93
(Tom Dascombe) *trckd ldr: pushed along and lost position ins 2f out: wknd* **155/10**

9 ½ **Kool Kompany (IRE)**[32] 5527 5-9-6 0 ........ SeanLevey 3 92
(Richard Hannon) *midfield: outpcd over 1f out: unable to get on terms* **135/10**

10 3 ½ **Diplomat (GER)**[49] 4939 6-9-6 0 ........ FabriceVeron 1 84
(Mario Hofer, Germany) *midfield on inner: pushed along turning in: wknd fnl 1 1/2f* **46/1**

1m 35.28s (-0.05)
**WFA** 3 from 4yo+ 5lb 10 Ran SP% **247.4**

**Owner** Stall Frohnbach **Bred** K H Schmoock **Trained** Germany

**FOCUS**

A small improvement from the winner.

# 6719 BRIGHTON (L-H)

Monday, September 4

**OFFICIAL GOING: Good (good to firm in places) changing to good after race 1 (2.00)**

Wind: medium, half against Weather: cloudy

## 6747 EBF MAIDEN FILLIES' STKS (PLUS 10 RACE) 5f 215y
2:00 (2:01) (Class 5) 2-Y-0 £3,234 (£962; £481; £240) Stalls Centre

Form RPR

04 1 **Wear It Well**[35] 5476 2-9-0 0 ........ DaneO'Neill 2 74
(Henry Candy) *mde all: rdn over 1f out: hrd pressed ins fnl f: fnd ex and holding chalr fnl 100yds: r.o* **8/1**[3]

42 2 ½ **Daybreak**[24] 5885 2-9-0 0 ........ AdamKirby 9 73
(Hughie Morrison) *hld up in tch in midfield: effrt 2f out: rdn to chse wnr over 1f out: chal and drvn ins fnl f: kpt on but a hld* **1/2**[1]

3 1 ½ **Princess Harley (IRE)** 2-9-0 0 ........ PatCosgrave 3 68+
(Mick Quinn) *awkward leaving stalls and s.i.s: hld up in last pair: c nrest stands rail and hdwy over 2f out: nt clr run and sltly impeded over 1f out: styd on wl ins fnl f: swtchd lft and wnt 3rd last strides* **25/1**

06 4 nk **Lady Godiva (IRE)**[24] 5885 2-8-11 0 ........ HollieDoyle(3) 4 67
(Richard Hannon) *t.k.h: chsd ldrs: effrt u.p over 1f out: wnt 3rd 100yds out: kpt on same pce after: lost 3rd last strides* **10/1**

02 5 ½ **Havana Heart**[14] 6262 2-9-0 0 ........ CharlesBishop 10 66
(Ismail Mohammed) *chsd ldrs: wnt 2nd over 1f out tl unable qck u.p over 1f out: lost 3rd and styd on same pce ins fnl f* **9/1**

6 3 ½ **Musical Theatre** 2-9-0 0 ........ OisinMurphy 7 55
(David Simcock) *t.k.h: hld up in tch in last quartet: effrt whn n.m.r 2f out: hdwy over 1f out: no imp ins fnl f* **6/1**[2]

0 7 1 ¾ **Harbour Seal**[33] 5534 2-9-0 0 ........ (h[1]) RobHornby 1 50
(Henry Spiller) *chsd ldr tl over 2f out: lost pl u.p over 1f out: wknd ins fnl f* **40/1**

0 8 4 **Foxangel**[17] 6132 2-9-0 0 ........ (h) OscarPereira 5 38
(Jose Santos) *chsd ldrs: rdn 2f out: sn lost pl: bhd ins fnl f* **50/1**

0 9 2 ½ **Happy Ending (IRE)**[28] 5710 2-9-0 0 ........ KieranO'Neill 6 31
(Seamus Mullins) *a towards rr: pushed along over 2f out: outpcd and bhd over 1f out* **66/1**

10 1 ¾ **Living In The Now** 2-8-11 0 ........ CallumShepherd(3) 8 25
(Charles Hills) *dwlt: a rr: lost tch 2f out* **20/1**

1m 12.3s (2.10) **Going Correction** +0.30s/f (Good) 10 Ran SP% **125.7**
Speed ratings (Par 92): **98,97,95,94,94 89,87,81,78,76**
CSF £13.05 TOTE £10.60: £2.30, £1.02, £5.90; EX 20.30 Trifecta £342.40.
**Owner** Andrew Whitlock Racing Ltd **Bred** David John Brown **Trained** Kingston Warren, Oxon

**FOCUS**

Race distance increased by 4yds. A drizzly day and easing underfoot conditions. This was an ordinary fillies' maiden in which they came middle to stands' side up the home straight. The winner looks an improver.

## 6748 IAN CARNABY (S) H'CAP 5f 215y
2:30 (2:31) (Class 6) (0-60,62) 3-Y-0+ £2,264 (£673; £336; £168) Stalls Centre

Form RPR

5024 1 **Lady Morel (IRE)**[13] 6283 3-9-0 55 ........ OisinMurphy 15 60
(Joseph Tuite) *in tch in midfield: rdn and effrt over 1f out: chsd clr ldr 1f out: styd on strly fnl 100yds: led last strides* **13/2**[3]

00-0 2 nk **Miss Uppity**[220] 445 4-8-0 46 oh1 ........ ManuelFernandes(7) 5 50
(Ivan Furtado) *led: rdn and wnt clr over 1f out: kpt drifting lft u.p ins fnl f: worn down towards fin and hdd last strides* **9/1**

0240 3 nse **Time Medicean**[16] 6197 11-9-3 56 ........ GeorgeDowning 7 60
(Tony Carroll) *in tch in midfield: wnt rt over 2f out: effrt over 1f out: hdwy 1f out: styd on strly u.p fnl 100yds: ev ch nr fin: nt quite get to ldrs* **13/2**[3]

0640 4 ½ **Rebel Heart**[24] 5892 3-8-11 52 ........ (v) WilliamCarson 10 54
(Bill Turner) *chsd ldrs: effrt 2f out: chsd clr ldr over 1f out tl 1f out: styd on u.p ins fnl f* **8/1**

-600 5 1 **Solitary Sister (IRE)**[18] 6112 3-8-4 52 ........ (v[1]) NicolaCurrie(7) 9 51
(Richard Spencer) *flashing tail leaving stalls: towards rr: edgd rt ent fnl 2f: swtchd lft and hdwy over 1f out: styd on wl ins fnl f: nvr trbld ldrs* **20/1**

03 6 ½ **Blackadder**[7] 6507 5-8-4 46 oh1 ........ (h) NoelGarbutt(3) 13 44
(Mark Gillard) *in rr: nt clr run and swtchd sharply lft 2f out: hdwy 1f out: r.o strly ins fnl f: nvr trbld ldrs* **25/1**

2100 7 ½ **Strictly Carter**[24] 5892 4-9-7 60 ........ RobertWinston 2 56
(Alan Bailey) *in tch in midfield: effrt to go prom in chsng gp over 1f out: no ex and no imp wl ins fnl f* **9/2**[1]

50-5 8 ¾ **Noneedtotellme (IRE)**[34] 5512 4-8-7 46 oh1 ........ RobHornby 6 40
(James Unett) *towards rr: rdn 2f out: hdwy jst over 1f out: styd on ins fnl f: nvr trbld ldrs* **25/1**

55/0 9 2 ½ **Almoqatel (IRE)**[55] 4713 5-8-7 46 oh1 ........ RyanPowell 8 32
(Tony Newcombe) *chsd ldr tl hung lft: rdn and lost 2nd over 1f out: lost pl and eased wl ins fnl f* **25/1**

2400 10 3 ¾ **Hurricane Alert**[24] 5871 5-8-11 53 ........ DavidEgan(3) 11 27
(Mark Hoad) *midfield: carried rt over 2f out: rdn ent fnl 2f: sn struggling and lost pl over 1f out: wknd fnl f* **16/1**

1050 11 9 **Perfect Pastime**[23] 5936 9-9-9 62 ........ (p) PatCosgrave 12 9
(Jim Boyle) *hld up towards rr: effrt and carried rt ent over 2f: sn rdn and no hdwy: wknd over 1f out* **12/1**

6-00 12 ½ **Sweet Sienna**[11] 6339 3-8-5 46 oh1 ........ JimmyQuinn 1
(Dean Ivory) *t.k.h: chsd ldrs: pushed along 2f out: sn lost pl: eased ins fnl f* **50/1**

-200 13 ½ **Lucky Di**[10] 6373 7-8-13 52 ........ CharlesBishop 3
(Peter Hedger) *rrd as stalls opened and slowly away: in tch in rr: rdn and no hdwy over 2f out: wknd over 1f out* **6/1**[2]

0-60 14 5 **Angelical Eve (IRE)**[46] 5050 3-8-8 52 ........ HectorCrouch(3) 14
(George Baker) *a towards rr: effrt whn nt clr run and hmpd over 2f out: no ch after: eased ins fnl f* **20/1**

200 15 28 **Take A Drop (IRE)**[11] 6341 4-8-7 46 ........ (b[1]) KieranO'Neill 4
(Seamus Mullins) *wl in tch in midfield tl lost pl qckly 1/2-way: bhd and heavily eased fnl f: t.o* **40/1**

1m 11.97s (1.77) **Going Correction** +0.30s/f (Good)
**WFA** 3 from 4yo+ 2lb 15 Ran SP% **119.3**
Speed ratings (Par 101): **100,99,99,98,97 96,96,95,91,86 74,74,73,66,29**
CSF £56.80 CT £409.43 TOTE £7.80: £2.40, £3.30, £2.80; EX 77.00 Trifecta £1048.20.The winner was bought in for £6,000
**Owner** Felstead Court Flyers **Bred** Stephanie Hanly **Trained** Lambourn, Berks

**FOCUS**

Race distance increased by 4yds. This was a strongly run selling handicap and it saw changing fortunes near the finish.

## 6749 MARATHONBET LIVE CASINO NURSERY H'CAP 5f 215y
3:00 (3:00) (Class 5) (0-70,72) 2-Y-0 £3,234 (£962; £481; £240) Stalls Centre

Form RPR

3350 1 **Diamond Dougal (IRE)**[10] 6375 2-9-1 64 ........ CharlesBishop 2 71
(Mick Channon) *hld up in tch: clsd and nt clr run over 1f out: nudged his way through and effrt to chal 1f out: wnt clr w ldr and led 100yds out: r.o wl: pushed out* **11/2**[3]

2165 2 ¾ **Queen Of Kalahari**[27] 5751 2-9-5 71 ........ CallumShepherd(3) 9 76
(Charles Hills) *chsd ldr over 4f out: sn led: rdn over 1f out: hrd pressed 1f out: c clr w wnr but hdd 100yds out: r.o but a hld after* **6/1**

665 3 3 ½ **General Marius (IRE)**[17] 6147 2-9-5 68 ........ (b[1]) HarryBentley 8 62
(Roger Varian) *in tch: effrt to r on stands rail over 2f out: outpcd and hung lft u.p over 1f out: kpt on to pass btn rivals ins fnl f: no threat to ldng pair* **9/2**[2]

040 4 ¾ **Blessed To Empress (IRE)**[20] 6036 2-9-3 66 ........ OisinMurphy 5 58
(Amy Murphy) *restless in stalls:t.k.h: in tch: pushed lft over 2f out: rdn to chal over 1f out tl nudged lft ent fnal f and sn outpcd: wknd ins fnl f* **7/1**

105 5 1 **Boomerang Betty (IRE)**[44] 5144 2-9-8 71 ........ DougieCostello 7 60
(Jamie Osborne) *stdd s: hld up in tch in rr: swtchd lft and hdwy over 2f out: rdn to press ldrs over 1f out: no ex and outpcd 1f out: wknd ins fnl f* **11/2**[3]

5511 6 hd **Princess Lyla (IRE)**[17] 6154 2-9-0 68 ........ FinleyMarsh(5) 6 56
(Richard Hughes) *t.k.h: led for 2f: rdn stl pressing ldr over 1f out tl no ex ent fnl f: wknd ins fnl f* **3/1**[1]

5302 7 3 ½ **Bodybuilder**[37] 5408 2-9-3 69 ........ HollieDoyle(3) 4 46
(Richard Hannon) *t.k.h: chsd ldr for over 1f out: sn dropped towards rr: bhd and rdn 2f out: no imp: wknd ins fnl f* **8/1**

1m 12.27s (2.07) **Going Correction** +0.30s/f (Good) 7 Ran SP% **111.8**
Speed ratings (Par 95): **98,97,92,91,90 89,85**
CSF £36.03 CT £157.85 TOTE £7.30: £3.60, £2.10; EX 38.10 Trifecta £452.20.
**Owner** Insignia Racing (flag) **Bred** Con Marnane **Trained** West Ilsley, Berks

**FOCUS**

Race distance increased by 4yds. A modest nursery lacking depth in which the first two pulled clear.

## 6750 ROUTE MOBILE MAIDEN FILLIES' STKS 1m 1f 207y
3:30 (3:31) (Class 5) 3-Y-0+ £3,234 (£962) Stalls High

Form RPR

2- 1 **Alwaysandforever (IRE)**[363] 6206 3-9-0 0 ........ RyanMoore 3 87
(Luca Cumani) *mde all: rdn over 1f out: reminder and stretched clr over 1f out: r.o wl: eased towards fin: easily* **2/13**[1]

303 **2** *14* **Sugardrop**[20] 6027 3-9-0 74 ........ SteveDrowne 2 68
(Amanda Perrett) *trckd rival: effrt 2f out: sn rdn and outpcd: wl btn and eased wl ins fnl f* **5/1**[2]

2m 7.55s (3.95) **Going Correction** +0.30s/f (Good) 2 Ran SP% **103.3**
Speed ratings (Par 100): **96,84**
TOTE £1.20.
**Owner** M Tabor, Mrs John Magnier & Derrick Smith **Bred** G Morrin **Trained** Newmarket, Suffolk

**FOCUS**
Race distance increased by 4yds. An uneventful match, but the form is hard to guage.

## 6751 LOVE FAIRS ANTIQUE FAIR 22 OCTOBER H'CAP (DIV I) 7f 211y
**4:00** (4:01) (Class 6) (0-55,56) 3-Y-0+ **£2,264** (£673; £336; £168) **Stalls** Centre

Form RPR

3655 **1** **Captain Marmalade (IRE)**[7] 6503 5-8-13 **50** ........(h) HollieDoyle(3) 1 58
(Jimmy Fox) *stdd s: t.k.h: hld up in tch in rr: clsd and swtchd lft over 1f out: sn pushed into ld: sn rdn clr and r.o wl: comf* **11/2**[3]

4262 **2** *4 ½* **Chough**[28] 5713 3-9-3 **56** ........ AdamKirby 7 53
(Hughie Morrison) *stdd bk to last pair after 1f: hld up in tch: effrt over 2f out: hdwy to chse ldrs u.p over 1f out: chsd clr wnr ins fnl f: no imp* **2/1**[1]

6064 **3** *¾* **African Quest**[26] 5791 3-8-4 **46** oh1 ........ NoelGarbutt(3) 9 41
(Gary Moore) *dwlt: in tch in rr: hdwy 1/2-way: chsd ldrs 4f out: rdn 3f out: drvn over 1f out: kpt on same pce ins fnl f* **22/1**

040 **4** *½* **Good Business (IRE)**[31] 5611 3-8-13 **55** ........ DavidEgan(3) 3 49
(Jeremy Noseda) *dwlt: wl in tch in midfield: chsd ldrs 4f out: pushed into ld 2f out: edgd rt over 1f out: sn hdd and unable qck: wknd and lost 2 pls ins fnl f* **15/2**

4043 **5** *2 ½* **Limerick Lord (IRE)**[26] 5791 5-8-9 **46** ........(p) ShelleyBirkett(3) 10 35
(Julia Feilden) *t.k.h: led tl 2f out: sn rdn and hung lft whn sltly impeded over 1f out: wknd ins fnl f* **11/2**[3]

4611 **6** *1* **The Special One (IRE)**[26] 5792 4-9-2 **55** ........(t) FinleyMarsh(5) 8 42
(Ali Stronge) *chsd ldrs: rdn and unable qck over 1f out: wknd ins fnl f* **5/1**[2]

3040 **7** *14* **Harlequin Rock**[13] 6296 4-9-7 **55** ........ WilliamCarson 4 10
(Mick Quinn) *t.k.h: hld up in tch in midfield: rdn and lost pl 2f out: bhd and eased ins fnl f* **16/1**

5635 **8** *10* **Lesanti**[12] 6324 3-8-10 **52** ........ CallumShepherd(3) 5
(Ed de Giles) *t.k.h: chsd ldr tl over 2f out: sn struggling and lost pl over 1f out: bhd and eased fnl f* **8/1**

1m 37.64s (1.64) **Going Correction** +0.30s/f (Good)
**WFA** 3 from 4yo+ 5lb 8 Ran SP% **113.9**
Speed ratings (Par 101): **103,98,97,97,94 93,79,69**
CSF £16.78 CT £224.22 TOTE £7.40: £2.40, £1.10, £6.00; EX 20.50 Trifecta £483.20.
**Owner** Mrs Sarah-Jane Fox **Bred** Miss C Magnier **Trained** Collingbourne Ducis, Wilts

**FOCUS**
Race distance increased by 4yds. An ordinary handicap, run at a solid pace, perhaps too solid with the first three coming from the rear. The winner has been rated near his best.

## 6752 LOVE FAIRS ANTIQUE FAIR 22 OCTOBER H'CAP (DIV II) 7f 211y
**4:30** (4:32) (Class 6) (0-55,55) 3-Y-0+ **£2,264** (£673; £336; £168) **Stalls** Centre

Form RPR

2204 **1** **With Approval (IRE)**[13] 6284 5-9-7 **55** ........(p) PatCosgrave 5 62
(Laura Mongan) *chsd ldr tl rdn to ld wl over 1f out: hld on wl u.p ins fnl f: rdn out* **10/3**[2]

0325 **2** *¾* **De Vegas Kid (IRE)**[5] 6587 3-8-12 **51** ........ GeorgeDowning 7 55
(Tony Carroll) *hld up in tch in midfield: effrt ent fnl 2f: rdn to chse ldrs and nt clr run ent fnl f: swtchd lft and pressed wnr ins fnl f: kpt on u.p but a hld* **9/4**[1]

2326 **3** *2 ½* **Lawfilly**[25] 5817 3-8-9 **55** ........ NicolaCurrie(7) 2 54
(Richard Hughes) *stdd and awkward leaving stalls: hld up in tch: swtchd rt and pushed along over 2f out: clsd to chse wnr over 1f out: rdn 1f out: fnd little and sn lost 2nd: wknd fnl 100yds* **4/1**[3]

0001 **4** *¾* **Lutine Charlie (IRE)**[25] 5817 10-8-12 **46** ........ JFEgan 9 44
(Emma Owen) *sn led: rdn and hdd wl over 1f out: styd pressing ldrs tl no ex 1f out: wknd ins fnl f* **8/1**

040 **5** *4 ½* **Performance Art (IRE)**[43] 4754 3-8-7 **46** ........ KieranO'Neill 3 32
(Seamus Mullins) *chsd ldrs: rdn ent fnl 2f: outpcd over 1f out: swtchd lft and tried to rally 1f out: sn wknd* **25/1**

0-00 **6** *7* **Arquus (IRE)**[90] 3435 4-9-0 **51** ........ CallumShepherd(3) 4 22
(Ed de Giles) *t.k.h: chsd ldrs: effrt over 2f out: unable qck and btn over 1f out: wknd qckly ins fnl f* **12/1**

544 **7** *3 ¾* **Alketios (GR)**[69] 4180 6-9-6 **54** ........(t[1]) DaneO'Neill 6 17
(Chris Gordon) *trckd ldrs: effrt ent fnl 2f: unable qck over 1f out and btn 1f out: eased ins fnl f* **7/1**

-000 **8** *7* **Turaathy (IRE)**[28] 5713 4-9-2 **50** ........(p[1]) SteveDrowne 8
(Tony Newcombe) *s.i.s: nvr gng wl in rr thrght: eased fnl f* **25/1**

1m 38.25s (2.25) **Going Correction** +0.30s/f (Good)
**WFA** 3 from 4yo+ 5lb 8 Ran SP% **112.8**
Speed ratings (Par 101): **100,99,96,96,91 84,80,73**
CSF £10.94 CT £29.29 TOTE £3.40: £1.30, £1.10, £1.60; EX 12.10 Trifecta £37.30.
**Owner** Mrs P J Sheen **Bred** Yeomanstown Stud **Trained** Epsom, Surrey

**FOCUS**
Race distance increased by 4yds. The second division of this handicap saw a slow-motion finish nearer the stands' rail. It was 0.61sec slower than the preceding race and the form looks ordinary.

## 6753 BRIGHTON LIONS FIREWORK NIGHT 5 NOVEMBER H'CAP 6f 210y
**5:00** (5:00) (Class 5) (0-70,72) 3-Y-0+ **£2,911** (£866; £432; £216) **Stalls** Centre

Form RPR

132 **1** **Black Caesar (IRE)**[65] 4373 6-9-6 **72** ........ SebastianWoods(7) 8 85
(Philip Hide) *chsd clr ldr: clsd and swtchd rt over 1f out: sn rdn to ld: r.o strly and drew clr ins fnl f: easily* **7/2**[2]

0635 **2** *6* **Miss Icon**[28] 5711 3-9-4 **67** ........ DanielMuscutt 3 62
(Patrick Chamings) *racd off the pce in 3rd: effrt over 2f out: clsd to chsd wnr u.p jst over 1f out: totally outpcd fnl f but kpt on to hold 2nd* **9/2**[3]

6540 **3** *1* **Pass The Cristal (IRE)**[8] 6485 3-9-0 **63** ........ DougieCostello 1 56
(William Muir) *t.k.h: hld up off the pce in midfield: effrt 2f out: rdn over 1f out: kpt on u.p ins fnl f: wnt 3rd last strides: no ch w wnr* **14/1**

0300 **4** *nk* **Gala Celebration (IRE)**[11] 6345 3-9-1 **64** ........(b[1]) FergusSweeney 11 56
(John Gallagher) *t.k.h: led and sn wl clr: rdn and hdd over 1f out: 3rd and btn 1f out: kpt on same pce: lost 3rd last strides* **9/1**

6042 **5** *2* **Tulip Dress**[11] 6345 4-9-4 **63** ........ RyanTate 9 52
(Anthony Carson) *stdd after s: hld up off the pce in last pair: effrt over 2f out: styd on same pce ins fnl f: nvr trbld ldrs* **3/1**[1]

1523 **6** *1 ¼* **Zavikon**[18] 6097 3-9-4 **67** ........ PatCosgrave 10 51
(Richard Hughes) *stdd after s: hld up off the pce in last pair: shkn up over 1f out: no imp fnl f: nvr trbld ldrs* **7/2**[2]

30-5 **7** *11* **German Whip**[14] 6263 4-9-7 **69** ........ HectorCrouch(3) 2 26
(Gary Moore) *hld up off the pce in midfield: rdn over 2f out: no imp and dropped to last over 1f out: eased towards fin* **10/1**

1m 24.15s (1.05) **Going Correction** +0.30s/f (Good)
**WFA** 3 from 4yo+ 4lb 7 Ran SP% **113.4**
Speed ratings (Par 103): **106,99,98,97,95 93,81**
CSF £19.19 CT £192.00 TOTE £3.80: £1.50, £2.80; EX 21.70 Trifecta £276.60.
**Owner** The Long Furlong **Bred** Miss Hilary Mullen **Trained** Findon, W Sussex

**FOCUS**
Race distance increased by 4yds. A fair handicap won by a course regular.

## 6754 SANTA FUN RUN 25 NOVEMBER AMATEUR RIDERS' H'CAP 1m 1f 207y
**5:30** (5:31) (Class 6) (0-60,59) 3-Y-0+ **£2,183** (£677; £338; £169) **Stalls** High

Form RPR

6532 **1** **Edge (IRE)**[12] 6306 6-10-12 **50** ........(b) MissSBrotherton 3 58
(Bernard Llewellyn) *t.k.h: hld up wl in tch: clsd to trck ldrs and nt clr run ent fnl 2f: clsd to join ldr ent fnl f: urged along to ld last strides* **6/4**[1]

-035 **2** *hd* **Oceanus (IRE)**[105] 2903 3-11-0 **58** ........ MrRBirkett 1 65
(Julia Feilden) *t.k.h: led for 2f: styd trcking ldrs: nt clr run 2f out: gap opened and rdn and qcknd to ld over 1f out: jnd ent fnl f: drvn and kpt on: hdd last strides* **9/2**[3]

3000 **3** *4 ½* **Jazri**[12] 6305 6-10-3 **46** ........(p) MrWillPettis(5) 8 43
(Milton Bradley) *stdd s: t.k.h: hld up in tch in rr: swtchd rt and effrt over 2f out: no imp tl styd on to pass btn horses ins fnl f: no threat to ldng pair* **14/1**

050 **4** *½* **Dancing Dragon (IRE)**[28] 5722 3-10-12 **56** ........ MrSWalker 4 53
(George Baker) *t.k.h: hld up wl in tch: effrt over 2f out: no imp u.p over 1f out: kpt on same pce ins fnl f* **7/2**[2]

6003 **5** *3 ½* **Master Of Heaven**[4] 6621 4-10-8 **53** ........(p) MissSStevens(7) 6 42
(Jim Boyle) *t.k.h: chsd ldr after 1f tl led 8f out: hdd over 1f out: rdn and outpcd over 1f out: wknd ins fnl f* **15/2**

4604 **6** *hd* **Knight Of The Air**[8] 6475 5-10-10 **55** ........(t) MrsCPownall(7) 7 44
(Joseph Tuite) *chsd ldrs: wnt 2nd 7f out tl led over 4f out: hdd over 1f out: unable qck and wknd ins fnl f* **8/1**

0030 **7** *3 ½* **My Lord**[192] 893 9-11-2 **59** ........ MissMBryant(5) 2 41
(Paddy Butler) *t.k.h: chsd ldr for 1f: styd chsng ldrs: rdn 2f out: lost pl over 1f out: wknd ins fnl f* **50/1**

2m 13.7s (10.10) **Going Correction** +0.30s/f (Good)
**WFA** 3 from 4yo+ 6lb 7 Ran SP% **111.9**
Speed ratings (Par 101): **71,70,67,66,64 63,61**
CSF £8.14 CT £63.46 TOTE £2.00: £1.60, £2.20; EX 9.00 Trifecta £47.20.
**Owner** D Maddocks & Partner **Bred** Swordlestown Stud **Trained** Fochriw, Caerphilly
■ Stewards' Enquiry : Mrs C Pownall caution: failed to take all reasonable and permissible measures to obtain the best possible placing

**FOCUS**
Race distance increased by 4yds. They kept far side in this weak handicap for amateur riders and went just an ordinary pace. The winner has been rated in line with recent form.
T/Plt: £86.40 to a £1 stake. Pool: £74,852.78 - 631.90 winning units. T/Qpdt: £14.70 to a £1 stake. Pool: £3,798.82 - 191.18 winning units. **Steve Payne**

# 6559 RIPON (R-H)
### Monday, September 4

**OFFICIAL GOING: Good to firm (good in places; 8.3)**
Wind: light half behind Weather: overcast

## 6755 THEAKSTONS POP-UP BEER FESTIVAL 30TH SEPTEMBER MAIDEN STKS 5f
**2:10** (2:13) (Class 5) 2-Y-O **£3,557** (£1,058; £529; £264) **Stalls** High

Form RPR

242 **1** **Mokaatil**[24] 5891 2-9-5 96 ........ JimCrowley 5 86+
(Owen Burrows) *trckd ldrs: pushed along to ld ent fnl f: rdn out fnl 110yds* **2/5**[1]

02 **2** *1 ¾* **Harrogate (IRE)**[14] 6264 2-9-5 0 ........ DanielTudhope 10 76
(James Bethell) *led: rdn 2f out: hdd ent fnl f: one pce fnl 110yds* **11/4**[2]

52 **3** *1 ½* **Biddy Brady (USA)**[19] 6055 2-9-0 0 ........ DavidAllan 6 66
(Tim Easterby) *prom: pushed along and outpcd 2f out: kpt on ins fnl f* **11/2**[3]

05 **4** *6* **Gorse (IRE)**[9] 6432 2-9-5 0 ........ ShaneGray 4 49+
(Ann Duffield) *sltly awkward s: midfield: rdn 2f out: one pce and nvr threatened ldng trio* **14/1**

44 **5** *shd* **Call Dawn**[18] 6086 2-8-7 0 ........ HarrisonShaw(7) 8 44
(Michael Easterby) *hld up: pushed along over 2f out: one pce and nvr threatened* **22/1**

00 **6** *1 ½* **Siena Flyer (IRE)**[18] 6086 2-9-0 0 ........ JackGarritty 1 38
(Jedd O'Keeffe) *hld up: nvr threatened* **66/1**

00 **7** *7* **Tea Rattle**[54] 4740 2-8-7 0 ........ RPWalsh(7) 2 13
(Scott Dixon) *dwlt: sn in tch: rdn over 2f out: edgd lft over 1f out and wknd* **66/1**

60 **8** *1 ½* **Sabellum (IRE)**[18] 6086 2-9-0 0 ........ PaulHanagan 3 8
(Richard Fahey) *hld up: rdn along 3f out: sn btn* **33/1**

58.53s (-1.47) **Going Correction** -0.175s/f (Firm) 8 Ran SP% **130.4**
Speed ratings (Par 95): **104,101,98,89,89 86,75,73**
CSF £2.35 TOTE £1.30: £1.10, £1.10, £1.50; EX 2.30 Trifecta £4.30.
**Owner** Hamdan Al Maktoum **Bred** Biddestone Stud **Trained** Lambourn, Berks

**FOCUS**
The watered ground (2mm overnight Thursday and 4mm overnight Friday into Saturday) was given as good to firm, good in places (GoingStick: 8.3). The rail on the bend from the back straight to the home straight was dolled out 3yds, adding 6yds to races on the round course. This proved fairly straightforward for the odds-on favourite who didn't need to run to his mark to win.

## 6756 SIS CELEBRATING 30 YEARS IN RACING NURSERY H'CAP 5f
**2:40** (2:40) (Class 5) (0-75,78) 2-Y-O **£3,557** (£1,058; £529; £264) **Stalls** High

Form RPR

4305 **1** **Life For Rent**[6] 6547 2-8-13 **66** ........ DavidAllan 7 68
(Tim Easterby) *mde all: pressed for ld fr early stage: rdn 2f out: kpt on* **7/2**[2]

3333 **2** *nk* **Qaaraat**[11] 6338 2-9-7 **74** ........ JimCrowley 8 77
(Ed Dunlop) *trckd ldrs: pushed along whn n.m.r appr fnl f: swtchd rt ins fnl f: nt in clr tl fnl 50yds: kpt on wl* **9/2**[3]

0046 **3** *nk* **Daffy Jane**[42] 5210 2-8-7 **60** ........ SilvestreDeSousa 2 60
(Nigel Tinkler) *in tch on outer: rdn over 2f out: hdwy over 1f out: kpt on fnl f* **11/1**

203 **4** *nk* **Undercover Brother**[19] 6055 2-9-6 **73** ........ DanielTudhope 1 72
(David O'Meara) *pressed ldr: rdn 2f out: kpt on same pce fnl f* **13/2**

3021 **5** *3* **Porchy Party (IRE)**[6] 6547 2-9-6 **78** 6ex........................(p) JaneElliott(5) 4 66
(Tom Dascombe) *prom: rdn 2f out: edgd lft appr fnl f: wknd fnl 75yds* **3/1**[1]

6423 **6** *2* **Seen The Lyte (IRE)**[17] 6128 2-9-0 **67**........................ JasonHart 5 48
(John Quinn) *hld up in tch: racd keenly: pushed along whn bit short of room appr fnl f: wknd ins fnl f* **9/2**[3]

0020 **7** *2 1/2* **Bahuta Acha**[107] 2816 2-8-13 **66**........................ SamJames 3 38
(David Loughnane) *squeezed out s: a towards rr* **22/1**

3256 **8** *1* **Donny Belle**[46] 5057 2-9-2 **69**........................ TomEaves 6 37+
(David Brown) *pressed ldr: rdn 2f out: already lost pl whn short of room appr fnl f: wknd* **25/1**

59.29s (-0.71) **Going Correction** -0.175s/f (Firm) **8** Ran SP% **113.4**
Speed ratings (Par 95): **98,97,97,96,91 88,84,82**
CSF £19.31 CT £155.33 TOTE £4.60: £1.20, £2.40, £2.30; EX 21.70 Trifecta £226.00.
**Owner** Reality Partnerships **Bred** Habton Farms **Trained** Great Habton, N Yorks

**FOCUS**
There was a bunched finish to this modest nursery.

## 6757 FOLLOW @RIPONRACES ON TWITTER H'CAP — 1m 4f 10y
**3:10** (3:10) (Class 4) (0-80,81) 3-Y-O+ **£5,175** (£1,540; £769; £384) **Stalls** Centre

Form RPR

212 **1** **Zack Mayo**[28] 5706 3-9-1 **77**........................ SilvestreDeSousa 3 90+
(Philip McBride) *prom: led over 8f out: pushed clr over 2f out: rdn over 1f out: kpt on: comf* **6/5**[1]

4043 **2** *3 3/4* **Busy Street**[25] 5830 5-9-8 **76**........................ BenCurtis 8 81
(Sally Haynes) *trckd ldr: rdn over 3f out: styd on but no ch wnr* **12/1**

1640 **3** *3/4* **Redicean**[9] 6445 3-9-5 **81**........................ DanielTudhope 9 86
(David O'Meara) *trckd ldrs: rdn over 3f out: kpt on same pce* **4/1**[2]

0255 **4** *1/2* **Theos Lolly (IRE)**[15] 6232 4-9-3 **78**........................ ConnorMurtagh(7) 6 81
(Richard Fahey) *led: hdd over 8f out: trckd ldr: rdn 3f out: plugged on* **12/1**

3352 **5** *2 1/4* **Sellingallthetime (IRE)**[17] 6126 6-9-4 **72**........................(p) PaulHanagan 1 72
(Michael Appleby) *trckd ldrs: short of room and shuffled to midfield over 6f out: rdn over 3f out: hung rt: plugged on* **10/1**

2164 **6** *1/2* **King's Coinage (IRE)**[16] 6210 3-8-11 **73**........................(h) JamesSullivan 5 73
(Ruth Carr) *hld up: rdn along 3f out: sme hdwy 2f out: one pce and nvr threatened* **15/2**[3]

655 **7** *1/2* **Itlaaq**[27] 5737 11-8-10 **71**........................(tp) RyanTimby(7) 10 69
(Michael Easterby) *midfield on outside: hdwy and chsd ldrs 4f out: rdn over 3f out: wknd over 1f out* **50/1**

1163 **8** *1/2* **Tapis Libre**[12] 6317 9-9-5 **80**........................ HarrisonShaw(7) 11 77
(Jacqueline Coward) *a towards rr* **25/1**

00 **9** *nse* **Up Ten Down Two (IRE)**[24] 5872 8-8-10 **67**........ RachelRichardson(3) 7 64
(Michael Easterby) *hld up in rr: pushed along 3f out: sme hdwy over 1f out: short of room ins fnl f* **66/1**

023 **10** *1 3/4* **Tamayuz Magic (IRE)**[30] 5667 6-9-11 **79**........................ CamHardie 4 73
(Michael Easterby) *midfield: rdn over 3f out: wknd over 1f out* **14/1**

0035 **11** *7* **Dutch Artist (IRE)**[32] 5578 5-9-1 **72**........................ JoshDoyle(3) 2 55
(Alan Brown) *dwlt: midfield on inner: rdn 3f out: wknd over 1f out* **50/1**

2m 35.32s (-1.38) **Going Correction** +0.025s/f (Good)
**WFA** 3 from 4yo+ 8lb **11** Ran SP% **117.6**
Speed ratings (Par 105): **105,102,102,101,100 99,99,99,99,97 93**
CSF £17.35 CT £48.09 TOTE £2.00: £1.10, £3.20, £1.90; EX 15.70 Trifecta £60.50.
**Owner** Mrs Sarah Hamilton & Chris Budgett 1 **Bred** Mrs S Hamilton & Kirtlington Stud Ltd **Trained** Newmarket, Suffolk

**FOCUS**
Race distance increased by 6yds. They went steady early and few got into it. The placed horses set the standard.

## 6758 DAVID CHAPMAN MEMORIAL H'CAP — 5f
**3:40** (3:40) (Class 3) (0-95,93) 3-Y-O+ **£7,762** (£2,310; £1,154; £577) **Stalls** High

Form RPR

0151 **1** **Tarboosh**[12] 6314 4-9-4 **87**........................ PaulMulrennan 8 96
(Paul Midgley) *trckd ldrs: racd keenly: pushed along and angled rt appr fnl f: rdn and kpt on wl: led 25yds out* **9/2**[2]

1121 **2** *1/2* **Muatadel**[19] 6062 4-8-10 **79**........................ TonyHamilton 6 86
(Roger Fell) *prom: rdn 2f out: led ins fnl f: kpt on but hdd 25yds out* **6/1**

1422 **3** *nk* **Arzaak (IRE)**[26] 5811 3-9-1 **85**........................(b) SilvestreDeSousa 2 91
(Chris Dwyer) *chsd ldrs: rdn 2f out: ev ch ins fnl f: kpt on* **11/2**[3]

4005 **4** *1 3/4* **Stanghow**[9] 6412 5-9-2 **85**........................ CamHardie 7 85
(Antony Brittain) *led: pushed along over 2f out: rdn over 1f out: hdd ins fnl f: no ex* **7/1**

0135 **5** *nse* **Silvanus (IRE)**[9] 6411 12-8-10 **79**........................ GrahamLee 3 79
(Paul Midgley) *hld up in rr: rdn along 2f out: kpt on ins fnl f: nrst fin* **22/1**

0001 **6** *1/2* **Excessable**[52] 4867 4-9-5 **91**........................ RachelRichardson(3) 9 89
(Tim Easterby) *trckd ldrs: rdn 2f out: hung rt and one pce ins fnl f* **8/1**

440 **7** *hd* **Olivia Fallow (IRE)**[14] 6267 5-8-8 **77**........................ JoeDoyle 4 74
(Paul Midgley) *chsd ldrs: rdn 2f out: one pce* **12/1**

4416 **8** *1 1/4* **Lexington Place**[12] 6314 7-8-5 **74**........................ JamesSullivan 1 67
(Ruth Carr) *hld up towards outer: rdn over 2f out: one pce and nvr threatened* **16/1**

312- **9** *7* **Aleef (IRE)**[287] 8050 4-9-10 **93**........................(h) DanielTudhope 5 60
(David O'Meara) *dwlt sltly and bmpd s: hld up in rr: rdn 2f out: sn wknd and bhd* **10/3**[1]

58.23s (-1.77) **Going Correction** -0.175s/f (Firm)
**WFA** 3 from 4yo+ 1lb **9** Ran SP% **112.5**
Speed ratings (Par 107): **107,106,105,102,102 102,101,99,88**
CSF £30.57 CT £150.22 TOTE £5.30: £2.00, £1.90, £1.80; EX 30.30 Trifecta £167.60.
**Owner** The Guys & Dolls & Sandfield Racing **Bred** Landmark Racing Limited **Trained** Westow, N Yorks

**FOCUS**
The first two are improvers and the third is as consistent as they come, so this is solid form for the grade.

## 6759 SIS TRADING SERVICES FILLIES' H'CAP — 6f
**4:10** (4:11) (Class 4) (0-85,86) 3-Y-O+ **£5,175** (£1,540; £769; £384) **Stalls** High

Form RPR

0400 **1** **Hope Solo (IRE)**[25] 5828 3-9-4 **79**........................(p1) DanielTudhope 8 89
(Tim Easterby) *mde all: pushed clr over 1f out: kpt on: comf* **10/1**

2261 **2** *2 3/4* **Pepita (IRE)**[22] 5965 3-9-8 **83**........................ AndreaAtzeni 4 83
(Richard Hannon) *hld up in tch: rdn over 2f out: hdwy over 1f out: kpt on same pce: wnt 2nd post* **2/1**[1]

0240 **3** *nse* **Rose Marmara**[15] 6237 4-8-11 **70**........................(t) JamesSullivan 5 70
(Brian Rothwell) *chsd ldr: rdn over 2f out: one pce: lost 2nd post* **10/1**

3-40 **4** *3* **Mistime (IRE)**[10] 6382 3-9-5 **80**........................ PJMcDonald 2 70
(Mark Johnston) *chsd ldrs on outer: rdn over 2f out: wknd over 1f out* **7/1**[3]

3140 **5** *4 1/2* **Rose Berry**[38] 5355 3-9-8 **83**........................(h) SilvestreDeSousa 3 59
(Chris Dwyer) *hld up: rdn over 2f out: wknd over 1f out* **3/1**[2]

232- **6** *1 1/2* **Thankyou Stars**[370] 6003 4-9-2 **75**........................ JackGarritty 7 46
(Jonathan Portman) *in tch: rdn over 2f out: wknd over 1f out* **33/1**

1m 11.52s (-1.48) **Going Correction** -0.175s/f (Firm)
**WFA** 3 from 4yo 2lb **6** Ran SP% **92.0**
Speed ratings (Par 102): **102,98,98,94,88 86**
Perfect Madge was withdrawn. Price at time of withdrawal 7-2. Rule 4 applies to all bets - deduction 20p in the pound. CSF £20.08 CT £94.67 TOTE £9.10: £3.90, £1.10; EX 21.80 Trifecta £111.90.
**Owner** Clipper Logistics **Bred** Old Long Hill Ballinteskin Stud Ltd **Trained** Great Habton, N Yorks

**FOCUS**
One-way traffic here, as the winner controlled the pace throughout and was always in command. She has been rated back to her best.

## 6760 SIS TRUSTED DELIVERY PARTNER MAIDEN STKS — 1m 1f 170y
**4:40** (4:40) (Class 5) 3-4-Y-O **£3,557** (£1,058; £529; £264) **Stalls** Low

Form RPR

54 **1** **Ludorum (IRE)**[15] 6236 3-9-5 0........................ PaulHanagan 1 66+
(Richard Fahey) *trckd ldrs: pushed along over 2f out: briefly n.m.r over 1f out: squeezed through gap to chal ins fnl f: rdn and kpt on: led towards fin* **11/4**[2]

25 **2** *1/2* **Gakku**[102] 3006 3-9-0 0........................(b1) AndreaAtzeni 3 60+
(Roger Varian) *dwlt: hld up in tch: hdwy and trckd ldrs over 3f out: rdn over 2f out: led 1f out: one pce and hdd towards fin* **1/3**[1]

0320 **3** *6* **Medici Moon**[27] 5761 3-9-5 52........................ DavidAllan 4 53
(Scott Dixon) *led: hung lft and rn wd on bhd 5f out: rdn 3f out: hdd 1f out: wknd* **40/1**

44 **4** *2 3/4* **Royal Headley (IRE)**[128] 2143 3-9-2 0........................ JoshDoyle(3) 2 47
(David O'Meara) *trckd ldrs: rdn to chal 2f out: wknd fnl f* **12/1**[3]

6 **5** *34* **The Foozler**[17] 6129 4-9-11 0........................ TomEaves 5
(Peter Niven) *prom: rdn over 3f out: wknd over 2f out: sn t.o* **100/1**

2m 6.38s (0.98) **Going Correction** +0.025s/f (Good)
**WFA** 3 from 4yo 6lb **5** Ran SP% **112.8**
Speed ratings (Par 103): **97,96,91,89,62**
CSF £4.16 TOTE £4.30: £1.40, £1.10; EX 4.80 Trifecta £15.20.
**Owner** Highclere Thoroughbred Racing - Lord Byron **Bred** Mount Coote Stud **Trained** Musley Bank, N Yorks

**FOCUS**
Race distance increased by 6yds. A weak maiden in which they went steady early and it developed into a bit of a dash inside the final 3f.
T/Jkpt: Not won. T/Plt: £12.60 to a £1 stake. Pool: £83,973.68 - 4829.65 winning units. T/Qpdt: £4.10 to a £1 stake. Pool: £5,403.75 - 958.21 winning units. **Andrew Sheret**

# 6438 WINDSOR (R-H)
Monday, September 4

**OFFICIAL GOING: Good to soft (6.8)**
Wind: Almost nil Weather: Overcast becoming fine, quite humid

## 6761 BATEAUX WINDSOR NOVICE STKS (PLUS 10 RACE) — 6f 12y
**1:50** (1:50) (Class 4) 2-Y-O **£3,946** (£1,174; £586; £293) **Stalls** Low

Form RPR

33 **1** **Take Me With You (USA)**[73] 4028 2-8-11 0........................ JamieSpencer 10 96+
(Jeremy Noseda) *mde all: tk field to far side fr 1/2-way: sn clr: pushed out* **4/11**[1]

6 **2** *9* **Sergio Leone (IRE)**[24] 5887 2-9-2 0........................ SeanLevey 11 71
(Richard Hannon) *a in 2nd: drew clr of rest fr 2f out but easily lft bhd by wnr* **5/1**[2]

**3** *5* **Despacito** 2-8-6 0........................ JennyPowell(5) 6 51
(Brendan Powell) *in tch: outpcd fr 1/2-way: no ch after: plugged on* **100/1**

05 **4** *1 1/2* **Motown Mick (IRE)**[45] 5105 2-9-2 0........................ TomMarquand 3 52
(Richard Hannon) *hld up in tch: outpcd fr 1/2-way: no ch after* **16/1**

6 **5** *2* **Authentic Art**[33] 5531 2-9-2 0........................ FranBerry 8 46
(Ralph Beckett) *dwlt: pushed along to stay in tch bef 1/2-way: sn lft bhd* **16/1**

1 **6** *nk* **Greeneyedafghan**[32] 5561 2-9-5 0........................ MartinDwyer 1 48
(William Muir) *chsd ldrs: outpcd fr 1/2-way: steadily fdd* **9/1**[3]

0 **7** *1/2* **Best Company (IRE)**[18] 6108 2-8-13 0........................ JackDuern(3) 2 43
(Dean Ivory) *mostly in last: struggling bef 1/2-way* **125/1**

1m 13.82s (0.82) **Going Correction** +0.425s/f (Yiel) **7** Ran SP% **113.5**
Speed ratings (Par 97): **111,99,92,90,87 87,86**
CSF £2.62 TOTE £1.30: £1.10, £2.30; EX 2.90 Trifecta £79.80.
**Owner** Phoenix Thoroughbred Limited **Bred** Mane Chance Llc **Trained** Newmarket, Suffolk

**FOCUS**
More than 11mm of rain overnight turned the ground soft. A fair novice, with the heavy odds-on favourite winning as she pleased. They headed far side in the straight.

## 6762 CALL STAR SPORTS ON 08000 521 321 NURSERY H'CAP — 1m 31y
**2:20** (2:20) (Class 5) (0-75,76) 2-Y-O **£2,911** (£866; £432; £216) **Stalls** Low

Form RPR

235 **1** **Simpson (IRE)**[53] 4805 2-9-10 **76**........................ JamieSpencer 6 81+
(Ed Walker) *trckd ldng pair: stl gng easily 2f out: produced to ld jst ins fnl f: sn drvn and kpt on* **9/4**[2]

2411 **2** *1* **Go Now Go Now (IRE)**[18] 6087 2-9-6 **72**........................ FrannyNorton 2 74
(Mark Johnston) *led after 1f: rdn over 2f out: hdd jst ins fnl f: kpt on* **2/1**[1]

5146 **3** *nse* **Shazzab (IRE)**[24] 5875 2-9-1 **70**........................(p1) AdamMcNamara(3) 1 72
(Richard Fahey) *chsd ldng trio: pushed along bef 1/2-way: drvn to cl 2f out: tried to chal 1f out: kpt on and nrly snatched 2nd* **6/1**[3]

500 **4** *3* **Rustang (FR)**[17] 6133 2-9-1 **67**........................(h1) ShaneKelly 7 62
(Richard Hughes) *hld up in detached last: urged along 3f out: limited rspnse but passed two rivals fr over 1f out* **16/1**

0642 **5** *1 1/4* **Bombshell Bay**[20] 6022 2-8-12 **64**........................ SeanLevey 3 56
(Richard Hannon) *led 1f: pressed ldr: upsides 3f out: drvn and steadily fdd jst over 2f out* **13/2**

2255 **6** *3 3/4* **The Love Doctor (IRE)**[27] 5742 2-9-3 **69**........................ JamesDoyle 4 53
(David Evans) *pushed along in 5th by 1/2-way: struggling over 2f out: sn btn* **13/2**

1m 46.87s (2.17) **Going Correction** +0.425s/f (Yiel) **6** Ran SP% **110.9**
Speed ratings (Par 95): **106,105,104,101,100 96**
CSF £6.98 TOTE £2.60: £2.30, £1.40; EX 8.10 Trifecta £30.20.
**Owner** R A Pegum **Bred** Irish National Stud **Trained** Upper Lambourn, Berks

**FOCUS**
A fair nursery, they again headed far side in the straight.

## 6763 STARSPORTSBET.CO.UK H'CAP 1m 3f 99y
2:50 (2:55) (Class 5) (0-75,76) 3-Y-O+ £2,975 (£885; £442; £221) Stalls Centre

Form RPR
455 1 **Romanor**[32] 5559 3-9-4 **76**....(h) JamieSpencer 2 83
(Ed Walker) *hld up in last: effrt and swift prog wl over 1f out: hrd rdn to chal ins fnl f: led last strides* 7/2[2]
-423 2 hd **Lester Kris (IRE)**[94] 3286 3-9-2 **74**.... TomMarquand 3 80
(Richard Hannon) *led 5f: led again over 4f out but pressed after: styd in centre fr 3f out: drvn 2f out: kpt on wl but hdd last strides* 6/1
0001 3 1 1/4 **Essenaitch (IRE)**[14] 6273 4-9-5 **70**.... FranBerry 1 74
(David Evans) *t.k.h: cl up: rdn to join ldr 2f out: stl upsides ins fnl f: no ex last 100yds* 11/2[3]
02 4 2 **Milky Way (IRE)**[53] 4804 5-9-9 **74**.... ShaneKelly 6 74
(Gary Moore) *trckd ldrs: rdn 3f out: kpt on and stl in tch over 1f out: one pce after* 2/1[1]
4-50 5 1 3/4 **Warrior Prince**[39] 5313 4-9-6 **71**.... JamesDoyle 4 69
(Ed Dunlop) *hld up in 5th: shkn up over 2f out: no prog over 1f out: fdd* 10/1
0040 6 nse **House Of Commons (IRE)**[30] 5664 4-9-5 **70**.... LukeMorris 7 67
(Michael Appleby) *t.k.h: pressed ldr: led after 5f to over 4f out: w ldr after to 2f out: steadily wknd u.p* 8/1
05-0 7 2 1/4 **Bazooka (IRE)**[191] 47 6-9-4 **69**.... DavidProbert 5 63
(David Flood) *rn wout one shoe: hld up in 6th: taken to far rail and drvn over 2f out: no prog and wknd over 1f out* 20/1

2m 34.39s (4.89) **Going Correction** +0.425s/f (Yiel)
**WFA** 3 from 4yo+ 7lb 7 Ran SP% **110.2**
Speed ratings (Par 103): **99,98,97,96,95 95,93**
CSF £22.60 TOTE £4.20: £1.90, £2.60; EX 22.90 Trifecta £100.80.
**Owner** P K Siu **Bred** Bba 2010 Ltd **Trained** Upper Lambourn, Berks

**FOCUS**
Run at a crawl, they headed far side again and it was the two 3yos who came out best. The race has been rated around the third.

## 6764 FOLLOW US ON TWITTER @STARSPORTS_BET H'CAP 5f 21y
3:20 (3:22) (Class 4) (0-80,80) 3-Y-O+ £4,690 (£1,395; £697; £348) Stalls Low

Form RPR
2141 1 **Vimy Ridge**[22] 5967 5-9-0 **78**....(t) JoshuaBryan(5) 1 89
(Alan Bailey) *trckd ldng pair: easily clsd fr 2f out to ld over 1f out: pushed out: comf* 5/4[1]
0302 2 2 **Monumental Man**[13] 6278 8-8-13 **77**....(p) PaddyBradley(5) 2 80
(Michael Attwater) *led 100yds: chsd ldr: clsng to chal whn wnr eased past over 1f out: vain chse after* 8/1
0323 3 2 1/4 **Wiley Post**[22] 5967 4-8-12 **71**....(b) DavidProbert 4 66
(Tony Carroll) *pushed along in last after 2f and struggling to stay in tch: kpt on u.p fr over 1f out: n.d* 11/4[2]
6401 4 1 1/4 **Waseem Faris (IRE)**[19] 6072 8-9-7 **80**.... PatDobbs 9 70
(Ken Cunningham-Brown) *hld up in 4th: cajoled along 2f out: no prog then or whn rdn over 1f out* 4/1[3]
-360 5 7 **Shackled N Drawn (USA)**[14] 6276 5-8-11 **70**.... TomMarquand 6 35
(Peter Hedger) *dwlt: tk fierce hold: led after 100yds and sn clr: hdd & wknd rapidly over 1f out* 12/1

1m 2.0s (1.70) **Going Correction** +0.425s/f (Yiel)
**WFA** 3 from 4yo+ 1lb 5 Ran SP% **109.9**
Speed ratings (Par 105): **103,99,96,94,83**
CSF £11.60 TOTE £1.80: £1.10, £3.30; EX 10.30 Trifecta £23.30.
**Owner** Dr S P Hargreaves **Bred** Mrs Sheila Oakes **Trained** Newmarket, Suffolk

**FOCUS**
Four of the nine originally declared runners came out and the in-form favourite won readily. They raced centre-field this time.

## 6765 CALL STAR SPREADS ON 0808 234 9709 MAIDEN STKS 1m 3f 99y
3:50 (3:53) (Class 5) 3-Y-O £2,975 (£885; £442; £221) Stalls Centre

Form RPR
1 **Royal Line** 3-9-5 0.... JamesDoyle 1 90+
(John Gosden) *dwlt: rn green in last: nudged along fr 5f out: suddenly picked up and clsd qckly over 2f out to ld over 1f out: cruised clr* 4/6[1]
6 2 2 3/4 **Lazarus (IRE)**[27] 5757 3-9-5 0....(t) JamieSpencer 7 76
(Amy Murphy) *in tch in rr: outpcd and dropped to last over 2f out: rallied over 1f out: shkn up and styd on to take 2nd nr fin* 33/1
0542 3 1/2 **Saniyaat**[20] 6044 3-9-0 75....(v) LukeMorris 6 70
(George Peckham) *t.k.h: trckd ldr: disp ld briefly wl over 1f out: sn outpcd by wnr u.p: lost 2nd nr fin* 11/2[3]
0 4 nk **Towie (IRE)**[16] 6194 3-9-5 0.... SeanLevey 2 74
(Hughie Morrison) *trckd ldr: disp ld briefly wl over 1f out: sn outpcd: one pce after* 5/1[2]
2243 5 2 1/2 **Steaming (IRE)**[32] 5563 3-9-5 77.... PatDobbs 5 70
(Ralph Beckett) *hld up in tch: shkn up and cl up 2f out: rdn and wknd over 1f out* 8/1
00 6 6 **Kirkland Forever**[16] 6194 3-9-0 0.... FranBerry 4 55
(Brendan Powell) *led to wl over 1f out: wknd qckly* 50/1

2m 38.27s (8.77) **Going Correction** +0.425s/f (Yiel) 6 Ran SP% **108.1**
Speed ratings (Par 101): **85,83,82,82,80 76**
CSF £23.40 TOTE £1.40: £1.10, £9.50; EX 20.00 Trifecta £41.10.
**Owner** HH Sheikha Al Jalila Racing **Bred** Darley **Trained** Newmarket, Suffolk

**FOCUS**
An ordinary maiden, but a winner of significant potential.

## 6766 STARSPREADS.COM H'CAP (DIV I) 1m 2f
4:20 (4:23) (Class 5) (0-70,71) 3-Y-O £2,975 (£885; £442; £221) Stalls Centre

Form RPR
-243 1 **Crushed (IRE)**[27] 5753 3-9-2 **70**.... GeorgiaCox(5) 10 80+
(William Haggas) *led after 2f and mde most fr then on: pushed along over 3f out: jnd and carried lft wl over 2f out: rdn to assert wl over 1f out: styd on wl* 2/1[1]
1200 2 2 1/2 **Ingleby Mackenzie**[13] 6291 3-8-12 **64**.... AdamMcNamara(3) 9 68
(Mick Channon) *trckd ldrs: chal over 3f out: rdn in 3rd after: no imp 2f out: styd on over 1f out to take 2nd ins fnl f: no threat to wnr* 14/1
6654 3 2 1/2 **Broughtons Knight**[13] 6293 3-8-12 **61**....(p1) JamieSpencer 2 60
(Henry Spiller) *hld up: prog to trck ldrs after 4f: hdwy to join wnr jst over 3f out and then steered lft towards far rail: rdn and no rspnse 2f out: hld after and lost 2nd ins fnl f* 5/1[2]
213 4 1 3/4 **Flood Defence (IRE)**[38] 5359 3-9-0 **66**.... GeorgeWood(3) 3 62
(Chris Wall) *hld up in last pair: struggling and detached over 3f out: n.d after but kpt on fr over 1f out to snatch 4th last strides* 5/1[2]
2241 5 nk **Sandy Shores**[9] 6439 3-9-6 **69**....(b) TomMarquand 4 64
(Brian Meehan) *t.k.h: hld up: rdn 3f out: one pce and nvr able to threaten ldrs* 11/2[3]
3600 6 hd **Miss M (IRE)**[31] 5591 3-8-9 **58**.... MartinDwyer 5 53
(William Muir) *hld up: rdn 3f out: one pce and nvr able to threaten ldrs* 50/1
0624 7 4 1/2 **Evening Hill**[42] 5218 3-9-8 **71**....(p1) ShaneKelly 7 57
(Richard Hughes) *t.k.h: led 2f: chsd wnr to over 3f out: wknd* 5/1[2]
20-6 8 40 **Lucky Esteem**[28] 5712 3-9-4 **67**....(t) FranBerry 6
(Neil Mulholland) *cl up tl wknd qckly over 3f out: bhd and eased 2f out: t.o* 20/1

2m 12.44s (3.74) **Going Correction** +0.425s/f (Yiel) 8 Ran SP% **112.1**
Speed ratings (Par 101): **102,100,98,96,96 96,92,60**
CSF £31.89 CT £121.99 TOTE £2.80: £1.40, £3.20, £1.40; EX 28.20 Trifecta £137.10.
**Owner** B Haggas **Bred** J Manogue **Trained** Newmarket, Suffolk

**FOCUS**
Division one of a modest handicap rated around the second, but a winner with the potential to do better. They headed far side in the straight.

## 6767 STARSPREADS.COM H'CAP (DIV II) 1m 2f
4:50 (4:51) (Class 5) (0-70,70) 3-Y-O £2,975 (£885; £442; £221) Stalls Centre

Form RPR
-311 1 **Oh It's Saucepot**[25] 5854 3-9-4 **70**.... GeorgeWood(3) 10 84+
(Chris Wall) *hld up: prog and rdn over 3f out: clsd to ld wl over 1f out: styd on strly and drew clr* 3/1[2]
5-65 2 4 1/2 **Poseidon (IRE)**[67] 4267 3-9-6 **69**.... JamieSpencer 4 74
(Ed Walker) *hld up: coaxed along to try to make prog 3f out: drvn 2f out: styd on after to take 2nd last 50yds: no ch w wnr* 10/3[3]
4533 3 3/4 **Time To Sea (IRE)**[17] 6144 3-9-1 **64**.... LiamKeniry 7 68
(John Butler) *racd quite freely: led: stl gng strly over 3f out: rdn and hdd wl over 1f out: no ex and lost 2nd fnl 50yds* 5/1
2322 4 2 1/4 **Prosecution**[13] 6281 3-9-4 **70**....(b1) CharlieBennett(3) 9 69
(Hughie Morrison) *trckd ldrs: wnt 2nd 3f out to 2f out: steadily wknd* 11/4[1]
5044 5 12 **Queen Moon (IRE)**[17] 6139 3-8-4 **60**.... JasonWatson(7) 3 35
(Andrew Balding) *t.k.h: chsd ldr to 3f out: sn wknd* 28/1
0553 6 6 **Broad Appeal**[21] 6006 3-8-7 **61**....(p1) MitchGodwin(5) 1 24
(Jonathan Portman) *hld up: rdn 3f out: no prog and sn btn* 11/1
005 7 33 **Afterburner**[17] 6150 3-9-2 **65**.... JamesDoyle 5
(Hugo Palmer) *chsd ldrs tl wknd qckly over 3f out: eased and t.o* 11/1
6000 8 130 **Moorea**[37] 5409 3-8-7 **56** oh11.... MartinDwyer 6
(John Bridger) *prom 4f: lost pl rapidly and last 5f out: sn t.o: virtually p.u 3f out* 100/1

2m 12.17s (3.47) **Going Correction** +0.425s/f (Yiel) 8 Ran SP% **112.5**
Speed ratings (Par 101): **103,99,98,97,87 82,56,**
CSF £12.99 CT £46.32 TOTE £3.60: £1.40, £1.50, £1.70; EX 14.60 Trifecta £56.20.
**Owner** The Eight Of Diamonds **Bred** Mrs C J Walker **Trained** Newmarket, Suffolk

**FOCUS**
The right horses came to the fore in division two of this handicap. The winner is on the upgrade.

## 6768 FOLLOW US ON TWITTER @STARSPREADS_BET H'CAP 6f 12y
5:20 (5:20) (Class 5) (0-75,75) 3-Y-O £2,975 (£885; £442; £221) Stalls Low

Form RPR
3462 1 **Zebulon (IRE)**[16] 6197 3-9-7 **75**.... SeanLevey 6 82
(Richard Hannon) *trckd ldr: rdn over 2f out: led wl over 1f out: drvn out* 9/4[2]
0443 2 1 1/4 **Kodicat (IRE)**[38] 5375 3-9-1 **69**.... JamieSpencer 2 72
(Kevin Ryan) *sltly awkward s: hld up in last pair: cajoled along to cl 2f out: plld out and drvn to take 2nd fnl f: fnd little and nvr chal wnr* 15/8[1]
0346 3 3 1/4 **Coastal Cyclone**[41] 5253 3-9-5 **73**.... DavidProbert 5 66
(Harry Dunlop) *fast away: led: rdn and hdd wl over 1f out: wknd fnl f* 5/1
31 4 4 1/2 **Kings Academy**[22] 5962 3-8-13 **67**....(t) LukeMorris 1 50
(Paul Cole) *hld up in last pair: urged along 1/2-way: no prog 2f out: sn wknd and eased* 11/4[3]

1m 15.3s (2.30) **Going Correction** +0.425s/f (Yiel) 4 Ran SP% **108.9**
Speed ratings (Par 101): **101,99,95,89**
CSF £6.83 TOTE £2.20; EX 7.70 Trifecta £22.50.
**Owner** Mrs J Wood **Bred** Kevin & Meta Cullen **Trained** East Everleigh, Wilts

**FOCUS**
A modest sprint handicap rated around the second.
T/Plt: £25.90 to a £1 stake. Pool: £68,950.85 - 1939.35 winning units. T/Qpdt: £17.10 to a £1 stake. Pool: £4,381.64 - 189.33 winning units. **Jonathan Neesom**

6769 - 6774a (Foreign Racing) - See Raceform Interactive

# 6472 GOODWOOD (R-H)
## Tuesday, September 5

**OFFICIAL GOING: Good changing to good to soft after race 2 (2.05) changing to soft after race 3 (2.40)**
Wind: medium, across Weather: rain

## 6775 "READ SILVESTRE DE SOUSA AT 188BET" MAIDEN STKS 1m 1f 197y
1:30 (1:31) (Class 5) 3-Y-O+ £4,528 (£1,347; £673; £336) Stalls Low

Form RPR
-343 1 **Red Royalist**[11] 6390 3-9-5 77....(p) MartinDwyer 2 77
(Marcus Tregoning) *trckd ldrs: rdn over 2f out: styd on ins fnl f: led fnl stride* 8/1
333 2 nk **Hats Off To Larry**[10] 6413 3-9-5 75.... CharlesBishop 1 76
(Mick Channon) *tall: swtg: racd keenly: w ldr tl dropped to cl 3rd over 3f out: led over 1f out: sn rdn: kpt on fnl f: hdd fnl stride* 11/2
33 3 1 1/4 **Fearsome**[15] 6277 3-9-5 0.... OisinMurphy 5 74
(Ralph Beckett) *athletic: lw: led: rdn and hdd over 1f out: kpt on same pce fnl f* 5/2[2]
54 4 nk **Ancient Longing**[17] 6194 3-9-0 0.... KieranShoemark 7 68
(Roger Charlton) *trckd ldrs: rdn and ev ch 2f out: kpt on same pce ins fnl f* 15/8[1]
5 5 2 3/4 **Psychotic**[19] 6103 4-9-8 0.... DidierGengoul(3) 6 66+
(David Menuisier) *trckd ldrs: swtchd rt whn nt clr run 3f out: sn rdn: kpt on but nt pce to get on terms* 5/1[3]
0 6 20 **Dance Rock**[20] 2721 4-9-11 0.... RobertWinston 4 26
(Neil Mulholland) *str: s.i.s: last: nvr gng pce to get involved fr 3f out* 25/1

2m 13.42s (5.32) **Going Correction** +0.675s/f (Yiel)
**WFA** 3 from 4yo 6lb 6 Ran SP% **110.4**
Speed ratings (Par 103): **105,104,103,103,101 85**
CSF £47.85 TOTE £7.40: £3.00, £2.40; EX 29.40 Trifecta £64.70.

**Owner** R C C Villers **Bred** J A And M A Knox **Trained** Whitsbury, Hants

**FOCUS**

It was dry overnight, but a showery day. The runners came stands' side in the straight and, of the principals, the winner challenged furthest away from the stands' rail. Just a fair maiden won by the form pick..

## 6776 ROA/RACING POST OWNERS JACKPOT EBF FILLIES' NOVICE STKS (PLUS 10 RACE) 7f

2:05 (2:06) (Class 5) 2-Y-O **£4,528** (£1,347; £673; £336) **Stalls** Low

Form RPR

5 **1** **Juliet Foxtrot**[24] 5938 2-9-0 0 JimCrowley 4 88+
(Charles Hills) *athletic: trckd ldrs: travelling best whn ldng wl over 1f out: pushed clr: easily* **8/11**[1]

06 **2** *7* **Richenza (FR)**[45] 5154 2-9-0 0 PatDobbs 1 71
(Ralph Beckett) *leggy: hld up last pair: hdwy over 2f out: chsd wnr ent fnl f: kpt on but nvr any threat* **8/1**

5 **3** *1* **Rasima**[20] 6064 2-9-0 0 AndreaAtzeni 3 68
(Roger Varian) *cmpt: trckd ldrs: rdn over 2f out: nt pce to chal but styd on nicely to go 3rd ins fnl f* **11/4**[2]

65 **4** *5* **Still Got It**[6] 6583 2-9-0 0 JFEgan 7 56
(Mick Channon) *cmpt: in tch: rdn over 2f out: sn one pce: wnt 4th ins fnl f* **20/1**

0 **5** *½* **Grasmere (IRE)**[14] 6292 2-9-0 0 RobertWinston 5 54
(Alan Bailey) *lengthy: led: rdn and hdd wl over 1f out: wknd ins fnl f* **66/1**

**6** *2* **Midas Maggie** 2-9-0 0 SteveDrowne 6 49
(Charles Hills) *athletic: lw: s.i.s: last pair: rdn over 2f out: nvr threatened: wknd fnl f* **25/1**

00 **7** *hd* **Sunday Best**[27] 5795 2-9-0 0 RobHornby 2 49
(Jonathan Portman) *w'like: trckd ldrs: effrt 2f out: wknd fnl f* **100/1**

32 **8** *6* **Not After Midnight (IRE)**[96] 3244 2-9-0 0 GeorgeDowning 9 34
(Daniel Kubler) *w'like: racd keenly: trckd ldr tl rdn 2f out: sn wknd* **15/2**[3]

1m 30.89s (3.89) **Going Correction** +0.675s/f (Yiel) **8** Ran SP% **118.5**

Speed ratings (Par 92): **104,96,94,89,88 86,86,79**

CSF £7.91 TOTE £1.50: £1.02, £2.00, £1.30; EX 7.50 Trifecta £16.90.

**Owner** K Abdullah **Bred** Juddmonte Farms Ltd **Trained** Lambourn, Berks

**FOCUS**

Add 10yds to race distance. After this race the going was changed to good to soft (from good to soft on the straight course and good on the round course). They came up the middle this time. There didn't seem to be much depth to this fillies' novice, but the winner looked quite good with the race rated around the third.

## 6777 188BET.CO.UK EBF PETER WILLETT MAIDEN STKS (PLUS 10 RACE) (SIRE-RESTRICTED RACE) 1m

2:40 (2:40) (Class 2) 2-Y-O

**£15,562** (£4,660; £2,330; £1,165; £582; £292) **Stalls** Low

Form RPR

**1** **Showroom (FR)** 2-9-5 0 PJMcDonald 2 87+
(Mark Johnston) *lengthy: mde all: qcknd clr over 1f out: quite impressive* **7/2**[1]

35 **2** *5* **Ship Of The Fen**[26] 5840 2-9-5 0 JimCrowley 11 75
(Martyn Meade) *prom: outpcd by wnr over 1f out: sn hld but kpt on wl for 2nd fnl f* **8/1**

0 **3** *1¼* **Knightly Spirit**[18] 6142 2-9-5 0 AndreaAtzeni 3 72
(Roger Varian) *cmpt: hld up towards rr: hdwy 3f out: rdn to chal for hld 2nd over 1f out: kpt on same pce fnl f* **9/2**[3]

**4** *1¼* **Sherzy Boy** 2-9-5 0 SeanLevey 5 70+
(Richard Hannon) *w'like: bit bkwd: mid-div: hdwy 3f out: sn rdn: styd on ins fnl f but nt pce to get involved* **25/1**

06 **5** *1¾* **Berkshire Royal**[24] 5934 2-9-5 0 RobHornby 1 66
(Andrew Balding) *trckd ldrs: rdn over 2f out: sn edgd lft: nt pce to chal: no ex whn lost 4th fnl 100yds* **50/1**

4 **6** *1½* **Mt Augustus**[26] 5840 2-9-5 0 DaneO'Neill 6 62
(Henry Candy) *trckd wnr: rdn jst over 2f out: sn one pce* **4/1**[2]

**7** *nk* **Silver Crescent** 2-9-5 0 PatDobbs 4 62+
(Ralph Beckett) *str: bit bkwd: mid-div: rdn whn outpcd 2f out: n.d after* **12/1**

**8** *2¾* **Gift Of Hera** 2-9-0 0 MartinDwyer 9 51+
(Sylvester Kirk) *str: bit bkwd: s.i.s: rdn over 2f out: a towards rr* **25/1**

62 **9** *3¼* **Great Vizier**[19] 6093 2-9-5 0 CharlesBishop 8 48
(Eve Johnson Houghton) *mid-div: rdn over 2f out: nvr threatened: wknd ent fnl f* **10/1**

4 **10** *9* **Poucor**[19] 6093 2-9-5 0 JFEgan 7 29
(Mick Channon) *w'like: leggy: mid-div: rdn 2f out: wknd over 1f out* **33/1**

**11** *2¾* **Highland Sky (IRE)** 2-9-5 0 JamieSpencer 10 23+
(David Simcock) *str: lw: dwlt: a in rr* **11/2**

1m 43.9s (4.00) **Going Correction** +0.675s/f (Yiel) **11** Ran SP% **116.3**

Speed ratings (Par 101): **107,102,100,99,97 96,95,93,89,80 78**

CSF £30.30 TOTE £4.20: £1.80, £2.40, £1.90; EX 32.80 Trifecta £208.40.

**Owner** Highclere T'Bred Racing- Nick Skelton **Bred** Petra Bloodstock Agency Ltd **Trained** Middleham Moor, N Yorks

**FOCUS**

Add 10yds to race distance. The going changed again after this race to soft (from good to soft). They raced middle to stands' side. A valuable maiden for EBF eligible 2yos sired by a winner over 11.5f or further.

## 6778 DOCKER HUGHES FILLIES' NURSERY H'CAP 6f

3:15 (3:15) (Class 2) 2-Y-O **£12,938** (£3,850; £1,924; £962) **Stalls** High

Form RPR

5660 **1** **Neola**[12] 6354 2-9-7 **89** JFEgan 3 92
(Mick Channon) *hld up in tch: hdwy over 2f out: led ent fnl f: r.o wl: rdn out* **7/2**[1]

011 **2** *¾* **Golden Salute (IRE)**[41] 5270 2-8-11 **79** DavidProbert 8 80
(Andrew Balding) *leggy: athletic: trckd ldr: str chal 2f out: rdn and ev ch ent fnl f: kpt on but no ex towards fin* **9/2**[2]

3331 **3** *½* **Shania Says (IRE)**[22] 6010 2-8-1 **69** FrannyNorton 4 68
(Tony Carroll) *led: rdn whn strly pressed fr 2f out: hdd ent fnl f: kpt on but no ex fnl 75yds* **6/1**

005 **4** *3* **Toomer**[17] 6183 2-7-13 **70** HollieDoyle(3) 6 60
(Richard Hannon) *last pair: rdn and hdwy over 1f out: kpt on to go 4th ins fnl f but nt pce to trble ldrs* **11/2**[3]

4005 **5** *¾* **Campion**[12] 6338 2-8-8 **76** (h[1]) TomMarquand 7 64
(Richard Hannon) *trckd ldrs: rdn 2f out: fdd ins fnl f* **25/1**

4120 **6** *4* **Faithful Promise**[13] 6330 2-8-12 **80** PJMcDonald 1 56
(Mark Johnston) *lw: trckd ldr: rdn 2f out: wknd ins fnl f* **7/2**[1]

054 **7** *¾* **Titchy Digits**[19] 6100 2-8-0 **71** DavidEgan(3) 5 45
(Michael Attwater) *untidily away and squeezed up s: last: sme prog over 2f out: sn rdn: wknd fnl f* **16/1**

410 **8** *2¾* **Armum (IRE)**[74] 4028 2-8-13 **81** (t[1]) AntonioFresu 2 47
(Ed Dunlop) *tk str hold on way to s: hld up in tch: effrt over 2f out: wknd over 1f out* **9/1**

1m 14.21s (2.01) **Going Correction** +0.50s/f (Yiel) **8** Ran SP% **112.0**

Speed ratings (Par 98): **106,105,104,100,99 94,93,89**

CSF £18.47 CT £89.31 TOTE £4.20: £1.30, £1.60, £2.10; EX 20.90 Trifecta £116.70.

**Owner** Bastian Family **Bred** E & R Bastian **Trained** West Ilsley, Berks

**FOCUS**

They raced middle to stands' side. A Class 2, but the top weight had an official rating of 89, so essentially a Class 3.

## 6779 ROYAL SUSSEX REGIMENT H'CAP 2m

3:50 (3:50) (Class 2) (0-105,92) 3-Y-O+ **£16,172** (£4,812; £2,405; £1,202) **Stalls** Low

Form RPR

3032 **1** **Arthur Mc Bride (IRE)**[3] 6680 8-9-5 **83** (t) LiamKeniry 5 91
(Nigel Twiston-Davies) *lw: mde all: drifted rt u.p whn chal jst over 1f out: styd on strly to assert fnl 120yds: won gng away* **3/1**[2]

3322 **2** *2½* **Aurora Gray**[34] 5524 4-9-7 **85** JimCrowley 3 90
(Hughie Morrison) *trckd wnr: rdn for str chal jst over 1f out: edging into wnr but carried v sltly rt fnl f: no ex fnl 120yds* **11/4**[1]

2003 **3** *3¼* **Jacob Cats**[17] 6201 8-9-10 **88** (v) HarryBentley 2 89
(William Knight) *s.i.s: last but in tch: hdwy 2f out: sn rdn to chse ldng pair: styd on same pce fnl f* **20/1**

2243 **4** *2½* **Fleeting Visit**[13] 6323 4-9-6 **84** (p) CharlesBishop 1 82
(Eve Johnson Houghton) *lw: trckd ldrs: rdn over 2f out: nt pce to mount chal: no ex ins fnl f* **4/1**[3]

4-33 **5** *3¼* **Arty Campbell (IRE)**[8] 6508 7-9-4 **82** (p) DavidProbert 6 76
(Bernard Llewellyn) *hld up but in tch: hdwy 4f out: effrt over 2f out: wknd over 1f out* **10/1**

0020 **6** *11* **Mister Manduro (FR)**[30] 5682 3-9-3 **92** PJMcDonald 7 75
(Mark Johnston) *trckd wnr tl rdn over 2f out: wknd over 1f out* **11/4**[1]

3m 42.34s (13.34) **Going Correction** +0.675s/f (Yiel)

**WFA** 3 from 4yo+ 11lb **6** Ran SP% **112.2**

Speed ratings (Par 109): **93,91,90,88,87 81**

CSF £11.65 CT £132.01 TOTE £3.50: £1.50, £1.80; EX 10.90 Trifecta £60.10.

**Owner** John Gaughan & Rob Rexton **Bred** Pat Kinsella **Trained** Naunton, Gloucs

**FOCUS**

They raced up the middle in the straight. Again a Class 2, but essentially a Class 3 on official ratings. Few got into this, with the winner left alone up front which was an advantage on the day.

## 6780 THOMAS BUTCHER 21ST BIRTHDAY H'CAP 6f

4:25 (4:25) (Class 4) (0-80,80) 3-Y-O+ **£6,469** (£1,925; £962; £481) **Stalls** High

Form RPR

4216 **1** **The Daley Express (IRE)**[33] 5564 3-9-5 **80** FrannyNorton 1 90
(Ronald Harris) *lw: racd centre: hld up: hdwy over 2f out: chal gng wl ent fnl f: led fnl 120yds: qcknd clr: readily* **7/2**[2]

4222 **2** *½* **Jashma (IRE)**[11] 6373 3-8-9 **70** (p[1]) ShaneKelly 4 77
(Richard Hughes) *trckd ldr in center: rdn to ld ent fnl f: hdd fnl 120yds: nt pce of wnr* **10/3**[1]

0-20 **3** *2¼* **Francisco**[17] 6192 5-9-7 **80** DavidProbert 2 79
(Tony Carroll) *racd center: hld up: rdn and hdwy over 1f out: r.o wl to go 3rd fnl 100yds but no threat to front pair* **7/2**[2]

4-14 **4** *¾* **Joe Packet**[81] 3777 10-8-13 **79** Pierre-LouisJamin(7) 6 75
(Jonathan Portman) *racd center: hld up: hdwy over 1f out: swtchd rt ent fnl f: kpt on same pce fnl 100yds* **7/1**

2260 **5** *1½* **Love Oasis**[11] 6392 3-9-2 **77** PJMcDonald 3 68
(Mark Johnston) *led center gp: prom overall: rdn to ld over 1f out: hdd ent fnl f: no ex* **7/1**

6536 **6** *9* **Artscape**[10] 6442 5-8-13 **72** RobertWinston 7 44
(Dean Ivory) *racd alone on stands' side: overall ldr tl rdn 2f out: hung rt and wknd ent fnl f* **6/1**[3]

5650 **7** *1½* **Bridge Builder**[29] 5711 7-8-8 **67** (p) TomMarquand 5 20
(Peter Hedger) *trckd ldr in center tl rdn: 2f out: wknd ent fnl f* **25/1**

1m 15.26s (3.06) **Going Correction** +0.50s/f (Yiel)

**WFA** 3 from 4yo+ 2lb **7** Ran SP% **110.7**

Speed ratings (Par 105): **99,98,95,94,92 80,78**

CSF £14.51 CT £39.94 TOTE £3.90: £1.90, £2.30; EX 13.90 Trifecta £33.80.

**Owner** The W H O Society **Bred** Allevamento Ficomontanino Srl **Trained** Earlswood, Monmouths

**FOCUS**

They raced middle to stands' side. A fair sprint handicap with the winner looking capable of better.

## 6781 "PLAY CASINO AT 188BET" H'CAP 1m 3f 44y

5:00 (5:01) (Class 5) (0-70,69) 4-Y-O+ **£4,528** (£1,347; £673; £336) **Stalls** High

Form RPR

0013 **1** **Overhaugh Street**[14] 6280 4-8-12 **60** LiamKeniry 1 70
(Ed de Giles) *mde all: styd on strly to assert ins fnl f: rdn out* **7/1**

0361 **2** *2¾* **Maestro Mac (IRE)**[27] 5809 4-9-6 **68** PatCosgrave 9 73
(Tom Clover) *in tch: rdn and hdwy over 2f out: sn chsng wnr: styd on but hld ins fnl f* **4/1**[3]

10-0 **3** *2½* **The Way You Dance (IRE)**[51] 1364 5-9-0 **62** (p) RobertWinston 8 63
(Neil Mulholland) *s.i.s: last: rdn 3f out: hdwy fr 2f out: wnt 3rd ent fnl f: styd on same pce* **25/1**

4306 **4** *5* **Art Of Swing (IRE)**[40] 5320 5-9-5 **67** TomQueally 7 60
(Gary Moore) *trckd ldrs: swtchd to stands' side rails 3f out: sn rdn and hung rt: wknd ent fnl f* **7/1**

5542 **5** *1¼* **Hard Toffee (IRE)**[9] 6479 6-9-7 **69** RobertTart 2 60
(Conrad Allen) *trckd wnr tl rdn wl over 2f out: wknd ins fnl f* **3/1**[2]

0056 **6** *shd* **Archangel Raphael (IRE)**[55] 4755 5-9-6 **68** PatDobbs 3 58
(Amanda Perrett) *in tch: effrt 3f out: wknd ent fnl f* **8/1**

6044 **7** *2¾* **Archimento**[15] 6258 4-9-6 **68** (t) DavidProbert 6 54
(Philip Hide) *hld up: rdn over 3f out: little imp: wknd ent fnl f* **11/4**[1]

2m 34.54s (8.04) **Going Correction** +0.675s/f (Yiel) **7** Ran SP% **111.6**

Speed ratings (Par 103): **97,95,93,89,88 88,86**

CSF £33.18 CT £646.49 TOTE £7.00: £2.80, £2.50; EX 32.50 Trifecta £490.40.

**Owner** Sharron & Robert Colvin **Bred** World Racing Network **Trained** Ledbury, H'fords

**FOCUS**

Add 10yds to race distance. The main action was up the middle in the straight. It was misty, making it hard to see the opening stages, but it was clear enough that the winner made all. He has been rated back to early levels.

T/Plt: £38.30 to a £1 stake. Pool: £88,268.52 - 1,681.49 winning units T/Qpdt: £7.40 to a £1 stake. Pool: £7,720.74 - 763.89 winning units **Tim Mitchell**

# [6688]HAMILTON (R-H)

Tuesday, September 5

**OFFICIAL GOING: Soft (heavy in places; 5.7)**

Wind: fresh across Weather: cloudy

## 6782 ALWAYS TRYING MAIDEN STKS 1m 68y

1:50 (1:52) (Class 5) 3-4-Y-0 £5,175 (£1,540; £769; £384) Stalls Low

Form RPR

5- **1** **Crystal River**[301] 7855 3-9-0 0 JoeFanning 4 79
(William Haggas) *trckd ldr in 2nd: led over 2f out: pushed clr over 1f out* **Evs**[2]

2 **2** 13 **Bombay (IRE)**[8] 6522 3-9-5 0 DanielTudhope 2 68
(David O'Meara) *in tch in 3rd: trckd ldr over 2f out: sn rdn: wknd fnl f* **5/6**[1]

2060 **3** 14 **Irvine Lady (IRE)**[3] 6690 4-9-5 45 (p) JamesSullivan 1 23
(R Mike Smith) *led: rdn whn hdd over 2f out: wknd* **100/1**

0 **4** 3 **Farage (IRE)**[17] 6194 3-8-9 0 RowanScott(5) 3 16
(John Patrick Shanahan, Ire) *v.s.a: a rr* **40/1**[3]

1m 53.82s (5.42) **Going Correction** +0.80s/f (Soft)
**WFA** 3 from 4yo 5lb 4 Ran SP% **108.0**
Speed ratings (Par 103): **104,91,77,74**
CSF £2.11 TOTE £1.80; EX 2.10 Trifecta £5.50.
**Owner** Somerville Lodge Limited **Bred** Darley **Trained** Newmarket, Suffolk

**FOCUS**
Add 8yds to race distance. Pretty testing conditions and they came home at long intervals in a maiden with little depth. Only two mattered.

## 6783 DRINKS EXPRESS H'CAP 1m 68y

2:25 (2:25) (Class 6) (0-65,67) 3-Y-O+ £3,234 (£962; £481; £240) Stalls Low

Form RPR

6051 **1** **Fleetfoot Jack (IRE)**[11] 6381 3-9-8 66 (p) DanielTudhope 2 73+
(David O'Meara) *midfield: pushed along and in tch whn bit short of room 2f out: in clr appr fnl f: sn rdn to chse ldr: led 110yds out: styd on* **5/2**[1]

1135 **2** 1 1/4 **Carlovian**[18] 6131 4-9-0 53 (p) JasonHart 3 57
(Mark Walford) *led for 1f: trckd ldr: rdn 3f out: styd on ins fnl f* **5/1**

5554 **3** 1/2 **Cliff Bay (IRE)**[11] 6381 3-9-6 64 JoeFanning 5 66
(Keith Dalgleish) *hld up: racd quite keenly: stdy hdwy fr over 3f out: rdn 2f out: kpt on ins fnl f* **9/1**

555 **4** 1 **Mr Cool Cash**[7] 6549 5-10-0 67 ConnorBeasley 1 68
(Richard Guest) *trckd ldr: led wl over 2f out: rdn over 1f out: hdd 110yds out: wknd* **4/1**[3]

032 **5** 2 **Green Howard**[22] 6003 9-9-5 58 (p) DuranFentiman 10 55
(Rebecca Bastiman) *hld up: rdn and hdwy on outer over 3f out: chsd ldrs over 2f out: hung rt over 1f out: wknd fnl 110yds* **12/1**

0-24 **6** 1/2 **Retribution**[35] 5509 3-9-6 64 PaulMulrennan 4 58
(David Lanigan) *hld up in midfield: pushed along and hdwy 3f out: rdn to chse ldr 2f out: wknd ins fnl f* **3/1**[2]

2000 **7** 8 **Secret City (IRE)**[34] 5543 11-8-7 51 oh6 (b) RowanScott(5) 6 29
(Rebecca Bastiman) *midfield: rdn along over 4f out: wknd over 2f out* **100/1**

-350 **8** 13 **Midnight Man (FR)**[80] 3819 3-8-13 60 (v[1]) CliffordLee(3) 8 8
(K R Burke) *led after 1f: rdn whn hdd wl over 2f out: wknd* **16/1**

1m 56.93s (8.53) **Going Correction** +0.80s/f (Soft)
**WFA** 3 from 4yo+ 5lb 8 Ran SP% **114.8**
Speed ratings (Par 101): **89,87,87,86,84 83,75,62**
CSF £15.54 CT £95.55 TOTE £2.80: £1.10, £1.70, £2.70; EX 15.60 Trifecta £80.50.
**Owner** F Gillespie **Bred** Marston Stud **Trained** Upper Helmsley, N Yorks

**FOCUS**
Add 8yds to race distance. Sound enough form with the placed horses pinning the level, with the pace a good one considering the ground.

## 6784 BB FOODSERVICE "HOPES N DREAMS" (S) STKS 1m 1f 35y

3:00 (3:00) (Class 4) 3-5-Y-O £6,469 (£1,925; £962; £481) Stalls Low

Form RPR

1305 **1** **What Wonders Weave (IRE)**[17] 6196 3-8-3 71 RowanScott(5) 1 73+
(John Patrick Shanahan, Ire) *hld up in tch: pushed along and hdwy over 2f out: rdn to ld appr fnl f: kpt on* **13/8**[1]

3224 **2** 2 1/4 **Greenview Paradise (IRE)**[43] 5212 3-8-3 65 PaulHanagan 8 62
(Richard Fahey) *led: jnd 4f out: rdn over 2f out: hdd appr fnl f: one pce ins fnl f* **7/2**[2]

0300 **3** shd **Bonnie Gals**[63] 4473 3-8-3 57 JoeFanning 3 61
(Keith Dalgleish) *hld up: hdwy and stl gng wl 2f out: rdn to chse ldrs over 1f out: kpt on same pce* **20/1**

330 **4** 8 **Shambra (IRE)**[25] 5895 3-8-8 63 (h[1]) ConnorBeasley 2 50
(Roger Fell) *dwlt: sn in tch: rdn over 2f out: wknd over 1f out* **15/2**

0-05 **5** 1 3/4 **Another Go (IRE)**[89] 3486 4-9-0 71 BenCurtis 5 47
(Sally Haynes) *trckd ldr: jnd ldr 4f out: rdn over 2f out: wknd over 1f out* **4/1**[3]

3520 **6** 2 1/2 **Beauden Barrett**[10] 6431 4-9-0 70 (tp) JasonHart 4 42
(John Quinn) *trckd ldr: rdn over 2f out: wknd over 1f out* **15/2**

2m 6.89s (7.19) **Going Correction** +0.80s/f (Soft)
**WFA** 3 from 4yo+ 6lb 6 Ran SP% **108.6**
Speed ratings (Par 105): **100,98,97,90,89 87**
CSF £6.91 TOTE £2.40: £1.30, £2.00; EX 7.60 Trifecta £31.50.There was no bid for the winner.
**Owner** Thistle Bloodstock Limited **Bred** Thistle Bloodstock Limited **Trained** Kells, Co Kilkenny

**FOCUS**
Add 8yds to race distance. The 3yos predictably dominated this seller, which has been rated around the third.

## 6785 VISIT THE ALL NEW RACING UK.COM H'CAP (DIV I) 6f 6y

3:35 (3:35) (Class 6) (0-65,67) 3-Y-O+ £3,234 (£962; £481; £240) Stalls High

Form RPR

0621 **1** **Dodgy Bob**[13] 6318 4-9-7 63 (v) PhilDennis(3) 5 71
(Michael Mullineaux) *prom: led wl over 1f out: sn pushed along: rdn and kpt on fnl f* **4/1**[2]

2212 **2** 2 **Melaniemillie**[6] 6571 3-8-13 54 JamesSullivan 7 56
(Ruth Carr) *hld up in tch: smooth hdwy on outside over 1f out: rdn to chal ins fnl f: one pce and sn hld in 2nd* **6/4**[1]

0000 **3** nk **Reflation**[3] 6688 5-8-7 46 (p) JoeFanning 11 47
(Patrick Holmes) *chsd ldrs: rdn over 2f out: kpt on ins fnl f* **16/1**

-646 **4** 2 **Excellent World (IRE)**[21] 6046 4-8-11 50 BarryMcHugh 8 45
(Tony Coyle) *prom: rdn over 2f out: wknd fnl 110yds* **7/1**

1534 **5** 1 1/4 **Cheeni**[11] 6384 5-8-8 47 (p) PatrickMathers 6 38
(Jim Goldie) *chsd ldrs: rdn over 2f out: wknd ins fnl f* **6/1**

4666 **6** 18 **Reckless Serenade (IRE)**[92] 3384 3-9-11 66 ConnorBeasley 9 3
(Keith Dalgleish) *led: rdn over 2f out: hdd wl over 1f out: wknd and eased* **9/2**[3]

1m 17.13s (4.93) **Going Correction** +0.80s/f (Soft)
**WFA** 3 from 4yo+ 2lb 6 Ran SP% **110.8**
Speed ratings (Par 101): **99,96,95,93,91 67**
CSF £10.19 CT £77.44 TOTE £6.00: £1.50, £1.50; EX 9.80 Trifecta £38.10.
**Owner** J P Daly And S & M Ashbrooke **Bred** Whatton Manor Stud & Robert Cornelius **Trained** Alpraham, Cheshire

**FOCUS**
A moderate sprint, but the in-form runners came to the fore and there may be more to come from the winner.

## 6786 VISIT THE ALL NEW RACING UK.COM H'CAP (DIV II) 6f 6y

4:10 (4:11) (Class 6) (0-65,67) 3-Y-O+ £3,234 (£962; £481; £240) Stalls High

Form RPR

1050 **1** **Souls In The Wind (IRE)**[10] 6442 3-9-7 67 RowanScott(5) 1 73
(John Patrick Shanahan, Ire) *dwlt: sn midfield: pushed along and hdwy 2f out: rdn to ld ins fnl f: kpt on* **12/1**

04 **2** 3/4 **Avenue Of Stars**[16] 6237 4-9-11 64 (p) AndrewMullen 8 68
(Karen McLintock) *prom: rdn over 2f out: led over 1f out: edgd lft 1f out: hdd ins fnl f: one pce* **4/1**[1]

6356 **3** 3/4 **Eltanin (IRE)**[24] 5919 3-9-8 63 (v) JasonHart 9 65
(John Quinn) *prom: rdn over 2f out: kpt on same pce fnl f* **9/2**[2]

3220 **4** 1 **Jacksonfire**[12] 6345 5-8-11 53 (p) PhilDennis(3) 4 52
(Michael Mullineaux) *dwlt: hld up: rdn along over 2f out: hdwy appr fnl f: kpt on* **6/1**

1504 **5** 1 1/4 **Be Bold**[4] 6660 5-9-10 63 ConnorBeasley 10 58
(Rebecca Bastiman) *led: racd towards stands' side and wd of main gp centre: rdn over 2f out: edgd lft and hdd over 1f out: no ex fnl f* **11/2**[3]

006 **6** hd **Sir Domino (FR)**[11] 6384 5-8-13 52 JackGarritty 6 48+
(Patrick Holmes) *trckd ldrs: rdn over 2f out: hmpd 1f out: no ex* **20/1**

1513 **7** 2 1/4 **Racquet**[13] 6318 4-10-0 67 JamesSullivan 5 54
(Ruth Carr) *trckd ldrs: racd keenly: rdn 2f out: wknd fnl f* **9/2**[2]

0006 **8** nse **Mr Conundrum**[7] 6550 4-8-7 46 oh1 (p) PaddyAspell 3 33
(Lynn Siddall) *hld up: rdn over 2f out: nvr threatened* **50/1**

2100 **9** 3 1/4 **Dutch Dream**[11] 6384 4-9-0 53 PaulHanagan 7 31
(Linda Perratt) *dwlt: a towards rr* **14/1**

-546 **10** nse **Urban Spirit (IRE)**[99] 3151 3-8-7 48 (p[1]) BarryMcHugh 2 25
(Roger Fell) *prom: racd quite keenly: rdn over 2f out: wknd over 1f out* **11/1**

1m 17.31s (5.11) **Going Correction** +0.80s/f (Soft)
**WFA** 3 from 4yo+ 2lb 10 Ran SP% **115.4**
Speed ratings (Par 101): **97,96,95,93,92 91,88,88,84,84**
CSF £59.01 CT £259.19 TOTE £12.20: £4.40, £2.00, £1.80; EX 71.00 Trifecta £399.90.
**Owner** Thistle Bloodstock Limited **Bred** Mrs C L Weld **Trained** Kells, Co Kilkenny

**FOCUS**
More competitive than the first division. The winner has been rated back to the best of her UAE form.

## 6787 EBF STALLIONS FLOWER OF SCOTLAND FILLIES' H'CAP 6f 6y

4:45 (4:45) (Class 3) (0-95,94) 3-Y-O+ £12,450 (£3,728; £1,864; £932; £466; £234) Stalls High

Form RPR

0141 **1** **Guishan**[10] 6412 7-9-10 94 (p) AlistairRawlinson 6 101
(Michael Appleby) *mde all: rdn 2f out: pressed ins fnl f: wandered but hld on wl* **15/8**[1]

4253 **2** nk **Southern Belle (IRE)**[26] 5828 4-9-9 93 PhillipMakin 8 99
(Robert Cowell) *trckd ldrs: rdn over 1f out: chal ins fnl f: kpt on but a jst hld* **5/1**[3]

1530 **3** 1 1/4 **Savannah Slew**[16] 6234 3-9-1 87 (b) PaulMulrennan 7 89
(James Given) *slowly away: sn hld up in tch: pushed along and hdwy to chse ldrs 2f out: rdn over appr fnl f: kpt on* **11/2**

4312 **4** 4 1/2 **Rutherford (IRE)**[11] 6382 3-8-11 83 ShaneGray 1 71
(Kevin Ryan) *chsd ldrs: rdn over 2f out: wknd ins fnl f* **7/2**[2]

6453 **5** hd **Courier**[11] 6382 5-8-13 83 BarryMcHugh 4 70
(Marjorie Fife) *prom: rdn over 2f out: wknd ins fnl f* **8/1**

5404 **6** 1 1/4 **Yeah Baby Yeah (IRE)**[10] 6454 4-9-1 85 (p) TomEaves 3 68
(Gay Kelleway) *hld up: rdn over 2f out: nvr threatened* **28/1**

231 **7** 3 3/4 **Made Of Honour (IRE)**[97] 3194 3-8-6 78 JoeyHaynes 5 49
(K R Burke) *hld up in tch towards outer: rdn over 2f out: wknd over 1f out* **11/1**

1m 15.43s (3.23) **Going Correction** +0.80s/f (Soft)
**WFA** 3 from 4yo+ 2lb 7 Ran SP% **111.9**
Speed ratings (Par 104): **110,109,107,101,101 100,95**
CSF £11.07 CT £41.71 TOTE £2.50: £1.60, £2.80; EX 13.20 Trifecta £35.90.
**Owner** Brian D Cantle **Bred** B D Cantle **Trained** Oakham, Rutland

**FOCUS**
A useful fillies' sprint with the bang in-form favourite triumphing. She is better than ever.

## 6788 RACING UK PROFITS RETURNED TO RACING H'CAP 1m 4f 15y

5:20 (5:21) (Class 6) (0-60,59) 4-Y-O+ £3,234 (£962; £481; £240) Stalls Low

Form RPR

3660 **1** **London Glory**[38] 5413 4-9-6 58 (b) JoeFanning 10 67
(David Thompson) *midfield: smooth hdwy over 3f out to trck ldr 2f out: pushed along into narrow ld over 1f out: edgd lft and briefly bmpd into hanging runner-up ent fnl f: continued to edge lft: styd on pushed out* **10/1**

5052 **2** 1/2 **Paddy's Rock (IRE)**[12] 6352 6-9-1 56 (p) JoshDoyle(3) 7 64
(Lynn Siddall) *hld up: rdn along over 4f out: hdwy over 2f out: hung rt but chal strly appr fnl f: briefly bmpd into wandering wnr: one pce towards fin* **7/2**[2]

3060 **3** 12 **Hellavashock**[12] 6352 4-8-4 47 (b) RowanScott(5) 3 37
(Alistair Whillans) *midfield: rdn to trck ldrs over 2f out: wknd in poor 3rd fnl f* **9/1**

1335 **4** 5 **Highway Robber**[12] 6352 4-9-1 53 PaulMulrennan 9 36
(Wilf Storey) *trckd ldr: rdn to ld over 2f out: hdd over 1f out: sn wknd* **4/1**[3]

045 **5** 1 1/2 **Poppyinthepark**[10] 6413 4-9-0 57 CallumRodriguez(5) 5 37
(Richard Ford) *in tch: rdn along 3f out: wknd appr fnl f* **16/1**

0016 **6** 6 **Adherence**[24] 5951 4-9-5 57 BarryMcHugh 2 28
(Tony Coyle) *hld up: rdn along over 4f out: sn btn* **8/1**

0303 **7** 6 **Dream Free**[15] 6270 4-9-7 59 (b) JasonHart 11 21
(Mark Walford) *led: rdn whn hdd over 2f out: wknd* **11/1**

0000 **8** 6 **Swiss Lait**[12] 6346 6-8-7 45 JamesSullivan 1
(Patrick Holmes) *trckd ldr: rdn over 3f out: wknd over 2f out* **40/1**

-605 9 1 **Anna's Legacy**[12] 6350 4-8-0 **45**....................(h[1]) SeanMooney(7) 6
(Jim Goldie) *a outpcd in rr* **66/1**

-013 10 19 **Champagne Rules**[21] 6035 6-9-0 **52**.................... PaddyAspell 4
(Sharon Watt) *s.i.s: hld up: bmpd 6f out: rdn 3f out: sn wknd* **3/1**[1]

2m 49.41s (10.81) **Going Correction** +0.80s/f (Soft) **10** Ran SP% **115.6**
Speed ratings (Par 101): **95,94,86,83,82 78,74,70,69,57**
CSF £44.59 CT £332.09 TOTE £9.30: £2.90, £1.50, £2.30; EX 51.50 Trifecta £570.20.
**Owner** Wayne Fleming **Bred** F L Li **Trained** Bolam, Co Durham
■ Stewards' Enquiry : Joe Fanning caution: careless riding

**FOCUS**
Add 8yds to race distance. A moderate handicap run at a decent gallop and two drew well clear. There was late contact, but it didn't alter the result.

## 6789 RACING UK HD ON SKY 432 H'CAP 1m 3f 15y
**5:55** (5:58) (Class 5) (0-75,77) 4-Y-0+ **£5,175** (£1,540; £769; £384) **Stalls** Low

Form RPR

3122 1 **Indian Chief (IRE)**[26] 5824 7-9-12 **76**.................... DanielTudhope 8 89+
(Rebecca Bastiman) *hld up: smooth hdwy over 3f out: sn trckd ldrs: nudged along to ld appr fnl f: cruised clr: v easily* **5/2**[2]

2254 2 7 **Henpecked**[17] 6208 7-9-6 **70**....................(p) PaulHanagan 7 69
(Alistair Whillans) *midfield: rdn and hdwy over 3f out: led over 2f out: hdd appr fnl f: plugged on but no ch w wnr* **10/1**

104 3 1 **Invictus (GER)**[25] 5872 5-9-2 **66**....................(p) PaulMulrennan 9 63
(David Loughnane) *trckd ldr: rdn to ld over 3f out: hdd 2f out: one pce* **16/1**

421 4 nk **State Sovereignty**[18] 6129 5-9-10 **77**.................... CliffordLee(3) 5 74
(Michael Scudamore) *trckd ldrs: racd keenly: rdn over 2f out: sn one pce* **5/4**[1]

0422 5 3 ¾ **Yensir**[20] 6060 4-9-4 **68**.................... GrahamLee 1 59
(Grant Tuer) *midfield: racd quite keenly: rdn over 2f out: wknd over 1f out* **5/1**[3]

1330 6 3 **Deep Resolve (IRE)**[29] 5701 6-9-3 **67**....................(b) BenCurtis 6 52
(Sally Haynes) *hld up: rdn along over 3f out: sn btn* **25/1**

0000 7 3 **Spes Nostra**[50] 4959 9-8-7 **64**....................(b) JamieGormley(7) 3 44
(Iain Jardine) *led: rdn whn hdd over 3f out: wknd fnl 2f* **22/1**

2m 32.87s (7.27) **Going Correction** +0.80s/f (Soft) **7** Ran SP% **112.8**
Speed ratings (Par 103): **105,99,99,98,96 94,91**
CSF £26.24 CT £325.30 TOTE £3.40: £1.60, £3.50; EX 25.50 Trifecta £123.70.
**Owner** Castle Construction (NE) Ltd **Bred** Paget Bloodstock **Trained** Cowthorpe, N Yorks

**FOCUS**
Add 8yds to race distance. An ordinary handicap that set up perfectly for the winner, who never had to come off the bridle. He has been rated to his old British form from the spring of 2015.
T/Plt: £34.90 to a £1 stake. Pool: £54,046.68 - 1,128.49 winning units T/Qpdt: £6.50 to a £1 stake. Pool: £4,172.30 - 471.81 winning units **Andrew Sheret**

# 6575 KEMPTON (A.W) (R-H)
### Tuesday, September 5

**OFFICIAL GOING: Polytrack: standard to slow (watered)**
Wind: Moderate, across Weather: Rain before racing; gradually brightening

## 6790 WATCH RACING UK ON TALKTALK TV NURSERY H'CAP (JOCKEY CLUB GRASSROOTS NURSERY QUALIFIER) 6f (P)
**5:50** (5:52) (Class 6) (0-60,60) 2-Y-0 **£2,264** (£673; £336; £168) **Stalls** Low

Form RPR

0456 1 **Roman Spinner**[18] 6154 2-8-12 **51**....................(t) LukeMorris 6 57
(Rae Guest) *trckd ldr: led 2f out: drvn over 1f out: kpt on wl* **5/1**[2]

036 2 1 ½ **Vegas Boy (IRE)**[6] 6585 2-9-4 **57**....................(t) TimmyMurphy 12 58+
(Jamie Osborne) *hld up in rr fr wd draw: prog 2f out: rdn and kpt on to chse wnr last 100yds: no imp after* **6/4**[1]

300 3 1 ½ **Casey Banter**[18] 6140 2-8-7 **49**.................... ShelleyBirkett(3) 2 46
(Julia Feilden) *nt that wl away but sn trckd ldrs: chal on inner 2f out: chsd wnr after but sn hld: lost 2nd last 100yds* **20/1**

2430 4 ¾ **Roses In June (IRE)**[20] 6063 2-8-5 **47**.................... HollieDoyle(3) 3 41
(J S Moore) *wl in tch: rdn and nt qckn wl over 1f out: one pce after* **10/1**

000 5 2 ¾ **Saria**[87] 3576 2-9-0 **53**.................... GeorgeDowning 5 39
(Tony Carroll) *in tch: outpcd 2f out: no ch over 1f out: kpt on late* **10/1**

600 6 nk **Uncovered**[28] 5749 2-8-10 **49**.................... RichardKingscote 1 34
(Tom Dascombe) *pushed up to ld: hdd 2f out: wknd over 1f out* **7/1**[3]

0052 7 1 **Watch Tan**[25] 5893 2-9-2 **55**....................(h) TrevorWhelan 9 37
(George Baker) *taken down early: stdd s: hld up in rr: pushed along on inner 2f out: no prog whn reminders 1f out: nvr in it* **14/1**

054 8 2 ¾ **Grand Acclaim (IRE)**[27] 5779 2-9-5 **58**.................... MartinHarley 10 32
(Harry Dunlop) *taken down early: a in rr: detached in last pair 2f out: no ch after* **12/1**

0564 9 1 **Cruel Clever Cat**[34] 5546 2-8-4 **50**.................... RhiainIngram(7) 8 21
(John Gallagher) *trapped out wd: chsd ldrs: wknd over 2f out* **16/1**

000 10 5 **Bucks Frizz (IRE)**[39] 5356 2-8-9 **48**.................... AdamBeschizza 7 4
(David Evans) *trapped out wd in rr: struggling 1/2-way: sn bhd* **25/1**

1m 13.74s (0.64) **Going Correction** 0.0s/f (Stan) **10** Ran SP% **116.2**
Speed ratings (Par 93): **95,93,91,90,86 85,84,80,79,72**
CSF £12.78 CT £141.18 TOTE £5.50: £1.40, £1.60, £3.70; EX 16.90 Trifecta £135.10.
**Owner** Reprobates Too **Bred** Ashbrittle Stud **Trained** Newmarket, Suffolk

**FOCUS**
No great pace on early and it developed into a bit of a dash up the straight. The form has been rated around the placed horses.

## 6791 32RED CASINO MAIDEN STKS 6f (P)
**6:20** (6:22) (Class 5) 3-Y-0+ **£2,911** (£866; £432; £216) **Stalls** Low

Form RPR

35 1 **Razzmatazz**[23] 5969 3-9-0 **0**.................... SamHitchcott 10 71
(Clive Cox) *pressed ldr and sn clr of rest: led over 2f out: rdn clr over 1f out: ld dwindled nr fin but nvr in any danger* **50/1**

2 1 **La Figlia (IRE)** 3-9-0 **0**.................... RyanMoore 9 67+
(Jeremy Noseda) *chsd clr ldng trio after 2f: shkn up over 2f out: prog to go 3rd over 1f out: drvn and styd on to take 2nd ins fnl f: clsd on wnr but nvr in time* **5/6**[1]

232 3 1 **Ptarmigan Ridge**[24] 5937 3-9-2 **74**.................... GeorgeWood(3) 12 69+
(James Fanshawe) *trapped out wd in midfield and off the pce: rdn and prog over 2f out: styd on wl fr over 1f out to take 3rd nr fin* **7/1**[3]

6 4 2 ½ **Majorette**[137] 1948 3-8-11 **0**.................... NoelGarbutt(3) 2 56
(Martin Smith) *led and sn clr w one rival: hdd over 2f out: wknd and lost 2 pls fnl f* **33/1**

2-4 5 ½ **Creek Walk (USA)**[84] 3682 3-9-0 **0**.................... PaddyBradley(5) 7 60+
(Saeed bin Suroor) *hld up wl in rr and off the pce: pushed along over 2f out: sme prog and rdn fnl f: styd on but too late to threaten* **9/4**[2]

442 6 ½ **Mohsen**[17] 6184 3-9-5 **73**.................... JimCrowley 8 58+
(Marcus Tregoning) *hld up in last pair and wl off the pce: pushed along on outer over 2f out: styd on wl fr over 1f out: nrst fin* **10/1**

00 7 nk **Treacherous**[11] 6368 3-9-2 **0**.................... CallumShepherd(3) 5 57+
(Ed de Giles) *taken down early: dwlt: hld up in rr and wl off the pce: pushed along on inner 2f out: kpt on steadily after: nrst fin* **66/1**

6000 8 nk **Banta Bay**[13] 6324 3-9-5 **45**.................... KierenFox 4 56?
(John Best) *chsd clr ldng pair to over 1f out: wknd fnl f: lost several pls nr fin* **100/1**

0306 9 5 **Mulsanne Chase**[40] 5326 3-9-5 **69**.................... LukeMorris 11 40
(Brian Barr) *hld up wl in rr and wl off the pce: brief effrt over 2f out: sn no prog* **66/1**

04 10 6 **Emilysbutterscotch**[22] 6009 3-9-0 **0**.................... AdamBeschizza 3 16
(Rae Guest) *t.k.h early: hld up: wknd 2f out* **66/1**

-06 11 11 **Charlie Alpha (IRE)**[128] 2171 3-8-12 **0**.................... RhiainIngram(7) 6
(Roger Ingram) *a wl in rr: t.o* **100/1**

0 12 3 ¼ **Val's Magic Touch**[22] 6009 3-9-0 **0**.................... TimmyMurphy 1
(John O'Shea) *t.k.h early: chsd clr ldng pair 2f: sn lost pl: t.o* **100/1**

1m 12.3s (-0.80) **Going Correction** 0.0s/f (Stan) **12** Ran SP% **119.3**
Speed ratings (Par 103): **105,103,102,99,98 97,97,96,90,82 67,63**
CSF £94.99 TOTE £35.30: £9.60, £1.10, £1.80; EX 185.10 Trifecta £988.00.
**Owner** Mrs J Dermot Cantillon & Partners **Bred** Bond Thoroughbred Corporation **Trained** Lambourn, Berks

**FOCUS**
A modest sprint maiden and a turn-up, but not hard to have doubts over the form.

## 6792 32RED ON THE APP STORE H'CAP 1m (P)
**6:50** (6:50) (Class 5) (0-75,78) 3-Y-0 **£2,911** (£866; £432; £216) **Stalls** Low

Form RPR

4205 1 **Tamayef (IRE)**[17] 6195 3-9-7 **75**.................... JamesDoyle 2 86
(Hugo Palmer) *sn in tch: rdn and prog over 2f out: drvn to cl over 1f out: led last 100yds: kpt on wl* **3/1**[2]

0341 2 ½ **Noble Masterpiece**[9] 6485 3-9-10 **78** 6ex.................... StevieDonohoe 8 88
(Sir Michael Stoute) *taken down early: t.k.h: hld up in last: gd prog fr jst over 2f out: swtchd towards inner and rdn to chal ins fnl f: styd on but jst hld* **11/4**[1]

2200 3 2 **Falbon**[20] 6068 3-9-8 **76**.................... DanielMuscutt 4 81
(Marco Botti) *led 1f: chsd ldr: rdn to ld again over 1f out: hdd and no ex last 100yds* **11/2**

0631 4 4 ½ **Habbad (FR)**[17] 6182 3-9-7 **75**....................(p) TomMarquand 10 70
(Richard Hannon) *hld up in last: urged along over 2f out: prog wl over 1f out: rchd 4th fnl f but no ch: eased nr fin* **10/1**

1053 5 ¾ **Masterofdiscovery**[13] 6310 3-8-12 **73**....................(b) WilliamCox(7) 1 66
(Clive Cox) *chsd ldrs: rdn on inner over 2f out: no imp over 1f out* **12/1**

0460 6 nk **Warrior's Spirit (IRE)**[11] 6397 3-9-7 **75**.................... SeanLevey 6 67
(Richard Hannon) *hld up in rr: pushed along over 2f out: kpt on steadily fr over 1f out: nvr involved* **16/1**

20-0 7 2 **Desert Grey (IRE)**[27] 5797 3-9-2 **70**....................(bt[1]) KieranShoemark 12 58
(Roger Charlton) *led after 1f fr wd draw: hdd over 1f out: wknd qckly fnl f* **33/1**

0060 8 1 ½ **Weloof (FR)**[11] 6387 3-9-5 **73**....................(t[1]) RichardKingscote 9 57
(Ed Dunlop) *chsd ldrs: rdn over 2f out: steadily wknd* **14/1**

4025 9 1 **My Illusionist**[40] 5332 3-9-5 **73**.................... LukeMorris 3 55
(Harry Dunlop) *chsd ldrs: urged along and lost pl over 2f out: n.d after* **50/1**

3602 10 1 **Quothquan (FR)**[83] 3721 3-9-2 **73**.................... GeorgeWood(3) 7 53
(Michael Madgwick) *hld up towards rr: rdn and no prog over 2f out: sn no ch* **5/1**[3]

3210 11 8 **Accomplice**[15] 6274 3-8-13 **67**.................... RobHornby 11 28
(Michael Blanshard) *in tch in midfield tl wknd qckly jst over 2f out: t.o* **33/1**

1m 38.26s (-1.54) **Going Correction** 0.0s/f (Stan) **11** Ran SP% **120.9**
Speed ratings (Par 101): **107,106,104,100,99 98,96,95,94,93 85**
CSF £11.92 CT £45.19 TOTE £4.10: £1.60, £1.50, £2.00; EX 15.90 Trifecta £77.70.
**Owner** Commission Air Limited **Bred** Tally-Ho Stud **Trained** Newmarket, Suffolk

**FOCUS**
The first three finished clear and this looks solid form for the grade.

## 6793 32RED H'CAP 1m 7f 218y(P)
**7:20** (7:20) (Class 3) (0-95,97) 4-Y-0+
**£7,158** (£2,143; £1,071; £535; £267; £134) **Stalls** Low

Form RPR

-150 1 **Cartwright**[77] 3928 4-9-7 **93**.................... LukeMorris 5 101
(Sir Mark Prescott Bt) *trckd ldng pair: wnt 2nd over 2f out: drvn to ld over 1f out: kpt on u.p fnl f* **11/2**

2001 2 1 **Velvet Revolution**[13] 6323 4-9-0 **86**.................... MartinHarley 3 93
(Marco Botti) *patiently rdn towards rr: effrt over 2f out: rdn on inner to press wnr ins fnl f: nt qckn last 100yds* **11/4**[2]

2125 3 hd **King Calypso**[27] 5799 6-8-9 **81**.................... TomQueally 9 87
(Denis Coakley) *trckd ldng trio: rdn over 2f out: tried to chal over 1f out: kpt on same pce fnl f* **14/1**

3141 4 1 ½ **Clowance One**[27] 5799 5-9-4 **90**....................(b) KieranShoemark 7 94
(Roger Charlton) *effrt to ld after 1f but pressed: stdd and hdd after 4f: led again wl over 2f out and drvn for home: hdd and one pce over 1f out* **13/8**[1]

6066 5 1 ½ **Gavlar**[24] 5912 6-8-13 **88**....................(v) CallumShepherd(3) 6 90
(William Knight) *bmpd by rival sn after s: hld up in last trio: effrt bnd 3f out where wd: nt qckn over 2f out and outpcd: tried to cl over 1f out: one pce* **9/2**[3]

000- 6 5 **Shades Of Silver**[433] 3784 7-8-13 **85**.................... LiamKeniry 8 81
(Ed de Giles) *hld up in last: pushed along over 3f out: outpcd over 2f out: nvr on terms after* **33/1**

2100 7 27 **Zain Arion (IRE)**[12] 6357 4-8-12 **84**.................... JFEgan 4 48
(John Butler) *led 1f: pestered ldr tl led again after 4f: hdd & wknd rapidly wl over 2f out: t.o* **20/1**

3m 28.99s (-1.11) **Going Correction** 0.0s/f (Stan) **7** Ran SP% **112.7**
Speed ratings (Par 107): **102,101,101,100,99 97,83**
CSF £20.37 CT £197.79 TOTE £5.10: £2.70, £1.40; EX 22.30 Trifecta £147.40.
**Owner** Exors Of The Late J L C Pearce **Bred** Meon Valley Stud **Trained** Newmarket, Suffolk


The Form Book Flat, Raceform Ltd, Newbury, RG14 5SJ

**FOCUS**
Quite a competitive staying race.

## 6794 32RED.COM H'CAP 6f (P)
**7:50** (7:51) (Class 4) (0-85,85) 4-Y-0+ **£4,690** (£1,395; £697; £348) **Stalls** Low

Form RPR
0004 1 **Exceed The Limit**[27] 5811 4-9-5 **83**...(p) TomMarquand 2 91
(Robert Cowell) *trckd ldr 1f then stdd: styd cl up: shkn up to ld over 1f out: hrd pressed fnl f: drvn and hld on wl* **7/1**
/050 2 *nk* **Secondo (FR)**[15] 6275 7-9-4 **82**... OisinMurphy 7 89
(Joseph Tuite) *hld up in last: prog on inner fr 2f out: drvn to press wnr last 100yds: nt qckn nr fin* **4/1**[3]
425 3 1 ¾ **Clear Spring (IRE)**[24] 5929 9-9-7 **85**... LukeMorris 1 86
(John Spearing) *hld up in 6th: effrt to chal over 1f out: sn nt qckn: kpt on same pce fnl f* **6/1**
2142 4 *nse* **Nezar (IRE)**[88] 3518 6-9-0 **78**... RobertWinston 6 81+
(Dean Ivory) *trckd ldrs: clsd on outer to chal over 1f out: nt qckn and lost 2nd last 100yds: eased fnl strides and lost 3rd* **7/2**[2]
6050 5 *nk* **Dutiful Son (IRE)**[20] 6068 7-8-11 **75**... HarryBentley 5 75
(Simon Dow) *trckd ldr after 1f: rdn to chal 2f out: one pce jst over 1f out* **3/1**[1]
0425 6 1 ¾ **Captain Lars (SAF)**[17] 6185 8-9-1 **82**...(v) AaronJones(3) 3 77
(Derek Shaw) *t.k.h: hld up in 5th: effrt 2f out: already hld whn n.m.r jst over 1f out: fdd* **7/1**
020 7 4 **Razin' Hell**[46] 5098 6-9-4 **85**...(v) LewisEdmunds(3) 4 67
(John Balding) *t.k.h: led at mod pce: tried to kick on over 2f out: hdd & wknd over 1f out* **12/1**

1m 13.1s **Going Correction** 0.0s/f (Stan) 7 Ran SP% **114.2**
Speed ratings (Par 105): **100,99,97,97,96 94,89**
CSF £34.77 TOTE £8.30: £3.40, £3.20; EX 42.90 Trifecta £226.60.
**Owner** Sultan Ali **Bred** Wood Hall Stud **Trained** Six Mile Bottom, Cambs

**FOCUS**
Not a bad sprint, but it was steadily run early on.

## 6795 100% PROFIT BOOST AT 32REDSPORT.COM H'CAP 7f (P)
**8:20** (8:20) (Class 5) (0-75,77) 4-Y-0+ **£2,911** (£866; £432; £216) **Stalls** Low

Form RPR
2431 1 **Siege Of Boston (IRE)**[5] 6620 4-9-11 **77** 6ex...(t) JFEgan 1 88
(John Butler) *hld up in rr: gd prog on inner 2f out: rdn to ld over 1f out: clr fnl f: readily* **11/4**[1]
0360 2 3 ¼ **Ubla (IRE)**[14] 6288 4-8-8 **63**...(p) DavidEgan(3) 5 65
(Jane Chapple-Hyam) *t.k.h: trckd ldr: led jst over 2f out: rdn and hdd over 1f out: no ch w wnr but kpt on for 2nd* **17/2**
35 3 ½ **Miracle Garden**[5] 6637 5-9-7 **73**...(p) StevieDonohoe 2 74
(Ian Williams) *trckd ldng pair: hrd rdn and nt qckn 2f out: one pce fnl f and jst hld on for 3rd* **5/1**
3-04 4 *nse* **Luang Prabang (IRE)**[31] 5656 4-9-2 **68**... JamesDoyle 7 69
(Chris Wall) *in tch: rdn over 2f out: kpt on fnl f to press for 3rd nr fin* **6/1**
2001 5 1 ½ **Bluff Crag**[14] 6288 4-9-2 **73**... FinleyMarsh(5) 3 69
(Richard Hughes) *trckd ldrs: shkn up and nt qckn over 2f out: tried to cl briefly over 1f out: one pce after* **7/2**[3]
0256 6 1 ½ **Cadeaux Boxer**[18] 6134 4-9-5 **71**...(h) JohnFahy 4 63
(Martin Smith) *led to jst over 2f out: steadily wknd over 1f out* **10/3**[2]
0045 7 1 ¾ **Plucky Dip**[14] 6290 6-9-3 **76**... JackOsborn(7) 6 64
(John Ryan) *hld up in last: detached 1/2-way: rdn and no prog over 2f out: no ch after* **33/1**
2205 8 8 **Tibibit**[46] 5118 4-9-2 **68**... LukeMorris 9 34
(Henry Tett) *s.i.s: sn rcvrd and in tch: shkn up and wknd jst over 2f out: eased fnl f* **25/1**

1m 25.24s (-0.76) **Going Correction** 0.0s/f (Stan) 8 Ran SP% **120.2**
Speed ratings (Par 103): **104,100,99,99,97 96,94,85**
CSF £28.67 CT £115.80 TOTE £3.70: £1.80, £3.10, £1.40; EX 37.00 Trifecta £172.40.
**Owner** Mark McKay **Bred** Willie McKay **Trained** Newmarket, Suffolk

**FOCUS**
A nice performance from the winner, who is now 3-5 on the AW and looks progressive.

## 6796 VERNON KAY NOW HERE ON SATURDAY H'CAP 1m 3f 219y(P)
**8:50** (8:50) (Class 6) (0-60,62) 4-Y-0+ **£2,264** (£673; £336; £168) **Stalls** Low

Form RPR
2006 1 **The Ginger Berry**[83] 3726 7-9-6 **62**...(h) GeorgeWood(3) 5 69
(Dr Jon Scargill) *wl in tch: smooth prog to trck ldr 2f: pushed into ld over 1f out and sn 2 l clr: idled last 75yds but a holding on* **10/1**
-010 2 *nk* **Howardian Hills (IRE)**[20] 6069 4-9-6 **59**... KieranShoemark 11 64
(Victor Dartnall) *v awkward s and slowly away: hld up in last pair: gd prog on inner 2f out: rdn and styd on wl fnl f: nvr quite able to chal* **8/1**[3]
3600 3 ½ **Jersey Bull (IRE)**[48] 5024 5-9-7 **60**...(h) LiamKeniry 10 64
(Michael Madgwick) *hld up in rr: prog over 2f out: rdn to chal on inner over 1f out: sn nt pce of wnr: styd on wl nr fin* **25/1**
/050 4 ½ **Garcon De Soleil**[29] 5716 4-8-7 **46** oh1... RobHornby 4 51
(Michael Blanshard) *towards rr: rdn over 2f out: limited prog and stl in rr jst over 1f out: fin strly and gaining at fin* **17/2**
65-0 5 ½ **Meetings Man (IRE)**[41] 5274 10-9-7 **60**...(p) TomMarquand 7 62
(Ali Stronge) *led after 2f: rdn and hdd over 1f out: one pce and lost pls ins fnl f* **25/1**
0345 6 ½ **Vexillum (IRE)**[13] 6309 8-8-4 **46** oh1...(p[1]) HollieDoyle(3) 8 47
(Neil Mulholland) *slowly away: hld up in last: cajoled along wl over 2f out: kpt on fr over 1f out: nvr rchd ldrs* **14/1**
5524 7 3 ½ **Tuolumne Meadows**[20] 6069 4-9-7 **60**...(v[1]) JamesDoyle 9 56
(Tony Newcombe) *wl plcd: drvn and nt qckn over 2f out: no prog after* **13/8**[1]
2022 8 4 **Rianna Star**[14] 6280 4-8-13 **55**... HectorCrouch(3) 2 44
(Gary Moore) *prom: rdn over 3f out: wknd over 1f out* **4/1**[2]
0200 9 1 **Star Links (USA)**[41] 5296 11-8-7 **46** oh1...(p) LukeMorris 3 34
(John Butler) *t.k.h early: prom tl wknd over 1f out* **20/1**
152 10 ½ **Wassail**[13] 6309 4-8-9 **51**... CallumShepherd(3) 1 38
(Ed de Giles) *led 2f: chsd ldr: drvn 4f out: wknd u.p 2f out* **8/1**[3]
120- 11 20 **Zarliman (IRE)**[334] 5021 7-8-10 **56**...(p) RhiainIngram(7) 6 11
(Roger Ingram) *in tch to 3f out: wknd qckly: t.o* **33/1**

2m 35.32s (0.82) **Going Correction** 0.0s/f (Stan) 11 Ran SP% **122.0**
Speed ratings (Par 101): **97,96,96,96,95 95,93,90,89,89 76**
CSF £86.36 CT £1968.55 TOTE £11.00: £3.50, £2.20, £5.60; EX 92.60 Trifecta £4098.60.
**Owner** Silent Partners **Bred** Strawberry Fields Stud **Trained** Newmarket, Suffolk

**FOCUS**
A moderate contest with the winner and third setting the level.
T/Jkpt: Not Won. T/Plt: £93.30 to a £1 stake. Pool: £92,183.63 - 721.20 winning units T/Qpdt: £63.80 to a £1 stake. Pool: £7,454.45 - 86.43 winning units **Jonathan Neesom**

# LAYTOWN
Tuesday, September 5

**OFFICIAL GOING: Sand: standard**

## 6797a AT THE RACES H'CAP 6f
**5:05** (5:06) (50-75,72) 4-Y-0+ **£6,054** (£1,877; £894; £402; £157)

RPR
1 **Coreczka (IRE)**[36] 5469 6-10-1 **64**... OisinOrr(5) 6 73
(Miss Clare Louise Cannon, Ire) *dwlt: in rr: pushed along bef 1/2-way: hdwy far side after 1/2-way to chal in 2nd over 1f out: rdn to ld ins fnl f and styd on wl clsng stages* **10/1**
2 ¾ **My Good Brother (IRE)**[6] 6602 8-10-6 **64**... ColinKeane 10 71
(T G McCourt, Ire) *dwlt and wnt sltly rt s: sn chsd ldrs: travelling wl fr 1/2-way and impr to chal 2f out: rdn to ld 1 1/2f out where edgd sltly lft: strly pressed and hdd ins fnl f: no ex cl home* **3/1**[1]
3 ½ **Bien Chase (IRE)**[18] 6169 6-10-10 **68**... WJLee 8 73
(Adrian McAllister, Ire) *hld up: 8th 1/2-way: prog under 2f out to chse ldrs over 1f out: rdn into 3rd ins fnl f and kpt on same pce: nt trble wnr* **7/1**[3]
4 2 ¼ **Guanabara Bay (IRE)**[31] 5674 4-10-13 **71**... DeclanMcDonogh 7 69
(Adrian McGuinness, Ire) *hld up: 7th 1/2-way: r.o in 8th ins fnl f into 4th cl home: nrst fin* **8/1**
5 ¾ **Prove The Point (IRE)**[20] 6081 4-10-11 **69**...(t) GaryCarroll 4 65
(Michael Mulvany, Ire) *chsd ldrs: rdn 2f out and no imp on ldrs ent fnl f: kpt on same pce* **14/1**
6 2 ½ **Mo Henry**[29] 5728 5-10-13 **71**... ShaneFoley 5 59
(Adrian Paul Keatley, Ire) *chsd ldrs: effrt on terms briefly under 2f out: sn no ex u.p and wknd ins fnl f* **11/2**[2]
7 1 ½ **Captain Bob (IRE)**[66] 4373 6-11-0 **72**... DougieCostello 1 55
(Jamie Osborne) *pushed along early: sn settled bhd ldrs: rdn fr 1/2-way and sn wknd* **8/1**
8 1 ¼ **Swiss Cross**[7] 6555 10-10-11 **69**...(t) ChrisHayes 3 48
(Phil McEntee) *chsd ldr: effrt on terms briefly under 2f out tl sn no ex: wknd between horses fr over 1f out* **7/1**[3]
9 1 ¾ **Pillar**[6] 6602 4-10-1 **59**... SeamieHeffernan 2 32
(Adrian McGuinness, Ire) *sn led: narrow advantage at 1/2-way: rdn 2f out and sn jnd: hdd u.p 1 1/2f out: wknd qckly* **10/1**
10 ½ **Cappadocia (IRE)**[35] 5519 7-10-8 **69**... GaryHalpin(3) 9 41
(John James Feane, Ire) *towards rr thrght: rdn and no imp after 1/2-way: one pce fnl 2f* **12/1**

1m 12.01s 10 Ran SP% **120.1**
CSF £41.41 CT £232.85 TOTE £14.80: £3.70, £1.60, £1.80; DF 64.80 Trifecta £583.30.
**Owner** G N Cannon **Bred** A & M Hennessy & P Madigan **Trained** Bangor, Co Down

**FOCUS**
A good ride on the winner in a race where the leaders Pillar and Swiss Cross just went a bit too hard up front.

## 6798a FOLLOW @THEMELBOURNE10 ON FACEBOOK H'CAP 6f
**5:35** (5:36) (45-65,63) 4-Y-0+ **£5,528** (£1,714; £816; £367; £143)

RPR
1 **Red All Star (IRE)**[39] 5385 7-9-12 **47**...(t) ColinKeane 4 54
(Gerard Keane, Ire) *on toes befhand: disp early tl sn led narrowly: rdn 1 1/2f out and sn jnd: regained narrow advantage u.p wl ins fnl f and kpt on wl to hold on: all out* **9/2**[2]
2 *nk* **Boxer Dunford (IRE)**[29] 5728 4-9-11 **49**... RossCoakley(3) 10 55
(D P Coakley, Ire) *chsd ldrs: tk clsr order bhd ldrs bef 1/2-way: rdn in 3rd over 1f out where hung lft briefly: r.o u.p wl ins fnl f into 2nd cl home: nrst fin* **14/1**
3 *hd* **Free To Roam (IRE)**[6] 6600 4-9-7 **47**... OisinOrr(5) 5 52
(Adrian McGuinness, Ire) *towards rr: hdwy 2f out to chse ldrs: rdn into 4th over 1f out and r.o u.p into 3rd cl home: nrst fin* **13/2**
4 *hd* **Rosenborg Rider (IRE)**[22] 5994 4-11-0 **63**... DeclanMcDonogh 1 68
(Adrian McGuinness, Ire) *disp early tl sn settled bhd ldr: cl 2nd at 1/2-way: rdn under 2f out and sn disp ld: hdd narrowly wl ins fnl f and no ex cl home where dropped to 4th* **11/4**[1]
5 3 ¼ **Full Shilling (IRE)**[6] 6599 9-10-5 **54**... RobbieColgan 2 48
(Mrs Ann Mooney, Ire) *chsd ldrs: pushed along bef 1/2-way and sn dropped to 6th: rdn fr 1/2-way and no imp on ldrs over 1f out: kpt on one pce in 5th ins fnl f* **16/1**
6 ½ **Catwilldo (IRE)**[6] 6602 7-10-0 **52**... RobbieDowney(3) 3 45
(Garvan Donnelly, Ire) *towards rr: rdn in 8th under 2f out and no imp on ldrs ent fnl f: kpt on one pce in 6th clsng stages* **12/1**
7 *nk* **Strategic Heights (IRE)**[16] 6246 8-11-0 **63**... DougieCostello 9 55
(Jamie Osborne) *chsd ldrs: rdn in 3rd 2f out and sn no ex: wknd fnl f* **11/2**[3]
8 ½ **Annagassan**[6] 6602 4-9-10 **45**... SeamieHeffernan 7 35
(Donal Kinsella, Ire) *towards rr: rdn in 9th 2f out and no imp: kpt on one pce ins fnl f* **33/1**
9 4 ½ **Duckanddive (IRE)**[18] 6169 4-9-5 **45**... KillianLeonard(5) 8 21
(Mrs Denise Foster, Ire) *sn trckd ldr briefly early: lost pl bef 1/2-way: rdn and wknd fr over 2f out* **10/1**
10 6 **Shabra Emperor (IRE)**[60] 4592 8-10-10 **59**...(t) ConorHoban 6 16
(Anthony McCann, Ire) *dwlt and sltly awkward s: in rr and pushed along bef 1/2-way: no imp whn wandered sltly under 2f out: nvr a factor* **13/2**

1m 12.09s 10 Ran SP% **119.2**
CSF £67.09 CT £423.76 TOTE £5.50: £1.80, £4.60, £2.10; DF 73.00 Trifecta £514.00.
**Owner** Gaeltacht Partnership **Bred** Pat Reynolds **Trained** Trim, Co Meath

**FOCUS**
A terrific finish after several entered the final furlong with a chance.

## 6799a GILNA'S COTTAGE INN MAIDEN 7f
**6:05** (6:05) 4-Y-0+ **£6,581** (£2,040; £972; £438; £170)

RPR
1 **Silk Cravat**[23] 5975 4-10-3 71... ColinKeane 2 73
(G M Lyons, Ire) *a.p: narrow advantage bef 1/2-way: travelling wl after 1/2-way and extended ld over 1f out: shkn up ins fnl f and kpt on wl under hands and heels clsng stages where pressed: nt extended* **13/8**[1]
2 ½ **Haraz (IRE)**[17] 6181 4-10-3 69... DougieCostello 4 72
(Jamie Osborne) *chsd ldrs early tl dropped to 6th at 1/2-way: hdwy in 5th after 1/2-way: nt clr run gng wl bhd ldrs fr over 1f out where checked: wnt 2nd wl ins fnl f and r.o to press wnr cl home: a hld* **5/1**[3]

3 2 ¼ **Live Twice**[17] 6220 4-9-12 61 ColmO'Donoghue 5 61
(P D Deegan, Ire) *w ldrs: cl 2nd bef 1/2-way: rdn 3f out and no imp on wnr u.p in 2nd ent fnl f: no ex in 3rd wl ins fnl f* **8/1**

4 2 ¼ **Sea Captain (IRE)**[24] 1810 5-10-3 46 RoryCleary 3 60
(Andrew Lee, Ire) *wnt sltly rt s: sn led narrowly tl jnd and hdd bef 1/2-way: u.p disputing 4th 2f out: no imp on wnr in 5th over 1f out: kpt on same pce in 4th wl ins fnl f* **40/1**

5 3 **Dandy Rock (IRE)**[18] 6169 4-10-3 64 (t) ChrisHayes 8 52
(T Hogan, Ire) *hooded to load: towards rr early tl impr to chse ldrs at 1/2-way: rdn over 2f out and no ex over 1f out: wknd ins fnl f* **7/2**[2]

6 5 **Jack Blue (IRE)**[60] 4594 5-10-3 52 MarkEnright 10 38
(Mrs John Harrington, Ire) *s.i.s and towards rr: rdn in 7th fr 1/2-way and no imp on ldrs in mod 6th under 2f out: one pce after* **20/1**

7 9 ½ **Ceyhan**[20] 6076 5-10-3 65 DeclanMcDonogh 7 13
(Jamie Osborne) *chsd ldrs on outer: 4th bef 1/2-way: rdn and wknd after 1/2-way* **12/1**

8 6 **Lucky Robin (IRE)**[31] 5-10-3 0 (t) EmmetMcNamara 9
(W J Burke, Ire) *s.i.s and towards rr thrght: no imp trailing bef 1/2-way: nvr a factor* **33/1**

9 12 **Tizme (IRE)**[10] 5-9-9 0 (t) RachaelBlackmore(3) 6
(Miss Denise Marie O'Shea, Ire) *mid-div early tl sn dropped towards rr: no imp fr bef 1/2-way: wknd* **6/1**

10 23 **Kingspan Ellie (IRE)**[23] 5-9-9 0 (t[1]) ConorMaxwell(3) 1
(G T Cuthbert, Ire) *v s.i.s and detached in rr thrght: nvr a factor* **50/1**

1m 23.82s **10 Ran SP% 122.2**
CSF £10.34 TOTE £2.60: £1.02, £1.40, £2.40; DF 8.70 Trifecta £46.00.
**Owner** Gaelic Thoroughbreds **Bred** Barton Stud Partnership **Trained** Dunsany, Co Meath

**FOCUS**
An ordinary maiden for sure, although it turned into an interesting race between a couple of characters.

## 6800a SCOTCH HALL SHOPPING CENTRE CLAIMING RACE 7f
6:35 (6:36) 4-Y-0+ **£5,528** (£1,714; £816; £367; £143)

RPR

1 **Tom Dooley (IRE)**[8] 6535 6-10-3 63 WJLee 8 67
(Richard John O'Brien, Ire) *hld up in tch: 6th 1/2-way: hdwy travelling wl over 2f out: shkn up in 3rd over 1f out and sn rdn in 2nd: styd on wl to ld ins fnl f: won gng away: comf* **3/1**[1]

2 3 ¾ **Arlecchino's Rock**[16] 6246 4-10-3 54 ColmO'Donoghue 3 57
(Patrick Martin, Ire) *led and disp: narrow advantage at 1/2-way: rdn and strly pressed ins fnl f where sn hdd: no imp on wnr clsng stages* **20/1**

3 1 ¾ **Mzuri (IRE)**[6] 6597 5-10-0 52 ColinKeane 5 49
(Adrian McGuinness, Ire) *chsd ldrs: 4th 1/2-way: outpcd briefly over 2f out where lost pl: sn rdn and clsd u.p into 4th ins fnl f: kpt on into 3rd fnl stride: nt trble wnr* **10/3**[2]

4 nse **Tidal's Baby**[26] 5817 8-10-3 58 DougieCostello 1 52
(Jamie Osborne) *wnt sltly rt s: chsd ldrs: 3rd 1/2-way: impr into 2nd gng wl after 1/2-way: rdn in 2nd over 1f out and sn no imp on wnr: wknd in 3rd wl ins fnl f: denied 3rd fnl stride* **9/2**

5 shd **Modern Tutor**[6] 6600 8-9-12 44 DonaghO'Connor(5) 6 52
(Miss Nicole McKenna, Ire) *hld up: 7th 1/2-way: rdn in rr after 1/2-way and clsd u.p into 5th 1f out: kpt on clsng stages: jst hld for 4th* **33/1**

6 3 ¾ **Our Max**[73] 4110 7-10-3 58 (t) LeighRoche 9 42
(Georgios Pakidis, Ire) *towards rr: last at 1/2-way: tk clsr order after 1/2-way: rdn in 6th 2f out and no ex disputing 4th 1f out: one pce after* **4/1**[3]

7 2 ¾ **Emperor Bob (IRE)**[19] 6120 5-9-12 48 KillianLeonard(5) 10 34
(Patrick J McKenna, Ire) *towards rr: 8th 1/2-way: rdn and no imp after 1/2-way: one pce fnl 2f* **8/1**

8 2 ¾ **Freedom Square (IRE)**[23] 4286 6-10-3 47 (t) ConorHoban 4 27
(Mark Michael McNiff, Ire) *dwlt: sn chsd ldrs: 5th 1/2-way: rdn over 2f out and sme hdwy far side: no ex 1 1/2f out: sn wknd* **25/1**

9 4 ¼ **Dovil's Duel (IRE)**[6] 6600 6-10-3 59 (t) JackKennedy 2 15
(Gavin Cromwell, Ire) *hooded to load: led and disp: cl 2nd after 1/2-way and sn lost pl: wknd fnl 2f* **16/1**

1m 24.01s **9 Ran SP% 114.8**
CSF £64.31 TOTE £3.40: £1.40, £3.80, £1.30; DF 45.50 Trifecta £179.90.
**Owner** Ballingarry Partnership **Bred** Ballylinch Stud **Trained** Ballingarry, Co Limerick

**FOCUS**
The winner has been a revelation, but with the handicapper getting to grips with him, this seemed a logical type of race to aim for.

## 6801a O'NEILLS SPORTS (Q.R.) H'CAP 7f
7:05 (7:08) (50-80,80) 4-Y-0+ **£6,581** (£2,040; £972; £438; £170)

RPR

1 **Rivellino**[18] 6164 7-11-9 76 MsLO'Neill(5) 1 85
(Adrian McGuinness, Ire) *chsd ldrs: tk clsr order fr 1/2-way and disp ld fr over 2f out: rdn to ld 1 1/2f out: strly pressed u.p wl ins fnl f: all out cl home: jst hld on* **11/2**[3]

2 hd **Seanie (IRE)**[25] 5899 8-11-10 72 (t) MrDerekO'Connor 9 80+
(David Marnane, Ire) *wnt rt s: chsd ldrs: disp 5th bef 1/2-way: rdn into 3rd 1 1/2f out and r.o u.p to strly press wnr clsng stages: jst failed* **8/1**

3 2 ¼ **Fastidious**[28] 5763 8-10-13 66 MrTHamilton(5) 8 63
(M D O'Callaghan, Ire) *hooded to load: sltly impeded s: sn chsd ldrs: cl 2nd at 1/2-way: rdn in 3rd 2f out and no imp on ldrs u.p in 4th over 1f out: kpt on clsng stages into 3rd fnl strides: nvr trbld ldrs* **25/1**

4 nk **Shepherd's Purse**[18] 6164 5-11-12 79 MrJCBarry(5) 5 80
(Joseph G Murphy, Ire) *cl up and led narrowly bef 1/2-way: jnd fr over 2f out and hdd 1 1/2f out: no ex u.p in 3rd wl ins fnl f: denied 3rd fnl strides* **9/2**[2]

5 5 **An Saighdiur (IRE)**[17] 6215 10-12-1 80 MrRPQuinlan(3) 2 68
(Andrew Slattery, Ire) *broke wl to ld narrowly: jnd and hdd bef 1/2-way: rdn bhd ldrs over 2f out and no imp u.p in 5th over 1f out: one pce fnl f: jst hld 5th* **8/1**

6 shd **Palawan**[26] 5821 4-11-12 77 (t[1]) MissKHarrington(3) 3 64
(Jamie Osborne) *hld up: 7th 1/2-way: rdn in 6th under 2f out and no imp on ldrs over 1f out: kpt on one pce: jst failed for 5th* **16/1**

7 3 **Korbous (IRE)**[19] 6120 8-12-3 79 MsKWalsh 10 58
(Richard Brabazon, Ire) *sltly impeded s: w.w: last bef 1/2-way: rdn in 8th under 2f out and no imp u.p in 7th ent fnl f: one pce after* **7/2**[1]

8 1 **Burn The Boats (IRE)**[8] 6535 8-11-5 70 MrFinianMaguire(3) 4 47
(John James Feane, Ire) *chsd ldrs: disp 5th bef 1/2-way: rdn over 2f out and sn wknd* **14/1**

9 shd **Knockmaole Boy (IRE)**[10] 5582 5-12-4 80 (t) MrJJCodd 6 56
(Gordon Elliott, Ire) *wnt rt s and bmpd rival: hld up: 8th 1/2-way: rdn over 2f out and sn no ex: wknd* **7/1**

10 8 ½ **Usa (IRE)**[6] 6604 10-10-13 66 MrDJBenson(5) 7 14
(S J Mahon, Ire) *bmpd s and towards rr: 9th bef 1/2-way: rdn and wknd in rr after 1/2-way* **7/1**

1m 24.05s **10 Ran SP% 119.4**
CSF £50.29 CT £1050.99 TOTE £7.00: £2.00, £3.00, £5.80; DF 58.90 Trifecta £2945.80.
**Owner** Ms Siobhan Gallagher **Bred** Castlemartin Sky & Skymarc Farm **Trained** Lusk, Co Dublin

**FOCUS**
The winner got first run, but was resolute too and deserved to score. The third has been rated close to his recent form.

## 6802a HIBERNIA STEEL (Q.R.) RACE 7f
7:35 (7:37) 4-Y-0+ **£7,897** (£2,448; £1,166; £525; £205)

RPR

1 **Monteverdi (FR)**[67] 4294 4-11-11 80 MissKHarrington(3) 7 80+
(Jamie Osborne) *got upset in stalls: sltly awkward s: sn chsd ldrs: impr travelling wl to dispute ld fr 1/2-way: led narrowly gng best under 2f out: rdn 1f out and styd on wl: comf* **7/4**[1]

2 3 **Edification**[3] 3415 4-12-0 82 MrPWMullins 8 72
(R P McNamara, Ire) *hooded to load: chsd ldrs: impr to dispute 2nd bef 1/2-way: disp ld gng wl over 2f out: rdn and hdd under 2f out: no imp on easy wnr ins fnl f: kpt on same pce* **9/2**[3]

3 ½ **Zanjabeel**[6] 6603 4-12-0 80 (t) MrJJCodd 3 71
(Gordon Elliott, Ire) *chsd ldrs early tl dropped to 7th fr 1/2-way: prog to chse ldrs under 2f out: sn rdn in 4th and no imp on easy wnr u.p in 3rd ins fnl f: kpt on same pce* **9/2**[3]

4 2 ¾ **Military Hill (IRE)**[19] 6120 4-11-9 69 MrTHamilton(5) 1 63
(Adrian McGuinness, Ire) *disp early tl led after 1f: jnd fr 1/2-way: rdn and hdd over 2f out: no ex in 4th ins fnl f: kpt on one pce clsng stages* **10/1**

5 2 **Molans Mare (IRE)**[16] 6246 7-10-11 44 MsLO'Neill(5) 9 46
(Keith Henry Clarke, Ire) *w.w towards rr: pushed along in 8th fr 1/2-way and sme hdwy u.p into 5th over 1f out: kpt on one pce ins fnl f* **33/1**

6 1 ¼ **Possible Future**[43] 5222 4-11-9 72 (t) MrJCBarry(5) 5 54
(Karl Thornton, Ire) *towards rr: pushed along in 6th fr 1/2-way: rdn 2f out and sn wandered sltly in 7th briefly: no ex in 6th over 1f out: one pce after* **16/1**

7 11 **Atlantic Jet (IRE)**[6] 6600 4-11-4 44 (t) MrFinianMaguire(3) 4 18
(Eugene M O'Sullivan, Ire) *disp early tl hdd narrowly after 1f: rdn bhd ldrs over 2f out and sn wknd* **50/1**

8 13 **Vitalized (IRE)**[6] 6604 5-11-4 57 (t) MrDJBenson(5) 2
(Damian Joseph English, Ire) *towards rr thrght: rdn in 8th fr 1/2-way and no imp: sn wknd: eased trailing in 8th fr over 1f out* **33/1**

9 24 **Il Piccolo Grande (IRE)**[16] 6244 4-12-0 65 MsKWalsh 6
(G M Lyons, Ire) *loaded wout rdr: s.i.s and sn detached in rr where rdn briefly: sn eased and t.o: nvr a factor* **3/1**[2]

1m 24.71s **9 Ran SP% 120.5**
Pick Six: Not Won. Pool of 2,727.81 carried forward to Gowran Park on Wednesday the 6th of September. Tote Aggregates - 2016: 142,067.00, 2017: 252,414.00 CSF £10.49 TOTE £2.80: £1.20, £1.50, £1.40; DF 13.20 Trifecta £47.10.
**Owner** Melbourne 10 Racing **Bred** S A Haras Du Mezeray & Ship Commodities **Trained** Upper Lambourn, Berks

**FOCUS**
The winner was entitled to go close with his rating and did a little bit more than that. The fifth anchors the form.
T/Jkpt: @875.00 - Pool: @3,822.32 T/Plt: @265.60 - Pool: @26,645.74 **Brian Fleming**

# 5195 MAISONS-LAFFITTE (R-H)
Tuesday, September 5

**OFFICIAL GOING: Turf: soft**

## 6803a PRIX ESMERALDA (CONDITIONS) (2YO FILLIES) (STRAIGHT) (TURF) 7f 110y
3:05 2-Y-0
**£17,675** (£7,145; £5,264; £3,384; £2,068; £1,316)

RPR

1 **Red Line (FR)**[31] 5679 2-8-11 0 CristianDemuro 3 92
(A De Watrigant, France) **6/4**[1]

2 1 ½ **Crown Vallary (FR)**[18] 6171 2-8-11 0 TonyPiccone 1 88
(K R Burke) *wl into stride: led early: rdn 2f out: hdd over 1f out: styd on wl fnl f but no ch w wnr* **4/1**[3]

3 2 ½ **Estijlaa**[24] 2-8-8 0 (b) AurelienLemaitre 6 80
(F Head, France) **29/10**[2]

4 ½ **La Canche (FR)**[18] 6171 2-8-8 0 EddyHardouin 4 78
(T Clout, France) **77/10**

5 3 ½ **La Miss (FR)**[28] 2-8-8 0 StephanePasquier 7 70
(Y Gourraud, France) **22/5**

6 3 ½ **Ma Petite Toscane (FR)**[55] 2-8-8 0 JeromeMoutard 5 62
(T Castanheira, France) **33/1**

PARI-MUTUEL (all including 1 euro stake): WIN 2.50; PLACE 1.60, 2.10; SF 8.20.
**Owner** Jean-Pierre-Joseph Dubois **Bred** J-P-J Dubois **Trained** France

## 6804a PRIX DE LA COCHERE - FONDS EUROPEEN DE L'ELEVAGE (LISTED RACE) (3YO+ FILLIES & MARES) (RND) (TURF) 1m
3:40 3-Y-0+ **£22,222** (£8,888; £6,666; £4,444; £2,222)

RPR

1 **Usherette (IRE)**[37] 5460 5-9-4 0 MickaelBarzalona 7 105
(A Fabre, France) *settled midfield: hdwy over 2f out: drvn to get on terms 1f out: styd on strly ins fnl f to assert cl home* **11/10**[1]

2 snk **Game Theory (IRE)**[79] 3883 5-9-4 0 StephanePasquier 3 105
(N Clement, France) **124/10**

3 ½ **Ettisaal**[44] 5196 3-8-9 0 AurelienLemaitre 6 99
(F Head, France) **2/1**[2]

4 hd **Silver Meadow (IRE)**[94] 3319 4-9-0 0 Pierre-CharlesBoudot 5 100
(F-H Graffard, France) **137/10**

5 ¾ **Silver Cape (FR)**[38] 5449 3-8-9 0 EddyHardouin 4 97
(T Clout, France) **34/1**

6 snk **Silver Step (FR)**[44] 5197 4-9-4 0 (h) CristianDemuro 8 101
(Mme Pia Brandt, France) **112/10**

7 nk **High Quality (IRE)**[62] 4-9-0 0 MaximeGuyon 1 97
(A Fabre, France) **96/10**[3]


The Form Book Flat, Raceform Ltd, Newbury, RG14 5SJ

8 5 **Conselice**[24] 5927 4-9-0 0 ........ TonyPiccone 2 85
(K R Burke) *keen early: dropped in bhd ldrs: remained keen: rdn over 2f out: sn btn and eased ins fnl f* **28/1**

1m 43.5s (1.20)
**WFA** 3 from 4yo+ 5lb **8** Ran SP% **119.2**
PARI-MUTUEL (all including 1 euro stake): WIN 2.10; PLACE 1.10, 1.70, 1.20; DF 11.30; SF 12.50.
**Owner** Godolphin SNC **Bred** Darley **Trained** Chantilly, France

6805 - (Foreign Racing) - See Raceform Interactive

## 6502 CHEPSTOW (L-H)
Wednesday, September 6

**OFFICIAL GOING: Good to soft (7.0)**
Wind: moderate breeze, across them in the straight Weather: sunny

### 6806 BLOODWISE BIG WELSH CAR SHOW 17TH SEPTEMBER FILLIES' NOVICE STKS (PLUS 10 RACE) 5f 16y
**2:10** (2:10) (Class 5) 2-Y-O **£3,234** (£962; £481; £240) **Stalls** Centre

Form RPR
024 1 **Awesome**[81] 3807 2-9-0 73 ........ AdamKirby 4 79
(Clive Cox) *mde virtually all: hrd pressed 2f out: drvn over 1f out: asserted nr fin* **13/2**

4 2 ½ **Shaya (IRE)**[54] 4841 2-9-0 0 ........ EdwardGreatrex 8 77
(Roger Fell) *cl up: chal 2f out: sn shkn up: kpt on and ev ch fnl f: hld nr fin* **14/1**

6 3 1 ¼ **Kaaba Stone (IRE)**[8] 6559 2-9-0 0 ........ JamieSpencer 5 73
(David Simcock) *towards rr: hdwy 2f out: sn rdn: swtchd rt appr fnl f: r.o wl towards fin* **11/4**[2]

23 4 2 **Global Rose (IRE)**[41] 5327 2-9-0 0 ........ LukeMorris 2 66
(Gay Kelleway) *t.k.h: trckd ldrs: rdn 1/2-way: sn hung rt: one pce fnl f* **9/2**[3]

0 5 ½ **Kodina**[19] 6138 2-8-11 0 ........ CallumShepherd(3) 1 64
(Charles Hills) *prom: rdn over 1f out: fdd fnl f* **14/1**

20 6 2 ¾ **Mushahadaat (IRE)**[35] 5528 2-9-0 0 ........ DaneO'Neill 9 54
(Brian Meehan) *chsd ldrs: drvn and unable qck 2f out: wknd fnl f* **15/8**[1]

5255 7 4 ½ **Highland Mary**[18] 6178 2-9-0 72 ........(v[1]) SeanLevey 7 38
(Richard Hannon) *prom: pushed along 2f out: wkng whn n.m.r over 1f out* **20/1**

00 8 1 **Eastern Sunrise**[32] 5660 2-9-0 0 ........ TomMarquand 3 34
(Richard Hannon) *jinked lft s: pushed along over 3f out: a in rr* **25/1**

0 9 5 **Miss Condi**[43] 5246 2-9-0 0 ........ TimmyMurphy 6 16
(Martin Keighley) *outpcd and a in rr* **150/1**

58.79s (-0.51) **Going Correction** +0.075s/f (Good) **9** Ran SP% **115.6**
Speed ratings (Par 92): **107,106,104,101,100 95,88,87,79**
CSF £88.59 TOTE £5.90: £2.10, £4.70, £1.60; EX 65.60 Trifecta £2151.00.
**Owner** Carmel Stud **Bred** Carmel Stud **Trained** Lambourn, Berks

**FOCUS**
An ordinary novice, little got into it with the market leaders found wanting for pace. The winner has been rated near her best to date.

### 6807 CSP H'CAP 7f 16y
**2:40** (2:42) (Class 5) (0-70,71) 3-Y-O+ **£3,234** (£962; £481; £240) **Stalls** Centre

Form RPR
4043 1 **Wahaab (IRE)**[9] 6502 6-9-4 63 ........(t[1]) TimmyMurphy 10 71
(Sophie Leech) *t.k.h early: hld up: shkn up over 2f out: hdwy over 1f out: rdn to ld fnl 100yds* **33/1**

1400 2 ¾ **Champagne Bob**[18] 6197 5-8-12 62 ........ JoshuaBryan(5) 14 68
(Richard Price) *t.k.h: trckd ldrs: rdn over 2f out: led narrowly over 1f out: hdd and unable qck fnl 100yds* **14/1**

2042 3 2 **Amood (IRE)**[27] 5827 6-9-12 71 ........ EdwardGreatrex 13 72+
(Archie Watson) *sn led: rdn over 2f out: narrowly hdd over 1f out: ev ch ins fnl f tl wknd fnl 100yds* **7/4**[1]

-461 4 ½ **Hedging (IRE)**[13] 6345 3-9-5 68 ........(p) CharlesBishop 6 66
(Eve Johnson Houghton) *wnt rt leaving stalls: midfield: rdn over 2f out: nt clr run early ins fnl f: r.o* **7/2**[2]

6501 5 ½ **Doctor Bong**[13] 6342 5-8-10 55 ........(b) LukeMorris 5 53
(Grace Harris) *midfield: clsd 3f out: rdn 2f out: nt qckn over 1f out: fdd ins fnl f* **16/1**

3230 6 nk **Zephyros (GER)**[20] 6092 6-9-4 63 ........ SeanLevey 2 60
(David Bridgwater) *hld up: shkn up 2f out: kpt on steadily fnl f* **20/1**

3113 7 nse **Sweet Pursuit**[20] 6106 3-9-3 66 ........ WilliamCarson 12 61
(Rod Millman) *chsd ldrs: rdn 3f out: kpt on u.p fnl f* **7/1**[3]

2-20 8 1 **Waqt (IRE)**[20] 6103 3-9-3 66 ........ DaneO'Neill 11 59
(Marcus Tregoning) *led early: cl up: drvn over 2f out: fdd fr over 1f out* **9/1**

0 9 2 ¼ **Nutini (IRE)**[14] 6310 4-9-4 63 ........(p) LiamKeniry 3 52
(Malcolm Saunders) *cl up: rdn over 2f out: wknd fnl f* **16/1**

3462 10 7 **Bella's Venture**[15] 6283 4-8-11 56 ........ TomMarquand 8 27
(John Gallagher) *sltly hmpd s: rdn over 3f out: drvn and lost tch over 1f out* **12/1**

1m 23.35s (0.15) **Going Correction** +0.075s/f (Good)
**WFA** 3 from 4yo+ 4lb **10** Ran SP% **114.9**
Speed ratings (Par 103): **102,101,98,98,97 97,97,96,93,85**
CSF £426.38 CT £1246.96 TOTE £13.00: £5.30, £4.10, £1.10; EX 179.80 Trifecta £407.70.
**Owner** Out Of Bounds & Mike Harris Racing Club **Bred** Shadwell Estate Company Limited **Trained** Elton, Gloucs

**FOCUS**
Run at a steady gallop, a couple of the leading fancies disappointed and it went to the complete outsider. The race has been rated around the second.

### 6808 NETWORK PRODUCTIONS MAIDEN STKS 7f 16y
**3:10** (3:10) (Class 5) 3-Y-O+ **£3,234** (£962; £481; £240) **Stalls** Centre

Form RPR
044 1 **Katheefa (USA)**[18] 6184 3-9-6 71 ........ DaneO'Neill 3 73
(Charles Hills) *chsd ldrs: wnt 2nd 2f out: shkn up to ld over 1f out: sn in command: rdn out* **9/4**[2]

53 2 1 ¾ **Cherished (IRE)**[24] 5969 3-9-1 0 ........ TimmyMurphy 2 63
(Geoffrey Deacon) *t.k.h early: led: drvn wl over 1f out: sn hdd: kpt on same pce* **13/2**[3]

32 3 1 ½ **Majboor (IRE)**[20] 6103 3-9-6 0 ........ LiamKeniry 5 65
(Dominic Ffrench Davis) *trckd ldr tl drvn and lost 2nd 2f out: one pce after* **4/6**[1]

0 4 5 **Thechampagnesonice**[43] 5247 4-9-5 0 ........ SteveDrowne 4 49
(Malcolm Saunders) *t.k.h: in tch: rdn 3f out: outpcd by ldrs 2f out: no ch after* **33/1**

0 5 7 **Jumbo's Boy**[12] 6368 3-9-1 0 ........ JoshuaBryan(5) 6 33
(Peter Bowen) *prom: drvn 2f out: sn wknd* **40/1**

0 6 7 **Nitro**[51] 4964 3-9-1 0 ........ MitchGodwin(5) 1 15
(Roy Brotherton) *in rr: rdn over 4f out: no ch fnl 3f* **200/1**

7 2 ¼ **Cymru Lady** 3-9-1 0 ........ CharlesBishop 7 4
(Nikki Evans) *dwlt: a bhd* **40/1**

1m 23.54s (0.34) **Going Correction** +0.075s/f (Good)
**WFA** 3 from 4yo 4lb **7** Ran SP% **112.4**
Speed ratings (Par 103): **101,99,97,91,83 75,73**
CSF £15.52 TOTE £2.70: £1.20, £2.60; EX 12.60 Trifecta £23.40.
**Owner** Hamdan Al Maktoum **Bred** Shadwell Farm LLC **Trained** Lambourn, Berks

**FOCUS**
Only three mattered in this modest maiden and the odds-on favourite was put in his place. A small personal best from the winner.

### 6809 REECER PORTABLE BUILDINGS H'CAP 1m 14y
**3:40** (3:40) (Class 4) (0-85,86) 3-Y-O+ **£5,175** (£1,540; £769; £384) **Stalls** Centre

Form RPR
1143 1 **Rigoletto (SWI)**[21] 6073 3-9-8 86 ........ JamieSpencer 2 98+
(Luca Cumani) *chsd ldrs: led after 1f: mde rest: shkn up over 1f out: sn qcknd clr: comf* **5/4**[1]

1320 2 4 **Redgrave (IRE)**[18] 6203 3-9-4 82 ........(h) LukeMorris 1 84
(Charles Hills) *hld up: shkn up 3f out: drvn and hung lft over 1f out: styd on to go 2nd wl ins fnl f: no threat to wnr* **9/1**

5050 3 nk **Eltezam (IRE)**[14] 6322 4-9-12 85 ........ AdamKirby 6 87
(Amanda Perrett) *led 1f: trckd wnr: drvn over 2f out: outpcd by wnr over 1f out: kpt on: lost 2nd wl ins fnl f* **16/1**

516 4 ½ **Zymyran**[12] 6404 3-9-7 85 ........(h) SeanLevey 4 85
(David Simcock) *s.i.s: hld up: hdwy 3f out: drvn over 1f out: disp hld 2nd ins fnl f tl nr fin* **9/2**[3]

13-2 5 2 ¾ **Ehtiraas**[47] 5125 4-9-10 83 ........ DaneO'Neill 7 78
(Owen Burrows) *trckd ldng pair: drvn and lost 3rd 3f out: wknd fnl f* **9/4**[2]

0001 6 6 **Mister Musicmaster**[14] 6310 8-8-12 71 ........ SteveDrowne 8 52
(Ron Hodges) *in rr: drvn 2f out: wknd over 1f out* **20/1**

1m 35.35s (-0.85) **Going Correction** +0.075s/f (Good)
**WFA** 3 from 4yo+ 5lb **6** Ran SP% **114.0**
Speed ratings (Par 105): **107,103,102,102,99 93**
CSF £13.90 CT £121.95 TOTE £2.20: £1.60, £2.80; EX 12.30 Trifecta £57.70.
**Owner** Simon Capon **Bred** Stall Schloss Berg **Trained** Newmarket, Suffolk

**FOCUS**
A useful 3yo handicap and, with little early pace on, the favourite was wisely taken to the front. The race has been rated around the second.

### 6810 DAVIES, LOVELL AND SUTTON ON COURSE BOOKMAKERS H'CAP 5f 16y
**4:10** (4:10) (Class 5) (0-70,69) 3-Y-O+ **£3,234** (£962; £481; £240) **Stalls** Centre

Form RPR
3032 1 **David's Beauty (IRE)**[18] 6179 4-8-8 53 ........(b) LukeMorris 2 59
(Brian Baugh) *cl up: drvn over 1f out: r.o u.p to ld last strides* **13/2**

3445 2 hd **Zipedeedodah (IRE)**[10] 6478 5-9-5 69 ........(t) JoshuaBryan(5) 4 74
(Joseph Tuite) *chsd ldrs: shkn up to ld over 1f out: drvn and edgd rt fnl f: hdd last strides* **6/1**[3]

4033 3 ½ **Kingstreet Lady**[12] 6372 4-8-5 50 ........(p[1]) EdwardGreatrex 6 53
(Richard Price) *towards rr: drvn over 1f out: r.o ins fnl f: clsng nr fin* **11/1**

0332 4 nk **John Joiner**[5] 6652 5-8-11 56 ........ FrannyNorton 3 58
(Peter Hedger) *s.s: in rr: hdwy 1/2-way: rdn over 1f out: drvn and unable qck ins fnl f* **15/8**[1]

5435 5 ½ **Bonjour Steve**[20] 6099 6-9-3 62 ........(p) DavidProbert 10 62
(Richard Price) *s.i.s: in rr: drvn 1/2-way: r.o fnl f: nrst fin* **3/1**[2]

0133 6 3 ¼ **Quantum Dot (IRE)**[15] 6278 6-9-0 62 ........(b) CallumShepherd(3) 1 51
(Ed de Giles) *led: rdn 2f out: hdd over 1f out: wknd ins fnl f* **13/2**

640 7 nk **Picc And Go**[65] 4445 4-8-7 52 ........ KieranO'Neill 7 40
(Matthew Salaman) *chsd ldrs: rdn over 2f out: hung rt and wknd fnl f* **66/1**

59.44s (0.14) **Going Correction** +0.075s/f (Good) **7** Ran SP% **110.6**
Speed ratings (Par 103): **101,100,99,99,98 93,92**
CSF £41.36 CT £399.21 TOTE £6.90: £3.40, £2.10; EX 41.60 Trifecta £256.20.
**Owner** G B Hignett **Bred** Miss Sinead Looney **Trained** Audley, Staffs
■ Diminutive was withdrawn. Rule 4 does not apply.

**FOCUS**
A moderate but competitive sprint. The winner put up her best effort since February.

### 6811 ANDREA AND MARTIN BIG WEDDING DAY H'CAP 1m 2f
**4:40** (4:40) (Class 5) (0-75,77) 4-Y-O+ **£3,234** (£962; £481; £240) **Stalls** Low

Form RPR
103 1 **Sparte Quercus (IRE)**[13] 6344 4-9-7 73 ........ FrannyNorton 5 86
(Ed Dunlop) *trckd ldrs: wnt 2nd 2f out: led appr fnl f: shkn up and r.o strly* **11/4**[1]

344 2 4 ½ **Angelical (IRE)**[20] 6109 4-8-6 58 ........ KieranO'Neill 4 62
(Daniel Mark Loughnane) *led: rdn 3f out: drvn and hdd appr fnl f: one pce and no ch w wnr* **6/1**

1231 3 2 **Seven Clans (IRE)**[19] 6144 5-9-2 68 ........(b) AdamKirby 1 68
(Neil Mulholland) *midfield: rdn and unable qck 3f out: styd on to go 3rd ins fnl f* **3/1**[2]

513 4 nk **Priors Brook**[29] 5747 6-9-6 77 ........ JoshuaBryan(5) 8 76
(Andrew Balding) *trckd ldr: drvn and lost 2nd 2f out: one pce* **7/2**[3]

0266 5 3 **Glorious Poet**[16] 6273 4-9-4 70 ........ LukeMorris 6 63
(John Spearing) *wnt to post early: hld up and t.k.h: rdn 3f out: outpcd 2f out: modest late hdwy* **8/1**

5126 6 ¾ **Rowlestonerendezvu**[14] 6307 4-8-7 59 ........ DavidProbert 2 51
(Tony Carroll) *wnt to post early: s.i.s: towards rr: hdwy 4f out: rdn over 2f out: wknd fnl f* **7/1**

536- 7 21 **Cry Fury**[14] 6424 9-8-7 59 ........(t) EdwardGreatrex 7 9
(Matt Sheppard) *dwlt bdly: in rr: effrt on outer 4f out: no imp: lost tch 2f out: t.o* **40/1**

000- 8 16 **Peak Hill**[366] 6190 4-8-8 60 ........ TomMarquand 3
(Adrian Wintle) *trckd ldrs: rdn 4f out: sn wknd: t.o* **66/1**

2m 7.92s (-2.68) **Going Correction** -0.125s/f (Firm) **8** Ran SP% **115.7**
Speed ratings (Par 103): **105,101,99,99,97 96,79,66**
CSF £20.09 CT £52.20 TOTE £3.80: £1.10, £2.40, £1.20; EX 22.10 Trifecta £94.70.
**Owner** S F Hui **Bred** Daniel Chassagneux **Trained** Newmarket, Suffolk

**FOCUS**
A modest handicap but a progressive winner. The race has been rated around the second.

## 6812 DAILY RACING SPECIALS AT 188BET APPRENTICE H'CAP — 1m 4f
5:10 (5:10) (Class 6) (0-65,67) 3-Y-O — £2,587 (£770; £384; £192) Stalls Low

Form — RPR

0-22 **1** **Meyandi**[41] 5320 3-9-9 **66** .......... JoshuaBryan(3) 5 — 79+
(Andrew Balding) *chsd ldrs: led after 4f: increased pce 3f out: drvn 2f out: stdy on wl* **5/2**[2]

-401 **2** 3¼ **Mirimar (IRE)**[32] 5653 3-9-10 **64** .......... EdwardGreatrex 1 — 72+
(Ed Vaughan) *t.k.h: prom: wnt 2nd 3f out: sn drvn: styd on but a hld by wnr* **7/2**[3]

5-22 **3** 6 **Starshell (IRE)**[99] 3178 3-9-5 **64** .......... ManuelFernandes(5) 8 — 62
(Sir Mark Prescott Bt) *in tch towards rr: hdwy 3f out: rdn and unable qck over 2f out: styd on to go modest 3rd ins fnl f* **2/1**[1]

-653 **4** 1 **Katabatika**[22] 6032 3-8-11 **56** .......... WilliamCox(5) 3 — 53
(Hughie Morrison) *s.i.s: hld up: hdwy into midfield after 5f: drvn over 2f out: in modest 3rd 2f out tl ins fnl f* **12/1**

6005 **5** 2½ **Celtik Secret**[26] 5867 3-8-11 **58** .......... TheodoreLadd(7) 2 — 51
(Hughie Morrison) *hld up: rdn over 2f out: styd on but nvr any threat* **33/1**

2554 **6** 4 **Malt Teaser (FR)**[27] 5843 3-9-7 **64** .......... PaddyPilley(3) 6 — 50
(John Best) *trckd ldrs: drvn 3f out: wknd 2f out* **14/1**

6446 **7** 1 **Helf (IRE)**[21] 6075 3-9-8 **67** .......... RossaRyan(5) 9 — 52
(Richard Hannon) *t.k.h early: led 4f: lost 2nd 3f out: sn rdn and nt qckn: wknd fnl f* **16/1**

064 **8** 1 **Zihaam**[7] 6573 3-9-4 **63** .......... (p) BenSanderson(5) 7 — 46
(Roger Fell) *s.i.s: sn in midfield: rdn over 4f out: wknd 2f out* **16/1**

0540 **9** 13 **Sakurajima (IRE)**[15] 6293 3-9-9 **63** .......... (t) CallumShepherd 10 — 25
(Charles Hills) *hld up: rdn 3f out: wknd 2f out* **20/1**

2m 37.64s (-1.36) **Going Correction** -0.125s/f (Firm) — **9** Ran SP% **118.0**
Speed ratings (Par 99): **99,96,92,92,90 87,87,86,77**
CSF £12.09 CT £20.39 TOTE £4.00: £1.30, £1.40, £1.70; EX 12.50 Trifecta £21.50.
**Owner** Mick and Janice Mariscotti **Bred** I Robinson & B Holland **Trained** Kingsclere, Hants

**FOCUS**
Run at a steady pace, little got into it and the first two were clear. There is more to come from the pair.
T/Plt: £169.10 to a £1 stake. Pool: £82,345.84 - 355.40 winning units. T/Qpdt: £30.60 to a £1 stake. Pool: £6,066.23 - 146.24 winning units. **Richard Lowther**

# 6790 KEMPTON (A.W) (R-H)
### Wednesday, September 6

**OFFICIAL GOING: Polytrack: standard to slow (watered)**
Wind: Breeze across Weather: Fine

## 6813 32RED CASINO H'CAP (DIV I) — 7f (P)
5:20 (5:23) (Class 6) (0-55,55) 3-Y-O+ — £2,264 (£673; £336; £168) Stalls Low

Form — RPR

5036 **1** **Chetan**[20] 6112 5-9-5 **54** .......... (t) BenCurtis 3 — 63
(Charlie Wallis) *hld up in mid-div on outer: shkn up over 3f out: rdn wl over 2f out and no immediate rspnse: swtchd to wd outside and began to pick up over 1f out: styd on wl and led 125yds out: in control and pushed out fnl 55yds* **2/1**[1]

-000 **2** 2¼ **Fever Few**[20] 6113 8-9-3 **55** .......... SimonPearce(3) 7 — 58
(Chris Wall) *chsd ldrs in 3rd on outer: rdn 2f out: led jst ins fnl f: hdd 125yds out: one pce after to hold 2nd* **10/1**[2]

0450 **3** ¾ **Locommotion**[89] 3522 5-9-4 **53** .......... JohnFahy 10 — 54
(Matthew Salaman) *chsd ldr and carried hd high: rdn 2f out and sn led: kpt on tl hdd jst ins fnl f: styd on one pce ins fnl f* **20/1**

2440 **4** 1¾ **Black Truffle (FR)**[28] 5792 7-8-9 **51** .......... (v) NicolaCurrie(7) 14 — 47
(Mark Usher) *hld up in rr-div on outer: shkn up and angled to inner over 2f out: rdn 2f out: styd on one pce and tk 3rd fnl 100yds* **16/1**

6052 **5** ½ **Morello (IRE)**[14] 6324 3-9-1 **54** .......... FranBerry 2 — 47
(Henry Candy) *gd early pce: sn taken bk and settled bhd ldrs on inner: rdn wl over 1f out: tk 3rd ent fnl f where ev ch: sn one pce and lost 3rd fnl 100yds* **2/1**[1]

6514 **6** ½ **Gypsy Rider**[81] 3823 8-8-11 **49** .......... TimClark(3) 1 — 42
(Henry Tett) *in rr-div on inner: rdn 2f out and stuck to rail: kpt on one pce fr over 1f out* **16/1**

6050 **7** 4 **Posh Bounty**[20] 6106 6-9-4 **53** .......... JimmyQuinn 11 — 36
(Paul Burgoyne) *sn c across fr wd draw so sit in rr: rdn 2f out and wnt to inner: plenty to do whn n.m.r ent fnl f: shuffled along after* **33/1**

0000 **8** 1½ **Champagne Freddie**[9] 6503 4-9-5 **54** .......... MartinHarley 4 — 33
(John O'Shea) *chsd ldrs in 4th: niggled along wl over 2f out: rdn 2f out: kpt on tl no ex ent fnl f: one pce after* **14/1**[3]

0500 **9** 1¼ **Deer Song**[10] 6478 4-8-12 **52** .......... JaneElliott(5) 9 — 27
(John Bridger) *hld up in rr: rdn over 2f out: struggling fr over 1f out: kpt on one pce after* **33/1**

0000 **10** ¾ **Parisian Chic (IRE)**[23] 6004 3-8-10 **54** .......... (v[1]) PaddyBradley(5) 6 — 25
(Lee Carter) *s.s and in rr: rdn over 2f out: sn struggling and lost tch wl over 1f out: plugged on ins fnl f* **14/1**[3]

0600 **11** 6 **Whaleweigh Station**[104] 3001 6-9-3 **52** .......... SilvestreDeSousa 12 — 9
(J R Jenkins) *sn led: rdn over 2f out: hdd 2f out: sn wknd and ease ins fnl f* **16/1**

1m 25.94s (-0.06) **Going Correction** +0.075s/f (Slow)
**WFA** 3 from 4yo+ 4lb — **11** Ran SP% **117.4**
Speed ratings (Par 101): **103,100,99,97,97 96,91,90,88,87 81**
CSF £23.99 CT £313.76 TOTE £3.10: £1.10, £2.70, £4.60; EX 24.50 Trifecta £362.50.
**Owner** Roger & Val Miles, Tony Stamp **Bred** Andrew W Robson **Trained** Ardleigh, Essex
■ Never Folding was withdrawn. Price at time of withdrawal 4-1. Rule 4 applies to all bets - Deduction 20p in the pound.

**FOCUS**
The going was standard to slow. A modest Class 6 where C&D form came to the fore and there was a well-punted winner. The race has been rated around the third.

## 6814 32RED CASINO H'CAP (DIV II) — 7f (P)
5:55 (5:56) (Class 6) (0-55,61) 3-Y-O+ — £2,264 (£673; £336; £168) Stalls Low

Form — RPR

6434 **1** **Queens Royale**[16] 6265 3-9-2 **55** .......... RobertWinston 5 — 61
(Michael Appleby) *sn led and mde all: rdn 2f out: kpt on wl ins fnl f: pushed out nr fin* **5/2**[1]

340 **2** ½ **Magic Mirror**[70] 4214 4-9-5 **54** .......... (v) FranBerry 7 — 61
(Mark Rimell) *hld up in last: c to outer wl over 2f out: sn shkn up: rdn w plenty to do wl over 1f out: qcknd up wl and rapid prog: effrt flattened out sltly fnl 110yds: stl clsng on ldng pair and tk 2nd nr fin* **3/1**[2]

4002 **3** 1 **Arcanista (IRE)**[14] 6318 4-9-3 **52** .......... (p) SilvestreDeSousa 1 — 56
(Chris Dwyer) *racd in 3rd on inner: rdn over 1f out in 2nd: styd on chsng wnr tl one pce and lost 2nd nr fin* **4/1**[3]

0-30 **4** ½ **Royal Caper**[81] 3823 7-8-12 **50** .......... RosieJessop(3) 4 — 53
(Miss Joey Ellis) *hld up in mid-div on inner: tk clsr order 2f out and sn rdn: kpt on over 1f out: one pce ins fnl f: lost 3rd fnl 150yds* **5/1**

000 **5** nk **Frangarry (IRE)**[20] 6114 5-9-3 **52** .......... JimmyQuinn 6 — 54
(Alan Bailey) *hld up in mid-div between horses: rdn 2f out: n.m.r ent fnl f and swtchd lft: kpt on one pce after* **16/1**

-000 **6** 1 **Jasmincita (IRE)**[135] 2017 3-9-0 **53** .......... (p[1]) TrevorWhelan 3 — 50
(George Baker) *in last trio on inner: rdn 2f out and wnt to inner: sme prog tl no ex fr jst over 1f out* **50/1**

4000 **7** 1¾ **Little Indian**[20] 6112 7-9-1 **50** .......... TomQueally 14 — 44
(J R Jenkins) *in rr: rdn 2f out: plenty to do ent fnl f in 8th: nt qckn and shuffled along ins fnl f* **33/1**

466 **8** ½ **Bird For Life**[72] 4164 3-8-8 **54** .......... NicolaCurrie(7) 12 — 45
(Mark Usher) *mid-div on outer and racd wd on bnd: rdn over 2f out: dropped to last 2f out: plugged on fr over 1f out* **50/1**

6640 **9** ½ **Welsh Inlet (IRE)**[21] 6076 9-9-3 **52** .......... WilliamCarson 11 — 44
(John Bridger) *bhd ldrs: struggling whn rdn along over 2f out: no ex over 1f out and wknd* **20/1**

5156 **10** 8 **Jazz Legend (USA)**[26] 5892 4-8-13 **53** .......... (h) BenRobinson(5) 8 — 23
(Mandy Rowland) *pressed ldr and t.k.h: rdn 2f out and wnt bkwards: in last 1f out and pushed out* **16/1**

1m 26.51s (0.51) **Going Correction** +0.075s/f (Slow)
**WFA** 3 from 4yo+ 4lb — **10** Ran SP% **113.6**
Speed ratings (Par 101): **100,99,98,97,97 96,94,93,93,83**
CSF £9.39 CT £27.93 TOTE £3.70: £2.00, £1.30, £1.30; EX 11.60 Trifecta £41.00.
**Owner** Wayne Brackstone, Steve Whitear **Bred** W Brackstone & S J Whitear **Trained** Oakham, Rutland

**FOCUS**
Division two of the Class 6 contest looked the more interesting contest and was won from the front as the market principals came to the fore. It was run just over half a second slower than the first division.

## 6815 WATCH RACING UK ON VIRGIN 536 NURSERY H'CAP (JOCKEY CLUB GRASSROOTS NURSERY QUALIFIER) — 7f (P)
6:25 (6:28) (Class 6) (0-60,62) 2-Y-O — £2,587 (£770; £384; £192) Stalls Low

Form — RPR

0001 **1** **Mountain Peak**[21] 6063 2-9-9 **62** .......... LiamKeniry 11 — 68+
(Ed Walker) *sn led and mde all: pressed over 2f out: sn shkn up and qcknd up wl: rdn over 1f out: 3 l ld ent fnl f: plcd horses clsng nr fin: rdn out* **5/1**[2]

5661 **2** 1¼ **Data Protection**[12] 6366 2-9-4 **60** .......... HectorCrouch(3) 9 — 63
(William Muir) *tk false step leaving stalls: in rr-div: rdn wl over 2f out and prog fr over 1f out: kpt on wl between horses ins fnl f to take 2nd nr fin* **9/1**[3]

0042 **3** ¾ **Ray Purchase**[6] 6625 2-8-9 **48** .......... ShaneKelly 2 — 49
(Keith Dalgleish) *chsd ldrs: racd a little keen at times: rdn wl over 1f out in 2nd: styd on ins fnl f: lost 2nd nr fin* **5/1**[2]

0020 **4** ½ **Shoyd**[7] 6585 2-9-6 **62** .......... HollieDoyle(3) 12 — 62
(Richard Hannon) *covered up between horses chsng ldrs: rdn to chse wnr wl over 1f out: kpt on ins fnl f* **9/1**[3]

5000 **5** 1¾ **Tarnemah (IRE)**[7] 6585 2-8-13 **52** .......... HarryBentley 1 — 47
(George Peckham) *chsd ldr on outer: rdn 2f out and stuck to inner: 3rd wl over 1f out: plugged on one pce ins fnl f* **25/1**

0034 **6** 4 **Super Florence (IRE)**[7] 6585 2-9-8 **61** .......... CharlesBishop 10 — 45
(Eve Johnson Houghton) *tk fierce hold in rr-div: settled by 4f out: shkn up over 3f out and prog chsng ldrs: rdn 2f out: plugged on: can do bttr* **10/1**

5002 **7** ¾ **Mouchee (IRE)**[7] 6585 2-9-4 **57** .......... SilvestreDeSousa 4 — 39
(David Evans) *racd on 4th out wd: lost a few pls on bnd wl over 3f out: shkn up over 2f out: no imp on ldrs and one pce fr over 1f out* **15/8**[1]

0060 **8** nk **Daffrah**[22] 6022 2-9-5 **58** .......... MartinHarley 3 — 39
(James Tate) *racd in mid-div on inner: rdn 2f out: one pce over 1f out* **20/1**

0600 **9** 3½ **My Guy (IRE)**[21] 6063 2-8-9 **48** .......... (p) JohnFahy 5 — 20
(J S Moore) *racd in last: rdn over 2f out: sn hld and plugged on* **66/1**

540 **10** 1½ **Blazing Beryl (IRE)**[23] 6005 2-9-7 **60** .......... OisinMurphy 7 — 28
(Brian Meehan) *in rr: rdn along at 1/2-way: no ex and nudged out fr 2f out* **16/1**

0500 **11** 2¼ **Afterthisone**[21] 6063 2-8-6 **45** .......... (h[1]) RobHornby 6 — 7
(Robin Dickin) *in rr: rdn wl over 2f out: no ex over 1f out: nudged out after* **100/1**

005 **12** 6 **Compton Grace**[28] 5779 2-8-13 **52** .......... JFEgan 8
(Mick Channon) *chsd ldr on outer: rdn over 2f out: sn no ex and wknd* **50/1**

1m 27.16s (1.16) **Going Correction** +0.075s/f (Slow) — **12** Ran SP% **116.1**
Speed ratings (Par 93): **96,94,93,93,91 86,85,85,81,79 77,70**
CSF £46.06 CT £239.50 TOTE £5.80: £1.60, £2.90, £1.80; EX 49.40 Trifecta £217.90.
**Owner** Ebury Racing **Bred** Mrs Hugh Maitland-Jones **Trained** Upper Lambourn, Berks

**FOCUS**
An interesting nursery run a little slower than the two Class 6 contests that opened the card. The race has been rated around the placed horses.

## 6816 32RED ON THE APP STORE NOVICE AUCTION STKS — 6f (P)
6:55 (6:57) (Class 5) 2-Y-O — £3,234 (£962; £481; £240) Stalls Low

Form — RPR

5 **1** **Ortiz**[44] 5216 2-8-11 0 .......... HarryBentley 10 — 75+
(Henry Candy) *chsd ldr on outer: upsides ldr and shkn up 2f out: led over 1f out: sn rdn: extended advantage being pushed out wl ins fnl f* **10/11**[1]

0330 **2** 2 **Iconic Knight (IRE)**[33] 5596 2-9-2 74 .......... LiamKeniry 3 — 74
(Ed Walker) *racd on inner bhd ldrs: n.m.r on heels 2f out and t.k.h: shkn up and chal between horses wl over 1f out: ev ch ent fnl f where tk 2nd: one pce wl ins fnl f* **5/2**[2]

2346 **3** 2 **Joegogo (IRE)**[39] 5430 2-9-2 71 .......... SilvestreDeSousa 8 — 68
(David Evans) *led: rdn wl over 1f out: hdd over 1f out: plugged on one pce after* **5/2**[2]

**4** 2¾ **Shamrock Emma (IRE)** 2-8-11 0 .......... PatDobbs 7 — 55
(John Best) *settled bhd ldrs: rdn wl over 1f out: kpt on nicely tl shuffled along ins fnl f* **25/1**

00 **5** 2¾ **Disapproval (IRE)**[81] 3821 2-8-11 0 .......... (h[1]) GeorgeDowning 4 — 47
(Daniel Kubler) *racd in mid-div: rdn over 2f out w plenty to do: plugged on fr over 1f out: kpt on one pce ins fnl f* **33/1**

00 **6** 1½ **Pammi**[26] 5885 2-8-11 0 .......... RyanTate 2 — 42
(Anthony Carson) *racd in 3rd on inner: rdn 2f out: one pce fr over 1f out and sn no ex ent fnl f: wknd qckly* **66/1**

00 **7** *2* **Landue**[64] 4465 2-8-9 0 TylerSaunders(7) 1 41
(Marcus Tregoning) *in last trio detached fr main gp: shkn up fr 2f out: nvr involved* **16/1**[3]

**8** *3* **Soft Sand** 2-9-2 0 TomQueally 11 32
(Peter Crate) *in last trio detached fr main gp: shkn up fr 2f out: nvr involved* **50/1**

P **9** *2 ½* **Tipi**[6] 6636 2-9-2 0 BenCurtis 6 25
(Charlie Wallis) *racd in mid-div: rdn along over 2f out: sn wknd* **100/1**

**10** *2* **Ragstone Sand (IRE)** 2-9-2 0 ShaneKelly 5 19
(Murty McGrath) *in last trio detached fr main gp: shkn up fr 2f out: nvr involved* **50/1**

1m 13.96s (0.86) **Going Correction** +0.075s/f (Slow) **10** Ran SP% **128.6**
Speed ratings (Par 95): **97,94,91,88,84 82,79,75,72,69**
CSF £3.92 TOTE £2.30: £1.10, £1.40, £1.30; EX 6.30 Trifecta £10.10.
**Owner** Paul G Jacobs **Bred** Whitley Stud **Trained** Kingston Warren, Oxon

**FOCUS**
An ordinary novice, with the front three in the market having it between them. The race has been rated around the balance of the placed horses.

## 6817 32RED.COM MAIDEN STKS 1m (P)
7:25 (7:28) (Class 5) 3-Y-0+ **£2,911** (£866; £432; £216) Stalls Low

Form RPR

0 **1** **Clearly**[44] 5220 3-9-0 0 JamesDoyle 1 74+
(John Gosden) *green bhd stalls: loaded wout rdr: sluggish s: settled in rr-div on rail: shkn up in 7th jst over 1f out w plenty to do: qcknd up smartly ins fnl f and led nr fin: impressive* **7/1**[3]

42 **2** *hd* **Tamih (IRE)**[68] 4309 3-9-5 0 AndreaAtzeni 3 78+
(Roger Varian) *racd in 3rd on inner: rdn over 1f out and sn led: kpt on wl tl hdd cl home: fought bk nr fin* **1/1**[1]

30 **3** *1 ¼* **Jafetica**[30] 5721 3-9-0 0 (h) TomQueally 7 70+
(James Fanshawe) *settled in mid-div between horses: tk clsr order on outer 2f out: rdn over 1f out: kpt on nicely and tk 3rd wl ins fnl f* **25/1**

02 **4** *shd* **Zain Star (IRE)**[28] 5794 3-9-5 0 JFEgan 12 75
(John Butler) *between horses chsng ldrs: rdn over 2f out: kpt on ins fnl f* **3/1**[2]

56 **5** *3* **Circuit Judge**[20] 6103 3-9-5 0 SilvestreDeSousa 8 68
(William Knight) *pressed ldr in 2nd: rdn over 1f out: kpt on wl tl wknd ins fnl f* **25/1**

5 **6** *1 ½* **Freedom Fighter (IRE)**[22] 6031 7-9-10 0 (t) TimmyMurphy 4 65
(Tim Pinfield) *sn led: shkn up and clr ld over 3f out: rdn ent 2f out: hdd over 1f out: plugged on* **100/1**

5 **7** *½* **Fintech (IRE)**[6] 6633 3-9-5 0 (t) AdamBeschizza 9 63
(Mrs Ilka Gansera-Leveque) *racd in mid-div: rdn wl over 1f out on outer kpt on one pce ins fnl f* **25/1**

**8** *hd* **Calm Charm (IRE)** 3-8-11 0 GeorgeWood(3) 5 58+
(Chris Wall) *in rr-div on inner: shkn up wl over 1f out: kpt on nicely ent fnl f under hands and heels: likely improver* **66/1**

6 **9** *1 ¼* **Manners Maketh Man (IRE)**[12] 6368 3-9-5 0 HarryBentley 14 60
(Ralph Beckett) *in rr-div: shuffled along fr over 1f out and one pce ins fnl f* **25/1**

0 **10** *nse* **Sky Marshal (IRE)**[20] 6103 3-9-5 0 LiamKeniry 6 62+
(Ed Walker) *broke wl but restrained into rr: shkn up wl over 1f out and in last over 1f out: shuffled along between horses ins fnl f: nvr involved* **66/1**

**11** *1 ½* **Lady Of Steel** 3-9-0 0 DanielMuscutt 10 51
(John Butler) *in rr: shkn up wl over 3f out: in last 2f out and shkn up: shuffled along over 1f out: kpt on one pce after: nvr nrr* **80/1**

**12** *2 ¼* **Perfect Art** 3-9-0 0 PatDobbs 2 46
(Ralph Beckett) *between horses chsng ldrs: rdn 2f out and stl in contention: wknd over 1f out* **12/1**

**13** *1 ¾* **Peter Stuyvesant (IRE)** 3-9-5 0 OisinMurphy 11 46
(Denis Coakley) *in rr-div on outer: rdn along over 2f out: no ex fr over 1f out* **50/1**

0 **14** *3 ¼* **Maid Of Rock (IRE)**[15] 6287 3-9-0 0 AntonioFresu 13 34
(Mike Murphy) *chsd ldrs on outer: shkn up 2f out and fnd nil: wknd after* **125/1**

1m 41.22s (1.42) **Going Correction** +0.075s/f (Slow)
**WFA** 3 from 7yo 5lb **14** Ran SP% **118.5**
Speed ratings (Par 103): **95,94,93,93,90 88,88,88,87,86 85,83,81,78**
CSF £13.26 TOTE £7.80: £2.60, £1.02, £6.80; EX 17.50 Trifecta £221.80.
**Owner** Godolphin **Bred** Darley **Trained** Newmarket, Suffolk

**FOCUS**
Not a great deal of depth, but potentially a smart winner.

## 6818 100% PROFIT BOOST AT 32REDSPORT.COM FILLIES' H'CAP 1m (P)
7:55 (7:57) (Class 5) (0-75,77) 3-Y-0+ **£2,911** (£866; £432; £216) Stalls Low

Form RPR

0642 **1** **Ventura Blues (IRE)**[7] 6576 3-9-12 **77** (p) PatDobbs 12 86
(Richard Hannon) *in rr-div: shkn up and scythed way through pack fr 2f out: qcknd up ent fnl f: pushed out to ld fnl 110yds: snugly* **11/4**[1]

-203 **2** *½* **Narjes**[28] 5797 3-9-7 **72** (h) TomQueally 3 80
(James Fanshawe) *chsd ldr in 3rd: rdn on inner wl over 1f out: led 150yds out: hdd 110yds out: kpt on to hold 2nd* **11/4**[1]

5160 **3** *¾* **Scala Regia (FR)**[19] 6160 3-9-3 **68** (b[1]) LukeMorris 1 74
(Sir Mark Prescott Bt) *pushed along leaving stalls and sn led: hdd 5f out: rdn 2f out and led wl over 1f out: kpt on tl hdd 150yds out: stuck on but nt pce of front pair* **14/1**

2414 **4** *3 ½* **Carol (IRE)**[54] 4845 3-9-11 **76** JamesDoyle 4 74
(Ed Dunlop) *t.k.h bhd ldrs: shkn up over 2f out: rdn 2f out: ev ch ent fnl f: wknd and lft bhd by ldng trio ins fnl f* **8/1**[2]

414 **5** *¾* **The Yellow Bus**[36] 5510 4-9-6 **73** DarraghKeenan(7) 7 70
(John Butler) *hld up in rr-div on inner: rdn 2f out: kpt on one pce past btn horses fr over 1f out: nvr nrr* **12/1**

105 **6** *2* **Sea Tea Dea**[28] 5813 3-9-2 **67** RyanTate 2 58
(Anthony Carson) *plld hrd bhd ldrs: settled bttr by 1/2-way: rdn 2f out: chsd ldng over 1f out: kpt on tl no ex and wknd fnl f* **20/1**

0460 **7** *nk* **Braztime**[41] 5331 3-9-11 **76** SeanLevey 9 66
(Richard Hannon) *pressed ldr tl racd in 2nd 5f out: rdn 2f out: kpt on tl no ex and wknd fnl f* **20/1**

106 **8** *½* **Hidden Charms (IRE)**[41] 5324 3-9-7 **72** HarryBentley 13 61
(David Simcock) *hld up in rr: shkn up wl over 2f out: no imp on ldr but kpt on ins fnl f* **14/1**

6206 **9** *3* **Delirium (IRE)**[13] 6340 3-7-13 **55** oh2 (p) JaneElliott(5) 10 37
(Ed de Giles) *chsd ldrs out wd: rdn wl over 2f out: one pce fr over 1f out* **40/1**

-440 **10** *½* **South Sea Belle (IRE)**[20] 6106 3-9-5 **70** (t) KieranShoemark 11 51
(David Menuisier) *hld up in rr: rdn over 2f out: kpt on one pce fr over 1f out* **33/1**

4240 **11** *3 ¾* **Skidby Mill (IRE)**[132] 2116 7-10-0 **74** OisinMurphy 5 47
(Laura Mongan) *in mid-div on inner and t.k.h: shkn up 2f out and no rspnse: pushed out after* **50/1**

1066 **12** *1* **Harmonise**[54] 4845 3-9-8 **73** SilvestreDeSousa 6 42
(Mick Channon) *early spd tl t.k.h bhd ldrs: tk up ld 5f out and sn 1 l up: rdn and hdd wl over 1f out: dropped bk through pack jst over 1f out* **11/1**[3]

-546 **13** *3* **Many A Tale**[23] 6015 3-9-5 **70** (p[1]) BenCurtis 8 32
(Ismail Mohammed) *racd in rr-div on outer: rdn over 2f out: struggling over 1f out: sn no ex* **14/1**

1m 38.63s (-1.17) **Going Correction** +0.075s/f (Slow)
**WFA** 3 from 4yo+ 5lb **13** Ran SP% **117.3**
Speed ratings (Par 100): **108,107,106,103,102 100,100,99,96,96 92,91,88**
CSF £7.97 CT £91.64 TOTE £3.40: £1.40, £1.20, £3.90; EX 12.30 Trifecta £86.90.
**Owner** Middleham Park Racing VI **Bred** George Kent **Trained** East Everleigh, Wilts

**FOCUS**
A competitive mile handicap, decent for a Class 5 event, and the winner may turn up in the London Mile final in three days' time.

## 6819 32RED H'CAP 1m 3f 219y(P)
8:25 (8:26) (Class 4) (0-80,80) 3-Y-0+ **£4,690** (£1,395; £697; £348) Stalls Low

Form RPR

3522 **1** **Royal Reserve**[10] 6467 4-9-11 **79** MartinHarley 7 89+
(David O'Meara) *hld up in last: shkn up wl over 2f out and rapid prog on outer: rdn and swept into led 2f out: kpt on wl ins fnl f* **11/4**[2]

2141 **2** *¾* **Solo Mission**[18] 6210 3-9-4 **80** (b[1]) TomQueally 4 88
(William Haggas) *led for 2f: racd in 2nd after: rdn 2f out whn wnr swept past: kpt on wl ins fnl f but no ch w wnr* **6/5**[1]

4425 **3** *2 ½* **Saumur**[65] 4442 5-9-3 **71** OisinMurphy 8 75
(Denis Coakley) *hld up in 5th: hemmed in 2f out and sltly hmpd: rdn over 1f out: 5th ent fnl f: pushed along tl rdn out for 3rd nr fin: can do bttr* **16/1**

260 **4** *nk* **Clovelly Bay (IRE)**[19] 6135 6-8-13 **74** TylerSaunders(7) 2 78
(Marcus Tregoning) *racd in 3rd: rdn 2f out bhd horses and n.m.r: sn edgd lft and sltly hmpd rival: kpt on one pce tl lost 3rd nr fin* **7/1**

2603 **5** *6* **Artful Rogue (IRE)**[28] 5798 6-9-12 **80** KieranShoemark 3 74
(Amanda Perrett) *racd in 5th: rdn 2f out on outer: no imp on ldrs whn nudged out ins fnl f* **5/1**[3]

156/ **6** *¾* **Marju's Quest (IRE)**[18] 2208 7-8-11 **68** HollieDoyle(3) 6 61
(Adrian Wintle) *led after 2f: t.k.h: slowed tempo at 1/2-way: shkn up over 3f out: rdn over 2f out: hdd 2f out: wknd and dropped to 6th over 1f out: plugged on* **33/1**

4456 **7** *½* **Rubensian**[15] 6294 4-9-8 **76** (p[1]) SeanLevey 1 68
(David Simcock) *racd in 6th on inner: rdn 2f out: one pce and wknd fr 1f out* **14/1**

2m 35.36s (0.86) **Going Correction** +0.075s/f (Slow)
**WFA** 3 from 4yo+ 8lb **7** Ran SP% **116.8**
Speed ratings (Par 105): **100,99,97,97,93 93,92**
CSF £6.69 CT £41.38 TOTE £2.90: £1.30, £1.60; EX 8.50 Trifecta £79.70.
**Owner** Royal Guinness Reserve Partnership **Bred** New England, Myriad & Watership Down **Trained** Upper Helmsley, N Yorks

**FOCUS**
The highest class race on the card was won by a smart jockey on a useful AW performer. He is better than ever on sand.

## 6820 LIVE RACING UK ON FACEBOOK NOW H'CAP 1m 7f 218y(P)
8:55 (8:55) (Class 6) (0-60,60) 3-Y-0+ **£2,264** (£673; £252; £252) Stalls Low

Form RPR

0035 **1** **Franny Nisbet**[12] 6376 3-9-2 **59** MartinDwyer 11 64
(William Muir) *wnt lft s and settled in rr-div: shkn up over 3f out: rdn 3f out and swtchd to outer: plenty to do over 1f out in rr of pack: kpt on wl ins fnl f and led post* **14/1**

4524 **2** *shd* **General Allenby**[12] 6376 3-8-7 **50** (be) KierenFox 1 55
(Henry Tett) *cl up: rdn over 2f out and swtchd to inner: kpt on wl and led 110yds out: hdd post* **9/2**[1]

3030 **3** *½* **Black Prince (FR)**[44] 5209 3-8-10 **53** (t) JFEgan 3 57
(Anthony Honeyball) *hld up in rr: rdn over 2f out w plenty to do: kpt on strly ins fnl f tl dead-heated for 3rd post* **5/1**[2]

0000 **3** *dht* **Alternate Route**[15] 6293 3-8-13 **56** (p[1]) LukeMorris 4 60
(Sir Mark Prescott Bt) *mid-div on inner: rdn over 2f out in centre: kpt on wl ins fnl f to force dead-heat for 3rd post* **6/1**[3]

5023 **5** *shd* **Percy Thrower (IRE)**[18] 6180 3-8-11 **57** CallumShepherd(3) 12 61
(Charles Hills) *sn led: clr ldr at 1/2-way: ld reduced and rdn 3f out: battled on whn pressed over 1f out tl no ex and wknd nr fin* **13/2**

5335 **6** *¾* **Macksville (IRE)**[13] 6343 4-9-13 **59** (p) RyanTate 9 60
(James Eustace) *hld up in rr-div on inner: shkn up wl over 3f out: prog fr over 1f: kpt on one pce fnl 150yds* **13/2**

3-25 **7** *½* **Intimidator (IRE)**[70] 4217 6-9-12 **58** DanielMuscutt 10 59
(Miss Joey Ellis) *in rr-div on outer: shkn up and tk clsr order over 3f out on inner: rdn wl over 2f out and gd prog: chsd ldng pair ins fnl f: no ex fnl 150yds and wknd* **8/1**

0 **8** *nse* **Ballyfarsoon (IRE)**[37] 5483 6-9-9 **55** (p) JamesDoyle 8 56
(Ian Williams) *chsd ldrs: rdn 3f out: kpt on one pce on outer ins fnl f* **16/1**

0440 **9** *1* **See And Be Seen**[13] 6343 7-9-9 **60** (p) MitchGodwin(5) 7 59
(Sylvester Kirk) *mid-div on outer: rdn over 2f out on outer: kpt on one pce fr over 1f out* **12/1**

0000 **10** *2 ¼* **Breton Belle (IRE)**[27] 5846 3-8-6 **52** HollieDoyle(3) 6 51
(David Simcock) *racd in mid-div: rdn over 2f out on inner: kpt on tl no ex and one pce fnl f* **33/1**

2530 **11** *2 ¼* **Topalova**[16] 6259 4-9-2 **48** JoeyHaynes 14 42
(Mark H Tompkins) *chsd ldrs and plld hrd at times: rdn over 2f out: no ex fr over 1f out* **25/1**

0600 **12** *29* **Lady Prima**[23] 6006 3-8-5 **48** KieranO'Neill 5 9
(Mike Murphy) *led for 1f: settled bhd ldr on rail: sddle slipped wl over 2f out and eased: t.o* **33/1**

003- **13** *14* **Storm Hawk (IRE)**[532] 1043 10-9-6 **52** (v) TomQueally 2
(Emma Owen) *racd in last and niggled along to keep tch: no ex and eased fr over 2f out: t.o* **80/1**

3m 31.63s (1.53) **Going Correction** +0.075s/f (Slow)
**WFA** 3 from 4yo+ 11lb **13** Ran SP% **118.1**
Speed ratings (Par 101): **99,98,98,98,98 98,98,98,97,96 95,80,73**
WIN: FN 18.10; PL: FN 5.60, AR 1.10, GA 1.50, BP 1.20; EX: 120.30; CSF: 73.17; TC: 214.77, 184.14; TF: FN/GA/AR 1677.70, FN/GA/BP 858.90;.
**Owner** Purple And Lilac Racing V **Bred** Newsells Park Stud **Trained** Lambourn, Berks

**FOCUS**
A thrilling finale as the stayers served up a blanket finish. It was dominated by the 3yos.

T/Jkpt: Not Won T/Plt: £11.90 to a £1 stake. Pool: £83,445.70 - 5,110.15 winning units. T/Qpdt: £4.60 to a £1 stake. Pool: £8,818.70 - 1,409.98 winning units. **Cathal Gahan**

# 6582 LINGFIELD (L-H)

## Wednesday, September 6

**OFFICIAL GOING: Good to soft (7.3)**

Wind: Moderate, half against in home straight Weather: Fine but cloudy

## 6821 US OPEN TENNIS AT 188BET CLAIMING STKS — 1m 3f 133y

1:50 (1:50) (Class 6) 3-4-Y-O — **£2,264** (£673; £336; £168) **Stalls** High

Form — RPR

P631 **1** **Ejayteekay**[22] 6034 4-9-4 72 ........ CharlieBennett(3) 7 — 63+
(Hughie Morrison) *trckd ldrs: prog to go 2nd 3f out: chal over 2f out: drvn to ld over 1f out: drew clr last 100yds* **5/4**[1]

1300 **2** 2½ **Outcrop (IRE)**[7] 6579 3-9-4 75 ........ OisinMurphy 4 — 65+
(Hughie Morrison) *led: rdn over 2f out: hdd over 1f out: pressed wnr tl no ex last 100yds* **6/4**[2]

5526 **3** 5 **Bizet (IRE)**[7] 6587 3-8-3 51 ........(v) JackOsborn(7) 8 — 49
(John Ryan) *racd wd: in tch: pushed along over 4f out: prog u.p to take 3rd over 2f out: no imp on ldng pair after* **12/1**

0306 **4** 4 **Light Gunner (IRE)**[28] 5780 3-9-2 48 ........ TimClark(3) 2 — 52
(Henry Tett) *hld up in 7th: pushed along 3f out: rdn and prog to take 4th 2f out: no hdwy after* **25/1**

6545 **5** 3½ **Kaisan**[20] 6095 4-9-10 59 ........(bt) DanielMuscutt 6 — 42
(Bernard Llewellyn) *chsd ldr: urged along fr 1/2-way: lost 2nd 4f out: wknd over 2f out* **16/1**

0010 **6** 1¾ **Tojosimbre**[18] 6180 3-9-1 49 ........(t) ShaneKelly 5 — 39
(Richard Hughes) *in tch: hrd rdn and no prog over 2f out: sn wknd* **12/1**

1466 **7** 1½ **Ladofash**[98] 3220 3-8-10 61 ........(p[1]) SilvestreDeSousa 3 — 32
(Chris Gordon) *chsd ldng pair: wnt 2nd 4f out to 3f out: wknd qckly* **8/1**[3]

0000 **8** 8 **Greyjoy (IRE)**[21] 6076 3-8-2 40 ........ ShariqMohd(7) 1 — 18
(Sylvester Kirk) *dwlt: a last: lost tch 4f out: bhd after* **66/1**

2m 32.68s (1.18) **Going Correction** +0.025s/f (Good)
**WFA** 3 from 4yo 8lb — **8 Ran SP% 122.2**
Speed ratings (Par 101): **97,95,92,89,87 85,84,79**
CSF £3.67 TOTE £2.00: £1.10, £1.10, £4.10; EX 3.80 Trifecta £22.60.
**Owner** Miss Magdalena Gut **Bred** Pinehurst Stud **Trained** East Ilsley, Berks

**FOCUS**
With 5mm of overnight rain the official description of the ground was eased in the morning to "good to soft". A typically uncompetitive claimer, which the betting rightly suggested only concerned the Hughie Morrison pair.

## 6822 AMBANT FINE ART AND SPECIE H'CAP — 1m 2f

2:20 (2:20) (Class 4) (0-85,83) 3-Y-O — **£4,690** (£1,395; £697; £348) **Stalls** Low

Form — RPR

2461 **1** **Turnpike Trip**[16] 6277 3-9-7 81 ........ FergusSweeney 5 — 86
(Henry Candy) *trckd ldr: shkn up to chal over 2f out: rdn to take narrow ld over 1f out: kpt on and a holding on* **3/1**[3]

-122 **2** ½ **Harbour Rock**[26] 5868 3-9-7 81 ........ OisinMurphy 4 — 85
(David Simcock) *hld up in last: shkn up 3f out: wnt 3rd 2f out but sn under maximum press: kpt on to take 2nd nr fin and clsd on wnr: nvr doing it qckly enough* **2/1**[2]

5423 **3** nk **Pirate Look (IRE)**[61] 4580 3-9-5 79 ........(p) AndreaAtzeni 3 — 82
(Marco Botti) *led: shkn up and pressed over 2f out: narrowly hdd over 1f out: kpt on but lost 2nd nr fin* **13/8**[1]

2051 **4** 15 **Duchess Of Fife**[24] 5961 3-8-7 67 oh1 ........(v) SilvestreDeSousa 2 — 54
(William Knight) *t.k.h: hld up in 3rd: shkn up 3f out: fnd nil and wknd 2f out: eased and t.o* **7/1**

2m 9.89s (-0.61) **Going Correction** +0.025s/f (Good) — **4 Ran SP% 108.9**
Speed ratings (Par 103): **103,102,102,90**
CSF £9.27 TOTE £4.10; EX 9.00 Trifecta £13.10.
**Owner** Mrs David Blackburn **Bred** Mrs M J Blackburn **Trained** Kingston Warren, Oxon

**FOCUS**
A disappointing turnout for this fair handicap, but it resulted in a good, tight finish.

## 6823 OILFIELD OFFSHORE UNDERWRITING MEDIAN AUCTION MAIDEN STKS — 1m 3f 133y

2:50 (2:50) (Class 6) 3-4-Y-O — **£2,264** (£673; £336; £168) **Stalls** High

Form — RPR

52 **1** **Star Guide**[14] 6320 3-9-1 0 ........ MartinDwyer 5 — 71
(Sylvester Kirk) *t.k.h: trckd ldr: wd bnd over 3f out: sn led: pressed and shkn up over 2f out: pushed along and asserted over 1f out: kpt on wl* **5/1**[3]

56 **2** 1 **Sula Island**[30] 5721 3-9-1 0 ........ FergusSweeney 4 — 69
(Alan King) *t.k.h: hld up in last: wd bnd over 3f out: pressed wnr over 2f out: nt qckn over 1f out: kpt on same pce after* **5/2**[2]

60 **3** 1 **Golden Set**[18] 6194 3-9-1 0 ........ JimCrowley 1 — 68
(James Fanshawe) *led at mod pce: wd bnd over 3f out: sn hdd and dropped to last: rallied over 1f out: kpt on to take 3rd last strides* **8/1**

0433 **4** nk **War At Sea (IRE)**[20] 6110 3-9-6 77 ........(h) OisinMurphy 3 — 72
(David Simcock) *t.k.h: trckd ldng pair: shkn up 3f out and nt qckn: kpt on but nvr pce to chal seriously: lost 3rd last strides* **10/11**[1]

2m 37.81s (6.31) **Going Correction** +0.025s/f (Good) — **4 Ran SP% 108.7**
Speed ratings (Par 101): **79,78,77,77**
CSF £17.00 TOTE £4.40; EX 20.10 Trifecta £44.60.
**Owner** J C Smith **Bred** Littleton Stud **Trained** Upper Lambourn, Berks

**FOCUS**
They went slow in this maiden, meaning it was a messy race and the form is likely to be weak.

## 6824 HAYDOCK SPRINT BETTING AT 188BET MAIDEN AUCTION FILLIES' STKS (PLUS 10 RACE) — 7f

3:20 (3:21) (Class 5) 2-Y-O — **£2,911** (£866; £432; £216) **Stalls** Centre

Form — RPR

6 **1** **Claudine (IRE)**[12] 6394 2-8-6 0 ........ HarryBentley 1 — 65
(Henry Candy) *chsd ldrs in centre: rdn over 2f out: clsd over 1f out: drvn ahd 100yds out: jst fended off host of fast finers* **16/1**

4 **2** ½ **Vera Drake (FR)**[22] 6042 2-8-11 0 ........ TonyHamilton 2 — 69
(Richard Fahey) *dwlt: towards rr: rdn wl over 2f out: rapid prog on outer jst over 1f out: fin wl to take 2nd last strides* **5/1**[3]

**3** nk **Apple Anni (IRE)** 2-8-11 0 ........ JFEgan 6 — 68+
(Mick Channon) *in tch: rdn to chse ldrs over 2f out: swtchd rt to nr side rail ins fnl f and drvn to chal: jst outpcd* **14/1**

**4** nse **Lady Of Aran (IRE)** 2-8-11 0 ........ StevieDonohoe 3 — 68
(Charlie Fellowes) *dwlt: wl in rr: pushed along in last trio over 2f out: rapid prog on outer over 1f out: styd on nr fin: jst outpcd* **16/1**

**5** ½ **Tesorina (IRE)** 2-8-6 0 ........ KierenFox 10 — 62
(William Knight) *dwlt: mostly in last pair: shkn up wl over 2f out: rapid prog on wd outside jst over 1f out: clsd nr fin: jst outpcd* **33/1**

62 **6** shd **Isabella Mayson**[35] 5534 2-8-6 0 ........ MartinDwyer 5 — 62
(Stuart Kittow) *pressed ldr: rdn to chal over 2f out: narrow ld over 1f out: hdd 100yds out: swamped by fast finers last strides* **9/2**[2]

00 **7** ½ **Courteous Crown**[20] 6100 2-8-3 0 ........ HollieDoyle(3) 8 — 60
(Richard Hannon) *mde most: rdn and pressed over 2f out: narrowly hdd over 1f out: stl upsides ins fnl f: fdd and lost several pls last 75yds* **25/1**

3 **8** 2 **Golden Image**[20] 6100 2-8-6 0 ........ RobHornby 7 — 55
(Jonathan Portman) *pressed ldrs: rdn over 2f out: fdd over 1f out* **5/2**[1]

6 **9** 4½ **Golden Deal (IRE)**[30] 5717 2-8-11 0 ........(h) OisinMurphy 12 — 48
(Richard Phillips) *prom tl steadily wknd over 2f out* **25/1**

00 **10** 2 **Gainsay**[30] 5717 2-8-8 0 ........ GeorgeWood(3) 13 — 43
(Jonathan Portman) *chsd ldrs: drvn and effrt against nr side rail 3f out: wknd over 2f out* **66/1**

**11** shd **Chanson De La Mer (IRE)** 2-8-3 0 ow2 ........ GeorgiaCox(5) 9 — 40
(David Menuisier) *nvr bttr than midfield: wknd over 2f out* **12/1**

045 **12** 6 **Ruby's Gem**[19] 6140 2-8-6 71 ........ SilvestreDeSousa 4 — 22+
(Philip McBride) *hld up in rr: wknd over 2f out: eased* **9/2**[2]

**13** 1¼ **Mayhem Maybe (IRE)** 2-8-6 0 ........ JimmyQuinn 11 — 19
(Gay Kelleway) *t.k.h: in tch to 3f out: sn struggling* **33/1**

1m 25.89s (2.59) **Going Correction** +0.20s/f (Good) — **13 Ran SP% 122.8**
Speed ratings (Par 92): **93,92,92,92,91 91,90,88,83,81 80,74,72**
CSF £92.66 TOTE £16.70: £5.30, £1.80, £4.80; EX 88.70 Trifecta £952.70.
**Owner** Henry Candy & Partners III **Bred** H Calvey & T Kirwan **Trained** Kingston Warren, Oxon

**FOCUS**
No more than an ordinary maiden and they finished in a bit of a heap.

## 6825 OILFIELD INSURANCE AGENCIES NURSERY H'CAP — 6f

3:50 (3:51) (Class 5) (0-70,70) 2-Y-O — **£2,911** (£866; £432; £216) **Stalls** Centre

Form — RPR

5426 **1** **Global Exceed**[21] 6063 2-8-11 60 ........(b) SilvestreDeSousa 6 — 69
(Ed Dunlop) *racd on outer: chsd ldrs: clsd 2f out: rdn to ld jst over 1f out: hanging and racd awkwardly after but drvn clr* **4/1**[2]

2042 **2** 2½ **Kodiac Express (IRE)**[5] 6651 2-9-1 69 ........ GeorgeBuckell(5) 7 — 71
(Mike Murphy) *mde most towards centre: hdd jst over 1f out: outpcd after* **6/1**

6356 **3** hd **Peace Prevails**[29] 5751 2-9-2 65 ........(p[1]) TonyHamilton 1 — 66
(Richard Fahey) *racd on outer: wl in tch: rdn 2f out: one pce fr over 1f out* **16/1**

4551 **4** nk **W G Grace (IRE)**[15] 6285 2-9-2 65 ........ JamesDoyle 10 — 65
(Mark Johnston) *racd against nr side rail: on terms w ldrs: stl there over 1f out: sn lft bhd* **5/1**[3]

050 **5** ¾ **Couldn't Could She**[28] 5786 2-8-13 62 ........ RoystonFfrench 2 — 61
(Adam West) *sn rdn in last: struggling thrght and stl last 1f out: styd on to pass several rivals last 100yds* **50/1**

6612 **6** ½ **Song Of Summer**[29] 5751 2-9-5 68 ........ OisinMurphy 11 — 64
(Archie Watson) *chsd ldrs and racd towards nr side: rdn and fdd over 1f out* **11/4**[1]

054 **7** shd **Stormy Sand (IRE)**[19] 6147 2-9-6 69 ........(t[1]) AndreaAtzeni 12 — 65
(Marco Botti) *racd towards nr side: chsd ldrs: rdn 2f out: steadily fdd* **5/1**[3]

633 **8** ¾ **Retained (FR)**[63] 4496 2-9-4 67 ........ PatDobbs 5 — 61
(John Best) *in tch in rr: rdn and no prog 2f out: one pce after* **12/1**

246 **9** hd **Zain Flash**[82] 3769 2-9-4 67 ........ JFEgan 8 — 60
(David Evans) *pressed ldr to 2f out: wknd over 1f out* **16/1**

1m 12.61s (1.41) **Going Correction** +0.20s/f (Good) — **9 Ran SP% 115.7**
Speed ratings (Par 95): **98,94,94,94,93 92,92,91,90**
CSF £28.32 CT £347.94 TOTE £3.80: £1.70, £2.10, £3.80; EX 25.90 Trifecta £236.20.
**Owner** Dr Johnny Hon **Bred** The Blue Maiden Partnership **Trained** Newmarket, Suffolk

**FOCUS**
A modest nursery on paper, but the winner clearly has potential to progress out of 0-70 company.

## 6826 188BET MAIDEN STKS (DIV I) — 6f

4:20 (4:21) (Class 5) 2-Y-O — **£2,911** (£866; £432; £216) **Stalls** Centre

Form — RPR

2 **1** **Ragstone Road (IRE)**[21] 6071 2-9-5 0 ........ ShaneKelly 7 — 77
(Richard Hughes) *trckd ldrs: chal fr 2f out and upsides: rdn to ld 100yds out: quite readily* **11/10**[1]

04 **2** ½ **City Gent**[14] 6304 2-9-5 0 ........ PatDobbs 1 — 76
(Ralph Beckett) *pressed ldrs: narrow ld over 1f out: rdn and hdd last 100yds: kpt on* **10/1**

0 **3** 2¼ **Laubali**[21] 6071 2-9-5 0 ........ JimCrowley 13 — 69
(Owen Burrows) *w ldrs: led 2f out to over 1f out: one pce fnl f* **7/1**[3]

04 **4** 2¼ **Expelled**[27] 5844 2-9-5 0 ........ DanielMuscutt 3 — 62+
(James Fanshawe) *in tch: swtchd to nr side rail 2f out: shkn up and kpt on to take 4th last strides: nvr on terms w ldrs* **9/2**[2]

0 **5** ½ **Mutabaahy (IRE)**[99] 3169 2-9-5 0 ........(h[1]) KieranShoemark 4 — 61
(Ed Dunlop) *dwlt: towards rr: shkn up over 2f out: sme prog over 1f out: no hdwy fnl f* **25/1**

3 **6** 2¾ **Katie Lee (IRE)**[28] 5779 2-8-9 0 ........ GeorgiaCox(5) 10 — 47
(Henry Candy) *chsd ldrs: rdn 1/2-way: steadily wknd* **10/1**

**7** ¾ **Dracarys** 2-9-5 0 ........ OscarPereira 6 — 50
(Jose Santos) *rn green and outpcd in last pair: nvr on terms but kpt on fnl f* **66/1**

3 **8** nk **Bbob Alula**[18] 6178 2-9-5 0 ........(t) JFEgan 12 — 49
(Bill Turner) *led to 2f out: sn wknd* **16/1**

**9** 1¼ **Seaquinn** 2-8-7 0 ........ LeviWilliams(7) 8 — 40
(John Best) *towards rr: rn green and hung bdly lft fr 2f out: no prog* **66/1**

**10** 5 **Arigato** 2-9-5 0 ........ MartinLane 5 — 30
(William Jarvis) *dwlt: rn green and a bhd in last pair* **25/1**

1m 12.53s (1.33) **Going Correction** +0.20s/f (Good) — **10 Ran SP% 113.0**
Speed ratings (Par 95): **99,98,95,92,91 88,87,86,84,78**
CSF £12.25 TOTE £2.10: £1.20, £2.40, £1.90; EX 11.80 Trifecta £59.50.
**Owner** Gallagher Bloodstock Limited **Bred** Miss Debbie Kitchin **Trained** Upper Lambourn, Berks

■ Count Otto was withdrawn. Price at time of withdrawal 33-1. Rule 4 does not apply.

**FOCUS**
This looked the weaker of the two divisions.

## 6827 188BET MAIDEN STKS (DIV II) 6f
4:55 (4:55) (Class 5) 2-Y-O £2,911 (£866; £432; £216) Stalls Centre

Form RPR
2 **1** **Society Power (IRE)**[16] 6272 2-9-5 0 PatCosgrave 4 81+
(William Haggas) *in tch in midfield: shkn up over 2f out: prog on outer over 1f out: drvn and kpt on to ld last 75yds: mde heavy weather of it* **5/6**[1]

62 **2** ½ **Manthoor (IRE)**[27] 5851 2-9-5 0 JimCrowley 12 79
(Owen Burrows) *trckd ldrs and racd towards nr side: rdn to chal over 1f out: styd on and snatched 2nd last stride* **6/1**

422 **3** *shd* **Jupiter**[23] 6005 2-9-5 78 FergusSweeney 10 79
(Henry Candy) *racd against nr side rail: led 2f: led again 2f out: drvn over 1f out: hdd and no ex last 75yds* **5/1**[3]

2 **4** 2 ¾ **Mountain Guard (IRE)**[19] 6146 2-9-5 0 AndreaAtzeni 7 70
(Roger Varian) *pressed ldrs: rdn to chal over 1f out: fdd ins fnl f* **4/1**[2]

0 **5** 1 ¾ **Dance Emperor (IRE)**[21] 6071 2-9-5 0 DanielMuscutt 3 65
(Ed Walker) *in tch in midfield: taken to wd outside and pushed along 2f out: tk 5th fnl f: nt disgracd* **66/1**

4 **6** 2 ¼ **Cristal Pallas Cat (IRE)**[14] 6319 2-9-0 0 RhiainIngram(5) 5 58
(Roger Ingram) *pressed ldr: led after 2f to 2f out: wknd* **50/1**

06 **7** 1 **Insurgence**[21] 6071 2-9-2 0 GeorgeWood(3) 1 55
(James Fanshawe) *in tch in midfield: pushed along over 2f out: steadily wknd* **25/1**

06 **8** *nse* **Amaretto**[30] 5709 2-9-5 0 JackMitchell 6 55
(Jim Boyle) *hld up towards rr and racd nr side: pushed along over 2f out: shkn up briefly over 1f out: no prog* **66/1**

6 **9** 6 **River Rule**[37] 5476 2-9-0 0 AdamBeschizza 11 32
(Stuart Williams) *a in last pair and nvr on terms* **66/1**

**10** 9 **Gowing Gowing Gone (IRE)** 2-9-0 0 StevieDonohoe 8 5
(Richard Spencer) *a in last pair: wknd over 2f out: sn bhd* **20/1**

1m 11.63s (0.43) **Going Correction** +0.20s/f (Good) 10 Ran SP% **120.6**
Speed ratings (Par 95): **105,104,104,100,98 95,93,93,85,73**
CSF £6.45 TOTE £1.70: £1.10, £1.80, £1.80; EX 6.40 Trifecta £18.30.
**Owner** Sheikh Rashid Dalmook Al Maktoum **Bred** Tally-Ho Stud **Trained** Newmarket, Suffolk

**FOCUS**
On paper this looked stronger than the first division and there could be a decent type among those that hit the frame. There is more to come from the winner.

## 6828 PREMIER LEAGUE BETTING AT 188BET MEDIAN AUCTION MAIDEN FILLIES' STKS 7f
5:25 (5:30) (Class 6) 3-5-Y-O £2,264 (£673; £336; £168) Stalls Centre

Form RPR
3236 **1** **Hindsight**[67] 4378 3-9-0 72 AlistairRawlinson 1 61+
(Michael Appleby) *t.k.h: pressed ldrs: led 2f out gng easily: pushed out fnl f* **1/4**[1]

5650 **2** 1 ¾ **Cool Echo**[27] 5855 3-9-0 56 (v) FergusSweeney 7 56
(J R Jenkins) *reluctant to enter stall: hld up: prog and swtchd to nr side rail 1/2-way: chal 2f out: pressed wnr after and clr of rest: safely hld fnl f* **15/2**[3]

-463 **3** 6 **Assertor**[12] 6368 3-9-0 55 GeorgeDowning 4 40
(Tony Carroll) *w ldr: led 3f out to 2f out: fdd* **6/1**[2]

0 **4** ¾ **Danica Ashton**[15] 6295 3-9-0 0 StevieDonohoe 2 38
(Miss Joey Ellis) *slowly away: detached in last: drvn 2f out: hung lft and stl green over 1f out: tk modest 4th nr fin* **50/1**

0000 **5** ½ **Shamonix (IRE)**[23] 6009 3-9-0 40 DanielMuscutt 5 37
(Mark Usher) *chsd ldrs tl wknd 2f out* **50/1**

06 **6** 12 **Make Sail**[67] 4368 3-9-0 0 PatCosgrave 6 6
(Tony Carroll) *led to 3f out: wknd rapidly* **25/1**

6 **7** 10 **Musical Fire**[21] 6066 3-9-0 0 KieranShoemark 3
(Peter Hedger) *spd 3f: sn wknd and bhd: t.o* **20/1**

1m 25.38s (2.08) **Going Correction** +0.20s/f (Good) 7 Ran SP% **118.6**
Speed ratings (Par 98): **96,94,87,86,85 72,60**
CSF £3.04 TOTE £1.20: £1.02, £3.10; EX 4.60 Trifecta £8.10.
**Owner** Manor Farm Stud & Hoermann Equine **Bred** Manor Farm Stud (rutland) **Trained** Oakham, Rutland

**FOCUS**
A weak, uncompetitive fillies' maiden which provided a good opportunity for the 72-rated favourite to get off the mark. The race has been rated around the second.
T/Plt: £243.40 to a £1 stake. Pool: £67,059.88 - 201.06 winning units. T/Qpdt: £69.30 to a £1 stake. Pool: £4,224.12 - 45.10 winning units. **Jonathan Neesom**

6829 - 6843a (Foreign Racing) - See Raceform Interactive

# 6681 CHELMSFORD (A.W) (L-H)
Thursday, September 7

**OFFICIAL GOING: Standard: polytrack**
Wind: virtually nil Weather: overcast

## 6844 BET TOTEPLACEPOT AT BETFRED.COM NOVICE AUCTION STKS (PLUS 10 RACE) 6f (P)
5:40 (5:43) (Class 4) 2-Y-O £7,115 (£2,117; £1,058; £529) Stalls Centre

Form RPR
1 **1** **Hikmaa (IRE)**[28] 5834 2-8-12 0 (t[1]) AdamBeschizza 3 77+
(Ed Vaughan) *hld up in tch in midfield: swtchd rt and effrt over 1f out: hdwy to chse ldr ins fnl f: r.o wl to ld towards fin: sn in command* **4/6**[1]

3422 **2** ¾ **Gold Filigree (IRE)**[23] 6021 2-8-11 73 ShaneKelly 7 74
(Richard Hughes) *t.k.h early: led tl 4f out: styd upsides ldr tl led again over 1f out: sn rdn and kicked clr: drvn ins fnl f: hdd and nt match pce of wnr towards fin* **3/1**[2]

4 **3** 2 ½ **Priscilla's Dream**[27] 5885 2-8-4 0 LukeMorris 5 59
(Philip McBride) *t.k.h early: jostling w rival leaving stalls: chsd ldrs: shkn up wl over 1f out: sn drvn: kpt on to go 3rd ins fnl f: nvr enough pce to threaten ldng pair* **5/1**[3]

304 **4** 2 **Weeton (IRE)**[22] 6056 2-8-13 76 JoeDoyle 8 62
(Julie Camacho) *taken down early: t.k.h: chsd ldrs tl wnt 2nd 5f out: led 4f out tl rdn and hdd over 1f out: outpcd and hung lft 1f out: lost 2nd and wknd ins fnl f* **10/1**

0 **5** 1 ¼ **Shadow Seeker (IRE)**[56] 4815 2-8-10 0 KieranO'Neill 2 56
(Paul D'Arcy) *t.k.h early: chsd ldrs: rdn over 1f out: unable qck: btn and wkng whn nt clr run ins fnl f* **50/1**

65 **6** 1 **Agent Of Fortune**[19] 6199 2-7-13 0 (h) JaneElliott(5) 1 47
(Christine Dunnett) *chsd ldr early: stdd bk and hmpd sn after: in tch in last trio: rdn over 1f out: sn struggling and btn: kpt on same pce ins fnl f* **80/1**

45 **7** *nk* **Follow The Feeling (USA)**[12] 6433 2-8-2 0 GeorgiaCox(5) 6 49
(Henry Spiller) *t.k.h early: jostling w rival leaving stalls: hld up in tch: effrt wl over 1f out: sn outpcd: wl hld and kpt on same pce ins fnl f* **25/1**

**8** 1 **Roof Garden** 2-8-11 0 JoeyHaynes 4 50
(Mark H Tompkins) *rn green: in tch in rr but sn pushed along: rdn and wandered over 1f out: sn btn and bhd ins fnl f* **66/1**

1m 13.14s (-0.56) **Going Correction** -0.025s/f (Stan) 8 Ran SP% **119.3**
Speed ratings (Par 97): **102,101,97,95,93 92,91,90**
CSF £3.09 TOTE £1.50: £1.10, £1.10, £1.60; EX 3.10 Trifecta £7.70.
**Owner** Sheikh Hamed Dalmook Al Maktoum **Bred** L Wright **Trained** Newmarket, Suffolk

**FOCUS**
Just an ordinary race, but quite a taking winner. The runner-up helps set the opening level, with the third appearing to replicate her debut form.

## 6845 BET TOTEJACKPOT AT BETFRED.COM NURSERY H'CAP 1m (P)
6:10 (6:14) (Class 6) (0-65,65) 2-Y-O £3,234 (£962; £481; £240) Stalls Low

Form RPR
535 **1** **Sunbreak (IRE)**[34] 5608 2-9-7 65 JoeFanning 4 74
(Mark Johnston) *mde all and dictated stdy gallop: gng best and shkn up over 1f out: readily asserted and in command ins fnl f: easily* **3/1**[2]

0001 **2** 1 ¾ **Dream Of Delphi (IRE)**[8] 6585 2-8-5 54 6ex (b) GeorgiaCox(5) 1 59
(William Haggas) *t.k.h: trckd ldrs: swtchd lft and effrt on inner to chse wnr over 1f out: clr 2nd and 2 l down 1f out: kpt on but nvr threatening wnr* **1/1**[1]

0441 **3** 5 **Four Fifty Three**[23] 6022 2-9-2 60 JoeyHaynes 5 53
(Mark H Tompkins) *t.k.h: hld up in tch in last pair: effrt wl over 1f out: sn rdn and unable qck: no ch w ldng pair but kpt on to go 3rd ins fnl f* **8/1**

000 **4** ½ **Cherubic**[24] 6005 2-8-12 56 (b[1]) LukeMorris 3 48
(Charles Hills) *awkward leaving stalls: t.k.h: hld up in tch in last pair: effrt over 1f out: sn drvn and outpcd: no ch w ldng pair fnl f: plugged on to go 4th towards fin* **25/1**

0515 **5** 1 ¾ **That's My Girl (IRE)**[19] 6200 2-9-7 65 SeanLevey 2 52
(Richard Hannon) *trckd ldr: rdn 2f out: lost 2nd and unable qck over 1f out: wknd ins fnl f* **4/1**[3]

1m 41.24s (1.34) **Going Correction** -0.025s/f (Stan) 5 Ran SP% **110.0**
Speed ratings (Par 93): **92,90,85,84,83**
CSF £6.44 TOTE £3.60: £2.70, £1.10; EX 6.80 Trifecta £22.00.
**Owner** Sheikh Hamdan bin Mohammed Al Maktoum **Bred** Godolphin **Trained** Middleham Moor, N Yorks

**FOCUS**
Two finished clear in this modest nursery. The third has been rated just over a length below form.

## 6846 BET TOTEQUADPOT AT BETFRED.COM H'CAP (DIV I) 1m (P)
6:40 (6:43) (Class 6) (0-60,60) 3-Y-O+ £3,234 (£962; £481; £240) Stalls Low

Form RPR
2656 **1** **Fantasy Gladiator**[28] 5854 11-9-8 58 (be[1]) LukeMorris 2 65
(Michael Appleby) *broke wl but racing lazily and rousted along early: in tch in rr: nt clr run over 2f out: swtchd rt and hdwy 2f out: chsd ldrs over 1f out: styd on wl ins fnl f to ld towards fin* **5/2**[1]

6013 **2** ½ **La Isla Bonita**[24] 6016 3-9-5 60 StevieDonohoe 8 65
(Richard Spencer) *pressed ldr: rdn to chal over 1f out: sn drvn and sustained duel w ldr after: styd on u.p to ld wl ins fnl f: hdd and no ex towards fin* **3/1**[2]

0653 **3** ¾ **Break The Silence**[10] 6529 3-8-10 51 JoeFanning 7 54
(Scott Dixon) *led: rdn and hrd pressed over 1f out: sustained duel w chalr tl hdd wl ins fnl f: styd on same pce towards fin* **3/1**[2]

4055 **4** 5 **Hidden Stash**[65] 4463 3-8-9 53 HollieDoyle(3) 9 45
(William Stone) *chsd ldrs: 3rd and rdn over 1f out: outpcd and dropped to 4th over 1f out: wknd ins fnl f* **10/1**

065 **5** 3 ¼ **Sir Jamie**[76] 4143 4-9-1 51 WilliamCarson 4 36
(Tony Carroll) *t.k.h: hld up in tch in midfield: effrt over 1f out: sn outpcd and btn: wknd ins fnl f* **14/1**

U0-5 **6** 4 ½ **Sovrano Dolce (IRE)**[22] 6066 4-9-4 59 GeorgeBuckell(5) 1 34
(Mike Murphy) *chsd ldrs: rdn over 2f out: sn struggling and outpcd: wknd over 1f out* **28/1**

-000 **7** 5 **Golden Harbour (FR)**[44] 5239 3-8-5 46 oh1 (t) KieranO'Neill 6 8
(Alex Hales) *s.i.s: in tch towards rr: rdn over 3f out: drvn and lost pl over 1f out: wkng whn hung rt u.p 1f out* **33/1**

4000 **8** 8 **Eternal Dream**[22] 6067 3-9-0 55 (p[1]) MartinHarley 5
(William Knight) *taken down early: t.k.h: hld up in tch in midfield: lost pl qckly wl over 1f out: wl bhd ins fnl f* **6/1**[3]

20-0 **9** 30 **Lazizah**[65] 4461 4-9-2 52 MartinDwyer 3
(Marcus Tregoning) *a towards rr: dropped to last over 3f out: racd awkwardly and lost tch over 2f out: eased wl over 1f out* **10/1**

1m 40.28s (0.38) **Going Correction** -0.025s/f (Stan)
**WFA** 3 from 4yo+ 5lb 9 Ran SP% **124.1**
Speed ratings (Par 101): **97,96,95,90,87 83,78,70,40**
CSF £11.11 CT £24.56 TOTE £3.30: £1.40, £1.50, £1.60; EX 15.90 Trifecta £30.50.
**Owner** The Fantasy Fellowship **Bred** R S A Urquhart **Trained** Oakham, Rutland

**FOCUS**
The first three finished clear in this low-grade handicap. The second and third help set the opening level.

## 6847 BET TOTEQUADPOT AT BETFRED.COM H'CAP (DIV II) 1m (P)
7:10 (7:11) (Class 6) (0-60,59) 3-Y-O+ £3,234 (£962; £481; £240) Stalls Low

Form RPR
3024 **1** **Bradfield Magic (IRE)**[14] 6340 3-9-2 59 CallumShepherd(3) 1 63
(Charles Hills) *trckd ldrs: effrt on inner over 1f out: sn chalng u.p: sustained effrt to ld last strides* **2/1**[1]

4450 **2** *hd* **Touch The Clouds**[28] 5850 6-8-7 45 HollieDoyle(3) 8 50
(William Stone) *led: rdn and hrd pressed over 1f out: sustained duel w chalrs and kpt on wl u.p: hdd last strides* **14/1**

U506 **3** 1 ¼ **Belgravian (FR)**[26] 5935 3-9-3 57 (tp) LukeMorris 2 58
(Archie Watson) *t.k.h: pressed ldr: rdn and ev ch over 1f out: hrd drvn ins fnl f: unable qck and outpcd fnl 100yds* **10/3**[2]

00 **4** 5 **Lord Of The Storm**[128] 2257 9-9-8 57 KierenFox 5 48
(Michael Attwater) *s.i.s: hld up in tch in last pair: effrt on inner and hdwy into midfield over 1f out: 4th and no imp fnl f* **7/1**[3]

050 **5** 1 ¼ **Chocolate Account (USA)**[48] 5118 3-8-5 45 JoeFanning 3 32
(Ed Dunlop) *t.k.h: hld up in tch in midfield: effrt to go 4th but ldng trio gng clr over 1f out: no imp and wl hld fnl f* **8/1**

4000 **6** 2 ¼ **Caribbean Spring (IRE)**[21] 6112 4-9-5 59 JaneElliott(5) 9 42
(George Margarson) *dwlt and pushed along leaving stalls: in tch in rr: effrt wl over 1f out: sn outpcd and wknd fnl f* **8/1**

5054 **7** 3 ¼ **Cloud Nine (FR)**[52] 4968 4-9-1 **50**.......... WilliamCarson 7 25
(Tony Carroll) *dwlt: in tch in midfield: hdwy to chse ldrs 1/2-way: rdn over 2f out: sn struggling and wknd over 1f out* **10/1**

000 **8** 1 ½ **Poet's Quest**[20] 6150 3-8-6 **46**.......... RobHornby 6 17
(Dean Ivory) *chsd ldrs tl 1/2-way: steadily lost pl: wknd over 1f out and sn bhd* **16/1**

5300 **9** ½ **Circulate**[24] 6016 3-9-3 **57**..........(b) KieranO'Neill 4 27
(Tom Clover) *t.k.h: hld up in tch: nt clr run over 2f out: swtchd rt and effrt 2f out: sn drvn and outpcd: bhd whn swtchd lft 1f out* **25/1**

1m 40.29s (0.39) **Going Correction** -0.025s/f (Stan)
**WFA** 3 from 4yo+ 5lb **9** Ran SP% **116.6**
Speed ratings (Par 101): **97,96,95,90,89 87,83,82,81**
CSF £32.94 CT £91.88 TOTE £2.70: £1.40, £3.50, £1.80; EX 30.70 Trifecta £130.70.
**Owner** Chris Wright And The Bradfieldians **Bred** Stratford Place Stud **Trained** Lambourn, Berks

**FOCUS**
The pace held up in this weak handicap. The time was almost identical to that for the previous division. The winner has been rated in keeping with her Salisbury effort.

## 6848 BET TOTEEXACTA AT BETFRED.COM H'CAP 1m 2f (P)
**7:40** (7:41) (Class 4) (0-80,82) 3-Y-O+ **£8,086** (£2,406; £1,202; £601) **Stalls** Low

Form RPR

2306 **1** **Ourmullion**[27] 5888 3-8-11 **73**..........(p[1]) JosephineGordon 8 82
(John Best) *rn in snatches: wl in tch in midfield: effrt and hdwy over 1f out: styd on strly to ld 75yds out: rdn out* **20/1**

0541 **2** ¾ **Ice Dancing (IRE)**[20] 6160 3-9-3 **79**..........(h) LouisSteward 5 86
(Michael Bell) *taken down early: chsd ldrs: trcking ldng pair whn nt clr run and swtchd lft wl over 1f out: sn chalng: kpt on wl and sustained effrt: jst outpcd by wnr towards fin* **9/2**[1]

4150 **3** *shd* **Jufn**[33] 5643 4-9-8 **78**..........(h) LiamKeniry 7 84
(John Butler) *taken down early: led: rdn and qcknd 2f out: hrd pressed and drvn over 1f out: sustained duel w chalr tl jst outpcd by wnr fnl 75yds* **5/1**[2]

-031 **4** 1 ¼ **Graceful James (IRE)**[30] 5747 4-9-12 **82**.......... KieranO'Neill 12 85+
(Jimmy Fox) *t.k.h: hld up in tch in midfield: effrt over 2f out: no imp u.p tl hdwy ins fnl f: styd on wl fnl 100yds: nt rch ldrs* **9/2**[1]

-155 **5** 1 ¼ **Tan Arabiq**[20] 6143 4-8-12 **68**.......... LukeMorris 1 69
(Michael Appleby) *t.k.h: wl in tch in midfield: effrt u.p to chse ldrs over 1f out: unable qck 1f out wknd ins fnl f* **7/1**[3]

1525 **6** *hd* **X Rated (IRE)**[32] 5686 3-9-2 **78**.......... JoeFanning 11 79
(Mark Johnston) *chsd ldr: rdn and pressing wnr 2f out: unable qck ent fnl f: wknd ins fnl f* **10/1**

4453 **7** 3 **The Gay Cavalier**[9] 6557 6-8-12 **68**..........(t) JackMitchell 2 62
(John Ryan) *s.i.s: rousted along early: in tch towards rr: effrt u.p over 1f out: styd on ins fnl f: nvr trbld ldrs* **10/1**

000 **8** 1 ¾ **Dolphin Village (IRE)**[19] 6202 7-9-3 **76**..........(h) CharlieBennett[(3)] 6 67
(Shaun Harris) *dwlt: sn rcvrd and in tch in midfield: rdn and struggling to qckn over 2f out: outpcd and wl hld over 1f out: plugged on* **25/1**

1244 **9** 1 ¼ **Light Of Joy (USA)**[15] 6307 3-9-2 **78**.......... StevieDonohoe 9 67
(David Lanigan) *hld up in tch in last quartet: effrt wl over 1f out: no imp and wl hld whn drifted lft 1f out* **8/1**

2005 **10** 1 **Boycie**[17] 6273 4-9-1 **78**.......... TinaSmith[(7)] 10 64
(Richard Hannon) *hmpd sn after s: in tch towards rr: effrt on inner over 1f out: no imp: nvr trbld ldrs* **25/1**

6343 **11** 1 ¼ **Bridge Of Sighs**[28] 5843 5-9-2 **72**..........(p[1]) DanielMuscutt 4 56
(Lee Carter) *hld up in tch in last quartet: effrt over 1f out: no imp and wl hld fnl f* **14/1**

0134 **12** 14 **Sunglider (IRE)**[22] 6059 4-9-9 **79**..........(vt) MartinHarley 3 35
(David O'Meara) *in tch in midfield: rdn over 2f out: sn struggling and dropped to rr wl over 1f out: bhd and eased ins fnl f* **10/1**

0-26 **13** 7 **Classic Villager**[52] 4976 5-9-10 **80**.......... DaneO'Neill 13 22
(Dean Ivory) *chsd ldrs on outer: rdn over 3f out: steadily lost pl and bhd wl over 1f out: sn eased: burst blood vessel* **25/1**

2m 7.02s (-1.58) **Going Correction** -0.025s/f (Stan)
**WFA** 3 from 4yo+ 6lb **13** Ran SP% **126.9**
Speed ratings (Par 105): **105,104,104,103,102 102,99,98,97,96 95,84,78**
CSF £109.98 CT £536.09 TOTE £18.80: £5.50, £2.30, £1.90; EX 154.20 Trifecta £1922.90.
**Owner** David & Elaine Long **Bred** Best Breeding **Trained** Oad Street, Kent

**FOCUS**
A fair handicap and the form looks sound enough. It's been rated around the third to a length pb.

## 6849 BET TOTETRIFECTA AT BETFRED.COM H'CAP 1m 6f (P)
**8:10** (8:11) (Class 4) (0-85,85) 3-Y-O+ **£8,086** (£2,406; £1,202; £601) **Stalls** Low

Form RPR

252 **1** **Chocolate Box (IRE)**[19] 6210 3-8-7 **73**..........(p) LukeMorris 7 84
(Luca Cumani) *in tch in midfield: clsd to trck ldrs 4f out: wnt 2nd 3f out and sn wnt clr w ldr: drvn over 1f out: edgd lft u.str.p and clsd to chal whn bmpd ldr towards fin: sn led: styd on* **5/1**[2]

5021 **2** *nk* **Renfrew Street**[15] 6317 4-9-13 **84**.......... JoeFanning 2 95
(Mark Johnston) *chsd ldr for 3f: styd chsng ldrs tl wnt 2nd again over 5f out: led over 3f out: wnt wl clr w wnr over 2f out: rdn over 1f out: kpt on wl: hrd pressed and bmpd towards fin: sn hdd* **8/1**

2265 **3** 13 **New World Power (JPN)**[20] 6135 4-9-11 **82**.......... ShaneKelly 8 74
(David Simcock) *stdd s: hld up in last pair: nt clr run as ldng pair kicked clr over 2f out: swtchd rt and hdwy 2f out: wnt 3rd 1f out: no ch w ldng pair* **7/1**[3]

1344 **4** 4 ½ **Wefait (IRE)**[19] 6196 3-9-0 **80**.......... SeanLevey 6 66
(Richard Hannon) *in tch in midfield: rdn and outpcd in 4th over 2f out: no ch over 1f out: wknd* **10/1**

524- **5** 6 **Dharoos (IRE)**[316] 7627 4-9-10 **81**.......... LiamKeniry 3 59
(Nigel Hawke) *hld up in tch in midfield: rdn 5f out: struggling and outpcd wl over 2f out: no ch after* **33/1**

12P4 **6** 1 ¼ **Lost The Moon**[101] 3138 4-9-8 **79**.......... JoeyHaynes 9 55
(Mark H Tompkins) *stdd s: hld up in last pair: rdn and outpcd wl over 2f out: no ch after* **40/1**

2104 **7** 13 **Maghfoor**[21] 6090 3-9-5 **85**..........(p[1]) DaneO'Neill 5 43
(Saeed bin Suroor) *hld up in tch in midfield: effrt jst over 3f out: sn u.p and outpcd by ldng pair over 2f out: no ch after: eased ins fnl f: t.o* **1/1**[1]

2136 **8** 6 **Padrinho (IRE)**[21] 6107 3-8-6 **72**.......... JosephineGordon 1 21
(John Best) *chsd ldrs: rdn over 5f out: outpcd and wl btn in 3rd over 2f out: wknd over 1f out: eased ins fnl f: t.o* **14/1**

0366 **9** 16 **Tetradrachm**[68] 4355 4-9-7 **78**..........(p) TomEaves 10 5
(David Simcock) *led tl over 3f out: sn rdn and outpcd and wl btn over 2f out: wknd and eased ins fnl f: t.o* **25/1**

-030 **P** **Going Up (IRE)**[29] 5799 4-9-10 **81**..........(h[1]) MartinHarley 4
(Rae Guest) *swtchd rt to outside sn after s: hdwy to chse ldr 3f out tl over 5f out: eased and p.u 4f out: burst blood vessel* **14/1**

2m 59.24s (-3.96) **Going Correction** -0.025s/f (Stan)
**WFA** 3 from 4yo 9lb **10** Ran SP% **121.9**
Speed ratings (Par 105): **110,109,102,99,96 95,88,84,75,**
CSF £45.98 CT £287.65 TOTE £6.00: £1.90, £2.40, £1.90; EX 36.90 Trifecta £231.10.
**Owner** Dahab Racing **Bred** Lisieux Stud **Trained** Newmarket, Suffolk
■ Stewards' Enquiry : Luke Morris caution: careless riding

**FOCUS**
A fair staying handicap, in which the pace didn't increase until after halfway and the first two quickly drew a mile clear going into home turn. Several of these weren't seen to best effect, and it's a tricky race to rate.

## 6850 BET TOTEWIN AT BETFRED.COM H'CAP 6f (P)
**8:40** (8:43) (Class 6) (0-65,67) 3-Y-O+ **£3,234** (£962; £481; £240) **Stalls** Centre

Form RPR

0012 **1** **Newstead Abbey**[7] 6635 7-9-7 **65**..........(p) TomEaves 3 72+
(Michael Herrington) *chsd ldrs: sn stdd to trck ldrs and travelled strly: nt clr run over 2f out tl rdn and hdwy to chse ldr jst over 1f out: styd on u.p to ld last stride* **5/4**[1]

0203 **2** *shd* **Nellie's Dancer**[21] 6112 3-8-7 **53**..........(p) JosephineGordon 12 60
(Scott Dixon) *w ldr tl led over 2f out: forged ahd and edgd lft u.p over 1f out: kpt on wl: hdd last stride* **12/1**

454 **3** 2 **Dream Start**[29] 5793 3-8-13 **59**..........(t) StevieDonohoe 6 60
(John Ryan) *wnt rt: cannoned into rival leaving stalls and v.s.a: bhd: hdwy and swtchd lft over 1f out: wnt 3rd and swtchd lft again ins fnl f: styd on but nvr getting to ldng pair* **7/1**[2]

4650 **4** 3 ¼ **Quite A Story**[20] 6157 5-8-12 **59**.......... CharlieBennett[(3)] 9 50
(Patrick Chamings) *taken down early: trckd ldrs: effrt and unable qck over 1f out: 3rd but no imp 1f out: sn wknd* **12/1**

0410 **5** ½ **Firesnake (IRE)**[23] 6046 4-8-7 **56**..........(v) CallumRodriguez[(5)] 11 46
(Lisa Williamson) *chsd ldrs: unable qck u.p over 1f out: wknd ins fnl f* **7/1**[2]

1306 **6** 2 **Soaring Spirits (IRE)**[30] 5750 7-9-2 **63**..........(v) JackDuern[(3)] 8 47
(Dean Ivory) *bmpd and squeezed for room sn after s: sn rdn along towards rr: reminders sme hdwy u.p and hung lft ins fnl f: styd on: nvr trbld ldrs* **14/1**

0050 **7** 1 ¼ **Classic Flyer**[10] 6531 5-8-7 **51** oh4..........(b) JimmyQuinn 4 31
(Christine Dunnett) *hmpd s: hld up in midfield: effrt 2f out: no imp over 1f out: wl hld styd on same pce ins fnl f* **50/1**

-535 **8** *hd* **Upper Lambourn (IRE)**[203] 761 9-8-7 **51** oh6.......... DannyBrock 14 30
(Denis Quinn) *chsd ldrs on outer: lost pl u.p over 1f out: wknd ins fnl f* **50/1**

2060 **9** 1 **Encapsulated**[73] 4162 7-8-6 **55**.......... RhiainIngram[(5)] 2 31
(Roger Ingram) *taken down early and led rdrless to post: broke okay but sn dropped to rr: grad switching to outer fr over 3f out: v wd bnd 2f out: no imp over 1f out* **20/1**

-350 **10** 1 ¼ **Welsh Rose**[24] 6015 4-9-6 **64**..........(h) LukeMorris 10 37
(Archie Watson) *tk v t.k.h to post: led tl over 2f out: rdn and unable qck over 1f out: racd awkwardly and btn 1f out: wl btn and eased ins fnl f* **7/1**[2]

00 **11** *nk* **Louis Vee (IRE)**[73] 4149 9-8-0 **51** oh6..........(p) NicolaCurrie[(7)] 1 23
(John O'Shea) *hld up in midfield: rdn over 2f out: no imp and wknd over 1f out: no ch whn nt clr run and hmpd ins fnl f* **33/1**

55 **12** ½ **Something Lucky (IRE)**[90] 3545 5-8-9 **56**..........(t[1]) HollieDoyle[(3)] 5 26
(Daniel Steele) *hmpd leaving stalls and slowly away: nt rcvr a in rr: no ch whn nt clr run and swtchd rt 1f out* **10/1**[3]

1m 13.01s (-0.69) **Going Correction** -0.025s/f (Stan)
**WFA** 3 from 4yo+ 2lb **12** Ran SP% **124.7**
Speed ratings (Par 101): **103,102,100,95,95 92,90,90,89,87 87,86**
CSF £18.94 CT £86.88 TOTE £2.00: £1.30, £3.40, £3.40; EX 20.80 Trifecta £118.60.
**Owner** Tony Culhane Racing Club **Bred** Grasshopper 2000 Ltd **Trained** Cold Kirby, N Yorks

**FOCUS**
A moderate sprint handicap.

## 6851 WICKHAM ENGINEERING MAIDEN STKS 1m 2f (P)
**9:10** (9:11) (Class 4) 3-Y-O+ **£8,086** (£2,406; £1,202; £601) **Stalls** Low

Form RPR

3 **1** **Airway**[70] 4274 3-9-2 0.......... GeorgeWood[(3)] 1 83
(James Fanshawe) *trckd ldrs: effrt to chse ldr 2f out: led ent fnl f: r.o wl whn pressed and a holding runner up ins fnl f: pushed out* **7/4**[2]

2 **2** ¾ **Ennjaaz (IRE)**[17] 6277 3-9-5 0.......... JimmyQuinn 4 81
(Saeed bin Suroor) *rn green: awkward and hmpd leaving stalls: slowly away: sn swtchd rt and hdwy to chse ldrs after 2f: effrt in 3rd 2f out: wnt 2nd and pressing wnr ins fnl f: kpt on but a hld* **10/11**[1]

453 **3** 7 **Munthany (USA)**[31] 5707 3-9-5 74.......... DaneO'Neill 2 67
(Charles Hills) *led: rdn over 1f out: hdd ent fnl f: sn outpcd and wknd ins fnl f* **4/1**[3]

4 **4** 1 ¾ **Kai Tak And Back**[9] 6548 3-9-5 0.......... MartinDwyer 8 64
(William Muir) *hld up in tch in midfield: unable qck u.p over 1f out: wknd ins fnl f* **25/1**

-020 **5** 1 ¾ **Velvet Voice**[23] 6048 3-9-0 61.......... JoeyHaynes 7 55
(Mark H Tompkins) *hld up in tch: effrt over 1f out: sn rdn and outpcd: wknd ins fnl f* **25/1**

4 **6** 3 ½ **Grantchester (IRE)**[30] 5746 3-9-5 0.......... RyanTate 5 53
(James Eustace) *hld up in tch: effrt and struggling over 2f out: wknd over 1f out:* **20/1**

**7** 4 ½ **Fire Whirl** 3-8-12 0.......... AbbieWibrew[(7)] 3 44
(William Knight) *bmpd and pushed lft s: hld up in last pair: swtchd rt and wd bnd 3f out: drifting bk lft and struggling 2f out: no ch over 1f out* **40/1**

0630 **8** 2 **Ripper Street (IRE)**[7] 6621 3-9-0 47..........(h) JaneElliott[(5)] 6 40
(Christine Dunnett) *t.k.h: pressed ldr tl 2f out: sn lost pl u.p: wknd fnl f* **100/1**

2m 8.19s (-0.41) **Going Correction** -0.025s/f (Stan) **8** Ran SP% **124.6**
Speed ratings (Par 105): **100,99,93,92,91 88,84,83**
CSF £3.94 TOTE £2.80: £1.10, £1.02, £1.40; EX 4.30 Trifecta £7.40.
**Owner** Dr Catherine Wills & Frederik Tylicki **Bred** St Clare Hall Stud **Trained** Newmarket, Suffolk

**FOCUS**
A maiden lacking depth. Two sons of Poet's Voice fought out the finish, clear of the rest. The first two have been rated as improving on their debuts.
T/Plt: £14.30 to a £1 stake. Pool: £98,981.93 - 5030.63 winning units. T/Qpdt: £13.90 to a £1 stake. Pool: £8,606.71 - 455.65 winning units. **Steve Payne**

# [5924] HAYDOCK (L-H)

Thursday, September 7

**OFFICIAL GOING: Good to soft (7.8)**

Wind: light breeze, against in straight Weather: overcast, cool

## 6852 32RED CASINO MAIDEN STKS (PLUS 10 RACE) 1m 3f 140y

2:00 (2:01) (Class 3) 3-Y-O £9,703 (£2,887; £1,443; £721) Stalls Centre

Form RPR

-325 1 **Fibonacci**[81] 3860 3-9-5 84 ........ JamesDoyle 1 74+
(Hugo Palmer) *trckd ldrs: tk clsr order gng wl over 3f out: pushed along briefly 2f out: hdwy to ld over 1f out: qckn clr under hand riding ent fnl f: readily* **4/7**[1]

052 2 3 1/4 **Line Of Beauty**[23] 6027 3-9-0 74 ........ AndreaAtzeni 3 64
(Simon Crisford) *led at stdy gallop: qcknd pce 4f out: 2 l ahd 3f out: pushed along 2f out: rdn and hdd over 1f out: kpt on fnl f* **7/2**[2]

652 3 1/2 **Ididitforyoooo (IRE)**[35] 5577 3-9-5 66 ........ JimmyFortune 5 68
(Brian Meehan) *hld up in 4th: pushed along to cl on first three 3f out: rdn 2f out: wnt 3rd over 1f out: r.o fnl f: gaining on runner-up nr fin* **10/1**

03 4 3 1/2 **Sky Eagle (IRE)**[23] 6031 3-9-5 0 ........ PatCosgrave 4 62
(Ed Walker) *chsd ldr: pushed along 3f out: lost pl and rdn 2f out: dropped to 4th over 1f out: no ex* **8/1**[3]

5 42 **Keem Bay** 3-8-11 0 ........ PhilDennis[(3)] 2
(Michael Mullineaux) *in rr: pushed along and lost tch fr 4f out* **150/1**

2m 34.23s (1.23) **Going Correction** +0.025s/f (Good) 5 Ran SP% **106.7**
Speed ratings (Par 105): **96,93,93,91,63**
CSF £2.59 TOTE £1.30: £1.10, £2.20; EX 2.70 Trifecta £5.70.
**Owner** Al Asayl Bloodstock Ltd **Bred** Al Asayl Bloodstock Ltd **Trained** Newmarket, Suffolk

**FOCUS**
All races run over the Inner Home Straight. Actual race distance 1m 3f 154yds. This is pretty straightforward maiden form. Afterwards the riders backed up the official going description. The runner-up has been rated close to her turf form, with the third to his maiden form.

## 6853 32RED EBFSTALLIONS.COM NOVICE STKS (PLUS 10 RACE) (C&G) 6f

2:30 (2:33) (Class 4) 2-Y-O £4,528 (£1,347; £673; £336) Stalls Centre

Form RPR

223 1 **Ginbar (IRE)**[18] 6231 2-9-0 79 ........ RichardKingscote 8 80+
(Tom Dascombe) *mde all on stands' rails: 1 l clr 2f out: pushed along: reminder and qcknd clr over 1f out: extended advantage ins fnl f: easily* **11/8**[1]

2 4 **Knighted (IRE)** 2-9-0 0 ........ TomEaves 4 70+
(Kevin Ryan) *hld up in last: hdwy on outer over 2f out: pushed along into 2nd over 1f out: drvn and r.o wl fnl f: no ch w wnr* **11/4**[2]

3 2 3/4 **Desert Doctor (IRE)** 2-9-0 0 ........ JamieSpencer 1 60
(Ed Walker) *broke wl: prom: 1 l bhd wnr 2f out: sn pushed along: lost 2nd pl over 1f out and rn green: styd on to secure 3rd pl ins fnl f* **4/1**[3]

4 1 1/2 **Deecider** 2-9-0 0 ........ JamesDoyle 6 55
(Tom Dascombe) *hld up: prog to trck ldrs 1/2-way: pushed along over 2f out: sn drvn: reminders over 1f out: one pce fnl f* **8/1**

0 5 2 1/2 **Snaffled (IRE)**[138] 1966 2-9-0 0 ........ PJMcDonald 7 48
(David Brown) *t.k.h: prom: trckd ldrs 1/2-way: pushed along in 3rd over 1f out: wknd and lost pl ent fnl f* **50/1**

6 4 1/2 **Sapper** 2-9-0 0 ........ PatCosgrave 3 34
(Ed Walker) *mid-div: dropped to last 1/2-way: pushed along and reminders over 1f out: no imp* **16/1**

6 7 1/2 **Cavalry Regiment**[30] 5755 2-9-0 0 ........ JasonHart 5 33
(John Quinn) *hld up: pushed along 2f out: sn drvn: wknd over 1f out* **33/1**

1m 15.04s (1.24) **Going Correction** +0.15s/f (Good) 7 Ran SP% **110.7**
Speed ratings (Par 97): **97,91,88,86,82 76,76**
CSF £4.90 TOTE £2.20: £1.40, £1.70; EX 5.80 Trifecta £15.70.
**Owner** The BGW Partnership & Partner **Bred** Rockfield Farm **Trained** Malpas, Cheshire

**FOCUS**
The stands' rail proved the place to be and it was easy for the favourite. The winner has been rated to his best.

## 6854 32RED.COM EBF NOVICE STKS (PLUS 10 RACE) (C&G) 7f 212y

3:00 (3:02) (Class 4) 2-Y-O £4,528 (£1,347; £673; £336) Stalls Low

Form RPR

1 **The Revenant** 2-9-0 0 ........ PatCosgrave 5 83+
(Hugo Palmer) *slowly away but sn rcvrd to r in midfield: hdwy to trck ldrs gng wl over 2f out: pushed along and qcknd wl to ld over 1f out: pressed by runner-up ent fnl f: rdn and r.o wl: on top nr fin* **11/2**[3]

63 2 3/4 **Global Conqueror**[22] 6057 2-9-0 0 ........ AndreaAtzeni 4 81
(Simon Crisford) *trckd ldrs: wnt 3rd 4f out: ev ch 2f out: passed by wnr over 1f out: rdn and chal wnr ent fnl f: r.o wl: hld nr fin* **3/1**[2]

3 3 2 1/4 **Ghostwatch (IRE)**[20] 6142 2-9-0 0 ........ JamesDoyle 9 76+
(Charlie Appleby) *trckd ldrs: prog into 4th 3f out: rdn 2f out: r.o fnl f but nt pce of first two* **4/6**[1]

4 2 1/4 **Kings Full (IRE)** 2-9-0 0 ........ TomEaves 7 71+
(Kevin Ryan) *hld up: hdwy 3f out: rdn over 1f out: r.o to take 4th ins fnl f* **10/1**

0 5 3/4 **Bertog**[33] 5631 2-9-0 0 ........ PaulMulrennan 3 69
(John Mackie) *prom: led briefly after 1 f: sn settled in 2nd: led 4f out: rdn and hdd over 1f out: no ex ent fnl f* **100/1**

6 6 3 1/2 **French Resistance (IRE)**[13] 6380 2-9-0 0 ........ TonyHamilton 8 62
(Roger Fell) *mid-div on inner: pushed along 3f out: one pce fnl 2 fs* **150/1**

7 1 3/4 **Adjutant** 2-9-0 0 ........ DanielTudhope 1 58
(David O'Meara) *trckd ldrs: pushed along and lost pl 2f out: wknd* **50/1**

8 1 3/4 **Pentland Hills (IRE)** 2-9-0 0 ........ RichardKingscote 11 54
(Chris Wall) *hld up: effrt and pushed along 3f out: one pce ent fnl f* **50/1**

9 1 1/4 **Creel** 2-9-0 0 ........ PhillipMakin 6 51
(David Brown) *hld up: pushed along 3f out: no imp* **100/1**

10 1 **Twisted Logic (IRE)** 2-9-0 0 ........ PJMcDonald 2 49
(Keith Dalgleish) *led tl hdd briefly after 1 f: sn regained ld: pushed along and hdd 4f out: drvn and wknd* **40/1**

11 4 **Duffy** 2-9-0 0 ........ PaulHanagan 10 40
(Richard Fahey) *a in rr: pushed along over 4f out: nvr a factor* **25/1**

1m 43.99s (0.29) **Going Correction** +0.025s/f (Good) 11 Ran SP% **122.3**
Speed ratings (Par 97): **99,98,96,93,93 89,87,86,84,83 79**
CSF £22.97 TOTE £7.70: £2.20, £1.40, £1.02; EX 24.00 Trifecta £41.70.
**Owner** Al Asayl Bloodstock Ltd **Bred** Al Asayl Bloodstock Ltd **Trained** Newmarket, Suffolk

**FOCUS**
Actual race distance 1m 3yds. A fair novice event that served up a decent test.

## 6855 32RED.COM H'CAP 7f 212y

3:30 (3:31) (Class 4) (0-80,82) 3-Y-O+ £5,822 (£1,732; £865; £432) Stalls Low

Form RPR

34-3 1 **Heaven's Rock (IRE)**[17] 6265 3-8-8 69 ........ RichardKingscote 11 76
(Tom Dascombe) *trckd ldrs: hdwy to ld 2f out: sn rdn: 1 l clr 1f out: hld on wl u.p ins fnl f* **9/1**

6361 2 1/2 **Trilliant (IRE)**[63] 4525 3-9-7 82 ........ PatCosgrave 9 88
(Ed Walker) *hld up: drvn over 2f out: hdwy on outer over 1f out: rdn ent fnl f: r.o strly to take 2nd last 100yds: clsng on wnr nr fin* **9/2**[2]

001 3 1/2 **Parole (IRE)**[12] 5698 5-8-8 67 ........(t) RachelRichardson[(3)] 3 73
(Tim Easterby) *trckd ldrs: pushed along and ev ch 3f out: drvn 2f out: rdn over 1f out: r.o to take 2nd ent fnl f: kpt on but lost 2nd pl 100yds out* **11/1**

3025 4 shd **Rashford's Double (IRE)**[18] 6235 3-9-5 80 ........(p) TonyHamilton 12 84
(Richard Fahey) *trckd ldrs: pushed along 2f out: rdn into 4th 1f out: r.o fnl f* **20/1**

3500 5 1/2 **Archie (IRE)**[20] 6134 5-9-9 79 ........ JamieSpencer 2 83+
(Tom Clover) *hld up: plenty to do over 2f out: swtchd and hdwy over 1f out: r.o fnl f: nvr nrr* **4/1**[1]

1020 6 1 1/2 **Sir Reginald Brown**[55] 4868 3-8-9 77 ........ ConnorMurtagh[(7)] 4 77
(Richard Fahey) *t.k.h: mid-div on inner: pushed along 2f out: sn rdn: hdwy ent fnl f: r.o one pce* **8/1**[3]

1-00 7 3/4 **Maifalki (FR)**[140] 1911 4-9-9 79 ........ JasonHart 6 79
(Mark Walford) *mid-div: pushed along over 2f out: reminders and effrt whn n.m.r over 1f out: eased fnl f* **25/1**

0014 8 3/4 **Wasm**[30] 5760 3-9-0 75 ........ ConnorBeasley 8 71
(Roger Fell) *hld up: lugged rt 3f out: sn pushed along: mod late hdwy* **22/1**

-400 9 3/4 **Different Journey**[17] 6266 4-8-13 69 ........ CamHardie 1 65
(Michael Easterby) *mid-div: pushed along over 3f out: no imp* **100/1**

220P 10 2 1/4 **Pumaflor (IRE)**[10] 6516 5-9-11 81 ........(p) DanielTudhope 7 72
(David O'Meara) *prom: taken rt to r alone in centre of crse 4f out: ev ch 2f out: drvn and lost pl over 1f out* **8/1**[3]

03 11 8 **Pecheurs De Perles (IRE)**[26] 5928 3-9-5 80 ........ PaulHanagan 5 51
(Iain Jardine) *led: pushed along 3f out: rdn and hdd 2f out: wknd* **4/1**[1]

1615 12 11 **Wigan Warrior**[26] 5928 3-9-2 77 ........ TomEaves 10 23
(David Brown) *slowly away: rcvrd to r in mid-div: pushed along 3f out: sn wknd* **33/1**

1m 42.53s (-1.17) **Going Correction** +0.025s/f (Good)
**WFA** 3 from 4yo+ 5lb 12 Ran SP% **115.6**
Speed ratings (Par 105): **106,105,105,104,104 102,102,101,100,98 90,79**
CSF £45.08 CT £461.54 TOTE £8.40: £2.60, £1.90, £2.90; EX 59.40 Trifecta £338.10.
**Owner** Tom Cleverley & Stephen Mound **Bred** Pat O'Donovan **Trained** Malpas, Cheshire

**FOCUS**
Actual race distance 1m 3yds. They were soon strung out in this competitive handicap. The third and fourth help set an ordinary standard.

## 6856 32RED.COM EBF STALLIONS CONDITIONS STKS 6f 212y

4:00 (4:01) (Class 3) 3-Y-O+ £9,703 (£2,887; £1,443; £721) Stalls Low

Form RPR

-030 1 **Donjuan Triumphant (IRE)**[33] 5640 4-9-1 104 ........(h) PJMcDonald 5 112
(Andrew Balding) *mde all: 1 l clr 3f out: pushed along and stl 1 l ahd 2f out: rdn and readily maintained advantage fnl f* **4/1**[2]

550- 2 1 1/4 **Yattwee (USA)**[369] 6109 4-9-1 102 ........ PatCosgrave 6 109
(Saeed bin Suroor) *chsd wnr thrght: 1 l down 3f and 2f out: sn pushed along: rdn ent fnl f: kpt on: but nvr clsng gap on wnr* **4/1**[2]

4104 3 3 1/2 **Solomon's Bay (IRE)**[34] 5593 3-9-4 107 ........(b[1]) JamesDoyle 2 105
(Roger Varian) *racd in 4th: drvn into 3rd over 1f out: cocked jaw ins fnl f: one pce: jst hld on for 3rd* **10/1**

4255 4 shd **So Beloved**[13] 6401 7-9-1 111 ........(h) DanielTudhope 4 99
(David O'Meara) *t.k.h: hld up: hdwy over 1f out: reminders and one pce fnl f: jst hld for 3rd* **5/4**[1]

3000 5 3/4 **Yuften**[40] 5393 6-9-5 102 ........ AndreaAtzeni 7 101
(Roger Charlton) *hld up: pushed along 2f out: briefly relegated to last: one pce fr over 1f out* **8/1**[3]

5001 6 2 **Accession (IRE)**[26] 5942 8-9-5 100 ........ MartinLane 1 96
(Charlie Fellowes) *trckd ldrs: pushed along 2f out: sn rdn and wknd* **18/1**

1m 27.36s (-3.34) **Going Correction** -0.20s/f (Firm)
**WFA** 3 from 4yo+ 4lb 6 Ran SP% **109.9**
Speed ratings (Par 107): **111,109,105,105,104 102**
CSF £19.18 TOTE £5.20: £2.00, £1.40; EX 22.90 Trifecta £102.40.
**Owner** King Power Racing Co Ltd **Bred** Patrick Cosgrove & Dream Ahead Syndicate **Trained** Kingsclere, Hants

**FOCUS**
Actual race distance 7f 3yds. This decent conditions event proved tactical. It's been rated around the first two.

## 6857 £10 FREE AT 32RED.COM H'CAP 1m 3f 140y

4:35 (4:37) (Class 2) (0-105,102) 3-Y-O+ £12,938 (£3,850; £1,924; £962) Stalls Centre

Form RPR

0140 1 **Marmajuke Bay**[20] 6151 4-8-13 87 ........(p) SteveDrowne 1 95
(Mark Usher) *trckd ldrs: hdwy 3f out: pushed along to ld 2f out: 1 l ld whn rdn over 1f out: r.o wl fnl f: on top nr fin* **15/2**

3261 2 2 **Azari**[26] 5924 5-9-8 96 ........(p) RichardKingscote 4 101
(Tom Dascombe) *slowly away: hld up: hdwy 3f out: pushed along whn n.m.r 2f out: sn in clr and chsd ldr ent fnl f: rdn and r.o but a hld by wnr* **4/1**[3]

4056 3 3 1/2 **Tawdeea**[41] 5353 5-9-10 98 ........(p) DanielTudhope 3 97
(David O'Meara) *hld up: hdwy 3f out: pushed along over 2f out: sn rdn: r.o to take 3rd ins fnl f* **10/3**[1]

4-66 4 1 1/2 **Agent Murphy**[12] 6440 6-10-0 102 ........ JimmyFortune 5 98
(Brian Meehan) *led: 1 l clr 3f out: drvn and hdd 2f out: rdn and wknd over 1f out* **9/1**

-524 5 1 **Niblawi (IRE)**[26] 5913 5-9-5 93 ........ PaulHanagan 2 88
(Neil Mulholland) *mid-div: hdwy and ev ch 3f out: sn rdn: no ex fr over 1f out* **7/2**[2]

0260 6 2 1/2 **Sennockian Star**[13] 6383 7-8-13 87 ........ PJMcDonald 7 78
(Mark Johnston) *prom: pushed along in 2nd 4f out: rdn over 3f out: wknd over 2f out* **22/1**

052- 7 6 **Percy Street**[158] 7538 4-9-10 98 ........ JamieSpencer 8 79
(Nicky Henderson) *mid-div: hdwy to go 2nd 6f out: taken wd 4f out: pushed along 3f out: rdn and wknd 2f out* **11/1**

4460 **8** 7 **Galapiat**41 5353 4-10-0 **102** JamesDoyle 6 71
(Mark Johnston) *hld up: taken wd 4f out: rdn 3f out: fdd* **7/1**
2m 32.18s (-0.82) **Going Correction** +0.025s/f (Good) 8 Ran SP% **112.2**
Speed ratings (Par 109): **103,101,99,98,97 96,92,87**
CSF £36.11 CT £118.17 TOTE £8.30: £2.30, £1.50, £1.20; EX 41.50 Trifecta £190.10.
**Owner** The Ridgeway Alchemist's **Bred** The Welldiggers Partnership **Trained** Upper Lambourn, Berks

**FOCUS**
Actual race distance 1m 3f 154yds. This was a good-quality handicap and it was run at a fair pace. Another step forward from the winner, with the runner-up confirming his latest improved C&D effort.

## 6858 32RED CASINO H'CAP (FOR GENTLEMAN AMATEUR RIDERS) 1m 3f 140y
**5:05** (5:05) (Class 5) (0-70,72) 4-Y-0+ **£3,431** (£1,064; £531; £266) **Stalls** Centre

Form RPR
4331 **1** **Take Two**25 5968 8-11-5 **72** MrJBrace(5) 9 79
(Alex Hales) *hld up in last: 4 l bhd pack: latched on to rest 4f out: hdwy 3f out: rdn 2f out: led wl over 1f out: 2 l clr ent fnl f: jnd by runner-up last 100yds: briefly hdd: rallied to ld nr fin: all out* **9/2**3
2412 **2** nse **Thorntoun Care**9 6551 6-11-3 **68** (p) MrBLynn(3) 5 75
(Iain Jardine) *hld up: hdwy on inner gng wl 3f out: trckd ldr 2f out: sn angled out and chsd wnr: rdn fnl f: sn alongside wnr: led briefly: hdd nr fin* **4/1**2
06-4 **3** 4 ½ **Manny Owens (IRE)**42 5320 5-11-3 **65** (t) MrJamesKing 3 65
(Jonjo O'Neill) *trckd ldrs: hdwy to ld over 4f out: 1 l clr and pushed along 2f out: rdn and hdd over 1f out: kpt on one pce to secure 3rd* **10/1**
005 **4** 3 ¼ **Modernism**12 6416 8-11-10 **72** (p) MrSWalker 2 66
(Ian Williams) *mid-div: trckd ldrs 3f out: pushed along 2f out: sn rdn and no ex* **7/1**
**5** 5 **Mais Si**21 6122 4-11-7 **69** (b) MrJJCodd 8 55
(Gordon Elliott, Ire) *mid-div on outer: pushed along 3f out: rdn 2f out: no ex* **10/3**1
1500 **6** 4 **Marmion**47 5163 5-11-0 **69** MrJMAndrews(7) 1 48
(Les Eyre) *t.k.h: led tl hdd over 4f out: rdn and wknd over 2f out* **28/1**
1312 **7** 5 **Diamonds A Dancing**20 6153 7-11-5 **72** (h) MrTGillard(5) 6 43
(Donald McCain) *prom: rdn in 2nd 3f out: wknd and lost pl 2f out* **4/1**2
2620 **8** 1 ¾ **King Of The Celts (IRE)**31 5701 9-11-2 **64** (p) MrWEasterby 7 32
(Tim Easterby) *trckd ldrs: pushed along and lost pl wl over 3f out: fdd* **28/1**
2m 34.93s (1.93) **Going Correction** +0.025s/f (Good) 8 Ran SP% **109.7**
Speed ratings (Par 103): **94,93,90,88,85 82,79,78**
CSF £20.91 CT £154.76 TOTE £5.00: £1.90, £1.70, £2.90; EX 19.70 Trifecta £145.70.
**Owner** Edging Ahead **Bred** Steven & Petra Wallace **Trained** Edgcote, Northamptonshire

**FOCUS**
Actual race distance 1m 3f 154yds. This modest handicap, confined to gentleman amateurs, was run at a muddling pace. The winner has been rated to his best since 2013.
T/Plt: £19.80 to a £1 stake. Pool: £58,820.49 - 2165.15 winning units. T/Qpdt: £21.70 to a £1 stake. Pool: £3,968.90 - 134.77 winning units. **Keith McHugh**

# 6393 SALISBURY (R-H)
Thursday, September 7

**OFFICIAL GOING: Good to soft (good in places) changing to good (good to soft in places) after race 1 (1.50)**
Wind: mild breeze, half-across Weather: cloudy

## 6859 FRANK MURRAY MEMORIAL EBF NOVICE STKS (PLUS 10 RACE) 1m
**1:50** (1:51) (Class 4) 2-Y-O **£5,822** (£1,732; £865; £432) **Stalls** Low

Form RPR
33 **1** **Al Jellaby**48 5105 2-9-2 0 AdamKirby 11 84+
(Clive Cox) *travelled wl in mid-div: hdwy over 3f out: rdn to chal over 1f out: kpt on wl to ld towards fin* **5/1**
1 **2** nk **White Mocha (USA)**27 5876 2-9-8 0 JosephineGordon 5 89
(Hugo Palmer) *wnt rt s: trckd ldr: led jst over 2f out: rdn over 1f out: kpt on: hdd towards fin* **5/2**1
0331 **3** 2 ½ **Yaafour**26 5934 2-9-8 84 RyanMoore 6 84
(Richard Hannon) *led: rdn and hdd jst over 2f out: kpt on tl no ex ins fnl f* **4/1**2
5 **4** 4 ½ **Nebuchadnezzar (FR)**48 5106 2-9-2 0 FergusSweeney 1 68
(Alan King) *hld up towards rr: hdwy 3f out: rdn 2f out: styd on into 4th jst over 1f out: nt pce of ldrs* **14/1**
**5** 1 ½ **Red Miracle** 2-8-11 0 WilliamCarson 3 60
(Rod Millman) *mid-div: hdwy 3f out: sn rdn: styd on same pce fnl 2f* **100/1**
01 **6** nk **Enzo (IRE)**16 6279 2-9-8 0 (t) LiamKeniry 7 70
(Ed Walker) *mid-div: hmpd 3f out: rdn over 1f out: little imp* **20/1**
**7** 2 **Pippin** 2-9-2 0 OisinMurphy 13 60+
(Hughie Morrison) *s.i.s: sn swtchd rt: towards rr and pushed along whn hmpd 3f out: sme prog sn after but nvr threatened to get on terms w ldrs* **25/1**
05 **8** ¾ **The Night King**10 6505 2-9-2 0 GrahamLee 2 58+
(Mick Channon) *hmpd 3f out: a towards rr* **10/1**
2 **9** 5 **Nuits St Georges (IRE)**28 5840 2-9-2 0 KieranShoemark 10 47+
(David Menuisier) *in tch whn bdly hmpd 3f out: nvr rcvrd* **5/1**
0 **10** 26 **Amenhotepthethird**54 4909 2-8-13 0 GeorgeWood(3) 8
(Mark Gillard) *struggling in rr fr over 3f out: wknd over 2f out: t.o* **250/1**
6 **11** 13 **Swiss Psalm**149 1694 2-8-11 0 RobHornby 12
(Mark Gillard) *trckd ldrs: rdn 3f out: sn wknd: t.o* **250/1**
02 **P** **Abandon Ship (IRE)**20 6142 2-9-2 0 JimCrowley 9
(Paul Cole) *prom whn lost action and p.u 3f out: fatally injured* **9/2**3
1m 44.83s (1.33) **Going Correction** +0.175s/f (Good) 12 Ran SP% **118.1**
Speed ratings (Par 97): **100,99,97,92,91 90,88,88,83,57 44,**
CSF £17.41 TOTE £5.50: £1.90, £1.40, £1.40; EX 20.30 Trifecta £100.60.
**Owner** AlMohamediya Racing **Bred** Niarchos Family **Trained** Lambourn, Berks

**FOCUS**
The ground had dried a touch and was changed to good, good to soft in places after the opener, and general opinion amongst those who rode in the opener was that it was still on the slow side. A fair novice and the first three came clear. A step forward from the first two, with the third rated just below his latest effort.

## 6860 IRISH YEARLING SALES NURSERY H'CAP 6f 213y
**2:20** (2:22) (Class 5) (0-70,71) 2-Y-O **£3,396** (£1,010; £505; £252) **Stalls** Centre

Form RPR
0445 **1** **Move To The Front (IRE)**30 5752 2-9-4 **67** (v1) AdamKirby 2 74
(Clive Cox) *a.p: shkn up briefly over 3f out: led over 2f out: edgd rt ins fnl f: kpt on strly: rdn out* **10/1**
663 **2** 1 ¾ **Dandiesque (IRE)**20 6147 2-9-3 **66** RyanMoore 4 69
(Richard Hannon) *pushed along early: mid-div: hdwy 2f out: sn rdn: nt beat of runs whn swtchd lft jst over 1f out: r.o to go 2nd fnl 75yds* **8/1**3
3005 **3** hd **Chai Chai (IRE)**13 6375 2-9-8 **71** OisinMurphy 8 72
(Andrew Balding) *mid-div: hdwy and rdn whn tight for room wl over 1f out: kpt on wl but drifting sltly rt ins fnl f: wnt 3rd cl home* **4/1**2
5311 **4** hd **Shovel It On (IRE)**23 6036 2-9-7 **70** JimCrowley 12 71
(David Evans) *mid-div: hdwy 3f out: rdn 2f out sn drifted rt: chsd wnr jst ins fnl f tl no ex fnl 75yds* **7/2**1
455 **5** nk **Tiny Tempest (IRE)**16 6279 2-9-2 **65** CharlesBishop 3 65
(Eve Johnson Houghton) *mid-div: hdwy 3f out: nt clrest of runs over 2f out: rdn to chal wl over 1f out tl jst ins fnl f: no ex fnl 100yds* **14/1**
302 **6** 1 ¼ **Trogon (IRE)**16 6279 2-9-8 **71** GrahamLee 10 68
(Mick Channon) *mid-div: rdn over 2f out: kpt on ins fnl f but nt pce to threaten* **11/1**
654 **7** 1 **Reverberation**29 5786 2-9-1 **69** MitchGodwin(5) 7 63
(Sylvester Kirk) *in tch: rdn and hdwy over 2f out: kpt on same pce fnl f* **20/1**
3404 **8** shd **Rainbow Jazz (IRE)**9 6552 2-9-7 **70** (p) TomQueally 1 64
(Mark Usher) *s.i.s: towards rr: stdy prog fr over 2f out: rdn over 1f out: no further imp fnl f* **20/1**
050 **9** ½ **Sotomayor**28 5840 2-9-2 **65** TomMarquand 11 57
(Richard Hannon) *s.i.s: towards rr: sn pushed along: sme late prog: n.d* **16/1**
430 **10** 3 ¼ **Golden Footsteps (IRE)**22 6064 2-9-7 **70** LiamKeniry 5 54
(Ed Walker) *racd keenly: trckd ldrs: nt clr run over 2f out: sn rdn: wknd jst over 1f out* **10/1**
40 **11** ¾ **Fenagh (IRE)**22 6064 2-9-4 **67** (p1) HarryBentley 13 49
(David Loughnane) *sn pushed along towards rr of midfield: nvr threatened to get involved* **20/1**
053 **12** nk **Adulate**17 6260 2-9-8 **71** (b) JosephineGordon 14 52
(Hugo Palmer) *led: rdn and hdd over 2f out: wknd over 1f out* **16/1**
0330 **13** 3 ¾ **Merchant Marine (IRE)**55 4858 2-9-5 **68** (v) PatDobbs 6 39
(Ralph Beckett) *mid-div: rdn over 2f out: sn wknd* **16/1**
1m 30.81s (2.21) **Going Correction** +0.175s/f (Good) 13 Ran SP% **118.4**
Speed ratings (Par 95): **94,92,91,91,91 89,88,88,87,84 83,83,78**
CSF £84.22 CT £384.56 TOTE £10.90: £3.30, £2.10, £1.80; EX 98.30 Trifecta £398.60.
**Owner** Paul & Clare Rooney **Bred** Redpender Stud Ltd **Trained** Lambourn, Berks
■ Stewards' Enquiry : Liam Keniry caution: careless riding

**FOCUS**
An ordinary nursery but it was run at a good gallop and the form looks sound for the grade. The fourth has been rated to his mark.

## 6861 BRITISH EBF QUIDHAMPTON MAIDEN FILLIES' STKS (PLUS 10 RACE) (DIV I) 6f 213y
**2:50** (2:53) (Class 2) 2-Y-O
**£12,450** (£3,728; £1,864; £932; £466; £234) **Stalls** Centre

Form RPR
**1** **Herecomesthesun (IRE)** 2-9-0 0 EdwardGreatrex 4 84+
(Archie Watson) *trckd ldrs: rdn to chal 2f out: kpt on wl fnl f: led fnl 75yds: won gng away* **11/1**3
23 **2** 1 ½ **Blanchefleur (IRE)**13 6385 2-9-0 0 RyanMoore 1 80
(Richard Hannon) *trckd ldrs: swtchd lft 2f out: rdn to ld over 1f out: kpt on but no ex whn hdd fnl 75yds* **13/8**2
2 **3** 2 ¼ **Fille De Reve**29 5795 2-9-0 0 JimCrowley 7 74
(Ed Walker) *racd keenly: mid-div: swtchd lft and hdwy 2f out: sn rdn to chse ldrs: kpt on but nt pce of front pair fnl f* **5/4**1
0 **4** 2 **Admired**13 6385 2-9-0 0 OisinMurphy 5 68
(Sir Michael Stoute) *led for over 3f: prom: led jst over 2f out: rdn and hdd over 1f out: no ex fnl 120yds* **20/1**
0 **5** 1 ¼ **Narodowa**13 6385 2-9-0 0 TomQueally 10 65
(David Lanigan) *s.i.s: last pair: hdwy over 3f out: rdn over 1f out: kpt on ins fnl f: wnt 5th towards fin* **100/1**
**6** nk **Snax** 2-9-0 0 FrannyNorton 3 64
(Mark Johnston) *prom: led over 3f out tl rdn over 2f out: fdd ins fnl f* **14/1**
**7** 1 ¼ **Gather** 2-9-0 0 PatDobbs 8 61
(Amanda Perrett) *hld up mid-div: outpcd over 2f out: kpt on ins fnl f: nvr trbld ldrs* **25/1**
**8** hd **Sea The Sunrise** 2-9-0 0 KieranShoemark 9 60
(David Menuisier) *s.i.s: last pair: outpcd 2f out: n.d* **20/1**
**9** ½ **Halima Hatun (USA)** 2-9-0 0 TomMarquand 6 59
(Ismail Mohammed) *trckd ldrs: rdn over 2f out: keeping on at same pce in hld 5th whn appeared to lose action fnl 120yds* **20/1**
**10** 11 **Kahlo (IRE)** 2-9-0 0 GeorgeWood 2 29
(Jonathan Portman) *s.i.s: sn mid-div: rdn over 2f out: wknd over 1f out* **50/1**
06 **11** 17 **Paulamey**126 2343 2-9-0 0 RobertTart 11
(David Evans) *sn pushed along in mid-div: bhd fnl 2f* **200/1**
1m 29.88s (1.28) **Going Correction** +0.175s/f (Good) 11 Ran SP% **119.1**
Speed ratings (Par 98): **99,97,94,92,91 90,89,89,88,75 56**
CSF £28.06 TOTE £12.00: £3.00, £1.10, £1.10; EX 31.60 Trifecta £58.40.
**Owner** Carmel Stud **Bred** Mrs Clodagh McStay **Trained** Upper Lambourn, W Berks

**FOCUS**
Division one of a useful fillies' maiden. The form stacks up well rated around the second and third.

## 6862 BRITISH EBF QUIDHAMPTON MAIDEN FILLIES' STKS (PLUS 10 RACE) (DIV II) 6f 213y
**3:20** (3:23) (Class 2) 2-Y-O
**£12,450** (£3,728; £1,864; £932; £466; £234) **Stalls** Centre

Form RPR
4 **1** **Clairette (IRE)**26 5938 2-9-0 0 KieranShoemark 9 83+
(Roger Charlton) *mde all: rdn clr over 1f out: in command after* **10/11**1
3 **2** 1 ½ **Goodnight Girl (IRE)**27 5885 2-9-0 0 GeorgeWood 4 79
(Jonathan Portman) *trckd wnr: rdn over 2f out: outpcd over 1f out: sn edgd lft: kpt on but a being hld fnl f* **5/1**3
50 **3** 2 **Shaherezada (IRE)**29 5795 2-9-0 0 AdamKirby 8 74
(Clive Cox) *hld up: hdwy over 3f out: sn rdn: kpt on to go 3rd ins fnl f but no threat to front pair* **12/1**
**4** ¾ **Melodies** 2-9-0 0 JimCrowley 5 72+
(Ed Dunlop) *hld up: pushed along and stdy prog fr 2f out: kpt on ins fnl f: snatched 4th cl home* **33/1**
**5** ½ **Marble Statue** 2-9-0 0 OisinMurphy 3 70
(Ralph Beckett) *trckd wnr tl rdn over 2f out: kpt chsng front pair tl no ex ins fnl f: lost 4th cl home* **10/1**

5 **6** *3 ½* **Final Set (IRE)**[29] 5795 2-9-0 0 ........ RyanMoore 7 61
(Sir Michael Stoute) *cl up: rdn over 2f out: nt pce to mount chal: wknd ent fnl f* **10/3**[2]

**7** *2 ¼* **Parmenter** 2-9-0 0 ........ FergusSweeney 1 55
(Alan King) *s.i.s: last pair: rdn wl over 2f out: nvr gng pce to get involved* **66/1**

**8** *6* **Shikoba (IRE)** 2-9-0 0 ........ HarryBentley 10 38
(Simon Crisford) *in tch: rdn over 2f out: wknd over 1f out: eased ins fnl f* **20/1**

**9** *1 ¼* **Nyala** 2-9-0 0 ........ GeorgeDowning 2 35
(Daniel Kubler) *sn pushed along in tch: rdn over 2f out: sn wknd* **100/1**

**10** *¾* **Empress Rose** 2-9-0 0 ........ FranBerry 6 33
(Richard Hughes) *s.i.s: last pair: rdn over 2f out* **50/1**

1m 29.97s (1.37) **Going Correction** +0.175s/f (Good) **10** Ran SP% **121.1**
Speed ratings (Par 98): **99,97,95,94,93 89,87,80,78,77**
CSF £6.01 TOTE £1.70: £1.10, £1.30, £3.30; EX 6.20 Trifecta £35.30.
**Owner** D J Deer **Bred** Kildaragh Stud **Trained** Beckhampton, Wilts

**FOCUS**
The time was fractionally slower than division one, but Clairette ran out a taking winner and would likely have won the first leg also. The runner-up rates an improver, but the level is fluid.

## 6863 BATHWICK TYRES DICK POOLE FILLIES' STKS (GROUP 3) 6f
**3:50** (3:56) (Class 1) 2-Y-O
**£24,101** (£9,137; £4,573; £2,278; £1,143; £573) **Stalls** Low

Form RPR

631 **1** **Anna Nerium**[40] 5420 2-9-0 80 ........ TomMarquand 6 100
(Richard Hannon) *mid-div: sltly outpcd and pushed along over 3f out: rdn and hdwy over 2f out: str run fnl 120yds: led cl home* **40/1**

3121 **2** *nk* **Eirene**[20] 6136 2-9-0 101 ........ AdamKirby 4 99
(Dean Ivory) *mid-div: hdwy over 2f out: led jst ins fnl f: sn rdn: edgd rt: no ex whn ct cl home: jst hld on for 2nd* **7/2**[1]

115 **3** *shd* **Special Purpose (IRE)**[14] 6354 2-9-0 99 ........ OisinMurphy 11 99
(William Haggas) *mid-div: hdwy over 2f out: sn rdn: r.o ins fnl f: nrly snatched 2nd fnl stride* **7/2**[1]

210 **4** *1* **One Minute (IRE)**[20] 6136 2-9-0 87 ........ RyanMoore 8 96
(William Haggas) *mid-div: rdn and hdwy over 1f out: kpt on ins fnl f: wnt 4th towards fin* **9/1**[3]

21 **5** *1 ¼* **Oriental Song (IRE)**[69] 4312 2-9-0 0 ........ JimCrowley 2 92
(Owen Burrows) *chsd ldrs: rdn wl over 1f out: kpt on but nt quite pce to chal: short of room cl home* **7/2**[1]

1 **6** *½* **Crossing The Line**[34] 5608 2-9-0 0 ........ JimmyQuinn 10 91
(Andrew Balding) *hld up towards rr: rdn over 2f out: hdwy over 1f out: kpt on but no threat fnl f* **12/1**

1013 **7** *shd* **Mrs Gallagher**[20] 6136 2-9-0 90 ........ JosephineGordon 5 90
(William Jarvis) *rrd leaving stalls: plld hrd and sn pressing ldr: rdn 2f out: led v briefly ent fnl f: edgd rt: no ex fnl 12yds* **14/1**

131 **8** *½* **Bambino Lola**[13] 6394 2-9-0 84 ........ RoystonFfrench 9 89
(Adam West) *towards rr: rdn over 2f out: hdwy over 1f out: kpt on fnl f but nt pce to threaten* **14/1**

1504 **9** *2* **Reflect Alexander (IRE)**[5] 6678 2-9-0 82 ........ RobertTart 7 83
(David Evans) *sn pushed along in mid-div: rdn over 2f out: nt pce to get on terms: fdd ins fnl f* **80/1**

1310 **10** *1* **Izzy Bizu (IRE)**[12] 6418 2-9-0 96 ........ FrannyNorton 1 80
(Mark Johnston) *led: rdn over 1f out: hdd ent fnl f: wknd fnl 120yds* **8/1**[2]

001 **11** *½* **Tricksy Spirit**[12] 6417 2-9-0 80 ........ JFEgan 14 78
(Mick Channon) *s.i.s: a towards rr* **66/1**

0210 **12** *9* **Misty Spirit**[20] 6136 2-9-0 77 ........ FranBerry 3 51
(David Elsworth) *chsd ldrs: jinked rt over 2f out: wknd over 1f out* **40/1**

6160 **13** *6* **Listen Alexander (IRE)**[20] 6136 2-9-0 80 ........ CharlesBishop 13 33
(David Evans) *a towards rr* **100/1**

1m 15.3s (0.50) **Going Correction** +0.175s/f (Good) **13** Ran SP% **117.4**
Speed ratings (Par 102): **103,102,102,101,99 98,98,98,95,94 93,81,73**
CSF £173.15 TOTE £30.20: £7.30, £1.80, £1.90; EX 260.70 Trifecta £2268.60.
**Owner** Exors Of The Late R J McCreery **Bred** Stowell Hill Ltd **Trained** East Everleigh, Wilts

**FOCUS**
A big-price winner, but no great surprise as she looked a filly of potential and the form looks sound for the level, with the right horses finishing in behind the winner. A big step forward from the winner, while the second and third and a few down the field suggest this is par for the grade.

## 6864 BRITISH STALLION STUDS EBF "LOCHSONG" FILLIES' H'CAP 6f
**4:20** (4:26) (Class 2) (0-100,97) 3-Y-O+
**£13,695** (£4,100; £2,050; £1,025; £512; £257) **Stalls** Low

Form RPR

3411 **1** **Thafeera (USA)**[20] 6149 3-8-12 87 ........ JimCrowley 8 102
(Charles Hills) *travelled strly: trckd ldr: led over 1f out: edgd rt but sn wl in command: readily* **9/4**[1]

-405 **2** *3* **Kassia (IRE)**[12] 6428 4-9-10 97 ........ GrahamLee 1 102
(Mick Channon) *trckd ldrs: rdn 2f out: kpt on to go 2nd ins fnl f but nvr any threat to wnr* **15/2**[3]

6251 **3** *1 ¼* **Rely On Me (IRE)**[13] 6392 3-8-10 85 ........ (p) OisinMurphy 7 86
(Andrew Balding) *led: rdn 2f out: hdd over 1f out: no ex fnl 120yds* **8/1**

6020 **4** *nk* **Clear Water (IRE)**[14] 6358 4-9-0 87 ........ FrannyNorton 2 87
(Michael Wigham) *sn mid-div: hdwy 2f out: sn rdn: wnt 4th ent fnl f: swtchd lft fnl 120yds: kpt on but nt pce to get on terms* **14/1**

4310 **5** *1 ¼* **Pixeleen**[54] 4889 5-9-5 92 ........ AdamKirby 6 88
(Malcolm Saunders) *trckd ldrs: rdn over 2f out: nt pce to get on terms: no ex fnl f* **12/1**

2011 **6** *hd* **Under The Covers**[13] 6371 4-9-4 91 ........ SamHitchcott 4 86
(Ronald Harris) *s.i.s: last pair: hdwy 2f out: sn rdn: kpt on same pce fnl f* **12/1**

3050 **7** *¾* **Stellarta**[12] 6412 6-9-1 88 ........ TomMarquand 10 81
(Michael Blanshard) *last pair: struggling over 2f out: nvr threatened to get involved* **18/1**

3204 **8** *½* **Bounce**[23] 6039 4-9-7 94 ........ HarryBentley 9 85
(Henry Candy) *mid-div: rdn over 2f out: nvr any imp: fdd ins fnl f* **4/1**[2]

2000 **9** *2* **Poet's Princess**[14] 6358 3-8-5 83 ........ GeorgeWood(3) 5 68
(Hughie Morrison) *trckd ldrs: rdn over 2f out: nt pce to chal: wknd ins fnl f* **12/1**

1040 **10** *nk* **Buying Trouble (USA)**[18] 6234 4-9-8 95 ........ JFEgan 3 79
(David Evans) *mid-div: rdn over 2f out: wknd over 1f out* **16/1**

1m 14.47s (-0.33) **Going Correction** +0.175s/f (Good)
**WFA** 3 from 4yo+ 2lb **10** Ran SP% **114.5**
Speed ratings (Par 96): **109,105,103,102,101 101,100,99,96,96**
CSF £19.03 CT £116.64 TOTE £2.60: £1.20, £2.30, £2.70; EX 18.50 Trifecta £77.50.
**Owner** Hamdan Al Maktoum **Bred** Shadwell Farm LLC **Trained** Lambourn, Berks

**FOCUS**
A useful fillies' sprint won by a highly progressive filly. The third has been rated close to her Newmarket latest, with the fourth a length off this year's form.

## 6865 LESTER BRUNT WEALTH MANAGEMENT H'CAP 1m 4f 5y
**4:50** (4:51) (Class 4) (0-85,86) 3-Y-O+ **£5,175** (£1,540; £769; £384) **Stalls** Low

Form RPR

-103 **1** **Opinionate**[19] 6202 3-9-0 80 ........ JimCrowley 5 93+
(Amanda Perrett) *travelled wl in tch: hdwy over 2f out: led over 1f out: edgd rt: rdn clr: comf* **11/4**[2]

2512 **2** *3* **Tomorrow Mystery**[16] 6291 3-9-2 82 ........ DougieCostello 9 89
(Jamie Osborne) *led tl over 3f out: led 2f out: sn rdn: hdd over 1f out: styd on but wl hld by wnr ins fnl f* **10/1**

5511 **3** *nk* **Uber Cool (IRE)**[33] 5667 3-8-10 81 ........ PaddyBradley(5) 1 88+
(Jane Chapple-Hyam) *in tch: hdwy over 2f out: sn rdn: squeezed through gap to chse ldng pair over 1f out: styd on same pce fnl f* **2/1**[1]

210 **4** *4* **Opposition**[54] 4908 4-9-12 84 ........ RyanMoore 6 83
(Ed Dunlop) *hld up: rdn wl over 2f out: styd on to go 4th ins fnl f but nvr gng pce to get involved* **10/1**

1511 **5** *4* **Langlauf (USA)**[78] 3968 4-9-11 86 ........ (p) GeorgeWood(3) 8 79
(Rod Millman) *trckd ldr: led over 3f out: rdn and hdd 2f out: fdd ins fnl f* **16/1**

1552 **6** *1 ¾* **Comrade Conrad (IRE)**[20] 6135 3-9-1 81 ........ (p[1]) KieranShoemark 7 72
(Roger Charlton) *trckd ldrs: rdn over 2f out: wknd ent fnl f* **4/1**[3]

0- **7** *7* **Sabre Squadron (IRE)**[325] 7412 4-9-8 80 ........ FergusSweeney 2 59
(Alan King) *hld up: rdn over 2f out: nvr any imp: wknd fnl f* **20/1**

51/5 **8** *¾* **Sleep Easy**[21] 6096 5-9-10 82 ........ (tp) AdamKirby 3 60
(Neil Mulholland) *s.i.s: struggling in detached last early: latched onto main gp 5f out: rdn 3f out: sn outpcd* **16/1**

3/-P **9** *dist* **Stock Hill Fair**[103] 3086 9-9-7 79 ........ (t) PatDobbs 4
(Brendan Powell) *trckd ldrs: rdn over 3f out: sn btn: virtually p.u fnl f* **33/1**

2m 37.54s (-0.46) **Going Correction** +0.125s/f (Good)
**WFA** 3 from 4yo+ 8lb **9** Ran SP% **117.6**
Speed ratings (Par 105): **106,104,103,101,98 97,92,92,**
CSF £31.17 CT £66.60 TOTE £3.40: £1.10, £3.10, £1.50; EX 39.00 Trifecta £119.90.
**Owner** K Abdullah **Bred** Millsec Limited **Trained** Pulborough, W Sussex

**FOCUS**
A useful handicap run at a good gallop and, as expected, the 3yos dominated. Another step up from the second.

## 6866 SHADWELL STUD RACING EXCELLENCE APPRENTICE H'CAP (WHIPS SHALL BE CARRIED BUT NOT USED) 1m
**5:20** (5:20) (Class 5) (0-70,71) 3-Y-O+ **£4,528** (£1,347; £673; £336) **Stalls** Low

Form RPR

504 **1** **The Groove**[30] 5757 4-9-5 63 ........ ManuelFernandes 8 69
(Fergal O'Brien) *sn trcking ldr: led narrowly fr 2f out: kpt on gamely: jst hld on* **9/1**

6450 **2** *nse* **Poetic Force (IRE)**[21] 6111 3-9-2 70 ........ (t) SophieRalston(5) 3 75+
(Tony Carroll) *hld up: hdwy over 1f out: str run ins fnl f: jst failed* **4/1**[2]

4266 **3** *shd* **Famous Dynasty (IRE)**[27] 5867 3-8-6 58 ........ NicolaCurrie(3) 10 63
(Michael Blanshard) *in tch: hdwy 2f out: ev ch thrght fnl f: jst hld* **10/1**

1315 **4** *2* **Fantasy Queen**[14] 6340 4-9-11 69 ........ (p[1]) MillyNaseb 7 70
(Eve Johnson Houghton) *hld up: pushed along over 2f out: no imp tl r.o ins fnl f: wnt 4th towards fin but nt threat to ldrs* **8/1**[3]

5005 **5** *1* **Jet Setter (IRE)**[19] 6181 3-8-9 61 ........ AledBeech(3) 9 59
(Tony Carroll) *hld up: pushed along over 2f out: no imp tl r.o ins fnl f: nvr threatened ldrs* **20/1**

1265 **6** *nk* **Many Dreams (IRE)**[28] 5843 4-9-7 68 ........ RossaRyan(3) 6 66
(Gary Moore) *racd keenly: trckd ldrs: str chal 2f out: ev ch ent fnl f: fdd* **4/1**[2]

1353 **7** *nk* **Ashazuri**[20] 6139 3-8-12 66 ........ (h) Pierre-LouisJamin(5) 4 63
(Jonathan Portman) *hmpd s: sn racing keenly trcking ldrs: chal 3f out: ev ch 2f out: fdd ins fnl f* **7/2**[1]

05-4 **8** *2* **Al's Memory (IRE)**[10] 6503 8-9-4 62 ........ KatherineGlenister 1 55
(David Evans) *led tl 2f out: wknd over 1f out* **12/1**

0000 **9** *½* **Beepeecee**[10] 6502 3-8-10 62 ........ StephenCummins(3) 5 53
(Richard Hughes) *in tch: hdwy over 2f out whn swtchd rt: ch over 1f out: wknd ins fnl f* **16/1**

000 **10** *1 ½* **Fort Jefferson**[32] 5686 4-9-6 71 ........ MichaelColes(7) 2 60
(Andrew Balding) *s.i.s: racd keenly and sn prom: wknd over 1f out* **10/1**

1m 45.73s (2.23) **Going Correction** +0.175s/f (Good)
**WFA** 3 from 4yo+ 5lb **10** Ran SP% **119.9**
Speed ratings (Par 103): **95,94,94,92,91 91,91,89,88,87**
CSF £46.26 CT £385.76 TOTE £13.90: £3.70, £1.70, £2.90; EX 65.30 Trifecta £805.40.
**Owner** The Groovy Gang **Bred** Cheveley Park Stud Ltd **Trained** Naunton, Gloucs

**FOCUS**
A modest apprentice handicap and with whips not allowed to be used, jockeyship made all the difference in the outcome. The third helps set the standard.
T/Jkpt: Not won. T/Plt: £11.90 to a £1 stake. Pool: £79,613.18 - 4870.11 winning units. T/Qpdt: £2.80 to a £1 stake. Pool: £6,534.51 - 1720.18 winning units. **Tim Mitchell**

# 5911 ASCOT (R-H)
## Friday, September 8

**OFFICIAL GOING: Soft (str 6.7, rnd 6.6)**
Wind: Moderate, half against in straight Weather: Overcast gradually brightening

## 6867 TWININGS NOVICE AUCTION STKS (PLUS 10 RACE) (DIV I) 6f
**1:30** (1:31) (Class 4) 2-Y-O **£6,469** (£1,925; £962; £481) **Stalls** High

Form RPR

3 **1** **Speak In Colours**[31] 5755 2-9-2 0 ........ RyanMoore 1 82
(Marco Botti) *t.k.h: hld up: quick prog to ld over 1f out: on top fnl f: rdn out* **9/4**[1]

30 **2** *1 ½* **Lady Dancealot (IRE)**[37] 5528 2-8-11 0 ........ SilvestreDeSousa 4 73
(David Elsworth) *hld up in rr: prog on outer of gp over 2f out: rdn over 1f out: chsd wnr fnl f: styd on but readily hld* **5/2**[2]

4 **3** *1* **Scenery**[14] 6394 2-9-2 0 ........ TomQueally 5 75
(Eve Johnson Houghton) *t.k.h: trckd ldrs: rdn over 1f out and edgd rt: kpt on same pce fnl f* **10/1**

130 **4** *nse* **Wasim (IRE)**[34] 5631 2-9-8 86 ........ (h[1]) SeanLevey 6 80
(Ismail Mohammed) *taken down early: pressed ldr: led 2f out to over 1f out: one pce after* **5/1**[3]

30 **5** *2* **Immortal Romance (IRE)**[25] 6005 2-9-2 0 ........ DanielTudhope 3 68
(Michael Bell) *trckd ldrs: pushed along and cl up over 1f out: fdd fnl f: nt disgracd* **8/1**

6 ¾ **Restless Rose** 2-8-11 0 AdamBeschizza 8 61
(Stuart Williams) *t.k.h: hld up in last: rdn and no significant prog 2f out* **33/1**

366 7 ¾ **Jack Regan**[42] 5380 2-9-2 75 JimCrowley 9 64
(Charles Hills) *hld up in rr: rdn and no prog 2f out: wl hld after* **15/2**

00 8 *hd* **Caviar Royale**[7] 6654 2-9-2 0 JimmyFortune 2 63
(Brian Meehan) *led to 2f out: pushed along and sn lost pl* **50/1**

1m 19.93s (5.43) **Going Correction** +0.775s/f (Yiel) 8 Ran SP% **112.9**
Speed ratings (Par 97): **94,92,90,90,87 86,85,85**
CSF £7.85 TOTE £3.00: £1.30, £1.20, £2.30; EX 8.60 Trifecta £55.80.
**Owner** Scuderia Archi Romani **Bred** Scuderia Archi Romani **Trained** Newmarket, Suffolk

**FOCUS**
Course at full width; distances as advertised. A rainy day, and soft ground, but it didn't look too demanding in this opener. They raced up the middle. This looked an ordinary novice event but some nice enough prospects. The winner has been rated as finding a little on his debut effort.

## 6868 TWININGS NOVICE AUCTION STKS (PLUS 10 RACE) (DIV II) 6f
**2:05** (2:08) (Class 4) 2-Y-O **£6,469** (£1,925; £962; £481) **Stalls** High

Form RPR

3 1 **Odyssa (IRE)**[25] 6010 2-8-11 0 ShaneKelly 8 81+
(Richard Hughes) *w'like: wnt rt s: trckd ldr: led wl over 1f out: sn pushed clr: readily* **7/2**[2]

20 2 3 ¼ **Last Enchantment (IRE)**[37] 5528 2-8-11 0 TomQueally 5 71
(Eve Johnson Houghton) *t.k.h: trckd ldrs: rdn over 1f out: chsd wnr fnl f: styd on but no ch* **7/1**

3 3 ¼ **Fashion Sense (IRE)** 2-8-8 0 HectorCrouch(3) 9 61
(Clive Cox) *leggy: athletic: led to wl over 1f out: sn lft bhd but hld on wl enough for 3rd* **9/2**[3]

56 4 2 **Montague (IRE)**[90] 3591 2-9-2 0 DougieCostello 6 60
(Jamie Osborne) *t.k.h: trckd ldrs: readily lft bhd fr over 1f out* **9/2**[3]

40 5 1 ¼ **Achianna (USA)**[14] 6394 2-8-11 0 WilliamCarson 2 52
(Rod Millman) *rrd s and slowly away: mostly in last: pushed along and passed wkng rivals fr over 1f out* **66/1**

6 3 ¾ **Society Lilly (IRE)** 2-8-11 0 JimCrowley 1 40
(Hugo Palmer) *leggy: chsd ldng pair to jst over 2f out: nudged along and wknd* **5/2**[1]

7 *nk* **United Kingdom** 2-9-2 0 RaulDaSilva 3 44
(Paul Cole) *taken down early: in tch 4f: shkn up and wknd* **12/1**

8 4 ½ **Saphil (IRE)** 2-9-2 0 FranBerry 4 31
(John Ryan) *cmpt: slowly away: rn green in rr: wknd 2f out* **25/1**

1m 19.98s (5.48) **Going Correction** +0.775s/f (Yiel) 8 Ran SP% **112.7**
Speed ratings (Par 97): **94,89,85,82,81 76,75,69**
CSF £27.19 TOTE £3.50: £1.40, £1.90, £1.50; EX 23.80 Trifecta £62.60.
**Owner** The Low Flyers **Bred** Padraig O'Reilly **Trained** Upper Lambourn, Berks
■ Desert Trip was withdrawn. Price at time of withdrawal 12-1. Rule 4 \n\x\x applies to bets placed prior to withdrawal but not to SP bets - deduction 5p in the pound

**FOCUS**
They raced middle to stands' side. There didn't look much depth to this. A nice step forward from the winner.

## 6869 CHARBONNEL ET WALKER BRITISH EBF MAIDEN STKS (PLUS 10 RACE) (SIRE-RESTRICTED RACE) 7f
**2:40** (2:40) (Class 3) 2-Y-O **£7,762** (£2,310; £1,154; £577) **Stalls** High

Form RPR

1 **Herculean** 2-9-5 0 RyanMoore 5 88+
(Roger Charlton) *str: scope: lw: trckd ldrs: nudged along 3f out: prog between rivals to ld over 1f out and in command after: rdn out last 100yds: promising* **11/10**[1]

2 1 ¾ **Wadilsafa** 2-9-5 0 JimCrowley 2 84+
(Owen Burrows) *leggy: athletic: trckd ldng pair: shkn up as wnr wnt past 2f out: styd on after to take 2nd ins fnl f: no real threat* **9/2**[3]

3 3 ½ **Archie McKellar**[32] 5710 2-9-5 0 PatDobbs 1 82
(Ralph Beckett) *swtg: s.s: hld up in last: prog over 2f out: chsd wnr jst over 1f out: kpt on but no imp and lost 2nd ins fnl f* **7/1**

4 3 ½ **Para Mio (IRE)** 2-9-5 0 ShaneKelly 3 74
(Seamus Durack) *unf: t.k.h: hld up: swtchd rt 2f out: no prog over 1f out and readily lft bhd* **40/1**

32 5 1 ½ **Merlin Magic**[21] 6132 2-9-5 0 SilvestreDeSousa 9 70
(David Elsworth) *led against nr side rail: hdd & wknd over 1f out* **5/2**[2]

6 2 ½ **Airmax (GER)** 2-9-0 0 PatrickO'Donnell(5) 7 64
(Ralph Beckett) *w'like: bit bkwd: dwlt: hld up: shkn up and no prog 2f out: sn btn* **50/1**

0 7 *nk* **Bodie And Doyle**[21] 6133 2-9-5 0 DavidProbert 6 63
(Andrew Balding) *w'like: w ldr to 2f out: wknd quite qckly* **50/1**

8 ¾ **Nelson River** 2-9-2 0 HectorCrouch(3) 4 61
(Clive Cox) *str: bit bkwd: rn green and a towards rr: wknd jst over 2f out* **33/1**

1m 33.29s (5.69) **Going Correction** +0.775s/f (Yiel) 8 Ran SP% **116.2**
Speed ratings (Par 99): **98,96,95,91,89 86,86,85**
CSF £6.60 TOTE £1.90: £1.02, £1.70, £1.70; EX 5.80 Trifecta £22.50.
**Owner** K Abdullah **Bred** Juddmonte Farms Ltd **Trained** Beckhampton, Wilts

**FOCUS**
They raced stands' side. Two well-bred newcomers with big-race entries filled the first two places. There's every chance the form proves a few lengths better than rated, but those down the field are the key.

## 6870 LEO BANCROFT SIGNATURE HAIR CARE CLASSIFIED STKS 1m (S)
**3:15** (3:15) (Class 3) 3-Y-O+ **£9,703** (£2,887; £1,443; £721) **Stalls** High

Form RPR

21- 1 **Cape Byron**[324] 7468 3-8-12 90 AndreaAtzeni 3 103+
(Roger Varian) *h.d.w: trckd ldrs gng wl: led wl over 1f out: sn shkn up: edgd lft fnl f and hrd pressed last 100yds: styd on wl* **13/8**[1]

1531 2 *nk* **Fire Brigade**[27] 5928 3-8-12 90 SilvestreDeSousa 5 102
(Michael Bell) *lw: hld up in last: swtchd to nr side rail and gd prog 2f out to chse wnr over 1f out: str chal last 100yds: styd on wl but a hld* **15/8**[2]

6616 3 7 **Fox Trotter (IRE)**[13] 6419 5-9-3 86 FrankieDettori 7 87
(Brian Meehan) *taken down early: trckd ldng pair: pushed along 3f out: outpcd fr 2f out: kpt on to win battle for modest 3rd* **12/1**

5034 4 ½ **Maths Prize**[37] 5548 3-8-12 89 (p) RyanMoore 1 85
(Roger Charlton) *pressed ldr to 2f out: sn btn* **20/1**

2631 5 *nk* **Musawaat**[13] 6426 3-8-12 90 JimCrowley 6 84
(Charles Hills) *lw: wl in tch: shkn up over 2f out: easily lft bhd fr wl over 1f out* **7/1**[3]

3243 6 ¾ **Dr Julius No**[13] 6422 3-8-12 90 (p[1]) ShaneKelly 2 82
(Richard Hughes) *hld up in tch: shkn up and no prog over 2f out: wknd wl over 1f out* **20/1**

0004 7 2 **Medieval (IRE)**[37] 5530 3-8-12 90 (b) DavidProbert 8 78
(Paul Cole) *led to wl over 1f out: sn wknd* **12/1**

1m 46.2s (5.40) **Going Correction** +0.775s/f (Yiel)
**WFA** 3 from 4yo+ 5lb 7 Ran SP% **110.3**
Speed ratings (Par 107): **104,103,96,96,95 95,93**
CSF £4.49 TOTE £2.20: £1.30, £2.30; EX 5.70 Trifecta £31.40.
**Owner** Sheikh Mohammed Obaid Al Maktoum **Bred** Darley **Trained** Newmarket, Suffolk

**FOCUS**
The runners were switched from the stands' side to race up the middle, before drifting back to the stands' rail; odd that they didn't just stay in the one place. Anyway, the first two pulled a long way clear, and smart-looking performances from both. The level is hard to pin down and could be better than rated, but the race lacked some depth.

## 6871 GARDEN FOR ALL SEASONS MAIDEN STKS (PLUS 10 RACE) 1m 3f 211y
**3:50** (3:50) (Class 3) 3-Y-O **£9,703** (£2,887; £1,443; £721) **Stalls** Low

Form RPR

-222 1 **Reverend Jacobs**[20] 6194 3-9-5 78 RyanMoore 2 78
(William Haggas) *trckd ldr 2f: styd cl up: gap appeared and shkn up between rivals to ld over 1f out: hrd pressed ins fnl f: drvn and edgd lft: jst hld on* **8/13**[1]

2 *shd* **Hang Man (IRE)** 3-9-5 0 AdamBeschizza 1 77
(Ed Vaughan) *dwlt: hld up in last: swtchd to outer 2f out: rdn and prog over 1f out: str chal ins fnl f: upsides nr fin: jst denied* **33/1**

2243 3 ¾ **Count Simon (IRE)**[20] 6196 3-9-5 72 DavidProbert 5 76
(Andrew Balding) *led: rdn over 2f out: hdd over 1f out: kpt on fnl f but nt qckn* **6/1**[3]

P02 4 1 **War Brigade (FR)**[24] 6031 3-9-5 0 (h) FranBerry 3 74
(David Simcock) *hld up in 4th: shkn up to take 2nd briefly 2f out: sn rdn and fnd little: kpt on same pce fnl f* **20/1**

-562 5 8 **Uptown Funk (IRE)**[62] 4623 3-9-5 67 (t[1]) FrankieDettori 4 65
(John Gosden) *chsd ldr after 2f to 2f out: wknd quite qckly* **11/4**[2]

2m 42.62s (10.12) **Going Correction** +1.00s/f (Soft) 5 Ran SP% **110.6**
Speed ratings (Par 105): **106,105,105,104,99**
CSF £21.54 TOTE £1.40: £1.10, £9.20; EX 19.50 Trifecta £49.40.
**Owner** Bernard Kantor **Bred** West Stow Stud Ltd **Trained** Newmarket, Suffolk

**FOCUS**
An ordinary maiden; there was less than 2l separating the first four at the line. It's been rated around the third.

## 6872 VICTORIA RACING CLUB H'CAP 1m 3f 211y
**4:25** (4:26) (Class 3) (0-95,95) 3-Y-O+ **£9,703** (£2,887; £1,443; £721) **Stalls** Low

Form RPR

3561 1 **Great Hall**[27] 5913 7-9-12 **95** FranBerry 4 103
(Mick Quinn) *hld up in 5th: prog on inner 2f out: rdn to ld ins fnl f: edgd lft but kpt on wl* **9/1**

2-10 2 ½ **Alqamar**[77] 4032 3-8-10 **87** (p) RyanMoore 5 94
(Charlie Appleby) *swtg: trckd ldng trio: pushed along on outer jst over 2f out: urged along and clsd to ld jst over 1f out: hdd ins fnl f: rdn and little rspnse after* **10/11**[1]

-614 3 2 ¼ **Roar (IRE)**[48] 5166 3-8-4 **81** oh3 JoeyHaynes 8 84
(Brian Ellison) *trckd ldr: rdn to ld 2f out: hdd and one pce jst over 1f out* **9/1**

3012 4 ¾ **Gawdawpalin (IRE)**[27] 5913 4-9-8 **91** MartinDwyer 6 93
(Sylvester Kirk) *t.k.h: hld up in 6th: rdn to cl on ldrs over 2f out: kpt on same pce fr over 1f out and nvr pce to threaten* **9/2**[2]

-012 5 1 ¾ **Star Of The East (IRE)**[15] 6344 3-8-7 **84** DavidProbert 7 83
(Mark Johnston) *led to 2f out: fdd* **5/1**[3]

40-0 6 12 **Poyle Thomas**[21] 6135 8-9-0 **88** PatrickO'Donnell(5) 1 68
(Michael Madgwick) *awkward s: hld up in last: pushed along and lost tch over 2f out: eased whn no ch fnl f* **50/1**

5016 7 ¾ **Mutadaffeq (IRE)**[19] 6232 4-9-7 **90** DanielTudhope 3 69
(David O'Meara) *trckd ldng pair to jst over 2f out: wknd qckly: eased fnl f* **25/1**

2m 41.86s (9.36) **Going Correction** +1.00s/f (Soft)
**WFA** 3 from 4yo+ 8lb 7 Ran SP% **113.0**
Speed ratings (Par 107): **108,107,106,105,104 96,96**
CSF £17.33 CT £77.97 TOTE £7.30: £3.30, £1.10; EX 20.80 Trifecta £201.40.
**Owner** M Quinn **Bred** Aston House Stud **Trained** Newmarket, Suffolk

**FOCUS**
A useful handicap. It's been rated around the winner and fourth.

## 6873 WEATHERBYS H'CAP 1m (S)
**5:00** (5:01) (Class 2) (0-105,104) 3-Y-O+
**£18,675** (£5,592; £2,796; £1,398; £699; £351) **Stalls** High

Form RPR

5-03 1 **Leader Writer (FR)**[27] 5914 5-8-12 **92** (p) FranBerry 9 102
(Henry Spiller) *t.k.h and sn hld up: stdy prog 2f out: pushed into ld ins fnl f: shkn up and sn drew clr* **10/1**

0450 2 2 ¼ **Storm Ahead (IRE)**[34] 5643 4-8-10 **90** oh2 (p[1]) HayleyTurner 2 95
(Marcus Tregoning) *hld up in tch: prog on outer of gp over 2f out: drvn to dispute ld over 1f out: outpcd by wnr ins fnl f: styd on* **12/1**

0506 3 ¾ **Big Baz (IRE)**[15] 6355 7-9-2 **96** DougieCostello 12 99
(William Muir) *dwlt: sn pressed ldrs: rdn to ld over 1f out to ins fnl f: one pce* **9/1**

1104 4 *nk* **Afaak**[55] 4904 3-8-7 **92** DavidProbert 7 94
(Charles Hills) *lw: hld up in rr: effrt 2f out: hrd rdn and nt qckn over 1f out: r.o ins fnl f: gaining on 3rd cl home* **9/4**[1]

2210 5 2 ½ **Truth Or Dare**[13] 6419 6-8-11 **91** TedDurcan 8 88
(James Bethell) *hld up in last trio: prog on outer of gp over 2f out: tried to chal over 1f out: sn rdn and wknd fnl f* **9/1**

1-03 6 2 ½ **Sacred Act**[143] 1860 6-9-2 **96** DanielTudhope 6 87
(Michael Bell) *trckd ldrs: stl rt there over 1f out: wknd qckly* **8/1**[3]

-102 7 2 **Eagle Creek (IRE)**[19] 6235 3-8-10 **95** AndreaAtzeni 4 80
(Simon Crisford) *lw: led to over 1f out: wknd* **8/1**[3]

0-10 8 1 ¾ **Banksea**[79] 3963 4-9-10 **104** RyanMoore 5 86
(Luca Cumani) *hld up towards rr: rdn 2f out: no imp on ldrs over 1f out: wknd ins fnl f* **6/1**[2]

-000 9 5 **Emell**[109] 2907 7-8-10 **95** (v) MitchGodwin(5) 10 66
(Tim Vaughan) *t.k.h: pressed ldr over 3f out: sn wknd* **50/1**

0053 10 3 ¾ **Secret Art (IRE)**[26] 5966 7-8-12 **92** SilvestreDeSousa 3 54
(William Knight) *trckd ldrs: rdn and wknd 2f out: heavily eased fnl f* **12/1**

5564 11 2 ¼ **Captain Cat (IRE)**[184] 1079 8-8-13 **93** GeorgeDowning 11 50
(Tony Carroll) *dwlt: a in rr: struggling over 2f out: sn bhd* **66/1**

1m 46.42s (5.62) **Going Correction** +0.775s/f (Yiel)
**WFA** 3 from 4yo+ 5lb 11 Ran SP% **115.2**
Speed ratings (Par 109): **102,99,99,98,96 93,91,89,84,81 78**
CSF £121.33 CT £1144.81 TOTE £10.10: £3.10, £3.80, £2.70; EX 152.30 Trifecta £1196.60.



The Form Book Flat, Raceform Ltd, Newbury, RG14 5SJ

**Owner** G B Partnership **Bred** G Heald **Trained** Newmarket, Suffolk
■ Stewards' Enquiry : Mitch Godwin caution; careless riding
**FOCUS**
They raced up the middle. A decent handicap. The runner-up has been rated to his best, with the third to his recent effort.

## 6874 BIBENDUM WINE H'CAP 6f
5:30 (5:33) (Class 4) (0-80,80) 3-Y-O+ £6,469 (£1,925; £962; £481) Stalls High

Form RPR
0000 1 **Mullionheir**[20] 6192 5-9-3 **76** SilvestreDeSousa 11 87
(John Best) *hld up in rr: swtchd to wd outside and gd prog 2f out: led over 1f out and drvn for home: hld on wl* **5/1**[3]
1502 2 ½ **Alaadel**[36] 5564 4-9-3 **76** (bt[1]) JimCrowley 15 85
(William Haggas) *lw: hld up: prog nr side 2f out: had to squeeze through against rail fr jst over 1f out: tk 2nd last 100yds and fin wl but too late* **2/1**[1]
630- 3 2 **Peter Park**[347] 6831 4-8-6 **72** AmeliaGlass(7) 17 75
(Clive Cox) *led at str pce: edgd lft towards nr side rail fr 2f out: hdd over 1f out: no ex and lost 2nd last 100yds* **33/1**
3526 4 2 **Cool Bahamian (IRE)**[13] 6429 6-9-5 **78** (b) JimmyFortune 3 74
(Eve Johnson Houghton) *prom on outer: rdn and jst abt on terms over 1f out: one pce after* **10/1**
0304 5 nse **Duke Cosimo**[27] 5947 7-8-10 **72** GeorgeWood(3) 9 68
(Michael Herrington) *in tch: drvn and struggling over 2f out: nvr any ch but kpt on quite wl fnl f* **10/1**
1440 6 1 ¼ **North Creek**[22] 6111 4-9-0 **73** ShaneKelly 1 65
(Chris Wall) *hld up on outer: hrd rdn and no prog wl over 1f out: btn after but plugged on last 100yds* **12/1**
0320 7 1 ½ **Perfect Symphony (IRE)**[18] 6265 3-9-0 **75** AdamBeschizza 8 62
(Kevin Ryan) *wl in tch: drvn wl over 1f out: sn wknd* **11/1**
0205 8 nk **Harwoods Volante (IRE)**[15] 6348 6-9-6 **79** FranBerry 14 65
(David O'Meara) *trckd ldrs: shkn up wl over 1f out and in tch: sn wknd* **12/1**
4-13 9 3 ½ **African Friend (IRE)**[18] 6267 4-9-4 **77** DaneO'Neill 6 52
(Henry Candy) *tk fierce hold: trckd ldr and tried to get cover: rdn 2f out: wknd over 1f out* **9/2**[2]
0-06 10 10 **Drop Kick Murphi (IRE)**[204] 765 3-9-3 **78** JoeyHaynes 2 21
(Christine Dunnett) *led small gp on outer to over 2f out: wknd rapidly: t.o* **50/1**
0630 11 2 ½ **Picket Line**[22] 6099 5-8-11 **70** (p) HayleyTurner 12 5
(Geoffrey Deacon) *nvr gng wl: drvn in last bef 1/2-way: t.o* **33/1**

1m 18.34s (3.84) **Going Correction** +0.775s/f (Yiel)
**WFA** 3 from 4yo+ 2lb 11 Ran SP% **117.9**
Speed ratings (Par 105): **105,104,101,99,98 97,95,94,90,76 73**
CSF £15.19 CT £302.39 TOTE £5.00: £1.40, £1.80, £9.00; EX 21.50 Trifecta £390.30.
**Owner** Simon Malcolm **Bred** D R Tucker **Trained** Oad Street, Kent
**FOCUS**
A fair sprint handicap in which they raced middle to stands' side. The third has been rated to form.
T/Plt: £9.30 to a £1 stake. Pool: £86,872.39 - 6,746.83 winning units. T/Qpdt: £4.10 to a £1 stake. Pool: £5,962.22 - 1,053.86 winning units. **Jonathan Neesom**

# 6852 HAYDOCK (L-H)
Friday, September 8

**OFFICIAL GOING: Soft (7.3)**
Wind: breezy, against in straight Weather: sunny intervals, cool under cloud cover

## 6875 32RED CASINO EBF FILLIES' NOVICE STKS (PLUS 10 RACE) 7f 212y
1:50 (1:52) (Class 5) 2-Y-O £3,557 (£1,058; £529; £264) Stalls Low

Form RPR
43 1 **Amazing Michele (FR)**[20] 6183 2-9-0 0 TonyHamilton 6 78+
(Richard Fahey) *niggled early: mid-div: 4th 3f out: trckd ldrs gng wl 2f out: swtchd to chal over 1f out: sn led: kpt up to work and asserted ent fnl f: comf* **4/1**[3]
2 1 ½ **Beckton** 2-9-0 0 TomMarquand 8 73
(Robyn Brisland) *hld up: pushed along 4f out: rdn 3f out: drvn and hdwy over 2f out: r.o to take 2nd ins fnl f* **14/1**
4 3 1 ¼ **Cavatina**[23] 6064 2-9-0 0 PatCosgrave 5 70
(William Haggas) *trckd ldrs: gng wl on outer 2f out: sn 2nd and ev ch: drvn over 1f out: one pce and lost 2nd ins fnl f* **15/8**[1]
6533 4 ¾ **Fleeting Freedom**[27] 5939 2-8-9 75 JoshuaBryan(5) 1 68
(Alan Bailey) *led: pushed along 2f out: drvn over 1f out: sn hdd: no ex fnl f* **11/4**[2]
63 5 ¾ **Rayna's World (IRE)**[25] 5999 2-9-0 0 GrahamLee 7 67
(Philip Kirby) *racd in last: hdwy 3f out: pushed along over 2f out: reminder over 1f out: briefly n.m.r ent fnl f: one pce* **13/2**
00 6 4 **Miss Perception**[50] 5056 2-9-0 0 RichardKingscote 2 58
(Tom Dascombe) *in rr: pushed along early: reminders 3f and 2f out: sn drvn along and no imp* **28/1**
3 7 2 ¾ **Coast Guard**[13] 6410 2-9-0 0 BenCurtis 3 52
(Tom Dascombe) *chsd ldr: cl up 3f out: pushed along over 2f out: sn rdn and wknd* **16/1**

1m 48.41s (4.71) **Going Correction** +0.575s/f (Yiel) 7 Ran SP% **110.8**
Speed ratings (Par 92): **99,97,96,95,94 90,88**
CSF £51.40 TOTE £4.60: £2.00, £6.60; EX 49.50 Trifecta £129.40.
**Owner** Nick Bradley Racing 40 & Partner **Bred** Tony Grey **Trained** Musley Bank, N Yorks
**FOCUS**
All races run on Inner Home Straight. Distance increased by 11yds. Pat Cosgrave described the ground as "proper soft" while Tony Hamilton felt it was "very soft." An ordinary fillies' novice run at a fair pace and the early leaders folded late on.

## 6876 32RED EBF FILLIES' NOVICE STKS (PLUS 10 RACE) 6f
2:25 (2:26) (Class 5) 2-Y-O £3,557 (£1,058; £529; £264) Stalls Centre

Form RPR
03 1 **Pulitzer**[37] 5528 2-9-0 0 JosephineGordon 2 72
(Hugo Palmer) *prom: hdwy to chal ldrs gng wl 2f out: led over 1f out: shkn up and r.o to settle issue ins fnl f: readily* **2/1**[1]
52 2 ¾ **Forever In Love**[25] 6010 2-9-0 0 (v[1]) RichardKingscote 8 70
(Sir Michael Stoute) *mid-div: pushed along and n.m.r 2f out: swtchd and rdn over 1f out: hdwy to chse wnr 1f out: r.o wl fnl f* **2/1**[1]
50 3 nk **Bee Ina Bonnet**[10] 6559 2-9-0 0 DavidNolan 13 69
(Tim Easterby) *mid-div: hdwy 2f out: pushed along and ev ch over 1f out: kpt on ins fnl f* **50/1**
4 nk **Chantresse (IRE)** 2-9-0 0 PJMcDonald 3 68
(K R Burke) *mid-div: niggled briefly after 2 fs: pushed along 2f out: hdwy over 1f out: r.o ins fnl f: nvr nrr* **16/1**
5 1 **Mzoon (IRE)** 2-9-0 0 StevieDonohoe 4 65+
(Charlie Fellowes) *hld up: hdwy 1/2-way: sn trcking ldrs: pushed along 2f out: drvn ent fnl f: kpt on* **7/1**[3]
0 6 nk **Helen Sherbet**[37] 5534 2-8-11 0 CliffordLee(3) 7 64
(K R Burke) *trckd ldrs: effrt and swtchd to outer 2f out: rdn over 1f out: one pce* **33/1**
7 ¾ **Agent Error (IRE)** 2-9-0 0 TonyHamilton 1 62
(David Simcock) *hld up: swtchd rt after 1f: effrt and pushed along over 1f out: kpt on fnl f* **25/1**
8 ½ **Scenic River** 2-8-11 0 RachelRichardson(3) 9 61
(Tim Easterby) *slowly away: rcvrd to go mid-div 1/2-way: pushed along over 1f out: no ex fnl f* **33/1**
5 9 1 ¾ **Long Embrace**[25] 6010 2-9-0 0 HarryBentley 12 55
(Simon Crisford) *prom: led over 2f out: drvn and hdd over 1f out: sn rdn and wknd* **11/2**[2]
10 6 **Blue Harmony** 2-8-7 0 PatrickO'Hanlon(7) 11 37
(K R Burke) *prom: pushed along and lost pl over 2f out: wknd* **50/1**
11 15 **Amazing Amaya** 2-8-11 0 LewisEdmunds(3) 10
(Derek Shaw) *led: drvn and hdd over 2f out: wknd qckly* **100/1**

1m 18.2s (4.40) **Going Correction** +0.525s/f (Yiel) 11 Ran SP% **115.1**
Speed ratings (Par 92): **91,90,89,89,87 87,86,85,83,75 55**
CSF £5.16 TOTE £2.90: £1.10, £1.80, £10.50; EX 7.80 Trifecta £152.30.
**Owner** W J and T C O Gredley **Bred** Stiftung Gestut Fahrhof **Trained** Newmarket, Suffolk
■ Polyphony was withdrawn. Price at time of withdrawal 33-1. Rule 4 does \n\x\x not apply
**FOCUS**
A fair novice. The first two have been rated as finding a little on their previous form.

## 6877 32RED H'CAP 6f
3:00 (3:03) (Class 4) (0-85,85) 3-Y-O+ £5,822 (£1,732; £865; £432) Stalls Centre

Form RPR
6346 1 **Hyperfocus (IRE)**[41] 5423 3-9-5 **85** JosephineGordon 4 96+
(Hugo Palmer) *trckd ldrs: hdwy to chal 2f out: shkn up and led over 1f out: drvn clr ins fnl f: comf* **11/2**[3]
4606 2 1 ¾ **Toofi (FR)**[27] 5929 6-9-6 **84** (p) DanielMuscutt 10 89
(John Butler) *prom: pushed along and ev ch 1f out: sn rdn: r.o wl fnl f: tk 2nd pl nr fin* **10/1**
040 3 nse **Somewhere Secret**[27] 5929 3-8-4 **73** (p[1]) PhilDennis(3) 11 78
(Michael Mullineaux) *cl up: led over 2f out: hdd over 1f out: kpt on fnl f: lost 2nd pl nr fin* **50/1**
2064 4 nse **Englishman**[18] 6275 7-9-4 **82** RichardKingscote 7 87+
(Milton Bradley) *hld up: pushed along and hdwy over 1f out: r.o strly fnl f: nvr nrr* **11/2**[3]
0041 5 nk **Russian Realm**[27] 5929 7-9-5 **83** GrahamLee 8 87
(Paul Midgley) *wnt to s early: hld up: pushed along over 1f out: rdn and r.o fnl f* **9/2**[1]
2101 6 ½ **Manshood (IRE)**[15] 6348 4-9-7 **85** (b) MartinLane 6 87
(Paul Midgley) *trckd ldrs: pushed along 2f out: rdn and hdwy 1f out: one pce fnl f* **5/1**[2]
1316 7 1 ¼ **Sitar**[24] 6040 3-8-6 **72** (h) TomMarquand 2 70
(James Fanshawe) *hld up: drvn over 1f out: hdwy ent fnl f: sn rdn and one pce* **20/1**
3100 8 hd **Meshardal (GER)**[13] 6429 7-8-10 **77** (p) LewisEdmunds(3) 5 74
(Ruth Carr) *mid-div: pushed along 2f out: drvn over 1f out: sn rdn: no imp* **18/1**
2216 9 5 **Cosmic Chatter**[21] 6141 7-8-10 **79** (p) CallumRodriguez(5) 9 60
(Ruth Carr) *hld up: effrt into mid-div 1/2-way: pushed along 2f out: sn rdn and no ex* **11/2**[3]
4050 10 2 **Laughton**[42] 5379 4-9-0 **78** (t[1]) HarryBentley 3 53
(Kevin Ryan) *mid-div: pushed along and hdwy on outer over 1f out: rdn and wknd fnl f* **9/1**
-300 11 4 ½ **Van Gerwen**[111] 2821 4-8-13 **77** PJMcDonald 1 38
(Les Eyre) *led: niggled over 2f out: sn rdn and hdd: wknd* **50/1**

1m 16.12s (2.32) **Going Correction** +0.525s/f (Yiel)
**WFA** 3 from 4yo+ 2lb 11 Ran SP% **114.0**
Speed ratings (Par 105): **105,102,102,102,102 101,99,99,92,90 84**
CSF £56.41 CT £2480.33 TOTE £6.70: £2.60, £2.90, £9.20; EX 67.20 Trifecta £3997.00.
**Owner** MPH Racing - II **Bred** Stephanie Von Schilcher & Gavan Kinch **Trained** Newmarket, Suffolk
**FOCUS**
A useful handicap won readily by a promising 3yo sprinter. The runner-up has been rated close to this year's C&D form.

## 6878 32RED.COM H'CAP 5f
3:35 (3:36) (Class 4) (0-85,85) 3-Y-O+ £5,822 (£1,732; £865; £432) Stalls Centre

Form RPR
3220 1 **Major Pusey**[18] 6275 5-9-5 **83** (t[1]) FergusSweeney 8 91
(John Gallagher) *a.p: disp ld 2f out: pushed along to ld on own wl over 1f out: drvn and asserted ent fnl f: readily* **7/2**[1]
0142 2 1 ¼ **Magical Dreamer (IRE)**[31] 5758 3-9-2 **81** DanielMuscutt 6 85
(James Fanshawe) *prom: disp ld 2f out: pushed along and relegated to 2nd wl over 1f out: rdn and kpt on fnl f* **9/2**[2]
0300 3 1 **Rasheeq (IRE)**[20] 6205 4-9-4 **85** RachelRichardson(3) 2 85
(Tim Easterby) *mid-div: trckd ldrs 2f out: pushed along over 1f out: rdn and r.o wl to take 3rd ins fnl f* **5/1**[3]
51 4 ¾ **Memories Galore (IRE)**[18] 6267 5-9-6 **84** (p) TonyHamilton 4 81
(Roger Fell) *trckd ldrs: pushed along and hdwy over 1f out: sn ev ch: rdn and one pce fnl f* **8/1**
030 5 nk **Elysian Flyer (IRE)**[18] 6267 5-9-1 **79** GrahamLee 7 75
(Paul Midgley) *led: hdd 2f out: rdn and weakend over 1f out* **5/1**[3]
2150 6 ¾ **Peachey Carnehan**[6] 6679 3-8-4 **72** (p[1]) PhilDennis(3) 12 65
(Michael Mullineaux) *in rr: hdwy 1/2-way: pushed along 2f out: rdn over 1f out: no imp* **20/1**
4650 7 hd **Invincible Ridge (IRE)**[13] 6411 9-8-11 **75** NeilFarley 3 68
(Eric Alston) *chsd ldrs: drvn and wknd over 2f out* **18/1**
51-0 8 2 ½ **Four Dragons**[13] 6411 3-8-8 **73** RichardKingscote 11 57
(Tom Dascombe) *prom: pushed along 2f out: rdn and wknd over 1f out* **15/2**
5625 9 2 ¼ **Top Boy**[42] 5354 7-9-4 **82** (v) MartinLane 1 58
(Derek Shaw) *a in rr: rdn over 2f out: no rspnse* **16/1**

1m 2.64s (1.84) **Going Correction** +0.525s/f (Yiel)
**WFA** 3 from 4yo+ 1lb 9 Ran SP% **112.5**
Speed ratings (Par 105): **106,104,102,101,100 99,99,95,91**
CSF £18.45 CT £76.92 TOTE £4.00: £1.40, £1.70, £2.10; EX 20.70 Trifecta £94.20.
**Owner** C R Marks (banbury) **Bred** C R Marks (Banbury) **Trained** Chastleton, Oxon

**FOCUS**
A useful sprint with the right horses coming to the fore. The winner has been rated back to his best, with the runner-up to form.

## 6879 32RED ON THE APP STORE H'CAP 6f 212y
4:10 (4:10) (Class 3) (0-90,92) 3-Y-0+
£8,715 (£2,609; £1,304; £652; £326; £163) Stalls Low

Form RPR
6000 1 **Muntadab (IRE)**[7] 6662 5-9-12 92 TonyHamilton 2 100
(Roger Fell) *mde virtually all: pushed along and briefly hdd 2f out: sn regained ld: plld 1 l clr over 1f out: rdn and r.o wl fnl f* 7/1
1000 2 1 ½ **Explain**[13] 6414 5-9-3 86 (b) LewisEdmunds(3) 1 90
(Ruth Carr) *mid-div: trckd ldrs 3f out: pushed along 2f out: rdn and hdwy over 1f out: r.o u.p to take 2nd ent fnl f: kpt on* 12/1
3524 3 ½ **Calder Prince (IRE)**[13] 6414 4-9-10 90 RichardKingscote 6 93
(Tom Dascombe) *chsd ldr: led briefly 2f out: sn hdd and pushed along: rdn over 1f out: no ex ins fnl f* 9/4[1]
3526 4 ½ **Noble Peace**[20] 6192 4-9-6 86 HarryBentley 7 87
(Henry Candy) *hld up: pushed along and hdwy over 2f out: rdn over 1f out: kpt on fnl f* 3/1[2]
13-0 5 2 ¾ **My Amigo**[159] 1515 4-9-5 85 PJMcDonald 8 79
(K R Burke) *in rr: swtchd to stands' side and drvn over 2f out: rdn and hdwy over 1f out: no ex fnl f* 14/1
0615 6 3 ¼ **Theodorico (IRE)**[20] 6192 4-9-10 90 BenCurtis 4 76
(David Loughnane) *t.k.h: trckd ldrs: pushed along in 3rd 3f out: rdn over 2f out: wknd over 1f out* 15/2
1240 7 2 ½ **Navarone (IRE)**[33] 5683 3-8-8 78 (h[1]) StevieDonohoe 5 55
(Richard Fahey) *hld up: hdwy over 2f out: rdn and weakend over 1f out* 20/1
0406 8 3 ½ **Twin Appeal (IRE)**[13] 6414 6-9-2 87 (b) JaneElliott(5) 3 57
(David Barron) *trckd ldrs: rdn and lost pl 2f out: wknd* 6/1[3]

1m 31.43s (0.73) **Going Correction** +0.325s/f (Good)
**WFA** 3 from 4yo+ 4lb 8 Ran SP% 113.4
Speed ratings (Par 107): **108,106,105,105,102 98,95,91**
CSF £83.62 CT £248.39 TOTE £7.00: £1.90, £4.50, £1.30; EX 120.20 Trifecta £666.40.
**Owner** Fell & High Hopes Partnership **Bred** Mrs James Wigan **Trained** Nawton, N Yorks

**FOCUS**
Distance increased by 11yds. A pretty ordinary handicap for the grade. The level is a bit fluid.

## 6880 £10 FREE AT 32RED.COM H'CAP 1m 6f
4:45 (4:45) (Class 4) (0-80,82) 3-Y-0+
£5,822 (£1,732; £865; £432) Stalls Centre

Form RPR
5200 1 **Nordic Combined (IRE)**[21] 6126 3-8-6 68 JosephineGordon 9 75
(Brian Ellison) *hld up: pushed along and hdwy 3f out: reminder 2f out: rdn to cl on ldr over 1f out: led ent fnl f: styd on wl* 20/1
-221 2 ½ **Astute Boy (IRE)**[17] 6293 3-8-12 74 MartinLane 7 80
(Ed Vaughan) *mid-div: hdwy 3f out: rdn over 2f out: led over 1f out: hdd ent fnl f: kpt on gamely* 4/1[2]
30-4 3 1 ¼ **Always Resolute**[16] 6317 6-9-9 76 ConnorKing 11 81
(Brian Ellison) *hld up: hdwy on outer 3f out: sn drvn: clsd on ldrs over 1f out: styd on u.p to take 3rd ent fnl f* 14/1
3435 4 4 ½ **Monaco Rose**[25] 6013 4-8-12 72 (h) SebastianWoods(7) 6 70
(Richard Fahey) *hld up: plenty to do 3f out: rdn over 2f out: styd on to pass btn horses fnl 2 fs* 14/1
0201 5 ¾ **Incus**[14] 6370 4-8-7 65 oh1 JaneElliott(5) 3 62
(Ed de Giles) *prom: led over 2f out: rdn and hdd over 1f out: no ex ent fnl f* 16/1
21 6 1 **Fulham (IRE)**[195] 925 3-9-1 77 TomMarquand 12 73
(Robyn Brisland) *hld up: effrt 3f out: rdn over 2f out: sme late hdwy* 14/1
5231 7 ½ **High On Light**[28] 5873 4-9-7 77 RachelRichardson(3) 1 72
(David Barron) *led: narrow ld 3f out: pushed along and hdd over 2f out: sn drvn and no ex* 7/1[3]
-231 8 1 **Hawridge Flyer**[24] 6031 3-9-3 79 PatCosgrave 8 73
(Stuart Kittow) *hld up: pushed along 4f out: rdn and hdwy over 3f out: ev ch over 2f out: no ex fnl 2 fs* 3/1[1]
0005 9 3 **Intense Tango**[14] 6391 6-9-12 82 (t) CliffordLee(3) 4 72
(K R Burke) *pushed along vigorously to secure pl in mid-div: drvn 1/2-way and 4f out: sn rdn: hdwy and ch over 2f out: wknd over 1f out* 16/1
012 10 ¾ **Takbeer (IRE)**[28] 5873 5-9-7 74 (p) RichardKingscote 5 62
(Nikki Evans) *trckd ldrs: cl up whn reminder 3f out: rdn and wknd over 2f out* 10/1
4224 11 26 **Normandie Attack (FR)**[30] 5799 3-9-1 77 (v) StevieDonohoe 10 31
(Charlie Fellowes) *mid-div: rdn and wknd 3f out* 8/1
005 12 9 **Foresee (GER)**[48] 5166 4-9-0 67 GrahamLee 2 6
(Tony Carroll) *in rr: lost tch and rdr looking down 3f out: eased* 50/1

3m 14.8s **Going Correction** +0.575s/f (Yiel)
**WFA** 3 from 4yo+ 9lb 12 Ran SP% 116.2
Speed ratings (Par 105): **86,85,85,82,82 81,81,80,78,78 63,58**
CSF £96.54 CT £1182.59 TOTE £23.00: £5.70, £1.90, £3.70; EX 125.80 Trifecta £1699.50 Part won..
**Owner** Dan Gilbert **Bred** Dan Gilbert **Trained** Norton, N Yorks

**FOCUS**
Distance increased by 17yds. Something of a slow-motion finish to this modest handicap. The 3yos predictably came to the fore. A pb from the winner.

## 6881 32RED CASINO H'CAP 1m 2f 42y
5:20 (5:20) (Class 3) (0-95,95) 3-Y-0+
£8,715 (£2,609; £1,304; £652; £326; £163) Stalls Centre

Form RPR
4000 1 **Awake My Soul (IRE)**[13] 6449 8-9-0 85 PJMcDonald 4 93
(Tom Tate) *led: 1 l clr 4f out: hdd by runner-up 2f out: rdn and rallied over 1f out: regained ld u.p ins fnl f: r.o resolutely* 8/1
6403 2 ½ **Star Of Rory (IRE)**[29] 5841 3-8-10 87 (v[1]) RichardKingscote 3 94
(Tom Dascombe) *a cl up: led 2f out: sn drvn: rdn over 1f out: hdd by rallying wnr ins fnl f: kpt on but hld nr fin* 5/1[3]
0512 3 2 **Michael's Mount**[18] 6273 4-8-10 81 (b) GrahamLee 7 84
(Ed Dunlop) *hld up: hdwy on outer 3f out: clsd on ldrs 2f out: rdn over 1f out: kpt on to take 3rd pl ins fnl f* 14/1
0134 4 1 **Zwayyan**[34] 5634 4-9-6 91 PatCosgrave 5 92
(William Haggas) *hld up: hdwy 3f out: trcking ldrs 2f out: sn drvn into 3rd pl: rdn 1f out: no ex and lost 3rd pl ins fnl f* 10/3[2]
4314 5 4 **In First Place**[20] 6176 3-8-1 81 SammyJoBell(3) 2 75
(Richard Fahey) *mid-div: hdwy into 3rd pl 4f out: cl up and drvn 2f out: rdn and wknd over 1f out* 14/1
4123 6 16 **Al Destoor**[34] 5634 7-9-6 91 (t) DavidNolan 9 52
(Jennie Candlish) *trckd ldrs: pushed along and lost pl 3f out: no ex fnl 2 fs* 10/1
121 7 6 **Don't Give Up**[25] 6007 3-9-4 95 MartinLane 1 45
(Saeed bin Suroor) *in rr: drvn briefly 5f out: pushed along 4f out: drvn and sme hdwy 3f out: reminders over 2f out: no ex: eased* 2/1[1]
4464 8 2 ¼ **Energia Fox (BRZ)**[33] 5686 7-8-10 81 TonyHamilton 6 26
(Richard Fahey) *a in rr: lost tch fr over 2f out* 50/1
04 9 2 ½ **Storm Rock**[30] 5781 5-8-11 82 HarryBentley 8 22
(Harry Dunlop) *mid-div: hdwy into 4th pl 3f out: drvn over 2f out: sn rdn and wknd* 16/1
635- 10 hd **Dwight D**[407] 4797 4-8-9 83 CliffordLee(3) 10 22
(Stuart Coltherd) *mid-div: pushed along and lost pl 4f out: drvn 3f out: fdd* 50/1

2m 16.4s (3.70) **Going Correction** +0.575s/f (Yiel)
**WFA** 3 from 4yo+ 6lb 10 Ran SP% 116.4
Speed ratings (Par 107): **108,107,106,105,102 89,84,82,80,80**
CSF £47.69 CT £552.64 TOTE £9.30: £2.80, £2.60, £3.60; EX 61.30 Trifecta £1016.40.
**Owner** T T Racing **Bred** Grundy Bloodstock Srl **Trained** Tadcaster, N Yorks

**FOCUS**
Distance increased by 33yds. Little got into this, the first two duelling from a fair way out. The winner has been rated to this year's form.
T/Plt: £339.60 to a £1 stake. Pool: £79,023.37 - 169.86 winning units. T/Qpdt: £59.20 to a £1 stake. Pool: £6,696.07 - 83.60 winning units. **Keith McHugh**

# 6813 KEMPTON (A.W) (R-H)
Friday, September 8

**OFFICIAL GOING: Polytrack: standard to slow (watered)**
Wind: light, across Weather: dry

## 6882 32RED.COM APPRENTICE H'CAP 1m (P)
5:50 (5:51) (Class 4) (0-85,85) 3-Y-0+
£5,175 (£1,540; £769; £384) Stalls Low

Form RPR
2210 1 **Jalela**[24] 6026 3-8-13 84 RossaRyan(7) 4 91
(Richard Hannon) *led for 1f: trckd ldr tl effrt to press ldr over 1f out: kpt on but looked hld tl styd on u.p fnl 75yds: led cl home* 14/1
200 2 nk **Archer's Arrow (USA)**[41] 5416 3-9-0 78 CallumShepherd 11 84
(Saeed bin Suroor) *styd wd early: chsd ldr over 6f out: rdn to ld over 1f out: kpt on u.p and looked to be holding wnr tl worn down and hdd cl home* 14/1
2315 3 hd **Cool Team (IRE)**[29] 5849 3-8-8 79 (tp) NicolaCurrie(7) 3 85+
(Hugo Palmer) *hld up in tch towards rr: rdn and hdwy over 1f out: chsd ldrs and swtchd rt ins fnl f: styd on wl and gng on strly at fin: nt quite rch ldrs* 5/1[3]
4-00 4 1 ¾ **Run To The Hills (USA)**[16] 6322 4-9-10 83 HectorCrouch 1 86
(George Peckham) *trckd ldrs tl shuffled bk to midfield 1/2-way: swtchd rt and effrt to chse ldrs wl over 1f out: no ex 1f out and keeping on same pce whn squeezed for room ins fnl f* 10/1
5305 5 nse **Ernststavroblofeld (USA)**[17] 6289 3-9-5 83 KieranShoemark 5 85
(Martyn Meade) *t.k.h: hld up wl in tch in midfield: effrt u.p over 1f out: hdwy ins fnl f: styd on u.p fnl 100yds: nvr getting on terms w ldrs* 11/4[1]
0053 6 hd **Zamjar**[17] 6282 3-8-13 77 LouisSteward 2 79+
(Ed Dunlop) *stdd after s: hld up in tch towards rr: rdn and hdwy over 1f out: chsd ldrs but keeping on same pce whn short of room and hmpd 100yds out: no imp after* 12/1
350 7 1 ¼ **Dream Of Summer (IRE)**[78] 4001 4-9-6 79 AaronJones 10 79
(Jeremy Noseda) *led after 1f: clr over 3f out: rdn and hdd over 1f out: unable qck u.p and wknd ins fnl f* 11/1
4554 8 hd **Mister Music**[14] 6378 8-8-11 73 GeorgiaCox(3) 6 72
(Tony Carroll) *hld up in tch towards rr: effrt ent fnl 2f: hdwy 1f out: swtchd rt and styd on ins fnl f: nvr trbld ldrs* 10/1
0341 9 2 ½ **Wannabe Friends**[14] 6378 4-9-2 80 FinleyMarsh(5) 7 73
(Richard Hughes) *v.s.a: grad rcvrd and tagged onto bk of field after 2f: effrt ent fnl 2f: kpt on ins fnl f: nvr threatened ldrs* 9/2[2]
6006 10 16 **Morning Suit (USA)**[19] 6235 3-9-2 83 RichardOliver(3) 8 39
(Mark Johnston) *in tch in midfield on outer: rdn over 2f out: sn dropped away and wl btn: wl bhd fnl f* 20/1

1m 39.21s (-0.59) **Going Correction** 0.0s/f (Stan)
**WFA** 3 from 4yo+ 5lb 10 Ran SP% 113.8
Speed ratings (Par 105): **102,101,101,99,99 99,98,98,95,79**
CSF £188.91 CT £1147.67 TOTE £10.20: £2.90, £4.30, £1.80; EX 89.00 Trifecta £528.80.
**Owner** Al Shaqab Racing **Bred** The Pocock Family **Trained** East Everleigh, Wilts

**FOCUS**
One of the stronger apprentice handicaps, though it lacked horses with recent winning form.

## 6883 32RED ON THE APP STORE/BRITISH STALLION STUDS EBF NOVICE STKS (PLUS 10 RACE) 1m (P)
6:20 (6:22) (Class 4) 2-Y-O
£4,269 (£1,270; £634; £317) Stalls Low

Form RPR
1 1 **Roaring Lion (USA)**[21] 6142 2-9-8 0 OisinMurphy 4 92+
(John Gosden) *pressed ldr tl led jst over 2f out: rdn and asserted over 1f out: rn green and hung lft but r.o strly ins fnl f: v readily* 4/5[1]
0 2 6 **Compliance (IRE)**[22] 6108 2-9-2 0 MartinHarley 5 71
(James Tate) *chsd ldrs: effrt wl over 1f out: wnt 2nd jst ins fnl f but wnr gng clr: kpt on same pce u.p after* 25/1
3 hd **Dragon Mountain** 2-9-2 0 TedDurcan 6 71
(Hugo Palmer) *hld up in tch towards rr: clsd and swtchd rt wl over 1f out: rdn and hdwy on inner over 1f out: styd on and pressing for 2nd towards fin: no ch w wnr* 16/1
04 4 ¾ **Verstappen (IRE)**[26] 5960 2-9-2 0 AndreaAtzeni 1 69
(Marco Botti) *t.k.h: chsd ldrs: rdn 2f out: unable qck over 1f out: no ch w wnr and kpt on same pce ins fnl f* 14/1
3 5 shd **La La Land (IRE)**[37] 5547 2-9-2 0 JamieSpencer 7 68
(Jamie Osborne) *in tch in midfield: effrt 2f out: outpcd and edgd rt over 1f out: rallied and styd on ins fnl f: no ch w wnr* 11/2[3]
3 6 hd **Eyecatcher (IRE)**[21] 6159 2-9-2 0 TimmyMurphy 8 68
(Simon Crisford) *sn stdd to last pair: pushed along 2f out: hdwy ent fnl f: styd on wl ins fnl f: nvr trbld ldrs* 20/1
0 7 1 **Dream Mount (IRE)**[34] 5631 2-9-2 0 TomQueally 2 66
(Marco Botti) *led tl jst over 2f out: rdn and unable qck w wnr over 1f out: lost 2nd jst ins fnl f: wknd fnl 100yds* 40/1
20 8 nse **Camomile Lawn (IRE)**[55] 4909 2-8-11 0 PatDobbs 10 60
(Ralph Beckett) *dwlt: steadily rcvrd and in midfield after 2f: rdn ent fnl 2f: sn outpcd: no ch w wnr and kpt on same pce ins fnl f* 14/1

9 3/4 **Tabernas (IRE)** 2-9-2 0 JamesDoyle 3 64+
(Charlie Appleby) *dwlt: sn rcvrd and in tch in midfield: rdn 3f out: outpcd whn sltly impeded over 1f out: no ch w wnr and kpt on same pce after* **5/1**[2]

10 1/2 **Feragust** 2-8-13 0 MarcMonaghan(3) 9 62
(Marco Botti) *in tch towards rr: rdn jst over 2f out: sn outpcd and wl hld over 1f out* **66/1**

11 2 1/4 **Vision Clear (GER)** 2-9-2 0 KieranShoemark 11 57
(Ed Dunlop) *dwlt and rn green in tch in rr: rdn over 2f out: sn struggling and wl btn over 1f out* **66/1**

1m 40.38s (0.58) **Going Correction** 0.0s/f (Stan) 11 Ran SP% **120.9**
Speed ratings (Par 97): **97,91,90,90,89 89,88,88,87,87 85**
CSF £34.38 TOTE £1.50: £1.10, £5.50, £3.90; EX 22.60 Trifecta £187.90.

**Owner** Qatar Racing Limited **Bred** Ranjan Racing Inc **Trained** Newmarket, Suffolk

**FOCUS**
This novice affair revolved around the favourite, who was the only previous winner in the race.

## 6884 32RED CASINO/BRITISH STALLION STUDS EBF NOVICE STKS (PLUS 10 RACE) (DIV I) 7f (P)
**6:50** (6:54) (Class 4) 2-Y-O **£4,269** (£1,270; £634; £317) **Stalls** Low

Form RPR

1 **Morlock (IRE)** 2-9-2 0 JamesDoyle 3 82+
(Charlie Appleby) *led for over 1f: styd chsng ldrs: effrt on inner to chal and rdn over 1f out: led ins fnl f: styd on: rdn out* **11/8**[1]

2 1/2 **Barton Mills** 2-9-2 0 MartinHarley 4 81+
(William Haggas) *t.k.h early: chsd ldrs: effrt 2f out: rdn to qckn to ld over 1f out: hdd ins fnl f: kpt on but a hld* **8/1**

0 3 2 1/2 **Exprompt (FR)**[42] 5365 2-9-2 0 FranBerry 11 74
(Hugo Palmer) *dwlt: styd wd and grad rcvrd to ld over 5f out: rdn 2f out: hdd over 1f out: outpcd by ldng pair but hld on to 3rd ins fnl f* **12/1**

4 1/2 **Reshaan (IRE)** 2-9-2 0 SeanLevey 9 73+
(Richard Hannon) *hld up in tch in midfield: effrt 2f out: 4th over 1f out: kpt on ins fnl f: nvr enough pce to threaten ldng pair* **14/1**

5 3/4 **Fennaan (IRE)** 2-9-2 0 (t[1]) RobertTart 6 71+
(John Gosden) *rn green in last trio: pushed along over 2f out: clsd and swtchd rt ent fnl f: hdwy ins fnl f: styd on wl towards fin: nvr trbld ldrs* **8/1**

23 6 hd **Warsaan**[35] 5608 2-9-2 0 JimCrowley 10 70+
(Owen Burrows) *t.k.h early: hld up in tch in last trio: effrt 2f out: hdwy ent fnl f: styd on wl fnl 100yds: nvr trbld ldrs* **4/1**[2]

7 hd **Compulsive (IRE)** 2-9-2 0 AndreaAtzeni 2 70
(Roger Varian) *in tch in midfield: effrt 2f out: unable qck and styd on same pce ins fnl f* **6/1**[3]

8 1 1/4 **Roman Warrior** 2-9-2 0 SilvestreDeSousa 8 66
(Harry Dunlop) *hld up in tch in rr: effrt and drifting rt over 1f out: kpt on same pce ins fnl f: nvr trbld ldrs* **50/1**

0 9 1 1/2 **Sa'ada (USA)**[22] 6108 2-8-8 0 HectorCrouch(3) 5 57
(George Peckham) *chsd ldrs: wnt 2nd 5f out tl rdn and unable qck ent fnl 2f: lost pl over 1f out: wknd ins fnl f* **150/1**

0 10 3 **Mandarin Princess**[21] 6140 2-8-11 0 DavidProbert 1 49
(Philip McBride) *in tch in midfield: rdn ent fnl 2f: sn outpcd and bhd 1f out: wknd ins fnl f* **33/1**

1m 27.95s (1.95) **Going Correction** 0.0s/f (Stan) 10 Ran SP% **118.5**
Speed ratings (Par 97): **88,87,84,84,83 82,82,81,79,76**
CSF £13.69 TOTE £2.40: £1.20, £2.00, £2.70; EX 13.80 Trifecta £98.70.

**Owner** Godolphin **Bred** Albert Conneally **Trained** Newmarket, Suffolk

**FOCUS**
An informative maiden and a lot to like about the performances of the first two home. The opening level is fluid.

## 6885 32RED CASINO/BRITISH STALLION STUDS EBF NOVICE STKS (PLUS 10 RACE) (DIV II) 7f (P)
**7:20** (7:26) (Class 4) 2-Y-O **£4,269** (£1,270; £634; £317) **Stalls** Low

Form RPR

2 1 **Symbolization (IRE)**[28] 5887 2-9-2 0 JamesDoyle 3 91+
(Charlie Appleby) *trckd ldrs: effrt and qcknd to ld over 1f out: r.o strly ins fnl f: readily* **4/9**[1]

2 1 1/2 **Glendevon (USA)** 2-9-2 0 JamieSpencer 9 87+
(Richard Hughes) *rn green: stdd s: t.k.h: hld up in tch towards rr: hdwy to chse ldrs wl over 1f out: wnt 2nd and swtchd lft ins fnl f: r.o wl for clr 2nd but nvr threatening wnr* **10/1**

2 3 4 **Tanseeq**[22] 6108 2-9-2 0 JimCrowley 7 74
(William Haggas) *led: rdn ent fnl 2f: hdd and unable qck over 1f out: lost 2nd and outpcd ins fnl f* **11/2**[2]

4 1 1/2 **Bobby Biscuit (USA)** 2-9-2 0 JFEgan 4 70
(Simon Dow) *in tch in midfield: effrt 2f out: kpt on ins fnl f: no threat to ldrs* **20/1**

5 5 1 1/2 **Connaught Ranger (IRE)**[32] 5710 2-9-2 0 TomQueally 6 66
(Denis Coakley) *t.k.h: hld up towards rr: effrt over 2f out: styd on ins fnl f: nvr trbld ldrs* **50/1**

0 6 1/2 **Apex Predator (IRE)**[21] 6133 2-9-2 0 DavidProbert 11 65
(Seamus Durack) *chsd ldr over 5f out tl unable qck and lost pl over 1f out: wknd ins fnl f* **66/1**

7 1 1/2 **Blue Whisper** 2-9-2 0 RyanTate 1 61
(James Eustace) *dwlt: in tch in midfield: rdn ent fnl 2f: sn outpcd and wknd over 1f out* **50/1**

2 8 1/2 **Bowler Hat**[21] 6147 2-9-2 0 FranBerry 10 59
(Hugo Palmer) *trckd ldrs: rdn ent fnl 2f: outpcd whn sltly impeded over 1f out: wknd fnl f* **6/1**[3]

9 6 **William Of Wykeham (IRE)** 2-9-2 0 TedDurcan 5 43
(Sir Michael Stoute) *s.i.s: rn green and a rr* **16/1**

10 17 **Dorian Gray (IRE)** 2-9-2 0 OisinMurphy 8
(Hughie Morrison) *rn v green: a bhd: lost tch over 2f out: t.o* **33/1**

1m 26.26s (0.26) **Going Correction** 0.0s/f (Stan) 10 Ran SP% **127.0**
Speed ratings (Par 97): **98,96,91,90,88 87,86,85,78,59**
CSF £7.08 TOTE £1.30: £1.02, £2.60, £1.60; EX 8.50 Trifecta £30.10.

**Owner** Godolphin **Bred** Godolphin **Trained** Newmarket, Suffolk

**FOCUS**
This maiden lacked depth and was all about the odds-on favourite. The winner has been rated up a little bit on his debut effort.

## 6886 LONGINES IRISH CHAMPIONS WEEKEND EBF FILLIES' CONDITIONS STKS (PLUS 10 RACE) 7f (P)
**7:50** (7:50) (Class 3) 2-Y-O **£9,337** (£2,796; £1,398; £699; £349) **Stalls** Low

Form RPR

15 1 **Poetic Charm**[27] 5941 2-9-2 0 JamesDoyle 3 88+
(Charlie Appleby) *trckd ldrs: effrt and qcknd to ld over 1f out: styd on wl and a doing enough ins fnl f: rdn out* **2/7**[1]

410 2 1 **Jousi**[27] 5941 2-9-2 84 AndreaAtzeni 5 85
(Hugo Palmer) *stdd s: t.k.h: hld up in tch in rr: effrt wl over 1f out: swtchd lft 1f out: chsd ldng pair ins fnl f: styd on to go 2nd last strides: nvr getting on terms w wnr* **9/2**[2]

6 3 hd **Club Tropicana**[12] 6480 2-8-12 0 DaneO'Neill 4 80
(Richard Spencer) *pressed ldr: rdn and ev ch wl over 1f out: chsd wnr ent fnl f: styd on same pce: lost 2nd last strides* **12/1**[3]

30 4 5 **Moggy (USA)**[71] 4253 2-8-12 0 PatDobbs 2 67
(Richard Hughes) *led and set stdy gallop: rdn ent fnl 2f: hdd over 1f out: outpcd and btn 1f out: wknd ins fnl f* **50/1**

10 5 hd **Santorini Sun (IRE)**[13] 6418 2-9-2 0 SilvestreDeSousa 1 70
(Mick Channon) *trckd ldrs: swtchd rt and effrt to chal wl over 1f out: outpcd and edgd rt 1f out: wknd ins fnl f* **14/1**

1m 27.85s (1.85) **Going Correction** 0.0s/f (Stan) 5 Ran SP% **112.3**
Speed ratings (Par 96): **89,87,87,81,81**
CSF £2.10 TOTE £1.10: £1.02, £1.80; EX 2.20 Trifecta £5.90.

**Owner** Godolphin **Bred** Godolphin **Trained** Newmarket, Suffolk

**FOCUS**
An uncompetitive event and a straightforward win for the long odds-on favourite. The winner didn't need to match her latest effort, but the third took a nice step forward.

## 6887 32RED H'CAP (LONDON MIDDLE DISTANCE SERIES QUALIFIER) 2f 219y(P)
**8:20** (8:25) (Class 3) (0-95,96) 3-Y-O+
**£7,470** (£2,236; £1,118; £559; £279; £140) **Stalls** Low

Form RPR

0034 1 **Western Duke (IRE)**[39] 5475 3-8-11 87 OisinMurphy 3 95
(Ralph Beckett) *chsd ldrs: effrt to chal over 1f out: led ins fnl f: styd on wl rdn out* **25/1**

5131 2 1/2 **Arab Moon**[30] 5798 3-9-0 90 SilvestreDeSousa 8 97+
(William Knight) *stdd s: hld up towards rr: hdwy into midfield 1/2-way: shifting lft and hdwy u.p over 1f out: styd on strly to chse wnr wl ins fnl f: clsng towards fin* **7/2**[2]

010 3 1/2 **Bush House (IRE)**[13] 6445 3-8-10 86 (b) JimCrowley 5 92
(Hugo Palmer) *chsd ldrs: effrt 2f out: kpt on wl u.p ins fnl f* **11/2**[3]

11 4 hd **Mountain Hunter (USA)**[13] 6422 3-9-6 96 WilliamCarson 4 102
(Saeed bin Suroor) *trckd ldrs and travelled strly: rdn and qcknd to ld but hrd pressed over 1f out: hdd ins fnl f: styd on same pce after: lost 2 pls towards fin* **6/4**[1]

6500 5 1/2 **Al Hamdany (IRE)**[34] 5634 3-8-13 89 DaneO'Neill 9 94
(Marco Botti) *t.k.h: early: hld up in tch in midfield: effrt 2f out: hdwy 1f out: kpt on wl ins fnl f: nvr quite getting on terms w ldrs* **33/1**

6 6 1 **Breden (IRE)**[25] 6007 7-9-3 86 (h) RobertTart 6 88
(Linda Jewell) *s.i.s: hld up in tch towards rr: rdn 2f out: hdwy u.p over 1f out: kpt on wl ins fnl f: nvr trbld ldrs* **50/1**

5564 7 nk **Banish (USA)**[30] 5798 4-9-0 83 (vt) JamesDoyle 1 85
(Hugo Palmer) *hld up in tch in midfield: swtchd rt and hdwy ent fnl 2f: chsd ldrs u.p 1f out: kpt on same pce and no imp ins fnl f* **14/1**

1216 8 1/2 **Kasperenko**[27] 5915 3-9-5 95 (b) TomQueally 12 97+
(David Lanigan) *s.i.s: bhd: rdn and swtchd lft jst over 1f out: styd on ins fnl f: nvr trbld ldrs* **11/1**

4560 9 1/2 **Sam Missile (IRE)**[21] 6151 4-9-9 92 TimmyMurphy 10 92
(James Fanshawe) *t.k.h: hld up in tch in midfield on outer: effrt over 2f out: styd on same pce and no imp u.p fr over 1f out* **14/1**

5/40 10 nk **Castlelyons (IRE)**[41] 5397 5-9-4 87 LiamKeniry 13 87
(Robert Stephens) *stdd s: t.k.h: hld up in last trio: effrt 2f out: rdn over 1f out: hdwy ins fnl f: styd on wl fnl 100yds: nvr trbld ldrs* **20/1**

4250 11 2 1/4 **Beardwood**[13] 6449 5-9-3 86 (p) FranBerry 7 82
(Mark Johnston) *hld up in tch in midfield: rdn and unable qck over 2f out: lost pl over 1f out: wknd ins fnl f* **33/1**

2000 12 3 **Manjaam (IRE)**[27] 5913 4-9-9 92 AndreaAtzeni 11 83
(Ed Dunlop) *hld up towards rr: hdwy into midfield 4f out: rdn and unable qck ent fnl 2f: wknd ins fnl f* **25/1**

6053 13 nk **Azam**[30] 5803 3-8-10 86 AlistairRawlinson 2 77
(Michael Appleby) *led: rdn and hdd over 1f out: sn outpcd and btn: wknd ins fnl f* **25/1**

2m 18.48s (-3.42) **Going Correction** 0.0s/f (Stan)
**WFA** 3 from 4yo+ 7lb 13 Ran SP% **123.4**
Speed ratings (Par 107): **112,111,111,111,110 110,109,109,109,108 107,105,104**
CSF £108.09 CT £579.79 TOTE £31.00: £5.90, £1.50, £2.00; EX 170.40 Trifecta £2183.90.

**Owner** London City Bloodstock **Bred** Epona Bloodstock Ltd **Trained** Kimpton, Hants

**FOCUS**
The latest qualifier in this series was much more competitive than the market suggested.

## 6888 KURT & JESSICA HIGGINS WEDDING H'CAP (JOCKEY CLUB GRASSROOTS FLAT SPRINT SERIES QUALIFIER) 6f (P)
**8:50** (8:53) (Class 5) (0-70,72) 3-Y-O+ **£3,234** (£962; £481; £240) **Stalls** Low

Form RPR

132 1 **Robbie Roo Roo**[8] 6638 4-8-13 60 (vt) AdamBeschizza 9 69
(Mrs Ilka Gansera-Leveque) *t.k.h: early: hld up in midfield: effrt 2f out: chsd clr ldng pair u.p jst over 1f out: styd on wl to ld last strides* **5/1**

0044 2 hd **Mishaal (IRE)**[12] 6464 7-9-7 68 KieranShoemark 3 76
(Michael Herrington) *chsd ldr for over 1f: chsd ldrs tl effrt to chse clr ldr 2f out: styd on to ld ins fnl f: hrd pressed wl ins fnl f: hdd last strides* **11/4**[1]

5566 3 4 **Diable D'Or (IRE)**[16] 6310 3-9-8 71 (b[1]) OisinMurphy 1 66
(Eve Johnson Houghton) *wnt lft s: t.k.h: sn led: rdn and clr over 1f out: hdd ins fnl f: sn btn and wknd fnl 100yds* **3/1**[2]

5432 4 3/4 **Showmethewayavrilo**[8] 6615 4-9-3 67 CharlieBennett(3) 6 60
(Malcolm Saunders) *t.k.h: hld up in last trio: swtchd lft over 2f out: hdwy u.p and switching rt over 1f out: no ch w ldng pair but kpt on ins fnl f* **11/2**

6005 5 1 3/4 **Fleeting Glimpse**[21] 6156 4-8-10 57 DavidProbert 2 44
(Patrick Chamings) *taken down early: bmpd s: t.k.h: hld up in tch in midfield: effrt 2f out: drvn to chse ldrs but nt on terms over 1f out: wl hld 1f out: wknd ins fnl f* **40/1**

5050 6 ½ **Fareeq**20 6197 3-9-9 72 ...(t) WilliamCarson 8 58
(Charlie Wallis) *bhd and sn pushed along: styd on ins fnl f: nvr trbld ldrs* 25/1

6634 7 ½ **Otomo**17 6282 3-9-8 71 ...(h) LiamKeniry 7 55
(Philip Hide) *bmpd: short of room and lost pl sn after s: hdwy to join ldr over 4f out tl lost 2nd and no rspnse to press 2f out: wknd over 1f out* 33/1

21 8 4 ½ **Miami Sunset**17 6295 3-9-9 72 ... SilvestreDeSousa 5 42
(Philip McBride) *hld up in tch in last trio: effrt jst over 2f out: no prog and wl btn over 1f out* 7/2³

0300 9 33 **Aragon Knight**168 1339 4-9-0 66 ...(h) PaddyBradley(5) 4
(Daniel Steele) *t.k.h: chsd ldrs tl lost pl qckly and bhd 2f out: lost tch and eased ins fnl f: t.o* 50/1

1m 12.07s (-1.03) **Going Correction** 0.0s/f (Stan)
**WFA** 3 from 4yo+ 2lb 9 Ran SP% **117.1**
Speed ratings (Par 103): **106,105,100,99,97 96,95,89,45**
CSF £18.95 CT £48.91 TOTE £5.30: £1.70, £1.50, £1.40; EX 19.10 Trifecta £76.50.
**Owner** Mrs I Gansera-Leveque **Bred** John James **Trained** Newmarket, Suffolk

**FOCUS**
An ordinary sprint handicap, though it was run at strong pace and played into the hands of the consistent winner, who stays further. A pb from the winner, with the runner-up rated close to this year's turf form.

## 6889 100% PROFIT BOOST AT 32REDSPORT.COM H'CAP 1m 7f 218y(P)
9:20 (9:20) (Class 5) (0-75,77) 4-Y-0+ £3,234 (£962; £481; £240) Stalls Low

Form RPR

06-6 1 **Mere Anarchy (IRE)**51 1002 6-9-1 66 ... DaneO'Neill 10 75
(Robert Stephens) *hld up in midfield: clsd to chse ldrs and travelling wl 3f out: effrt to chal over 1f out: sustained effrt to ld wl ins fnl f: styd on* 33/1

2 ½ **Allee Bleue (IRE)**154 7-9-4 69 ... TomQueally 3 77
(Philip Hobbs) *hld up in midfield: clsd to chse ldrs 3f out: pressing ldr and switching lft 2f out: rdn to ld over 1f out: kpt on u.p tl hdd and one pce wl ins fnl f* 9/2²

0300 3 1 ½ **Age Of Wisdom (IRE)**16 6323 4-9-2 70 ...(p¹) HectorCrouch(3) 4 76
(Gary Moore) *hld up in midfield: swtchd lft over 2f out: swtchd rt and rdn to chal wl over 1f out: no ex and jst outpcd fnl 100yds* 5/1³

0014 4 1 ¾ **Whitecliff Park (IRE)**16 6323 4-9-7 72 ...(p) SilvestreDeSousa 12 76
(Brian Ellison) *hld up towards rr: swtchd lft and effrt 2f out: hdwy u.p on outer over 1f out: chsd clr ldng trio 1f out: styd on but nvr getting on terms* 7/2¹

3205 5 4 ½ **Spiritoftomintoul**35 5590 8-8-13 64 ...(t) GeorgeDowning 11 63
(Tony Carroll) *hld up last trio: clsd 4f out: rdn over 2f out: nvr getting on terms w ldrs: kpt on u.p ins fnl f* 25/1

250- 6 hd **Jack Bear**95 7215 6-9-12 77 ... FranBerry 2 75
(Harry Whittington) *hld up towards rr: effrt on inner and swtchd lft over 2f out: no imp u.p over 1f out: wl hld and kpt on same pce ins fnl f* 12/1

2621 7 shd **Fitzwilly**10 6565 7-9-4 72 6ex ... CallumShepherd(3) 5 70
(Mick Channon) *chsd ldrs: wnt 2nd and clsd 4f out: rdn to ld 3f out: hdd over 1f out: wknd ins fnl f* 14/1

013/ 8 4 **Aviator (GER)**575 7140 9-9-7 72 ... RyanTate 7 65
(James Eustace) *hld up in midfield: rdn 3f out: drvn to chse ldrs over 2f out but sn unable qck: wknd over 1f out* 20/1

5-64 9 24 **Linguine (FR)**18 6259 7-9-5 70 ...(b) OisinMurphy 6 35
(Seamus Durack) *chsd ldr tl led after 2f: rdn and hdd 3f out: sn u.p and btn: eased over 1f out: t.o* 14/1

-103 10 28 **Avenue Des Champs**18 6259 5-8-9 65 ...(p) PaddyBradley(5) 9
(Jane Chapple-Hyam) *chsd ldrs: wnt 2nd 10f out tl 4f out: dropped out and btn over 2f out: eased over 1f out: t.o* 9/1

0-43 11 31 **Spice Fair**36 5566 10-9-5 70 ... LiamKeniry 1
(Mark Usher) *hld up in rr: reminders 7f out: nvr gng wl after: lost tch and eased over 3f out: t.o* 20/1

000- 12 30 **Diamond Joel**38 6565 5-9-5 70 ...(p¹) DougieCostello 8
(David Dennis) *led for 2f: chsd ldr tl 10f out: lost pl 5f out: bhd and eased over 3f out: t.o* 100/1

0311 U **Golly Miss Molly**72 4217 6-9-3 68 ...(b) MartinLane 13
(Martin Bosley) *stmbld bdly and uns rdr leaving stalls* 7/1

3m 24.93s (-5.17) **Going Correction** 0.0s/f (Stan) 13 Ran SP% **117.9**
Speed ratings (Par 103): **112,111,111,110,107 107,107,105,93,79 64,49,**
CSF £166.87 CT £894.78 TOTE £37.40: £8.40, £2.20, £2.10; EX 281.30 Trifecta £3194.90 Part won..
**Owner** R Stephens **Bred** J Hanly & C Neilan **Trained** Penhow, Newport
■ Stewards' Enquiry : Tom Queally two-day ban: used whip above the permitted level (Sep 22-23)

**FOCUS**
A fair staying handicap. There was early drama as the hat-trick seeking Golly Miss Molly unseated her rider leaving the stalls. The winner has been rated as improving on his maiden form.
T/Plt: £26.40 to a £1 stake. Pool: £63,157.10 - 1,745.91 winning units. T/Qpdt: £4.10 to a £1 stake. Pool: £6,791.70 - 1,207.34 winning units. **Steve Payne**

6624

# MUSSELBURGH (R-H)
Friday, September 8

**OFFICIAL GOING: Good to firm (good in places; 6.8)**
Wind: fresh half against Weather: cloudy

## 6890 MITSUBISHI ELECTRIC NOVICE AUCTION STKS 7f 33y
4:30 (4:31) (Class 5) 2-Y-O £3,881 (£1,155; £577; £288) Stalls Low

Form RPR

3204 1 **Arabian Jazz (IRE)**22 6087 2-8-4 67 ... TristanPrice(7) 2 68
(Michael Bell) *chsd ldr: rdn over 2f out: kpt on: led 75yds out* 4/1³

53 2 ¾ **Spray The Sea (IRE)**57 4792 2-9-2 0 ... ConnorBeasley 8 71
(Bryan Smart) *led: racd quite keenly: rdn 2f out: drvn ins fnl f: one pce and hdd fnl 75yds* 11/4¹

202 3 2 ¼ **Oswald (IRE)**29 5847 2-9-2 73 ... PaulMulrennan 1 65
(Robyn Brisland) *dwlt sltly: sn in tch: rdn to chse ldrs 2f out: one pce in 3rd fnl f* 7/1

4 ¾ **How Bizarre** 2-9-2 0 ... TomEaves 4 63+
(Kevin Ryan) *s.i.s: hld up in rr: racd keenly: pushed along and hdwy 2f out: hung rt but kpt on ins fnl f: nrst fin* 11/1

5 1 ¾ **Canadian George (FR)** 2-9-2 0 ... JamesSullivan 6 59+
(Keith Dalgleish) *hld up in tch: pushed along over 2f out: keeping on same pce whn hmpd on rail fnl 50yds* 20/1

6 nse **Pelice (IRE)** 2-8-11 0 ... JoeFanning 5 56+
(Mark Johnston) *chsd ldr: outpcd and lost pl 4f out: keeping on again whn hmpd fnl 50yds* 7/2²

552 7 ¾ **Mi Capricho (IRE)**9 6590 2-8-11 0 ... RowanScott(5) 3 56
(Keith Dalgleish) *in tch: rdn and outpcd over 2f out: no threat after* 6/1

8 ½ **Southpark** 2-9-2 0 ... JackGarritty 7 59+
(Richard Fahey) *dwlt: hld up: pushed along and attempting to make hdwy whn short of room 3f out tl 2f out: short of room again ins fnl f* 16/1

1m 29.32s (0.32) **Going Correction** -0.15s/f (Firm) 8 Ran SP% **114.7**
Speed ratings (Par 95): **92,91,88,87,85 85,84,84**
CSF £15.49 TOTE £3.50: £1.60, £2.00, £2.40; EX 17.60 Trifecta £111.60.
**Owner** Ontoawinner, K Stewart & Partner **Bred** Andrew Lennon **Trained** Newmarket, Suffolk

**FOCUS**
A fair juvenile novice contest. They went a decent gallop on ground officially described as good to firm, good in places.

## 6891 PDM H'CAP 5f 1y
5:05 (5:05) (Class 5) (0-75,77) 3-Y-O+ £3,234 (£962; £481; £240) Stalls High

Form RPR

3202 1 **Landing Night (IRE)**9 6574 5-9-0 71 ...(tp) RowanScott(5) 5 81
(Rebecca Menzies) *dwlt sltly: hld up: rdn along and gd hdwy on outer over 1f out: edgd lft but kpt on wl: led 50yds out* 4/1²

312 2 ¾ **Noah Amor (IRE)**6 6670 4-9-5 71 ... ConnorBeasley 1 78
(David O'Meara) *out sharply to get across fr outside stall and ld on rail: rdn 2f out: kpt on but hdd 50yds out* 3/1¹

5225 3 2 ¾ **Oriental Lilly**34 5636 3-8-4 64 ... SeanMooney(7) 8 61
(Jim Goldie) *dwlt: hld up: pushed along and outpcd in rr 1/2-way: kpt on ins fnl f: wnt 3rd nr fin* 16/1

3012 4 nk **Liberatum**6 6679 3-9-3 70 ... JamesSullivan 2 66
(Ruth Carr) *trckd ldrs: rdn over 1f out: one pce ins fnl f: lost 3rd nr fin* 9/2³

6450 5 nk **Economic Crisis (IRE)**9 6593 8-9-1 67 ... JoeDoyle 4 62
(Colin Teague) *hld up: rdn 2f out: hdwy appr fnl f: one pce ins fnl f* 20/1

0156 6 1 ½ **Just Us Two (IRE)**13 6430 5-9-11 77 ...(p¹) JoeFanning 6 67
(Robert Cowell) *hld up: pushed along 2f out: bit short of room and swtchd rt fnl 50yds: nvr threatened* 7/1

3001 7 ¾ **One Boy (IRE)**15 6351 6-9-5 71 ... PaulMulrennan 7 58
(Paul Midgley) *chsd ldr: rdn to chal over 1f out: wknd ins fnl f* 7/1

204 8 nk **Alsvinder**18 6267 4-9-10 76 ... TomEaves 3 62
(David O'Meara) *dwlt: sn chsd ldrs towards outer: rdn 2f out: hung rt and wknd appr fnl f* 10/1

2104 9 5 **Liquid (IRE)**13 6430 3-9-6 73 ... JackGarritty 9 41
(David Barron) *prom: rdn over 2f out: wknd over 1f out and eased* 12/1

59.94s (-0.46) **Going Correction** +0.05s/f (Good)
**WFA** 3 from 4yo+ 1lb 9 Ran SP% **115.6**
Speed ratings (Par 103): **105,103,99,98,98 96,94,94,86**
CSF £16.45 CT £172.61 TOTE £5.20: £1.70, £1.90, £4.40; EX 25.90 Trifecta £601.70.
**Owner** John Dance **Bred** Mrs Claire Doyle **Trained** Mordon, Durham

**FOCUS**
A fair sprint handicap. The favourite set a decent gallop from an awkward draw. The winner has been rated a bit up on this year's form, with the runner-up to his latest.

## 6892 TURCAN CONNELL H'CAP 1m 4f 104y
5:35 (5:35) (Class 6) (0-65,66) 3-Y-O £2,587 (£770; £384; £192) Stalls Low

Form RPR

0506 1 **Costa Percy**18 2686 3-9-2 59 ... JoeFanning 8 66
(Jennie Candlish) *mde all: rdn over 2f out: drvn and pressed fnl f: hld on gamely* 7/2²

2401 2 nk **High Wells**8 6611 3-9-9 66 6ex ...(b) PaulMulrennan 3 73
(Seamus Durack) *hld up in rr: pushed along and gd hdwy 2f out: rdn to chal fnl f: styd on but a jst hld* 2/1¹

3052 3 1 ¾ **Rosemay (FR)**9 6594 3-9-0 64 ... JamieGormley(7) 2 68
(Iain Jardine) *hld up in tch: pushed along over 2f out: rdn and hdwy appr fnl f: kpt on* 9/2³

4454 4 4 **Elite Icon**15 6352 3-8-3 46 ... JamesSullivan 7 44
(Iain Jardine) *chsd ldr on outer: wnt prom 7f out: rdn over 2f out: wknd ins fnl f* 9/2³

3542 5 3 ¼ **Knightsbridge Liam (IRE)**22 6088 3-8-5 55 ... HarrisonShaw(7) 5 48
(Michael Easterby) *hld up in tch on outer: racd keenly: hdwy and prom over 4f out: rdn over 2f out: wknd ins fnl f* 8/1

5155 6 3 **American Craftsman (IRE)**25 6002 3-9-6 63 ...(p) JackGarritty 6 51
(Jedd O'Keeffe) *trckd ldrs: shuffled bk a bit 6f out: rdn over 2f out: wknd ins fnl f* 16/1

0500 7 6 **Chionodoxa**46 5209 3-8-2 45 ... DuranFentiman 1 24
(Tim Easterby) *trckd ldr: rdn along over 3f out: wknd over 1f out* 50/1

4600 8 1 ½ **Mister Moosah (IRE)**11 6518 3-9-4 61 ... TomEaves 4 38
(Micky Hammond) *hld up in tch: rdn over 2f out: wknd over 1f out* 33/1

2m 43.38s (1.38) **Going Correction** -0.15s/f (Firm) 8 Ran SP% **113.8**
Speed ratings (Par 99): **89,88,87,84,82 80,76,75**
CSF £10.81 CT £30.58 TOTE £5.60: £1.60, £1.10, £3.00; EX 13.10 Trifecta £54.00.
**Owner** Paul & Clare Rooney **Bred** G B Partnership **Trained** Basford Green, Staffs

**FOCUS**
A modest middle-distance 3yo handicap. The second favourite made all at decent tempo. Straightforward form for the grade, rated around the second, third and fourth.

## 6893 CALA HOMES H'CAP 1m 2y
6:05 (6:05) (Class 5) (0-70,74) 3-Y-O+ £3,234 (£962; £481; £240) Stalls Low

Form RPR

5121 1 **Masarzain (IRE)**9 6591 4-10-2 74 6ex ... EdwardGreatrex 10 88
(Archie Watson) *sn trckd ldrs on outer: pushed along to ld appr fnl f: kpt on wl to draw clr: easily* 13/8¹

1503 2 5 **Inglorious**8 6627 3-9-4 67 ...(p) ConnorBeasley 4 69
(Keith Dalgleish) *led narrowly: rdn over 2f out: hdd appr fnl f: kpt on ins fnl f but no ch w easy wnr* 12/1

4041 3 ¾ **Armagnac (IRE)**7 6664 3-8-8 64 ... TristanPrice(7) 2 64
(Michael Bell) *midfield on inner: rdn to chse ldrs 2f out: bit short of room and angled lft ent fnl f: kpt on* 7/1³

0611 4 ½ **Edgar Allan Poe (IRE)**59 4721 3-9-8 71 ... JoeFanning 3 70
(Rebecca Bastiman) *trckd ldrs: rdn and ev ch over 1f out: wknd fnl 75yds* 9/2²

044 5 2 **Lil Sophella (IRE)**9 6591 8-9-9 67 ... JackGarritty 7 62
(Patrick Holmes) *dwlt: hld up in rr: rdn along over 2f out: kpt on fnl f: nvr threatened* 16/1

6402 6 hd **Argaki (IRE)**15 6346 7-8-11 60 ... RowanScott(5) 6 55
(Keith Dalgleish) *hld up: rdn over 2f out: kpt on fnl f: nvr threatened* 15/2

2301 7 2 ¼ **Kicking The Can (IRE)**77 4059 6-8-9 60 ... NatalieHambling(7) 9 49
(Noel Wilson) *midfield: rdn over 2f out: wknd ins fnl f* 20/1

0102 8 5 **Ellaal**9 6591 8-9-4 62 ...(p) JamesSullivan 5 40
(Ruth Carr) *pressed ldr: racd quite keenly: rdn over 2f out: wknd over 1f out* 8/1

1600 **9** *18* **Ching Ching Lor (IRE)**[12] 6470 3-8-13 **62**....................(v[1]) TomEaves 1
(Declan Carroll) *hld up: rdn over 2f out: wknd over 1f out and sn bhd* **33/1**
1m 39.01s (-2.19) **Going Correction** -0.15s/f (Firm)
**WFA** 3 from 4yo+ 5lb **9** Ran SP% **112.9**
Speed ratings (Par 103): **104,99,98,97,95 95,93,88,70**
CSF £22.60 CT £108.08 TOTE £2.20: £1.20, £3.80, £2.00; EX 24.30 Trifecta £116.30.
**Owner** Masarzain Partnership **Bred** Mrs Josephine Hughes **Trained** Upper Lambourn, W Berks

**FOCUS**
A fair handicap. The clear favourite outclassed this opposition in a decent time. Another step forward from the winner, with the runner-up rated close to form.

## 6894 ST ANDREWS TIMBER H'CAP — 7f 33y
**6:35** (6:36) (Class 4) (0-85,86) 3-Y-0+ **£5,175** (£1,540; £769; £384) **Stalls** Low

Form RPR
1016 **1** **Dark Profit (IRE)**[6] 6672 5-9-9 **83**..............................(p) ConnorBeasley 3 92
(Keith Dalgleish) *trckd ldr: rdn to ld over 1f out: kpt on wl* **7/2**[2]
0525 **2** *2* **Roaring Forties (IRE)**[17] 6297 4-8-12 **77**..................... RowanScott(5) 1 80
(Rebecca Bastiman) *slowly away: sn midfield on inner: rdn and hdwy to chse ldr appr fnl f: kpt on* **9/1**
0502 **3** *hd* **Royal Connoisseur (IRE)**[34] 5646 6-8-4 **71**.......... ConnorMurtagh(7) 5 73
(Richard Fahey) *hld up: racd keenly: pushed along over 2f out: swtchd rt and hdwy appr fnl f: rdn and kpt on* **14/1**
5401 **4** *½* **Sakhee's Return**[9] 6570 5-9-7 **81** 6ex.........................(t) DuranFentiman 4 82
(Tim Easterby) *racd keenly in midfield: rdn and hdwy to chse ldr appr fnl f: one pce fnl 110yds* **8/1**
5133 **5** *1 ¼* **Magical Effect (IRE)**[9] 6570 5-9-12 **86**.................... JamesSullivan 7 84
(Ruth Carr) *trckd ldr: racd keenly: rdn 2f out: sn one pce: hld whn hmpd 110yds out* **7/4**[1]
6506 **6** *3 ½* **Thomas Cranmer (USA)**[13] 6426 3-9-6 **84**...................... JoeFanning 6 73
(Mark Johnston) *led: rdn along over 2f out: hdd over 1f out: wknd fnl f* **4/1**[3]
5236 **7** *nk* **Jabbaar**[79] 3976 4-8-6 **73**............................................ JamieGormley(7) 2 60
(Iain Jardine) *hld up in rr: rdn along over 2f out: sn btn* **14/1**
1m 29.17s (0.17) **Going Correction** -0.15s/f (Firm)
**WFA** 3 from 4yo+ 4lb **7** Ran SP% **113.0**
Speed ratings (Par 105): **93,90,90,89,88 84,84**
CSF £33.09 TOTE £4.20: £2.20, £4.70; EX 36.90 Trifecta £315.70.
**Owner** Weldspec Glasgow Limited **Bred** Mrs S M Rogers & Sir Thomas Pilkington **Trained** Carluke, S Lanarks

**FOCUS**
The feature contest was a decent handicap. They went a steady gallop and the second favourite was well on top from over 1f out. Another step forward from the winner, with the runner-up rated a bit off his recent C&D effort.

## 6895 REALM CONSTRUCTION-CIVIL ENGINEERING AND GROUNDWORKS H'CAP — 1m 5f 216y
**7:05** (7:05) (Class 5) (0-70,72) 4-Y-0+ **£3,234** (£962; £481; £240) **Stalls** Low

Form RPR
-061 **1** **Chebsey Beau**[27] 5923 7-9-7 **68**.......................................... JasonHart 6 81
(John Quinn) *racd in 3rd but wl bhd ldng pair: rdn along and briefly outpcd in 4th over 3f out: gd hdwy 2f out: led ins fnl f: styd on* **13/2**[3]
0011 **2** *1 ¼* **Brandon Castle**[14] 6398 5-9-11 **72**.......................(t) EdwardGreatrex 2 82
(Archie Watson) *racd keenly: led for 2f: chsd ldr: wl clr of remainder: led again over 5f out: clr over 2f out: rdn and reduced advantage appr fnl f: hdd ins fnl f: one pce* **6/5**[1]
2511 **3** *6* **Canny Style**[35] 5599 4-9-10 **71**............................................ TomEaves 7 73
(Kevin Ryan) *midfield: rdn and hdwy over 2f out: one pce in 3rd over 1f out* **6/1**[2]
3434 **4** *1* **Stoneham**[20] 5259 6-9-0 **68**.......................................(h) JamieGormley(7) 3 68
(Iain Jardine) *hld up: rdn along 3f out: kpt on fr over 1f out: nvr threatened* **8/1**
2360 **5** *10* **Schmooze (IRE)**[15] 6352 8-8-2 **49**................................ JamesSullivan 5 35
(Linda Perratt) *a towards rr* **20/1**
6132 **6** *1 ¼* **Jonny Delta**[9] 6592 10-8-5 **59**....................................... SeanMooney(7) 8 43
(Jim Goldie) *led after 2f: set str pce: hdd over 5f out: wknd fnl 2f* **7/1**
3232 **7** *15* **Tectonic (IRE)**[9] 6595 8-9-1 **62**.......................................(p) JoeFanning 4 25
(Keith Dalgleish) *hld up: hdwy into midfield over 4f out: rdn over 3f out: wknd fnl 2f* **8/1**
6056 **R** **Russian Royale**[10] 6565 7-8-5 **57**................................... RowanScott(5) 1
(Micky Hammond) *ref to r* **33/1**
3m 1.12s (-4.18) **Going Correction** -0.15s/f (Firm) **8** Ran SP% **115.5**
Speed ratings (Par 103): **105,104,100,100,94 93,85,**
CSF £14.90 CT £50.16 TOTE £8.60: £2.50, £1.10, £2.00; EX 15.40 Trifecta £79.60.
**Owner** Kent, Greaves, Dawson **Bred** Mickley Stud & M A Greaves **Trained** Settrington, N Yorks

**FOCUS**
A modest staying handicap. They went a contested gallop and the favourite paid the price in the final furlong. The winner has been rated back to his old Flat form.

## 6896 NEVER MISS A RACE ON RACING UK H'CAP — 5f 1y
**7:35** (7:36) (Class 6) (0-60,68) 3-Y-0+ **£2,587** (£770; £384; £192) **Stalls** High

Form RPR
2441 **1** **Hamidans Girl (IRE)**[12] 6469 3-10-2 **68** 6ex................ PaulMulrennan 6 79+
(Keith Dalgleish) *trckd ldrs: pushed along over 1f out: led 110yds out: kpt on wl pushed out: comf* **5/2**[1]
-562 **2** *2* **The Night Before**[12] 6469 3-9-4 **56**................................ JoeFanning 1 60
(Robert Cowell) *prom: led 2f out: rdn over 1f out: hdd 110yds out: kpt on but no ch wnr* **11/4**[2]
400 **3** *¾* **Thornaby Princess**[8] 6631 6-8-9 **46**...................................(p) JoeDoyle 2 47
(Colin Teague) *prom: rdn 2f out: kpt on* **18/1**
030 **4** *½* **Lizzy's Dream**[22] 6114 9-8-8 **45**............................... ConnorBeasley 8 45
(Rebecca Bastiman) *in tch: rdn and outpcd 2f out: kpt on ins fnl f* **12/1**
063 **5** *nk* **Dawoodi**[6] 6694 3-9-6 **58**....................................................(h) TomEaves 5 56
(Linda Perratt) *dwlt: sn in tch: rdn to chse ldr over 1f out: wknd fnl 110yds* **16/1**
504 **6** *½* **Thorntoun Lady (USA)**[13] 6437 7-9-3 **54**...................... JamesSullivan 4 51
(Jim Goldie) *dwlt: hld up: rdn along 1/2-way: kpt on ins fnl f: nvr threatened* **7/2**[3]
240 **7** *1 ¼* **Archie Stevens**[66] 4458 7-9-3 **54**.......................................... JackGarritty 7 46
(Clare Ellam) *led: rdn whn hdd 2f out: wknd fnl f* **18/1**
3605 **8** *1 ¾* **Brendan (IRE)**[8] 6631 4-8-8 **45**.................................. EdwardGreatrex 3 31
(Jim Goldie) *dwlt: a outpcd towards rr* **9/1**
1m 0.12s (-0.28) **Going Correction** +0.05s/f (Good)
**WFA** 3 from 4yo+ 1lb **8** Ran SP% **111.6**
Speed ratings (Par 101): **104,100,99,98,98 97,95,92**
CSF £9.06 CT £93.27 TOTE £2.70: £1.10, £1.30, £4.30; EX 11.90 Trifecta £126.30.
**Owner** Middleham Park Racing LXVII **Bred** Patrick Byrnes **Trained** Carluke, S Lanarks

**FOCUS**
A modest sprint handicap. The favourite came through to win readily from the right horse in second. The third has been rated to the best of her 2017 form.
T/Plt: £33.80 to a £1 stake. Pool: £50,278.909 - 1,084.58 winning units. T/Qpdt: £15.80 to a £1 stake. Pool: £3,795.66 - 177.26 winning units. **Andrew Sheret**

# 5831 NEWCASTLE (A.W) (L-H)
## Friday, September 8

**OFFICIAL GOING: Tapeta: standard**
Wind: Breezy, half against in races on straight course and in over 3f of home straight in races on round c Weather: Cloudy, bright

## 6897 GOWLAND & DAWSON/EBF NOVICE STKS (PLUS 10 RACE) — 6f (Tp)
**1:40** (1:43) (Class 4) 2-Y-0 **£4,528** (£1,347; £673; £336) **Stalls** Centre

Form RPR
4 **1** **Rastacap**[10] 6559 2-8-11 0.............................................. FrannyNorton 3 79+
(Mark Johnston) *mde all: rdn over 1f out: kpt on strly to go clr fnl f: unchal* **4/1**[3]
2R **2** *2 ½* **Chief Justice**[16] 6326 2-9-2 0........................................ PaulHanagan 12 77
(Richard Fahey) *s.i.s: sn pushed along in rr: smooth hdwy to chse wnr ent fnl f: kpt on: nt pce to chal* **2/1**[1]
55 **3** *1 ¼* **Saisons D'Or (IRE)**[18] 6264 2-9-2 0............................... JackGarritty 5 73
(Jedd O'Keeffe) *t.k.h early: trckd ldrs: effrt and chsd wnr over 1f out to ent fnl f: kpt on same pce* **9/1**
**4** *nk* **Sarookh (USA)** 2-9-2 0................................................... JackMitchell 2 72
(Roger Varian) *hld up on far side of gp: stdy hdwy over 2f out: effrt and rdn over 1f out: kpt on same pce ins fnl f* **7/2**[2]
**5** *1 ¼* **Royal Pursuit (USA)** 2-9-2 0.............................................. KevinStott 9 68
(Kevin Ryan) *t.k.h: trckd wnr to over 1f out: rdn and wknd ins fnl f* **8/1**
**6** *nk* **Farhh Away** 2-9-2 0....................................................... PaulMulrennan 6 67+
(Michael Dods) *s.i.s: hld up in midfield: shkn up 2f out: kpt on steadily fnl f: bttr for r* **12/1**
60 **7** *1 ¼* **Blacklooks (IRE)**[7] 6653 2-9-2 0.................................... PhillipMakin 4 64
(Ivan Furtado) *trckd ldrs: rdn over 2f out: wknd ins fnl f* **28/1**
**8** *2 ½* **Swiss Marlin** 2-8-11 0........................................................ JasonHart 7 51
(John Quinn) *t.k.h early: hld up: rdn and outpcd over 3f out: rallied fnl f: nvr able to chal* **40/1**
0 **9** *1* **Little Red Berry (IRE)**[13] 6432 2-8-11 0.............................. JoeDoyle 8 48
(James Given) *hld up in midfield on nr side of gp: rdn over 2f out: no imp fr over 1f out* **50/1**
60 **10** *½* **Gembari**[7] 6654 2-8-9 0............................................ ManuelFernandes(7) 10 52
(Ivan Furtado) *bhd and sn pushed along: outpcd over 3f out: edgd lft 2f out: sn no imp* **33/1**
60 **11** *1* **Lord Caprio (IRE)**[16] 6311 2-9-2 0..................................... TomEaves 13 49
(Ben Haslam) *hld up: rdn over 2f out: shortlived effrt over 1f out: sn no imp* **150/1**
0 **12** *5* **Displaying Amber**[25] 6010 2-8-11 0................................. CamHardie 11 29
(Ben Haslam) *hld up: rdn over 2f out: hld whn checked over 1f out* **100/1**
00 **13** *1 ½* **True North (IRE)**[11] 6525 2-9-2 0...................................... LukeMorris 1 29
(Sir Mark Prescott Bt) *bhd: struggling over 3f out: sn btn* **80/1**
1m 14.75s (2.25) **Going Correction** +0.325s/f (Slow) **13** Ran SP% **118.0**
Speed ratings (Par 97): **98,94,93,92,90 90,88,85,84,83 82,75,73**
CSF £11.83 TOTE £4.10: £1.50, £1.30, £2.30; EX 16.30 Trifecta £98.00.
**Owner** Hugh Hart **Bred** H C Hart **Trained** Middleham Moor, N Yorks

**FOCUS**
A breezy day with the wind partly against them up the straight. The time for the opener on standard Tapeta was 4.55sec slower than standard. A fair race which should produce winners. The third has been rated close to his Thirsk 6f form.

## 6898 STONBURY H'CAP — 2m 56y (Tp)
**2:15** (2:15) (Class 6) (0-60,61) 3-Y-0+ **£3,234** (£962; £481; £240) **Stalls** Low

Form RPR
3265 **1** **Hallstatt (IRE)**[19] 6233 11-10-3 **61**..........................(t) LukeMorris 4 68
(John Mackie) *hld up towards rr: rdn and outpcd over 4f out: rallied 2f out: sustained run fnl f to ld towards fin* **14/1**
6061 **2** *nk* **Shine Baby Shine**[11] 6530 3-8-12 **53** 6ex.................... PatrickMathers 3 62
(Philip Kirby) *missed break: sn pushed along in rr: gd hdwy on outside to ld over 2f out: rdn and kpt on fnl f: hdd towards fin* **7/4**[1]
-026 **3** *1 ¾* **Traditional Dancer (IRE)**[37] 5257 5-9-8 **52**..............(b) PaulHanagan 13 57
(Iain Jardine) *hld up in midfield: stdy hdwy to chse ldrs 6f out: led briefly gng wl over 2f out: sn rdn: rallied over 1f out: one pce ins fnl f* **9/4**[2]
0502 **4** *1* **Jan Smuts (IRE)**[10] 6565 9-9-0 **51**........................(tp) ConnorMurtagh(7) 6 54
(Wilf Storey) *hld up: smooth hdwy to chal over 2f out: rdn and one pce last 100yds* **9/1**[3]
6360 **5** *10* **Treble Strike (USA)**[93] 3459 4-10-3 **61**......................... FrannyNorton 1 52
(David C Griffiths) *in tch: drvn and outpcd over 4f out: rallied over 1f out: nvr able to chal* **33/1**
0450 **6** *2 ½* **Wee Bogus**[9] 6592 4-9-13 **57**...........................................(p[1]) PhillipMakin 12 45
(Alistair Whillans) *trckd ldrs: led over 3f out to over 2f out: rdn and wknd over 1f out* **25/1**
0230 **7** *shd* **Desktop**[11] 6530 5-9-11 **55**................................................... CamHardie 11 43
(Antony Brittain) *t.k.h: hld up in midfield: drvn and outpcd over 3f out: btn fnl 2f* **33/1**
5-60 **8** *2 ¾* **Kisumu**[8] 3566 5-9-11 **58**.......................................(p) AdamMcNamara(3) 7 43
(Micky Hammond) *hld up: effrt and swtchd lft over 2f out: sn no imp: btn over 1f out* **33/1**
5363 **9** *17* **Mcvicar**[19] 6233 8-9-12 **56**.................................................(p) SamJames 5 21
(John Davies) *led 3f: cl up tl rdn and wknd over 2f out* **12/1**
0/03 **10** *12* **Ferngrove (USA)**[21] 6129 6-9-2 **46**.............................(t) PaddyAspell 8
(Susan Corbett) *t.k.h: hld up on outside: hdwy to ld after 3f: hdd over 3f out: wknd over 2f out* **33/1**
0400 **11** *15* **Silk Trader (IRE)**[99] 3243 3-8-4 **45**................................(t[1]) AndrewMullen 9
(Sharon Watt) *hld up in tch on ins: struggling over 4f out: sn wknd* **66/1**
4652 **12** *55* **Byronegetonefree**[41] 5413 6-9-7 **51**................................... JasonHart 14
(Stuart Coltherd) *prom on ins: drvn and outpcd over 4f out: lost tch fnl 2f: t.o* **9/1**[3]
-260 **13** *5* **Single Estate**[79] 3977 3-8-8 **49**................................................ JoeDoyle 2
(Simon Waugh) *hld up: drvn and struggling over 4f out: lost tch over 2f out: t.o* **33/1**
3m 38.57s (3.37) **Going Correction** +0.225s/f (Slow)
**WFA** 3 from 4yo+ 11lb **13** Ran SP% **121.5**
Speed ratings (Par 101): **100,99,98,98,93 92,92,90,82,76 68,41,38**
CSF £37.46 CT £81.83 TOTE £13.60: £3.60, £1.20, £1.90; EX 56.60 Trifecta £283.20.
**Owner** NSU Leisure & Mrs Carolyn Seymour **Bred** Darley **Trained** Church Broughton , Derbys

**FOCUS**
A low-grade staying event. The first four finished clear after a fine finish. The winner has been rated just above this year's form.

## 6899 ESH CONSTRUCTION MAIDEN STKS 1m 5y (Tp)
2:50 (2:51) (Class 5) 3-Y-O+ £3,881 (£1,155; £577; £288) Stalls Centre

Form RPR

1 **Breeze (IRE)**[22] 6121 3-9-0 72 (b) PhillipMakin 5 75
(J A Stack, Ire) *in tch: stdy hdwy 2f out: rdn to ld ins fnl f: kpt on: jst lasted* 7/1

244 2 nse **Subhaan**[22] 6103 3-9-5 74 JackMitchell 7 80
(Roger Varian) *prom: drvn along 2f out: rallied and pressed wnr ins fnl f: kpt on wl* 5/2[2]

406 3 1 ¼ **Pequeninha**[17] 6287 3-9-0 0 AndrewMullen 6 72
(David Simcock) *hld up: rdn and effrt 2f out: kpt on ins fnl f: nt rch first two* 20/1

3303 4 ¾ **Portledge (IRE)**[19] 6235 3-9-5 74 (b) PaulHanagan 3 75
(James Bethell) *t.k.h: trckd ldrs: led over 2f out: rdn and hdd ins fnl f: kpt on same pce* 11/2[3]

53 5 1 ¼ **Naaeebb (USA)**[18] 6268 3-9-5 0 KevinStott 2 72
(Saeed bin Suroor) *w ldr: drvn 2f out: outpcd ins fnl f* 7/4[1]

-320 6 ½ **Luminous**[49] 5131 3-9-0 70 RyanPowell 1 66
(Simon Crisford) *led to over 2f out: rallied: drvn and wknd ins fnl f* 33/1

4 7 6 **Isstoora (IRE)**[17] 6287 3-9-0 0 LukeMorris 4 52
(Marco Botti) *hld up: pushed along and effrt over 2f out: wknd fr over 1f out* 6/1

06 8 9 **Major Minus**[11] 6522 3-9-5 0 JasonHart 9 35
(Tim Easterby) *dwlt: hld up: drvn and outpcd over 3f out: btn fnl 2f* 125/1

63 9 ½ **Global Roar**[11] 6522 4-9-10 0 JimmyQuinn 8 35
(John Weymes) *in tch: drvn and outpcd 3f out: sn wknd* 66/1

1m 41.2s (2.60) **Going Correction** +0.325s/f (Slow)
**WFA** 3 from 4yo 5lb 9 Ran SP% 117.1
Speed ratings (Par 103): **100,99,98,97,96 96,90,81,80**
CSF £24.79 TOTE £6.50: £1.80, £1.30, £6.30; EX 27.60 Trifecta £221.00.
**Owner** P Vela & Mrs John Magnier **Bred** Barronstown Stud **Trained** Golden, Co. Tipperary

**FOCUS**
The first two finished wide apart in what looked a fair maiden. The fourth helps set the standard.

## 6900 MMB BLAYDON RACE NURSERY H'CAP 1m 5y (Tp)
3:25 (3:25) (Class 2) 2-Y-O
£15,562 (£4,660; £2,330; £1,165; £582; £292) Stalls Centre

Form RPR

111 1 **Codicil**[25] 6008 2-8-10 79 LukeMorris 4 83
(Sir Mark Prescott Bt) *trckd ldrs: rdn to ld over 1f out: sn edgd rt: hrd pressed whn veered lft ins fnl f: hld on wl cl home* 9/4[1]

2032 2 shd **Weellan**[27] 5918 2-8-3 72 (p[1]) JimmyQuinn 3 76
(John Quinn) *t.k.h: hld up: stdy hdwy over 2f out: effrt and pressed wnr ins fnl f: sn ev ch and carried lft: kpt on: hld nr fin* 8/1

612 3 2 **Footsteps Forever (IRE)**[45] 5255 2-8-8 77 FrannyNorton 5 76
(Mark Johnston) *cl up: rdn over 2f out: outpcd over 1f out: rallied fnl f: kpt on: nt rch first two* 9/1

3123 4 shd **Kit Marlowe**[6] 6683 2-9-0 83 JasonHart 1 82
(Mark Johnston) *led: rdn over 2f out: hdd over 1f out: kpt on same pce ins fnl f* 14/1

3652 5 3 **Poet's Dawn**[10] 6561 2-8-3 72 CamHardie 7 65
(Tim Easterby) *hld up: effrt and rdn over 2f out: edgd lft and no imp fr over 1f out* 25/1

1212 6 ½ **Indomeneo**[24] 6029 2-8-11 80 PaulHanagan 6 71
(Richard Fahey) *in tch: drvn and outpcd over 2f out: n.d after* 9/2[3]

3116 7 2 ¼ **Curiosity (IRE)**[38] 5501 2-9-7 90 JackMitchell 2 77
(Hugo Palmer) *hld up on far side of gp: stdy hdwy over 2f out: drvn over 1f out: wknd fnl f* 3/1[2]

2133 8 ¾ **Star Of Zaam (IRE)**[8] 6636 2-8-2 71 (p) AndrewMullen 8 56
(K R Burke) *hld up in tch on nr side of gp: drvn and outpcd over 2f out: btn over 1f out* 10/1

1m 43.65s (5.05) **Going Correction** +0.325s/f (Slow) 8 Ran SP% 114.7
Speed ratings (Par 101): **87,86,84,84,81 81,79,78**
CSF £21.16 CT £135.79 TOTE £3.00: £1.10, £3.10, £3.00; EX 21.70 Trifecta £162.20.
**Owner** Cheveley Park Stud **Bred** Cheveley Park Stud Ltd **Trained** Newmarket, Suffolk

**FOCUS**
A valuable nursery which used to be run on August Bank Holiday Monday. They split into two groups of four early on before merging down the middle at halfway, the first two coming from the group nearer the far side.

## 6901 FASTFLOW PIPELINE SERVICES H'CAP 1m 4f 98y (Tp)
4:00 (4:02) (Class 6) (0-65,66) 3-Y-O+ £3,234 (£962; £481; £240) Stalls High

Form RPR

0030 1 **Sir Runs A Lot**[45] 5267 5-9-1 54 (b[1]) SamJames 11 59+
(David Barron) *t.k.h early: trckd ldrs: led gng wl over 2f out: rdn clr over 1f out: hld on wl towards fin* 8/1

325U 2 nk **Padleyourowncanoe**[11] 6524 3-8-12 59 (b) LukeMorris 7 65
(Daniel Mark Loughnane) *t.k.h: hld up midfield: effrt and pushed along over 2f out: styd on wl fnl f to take 2nd cl home* 8/1

4532 3 nse **Good Time Ahead (IRE)**[18] 6270 3-9-1 62 JimmyQuinn 12 67
(Philip Kirby) *prom: effrt and rdn over 2f out: chsd wnr over 1f out: kpt on fnl f: no ex and lost 2nd nr fin* 4/1[1]

4405 4 1 ¼ **Major Rowan**[29] 5832 6-9-12 65 PhillipMakin 1 67
(John Davies) *hld up: smooth hdwy on outside over 2f out: effrt and rdn wl over 1f out: one pce fnl f* 22/1

3640 5 1 ¼ **Surround Sound**[18] 6270 7-9-4 57 (tp) CamHardie 8 57
(Tim Easterby) *missed break: hld up: hdwy over 3f out: rdn over 2f out: kpt on fnl f: nt pce to chal* 14/1

0450 6 2 ½ **Carthage (IRE)**[52] 5008 6-9-8 66 BenRobinson(5) 13 62
(Brian Ellison) *hld up: rdn and hdwy over 3f out: no imp fr 2f out* 8/1

6055 7 6 **Warfare**[16] 6316 8-9-9 62 (p) BarryMcHugh 5 49
(Tim Fitzgerald) *hld up midfield on outside: hdwy and cl up 1/2-way: rdn to chal over 2f out: wknd over 1f out* 20/1

0/50 8 shd **Rock A Doodle Doo (IRE)**[27] 5951 10-9-1 61 PaulaMuir(7) 6 48
(Sean Regan) *in tch: lost grnd 5f out: struggling fr 3f out* 100/1

4342 9 1 ½ **Tred Softly (IRE)**[48] 4169 4-9-5 58 (b) JasonHart 10 42
(John Quinn) *hld up midfield: stdy hdwy over 2f out: rdn and wknd over 1f out* 15/2[3]

1410 10 10 **Metronomic (IRE)**[41] 5404 3-9-3 64 AndrewMullen 14 33
(Peter Niven) *led to over 4f out: rdn and wknd over 2f out* 12/1

252 11 7 **Spirit Of The Vale (IRE)**[12] 6470 4-9-3 56 (h[1]) KevinStott 9 13
(Oliver Greenall) *hld up: pushed along and effrt 3f out: sn no imp: hld whn checked wl over 1f out* 5/1[2]

36-3 12 shd **Le Deluge (FR)**[37] 5539 7-9-8 64 (t) AdamMcNamara(3) 3 21
(Micky Hammond) *t.k.h: hld up midfield: hdwy to ld over 4f out: rdn and hdd over 2f out: edgd lft and wknd wl over 1f out* 25/1

60-0 13 47 **Quiet Weekend**[34] 5632 3-8-4 51 oh1 (t) FrannyNorton 4
(James Bethell) *in tch: drvn and outpcd over 4f out: sn struggling: lost tch fnl 3f: t.o* 22/1

6000 14 16 **Danny Mc D**[9] 6591 4-9-2 55 (p) PaulHanagan 2
(Iain Jardine) *hld up on ins: struggling over 4f out: lost tch fnl 3f: t.o* 50/1

2m 43.26s (2.16) **Going Correction** +0.225s/f (Slow)
**WFA** 3 from 4yo+ 8lb 14 Ran SP% 116.4
Speed ratings (Par 101): **101,100,100,99,99 97,93,93,92,85 81,80,49,38**
CSF £62.27 CT £296.06 TOTE £8.50: £2.70, £2.70, £1.70; EX 101.20 Trifecta £805.70.
**Owner** Harrowgate Bloodstock Ltd **Bred** Immobiliare Casa Paola SRL **Trained** Maunby, N Yorks

**FOCUS**
A moderate handicap. The winner has been rated in line with this year's turf best.

## 6902 TURNER & TOWNSEND H'CAP (DIV I) 7f 14y (Tp)
4:35 (4:37) (Class 6) (0-60,60) 3-Y-O+ £3,234 (£962; £481; £240) Stalls Centre

Form RPR

2325 1 **Masquerade Bling (IRE)**[22] 6101 3-9-2 56 (p[1]) AndrewMullen 13 62
(Daniel Mark Loughnane) *t.k.h: hld up towards rr: effrt whn n.m.r and stmbld wl over 1f out: sn swtchd rt: hdwy to ld wl ins fnl f: pushed out* 7/1[3]

0000 2 1 ¼ **Broughtons Fancy**[11] 6528 4-9-3 53 KevinStott 5 58
(Karen Tutty) *in tch: hdwy to ld over 1f out: rdn and hdd wl ins fnl f: kpt on same pce* 22/1

5204 3 ¾ **Darvie**[20] 6182 3-9-2 56 PaddyAspell 8 57
(David Barron) *s.i.s: hld up: smooth hdwy on nr side of gp to chse ldrs over 1f out: rdn and one pce ins fnl f* 8/1

6600 4 ½ **Mr Coco Bean (USA)**[57] 4789 3-9-6 60 (h[1]) ShaneGray 7 60
(Ann Duffield) *hld up: pushed along over 2f out: hdwy on far side of gp over 1f out: kpt on ins fnl f: nrst fin* 14/1

2006 5 1 **Grey Destiny**[11] 6529 7-9-9 59 CamHardie 9 62
(Antony Brittain) *slowly away: hld up: effrt whn nt clr run over 1f out: kpt on strly fnl f: nrst fin* 14/1

2100 6 ½ **Isntshesomething**[8] 6620 5-9-7 57 (v) FrannyNorton 11 55
(Richard Guest) *trckd ldr: effrt and drvn over 1f out: outpcd ins fnl f* 11/1

-100 7 1 **Great Colaci**[22] 6112 4-9-4 54 PatrickMathers 12 50
(Gillian Boanas) *led: rdn over 2f out: hdd over 1f out: wknd ins fnl f* 6/1[2]

005 8 hd **Simmo's Partytrick (IRE)**[60] 4693 4-9-2 52 SamJames 14 47
(Geoffrey Harker) *hld up on nr side of gp: effrt and pushed along over 2f out: no imp fr over 1f out* 25/1

435 9 ¾ **Regal Decree**[13] 6437 3-8-11 54 (b) AdamMcNamara(3) 2 45
(Jedd O'Keeffe) *in tch on far side of gp: rdn over 2f out: flashed tail and outpcd over 1f out* 11/2[1]

60 10 1 ¼ **Kelpie Spirit (IRE)**[42] 5374 3-8-10 50 JimmyQuinn 3 38
(John Weymes) *hld up: rdn over 2f out: nt clr run over 1f out: nvr rchd ldrs* 66/1

406 11 shd **Excellent Story**[34] 5670 3-9-6 60 PhillipMakin 10 48
(John Davies) *in tch: effrt whn checked 2f out: sn drvn and outpcd* 12/1

0020 12 1 ½ **Steel Helmet (IRE)**[41] 5417 3-9-1 60 BenRobinson(5) 6 44
(Brian Ellison) *cl up: rdn over 2f out: wknd over 1f out* 11/2[1]

4530 13 nk **Tango Sky (IRE)**[24] 6041 8-9-5 55 LukeMorris 1 40
(Paul Midgley) *hld up on far side of gp: rdn over 2f out: wknd over 1f out* 16/1

-200 14 12 **Vecheka (IRE)**[24] 6045 6-9-1 54 (t[1]) JoshDoyle(3) 4 9
(Kenny Johnson) *t.k.h: cl up tl rdn and wknd over 2f out* 40/1

1m 28.1s (1.90) **Going Correction** +0.325s/f (Slow)
**WFA** 3 from 4yo+ 4lb 14 Ran SP% 116.0
Speed ratings (Par 101): **102,100,99,99,98 97,96,96,95,93 93,91,91,77**
CSF £155.55 CT £1290.70 TOTE £8.20: £3.20, £5.80, £2.40; EX 159.00 Trifecta £2221.60.
**Owner** C E Weare **Bred** David McGuinness **Trained** Rock, Worcs

**FOCUS**
Slightly the slower division, and very moderate form. Straightforward form.

## 6903 TURNER & TOWNSEND H'CAP (DIV II) 7f 14y (Tp)
5:10 (5:11) (Class 6) (0-60,59) 3-Y-O+ £3,234 (£962; £481; £240) Stalls Centre

Form RPR

0546 1 **Broctune Papa Gio**[13] 6435 10-9-3 52 (p[1]) PatrickMathers 2 60
(Gillian Boanas) *prom on far side of gp: led over 2f out: rdn over 1f out: hld on wl fnl f* 10/1

2423 2 hd **Jack Blane**[8] 6630 3-9-4 57 (p) AndrewMullen 9 63
(Keith Dalgleish) *in tch: effrt and edgd lft over 1f out: pressed wnr ins fnl f: kpt on: jst hld* 11/4[1]

315 3 2 ¾ **State Residence (IRE)**[9] 6572 3-9-0 56 (vt) JoshDoyle(3) 1 55
(David O'Meara) *hld up: rdn and hdwy over 1f out: tk 3rd ins fnl f: kpt on: nt rch first two* 9/1

000 4 ½ **Fikhaar**[21] 6150 3-9-5 58 KevinStott 8 55
(Kevin Ryan) *t.k.h: cl up: effrt and chsd wnr over 1f out to ins fnl f: one pce* 5/1[2]

2036 5 2 ½ **Rose Eclair**[18] 6271 4-9-10 59 (p) CamHardie 14 52
(Tim Easterby) *hld up: effrt and hdwy wl over 1f out: no further imp fnl f* 14/1

4404 6 1 ½ **Cool Strutter (IRE)**[21] 6131 5-9-4 53 SamJames 3 42
(Karen Tutty) *hld up: rdn and hdwy over 1f out: kpt on fnl f: nvr able to chal* 5/1[2]

5655 7 1 **Windforpower (IRE)**[9] 6571 7-9-7 56 (p) BarryMcHugh 6 43+
(Tracy Waggott) *t.k.h: trckd ldrs tl rdn and wknd over 1f out* 20/1

5145 8 nk **Mr Potter**[165] 1408 4-9-8 57 (e[1]) FrannyNorton 13 43
(Richard Guest) *hld up: pushed along over 2f out: sn no imp: btn over 1f out* 8/1[3]

6066 9 3 ½ **Peny Arcade**[21] 6131 3-8-11 50 PaulHanagan 7 25
(Alistair Whillans) *led to over 2f out: rdn and wknd over 1f out* 12/1

553- 10 2 ¼ **Dream Revival**[487] 2107 4-9-7 56 PaddyAspell 4 28
(Paul Collins) *in tch: struggling over 2f out: sn btn* 33/1

0000 11 2 ¼ **Baby Helmet**[47] 5182 3-9-2 55 ShaneGray 10 19
(Karen Tutty) *in tch: rdn over 3f out: wknd over 2f out* 40/1

1m 27.87s (1.67) **Going Correction** +0.325s/f (Slow)
**WFA** 3 from 4yo+ 4lb 11 Ran SP% 114.7
Speed ratings (Par 101): **103,102,99,99,96 94,93,93,89,86 83**
CSF £35.98 CT £265.68 TOTE £9.90: £2.70, £2.30, £2.40; EX 47.00 Trifecta £468.90.
**Owner** Thwaites Young & Alessi **Bred** Lesley Winn And Reveley Farms **Trained** Lingdale, Redcar & Cleveland

■ Stewards' Enquiry : Patrick Mathers four-day ban: used whip above the permitted level (Sep 22-26)

**FOCUS**

This was run in a time 0.23sec quicker than the first division. Very ordinary form. Straightforward form, with the third rated a bit below his recent win.

**6904** **NWG MAIDEN STKS** **5f (Tp)**
**5:40** (5:42) (Class 5) 3-Y-O+ **£2,911** (£866; £432; £216) **Stalls** Centre

Form RPR

202 **1** **Nuns Walk**[9] 6568 3-9-0 0 PhillipMakin 2 65
(Tim Easterby) *cl up on far side of gp: rdn to ld over 1f out: flashed tail ins fnl f: kpt on wl* **6/4**[1]

0 **2** ½ **Lady Of The Lamp (IRE)**[20] 6184 3-9-0 0 FrannyNorton 6 64
(Rae Guest) *led: rdn and hdd over 1f out: rallied: kpt on same pce wl ins fnl f* **3/1**[2]

5000 **3** 3 **Seebring (IRE)**[22] 6091 3-9-0 52 BenRobinson(5) 1 58
(Brian Ellison) *in tch: drvn and outpcd wl over 1f out: rallied ins fnl f: kpt on: nt rch first two* **16/1**

0432 **4** shd **Angel Palanas**[26] 5962 3-8-12 59 (p) RussellHarris(7) 8 57
(K R Burke) *prom: drvn and effrt 2f out: kpt on same pce ins fnl f* **9/2**[3]

6 **5** 3¾ **High Anxiety**[95] 3383 3-9-0 0 JimmyQuinn 5 39
(John Weymes) *t.k.h early: cl up tl rdn and wknd over 1f out* **33/1**

630 **6** 2¾ **Canadian Royal**[9] 6581 3-9-5 68 (t) LukeMorris 9 34
(Stuart Williams) *hld up on nr side of gp: drvn over 3f out: no imp fr 2f out* **5/1**

40 **7** nk **Swing Time (IRE)**[20] 6184 3-9-5 0 BarryMcHugh 4 33
(Eric Alston) *dwlt: hld up: rdn and struggling over 2f out: sn btn* **100/1**

4 **8** 2 **Kaylen's Mischief**[11] 6522 4-9-6 0 PaddyAspell 7 26
(Philip Kirby) *awkward s: hld up: struggling over 2f out: sn btn* **18/1**

0 **9** 1¾ **Eureka Springs**[43] 5335 4-9-1 0 AndrewMullen 3 14
(Lisa Williamson) *in tch tl rdn and wknd over 1f out* **150/1**

1m 0.76s (1.26) **Going Correction** +0.325s/f (Slow)
**WFA** 3 from 4yo 1lb **9** Ran SP% **115.6**
Speed ratings (Par 103): **102,101,96,96,90 85,85,82,79**
CSF £6.07 TOTE £2.40: £1.40, £1.10, £6.30; EX 7.40 Trifecta £52.70.
**Owner** Habton Farms **Bred** Cockrill Emmerson & Woodley **Trained** Great Habton, N Yorks

**FOCUS**

A pretty ordinary sprint maiden in which the first two pulled clear. The winner has been rated a shade off her Catterick figure.

T/Jkpt: Not won. T/Plt: £95.80 to a £1 stake. Pool: £69,538.63 - 529.83 winning units. T/Qpdt: £29.50 to a £1 stake. Pool: £4,767.33 - 119.30 winning units. **Richard Young**

6905 - 6911a (Foreign Racing) - See Raceform Interactive

## 6648 SAINT-CLOUD (L-H)

### Friday, September 8

**OFFICIAL GOING: Turf: good**

**6912a** **PRIX LA ROCHETTE (GROUP 3) (2YO) (TURF)** **7f**
**1:10** 2-Y-O **£34,188** (£13,675; £10,256; £6,837)

RPR

**1** **Glorious Journey**[90] 3590 2-9-0 0 JamesDoyle 2 108+
(Charlie Appleby) *mde all: kpt on wl whn asked fnl 2f: a in full control* **6/4**[2]

**2** 1¼ **Feralia (FR)**[38] 5694 2-8-10 0 Jean-BernardEyquem 1 101
(J-C Rouget, France) *hld up in tch: rdn in 2nd over 1f out: kpt on fnl f but a hld by wnr* **1/1**[1]

**3** 3½ **A Quiet Man (IRE)**[19] 6247 2-9-0 0 TonyPiccone 3 95
(F Chappet, France) *restrained early: trckd wnr: rdn and outpcd fnl 2f: fdd* **3/1**[3]

**4** 2 **Calva D'Auge (FR)**[10] 2-9-0 0 Francois-XavierBertras 4 90
(B De Montzey, France) *hld up and nvr out of last: no imp in st: wl btn* **14/1**

1m 26.42s (-5.78) **4** Ran SP% **121.7**
PARI-MUTUEL (all including 1 euro stake): WIN 2.50; PLACE 1.10, 1.20; SF 4.50.
**Owner** HH Sheikha Al Jalila Racing **Bred** Normandie Stud Ltd **Trained** Newmarket, Suffolk

**6913a** **PRIX DE LUTECE (GROUP 3) (3YO) (TURF)** **1m 7f**
**1:40** 3-Y-O **£34,188** (£13,675; £10,256; £6,837; £3,418)

RPR

**1** **Darbuzan (FR)**[26] 5982 3-8-11 0 ChristopheSoumillon 3 104
(M Delzangles, France) *a cl up: led gng strly 2f out: shkn up over 1f out: styd on: idled and rdn towards fin: jst lasted* **1/2**[1]

**2** snk **Monreal (IRE)**[33] 3-8-11 0 FabriceVeron 1 104
(Jean-Pierre Carvalho, Germany) *led early then trckd new ldr: rdn 2f out: angled out and styd on: clsd fnl f and up for 2nd cl home: nt quite rch wnr* **68/10**

**3** nse **Casterton (IRE)**[38] 3-8-11 0 Pierre-CharlesBoudot 5 104
(A Fabre, France) *hld up in last: rdn early in st: styd on steadily down outer fnl 2f but nt quite rch wnr: jst pipped for 2nd* **53/10**[2]

**4** 2½ **Galipad**[26] 5982 3-8-11 0 MaximeGuyon 4 101
(A Fabre, France) *sn led: rdn and hdd 2f out: no ex fnl f: fdd* **6/1**[3]

**5** ¾ **Light Pillar (IRE)**[26] 5982 3-8-11 0 StephanePasquier 2 100
(A Fabre, France) *midfield: rdn and outpcd fnl 2f: dropped to last* **11/1**

3m 18.4s **5** Ran SP% **118.0**
PARI-MUTUEL (all including 1 euro stake): WIN 1.50; PLACE 1.10, 1.50; SF 6.00.
**Owner** Princess Zahra Aga Khan **Bred** Princess Zahra Aga Khan **Trained** France

**6914a** **PRIX DES TOURELLES - FONDS EUROPEEN DE L'ELEVAGE (LISTED RACE) (3YO+ FILLIES & MARES) (TURF)** **1m 4f**
**2:40** 3-Y-O+ **£22,222** (£8,888; £6,666; £4,444; £2,222)

RPR

**1** **Cap Verite (IRE)**[15] 6364 3-8-10 0 StephanePasquier 1 100+
(N Clement, France) **48/10**[3]

**2** snk **Pleasant Surprise (IRE)**[34] 5658 3-8-10 0 JamieSpencer 3 100
(Luca Cumani) *travelled strly in midfield: smooth hdwy on outer early in st: led over 1f out: rdn and fnd little fnl f: worn down and hdd last strides* **3/1**[1]

**3** hd **Sisene (IRE)**[52] 5014 4-9-4 0 (p) EddyHardouin 5 99
(P Monfort, France) **45/1**

**4** 1 **Mahati (FR)**[46] 5229 4-9-4 0 Pierre-CharlesBoudot 9 97
(A Fabre, France) **9/1**

**5** 1 **Cosmica Sidera (IRE)**[142] 4-9-4 0 GregoryBenoist 2 95
(D Smaga, France) **17/1**

**6** ½ **Gipoia (FR)**[68] 4424 3-8-10 0 VincentCheminaud 7 96
(M Delzangles, France) **12/1**

**7** nse **Style Icon (FR)**[17] 6299 3-8-10 0 AlexisBadel 8 96
(H-F Devin, France) **11/2**

**8** 1½ **Great White Shark (FR)**[34] 5630 3-8-11 0 ow1 ChristopheSoumillon 6 94
(James Fanshawe) *trckd ldr: rdn to chal early in st: no ex over 1f out: wknd* **63/10**

**9** ½ **Jollify (IRE)**[159] 1530 4-9-4 0 MickaelBarzalona 4 91
(A Fabre, France) *midfield: rdn into st: outpcd and no imp fnl 2f: dropped to last* **19/5**[2]

2m 35.18s (-5.22)
**WFA** 3 from 4yo 8lb **9** Ran SP% **117.6**
PARI-MUTUEL (all including 1 euro stake): WIN 5.80; PLACE 1.90, 1.60, 5.80; DF 11.50; SF 25.20.
**Owner** S E Sangster **Bred** Rabbah Bloodstock Limited **Trained** Chantilly, France

**6915a** **PRIX DE BOULOGNE (LISTED RACE) (4YO+) (TURF)** **1m 2f**
**3:10** 4-Y-O+ **£22,222** (£8,888; £6,666; £4,444; £2,222)

RPR

**1** **Uele River**[13] 6440 5-8-10 0 MickaelBarzalona 4 101
(Henry Candy) *trckd ldr: rdn to chal 2f out and sn led: jnd ent fnl f: hdd but styd on gamely and battled to get bk up: jst prevailed* **269/10**

**2** hd **Kourkan (FR)**[82] 3880 4-9-4 0 ChristopheSoumillon 5 109
(J-M Beguigne, France) **23/10**[1]

**3** 1½ **Arthenus**[27] 5925 5-9-0 0 (p) Pierre-CharlesBoudot 6 102
(James Fanshawe) *prom: rdn into st: styd on fnl 2f and up for 3rd fnl strides: nt quite pce of front pair* **48/10**[3]

**4** snk **Shutterbug (FR)**[21] 6173 5-9-0 0 (b) AntoineHamelin 2 102
(M Figge, Germany) **5/1**

**5** 2½ **Gianyar (FR)**[25] 4-9-0 0 ClementLecoeuvre 3 97
(E Lellouche, France) **22/1**

**6** 3 **Per Un Dixir (IRE)**[117] 2663 4-9-4 0 CristianDemuro 1 95
(P Bary, France) **8/1**

**7** 6 **Octoking (FR)**[100] 5-9-0 0 (p) FranckBlondel 8 79
(R Martens, France) **12/1**

**P** **Alignement**[24] 6052 4-9-0 0 MaximeGuyon 7
(C Laffon-Parias, France) **14/5**[2]

2m 4.08s (-11.92) **8** Ran SP% **117.3**
PARI-MUTUEL (all including 1 euro stake): WIN 27.90; PLACE 4.00, 1.40, 1.80; DF 39.70; SF 97.90.
**Owner** Mrs Alison Ruggles **Bred** Mrs A R Ruggles **Trained** Kingston Warren, Oxon

## 6867 ASCOT (R-H)

### Saturday, September 9

**OFFICIAL GOING: Good to soft (soft in places) changing to soft after race 4 (3.20)**

Wind: Light, against Weather: Fine but cloudy, heavy shower middle of meeting, Race 6 (4.30) run in thunderstorm

**6916** **SODEXO BRITISH EBF NOVICE STKS (PLUS 10 RACE) (DIV I)** **7f**
**1:35** (1:35) (Class 4) 2-Y-O **£6,469** (£1,925; £962; £481) **Stalls** High

Form RPR

**1** **Fajjaj (IRE)** 2-9-2 0 JosephineGordon 3 81+
(Hugo Palmer) *trckd ldng pair: led 2f out but tended to be green in front: hdd 1f out and sn a l down: picked up really wl last 75yds and r.o to ld nr fin* **3/1**[2]

**2** ½ **Court Of Justice (FR)** 2-9-2 0 JamieSpencer 1 79+
(David Simcock) *dwlt and wnt rt s: hld up in last: swift prog on outer 2f out to ld 1f out: drvn a l clr 100yds out: kpt on but hdd nr fin* **2/1**[1]

6 **3** 2¼ **Danceteria (FR)**[15] 6374 2-9-2 0 KieranShoemark 2 73
(David Menuisier) *taken down early: t.k.h: trckd ldrs: chal and upsides fr 2f out to 1f out: one pce after* **10/1**

**4** 2 **Elusif (IRE)** 2-9-2 0 AndreaAtzeni 4 68
(Marco Botti) *hld up in tch: shkn up 2f out: sn outpcd: n.d after but plugged on fnl f* **8/1**

6 **5** 1¼ **Soldiers Bay (IRE)**[22] 6133 2-9-2 0 JimmyFortune 8 65
(Brian Meehan) *mde most to 2f out: steadily wknd over 1f out* **4/1**[3]

56 **6** shd **Robinson Crusoe (IRE)**[22] 6132 2-8-13 0 HollieDoyle(3) 7 66
(Richard Hannon) *dwlt: hld up in tch: nt clr run over 1f out then wknd out of it* **11/1**

**7** nse **Roundhead** 2-9-2 0 TomMarquand 5 65
(Richard Hannon) *w ldr to 2f out: wknd jst over 1f out* **20/1**

54 **8** hd **Affluence (IRE)**[13] 6472 2-8-13 0 NoelGarbutt(3) 9 64
(Martin Smith) *chsd ldrs: pushed along wl over 2f out: wknd over 1f out* **50/1**

1m 34.2s (6.60) **Going Correction** +0.775s/f (Yiel) **8** Ran SP% **113.6**
Speed ratings (Par 97): **93,92,89,87,86 86,85,85**
CSF £9.28 TOTE £3.80: £1.40, £1.10, £2.60; EX 10.50 Trifecta £89.40.
**Owner** Al Shaqab Racing **Bred** Wansdyke Farms Ltd & J M Burke **Trained** Newmarket, Suffolk

**FOCUS**

A fair novice and two promising newcomers came clear late.

**6917** **LAVAZZA FILLIES' NOVICE STKS (PLUS 10 RACE)** **7f 213y(R)**
**2:10** (2:11) (Class 4) 2-Y-O **£6,469** (£1,925; £962; £481) **Stalls** Low

Form RPR

2 **1** **Soliloquy**[15] 6386 2-9-0 0 JamieSpencer 3 84+
(Charlie Appleby) *mde all: pushed along 2f out: more than a l ahd after: rdn fnl f: clsd on by runner-up nr fin* **4/7**[1]

**2** ½ **Sheikha Reika (FR)** 2-9-0 0 AndreaAtzeni 2 83+
(Roger Varian) *trckd ldng pair: rdn and no prog over 1f out: styd on wl fnl f: tk 2nd last 75yds and clsd on wnr nr fin* **4/1**[2]

2 **3** 1¼ **Lubinka (IRE)**[21] 6183 2-9-0 0 JosephineGordon 4 80
(Peter Chapple-Hyam) *trckd ldrs: moved up to chse wnr 2f out: rdn and lost 2nd over 1f out: kpt on same pce* **11/2**[3]

**4** nk **Respectable** 2-9-0 0 PatDobbs 5 79
(Ralph Beckett) *hld up in last trio: prog on outer 2f out: chsd wnr over 1f out: unable to chal fnl f: fdd last 75yds* **20/1**

**5** 1¼ **Trump Alexander (IRE)** 2-9-0 0 TomMarquand 8 76
(Richard Hannon) *chsd wnr to 2f out: one pce u.p after* **20/1**

0 **6** 5 **Arthenia (IRE)**[22] 6132 2-9-0 0 JimmyFortune 7 65
(Charles Hills) *hld up in last: pushed along over 2f out: no imp on ldrs over 1f out: fdd* **25/1**

7 3 ¾ **Arabian Sea (USA)** 2-9-0 0 ........ KieranShoemark 1 56
(Roger Charlton) *a in last trio: wknd 2f out* **33/1**

1m 47.51s (6.81) **Going Correction** +0.775s/f (Yiel) 7 Ran SP% **115.3**
Speed ratings (Par 94): **96,95,94,93,92 87,83**
CSF £2.99 TOTE £1.50: £1.10, £2.50; EX 3.90 Trifecta £7.30.
**Owner** Godolphin **Bred** Godolphin **Trained** Newmarket, Suffolk

**FOCUS**
A useful fillies' novice and they finished in market order. A slight step forward from the winner, with the third and sixth helping to set the opening level.

## 6918 CUNARD H'CAP 7f
**2:45** (2:46) (Class 2) 3-Y-0+
**£49,800** (£14,912; £7,456; £3,728; £1,864; £936) **Stalls** High

Form RPR
0620 1 **Remarkable**42 5393 4-9-8 **107** ........(b) KieranShoemark 15 116
(John Gosden) *in tch in midfield: bmpd by rival over 5f out: rdn over 2f out: prog over 1f out: led jst ins fnl f: a in command nr fin* **10/1**
1102 2 ½ **Mjjack (IRE)**42 5393 3-8-9 **98** ........ RoystonFfrench 6 103
(K R Burke) *mde most: rdn 2f out: hdd jst ins fnl f: kpt on wl but a hld* **6/1**1
0000 3 1 ¼ **Heaven's Guest (IRE)**42 5393 7-8-5 **90** ........ PatrickMathers 3 94
(Richard Fahey) *trckd ldrs: rdn 2f out: styd on but nvr quite able to chal: jst won battle for 3rd* **20/1**
P061 4 nse **Raising Sand**28 5914 5-8-13 **98** ........ DougieCostello 14 102
(Jamie Osborne) *s.s: hld up in last pair: prog 2f out: rdn over 1f out: styd on wl fnl f and nrly snatched 3rd* **12/1**
6553 5 nk **Firmament**16 6355 5-9-10 **109** ........ PhillipMakin 11 112
(David O'Meara) *hld up in last: prog 2f out: rdn and styd on wl fnl f but too late to threaten ldrs* **9/1**
2112 6 shd **Lualiwa**28 5916 3-8-3 **95** ........ DavidEgan(3) 13 96
(Kevin Ryan) *w ldrs and led those that racd on nr side of gp: stl on terms over 1f out: one pce* **17/2**3
0603 7 nse **Birchwood (IRE)**36 5594 4-9-6 **105** ........ JamieSpencer 10 108
(Richard Fahey) *hld up in rr: promising prog 2f out: clsd on ldrs and drvn 1f out: effrt flattened out last 100yds* **7/1**2
2010 8 ½ **Bertiewhittle**14 6419 9-8-3 **93** ........ RowanScott(5) 5 94
(David Barron) *dwlt: sn in midfield: drvn on outer of gp and clsd on ldrs 2f out: one pce fnl f* **33/1**
1523 9 shd **Breakable**7 6676 6-8-12 **97** ........ AndrewMullen 18 98
(Tim Easterby) *pressed ldrs on nr side of gp: rdn over 2f out and struggling: kpt on again fnl f but n.d* **25/1**
4000 10 1 ½ **Shady McCoy (USA)**14 6419 7-7-13 **87** ........ GeorgeWood(3) 8 84
(Ian Williams) *trckd ldrs: rdn and fnd little 2f out: one pce after* **12/1**
0010 11 2 ½ **Squats (IRE)**7 6685 5-8-9 **99** ........ GeorgiaCox(5) 16 89
(William Haggas) *t.k.h early: chsd ldrs: lost pl over 2f out: sn struggling* **6/1**1
3023 12 2 ¾ **Glory Awaits (IRE)**13 6483 7-8-4 **89** ........(b) JoeyHaynes 7 72
(David Simcock) *t.k.h: w ldr: stl rt there wl over 1f out: wknd* **20/1**
6050 13 nk **Summer Icon**60 4718 4-8-7 **92** ........ RobHornby 19 74
(Mick Channon) *dwlt: nvr beyond midfield on nr side of gp: wknd 2f out* **66/1**
5063 14 ¾ **Von Blucher (IRE)**42 5434 4-8-12 **97** ........(t) PJMcDonald 9 77
(Rebecca Menzies) *hld up in midfield: rdn and no imp jst over 2f out: wknd over 1f out* **14/1**
2051 15 3 ¼ **Masham Star (IRE)**7 6685 3-8-9 **98** ........ FranBerry 2 67
(Mark Johnston) *prom on outer of gp: chal and w ldr jst over 2f out: wknd rapidly wl over 1f out* **12/1**
0600 16 3 ½ **Top Score**42 5393 3-9-3 **106** ........ JosephineGordon 12 66
(Saeed bin Suroor) *s.v.s: tk fierce hold and sn ct up: bmpd rival over 5f out: wknd over 2f out* **22/1**
-200 17 15 **Early Morning (IRE)**28 5914 6-8-13 **98** ........ JimmyFortune 20 19
(Harry Dunlop) *t.k.h: prom on nr side of gp to 1/2-way: wknd qckly: t.o* **50/1**

1m 30.29s (2.69) **Going Correction** +0.775s/f (Yiel)
**WFA** 3 from 4yo+ 4lb 17 Ran SP% **124.5**
Speed ratings (Par 109): **115,114,113,112,112 112,112,111,111,110 107,104,103,102,99 95,77**
CSF £64.25 CT £1251.08 TOTE £11.60: £2.60, £2.10, £5.80, £2.80; EX 93.90 Trifecta £3417.40.

**Owner** Cheveley Park Stud **Bred** Cheveley Park Stud Ltd **Trained** Newmarket, Suffolk
■ Stewards' Enquiry : Georgia Cox caution: careless riding
Josephine Gordon caution: entered the wrong stall

**FOCUS**
Racing centre-field, plenty had their chance in this strong handicap and the form looks good.

## 6919 RITZ CLUB EBF "BREEDERS SERIES" FILLIES' H'CAP 1m (S)
**3:20** (3:20) (Class 2) (0-100,98) 3-Y-0+ **£19,407** (£5,775; £2,886; £1,443) **Stalls** High

Form RPR
5-10 1 **Amabilis**39 5506 3-9-5 **94** ........ PatDobbs 7 105
(Ralph Beckett) *dwlt: hld up in last: stl cantering 3f out: prog 2f out: shkn up to cl over 1f out: led jst ins fnl f: rdn clr: v readily* **11/2**2
0020 2 3 ½ **Havre De Paix (FR)**42 5393 5-9-6 **90** ........ KieranShoemark 10 94
(David Menuisier) *mde most: rdn 2f out: kpt on but hdd jst ins fnl f and readily lft bhd by wnr* **11/4**1
1110 3 1 **Whispered Kiss**16 6358 4-9-1 **85** ........ AntonioFresu 3 87
(Mike Murphy) *cl up: chsd ldr over 2f out and sn rdn to chal: hld over 1f out and sn lost 2nd: one pce after* **11/1**
5113 4 2 **Seduce Me**29 5889 3-9-1 **90** ........(p) JoeyHaynes 8 86
(K R Burke) *hld up in tch: shkn up 3f out: prog to chse ldng pair 2f out to over 1f out: fdd ins fnl f* **8/1**
3361 5 6 **Stellar Surprise**30 5856 3-8-5 **83** ........(t) AaronJones(3) 5 65
(Stuart Williams) *hld up: effrt over 2f out to chse ldrs over 1f out: wknd fnl f* **14/1**
0313 6 11 **Black Bess**15 6377 4-9-2 **91** ........ PaddyBradley(5) 12 49
(Jim Boyle) *w ldr to 3f out: wknd over 2f out: sn bhd* **8/1**
1-30 7 14 **Somethingthrilling**224 465 5-9-2 **91** ........ JoshuaBryan(5) 1 17
(David Elsworth) *chsd ldrs 5f: wknd qckly: t.o* **16/1**
1112 8 ¾ **Peach Melba**9 6629 3-9-2 **91** ........ PJMcDonald 13 14
(Mark Johnston) *racd towards nr side of gp: rdn and struggling 3f out: t.o* **11/2**2
-016 9 2 ½ **Soul Silver (IRE)**39 5506 3-9-0 **92** ........ GeorgeWood(3) 11 9
(David Simcock) *chsd ldrs 5f: wknd qckly: t.o* **6/1**3

1m 47.89s (7.09) **Going Correction** +0.775s/f (Yiel)
**WFA** 3 from 4yo+ 5lb 9 Ran SP% **114.8**
Speed ratings (Par 96): **95,91,90,88,82 71,57,56,54**
CSF £20.87 CT £161.73 TOTE £5.80: £2.20, £1.50, £3.40; EX 22.80 Trifecta £199.60.
**Owner** K Abdullah **Bred** Juddmonte Farms Ltd **Trained** Kimpton, Hants

**FOCUS**
A few of the fancied runners failed to give their running in a race where the ground made it hard work for these fillies and mares. It's been rated around the runner-up to her July C&D form.

## 6920 APPLETISER STKS (HERITAGE H'CAP) 1m 3f 211y
**3:55** (3:55) (Class 2) 3-Y-0
**£62,250** (£18,640; £9,320; £4,660; £2,330; £1,170) **Stalls** Low

Form RPR
414 1 **Duke Of Bronte**44 5328 3-8-3 **84** ........ GeorgeWood(3) 14 93
(Rod Millman) *wl plcd on outer: shkn up and clsd fr 2f out: rdn to ld jst over 1f out: kpt on* **16/1**
3262 2 nk **Melting Dew**20 6232 3-8-9 **87** ow1 ........(p1) PatDobbs 10 95
(Sir Michael Stoute) *trckd ldr: led 2f out: rdn and hdd jst over 1f out: kpt on wl to press wnr again nr fin* **16/1**
1511 3 1 ¼ **Mam'Selle (IRE)**21 6196 3-8-9 **87** ........ TomMarquand 4 93+
(William Haggas) *settled in rr: 11th 3f out: rdn and prog on outer 2f out: styd on to take 3rd last 75yds* **14/1**
3125 4 1 **Londinium**15 6399 3-9-2 **94** ........ PJMcDonald 9 98
(Mark Johnston) *trckd ldng pair: cl up 2f out: rdn and nt qckn over 1f out: lost 3rd last 75yds* **10/1**
0224 5 ½ **First Nation**38 5525 3-9-4 **96** ........ JamieSpencer 15 100
(Charlie Appleby) *nt that wl away: r wd early and sn trckd ldrs: chal 2f out: nt qckn over 1f out: one pce after* **11/2**3
2311 6 ¾ **Torcello (IRE)**15 6389 3-8-7 **85** ........ RobHornby 7 87
(Andrew Balding) *t.k.h early: wl in tch: hrd rdn and nt qckn 2f out: styd on again fnl f* **5/1**2
2600 7 1 ½ **Speedo Boy (FR)**15 6399 3-9-6 **98** ........ PhillipMakin 8 98
(Ian Williams) *hld up and nvr beyond midfield: shkn up 2f out: kpt on but n.d and nvr really involved* **16/1**
3514 8 ½ **Rake's Progress**28 5915 3-8-0 **81** ........ DavidEgan(3) 11 80
(Heather Main) *led to 2f out: steadily wknd* **7/1**
1232 9 ¾ **To Dibba**16 6349 3-8-13 **91** ........ FranBerry 12 89
(Roger Varian) *dwlt: racd on outer in midfield: rdn 2f out: one pce and no real prog* **9/2**1
1132 10 2 ½ **Anythingtoday (IRE)**13 6474 3-9-7 **99** ........(p) JosephineGordon 1 93
(Hugo Palmer) *hld up in last trio: shkn up over 2f out: no great prog and nvr involved* **16/1**
1210 11 ½ **Glenys The Menace (FR)**14 6445 3-8-7 **85** ........ MartinDwyer 5 78
(John Best) *dwlt: hld up in last trio: shkn up over 2f out: no great prog and nvr involved* **12/1**
5432 12 10 **Mister Belvedere**35 5630 3-8-9 **87** ........ AndrewMullen 6 64
(Michael Dods) *wl in tch on inner: drvn over 2f out: wknd qckly over 1f out* **50/1**
2221 13 1 **Seafarer (IRE)**16 6344 3-8-9 **94** ow1 ........ TylerSaunders(7) 3 70
(Marcus Tregoning) *dwlt: tk no interest and sn t.o* **10/1**
0300 14 7 **Bear Valley (IRE)**7 6671 3-8-8 **86** ........ RoystonFfrench 2 50
(Mark Johnston) *in tch in rr: no prog over 2f out: wknd qckly and eased: t.o* **25/1**

2m 39.13s (6.63) **Going Correction** +0.775s/f (Yiel) 14 Ran SP% **124.6**
Speed ratings (Par 107): **108,107,106,106,105 105,104,104,103,101 101,94,94,89**
CSF £259.16 CT £3667.58 TOTE £22.10: £7.10, £4.70, £3.50; EX 427.10 Trifecta £3961.80.
**Owner** Perfect Match **Bred** Harts Farm Stud **Trained** Kentisbeare, Devon

**FOCUS**
A good 3yo handicap, although several may not have handled conditions. The fourth and fifth help set the standard.

## 6921 SODEXO BRITISH EBF NOVICE STKS (PLUS 10 RACE) (DIV II) 7f
**4:30** (4:34) (Class 4) 2-Y-0 **£6,469** (£1,925; £962; £481)

Form RPR
1 **Elector** 2-9-2 0 ........ PatDobbs 5 78+
(Sir Michael Stoute) *trckd ldrs: shkn up 2f out: clsd to chal fnl f: led nr fin* **7/1**
0 2 ½ **Agar's Plough**15 6388 2-9-2 0 ........ PJMcDonald 1 77
(Ed Dunlop) *trckd ldrs: prog on outer of gp to ld over 1f out: rn green and hung lft fnl f: hrd pressed whn hung rt and hdd nr fin* **5/1**3
3 ½ **Dream Warrior** 2-9-2 0 ........ JamieSpencer 7 76
(Charlie Appleby) *hld up in tch: shkn up 2f out: clsd 1f out: styd on but nvr quite able to chal* **5/6**1
6 4 2 ¾ **Antagonist**33 5710 2-9-2 0 ........ KieranShoemark 8 69
(Roger Charlton) *hld up in last: shkn up and effrt over 1f out: kpt on fnl f but nvr on terms* **9/2**2
3 5 nse **Aegean Legend**42 5408 2-9-2 0 ........ JosephineGordon 4 69
(John Bridger) *trckd ldr: led 2f out to over 1f out: wknd fnl f* **20/1**
6 2 ¾ **Walk On Walter (IRE)** 2-9-2 0 ........ FranBerry 3 62
(David Simcock) *hld up in rr: shkn up and no prog 2f out* **16/1**
00 7 ½ **Carlini (IRE)**24 6057 2-9-2 0 ........ JimmyFortune 2 61
(Brian Meehan) *led to 2f out: steadily wknd* **33/1**

1m 41.88s (14.28) **Going Correction** +0.775s/f (Yiel) 7 Ran SP% **115.5**
Speed ratings (Par 97): **49,48,47,44,44 41,40**
CSF £42.13 TOTE £6.70: £2.50, £2.20; EX 36.00 Trifecta £66.60.
**Owner** The Queen **Bred** The Queen **Trained** Newmarket, Suffolk

**FOCUS**
This was started by flag due to thunder, lightning and heavy rain. A useful novice and like the first division it went to a newcomer. They raced down the centre. It's been rated cautiously.

## 6922 CHAPEL DOWN H'CAP 6f
**5:05** (5:06) (Class 2) (0-105,105) 3-Y-0+
**£18,675** (£5,592; £2,796; £1,398; £699; £351) **Stalls** High

Form RPR
2403 1 **Ice Lord (IRE)**36 5612 5-8-2 **86** ........ HollieDoyle(3) 12 99
(Chris Wall) *awkward s: hanging bdly rt first f and wl bhd in last: prog fr 1/2-way: passed tiring rivals fr 2f out to chse ldr fnl f: styd on to ld last 75yds: remarkable* **6/1**2
0206 2 1 ¼ **Gulliver**19 6275 3-8-5 **88** ........(t) JosephineGordon 2 97
(Hugo Palmer) *chsd ldrs but sn urged along: wnt 2nd sn after 1/2-way: led wl over 1f out: hung bdly lft and rt continuously after: hdd last 75yds* **14/1**
4514 3 6 **Get Knotted (IRE)**21 6186 5-9-4 **99** ........(p) AndrewMullen 3 89
(Michael Dods) *dwlt: towards rr: rdn sn after 1/2-way and struggling: kpt on fr 2f out to snatch modest 3rd last strides* **6/1**2
31 4 nk **Jordan Sport**29 5890 4-9-3 **98** ........(h) JamieSpencer 11 87
(David Simcock) *led at str pce: hdd wl over 1f out and impeded sn after: wknd fnl f and lost modest 3rd last strides* **11/4**1
1202 5 4 ½ **Bossipop**14 6412 4-8-9 **90** ........(b) PJMcDonald 7 64
(Tim Easterby) *pressed ldrs over 3f: steadily wknd* **7/1**

-344 **6** 3 3/4 **Nobly Born**[28] 5916 3-9-0 **97** JimmyFortune 19 59+
(John Gosden) *hld up in midfield: gng nticeably bttr than many 3f out: shkn up and limited rspnse 2f out: eased whn no ch fnl f* **13/2**[3]

006 **7** 1 1/4 **Doc Sportello (IRE)**[28] 5911 5-9-3 **98** PatDobbs 18 56
(Tony Carroll) *dwlt: hld up in rr: shkn up over 2f out: no prog and sn no ch* **18/1**

0-60 **8** 1 1/2 **Repton (IRE)**[14] 6419 3-8-10 **93** TomMarquand 8 47
(Richard Hannon) *rdn in rr 1/2-way: sn wl btn* **18/1**

0006 **9** 1 **Magnus Maximus**[135] 2114 6-9-3 **103** FinleyMarsh(5) 17 53
(Robyn Brisland) *pressed ldr to over 3f out: wknd qckly* **16/1**

-000 **10** 1/2 **Outback Traveller (IRE)**[35] 5640 6-9-5 **100** FranBerry 1 49+
(Robert Cowell) *hld up in midfield: effrt over 2f out: no prog wl over 1f out: sn wknd* **14/1**

5630 **11** hd **Poet's Society**[7] 6677 3-8-4 **87** RoystonFfrench 20 35
(Mark Johnston) *racd alone against nr side rail: nvr remotely on terms* **25/1**

6034 **12** 2 1/2 **Barrington (IRE)**[39] 5513 3-8-12 **95** (t) SteveDrowne 4 35
(Charles Hills) *pressed ldrs to 1/2-way: sn wknd* **50/1**

1000 **13** 2 3/4 **Blaine**[28] 5911 7-8-9 **95** (b) JoshuaBryan(5) 14 26
(Brian Barr) *a in rr: rdn and struggling fr 1/2-way* **25/1**

1m 17.89s (3.39) **Going Correction** +0.775s/f (Yiel)
**WFA** 3 from 4yo+ 2lb **13** Ran SP% **120.5**
Speed ratings (Par 109): **108,106,98,97,91 86,85,83,81,81 81,77,74**
CSF £86.31 CT £553.68 TOTE £6.90: £2.40, £4.50, £2.20; EX 85.60 Trifecta £990.30.
**Owner** Hintlesham Racing **Bred** Corduff Stud Ltd & J F Gribomont **Trained** Newmarket, Suffolk

**FOCUS**
The main action unfolded nearer the far side in this useful sprint handicap, with the first two coming clear after the race fell apart. The winner has been rated in line with his better form.

## 6923 SUPERSTARS H'CAP 5f
**5:40** (5:40) (Class 3) (0-90,92) 3-Y-O+ **£9,703** (£2,887; £1,443; £721) **Stalls** High

Form RPR

2600 **1** **Pettochside**[19] 6275 8-8-10 **82** HollieDoyle(3) 11 90
(John Bridger) *chsd ldrs in centre: rdn over 1f out: styd on wl fnl f to ld last 75yds* **9/2**[3]

5000 **2** 1 **Robot Boy (IRE)**[17] 6325 7-9-7 **90** FranBerry 2 94
(David Barron) *racd alone towards far side: on terms: overall ldr wl over 1f out gng strly: drvn fnl f: hdd and nt qckn last 75yds* **9/1**

1531 **3** 3/4 **Miningggold**[7] 6669 4-8-8 **77** (p) AndrewMullen 7 79
(Michael Dods) *chsd ldrs in centre: rdn over 1f out: kpt on to take 3rd ins fnl f: nt pce to chal* **12/1**

0001 **4** nk **Mont Kiara (FR)**[36] 5612 4-9-2 **85** JamieSpencer 12 86
(Kevin Ryan) *stdd s and awkwardly away: hld up in last: coaxed along to make prog over 1f out: sn drvn and hanging: styd on fnl f to take 4th nr fin: no ch to chal* **7/2**[1]

4125 **5** 1/2 **Dark Defender**[35] 5647 4-9-1 **89** (b) RowanScott(5) 6 88
(Keith Dalgleish) *overall ldr in centre: hdd wl over 1f out: one pce* **7/1**

143 **6** nk **Turanga Leela**[56] 4889 3-8-8 **83** (v) FinleyMarsh(5) 8 81
(Ian Williams) *pressed overall ldr in centre to 2f out: one pce over 1f out* **10/1**

-205 **7** 3/4 **Ladweb**[22] 6137 7-8-12 **81** JoeyHaynes 1 76
(John Gallagher) *racd alone far side: on terms w ldrs: rdn 2f out: one pce over 1f out* **16/1**

5116 **8** 3/4 **Ocelot**[21] 6177 3-8-12 **82** TomMarquand 5 74
(Robert Cowell) *in tch in centre: rdn and no prog 2f out: one pce after* **20/1**

1604 **9** 1/2 **Shamshon (IRE)**[7] 6695 6-9-5 **88** (t) PJMcDonald 3 79
(Stuart Williams) *a in rr in centre: rdn and no prog 2f out* **4/1**[2]

0000 **10** 19 **Afandem (IRE)**[17] 6325 3-9-7 **91** JosephineGordon 14 13
(Hugo Palmer) *pushed along in centre by 1/2-way to stay in tch: wknd rapidly u.p wl over 1f out: t.o* **12/1**

1m 3.78s (3.28) **Going Correction** +0.775s/f (Yiel)
**WFA** 3 from 4yo+ 1lb **10** Ran SP% **118.0**
Speed ratings (Par 107): **104,102,101,100,99 99,98,97,96,65**
CSF £45.30 CT £469.20 TOTE £5.30: £1.70, £2.50, £3.10; EX 45.80 Trifecta £502.20.
**Owner** P Cook **Bred** New Hall Stud **Trained** Liphook, Hants

**FOCUS**
A decent sprint, they mainly raced down the centre. The winner has been rated back to his July C&D form.
T/Plt: £222.90 to a £1 stake. Pool: £90,607.46 - 406.34 winning units. T/Qpdt: £229.90 to a £1 stake. Pool: £6,381.24 - 27.75 winning units. **Jonathan Neesom**

# 6875 HAYDOCK (L-H)
## Saturday, September 9

**OFFICIAL GOING: Heavy**
Wind: Moderate, against in straight of over 4f Weather: Fine

## 6924 EBF BREEDERS' SERIES 32RED FILLIES' H'CAP 1m 2f 100y
**1:20** (1:20) (Class 2) (0-100,94) 3-Y-O+
**£18,675** (£5,592; £2,796; £1,398; £699; £351) **Stalls** Centre

Form RPR

1163 **1** **Company Asset (IRE)**[16] 6349 4-9-5 **89** TomEaves 5 103+
(Kevin Ryan) *stdd s: hld up: smooth hdwy to ld on bit 2f out: asserted over 1f out: clr whn eased down ins fnl f* **9/1**

5341 **2** 6 **Empress Ali (IRE)**[22] 6152 6-9-6 **90** JamesSullivan 9 91
(Tom Tate) *hld up: rdn and hdwy to chse ldrs over 2f out: kpt on to take 2nd 1f out: no ch w wnr* **5/1**[2]

111 **3** 1 1/4 **Time Chaser**[30] 5841 3-9-1 **91** JamesDoyle 8 91
(Roger Charlton) *led early: dropped in bhd ldrs sn after: tk clsr order and prom on outer 6f out: led 3f out: rdn and hdd 2f out: unable to go w wnr whn lost 2nd 1f out: no ex ins fnl f* **1/1**[1]

2606 **4** 3 3/4 **Lucy The Painter (IRE)**[23] 6104 5-9-4 **88** (p[1]) AdamKirby 2 80
(Ed de Giles) *pushed along sn after s: towards rr: rdn and outpcd over 2f out: kpt on u.p fnl f but no ch* **12/1**

1105 **5** 4 **Curlew River**[7] 6675 3-9-4 **94** RichardKingscote 7 80
(Mark Johnston) *sn led: rdn and hdd 3f out: wknd 2f out* **17/2**

1503 **6** 1/2 **Appointed**[7] 6671 3-8-12 **91** RachelRichardson(3) 4 76
(Tim Easterby) *handy: effrt wl over 2f out: wknd wl over 1f out* **7/1**[3]

2200 **7** 3 **Sophie P**[43] 5381 4-9-10 **94** SilvestreDeSousa 1 73
(R Mike Smith) *racd keenly: prom: rdn 3f out: wknd over 2f out* **25/1**

2m 18.19s (2.69) **Going Correction** +0.475s/f (Yiel)
**WFA** 3 from 4yo+ 6lb **7** Ran SP% **111.2**
Speed ratings (Par 96): **108,103,102,99,96 95,93**
CSF £49.88 CT £81.32 TOTE £8.20: £3.10, £2.50; EX 50.80 Trifecta £116.00.
**Owner** Hambleton Racing Ltd XVI **Bred** Newlands House Stud **Trained** Hambleton, N Yorks

**FOCUS**
All races on Stands Side Home Straight. Race distance increased by 6yds. They were racing on fresh ground which hadn't been used for five weeks, but after riding in the opener James Doyle said: "The ground is bottomless, it's very soft and testing" and Jimmy Sullivan said: "It is very soft - it is not dead but it's hard work." Several of these were below par and the time was just over 10sec slower than standard. There was a very easy winner of this good fillies and mares' event. The runner-up has been rated a bit off her recent form.

## 6925 32RED CASINO ASCENDANT STKS (LISTED RACE) 1m 37y
**1:50** (1:51) (Class 1) 2-Y-O
**£14,461** (£5,482; £2,743; £1,366; £685; £344) **Stalls** Low

Form RPR

41 **1** **Chilean**[9] 6616 2-9-2 **0** SilvestreDeSousa 6 105+
(Martyn Meade) *racd keenly early on: sn covered up bhd ldrs: str run on outer to ld over 1f out: styd on powerfully to draw clr ins fnl f* **6/1**

314 **2** 3 1/2 **Learn By Heart**[21] 6190 2-9-2 **97** JimCrowley 3 97
(William Haggas) *prom: led 2f out: rdn and hdd over 1f out: no ch w wnr fnl f* **4/1**[2]

16 **3** 1/2 **Dee Ex Bee**[17] 6326 2-9-2 **0** AdamKirby 2 96
(Mark Johnston) *led: rdn and hdd 2f out: kpt on same pce fr over 1f out* **3/1**[1]

41 **4** 1/2 **Dark Acclaim (IRE)**[44] 5314 2-9-2 **0** DanielMuscutt 1 95
(Marco Botti) *missed break: sn trckd ldrs: rdn and ch 2f out: kpt on same pce fr over 1f out* **9/2**[3]

41 **5** 2 1/4 **Dubhe**[30] 5840 2-9-2 **0** JamesDoyle 7 90
(Charlie Appleby) *prom: rdn over 2f out: one pce fr over 1f out* **9/2**[3]

1 **6** 2 1/2 **Yabass (IRE)**[27] 5964 2-9-2 **0** EdwardGreatrex 4 84
(Archie Watson) *hld up: rdn 2f out: no imp* **12/1**

1021 **7** 1 1/4 **Veejay (IRE)**[11] 6561 2-9-2 **89** GrahamLee 5 82
(Mick Channon) *hld up: rdn over 2f out: no imp* **10/1**

1m 47.73s (3.03) **Going Correction** +0.475s/f (Yiel) **7** Ran SP% **112.4**
Speed ratings (Par 103): **103,99,99,98,96 93,92**
CSF £28.98 TOTE £6.60: £3.10, £2.00; EX 31.50 Trifecta £92.60.
**Owner** Sefton Lodge (Thoroughbred Racing) **Bred** Ed's Stud Ltd **Trained** Newmarket, Suffolk

**FOCUS**
Race distance increased by 6yds. Havana Gold is the best winner of this Listed event, while high-class filly Chriselliam was second in it. Chilean looks a smart prospect. It's been rated in line with the race averages.

## 6926 32RED SPRINT CUP STKS (BRITISH CHAMPIONS SERIES) (GROUP 1) 6f
**2:25** (2:25) (Class 1) 3-Y-O+
**£147,446** (£55,900; £27,976; £13,936; £6,994; £3,510) **Stalls** Centre

Form RPR

2121 **1** **Harry Angel (IRE)**[56] 4907 3-9-1 **119** AdamKirby 8 128
(Clive Cox) *racd enthusiastically: mde all: rdn over 1f out: edgd lft and drew clr ins fnl f: impressive* **2/1**[1]

2120 **2** 4 **Tasleet**[56] 4907 4-9-3 **116** (p) JimCrowley 5 116
(William Haggas) *wnt sltly rt and bmpd rival s: a.p: rdn and unable qck over 1f out: styd on ins fnl f but nt pce of wnr* **9/2**[2]

-510 **3** 1 1/2 **The Tin Man**[56] 4907 5-9-3 **117** TomQueally 9 112
(James Fanshawe) *hld up: hdwy 2f out: rdn to chse ldrs over 1f out: styd on ins fnl f: nt pce of front two* **11/2**

3-13 **4** 2 1/2 **Blue Point (IRE)**[78] 4030 3-9-1 **116** JamesDoyle 1 104
(Charlie Appleby) *w wnr tl rdn and unable qck over 1f out: styd on same pce ins fnl f* **15/2**

3052 **5** 2 **Cougar Mountain (IRE)**[27] 5974 6-9-3 **110** (tp) BenCurtis 10 98
(A P O'Brien, Ire) *hld up in midfield: pushed along over 2f out: rdn over 1f out: kpt on ins fnl f: nvr able to chal* **40/1**

0025 **6** 1/2 **Mr Lupton (IRE)**[27] 5974 4-9-3 **108** RichardKingscote 11 97
(Richard Fahey) *hld up: rdn over 1f out: kpt on u.p ins fnl f: no imp on ldrs* **50/1**

U640 **7** 1/2 **Growl**[21] 6206 5-9-3 **109** (p) GrahamLee 7 95
(Richard Fahey) *in tch: rdn and outpcd over 1f out: sn edgd lft u.p: kpt on same pce ins fnl f* **25/1**

0104 **8** 1/2 **Kimberella**[7] 6668 7-9-3 **110** PaulMulrennan 6 94
(Richard Fahey) *dwlt and bmpd s: midfield: rdn and lost pl over 1f out: n.d after* **40/1**

1031 **9** nk **Brando**[34] 5690 5-9-3 **116** TomEaves 4 93
(Kevin Ryan) *hld up: rdn over 1f out: nvr able to trble ldrs* **5/1**[3]

0321 **10** 3/4 **Queen Kindly**[20] 6234 3-8-12 **103** PaulHanagan 3 87
(Richard Fahey) *trckd ldrs tl rdn and outpcd over 1f out: wknd wl ins fnl f* **33/1**

0114 **11** 3 3/4 **Magical Memory (IRE)**[34] 5690 5-9-3 **110** SilvestreDeSousa 2 79
(Charles Hills) *trckd ldrs tl lost pl 2f out: rdn and wknd over 1f out: wl btn ins fnl f* **12/1**

1m 13.9s (0.10) **Going Correction** +0.45s/f (Yiel)
**WFA** 3 from 4yo+ 2lb **11** Ran SP% **116.6**
Speed ratings (Par 117): **117,111,109,106,103 103,102,101,101,100 95**
CSF £10.17 CT £42.77 TOTE £2.70: £1.50, £1.60, £2.30; EX 12.60 Trifecta £65.20.
**Owner** Godolphin **Bred** Cbs Bloodstock **Trained** Lambourn, Berks

**FOCUS**
With the wet forecast in mind this race was rescheduled earlier in the week, having due to be run as the sixth race on the card. It lacked last year's winner Quiet Reflection (not ready in time), Limato (ground) and Caravaggio (rerouted to the Curragh) but was still a good-quality renewal, and we were treated to a brilliant winner. A small group of three raced a little wider out than the others and the early pace looked only steady, but the time was only 3.4sec off the standard. The winner rates up with the top recent sprinters. The runner-up has been rated a length off his soft ground form.

## 6927 32RED BE FRIENDLY H'CAP 5f
**3:00** (3:03) (Class 2) (0-100,100) 3-Y-O+**£19,407** (£5,775; £2,886; £1,443) **Stalls** Centre

Form RPR

0025 **1** **Mayleaf Shine (IRE)**[14] 6450 3-8-7 **87** (h) JamesSullivan 6 98
(Iain Jardine) *hld up: rdn and hdwy over 1f out: edgd lft and led fnl 150yds: sn edgd rt: in command nr fin* **7/1**[3]

3300 **2** 1 **Soie D'Leau**[14] 6412 5-8-10 **89** SilvestreDeSousa 10 96
(Kristin Stubbs) *led: rdn over 1f out: hdd fnl 150yds: hld nr fin* **11/2**[2]

0330 **3** 1 1/2 **Confessional**[7] 6677 10-8-8 **87** (e) DavidProbert 5 89
(Tim Easterby) *hld up: hdwy 2f out: rdn over 1f out: styd on towards fin: nt rch front two* **8/1**

4111 **4** 3/4 **Holmeswood**[14] 6450 3-9-3 **97** PaulMulrennan 1 96+
(Michael Dods) *hld up: rdn and hdwy over 1f out: kpt on ins fnl f: no ex fnl 75yds* **9/2**[1]

2050 **5** *hd* **Monsieur Joe (IRE)**[7] 6695 10-8-10 **89** TomQueally 9 88
(Paul Midgley) *hld up: rdn over 1f out: styd on ins fnl f: nvr able to chal* **20/1**

2303 **6** *nk* **Orvar (IRE)**[21] 6177 4-8-11 **90** PaulHanagan 12 88
(Robert Cowell) *prom: rdn and unable qck over 1f out: kpt on same pce ins fnl f* **20/1**

3046 **7** *1 3/4* **Copper Knight (IRE)**[14] 6450 3-9-1 **98** (t) RachelRichardson(3) 4 89
(Tim Easterby) *chsd ldrs: ch wl over 1f out: sn unable qck: fdd fnl 100yds* **10/1**

0130 **8** *2* **Reflektor (IRE)**[14] 6412 4-9-1 **94** RichardKingscote 8 78
(Tom Dascombe) *prom: pushed along over 2f out: wknd over 1f out* **15/2**

0302 **9** *3 3/4* **Distant Past**[16] 6348 6-8-10 **89** (p) TomEaves 2 60
(Kevin Ryan) *restless in stalls: in tch: rdn over 2f out: wknd over 1f out* **11/1**

0231 **10** *1/2* **Midnight Malibu (IRE)**[12] 6512 4-8-7 **86** oh1 BenCurtis 3 55
(Tim Easterby) *w ldr tl rdn 2f out: wknd over 1f out* **11/1**

000U **11** *nk* **Boom The Groom (IRE)**[12] 6512 6-9-4 **97** RobertWinston 13 65
(Tony Carroll) *hld up: rdn 2f out: lft bhd fnl f* **25/1**

3034 **12** *4* **Green Door (IRE)**[9] 6640 6-9-7 **100** (v) AdamKirby 7 53
(Robert Cowell) *cl up: pushed along 2f out: wknd over 1f out* **12/1**

1m 1.84s (1.04) **Going Correction** +0.45s/f (Yiel)
**WFA** 3 from 4yo+ 1lb **12** Ran SP% **115.8**
Speed ratings (Par 109): **109,107,105,103,103 103,100,97,91,90 89,83**
CSF £42.79 CT £321.16 TOTE £6.80: £2.20, £2.40, £2.40; EX 44.20 Trifecta £174.10.
**Owner** R S Solomon & Partner **Bred** Eamonn Phelan & Reuben Solomon **Trained** Carrutherstown, D'fries & G'way

**FOCUS**
A competitive sprint handicap. A length pb from the winner, with the runner-up close to this year's best.

## 6928 32RED MILE (REGISTERED AS THE SUPERIOR MILE STKS) (GROUP 3) 1m 37y
3:35 (3:40) (Class 1) 3-Y-0+
**£35,727** (£13,545; £6,778; £3,376; £1,694; £850) **Stalls** Low

Form RPR

6411 **1** **Ballet Concerto**[23] 6105 4-9-6 111 RichardKingscote 7 120
(Sir Michael Stoute) *chsd ldr: rdn to ld 1f out: styd on: in control nr fin* **8/1**[3]

2520 **2** *1 1/4* **Kaspersky (IRE)**[21] 6193 6-9-3 113 PaulMulrennan 2 114
(Jane Chapple-Hyam) *led: rdn over 1f out: sn hdd: kpt on u.p: hld nr fin* **14/1**

0-14 **3** *3/4* **Morando (FR)**[23] 6119 4-9-3 112 HarryBentley 9 112+
(Roger Varian) *hld up: rdn over 4f out: hdwy 2f out: styd on for press ins fnl f: unable to mount serious chal* **9/2**[2]

1153 **4** *2 1/2* **Sovereign Debt (IRE)**[14] 6444 8-9-8 114 JamesSullivan 5 112
(Ruth Carr) *trckd ldrs: rdn 2f out: styd on same pce ins fnl f* **12/1**

5041 **5** *1* **Mitchum Swagger**[36] 5616 5-9-3 106 (p) TomQueally 8 104
(David Lanigan) *in rr: hdwy 2f out: rdn to chse ldrs over 1f out: sn hung lft: one pce ins fnl f* **8/1**[3]

2515 **6** *hd* **Benbatl**[42] 5394 3-9-1 114 (t) WilliamCarson 3 106
(Saeed bin Suroor) *s.i.s: sn trckd ldrs: rdn over 2f out: edgd lft u.p over 1f out: one pce fnl f* **3/1**[1]

0010 **7** *7* **Rusumaat (IRE)**[15] 6401 3-8-12 109 JimCrowley 10 87
(Mark Johnston) *racd wd and prom early on: sn restrained: rdn over 2f out: wknd over 1f out* **18/1**

-101 **8** *18* **Flaming Spear (IRE)**[16] 6355 5-9-3 107 RobertWinston 4 46
(Kevin Ryan) *hld up: rdn over 2f out: lft bhd over 1f out* **9/2**[2]

3040 **9** *1 1/4* **Victory Bond**[16] 6355 4-9-3 105 (b[1]) SilvestreDeSousa 6 43
(William Haggas) *prom tl rdn and wknd over 2f out* **8/1**[3]

1m 45.93s (1.23) **Going Correction** +0.475s/f (Yiel)
**WFA** 3 from 4yo+ 5lb **9** Ran SP% **114.3**
Speed ratings (Par 113): **112,110,110,107,106 106,99,81,80**
CSF £110.73 TOTE £8.40: £2.90, £3.70, £1.60; EX 125.70 Trifecta £922.40.
**Owner** Saeed Suhail **Bred** Meon Valley Stud **Trained** Newmarket, Suffolk
■ You're Fired was withdrawn. Price at time of withdrawal 33-1. Rule 4 does not apply.

**FOCUS**
Race distance increased by 6yds. This decent Group 3 was run at a good clip, courtesy of the runner-up, and not many were able to get involved. They came down the centre of the track in the straight. It's been rated around the first two.

## 6929 32RED CASINO H'CAP 1m 6f
4:10 (4:11) (Class 2) (0-105,100) 3-Y-0 **£38,814** (£11,550; £5,772; £2,886) **Stalls** Low

Form RPR

3111 **1** **Sepal (USA)**[15] 6383 4-8-1 **84** JamieGormley(7) 10 93
(Iain Jardine) *in tch: rdn and bit outpcd over 2f out: hdwy over 1f out: led 110yds out: styd on wl* **11/4**[1]

4230 **2** *3* **Graceland (FR)**[7] 6675 5-9-1 **91** LouisSteward 6 96
(Michael Bell) *in tch: racd quite keenly: rdn to chse ldr wl over 1f out: led ins fnl f: hdd 110yds out: one pce* **6/1**

0553 **3** *2* **Jaameh (IRE)**[14] 6427 4-9-6 **96** JimCrowley 12 98
(Mark Johnston) *midfield: rdn and outpcd 3f out: styd on wl fnl f: wnt modest 3rd post* **11/2**[3]

-500 **4** *nse* **Cleonte (IRE)**[35] 5638 4-9-3 **93** (p) DavidProbert 8 95
(Andrew Balding) *hld up: rdn along 3f out: plugged on fnl f: nvr threatened* **12/1**

1152 **5** *nk* **Great Fighter**[29] 5882 7-8-6 **85** (v) PhilDennis(3) 4 87
(Jim Goldie) *dwlt: hld up: rdn and hdwy over 2f out: edgd lft over 1f out: one pce ins fnl f* **16/1**

3361 **6** *hd* **Compton Mill**[45] 5287 5-8-3 **82** CharlieBennett(3) 7 84
(Hughie Morrison) *midfield: rdn over 2f out: one pce and nvr threatened* **9/2**[2]

0343 **7** *1/2* **Ravenous**[22] 6151 6-8-3 **79** PaulHanagan 3 80
(Luke Dace) *led: pushed along and qcknd 5 l clr over 3f out: rdn and reduced advantage over 1f out: hdd ins fnl f: wknd* **7/1**

0410 **8** *1 1/2* **Pumblechook**[15] 6383 4-8-11 **87** HarryBentley 2 86
(Mark Johnston) *trckd ldr: rdn along 3f out: wknd fnl f* **9/1**

1150 **9** *8* **Mukhayyam**[15] 6399 5-9-0 **93** (p) RachelRichardson(3) 9 82
(Tim Easterby) *trckd ldr: racd keenly: rdn over 3f out: wknd 2f out* **20/1**

3m 13.22s (11.22) **Going Correction** +0.90s/f (Soft) **9** Ran SP% **115.4**
Speed ratings (Par 109): **103,101,100,100,99 99,99,98,94**
CSF £19.37 CT £84.59 TOTE £3.50: £1.70, £2.00, £1.80; EX 20.70 Trifecta £60.00.
**Owner** I J Jardine **Bred** Juddmonte Farms Inc **Trained** Carrutherstown, D'fries & G'way

**FOCUS**
Race distance increased by 23yds. Formerly known as the Old Borough Cup, this valuable handicap was run in heavy rain. The leader kicked clear in the straight, having led them down the middle, and they got racing early. It was 2sec slower than the following 3yo handicap. The runner-up helps set the standard.

## 6930 32RED.COM H'CAP 1m 6f
4:45 (4:45) (Class 2) 3-Y-0
**£62,250** (£18,640; £9,320; £4,660; £2,330; £1,170) **Stalls** Low

Form RPR

0511 **1** **Taxmeifyoucan (IRE)**[7] 6692 3-8-4 **84** (v) JamesSullivan 6 93
(Keith Dalgleish) *midfield: rdn over 3f out: gd hdwy on outer over 1f out: edgd lft ins fnl f: styd on wl: led towards fin* **16/1**

1406 **2** *1/2* **Face The Facts (IRE)**[58] 4811 3-8-10 **90** RobertTart 10 98
(John Gosden) *s.i.s: hld up: hdwy on outside to trck ldrs 6f out: rdn to ld over 3f out: edgd lft to far rail 2f out: sn pressed: styd on gamely but hdd towards fin* **17/2**

-315 **3** *1/2* **Time To Study (FR)**[78] 4032 3-9-4 **98** AdamKirby 2 105
(Mark Johnston) *midfield: bmpd along and lost pl over 4f out: rdn and hdwy over 2f out: chsd ldrs appr fnl f: styd on* **11/2**[2]

3136 **4** *2 3/4* **Winston C (IRE)**[14] 6445 3-8-8 **88** HarryBentley 8 92+
(Michael Bell) *trckd ldr: rdn to chal strly wl over 1f out: wknd fnl 110yds* **6/1**[3]

6431 **5** *11* **Orsino (IRE)**[23] 6107 3-8-0 **80** oh6 JimmyQuinn 9 69
(Andrew Balding) *trckd ldrs: rdn along over 3f out: wknd over 1f out* **22/1**

131 **6** *nk* **Great Sound (IRE)**[22] 6135 3-8-12 **92** GrahamLee 7 81
(John Gosden) *hld up in rr: wnt in snatches: rdn over 4f out: nvr threatened* **7/1**

5311 **7** *3/4* **Joshua Reynolds**[44] 5328 3-8-13 **93** (b) JimCrowley 5 81
(John Gosden) *hld up: rdn over 4f out: nvr threatened* **11/4**[1]

5151 **8** *1/2* **Mistress Quickly (IRE)**[50] 5108 3-8-9 **89** PaulHanagan 4 76
(Ralph Beckett) *t.k.h early: settled in tch after 2f: rdn over 3f out: wknd over 1f out* **8/1**

1261 **9** *1* **Hochfeld (IRE)**[14] 6427 3-9-7 **101** RichardKingscote 3 87
(Mark Johnston) *led: rdn whn hdd over 3f out: wknd over 2f out* **11/1**

1214 **10** *2 1/4* **Archi's Affaire**[15] 6383 3-8-9 **89** PaulMulrennan 1 72
(Michael Dods) *trckd ldr: rdn over 3f out: wknd fnl 2f* **11/1**

3m 11.24s (9.24) **Going Correction** +0.90s/f (Soft) **10** Ran SP% **117.4**
Speed ratings (Par 107): **109,108,108,106,100 100,99,99,99,97**
CSF £145.90 CT £854.60 TOTE £12.20: £4.10, £2.70, £2.40; EX 231.50 Trifecta £2197.70.
**Owner** Straightline Bloodstock **Bred** E Lonergan **Trained** Carluke, S Lanarks
■ Stewards' Enquiry : James Sullivan two-day ban: used whip above permitted level (Sep 23-25)

**FOCUS**
Race distance increased by 23yds. This valuable handicap was run at a good gallop in a time 2sec quicker than the preceding event for older horses. It's been won by young stayers of the calibre of Nearly Caught and Mizzou, but there didn't look anything of that level in this field. They came down the centre of the track initially and the first four came clear. Another step forward from the winner, with the runner-up rated to his Queen's Vase form.
T/Jkpt: Not Won. T/Plt: £175.30 to a £1 stake. Pool: £105,462.00 - 601.55 winning units. T/Qpdt: £13.10 to a £1 stake. Pool: £8,906.17 - 679.15 winning units. **Darren Owen**

# 6882 KEMPTON (A.W) (R-H)
Saturday, September 9
**OFFICIAL GOING: Polytrack: standard to slow (watered)**
Wind: light, across Weather: bright spells and showers

## 6931 TOTEPLACEPOT SEPTEMBER STKS (GROUP 3) 1m 3f 219y(P)
2:05 (2:05) (Class 1) 3-Y-0+
**£36,861** (£13,975; £6,994; £3,484; £1,748; £877) **Stalls** Low

Form RPR

2631 **1** **Chemical Charge (IRE)**[57] 4849 5-9-5 114 OisinMurphy 3 112+
(Ralph Beckett) *t.k.h: chsd ldr tl over 8f out: styd chsng ldrs: effrt 2f out: 4th and nt clr run whn swtchd lft over 1f out: str run u.p ins fnl f: led last strides* **13/8**[1]

6030 **2** *hd* **Scarlet Dragon**[14] 6447 4-9-5 108 (h) CharlesBishop 4 111
(Eve Johnson Houghton) *t.k.h: hld up wl in tch: effrt to chal 2f out: sn rdn: led 1f out: forged ahd ins fnl f: kpt on u.p: hdd last strides* **7/1**[3]

1650 **3** *3/4* **Wild Hacked (USA)**[14] 6447 4-9-5 106 LukeMorris 6 110
(Marco Botti) *chsd ldng pair tl wnt 2nd over 8f out: led ent fnl 2f: sn rdn: hdd 1f out: kpt on same pce u.p fnl 100yds* **8/1**

23-1 **4** *nk* **Danehill Kodiac (IRE)**[21] 6201 4-9-5 103 SeanLevey 1 109
(Richard Hannon) *led and set stdy gallop: hdd and rdn ent fnl 2f: kpt on wl u.p and stl ev ch: jst outpcd fnl 100yds* **7/1**[3]

0442 **5** *1 1/2* **Law And Order (IRE)**[14] 6440 3-8-11 104 MartinHarley 2 107
(James Tate) *stdd s: t.k.h: hld up in tch in rr: shkn up 2f out: effrt and swtchd rt over 1f out: kpt on ins fnl f but nvr getting on terms w ldrs* **14/1**

361 **6** *1 1/4* **Midterm**[12] 6514 4-9-5 110 TedDurcan 5 105
(Sir Michael Stoute) *stdd s: hld up in tch: swtchd lft and effrt over 2f out: no imp and drifting rt over 1f out: bhd ins fnl f* **11/4**[2]

2m 34.55s (0.05) **Going Correction** 0.0s/f (Stan)
**WFA** 3 from 4yo+ 8lb **6** Ran SP% **107.5**
Speed ratings (Par 113): **99,98,98,98,97 96**
CSF £12.20 TOTE £2.30: £1.20, £3.80; EX 11.10 Trifecta £48.90.
**Owner** Qatar Racing Limited **Bred** Viktor Timoshenko **Trained** Kimpton, Hants

**FOCUS**
In recent years this Group 3 has proved to be a decent guide to the following spring's Dubai Carnival, with Prince Bishop taking the Dubai World Cup and Jack Hobbs the Sheema Classic after scoring here. This looked an interesting renewal, although a few of these had questions to answer and it produced an exciting finish. The fourth has been rated as running as well as ever.

## 6932 TOTESCOOP6 NURSERY H'CAP (JOCKEY CLUB GRASSROOTS NURSERY QUALIFIER) 7f (P)
2:40 (2:40) (Class 4) (0-80,80) 2-Y-0 **£5,175** (£1,540; £769; £384) **Stalls** Low

Form RPR

244 **1** **Fabulous Red**[30] 5834 2-9-4 **77** OisinMurphy 2 79
(Ed Dunlop) *taken down early and led to post: trckd ldrs: nt clr run over 2f out: swtchd 2f out: sn rdn and hdwy to chal over 1f out: led 100yds out: styd on wl and forged ahd towards fin: rdn out* **5/2**[1]

6256 **2** *3/4* **Collateral (IRE)**[14] 6438 2-9-1 **74** MartinHarley 3 74
(James Tate) *hld up wl in tch: effrt over 2f out: hdwy to chal over 1f out: drvn to ld ins fnl f: sn hdd and styd on same pce u.p fnl 100yds* **7/1**



The Form Book Flat, Raceform Ltd, Newbury, RG14 5SJ

2403 **3** *nse* **Tig Tog (IRE)**[15] 6375 2-9-2 **75** SeanLevey 7 75
(Richard Hannon) *pressed ldr tl led 2f out: sn rdn and hrd pressed: hdd ins fnl f: kpt on same pce u.p fnl 100yds* **7/2**[2]

330 **4** *1 1/4* **Retained (FR)**[3] 6825 2-8-6 **68** ow1 HectorCrouch(3) 4 64
(John Best) *stdd after s: t.k.h early: hld up in tch in last pair: effrt over 2f out: nt clrest of runs and swtchd rt 2f out: hdwy and drvn to chal over 1f out: jst getting outpcd whn squeezed for room ins fnl f* **6/1**[3]

1632 **5** *nk* **Tunes Of Glory**[15] 6367 2-9-7 **80** LukeMorris 5 76
(Sir Mark Prescott Bt) *bmpd s: t.k.h: stdd after s and hld up in last pair: effrt 2f out: pressing ldrs u.p jst over 1f out: no ex and outpcd ins fnl f* **5/2**[1]

4140 **6** *3 1/2* **Royal Liberty**[59] 4758 2-9-0 **73** FrannyNorton 6 59
(Mark Johnston) *bmpd s: sn led: rdn and wandered 2f out: lost pl over 1f out: wknd ins fnl f* **25/1**

1m 26.53s (0.53) **Going Correction** 0.0s/f (Stan) 6 Ran SP% **110.0**
Speed ratings (Par 97): **96,95,95,93,93 89**
CSF £19.36 TOTE £3.00: £1.90, £3.30; EX 21.60 Trifecta £87.30.
**Owner** The Hon R J Arculli **Bred** The Hon R J Arculli **Trained** Newmarket, Suffolk

**FOCUS**
Not the strongest race of it's type, but a competitive looking nursery and another good finish. It's been rated around those close up.

## 6933 TOTEQUADPOT LONDON MILE H'CAP (SERIES FINAL) 1m (P)
**3:15** (3:17) (Class 2) 3-Y-0+

**£37,350** (£11,184; £5,592; £2,796; £1,398; £702) **Stalls** Low

Form RPR

2411 **1** **Brilliant Vanguard (IRE)**[12] 6520 4-9-4 **89** (p) KevinStott 8 97+
(Kevin Ryan) *hld up in tch in midfield: swtchd lft over 2f out: rdn and hdwy over 1f out: edging rt and led ins fnl f: r.o wl* **8/1**[2]

0044 **2** *1/2* **The Warrior (IRE)**[17] 6322 5-9-0 **85** FrannyNorton 7 92+
(Amanda Perrett) *hld up in midfield: clsd jst over 2f out: chsd ldrs and nt clr run whn swtchd lft over 1f out: squeezed between horses to chse wnr wl ins fnl f: kpt on* **11/1**

2024 **3** *1/2* **Golden Wedding (IRE)**[7] 6700 5-8-11 **82** CharlesBishop 5 88
(Eve Johnson Houghton) *in tch in midfield: effrt over 2f out: hdwy to chse ldrs whn squeezed for room jst ins fnl f: styd on u.p to go 3rd wl ins fnl f* **14/1**

6421 **4** *1* **Ventura Blues (IRE)**[3] 6818 3-8-10 **86** 6ex (p) SeanLevey 6 89
(Richard Hannon) *t.k.h: hld up in tch in last quartet: rdn and hdwy whn carried lft over 1f out: styd on wl ins fnl f: nt rch ldrs* **6/1**[1]

5340 **5** *1/2* **Reaver (IRE)**[14] 6422 4-8-6 **80** (v[1]) HectorCrouch(3) 1 83
(Eve Johnson Houghton) *dwlt: sn rcvrd and in tch in midfield: clsd to chse ldrs and swtchd rt 2f out: sn drvn and ev ch over 1f out: wnt lft and then rt whn led jst ins fnl f: sn hdd: wknd towards fin* **11/1**

1143 **6** *1/2* **Commodity (IRE)**[26] 6014 4-8-13 **84** TedDurcan 16 85+
(Sir Michael Stoute) *led and crossed over to r on inner: rdn and hrd pressed 2f out: carried lft jst over 1f out: hdd jst ins fnl f: outpcd fnl 100yds* **12/1**

-126 **7** *1* **Lastmanlastround (IRE)**[79] 4001 4-8-10 **81** OisinMurphy 9 80
(Rae Guest) *t.k.h: chsd ldrs: rdn and ev ch 2f out tl no ex jst ins fnl f: wknd fnl 100yds* **20/1**

4500 **7** *dht* **Presumido (IRE)**[17] 6322 7-8-11 **82** LukeMorris 11 81
(Simon Dow) *hld up in tch in midfield: effrt over 2f out: hdwy whn carried lft over 1f out: kpt on u.p ins fnl f: nvr threatened ldrs* **50/1**

3415 **9** *1/2* **Mazyoun**[17] 6322 3-9-0 **90** (b) PatCosgrave 10 92+
(Hugo Palmer) *stdd after s: hld up in tch in last pair: nt clr run wl over 1f out: gd hdwy ent fnl f: running on whn nt clr run and eased fnl 100yds* **10/1**[3]

1000 **10** *nk* **Gossiping**[36] 5594 5-9-10 **95** (p) ShaneKelly 14 92
(Gary Moore) *stdd s: hld up in tch in rr: effrt on inner and hdwy over 1f out: kpt on u.p but nt clrest of runs at times ins fnl f: nvr trbld ldrs* **25/1**

3016 **11** *1/2* **Georgian Bay (IRE)**[17] 6322 7-9-0 **88** (v) CliffordLee(3) 15 84
(K R Burke) *hld up in midfield: effrt on outer over 2f out: hmpd 1f out: kpt on but nvr getting on terms w ldrs* **14/1**

5200 **12** *1 1/4* **Mustarrid (IRE)**[28] 5926 3-9-2 **92** DaneO'Neill 2 88+
(Richard Hannon) *dwlt: sn pushed up and racd in tch in midfield: effrt 2f out: unable qck ent fnl f: btn whn nt clr run and eased ins fnl f* **8/1**[2]

0004 **13** *1/2* **Ripoll (IRE)**[33] 5719 4-8-7 **83** (t) MitchGodwin(5) 4 75
(Sylvester Kirk) *dwlt: hld up in midfield: effrt 2f out: sn u.p: no imp* **20/1**

1134 **14** *3 1/2* **Chiefofchiefs**[26] 6007 4-9-3 **88** (p) StevieDonohoe 13 72
(Charlie Fellowes) *in tch in midfield on outer: lost pl u.p and bhd: wl hld whn squeezed for room jst over 1f out* **6/1**[1]

4301 **15** *1* **Timeless Art (IRE)**[17] 6322 4-9-0 **85** (e) MartinHarley 12 67
(K R Burke) *styd wd early: chsd ldr tl jst over 2f out: losing pl whn squeezed for room and hmpd jst over 1f out: wknd* **14/1**

120 **16** *3/4* **Believe It (IRE)**[13] 6475 5-8-11 **89** (b) StephenCummins(7) 3 69
(Richard Hughes) *t.k.h: chsd ldrs tl lost pl u.p over 1f out: wknd fnl f* **25/1**

1m 37.45s (-2.35) **Going Correction** 0.0s/f (Stan)
**WFA** 3 from 4yo+ 5lb 16 Ran SP% **123.4**
Speed ratings (Par 109): **111,110,110,109,108 108,107,107,106,106 105,104,103,100,99 98**
CSF £87.52 CT £1234.45 TOTE £8.40: £2.80, £2.80, £3.60, £1.80; EX 97.40 Trifecta £1379.70.
**Owner** J C G Chua & C K Ong **Bred** Frank Moynihan **Trained** Hambleton, N Yorks
■ Stewards' Enquiry : Franny Norton three-day ban: careless riding (Sep 23-26)
Hector Crouch caution: careless riding

**FOCUS**
A valuable prize for the final of this series and it produced a strong handicap typical of most previous runnings. The pace was good, as it usually is, and although the winner scored decisively, there was a bunched finish for the minor placings. The third seems the key to the level.

## 6934 TOTEPOOLLIVEINFO.COM NURSERY H'CAP 1m (P)
**3:50** (3:52) (Class 4) (0-85,82) 2-Y-0 **£5,175** (£1,540; £769; £384) **Stalls** Low

Form RPR

0122 **1** **Tadleel**[14] 6425 2-9-7 **82** DaneO'Neill 3 86
(Ed Dunlop) *hld up in tch: rdn and qcknd to ld over 1f out: styd on wl ins fnl f* **13/2**

310 **2** *1* **Jazeel (IRE)**[17] 6326 2-9-7 **82** CharlesBishop 5 84
(Mick Channon) *hld up in tch in last trio: rdn and hdwy over 1f out: chsd wnr ins fnl f: kpt on wl but nvr quite getting on terms* **8/1**

5102 **3** *2 1/4* **Di Fede (IRE)**[43] 5366 2-9-7 **82** OisinMurphy 2 79
(Ralph Beckett) *broke wl: stdd to trck ldng pair: swtchd rt and effrt 2f out: chsd wnr over 1f out: no imp: lost 2nd ins fnl f: wknd towards fin* **11/4**[1]

0051 **4** *nk* **El Borracho (IRE)**[15] 6395 2-8-8 **69** TedDurcan 7 65
(Simon Dow) *stdd after s: hld up in rr: swtchd lft and effrt wl over 1f out: hdwy 1f out: styd on ins fnl f: nvr trbld ldrs* **15/2**

014 **5** *1/2* **Al Ozzdi**[18] 6279 2-9-0 **75** (t) PatCosgrave 6 70
(Simon Crisford) *t.k.h: hld up in tch in last trio: effrt over 1f out: no imp and styd on same pce fr over 1f out* **7/1**

3031 **6** *1/2* **We Are The World**[18] 6286 2-9-4 **79** (p) LukeMorris 1 72
(Archie Watson) *sn led: rdn ent fnl 2f: hdd over 1f out: sn outpcd and wknd ins fnl f* **9/2**[2]

1033 **7** *1 3/4* **Finsbury Park**[14] 6425 2-9-4 **79** ShaneKelly 4 68
(Robyn Brisland) *pressed ldr: rdn ent fnl 2f: sn struggling and outpcd over 1f out: bhd ins fnl f* **6/1**[3]

1m 39.06s (-0.74) **Going Correction** 0.0s/f (Stan) 7 Ran SP% **107.8**
Speed ratings (Par 97): **103,102,99,99,98 98,96**
CSF £49.41 TOTE £5.70: £3.00, £4.30; EX 40.50 Trifecta £145.20.
**Owner** Hamdan Al Maktoum **Bred** Anthony Byrne **Trained** Newmarket, Suffolk

**FOCUS**
There was a downpour before and during this race. A tightly knit nursery handicap but the winner scored with authority. The time was unsurprisingly 1.61 secs slower than the preceding handicap.

## 6935 TOTEPOOL SIRENIA STKS (GROUP 3) 6f (P)
**4:25** (4:27) (Class 1) 2-Y-O

**£25,519** (£9,675; £4,842; £2,412; £1,210; £607) **Stalls** Low

Form RPR

1422 **1** **Invincible Army (IRE)**[14] 6446 2-9-1 109 MartinHarley 2 109
(James Tate) *t.k.h: trckd ldng pair: effrt to chse ldr and swtchd lft over 1f out: rdn and clsd to ld ins fnl f: r.o wl: comf* **11/8**[1]

2041 **2** *1 1/2* **Corinthia Knight (IRE)**[29] 5891 2-9-1 93 OisinMurphy 1 104
(Archie Watson) *led: rdn ent fnl 2f: hdd ins fnl f: sn outpcd by wnr but kpt on for clr 2nd* **11/4**[2]

0113 **3** *3 3/4* **Lake Volta (IRE)**[12] 6521 2-9-1 98 FrannyNorton 5 93
(Mark Johnston) *t.k.h: chsd ldr: rdn ent fnl 2f: outpcd and lost 2nd over 1f out: wl hld and kpt on same pce fnl f* **10/1**

1 **4** *1 3/4* **Eqtidaar (IRE)**[22] 6146 2-9-1 0 DaneO'Neill 8 88
(Sir Michael Stoute) *dwlt: sn rcvrd and in tch in midfield: effrt ent fnl 2f: 4th and no imp u.p over 1f out: wknd ins fnl f* **7/2**[3]

1310 **5** *shd* **Green Fortune**[17] 6330 2-9-1 87 (b[1]) PatCosgrave 3 87
(William Haggas) *dwlt and pushed along early: in tch in last trio: effrt 2f out: sn drvn and no imp: wl hld over 1f out* **25/1**

166 **6** *1 3/4* **True Blue Moon (IRE)**[70] 4386 2-9-1 0 SeanLevey 6 82
(Joseph Patrick O'Brien, Ire) *hld up in tch in rr: effrt over 2f out: sn u.p and no hdwy: wl btn over 1f out* **12/1**

1020 **7** *5* **Declarationoflove (IRE)**[14] 6448 2-9-1 84 KieranO'Neill 7 67
(Tom Clover) *in tch in midfield: rdn over 2f out: sn struggling and outpcd: wl btn over 1f out* **50/1**

0150 **8** *2 1/4* **Connery (IRE)**[49] 5150 2-9-1 84 LukeMorris 9 60
(Sylvester Kirk) *hld up in tch in last trio: wd bnd 3f out and sn rdn: bhd over 1f out* **100/1**

1m 11.02s (-2.08) **Going Correction** 0.0s/f (Stan) 2y crse rec 8 Ran SP% **114.6**
Speed ratings (Par 105): **113,111,106,103,103 101,94,91**
CSF £5.26 TOTE £2.20: £1.20, £1.10, £2.30; EX 6.30 Trifecta £27.30.
**Owner** Saeed Manana **Bred** Rabbah Bloodstock Limited **Trained** Newmarket, Suffolk

**FOCUS**
The best recent winners of this Group 3 have been Hooray and The Last Lion, the subsequent winners of the Group 1 Cheveley Park and Middle Park Stakes respectively. This renewal did not look the strongest but gave an opportunity for one with solid Group race form, and he gained due reward. The winner has been rated roughly to his Gimcrack level. The fifth is a possible anchor for the form.

## 6936 TOTEEXACTA H'CAP 7f (P)
**5:00** (5:00) (Class 4) (0-85,87) 3-Y-0+ **£5,822** (£1,732; £865; £432) **Stalls** Low

Form RPR

1-50 **1** **Accidental Agent**[120] 2565 3-9-6 **85** CharlesBishop 1 95+
(Eve Johnson Houghton) *hld up in tch in last pair: rdn and gd hdwy over 1f out: chsd ldrs and swtchd rt jst ins fnl f: sn led and in command: rdn out* **8/1**

-500 **2** *1 3/4* **Leontes**[15] 6371 3-9-3 **82** OisinMurphy 12 87
(Andrew Balding) *chsd ldr: effrt ent fnl 2f: pressing ldr and drvn over 1f out: outpcd by wnr jst ins fnl f: wnt 2nd 100yds out: kpt on but no threat to wnr* **16/1**

/0-0 **3** *1* **Marylebone**[133] 2133 4-9-5 **80** (t[1]) PatCosgrave 2 85
(Ed Walker) *hld up in tch in midfield: effrt jst over 2f out: rdn and hdwy over 1f out: styd on ins fnl f: snatched 3rd last strides: no threat to wnr* **6/1**[2]

11-0 **4** *hd* **Finelcity (GER)**[18] 6289 4-9-7 **85** (v) HectorCrouch(3) 8 89
(Harry Dunlop) *sn led: rdn wl over 1f out: hdd ins fnl f: nt match pce of wnr and lost 2nd 100yds out: kpt on same pce* **10/1**

2352 **5** *1/2* **Plant Pot Power (IRE)**[14] 6426 3-9-5 **84** SeanLevey 3 85
(Richard Hannon) *t.k.h: hld up in tch in last trio: hdwy u.p over 1f out: kpt on ins fnl f: no threat to wnr* **9/2**[1]

0513 **6** *3/4* **Phalaborwa**[17] 6321 3-9-6 **85** AdamBeschizza 6 84
(Ed Vaughan) *t.k.h: chsd ldrs: unable qck u.p over 1f out: kpt on same pce ins fnl f* **9/2**[1]

206 **7** *1* **Ghalib (IRE)**[49] 5159 5-9-12 **87** (bt) FrannyNorton 4 85
(Amy Murphy) *chsd ldrs: effrt jst over 2f out: unable qck over 1f out: wknd ins fnl f* **20/1**

31 **8** *2 1/4* **Yabrave**[42] 5431 3-9-0 **84** CameronNoble(5) 10 74+
(Roger Varian) *s.i.s: swtchd rt and hld up in rr: swtchd rt and effrt u.p over 1f out: no imp: nvr trbld ldrs* **7/1**[3]

1252 **9** *3/4* **Mulzim**[23] 6113 3-8-12 **77** DaneO'Neill 5 65
(Ed Dunlop) *hld up in tch in midfield: effrt on inner jst over 2f out: drvn and no hdwy over 1f out: wknd ins fnl f* **8/1**

6036 **10** *3* **Professor**[30] 5842 7-9-4 **79** (p) LukeMorris 7 61
(Michael Attwater) *hld up in tch towards rr on outer: rdn over 2f out: sn struggling and bhd over 1f out* **20/1**

3164 **11** *hd* **Moonwise (IRE)**[63] 4617 3-8-8 **78** PatrickO'Donnell(5) 9 57
(Ralph Beckett) *plld hrd: hld up in tch in midfield on outer: rdn ent fnl 2f: sn struggling and dropped to rr over 1f out: wknd ins fnl f* **12/1**

1m 24.84s (-1.16) **Going Correction** 0.0s/f (Stan)
**WFA** 3 from 4yo+ 4lb 11 Ran SP% **117.6**
Speed ratings (Par 105): **106,104,102,102,102 101,100,97,96,93 92**
CSF £128.16 CT £831.82 TOTE £9.10: £2.80, £4.20, £2.10; EX 140.80 Trifecta £753.50.
**Owner** Mrs R F Johnson Houghton **Bred** Mrs R F Johnson Houghton **Trained** Blewbury, Oxon

**FOCUS**

Another competitive contest which was run 1.69 secs faster than the earlier nursery over the trip. The winner swept through his rivals for an easy success. The fourth has been rated close to his 3yo form.

## 6937 TOTETRIFECTA H'CAP (JOCKEY CLUB GRASSROOTS FLAT MIDDLE DISTANCE SERIES QUALIFIER) 1m 2f 219y(P)

5:30 (5:31) (Class 4) (0-80,82) 3-Y-O+ £5,822 (£1,732; £865; £432) Stalls Low

Form RPR

2210 1 **Therthaar**30 5820 4-9-7 77 HectorCrouch(3) 7 83
(Ismail Mohammed) *chsd ldr tl clsd to join ldr 7f out: rdn to ld over 1f out: edgd lft u.p and hdd ent fnl f: rallied u.p to ld again ins fnl f: hld on: all out* **7/1**

0344 2 hd **Pioneertown (IRE)**15 6398 3-8-12 72 LukeMorris 2 77
(Sir Mark Prescott Bt) *t.k.h: hld up in tch in midfield: rdn over 2f out: swtchd rt 2f out: pressing ldrs and drvn over 1f out: ev ch ins fnl f: styd on wl to snatch 2nd last stride: nt quite rch wnr* **4/1**2

5113 3 shd **Koeman**14 6423 3-9-8 82 CharlesBishop 4 87
(Mick Channon) *wl in tch in midfield: effrt over 2f out: rdn and ev ch between rivals over 1f out: led ins fnl f: sn hdd: kpt on: lost 2nd last stride* **5/2**1

5300 4 ¾ **Tangramm**59 4751 5-9-12 79 PatCosgrave 1 83
(Dean Ivory) *stdd s: hld up in tch in last pair: effrt on outer over 2f out: hdwy to ld ent fnl f: sn hdd: no ex and wknd towards fin* **20/1**

1263 5 ½ **Eskendash (USA)**19 6273 4-9-11 78 RobHornby 5 81
(Pam Sly) *stdd s: t.k.h: hld up in tch in last pair: rdn over 2f out: hdwy u.p to chse ldrs 1f out: kpt on* **5/2**1

4131 6 ¾ **Bonnie Arlene (IRE)**9 6628 3-9-2 76 FrannyNorton 6 79
(Mark Johnston) *chsd ldrs: rdn over 2f out: drvn and pressing ldrs over 1f out: no ex and outpcd whn nt clrest of runs ins fnl f* **6/1**3

0600 7 7 **Rita's Man (IRE)**9 6620 3-8-10 70 KieranO'Neill 8 61
(Richard Hannon) *t.k.h: led and set stdy gallop: jnd 7f out: rdn and hdd over 2f out: lost pl and btn over 1f out: wknd ins fnl f* **25/1**

2m 22.95s (1.05) **Going Correction** 0.0s/f (Stan)
**WFA** 3 from 4yo+ 7lb **7** Ran SP% **112.5**
Speed ratings (Par 105): **96,95,95,95,94 94,89**
CSF £33.74 CT £88.49 TOTE £8.80: £3.10, £2.00; EX 54.70 Trifecta £173.70.
**Owner** Sultan Ali **Bred** Cheveley Park Stud Ltd **Trained** Newmarket, Suffolk

**FOCUS**

An interesting handicap with several progressive 3yos taking on their seniors and it produced a terrific close finish.
T/Plt: £1,277.10 to a £1 stake. Pool: £58,750.43 - 33.58 winning units. T/Qpdt: £165.60 to a £1 stake. Pool: £4,141.21 - 18.50 winning units. **Steve Payne**

# 6658 THIRSK (L-H)

Saturday, September 9

**OFFICIAL GOING: Soft (good to soft in places) changing to soft after race 2 (2.15)**

Wind: Light across Weather: Cloudy with showers

## 6938 JENNY ROBERTS ORIGINAL BRITISH MILLINERY - EBF NOVICE STKS (PLUS 10 RACE) (DIV I) 7f

1:45 (1:48) (Class 4) 2-Y-O £4,269 (£1,270; £634; £317) Stalls Low

Form RPR

44 1 **Poets Dream (IRE)**19 6260 2-9-2 0 BarryMcHugh 6 78
(Mohamed Moubarak) *t.k.h: mde all: pushed along 2f out: sn rdn clr: kpt on strly* **7/1**

65 2 3½ **Barefoot Baby (IRE)**17 6311 2-8-11 0 TonyHamilton 4 64
(Richard Fahey) *trckd ldrs: hdwy on inner 3f out: rdn over 1f out: kpt on to chse wnr ins fnl f: sn no imp* **14/1**

0 3 ¾ **Salire (IRE)**33 5702 2-8-11 0 JackGarritty 12 62
(Ann Duffield) *cl up: pushed along 3f out: chsng wnr and rdn 2f out: drvn over 1f out: kpt on same pce* **150/1**

4 1½ **Alkhawaneej Boy (IRE)** 2-9-2 0 ShaneGray 3 64+
(Kevin Ryan) *dwlt and in rr: hdwy on wd outside over 2f out: rdn over 1f out: kpt on wl fnl f: nrst fin* **10/1**

6 5 hd **A Bit Of A Touch (IRE)**24 6057 2-9-2 0 DavidNolan 7 63
(Richard Fahey) *trckd ldrs: hdwy over 2f out: rdn along wl over 1f out: sn edgd lft and no imp appr fnl f* **7/2**2

6 1½ **Aphaea** 2-8-11 0 CamHardie 11 54+
(Michael Easterby) *dwlt and towards rr: hdwy over 2f out: rdn along over 1f out: kpt on fnl f* **50/1**

7 1 **She's Royal** 2-8-11 0 ConnorBeasley 9 52
(Bryan Smart) *midfield: hdwy 3f out: rdn along 2f out: kpt on same pce* **40/1**

5 8 2¼ **Bollin Joan**8 6659 2-8-11 0 JasonHart 10 46
(Tim Easterby) *dwlt and towards rr: hdwy on inner over 2f out: rdn wl over 1f out: n.d* **25/1**

9 nk **Conversant (IRE)** 2-9-2 0 JackMitchell 1 51
(Hugo Palmer) *trckd ldrs: hdwy 3f out: rdn to chse ldng pair 2f out: edgd rt over 1f out: sn wknd* **2/1**1

1 10 6 **Highest Rank (IRE)**17 6311 2-9-1 0 PatrickO'Hanlon(7) 2 42
(K R Burke) *trckd ldng pair: pushed along over 2f out: sn rdn and wknd* **4/1**3

00 11 1¾ **Taifbalady (IRE)**65 4526 2-9-2 0 JoeFanning 5 31
(Mark Johnston) *in tch: rdn along 3f out: sn outpcd* **33/1**

12 2½ **Dicktation** 2-8-13 0 LewisEdmunds(3) 13 25
(Richard Whitaker) *a towards rr* **66/1**

13 21 **Northern Force** 2-8-9 0 BenSanderson(7) 8
(Roger Fell) *s.i.s: green and a bhd* **50/1**

1m 31.66s (4.46) **Going Correction** +0.775s/f (Yiel) **13** Ran SP% **119.1**
Speed ratings (Par 97): **105,101,100,98,98 96,95,92,92,85 83,80,56**
CSF £94.97 TOTE £7.90: £2.00, £2.90, £20.60; EX 62.30.
**Owner** Al Thumama Racing **Bred** Rabbah Bloodstock Limited **Trained** Exning, Suffolk

**FOCUS**

Home bend dolled out adding 10yds to races 1, 2, 3, 4, 5 and 7. After a further 3mm of overnight rain the going was changed to soft, good to soft in places. The first division of a fair novice and very few got into it, with the first three home being up there throughout.

## 6939 JENNY ROBERTS ORIGINAL BRITISH MILLINERY - EBF NOVICE STKS (PLUS 10 RACE) (DIV II) 7f

2:15 (2:17) (Class 4) 2-Y-O £4,269 (£1,270; £634; £317) Stalls Low

Form RPR

1 **Air Raid** 2-9-2 0 JackGarritty 12 81+
(Jedd O'Keeffe) *trckd ldng pair: hdwy over 2f out: sn cl up: rdn to take slt ld jst over 1f out: rdn and green ins fnl f: kpt on wl towards fin* **12/1**

23 2 ¾ **Qianlong**19 6272 2-9-2 0 JackMitchell 5 79
(Roger Varian) *trckd ldr: hdwy and cl up over 2f out: led wl over 1f out: sn jnd and rdn: hdd jst over 1f out: drvn and rallied to have ev ch ins fnl f: no ex fnl 75yds* **6/4**1

312 3 3¼ **Travelcard (USA)**21 6199 2-9-3 78 JoeFanning 3 72
(Mark Johnston) *led: pushed along and jnd wl over 2f out: hdd wl over 1f out: sn rdn and grad wknd* **2/1**2

36 4 1¼ **Delph Crescent (IRE)**34 5680 2-9-2 0 TonyHamilton 1 68
(Richard Fahey) *trckd ldng pair on inner: pushed along 3f out: rdn 2f out: sn drvn and kpt on same pce* **8/1**3

5 9 **Dawn Breaking** 2-8-13 0 LewisEdmunds(3) 8 45
(Richard Whitaker) *towards rr: hdwy over 2f out: sn rdn along and plugged on: n.d* **33/1**

6 1 **Daffy Grey (IRE)** 2-9-2 0 CamHardie 7 43
(Michael Easterby) *s.i.s and bhd: sme late hdwy* **40/1**

00 7 hd **The Gingerbreadman**30 5834 2-8-9 0 PaulaMuir(7) 10 42
(Chris Fairhurst) *a towards rr* **125/1**

8 1 **Gullane One (IRE)** 2-9-2 0 DuranFentiman 11 40
(Tim Easterby) *chsd ldrs: rdn along 3f out: sn outpcd* **33/1**

9 1¾ **Snowdon** 2-8-11 0 ConnorBeasley 13 30
(Michael Dods) *a in rr* **9/1**

06 10 2¾ **Jaycols Star**48 5179 2-9-2 0 DavidNolan 6 29
(Philip Kirby) *a towards rr* **50/1**

0 11 1 **Cuppacoco**32 5735 2-8-11 0 ShaneGray 4 21
(Ann Duffield) *chsd ldrs on inner: rdn along 3f out: sn outpcd and bhd* **66/1**

12 8 **Power Sail** 2-8-13 0 AdamMcNamara(3) 9 6
(Tim Easterby) *a in rr* **40/1**

1m 32.34s (5.14) **Going Correction** +0.775s/f (Yiel) **12** Ran SP% **117.1**
Speed ratings (Par 97): **101,100,96,95,84 83,83,82,80,77 75,66**
CSF £29.28 TOTE £14.40: £3.20, £1.10, £1.10; EX 41.30 Trifecta £124.50.
**Owner** Paul & Dale Chapman Racing **Bred** Meon Valley Stud **Trained** Middleham Moor, N Yorks

**FOCUS**

Race distance increased by 10yds. The second division was run 0.68sec slower than the first leg, and once again those that raced prominently had the advantage. The going was changed to soft before this race. It's been rated around the balance of the second, third and fourth.

## 6940 BARKERS OF NORTHALLERTON NURSERY H'CAP 7f 218y

2:50 (2:50) (Class 5) (0-75,73) 2-Y-O £3,881 (£1,155; £577; £288) Stalls Low

Form RPR

4503 1 **Che Bella (IRE)**26 5990 2-9-2 68 JoeFanning 5 81+
(Keith Dalgleish) *trckd ldrs: smooth hdwy on outer 3f out: cl up 2f out: sn chal: rdn to ld ent fnl f: kpt on strly* **7/1**3

4355 2 3 **El Chapo**14 6425 2-9-0 66 BarryMcHugh 2 72
(Richard Fahey) *trckd ldrs: hdwy 3f out: sn cl up: rdn to ld wl over 1f out: sn jnd: hdd and drvn appr fnl f: kpt on same pce* **7/1**3

3250 3 5 **Dontgiveuponbob**14 6425 2-9-3 72 AdamMcNamara(3) 12 67
(Richard Fahey) *towards rr: hdwy wl over 2f out: rdn over 1f out: kpt on fnl f* **10/1**

2611 4 nk **Kikini Bamalaam (IRE)**9 6626 2-9-3 69 ConnorBeasley 7 63
(Keith Dalgleish) *hld up: hdwy 1/2-way: chsd ldrs over 2f out: rdn along wl over 1f out: sn drvn and kpt on same pce* **8/1**

566 5 2½ **Zoffinia (IRE)**21 6183 2-8-5 60 SammyJoBell(3) 11 49
(Richard Fahey) *towards rr: hdwy wl over 2f out: rdn along wl over 1f out: sn one pce* **18/1**

3341 6 nk **Faradays Spark (IRE)**22 6127 2-8-10 62 TonyHamilton 13 50
(Richard Fahey) *towards rr: hdwy over 2f out: rdn along wl over 1f out: n.d* **7/1**3

0000 7 shd **Progressive Jazz (IRE)**32 5752 2-7-9 52 oh2 RhiainIngram(5) 9 40
(K R Burke) *chsd ldrs: rdn along over 2f out: sn wknd* **50/1**

0030 8 ½ **Hamba Moyo (IRE)**9 6625 2-8-4 56 (p) JoeDoyle 6 43
(Tim Easterby) *chsd ldr: rdn along 3f out: wknd fnl 2f* **66/1**

0223 9 2¼ **Mr Carbonator**23 6087 2-8-7 59 ShaneGray 14 41
(Philip Kirby) *a in rr* **5/1**1

0004 10 1½ **Foxy's Spirit**21 6204 2-8-3 55 DuranFentiman 4 34
(Tim Easterby) *led: rdn along over 2f out: hdd wl over 1f out: sn drvn and wknd* **40/1**

0160 11 1 **Jackontherocks**23 6087 2-9-0 71 CallumRodriguez(5) 15 47
(Michael Dods) *racd wd early: a towards rr* **15/2**

330 12 29 **Astraea**43 5380 2-9-5 71 CamHardie 8
(Michael Easterby) *dwlt: a in rr* **22/1**

4033 13 17 **Burnieboozle (IRE)**9 6625 2-9-1 67 JasonHart 10
(John Quinn) *in tch on outer: rdn along over 3f out: sn wknd* **6/1**2

1m 45.72s (5.62) **Going Correction** +0.775s/f (Yiel) **13** Ran SP% **115.9**
Speed ratings (Par 95): **102,99,94,93,91 90,90,90,88,86 85,56,39**
CSF £52.20 CT £506.77 TOTE £8.40: £2.70, £2.40, £3.20; EX 63.80 Trifecta £304.30.
**Owner** Weldspec Glasgow Limited **Bred** Eimear Mulhern **Trained** Carluke, S Lanarks

**FOCUS**

Race distance increased by 10yds. A fair nursery and they finished well strung out. It's been rated at something like face value.

## 6941 EBF STALLIONS MAIDEN FILLIES' STKS 7f 218y

3:30 (3:30) (Class 4) 3-Y-O+ £6,469 (£1,925; £962; £481) Stalls Low

Form RPR

32 1 **Caravela (IRE)**20 6236 3-9-0 0 JoeFanning 5 78
(Mick Channon) *trckd ldr: cl up over 2f out: rdn along and swtchd lft over 1f out: styd on u.p fnl f: led last 50yds* **11/8**1

5-22 2 1 **Ambrosia**18 6287 3-9-0 73 (p) JackMitchell 1 76
(Roger Varian) *t.k.h: led: pushed along over 2f out: rdn and edgd rt over 1f out: drvn and flashed tail ins fnl f: hdd and no ex last 50yds* **11/4**3

55 3 3½ **Teomaria**20 6236 3-9-0 0 JackGarritty 2 68
(K R Burke) *plld hrd early: restrained in tch: hdwy on outer 3f out: chsd ldng pair and rdn along 2f out: sn drvn and kpt on same pce* **12/1**

022 **4** *6* **Cape To Cuba**[72] 4275 3-9-0 79 TonyHamilton 4 54
(James Fanshawe) *hld up in tch: pushed along wl over 2f out: sn rdn and outpcd fnl 2f* **2/1**[2]

1m 47.38s (7.28) **Going Correction** +0.775s/f (Yiel) **4** Ran SP% **109.8**
Speed ratings (Par 102): **94,93,89,83**
CSF £5.52 TOTE £2.00; EX 4.80 Trifecta £24.50.
**Owner** Jon and Julia Aisbitt **Bred** Jon And Julia Aisbitt **Trained** West Ilsley, Berks

**FOCUS**
Race distance increased by 10yds. A fair maiden. The runner-up has been rated to form.

## 6942 EBF H'CAP 7f 218y
**4:05** (4:07) (Class 3) (0-95,87) 3-Y-O **£9,703** (£2,887; £1,443; £721) **Stalls** Low

Form RPR
312 **1** **Kryptos**[24] 6073 3-9-0 **87** NicolaCurrie(7) 4 100
(John Berry) *trckd ldr: hdwy over 2f out: led wl over 1f out: sn rdn clr: styd on strly* **5/2**[2]

1202 **2** *5* **Mountain Angel (IRE)**[13] 6483 3-9-4 **84** JackMitchell 7 85
(Roger Varian) *hld up in rr: hdwy 3f out: rdn to chse wnr and edgd lft over 1f out: sn drvn and kpt on same pce* **1/1**[1]

-505 **3** *3 3/4* **Andok (IRE)**[66] 4507 3-9-2 **82** TonyHamilton 2 74
(Richard Fahey) *trckd ldr: hdwy over 2f out: rdn wl over 1f out: sn drvn and one pce* **7/2**[3]

2-0 **4** *nk* **Mushaireb**[160] 1518 3-9-1 **81** BarryMcHugh 3 73
(Richard Fahey) *hld up: hdwy 2f out: rdn wl over 1f out: n.d* **12/1**

15-0 **5** *4 1/2* **Jacquard (IRE)**[10] 6570 3-9-4 **84** JoeFanning 6 65
(Mark Johnston) *led: rdn along over 2f out: hdd wl over 1f out: sn drvn and wknd* **25/1**

1m 45.96s (5.86) **Going Correction** +0.775s/f (Yiel) **5** Ran SP% **112.3**
Speed ratings (Par 105): **101,96,92,91,87**
CSF £5.56 TOTE £3.10: £1.50, £1.10; EX 5.80 Trifecta £11.50.
**Owner** Tony Fordham **Bred** Juddmonte Farms Ltd **Trained** Newmarket, Suffolk

**FOCUS**
Race distance increased by 10yds. Not a strong field for the grade, but the winner won as he liked and remains on an upward curve.

## 6943 PERSONAL TOUCHES H'CAP 6f
**4:40** (4:43) (Class 4) (0-80,82) 4-Y-O+ **£6,469** (£1,925; £962; £481) **Stalls** Centre

Form RPR
2340 **1** **Kenny The Captain (IRE)**[28] 5947 6-8-11 **73** SammyJoBell(3) 15 86
(Tim Easterby) *trckd ldrs: hdwy on outer to chse ldr over 2f out: rdn to ld 1 1/2f out: clr ins fnl f: kpt on strly* **7/2**[1]

0043 **2** *2 3/4* **Quick Look**[14] 6411 4-9-4 **77** CamHardie 1 81
(Michael Easterby) *trckd ldrs on inner: hdwy 2f out: rdn over 1f out: kpt on ins fnl f* **11/1**

5360 **3** *2 1/4* **B Fifty Two (IRE)**[19] 6267 8-8-11 **70** (t) BarryMcHugh 5 67
(Marjorie Fife) *chsd ldrs: hdwy over 2f out: rdn along wl over 1f out: drvn and kpt on fnl f* **9/1**

3230 **4** *3 1/4* **Pomme De Terre (IRE)**[17] 6314 5-9-2 **80** (b) CallumRodriguez(5) 14 66
(Michael Dods) *led: pushed clr 1/2-way: rdn along 2f out: hdd 1 1/2f out: sn drvn and wknd fnl f* **11/2**[2]

0530 **5** *5* **Market Choice (IRE)**[11] 6546 4-8-7 **66** JoeFanning 9 36
(Tracy Waggott) *hld up: hdwy whn n.m.r and swtchd rt 2f out: sn rdn and kpt on: nvr rch ldrs* **13/2**[3]

2034 **6** *2 1/2* **Fredricka**[37] 5564 6-9-5 **78** (b[1]) RenatoSouza 6 40
(Ivan Furtado) *dwlt and towards rr: hdwy 2f out: sn rdn and nvr nr ldrs* **25/1**

00 **7** *3/4* **Majdool (IRE)**[81] 3946 4-8-9 **75** (h[1]) NatalieHambling(7) 16 35
(Noel Wilson) *in tch on outer: pushed along over 2f out: sn rdn and wknd over 1f out* **50/1**

6400 **8** *nse* **Money Team (IRE)**[84] 3847 6-9-0 **73** ShaneGray 3 33
(David Barron) *dwlt: a in rr* **16/1**

0250 **9** *1/2* **Aprovado (IRE)**[28] 5947 5-9-9 **82** ConnorBeasley 8 40
(Michael Dods) *chsd ldrs: rdn along over 2f out: sn drvn and wknd* **12/1**

0506 **10** *1 3/4* **Zylan (IRE)**[8] 6663 5-9-5 **78** TonyHamilton 11 31
(Roger Fell) *a towards rr* **11/1**

4545 **11** *3 3/4* **Secret Missile**[98] 3332 7-8-10 **69** (v[1]) JoeDoyle 12 10
(David C Griffiths) *chsd ldr: rdn along 1/2-way: sn wknd* **28/1**

1m 15.02s (2.32) **Going Correction** +0.675s/f (Yiel) **11** Ran SP% **100.4**
Speed ratings (Par 105): **111,107,104,100,93 90,89,88,88,85 80**
CSF £28.84 CT £170.31 TOTE £3.70: £1.50, £2.70, £2.60; EX 30.80 Trifecta £329.80.
**Owner** Reality Partnerships V **Bred** Joe Foley & John Grimes **Trained** Great Habton, N Yorks
■ Favourite Treat was withdrawn. Price at time of withdrawal 4-1. Rule 4 applies to all bets. Deduction - 20p in the pound.

**FOCUS**
A competitive sprint handicap, but a decisive winner, and again it paid to race prominently. The runner-up has been rated to this year's form.

## 6944 CALVERTS CARPETS HAMBLETON CUP H'CAP 1m 4f 8y
**5:15** (5:15) (Class 4) (0-85,84) 3-Y-O+ **£6,469** (£1,925; £962; £481) **Stalls** High

Form RPR
112 **1** **Barwell (IRE)**[21] 6187 3-8-10 **81** CallumRodriguez(5) 7 95+
(Michael Dods) *trckd ldrs: hdwy over 3f out: led wl over 1f out: sn rdn clr: styd on* **11/10**[1]

6640 **2** *3 1/2* **Lopes Dancer (IRE)**[41] 5455 5-9-2 **74** JoeFanning 4 81
(Sally Haynes) *hld up in rr: hdwy on inner over 3f out: swtchd rt to outer and chsd ldrs over 2f out: rdn to chse wnr ent fnl f: sn drvn: carried hd high and no imp* **16/1**

1054 **3** *1 3/4* **Swaheen**[28] 5924 5-9-8 **80** (p) JoeDoyle 3 84
(Julie Camacho) *trckd ldrs: hdwy on inner and cl up over 2f out: rdn wl over 1f out: sn drvn and kpt on same pce* **6/1**[2]

30-4 **4** *2* **Henry Smith**[49] 5164 5-9-6 **81** (be) LewisEdmunds(3) 1 82
(John Weymes) *trckd ldng pair: hdwy over 3f out: rdn to ld over 2f out: drvn and hdd wl over 1f out: sn wknd* **25/1**

633 **5** *shd* **Royal Shaheen (FR)**[14] 6416 4-9-6 **78** (v) BarryMcHugh 2 79
(Alistair Whillans) *led: rdn along over 3f out: hdd over 2f out: sn drvn and grad wknd* **10/1**

4351 **6** *3 3/4* **Sheriff Of Nawton (IRE)**[11] 6551 6-8-12 **70** TonyHamilton 9 65
(Roger Fell) *hld up towards rr: hdwy 5f out: chsd ldrs 3f out: rdn along over 2f out: sn drvn and one pce* **13/2**[3]

3244 **7** *nk* **Chancery (USA)**[26] 6000 9-9-10 **82** (p) DavidNolan 8 76
(David O'Meara) *hld up in rr: hdwy 3f out: sn in tch and rdn along over 2f out: drvn wl over 1f out: no further prog* **9/1**

25-5 **8** *14* **Craggaknock**[84] 991 6-9-9 **81** JasonHart 10 53
(Mark Walford) *towards rr: racd wd in bk st: rdn along over 4f out: outpcd and bhd fr wl over 2f out* **12/1**

66 **9** *41* **Highland Castle**[26] 6000 9-9-3 **75** (t) NeilFarley 11
(Lucinda Egerton) *a in rr: outpcd and bhd fnl 3f* **125/1**

0-55 **10** *2* **Icefall (IRE)**[31] 5803 4-9-11 **83** CamHardie 5
(Tim Easterby) *a in rr: outpcd and bhd fnl 3f* **40/1**

1460 **11** *1 1/2* **Be Perfect (USA)**[15] 6383 8-9-12 **84** (b) JackGarritty 6
(Ruth Carr) *trckd ldr: cl up 1/2-way: rdn along over 3f out: sn lost pl and bhd* **33/1**

2m 43.64s (7.44) **Going Correction** +0.775s/f (Yiel)
**WFA** 3 from 4yo+ 8lb **11** Ran SP% **117.9**
Speed ratings (Par 105): **106,103,102,101,101 98,98,89,61,60 59**
CSF £21.48 CT £81.38 TOTE £1.90: £1.30, £3.80, £1.70; EX 19.90 Trifecta £93.40.
**Owner** Tullpark Limited **Bred** Tullpark Ltd **Trained** Denton, Co Durham

**FOCUS**
Race distance increased by 10yds. A decent handicap, but not all that competitive, and an improving 3yo proved far too good. The runner-up has been rated close to form.

## 6945 CHRISTMAS PARTY NIGHTS @THIRSKRACES BOOK NOW H'CAP 5f
**5:45** (5:45) (Class 4) (0-85,86) 3-Y-O **£3,357** (£3,357; £769; £384) **Stalls** Centre

Form RPR
0212 **1** **Erissimus Maximus (FR)**[22] 6137 3-9-5 **83** (b) JoeFanning 2 88
(Chris Dwyer) *trckd ldrs: hdwy and cl up over 1f out: sn rdn: drvn to ld last 100yds and edgd rt: jnd on line* **3/1**[2]

1431 **1** *dht* **Sheepscar Lad (IRE)**[7] 6670 3-8-12 **79** LewisEdmunds(3) 7 84
(Nigel Tinkler) *trckd ldrs: hdwy over 1f out: effrt and nt clr run ins fnl f: swtchd lft and rdn last 50yds: qcknd wl to join ldr on line* **5/1**[3]

1604 **3** *1/2* **Yorkshiredebut (IRE)**[7] 6679 3-8-12 **76** NeilFarley 3 79
(Paul Midgley) *led: rdn along and jnd over 1f out: drvn and edgd rt ins fnl f: hdd last 100yds: no ex nr fin* **14/1**

4623 **4** *1/2* **Harome (IRE)**[12] 6519 3-9-2 **80** TonyHamilton 8 81
(Roger Fell) *wnt lft s: trckd ldr: rdn to chal wl over 1f out: drvn and ev ch ent fnl f: kpt on same pce towards fin* **7/1**

1-13 **5** *3/4* **Storm Over (IRE)**[22] 6137 3-9-8 **86** ShaneGray 6 85+
(Robert Cowell) *hld up: hdwy over 1f out: rdn ent fnl f: kpt on same pce* **9/4**[1]

1536 **6** *nk* **Foxy Boy**[28] 5920 3-8-9 **73** ConnorBeasley 1 71
(Michael Dods) *trckd ldrs: hdwy over 1f out: rdn ins fnl f: kpt on same pce towards fin* **7/1**

-304 **7** *14* **Plata O Plomo**[125] 2425 3-9-7 **85** DavidNolan 5 32
(David O'Meara) *trckd ldr: cl up 1/2-way: rdn along 2f out: hld whn n.m.r over 1f out: sn wknd* **12/1**

1m 2.5s (2.90) **Going Correction** +0.675s/f (Yiel) **7** Ran SP% **111.8**
Speed ratings (Par 103): **103,103,102,101,100 99,77**
WIN: SL 3.00, EM 1.70; PL: SL 2.70, EM 1.50; EX: SL/EM 11.40 EM/SL 8.50 CSF: EM/SL 8.71, SL/EM 9.71 TC: EM/SL/YD 87.13, SL/EM/YD 95.49; TF: SL/EM/YD 131.20 EM/SL/YD 89.40.
**Owner** Leeds Plywood And Doors Ltd **Bred** Stockvale Bloodstock Ltd **Trained** Langton, N Yorks
**Owner** P Venner **Bred** Derek Clee **Trained** Newmarket, Suffolk

**FOCUS**
A useful 3yo sprint handicap, in which they went a good pace, and there was a thrilling finish. The third is the key to the form, as she's been rated to her standout Catterick win for now.
T/Plt: £131.80 to a £1 stake. Pool: £48,568.05 - 268.92 winning units. T/Qpdt: £20.50 to a £1 stake. Pool: £2,556.89 - 91.86 winning units. **Joe Rowntree**

# 6632 WOLVERHAMPTON (A.W) (L-H)
Saturday, September 9

**OFFICIAL GOING: Tapeta: standard**
Wind: breezy Weather: overcast

## 6946 CELEBRATE CHRISTMAS AT WOLVERHAMPTON APPRENTICE H'CAP (DIV I) 1m 142y (Tp)
**4:55** (4:58) (Class 6) (0-65,67) 3-Y-O+ **£2,587** (£770; £384; £192) **Stalls** Low

Form RPR
163 **1** **Bell Heather (IRE)**[9] 6638 4-9-5 **61** ConnorMurtagh(3) 1 69+
(Patrick Morris) *hld up: hdwy over 1f out: 3 l bhd runner-up ent fnl f: str run u.p to ld last stride* **13/2**[3]

0446 **2** *shd* **Solent Meads (IRE)**[19] 6257 3-9-6 **65** (b) PaddyPilley 6 73
(Daniel Kubler) *led tl hdd after 2f: remained prom: led again wl over 1f out: pushed 3 l clr ent fnl f: kpt on but ct in last stride* **9/1**

205 **3** *5* **Sunshineandbubbles**[13] 6479 4-8-10 **54** (p) RossaRyan(5) 9 51
(Daniel Mark Loughnane) *trckd ldrs: hdwy 2f out: 2nd over 1f out: sn drvn: one pce fnl f* **22/1**

5000 **4** *nk* **Masonic (IRE)**[29] 5895 3-9-4 **63** (h[1]) JaneElliott 8 60
(Robyn Brisland) *mid-div: hdwy into 4th over 1f out: no ex fnl f* **8/1**

6052 **5** *1* **Upended**[32] 5761 3-8-9 **61** SebastianWoods(7) 12 56
(Chris Wall) *hld up in last: hdwy on inner 2f out: r.o ins fnl f: nrst fin* **9/1**

0-06 **6** *shd* **Four Kingdoms (IRE)**[100] 3243 3-8-2 **51** oh4 ow3 RussellHarris(7) 3 48
(K R Burke) *hld up: pushed along 2f out: rdn over 1f out: one pce* **25/1**

064 **7** *3* **Celtic Artisan (IRE)**[19] 6266 6-9-8 **64** (bt) PatrickVaughan(3) 5 52
(Rebecca Menzies) *trckd ldrs: 3rd 3f out: pushed along 2f out: sn rdn and wknd* **4/1**[1]

45 **8** *1 1/2* **Stormbound (IRE)**[12] 6541 8-10-0 **67** (b) MeganNicholls 7 52
(Paul Cole) *hld up: hdwy 2f out: drvn over 1f out: no ex* **13/2**[3]

000 **9** *hd* **Twiggy**[13] 6470 3-9-5 **64** (h) BenRobinson 13 48
(Iain Jardine) *mid-div: drvn over 1f out: one pce fnl f* **25/1**

000 **10** *5* **Kafoo**[26] 5991 4-9-3 **63** KeelanBaker(7) 10 37
(Michael Appleby) *mid-div: hdwy and rdn over 1f out: no ex fnl f* **22/1**

-004 **11** *1* **My Fantasea (IRE)**[17] 6310 4-9-9 **65** (v[1]) KatherineGlenister(3) 2 37
(David Evans) *t.k.h: prom tl led after 2f: hdd wl over 1f out: sn wknd* **5/1**[2]

2620 **12** *nk* **Chelwood Gate (IRE)**[22] 6153 7-9-13 **66** (v) GeorgeBuckell 4 37
(Conor Dore) *hld up: pushed along 3f out: no prog fnl 2f* **20/1**

1m 49.05s (-1.05) **Going Correction** -0.225s/f (Stan)
**WFA** 3 from 4yo+ 6lb **12** Ran SP% **114.7**
Speed ratings (Par 101): **95,94,90,90,89 89,86,85,85,80 79,79**
CSF £56.03 CT £1228.16 TOTE £6.40: £2.60, £3.20, £5.90; EX 71.80 Trifecta £1689.20.
**Owner** Dr Marwan Koukash **Bred** Tinnakill Bloodstock & Joe Osborne **Trained** Prescot, Merseyside

**FOCUS**
The first division of a modest apprentice riders' handicap. They went a slightly muddling gallop on standard Tapeta. The winner has been rated to her recent best.

## 6947 CELEBRATE CHRISTMAS AT WOLVERHAMPTON APPRENTICE H'CAP (DIV II) — 1m 142y (Tp)
**5:25** (5:27) (Class 6) (0-65,66) 3-Y-O+ — **£2,587** (£770; £384; £192) **Stalls** Low

Form — RPR

4002 **1** **Jack Of Diamonds (IRE)**[23] 6101 8-9-6 **64**.................. RossaRyan(5) 1 — 71
(Roger Teal) *mid-div: hdwy 2f out: pushed along into 3rd over 1f out: sn rdn: led ent fnl f: r.o wl* **2/1**[1]

-006 **2** 1 ½ **Eium Mac**[72] 4263 8-8-12 **51** oh1........................................(b) JaneElliott 2 — 55
(Neville Bycroft) *led: hdd over 1f out: sn rdn and relegated to 3rd: rallied to take 2nd ins fnl f* **20/1**

5650 **3** nk **Know Your Name**[9] 6638 6-9-5 **63**................................. WilliamCox(5) 4 — 66
(Donald McCain) *trckd ldr: pushed into ld over 1f out: rdn and hdd ent fnl f: one pce* **12/1**

0-45 **4** nk **Champagne Pink (FR)**[30] 5829 3-8-10 **62**.........(h) PatrickO'Hanlon(7) 11 — 65
(K R Burke) *hld up: rdn and hdwy over 1f out: r.o ins fnl f: nvr nrr* **16/1**

0004 **5** 1 **Sir Lancelott**[29] 5897 5-9-6 **59**.........................(p) BenRobinson 10 — 59
(Adrian Nicholls) *trckd ldrs: drvn over 1f out: rdn and no ex fnl f* **12/1**

4000 **6** hd **Gog Elles (IRE)**[13] 6496 3-7-13 **51** oh5..............................(p) TinaSmith(7) 6 — 52
(J S Moore) *trckd ldrs: 3rd over 1f out: briefly n.m.r: one pce fnl f* **28/1**

325 **7** ¾ **Top Offer**[6] 6725 8-9-2 **58**.........................................(v) ConnorMurtagh(3) 3 — 56
(Patrick Morris) *mid-div: drvn 2f out: effrt u.p over 1f out: no ex ins fnl f* **9/1**

0510 **8** 1 **Flying Fantasy**[23] 6111 5-9-7 **65**............................(p) GabrieleMalune(5) 8 — 61
(Michael Appleby) *hld up: pushed along 2f out: drvn over 1f out: sn rdn and one pce* **6/1**[2]

3404 **9** 2 **Ravenhoe (IRE)**[19] 6263 4-9-13 **66**.................................. RichardOliver 7 — 58
(Mark Johnston) *hld up: drvn 2f out: rdn over 1f out: one pce fnl f* **9/1**

2024 **10** ½ **Dream Magic (IRE)**[40] 5485 3-9-0 **66**..................................... TobyEley(7) 9 — 57
(Daniel Mark Loughnane) *racd in last: drvn 2f out: rdn over 1f out: no imp* **7/1**[3]

6300 **11** 3 ½ **Secret Glance**[59] 4747 5-9-4 **57**..................................... PaddyPilley 12 — 41
(Adrian Wintle) *hld up: pushed along 2f out: rdn over 1f out: no imp: eased* **25/1**

0000 **12** 2 **Multitask**[18] 6288 7-9-5 **65**...................................... JasonWatson(7) 5 — 45
(Gary Moore) *hld up: rn v wd 2f out: no ch after* **10/1**

1m 48.72s (-1.38) **Going Correction** -0.225s/f (Stan)
**WFA** 3 from 4yo+ 6lb — **12** Ran SP% **122.5**
Speed ratings (Par 101): **97,95,95,95,94 94,93,92,90,90 87,85**
CSF £52.55 CT £355.40 TOTE £2.50: £1.60, £6.10, £3.80; EX 54.00 Trifecta £716.10.
**Owner** Inside Track Racing Club **Bred** Gigginstown House Stud **Trained** Great Shefford, Berks

**FOCUS**
The second division of a modest apprentice riders' handicap. The winning time was marginally quicker off a more even tempo. The winner has been rated as just repeating his last turf form.

## 6948 JOIN AT THE RACES ON FACEBOOK H'CAP — 1m 1f 104y (Tp)
**6:00** (6:00) (Class 5) (0-72,73) 3-Y-O+ — **£2,911** (£866; £432; £216) **Stalls** Low

Form — RPR

43-0 **1** **Barnaby Brook (CAN)**[12] 6523 7-8-13 **61**.........................(b) BenCurtis 4 — 69+
(Tom Dascombe) *trckd ldrs: rdn and hdwy over 1f out: r.o wl to ld ins fnl f: sn clr: readily* **14/1**

2253 **2** 1 ¾ **Sir Gnet (IRE)**[22] 6160 3-8-12 **66**.........................................(h) DavidProbert 1 — 70
(Ed Dunlop) *mid-div: pushed along 2f out: hdwy over 1f out: rdn and r.o wl fnl f: tk 2nd last 25yds* **7/4**[1]

6650 **3** ½ **Mighty Lady**[17] 6323 4-9-5 **72**........................................... JaneElliott(5) 5 — 75+
(Robyn Brisland) *last early: pushed along on outer 2f out: hdwy and rdn over 1f out: r.o wl fnl f: tk 3rd last stride: nvr nrr* **16/1**

2411 **4** ½ **Alnasl (IRE)**[10] 6594 3-9-5 **73**.................................(h) EdwardGreatrex 10 — 75
(Archie Watson) *led: drvn 2f out: sn 2 l clr: rdn over 1f out: hdd ins fnl f: no ex and lost two pls nr fin* **5/2**[2]

2150 **5** ½ **Archipeligo**[14] 6431 6-9-3 **72**..........................(p) ConnorMurtagh(7) 11 — 73
(Iain Jardine) *mid-div: rdn and hdwy over 1f out: r.o fnl f* **10/1**

652 **6** nse **Maraakib (IRE)**[11] 6557 5-9-6 **71**...................................(p) JoshDoyle(3) 7 — 72
(David O'Meara) *chsd ldr: pushed along in 2nd 2f out: rdn and hdd for 2nd ent fnl f: grad wknd* **6/1**[3]

0000 **7** 2 ¾ **Accurate**[9] 6637 4-9-6 **68**.......................................... GeorgeDowning 9 — 63
(Ian Williams) *mid-div: pushed along in 4th 2f out: wknd and lost pl over 1f out* **25/1**

4-00 **8** ½ **Miss Minuty**[17] 6307 5-9-1 **70**...................................... JasonWatson(7) 8 — 64
(Jeremy Scott) *hld up: rdn over 1f out: mod late hdwy* **20/1**

0000 **9** 1 ¼ **Idol Deputy (FR)**[22] 6158 11-9-7 **69**...................................(p) RyanPowell 6 — 60
(James Bennett) *mid-div: effrt and pushed along 2f out: no imp ent fnl f* **40/1**

6504 **10** nk **Northdown**[22] 6160 3-9-3 **71**......................................(p) FergusSweeney 12 — 62
(David Lanigan) *trckd ldrs: pushed along 2f out: wknd over 1f out* **16/1**

522- **11** 16 **Vastly (USA)**[352] 6702 8-9-8 **70**......................................(t) TimmyMurphy 3 — 27
(Sophie Leech) *a in rr* **20/1**

1m 58.38s (-2.42) **Going Correction** -0.225s/f (Stan)
**WFA** 3 from 4yo+ 6lb — **11** Ran SP% **122.6**
Speed ratings (Par 103): **101,99,99,98,98 98,95,95,94,93 79**
CSF £38.82 CT £429.59 TOTE £16.20: £3.90, £1.10, £4.60; EX 53.40 Trifecta £954.20.
**Owner** G C Myddelton **Bred** Adena Springs **Trained** Malpas, Cheshire

**FOCUS**
A fair handicap. They went a decent gallop and it is sound form. A small pb from the runner-up.

## 6949 FOLLOW @ATTHERACES ON TWITTER CLAIMING STKS — 7f 36y (Tp)
**6:30** (6:30) (Class 5) 3-Y-O+ — **£3,234** (£962; £481; £240) **Stalls** High

Form — RPR

0-00 **1** **Unforgiving Minute**[64] 4563 6-9-9 **85**.................................. AdamKirby 3 — 92
(John Butler) *chsd ldrs 6 l in arrrs: clsd 3f out: hdwy and pushed along to ld over 1f out: drvn clr ent fnl f: wnt lft: briefly hmpd 3rd horse 75yds out: hld on wl* **7/4**[1]

0236 **2** 1 **Tatlisu (IRE)**[13] 6464 7-9-5 **89**................................ AdamMcNamara(3) 1 — 89
(Richard Fahey) *hld up: pushed along over 1f out: hdwy into 2nd ent fnl f: sn drvn and relegated to 3rd: rdn and regained 2nd nr fin* **6/1**[3]

1343 **3** hd **Horsted Keynes (FR)**[13] 6484 7-9-7 **92**.......................... GeorgeBuckell(5) 2 — 94
(David Simcock) *hld up: hdwy over 1f out: 4th 1f out: drvn into 2nd ins fnl f: briefly hmpd by wnr 75yds out: nt rcvr* **15/8**[2]

1000 **4** 3 ¾ **Michele Strogoff**[12] 6515 4-9-12 **85**.....................................(b) BenCurtis 7 — 83
(Tony Coyle) *chsd ldr: led wl over 1f out: sn hdd and rdn: one pce fnl f* **12/1**

0502 **5** ½ **Al Khan (IRE)**[13] 6464 8-9-6 **84**.........................................(p) TomEaves 5 — 76
(Kevin Ryan) *mid-div: drvn over 1f out: sn rdn: no ex fnl f* **15/2**

3010 **6** 4 **Joey's Destiny (IRE)**[46] 5245 7-8-6 **79**.......................... WilliamCox(7) 9 — 59
(Antony Brittain) *hld up: drvn and effrt on inner 2f out: struggling to go pce whn bdly hmpd by wkng rival over 1f out: no ch after* **12/1**

0055 **7** 11 **Awesome Allan (IRE)**[19] 6276 3-9-1 **73**.............. KatherineGlenister(7) 4 — 43
(David Evans) *led tl hdd wl over 1f out: wknd qckly* **50/1**

1m 27.15s (-1.65) **Going Correction** -0.225s/f (Stan)
**WFA** 3 from 4yo+ 4lb — **7** Ran SP% **114.5**
Speed ratings (Par 103): **100,98,98,94,93 89,76**
CSF £12.95 TOTE £2.50: £1.70, £2.40; EX 13.60 Trifecta £35.60.Joey's Destiny was claimed by Mr Kevin Frost for £5,000
**Owner** Power Geneva Ltd **Bred** Equine Breeding Limited **Trained** Newmarket, Suffolk
■ Stewards' Enquiry : Adam Kirby two-day ban: careless riding (Sep 23-25)

**FOCUS**
A decent claimer. They went a strong gallop and it got rough up the far rail in the closing stages. The winner has been rated to last year's course form.

## 6950 SUN BETS DOWNLOAD THE APP EBF NOVICE STKS — 5f 21y (Tp)
**7:00** (7:01) (Class 5) 2-Y-O — **£3,234** (£962; £481; £240) **Stalls** Low

Form — RPR

5432 **1** **Expecting**[17] 6304 2-8-13 **76**.......................................... CallumShepherd(3) 4 — 77
(Charles Hills) *mde all: pushed along over 1f out: rdn and 1 l clr ent fnl f: r.o wl: on top nr fin* **7/2**[2]

42 **2** 1 ¼ **Midsummer Knight**[96] 3406 2-9-2 **0**......................... SilvestreDeSousa 5 — 73
(Mick Channon) *chsd wnr thrght: drvn over 1f out: 1 l bhd ent fnl f: rdn and r.o: a hld* **5/2**[1]

6 **3** 1 **Bakht Khan (IRE)**[30] 5825 2-9-2 **0**...................................... TomEaves 1 — 69
(Kevin Ryan) *trckd ldrs: pushed along in 3rd over 1f out: rdn fnl f: kpt on* **11/2**

2016 **4** 2 ½ **Hello Girl**[19] 6262 2-9-1 **77**.................................................. DavidProbert 6 — 59
(Dean Ivory) *trckd ldrs: drvn in 4th over 1f out: rdn ent fnl f: no ex* **4/1**[3]

0 **5** 1 ½ **Violet Beauregarde**[44] 5327 2-8-11 **0**.....................(h[1]) StevieDonohoe 3 — 50
(Harry Dunlop) *hld up: pushed along over 1f out: briefly rdn 1f out: one pce fnl f* **50/1**

00 **6** 2 ¼ **Calvin's Gal (IRE)**[9] 6636 2-8-11 **0**..................................... DannyBrock 8 — 41
(Luke McJannet) *hld up: drvn and racd wd over 1f out: sn rdn and no imp* **100/1**

501 **7** ½ **Royal Diplomat (IRE)**[12] 6525 2-9-6 **82**...................... AdamMcNamara(3) 9 — 52
(Richard Fahey) *prom: rdn over 1f out: lost pl and wknd ent fnl f* **9/2**

0 **8** shd **Poppy Jag (IRE)**[66] 4502 2-8-11 **0**.................................... RyanPowell 11 — 39
(Kevin Frost) *racd wd: prom: pushed along 2f out: wknd fnl f* **100/1**

**9** ¾ **Kylie Style** 2-8-8 **0**.......................................................... JackDuern(3) 7 — 37
(Steph Hollinshead) *slowly away: in rr: pushed along 2f out: rdn over 1f out: no imp* **100/1**

642 **10** 3 ¼ **Arizona Mist (IRE)**[49] 5162 2-8-11 **72**............................ PaulMulrennan 10 — 34
(Simon Crisford) *t.k.h: restrained in midfield: pushed along over 1f out: one pce and eased fnl f* **15/2**

0U5 **11** hd **Peas On Earth**[75] 4160 2-8-11 **0**.................................... PatrickMathers 2 — 24
(Derek Shaw) *in rr: pushed along 2f out: rdn over 1f out: no imp* **50/1**

1m 1.04s (-0.86) **Going Correction** -0.225s/f (Stan) — **11** Ran SP% **123.0**
Speed ratings (Par 95): **97,95,93,89,87 83,82,82,81,76 75**
CSF £13.38 TOTE £4.80: £1.60, £1.30, £1.90; EX 15.60 Trifecta £78.70.
**Owner** Kangyu International Racing (HK) Limited **Bred** D J And Mrs Deer **Trained** Lambourn, Berks

**FOCUS**
A fair juvenile novice sprint contest. They went a decent gallop and two well-drawn colts at the head of the betting fought it out. Straightforward form rated around the first two.

## 6951 FOLLOW SUN BETS ON INSTAGRAM NURSERY H'CAP — 6f 20y (Tp)
**7:30** (7:32) (Class 5) (0-75,77) 2-Y-O — **£3,234** (£962; £481; £240) **Stalls** Low

Form — RPR

4402 **1** **Central City (IRE)**[22] 6128 2-9-7 **75**.................................... JackMitchell 6 — 81
(Hugo Palmer) *trckd ldrs: pushed along and hdwy to ld 1f out: rdn and c clr ins fnl f: comf* **4/1**[2]

0556 **2** 2 ¼ **Gabrial The Devil (IRE)**[32] 5752 2-8-12 **66**......................... PhillipMakin 10 — 65
(David O'Meara) *cl up in 2nd: led wl over 1f out: hdd and rdn 1f out: kpt on fnl f* **25/1**

6104 **3** ¾ **Milton Road**[7] 6684 2-9-6 **77**.......................................... CallumShepherd(3) 5 — 74+
(Mick Channon) *hld up: drvn and hdwy over 1f out: r.o strly to take 3rd ins fnl f* **8/1**

3420 **4** 1 **Alaska (IRE)**[25] 6036 2-9-1 **74**........................................ MitchGodwin(5) 8 — 68
(Sylvester Kirk) *mid-div: pushed along 2f out: rdn over 1f out: r.o over 1f out: r.o fnl f* **12/1**

450 **5** hd **Shootingthe Breeze**[30] 5844 2-8-12 **66**.............(p[1]) RichardKingscote 9 — 59
(Tom Dascombe) *led: pushed along and hdd wl over 1f out: sn drvn: rdn and wknd fnl f* **14/1**

053 **6** 1 ½ **Leaderofthepack**[26] 6012 2-8-12 **69**.......................... AdamMcNamara(3) 7 — 58
(Bryan Smart) *trckd ldrs: pushed along in 4th 2f out: rdn over 1f out: wknd* **20/1**

4510 **7** nk **Danehill Desert (IRE)**[49] 5150 2-9-0 **75**................... ConnorMurtagh(7) 12 — 63
(Richard Fahey) *mid-div on outer: drvn 2f out: effrt and rdn over 1f out: no ex* **16/1**

5011 **8** 1 **Flo's Melody**[12] 6517 2-8-11 **65**...................................... PaulMulrennan 11 — 50
(Richard Fahey) *in rr: pushed along 2f out: rdn over 1f out: no imp* **16/1**

5451 **9** ½ **Just For Fun**[9] 6634 2-8-11 **65**....................................(b) PatrickMathers 3 — 49
(Richard Fahey) *slowly away: pushed along to r in mid-div: drvn over 1f out: no imp* **6/1**[3]

3233 **10** 2 ¾ **Indian Warrior**[29] 5865 2-9-5 **73**................................. SilvestreDeSousa 2 — 48
(Ed Dunlop) *mid-div: drvn and wknd over 1f out: eased* **3/1**[1]

2116 **11** 7 **Mr Wagyu (IRE)**[43] 5373 2-9-6 **74**........................................ AdamKirby 4 — 28
(John Quinn) *in rr: last 2f out: sn lost tch* **6/1**[3]

1m 13.19s (-1.31) **Going Correction** -0.225s/f (Stan) — **11** Ran SP% **119.4**
Speed ratings (Par 95): **99,96,95,93,93 91,91,89,89,85 76**
CSF £100.04 CT £790.14 TOTE £5.40: £2.20, £6.80, £2.70; EX 134.80 Trifecta £572.60.
**Owner** Lit Lung Lee **Bred** Mattock Stud **Trained** Newmarket, Suffolk
■ Stewards' Enquiry : Callum Shepherd two-day ban: Careless riding (Sep 23-25)
Mitch Godwin caution: careless riding

**FOCUS**
A fair nursery handicap. They went a decent gallop and a well-supported second favourite won convincingly in a good time. The second and third help set the level.

## 6952 SUNBETS.CO.UK H'CAP — 1m 4f 51y (Tp)
**8:00** (8:00) (Class 3) (0-90,89) 3-Y-O **£7,561** (£2,263; £1,131; £566; £282) **Stalls** Low

Form — RPR

31 **1** **Gold Star**[21] 6194 3-9-0 **88**.................................................. DavidEgan(3) 6 — 104+
(Saeed bin Suroor) *cl 2nd gng wl: pushed along to ld 2f out: drvn and qcknd clr over 1f out: kpt up to work to extend advantage ins fnl f: easily* **5/6**[1]

621 **2** *3 3/4* **Abjar**[29] 5894 3-8-10 **81** RichardKingscote 2 89
(Sir Michael Stoute) *led: pushed along 3f out: hdd 2f out: sn rdn and lft bhd by wnr: kpt on fnl f* **4/1**[2]

2P54 **3** *3 1/4* **Plutocracy (IRE)**[56] 4908 7-9-10 **87** (p) AdamKirby 1 89
(Gary Moore) *hld up: effrt and pushed along 2f out: hdwy into 3rd over 1f out: rdn and r.o fnl f* **18/1**

2052 **4** *2 1/4* **Batts Rock (IRE)**[56] 4908 4-9-9 **86** (p) StevieDonohoe 4 84
(Michael Bell) *hld up in last: wnt 5th 3f out: pushed along 2f out: racd wd and rdn over 1f out: styd on to take 4th ins fnl f* **8/1**[3]

3140 **5** *2* **Afonso De Sousa (USA)**[13] 6482 7-9-12 **89** AlistairRawlinson 3 84
(Michael Appleby) *trckd ldrs: pushed along in 3rd 2f out: rdn and lost pl over 1f out: no ex* **50/1**

6-15 **6** *3* **Angrywhitepyjamas (IRE)**[56] 4882 4-9-7 **84** MartinDwyer 5 74
(William Muir) *mid-div: pushed along 3f out: rdn in 4th 2f out: wknd over 1f out* **18/1**

21-5 **7** *7* **Laqab (IRE)**[13] 6482 4-9-5 **82** SilvestreDeSousa 7 65+
(Roger Varian) *t.k.h: hld up: plld way to front rnk after 4f: restrained but ref to settle: dropped to last 3f out: sn pushed along and lost tch* **4/1**[2]

2m 35.42s (-5.38) **Going Correction** -0.225s/f (Stan)
**WFA** 3 from 4yo+ 8lb **7** Ran SP% **118.2**
Speed ratings (Par 107): **108,105,103,101,100 98,93**
CSF £4.87 TOTE £1.70: £1.40, £1.90; EX 5.10 Trifecta £38.10.
**Owner** Godolphin **Bred** Darley **Trained** Newmarket, Suffolk

**FOCUS**
The feature contest was a decent middle-distance handicap. They appeared to go a muddling gallop but the winning time still compliments a splendid winning performance from the favourite.

## 6953 UNIVERSITY OF WOLVERHAMPTON RACING H'CAP 1m 4f 51y (Tp)
**8:30** (8:33) (Class 6) (0-60,60) 3-Y-O+ **£2,587** (£770; £384; £192) **Stalls** Low

Form RPR

3040 **1** **Hussar Ballad (USA)**[28] 5950 8-9-5 **60** WilliamCox(7) 2 70
(Antony Brittain) *hld up: gd hdwy on outer over 2f out: clsd qckly on ldrs over 1f out: sn led: reminder and c clr ins fnl f: easily* **7/1**[3]

2335 **2** *3 1/2* **Powered (IRE)**[12] 6509 4-9-7 **58** DavidEgan(3) 7 61
(David Evans) *hld up: hdwy 2f out: pushed along over 1f out: rdn and wnt 2nd ent fnl f: r.o wl but no ch w wnr* **17/2**

065 **3** *1 3/4* **The Last Melon**[29] 5894 5-9-8 **56** RyanPowell 9 57
(James Bennett) *trckd ldrs: pushed along in 3rd 2f out: relegated to 5th over 1f out: rallied to regain 3rd ins fnl f* **33/1**

3006 **4** *1* **Yasir (USA)**[12] 6530 9-8-11 **52** KatherineGlenister(7) 4 51
(Conor Dore) *hld up: pushed along over 2f out: hdwy over 1f out: rdn and r.o wl fnl f* **20/1**

4064 **5** *nk* **Star Ascending (IRE)**[12] 6524 5-9-4 **52** (p) TomEaves 6 51
(Jennie Candlish) *cl 2nd: drvn 2f out: rdn and wknd over 1f out* **9/1**

1060 **6** *hd* **Infiniti (IRE)**[19] 6270 4-9-3 **56** JaneElliott(5) 12 54
(Barry Leavy) *led: rdn and hdd over 1f out: wknd fnl f* **14/1**

005 **7** *1 1/2* **Callaghan (GER)**[17] 6305 4-9-2 **50** (t) StevieDonohoe 1 46
(Tom Gretton) *hld up: drvn 2f out: rdn over 1f out: one pce* **28/1**

0120 **8** *1/2* **Filament Of Gold (USA)**[54] 4967 6-9-7 **55** (p) AdamKirby 3 50
(Roy Brotherton) *mid-div: niggled 3f out: hdwy and pushed along 2f out: one pce fnl f* **10/1**

0401 **9** *6* **Tingo In The Tale (IRE)**[22] 6153 8-9-2 **57** (p) TobyEley(7) 11 42
(Tony Forbes) *trckd ldrs: rdn in 4th 3f out: wknd 2f out* **11/1**

5521 **10** *9* **Frozon**[30] 5850 4-9-4 **57** (h) BenRobinson(5) 8 28
(Brian Ellison) *t.k.h: mid-div: drvn 3f out: rdn over 1f out: no ex: eased* **3/1**[1]

3300 **11** *4* **Stonecoldsoba**[52] 1985 4-9-11 **59** SilvestreDeSousa 10 24
(Denis Quinn) *hld up: rdn 3f out: no imp* **7/2**[2]

5235 **12** *71* **Life Of Luxury**[18] 6294 4-9-10 **58** WilliamCarson 5
(Mark Brisbourne) *mid-div: drvn and lost pl 3f out: sn dropped rt out* **8/1**

2m 37.38s (-3.42) **Going Correction** -0.225s/f (Stan) **12** Ran SP% **126.6**
Speed ratings (Par 101): **102,99,98,97,97 97,96,96,92,86 83,36**
CSF £68.54 CT £1887.20 TOTE £8.40: £2.10, £2.90, £7.10; EX 72.00 Trifecta £2566.50.
**Owner** Antony Brittain **Bred** Darley **Trained** Warthill, N Yorks

**FOCUS**
A moderate middle-distance handicap. They went a respectable gallop and two of the more likelier types came to the fore. The second and third help pin the level.
T/Plt: £410.20 to a £1 stake. Pool: £55,519.44 - 98.80 winning units. T/Qpdt: £29.70 to a £1 stake. Pool: £9,408.74 - 233.78 winning units. **Keith McHugh**

6954 - (Foreign Racing) - See Raceform Interactive

# 6115 LEOPARDSTOWN (L-H)
Saturday, September 9

**OFFICIAL GOING: Inner track - good to yielding (good in places); outer track - good (good to yielding in places)**

## 6955a WILLIS TOWERS WATSON CHAMPIONS JUVENILE STKS (GROUP 3) (INNER TRACK) 1m
**4:00** (4:00) 2-Y-O

**£50,427** (£16,239; £7,692; £3,418; £1,709; £854)

RPR

**1** **Nelson (IRE)**[23] 6118 2-9-3 0 DonnachaO'Brien 7 109
(A P O'Brien, Ire) *trckd ldr in 2nd tl led after 1f: rdn to extend advantage 2f out: clr appr fnl f: styd on strly* **11/2**

**2** *3* **Kew Gardens (IRE)**[17] 6331 2-9-3 0 SeamieHeffernan 5 102+
(A P O'Brien, Ire) *racd in mid-div: pushed along in 8th 3f out: stl only 8th ent fnl f: styd on strly into 2nd cl home: nt trble wnr* **10/1**

**3** *3/4* **Delano Roosevelt (IRE)**[44] 5343 2-9-3 0 RyanMoore 6 100+
(A P O'Brien, Ire) *hld up: 9th at 1/2-way: prog and swtchd rt appr fnl f in 7th: styd on strly into 3rd cl home: nrst fin* **11/10**[1]

**4** *1/2* **Riyazan (IRE)**[33] 5724 2-9-3 0 PatSmullen 10 99
(M Halford, Ire) *hld up: clsr on outer at 1/2-way in mid-div: gd prog over 1f out: chsd clr ldr in 2nd ent fnl f: no imp and dropped to 4th cl home* **5/1**[3]

**5** *2* **Camelback (USA)**[20] 6240 2-9-3 102 ColinKeane 9 95
(G M Lyons, Ire) *chsd ldrs: gd hdwy to press ldrs in 3rd after 3f: rdn briefly into 2nd appr fnl f: sn no imp: wknd fnl 100yds* **14/1**

**6** *nk* **Medal Of Honour**[13] 6493 2-9-3 87 (t) WayneLordan 1 94
(Joseph Patrick O'Brien, Ire) *racd in mid-div: 7th at 1/2-way: bit short of room on inner under 2f out: swtchd rt and kpt on same pce ins fnl f* **50/1**

**7** *2 1/2* **Mattymolls Gaga (IRE)**[29] 5903 2-9-3 93 ColmO'Donoghue 4 88
(Mrs John Harrington, Ire) *led for 1f: chsd ldrs in 3rd tl pushed along and nt qckn over 1f out in 4th: wknd ins fnl f* **33/1**

**8** *nk* **Theobald (IRE)**[44] 5345 2-9-3 103 KevinManning 8 88
(J S Bolger, Ire) *sn trckd ldr in 2nd: pushed along over 2f out: nt qckn appr fnl f: sn no ex* **9/2**[2]

**9** *3 1/2* **Sirjack Thomas (IRE)**[12] 6532 2-9-3 86 WJLee 3 80
(Madeleine Tylicki, Ire) *t.k.h early to chse ldrs: 6th at 1/2-way: bit short of room under 2f out: no imp appr fnl f: wknd* **33/1**

**10** *7 1/2* **Verbitude (IRE)**[167] 1383 2-9-3 0 RonanWhelan 2 62
(J S Bolger, Ire) *in rr thrght: nvr a factor: detached appr fnl f: eased fnl 100yds* **66/1**

1m 47.35s (6.15) **Going Correction** +0.85s/f (Soft) **10** Ran SP% **122.9**
Speed ratings: **103,100,99,98,96 96,93,93,90,82**
CSF £60.39 TOTE £7.80: £2.10, £2.80, £1.02; DF 41.70 Trifecta £72.70.
**Owner** Mrs John Magnier & Michael Tabor & Derrick Smith **Bred** Orpendale, Chelston & Wynatt **Trained** Cashel, Co Tipperary

**FOCUS**
Race run on Inner Track. A good performance from the winner, looking like a proper horse now since front-running tactics have been employed. The principals all look improvers.

## 6956a IRISH STALLION FARMS EBF "PETINGO" H'CAP (PREMIER HANDICAP) (INNER TRACK) 1m 4f 180y
**4:35** (4:37) 3-Y-O+

**£75,641** (£24,358; £11,538; £5,128; £2,564; £1,282)

RPR

**1** **Laws Of Spin (IRE)**[16] 6361 4-9-4 **97** (t) ChrisHayes 8 101
(W P Mullins, Ire) *racd in mid-div: gd prog towards outer 2f out to chse ldrs: wnt 3rd appr fnl f: styd on wl to ld ins fnl 50yds: hld on wl* **14/1**

**2** *hd* **Machine Learner**[22] 6135 4-8-10 **89** (v) DeclanMcDonogh 4 93
(Joseph Tuite) *racd in mid-div on inner: chse ldrs fr 1/2-way: short of room under 2f out: wnt 4th ent fnl f: styd on strly into 2nd cl home: jst hld* **8/1**[2]

**3** *nk* **Clongowes (IRE)**[16] 6361 3-8-11 **98** KevinManning 11 104
(J S Bolger, Ire) *sn pressed ldr in 2nd: rdn to ld fnl 100yds: hdd ins fnl 50yds and dropped to 3rd cl home* **16/1**

**4** *shd* **Artful Artist (IRE)**[9] 7708 8-7-13 **83** oh2 (t) KillianLeonard(5) 14 86+
(A J Martin, Ire) *racd towards rr: prog on inner under 2f out: wnt 6th ent fnl f: kpt on wl into 4th cl home: nrst fin* **14/1**

**5** *1/2* **Le Vagabond (FR)**[22] 6165 5-9-3 **96** WJLee 5 99+
(E J O'Grady, Ire) *racd in mid-div: wnt 11th appr fnl f: kpt on strly into 5th cl home: nrst fin* **14/1**

**6** *hd* **Song Of Namibia (IRE)**[65] 4550 6-9-2 **95** (p) GaryCarroll 20 97+
(G M Lyons, Ire) *hld up: rdn and prog 2f out on outer: kpt on wl ins fnl f: nvr nrr* **20/1**

**7** *hd* **Daybreak Boy (IRE)**[48] 5193 4-8-11 **90** PatSmullen 2 92
(Henry De Bromhead, Ire) *trckd ldrs in 3rd: rdn in 4th under 2f out: no imp ins fnl f: kpt on same pce* **10/1**[3]

**8** *nse* **Landsman (IRE)**[15] 6399 4-8-9 **88** (t) ShaneFoley 1 90
(A J Martin, Ire) *racd in mid-div: hmpd and lost position after 2f: kpt on wl towards inner fr under 2f out: nvr nrr* **16/1**

**9** *3/4* **Tara Dylan (IRE)**[15] 6408 5-7-11 **83** oh4 (h) SeanDavis(7) 6 84
(Thomas Mullins, Ire) *racd in mid-div: rdn under 2f out: kpt on same pce ins fnl f* **33/1**

**10** *1/2* **St Stephens Green (IRE)**[21] 6222 6-8-7 **86** ow1 ColmO'Donoghue 3 86
(Emmet Mullins, Ire) *sn led: strly pressed over 1f out: hdd fnl 100yds: wknd clsng stages* **8/1**[2]

**11** *nk* **Utah (IRE)**[79] 3998 3-8-9 **96** SeamieHeffernan 12 97
(A P O'Brien, Ire) *chsd ldrs: clsr in 3rd 3f out: no imp ent fnl f: wknd* **10/1**[3]

**12** *1/2* **Dalton Highway (IRE)**[10] 6603 4-8-4 **83** (v) LeighRoche 13 82
(D K Weld, Ire) *hld up: pushed along towards rr 3f out: kpt on wl ins fnl f: nvr nrr* **25/1**

**13** *hd* **Renneti (FR)**[21] 6214 8-10-3 **110** RWalsh 9 108
(W P Mullins, Ire) *hld up: rdn and sme prog under 3f out: kpt on same pce fr over 1f out: nvr on terms* **12/1**

**14** *nk* **Moonmeister (IRE)**[15] 6399 6-8-10 **89** (t) ConorHoban 15 87
(A J Martin, Ire) *towards rr whn sltly hmpd after 2f: prog under 2f out on inner: kpt on wl tl no ex ins fnl 100yds* **33/1**

**15** *nse* **Snow Falcon (IRE)**[16] 6361 7-8-13 **97** OisinOrr(5) 18 95
(Noel Meade, Ire) *sn chsd ldrs: pushed along in 7th 3f out: sltly hmpd and swtchd rt 2f out: no imp ent fnl f* **3/1**[1]

**16** *hd* **Sea The Lion (IRE)**[16] 6361 6-8-7 **86** RonanWhelan 17 83
(Jarlath P Fahey, Ire) *a towards rr: hdwy over 1f out: kpt on strly under hands and heels ins fnl f: nvr nrr* **12/1**

**17** *3 3/4* **Percy (IRE)**[24] 6079 3-8-10 **97** ColinKeane 16 90
(G M Lyons, Ire) *chsd ldrs: clsr in 4th 6f out: rdn and wknd over 2f out: no ex* **16/1**

**18** *3 3/4* **Tilly's Chilli (IRE)**[32] 5766 3-7-13 **91** oh3 TomMadden(5) 10 78
(Mrs John Harrington, Ire) *chsd ldrs: rdn in 7th 3f out: wknd under 2f out* **33/1**

**19** *2 3/4* **De Coronado (USA)**[22] 6165 4-8-5 **84** (t) WayneLordan 7 65
(A P O'Brien, Ire) *bit slowly away and a towards rr: nvr a factor* **22/1**

**20** *15* **Elusive Duchess (IRE)**[52] 5042 3-7-11 **91** oh5 DannySheehy(7) 19 50
(Adrian Paul Keatley, Ire) *racd in rr of mid-div: wknd to rr over 2f out and sn detached* **50/1**

2m 47.68s (-0.42)
**WFA** 3 from 4yo+ 8lb **20** Ran SP% **142.2**
CSF £129.34 CT £1892.41 TOTE £21.50: £4.00, £2.00, £3.40, £4.20; DF 258.00 Trifecta £1270.70.
**Owner** Ballylinch Stud **Bred** Ballylinch Stud **Trained** Muine Beag, Co Carlow

**FOCUS**
Race run on Inner Track. A stop-start sort of gallop ensured a driving finish and those coming off the pace had the advantage.

## 6957a KPMG ENTERPRISE STKS (GROUP 3) (INNER TRACK) 1m 4f
**5:05** (5:05) 3-Y-O+

**£50,427** (£16,239; £7,692; £3,418; £1,709; £854)

RPR

**1** **Eziyra (IRE)**[32] 5766 3-9-1 107 (h) PatSmullen 2 108+
(D K Weld, Ire) *settled 4th: pushed along under 3f out: clsr on outer 2f out: wnt 2nd over 1f out: styd on wl to ld fnl 100yds: kpt on wl cl home* **9/10**[1]

**2** *3/4* **Exemplar (IRE)**[61] 4707 3-9-1 106 (bt[1]) SeamieHeffernan 6 107+
(A P O'Brien, Ire) *racd in rr: prog whn hung rt 2f out towards stands' side: 5th ent fnl f: styd on strly into 2nd cl home: nrst fin* **14/1**

**3** *shd* **Glamorous Approach (IRE)**[13] 6490 4-9-6 100 (p) KevinManning 1 103
(J S Bolger, Ire) *led early but sn hdd: chsd ldrs in 3rd: rdn into 2nd 2f out: dropped to 3rd over 1f out: kpt on wl for press fnl 100yds* **16/1**

4 shd **Cannonball (IRE)**32 5775 3-9-1 99 ColinKeane 3 107
(G M Lyons, Ire) *hld up in 5th: gd run through on inner appr fnl f into 4th: kpt on strly clsng stages* **10/1**

5 2 **Spanish Steps (IRE)**17 6327 3-9-4 110 RyanMoore 4 106
(A P O'Brien, Ire) *sn led: rdn over 2f out: hdd fnl 100yds: no ex fnl 50yds and wknd to 5th* **9/2**3

6 4 3/4 **US Army Ranger (IRE)**39 5503 4-9-9 110 DonnachaO'Brien 5 95
(A P O'Brien, Ire) *sn chsd ldr in 2nd: rdn and nt qckn under 2f out: dropped to rr ent fnl f: eased fnl 100yds* **7/2**2

2m 41.52s (6.22) **Going Correction** +0.85s/f (Soft)
**WFA** 3 from 4yo 8lb **6** Ran SP% **114.7**
Speed ratings: **113,112,112,112,111 107**
CSF £15.97 TOTE £1.50: £1.02, £3.60; DF 14.60 Trifecta £68.70.

**Owner** H H Aga Khan **Bred** His Highness The Aga Khan's Studs S C **Trained** Curragh, Co Kildare

**FOCUS**
Race run on Inner Track. The stop-start nature of the gallop didn't suit the favourite and she did well to win. It's been rated around the balance of the first three and fifth.

## 6958a COOLMORE FASTNET ROCK MATRON STKS (GROUP 1) (F&M) (OUTER TRACK) 1m
**5:35** (5:37) 3-Y-O+

**£176,495** (£56,837; £26,923; £11,965; £5,982; £2,991)

RPR

1 **Hydrangea (IRE)**37 5571 3-9-0 111 (p) WayneLordan 9 118
(A P O'Brien, Ire) *trckd ldr in 2nd: pushed along over 2f out: dropped to 3rd over 1f out: rallied wl for press in 2nd ins fnl f: kpt on gamely to ld cl home* **20/1**

2 hd **Winter (IRE)**37 5571 3-9-0 119 RyanMoore 3 118+
(A P O'Brien, Ire) *chsd ldrs in 3rd: clsr in 2nd under 2f out: rdn to ld narrowly appr fnl f: sn strly pressed: hdd cl home* **1/1**1

3 3/4 **Persuasive (IRE)**41 5460 4-9-5 112 FrankieDettori 11 117+
(John Gosden) *racd in mid-div: 7th at 1/2-way: prog into 5th over 1f out: kpt on strly fnl 100yds into 3rd cl home: nrst fin* **6/1**3

4 3/4 **Wuheida**34 5693 3-9-0 111 JamesDoyle 6 114
(Charlie Appleby) *chsd ldrs in 4th: rdn to briefly press ldr in 2nd over 1f out: no ex ins fnl 100yds: dropped to 4th clsng stages* **12/1**

5 2 1/2 **Qemah (IRE)**41 5460 4-9-5 114 GregoryBenoist 12 109+
(J-C Rouget, France) *racd in rr: racd keenly: 9th 2f out: wnt 8th ent fnl f: kpt on wl into 5th clsng stages: nvr nrr* **5/1**2

6 nk **Roly Poly (USA)**41 5460 3-9-0 112 (p) SeamieHeffernan 8 108
(A P O'Brien, Ire) *led: strly pressed over 1f out and sn hdd: no ex in 4th ent fnl f: wknd fnl 100yds* **13/2**

7 hd **Rhododendron (IRE)**83 3881 3-9-0 116 PBBeggy 10 107
(A P O'Brien, Ire) *bit slowly away and racd towards rr: 8th at 1/2-way: prog on inner under 2f out: no imp ins fnl f: kpt on same pce* **12/1**

8 1/2 **Intricately (IRE)**23 6119 3-9-0 107 (b1) DonnachaO'Brien 2 106
(Joseph Patrick O'Brien, Ire) *racd in mid-div: 6th at 1/2-way: rdn and no imp over 1f out: kpt on same pce* **50/1**

9 4 1/4 **Diamond Fields (IRE)**23 6119 4-9-5 105 ChrisHayes 4 97
(J A Stack, Ire) *a towards rr: no imp under 2f out* **100/1**

10 2 1/4 **Bean Feasa**56 4928 3-9-0 101 (t) KevinManning 1 91
(J S Bolger, Ire) *racd in mid-div: 5th at 1/2-way: wknd over 1f out* **100/1**

1m 41.89s (0.69) **Going Correction** +0.525s/f (Yiel)
**WFA** 3 from 4yo+ 5lb **10** Ran SP% **118.4**
Speed ratings: **117,116,116,115,112 112,112,111,107,105**
CSF £40.89 CT £153.61 TOTE £27.30: £4.60, £1.02, £2.00; DF 55.80 Trifecta £580.50.

**Owner** Derrick Smith & Mrs John Magnier & Michael Tabor **Bred** Beauty Is Truth Syndicate **Trained** Cashel, Co Tipperary

**FOCUS**
Race run on Outer Track. An extraordinary finish, as the favourite had everything go perfectly for her only to run out of steam late on. A small personal best from the winner, with the standard set by the third, fourth and eighth.

## 6959a CLIPPER LOGISTICS BOOMERANG STKS (GROUP 2) (OUTER TRACK) 1m
**6:10** (6:10) 3-Y-O+

**£100,854** (£32,478; £15,384; £6,837; £3,418; £1,709)

RPR

1 **Suedois (FR)**15 6401 6-9-8 112 DanielTudhope 1 112
(David O'Meara) *hld up in 5th: rdn to chse ldrs in 4th under 2f out: styd on strly between horses ins fnl f to ld cl home* **10/3**3

2 1/2 **True Valour (IRE)**23 6119 3-9-3 108 ShaneFoley 6 110
(J P Murtagh, Ire) *hld up in 6th: swtchd rt 2f out: gd prog on outer into 4th fnl 100yds: kpt on wl into 2nd on line* **25/1**

3 hd **Psychedelic Funk**17 6334 3-9-3 105 (b1) ColinKeane 3 110
(G M Lyons, Ire) *trckd ldr in 2nd: rdn to press ldr fnl 150yds and led ins fnl 100yds: hdd cl home and dropped to 3rd on line* **12/1**

4 shd **Sir John Lavery (IRE)**32 5765 3-9-3 111 RyanMoore 2 111+
(A P O'Brien, Ire) *racd in rr: clsr whn bit short of room under 2f out: again n.m.r ins fnl f and swtchd rt in 6th: styd on strly on outer into 4th cl home: nrst fin* **11/8**1

5 1/2 **Whitecliffsofdover (USA)**32 5765 3-9-3 107 (bt) SeamieHeffernan 5 108
(A P O'Brien, Ire) *sn led: rdn over 1f out: strly pressed ins fnl f: hdd ins fnl 100yds: dropped to 5th cl home* **20/1**

6 1 **Alexios Komnenos (IRE)**23 6119 3-9-3 108 ChrisHayes 4 106
(J A Stack, Ire) *settled in 4th: rdn into 3rd over 1f out: nt qckn fnl 100yds and dropped to 5th clsng stages* **3/1**2

7 12 **Custom Cut (IRE)**23 6119 8-9-8 107 JamesDoyle 7 79
(David O'Meara) *trckd ldrs in 3rd: rdn and nt qckn over 1f out: sn dropped to rr and eased* **14/1**

1m 42.39s (1.19) **Going Correction** +0.525s/f (Yiel)
**WFA** 3 from 6yo+ 5lb **7** Ran SP% **113.2**
Speed ratings: **115,114,114,114,113 112,100**
CSF £71.15 TOTE £4.60: £2.20, £5.80; DF 93.60 Trifecta £337.30.

**Owner** George Turner & Clipper Logistics **Bred** Mme Elisabeth Vidal **Trained** Upper Helmsley, N Yorks

**FOCUS**
Race run on Outer Track. Six horses separated by 2l with the form rated around the second to fifth horses.

## 6960a QIPCO IRISH CHAMPION STKS (GROUP 1) (OUTER TRACK) 1m 2f
**6:45** (6:46) 3-Y-O+

**£608,974** (£202,991; £96,153; £42,735; £21,367; £10,683)

RPR

1 **Decorated Knight**17 6328 5-9-7 119 AndreaAtzeni 10 121
(Roger Charlton) *racd in rr: stl in last under 2f out: prog on outer ent fnl f in 8th: styd on strly to ld ins fnl 100yds: kpt on wl* **25/1**

2 1/2 **Poet's Word (IRE)**36 5592 4-9-7 113 JamesDoyle 9 120
(Sir Michael Stoute) *racd in mid-div: towards rr at 1/2-way: 9th under 2f out: styd on wl towards outer into 5th ent fnl f: briefly on terms fnl 100yds but sn hdd: kpt on wl* **10/1**

3 1 3/4 **Eminent (IRE)**25 6053 3-9-1 116 FrankieDettori 1 117
(Martyn Meade) *led and sn 3 l clr: ld reduced 3f out: rdn under 2f out: strly pressed ins fnl f and hdd fnl 100yds: no ex clsng stages in 3rd* **3/1**2

4 3/4 **Moonlight Magic**51 5087 4-9-7 112 (t) KevinManning 5 115
(J S Bolger, Ire) *chsd ldrs in 4th: rdn to trck ldr in 2nd over 1f out: no ex fnl 100yds where dropped to 4th: kpt on same pce* **33/1**

5 3/4 **The Taj Mahal (IRE)**28 5953 3-9-1 112 DonnachaO'Brien 4 114
(A P O'Brien, Ire) *racd in mid-div: prog towards outer over 1f out: bit short of room fnl 100yds: kpt on wl into 5th cl home* **50/1**

6 shd **Cliffs Of Moher (IRE)**17 6328 3-9-1 118 (t) SeamieHeffernan 6 116+
(A P O'Brien, Ire) *hld up in 8th: gd prog on inner into mid-div 2f out: sn short of room in 5th: again denied room ent fnl f: kpt on wl under hands and heels clsng stages* **9/1**3

7 nse **Churchill (IRE)**17 6328 3-9-1 123 RyanMoore 2 115+
(A P O'Brien, Ire) *chsd ldrs in 3rd: pushed along in 4th whn sltly hmpd under 2f out: 3rd ent fnl f: sn no ex: eased clsng stages* **8/11**1

8 1 **Zhukova (IRE)**69 4419 5-9-4 115 PatSmullen 3 108
(D K Weld, Ire) *racd in mid-div: rdn to chse ldrs over 1f out: no imp fnl 100yds: kpt on same pce* **10/1**

9 3 1/2 **The Grey Gatsby (IRE)**30 5862 6-9-7 110 DeclanMcDonogh 7 104
(D K Weld, Ire) *a towards rr: rdn and no imp under 2f out: kpt on one pce* **66/1**

10 4 1/2 **Success Days (IRE)**42 5436 5-9-7 114 (t) ShaneFoley 8 95
(K J Condon, Ire) *chsd clr ldr in 2nd tl rdn and edgd lft under 2f out: nt qckn over 1f out and sn wknd* **40/1**

2m 8.36s (0.16) **Going Correction** +0.525s/f (Yiel)
**WFA** 3 from 4yo+ 6lb **10** Ran SP% **123.8**
Speed ratings: **120,119,118,117,117 116,116,116,113,109**
CSF £256.02 CT £988.36 TOTE £26.60: £5.00, £3.10, £1.80; DF 234.10 Trifecta £1392.90.

**Owner** Saleh Al Homaizi & Imad Al Sagar **Bred** Saleh Al Homaizi & Imad Al Sagar **Trained** Beckhampton, Wilts

**FOCUS**
Race run on Outer Track. Difficult to know what to make of this Group 1, a tactical affair and an outcome which suggests it was a sub-standard contest. Personal bests for both the front two, with a good standard set around the third, fourth and fifth.

## 6961a IRISH STALLION FARMS EBF "SOVEREIGN PATH" H'CAP (PREMIER HANDICAP) (OUTER TRACK) 7f
**7:20** (7:20) 3-Y-O+

**£75,641** (£24,358; £11,538; £5,128; £2,564; £1,282)

RPR

1 **Burnt Sugar (IRE)**14 6419 5-9-4 **95** DeclanMcDonogh 12 107+
(Roger Fell) *racd in mid-div: prog on outer over 1f out: rapid hdwy to ld fnl 150yds: styd on strly* **7/1**3

2 2 **Silverkode (IRE)**42 5444 3-9-4 **99** GaryCarroll 10 104
(Joseph G Murphy, Ire) *racd in mid-div: tk clsr order under 2f out: rdn to dispute ins fnl f: hdd fnl 150yds and nt qckn w wnr: kpt on same pce* **5/1**2

3 1 **Withernsea (IRE)**36 5594 6-9-8 **99** DonnachaO'Brien 1 103
(Richard Fahey) *racd in mid-div: rdn over 2f out: clsr ent fnl f: styd on wl into 3rd ins fnl 100yds: nvr nrr* **4/1**1

4 1 3/4 **Have A Nice Day**21 6215 7-8-13 **90** (b1) RonanWhelan 5 89
(John James Feane, Ire) *chsd ldrs in 4th: 3rd at 1/2-way: rdn dispute appr fnl f and sn led: hdd fnl 150yds: no ex and sn dropped to 4th* **16/1**

5 1/2 **Texas Rock (IRE)**21 6215 6-9-12 **103** (p) WJLee 18 101
(M C Grassick, Ire) *racd in mid-div: rdn and prog towards outer over 1f out: kpt on wl fnl f into 5th clsng stages: nvr nrr* **12/1**

6 1/2 **Glastonbury Song (IRE)**80 3959 3-9-10 **105** ColinKeane 7 99
(G M Lyons, Ire) *hld up: prog on inner under 2f out: chsd ldrs appr fnl f in 4th: no imp fnl 100yds: kpt on same pce* **11/1**

7 nse **Elusive Time (IRE)**13 6491 9-8-13 **93** (p) RossCoakley(3) 9 89
(Takashi Kodama, Ire) *chsd ldrs: pushed along in 5th under 2f out: nt qckn ins fnl f: kpt on same pce* **20/1**

8 1/2 **Baraweez (IRE)**7 6685 7-9-5 **96** ChrisHayes 17 91+
(Brian Ellison) *racd in rr of mid-div: prog appr fnl f: styd on wl clsng stages: nvr on terms* **9/1**

9 nk **Tempera**9 6642 3-9-2 **97** PatSmullen 16 89+
(D K Weld, Ire) *racd towards rr: pushed along over 2f out: kpt on wl ins fnl f: nvr nrr* **9/1**

10 1 **Geological (IRE)**22 6164 5-9-1 **97** DonaghO'Connor(5) 2 88
(Damian Joseph English, Ire) *led tl hdd after 2f: trckd ldrs tl nt qckn appr fnl f: no ex* **40/1**

11 3/4 **Marshall Jennings (IRE)**32 5765 5-9-10 **101** ColmO'Donoghue 3 90
(Mrs John Harrington, Ire) *chsd ldrs in 3rd: 2nd at 1/2-way: rdn to dispute under 2f out tl hdd appr fnl f: wknd* **16/1**

12 nk **Turbine (IRE)**13 6491 4-8-12 **89** (tp) SeamieHeffernan 14 78
(Denis Gerard Hogan, Ire) *trckd ldr tl led after 2f: hdd appr fnl f: wknd* **14/1**

13 1 **Stormy Belle (IRE)**13 6491 3-8-11 **92** LeighRoche 11 76
(P A Fahy, Ire) *sn chsd ldrs in 5th: rdn and nt qckn appr fnl f: sn one pce* **25/1**

14 nse **Remarkable Lady (IRE)**13 6491 4-9-3 **94** (tp) WayneLordan 8 80
(H Rogers, Ire) *racd towards rr: rdn along in rr under 2f out: kpt on ins fnl f: nvr on terms* **28/1**

15 1 **Elusive Beauty (IRE)**9 6642 3-8-12 **93** (v) ShaneFoley 15 74
(K J Condon, Ire) *bit slowly away and racd towards rr: gd hdwy on inner over 1f out to chse ldrs whn short of room ent fnl f and checked: sn eased* **33/1**

16 nse **Holy Cat (IRE)**22 6164 3-8-4 **92** (v1) SeanDavis(7) 4 73
(M D O'Callaghan, Ire) *chsd ldrs on inner whn hmpd after 2f and dropped to mid-div: rdn and no imp appr fnl f* **16/1**

17 *hd* **Noivado (IRE)**[100] 3268 3-9-5 **100** KevinManning 6 80
(G M Lyons, Ire) *chsd ldrs on inner: swtchd off rails over 2f out: nt qckn appr fnl f: wknd* **25/1**

18 *½* **Duchess Of France (IRE)**[9] 6642 4-8-6 **90** (t) DannySheehy(7) 13 71
(Adrian Paul Keatley, Ire) *racd in rr of mid-div: pushed along under 2f out: no imp appr fnl f: sn no ex* **20/1**

1m 27.79s (-0.91) **Going Correction** +0.125s/f (Good)
**WFA** 3 from 4yo+ 4lb **18 Ran SP% 135.6**
Speed ratings: **110,107,106,104,104 103,103,102,102,101 100,100,98,98,97 97,97,96**
Not Won. Pool of 125,417.29 carried forward to Curragh on Sunday 10th September. Tote Aggregates: 2016: 968,977.00 2017: 785,940.00 CSF £42.22 CT £175.39 TOTE £8.60: £2.10, £1.70, £1.30, £3.90; DF 55.70 Trifecta £377.20.
**Owner** Middleham Park Racing XL & Partner **Bred** Ballylinch Stud **Trained** Nawton, N Yorks

**FOCUS**
Race run on Outer Track. A concluding example on the day of the advantage of coming wide from off the pace as the winner stormed to victory. The third helps set the standard, with the fourth, sixth, ninth and tenth all rated close to their recent form.
T/Jkpt: @5,157.70. Pool: @29,427.62 - 4.0 winning units. T/Plt: @305.90. Pool: @43,414.05 - 99.33 winning units. **Alan Hewison**

## 3103 BORDEAUX LE BOUSCAT (R-H)
Saturday, September 9

**OFFICIAL GOING: Turf: very soft**

### 6963a PRIX MILLKOM (LISTED RACE) (3YO) (TURF) 1m
**1:50** 3-Y-O **£23,504** (£9,401; £7,051; £4,700; £2,350)

RPR

1 **Miss Julia Star (FR)**[44] 3-8-13 0 (p) AntoineHamelin 6 102
(B De Montzey, France) **114/10**

2 *nk* **Argentic (FR)**[39] 5522 3-9-2 0 MaximeGuyon 9 104+
(F Head, France) **31/5**[3]

3 *nk* **D'bai (IRE)**[42] 5392 3-9-2 0 (b) MickaelBarzalona 8 103+
(Charlie Appleby) **6/5**[1]

4 *7* **Manahir (FR)**[46] 3-9-2 0 Pierre-CharlesBoudot 1 87
(H-A Pantall, France) **26/5**[2]

5 *nk* **Charlot The Kid (FR)** 3-9-2 0 Francois-XavierBertras 5 87
(C Delcher-Sanchez, France) **171/10**

6 *3½* **Skalleto (FR)**[45] 3-9-2 0 AnthonyCrastus 2 78
(P Sogorb, France) **148/10**

7 *nk* **Time's Arrow (IRE)**[50] 5115 3-9-2 0 StephanePasquier 7 78
(P Sogorb, France) **39/1**

8 *11* **Waltz Key (FR)**[70] 3-8-13 0 ChristopheSoumillon 4 49
(J-C Rouget, France) **26/5**[2]

9 *1* **Livrable**[105] 3103 3-9-2 0 JulienAuge 3 50
(C Ferland, France) **269/10**

1m 41.04s **9 Ran SP% 117.6**
PARI-MUTUEL (all including 1 euro stake): WIN 12.40; PLACE 2.10, 1.90, 1.30; DF 25.30; SF 59.80.
**Owner** Bruno De Montzey **Bred** Mme E Vayssier & J Vayssier **Trained** France

6963a (Foreign Racing) - See Raceform Interactive

## 6444 YORK (L-H)
Sunday, September 10

**OFFICIAL GOING: Good to soft (soft in places; overall 6.0; home straight; far side 6.1, centre 6.2, stands' side 6.3)**
Wind: Strong and blustery behind Weather: Cloudy with showers

### 6964 TOM O'RYAN MEMORIAL APPRENTICE H'CAP (A LEG OF THE GO RACING IN YORKSHIRE FUTURE STARS SERIES) 7f
**1:55** (1:56) (Class 4) (0-80,81) 4-Y-O+ **£7,762** (£2,310; £1,154; £577) **Stalls** Low

Form RPR

4364 1 **Dark Intention (IRE)**[42] 5455 4-8-12 **74** CallumRodriguez(3) 16 85+
(Lawrence Mullaney) *towards rr and pushed along 1/2-way: swtchd rt and hdwy over 2f out: rdn to chse ldrs over 1f out: styd on wl fnl f to ld last 50 yds* **13/2**[1]

6443 2 *2¼* **Roll On Rory**[8] 6672 4-9-4 **77** (v) CliffordLee 3 82
(Jason Ward) *led: pushed along and jnd 3f out: rdn wl over 1f out: drvn ent fnl f: hdd and no ex last 50 yds* **7/1**[2]

341 3 *½* **Short Work**[21] 6238 4-8-9 **68** (b) ShelleyBirkett 1 72
(David O'Meara) *prom: hdwy and cl up over 2f out: rdn to chal over 1f out: drvn and ev ch ins fnl f: kpt on same pce towards fin* **14/1**

6062 4 *2¼* **Lagenda**[11] 6570 4-9-8 **81** (b) LewisEdmunds 11 79
(Kevin Ryan) *trckd ldrs: pushed along wl over 2f out: rdn wl over 1f out: kpt on u.p fnl f* **8/1**[3]

0502 5 *nse* **God Willing**[9] 6663 6-9-0 **78** (b) GerO'Neill(5) 12 76
(Declan Carroll) *trckd ldrs: hdwy over 2f out: rdn over 1f out: drvn and kpt on same pce fnl f* **8/1**[3]

4162 6 *5* **Cliff (IRE)**[12] 6546 7-8-1 **67** FayeMcManoman(7) 2 52
(Nigel Tinkler) *midfield: hdwy over 2f out: rdn over 1f out: nvr able to chal* **16/1**

5030 7 *1½* **Chaplin Bay (IRE)**[9] 6663 5-8-5 **67** (p) JaneElliott(3) 9 48
(Ruth Carr) *sltly hmpd s and rr: hdwy over 2f out: sn rdn and kpt on fnl f: nvr nr ldrs* **16/1**

4140 8 *2¾* **Destroyer**[20] 6266 4-9-6 **79** KieranShoemark 6 53
(Tom Tate) *chsd ldrs: rdn along over 2f out: drvn wl over 1f out: grad wknd* **12/1**

4414 9 *½* **Tadaawol**[11] 6570 4-8-12 **78** (p) BenSanderson(7) 14 50
(Roger Fell) *rr tl sme late hdwy* **9/1**

3323 10 *1¾* **Chiswick Bey (IRE)**[14] 6464 9-8-3 **67** ConnorMurtagh(5) 8 35
(Richard Fahey) *towards rr: rdn along over 2f out: plugged on: nvr a factor* **25/1**

4105 11 *hd* **Art Echo**[37] 5610 4-9-5 **78** (t) CharlieBennett 10 45
(John Mackie) *nvr bttr than midfield* **12/1**

0432 12 *shd* **Quick Look**[1] 6943 4-8-11 **77** RyanTimby(7) 20 44
(Michael Easterby) *chsd ldrs: rdn along over 2f out: sn wknd* **20/1**

2425 13 *2* **Alpine Dream (IRE)**[10] 6629 4-8-11 **75** (b) JamieGormley(5) 15 37
(Tim Easterby) *a towards rr* **16/1**

5332 14 *1¾* **Ticks The Boxes (IRE)**[26] 6049 5-8-9 **71** ow3 (p) RobJFitzpatrick(3) 7 28
(John Wainwright) *dwlt: a in rr* **25/1**

0516 15 *9* **Mywayistheonlyway (IRE)**[33] 5739 4-9-3 **76** PhilDennis 19 10
(Grant Tuer) *midfield: hdwy on wd outside to chse ldrs over 2f out: sn rdn along and wknd over 1f out* **50/1**

6000 16 *10* **In The Red (IRE)**[15] 6442 4-8-13 **75** LuluStanford(3) 13
(Martin Smith) *a towards rr* **16/1**

6012 17 *15* **Jacob's Pillow**[27] 5994 6-8-13 **75** RowanScott(3) 17
(Rebecca Bastiman) *chsd ldrs: rdn along wl over 2f out: sn wknd* **20/1**

2-33 18 *2¼* **Garter (IRE)**[221] 505 4-8-5 **67** MeganNicholls(3) 18
(Richard Fahey) *a towards rr* **20/1**

1m 26.74s (1.44) **Going Correction** +0.30s/f (Good) **18 Ran SP% 127.6**
Speed ratings (Par 105): **103,100,99,97,97 91,89,86,86,84 83,83,81,79,69 57,40,38**
CSF £46.51 CT £658.88 TOTE £7.10: £2.10, £2.10, £4.30, £2.60; EX 60.40 Trifecta £1486.40.
**Owner** Ian Buckley **Bred** Desert Star Phoenix Jvc **Trained** Great Habton, N Yorks

**FOCUS**
Callum Rodriguez, who rode the first winner, said it was "good to soft". The time confirmed that view as it was 4.74 seconds slower than standard, despite a fresh wind mainly behind the runners in the straight, where they came down the centre of the track. This big-field event was largely dominated those racing prominently, the winner an exception.

### 6965 HANSON SPRINGS H'CAP 1m 2f 56y
**2:30** (2:32) (Class 3) (0-90,88) 3-Y-O+ **£12,291** (£3,657; £1,827; £913) **Stalls** Low

Form RPR

104 1 **Carnageo (FR)**[17] 6349 4-9-6 **84** (b) PaulHanagan 1 92
(Richard Fahey) *trckd ldrs: hdwy over 2f out: rdn over 1f out: drvn to ld last 100 yds: edgd lft towards fin: hld on wl* **12/1**

1210 2 *hd* **Save The Bees**[15] 6449 9-8-12 **83** GerO'Neill(7) 7 90
(Declan Carroll) *led: styd nr far rail home st: rdn over 2f out: drvn over 1f out: hdd last 100 yds: kpt on gamely towards fin* **14/1**

1221 3 *2* **Indian Chief (IRE)**[5] 6789 7-9-4 **82** 6ex ConnorBeasley 8 85
(Rebecca Bastiman) *hld up in rr: hdwy wl over 2f out: chsd ldrs over 1f out: rdn to chse ldng pair and edgd lft ins fnl f: kpt on same pce towards fin* **5/1**[1]

4106 4 *1¾* **Dance King**[16] 6399 7-9-8 **86** (tp) JamesSullivan 15 86
(Tim Easterby) *dwlt: hld up towards rr: hdwy over 2f out: rdn over 1f out: kpt on wl fnl f: nrst fin* **9/1**

2454 5 *1½* **Innocent Touch (IRE)**[13] 6515 6-9-10 **88** TonyHamilton 3 85
(Richard Fahey) *trckd ldr: c wd to centre home st: cl up 3f out: rdn along wl over 1f out: drvn appr fnl f: grad wknd* **11/2**[2]

2030 6 *½* **Parish Boy**[8] 6701 5-8-13 **77** JosephineGordon 4 73
(David Loughnane) *t.k.h: hld up towards rr: hdwy wl over 2f out: chsd ldrs wl over 1f out: sn rdn and kpt on same pce fnl f* **14/1**

4123 7 *½* **Visitant**[37] 5609 4-9-7 **85** PatrickMathers 6 80
(David Thompson) *chsd ldrs: hdwy on outer 3f out: rdn along over 2f out: drvn wl over 1f out: kpt on same pce* **13/2**[3]

21- 8 *3* **Trading Point (FR)**[331] 7317 3-8-12 **82** PhillipMakin 5 72
(John Quinn) *trckd ldrs: hdwy over 3f out: cl up centre 2f out: rdn and ev ch ent fnl f: sn drvn and wknd* **7/1**

00-5 9 *10* **Trendsetter (IRE)**[237] 266 6-9-7 **88** AaronJones(3) 14 58
(Micky Hammond) *hld up: a in rr* **50/1**

2003 10 *8* **Jacbequick**[12] 6563 6-9-3 **84** (p) JoshDoyle(3) 10 39
(David O'Meara) *chsd ldrs: rdn along 3f out: wknd over 2f out* **20/1**

0542 11 *1½* **Briyouni (FR)**[20] 6266 4-9-1 **79** (p) TomEaves 11 31
(Kevin Ryan) *prom: rdn along over 3f out: wknd 2f out* **10/1**

3435 12 *23* **Boots And Spurs**[22] 6209 8-8-12 **81** (v) GeorgeBuckell(5) 13
(Scott Dixon) *in tch on outer: rdn along 3f out: sn wknd* **20/1**

2m 14.3s (1.80) **Going Correction** +0.30s/f (Good)
**WFA** 3 from 4yo+ 6lb **12 Ran SP% 109.5**
Speed ratings (Par 107): **104,103,102,100,99 99,98,96,88,82 80,62**
CSF £144.66 CT £820.48 TOTE £11.70: £3.60, £3.00, £2.10; EX 131.40 Trifecta £568.40.
**Owner** The Up For Anything Syndicate **Bred** Viktor Timoshenko **Trained** Musley Bank, N Yorks

■ Grapevine was withdrawn. Price at time of withdrawal 10-1. Rule 4 applies to all bets - deduction 5p in the pound.

**FOCUS**
Race run over an additional 22yds. Decent handicap form. They all came down the middle except the runner-up, who stayed on the rail.

### 6966 BETFRED SUPPORTS YORK AGAINST CANCER GARROWBY STKS (LISTED RACE) 6f
**3:00** (3:00) (Class 1) 3-Y-O+
**£28,355** (£10,750; £5,380; £2,680; £1,345; £675) **Stalls** High

Form RPR

3200 1 **Tommy Taylor (USA)**[22] 6198 3-9-0 **100** TomEaves 4 108
(Kevin Ryan) *cl up on outer: chal wl over 1f out and sn rdn: drvn to ld ins fnl f: sn edgd rt: jst hld on* **14/1**

3-14 2 *nse* **Downforce (IRE)**[106] 3099 5-9-5 **110** WJLee 9 111+
(W McCreery, Ire) *chsd ldrs: hdwy 2f out: nt clr run and swtchd lft ent fnl f: sn rdn to chal: drvn and ev ch last 75yds: jst failed* **6/1**

0500 3 *3½* **Mobsta (IRE)**[36] 5640 5-9-2 **98** GrahamLee 5 97
(Mick Channon) *in rr and rdn along 1/2-way: hdwy over 1f out: swtchd lft to outer and drvn ent fnl f: styd on wl to take 3rd nr fin* **25/1**

4232 4 *nk* **Steady Pace**[15] 6428 4-9-2 **108** JosephineGordon 8 96
(Saeed bin Suroor) *cl up: rdn along wl over 1f out: drvn and kpt on same pce fnl f* **7/2**[2]

401 5 *hd* **Lancelot Du Lac (ITY)**[36] 5640 7-9-2 **107** (h) PatCosgrave 2 95
(Dean Ivory) *led: rdn along over 1f out: drvn and edgd rt ent fnl f: sn hdd and edgd lft: hld whn n.m.r last 150yds: one pce towards fin* **3/1**[1]

-200 6 *3¼* **Don't Touch**[16] 6401 5-9-2 **109** (v) TonyHamilton 7 85
(Richard Fahey) *cl up on stands' rail: rdn along wl over 1f out: drvn and wknd ent fnl f* **9/2**[3]

511- 7 *nse* **Spiritual Lady**[317] 7667 3-8-9 **105** DavidProbert 6 80
(Philip McBride) *trckd ldrs: hdwy over 1f out: ev ch whn n.m.r ent fnl f: sn squeezed out and wknd* **9/1**

1m 12.62s (0.72) **Going Correction** +0.30s/f (Good)
**WFA** 3 from 4yo+ 2lb **7 Ran SP% 100.2**
Speed ratings (Par 111): **107,106,102,101,101 97,97**
CSF £70.81 TOTE £14.90: £4.50, £2.50; EX 82.90 Trifecta £2282.90.
**Owner** Mrs Angie Bailey **Bred** Dr John A Chandler **Trained** Hambleton, N Yorks

■ Intisaab was withdrawn. Price at time of withdrawal 7-1. Rule 4 applies to all bets - deductuion 10p in the pound.

**FOCUS**
A fair Listed sprint in which two pulled clear.

## 6967 JUDITH MARSHALL MEMORIAL BRITISH EBF NOVICE STKS (PLUS 10 RACE) (SIRE-RESTRICTED RACE) 7f
3:35 (3:35) (Class 3) 2-Y-O £7,762 (£2,310; £1,154; £577) Stalls Low

| Form | | | | RPR |
|---|---|---|---|---|
| | 1 | | **Elarqam** 2-9-2 0 DaneO'Neill 4 | 94+ |
| | | | (Mark Johnston) *wnt rt s: trckd ldrs: hdwy over 2f out: rdn to chse ldr over 1f out: led ent fnl f: sn clr: kpt on strly* **10/11**[1] | |
| 2 | 2 | 3 ¾ | **Ayutthaya (IRE)**[16] 6380 2-9-2 0 TomEaves 2 | 84 |
| | | | (Kevin Ryan) *led: pushed along over 2f out: rdn and edgd rt over 1f out: hdd and drvn ent fnl f: kpt on: no ch w wnr* **2/1**[2] | |
| 5 | 3 | 3 | **Buckstopper Kit (USA)**[16] 6380 2-9-2 0 (b[1]) PaulHanagan 7 | 77 |
| | | | (Richard Fahey) *chsd ldrs: rdn along over 2f out: kpt on fnl f* **12/1** | |
| 451 | 4 | 1 ¼ | **Fighting Irish (IRE)**[43] 5430 2-9-8 77 JosephineGordon 1 | 79 |
| | | | (Harry Dunlop) *trckd ldr: cl up 1/2-way: rdn along 2f out: drvn over 1f out: grad wknd* **7/1**[3] | |
| 0 | 5 | 15 | **The Knot Is Tied (IRE)**[9] 6658 2-9-2 0 JamesSullivan 5 | 36 |
| | | | (Tim Easterby) *sn outpcd and bhd* **33/1** | |
| | 6 | hd | **Enforcement (IRE)** 2-9-2 0 TimmyMurphy 3 | 35 |
| | | | (Martin Keighley) *chsd ldrs: pushed along 3f out: rdn over 2f out: sn wknd* **33/1** | |

1m 26.77s (1.47) **Going Correction** +0.30s/f (Good) 6 Ran SP% **111.8**
Speed ratings (Par 99): **103,98,95,93,76 76**
CSF £2.88 TOTE £1.90: £1.30, £1.20; EX 3.10 Trifecta £14.80.
**Owner** Hamdan Al Maktoum **Bred** Floors Farming **Trained** Middleham Moor, N Yorks

**FOCUS**
A decent novice event confined to the progeny of stallions who won at 9.5f plus, with a clear-cut winner. The runners came down the centre of the straight at first before ending up near the stands' rail. The runner-up and fourth suggest this sort of opening level is sensible.

## 6968 TRANSCORE LTD 27TH ANNIVERSARY H'CAP 2m 56y
4:10 (4:10) (Class 4) (0-85,83) 3-Y-O+ £7,762 (£2,310; £1,154; £577) Stalls Low

| Form | | | | RPR |
|---|---|---|---|---|
| 40-3 | 1 | | **Blue Hussar (IRE)**[115] 2770 6-9-10 79 PJMcDonald 12 | 89 |
| | | | (Micky Hammond) *trckd ldrs: hdwy over 4f out: cl up 3f out: sn led: rdn clr over 1f out: kpt on strly u.p fnl f* **12/1** | |
| 3520 | 2 | 3 | **Shearling**[17] 6357 4-9-5 79 BenRobinson(5) 10 | 85 |
| | | | (Brian Ellison) *hld up in rr: hdwy 5f out: effrt on wd outside over 2f out: rdn wl over 1f out: drvn to chse wnr ins fnl f: no imp towards fin* **6/1**[2] | |
| 0442 | 3 | ¾ | **Transpennine Star**[34] 5700 4-8-12 72 (p) CallumRodriguez(5) 11 | 77 |
| | | | (Michael Dods) *trckd ldng pair: hdwy over 5f out: cl up over 3f out: sn led: rdn along and hdd wl over 2f out: drvn over 1f out: kpt on same pce fnl f* **8/1**[3] | |
| 1121 | 4 | 3 ¼ | **Graceful Lady**[43] 5438 4-9-0 76 DarraghKeenan(7) 7 | 77 |
| | | | (Robert Eddery) *dwlt and hld up in rr: hdwy over 3f out: effrt on wd outside 2f out: sn chsng ldrs and rdn: drvn and one pce appr fnl f* **6/1**[2] | |
| 6215 | 5 | 4 ½ | **Di Alta (IRE)**[34] 5715 3-9-2 82 PatCosgrave 5 | 80 |
| | | | (Ed Walker) *hld up: hdwy and in tch 7f out: chsd ldrs over 4f out: rdn along 3f out: drvn and plugged on one pce fnl 2f* **6/1**[2] | |
| -055 | 6 | nk | **Cousin Khee**[26] 6038 10-8-12 70 CharlieBennett(3) 14 | 65 |
| | | | (Hughie Morrison) *hld up in midfield: hdwy over 4f out: chsd ldrs over 2f out: sn rdn and kpt on one pce* **20/1** | |
| 6430 | 7 | 2 | **Aramist (IRE)**[18] 6317 7-9-0 69 BenCurtis 8 | 62 |
| | | | (Sally Haynes) *in tch: hdwy 4f out: rdn along 3f out: drvn over 2f out: sn no imp* **20/1** | |
| 1645 | 8 | 6 | **Zenafire**[8] 6680 8-8-13 71 (p) SammyJoBell(3) 1 | 57 |
| | | | (Sarah Hollinshead) *midfield: pushed along 5f out: rdn along over 3f out: sn drvn and wknd* **16/1** | |
| /411 | 9 | 1 | **Attention Seaker**[24] 6090 7-9-1 70 (t) JasonHart 4 | 55 |
| | | | (Tim Easterby) *hld up: hdwy into midfield on inner over 5f out: rdn along to chse ldrs over 3f out: sn outpcd* **6/1**[2] | |
| 0-50 | 10 | ¾ | **Wind Place And Sho**[18] 6323 5-10-0 83 GrahamLee 9 | 67 |
| | | | (James Eustace) *trckd ldr: cl up 5f out: rdn along 4f out: sn drvn and wknd* **16/1** | |
| 142 | 11 | 4 | **Kashmiri Sunset**[18] 6317 6-9-1 77 (tp) JamieGormley(7) 2 | 56 |
| | | | (Iain Jardine) *a in rr* **5/1**[1] | |
| 5360 | 12 | shd | **Mysterial**[14] 6467 7-8-6 64 PhilDennis(3) 3 | 43 |
| | | | (Declan Carroll) *led: rdn along over 4f out: hdd jst over 3f out: sn drvn and wknd* **25/1** | |

3m 41.31s (6.81) **Going Correction** +0.30s/f (Good)
**WFA** 3 from 4yo+ 11lb 12 Ran SP% **117.7**
Speed ratings (Par 105): **94,92,92,90,88 88,87,84,83,83 81,81**
CSF £79.48 CT £620.98 TOTE £12.10: £3.20, £2.40, £2.80; EX 100.90 Trifecta £983.10.
**Owner** R M Howard **Bred** Lynch Bages Ltd & Camas Park Stud **Trained** Middleham, N Yorks

**FOCUS**
Race run over an additional 22yds. A fair staying handicap which wasn't truly run. Three raced a way clear of the rest down the far side, and this time the runners stayed on the inner up the home straight.

## 6969 PETER SUTTON MEMORIAL BRITISH EBF NOVICE STKS (PLUS 10 RACE) 5f 89y
4:45 (4:49) (Class 3) 2-Y-O £7,762 (£2,310; £1,154; £577) Stalls High

| Form | | | | RPR |
|---|---|---|---|---|
| 421 | 1 | | **May Girl**[45] 5327 2-8-10 75 JonathanFisher(7) 7 | 85 |
| | | | (Robert Cowell) *dwlt: sn cl up nr stands rail: led 1/2-way: rdn and hung lft over 1f out: sn corrected and kpt on wl towards fin* **16/1** | |
| | 2 | ½ | **Pretty Baby (IRE)** 2-8-11 0 PatCosgrave 2 | 77+ |
| | | | (William Haggas) *trckd ldrs: hdwy 2f out: rdn to chse wnr ins fnl f: kpt on wl towards fin* **7/4**[1] | |
| | 3 | 2 ¾ | **Militia** 2-9-2 0 PaulHanagan 3 | 73 |
| | | | (Richard Fahey) *.led: hdd 1/2-way: cl up: rdn along wl over 1f out: grad wknd* **8/1**[3] | |
| | 4 | 2 ¾ | **Fool For You (IRE)** 2-8-11 0 PJMcDonald 6 | 59 |
| | | | (Richard Fahey) *dwlt and rr: hdwy wl over 1f out: sn rdn: green and edgd lft ent fnl f: kpt on same pce* **20/1** | |
| 5310 | 5 | 2 | **Savalas (IRE)**[18] 6330 2-9-8 81 TomEaves 1 | 63 |
| | | | (Kevin Ryan) *trckd ldrs: pushed along over 2f out: sn rdn and wknd wl over 1f out* **5/1**[2] | |
| 1 | 6 | 23 | **Equilateral**[22] 6178 2-9-8 0 SteveDrowne 5 | |
| | | | (Charles Hills) *trckd ldrs: pushed along 2f out: hld whn n.m.r and squeezed out wl over 1f out: sn wknd and eased* **7/4**[1] | |

1m 5.27s (1.17) **Going Correction** +0.30s/f (Good) 6 Ran SP% **111.1**
Speed ratings (Par 99): **102,101,96,92,89 52**
CSF £43.74 TOTE £9.60: £3.20, £1.70; EX 46.60 Trifecta £220.50.
**Owner** Bottisham Heath Stud **Bred** Bottisham Heath Stud **Trained** Six Mile Bottom, Cambs

**FOCUS**
Just a fair novice race, with the joint favourite not running his race. The level is a bit fluid and could be better.

## 6970 COOPERS MARQUEES H'CAP 6f
5:20 (5:21) (Class 3) (0-95,97) 3-Y-O £9,703 (£2,887; £1,443; £721) Stalls High

| Form | | | | RPR |
|---|---|---|---|---|
| 2320 | 1 | | **Major Jumbo**[15] 6450 3-9-6 90 KevinStott 4 | 100 |
| | | | (Kevin Ryan) *mde all: pushed along over 2f out: rdn and strly pressed appr fnl f: edgd lft ins fnl f: hld on wl* **9/1** | |
| 212 | 2 | nk | **Dakota Gold**[22] 6198 3-9-13 97 ConnorBeasley 9 | 106 |
| | | | (Michael Dods) *s.i.s: hld up: hdwy and in tch 1/2-way: rdn and hdwy to chal strly appr fnl f: kpt on: carried sltly lft by wnr fnl 110yds: a jst hld* **5/2**[1] | |
| 1624 | 3 | 3 | **Muscika**[16] 6392 3-8-13 83 (p[1]) PhillipMakin 3 | 82 |
| | | | (David O'Meara) *trckd ldrs: rdn over 2f out: one pce and edgd lft ins fnl f* **8/1**[3] | |
| 4001 | 4 | nk | **Hope Solo (IRE)**[6] 6759 3-9-1 85 6ex (p) JamesSullivan 2 | 83 |
| | | | (Tim Easterby) *prom: rdn over 2f out: no ex and edgd lft ins fnl f* **14/1** | |
| 5601 | 5 | 2 ¼ | **Hee Haw (IRE)**[13] 6519 3-9-0 84 GrahamLee 7 | 75 |
| | | | (Paul Midgley) *in tch: rdn over 2f out: wknd ins fnl f* **8/1**[3] | |
| -034 | 6 | 8 | **Shamsaya (IRE)**[31] 5828 3-9-1 85 PaulHanagan 5 | 51 |
| | | | (Simon Crisford) *hld up: sn pushed along: a towards rr* **17/2** | |
| 3U11 | 7 | 1 | **Gnaad (IRE)**[9] 6652 3-8-7 77 JosephineGordon 8 | 39 |
| | | | (Alan Bailey) *trckd ldrs: rdn over 2f out: wknd over 1f out* **8/1**[3] | |
| 1530 | 8 | 4 | **Pennsylvania Dutch**[15] 6450 3-9-0 84 PatCosgrave 10 | 34 |
| | | | (William Haggas) *hld up: rdn over 2f out: sn btn and bhd* **9/2**[2] | |
| 0000 | 9 | 8 | **Private Matter**[29] 5916 3-9-7 91 (h) TonyHamilton 1 | 15 |
| | | | (Richard Fahey) *dwlt: a towards rr* **12/1** | |

1m 12.18s (0.28) **Going Correction** +0.30s/f (Good) 9 Ran SP% **115.0**
Speed ratings (Par 105): **110,109,105,105,102 91,90,84,74**
CSF £31.67 CT £191.94 TOTE £9.30: £2.20, £1.50, £2.60; EX 31.10 Trifecta £349.70.
**Owner** T A Rahman **Bred** D R Botterill **Trained** Hambleton, N Yorks

**FOCUS**
A good sprint handicap confined to 3yos. The first two drifted over to the far rail under pressure, finishing clear.
T/Jkpt: Not won. T/Plt: £567.90 to a £1 stake. Pool: £139,673.66 - 179.53winning units. T/Qpdt: £73.90 to a £1 stake. Pool: £7,649.95 - 76.60 winning units. **Joe Rowntree**

# 6486 CURRAGH (R-H)
Sunday, September 10

**OFFICIAL GOING: Straight course - soft; round course - yielding to soft changing to straight course - soft to heavy, round course - soft after race 2 (2.35)**

## 6971a IRISH STALLION FARMS EBF "BOLD LAD" SPRINT H'CAP (PREMIER HANDICAP) 6f
2:00 (2:02) 3-Y-O+
£75,641 (£24,358; £11,538; £5,128; £2,564; £1,282)

| | | | RPR |
|---|---|---|---|
| 1 | | **Ice Age (IRE)**[20] 6275 4-9-6 96 CharlesBishop 19 | 106+ |
| | | (Eve Johnson Houghton) *led and disp early: gng wl w narrow advantage nr side after 1/2-way: rdn over 1f out and kpt on wl to assert ins fnl f* **15/2**[2] | |
| 2 | 1 ¼ | **Al Qahwa (IRE)**[22] 6206 4-9-7 97 (p) DanielTudhope 18 | 103 |
| | | (David O'Meara) *chsd ldrs: pushed along in 4th fr 1/2-way: rdn into 2nd nr side 1f and kpt on wl wout matching wnr: a hld* **12/1** | |
| 3 | 1 | **Blairmayne (IRE)**[8] 6704 4-7-13 80 oh6 KillianLeonard(5) 17 | 83 |
| | | (Miss Natalia Lupini, Ire) *chsd ldrs: disp 6th at 1/2-way: rdn into 3rd ins fnl f and no imp on wnr: kpt on same pce* **50/1** | |
| 4 | 1 ½ | **Tithonus (IRE)**[18] 6325 6-9-2 95 (bt) GaryHalpin(3) 9 | 93+ |
| | | (Denis Gerard Hogan, Ire) *w ldrs: disp cl 2nd at 1/2-way: rdn after 1/2-way and no imp on wnr ent fnl f: kpt on same pce in 4th wl ins fnl f* **9/1** | |
| 5 | hd | **Swish (IRE)**[8] 6703 3-8-5 86 (p) DavidEgan(3) 16 | 83 |
| | | (John James Feane, Ire) *mid-div: sme late hdwy over 1f out to chse ldrs nr side: swtchd rt ins fnl f and kpt on same pce in 5th clsng stages: nt trble wnr* **40/1** | |
| 6 | 2 | **Gin In The Inn (IRE)**[36] 5637 4-9-1 91 ChrisHayes 4 | 82+ |
| | | (Richard Fahey) *w.w towards rr: sme hdwy fr under 2f out to chse ldrs ent fnl f: kpt on same pce ins fnl f: nvr trbld ldrs* **18/1** | |
| 7 | ½ | **Ma Fee Heela (FR)**[35] 5688 3-8-11 89 (v[1]) PatSmullen 15 | 78 |
| | | (M D O'Callaghan, Ire) *dwlt and towards rr early: tk clsr order in 14th fr 1/2-way: sme hdwy under 2f out where rdn: no imp on ldrs ent fnl f: kpt on one pce* **16/1** | |
| 8 | ½ | **Patuano (IRE)**[24] 6116 3-8-1 86 NathanCrosse(7) 11 | 74 |
| | | (W McCreery, Ire) *in tch: disp 9th at 1/2-way: rdn 2f out and no imp ent fnl f: kpt on one pce* **16/1** | |
| 9 | ¾ | **Comhghairdeas (IRE)**[10] 6639 3-8-8 86 7ex SilvestreDeSousa 21 | 71 |
| | | (Andrew Slattery, Ire) *hooded to load: chsd ldrs nr side: 5th 1/2-way: rdn 2f out and no ex u.p over 1f out: one pce after* **14/1** | |
| 10 | nk | **Raucous**[15] 6419 4-9-12 102 (p) RyanMoore 22 | 86 |
| | | (William Haggas) *mid-div: tk clsr order nr side 1 1/2f out where n.m.r bhd horses briefly: sn rdn and no ex* **7/1**[1] | |
| 11 | nk | **George Bowen (IRE)**[22] 6206 5-9-2 92 (p) DavidNolan 5 | 75+ |
| | | (Richard Fahey) *sn settled in rr of mid-div: pushed along fr bef 1/2-way and sme hdwy u.p over 1f out: kpt on one pce* **12/1** | |
| 12 | shd | **Enter The Red (IRE)**[14] 6489 8-7-11 80 oh4 (b) DannySheehy(7) 13 | 63 |
| | | (Aidan Anthony Howard, Ire) *w ldrs: disp cl 2nd at 1/2-way: rdn after 1/2-way and remained prom tl wknd 1f out* **16/1** | |
| 13 | ¾ | **Snap Shots (IRE)**[22] 6206 5-9-3 93 (p) DeclanMcDonogh 2 | 74+ |
| | | (Tony Coyle) *hooded to load: chsd ldrs far side: disp 6th at 1/2-way: rdn after 1/2-way and no ex u.p over 1f out: wknd* **14/1** | |
| 14 | ¾ | **Celebration**[57] 4925 4-9-5 95 ColinKeane 6 | 73+ |
| | | (G M Lyons, Ire) *w.w towards rr: pushed along under 2f out and nt clr run over 1f out where swtchd rt and sme hdwy: short of room between horses ins fnl f and no imp after* **8/1**[3] | |
| 15 | ½ | **Art Obsession (IRE)**[22] 6205 6-8-6 82 LeighRoche 12 | 59 |
| | | (Paul Midgley) *in rr of mid-div: pushed along fr bef 1/2-way and no imp over 1f out* **25/1** | |
| 16 | ¾ | **Rapid Applause**[14] 6489 5-8-4 87 (v[1]) SeanDavis(7) 23 | 61 |
| | | (M D O'Callaghan, Ire) *in tch: disp 9th nr side at 1/2-way: rdn 2f out and no imp over 1f out where n.m.r: wknd ins fnl f* **20/1** | |

17 ½ **Maarek**[10] 6639 10-9-4 **94**............................ SeamieHeffernan 1 67+
(Miss Evanna McCutcheon, Ire) *chsd ldrs far side early: pushed along bef 1/2-way and sn no imp in mid-div: wknd* **16/1**

18 1¾ **Ducky Mallon (IRE)**[24] 6116 6-8-8 **84**.........................(t) NGMcCullagh 8 51+
(Donal Kinsella, Ire) *mid-div: 11th 1/2-way: rdn after 1/2-way and no imp over 1f out: wknd* **12/1**

19 ¾ **Rattling Jewel**[14] 6489 5-9-0 **90**...............................(p) WayneLordan 3 55+
(Miss Nicole McKenna, Ire) *chsd ldrs early: pushed along bef 1/2-way and sn wknd* **14/1**

20 1¼ **Reckless Endeavour (IRE)**[23] 6164 4-9-7 **97**................ GaryCarroll 10 58+
(G M Lyons, Ire) *towards rr thrght: rdn and no imp after 1/2-way* **33/1**

21 ½ **Poyle Vinnie**[36] 5640 7-9-8 **98**.................................. AlistairRawlinson 7 57+
(Michael Appleby) *dwlt: towards rr far side for most: tk clsr order after 1/2-way: rdn over 1f out and no imp: eased wl ins fnl f* **20/1**

22 4½ **Alfredo Arcano (IRE)**[23] 6164 3-8-6 **83** ow1..........(bt[1]) SamHitchcott 14 28
(David Marnane, Ire) *in rr of mid-div: pushed along fr bef 1/2-way and sn wknd to rr: eased fnl f* **25/1**

1m 14.38s (-1.12) **Going Correction** +0.075s/f (Good)
**WFA** 3 from 4yo+ 2lb **22** Ran SP% **141.8**
Speed ratings: **110,108,107,105,104 102,101,100,99,99 98,98,97,96,96 95,94,92,91,89 88,82**
CSF £98.45 CT £2566.42 TOTE £7.00: £2.30, £3.30, £20.60, £2.10; DF 95.10.
**Owner** Eden Racing III **Bred** Piercetown Stud **Trained** Blewbury, Oxon

**FOCUS**
Soft ground on the straight course, yielding-to-soft on the round course. British stables have plundered this big sprint handicap every year since the Champions Weekend was inaugurated. The stands' side dominated emphatically, the first three coming from 19, 18 and 17 respectively. The runner-up has been rated to his best.

## 6972a MOYGLARE "JEWELS" BLANDFORD STKS (GROUP 2) (F&M) 1m 2f
**2:35** (2:36) 3-Y-0+

**£100,854** (£32,478; £15,384; £6,837; £3,418; £1,709)

RPR

1 **Shamreen (IRE)**[21] 6243 4-9-6 107.................................. PatSmullen 4 111+
(D K Weld, Ire) *mde all: narrow advantage at 1/2-way: stl gng wl into st: rdn 1 1/2f out and sn extended advantage: styd on wl ins fnl f: comf* **9/1**

2 3 **Beautiful Morning**[14] 6490 4-9-6 102.......................... ColmO'Donoghue 5 105
(Mrs John Harrington, Ire) *settled bhd ldr: cl 2nd at 1/2-way: rdn in 2nd over 2f out and no imp on wnr ins fnl f: kpt on wl clsng stages to hold 2nd* **16/1**

3 nk **Rain Goddess (IRE)**[14] 6490 3-9-0 110.........................(t) RyanMoore 3 105+
(A P O'Brien, Ire) *chsd ldrs: 5th 1/2-way: pushed along disputing 4th 2f out: n.m.r between horses over 1f out and lost pl briefly: sn rdn into 3rd and kpt on clsng stages: jst hld for 2nd: nt trble wnr* **5/1**[3]

4 1¼ **Sea Of Grace (IRE)**[29] 5927 3-9-0 109......................... DanielTudhope 7 103+
(William Haggas) *hld up: 7th 1/2-way: prog gng wl on outer over 2f out to chse ldrs: rdn 1 1/2f out and no imp on wnr disputiing 3rd ins fnl f: kpt on same pce* **5/4**[1]

5 shd **Rosental**[25] 6074 5-9-6 99............................................ AdamKirby 2 102
(Luca Cumani) *chsd ldrs: disp 3rd at 1/2-way: pushed along 2f out and sn no imp on wnr u.p in 3rd: one pce wl ins fnl f* **50/1**

6 1½ **Smart Call (SAF)**[21] 6248 6-9-6 110......................... DonnachaO'Brien 9 99
(Sir Michael Stoute) *chsd ldrs: disp 3rd at 1/2-way: pushed along into st and sn no imp on wnr: wknd ins fnl f* **8/1**

7 2¼ **Santa Monica**[31] 5862 4-9-6 99................................ DeclanMcDonogh 1 94
(Charles O'Brien, Ire) *hld up in tch: 6th 1/2-way: pushed along over 2f out and no imp on ldrs u.p ent fnl f: kpt on one pce* **80/1**

8 3¼ **Alluringly (USA)**[17] 6356 3-9-0 105.............................. WayneLordan 6 89
(A P O'Brien, Ire) *towards rr: rdn in 8th under 3f out and no imp: one pce fnl 2f* **18/1**

9 7 **Seventh Heaven (IRE)**[127] 2398 4-9-6 119.............. SeamieHeffernan 8 74
(A P O'Brien, Ire) *a bhd: last at 1/2-way: pushed along and no imp fr over 2f out: wknd and eased ins fnl f* **10/3**[2]

2m 12.84s (3.54) **Going Correction** +0.325s/f (Good)
**WFA** 3 from 4yo+ 6lb 9 Ran SP% **119.6**
Speed ratings: **98,95,95,94,94 93,91,88,83**
CSF £144.60 TOTE £8.80: £2.60, £5.00, £2.20; DF 128.60 Trifecta £582.70.
**Owner** H H Aga Khan **Bred** His Highness The Aga Khan's Studs S C **Trained** Curragh, Co Kildare

**FOCUS**
A smart performance by the winner who had to cope with stronger opposition than when winning the same race in 2016. The second and fifth have been rated as stepping up, with the third and fourth below their best.

## 6973a DERRINSTOWN STUD FLYING FIVE STKS (GROUP 2) 5f
**3:05** (3:08) 3-Y-0+

**£151,282** (£48,717; £23,076; £10,256; £5,128; £2,564) **Stalls** Centre

RPR

1 **Caravaggio (USA)**[35] 5690 3-9-3 121................................ RyanMoore 8 116+
(A P O'Brien, Ire) *in tch nr side: 8th bef 1/2-way: pushed along fr 1/2-way and hdwy over 1f out: sn swtchd rt into 2nd and styd on wl to ld wl ins fnl f: comf* **10/11**[1]

2 1 **Alphabet**[10] 6640 3-9-0 92.........................................(t) SeamieHeffernan 7 109
(A P O'Brien, Ire) *cl up and sn led: rdn over 1f out: reduced advantage ins fnl f where pressed and hdd wl ins fnl f: no ch w wnr clsng stages* **50/1**

3 1¼ **Son Of Rest**[10] 6640 3-9-3 111........................................ ChrisHayes 12 108+
(J A Stack, Ire) *in tch nr side: 6th bef 1/2-way: pushed along under 2f out: sn rdn and clsd u.p into nvr threatening 3rd clsng stages: nvr trbld ldrs* **9/1**

4 ¾ **Caspian Prince (IRE)**[57] 4927 8-9-4 115............(t) DeclanMcDonogh 11 105
(Tony Coyle) *chsd ldrs nr side: disp 2nd at 1/2-way: rdn under 2f out and no ex u.p in 3rd ins fnl f: denied 3rd clsng stages* **5/1**[2]

5 1¼ **Cotai Glory**[16] 6402 5-9-4 112.................................. SilvestreDeSousa 3 100
(Charles Hills) *broke wl to ld narrowly tl sn hdd and settled bhd ldr: disp 2nd at 1/2-way: rdn over 1f out and sn no ex u.p : one pce in 5th wl ins fnl f* **13/2**[3]

6 ½ **Ardhoomey (IRE)**[10] 6640 5-9-4 108...............................(t) ColinKeane 5 99
(G M Lyons, Ire) *hld up in tch nr side: 7th 1/2-way: pushed along 1 1/2f out: sn n.m.r and checked sltly 1f out: rdn into 6th wl ins fnl f and kpt on clsng stages* **10/1**

7 1¾ **Gorane (IRE)**[10] 6640 3-9-0 99.................................... DanielTudhope 2 89
(Henry De Bromhead, Ire) *chsd ldrs far side: 5th 1/2-way: rdn under 2f out and sn no ex: wknd ins fnl f* **14/1**

8 shd **Tis Marvellous**[64] 4635 3-9-3 104...................................(t) AdamKirby 4 92
(Clive Cox) *chsd ldrs nr side: 4th 1/2-way: rdn 2f out and no ex bhd ldrs 1f out where n.m.r briefly: wknd* **16/1**

9 3½ **Spirit Quartz (IRE)**[57] 4927 9-9-4 104......................... JulianResimont 1 79
(Barry John Murphy, Ire) *sltly awkward s: chsd ldrs far side early: pushed along in mid-div fr bef 1/2-way and sn no imp on ldrs: one pce fnl 2f* **50/1**

10 1¼ **Duke Of Firenze**[36] 5640 8-9-4 106........................................ FranBerry 9 75
(David C Griffiths) *towards rr thrght: 10th bef 1/2-way: pushed along over 1f out and no imp: one pce after* **25/1**

11 4¾ **Pious Alexander (IRE)**[46] 5308 3-9-0 87......................... WayneLordan 6 55
(Edward Lynam, Ire) *a bhd: last at 1/2-way: wknd over 1f out* **66/1**

1m 0.54s (-2.36) **Going Correction** +0.075s/f (Good)
**WFA** 3 from 5yo+ 1lb **11** Ran SP% **123.3**
Speed ratings: **121,119,117,116,114 113,110,110,104,102 95**
CSF £81.38 TOTE £1.70: £1.02, £7.80, £3.30; DF 37.30 Trifecta £242.30.
**Owner** Mrs John Magnier & Michael Tabor & Derrick Smith **Bred** Windmill Manor Farms Inc Et Al **Trained** Cashel, Co Tipperary

**FOCUS**
This represented a good opportunity for \bCaravaggio\p to get back on track after his three-year-old career was somewhat derailed in the July Cup and most recently in the Prix Maurice de Gheest at Deauville. It wasn't quite the speed test that was expected as the soft ground made this more about stamina than anything else. He came through the ground well and won comfortably but he has yet to prove himself as the lightning quick racehorse he was described as at the beginning of the season by Aidan O'Brien. The runner-up anchors the form.

## 6974a MOYGLARE STUD STKS (GROUP 1) (FILLIES) 7f
**3:40** (3:42) 2-Y-0

**£170,512** (£56,837; £26,923; £11,965; £5,982; £2,991)

RPR

1 **Happily (IRE)**[21] 6242 2-9-0 109..............................(t) DonnachaO'Brien 10 112
(A P O'Brien, Ire) *broke wl to ld early tl sn hdd and settled bhd ldr: 3rd after 1f: rdn 2f out and pressed wnr in 2nd ent fnl f: kpt on wl u.p ins fnl f to ld fnl strides* **13/2**

2 shd **Magical (IRE)**[21] 6242 2-9-0 109........................................ RyanMoore 2 112
(A P O'Brien, Ire) *cl up bhd ldr early tl sn led: rdn 1 1/2f out where pressed: all out wl ins fnl f where strly pressed and hdd fnl strides* **9/4**[2]

3 3¾ **September (IRE)**[21] 6242 2-9-0 0................................ SeamieHeffernan 9 102
(A P O'Brien, Ire) *dwlt sltly: hld up in tch: 6th 1/2-way: tk clsr order in 4th after 1/2-way: rdn on outer 2f out and clsd u.p into 3rd ent fnl f: no imp on ldrs wl ins fnl f: kpt on same pce* **4/1**[3]

4 2 **Muirin (IRE)**[28] 5972 2-9-0 0...................................... DeclanMcDonogh 7 97
(Edward Lynam, Ire) *chsd ldrs: 4th 1/2-way: sn lost pl and rdn: u.p in 5th ent fnl f where no imp on ldrs: kpt on same pce into 4th cl home* **10/1**

5 ¾ **Alpha Centauri (IRE)**[79] 4028 2-9-0 108.................. ColmO'Donoghue 6 96
(Mrs John Harrington, Ire) *chsd ldrs tl wnt 2nd after 1f: rdn over 2f out and sn no imp on ldr u.p in 3rd: wknd in 4th ins fnl f: denied 4th cl home* **2/1**[1]

6 1½ **Gasta (IRE)**[14] 6488 2-9-0 90........................................... RonanWhelan 4 92
(J S Bolger, Ire) *s.i.s and in rr early: 7th 1/2-way: rdn 2f out and no imp on ldrs: kpt on one pce in 6th ins fnl f* **66/1**

7 2¼ **Ballet Shoes (IRE)**[14] 6487 2-9-0 104............................ WayneLordan 8 86
(A P O'Brien, Ire) *chsd ldrs: 5th 1/2-way: pushed along over 2f out and sn no ex u.p: wknd over 1f out* **14/1**

8 ½ **Active Approach**[33] 5762 2-9-0 0.................................. KevinManning 5 85
(J S Bolger, Ire) *dwlt: sn settled in rr: last at 1/2-way: rdn and no imp over 2f out: one pce after* **33/1**

1m 26.93s (-3.87) **Going Correction** -0.25s/f (Firm) 8 Ran SP% **117.6**
Speed ratings: **112,111,107,105,104 102,100,99**
CSF £22.23 CT £68.18 TOTE £13.60: £1.70, £1.10, £1.80; DF 19.40 Trifecta £48.90.
**Owner** Derrick Smith & Mrs John Magnier & Michael Tabor **Bred** Orpendale And Chelston Ireland **Trained** Cashel, Co Tipperary

**FOCUS**
Aidan O'Brien's strength-in-depth with his juvenile fillies was perfectly illustrated here, a one-two-three accomplished in spite of the withdrawal of Ryan Moore's intended mount. The third has been rated to her Debutante form, with the first two improving from their runs in that race.

## 6975a GOFFS VINCENT O'BRIEN NATIONAL STKS (GROUP 1) (ENTIRE COLTS & FILLIES) 7f
**4:15** (4:15) 2-Y-0

**£170,512** (£56,837; £26,923; £11,965; £5,982; £2,991)

RPR

1 **Verbal Dexterity (IRE)**[71] 4386 2-9-3 110...................... KevinManning 4 119
(J S Bolger, Ire) *led briefly tl sn hdd and settled bhd ldr: disp ld fr 1/2-way: rdn w narrow ld briefly over 2f out tl sn hdd: regained advantage u.p far side ins fnl f and styd on strly clsng stages* **5/2**[2]

2 3½ **Beckford**[28] 5973 2-9-3 113.............................................. PatSmullen 6 110
(Gordon Elliott, Ire) *chsd ldrs: disp cl 3rd fr 1/2-way: gng best on outer 2f out and sn led narrowly: rdn 1f out and hdd u.p ins fnl f: no imp on wnr clsng stages* **6/4**[1]

3 2¾ **Rostropovich (IRE)**[21] 6240 2-9-3 107..........................(t) RyanMoore 5 103
(A P O'Brien, Ire) *w ldrs and sn led narrowly tl jnd bef 1/2-way: hdd over 2f out where rdn: no ex u.p in 3rd 1 1/2f out: kpt on same pce ins fnl f* **7/1**[3]

4 4½ **Coat Of Arms (IRE)**[21] 6240 2-9-3 106..................... DonnachaO'Brien 1 92
(A P O'Brien, Ire) *w.w: cl 6th at 1/2-way: rdn in 5th 1 1/2f out and no imp on ldrs: kpt on one pce in mod 4th ins fnl f* **8/1**

5 ½ **Lethal Steps**[30] 5903 2-9-3 97............................................ ColinKeane 7 91
(G M Lyons, Ire) *w.w towards rr: last at 1/2-way: rdn over 2f out and no imp on ldrs: kpt on one pce into mod 5th wl ins fnl f: nvr trbld ldrs* **16/1**

6 2½ **Brother Bear (IRE)**[57] 4926 2-9-3 106..................... ColmO'Donoghue 3 84
(Mrs John Harrington, Ire) *cl up tl sn settled bhd ldrs in 4th: disp cl 3rd fr 1/2-way: rdn over 2f out and sn no ex: wknd over 1f out* **7/1**[3]

7 6 **Berkeley Square (IRE)**[21] 6240 2-9-3 102............... SeamieHeffernan 8 69
(A P O'Brien, Ire) *w.w: cl 5th at 1/2-way: rdn over 2f out and sn no ex: wknd over 1f out: eased wl ins fnl f* **20/1**

1m 27.32s (-3.48) **Going Correction** -0.25s/f (Firm) 7 Ran SP% **115.3**
Speed ratings: **109,105,101,96,96 93,86**
CSF £6.78 CT £21.35 TOTE £3.40: £1.90, £1.30; DF 7.50 Trifecta £32.70.
**Owner** Mrs J S Bolger **Bred** J S Bolger & John Corcoran **Trained** Coolcullen, Co Carlow

**FOCUS**
Something of a Hamlet without the Prince scenario here, with Gustav Klimt taken out by Aidan O'Brien. The winner battled away well and is in good hands for a 2018 Classic campaign. The form could be rated 3lb higher, but with the runner-up appearing to not get home and the third's latest form not bombproof, it's probably worth being cautious.

## 6976a COMER GROUP INTERNATIONAL IRISH ST. LEGER (GROUP 1) 1m 6f
4:50 (4:52) 3-Y-O+
£243,589 (£81,196; £38,461; £17,094; £8,547; £4,273)

RPR

1 **Order Of St George (IRE)**22 6214 5-9-10 120................ RyanMoore 5 125+
(A P O'Brien, Ire) *sweated up befhand: hld up in tch: 6th 1/2-way: gd hdwy to ld over 3f out: drvn clr under 2f out where edgd rt: in command and wl clr ent fnl f: styd on strly: easily* **2/5**1

2 9 **Torcedor (IRE)**80 3996 5-9-10 110........................(p) ColmO'Donoghue 3 112
(Mrs John Harrington, Ire) *chsd ldrs: 5th 1/2-way: rdn in 6th 3f out and clsd u.p into 2nd over 1f out where no imp on easy wnr: kpt on wl* **14/1**

3 4 ½ **Mount Moriah**36 5639 3-9-1 106.................................. HarryBentley 2 108
(Ralph Beckett) *chsd ldr early tl settled in 3rd after 1f: lost pl appr st: pushed along in 5th fr 3f out: rdn into 4th under 2f out and no imp on easy wnr: kpt on u.p into mod 3rd cl home* **14/1**

4 ¾ **Wicklow Brave**22 6214 8-9-10 113................................ ChrisHayes 7 105
(W P Mullins, Ire) *hld up towards rr: hdwy fr over 4f out to chse ldrs in 4th fr 3f out: rdn in 2nd over 2f out and no imp on easy wnr: dropped to 3rd over 1f out: one pce after and denied mod 3rd cl home* **11/1**3

5 10 **Lord Yeats**15 6447 4-9-10 108........................................ PaulMulrennan 1 91
(Jedd O'Keeffe) *broke wl to ld: narrow advantage at 1/2-way: rdn and hdd over 3f out: sn wknd* **28/1**

6 2 ¾ **Twilight Payment (IRE)**22 6214 4-9-10 106............(tp) KevinManning 9 87
(J S Bolger, Ire) *chsd ldrs tl impr into 2nd after 1f: cl 2nd at 1/2-way: rdn over 3f out and sn no imp on easy wnr u.p in 3rd: wknd* **20/1**

7 4 ½ **The Tartan Spartan (IRE)**8 6675 4-9-10 102............ RonanWhelan 10 81
(John Patrick Shanahan, Ire) *settled in rr: tk clsr order after 1/2-way and impr on outer into 7th 3f out: sn rdn and no imp on ldrs: one pce fnl 2f* **66/1**

8 1 ½ **Dartmouth**16 6400 5-9-10 115..................................... SeamieHeffernan 6 78
(Sir Michael Stoute) *hooded to load: hld up: rdn in 8th under 4f out and no imp in 9th into st: one pce fnl 2f* **5/1**2

9 ½ **Benkei (IRE)**6 5625 7-9-10 96........................................ ColinKeane 8 78
(H Rogers, Ire) *chsd ldrs: clsr in 4th after 5f: pushed along bhd ldrs 5f out and wknd u.p over 3f out* **66/1**

10 35 **Western Hymn**59 4814 6-9-10 110...........................(p) PatSmullen 4 29
(John Gosden) *hld up: 7th 1/2-way: dropped to rr bef st where pushed along: sn wknd: eased over 1f out* **14/1**

3m 7.82s (-1.58) **Going Correction** +0.325s/f (Good)
**WFA** 3 from 4yo+ 9lb **10** Ran SP% **127.6**
Speed ratings: **117,111,109,108,103 101,99,98,97,77**
CSF £9.55 CT £52.02 TOTE £1.60: £1.02, £2.50, £3.90; DF 9.00 Trifecta £72.50.
**Owner** M Tabor/D Smith/Mrs Magnier/L J Williams **Bred** Paget Bloodstock **Trained** Cashel, Co Tipperary

**FOCUS**
No worries this time for the odds-on favourite and 2015 winner who was sensationally defeated here in 2016.

## 6977a TATTERSALLS IRELAND SUPER AUCTION SALE STKS (PLUS 10 RACE) 6f 63y
5:25 (5:28) 2-Y-O
£126,068 (£49,145; £23,504; £14,957; £8,547; £4,273)

RPR

1 **Snazzy Jazzy (IRE)**20 6272 2-9-5 0............................... AdamKirby 24 98
(Clive Cox) *chsd ldrs nr side: cl 6th at 1/2-way: hdwy after 1/2-way to chal 1 1/2f out: rdn to ld ins fnl f and kpt on wl to assert clsng stages* **4/1**2

2 3 **Pretty Boy Floyd (IRE)**23 6163 2-8-13 73.................(v1) ConorHoban 23 83
(Sarah Dawson, Ire) *sn led: 1 l clr at 1/2-way: rdn after 1/2-way and strly pressed 1 1/2f out: hdd u.p ins fnl f and kpt on wl wout matching wnr clsng stages* **66/1**

3 3 **Dragons Tail (IRE)**29 5939 2-9-3 91.............................. ShaneFoley 13 78+
(Tom Dascombe) *mid-div: hdwy after 1/2-way: rdn into 6th 1f out and kpt on u.p into nvr threatening 3rd fnl strides* **14/1**

4 shd **The Broghie Man**52 5084 2-8-11 0............................. KevinManning 21 72
(Brendan W Duke, Ire) *w ldrs: pushed along in 2nd after 1/2-way and ev ch almost on terms u.p over 1f out: no imp on wnr in 3rd wl ins fnl f: denied 3rd fnl strides* **8/1**3

5 nk **Camacho Chief (IRE)**8 6693 2-8-13 84.................... PaulMulrennan 19 73
(Michael Dods) *chsd ldrs nr side: disp 7th at 1/2-way: sn pushed along and rdn into 4th briefly ins fnl f: no ex and one pce in 5th clsng stages* **12/1**

6 1 ½ **Goodthingstaketime (IRE)**21 6241 2-8-6 99................ ChrisHayes 26 62
(J A Stack, Ire) *in tch: disp 8th at 1/2-way: tk clsr order after 1/2-way: nt clr run briefly under 2f out: sn rdn in 5th and no ex ins fnl f: one pce clsng stages* **13/8**1

7 5 ½ **Controversial Lady (IRE)**15 6452 2-8-8 77.................. LeighRoche 9 48+
(J S Moore) *mid-div: sme hdwy after 1/2-way: kpt on one pce ins fnl f: nvr nrr* **40/1**

7 dht **Nailed On Nina (IRE)**23 6163 2-8-6 0.......................... MarkGallagher 1 46+
(P M Mooney, Ire) *mid-div far side: hdwy under 2f out to chse ldrs: rdn and no ex ins fnl f: one pce clsng stages* **66/1**

9 nk **Shovel It On (IRE)**3 6860 2-8-13 70..................... DeclanMcDonogh 2 52+
(David Evans) *in tch far side: rdn after 1/2-way and no imp over 1f out: kpt on one pce* **33/1**

10 1 ¼ **Helvetian**13 6521 2-9-3 97.............................................. RonanWhelan 7 52+
(Mick Channon) *prom tl sn settled bhd ldrs: rdn and no ex after 1/2-way: one pce fnl 2f* **14/1**

11 ½ **Stormy Tale (IRE)**35 5687 2-8-6 58.........................(h1) DannySheehy 30 40
(Michael Mulvany, Ire) *dwlt and towards rr: pushed along and tk clsr order bef 1/2-way: kpt on one pce fnl 2f* **66/1**

12 3 **Ventura Gold (IRE)**10 6626 2-9-1 72.............................. DavidNolan 10 40+
(Richard Fahey) *in rr of mid-div: rdn after 1/2-way and kpt on one pce fnl 2f* **50/1**

13 hd **Verhoyen**58 4873 2-8-11 93.......................................... WayneLordan 11 36+
(M C Grassick, Ire) *hld up: rdn after 1/2-way and no imp: kpt on one pce fnl 2f* **20/1**

14 shd **Austin Powers (IRE)**14 6481 2-9-1 73............................ FranBerry 28 39
(Mark Johnston) *in tch nr side: rdn and no ex after 1/2-way: one pce fnl 2f* **50/1**

15 1 **Masucci (IRE)**14 6493 2-9-5 85...................................(b1) ColinKeane 14 40+
(G M Lyons, Ire) *chsd ldrs diwn centre: disp cl 3rd at 1/2-way: wknd over 1f out* **20/1**

16 2 ½ **Summerseat Mist (IRE)**56 4933 2-8-10 72................(v1) SeanDavis 27 24
(M D O'Callaghan, Ire) *dismntd bef s: s.i.s and in rr early: tk clsr order and pushed along towards rr fr 1/2-way: kpt on one pce fnl 2f* **66/1**

17 ½ **Gangland**14 6466 2-9-1 67...............................(h) DonnachaO'Brien 22 28
(Richard Fahey) *in tch: rdn and wknd after 1/2-way* **50/1**

18 hd **Wolfofbaggotstreet (IRE)**21 6241 2-9-5 94................. NGMcCullagh 6 31+
(J P Murtagh, Ire) *dwlt and towards rr early: kpt on one pce fnl 2f: nvr a factor* **20/1**

19 ½ **Phoenix Lightning (IRE)**37 5600 2-8-13 74...............(p1) PatSmullen 5 24+
(Richard Fahey) *hld up: rdn and no imp after 1/2-way* **20/1**

20 1 ½ **Little Luna (IRE)**74 4225 2-8-6 0...........................(t1) KillianLeonard 20 12
(John Geoghegan, Ire) *towards rr: rdn and no imp after 1/2-way: kpt on one pce fnl 2f* **100/1**

21 shd **Ballot Box**16 6405 2-8-10 75............................... ColmO'Donoghue 16 16+
(Mrs John Harrington, Ire) *towards rr for most: rdn and no imp after 1/2-way: kpt on one pce ins fnl f* **33/1**

22 ¾ **Optimum Time (IRE)**59 4805 2-9-1 80.......................... CharlesBishop 25 19
(Eve Johnson Houghton) *in tch: pushed along in 13th bef 1/2-way and sn no ex: wknd* **25/1**

23 ½ **Youareiffraaj (IRE)**14 6488 2-8-13 0.............................. GaryHalpin 12 15+
(John James Feane, Ire) *mid-div: rdn and wknd after 1/2-way* **33/1**

24 2 **Brockey Rise (IRE)**12 6547 2-9-3 70.......................(v) GaryCarroll 18 14+
(David Evans) *hld up: pushed along in rr of mid-div fr 1/2-way and sn wknd* **66/1**

25 ¾ **Villa Tora**16 6379 2-8-8 70................................................. DavidEgan 17 +
(Mark Johnston) *chsd ldrs: disp cl 3rd at 1/2-way: rdn 2f out and sn no ex: wknd* **50/1**

26 4 ¾ **Kraka (IRE)**30 5874 2-9-3 80.................................... RichardKingscote 3 +
(Tom Dascombe) *in tch: 11th 1/2-way: sn rdn and wknd 2f out* **14/1**

27 1 **Freescape**23 6163 2-9-1 0................................................... OisinOrr 8 +
(David Marnane, Ire) *in rr of mid-div far side: rdn and no imp after 1/2-way: wknd* **20/1**

28 18 **Villa Savina (IRE)**48 5216 2-8-8 0.............................. SamHitchcott 15 +
(Clive Cox) *in tch: pushed along fr bef 1/2-way and sn wknd* **12/1**

29 nse **Our Man In Havana**35 5685 2-9-1 73.................... SeamieHeffernan 29
(Tom Dascombe) *chsd ldrs: disp cl 3rd at 1/2-way: rdn after 1/2-way and sn no ex: wknd fnl 2f* **40/1**

1m 18.95s (-0.15) **Going Correction** +0.075s/f (Good) **29** Ran SP% **162.2**
Speed ratings: **104,100,96,95,95 93,86,86,85,84 83,79,79,79,77 74,73,73,72,70 70,69,68,66,65 58,57,33,33**
CSF £297.19 TOTE £5.50: £2.20, £19.90, £6.00; DF 962.30 Trifecta £3733.40.
**Owner** Mrs Olive Shaw **Bred** Bluegate Stud **Trained** Lambourn, Berks

**FOCUS**
A great opportunity for some ordinary horses to pick up significant prize money. High numbers dominated, as in the big sprint handicap early in the day. The runner-up almost certainly governs the level of the form.

## 6978a IRISH STALLION FARMS EBF "NORTHFIELDS" H'CAP (PREMIER HANDICAP) 1m 2f
5:55 (6:01) 3-Y-O+
£75,641 (£24,358; £11,538; £5,128; £2,564; £1,282)

RPR

1 **Panstarr**25 6081 3-8-4 **88**.............................................. RoryCleary 10 96
(J S Bolger, Ire) *mde all: pushed along 2 l clr into st: sn rdn and kpt on wl u.p ins fnl f: all out clsng stages: jst hld on* **8/1**

2 nk **Mawaany (IRE)**37 5622 4-9-0 **92**................................ ColinKeane 15 98+
(G M Lyons, Ire) *mid-div: sme hdwy to chse ldrs 3f out: rdn in 4th 2f out and r.o wl u.p nr side ins fnl f into nvr nrr 2nd fnl strides: jst failed* **7/2**1

3 ½ **Spruce Meadows (IRE)**23 6165 4-8-9 **90**..............(p) GaryHalpin(3) 9 95
(John James Feane, Ire) *sn trckd ldr: rdn in 2nd over 3f out and pressed wnr u.p ins fnl f: denied 2nd fnl strides* **14/1**

4 hd **Apparition (IRE)**13 6537 3-8-4 **88** oh1.......................... WayneLordan 1 94+
(Joseph Patrick O'Brien, Ire) *mid-div: pushed along in 7th into st and sme hdwy far side 1 1/2f out: u.p in 4th wl ins fnl f: kpt on clsng stages* **8/1**

5 3 ½ **Maudlin Magdalen (IRE)**23 7478 7-7-12 **83**..........(t) SeanDavis(7) 17 81
(Donal Kinsella, Ire) *chsd ldrs: 3rd over 3f out: sn rdn bhd ldrs and no ex under 2f out: one pce ins fnl f* **16/1**

6 nk **Breathe Easy (IRE)**14 6491 7-8-11 **89**.......................... RonanWhelan 5 86+
(Gavin Cromwell, Ire) *dwlt and awkward s: settled in rr early: rdn towards rr appr st and kpt on u.p fnl f: nvr nrr* **7/1**3

7 hd **Jet Streaming (IRE)**39 5552 3-7-11 **88** oh2............... DannySheehy(7) 3 86
(Adrian Paul Keatley, Ire) *chsd ldr and racd keenly early: sn settled bhd ldrs: niggled along in 6th after 1/2-way: rdn over 3f out and no imp on ldrs: one pce fnl f* **7/1**3

8 1 **First Flight (IRE)**15 6449 6-9-1 **96**............................ DavidEgan(3) 4 91
(Heather Main) *hld up in tch: rdn and no ex into st: one pce fnl 2f* **6/1**2

9 3 **The Mouse Doctor (IRE)**28 5976 4-8-7 **85**.................(t) ShaneFoley 16 74
(A J Martin, Ire) *hld up: last at 1/2-way: rdn in 12th under 2f out and kpt on one pce ins fnl f* **8/1**

10 1 ¼ **Ace Of Diamonds (IRE)**13 6538 4-8-4 **82** oh3............... LeighRoche 6 69
(D K Weld, Ire) *hld up towards rr: pushed along over 3f out and no imp into st: kpt on one pce fnl 2f* **12/1**

11 1 **Master Speaker (IRE)**14 6489 7-8-6 **89**...............(tp) KillianLeonard(5) 8 74
(M J Tynan, Ire) *hld up towards rr: pushed along in 10th into st and sn no ex: one pce fnl 2f* **25/1**

12 20 **Stronger Than Me (IRE)**91 3633 9-9-5 **97**........... DeclanMcDonogh 12 42
(W T Farrell, Ire) *hld up in tch: tk clsr order after 1/2-way: pushed along in 4th over 3f out and sn no ex u.p: wknd 2f out: no imp whn sltly hmpd 1 1/2f out and eased* **25/1**

13 1 ¾ **Sea Swift (IRE)**18 6337 4-9-3 **95**..................................(h) PatSmullen 2 36
(D K Weld, Ire) *chsd ldrs: pushed along over 3f out and sn no ex u.p in 6th: wknd under 2f out and sn sltly hmpd: eased over 1f out* **16/1**

2m 13.7s (4.40) **Going Correction** +0.325s/f (Good)
**WFA** 3 from 4yo+ 6lb **13** Ran SP% **128.7**
Speed ratings: **95,94,94,94,91 91,91,90,87,86 86,70,68**
Pick Six: 17,588.80 - Pool: 276,396.20 - 11 Winning Units. Tote Aggregate: 2017: 727,095.00 - 2016: 823,112.00 CSF £38.92 CT £404.92 TOTE £11.30: £3.10, £2.00, £5.30; DF 48.10 Trifecta £823.70.
**Owner** Godolphin **Bred** Darley **Trained** Coolcullen, Co Carlow

**FOCUS**
Quite a few defections on account of the deteriorating ground, but still a good competitive handicap won by a tough and improving filly. The third sets the standard to his best.
T/Jkpt: @90.30. Pool: @25,000.00 T/Plt: @38.40. Pool: @52,870.83 **Brian Fleming**

## 6728 CHANTILLY (R-H)
Sunday, September 10

**OFFICIAL GOING: Turf: soft; polytrack: standard**

### 6979a QATAR PRIX DU PETIT COUVERT (GROUP 3) (3YO+) (TURF) 5f
12:50 3-Y-O+ £34,188 (£13,675; £10,256; £6,837; £3,418)

RPR

1 **Lady Macapa**50 5149 4-8-10 0 LukeMorris 4 110
(Clive Cox) *prom: rdn 2 1/2f out: led 2f out: hdd over 1f out: drvn and rallied to ld again 1f out: kpt on gamely* **186/10**

2 *nk* **Gold Vibe (IRE)**9 4-9-0 0 ChristopheSoumillon 8 113+
(P Bary, France) *hld up towards rr: stdy hdwy fr under 2f out: rdn over 1f out: styd on wl fnl f: ev ch clsng stages: jst hld* **51/10**2

3 *shd* **Fashion Queen**85 3835 3-8-9 0 MaximeGuyon 9 109+
(David O'Meara) *in tch: pushed along under 3f out: rdn 2f out: hdwy to press ldrs under 1f out: kpt on wl* **91/10**

4 *1 1/2* **Kyllang Rock (IRE)**26 6039 3-8-13 0 (b) MartinHarley 7 108
(James Tate) *hld up towards rr of midfield: hdwy fr over 2f out: rdn under 2f out: led over 1f out: sn drvn: hdd 1f out: wknd last 150yds* **78/10**3

5 *1* **Largent Du Bonheur (FR)**24 4-9-0 0 (b) Christophe-PatriceLemaire 5 104
(M Delzangles, France) *in tch: rdn and kpt on same pce fr over 2f out* **108/10**

6 *1 3/4* **Cox Bazar (FR)**43 5450 3-8-13 0 JulienAuge 10 98
(C Ferland, France) *led: rdn and hdd 2f out: wknd fnl f* **6/5**1

7 *1 1/4* **Evil Spell**91 3632 5-8-10 0 MickaelBarzalona 6 89
(Robert Cowell) *bmpd s: outpcd in rr: kpt on fr over 1f out: nvr a factor* **42/1**

8 *2 1/2* **Facilitate**31 3-8-9 0 VincentCheminaud 1 80
(D Smaga, France) *in tch: rdn over 2f out: wknd 1 1/2f out* **81/10**

9 *1 1/4* **California Tee**43 5450 3-8-9 0 (b) AntoineHamelin 3 76
(Matthieu Palussiere, France) *a towards rr* **30/1**

10 *1 3/4* **Mubaalegh**31 3-8-13 0 AlexisBadel 2 73
(J E Hammond, France) *in tch in midfield: rdn and unable qck 2f out: sn lost pl and wl btn* **16/1**

59.89s (1.59) **Going Correction** +0.60s/f (Yiel)
**WFA** 3 from 4yo+ 1lb 10 Ran SP% **119.1**
Speed ratings: **111,110,110,107,106 103,101,97,95,92**
PARI-MUTUEL (all including 1 euro stake): WIN 19.60; PLACE 4.40, 2.20, 3.20; DF 49.30; SF 92.60.
**Owner** Michael Johnson & John Law **Bred** Peter Winkworth **Trained** Lambourn, Berks

**FOCUS**
Personal bests from the winner and third, with the fourth and fifth setting the standard.

### 6980a QATAR PRIX NIEL (GROUP 2) (3YO COLTS & FILLIES) (TURF) 1m 4f
1:50 3-Y-O £63,333 (£24,444; £11,666; £7,777; £3,888)

RPR

1 **Cracksman**18 6327 3-9-2 0 FrankieDettori 3 118+
(John Gosden) *chsd ldr: pushed along under 3f out: rdn to ld 2f out: drew clr ins fnl f: comf* **2/5**1

2 *3 1/2* **Avilius**26 6053 3-9-2 0 MickaelBarzalona 2 113
(A Fabre, France) *in tch in 3rd: rdn to chse ldr 2f out: kpt on: no imp on wnr fnl f* **78/10**

3 *1* **Finche**56 4941 3-9-2 0 VincentCheminaud 4 111
(A Fabre, France) *led: outpcd and dropped to 3rd 2f out: kpt on fnl f* **42/10**2

4 *4* **Ice Breeze**58 4878 3-9-2 0 Pierre-CharlesBoudot 5 105+
(P Bary, France) *hld up in 4th: rdn and no imp fr over 2f out* **77/10**3

5 *3/4* **Walsingham (GER)**35 3-9-2 0 CristianDemuro 1 103+
(Waldemar Hickst, Germany) *a in rr* **206/10**

2m 37.78s (6.78) **Going Correction** +0.60s/f (Yiel) 5 Ran SP% **118.1**
Speed ratings: **101,98,98,95,94**
PARI-MUTUEL (all including 1 euro stake): WIN 1.40; PLACE 1.10, 1.10, SF 4.80.
**Owner** A E Oppenheimer **Bred** Hascombe And Valiant Studs **Trained** Newmarket, Suffolk

**FOCUS**
Not an overly strong edition of the race in terms of depth, even though there's no doubting the winner is top notch, and little changed in the race.

### 6981a QATAR PRIX VERMEILLE (GROUP 1) (3YO+ FILLIES & MARES) (TURF) 1m 4f
3:15 3-Y-O+ £170,931 (£68,384; £34,192; £17,081; £8,555)

RPR

1 **Bateel (IRE)**35 5691 5-9-3 0 Pierre-CharlesBoudot 4 117+
(F-H Graffard, France) *midfield: gd hdwy fr over 2f out: rdn 2f out: led under 2f out: drvn over 1f out: strly pressed ins fnl f: fnd ex to assert last 100yds: readily* **53/10**2

2 *2 1/2* **Journey**70 4419 5-9-3 0 FrankieDettori 2 113
(John Gosden) *trckd ldrs: smooth hdwy to ld 2f out: rdn and hdd under 2f out: kpt on wl to press ldr ins fnl f: no ex and hld last 100yds* **41/10**1

3 *3* **Left Hand**21 6248 4-9-3 0 (p) MaximeGuyon 5 108
(C Laffon-Parias, France) *hld up towards rr of midfield: sltly hmpd 5f out: rdn and hdwy fr over 2f out: sltly hmpd under 2f out: chsd ldrs 1 1/2f out: kpt on same pce fnl f* **71/10**3

4 *1/2* **Traffic Jam (IRE)**35 5691 4-9-3 0 StephanePasquier 6 107
(N Clement, France) *in tch in midfield: rdn over 3f out: drvn and kpt on same pce fr over 2f out* **103/10**

5 *1/2* **Strathspey**22 6227 3-8-9 0 MickaelBarzalona 11 107
(A Fabre, France) *hld up towards rr: sltly hmpd 5f out: rdn and kpt on steadily fr 3 1/2f out: n.d* **163/10**

6 *1 1/4* **God Given**28 5981 3-8-9 0 JamieSpencer 10 105
(Luca Cumani) *chsd ldr: rdn under 4f out: ev ch 2f out: wknd steadily fr under 2f out* **121/10**

7 *10* **Ajman Princess (IRE)**21 6248 4-9-3 0 (p) AndreaAtzeni 3 88
(Roger Varian) *led: rdn under 3f out: hdd under 2f out: sn wknd* **132/10**

8 *2* **The Black Princess (FR)**64 4613 4-9-3 0 JimCrowley 9 85
(John Gosden) *towards rr of midfield: hmpd 5f out: rdn 2 1/2f out: wknd under 2f out* **53/10**2

9 *10* **Baiyouna (FR)**40 3-8-10 0 ow1 ChristopheSoumillon 1 71+
(A De Royer-Dupre, France) *hld up in rr: bdly hmpd 5f out: sn bhd* **156/10**

10 *dist* **Endless Time (IRE)**38 5569 5-9-3 0 (p) JamesDoyle 8 +
(Charlie Appleby) *dwlt: sn in tch in midfield: rdn and no rspnse 3 1/2f out: sn eased* **19/2**

11 *dist* **Blond Me (IRE)**38 5571 5-9-3 0 OisinMurphy 7 +
(Andrew Balding) *towards rr of midfield: stmbld 5f out: sn dropped to rr and btn: eased fr over 2f out* **97/10**

2m 32.9s (1.90) **Going Correction** +0.60s/f (Yiel)
**WFA** 3 from 4yo+ 8lb 11 Ran SP% **117.9**
Speed ratings: **117,115,113,113,112 111,105,103,97,**
PARI-MUTUEL (all including 1 euro stake): WIN 6.30; PLACE 2.00, 2.00, 2.30; DF 15.50; SF 30.50.
**Owner** Al Asayl Bloodstock Ltd **Bred** Sheikh Sultan Bin Khalifa Al Nayhan **Trained** France

**FOCUS**
Good form, with the right horses coming to the fore, and there was no hanging around which ensured a true test. The fifth and sixth are the best guides to the level.

### 6982a QATAR PRIX DU MOULIN DE LONGCHAMP (GROUP 1) (3YO+ NO GELDINGS) (TURF) 1m
3:55 3-Y-O+ £219,769 (£87,923; £43,961; £21,961; £11,000)

RPR

1 **Ribchester (IRE)**39 5527 4-9-3 0 JamesDoyle 8 123+
(Richard Fahey) *chsd ldr: rdn to ld under 2f out: drvn and kpt on strly fnl f* **1/1**1

2 *3/4* **Taareef (USA)**28 5980 4-9-3 0 ChristopheSoumillon 7 121+
(J-C Rouget, France) *in tch: rdn over 2f out: ev ch appr fnl f: kpt on fnl f: a hld by wnr* **4/1**2

3 *3 1/2* **Massaat (IRE)**22 6193 4-9-3 0 JimCrowley 4 113
(Owen Burrows) *trckd ldrs: rdn 2f out: wknd steadily ins fnl f* **91/10**

4 *nk* **Robin Of Navan (FR)**70 4423 4-9-3 0 CristianDemuro 5 112
(Harry Dunlop) *led: rdn 2f out: hdd under 2f out: wknd steadily fr over 1f out* **148/10**

5 *nk* **Inns Of Court (IRE)**28 5980 3-8-13 0 MickaelBarzalona 6 112+
(A Fabre, France) *hld up towards rr: rdn and kpt on steadily fr 2 1/2f out: nvr gng pce to chal* **8/1**

6 *1 1/4* **Lightning Spear**15 6420 6-9-3 0 OisinMurphy 1 109+
(David Simcock) *hld up in midfield: rdn over 2f out: hmpd 1f out: no ex fnl f* **9/1**

7 *1 3/4* **Lady Frankel**26 6054 3-8-9 0 Pierre-CharlesBoudot 3 101+
(A Fabre, France) *a in rr* **76/10**3

1m 40.75s (2.75) **Going Correction** +0.60s/f (Yiel)
**WFA** 3 from 4yo+ 5lb 7 Ran SP% **119.0**
Speed ratings: **110,109,105,105,105 103,102**
PARI-MUTUEL (all including 1 euro stake): WIN 1.60; PLACE 1.10, 1.50, 1.90; DF 4.60; SF 8.20.
**Owner** Godolphin **Bred** A Thompson & M O'Brien **Trained** Musley Bank, N Yorks

**FOCUS**
Not a particularly strong edition of this but the form looks sound enough, with the class of the race seeing off a pair of progressive 4yos. It paid to race prominently, those held up not landing a blow.

### 6983a QATAR PRIX FOY (GROUP 2) (4YO+ NO GELDINGS) (TURF) 1m 4f
4:35 4-Y-O+ £63,333 (£24,444; £11,666; £7,777; £3,888)

RPR

1 **Dschingis Secret (GER)**28 5983 4-9-2 0 AdriedeVries 4 120+
(Markus Klug, Germany) *in tch: rdn 1 1/2f out: led over 1f out: styd on strly last 100yds: readily* **54/10**

2 *1 1/2* **Cloth Of Stars (IRE)**132 2249 4-9-2 0 MickaelBarzalona 5 117+
(A Fabre, France) *hld up towards rr: stdy hdwy fr 2f out: rdn 1 1/2f out: nt clr run 1f out: styd on fnl f: wnt 2nd clsng stages: no ch w wnr* **17/10**1

3 *nk* **Talismanic**58 4879 4-9-2 0 VincentCheminaud 6 117
(A Fabre, France) *hld up towards rr: rdn and hdwy fr 2f out: ev ch 1f out: no ex last 100yds* **193/10**

4 *1 3/4* **Satono Diamond (JPN)**133 2203 4-9-2 0 Christophe-PatriceLemaire 1 114
(Yasutoshi Ikee, Japan) *chsd ldr: rdn to ld narrowly 1 1/2f out: hdd over 1f out: wknd last 150yds* **19/10**2

5 *1 1/2* **Silverwave (FR)**70 4423 5-9-2 0 Pierre-CharlesBoudot 2 112
(P Bary, France) *t.k.h: in tch: rdn under 2f out: wknd appr fnl f* **16/5**3

6 *hd* **Satono Noblesse (JPN)**183 7-9-2 0 YugaKawada 3 111
(Yasutoshi Ikee, Japan) *led: rdn 2f out: hdd 1 1/2f out: wknd fnl f* **31/1**

2m 35.86s (4.86) **Going Correction** +0.60s/f (Yiel) 6 Ran SP% **119.0**
Speed ratings: **107,106,105,104,103 103**
PARI-MUTUEL (all including 1 euro stake): WIN 6.40; PLACE 2.50, 1.60; SF 24.00.
**Owner** Horst Pudwill **Bred** Gestut Park Wiedingen **Trained** Germany

**FOCUS**
Bit of a messy race, with Japanese pacemaker Satono Noblesse not doing a very good job, and it was the progressive German runner who came out on top. The winner's previous form could be rated 120. The sixth helps set the level.

### 6984a QATAR PRIX GLADIATEUR (GROUP 3) (4YO+) (TURF) 1m 7f
5:10 4-Y-O+ £34,188 (£13,675; £10,256; £6,837; £3,418)

RPR

1 **Vazirabad (FR)**105 3119 5-9-4 0 ChristopheSoumillon 6 119+
(A De Royer-Dupre, France) *dwlt: hld up in midfield: smooth hdwy fr 3f out: rdn to ld narrowly over 1f out: drvn to assert last 100yds: cosily* **9/10**1

2 *3/4* **Holdthasigreen (FR)**21 6250 5-9-0 0 (p) TonyPiccone 8 112
(C Le Lay, France) *chsd ldr: led after 6f: rdn 2f out: hdd over 1f out: rallied to press ldr ins fnl f: no ex and hld last 100yds* **56/10**2

3 *7* **Trip To Rhodos (FR)**105 8-8-11 0 TheoBachelot 3 101
(Pavel Tuma, Czech Republic) *trckd ldrs: rdn and outpcd 3f out: kpt on steadily fr 1 1/2f out* **31/1**

4 *3 1/2* **Flymetothestars**15 6447 4-8-11 0 LukeMorris 5 96
(Sir Mark Prescott Bt) *hld up towards rr: rdn and kpt on steadily fr under 3f out: nvr gng pce to chal* **57/10**3

5 *2* **Ming Dynasty (FR)**27 5-8-11 0 VincentCheminaud 7 94
(M Delzangles, France) *dwlt: hld up in rr: rdn and kpt on steadily fr 2f out: n.d* **29/1**

6 *6* **Nearly Caught (IRE)**21 6250 7-9-0 0 JamesDoyle 4 90
(Hughie Morrison) *led: hdd after 6f: rdn 5f out: wknd under 2f out* **7/1**

7 *hd* **Vent De Force**49 5198 6-8-11 0 OlivierPeslier 2 87
(Hughie Morrison) *a towards rr* **158/10**

8 *dist* **Sirius (GER)**28 5983 6-9-0 0 MaximeGuyon 1
(Andreas Suborics, Germany) *midfield: pushed along under 3f out: wknd under 2f out: eased fr 1 1/2f out* **74/10**

3m 18.13s (2.03) **Going Correction** +0.60s/f (Yiel) 8 Ran SP% **119.5**
Speed ratings: **118,117,113,112,110 107,107,**
PARI-MUTUEL (all including 1 euro stake): WIN 1.90; PLACE 1.10, 1.50, 3.70; DF 5.30; SF 6.60.
**Owner** H H Aga Khan **Bred** Haras De Son Altesse L'Aga Khan Scea **Trained** Chantilly, France

**FOCUS**
It's been rated around the first three to their recent form.

6254 **DUSSELDORF** (R-H)

Sunday, September 10

**OFFICIAL GOING: Turf: soft**

## 6985a GROSSER PREIS VON ENGEL & VOLKERS DUSSELDORF - 93RD JUNIOREN-PREIS (LISTED RACE) (2YO) (TURF) 1m

2:20 2-Y-O £11,965 (£5,555; £2,564; £1,282)

RPR

1 **Alounak (FR)**[22] 6229 2-9-2 0 MarcLerner 4 95
(Jean-Pierre Carvalho, Germany) 9/5[2]

2 *hd* **Royal Youmzain (FR)**[63] 2-9-0 0 EduardoPedroza 5 93
(A Wohler, Germany) 3/5[1]

3 *3/4* **Dina (GER)** 2-8-10 0 MartinSeidl 1 87
(Markus Klug, Germany) 48/10

4 *nk* **Move Over**[16] 6367 2-9-0 0 (b) DanielePorcu 3 90
(Richard Hannon) *ld early: pushed along to hold advantage over 2f out: rdn and hdd 1f out: rallied and styd on towards fin* 41/10[3]

1m 39.52s (-1.64) 4 Ran SP% **135.1**
PARI-MUTUEL (all including 10 euro stake): WIN: 28; PLACE: 10, 10; SF: 34.

**Owner** Darius Racing **Bred** Framont Limited & S.C.E.A. Des Prairies **Trained** Germany

## 6986a PREIS DER HOLSCHBACH IMMOBILIEN GRUPPE - BBAG AUKTIONSRENNEN DUSSELDORF (CONDITIONS) (2YO) (TURF) 7f

3:20 2-Y-O £21,367 (£9,401; £5,128; £3,418; £1,709; £1,709)

RPR

1 **Kronprinz (GER)** 2-9-0 0 AndraschStarke 1
(P Schiergen, Germany) 148/10

2 *1/2* **Ernesto (GER)** 2-9-0 0 MartinSeidl 6
(Markus Klug, Germany) 30/1

3 *hd* **Shaolin (GER)** 2-9-0 0 MmeYvonneDonze 7
(P Schiergen, Germany) 35/1

4 *1/2* **Klungel (GER)** 2-9-0 0 AndreasHelfenbein 5
(Markus Klug, Germany) 96/10

5 *2 1/2* **Zabaletaswansong (GER)**[46] 5292 2-9-0 0 JozefBojko 4
(Richard Hannon) *pushed along to contest ld early: dropped to midfield after 1f: pushed along to take clsr order over 2f out: drvn over 1f out: styd on one pce ins fnl f* 113/10

6 *1 1/4* **Northern Fox (GER)** 2-9-0 0 SibylleVogt 10
(Yasmin Almenrader, Germany) 239/10

7 *1 1/4* **Emerald Master (GER)** 2-9-0 0 EduardoPedroza 2
(Mario Hofer, Germany) 16/5[2]

8 *1 1/4* **Theo (GER)**[41] 2-9-0 0 MarcLerner 14
(Waldemar Hickst, Germany) 37/10[3]

9 *hd* **Ivo (GER)** 2-9-0 0 TomSchurig 8
(P Vovcenko, Germany) 212/10

10 *2* **Northern Hollow (GER)** 2-9-0 0 MaximPecheur 11
(Markus Klug, Germany) 178/10

11 *hd* **Numerion (GER)**[91] 2-9-2 0 DanielePorcu 3
(S Smrczek, Germany) 124/10

12 *1/2* **Apollo (GER)** 2-9-0 0 FrauRebeccaDanz 12
(J Hirschberger, Germany) 30/1

13 *1 1/2* **Legacy (GER)**[63] 2-9-0 0 FilipMinarik 13
(Jean-Pierre Carvalho, Germany) 14/5[1]

14 *9* **El Footstep (GER)** 2-9-0 0 (p) AlexanderPietsch 9
(Mario Hofer, Germany) 157/10

1m 28.28s 14 Ran SP% **131.8**
PARI-MUTUEL (all including 10 euro stake): WIN: 158; PLACE: 42, 62, 89; SF: 3941.

**Owner** Abdulmagid A Alyousfi **Bred** Gestut Etzean **Trained** Germany

## 6987a GROSSE EUROPA MEILE DES PORSCHE ZENTRUM DUSSELDORF (GROUP 3) (3YO+) (TURF) 1m

4:25 3-Y-O+ £27,350 (£10,256; £5,128; £2,564; £1,709)

RPR

1 **Delectation**[58] 4857 3-8-9 0 EduardoPedroza 6 110+
(A Wohler, Germany) *hld up towards rr: rdn and gd hdwy fr 2 1/2f out: led 1f out: qcknd clr ins fnl f: comf* 8/5[2]

2 *3 1/2* **Millowitsch (GER)**[14] 6495 4-9-3 0 AndreasHelfenbein 5 106
(Markus Klug, Germany) *chsd ldr: rdn to ld 2 1/2f out: hdd 1f out: kpt on same pce fnl f* 7/5[1]

3 *2 1/2* **Arazza (GER)**[21] 6254 3-8-7 0 MaximPecheur 3 94
(J Hirschberger, Germany) *midfield: dropped towards rr 5f out: rdn and hdwy fr 2 1/2f out: chsd ldrs appr fnl f: no ex ins fnl f* 17/2

4 *2* **Kick And Rush (GER)**[21] 6255 3-8-10 0 AlexanderPietsch 7 93
(Mario Hofer, Germany) *hld up towards rr: hdwy into midfield 5f out: rdn and no imp fr 2 1/2f out* 9/1

5 *2* **Cashman (FR)**[23] 6173 4-9-1 0 JozefBojko 1 89
(A Wohler, Germany) *led: rdn under 3f out: hdd 2 1/2f out: wknd 1 1/2f out* 84/10[3]

6 *1 1/2* **Wildpark (GER)**[315] 6-9-1 0 AndraschStarke 4 86
(D Moser, Germany) *in tch: rdn and outpcd under 3f out: wknd 1 1/2f out* 17/2

7 *15* **Capitano (GER)**[28] 4-9-1 0 FilipMinarik 2 51
(J Hirschberger, Germany) *in tch: rdn 3f out: lost pl 2 1/2f out: sn struggling: eased fnl f* 84/10[3]

1m 38.62s (-2.54)
**WFA** 3 from 4yo+ 5lb 7 Ran SP% **132.5**
PARI-MUTUEL (all including 10 euro stake): WIN: 26; PLACE: 17, 14; SF: 40.

**Owner** Australian Bloodstock Stable **Bred** Crossfields Bloodstock Ltd **Trained** Germany

6988 - 6999a (Foreign Racing) - See Raceform Interactive

6747 **BRIGHTON** (L-H)

Monday, September 11

**OFFICIAL GOING: Good to soft (soft in places; 7.0)**
Wind: strong, across Weather: windy, bright spells and blustery showers

## 7000 CALL STAR SPORTS ON 08000 521 321 FILLIES' H'CAP 5f 215y

2:25 (2:25) (Class 5) (0-75,77) 3-Y-O+ £2,911 (£866; £432; £216) **Stalls Centre**

Form RPR

2664 1 **Storm Cry**[20] 6290 3-9-7 **77** DavidProbert 3 86
(Mark Johnston) *racd in 4th: effrt over 1f out: hdwy to chse ldr and edgd lft 1f out: styd on to ld 75yds out: sn in command and eased cl home* 5/2[2]

2514 2 *1 1/2* **Monteamiata (IRE)**[35] 5711 3-9-5 **75** LiamKeniry 6 79
(Ed Walker) *dwlt: sn rcvrd to chse ldr: clsd and rdn over 1f out: lost 2nd 1f out: styd on same pce ins fnl f: snatched 2nd again on post* 2/1[1]

26 3 *nse* **Flowing Clarets**[26] 6072 4-8-7 **61** KieranO'Neill 4 65
(John Bridger) *led: clr 1/2-way: rdn 2f out: drvn ins fnl f: hdd 75yds out: no ex: wknd towards fin and lost 2nd on post* 9/2

2252 4 *hd* **Whitecrest**[12] 6586 9-9-3 **71** LukeMorris 5 74
(John Spearing) *chsd ldng pair: rdn over 2f out: unable qck and dropped to 4th over 1f out: rallied ins fnl f: styd on u.p fnl 100yds and pressing for 2nd cl home* 7/2[3]

6036 5 *8* **Pretty Bubbles**[29] 5965 8-9-7 **75** (v) FergusSweeney 2 53
(J R Jenkins) *stdd s: hld up in rr: sltly impeded 4f out: effrt on inner ent fnl 2f: no imp over 1f out: wknd and wl btn whn eased towards fin* 10/1

1m 12.5s (2.30) **Going Correction** +0.475s/f (Yiel)
**WFA** 3 from 4yo+ 2lb 5 Ran SP% **111.4**
Speed ratings (Par 100): **103,101,100,100,90**
CSF £8.03 TOTE £2.70: £1.50, £1.40; EX 8.40 Trifecta £21.60.

**Owner** A D Spence & Mr And Mrs P Hargreaves **Bred** Mr & Mrs P Hargreaves & Mr A D Spence **Trained** Middleham Moor, N Yorks

**FOCUS**

Rail moved out between the 6f and 2.5f, adding 5yds to each race distance. They stayed towards the far side in what was a modest opening race. Straightforward form.

## 7001 FOLLOW US ON TWITTER @ STARSPORTS_BET EBF NOVICE STKS 6f 210y

2:55 (2:57) (Class 5) 2-Y-O £2,911 (£866; £432; £216) **Stalls Centre**

Form RPR

54 1 **Rastrelli (FR)**[17] 6374 2-8-13 0 GeorgeWood(3) 4 81+
(Charlie Appleby) *trckd ldng pair: swtchd rt and chal between horses over 1f out: led ent fnl f: r.o wl and drew clr ins fnl f: easily* 6/5[1]

2 *4* **Illusional** 2-9-2 0 DavidProbert 2 70
(Mark Johnston) *led: rdn and rn green 2f out: hdd ent fnl f: easily outpcd by wnr but kpt on for clr 2nd ins fnl f* 7/2[3]

56 3 *1 1/4* **Ashington**[11] 6616 2-8-9 0 GabrieleMalune(7) 3 67+
(Luca Cumani) *hld up wl in tch in last pair: effrt in 4th and swtchd rt over 1f out: sn outpcd: wnt 3rd ins fnl f: kpt on but no ch w wnr: eased towards fin* 16/1

52 4 *1 3/4* **Sarstedt**[47] 5292 2-9-2 0 DaneO'Neill 5 62
(Henry Candy) *t.k.h: sn pressing ldr: rdn and outpcd in 3rd jst over 1f out: wknd ins fnl f* 15/8[2]

00 5 *10* **Swift Fox**[24] 6133 2-8-13 0 HectorCrouch(3) 6 36
(Gary Moore) *wl in tch in midfield: effrt over 2f out: sn struggling and btn whn hung lft over 1f out: wknd fnl f* 33/1

56 6 *13* **Kalakchee**[20] 6286 2-9-2 0 (h) KieranShoemark 1
(Amy Murphy) *awkward as stalls opened and slowly away: hld up in tch in rr: pushed along over 2f out: rdn 2f out: sn lost tch and eased ins fnl f* 66/1

1m 26.13s (3.03) **Going Correction** +0.475s/f (Yiel) 6 Ran SP% **112.8**
Speed ratings (Par 95): **101,96,95,93,81 66**
CSF £5.96 TOTE £1.90: £1.10, £2.30; EX 7.10 Trifecta £40.50.

**Owner** Godolphin **Bred** T De La Heronniere Et Al **Trained** Newmarket, Suffolk

**FOCUS**

Add 5yds. They again stayed far side. This might prove a fair enough race, and the 3rd looks the key.

## 7002 STACATRUC FORKLIFTS UP THE H'CAP 6f 210y

3:25 (3:27) (Class 5) (0-75,78) 3-Y-O+ £2,911 (£866; £432; £216) **Stalls Centre**

Form RPR

2015 1 **Good Luck Charm**[17] 6378 8-9-2 **73** (b) HectorCrouch(3) 8 81
(Gary Moore) *hld up in tch in midfield: clsd to trck ldrs over 2f out: rdn to chal over 1f out: led and edgd lft ent fnl f: styd on* 12/1

2531 2 *1* **King Of Swing**[9] 6681 4-8-13 **72** (h) FinleyMarsh(5) 1 77
(Richard Hughes) *hld up in rr: swtchd rt but stl plenty to do 2f out: hdwy to chse clr ldng pair and wandered ins fnl f: clsd and swtchd rt wl ins fnl f: rdr dropped rein but r.o strly to go 2nd nr fin* 3/1[2]

1321 3 *1/2* **Black Caesar (IRE)**[7] 6753 6-9-3 **78** 6ex SebastianWoods(7) 7 82
(Philip Hide) *trckd ldrs tl led 2f out: sn rdn and hrd pressed: hdd ent fnl f: kpt on same pce and a hld ins fnl f: lost 2nd nr fin* 2/1[1]

0430 4 *2* **Sarangoo**[10] 6656 9-9-3 **71** DaneO'Neill 2 70
(Malcolm Saunders) *trckd ldng trio: clsd and nt clr run over 2f out: effrt ent fnl 2f: chsd clr ldng pair but unable qck u.p over 1f out: kpt on same pce ins fnl f* 10/1

6123 5 *3/4* **Field Of Vision (IRE)**[16] 6442 4-9-2 **75** JoshuaBryan(5) 6 72
(Joseph Tuite) *off the pce in last: rdn and stl plenty to do 2f out: hdwy ins fnl f: styd on wl fnl 100yds: nt rch ldrs* 11/2[3]

505 6 *1/2* **East Coast Lady (IRE)**[34] 5750 5-8-13 **67** KieranShoemark 3 63
(William Stone) *led for 2f: chsd ldr tl 2f out: outpcd and edging rt over 1f out: wl hld and kpt on same pce ins fnl f* 14/1

3230 7 *2* **Live Dangerously**[17] 6378 7-8-7 **61** oh5 KieranO'Neill 4 51
(John Bridger) *stdd after s: a in last trio: no imp u.p over 1f out: n.d* 10/1

0004 8 *18* **El Torito (IRE)**[39] 5560 3-9-1 **73** (p) PatCosgrave 5 15
(Jim Boyle) *hung lft thrght: chsd ldr tl led 5f out: hdd 2f out: sn dropped out: bhd and eased ins fnl f* 8/1

1m 25.4s (2.30) **Going Correction** +0.475s/f (Yiel)
**WFA** 3 from 4yo+ 4lb 8 Ran SP% **117.4**
Speed ratings (Par 103): **105,103,103,101,100 99,97,76**
CSF £49.39 CT £105.66 TOTE £13.40: £2.90, £1.50, £1.40; EX 77.70 Trifecta £190.90.

**Owner** Heart Of The South Racing **Bred** John And Caroline Penny **Trained** Lower Beeding, W Sussex

**FOCUS**
Add 5yds. They raced far side in this modest handicap. The winner has been rated in line with his best from the last two years.

## 7003 STARSPORTSBET.CO.UK H'CAP 1m 3f 198y
3:55 (3:57) (Class 6) (0-60,61) 3-Y-O £2,587 (£770; £384; £192) Stalls High

Form RPR
50-0 1 **Send Up (IRE)**[20] 6287 3-9-7 58 LukeMorris 4 67+
(Sir Mark Prescott Bt) *hld up in tch: rdn wl over 3f out: pressed ldng pair over 1f out: kpt on to chal 1f out: led ins fnl f: forged ahd under hands and heels riding towards fin* **15/2**

0234 2 ½ **Broughtons Admiral**[27] 6048 3-9-7 58 (p[1]) RobertWinston 7 65
(Henry Spiller) *hld up wl in tch: clsd to press ldrs 5f out tl led wl over 1f out: edging lft ent fnl f: drvn and hdd ins fnl f: styd on same pce after* **4/5[1]**

0125 3 6 **Ablaze**[21] 6259 3-9-5 56 PatCosgrave 2 53
(Laura Mongan) *led for 1f: chsd ldr tl led again over 3f out: rdn and hdd over 1f out: getting outpcd whn hung lft and n.m.r jst over 1f out: wknd ins fnl f* **3/1[2]**

0643 4 15 **African Quest**[7] 6751 3-8-5 45 NoelGarbutt(3) 1 18
(Gary Moore) *t.k.h: trckd ldrs: rdn over 3f out: outpcd and btn over 2f out: wknd over 1f out* **13/2[3]**

-054 5 nk **Vaudieu**[124] 2515 3-9-4 58 (b) JackDuern(3) 5 31
(Dean Ivory) *dwlt: hdwy to ld after 1f: hdd over 3f out: rdn and dropped out ent fnl 2f: sn wknd* **28/1**

2m 41.82s (9.12) **Going Correction** +0.475s/f (Yiel) 5 Ran SP% **109.1**
Speed ratings (Par 99): **88,87,83,73,73**
CSF £14.01 TOTE £5.20: £2.50, £1.30; EX 13.40 Trifecta £19.10.
**Owner** Old Harrovian Racing Club **Bred** Barronstown Stud **Trained** Newmarket, Suffolk

**FOCUS**
Add 5yds. They stayed far side in the straight. This only seriously concerned three horses, but the first two pulled clear.

## 7004 LOVE FAIRS ANTIQUE FAIR 22 OCT H'CAP 1m 1f 207y
4:25 (4:26) (Class 5) (0-75,76) 3-Y-O+ £2,911 (£866; £432; £216) Stalls High

Form RPR
-032 1 **Oden**[14] 6518 3-9-6 76 (p) JackMitchell 6 88+
(Roger Varian) *pressed ldr tl led over 6f out: gng best over 2f out: shkn up over 1f out: edging lft but clr 1f out: styd on and in n.d ins fnl f: easily* **2/1[1]**

3253 2 5 **Prerogative (IRE)**[21] 6258 3-9-4 74 (p) TomMarquand 5 75
(Richard Hannon) *led tl over 6f out: rdn over 3f out: drvn and outpcd by wnr over 1f out: wl hld but plugged on to hold 2nd ins fnl f* **7/2[2]**

53 3 hd **Haulani (USA)**[49] 5218 3-9-0 73 (bt[1]) HectorCrouch(3) 3 74
(Philip Hide) *t.k.h: trckd ldrs: effrt on inner 3f out: outpcd by wnr and hung lft over 1f out: battling for wl hld 2nd ins fnl f: plugged on u.p* **2/1[1]**

1611 4 1 ¼ **Av A Word**[13] 6557 3-9-2 72 (p) LukeMorris 2 70
(Daniel Kubler) *s.i.s: in tch in rr: effrt over 2f out: no imp u.p over 1f out: wl hld 4th ins fnl f: eased towards fin* **11/2[3]**

0044 5 3 ½ **Pink Ribbon (IRE)**[13] 6557 5-8-10 65 (p) MitchGodwin(5) 4 55
(Sylvester Kirk) *hld up wl in tch: rdn and dropped to rr over 2f out: sn drvn and no imp: wl btn and hung lft over 1f out: eased towards fin* **12/1**

2m 7.92s (4.32) **Going Correction** +0.475s/f (Yiel)
**WFA** 3 from 5yo 6lb 5 Ran SP% **112.0**
Speed ratings (Par 103): **101,97,96,95,93**
CSF £9.49 TOTE £3.00: £1.90, £1.70; EX 10.10 Trifecta £20.20.
**Owner** Saleh Al Homaizi & Imad Al Sagar **Bred** Saleh Al Homaizi & Imad Al Sagar **Trained** Newmarket, Suffolk

**FOCUS**
Add 5yds. The main action unfolded towards the far side, and nothing could live with the progressive winner.

## 7005 BRIGHTON LIONS FIREWORK NIGHT 5 NOV H'CAP 7f 211y
4:55 (4:55) (Class 6) (0-60,62) 3-Y-O £2,587 (£770; £384; £192) Stalls Centre

Form RPR
2-00 1 **Buskin River (IRE)**[24] 6153 3-9-11 62 RyanTate 9 68
(James Eustace) *wl in tch in midfield: effrt to chse ldrs 2f out: drvn and ev ch ent fnl f: led ins fnl f: styd on: rdn out* **6/1[3]**

0056 2 nk **Dawn Goddess**[20] 6281 3-8-5 45 NoelGarbutt(3) 8 50
(Gary Moore) *s.i.s: hld up in tch: rdn and hdwy to join ldrs and r against stands' rail over 3f out: led over 2f out: drvn over 1f out: hdd ins fnl f: kpt on but hld cl home* **16/1**

6005 3 2 ¾ **Solitary Sister (IRE)**[7] 6748 3-8-8 52 (v) NicolaCurrie(7) 3 51
(Richard Spencer) *s.i.s and flashing tail early: hld up in tch in rr: rdn and hdwy on inner over 2f out: ev ch and flashing tail u.p whn drifted to far rail over 1f out: wknd ins fnl f* **8/1**

3353 4 nse **Oakley Pride (IRE)**[32] 5852 3-9-4 55 (t[1]) LukeMorris 11 54
(Gay Kelleway) *wl in tch in midfield: c towards stands' rail and effrt over 2f out: chsd ldng trio 1f out: hung lft and kpt on same pce ins fnl f* **16/1**

U512 5 4 ½ **Captain Sedgwick (IRE)**[35] 5714 3-9-2 53 JimmyQuinn 6 42
(John Spearing) *wl in tch in midfield: effrt over 2f out: no imp u.p over 1f out: wknd ins fnl f* **9/2[2]**

1310 6 3 ½ **Luxford**[40] 5545 3-9-5 56 MartinDwyer 12 36
(John Best) *led: hdd over 2f out: rdn and unable qck 2f out: lost pl over 1f out: wknd fnl f* **9/2[2]**

6-03 7 2 ¼ **Latest Quest (IRE)**[139] 2056 3-8-10 52 MitchGodwin(5) 5 27
(Sylvester Kirk) *wl in tch in midfield: effrt over 2f out: no imp and btn over 1f out: wknd fnl f* **12/1**

4033 8 1 **Zoffanist (IRE)**[12] 6587 3-9-3 54 JackMitchell 13 27
(Amanda Perrett) *pressed ldrs: rdn 3f out: lost pl and btn wl over 1f out: wknd over 1f out* **7/2[1]**

0253 9 3 **Ronni Layne**[34] 5761 3-8-13 50 KieranShoemark 4 16
(Conrad Allen) *pressed ldr tl 3f out: sn struggling and lost pl 2f out: bhd ins fnl f* **17/2**

041 10 21 **Garth Rockett**[41] 5512 3-9-2 58 (p) JennyPowell(5) 1
(Brendan Powell) *chsd ldrs: rdn over 2f out: sn struggling and bhd 2f out: eased ins fnl f: t.o* **14/1**

1m 39.25s (3.25) **Going Correction** +0.475s/f (Yiel) 10 Ran SP% **120.6**
Speed ratings (Par 99): **102,101,98,98,94 90,88,87,84,63**
CSF £100.06 CT £800.34 TOTE £6.80: £2.00, £5.80, £3.00; EX 144.70 Trifecta £984.80.
**Owner** David Batten & Mrs James Eustace **Bred** Cbs Bloodstock **Trained** Newmarket, Suffolk

**FOCUS**
Add 5yds. The runners were all over the place in the straight, with the winner up the middle, the runner-up against the stands' rail and the third alone on the far side. That trio came into this a combined 0-19, so moderate stuff.

## 7006 SANTA FUN RUN 25 NOV APPRENTICE H'CAP 7f 211y
5:25 (5:25) (Class 6) (0-60,61) 4-Y-O+ £2,587 (£770; £384; £192) Stalls Centre

Form RPR
3040 1 **Intimately**[26] 6076 4-9-10 57 GeorgeWood 3 63
(Jonathan Portman) *stdd s: hld up wl in tch in last pair: clsd and nt clr run over 2f out: swtchd lft and hdwy to chse ldrs whn bumping w rival over 1f out: rdn to ld ent fnl f: styd on: rdn out* **7/1**

-202 2 ¾ **World Record (IRE)**[21] 6263 7-9-10 57 KieranShoemark 8 61
(Mick Quinn) *mostly chsd ldr: rdn and clsd to ld over 1f out: sn drvn and hdd: kpt on but a hld ins fnl f* **11/4[1]**

6500 3 1 ¼ **Port Lairge**[27] 6035 7-8-12 45 (b) PhilDennis 4 46
(Michael Chapman) *dwlt: wl in tch in last trio: hdwy on outer to go prom in chsng gp 3f out: clsd and chsd ldrs u.p over 1f out: kpt on same pce ins fnl f* **10/1**

1303 4 ½ **Papou Tony**[20] 6284 4-10-0 61 HectorCrouch 1 61
(George Baker) *hld up in tch in last pair: rdn and hdwy over 2f out: chsng ldrs whn bumping w wnr over 1f out: sn ev ch: hung lft 1f out: no ex and wknd wl ins fnl f* **10/3[2]**

/000 5 ¾ **Rolling Dice**[25] 6101 6-9-10 57 (v[1]) CallumShepherd 9 56
(Dominic Ffrench Davis) *hld up wl in tch in midfield: clsd 2f out: rdn to press ldrs over 1f out: unable qck and wknd ins fnl f* **6/1[3]**

0304 6 2 ¼ **Nonno Giulio (IRE)**[9] 6681 6-9-4 58 (b) NicolaCurrie(7) 7 51
(Conor Dore) *t.k.h: hld up wl in tch in midfield: clsd 2f out: rdn and ev ch over 1f out: sn outpcd and wknd ins fnl f* **6/1[3]**

0036 7 9 **The Firm (IRE)**[20] 6296 8-9-1 55 (b) GinaMangan(7) 6 28
(J R Jenkins) *t.k.h: chsd ldrs tl led 5f out: sn clr: rdn and edgd rt over 1f out: sn hdd and dropped out: fdd ins fnl f* **25/1**

0506 8 3 ¾ **Megalala (IRE)**[44] 5405 16-8-10 46 MitchGodwin(3) 5 10
(John Bridger) *led tl 5f out: rdn and lost pl over 2f out: bhd fnl 2f* **20/1**

0356 9 7 **Ede's The Mover**[53] 5062 4-9-2 52 PaddyBradley(3) 10
(Pat Phelan) *dwlt: in tch in midfield: rdn over 2f out: sn struggling: bhd fnl 2f: eased ins fnl f* **10/1**

1m 38.95s (2.95) **Going Correction** +0.475s/f (Yiel) 9 Ran SP% **117.6**
Speed ratings (Par 101): **104,103,102,101,100 98,89,85,78**
CSF £27.12 CT £197.24 TOTE £7.50: £2.20, £1.10, £3.50; EX 31.70 Trifecta £207.70.
**Owner** Whitcoombe Park Racing **Bred** S Emmet And Miss R Emmet **Trained** Upper Lambourn, Berks
■ Stewards' Enquiry : Kieran Shoemark four-day ban: used whip above permitted level (Sep 25-28)

**FOCUS**
Add 5yds. They raced middle to far side in this moderate handicap. It's been rated around the balance of the front three's 2017 form.
T/Jkpt: £38,336.20 to a £1 stake. Pool: £95,840.57 - 2.5 winning units T/Plt: £47.10 to a £1 stake. Pool: £86,342.76 - 1,337.99 winning units T/Qpdt: £19.50 to a £1 stake. Pool: - 225.77 winning units **Steve Payne**

7007 - 7010a (Foreign Racing) - See Raceform Interactive

# 6803 MAISONS-LAFFITTE (R-H)
Monday, September 11

**OFFICIAL GOING: Turf: very soft**

## 7011a PRIX SARACA (LISTED RACE) (2YO) (TURF) 6f 110y
1:20 (1:20) 2-Y-O £25,641 (£10,256; £7,692; £5,128; £2,564)

RPR
1 **Sonjeu (FR)**[37] 5679 2-8-13 0 MaximeGuyon 8 95
(C Ferland, France) **61/10[3]**
2 nk **Beau Ideal**[44] 2-9-2 0 MickaelBarzalona 2 97
(A Fabre, France) *hld up towards rr: gd hdwy 2f out: rdn to chal 1f out: drvn ins fnl f: jst failed* **6/5[1]**
3 ½ **Fastidious (FR)**[37] 5679 2-9-2 0 ChristopheSoumillon 3 96
(Louis Baudron, France) **36/5**
4 1 ¼ **So Hi Society (IRE)**[18] 6354 2-8-13 0 CristianDemuro 4 90
(Archie Watson) *hld up towards rr: pushed along to chal over 2f out: sltly short of room against rail over 1f out and swtchd: styd on ins fnl f* **43/10[2]**
5 nse **Yayajonh (FR)**[37] 5679 2-9-2 0 HugoJourniac 5 92
(Jane Soubagne, France) **199/10**
6 3 **Salt Lake City (FR)**[6] 2-9-2 0 OlivierPeslier 7 84
(Robert Collet, France) **164/10**
7 4 **Yori (IRE)**[38] 2-8-13 0 AnthonyCrastus 9 70
(P Vovcenko, Germany) **26/1**
8 2 ½ **Sagres**[27] 6051 2-8-13 0 (b) Pierre-CharlesBoudot 6 63
(F-H Graffard, France) **111/10**
9 ¾ **Blue Tango (GER)**[43] 5461 2-9-2 0 AlexisBadel 1 64
(M Munch, Germany) **177/10**

1m 18.7s 9 Ran SP% **118.4**
PARI-MUTUEL (all including 1 euro stake): WIN 7.10; PLACE 1.60, 1.30, 1.70; DF 5.80; SF 16.70.
**Owner** Wertheimer & Frere **Bred** S Vidal **Trained** France

## 7012a PRIX PHAREL (MAIDEN) (2YO COLTS & GELDINGS) (TURF) 6f 110y
1:50 (1:20) 2-Y-O £11,538 (£4,615; £3,461; £2,307; £1,153)

RPR
1 **True Romance (FR)**[38] 5626 2-9-2 0 MaximeGuyon 2 87
(F-H Graffard, France) **21/10[1]**
2 3 **Cabotin (FR)**[16] 6453 2-9-2 0 Pierre-CharlesBoudot 3 79
(A Fabre, France) **27/10[2]**
3 nk **The Lamplighter (FR)**[37] 5641 2-9-2 0 TheoBachelot 5 78
(George Baker) *wl into stride: led early: pushed along over 2f out to hold advantage: rdn and hdd 1f out: styd on one pce fnl f* **269/10**
4 ¾ **Wilderness Now (IRE)**[30] 5952 2-9-2 0 ChristopheSoumillon 9 76
(F Chappet, France) **49/10[3]**
5 shd **Arrogant (IRE)**[17] 6403 2-9-2 0 MickaelBarzalona 6 76
(Jose Santos) *sn trcking ldrs: rdn to chal 2f out: drvn over 1f out: styd on same pce fnl f* **131/10**
6 shd **Marsh Harbour (FR)**[32] 5989 2-9-2 0 OlivierPeslier 11 75
(Mario Hofer, Germany) **194/10**
7 1 ¾ **Anotherfortheroad** 2-9-2 0 AntoineHamelin 10 71
(Matthieu Palussiere, France) **111/10**

8 1 3/4 **French Bere (FR)** 2-8-11 0 StephanePasquier 4 61
(N Clement, France) 188/10
9 1 1/4 **Easyrider (FR)**[30] 5952 2-8-10 0 JeromeMoutard(6) 7 62
(J-M Lefebvre, France) 43/1
10 7 **Zafeeno (FR)** 2-8-11 0 AlexisBadel 1 38
(H-A Pantall, France) 29/1
11 20 **Maktava (FR)**[106] 2-9-2 0 GregoryBenoist 8
(D Smaga, France) 132/10

1m 20.3s 11 Ran SP% 117.8
PARI-MUTUEL (all including 1 euro stake): WIN 3.10; PLACE 1.50, 1.70, 4.70; DF 3.80; SF 8.80.
**Owner** S Hadida, Haras Des Adelis & T De La Heronniere **Bred** T De La Heronniere & Mme D De La Heronniere **Trained** France

# 6567 CATTERICK (L-H)

Tuesday, September 12

**OFFICIAL GOING: Good to soft (soft in places; 7.6)**
Wind: Fresh; half behind Weather: Fine

## 7013 IRISH STALLION FARMS EBF NOVICE MEDIAN AUCTION STKS 5f 212y
1:45 (1:45) (Class 5) 2-Y-O £3,881 (£1,155; £577; £288) Stalls Low

Form RPR
33 1 **Captain Jameson (IRE)**[20] 6312 2-9-2 0 JasonHart 3 83+
(John Quinn) *mde most: hdd briefly 3f out: rdn over 2f out: strly pressed ent fnl f: kpt on wl* 6/1[3]
44 2 1 1/4 **Mont Kinabalu (IRE)**[61] 4792 2-9-2 0 KevinStott 6 79
(Kevin Ryan) *hld up in tch: pushed along over 3f out: hdwy over 2f out: rdn to chal strly ent fnl f: one pce fnl 75yds* 5/2[1]
3240 3 6 **Charnock Richard**[19] 6353 2-9-2 83 TomEaves 7 61
(David Brown) *pressed ldr: rdn over 2f out: wknd fnl f* 11/4[2]
03 4 2 3/4 **The Great Dandini (IRE)**[27] 6071 2-9-2 0 (t[1]) RobertWinston 5 52
(Seamus Durack) *chsd ldrs: rdn over 2f out: wknd appr fnl f* 5/2[1]
05 5 1 1/2 **Bertie Wallace (IRE)**[28] 6042 2-9-2 0 GrahamLee 2 47
(Keith Dalgleish) *trckd ldrs: rdn over 2f out: wknd over 1f out* 28/1
60 6 1 1/4 **Sir Derrick (IRE)**[17] 6432 2-8-13 0 RachelRichardson(3) 1 43
(Tim Easterby) *dwlt: hld up in tch: rdn over 2f out: wknd over 1f out* 25/1
7 8 **Blyton Lass** 2-8-11 0 PaulMulrennan 4 14
(James Given) *a in rr* 33/1
8 6 **Boudica Bay (IRE)** 2-8-11 0 NeilFarley 8
(Eric Alston) *a outpcd in rr* 50/1

1m 14.07s (0.47) **Going Correction** +0.175s/f (Good) 8 Ran SP% 110.3
Speed ratings (Par 95): **103,101,93,89,87 86,75,67**
CSF £19.69 TOTE £7.30: £1.90, £1.40, £1.80; EX 22.60 Trifecta £55.30.
**Owner** The Jam Partnership **Bred** Yeomanstown Stud **Trained** Settrington, N Yorks

**FOCUS**
There was 4.5mm of rain on Saturday and another 8mm overnight Sunday, but it had been dry over the previous 24 hours and the going was given as good to soft, soft in places (GoingStick: 7.6). After riding in the first race Rachel Richardson felt it was "soft ground", Tom Eaves described it as "good to soft" and Graham Lee described conditions as "not that bad, a little bit dead but good to soft." The rail on the bend turning into the home straight was dolled out 4yds, and the Parade ring bend was dolled out 2yds. Race distance increased by 12yds. A fair maiden in which the first two drew right away. They stayed on the inside in the straight.

## 7014 ALL NEW RACINGUK.COM H'CAP 5f
2:15 (2:19) (Class 6) (0-65,73) 3-Y-O £2,264 (£673; £336; £168) Stalls Low

Form RPR
0116 1 **Ebitda**[13] 6574 3-9-2 64 GeorgeBuckell(5) 2 72
(Scott Dixon) *prom: rdn to ld 1f out: kpt on* 9/1
2202 2 1/2 **Vintage Dream (IRE)**[10] 6694 3-9-2 59 (be[1]) PatrickMathers 1 65
(Noel Wilson) *led: rdn 2f out: hdd 1f out: kpt on but a hld* 11/1
626 3 3 3/4 **Charlie's Dreamer**[22] 6268 3-9-5 62 LukeMorris 9 55
(Michael Appleby) *hld up: sn pushed along: hdwy appr fnl f: kpt on: wnt modest 3rd post* 14/1
4411 4 hd **Hamidans Girl (IRE)**[4] 6896 3-10-2 73 6ex PaulMulrennan 11 65
(Keith Dalgleish) *trckd ldrs: pushed along over 1f out: wknd ins fnl f: lost 3rd nr fin* 5/2[1]
003 5 3/4 **Bithynia (IRE)**[15] 6526 3-9-3 60 (t[1]) JoeFanning 6 49
(Christopher Kellett) *chsd ldrs: rdn over 2f out: wknd ins fnl f* 12/1
454 6 nk **Bay Station**[16] 6469 3-9-2 59 (p) PJMcDonald 8 47
(Jason Ward) *hld up: rdn over 2f out: minor late hdwy: nvr threatened* 13/2[3]
6044 7 3 1/4 **Glyder**[19] 6339 3-9-2 59 RoystonFfrench 3 36
(John Holt) *chsd ldrs: rdn over 2f out: wknd fnl f* 13/2[3]
5012 8 1 1/2 **Hot Hannah**[18] 6384 3-9-4 66 CallumRodriguez(5) 10 37
(Michael Dods) *prom: rdn 2f out: wknd fnl f* 7/2[2]
6005 9 2 1/2 **Verdi (IRE)**[13] 6582 3-7-10 46 ow1 (b) JackOsborn(7) 4 8
(John Ryan) *awkward s: a outpcd in rr* 80/1

1m 0.45s (0.65) **Going Correction** +0.175s/f (Good) 9 Ran SP% 111.4
Speed ratings (Par 99): **101,100,94,93,92 92,87,84,80**
CSF £97.32 CT £1344.16 TOTE £9.40: £2.60, £2.70, £2.70; EX 62.90 Trifecta £639.00.
**Owner** Chesterfield Estates **Bred** Selwood, Hoskins & Trickledown **Trained** Babworth, Notts

**FOCUS**
A modest sprint but a progressive winner.

## 7015 2017 CATTERICK TWELVE FURLONG SERIES H'CAP 1m 4f 13y
2:45 (2:45) (Class 6) (0-65,65) 4-Y-O+ £3,234 (£962; £481; £240) Stalls Centre

Form RPR
3050 1 **Wotabreeze (IRE)**[16] 6467 4-9-7 65 (p[1]) JasonHart 11 73
(John Quinn) *midfield: pushed along and hdwy over 2f out: rdn to ld appr fnl f: kpt on* 7/1[3]
5131 2 1 1/4 **Mr Sundowner (USA)**[13] 6592 5-8-11 58 (t) SammyJoBell(3) 2 64
(Wilf Storey) *midfield: pushed along and hdwy over 2f out: chsd ldrs over 1f out: kpt on ins fnl f* 5/1[1]
042 3 2 **Steccando (IRE)**[22] 6269 4-8-13 57 BenCurtis 1 60
(Sally Haynes) *in tch: rdn and hdwy over 2f out: chal strly over 1f out: no ex fnl 110yds* 5/1[1]
0020 4 2 **Annoushka**[42] 5508 4-8-6 50 (t) AdamBeschizza 14 50
(Mrs Ilka Gansera-Leveque) *sn led: rdn over 2f out: hdd appr fnl f: no ex* 16/1
0-3P 5 1/2 **Shamar (FR)**[10] 6709 9-9-5 63 (t) TonyHamilton 13 62
(R K Watson, Ire) *hld up in midfield: rdn 3f out: styd on fnl f: nvr threatened* 6/1[2]

6000 6 1 **Patent**[28] 6035 4-8-2 46 oh1 (b) JamesSullivan 3 43
(Peter Niven) *hld up in midfield: rdn over 3f out: styd on fnl f: nvr threatened* 18/1
2-00 7 2 1/4 **Optima Petamus**[53] 5096 5-9-5 63 JackGarritty 12 57
(Patrick Holmes) *hld up: rdn along 3f out: sme late hdwy: nvr threatened* 28/1
1200 8 1/2 **Gold Merlion (IRE)**[14] 6556 4-9-7 65 JoeFanning 5 58
(Mark Johnston) *prom: rdn over 3f out: wknd over 1f out* 16/1
0355 9 1 1/4 **Falcon's Fire (IRE)**[32] 5883 4-9-6 64 (b[1]) AndrewMullen 4 55
(Keith Dalgleish) *trckd ldrs: rdn to chse ldr over 2f out: wknd over 1f out* 10/1
6556 10 4 **Aqua Libre**[18] 6369 4-9-6 64 CamHardie 9 48
(Jennie Candlish) *hld up: nvr threatened* 14/1
400 11 12 **Lopito De Vega (IRE)**[16] 6470 5-9-1 59 FrannyNorton 7 24
(David C Griffiths) *trckd ldrs: rdn along over 3f out: wknd over 2f out* 7/1[3]
-553 12 4 1/2 **Duke Of Sonning**[56] 4545 5-9-0 58 (b) DuranFentiman 15 16
(Shaun Harris) *s.i.s: sn pushed along in rr: a bhd* 25/1
0-00 13 95 **Belle Peinture (FR)**[42] 5498 6-8-2 46 oh1 (p) JoeDoyle 8
(Alan Lockwood) *prom: rdn along and lost pl over 6f out: sn struggling in rr: t.o fnl 3f* 100/1

2m 40.23s (1.33) **Going Correction** +0.175s/f (Good) 13 Ran SP% 113.7
Speed ratings (Par 101): **102,101,99,98,98 97,96,95,94,92 84,81,17**
CSF £39.08 CT £190.45 TOTE £5.70: £1.60, £2.40, £1.70; EX 32.70 Trifecta £54.00.
**Owner** The New Century Partnership **Bred** Triermore Stud **Trained** Settrington, N Yorks

**FOCUS**
Race distance increased by 18yds. An ordinary handicap.

## 7016 BOOK NOW FOR SATURDAY 23RD SEPTEMBER H'CAP 7f 6y
3:15 (3:17) (Class 4) (0-80,81) 3-Y-O £6,469 (£1,925; £962; £481) Stalls Low

Form RPR
1002 1 **Our Charlie Brown**[12] 6627 3-9-2 74 JamesSullivan 2 81
(Tim Easterby) *in tch: pushed along and hdwy on inner over 2f out: rdn to ld over 1f out: kpt on* 7/2[2]
3242 2 1 **Heir Of Excitement (IRE)**[20] 6315 3-9-5 77 (p) ShaneGray 9 81
(Kevin Ryan) *chsd ldrs towards outer: rdn and ev ch over 1f out: one pce fnl 110yds* 5/1[3]
2500 3 1 1/4 **Tai Sing Yeh (IRE)**[66] 4634 3-9-7 79 (t) LukeMorris 5 80
(Charles Hills) *trckd ldr: rdn over 2f out: kpt on same pce* 6/1
41-4 4 3/4 **Mamdood (IRE)**[59] 4912 3-8-13 78 (t[1]) JamieGormley(7) 3 77
(Susan Corbett) *hld up: pushed along 2f out: hmpd and swtchd lft appr fnl f: kpt on: short of room again fnl 75yds: nvr able to chal* 14/1
2101 5 nse **Aimez La Vie (IRE)**[46] 5376 3-9-9 81 PaulHanagan 7 79
(Richard Fahey) *trckd ldr: pushed along to chal 2f out: wknd ins fnl f* 10/3[1]
5210 6 1 1/2 **Acadian Angel (IRE)**[19] 6358 3-9-5 77 JasonHart 6 71
(John Quinn) *dwlt: hld up in tch: rdn along over 2f out: no imp and nvr threatened* 13/2
4651 7 3 1/2 **Malcolm The Pug (IRE)**[13] 6582 3-8-9 67 TomEaves 8 52
(David Brown) *sn led: rdn over 2f out: hdd over 1f out: sn wknd* 20/1
656 8 1 3/4 **Betty Grable (IRE)**[24] 6184 3-7-13 60 SammyJoBell(3) 1 40
(Wilf Storey) *hld up: nvr threatened* 11/1

1m 27.22s (0.22) **Going Correction** +0.175s/f (Good) 8 Ran SP% 109.3
Speed ratings (Par 103): **105,103,102,101,101 99,95,93**
CSF £19.36 CT £91.02 TOTE £5.00: £1.60, £1.70, £1.80; EX 14.60 Trifecta £110.60.
**Owner** Ontoawinner, SDH Project Services Ltd 2 **Bred** North Bradon Stud & D R Tucker **Trained** Great Habton, N Yorks

**FOCUS**
Race distance increased by 12yds. A fair handicap fought out by a couple of old foes.

## 7017 BET AT RACINGUK.COM H'CAP (DIV I) 5f 212y
3:45 (3:45) (Class 6) (0-65,65) 3-Y-O+ £2,264 (£673; £336; £168) Stalls Low

Form RPR
0501 1 **Indian Pursuit (IRE)**[13] 6571 4-9-10 65 JasonHart 11 71
(John Quinn) *chsd ldrs: rdn over 2f out: chal fnl f: edgd rt: led narrowly 50yds out: kpt on* 15/2[3]
0020 2 shd **Meandmyshadow**[17] 6435 9-9-4 62 (b) JoshDoyle(3) 12 68
(Alan Brown) *led: pushed along over 3f out: wandered u.p fr over 1f out: hdd 50yds out: kpt on* 9/1
2130 3 1 3/4 **Cupid's Arrow (IRE)**[22] 6265 3-9-5 62 JamesSullivan 4 63
(Ruth Carr) *racd keenly in tch: rdn to chse ldr over 1f out: keeping on whn short of room between 1st and 2nd 75yds out* 5/1[2]
1003 4 2 **Uncle Charlie (IRE)**[20] 6313 3-9-8 65 ShaneGray 8 59
(Ann Duffield) *hld up in midfield: rdn over 2f out: hdwy over 1f out: kpt on fnl f* 8/1
0063 5 nk **Robbian**[28] 6041 6-8-7 51 NoelGarbutt(3) 1 45
(Charles Smith) *midfield: rdn along over 2f out: kpt on fnl f* 20/1
5000 6 1 **Blistering Dancer (IRE)**[52] 5145 7-7-12 46 oh1 (b) JamieGormley(7) 10 37
(Tony Carroll) *prom: rdn over 2f out: wknd over 1f out* 66/1
1140 7 1 1/4 **Clear As A Bell (IRE)**[22] 6265 3-9-4 64 RachelRichardson(3) 6 52
(Tim Easterby) *hld up: minor late hdwy: nvr threatened* 11/1
042 8 nse **Avenue Of Stars**[7] 6786 4-9-9 64 (p) AndrewMullen 7 51
(Karen McLintock) *midfield: rdn over 2f out: wknd over 1f out* 4/1[1]
4016 9 3/4 **Le Manege Enchante (IRE)**[24] 6197 4-9-2 57 (v) PatrickMathers 5 41
(Derek Shaw) *hld up: nvr threatened* 15/2[3]
-005 10 7 **Traveltalk (IRE)**[45] 5411 3-9-7 64 (p) BenCurtis 2 27
(Brian Ellison) *a towards rr* 12/1
000- 11 12 **Clouded Gold**[375] 6105 5-8-5 46 oh1 LukeMorris 3
(Michael Appleby) *midfield: rdn 3f out: wknd over 1f out* 18/1
265 12 1 1/4 **Sarabi**[15] 6527 4-8-12 60 (p) RPWalsh(7) 9
(Scott Dixon) *dwlt: sn prom on outer: rdn over 2f out: wknd over 1f out* 25/1

1m 14.4s (0.80) **Going Correction** +0.175s/f (Good)
**WFA** 3 from 4yo+ 2lb 12 Ran SP% 112.7
Speed ratings (Par 101): **101,100,98,95,95 94,92,92,91,82 66,64**
CSF £68.04 CT £374.13 TOTE £5.50: £2.20, £3.60, £1.90; EX 78.30 Trifecta £426.70.
**Owner** Malcolm Walker **Bred** Sean Gorman **Trained** Settrington, N Yorks

**FOCUS**
Race distance increased by 12yds. It didn't pay to be too far off the pace in this sprint handicap.

## 7018 BET AT RACINGUK.COM H'CAP (DIV II) 5f 212y
4:15 (4:16) (Class 6) (0-65,64) 3-Y-O+ £2,264 (£673; £336; £168) Stalls Low

Form RPR
0302 1 **Bold Spirit**[13] 6572 6-8-11 54 (t) PhilDennis(3) 1 61
(Declan Carroll) *trckd ldrs: rdn to chal ent fnl f: led 50yds out: kpt on* 9/2[2]

5443 **2** 1 3/4 **Rapid Ranger**[13] 6596 3-9-1 **60**....................(h) JoshDoyle(3) 7 62
(David O'Meara) *hld up: stl lot to do 2f out: pushed along and hdwy over 1f out: hung lft ent fnl f: r.o wl fnl 110yds: wnt 2nd nr fin* **9/1**

0021 **3** nk **Spirit Of Zebedee (IRE)**[13] 6572 4-9-9 **63**....................(p) JasonHart 4 65
(John Quinn) *led narrowly: rdn over 2f out: drvn whn hdd 50yds out: no ex: rdr dropped hands nr fin and lost 2nd* **9/4**[1]

0660 **4** 1 **Tanawar (IRE)**[14] 6549 7-9-8 **62**....................(b) JamesSullivan 9 60
(Ruth Carr) *pressed ldr: rdn over 2f out: no ex ins fnl f* **17/2**

0664 **5** 3/4 **Trick Of The Lyte (IRE)**[12] 6630 3-8-6 **48**.................... AndrewMullen 8 44
(John Quinn) *chsd ldrs: rdn over 2f out: no ex fnl f* **13/2**[3]

5000 **6** 1 3/4 **Extrasolar**[14] 6546 7-9-10 **64**....................(t) PhillipMakin 11 54
(Geoffrey Harker) *hld up in midfield: hdwy over 2f out: rdn and one pce fr over 1f out* **17/2**

1405 **7** 3 3/4 **Kodimoor (IRE)**[15] 6531 4-9-6 **60**.................... JoeFanning 3 44
(Christopher Kellett) *pressed ldr: rdn over 2f out: wknd appr fnl f* **11/1**

0-00 **8** 2 **Barkston Ash**[14] 6546 9-9-8 **62**....................(p) NeilFarley 5 35
(Eric Alston) *midfield: sn pushed along: wknd over 1f ot* **16/1**

5-00 **9** 2 1/4 **Paco Lady**[137] 2121 3-8-5 **47**.................... RoystonFfrench 10 13
(Ivan Furtado) *hld up: nvr threatened* **66/1**

0120 **10** 6 **Kyllach Me (IRE)**[83] 3979 5-8-12 **59**....................(v) HarryRussell(7) 2 7
(Bryan Smart) *dwlt: a towards rr* **25/1**

1m 14.47s (0.87) **Going Correction** +0.175s/f (Good)
**WFA** 3 from 4yo+ 2lb **10** Ran SP% **112.9**
Speed ratings (Par 101): **101,98,98,96,95 93,88,85,82,74**
CSF £43.10 CT £114.88 TOTE £6.10: £2.40, £2.60, £1.10; EX 42.00 Trifecta £126.40.
**Owner** Mrs Sarah Bryan **Bred** The Queen **Trained** Malton, N Yorks

■ Stewards' Enquiry : Jason Hart seven-day ban: failing to take all reasonable and permissible measures to obtain the best possible placing

**FOCUS**
Race distance increased by 12yds. This was run in a similar time to the first division.

## 7019 WISE BETTING AT RACINGUK.COM H'CAP 1m 5f 192y
**4:45** (4:48) (Class 5) (0-75,76) 3-Y-O **£2,911** (£866; £432; £216) **Stalls** Low

Form RPR
6412 **1** **Vindicator (IRE)**[31] 5951 3-9-7 **76**....................(p) CallumRodriguez(5) 6 86+
(Michael Dods) *hld up in tch: pushed along and hdwy on outer wl over 2f out: rdn to ld over 1f out: styd on wl* **10/3**[2]

0111 **2** 1 3/4 **Wolfcatcherjack (IRE)**[12] 6632 3-9-12 **76**.................... LukeMorris 3 83
(Sir Mark Prescott Bt) *hld up in tch: rdn along wl over 2f out: styd on fr over 1f out: wnt 2nd ins fnl f but nvr getting to wnr* **7/4**[1]

2254 **3** 2 3/4 **Duke's Girl**[26] 6107 3-9-3 **67**.................... LouisSteward 4 70
(Michael Bell) *trckd ldrs: rdn to chse ldr over 2f out: one pce in 3rd ins fnl f* **5/1**[3]

1215 **4** 1/2 **Sheriff Garrett (IRE)**[17] 6415 3-9-7 **71**....................(p) JamesSullivan 2 75+
(Tim Easterby) *trckd ldrs: racd keenly: short of room on inner over 2f out and shuffled towards rr: sn rdn: styd on fnl f* **9/1**

0230 **5** 1 3/4 **Cornerstone Lad**[44] 5454 3-9-0 **64**.................... AndrewMullen 5 64
(Micky Hammond) *hld up in rr: racd keenly: pushed along whn bit short of room on inner over 2f out: plugged on nvr threatened* **14/1**

0600 **6** 2 **Riviere Argentee (FR)**[12] 6649 3-9-1 **65**....................(v[1]) BenCurtis 1 62
(K R Burke) *prom: led over 3f out: rdn over 2f out: hdd over 1f out: wknd* **50/1**

5223 **7** 6 **Mambo Dancer**[13] 6573 3-9-5 **69**.................... JoeFanning 7 57
(Mark Johnston) *led: hdd over 3f out: already wkng whn short of room over 2f out* **5/1**[3]

3m 6.04s (2.44) **Going Correction** +0.175s/f (Good) **7** Ran SP% **111.4**
Speed ratings (Par 101): **100,99,97,97,96 95,91**
CSF £9.06 CT £26.02 TOTE £4.40: £1.60, £1.50; EX 10.60 Trifecta £46.50.
**Owner** Pat & Gary Cahill **Bred** Gearoid Cahill **Trained** Denton, Co Durham

**FOCUS**
Race distance increased by 18yds. A fair handicap, and improvers finished 1-2.

## 7020 RACING AGAIN 23RD SEPTEMBER H'CAP 5f
**5:15** (5:16) (Class 6) (0-65,64) 4-Y-0+ **£2,587** (£770; £384; £192) **Stalls** Low

Form RPR
4531 **1** **Lydiate Lady**[15] 6531 5-8-9 **52**.................... NeilFarley 3 59
(Eric Alston) *mde all: pressed thrght: rdn 1/2-way: hld on wl* **9/1**

5303 **2** 1/2 **Compton River**[19] 6351 5-9-4 **64**.................... AdamMcNamara(3) 2 69
(Bryan Smart) *prom: rdn to chal strly wl over 1f out: one pce fnl 50yds* **9/1**

220 **3** 1 1/4 **Cruise Tothelimit (IRE)**[53] 5098 9-9-2 **64**........(bt) CallumRodriguez(5) 6 65
(Patrick Morris) *pressed ldr: rdn 1/2-way: one pce fnl f* **16/1**

0040 **4** 1/2 **Nora Batt (IRE)**[10] 6704 4-8-8 **51**.................... BenCurtis 8 50
(John W Nicholson, Ire) *chsd ldrs: rdn 1/2-way: kpt on same pce* **15/2**

0000 **5** 1 1/4 **Coiste Bodhar (IRE)**[92] 3667 6-9-0 **64**.................... RPWalsh(7) 10 58
(Scott Dixon) *midfield: rdn 1/2-way: kpt on same pce: nvr threatened ldrs* **25/1**

6455 **6** shd **Mitchum**[10] 6688 8-7-13 **49**....................(h[1]) JamieGormley(7) 7 43+
(Ron Barr) *outpcd towards rr tl kpt on fnl f* **9/2**[2]

5000 **7** 1 1/4 **Lackaday**[12] 6631 5-8-13 **56**....................(b) PatrickMathers 12 46
(Noel Wilson) *hld up in midfield: rdn along 1/2-way: one pce and nvr threatened* **12/1**

3014 **8** nse **Whipphound**[10] 6688 9-8-10 **53**....................(b) JamesSullivan 4 42
(Ruth Carr) *hld up: nvr threatened* **11/2**[3]

0-02 **9** 3 1/4 **Miss Uppity**[8] 6748 4-8-2 **45**.................... JoeFanning 11 23
(Ivan Furtado) *hld up: rdn along and outpcd 3f out: nvr threatened* **7/2**[1]

6464 **10** shd **Excellent World (IRE)**[7] 6785 4-8-7 **50**.................... BarryMcHugh 9 27
(Tony Coyle) *dwlt: hld up: nvr threatened* **11/1**

0060 **11** 3 **Oddsocks (IRE)**[12] 6635 5-8-2 **45**....................(b[1]) AndrewMullen 1 12
(Tony Carroll) *a towards rr* **100/1**

/0-0 **12** 7 **Excellent Addition (IRE)**[81] 4059 7-8-4 **47**............(t) DuranFentiman 13
(Lee James) *a towards rr* **150/1**

1m 0.33s (0.53) **Going Correction** +0.175s/f (Good) **12** Ran SP% **115.0**
Speed ratings (Par 101): **102,101,99,98,96 96,94,94,88,88 84,72**
CSF £84.26 CT £1274.81 TOTE £10.20: £2.70, £2.80, £4.80; EX 50.20 Trifecta £674.20.
**Owner** The Scotch Piper Racing **Bred** Catridge Farm Stud **Trained** Longton, Lancs

**FOCUS**
Few got into this, the pace holding up well, and the winner built on her Southwell success.
T/Jkpt: Not won. T/Plt: £113.50 to a £1 stake. Pool: £59,255.68 - 381.00 winning units T/Qpdt: £6.80 to a £1 stake. Pool: £5,034.04 - 544.10 winning units **Andrew Sheret**

# 5956 LEICESTER (R-H)
Tuesday, September 12

**OFFICIAL GOING: Good to soft (7.2)**
Wind: medium, behind Weather: fine

## 7021 BRITISH STALLION STUDS APOLLO EBF FILLIES' NOVICE STKS (PLUS 10 RACE) (DIV I) 7f
**2:25** (2:28) (Class 4) 2-Y-O **£6,469** (£1,925; £962; £481) **Stalls** High

Form RPR
3 **1** **Aim Of Artemis (IRE)**[25] 6138 2-9-0 0.................... RyanMoore 2 85+
(Sir Michael Stoute) *hld up in tch in midfield: pushed along and dropped to last trio 4f out: rdn and hdwy whn swtchd lft over 1f out: drvn to chse clr ldng pair 1f out: styd on strly to ld towards fin* **11/4**[2]

41 **2** 1/2 **Shepherd Market (IRE)**[26] 6093 2-9-3 0.................... AdamKirby 9 87
(Clive Cox) *led: rdn and hrd pressed over 1f out: hdd 1f out: battled on gamely u.p to ld again wl ins fnl f: hdd and no ex towards fin* **7/2**[3]

42 **3** nk **Tivoli (IRE)**[18] 6385 2-9-0 0.................... FrankieDettori 10 83
(John Gosden) *travelled strly: trckd ldrs: effrt and rdn to ld over 1f out: led 1f out: sn drvn: hdd and one pce wl ins fnl f* **6/4**[1]

363 **4** 2 **Ziarah (IRE)**[18] 6386 2-9-0 79.................... MartinHarley 6 78
(James Tate) *hld up wl in tch in midfield: effrt 2f out: unable qck u.p over 1f out: kpt on same pce ins fnl f* **7/1**

4 **5** 2 3/4 **Hula Girl**[25] 6138 2-9-0 0.................... JimCrowley 5 71
(Charles Hills) *chsd ldr tl unable qck and lost pl over 1f out: wknd ins fnl f* **12/1**

0 **6** 1 1/4 **Railport Dolly**[28] 6037 2-9-0 0....................(h[1]) AlistairRawlinson 1 68
(Michael Appleby) *chsd ldrs: rdn ent fnl 2f: unable qck and lost pl over 1f out: wknd ins fnl f* **100/1**

**7** 1 1/4 **Preening** 2-9-0 0.................... AndreaAtzeni 3 65
(James Fanshawe) *hld up wl in tch in midfield: rdn over 2f out: sn outpcd: wl hld but kpt on again ins fnl f* **33/1**

**8** 4 1/2 **Grace's Secret** 2-9-0 0.................... LiamKeniry 4 54
(Ed Walker) *s.i.s: in tch in rr: effrt over 2f out: sn struggling and btn 2f out: bhd fnl f* **66/1**

**9** 1 1/2 **Fayrouz** 2-9-0 0.................... SilvestreDeSousa 11 50
(Ismail Mohammed) *stdd and swtchd rt after s: hld up wl in tch in rr: shkn up over 2f out: sn rdn and struggling: wknd and bhd fnl f* **40/1**

50 **10** 1 **Ferrier**[16] 6480 2-9-0 0.................... RyanPowell 7 47
(Sir Mark Prescott Bt) *s.i.s and rousted along early: sn rcvrd and in tch in midfield: rdn 3f out: lost pl and bhd over 1f out* **200/1**

1m 24.9s (-1.30) **Going Correction** -0.025s/f (Good) **10** Ran SP% **117.4**
Speed ratings (Par 94): **106,105,105,102,99 98,96,91,89,88**
CSF £12.81 TOTE £4.10: £1.60, £1.50, £1.10; EX 16.80 Trifecta £39.90.
**Owner** Ballymacoll Stud **Bred** Ballymacoll Stud Farm Ltd **Trained** Newmarket, Suffolk

**FOCUS**
Following 7mm of rain overnight the going had eased slightly to good to soft all over (GoingStick 7.2). The first division of an interesting fillies' novice event in which they came up the centre and those with previous experience dominated. The time was 2.2sec outside standard, suggesting the official going description was about right. After riding in the opener Jim Crowley said: "The ground is on the slow side", Andrea Atzeni and Adam Kirby said: "It is good to soft ground" and Martin Harley said: "It is soft".

## 7022 BRITISH STALLION STUDS APOLLO EBF FILLIES' NOVICE STKS (PLUS 10 RACE) (DIV II) 7f
**2:55** (2:57) (Class 4) 2-Y-O **£6,469** (£1,925; £962; £481) **Stalls** High

Form RPR
**1** **Orsera (IRE)** 2-9-0 0....................(h[1]) JackMitchell 3 77+
(Peter Chapple-Hyam) *t.k.h: trckd ldrs: effrt to chal over 1f out: sn rdn: led ins fnl f: styd on wl and forged ahd towards fin* **20/1**

**2** 1 **Verve (IRE)** 2-9-0 0.................... JamesDoyle 4 75+
(Hugo Palmer) *hld up in tch in midfield: clsd to chse ldrs 2f out: rdn to chal jst over 1f out: kpt on u.p sustained chal tl no ex and one pce towards fin* **6/4**[1]

**3** nk **Beautiful Memory (IRE)** 2-9-0 0.................... OisinMurphy 5 74
(Saeed bin Suroor) *trckd ldr tl rdn to ld over 1f out: sn hrd pressed: hdd ins fnl f: kpt on and stl ev ch tl no ex and one pce towards fin* **11/4**[2]

**4** 2 1/4 **Romaana** 2-9-0 0.................... AndreaAtzeni 8 68
(Simon Crisford) *hld up in tch in midfield: clsd to trck ldrs and shkn up ent fnl 2f: rdn and unable qck over 1f out: kpt on same pce ins fnl f* **8/1**

04 **5** shd **Lady Willpower**[25] 6146 2-9-0 0.................... FranBerry 6 68
(John Quinn) *led tl rdn and hdd over 1f out: 4th and outpcd 1f out: edgd rt and kpt on same pce ins fnl f* **50/1**

**6** 2 3/4 **Savaanah (IRE)** 2-9-0 0.................... SilvestreDeSousa 1 61
(Roger Varian) *stdd s and dropped in bhd: hld up in tch in last pair: effrt and shkn up 2f out: no imp whn squeezed for room: impeded and wnt rt over 1f out: wl hld and kpt on same pce after* **5/1**[3]

**7** 1 1/2 **Revalue** 2-9-0 0.................... RyanMoore 9 57
(Charles Hills) *t.k.h: trckd ldrs: rdn 2f out: sn wandered rt and outpcd: wknd fnl f* **8/1**

**8** 8 **Astrofire** 2-9-0 0.................... JoeyHaynes 7 37
(Mark H Tompkins) *s.i.s: in tch in rr: pushed along 1/2-way: wknd 2f out: bhd fnl f* **150/1**

0 **9** 17 **Night Myth (IRE)**[13] 6584 2-9-0 0.................... TomMarquand 10
(Richard Hannon) *chsd ldrs early: rdn over 4f out: lost pl 1/2-way: bhd fnl 2f: sn lost tch: t.o* **40/1**

1m 25.84s (-0.36) **Going Correction** -0.025s/f (Good) **9** Ran SP% **115.4**
Speed ratings (Par 94): **101,99,99,96,96 93,91,82,63**
CSF £49.94 TOTE £25.40: £6.10, £1.10, £1.50; EX 78.90 Trifecta £267.80.
**Owner** Eledy Srl **Bred** Eledy Srl **Trained** Newmarket, Suffolk

**FOCUS**
Those with previous experience hadn't shown as much as those in the first division, so it was no surprise that the finish of this race was dominated by newcomers, but still a surprise result. Again they came up the middle and the winning time was just under a second slower than the first leg.

## 7023 DALE HALL & HICKMAN ASSOCIATES (S) STKS 7f
**3:25** (3:26) (Class 6) 2-Y-O **£3,234** (£962; £481; £240) **Stalls** High

Form RPR
6422 **1** **Felisa**[15] 6517 2-8-4 60.................... DavidEgan(3) 2 64
(David Evans) *trckd ldr tl rdn to ld over 1f out: hung rt but in command ins fnl f: styd on: eased cl home* **7/2**[3]

654 **2** 2¾ **Still Got It**[7] 6776 2-8-7 0 ........ RobHornby 6 57
(Mick Channon) *stdd s: hld up in tch in last pair: effrt ent fnl 2f: hdwy u.p over 1f out: chsd clr wnr ent fnl f: styd on for clr 2nd but no threat to wnr* **4/1**

0020 **3** 2 **Grimeford Lane (IRE)**[35] 5756 2-8-12 67 ........ (p[1]) ConnorBeasley 9 57
(Michael Dods) *hld up in tch in midfield: shkn up ent fnl 2f: drvn and edging rt over 1f out: wnt 3rd 1f out: kpt on same pce and no imp ins fnl f* **11/4**[1]

0520 **4** 5 **Watch Tan**[7] 6790 2-8-7 55 ........ (h) SilvestreDeSousa 8 40
(George Baker) *taken down early: hld up in tch in last pair: effrt over 2f out: sn struggling: hdwy to pass btn horse u.p 1f out: wnt modest 4th ins fnl f: nvr trbld ldrs* **16/1**

3020 **5** 2 **Bodybuilder**[8] 6749 2-8-12 69 ........ TomMarquand 7 40
(Richard Hannon) *trckd ldrs: rdn 1/2-way: unable qck and lost pl jst over 2f out: wknd over 1f out* **10/1**

3 **6** *hd* **Little Poem**[32] 5886 2-8-7 0 ........ (h) AntonioFresu 3 34
(Marco Botti) *t.k.h: hld up in tch in midfield: rdn over 2f out: sn struggling and dropped to rr: wl btn over 1f out* **3/1**[2]

6020 **7** 2¼ **Red Snapper**[13] 6585 2-8-7 55 ........ MartinDwyer 5 29
(William Stone) *led tl rdn and hdd over 1f out: sn outpcd and btn 4th 1f out: wknd* **25/1**

00 **8** 16 **Koin**[16] 6480 2-8-7 0 ........ JoeyHaynes 4
(Mark H Tompkins) *chsd ldrs tl 3f out: sn struggling and lost pl: wl bhd and eased ins fnl f* **66/1**

1m 25.82s (-0.38) **Going Correction** -0.025s/f (Good) **8** Ran SP% **114.2**
Speed ratings (Par 93): **101,97,95,89,87 87,84,66**
CSF £17.88 TOTE £4.40: £1.50, £1.60, £1.20; EX 19.10 Trifecta £45.00.The winner was bought in for 7,500 guineas. Still Got It was claimed by Daniel Mark Loughnane for £7,000.
**Owner** Mark Windsor, Richard Kent **Bred** Mickley Stud & Mark Winsor **Trained** Pandy, Monmouths

**FOCUS**
A moderate seller with a few of these having something to prove and not form to dwell on. Again they came up the centre and the first three pulled clear.

## 7024 GATELEYS PLC H'CAP 1m 3f 179y
3:55 (3:56) (Class 4) (0-80,81) 3-Y-0+ £6,469 (£1,925; £962; £481) Stalls Low

Form RPR

2411 **1** **Maori Bob (IRE)**[16] 6467 3-8-12 78 ........ LuluStanford(5) 5 87+
(Michael Bell) *dwlt and pushed along early: in tch in last quartet: hdwy over 2f out: rdn to chse ldr over 1f out: led 1f out: pushed along hands and heels and a in command ins fnl f: quite comf* **9/2**[2]

3011 **2** ¾ **Medalla De Oro**[29] 6006 3-9-3 78 ........ (h) JackMitchell 7 85
(Peter Chapple-Hyam) *racd keenly: led: rdn over 2f out: drvn and hdd 1f out: kpt on u.p but a hld by wnr ins fnl f* **6/1**[3]

3316 **3** ¾ **Harebell (IRE)**[36] 5715 3-9-6 81 ........ PatDobbs 9 87
(Ralph Beckett) *stdd s: hld up in tch in last quartet: rdn and hdwy on inner ent fnl 2f: chsd ldrs and swtchd lft jst ins fnl f: kpt on but nvr threatening wnr* **10/1**

0215 **4** 2¼ **The New Pharaoh (IRE)**[33] 5830 6-9-8 75 ........ TedDurcan 6 76
(Chris Wall) *stdd s: hld up in tch in last pair: rdn 2f out: nt clr run and switching lft over 1f out: hdwy ins fnl f: styd on to snatch 4th on post: no threat to ldrs* **12/1**

5003 **5** *nse* **Sean O'Casey (IRE)**[24] 6176 4-9-11 78 ........ SilvestreDeSousa 4 79
(Michael Appleby) *t.k.h: chsd ldr for 2f: styd prom: rdn to chse ldr again over 2f out tl over 1f out: sn outpcd: kpt on same pce fnl f* **8/1**

1504 **6** ¾ **Near Kettering**[18] 6389 3-9-4 79 ........ RyanMoore 2 80
(Luca Cumani) *hld up wl in tch in midfield: swtchd lft and effrt over 2f out: no imp u.p 2f out: kpt on same pce after* **4/1**[1]

0232 **7** ¾ **Phoenix Dawn**[26] 6107 3-8-9 70 ........ MartinDwyer 3 70
(Brendan Powell) *chsd ldr after 2f tl over 2f out: sn outpcd u.p: hld and kpt on same pce fr over 1f out* **11/1**

4/1- **8** ¾ **Captain Navarre**[535] 1093 5-9-12 79 ........ StevieDonohoe 1 77
(Charlie Fellowes) *wl in tch in midfield: rdn 3f out: outpcd and dropped towards rr 2f out: kpt on same pce and no imp after* **6/1**[3]

2240 **9** ½ **All My Love (IRE)**[76] 4216 5-9-9 76 ........ RobHornby 8 73
(Pam Sly) *chsd ldng trio on outer: rdn and losing pl whn squeezed for room over 2f out: wl hld and kpt on same pce fnl 2f* **25/1**

6065 **10** 2 **Caponova (IRE)**[31] 5924 4-9-11 78 ........ RichardKingscote 10 72
(Tom Dascombe) *stdd and dropped in bhd after s: hld up in tch in last pair: effrt u.p jst over 2f out: no prog: n.d* **11/1**

2m 35.0s (1.10) **Going Correction** +0.225s/f (Good)
**WFA** 3 from 4yo+ 8lb **10** Ran SP% **115.2**
Speed ratings (Par 105): **105,104,104,102,102 101,101,100,100,99**
CSF £31.28 CT £255.85 TOTE £4.70: £1.70, £2.50, £3.30; EX 22.00 Trifecta £202.00.
**Owner** P Philipps, C Philipps, T Redman **Bred** Peter Molony **Trained** Newmarket, Suffolk

**FOCUS**
A fair middle-distance handicap with a few of these coming into it in form, including a couple bidding for a hat-trick. They finished 1-2, so the form looks rock-solid.

## 7025 WEATHERBYS H'CAP 7f
4:25 (4:25) (Class 3) (0-95,94) 3-Y-0+ £8,345 (£2,483; £1,240; £620) Stalls High

Form RPR

2052 **1** **Graphite Storm**[24] 6192 3-9-1 89 ........ AdamKirby 3 99+
(Clive Cox) *stdd s: hld up off the pce in last pair: rdn and clsd wl over 1f out: chal u.p ent fnl f: led 150yds out: styd on wl: rdn out* **9/4**[1]

140 **2** 1¼ **Easy Tiger**[17] 6419 5-8-13 83 ........ LiamKeniry 1 89
(Malcolm Saunders) *led: rdn and forged ahd over 1f out: sn hrd pressed: hdd and one pced fnl 150yds* **6/1**

442 **3** 2 **Qeyaadah (IRE)**[24] 6186 4-9-2 86 ........ SilvestreDeSousa 7 87
(Michael Appleby) *chsd ldr: rdn and ev ch over 1f out: sn drvn and outpcd: rallied and edgd rt ins fnl f: kpt on to go 3rd towards fin* **7/2**[3]

5322 **4** ¾ **War Glory (IRE)**[10] 6676 4-9-9 93 ........ RyanMoore 4 92
(Richard Hannon) *hld up off the pce in midfield: clsd 2f out: drvn to press ldrs jst over 1f out: no ex and outpcd ins ins fnl f: lost 3rd towards fin* **3/1**[2]

0004 **5** 1¼ **Smokey Lane (IRE)**[18] 6371 3-9-6 94 ........ TimmyMurphy 8 87
(Christian Williams) *racd away fr rivals: chsd ldrs: effrt and unable qck over 1f out: wl hld and kpt on same pce fnl f* **33/1**

-100 **6** 8 **Taurean Star (IRE)**[87] 3837 4-9-7 91 ........ JamesDoyle 2 65
(Michael Bell) *stdd s: hld up off the pce in rr: effrt over 2f out: no imp u.p over 1f out: bhd and eased wl ins fnl f* **13/2**

1m 24.6s (-1.60) **Going Correction** -0.025s/f (Good)
**WFA** 3 from 4yo+ 4lb **6** Ran SP% **108.6**
Speed ratings (Par 107): **108,106,104,103,102 92**
CSF £14.90 CT £39.06 TOTE £2.70: £1.60, £2.60; EX 14.50 Trifecta £55.70.
**Owner** Mrs Olive Shaw **Bred** Mrs O A Shaw **Trained** Lambourn, Berks

**FOCUS**
A decent and tight handicap despite the small field and they went a good pace. Four of the six came up the centre the whole way and a couple raced more towards the nearside early, though one of them soon joined the main bunch.

## 7026 BRITISH STALLION STUDS EBF FILBERT NOVICE STKS (PLUS 10 RACE) 1m 53y
4:55 (4:57) (Class 4) 2-Y-0 £6,469 (£1,925; £962; £481) Stalls Low

Form RPR

2 **1** **Morning Wonder (IRE)**[42] 5492 2-9-2 0 ........ RyanMoore 7 78+
(Kevin Ryan) *pressed ldr: rdn ent fnl 2f: led over 1f out: drvn and pressed ins fnl f: styd on and a holding runner up: drvn out* **5/2**[2]

**2** ¾ **Setting Sail** 2-9-2 0 ........ JamesDoyle 9 76
(Charlie Appleby) *dropped in sn after s: hld up in tch in last trio: rdn and hdwy jst over 2f out: chsd ldrs over 1f out: pressed wnr u.p ins fnl f: kpt on but a hld* **9/2**[3]

**3** 1½ **Starcaster** 2-9-2 0 ........ JimCrowley 4 73+
(Hughie Morrison) *dwlt: hld up in tch in rr: rdn and hdwy on outer 2f out: chsd ldng pair jst ins fnl f: edgd rt and no imp fnl 100yds: eased nr fin* **25/1**

**4** 2¾ **Regal Director (IRE)** 2-9-2 0 ........ AndreaAtzeni 6 67
(Simon Crisford) *t.k.h: led and set stdy gallop: rdn and hdd over 1f out: unable qck and btn 1f out: wknd ins fnl f* **10/1**

0 **5** *shd* **Ghazan (IRE)**[36] 5709 2-9-2 0 ........ AdamKirby 5 67
(Clive Cox) *t.k.h: chsd ldrs: rdn ent fnl 2f: 5th and outpcd whn swtchd lft over 1f out: kpt on same pce fnl f* **20/1**

1 **6** ¾ **Lynwood Gold (IRE)**[14] 6553 2-9-8 0 ........ OisinMurphy 3 71
(Mark Johnston) *s.i.s and rousted along leaving stalls: sn rcvrd and wl in tch in midfield: effrt whn hemmed in over 2f out: 6th and no imp u.p over 1f out: kpt on same pce fnl f* **7/4**[1]

55 **7** 1¾ **Onefootinfront**[25] 6159 2-9-2 0 ........ SteveDrowne 8 61
(Daniel Mark Loughnane) *wl in tch in midfield on outer: rdn over 2f out: sn outpcd: wl hld and kpt on same pce fr over 1f out* **100/1**

**8** *nk* **The Fiddler** 2-8-13 0 ........ GeorgeWood(3) 1 60
(Chris Wall) *hld up in tch in last trio: rdn and nt clr run whn swtchd lft 2f out: no prog: nvr trbld ldrs* **50/1**

**9** 11 **Global Angel** 2-9-2 0 ........ FranBerry 10 36
(Ed Dunlop) *chsd ldrs on outer tl rdn and lost pl over 2f out: bhd and eased ins fnl f* **66/1**

1m 47.99s (2.89) **Going Correction** +0.225s/f (Good) **9** Ran SP% **105.3**
Speed ratings (Par 97): **94,93,91,89,88 88,86,86,75**
CSF £10.91 TOTE £3.20: £1.20, £1.90, £4.60; EX 12.50 Trifecta £156.90.
**Owner** Sultan Ali **Bred** Rabbah Bloodstock Limited **Trained** Hambleton, N Yorks
■ Future Score was withdrawn. Price at time of withdrawal 8/1. Rule 4 applies to all bets - deduction 10p in the pound.

**FOCUS**
A fascinating novice event and some eye-catching performances from a few of the newcomers, but experience may have proved key.

## 7027 EBF STALLIONS PRESTWOLD CONDITIONS STKS 5f
5:25 (5:26) (Class 3) 3-Y-0+ £10,081 (£3,017; £1,508; £755; £376) Stalls High

Form RPR

0-60 **1** **Waady (IRE)**[108] 3079 5-8-12 106 ........ (h) JimCrowley 1 107
(John Gosden) *w ldrs: rdn and ev ch over 1f out: led ins fnl f: forged ahd and edgd lft 100yds out: styd on* **9/4**[2]

5020 **2** 1½ **Kachy**[39] 5595 4-8-12 107 ........ (t[1]) RichardKingscote 3 102
(Tom Dascombe) *led but hrd pressed thrght: rdn over 1f out: hdd ins fnl f: kpt on same pce fnl 100yds* **5/4**[1]

0606 **3** ½ **Gracious John (IRE)**[10] 6677 4-8-5 95 ........ KatherineGlenister(7) 5 100
(David Evans) *outpcd in 4th: pushed along 3f out: rdn and clsd over 1f out: swtchd rt ins fnl f: styd on to snatch 3rd nr fin* **16/1**

5114 **4** ½ **Ornate**[17] 6428 4-8-12 108 ........ (h) RyanMoore 4 98
(Robert Cowell) *t.k.h: sn w ldr: rdn and ev ch 2f out tl no ex u.p ins fnl f: wknd towards fin* **11/4**[3]

4050 **5** 13 **Percy Toplis**[26] 6114 3-8-12 43 ow1 ........ (b[1]) TrevorWhelan 2 52
(Christine Dunnett) *sn outpcd in rr: nvr on terms: eased ins fnl f* **250/1**

59.26s (-0.74) **Going Correction** -0.025s/f (Good)
**WFA** 3 from 4yo+ 1lb **5** Ran SP% **108.2**
Speed ratings (Par 107): **104,101,100,100,79**
CSF £5.25 TOTE £4.10: £1.60, £1.10; EX 6.00 Trifecta £25.50.
**Owner** Hamdan Al Maktoum **Bred** Knocklong House Stud **Trained** Newmarket, Suffolk

**FOCUS**
Only three appeared to matter according to the market in this decent conditions sprint and the trio raced alongside each other for much of the way. They stayed nearside this time. The level revolves around the 3rd.

## 7028 SWAN APPRENTICE H'CAP 1m 2f
5:55 (5:55) (Class 6) (0-65,66) 4-Y-0+ £3,234 (£962; £481; £240) Stalls Low

Form RPR

6560 **1** **Big Time Dancer (IRE)**[17] 6434 4-9-8 61 ........ (p) BenRobinson 3 67
(Brian Ellison) *hld up in tch in midfield: effrt on inner over 2f out: pressed ldrs over 1f out: ev ch ins fnl f: styd on wl to ld on post* **8/1**

3403 **2** *nse* **Zaria**[19] 6341 6-8-7 51 ........ (p) GabrieleMalune(5) 8 57
(Richard Price) *chsd ldrs: rdn to chse ldr 2f out: sn ev ch: led 1f out: edgd rt but kpt on u.p: hdd post* **10/1**

5113 **3** ¾ **Inflexiball**[27] 6060 5-9-9 62 ........ KieranShoemark 6 67
(John Mackie) *hld up in tch towards rr: effrt over 2f out: hdwy to chse ldrs u.p over 1f out: kpt on ins fnl f* **7/1**

2550 **4** *hd* **Stoneboat Bill**[28] 6035 5-9-6 62 ........ GerO'Neill(3) 5 66
(Declan Carroll) *stdd s: hld up in tch in rr: effrt on outer and edgd rt over 2f out: hdwy over 1f out: styd on strly ins fnl f: nt rch ldrs* **6/1**[3]

2555 **5** ¾ **Moojaned (IRE)**[15] 6524 6-9-0 58 ........ RossaRyan(5) 13 61
(John Flint) *led and grad crossed to inner: rdn over 2f out: drvn over 1f out: hdd 1f out: keeping on same pce and hld whn squeezed for room wl ins fnl f* **7/1**

3422 **6** 2¾ **Castle Talbot (IRE)**[33] 5854 5-9-12 65 ........ (p) DavidEgan 11 63
(Tom Clover) *t.k.h: hld up wl in tch in midfield: effrt over 2f out: kpt on same pce u.p fr over 1f out* **5/1**[1]

3225 **7** ¾ **Sir Jack**[24] 6188 4-9-10 63 ........ CliffordLee 12 60
(Tony Carroll) *hld up in tch in midfield: rdn 3f out: hdwy u.p to chse ldrs over 1f out: no ex 1f out: wknd ins fnl f* **11/2**[2]

**8** ¾ **Missguided (IRE)**[80] 4113 4-9-10 63 ........ CallumShepherd 14 58
(Alex Hales) *stdd s: hld up in tch towards rr: hdwy on inner over 2f out: n.m.r 2f out: chsd ldrs and rdn over 1f out: no ex 1f out: wknd ins fnl f* **9/1**

606R **9** *1* **Balmont Belle (IRE)**[25] 6153 7-8-9 **51** oh6................ RhiainIngram(3) 7 44
(Barry Leavy) *hld up in tch towards rr: effrt and no imp whn edgd rt 3f out: kpt on to pass btn rivals ins fnl f: nvr trbld ldrs* **100/1**

006 **10** *hd* **Midnight Mood**[34] 5790 4-8-10 **54**..................(p[1]) StephenCummins(5) 1 47
(Dominic Ffrench Davis) *t.k.h: hld up wl in tch in midfield: rdn over 2f out: sn outpcd: wknd over 1f out* **16/1**

3645 **11** *1* **Scent Of Power**[66] 4625 5-8-12 **51** oh5......................(t) RichardOliver 15 42
(Barry Leavy) *chsd ldrs: wnt 2nd 1/2-way tl 2f out: sn lost pl: wknd fnl f* **25/1**

-000 **12** *4* **Rock'n Gold**[33] 5843 4-9-9 **65**.......................................... FinleyMarsh(3) 9 49
(Adrian Wintle) *hld up in tch in midfield: effrt over 2f out: no imp and btn whn nt clr run and swtchd lft over 1f out: wknd* **66/1**

-554 **13** *1 1/4* **Navajo Storm (IRE)**[21] 6294 4-9-0 **53**.................................. JaneElliott 2 35
(Michael Appleby) *t.k.h: chsd ldr tl 1/2-way: rdn over 2f out: lost pl and btn over 1f out: wknd fnl f* **18/1**

6000 **14** *1* **May Mist**[70] 4469 5-8-13 **52**................................................ EoinWalsh 10 32
(Trevor Wall) *stdd s: hld up in tch towards rr: rdn and no hdwy over 3f out: n.d* **100/1**

2m 11.2s (3.30) **Going Correction** +0.225s/f (Good) **14** Ran SP% **120.0**
Speed ratings (Par 101): **95,94,94,94,93 91,90,90,89,89 88,85,84,83**
CSF £84.40 CT £594.64 TOTE £8.60: £2.90, £3.30, £3.00; EX 117.10 Trifecta £922.60.
**Owner** Andy Bell Anna Noble Arnie Flower **Bred** Gerard Callanan **Trained** Norton, N Yorks
■ Stewards' Enquiry : Ben Robinson nine-day ban: used whip above the permitted level (Sep 26-Oct 4)

**FOCUS**
A moderate albeit open and competitive apprentice handicap to end. A tight finish and last year's first and second finished fourth and third this time. The winner, a big class dropper, was well in on last August's form and has been rated back within 3lb or so of that.
T/Plt: £13.60 to a £1 stake. Pool: £64,198.80 - 3,431.63 winning units T/Qpdt: £9.10 to a £1 stake. Pool: £3,917.96 - 318.10 winning units **Steve Payne**

6897 **NEWCASTLE (A.W)** (L-H)
Tuesday, September 12

**OFFICIAL GOING: Tapeta: standard**
Wind: Breezy, half against in races on straight course and in over 3f of home straight in races on the rou Weather: Overcast 1-4, raining from race 3

## 7029 JAMES T. BLAKEMAN SUPREME SAUSAGE NURSERY H'CAP (DIV I) 7f 14y (Tp)
**5:45** (5:45) (Class 6) (0-60,62) 2-Y-O **£2,264** (£673; £336; £168) **Stalls** Centre

Form RPR

554 **1** **Sulafaat (IRE)**[19] 6347 2-9-9 **62**..................................... FrannyNorton 10 70
(Mark Johnston) *mde all: clr w runner-up over 1f out: sn hrd pressed: hld on wl towards fin* **9/4**[1]

4056 **2** *hd* **Archie Perkins (IRE)**[12] 6625 2-9-1 **57**................... LewisEdmunds(3) 3 64
(Nigel Tinkler) *pressed wnr: ev ch and clr of rest over 1f out: kpt on fnl f: hld nr fin* **5/1**[3]

0604 **3** *5* **Highland Bobby**[12] 6634 2-9-8 **61**........................................ DavidNolan 5 56
(David O'Meara) *hld up: effrt and pushed along 2f out: chsd clr ldng pair ins fnl f: kpt on: nt pce to chal* **6/1**

3500 **4** *hd* **Marsh Storm (IRE)**[12] 6634 2-9-6 **59**.............................. PJMcDonald 11 53
(K R Burke) *trckd ldrs: drvn along over 2f out: one pce and lost 3rd ins fnl f* **9/1**

0233 **5** *shd* **Rock On Bertie (IRE)**[13] 6585 2-9-2 **55**............................(p) TomEaves 8 49
(Nigel Tinkler) *t.k.h: hld up: effrt and rdn over 2f out: one pce fr over 1f out* **4/1**[2]

0060 **6** *1 1/2* **Mountain Meadow**[35] 5756 2-8-13 **52**.......................(p[1]) PaulHanagan 1 42
(Richard Fahey) *in tch on far side of gp: drvn and outpcd over 2f out: rallied fnl f: no imp* **18/1**

6033 **7** *hd* **Sandama (IRE)**[29] 6011 2-9-1 **54**...................................... TonyHamilton 4 44
(Richard Fahey) *hld up: drvn and struggling wl over 2f out: rallied ins fnl f: nvr on terms* **12/1**

0043 **8** *3 1/2* **Angie B (IRE)**[31] 5945 2-8-9 **48**.......................................... CamHardie 12 29
(John Wainwright) *t.k.h: hld up in tch: struggling over 2f out: sn btn* **25/1**

000 **9** *2 3/4* **Lady Cashmere (IRE)**[18] 6380 2-8-0 **46** ow1.....(v[1]) ConnorMurtagh(7) 6 20
(Alistair Whillans) *trckd ldrs: rdn and lost pl over 2f out: sn btn* **50/1**

0000 **10** *13* **Harbour Rose**[35] 5756 2-8-11 **50**.....................................(h[1]) PaddyAspell 2
(Philip Kirby) *hld up: drvn and outpcd 3f out: btn fnl 2f* **100/1**

000 **11** *2* **Your Just Desserts (IRE)**[55] 5015 2-8-6 **45**........................ JoeDoyle 9
(Micky Hammond) *hld up midfield: rdn wl over 2f out: sn wknd* **25/1**

1m 25.56s (-0.64) **Going Correction** -0.075s/f (Stan) **11** Ran SP% **115.3**
Speed ratings (Par 93): **100,99,94,93,93 92,91,87,84,69 67**
CSF £12.68 CT £60.01 TOTE £3.40: £1.40, £2.00, £1.90; EX 17.80 Trifecta £86.50.
**Owner** Hamdan Al Maktoum **Bred** Shadwell Estate Company Limited **Trained** Middleham Moor, N Yorks
■ Stewards' Enquiry : P J McDonald two-day ban; used whip without allowing the filly time to respond (tba)

**FOCUS**
The first division of a modest nursery handicap, and the winner improved.

## 7030 JAMES T. BLAKEMAN SUPREME SAUSAGE NURSERY H'CAP (DIV II) 7f 14y (Tp)
**6:15** (6:16) (Class 6) (0-60,62) 2-Y-O **£2,264** (£673; £336; £168) **Stalls** Centre

Form RPR

660 **1** **Crown Of Cortez**[13] 6590 2-9-4 **57**..........................(b[1]) TonyHamilton 10 62
(Richard Fahey) *hld up in tch on nr side of gp: effrt and hdwy 2f out: led appr fnl f: rdn and kpt on wl* **6/1**[3]

6404 **2** *1/2* **Foxy Lady**[12] 6626 2-9-6 **59**.................................................. JoeDoyle 5 63
(Kevin Ryan) *trckd ldrs: led briefly over 1f out: sn rdn: ev ch fnl f: hld last 50yds* **7/2**[1]

660 **3** *2 3/4* **What Do You Think (IRE)**[41] 5537 2-9-2 **55**.............. PaulMulrennan 8 52
(Michael Dods) *hld up: hdwy over 2f out: rdn and chsd ldng pair over 1f out: kpt on ins fnl f: nt pce to chal* **6/1**[3]

0000 **4** *2 1/4* **Admiral Spice (IRE)**[37] 5685 2-9-4 **62**...............(p[1]) PaddyPilley(5) 1 54
(Tom Dascombe) *in tch on far side of gp: effrt and drvn over 2f out: kpt on same pce fr over 1f out* **7/1**

064 **5** *1* **Racing Radio (IRE)**[15] 6517 2-9-3 **56**............................ PaddyAspell 11 45
(David Barron) *hld up: pushed along over 2f out: hdwy nr side of gp over 1f out: edgd lft: kpt on fnl f: no imp* **18/1**

0004 **6** *1 1/2* **Ladycammyofclare (IRE)**[12] 6625 2-8-8 **47**................... FrannyNorton 9 32
(Mark Johnston) *trckd ldrs: drvn over 2f out: wknd ins fnl f* **11/1**

060 **7** *1 3/4* **Stark Reality (IRE)**[17] 6432 2-8-13 **52**.................................. TomEaves 7 33
(Nigel Tinkler) *dwlt: hld up: rdn along over 2f out: hdwy over 1f out: kpt on: nvr able to chal* **33/1**

006 **8** *3 1/2* **Duggary**[32] 5876 2-9-7 **60**.................................................. DavidNolan 6 32
(Kevin Frost) *w ldrs to 1/2-way: sn rdn along: wknd over 1f out* **15/2**

3P15 **9** *hd* **Society's Dream (IRE)**[12] 6625 2-9-0 **53**............................ PJMcDonald 4 25
(K R Burke) *t.k.h: cl up: led 1/2-way to over 1f out: sn wknd* **5/1**[2]

000 **10** *3/4* **Partry Flyer (IRE)**[17] 6410 2-8-6 **45**...............................(v[1]) CamHardie 2 15
(Oliver Greenall) *dwlt: hld up: rdn and effrt over 2f out: hmpd wl over 1f out: sn btn* **50/1**

605 **11** *20* **American Ruby (USA)**[29] 5999 2-8-10 **49**............................ JasonHart 3
(Roger Fell) *racd on far side of gp: slt ld to 1/2-way: rdn and wknd qckly over 2f out: t.o* **28/1**

1m 25.86s (-0.34) **Going Correction** -0.075s/f (Stan) **11** Ran SP% **113.7**
Speed ratings (Par 93): **98,97,94,91,90 88,86,82,82,81 58**
CSF £25.87 CT £133.34 TOTE £5.90: £2.30, £1.50, £2.40; EX 23.30 Trifecta £123.80.
**Owner** Cheveley Park Stud **Bred** Cheveley Park Stud Ltd **Trained** Musley Bank, N Yorks

**FOCUS**
The second division of a modest nursery, but another improved winner.

## 7031 Q PLATINUM FISH & CHIPS H'CAP 1m 4f 98y (Tp)
**6:45** (6:45) (Class 3) (0-90,86) 3-Y-O **£7,439** (£2,213; £1,106; £553) **Stalls** High

Form RPR

2214 **1** **Humble Hero (IRE)**[66] 4612 3-9-5 **84**............................... PatCosgrave 3 93+
(William Haggas) *hld up: smooth hdwy over 2f out: effrt and rdn over 1f out: led ins fnl f: hung rt: styd on wl* **5/4**[1]

1204 **2** *1 1/2* **Amlad (IRE)**[23] 6232 3-9-7 **86**........................................ PaulMulrennan 1 92
(Ed Dunlop) *cl up in chsng gp: hdwy to chse ldr over 4f out: led and pushed along over 2f out: hdd ins fnl f* **4/1**[3]

3012 **3** *1 1/4* **Doctor Bartolo (IRE)**[24] 6189 3-9-4 **83**...................... WilliamCarson 2 87
(Charles Hills) *hld up: stdy hdwy over 3f out: effrt and ev ch 2f out: sn rdn: kpt on same pce fnl f* **7/2**[2]

1422 **4** *23* **New Society (IRE)**[33] 5832 3-8-9 **74**................................ PJMcDonald 5 41
(James Bethell) *chsd clr ldr: rdn over 2f out: sn wknd: t.o* **9/2**

5605 **5** *22* **Voski (USA)**[13] 6573 3-8-7 **72**......................................(b[1]) FrannyNorton 4 4
(Mark Johnston) *t.k.h: led: clr after 2f to over 3f out: hdd over 2f out: sn wknd and eased* **16/1**

2m 40.2s (-0.90) **Going Correction** +0.075s/f (Slow) **5** Ran SP% **110.7**
Speed ratings (Par 105): **106,105,104,88,74**
CSF £6.63 TOTE £1.80: £1.30, £2.00; EX 7.00 Trifecta £16.80.
**Owner** Mrs S Magnier/M Tabor/M Jooste & D Smith **Bred** Lynch Bages & Camas Park Stud **Trained** Newmarket, Suffolk

**FOCUS**
The feature contest was a decent little middle-distance 3yo handicap and the winner is progressive.

## 7032 42ND STREET CLASSIC SAUSAGE FISH & CHIPS FILLIES' H'CAP 1m 4f 98y (Tp)
**7:15** (7:16) (Class 5) (0-75,77) 3-Y-O+ **£2,911** (£866; £432; £216) **Stalls** High

Form RPR

2642 **1** **Sileel (USA)**[12] 6623 3-9-2 **73**.......................................(v) PJMcDonald 5 78
(Ed Dunlop) *mde all: set stdy pce: rdn wl over 1f out: styd on wl fnl f* **7/2**[1]

2542 **2** *3/4* **Henpecked**[7] 6789 7-9-7 **70**.........................................(p) PaulHanagan 7 74+
(Alistair Whillans) *hld up: hdwy on outside wl over 1f out: chsd wnr ins fnl f: r.o* **7/2**[1]

424 **3** *3/4* **Alfa Queen (IRE)**[25] 6161 3-8-13 **70**..................................... KevinStott 4 72
(Iain Jardine) *in tch: rdn over 1f out: r.o ins fnl f: nrst fin* **11/1**

-365 **4** *shd* **Nurse Nightingale**[89] 3759 3-8-6 **70**........................... TristanPrice(7) 6 73+
(Michael Bell) *t.k.h early: hld up in tch: effrt and pushed along over 1f out: r.o fnl f: nt pce to chal* **7/1**[3]

4-04 **5** *shd* **Nepeta (USA)**[14] 6551 3-8-11 **68**.................................... FrannyNorton 9 70
(Mark Johnston) *chsd wnr 4f: cl up: rdn over 2f out: rallied: kpt on same pce ins fnl f* **6/1**[2]

1611 **6** *1/2* **Maulesden May (IRE)**[31] 5921 4-10-0 **77**......................... GrahamLee 1 78
(Keith Dalgleish) *cl up: wnt 2nd after 4f: effrt and rdn over 1f out: wknd ins fnl f* **7/1**[3]

3352 **7** *1/2* **Wor Lass**[12] 6628 9-9-7 **75**.............................................. RowanScott(5) 8 75
(Donald Whillans) *dwlt: hld up towards rr: effrt and pushed along over 2f out: hdwy over 1f out: no imp fnl f* **8/1**

3102 **8** *4* **Fire Leopard**[13] 6573 3-9-4 **75**........................................(h) PhillipMakin 2 69
(David O'Meara) *plld hrd early: hld up: drvn along over 2f out: sn no imp: btn over 1f out* **17/2**

6-04 **9** *hd* **Struck By The Moon**[17] 6413 3-8-4 **61**............................... LukeMorris 3 55
(Charles Hills) *t.k.h: in tch: hdwy on outside over 3f out: rdn and wknd over 1f out* **16/1**

2m 45.99s (4.89) **Going Correction** +0.075s/f (Slow)
**WFA** 3 from 4yo+ 8lb **9** Ran SP% **119.6**
Speed ratings (Par 100): **86,85,85,84,84 84,84,81,81**
CSF £15.74 CT £124.26 TOTE £4.50: £1.90, £1.70, £2.70; EX 17.70 Trifecta £179.50.
**Owner** Abdullah Saeed Al Naboodah **Bred** Camas Park Stud **Trained** Newmarket, Suffolk

**FOCUS**
A fair middle-distance fillies' handicap. The winner controlled the race from the front at her own tempo.

## 7033 GOLDENSHEAF BATTER FLOUR FISH & CHIPS EBF MAIDEN FILLIES' STKS (PLUS 10 RACE) 7f 14y (Tp)
**7:45** (7:46) (Class 5) 2-Y-O **£2,911** (£866; £432; £216) **Stalls** Centre

Form RPR

4 **1** **Chrisellaine (IRE)**[29] 5990 2-9-0 0.................................. PJMcDonald 11 74+
(Charles Hills) *t.k.h: hld up midfield: effrt and hdwy on nr side of gp over 1f out: led ins fnl f: pushed clr: comf* **3/1**[1]

6 **2** *2* **Sharp Reminder**[27] 6064 2-9-0 0........................................ LukeMorris 8 69
(James Tate) *t.k.h: prom on nr side of gp: effrt and ev ch ins fnl f: sn chsng wnr: r.o* **5/1**[3]

63 **3** *hd* **Champarisi**[22] 6264 2-9-0 0............................................ JackGarritty 10 68
(Grant Tuer) *trckd ldr: effrt and ev ch over 1f out to ins fnl f: kpt on* **10/1**

2 **4** *nse* **Grise Lightning (FR)**[19] 6347 2-9-0 0............................. PaulHanagan 5 68
(Richard Fahey) *prom on far side of gp: rdn over 2f out: rallied and ev ch briefly ins fnl f: one pce* **7/2**[2]

632 **5** *1/2* **Formiga (IRE)**[17] 6456 2-9-0 0.......................................... OscarPereira 6 67
(Jose Santos) *led: rdn 2f out: hdd ins fnl f: sn outpcd* **40/1**

0 **6** *2* **Daddys Poppit (USA)**[25] 6138 2-9-0 0............................. PatCosgrave 1 62
(William Haggas) *hld up: pushed along over 2f out: effrt over 1f out: sn no imp* **11/2**

**7** *1/2* **North Bay Sunrise (IRE)** 2-9-0 0.............................. AdamBeschizza 2 60+
(Ed Vaughan) *hld up: rdn over 2f out: hdwy fnl f: kpt on: nt pce to chal* **25/1**

8 1 3/4 **Military Madame (IRE)** 2-9-0 0 JasonHart 3 56
(John Quinn) *s.i.s: hld up: hdwy on far side of gp and in tch over 2f out: wknd wl over 1f out* 25/1

0 9 3/4 **Alacritas**91 3697 2-9-0 0 TomEaves 9 54
(David Simcock) *t.k.h: hld up: drvn and outpcd over 2f out: sn btn* 33/1

0 10 2 1/2 **Chef United**22 6264 2-9-0 0 TonyHamilton 4 48
(Roger Fell) *hld up: drvn and struggling over 2f out: sn btn* 150/1

0 11 7 **Shesaidyes (IRE)**16 6480 2-9-0 0 PaulMulrennan 7 30
(Henry Spiller) *t.k.h: hld up midfield: struggling over 2f out: sn wknd* 15/2

1m 28.49s (2.29) **Going Correction** -0.075s/f (Stan) 11 Ran SP% **113.9**
Speed ratings (Par 92): **83,80,80,80,79 77,77,75,74,71 63**
CSF £16.62 TOTE £3.50: £1.30, £1.90, £2.90; EX 16.70 Trifecta £142.90.
**Owner** Ballylinch Stud **Bred** Ballylinch Stud **Trained** Lambourn, Berks

**FOCUS**
An ordinary juvenile fillies' maiden. They went a modest gallop and but the favourite still confirmed her superiority.

## 7034 Q TORENO FISH & CHIPS H'CAP 1m 5y (Tp)
8:15 (8:19) (Class 5) (0-75,77) 3-Y-0+ £2,911 (£866; £432; £216) Stalls Centre

Form RPR

1030 1 **Auspicion**19 6349 5-9-10 74 AndrewMullen 5 83
(Tom Tate) *hld up: rdn and hdwy over 1f out: led ins fnl f: drvn out* 15/2[3]

306 2 1 1/4 **Four Wishes**26 6091 3-8-8 63 (b1) JasonHart 11 68
(Tim Easterby) *prom on nr side of gp: hdwy to ld wl over 1f out: hdd ins fnl f: kpt on* 25/1

6324 3 1 1/4 **Gerry The Glover (IRE)**57 4959 5-9-13 77 (p) ConnorKing 7 80
(Brian Ellison) *missed break: hld up: rdn and hdwy wl over 1f out: kpt on ins fnl f: tk 3rd cl home* 6/1[1]

3220 4 nse **Totally Magic (IRE)**14 6564 5-8-12 65 LewisEdmunds(3) 4 68
(Richard Whitaker) *in tch: effrt and drvn over 1f out: kpt on ins fnl f* 6/1[1]

0 5 hd **Rock Warbler (IRE)**25 6143 4-9-9 73 (t) KevinStott 13 75
(Oliver Greenall) *hld up on nr side of gp: hdwy over 1f out: effrt and disp ld briefly ins fnl f: sn no ex* 7/1[2]

0020 6 2 1/2 **Acrux**13 6570 4-9-10 74 (h) PhillipMakin 9 71
(David O'Meara) *. hld up: hdwy nr side over 2f out: rdn and outpcd whn checked appr fnl f: sn no imp* 8/1

1504 7 1 3/4 **Racemaker**14 6564 3-9-3 72 NeilFarley 3 64
(Andrew Crook) *w ldrs: led over 2f out to over 1f out: outpcd ins fnl f* 40/1

0246 8 1 3/4 **Tailor's Row (USA)**21 6289 3-9-3 72 FrannyNorton 6 60
(Mark Johnston) *t.k.h: led to over 2f out: rdn and wknd over 1f out* 15/2[3]

4225 9 3 1/2 **Yensir**7 6789 4-9-4 68 GrahamLee 2 49
(Grant Tuer) *dwlt: sn prom on far side of gp: rdn over 2f out: wknd wl over 1f out* 11/1

0354 10 1 **Gun Case**17 6435 5-8-12 62 (p) PaulHanagan 1 40
(Alistair Whillans) *w ldrs on far side of gp: rdn over 2f out: wknd over 1f out* 7/1[2]

5044 11 7 **Tafteesh (IRE)**102 3289 4-8-5 62 HarrisonShaw(7) 8 24
(Michael Easterby) *hld up in tch on far side of gp: rdn and outpcd over 2f out: hung lft and sn wknd* 33/1

6000 12 3 3/4 **Fire Diamond**21 6288 4-9-2 66 (vt1) PaulMulrennan 10 20
(Tom Dascombe) *t.k.h: in tch: drvn and outpcd over 2f out: sn wknd* 25/1

5010 13 2 1/2 **Table Manners**66 4608 5-8-10 63 SammyJoBell(3) 14 11
(Wilf Storey) *hld up: rdn over 2f out: sn wknd* 20/1

1m 36.28s (-2.32) **Going Correction** -0.075s/f (Stan) course record
**WFA** 3 from 4yo+ 5lb 13 Ran SP% **114.4**
Speed ratings (Par 103): **108,106,105,105,105 102,101,99,95,94 87,84,81**
CSF £185.58 CT £1232.59 TOTE £7.90: £2.80, £7.00, £2.60; EX 200.50 Trifecta £1751.20.
**Owner** David Storey & T P Tate **Bred** Lael Stables **Trained** Tadcaster, N Yorks

**FOCUS**
A fair, wide-open handicap. The winner has been rated as running his best race since early as a 4yo.

## 7035 MARTYN EDWARDS FRYING RANGE FISH & CHIPS MEDIAN AUCTION MAIDEN STKS 7f 14y (Tp)
8:45 (8:47) (Class 6) 3-5-Y-0 £2,264 (£673; £336; £168) Stalls Centre

Form RPR

350 1 **Amazing Grazing (IRE)**35 5757 3-8-10 68 PatrickVaughan(7) 5 66+
(David O'Meara) *trckd ldrs: shkn up to ld over 1f out: rdn out fnl f* 7/4[2]

2044 2 1 **Joys Delight**12 6638 3-8-12 61 AndrewMullen 1 57
(Daniel Mark Loughnane) *hld up in tch on nr side of gp: effrt and hdwy over 1f out: chsd wnr ins fnl f: r.o fin* 11/10[1]

0020 3 3/4 **Starboard Watch**17 6435 3-8-12 60 JamesSullivan 3 55
(James Given) *stdd in tch: smooth hdwy over 2f out: effrt and disp 2nd pl briefly ins fnl f: edgd lft and sn one pce* 11/2[3]

00 4 1 3/4 **Compass Rose (IRE)**56 5003 3-8-12 0 LukeMorris 2 50?
(Scott Dixon) *led at ordinary gallop: rdn and hdd over 1f out: outpcd ins fnl f* 50/1

0 5 1/2 **Intoxikating**92 3669 3-8-10 0 (t) GinaMangan(7) 4 54?
(Gay Kelleway) *t.k.h: trckd ldr to over 1f out: edgd lft and sn outpcd: btn ins fnl f* 12/1

1m 27.84s (1.64) **Going Correction** -0.075s/f (Stan) 5 Ran SP% **109.0**
Speed ratings (Par 101): **87,85,85,83,82**
CSF £3.94 TOTE £2.60: £1.20, £1.10; EX 4.20 Trifecta £6.50.
**Owner** A Barnes **Bred** Naoise Conroy **Trained** Upper Helmsley, N Yorks

**FOCUS**
A modest maiden, and not a race that will live long in the memory, but the right three horses came to the fore off an ordinary gallop. It's been rated around the 2nd.

## 7036 KFE & CF CAPITAL FINANCE FISH & CHIPS H'CAP 5f (Tp)
9:15 (9:17) (Class 6) (0-60,58) 3-Y-0+ £2,264 (£673; £336; £168) Stalls Centre

Form RPR

6554 1 **Groundworker (IRE)**12 6631 6-9-3 54 (t) PaulMulrennan 1 61
(Paul Midgley) *trckd ldrs: rdn to ld over 1f out: sn hrd pressed: kpt on wl fnl f* 5/1[2]

0000 2 3/4 **Young Tiger**45 5419 4-8-10 47 (h1) AndrewMullen 6 51
(Tom Tate) *t.k.h early: cl up: effrt and ev ch over 1f out to ins fnl f: kpt on: hld nr fin* 10/1

2560 3 1/2 **Canford Bay (IRE)**16 6469 3-9-1 53 PhillipMakin 12 56
(Antony Brittain) *prom on nr side of gp: effrt and rdn over 1f out: kpt on ins fnl f* 8/1

0045 4 3/4 **Imperial Legend (IRE)**18 6384 8-9-4 58 (p) RachelRichardson(3) 7 58
(Alan Brown) *in tch: effrt and rdn over 1f out: kpt on same pce ins fnl f* 11/1

0550 5 2 1/4 **Lotara**14 6546 5-8-10 50 (v1) PhilDennis(3) 9 42
(Jim Goldie) *hld up: rdn over 2f out: hdwy towards far side of gp over 1f out: kpt on: nt pce to chal* 6/1

3503 6 1/2 **Pearl Noir**15 6531 7-8-10 54 (b) RPWalsh(7) 4 44
(Scott Dixon) *led at decent gallop: rdn and hdd over 1f out: wknd ins fnl f* 11/1

3056 7 1 **Luv U Always**13 6596 3-8-5 50 (p) JamieGormley(7) 2 36
(Iain Jardine) *hld up: in tch: effrt and rdn 2f out: wknd appr fnl f* 40/1

5210 8 1/2 **Tea El Tee (IRE)**24 6174 3-9-5 57 (v) TomEaves 5 42
(Gay Kelleway) *dwlt: hld up: drvn along 1/2-way: sme hdwy over 1f out: nvr rchd ldrs* 14/1

6622 9 1 1/2 **Boogie Babe**25 6148 3-9-3 55 PaulHanagan 8 34
(Richard Fahey) *hld up: drvn and outpcd 1/2-way: nvr rchd ldrs* 11/2[3]

0003 10 shd **Seebring (IRE)**4 6904 3-9-0 52 BenCurtis 11 31
(Brian Ellison) *bhd: rdn and outpcd 1/2-way: sn btn* 3/1[1]

0-00 11 1 3/4 **Equipe**16 6469 3-8-7 45 (h1) CamHardie 3 17
(Richard Whitaker) *reluctant to enter stalls: bhd and sn outpcd: sn btn* 100/1

00-0 12 20 **Suraat (IRE)**24 6184 3-8-12 50 LukeMorris 10
(Robert Cowell) *dwlt and blkd s: bhd: struggling 1/2-way: btn and eased over 1f out* 33/1

58.81s (-0.69) **Going Correction** -0.075s/f (Stan)
**WFA** 3 from 4yo+ 1lb 12 Ran SP% **121.2**
Speed ratings (Par 101): **102,100,100,98,95 94,92,92,89,89 86,54**
CSF £55.23 CT £408.10 TOTE £9.40: £2.70, £3.50, £3.00; EX 95.90 Trifecta £648.30.
**Owner** Blackburn Family **Bred** Knockainey Stud **Trained** Westow, N Yorks

**FOCUS**
A moderate sprint handicap but straightforward form.
T/Plt: £24.80 to a £1 stake. Pool: £79,779.40 - 2,346.79 winning units T/Qpdt: £12.40 to a £1 stake. Pool: £7,580.69 - 451.40 winning units **Richard Young**

7037 - 7040a (Foreign Racing) - See Raceform Interactive

# 6545 CARLISLE (R-H)
Wednesday, September 13

**OFFICIAL GOING: Heavy (6.9)**
Wind: Fresh, half against in over 2f of home straight Weather: Overcast, dry

## 7041 WATCH RACING UK ANYWHERE NURSERY H'CAP (JOCKEY CLUB GRASSROOTS NURSERY QUALIFIER) 5f 193y
2:10 (2:12) (Class 5) (0-75,77) 2-Y-0 £3,396 (£1,010; £505; £252) Stalls Low

Form RPR

0422 1 **Lucky Lucky Man (IRE)**15 6545 2-9-3 71 TonyHamilton 5 82
(Richard Fahey) *in tch: hdwy over 2f out: led wl over 1f out: sn pushed clr: readily* 13/2[3]

3501 2 4 1/2 **Diamond Dougal (IRE)**9 6749 2-9-2 70 6ex GrahamLee 4 68
(Mick Channon) *hld up: hdwy over 2f out: effrt and chsd (clr) wnr ins fnl f: kpt on: no imp* 8/1

0000 3 1/2 **Mabo**19 6379 2-8-8 62 BarryMcHugh 7 58
(Richard Fahey) *bhd: effrt and racd alone far side over 2f out: rdn and ch over 1f out: one pce ins fnl f* 12/1

0042 4 3/4 **Excellent Times**29 6043 2-8-6 60 AndrewMullen 2 54
(Tim Easterby) *blkd s: hld up: hdwy on outside over 2f out: rdn and one pce fr over 1f out* 13/2[3]

0200 5 hd **Bahuta Acha**9 6756 2-8-12 66 LukeMorris 11 64+
(David Loughnane) *dwlt: sn in tch: no room and lost pl over 2f out: no room tl swtchd rt and hdwy over 1f out: kpt on fnl f: nrst fin* 50/1

653 6 hd **Skyva**16 6525 2-8-9 63 (h) CamHardie 1 56
(Brian Ellison) *hld up midfield: effrt and rdn over 2f out: kpt on same pce fnl f* 18/1

6406 7 1 1/2 **Fastalong (IRE)**15 6561 2-8-1 58 RachelRichardson(3) 10 49
(Tim Easterby) *hld up: nt clr run over 2f out: effrt and swtchd rt wl over 1f out: kpt on: no imp* 28/1

050 8 3/4 **Lady Sandy (IRE)**14 6567 2-8-4 58 FrannyNorton 3 46
(David Barron) *s.i.s: hld up: nt clr run over 2f out: hdwy over 1f out: sn no imp* 20/1

4030 9 1 3/4 **Admiral Rooke (IRE)**27 6087 2-8-8 67 CallumRodriguez(5) 14 50
(Michael Dods) *hld up midfield: nt clr run over 2f out: rdn over 1f out: sn wknd* 11/2[2]

1332 10 1 3/4 **Havana Star (IRE)**19 6379 2-9-7 75 (p1) KevinStott 8 56
(Kevin Ryan) *w ldrs to 1/2-way: rdn and wknd 2f out* 2/1[1]

040 11 2 1/4 **Acromatic (IRE)**77 4205 2-8-7 61 (b1) JasonHart 9 30
(John Quinn) *hld up in tch: rdn over 2f out: wknd over 1f out* 25/1

4546 12 7 **Ryedale Encore**13 6626 2-8-7 61 DuranFentiman 13 9
(Tim Easterby) *led to over 2f out: sn rdn and wknd* 33/1

005 13 3/4 **The Auld Hoose (IRE)**14 6567 2-8-2 59 SammyJoBell(3) 6 4
(Richard Fahey) *w ldrs: led over 2f out to wl over 1f out: sn wknd* 18/1

1m 17.69s (3.99) **Going Correction** +0.70s/f (Yiel) 13 Ran SP% **121.7**
Speed ratings (Par 95): **101,95,94,93,93 92,90,89,87,85 82,72,71**
CSF £55.22 CT £622.63 TOTE £4.80: £2.10, £2.80, £4.00; EX 35.10 Trifecta £326.40.
**Owner** The Musley Bank Partnership & Partner **Bred** Ms Sarah-Anne Heffernan **Trained** Musley Bank, N Yorks

**FOCUS**
Following 15mm of overnight rain the going was changed to heavy, and the meeting had to pass an early inspection. Due to rail realignments races 2, 3, 4, 5 & 6 were increased by 14yds and races 7 & 8 increased by 25yds. A fair nursery, with all bar one of the field coming down the stands' rail, and a big step up from the winner.

## 7042 WATCH RACING UK ON SKY 432 H'CAP 7f 173y
2:40 (2:42) (Class 5) (0-70,71) 3-Y-0+ £3,234 (£962; £481; £240) Stalls Low

Form RPR

4103 1 **Ventura Secret (IRE)**15 6564 3-8-13 67 RachelRichardson(3) 14 75
(Tim Easterby) *pressed ldr: led over 2f out: rdn and edgd lft 1f out: hld on wl* 4/1[2]

0423 2 1/2 **Jay Kay**15 6549 8-8-13 66 (h) PatrickO'Hanlon(7) 4 74
(K R Burke) *hld up in tch: hdwy to press wnr over 2f out: rdn over 1f out: kpt on fnl f: hld nr fin* 7/1[3]

1112 3 3 1/2 **Im Dapper Too**21 6316 6-9-11 71 SamJames 6 71
(John Davies) *prom: effrt and rdn 2f out: kpt on same pce appr fnl f* 7/2[1]

6051 4 5 **Thornaby Nash**15 6549 6-8-5 56 (p) GemmaTutty(5) 12 44
(Karen Tutty) *in tch: effrt whn nt clr run briefly 2f out: drvn and outpcd appr fnl f* 8/1

315 5 1 3/4 **Dreamofdiscovery (IRE)**27 6091 3-8-11 62 (p) JoeDoyle 10 45
(Julie Camacho) *s.i.s: hld up: rdn over 3f out: hdwy over 1f out: kpt on: no imp* 12/1

23-0 6 2 1/4 **Oregon Gift**18 6435 5-8-7 58 BenRobinson(5) 1 37
(Brian Ellison) *led to over 2f out: racd in centre of trck in st: wknd over 1f out* 25/1



The Form Book Flat, Raceform Ltd, Newbury, RG14 5SJ

1245 **7** *1 ½* **Crazy Tornado (IRE)**[14] 6591 4-9-10 **70**..........................(h) GrahamLee 8 46
(Keith Dalgleish) *hld up: rdn over 3f out: sme hdwy in centre of crse over 1f out: n.d* **9/1**

4500 **8** *1* **Ingleby Spring (IRE)**[11] 6690 5-8-10 **56** oh2................. TonyHamilton 2 30
(Richard Fahey) *s.i.s: sn midfield: drvn and outpcd over 2f out: n.d after* **16/1**

2106 **9** *3 ¼* **Remember Rocky**[14] 6591 8-8-8 **61**......................(b) ConnorMurtagh(7) 9 27
(Lucy Normile) *bhd: struggling 1/2-way: nvr on terms* **16/1**

0600 **10** *2* **Foresight (FR)**[14] 6591 4-8-11 **57**.......................................(t) KevinStott 7 18
(Kevin Ryan) *hld up: drvn and outpcd over 3f out: btn fnl 2f* **14/1**

0030 **11** *2* **Jordan James (IRE)**[75] 4304 4-9-6 **66**...........................(p) LukeMorris 3 23
(Brian Ellison) *prom: rdn in centre of crse over 2f out: sn wknd* **10/1**

-140 **12** *9* **African Grey**[144] 1968 3-8-2 **60**................................. JamieGormley(7) 13
(Martin Todhunter) *hld up on outside: drvn and struggling over 3f out: sn btn* **50/1**

1m 44.7s (4.70) **Going Correction** +0.70s/f (Yiel)
**WFA** 3 from 4yo+ 5lb **12** Ran SP% **116.9**
Speed ratings (Par 103): **104,103,100,95,93 91,89,88,85,83 81,72**
CSF £31.76 CT £109.25 TOTE £5.70: £1.80, £2.00, £1.30; EX 37.10 Trifecta £126.50.
**Owner** Middleham Park Racing LXI & Partner **Bred** Audrey Frances Stynes **Trained** Great Habton, N Yorks

**FOCUS**
Race distance increased by 14yds. A fair handicap and the form makes sense.

## 7043 BRITISH STALLION STUDS EBF MAIDEN STKS (PLUS 10 RACE) (SIRE-RESTRICTED RACE) 7f 173y
**3:10** (3:11) (Class 4) 2-Y-O **£6,469** (£1,925; £962; £481) **Stalls** Low

Form RPR

6 **1** **Wax And Wane**[49] 5301 2-9-5 0............................................. BenCurtis 1 80+
(K R Burke) *hld up: hdwy to press ldr 2f out: swtchd rt 1f out: led wl ins fnl f: kpt on strly* **9/1**

2 **2** *¾* **Soldier To Follow**[31] 5964 2-9-5 0.................................. DavidProbert 2 78
(Andrew Balding) *hld up in tch: hdwy to ld on outside 2f out: drifted lft over 1f out: hdd and no ex wl ins fnl f* **13/8**[1]

00 **3** *4* **Dr Richard Kimble (IRE)**[19] 6380 2-9-5 0.......................... JasonHart 5 69
(Mark Johnston) *led: rdn and hdd 2f out: kpt on same pce over 1f out* **66/1**

4 **4** *½* **Voice Of The North**[16] 6510 2-9-5 0............................... FrannyNorton 6 68
(Mark Johnston) *cl up: rdn and ev ch over 2f out: outpcd fr over 1f out* **7/4**[2]

2 **5** *2 ¾* **Ormesher**[21] 6312 2-9-5 0..................................................... DavidNolan 3 61
(Donald McCain) *trckd ldrs: rdn and outpcd 2f out: btn fnl f* **5/1**[3]

44 **6** *3 ¾* **Iconic Code**[15] 6553 2-9-0 0............................................... GrahamLee 8 48
(Mick Channon) *prom: rdn whn checked appr 2f out: sn wknd* **14/1**

**7** *29* **Contrebasse** 2-9-5 0............................................................... DavidAllan 7
(Tim Easterby) *s.s: bhd: hdwy 1/2-way: drvn and wknd fr 3f out: t.o* **20/1**

1m 45.9s (5.90) **Going Correction** +0.70s/f (Yiel) **7** Ran SP% **114.0**
Speed ratings (Par 97): **98,97,93,92,90 86,57**
CSF £24.03 TOTE £10.80: £3.40, £1.70; EX 29.40 Trifecta £240.60.
**Owner** Tim Dykes **Bred** Stowell Hill Partners **Trained** Middleham Moor, N Yorks

**FOCUS**
Race distance increased by 14yds. A fair maiden, the winner stepping up a good deal from his debut.

## 7044 ANDERSONS H'CAP 7f 173y
**3:40** (3:41) (Class 3) (0-95,93) 3-Y-O+ **£8,086** (£2,406; £1,202; £601) **Stalls** Low

Form RPR

5240 **1** **King's Pavilion (IRE)**[39] 5668 4-9-2 **85**........................ BenCurtis 10 96
(David Barron) *hld up: hdwy over 2f out: led over 1f out: rdn clr fnl f* **9/2**[2]

000 **2** *3 ½* **Instant Attraction (IRE)**[47] 5382 6-9-3 **86**.................. JackGarritty 9 89
(Jedd O'Keeffe) *led 3f: pressed ldr: regained ld over 2f out: hdd over 1f out: kpt on same pce fnl f* **8/1**

2010 **3** *2* **Mohab**[18] 6422 4-9-3 **86**........................................................(p) KevinStott 8 84
(Kevin Ryan) *s.i.s: hld up: rdn over 2f out: hdwy on outside over 1f out: kpt on: nt pce to chal* **7/1**[3]

605 **4** *1* **Highland Colori (IRE)**[31] 5966 9-9-5 **88**....................(v) DavidProbert 4 84
(Andrew Balding) *pressed ldr: led after 3f to over 2f out: drvn and outpcd fr over 1f out* **12/1**

405 **5** *nk* **Candelisa (IRE)**[20] 6349 4-9-6 **89**....................................(p) GrahamLee 5 84
(Jedd O'Keeffe) *trckd ldrs: effrt and drvn along 2f out: no ex fnl f* **15/2**

0060 **6** *1 ¾* **Father Bertie**[16] 6520 5-9-3 **86**........................................(tp) DavidAllan 6 77
(Tim Easterby) *t.k.h: trckd ldrs: drvn over 2f out: wknd over 1f out* **7/1**[3]

46-0 **7** *1 ¼* **Clef**[109] 3094 3-8-7 **81**........................................................ BarryMcHugh 7 68
(Richard Fahey) *hld up in tch: rdn over 2f out: wknd over 1f out* **25/1**

1151 **8** *2 ¾* **Zodiakos (IRE)**[32] 5949 4-9-3 **86**................................(p) TonyHamilton 11 68
(Roger Fell) *trckd ldrs on outside: drvn along over 2f out: wknd over 1f out* **9/2**[2]

0124 **9** *9* **Saint Equiano**[39] 5669 3-8-12 **86**.......................................... PhillipMakin 1 53
(Keith Dalgleish) *plld hrd: hld up: effrt on outside over 2f out: sn wknd* **4/1**[1]

1m 44.03s (4.03) **Going Correction** +0.70s/f (Yiel)
**WFA** 3 from 4yo+ 5lb **9** Ran SP% **115.8**
Speed ratings (Par 107): **107,103,101,100,100 98,97,94,85**
CSF £40.32 CT £249.12 TOTE £3.90: £1.50, £2.40, £2.30; EX 48.70 Trifecta £235.00.
**Owner** Laurence O'Kane **Bred** Darley **Trained** Maunby, N Yorks

**FOCUS**
Race distance increased by 14yds. A competitive handicap, albeit not the strongest for the grade, and a decisive back-to-form winner.

## 7045 WATCH RACING UK ON THE GO EBF FILLIES' NOVICE STKS (PLUS 10 RACE) 6f 195y
**4:10** (4:16) (Class 5) 2-Y-O **£3,234** (£962; £481; £240) **Stalls** Low

Form RPR

436 **1** **Bungee Jump (IRE)**[11] 6666 2-9-0 74.................................... KevinStott 3 77+
(Kevin Ryan) *plld hrd: mde all: rdn clr fr over 1f out: unchal* **11/10**[1]

6 **2** *5* **The Cliff Horse (IRE)**[18] 6433 2-9-0 0.............................. JackGarritty 4 62
(Donald McCain) *pressed wnr thrght: rdn over 2f out: one pce fr over 1f out* **7/1**

05 **3** *6* **Calling Rio (IRE)**[11] 6666 2-9-0 0........................................ SamJames 6 46
(David Loughnane) *trckd ldrs: drvn over 2f out: wknd over 1f out* **16/1**

356 **4** *2 ¼* **Ann Without An E**[12] 6659 2-9-0 82...................................... GrahamLee 7 41
(Mick Channon) *hld up: rdn along over 3f out: shortlived effrt 2f out: sn btn* **10/3**[2]

**5** *1 ¾* **Isle Of Avalon (IRE)** 2-9-0 0............................................... LukeMorris 5 36
(Sir Mark Prescott Bt) *dwlt: bhd: rdn over 3f out: nvr rchd ldrs* **7/2**[3]

**6** *11* **Shakiah (IRE)** 2-9-0 0........................................................... PaddyAspell 2 7
(Sharon Watt) *dwlt: plld hrd in tch: struggling over 2f out: sn btn* **40/1**

**7** *19* **Isabella Ruby** 2-9-0 0...........................................................(h[1]) JoeDoyle 1
(Lisa Williamson) *in tch: drvn along over 3f out: wknd over 2f out: t.o* **40/1**

1m 32.62s (5.52) **Going Correction** +0.70s/f (Yiel) **7** Ran SP% **116.2**
Speed ratings (Par 92): **96,90,83,80,78 66,44**
CSF £10.32 TOTE £2.20: £1.80, £3.60; EX 11.30 Trifecta £52.70.
**Owner** Nick Bradley Racing 7 & Partner **Bred** Roundhill Stud **Trained** Hambleton, N Yorks

**FOCUS**
Race distance increased by 14yds. An ordinary novice event and they finished well strung out, but an improved showing from the winner.

## 7046 WATCH RACING UK ON BTTV H'CAP 6f 195y
**4:40** (4:42) (Class 5) (0-70,71) 3-Y-O+ **£3,234** (£962; £481; £240) **Stalls** Low

Form RPR

0002 **1** **Tagur (IRE)**[13] 6630 3-8-13 **59**............................................... KevinStott 3 68
(Kevin Ryan) *cl up: hdwy over 2f out: rdn to ld ins fnl f: styd on strly* **7/1**

0502 **2** *2 ½* **Reinforced**[15] 6550 4-9-10 **66**........................................(tp) AndrewMullen 7 70
(Michael Dods) *led: rdn along 2f out: hdd ins fnl f: kpt on same pce* **9/2**[3]

5133 **3** *½* **Redarna**[21] 6315 3-8-8 **61**...................................... ConnorMurtagh(7) 6 61+
(Dianne Sayer) *dwlt: hld up: effrt whn nt clr run over 2f out to over 1f out: sn rdn: kpt on fnl f: nt rch first two* **3/1**[1]

554 **4** *5* **Mr Cool Cash**[8] 6783 5-9-10 **66**................................... ConnorBeasley 10 55
(Richard Guest) *in tch: effrt and rdn over 2f out: wknd appr fnl f* **13/2**

4002 **5** *1 ¾* **Champagne Bob**[7] 6807 5-9-1 **62**................................ BenRobinson(5) 2 47
(Richard Price) *dwlt: hld up: drvn over 3f out: hdwy over 1f out: no imp fnl f* **11/2**

-000 **6** *3 ¼* **Niqnaaqpaadiwaaq**[34] 5827 5-8-10 **52** oh1......................... NeilFarley 11 28
(Eric Alston) *cl up: rdn over 2f out: wknd over 1f out* **12/1**

3045 **7** *½* **Dellaguista (IRE)**[29] 6047 3-9-11 **71**.................................... DavidAllan 1 44
(Tim Easterby) *hld up: drvn along over 2f out: sn btn* **4/1**[2]

000 **8** *1 ¾* **Yair Hill (IRE)**[27] 6092 9-8-7 **52** oh7......................... RachelRichardson(3) 4 22
(Thomas Cuthbert) *trckd ldrs: rdn over 2f out: wknd wl over 1f out* **50/1**

1m 31.61s (4.51) **Going Correction** +0.70s/f (Yiel)
**WFA** 3 from 4yo+ 4lb **8** Ran SP% **114.1**
Speed ratings (Par 103): **102,99,98,92,90 87,86,84**
CSF £38.20 CT £114.52 TOTE £7.60: £2.10, £1.70, £1.70; EX 35.50 Trifecta £99.20.
**Owner** Andy Turton & John Blackburn **Bred** Corrin Stud **Trained** Hambleton, N Yorks

**FOCUS**
Race distance increased by 14yds. A fair handicap and it paid to race prominently.

## 7047 WATCH RACING UK ON YOUVIEW NOW H'CAP (DIV I) 1m 6f 32y
**5:10** (5:11) (Class 6) (0-65,67) 3-Y-O+ **£2,911** (£866; £432; £216) **Stalls** Low

Form RPR

2021 **1** **Question Of Faith**[14] 6569 6-9-5 **61**....................... CallumRodriguez(5) 9 67
(Martin Todhunter) *dwlt: hld up: smooth hdwy over 4f out: chsd ldr over 2f out: swtchd rt and led wl ins fnl f: staed on wl* **5/2**[2]

0020 **2** *½* **In Focus (IRE)**[23] 6269 6-8-9 **53**............................(h) JamieGormley(7) 11 58
(Dianne Sayer) *led: rdn 2f out: hdd wl insdide fnl f: kpt on same pce* **16/1**

00/0 **3** *¾* **New Youmzain (FR)**[44] 5468 8-10-0 **65**......................... AndrewMullen 3 69
(Lucy Normile) *hedl up in tch: drven and outpcd over 4f out: rallied and swtchd rt over 1f out: styd on wl: nrst fin* **66/1**

-223 **4** *9* **Starshell (IRE)**[7] 6812 3-9-4 **64**............................................ LukeMorris 1 59
(Sir Mark Prescott Bt) *prom: drvn along over 5f out: rallied: effrt over 2f out: wknd over 1f out* **5/6**[1]

34/6 **5** *3 ¼* **Bourne**[21] 6317 11-10-2 **67**.................................................(b) DavidNolan 7 55
(Donald McCain) *hld up: drvn and outpcd over 6f out: sme late hdwy: nvr on terms* **20/1**

403 **6** *8* **Little Jo**[15] 6548 3-8-6 **52** ow3................................................. GrahamLee 8 32
(Chris Grant) *chsd ldr util rdn and wknd over 2f out* **10/1**[3]

0300 **7** *4 ½* **Grey Mist**[18] 6436 3-9-2 **62**...............................................(p) DavidAllan 4 36
(Tim Easterby) *dwlt: hel;d up: rdn and outpcd over 4f out: btn fnl 2f* **10/1**[3]

3m 20.81s (13.31) **Going Correction** +0.70s/f (Yiel)
**WFA** 3 from 6yo+ 9lb **7** Ran SP% **113.4**
Speed ratings (Par 101): **89,88,88,83,81 76,74**
CSF £38.94 CT £2059.99 TOTE £2.70: £2.30, £7.60; EX 30.00 Trifecta £344.50.
**Owner** K Fitzsimons & G Fell **Bred** Sir Robert Ogden **Trained** Orton, Cumbria

**FOCUS**
Race distance increased by 25yds. This has been rated as straightforward form around the winner and runner-up.

## 7048 WATCH RACING UK ON YOUVIEW NOW H'CAP (DIV II) 1m 6f 32y
**5:40** (5:43) (Class 6) (0-65,65) 3-Y-O+ **£2,911** (£866; £432; £216) **Stalls** Low

Form RPR

4544 **1** **Elite Icon**[5] 6892 3-7-9 **48** ow2................................ JamieGormley(7) 11 59+
(Iain Jardine) *hld up: outpcd and detached after 3f: rallied over 4f out: effrt and led over 1f out: styd on strly fnl f* **4/1**[2]

4512 **2** *3* **Bodacious Name (IRE)**[36] 5740 3-9-3 **63**........................ JasonHart 10 70
(John Quinn) *hld up in tch: smooth hdwy over 3f out: ev ch over 2f out: sn rdn and outpcd: rallied and chsd wnr ins fnl f: kpt on* **15/8**[1]

0602 **3** *1 ¾* **Tyrolean**[19] 6370 4-10-0 **65**............................................(p[1]) LukeMorris 2 68
(Seamus Durack) *cl up: led 3f out to over 1f out: sn rdn and edgd lft: lost 2nd and no ex ins fnl f* **10/1**

3413 **4** *5* **Ocean Gale**[19] 6370 4-9-0 **51**........................................... DavidProbert 8 47
(Richard Price) *hld up: rdn and hdwy on outside over 3f out: no imp fr 2f out* **16/1**

4252 **5** *½* **Eyreborn (IRE)**[11] 6692 3-8-13 **64**.............................. RowanScott(5) 7 62
(Keith Dalgleish) *hld up bhd ldng gp: drvn and outpcd over 4f out: rallied over 1f out: no imp* **11/2**

0640 **6** *7* **Zihaam**[7] 6812 3-9-2 **62**........................................................ TonyHamilton 6 50
(Roger Fell) *cl up: drvn and outpcd over 2f out: btn over 1f out* **20/1**

3555 **7** *¾* **Lady Natasha (IRE)**[33] 5872 4-9-6 **57**................................. BenCurtis 5 43
(K R Burke) *hld up in tch: drvn and outpcd over 3f out: btn fnl 2f* **12/1**

5600 **8** *11* **Chelsea's Boy (IRE)**[15] 6551 4-10-0 **65**............................ GrahamLee 3 36
(Donald McCain) *led to 3f out: rdn and sn wknd* **40/1**

061 **9** *53* **Mick The Poser (IRE)**[20] 6352 3-8-3 **49**.....................(p) AndrewMullen 9
(Jennie Candlish) *t.k.h: sn prom on outside: drvn and outpcd over 3f out: lost tch over 2f out: eased* **9/2**[3]

3m 19.0s (11.50) **Going Correction** +0.70s/f (Yiel)
**WFA** 3 from 4yo+ 9lb **9** Ran SP% **118.2**
Speed ratings (Par 101): **95,93,92,89,89 85,84,78,48**
CSF £12.22 CT £70.48 TOTE £5.10: £1.80, £1.10, £2.50; EX 16.10 Trifecta £134.70.
**Owner** I J Jardine **Bred** C A Cyzer **Trained** Carrutherstown, D'fries & G'way

**FOCUS**
Race distance increased by 25yds. The second division was run in 1.81sec quicker than the first leg.

T/Jkpt: Not won. T/Plt: £120.00 to a £1 stake. Pool: £55,881.06. 339.78 winning units. T/Qpdt: £28.70 to a £1 stake. Pool: £3,260.01. 83.95 winning units. **Richard Young**

# 6181 DONCASTER (L-H)

Wednesday, September 13

**OFFICIAL GOING: Soft (good to soft in places; 6.9)**

Wind: Strong against Weather: Bright and breezy

## 7049 IRISH STALLION FARMS EBF CONDITIONS STKS (PLUS 10 RACE) 6f 2y

**2:20** (2:20) (Class 2) 2-Y-O **£11,205** (£3,355; £1,677; £838) **Stalls** High

Form RPR

31 **1** **Shababy**[25] 6199 2-8-13 0 JimCrowley 2 107+
(Owen Burrows) *.trckd ldr towards centre: hdwy over 2f out: led wl over 1f out: sn rdn clr: kpt on strly* **13/8**[2]

1214 **2** *7* **John Kirkup**[21] 6330 2-8-11 92 PaulMulrennan 4 84
(Michael Dods) *racd towards stands rail: hdwy wl over 1f out: sn rdn: kpt on u.p fnl f: tk 2nd towards fin: no ch w wnr* **9/2**[3]

210 **3** *1* **Beatbox Rhythm (IRE)**[21] 6326 2-8-13 89 PJMcDonald 1 83
(K R Burke) *racd towards centre: led: rdn along over 2f out: hdd wl over 1f out: sn drvn and kpt on same pce* **8/1**

1111 **4** *9* **Demons Rock (IRE)**[21] 6330 2-8-11 102 RichardKingscote 3 54
(Tom Dascombe) *racd nr stands rail: cl up: pushed along over 2f out: sn rdn: wknd wl over 1f out* **6/4**[1]

1m 13.77s (0.17) **Going Correction** +0.275s/f (Good) **4** Ran SP% **107.4**
Speed ratings (Par 101): **109,99,98,86**
CSF £8.53 TOTE £2.30; EX 8.00 Trifecta £24.40.
**Owner** Hamdan Al Maktoum **Bred** Bearstone Stud Ltd **Trained** Lambourn, Berks

**FOCUS**
The round course railed out from about 1m2f until round joins the straight. The runners faced a strong headwind off the final bend. After winning the first Jim Crowley said the going was 'soft ground and drying all the time'. There was a deeply impressive winner of this interesting little conditions event, although it did fall apart somewhat. It has been rated cautiously around the 2nd/3rd. The main action was nearer the stands' side.

## 7050 OWLERTON GREYHOUND STADIUM NURSERY H'CAP 7f 6y

**2:50** (2:50) (Class 2) 2-Y-O **£11,644** (£3,465; £1,731; £865) **Stalls** High

Form RPR

210 **1** **Nobleman's Nest**[18] 6446 2-8-13 **85** SilvestreDeSousa 7 93+
(Simon Crisford) *hld up: hdwy to trck ldrs 1/2-way: cl up over 2f out: led wl over 1f out: rdn appr fnl f: kpt on strly* **5/2**[1]

3221 **2** *1 ½* **Crownthorpe**[11] 6699 2-8-10 **82** PaulMulrennan 5 86
(Richard Fahey) *hld up in tch: hdwy over 2f out: rdn to chse wnr over 1f out: drvn ins fnl f: kpt on same pce* **4/1**[2]

1131 **3** *2 ½* **Placebo Effect (IRE)**[13] 6625 2-8-0 **72** oh2 JamesSullivan 8 70
(Ollie Pears) *hld up towards rr: hdwy 3f out: chsd ldrs 2f out: rdn over 1f out: drvn and kpt on same pce fnl f* **8/1**[3]

1150 **4** *½* **Guzman (IRE)**[20] 6353 2-8-7 **79** (h) PaulHanagan 6 76
(Richard Fahey) *trckd ldrs: pushed along over 2f out: sn rdn and kpt on same pce appr fnl f* **8/1**[3]

0054 **5** *3 ¼* **Toomer**[8] 6778 2-8-0 **72** oh2 KieranO'Neill 3 61+
(Richard Hannon) *led: rdn along over 2f out: sn edgd lft and hdd wl over 1f out: grad wknd* **14/1**

4136 **6** *2 ½* **Benadalid**[18] 6432 2-8-5 **77** ShaneGray 2 59+
(Chris Fairhurst) *prom: rdn along wl over 2f out: sn wknd* **20/1**

041 **7** *2 ¾* **Rum Runner**[12] 6653 2-8-12 **84** SeanLevey 4 60+
(Richard Hannon) *prom: pushed along 3f out: sn rdn and wknd 2f out* **4/1**[2]

2050 **8** *3 ½* **Inviolable Spirit (IRE)**[20] 6353 2-8-6 **78** PatrickMathers 9 45
(Richard Fahey) *t.k.h: a towards rr* **11/1**

240 **9** *½* **Bomad**[26] 6147 2-7-13 **74** ow2 AaronJones(3) 11 40
(Derek Shaw) *cl up: rdn along over 2f out: sn wknd* **66/1**

1m 27.51s (1.21) **Going Correction** +0.275s/f (Good) **9** Ran SP% **112.0**
Speed ratings (Par 101): **104,102,99,98,95 92,89,85,84**
CSF £11.80 CT £66.46 TOTE £3.10: £1.20, £1.70, £2.70; EX 12.20 Trifecta £46.40.
**Owner** Mrs P Good **Bred** Mrs P Good **Trained** Newmarket, Suffolk

**FOCUS**
Probably a fair handicap, with the first three appearing to run up to their best. The early gallop didn't look overly strong but soon evened out.

## 7051 PEPSI MAX SCARBROUGH STKS (LISTED RACE) 5f 3y

**3:20** (3:20) (Class 1) 2-Y-O+

**£22,684** (£8,600; £4,304; £2,144; £1,076; £540) **Stalls** High

Form RPR

1030 **1** **Encore D'Or**[29] 6025 5-9-11 104 RyanMoore 4 106
(Robert Cowell) *towards rr: hdwy 2f out: rdn over 1f out: swtchd lft and chal ins fnl f: drvn and kpt on to ld last 100 yds* **13/2**

351 **2** *1* **Razzmatazz**[8] 6791 3-9-5 0 SamHitchcott 2 98
(Clive Cox) *dwlt: sn chsng ldrs: hdwy over 2f out: cl up over 2f out: rdn to ld over 1f out: drvn ins fnl f: hdd and no ex last 100 yds* **33/1**

0-00 **3** *1* **Go On Go On Go On**[11] 6668 4-9-6 93 AdamKirby 1 94
(Clive Cox) *chsd ldr: hdwy 1/2-way: cl up 2f out: sn rdn and ev ch: drvn and kpt on same pce fnl f* **11/1**

2002 **4** *hd* **Final Venture**[11] 6668 5-10-0 109 (h) OisinMurphy 3 101
(Paul Midgley) *dwlt and rr: hdwy on outer 2f out: sn rdn: kpt on fnl f* **6/4**[1]

0033 **5** *2 ¼* **Thesme**[21] 6325 5-9-6 100 FrankieDettori 6 85
(Nigel Tinkler) *racd nr stands rail: clr ldr: pushed along over 2f out: jnd and rdn wl over 1f out: sn drvn and hdd: sn wknd* **9/4**[2]

5116 **6** *1 ¼* **Desert Law (IRE)**[11] 6668 9-9-11 100 PaulMulrennan 5 86
(Paul Midgley) *racd nr stands rail: chsd clr ldr: rdn along 2f out: sn drvn and wknd* **6/1**[3]

1m 1.91s (1.41) **Going Correction** +0.275s/f (Good)
**WFA** 3 from 4yo+ 1lb **6** Ran SP% **109.7**
Speed ratings: **99,97,95,95,91 89**
CSF £135.69 TOTE £7.30: £3.10, £9.30; EX 131.50 Trifecta £371.00.
**Owner** Mrs Morley,G Johnson,Newsells Park Stud **Bred** Newsells Park Stud **Trained** Six Mile Bottom, Cambs

**FOCUS**
This year's Listed Scarbrough Stakes was run at a blistering pace and the first pair dominated the finish towards the centre. The level is fluid but the winner has been rated to his AW best.

## 7052 CLIPPER LOGISTICS LEGER LEGENDS CLASSIFIED STKS 1m (S)

**3:50** (3:53) (Class 5) 3-Y-O+ **£6,469** (£1,925; £962; £481) **Stalls** High

Form RPR

0563 **1** **Off Art**[18] 6434 7-11-2 70 BrianHarding 3 76
(Tim Easterby) *trckd ldrs: hdwy 3f out: cl up 2f out: rdn over 1f out: drvn ins fnl f: kpt on wl to ld last 75 yds* **5/1**[2]

0455 **2** *½* **Fire Palace**[30] 6006 3-10-11 69 AdrianNicholls 5 74
(Robert Eddery) *midfield: hdwy 1/2-way: tk slt ld on outer 2f out and sn rdn: drvn ins fnl f: edgd lft and hdd last 75 yds* **10/1**

3626 **3** *½* **Character Onesie (IRE)**[16] 6516 5-11-2 70 IanMongan 6 74
(Richard Fahey) *dwlt: sn in tch: hdwy over 3f out: cl up 2f out: rdn wl over 1f out and ev ch tl drvn ins fnl f and kpt on same pce towards fin* **9/2**[1]

2560 **4** *¾* **Detachment**[120] 2701 4-11-2 70 OlliePears 10 72
(Les Eyre) *hld up in rr: hdwy 1/2-way: trckd ldrs over 2f out: effrt and nt clr run over 1f out: swtchd rt to stands rail and rdn ent fnl f: sn drvn and kpt on same pce* **8/1**[3]

4032 **5** *1 ½* **Haraz (IRE)**[8] 6799 4-11-2 69 (b) LukeHarvey 16 69+
(Jamie Osborne) *hld up towards rr: hdwy over 3f out: sn n.m.r and pushed along: rdn over 2f out: styd on fr over 1f out: nt rch ldrs* **9/1**

4530 **6** *2 ½* **The Gay Cavalier**[6] 6848 6-11-2 67 (tp) DaraghO'Donohoe 9 63
(John Ryan) *hld up towards rr: hdwy on wd outside wl over 2f out: sn rdn and kpt on fnl f* **20/1**

063 **7** *4* **Soldier Blue (FR)**[45] 5458 3-10-11 69 GeorgeDuffield 12 53
(Brian Ellison) *.hld up towards rr: hdwy 1/2-way: rdn along and in tch over 2f out: sn drvn and one pce* **9/2**[1]

0003 **8** *2 ½* **Mustaqbal (IRE)**[29] 6049 5-11-2 67 (p) DaleGibson 15 48
(Michael Dods) *a towards rr* **12/1**

5630 **9** *½* **Hitman**[25] 6181 4-11-2 68 TomMcLaughlin 4 47
(Rebecca Bastiman) *t.k.h: chsd ldrs: rdn along over 2f out: sn drvn and wknd* **20/1**

2253 **10** *2* **Patching**[17] 6485 3-10-11 67 (b) GaryBardwell 2 41
(Giles Bravery) *t.k.h: chsd ldr on outer: rdn along 3f out: sn wknd* **16/1**

4040 **11** *3* **Undiscovered Angel (FR)**[33] 5910 3-10-11 70 TonyClark 7 34
(K R Burke) *led: rdn along 3f out: hdd over 2f out: sn wknd* **33/1**

5450 **12** *1 ¾* **Secret Missile**[4] 6943 7-11-2 69 RodneyLappin 8 31
(David C Griffiths) *prom: rdn along and lost pl wl over 3f out: sn in rr* **66/1**

5313 **13** *5* **Diamond Runner (IRE)**[25] 6188 5-11-2 59 (b) JamieMackay 14 20
(Lawrence Mullaney) *chsd ldrs: rdn along over 3f out: sn wknd* **16/1**

1006 **14** *28* **Poor Duke (IRE)**[20] 6341 7-11-2 55 (v) TonyCulhane 11
(Michael Mullineaux) *a in rr: rdn along and outpcd fr over 3f out* **100/1**

1m 44.84s (5.54) **Going Correction** +0.275s/f (Good)
**WFA** 3 from 4yo+ 5lb **14** Ran SP% **117.6**
Speed ratings (Par 103): **83,82,82,81,79 77,73,70,70,68 65,63,58,30**
CSF £50.08 TOTE £6.40: £2.20, £3.40, £2.40; EX 63.60 Trifecta £473.80.
**Owner** D B & Mrs C Lamplough **Bred** D B Lamplough **Trained** Great Habton, N Yorks

**FOCUS**
While this race featured jockeys that rarely now ride in public, it was competitive and the form can be reliable for the level, although the winning time was nothing special. The winner has been rated to this year's form.

## 7053 WILLIAM HILL GET THE APP ON GOOGLE PLAY H'CAP 7f 6y

**4:20** (4:22) (Class 2) (0-100,98) 3-Y-O

**£12,450** (£3,728; £1,864; £932; £466; £234) **Stalls** High

Form RPR

115 **1** **Lahore (USA)**[17] 6497 3-8-9 **86** SilvestreDeSousa 6 103+
(Roger Varian) *dwlt and hld up in rr: smooth hdwy over 2f out: led 11/2f out: sn rdn clr: readily* **7/2**[1]

4211 **2** *4* **Bengal Lancer**[19] 6397 3-8-1 **85** ManuelFernandes(7) 3 90
(Ian Williams) *prom: cl up 3f out: rdn to ld 2f out: hdd and drvn 11/2f out: kpt on same pce fnl f* **9/2**[2]

1542 **3** *½* **Night Circus (IRE)**[32] 5943 3-9-1 **92** AdamKirby 5 96
(Charlie Appleby) *trckd ldrs: pushed along wl over 2f out: rdn wl over 1f out: drvn and kpt on fnl f: tk 3rd nr line* **8/1**

0141 **4** *nk* **Important Mission (USA)**[29] 6026 3-9-0 **91** RyanMoore 1 94
(William Haggas) *dwlt: in tch: hdwy on outer to chse ldrs 2f out and sn rdn: drvn over 1f out: kpt on same pce fnl f* **13/2**

3001 **5** *½* **Hyde Park**[17] 6484 3-9-7 **98** (t) FrankieDettori 4 100
(John Gosden) *trckd ldrs: hdwy over 2f out: rdn along wl over 1f out: drvn and kpt on same pce fnl f* **11/2**[3]

3343 **6** *3* **High Acclaim (USA)**[12] 6655 3-8-10 **87** (p) OisinMurphy 7 81
(Roger Teal) *racd nr stands rail: cl up: led 1/2-way: rdn along over 2f out: sn hdd & wknd* **16/1**

2303 **7** *1 ¼* **Six Strings**[25] 6186 3-8-11 **88** PaulHanagan 8 79
(Richard Fahey) *in tch: pushed along 3f out: rdn over 2f out: n.d* **6/1**

1215 **8** *7* **Pillar Of Society (IRE)**[12] 6655 3-8-12 **89** SeanLevey 2 62
(Richard Hannon) *racd towards centre: led: hdd 1/2-way and sn riodden along: wknd wl over 2f out* **8/1**

1m 26.66s (0.36) **Going Correction** +0.275s/f (Good) **8** Ran SP% **111.5**
Speed ratings (Par 107): **108,103,102,102,101 98,97,89**
CSF £18.16 CT £112.22 TOTE £3.90: £1.50, £1.70, £2.70; EX 19.70 Trifecta £139.90.
**Owner** Prince A A Faisal **Bred** Nawara Stud Company Ltd **Trained** Newmarket, Suffolk

**FOCUS**
This decent 3yo handicap looked wide open, but it proved one-way traffic. The 2nd has been rated close to his Salisbury win.

## 7054 SPORTS ID - STRENGTH IN SPORT CONDITIONS STKS 1m 2f 43y

**4:50** (4:50) (Class 2) 3-Y-O+ **£11,827** (£3,541; £1,770; £885) **Stalls** Low

Form RPR

3322 **1** **Mount Logan (IRE)**[16] 6514 6-9-2 110 (p) AndreaAtzeni 3 111
(Roger Varian) *trckd ldr: hdwy and cl up over 2f out: pushed along to take slt ld wl over 1f out: sn rdn: drvn ent fnl f: kpt on wl towards fin* **2/1**[2]

6504 **2** *1* **Red Verdon (USA)**[74] 4360 4-9-2 107 JimCrowley 5 109
(Ed Dunlop) *led: pushed along 3f out: jnd and rdn over 2f out: hdd wl over 1f out and sn drvn: rallied ins fnl f: no ex towards fin* **5/1**[3]

564- **3** *1* **Sumbal (IRE)**[326] 7545 5-9-2 106 OisinMurphy 2 107
(David Simcock) *dwlt and hld up in rr: hdwy on outer over 2f out: rdn wl over 1f out: drvn and ch ent fnl f: kpt on same pce* **9/1**

-433 **4** *hd* **Mirage Dancer**[21] 6327 3-8-10 111 ...................... RyanMoore 1 108
(Sir Michael Stoute) *trckd ldng pair: niggled along over 2f out: effrt and n.m.r over 1f out: sn swtchd rt and drvn: kpt on same pce* **11/10**[1]

2m 14.22s (4.82) **Going Correction** +0.775s/f (Yiel)
**WFA** 3 from 4yo+ 6lb **4** Ran SP% **107.6**
Speed ratings (Par 109): **111,110,109,109**
CSF £10.98 TOTE £2.80; EX 11.60 Trifecta £26.00.
**Owner** Sheikh Mohammed Obaid Al Maktoum **Bred** Ladyswood Stud & Canning Downs Stud Aus **Trained** Newmarket, Suffolk

**FOCUS**
Add 6yds. This quality conditions event was predictably tactical and it's muddling form, but the winner has been rated close to his best.

## 7055 1STSECURITYSOLUTIONS.CO.UK H'CAP — 5f 3y
**5:20** (5:23) (Class 4) (0-85,85) 3-Y-O+ **£6,469** (£1,925; £962; £481) **Stalls** High

Form RPR
403 **1** **Somewhere Secret**[5] 6877 3-8-5 **73** ...................... (p) PhilDennis(3) 3 81
(Michael Mullineaux) *chsd ldrs on outer: hdwy wl over 1f out: rdn to chal ins fnl f: sn drvn and edgd rt: kpt on wl to ld last 75 yds* **11/1**

5231 **2** *hd* **Suwaan (IRE)**[14] 6596 3-8-7 **72** ...................... PaulHanagan 2 79
(Ruth Carr) *trckd ldrs: smooth hdwy to ld over 1f out: rdn ent fnl f: sn drvn and edgd lft: hdd last 75 yds: no ex* **16/1**

1212 **3** *1 1/4* **Muatadel**[9] 6758 4-9-1 **79** ...................... PJMcDonald 11 82
(Roger Fell) *.in tch: hdwy to chse ldrs wl over 1f out: sn rdn and kpt on fnl f* **11/4**[1]

6444 **4** *3/4* **Foxtrot Knight**[14] 6574 5-8-8 **72** ...................... JamesSullivan 7 72
(Ruth Carr) *midfield: hdwy wl over 1f out: sn rdn and kpt on fnl f* **16/1**

3344 **5** *1/2* **Fumbo Jumbo (IRE)**[14] 6593 4-9-5 **83** ...................... PaulMulrennan 14 81+
(Michael Dods) *towards rr: pushed along 2f out: sn rdn and styd on wl fnl f* **15/2**[3]

0006 **6** *shd* **Venturous (IRE)**[25] 6185 4-9-4 **82** ...................... SilvestreDeSousa 4 80+
(David Barron) *s.i.s and lost 5 l s: bhd: hdwy over 2f out: rdn to chse ldrs over 1f out: drvn and n.m.r ins fnl f: kpt on same pce* **11/2**[2]

545 **7** *1/2* **Singeur (IRE)**[25] 6205 10-9-3 **81** ...................... DuranFentiman 8 77
(Rebecca Bastiman) *midfield: hdwy wl over 1f out: sn rdn and kpt on fnl f* **14/1**

0-50 **8** *hd* **Tilly Trotter (IRE)**[54] 5117 3-9-1 **80** ...................... PatrickMathers 6 75
(Declan Carroll) *dwlt: sn chsng ldrs: hdwy 2f out: rdn over 1f out: drvn and one pce fnl f* **20/1**

4441 **9** *3/4* **Penny Dreadful**[14] 6574 5-8-2 **73** ...................... (p) RPWalsh(7) 5 66
(Scott Dixon) *cl u towards stands rail: rdn to rake slt ld 2f out: drvn and hdd over 1f out: wknd fnl f* **16/1**

1000 **10** *1/2* **Tylery Wonder (IRE)**[25] 6185 7-9-2 **80** ...................... (b) OisinMurphy 16 71
(Paul Midgley) *racd towards stands rail: chsd ldrs: rdn along 2f out: sn drvn and wknd* **9/1**

0346 **11** *3/4* **Fredricka**[4] 6943 6-8-7 **78** ...................... (p) ManuelFernandes(7) 10 66
(Ivan Furtado) *hld up towards rr: hdwy wl over 1f out: sn rdn and styng on whn n.m.r ins fnl f: sn eased* **25/1**

0200 **12** *3/4* **Bronze Beau**[14] 6574 10-8-1 **72** ...................... (tp) FayeMcManoman(7) 9 58
(Kristin Stubbs) *racd centre: led: hdd 3f out: sn rdn and wknd fnl 2f* **66/1**

004 **13** *nk* **Crosse Fire**[14] 6574 5-8-7 **71** oh3 ...................... (v) KieranO'Neill 12 55
(Scott Dixon) *prom towards stands rail: led after 2f: rdn along and hdd 2f out: sn drvn and wknd* **33/1**

0226 **14** *nse* **Bogart**[14] 6593 8-9-4 **82** ...................... (tp) TomEaves 15 66
(Kevin Ryan) *a in rr* **9/1**

0660 **15** *6* **Fast Act (IRE)**[32] 5920 5-9-0 **78** ...................... ShaneGray 13 41
(Kevin Ryan) *.racd towards stands rail: chsd ldrs: rdn along 1/2-way: sn wknd* **33/1**

1m 1.09s (0.59) **Going Correction** +0.275s/f (Good)
**WFA** 3 from 4yo+ 1lb **15** Ran SP% **122.4**
Speed ratings (Par 105): **106,105,103,102,101 101,100,100,99,98 97,96,95,95,85**
CSF £167.64 CT £641.90 TOTE £13.50: £4.10, £5.40, £1.60; EX 279.40 Trifecta £1475.60.
**Owner** Mia Racing **Bred** Mia Racing **Trained** Alpraham, Cheshire

**FOCUS**
This looked a really competitive sprint handicap, and the pace was sound from the outset. However, it was noticeable that the first pair home were more towards the inside rail, plus they were two of the three 3yos in the field. A pb from the winner.
T/Plt: £1,010.30 to a £1 stake. Pool: £99,072.54. 71.58 winning units. T/Qpdt: £169.10 to a £1 stake. Pool: £6,767.47. 29.60 winning units. **Joe Rowntree**

# 6931 KEMPTON (A.W) (R-H)
Wednesday, September 13

**OFFICIAL GOING: Polytrack: standard to slow**
Wind: Moderate across (away from stands) Weather: Fine

## 7056 100% PROFIT BOOST AT 32REDSPORT.COM CLASSIFIED CLAIMING STKS — 6f (P)
**5:45** (5:48) (Class 5) 3-Y-O+ **£2,911** (£866; £432; £216) **Stalls** Low

Form RPR
-562 **1** **Red Trooper (FR)**[14] 6582 4-8-7 71 ...................... JosephineGordon 6 69
(George Baker) *chsd ldrs: urged along over 2f out: prog to press ldr jst over 1f out: led ins fnl f: kpt on* **6/1**[2]

0442 **2** *nk* **Mishaal (IRE)**[5] 6888 7-9-1 70 ...................... KieranShoemark 4 76
(Michael Herrington) *trckd ldng pair: clsd to ld over 1f out: hdd u.p ins fnl f: pressed wnr after but edgd lft and nt qckn* **11/8**[1]

14 **3** *2 3/4* **Kings Academy**[9] 6768 3-9-7 72 ...................... (p) RaulDaSilva 7 75
(Paul Cole) *chsd ldrs: rdn over 2f out: kpt on fr over 1f out to take 3rd ins fnl f: no threat to ldng pair* **25/1**

5300 **4** *1* **Yeeoow (IRE)**[54] 5132 8-8-11 73 ...................... (p) MartinHarley 1 60
(K R Burke) *led to over 1f out: fdd ins fnl f* **9/1**

0600 **5** *1/2* **Red Gunner**[13] 6620 3-8-10 68 ...................... ShelleyBirkett(3) 12 62+
(David O'Meara) *wl in rr fr wdst draw: urged along over 2f out: kpt on to take 5th ins fnl f: nvr a threat* **33/1**

2154 **6** *1* **Dealer's Choice (IRE)**[36] 5758 3-9-7 73 ...................... HarryBentley 10 67
(Roger Varian) *nvr bttr than midfield: rdn and no imp over 2f out: one pce* **8/1**

6630 **7** *nk* **The Big Lad**[16] 6527 5-9-5 72 ...................... (b) ShaneKelly 5 62
(Richard Hughes) *towards rr: effrt on inner over 2f out: plugged on one pce and n.d* **11/1**

3332 **8** *3/4* **Dream Farr (IRE)**[16] 6507 4-9-1 74 ...................... (t) LiamKeniry 9 56
(Ed Walker) *chsd ldr to 2f out: wknd sn after* **15/2**[3]

430 **9** *nk* **Major Crispies**[13] 6620 6-8-12 70 ...................... (bt) PatrickVaughan(7) 3 59
(David O'Meara) *rrd s and slowly away: mostly in last pair: racd awkwardly whn asked for effrt over 2f out: plodded on* **12/1**

1000 **10** *2 1/2* **Picture Dealer**[27] 6113 8-8-12 73 ...................... SimonPearce(3) 11 47
(Lydia Pearce) *a wl in rr: wd bnd 1/2-way: sn no ch* **33/1**

0000 **11** *shd* **Spiritofedinburgh (IRE)**[74] 4350 3-8-3 57 ...................... (p[1]) MartinDwyer 8 36
(Brendan Powell) *sn rdn to stay in tch: dropped to rr 2f out and wl btn after* **66/1**

1m 11.82s (-1.28) **Going Correction** 0.0s/f (Stan)
**WFA** 3 from 4yo+ 2lb **11** Ran SP% **116.5**
Speed ratings (Par 103): **108,107,103,102,101 100,100,99,98,95 95**
CSF £14.03 TOTE £5.70: £2.00, £1.20, £5.40; EX 19.70 Trifecta £157.60.The winner was subject to a friendly claim.
**Owner** PJL Racing 1 **Bred** Famille Niarchos **Trained** Manton, Wilts

**FOCUS**
A fair claimer, although the winner has been rated 10lb off his best.

## 7057 VISIT RACINGUK.COM NURSERY H'CAP (JOCKEY CLUB GRASSROOTS NURSERY QUALIFIER) — 7f (P)
**6:15** (6:16) (Class 6) (0-65,71) 2-Y-O **£2,264** (£673; £336; £168) **Stalls** Low

Form RPR
5351 **1** **Sunbreak (IRE)**[6] 6845 2-9-13 **71** 6ex ...................... JoeFanning 5 74
(Mark Johnston) *mde all: urged along over 1f out: pressed on both sides fnl f but a looked to be in command: rdn out* **1/1**[1]

6036 **2** *nk* **Panophobia**[15] 6552 2-9-4 **65** ...................... AdamMcNamara(3) 2 66
(Richard Fahey) *prom: rdn to dispute 2nd over 1f out: chal ins fnl f: kpt on but a hld* **17/2**

6405 **3** *hd* **Revenge**[13] 6634 2-8-11 **55** ...................... (b) MartinDwyer 13 56
(Tim Easterby) *spd fr wd draw to chse wnr: rdn 2f out: tried to chal fr over 1f out but a hld: lost 2nd last 75yds* **20/1**

0505 **4** *1 1/2* **Couldn't Could She**[7] 6825 2-9-4 **62** ...................... RoystonFfrench 11 59
(Adam West) *prom: rdn over 3f out: nvr pce to chal after but kpt on same pce* **66/1**

5656 **5** *shd* **Galactic (IRE)**[19] 6395 2-9-5 **66** ...................... HollieDoyle(3) 10 62+
(Richard Hannon) *mostly in last trio and pushed along over 3f out: rdn and prog fr 2f out: styd on fnl f: nrst fin* **10/1**

2125 **6** *1 1/4* **Give Em A Clump (IRE)**[13] 6613 2-8-13 **60** ...................... DavidEgan(3) 4 53
(David Evans) *plld hrd early in midfield: pushed along after 2f towards rr: struggling on outer over 2f out: suddenly styd on again fnl f* **8/1**[3]

0622 **7** *shd* **Laura Knight (IRE)**[13] 6634 2-9-7 **65** ...................... (p) PatDobbs 3 58
(Gary Moore) *t.k.h: hld up in midfield: lost pl and in rr over 2f out: effrt wl over 1f out: kpt on but nvr gng to rch ldrs* **6/1**[2]

6235 **8** *1/2* **Tranquil Soul**[19] 6366 2-9-8 **66** ...................... TedDurcan 7 57
(David Lanigan) *sltly awkward s: hld up in last: wd bnd 3f out: stl last 2f out: reminder over 1f out: prog past btn rivals fnl f but then eased last 50yds* **20/1**

1660 **9** *nk* **Our Kid (IRE)**[29] 6036 2-9-5 **63** ...................... (b[1]) AdamBeschizza 12 54
(Richard Fahey) *t.k.h: trapped out side in midfield: rdn 2f out: no prog* **25/1**

565 **10** *1/2* **Graffitista (IRE)**[23] 6272 2-9-5 **63** ...................... KieranShoemark 6 52
(George Scott) *wl in rr: pushed along 3f out: prog 2f out: no hdwy 1f out: wknd last 100yds* **14/1**

605 **11** *3 1/4* **Misty Breese (IRE)**[83] 3999 2-8-6 **50** ...................... (b[1]) JoeyHaynes 1 30
(Paul D'Arcy) *nvr bttr than midfield: wknd on inner over 1f out* **50/1**

6650 **12** *nk* **Catch The Pigeon**[14] 6585 2-8-10 **54** ...................... LiamKeniry 8 34
(Ed de Giles) *slowly away: a in rr: brief effrt on inner over 2f out: sn btn* **40/1**

1m 26.33s (0.33) **Going Correction** 0.0s/f (Stan) **12** Ran SP% **120.9**
Speed ratings (Par 93): **98,97,97,95,95 94,94,93,93,92 88,88**
CSF £9.35 CT £118.90 TOTE £2.10: £1.10, £2.90, £4.80; EX 13.30 Trifecta £128.80.
**Owner** Sheikh Hamdan bin Mohammed Al Maktoum **Bred** Godolphin **Trained** Middleham Moor, N Yorks

**FOCUS**
They didn't go a great gallop early and nothing got into it from off the pace. Modest bare form around 2-3-4.

## 7058 32RED CASINO H'CAP — 7f (P)
**6:45** (6:46) (Class 5) (0-70,70) 3-Y-O+ **£2,911** (£866; £432; £216) **Stalls** Low

Form RPR
6516 **1** **Daring Guest (IRE)**[48] 5341 3-8-12 **67** ...................... JaneElliott(5) 1 75
(George Margarson) *wl in tch: pushed along and threaded through rivals fr 2f out: rdn to ld jst over 1f out: styd on* **11/1**

1-36 **2** *1/2* **Medicean El Diablo**[13] 6620 4-9-7 **67** ...................... TomMarquand 10 76
(Jimmy Fox) *hld up and sn in last: drvn and gd prog fr jst over 2f out: chal jst over 1f out on inner: styd on but jst hld last 100yds* **8/1**

4413 **3** *1* **Easy Code**[33] 5870 4-9-4 **69** ...................... GeorgiaCox(5) 2 75
(William Haggas) *hld up in rr: shkn up and prog wl over 1f out: tk 3rd last 150yds: no imp ldng pair nr fin* **9/2**[1]

4003 **4** *nk* **Mezmaar**[22] 6288 8-9-6 **66** ...................... SteveDrowne 6 71
(Mark Usher) *trckd ldr after 1f: rdn to ld over 2f out: hdd and one pce jst over 1f out* **8/1**

100 **5** *1 1/2* **Chicago Star**[27] 6106 3-9-5 **69** ...................... ShaneKelly 11 68
(Mick Channon) *wl in rr: rdn over 2f out: styd on fr over 1f out on outer: nvr nrr* **33/1**

4515 **6** *1/2* **African Blessing**[17] 6485 4-9-3 **68** ...................... JoshuaBryan(5) 8 68
(Charlie Wallis) *chsd ldr 1f: styd cl up on inner: nt qckn wl over 1f out: one pce after* **20/1**

6603 **7** *1/2* **Gold Club**[26] 6156 6-9-6 **66** ...................... (t[1]) PatCosgrave 12 64
(Tom Clover) *chsd ldrs: rdn and cl up 2f out: steadily wknd fnl f* **20/1**

0144 **8** *3/4* **Paradwys (IRE)**[17] 6485 3-9-6 **70** ...................... (p) EdwardGreatrex 7 64
(Archie Watson) *in tch in midfield: rdn and no rspnse over 2f out: nvr on terms after* **8/1**

331 **9** *3 1/4* **Chatoyer (FR)**[16] 6502 3-9-3 **70** ...................... (h) HollieDoyle(3) 13 55
(Richard Hannon) *plld hrd on outer and chsd ldrs after 2f: wknd 2f out* **7/1**[3]

0400 **10** *1/2* **Know The Truth**[35] 5797 3-8-8 **65** ...................... JasonWatson(7) 5 49
(Andrew Balding) *dwlt: a in rr: brief effrt on inner over 2f out: sn no prog* **20/1**

0561 **11** *2 1/2* **Iftitah (IRE)**[13] 6638 3-8-11 **68** ...................... (bt) RossaRyan(7) 4 45
(George Peckham) *hld up: hmpd on inner after 1f: effrt over 2f out: sn no prog and wknd over 1f out* **5/1**[2]

0666 **12** *1* **Swanton Blue (IRE)**[13] 6615 4-9-9 **69** ...................... LiamKeniry 14 46
(Ed de Giles) *led to over 2f out: wknd* **50/1**

1-00 **13** *1 1/4* **Mississippi Miss**[29] 6026 3-9-3 **70** ...................... GeorgeWood(3) 3 41
(Dr Jon Scargill) *trapped out wd in midfield: pushed along 1/2-way: wdst of all in st and wknd* **9/1**

1m 25.32s (-0.68) **Going Correction** 0.0s/f (Stan)
**WFA** 3 from 4yo+ 4lb **13** Ran SP% **118.2**
Speed ratings (Par 103): **103,102,101,100,99 98,98,97,93,92 90,88,87**
CSF £88.24 CT £475.16 TOTE £12.90: £3.80, £3.00, £1.60; EX 146.20 Trifecta £1411.20.

**Owner** John Guest Racing **Bred** Ringfort Stud **Trained** Newmarket, Suffolk

**FOCUS**

They went quite steady early, but things picked up on the bend and it was the more patiently ridden runners who came to the fore.

## 7059 32RED.COM BREEDERS BACKING RACING EBF MAIDEN FILLIES' STKS 1m 3f 219y(P)

7:15 (7:16) (Class 5) 3-4-Y-O £4,204 (£1,251; £625; £312) Stalls Low

Form RPR

44 **1** **Romina**[37] 5721 3-9-0 0.....(h[1]) ShaneKelly 2 80
(Richard Hughes) *mde all: stl gng easily over 2f out: sent for home sn after: styd on and nvr gng to be ct fnl f* **11/4**[2]

4 **2** 1 1/4 **Symbol**[138] 2131 3-9-0 0..... DanielMuscutt 5 78
(James Fanshawe) *hld up disputing 4th: shkn up over 2f out and prog to take 2nd wl over 1f out: styd on but wnr nt stopping and nvr able to chal* **30/100**[1]

00 **3** 14 **Sonnet Rose (IRE)**[47] 5364 3-9-0 0..... SaleemGolam 1 56
(Conrad Allen) *chsd wnr to wl over 1f out: wknd qckly* **66/1**

0 **4** 7 **The Lady Rules**[41] 5577 3-9-0 0..... AdamBeschizza 6 44
(Mrs Ilka Gansera-Leveque) *restless in stalls: hld up disputing 4th: wknd qckly 2f out* **20/1**[3]

604 **5** 3 1/2 **Dartmoor Girl (IRE)**[35] 5796 3-9-0 47.....(b) RobHornby 3 39
(Mark Gillard) *disp 2nd pl to over 2f out: wknd qckly* **250/1**

**6** 5 **Kwikstep** 3-8-11 0..... EoinWalsh(3) 4 31
(Andi Brown) *s.v.s: ct up and in tch in last to 3f out: sn wknd* **25/1**

2m 34.89s (0.39) **Going Correction** 0.0s/f (Stan) **6 Ran SP% 114.1**
Speed ratings (Par 100): **98,97,87,83,80 77**
CSF £4.08 TOTE £5.80: £1.40, £1.02; EX 6.20 Trifecta £22.90.

**Owner** Normandie Stud Ltd **Bred** Normandie Stud Ltd **Trained** Upper Lambourn, Berks

**FOCUS**

A bit of a turn-up, at least judged by the market. The first two have been rated close to form.

## 7060 32RED H'CAP 1m 7f 218y(P)

7:45 (7:45) (Class 4) (0-80,78) 3-Y-O £4,690 (£1,395; £697; £348) Stalls Low

Form RPR

2461 **1** **Munstead Star**[21] 6320 3-9-5 76..... RobHornby 1 82+
(Andrew Balding) *hld up disputing 4th: shkn up and effrt over 2f out: chsd ldr over 1f out: drvn to ld last 150yds: styd on wl* **4/1**[3]

0422 **2** 1 1/4 **Master Archer (IRE)**[29] 6038 3-9-4 78.....(p) GeorgeWood(3) 7 82
(James Fanshawe) *trckd ldr: led jst over 2f out gng strly: rdn over 1f out: hdd last 150yds and no ex* **5/2**[1]

3213 **3** nk **Sussex Ranger (USA)**[19] 6376 3-9-2 76.....(p) HectorCrouch(3) 2 79+
(Gary Moore) *hld up disputing 6th: rdn and swtchd to inner 2f out: kpt on fr over 1f out: clsd on runner-up nr fin* **3/1**[2]

146 **4** 3/4 **Sure To Explore (IRE)**[30] 6013 3-9-4 75..... MartinDwyer 4 77
(William Muir) *chsd ldrs disputing 4th: tended to run in snatches fr 1/2-way: rdn over 2f out: kpt on same pce and nvr able to chal* **33/1**

6136 **5** 1 **Veiled Secret (IRE)**[19] 6376 3-9-4 75..... RyanPowell 3 76
(Sir Mark Prescott Bt) *led: stretched on over 3f out: rdn and hdd jst over 2f out: fnd nil and fdd fnl f* **7/1**

6053 **6** 1/2 **Lethal Impact (JPN)**[14] 6580 3-9-5 76.....(b[1]) MartinHarley 6 76
(David Simcock) *hld up disputing 6th: effrt on outer and wl in tch over 2f out: nt qckn over 1f out: fdd* **5/1**

5536 **7** 9 **Gee Sixty Six**[29] 6023 3-8-7 64..... JoeyHaynes 5 53
(Mark H Tompkins) *stdd s: plld hrd early: hld up in last: rdn once pce increased over 3f out: sn btn* **33/1**

2601 **8** 1 3/4 **Plage Depampelonne**[18] 6436 3-8-12 69.....(p) TedDurcan 8 56
(James Bethell) *trckd ldr to over 2f out: sn lost pl and btn: eased fnl f* **25/1**

3m 30.5s (0.40) **Going Correction** 0.0s/f (Stan) **8 Ran SP% 112.5**
Speed ratings (Par 103): **99,98,98,97,97 97,92,91**
CSF £13.87 CT £32.56 TOTE £5.60: £2.20, £1.10, £1.10; EX 16.20 Trifecta £33.70.

**Owner** Lady Gillian Brunton **Bred** Sir Gordon Brunton **Trained** Kingsclere, Hants

**FOCUS**

A fair staying contest.

## 7061 RACING POST READER'S AWARD; VOTE KEMPTON H'CAP (DIV I) 1m (P)

8:15 (8:17) (Class 6) (0-65,65) 3-Y-O+ £2,264 (£673; £336; £168) Stalls Low

Form RPR

0361 **1** **Chetan**[7] 6813 5-9-0 60 6ex.....(t) JoshuaBryan(5) 11 67
(Charlie Wallis) *sn trckd ldr: led 2f out: drvn clr fnl f: readily* **5/1**[1]

45-5 **2** 1 1/4 **Caledonia Duchess**[35] 5794 4-9-10 65..... TomMarquand 13 69
(Jo Hughes) *trckd ldrs on outer: rdn 2f out: chsd wnr fnl f: kpt on but nvr able to threaten* **12/1**

3630 **3** 3/4 **Doria Road (USA)**[39] 5666 3-9-2 62..... MartinHarley 2 63
(Kevin Ryan) *wl in tch: rdn and no prog over 2f out: styd on fr over 1f out to snatch 3rd last strides* **6/1**[2]

4166 **4** hd **Orithia (USA)**[62] 4804 3-9-4 64.....(b[1]) ShaneKelly 9 65
(Seamus Durack) *hld up in rr: prog on inner over 2f out: hdwy stalled over 1f out: styd on again fnl f: nrly snatched 3rd* **8/1**

0045 **5** 1/2 **D'Waterside**[32] 5935 3-8-12 58..... JosephineGordon 10 58
(David Loughnane) *won battle for ld: drvn 3f out: hdd 2f out: lost 2nd fnl f and fdd nr fin* **25/1**

-220 **6** shd **Captain Pugwash (IRE)**[19] 6387 3-9-5 65..... LiamKeniry 12 65
(Henry Spiller) *hld up in rr: rdn and nt qckn over 2f out: styd on fr over 1f out: nrst fin* **8/1**

4000 **7** shd **Zoffany Bay (IRE)**[82] 4050 3-9-5 65.....(b[1]) HarryBentley 7 64
(George Peckham) *hld up wl in rr: rdn over 2f out: no prog tl kpt on fr over 1f out: nrst fin but no ch* **11/1**

5216 **8** hd **Mordoree (IRE)**[35] 5783 3-8-11 60.....(p) HectorCrouch(3) 3 59
(Clive Cox) *hld up towards rr: prog on inner over 2f out: drvn to dispute 3rd ins fnl f: fdd nr fin* **9/1**

550 **9** 1 1/4 **St James's Park (IRE)**[50] 5243 4-9-8 63.....(b[1]) AntonioFresu 4 60
(Luke McJannet) *in tch: dropped to rr and rdn over 2f out: struggling after: styd on u.str.p last 150yds* **16/1**

0053 **10** 2 **Thecornishbarron (IRE)**[22] 6294 5-9-9 64..... StevieDonohoe 5 56
(John Ryan) *wl in tch: rdn and nt qckn over 2f out: steadily lost pl fnl f* **11/1**

0500 **11** 7 **Rightway (IRE)**[63] 4747 6-9-5 60..... RobertWinston 1 36
(Tony Carroll) *chsd ldng pair: rdn and wknd 2f out* **16/1**

2-04 **12** 1 **Shadow Beauty**[14] 6587 3-9-3 63.....(p[1]) DanielMuscutt 6 36
(Marco Botti) *chsd ldrs to over 2f out: sn wknd* **7/1**[3]

0-00 **13** 1 1/2 **Poyle Emily**[12] 6656 4-9-2 57.....(v[1]) FranBerry 8 28
(Michael Madgwick) *a in rr: fnd nil whn rdn over 2f out* **66/1**

1m 39.51s (-0.29) **Going Correction** 0.0s/f (Stan)
**WFA** 3 from 4yo+ 5lb **13 Ran SP% 117.1**
Speed ratings (Par 101): **101,99,99,98,98 98,98,97,96,94 87,86,85**
CSF £63.83 CT £381.84 TOTE £5.00: £1.90, £4.00, £2.40; EX 51.70 Trifecta £649.10.

**Owner** Roger & Val Miles, Tony Stamp **Bred** Andrew W Robson **Trained** Ardleigh, Essex

**FOCUS**

The early pace wasn't that quick and the first two raced in the first three virtually throughout.

## 7062 RACING POST READER'S AWARD; VOTE KEMPTON H'CAP (DIV II) 1m (P)

8:45 (8:46) (Class 6) (0-65,65) 3-Y-O+ £2,264 (£673; £336; £168) Stalls Low

Form RPR

4462 **1** **Solent Meads (IRE)**[4] 6946 3-9-5 65.....(b) GeorgeDowning 14 72
(Daniel Kubler) *spd fr wd draw and led after 1f: committed for home over 2f out and at least 2 l ahd: drvn over 1f out: clung on wl* **8/1**

0500 **2** 1/2 **Balgair**[51] 5218 3-9-5 65..... PatCosgrave 6 71+
(Tom Clover) *hld up wl in rr: prog wl over 1f out: r.o to take 2nd last 100yds: clsd on wnr fin: too late* **11/2**[2]

360 **3** 1 1/4 **True Colors**[24] 6236 3-9-1 64..... AdamMcNamara(3) 2 67
(Richard Fahey) *in tch: prog 2f out: chsd wnr 1f out: no imp and lost 2nd last 100yds* **14/1**

5605 **4** 1 1/4 **Hot Mustard**[21] 6310 7-9-1 56.....(h) MartinDwyer 1 57
(William Muir) *wl in tch: effrt on inner 2f out: kpt on one pce and nvr able to threaten* **20/1**

4012 **5** nk **Slow To Hand**[19] 6387 3-9-3 63.....(b) JosephineGordon 11 62
(William Jarvis) *chsd ldrs: rdn and nt qckn over 2f out: one pce and no imp after* **9/4**[1]

2223 **6** hd **Coverham (IRE)**[82] 4050 3-8-12 65..... RossaRyan(7) 12 64
(James Eustace) *chsd ldrs: nt qckn 2f out: kpt on same pce after* **7/1**

5056 **7** 1/2 **Candesta (USA)**[26] 6143 7-9-7 62..... FranBerry 4 61
(Julia Feilden) *led 1f: styd prom: chsd wnr 2f out to 1f out: wknd last 100yds* **16/1**

4-50 **8** 1/2 **Brasted (IRE)**[111] 2996 5-9-5 65.....(t) PaddyBradley(5) 10 63
(Lee Carter) *hld up in rr: pushed along and appeared to be hanging fr over 2f out: no prog tl kpt on fnl f: nvr in it* **50/1**

0010 **9** 1/2 **Red Dragon (IRE)**[27] 6102 7-8-12 53..... RobHornby 3 50
(Michael Blanshard) *hld up wl in rr: effrt on inner 2f out: one pce and nvr a threat* **20/1**

4064 **10** 1 **Widnes**[13] 6620 3-9-0 65.....(b) JoshuaBryan(5) 5 58
(Alan Bailey) *hld up but sn in midfield: rdn and no prog over 2f out* **6/1**[3]

0343 **11** nk **McDelta**[19] 6393 7-8-13 54.....(p) TimmyMurphy 8 48
(Geoffrey Deacon) *chsd wnr after 2f to 2f out: wknd* **20/1**

6260 **12** 5 **Auric Goldfinger (IRE)**[11] 6681 3-8-10 63.....(b) TinaSmith(7) 13 44
(Richard Hannon) *dwlt: racd wd in rr: shkn up and no rspnse over 2f out* **50/1**

3-60 **13** 4 1/2 **St Patrick's Day (IRE)**[246] 164 5-9-8 63.....(v) DougieCostello 7 35
(J R Jenkins) *hld up: a in last pair: wknd over 2f out* **33/1**

1m 39.2s (-0.60) **Going Correction** 0.0s/f (Stan)
**WFA** 3 from 5yo+ 5lb **13 Ran SP% 117.7**
Speed ratings (Par 101): **103,102,101,100,99 99,99,98,98,97 96,91,87**
CSF £46.31 CT £629.11 TOTE £7.20: £2.30, £2.30, £4.20; EX 53.80 Trifecta £1295.40.

**Owner** Peter Britton & Partner **Bred** Thomas McHugh **Trained** Lambourn, Berks

**FOCUS**

This was fairly steadily run and the winner dictated things in front. It was the quicker of the two divisions by 0.31sec.

## 7063 32RED ON THE APP STORE H'CAP 1m 3f 219y(P)

9:15 (9:15) (Class 5) (0-75,77) 3-Y-O £2,911 (£866; £432; £216) Stalls Low

Form RPR

0-21 **1** **Just In Time**[18] 6423 3-8-12 65..... MartinDwyer 9 76+
(Alan King) *hld up in 7th: shkn up on wd outside over 2f out: picked up really wl over 1f out and swept into the ld last 150yds: sn clr* **13/8**[1]

0554 **2** 1 1/2 **Sputnik Planum (USA)**[22] 6291 3-9-2 69.....(t) TedDurcan 10 76
(David Lanigan) *dwlt but sn pushed up to press ldng pair: chsd ldr 3f out and carried sltly lft 2f out: pressed new ldr 1f out: sn outpcd by wnr: styd on* **9/1**

0013 **3** 1 **Free Forum (IRE)**[33] 5867 3-9-0 67..... HarryBentley 8 72
(David Simcock) *trckd ldrs: rdn to cl and led over 1f out: hdd and outpcd last 150yds: lost 2nd nr fin* **11/2**[2]

605 **4** 1 1/2 **Hajaam (IRE)**[23] 6277 3-8-10 63..... StevieDonohoe 3 66
(Charlie Fellowes) *trckd ldrs in 6th: effrt towards inner 2f out: outpcd fnl f* **16/1**

6132 **5** 1/2 **Dangerous Ends**[22] 6288 3-9-3 70.....(p) JackMitchell 5 72
(Brett Johnson) *hld up in last trio: prog on inner 2f out: outpcd by ldrs fr jst over 1f out* **7/1**[3]

2251 **6** 1 1/4 **American History (USA)**[22] 6281 3-9-3 73.....(p) HectorCrouch(3) 13 73
(William Muir) *sn led: hung lft u.p over 2f out: hdd over 1f out: wknd* **14/1**

4232 **7** 1/2 **Lester Kris (IRE)**[9] 6763 3-9-7 74.....(p[1]) PatDobbs 1 73
(Richard Hannon) *mostly chsd ldr to 3f out: fdd fr 2f out* **8/1**

1510 **8** nk **Star Maker**[18] 6423 3-9-5 77..... MitchGodwin(5) 11 76
(Sylvester Kirk) *plld hrd: hld up: effrt 3f out: no real prog after* **10/1**

0400 **9** 1 **See The City (IRE)**[12] 6657 3-9-4 71.....(b[1]) RyanTate 6 68
(James Eustace) *chsd ldrs tl fdd fr 2f out* **50/1**

4-50 **10** 4 **Tuscany (IRE)**[45] 5458 3-9-3 70.....(b[1]) RaulDaSilva 7 61
(Paul Cole) *s.s: hld up in last pair: rdn and no prog over 2f out: sn btn* **40/1**

2556 **11** 22 **Our Boy (IRE)**[14] 6579 3-9-5 72..... FranBerry 4 28+
(David Evans) *t.k.h: hld up in last pair: wknd 3f out: eased and t.o* **20/1**

2m 34.9s (0.40) **Going Correction** 0.0s/f (Stan) **11 Ran SP% 117.9**
Speed ratings (Par 101): **98,97,96,95,95 94,93,93,92,90 75**
CSF £16.80 CT £68.36 TOTE £2.40: £1.10, £3.00, £2.00; EX 17.60 Trifecta £105.00.

**Owner** HP Racing Just In Time **Bred** Overbury Stallions Ltd And D Boocock **Trained** Barbury Castle, Wilts

**FOCUS**

Just a modest handicap but the winner looks progressive and is one to keep on side.

T/Plt: £13.00 to a £1 stake. Pool: £74,772.08. 4,185.29 winning units. T/Qpdt: £6.30 to a £1 stake. Pool: £6,988.53. 813.35 winning units. **Jonathan Neesom**

7064 - 7065a (Foreign Racing) - See Raceform Interactive

## 7037 LISTOWEL (L-H)

Wednesday, September 13

**OFFICIAL GOING: Heavy**

### 7066a EDMUND & JOSIE WHELAN MEMORIAL LISTOWEL STKS (LISTED RACE) 1m 1f

**3:05** (3:07) 3-Y-O+

**£25,213** (£8,119; £3,846; £1,709; £854; £427)

RPR

1 **Riven Light (IRE)**[13] 6645 5-9-9 105 KevinManning 4 103+
(W P Mullins, Ire) *hld up: tk clsr order over 2f out: travelled wl to ld appr fnl f and sn pushed clr: advantage reduced cl home* **11/8**[1]

2 ¾ **Zawraq (IRE)**[325] 7558 5-9-9 105 PatSmullen 2 101+
(D K Weld, Ire) *settled off ldrs: clsr in 4th at 1/2-way: pushed along and nt qckn under 2f out: wnt 3rd appr fnl f: kpt on wl under hands and heels into 2nd clsng stages: nt rch wnr* **11/2**[2]

3 2 **Dew Line (IRE)**[9] 6772 5-9-4 85 GaryCarroll 1 92
(Michael Mulvany, Ire) *sn led: hdd appr fnl f: sn no match for wnr: kpt on same pce and dropped to 3rd clsng stages* **33/1**

4 6 **Canary Row (IRE)**[21] 6334 7-9-12 97 (v) RonanWhelan 10 87
(P J Prendergast, Ire) *chsd ldrs in 3rd: pushed along over 2f out: nt qckn over 1f out in 4th: sn one pce* **7/1**[3]

5 1 ¼ **Dream Walker (FR)**[17] 6491 8-9-9 95 (t) ChrisHayes 9 82
(Brian Ellison) *racd towards rr: tk clsr order under 3f out on outer: no imp in 5th ent fnl f: kpt on one pce* **7/1**[3]

6 1 ¾ **Savannah Storm**[40] 5625 4-9-9 100 ColinKeane 8 78
(G M Lyons, Ire) *hld up: pushed along and no imp under 2f out: kpt on one pce under hands and heels fnl f* **12/1**

7 shd **Bengala (FR)**[60] 4928 3-8-12 94 (h) DeclanMcDonogh 5 73
(John M Oxx, Ire) *chsd ldrs in 4th whn checked ins 1st f: 5th at 1/2-way: rdn and nt qckn under 2f out: no ex appr fnl f* **11/2**[2]

8 4 ½ **Jeremys Joy (IRE)**[21] 6336 5-9-4 88 (h) RobbieDowney 6 63
(Keith Henry Clarke, Ire) *slowly away and detached early: in rr for most: modest late hdwy wout ever threatening* **25/1**

9 32 **Aussie Valentine (IRE)**[13] 6645 6-9-9 89 (tp) ColmO'Donoghue 7 1
(P D Deegan, Ire) *trckd ldr in 2nd: pushed along under 3f out: nt qckn and wknd 2f out: eased fnl f: struck into* **16/1**

2m 5.65s
**WFA** 3 from 4yo+ 6lb **9** Ran SP% **118.2**
CSF £9.45 TOTE £2.30: £1.30, £1.60, £5.60; DF 6.70 Trifecta £262.90.
**Owner** Mrs S Ricci **Bred** Stilvi Compania Financiera Sa **Trained** Muine Beag, Co Carlow

**FOCUS**
The front-running 3rd limits the level, but this fits with the winner to his latest and the runner-up in line with last year's sole start.

7067 - 7068a (Foreign Racing) - See Raceform Interactive

## 6912 SAINT-CLOUD (L-H)

Wednesday, September 13

**OFFICIAL GOING: Turf: very soft**

### 7069a PRIX DU SQUARE DES BATIGNOLLES (H'CAP) (4YO) (TURF) 1m 4f 110y

**5:40** 4-Y-O **£8,119** (£3,247; £2,435; £1,623; £811)

RPR

1 **Waldenon (FR)**[20] 6365 4-8-5 **0** AnnaelleDidon-Yahlali(10) 5 54
(S Jesus, France) **50/1**

2 shd **Calajani (FR)**[20] 6365 4-9-0 **0** MlleAlisonMassin(4) 11 57
(Andrew Hollinshead, France) **61/10**[3]

3 2 **Ernie (FR)**[306] 4-9-1 **0** (p) RonanThomas 4 51
(F Foresi, France) **83/10**

4 1 ¾ **Debt Of Honour (FR)**[20] 6365 4-9-6 **0** SebastienMaillot 8 53
(C Boutin, France) **97/10**

5 2 **Franko Folie (FR)**[20] 6365 4-9-6 **0** (p) Pierre-CharlesBoudot 7 50
(Gay Kelleway) *settled in 2nd: pushed up to chal over 2f out: drvn over 1f out: unable qck and styd on same pce fnl f* **3/1**[1]

6 1 ¼ **Ernestine (FR)**[20] 6365 4-9-4 **0** JeromeMoutard 3 46
(J-M Lefebvre, France) **10/1**

7 ¾ **Conte Fleurette (FR)**[47] 4-8-11 **0** ClaraCornet(8) 1 46
(Mlle V Mercader, France) **114/10**

8 6 **Gaea (FR)**[20] 6365 4-9-3 **0** (b) AntoineCoutier 12 34
(S Jesus, France) **8/1**

9 1 ¾ **Bella Noche (FR)**[117] 4-9-4 **0** (p) EddyHardouin 6 32
(P Monfort, France) **193/10**

10 5 **Kytalpha's Sun (FR)**[105] 4-9-6 **0** FabienLefebvre 2 26
(Mme A-C Trouve, France) **102/10**

11 15 **Nargis Queen (FR)** 4-9-6 **0** (p) CyrilleStefan 9
(P Baudry, France) **58/10**[2]

2m 58.94s **11** Ran SP% **118.0**
PARI-MUTUEL (all including 1 euro stake): WIN 51.50; PLACE 9.10, 2.90, 3.10; DF 125.60; SF 400.00.
**Owner** Michael Boudraa **Bred** Earl De La Belle Aumone **Trained** France

### 7070a PRIX DE FAUSSES REPOSES (CLAIMER) (4YO+) (TURF) 1m 4f

**6:10** 4-Y-O+ **£8,119** (£3,247; £2,435; £1,623; £811)

RPR

1 **Master Dan**[76] 6-9-1 0 (p) NicolasEven 7 73
(S Dehez, France) **239/10**

2 shd **Fair Trade (GER)**[500] 6-9-4 0 ThomasHuet 1 76
(Henk Grewe, Germany) **42/10**[2]

3 1 ¾ **Rodyana (FR)**[32] 4-8-11 0 (b) FabienLefebvre 6 66
(P Monfort, France) **26/1**

4 1 ¼ **Olivia Pope (FR)**[121] 4-9-2 0 FrankPanicucci 3 69
(E Lellouche, France) **71/10**

5 ¾ **Montesquieu (FR)**[186] 7-9-8 0 (p) AdrienMoreau 5 74
(M Boutin, France) **29/10**[1]

6 1 ½ **Chill Wind (FR)**[18] 6-9-0 0 PaulineProd'homme(4) 2 63
(D & P Prod'Homme, France) **57/10**

7 4 **Trigger Flash (FR)**[113] 6-8-11 0 MlleAlisonMassin(5) 11 55
(F Cheyer, France) **231/10**

8 12 **Mumgala (FR)**[34] 7-9-2 0 (b) ThierryThulliez 4 40
(F Vermeulen, France) **23/5**[3]

9 1 ¾ **Alcatraz (IRE)**[16] 6543 5-8-10 0 (p) HayleyTurner(5) 9 32
(George Baker) *dwlt: sn rcvrd to take clsr order: jnd ldr after 1f: remained cl up: pushed along over 2f out: little rspnse and eased ins fnl f* **103/10**

10 12 **Wind Law (FR)**[550] 10-8-11 0 ErwannLebreton 8 13
(J Schiestel Fils, France) **51/1**

11 7 **Mister Smart (FR)**[14] 7-8-13 0 ow2 (p) KyllanBarbaud 10 4
(N Caulliery, France) **175/10**

2m 47.91s (7.51) **11** Ran SP% **118.0**
PARI-MUTUEL (all including 1 euro stake): WIN 24.90; PLACE 7.40, 2.90, 9.00; DF 52.00; SF 138.50.
**Owner** Jean-Louis Dehez **Bred** Ed's Stud Ltd **Trained** France

7071 - 7078a (Foreign Racing) - See Raceform Interactive

## 6806 CHEPSTOW (L-H)

Thursday, September 14

**OFFICIAL GOING: Soft (good to soft in places; 6.2)**

Wind: variable breeze, partly behind them in the home straight Weather: sunny

### 7079 ST LEGER BETTING AT 188BET EBF NOVICE STKS 7f 16y

**1:10** (1:11) (Class 5) 2-Y-O **£3,234** (£962; £481; £240) **Stalls** Centre

Form RPR

1 **Statuario** 2-9-2 0 TomQueally 3 75+
(Eve Johnson Houghton) *midfield: impr 1/2-way: pushed along 2f out: led 150yds out: comf* **6/1**[3]

0 2 2 ½ **Beyond Equal**[20] 6394 2-9-2 0 MartinDwyer 7 69
(Stuart Kittow) *racd keenly: disp ld: rdn over 1f out: edgd rt and hdd 150yds out: unable qck* **33/1**

6223 3 nk **Polly's Gold (IRE)**[19] 6417 2-8-11 70 ShaneKelly 2 63
(Richard Hughes) *disp ld: rdn over 1f out: hdd 150yds out: no ex* **5/4**[1]

00 4 1 ¼ **Smugglers Top**[43] 5537 2-9-2 0 RichardKingscote 6 65+
(Tom Dascombe) *chsd ldrs: rdn 3f out: kpt on same pce fnl 2f* **16/1**

0 5 ½ **Mister Maestro**[62] 4826 2-9-2 0 TomMarquand 9 64
(Richard Hannon) *midfield: rdn 1/2-way: styd on u.p fnl 2f* **7/1**

6 1 ¼ **Grey Spirit (IRE)** 2-9-2 0 RyanPowell 4 61
(Sir Mark Prescott Bt) *s.s: rdn whn carried lft after 3f: styd on steadily fnl 2f: improve* **14/1**

7 6 **Glamorous Dream (IRE)** 2-8-11 0 RaulDaSilva 1 41
(Ronald Harris) *s.s: t.k.h in rr: hdwy 1/2-way: drvn over 2f out: wknd over 1f out* **22/1**

8 4 **Gunnar Julius (USA)** 2-9-2 0 PatCosgrave 10 36
(Ed Walker) *towards rr: swvd lft after 3f: rdn and sme hdwy 1/2-way: wknd appr fnl f* **5/1**[2]

0 9 nk **Blackwood**[38] 5709 2-9-2 0 RobHornby 12 35
(Michael Blanshard) *in tch: drvn 1/2-way: wknd 2f out* **50/1**

00 10 shd **Miss Condi**[8] 6806 2-8-11 0 JoeyHaynes 11 30
(Martin Keighley) *chsd ldrs: rdn 3f out: wknd 2f out* **100/1**

11 3 ¼ **Miniature Daffodil (IRE)** 2-9-2 0 TimmyMurphy 5 26
(Christian Williams) *prom 3f: sn wknd* **20/1**

12 11 **Boko Fittleworth (IRE)** 2-9-2 0 FranBerry 8
(Jonjo O'Neill) *v.s.a: rn green and a bhd* **16/1**

1m 25.51s (2.31) **Going Correction** +0.20s/f (Good) **12** Ran SP% **121.3**
Speed ratings (Par 95): **94,91,90,89,88 87,80,75,75,75 71,59**
CSF £199.91 TOTE £6.40: £2.00, £6.70, £1.10; EX 185.80 Trifecta £774.70.
**Owner** Michael G Cohen And David Cohen **Bred** David Cohen **Trained** Blewbury, Oxon

**FOCUS**
A modest novice but a promising debut from the winner.

### 7080 DAILY RACING SPECIALS AT 188BET MAIDEN STKS 7f 16y

**1:40** (1:41) (Class 5) 3-Y-O+ **£3,234** (£962; £481; £240) **Stalls** Centre

Form RPR

6 1 **Ashwass (USA)**[36] 5794 3-9-5 0 JackMitchell 9 91+
(Roger Varian) *led 2f: styd cl up: led again 1/2-way: pushed clr over 1f out: r.o strly: eased towards fin* **5/4**[1]

3 2 8 **Holiday Girl (IRE)**[14] 6614 3-9-0 82 TomQueally 1 65
(Eve Johnson Houghton) *trckd ldrs: rdn and wnt 2nd over 2f out: outpcd by wnr over 1f out: no ch after but in n.d of losing 2nd* **6/4**[2]

06 3 4 **Dance Rock**[9] 6775 4-9-9 0 (v[1]) TrevorWhelan 8 62
(Neil Mulholland) *towards rr: hdwy 3f out: rdn 2f out: sn wnt 3rd: styd on but no imp on ldng pair* **16/1**

00 4 2 **Sky Marshal (IRE)**[8] 6817 3-9-5 0 RichardKingscote 3 54
(Ed Walker) *midfield: rdn and clsd over 2f out: one pce and no ch w ldrs fr over 1f out* **20/1**

04 5 2 **Thechampagnesonice**[8] 6808 4-9-4 0 SteveDrowne 7 46
(Malcolm Saunders) *chsd ldrs: rdn over 2f out: sn one pce and hld* **25/1**

06 6 nk **Bleu Et Noir**[27] 6150 6-9-9 0 (h) KieranO'Neill 2 50
(Tim Vaughan) *t.k.h: hld up: detached in last after 2f: shkn up 2f out: styd on steadily* **16/1**

7 1 ¼ **Dilinger** 3-9-5 0 MartinDwyer 11 45
(Stuart Kittow) *t.k.h: prom: led after 2f tl 1/2-way: rdn and lost 2nd over 2f out: wkng whn hung lft over 1f out* **12/1**[3]

05 8 2 **Jumbo's Boy**[8] 6808 3-9-0 0 JoshuaBryan(5) 10 40
(Peter Bowen) *midfield tl rdn and dropped to rr 1/2-way: no ch whn hung rt ins fnl f* **66/1**

00-0 9 hd **Giveitsomeginger**[47] 5409 3-9-0 43 ShaneKelly 5 34
(Jo Hughes) *hld up towards rr: rdn and sme hdwy over 2f out: wknd over 1f out* **66/1**

10 8 **Lead A Dance (IRE)** 3-8-11 0 TimClark(3) 12 14
(John Butler) *s.i.s: clsd to chse ldrs after 2f: drvn over 2f out: sn wknd* **20/1**

1m 24.89s (1.69) **Going Correction** +0.20s/f (Good)
**WFA** 3 from 4yo+ 4lb **10** Ran SP% **120.3**
Speed ratings (Par 103): **98,88,84,82,79 79,77,75,75,66**
CSF £3.19 TOTE £2.80: £1.10, £1.02, £4.70; EX 3.50 Trifecta £18.90.
**Owner** Sheikh Ahmed Al Maktoum **Bred** Darley **Trained** Newmarket, Suffolk

**FOCUS**
A pretty weak maiden, no depth, but still impressive from the winner.

## 7081 188BET NURSERY H'CAP 5f 16y
2:15 (2:16) (Class 6) (0-60,66) 2-Y-O £2,587 (£770; £384; £192) Stalls Centre

Form RPR
460 1 **Owen The Law**[14] 6634 2-8-12 **51**....................(v[1]) FranBerry 10 55
(David Evans) *mde all: got over to stands' rail over 3f out: drvn over 1f out: hld on wl* **20/1**
4261 2 *nk* **Global Exceed**[8] 6825 2-9-13 **66** 6ex....................(b) FrannyNorton 5 69
(Ed Dunlop) *hld up: pushed along and hdwy 2f out: edgd rt and r.o fnl f: jst hld* **9/4**[1]
500 3 *1 ¼* **Cove Beach**[58] 4991 2-9-3 **61**.................... MitchGodwin[(5)] 2 59
(Paul Cole) *prom: rdn and ev ch over 1f out: hung rt ins fnl f: unable qck* **20/1**
005 4 *hd* **Madame Jo Jo**[22] 6304 2-9-2 **60**.................... JaneElliott[(5)] 1 58
(Sarah Hollinshead) *towards rr: rdn and clsd over 2f out: styd on same pce fnl f* **20/1**
4010 5 *½* **Just For The Craic (IRE)**[14] 6609 2-9-9 **62**.............. TrevorWhelan 14 58
(Neil Mulholland) *chsd ldrs: drvn 2f out: kpt on same pce* **20/1**
0405 6 *¾* **Red For Danger**[14] 6609 2-8-10 **49**....................(h) TomQueally 12 42
(Eve Johnson Houghton) *wnt to post early: chsd ldrs: drvn 2f out and lost pl: r.o again fnl f* **8/1**[3]
0040 7 *½* **Rio Santos**[15] 6585 2-8-10 **49**.................... JimmyQuinn 13 40
(Rod Millman) *missed break sltly: towards rr: rdn 2f out: drvn and r.o ins fnl f* **16/1**
0405 8 *½* **Lady Lintera (IRE)**[17] 6517 2-9-0 **53**....................(h) JoeyHaynes 15 43
(Ann Duffield) *wnt to post early: towards rr: rdn after 2f: hdwy over 1f out: no imp ins fnl f* **25/1**
5303 9 *¾* **Hope And Glory (IRE)**[14] 6634 2-9-1 **54**..........(p) RichardKingscote 4 41
(Tom Dascombe) *prom: rdn over 2f out: wknd fnl f* **7/2**[2]
024 10 *1 ½* **Zapateado**[31] 6012 2-9-7 **60**.................... ShaneKelly 7 42
(Richard Hughes) *midfield: shkn up over 1f out: kpt on steadily fnl f: nvr cl enough to chal* **12/1**
0604 11 *½* **Cent Flying**[14] 6609 2-9-2 **55**.................... MartinDwyer 9 35
(William Muir) *chsd ldrs: drvn 2f out: wknd appr fnl f* **8/1**[3]
506 12 *1* **Hollie's Dream**[15] 6583 2-9-2 **55**.................... SamHitchcott 3 31
(David Evans) *towards rr: rdn after 2f: btn over 1f out* **33/1**
0620 13 *nse* **Cranworth Phoenix**[33] 5933 2-8-10 **49**.................... RaulDaSilva 11 25
(Brian Barr) *midfield: rdn 1/2-way: outpcd over 1f out* **33/1**
6000 14 *1* **Alaskan Star (IRE)**[14] 6609 2-9-7 **60**....................(p) SteveDrowne 6 32
(Amanda Perrett) *chsd ldrs: rdn 1/2-way: wknd over 1f out* **25/1**
4304 15 *3 ¼* **Roses In June (IRE)**[9] 6790 2-8-8 **47**....................(b[1]) KieranO'Neill 8 8
(J S Moore) *midfield: sn rdn along and nvr gng: drvn 1/2-way: wknd 2f out* **25/1**

1m 1.22s (1.92) **Going Correction** +0.20s/f (Good) **15 Ran SP% 125.3**
Speed ratings (Par 93): **92,91,89,89,88 87,86,85,84,82 81,79,79,77,72**
CSF £59.59 CT £991.36 TOTE £26.70: £6.40, £1.80, £6.30; EX 94.40 Trifecta £2568.60 Part won..
**Owner** Principality Racing Partnership **Bred** Usk Valley Stud **Trained** Pandy, Monmouths

**FOCUS**
Moderate nursery form.

## 7082 188BET.CO.UK NURSERY H'CAP 1m 14y
2:50 (2:52) (Class 6) (0-60,60) 2-Y-O £2,587 (£770; £384; £192) Stalls Centre

Form RPR
0020 1 **Milan Reef (IRE)**[14] 6613 2-9-0 **53**.................... PatCosgrave 9 60
(David Loughnane) *mde virtually all: rdn over 1f out: r.o: drvn out towards fin* **13/2**
0402 2 *1 ¾* **Dark Blue (IRE)**[14] 6613 2-9-4 **57**.................... RaulDaSilva 3 60
(Mick Channon) *hld up: rdn and nt clr run over 3f out: drvn and hdwy 2f out: kpt on fnl f: wnt 2nd nr fin* **5/1**[3]
0054 3 *nk* **Tony Soprano (IRE)**[37] 5756 2-9-7 **60**.................... DaneO'Neill 8 62
(Martyn Meade) *t.k.h: chsd ldrs: rdn over 2f out: drvn and kpt on same pce fnl f: lost 2nd nr fin* **5/2**[1]
000 4 *2 ¾* **Puramente**[22] 6304 2-9-7 **60**.................... ShaneKelly 10 56+
(Jo Hughes) *s.i.s: towards rr: rdn over 3f out: hdwy over 1f out: styd on ins fnl f* **12/1**
0540 5 *¾* **Istanbul Pasha (IRE)**[29] 6063 2-8-12 **51**.................... FranBerry 6 46
(David Evans) *midfield: rdn and hdwy to chse ldrs 3f out: drvn 2f out: one pce fnl f* **8/1**
5400 6 *3* **Blazing Beryl (IRE)**[8] 6815 2-9-7 **60**....................(b[1]) TomMarquand 7 48
(Brian Meehan) *t.k.h: prom: drvn 3f out: outpcd by ldrs over 1f out: wknd ins fnl f* **20/1**
000 7 *1 ½* **Galloping Hogan (IRE)**[40] 5641 2-9-1 **59**.............. MitchGodwin[(5)] 5 44
(Sylvester Kirk) *t.k.h: prom: drvn over 2f out: wknd over 1f out* **8/1**
056 8 *hd* **Amarone Red (IRE)**[19] 6410 2-9-0 **53**..........(p[1]) RichardKingscote 4 37
(Tom Dascombe) *hld up: rdn 1/2-way: lost tch 2f out* **14/1**
0214 9 *6* **Atalanta Queen**[33] 5933 2-9-2 **60**....................(v[1]) JaneElliott[(5)] 1 31
(Michael Appleby) *chsd ldrs on outer: drvn over 2f out: edgd rt and wknd over 1f out* **9/2**[2]
5000 10 *24* **Afterthisone**[8] 6815 2-8-6 **45**....................(h) RobHornby 2
(Robin Dickin) *s.i.s: sn w ldrs: drvn over 3f out: wknd qckly: t.o* **100/1**

1m 37.72s (1.52) **Going Correction** +0.20s/f (Good) **10 Ran SP% 119.1**
Speed ratings (Par 93): **100,98,97,95,94 91,89,89,83,59**
CSF £39.92 CT £106.83 TOTE £6.40: £1.80, £1.90, £1.30; EX 40.60 Trifecta £161.70.
**Owner** Martin Godfrey **Bred** Pat Beirne **Trained** Market Drayton, Shropshire

**FOCUS**
Lowly nursery form and, as in the previous race, the winner made all against the stands' rail.

## 7083 GET 1/4 ODDS AT 188BET H'CAP 1m 14y
3:25 (3:26) (Class 5) (0-75,77) 3-Y-O+ £3,234 (£962; £481; £240) Stalls Centre

Form RPR
1434 1 **Alemaratalyoum (IRE)**[32] 5961 3-9-5 **75**.................... FrannyNorton 9 83
(Ed Dunlop) *midfield: hdwy 3f out: rdn wl over 1f out: r.o u.p to ld fnl 100yds* **6/1**[2]
0406 2 *1 ¼* **House Of Commons (IRE)**[10] 6763 4-9-5 **70**.......... AlistairRawlinson 1 76
(Michael Appleby) *led: drvn 2f out: hdd and no ex fnl 100yds* **12/1**
6130 3 *hd* **Mouille Point**[57] 5033 3-9-7 **77**.................... TomMarquand 14 82
(Richard Hannon) *hld up: drvn over 2f out: hdwy over 1f out: r.o wl fnl f* **12/1**
4-50 4 *¾* **Mesophere**[166] 1499 3-8-11 **67**.................... ShaneKelly 10 70
(Harry Fry) *chsd ldrs: rdn over 2f out: in 2nd over 1f out tl ent fnl f: one pce* **14/1**
0431 5 *1 ¾* **Wahaab (IRE)**[8] 6807 6-9-4 **69** 6ex....................(t) TimmyMurphy 2 69
(Sophie Leech) *t.k.h: hld up: rdn and hdwy over 2f out: r.o fnl f but nvr able to rch ldrs* **12/1**
-040 6 *2 ¼* **Unison (IRE)**[12] 6701 7-9-10 **75**.................... RyanTate 12 70
(Jeremy Scott) *prom 2f: midfield after tl rdn and dropped towards rr 3f out: styd on again fnl f* **8/1**
00 7 *hd* **Nutini (IRE)**[8] 6807 4-8-12 **63**....................(p) SteveDrowne 5 57
(Malcolm Saunders) *trckd ldr: rdn over 2f out: lost 2nd over 1f out: sn wknd: girths slipped bk ins fnl f* **20/1**
-426 8 *nse* **Medicean Ballet (IRE)**[24] 6274 3-9-5 **75**.................... DaneO'Neill 7 68
(Henry Candy) *hld up: rdn over 3f out: no hdwy fnl 2f* **7/1**[3]
0203 9 *½* **Spirit Of Belle**[30] 6034 3-8-9 **72**.................... KatherineGlenister[(7)] 4 64
(David Evans) *chsd ldrs: rdn and unable qck over 3f out: wknd fnl f* **8/1**
0014 10 *5* **Native Soldier (IRE)**[26] 6195 3-9-2 **77**....................(p) MitchGodwin[(5)] 8 57
(John Flint) *chsd ldrs: drvn over 2f out: grad wknd* **5/1**[1]
2452 11 *7* **Right About Now (IRE)**[40] 5656 3-9-1 **71**..........(p[1]) RichardKingscote 6 35
(Ismail Mohammed) *midfield: rdn and lost pl over 3f out: wknd over 1f out* **10/1**
6314 12 *5* **Habbad (FR)**[9] 6792 3-9-1 **71**....................(p) TomQueally 3 24
(Richard Hannon) *chsd ldrs: rdn over 2f out: wknd over 1f out: eased ins fnl f* **8/1**
0313 13 *1 ¾* **Fit For The Job (IRE)**[21] 5559 5-9-11 **76**....................(p) FranBerry 13 26
(Jonjo O'Neill) *s.i.s: t.k.h in rr: rdn over 2f out: wknd over 1f out: eased ins fnl f* **16/1**

1m 36.72s (0.52) **Going Correction** +0.20s/f (Good)
**WFA** 3 from 4yo+ 5lb **13 Ran SP% 126.3**
Speed ratings (Par 103): **105,103,103,102,101 98,98,98,98,93 86,81,79**
CSF £80.88 CT £891.32 TOTE £7.40: £2.80, £5.20, £2.80; EX 112.20 Trifecta £2721.80 Part won..
**Owner** Mohammed Jaber **Bred** Ammerland Verwaltung Gmbh & Co Kg **Trained** Newmarket, Suffolk

**FOCUS**
An ordinary handicap and the main action again unfolded nearer the stands' side.

## 7084 READ SILVESTRE DE SOUSA AT 188BET H'CAP 6f 16y
3:55 (3:57) (Class 4) (0-85,86) 3-Y-O+ £5,175 (£1,540; £769; £384) Stalls Centre

Form RPR
0500 1 **Goring (GER)**[24] 6275 5-9-5 **83**....................(p[1]) TomQueally 2 89
(Eve Johnson Houghton) *mde virtually all: jnd over 2f out: drvn over 1f out: edgd rt ins fnl f: asserted cl home* **11/4**[1]
253 2 *nk* **Clear Spring (IRE)**[9] 6794 9-9-7 **85**.................... ShaneKelly 3 90
(John Spearing) *broke wl: sn hld up in 5th: rdn 2f out: drvn and r.o wl fnl f: wnt 2nd cl home* **9/2**[3]
303 3 *shd* **Letmestopyouthere (IRE)**[17] 6506 3-8-11 **82**.......... JoshuaBryan[(5)] 4 87
(David Evans) *trckd wnr: chal over 2f out: r.o u.p and ev ch: carried sltly rt ins fnl f: no ex and lost 2nd cl home* **5/1**
2161 4 *2 ¼* **The Daley Express (IRE)**[9] 6780 3-9-6 **86** 6ex.......... FrannyNorton 6 83
(Ronald Harris) *t.k.h: trckd ldrs: drvn and edgd lft appr fnl f: unable qck* **7/2**[2]
6505 5 *nk* **Glory Of Paris (IRE)**[29] 6073 3-8-7 **73**.................... JimmyQuinn 1 70
(Rod Millman) *hld up bhd ldrs: drvn over 1f out: wknd fnl f* **6/1**
640 6 *1* **Signore Piccolo**[26] 6185 6-9-6 **84**....................(h) FranBerry 5 77
(David Loughnane) *hld up and plld hrd: rdn over 2f out: wkng whn hung lft over 1f out* **6/1**

1m 12.2s (0.20) **Going Correction** +0.20s/f (Good)
**WFA** 3 from 5yo+ 2lb **6 Ran SP% 112.3**
Speed ratings (Par 105): **106,105,105,102,102 100**
CSF £15.31 TOTE £3.30: £1.70, £1.90; EX 17.50 Trifecta £64.00.
**Owner** G C Stevens **Bred** Westminster Race Horses Gmbh **Trained** Blewbury, Oxon

**FOCUS**
They raced down the centre in this decent sprint. Straightforward form; the winner was back to his last winning mark.

## 7085 PLAY ROULETTE AT 188BET H'CAP 1m 4f
4:30 (4:34) (Class 6) (0-65,66) 3-Y-O+ £2,587 (£770; £384; £192) Stalls Low

Form RPR
1023 1 **Incredible Dream (IRE)**[17] 6509 4-9-6 **62**..........(p) JackDuern[(3)] 11 69
(Dean Ivory) *s.i.s: hld up: hdwy 5f out: drvn 4f out: styd on wl to ld ent appr fnl f: sn in command* **9/1**[2]
60-0 2 *3 ¼* **Big Sigh (IRE)**[201] 935 3-9-4 **65**.................... RichardKingscote 2 68
(Ismail Mohammed) *trckd ldrs: wnt 2nd 3f out: drvn to ld over 2f out: hdd ent fnl f: one pce* **14/1**[3]
5364 3 *3 ¼* **Turnbury**[51] 5249 6-9-3 **56**....................(p) RyanTate 9 53
(Nikki Evans) *chsd ldrs: rdn 4f out: ev ch 2f out tl one pce appr fnl f* **33/1**
-221 4 *½* **Meyandi**[8] 6812 3-9-0 **66**.................... JoshuaBryan[(5)] 6 64
(Andrew Balding) *led tl drvn and hdd over 2f out: one pce* **2/5**[1]
0044 5 *16* **Iley Boy**[17] 6509 3-8-5 **52**.................... MartinDwyer 5 26
(John Gallagher) *trckd ldr: drvn: hung lft and lost 2nd over 3f out: wknd over 1f out* **20/1**
564 6 *19* **Monar Lad (IRE)**[30] 6031 5-9-5 **58**.................... TimmyMurphy 4 17
(Dai Burchell) *midfield: drvn over 3f out: wknd over 2f out: t.o* **16/1**
552/ 7 *2* **Pershing**[29] 3791 6-9-4 **57**....................(h) TrevorWhelan 7
(Kevin Frost) *hld up: drvn and wknd 4f out: t.o* **28/1**
000 8 *3 ¼* **Breeze Up**[24] 6277 3-7-13 **51** oh6....................(p[1]) JaneElliott[(5)] 8
(Ed de Giles) *t.k.h in midfield: wknd 5f out: t.o* **40/1**
0102 9 *nk* **Howardian Hills (IRE)**[9] 6796 4-9-6 **59**.................... ShaneKelly 13
(Victor Dartnall) *t.k.h: a in rr: rdn and lost tch over 4f out: t.o* **16/1**
3-62 10 *9* **Casaclare (IRE)**[17] 6509 3-9-1 **62**....................(t) FranBerry 12
(Jonjo O'Neill) *hld up: hdwy into midfield after 4f: drvn 4f out: wknd over 2f out: virtualy p.u: t.o* **9/1**[2]

2m 41.77s (2.77) **Going Correction** +0.20s/f (Good)
**WFA** 3 from 4yo+ 8lb **10 Ran SP% 123.5**
Speed ratings (Par 101): **98,95,93,93,82 70,68,66,66,60**
CSF £125.30 CT £3970.54 TOTE £9.90: £2.00, £3.10, £7.60; EX 114.20 Trifecta £2349.00.
**Owner** Black Star Racing **Bred** Rabbah Bloodstock Limited **Trained** Radlett, Herts
■ Eastern Lady was withdrawn. Price at time of withdrawal 50/1. Rule 4 does not apply.

**FOCUS**
A number of these didn't look happy on the ground. This has been rated around the 2nd/3rd.
T/Plt: £50.40 to a £1 stake. Pool: £48,676.74 - 704.57 winning units T/Qpdt: £40.70 to a £1 stake. Pool: £3,532.92 - 64.20 winning units **Richard Lowther**

# 7049 DONCASTER (L-H)

Thursday, September 14

**OFFICIAL GOING: Straight course - good to soft (soft in places); round course - soft (good to soft in places; 7.2)**

Wind: Strong against Weather: Cloudy and blustery with showers

## 7086 DFS SILK SERIES LADY RIDERS' H'CAP (FOR PRO-AM LADY RIDERS) 6f 2y

**1:20** (1:21) (Class 3) (0-90,90) 3-Y-0+ **£12,938** (£3,850; £1,924; £962) **Stalls** High

Form RPR

4204 **1** **Buccaneers Vault (IRE)**[26] 6197 5-9-4 **73** GeorgiaCox 4 82
(Paul Midgley) *t.k.h early: hld up: towards rr whn n.m.r and pushed along wl over 2f out: rdn along and gd hdwy wl over 1f out: led appr fnl f: kpt on wl u.p fnl f* **9/1**

3401 **2** *1* **Kenny The Captain (IRE)**[5] 6943 6-9-10 **79** 6ex.. RachelRichardson 12 85
(Tim Easterby) *hld up: hdwy 2f out: rdn to chse ldrs over 1f out: drvn and kpt on fnl f* **4/1**[1]

U050 **3** *3/4* **Paddy Power (IRE)**[26] 6205 4-9-7 **76** MeganNicholls 8 79
(Richard Fahey) *awkward and dwlt s: towards rr: hdwy 1/2-way: chsd ldrs wl over 1f out: sn rdn and kpt on fnl f* **14/1**

1100 **4** *1/2* **Related**[13] 6662 7-10-2 **85** (b) HollieDoyle 9 87
(Paul Midgley) *cl up: led after 2f: rdn along 2f out: sn hdd and drvn: kpt on same pce fnl f* **12/1**

1006 **5** *shd* **Adam's Ale**[15] 6570 8-9-11 **80** (e) MissBeckySmith 11 81
(Marjorie Fife) *prom: hdwy to ld wl over 1f out: sn rdn and hdd appr fnl f: drvn and kpt on same pce fnl f* **16/1**

2404 **6** *nse* **Rebel Surge (IRE)**[24] 6261 4-10-5 **88** (p) JennyPowell 1 89
(Richard Spencer) *towards rr: hdwy on wd outside over 2f out: sn rdn along and chsd ldrs whn n.m.r over 1f out: drvn and kpt on fnl f* **16/1**

000 **7** *1/2* **Hoofalong**[22] 6325 7-10-7 **90** (b) MissJoannaMason 10 90
(Michael Easterby) *towards rr: hdwy 2f out: sn rdn along and kpt on fnl f* **9/2**[2]

0041 **8** *5* **Khelman (IRE)**[45] 5471 7-10-1 **84** SammyJoBell 2 68
(Richard Fahey) *hld up on outer: hdwy 1/2-way: rdn along to chse ldrs 2f out: sn drvn and grad wknd* **11/1**

0030 **9** *4* **Majestic Moon (IRE)**[47] 5396 7-9-12 **81** ShelleyBirkett 5 52
(Julia Feilden) *chsd ldrs: rdn along wl over 2f out: sn wknd* **16/1**

1411 **10** *shd* **Vimy Ridge**[10] 6764 5-9-10 **84** 6ex (t) MissJCooley(5) 14 55
(Alan Bailey) *dwlt and bhd: hdwy and in tch over 2f out: sn rdn along and n.d* **11/1**

4221 **11** *1/2* **Case Key**[26] 6197 4-9-6 **75** (p) JosephineGordon 3 44
(Michael Appleby) *in tch on outer: chsd ldrs 1/2-way: rdn along over 2f out: sn drvn and wknd* **15/2**[3]

1025 **12** *1 1/2* **Seamster**[22] 6303 10-9-2 **76** (t) LauraCoughlan(5) 7 40
(David Loughnane) *chsd ldrs: cl up over 3f out: rdn along over 2f out: sn wknd* **25/1**

20 **13** *6* **Tavener**[63] 4803 5-9-7 **76** (p) MissSBrotherton 13 21
(David C Griffiths) *led 2f: prom: rdn along over 2f out: sn drvn and wknd* **33/1**

1m 12.88s (-0.72) **Going Correction** +0.075s/f (Good) **13** Ran SP% **115.4**

Speed ratings (Par 107): **107,105,104,104,103 103,103,96,91,91 90,88,80**

CSF £43.16 CT £521.22 TOTE £10.30: £3.20, £1.70, £3.90; EX 53.40 Trifecta £720.60.

**Owner** Robert And Sheila Bradley **Bred** Kilfrush Stud **Trained** Westow, N Yorks

**FOCUS**

The round course was railed out from about the 1m2f point until the round course joins the straight track. The second day of the St Leger meeting started off with the final leg of a competitive set of races involving professional, apprentice and amateur female riders. Following her third-place finish, Megan Nicholls was the overall winner of the series. A decent field lined up and the pace was sound from the outset. The winner has been rated to his turf best.

## 7087 EBF BRITISH STALLION STUDS "CARRIE RED" FILLIES' NURSERY H'CAP 6f 111y

**1:50** (1:50) (Class 2) 2-Y-O **£25,204** (£7,544; £3,772; £1,888; £940) **Stalls** High

Form RPR

4160 **1** **Ellthea (IRE)**[26] 6228 2-9-0 **81** CliffordLee(3) 2 95+
(K R Burke) *trckd ldr: cl up 1/2-way: led 2f out: rdn and qcknd clr appr fnl f: kpt on strly* **8/1**

3232 **2** *3 3/4* **Clubbable**[12] 6693 2-8-11 **75** PaulHanagan 4 79
(Richard Fahey) *hld up in rr: hdwy 2f out: rdn over 1f out: drvn and kpt on fnl 2f: tk 2nd last 100yds: no ch w wnr* **7/4**[1]

0641 **3** *1* **She's Different (IRE)**[20] 6379 2-8-4 **68** AndrewMullen 1 69
(Nigel Tinkler) *trckd ldng pair: effrt on outer 2f out: sn rdn and ev ch: drvn appr fnl f: kpt on same pce* **5/1**[3]

2126 **4** *4* **Silver Starlight**[21] 6353 2-9-2 **80** DavidAllan 3 70
(Tim Easterby) *hld up: hdwy over 2f out: rdn along wl over 1f out: kpt on one pce* **6/1**

1100 **5** *1 1/2* **Poetic Steps (FR)**[12] 6693 2-9-2 **80** PJMcDonald 5 66
(Mark Johnston) *led: pushed along 1/2-way: rdn over 2f out: sn hdd: drvn and wknd* **12/1**

001 **6** *5* **The Mums**[27] 6138 2-9-7 **85** FrankieDettori 6 57
(John Gosden) *trckd ldrs: pushed along 3f out: rdn over 2f out: sn btn* **3/1**[2]

1m 19.89s (-0.01) **Going Correction** +0.075s/f (Good) **6** Ran SP% **111.1**

Speed ratings (Par 98): **103,98,97,93,91 85**

CSF £22.07 TOTE £8.80: £3.50, £1.60; EX 20.30 Trifecta £86.10.

**Owner** Mrs M Gittins **Bred** George Kent **Trained** Middleham Moor, N Yorks

**FOCUS**

The pace lifted sharply after halfway in this fair fillies' nursery.

## 7088 WILLIAM HILL MAY HILL STKS (GROUP 2) (FILLIES) 1m (S)

**2:25** (2:26) (Class 1) 2-Y-O

**£39,697** (£15,050; £7,532; £3,752; £1,883; £945) **Stalls** High

Form RPR

12 **1** **Laurens (FR)**[26] 6228 2-9-0 0 PJMcDonald 4 106+
(K R Burke) *trckd ldrs: hdwy 2f out: rdn to chse ldr ent fnl f: sn drvn: kpt on gamely to ld nr line* **11/4**[1]

51 **2** *hd* **Dark Rose Angel (IRE)**[26] 6183 2-9-0 0 PaulMulrennan 1 105
(Simon Crisford) *hld up: hdwy on wd outside wl over 1f out: chal ent fnl f: rdn to ld and edgd rt last 100yds: drvn: edgd lft and hdd nr line* **14/1**

2216 **3** *hd* **Nyaleti (IRE)**[25] 6249 2-9-0 113 JamesDoyle 7 105
(Mark Johnston) *led: pushed along and qcknd 2f out: rdn over 1f out: drvn ins fnl f: hdd last 100yds: kpt on* **4/1**[2]

2 **4** *nk* **Sizzling (IRE)**[14] 6643 2-9-0 0 RyanMoore 2 104
(A P O'Brien, Ire) *trckd ldrs: hdwy 2f out: rdn to chse ldr over 1f out: chal ent fnl f: sn drvn and ev ch: no ex last 75yds* **9/1**

1311 **5** *2 3/4* **Billesdon Brook**[19] 6418 2-9-0 100 SeanLevey 8 98
(Richard Hannon) *hld up: hdwy over 2f out: rdn along wl over 1f out: sn drvn and no imp* **4/1**[2]

111 **6** *1 1/2* **She Believes (IRE)**[20] 6375 2-9-0 95 LiamKeniry 5 95
(Sylvester Kirk) *hld up in rr: effrt over 2f out: sn rdn along and n.d* **16/1**

1611 **7** *1 3/4* **Tajaanus (IRE)**[33] 5941 2-9-0 102 JimCrowley 3 91
(Richard Hannon) *trckd ldr: cl up over 3f out: rdn along 2f out: sn wknd* **9/2**[3]

0513 **8** *1 1/2* **Miss Bar Beach (IRE)**[19] 6418 2-9-0 96 GrahamLee 6 88
(Keith Dalgleish) *trckd ldrs: pushed along 3f out: sn rdn and wknd* **22/1**

1m 40.06s (0.76) **Going Correction** +0.075s/f (Good) **8** Ran SP% **111.7**

Speed ratings (Par 104): **99,98,98,98,95 94,92,90**

CSF £40.72 TOTE £3.30: £1.40, £3.20, £1.60; EX 40.80 Trifecta £201.30.

**Owner** John Dance **Bred** Bloodstock Agency Ltd **Trained** Middleham Moor, N Yorks

**FOCUS**

Muddling form and it's hard to rate the bare level any higher.

## 7089 DFS PARK HILL STKS (GROUP 2) (F&M) 1m 6f 115y

**3:00** (3:01) (Class 1) 3-Y-O+

**£51,039** (£14,517; £14,517; £4,824; £2,421; £1,215) **Stalls** Low

Form RPR

1-03 **1** **Alyssa**[68] 4639 4-9-5 100 PatDobbs 2 105
(Ralph Beckett) *led: qcknd 3f out: pushed along 2f out: rdn jst over 1f out: hdd wl ins fnl f: rallied to ld again nr fin* **25/1**

1-33 **2** *1/2* **Aljezeera**[21] 6357 3-8-9 97 FrankieDettori 1 104
(Luca Cumani) *trckd ldrs: hdwy 3f out: pushed along over 2f out: rdn to chal over 1f out: drvn to take slt ld ins fnl f: hdd and no ex nr fin* **11/2**[2]

1113 **2** *dht* **Melodic Motion (IRE)**[42] 5569 3-8-9 102 OisinMurphy 6 104
(Ralph Beckett) *hld up in rr: hdwy 3f out: chsd ldrs 2f out: rdn over 1f out: ev ch ins fnl f: sn drvn and kpt on same pce towards fin* **9/2**[1]

2 **4** *3/4* **Detailed (IRE)**[10] 6772 3-8-9 92 AndreaAtzeni 3 103
(Joseph Patrick O'Brien, Ire) *hld up in rr: hdwy on inner wl over 2f out: rdn ent fnl f: sn ev ch: drvn and kpt on same pce towards fin* **13/2**[3]

-153 **5** *3/4* **Wild Irish Rose (IRE)**[37] 5766 3-8-9 102 SeanLevey 9 102
(A P O'Brien, Ire) *in tch: hdwy on inner wl over 2f out: rdn over 1f out: drvn and ch ent fnl f: kpt on same pce* **15/2**

2020 **6** *3 1/4* **Dubka**[19] 6447 4-9-5 102 RyanMoore 10 98
(Sir Michael Stoute) *hld up in midfield: hdwy 4f out: pushed along 3f out: rdn over 2f out: sn one pce* **9/2**[1]

0553 **7** *3/4* **Harlequeen**[12] 6675 4-9-5 101 (v) GrahamLee 5 97
(Mick Channon) *trckd ldrs: pushed along 4f out: rdn over 3f out: sn one pce* **28/1**

6243 **8** *3 1/2* **Natural Scenery**[19] 6447 4-9-5 107 (p) JimCrowley 8 92
(Saeed bin Suroor) *trckd wnr: effrt and cl up over 3f out: rdn along wl over 2f out: sn drvn and wknd* **9/2**[1]

1060 **9** *1/2* **Sweet Selection**[44] 5503 5-9-5 105 AdamKirby 7 91
(Hughie Morrison) *trckd ldrs: pushed along over 4f out: rdn over 3f out: sn wknd* **12/1**

2-53 **10** *1 3/4* **Groovejet**[20] 6391 6-9-5 95 StevieDonohoe 4 89
(Richard Spencer) *a towards rr* **50/1**

3m 11.59s (4.19) **Going Correction** +0.25s/f (Good)

**WFA** 3 from 4yo+ 10lb **10** Ran SP% **112.0**

Speed ratings (Par 115): **98,97,97,97,96 95,94,92,92,91**

WIN: 32.20; PL: ALY £7.30, ALJ £2.10, MM £1.60. EX: ALY/ALJ £127.40; ALY/MM £111.80. CSF: ALY/ALJ £74.62; ALY/MM £63.76. TRIFECTA: ALY/ALJ/MM £896.80; ALY/MM/ALJ £1,511.60.

**Owner** Miss K Rausing **Bred** Miss K Rausing **Trained** Kimpton, Hants

**FOCUS**

Add 6yds. A highly competitive Group 2 Park Hill, run at a sound pace, that threw up a cracking finish. It saw a 1-2 of sorts for Ralph Beckett. A small pb from the winner.

## 7090 WEATHERBYS RACING BANK £300,000 2-Y-O STKS 6f 111y

**3:35** (3:43) (Class 2) 2-Y-O

**£147,540** (£59,040; £29,520; £14,730; £7,380; £7,380) **Stalls** High

Form RPR

323 **1** **Laugh A Minute**[20] 6403 2-8-12 82 AndreaAtzeni 3 98
(Roger Varian) *dwlt: hld up in rr towards far side: smooth hdwy over 2f out: rdn over 1f out: led ins fnl f: styd on* **12/1**

6315 **2** *1 1/4* **Danzan (IRE)**[22] 6326 2-9-0 96 DavidProbert 15 97+
(Andrew Balding) *prom centre: cl up 1/2-way: led over 2f out: rdn and edgd lft over 1f out: drvn and edgd lft ins fnl f: hdd and no ex last 120yds* **12/1**

1534 **3** *3/4* **Alba Power (IRE)**[21] 6353 2-8-6 96 JosephineGordon 2 87
(Hugo Palmer) *trckd ldrs towards far side: hdwy 2f out: rdn over 1f out: ch and drvn ins fnl f: kpt on same pce* **9/1**

132 **4** *1/2* **Great Prospector (IRE)**[21] 6353 2-8-9 105 PaulHanagan 10 89
(Richard Fahey) *trckd ldrs: hdwy 2f out: rdn over 1f out: drvn and kpt on fnl f* **7/2**[1]

1346 **5** *nk* **Zap**[22] 6330 2-8-12 88 TonyHamilton 7 91
(Richard Fahey) *towards rr: hdwy over 2f out: rdn wl over 1f out: styd on wl fnl f* **33/1**

5043 **6** *3/4* **Elysium Dream**[26] 6200 2-8-4 83 HollieDoyle 18 81
(Richard Hannon) *stmbld and hmpd s: in rr: hdwy wl over 1f out: sn rdn and fin strly* **25/1**

5131 **7** *3/4* **Alfa McGuire (IRE)**[18] 6465 2-8-6 88 ConnorBeasley 16 81
(Bryan Smart) *chsd ldrs towards outer: rdn along 2f out: drvn over 1f out: kpt on same pce fnl f* **25/1**

3242 **8** *nk* **Queen's Sargent (FR)**[22] 6330 2-8-12 85 ShaneGray 6 86
(Kevin Ryan) *in tch towards far side: pushed along and sltly outpcd 2f out: sn rdn and kpt on fnl f* **33/1**

2411 **9** *hd* **Tangled (IRE)**[21] 6353 2-8-9 102 SeanLevey 9 82
(Richard Hannon) *in tch: hdwy to chse ldrs wl over 1f out: drvn ent fnl f: kpt on same pce* **9/2**[2]

1546 **10** *hd* **Jedi Master (IRE)**[12] 6699 2-8-6 83 PatrickMathers 12 79
(Richard Fahey) *towards rr: hdwy over 2f out: sn rdn and kpt on fnl f* **25/1**

0062 **11** *2 1/4* **Requinto Dawn (IRE)**[18] 6466 2-8-9 84 TomEaves 1 76
(Richard Fahey) *in rr: hdwy towards far side over 2f out: rdn wl over 1f out: sn no imp* **100/1**

26 **12** *1/2* **Faraasah (IRE)**[62] 4826 2-8-6 0 JasonHart 22 71+
(Brian Meehan) *racd wd early: led: hdd 1/2-way: rdn along over 2f out: grad wknd* **25/1**

**13** *1* **Sebastiano Ricci (IRE)**[10] 6769 2-9-2 0 RyanMoore 20 78
(Joseph Patrick O'Brien, Ire) *swtchd lft s: a towards rr* **33/1**

1040 **14** *nk* **Helvetian**[4] 6977 2-8-9 97 GrahamLee 14 71
(Mick Channon) *in tch: rdn along over 2f out: sn wknd* **40/1**

6601 **15** *2 ¼* **Neola**[9] 6778 2-8-4 89 BenCurtis 19 59
(Mick Channon) *racd towards stands' side: a towards rr* **8/1**[3]

142 **16** *½* **International Man**[29] 6057 2-8-12 82 JackGarritty 17 66
(Richard Fahey) *a towards rr* **40/1**

2223 **17** *1 ¾* **Cosa Nostra (IRE)**[12] 6674 2-8-9 82 BarryMcHugh 5 58
(Richard Fahey) *chsd ldrs towards far side: rdn along over 2f out: sn wknd* **100/1**

6 **18** *hd* **Medal Of Honour**[5] 6955 2-9-2 0 (t) WayneLordan 11 65
(Joseph Patrick O'Brien, Ire) *a towards rr* **40/1**

5013 **19** *1* **Areen Faisal (IRE)**[22] 6330 2-8-12 85 PhillipMakin 13 58
(David O'Meara) *racd centre: cl up: led 1/2-way: rdn along and hdd over 2f out: sn drvn and wknd wl over 1f out* **40/1**

100 **20** *1 ½* **Chookie Dunedin**[17] 6521 2-8-12 94 JimCrowley 8 54
(Keith Dalgleish) *racd towards far side: chsd ldrs: rdn along 3f out: grad wknd* **50/1**

5211 **21** *1 ¼* **Magic Jazz (IRE)**[12] 6693 2-8-6 80 JoeDoyle 4 44
(Kevin Ryan) *racd towards far side: chsd ldrs: rdn along wl 1/2-way: sn wknd* **25/1**

421 **22** *10* **Humble Gratitude**[12] 6689 2-8-9 86 (p[1]) MartinHarley 21 20
(K R Burke) *racd towards stands' side: a towards rr* **14/1**

1m 19.39s (-0.51) **Going Correction** +0.075s/f (Good) **22** Ran SP% **125.3**
Speed ratings (Par 101): **105,103,102,102,101 100,100,99,99,99 96,96,95,94,92 91,89,89,88,86 85,73**
CSF £125.16 TOTE £11.10: £3.90, £4.40, £3.30; EX 131.40 Trifecta £924.60.
**Owner** Sheikh Mohammed Obaid Al Maktoum **Bred** Whitsbury Manor Stud And Mrs M E Slade **Trained** Newmarket, Suffolk

**FOCUS**
As one would imagine for the money on offer, this looked a strong race and it was run at a good gallop. The first two home both enhance Wells Farhh Go's profile, as that colt has finished in front of the pair in recent starts. The winner is a big improver.

## 7091 CROWNHOTEL-BAWTRY.COM H'CAP — 1m 2f 43y
**4:05** (4:09) (Class 2) (0-105,102) 3-Y-O+**£15,562** (£4,660; £2,330; £1,165) **Stalls** Low

Form RPR

2145 **1** **Euginio (IRE)**[12] 6698 3-9-4 **102** AndreaAtzeni 4 109
(Richard Hannon) *trckd ldng pair: hdwy over 2f out: rdn to take narrow ld 1 1/2f out: drvn ins fnl f: kpt on wl towards fin* **11/4**[2]

3123 **2** *nk* **Another Eclipse (IRE)**[18] 6482 3-8-1 **88** oh1 GeorgeWood[(3)] 1 94
(David Simcock) *hld up in rr: hdwy over 2f out: rdn and edgd lft over 1f out: drvn to chal on outer ins fnl f: kpt on* **5/2**[1]

-264 **3** *¾* **Al Neksh**[20] 6399 4-8-12 **90** FrankieDettori 3 95
(William Haggas) *led: pushed along over 2f out: rdn and hdd 1 1/2f out: cl up: drvn and ev ch ent fnl f tl no ex last 75yds* **3/1**[3]

0313 **4** *hd* **Dark Red (IRE)**[19] 6449 5-9-4 **96** RyanMoore 5 100
(Ed Dunlop) *trckd ldr: pushed along over 2f out: rdn and cl up over 1f out: drvn and ev ch ent fnl f: no ex last 75yds* **5/2**[1]

2m 14.6s (5.20) **Going Correction** +0.25s/f (Good)
**WFA** 3 from 4yo+ 6lb **4** Ran SP% **108.8**
Speed ratings (Par 109): **89,88,88,88**
CSF £9.70 TOTE £4.10; EX 12.30 Trifecta £32.10.
**Owner** Saleh Al Homaizi & Imad Al Sagar **Bred** Arkle Bloodstock **Trained** East Everleigh, Wilts

**FOCUS**
Add 6yds. Not surprisingly this decent small-field handicap proved tactical.

## 7092 BREEDERS' SERIES EBF FILLIES' H'CAP — 1m 3f 197y
**4:35** (4:35) (Class 2) (0-100,93) 3-Y-O+
**£18,675** (£5,592; £2,796; £1,398; £699; £351) **Stalls** Low

Form RPR

331 **1** **What A Home (IRE)**[47] 5401 3-8-5 **80** PaulHanagan 1 89+
(William Haggas) *t.k.h: trckd ldr: hdwy 3f out: swtchd rt and rdn to take narrow ld jst over 2f out: drvn ins fnl f: kpt on wl towards fin* **1/1**[1]

4113 **2** *1 ½* **Pacharana**[28] 6104 4-9-12 **93** AdamKirby 3 98
(Luca Cumani) *trckd ldr: hdwy over 2f out and sn cl up: rdn over 1f out: drvn and ev ch ent fnl f: kpt on same pce towards fin* **12/1**

2152 **3** *¾* **Stoney Broke**[47] 5414 4-9-4 **85** DanielMuscutt 2 89
(James Fanshawe) *trckd ldrs: hdwy over 2f out: rdn to chse ldng pair over 1f out: drvn and kpt on same pce fnl f* **12/1**

4161 **4** *nse* **Camerone (IRE)**[22] 6307 3-8-13 **88** PatDobbs 5 92
(Ralph Beckett) *hld up: pushed along and sltly outpcd over 2f out: rdn wl over 1f out: swtchd lft and drvn ent fnl f: kpt on* **15/2**

4521 **5** *1 ¼* **Nathalie**[30] 6044 3-8-3 **81** GeorgeWood[(3)] 6 83
(James Fanshawe) *hld up in rr: hdwy over 2f out: rdn to chse ldrs over 1f out: sn drvn and no imp fnl f* **7/2**[2]

0212 **6** *2 ¼* **Renfrew Street**[7] 6849 4-9-3 **84** PJMcDonald 4 82
(Mark Johnston) *sn led: pushed along 3f out: rdn and hdd jst over 2f out: sn wknd* **7/1**[3]

2m 35.23s (0.33) **Going Correction** +0.25s/f (Good)
**WFA** 3 from 4yo 8lb **6** Ran SP% **111.9**
Speed ratings (Par 96): **108,107,106,106,105 104**
CSF £14.27 TOTE £1.70: £1.20, £4.30; EX 13.00 Trifecta £69.10.
**Owner** Sunderland Holding Inc **Bred** Tullpark Ltd **Trained** Newmarket, Suffolk

**FOCUS**
About 6 yards needs adding to this official distance. Despite a short-priced favourite lining up, this looked a strong race of its type. The runner-up has been rated to form, and the 3rd to her AW level.
T/Jkpt: Not Won. T/Plt: £401.10 to a £1 stake. Pool: £146,662.81 - 266.89 winning units T/Qpdt: £66.70 to a £1 stake. Pool: £12,210.69 - 135.45 winning units **Joe Rowntree**

# 6552 EPSOM (L-H)
Thursday, September 14

**OFFICIAL GOING: Good (6.9)**
Wind: medium to strong, against Weather: overcast, breezy

## 7093 IRISH STALLION FARMS EBF NOVICE MEDIAN AUCTION STKS — 7f 3y
**1:30** (1:31) (Class 5) 2-Y-O **£3,881** (£1,155; £577; £288) **Stalls** Low

Form RPR

3 **1** **Hollydaze (IRE)**[15] 6584 2-8-11 0 SilvestreDeSousa 7 80+
(Richard Hughes) *pressed ldr: travelling best 2f out: pushed into ld jst over 1f out: sn qcknd and asserted: in command ins fnl f: pushed out: comf* **4/1**[2]

3 **2** *2* **King Of The Sand (IRE)**[23] 6279 2-8-13 0 HectorCrouch[(3)] 2 79
(Gary Moore) *led: rdn 2f out: hdd and unable qck jst over 1f out: wl hld by wnr after: kpt on same pce for clr 2nd* **6/1**[3]

262 **3** *4* **Hateya (IRE)**[17] 6510 2-8-8 71 CharlieBennett[(3)] 4 63
(Jim Boyle) *chsd ldrs: lft 3rd over 5f out: rdn 2f out: outpcd and lost 3rd over 1f out: no ch w ldng pair after: wnt 3rd again ins fnl f* **6/1**[3]

5 **4** *½* **Rosedale Topping (IRE)**[40] 5655 2-8-11 0 HarryBentley 9 62
(Ed Vaughan) *in tch in midfield: 5th and rdn 3f out: hdwy to chse clr ldng pair but wanting to edge lft down the camber over 1f out: kpt on same pce and no imp after: lost 3rd ins fnl f* **14/1**

**5** *nk* **Dukeofwallingford** 2-9-2 0 EdwardGreatrex 10 66
(Eve Johnson Houghton) *in rr on main gp: effrt over 2f out: kpt on ins fnl f: no ch w ldng pair* **20/1**

52 **6** *2 ¾* **Lifeboat (IRE)**[78] 4218 2-8-13 0 CallumShepherd[(3)] 5 59+
(Charles Hills) *restless in stalls: awkward leaving stalls: sn chsng ldrs: lft 4th whn hmpd and carried rt over 5f out: effrt ent fnl 2f: wanting to edge lft down the camber and outpcd over 1f out: wknd ins fnl f* **13/8**[1]

6 **7** *2* **Port Of Call**[13] 6654 2-9-2 0 KieranShoemark 8 53
(Amanda Perrett) *hld up in rr of main gp: clsd and effrt over 2f out: a wanting to hang down the camber after: no imp: wknd fnl f* **6/1**[3]

6 **8** *8* **King Athelstan (IRE)**[17] 6510 2-9-2 0 RobertWinston 1 32
(John Best) *sn dropped to last pair and outpcd: nvr on terms after* **20/1**

60 **9** *1* **Quick Recovery**[13] 6654 2-8-11 0 (h[1]) FergusSweeney 6 24
(Jim Boyle) *v.s.a: a outpcd in rr* **66/1**

0 **10** *39* **Peggie Sue**[15] 6583 2-8-11 0 RoystonFfrench 3 +
(Adam West) *t.k.h: chsd ldrs: r.oto heels and stmbld over 5f out: sddle slipped and sn swtchd rt to wd outside: rdr unable to offer any assistance after: t.o and moving towards stands side 3f out* **66/1**

1m 24.4s (1.10) **Going Correction** +0.175s/f (Good) **10** Ran SP% **120.1**
Speed ratings (Par 95): **100,97,93,92,92 89,86,77,76,31**
CSF £28.08 TOTE £3.90: £1.30, £2.30, £1.80; EX 32.90 Trifecta £109.70.
**Owner** P D Merritt **Bred** O Costello & R Moorhead **Trained** Upper Lambourn, Berks

**FOCUS**
Rail out up to seven yards from 1m2f to winning post, adding 30 yards to all races of 1m+, 20 yards to 7f races and 10 yards to 6f races. A fair contest run at a steady pace which suited those handy. The first two are improvers.

## 7094 STELRAD RADIATOR H'CAP — 7f 3y
**2:00** (2:01) (Class 4) (0-80,82) 3-Y-O+
**£7,470** (£2,236; £1,118; £559; £279; £140) **Stalls** Low

Form RPR

4346 **1** **Scofflaw**[16] 6554 3-9-3 **80** AdamMcNamara[(3)] 4 89
(Richard Fahey) *hld up in tch in midfield: effrt 2f out: hdwy and rdn to ld over 1f out: styd on u.p to assert ins fnl f: rdn out* **7/1**[3]

0112 **2** *1 ¼* **Bumptious**[14] 6619 4-9-7 **77** (p) SilvestreDeSousa 5 84+
(Ismail Mohammed) *hld up in midfield: effrt on outer over 2f out: hdwy u.p over 1f out: chse wnr ins fnl f: hanging down the camber and no imp after* **9/4**[1]

234 **3** *1 ¼* **Gold Hunter (IRE)**[22] 6303 7-9-1 **76** (p) PaddyPilley[(5)] 10 80
(Steve Flook) *hld up in tch in midfield: effrt ent fnl 2f: rdn to chal over 1f out tl no ex ins fnl f: lost 2nd and wknd fnl 100yds* **20/1**

4653 **4** *3* **Munfallet (IRE)**[16] 6555 6-9-8 **78** KieranShoemark 8 74
(David Brown) *led tl 3f out: sn rdn: unable qckn and outpcd over 1f out: wl hld and battling for 4th 1f out: kpt on same pce ins fnl f* **10/1**

16-6 **5** *hd* **Colonel Frank**[40] 5642 3-9-8 **82** JimmyFortune 2 75
(Ed Walker) *jnd ldr after 1f tl led 3f out: rdn and hdd over 1f out: sn outpcd and battling for wl hld 4th 1f out: kpt on same pce ins fnl f* **8/1**

3213 **6** *½* **Black Caesar (IRE)**[3] 7002 6-9-1 **78** 6ex SebastianWoods[(7)] 3 72
(Philip Hide) *hld up in midfield: effrt ent fnl 2f: drvn and nt clrest of runs over 1f out: no threat to ldrs and kpt on same pce ins fnl f* **10/1**

2112 **7** *nse* **Lord Clenaghcastle (IRE)**[17] 6516 3-9-5 **82** HectorCrouch[(3)] 1 74
(Gary Moore) *in tch in midfield: clsd to chse ldrs 3f out: sn rdn and struggling to qckn: outpcd and btn over 1f out: plugged on same pce ins fnl f* **9/2**[2]

2133 **8** *1* **Limelite (IRE)**[20] 6397 3-8-12 **72** (p[1]) HarryBentley 6 64+
(Richard Hannon) *w ldrs tl stdd bk to chse ldng pair over 5f out: trcking ldr on inner 3f out: effrt over 1f out: nvr clr enough run to make any prog: stuck bhd rival and rdr nt given her a hrd time ins fnl f* **12/1**

0066 **9** *¾* **Outer Space**[23] 6297 6-9-8 **78** DougieCostello 11 67
(Jamie Osborne) *stdd and awkward leaving stalls: hld up in last trio: swtchd lft and effrt on inner over 2f out: switching bk rt and lost pl over 1f out: nt clrest of runs and no imp after* **25/1**

1001 **10** *hd* **Favourite Royal (IRE)**[16] 6555 3-9-6 **80** (p) RobertWinston 7 67
(Eve Johnson Houghton) *hld up in last trio: effrt on outer over 2f out: no imp and edging lft down the camber over 1f out: wl hld fnl f* **7/1**[3]

0040 **11** *½* **El Torito (IRE)**[3] 7002 3-8-10 **73** (h[1]) CharlieBennett[(3)] 9 58
(Jim Boyle) *sn outpcd in rr: clsd 3f out: no imp over 1f out: nvr trbld ldrs* **66/1**

1m 23.8s (0.50) **Going Correction** +0.175s/f (Good)
**WFA** 3 from 4yo+ 4lb **11** Ran SP% **121.0**
Speed ratings (Par 105): **104,102,101,97,97 96,96,95,94,94 94**
CSF £23.35 CT £320.77 TOTE £6.80: £1.70, £1.90, £6.00; EX 25.30 Trifecta £371.40.
**Owner** P Timmins & A Rhodes Haulage **Bred** Mrs M E Slade **Trained** Musley Bank, N Yorks

**FOCUS**
Due to rail movement add 20yds. This was competitive enough for the grade and run at a solid pace. The winner has been rated back to his best.

## 7095 FOCUS RIGGING H'CAP — 1m 113y
**2:35** (2:37) (Class 5) (0-75,75) 3-Y-O **£4,528** (£1,347; £673; £336) **Stalls** Low

Form RPR

4114 **1** **Alnasl (IRE)**[5] 6948 3-9-5 **73** (h) EdwardGreatrex 2 84
(Archie Watson) *mde all and dictated gallop: gng best over 2f out: rdn and readily wnt clr over 1f out: in n.d and r.o wl fnl f: unchal* **11/4**[1]

2443 **2** *3 ½* **Traveller (FR)**[16] 6558 3-9-4 **75** (t) CallumShepherd[(3)] 6 77
(Charles Hills) *hld up in last trio: effrt over 2f out: chsd clr wnr and hanging lft down the camber ins fnl f: kpt on but no imp on wnr* **5/1**[2]

2360 **3** *1* **Unit Of Assessment (IRE)**[22] 6310 3-9-2 **70** (t[1]) HarryBentley 1 70
(William Knight) *chsd ldrs: swtchd rt and rdn 3f out: outpcd by wnr 2f out: wnt 2nd but no threat to wnr 1f out: lost 2nd and kpt on same pce ins fnl f* **10/1**

1-50 **4** *½* **Diamond Bear (USA)**[92] 3727 3-9-2 **73** RosieJessop[(3)] 7 72
(Sir Mark Prescott Bt) *hld up in tch in midfield: swtchd to inner after 2f: effrt over 2f out: outpcd by wnr and trying to switch rt whn hemmed in over 1f out: no ch w wnr fnl f: kpt on to snatch 4th last strides* **8/1**

0146 **5** *nk* **Natajack**[36] 5802 3-8-13 **70**.......... AdamMcNamara(3) 3 68
(Richard Fahey) *chsd wnr: rdn over 2f out: sn outpcd by wnr: wl hld whn lost 2nd 1f out: plugged on same pce ins fnl f* **6/1**[3]
2060 **6** *8* **Lord Commander**[31] 6014 3-9-4 **72**.......... DavidNolan 5 52
(Richard Fahey) *stdd s: hld up in last pair: effrt wl over 2f out: sn struggling: bhd fnl f* **20/1**
0-00 **7** *11* **Beaconsfield**[52] 5221 3-8-7 **61** oh1.......... SilvestreDeSousa 4 17
(Hughie Morrison) *stdd s: hld up in last pair: effrt over 2f out: sn btn: bhd over 1f out* **6/1**[3]
1m 46.15s (0.05) **Going Correction** +0.175s/f (Good) **7** Ran SP% **96.9**
Speed ratings (Par 101): **106,102,102,101,101 94,84**
CSF £11.48 CT £65.31 TOTE £2.60: £2.10, £2.20; EX 8.40 Trifecta £45.70.
**Owner** K Sohi **Bred** Shadwell Estate Company Limited **Trained** Upper Lambourn, W Berks
■ Heart Of Gold was withdrawn. Price at time of withdrawal 9/2. Rule 4 applies to all bets - deduction 15p in the pound.
**FOCUS**
Due to rail movement add 30yds. The pace was honest for this open handicap.

## 7096 LEXUS JUMP JOCKEYS' DERBY H'CAP 1m 4f 6y
**3:10** (3:10) (Class 4) (0-85,85) 4-Y-0+
**£7,470** (£2,236; £1,118; £559; £279; £140) **Stalls** Centre

Form RPR
1131 **1** **C'Est No Mour (GER)**[17] 6513 4-11-6 **81**.......... LeightonAspell 5 89+
(Peter Hedger) *hld up in last trio: clsd 4f out and travelling strly: hdwy to chse ldrs over 1f out: rdn and qcknd to ld jst over 1f out: in command and r.o wl ins fnl f: comf* **9/4**[1]
221/ **2** *¾* **Altaayil (IRE)**[21] 1516 6-11-10 **85**.......... JamieMoore 4 91
(Gary Moore) *chsd ldrs: rdn: lost pl and nt clr run 2f out: swtchd rt and rallied over 1f out: chsd wnr wl ins fnl f: styd on but nvr threatening wnr* **12/1**
0446 **3** *2* **Bamako Du Chatelet (FR)**[24] 6259 6-10-10 **71** oh3.....(p) TomO'Brien 3 74
(Ian Williams) *chsd ldrs tl dropped to midfield over 8f out: rdn and hdwy to chal 2f out: 2nd but outpcd by wnr 1f out: styd on same pce and lost 2nd wl ins fnl f* **14/1**
223 **4** *3 ½* **Hollywood Road (IRE)**[17] 6513 4-11-10 **85**..........(b) ConorShoemark 1 82
(Don Cantillon) *hld up in tch in midfield: effrt over 2f out: no imp over 1f out: wl hld ins fnl f: plugged on to go 4th wl ins fnl f* **9/2**[3]
0441 **5** *2 ¼* **Croquembouche (IRE)**[25] 6232 8-11-9 **84**..........(p) NicodeBoinville 6 78
(Ed de Giles) *led: rdn ent fnl 2f: hdd jst over 1f out: sn outpcd: wknd ins fnl f* **7/1**
6050 **6** *2 ¾* **Captain Peacock**[24] 6273 4-11-5 **80**..........(b) BrendanPowell 2 69
(William Knight) *s.i.s: steadily rcvrd to chse ldrs 9f out: rdn and outpcd whn hung lft over 1f out: wknd fnl f* **20/1**
3300 **7** *6* **Ardamir (FR)**[36] 5798 5-11-3 **78**.......... TomCannon 7 58
(Laura Mongan) *hld up in last trio: swtchd lft and effrt over 2f out: sn no imp: wknd over 1f out* **25/1**
3541 **8** *1 ½* **Cordite (IRE)**[16] 6556 6-10-11 **72**..........(h) DougieCostello 9 49
(Jim Boyle) *taken down early: t.k.h: mostly chsd ldr tl 3f out: sn dropped out and bhd over 1f out* **7/2**[2]
010/ **9** *6* **Rossetti**[54] 5962 9-11-5 **80**..........(h) NoelFehily 8 48
(Neil Mulholland) *sn dropped to rr and nvr travelling wl: rdn 3f out: sn wl btn* **8/1**
2m 42.66s (3.76) **Going Correction** +0.175s/f (Good) **9** Ran SP% **117.8**
Speed ratings (Par 105): **94,93,92,89,88 86,82,81,77**
CSF £32.07 CT £314.87 TOTE £2.60: £1.20, £3.20, £3.70; EX 22.70 Trifecta £433.10.
**Owner** D Wilbrey **Bred** Graf U Grafin V Stauffenberg **Trained** Hook, Hampshire
**FOCUS**
Due to rail movement add 30yds. A fair handicap rated around the 3rd to his turf best; the winner progressed again.

## 7097 KOVARA KLASSIC H'CAP 1m 2f 17y
**3:45** (3:48) (Class 5) (0-75,75) 3-Y-0 **£4,528** (£1,347; £673; £336) **Stalls** Low

Form RPR
3223 **1** **Dream Machine (IRE)**[17] 6518 3-9-7 **75**.......... SilvestreDeSousa 7 82+
(Michael Bell) *stdd and dropped in after s: hld up in tch in rr: swtchd rt and effrt over 2f out: hdwy to chse ldr but hanging lft down camber over 1f out: led ins fnl f: sn in command but continued to hang lft: comf* **5/4**[1]
2420 **2** *1* **Music Lesson**[29] 6067 3-9-4 **72**.......... RobertWinston 3 75
(Hughie Morrison) *led: pushed along and qcknd 2f out: rdn over 1f out: hdd ins fnl f: styd on same pce after* **8/1**
2310 **3** *1 ¼* **Snookered (IRE)**[33] 5921 3-9-0 **68**.......... DavidNolan 2 69
(Richard Fahey) *taken down early: sn pressing ldr: rdn over 2f out: drvn and unable to match pce of ldr 2f out: 3rd and kpt on same pce ins fnl f* **8/1**
1221 **4** *hd* **Hawridge Glory (IRE)**[20] 6393 3-9-3 **71**.......... KieranShoemark 1 73+
(Rod Millman) *dwlt: sn rcvrd and in tch in midfield: effrt and trying to switch rt 2f out: nvr enough room and edging bk lft over 1f out: kpt on towards fin: no ch w wnr* **9/2**[2]
6020 **5** *nk* **Quothquan (FR)**[9] 6792 3-9-2 **73**.......... HectorCrouch(3) 5 73
(Michael Madgwick) *hld up in tch in last pair: effrt jst over 2f out: unable qck over 1f out: nt clrest run and swtchd rt ins fnl f: styd on towards fin: no threat to wnr* **16/1**
651 **6** *1 ¾* **Swaffham Bulbeck (IRE)**[42] 5577 3-9-0 **68**.......... AdamBeschizza 4 64
(Ed Vaughan) *chsd ldrs: effrt over 2f out: unable qck u.p over 1f out: wknd ins fnl f* **5/1**[3]
506 **7** *1* **Outofthequestion**[33] 5931 3-8-9 **63**.......... FergusSweeney 6 57
(Alan King) *hld up in tch: effrt over 2f out: no imp whn sltly squeezed for room over 1f out: bhd ins fnl f* **14/1**
2m 11.25s (1.55) **Going Correction** +0.175s/f (Good) **7** Ran SP% **114.1**
Speed ratings (Par 101): **100,99,98,98,97 96,95**
CSF £12.15 TOTE £2.20: £1.50, £3.70; EX 11.60 Trifecta £49.10.
**Owner** J Barnett & Timmy Hyde **Bred** Keatly Overseas Ltd **Trained** Newmarket, Suffolk
**FOCUS**
Due to rail movement add 30yds. The pace was steady for this fair handicap, and this has been rated around the front-running 2nd.

## 7098 FOLLOW @RACING_UK ON TWITTER NOW H'CAP 1m 113y
**4:15** (4:18) (Class 5) (0-75,81) 4-Y-0+ **£3,881** (£1,155; £577; £288) **Stalls** Low

Form RPR
000 **1** **Lady Perignon**[12] 6700 4-9-6 **74**.......... JimmyFortune 11 82
(Andrew Balding) *t.k.h: led after 1f: mde rest: rdn over 1f out: styd on wl u.p whn pressed ins fnl f: rdn out* **14/1**
1211 **2** *½* **Masarzain (IRE)**[6] 6893 4-9-13 **81** 6ex.......... EdwardGreatrex 8 88
(Archie Watson) *t.k.h: hld up in last trio: effrt over 2f out: swtchd rt and hdwy over 1f out: pressed wnr ins fnl f: kpt on but hld fnl 100yds* **2/1**[1]
2620 **3** *½* **Squiggley**[38] 5715 4-9-5 **73**.......... KieranShoemark 9 79
(Henry Candy) *pushed along leaving stalls: hld up in rr: rdn: hdwy and swtchd rt over 1f out: wnt 3rd ins fnl f: kpt on: nvr getting to ldrs* **13/2**[3]
660 **4** *1 ¼* **Duke Of North (IRE)**[23] 6288 5-8-11 **68**.......... CharlieBennett(3) 2 71
(Jim Boyle) *hld up in tch in midfield: swtchd lft and effrt u.p to chse ldrs over 1f out: styd on same pce ins fnl f* **50/1**
3430 **5** *¾* **Bridge Of Sighs**[7] 6848 5-8-13 **72**..........(p) PaddyBradley(5) 3 73
(Lee Carter) *hld up in midfield: rdn: lost pl and swtchd rt 2f out: hdwy ins fnl f: styd on fnl 100yds: no threat to ldrs* **25/1**
3113 **6** *nk* **Pacific Salt (IRE)**[27] 6143 4-9-3 **74**.......... CallumShepherd(3) 1 74
(Pam Sly) *t.k.h: chsd ldrs: effrt 2f out: unable qck over 1f out: styd on same pce ins fnl f* **8/1**
440 **7** *½* **Harlequin Striker (IRE)**[27] 6134 5-9-7 **75**.......... RobertWinston 4 74
(Dean Ivory) *led for 1f: chsd ldr tl 5f out: rdn to chse ldr again over 2f out: unable qck over 1f out: lost 2nd and wknd ins fnl f* **9/1**
4253 **8** *5* **Shifting Star (IRE)**[17] 6516 12-9-2 **70**..........(vt) WilliamCarson 5 58
(John Bridger) *chsd ldrs tl wnt 2nd 5f out tl over 2f out: sn lost pl u.p: bhd ins fnl f* **20/1**
0121 **9** *2 ¼* **Buzz Lightyere**[11] 6725 4-8-7 **61** oh1.......... SilvestreDeSousa 6 44
(Philip Hide) *pushed along leaving stalls: hld up in tch in last trio: effrt towards inner over 2f out: no imp u.p over 1f out: wl btn and eased ins fnl f* **7/2**[2]
5605 **U** **Groor**[17] 6516 5-9-7 **75**.......... HarryBentley 7
(Mohamed Moubarak) *stmbld bdly and uns rdr leaving stalls* **8/1**
1m 46.36s (0.26) **Going Correction** +0.175s/f (Good) **10** Ran SP% **118.3**
Speed ratings (Par 103): **105,104,104,103,102 102,101,97,95,**
CSF £42.23 CT £198.06 TOTE £18.20: £4.60, £1.30, £2.30; EX 67.20 Trifecta £493.80.
**Owner** Mrs Fitri Hay **Bred** Newsells Park Stud **Trained** Kingsclere, Hants
**FOCUS**
Due to rail movement add 30yds. A fair handicap and a back-to-form winner.

## 7099 WERNICK EVENTS H'CAP 6f 3y
**4:45** (4:50) (Class 5) (0-70,72) 3-Y-0+ **£4,528** (£1,347; £673; £336) **Stalls** High

Form RPR
2-25 **1** **Kowaiyess (IRE)**[153] 1762 3-9-5 **70**.......... AdamBeschizza 7 78
(Mohamed Moubarak) *t.k.h: pressed ldr tl led over 4f out: hung rt bnd over 3f out: rdn over 1f out: hanging lft down camber fnl f: hld on: all out* **25/1**
0064 **2** *nk* **Grandad's World (IRE)**[12] 6669 5-9-6 **72**.......... AdamMcNamara(3) 13 79
(Richard Fahey) *stuck wd early: chsd ldrs: clsd and swtchd lft 2f out: rdn and ev ch ent fnl f: hung lft down camber ins fnl f: kpt on but a jst hld* **6/1**[3]
0423 **3** *¾* **Amood (IRE)**[8] 6807 6-9-8 **71**..........(p) EdwardGreatrex 10 76+
(Archie Watson) *hld up off the pce in midfield: rdn 2f out: swtchd rt over 1f out: hdwy 1f out: hanging lft down camber but styd on to go 3rd wl ins fnl f: nt rch ldrs* **6/4**[1]
263 **4** *1 ¼* **Flowing Clarets**[3] 7000 4-8-12 **61**.......... WilliamCarson 11 62
(John Bridger) *chsd ldrs: wnt 2nd and swtchd lft over 3f out: rdn and ev ch 2f out tl no ex in 3rd 1f out: wknd fnl 100yds* **7/1**
06 **5** *1* **Topology**[29] 6076 4-8-13 **62**..........(v) HarryBentley 8 59
(Joseph Tuite) *midfield: effrt over 2f out: no imp tl hdwy ins fnl f: styd on towards fin: nvr trbld ldrs* **9/2**[2]
420 **6** *¾* **Viva Verglas (IRE)**[129] 2469 6-9-1 **71**.......... TobyEley(7) 9 66
(Daniel Mark Loughnane) *dwlt: sn in midfield: rdn and hdwy 2f out: carried lft ent fnl f: kpt on but no threat to ldrs* **25/1**
5624 **7** *nse* **Red Stripes (USA)**[27] 6156 5-8-11 **60**..........(b) RobertTart 12 55
(Lisa Williamson) *t.k.h: led and styd wd: hdd over 4f out: lost 2nd but styd chsng ldrs over 3f out: hung lft u.p down camber over 1f out: wknd ins fnl f* **12/1**
6563 **8** *½* **Flying Sakhee**[20] 6373 4-8-0 **56** oh6..........(b) ManuelFernandes(7) 6 49
(John Bridger) *sn outpcd and wl off the pce in last trio: styd on ins fnl f: nvr trbld ldrs* **20/1**
4355 **9** *2 ¼* **Bonjour Steve**[8] 6810 6-8-10 **62**..........(p) DavidEgan(3) 2 48
(Richard Price) *wl in tch in midfield: effrt and rdn to chse ldrs 2f out: unable qck over 1f out: wknd ins fnl f* **8/1**
0500 **10** *1 ½* **Perfect Pastime**[10] 6748 9-8-10 **62**.......... CharlieBennett(3) 1 43
(Jim Boyle) *sn wl off the pce in last pair: n.d* **50/1**
6500 **11** *24* **Bridge Builder**[9] 6780 7-9-4 **67**..........(v) KieranShoemark 3
(Peter Hedger) *sn outpcd and detached in last: lost tch 1/2-way: t.o and eased ins fnl f* **33/1**
1m 9.9s (0.50) **Going Correction** +0.175s/f (Good)
**WFA** 3 from 4yo+ 2lb **11** Ran SP% **121.1**
Speed ratings (Par 103): **103,102,101,99,98 97,97,96,93,91 59**
CSF £165.11 CT £380.04 TOTE £13.70: £4.90, £1.70, £1.60; EX 44.20 Trifecta £345.70.
**Owner** Al Jasra Racing **Bred** Shadwell Estate Company Limited **Trained** Exning, Suffolk
**FOCUS**
Due to rail movement add 6yds. Not a strong race for the grade but it was run at a strong pace, and the first two home were up with the gallop throughout.
T/Plt: £56.20 to a £1 stake. Pool: £55,324.78 - 717.88 winning units T/Qpdt: £7.70 to a £1 stake. Pool: £4,935.56 - 470.36 winning units **Steve Payne**

7100 - 7104a (Foreign Racing) - See Raceform Interactive

# 6674 CHESTER (L-H)
Friday, September 15

**OFFICIAL GOING: Soft (heavy in places) changing to heavy after race 2 (2.50)**
Wind: Moderate, half against in straight of just over 1f Weather: Fine

## 7105 SUPPORTING BRITISH STALLIONS EBF NOVICE STKS (PLUS 10 RACE) (C&G) 7f 127y
**2:15** (2:16) (Class 4) 2-Y-0
**£6,225** (£1,864; £932; £466; £233; £117) **Stalls** Low

Form RPR
2 **1** **Spud (IRE)**[13] 6674 2-9-0 0.......... FrannyNorton 1 95+
(Tom Dascombe) *mde all: pushed clr fr over 1f out: eased down towards fin: impressive* **30/100**[1]
66 **2** *15* **Manor Park**[13] 6674 2-9-0 0.......... FergusSweeney 4 60
(Alan King) *chsd ldrs: rdn to take 2nd 2f out: no ch w wnr fr over 1f out* **16/1**[3]
**3** *1 ¼* **Regular Income (IRE)** 2-9-0 0.......... RoystonFfrench 6 57
(Adam West) *unruly in preliminaries: missed break and v awkward s: bhd: rdn along and green: hdwy to chse ldrs 5f out: outpcd over 2f out: wanted to hang lft: kpt on to take 3rd jst ins fnl f: no ch w wnr* **33/1**
0 **4** *3 ¾* **Weinberg**[14] 6658 2-9-0 0.......... PaulMulrennan 3 49
(Donald McCain) *chsd wnr: rdn 3f out: lost 2nd 2f out: wknd 1f out* **66/1**

5 13 **Fanan** 2-9-0 0 PaulHanagan 2 19
(Simon Crisford) *dwlt and wnt rt s: bhd and rn green: detached tl 5f out and again whn outpcd fr 3f out* **4/1[2]**

6 6 **Kendergarten Kop (IRE)** 2-9-0 0 AlistairRawlinson 5
(Tom Dascombe) *chsd ldrs: lost pl 5f out: outpcd and bhd 3f out* **20/1**

1m 40.27s (6.47) **Going Correction** +1.05s/f (Soft) **6** Ran SP% **112.0**
Speed ratings (Par 97): **109,94,92,89,76 70**
CSF £6.68 TOTE £1.10: £1.02, £3.90; EX 5.40 Trifecta £53.40.
**Owner** Stuart Banks & Owen Promotions **Bred** John T Heffernan & Grainne Dooley **Trained** Malpas, Cheshire

**FOCUS**
Rail movements increase race distances as follows: Races 1, 2, 4 and 7 by 24 yards, races 3 and 5 by 26 yards and race 6 by 46 yards. A fair juvenile novice contest. They went a respectable gallop on ground officially described as soft, heavy in places. The race has been rated around the runner-up.

## 7106 #THEMBNATEAM NURSERY H'CAP 7f 1y
**2:50** (2:53) (Class 4) (0-85,79) 2-Y-0

**£6,225** (£1,864; £932; £466; £233; £117) **Stalls** Low

Form RPR

0053 1 **Chai Chai (IRE)**[8] 6860 2-8-13 **71** DavidProbert 8 76+
(Andrew Balding) *towards rr: hdwy over 2f out: styd on to ld fnl 150yds: pushed out and in command after* **4/1[2]**

3465 2 1 ¾ **Magnus (IRE)**[35] 5875 2-9-1 **73** AlistairRawlinson 3 74
(Tom Dascombe) *w ldr: led over 2f out: wandered and nrly 3 l clr over 1f out: hdd fnl 150yds: no ex towards fin* **7/2[1]**

543 3 4 ½ **Knowing Glance (IRE)**[54] 5179 2-8-13 **71** PaulHanagan 7 60
(Richard Fahey) *dwlt and bmpd s: midfield: hung lft over 2f out: hdwy over 1f out: disorganised and hung lft u.p ins fnl f: kpt on same pce* **6/1[3]**

5562 4 2 **Gabrial The Devil (IRE)**[6] 6951 2-8-8 **66** (h[1]) SamJames 9 50
(David O'Meara) *bhd: rdn 2f out: hdwy 1f out: styd on ins fnl f: nvr able to rch ldrs* **11/1**

440 5 1 ¾ **Gossip Column (IRE)**[22] 6353 2-9-0 **72** PaulMulrennan 6 52
(Charles Hills) *dwlt and bmpd s: midfield: rdn and outpcd 2f out: kpt on ins fnl f: nvr able to trble ldrs* **6/1[3]**

045 6 ¾ **Mariah's Melody (IRE)**[13] 6678 2-8-2 **60** AndrewMullen 1 38
(Lisa Williamson) *racd keenly: led: rdn 4f out: hdd over 2f out: wknd 1f out* **40/1**

1440 7 hd **Falmouth Light (FR)**[23] 6330 2-9-6 **78** FrannyNorton 2 56
(Mark Johnston) *trckd ldrs: pushed along 3f out: wknd over 1f out* **4/1[2]**

431 8 3 ¼ **The Throstles**[36] 5847 2-9-1 **73** DavidNolan 5 43
(Kevin Frost) *wnt rt s: trckd ldrs: rdn 3f out: wknd over 1f out: lame* **8/1**

1m 35.11s (8.61) **Going Correction** +1.10s/f (Soft) **8** Ran SP% **112.7**
Speed ratings (Par 97): **94,92,86,84,82 81,81,77**
CSF £17.84 CT £81.55 TOTE £4.10: £1.30, £1.50, £2.10; EX 17.50 Trifecta £121.70.
**Owner** King Power Racing Co Ltd **Bred** Diomed Bloodstock And Lki Bloodstock **Trained** Kingsclere, Hants

**FOCUS**
Race distance increased by 24 yards. A fair nursery handicap. They went a decent gallop and the favourite, proven on soft ground, benefited from a patient ride. The official going was changed to heavy following this contest. The race has been rated around the second.

## 7107 DEEPBRIDGE CAPITAL H'CAP 1m 2f 70y
**3:25** (3:25) (Class 3) (0-95,90) 3-Y-0 **£7,470** (£2,236; £1,118; £559) **Stalls** High

Form RPR

1314 1 **Alexander M (IRE)**[17] 6563 3-9-5 **88** FrannyNorton 3 98
(Mark Johnston) *mde all: stdd pce 3f out: shkn up 2f out: edgd lft whn strly pressed ins fnl f: sn stened up: hld on gamely nr fin* **4/1[3]**

2422 2 hd **Native Prospect**[29] 6094 3-8-12 **81** DavidProbert 4 90
(Andrew Balding) *racd in 2nd pl: keen whn pce stdd 3f out: rdn and unable qck whn lost 2nd over 1f out: rallied wl ins fnl f: clsd on wnr nr fin* **3/1[2]**

0211 3 ½ **Nathan**[27] 6189 3-9-7 **90** FergusSweeney 2 98+
(Alan King) *s.i.s: chsd ldrs: rdn to take 2nd over 1f out: str chal on inner sn after tl no ex nr fin* **4/5[1]**

5310 4 7 **Drumochter**[21] 6389 3-8-5 **74** PaulHanagan 5 68
(Charles Hills) *stdd s: hld up: outpcd over 1f out: sn lft bhd* **14/1**

2m 23.45s (12.25) **Going Correction** +1.15s/f (Soft) **4** Ran SP% **107.2**
Speed ratings (Par 105): **97,96,96,90**
CSF £15.10 TOTE £4.00; EX 11.40 Trifecta £17.10.
**Owner** Christinee Budden, M Budden, Matthew Budden **Bred** Christine E Budden & Partners **Trained** Middleham Moor, N Yorks

**FOCUS**
Race distance increased by 26 yards. A decent little 3yo handicap. The winner dictated a muddling tempo from the front and the race has been rated through the placed horses.

## 7108 ESL GROUP H'CAP 7f 1y
**3:55** (3:56) (Class 3) (0-95,96) 3-Y-0+

**£7,470** (£2,236; £1,118; £559; £279; £140) **Stalls** Low

Form RPR

0002 1 **Explain**[7] 6879 5-9-5 **86** (b) JamesSullivan 4 95
(Ruth Carr) *chsd ldrs: rdn to ld 1f out: styd on wl: in command towards fin* **4/1[3]**

6364 2 1 ½ **Luis Vaz De Torres (IRE)**[13] 6672 5-9-2 **83** (h) DavidNolan 11 88
(Richard Fahey) *midfield: hdwy over 1f out: tried to chal ins fnl f: wnt 2nd fnl 100yds: nt pce of wnr* **16/1**

0051 3 ½ **Penwortham (IRE)**[13] 6676 4-9-1 **89** (h) SebastianWoods(7) 5 93
(Richard Fahey) *midfield: waited for a run 2f out: hdwy sn after to chal: styd on same pce fnl 100yds* **3/1[1]**

5243 4 2 ¼ **Calder Prince (IRE)**[7] 6879 4-9-9 **90** DavidProbert 12 88
(Tom Dascombe) *hld up: rdn 2f out: hdwy ins fnl f: styd on: nt rch ldrs* **7/1**

3200 5 3 ½ **Gabrial The Tiger (IRE)**[13] 6672 5-8-9 **76** FrannyNorton 10 65
(Richard Fahey) *w ldr: rdn to ld 2f out: hdd 1f out: wknd ins fnl f* **8/1**

3363 6 shd **Rajar**[15] 6629 3-9-8 **93** (h) PaulHanagan 8 80
(Richard Fahey) *chsd ldrs: effrt whn bmpd over 1f out: wknd ins fnl f* **9/1**

5660 7 5 **Right Touch**[27] 6206 7-9-5 **93** ConnorMurtagh(7) 1 69
(Richard Fahey) *hld up: rdn over 1f out: no imp* **7/2[2]**

4262 8 2 ¾ **Chosen Character (IRE)**[12] 6725 9-8-3 **77** (vt) ElishaWhittington(7) 3 45
(Tom Dascombe) *a bhd: u.p 3f out: nvr on terms* **14/1**

1200 9 1 ½ **Call Out Loud**[20] 6414 5-8-9 **76** (vt) AlistairRawlinson 6 41
(Michael Appleby) *racd keenly: led: rdn and hdd 2f out: wknd over 1f out* **20/1**

1m 33.64s (7.14) **Going Correction** +1.20s/f (Soft)
**WFA** 3 from 4yo+ 4lb **9** Ran SP% **118.1**
Speed ratings (Par 107): **107,105,104,102,98 98,92,89,87**
CSF £66.53 CT £221.65 TOTE £4.10: £1.60, £4.70, £1.20; EX 93.60 Trifecta £830.50.
**Owner** The Beer Stalkers & Ruth Carr **Bred** Tibthorpe Stud **Trained** Huby, N Yorks

**FOCUS**
Race distance increased by 24 yards. The feature contest was a good handicap. They went decent gallop and it's sound form, rated around the placed horses.

## 7109 EWL MAIDEN FILLIES' STKS 1m 2f 70y
**4:30** (4:32) (Class 4) 3-Y-0+

**£6,225** (£1,864; £932; £466; £233; £117) **Stalls** High

Form RPR

22-3 1 **Song Maker**[56] 5118 3-9-0 82 (b[1]) PhillipMakin 9 76
(Charlie Appleby) *mde all: drew clr 3f out: abt 6 l clr 2f out: rdn over 1f out: reduced advantage ins fnl f: all out: hld on gamely* **15/8[2]**

252 2 nk **Gakku**[11] 6760 3-9-0 0 (b) FrannyNorton 6 75
(Roger Varian) *chsd clr ldr: rdn 3f out: styd on ins fnl f: clsd on wnr nr fin: jst failed* **5/4[1]**

3 2 ½ **River Icon**[20] 5-9-1 0 CallumRodriguez(5) 2 69
(Iain Jardine) *chsd ldrs: rdn over 3f out: outpcd over 2f out: styd on ins fnl f: nvr able to chal* **4/1[3]**

0- 4 hd **Ebqaa (IRE)**[295] 8081 3-9-0 0 TomEaves 5 70
(James Unett) *s.i.s: in rr: hdwy over 3f out: styd on ins fnl f: nvr able to chal* **25/1**

2 5 12 **Clemency**[20] 6413 6-9-6 0 PaulMulrennan 1 52
(Donald McCain) *s.i.s: hld up: pushed along and hdwy over 4f out: chsd ldrs over 3f out: wknd ins fnl f* **11/2**

4004 6 15 **Ejabah (IRE)**[18] 6526 3-9-0 48 JoeyHaynes 8 16
(Charles Smith) *hld up: rdn and outpcd over 2f out: eased whn wl btn ins fnl f* **50/1**

0000 7 10 **Zarkavon**[25] 6268 3-9-0 23 (p) JamesSullivan 3
(John Wainwright) *chsd ldrs tl rdn and wknd over 3f out* **100/1**

0000 8 2 ¼ **Just Heather (IRE)**[20] 6413 3-9-0 37 (p) ShaneGray 4
(John Wainwright) *midfield tl rdn and wknd over 3f out* **100/1**

2m 23.03s (11.83) **Going Correction** +1.25s/f (Soft)
**WFA** 3 from 5yo+ 6lb **8** Ran SP% **122.4**
Speed ratings (Par 102): **102,101,99,99,90 78,70,68**
CSF £4.99 TOTE £2.70: £1.10, £1.10, £1.20; EX 5.30 Trifecta £14.00.
**Owner** Godolphin **Bred** Michael E Wates **Trained** Newmarket, Suffolk

**FOCUS**
Race distance increased by 26 yards. A fair fillies' maiden and the right two horses produced a thrilling photo-finish, but the form may not be totally straightforward.

## 7110 #THEMBNATEAM H'CAP 1m 7f 196y
**5:05** (5:06) (Class 3) (0-95,93) 3-Y-0 **£7,470** (£2,236; £1,118; £559; £279) **Stalls** Low

Form RPR

-335 1 **Arty Campbell (IRE)**[10] 6779 7-8-9 **81** (p) WilliamCox(7) 2 87
(Bernard Llewellyn) *s.i.s: racd keenly: hld up: rdn 3f out: hdwy 2f out: styd on to ld jst over 1f out: edgd lft ins fnl f: hld on wl* **13/2[3]**

100 2 nk **Perfect Summer (IRE)**[62] 4921 7-8-10 **75** (p) AndrewMullen 4 80
(Ian Williams) *sn chsd ldr: rdn and lost 2nd wl over 7f out: rdn and outpcd over 4f out: rallied ins fnl f: styd on wl and clsd on wnr towards fin* **11/1**

1351 3 1 ¼ **Key Bid**[20] 6415 3-8-12 **88** (b) PhillipMakin 5 92+
(Charlie Appleby) *led: rdn over 1f out: sn hdd: swtchd rt ins fnl f: tried to rally: no ex towards fin* **8/13[1]**

5000 4 1 ¾ **Isharah (USA)**[23] 6329 4-9-10 **89** FrannyNorton 1 90
(Mark Johnston) *chsd ldrs: wnt 2nd wl over 7f out tl over 4f out: 2nd again briefly whn over 2f out: kpt on u.p ins fnl f but no real imp: eased whn one pce fnl 50yds* **16/1**

5000 5 14 **Suegioo (FR)**[23] 6329 8-10-0 **93** DavidNolan 3 87
(Richard Fahey) *hld up in rr: hdwy on outer 5f out: chsd ldr over 4f out: rdn and chalng 3f out: lost 2nd over 2f out: wknd over 1f out: eased whn btn ins fnl f* **4/1[2]**

3m 51.08s (23.08) **Going Correction** +1.30s/f (Soft)
**WFA** 3 from 4yo+ 11lb **5** Ran SP% **109.5**
Speed ratings (Par 107): **94,93,93,92,85**
CSF £60.73 TOTE £6.30: £2.30, £3.40; EX 46.70 Trifecta £122.60.
**Owner** Alex James & B J Llewellyn **Bred** Airlie Stud **Trained** Fochriw, Caerphilly

**FOCUS**
Race distance increased by 46 yards. A good little staying handicap and a race of changing fortunes from over 2f out in the demanding ground. The first two have been rated to form.

## 7111 STARDUST LIVERPOOL H'CAP (FOR GENTLEMAN AMATEUR RIDERS) 7f 127y
**5:40** (5:41) (Class 4) (0-80,80) 3-Y-0+

**£5,996** (£1,873; £936; £468; £234; £118) **Stalls** Low

Form RPR

0063 1 **Dark Devil (IRE)**[20] 6414 4-11-2 **80** MrBillyGarritty(5) 11 90+
(Richard Fahey) *chsd ldrs: led over 2f out: rdn over 1f out: pressed wl ins fnl f: kpt on gamely* **9/2[2]**

6203 2 ½ **Mia Cara**[22] 6340 3-9-9 **64** (v) MrJFlook(5) 8 72
(David Evans) *dwlt: towards rr: hdwy 3f out: effrt and swtchd lft over 1f out: sn 2nd: styd on and tried to chal wl ins fnl f: hld nr fin* **11/1**

6361 3 5 **Mr Red Clubs (IRE)**[19] 6475 8-11-4 **77** (p) MrFTett 4 74
(Henry Tett) *midfield: hdwy 3f out: big effrt over 1f out: kpt on same pce ins fnl f* **12/1**

3603 4 1 ¼ **B Fifty Two (IRE)**[6] 6943 8-10-8 **70** (t) MrBLynn(3) 3 64
(Marjorie Fife) *midfield: hdwy over 3f out: rdn and ch over 1f out: kpt on same pce ins fnl f* **7/2[1]**

11 5 8 **Miss Goldsmith (IRE)**[31] 6047 4-9-13 **63** MrSLee(5) 9 39
(Rebecca Menzies) *hld up: hdwy over 2f out: kpt on ins fnl f: no imp* **8/1**

360- 6 ½ **Swift Cedar (IRE)**[391] 5642 7-10-7 **73** MrCAJones(7) 2 48
(David Evans) *in rr: u.p over 1f out: kpt on ins fnl f: nvr a threat* **40/1**

1310 7 3 ¼ **Echo Of Lightning**[20] 6414 7-11-7 **80** (p) MrSWalker 7 47
(Brian Ellison) *chsd ldrs tl rdn and wknd 3f out* **5/1[3]**

1631 8 10 **Bell Heather (IRE)**[6] 6946 4-10-5 **69** MrMEnnis(5) 10 13
(Patrick Morris) *in tch: bucking and wnt wd over 6f out: sn t.o: plugged on ins fnl f* **14/1**

0000 9 1 **Maggie Pink**[48] 5399 8-10-6 **70** MrJamesKendrick(5) 12 12
(Michael Appleby) *chsd ldr: led over 3f out: rdn and hdd over 2f out: sn wknd* **33/1**

/1-0 10 4 **Korbous (IRE)**[10] 6801 8-11-6 **79** MrRBirkett 1 12
(Richard Brabazon, Ire) *midfield tl wknd over 3f out* **5/1[3]**

6503 **11** *21* **Know Your Name**[6] 6947 6-10-4 **63**..........................(p[1]) MrJamesKing 6
(Donald McCain) *led: rdn and hdd over 3f out: sn wknd* **25/1**

1m 43.92s (10.12) **Going Correction** +1.35s/f (Soft)
**WFA** 3 from 4yo+ 5lb **11** Ran SP% **116.8**
Speed ratings (Par 105): **103,102,97,96,88 87,84,74,73,69 48**
CSF £51.76 CT £567.95 TOTE £4.60: £1.80, £3.50, £3.40; EX 65.50 Trifecta £530.50.
**Owner** Arnold, Leitao, Woodward & Wrigley **Bred** Yeomanstown Stud **Trained** Musley Bank, N Yorks

**FOCUS**
Race distance increased by 24 yards. A fair amateur riders' handicap. They went a contested gallop and it's sound form under the conditions.
T/Plt: £159.20 to a £1 stake. Pool: £57,144.50 - 261.87 winning units T/Qpdt: £84.20 to a £1 stake. Pool: £3,632.84 - 31.90 winning units **Darren Owen**

# 7086 DONCASTER (L-H)

Friday, September 15

**OFFICIAL GOING: Straight course - good to soft (good in places); round course - good to soft (7.5)**
Wind: Strong against Weather: Cloudy asnd breezy

## 7112 WEATHERBYS BANK FOREIGN EXCHANGE FLYING SCOTSMAN STKS (LISTED RACE) 7f 6y

**1:20** (1:22) (Class 1) 2-Y-O
**£17,013** (£6,450; £3,228; £1,608; £807; £405) **Stalls** Centre

Form RPR
132 **1** **Tip Two Win**[18] 6521 2-9-0 98.......................................... AdamKirby 2 105
(Roger Teal) *hld up towards rr: hdwy on inner 1/2-way: rdn and qcknd to ld 2f out: sn edgd rt: clr ent fnl f: kpt on wl* **11/2**[3]
143 **2** *2* **Tigre Du Terre (FR)**[21] 6396 2-9-0 99.......................................... RyanMoore 4 100
(Richard Hannon) *trckd ldrs: pushed along and outpcd over 2f out: rdn wl over 1f out: styd on fnl f* **15/8**[1]
1450 **3** *nk* **Aqabah (USA)**[62] 4906 2-9-0 104.......................................... JamesDoyle 3 99
(Charlie Appleby) *cl up: effrt to chal over 2f out: sn rdn and chsd wnr tl drvn and kpt on same pce fnl f* **7/2**[2]
41 **4** *1 3/4* **Soldier's Minute**[16] 6590 2-9-0 0.......................................... ConnorBeasley 1 95
(Keith Dalgleish) *trckd ldrs: rdn along 2f out: drvn over 1f out: kpt on same pce* **12/1**
254 **5** *3/4* **Zaaki**[23] 6326 2-9-0 101.......................................... StevieDonohoe 6 93
(Mohamed Moubarak) *dwlt and towards rr: hdwy over 2f out: rdn to chse ldrs and edgd lft over 1f out: sn no imp* **11/2**[3]
6415 **6** *4 1/2* **Major Peirson (IRE)**[56] 5109 2-9-0 87.......................................... DougieCostello 8 82
(Jo Hughes) *sn led: pushed along wl over 2f out: sn rdn: hdd 2f out and sn wknd* **33/1**
61 **7** *5* **Zoffalee (FR)**[40] 5680 2-9-0 0.......................................... LukeMorris 5 69
(Tom Dascombe) *t.k.h early: hld up: pushed along 3f out: rdn: green and wandered wl over 1f out: sn outpcd and bhd* **16/1**
6100 **8** *2* **De Bruyne Horse**[13] 6696 2-9-4 100..........................(p) SilvestreDeSousa 7 73
(Richard Hannon) *trckd ldrs: hdwy and cl up over 2f out: rdn and hld whn n.m.r over 1f out: sn wknd and eased* **10/1**

1m 25.58s (-0.72) **Going Correction** 0.0s/f (Good) **8** Ran SP% **113.4**
Speed ratings (Par 103): **104,101,101,99,98 93,87,85**
CSF £15.95 TOTE £5.70: £1.70, £1.10, £1.60; EX 15.80 Trifecta £60.30.
**Owner** Mrs Anne Cowley **Bred** Mrs Anne Cowley **Trained** Great Shefford, Berks

**FOCUS**
Frankel routed two rivals in this race in 2010, three years before it acquired Listed status and the Flying Scotsman name. Run at a decent pace, this looked an up-to-scratch renewal and has been rated around the runner-up. Having ridden in it both James Doyle and Connor Beasley felt the ground was riding "dead", while Luke Morris and Silvestre de Sousa were of the view it was "on the soft side of good". Times suggest it was riding faster than the official description.

## 7113 JAPAN RACING ASSOCIATION SCEPTRE STKS (GROUP 3) (F&M) 7f 6y

**1:50** (1:53) (Class 1) 3-Y-O+
**£34,026** (£12,900; £6,456; £3,216; £1,614; £810) **Stalls** Centre

Form RPR
6223 **1** **Music Box (IRE)**[15] 6642 3-8-12 101.......................................... RyanMoore 6 110
(A P O'Brien, Ire) *hld up in rr: hdwy in centre 3f out: chsd ldrs 2f out: rdn to ld over 1f out: drvn ins fnl f: kpt on wl* **8/1**
11-2 **2** *1* **Eternally**[42] 5597 4-9-2 104.......................................... FrankieDettori 13 109
(John Gosden) *racd towards stands' rail: sn led: rdn along and hdd over 1f out: drvn and edgd lft ins fnl f: kpt on wl towards fin* **6/1**[3]
1163 **3** *1/2* **Tomyris**[42] 5597 3-8-12 104.......................................... AndreaAtzeni 12 106
(Roger Varian) *racd towards stands' rail: trckd ldrs: pushed along 2f out: rdn and hdwy over 1f out: edgd lft and kpt on u.p fnl f* **11/2**[2]
-401 **4** *1 3/4* **Talaayeb**[21] 6401 3-9-1 110.......................................... DaneO'Neill 8 104
(Owen Burrows) *racd centre: hld up in tch: hdwy over 2f out: rdn wl over 1f out: drvn appr fnl f and kpt on same pce* **7/2**[1]
2031 **5** *1 1/4* **On Her Toes (IRE)**[49] 5352 3-8-12 102.......................................... JoeFanning 2 98
(William Haggas) *racd centre: prom: cl up over 2f out: rdn wl over 1f out and ev ch tl drvn and wknd appr fnl f* **11/1**
0321 **6** *1 1/4* **Pirouette**[26] 6254 4-9-2 107..........................(b) RobertWinston 4 96
(Hughie Morrison) *prom towards centre: cl up 1/2-way: rdn along 2f out: grad wknd* **9/1**
5230 **7** *3/4* **Breakable**[6] 6918 6-9-2 97.......................................... DavidAllan 9 94
(Tim Easterby) *racd towards stands' side: towards rr: effrt over 2f out: sn rdn along: kpt on fnl f: n.d* **33/1**
0045 **8** *hd* **Smoulder**[15] 6642 3-8-12 92..........................(h) SilvestreDeSousa 10 92
(A P O'Brien, Ire) *a towards rr* **40/1**
1453 **9** *1* **Classical Times**[26] 6234 3-8-12 96.......................................... JackMitchell 11 89
(Peter Chapple-Hyam) *racd nr stands' side: a towards rr* **20/1**
-002 **10** *3/4* **Drumfad Bay (IRE)**[15] 6642 3-8-12 96.......................................... StevieDonohoe 3 87
(Mrs John Harrington, Ire) *hmpd s: sn trcking ldrs centre: rdn along wl over 2f out: sn drvn and wknd* **20/1**
-130 **11** *10* **Sibilance**[86] 3964 3-8-12 93.......................................... OisinMurphy 5 60
(Ralph Beckett) *midfield: rdn along wl over 2f out: sn outpcd* **25/1**
1111 **12** *1 1/4* **Whatsthemessage (IRE)**[13] 6691 3-8-12 91.......................................... GrahamLee 1 57
(Keith Dalgleish) *racd centre: prom: rdn along over 2f out: sn wknd* **33/1**
2611 **13** *10* **Unforgetable Filly**[89] 3882 3-9-3 109.......................................... JamesDoyle 7 35
(Hugo Palmer) *a in rr* **7/1**

1m 24.72s (-1.58) **Going Correction** 0.0s/f (Good)
**WFA** 3 from 4yo+ 4lb **13** Ran SP% **115.5**
Speed ratings (Par 113): **109,107,107,105,103 102,101,101,100,99 87,86,75**
CSF £48.40 TOTE £7.60: £2.40, £2.20, £2.30; EX 39.60 Trifecta £207.00.
**Owner** M Tabor, Mrs J Magnier & D Smith **Bred** Bernard Cooke **Trained** Cashel, Co Tipperary

**FOCUS**
A good, competitive edition of this Group 3 and it was run in a respectable 1.72sec outside the standard. There was a difference of opinion among the jockeys early on before the whole field congregated centre to stands' side. For the 11th time in the last dozen runnings it went to a 3yo, who made up all bar three of the field this year. The winner improved in line with recent progress.

## 7114 WAINWRIGHTS FLYING CHILDERS STKS (GROUP 2) 5f 3y

**2:25** (2:25) (Class 1) 2-Y-O
**£39,697** (£15,050; £7,532; £3,752; £1,883; £945) **Stalls** Centre

Form RPR
113 **1** **Heartache**[54] 5195 2-8-12 107.......................................... RyanMoore 1 110
(Clive Cox) *racd centre: trckd ldrs: hdwy 2f out: rdn to chal over 1f out: drvn ins fnl f: led last 75yds* **6/4**[2]
0112 **2** *1/2* **Havana Grey**[26] 6249 2-9-1 113.......................................... PJMcDonald 8 111+
(K R Burke) *racd wd towards stands' side: led: rdn along over 1f out: drvn and edgd lft ins fnl f: hdd and no ex last 75yds* **1/1**[1]
211 **3** *4 1/2* **May Girl**[5] 6969 2-8-12 75.......................................... AndreaAtzeni 3 92
(Robert Cowell) *prom centre: cl up 2f out: rdn over 1f out: drvn ent fnl f: kpt on same pce* **10/1**[3]
6451 **4** *1/2* **Pursuing The Dream (IRE)**[31] 6051 2-8-12 100......... DougieCostello 4 90
(Jamie Osborne) *dwlt and in rr: hdwy wl over 1f out: sn rdn and kpt on fnl f* **12/1**
1300 **5** *3* **Roland Rocks (IRE)**[45] 5501 2-9-1 93.......................................... GeraldMosse 9 82
(John Ryan) *in rr: hdwy wl over 1f out: sn rdn: kpt on fnl f* **20/1**
422 **6** *2 1/4* **Midsummer Knight**[6] 6950 2-9-1 0.......................................... SilvestreDeSousa 6 74
(Mick Channon) *chsd ldrs centre: rdn along 2f out: sn drvn and outpcd* **40/1**
0511 **7** *nk* **Spoof**[14] 6651 2-9-1 80..........................(h) CallumShepherd 5 73
(Charles Hills) *t.k.h: chsd ldrs: rdn along over 2f out: sn wknd* **28/1**
1143 **8** *3/4* **Yogi's Girl (IRE)**[13] 6678 2-8-12 90.......................................... StevieDonohoe 7 68
(David Evans) *racd in tch centre: rdn along over 2f out: sn wknd* **25/1**
1040 **9** *3* **Wings Of The Rock (IRE)**[28] 6136 2-8-12 83..........................(h) LukeMorris 2 57
(Scott Dixon) *t.k.h: chsd ldrs centre: rdn along over 2f out: sn wknd* **50/1**

58.73s (-1.77) **Going Correction** 0.0s/f (Good) **9** Ran SP% **123.2**
Speed ratings (Par 107): **114,113,106,105,100 96,96,95,90**
CSF £3.40 TOTE £2.50: £1.10, £1.02, £2.90; EX 4.00 Trifecta £18.60.
**Owner** The Hot To Trot Syndicate - Heartache **Bred** Whitsbury Manor Stud **Trained** Lambourn, Berks

**FOCUS**
The action was up the middle and two really good sprint juveniles pulled well clear. The contest has been rated towards the better end of the race average.

## 7115 WILLIAM HILL MALLARD H'CAP 1m 6f 115y

**3:00** (3:00) (Class 2) (0-110,108) 3-Y-O+**£25,876** (£7,700; £3,848; £1,924) **Stalls** Low

Form RPR
3153 **1** **Time To Study (FR)**[6] 6930 3-8-8 **98**.......................................... PJMcDonald 7 108
(Mark Johnston) *trckd ldr: hdwy to take slt ld 3f out: sn jnd and rdn: drvn ent fnl f: rdr dropped rein last 50yds: hld on gamely towards fin* **11/8**[1]
0222 **2** *hd* **Byron Flyer**[34] 5912 6-8-13 **93**..........................(p[1]) RyanMoore 6 102
(Ian Williams) *trckd ldrs: smooth hdwy over 3f out: sn cl up: chal 2f out: rdn over 1f out: drvn to dispute ld ins fnl f: ev ch tl no ex nr line* **6/1**[2]
-000 **3** *5* **Shrewd**[23] 6329 7-8-9 **96**.......................................... JamieGormley(7) 4 98
(Iain Jardine) *hld up in rr: hdwy 4f out: chsd ldrs over 2f out: rdn wl over 1f out: kpt on same pce fnl f* **9/1**
-300 **4** *1 1/4* **Seamour (IRE)**[20] 6447 6-9-7 **101**..........................(p) AdamKirby 2 101
(Brian Ellison) *trckd ldrs on inner: pushed along 3f out: rdn and hdwy to chse ldng pair wl over 1f out: sn drvn and kpt on same pce* **13/2**[3]
1630 **5** *3* **Elidor**[20] 6447 7-10-0 **108**.......................................... SilvestreDeSousa 3 104
(Mick Channon) *hld up in rr: hdwy wl over 2f out: sn rdn along: plugged on fnl f: n.d* **20/1**
0-04 **6** *3 3/4* **Penglai Pavilion (USA)**[23] 6329 7-9-6 **100**..........................(p) JamesDoyle 5 92
(Charlie Appleby) *led: pushed along and qcknd 4f out: rdn and hdd narrowly 3f out: drvn to chse ldng pair wl over 1f out: grad wknd* **6/1**[2]
3340 **7** *1* **Lord George (IRE)**[54] 5198 4-9-0 **97**.......................................... GeorgeWood(3) 1 87
(James Fanshawe) *trckd ldr on inner: pushed along over 4f out: rdn wl over 3f out: sn wknd* **15/2**

3m 10.18s (2.78) **Going Correction** +0.30s/f (Good)
**WFA** 3 from 4yo+ 10lb **7** Ran SP% **110.5**
Speed ratings (Par 109): **104,103,101,100,98 96,96**
CSF £9.22 TOTE £2.10: £1.40, £2.40; EX 8.40 Trifecta £56.50.
**Owner** Abdulla Al Mansoori **Bred** E A R L Haras Du Quesnay **Trained** Middleham Moor, N Yorks

**FOCUS**
A quality staying handicap and sound form, although the field was smaller than this race usually attracts. There was a terrific finish as two pulled clear.

## 7116 DONCASTER CUP STKS (GROUP 2) (BRITISH CHAMPIONS SERIES) 2m 1f 197y

**3:35** (3:35) (Class 1) 3-Y-O+
**£56,710** (£21,500; £10,760; £5,360; £2,690; £1,350) **Stalls** Low

Form RPR
6232 **1** **Desert Skyline (IRE)**[26] 6250 3-8-5 110..........................(p) SilvestreDeSousa 6 115
(David Elsworth) *hld up in rr: stdy hdwy over 3f out: trckd ldrs 2f out: rdn to chal ent fnl f: led last 120yds: kpt on strly* **2/1**[1]
/120 **2** *1 1/2* **Thomas Hobson**[21] 6400 7-9-3 110.......................................... RyanMoore 5 113
(W P Mullins, Ire) *hld up towards rr: smooth hdwy over 3f out: cl up 2f out: rdn to ld appr fnl f: sn drvn: hdd last 120yds: kpt on* **4/1**[2]
3604 **3** *hd* **Sheikhzayedroad**[21] 6400 8-9-3 114..........................(h) MartinHarley 7 112
(David Simcock) *trckd ldrs: hdwy over 3f out: led 2f out and sn rdn: hdd appr fnl f: sn drvn and kpt on* **5/1**[3]
0036 **4** *1/2* **Clever Cookie**[20] 6447 9-9-3 106..........................(p) GrahamLee 3 111
(Peter Niven) *hld up in tch: hdwy 4f out: trckd ldrs 3f out: effrt over 2f out: rdn and ev ch over 1f out: drvn and kpt on fnl f* **33/1**
3505 **5** *8* **High Jinx (IRE)**[21] 6400 9-9-3 109.......................................... DavidAllan 8 102
(Tim Easterby) *rdn along s: sn cl up and led after 1f: pushed along over 4f out: rdn along over 3f out: sn hdd and drvn: lost pl over 2f out: plugged on u.p fnl f* **20/1**
121 **6** *1 3/4* **Montaly**[21] 6400 6-9-6 113.......................................... OisinMurphy 9 103
(Andrew Balding) *hld up towards rr: hdwy over 3f out: rdn along 2f out: sn drvn and n.d* **15/2**
-345 **7** *6* **She Is No Lady**[45] 5503 5-9-0 110.......................................... JamesDoyle 1 91
(Ralph Beckett) *trckd ldrs: pushed along on inner 4f out: rdn over 3f out: sn drvn and wknd* **7/1**
-566 **8** *20* **Pallasator**[26] 6250 8-9-3 109..........................(p[1]) RosieJessop 4 72
(Sir Mark Prescott Bt) *trckd ldrs: hdwy and cl up 6f out: led over 3f out: rdn along and hdd 2f out: sn drvn and wknd* **16/1**

3541 **9** *12* **Fun Mac (GER)**[54] 5198 6-9-3 103..............................(bt) AdamKirby 2 58
(Hughie Morrison) *led 1f: cl up: rdn along over 4f out: sn wknd* **22/1**

3m 51.88s (-3.12) **Going Correction** +0.30s/f (Good)
**WFA** 3 from 5yo+ 12lb **9** Ran SP% **112.2**
Speed ratings (Par 115): **118,117,117,117,113 112,110,101,95**
CSF £9.16 TOTE £2.60: £1.20, £1.70, £1.70; EX 10.60 Trifecta £35.50.
**Owner** C Benham/ D Whitford/ L Quinn/ K Quinn **Bred** Tinnakill Bloodstock & Cannings **Trained** Newmarket, Suffolk

**FOCUS**
This race fell apart to a point to only seriously concern the first four, who came from off the pace, but still good staying form from them and a small personal best from the winner. They stayed far side in the straight.

## 7117 GARY REID MEMORIAL BRITISH STALLION STUDS EBF MAIDEN STKS (PLUS 10 RACE) 1m (S)
**4:05** (4:07) (Class 3) 2-Y-O **£9,703** (£2,887; £1,443; £721) **Stalls** Centre

Form RPR
343 **1** **Blue Laureate**[18] 6505 2-9-0 78.............................. AdamKirby 8 87+
(Clive Cox) *trckd ldr: led 1/2-way: rdn clr over 1f out: kpt on strly* **16/1**
6 **2** *4 ½* **Sha La La La Lee**[21] 6403 2-9-0 0.............................. MartinHarley 1 77
(Tom Dascombe) *led: hdd 1/2-way: rdn along wl over 1f out: drvn and kpt on fnl f: no ch w wnr* **10/1**
**3** *¾* **Ghaiyyath (IRE)** 2-9-0 0.............................. JamesDoyle 7 75+
(Charlie Appleby) *trckd ldrs: pushed along over 2f out: rdn wl over 1f out: kpt on same pce* **6/5**[1]
**4** *1 ¼* **Tiffin Top** 2-9-0 0.............................. FrankieDettori 11 72+
(John Gosden) *trckd ldrs: pushed along 2f out: rdn and green over 1f out: kpt on same pce* **7/1**[3]
**5** *¾* **Ace Ventura** 2-9-0 0.............................. AndreaAtzeni 10 71+
(Roger Varian) *dwlt and hld up in rr: green and pushed along over 2f out: hdwy wl over 1f out: kpt on fnl f* **13/2**[2]
4 **6** *½* **Sherzy Boy**[10] 6777 2-9-0 0.............................. RyanMoore 5 70
(Richard Hannon) *trckd ldrs: effrt over 2f out: sn rdn along and kpt on same pce* **15/2**
**7** *1 ½* **Quantatmental (IRE)** 2-9-0 0.............................. PJMcDonald 9 66
(Tom Dascombe) *dwlt: t.k.h in rr: hdwy over 2f out: green and sn rdn along: n.d* **66/1**
**8** *2* **Thunderhooves** 2-9-0 0.............................. GeraldMosse 3 61
(John Ryan) *towards rr: hdwy and in tch over 2f out: sn rdn and wknd* **40/1**
**9** *1* **Military Law** 2-9-0 0.............................. OisinMurphy 6 59
(John Gosden) *dwlt and towards rr: hdwy and in tch 1/2-way: rdn along and green over 2f out: sn wknd* **8/1**
**10** *¾* **Dagueneau (IRE)** 2-9-0 0.............................. LukeMorris 2 57
(Ed Dunlop) *towards rr: hdwy and in tch over 3f out: sn rdn along and wknd* **80/1**

1m 41.16s (1.86) **Going Correction** 0.0s/f (Good) **10** Ran SP% **114.3**
Speed ratings (Par 99): **90,85,84,83,82 82,80,78,77,77**
CSF £160.99 TOTE £13.80: £3.30, £2.40, £1.10; EX 122.60 Trifecta £1088.30.
**Owner** Cavendish Bloodstock Racing & Partner **Bred** Cavendish Bloodstock **Trained** Lambourn, Berks

**FOCUS**
Leger hopeful The Anvil was third in this last year. A decent maiden on paper, but it wasn't run at a great gallop and it proved difficult to make up ground. Only three of these had run before, but two of them finished 1-2. The winner was showing much improved form.

## 7118 LAKESIDE VILLAGE OUTLET SHOPPER H'CAP 6f 111y
**4:35** (4:35) (Class 2) (0-105,97) 3-Y-O+ **£12,938** (£3,850; £1,924; £962) **Stalls** Centre

Form RPR
0300 **1** **Amazour (IRE)**[76] 4353 5-9-7 **97**..............................(p[1]) JamesDoyle 4 104
(Ismail Mohammed) *dwlt and towards rr: swtchd lft and hdwy over 2f out: rdn to chal over 1f out: drvn to ld ins fnl f: jst hld on* **9/2**[2]
0001 **2** *shd* **Muntadab (IRE)**[7] 6879 5-9-6 **96** 6ex.............................. TonyHamilton 1 102
(Roger Fell) *led: rdn wl over 1f out: drvn and hdd ins fnl f: kpt on: jst hld* **3/1**[1]
650 **3** *½* **Dougan**[25] 6275 5-9-0 **90**.............................. AdamKirby 5 95
(David Evans) *trckd ldrs: hdwy wl over 1f out: rdn to chal ent fnl f: sn drvn and ev ch tl nt qckn nr fin* **9/2**[2]
0210 **4** *¾* **Northgate Lad (IRE)**[22] 6355 5-8-11 **92**.............................. BenRobinson(5) 9 95
(Brian Ellison) *cl up: rdn wl over 1f out: ev ch: drvn ent fnl f: kpt on same pce* **8/1**
0152 **5** *2 ¼* **Aventinus (IRE)**[31] 6026 3-8-9 **89**.............................. JackMitchell 3 84
(Hugo Palmer) *trckd ldrs: hdwy and cl up 2f out: rdn over 1f out: ev ch: drvn ent fnl f: sn wknd* **9/2**[2]
-003 **6** *1* **Medici Banchiere**[63] 4868 3-8-10 **90**.............................. PJMcDonald 8 82
(K R Burke) *cl up: rdn along 2f out: grad wknd* **11/2**[3]
6040 **7** *11* **Tropics (USA)**[34] 5911 9-9-7 **97**.............................. RobertWinston 6 60
(Dean Ivory) *a in rr* **16/1**

1m 18.23s (-1.67) **Going Correction** 0.0s/f (Good)
**WFA** 3 from 4yo+ 4lb **7** Ran SP% **111.9**
Speed ratings (Par 109): **109,108,108,107,104 103,91**
CSF £17.57 CT £62.11 TOTE £4.80: £2.60, £2.10; EX 14.60 Trifecta £43.00.
**Owner** Sheikh Juma Dalmook Al Maktoum **Bred** J F Tuthill **Trained** Newmarket, Suffolk

**FOCUS**
They raced up the middle. Not as many runners as you might expect for this sort of race, with the winner back to form and the runner-up close to his best.

## 7119 COOPERS MARQUEES CLASSIFIED STKS 1m 2f 43y
**5:10** (5:11) (Class 3) 3-Y-O+
**£9,337** (£2,796; £1,398; £699; £349; £175) **Stalls** Low

Form RPR
0041 **1** **Pivoine (IRE)**[16] 6579 3-8-12 83..............................(v) RyanMoore 7 91+
(Sir Michael Stoute) *trckd ldrs: hdwy 3f out: sn chsng ldr: cl up on inner 2f out: rdn to ld over 1f out: kpt on* **9/4**[1]
1 **2** *½* **Lawless Secret**[39] 5721 3-8-9 85..............................(h) OisinMurphy 9 87+
(Simon Crisford) *hld up: hdwy over 2f out: rdn wl over 1f out: styd on wl fnl f* **11/4**[2]
1163 **3** *3 ¼* **Three Duchesses**[19] 6477 3-8-2 85.............................. TristanPrice(7) 3 80
(Michael Bell) *hld up in rr: gd hdwy on outer over 3f out: led wl over 2f out: rdn 2f out: hdd over 1f out: one pce fnl f* **9/1**
0025 **4** *1 ¾* **Zealous (IRE)**[44] 5540 4-9-4 72.............................. JoeFanning 6 79+
(Sally Haynes) *hld up in rr: hdwy wl over 2f out: n.m.r and swtchd lft to inner and rdn wl over 1f out: kpt on fnl f: n.d* **20/1**
12-0 **5** *¾* **Rebel Cause (IRE)**[36] 5849 4-9-4 81.............................. StevieDonohoe 5 77
(Richard Spencer) *trckd ldrs: pushed along over 3f out: rdn wl over 2f out: sn one pce* **20/1**
1144 **6** *shd* **Helovaplan (IRE)**[32] 6001 3-8-12 82.............................. ConnorBeasley 2 78
(Bryan Smart) *hld up in tch: effrt and n.m.r over 2f out: sn swtchd rt to outer and rdn: no imp* **16/1**
1112 **7** *13* **Swilly Sunset**[13] 6701 4-9-4 85.............................. SilvestreDeSousa 8 51+
(Anthony Carson) *trckd ldr: pushed along 3f out: rdn over 2f out: sn btn and eased* **3/1**[3]
2110 **8** *25* **Turning Gold**[56] 5115 3-8-12 83..............................(b) LukeMorris 1
(Sir Mark Prescott Bt) *led: rdn along over 3f out: sn hdd & wknd* **14/1**

2m 10.72s (1.32) **Going Correction** +0.30s/f (Good)
**WFA** 3 from 4yo 6lb **8** Ran SP% **114.5**
Speed ratings (Par 107): **106,105,103,101,101 100,90,70**
CSF £8.62 TOTE £3.00: £1.40, £1.40, £2.50; EX 10.60 Trifecta £80.10.
**Owner** Ballymacoll Stud **Bred** Ballymacoll Stud Farm Ltd **Trained** Newmarket, Suffolk
■ Stewards' Enquiry : Tristan Price 2 day ban: careless riding as he had allowed his mount to drift left away from the whip (29 Sep/1 Oct)

**FOCUS**
A useful classified race. The first two are progressive and the fourth looks the key to the form.
T/Jkpt: Not Won. T/Plt: £6.50 to a £1 stake. Pool: £173,411.48 - 19,345,39 winning units T/Qpdt: £2.50 to a £1 stake. Pool: £13,813.33 - 4,060,94 winning units **Joe Rowntree**

# 6859 SALISBURY (R-H)
Friday, September 15

**OFFICIAL GOING: Soft (good to soft in places including whole loop section) changing to soft after race 1 (4:25)**
Wind: light breeze half against Weather: sunny periods

## 7120 BOOKER WHOLESALE NOVICE MEDIAN AUCTION STKS 1m
**4:25** (4:30) (Class 5) 2-Y-O **£4,043** (£1,203; £601; £300) **Stalls** Low

Form RPR
2 **1** **Alternative Fact**[28] 6140 2-9-2 0.............................. KieranShoemark 2 90+
(Ed Dunlop) *mde all: rdn clr 2f out: kpt on strly* **4/1**[3]
5 **2** *6* **Deyaarna (USA)**[21] 6388 2-9-2 0.............................. EdwardGreatrex 4 77
(Saeed bin Suroor) *trckd ldng pair: rdn over 2f out: chsd wnr over 1f out: kpt on but nvr any threat* **7/4**[1]
0 **3** *3* **Westbrook Bertie**[14] 6653 2-9-2 0.............................. GeorgeDowning 12 70
(Mick Channon) *mid-div: rdn and hdwy over 2f out: r.o wl fnl f: nvr any threat to front pair but snatched 3rd fnl stride* **33/1**
**4** *nse* **Rashdan (FR)** 2-9-2 0.............................. JosephineGordon 6 70+
(Hugo Palmer) *trckd wnr: rdn over 2f out: sn outpcd by wnr: no ex ins fnl f: lost 3rd fnl stride* **7/2**[2]
**5** *3 ½* **Jackfinbar (FR)** 2-9-2 0.............................. TomQueally 11 63
(Harry Dunlop) *s.i.s: sn hing rt: racd green towards rr: rdn and hdwy over 2f out: styd on same pce fr over 1f out* **33/1**
006 **6** *5* **Mafeking**[52] 5246 2-8-11 0.............................. FinleyMarsh(5) 7 52
(Harry Dunlop) *in tch: rdn over 3f out: sn one pce* **66/1**
**7** *nk* **Construct** 2-9-2 0.............................. PatDobbs 8 51
(Ralph Beckett) *mid-div: hdwy over 3f out: rdn over 2f out: nvr threatened ldrs: wknd fnl f* **6/1**
**8** *hd* **Munstead Gold** 2-8-11 0.............................. JoshuaBryan(5) 13 50
(Andrew Balding) *hld up towards rr: styd on steadily fnl 2f but nvr any danger* **33/1**
**9** *2 ½* **French Kiss (IRE)** 2-8-13 0.............................. CharlieBennett(3) 10 45
(Hughie Morrison) *towards rr: sme late prog: nvr a factor* **33/1**
03 **10** *3 ¼* **Tulane (IRE)**[38] 5749 2-9-2 0.............................. TimmyMurphy 14 38
(Richard Phillips) *towards rr of midfield: rdn over 2f out: hung rt and wknd over 1f out* **40/1**
**11** *½* **Gendarme (IRE)** 2-9-2 0.............................. TomMarquand 15 37
(Richard Hannon) *chsd ldrs: sn pushed along: grad lost pl fr 3f out* **16/1**
**12** *4 ½* **Danish Dancer (IRE)** 2-9-2 0..............................(b[1]) LiamKeniry 9 27
(Ed Walker) *mid-div: rdn over 3f out: wknd 2f out* **50/1**
**13** *shd* **Sunny Lane (IRE)** 2-8-11 0.............................. LiamJones 1 22
(J S Moore) *trckd ldrs: rdn and edgd lft wl over 2f out: sn wknd* **66/1**
**14** *26* **Sky Rocket** 2-8-13 0.............................. HollieDoyle(3) 3
(Sylvester Kirk) *s.i.s: racd green: a in rr: struggling 1/2-way: sn lost tch* **33/1**

1m 48.49s (4.99) **Going Correction** +0.60s/f (Yiel) **14** Ran SP% **120.8**
Speed ratings (Par 95): **99,93,90,89,86 81,81,80,78,75 74,70,70,44**
CSF £10.57 TOTE £3.90: £1.70, £1.10, £10.00; EX 11.50 Trifecta £205.10.
**Owner** The Alternative Lot **Bred** Rabbah Bloodstock Limited **Trained** Newmarket, Suffolk

**FOCUS**
The going was officially described as soft, good to soft in places on the straight course and good to soft on the loop. It was a bright and sunny afternoon. A fair maiden and an impressive all-the-way winner.

## 7121 HARRIET HODGKINSON 21ST BIRTHDAY NURSERY H'CAP 6f 213y
**5:00** (5:00) (Class 5) (0-75,74) 2-Y-O **£3,396** (£1,010; £505; £252) **Stalls** Centre

Form RPR
036 **1** **Ojala (IRE)**[15] 6636 2-8-12 **70**.............................. PaddyBradley(5) 7 76
(Simon Dow) *mde all: drifted lft whn rdn ent fnl f: kpt on wl to assert fnl 120yds* **8/1**
0260 **2** *1 ¼* **Zalshah**[14] 6651 2-9-4 **71**.............................. TomMarquand 6 74
(Richard Hannon) *hld up: smooth hdwy 2f out: rdn to chal ent fnl f: kpt on but no ex towards fin* **10/1**
1630 **3** *2 ½* **Alifax**[31] 6050 2-9-6 **73**.............................. TimmyMurphy 1 70
(Jamie Osborne) *trckd ldrs: chal 3f out rdn over 1f out: no ex ins fnl f* **4/1**[3]
6632 **4** *4* **Dandiesque (IRE)**[8] 6860 2-8-10 **66**..............................(p[1]) HollieDoyle(3) 3 53
(Richard Hannon) *hmpd s: last pair but wl in tch: pushed along over 3f out: rdn over 2f out: nt pce to chal* **7/2**[2]
4315 **5** *1 ¾* **Ragstone View (IRE)**[30] 6065 2-9-2 **74**.............................. FinleyMarsh(5) 4 57
(Richard Hughes) *hmpd s: trckd ldrs: rdn over 2f out: sn one pce* **4/1**[3]
4112 **6** *10* **Go Now Go Now (IRE)**[11] 6762 2-9-5 **72**.............................. KieranShoemark 2 42+
(Mark Johnston) *stmbld bdly leaving stalls: trckd wnr tl rdn 3f out: sn looking hld: wknd ent fnl f* **11/4**[1]

1m 34.58s (5.98) **Going Correction** +0.60s/f (Yiel) **6** Ran SP% **109.1**
Speed ratings (Par 95): **89,87,84,80,78 66**
CSF £73.09 TOTE £9.90: £4.90, £4.80; EX 66.90 Trifecta £505.20.
**Owner** Robert Moss **Bred** Ballyphilip Stud **Trained** Ashtead, Surrey

**FOCUS**
An unsatisfactory nursery, in which the favourite stumbled at the start and interfered with two others. The improving winner was never headed and made a successful handicap debut.

## 7122 ROA/RACING POST OWNERS JACKPOT H'CAP 6f
**5:30** (5:34) (Class 6) (0-65,66) 3-Y-O **£3,234** (£962; £481; £240) **Stalls** Low

Form RPR

0244 **1** **Twilight Spirit**[14] 6656 3-8-13 **57**.............................(b[1]) TomMarquand 12 66
(Tony Carroll) *mid-div: pushed along and hdwy fr 3f out: drvn for str chal ent fnl f: disp ld fnl 120yds: won on nod* **6/1**[3]

5504 **2** *nse* **Vixen (IRE)**[29] 6106 3-8-9 **53**.................................(h) JosephineGordon 9 62
(Eve Johnson Houghton) *trckd ldrs: tk narrow advantage 3f out: sn rdn: edgd sltly rt over 1f out: kpt on whn jnd fnl 120yds: lost on nod* **9/2**[2]

0246 **3** *3* **Violet's Lads (IRE)**[14] 6656 3-8-10 **61**.............. RossaRyan(7) 16 61
(Brett Johnson) *hld up towards rr: stmbld bdly wl over 3f out: hdwy wl over 2f out: rdn over 1f out: drifted sltly rt but kpt on ins fnl f: snatched 3rd fnl stride* **25/1**

3514 **4** *nk* **Wotadoll**[37] 5812 3-8-12 **56**................................................ PatCosgrave 1 55
(Dean Ivory) *mid-div: hdwy over 3f out: nt clr run briefly over 2f out: sn rdn: ev ch fr wl over 1f out tl no ex fnl 100yds: lost 3rd fnl stride* **8/1**

254 **5** *1 ¾* **Charleston Belle**[34] 5937 3-9-7 **65**...................................... PatDobbs 4 59
(Giles Bravery) *s.i.s: towards rr: hdwy fr 2f out: rdn over 1f out: kpt on ins fnl f but nt pce to get involved* **16/1**

5-55 **6** *2 ¾* **Delahay**[132] 2393 3-8-6 **53**................................................ HollieDoyle(3) 8 38
(Michael Blanshard) *mid-div: rdn over 2f out: kpt on same pce fnl f* **33/1**

0621 **7** *nk* **Deciding Vote**[36] 5855 3-9-5 **63**........................................ HarryBentley 10 48
(Chris Wall) *mid-divsion: hdwy over 2f out: rdn to chse ldrs wl over 1f out: nt quite pce to chal: wknd ins fnl f* **4/1**[1]

0525 **8** *3 ¼* **Morello (IRE)**[9] 6813 3-8-10 **54**................................ KieranShoemark 11 29
(Henry Candy) *hld up towards rr: rdn 2f out: kpt on fnl f: n.d* **16/1**

6-60 **9** *¾* **Dontforgettocall**[161] 1605 3-9-0 **58**.........................(b[1]) EdwardGreatrex 7 31
(Joseph Tuite) *prom: led briefly 3f out: sn rdn w ev ch: wknd ent fnl f* **25/1**

6404 **10** *1 ¼* **Rebel Heart**[11] 6748 3-8-5 **52**.......................................... CharlieBennett(3) 3 21
(Bill Turner) *pressed ldr: rdn and ev ch 2f out: wknd jst over 1f out* **10/1**

5006 **11** *1* **Grecian Divine (IRE)**[112] 3035 3-9-8 **66**........................... LiamJones 14 32
(Joseph Tuite) *towards rr: swtchd lft and rdn 2f out: nvr threatened to get on terms* **50/1**

2051 **12** *1* **Incentive**[31] 6028 3-9-7 **65**.................................................(p) LiamKeniry 2 28
(Stuart Kittow) *in tch tl bdly hmpd wl over 2f out: n.d after* **8/1**

0000 **13** *2 ½* **Eternal Dream**[8] 6846 3-8-11 **55**.......................................... TomQueally 6 10
(William Knight) *prom tl over 3f out: sn wknd* **33/1**

5320 **14** *shd* **Nuzha**[72] 4500 3-9-2 **65**.................................................(p) RhiainIngram(5) 5 20
(Karen George) *led tl 3f out: sn rdn: wkng whn hmpd over 1f out* **33/1**

3004 **15** *1 ¾* **Gala Celebration (IRE)**[11] 6753 3-9-1 **64**...........(v[1]) GeorgeBuckell(5) 13 14
(John Gallagher) *v.s.a: a in rr* **14/1**

1m 17.83s (3.03) **Going Correction** +0.60s/f (Yiel) **15 Ran SP% 120.7**
Speed ratings (Par 99): **103,102,98,98,96 92,92,87,86,85 83,82,79,79,76**
CSF £30.55 CT £657.58 TOTE £7.50: £4.10, £2.40, £7.70; EX 40.50 Trifecta £809.30.
**Owner** Godfrey Wilson **Bred** Mrs C R D Wilson **Trained** Cropthorne, Worcs

**FOCUS**
A moderate 3yo sprint handicap. Three of the runners were wearing first-time headgear. The first two home fought out a good finish and pulled clear, with the winner achieving a minor personal best.

## 7123 BRITISH STALLION STUDS EBF FILLIES' NURSERY H'CAP 6f
**6:05** (6:07) (Class 3) (0-90,83) 2-Y-O **£9,056** (£2,695; £1,346; £673) **Stalls** Low

Form RPR

0304 **1** **Daddies Girl (IRE)**[21] 6395 2-8-13 **75**.............................. SteveDrowne 6 83
(Rod Millman) *a.p: rdn over 2f out: led jst over 1f out: kpt on wl and in command fnl f* **5/1**

1220 **2** *2 ½* **Validator**[28] 6136 2-9-7 **83**............................................. PatCosgrave 8 84
(William Haggas) *racd apart fr main gp clsr to stands' side rails tl jnd 3f out: prom: led over 3f out: rdn and hdd jst over 1f out: no ex fnl f* **11/4**[1]

3123 **3** *¾* **Travelcard (USA)**[6] 6939 2-9-2 **78**............................. KieranShoemark 4 76
(Mark Johnston) *chsd ldrs: rdn over 2f out: wnt 3rd over 1f out: kpt on same pce fnl f* **7/2**[2]

4100 **4** *¾* **Armum (IRE)**[10] 6778 2-9-5 **81**.......................................(t[1]) AntonioFresu 2 77
(Ed Dunlop) *awkwardly away: last pair: rdn over 2f out: no imp tl kpt on into 4th ins fnl f: clsng on ldrs at fin* **20/1**

3350 **5** *1 ¼* **Glaceon (IRE)**[55] 5150 2-9-1 **77**............................................ SeanLevey 7 69
(Richard Hannon) *trckd ldrs: rdn over 2f out: kpt on same pce fnl f* **6/1**

244 **6** *hd* **Indicia**[32] 6010 2-9-2 **78**.......................................................... PatDobbs 1 70
(Charles Hills) *last pair: rdn over 2f out: kpt on ins fnl f but nt pce to get involved* **9/2**[3]

3420 **7** *8* **Miss Mo Brown Bear (IRE)**[30] 6057 2-8-7 **69**..........(p) TomMarquand 5 37
(Richard Hannon) *led tl over 3f out: rdn over 2f out: wknd ent fnl f* **8/1**

1m 18.5s (3.70) **Going Correction** +0.60s/f (Yiel) **7 Ran SP% 113.9**
Speed ratings (Par 96): **99,95,94,93,92 91,81**
CSF £18.99 CT £53.54 TOTE £7.00: £3.20, £1.70; EX 21.90 Trifecta £96.30.
**Owner** Daddies Girl Partnership **Bred** William Blake **Trained** Kentisbeare, Devon
■ Falcon's Vision was withdrawn. Price at time of withdrawal 9/2. Rule 4 applies to bets struck at board prices prior to withdrawal but not to SP bets - deduction 15p in the pound. New market formed

**FOCUS**
An informative fillies' nursery with the favourite returning to form in a handicap after disappointing in Listed company last time.

## 7124 BATHWICK TYRES "PERSIAN PUNCH" CONDITIONS STKS 1m 6f 44y
**6:35** (6:36) (Class 2) 3-Y-O+

**£12,450** (£3,728; £1,864; £932; £466; £234) **Stalls** Far side

Form RPR

1324 **1** **On To Victory**[20] 6445 3-8-10 103.................................... TomMarquand 1 107+
(Eve Johnson Houghton) *trckd clr ldr: clsd on ldr over 5f out: led over 1f out: styd on wl: rdn out* **8/11**[1]

5-60 **2** *2 ½* **Battersea**[20] 6447 6-9-5 103.............................................. HarryBentley 4 104
(Roger Varian) *trckd ldr in chsng gp: nt clr run fr 3f out: rdn over 2f out: swtchd rt over 1f out: sn chsng wnr: styd on but a being hld* **3/1**[2]

4003 **3** *3 ¼* **Lustrous Light (IRE)**[63] 4863 4-9-5 97................................. PatDobbs 5 100
(Ralph Beckett) *hld up in chsng gp: rdn 2f out: styd on but nt pce to get on terms: wnt 3rd cl home* **12/1**

**4** *hd* **Top Ville Ben (IRE)**[141] 5-9-5 0..................................... TimmyMurphy 2 100
(Philip Kirby) *racd keenly: led: sn clr: rdn and hdd over 1f out: no ex ins fnl f: lost 3rd cl home* **40/1**

2000 **5** *2 ¼* **Prince Of Arran**[21] 6400 4-9-5 106...................................... TomQueally 7 97
(Charlie Fellowes) *trckd ldrs: rdn wl over 1f out: styd on but nt pce to get on terms* **6/1**[3]

**6** *48* **Lady Buttons**[139] 7-9-0 0..................................................... JimmyQuinn 6 29
(Philip Kirby) *trckd ldrs: rdn 3f out: wknd 2f out: eased ins fnl f* **33/1**

3m 17.51s (10.11) **Going Correction** +0.60s/f (Yiel)
**WFA** 3 from 4yo+ 9lb **6 Ran SP% 110.3**
Speed ratings (Par 109): **95,93,91,91,90 62**
CSF £2.98 TOTE £1.60: £1.50, £1.40; EX 3.30 Trifecta £9.50.
**Owner** HP Racing On To Victory **Bred** The Aston House Stud **Trained** Blewbury, Oxon

**FOCUS**
A couple of key non-runners and a straightforward success for the ultra-consistent winner, who justified odds-on favouritism and still looks on the upgrade.

## 7125 BRITISH EBF MERCEDES-BENZ OF SALISBURY MAIDEN STKS 1m 1f 201y
**7:05** (7:06) (Class 5) 3-Y-O **£4,204** (£1,251; £625; £312) **Stalls** Low

Form RPR

3520 **1** **Italian Heiress**[34] 5915 3-8-11 81.................................. HectorCrouch(3) 4 85
(Clive Cox) *trckd ldr: led over 2f out: rdn whn strly pressed over 1f out: kpt on wl to assert clsng stages* **3/1**[2]

52- **2** *¾* **Ajman King (IRE)**[338] 7283 3-9-5 0..................................... HarryBentley 1 88+
(Roger Varian) *s.i.s: last pair but in tch: hdwy over 2f out: rdn for str chal over 1f out: kpt on w ev ch tl no ex clsng stages* **8/11**[1]

03 **3** *1 ½* **Tranquil Star (IRE)**[126] 2564 3-9-0 0.................................. TomQueally 6 80
(Jeremy Noseda) *in tch: hdwy over 2f out: sn rdn: chsd ldng pair over 1f out: kpt on ins fnl f* **11/2**[3]

0-54 **4** *10* **Clemento (IRE)**[98] 3533 3-9-5 73.............................. KieranShoemark 5 65
(Roger Charlton) *hld up but in tch: rdn 3f out: wnt 4th ins fnl f but nvr gng pce to threaten ldrs* **14/1**

00 **5** *3 ½* **Crystal Sunstone**[15] 6633 3-9-5 0...................................... CharlesBishop 7 58
(Eve Johnson Houghton) *trckd ldr: rdn and ev ch briefly jst over 2f out: wknd ent fnl f* **50/1**

4 **6** *8* **Eastern (IRE)**[15] 6614 3-9-0 0................................................ LiamKeniry 2 37
(Andrew Balding) *led: rdn and hdd over 2f out: wknd over 1f out* **14/1**

2m 14.95s (5.05) **Going Correction** +0.60s/f (Yiel) **6 Ran SP% 113.6**
Speed ratings (Par 101): **103,102,101,93,90 84**
CSF £5.67 TOTE £3.60: £2.10, £1.10; EX 6.70 Trifecta £18.50.
**Owner** Cheveley Park Stud **Bred** Cheveley Park Stud Ltd **Trained** Lambourn, Berks

**FOCUS**
A fair maiden and the first three pulled nicely clear of a 73-rated rival.
T/Plt: £108.90 to a £1 stake. Pool: £56,494.65 - 378.46 winning units T/Qpdt: £7.10 to a £1 stake. Pool: £10,872.76 - 1119.50 winning units **Tim Mitchell**

# 6695 SANDOWN (R-H)
Friday, September 15

**OFFICIAL GOING: Good (good to firm in places back straight; rnd 7.3; spr 6.7)**
Wind: Moderate, half against Weather: Fine but cloudy

## 7126 WALL STREET JOURNAL EBF MAIDEN STKS 5f 10y
**1:30** (1:32) (Class 5) 2-Y-O **£3,881** (£1,155; £577; £288) **Stalls** Low

Form RPR

522 **1** **Swing Out Sister (IRE)**[27] 6178 2-9-0 74...................... SamHitchcott 8 76
(Clive Cox) *chsd ldng trio: clsd on outer to ld wl over 1f out: sn drvn: hld on wl fnl f* **4/1**[3]

54 **2** *1* **Wafeer (IRE)**[50] 5314 2-9-5 0........................................... SeanLevey 13 77
(Richard Hannon) *nt that wl away fr wd draw: sn in tch in midfield: rdn and prog fr 2f out: styd on fnl f: nvr quite able to chal but tk 2nd last stride* **5/2**[1]

0222 **3** *nse* **Time For Wine (IRE)**[22] 6338 2-8-11 72......................... DavidEgan(3) 4 72
(David Evans) *trckd ldng pair: rdn to chse wnr over 1f out: kpt on but a hld fnl f: lost 2nd last stride* **3/1**[2]

60 **4** *½* **By Royal Approval (IRE)**[20] 6432 2-8-12 0............ GabrieleMalune(7) 2 75
(Michael Appleby) *hld up in 8th and off the pce: sme prog and reminder over 1f out: styd on and reminder ins fnl f: tk 4th nr fin: likely to do bttr* **50/1**

6 **5** *1 ¼* **Section Onesixsix (IRE)**[12] 6719 2-9-0 0......................... CharlesBishop 7 66
(Mick Channon) *chsd ldrs: rdn to cl fr 2f out: kpt on same pce fnl f and nvr able to chal* **33/1**

4503 **6** *3 ¼* **Gaelic Spirit (IRE)**[13] 6682 2-9-0 70........................... EdwardGreatrex 1 54
(Joseph Tuite) *led against rail to wl over 1f out: wknd fnl f* **10/1**

0603 **7** *nse* **Mother Of Dragons (IRE)**[12] 6719 2-9-0 77................(bt[1]) FranBerry 12 54
(Joseph Tuite) *hld up off the pce in 9th: shkn up 2f out: nvr on terms but kpt on fnl f: nt disgracd* **16/1**

**8** *1* **Mighty Mac (IRE)** 2-9-5 0..................................................... PatDobbs 5 55
(Ralph Beckett) *green preliminaries: sn wl off the pce in 10th: shkn up and prog against rail 2f out: nvr rchd ldrs and no hdwy fnl f: nt disgracd* **10/1**

00 **9** *2 ¼* **Hold Your Breath**[20] 6417 2-9-0 0................................. SteveDrowne 10 42
(Tony Carroll) *hld up and sn virtually t.o in 11th: pushed along and kpt on fr 2f out: possible improver* **66/1**

**10** *3 ¾* **Rose Of Shiraz** 2-9-0 0.................................................... KieranO'Neill 6 29
(J S Moore) *nvr beyond midfield and urged along bef 1/2-way: wl btn over 1f out* **50/1**

46 **11** *2* **Cardaw Lily (IRE)**[116] 2905 2-9-0 0.................................. ShaneKelly 3 22
(Richard Hughes) *w ldr to 1/2-way: wknd rapidly and eased* **7/1**

**12** *6* **Stylish Grace (FR)** 2-9-0 0................................................. LiamJones 9
(J S Moore) *s.s: immediately t.o* **50/1**

1m 1.19s (-0.41) **Going Correction** -0.025s/f (Good) **12 Ran SP% 120.5**
Speed ratings (Par 95): **102,100,100,99,97 92,92,90,87,81 77,68**
CSF £14.33 TOTE £4.60: £1.60, £1.60; EX 17.80 Trifecta £38.70.
**Owner** S R Hope & S W Barrow **Bred** Deer Forest Stud **Trained** Lambourn, Berks

**FOCUS**
Ordinary maiden form, with the leaders going too fast early. The form looks straightforward through the winner and third.

## 7127 MOLSON COORS H'CAP 5f 10y
**2:00** (2:02) (Class 5) (0-75,77) 3-Y-O+ **£3,881** (£1,155; £577; £288) **Stalls** Low

Form RPR

2222 **1** **Jashma (IRE)**[10] 6780 3-9-3 **70**.............................................(p) ShaneKelly 4 78
(Richard Hughes) *trckd ldrs in 5th: plld towards outer and prog 2f out: rdn to ld jst over 1f out: hung lft but styd on* **9/2**[2]

2564 **2** *1* **Taajub (IRE)**[24] 6278 10-8-13 **68**..................................... HectorCrouch(3) 5 72
(Peter Crate) *walked to post early: racd on outer in midfield: rdn and prog fr 2f out: chsd wnr ins fnl f: hung lft after and nvr able to chal* **20/1**

0050 **3** *shd* **Merdon Castle (IRE)**[14] 6652 5-9-2 **68**............................ SaleemGolam 8 72
(Jane Chapple-Hyam) *dwlt: pushed along in last and struggling to go the pce: drvn and prog over 1f out on outer: styd on to take 3rd ins fnl f* **16/1**

3463 **4** ¾ **Coastal Cyclone**[11] 6768 3-9-6 **73** (b[1]) HarryBentley 6 74
(Harry Dunlop) *s.i.s: towards rr and racd against rail: prog over 1f out: styd on ins fnl f but too late to threaten* **12/1**

3022 **5** 1 **Monumental Man**[11] 6764 8-9-6 **77** (p) PaddyBradley(5) 2 75
(Michael Attwater) *t.k.h: trckd ldng pair and racd against rail early: rdn and nt qckn over 1f out: kpt on same pce fnl f* **9/1**

4452 **6** 1 **Zipedeedodah (IRE)**[9] 6810 5-8-11 **68** (t) JoshuaBryan(5) 9 62
(Joseph Tuite) *trckd ldng pair: wnt 2nd 2f out but wnr sn wnt past: fdd fnl f* **7/1**

0546 **7** ½ **Big Lachie**[29] 6113 3-9-6 **73** SteveDrowne 3 65
(Daniel Mark Loughnane) *dwlt: sn pushed along in last pair: effrt u.p over 1f out: kpt on but nvr pce to threaten* **10/1**

3206 **8** 1¼ **Lydia's Place**[13] 6695 4-9-8 **77** DavidEgan(3) 11 65
(Richard Guest) *taken down early: gd spd fr wd draw: led but styd away fr rail: hdd & wknd jst over 1f out* **8/1**

3630 **9** 1¾ **Dashing Poet**[94] 3692 3-8-7 **63** HollieDoyle(3) 1 45
(Heather Main) *racd against rail: chsd ldr to 2f out: sn btn* **6/1**[3]

11 **10** 5 **Melonade**[69] 4619 3-9-5 **72** BenCurtis 10 36
(David Barron) *racd on outer: in rr: pushed along 1/2-way: rdn and struggling over 1f out: wl btn whn j. path jst ins fnl f* **7/2**[1]

1m 0.81s (-0.79) **Going Correction** -0.025s/f (Good)
**WFA** 3 from 4yo+ 1lb **10** Ran SP% **115.7**
Speed ratings (Par 103): **105,103,103,102,100 98,98,96,93,85**
CSF £88.56 CT £1319.30 TOTE £4.90: £1.70, £5.40, £4.20; EX 82.90 Trifecta £1397.50.
**Owner** M Clarke, S Geraghty, J Jeffries **Bred** Jonathan David Clague **Trained** Upper Lambourn, Berks

**FOCUS**
A modest sprint that went to one of the 3yos who recorded a small personal best.

## 7128 SUPPORTING BRITISH STALLIONS EBF NOVICE STKS 1m

**2:35** (2:39) (Class 5) 2-Y-O **£3,881** (£1,155; £577; £288) **Stalls** Low

Form RPR

6 **1** **Crossed Baton**[28] 6142 2-9-2 0 HarryBentley 4 84+
(John Gosden) *cl up: rdn over 1f out and plld off rail: r.o fnl f to ld last 100yds: readily* **2/1**[1]

**2** 1 **Stephensons Rocket (IRE)** 2-9-2 0 PatCosgrave 12 82
(Ed Walker) *awkward s: t.k.h and sn trckd ldng pair: quick move to ld wl over 1f out gng strly: rn green in front: hdd and outpcd last 100yds* **14/1**

3 **3** 2 **Cassini (IRE)**[36] 5840 2-9-2 0 (t) RobertTart 13 77
(John Gosden) *chsd ldrs: shkn up 2f out: nt pce to chal but styd on to take 3rd wl ins fnl f* **9/2**[3]

3 **4** 2 **Zaajer**[14] 6654 2-9-2 0 FranBerry 1 72
(Owen Burrows) *led: gng strly over 2f out: hdd and shkn up wl over 1f out: fnd nil* **11/4**[2]

**5** 2¾ **House Edge** 2-9-2 0 JamieSpencer 5 66+
(Michael Bell) *hld up in last quartet: pushed along over 2f out: styd on wl fnl f: gng on at fin* **25/1**

**6** hd **Mekong** 2-9-2 0 TedDurcan 8 66
(Sir Michael Stoute) *in tch in midfield: pushed along and no prog over 2f out: reminder over 1f out: styd on wl fnl f* **9/1**

03 **7** hd **Global Style (IRE)**[17] 6553 2-9-2 0 BenCurtis 14 65
(Ed Dunlop) *chsd ldrs rdn over 2f out: steadily fdd fr over 1f out* **16/1**

00 **8** ¾ **Ocean Side**[14] 6654 2-9-2 0 SeanLevey 2 63
(Richard Hannon) *pressed ldr to 2f out: sn wknd* **50/1**

**9** ¾ **Diocletian (IRE)** 2-9-2 0 MartinDwyer 11 62
(Andrew Balding) *s.s: hld up in last pair: sme prog 2f out and stl gng wl enough: nvr any ch and rn out of room nr fin* **33/1**

**9** dht **Institution (IRE)** 2-9-2 0 SteveDrowne 3 62+
(Charles Hills) *s.s: hld up in rr: pushed along and sme prog 2f out: no hdwy over 1f out* **25/1**

**11** 1½ **Spice War** 2-9-2 0 JasonHart 6 58
(Brian Meehan) *nvr bttr than midfield: pushed along firmly and no prog 2f out: n.m.r and lost pl nr fin* **25/1**

**12** 2½ **Kabrit (IRE)** 2-9-2 0 RobHornby 7 53
(Andrew Balding) *hld up in last pair: stl there over 1f out: only jst sing to run on as r fin* **50/1**

**13** ¾ **Baasha** 2-9-2 0 ShaneKelly 9 51
(Ed Dunlop) *dwlt: a in rr: shkn up and no prog over 2f out* **66/1**

0 **14** 6 **Compass Point**[25] 6260 2-9-2 0 JohnFahy 10 37
(Laura Mongan) *trapped out wd: chsd ldrs: wknd over 2f out: bhd fnl f* **66/1**

1m 44.65s (1.35) **Going Correction** -0.025s/f (Good) **14** Ran SP% **122.1**
Speed ratings (Par 95): **92,91,89,87,84 84,83,83,82,82 80,78,77,71**
CSF £30.80 TOTE £3.00: £1.40, £3.20, £1.60; EX 30.90 Trifecta £154.20.
**Owner** K Abdullah **Bred** Juddmonte Farms Ltd **Trained** Newmarket, Suffolk
■ Atomic Jack was withdrawn. Price at time of withdrawal 100/1. Rule 4 does not apply

**FOCUS**
Add 17yds to race distance. A decent maiden, with the right horses coming to the fore and the race has been rated through the third. Little got involved from off the pace.

## 7129 INKERMAN LONDON H'CAP 1m

**3:10** (3:10) (Class 3) (0-95,95) 3-Y-O+
**£8,092** (£2,423; £1,211; £605; £302; £152) **Stalls** Low

Form RPR

-320 **1** **The Grape Escape (IRE)**[85] 3997 3-9-2 **92** SeanLevey 10 106
(Richard Hannon) *trckd ldr 2f: styd prom on inner: nt clr run 2f out tl swtchd out to chsd wnr fnl f: carried lft sn after: pushed along and r.o wl to ld last strides* **6/1**[2]

321 **2** hd **Sharja Bridge**[28] 6150 3-9-5 **95** HarryBentley 6 110+
(Roger Varian) *trckd ldrs: prog to ld over 1f out: drvn and edgd lft ins fnl f: styd on wl but hdd last strides* **9/4**[1]

6121 **3** 3 **Almoreb (IRE)**[15] 6617 3-9-2 **92** TedDurcan 7 100
(Richard Hannon) *hld up in midfield: rdn 2f out: prog on outer over 1f out: styd on to take 3rd ins fnl f: no ch w ldng pair* **8/1**[3]

0530 **4** 2½ **Secret Art (IRE)**[7] 6873 7-9-7 **92** MartinDwyer 8 95
(William Knight) *pressed ldr after 2f: chal fr 3f out to over 1f out: wknd ins fnl f* **20/1**

1125 **5** 1 **See The Master (IRE)**[20] 6422 3-8-7 **83** SamHitchcott 3 83+
(Clive Cox) *hld up in rr: pushed along over 2f out: prog and rdn over 1f out: kpt on but nvr pce to rch ldrs* **12/1**

1130 **6** hd **Frank Bridge**[20] 6419 4-9-6 **91** CharlesBishop 2 91
(Eve Johnson Houghton) *trckd ldrs: rdn and rt on terms 2f out: fdd over 1f out* **16/1**

0131 **7** ¾ **Angel Down**[33] 5966 3-8-10 **86** FranBerry 5 84
(Henry Candy) *chsd ldrs: rdn and no prog 2f out: wknd over 1f out* **8/1**[3]

0433 **8** ¾ **Calvados Spirit**[60] 4976 4-8-11 **85** (h) HectorCrouch(3) 9 82
(William Muir) *led: rdn over 2f out: hdd & wknd over 1f out* **40/1**

00 **9** 1¼ **Mr Bossy Boots (IRE)**[13] 6685 6-8-9 **83** (t) DavidEgan(3) 11 77
(Amanda Perrett) *dwlt: a in rr: shkn up and no prog over 2f out* **50/1**

0030 **10** ½ **Sir Roderic (IRE)**[13] 6676 4-9-1 **86** (t) WilliamCarson 1 79
(Rod Millman) *a towards rr: rdn and no prog over 2f out* **12/1**

6163 **11** 1¾ **Fox Trotter (IRE)**[7] 6870 5-9-1 **86** JasonHart 4 75
(Brian Meehan) *stdd s: hld up in last pair: rdn and no prog over 2f out* **14/1**

1651 **12** ½ **Pensax Boy**[32] 6014 5-9-2 **87** SteveDrowne 13 75
(Daniel Mark Loughnane) *chsd ldrs but trapped out wd: wknd 2f out* **25/1**

53 **13** 7 **Manson**[31] 6024 4-9-9 **94** (p) BenCurtis 12 66
(Dominic Ffrench Davis) *dwlt: a wl in rr: rdn and wknd over 2f out* **11/1**

1m 42.62s (-0.68) **Going Correction** -0.025s/f (Good)
**WFA** 3 from 4yo+ 5lb **13** Ran SP% **116.6**
Speed ratings (Par 107): **102,101,98,96,95 95,94,93,92,91 90,89,82**
CSF £18.45 CT £110.17 TOTE £6.80: £2.30, £1.30, £2.70; EX 23.90 Trifecta £144.00.
**Owner** John Manley **Bred** John Manley **Trained** East Everleigh, Wilts

**FOCUS**
Add 17yds to race distance. The 3yos dominated this useful handicap and the form looks strong. it paid to race handily.

## 7130 KINGSWAY CLAIMS FILLIES' H'CAP 7f

**3:45** (3:47) (Class 4) (0-85,84) 3-Y-O+ **£5,822** (£1,732; £865; £432) **Stalls** Low

Form RPR

-210 **1** **Crafty Madam (IRE)**[96] 3621 3-8-8 **72** SamHitchcott 4 83
(Clive Cox) *t.k.h early: sn restrained into 6th: prog on outer over 2f out: rdn to ld wl over 1f out: drvn and kpt on wl whn clr fnl f* **7/1**[3]

0110 **2** 2¾ **Always Thankful**[13] 6697 3-8-8 **75** (p) HectorCrouch(3) 1 79
(Ismail Mohammed) *hld up in midfield: rdn over 2f out: prog to take 3rd jst over 1f out: kpt on and snatched 2nd last stride* **7/1**[3]

0244 **3** hd **Snow Squaw**[25] 6274 3-8-5 **72** (p) DavidEgan(3) 7 75
(David Elsworth) *t.k.h and swift move to press ldr after 1f: led over 2f out to wl over 1f out: readily hld by wnr after: lost 2nd last stride* **5/1**[2]

6020 **4** 1¾ **Brogan**[69] 4617 3-9-3 **81** (p[1]) BenCurtis 3 79
(Tom Dascombe) *trckd ldrs: rdn 2f out: one pce and no threat fr over 1f out* **8/1**

1455 **5** ¾ **La Celebs Ville (IRE)**[25] 6274 4-9-2 **76** (p) FranBerry 9 74
(Tom Dascombe) *hld up in last pair: effrt and rdn on outer 2f out: plugged on same pce and no ch* **20/1**

4415 **6** ¾ **Caridade (USA)**[22] 6358 3-9-2 **80** KevinStott 8 74
(Kevin Ryan) *trckd ldr 1f: styd cl up: shkn up over 2f out and sn lost pl: drvn and wl btn over 1f out* **11/8**[1]

4435 **7** 1 **First Experience**[20] 6439 6-8-13 **73** (v) KierenFox 6 66
(Lee Carter) *hld up in last pair: rdn and no real prog over 2f out* **16/1**

15 **8** 3 **Mulhimatty**[119] 2802 3-9-6 **84** DanielMuscutt 5 67
(Charles Hills) *led at str pce: hdd over 2f out: sn wknd* **10/1**

1m 29.3s (-0.20) **Going Correction** -0.025s/f (Good)
**WFA** 3 from 4yo+ 4lb **8** Ran SP% **114.6**
Speed ratings (Par 102): **100,96,96,94,93 92,91,88**
CSF £54.77 CT £268.61 TOTE £8.50: £2.50, £2.60, £1.90; EX 56.00 Trifecta £221.80.
**Owner** Con Harrington **Bred** Con Harrington **Trained** Lambourn, Berks

**FOCUS**
Add 17yds to race distance. Ordinary form rated around the third, with the favourite disappointing, but a progressive winner for a red-hot yard. The leaders went too hard early.

## 7131 DIRECTORSHIP H'CAP 1m

**4:15** (4:20) (Class 4) (0-80,82) 3-Y-O+ **£5,822** (£1,732; £865; £432) **Stalls** Low

Form RPR

126 **1** **Fastar (IRE)**[21] 6387 3-9-3 **78** CharlesBishop 9 87
(Brian Meehan) *hld up bhd ldrs disputing 5th: prog towards outer to chal over 2f out: drvn to ld over 1f out: kpt on wl u.p* **7/1**[3]

2136 **2** 1 **Badenscoth**[16] 6576 3-9-1 **79** (h) JackDuern(3) 7 86
(Dean Ivory) *taken down early: hld up in last trio: gd prog on wd outside over 2f out though sltly unbalanced: drvn to chal jst over 1f out: kpt on to take 2nd nr fin* **12/1**

1242 **3** ½ **Call Me Grumpy (IRE)**[29] 6111 3-9-0 **78** DavidEgan(3) 14 84
(Roger Varian) *trapped out wd towards rr: stdy prog fr 1/2-way: clsd to ld on outer 2f out: rdn over 1f out: kpt on but lost 2nd nr fin* **10/3**[1]

6033 **4** 1¾ **Grand Inquisitor**[13] 6700 5-9-10 **80** (p) FranBerry 3 83
(Ian Williams) *hld up in last: prog on outer over 2f out: drvn and kpt on to take 4th jst over 1f out: no imp ldng trio after* **4/1**[2]

0506 **5** 1½ **Directorship**[13] 6700 11-9-1 **74** HectorCrouch(3) 2 73
(Patrick Chamings) *sn in midfield: lost pl 3f out and last 2f out: rallied over 1f out: styd on wl to take 5th nr fin: has been retired* **12/1**

6664 **6** 1¾ **Sea Shack**[30] 6068 3-9-0 **75** MartinDwyer 8 69
(William Knight) *taken down early: w ldrs at str pce: upsides 3f out: steadily wknd fr 2f out* **7/1**[3]

1510 **7** hd **Sir Plato (IRE)**[18] 6516 3-9-7 **82** WilliamCarson 11 76
(Rod Millman) *led 1f but sn dropped to 4th: lost pl fr over 2f out and in rr over 1f out: plugged on again fnl f* **20/1**

1250 **8** ¾ **Derek Duval (USA)**[28] 6145 3-9-3 **78** (t) BenCurtis 6 70
(Stuart Williams) *nvr bttr than midfield: rdn and no prog over 2f out* **7/1**[3]

5/44 **9** ¾ **Ogbourne Downs**[23] 4976 7-8-12 **73** PaddyPilley(5) 10 64
(Ben Pauling) *hld up towards rr: prog towards outer over 2f out: drvn and wknd over 1f out* **33/1**

5523 **10** hd **Miss Pacific**[36] 5856 3-8-9 **70** ShaneKelly 15 60
(William Jarvis) *slowly away: nvr really gng in last pair: modest late prog* **12/1**

0360 **11** 1 **Top Beak (IRE)**[13] 6701 4-9-5 **75** (t) RobHornby 12 64
(Michael Attwater) *w ldrs at str pce: led 3f out to 2f out: wknd* **33/1**

5661 **12** 6 **Blaze Of Hearts (IRE)**[24] 6294 4-9-5 **75** TedDurcan 13 50
(Dean Ivory) *led after 1f: set str pce but pressed: hdd 3f out: wknd u.p 2f out: heavily eased fnl f* **16/1**

6060 **13** 9 **Ready (IRE)**[88] 3920 7-9-5 **75** DannyBrock 4 29
(Mark Pattinson) *chsd ldrs tl wknd 3f out: t.o* **33/1**

-156 **14** 5 **Music Major**[163] 1553 4-8-13 **69** KierenFox 5 12
(Michael Attwater) *nvr bttr than midfield: wknd qckly u.p over 2f out: t.o* **66/1**

1m 42.99s (-0.31) **Going Correction** -0.025s/f (Good)
**WFA** 3 from 4yo+ 5lb **14** Ran SP% **124.6**
Speed ratings (Par 105): **100,99,98,96,95 93,93,92,91,91 90,84,75,70**
CSF £86.90 CT £347.68 TOTE £9.00: £2.80, £3.70, £1.80; EX 112.60 Trifecta £664.10.
**Owner** Biddestone Racing Partnership XVIII **Bred** Ringfort Stud **Trained** Manton, Wilts
■ Palmerston was withdrawn. Price at time of withdrawal 17/2. Rule 4 applies to bets struck at board prices prior to withdrawal but not to SP bets - deduction 10p in the pound. New market formed

**FOCUS**
Add 17yds to race distance. A competitive handicap and solid form. They went a decent gallop and the main action unfolded more towards the centre.

## 7132 FALCON GREEN PERSONNEL H'CAP 1m 1f 209y
**4:45** (4:48) (Class 4) (0-85,87) 3-Y-O+ £5,822 (£1,732; £865; £432) **Stalls** Low

Form RPR
2021 **1** **Capton**[27] 6195 4-9-10 **82** FranBerry 6 91
(Henry Candy) *mde all: taken wl away fr ins in st: rdn 2f out: styd on wl and clr fnl f* **10/3**[1]
031 **2** 2 1/4 **Sparte Quercus (IRE)**[9] 6811 4-9-4 **79** 6ex DavidEgan(3) 7 83
(Ed Dunlop) *t.k.h: hld up in midfield: prog to chse wnr over 2f out: rdn and no imp fr over 1f out* **7/2**[2]
5110 **3** 1/2 **Fair Power (IRE)**[44] 5525 3-9-4 **82** RobertTart 5 86
(Sylvester Kirk) *sn in last: shoved along and struggling over 4f out: stl last 2f out: styd on wl fr over 1f out to take 3rd nr fin* **11/1**
6600 **4** nk **Zamperini (IRE)**[22] 3785 5-9-4 **76** JimmyFortune 10 78
(Mike Murphy) *hld up towards rr: brought wd in st: rdn and no rspnse jst over 2f out: styd on fnl f to take 4th last strides* **25/1**
145 **5** nk **Zzoro (IRE)**[77] 4316 4-10-1 **87** MartinDwyer 2 88
(Amanda Perrett) *t.k.h: hld up bhd ldrs: brought wd in st: rdn to chse ldng pair 2f out: hld fnl f: fdd last 150yds* **16/1**
2-00 **6** 1 3/4 **So Celebre (GER)**[27] 6195 4-9-1 **73** BenCurtis 3 71
(Ian Williams) *rousted along early but stl in rr: rdn and no prog over 2f out* **16/1**
031 **7** nk **Casement (IRE)**[21] 6368 3-9-4 **82** ShaneKelly 4 80
(Roger Charlton) *hld up in tch: clsd on ldrs gng wl whn nt clr run wl over 2f out and lost pl: tried to rally over 1f out but wandered and then fdd* **10/3**[1]
-126 **8** 1 3/4 **Regicide (IRE)**[72] 4498 4-10-0 **86** DanielMuscutt 9 80
(James Fanshawe) *hld up in rr: rdn and no prog over 2f out* **10/1**
2133 **9** 3/4 **Fast And Hot (IRE)**[27] 6189 4-9-8 **80** (b) KieranO'Neill 1 72
(Richard Hannon) *chsd ldng pair: stl in tch 2f out: wknd over 1f out* **8/1**[3]
2240 **10** 7 **Inke (IRE)**[32] 6013 5-9-3 **75** (p) WilliamCarson 8 53
(Jim Boyle) *chsd wnr to over 2f out: wknd u.p* **50/1**

2m 8.32s (-2.18) **Going Correction** -0.025s/f (Good)
**WFA** 3 from 4yo+ 6lb 10 Ran SP% **114.5**
Speed ratings (Par 105): **107,105,104,104,104 102,102,101,100,95**
CSF £14.81 CT £112.87 TOTE £4.20: £1.60, £1.30, £2.80; EX 16.20 Trifecta £150.90.
**Owner** W P Wyatt **Bred** Dunchurch Lodge Stud Company **Trained** Kingston Warren, Oxon

**FOCUS**
Add 17yds to race distance. A useful handicap, they raced centre field and some progressive types came to the fore. They didn't go much of a gallop, though.
T/Plt: £64.30 to a £1 stake. Pool: £68,313.53 - 775.12 winning units T/Qpdt: £16.10 to a £1 stake. Pool: £6,013.21 - 275.48 winning units **Jonathan Neesom**

7133 - 7136a (Foreign Racing) - See Raceform Interactive

# 7105 CHESTER (L-H)
Saturday, September 16

**OFFICIAL GOING: Heavy (5.6)**
Wind: Moderate, half against in straight of over 1f Weather: Cloudy

## 7137 #THEMBNATEAM H'CAP 5f 15y
**1:30** (1:31) (Class 4) (0-80,80) 3-Y-O+
£7,470 (£2,236; £1,118; £559; £279; £140) **Stalls** Low

Form RPR
3110 **1** **Show Palace**[24] 6314 4-9-5 **78** FrannyNorton 2 88
(Jennie Candlish) *chsd ldrs: effrt to take 2nd over 1f out: r.o to ld fnl 75yds: in command after* **11/4**[1]
6222 **2** 1 1/2 **Desert Ace (IRE)**[24] 6314 6-9-5 **78** (p) TomEaves 3 83
(Iain Jardine) *led: rdn over 1f out: hdd fnl 75yds: no ex nr fin* **9/2**[2]
1120 **3** 1 3/4 **Come On Dave (IRE)**[21] 6411 8-9-4 **77** (v) JosephineGordon 6 76
(John Butler) *midfield: rdn over 1f out: hdwy ins fnl f: styd on: nt rch ldrs* **16/1**
0032 **4** 1 1/4 **Ballesteros**[21] 6411 8-9-1 **74** PaulHanagan 8 69
(Richard Fahey) *chsd ldrs: rdn and unable qck over 1f out: styd on same pce ins fnl f* **13/2**
3122 **5** 2 1/2 **Noah Amor (IRE)**[8] 6891 4-9-1 **74** PhillipMakin 1 60
(David O'Meara) *chsd ldr: rdn and lost 2nd over 1f out: hung lft ent fnl f: sn fdd* **11/2**[3]
2021 **6** nk **Landing Night (IRE)**[8] 6891 5-9-4 **77** (tp) PJMcDonald 5 62
(Rebecca Menzies) *midfield: rdn and sme hdwy on inner over 1f out: no imp on ldrs* **10/1**
055 **7** 1 **Casterbridge**[37] 5827 5-8-11 **70** (p[1]) NeilFarley 9 51
(Eric Alston) *hld up: rdn over 1f out: nvr able to trble ldrs* **25/1**
4256 **8** 2 **Captain Lars (SAF)**[11] 6794 8-9-5 **78** (v) PatrickMathers 4 52
(Derek Shaw) *towards rr: rdn 1/2-way: nvr able to get on terms* **8/1**
6605 **9** 4 **Impart**[14] 6679 3-9-2 **79** (p[1]) JoshDoyle(3) 7 39
(David O'Meara) *hld up: sn in midfield: effrt on outer 1/2-way: no imp on ldrs: wknd over 1f out* **25/1**
0020 **10** 1 3/4 **Blithe Spirit**[14] 6677 6-9-2 **80** CallumRodriguez(5) 11 34
(Eric Alston) *midfield: rdn and lost pl 1/2-way: rn wd whn bhd on bnd wl over 1f out: nvr a threat* **16/1**
530- **11** 2 **Bondi Beach Boy**[310] 7892 8-9-5 **78** DavidAllan 12 25
(Antony Brittain) *dwlt: in rr: u.p 1/2-way: nvr a threat* **50/1**

1m 5.83s (4.83) **Going Correction** +1.10s/f (Soft)
**WFA** 3 from 4yo+ 1lb 11 Ran SP% **115.2**
Speed ratings (Par 105): **105,102,99,97,93 93,91,88,82,79 76**
CSF £13.91 CT £164.45 TOTE £3.40: £1.50, £1.60, £4.00; EX 17.00 Trifecta £185.10.
**Owner** P and Mrs G A Clarke **Bred** M C Humby **Trained** Basford Green, Staffs

**FOCUS**
The rail between the 6f and 1f point was moved out a further 3 yards after racing on Friday. Add 30 yards to this official distance. With the ground given as heavy, not many of these got involved and being drawn low proved key. Franny Norton reported after the opener "It's a bit more holding today than yesterday." The winner has been rated in line with his summer progress.

## 7138 32RED CASINO NURSERY H'CAP 5f 15y
**2:05** (2:05) (Class 3) (0-95,89) 2-Y-O
£11,205 (£3,355; £1,677; £838; £419; £210) **Stalls** Low

Form RPR
0215 **1** **Porchy Party (IRE)**[12] 6756 2-8-8 **76** (p) BenCurtis 1 81
(Tom Dascombe) *trckd ldrs: rdn 2f out: r.o to ld wl ins fnl f: powered away towards fin* **3/1**[1]
261 **2** 1 3/4 **Mable Lee (IRE)**[43] 5614 2-8-3 **71** JosephineGordon 5 70
(Iain Jardine) *trckd ldrs: rdn and sltly outpcd over 1f out: rallied ins fnl f: styd on to take 2nd fnl strides: nt pce of wnr* **10/3**[2]
0242 **3** nk **Simmy's Copshop**[28] 6207 2-9-7 **89** PaulHanagan 8 87
(Richard Fahey) *racd off the pce: hdwy over 1f out: chsd ldrs ins fnl f: styd on towards fin* **5/1**[3]
101 **4** 1/2 **Viscount Loftus (IRE)**[27] 6231 2-9-5 **87** FrannyNorton 2 83
(Mark Johnston) *disp ld: rdn over 1f out: hdd wl ins fnl f: styd on same pce towards fin* **3/1**[1]
4125 **5** nk **Angel Force (IRE)**[21] 6448 2-9-3 **85** (h) DavidAllan 6 80
(David C Griffiths) *racd keenly: disp ld: rdn over 1f out: hdd wl ins fnl f: kpt on same pce towards fin* **10/1**
5340 **6** 1 1/4 **Mr Greenlight**[23] 6353 2-8-6 **74** PatrickMathers 3 65
(Tim Easterby) *dwlt: in rr: rdn over 1f out: kpt on ins fnl f: nvr able to chal* **8/1**
3463 **7** 1 **Joegogo (IRE)**[10] 6816 2-7-13 **70** DavidEgan(3) 11 57
(David Evans) *racd off the pce: effrt over 1f out: no imp on ldrs: one pce ins fnl f* **20/1**

1m 6.57s (5.57) **Going Correction** +1.15s/f (Soft) 7 Ran SP% **114.7**
Speed ratings (Par 99): **101,98,97,96,96 94,92**
CSF £13.38 CT £47.24 TOTE £3.80: £2.20, £1.90; EX 14.00 Trifecta £92.70.
**Owner** R F H Partnership 1 **Bred** Seamus O'Neill **Trained** Malpas, Cheshire
■ Stewards' Enquiry : Ben Curtis 4 day ban: using his whip above the permitted level (1-4 Oct)

**FOCUS**
Add 30 yards to this official distance. It looked like the leading pair went off too quickly considering neither could hold on when challenged.

## 7139 32RED.COM STAND CUP STKS (LISTED RACE) 1m 4f 63y
**2:40** (2:42) (Class 1) 3-Y-O+ £22,684 (£8,600; £4,304; £2,144; £1,076) **Stalls** Low

Form RPR
51-3 **1** **Duretto**[127] 2571 5-9-3 112 GrahamLee 2 107
(Andrew Balding) *stdd s: hld up: hdwy and swtchd lft over 1f out: led jst ins fnl f: edgd rt towards fin: kpt on wl* **11/10**[1]
-500 **2** 1/2 **Across The Stars (IRE)**[21] 6440 4-9-3 110 (h) TedDurcan 3 106
(Sir Michael Stoute) *hld up: effrt 2f out: carried hd to one side whn u.p over 1f out: styd on to take 2nd wl ins fnl f: nt pce of wnr: clsd nr fin* **6/1**[3]
4450 **3** 1 3/4 **Rich Legacy (IRE)**[44] 5569 3-8-5 101 JosephineGordon 5 97
(Ralph Beckett) *prom: w ldr 2f out: rdn to nose ahd over 1f out: hdd jst ins fnl f: kpt on same pce towards fin* **9/1**
5421 **4** 2 **My Reward**[14] 6675 5-9-6 100 DavidAllan 4 103
(Tim Easterby) *led: pressed 2f out: rdn and hdd over 1f out: no ex fnl 150yds* **8/1**
2310 **5** 1/2 **Soldier In Action (FR)**[21] 6447 4-9-3 109 FrannyNorton 1 99
(Mark Johnston) *prom: rdn 2f out: outpcd over 1f out: n.d after* **11/4**[2]

2m 53.4s (14.90) **Going Correction** +1.20s/f (Soft)
**WFA** 3 from 4yo+ 7lb 5 Ran SP% **109.7**
Speed ratings (Par 111): **98,97,96,95,94**
CSF £8.08 TOTE £1.80: £1.40, £2.70; EX 6.50 Trifecta £29.90.
**Owner** Lord Blyth **Bred** Lord Blyth **Trained** Kingsclere, Hants

**FOCUS**
Add 58 yards to the official distance. This middle-distance Listed contest wasn't run at a quick tempo, so it was an impressive effort by the winner who didn't need to be at his best.

## 7140 32RED.COM H'CAP 7f 127y
**3:15** (3:17) (Class 3) (0-90,91) 3-Y-O+
£12,450 (£3,728; £1,864; £932; £466; £234) **Stalls** Low

Form RPR
1121 **1** **Dan Troop**[49] 5400 3-8-13 **90** ConnorMurtagh(7) 1 101
(Richard Fahey) *chsd ldr: rdn to ld over 1f out: kpt on: doing enough towards fin* **5/2**[1]
2401 **2** 1/2 **King's Pavilion (IRE)**[3] 7044 4-9-11 **91** 6ex BenCurtis 5 100
(David Barron) *s.i.s: hld up: rdn and hdwy 2f out: wnt 2nd ins fnl f: styd on and clsd on wnr towards fin* **7/2**[2]
002 **3** 2 1/4 **Instant Attraction (IRE)**[3] 7044 6-9-6 **86** JackGarritty 8 90
(Jedd O'Keeffe) *midfield: rdn and hdwy over 2f out: styd on towards fin: nt pce of front two* **7/1**[3]
4140 **4** 1 **Tadaawol**[6] 6964 4-8-12 **78** (p) FrannyNorton 7 80
(Roger Fell) *led: rdn and hdd over 1f out: styd on same pce fnl 100yds* **10/1**
0200 **5** hd **Fingal's Cave (IRE)**[14] 6676 5-9-5 **90** CallumRodriguez(5) 11 91
(Philip Kirby) *hld up: rdn over 1f out: styd on ins fnl f: gng on at fin: nvr nrr* **16/1**
3056 **6** 1 1/4 **Ice Slice (IRE)**[52] 5294 6-9-9 **89** RyanTate 6 87
(James Eustace) *jst abt in midfield: rdn and hdwy over 1f out: nt rch ldrs: one pce ins fnl f* **7/1**[3]
1321 **7** 1 1/4 **Kenstone (FR)**[21] 6414 4-9-0 **87** (p) WilliamCox(7) 4 82
(Adrian Wintle) *chsd ldrs: rdn over 1f out: wknd ins fnl f* **7/1**[3]
1606 **8** 3 3/4 **Alejandro (IRE)**[86] 4017 8-9-9 **89** JosephineGordon 9 76
(David Loughnane) *hld up: struggling over 2f out: nvr a threat* **33/1**
2400 **9** 2 1/4 **Heir To A Throne (FR)**[21] 6414 4-8-13 **79** (p) ShaneGray 3 61
(Kevin Ryan) *midfield: rdn 3f out: wknd 2f out* **16/1**
1300 **10** 8 **Shouranour (IRE)**[17] 6570 7-9-1 **84** (b) JoshDoyle(3) 2 47
(Alan Brown) *prom: rdn 3f out: lost pl 2f out: wknd jst over 1f out* **12/1**

1m 41.94s (8.14) **Going Correction** +1.25s/f (Soft)
**WFA** 3 from 4yo+ 4lb 10 Ran SP% **119.8**
Speed ratings (Par 107): **109,108,106,105,105 103,102,98,96,88**
CSF £11.39 CT £56.65 TOTE £2.90: £1.10, £1.80, £3.10; EX 18.40 Trifecta £89.40.
**Owner** Mrs Janis Macpherson **Bred** Liam Sheridan **Trained** Musley Bank, N Yorks

**FOCUS**
Add 37 yards to the official distance. There was a decent pace set considering the conditions, and the winner was probably value for more than the margin of success.

## 7141 INNOSPEC / EBF STALLIONS NOVICE STKS (PLUS 10 RACE) 6f 17y
**3:50** (3:53) (Class 4) 2-Y-O
£6,225 (£1,864; £932; £466; £233; £117) **Stalls** Low

Form RPR
42 **1** **Shaya (IRE)**[10] 6806 2-8-11 0 FrannyNorton 6 74
(Roger Fell) *chsd ldr: led 2f out: rdn and tail flashed whn strly pressed and jnd fnl 100yds: fnd ex nr fin* **13/8**[1]
**2** 1/2 **Gabrial The Saint (IRE)** 2-9-2 0 PaulHanagan 9 78
(Richard Fahey) *missed break: in midfield after 2f: hdwy 2f out: rdn to take 2nd over 1f out: moved upsides to chal strly fnl 100yds: hld nr fin: can improve* **5/1**[3]

0 **3** *7* **Flere Imsaho (IRE)**[42] 6665 2-8-11 0 PaddyPilley(5) 3 57
(Tom Dascombe) *chsd ldrs: rdn over 2f out: styd on same pce for press fr over 1f out* **14/1**

55 **4** *nse* **Gabrials Centurion (IRE)**[14] 6674 2-9-2 0 PhillipMakin 8 56
(David O'Meara) *hld up: rdn 2f out: hdwy over 1f out: kpt on ins fnl f: no imp on front two: one to nte* **9/2**[2]

0 **5** *nk* **Isabella Ruby**[3] 7045 2-8-4 0 (h) ConnorMurtagh(7) 10 50
(Lisa Williamson) *chsd ldrs: rdn wl over 1f out: one pce fnl f* **100/1**

00 **6** *4* **Harbour Seal**[12] 6747 2-8-11 0 (h) BenCurtis 2 38
(Henry Spiller) *led: rdn and hdd 2f out: wknd fnl f* **20/1**

05 **7** *hd* **Grasmere (IRE)**[11] 6776 2-8-11 0 JosephineGordon 7 38
(Alan Bailey) *in tch: pushed along 3f out: lost pl over 2f out: n.d after* **16/1**

4 **8** *3 ¼* **Deecider**[9] 6853 2-9-2 0 PJMcDonald 4 33
(Tom Dascombe) *missed break: rdn along thrght: a bhd* **5/1**[3]

54 **9** *6* **Finnion Fox**[24] 6311 2-9-2 0 DavidAllan 12 15
(Tim Easterby) *towards rr: u.p over 2f out: eased whn wl btn wl ins fnl f* **9/1**

1m 23.13s (9.33) **Going Correction** +1.30s/f (Soft) **9** Ran SP% **117.9**
Speed ratings (Par 97): **89,88,79,78,78 73,72,68,60**
CSF £10.20 TOTE £2.60: £1.10, £1.70, £3.60; EX 11.60 Trifecta £112.80.
**Owner** Nick Bradley Racing 6 & Partner **Bred** Shadwell Estate Company Limited **Trained** Nawton, N Yorks

**FOCUS**
Add 37 yards to the official distance. Not a strong looking race of its type and two came clear.

## 7142 IDEAL RECRUIT H'CAP — 1m 2f 70y
4:25 (4:25) (Class 4) (0-80,80) 3-Y-0+
**£7,470** (£2,236; £1,118; £559; £279; £140) **Stalls** High

Form RPR

4306 **1** **Bahama Moon (IRE)**[21] 6416 5-9-7 **77** BenCurtis 7 88
(David Barron) *midfield: hdwy 3f out: led 2f out: drew clr over 1f out: styd on wl* **7/2**[1]

4366 **2** *2 ¼* **Marsh Pride**[49] 5414 5-9-9 **79** PJMcDonald 10 84
(K R Burke) *hld up: impr into midfield 7f out: rdn over 3f out: hdwy over 2f out: wnt 2nd over 1f out: styd on ins fnl f: nt trble wnr* **6/1**[3]

2360 **3** *1 ¾* **Jabbaar**[8] 6894 4-9-3 **73** PhillipMakin 9 75
(Iain Jardine) *hld up: hdwy on wd outside wl over 1f out: looked ill at ease on trck: tk 3rd wl ins fnl f: kpt on under hand ride: nt trble front two* **14/1**

0350 **4** *1 ½* **Gabrial's Kaka (IRE)**[21] 6414 7-9-6 **76** PaulHanagan 11 75
(Richard Fahey) *midfield: rdn and hdwy over 1f out: kpt on ins fnl f: no imp* **13/2**

2000 **5** *2 ¾* **Throckley**[21] 6434 6-9-9 **79** (t) SamJames 3 73
(John Davies) *midfield: hdwy 2f out: rdn to chse ldrs over 1f out: one pce ins fnl f* **9/2**[2]

3340 **6** *¾* **Outback Blue**[21] 6416 4-8-12 **71** (vt) DavidEgan(3) 5 64
(David Evans) *missed break: rdn and bhd: stdy hdwy u.p over 2f out: nvr a threat* **8/1**

0000 **7** *1* **Vettori Rules**[20] 6482 4-9-8 **78** JosephineGordon 2 69
(Gay Kelleway) *dwlt: hld up: rdn over 2f out: kpt on ins fnl f: nvr a threat* **16/1**

3300 **8** *½* **Celestation**[42] 5650 3-9-0 **75** FrannyNorton 1 66
(Mark Johnston) *led: rdn and hdd over 2f out: wknd ins fnl f* **8/1**

0350 **9** *1* **Dutch Artist (IRE)**[12] 6757 5-8-10 **69** (b1) JoshDoyle(3) 4 57
(Alan Brown) *chsd ldr: led over 2f out: sn hdd: unable to go w wnr: wknd 1f out* **25/1**

4640 **10** *7* **Energia Fox (BRZ)**[8] 6881 7-9-8 **78** PatrickMathers 8 52
(Richard Fahey) *chsd ldrs: rdn 2f out: wknd over 1f out* **20/1**

04 **11** *55* **Staff College (FR)**[35] 5931 3-9-2 **77** TedDurcan 6
(Henry Spiller) *chsd ldrs: pushed along 5f out: rdn and wknd over 3f out: eased whn wl btn over 2f out: t.o* **11/1**

2m 24.84s (13.64) **Going Correction** +1.35s/f (Soft)
**WFA** 3 from 4yo+ 5lb **11** Ran SP% **119.7**
Speed ratings (Par 105): **99,97,95,94,92 91,91,90,89,84 40**
CSF £24.82 CT £267.20 TOTE £3.90: £1.50, £2.00, £5.50; EX 26.80 Trifecta £378.10.
**Owner** D G Pryde & D Van Der Hoeven **Bred** Ammerland Verwaltung Gmbh & Co Kg **Trained** Maunby, N Yorks

**FOCUS**
Add 39 yards to the official distance. Probably just a fair handicap, but the form can prove strong for the coming weeks.

## 7143 CHRISTMAS PARTIES WITH HORSERADISH CATERING H'CAP — 1m 6f 87y
5:00 (5:01) (Class 3) (0-90,87) 4-Y-0+
**£11,205** (£3,355; £1,677; £838; £419; £210) **Stalls** Low

Form RPR

2222 **1** **Kajaki (IRE)**[21] 6427 4-8-13 **79** (p) TomEaves 9 89
(Kevin Ryan) *chsd ldr: led over 2f out: rdn over 1f out: drew clr ins fnl f: styd on strly* **9/2**[3]

0621 **2** *4 ½* **St Mary's**[14] 6680 4-8-10 **83** WilliamCox(7) 4 87+
(Andrew Balding) *hld up: checked over 3f out: rdn and hdwy over 2f out w work to do: wnt 2nd wl ins fnl f: styd on: nt trble wnr* **5/2**[1]

2110 **3** *1* **Berrahri (IRE)**[35] 5912 6-9-5 **85** JosephineGordon 7 88
(John Best) *led: rdn and hdd over 2f out: unable to go w wnr over 1f out: lost 2nd wl ins fnl f: styd on same pce* **4/1**[2]

4610 **4** *4 ½* **Plymouth Sound**[28] 6176 5-8-10 **79** (v) DavidEgan(3) 1 76
(Bernard Llewellyn) *midfield: rdn and hdwy on inner to chse ldrs over 2f out: one pce over 1f out* **20/1**

0406 **5** *hd* **Gabrial's Star**[14] 6680 8-8-9 **75** (b) PatrickMathers 5 72
(Richard Fahey) *hld up: hdwy 5f out: rdn over 3f out: sn chsd ldrs: lost pl over 2f out: n.d after* **14/1**

5400 **6** *½* **Gabrial's King (IRE)**[14] 6680 8-9-3 **83** PaulHanagan 6 79
(Richard Fahey) *chsd ldrs: rdn over 2f out: outpcd after* **14/1**

2606 **7** *15* **Sennockian Star**[9] 6857 7-9-5 **85** FrannyNorton 2 62
(Mark Johnston) *chsd ldrs tl rdn and wknd over 3f out* **12/1**

4120 **8** *3* **Nabhan**[19] 6508 5-8-12 **78** (tp) PJMcDonald 8 51
(Bernard Llewellyn) *in rr: hdwy 3f out: no imp on ldrs: rdn and wknd over 2f out* **20/1**

1515 **9** *13* **West Drive (IRE)**[33] 6000 4-9-7 **87** (v1) JackMitchell 3 43
(Roger Varian) *racd keenly: stdd into midfield early: rdn over 3f out: sn wknd* **9/2**[3]

3m 30.23s (23.23) **Going Correction** +1.40s/f (Soft) **9** Ran SP% **115.5**
Speed ratings (Par 107): **89,86,85,83,83 82,74,72,65**
CSF £16.16 CT £46.96 TOTE £4.90: £1.70, £1.30, £1.70; EX 21.10 Trifecta £74.80.
**Owner** F Gillespie **Bred** Epona Bloodstock Ltd **Trained** Hambleton, N Yorks

**FOCUS**
Add 70 yards to the official distance. An intriguing finale to the meeting, in what were demanding conditions. The race was run at a crawl early and few made any impression.

T/Plt: £34.30 to a £1 stake. Pool: £96,265.20 - 2046.29 winning units. T/Qpdt: £6.90 to a £1 stake. Pool: £6,087.28 - 644.12 winning units. **Darren Owen**

# 7112 DONCASTER (L-H)
Saturday, September 16

**OFFICIAL GOING: Good to soft (good in places on straight course)**
Wind: fresh behind Weather: overcast

## 7144 WILLIAM HILL PORTLAND H'CAP — 5f 143y
1:50 (1:51) (Class 2) 3-Y-0+
**£37,350** (£11,184; £5,592; £2,796; £1,398; £702) **Stalls** Centre

Form RPR

0253 **1** **Spring Loaded (IRE)**[14] 6677 5-8-9 **92** JoeyHaynes 22 106
(Paul D'Arcy) *chsd ldrs towards stands' side: rdn to ld 1f out: edgd lft but r.o strly to draw clr* **12/1**

1202 **2** *3 ½* **Vibrant Chords**[28] 6185 4-9-0 **97** AdamKirby 8 99
(Henry Candy) *midfield towards outside of stands' side gp: rdn and hdwy 2f out: kpt on to go 2nd fnl 75yds but no ch w wnr: 2nd of 15 in gp* **7/1**[1]

1004 **3** *¾* **Justanotherbottle (IRE)**[21] 6450 3-8-8 **93** AntonioFresu 18 93
(Declan Carroll) *prom stands' side: led over 2f out: sn rdn: hdd 1f out: edgd lft: one pce and lost 2nd fnl 75yds: 3rd of 15 in gp* **22/1**

2243 **4** *1* **Lexington Abbey**[35] 5911 6-9-0 **97** (p) RyanMoore 15 94
(Kevin Ryan) *prom stands' side: rdn 2f out: carried lft jst ins fnl f: kpt on same pce: 4th of 15 in gp* **10/1**[3]

3420 **5** *hd* **Pipers Note**[14] 6668 7-9-4 **101** JamesSullivan 11 97
(Ruth Carr) *hld up stands' side: rdn along over 2f out: kpt on ins fnl f: nrst fin: 5th of 15 in gp* **25/1**

3324 **6** *nse* **A Momentofmadness**[24] 6325 4-8-12 **95** JimCrowley 20 91+
(Charles Hills) *prom stands' side: rdn 2f out: keeping on same pce whn hmpd fnl 50yds: 6th of 15 in gp* **14/1**

0000 **7** *nk* **Captain Colby (USA)**[46] 5513 5-8-9 **92** (b) DavidProbert 16 87
(Ed Walker) *dwlt: outpcd in rr stands' side tl kpt on wl fr appr fnl f: nrst fin: 7th of 15 in gp* **16/1**

1213 **8** *nk* **Merlin**[28] 6198 3-8-7 **95** GeorgeWood(3) 1 89
(Michael Bell) *chsd ldrs far side: rdn to ld gp 2f out: briefly hdd in gp ins fnl f: kpt on same pce: 1st of 7 in gp* **11/1**

0500 **9** *shd* **Duke Of Firenze**[6] 6973 8-9-4 **106** FinleyMarsh(5) 17 100
(David C Griffiths) *in tch stands' side: rdn along 2f out: kpt on same pce and nvr threatened: 8th of 15 in gp* **33/1**

042 **10** *shd* **Hakam (USA)**[64] 4830 5-8-10 **96** (p1) LewisEdmunds(3) 19 89
(Michael Appleby) *dwlt: outpcd in rr towards stands' side tl kpt on fr appr fnl f: nrst fin: 9th of 15 in gp* **20/1**

2201 **11** *1* **Major Pusey**[8] 6878 5-8-5 **88** (t) MartinDwyer 12 78
(John Gallagher) *midfield stands' side: sn pushed along: nvr threatened: 10th of 15 in gp* **16/1**

015 **12** *½* **Lancelot Du Lac (ITY)**[6] 6966 7-9-10 **107** (h) FrankieDettori 2 95
(Dean Ivory) *in tch towards far side: rdn and hdwy 2f out: briefly led gp ins fnl f: wknd fnl 75yds: 2nd of 7 in gp* **12/1**

0500 **13** *shd* **Move In Time**[24] 6325 9-8-6 **89** SamJames 14 77
(David O'Meara) *prom stands' side: rdn and outpcd 2f out: no threat after: 11th of 15 in gp* **25/1**

12-0 **14** *2 ½* **Aleef (IRE)**[12] 6758 4-8-5 **91** (h) ShelleyBirkett(3) 21 71
(David O'Meara) *led stands' side and overall ldr: hdd over 2f out: sn rdn: wknd fnl f: 12th of 15 in gp* **33/1**

153 **15** *½* **Evergate**[21] 6450 3-8-7 **92** HayleyTurner 4 70
(Robert Cowell) *hld up far side: nvr threatened: 3rd of 7 in gp* **14/1**

6013 **16** *1 ¼* **Stake Acclaim (IRE)**[26] 6275 5-9-4 **101** RobertWinston 10 99+
(Dean Ivory) *chsd ldrs stands' side: rdn over 2f out: bdly hmpd jst ins fnl f: no ch after and eased: 13th of 15 in gp* **8/1**[2]

2000 **17** *nk* **Eastern Impact (IRE)**[28] 6206 6-9-0 **100** (p) AdamMcNamara(3) 6 73
(Richard Fahey) *chsd ldrs far side: rdn over 2f out: wknd over 1f out: 4th of 7 in gp* **20/1**

0116 **18** *1 ½* **Under The Covers**[9] 6864 4-8-8 **91** SamHitchcott 3 59
(Ronald Harris) *led far side: rdn whn hdd 2f out: sn wknd: 5th of 7 in gp* **40/1**

0000 **19** *nk* **Harry Hurricane**[42] 5640 5-8-13 **96** (b) TrevorWhelan 7 63
(George Baker) *hld up far side: nvr threatened: 6th of 7 in gp* **12/1**

0115 **20** *1 ¼* **Compas Scoobie**[19] 6512 4-8-12 **95** (v) AndreaAtzeni 9 58
(Roger Varian) *dwlt: hld up stands' side: nvr threatened: 14th of 15 in gp* **14/1**

1000 **21** *1 ½* **Line Of Reason (IRE)**[14] 6668 7-9-5 **102** OisinMurphy 5 60
(Paul Midgley) *chsd ldrs far side: rdn over 2f out: wknd over 1f out: last of 7 in gp* **33/1**

2025 **22** *11* **Bossipop**[7] 6922 4-8-7 **90** (b) JasonHart 13 12
(Tim Easterby) *chsd ldrs stands' side: rdn over 2f out: sn wknd: eased* **33/1**

1m 6.81s (-1.99) **Going Correction** 0.0s/f (Good)
**WFA** 3 from 4yo+ 2lb **22** Ran SP% **131.6**
Speed ratings (Par 109): **113,108,107,106,105 105,105,104,104,104 103,102,102,99,98 96,96,94,94,92 90,75**
CSF £85.29 CT £1915.29 TOTE £13.70: £2.90, £2.20, £5.40, £2.70; EX 112.10 Trifecta £3725.40.
**Owner** Rowley Racing **Bred** Swordlestown Little **Trained** Newmarket, Suffolk
■ Stewards' Enquiry : Antonio Fresu 4 day ban: careless riding (1-4 Oct)

**FOCUS**
Those who rode in the opener felt the ground was on the soft side and dead. Racing in three groups initially, those nearer the stands' side were on top from an early stage and the race produced a clear-cut winner, who has been rated to the balance of his AW form.

## 7145 ALAN WOOD PLUMBING AND HEATING PARK STKS (GROUP 2) — 7f 6y
2:25 (2:26) (Class 1) 3-Y-0+
**£56,710** (£21,500; £10,760; £5,360; £2,690; £1,350) **Stalls** Centre

Form RPR

6062 **1** **Aclaim (IRE)**[41] 5690 4-9-4 113 (t) OisinMurphy 8 118
(Martyn Meade) *trckd ldrs: pushed along whn swtchd lft over 1f out: rdn to chal ins fnl f: led 110yds out: kpt on wl* **3/1**[2]

-632 **2** *¾* **Nathra (IRE)**[14] 6697 4-9-1 108 FrankieDettori 3 113
(John Gosden) *chsd ldrs: rdn along over 2f out: chal strly jst ins fnl f: kpt on* **13/2**

-112 **3** *1* **Home Of The Brave (IRE)**[46] 5502 5-9-4 115 (t) JamesDoyle 5 113
(Hugo Palmer) *racd keenly: led narrowly: rdn along whn hdd over 1f out: kpt on same pce ins fnl f* **9/4**[1]

6210 **4** *shd* **Spirit Of Valor (USA)**[46] 5502 3-9-4 116........................(bt) RyanMoore 1 115
(A P O'Brien, Ire) *stmbld sltly s but sn w ldr: rdn to ld over 1f out: strly pressed jst ins fnl f: hdd 110yds out: no ex* **13/2**

5314 **5** *3/4* **Breton Rock (IRE)**[28] 6193 7-9-7 113.............................. AndreaAtzeni 4 114
(David Simcock) *hld up in rr: rdn along and hdwy appr fnl f: kpt on same pce: nvr threatened* **6/1**[3]

0205 **6** *1/2* **Sir Dancealot (IRE)**[28] 6193 3-9-1 110.............................. JimCrowley 6 109+
(David Elsworth) *hld up: hung lft but hdwy appr fnl f: rdn and kpt on same pce ins fnl f: nvr threatened* **8/1**

1103 **7** *2 3/4* **Viscount Barfield**[20] 6476 4-9-4 105..............................(h) DavidProbert 7 102
(Andrew Balding) *racd keenly in midfield: rdn 2f out: wknd ins fnl f* **28/1**

-000 **8** *1/2* **Peace Envoy (FR)**[62] 4935 3-9-1 106.............................. SeamieHeffernan 2 100
(A P O'Brien, Ire) *midfield: rdn and hdwy over 1f out: wknd fnl f* **25/1**

1m 25.59s (-0.71) **Going Correction** 0.0s/f (Good)
**WFA** 3 from 4yo+ 3lb **8** Ran SP% **115.1**
Speed ratings (Par 115): **104,103,102,101,101 100,97,96**
CSF £23.01 TOTE £3.80: £1.40, £2.10, £1.20; EX 23.90 Trifecta £63.90.
**Owner** Canning Downs & Partner **Bred** D Farrington And Canning Downs **Trained** Newmarket, Suffolk

**FOCUS**
Sound form, but the pace looked steady and the first four finishers raced in the first four pretty much throughout. They all gradually edged towards the far side.

## 7146 HOWCROFT INDUSTRIAL SUPPLIES CHAMPAGNE STKS (GROUP 2) (C&G) 7f 6y
**3:00** (3:00) (Class 1) 2-Y-O
**£42,532** (£16,125; £8,070; £4,020; £2,017; £1,012) **Stalls** Centre

Form RPR

5 **1** **Seahenge (USA)**[46] 5501 2-9-0 0.............................. DonnachaO'Brien 6 110
(A P O'Brien, Ire) *hld up: pushed along and gd hdwy appr fnl f: rdn to ld 75yds out: kpt on* **8/1**

1011 **2** *nk* **Hey Gaman**[28] 6190 2-9-0 103.............................. MartinHarley 7 109
(James Tate) *led: rdn 2f out: drvn and pressed fnl f: hdd 75yds out: edgd rt and one pce* **6/1**

11 **3** *nk* **Mythical Magic (IRE)**[34] 5978 2-9-0 0.............................. JamesDoyle 8 108
(Charlie Appleby) *trckd ldrs: racd quite keenly: rdn to chal appr fnl f: keeping on same pce whn carried rt by runner-up towards fin* **9/4**[1]

12 **4** *4* **Red Mist**[28] 6190 2-9-0 0.............................. AndreaAtzeni 5 98
(Simon Crisford) *trckd ldrs: racd quite keenly: rdn to chal over 1f out: wknd ins fnl f* **7/2**[3]

1 **5** *4* **Dream Today (IRE)**[22] 6403 2-9-0 0.............................. OisinMurphy 2 88
(Mark Johnston) *prom: rdn over 2f out: hung lft and outpcd over 1f out: edgd rt and wknd ins fnl f* **10/3**[2]

04 **6** *3* **Island Sound**[19] 6505 2-9-0 0.............................. GeorgeWood 1 81
(Heather Main) *in tch: rdn over 2f out: wknd over 1f out* **100/1**

**7** *22* **Mendelssohn (USA)**[34] 5971 2-9-0 0.............................. RyanMoore 3 26
(A P O'Brien, Ire) *trckd ldrs: rdn 2f out: sn wknd* **9/1**

1m 25.78s (-0.52) **Going Correction** 0.0s/f (Good) **7** Ran SP% **112.5**
Speed ratings (Par 107): **102,101,101,96,92 88,63**
CSF £52.36 TOTE £9.30: £4.00, £2.90; EX 49.50 Trifecta £179.00.
**Owner** Michael Tabor & Derrick Smith & Mrs John Magnier **Bred** K & G Stables **Trained** Cashel, Co Tipperary
■ Stewards' Enquiry : Martin Harley caution: careless riding (allowed colt to shift right away from the whip)

**FOCUS**
Not a strong edition of this race (the worst since 1998 on RPRs), they went a pretty steady gallop, racing down the centre, and there was little between the first three.

## 7147 WILLIAM HILL ST LEGER STKS (GROUP 1) (BRITISH CHAMPIONS SERIES) (C&F) 1m 6f 115y
**3:35** (3:37) (Class 1) 3-Y-O
**£396,970** (£150,500; £75,320; £37,520; £18,830; £9,450) **Stalls** Low

Form RPR

4361 **1** **Capri (IRE)**[77] 4387 3-9-1 120.............................. RyanMoore 9 121
(A P O'Brien, Ire) *in tch: trckd ldrs over 4f out: led narrowly 3f out: sn rdn along: drvn ent fnl f: styd on wl* **3/1**[1]

1331 **2** *1/2* **Crystal Ocean**[42] 5639 3-9-1 114.............................. JimCrowley 1 120
(Sir Michael Stoute) *hld up: hdwy gng wl over 3f out: rdn over 1f out: qcknd to chal jst ins fnl f: one pce and hld fnl 110yds* **5/1**[3]

1211 **3** *shd* **Stradivarius (IRE)**[46] 5503 3-9-1 116.............................. JamesDoyle 6 119
(John Gosden) *midfield: hdwy on inner over 4f out: pushed along to chal over 3f out: rdn over 2f out: one pce fnl 110yds* **9/2**[2]

4012 **4** *1 1/2* **Rekindling**[28] 6214 3-9-1 114.............................. DonnachaO'Brien 10 117
(Joseph Patrick O'Brien, Ire) *hld up: pushed along and sme hdwy over 2f out: rdn over 1f out: styd on wl: wnt 4th fnl 50yds* **10/1**

5142 **5** *1 1/4* **Coronet**[23] 6356 3-8-12 113.............................. FrankieDettori 7 112
(John Gosden) *midfield: hdwy to chse ldrs 3f out: sn rdn: wknd ins fnl f* **8/1**

1522 **6** *2 1/4* **Count Octave**[21] 6421 3-9-1 104.............................. OisinMurphy 8 112
(Andrew Balding) *hld up in midfield: rdn along 3f out: kpt on same pce and nvr threatened* **20/1**

2341 **7** *11* **Raheen House (IRE)**[65] 4811 3-9-1 110.............................. AdamKirby 11 97
(Brian Meehan) *hld up in midfield: hdwy and in tch on outer 3f out: sn rdn: wknd over 1f out* **14/1**

1032 **8** *9* **Venice Beach (IRE)**[24] 6327 3-9-1 113.................(tp) SeamieHeffernan 3 85
(A P O'Brien, Ire) *chsd clr ldr: clsr over 5f out: disp ld over 4f out: sn rdn: wknd over 2f out* **12/1**

1054 **9** *1 1/2* **Douglas Macarthur (IRE)**[24] 6327 3-9-1 114......... EmmetMcNamara 5 83
(A P O'Brien, Ire) *chsd clr ldr: clsr over 5f out: led narrowly over 4f out: rdn whn hdd 3f out: wknd* **33/1**

1111 **10** *1 3/4* **Defoe (IRE)**[28] 6191 3-9-1 113.............................. AndreaAtzeni 2 81
(Roger Varian) *hld up: rdn and sme hdwy on outer over 2f out: wknd 2f out: eased* **6/1**

-300 **11** *31* **The Anvil (IRE)**[77] 4387 3-9-1 108.............................. MichaelHussey 4 39
(A P O'Brien, Ire) *led and sn clr: rdn along and reduced advantage over 5f out: hdd over 4f out: wknd and t.o* **66/1**

3m 4.04s (-3.36) **Going Correction** +0.225s/f (Good) **11** Ran SP% **117.9**
Speed ratings (Par 115): **117,116,116,115,115 114,108,103,102,101 85**
CSF £17.42 CT £67.23 TOTE £3.90: £1.50, £2.00, £1.90; EX 21.40 Trifecta £95.40.
**Owner** Derrick Smith & Mrs John Magnier & Michael Tabor **Bred** Lynch Bages Ltd & Camas Park Stud **Trained** Cashel, Co Tipperary

**FOCUS**
A strong edition of the St Leger and the form reads well, with the Irish Derby and Goodwood Cup winners finishing first and third, and perhaps the best long-term prospect splitting them. There was no hanging around, with Ballydoyle pacemaker The Anvil charging off, albeit he was largely ignored and allowed to go clear, but the race for home began early in the straight and it was a thorough test at the distance.

## 7148 NAPOLEONS CASINOS & RESTAURANTS NURSERY H'CAP 1m (S)
**4:10** (4:11) (Class 2) 2-Y-O
**£11,827** (£3,541; £1,770; £885; £442; £222) **Stalls** Centre

Form RPR

1022 **1** **Westerland**[14] 6684 2-9-0 86..............................(p) FrankieDettori 3 94
(John Gosden) *dwlt but sn prom: racd quite keenly: pushed along to ld wl over 2f out: rdn whn jnd appr fnl f: drvn and kpt on wl fnl f* **13/8**[1]

131 **2** *shd* **Regimented (IRE)**[19] 6505 2-8-12 84.............................. JimCrowley 5 92
(Richard Hannon) *hld up in tch: pushed along and hdwy over 2f out: rdn to join ldr appr fnl f: kpt on wl: btn on nod* **9/2**[3]

105 **3** *3 1/2* **Ventura Knight (IRE)**[14] 6684 2-9-7 93.............................. OisinMurphy 4 93
(Mark Johnston) *trckd ldrs: rdn along wl over 2f out: one pce in 3rd fnl f* **16/1**

5101 **4** *2* **Maksab (IRE)**[21] 6425 2-8-13 85.............................. AndreaAtzeni 2 81
(Mick Channon) *sn trckd ldrs: rdn along over 2f out: wknd ins fnl f* **9/2**[3]

6211 **5** *1 1/2* **Rhosneigr (IRE)**[36] 5875 2-8-11 83.............................. SteveDrowne 1 75
(Charles Hills) *sn led: pushed along whn hdd wl over 2f out: sn rdn: wknd appr fnl f* **7/2**[2]

6510 **6** *4* **Ventura Dragon (IRE)**[23] 6353 2-8-8 80.............................. BarryMcHugh 6 64
(Richard Fahey) *hld up: rdn over 2f out: wknd over 1f out* **10/1**

1m 39.37s (0.07) **Going Correction** 0.0s/f (Good) **6** Ran SP% **111.7**
Speed ratings (Par 101): **99,98,95,93,91 87**
CSF £9.17 TOTE £2.10: £1.40, £2.90; EX 8.60 Trifecta £60.60.
**Owner** K Abdullah **Bred** Juddmonte Farms Ltd **Trained** Newmarket, Suffolk

**FOCUS**
A useful nursery, although not many runners. They gradually edged towards the stands' side.

## 7149 P J TOWEY CONSTRUCTION LTD H'CAP 1m (S)
**4:45** (4:45) (Class 2) (0-110,105) 3-Y-O+
**£15,562** (£4,660; £2,330; £1,165; £582; £292) **Stalls** Centre

Form RPR

3121 **1** **Kryptos**[7] 6942 3-8-3 95.............................. NicolaCurrie(7) 7 106+
(John Berry) *trckd ldrs: racd quite keenly: pushed along and qcknd to ld appr fnl f: kpt on wl* **9/2**[3]

3512 **2** *1 3/4* **Battered**[22] 6404 3-8-13 98..............................(b) RyanMoore 5 104
(William Haggas) *dwlt: hld up in rr: pushed along and hdwy 2f out: rdn to chse ldr 1f out: kpt on but a hld* **11/4**[1]

-600 **3** *3/4* **You're Fired (IRE)**[168] 1494 6-9-3 105.................... PatrickO'Hanlon(7) 10 109
(K R Burke) *hld up: rdn along 2f out: kpt on fnl f: wnt 3rd fnl 110yds* **25/1**

-050 **4** *1 3/4* **Battle Of Marathon (USA)**[32] 6024 5-9-2 97.................... AdamKirby 1 97
(John Ryan) *trckd ldrs: rdn to ld over 1f out: hdd appr fnl f: no ex ins fnl f* **40/1**

5063 **5** *nk* **Big Baz (IRE)**[8] 6873 7-9-0 95.............................. DougieCostello 6 95
(William Muir) *midfield: pushed along and outpcd whn bit short of room appr fnl f: kpt on ins fnl f* **13/2**

465B **6** *1* **Just Hiss**[28] 6209 4-8-10 91 oh1.............................. JasonHart 8 88
(Tim Easterby) *prom: rdn and outpcd over 1f out: plugged on ins fnl f* **22/1**

1000 **7** *1 1/4* **Master Carpenter (IRE)**[14] 6698 6-9-5 100.................... OisinMurphy 9 94
(Rod Millman) *hld up: rdn over 2f out: nvr threatened* **14/1**

000- **8** *1/2* **Bronze Angel (IRE)**[336] 7354 8-9-7 102........................(p) HayleyTurner 4 95
(Marcus Tregoning) *hld up: rdn along over 2f out: nvr threatened* **25/1**

0403 **9** *1 3/4* **Sinfonietta (FR)**[20] 6491 5-8-5 91 oh1.............................. FinleyMarsh(5) 3 80
(David Menuisier) *pressed ldr: rdn to ld 2f out: hdd over 1f out: wknd* **5/1**

0030 **10** *7* **Muntazah**[32] 6024 4-9-7 102.............................. JimCrowley 2 75
(Owen Burrows) *led narrowly: rdn whn hdd 2f out: wknd and eased* **4/1**[2]

1m 37.29s (-2.01) **Going Correction** 0.0s/f (Good)
**WFA** 3 from 4yo+ 4lb **10** Ran SP% **116.0**
Speed ratings (Par 109): **110,108,107,105,105 104,103,102,100,93**
CSF £16.39 CT £284.95 TOTE £4.90: £1.70, £1.50, £4.20; EX 15.90 Trifecta £349.60.
**Owner** Tony Fordham **Bred** Juddmonte Farms Ltd **Trained** Newmarket, Suffolk

**FOCUS**
A decent handicap and the main action was middle to stands' side. The first two continue to progress.

## 7150 MARRA FALCONS H'CAP 1m 3f 197y
**5:55** (5:55) (Class 2) (0-110,102) 3-Y-O+
**£12,450** (£3,728; £1,864; £932; £466; £234) **Stalls** Low

Form RPR

2-11 **1** **Game Starter (IRE)**[43] 5609 3-9-1 100..........................(p) OisinMurphy 2 112+
(Saeed bin Suroor) *led: hdd over 4f out: pushed along to ld again over 2f out: rdn over 1f out: edgd lft ins fnl f: kpt on wl: comf* **5/6**[1]

6010 **2** *3 1/2* **Amazing Red (IRE)**[22] 6399 4-8-11 89.............................. DavidProbert 1 94
(Ed Dunlop) *hld up in tch: racd quite keenly: pushed along and hdwy 2f out: rdn over 1f out: styd on fnl f: wnt 2nd nr fin* **11/2**[3]

5050 **3** *nk* **Restorer**[35] 5925 5-9-6 98.............................. AdamKirby 4 103
(William Muir) *trckd ldrs: rdn to chse ldr 2f out: no ex ins fnl f: lost 2nd nr fin* **12/1**

0133 **4** *7* **King Bolete (IRE)**[21] 6440 5-9-10 102..........................(p) AndreaAtzeni 3 95
(Roger Varian) *prom: led over 4f out: rdn whn hdd over 2f out: hung lft and wknd* **5/1**[2]

411- **5** *1* **Nietzsche**[185] 6561 4-8-5 88 oh2..............................(h) BenRobinson(5) 5 80
(Brian Ellison) *dwlt: hld up: racd keenly: rdn over 2f out: wknd over 1f out* **20/1**

563 **6** *shd* **Tawdeea**[9] 6857 5-9-4 96..............................(p) JimCrowley 6 88
(David O'Meara) *trckd ldrs: rdn over 3f out: wknd over 2f out* **7/1**

2m 36.76s (1.86) **Going Correction** +0.225s/f (Good)
**WFA** 3 from 4yo+ 7lb **6** Ran SP% **111.6**
Speed ratings (Par 109): **102,99,99,94,94 94**
CSF £5.79 TOTE £1.60: £1.10, £2.40; EX 6.30 Trifecta £31.50.
**Owner** Godolphin **Bred** Darley **Trained** Newmarket, Suffolk

**FOCUS**
The only 3yo proved too progressive for his rivals with the race rated through the runner-up.
T/Jkpt: Not won. T/Plt: £112.90 to a £1 stake. Pool: £257,097.11 - 1660.97 winning units.
T/Qpdt: £32.40 to a £1 stake. Pool: £13,756.29 - 313.40 winning units. **Andrew Sheret**

# 6821 LINGFIELD (L-H)

Saturday, September 16

**OFFICIAL GOING: Soft (good to soft in places) changing to good to soft (soft in places) after race 1 (1.55)**

Wind: light breeze Weather: cloudy, mild

## 7151 STONEGATE FOUNDATION FILLIES' H'CAP — 1m 3f 133y

1:55 (1:55) (Class 5) (0-70,72) 3-Y-O+ — £2,911 (£866; £432; £216) Stalls High

Form — RPR

0-11 **1** **Hermosa Vaquera (IRE)**[17] 6589 7-8-9 58 ............... HectorCrouch(3) 3 — 64
(Gary Moore) *hld up: hdwy to cl on ldrs 3f out: pushed along and ev ch 2f out: rdn over 1f out: led 100yds out: r.o wl to assert nr fin* **6/1**

6311 **2** ½ **Ejayteekay**[10] 6821 4-9-9 72 ............... CharlieBennett(3) 4 — 77
(Hughie Morrison) *hld up: hdwy 3f out: sn ev ch: pushed along and almost alongside ldr 2f out: rdn ent fnl f: sn led: hdd 100yds out: kpt on wl* **5/2[2]**

0022 **3** ½ **Rainbow Rising (FR)**[17] 6578 3-9-4 71 ............... KieranShoemark 1 — 75
(David Menuisier) *led: rdn 2f out: narrow ld ent fnl f: sn hdd: kpt on* **9/4[1]**

361 **4** 3¾ **Miss Inga Sock (IRE)**[44] 5555 5-9-3 68 ............... GeorgiaCox(5) 7 — 66
(Eve Johnson Houghton) *hld up: pushed along in last 3f out: rdn 2f out: hdwy into 4th ent fnl f: one pce: lost shoe* **6/1**

1165 **5** 1¼ **Multigifted**[43] 5607 4-9-10 70 ............... (t) LiamKeniry 6 — 66
(Michael Madgwick) *prom: pushed along 3f out: lost pl and rdn 2f out: no ex fnl f* **14/1**

334 **6** 10 **Perfect Spy**[16] 6633 3-9-0 67 ............... PatCosgrave 5 — 47
(Luca Cumani) *t.k.h: prom early: restrained in 3rd: hdwy and ev ch 3f out: sn pushed along: wknd 2f out: eased whn btn* **5/1[3]**

2m 34.99s (3.49) **Going Correction** -0.225s/f (Firm)
**WFA** 3 from 4yo+ 7lb — **6 Ran SP% 111.2**
Speed ratings (Par 100): **79,78,78,75,75 68**
CSF £20.94 TOTE £6.30: £2.80, £1.80; EX 19.40 Trifecta £66.10.
**Owner** Michael Baldry **Bred** James Burns And A Moynan **Trained** Lower Beeding, W Sussex

**FOCUS**
This modest fillies' handicap was run at an ordinary pace, which began to lift seriously from 3f out.

## 7152 STONEGATE HOMES H'CAP — 1m 6f

2:30 (2:30) (Class 6) (0-60,61) 3-Y-O+ — £2,264 (£673; £336; £168) Stalls Low

Form — RPR

5413 **1** **Our Cilla**[44] 5581 3-8-5 54 ............... (b) MillyNaseb(7) 2 — 63
(Julia Feilden) *hld up in last: hdwy on inner 3f out: rdn and clsd on ldrs 2f out: wnt 2nd over 1f out: led ent fnl f: styd on wl: comf* **10/3[2]**

235 **2** 2 **Perla Blanca (USA)**[25] 6293 3-9-4 60 ............... KieranShoemark 6 — 66
(Marcus Tregoning) *hld up: pushed along 3f out: drvn and hdwy over 2f out: sn led: rdn 2f out: 1 l ld over 1f out: clsd down and hdd by wnr ent fnl f: no ex* **3/1[1]**

-032 **3** 4½ **Ravenswood**[17] 6589 4-9-6 54 ............... RobHornby 3 — 53
(Patrick Chamings) *trckd ldrs: drvn 3f out: rdn and effrt 2f out: styd on fnl f: tk 3rd pl nr fin* **11/2[3]**

600 **4** nk **Percipio**[59] 5022 3-8-8 50 ............... FergusSweeney 1 — 50
(Alan King) *hld up: pushed along and hdwy 3f out: racd alone on inner and ev ch 2f out: rdn and weakend fnl f: lost 3rd nr fin* **20/1**

3605 **5** 6 **Avantgardist (GER)**[21] 6443 3-9-0 61 ............... (b) PaddyBradley(5) 7 — 53
(Pat Phelan) *chsd ldr: pushed along 3f out: drvn 2f out and briefly n.m.r: rdn and no ex fr over 1f out* **25/1**

0235 **6** 3½ **Percy Thrower (IRE)**[10] 6820 3-8-12 57 ............... CallumShepherd(3) 4 — 45
(Charles Hills) *led: 2 l clr over 3f out: rdn and hdd over 2f out: wknd* **6/1**

0005 **7** 13 **Tatawu (IRE)**[17] 6589 5-9-2 50 ............... (b) WilliamCarson 5 — 19
(Peter Hiatt) *mid-div: rdn 3f out: wknd and lost pl over 2f out* **33/1**

1432 **8** 57 **Snowy Winter (USA)**[16] 6611 3-9-5 61 ............... (t) EdwardGreatrex 8
(Archie Watson) *chsd ldrs: pushed along briefly 5f out: drvn 3f out: rdn over 2f out: wknd qckly and lost tch* **10/3[2]**

3m 6.27s (-3.73) **Going Correction** -0.225s/f (Firm)
**WFA** 3 from 4yo+ 8lb — **8 Ran SP% 112.4**
Speed ratings (Par 101): **101,99,97,97,93 91,84,51**
CSF £13.14 CT £51.22 TOTE £4.10: £1.50, £1.10, £2.00; EX 15.00 Trifecta £74.50.
**Owner** Mrs C T Bushnell **Bred** Meon Valley Stud **Trained** Exning, Suffolk

**FOCUS**
The main action developed down the middle of the home straight in this staying handicap and the form looks okay.

## 7153 BRITISH STALLION STUDS EBF FILLIES' NOVICE STKS (PLUS 10 RACE) — 7f 135y

3:05 (3:07) (Class 4) 2-Y-O — £6,301 (£1,886; £943; £472; £235) Stalls Centre

Form — RPR

22 **1** **Give And Take**[25] 6292 2-9-0 0 ............... PatCosgrave 8 — 87+
(William Haggas) *mde all: qcknd 3 l clr over 1f out: pushed along and extended advantage ins fnl f: easily* **4/5[1]**

4 **2** 4½ **Lady Of Aran (IRE)**[10] 6824 2-9-0 0 ............... StevieDonohoe 13 — 73
(Charlie Fellowes) *prom: rdn in 2nd over 1f out: kpt on fnl f but no ch w wnr* **5/1[3]**

**3** 2¼ **Lunar Maria** 2-9-0 0 ............... MartinLane 12 — 68
(Charlie Appleby) *trckd ldrs: pushed along and wnt 3rd over 1f out: one pce fnl f* **7/2[2]**

**4** 2½ **River Cafe (IRE)** 2-8-9 0 ............... MitchGodwin(5) 14 — 62
(Sylvester Kirk) *hld up: drvn and hdwy over 1f out: styd on wl fnl f* **33/1**

60 **5** 1¼ **Becky Sharp**[15] 6653 2-8-9 0 ............... PaddyBradley(5) 6 — 59
(Jim Boyle) *prom: pushed along 2f out: rdn over 1f out: no ex* **50/1**

0 **6** 1 **Obrigada**[31] 6064 2-9-0 0 ............... KieranShoemark 5 — 57
(Tom Clover) *hld up: pushed along and effrt 2f out: one pce fnl f* **20/1**

**7** 1 **Livvys Dream (IRE)** 2-9-0 0 ............... DanielMuscutt 7 — 54
(Charles Hills) *hld up: pushed along over 1f out: one pce* **14/1**

65 **8** ½ **Roseau City**[36] 5885 2-9-0 0 ............... DaneO'Neill 10 — 53
(David Elsworth) *hld up: drvn in rr 2f out: kpt on one pce* **20/1**

6 **9** 5 **Miss Paris**[44] 5573 2-9-0 0 ............... LiamKeniry 2 — 41
(Charles Hills) *hld up: pushed along 2f out: wknd over 1f out* **33/1**

0 **10** shd **Miss Recycled**[17] 6584 2-8-9 0 ............... JaneElliott(5) 4 — 41
(Michael Madgwick) *prom: pushed along and wknd over 1f out* **66/1**

**11** nse **Ipsilante** 2-8-11 0 ............... HectorCrouch(3) 9 — 41
(Jonathan Portman) *hld up: pushed along and effrt 2f out: wknd ent fnl f* **33/1**

**12** 3 **Indiscretion (IRE)** 2-9-0 0 ............... RobHornby 3 — 34
(Jonathan Portman) *hld up: hdwy 3f out: pushed along 2f out: wknd over 1f out* **25/1**

1m 33.4s (1.10) **Going Correction** +0.325s/f (Good) — **12 Ran SP% 126.8**
Speed ratings (Par 94): **107,102,100,97,96 95,94,94,89,88 88,85**
CSF £5.04 TOTE £1.70: £1.02, £1.90, £1.60; EX 5.70 Trifecta £11.60.
**Owner** Nicholas Jones **Bred** Coln Valley Stud **Trained** Newmarket, Suffolk

**FOCUS**
This proved one-way traffic for the winner.

## 7154 BRITISH STALLION STUDS EBF CONDITIONS STKS — 7f

3:40 (3:42) (Class 3) 3-Y-O+ — £9,766 (£2,923; £1,461; £731; £364) Stalls Centre

Form — RPR

2-20 **1** **Dream Of Dreams (IRE)**[21] 6428 3-8-13 102 ............ KieranShoemark 3 — 109
(Sir Michael Stoute) *trckd ldr: led narrowly over 3f out: pushed along 2f out: rdn over 1f out: qcknd clr ent fnl f: r.o strly: comf* **7/2[3]**

6620 **2** 5 **Mutawathea**[63] 4905 6-9-2 101 ............... (p) MartinLane 1 — 97
(Simon Crisford) *prom: cl 2nd over 3f out: pushed along 2f out: rdn over 1f out: nt keep tabs on wnr ent fnl f: but kpt on* **9/2**

3004 **3** ½ **Oh This Is Us (IRE)**[21] 6420 4-9-9 108 ............... SeanLevey 5 — 103
(Richard Hannon) *hld up: hdwy 2f out: sn rdn and ever ch in cl 3rd: no ex fnl f* **9/4[2]**

0500 **4** ½ **Summer Icon**[7] 6918 4-8-11 90 ............... ShaneKelly 2 — 89
(Mick Channon) *hld up: pushed along and hdwy 2f out: rdn over 1f out: one pce fnl f* **16/1**

4260 **5** 5 **Ibn Malik (IRE)**[14] 6685 4-9-2 103 ............... DaneO'Neill 4 — 87
(Charles Hills) *led: hdd over 3f out: sn pushed along and struggling: rdn 2f out: wknd and eased fnl f* **2/1[1]**

1m 24.54s (1.24) **Going Correction** +0.325s/f (Good)
**WFA** 3 from 4yo+ 3lb — **5 Ran SP% 110.4**
Speed ratings (Par 107): **105,99,98,98,92**
CSF £18.73 TOTE £4.10: £1.80, £2.90; EX 25.40 Trifecta £46.70.
**Owner** Saeed Suhail **Bred** Prostock Ltd **Trained** Newmarket, Suffolk

**FOCUS**
A high-quality little conditions event but not the most convincing field.

## 7155 HETTIE LEIGHTON BIRTHDAY CELEBRATIONS FILLIES' H'CAP — 6f

4:15 (4:17) (Class 4) (0-85,85) 3-Y-O+ — £4,690 (£1,395; £697; £348) Stalls Centre

Form — RPR

6640 **1** **Rosabelle**[46] 5513 3-8-9 80 ............... (b[1]) JoshuaBryan(5) 4 — 90
(Alan Bailey) *prom: led 2f out: rdn over 1f out: sn 1 l clr: kpt up to work ins fnl f and extended advantage: readily* **7/1**

2163 **2** 2 **Beck And Call**[26] 6276 3-8-6 77 ............... GeorgiaCox(5) 3 — 81
(Henry Candy) *mid-div: pushed along and hdwy on outer 2f out: 2nd whn rdn over 1f out: kpt on but hld ins fnl f* **7/2[2]**

2150 **3** ¾ **Curious Fox**[21] 6429 4-9-5 83 ............... KieranShoemark 1 — 84
(Anthony Carson) *slowly away: in rr: pushed along 2f out: hdwy over 1f out: rdn into 3rd ent fnl f: no further prog* **5/1**

2361 **4** ½ **Hindsight**[10] 6828 3-8-6 72 ............... TomMarquand 7 — 72
(Michael Appleby) *mid-div: pushed along 2f out: rdn over 1f out: tk 4th ins fnl f: no ex nr fin* **5/1**

2612 **5** 2¾ **Pepita (IRE)**[12] 6759 3-9-3 83 ............... SeanLevey 5 — 74
(Richard Hannon) *led: pushed along over 2f out: hdd 2f out: sn rdn and wknd* **4/1[3]**

4023 **6** ¾ **Angel Of Darkness**[23] 6358 3-9-2 85 ............... CallumShepherd(3) 2 — 73
(Charles Hills) *trckd ldrs: drvn 2f out: rdn and wknd over 1f out: eased* **10/3[1]**

0130 **7** 2¾ **Chupalla**[24] 6321 3-9-2 82 ............... FranBerry 6 — 62
(David Evans) *prom: pushed along over 2f out: sn rdn and lost pl: eased* **16/1**

1m 12.32s (1.12) **Going Correction** +0.325s/f (Good)
**WFA** 3 from 4yo 2lb — **7 Ran SP% 117.0**
Speed ratings (Par 102): **105,102,101,100,97 96,92**
CSF £32.78 TOTE £8.30: £3.30, £2.10; EX 43.40 Trifecta £234.40.
**Owner** P T Tellwright **Bred** P T Tellwright **Trained** Newmarket, Suffolk

**FOCUS**
A fair fillies' sprint handicap and sound enough form.

## 7156 IMAGINATION STATION H'CAP — 7f

4:50 (4:50) (Class 4) (0-85,85) 3-Y-O+ — £4,690 (£1,395; £697; £348) Stalls Centre

Form — RPR

4032 **1** **Ower Fly**[31] 6068 4-9-2 83 ............... (b) HollieDoyle(3) 5 — 94
(Richard Hannon) *mde all: narrow advantage tl wnt 3 l clr 1/2-way: in command 2f out: pushed along over 1f out: stl clr whn rdn ent fnl f: r.o wl and gng away at fin: readily* **4/1[2]**

0060 **2** 4 **Intense Style (IRE)**[28] 6209 5-8-8 77 ............... JaneElliott(5) 7 — 78
(Les Eyre) *prom: 3 l bhd wnr in 2nd 1/2-way: rdn over 1f out: kpt on fnl f: but nvr any ch w wnr* **4/1[2]**

1431 **3** 4 **Hajjam**[35] 5948 3-8-11 78 ............... (h) KieranShoemark 3 — 70
(David O'Meara) *mid-div: drvn into 3rd 2f out: rdn over 1f out: no ex fnl f* **5/2[1]**

6510 **4** 1½ **Coral Sea**[18] 6555 3-9-1 82 ............... (h) DaneO'Neill 6 — 67
(Charles Hills) *hld up: pushed along 3f out: rdn 2f out: styd on fnl f: tk 4th nr fin* **8/1**

1134 **5** nk **Family Fortunes**[22] 6397 3-9-4 85 ............... PatDobbs 1 — 70
(Sylvester Kirk) *mid-div: effrt on outer 3f out: drvn 2f out: rdn ent fnl f: no ex: lost 4th nr fin* **9/2[3]**

0550 **6** 7 **Awesome Allan (IRE)**[7] 6949 3-8-6 73 ............... AdamBeschizza 8 — 39
(David Evans) *cl 2nd tl wnr drew 3 l clr 1/2-way: drvn 2f out: rdn over 1f out: wknd* **20/1**

0060 **7** 1¼ **Dutch Uncle**[24] 6322 5-9-1 79 ............... TomMarquand 2 — 43
(Robert Cowell) *hld up: pushed along over 3f out: rdn over 2f out: wknd* **12/1**

5020 **8** 14 **Sans Souci Bay**[14] 6686 3-9-2 83 ............... (b) KieranO'Neill 4 — 10
(Richard Hannon) *v.s.a losing several l: latched on to pack 1/2-way: sn rdn: wknd over 2f out: eased* **12/1**

1m 24.39s (1.09) **Going Correction** +0.325s/f (Good)
**WFA** 3 from 4yo+ 3lb — **8 Ran SP% 118.0**
Speed ratings (Par 105): **106,101,96,95,94 86,85,69**
CSF £21.15 CT £48.34 TOTE £3.90: £1.40, £1.60, £1.60; EX 23.50 Trifecta £88.30.
**Owner** Green Pastures Farm **Bred** Green Pastures Farm **Trained** East Everleigh, Wilts



The Form Book Flat, Raceform Ltd, Newbury, RG14 5SJ

**FOCUS**
This was a fair handicap on paper, but it fell apart from 2f out. The winner has been rated to his AW form.

## 7157 TOMLIN 20TH ANNIVERSARY H'CAP (DIV I) 7f 135y
**5:25** (5:26) (Class 5) (0-70,71) 3-Y-0+ **£2,911** (£866; £432; £216) **Stalls** Centre

Form RPR
4614 **1** **Hedging (IRE)**[10] 6807 3-9-6 **68**....................(p) CharlesBishop 4 75
(Eve Johnson Houghton) *trckd ldrs: hdwy gng wl 3f out: led 2f out: rdn over 1f out: 1 l clr ent fnl f: styd on wl* **7/2**[2]
6-00 **2** 1 ½ **Spun Gold**[130] 2506 3-9-2 **64**.................... StevieDonohoe 1 67
(Charlie Fellowes) *mid-div: hdwy 3f out: pushed along in 3rd 2f out: rdn over 1f out: rn to take 2nd ins fnl f* **25/1**
000 **3** ½ **Highway One (USA)**[22] 6378 3-9-9 **71**.................... PatCosgrave 2 73
(George Baker) *prom: led 1/2-way: pushed along over 2f out: rdn and hdd 2f out: 2nd 1f out: no ex and lost 2nd ins fnl f* **16/1**
604 **4** 1 **Duke Of North (IRE)**[2] 7098 5-9-7 **68**.................... CharlieBennett(3) 3 67
(Jim Boyle) *hld up: hdwy 3f out: rdn into 4th over 1f out: kpt on fnl f* **5/1**[3]
3306 **5** 2 ½ **Art's Desire (IRE)**[16] 6638 3-9-2 **64**.................... LiamKeniry 10 58
(Ed Walker) *mid-div: pushed along 3f out: rdn 2f out: sme late hdwy* **8/1**
0564 **6** ¾ **Tigerwolf (IRE)**[18] 6555 4-9-10 **71**.................... CallumShepherd(3) 6 63
(Mick Channon) *trckd ldrs: cl up 2f out: sn drvn: one pce* **11/2**
4503 **7** 10 **Locommotion**[10] 6813 5-8-10 **54** oh2....................(t[1]) JohnFahy 8 22
(Matthew Salaman) *dwlt losing several l: pushed along to join pack 1/2-way: drvn over 2f out: sn rdn and no ex* **20/1**
350 **8** ½ **Western Safari (IRE)**[25] 6287 3-9-1 **63**.................... SeanLevey 9 30
(Richard Hannon) *hld up: drvn 3f out: no imp* **20/1**
5063 **9** 8 **Scarlet Thrush (IRE)**[52] 5286 3-8-12 **60**....................(b) DannyBrock 5 9
(Luke McJannet) *prom: drvn 1/2-way: rdn over 3f out: wknd* **50/1**
1116 **10** 1 **Arctic Flower (IRE)**[21] 6439 4-9-0 **63**.................... JoshuaBryan(5) 7 9
(John Bridger) *led: hdd 1/2-way: drvn over 2f out: wknd* **10/3**[1]
0304 **11** 9 **Higgy's Heartbeat**[19] 6502 3-8-6 **57**.................... JackDuern(3) 11
(Dean Ivory) *trckd ldrs: rdn 3f out: wknd 2f out: eased* **12/1**
2000 **12** 3 ¾ **Like No Other**[39] 5739 4-9-7 **70**....................(b) JaneElliott(5) 12
(Les Eyre) *prom: rdn and wknd 2f out* **25/1**

1m 34.08s (1.78) **Going Correction** +0.325s/f (Good)
**WFA** 3 from 4yo+ 4lb **12** Ran SP% **121.2**
Speed ratings (Par 103): **104,102,102,101,98 97,87,87,79,78 69,65**
CSF £97.61 CT £933.53 TOTE £4.00: £1.50, £6.80, £4.80; EX 115.70 Trifecta £1690.50.
**Owner** The Picnic Partnership **Bred** Old Carhue & Graeng Bloodstock **Trained** Blewbury, Oxon

**FOCUS**
An ordinary handicap in which they came down the middle of the course.

## 7158 TOMLIN 20TH ANNIVERSARY H'CAP (DIV II) 7f 135y
**6:00** (6:02) (Class 5) (0-70,70) 3-Y-0+ **£2,911** (£866; £432; £216) **Stalls** Centre

Form RPR
2665 **1** **Glorious Poet**[10] 6811 4-9-8 **68**.................... WilliamCarson 10 82
(John Spearing) *mde all: led early gp of two on stands' side: lft alone after 3f: 2 l clr 2f out: drvn over 1f out: 3 l clr 1f out: kpt up to work and extended advantage ins fnl f: comf* **7/1**[3]
3222 **2** 5 **Lucky Louie**[32] 6034 4-9-2 **69**....................(p) RossaRyan(7) 1 71
(Roger Teal) *mid-div: hdwy 2f out: rdn into 2nd over 1f out: r.o fnl f but nvr a threat to wnr* **3/1**[1]
2300 **3** 1 ¼ **Live Dangerously**[5] 7002 7-8-10 **56**....................(p) KieranO'Neill 2 55
(John Bridger) *led main gp in centre: pushed along in 2nd 3f out: rdn 2f out: relegated to 3rd over 1f out: kpt on fnl f* **8/1**
3226 **4** 1 ½ **Zorba The Greek**[20] 6479 5-9-10 **70**....................(b) AdamBeschizza 12 66
(Ed Vaughan) *trckd wnr on stands' side tl jnd main gp and chsd ldr in centre after 3 fs: pushed along 2f out: rdn and dropped to 4th over 1f out: one pce* **8/1**
0-25 **5** ¾ **Sentinel**[16] 6620 3-8-10 **60**.................... StevieDonohoe 11 54
(Charlie Fellowes) *trckd ldrs: drvn 3f out: rdn over 1f out: no ex fnl f* **6/1**[2]
2656 **6** 2 ½ **Many Dreams (IRE)**[9] 6866 4-9-3 **66**.................... HectorCrouch(3) 8 54
(Gary Moore) *mid-div: drvn 2f out: rdn over 1f out: no ex fnl f* **7/1**[3]
0005 **7** 3 **Gabrielle**[37] 5857 4-9-0 **60**....................(h) MartinLane 3 41
(Dr Jon Scargill) *hld up: pushed along 3f out: drvn 2f out: one pce* **20/1**
4403 **8** ½ **Equal Rights**[107] 3250 3-8-6 **56**....................(p) EdwardGreatrex 9 36
(Eve Johnson Houghton) *trckd ldrs: pushed along 3f out: rdn over 2f out: wknd over 1f out* **10/1**
-044 **9** 1 ¾ **Luang Prabang (IRE)**[11] 6795 4-9-1 **64**.................... HollieDoyle(3) 7 40
(Chris Wall) *mid-div: pushed along and lost pl 2f out: rdn over 1f out: no ex* **9/1**
4524 **10** 6 **Rattle On**[37] 5823 4-9-1 **61**....................(p) PatCosgrave 6 23
(Jim Boyle) *awkward leaving stalls: sn rcvrd to chse ldrs: rdn 2f out: weakend over 1f out* **10/1**
000 **11** 51 **Dynamic Girl (IRE)**[44] 5558 4-9-0 **60**....................(p) KieranShoemark 5
(Brendan Powell) *slowly away and received reminder: in rr: pushed along 3f out: sn rdn and no rspnse: heavily eased* **25/1**

1m 33.81s (1.51) **Going Correction** +0.325s/f (Good)
**WFA** 3 from 4yo+ 4lb **11** Ran SP% **123.3**
Speed ratings (Par 103): **105,100,98,97,96 94,91,90,88,82 31**
CSF £29.71 CT £182.82 TOTE £8.70: £2.60, £1.60, £2.70; EX 39.00 Trifecta £128.20.
**Owner** Randolph & Mortimer Racing **Bred** Bolton Grange **Trained** Kinnersley, Worcs

**FOCUS**
The second division of an ordinary handicap and it was messy.
T/Plt: £54.80 to a £1 stake. Pool: £65,473.41 - 872.02 winning units. T/Qpdt: £12.60 to a £1 stake. Pool: £4,882.00 - 284.50 winning units. **Keith McHugh**

# 6890 MUSSELBURGH (R-H)
## Saturday, September 16

**OFFICIAL GOING: Good (good to soft in places) changing to good to soft after race 1 (2.55) changing to soft after race 2 (3.30)**
Wind: Breezy, half against Weather: Overcast, raining during race 2

## 7159 COAST TO COAST NURSERY H'CAP 5f 1y
**2:55** (2:57) (Class 5) (0-70,69) 2-Y-0 **£3,234** (£962; £481; £240) **Stalls** High

Form RPR
0463 **1** **Daffy Jane**[12] 6756 2-8-13 **61**.................... SilvestreDeSousa 6 68
(Nigel Tinkler) *cl up: led 1/2-way: rdn and edgd lft over 1f out: kpt on wl fnl f* **9/2**[1]
0550 **2** 1 ¼ **Savannah's Show**[29] 6154 2-8-8 **56**.................... ConnorBeasley 2 58
(Richard Guest) *in tch on outside: effrt and pressed wnr over 1f out: kpt on fnl f: hld last 75yds* **20/1**
605 **3** nk **Eller Brook**[30] 6085 2-8-12 **60**.................... PaulMulrennan 7 61
(Michael Dods) *hld up: hdwy whn nt clr run wl over 1f out: kpt on ins fnl f: nrst fin* **8/1**
5050 **4** 1 ¾ **Lord Of The Glen**[22] 6379 2-8-2 **53** ow1....................(p) PhilDennis(3) 9 48
(Jim Goldie) *hld up: effrt and rdn over 1f out: kpt on ins fnl f: nvr able to chal* **20/1**
4244 **5** 1 **Dyson's Girl**[43] 5614 2-9-0 **62**....................(p[1]) KevinStott 5 53
(Bryan Smart) *hld up in tch: effrt and rdn over 1f out: outpcd fnl f* **11/2**[2]
0542 **6** 1 ¼ **Hypnotic Dancer (IRE)**[29] 6154 2-8-7 **55**....................(t) AndrewMullen 12 42
(Keith Dalgleish) *prom: effrt and rdn 2f out: wknd fnl f* **8/1**
1465 **7** ½ **Aquadabra (IRE)**[15] 6651 2-9-0 **69**.................... JamieGormley(7) 8 54
(Mick Channon) *hld up in midfield: effrt whn nt clr run over 1f out to ent fnl f: sn n.d* **13/2**[3]
00 **8** 1 ¾ **Rocket Man Dan (IRE)**[18] 6547 2-9-2 **64**....................(p[1]) JoeFanning 14 51+
(Keith Dalgleish) *dwlt: t.k.h: hld up: effrt whn nt clr run over 1f out: sn no imp* **9/1**
30 **9** nk **Me Before You (IRE)**[31] 6056 2-8-10 **65**....................(h[1]) PatrickVaughan(7) 10 42
(David O'Meara) *prom: effrt and rdn 2f out: wknd fnl f* **25/1**
030 **10** 1 ¾ **Alaskan Beauty (IRE)**[40] 5702 2-8-12 **63**.................... RachelRichardson(3) 13 34
(Tim Easterby) *prom: nt clr run over 2f out: rdn and wknd over 1f out* **12/1**
066 **11** nk **Orient Princess**[49] 5398 2-8-2 **50**.................... CamHardie 1 20
(Paul Midgley) *in tch on outside: effrt over 2f out: edgd rt and wknd over 1f out* **33/1**
0050 **12** 10 **Oriental Power**[16] 6626 2-8-3 **51** oh3 ow3.................... JoeDoyle 4
(Jim Goldie) *s.i.s: bhd and outpcd: nvr on terms* **100/1**
366 **13** 1 ¾ **Royal Crown (IRE)**[105] 3328 2-9-3 **65**.................... DavidNolan 3
(David O'Meara) *bhd: struggling over 2f out: sn btn* **20/1**
5350 **14** ½ **Shay C**[43] 5603 2-9-2 **64**.................... TonyHamilton 11
(Declan Carroll) *led to 1/2-way: rdn and wknd wl over 1f out* **12/1**

1m 1.47s (1.07) **Going Correction** +0.10s/f (Good) **14** Ran SP% **116.6**
Speed ratings (Par 95): **95,93,92,89,88 86,85,82,82,79 78,62,59,59**
CSF £100.11 CT £702.64 TOTE £6.00: £2.40, £6.50, £2.10; EX 109.80 Trifecta £1534.70.
**Owner** W Burton & D Fielding **Bred** Mrs G S Rees And Douglas McMahon **Trained** Langton, N Yorks

■ Stewards' Enquiry : Kevin Stott caution: careless riding

**FOCUS**
The bottom bend was moved out to give fresher ground, adding 7yds to races 2, 3, 4, 5, 7 and 8. Officially the going was given as good, good to soft in places. A modest nursery, but a progressive winner with the second running to her mark.

## 7160 LG PHARMACY LTD LUCKY GALLOP EBF MAIDEN STKS (PLUS 10 RACE) (SIRE-RESTRICTED RACE) 1m 2y
**3:30** (3:30) (Class 3) 2-Y-0 **£7,762** (£2,310; £1,154; £577) **Stalls** Low

Form RPR
54 **1** **Dubai Empire (FR)**[22] 6403 2-9-5 0.................... TomQueally 2 78+
(John Quinn) *s.i.s: chsd ldng pair: effrt 3f out: rdn to ld ins fnl f: edgd rt: styd on wl* **11/10**[1]
502 **2** ¾ **Gamesters Icon**[15] 6659 2-9-0 72.................... PaulMulrennan 3 71
(Bryan Smart) *led: rdn and hrd pressed fr 3f out: hdd ins fnl f: kpt on: hld nr fin* **9/1**
543 **3** ¾ **Mail Order**[14] 6666 2-9-0 72.................... JoeFanning 4 69
(Mark Johnston) *chsd ldr: effrt and ev ch over 2f out to ins fnl f: kpt on same pce* **5/1**[3]
**4** 3 ½ **Dalileo (IRE)** 2-9-5 0.................... SilvestreDeSousa 1 67
(Mark Johnston) *s.i.s: rn green in rr: hdwy on outside and cl up over 3f out: outpcd 2f out: n.d after* **2/1**[2]

1m 45.01s (3.81) **Going Correction** +0.40s/f (Good) **4** Ran SP% **107.6**
Speed ratings (Par 99): **96,95,94,91**
CSF £10.11 TOTE £1.80; EX 9.50 Trifecta £14.50.
**Owner** Ahmad Abdulla Al Shaikh **Bred** E A R L Haras Du Quesnay **Trained** Settrington, N Yorks

**FOCUS**
Race distance increased by 7yds. An interesting maiden with the future in mind. It was run in a heavy shower and straightforward form.

## 7161 EBF STALLIONS BREEDING WINNERS SCOTTISH PREMIER SERIES FILLIES' H'CAP 1m 2y
**4:05** (4:06) (Class 4) (0-85,86) 3-Y-0+ **£8,086** (£2,406; £1,202; £601) **Stalls** Low

Form RPR
1611 **1** **Set In Stone (IRE)**[29] 6134 3-9-7 **86**.................... RowanScott(5) 2 97
(John Patrick Shanahan, Ire) *trckd ldrs: effrt and swtchd lft over 2f out: led over 1f out: rdn out* **6/4**[1]
0354 **2** 2 **Invermere**[14] 6691 4-9-2 **72**.................... TonyHamilton 3 78
(Richard Fahey) *pressed ldr: led gng wl over 2f out: rdn: edgd rt and hdd over 1f out: rallied: one pce ins fnl f* **4/1**[2]
05/5 **3** 3 ¾ **Midnitemudcrabs (IRE)**[10] 6829 4-9-5 **75**....................(p) DavidNolan 1 72
(John James Feane, Ire) *led: rdn and hdd over 2f out: rallied: one pce fnl f* **9/1**
0544 **4** 1 ½ **Forever A Lady (IRE)**[16] 6629 4-8-13 **69**.................... AndrewMullen 4 63
(Keith Dalgleish) *prom on outside: drvn and outpcd over 2f out: rallied ins fnl f: sn no imp* **20/1**
4346 **5** 2 **Hidden Rebel**[58] 5072 5-9-12 **82**....................(b[1]) PaulMulrennan 5 71
(Alistair Whillans) *s.i.s: hld up in tch: effrt and rdn over 2f out: no imp over 1f out: btn whn flashed tail ins fnl f* **8/1**[3]
-126 **6** 3 ½ **Contentment**[71] 4564 3-9-4 **78**....................(t) JoeFanning 6 59
(William Haggas) *hld up in tch on outside: drvn along over 2f out: edgd rt and wknd wl over 1f out* **4/1**[2]
06 **7** 3 ¼ **Alexandrakollontai (IRE)**[28] 6208 7-9-2 **79**..........(b) JamieGormley(7) 7 53
(Alistair Whillans) *broke wl but sn dropped rr: drvn and struggling over 2f out: sn btn* **20/1**

1m 42.75s (1.55) **Going Correction** +0.40s/f (Good)
**WFA** 3 from 4yo+ 4lb **7** Ran SP% **110.6**
Speed ratings (Par 102): **108,106,102,100,98 95,92**
CSF £7.04 TOTE £2.30: £1.30, £2.30; EX 8.60 Trifecta £41.50.
**Owner** Thistle Bloodstock Limited **Bred** Thistle Bloodstock Limited **Trained** Kells, Co Kilkenny

**FOCUS**
Race distance increased by 7yds. The going was changed to soft before this race. A decent handicap run at a good pace, the winner continuing her improvement.

## 7162 DEUCHERS IPA H'CAP 1m 208y
**4:40** (4:40) (Class 4) (0-80,82) 3-Y-0 **£7,762** (£2,310; £1,154; £577) **Stalls** Low

Form RPR
5150 **1** **Heatongrad (IRE)**[42] 5650 3-8-12 **71**.................... TonyHamilton 11 80
(Richard Fahey) *cl up: led gng wl over 2f out: rdn over 1f out: hld on wl fnl f* **25/1**

0466 **2** *nk* **Rock N Rolla (IRE)**[43] 5601 3-9-1 **74**........................ ConnorBeasley 4 82
(Keith Dalgleish) *prom: effrt and chsd wnr wl over 1f out: kpt on fnl f: hld nr fin* **20/1**

3051 **3** *nk* **What Wonders Weave (IRE)**[11] 6784 3-8-7 **71**.............. RowanScott(5) 5 79+
(John Patrick Shanahan, Ire) *t.k.h: hld up in midfield: effrt over 2f out: kpt on fnl f: nrst fin* **5/1**[3]

2103 **4** *5* **Everything For You (IRE)**[20] 6468 3-9-7 **80**....................(p) KevinStott 9 77
(Kevin Ryan) *s.i.s: sn pushed along in rr: drvn over 3f out: hdwy over 1f out: kpt on fnl f: no imp* **10/3**[2]

2614 **5** *3 ¼* **Fayez (IRE)**[16] 6617 3-9-9 **82**.................................... DavidNolan 1 72
(David O'Meara) *hld up on ins: checked bnd over 4f out: effrt over 2f out: wknd ins fnl f* **9/1**

3501 **6** *1* **Born To Boom (IRE)**[24] 6315 3-8-11 **73**......................... CliffordLee(3) 2 61
(K R Burke) *dwlt: rcvrd and sn led: drvn and hdd over 2f out: wknd wl over 1f out* **13/2**

6420 **7** *1* **Akkadian Empire**[35] 5950 3-8-12 **71**..........................(h) PaulMulrennan 6 57
(Iain Jardine) *hld up on outside: pushed along over 2f out: edgd rt and outpcd over 1f out: sn btn* **14/1**

1535 **8** *hd* **Brother McGonagall**[24] 6315 3-8-12 **74**............. RachelRichardson(3) 8 60
(Tim Easterby) *hld up: drvn along over 2f out: sn n.d* **16/1**

11-3 **9** *3* **Under Control (IRE)**[17] 6576 3-9-4 **77**............................. JoeFanning 7 56
(William Haggas) *dwlt: hld up on outside: drvn over 2f out: edgd rt and wknd wl over 1f out* **3/1**[1]

0364 **10** *nk* **Supreme Power (IRE)**[18] 6549 3-8-4 **63** oh1 ow2...... RoystonFfrench 3 42
(Tracy Waggott) *trckd ldrs: lost pl over 2f out: sn wknd* **25/1**

0514 **11** *5* **Akamanto (IRE)**[35] 5921 3-8-2 **68**............................ JamieGormley(7) 10 36
(R Mike Smith) *sn towards rr on outside: struggling over 3f out: sn wknd* **33/1**

1m 56.03s (2.13) **Going Correction** +0.40s/f (Good) **11** Ran SP% **116.0**
Speed ratings (Par 103): **106,105,105,101,98 97,96,96,93,93 88**
CSF £424.94 CT £2955.85 TOTE £30.10: £7.30, £5.10, £2.10; EX 440.90 Trifecta £2593.80.
**Owner** Middleham Park Racing XXXV & Partner **Bred** M Morgan **Trained** Musley Bank, N Yorks
■ Stewards' Enquiry : Rowan Scott two-day ban: used whip above the permitted level (Oct 1-2)

**FOCUS**
Race distance increased by 7yds. A competitive handicap for the grade and the first three were clear of the rest.

## 7163 CALEDONIAN CUP H'CAP — 1m 5f 216y
**5:15** (5:17) (Class 3) (0-90,85) 3-Y-O

**£15,562** (£4,660; £2,330; £1,165; £582; £292) **Stalls Low**

Form RPR

1210 **1** **Tor**[21] 6445 3-9-0 **85**.............................................. JamieGormley(7) 6 93
(Iain Jardine) *trckd ldrs: effrt and chsd ldr over 1f out: kpt on wl fnl f to ld last stride* **5/2**[1]

2120 **2** *nse* **Dominating (GER)**[21] 6445 3-9-5 **83**................................... JoeFanning 1 91+
(Mark Johnston) *cl up: led over 2f out: rdn fnl f: kpt on: hdd last stride* **5/1**[3]

1412 **3** *2 ¼* **Solo Mission**[10] 6819 3-9-5 **83**......................................(p) TomQueally 7 88
(William Haggas) *in tch on outside: hdwy to ld and maintained stdy pce 1/2-way: drvn and hdd over 2f out: rallied: outpcd over 1f out* **4/1**[2]

0125 **4** *2 ¼* **Star Of The East (IRE)**[8] 6872 3-9-6 **84**.................. RoystonFfrench 3 86
(Mark Johnston) *led at stdy gallop to 1/2-way: prom: effrt and drvn over 2f out: no imp over 1f out* **17/2**

3442 **5** *5* **Pioneertown (IRE)**[7] 6937 3-8-9 **73**................................ LukeMorris 5 68
(Sir Mark Prescott Bt) *t.k.h: hld up in tch: stdy hdwy over 4f out: drvn over 2f out: edgd rt and wknd over 1f out* **5/1**[3]

5335 **6** *1 ½* **Somnambulist**[28] 6210 3-8-4 **68**..................................(h) AndrewMullen 2 61
(Keith Dalgleish) *hld up: drvn and outpcd over 3f out: n.d after* **25/1**

2433 **7** *8* **Amelia Dream**[21] 6415 3-8-8 **72**............................... SilvestreDeSousa 4 54
(Mick Channon) *plld hrd: hld up in tch on ins: checked 1/2-way: drvn and outpcd over 4f out: btn 2f out: sn eased* **11/2**

3m 14.95s (9.65) **Going Correction** +0.40s/f (Good) **7** Ran SP% **111.7**
Speed ratings (Par 105): **88,87,86,85,82 81,77**
CSF £14.49 TOTE £2.60: £1.80, £2.40; EX 14.70 Trifecta £50.40.
**Owner** I Wilson **Bred** Iain Wilson **Trained** Carrutherstown, D'fries & G'way

**FOCUS**
Race distance increased by 7yds. An open-looking handicap, albeit not the strongest for the grade, and the two protagonists recorded a personal best.

## 7164 THREE HOP H'CAP — 5f 1y
**5:45** (5:45) (Class 6) (0-60,59) 3-Y-O+ **£3,234** (£962; £481; £240) **Stalls High**

Form RPR

635 **1** **Dawoodi**[8] 6896 3-9-2 **55**...........................................(h) DavidNolan 3 62
(Linda Perratt) *hld up: smooth hdwy on outside over 1f out: rdn to ld ins fnl f: kpt on wl* **14/1**

6060 **2** *1 ¼* **Lady Molly (IRE)**[17] 6594 3-8-6 **45**...........................(b[1]) AndrewMullen 10 48
(Keith Dalgleish) *w ldrs: rdn over 2f out: ev ch whn hung rt ins fnl f: kpt on: nt pce of wnr* **10/1**

-203 **3** *shd* **Red Forever**[16] 6631 6-8-5 **46**..........................(h[1]) RachelRichardson(3) 5 48
(Thomas Cuthbert) *dwlt: hld up: smooth hdwy whn nt clr run over 1f out: rdn and r.o wl fnl f: nrst fin* **11/2**[3]

3003 **4** *¾* **Twentysvnthlancers**[15] 6660 4-9-7 **59**......................... PaulMulrennan 9 58
(Paul Midgley) *led: rdn over 2f out: hdd and no ex ins fnl f* **5/1**[2]

2000 **5** *1 ¾* **Vecheka (IRE)**[8] 6902 6-8-12 **50**..................................(e[1]) TonyHamilton 6 43
(Kenny Johnson) *hld up: effrt whn nt clr run over 1f out: edgd rt and no imp fnl f* **28/1**

5345 **6** *nse* **Cheeni**[11] 6785 5-8-6 **47**.............................................(v[1]) PhilDennis(3) 7 40
(Jim Goldie) *in tch: effrt and cl up over 1f out: no ex ins fnl f* **7/1**

6550 **7** *nk* **Windforpower (IRE)**[8] 6903 7-9-1 **53**.........................(p) RoystonFfrench 11 45
(Tracy Waggott) *w ldrs to 1/2-way: rdn and no ex fr over 1f out* **8/1**

2001 **8** *hd* **See Vermont**[16] 6631 9-9-7 **59**...............................(b) SilvestreDeSousa 2 50
(Rebecca Bastiman) *bhd on outside: effrt and rdn over 2f out: wknd over 1f out* **3/1**[1]

0212 **9** *1* **Knockamany Bends (IRE)**[14] 6688 7-8-11 **49**.............(p[1]) KevinStott 12 37
(John Wainwright) *chsd ldrs: drvn over 2f out: wknd wl over 1f out* **6/1**

0000 **10** *4 ½* **Fintry Flyer**[17] 6596 3-8-6 **45**..........................................(p[1]) JoeDoyle 8 16
(Jim Goldie) *cl up on outside: rdn over 2f out: wknd over 1f out* **50/1**

1m 2.45s (2.05) **Going Correction** +0.40s/f (Good)
**WFA** 3 from 4yo+ 1lb **10** Ran SP% **116.1**
Speed ratings (Par 101): **99,97,96,95,92 92,92,91,90,83**
CSF £145.30 CT £887.64 TOTE £13.90: £3.00, £3.80, £1.50; EX 186.90 Trifecta £1211.00.
**Owner** John Murphy **Bred** Hesmonds Stud Ltd **Trained** East Kilbride, S Lanarks

**FOCUS**
A moderate handicap. The third horse pins the level.

## 7165 ALL-NEW RACINGUK.COM H'CAP (DIV I) — 7f 33y
**6:15** (6:17) (Class 6) (0-60,60) 3-Y-O+ **£3,234** (£962; £481; £240) **Stalls Low**

Form RPR

0000 **1** **Hitchcock**[26] 6271 3-8-13 **55**.......................................(b) KevinStott 3 67
(Kevin Ryan) *led 2f: w ldr: led over 2f out: drew clr fr over 1f out: eased last 100yds* **8/1**[3]

0656 **2** *6* **Quiet Moment (IRE)**[16] 6630 3-8-8 **50**..........................(h) JoeFanning 10 45
(Keith Dalgleish) *trckd ldrs on outside: drvn along over 2f out: chsd (clr) wnr appr fnl f: r.o* **12/1**

**3** *1 ¼* **D K Travel (IRE)**[16] 6644 3-8-5 **47**..................................(t[1]) LukeMorris 9 39
(John James Feane, Ire) *t.k.h early: hld up in tch: effrt and rdn over 2f out: kpt on ins fnl f: no imp* **6/1**[2]

1340 **4** *nk* **Harbour Patrol (IRE)**[21] 6437 5-8-13 **52**..............(b) SilvestreDeSousa 2 44
(Rebecca Bastiman) *hld up: rdn and effrt on wd outside over 2f out: kpt on fnl f: no imp* **2/1**[1]

0615 **5** *1 ¼* **Cosmic Sky**[16] 6630 3-8-8 **53**...........................(h) RachelRichardson(3) 7 41
(Tim Easterby) *w ldr: led after 2f to over 2f out: lost 2nd appr fnl f: sn btn* **8/1**[3]

1000 **6** *½* **Great Colaci**[8] 6902 4-9-0 **53**.......................................(p[1]) DavidNolan 1 41
(Gillian Boanas) *prom: drvn along over 2f out: wknd over 1f out* **6/1**[2]

1400 **7** *2 ¾* **Gaelic Wizard (IRE)**[21] 6437 9-8-10 **54**..................(v) GemmaTutty(5) 5 35
(Karen Tutty) *t.k.h: hld up: rdn along over 2f out: kpt on fnl f: no imp* **11/1**

6600 **8** *¾* **Whip Up A Frenzy (IRE)**[29] 6131 5-8-1 **47**................ ZakWheatley(7) 6 26
(David O'Meara) *hld up towards rr: drvn along over 2f out: sn n.d: btn over 1f out* **16/1**

3046 **9** *½* **Red Shadow**[14] 6690 8-8-2 **46** oh1...........................(v) RowanScott(5) 11 24
(Alistair Whillans) *hld up in midfield on outside: drvn along over 2f out: sn wknd* **20/1**

/U-5 **10** *13* **Knotty Jack (IRE)**[14] 6667 5-8-7 **46** oh1....................... AndrewMullen 4
(Chris Grant) *s.i.s: hld up: rdn and outpcd over 2f out: sn btn* **50/1**

1m 31.88s (2.88) **Going Correction** +0.40s/f (Good)
**WFA** 3 from 4yo+ 3lb **10** Ran SP% **112.8**
Speed ratings (Par 101): **99,92,90,90,88 88,85,84,83,68**
CSF £96.02 CT £626.40 TOTE £8.40: £2.70, £3.60, £2.30; EX 104.20 Trifecta £680.60.
**Owner** Mrs Angie Bailey **Bred** Mrs A Shone **Trained** Hambleton, N Yorks

**FOCUS**
Race distance increased by 7yds. The first division of a moderate handicap and a wide-margin winner, who has been rated back near to his debut form.

## 7166 ALL-NEW RACINGUK.COM H'CAP (DIV II) — 7f 33y
**6:45** (6:46) (Class 6) (0-60,59) 3-Y-O+ **£3,234** (£962; £481; £240) **Stalls Low**

Form RPR

0010 **1** **Riponian**[14] 6690 7-9-2 **54**.......................................(t) JoeyHaynes 8 62
(Susan Corbett) *mde all: rdn over 1f out: kpt on strly fnl f* **6/1**[3]

4304 **2** *3* **Champion Harbour (IRE)**[24] 6315 3-9-0 **55**.................. TonyHamilton 7 55
(Richard Fahey) *hld up on ins: effrt 2f out: chsd wnr ent fnl f: kpt on same pce last 100yds* **5/2**[1]

3153 **3** *2 ½* **State Residence (IRE)**[8] 6903 3-9-1 **56**......................(vt) DavidNolan 3 49
(David O'Meara) *trckd ldrs: wnt 2nd over 2f out to ent fnl f: kpt on same pce* **5/2**[1]

0060 **4** *1* **Little Kingdom (IRE)**[21] 6437 3-8-6 **47**..................... RoystonFfrench 10 38
(Tracy Waggott) *t.k.h in tch: hld up on outside: effrt and rdn over 2f out: outpcd fr over 1f out* **9/1**

0-03 **5** *2 ¾* **Jebel Tara**[14] 6688 12-8-3 **46**................................(bt) RowanScott(5) 11 31
(Alistair Whillans) *chsd wnr to over 2f out: sn rdn and wknd* **8/1**

0500 **6** *¾* **Jacob Black**[37] 5836 6-9-3 **55**....................................(vt[1]) PaddyAspell 5 38
(Kenny Johnson) *s.i.s and detached in last pl: stdy hdwy 3f out: shkn up briefly over 1f out: sn no imp: btn fnl f* **20/1**

4503 **7** *4 ½* **Willbeme**[17] 6572 9-9-7 **59**...........................................(t) LukeMorris 12 31
(Simon West) *t.k.h: trckd ldrs: drvn over 2f out: sn wknd* **11/2**[2]

1m 32.82s (3.82) **Going Correction** +0.40s/f (Good)
**WFA** 3 from 4yo+ 3lb **7** Ran SP% **112.7**
Speed ratings (Par 101): **94,90,87,86,83 82,77**
CSF £20.76 CT £46.40 TOTE £7.60: £3.10, £1.60; EX 25.10 Trifecta £83.40.
**Owner** Girsonfield Racing Club **Bred** W B Imison **Trained** Otterburn, Northumberland
■ Stewards' Enquiry : Paddy Aspell 10 day ban: failing to take all reasonable and permissible measures throughout the race (30 Sep, 1-7/9/10 Oct)

**FOCUS**
Race distance increased by 7yds. An all-the-way winner of the second division, with the time 0.94sec slower than the first leg.
T/Plt: £2050.50 to a £1 stake. Pool: £48,735.59 - 17.35 winning units. T/Qpdt: £254.80 to a £1 stake. Pool: £4,925.18 - 14.30 winning units. **Richard Young**

7167 - 7170a (Foreign Racing) - See Raceform Interactive

# 6829 GOWRAN PARK (R-H)
Saturday, September 16

**OFFICIAL GOING: Soft to heavy**

## 7171a DENNY CORDELL LAVARACK & LANWADES STUD FILLIES STKS (GROUP 3) — 1m 1f 100y
**4:20** (4:20) 3-Y-O+

**£36,559** (£11,773; £5,576; £2,478; £1,239; £619)

RPR

**1** **Laganore (IRE)**[62] 4934 5-9-5 104............................... ColinKeane 11 108+
(A J Martin, Ire) *racd in rr: clsr travelling wl 2f out: trckd ldr in 2nd appr fnl f: rdn to ld fnl 150yds: pushed out clsng stages: comf* **7/2**[1]

**2** *2* **I'm So Fancy (IRE)**[16] 6642 3-9-0 93............................... ShaneFoley 7 105
(Mrs John Harrington, Ire) *racd in mid-div: gd hdwy on stands' side 2f out and sn led: trckd appr fnl f: hdd fnl 150yds and nt qckn w wnr: kpt on wl in clr 2nd* **14/1**

**3** *8 ½* **Wilamina (IRE)**[27] 6248 4-9-5 102.............................. ChrisHayes 9 86
(Martyn Meade) *chsd ldrs in 5th: clsr in 4th 4f out: rdn to trck ldr in 2nd 2f out: nt qckn appr fnl f in 3rd: sn no ex w principals* **7/1**

**4** *4 ¾* **Key To My Heart (IRE)**[20] 6490 3-9-0 102....................(b) GaryCarroll 6 78
(A P O'Brien, Ire) *led tl hdd under 2f out: sn one pce* **7/1**

**5** *1 ¼* **Alluringly (USA)**[6] 6972 3-9-0 104..............................(v[1]) PBBeggy 1 75
(A P O'Brien, Ire) *racd towards rr: rdn in mid-div 2f out: no imp appr fnl f: kpt on one pce* **11/2**[2]

6 6 ½ **Glamorous Approach (IRE)**[7] 6957 4-9-5 102.........(p) KevinManning 4 61
(J S Bolger, Ire) *chsd ldrs in 4th: rdn in 5th under 4f out: nt qckn under 2f out: sn no ex* **13/2**[3]

7 nk **Bumbasina (IRE)**[24] 6334 3-9-0 92.......................................... WJLee 10 61
(W McCreery, Ire) *racd towards rr: pushed along under 3f out: rdn in 9th 2f out: kpt on one pce: nvr on terms* **12/1**

8 2 ¾ **Remarkable Lady (IRE)**[7] 6961 4-9-5 92...........(tp) DeclanMcDonogh 5 55
(H Rogers, Ire) *racd in mid-div: pushed along in rr over 3f out: nvr a factor* **50/1**

9 7 **Pocketfullofdreams (FR)**[24] 6334 3-9-0 96..............(h) NGMcCullagh 3 41
(A P O'Brien, Ire) *t.k.h and chsd ldrs in 3rd: sn clsr in 2nd: rdn and nt qckn 2f out: sn wknd* **20/1**

10 25 **Dabulena (IRE)**[116] 2934 3-9-0 95...................................... PatSmullen 8
(D K Weld, Ire) *quite keen early to trck ldr in 2nd: sn 3rd: rdn over 2f out and sn wknd: eased fr over 1f out: lost shoe/action* **7/2**[1]

11 29 **Ionization (IRE)**[16] 6642 4-9-5 91.................................... RonanWhelan 2
(John Patrick Shanahan, Ire) *racd in mid-div on inner: rdn and bit clsr 3f out: wknd qckly to rr under 2f out: eased fr over 1f out* **33/1**

2m 6.67s (-0.33)
**WFA** 3 from 4yo+ 5lb 11 Ran SP% **122.2**
CSF £57.79 TOTE £4.40: £1.30, £4.40, £2.70; DF 60.60 Trifecta £408.80.
**Owner** Newtown Anner Stud Farm Ltd **Bred** Newtown Anner Stud Farm Ltd **Trained** Summerhill, Co. Meath

**FOCUS**
A deserved win at this level for this consistent mare, who has been rated in line with this year's best.

7172 - 7174a (Foreign Racing) - See Raceform Interactive

## 7011 MAISONS-LAFFITTE (R-H)
Saturday, September 16
**OFFICIAL GOING: Turf: very soft**

### 7175a PRIX DE BLAISON (MAIDEN) (2YO COLTS & GELDINGS) (STRAIGHT) (TURF) 7f 110y
1:05 2-Y-O **£11,538** (£4,615; £3,461; £2,307; £1,153)

RPR

1 **Baillolet (FR)**[37] 5989 2-9-2 0.......................................... CristianDemuro 1 85
(Mme Pia Brandt, France) **9/10**[1]

2 ½ **Infernal Majesty (FR)**[25] 2-9-2 0.................................... TheoBachelot 7 84
(S Wattel, France) **48/10**[3]

3 2 ½ **Checkpoint Charlie (IRE)**[38] 2-9-2 0.............................. JulienAuge 5 78
(E J O'Neill, France) **13/1**

4 2 **Smart Move (FR)**[39] 5776 2-9-2 0..................................... GeraldMosse 4 73
(F-H Graffard, France) **226/10**

5 3 **Day Of Rest (FR)**[29] 6170 2-9-2 0.................................... MaximeGuyon 3 66
(George Baker) **17/5**[2]

6 1 **The Gates Of Dawn (FR)**[35] 5952 2-9-2 0...........(b) AurelienLemaitre 6 64
(F Head, France) **58/10**

PARI-MUTUEL (all including 1 euro stake): WIN 1.90; PLACE 1.30, 2.00; SF 5.60.
**Owner** Gerard Augustin-Normand **Bred** Franklin Finance S.A. **Trained** France

### 7176a PRIX DU PRINCE D'ORANGE (GROUP 3) (3YO) (ROUND) (TURF) 1m 2f (S)
1:35 3-Y-O **£34,188** (£13,675; £10,256; £6,837; £3,418)

RPR

1 **Recoletos (FR)**[32] 6053 3-9-2 0.......................................... OlivierPeslier 1 114
(C Laffon-Parias, France) *racd freely: trckd ldr under restraint: led appr 3 1/2f out: qcknd more than 1 1/2f out: rdn ent fnl f: styd on gamely u.p: jst hld on* **6/4**[1]

2 nse **Plumatic**[104] 3368 3-9-2 0................................................ MaximeGuyon 3 114+
(A Fabre, France) *a cl up under a tight hold: pushed along but nt qckn 2f out: styd on under driving wl under 1 1/2f out: grad reeled in ldr fnl f: nt quite get up* **54/10**[3]

3 1 ¾ **Afandem (FR)**[35] 5953 3-9-2 0......................................... GregoryBenoist 2 110
(J-C Rouget, France) *led: hdd appr 3 1/2f out: remained cl up: rdn and nt qckn under 1 1/2f out: kpt on at same pce fnl f* **31/10**[2]

4 3 **Bay Of Poets (IRE)**[29] 6172 3-9-2 0.............................. CristianDemuro 5 104+
(Charlie Appleby) *w.w adrift of ldng trio: began to cl 2f out: rdn and no more imp 1 1/2f out: plugged on at one pce* **54/10**[3]

5 1 ¾ **Volfango (IRE)**[29] 6172 3-9-2 0.................................... AurelienLemaitre 6 101+
(F Head, France) *w.w in fnl pair: no imp whn asked to cl more than 2f out: kpt on ins fnl f: nvr in contention* **66/10**

6 1 ¾ **Devamani (FR)**[49] 3-9-2 0................................. ChristopheSoumillon 4 97+
(A De Royer-Dupre, France) *slowly away: settled in rr: rdn and short-lived effrt 2f out: nvr got involved* **17/2**

2m 14.3s (11.90) 6 Ran SP% **119.3**
PARI-MUTUEL (all including 1 euro stake): WIN 2.50; PLACE 1.70, 2.50; SF 13.70.
**Owner** Sarl Darpat France **Bred** Sarl Darpat France **Trained** Chantilly, France

**FOCUS**
A steadily run race in which the forwardly placed winner and 3rd set the standard, with a big pb from the 2nd.

### 7177a LA COUPE DE MAISONS-LAFFITTE (GROUP 3) (3YO+) (STRAIGHT) (TURF) 1m 2f (S)
3:15 3-Y-0+ **£34,188** (£13,675; £10,256; £6,837; £3,418)

RPR

1 **Garlingari (FR)**[20] 6499 6-9-2 0....................(p) StephanePasquier 4 114
(Mme C Barande-Barbe, France) *mde virtually all: sn led gp of four towards centre: hrd pressed whn drvn over 1f out: styd on strly fnl f* **21/10**[2]

2 ¾ **One Foot In Heaven (IRE)**[133] 2398 5-9-2 0.................. MaximeGuyon 3 113
(A De Royer-Dupre, France) *trckd ldr towards centre: shkn up to chal over 1f out: sn rdn and styd on: a looked 2nd best fnl f* **6/4**[1]

3 hd **Haggle**[27] 6248 4-8-13 0................................................ AlexisBadel 1 109
(H-F Devin, France) *trckd ldr in stands' side pair: drvn to cl appr 1 1/2f out: styd on to chse ldng pair into fnl f: kpt on wl* **41/10**[3]

4 3 **Furia Cruzada (CHI)**[27] 6248 6-9-3 0............................ GregoryBenoist 5 107
(S Kobayashi, France) *settled 3rd in gp towards centre: no imp whn asked to cl 1 1/2f out: one pce fnl f* **183/10**

5 6 **Royal Dolois (FR)**[12] 6773 5-9-2 0........................ Pierre-CharlesBoudot 6 94
(J-M Lefebvre, France) *led stands' side pair: drvn and 2nd overall appr 1 1/2f out: sn btn* **5/1**

6 3 ½ **Subway Dancer (IRE)**[32] 6052 5-9-2 0.................. VincentCheminaud 2 87
(Z Koplik, Czech Republic) *a in rr: rdn and no imp wl over 1 1/2f out: bhd fnl f* **167/10**

2m 7.2s (4.80) 6 Ran SP% **119.4**
PARI-MUTUEL (all including 1 euro stake): WIN 3.10; PLACE 1.40, 1.50; SF 6.80.
**Owner** Mme Corine Barande-Barbe **Bred** Mme C Barande Barbe & Mme J J Massy **Trained** France

## WOODBINE (L-H)
Saturday, September 16
**OFFICIAL GOING: Tapeta: fast, turf: firm**

### 7178a NORTHERN DANCER TURF STKS (GRADE 1) (3YO+) (TURF) 1m 4f (T)
10:31 3-Y-0+

**£130,120** (£36,144; £18,072; £10,843; £4,337; £1,807)

RPR

1 **Johnny Bear (CAN)**[17] 6-8-7 0...................................(b) LuisContreras 7 112
(Ashlee Brnjas, Canada) *trckd ldrs: rdn over 2f out: jnd ldr 100yds out: jst prevailed* **91/10**

2 hd **Hawkbill (USA)**[34] 5983 4-8-11 0...........................(p) ColmO'Donoghue 8 115
(Charlie Appleby) *led: rdn 2f out: jnd 100yds out: jst hld* **3/5**[1]

3 ¾ **Messi (GER)**[56] 7-8-9 0........................................................ JoseLOrtiz 4 112+
(H Graham Motion, U.S.A) *hld up towards rr of midfield: stdy hdwy fr 4f out: rdn 1 1/2f out: kpt on wl fnl f* **31/10**[2]

4 3 ¾ **Seeking Albert (CAN)**[27] 3-8-1 0 ow1...........................(b[1]) DJMoran 6 106
(Michael P De Paulo, Canada) *in tch in midfield: pushed along under 3f out: rdn and kpt on same pce fr 2f out* **41/1**

5 2 **English Illusion (CAN)**[17] 4-8-7 0....................... EuricoRosaDaSilva 1 101
(Daniel J Vella, Canada) *midfield: dropped to rr under 3f out: rdn and kpt on steadily ins fnl f* **36/1**

6 1 **Noble Thought (USA)**[27] 4-8-7 0..........................(b) PatrickHusbands 3 99
(Malcolm Pierce, Canada) *hld up towards rr: sme hdwy on outer appr 2f out: rdn 2f out: wknd ins fnl f* **15/2**[3]

7 1 **Pumpkin Rumble (USA)**[27] 6-8-7 0........................ JesseMCampbell 5 98
(Kevin Attard, Canada) *chsd ldr: rdn 2 1/2f out: wknd under 2f out* **35/1**

8 ¾ **Camp Creek (CAN)**[136] 4-8-7 0.................. RafaelManuelHernandez 2 96
(Kevin Attard, Canada) *a towards rr* **39/1**

2m 27.3s (-2.30)
**WFA** 3 from 4yo+ 7lb 8 Ran SP% **118.9**
PARI-MUTUEL (all including 2 cad stake): WIN 20.20; PLACE (1-2) 5.60, 2.60; SF 64.10.
**Owner** Colebrook Farms & Bear Stables Ltd **Bred** Tall Oaks Farm **Trained** North America

### 7179a RICOH WOODBINE MILE STKS (GRADE 1) (3YO+) (TURF) 1m (T)
11:34 3-Y-0+

**£289,156** (£96,385; £48,192; £24,096; £9,638; £4,819)

RPR

1 **World Approval (USA)**[35] 5955 5-8-12 0...............(b) JohnRVelazquez 1 123+
(Mark Casse, Canada) *disp ld: led 2 1/2f out: rdn 2f out: wnt clr appr fnl f: kpt on strly* **47/20**[1]

2 2 ½ **Lancaster Bomber (USA)**[45] 5527 3-8-0 0................. WayneLordan 10 109+
(A P O'Brien, Ire) *in tch in midfield on outer: short of room whn rdn under 2f out: kpt on wl fnl f: wnt 2nd 100yds out: no ch w wnr* **91/20**[3]

3 ½ **Long On Value (USA)**[41] 6-8-5 0.................................... JoelRosario 3 109+
(William Mott, U.S.A) *hld up in rr: stl in rr and travelling wl whn nt clr run over 1f out: swtchd to outside and drvn 1f out: styd on strly fnl f: nrst fin* **96/10**

4 nse **Mondialiste (IRE)**[21] 6444 7-8-9 0.......................................... JoseLOrtiz 8 113+
(David O'Meara) *hld up in rr: rdn over 2f out: drvn under 2f out: kpt on wl fnl f* **137/10**

5 ½ **Arod (IRE)**[154] 6-8-5 0............................................................ HarryBentley 9 108
(David Simcock) *hld up towards rr of midfield: rdn over 2f out: kpt on fnl f* **51/1**

6 ½ **Dutch Connection**[20] 6476 5-8-7 0.......................... MickaelBarzalona 11 108
(Charles Hills) *in tch in midfield: rdn and kpt on same pce fr over 1f out* **269/10**

7 ½ **Conquest Panthera (USA)**[28] 5-8-9 0..................... PatrickHusbands 7 109
(Mark Casse, Canada) *prom: rdn under 2f out: hung lft 1f out: wknd steadily ins fnl f* **11/1**

8 2 ¼ **Tower Of Texas (CAN)**[28] 6-8-9 0.....................(b) EuricoRosaDaSilva 2 104
(Roger L Attfield, Canada) *in tch in midfield: rdn over 3f out: chsd ldrs appr fnl f: wknd 150yds out* **107/10**

9 2 ¾ **Glenville Gardens (USA)**[28] 5-8-7 0............................ LuisContreras 12 96
(Sid Attard, Canada) *trckd ldrs on outer: wd into st: rdn over 2f out: wknd 1 1/2f out* **148/10**

10 3 **Best Bard (CAN)**[41] 7-8-5 0........................... RafaelManuelHernandez 4 87
(Norman McKnight, Canada) *in tch in midfield: rdn 2f out: wknd over 1f out* **138/1**

11 nse **Deauville (IRE)**[34] 5977 4-8-9 0.................................(p) JamieSpencer 6 91
(A P O'Brien, Ire) *prom: rdn 2 1/2f out: wknd over 1f out: eased ins fnl f* **33/10**[2]

12 ¾ **Dragon Bay (USA)**[27] 4-8-9 0...................................... GaryBoulanger 5 89
(Stuart C Simon, Canada) *disp ldr: pushed along and hdd 2 1/2f out: wknd 2f out* **68/1**

1m 33.05s
**WFA** 3 from 4yo+ 4lb 12 Ran SP% **118.2**
PARI-MUTUEL (all including 2 cad stake): WIN 6.70; PLACE (1-2) 3.90, 5.30; SHOW (1-2-3) 3.00, 4.00, 5.30; SF 42.00.
**Owner** Live Oak Plantation **Bred** Live Oak Stud **Trained** Canada

**FOCUS**
This was a muddling race with a sprint finish: 23.77 (2f), 22.68 (4f), 23.86 (6f), 22.74 (line).

7180 - 7189a (Foreign Racing) - See Raceform Interactive

## 6609 BATH (L-H)

Sunday, September 17

**OFFICIAL GOING: Good to soft (7.1)**
Wind: light across Weather: cloudy

### 7190 BRISTOL CONSERVATORY UPGRADES H'CAP (DIV I) 5f 160y
2:15 (2:15) (Class 6) (0-60,60) 3-Y-O+ £2,264 (£673; £336; £168) Stalls Centre

Form RPR

5004 **1** **Evening Starlight**[29] 6179 4-9-0 **53** SteveDrowne 12 61
(Ron Hodges) *a.p: rdn to ld over 1f out: sn strly chal: kpt on gamely: rdn out* **12/1**

0055 **2** ½ **Fleeting Glimpse**[9] 6888 4-8-12 **54** CharlieBennett(3) 13 60
(Patrick Chamings) *hld up towards rr: hdwy over 2f out: rdn for str chal fr over 1f out: ev ch fnl f: kpt on but no ex cl home* **16/1**

1202 **3** 1 ½ **Frank Cool**[29] 6174 4-9-5 **58** RobertWinston 8 59
(Tony Carroll) *squeezed up s: mid-div: hdwy 2f out: sn swtchd lft and rdn: kpt on ins fnl f but nt quite pce to chal* **5/2[1]**

0000 **4** 1 ½ **Tisa River (IRE)**[34] 6004 3-8-2 **46** oh1 (t[1]) HollieDoyle(3) 7 42
(Milton Bradley) *disp ld: rdn and hdd over 1f out: kpt on same pce fnl f* **22/1**

0325 **5** ½ **Fantasy Justifier (IRE)**[29] 6179 6-9-7 **60** LukeMorris 16 55
(Ronald Harris) *slowly away: in last pair: swtchd to far side and hdwy over 2f out: kpt on fnl f but nt pce to get on terms* **8/1**

1316 **6** ½ **Wild Flower (IRE)**[23] 6373 5-9-5 **58** KieranO'Neill 9 51
(Jimmy Fox) *disp ld: rdn and hdd over 1f out: kpt on same pce fnl f* **9/2[2]**

0603 **7** 2 ¼ **Head Space (IRE)**[18] 6582 9-8-9 **55** (v) JasonWatson(7) 3 41
(Brian Barr) *s.i.s: in last pair: kpt on fr over 1f out: nvr trbld ldrs* **25/1**

6400 **8** 1 ¾ **Picc And Go**[11] 6810 4-8-9 **48** JohnFahy 11 28
(Matthew Salaman) *s.i.s: towards rr: sme late prog: n.d* **33/1**

0006 **9** 1 **Blistering Dancer (IRE)**[5] 7017 7-8-5 **46** oh1 ow3(b) MitchGodwin(5) 10 26
(Tony Carroll) *trckd ldrs: rdn over 2f out: drifted lft over 1f out: wknd* **16/1**

0650 **10** 1 ¼ **Bingo George (IRE)**[22] 6437 4-8-4 **46** oh1 (b[1]) GeorgeWood(3) 6 19
(Mark Rimell) *chsd ldrs: rdn over 2f out: carried lft and tight for room over 1f out: one pce fnl f* **7/1[3]**

6040 **11** ½ **Diminutive (IRE)**[20] 6507 5-8-7 **46** oh1 (b) RobHornby 14 17
(Grace Harris) *mid-div: rdn 3f out: nvr threatened: wknd fnl f* **20/1**

0006 **12** 5 **Candelaria**[17] 6612 4-8-11 **50** (v[1]) ShaneKelly 5 4
(Jonjo O'Neill) *in tch: effrt over 2f out: wknd over 1f out* **20/1**

3520 **13** 1 ½ **Triple Dream**[17] 6635 12-8-7 **46** oh1 RyanPowell 15
(Milton Bradley) *mid-div on outer: rdn wl over 2f out: wknd over 1f out* **20/1**

44 **14** 10 **Mags Well (IRE)**[68] 4723 3-9-4 **59** LiamKeniry 2
(Geoffrey Deacon) *chsd ldrs: rdn over 2f out: sn wknd: eased fnl f* **14/1**

1m 13.93s (2.73) **Going Correction** +0.325s/f (Good)
**WFA** 3 from 4yo+ 2lb **14** Ran SP% **121.9**
Speed ratings (Par 101): **94,93,91,89,88 88,85,82,81,79 79,72,70,57**
CSF £170.32 CT £642.35 TOTE £13.80: £4.10, £4.80, £1.20; EX 199.80 Trifecta £531.40.
**Owner** R J Hodges **Bred** Worksop Manor Stud **Trained** Charlton Mackrell, Somerset

**FOCUS**
Owing to an infestation of chafer grubs on the home bend, the track could only stage races over distances short of 6f.\n\x\x This moderate sprint handicap looks straightforward rated around the third.

### 7191 BRISTOL CONSERVATORY UPGRADES H'CAP (DIV II) 5f 160y
2:45 (2:54) (Class 6) (0-60,60) 3-Y-O+ £2,264 (£673; £336; £168) Stalls Centre

Form RPR

2030 **1** **Langley Vale**[39] 5784 8-9-7 **60** RobertWinston 3 66
(Roger Teal) *hld up towards rr of midfield: hdwy fr 2f out: str chal ins fnl f: led fnl stride: drvn rt out* **8/1[3]**

2403 **2** nse **Time Medicean**[13] 6748 11-9-3 **56** GeorgeDowning 2 62
(Tony Carroll) *in tch: hdwy over 2f out: rdn to ld over 1f out: strly pressed ins fnl f: kpt on: hdd fnl stride* **9/1**

003 **3** nk **Angelito**[67] 4735 8-8-7 **49** EoinWalsh(3) 11 54
(Tony Newcombe) *s.i.s: towards rr: rdn and hdwy fr over 2f out: chal ins fnl f: kpt on but no ex cl home* **14/1**

0321 **4** 4 **David's Beauty (IRE)**[11] 6810 4-9-2 **55** (b) LukeMorris 7 47
(Brian Baugh) *trckd ldrs: rdn and ev ch 2f out tl jst over 1f out: kpt on same pce fnl f* **6/1[2]**

4013 **5** 1 **Cee Jay**[34] 6004 4-9-2 **58** CharlieBennett(3) 12 46
(Patrick Chamings) *towards rr of midfield: rdn wl over 2f out: no imp tl r.o ent fnl f* **10/1**

00 **6** hd **Captain Scooby**[30] 6148 11-8-9 **46** oh1 ow2 (b) JohnFahy 8 36
(Richard Guest) *dwlt: bhd: r.o fr over 1f out but nvr threatened to get on terms* **25/1**

0006 **7** nk **Silver Penny**[18] 6581 3-8-6 **47** (p) RyanPowell 16 34
(Jim Boyle) *led: rdn and hdd over 1f out: no ex fnl f* **11/1**

1150 **8** 1 ¼ **Termsnconditions (IRE)**[36] 5919 3-9-1 **56** (v[1]) KieranO'Neill 5 39
(Tim Vaughan) *chsd ldrs: rdn 3f out: one pce fnl 2f* **12/1**

5134 **9** hd **Whiteley (IRE)**[14] 6724 3-8-12 **56** DavidEgan(3) 15 38
(Mick Channon) *trckd ldrs: rdn over 2f out: fdd ins fnl f* **6/1[2]**

3001 **10** 2 **Kaaber (USA)**[33] 6041 6-8-8 **52** MitchGodwin(5) 6 27
(Michael Blake) *hld up towards rr: rdn 3f out: little imp: no ch whn hmpd ins fnl f* **4/1[1]**

0600 **11** hd **Arizona Snow**[99] 3569 5-8-7 **46** oh1 (p) RaulDaSilva 9 21
(Ronald Harris) *mid-div: rdn over 2f out: nvr threatened: wknd fnl f* **33/1**

5000 **12** ½ **Tally's Song**[17] 6615 4-8-7 **46** (p) RobHornby 14 19
(Grace Harris) *chsng ldrs whn squeezed up and lost pl after 1f: mid-div: rdn and hdwy 2f out: wknd ent fnl f* **50/1**

0500 **13** hd **Posh Bounty**[11] 6813 6-9-5 **58** LiamKeniry 13 30
(Paul Burgoyne) *s.i.s: a towards rr* **25/1**

6000 **14** shd **Striking For Gold**[20] 6507 3-8-0 **46** oh1 (p) JaneElliott(5) 4 18
(Sarah Hollinshead) *chsd ldrs: rdn 3f out: wknd over 1f out* **66/1**

6050 **15** 5 **Rapid Rise (IRE)**[18] 6581 3-9-5 **60** JosephineGordon 10 16
(Milton Bradley) *chsd ldrs: rdn over 2f out: wkng whn squeezed up over 1f out* **20/1**

1m 14.26s (3.06) **Going Correction** +0.325s/f (Good)
**WFA** 3 from 4yo+ 2lb **15** Ran SP% **120.3**
Speed ratings (Par 101): **92,91,91,86,84 84,84,82,82,79 79,78,78,78,71**
CSF £71.85 CT £1025.24 TOTE £8.30: £2.80, £3.00, £6.20; EX 81.40 Trifecta £1957.10.
**Owner** Mrs Muriel Forward & Dr G C Forward **Bred** Miss Brooke Sanders **Trained** Great Shefford, Berks

■ Amberine was withdrawn. Price at time of withdrawal 12-1. Rule 4 applies to board prices prior to withdrawal but not to SP bets - deduction 5p in the pound. New market formed.

■ Stewards' Enquiry : George Downing two-day ban: used whip above the permitted level (1st-2nd Oct)

**FOCUS**
The second division of a weak sprint handicap, rated around the placed horses.

### 7192 PK BUILDING H'CAP 5f 10y
3:15 (3:21) (Class 4) (0-80,82) 3-Y-O+ £4,690 (£1,395; £697; £348) Stalls Centre

Form RPR

311 **1** **Delagate This Lord**[25] 6308 3-9-2 **74** DavidEgan(3) 4 84+
(Michael Attwater) *slowly away: last pair: hdwy over 2f out: rdn to ld jst ins fnl f: r.o wl: readily* **2/1[1]**

6221 **2** 1 ¼ **Bellevarde (IRE)**[31] 6098 3-8-11 **66** JosephineGordon 8 71
(Richard Price) *disp ld: drvn ahd wl over 1f out: hdd jst ins fnl f: kpt on but nt pce of wnr* **13/2[3]**

63 **3** ½ **Red Alert**[16] 6652 3-9-5 **74** DougieCostello 7 77
(William Muir) *trckd ldrs: rdn over 2f out: nt pce to chal but kpt on ins fnl f* **14/1**

1113 **4** ½ **Pastfact**[20] 6511 3-9-4 **73** LiamKeniry 2 74+
(Malcolm Saunders) *outpcd in last early: hdwy 2f out: kpt on to go 4th ins fnl f* **8/1**

241 **5** 3 ½ **Fujin**[14] 6720 6-9-4 **75** (v) CharlieBennett(3) 6 64
(Shaun Harris) *disp ld tl rdn wl over 1f out: fdd ins fnl f* **10/1**

4332 **6** 1 ¼ **Secret Potion**[25] 6308 3-9-1 **70** LukeMorris 1 54
(Ronald Harris) *chsd ldrs: rdn 3f out: sn outpcd: fdd ins fnl f* **7/1**

1202 **7** hd **Patchwork**[30] 6141 3-9-13 **82** ShaneKelly 5 66
(Richard Hughes) *trckd ldrs: rdn 2f out: nt pce to chal: fdd ins fnl f* **3/1[2]**

1m 3.34s (0.84) **Going Correction** +0.325s/f (Good)
**WFA** 3 from 6yo+ 1lb **7** Ran SP% **111.0**
Speed ratings (Par 105): **106,104,103,102,96 94,94**
CSF £14.52 CT £133.36 TOTE £2.90: £1.40, £3.60; EX 16.40 Trifecta £133.00.
**Owner** Mrs M S Teversham **Bred** Mrs Monica Teversham **Trained** Epsom, Surrey

**FOCUS**
A modest sprint handicap. Sound form.

### 7193 SOUTHMEAD GLASS & GLAZING NURSERY H'CAP (DIV I) 5f 10y
3:45 (3:45) (Class 5) (0-75,77) 2-Y-O £3,234 (£962; £481; £240) Stalls Centre

Form RPR

5202 **1** **Jim Rockford**[20] 6525 2-9-3 **72** HectorCrouch(3) 2 77
(Ralph Beckett) *trcking ldrs whn squeezed up after 1f: dropped to last but in tch: rdn over 2f out: hdwy over 1f out: r.o to ld fnl 100yds: won gng away* **3/1[2]**

0126 **2** ¾ **Deviate (IRE)**[15] 6678 2-9-6 **77** PaddyPilley(5) 5 79
(Tom Dascombe) *led: rdn over 1f out: kpt on but no ex whn hdd fnl 100yds* **7/2[3]**

423 **3** 4 **Spanish Star (IRE)**[44] 5586 2-9-3 **69** LiamKeniry 3 57
(Patrick Chamings) *racd keenly: trckd ldr: rdn wl over 1f out: nt pce of front pair fnl f* **15/8[1]**

055 **4** nse **Fab (IRE)**[20] 6525 2-9-7 **73** DougieCostello 1 61
(Jamie Osborne) *awkwardly away: sn trcking ldr: rdn 2f out: nt pce of front pair fnl f* **7/1**

0640 **5** 2 ¾ **Hastenplace**[61] 4991 2-8-7 **59** LukeMorris 6 37
(Rod Millman) *chsd ldrs: rdn 3f out: one pce fnl 2f* **6/1**

1m 5.35s (2.85) **Going Correction** +0.325s/f (Good) **5** Ran SP% **108.8**
Speed ratings (Par 95): **90,88,82,82,77**
CSF £13.22 TOTE £3.70: £2.20, £1.60; EX 15.60 Trifecta £28.80.
**Owner** Chelsea Thoroughbreds-The Rockford Files **Bred** Mrs Fiona Denniff **Trained** Kimpton, Hants

■ Stewards' Enquiry : Hector Crouch 2 day ban: using his whip above the permitted level (1/2 Oct)

**FOCUS**
Not a bad sprint nursery in which two came clear.

### 7194 SOUTHMEAD GLASS & GLAZING NURSERY H'CAP (DIV II) 5f 10y
4:15 (4:17) (Class 5) (0-75,74) 2-Y-O £3,234 (£962; £481; £240) Stalls Centre

Form RPR

0213 **1** **Roundhay Park**[21] 6466 2-9-7 **74** TomEaves 3 79
(Nigel Tinkler) *hld up bhd ldrs: smooth hdwy over 2f out: led jst over 1f out: rdn clr: comf* **5/2[1]**

034 **2** 1 ¾ **Maygold**[24] 6338 2-8-11 **64** (h[1]) LiamKeniry 1 63
(Ed Walker) *trckd ldrs: led 2f out: sn rdn: hdd jst over 1f out: kpt on but nt pce of wnr* **5/1**

433 **3** 5 **Big Time Maybe (IRE)**[33] 6021 2-9-7 **74** (p[1]) RichardKingscote 5 55
(Tom Dascombe) *chsd ldrs: rdn in cl 3rd over 1f out: kpt on same pce fnl f* **7/2[3]**

1254 **4** 1 **Dreamboat Annie**[16] 6651 2-9-1 **68** SteveDrowne 4 45
(Mark Usher) *pushed along in last but in tch over 3f out: kpt on fnl f but nvr gng pce to threaten* **6/1**

220 **5** hd **Tonkolili (IRE)**[19] 6559 2-9-2 **72** HectorCrouch(3) 2 49
(William Muir) *disp ld tl rdn 2f out: sn hld: no ex fnl f* **10/1**

031 **6** hd **Zain Smarts (IRE)**[17] 6609 2-8-13 **69** DavidEgan(3) 6 45
(David Evans) *disp ld: rdn and hdd 2f out: sn drifted lft and hld: no ex fnl f* **10/3[2]**

1m 4.02s (1.52) **Going Correction** +0.325s/f (Good) **6** Ran SP% **113.9**
Speed ratings (Par 95): **100,97,89,87,87 86**
CSF £15.64 TOTE £3.50: £2.50, £3.20; EX 18.20 Trifecta £81.50.
**Owner** Leeds Plywood And Doors Ltd **Bred** James Munroe **Trained** Langton, N Yorks

**FOCUS**
The second division of the 5f nursery and again two pulled clear. The race has been rated around the runner-up

### 7195 PROFAB WINDOWS SUMMER SPRINT SERIES FINAL H'CAP 5f 160y
4:45 (4:45) (Class 2) 3-Y-O+ £13,232 (£3,960; £1,980; £991; £493) Stalls Centre

Form RPR

1114 **1** **Our Lord**[16] 6652 5-8-13 **82** DavidEgan(3) 12 91
(Michael Attwater) *mid-div: hdwy over 2f out: led over 1f out: hld on wl whn chal ins fnl f: drvn out* **7/2[1]**

0445 **2** nk **Storm Melody**[43] 5656 4-8-1 **70** GeorgeWood(3) 8 78
(Jonjo O'Neill) *slowly away: towards rr: nt clr run and swtchd rt 2 out: rdn and hdwy over 1f out: chal ins fnl f: kpt on* **4/1[2]**

3105 **3** 2 ¼ **Pixeleen**[10] 6864 5-9-10 **90** JosephineGordon 1 91
(Malcolm Saunders) *chsd ldrs: rdn over 1f out: kpt on ins fnl f but nt quite pce to chal* **9/2[3]**

5350 **4** 1 ½ **Essaka (IRE)**[17] 6615 5-7-7 **66** oh15 SophieRalston(7) 3 62?
(Tony Carroll) *s.i.s: towards rr: hdwy into midfield after 1f: rdn to chse ldrs over 1f out: kpt on same pce fnl f* **100/1**

1661 **5** 1 **Coronation Cottage**[17] 6612 3-8-2 **73** CharlieBennett(3) 7 65
(Malcolm Saunders) *led: rdn and hdd over 1f out: no ex fnl f* **9/1**

4324 **6** *1 3/4* **Showmethewayavrilo**[9] 6888 4-8-2 **68** ........ LukeMorris 6 55
(Malcolm Saunders) *chsd ldrs: rdn over 2f out: sn one pce* **7/1**
0114 **7** *shd* **Jaganory (IRE)**[17] 6615 5-7-9 **66** oh3 ........ (p) JaneElliott(5) 11 52
(Christopher Mason) *chsd ldrs: rdn 2f out: fdd ins fnl f* **16/1**
3436 **8** *1/2* **Prominna**[21] 6478 7-7-9 **66** oh10 ........ RhiainIngram(5) 4 51
(Tony Carroll) *chsd ldrs: rdn 3f out: one pce fnl 2f* **33/1**
1312 **9** *1/2* **Dandilion (IRE)**[17] 6612 4-7-11 **66** oh2 ........ (t) HollieDoyle(3) 5 49
(Alex Hales) *sn outpcd in rr: n.d* **6/1**
0233 **10** *1 1/2* **Burauq**[17] 6615 5-8-0 **66** oh14 ........ (v) RyanPowell 14 44
(Milton Bradley) *s.i.s: a towards rr* **66/1**
0250 **11** *nk* **Seamster**[3] 7086 10-8-3 **76** ........ (t) LauraCoughlan(7) 10 53
(David Loughnane) *mid-div: effrt over 2f out: wknd ent fnl f* **12/1**

1m 13.41s (2.21) **Going Correction** +0.325s/f (Good)
**WFA** 3 from 4yo+ 2lb **11** Ran SP% **116.2**
Speed ratings (Par 109): **98,97,94,92,91 88,88,88,87,85 85**
CSF £17.05 CT £64.98 TOTE £4.20: £1.80, £2.10, £2.00; EX 19.20 Trifecta £75.60.
**Owner** Mrs M S Teversham **Bred** Mrs Monica Teversham **Trained** Epsom, Surrey

**FOCUS**
An open edition of this series final.
T/Jkpt: Not won. T/Plt: £156.80 to a £1 stake. Pool: £124,881.78 - 581.31 winning units. T/Qpdt: £14.00 to a £1 stake. Pool: £8,797.46 - 462.23 winning units. **Tim Mitchell**

## 6366 FFOS LAS (L-H)
### Sunday, September 17

**OFFICIAL GOING: Heavy (soft in places; 5.1)**
Wind: slight crosswind in the home straight Weather: sunny spells

### 7196 BET WITH PETER SUTTON BOOKMAKERS ON COURSE NURSERY H'CAP 6f
**2:00** (2:01) (Class 6) (0-60,61) 2-Y-O **£2,911** (£866; £432; £216) **Stalls** Centre

Form RPR
1256 **1** **Give Em A Clump (IRE)**[4] 7057 2-9-7 **60** ........ (v) KieranShoemark 7 65
(David Evans) *racd keenly: prom tl led over 4f out: drvn 2f out: in command ent fnl f: r.o wl* **9/4**[1]
0454 **2** *2* **Kheleyf's Girl**[37] 5886 2-9-7 **60** ........ FranBerry 5 59
(David Evans) *prom: rdn over 2f out: wnt 2nd jst ins fnl f: kpt on but hld by wnr* **9/1**
0600 **3** *1/2* **Bullseye Bullet**[17] 6634 2-8-6 **52** ........ (p) NicolaCurrie(7) 3 50
(Mark Usher) *hld up bhd ldrs: clsd 1/2-way: rdn to chse wnr over 1f out: unable qck and lost 2nd jst ins fnl f* **18/1**
0564 **4** *1* **Inuk (IRE)**[32] 6063 2-8-11 **55** ........ (p[1]) FinleyMarsh(5) 4 50
(Richard Hughes) *hld up: rdn and swtchd lft over 1f out: kpt on same pce* **7/1**
0400 **5** *hd* **Rio Santos**[3] 7081 2-8-10 **49** ........ OisinMurphy 6 43
(Rod Millman) *hld up: drvn 2f out: styd on same pce fnl f* **5/2**[2]
000 **6** *shd* **Dark Freedom (IRE)**[40] 5755 2-9-5 **61** ........ CallumShepherd(3) 2 55
(Charles Hills) *s.i.s: hld up: rdn over 2f out: one pce appr fnl f* **8/1**
5054 **7** *nk* **Couldn't Could She**[4] 7057 2-9-3 **61** ........ BenRobinson(5) 1 54
(Adam West) *mounted in chute: t.k.h: led over 1f: chsd wnr: rdn and ev ch over 1f out: wknd appr fnl f* **10/3**[3]

1m 15.94s (5.94) **Going Correction** +0.825s/f (Soft) **7** Ran SP% **121.3**
Speed ratings (Par 93): **93,90,89,88,88 87,87**
CSF £25.03 TOTE £2.60: £1.70, £3.40; EX 17.40 Trifecta £233.20.
**Owner** Power Geneva Ltd & Partner **Bred** Pixies Syndicate **Trained** Pandy, Monmouths

**FOCUS**
Heavy ground officially and a time 7sec slower than RP Standard backed that up. This was a weak affair and positive pointers for the future and thin on the ground.

### 7197 EBF NOVICE STKS (PLUS 10 RACE) 7f 80y(R)
**2:30** (2:31) (Class 4) 2-Y-O **£5,175** (£1,540; £769; £384) **Stalls** Low

Form RPR
503 **1** **Yorbelucky**[23] 6367 2-9-2 **71** ........ FranBerry 6 74
(David Evans) *mde all: shkn up 2f out and sn drew clr: drvn appr fnl f: styd on wl* **4/1**[2]
14 **2** *2 3/4* **Christopher Wood (IRE)**[64] 4885 2-9-8 0 ........ PatDobbs 1 73
(Ralph Beckett) *trckd ldrs: rdn to go 2nd over 2f out: outpcd by wnr over 1f out: kpt on to hold 2nd* **1/2**[1]
3 **3** *nk* **Despacito**[13] 6761 2-8-11 0 ........ OisinMurphy 4 62
(Brendan Powell) *trckd wnr tl lost 2nd over 2f out: rdn over 1f out: lacked pce to trble wnr fnl f but pressed for 2nd* **20/1**
**4** *8* **Our Power (IRE)** 2-9-2 0 ........ TimmyMurphy 5 47
(Christian Williams) *s.i.s: hld up: hung lft whn rdn over 2f out: wknd over 1f out: wnt mod 4th ins fnl f* **12/1**
16 **5** *1 1/2* **Greeneyedafghan**[13] 6761 2-9-5 0 ........ MartinDwyer 3 46
(William Muir) *t.k.h: hld up: rdn wl over 2f out: no real imp: wknd over 1f out: lost mod 4th ins fnl f* **11/2**[3]

1m 43.84s (10.24) **Going Correction** +1.075s/f (Soft) **5** Ran SP% **114.5**
Speed ratings (Par 97): **84,80,80,71,69**
CSF £6.80 TOTE £4.90: £2.30, £1.02; EX 9.20 Trifecta £32.90.
**Owner** R S Brookhouse **Bred** R S Brookhouse **Trained** Pandy, Monmouths

**FOCUS**
Not a bad little nursery won by a horse who looks quite progressive now.

### 7198 PETERSON FAMILY SUPPORTING THE NSPCC CYMRU/WALES H'CAP 7f 80y(R)
**3:00** (3:06) (Class 6) (0-65,65) 3-Y-O+ **£3,234** (£962; £481; £240) **Stalls** Low

Form RPR
4441 **1** **Topmeup**[24] 6341 3-8-10 **57** ........ (v) FranBerry 3 62
(David Evans) *midfield: hdwy 3f out: drvn over 1f out: r.o gamely to ld fnl 50yds* **5/1**[2]
5041 **2** *hd* **The Groove**[10] 6866 4-9-7 **65** ........ TrevorWhelan 5 70
(Fergal O'Brien) *trckd ldrs: led narrowly over 2f out: drvn over 1f out: kpt on bravely: hdd fnl 50yds* **8/1**
0005 **3** *1/2* **Rolling Dice**[6] 7006 6-8-10 **57** ........ (b[1]) CallumShepherd(3) 10 61
(Dominic Ffrench Davis) *towards rr: hdwy over 2f out: drvn over 2f out: r.o fnl f: wnt 3rd last strides* **6/1**[3]
4-45 **4** *nk* **Swot**[23] 6393 5-8-6 **57** ........ (p) RossaRyan(7) 7 60
(Roger Teal) *midfield: rdn and hdwy over 2f out: nt qckn ins fnl f: lost 3rd last strides* **7/1**
1010 **5** *2 1/4* **Misu Pete**[39] 5793 5-9-0 **58** ........ (p) OisinMurphy 8 56
(Mark Usher) *trcked ldr tl lost 2nd 3f out: rdn 2f out: kpt on same pce* **13/2**
402 **6** *1/2* **Bryght Boy**[57] 5145 4-9-2 **60** ........ (p) KieranShoemark 1 57
(Ed Walker) *chsd ldrs: drvn and ev ch over 2f out: nt qckn: grad wknd fnl f* **11/4**[1]
0/0- **7** *2 3/4* **Birikyno**[468] 2969 6-8-4 **51** oh6 ........ NathanAlison(3) 12 41
(Matthew Salaman) *s.s: in rr: c wdst st: rdn 3f out: modest hdwy fnl f* **50/1**
0465 **8** *1 3/4* **Tally's Son**[24] 6341 3-8-4 **51** oh3 ........ (p[1]) EdwardGreatrex 2 36
(Grace Harris) *led: rdn and hdd over 2f out: sn wknd* **14/1**
5015 **9** *1* **Doctor Bong**[11] 6807 5-8-11 **55** ........ (b) PatDobbs 9 38
(Grace Harris) *chsd ldrs tl rdn and wknd over 1f out* **10/1**
0-00 **10** *1* **Zebs Lad (IRE)**[23] 6393 5-8-0 **51** ........ (p) GabrieleMalune(7) 4 32
(Nikki Evans) *s.s: in rr: hdwy over 2f out: sn drvn: wknd over 1f out* **25/1**
6013 **11** *3 1/2* **Barista (IRE)**[20] 6503 9-9-3 **61** ........ MartinDwyer 6 33
(Brian Forsey) *s.s: in rr: rdn and effrt on ins over 2f out: no real imp: wknd over 1f out* **8/1**

1m 40.66s (7.06) **Going Correction** +1.075s/f (Soft)
**WFA** 3 from 4yo+ 3lb **11** Ran SP% **127.2**
Speed ratings (Par 101): **102,101,101,100,98 97,94,92,91,90 86**
CSF £48.89 CT £260.51 TOTE £6.00: £2.10, £2.60, £2.10; EX 30.00 Trifecta £278.60.
**Owner** M W Lawrence **Bred** Whitwell Bloodstock **Trained** Pandy, Monmouths
■ Stewards' Enquiry : Callum Shepherd 3 day ban: weighing in at 2 lbs overweight (1-3 Oct)

**FOCUS**
A wide-open albeit ordinary handicap run at what looked a reasonable pace in the conditions and the winner looks a really tough little filly who takes her racing well.

### 7199 BBI GROUP SUPPORTING CHILDLINE WALES FILLIES' H'CAP 1m (R)
**3:30** (3:34) (Class 5) (0-70,71) 3-Y-O+ **£3,881** (£1,155; £432; £432) **Stalls** Low

Form RPR
5223 **1** **Fastnet Spin (IRE)**[27] 6274 3-9-7 **71** ........ (bt) FranBerry 6 77
(David Evans) *hld up: hdwy on outer 3f out: pushed along over 2f out: drvn to ld fnl 100yds: kpt on* **7/2**[1]
0310 **2** *1 1/4* **Born To Please**[39] 5790 3-7-10 **53** ........ NicolaCurrie(7) 2 56
(Mark Usher) *hld up: hdwy 3f out: drvn and edgd lft 2f out: led ent fnl f: hdd and unable qck fnl 100yds* **9/2**[2]
560 **3** *hd* **Waves (IRE)**[53] 5276 3-9-3 **67** ........ EdwardGreatrex 7 70
(Eve Johnson Houghton) *midfield: rdn and clsd 2f out: drvn and styd on fnl f* **11/2**[3]
-423 **3** *dht* **The Bear Can Fly**[26] 6283 3-8-13 **63** ........ KieranShoemark 10 66
(David Menuisier) *s.s: in rr: hdwy on outer 3f out: drvn over 2f out: wandered u.p: styd on fnl f* **7/2**[1]
-050 **5** *4* **Everdina**[206] 881 3-8-8 **58** ........ DavidProbert 12 51
(Ed Walker) *midfield: hdwy 3f out: drvn over 1f out: wknd fnl f* **10/1**
430 **6** *nk* **Cooperess**[39] 5791 4-8-7 **53** oh5 ........ MartinDwyer 5 46
(Dai Burchell) *chsd ldrs: wnt 2nd over 4f out: led 3f out: drvn 2f out: sn hung lft: hdd ent fnl f: wknd* **12/1**
0640 **7** *9* **Bois D'Ebene (IRE)**[24] 6345 3-8-6 **61** ........ BenRobinson(5) 11 33
(John O'Shea) *sn trcking ldrs: drvn and ev ch 2f out: nt qckn and sn wknd* **16/1**
4633 **8** *hd* **Assertor**[11] 6828 3-8-3 **58** ow3 ........ (h) FinleyMarsh(5) 3 30
(Tony Carroll) *chsd ldrs: rdn over 2f out: wknd qckly* **18/1**
-600 **9** *1 1/4* **Mistress Viz (IRE)**[27] 6257 3-7-13 **56** ........ AledBeech(7) 4 25
(Daniel Mark Loughnane) *midfield: effrt and sme hdwy over 3f out: wknd 2f out* **8/1**
3603 **10** *13* **Imperial Link**[24] 6342 5-8-0 **53** oh8 ........ (v) GabrieleMalune(7) 8
(John O'Shea) *led and racd keenly: rdn and hdd 3f out: wknd qckly* **10/1**
-000 **11** *60* **Saxony**[92] 3809 6-8-4 **53** oh8 ........ NathanAlison(3) 9
(Matthew Salaman) *t.k.h: chsd ldr over 3f: sn wknd: t.o* **66/1**

1m 49.34s (8.34) **Going Correction** +1.075s/f (Soft)
**WFA** 3 from 4yo+ 4lb **11** Ran SP% **127.6**
Speed ratings (Par 100): **101,99,99,99,95 95,86,86,84,71 11**
PL: 1.10 Waves, 0.80p The Bear Can Fly. TC: The Bear Can Fly; Fastnet Spin, Born To Please, Waves £46.22, Fastnet Spin, Born To Please, The Bear Can Fly £32.00 CSF £20.95 TOTE £4.60: £1.50, £1.90; EX 27.80.
**Owner** Dukes Head Racing **Bred** Rockhart Trading Ltd **Trained** Pandy, Monmouths

**FOCUS**
They went quite hard here and the field finished well strung out. The first four came clear in what looks an ordinary enough handicap.

### 7200 ARMY CADETS WALES SUPPORTING NSPCC SCHOOLS SERVICE H'CAP 2m (R)
**4:00** (4:01) (Class 3) (0-90,92) 3-Y-O+ **£7,762** (£2,310; £1,154; £577) **Stalls** Low

Form RPR
3230 **1** **Look My Way**[22] 6445 3-8-8 **79** ........ DavidProbert 1 96
(Andrew Balding) *mde all: hanging lft fr over 2f out but qckly drew wl clr: rchd ins rail over 1f out: in n.d and kpt up to work fnl f* **6/4**[1]
3035 **2** *22* **Champagne Champ**[30] 6151 5-10-0 **89** ........ OisinMurphy 5 86
(Rod Millman) *chsd wnr thrght: drvn 5f out: outpcd and no ch fr over 2f out: plugged on* **7/2**[3]
0440 **3** *6* **Desert God (IND)**[30] 6151 5-9-10 **92** ........ StephenCummins(7) 2 84
(Richard Hughes) *trckd ldrs tl outpcd 4f out: drvn over 3f out: sn wknd* **8/1**
111 **4** *2* **Rolling Maul (IRE)**[36] 5944 9-9-5 **85** ........ JoshuaBryan(5) 6 75
(Peter Bowen) *hld up in last: rdn along 6f out: drvn and lost tch 4f out: wnt poor 4th cl home* **7/4**[2]
-304 **5** *nk* **Norab (GER)**[20] 6508 6-8-4 **72** ........ (b) WilliamCox(7) 4 62
(Bernard Llewellyn) *chsd ldrs tl drvn and wknd 4f out: lost poor 4th cl home* **18/1**
00-6 **6** *29* **Shades Of Silver**[12] 6793 7-9-5 **83** ........ CallumShepherd(3) 3 47
(Ed de Giles) *hld up: drvn 5f out: wknd 4f out: t.o* **25/1**

3m 40.66s (10.66) **Going Correction** +1.075s/f (Soft)
**WFA** 3 from 5yo+ 10lb **6** Ran SP% **118.8**
Speed ratings (Par 107): **116,105,102,101,100 86**
CSF £7.89 TOTE £2.10: £1.10, £1.60; EX 6.60 Trifecta £31.70.
**Owner** Kingsclere Racing Club **Bred** Kingsclere Stud **Trained** Kingsclere, Hants

**FOCUS**
This decent staying event was over as a contest half way up the straight as the leader, the only 3yo in the contest, began to go further and further clear. He's a stayer on the up.

### 7201 IRISH STALLION FARMS EBF FILLIES' H'CAP 1m 2f (R)
**4:30** (4:32) (Class 4) (0-80,79) 3-Y-O+ **£6,469** (£1,925; £962; £481) **Stalls** Low

Form RPR
322 **1** **Lorelina**[20] 6515 4-9-7 **79** ........ WilliamCox(7) 4 88+
(Andrew Balding) *trckd ldrs: rdn 2f out: carried lft over 1f out: sn led: styd on wl* **1/1**[1]
2-53 **2** *3/4* **Bybrook**[35] 5957 4-9-7 **72** ........ (p[1]) OisinMurphy 5 78
(David Simcock) *trckd ldr: led narrowly 2f out: sn hung lft: hdd appr fnl f: kpt on u.p* **3/1**[2]

2634 **3** *2* **Cotinga**[23] 6369 3-9-3 **73** PatDobbs 6 75
(Ralph Beckett) *hld up: rdn to go 3rd 2f out: no imp on ldng pair tl styd on ins fnl f* **9/2**[3]
1414 **4** *12* **Pondering**[31] 6094 3-9-1 **71** (v) EdwardGreatrex 3 49
(Eve Johnson Houghton) *hld up: niggled along 5f out: drvn over 3f out: wknd over 1f out* **6/1**
4130 **5** *8* **Paradise Cove**[30] 6139 3-9-4 **74** KieranShoemark 1 36
(Charlie Fellowes) *t.k.h: led tl rdn and hdd 2f out: wknd qckly* **9/1**
2m 18.67s (9.27) **Going Correction** +1.075s/f (Soft)
**WFA** 3 from 4yo 5lb **5** Ran SP% **117.5**
Speed ratings (Par 102): **105,104,102,93,86**
CSF £4.74 TOTE £1.80: £1.10, £2.30; EX 5.60 Trifecta £12.10.
**Owner** Tim Wixted & Tony Anderson **Bred** Tony Anderson & Tim Wixted **Trained** Kingsclere, Hants
**FOCUS**
Ordinary fare for the grade and it turned into a match from around 2f out.

## 7202 WESTWALESPROPERTIES.CO.UK H'CAP 1m 3f 209y(R)
5:00 (5:03) (Class 5) (0-75,75) 3-Y-0+ **£3,881** (£1,155; £577; £288) **Stalls** Low

Form RPR
5-00 **1** **Bazooka (IRE)**[13] 6763 6-8-9 **65** RossaRyan(7) 7 72
(David Flood) *t.k.h in rr: sn in tch in 4th: swtchd lft and clsd over 2f out: r.o to ld early ins fnl f: drvn out* **12/1**
3332 **2** *¾* **Inconceivable (IRE)**[14] 6723 3-9-5 **75** PatDobbs 5 81
(Ralph Beckett) *trckd ldng pair: shkn up 3f out: rdn to ld over 1f out: hdd early ins fnl f: unable qck* **9/4**[2]
5610 **3** *6* **Eolian**[16] 6657 3-9-2 **72** (p) DavidProbert 2 69
(Andrew Balding) *led: sddle sn slipped: rdn and hdd over 1f out: no ex fnl f* **2/1**[1]
5342 **4** *3 ¼* **Pastoral Music**[17] 6610 4-9-7 **70** (p) OisinMurphy 4 61
(Hughie Morrison) *pressed ldr: rdn and lost 2nd over 2f out: wknd over 1f out* **11/4**[3]
2/4 **5** *10* **Prussian Eagle (IRE)**[5] 6034 6-9-5 **68** TimmyMurphy 6 43
(Evan Williams) *s.i.s: hld up and sn in last: clsd over 4f out: drvn over 2f out: sn wknd* **7/2**
2m 49.98s (12.58) **Going Correction** +1.075s/f (Soft)
**WFA** 3 from 4yo+ 7lb **5** Ran SP% **120.7**
Speed ratings (Par 103): **101,100,96,94,87**
CSF £42.36 TOTE £20.40: £5.00, £1.30; EX 57.10 Trifecta £195.80.
**Owner** Mrs Anne Cowley **Bred** Cyril Kiernan **Trained** Chiseldon, Wiltshire
**FOCUS**
A run of the mill event for the grade in which the front two came well clear in the final furlong.
T/Plt: £30.90 to a £1 stake. Pool: £99,369.26 - 2,340.19 winning units. T/Qpdt: £7.80 to a £1 stake. Pool: £8,402.68 - 795.10 winning units. **Richard Lowther**

# 4130 DORTMUND (R-H)
Sunday, September 17

**OFFICIAL GOING: Turf: good to soft**

## 7203a PREIS DES GESTUTS WITTEKINDSHOF - 133RD DEUTSCHES ST LEGER (GROUP 3) (3YO+) (TURF) 1m 6f
3:30 3-Y-0+ **£27,350** (£10,256; £5,128; £2,564; £1,709)

RPR
**1** **Oriental Eagle (GER)**[22] 3-8-13 0 JackMitchell 10 107
(J Hirschberger, Germany) *broke wl fr wd draw: grad tacked ins and led after 1f: mde rest: styd on gamely u.p fr 1 1/2f out: edgd lft thrght fnl f: a holding chalrs* **123/10**
**2** *1 ¼* **Moonshiner (GER)**[28] 6250 4-9-6 0 (b) FilipMinarik 4 102
(Jean-Pierre Carvalho, Germany) *hld up in midfield on inner: pushed along and clsd fr over 1 1/2f out: chsd wnr fnl f: a hld* **12/5**[2]
**3** *½* **Khan (GER)**[31] 3-8-13 0 AntoineHamelin 7 105+
(Henk Grewe, Germany) *w.w towards rr: hdwy more than 1 1/2f out: styd on strly fnl f: nvr nrr* **15/1**
**4** *nk* **Sound Check (GER)**[15] 4-9-6 0 AndraschStarke 1 101
(P Schiergen, Germany) *w.w in rr: tk clsr order fr 2 1/2f out: chsd ldng trio 1 1/2f out: styd on on fnl f: nt pce to get on terms* **6/5**[1]
**5** *¾* **Shadow Sadness (GER)**[9] 5-9-6 0 JozefBojko 2 100
(C Von Der Recke, Germany) *settled towards rr: hdwy 2f out: kpt on fnl f: nvr on terms* **198/10**
**6** *5* **Eagle Eyes (GER)**[15] 4-9-3 0 MarcLerner 5 90
(Jean-Pierre Carvalho, Germany) *led early: hdd after 1f: remained cl up: wknd wl over 1 1/2f out* **31/1**
**7** *11* **Alicante (GER)**[17] 3-8-9 0 AndreasHelfenbein 3 77
(Markus Klug, Germany) *settled in midfield on outer: drvn and no imp fr 2f out: sn wl btn* **17/1**
**8** *2 ½* **Near England (IRE)**[15] 6710 4-9-3 0 AdriedeVries 6 71
(Markus Klug, Germany) *settled in fnl pair: drvn along fr after 1/2-way: bhd fnl 2f* **43/10**[3]
**9** *47* **Summershine (IRE)**[36] 6-9-3 0 MaximPecheur 9
(Frau Anna Schleusner-Fruhriep, Germany) *cl up: lost pl more than 3 1/2f out: t.o fnl 2f* **148/10**
**10** *63* **Stamford Raffles**[30] 6151 4-9-6 0 PaddyBradley 8
(Jane Chapple-Hyam) *chsd ldrs: lost pl 4f out: wknd qckly: t.o over 2f out* **209/10**
3m 7.51s (2.01)
**WFA** 3 from 4yo+ 8lb **10** Ran SP% **131.9**
PARI-MUTUEL (all including 10 euro stake): WIN 133; PLACE: 31, 23; 34; SF: 1393.
**Owner** Gestut Auenquelle **Bred** Gestut Auenquelle **Trained** Germany

# 6255 HANOVER (L-H)
Sunday, September 17

**OFFICIAL GOING: Turf: good**

## 7204a GROSSER PREIS DER METALLBAU BURCKHARDT GMBH (LISTED RACE) (3YO+ FILLIES & MARES) (TURF) 1m
3:45 3-Y-0+ **£11,965** (£5,555; £2,564; £1,282)

RPR
**1** **Discursus**[41] 5731 3-8-9 0 AndreBest 8 102+
(H-A Pantall, France) *w.w towards rr: nudged along to cl over 2 1/2f out: 4th and rdn 2f out: styd on to ld ent last 1 1/2f: drvn clr: won easing down* **19/10**[1]
**2** *4 ¾* **Flemish Duchesse (FR)**[76] 4518 4-9-3 0 MarcoCasamento 1 94
(Andreas Suborics, Germany) **43/5**
**3** *3 ¼* **Scapina (GER)**[18] 6605 3-8-9 0 RenePiechulek 7 83
(Henk Grewe, Germany) **235/10**
**4** *shd* **Diamond Daisy (GER)** 4-9-0 0 EduardoPedroza 3 83
(Ferdinand J Leve, Germany) **123/10**
**5** *3 ¼* **Dalila (GER)**[14] 3-8-10 0 ow1 MrVinzenzSchiergen 4 76
(P Schiergen, Germany) **128/10**
**6** *2 ¼* **Wild Approach (GER)**[28] 6254 4-9-3 0 WladimirPanov 9 74
(D Moser, Germany) **14/5**[2]
**7** *hd* **Sunny Belle (IRE)**[18] 6605 3-8-9 0 DanielePorcu 10 69
(P Schiergen, Germany) **22/5**[3]
**8** *1 ½* **Vallante (GER)**[322] 7720 4-9-0 0 MartinSeidl 6 68
(J Hirschberger, Germany) **102/10**
**9** *1* **Stellar Surprise**[8] 6919 3-8-9 0 BauyrzhanMurzabayev 2 66
(Stuart Williams) *chsd ldrs fr s: sn pushed along to hold share of 4th: lost pl 1/2-way: rdn and short-lived effrt over 2f out: rdn and btn appr fnl f* **125/10**
**10** *3 ½* **Neve (GER)**[153] 5-9-0 0 StephenHellyn 5 56
(Yasmin Almenrader, Germany) **225/10**
1m 39.38s
**WFA** 3 from 4yo+ 4lb **10** Ran SP% **129.2**
PARI-MUTUEL (all including 10 euro stake): WIN: 29; PLACE: 19, 28, 47; SF: 217.
**Owner** Godolphin SNC **Bred** Darley **Trained** France

# 4131 SAN SIRO (R-H)
Sunday, September 17

**OFFICIAL GOING: Turf: heavy**

## 7205a PREMIO FEDERICO TESIO (GROUP 2) (3YO+) (TURF) 1m 3f
3:35 3-Y-0+ **£59,829** (£26,324; £14,358; £7,179)

RPR
**1** **Full Drago (ITY)**[65] 4879 4-9-1 0 DarioVargiu 2 110+
(Stefano Botti, Italy) *mde virtually all: sn 3l clr: kicked for home 3f out: hdd narrowly 2f out: rallied u.p to regain ld more than 1 1/2f out: responded gamely whn chal 1f out: asserted fnl 75yds* **98/100**[1]
**2** *1 ¾* **Way To Paris**[28] 6250 4-8-13 0 PierantonioConvertino 5 105
(Antonio Marcialis, Italy) *settled next to last: hdwy 2f out: chsd ldng pair 1 1/2f out: sn rdn: chal ldr 1f out: no ex fnl 75yds* **13/5**[3]
**3** *6* **Mac Mahon (ITY)**[65] 4878 3-8-9 0 CristianDemuro 1 97
(Stefano Botti, Italy) *chsd ldng pair: rdn to ld narrowly 2f out: hdd over 1 1/2f out: nt pce of front two fnl f* **23/20**[2]
**4** *3* **Aethos (IRE)**[15] 6711 3-8-7 0 SilvanoMulas 4 90
(Stefano Botti, Italy) *chsd ldr: rdn and outpcd fr 2f out: bhd fnl 1 1/2f* **183/10**
**5** *1 ¾* **Mushibest (ITY)**[78] 3-8-7 0 (b) LucaManiezzi 3 87
(Stefano Botti, Italy) *missed break: racd in rr: no imp whn rdn 3f out: nvr in contention* **98/100**[1]
2m 18.2s (-0.40)
**WFA** 3 from 4yo 6lb **5** Ran SP% **180.5**
PARI-MUTUEL (all including 1 euro stake): WIN 1.98 PLACE 1.21, 1.46 DF 3.48.
**Owner** Dioscuri Srl **Bred** Massimo Dragoni **Trained** Italy

# 7178 WOODBINE (L-H)
Sunday, September 17

**OFFICIAL GOING: Turf: firm**

## 7206a NATALMA STKS (GRADE 1) (2YO FILLIES) (TURF) 1m (T)
10:24 2-Y-0
**£90,361** (£36,144; £18,072; £7,530; £3,012; £1,506)

RPR
**1** **Capla Temptress (IRE)**[36] 5941 2-8-9 0 JoelRosario 7 101+
(Marco Botti) *bmpd and hmpd s: settled in fnl trio: smooth hdwy over 2f out: 6th and drvn 1 1/2f out: angled out between horses wl over 1f out: r.o wl fnl f: led fnl 30yds: cosily* **57/10**[3]
**2** *¾* **Dixie Moon (CAN)**[29] 2-8-9 0 EuricoRosaDaSilva 9 98
(Catherine Day-Phillips, Canada) *led: kicked 1l clr wl over 1 1/2f out: sn rdn and r.o: hdd fnl 30yds: no ex* **131/10**
**3** *hd* **Wonder Gadot (CAN)**[22] 2-8-9 0 PatrickHusbands 8 98
(Mark Casse, Canada) *a cl up: drvn to chse ldr 1 1/2f out: styd on fnl f: nvr quite on terms* **41/20**[1]
**4** *3 ¼* **March X Press (USA)**[32] 2-8-9 0 JoseLOrtiz 3 90
(Todd Pletcher, U.S.A) *hld up in midfield: shkn up to chse ldng gp 2f out: kpt on at same pce fnl f* **12/5**[2]
**5** *½* **Pretty Lady (USA)**[21] 2-8-9 0 GaryBoulanger 5 89
(Mark Casse, Canada) *wnt rt s and bmpd rival: in rr: tk clsr order after 1/2-way: kpt on at same pce u.p fnl 1 1/2f: nvr trbld ldrs* **46/1**
**6** *1* **Golden Orb (USA)**[42] 2-8-9 0 LuisContreras 6 87
(Christophe Clement, U.S.A) *bmpd s: chsd ldrs: 4th and drvn 2f out but no imp on ldrs: dropped away ins fnl f* **6/1**

7 1 3/4 **Mo Big Cat (CAN)**[22] 2-8-9 0 ................................(b) JesseMCampbell 2 83
(Mark Casse, Canada) *racd in fnl trio: short-lived effrt u.p 2f out: sn btn and wknd* **71/1**

8 1 **Delamar (USA)**[23] 2-8-9 0 ................................ JeromeLermyte 4 81
(Roger L Attfield, Canada) *chsd ldr: rdn and nt qckn 2f out: wknd ins fnl 1 1/2f* **159/10**

9 3 **Dooder (USA)**[38] 2-8-9 0 ................................ JohnRVelazquez 1 74
(Chad C Brown, U.S.A) *racd in midfield: rdn and lost pl more than 2f fr home: sn wknd* **43/5**

1m 35.12s **9** Ran SP% **118.4**
PARI-MUTUEL (all including 2 cad stake): WIN 13.40; PLACE (1-2) 7.50, 11.30; SHOW (1-2-3) 4.90, 6.30, 2.70; SF 152.10.
**Owner** Team Valor **Bred** Pier House Stud **Trained** Newmarket, Suffolk

**FOCUS**
A "win and you're in" contest for the Breeders' Cup Juvenile Fillies Turf.

7207 - 7209a (Foreign Racing) - See Raceform Interactive

# 7000 BRIGHTON (L-H)
## Monday, September 18

**OFFICIAL GOING: Good (good to soft in places; 7.8)**
Wind: light, behind Weather: light cloud, bright spells

## 7210 TOTEPOOL BETTING ON ALL UK RACING APPRENTICE (S) H'CAP 1m 1f 207y
**1:35** (1:36) (Class 6) (0-60,62) 3-Y-O+ **£2,264** (£673; £336; £168) **Stalls** High

Form RPR

0352 **1** **Oceanus (IRE)**[14] [6754] 3-9-5 **60** ................................ ShelleyBirkett 2 68
(Julia Feilden) *hld up in tch in midfield: clsd to trck ldrs and nt clrest of runs 2f out: hdwy and rdn to chal ent fnl f: led ins fnl f: r.o wl* **9/2[2]**

5321 **2** nk **Edge (IRE)**[14] [6754] 6-9-4 **54** ................................(b) KieranShoemark 8 60
(Bernard Llewellyn) *t.k.h: hld up in tch in last quartet: hdwy ent fnl 2f: rdn to ld ent fnl f: hdd ins fnl f: kpt on but a jst hld after* **4/1[1]**

0106 **3** 1 1/2 **Tojosimbre**[12] [6821] 3-8-3 **49** ................................(t[1]) FinleyMarsh(5) 7 54
(Richard Hughes) *stdd after s: hld up in last quartet: clsd towards inner and nt clr run whn swtchd rt over 1f out: swtchd sharply lft and chsd ldrs 1f out: kpt on same pce ins fnl f* **13/2[3]**

-653 **4** nse **Indiana Dawn**[27] [6296] 4-8-12 **51** ................................(p) JoshuaBryan(3) 1 54
(Robert Stephens) *taken down early: hld up in tch towards rr: hdwy 2f out: rdn to chse ldrs 1f out: kpt on same pce ins fnl f* **13/2[3]**

4662 **5** 1/2 **Saint Helena (IRE)**[40] [5782] 9-9-7 **62** ................................(b) WilliamCox(5) 9 64
(Mark Gillard) *in tch in midfield: effrt over 2f out: rdn and ev ch ent fnl f: jst getting outpcd whn squeezed for room ins fnl f: kpt on same pce after* **12/1**

-000 **6** 3 3/4 **Follow Me (IRE)**[147] [2018] 3-8-11 **55** ow3 ................ PaddyBradley(3) 6 51
(Lee Carter) *chsd ldr tl 7f out: sn pushed lft: continued chsng ldrs: rdn jst over 2f out: jst struggling to qckn whn squeezed for room ent fnl f: wknd ins fnl f* **25/1**

5003 **7** 1 **Port Lairge**[7] [7006] 7-8-10 **46** oh1 ................................(b) DavidEgan 5 39
(Michael Chapman) *s.i.s: bhd: rdn 3f out: hdwy towards inner over 1f out: kpt on ins fnl f: nvr trbld ldrs* **8/1**

0066 **8** 3/4 **Kitsey (IRE)**[58] [5142] 3-8-11 **52** ................................ HollieDoyle 10 45
(Richard Hannon) *in tch in midfield: rdn 4f out: lost pl and bhd whn drifted lft over 1f out: wl hld and plugged on same pce ins fnl f* **9/1**

0060 **9** 1 **Jump Around**[18] [6621] 3-8-5 **46** oh1 ................................(t) EdwardGreatrex 4 37
(Ali Stronge) *in tch towards rr: rdn 3f out: sn struggling: bhd and wl hld over 1f out* **20/1**

50-0 **10** 1 1/4 **Maysonri**[138] [2315] 3-8-6 **47** ................................(p) AaronJones 12 35
(Mark Hoad) *dwlt: steadily rcvrd to chse ldr after 7f: shifted lft over 6f out: rdn to ld 2f out: hdd jst over 1f out and sn impeded: wknd ins fnl f* **80/1**

0045 **11** 3 **Russian Ranger (IRE)**[38] [5898] 4-9-8 **58** ................................(b) GeorgeWood 3 40
(Jonathan Portman) *led for 2f: styd chsng ldrs: rdn to press ldrs jst over 2f out tl unable qck over 1f out: sn btn and wknd fnl f* **10/1**

0000 **12** 15 **Greyjoy (IRE)**[12] [6821] 3-7-12 **46** oh1 ................................ ShariqMohd(7) 11
(Sylvester Kirk) *t.k.h: hdwy to ld after 2: rdn and hdd 2f out: sn dropped out: bhd fnl f* **80/1**

2m 6.3s (2.70) **Going Correction** +0.15s/f (Good)
**WFA** 3 from 4yo+ 5lb **12** Ran SP% **113.8**
Speed ratings (Par 101): **95,94,93,93,93 90,89,88,87,86 84,72**
CSF £21.09 CT £114.25 TOTE £4.40: £1.70, £1.60, £2.70; EX 21.50 Trifecta £150.60.There was no bid for the winner.
**Owner** Miss J Feilden **Bred** Castlefarm Stud **Trained** Exning, Suffolk

**FOCUS**
All race distances as advertised. This selling handicap for apprentice riders got rough in the home straight, but it's straightforward form.

## 7211 TOTEQUADPOT AT TOTESPORT.COM MAIDEN AUCTION STKS 6f 210y
**2:10** (2:11) (Class 6) 2-Y-O **£2,749** (£818; £408; £204) **Stalls** Low

Form RPR

420 **1** **Groundnut**[61] [5030] 2-8-9 72 ................................(p[1]) GeorgeWood(3) 3 74
(Jonathan Portman) *hld up in midfield: effrt in 4th and swtchd rt wl over 1f out: str run 1f out: led 75yds out: sn in command and r.o wl* **3/1[3]**

5 **2** 1 3/4 **Pompey Chimes (IRE)**[17] [6654] 2-8-13 0 ................................ HectorCrouch(3) 4 73
(Gary Moore) *chsd ldr: effrt to cl and upsides 2f out: rdn to ld over 1f out: hdd 75yds out and nt match pce of wnr after: kpt on for clr 2nd* **9/4[2]**

**3** 2 3/4 **Ipcress File** 2-8-12 0 ................................ KieranO'Neill 8 62
(Scott Dixon) *chsd ldng pair: rdn jst over 2f out: 3rd and outpcd over 1f out: kpt on same pce fnl f* **33/1**

5 **4** 3/4 **Tesorina (IRE)**[12] [6824] 2-8-8 0 ................................ SilvestreDeSousa 2 56+
(William Knight) *stdd s: hld up in last pair: swtchd rt and effrt in centre over 2f out: 5th and no imp u.p over 1f out: wnt 4th nr fin: nvr trbld ldrs* **11/8[1]**

00 **5** 1/2 **Arachina (IRE)**[56] [5216] 2-8-9 0 ................................(v[1]) TomMarquand 9 55
(Harry Dunlop) *racd freely: led and sn clr: rdn and jnd 2f out: hdd over 1f out: sn outpcd and wknd ins fnl f* **50/1**

**6** 5 **Poetic Affair** 2-9-0 0 ................................ DavidProbert 5 47
(Mark Johnston) *midfield: rdn over 2f out: sn struggling and unable qck: wl btn over 1f out: wknd fnl f* **8/1**

0 **7** 23 **May Spirit**[97] [3689] 2-8-10 0 ................................ EdwardGreatrex 1
(Michael Blanshard) *t.k.h: hld up in last pair: rdn over 2f out: sn struggling: bhd and lost tch over 1f out* **66/1**

1m 24.56s (1.46) **Going Correction** +0.15s/f (Good) **7** Ran SP% **115.4**
Speed ratings (Par 93): **97,95,91,91,90 84,58**
CSF £10.39 TOTE £3.90: £1.60, £1.90; EX 11.30 Trifecta £130.30.
**Owner** Mrs J K Powell And D F Powell **Bred** Mrs J K Powell & Catridge Farm Stud **Trained** Upper Lambourn, Berks

**FOCUS**
An ordinary 2yo maiden rated around the balance of the front pair.

## 7212 JANE SAINES 60TH BIRTHDAY CELEBRATION H'CAP (DIV I) 6f 210y
**2:40** (2:42) (Class 6) (0-60,62) 3-Y-O+ **£2,264** (£673; £336; £168) **Stalls** Low

Form RPR

0006 **1** **Baltic Prince (IRE)**[25] [6345] 7-9-7 **60** ................................ GeorgeDowning 8 69+
(Tony Carroll) *mde all: rdn over 1f out: clr and in command 1f out: styd on strly: readily* **13/2**

0435 **2** 2 3/4 **Limerick Lord (IRE)**[14] [6751] 5-8-4 **46** ................................(p) ShelleyBirkett(3) 4 48
(Julia Feilden) *taken down early: chsd ldrs: effrt 2f out: chsd clr wnr 1f out and sn edgd lft: kpt on same pce and no imp* **6/1[3]**

001 **3** nse **Tifl**[21] [6507] 4-8-13 **55** ................................(bt) DavidEgan(3) 3 56
(Heather Main) *hld up in midfield: swtchd rt and effrt wl over 2f out: hdwy u.p over 1f out: kpt on and pressing for 2nd cl home: no ch w wnr* **8/1**

-030 **4** 1 1/4 **Latest Quest (IRE)**[7] [7005] 3-8-10 **52** ................................ TomMarquand 5 49
(Sylvester Kirk) *wl in tch in midfield: effrt on inner ent fnl 2f: unable qck ent fnl f: kpt on same pce after* **16/1**

0241 **5** nk **Lady Morel (IRE)**[14] [6748] 3-9-0 **56** ................................ OisinMurphy 10 52
(Joseph Tuite) *wl in tch: effrt 2f out: unable qck u.p over 1f out: kpt on same pce ins fnl f* **4/1[1]**

3233 **6** 2 1/4 **Justice Rock**[27] [6298] 4-8-11 **50** ................................(t) SilvestreDeSousa 7 41
(Phil McEntee) *hld up in tch in midfield: no hdwy u.p over 1f out: kpt on ins fnl f: no threat to wnr* **8/1**

-006 **7** 1/2 **Arquus (IRE)**[14] [6752] 4-8-9 **48** ................................ DavidProbert 9 38
(Ed de Giles) *chsd wnr: unable qck over 1f out: lost 2nd 1f out and sn hmpd: wknd ins fnl f* **20/1**

0000 **8** shd **Mr Andros**[21] [6528] 4-8-12 **51** ................................(tp) MartinDwyer 1 41
(Brendan Powell) *hld up in tch towards rr: effrt on inner over 2f out: hdwy over 1f out: no imp fnl f* **25/1**

5/00 **9** 1 1/2 **Almoqatel (IRE)**[14] [6748] 5-8-7 **46** oh1 ................................ KieranO'Neill 6 32
(Tony Newcombe) *chsd ldng trio: unable qck u.p and lost pl over 1f out: wknd ins fnl f* **33/1**

1126 **10** nk **Tigerfish (IRE)**[39] [5848] 3-8-11 **58** ................................(p) JoshuaBryan(5) 12 42
(William Stone) *in tch in midfield: lost pl u.p over 1f out: wknd fnl f* **5/1[2]**

00 **11** nse **Bed Of Diamonds**[40] [5787] 3-8-4 **46** oh1 ................................ RoystonFfrench 2 30
(Adam West) *s.i.s: in tch in rr: no hdwy u.p over 1f out: n.d* **50/1**

0-30 **12** 4 **Lady Gwhinnyvere (IRE)**[40] [5783] 3-8-4 **46** oh1 ................ JimmyQuinn 15 19
(John Spearing) *a towards rr: rdn 2f out: sn btn and bhd fnl f* **25/1**

050 **13** 2 1/2 **Pulsating (IRE)**[122] [2793] 3-8-12 **57** ................................ HollieDoyle(3) 11 23
(Daniel Steele) *midfield: effrt over 2f out: struggling towards rr and swtchd rt over 1f out: sn wl btn: bhd fnl f* **12/1**

050 **14** 14 **Golden Cannon**[107] [3329] 6-9-5 **58** ................................ DannyBrock 13
(Sheena West) *hld up in rr: hung lft and btn 2f out: eased over 1f out* **50/1**

1m 23.73s (0.63) **Going Correction** +0.15s/f (Good)
**WFA** 3 from 4yo+ 3lb **14** Ran SP% **119.4**
Speed ratings (Par 101): **102,98,98,97,97 94,93,93,92,91 91,87,84,68**
CSF £41.39 CT £319.95 TOTE £8.20: £3.10, £2.20, £2.90; EX 53.00 Trifecta £935.70.
**Owner** A Mills **Bred** William Pilkington **Trained** Cropthorne, Worcs

**FOCUS**
This looked competitive for the class yet few landed a serious blow. The winner has been rated close to last year's C&D form.

## 7213 JANE SAINES 60TH BIRTHDAY CELEBRATION H'CAP (DIV II) 6f 210y
**3:10** (3:10) (Class 6) (0-60,62) 3-Y-O+ **£2,264** (£673; £336; £168) **Stalls** Low

Form RPR

6116 **1** **The Special One (IRE)**[14] [6751] 4-9-6 **55** ................................ TomMarquand 1 61
(Ali Stronge) *hld up towards rr: swtchd rt and stl plenty to do over 2f out: str run u.p over 1f out: led wl ins fnl f: sn in command and gng away at fin* **6/1**

0014 **2** 1 3/4 **Lutine Charlie (IRE)**[14] [6752] 10-8-11 **46** ................................ MartinDwyer 10 47
(Emma Owen) *chsd ldr: rdn ent fnl 2f: outpcd by ldr 2f out: lost 2nd but kpt on steadily ins fnl f: no ch w wnr but wnt 2nd again nr fin* **12/1**

4620 **3** 1/2 **Bella's Venture**[12] [6807] 4-9-4 **53** ................................ FergusSweeney 3 53
(John Gallagher) *led: rdn and kicked clr 2f out: drvn over 1f out: hdd wl ins fnl f: immediately outpcd by wnr: lost 2nd nr fin* **15/2**

0053 **4** 1 1/4 **Solitary Sister (IRE)**[7] [7005] 3-8-7 **52** ................................(v) NicolaCurrie(7) 11 48
(Richard Spencer) *hld up in midfield: pushed along and clsd over 1f out: chsd ldrs ins fnl f: flashed tail whn tapped w whip and kpt on same pce towards fin* **9/2[3]**

036 **5** nk **Blackadder**[14] [6748] 5-8-11 **46** ow1 ................................ FranBerry 9 42
(Mark Gillard) *sn dropped to rr: rdn and effrt in centre over 2f out: hdwy 2f out: edgd lft 1f out: chsd ldrs and kpt on same pce ins fnl f* **14/1**

3034 **6** 4 1/2 **Papou Tony**[7] [7006] 4-9-12 **61** ................................ LiamKeniry 13 45
(George Baker) *pushed along leaving stalls: hld up in midfield: effrt over 2f out: no imp over 1f out: wl hld but passed btn horses ins fnl fur* **4/1[2]**

663- **7** 1/2 **Touch Of Color**[326] [7642] 4-9-2 **54** ................................ AdamMcNamara(3) 4 36
(Richard Fahey) *in tch in midfield: rdn 3f out: unable qck u.p 2f out: wl hld over 1f out* **7/2[1]**

4200 **8** 2 **Ixelles Diamond (IRE)**[88] [4010] 6-9-1 **55** ................................ PaddyBradley(5) 6 32
(Lee Carter) *in tch in midfield: rdn over 2f out: lost pl and bhd over 1f out* **25/1**

0045 **9** nk **Suni Dancer**[40] [5792] 6-9-1 **50** ................................ GeorgeDowning 5 26
(Tony Carroll) *hld up in last trio: effrt over 2f out: drvn and no hdwy over 1f out: nvr trbld ldrs* **10/1**

5R/0 **10** 1/2 **Dylan's Centenary**[32] [6112] 6-8-11 **46** ................................ SilvestreDeSousa 2 21
(Phil McEntee) *hld up in midfield: effrt towards inner over 2f out: no imp over 1f out: wknd* **25/1**

0000 **11** 2 1/4 **Nonnie And Norny**[61] [5040] 3-8-7 **45** ................................ DannyBrock 12 13
(Shaun Harris) *chsd ldrs: rdn over 2f out: sn struggling and lost pl over 1f out: wknd* **100/1**

1m 23.84s (0.74) **Going Correction** +0.15s/f (Good)
**WFA** 3 from 4yo+ 3lb **11** Ran SP% **118.6**
Speed ratings (Par 101): **101,99,98,97,96 91,90,88,88,87 85**
CSF £74.94 CT £560.76 TOTE £6.70: £2.30, £3.40, £2.60; EX 96.50 Trifecta £521.30.
**Owner** BGC Racing **Bred** Barouche Stud Ireland Ltd **Trained** Eastbury, Berks

**FOCUS**
This second division of the 7f handicap was run at a brisk pace. The winner has been rated back to her best.

## 7214 PARK LANE GROUP H'CAP 5f 215y
**3:45** (3:45) (Class 4) (0-80,82) 3-Y-O+ **£4,690** (£1,395; £697; £348) **Stalls** Low

Form RPR

0430 **1** **Marie Of Lyon**[24] [6382] 3-9-6 **82** ................................ AdamMcNamara(3) 6 91
(Richard Fahey) *hld up in tch: clsd to chse ldrs on outer ent fnl 2f: edgd lft u.p over 1f out: led jst ins fnl f: r.o wl* **3/1[1]**

2524 **2** 1 ½ **Whitecrest**[7] 7000 9-9-0 **71** ........ WilliamCarson 1 75
(John Spearing) *in tch in midfield: swtchd rt over 2f out: hemmed in and nt clr run 2f out: bmpd over 1f out: in the clr and hdwy u.p 1f out: chsd wnr wl ins fnl f: kpt on but nvr getting on terms* **9/2**[3]

2050 **3** 1 ¼ **Ladweb**[9] 6923 7-9-7 **78** ........ KieranShoemark 3 78
(John Gallagher) *t.k.h: led for over 1f out: chsd ldr after tl rdn to ld over 1f out: drvn and hdd jst ins fnl f: lost 2nd and wknd wl ins fnl f* **4/1**[2]

6100 **4** ½ **Highly Sprung (IRE)**[29] 6237 4-9-3 **74** ........ DavidProbert 2 72
(Mark Johnston) *s.i.s: hld up in tch in rr: hdwy u.p to chse ldrs whn nt clr run and swtchd rt over 1f out: kpt on same pce ins fnl f* **8/1**

0300 **5** 4 ½ **Majestic Moon (IRE)**[4] 7086 7-9-7 **81** ........(b) ShelleyBirkett(3) 5 65
(Julia Feilden) *led over 4f out tl rdn and hdd over 1f out: sn outpcd: wknd ins fnl f* **4/1**[2]

-000 **6** 8 **Fang**[48] 5513 4-9-1 **72** ........ FranBerry 4 30
(William Jarvis) *chsd ldrs: rdn and pressed ldrs 2f out tl no ex and lost pl ent fnl f: bhd and eased fnl 100yds* **6/1**

1m 10.07s (-0.13) **Going Correction** +0.15s/f (Good)
**WFA** 3 from 4yo+ 2lb **6** Ran SP% **108.6**
Speed ratings (Par 105): **106,104,102,101,95 85**
CSF £15.42 TOTE £3.40: £2.00, £2.40; EX 16.40 Trifecta £75.80.
**Owner** Clipper Logistics **Bred** Limestone Stud **Trained** Musley Bank, N Yorks

**FOCUS**
A fair little sprint handicap, rated around the runner-up.

## 7215 WOODCOTE FLYING CLUB H'CAP — 1m 3f 198y
4:15 (4:16) (Class 6) (0-55,54) 3-Y-O+ £2,264 (£673; £336; £168) Stalls High

Form RPR

3203 **1** **Esspeegee**[21] 6530 4-9-1 **45** ........(p) JimmyQuinn 5 56
(Alan Bailey) *chsd ldrs: chsd ldr wl over 2f out: sn rdn: led over 1f out: styd on wl ins fnl f: rdn out* **5/1**[2]

6601 **2** ½ **Kilim**[27] 6280 4-8-13 **50** ........(t) NicolaCurrie(7) 8 60
(John Berry) *hld up in tch towards rr: hdwy on outer over 3f out: rdn to chal over 1f out: kpt on u.p but a hld ins fnl f* **9/2**[1]

060 **3** 5 **Midnight Mood**[6] 7028 4-9-10 **54** ........ LiamKeniry 9 56
(Dominic Ffrench Davis) *hld up in midfield: rdn 4f out: chsd ldrs 2f out: 4th and no imp: kpt on same pce and wnt 3rd wl ins fnl f* **8/1**

6406 **4** 3 ¼ **Haldaw**[39] 5846 3-8-13 **53** ........ DavidEgan(3) 7 51
(Mick Channon) *chsd ldrs tl wnt 2nd over 4f out: rdn to ld 3f out: hung lft to inner rail and hdd over 1f out: wknd and lost 3rd wl ins fnl f* **7/1**

006 **5** 4 ½ **Sampaquita (FR)**[28] 6277 3-8-11 **51** ........ HectorCrouch(3) 14 42
(Gary Moore) *hld up in tch in midfield: effrt wl over 2f out: 5th and no imp over 1f out: wknd ins fnl f* **10/1**

006P **6** 5 **Jeremy's Jet (IRE)**[21] 6530 6-9-2 **46** ........(t) GeorgeDowning 4 28
(Tony Carroll) *hld up in tch towards rr: rdn and hdwy over 2f out: 6th and no imp over 1f out: wknd ins fnl f* **11/2**[3]

-000 **7** 5 **House Of Frauds (IRE)**[104] 3426 9-8-12 **45** ........ EoinWalsh(3) 12 19
(Tony Newcombe) *stdd s: hld up in rr: swtchd rt and effrt 3f out: no imp 2f out: sn wknd* **25/1**

0 **8** 3 ¾ **Kingwilliamstown**[37] 5931 3-8-8 **45** ........ OscarPereira 13 14
(Jose Santos) *chsd ldrs: rdn 3f out: sn struggling and lost pl over 2f out: wl bhd fnl f* **9/1**

43-0 **9** 7 **Trust The Man (IRE)**[252] 141 4-9-6 **50** ........(tp[1]) RoystonFfrench 2 7
(Adam West) *chsd ldr tl over 4f out: sn rdn and lost pl: bhd 2f out: wknd* **33/1**

0060 **10** 18 **Barbary Prince**[19] 6589 5-8-12 **45** ........(b[1]) CharlieBennett(3) 11
(Shaun Harris) *hood removed late and s.i.s: t.k.h: hld up in last pair: short-lived effrt over 3f out: sn btn and bhd: t.o* **50/1**

-0P0 **11** 44 **Krafty One**[26] 6306 5-9-4 **48** ........(p) KieranShoemark 1
(Michael Scudamore) *midfield: rdn over 2f out: no rspnse and sn btn: t.o and virtually p.u ins fnl f* **33/1**

2601 **12** 7 **Altaira**[26] 6305 6-9-9 **53** ........(b) WilliamCarson 3
(Tony Carroll) *led tl 3f out: sn dropped out: t.o and virtually p.u ins fnl f* **6/1**

2m 34.29s (1.59) **Going Correction** +0.15s/f (Good)
**WFA** 3 from 4yo+ 7lb **12** Ran SP% **118.9**
Speed ratings (Par 101): **100,99,96,94,91 87,84,82,77,65 36,31**
CSF £26.96 CT £180.41 TOTE £5.40: £2.40, £2.20, £2.30; EX 22.90 Trifecta £169.60.
**Owner** The Skills People Group Ltd **Bred** Trinity Park Stud **Trained** Newmarket, Suffolk

**FOCUS**
An open-looking handicap. The first pair came clear towards the stands' side and the winner posted his best effort yet on turf.

## 7216 BRIGHTON LIONS FIREWORK NIGHT NOVEMBER 5TH H'CAP — 7f 211y
4:45 (4:46) (Class 6) (0-65,65) 3-Y-O+ £2,264 (£673; £336; £168) Stalls Low

Form RPR

1330 **1** **Andalusite**[20] 6555 4-9-4 **62** ........(v) FergusSweeney 16 70
(John Gallagher) *w ldr tl led 6f out: clr 4f out: shkn up 2f out: sn rdn and stl clr over 1f out: kpt on wl and in command ins fnl f* **12/1**

6533 **2** 2 **Break The Silence**[11] 6846 3-8-3 **51** ........ KieranO'Neill 8 54
(Scott Dixon) *led for 2f: chsd wnr: rdn jst over 2f out: no imp on wnr and kpt on same pce u.p fnl f* **9/1**

2041 **3** hd **With Approval (IRE)**[14] 6752 5-9-0 **58** ........(p) PatCosgrave 14 61
(Laura Mongan) *chsd ldrs: effrt over 2f out: no imp on wnr and kpt on same pce u.p ins fnl f* **5/1**[2]

-361 **4** ¾ **Appease**[27] 6296 8-8-4 **51** oh2........(p) ShelleyBirkett(3) 6 52
(Julia Feilden) *in tch in midfield: effrt over 2f out: hdwy and battling for placings 1f out: kpt on same pce ins fnl f: fin lame* **7/1**

5036 **5** nk **False Id**[16] 6681 4-8-10 **54** ........ EdwardGreatrex 7 55
(Daniel Steele) *hld up in tch in last trio: swtchd lft 2f out: hdwy u.p over 1f out: battling for placings 1f out: kpt on same pce ins fnl f* **16/1**

2663 **6** nk **Famous Dynasty (IRE)**[11] 6866 3-8-4 **59** ........ NicolaCurrie(7) 12 59
(Michael Blanshard) *dwlt: sn rcvrd and in tch in midfield: rdn over 2f out: no imp tl styd on ins fnl f: no threat to wnr* **7/1**

1500 **7** 1 **Galinthias**[20] 6557 5-9-7 **65** ........ HarryBentley 3 63
(Simon Dow) *wl in tch in midfield: rdn and hdwy over 2f out: chsd ldrs but no imp over 1f out: wknd ins fnl f* **11/2**[3]

00-0 **8** 1 ¾ **Designamento (IRE)**[31] 6153 3-8-0 **51** oh6........ DavidEgan(3) 13 46
(Ed de Giles) *chsd ldrs: rdn over 2f out: unable qck over 1f out: losing pl whn nt clr run and hmpd jst ins fnl f: wknd fnl 100yds* **28/1**

5050 **9** hd **Gannicus**[36] 5968 6-9-0 **58** ........(tp) MartinDwyer 1 51
(Brendan Powell) *dwlt and bustled along early: towards rr: effrt over 2f out: hdwy over 1f out: no imp 1f out: wknd ins fnl f* **16/1**

6551 **10** ½ **Captain Marmalade (IRE)**[14] 6751 5-8-10 **57** ........(h) HollieDoyle(3) 2 49
(Jimmy Fox) *stdd s and dropped in bhd after s: hld up in rr: effrt over 2f out: no real imp whn nt clr run and swtchd rt over 1f out: hmpd jst ins fnl f: nvr trbld ldrs* **9/2**[1]

1406 **11** 3 ¾ **Moonstone Rock**[32] 6102 3-8-7 **58** ........(b) CharlieBennett(3) 4 41
(Jim Boyle) *dwlt: hdwy into midfield over 4f out: effrt over 2f out: sn rdn and no imp: lost pl and bhd 1f out: wknd ins fnl f* **25/1**

2600 **12** 1 **Auric Goldfinger (IRE)**[5] 7062 3-8-8 **63** ........(b) RossaRyan(7) 9 44
(Richard Hannon) *in tch in midfield: rdn over 2f out: unable qck and sn lost pl: bhd 1f out* **25/1**

1m 36.8s (0.80) **Going Correction** +0.15s/f (Good)
**WFA** 3 from 4yo+ 4lb **12** Ran SP% **115.8**
Speed ratings (Par 101): **102,100,99,99,98 98,97,95,95,95 91,90**
CSF £110.43 CT £623.32 TOTE £12.10: £3.30, £2.70, £1.40; EX 123.40 Trifecta £540.70.
**Owner** The LAM Partnership **Bred** Pinnacle Bloodstock Ltd **Trained** Chastleton, Oxon
■ Spiritual Star was withdrawn not under orders. Rule 4 does not apply.

**FOCUS**
This moderate handicap was another truly run affair and again they shunned the far rail. A personal best from the class-dropping winner.

## 7217 SANTA FUN RUN NOVEMBER 25TH H'CAP — 5f 60y
5:15 (5:15) (Class 5) (0-70,71) 3-Y-O+ £2,911 (£866; £432; £216) Stalls Low

Form RPR

416 **1** **Bella Alissa**[62] 4990 3-9-4 **68** ........(p) PatCosgrave 1 78
(Robert Cowell) *in tch in midfield: clsd on inner 1/2-way: rdn to chal over 1f out: led ins fnl f: r.o wl* **16/1**

1532 **2** 1 **The Big Short**[22] 6478 3-9-2 **66** ........ SilvestreDeSousa 7 73
(Charles Hills) *sn led: edgd lft u.p and hrd pressed over 1f out: hdd and no ex ins fnl f* **13/8**[1]

0013 **3** 2 ¾ **Everkyllachy (IRE)**[15] 6724 3-8-6 **59** ........(b) HollieDoyle(3) 5 56
(J S Moore) *sn in last pair: rdn over 2f out: nt clr run over 1f out: hdwy 1f out: r.o strly ins fnl f: snatched 3rd on post* **5/1**[3]

4526 **4** nse **Zipedeedodah (IRE)**[3] 7127 5-9-2 **70** ........(t) JoshuaBryan(5) 2 67
(Joseph Tuite) *broke wl: sn hdd and chsd ldr for 2f: styd prom: pressing ldr again wl over 1f out: sn carried lft and rdn: no ex 1f out: wknd ins fnl f* **7/2**[2]

5036 **5** 1 ½ **Pearl Noir**[6] 7036 7-8-11 **60** ........(b) KieranO'Neill 6 51
(Scott Dixon) *missed break and short of room early: hdwy to chse ldr after 2f tl wl over 1f out: 4th and outpcd over 1f out: wknd ins fnl f* **9/1**

2045 **6** 1 ¾ **Stringybark Creek**[17] 6660 3-8-6 **56** oh3........ EdwardGreatrex 4 41
(Daniel Steele) *midfield: rdn over 2f out: sn outpcd and wknd u.p over 1f out* **33/1**

50 **7** 2 ¼ **Something Lucky (IRE)**[11] 6850 5-8-7 **56** ........(t[1]) RoystonFfrench 3 33
(Daniel Steele) *in tch in last pair: effrt and c nrest stands' rail over 2f out: no imp u.p: wknd over 1f out* **25/1**

44 **8** 4 ½ **Sandfrankskipsgo**[28] 6276 8-9-8 **71** ........ ShaneKelly 8 33
(Peter Crate) *chsd ldrs: rdn over 2f out: sn struggling: wknd over 1f out* **13/2**

1m 2.58s (0.28) **Going Correction** +0.15s/f (Good)
**WFA** 3 from 5yo+ 1lb **8** Ran SP% **113.0**
Speed ratings (Par 103): **103,101,97,96,94 91,88,80**
CSF £41.57 CT £155.89 TOTE £8.50: £3.30, £1.10, £1.60; EX 23.10 Trifecta £104.20.
**Owner** Saleh Al Homaizi & Imad Al Sagar **Bred** Saleh Al Homaizi & Imad Al Sagar **Trained** Six Mile Bottom, Cambs
■ Stewards' Enquiry : Shane Kelly caution: careless riding

**FOCUS**
Not a bad sprint handicap with the winner unexposed and improving.
T/Jkpt: Not Won. T/Plt: £123.90 to a £1 stake. Pool: £77,333.53 - 455.34 winning units. T/Qpdt: £26.70 to a £1 stake. Pool: £7,307.28 - 201.83 winning units. **Steve Payne**

# [7041] CARLISLE (R-H)
Monday, September 18

**OFFICIAL GOING: Heavy (6.4)**
Wind: Almost nil Weather: Overcast, light rain

## 7218 WATCH RACING UK ON BTTV APPRENTICE H'CAP — 5f
1:45 (1:47) (Class 6) (0-65,67) 3-Y-O+ £2,911 (£866; £432; £216) Stalls Low

Form RPR

1 **1** **Passionatta (IRE)**[25] 6339 3-8-6 **51** oh1........(v) RowanScott(3) 6 63
(J P Murtagh, Ire) *uns rdr and loose bef s: mde all: rdn: edgd lft and clr over 1f out: kpt on wl fnl f: unchal* **11/2**[2]

0004 **2** 2 ½ **Desperados Destiny**[39] 5837 3-9-5 **67** ........(p) CallumRodriguez(6) 3 70
(Michael Dods) *in tch: hdwy to chse wnr over 2f out: sn rdn: kpt on fnl f: no imp* **7/1**[3]

4324 **3** 3 ½ **Angel Palanas**[10] 6904 3-8-7 **59** ........(p) RussellHarris(10) 11 49
(K R Burke) *trckd ldrs: effrt and rdn over 2f out: kpt on same pce fr over 1f out* **9/1**

2204 **4** 5 **Jacksonfire**[13] 6786 5-8-10 **51** ........(p) PhilDennis 1 23
(Michael Mullineaux) *midfield: effrt and drvn along over 2f out: kpt on fnl f: no imp* **7/1**[3]

1315 **5** ¾ **Yes You (IRE)**[20] 6546 3-9-1 **65** ........ JamieGormley(8) 5 35
(Iain Jardine) *bhd: rdn along over 2f out: kpt on fnl f: nvr able to chal* **7/4**[1]

0003 **6** 2 ¼ **Reflation**[13] 6785 5-8-8 **51** oh6 ow1........ RobJFitzpatrick(3) 2 14
(Patrick Holmes) *dwlt and rdr lost iron briefly: bhd: drvn along 1/2-way: sme late hdwy: nvr on terms* **33/1**

1560 **7** 1 **Jazz Legend (USA)**[12] 6814 4-8-7 **52** ........(h) BenRobinson(3) 10 9
(Mandy Rowland) *chsd wnr to over 2f out: rdn and wknd over 1f out* **50/1**

066 **8** ¾ **Sir Domino (FR)**[13] 6786 5-8-2 **51** oh3........ PaulaMuir(8) 12
(Patrick Holmes) *midfield on outside: drvn along over 2f out: edgd rt and wknd over 1f out* **20/1**

2120 **9** 1 ¼ **Knockamany Bends (IRE)**[2] 7164 7-8-10 **51** oh2..(p) LewisEdmunds 7
(John Wainwright) *prom: drvn along over 2f out: wknd wl over 1f out* **14/1**

0140 **10** nk **Whipphound**[6] 7020 9-8-9 **53** ........(b) JaneElliott(3) 9
(Ruth Carr) *dwlt: bhd and pushed along: hung lft over 2f out: hung rt and wknd over 1f out* **9/1**

0466 **11** 9 **Goninodaethat**[18] 6631 9-8-6 **57** ........ SeanMooney(10) 4
(Jim Goldie) *bhd: struggling over 2f out: sn btn* **20/1**

1m 3.42s (2.62) **Going Correction** +0.60s/f (Yiel)
**WFA** 3 from 4yo+ 1lb **11** Ran SP% **117.8**
Speed ratings (Par 101): **103,99,93,85,84 80,79,77,75,75 60**
CSF £41.76 CT £352.69 TOTE £6.90: £2.50, £2.40, £2.50; EX 51.90 Trifecta £597.70.
**Owner** JP Murtagh Racing **Bred** Andy Collins & Intense Focus Syndicate **Trained** Coolaghknock Glebe,Co Kildare

**FOCUS**
There had been 25mm of rain over the previous week and the going was given as heavy (GoingStick: 6.4). The rail was at its innermost position, except for the bend after the winning post, which was out by 4yds, increasing the distance of races over 1m3f (races 2 & 3) by 4yds. A low-grade sprint and they finished well strung out in the testing ground.

## 7219 WATCH RACING UK ON YOUVIEW NOW H'CAP (DIV I) 1m 3f 39y
2:20 (2:20) (Class 6) (0-60,61) 3-Y-O+ £2,911 (£866; £432; £216) Stalls High

Form RPR

5 **1** **Les Arceaux (IRE)**[83] 4190 3-8-13 **55** BenCurtis 7 64
(J P Murtagh, Ire) *hld up: rdn and hdwy over 2f out: edgd rt over 1f out: drvn to ld ins fnl f: kpt on strly* **9/4**[1]

1630 **2** *2* **Rubis**[48] 5498 4-9-3 **60** ConnorMurtagh(7) 1 65
(Richard Fahey) *hld up on ins: hdwy over 2f out: rdn and led over 1f out: hdd ins fnl f: kpt on same pce* **17/2**

0-60 **3** *3/4* **Unonothinjonsnow**[21] 6529 3-8-4 **46** oh1 JoeFanning 10 51
(Richard Guest) *stdd s: hld up: hdwy to chse ldrs over 2f out: rdn and ev ch over 1f out: kpt on same pce ins fnl f* **9/1**

0522 **4** *1 1/2* **Paddy's Rock (IRE)**[13] 6788 6-9-6 **59** (p) JoshDoyle(3) 2 61
(Lynn Siddall) *dwlt: sn pushed along in rr: rdn 3f out: hdwy over 1f out: kpt on fnl f: nvr able to chal* **4/1**[2]

5000 **5** *1 1/2* **Chionodoxa**[10] 6892 3-8-1 **46** oh1 (p[1]) RachelRichardson(3) 4 46
(Tim Easterby) *trckd ldrs: chal 3f out: rdn and outpcd over 1f out: btn fnl f* **33/1**

3024 **6** *2 3/4* **Quoteline Direct**[26] 6316 4-9-11 **61** (h) PJMcDonald 11 56
(Micky Hammond) *hld up in midfield: smooth hdwy to ld 3f out: rdn and hdd over 1f out: sn wknd* **8/1**

50-6 **7** *3* **Heaven Scent**[48] 5493 4-8-13 **49** (bt) TomEaves 8 40
(Donald McCain) *mounted on crse: trckd ldrs: rdn along over 2f out: wknd over 1f out* **25/1**

3630 **8** *3* **Mcvicar**[10] 6898 8-9-5 **55** (p) SamJames 13 41
(John Davies) *hld up towards rr: drvn along wl over 2f out: sn no imp: btn over 1f out* **17/2**

5034 **9** *2 1/2* **Colour Contrast (IRE)**[16] 6690 4-8-10 **53** JamieGormley(7) 3 36
(Iain Jardine) *hld up: drvn and outpcd over 2f out: sn btn* **11/2**[3]

000- **10** *hd* **Papagayo (IRE)**[422] 4648 5-8-13 **49** GrahamLee 12 31
(Barry Murtagh) *bhd: rdn over 3f out: btn fnl 2f* **80/1**

0-00 **11** *15* **Chookie Valentine**[16] 6690 4-8-10 **46** oh1 (p) ConnorBeasley 6 6
(Keith Dalgleish) *midfield: effrt and drvn wl over 2f out: sn wknd* **50/1**

0006 **12** *shd* **Wolf Heart (IRE)**[19] 6592 9-8-10 **46** oh1 (v[1]) JoeDoyle 5 6
(Lucy Normile) *led to 3f out: sn drvn and lost pl: eased whn no ch over 1f out* **80/1**

-066 **13** *1 1/4* **Hazy Manor (IRE)**[19] 6594 3-8-5 **47** (p) ShaneGray 9 6
(Julia Brooke) *pressed ldr tl rdn and wknd over 2f out: eased whn btn over 1f out* **66/1**

2m 34.48s (11.38) **Going Correction** +0.80s/f (Soft)
**WFA** 3 from 4yo+ 6lb 13 Ran SP% **121.0**
Speed ratings (Par 101): **90,88,88,86,85 83,81,79,77,77 66,66,65**
CSF £22.05 CT £150.27 TOTE £3.50: £2.30, £3.00, £5.00; EX 21.70 Trifecta £206.40.
**Owner** JP Murtagh Racing **Bred** B Walsh **Trained** Coolaghknock Glebe,Co Kildare

**FOCUS**
Race distance increased by 4yds. Despite the conditions they went a decent pace.

## 7220 WATCH RACING UK ON YOUVIEW NOW H'CAP (DIV II) 1m 3f 39y
2:50 (2:50) (Class 6) (0-60,62) 3-Y-O+ £2,911 (£866; £432; £216) Stalls High

Form RPR

3304 **1** **Shambra (IRE)**[13] 6784 3-9-6 **62** (h) TonyHamilton 5 69
(Roger Fell) *mde all: rdn 2f out: hrd pressed ins fnl f: styd on gamely towards fin* **10/1**

0000 **2** *nk* **Royal Icon**[23] 6435 3-8-13 **55** TomEaves 9 62
(Kevin Ryan) *hld up: rdn and hdwy over 2f out: swtchd rt over 1f out: sn chsng wnr: disp ld ins fnl f: kpt on: hld nr fin* **12/1**

4600 **3** *2 1/4* **Leopard (IRE)**[20] 6549 3-8-13 **55** BarryMcHugh 3 58
(Tony Coyle) *t.k.h: hld up: effrt and rdn wl over 1f out: kpt on fnl f: nrst fin* **9/1**

4600 **4** *2 3/4* **Inspector Norse**[62] 5002 6-8-11 **50** RachelRichardson(3) 7 48
(Tim Easterby) *prom: effrt and rdn over 2f out: outpcd fr over 1f out* **8/1**

004 **5** *1 1/2* **Melanna (IRE)**[45] 5607 6-9-10 **60** GrahamLee 12 56
(Richard Ford) *chsd wnr: effrt and rdn over 2f out: edgd rt over 1f out: wknd ins fnl f* **7/1**[3]

00 **6** *1 1/2* **Hot Gossip (IRE)**[34] 6048 3-8-4 **46** oh1 JamesSullivan 1 41
(Dianne Sayer) *hld up in midfield: drvn along over 2f out: no imp fr over 1f out* **18/1**

5125 **7** *hd* **Sakhalin Star (IRE)**[19] 6592 6-9-10 **60** (p[1]) ConnorBeasley 4 53
(Richard Guest) *hld up: stdy hdwy over 3f out: drvn and outpcd wl over 1f out* **9/2**[2]

3660 **8** *1/2* **Red Star Dancer (IRE)**[35] 5997 3-8-11 **53** BenCurtis 6 47
(David Barron) *hld up in midfield: lost pl after 3f: drvn over 3f out: no imp fr 2f out* **3/1**[1]

0005 **9** *1 1/2* **Cool Run Girl (IRE)**[24] 6381 3-7-11 **46** oh1 (t) JamieGormley(7) 2 37
(Iain Jardine) *in tch: rdn over 2f out: wknd over 1f out* **14/1**

/00- **10** *nk* **Anginola (IRE)**[21] 378 8-8-10 **46** oh1 (v) ShaneGray 11 36
(Julia Brooke) *hld up: drvn along over 2f out: sn wknd* **50/1**

00-3 **11** *nk* **Toola Boola**[156] 1469 7-9-4 **54** JackGarritty 10 43
(Jedd O'Keeffe) *hld up: drvn along over 3f out: wknd fr 2f out* **8/1**

-000 **12** *21* **Dark Illustrator**[16] 6690 4-8-10 **46** oh1 PaddyAspell 8 4
(Lynn Siddall) *hld up: drvn and struggling over 3f out: lost tch fr 2f out* **66/1**

2m 38.27s (15.17) **Going Correction** +0.80s/f (Soft)
**WFA** 3 from 4yo+ 6lb 12 Ran SP% **120.1**
Speed ratings (Par 101): **76,75,74,72,71 69,69,69,68,68 67,52**
CSF £125.91 CT £1130.98 TOTE £8.50: £2.40, £2.90, £3.00; EX 81.70 Trifecta £846.80.
**Owner** R G Fell **Bred** John O'Kelly Bloodstock Services **Trained** Nawton, N Yorks

**FOCUS**
Race distance increased by 4yds. Not as strong an early gallop this time and the winner dominated from the front, recording a time 3.79sec slower than the winner of the first division. She achieved a small personal best.

## 7221 WATCH RACING UK ANYWHERE NOVICE AUCTION STKS 6f 195y
3:20 (3:20) (Class 5) 2-Y-O £3,396 (£1,010; £505; £252) Stalls Low

Form RPR

**1** **Ocean Voyage (IRE)** 2-8-11 0 PaulHanagan 1 70
(Richard Fahey) *hld up in tch: drvn and outpcd over 2f out: rallied and edgd lft over 1f out: ev ch last 75yds: led nr fin* **10/1**

12 **2** *nse* **Book Of Dreams (IRE)**[22] 6465 2-9-9 0 PJMcDonald 2 82
(Mark Johnston) *pressed ldr: led over 2f out: rdn and hung lft over 1f out: kpt on wl fnl f: hdd nr fin* **85/40**[2]

0 **3** *5* **Southpark**[10] 6890 2-9-2 0 TonyHamilton 7 63
(Richard Fahey) *hld up in tch: effrt and pushed along over 2f out: effrt and wnt 2nd briefly over 1f out: outpcd by first two ins fnl f* **12/1**

63 **4** *2 3/4* **Divine Intuition (IRE)**[60] 5058 2-9-2 0 TomQueally 5 56
(Kevin Ryan) *t.k.h early: trckd ldrs: effrt and disp 2nd pl briefly over 1f out: wknd ins fnl f* **7/2**[3]

532 **5** *1/2* **Spray The Sea (IRE)**[10] 6890 2-9-2 72 ConnorBeasley 3 54
(Bryan Smart) *led to over 2f out: chsd wnr to over 1f out: sn rdn and wknd* **2/1**[1]

0 **6** *27* **Sentimental Gent (FR)**[28] 6264 2-9-2 0 TomEaves 4
(Kevin Ryan) *hld up: drvn and struggling over 2f out: sn btn: t.o* **40/1**

**7** *1 1/2* **Kenmare River** 2-9-2 0 JackGarritty 6
(Jedd O'Keeffe) *s.i.s: hld up: rdn and struggling 3f out: sn btn: t.o* **25/1**

1m 33.04s (5.94) **Going Correction** +0.80s/f (Soft) 7 Ran SP% **110.6**
Speed ratings (Par 95): **98,97,92,89,88 57,55**
CSF £29.61 TOTE £8.50: £5.90, £1.30; EX 28.70 Trifecta £178.90.
**Owner** Alan Harte **Bred** Egmont Stud **Trained** Musley Bank, N Yorks

**FOCUS**
A fair novice race, but awful ground for inexperienced 2yos.

## 7222 WATCH RACING UK ON SKY 432 FILLIES' NURSERY H'CAP (JOCKEY CLUB GRASSROOTS NURSERY QUALIFIER) 6f 195y
3:55 (3:55) (Class 5) (0-70,69) 2-Y-O £3,396 (£1,010; £505; £252) Stalls Low

Form RPR

043 **1** **Powerful Society (IRE)**[21] 6510 2-9-7 **69** PaulHanagan 4 70
(Richard Fahey) *dwlt: hld up: rdn over 2f out: hdwy over 1f out: led and edgd lft ins fnl f: kpt on strly* **9/4**[1]

5020 **2** *3/4* **Claramara (IRE)**[18] 6626 2-9-2 **64** PJMcDonald 7 64
(Mark Johnston) *hld up in tch: pushed along over 2f out: hdwy over 1f out: ev ch ins fnl f: sn chsng wnr: kpt on fnl f* **10/1**

404 **3** *hd* **Show Princess**[23] 6433 2-9-1 **63** DougieCostello 2 62
(Michael Appleby) *trckd ldrs: rdn and led over 1f out: hdd whn checked ins fnl f: kpt on same pce nr fin* **20/1**

233 **4** *1/2* **Elysee Star**[23] 6433 2-9-2 **64** GrahamLee 1 62
(Ben Haslam) *hld up: effrt and hdwy on outside over 1f out: drvn and ev ch briefly ins fnl f: kpt on same pce* **11/2**[3]

4060 **5** *1/2* **Fastalong (IRE)**[5] 7041 2-8-10 **58** DavidAllan 5 55
(Tim Easterby) *trckd ldrs: drvn along over 2f out: outpcd over 1f out: kpt on ins fnl f* **7/2**[2]

4530 **6** *1 1/4* **Collateral Beauty**[30] 6200 2-9-4 **66** JackGarritty 3 61
(Richard Fahey) *led to over 1f out: rdn and no ex whn hmpd wl ins fnl f* **11/2**[3]

0063 **7** *1 1/4* **Plansina**[21] 6517 2-8-2 **53** RachelRichardson(3) 6 43
(Tim Easterby) *t.k.h early: pressed ldr to over 1f out: sn drvn and outpcd* **9/1**

0500 **8** *4 1/2* **Lil Gem (IRE)**[38] 5878 2-8-2 **50** JoeFanning 8 29
(Keith Dalgleish) *hld up: rdn and outpcd over 2f out: btn over 1f out* **20/1**

1m 34.25s (7.15) **Going Correction** +0.80s/f (Soft) 8 Ran SP% **112.4**
Speed ratings (Par 92): **91,90,89,89,88 87,85,80**
CSF £24.95 CT £354.87 TOTE £3.00: £1.20, £2.90, £4.60; EX 18.90 Trifecta £126.30.
**Owner** Crown Select **Bred** Gigginstown House Stud **Trained** Musley Bank, N Yorks
■ Stewards' Enquiry : Paul Hanagan two-day ban: careless riding

**FOCUS**
A competitive fillies' nursery in which they finished in a bit of a heap.

## 7223 WATCH RACING UK ON VIRGIN 536 H'CAP 6f 195y
4:25 (4:27) (Class 4) (0-80,78) 3-Y-O+ £5,498 (£1,636; £817; £408) Stalls Low

Form RPR

3315 **1** **Beverley Bullet**[33] 6060 4-8-10 **62** (p) JoeFanning 2 71
(Lawrence Mullaney) *pressed ldr: led over 2f out: rdn and edgd rt over 1f out: styd on strly fnl f* **9/2**[3]

2620 **2** *2 1/2* **Flyboy (IRE)**[20] 6555 4-9-12 **78** (b) JackGarritty 6 80
(Richard Fahey) *t.k.h: hld up: hdwy on outside to chse wnr over 1f out: drvn and one pce fnl f* **11/2**

1333 **3** *nk* **Redarna**[5] 7046 3-8-6 **61** JamesSullivan 4 61
(Dianne Sayer) *t.k.h: trckd ldrs: drvn and outpcd over 2f out: rallied over 1f out: kpt on ins fnl f* **11/4**[1]

5025 **4** *2 1/2* **God Willing**[8] 6964 6-9-5 **78** GerO'Neill(7) 8 73
(Declan Carroll) *hld up: drvn and outpcd over 2f out: rallied ins fnl f: no imp* **7/2**[2]

1404 **5** *hd* **Tadaawol**[2] 7140 4-9-12 **78** (p) TonyHamilton 5 72
(Roger Fell) *led: rdn and hdd over 2f out: rallied: wknd ins fnl f* **9/2**[3]

1306 **6** *1 3/4* **Gilmer (IRE)**[49] 5471 6-9-11 **77** TomEaves 3 67
(James Ewart) *prom: drvn and outpcd over 2f out: btn over 1f out* **22/1**

5316 **7** *1 1/4* **Specialv (IRE)**[31] 6149 4-9-3 **69** (p) BenCurtis 7 55
(Brian Ellison) *hld up: drvn and struggling over 2f out: sn btn* **12/1**

1m 31.8s (4.70) **Going Correction** +0.80s/f (Soft)
**WFA** 3 from 4yo+ 3lb 7 Ran SP% **112.7**
Speed ratings (Par 105): **105,102,101,98,98 96,95**
CSF £28.16 CT £78.92 TOTE £4.30: £2.20, £2.50; EX 30.90 Trifecta £75.70.
**Owner** Mrs Jean Stapleton & Rob Wilson **Bred** Keith Trowbridge **Trained** Great Habton, N Yorks

**FOCUS**
The soft-ground professionals came to the fore here and a personal best from the winner.

## 7224 WATCH RACING UK ON THE GO MAIDEN FILLIES' STKS 1m 1f
4:55 (4:55) (Class 5) 3-Y-O+ £3,234 (£962; £481) Stalls Low

Form RPR

**1** **She's Pukka** 3-9-0 0 GrahamLee 3 71
(Iain Jardine) *dwlt: chsd ldrs: pushed along over 2f out: hdwy over 1f out: led ins fnl f: styd on strly* **9/2**[3]

344 **2** *1 1/2* **Relevant (IRE)**[34] 6027 3-9-0 67 DanielTudhope 1 68
(K R Burke) *pressed ldr: led over 2f out: rdn over 1f out: hdd ins fnl f: kpt on same pce* **1/1**[1]

40- **3** *hd* **For The Roses**[24] 6407 3-9-0 68 (t) BenCurtis 4 67
(J P Murtagh, Ire) *led at ordinary gallop: rdn and hdd over 2f out: rallied and ev ch over 1f out to ins fnl f: kpt on same pce* **6/4**[2]

2m 7.68s (10.08) **Going Correction** +0.80s/f (Soft)
**WFA** 3 from 6yo 5lb 3 Ran SP% **108.2**
Speed ratings (Par 100): **87,85,85**
CSF £9.26 TOTE £4.10; EX 5.80 Trifecta £8.50.
**Owner** Paul & Clare Rooney **Bred** Hall Of Fame Stud Ltd **Trained** Carrutherstown, D'fries & G'way

**FOCUS**
An ordinary maiden and ability to handle the ground was probably the determining factor. The race has been rated around the pair with experience.

## 7225 WATCH RACING UK ON TALKTALK H'CAP (JOCKEY CLUB GRASSROOTS MIDDLE DISTANCE QUALIFIER) 1m 1f
**5:25** (5:27) (Class 5) (0-75,74) 3-Y-O+ **£3,396** (£1,010; £505; £252) **Stalls** Low

Form RPR
2200 **1** **Billy Bond**[35] 6003 5-8-7 **55** oh2..........(b) JoeFanning 2 66
(Richard Fahey) *t.k.h early: chsd ldr: led gng wl over 2f out: pushed clr over 1f out: edgd rt: kpt on wl fnl f* **20/1**
2530 **2** 2½ **Abushamah (IRE)**[23] 6434 6-9-9 **71**.......... JamesSullivan 9 77
(Ruth Carr) *hld up: pushed along over 2f out: hdwy to chse (clr) wnr over 1f out: kpt on ins fnl f* **10/1**
36 **3** 4½ **Polar Forest**[20] 6551 7-9-6 **68**..........(e) ConnorBeasley 5 64
(Richard Guest) *dwlt: hld up: rdn over 3f out: hdwy 2f out: kpt on fnl f: nvr able to chal* **18/1**
0013 **4** ½ **Parole (IRE)**[11] 6855 5-9-2 **67**..........(t) RachelRichardson(3) 12 62
(Tim Easterby) *prom: drvn and outpcd over 2f out: no imp fr over 1f out* **7/2**[2]
3304 **5** 2¾ **Miningrocks (FR)**[23] 6431 5-9-4 **73**.......... GerO'Neill(7) 3 62
(Declan Carroll) *led to over 2f out: outpcd and edgd rt over 1f out: btn fnl f* **8/1**
4040 **6** 2½ **Toboggan's Fire**[25] 6349 4-9-12 **74**.......... ShaneGray 6 58
(Ann Duffield) *bhd: drvn over 3f out: sme late hdwy: nvr on terms* **16/1**
360- **7** 2¼ **Topamichi**[331] 7531 7-9-2 **67**.......... LewisEdmunds(3) 7 47
(Michael Appleby) *hld up in midfield: stdy hdwy over 3f out: rdn and outpcd over 2f out: sn n.d* **9/4**[1]
6526 **8** 18 **Maraakib (IRE)**[9] 6948 5-9-9 **71**..........(p) DanielTudhope 1 13
(David O'Meara) *trckd ldrs tl rdn and wknd over 2f out* **15/2**[3]
6-46 **9** 3¼ **Page Of Wands**[249] 195 4-8-6 **61**.......... ConnorMurtagh(7) 10
(George Bewley) *hld up: struggling over 4f out: btn over 2f out* **66/1**
22 **10** 4½ **Haroon (IRE)**[20] 6548 3-9-5 **72**..........(t) BarryMcHugh 11
(Tony Coyle) *dwlt: bhd and pushed along: struggling over 3f out: sn wknd* **10/1**
5600 **11** 6 **Fidelma Moon (IRE)**[23] 6435 5-8-9 **57** oh4 ow2.......... BenCurtis 13
(Tracy Waggott) *midfield on outside: struggling wl over 2f out: sn wknd* **66/1**
345 **12** 25 **Konig Dax (GER)**[63] 4959 7-9-12 **74**..........(t) TomEaves 4
(Alistair Whillans) *midfield on ins: lost pl 4f out: sn struggling: t.o* **25/1**

2m 6.35s (8.75) **Going Correction** +0.80s/f (Soft)
**WFA** 3 from 4yo+ 5lb **12 Ran SP% 116.8**
Speed ratings (Par 103): **93,90,86,86,83 81,79,63,60,56 51,29**
CSF £199.42 CT £3694.93 TOTE £18.10: £3.90, £2.80, £5.00; EX 123.30 Trifecta £1781.10.
**Owner** Mr & Mrs P Ashton **Bred** Mr & Mrs P Ashton **Trained** Musley Bank, N Yorks

**FOCUS**
Few got involved here with the winner rated close to last winter's AW form.
T/Plt: £282.60 to a £1 stake. Pool: £55,066.77 - 142.23 winning units T/Qpdt: £46.10 to a £1 stake. Pool: £5,252.99 - 84.20 winning units **Richard Young**

# 7079 CHEPSTOW (L-H)
## Tuesday, September 19

**OFFICIAL GOING: Good to soft changing to good to soft (soft in places) after race 2 (2:10)**
Wind: light crosswind Weather: fine

## 7226 CRICKET BETTING AT 188BET/EBF FILLIES' NOVICE STKS (PLUS 10 RACE) 7f 16y
**1:40** (1:41) (Class 5) 2-Y-O **£3,881** (£1,155; £577; £288) **Stalls** Centre

Form RPR
040 **1** **Zoraya (FR)**[22] 6542 2-9-0 0.......... RaulDaSilva 7 74
(Paul Cole) *midfield: rdn over 2f out: chsd ldrs over 1f out: wnt 3rd ent fnl f: r.o to ld cl home* **20/1**
302 **2** nk **Frolic**[17] 6666 2-9-0 77.......... LukeMorris 4 73
(Sir Mark Prescott Bt) *led: rdn over 1f out: drvn fnl f: ct cl home* **7/2**[2]
00 **3** 1½ **Lamb Chop**[57] 5216 2-9-0 0..........(p[1]) WilliamCarson 11 69
(Rod Millman) *prom: racd alone stands' side tl edgd over to join main body over 4f out: rdn over 2f out: r.o u.p fnl f* **66/1**
0 **4** 1 **Parmenter**[12] 6862 2-9-0 0.......... FergusSweeney 8 67+
(Alan King) *hld up towards rr: pushed along: swtchd rt and hdwy 2f out: styd on steadily fnl f: nt rch ldrs* **33/1**
32 **5** 1¾ **Goodnight Girl (IRE)**[12] 6862 2-8-11 0.......... GeorgeWood(3) 1 62
(Jonathan Portman) *trckd ldrs: rdn over 2f out: drvn over 1f out: no ex fnl f* **11/8**[1]
54 **6** 1¼ **Diva Star**[25] 6386 2-9-0 0.......... MartinDwyer 5 59
(Marcus Tregoning) *t.k.h towards rr: hdwy to chse ldrs 3f out: sn drvn: nt run on and hld fnl f* **4/1**[3]
**7** 2¾ **Edge Of The World (IRE)** 2-9-0 0.......... OisinMurphy 9 52
(Ralph Beckett) *dwlt: in rr: rdn 3f out: no imp tl sme hdwy fnl f* **15/2**
4052 **8** ¾ **Fusion Central (IRE)**[22] 6504 2-8-7 68.......... RossaRyan(7) 6 51
(Richard Hannon) *prom: rdn over 2f out: wknd over 1f out* **11/1**
06 **9** 8 **Hurricane Lil (IRE)**[24] 6417 2-9-0 0.......... TrevorWhelan 10 31
(George Baker) *prom: rdn over 2f out: wknd wl over 1f out* **25/1**
00 **10** ¾ **Pollyissimo**[32] 6138 2-9-0 0.......... ShaneKelly 3 29
(Richard Hughes) *t.k.h in midfield: rdn and lost pl 1/2-way: no ch fnl 2f* **66/1**
**11** 3¾ **Supermoss** 2-8-9 0.......... MitchGodwin(5) 2 19
(Heather Main) *midfield: clsd after 4f: rdn over 2f out: wknd over 1f out* **100/1**

1m 27.58s (4.38) **Going Correction** +0.575s/f (Yiel) **11 Ran SP% 119.9**
Speed ratings (Par 92): **97,96,94,93,91 90,87,86,77,76 72**
CSF £87.86 TOTE £23.40: £6.10, £1.40, £22.10; EX 106.10 Trifecta £1990.10.
**Owner** The Fairy Story Partnership **Bred** Jedburgh Stud & Deepwood Farm Stud **Trained** Whatcombe, Oxon

**FOCUS**
An ordinary novice in which the short-price favourite disappointed.

## 7227 TICKET GIVEAWAYS AT 188BET MAIDEN FILLIES' STKS 7f 16y
**2:10** (2:11) (Class 5) 3-Y-O+ **£3,234** (£962; £481; £240) **Stalls** Centre

Form RPR
2223 **1** **Spinnaka (IRE)**[33] 6103 3-9-0 75..........(v[1]) LukeMorris 4 81
(Luca Cumani) *wnt rt leaving stalls: prom: wnt 2nd over 4f out: led over 2f out: drvn over 1f out: hld on nr fin* **2/1**[2]
**2** hd **Diagnostic** 3-9-0 0.......... PatCosgrave 5 80
(William Haggas) *s.s: t.k.h and hld up: hdwy over 4f out: drvn to chse wnr over 1f out: r.o: clsng towards fin* **6/4**[1]
2 **3** 11 **Natheer (USA)**[34] 6066 3-9-0 0.......... DaneO'Neill 1 52
(Roger Varian) *hld up: hdwy over 2f out: drvn and ch over 1f out: sn outpcd by ldng pair: kpt on same pce to hold modest 3rd* **7/2**[3]
40- **4** ¾ **Tazmania (IRE)**[321] 7763 3-9-0 0.......... SamHitchcott 6 50
(Clive Cox) *chsd ldrs: rdn over 2f out: one pce* **14/1**
404- **5** 2 **Rockshine**[342] 7284 3-9-0 68.......... PatDobbs 2 45
(Richard Hannon) *prom tl lost pl 1/2-way: rdn 2f out: styd on but no threat* **20/1**
532 **6** 2½ **Cherished (IRE)**[13] 6808 3-9-0 68.......... TimmyMurphy 3 38
(Geoffrey Deacon) *t.k.h: led over 1f: styd prom: drvn 2f out: wknd appr fnl f* **10/1**
**7** 5 **Stockhill Star** 3-9-0 0.......... MartinDwyer 7 25
(Brendan Powell) *dwlt and half rrd s: plld hrd: hdwy to ld over 5f out: rdn and hdd over 2f out: rn green and wknd qckly* **66/1**
**8** 21 **Miss Quoted**[9] 5-9-3 0.......... SteveDrowne 8
(Seamus Mullins) *a in rr: lost tch 3f out: t.o* **100/1**

1m 27.6s (4.40) **Going Correction** +0.575s/f (Yiel)
**WFA** 3 from 5yo 3lb **8 Ran SP% 118.6**
Speed ratings (Par 100): **97,96,84,83,81 78,72,48**
CSF £5.58 TOTE £2.90: £1.10, £1.10, £1.40; EX 6.90 Trifecta £17.90.
**Owner** Fittocks Stud & Andrew Bengough **Bred** Ballylinch Stud **Trained** Newmarket, Suffolk

**FOCUS**
Two drew clear in this ordinary maiden, with the winner's experience making the difference. She has been rated to form.

## 7228 188BET NURSERY H'CAP 6f 16y
**2:45** (2:45) (Class 5) (0-70,70) 2-Y-O **£3,234** (£962; £481; £240) **Stalls** Centre

Form RPR
054 **1** **Motown Mick (IRE)**[15] 6761 2-9-7 **70**.......... TomMarquand 9 74
(Richard Hannon) *chsd ldrs: drvn over 2f out: stl 5th ent fnl f: r.o to ld fnl 75yds* **5/1**[3]
0005 **2** 1 **Saria**[14] 6790 2-8-2 **51**.......... KieranO'Neill 1 52
(Tony Carroll) *towards rr: hdwy 1/2-way: drvn over 2f out: ev ch over 1f out tl unable qck nr fin* **20/1**
5514 **3** ¾ **W G Grace (IRE)**[13] 6825 2-9-2 **65**.......... FrannyNorton 8 64
(Mark Johnston) *pressed ldr: drvn to ld ins fnl f: hdd fnl 75yds: no ex* **9/2**[2]
5012 **4** 2¼ **Diamond Dougal (IRE)**[6] 7041 2-9-7 **70**.......... DaneO'Neill 4 62
(Mick Channon) *wnt rt leaving stalls: chsd ldrs: rdn to ld over 1f out: hdd ins fnl f: wknd fnl 50yds* **5/2**[1]
0320 **5** 2 **Bhindi**[24] 6417 2-9-5 **68**.......... CharlesBishop 3 54
(Eve Johnson Houghton) *led: drvn 2f out: hdd over 1f out: wknd ins fnl f* **11/2**
5116 **6** ¾ **Princess Lyla (IRE)**[15] 6749 2-9-5 **68**.......... ShaneKelly 2 52
(Richard Hughes) *t.k.h in midfield: rdn over 2f out: one pce* **15/2**
600 **7** 2 **Swissal (IRE)**[29] 6272 2-9-2 **65**.......... LukeMorris 7 43
(David Dennis) *s.s: towards rr: rdn and hdwy over 2f out: one pce appr fnl f* **25/1**
0460 **8** 8 **Comselle**[18] 6651 2-9-0 **63**.......... OisinMurphy 6 17
(Stuart Kittow) *t.k.h towards rr: pushed along over 2f out: wknd over 1f out* **16/1**
5100 **9** ¾ **Brockey Rise (IRE)**[9] 6977 2-9-0 **70**..........(v) KatherineGlenister(7) 5 22
(David Evans) *bmpd leaving stalls: t.k.h: prom tl lost pl over 3f out: rdn and lft bhd over 2f out* **8/1**

1m 15.43s (3.43) **Going Correction** +0.575s/f (Yiel) **9 Ran SP% 116.2**
Speed ratings (Par 95): **100,98,97,94,92 91,88,77,76**
CSF £97.27 CT £486.42 TOTE £8.10: £2.60, £5.60, £1.60; EX 139.10 Trifecta £682.90.
**Owner** N Woodcock & M Daniels **Bred** Top Row Partnership **Trained** East Everleigh, Wilts

**FOCUS**
Modest nursery form.

## 7229 188BET.CO.UK H'CAP 7f 16y
**3:15** (3:15) (Class 4) (0-85,84) 3-Y-O+ **£5,175** (£1,540; £769; £384) **Stalls** Centre

Form RPR
2440 **1** **Berkshire Boy (IRE)**[103] 3504 3-9-2 **82**..........(b) RobHornby 1 91
(Andrew Balding) *trckd ldrs: led 3f out: drvn and edgd rt over 1f out: r.o* **9/2**
4426 **2** 1¾ **Mohsen**[14] 6791 3-8-7 **73**.......... MartinDwyer 2 77
(Marcus Tregoning) *hld up: pushed along and hdwy over 2f out: drvn to chse wnr wl over 1f out: hld whn edgd rt ins fnl f* **12/1**
0411 **3** 1 **Salt Whistle Bay (IRE)**[32] 6143 3-8-12 **78**.......... OisinMurphy 8 79
(Rae Guest) *trckd ldrs: rdn over 2f out: wandered u.p and kpt on fnl f* **7/2**[2]
3525 **4** nk **Plant Pot Power (IRE)**[10] 6936 3-9-1 **84**.......... HollieDoyle(3) 7 84+
(Richard Hannon) *s.s: hld up: hdwy 2f out: rdn over 1f out: r.o fnl f* **3/1**[1]
3202 **5** 2½ **Redgrave (IRE)**[13] 6809 3-9-0 **80**..........(h) LukeMorris 6 74
(Charles Hills) *chsd ldrs: hung sltly lft over 3f out: clsd to dispute 2nd 2f out: drvn over 1f out: one pce fnl f* **4/1**[3]
5066 **6** 6 **Thomas Cranmer (USA)**[11] 6894 3-9-3 **83**.......... FrannyNorton 4 61
(Mark Johnston) *cl up: rdn over 2f out: wknd over 1f out* **18/1**
0413 **7** 3 **Another Boy**[25] 6378 4-8-6 **74**..........(p) PatrickO'Donnell(5) 5 44
(Ralph Beckett) *led 4f: sn rdn: styd prom tl wknd over 1f out* **7/1**
4304 **8** shd **Sarangoo**[8] 7002 9-8-3 **71**.......... GeorgiaCox(5) 3 41
(Malcolm Saunders) *t.k.h: chsd ldrs tl rdn and dropped rr over 3f out: lost tch over 1f out* **20/1**

1m 26.11s (2.91) **Going Correction** +0.575s/f (Yiel)
**WFA** 3 from 4yo+ 3lb **8 Ran SP% 115.6**
Speed ratings (Par 105): **106,104,102,102,99 92,89,89**
CSF £56.48 CT £211.65 TOTE £5.30: £1.90, £3.00, £1.70; EX 64.50 Trifecta £326.40.
**Owner** Berkshire Parts & Panels Ltd **Bred** Ms Vanessa Teehan **Trained** Kingsclere, Hants

**FOCUS**
Fair handicap form with the winner recording a clear personal best.

## 7230 NFL BETTING AT 188BET (S) STKS 1m 2f
**3:50** (3:50) (Class 6) 3-Y-O **£2,587** (£770; £384; £192) **Stalls** Low

Form RPR
3002 **1** **Outcrop (IRE)**[13] 6821 3-9-3 72.......... OisinMurphy 4 69+
(Hughie Morrison) *wnt to post early: mde all: sn several l clr: given breather on home turn 5f out: rdn and increased pce 3f out: pressed fnl 2f: styd on u.p and a holding runner-up* **10/11**[1]
3634 **2** 1 **Pacofilha**[20] 6578 3-8-9 67.......... RaulDaSilva 1 59+
(Paul Cole) *chsd ldrs: wnt 2nd over 3f out: rdn to press wnr 2f out: kpt on u.p but a being hld* **11/10**[2]

1000 **3** *6* **London Grammar (IRE)**[45] 5653 3-8-10 54............. PaddyBradley[(5)] 7 54
(Ralph J Smith) *hld up: hdwy 4f out: drvn and wnt 3rd 2f out: kpt on but little imp on first two* **14/1**[3]

0405 **4** *7* **Performance Art (IRE)**[15] 6752 3-8-9 42..................(p[1]) KieranO'Neill 5 34
(Seamus Mullins) *chsd ldng pair: rdn 4f out: lost 3rd 2f out: grad wknd* **25/1**

06 **5** *23* **Nitro**[13] 6808 3-8-9 0.......................................... MitchGodwin[(5)] 6
(Roy Brotherton) *hld up in 5th: rdn 5f out: wknd over 3f out: t.o* **80/1**

600- **6** *4* **Sam The Rebel**[343] 7259 3-9-0 43................................ WilliamCarson 3
(Mike Hammond) *plld hrd: chsd wnr: clsd 5f out: drvn and lost 2nd over 3f out: sn wknd* **40/1**

06- **7** *18* **Myhorsewithnoname (IRE)**[358] 6828 3-8-11 0.......(v[1]) AaronJones[(3)] 2
(Mark Hoad) *hld up: rdn over 4f out: sn lost tch: t.o* **66/1**

2m 13.52s (2.92) **Going Correction** +0.35s/f (Good) 7 Ran SP% **115.7**
Speed ratings (Par 99): **102,101,96,90,72 69,54**
CSF £2.20 TOTE £1.70: £1.10, £1.10; EX 2.20 Trifecta £5.10.Outcrop sold for 16,000gns to Jennie Candlish. Pacofilha was claimed by Mr J.L.Flint for £10,000.
**Owner** J H Richmond-Watson **Bred** J H Richmond-Watson **Trained** East Ilsley, Berks
■ Stewards' Enquiry : William Carson five-day ban: using whip when out of contention (3-7 Oct)
Oisin Murphy two-day ban: excessive use of whip (Oct 3-4)

**FOCUS**
Effectively a match and the big two had it to themselves from some way out.

## 7231 READ SILVESTRE DE SOUSA AT 188BET H'CAP 1m 4f
**4:20** (4:20) (Class 4) (0-85,84) 3-Y-0+ **£5,175** (£1,540; £769; £384) **Stalls** Low

Form RPR

513 **1** **Fools And Kings**[33] 6094 3-8-10 **78**.......................... GeorgeWood[(3)] 1 87+
(Robyn Brisland) *hld up: rdn and hdwy 2f out: r.o to ld ins fnl f: pushed out* **8/1**

-216 **2** *1 ¾* **Knight Destroyer (IRE)**[22] 5153 3-8-12 **77**........................ FranBerry 9 83
(Jonjo O'Neill) *hld up: hdwy 3f out: drvn 2f out: ev ch 1f out: styd on same pce* **12/1**

4331 **3** *nk* **Sable Island (IRE)**[24] 6413 3-8-13 **78**............................... PatDobbs 8 83
(Sir Michael Stoute) *chsd ldrs: led wl over 2f out: sn drvn: hdd and unable qck ins fnl f* **7/2**[2]

-566 **4** *nse* **Murgan**[22] 6508 5-9-6 **78**..........................................(t[1]) OisinMurphy 3 82
(Stuart Kittow) *chsd ldrs: rdn and sltly outpcd over 3f out: styd on fnl f* **11/1**

50-0 **5** *1* **Argus (IRE)**[50] 5488 5-9-12 **84**.........................................(h) JohnFahy 6 86
(Alexandra Dunn) *hld up: drvn and clsd on outer over 2f out: kpt on same pce* **20/1**

1034 **6** *¾* **See Of Rome**[24] 6415 3-9-5 **84**......................................(p[1]) ShaneKelly 2 86
(Richard Hughes) *prom: rdn 2f out: nt clr run over 1f out: styd on steadily fnl f* **9/2**[3]

5615 **7** *8* **Earthly (USA)**[31] 6176 3-8-4 **76**.................................... WilliamCox[(7)] 5 65
(Bernard Llewellyn) *midfield: rdn over 2f out: wknd over 1f out* **16/1**

1110 **8** *1 ¼* **Ya Jammeel**[17] 6680 4-9-6 **78**........................................ FrannyNorton 7 64
(Mick Channon) *led 100yds: trckd ldr tl led again 3f out: sn drvn and hdd: wknd fnl f* **10/3**[1]

33-1 **9** *9* **Time To Blossom**[24] 6431 4-9-9 **81**.................................... DaneO'Neill 4 53
(Simon Crisford) *s.i.s: led after 100yds: rdn and hdwy 3f out: sn wknd* **11/2**

2m 42.61s (3.61) **Going Correction** +0.35s/f (Good)
**WFA** 3 from 4yo+ 7lb 9 Ran SP% **116.6**
Speed ratings (Par 105): **101,99,99,99,98 98,93,92,86**
CSF £99.27 CT £398.96 TOTE £8.20: £2.00, £3.60, £2.70; EX 85.00 Trifecta £611.30.
**Owner** Paul Hancock **Bred** Mrs D O'Brien **Trained** Newmarket, Suffolk

**FOCUS**
An ordinary handicap won by a progressive sort, with the closers coming to the fore late on.

## 7232 PLAY CASINO AT 188BET H'CAP (DIV I) 2m
**4:55** (4:55) (Class 6) (0-65,67) 3-Y-0+ **£2,587** (£770; £384; £192) **Stalls** Low

Form RPR

1-36 **1** **Master Dancer**[89] 4000 6-9-9 **64**.............................(p) MitchGodwin[(5)] 11 75
(Tim Vaughan) *s.s: hld up in rr: hdwy on inner 4f out: swtchd rt and drvn 3f out: led wl over 1f out: sn clr: styd on wl* **14/1**

5400 **2** *10* **Ivanhoe**[27] 6309 7-9-8 **58**................................................ SteveDrowne 2 57
(Michael Blanshard) *towards rr: hdwy over 3f out: styd on u.p to go 2nd ins fnl f: no ch w wnr* **20/1**

0351 **3** *1* **Franny Nisbet**[13] 6820 3-9-1 **61**...................................... MartinDwyer 8 61
(William Muir) *hld up in last: drvn and hdwy on outer 3f out: hung lft fr 2f out: styd on to go 3rd ins fnl f* **7/2**[1]

0524 **4** *½* **Leapt**[25] 6370 3-9-7 **67**.................................................(h) ShaneKelly 13 66
(Richard Hughes) *wnt to post early: prom: led after 2f tl after 4f: chsd ldr: led again over 2f out tl wl over 1f out: nt run on: lost 2 pls ins fnl f* **7/2**[1]

0665 **5** *1 ¼* **Artic Nel**[31] 6180 3-8-7 **53**............................................. LukeMorris 3 51
(Ian Williams) *chsd ldrs: drvn over 3f out: kpt on same pce* **9/2**[2]

/00- **6** *shd* **Racing Spirit**[20] 1322 5-8-9 **45**...................................... DannyBrock 1 41
(Dave Roberts) *midfield: rdn over 4f out: one pce: hld whn n.m.r 2f out* **16/1**

/630 **7** *4* **Wintour Leap**[56] 5244 6-9-8 **58**...................................... DaneO'Neill 7 49
(Robert Stephens) *towards rr: rdn over 4f out: no real imp* **14/1**

4540 **8** *3* **Taste The Wine (IRE)**[17] 5716 11-8-6 **49**...............(tp) WilliamCox[(7)] 9 36
(Bernard Llewellyn) *hld up: hdwy 6f out: one pce fnl 3f* **25/1**

01 **9** *1 ¼* **Tsundoku (IRE)**[53] 5361 6-9-4 **54**..................................... JohnFahy 10 40
(Alexandra Dunn) *chsd ldrs: hdwy to ld after 4f: rdn 3f out: hdd over 2f out: wknd over 1f out* **9/2**[2]

0000 **10** *57* **Tarakkom (FR)**[97] 3724 5-8-10 **46**................................... RobHornby 12
(Peter Hiatt) *chsd ldrs: dropped to midfield after 5f: rdn 4f out: sn wknd: t.o* **33/1**

6045 **11** *40* **Dartmoor Girl (IRE)**[6] 7059 3-8-1 **47**.........................(b) RaulDaSilva 4
(Mark Gillard) *wnt to post early: led 2f: styd prom tl wknd 4f out: t.o* **50/1**

325- **12** *14* **Atalanta Bay (IRE)**[382] 6090 7-9-5 **62**....................... TylerSaunders[(7)] 5 +
(Marcus Tregoning) *hld up: sddle sn slipped and wnt prom after 3f: wknd 4f out: virtually p.u: t.o* **12/1**[3]

3m 42.41s (3.51) **Going Correction** +0.35s/f (Good)
**WFA** 3 from 5yo+ 10lb 12 Ran SP% **121.2**
Speed ratings (Par 101): **105,100,99,99,98 98,96,95,94,65 45,38**
CSF £271.45 CT £1206.85 TOTE £12.30: £3.40, £4.70, £2.10; EX 212.70 Trifecta £852.20.
**Owner** select-racing-club.co.uk & C Davies **Bred** D J Bloodstock, G Roddick & Wrottesley Ltd **Trained** Aberthin, Vale of Glamorgan
■ Stewards' Enquiry : Danny Brock two-day ban: used whip above shoulder height

**FOCUS**
What had looked quite an open staying handicap was taken apart by the top weight.

## 7233 PLAY CASINO AT 188BET H'CAP (DIV II) 2m
**5:25** (5:25) (Class 6) (0-65,64) 3-Y-0+ **£2,587** (£770; £384; £192) **Stalls** Low

Form RPR

4-52 **1** **Kozier (GER)**[25] 6376 3-8-10 **59**................................... HollieDoyle[(3)] 1 71
(Alan King) *t.k.h early: chsd ldrs: rdn 3f out: wnt 2nd 2f out: led over 1f out: drvn and styd on* **1/1**[1]

0003 **2** *2 ½* **Alternate Route**[13] 6820 3-8-10 **56**................................(p) LukeMorris 2 65
(Sir Mark Prescott Bt) *midfield: clsd 1/2-way: wnt 2nd 4f out: drvn to ld over 3f out: hdd over 1f out: kpt on same pce u.p* **9/2**[2]

5242 **3** *4 ½* **General Allenby**[13] 6820 3-8-5 **51**..............................(be) RaulDaSilva 10 55
(Henry Tett) *hld up: hdwy on outer over 5f out: drvn over 3f out: hld in 3rd whn edgd rt over 1f out* **5/1**[3]

6244 **4** *6* **Goldslinger (FR)**[26] 6343 5-9-11 **64**............................... JackDuern[(3)] 3 58
(Dean Ivory) *chsd ldrs tl led after 5f: hdd over 3f out: one pce* **9/1**

3202 **5** *¾* **Miskin**[43] 5716 8-9-7 **57**...................................................(h) DaneO'Neill 8 51
(Robert Stephens) *midfield: hdwy into 2nd gng wl 3f out: sn drvn: lost 2nd 2f out: nt run on* **11/1**

6/00 **6** *4 ½* **Kalimantan (IRE)**[69] 4756 7-8-13 **49**.........................(v[1]) KieranO'Neill 12 37
(Tim Vaughan) *trckd ldr 5f: styd prom: rdn 4f out: wknd 2f out* **25/1**

/560 **7** *11* **Flannery (IRE)**[22] 6509 6-8-4 **45** ow2....................(t) MitchGodwin[(5)] 7 20
(Tim Vaughan) *hld up: drvn 4f out: wknd over 2f out* **50/1**

6505 **8** *¾* **Rob's Legacy**[13] 6530 4-8-9 **45**........................................(b) DannyBrock 4 19
(Shaun Harris) *chsd along to ld after 100yds: hdd after 5f: rdn and lost 2nd 4f out: wknd over 2f out* **50/1**

400/ **9** *¾* **Cropley (IRE)**[303] 51 8-9-9 **59**..................................... CharlesBishop 9 32
(Dai Burchell) *chsd ldrs tl lost pl 1/2-way: rdn and wknd over 5f out* **40/1**

6436 **10** *19* **Petrify**[33] 5716 7-8-10 **53**...........................................(tp) WilliamCox[(7)] 11
(Bernard Llewellyn) *s.s: in rr tl hdwy into midfield after 5f: rdn over 4f out: wknd 3f out: t.o* **25/1**

1-40 **11** *1 ½* **Work (IRE)**[97] 3724 4-9-8 **58**.......................................(bt) PatDobbs 6 7
(David Pipe) *hld up towards rr: sme hdwy 5f out: rdn over 3f out: wknd over 2f out: t.o* **25/1**

6/0 **12** *16* **Lake Shore Drive (IRE)**[46] 5590 5-9-6 **56**...................... TimmyMurphy 5
(Johnny Farrelly) *hld up and bhd: lost tch 5f out: t.o* **20/1**

3m 42.09s (3.19) **Going Correction** +0.35s/f (Good)
**WFA** 3 from 4yo+ 10lb 12 Ran SP% **125.8**
Speed ratings (Par 101): **106,104,102,99,99 96,91,91,90,81 80,72**
CSF £5.48 CT £17.70 TOTE £1.80: £1.10, £2.00, £2.90; EX 7.50 Trifecta £26.80.
**Owner** The Barbury Lions 2 **Bred** Dr W Spangler **Trained** Barbury Castle, Wilts

**FOCUS**
The stronger of the two divisions and the 3yos predictably dominated, including the class-dropping winner.
T/Plt: £63.40 to a £1 stake. Pool: £68,521.65 - 788.36 winning units T/Qpdt: £15.00 to a £1 stake. Pool: £6,945.70 - 340.53 winning units **Richard Lowther**

# 7029 NEWCASTLE (A.W) (L-H)
Tuesday, September 19

**OFFICIAL GOING: Tapeta: standard**
Wind: Breezy, half against in races on straight course and in over 3f of home straight on races on round c Weather: Fine, dry

## 7234 DAILY RACING SPECIALS AT 188BET H'CAP 1m 4f 98y (Tp)
**5:40** (5:40) (Class 4) (0-85,85) 3-Y-0+ **£4,851** (£1,443; £721; £360) **Stalls** High

Form RPR

6402 **1** **Lopes Dancer (IRE)**[10] 6944 5-9-0 **75**............................... JoeFanning 7 83
(Sally Haynes) *prom: rdn to ld over 1f out: hrd pressed fnl f: hld on gamely cl home* **13/2**

1324 **2** *shd* **Cape Peninsular**[52] 5414 4-9-8 **83**.............................. MartinHarley 9 91
(James Tate) *hld up midfield: smooth hdwy over 2f out: rdn to dispute ld ins fnl f: kpt on: jst hld* **5/2**[1]

321- **3** *1 ¾* **Rasmee**[347] 7106 4-9-5 **80**........................................... RobertWinston 6 85+
(Roger Charlton) *hld up: smooth hdwy on outside over 2f out: rdn to chse ldrs over 1f out: kpt on ins fnl f* **7/2**[2]

5640 **4** *1* **Banish (USA)**[11] 6887 4-9-6 **81**.................................(vt) JamesDoyle 10 85
(Hugo Palmer) *dwlt and swtchd lft s: hld up: rdn and hdwy on wd outside over 2f out: kpt on same pce ins fnl f* **5/1**[3]

1505 **5** *¾* **Archipeligo**[10] 6948 6-8-3 **71**................................... JamieGormley[(7)] 3 73
(Iain Jardine) *hld up: smooth hdwy over 2f out: rdn over 1f out: kpt on same pce ins fnl f* **20/1**

6500 **6** *3 ¼* **Aardwolf (USA)**[35] 6026 3-9-3 **85**................................... PJMcDonald 8 83
(Mark Johnston) *trckd ldr: led over 2f out to over 1f out: sn wknd* **12/1**

2161 **7** *shd* **Monsieur Glory**[19] 6610 4-9-3 **78**................................... HarryBentley 1 75
(Tom Clover) *hld up in tch: drvn along 3f out: rallied: wknd over 1f out* **16/1**

-550 **8** *½* **Icefall (IRE)**[10] 6944 4-9-6 **81**....................................(p[1]) DavidAllan 2 77
(Tim Easterby) *hld up midfield: drvn and outpcd wl over 2f out: n.d after* **66/1**

2440 **9** *13* **Chancery (USA)**[10] 6944 9-9-4 **79**...............................(p) DavidNolan 5 54
(David O'Meara) *hld up: effrt and rdn over 2f out: sn struggling* **28/1**

2560 **10** *4 ½* **Luv U Whatever**[29] 6269 7-9-3 **78**................................ BarryMcHugh 4 46
(Marjorie Fife) *chsd ldrs: drvn over 3f out: wknd over 2f out* **50/1**

4600 **11** *nk* **Be Perfect (USA)**[10] 6944 8-9-8 **83**.........................(b) JamesSullivan 12 51
(Ruth Carr) *led to over 2f out: rdn and wknd over 1f out* **33/1**

1646 **12** *25* **King's Coinage (IRE)**[15] 6757 3-8-4 **72**........................(h) JoeDoyle 11 1
(Ruth Carr) *prom on outside: drvn and outpcd over 3f out: struggling fnl 2f* **11/1**

2m 36.82s (-4.28) **Going Correction** -0.125s/f (Stan)
**WFA** 3 from 4yo+ 7lb 12 Ran SP% **117.3**
Speed ratings (Par 105): **109,108,107,107,106 104,104,104,95,92 92,75**
CSF £21.73 CT £67.29 TOTE £8.30: £3.00, £1.40, £1.40; EX 27.80 Trifecta £116.10.
**Owner** D G Clayton Racing **Bred** Carol Burke & Lope De Vega Syndicate **Trained** Melsonby, N Yorks

**FOCUS**
A fairly decent middle-distance handicap. They went a respectable gallop on standard Tapeta and the right horses came to the fore in a good time.

## 7235 READ SILVESTRE DE SOUSA AT 188BET H'CAP (DIV I) 1m 2f 42y (Tp)
**6:10** (6:14) (Class 6) (0-65,65) 3-Y-0+ **£2,587** (£770; £384; £192) **Stalls** High

Form RPR

5025 **1** **My Brother Mike (IRE)**[19] 6611 3-9-1 **61**........................ DavidNolan 14 72+
(Kevin Frost) *hld up in tch: smooth hdwy to ld over 1f out: rdn clr fnl f* **6/1**[2]

-454 **2** 4 ½ **Champagne Pink (FR)**[10] 6947 3-8-13 **62**....................(h) CliffordLee(3) 8 65
(K R Burke) *chsd ldrs: effrt and wnt 2nd over 1f out: kpt on fnl f: nt pce of wnr* **6/1**[2]

3400 **3** ½ **Restive (IRE)**[92] 3898 4-9-3 **65**.................................. JamieGormley(7) 10 66
(Iain Jardine) *hld up in tch: stdy hdwy over 2f out: effrt and rdn over 1f out: kpt on fnl f: no imp* **7/2**[1]

0620 **4** hd **Getgo**[23] 6471 3-9-5 **65**....................................(b) JamesDoyle 2 67
(David Lanigan) *hld up on ins: effrt and rdn over 2f out: kpt on same pce ins fnl f* **15/2**

0130 **5** 1 ½ **Champagne Rules**[14] 6788 6-8-11 **52**.............................(t) PaddyAspell 4 50
(Sharon Watt) *hld up in midfield on outside: stdy hdwy over 2f out: effrt and disp 2nd pl over 1f out: drifted rt: outpcd ins fnl f* **40/1**

1550 **6** ½ **London Master**[32] 6144 3-9-3 **63**................................. AdamBeschizza 12 61
(Chris Wall) *hld up in midfield: effrt and rdn over 2f out: no imp over 1f out* **7/1**

0204 **7** ¾ **Adventureman**[22] 6523 5-9-2 **57**....................................(b) JamesSullivan 9 53
(Ruth Carr) *t.k.h early: pressed ldr: led over 3f out to over 1f out: sn outpcd* **16/1**

3401 **8** 1 ¾ **Savannah Moon (IRE)**[27] 6316 3-9-4 **64**......................... TomEaves 1 58+
(Kevin Ryan) *hld up: hdwy over 2f out: sn rdn: no imp wl over 1f out* **13/2**[3]

4000 **9** 4 **Different Journey**[12] 6855 4-9-9 **64**............................... CamHardie 6 49
(Michael Easterby) *hld up in tch: rdn over 2f out: wknd wl over 1f out* **20/1**

500 **10** hd **Stolen Angel (IRE)**[32] 6150 3-8-13 **59**.......................... DavidAllan 11 45
(Antony Brittain) *unruly bef s: t.k.h in rr: rdn over 2f out: sn wknd* **22/1**

6-30 **11** 3 ¼ **Le Deluge (FR)**[11] 6901 7-9-7 **62**....................................(t) PJMcDonald 13 41+
(Micky Hammond) *s.i.s: hld up: pushed along whn hung lft over 2f out: sn btn* **25/1**

3600 **12** 2 ¼ **Mysterial**[9] 6968 7-9-6 **64**..............................................(v) PhilDennis(3) 5 39
(Declan Carroll) *t.k.h: led to over 3f out: wknd fr 2f out* **22/1**

5-00 **13** 30 **Royal Flute**[155] 1830 3-8-8 **54**........................................(p1) JosephineGordon 3
(Mark Walford) *unruily in paddock: bhd: struggling over 4f out: btn and eased fnl 2f* **80/1**

2m 8.68s (-1.72) **Going Correction** -0.125s/f (Stan)
**WFA** 3 from 4yo+ 5lb **13** Ran SP% **115.3**
Speed ratings (Par 101): **101,97,97,96,95 95,94,93,90,89 87,85,61**
CSF £36.46 CT £145.21 TOTE £7.40: £2.40, £2.30, £1.70; EX 49.80 Trifecta £230.70.
**Owner** J T Stimpson **Bred** D & J Dwan **Trained** Market Drayton, Shropshire

**FOCUS**
The first division of a modest handicap. They went a respectable gallop and it is sound form.

## 7236 READ SILVESTRE DE SOUSA AT 188BET H'CAP (DIV II) 1m 2f 42y (Tp)
6:40 (6:45) (Class 6) (0-65,65) 3-Y-0+ £2,587 (£770; £384; £192) Stalls High

Form RPR

06-1 **1** **Bahkit (IRE)**[22] 6518 3-9-4 **64**............................................ JoeDoyle 11 70
(Sally Haynes) *t.k.h: led and sn 3 l clr: rdn and hdd over 1f out: rallied and regained ld ins fnl f: hld on gamely* **2/1**[1]

0640 **2** shd **Perceived**[23] 6470 5-9-8 **63**.............................................. CamHardie 14 68
(Antony Brittain) *hld up on outside: hdwy over 2f out: effrt and disp ld fr over 1f out: kpt on fnl f: jst hld* **25/1**

3303 **3** ½ **Lord Kitten (USA)**[23] 6470 3-9-3 **63**...........................(tp) JamesDoyle 13 68
(David Lanigan) *trckd ldrs: rdn to ld over 1f out: hdd ins fnl f: no ex nr fin* **11/4**[2]

5425 **4** nk **Knightsbridge Liam (IRE)**[11] 6892 3-8-9 **55**............. JamesSullivan 10 59+
(Michael Easterby) *s.i.s: hld up: stdy hdwy over 2f out: effrt and swtchd rt over 1f out: styd on wl fnl f* **11/2**[3]

3550 **5** 2 **Falcon's Fire (IRE)**[7] 7015 4-9-4 **64**...............................(b) RowanScott(5) 4 64
(Keith Dalgleish) *chsd wnr to over 1f out: sn drvn and one pce* **20/1**

520 **6** shd **Spirit Of The Vale (IRE)**[11] 6901 4-9-1 **56**.....................(t) KevinStott 7 56
(Oliver Greenall) *hld up: stdy hdwy over 2f out: effrt and rdn over 1f out: outpcd ins fnl f* **12/1**

0550 **7** 1 **Warfare**[11] 6901 8-9-5 **60**....................................................(p) BarryMcHugh 9 58
(Tim Fitzgerald) *hld up on outside: smooth hdwy and prom 3f out: rdn and wknd over 1f out* **9/1**

3030 **8** ¾ **Dream Free**[14] 6788 4-9-2 **57**..........................................(p) JasonHart 5 53
(Mark Walford) *t.k.h: in tch: rdn over 2f out: wknd over 1f out* **14/1**

3500 **9** 4 **Midnight Man (FR)**[14] 6783 3-8-11 **57**............................ PJMcDonald 3 47
(K R Burke) *hld up: rdn over 2f out: sn no imp* **40/1**

3650 **10** 5 **Stun Gun**[13] 4169 7-9-1 **56**...............................................(p) TonyHamilton 8 36
(Derek Shaw) *hld up midfield: drvn and outpcd over 2f out: btn over 1f out* **66/1**

-000 **11** 4 **Galilee Chapel (IRE)**[43] 5701 8-9-3 **65**...................(b) RhonaPindar(7) 12 38
(Alistair Whillans) *t.k.h: hld up: stdy hdwy over 3f out: rdn and wknd 2f out* **25/1**

2m 10.85s (0.45) **Going Correction** -0.125s/f (Stan)
**WFA** 3 from 4yo+ 5lb **11** Ran SP% **116.1**
Speed ratings (Par 101): **93,92,92,92,90 90,89,89,86,82 78**
CSF £62.68 CT £141.72 TOTE £3.00: £1.60, £5.40, £1.40; EX 59.40 Trifecta £224.20.
**Owner** Mrs J Porter **Bred** Miss Elaine Marie Smith **Trained** Melsonby, N Yorks

**FOCUS**
The second division of a modest handicap. The winning time was over two seconds slower.

## 7237 188BET/EBF BRITISH STALLIONS STUDS NOVICE STKS 1m 5y (Tp)
7:10 (7:14) (Class 5) 2-Y-0 £3,396 (£1,010; £505; £252) Stalls Centre

Form RPR

0 **1** **Tansheet (IRE)**[32] 6132 2-9-2 0.................................... RichardKingscote 2 73+
(William Haggas) *prom on outside: shkn up to ld over 1f out: kpt on wl: comf* **5/1**[3]

**2** 1 ½ **Photonics (IRE)** 2-9-2 0..................................................... PJMcDonald 10 69
(Hugo Palmer) *dwlt: hld up towards rr: rdn and hdwy over 1f out: chsd wnr wl ins fnl f: r.o* **8/1**

4 **3** nk **Going Native**[25] 6385 2-8-11 0............................................. LiamKeniry 5 64
(Ed Walker) *t.k.h: led to over 1f out: kpt on same pce ins fnl f* **16/1**

0 **4** nk **Tabernas (IRE)**[11] 6883 2-9-2 0......................................... JamesDoyle 3 68
(Charlie Appleby) *trckd ldrs: drvn over 2f out: rallied and ev ch briefly over 1f out: one pce ins fnl f* **9/2**[2]

02 **5** ½ **Compliance (IRE)**[11] 6883 2-9-2 0..................................... MartinHarley 8 67
(James Tate) *prom: effrt and ev ch briefly over 1f out: one pce ins fnl f* **10/3**[1]

0 **6** ¾ **Vision Clear (GER)**[11] 6883 2-9-2 0.................................. GrahamLee 6 65
(Ed Dunlop) *hld up in tch: rdn over 2f out: no imp ins fnl f* **100/1**

0 **7** shd **Broken Force (USA)**[25] 6403 2-9-2 0................................. BenCurtis 11 65
(K R Burke) *t.k.h: hld up midfield: effrt and pushed along over 1f out: sn no imp* **8/1**

**8** nk **Finisher (USA)** 2-9-2 0............................................................ TomEaves 9 64+
(Kevin Ryan) *dwlt: hld up: rdn over 2f out: kpt on ins fnl f: nvr able to chal* **15/2**

**9** 1 **Encryption (IRE)** 2-9-2 0...................................................... DavidNolan 1 62
(George Scott) *hld up midfield: rdn over 2f out: no imp fr over 1f out* **11/1**

00 **10** ¾ **Thunder North (IRE)**[33] 6108 2-9-2 0........................... PaulMulrennan 12 60+
(David Lanigan) *hld up: rdn over 2f out: hung lft over 1f out: sn btn* **50/1**

56 **11** ¾ **Amazing Rock (SWI)**[20] 6590 2-9-2 0.............................. JoeFanning 4 58
(Mark Johnston) *trckd ldrs: effrt and ev ch briefly wl over 1f out: sn wknd* **50/1**

50 **12** 3 ½ **Tommy Shelby (FR)**[19] 6636 2-9-2 0............................... TonyHamilton 13 50+
(Richard Fahey) *stdd s: hld up: rdn and outpcd 3f out: sn n.d* **80/1**

**13** 2 ¼ **Making Miracles** 2-9-2 0........................................................ JasonHart 7 45
(Mark Johnston) *missed break: bhd: rdn over 3f out: wknd over 2f out* **28/1**

1m 40.22s (1.62) **Going Correction** +0.025s/f (Slow) **13** Ran SP% **115.7**
Speed ratings (Par 95): **92,90,90,89,89 88,88,88,87,86 85,82,80**
CSF £42.18 TOTE £5.70: £2.00, £2.50, £2.90; EX 56.30 Trifecta £565.80.
**Owner** Hamdan Al Maktoum **Bred** Shadwell Estate Company Limited **Trained** Newmarket, Suffolk

**FOCUS**
An ordinary juvenile novice contest in terms of prior form, but some interesting debutants and unexposed sorts on view. They at best a respectable gallop.

## 7238 188BET.CO.UK/EBF FILLIES' NOVICE STKS (PLUS 10 RACE) 6f (Tp)
7:40 (7:43) (Class 5) 2-Y-0 £3,396 (£1,010; £505; £252) Stalls Centre

Form RPR

10 **1** **Peace Trail**[24] 6418 2-9-7 0.................................................. JamesDoyle 13 85
(Charlie Appleby) *wore hood in paddock: racd in stands' side gp: mde all and overall ldr: rdn over 1f out: styd on strly fnl f* **11/4**[2]

**2** 1 ¼ **Cirrus Minor (FR)** 2-8-11 0.............................................. CliffordLee(3) 6 74
(K R Burke) *cl up in centre: effrt and chsd wnr 2f out: kpt on ins fnl f: nt pce to chal* **50/1**

**3** 1 ¼ **Mountain Breath** 2-9-0 0....................................................... JasonHart 12 70
(Chris Fairhurst) *prom in stands' side gp: effrt and pushed along 2f out: kpt on fnl f: nt pce to chal* **250/1**

**4** ¾ **Alwasmiya** 2-9-0 0.................................................................. HarryBentley 9 67
(Simon Crisford) *wore hood in paddock: cl up centre: effrt and disp 2nd pl over 1f out: kpt on same pce ins fnl f* **11/8**[1]

2 **5** ½ **Zip Along (IRE)**[33] 6085 2-9-0 0...................................... TonyHamilton 10 66
(Richard Fahey) *cl up stands' side: rdn along 2f out: kpt on fnl f: nvr able to chal* **16/1**

**6** hd **High Seas (IRE)** 2-9-0 0.................................................. JosephineGordon 4 65
(Hugo Palmer) *in tch centre: drvn along over 2f out: no imp fr over 1f out* **22/1**

3 **7** 2 **Qafilah (IRE)**[20] 6583 2-9-0 0....................................... RichardKingscote 8 59
(Charles Hills) *s.i.s: hld up centre: pushed along and outpcd over 2f out: rallied over 1f out: no imp* **9/1**

**8** ¾ **Lulu Star (IRE)** 2-9-0 0....................................................... DavidNolan 11 56
(Richard Fahey) *hld up in tch stands' side: effrt 2f out: kpt on same pce fnl f* **40/1**

**9** hd **Alhawdaj (USA)** 2-9-0 0.................................................... PJMcDonald 2 56
(Mark Johnston) *led centre gp to 2f out: rdn and wknd fnl f* **11/1**

**10** ¾ **La Cabana** 2-9-0 0.................................................................. JackGarritty 7 53
(Richard Fahey) *s.i.s: hld up centre: rdn and outpcd over 2f out: n.d after* **80/1**

0 **11** ¾ **Faay (IRE)**[25] 6385 2-9-0 0............................................... PaulMulrennan 5 51
(Ed Dunlop) *t.k.h: in tch centre: flashed tailed repeatedly early on: shkn up and outpcd over 1f out: btn fnl f* **66/1**

00 **12** ¾ **Chef United**[7] 7033 2-9-0 0.............................................. ConnorBeasley 3 49
(Roger Fell) *bhd centre: rdn and outpcd over 2f out: sn btn* **250/1**

4 **13** 5 **Swiss Chocolate (IRE)**[39] 5891 2-9-0 0.......................... MartinHarley 1 33
(William Haggas) *cl up centre: rdn over 2f out: wknd over 1f out* **13/2**[3]

1m 13.01s (0.51) **Going Correction** +0.025s/f (Slow) **13** Ran SP% **118.6**
Speed ratings (Par 92): **97,95,93,92,92 91,89,88,87,86 85,84,78**
CSF £145.02 TOTE £3.40: £1.20, £12.10, £13.20; EX 82.90 Trifecta £2194.00.
**Owner** Godolphin **Bred** Mrs R D Peacock **Trained** Newmarket, Suffolk

**FOCUS**
A fair juvenile fillies' novice contest. The second favourite made all at her own respectable tempo up the seemingly favoured stands' rail.

## 7239 PLAY CASINO AT 188BET NURSERY H'CAP 1m 5y (Tp)
8:10 (8:12) (Class 6) (0-65,67) 2-Y-0 £2,587 (£770; £384; £192) Stalls Centre

Form RPR

0562 **1** **Archie Perkins (IRE)**[7] 7029 2-8-10 **57**........................ LewisEdmunds(3) 1 63
(Nigel Tinkler) *cl up: rdn to ld over 1f out: edgd rt ins fnl f: kpt on wl* **7/4**[1]

5303 **2** ¾ **Far Dawn**[19] 6613 2-9-5 **63**................................................. HarryBentley 5 67
(Simon Crisford) *hld up in tch: rdn over 2f out: effrt over 1f out: pressed wnr ins fnl f: kpt on: hld nr fin* **9/4**[2]

0004 **3** ¾ **Admiral Spice (IRE)**[7] 7030 2-9-4 **62**....................(p) RichardKingscote 9 65
(Tom Dascombe) *in tch: rdn over 2f out: sn hung lft: kpt on ins fnl f: nrst fin* **6/1**[3]

541 **4** hd **Lady Alavesa**[47] 5562 2-9-6 **64**............................................. TomEaves 12 66
(Gay Kelleway) *s.i.s: hld up: rdn over 2f out: hdwy and edgd rt over 1f out: kpt on ins fnl f* **16/1**

5005 **5** nse **Starboy (IRE)**[59] 5143 2-9-8 **66**........................................ MartinHarley 7 68
(George Scott) *missed break: hld up: stdy hdwy over 2f out: rdn and kpt on ins fnl f* **25/1**

043 **6** 1 **Kylie Rules**[40] 5833 2-9-9 **67**............................................... ShaneGray 3 67
(Ann Duffield) *led: rdn and hdd over 1f out: outpcd ins fnl f* **20/1**

005 **7** nk **Echo (IRE)**[23] 6465 2-8-11 **55**.............................................. JackGarritty 2 54
(Jedd O'Keeffe) *dwlt: sn rdn along in midfield: effrt and edgd lft over 1f out: sn no imp* **20/1**

006 **8** nk **Troop**[23] 6465 2-8-10 **54**......................................................(p1) GrahamLee 8 53
(Ann Duffield) *hld up: pushed along over 2f out: hdwy over 1f out: nvr able to chal* **66/1**

0060 **9** 6 **Saxonroad Boy (USA)**[19] 6626 2-8-7 **51**...................(p1) BarryMcHugh 11 36
(Richard Fahey) *hld up: rdn and outpcd over 2f out: sn n.d* **25/1**

000 **10** 3 **Bee Machine (IRE)**[73] 4598 2-8-1 **45**............................. PatrickMathers 4 24
(Declan Carroll) *plld hrd: in tch: rdn over 2f out: wknd over 1f out* **25/1**

5004 **11** 4 ½ **Marsh Storm (IRE)**[7] 7029 2-9-1 **59**................................ PJMcDonald 6 28
(K R Burke) *t.k.h: cl up: lost pl over 2f out: sn btn* **14/1**

0004 **12** 4 **Cherubic**[12] 6845 2-8-10 **54**................................................(b) JoeFanning 13 14
(Charles Hills) *hld up: drvn and struggling over 2f out: sn btn* **22/1**

1m 39.62s (1.02) **Going Correction** +0.025s/f (Slow) **12** Ran SP% **120.9**
Speed ratings (Par 93): **95,94,93,93,93 92,91,91,85,82 78,74**
CSF £5.09 CT £19.71 TOTE £2.70: £1.40, £1.30, £1.90; EX 7.70 Trifecta £20.30.
**Owner** J Raybould & S Perkins **Bred** Helen Lyons **Trained** Langton, N Yorks


The Form Book Flat, Raceform Ltd, Newbury, RG14 5SJ

**FOCUS**
A modest nursery. The right three horses came to the fore off a respectable tempo.

## 7240 GET 1/4 ODDS AT 188BET H'CAP 1m 5y (Tp)
8:40 (8:42) (Class 6) (0-60,60) 3-Y-O+ £2,587 (£770; £384; £192) Stalls Centre

Form RPR
3044 **1** **Kilbaha Lady (IRE)**[18] 6664 3-9-2 **60**.....................(t) LewisEdmunds(3) 5 67
(Nigel Tinkler) *hld up towards rr: hdwy over 1f out: rdn to ld ins fnl f: kpt on wl* **7/1**[3]
6R-2 **2** *nk* **Honey Badger**[28] 6296 6-9-4 **55**.....................(p) TomEaves 12 61
(Michael Herrington) *hld up on nr side of gp: hdwy and ev ch over 1f out to ins fnl f: kpt on: hld nr fin* **10/1**
-600 **3** *hd* **American Hustle (IRE)**[19] 5002 5-9-2 **53**..................... BenCurtis 2 59
(Brian Ellison) *hld up: effrt on far side of gp over 1f out: rdn and kpt on ins fnl f: nrst fin* **20/1**
0514 **4** *nk* **Thornaby Nash**[6] 7042 6-9-0 **56**.....................(p) GemmaTutty(5) 1 61
(Karen Tutty) *t.k.h: cl up on far side of gp: led over 1f out to ins fnl f: kpt on same pce* **12/1**
500 **5** *nk* **Intiwin (IRE)**[26] 6346 5-9-6 **57**..................... DavidNolan 4 62
(Linda Perratt) *hld up: hdwy on far side ofd gp over 1f out: ev ch briefly ins fnl f: kpt on: hld nr fin* **25/1**
3064 **6** *nk* **Luath**[22] 6528 4-9-9 **60**..................... JamesSullivan 10 64
(Suzzanne France) *cl up on nr side of gp: effrt and ev ch briefly over 1f out: one pce ins fnl f* **17/2**
0065 **7** *3/4* **Grey Destiny**[11] 6902 7-9-7 **58**..................... CamHardie 11 60
(Antony Brittain) *missed break: hld up: rdn and hdwy over 1f out: kpt on fnl f: no imp* **9/1**
0026 **8** *3/4* **Lozah**[21] 6549 4-9-5 **56**..................... TonyHamilton 14 57
(Roger Fell) *hld up: rdn and hdwy over 1f out: no imp ins fnl f* **11/2**[2]
6004 **9** *1 1/2* **Mr Coco Bean (USA)**[11] 6902 3-9-3 **58**.....................(h) ShaneGray 3 55
(Ann Duffield) *t.k.h: cl up: led over 2f out to over 1f out: sn lost pl* **10/1**
5-00 **10** *5* **Nargiza (USA)**[28] 6281 3-9-2 **57**..................... AdamBeschizza 9 43
(Chris Wall) *prom on nr side of gp: effrt over 2f out: wknd over 1f out* **20/1**
4400 **11** *3/4* **Kensington Palace (IRE)**[36] 5991 4-9-2 **53**.....................(p) BarryMcHugh 7 38
(Marjorie Fife) *led at modest gallop: rdn and hdd over 2f out: wknd over 1f out* **25/1**
4232 **12** *3 1/2* **Jack Blane**[11] 6903 3-9-4 **59**.....................(p) GrahamLee 8 36
(Keith Dalgleish) *t.k.h: cl up tl rdn and wknd over 1f out* **3/1**[1]
36-0 **13** *4 1/2* **Mayleen (IRE)**[117] 2993 3-9-5 **60**..................... DougieCostello 6 27
(Ann Duffield) *t.k.h in midfield: drvn and outpcd over 2f out: sn btn* **50/1**

1m 40.52s (1.92) **Going Correction** +0.025s/f (Slow)
**WFA** 3 from 4yo+ 4lb **13** Ran SP% **118.5**
Speed ratings (Par 101): **91,90,90,90,89 89,88,88,86,81 80,77,72**
CSF £68.68 CT £1387.71 TOTE £7.60: £2.50, £3.20, £6.40; EX 57.10 Trifecta £2459.10.
**Owner** The Dapper Partnership **Bred** Helen Lyons **Trained** Langton, N Yorks

**FOCUS**
A moderate handicap. They went a muddling gallop and finished in a bit of a heap.

## 7241 BEST ODDS GUARANTEED AT 188BET FILLIES' H'CAP 7f 14y (Tp)
9:10 (9:11) (Class 5) (0-75,73) 3-Y-O+ £3,234 (£962; £481; £240) Stalls Centre

Form RPR
3124 **1** **Castle Hill Cassie (IRE)**[32] 6149 3-9-6 **72**..................... GrahamLee 7 81
(Ben Haslam) *hld up: hdwy to ld over 1f out: sn rdn: kpt on strly fnl f* **14/1**
15 **2** *nk* **Express Lady (IRE)**[80] 4351 3-9-7 **73**.....................(t[1]) JosephineGordon 8 81
(Hugo Palmer) *hld up on nr side of gp: hdwy to chse wnr over 1f out: kpt on ins fnl f: hld nr fin* **4/1**[2]
5221 **3** *1 1/2* **Lady In Question (IRE)**[21] 6550 3-9-0 **73**..................... ConnorMurtagh(7) 5 77
(Richard Fahey) *in tch: effrt and rdn over 1f out: kpt on same pce ins fnl f* **4/1**[2]
0520 **4** *1 1/4* **Outfox**[24] 6435 3-8-10 **62**..................... TomEaves 3 63
(Bryan Smart) *s.i.s: sn in tch: rdn and outpcd over 2f out: rallied ins fnl f: no imp* **40/1**
2204 **5** *nk* **Totally Magic (IRE)**[7] 7034 5-8-13 **65**.....................(p) LewisEdmunds(3) 1 66
(Richard Whitaker) *rrd as stalls opened and lost grnd s: sn prom on far side of gp: led over 2f out to over 1f out: no ex ins fnl f* **11/4**[1]
164 **6** *1* **Wahiba (GER)**[62] 5039 4-9-3 **69**..................... MarcMonaghan(3) 6 67
(Marco Botti) *prom: effrt and rdn over 2f out: outpcd appr fnl f* **16/1**
5334 **7** *nk* **Bush Beauty (IRE)**[21] 6550 6-8-5 **54**..................... JamesSullivan 9 51
(Eric Alston) *dwlt: hld up: rdn over 2f out: kpt on ins fnl f: no imp* **12/1**
3045 **8** *3 1/4* **The Lacemaker**[54] 5325 3-9-4 **70**..................... PJMcDonald 10 57
(Ed Dunlop) *hld up: rdn along over 2f out: sn no imp* **10/1**[3]
0542 **9** *1 1/2* **Conqueress (IRE)**[24] 6439 3-9-0 **66**.....................(p) RichardKingscote 4 49
(Tom Dascombe) *mde most to over 2f out: rdn and wknd over 1f out* **10/1**[3]
4432 **10** *64* **Halinka (IRE)**[18] 6664 3-8-11 **68**..................... CameronNoble(5) 2
(Roger Varian) *plld hrd and sddle sn slipped forward: racd on far side of gp: disp ld to over 2f out: sn lost pl and eased: t.o* **11/1**

1m 25.7s (-0.50) **Going Correction** +0.025s/f (Slow)
**WFA** 3 from 4yo+ 3lb **10** Ran SP% **115.9**
Speed ratings (Par 100): **103,102,100,99,99 98,97,93,92,19**
CSF £68.93 CT £271.82 TOTE £15.70: £5.80, £2.10, £1.40; EX 93.10 Trifecta £272.40.
**Owner** Ontoawinner Trojan Horse J Pak & Partner **Bred** Yeomanstown Stud **Trained** Middleham Moor, N Yorks

**FOCUS**
An ordinary fillies' handicap. They went a respectable gallop and it is sound form.
T/Jkpt: Not Won T/Plt: £141.40 to a £1 stake. Pool: £84,956.74 - 438.51 winning units T/Qpdt: £37.70 to a £1 stake. Pool: £10,299.17 - 201.92 winning units **Richard Young**

# 6431 REDCAR (L-H)
Tuesday, September 19

**OFFICIAL GOING: Soft (6.9)**
Wind: light across Weather: sunny

## 7242 WATCH RACING UK ANYWHERE NOVICE AUCTION STKS 5f
1:20 (1:21) (Class 6) 2-Y-O £2,749 (£818; £408; £204) Stalls Centre

Form RPR
620 **1** **Dandy's Beano (IRE)**[34] 6055 2-8-11 75..................... KevinStott 4 75+
(Kevin Ryan) *trckd ldrs: pushed along to chal ent fnl f: led 110yds out: edgd rt: kpt on* **3/1**[2]
523 **2** *2* **Biddy Brady (USA)**[15] 6755 2-8-11 68..................... DavidAllan 10 68
(Tim Easterby) *sn led: rdn 2f out: hdd 110yds out: one pce* **4/1**[3]
62 **3** *1 1/2* **Kyllachy Dragon (IRE)**[34] 6056 2-9-0 0..................... DavidNolan 9 65
(Iain Jardine) *trckd ldr: rdn 2f out: one pce fnl f* **5/2**[1]
**4** *1 3/4* **Gleaming Sun** 2-8-5 0..................... HarrisonShaw(7) 8 57
(Michael Easterby) *midfield: rdn 2f out: kpt on* **100/1**
**5** *1* **Hedonism (IRE)** 2-8-11 0..................... JosephineGordon 1 53
(Hugo Palmer) *hld up: sn pushed along: kpt on fnl f: nrst fin* **7/1**
00 **6** *1 1/4* **Barney Bullet (IRE)**[24] 6432 2-9-2 0..................... PatrickMathers 2 53
(Noel Wilson) *hld up: rdn along 1/2-way: nvr threatened* **40/1**
50 **7** *hd* **Arctic Treasure (IRE)**[24] 6432 2-9-0 0..................... TonyHamilton 5 50
(Richard Fahey) *dwlt: hld up: pushed along 3f out: sme late hdwy: nvr threatened* **8/1**
46 **8** *3/4* **Bonanza Bowls**[21] 6545 2-9-2 0..................... ConnorBeasley 6 50
(Bryan Smart) *in tch: rdn along 1/2-way: wknd fnl f* **16/1**
3550 **9** *1* **Monkey Magic**[35] 6043 2-8-11 53..................... TomEaves 7 41
(Nigel Tinkler) *trckd ldr: rdn 2f out: wknd appr fnl f* **40/1**
**10** *3 3/4* **Warrior's Valley** 2-8-12 0..................... PJMcDonald 3 28
(David C Griffiths) *wnt lft s and slow into stride: hld up: rdn along 1/2-way: wknd over 1f out* **25/1**

1m 0.3s (1.70) **Going Correction** +0.225s/f (Good) **10** Ran SP% **112.8**
Speed ratings (Par 93): **95,91,89,86,85 83,82,81,79,73**
CSF £14.46 TOTE £3.30: £1.40, £1.30, £1.50; EX 14.90 Trifecta £43.50.
**Owner** Hambleton Racing Ltd XLVII **Bred** Ruskerne Ltd **Trained** Hambleton, N Yorks

**FOCUS**
It was dry all day Monday and overnight, but the going was still given as soft (GoingStick: 6.9). A modest novice race with the winner in keeping with her Nottingham form.

## 7243 WEATHERBYS RACING BANK NURSERY H'CAP 7f
1:50 (1:50) (Class 5) (0-75,73) 2-Y-O £3,234 (£962; £481; £240) Stalls Centre

Form RPR
364 **1** **Dark Liberty (IRE)**[35] 6037 2-9-5 **71**..................... GrahamLee 8 77+
(Simon Crisford) *trckd ldrs: led over 2f out: rdn appr fnl f: edgd lft ins fnl f: kpt on* **9/1**
6163 **2** *3/4* **Byron's Choice**[25] 6379 2-9-7 **73**..................... PaulMulrennan 6 77
(Michael Dods) *keen early: hld up in tch: hdwy to trck ldrs over 2f out: rdn over 1f out: kpt on* **7/2**[2]
1313 **3** *3/4* **Placebo Effect (IRE)**[6] 7050 2-9-3 **69**..................... AndrewMullen 3 71
(Ollie Pears) *dwlt: hld up: stdy hdwy over 2f out: rdn to chse ldr over 1f out: sltly hmpd and swtchd rt ins fnl f: kpt on* **9/4**[1]
034 **4** *3* **Emerald Rocket (IRE)**[24] 6432 2-8-13 **65**..................... PJMcDonald 10 60
(K R Burke) *dwlt: hld up: rdn and hdwy over 2f out: chsd ldr over 1f out: wknd ins fnl f* **5/1**[3]
000 **5** *2 1/2* **Graphite Girl (IRE)**[27] 6312 2-8-0 **55** ow2..................... RachelRichardson(3) 2 44
(Tim Easterby) *prom: led 5f out: rdn whn hdd over 1f out: wknd fnl f* **66/1**
6024 **6** *2 1/2* **Super Major (IRE)**[32] 6128 2-9-1 **72**..................... CallumRodriguez(5) 4 54
(Michael Dods) *trckd ldrs: rdn over 2f out: wknd over 1f out* **13/2**
5426 **7** *3/4* **Reinbeau Prince**[33] 6087 2-9-3 **69**..................... TonyHamilton 9 49
(Richard Fahey) *chsd ldrs: rdn over 2f out: wknd over 1f out* **11/1**
0640 **8** *7* **Mountain Approach (IRE)**[19] 6625 2-8-9 **61**.....................(b) PatrickMathers 7 24
(Richard Fahey) *prom: racd keenly: rdn over 2f out: sn wknd* **20/1**
1600 **9** *8* **Jackontherocks**[10] 6940 2-9-2 **68**..................... ConnorBeasley 11 11
(Michael Dods) *midfield on outer: rdn over 3f out: wknd over 2f out* **20/1**
3326 **10** *6* **Sorority**[32] 6128 2-9-2 **68**..................... JoeFanning 5
(Mark Johnston) *led narrowly: hdd 5f out: rdn 3f out: sn wknd and bhd* **25/1**

1m 26.47s (1.97) **Going Correction** +0.225s/f (Good) **10** Ran SP% **116.2**
Speed ratings (Par 95): **97,96,95,91,89 86,85,77,68,61**
CSF £38.66 CT £98.88 TOTE £9.10: £3.60, £1.30, £1.20; EX 47.70 Trifecta £89.70.
**Owner** Sheikh Rashid Dalmook Al Maktoum **Bred** Yeomanstown Stud **Trained** Newmarket, Suffolk

**FOCUS**
The early gallop wasn't that strong, but it gradually picked up with the winner moving as though on a good mark.

## 7244 WEATHERBYS BANK FOREIGN EXCHANGE H'CAP (DIV I) 5f 217y
2:20 (2:20) (Class 5) (0-75,77) 3-Y-O+ £3,234 (£962; £481; £240) Stalls Centre

Form RPR
2023 **1** **Penny Pot Lane**[21] 6550 4-8-10 **67**..................... LewisEdmunds(3) 4 76
(Richard Whitaker) *prom: rdn over 2f out: led over 1f out: kpt on* **7/1**
0302 **2** *3/4* **Interlink (USA)**[22] 6527 4-8-13 **67**..................... BenCurtis 3 73
(Michael Appleby) *prom: led narrowly over 3f out: rdn over 2f out: hdd over 1f out: kpt on* **13/2**[3]
6015 **3** *nk* **Geoff Potts (IRE)**[27] 6314 4-9-2 **70**..................... DavidNolan 5 75
(Richard Fahey) *trckd ldrs: rdn over 2f out: chal ent fnl f: kpt on* **3/1**[1]
2203 **4** *nk* **Point Of Woods**[17] 6669 4-8-2 **63**.....................(p) ConnorMurtagh(7) 6 67
(Tina Jackson) *midfield: rdn 2f out: chsd ldrs over 1f out: kpt on* **14/1**
5012 **5** *1/2* **Summerghand (IRE)**[22] 6511 3-9-6 **76**..................... DanielTudhope 11 78+
(David O'Meara) *s.i.s: hld up: rdn and hdwy into midfield 2f out: kpt on same pce* **11/2**[2]
3045 **6** *1/2* **Duke Cosimo**[11] 6874 7-9-2 **70**..................... TomEaves 2 71
(Michael Herrington) *midfield: rdn over 2f out: kpt on same pce and nvr threatened* **15/2**
2160 **7** *1/2* **Cosmic Chatter**[11] 6877 7-9-9 **77**.....................(p) JackGarritty 8 76
(Ruth Carr) *trckd ldrs: rdn over 2f out: no ex fnl f* **12/1**
1200 **8** *1 1/4* **Samarmadi**[32] 6141 3-9-5 **75**..................... JosephineGordon 1 70
(Hugo Palmer) *slowly away: hld up in rr: rdn over 2f out: nvr threatened* **14/1**
0000 **9** *1/2* **See The Sun**[41] 5804 6-8-12 **66**..................... DavidAllan 7 60
(Tim Easterby) *led narrowly: hdd over 3f out: sn rdn along: remained cl up tl wknd appr fnl f* **14/1**
3560 **10** *nk* **Lexington Sky (IRE)**[22] 6527 3-9-3 **73**..................... TonyHamilton 10 66
(Roger Fell) *hld up: rdn over 2f out: nvr threatened* **33/1**
5130 **11** *nk* **Racquet**[14] 6786 4-8-13 **67**..................... JamesSullivan 9 59
(Ruth Carr) *midfield: rdn over 2f out: wknd fnl f* **25/1**

1m 12.25s (0.45) **Going Correction** +0.225s/f (Good)
**WFA** 3 from 4yo+ 2lb **11** Ran SP% **112.5**
Speed ratings (Par 103): **106,105,104,104,103 102,102,100,99,99 99**
CSF £49.61 CT £164.24 TOTE £8.00: £3.50, £1.90, £1.50; EX 59.30 Trifecta £350.40.
**Owner** A Melville **Bred** Hellwood Stud Farm & G P Clarke **Trained** Scarcroft, W Yorks

**FOCUS**
The pace held up pretty well here, the first two racing in the front rank throughout, and it was been rated through the runner-up's turf form this year.

## 7245 WEATHERBYS BANK FOREIGN EXCHANGE H'CAP (DIV II) 5f 217y
2:55 (2:56) (Class 5) (0-75,75) 3-Y-O+ £3,234 (£962; £481; £240) Stalls Centre

Form RPR
413 **1** **Short Work**[9] 6964 4-9-0 **68**.....................(b) DanielTudhope 1 81
(David O'Meara) *mde all: rdn 2f out: kpt on wl to draw clr fnl f* **11/8**[1]

1345 **2** 3 **Metisian**[27] 6313 3-8-12 **68**....(p[1]) PaulMulrennan 3 71+
(Jedd O'Keeffe) *slowly away: hld up: rdn and hdwy over 2f out: kpt on fnl f: wnt 2nd towards fin: no ch w wnr* **13/2**[2]

4005 **3** ½ **Honeysuckle Lil (IRE)**[25] 6382 5-8-10 **67**....(p) RachelRichardson[(3)] 6 69
(Tim Easterby) *trckd ldrs: rdn over 2f out: chsd ldr 1f out: one pce: lost 2nd towards fin* **12/1**

6134 **4** 1¾ **Danish Duke (IRE)**[22] 6527 6-9-1 **69**....(p) JamesSullivan 10 65
(Ruth Carr) *hld up: rdn over 2f out: hdwy over 1f out: kpt on ins fnl f* **16/1**

3200 **5** 1 **Perfect Symphony (IRE)**[11] 6874 3-9-3 **73**....(p) TomEaves 7 66
(Kevin Ryan) *prom: rdn over 2f out: wknd ins fnl f* **20/1**

6046 **6** ¾ **Madrinho (IRE)**[66] 4887 4-9-6 **74**....(p[1]) BarryMcHugh 5 65
(Neville Bycroft) *midfield: rdn over 2f out: no imp* **12/1**

1305 **7** 1¾ **Round The Island**[18] 6663 4-8-10 **67**.... LewisEdmunds[(3)] 8 52
(Richard Whitaker) *prom: rdn over 2f out: chal strly over 1f out: hung rt appr fnl f: wknd* **8/1**[3]

4431 **8** 3¼ **Manatee Bay**[21] 6546 7-8-10 **71**....(v) NatalieHambling[(7)] 4 46
(Noel Wilson) *hld up in midfield: rdn along 3f out: sn struggling* **9/1**

5305 **9** 1¼ **Market Choice (IRE)**[10] 6943 4-8-10 **64**....(p) PJMcDonald 9 35
(Tracy Waggott) *chsd ldrs: rdn 3f out: wknd over 1f out* **28/1**

6616 **10** 1¼ **Alfie's Angel (IRE)**[26] 6348 3-9-5 **75**.... GrahamLee 11 42
(Bryan Smart) *a towards rr* **16/1**

10-4 **11** 5 **Gypsy Major**[46] 5620 5-8-7 **61** oh1....(v) AndrewMullen 2 12
(John Weymes) *midfield: rdn 3f out: sn wknd* **50/1**

1m 12.45s (0.65) **Going Correction** +0.225s/f (Good)
**WFA** 3 from 4yo+ 2lb **11** Ran SP% **113.9**
Speed ratings (Par 103): **104,100,99,97,95 94,92,88,86,84 78**
CSF £9.36 CT £76.06 TOTE £2.10: £1.10, £2.50, £3.10; EX 11.00 Trifecta £88.20.
**Owner** N D Crummack Ltd & Arthur Rhodes **Bred** Downfield Cottage Stud **Trained** Upper Helmsley, N Yorks

**FOCUS**
Marginally the slower of the two divisions by 0.20sec, but a good performance from the well-backed winner who is back to something like his 3yo form.

## 7246 RACING UK STRAIGHT MILE SERIES H'CAP (RACING UK STRAIGHT MILE SERIES QUALIFIER) 7f 219y
**3:25** (3:25) (Class 4) (0-85,86) 3-Y-O+ **£6,469** (£1,925; £962; £481) **Stalls** Centre

Form RPR

311 **1** **Kynren (IRE)**[31] 6203 3-9-3 **85**.... BenCurtis 4 98+
(David Barron) *trckd ldr: pushed along to ld over 1f out: kpt on wl to draw clr: readily* **2/1**[1]

2664 **2** 3 **Fashaak (IRE)**[32] 6143 4-8-12 **76**.... JFEgan 6 81
(John Butler) *in tch: rdn over 2f out: hdwy over 1f out: wnt 2nd ins fnl f: kpt on but no ch wnr* **12/1**

-060 **3** ¾ **Woody Bay**[35] 6049 7-8-9 **73**.... JasonHart 7 76
(Mark Walford) *midfield: rdn over 2f out: hdwy over 1f out: kpt on* **40/1**

1150 **4** 4 **Showboating (IRE)**[45] 5668 9-9-2 **83**.... LewisEdmunds[(3)] 5 77
(John Balding) *led: rdn along 3f out: hdd over 1f out: wknd ins fnl f* **28/1**

0046 **5** 2 **Silvery Moon (IRE)**[80] 4377 10-9-1 **82**.... RachelRichardson[(3)] 10 71
(Tim Easterby) *hld up: rdn along 3f out: kpt on ins fnl f: kpt on ins fnl f: nvr threatened* **10/1**

0606 **6** 3¾ **Father Bertie**[6] 7044 5-9-8 **86**....(tp) DavidAllan 8 67
(Tim Easterby) *prom: rdn 3f out: wknd over 1f out* **9/2**[2]

553 **7** 2¼ **Omeros**[19] 6617 3-9-0 **82**....(h[1]) JosephineGordon 11 58
(Hugo Palmer) *midfield: rdn and outpcd over 3f out: sn btn* **5/1**[3]

3620 **8** 1 **Finn Class (IRE)**[45] 5668 6-9-7 **85**....(p) PaulMulrennan 2 58
(Michael Dods) *a towards rr* **9/1**

121- **9** 3¼ **Poet's Beauty (IRE)**[431] 4368 4-9-7 **85**....(p) KevinStott 9 51
(Ismail Mohammed) *chsd ldrs: rdn over 3f out: wknd 2f out* **8/1**

0060 **P** **Morning Suit (USA)**[11] 6882 3-8-13 **81**.... JoeFanning 1
(Mark Johnston) *dwlt: hld up: wnt wrong 3f out and p.u* **33/1**

1m 38.48s (1.88) **Going Correction** +0.225s/f (Good)
**WFA** 3 from 4yo+ 4lb **10** Ran SP% **114.9**
Speed ratings (Par 105): **99,96,95,91,89 85,83,82,79,**
CSF £27.43 CT £727.95 TOTE £2.60: £1.10, £4.30, £7.00; EX 25.20 Trifecta £675.40.
**Owner** Elliott Brothers & Peacock & Partner **Bred** Rathasker Stud **Trained** Maunby, N Yorks

**FOCUS**
This proved straightforward for the progressive winner with the runner-up rated to this year's form.

## 7247 MARKET CROSS JEWELLERS MAIDEN STKS 5f 217y
**4:00** (4:03) (Class 5) 3-Y-O+ **£3,234** (£962; £481; £240) **Stalls** Centre

Form RPR

22 **1** **Van Velde (IRE)**[17] 6667 3-9-5 0....(p) JasonHart 1 60+
(John Quinn) *dwlt: sn trckd ldrs: rdn to ld over 1f out: edgd rt ins fnl f: kpt on* **6/4**[1]

53 **2** 2½ **Essential**[183] 1287 3-9-5 0.... DanielTudhope 4 52
(George Scott) *prom: rdn over 2f out: edgd lft appr fnl f: kpt on same pce* **7/4**[2]

0420 **3** shd **Mighty Bond**[24] 6437 5-9-7 47....(p) BenCurtis 6 52
(Tracy Waggott) *led: rdn over 2f out: hdd 2f out: kpt on same pce* **16/1**

0254 **4** 1½ **Gunmaker (IRE)**[40] 5855 3-9-5 66.... TomEaves 5 47
(David Simcock) *dwlt: hld up: hdwy and prom 3f out: led on bit 2f out: rdn and hdd over 1f out: wknd ins fnl f* **7/2**[3]

0 **5** 2¼ **Spring Beauty**[38] 5946 3-8-11 0.... PhilDennis[(3)] 7 35
(John Weymes) *trckd ldrs: keen early: rdn and outpcd over 2f out: kpt on ins fnl f* **33/1**

0060 **6** 3¾ **Kylla**[50] 5472 4-8-13 34....(p[1]) JoshDoyle[(3)] 3 23
(Alan Brown) *in tch: rdn 3f out: wknd over 1f out* **100/1**

0 **7** 8 **Subotal (IRE)**[155] 1830 4-9-7 0.... ConnorBeasley 2 2
(Richard Guest) *slowly away: a rr* **50/1**

4000 **8** 5 **Hamriyah**[25] 6381 3-9-5 50....(b[1]) TonyHamilton 8
(Tim Easterby) *midfield: rdn along over 3f out: wknd fnl 2f* **20/1**

1m 14.25s (2.45) **Going Correction** +0.225s/f (Good)
**WFA** 3 from 4yo+ 2lb **8** Ran SP% **115.1**
Speed ratings (Par 103): **92,88,88,86,83 78,67,61**
CSF £4.30 TOTE £2.10: £1.10, £1.10, £3.60; EX 4.90 Trifecta £24.00.
**Owner** JJ Quinn Racing Ltd **Bred** Woodcock Moon Partnership **Trained** Settrington, N Yorks

**FOCUS**
Modest sprint maiden form, as one would expect at this time of year.

## 7248 RACING UK PROFITS RETURNED TO RACING H'CAP 1m 5f 218y
**4:30** (4:31) (Class 6) (0-65,65) 3-Y-O+ **£2,897** (£855; £427) **Stalls** Low

Form RPR

2406 **1** **Jan De Heem**[24] 6431 7-8-13 **57**....(p) ConnorMurtagh[(7)] 3 63
(Tina Jackson) *midfield: hdwy to trck ldr gng wl 2f out: pushed along to ld ins fnl f: drvn out and edgd rt fnl 110yds* **8/1**[3]

3041 **2** nk **Stanarley Pic**[38] 5951 6-9-10 **61**.... NeilFarley 5 67
(Sally Haynes) *led: rdn over 2f out: hdd ins fnl f: styd on* **4/1**[1]

0006 **3** ½ **Patent**[7] 7015 4-8-9 **46** oh1....(b) JasonHart 9 51
(Peter Niven) *hld up: hdwy 4f out: rdn to chse ldrs over 2f out: styd on fnl f* **16/1**

4640 **4** 1¼ **Silver Gleam (IRE)**[21] 6565 3-8-2 **47**.... DuranFentiman 1 52
(Chris Fairhurst) *hld up: rdn and clsr 2f out: styd on fnl f* **14/1**

4453 **5** 2 **Princess Nearco (IRE)**[21] 6551 3-9-1 **60**....(p) JackGarritty 6 63
(Patrick Holmes) *dwlt: sn midfield: hdwy to trck ldrs 6f out: rdn to chse ldr over 3f out: wknd ins fnl f* **5/1**[2]

0-60 **6** 2¼ **Legalized**[22] 6530 3-8-3 **48**.... AndrewMullen 12 48
(James Given) *hld up: rdn along over 3f out: nvr threatened* **12/1**

3000 **7** 11 **Grey Mist**[6] 7047 3-9-0 **62**....(b[1]) RachelRichardson[(3)] 10 48
(Tim Easterby) *prom: rdn over 3f out: wknd over 2f out* **25/1**

4465 **8** ½ **Celtic Power**[31] 5923 5-8-3 **47**....(b) SeanMooney[(7)] 4 30
(Jim Goldie) *in tch: rdn over 3f out: wknd over 2f out* **9/1**

3035 **9** hd **Cavalieri (IRE)**[20] 6569 7-9-6 **57**....(tp) KevinStott 7 40
(Philip Kirby) *midfield: rdn over 3f out: wknd over 2f out* **12/1**

444 **10** 6 **Royal Headley (IRE)**[15] 6760 3-9-6 **65**.... DanielTudhope 2 42
(David O'Meara) *trckd ldrs: rdn over 3f out: wknd over 2f out* **4/1**[1]

0-03 **11** 49 **Parkwarden (IRE)**[29] 4839 3-8-3 **48** ow1.... ShaneGray 11
(Chris Grant) *prom: rdn along and lost pl 7f out: dropped to rr over 5f out: wknd and t.o over 4f out* **33/1**

013/ **12** 77 **Harvey's Hope**[586] 7678 11-8-12 **54**.... CallumRodriguez[(5)] 8
(Paul Collins) *midfield: dropped to rr 6f out: wknd and t.o fnl 5f* **16/1**

3m 9.63s (4.93) **Going Correction** +0.225s/f (Good)
**WFA** 3 from 4yo+ 8lb **12** Ran SP% **118.4**
Speed ratings (Par 101): **94,93,93,92,91 90,84,83,83,80 52,8**
CSF £39.89 CT £509.96 TOTE £8.00: £2.60, £1.40, £4.70; EX 45.10 Trifecta £593.80.
**Owner** H L Thompson & D Tucker **Bred** Larksborough Stud Limited **Trained** Liverton, Cleveland

**FOCUS**
A moderate handicap with the winner rated to the best of this year's form.

## 7249 WATCH RACING UK ON THE GO APPRENTICE H'CAP 7f
**5:05** (5:05) (Class 5) (0-70,71) 3-Y-O+ **£3,234** (£962; £481; £240) **Stalls** Centre

Form RPR

0365 **1** **Rose Eclair**[11] 6903 4-8-6 **57**.... HannahWorrall[(7)] 3 67
(Tim Easterby) *mde all: sn clr: rdn over 2f out: kpt on wl: unchal* **12/1**

3066 **2** 3½ **Grinty (IRE)**[29] 6265 3-9-3 **64**.... CallumRodriguez 2 64
(Michael Dods) *hld up: rdn and hdwy 2f out: wnt 2nd ins fnl f: kpt on but no ch wnr* **5/1**[2]

0005 **3** 2½ **Tadaany (IRE)**[42] 5739 5-9-13 **71**.... JaneElliott 7 66
(Ruth Carr) *chsd clr ldr: rdn over 2f out: lost 2nd ins fnl f: no ex* **11/2**[3]

0564 **4** ¾ **Sunnua (IRE)**[35] 6049 4-8-8 **59**....(p) SebastianWoods[(7)] 4 52
(Richard Fahey) *hld up in midfield: rdn over 3f out: plugged on fr over 1f out: nvr threatened* **5/1**[2]

0231 **5** 1 **Insurplus (IRE)**[24] 6435 4-8-13 **62**.... SeanMooney[(5)] 1 52
(Jim Goldie) *hld up: rdn 3f out: nvr threatened* **9/2**[1]

0-26 **6** ½ **Connemera Queen**[58] 5185 4-9-9 **67**.... JoshuaBryan 6 56
(John Butler) *midfield: rdn over 3f out: no imp* **13/2**

3000 **7** 5 **Kommander Kirkup**[17] 6669 6-9-1 **62**.... ConnorMurtagh[(3)] 8 38
(Michael Herrington) *midfield: rdn over 3f out: wknd fnl f* **33/1**

0222 **8** 2½ **Fine Example**[34] 6076 4-9-13 **71**....(b) MeganNicholls 11 40
(Kevin Ryan) *chsd clr ldr: rdn along over 3f out: wknd over 1f out* **8/1**

020 **9** ½ **Dark Forest**[26] 6348 4-9-5 **68**....(p) HarrisonShaw[(5)] 10 36
(Marjorie Fife) *midfield: rdn over 3f out: wknd over 1f out* **14/1**

5100 **P** **Flying Fantasy**[10] 6947 5-9-5 **68**....(p) GabrieleMalune[(5)] 9
(Michael Appleby) *dwlt: hld up in rr: rdn and wknd qckly 4f out: p.u (bled fr nose)* **12/1**

1m 26.33s (1.83) **Going Correction** +0.225s/f (Good)
**WFA** 3 from 4yo+ 3lb **10** Ran SP% **116.3**
Speed ratings (Par 103): **98,94,91,90,89 88,82,80,79,**
CSF £70.86 CT £373.80 TOTE £14.20: £3.50, £1.90, £2.20; EX 82.80 Trifecta £1147.10.
**Owner** James Bowers **Bred** J Bowers **Trained** Great Habton, N Yorks

**FOCUS**
Few got into this, the winner having things under control from some way out. He has been rated to this year's form.
T/Plt: £9.40 to a £1 stake. Pool: £59,023.36 - 4,543.31 winning units T/Qpdt: £4.90 to a £1 stake. Pool: £3,532.68 - 528.59 winning units **Andrew Sheret**

# 6479 YARMOUTH (L-H)
## Tuesday, September 19

**OFFICIAL GOING: Soft (6.3)**
Wind: light, half behind Weather: fine

## 7250 BRITISH STALLION STUDS EBF NOVICE STKS (PLUS 10 RACE) 6f 3y
**2:00** (2:03) (Class 4) 2-Y-O **£6,469** (£1,925; £962; £481) **Stalls** Centre

Form RPR

**1** **Mutaaqeb** 2-9-2 0.... JimCrowley 10 80+
(Owen Burrows) *s.i.s: hld up in tch in last pair: shkn up and swtchd rt over 2f out: rdn and hdwy over 1f out. chsd ldr jst ins fnl f: r.o wl to ld cl home* **3/1**[1]

**2** nk **Rule Of Honour** 2-8-13 0.... HectorCrouch[(3)] 2 79+
(Ismail Mohammed) *trckd ldrs: shkn up to chse ldr wl over 1f out: sn rdn to chal: led 1f out: drvn ins fnl f: kpt on u.p: hdd nr fin* **6/1**

00 **3** 3½ **Equilibrium**[16] 6719 2-8-11 0.... PaoloSirigu 3 64
(Robert Eddery) *led: rdn and hrd pressed over 1f out: hdd 1f out: outpcd by ldng pair but battled on gamely to hold 3rd ins fnl f* **100/1**

**4** nk **Society Prince (IRE)** 2-9-2 0.... TomQueally 6 68
(James Fanshawe) *hld up wl in tch in midfield: shkn up and effrt over 1f out: hdwy and rdn to chse ldrs 1f out: outpcd by ldng pair and kpt on same pce ins fnl f* **16/1**

00 **5** ¾ **Mandarin Princess**[11] 6884 2-8-11 0.... DavidProbert 9 60
(Philip McBride) *chsd ldrs: rdn 2f out: unable qck and outpcd over 1f out: no ch w ldng pair but kpt on ins fnl f* **33/1**

06 **6** shd **Mashaheer**[24] 6424 2-9-2 0.... RyanMoore 1 65
(William Haggas) *chsd ldr tl unable qck u.p over 1f out: no ch w ldng pair and kpt on same pce ins fnl f* **9/2**[3]

000 **7** ½ **True North (IRE)**[11] 6897 2-8-9 0.... ManuelFernandes[(7)] 11 64
(Sir Mark Prescott Bt) *in tch in midfield: shkn up and outpcd over 1f out: no ch w ldng pair but kpt on wl ins fnl f* **100/1**

**8** ¾ **Zizum**[40] 5858 2-9-2 0.... KieranShoemark 8 61
(George Scott) *hld up in tch towards rr: pushed along over 1f out: kpt on ins fnl f: nvr trbld ldrs* **20/1**

5 **9** *nse* **Turquoise Bay (USA)**[33] 6108 2-9-2 0 SilvestreDeSousa 7 61
(Chris Dwyer) *short of room and hmpd sn after s: hld up in tch in rr: effrt and swtchd lft over 1f out: hdwy u.p to chse ldrs 1f out: sn btn and wknd ins fnl f* **4/1**[2]

**10** *nk* **Scapusc** 2-9-2 0 (t[1]) DanielMuscutt 4 60
(Marco Botti) *wl in tch in midfield: rdn over 2f out: lost pl and towards rr over 1f out: kpt on same pce and no imp after* **9/1**

**11** *3 ¼* **Matchmaking (GER)** 2-9-2 0 RyanPowell 12 51
(Sir Mark Prescott Bt) *s.i.s: a rr and sn pushed along: n.d* **40/1**

0 **12** *2 ½* **Protected Guest**[66] 4885 2-9-2 0 MartinLane 5 43
(George Margarson) *s.i.s: hld up towards rr: hdwy into midfield 4f out: rdn over 2f out: lost pl over 1f out: bhd fnl f* **9/1**

1m 12.9s (-1.50) **Going Correction** -0.175s/f (Firm) 12 Ran SP% **115.5**
Speed ratings (Par 97): **103,102,97,97,96 96,95,94,94,94 89,86**
CSF £19.72 TOTE £3.90: £2.00, £2.40, £21.20; EX 24.30 Trifecta £3994.40.
**Owner** Hamdan Al Maktoum **Bred** Shadwell Estate Company Limited **Trained** Lambourn, Berks

**FOCUS**
There was 4mm of rain overnight and the ground was soft. They raced up the middle, but with the first three more towards the stands' side than some in the closing stages. A couple of promising newcomers pulled clear.

## 7251 VINCE SULLIVAN MEMORIAL NURSERY H'CAP 1m 3y
**2:35** (2:35) (Class 4) (0-85,81) 2-Y-O **£4,528** (£1,347; £673; £336) **Stalls** Centre

Form RPR

635 **1** **Rayna's World (IRE)**[11] 6875 2-8-7 **67** JimmyQuinn 3 76+
(Philip Kirby) *chsd ldrs: wnt 2nd 5f out tl led over 2f out: sn jnd but gng best tl reminders and readily asserted 1f out: sn clr and r.o wl: comf* **9/1**

2166 **2** *4 ½* **Midnight Wilde**[17] 6684 2-9-2 **76** SilvestreDeSousa 2 75
(John Ryan) *midfield: clsd to join ldr and rdn 2f out: drvn over 1f out: easily brushed aside by wnr 1f out: plugged on same pce ins fnl f* **4/1**[2]

2351 **3** *3 ¼* **Simpson (IRE)**[15] 6762 2-9-7 **81** KieranShoemark 6 73
(Ed Walker) *t.k.h: hld up in midfield: clsd to chse ldrs over 2f out: 3rd and no imp over 1f out: wl hld and plugged on same pce ins fnl f* **6/4**[1]

0601 **4** *7* **Hemingford (IRE)**[42] 5756 2-8-10 **70** StevieDonohoe 4 47
(Charlie Fellowes) *led for over 1f: chsd ldr tl 5f out: rdn 3f out: struggling and btn 2f out: sn wknd* **5/1**[3]

3415 **5** *10* **Noble Manners (IRE)**[21] 6561 2-9-3 **77** JimCrowley 1 32
(Mark Johnston) *s.i.s: hld up in last pair: clsd over 2f out: sn rdn and btn: wl bhd and eased wl ins fnl f* **13/2**

6353 **6** *3* **Lucifugous (IRE)**[23] 6472 2-8-4 **64** JoeyHaynes 5 12
(Stuart Williams) *taken down early: stdd s: plld hrd and ref to settle: hdwy to ld over 6f out: sn clr: hdd over 2f out: sn dropped out: wl bhd and eased wl ins fnl f* **8/1**

1m 40.3s (-0.30) **Going Correction** -0.175s/f (Firm) 6 Ran SP% **111.1**
Speed ratings (Par 97): **94,89,86,79,69 66**
CSF £43.05 TOTE £10.00: £4.60, £2.00; EX 53.30 Trifecta £160.40.
**Owner** Ace Bloodstock & Rayna Fitzgerald **Bred** George Kent **Trained** East Appleton, N Yorks

**FOCUS**
They raced up the middle. This had the look of a race that fell apart, with the field strung out and most of them seemingly on an off day. The race has been rated around the second.

## 7252 DAN HAGUE, YARMOUTH'S NUMBER 1 BOOKMAKER H'CAP 1m 3f 104y
**3:05** (3:05) (Class 2) (0-100,97) 3-Y-O+ **£15,185** (£4,545; £2,272; £1,137; £566) **Stalls** Low

Form RPR

121 **1** **Zack Mayo**[15] 6757 3-8-9 **85** (p[1]) SilvestreDeSousa 3 96+
(Philip McBride) *chsd ldr tl rdn to ld 3f out: edgd rt over 1f out: hld on wl ins fnl f* **8/1**

111 **2** *½* **High End**[22] 6515 3-9-4 **97** DavidEgan[(3)] 5 106
(Saeed bin Suroor) *chsd ldng pair: chsd wnr wl over 2f out: wnt lft u.p 1f out: kpt on and pressing wnr wl ins fnl f: hld towards fin* **5/4**[1]

3124 **3** *3 ¼* **Eynhallow**[23] 6474 3-9-2 **92** KieranShoemark 1 96
(Roger Charlton) *hld up in tch in last pair: effrt over 2f out: chsd clr ldng pair: kpt on but nvr getting on terms w ldrs* **9/2**[2]

6110 **4** *6* **Intellect (IRE)**[24] 6445 3-9-2 **92** RyanMoore 2 86
(Sir Michael Stoute) *led: rdn and hdd 3f out: outpcd and btn 2f out: lost 3rd and wknd over 1f out* **5/1**[3]

1031 **5** *3 ½* **Opinionate**[12] 6865 3-8-12 **88** JimCrowley 4 76
(Amanda Perrett) *hld up in tch in last pair: effrt over 2f out: sn btn: bhd over 1f out* **5/1**[3]

2m 30.92s (2.22) **Going Correction** +0.40s/f (Good) 5 Ran SP% **107.1**
Speed ratings (Par 107): **107,106,104,99,97**
CSF £17.69 TOTE £5.90: £2.00, £1.80; EX 16.90 Trifecta £65.30.
**Owner** Mrs Sarah Hamilton & Chris Budgett 1 **Bred** Mrs S Hamilton & Kirtlington Stud Ltd **Trained** Newmarket, Suffolk

**FOCUS**
They raced up the middle in the straight. A decent handicap, but only the first two looked to run their race with the winner backing up his impressive Ripon win.

## 7253 LA CONTINENTAL CAFE/TIPSTERTABLES.COM OF GREAT YARMOUTH H'CAP 1m 3f 104y
**3:40** (3:40) (Class 6) (0-60,62) 3-Y-O+ **£3,234** (£962; £481; £240) **Stalls** Low

Form RPR

0040 **1** **Seventii**[19] 6622 3-7-11 **46** oh1 DarraghKeenan[(7)] 5 58
(Robert Eddery) *hld up wl in tch in midfield: clsd to trck ldrs and travelling strly over 3f out: led 2f out: sn rdn clr: r.o wl: comf* **18/1**

2342 **2** *5* **Broughtons Admiral**[8] 7003 3-9-2 **58** (p) StevieDonohoe 13 62
(Henry Spiller) *hld up in tch in midfield: effrt over 2f out: drvn over 1f out: kpt on u.p ins fnl f to go 2nd nr fin: no ch w wnr* **13/8**[1]

00-5 **3** *½* **Fortia**[19] 6623 3-9-3 **59** SilvestreDeSousa 6 62
(Dean Ivory) *chsd ldrfor 2f: chsd ldrs tl wnt 2nd again over 3f out: sn rdn: ev ch briefly 2f out: 2nd but nt match pce of wnr over 1f out: kpt on same pce u.p fnl f: lost 2nd nr fin* **7/1**[3]

053 **4** *1 ¼* **Dragonite (IRE)**[41] 5790 3-8-1 **46** DavidEgan[(3)] 3 47
(Daniel Mark Loughnane) *hld up in tch in midfield: rdn and hdwy 4f out: chsd ldrs and drvn over 2f out: unable qck over 1f out: no ch w wnr and kpt on same pce ins fnl f* **11/2**[2]

5535 **5** *½* **Sexy Secret**[49] 5509 6-8-11 **50** (p) SimonPearce[(3)] 7 49
(Lydia Pearce) *led: rdn 3f out: hdd 2f out: sn outpcd: wl hld and kpt on same pce fnl f* **10/1**

5263 **6** *4* **Bizet (IRE)**[13] 6821 3-8-2 **51** (v) JackOsborn[(7)] 8 45
(John Ryan) *hld up in tch in last trio: swtchd lft and effrt over 2f out: no imp u.p over 1f out: nvr trbld ldrs* **16/1**

0000 **7** *1 ½* **Clearance**[47] 5581 3-8-6 **48** JoeyHaynes 4 39
(Mark H Tompkins) *hld up in last pair: effrt 4f out: sme hdwy into midfield over 2f out: no imp and wl hld after: nvr trbld ldrs* **28/1**

4404 **8** *8* **Magic Beans**[24] 6436 3-8-11 **56** CharlieBennett[(3)] 12 34
(Hughie Morrison) *chsd ldrs: rdn over 3f out: unable qck and sn struggling: bhd over 1f out* **8/1**

0-01 **9** *5* **Seaborn (IRE)**[222] 637 3-9-6 **62** DavidProbert 10 32
(Tim Vaughan) *hld up in last pair: rdn over 3f out: drvn and swtchd lft over 2f out: sn btn: bhd and eased wl ins fnl f* **7/1**[3]

20/4 **10** *5* **Rathealy (IRE)**[172] 1182 6-9-3 **60** JacobMitchell[(7)] 11 21
(Christine Dunnett) *jostled leaving stalls: chsd ldr after 2f tl over 3f out: sn lost pl: bhd over 1f out* **100/1**

2m 32.53s (3.83) **Going Correction** +0.40s/f (Good)
**WFA** 3 from 6yo 6lb 10 Ran SP% **114.3**
Speed ratings (Par 101): **102,98,98,97,96 93,92,86,83,79**
CSF £46.66 CT £236.03 TOTE £20.80: £5.90, £1.20, £2.10; EX 58.70 Trifecta £433.80.
**Owner** Graham & Lynn Knight **Bred** Biddestone Stud Ltd **Trained** Newmarket, Suffolk

**FOCUS**
The main action was up the middle in the straight. Moderate stuff.

## 7254 PARKDEAN RESORTS THE BROADS MAIDEN STKS 6f 3y
**4:10** (4:12) (Class 5) 3-Y-O+ **£3,557** (£1,058; £529; £264) **Stalls** Centre

Form RPR

3 **1** **One Master**[31] 6184 3-9-0 0 RyanMoore 7 76+
(William Haggas) *trckd ldrs: effrt 2f out: sn rdn to chal: led 1f out: styd on strly and drew clr ins fnl f* **4/11**[1]

35 **2** *2 ¾* **Perfect Sense**[22] 6522 3-9-2 0 (v[1]) CallumShepherd[(3)] 5 72
(Saeed bin Suroor) *led: rdn 2f out: hdd 1f out: no ex and outpcd by wnr ins fnl f: kpt on same pce for clr 2nd after* **6/1**[2]

64 **3** *2* **Majorette**[14] 6791 3-8-11 0 NoelGarbutt[(3)] 2 61
(Martin Smith) *t.k.h: chsd ldr: rdn 2f out: 3rd and outpcd 1f out: no ch w wnr and kpt on same pce ins fnl f* **11/1**

50 **4** *¾* **Fintech (IRE)**[13] 6817 3-9-5 0 (t) SaleemGolam 3 64
(Mrs Ilka Gansera-Leveque) *hld up in tch: effrt over 1f out: 4th and edgd lft ins fnl f: kpt on same pce fnl 150yds: no ch w wnr* **20/1**

-200 **5** *nk* **Waqt (IRE)**[13] 6807 3-9-5 64 JimCrowley 4 63
(Marcus Tregoning) *chsd ldrs: effrt 2f out: unable qck u.p over 1f out: plugged on same pce fnl f* **6/1**[2]

0000 **6** *4 ½* **Tilsworth Lukey**[55] 5285 4-9-0 38 GinaMangan[(7)] 9 48?
(J R Jenkins) *stdd after s: hld up in last pair: effrt over 1f out: sn hung lft and btn: wknd fnl f* **150/1**

4335 **7** *2* **Tawaafoq**[16] 6724 3-9-5 65 TedDurcan 8 42
(Mick Quinn) *stdd s: t.k.h: hld up in tch in last pair: effrt 2f out: sn btn: bhd and eased wl ins fnl f* **7/1**[3]

**8** *23* **Eye Burner** 3-9-5 0 AlistairRawlinson 6
(J R Jenkins) *s.i.s: in tch in rr: hdwy into midfield 4f out: hung lft over 2f out: bhd and stl hanging bdly over 1f out: eased ins fnl f: t.o* **66/1**

1m 13.39s (-1.01) **Going Correction** -0.175s/f (Firm)
**WFA** 3 from 4yo 2lb 8 Ran SP% **129.6**
Speed ratings (Par 103): **99,95,92,91,91 85,82,51**
CSF £4.35 TOTE £1.30: £1.02, £1.80, £3.20; EX 4.80 Trifecta £26.30.
**Owner** Lael Stable **Bred** Lael Stables **Trained** Newmarket, Suffolk

**FOCUS**
The main action was middle to stands' side. A weak sprint maiden with the placed horses rated to form.

## 7255 MOULTON NURSERY OF ACLE H'CAP 6f 3y
**4:45** (4:45) (Class 5) (0-70,72) 3-Y-O+ **£3,881** (£1,155; £577; £288) **Stalls** Centre

Form RPR

2110 **1** **Ocean Temptress**[17] 6681 3-8-8 **66** (v) JackOsborn[(7)] 8 75
(John Ryan) *led and sn clr: rdn over 1f out: hrd pressed 1f out: hdd ins fnl f: battled bk gamely to ld again last strides* **11/2**

0530 **2** *hd* **Quatrieme Ami**[129] 2621 4-9-6 **69** DavidProbert 4 77
(Philip McBride) *prom in main gp: chsd clr ldr over 2f out: rdn and clsd over 1f out: chal 1f out: drvn to ld ins fnl f: hdd last strides* **15/2**

6000 **3** *2 ½* **Reedanjas (IRE)**[32] 6155 3-8-12 **66** DavidEgan[(3)] 6 66
(Gay Kelleway) *prom in main gp: effrt in 3rd over 2f out: kpt on u.p ins fnl f: nvr getting on terms w ldng pair* **16/1**

0635 **4** *2 ½* **Robbian**[7] 7017 6-8-4 **56** oh5 NoelGarbutt[(3)] 2 48
(Charles Smith) *taken down early: prom in main gp: rdn over 2f out: 4th and kpt on same pce u.p over 1f out* **14/1**

4406 **5** *¾* **North Creek**[11] 6874 4-9-7 **70** JimCrowley 3 60
(Chris Wall) *off the pce in last pair: effrt 2f out: 5th and stl plenty to do 1f out: kpt on but nvr getting on terms w ldrs* **11/4**[1]

025 **6** *6* **Blazed (IRE)**[31] 6184 3-9-5 **70** (t) KieranShoemark 1 40
(Roger Charlton) *stdd and swtchd rt after s: hld up in rr: swtchd rt and effrt 2f out: sn rdn and no prog: wknd fnl f* **9/2**[3]

0-00 **7** *1 ¼* **Mossy's Lodge**[160] 1729 4-9-0 **63** RyanTate 7 29
(Anthony Carson) *chsd clr wnr tl rdn and lost pl over 2f out: bhd over 1f out* **25/1**

-060 **8** *¾* **Drop Kick Murphi (IRE)**[11] 6874 3-9-7 **72** JoeyHaynes 5 36
(Christine Dunnett) *midfield: rdn and swtchd lft over 2f out: sn struggling: bhd over 1f out* **40/1**

/2-0 **9** *18* **Dream Bounty**[30] 6237 5-8-8 **57** SilvestreDeSousa 10
(Michael Appleby) *prom in main gp: rdn 1/2-way: lost pl and bhd over 1f out: eased ins fnl f* **3/1**[2]

1m 12.81s (-1.59) **Going Correction** -0.175s/f (Firm)
**WFA** 3 from 4yo+ 2lb 9 Ran SP% **115.8**
Speed ratings (Par 103): **103,102,99,96,95 87,85,84,60**
CSF £46.34 CT £624.03 TOTE £5.40: £2.00, £2.40, £4.00; EX 48.10 Trifecta £380.70.
**Owner** The Temptations **Bred** Old Mill Stud Ltd And Oomswell Ltd **Trained** Newmarket, Suffolk

**FOCUS**
They raced middle to stands' side. Few got into this modest sprint handicap with the form looking fluid.

## 7256 WAINWRIGHT GOLDEN ALE H'CAP 5f 42y
**5:15** (5:15) (Class 4) (0-85,85) 3-Y-O+ **£5,175** (£1,540; £769; £384) **Stalls** Centre

Form RPR

6300 **1** **Poet's Society**[10] 6922 3-9-6 **85** JimCrowley 4 92
(Mark Johnston) *mde all: rdn over 1f out: battled on wl u.p and forged ahd ins fnl f: rdn out* **7/2**[3]

1422 **2** *¾* **Magical Dreamer (IRE)**[11] 6878 3-9-3 **82** DanielMuscutt 3 86
(James Fanshawe) *trckd ldr: upsides and stl travelling strly over 1f out: effrt 1f out: unable qck u.p and one pced ins fnl f* **1/1**[1]

1641 **3** *2* **Annie Salts**[49] 5514 4-8-8 **72** (h) SilvestreDeSousa 5 69
(Chris Dwyer) *taken down early: hld up in tch in rr: clsd to trck ldng pair 2f out: swtchd rt and effrt ent fnl f: no imp u.p and eased towards fin* **3/1**[2]

1355 **4** *8* **Silvanus (IRE)**15 6758 12-8-13 77 TomQueally 6 46
(Paul Midgley) *taken down early: trckd ldrs: rdn over 2f out: dropped to last 2f out: wknd fnl f* **15/2**

1m 2.37s (-0.33) **Going Correction** -0.175s/f (Firm)
**WFA** 3 from 4yo+ 1lb **4** Ran SP% **109.0**
Speed ratings (Par 105): **95,93,90,77**
CSF £7.58 TOTE £3.30; EX 9.20 Trifecta £12.70.
**Owner** Sheikh Hamdan bin Mohammed Al Maktoum **Bred** Darley **Trained** Middleham Moor, N Yorks

**FOCUS**
They raced middle to far side. The winner has been rated to his best, but the second looks the one to take from this small-field event.
T/Plt: £160.30 to a £1 stake. Pool: £73,194.29 - 333.28 winning units T/Qpdt: £8.60 to a £1 stake. Pool: £4,239.22 - 360.98 winning units **Steve Payne**

7257 - 7260a (Foreign Racing) - See Raceform Interactive

## 5687 GALWAY (R-H)
### Tuesday, September 19

**OFFICIAL GOING: Soft**

## 7261a ARDILAUN HOTEL OYSTER STKS (LISTED RACE) 1m 4f
4:35 (4:36) 3-Y-O+
**£25,213** (£8,119; £3,846; £1,709; £854; £427)

RPR

**1** **Airlie Beach (IRE)**33 6122 7-9-7 0 PatSmullen 5 98+
(W P Mullins, Ire) *chsd ldrs: 5th 1/2-way: tk clsr order bhd ldrs gng wl 4f out: pushed along on outer over 2f out and led narrowly appr st: rdn 1 1/2f out and styd on wl ins fnl f* **2/1**1

**2** *1 ½* **Remarkable Lady (IRE)**3 7171 4-9-7 92 (tp) ShaneFoley 6 96+
(H Rogers, Ire) *hld up: 6th 1/2-way: hdwy on outer over 2f out: rdn in 2nd into st where pressed wnr: kpt on wl wout matching wnr ins fnl f* **8/1**

**3** *3* **Red Stars (IRE)**93 3874 4-9-7 98 (h) DeclanMcDonogh 3 91
(John M Oxx, Ire) *loaded wout rdr: chsd ldrs: disp 3rd at 1/2-way: rdn in 4th over 2f out and lost pl appr st: wnt 3rd u.p ins fnl f where no imp on ldrs: kpt on same pce* **11/2**3

**4** *1 ¼* **Pavlenko (JPN)**23 6490 3-9-0 93 SeamieHeffernan 11 90+
(A P O'Brien, Ire) *sn settled in rr: last at 1/2-way: pushed along in 8th under 2f out and sme hdwy u.p 1f out: kpt on into nvr threatening 4th wl ins fnl f: nvr trbld ldrs* **16/1**

**5** *1 ½* **Tara Dylan (IRE)**10 6956 5-9-7 81 (t) ColinKeane 9 87
(Thomas Mullins, Ire) *hld up: 7th 1/2-way: prog on outer over 2f out: rdn into 4th briefly ins fnl f where no imp on ldrs: one pce after and one pce in 5th clsng stages* **16/1**

**6** *1 ¼* **Dew Line (IRE)**6 7066 5-9-7 94 GaryCarroll 4 85
(Michael Mulvany, Ire) *broke wl to ld tl hdd after 1f and settled bhd ldrs: disp 3rd at 1/2-way: pushed along in 3rd over 4f out: sn rdn and no imp on ldrs u.p in 7th 2f out: kpt on one pce ins fnl f* **12/1**

**7** *1 ½* **Flaming Sea (IRE)**46 5623 4-9-7 83 WJLee 1 82
(Conor O'Dwyer, Ire) *cl up: 2nd 1/2-way: led narrowly between horses briefly over 2f out tl sn hdd: wknd u.p in 3rd fr over 1f out* **7/1**

**8** *½* **Jeremys Joy (IRE)**6 7066 5-9-7 87 (h) RobbieDowney 7 82
(Keith Henry Clarke, Ire) *dwlt and pushed along early: sn settled towards rr: 8th 1/2-way: pushed along under 3f out and no ex u.p 2f out: one pce after* **25/1**

**9** *2 ¼* **Pearl Of The West (IRE)**30 6245 3-9-0 90 KevinManning 8 79
(P A Fahy, Ire) *w ldrs tl led after 1f: 1 l clr at 1/2-way: rdn and hdd over 2f out: sn wknd qckly* **3/1**2

2m 45.97s (2.87)
**WFA** 3 from 4yo+ 7lb **9** Ran SP% **120.6**
CSF £20.14 TOTE £3.10: £1.30, £3.00, £1.50; DF 22.10 Trifecta £123.20.
**Owner** Supreme Horse Racing Club & Kenneth Sharp **Bred** Mrs J M Mullins **Trained** Muine Beag, Co Carlow

**FOCUS**
A fantastic way to draw the curtain on the career of brilliant race mare Airlie Beach.

7262 - 7263a (Foreign Racing) - See Raceform Interactive

## 6666 BEVERLEY (R-H)
### Wednesday, September 20

**OFFICIAL GOING: Soft (good to soft in places; 6.4)**
Wind: Light across Weather: Cloudy

## 7264 BET TOTEPLACEPOT AT BETFRED.COM CLAIMING STKS 5f
1:50 (1:50) (Class 6) 2-Y-O **£2,587** (£770; £384; £192) **Stalls Low**

Form RPR

4236 **1** **Seen The Lyte (IRE)**16 6756 2-8-8 65 BenRobinson(5) 5 65
(John Quinn) *cl up: rdn to chal wl over 1f out: led appr fnl f: drvn out* **5/2**3

0110 **2** *1* **Flo's Melody**11 6951 2-8-7 64 BarryMcHugh 4 55
(Richard Fahey) *trckd ldrs: pushed along over 2f out: swtchd rt and rdn over 1f out: drvn ins fnl f: kpt on* **9/4**2

5100 **3** *½* **Danehill Desert (IRE)**11 6951 2-9-2 73 SammyJoBell(3) 3 66
(Richard Fahey) *dwlt and towards rr: hdwy to trck ldrs on inner 1/2-way: n.m.r and swtchd lft over 1f out: sn rdn: chsd wnr ins fnl f: drvn and kpt on same pce* **2/1**1

4050 **4** *1 ¾* **Lady Lintera (IRE)**6 7081 2-8-11 53 (h) ShaneGray 6 51
(Ann Duffield) *towards rr: hdwy over 2f out: rdn wl over 1f out: kpt on fnl f* **33/1**

00 **5** *2 ¼* **Honey Gg**42 5801 2-8-6 0 PhilDennis(3) 1 41
(Declan Carroll) *slt ld: rdn along wl over 1f out: hdd appr fnl f: sn drvn and grad wknd* **50/1**

4220 **6** *¾* **Christmas Night**20 6634 2-8-13 63 AndrewMullen 7 43
(Ollie Pears) *dwlt and towards rr: hdwy over 2f out: rdn along wl over 1f out: kpt on fnl f* **10/1**

0000 **7** *1* **Dark Hedges**29 6285 2-8-2 47 ConnorMurtagh(7) 9 35
(Olly Williams) *chsd ldrs: rdn along over 2f out: sn wknd* **100/1**

005 **8** *8* **Free Spirited**70 4740 2-8-10 58 (p1) TonyHamilton 10 7
(Richard Fahey) *dwlt: t.k.h and sn chsng ldng pair on outer: rdn and hung rt 2f out: sn wknd* **14/1**

1m 6.52s (3.02) **Going Correction** +0.55s/f (Yiel) **8** Ran SP% **114.3**
Speed ratings (Par 93): **97,95,94,91,88 87,85,72**
CSF £8.51 TOTE £2.70: £1.10, £1.10, £1.30; EX 8.80 Trifecta £18.70.Flo's Melody was claimed for £6000 by Mr Barry Leavy
**Owner** Boys Of Buckley **Bred** Highest Praise Syndicate **Trained** Settrington, N Yorks

**FOCUS**
The going was given as soft, good to soft in places (GoingStick: 6.4). Modest form with the winner near her best.

## 7265 BET TOTEEXACTA AT BETFRED.COM EBF FILLIES' NOVICE STKS (PLUS 10 RACE) 7f 96y
2:20 (2:20) (Class 5) 2-Y-O **£3,881** (£1,155; £577; £288) **Stalls Low**

Form RPR

503 **1** **Bee Ina Bonnet**12 6876 2-9-0 69 TonyHamilton 5 71
(Tim Easterby) *trckd wnr: hdwy over 2f out: rdn to chal over 1f out: led ent fnl f: sn drvn and hld on wl towards fin* **7/1**

**2** *½* **Celestin's** 2-9-0 0 BenCurtis 7 70+
(William Haggas) *hld up in rr: swtchd to outer and hdwy over 2f out: rdn over 1f out: styd on to chal ins fnl f and ev ch: nt qckn towards fin* **10/3**3

**3** *4* **Tiara Gold** 2-9-0 0 DavidAllan 2 60
(Rae Guest) *dwlt: green and hld up in rr: hdwy on inner over 2f out: rdn over 1f out: kpt on same pce fnl f* **20/1**

4 **4** *1* **Sempre Presto (IRE)**19 6659 2-9-0 0 JackGarritty 4 58
(Richard Fahey) *sn pushed along and in tch: rdn along 3f out: outpcd over 2f out: kpt on u.p fnl f* **9/4**1

4365 **5** *shd* **Ruysch (IRE)**22 6552 2-9-0 71 (b1) PaulMulrennan 3 57
(Ed Dunlop) *led at gd clip: pushed along 2f out: sn jnd and rdn: drvn and hdd ent fnl f: sn wknd* **3/1**2

06 **6** *6* **Helen Sherbet**12 6876 2-8-11 0 CliffordLee(3) 1 43
(K R Burke) *chsd ldng pair: pushed along over 3f out: rdn over 2f out: sn drvn and wknd wl over 1f out* **9/2**

1m 37.32s (3.52) **Going Correction** +0.55s/f (Yiel) **6** Ran SP% **114.3**
Speed ratings (Par 92): **101,100,95,94,94 87**
CSF £30.98 TOTE £6.00: £4.00, £1.90; EX 30.90 Trifecta £219.90.
**Owner** Bearstone Stud Limited **Bred** Bearstone Stud Ltd **Trained** Great Habton, N Yorks

**FOCUS**
A fair fillies' event.

## 7266 BET TOTEQUADPOT AT BETFRED.COM NOVICE AUCTION STKS 7f 96y
2:55 (2:58) (Class 5) 2-Y-O **£3,881** (£1,155; £577; £288) **Stalls Low**

Form RPR

3 **1** **Apple Anni (IRE)**14 6824 2-8-11 0 JFEgan 7 76
(Mick Channon) *hld up towards rr: hdwy on inner 3f out: swtchd lft and effrt to chse ldng pair 2f out: rdn to ld appr fnl f: kpt on wl* **9/2**3

42 **2** *2 ¾* **Vera Drake (FR)**14 6824 2-8-11 0 TonyHamilton 5 69
(Richard Fahey) *chsd ldng pair: tk clsr order 3f out: led wl over 1f out: sn rdn: hdd and drvn appr fnl f: kpt on* **5/2**1

**3** *2 ¾* **Hyanna** 2-8-11 0 DavidAllan 2 63
(Tim Easterby) *dwlt and towards rr: hdwy 3f out: swtchd lft and rdn 2f out: kpt on to chse ldng pair fnl f* **33/1**

4 **4** *5* **How Bizarre**12 6890 2-9-2 0 TomEaves 3 55+
(Kevin Ryan) *slt ld: rdn along 3f out: hdd wl over 1f out: sn drvn and grad wknd* **11/2**

45 **5** *1 ½* **Firby (IRE)**46 5631 2-9-2 0 KevinStott 6 52
(James Bethell) *in tch: hdwy to chse ldrs 3f out: rdn along over 2f out: sn drvn and one pce* **4/1**2

**6** *4 ½* **Dragon Tattoo (IRE)** 2-8-11 0 BenCurtis 4 36
(Hugo Palmer) *dwlt: a towards rr* **10/1**

6 **7** *6* **Pelice (IRE)**12 6890 2-8-11 0 JoeFanning 8 21
(Mark Johnston) *in tch: rdn along 3f out: sn outpcd* **13/2**

5 **8** *12* **Allnite (IRE)**25 6410 2-9-2 0 RichardKingscote 1 +
(Tom Dascombe) *cl up: disp ld 1/2-way: rdn along 3f out: sn wknd* **11/1**

1m 37.17s (3.37) **Going Correction** +0.55s/f (Yiel) **8** Ran SP% **115.8**
Speed ratings (Par 95): **102,98,95,90,88 83,76,62**
CSF £16.43 TOTE £5.70: £1.50, £1.20, £9.70; EX 16.60 Trifecta £334.90.
**Owner** Mrs T Burns **Bred** Rathasker Stud **Trained** West Ilsley, Berks

**FOCUS**
With the two leaders taking each other on, this was run at a strong pace.

## 7267 BET TOTETRIFECTA AT BETFRED.COM H'CAP 1m 4f 23y
3:25 (3:26) (Class 4) (0-80,79) 3-Y-O+
**£6,225** (£1,864; £932; £466; £233; £117) **Stalls Low**

Form RPR

3341 **1** **Bolder Bob (IRE)**43 5753 3-9-0 77 BenCurtis 1 87+
(David Barron) *trckd ldng pair: tk cl order over 3f out: chal 2f out: led 11/2f out: rdn clr ent fnl f: kpt on strly* **8/11**1

0131 **2** *3 ¼* **Overhaugh Street**15 6781 4-8-9 65 oh2 LiamKeniry 8 69+
(Ed de Giles) *led 4f: chsd ldr tl led again over 2f out: sn rdn: hdd 11/2f out: sn drvn and kpt on same pce* **9/1**3

5006 **3** *¾* **Marmion**13 6858 5-8-10 66 (h) DavidAllan 4 69
(Les Eyre) *chsd ldrs: hdwy 3f out: rdn along over 2f out: drvn over 1f out: kpt on same pce* **20/1**

2000 **4** *nk* **Serenity Now (IRE)**33 6126 9-8-6 67 BenRobinson(5) 5 70
(Brian Ellison) *hld up in rr: rdn along 3f out: hdwy 2f out: kpt on u.p fnl f* **40/1**

1056 **5** *1 ½* **Auxiliary**40 5872 4-8-13 69 (p) JamesSullivan 6 69
(Patrick Holmes) *in tch: pushed along over 3f out: rdn wl over 2f out: sn drvn and no imp* **25/1**

0112 **6** *¾* **Medalla De Oro**8 7024 3-9-1 78 (h) PaulMulrennan 2 78
(Peter Chapple-Hyam) *cl up: led after 4f: rdn along 3f out: hdd over 2f out and sn wknd* **9/4**2

1630 **7** *1 ¼* **Tapis Libre**16 6757 9-9-2 79 HarrisonShaw(7) 3 76
(Jacqueline Coward) *hld up: a in rr* **18/1**

2m 44.77s (4.97) **Going Correction** +0.55s/f (Yiel)
**WFA** 3 from 4yo+ 7lb **7** Ran SP% **115.0**
Speed ratings (Par 105): **105,102,102,102,101 100,99**
CSF £8.57 CT £73.73 TOTE £1.60: £1.10, £4.70; EX 8.80 Trifecta £50.00.
**Owner** S Chappell **Bred** Gerry And John Rowley **Trained** Maunby, N Yorks

**FOCUS**
This proved pretty straightforward for the odds-on and improving favourite.

## 7268 BET TOTEWIN AT BETFRED.COM H'CAP 5f
4:00 (4:03) (Class 5) (0-75,77) 3-Y-O+ **£3,780** (£1,131; £565; £283; £141) **Stalls Low**

Form RPR

0010 **1** **One Boy (IRE)**12 6891 6-9-2 70 GrahamLee 3 79
(Paul Midgley) *hld up in tch on inner: hdwy 2f out: nt clr run and swtchd lft jst over 1f out: sn rdn and chal ins fnl f: drvn and kpt on to ld last 50yds* **16/1**

2630 **2** *1 ¼* **Flash City (ITY)**30 6267 9-9-0 **68**........ JackGarritty 2 72
(Ruth Carr) *chsd ldrs: hdwy wl over 1f out: rdn to ld appr fnl f: sn drvn: hdd and no ex last 50yds* **16/1**

0120 **3** *shd* **Jacob's Pillow**10 6964 6-9-7 **75**........(p) DuranFentiman 7 79
(Rebecca Bastiman) *cl up: rdn wl over 1f out: ev ch ent fnl f: sn drvn and kpt on same pce* **20/1**

5366 **4** *¾* **Foxy Boy**11 6945 3-8-12 **72**........ CallumRodriguez(5) 4 73
(Michael Dods) *dwlt and towards rr: in tch 1/2-way: hdwy to chse ldrs over 1f out: sn rdn and kpt on same pce fnl f* **7/1**

3000 **5** *nk* **Van Gerwen**12 6877 4-9-5 **73**........ JoeFanning 11 73
(Les Eyre) *chsd ldrs on outer: hdwy and cl up 2f out: sn rdn: drvn appr fnl f: kpt on same pce* **33/1**

2313 **6** *nk* **Dirchill (IRE)**27 6348 3-9-6 **75**........(b1) BenCurtis 6 74+
(David Barron) *dwlt and towards rr: rdn along wl over 1f out: sn drvn: kpt on fnl f* **3/1**1

5313 **7** *½* **Miningggold**11 6923 4-9-9 **77**........(p) PaulMulrennan 9 74
(Michael Dods) *chsd ldrs: rdn along wl over 1f out: sn drvn and no imp fnl f* **8/1**

2226 **8** *3* **Astrophysics**18 6670 5-9-0 **68**........ PaddyAspell 10 54
(Lynn Siddall) *a towards rr* **9/1**

3020 **9** *hd* **Savannah Beau**39 5930 5-9-0 **68**........(v) PhillipMakin 12 53
(Derek Shaw) *dwlt and swtchd rt s to inner rail: rr: hdwy wl over 1f out: sn rdn and n.d* **20/1**

2312 **10** *shd* **Suwaan (IRE)**7 7055 3-9-3 **72**........ JamesSullivan 8 57
(Ruth Carr) *t.k.h: chsd ldrs: rdn along wl over 1f out: sn wknd* **7/2**2

2060 **11** *½* **Lydia's Place**5 7127 4-9-6 **77**........ CliffordLee(3) 1 60
(Richard Guest) *led: rdn along wl over 1f out: drvn and hdd appr fnl f: sn wknd* **13/2**3

3060 **12** *hd* **Tan**21 6574 3-9-6 **75**........(t) BarryMcHugh 5 58
(Tony Coyle) *chsd ldrs: rdn along 2f out: sn wknd* **40/1**

1m 6.75s (3.25) **Going Correction** +0.55s/f (Yiel)
**WFA** 3 from 4yo+ 1lb **12** Ran SP% **120.8**
Speed ratings (Par 103): **96,94,93,92,92 91,90,86,85,85 84,84**
CSF £239.94 CT £5153.24 TOTE £17.50: £5.20, £3.90, £7.40; EX 244.20 Trifecta £4534.60.
**Owner** R Wardlaw & Partner **Bred** Tom Radley **Trained** Westow, N Yorks

**FOCUS**
A competitive sprint with the winner rated back to his best in the past two years.

## 7269 BET TOTEPLACE AT BETFRED.COM EBF NOVICE STKS 5f
4:35 (4:38) (Class 5) 2-Y-O £3,881 (£1,155; £577; £288) Stalls Low

Form RPR

01 **1** **Elnadim Star (IRE)**34 6085 2-9-4 0........ TomEaves 7 78
(Kevin Ryan) *hld up in rr: smooth hdwy 2f out: rdn to chse ldr ent fnl f: sn drvn: kpt on wl to ld last 50yds* **13/2**3

3233 **2** *½* **Palmer (IRE)**47 5615 2-9-2 72........ GrahamLee 1 74
(Bryan Smart) *cl up on inner: led wl over 1f out and sn rdn: drvn ins fnl f: hdd and no ex last 50yds* **7/1**

03 **3** *1 ¾* **Laubali**14 6826 2-9-2 0........ RichardKingscote 2 68
(Owen Burrows) *trckd ldrs: rdn along whn n.m.r wl over 1f out: chsd ldng pair ins fnl f: no imp towards fin* **7/2**2

00 **4** *4* **Magic Pulse (IRE)**74 4598 2-8-11 0........ ShaneGray 6 48
(Ann Duffield) *towards rr: hdwy on inner 2f out: chsd ldrs and n.m.r over 1f out: rdn and squeezed through ins fnl f: styd on* **50/1**

00 **5** *1 ½* **Cuppacoco**11 6939 2-8-11 0........ JackGarritty 4 43
(Ann Duffield) *slt ld: rdn along and hdd wl over 1f out: sn rdn and cl up tl drvn and wknd appr fnl f* **80/1**

5 **6** *¾* **Loulin**31 6231 2-9-2 0........ DavidNolan 3 45
(David O'Meara) *trckd ldrs on inner: hdwy 2f out: effrt and n.m.r over 1f out: rdn whn sltly hmpd appr fnl f: kpt on same pce* **14/1**

425 **7** *nse* **Albert Street (IRE)**28 6312 2-9-2 71........ PaulMulrennan 5 45
(Michael Dods) *t.k.h: trckd ldrs: n.m.r over 2f out: rdn whn n.m.r wl over 1f out: kpt on towards fin* **8/1**

2 **8** *4 ½* **Angel's Whisper (IRE)**25 6438 2-8-11 0........ JFEgan 8 24
(Jeremy Noseda) *trckd ldng pair: pushed along over 2f out: rdn and n.m.r over 1f out: sn drvn and hld* **2/1**1

5 **9** *3* **Enrolment**22 6559 2-8-11 0........ TonyHamilton 9 13
(Richard Fahey) *chsd ldrs on outer: rdn along 2f out: sn wknd* **8/1**

2 **10** *nse* **Paco Escostar**21 6567 2-8-11 0........ CamHardie 10 13
(Paul Midgley) *dwlt: a towards rr* **16/1**

1m 6.75s (3.25) **Going Correction** +0.55s/f (Yiel) **10** Ran SP% **119.4**
Speed ratings (Par 95): **96,95,92,86,83 82,82,75,70,70**
CSF £52.76 TOTE £7.10: £2.20, £2.30, £1.30; EX 49.40 Trifecta £184.20.
**Owner** Jaber Abdullah **Bred** Mrs M Marnane **Trained** Hambleton, N Yorks

**FOCUS**
A fair novice and a good performance from the penalised winner.

## 7270 COLLECT TOTEPOOL WINNINGS AT BETFRED SHOPS APPRENTICE CLASSIFIED STKS (RACING EXCELLENCE) (DIV I) 1m 100y
5:05 (5:08) (Class 6) 3-Y-O+ £2,587 (£770; £384; £192) Stalls Low

Form RPR

6320 **1** **John Caesar (IRE)**37 5997 6-9-7 53........(tp) BenRobinson 4 56
(Rebecca Bastiman) *trckd ldrs: hdwy 3f out: sn chsng ldr: rdn over 1f out: drvn to chal ins fnl f: rdn on wl to ld last 75yds* **7/2**2

004 **2** *1* **Cosmic Dust**37 6003 4-9-7 45........ WilliamCox 8 54
(Richard Whitaker) *led: rdn along wl over 1f out: drvn ins fnl f: hdd last 75yds: no ex* **25/1**

**3** *1 ¼* **Lucky Ellen (IRE)**158 1806 3-9-3 51........ PatrickVaughan 5 51
(Jennie Candlish) *dwlt and towards rr: hdwy 3f out: chsd ldrs wl over 1f out: sn rdn: drvn and kpt on fnl f* **11/4**1

4545 **4** *1* **Hellomoto**21 6594 3-9-3 55........(p) CameronNoble 7 49
(Kevin Ryan) *towards rr: hdwy 3f out: rdn along over 2f out: chsd ldrs over 1f out: sn drvn and kpt on same pce* **9/2**3

0045 **5** *2* **Little Pippin**27 6346 4-9-2 43........ SebastianWoods(5) 1 44
(Tony Coyle) *towards rr: hdwy 1/2-way: in tch over 2f out: rdn wl over 1f out: one pce* **9/1**

53-0 **6** *½* **Dream Revival**12 6903 4-9-7 52........ JamieGormley 3 43
(Paul Collins) *chsd ldrs: hdwy 3f out: rdn over 2f out: drvn over 1f out: grad wknd* **66/1**

0065 **7** *1 ¼* **King Kevin**95 3819 3-9-3 51........ CallumRodriguez 10 41
(Ed Dunlop) *nvr bttr than midfield* **5/1**

0500 **8** *8* **Pindaric**41 5831 3-9-3 50........ ConnorMurtagh 9 23
(Alan Lockwood) *trckd ldng pair: hdwy and cl up 3f out: rdn along over 2f out: sn drvn and wknd* **12/1**

600 **9** *1 ½* **Silk Mill Blue**59 5182 3-9-3 51........(p1) NatalieHambling 6 20
(Richard Whitaker) *a in rr* **16/1**

00-5 **10** *12* **Rebel Flame**243 331 3-9-3 55........ ManuelFernandes 2
(John Weymes) *cl up on inner: pushed along over 3f out: rdn wl over 2f out: sn wknd* **20/1**

1m 52.42s (4.82) **Going Correction** +0.55s/f (Yiel)
**WFA** 3 from 4yo+ 4lb **10** Ran SP% **117.4**
Speed ratings (Par 101): **97,96,94,93,91 91,90,82,80,68**
CSF £90.21 TOTE £3.50: £1.40, £5.40, £1.50; EX 63.10 Trifecta £343.30.
**Owner** Mrs K Hall & Mrs P Bastiman **Bred** Polish Belle Partnership **Trained** Cowthorpe, N Yorks

**FOCUS**
It paid to race prominently and it was the quicker of the two divisions by 0.69sec. The race makes sense around the winner on this year's form.

## 7271 COLLECT TOTEPOOL WINNINGS AT BETFRED SHOPS APPRENTICE CLASSIFIED STKS (RACING EXCELLENCE) (DIV II) 1m 100y
5:35 (5:36) (Class 6) 3-Y-O+ £2,587 (£770; £384; £192) Stalls Low

Form RPR

4200 **1** **Broughtons Story**23 6518 3-8-12 52........ JackOsborn(5) 1 56
(Henry Spiller) *hld up in tch: hdwy on inner over 2f out: effrt and n.m.r over 1f out: sn rdn to chal: squeezed through to ld last 75yds* **6/1**

0353 **2** *nk* **Kulgri**26 6381 3-9-3 50........ CallumRodriguez 2 55
(Kevin Ryan) *led: pushed along over 2f out: rdn over 1f out: drvn ins fnl f: hdd last 75yds* **8/1**

2200 **3** *1 ¼* **Catastrophe**22 6549 4-9-7 55........ WilliamCox 7 53
(John Quinn) *trckd ldrs: hdwy over 2f out: rdn on outer to chse ldng pair ent fnl f: sn drvn and kpt on* **5/1**3

0264 **4** *1 ½* **Rebel State (IRE)**34 6092 4-9-4 54........(p) HarrisonShaw(3) 10 49
(Jedd O'Keeffe) *hld up in rr: hdwy 2f out: rdn to chse ldrs on inner over 1f out: kpt on same pce* **7/2**1

0624 **5** *3 ¾* **Pitch High (IRE)**27 6341 3-9-3 52........ MillyNaseb 6 41
(Julia Feilden) *trckd ldr: pushed along over 2f out: rdn wl over 1f out: sn drvn and wknd* **4/1**2

3340 **6** *½* **Siyahamba (IRE)**36 6048 3-8-10 50........ HarryRussell(7) 4 40
(Bryan Smart) *towards rr: hdwy to chse ldrs over 3f out: rdn along over 2f out: sn btn* **16/1**

0604 **7** *shd* **Pontecarlo Boy**24 6471 3-9-3 43........(p) ConnorMurtagh 5 40
(Richard Whitaker) *prom on inner: pushed along 3f out: rdn over 2f out: sn drvn and wknd over 1f out* **16/1**

00-5 **8** *14* **Jackman**125 2758 3-9-3 44........ GerO'Neill 8 9
(Lee James) *dwlt: a in rr* **50/1**

0510 **P** **Euro Mac**22 6549 5-9-7 51........ JaneElliott 9
(Neville Bycroft) *prom: cl up 3f out: lost action and p.u over 2f out* **4/1**2

1m 53.11s (5.51) **Going Correction** +0.55s/f (Yiel)
**WFA** 3 from 4yo+ 4lb **9** Ran SP% **118.0**
Speed ratings (Par 101): **94,93,92,90,87 86,86,72,**
CSF £54.24 TOTE £4.10: £2.30, £2.00, £1.80; EX 47.00 Trifecta £196.20.
**Owner** Broughton Thermal Insulation **Bred** M E Broughton **Trained** Newmarket, Suffolk

**FOCUS**
The slower of the two divisions by 0.69sec and once again bagging the far rail proved crucial.
T/Jkpt: Not Won. T/Plt: £262.90 to a £1 stake. Pool: £58,368.74 - 162.06 winning units T/Qpdt: £116.60 to a £1 stake. Pool: £4,651.82 - 29.52 winning units **Joe Rowntree**

# 7126 SANDOWN (R-H)
Wednesday, September 20

**OFFICIAL GOING: Good (good to soft in places; rnd 7.0; spr 6.8)**
Wind: Nil Weather: White cloud

## 7272 QUARRY STREET CAPITAL SUPPORTS RACEHORSE REHABILITATION H'CAP (JC GRASSROOTS FLAT SPRINT SERIES) 5f 10y
1:30 (1:30) (Class 5) (0-75,77) 3-Y-O+ £3,881 (£1,155; £577; £288) Stalls High

Form RPR

0221 **1** **Operative**24 6478 4-9-6 **74**........ AdamKirby 3 83
(Ed de Giles) *lw: sltly missed break: hld up in mid-div between horses: shkn up and prog gng wl 2f out: rdn between horses over 1f out: led jst ins fnl f: drvn and kpt on wl fnl 100yds* **7/2**2

-130 **2** *¾* **African Friend (IRE)**12 6874 4-9-7 **75**........ FergusSweeney 4 81
(Henry Candy) *sluggish s: hld up in rr of pack: shkn up wl over 1f out and prog: swtchd lft and rdn over 1f out: led in centre ent fnl f: hdd jst ins fnl f: kpt on but a hld* **11/4**1

5642 **3** *2 ¾* **Taajub (IRE)**5 7127 10-8-11 **68**........(b) HectorCrouch(3) 8 64
(Peter Crate) *walked to post: cl up on outer: niggled along by 1/2-way: drifted lft wl over 1f out: kpt on hold 3rd* **8/1**

0640 **4** *1 ¼* **Mad Endeavour**20 6635 6-8-4 **61**........(b) DavidEgan(3) 6 53
(Stuart Kittow) *cl up w ldr: shkn up over 2f out: rdn over 1f out: kpt on one pce ins fnl f* **12/1**

-211 **5** *shd* **Piazon**189 1206 6-9-2 **77**........(tp1) DarraghKeenan(7) 5 69
(John Butler) *wnt to post early: led early: pressed fr 1/2-way: rdn 2f out: hdd over 1f out: no ex ins fnl f* **20/1**

014 **6** *¾* **Look Surprised**20 6612 4-8-9 **68**........ MitchGodwin(5) 1 57
(Roger Teal) *hld up bhd ldrs: prog and rdn 2f out: led over 1f out: hdd ent fnl f: no ex sn after* **10/1**

4634 **7** *2 ½* **Coastal Cyclone**5 7127 3-9-1 **70**........(b) OisinMurphy 9 50
(Harry Dunlop) *bhd ldrs: rdn wl over 1f out: nt qckn and kpt on one pce* **13/2**3

0332 **8** *6* **Little Miss Daisy**26 6372 3-8-8 **63**........ MartinDwyer 7 21
(William Muir) *blindfold removed late and completely missed break: a in rr* **12/1**

5366 **9** *6* **Artscape**15 6780 5-9-2 **70**........(p1) RobertWinston 2 7
(Dean Ivory) *lw: early spd and disp ld on farside rail: niggled along to hold pl at 1/2-way: wknd qckly wl over 2f out: no ex wl over 1f out and eased* **8/1**

1m 2.41s (0.81) **Going Correction** +0.25s/f (Good)
**WFA** 3 from 4yo+ 1lb **9** Ran SP% **113.7**
Speed ratings (Par 103): **103,101,97,95,95 94,90,80,70**
CSF £13.31 CT £70.06 TOTE £4.00: £1.20, £1.30, £2.20; EX 14.60 Trifecta £84.10.
**Owner** Gwyn & Samantha Powell & Partner **Bred** Whitsbury Manor Stud **Trained** Ledbury, H'fords

**FOCUS**
All distances as advertised. Following the opener Fergus Sweeney and Martin Dwyer described the ground as "soft", although others felt it wasn't quite as bad. The winner has been rated to his best.

## 7273 GG.CO.UK SUPPORTS THE RACEHORSE SANCTUARY EBF NOVICE STKS — 1m

**2:00** (2:00) (Class 5) 2-Y-O — **£3,881** (£1,155; £577; £288) **Stalls** Low

Form — RPR

42 **1** **Kitaabaat**[26] 6374 2-9-2 0 ... JimCrowley 4 — 85+
(Owen Burrows) *cl up bhd ldrs: swtchd to outer ent 2f out: upsides whn shkn up and led 2f out: sn rdn: qcknd up wl and 3 l ld ent fnl f: idled fnl 150yds w runner-up clsng qckly: drvn out to hold on* **9/4**[1]

**2** 3/4 **Sevenna Star (IRE)** 2-9-2 0 ... RobertTart 3 — 83+
(John Gosden) *tall: hld up in rr-div on rail: shkn up and gd prog on rail wl over 1f out: swtchd out lft ent fnl f: plenty to do whn picked up wl and began to cl on wnr wl ins fnl f: nrst fin* **7/1**

0 **3** 3 1/2 **Delsheer (FR)**[19] 6653 2-9-2 0 ... FrankieDettori 2 — 75
(Hugo Palmer) *chsd ldr on inner: upsides whn rdn 2f out: sn lft bhd by wnr: kpt on one pce ins fnl f to hold 3rd: no match for ldng pair* **11/1**

33 **4** hd **Adams Park**[26] 6374 2-8-13 0 ... DavidEgan(3) 9 — 75
(Roger Varian) *lw: squeezed up s: mid-div and wdst of all early: taken bk to inner and bhd ldrs after 3f: led over 2f out: sn rdn: kpt on one pce tl hdd 2f out: no ex after and plugged on in dual for 3rd fnl f* **5/1**[3]

6 **5** 2 1/4 **Falcon Eye (IRE)**[68] 4860 2-9-2 0 ... AdamKirby 10 — 70
(Charlie Appleby) *mid-div on outer tl carried lft by rival after 1f and wnt v wd: rdn over 2f out: one pce after* **7/2**[2]

**6** 3/4 **Birthright** 2-9-2 0 ... SeanLevey 1 — 68+
(Richard Hannon) *str: settled on rail in mid-div: rdn over 2f out: no imp over 1f out: kpt on one pce under hands and heels ins fnl f* **50/1**

**7** 1 1/2 **Unbridled Spirit** 2-9-2 0 ... OisinMurphy 6 — 64
(Andrew Balding) *w'like: mid-div bhd ldrs whn spooked and veered lft after 1f hampering rivals: rdn over 1f out: kpt on one pce* **33/1**

44 **8** 1 3/4 **Homerton**[33] 6142 2-9-2 0 ... TomQueally 12 — 60
(Robyn Brisland) *chsd ldrs: led 3f out: hdd over 2f out: sn no ex and wknd* **20/1**

**9** 2 1/2 **First Eleven** 2-9-2 0 ... KieranShoemark 5 — 55+
(John Gosden) *str: gd-bodied: bit bkwd: missed break by several l and detached in rr: grad reduced gap and in rr of pack 4f out: shkn up over 3f out: no imp over 2f: pushed out after* **5/1**[3]

0 **10** 2 3/4 **Newborough**[26] 6403 2-8-13 0 ... CallumShepherd(3) 7 — 48
(Charles Hills) *mid-div early: cannoned into by rival after 1f and wnt lft: in rr-div: shkn up over 2f out: rdn 2f out: sn no ex* **66/1**

0 **11** 3 1/2 **Global Angel**[8] 7026 2-9-2 0 ... JimmyQuinn 11 — 40
(Ed Dunlop) *w'like: in rr: niggled along fr over 3f out: no prog after* **100/1**

000 **12** 9 **The Naughty Step (IRE)**[23] 6510 2-8-11 48 ...(p[1]) PaddyBradley(5) 13 — 20
(Jim Boyle) *sn led: hdd over 3f out: wknd qckly after* **100/1**

1m 45.61s (2.31) **Going Correction** +0.175s/f (Good) — 12 Ran SP% **120.3**
Speed ratings (Par 95): **95,94,90,90,88 87,86,84,81,79 75,66**
CSF £18.47 TOTE £2.80: £1.20, £2.20, £3.00; EX 20.10 Trifecta £176.00.
**Owner** Hamdan Al Maktoum **Bred** Shadwell Estate Company Limited **Trained** Lambourn, Berks

**FOCUS**
A useful novice, with the first pair clear, and it's a race that should produce plenty of winners.

## 7274 MAX PATEL WEALTH MANAGER OF CHOICE CONDITIONS STKS (PLUS 10 RACE) — 7f

**2:35** (2:35) (Class 3) 2-Y-O — **£7,470** (£2,236; £1,118; £559) **Stalls** Low

Form — RPR

0 **1** **Wafy (IRE)**[40] 5887 2-8-12 0 ... JimCrowley 4 — 92+
(Charles Hills) *str: wnt lft s: racd in 3rd bhd 2nd: rdn along over 2f out: swtchd wdst over 1f out: led wl ins fnl f: in control cl home and gng on at fin* **13/2**[3]

1 **2** 1 1/2 **Il Primo Sole**[34] 6108 2-9-1 0 ... FrankieDettori 3 — 91
(John Gosden) *athletic: str: lw: wnt lft s: hld up bhd ldr and plld hrd at times: shkn up over 2f out to keep tabs w ldr: led jst ins fnl f: hdd wl ins fnl f: kpt on but no match for wnr* **4/7**[1]

1 **3** 3/4 **Last Voyage (USA)**[128] 2691 2-9-3 0 ... AdamKirby 1 — 91
(Charlie Appleby) *str: wnt sltly lft s and sn led: clr ld at 1/2-way: shkn up to increase pce over 2f out: rdn 2f out: hdd jst ins fnl f: kpt on tl no ex and wknd fnl 100yds* **7/2**[2]

21 **4** 5 **Ragstone Road (IRE)**[14] 6826 2-8-12 0 ... ShaneKelly 5 — 73
(Richard Hughes) *t.k.h gng to post: wnt markedly lft s: sn hld up in rr and t.k.h: rdn over 2f out: no ex by over 1f out and kpt on one pce* **11/1**

1m 30.76s (1.26) **Going Correction** +0.175s/f (Good) — 4 Ran SP% **107.5**
Speed ratings (Par 99): **99,97,96,90**
CSF £10.99 TOTE £8.80; EX 12.90 Trifecta £23.60.
**Owner** Hamdan Al Maktoum **Bred** Shadwell Estate Company Limited **Trained** Lambourn, Berks

**FOCUS**
An ordinary conditions race in terms of depth and it may not have taken too much winning with excuses for the beaten runners, but nonetheless a nice performance from the improved winner.

## 7275 RACEHORSE SANCTUARY FORTUNE STKS (LISTED RACE) — 1m

**3:05** (3:05) (Class 1) 3-Y-O+

**£20,982** (£7,955; £3,981; £1,983; £995; £499) **Stalls** Low

Form — RPR

1510 **1** **Khafoo Shememi (IRE)**[95] 3843 3-9-3 107 ... SeanLevey 5 — 111
(Richard Hannon) *lw: cl up bhd ldrs: rdn and led 1f out: kpt on wl cl home* **14/1**

2004 **2** 3/4 **Hors De Combat**[74] 4636 6-9-4 101 ... TomQueally 10 — 106
(Denis Coakley) *hld up in rr on outer: shkn up 2f out and smooth prog on outer over 1f out: rdn and ev ch fnl f: kpt on tl no ex nr fin but stuck on to take 2nd fnl strides* **16/1**

0240 **3** nk **Larchmont Lad (IRE)**[39] 5925 3-9-0 105 ... DanielTudhope 9 — 105
(David O'Meara) *chsd ldr on outer: rdn wl over 1f out and pressed ldr: wnr wnt by 1f out: kpt on tl lost 2nd fnl strides* **8/1**[3]

001 **4** hd **Naval Warfare (IRE)**[39] 5943 3-9-0 98 ... OisinMurphy 4 — 105
(Andrew Balding) *lw: sn led: rdn wl over 2f out: hdd 1f out: fought on wl ins fnl f but nt gng pce for plcd horses* **9/1**

-123 **5** 1/2 **Laidback Romeo (IRE)**[23] 6520 5-9-4 97 ... AdamKirby 7 — 104
(Clive Cox) *stmbld sltly leaving stalls: hld up in rr: rdn 2f out: no ex wl ins fnl f* **11/2**[2]

0313 **6** 1 1/4 **D'bai (IRE)**[11] 6963 3-9-0 111 ...(b) JimCrowley 6 — 101
(Charlie Appleby) *in rr-div and covered up between horses: shkn up and gng wl fr over 1f out: n.m.r and nvr really lened: eased wl ins fnl f: can do bttr* **7/4**[1]

2050 **7** 1/2 **Escobar (IRE)**[26] 6401 3-9-0 102 ...(tp[1]) FrankieDettori 1 — 100
(Hugo Palmer) *mid-div on rail: rdn over 2f out: no ex ent fnl f* **12/1**

0100 **8** 1/2 **Murad Khan (FR)**[36] 6024 4-9-4 102 ...(h) JackMitchell 8 — 99
(Hugo Palmer) *in rr-div on outer: rdn wl over 2f out: no prog fr over 1f out* **14/1**

6-05 **9** 4 1/2 **Richard Pankhurst**[25] 6420 5-9-4 110 ...(v[1]) KieranShoemark 2 — 88
(John Gosden) *swtg: hld up in last on rail: rdn 2f out and no rspnse: shuffled along fr 1f out* **9/1**

0600 **10** 3 1/4 **Kool Kompany (IRE)**[17] 6746 5-9-7 106 ... TomMarquand 3 — 84
(Richard Hannon) *bhd ldr on inner: rdn along wl over 2f out: began to weaken over 1f out: sn no ex and eased fnl f* **20/1**

1m 43.65s (0.35) **Going Correction** +0.175s/f (Good)
**WFA** 3 from 4yo+ 4lb — 10 Ran SP% **114.5**
Speed ratings (Par 111): **105,104,103,103,103 102,101,101,96,93**
CSF £212.37 TOTE £16.00: £3.70, £6.00, £2.90; EX 291.30 Trifecta £4158.00.
**Owner** Saeed Suhail **Bred** Mrs M McWey **Trained** East Everleigh, Wilts

**FOCUS**
A competitive-looking Listed race, 3yos filled three of the first four places with two of the outsiders coming to the fore. The race has been rated around the fifth.

## 7276 JACK PENNINGTON MEMORIAL FILLIES' H'CAP — 1m

**3:40** (3:40) (Class 4) (0-85,86) 3-Y-O — **£5,822** (£1,732; £865; £432) **Stalls** Low

Form — RPR

3012 **1** **UAE Queen**[30] 6274 3-8-13 77 ... JackMitchell 9 — 86+
(Roger Varian) *hld up in rr-div: rdn wl over 1f out and gd prog: 4th ent fnl f: kpt on wl last 110yds between horses to ld nr fin* **14/1**

3114 **2** 1/2 **Finale**[42] 5789 3-8-12 76 ... RobertWinston 8 — 84
(Hughie Morrison) *t.k.h in mid-div on outer: shkn up and prog over 2f out: rdn and led wl over 1f out: kpt on wl tl hdd nr fin* **14/1**

01 **3** shd **Clearly**[14] 6817 3-8-13 77 ... KieranShoemark 10 — 85+
(John Gosden) *str: stood stl in stalls: completely missed break: detached in rr tl tacked on to rr of gp over 3f out: shkn up over 2f out and swtchd to outer: rdn wl over 1f out: edgd rt and gd hdwy: ev ch 1f out: no ex nr fin* **10/1**

2101 **4** 1/2 **Jalela**[12] 6882 3-9-1 86 ... RossaRyan(7) 11 — 93
(Richard Hannon) *in rr-div on outer: rdn wl over 1f out and prog on outer: pressed ldr over 1f out: no ex nr fin and lost two pls* **9/1**

3-1 **5** 1 1/2 **Dynamic**[26] 6390 3-9-2 80 ... OisinMurphy 2 — 87+
(William Haggas) *lw: in mid-div between horses: gng wl whn shkn up to make prog wl over 1f out: hmpd whn rival c across sn after: plenty to do ent fnl f: shuffled along after* **2/1**[1]

4101 **6** 1 1/2 **Al Nafoorah**[18] 6700 3-9-4 82 ... AdamKirby 6 — 82
(Ed Dunlop) *hld up in rr on inner: shkn up and n.m.r on inner over 1f out: in clr 1f out: shuffled along after* **5/1**[2]

6406 **7** 2 **Darkroom Angel**[41] 5822 3-8-8 75 ... HectorCrouch(3) 5 — 70
(Philip Hide) *chsd ldrs: rdn along wl over 2f out: sn lost pl: plugged on after* **33/1**

3054 **8** 2 3/4 **Flying North**[26] 6377 3-9-3 81 ... TimmyMurphy 4 — 70
(Richard Hannon) *bhd ldrs on rail: rdn over 2f out: edgd rt and hmpd rival: one pce fr over 1f out* **25/1**

5-00 **9** 3 1/4 **Assanilka (FR)**[119] 2978 3-9-7 85 ...(p[1]) StevieDonohoe 7 — 66
(Harry Dunlop) *w ldr on outer: rdn wl over 2f out: u.p over 1f out and wandered abt hampering rival: wknd after* **50/1**

111U **10** nse **Madeleine Bond**[19] 6655 3-9-0 83 ... GeorgiaCox(5) 1 — 64
(Henry Candy) *in rr-div on inner: rdn wl over 2f out: sme prog whn squeezed up on rail 2f out: pushed out fr over 1f out* **11/2**[3]

6121 **11** 1 **Kyllachys Tale (IRE)**[30] 6274 3-9-4 82 ... TomMarquand 3 — 61
(Roger Teal) *led and set str pce: rdn over 2f out: swamped wl over 1f out: sn no ex and wknd* **12/1**

1m 44.79s (1.49) **Going Correction** +0.175s/f (Good) — 11 Ran SP% **114.2**
Speed ratings (Par 100): **99,98,98,97,96 94,92,90,86,86 85**
CSF £185.52 CT £1334.33 TOTE £13.60: £4.20, £4.50, £3.30; EX 165.50 Trifecta £1730.60.
**Owner** Sheikh Mohammed Obaid Al Maktoum **Bred** Fittocks Stud **Trained** Newmarket, Suffolk
■ Stewards' Enquiry : Timmy Murphy caution: careless riding

**FOCUS**
A useful fillies' handicap that was run at a good gallop and the closers prospered. It has been rated positively.

## 7277 MOLSON COORS H'CAP (JOCKEY CLUB GRASSROOTS FLAT MIDDLE DISTANCE SERIES QUALIFIER) — 1m 1f 209y

**4:15** (4:15) (Class 4) (0-85,86) 3-Y-O — **£5,822** (£1,732; £865; £432) **Stalls** Low

Form — RPR

0632 **1** **The Statesman**[18] 6671 3-9-3 81 ... JimCrowley 11 — 95
(Ian Williams) *broke wl on outer: sn taken bk and hld up in rr-div on outer: shkn up over 2f out and led wl over 1f out: rdn and kpt on wl whn pressed ins fnl f: a doing enough* **11/4**[1]

0015 **2** 1/2 **Jupiter Light**[74] 4640 3-9-7 85 ... FrankieDettori 2 — 98
(John Gosden) *settled in rr-div: rdn over 2f out: gd prog over 1f out on rail: pressed ldr wl ins fnl f: a being hld* **5/1**[3]

1001 **3** 5 **Mister Blue Sky (IRE)**[19] 6657 3-9-1 84 ... MitchGodwin(5) 4 — 87
(Sylvester Kirk) *sn led and t.k.h: rdn ent 2f out: hdd wl over 1f out: plugged on to hold 3rd ins fnl f* **4/1**[2]

610 **4** 1 1/2 **Lightly Squeeze**[32] 6189 3-9-0 78 ...(p) ShaneKelly 9 — 78
(Philip Hide) *hld up in rr: rdn over 3f out: kpt on past btn horses ins fnl f* **33/1**

046P **5** nk **Rosarno (IRE)**[18] 6701 3-9-0 78 ...(bt) RobertWinston 10 — 77
(Charles Hills) *chsd ldrs on outer: shkn up and prog over 2f out: briefly looked dangerous 2f out: nt qckn and styd on same pce* **14/1**

-163 **6** 4 1/2 **Music Seeker (IRE)**[55] 5323 3-9-6 84 ... RyanTate 7 — 74
(James Eustace) *between horses chsng ldrs: rdn over 2f out: no imp and nudged out ent fnl f* **4/1**[2]

0-25 **7** 6 **Trading Punches (IRE)**[104] 3505 3-9-8 86 ... SeanLevey 3 — 64
(David Brown) *bhd ldrs on inner: rdn 3f out: plugged on fr over 1f out* **11/1**

52-2 **8** 1/2 **Makkadangdang**[140] 2296 3-8-9 73 ... OisinMurphy 8 — 50
(Andrew Balding) *chsd ldr on outer: rdn wl over 2f out: nt qckn and grad wknd fr over 1f out* **9/1**

3510 **9** 13 **War Of Succession**[28] 6322 3-9-1 82 ... EoinWalsh(3) 6 — 33
(Tony Newcombe) *a in rr: pushed along ent st: struggling 3f out: no ex sn after* **100/1**

2m 10.48s (-0.02) **Going Correction** +0.175s/f (Good) — 9 Ran SP% **112.3**
Speed ratings (Par 103): **107,106,102,101,101 97,92,92,81**
CSF £16.02 CT £52.66 TOTE £2.60: £1.10, £1.90, £2.10; EX 18.60 Trifecta £45.30.
**Owner** Randolph & Mortimer Racing **Bred** Barry Walters **Trained** Portway, Worcs

**FOCUS**
A decent little handicap and the form looks solid.

## 7278 ALL NEW RACINGUK.COM FILLIES' H'CAP (DIV I) 1m 1f 209y
4:45 (4:45) (Class 5) (0-70,72) 3-Y-O+ £3,881 (£1,155; £577; £288) Stalls Low

Form RPR

134 **1** **Flood Defence (IRE)**[16] 6766 3-9-1 **66**........................ GeorgeWood(3) 5 73
(Chris Wall) *t.k.h early bhd ldrs: settled bttr after 3f: shkn up and gd prog fr over 2f out: rdn 2f out: upsides ldr ins fnl f tl led nr fin* **4/1**[3]

3206 **2** *nk* **Luminous**[12] 6899 3-9-5 **67**................................................ OisinMurphy 3 73
(Simon Crisford) *led after 1f on inner and dictated ordinary pce: rdn over 2f out: kpt on wl tl pressed by wnr ins fnl f: fought on tl no ex and hdd nr fin* **7/1**

6503 **3** *2* **Beatisa**[34] 6101 3-8-10 **58**............................................... StevieDonohoe 8 60
(Ed Walker) *lw: bhd ldr on inner: rdn over 2f out: kpt on to hold 3rd fr over 1f wout ever threatening front pair* **7/1**

0325 **4** *1* **Precious Angel (IRE)**[19] 6657 3-9-7 **69**............................... PatDobbs 6 69
(Richard Hannon) *led for 1f: settled bhd ldr on outer: rdn over 2f out: kpt on ins fnl f in duel for 3rd tl no ex nr fin* **7/2**[2]

2331 **5** *hd* **Becca Campbell (IRE)**[34] 6095 4-10-1 **72**..............(p) EdwardGreatrex 9 71
(Eve Johnson Houghton) *in rr-div between horses: rdn over 2f out and sme prog in 5th: plugged on ins fnl f* **3/1**[1]

200 **6** *3* **Della Valle (GER)**[51] 5477 4-9-6 **63**................................ AntonioFresu 7 56
(Mike Murphy) *settled in mid-div on outer: rdn over 2f out: one pce fr over 1f out* **20/1**

240 **7** *1 3/4* **Rum Swizzle**[69] 4804 5-10-0 **71**......................................... AdamKirby 10 61
(Harry Dunlop) *in rr-div: rdn over 2f out: no imp on ldrs sn after and pushed out fnl f* **20/1**

5300 **8** *5* **Everlasting Sea**[23] 6509 3-8-9 **57**..................................... MartinDwyer 1 38
(Stuart Kittow) *in rr: rdn over 2f out: nt qcknd and pushed out fr over 1f out* **33/1**

4444 **9** *1/2* **Luna Magic**[28] 6320 3-9-6 **68**........................................... TomQueally 4 48
(Lydia Pearce) *tk fierce hold for first 5f: rdn over 2f out: no ex sn after* **14/1**

2m 14.47s (3.97) **Going Correction** +0.175s/f (Good)
**WFA** 3 from 4yo+ 5lb **9** Ran SP% **111.4**
Speed ratings (Par 100): **91,90,89,88,88 85,84,80,80**
CSF £29.67 CT £182.59 TOTE £6.80: £2.10, £2.30, £2.10; EX 34.00 Trifecta £169.60.
**Owner** Horsetrader One **Bred** Mcr Bloodstock Ltd **Trained** Newmarket, Suffolk

**FOCUS**
Little pace on here and it paid to race handily. The form has been rated cautiously.

## 7279 ALL NEW RACINGUK.COM FILLIES' H'CAP (DIV II) 1m 1f 209y
5:15 (5:16) (Class 5) (0-70,72) 3-Y-O+ £3,881 (£1,155; £577; £288) Stalls Low

Form RPR

2060 **1** **Delirium (IRE)**[14] 6818 3-7-13 **51**...............................(p) DavidEgan(3) 8 59
(Ed de Giles) *hld up in mid-div between horses: briefly shkn up over 3f out: rdn over 2f out and no immediate prog: prog ent fnl f between horses: wnt to rail ins fnl f and kpt on wl to ld nr fin* **16/1**

5060 **2** *1/2* **Shimmering Light**[44] 5721 3-9-5 **68**..........................(v[1]) DanielTudhope 9 74
(Michael Bell) *hld up in rr on outer: smooth prog wdst of all over 2f out: rdn wl over 1f out and sn led: kpt on wl ins fnl f tl hdd nr fin* **16/1**

3145 **3** *1* **Millie's Kiss**[17] 6722 3-8-12 **68**...................................... RossaRyan(7) 5 72
(Philip McBride) *hld up in rr: briefly niggled along over 4f out: rdn over 2f out on outer: kpt on wl and ev ch ins fnl f: run petered out and nt pce of front two fnl 110yds* **13/2**

0241 **4** *3 1/4* **Bradfield Magic (IRE)**[13] 6847 3-8-9 **61**............. CallumShepherd(3) 10 59
(Charles Hills) *sluggish s: sn mde up grnd and settled bhd ldrs on outer: rdn over 2f out and kpt on: upsides ldr ent fnl f: sn no ex and wknd fnl 110yds* **12/1**

3202 **5** *1 3/4* **Ghinia (IRE)**[40] 5888 6-10-0 **72**........................................ RobHornby 2 65
(Pam Sly) *in rr on inner: shkn up and tk clsr order over 2f out: rdn over 1f out w wkng rival in front: swtchd off rail ins fnl f and plugged on one pce* **5/1**[2]

2-1 **6** *3* **Dubaitwentytwenty**[259] 40 3-9-5 **68**..........................(t[1]) JackMitchell 6 56
(Hugo Palmer) *led tl hdd at 1/2-way: remained cl up: rdn and led wl over 2f out: hdd over 1f out: sn fnd nil and pushed out fnl f* **5/1**[2]

544 **7** *1 1/2* **Ancient Longing**[15] 6775 3-9-5 **68**.............................. KieranShoemark 3 56
(Roger Charlton) *mid-div on inner: pushed along bhd ldr jst over 2f out: lft bhd ent fnl f: no ex and sn eased* **5/2**[1]

0522 **8** *hd* **Line Of Beauty**[13] 6852 3-9-7 **70**........................................ OisinMurphy 7 55
(Simon Crisford) *lw: bhd ldr between horses: urged along over 2f out: fnd nil: sn lft bhd and pushed out fr over 1f out* **6/1**[3]

0504 **9** *15* **Doodle Dandy (IRE)**[25] 6439 4-8-8 **52**................................ RyanPowell 4 6
(David Bridgwater) *t.k.h bhd ldr: plld way to front at 1/2-way: niggled along and hdd wl over 2f out: wknd qckly sn after: eased fnl 100yds* **20/1**

2m 13.13s (2.63) **Going Correction** +0.175s/f (Good)
**WFA** 3 from 4yo+ 5lb **9** Ran SP% **113.7**
Speed ratings (Par 100): **96,95,94,92,90 88,87,87,75**
CSF £237.60 CT £1827.88 TOTE £18.70: £3.70, £4.80, £2.50; EX 398.80 Trifecta £992.90.
**Owner** Mrs Samantha Powell **Bred** Old Carhue Stud **Trained** Ledbury, H'fords

**FOCUS**
The weaker of the two divisions, they didn't appear to go more than a fair gallop, but the closers dominated. The winner has been rated back to her best.
T/Plt: £1,382.80 to a £1 stake. Pool: £73,252.67 - 38.67 winning units T/Qpdt: £397.80 to a £1 stake. Pool: £4,462.40 - 8.30 winning units **Cathal Gahan**

# 7250 YARMOUTH (L-H)
Wednesday, September 20

**OFFICIAL GOING: Soft (good to soft in places) changing to good to soft (soft in places) after race 6 (4.55)**
Wind: light, behind Weather: fine

## 7280 HOBGOBLIN LEGENDARY RUBY ALE / EBF MAIDEN STKS (PLUS 10 RACE) (DIV I) 7f 3y
2:10 (2:13) (Class 4) 2-Y-O £4,528 (£1,347; £673; £336) Stalls Centre

Form RPR

**1** **Imperial Past** 2-9-5 0...............................................(t[1]) ColmO'Donoghue 7 73+
(Charlie Appleby) *pressed ldr tl pushed into ld over 1f out: rdn and kpt on wl ins fnl f: rdn out* **5/2**[1]

**2** *3/4* **Prime Minister (IRE)** 2-9-5 0.............................................. HarryBentley 5 71+
(Ed Vaughan) *hld up wl in tch in midfield: effrt to chse ldrs whn rn green and edgd lft over 1f out: kpt on same pce ins fnl f: wnt 2nd last stride* **9/2**[3]

**3** *shd* **Taghee** 2-9-2 0.......................................................... MarcMonaghan(3) 12 71+
(Marco Botti) *trckd ldrs: effrt and ev ch over 1f out: kpt on same pce ins fnl f: lost 2nd last stride* **20/1**

**4** *1/2* **Herdwick** 2-9-5 0.............................................................. RyanMoore 8 70
(Sir Michael Stoute) *trckd ldrs: effrt over 1f out: rdn ins fnl f: kpt on same pce fnl 100yds* **9/2**[3]

**5** *nk* **Tamkeen** 2-9-5 0................................................................ DaneO'Neill 9 69
(Owen Burrows) *dwlt: sn in tch in midfield: effrt 2f out: hdwy u.p to chse ldrs 1f out: kpt on same pce ins fnl f* **4/1**[2]

**6** *nk* **Mr Gent (IRE)** 2-9-5 0........................................................ PJMcDonald 3 68+
(Ed Dunlop) *hld up in tch in midfield: effrt over 1f out: trying to switch rt but hung lft 1f out: hdwy ins fnl f: kpt on fnl 75yds: nt clr run nr fin* **16/1**

0 **7** *4* **Arigato**[14] 6826 2-9-5 0...................................................... MartinLane 11 58
(William Jarvis) *led and set stdy gallop: rdn and hdd over 1f out: sn outpcd and wknd ins fnl f* **66/1**

**8** *1 1/2* **Archibald Leitch** 2-9-5 0...................................................... FranBerry 4 54
(David Evans) *dwlt: hld up in tch in last trio: pushed along ent fnl 2f: no imp and hung lft over 1f out: wl hld and one pced fnl f* **33/1**

**9** *10* **Timoshenko** 2-9-5 0............................................................ LukeMorris 1 29
(Sir Mark Prescott Bt) *a towards rr and sn rousted along: wknd 2f out* **25/1**

**10** *hd* **Saint Anthony** 2-9-5 0........................................................ JoeyHaynes 2 29
(Mark H Tompkins) *a rr: nt clr run and hmpd over 2f out: sn wknd* **66/1**

**11** *10* **Equo** 2-9-5 0.................................................................. AdamBeschizza 10 4
(Chris Wall) *stdd after s: in tch in midfield: rdn and lost pl over 2f out: wl bhd and eased ins fnl f* **28/1**

1m 30.68s (4.08) **Going Correction** +0.20s/f (Good) **11** Ran SP% **108.8**
Speed ratings (Par 97): **84,83,83,82,82 81,77,75,64,63 52**
CSF £10.96 TOTE £3.20: £1.40, £1.50, £4.90; EX 13.40 Trifecta £172.10.
**Owner** Godolphin **Bred** Godolphin **Trained** Newmarket, Suffolk
■ Jawan was withdrawn. Price at time of withdrawal 11-1. Rule 4 applies to all bets - deduction 5p in the pound.

**FOCUS**
Going changed to soft, good to soft in places before racing. The only runner with previous experience hadn't shown much and with six finishing close up, this might not be form to get too carried away with.

## 7281 HOBGOBLIN LEGENDARY RUBY ALE / EBF MAIDEN STKS (PLUS 10 RACE) (DIV II) 7f 3y
2:45 (2:46) (Class 4) 2-Y-O £4,528 (£1,347; £673; £336) Stalls Centre

Form RPR

**1** **Regal Reality** 2-9-5 0........................................................ RyanMoore 4 76
(Sir Michael Stoute) *mde all: rdn 2f out: fnd ex over 1f out: kpt on wl u.p whn pressed ins fnl f: rdn out* **9/4**[2]

**2** *1/2* **Rich Identity** 2-9-5 0........................................................ AndreaAtzeni 7 75
(Roger Varian) *dwlt: sn in tch in midfield: clsd to chsd ldrs over 1f out: swtchd lft and chsd wnr 1f out: str chal ins fnl f: kpt on wl but a hld* **11/2**[3]

3 **3** *2 1/4* **Dream Warrior**[11] 6921 2-9-5 0...................................... ColmO'Donoghue 2 69
(Charlie Appleby) *t.k.h: pressed wnr: rdn wl over 1f out: lost 2nd and unable qck u.p 1f out: outpcd but hld on to 3rd ins fnl f* **1/1**[1]

**4** *nk* **Grandscape** 2-9-5 0........................................................ PJMcDonald 8 68
(Ed Dunlop) *hld up in tch in midfield: effrt over 1f out: chsd ldrs 1f out: kpt on same pce and no imp ins fnl f* **33/1**

44 **5** *2* **Bajan Gold (IRE)**[26] 6367 2-9-5 0..................................... AdamBeschizza 3 63
(Stuart Williams) *stdd s: hld up in tch in rr: pushed along and swtchd lft 1f out: hdwy and kpt on wl ins fnl f: no threat to ldrs* **20/1**

**6** *shd* **Sheriff** 2-9-5 0.................................................................. LouisSteward 10 63
(Michael Bell) *hld up in tch towards rr: effrt 2f out: hdwy into midfield over 1f out: kpt on but no threat to ldrs ins fnl f* **25/1**

**7** *shd* **Comporta** 2-9-5 0........................................................ SilvestreDeSousa 9 63
(Ismail Mohammed) *hld up in tch in midfield: rdn and unable qck over 1f out: hld and kpt on same ins fnl f* **16/1**

**8** *hd* **Launceston Place (FR)** 2-9-5 0........................................... TedDurcan 5 62
(Henry Spiller) *trckd ldng pair: rdn and ev ch over 1f out tl outpcd and btn 1f out: wknd ins fnl f* **50/1**

**9** *1 3/4* **Go Fox** 2-9-5 0................................................................ PatCosgrave 6 58
(Tom Clover) *t.k.h: wl in tch in midfield: rdn 2f out: unable qck over 1f out: wknd ins fnl f* **66/1**

0 **10** *1/2* **Roof Garden**[13] 6844 2-9-5 0.............................................. JoeyHaynes 1 57
(Mark H Tompkins) *wl in tch in midfield: rdn over 2f out: outpcd and lost pl over 1f out: wknd ins fnl f* **100/1**

**11** *10* **Twister (IRE)** 2-9-5 0........................................................ LukeMorris 11 32
(Sir Mark Prescott Bt) *a rr and sn rousted along: wknd 2f out* **33/1**

1m 30.74s (4.14) **Going Correction** +0.20s/f (Good) **11** Ran SP% **121.0**
Speed ratings (Par 97): **84,83,80,80,78 78,78,77,75,75 63**
CSF £14.65 TOTE £3.30: £1.20, £1.70, £1.02; EX 16.10 Trifecta £30.10.
**Owner** Cheveley Park Stud **Bred** Cheveley Park Stud Ltd **Trained** Newmarket, Suffolk

**FOCUS**
This looked the stronger of the two divisions and the front pair both have plenty to recommend them.

## 7282 DANNY AND PEGGY WRIGHT MEMORIAL FILLIES' H'CAP 6f 3y
3:15 (3:16) (Class 5) (0-75,75) 3-Y-O+ £3,234 (£962; £481; £240) Stalls Centre

Form RPR

0633 **1** **Fortitude (IRE)**[33] 6149 3-9-7 **74**................................ JosephineGordon 3 82
(Hugo Palmer) *dwlt: t.k.h: sn rcvrd and hld up in tch in midfield: trckd ldrs travelling strly 2f out: rdn to ld 1f out: sn in command and r.o wl: comf* **3/1**[2]

543 **2** *2* **Dream Start**[13] 6850 3-8-6 **59**..................................(t) SilvestreDeSousa 2 61
(John Ryan) *chsd ldrs: rdn over 2f out: led 2f out: sn drvn and hdd 1f out: nt match pce of wnr but hld on for 2nd ins fnl f* **5/2**[1]

6263 **3** *1/2* **Charlie's Dreamer**[8] 7014 3-8-9 **62**.................................... LukeMorris 4 62
(Michael Appleby) *chsd ldr: rdn and ev ch 2f out: nt match pce of wnr and one pced ins fnl f* **10/1**

0023 **4** *1* **Arcanista (IRE)**[14] 6814 4-7-12 **56** oh4.......................(p) NicolaCurrie(7) 9 53
(Chris Dwyer) *t.k.h: hld up in tch: effrt 2f out: hung lft but kpt on ins fnl f: no threat to wnr* **16/1**

3160 **5** *nk* **Sitar**[12] 6877 3-9-4 **71**...................................................... DanielMuscutt 7 67
(James Fanshawe) *stdd after s: t.k.h: hld up in tch in rr: swtchd lft and effrt over 1f out: kpt on ins fnl f: no threat to wnr* **6/1**

0365 **6** *3/4* **Pretty Bubbles**[9] 7000 8-9-10 **75**..........................(v) AlistairRawlinson 1 69
(J R Jenkins) *hld up in tch: hdwy over 2f out: rdn to press ldrs wl over 1f out tl unable qck 1f out: wknd ins fnl f* **33/1**

1420 **7** 2 ¾ **Emily Goldfinch**[19] 6656 4-8-9 60 ........ DannyBrock 6 45
(Phil McEntee) *led tl hdd and rdn 2f out: unable qck and lost pl over 1f out: keeping on same pce and btn whn carried lft jst ins fnl f: wknd fnl 100yds* **10/1**

0222 **8** *hd* **Seyasah (IRE)**[29] 6295 3-9-0 67 ........ TedDurcan 8 51
(Chris Wall) *hld up in tch in last trio: effrt u.p over 1f out: no imp and wl hld 1f out* **5/1**[3]

1m 15.17s (0.77) **Going Correction** +0.20s/f (Good)
**WFA** 3 from 4yo+ 2lb **8 Ran SP% 111.5**
Speed ratings (Par 100): **102,99,98,97,96 95,92,92**
CSF £10.35 CT £61.30 TOTE £3.90: £1.80, £1.10, £2.80; EX 9.90 Trifecta £27.10.
**Owner** Isa Salman **Bred** Epona Bloodstock Ltd **Trained** Newmarket, Suffolk

**FOCUS**
A run-of-the-mill fillies' handicap, but the winner was far too strong for her rivals.

## 7283 EBF STALLIONS JOHN MUSKER FILLIES' STKS (LISTED RACE) 1m 2f 23y
**3:50** (3:51) (Class 1) 3-Y-O+

**£22,488** (£8,560; £4,284; £2,136; £1,072; £540) **Stalls** Low

Form RPR

-452 **1** **Beautiful Morning**[10] 6972 4-9-2 102 ........ ColmO'Donoghue 2 106+
(Mrs John Harrington, Ire) *trckd ldrs and travelled str thrght: led ent fnl 2f: rdn and readily qckn clr over 1f out: in command and r.o wl after: comf* **9/4**[1]

1-20 **2** 2 ½ **Vintage Folly**[80] 4424 3-8-11 102 ........ JosephineGordon 12 101
(Hugo Palmer) *in tch in midfield: effrt jst over 2f out: drvn to chse clr wnr over 1f out: kpt on wl for clr 2nd but no imp on wnr* **12/1**

2102 **3** 2 **High Hopes**[35] 6074 4-9-2 99 ........ JamieSpencer 9 97+
(David Simcock) *hld up in tch in rr: swtchd rt 4f out: effrt and rdn over 1f out: hdwy u.p 1f out: wnt 3rd and hung lft 100yds out: styd on but no threat to wnr* **8/1**

-132 **4** 1 ¼ **Indulged**[33] 6152 4-9-2 94 ........ RyanMoore 10 95
(James Fanshawe) *hld up in last pair: effrt 2f out: hdwy u.p 1f out: styd on to go 4th towards fin: nvr trbld ldrs* **9/2**[3]

1612 **5** ½ **Flood Warning**[123] 2827 3-8-11 94 ........ LukeMorris 7 94
(Clive Cox) *hld up in tch towards rr: hdwy over inner 3f out: drvn to chse ldrs 2f out: sn outpcd: wknd ins fnl f* **8/1**

5212 **6** *hd* **Titi Makfi**[25] 6449 3-8-11 100 ........ PJMcDonald 11 93
(Mark Johnston) *dwlt and bustled along early: rcvrd to chse ldrs after 2f out: rdn to press wnr 2f out: unable to match pce of wnr over 1f out: 3rd and btn 1f out: edgd lft and wknd ins fnl f* **7/2**[2]

6535 **7** 1 **Jelly Monger (IRE)**[34] 6104 5-9-2 85 ........ PatCosgrave 4 91
(Dominic Ffrench Davis) *hld up in tch in midfield: effrt ent fnl 2f: no imp over 1f out and kpt on same pce ins fnl f* **66/1**

3-15 **8** *nk* **Al Mayda (USA)**[33] 6152 3-8-11 77 ........(t[1]) HarryBentley 8 91?
(Hugo Palmer) *taken down early: chsd ldr: rdn and ever ch over 2f out tl outpcd over 1f out: btn whn squeezed for room and wknd ins fnl f* **40/1**

300 **9** 1 ¼ **Somethingthrilling**[11] 6919 5-9-2 90 ........ SilvestreDeSousa 3 88
(David Elsworth) *hld up in tch in midfield: clsd to chse ldrs 2f out: drvn and unable qck over 1f out: wl hld whn sltly short of room and wknd ins fnl f* **40/1**

3130 **10** 1 ¾ **Florenza**[23] 6520 4-9-2 90 ........ TedDurcan 1 85
(Chris Fairhurst) *led tl jst over 2f out: sn rdn and lost pl over 1f out: btn whn squeezed for room and wknd ins fnl f* **80/1**

6414 **11** 1 ½ **Ouja**[27] 6357 3-8-11 95 ........ AndreaAtzeni 5 83
(John Gosden) *hld up in tch towards rr: effrt over 2f out: no imp: bhd over 1f out* **9/1**

2m 9.09s (-1.41) **Going Correction** +0.15s/f (Good)
**WFA** 3 from 4yo+ 5lb **11 Ran SP% 118.7**
Speed ratings (Par 108): **111,109,107,106,106 105,105,104,103,102 101**
CSF £31.63 TOTE £3.20: £1.30, £2.80, £2.40; EX 34.40 Trifecta £244.10.
**Owner** Jon S Kelly **Bred** Newsells Park Stud **Trained** Moone, Co Kildare

**FOCUS**
An up-to-scratch renewal of this Listed event and the winner looked a cut above this grade.

## 7284 PARKLANDS LEISURE HOLIDAY DISTRIBUTORS H'CAP 1m 2f 23y
**4:25** (4:25) (Class 3) (0-90,89) 3-Y-O+ **£7,876** (£2,357; £1,178; £590) **Stalls** Low

Form RPR

0130 **1** **Swiftsure (IRE)**[47] 5598 3-9-1 85 ........ RyanMoore 1 90
(Sir Michael Stoute) *hld up in 3rd: effrt 3f out: chsd clr ldr ent fnl f: drvn and grad clsd over 1f out: led wl ins fnl f: styd on* **2/1**[2]

2163 **2** ½ **Rotherwick (IRE)**[18] 6698 5-9-10 89 ........(t) PJMcDonald 4 92
(Paul Cole) *stdd s: hld up in rr: effrt over 2f out: disputing 2nd bhd clr wnr 2f out: grad clsd u.p and ev ch ins fnl f: kpt on: snatched 2nd on post* **11/8**[1]

1320 **3** *nse* **Faithful Creek (IRE)**[147] 2086 5-9-4 83 ........(p) SilvestreDeSousa 3 86
(Michael Appleby) *led: rdn 3f out: drvn 2f out: hdd wl ins fnl f: kpt on but unable qck towards fin: lost 2nd on post* **9/2**[3]

5-16 **4** 7 **Solo Hunter**[96] 3785 6-9-10 89 ........(b) JosephineGordon 2 78
(Martyn Meade) *dwlt and rousted along early: chsd ldr rdn and dropped to last 2f out: wknd fnl f* **6/1**

2m 11.66s (1.16) **Going Correction** +0.15s/f (Good)
**WFA** 3 from 5yo+ 5lb **4 Ran SP% 107.9**
Speed ratings (Par 107): **101,100,100,94**
CSF £5.12 TOTE £2.30; EX 4.90 Trifecta £5.80.
**Owner** The Queen **Bred** Darley **Trained** Newmarket, Suffolk

**FOCUS**
A disappointing turnout for this 0-90 handicap, but the pace looked solid and it produced a tight finish.

## 7285 SEA-DEER H'CAP 1m 3y
**4:55** (4:56) (Class 4) (0-85,86) 3-Y-O+ **£5,175** (£1,540; £769; £384) **Stalls** Centre

Form RPR

2-1 **1** **Zabeel Prince (IRE)**[83] 4275 4-9-8 86 ........ AndreaAtzeni 6 104+
(Roger Varian) *t.k.h: trckd ldrs tl wnt 2nd 2f out: pushed into ld 1f out: sn readily wnt clr: v easily* **8/11**[1]

6210 **2** 3 ½ **London (FR)**[20] 6617 4-9-2 80 ........(h) JosephineGordon 4 87
(Phil McEntee) *led: rdn 2f out: drvn and hdd 1f out: sn brushed aside by wnr and kpt on same pce for clr 2nd* **20/1**

6506 **3** 3 ¼ **Hawatif (IRE)**[141] 2254 4-9-0 78 ........ DavidProbert 2 78
(Anthony Carson) *stdd s: hld up in last pair: effrt over 2f out: wnt modest 3rd over 1f out: styd on but no ch w wnr* **25/1**

0503 **4** 4 **Eltezam (IRE)**[14] 6809 4-9-5 83 ........ SilvestreDeSousa 3 73
(Amanda Perrett) *restless in stalls: chsd ldr tl 2f out: 3rd and outpcd u.p over 1f out: lost 3rd and wknd ins fnl f* **11/2**[3]

1210 **5** 9 **Honiara**[20] 6617 4-9-7 85 ........(p[1]) PJMcDonald 1 55
(Paul Cole) *stdd s: t.k.h: hld up in tch in last pair: effrt ent fnl 2f: no prog and btn over 1f out: wl btn and eased wl ins fnl f* **9/1**

0116 **6** 42 **Wealth Tax**[27] 6349 4-9-4 82 ........ LukeMorris 5
(Ed Dunlop) *in tch in midfield: rdn over 2f out: sn dropped to rr and lost tch: t.o and virtually p.u ins fnl f* **4/1**[2]

1m 41.83s (1.23) **Going Correction** +0.20s/f (Good) **6 Ran SP% 111.9**
Speed ratings (Par 105): **101,97,94,90,81 39**
CSF £17.60 TOTE £1.50: £1.10, £8.30; EX 16.50 Trifecta £105.80.
**Owner** Sheikh Mohammed Obaid Al Maktoum **Bred** Roundhill Stud **Trained** Newmarket, Suffolk

**FOCUS**
An uneventful handicap with no depth in which the red-hot favourite won as the market suggested he would.

## 7286 STANLEY THREADWELL MEMORIAL H'CAP 5f 42y
**5:25** (5:26) (Class 2) (0-105,97) 3-Y-£12,602 (£3,772; £1,886; £944; £470) **Stalls** Centre

Form RPR

5000 **1** **Equimou**[25] 6450 3-9-2 92 ........ JamieSpencer 2 99
(Robert Eddery) *stdd s: hld up in rr: swtchd lft and effrt jst over 1f out: hdwy under hands and heels riding to ld wl ins fnl f: r.o wl* **12/1**

1320 **2** ½ **Jumira Bridge**[69] 4816 3-9-6 96 ........ AndreaAtzeni 5 101
(Roger Varian) *hld up in tch: clsd to trck ldrs and nt clr run over 1f out: swtchd rt 1f out: hdwy u.p and ev ch 100yds out: kpt on: wnt 2nd last strides* **13/2**[3]

2122 **3** *nk* **Dakota Gold**[10] 6970 3-9-7 97 ........ ConnorBeasley 1 101
(Michael Dods) *restless in stalls: t.k.h: hld up in tch: effrt to chse ldrs over 1f out: drvn and ev ch 1f out: kpt on: unable qck towards fin* **11/10**[1]

4223 **4** *shd* **Arzaak (IRE)**[16] 6758 3-8-9 85 ........(b) SilvestreDeSousa 3 89
(Chris Dwyer) *taken down early: w ldr: rdn over 1f out: drvn to ld ins fnl f: hdd and no ex 50yds out: lost 2 pls cl home* **4/1**[2]

6063 **5** *nk* **Gracious John (IRE)**[8] 7027 4-8-13 95 ........ KatherineGlenister[(7)] 4 98
(David Evans) *led: rdn over 1f out: hdd ins fnl f: no ex and styd on at same pce fnl 100yds* **7/1**

4403 **6** 3 **Orient Class**[21] 6593 6-8-10 88 ........ HollieDoyle[(3)] 6 80
(Paul Midgley) *w ldr tl unable qck and lost pl over 1f out: wknd ins fnl f* **9/1**

1m 2.54s (-0.16) **Going Correction** +0.20s/f (Good)
**WFA** 3 from 4yo+ 1lb **6 Ran SP% 111.1**
Speed ratings (Par 109): **109,108,107,107,107 102**
CSF £81.32 TOTE £11.80: £3.60, £2.10; EX 70.30 Trifecta £348.00.
**Owner** Edwin S Phillips **Bred** Stratford Place Stud & Minster Stud **Trained** Newmarket, Suffolk

**FOCUS**
A good quality sprint handicap and a fine ride on the winner, who was causing a minor upset, but she has been rated back to her best.

## 7287 PARKDEAN RESORTS CREATING AMAZING MEMORIES H'CAP 6f 3y
**5:55** (5:56) (Class 4) (0-85,84) 3-Y-O **£5,175** (£1,540; £769; £384) **Stalls** Centre

Form RPR

31 **1** **Equitation**[32] 6184 3-9-0 77 ........ AndreaAtzeni 1 88+
(Roger Varian) *racd far side: stdd s: hld up in midfield overall: effrt to chal ent fnl f: rdn to ld 150yds out: r.o wl: 1st of 3 in gp* **3/1**[1]

1022 **2** ¾ **Stanhope**[26] 6392 3-9-7 84 ........(p[1]) FranBerry 5 90
(Mick Quinn) *racd stands' side: led gp and chsd ldrs overall: ev ch u.p over 1f out: chsd wnr and kpt on same pce wl ins fnl f: 1st of 5 in gp* **5/1**[2]

1405 **3** 1 **Rose Berry**[16] 6759 3-9-5 82 ........(h) SilvestreDeSousa 4 85
(Chris Dwyer) *taken down early: stdd s: hld up in rr: hdwy to chse ldrs 2f out: drvn and ev ch over 1f out: kpt on same pce ins fnl f: 2nd of 5 in gp* **12/1**

0232 **4** ¾ **Father McKenzie**[77] 4500 3-8-9 75 ........ HollieDoyle[(3)] 3 75
(James Eustace) *racd far side: chsd overall ldr: rdn to ld over 1f out: hdd 150yds: no ex: wknd and lost 2 pls wl ins fnl f: 2nd of 3 in gp* **11/2**[3]

3104 **5** ¾ **Comprise**[53] 5416 3-8-12 75 ........ JamieSpencer 2 73
(Michael Bell) *racd far side: overall ldr: rdn and hdd over 1f out: no ex 1f out: wknd ins fnl f: 3rd of 3 in gp* **5/1**[2]

5361 **6** ¾ **Jessinamillion**[18] 6694 3-8-10 73 ........ TedDurcan 8 69
(James Bethell) *racd stands side: hld up in rr: effrt 2f out: no imp over 1f out: kpt on same pce ins fnl f: 3rd of 5 in gp* **9/1**

1320 **7** 3 ¾ **Fantasy Keeper**[18] 6686 3-8-8 71 ........ LukeMorris 6 55
(Michael Appleby) *racd stands side: chsd ldrs overall: effrt over 2f out: lost pl and btn over 1f out: wknd fnl f: 4th of 5 in gp* **5/1**[2]

**8** 8 **Time Constraints (USA)**[188] 1230 3-8-12 75 ........ DavidProbert 7 33
(Anthony Carson) *racd stands side: in tch: rdn over 2f out: sn struggling and lost pl: bhd fnl f: 5th of 5 in gp* **20/1**

1m 13.99s (-0.41) **Going Correction** +0.20s/f (Good) **8 Ran SP% 112.8**
Speed ratings (Par 103): **110,109,107,106,105 104,99,89**
CSF £17.49 CT £154.15 TOTE £3.40: £1.40, £1.60, £3.70; EX 16.80 Trifecta £113.70.
**Owner** The Equitation Partnership **Bred** Newsells Park Stud **Trained** Newmarket, Suffolk

**FOCUS**
The field split into two groups for the concluding sprint handicap, but there didn't look to be much in the draw. The winner is on the upgrade.
T/Plt: £23.10 to a £1 stake. Pool: £76,996.87 - 2426.04 winning units. T/Qpdt: £13.90 to a £1 stake. Pool: £5,251.72 - 278.30 winning units. **Steve Payne**

7288 - 7289a (Foreign Racing) - See Raceform Interactive

# [5187]FAIRYHOUSE (R-H)
### Wednesday, September 20

**OFFICIAL GOING: Yielding (yielding to soft in places) changing to soft after race 1 (2.25) changing to soft to heavy after race 3 (3.30)**

## 7290a BALLYHANE BLENHEIM STKS (LISTED RACE) 6f
**3:30** (3:30) 2-Y-O

**£25,213** (£8,119; £3,846; £1,709; £854; £427)

RPR

**1** **Brick By Brick (IRE)**[18] 6705 2-9-3 93 ........ ShaneFoley 2 100
(Mrs John Harrington, Ire) *mde all: 1 l clr at 1/2-way: stl travelling wl over 2f out down centre: rdn nr side ins fnl f and styd on wl to assert clsng stages: comf* **5/1**[2]

**2** 2 ¾ **Gobi Desert**[31] 6239 2-9-3 0 ........ ColinKeane 3 92
(G M Lyons, Ire) *settled bhd ldr: 2nd at 1/2-way: rdn in 2nd far side under 2f out and no imp on wnr u.p ins fnl f: kpt on same pce* **8/11**[1]

**3** 1 ¼ **Golden Spell**[24] 6488 2-8-12 93 ........ SeamieHeffernan 4 83
(J P Murtagh, Ire) *chsd ldrs: disp 3rd at 1/2-way: rdn in 3rd 2f out and no imp on wnr u.p over 1f out: kpt on same pce* **8/1**

4 *1* **Sometimesadiamond (IRE)**[24] 6487 2-8-12 93.......... KevinManning 6 80+
(J S Bolger, Ire) *chsd ldrs early: 6th at 1/2-way: rdn over 2f out and no imp on ldrs u.p in 5th ent fnl f: kpt on same pce into nvr threatening 4th cl home* **6/1**[3]
5 *3/4* **Damselfly (IRE)**[12] 6905 2-8-12 78.................................. WayneLordan 1 78
(Joseph Patrick O'Brien, Ire) *hld up towards rr: 5th 1/2-way: pushed along over 2f out and sme hdwy into 4th u.p far side over 1f out where no imp on wnr: one pce wl ins fnl f and denied 4th cl home* **33/1**
6 *6 1/2* **My Silver Nails (IRE)**[18] 6705 2-8-12 79........................(h) GaryCarroll 7 58
(Michael Mulvany, Ire) *hld up in rr: last at 1/2-way: pushed along over 2f out and no ex u.p 2f out: one pce after* **16/1**
7 *41* **Sollertia (IRE)**[23] 6533 2-8-12 0......................................... PatSmullen 5
(Tracey Collins, Ire) *settled bhd ldr early: disp 3rd at 1/2-way: pushed along over 2f out and sn wknd to rr: eased fr over 1f out: t.o* **10/1**

1m 19.65s (7.15) **7** Ran SP% **117.9**
CSF £9.48 TOTE £5.80: £1.90, £1.02; DF 11.20 Trifecta £37.50.
**Owner** Anamoine Limited **Bred** Lismacue Mare Syndicate **Trained** Moone, Co Kildare
**FOCUS**
Two notable non-runners here, Fleet Review (rated 102 and would have put some substance to the form) and impressive Bellewstown maiden winner Abamanova. The winner bounced out, made all and never looked in danger at any stage.

7291 - 7304a (Foreign Racing) - See Raceform Interactive

## 7175 MAISONS-LAFFITTE (R-H)
Wednesday, September 20
**OFFICIAL GOING: Turf: heavy**

### 7305a PRIX BERTRAND DE TARRAGON (GROUP 3) (3YO+ FILLIES & MARES) (STRAIGHT) (TURF) 1m 1f
**4:05** 3-Y-O+ **£34,188** (£13,675; £10,256; £6,837; £3,418)

RPR
1 **Golden Legend (FR)**[17] 6732 3-8-11 0............................. AlexisBadel 9 109+
(H-F Devin, France) *hld up: rdn and hdwy 2f out: led ins fnl f: styd on* **31/5**[3]
2 *1 3/4* **Via Firenze (IRE)**[40] 5908 4-9-2 0.................................. MaximeGuyon 7 104
(Mme Pia Brandt, France) *midfield: rdn to ld 2f out: styd on but hdd ins fnl f and hld after* **9/2**[2]
3 *1 1/4* **Heuristique (IRE)**[108] 3367 3-8-11 0.................. Pierre-CharlesBoudot 2 103
(F-H Graffard, France) *in tch: rdn 2f out: styd on fnl f and up tor 3rd post: nt pce to chal* **11/5**[1]
4 *hd* **Araaja (IRE)**[32] 6227 3-8-11 0.................................... MickaelBarzalona 1 102
(A De Watrigant, France) *led: hdd 2f out and sn rdn: kpt on but nt pce of front pair fnl f: lost 3rd post* **32/5**
5 *1/2* **Dawn Of Hope (IRE)**[24] 6490 4-9-2 0.......................... CristianDemuro 5 100
(Roger Varian) *hld up: rdn and effrt 2f out: sn outpcd: styd on but wl hld* **87/10**
6 *3* **Dallas Affair**[73] 4665 3-8-11 0..................................... AurelienLemaitre 6 95
(F Head, France) *trckd ldr: rdn to chal 2f out: no ex fnl f: fdd* **7/1**
7 *1 3/4* **Djumay (GER)**[17] 3-8-11 0.............................................. EddyHardouin 4 91
(Andreas Suborics, Germany) *midfield: dropped bk and rdn in rr 2f out: plugged on but wl btn* **58/1**
8 *nk* **Game Theory (IRE)**[15] 6804 5-9-2 0........................ StephanePasquier 8 90
(N Clement, France) *sn prom: disputing whn rdn 2f out: no ex and wknd fnl f* **71/10**
9 *5* **Syrita (FR)**[31] 6248 4-9-2 0..............................................(p) OlivierPeslier 3 79
(M Nigge, France) *midfield: rdn and outpcd 2f out: last and btn whn eased ins fnl f* **187/10**

1m 54.75s (0.05) **9** Ran SP% **118.8**
**WFA** 3 from 4yo+ 5lb
PARI-MUTUEL (all including 1 euro stake): WIN 7.20; PLACE 2.00, 1.80, 1.40; DF 15.00; SF 37.40.
**Owner** Mme Henri Devin **Bred** Mme H Devin **Trained** France
**FOCUS**
The race has been rated around the balance of the first five home. The winner kept on well to score cosily.

### 7306a PRIX ECLIPSE (GROUP 3) (2YO) (TURF) 6f
**4:35** 2-Y-O **£34,188** (£13,675; £10,256; £6,837; £3,418)

RPR
1 **Sound And Silence**[17] 6728 2-8-11 0............................(p) JamesDoyle 1 110+
(Charlie Appleby) *travelled best: mde all: rdn 2f out: kpt on and drew clr fnl f: readily* **9/10**[1]
2 *3* **Coeur De Beaute (FR)**[36] 6051 2-8-8 0................ StephanePasquier 4 98
(M Delcher Sanchez, France) *trckd wnr: rdn and effrt 2f out: sn outpcd: kpt on for wl hld 2nd* **16/5**[2]
3 *1 3/4* **French Pegasus (FR)**[31] 6247 2-8-11 0............ Pierre-CharlesBoudot 3 96
(Y Barberot, France) *hld up: rdn 2f out: kpt on fnl f and jst prevailed for 3rd: nvr threatened wnr* **59/10**[3]
4 *hd* **Arecibo (FR)**[17] 6728 2-8-11 0........................................ MaximeGuyon 2 95
(C Laffon-Parias, France) *in tch: rdn and outpcd fnl 2f: jst denied 3rd* **63/10**
5 *4 1/2* **River Cannes (FR)**[31] 6251 2-8-8 0............................. MickaelBarzalona 5 79
(T Castanheira, France) *midfield: no ex over 1f out: dropped to last and wl btn* **67/10**

1m 13.81s (0.41) **5** Ran SP% **117.6**
PARI-MUTUEL (all including 1 euro stake): WIN 1.90; PLACE 1.10, 1.50, SF 4.30.
**Owner** Godolphin **Bred** Godolphin **Trained** Newmarket, Suffolk
**FOCUS**
A small field on desperate ground. The winner made all and had the run of things.

### 7307a L'EXPRESS (CLAIMER) (4YO+) (TURF) 4f
**5:35** 4-Y-O+ **£9,829** (£3,931; £2,948; £1,965; £982)

RPR
1 **Des Annees Folles (FR)**[21] 4-8-8 0.................(p) FrancoisRenaut(8) 11 67
(P Adda, France) **26/1**
2 *snk* **Bellcanto (GER)**[71] 4955 5-9-1 0..................................... LukasDelozier 1 65
(J Hirschberger, Germany) **135/10**
3 *1 1/2* **Maharad (FR)**[31] 7-9-2 0................................................. DavidBreux 2 60
(Ecurie Avant-Garde, Belgium) **77/10**
4 *hd* **Renounce (FR)**[9] 6-8-11 0...................................(b) DelphineSantiago(5) 9 56
(D De Waele, France) **108/10**
5 *1/2* **O Dee**[71] 4955 5-8-11 0.................................................. CristianDemuro 10 53
(J Phelippon, France) **12/5**[1]
6 *1/2* **Secretjim (FR)**[115] 4-8-13 0 ow2......................(b) ChristopheSoumillon 7 53
(Tim Devos, Belgium) **53/10**[3]
7 *1 1/4* **Moscow Eight (IRE)**[364] 11-8-11 0.............................. FabriceVeron 12 46
(E J O'Neill, France) **231/10**
8 *nk* **Kiri Sunrise (IRE)**[339] 4-9-1 0.............................. BorjaFayosMartin 4 48
(Ivan Lopez Santiago, Spain) **24/1**
9 *hd* **Normal Equilibrium**[25] 6411 7-8-7 0.......................... HayleyTurner(4) 3 40
(Ivan Furtado) *qckly into stride: disp ld early: nudged along 2f out: drvn over 1f out: wknd ins fnl f* **26/5**[2]
10 *shd* **Efily (FR)**[790] 4572 4-7-12 0..................(p) MlleMickaelleMichel(10) 6 36
(Z Koplik, Czech Republic) **109/10**
11 *1 3/4* **Smidgen (IRE)**[719] 6898 6-8-11 0................................ StephaneBreux 5 36
(T Van Den Troost, Belgium) **112/10**
12 *1 1/2* **Du Pyla (FR)**[321] 4-8-11 0....................................(p) VincentCheminaud 8 30
(Z Koplik, Czech Republic) **55/1**

PARI-MUTUEL (all incl 1 euro stake): WIN 27.00; PLACE 6.20, 4.10, 3.00; DF 101.80; SF 217.60.
**Owner** Michel Serre **Bred** L Fleury & M Fleury **Trained** France

### 7308a PRIX DE BETHEMONT (CLAIMER) (3YO) (TURF) 6f
**6:05** 3-Y-O **£9,829** (£3,931; £2,948; £1,965; £982)

RPR
1 **Sweeticon**[55] 3-8-4 0................................................... HayleyTurner(4) 1 60
(Antonio Marcialis, Italy) **5/2**[1]
2 *snk* **Lightoller (IRE)**[22] 6558 3-9-4 0.................................(b) AdrienFouassier 9 70
(P Monfort, France) **191/10**
3 *5* **Happy Dream (ITY)**[38] 3-8-11 0................................... AntoineHamelin 7 47
(J Parize, France) **129/10**
4 *nk* **King Of Spades (FR)**[16] 3-9-1 0.......................(b) ClementLecoeuvre(3) 8 53
(Gianluca Bietolini, Italy) **23/5**[3]
5 *1 3/4* **Sivinsk (FR)**[25] 6455 3-8-13 0 ow2...................... ChristopheSoumillon 2 42
(Simone Brogi, France) **51/10**
6 *1 1/4* **Mister Art (IRE)**[29] 3-8-11 0.............................................(b) TonyPiccone 5 36
(Matthieu Palussiere, France) **92/10**
7 *1 1/2* **Dolokhov**[277] 3-8-11 0.......................................(b) Pierre-CharlesBoudot 3 32
(J Phelippon, France) **4/1**[2]
8 *1 1/4* **Chatoyer (FR)**[7] 7058 3-9-1 0............................................. AlexisBadel 4 32
(J S Moore) *midfield: rdn 1/2-way: no ex and btn fnl 2f: wknd* **141/10**
9 *15* **If I Say So**[38] 3-9-3 0..................................................(p) AdrienMoreau(3) 6
(M Boutin, France) **13/1**

1m 12.41s (-0.99) **9** Ran SP% **118.6**
PARI-MUTUEL (all incl 1 euro stake): WIN 3.50; PLACE 1.50, 4.20, 3.30; DF 36.60; SF 45.00.
**Owner** Andreina Mosca Toselli **Bred** Az Agr San Felice Di Toselli Andreina **Trained** Italy

7309a (Foreign Racing) - See Raceform Interactive

## 5990 AYR (L-H)
Thursday, September 21
**7310 Meeting Abandoned -** Waterlogged

## 6844 CHELMSFORD (A.W) (L-H)
Thursday, September 21
**OFFICIAL GOING: Polytrack: standard**
Wind: Fresh half-behind Weather: Overcast turning to rain after race 2

### 7318 DOWNLOAD THE CHELMSFORD CITY RACECOURSE APP NURSERY H'CAP 5f (P)
**5:45** (5:46) (Class 4) (0-85,85) 2-Y-O **£7,115** (£2,117; £1,058; £529) **Stalls** Low

Form RPR
1300 1 **Encrypted**[26] 6448 2-9-6 **84**........................................ JosephineGordon 4 90
(Hugo Palmer) *chsd ldrs: hmpd wl over 3f out: rdn and edgd lft over 1f out: r.o to ld nr fin* **5/2**[1]
4100 2 *1/2* **Emilia James**[25] 6494 2-9-3 **81**............................... RichardKingscote 5 85
(Mark Johnston) *edgd rt s: chsd ldr: rdn over 1f out: edgd lft and led wl ins fnl f: hdd nr fin* **7/1**[3]
1402 3 *1 1/4* **Brandy Station (IRE)**[21] 6624 2-8-12 **76**........................... RobertTart 2 76
(Lisa Williamson) *led: rdn over 1f out: hdd and unable qck wl ins fnl f* **33/1**
1331 4 *1/2* **Shaheen (IRE)**[25] 6466 2-9-0 **78**..................................(t) FrankieDettori 1 76
(John Quinn) *chsd ldrs: rdn over 1f out: no ex wl ins fnl f* **5/2**[1]
130 5 *2* **Chatburn (IRE)**[28] 6353 2-9-5 **83**.................................. MartinHarley 10 74+
(David O'Meara) *s.i.s: in rr: rdn over 1f out: edgd lft and r.o ins fnl f: nvr nrr* **14/1**
2410 6 *1/2* **Dahik (IRE)**[93] 3929 2-9-5 **83**................................................ DaneO'Neill 9 72
(Roger Varian) *hmpd s: hdwy over 3f out: rdn over 1f out: no ex* **16/1**
2201 7 *1* **Global Passion (FR)**[19] 6682 2-8-12 **79**........................ CallumShepherd(3) 3 64
(Charles Hills) *hld up: racd keenly: rdn over 1f out: nvr on terms* **14/1**
0130 8 *1/2* **Gift In Time (IRE)**[29] 6330 2-9-4 **82**............................ AdamBeschizza 6 66
(James Given) *sn pushed along in rr: rdn over 1f out: n.d* **8/1**
144 9 *9* **Awsaaf**[32] 6231 2-9-0 **78**..................................................(h[1]) JimCrowley 7 29
(Simon Crisford) *hld up: wknd over 1f out: eased* **5/1**[2]

59.17s (-1.03) **Going Correction** -0.125s/f (Stan) **9** Ran SP% **119.6**
Speed ratings (Par 97): **103,102,100,99,96 95,93,93,78**
CSF £21.94 CT £474.82 TOTE £3.50: £1.10, £2.50, £7.40; EX 29.00 Trifecta £651.10.
**Owner** K Abdullah **Bred** Juddmonte Farms Ltd **Trained** Newmarket, Suffolk
**FOCUS**
Not a bad nursery with the winner rated in line with his previous win.

### 7319 BILL IVES MEMORIAL H'CAP 1m 6f (P)
**6:15** (6:16) (Class 5) (0-70,72) 3-Y-O+ **£5,175** (£1,540; £769; £384) **Stalls** Low

Form RPR
3356 1 **Macksville (IRE)**[15] 6820 4-9-2 **58**...................................(b[1]) RyanTate 10 65
(James Eustace) *sn pushed along in rr: hdwy over 1f out: r.o to ld wl ins fnl f* **14/1**
3654 2 *1 1/4* **Nurse Nightingale**[9] 7032 3-9-6 **70**.......................(h[1]) SilvestreDeSousa 6 77
(Michael Bell) *chsd ldr over 12f out tl led over 1f out: rdn and hdd wl ins fnl f* **5/1**
5625 3 *1 1/2* **Uptown Funk (IRE)**[13] 6871 3-9-3 **67**..................................(tp) RobertTart 2 72
(John Gosden) *hld up: hdwy over 1f out: rdn and r.o to go 3rd post: nt rch ldrs* **9/2**[3]
5542 4 *shd* **Sputnik Planum (USA)**[8] 7063 3-9-5 **69**..........................(t) TedDurcan 1 74
(David Lanigan) *trckd ldrs: rdn and edgd lft over 1f out: styd on same pce ins fnl f* **4/1**[2]
3212 5 *1/2* **Plato's Kode (IRE)**[22] 4989 3-9-1 **65**.........................(tp) RobertWinston 5 69
(Seamus Durack) *hld up in tch: rdn over 1f out: styd on same pce ins fnl f* **7/2**[1]

2/0- **6** *2* **Caged Lightning (IRE)**[513] 1760 7-9-10 **71**..............(p) FinleyMarsh(5) 3 70
(Steve Gollings) *prom: rdn whn hmpd over 1f out: styd on same pce* **28/1**
0440 **7** *3 ¼* **Indian Red**[111] 3291 3-8-12 **62**.............................. JoeyHaynes 8 59
(Mark H Tompkins) *s.i.s: hld up: rdn over 2f out: nt trble ldrs* **50/1**
-513 **8** *¾* **Kerrera**[22] 6578 4-9-12 **68**................................... JimCrowley 13 62
(Paul Webber) *hld up: rdn over 2f out: nvr nrr* **12/1**
464 **9** *2* **Conkering Hero (IRE)**[21] 6618 3-9-7 **71**.............. EdwardGreatrex 7 64
(Joseph Tuite) *led 1f: chsd ldrs: rdn over 2f out: wknd fnl f* **25/1**
23-0 **10** *3* **Unsuspected Girl (IRE)**[64] 5024 4-9-10 **66**..............(t[1]) LiamKeniry 11 53
(Graeme McPherson) *dwlt: hld up: rdn over 1f out: nvr on terms* **25/1**
0531 **11** *1 ¾* **Woofie (IRE)**[58] 5244 5-9-6 **62**........................ GeorgeDowning 14 46
(Laura Mongan) *led after 1f: rdn and hdd over 1f out: wknd fnl f* **25/1**
-505 **12** *6* **Warrior Prince**[17] 6763 4-9-12 **68**....................(t[1]) DavidProbert 12 44
(Ed Dunlop) *hld up: rdn over 2f out: nvr on terms* **25/1**
51-1 **13** *24* **Regal Gait (IRE)**[161] 1754 4-9-10 **69**...................... HectorCrouch(3) 4 11
(Harry Whittington) *hld up: rdn over 5f out: wknd over 2f out* **6/1**

2m 58.8s (-4.40) **Going Correction** -0.125s/f (Stan)
**WFA** 3 from 4yo+ 8lb **13** Ran SP% **126.5**
Speed ratings (Par 103): **107,106,105,105,105 103,102,101,100,98 97,94,80**
CSF £81.22 CT £381.81 TOTE £19.40: £4.30, £2.10, £2.40; EX 100.60 Trifecta £1517.80.
**Owner** G Carstairs & R Marker **Bred** T Boylan **Trained** Newmarket, Suffolk
**FOCUS**
This was run at a solid gallop. The winner had slipped to a fair mark and has been rated back to his best.

## 7320 CUNNINGTONS SOLICITORS H'CAP 6f (P)
**6:45** (6:51) (Class 6) (0-65,65) 3-Y-O+ **£3,234** (£962; £481; £240) **Stalls** Centre

Form RPR
3443 **1** **Harlequin Storm (IRE)**[38] 6009 3-9-4 **64**.................. RobertWinston 5 71
(Dean Ivory) *led: hdd over 4f out: led again 1/2-way: rdn and hung rt fr over 1f out: r.o* **6/1**[3]
-205 **2** *2* **Bahamian Paradise**[114] 3184 3-8-12 **61**................... CharlieBennett(3) 1 62
(Hughie Morrison) *sn pushed along to chse ldrs: rdn over 1f out: styd on same pce ins fnl f* **6/1**[3]
0306 **3** *½* **Billyoakes (IRE)**[39] 5962 5-8-12 **61**......................(p) JoshuaBryan(5) 3 61
(Charlie Wallis) *chsd ldrs: rdn over 2f out: styd on same pce ins fnl f* **10/1**
0005 **4** *¾* **Space War**[45] 5695 10-9-3 **64**.................................... DavidEgan(3) 2 61
(Michael Easterby) *hld up: hdwy 2f out: sn rdn: styd on same pce ins fnl f* **7/2**[1]
0054 **5** *1 ¼* **Fairway To Heaven (IRE)**[22] 6586 8-8-13 **62**.............. PaddyBradley(5) 8 56
(Lee Carter) *hmpd s: in rr: rdn: hung lft and r.o ins fnl f: nvr nrr* **10/1**
1440 **6** *1 ¼* **Nag's Wag (IRE)**[24] 6527 4-9-7 **65**............................. LiamKeniry 10 55
(Conor Dore) *trckd ldrs: pushed along 1/2-way: rdn over 1f out: wknd fnl f* **33/1**
0300 **7** *shd* **Kyllukey**[29] 6303 4-9-5 **63**.......................................... LukeMorris 4 52
(Milton Bradley) *prom: lost pl 4f out: sn drvn along: nt clr run and swtchd rt over 1f out: styd on ins fnl f* **10/1**
5056 **8** *2 ¼* **Corridor Kid (IRE)**[34] 6148 4-9-4 **62**............................(v) KierenFox 6 45
(Derek Shaw) *edgd rt s: hld up: rdn over 1f out: nvr on terms* **25/1**
0503 **9** *5* **Top Of The Bank**[21] 6635 4-9-7 **65**...................(p) JosephineGordon 11 33+
(Kristin Stubbs) *sn drvn along and prom: led over 4f out: hdd 1/2-way: w wnr: rdn and ev ch 2f out: wknd fnl f* **5/1**[2]
5536 **10** *nk* **Commanche**[21] 6635 8-9-6 **64**...........................(b) SilvestreDeSousa 12 31+
(Chris Dwyer) *sn drvn along to chse ldrs: wknd and eased over 1f out* **7/1**
05 **11** *1* **Q Cee**[53] 5081 4-9-2 **60**..............................................(b[1]) JoeyHaynes 9 24
(Eugene Stanford) *hmpd s: hld up: no ch whn hmpd over 1f out* **8/1**

1m 12.39s (-1.31) **Going Correction** -0.125s/f (Stan)
**WFA** 3 from 4yo+ 2lb **11** Ran SP% **125.1**
Speed ratings (Par 101): **103,100,99,98,97 95,95,92,85,85 83**
CSF £44.85 CT £367.85 TOTE £6.90: £2.20, £2.70, £3.40; EX 59.80 Trifecta £1050.30.
**Owner** Harlequin Direct Ltd & D Bloy **Bred** Rathasker Stud **Trained** Radlett, Herts
**FOCUS**
A modest sprint with the second, third and fourth setting the straightforward level.

## 7321 HAVENS HOSPICES H'CAP 7f (P)
**7:15** (7:20) (Class 4) (0-80,82) 3-Y-O+ **£8,086** (£2,406; £1,202; £601) **Stalls** Low

Form RPR
343 **1** **Gold Hunter (IRE)**[7] 7094 7-8-12 **76**.........................(p) PaddyPilley(5) 2 84
(Steve Flook) *hld up: hdwy 1/2-way: rdn to ld wl ins fnl f: edgd rt: styd on* **16/1**
4041 **2** *nk* **Rouge Nuage (IRE)**[21] 6637 7-9-2 **75**........................... JimmyQuinn 3 82
(Conrad Allen) *chsd ldrs: led 1/2-way: rdn over 1f out: hdd wl ins fnl f: styd on* **20/1**
1162 **3** *1* **Cainhoe Star**[21] 6620 4-8-12 **71**................................... LukeMorris 1 75
(Anthony Carson) *a.p: rdn over 1f out: styd on* **5/1**[2]
-313 **4** *½* **Blue On Blue (USA)**[78] 4500 3-9-1 **77**.....................(h) FrankieDettori 10 79+
(John Gosden) *hld up in tch: rdn over 1f out: edgd lft ins fnl f: r.o* **4/1**[1]
3323 **5** *nk* **Dark Side Dream**[19] 6686 5-9-4 **77**........................ AdamBeschizza 9 79
(Chris Dwyer) *led after 1f: hdd 1/2-way: rdn over 1f out: kpt on* **7/1**[3]
0223 **6** *nk* **Fieldsman (USA)**[20] 6663 5-9-8 **81**............................ DavidProbert 4 82
(David O'Meara) *hld up in tch: plld hrd: rdn over 1f out: styd on* **7/1**[3]
2434 **7** *½* **Envisaging (IRE)**[21] 6637 3-9-2 **78**...................(t) SilvestreDeSousa 6 77+
(James Fanshawe) *plld hrd and prom: stdd and lost pl over 5f out: rdn and hung rt over 1f out: r.o* **4/1**[1]
0450 **8** *1 ¼* **Plucky Dip**[16] 6795 6-9-2 **75**................................ JosephineGordon 5 72
(John Ryan) *led 1f: trckd ldrs: racd keenly: rdn over 1f out: nt clr run ins fnl f: styd on same pce* **20/1**
04-2 **9** *hd* **Tobrave (IRE)**[43] 5797 3-8-11 **76**.............................(h) DavidEgan(3) 14 71
(Roger Varian) *hld up: styd on fnl f: nvr nrr* **8/1**
4014 **10** *½* **Sakhee's Return**[13] 6894 5-9-7 **80**.......................(t) RobertWinston 7 75
(Tim Easterby) *hld up: hdwy over 1f out: nt clr run ins fnl f: one pce* **12/1**
0322 **11** *2 ½* **Nostalgie**[29] 6321 3-9-6 **82**......................................... MartinHarley 12 69
(James Tate) *hld up: rdn over 1f out: nvr on terms* **14/1**
0030 **12** *nse* **Steal The Scene (IRE)**[94] 3912 5-9-8 **81**................ DougieCostello 15 69
(Kevin Frost) *hld up: shkn up over 1f out: nvr on terms* **33/1**
06 **13** *4 ½* **Arlecchino's Leap**[38] 6014 5-9-8 **81**.............................(p) LiamKeniry 11 57
(Mark Usher) *hld up: rdn over 2f out: n.d* **50/1**
6- **14** *shd* **Chelsea Corsage (IRE)**[347] 7193 3-9-0 **76**.................. TomMarquand 8 50
(Paul D'Arcy) *hld up: rdn over 1f out: n.d* **25/1**

1m 25.87s (-1.33) **Going Correction** -0.125s/f (Stan)
**WFA** 3 from 4yo+ 3lb **14** Ran SP% **131.3**
Speed ratings (Par 105): **102,101,100,99,99 99,98,97,97,96 93,93,88,88**
CSF £321.55 CT £1265.47 TOTE £20.70: £5.40, £5.40, £2.10; EX 365.50 Trifecta £3373.80.
**Owner** Glyn Byard **Bred** Airlie Stud And Sir Thomas Pilkington **Trained** Leominster, Herefordshire

**FOCUS**
There was a lack of pace and it was an advantage to be prominent, so the winner did quite well to quicken up from midfield. He is up slightly on his form of the past two years.

## 7322 CHELMSFORD CITY RACECOURSE SUPPORTING HAVENS HOSPICES MEDIAN AUCTION MAIDEN STKS 1m (P)
**7:45** (7:47) (Class 4) 3-4-Y-O **£5,175** (£1,540; £769; £384) **Stalls** Low

Form RPR
4- **1** **Enigmatic (IRE)**[462] 3301 3-9-5 0............................ DougieCostello 6 69
(Jamie Osborne) *trckd ldrs: racd keenly: swtchd rt over 1f out: rdn to ld wl ins fnl f: r.o* **14/1**
**2** *½* **Swiss Vinnare** 3-9-5 0................................................ DannyBrock 2 68
(Phil McEntee) *s.i.s: hld up: pushed along and hdwy over 1f out: r.o* **50/1**
4 **3** *nk* **Yogiyogiyogi (IRE)**[140] 2330 3-8-11 0.......................... DavidEgan(3) 8 63
(Denis Coakley) *chsd ldrs: rdn and edgd lft over 1f out: sn led: hdd wl ins fnl f* **6/1**[3]
244 **4** *1 ¼* **Lewinsky (IRE)**[31] 6277 3-9-0 73............................. JosephineGordon 7 61
(Hugo Palmer) *w ldr tl settled into 2nd over 6f out: led over 2f out: rdn and hdd 1f out: no ex wl ins fnl f* **3/1**[2]
3-3 **5** *hd* **Deliberator**[140] 2330 3-9-5 0.................................. SilvestreDeSousa 5 65
(William Knight) *free to post: hld up: racd keenly: rdn and hung rt over 1f out: r.o: nt rch ldrs* **1/1**[1]
2534 **6** *1 ½* **Nuncio**[30] 6295 3-9-5 68............................................. GeorgeDowning 3 62
(Daniel Kubler) *hld up in tch: swtchd rt over 2f out: rdn over 1f out: styd on same pce ins fnl f* **6/1**[3]
0 **7** *1* **Saradani Bay**[49] 5577 3-9-5 0...................................... MartinHarley 9 60
(Rae Guest) *hld up: nvr on terms* **25/1**
0 **8** *6* **Lady Of Steel**[15] 6817 3-9-0 0.................................. DanielMuscutt 11 43
(John Butler) *hld up: rdn over 1f out: n.d* **33/1**
050 **9** *5* **Akuna Mattatta (IRE)**[211] 863 3-9-0 45........................ PaddyBradley(5) 1 38
(Ralph J Smith) *hld up: racd keenly: a in rr* **100/1**
04 **10** *shd* **Danica Ashton**[15] 6828 3-8-11 0.................................. RosieJessop(3) 4 32
(Miss Joey Ellis) *sn pushed along to ld: rdn and hdd over 2f out: wknd over 1f out* **100/1**

1m 39.46s (-0.44) **Going Correction** -0.125s/f (Stan) **10** Ran SP% **121.0**
Speed ratings (Par 105): **97,96,96,94,94 93,92,86,81,81**
CSF £539.51 TOTE £18.20: £5.50, £23.00, £2.30; EX 858.50 Trifecta £4992.50.
**Owner** Charles E Noell & Michael Buckley **Bred** Stonepark Farms **Trained** Upper Lambourn, Berks
**FOCUS**
Modest maiden form which has been rated cautiously.

## 7323 2018 MEMBERSHIP NOW AVAILABLE H'CAP 1m (P)
**8:15** (8:18) (Class 6) (0-60,67) 3-Y-O+ **£3,234** (£962; £481; £240) **Stalls** Low

Form RPR
3611 **1** **Chetan**[8] 7061 5-9-9 **67** 7ex......................................(t) JoshuaBryan(5) 3 77
(Charlie Wallis) *prom: pushed along 5f out: led over 1f out: rdn out* **3/1**[1]
-043 **2** *2 ½* **Prince Jai**[41] 5897 4-8-12 **51**...............................(b) RichardKingscote 7 55
(Ian Williams) *w ldr tl led over 2f out: rdn and hdd over 1f out: styd on same pce ins fnl f* **6/1**[3]
0504 **3** *nk* **Dukes Meadow**[21] 6622 6-8-6 **50**................................ RhiainIngram(5) 4 53
(Roger Ingram) *hld up: hdwy over 1f out: r.o* **8/1**
0400 **4** *½* **Captain Hawk**[21] 6638 3-9-3 **60**.........................(p) JosephineGordon 10 62
(Ian Williams) *hld up: hdwy: nt clr run and swtchd rt over 1f out: r.o* **10/1**
1032 **5** *¾* **Just Fab (IRE)**[21] 6621 4-8-9 **53**..........................(b) PaddyBradley(5) 1 55
(Lee Carter) *hld up: hdwy and nt clr run over 1f out: r.o* **12/1**
5040 **6** *nk* **Never Folding (IRE)**[36] 6069 3-8-12 **55**........................ RobertWinston 6 57
(Seamus Durack) *s.i.s: hld up: plld hrd: nt clr run and swtchd rt over 1f out: r.o ins fnl f: nvr nrr* **8/1**
2622 **7** *½* **Chough**[17] 6751 3-8-9 **55**.......................................... CharlieBennett(3) 15 54
(Hughie Morrison) *chsd ldrs: rdn and ev ch over 1f out: no ex ins fnl f* **10/1**
2200 **8** *hd* **Little Choosey**[19] 6673 7-9-4 **60**................................(bt) HollieDoyle(3) 9 58
(Roy Bowring) *chsd ldrs: rdn over 1f out: no ex ins fnl f* **16/1**
4660 **9** *2 ½* **Bird For Life**[15] 6814 3-8-0 **50**.................................. NicolaCurrie(7) 13 42
(Mark Usher) *hld up: rdn over 1f out: r.o towards fin: nvr nrr* **50/1**
0030 **10** *nk* **Born To Reason (IRE)**[41] 5897 3-8-12 **55**...............(h) DougieCostello 11 47
(Kevin Frost) *prom: rdn over 1f out: wknd fnl f* **14/1**
0300 **11** *¾* **Caledonia Laird**[21] 6638 6-9-6 **59**.........................(b) TomMarquand 16 49
(Jo Hughes) *hld up: rdn over 1f out: nvr trbld ldrs* **25/1**
5063 **12** *1 ½* **Belgravian (FR)**[14] 6847 3-8-13 **56**............................(tp) LukeMorris 5 43
(Archie Watson) *s.i.s: hld up: plld hrd: sme hdwy wl over 1f out: sn rdn: hung lft and hmpd: wknd fnl f* **9/2**[2]
000 **13** *9* **Three's A Crowd (IRE)**[87] 4164 3-9-0 **57**............... SilvestreDeSousa 14 23
(Ed de Giles) *s.i.s: hld up: nvr on terms* **20/1**
240 **14** *nse* **The Happy Hammer (IRE)**[19] 6681 11-9-5 **58**.............. JoeyHaynes 12 24
(Eugene Stanford) *hld up: rdn over 2f out: n.d* **33/1**
6540 **15** *1 ½* **Princess Ophelia**[52] 5485 3-9-3 **60**........................ AlistairRawlinson 8 22
(Michael Appleby) *led over 5f: hung lft and wknd over 1f out* **50/1**
R/00 **R** **Dylan's Centenary**[3] 7213 6-8-4 **46**................................ DavidEgan(3) 2
(Phil McEntee) *ref to r* **50/1**

1m 38.58s (-1.32) **Going Correction** -0.125s/f (Stan)
**WFA** 3 from 4yo+ 4lb **16** Ran SP% **135.5**
Speed ratings (Par 101): **101,98,98,97,96 96,96,95,93,93 92,90,81,81,80**
CSF £21.84 CT £143.12 TOTE £4.30: £1.40, £2.30, £2.30, £2.30; EX 34.00 Trifecta £251.00.
**Owner** Roger & Val Miles, Tony Stamp **Bred** Andrew W Robson **Trained** Ardleigh, Essex
**FOCUS**
A moderate handicap with the winner pretty much back to last year's best.

## 7324 BOOK YOUR CHRISTMAS PARTY HERE H'CAP (DIV I) 1m 2f (P)
**8:45** (8:48) (Class 6) (0-60,61) 3-Y-O+ **£3,234** (£962; £481; £240) **Stalls** Low

Form RPR
3336 **1** **Arcadian Sea (IRE)**[24] 6524 3-8-13 **54**...................... JosephineGordon 4 62
(William Jarvis) *hld up in tch: rdn to ld and edgd lft wl ins fnl f: styd on* **5/2**[1]
6561 **2** *1 ½* **Fantasy Gladiator**[14] 6846 11-9-11 **61**.....................(be) TomMarquand 2 65
(Michael Appleby) *s.i.s and sn pushed along: hdwy over 6f out: rdn over 1f out: ev ch ins fnl f: styd on same pce* **5/1**[2]
0035 **3** *1 ½* **Master Of Heaven**[17] 6754 4-8-9 **50**..........................(p) PaddyBradley(5) 3 51
(Jim Boyle) *led: rdn over 1f out: hdd and no ex wl ins fnl f* **10/1**
6032 **4** *1 ½* **Outlaw Torn (IRE)**[19] 6673 8-9-4 **54**.................................(e) RobHornby 1 52
(Richard Guest) *prom: chsd ldr over 2f out: rdn over 1f out: no ex ins fnl f* **7/1**
000- **5** *2 ½* **Diptych (USA)**[332] 7576 3-9-5 **60**......................................(p[1]) LukeMorris 11 55
(Sir Mark Prescott Bt) *sn chsng ldrs: drvn along over 3f out: edgd lft and styd on same pce fr over 1f out* **6/1**[3]

4003 **6** *hd* **Avocet (USA)**[21] 6622 4-8-3 **46**........ MillyNaseb(7) 5 39
(Julia Feilden) *hld up: hdwy over 2f out: rdn over 1f out: styd on same pce* **6/1**[3]

4406 **7** *1 3/4* **Sussex Girl**[20] 6664 3-8-12 **60**........ NicolaCurrie(7) 6 51
(John Berry) *hld up: sme hdwy over 1f out: no ex fnl f* **12/1**

0000 **8** *9* **Geordielad**[110] 3326 3-8-2 **46** oh1........ DavidEgan(3) 8 20
(Jamie Osborne) *hld up: rdn over 2f out: nvr on terms* **20/1**

0003 **9** *2* **Jazri**[17] 6754 6-8-7 **46** oh1........(p) HollieDoyle(3) 9 15
(Milton Bradley) *s.s: hld up: rdn over 4f out: n.d* **16/1**

0456 **10** *1 3/4* **Dor's Law**[21] 6622 4-9-2 **52**........ RobertWinston 12 18
(Dean Ivory) *wnt prom after 1f: chsd ldr over 6f out tl rdn over 2f out: wknd over 1f out* **14/1**

0660 **11** *5* **Coachella (IRE)**[28] 6342 3-8-5 **46** oh1........ SilvestreDeSousa 7
(Ed de Giles) *s.i.s: hld up: a in rr: wknd over 2f out* **10/1**

55-0 **12** *8* **Master Of Song**[21] 6622 10-8-10 **46** oh1........(b) JimmyQuinn 10
(Roy Bowring) *prom: hmpd over 8f out: wknd wl over 2f out* **50/1**

2m 5.7s (-2.90) **Going Correction** -0.125s/f (Stan)
**WFA** 3 from 4yo+ 5lb **12 Ran SP% 131.5**
Speed ratings (Par 101): **106,104,103,102,100 100,98,91,90,88 84,78**
CSF £16.33 CT £118.52 TOTE £3.00: £1.50, £2.00, £3.30; EX 17.80 Trifecta £131.60.
**Owner** The Arcadian Sea Partnership **Bred** Philip McAuliffe **Trained** Newmarket, Suffolk

**FOCUS**
The market proved a good guide here. The race has been rated though the placed horses.

## 7325 BOOK YOUR CHRISTMAS PARTY HERE H'CAP (DIV II) 1m 2f (P)
**9:15** (9:19) (Class 6) (0-60,60) 3-Y-O+ **£3,234** (£962; £481; £240) **Stalls Low**

Form RPR

4466 **1** **Estibdaad (IRE)**[21] 6632 7-9-1 **54**........(t) CallumShepherd(3) 13 61
(Paddy Butler) *led after 1f: rdn and edgd rt over 1f out: styd on* **12/1**

2654 **2** *2* **California Cliffs (IRE)**[23] 6560 3-8-9 **50**........ DavidProbert 4 54
(Rae Guest) *led 1f: trckd ldrs: racd keenly: rdn and ev ch over 1f out: styd on same pce ins fnl f* **12/1**

4602 **3** *2* **Tommy's Secret**[21] 6622 7-9-0 **50**........(p) MartinHarley 5 49
(Jane Chapple-Hyam) *hld up in tch: lost pl 5f out: hdwy and hung rt over 1f out: r.o* **3/1**[2]

600 **4** *nk* **Dixon**[76] 4569 3-9-2 **57**........ JoeyHaynes 1 57
(Mark H Tompkins) *hld up: hdwy u.p over 1f out: styd on* **14/1**

2361 **5** *1/2* **Bollin Ted**[25] 6470 3-9-5 **60**........ RobertWinston 9 59
(Tim Easterby) *plld hrd and prom: rdn and edgd rt over 1f out: styng on same pce whn hung lft ins fnl f* **11/4**[1]

0005 **6** *hd* **Bridal March**[44] 5761 3-8-7 **48**........(p) LukeMorris 8 47
(John Mackie) *hld up in tch: rdn over 2f out: styd on same pce fnl f* **28/1**

0554 **7** *nk* **Hidden Stash**[14] 6846 3-8-7 **51**........ HollieDoyle(3) 12 49
(William Stone) *chsd ldr after 1f tl 4f out: remained handy: rdn and nt clr run over 1f out: styng on same pce whn nt clr run ins fnl f* **25/1**

0004 **8** *1 1/4* **Neptune Star**[25] 6470 3-8-5 **46** oh1........ SilvestreDeSousa 3 42
(Michael Easterby) *hld up: plld hrd: swtchd rt over 5f out: hdwy to chse ldr 4f out: rdn and hung rt over 1f out: no ex fnl f* **4/1**[3]

6000 **9** *5* **Tawfeer**[41] 5897 3-8-9 **50**........(p) RobHornby 2 36
(James Unett) *hld up: rdn over 1f out: n.d* **66/1**

-603 **10** *3 1/2* **Unonothinjonsnow**[3] 7219 3-8-5 **46** oh1........ JimmyQuinn 10 25
(Richard Guest) *s.i.s: hld up: racd keenly: rdn over 1f out: n.d* **4/1**[3]

3/6- **11** *17* **Bowsers Bold**[351] 7063 6-9-0 **55**........ RhiainIngram(5) 11
(Roger Ingram) *s.i.s: hld up: wknd over 2f out* **66/1**

2m 9.69s (1.09) **Going Correction** -0.125s/f (Stan)
**WFA** 3 from 5yo+ 5lb **11 Ran SP% 124.0**
Speed ratings (Par 101): **90,88,86,86,86 86,85,84,80,77 64**
CSF £149.73 CT £552.73 TOTE £12.20: £3.30, £3.40, £1.50; EX 143.90 Trifecta £613.90.
**Owner** Miss M Bryant **Bred** John O'Connor **Trained** East Chiltington, E Sussex
■ Stewards' Enquiry : Callum Shepherd 2 day ban: careless riding (5/6 Oct)

**FOCUS**
This was steadily run, favouring those up front, and the time was 3.99sec slower than the first division.
T/Plt: £11,414.50 to a £1 stake. Pool: £104,763.77 - 6.70 winning units. T/Qpdt: £695.00 to a £1 stake. Pool: £15,178.32 - 16.16 winning units. **Colin Roberts**

# 6231 PONTEFRACT (L-H)
## Thursday, September 21

**OFFICIAL GOING: Good to soft (good in places) changing to soft after race 1 (2.20)**
Wind: Light half behind Weather: Heavy cloud and rain

## 7326 BOOK YOUR 23RD OCTOBER TOTEPOOL PACKAGE MEDIAN AUCTION MAIDEN STKS 5f 3y
**2:20** (2:23) (Class 5) 2-Y-0 **£3,234** (£962; £481; £240) **Stalls Low**

Form RPR

6 **1** **Jonboy**[28] 6347 2-9-5 0........ BenCurtis 6 80
(David Barron) *trckd ldrs: hdwy wl over 1f out: rdn ins fnl f: styd on strly to ld towards fin* **9/1**

43 **2** *1/2* **Black Friday**[41] 5879 2-9-5 0........ AndrewMullen 2 78
(Karen McLintock) *awkward s and towards rr: pushed along and hdwy on inner 1/2-way: chsd ldrs and n.m.r wl over 1f out: sn swtchd rt and rdn: styd on wl towards fin* **4/1**[3]

022 **3** *1/2* **Harrogate (IRE)**[17] 6755 2-9-5 78........ KevinStott 13 76
(James Bethell) *wnt rt s: sn cl up: rdn to chal over 1f out: drvn ins fnl f: led last 100yds: hdd and no ex towards fin* **11/2**

3 **4** *1 3/4* **Militia**[11] 6969 2-9-5 0........ JackGarritty 8 70
(Richard Fahey) *led: rdn along over 1f out: jnd and drvn ins fnl f: hdd last 100yds: one pce* **5/2**[1]

5324 **5** *3/4* **Rossall**[23] 6547 2-9-0 76........ CallumRodriguez(5) 11 67
(Michael Dods) *trckd ldng pair: pushed along 2f out: rdn wl over 1f out: drvn and no imp fnl f* **3/1**[2]

520 **6** *3 3/4* **Dangerous Lady**[23] 6559 2-9-0 69........ DuranFentiman 10 49
(Tim Easterby) *in tch: pushed along 1/2-way: rdn wl over 1f out: sn one pce* **25/1**

0 **7** *shd* **Kylie Style**[12] 6950 2-8-8 0 ow1........ PatrickVaughan(7) 3 50
(Steph Hollinshead) *a towards rr* **66/1**

**8** *3 3/4* **Mystical Mac (IRE)** 2-9-5 0........ GrahamLee 4 40
(Iain Jardine) *a towards rr* **33/1**

53 **9** *4* **Sovereign State**[42] 5839 2-9-5 0........ HarryBentley 9 26
(Robert Cowell) *dwlt: a towards rr* **14/1**

0 **10** *1/2* **Twelve A**[29] 6311 2-9-5 0........ SamJames 12 24
(David O'Meara) *a in rr* **66/1**

0 **11** *1 3/4* **Eeh Bah Gum (IRE)**[31] 6264 2-9-5 0........ PhillipMakin 1 18
(David O'Meara) *chsd ldrs: rdn along on inner over 2f out: wknd wl over 1f out* **50/1**

0 **12** *12* **Ms Tilly**[34] 6147 2-8-11 0........ AaronJones(3) 7
(David Brown) *sn outpcd and a bhd* **100/1**

1m 5.42s (2.12) **Going Correction** +0.50s/f (Yiel) **12 Ran SP% 118.3**
Speed ratings (Par 95): **103,102,101,98,97 91,91,85,78,78 75,56**
CSF £43.47 TOTE £10.50: £2.90, £1.60, £1.80; EX 51.00 Trifecta £389.40.
**Owner** Ron Hull **Bred** Michael Ng **Trained** Maunby, N Yorks

**FOCUS**
It started raining in the lead up to racing, but the the going was still officially good to soft, good in places (GoingStick 7.3). An ordinary sprint maiden in which the leaders may have done a bit too much early and set it up for a couple of closers. The winning time was 3.92sec outside standard, suggesting the ground was testing enough for these 2yos, and this was confirmed by the jockeys. The second, third and fourth help set the straightforward level.

## 7327 MATTY BOWN H'CAP 1m 6y
**2:50** (2:52) (Class 4) (0-80,81) 3-Y-O+ **£5,175** (£1,540; £769; £384) **Stalls Low**

Form RPR

2-04 **1** **Mushaireb**[12] 6942 3-9-2 **79**........ JackGarritty 3 89
(Richard Fahey) *t.k.h early: hld up in rr: smooth hdwy on inner 2f out: sn swtchd rt to outer and effrt to chse ldrs whn hung lft and rdr lost irons over 1f out: sn corrected and rdn: styd on strly to ld last 50yds* **8/1**

544 **2** *1 3/4* **Mr Cool Cash**[8] 7046 5-8-7 **66**........ ConnorBeasley 1 72
(Richard Guest) *in tch: hdwy 3f out: chsd ldr over 1f out: sn rdn: drvn to ld ent fnl f: hdd and no ex last 50yds* **9/2**[3]

3100 **3** *2 1/4* **Echo Of Lightning**[6] 7111 7-9-0 **80**........(p) BenSanderson(7) 12 81
(Roger Fell) *led: rdn clr wl over 1f out: hdd and drvn ent fnl f: kpt on same pce* **16/1**

536 **4** *1 3/4* **Trinity Star (IRE)**[25] 6471 6-8-7 **66** oh2........(b) AndrewMullen 7 63
(Michael Dods) *in rr: pushed along 1/2-way: hdwy over 2f out: rdn wl over 1f out: swtchd rt appr fnl f: kpt on wl towards fin* **14/1**

3432 **5** *1/2* **Election Day**[25] 6468 3-9-4 **81**........ FrannyNorton 6 77
(Mark Johnston) *prom on inner: hdwy to chse ldr 3f out: rdn along wl over 1f out: sn drvn and grad wknd* **7/2**[1]

3626 **6** *nk* **Spinart**[30] 6288 4-8-10 **69**........(p) GrahamLee 5 64
(Pam Sly) *hld up in tch: hdwy 3f out: rdn along wl over 1f out: sn one pce* **4/1**[2]

2265 **7** *5* **Lamloom (IRE)**[25] 6468 3-9-3 **80**........ PhillipMakin 9 63
(David O'Meara) *chsd ldr: pushed along 3f out: rdn over 2f out: sn wknd* **9/1**

0020 **8** *27* **Dandyleekie (IRE)**[23] 6564 5-8-8 **74**........(p) PatrickVaughan(7) 4
(David O'Meara) *chsd ldrs: rdn along 3f out: sn wknd and eased fnl 2f* **12/1**

1506 **9** *1 1/2* **Thaqaffa (IRE)**[23] 6555 4-9-5 **78**........ HarryBentley 10
(Amy Murphy) *chsd ldrs: pushed along 1/2-way: sn rdn and wknd 3f out: bhd and eased fnl 2f* **12/1**

-122 **10** *9* **Pushaq (IRE)**[52] 5484 4-9-4 **77**........ ShaneKelly 11
(Anthony McCann, Ire) *dwlt and towards rr: hdwy and in tch 1/2-way: rdn along over 3f out: sn lost pl and bhd whn eased fnl 2f* **16/1**

1m 48.0s (2.10) **Going Correction** +0.50s/f (Yiel)
**WFA** 3 from 4yo+ 4lb **10 Ran SP% 115.3**
Speed ratings (Par 105): **109,107,105,103,102 102,97,70,68,59**
CSF £43.41 CT £580.05 TOTE £7.30: £2.60, £1.60, £5.70; EX 46.70 Trifecta £396.10.
**Owner** Al Shaqab Racing **Bred** Lordship Stud **Trained** Musley Bank, N Yorks

**FOCUS**
The ground was changed to soft all over before this race. A fair handicap rated through the runner-up. The winner, second and fourth came from well back and there was a bit of drama passing the furlong pole.

## 7328 BOOK YOUR CHRISTMAS PARTY HERE ON 0113 2876387 H'CAP 1m 2f 5y
**3:25** (3:25) (Class 4) (0-85,87) 3-Y-O+ **£5,175** (£1,540; £769; £384) **Stalls Low**

Form RPR

335 **1** **Royal Shaheen (FR)**[12] 6944 4-9-4 **77**........(v) GrahamLee 1 86
(Alistair Whillans) *hld up: hdwy to trck ldrs on inner after 3f: smooth hdwy over 2f out: sn swtchd rt to chal: led over 1f out: pushed out* **4/1**[2]

3453 **2** *2 1/4* **Peterhouse (USA)**[36] 6061 5-8-12 **71**........ KevinStott 3 76
(Jason Ward) *pushed along in rr early: hdwy over 3f out: effrt on inner to chse ldrs 2f out: sn swtchd rt and rdn: kpt on to chse wnr ins fnl f: no imp* **5/1**[3]

600 **3** *3 3/4* **Kharbetation (IRE)**[24] 6520 4-10-0 **87**........ PhillipMakin 5 85
(David O'Meara) *led: rdn along 2f out: hdd and drvn over 1f out: kpt on same pce* **20/1**

2102 **4** *3* **Save The Bees**[11] 6965 9-9-3 **83**........ GerO'Neill(7) 8 75
(Declan Carroll) *cl up: pushed along over 3f out: rdn over 2f out: drvn and kpt on same pce fr wl over 1f out* **13/2**

1315 **5** *4* **Alfred Richardson**[24] 6518 3-8-10 **74**........ SamJames 4 59
(John Davies) *in tch whn stmbld and lost pl bnd after 1f: hdwy over 2f out: rdn wl over 1f out: nvr nr ldrs* **8/1**

541 **6** *10* **Ludorum (IRE)**[17] 6760 3-8-10 **74**........ JackGarritty 2 40
(Richard Fahey) *chsd ldrs: rdn along wl over 2f out: sn wknd* **7/2**[1]

4320 **7** *1* **Mister Belvedere**[12] 6920 3-9-4 **87**........ CallumRodriguez(5) 7 51
(Michael Dods) *in tch: hdwy to chse ldrs 4f out: rdn along 3f out: sn wknd* **8/1**

043 **8** *20* **Invictus (GER)**[16] 6789 5-8-10 **69** oh4........(p) BenCurtis 9
(David Loughnane) *prom: rdn along over 3f out: wknd over 2f out* **33/1**

3324 **9** *18* **Azzir (IRE)**[42] 5830 5-8-11 **73**........ CliffordLee(3) 6
(K R Burke) *a in rr: bhd and eased fr over 1f out* **7/1**

2m 17.44s (3.74) **Going Correction** +0.50s/f (Yiel)
**WFA** 3 from 4yo+ 5lb **9 Ran SP% 114.6**
Speed ratings (Par 105): **105,103,100,97,94 86,85,69,55**
CSF £24.15 CT £353.30 TOTE £4.90: £1.70, £1.70, £5.90; EX 22.10 Trifecta £523.40.
**Owner** Frank Lowe **Bred** SF Bloodstock LLC **Trained** Newmill-On-Slitrig, Borders

**FOCUS**
Another fair handicap and the pace looked solid in the conditions. The winner has been rated close to his old best.

## 7329 EBF "BREEDERS' SERIES' FILLIES" H'CAP 6f
**4:00** (4:03) (Class 2) (0-100,98) 3-Y-O+
**£18,675** (£5,592; £2,796; £1,398; £699; £351) **Stalls Low**

Form RPR

4301 **1** **Marie Of Lyon**[3] 7214 3-8-9 **88** 6ex........ AdamMcNamara(3) 1 97
(Richard Fahey) *mde all: rdn over 1f out: kpt on strly* **3/1**[2]

1241 **2** *2 1/4* **Tirania**[21] 6629 3-8-13 **89**........ PatDobbs 2 91
(William Haggas) *trckd ldrs on inner: hdwy 2f out: rdn over 1f out: drvn and kpt on fnl f* **5/2**[1]

0014 **3** *hd* **Hope Solo (IRE)**[11] 6970 3-8-10 **86**....................(p) KevinStott 7 87
(Tim Easterby) *cl up: rdn along wl over 1f out: drvn and kpt on same pce fnl f* **15/2**

5303 **4** *3 ¾* **Savannah Slew**[16] 6787 3-8-11 **87**....................(p[1]) AndrewMullen 9 76
(James Given) *dwlt and in rr: hdwy on inner over 2f out: rdn wl over 1f out: kpt on u.p fnl f* **8/1**

0030 **5** *4* **Megan Lily (IRE)**[27] 6382 3-8-13 **89**.................... JackGarritty 8 66
(Richard Fahey) *uns rdr on way to s: t.k.h: a in rr* **16/1**

4612 **6** *½* **Sandra's Secret (IRE)**[19] 6669 4-8-0 **79** oh2.................... JaneElliott(5) 4 54
(Les Eyre) *dwlt: in tch: pushed along over 2f out: rdn to chse ldrs wl over 1f out: wknd appr fnl f* **10/1**

2532 **7** *10* **Southern Belle (IRE)**[16] 6787 4-9-7 **95**.................... PhillipMakin 6 38
(Robert Cowell) *unruly in preliminaries: awkward s: t.k.h and sn chsng ldrs on outer: rdn 2f out: sn wknd and eased fnl f* **4/1**[3]

1m 18.66s (1.76) **Going Correction** +0.50s/f (Yiel)
**WFA** 3 from 4yo 2lb **7** Ran SP% **111.4**
Speed ratings (Par 109): **108,105,104,99,94 93,80**
CSF £10.34 CT £47.18 TOTE £3.70: £2.40, £1.40; EX 11.70 Trifecta £55.00.
**Owner** Clipper Logistics **Bred** Limestone Stud **Trained** Musley Bank, N Yorks

**FOCUS**
A decent prize for this fillies' handicap, but it was weakened by the absence of last year's winner Kassia and the unexposed Clon Coulis. Few ever got into it, a couple misbehaved beforehand and another couple pulled too hard in the race, so not strong form for the grade. Again the 3yos dominated this contest.

## 7330 TRADEWAY SHIPPING - SUZY WOODS CAN'T PICK A WINNER H'CAP 2m 1f 27y
**4:30** (4:33) (Class 5) (0-75,73) 3-Y-0+ **£3,234** (£962; £481; £240) **Stalls** Low

Form RPR

2463 **1** **La Fritillaire**[23] 6565 5-9-4 **63**....................(p[1]) AndrewMullen 8 71
(James Given) *trckd ldr: cl up over 5f out: led 4f out: rdn wl over 1f out: drvn ent fnl f: hld on gamely towards fin* **17/2**

4423 **2** *nse* **Transpennine Star**[11] 6968 4-9-8 **72**....................(p) CallumRodriguez(5) 1 79
(Michael Dods) *led: jnd over 5f out: pushed along and hdd 4f out: rdn over 2f out: drvn and rallied gamely to chal ins fnl f: ev ch: jst hld* **2/1**[1]

-632 **3** *4* **Almost Gemini (IRE)**[21] 6233 8-9-12 **71**....................(p) JackGarritty 2 74
(Kenneth Slack) *trckd ldrs: hdwy over 4f out: chsd ldng pair over 2f out and sn rdn: drvn over 1f out: no imp fnl f* **6/1**[3]

1050 **4** *3 ½* **Tuscan Gold**[32] 6233 10-9-3 **62**....................(p) FrannyNorton 13 62
(Micky Hammond) *s.i.s and in rr: stdy hdwy 7f out: in tch over 3f out: rdn along to chse ldrs 3f out: drvn 2f out and sn one pce* **25/1**

2004 **5** *7* **Madam Lilibet (IRE)**[32] 6233 8-8-11 **56**.................... PaddyAspell 5 50
(Sharon Watt) *in tch: pushed along over 4f out: rdn over 3f out: drvn and one pce fr over 2f out* **14/1**

5363 **6** *2 ¼* **Bulas Belle**[22] 6569 7-9-4 **70**.................... PatrickVaughan(7) 7 62
(Grant Tuer) *hld up in rr: sme hdwy over 5f out: rdn along 4f out: n.d* **8/1**

0200 **7** *10* **Saved By The Bell (IRE)**[35] 6090 7-9-13 **72**.................... ShaneKelly 3 55
(Lawrence Mullaney) *chsd ldng pair: rdn along 5f out: drvn over 3f out: sn wknd* **12/1**

3605 **8** *3* **Treble Strike (USA)**[13] 6898 4-8-9 **59**.................... MitchGodwin(5) 10 39
(David C Griffiths) *a in rr* **33/1**

44 **9** *2 ¼* **Maple Stirrup (IRE)**[23] 6565 5-8-2 **54** oh6.................... PaulaMuir(7) 11 32
(Patrick Holmes) *midfield: rdn along over 7f out: outpcd fr over 5f out* **50/1**

3342 **10** *16* **Tyrell (IRE)**[48] 5590 4-9-13 **72**....................(p[1]) BenCurtis 6 36
(Micky Hammond) *chsd ldng pair: rdn along 5f out: drvn over 3f out: sn wknd* **12/1**

0611 **11** *30* **Chebsey Beau**[13] 6895 7-9-11 **73**.................... AdamMcNamara(3) 9 10
(John Quinn) *midfield: sme hdwy on outer over 6f out: rdn along 5f out: sn wknd* **5/1**[2]

3m 57.17s (12.57) **Going Correction** +0.50s/f (Yiel) **11** Ran SP% **116.7**
Speed ratings (Par 103): **90,89,88,86,83 82,77,75,74,67 53**
CSF £25.21 CT £113.27 TOTE £9.60: £3.50, £1.20, £2.10; EX 33.50 Trifecta £209.50.
**Owner** Ingram Racing **Bred** Mrs P M Ignarski **Trained** Willoughton, Lincs

**FOCUS**
A modest staying handicap, but despite a true test of stamina a cracking duel between the front pair the whole way round, and there was nothing between them at the finish. The runner-up sets the standard.

## 7331 WATCH RACING UK IN HD MAIDEN STKS 1m 2f 5y
**5:05** (5:09) (Class 5) 3-Y-0+ **£3,234** (£962; £481; £240) **Stalls** Low

Form RPR

3 **1** **Misscarlett (IRE)**[37] 6044 3-9-0 0.................... BenCurtis 5 66+
(Sally Haynes) *mde all: rdn clr over 1f out: hung bdly rt ins fnl f: kpt on strly towards fin* **3/1**[2]

-005 **2** *4 ½* **Frankster (FR)**[86] 4170 4-9-10 56....................(t[1]) FrannyNorton 2 61
(Micky Hammond) *in tch: hdwy 3f out: rdn to chse ldrs over 1f out: drvn to chse wnr ins fnl f: sn edgd rt and no imp* **25/1**

20 **3** *2 ¼* **Heron (USA)**[76] 4569 3-9-5 0.................... JackMitchell 7 58
(Hugo Palmer) *trckd wnr: cl up over 4f out: rdn along over 2f out: drvn over 1f out: kpt on same pce* **9/2**

3332 **4** *3 ¾* **Hats Off To Larry**[16] 6775 3-9-5 75.................... GrahamLee 10 51+
(Mick Channon) *t.k.h early: trckd ldrs: hdwy 3f out: rdn along 2f out: drvn over 1f out: sn one pce* **2/1**[1]

5460 **5** *½* **Urban Spirit (IRE)**[16] 6786 3-9-5 45.................... JackGarritty 1 50?
(Roger Fell) *towards rr: hdwy over 3f out: rdn along on inner 2f out: kpt on u.p fnl f* **50/1**

05 **6** *7* **Good Man (IRE)**[53] 5458 4-9-10 0....................(p) AndrewMullen 3 35
(Karen McLintock) *midfield: pushed along over 3f out: rdn wl over 2f out: nvr nr ldrs* **25/1**

52 **7** *26* **Mesbaar**[21] 6633 3-9-5 0.................... HarryBentley 8 +
(Roger Varian) *hld up: sme hdwy 4f out: rdn along 3f out: drvn 2f out: sn outpcd and eased whn bhd over 1f out* **10/3**[3]

65 **8** *9* **The Foozler**[7] 6760 4-9-7 0.................... AdamMcNamara(3) 4
(Peter Niven) *prom: rdn along 5f out: sn lost pl and bhd* **125/1**

6-00 **9** *23* **Trois Bon Amis (IRE)**[125] 2790 3-9-5 56....................(t[1]) PaddyAspell 6
(Mark Campion) *a in rr* **100/1**

**10** *57* **Fashaar**[19] 6707 4-9-10 69.................... ShaneKelly 9
(Anthony McCann, Ire) *in tch on outer: rdn along 4f out: sn lost pl and bhd: virtually p.u over 1f out* **20/1**

2m 19.27s (5.57) **Going Correction** +0.50s/f (Yiel)
**WFA** 3 from 4yo 5lb **10** Ran SP% **115.8**
Speed ratings (Par 103): **97,93,91,88,88 82,61,54,36,**
CSF £76.71 TOTE £3.80: £1.20, £4.70, £1.50; EX 63.50 Trifecta £302.40.
**Owner** Mrs J Porter **Bred** Fontstown Stud **Trained** Melsonby, N Yorks

**FOCUS**
An uncompetitive older-horse maiden and the proximity of a 56-rated horse and a 45-rated horse in second and fifth respectively holds the form down, but the winner is value for more.

## 7332 NEVER MISS A RACE ON RACING UK APPRENTICE H'CAP 6f
**5:35** (5:36) (Class 5) (0-70,73) 3-Y-0+ **£3,234** (£962; £481; £240) **Stalls** Low

Form RPR

0231 **1** **Penny Pot Lane**[2] 7244 4-9-9 **73** 6ex.................... SebastianWoods(3) 5 82
(Richard Whitaker) *prom on inner: hdwy 2f out: sn led: rdn clr over 1f out: kpt on wl towards fin* **10/3**[2]

6021 **2** *¾* **My Girl Maisie (IRE)**[21] 6630 3-8-7 **59**.................... JackOsborn(3) 2 65
(Richard Guest) *trckd ldrs: hdwy on inner 2f out: swtchd rt and rdn to chse wnr over 1f out: drvn and kpt on wl fnl f* **3/1**[1]

1626 **3** *1 ¾* **Cliff (IRE)**[11] 6964 7-9-1 **67**.................... FayeMcManoman(5) 12 67
(Nigel Tinkler) *hld up in rr: hdwy on outer wl over 1f out: rdn and styd on wl fnl f: nrst fin* **11/2**[3]

2000 **4** *1* **Sophisticated Heir (IRE)**[21] 6637 7-9-1 **65**.................... TristanPrice(3) 4 62
(Kevin Frost) *chsd ldrs: hdwy 2f out and sn rdn: drvn and kpt on same pce fnl f* **25/1**

04 **5** *nk* **Roys Dream**[29] 6313 3-9-4 **67**.................... GabrieleMalune 10 63
(Paul Collins) *towards rr: hdwy wl over 1f out: sn rdn: kpt on fnl f: nrst fin* **11/1**

300 **6** *1 ½* **Major Crispies**[8] 7056 6-9-2 **70**....................(b) TommyO'Connor(7) 9 61
(David O'Meara) *trckd ldrs: hdwy on outer and cl up 1/2-way: rdn along 2f out: wknd over 1f out* **14/1**

3320 **7** *1 ¼* **Ticks The Boxes (IRE)**[11] 6964 5-9-2 **68**....................(p) TobyEley(5) 8 55
(John Wainwright) *chsd ldng pair: rdn along 2f out: sn drvn and grad wknd* **16/1**

0015 **8** *3 ½* **Prazeres**[23] 6558 3-8-8 **60**.................... JonathanFisher(3) 7 36
(Les Eyre) *led: rdn along over 2f out: hdd wl over 1f out: sn wknd* **16/1**

0050 **9** *2 ¼* **Caeser The Gaeser (IRE)**[26] 6435 5-8-12 **62**..(p) RobertDodsworth(3) 3 31
(Nigel Tinkler) *a in rr* **14/1**

5610 **10** *¾* **Ki Ki**[23] 6546 5-8-12 **66**.................... HarryRussell(7) 1 32
(Bryan Smart) *a towards rr* **14/1**

5000 **11** *1* **Taskeen (IRE)**[86] 4168 4-9-6 **67**.................... BenSanderson 11 30
(Roger Fell) *a in rr* **12/1**

1m 19.65s (2.75) **Going Correction** +0.50s/f (Yiel)
**WFA** 3 from 4yo+ 2lb **11** Ran SP% **115.1**
Speed ratings (Par 103): **101,100,97,96,95 93,92,87,84,83 82**
CSF £13.40 CT £53.41 TOTE £4.30: £1.60, £1.30, £2.20; EX 14.10 Trifecta £72.80.
**Owner** A Melville **Bred** Hellwood Stud Farm & G P Clarke **Trained** Scarcroft, W Yorks

**FOCUS**
A modest apprentice sprint handicap in which a couple of fillies held sway.
T/Plt: £188.50 to a £1 stake. Pool: £92,233.81 - 357.03 winning units T/Qpdt: £21.10 to a £1 stake. Pool: £7,952.42 - 278.66 winning units **Joe Rowntree**

# [7280]YARMOUTH (L-H)
Thursday, September 21

**OFFICIAL GOING: Good to soft (soft in places; 6.7)**
Wind: medium, against Weather: fine

## 7333 BRITISH STALLION STUDS EBF NOVICE STKS (PLUS 10 RACE) 1m 3y
**2:00** (2:03) (Class 4) 2-Y-0 **£4,528** (£1,347; £673; £336) **Stalls** Centre

Form RPR

22 **1** **Gabr**[27] 6403 2-9-2 0.................... JimCrowley 5 78+
(Sir Michael Stoute) *trckd ldr tl clsd and upsides over 1f out: pushed into ld 1f out: reminder and asserted ins fnl f: pushed out: comf* **4/9**[1]

5 **2** *1 ¾* **Istanbul Sultan (IRE)**[34] 6133 2-9-2 0.................... RyanMoore 3 74+
(William Haggas) *dwlt: in tch in last pair: effrt over 1f out: hdwy to chse ldrs over 1f out: kpt on same pce ins fnl f: wnt 2nd cl home* **9/2**[3]

0 **3** *hd* **Blooriedotcom (IRE)**[26] 6424 2-9-2 0.................... MartinHarley 4 73
(Peter Chapple-Hyam) *stdd after s: hld up in tch in rr: swtchd rt 2f out: rdn and hdwy to chse ldrs jst over 1f out: kpt on same pce: wnt 3rd last strides* **80/1**

5 **4** *nk* **Bowditch (IRE)**[27] 6374 2-9-2 0.................... JamesDoyle 6 73
(John Gosden) *led: rdn wl over 1f out: hdd 1f out: styd in same pce ins fnl f: lost 2 pls cl home* **4/1**[2]

05 **5** *9* **Snaffled (IRE)**[14] 6853 2-9-2 0.................... SeanLevey 1 51
(David Brown) *t.k.h: hld up wl in tch in midfield: swtchd lft over 2f out: rdn and outpcd over 1f out: wknd fnl f* **100/1**

**6** *9* **Volevo Lui** 2-9-2 0.................... DanielMuscutt 2 29
(Marco Botti) *chsd ldrs tl rdn and lost pl over 2f out: sn bhd: wknd over 1f out* **33/1**

1m 42.4s (1.80) **Going Correction** +0.10s/f (Good) **6** Ran SP% **112.6**
Speed ratings (Par 97): **95,93,93,92,83 74**
CSF £2.97 TOTE £1.30: £1.10, £2.00; EX 3.10 Trifecta £20.40.
**Owner** Hamdan Al Maktoum **Bred** Cheveley Park Stud Ltd **Trained** Newmarket, Suffolk

**FOCUS**
The second day of the Eastern meeting and it was dry overnight. They kept middle-to-stands' side in this fair novice contest and went a routine pace into a strong headwind.

## 7334 KEN LINDSAY MEMORIAL/EBF FILLIES' NOVICE STKS (PLUS 10 RACE) 6f 3y
**2:30** (2:32) (Class 4) 2-Y-0 **£4,528** (£1,347; £673; £336) **Stalls** Centre

Form RPR

**1** **Beauty Filly** 2-9-0 0.................... RyanMoore 10 79+
(William Haggas) *hld up in tch in midfield: effrt ent fnl 2f: rdn to chal over 1f out: led jst ins fnl f: r.o wl: rdn out* **6/4**[1]

1 **2** *1* **Flying Sparkle (IRE)**[80] 4440 2-9-3 0.................... JamieSpencer 1 79
(Michael Bell) *led tl over 2f out: chsd ldr tl rdn to ld again over 1f out: drvn and hdd ins fnl f: styd on same pce fnl 100yds* **11/4**[2]

**3** *nse* **Left Alone** 2-9-0 0.................... JamesDoyle 11 76+
(Hugo Palmer) *hld up in tch towards rr: nt clr run and swtchd rt over 1f out: hdwy and swtchd lft ins fnl f: r.o strly fnl 100yds* **5/1**[3]

00 **4** *½* **Rozanne (IRE)**[22] 6584 2-9-0 0.................... JFEgan 9 74
(Jeremy Noseda) *hld up in tch: rdn and hdwy ent fnl f: swtchd lft ins fnl f: styd on wl* **33/1**

**5** *1 ¼* **Bidding War** 2-9-0 0.................... MartinHarley 3 71
(James Tate) *in tch in last trio: rdn and hdwy over 2f out: chsd ldrs over 1f out: unable qck and kpt on same pce ins fnl f* **20/1**

0 **6** *1* **Image**[25] 6480 2-9-0 0.................... DavidProbert 6 68
(Philip McBride) *t.k.h: hld up wl in tch in midfield: effrt over 1f out: unable qck and kpt on same pce ins fnl f* **16/1**

0 **7** 1 ½ **Rupert's Lass**[45] 5717 2-9-0 0 LouisSteward 13 63
(Michael Bell) *sn bhd and reminder after 1f: hdwy whn pushed lft ent fnl f: kpt on ins fnl f: nvr trbld ldrs* **100/1**

0 **8** 1 ¼ **Agent Error (IRE)**[13] 6876 2-9-0 0 StevieDonohoe 2 59
(David Simcock) *t.k.h: chsd ldrs: rdn 2f out: unable qck and lost pl over 1f out: wknd ins fnl f* **28/1**

2300 **9** 1 ¼ **Angel Of The South (IRE)**[28] 6353 2-9-0 73 RobertWinston 4 56
(Dean Ivory) *chsd ldrs: swtchd to stands' rail 1/2-way: sn led: rdn and hdd over 1f out: sn outpcd: wknd ins fnl f* **11/1**

06 **10** 1 ½ **Wotamadam**[34] 6147 2-9-0 0 SilvestreDeSousa 5 51
(Dean Ivory) *in tch in midfield: rdn 2f out: unable qck and lost pl over 1f out: wknd ins fnl f* **66/1**

**11** ¾ **Connoisseur** 2-9-0 0 LukeMorris 12 49
(Sir Mark Prescott Bt) *midfield but sn bustled along: lost pl and bhd 1/2-way: n.d after* **100/1**

50 **12** nse **Long Embrace**[13] 6876 2-9-0 0 OisinMurphy 7 49
(Simon Crisford) *hld up in tch towards rr: effrt over 1f out: no real imp whn pushed lft ent fnl f: wknd ins fnl f* **33/1**

0 **13** 1 ½ **Miss Minding (IRE)**[25] 6480 2-9-0 0 (h1) LiamKeniry 8 44
(Ed Dunlop) *chsd ldrs: rdn over 1f out: losing pl whn wnt sharply lft ent fnl f: sn wknd* **50/1**

1m 15.53s (1.13) **Going Correction** +0.10s/f (Good) **13** Ran SP% **117.1**
Speed ratings (Par 94): **96,94,94,93,92 90,88,87,85,83 82,82,80**
CSF £4.85 TOTE £2.30: £1.02, £1.60, £2.20; EX 6.90 Trifecta £23.60.
**Owner** Sheikh Juma Dalmook Al Maktoum **Bred** Highbank Stud **Trained** Newmarket, Suffolk

**FOCUS**
An interesting fillies' novice event, run at a sound pace with the leaders coming nearside from halfway.

## 7335 PARKDEAN RESORTS STARLAND KREW NURSERY H'CAP 6f 3y
**3:00** (3:01) (Class 4) (0-80,82) 2-Y-O **£4,410** (£1,320; £660; £330; £164) **Stalls** Centre

Form RPR

4514 **1** **Fighting Irish (IRE)**[11] 6967 2-9-4 77 StevieDonohoe 1 90+
(Harry Dunlop) *mde all: rdn and qcknd clr over 1f out: r.o strly ins fnl f: readily* **7/1**

1404 **2** 5 **Royal Household**[27] 6375 2-9-0 76 HollieDoyle(3) 2 74
(Richard Hannon) *t.k.h: chsd ldrs tl wnt 2nd over 4f out: swtchd lft and effrt ent fnl 2f: nt match pce of wnr over 1f out: wl hld in clr 2nd and kpt on same pce ins fnl f* **15/8**[1]

4002 **3** 2 **New Empire**[48] 5596 2-9-4 80 DavidEgan(3) 5 72
(Peter Chapple-Hyam) *hld up in tch: effrt wl over 1f out: wnt 3rd 1f out: kpt on same pce and no ch w wnr fnl f* **17/2**

522 **4** 2 ¾ **Forever In Love**[13] 6876 2-8-11 70 (b1) RyanMoore 3 54
(Sir Michael Stoute) *s.i.s: in rr tl hdwy after 2f: chsd ldrs and rdn ent fnl 2f: unable qck and btn over 1f out: wknd ins fnl f* **3/1**[2]

4054 **5** hd **Hard Graft**[37] 6036 2-9-1 74 SeanLevey 6 57
(David Brown) *stdd s: t.k.h: hld up in tch in rr: effrt over 1f out: sn rdn and no hdwy: wl btn 1f out* **16/1**

4021 **6** nk **Central City (IRE)**[12] 6951 2-9-9 82 JamesDoyle 4 64
(Hugo Palmer) *chsd ldr tl over 1f out: lost pl u.p over 1f out: wl btn 1f out* **7/2**[3]

1m 13.95s (-0.45) **Going Correction** +0.10s/f (Good) **6** Ran SP% **110.9**
Speed ratings (Par 97): **107,100,97,94,93 93**
CSF £20.12 TOTE £8.70: £3.50, £1.10; EX 19.40 Trifecta £110.60.
**Owner** Daniel Macauliffe & Anoj Don **Bred** Kilcarn Stud **Trained** Lambourn, Berks

**FOCUS**
This was a competitive little nursery on paper, but the winner proved a class apart. He could be rated well into the 90s in due course.

## 7336 BATH SUMMER STAYING SERIES FINAL H'CAP 1m 6f 17y
**3:35** (3:35) (Class 2) 3-Y-O+ **£12,602** (£3,772; £1,886; £944; £470) **Stalls** High

Form RPR

3211 **1** **Hope Is High**[29] 6309 4-9-10 72 SilvestreDeSousa 12 79+
(John Berry) *stdd s: hld up in tch in rr: swtchd rt and effrt 2f out: hdwy to ld 1f out: hld on wl u.p ins fnl f: rdn out* **11/4**[1]

123 **2** ¾ **Innoko (FR)**[48] 5590 7-9-1 63 (p1) PatCosgrave 2 68
(Robert Stephens) *chsd ldrs: nt clr run 2f out tl gap opened and hdwy u.p jst over 1f out: pressing wnr ins fnl f: kpt on wl u.p but hld towards fin* **8/1**[3]

2253 **3** 1 ½ **Eben Dubai (IRE)**[29] 6305 5-8-2 50 (p1) LukeMorris 1 53
(John Flint) *t.k.h: hld up in tch in last trio: clsd and nt clr run over 3f out: swtchd rt over 2f out: stl nt clrest of runs and swtchd rt again over 1f out: styd on wl u.p to go 3rd towards fin* **9/1**

3312 **4** 1 **With Pleasure**[33] 6196 4-9-9 71 DanielMuscutt 7 73
(John Flint) *wl in tch in midfield: clsd to press ldrs and rdn 2f out: led over 1f out: hdd 1f out: 3rd and outpcd jst ins fnl f: styd on same pce after* **6/1**[2]

2055 **5** nk **Spiritoftomintoul**[13] 6889 8-9-1 63 (bt1) GeorgeDowning 6 64
(Tony Carroll) *hld up in tch towards rr: rdn and hdwy over 1f out: styd on same pce u.p ins fnl f* **12/1**

0413 **6** 2 **Affair**[21] 6611 3-8-0 56 oh2 KieranO'Neill 4 56
(Hughie Morrison) *chsd ldr tl rdn to ld ent fnl 2f: hdd and unable qck over 1f out: edgd rt and wknd jst ins fnl f* **11/1**

401 **7** ½ **Delannoy**[25] 6473 3-7-12 61 (v) DarraghKeenan(7) 8 63+
(Neil Mulholland) *hld up in tch: nt clr run and shuffled bk to rr jst over 2f out: nvr enough room to make any hdwy after tl swtchd rt wl ins fnl f: pushed along and sme hdwy towards fin* **20/1**

0156 **8** ½ **Grams And Ounces**[24] 6509 10-8-11 59 (tp) TimmyMurphy 10 56
(Grace Harris) *hld up in last pair: hdwy on outer 12f out: chsd ldrs 8f out: rdn and pressing ldrs ent fnl 2f tl unable qck over 1f out: wknd ins fnl f* **33/1**

520 **9** ½ **Wassail**[16] 6796 4-7-13 50 DavidEgan(3) 11 46
(Ed de Giles) *chsd ldrs: rdn 3f out: lost pl over 1f out: wknd ins fnl f* **25/1**

0331 **10** 1 **Desert Cross**[57] 5274 4-9-5 67 RyanMoore 3 65+
(Jonjo O'Neill) *hld up in tch in midfield: clsd on inner but nt clr run ent fnl 2f: nvr enough room to make any hdwy after and eased off ins fnl f* **6/1**[2]

3456 **11** ¾ **Vexillum (IRE)**[16] 6796 8-7-11 48 oh3 (p) HollieDoyle(3) 9 42
(Neil Mulholland) *stdd s: hld up in rr: hdwy into midfield on outer 8f out: rdn over 2f out: lost pl and bhd over 1f out: wknd ins fnl f* **28/1**

6016 **12** 6 **Dukinta (IRE)**[21] 6618 3-9-6 76 (v) FranBerry 5 63
(Hugo Palmer) *led tl rdn and hdd ent fnl 2f: lost pl and bhd 1f out: wknd ins fnl f* **10/1**

3m 14.9s (7.30) **Going Correction** +0.10s/f (Good)
**WFA** 3 from 4yo+ 8lb **12** Ran SP% **116.5**
Speed ratings (Par 109): **83,82,81,81,80 79,79,79,78,78 77,74**
CSF £22.86 CT £175.71 TOTE £3.70: £1.50, £2.60, £2.00; EX 28.00 Trifecta £112.20.
**Owner** Mrs Emma Berry & John Berry **Bred** Miss K Rausing **Trained** Newmarket, Suffolk

**FOCUS**
This series final was rescheduled from Bath last weekend. It was run at an uneven pace, but represents decent form for the class and the winner continues to progress.

## 7337 "GET ON" WITH DAN HAGUE H'CAP 1m 6f 17y
**4:10** (4:10) (Class 2) (0-100,100) 3-Y-O+ **£12,602** (£3,772; £1,886; £944; £470) **Stalls** High

Form RPR

5611 **1** **Great Hall**[13] 6872 7-10-0 100 FranBerry 8 108
(Mick Quinn) *hld up in rr: nt clr run over 2f out: effrt in 5th but stl plenty to do over 1f out: str run to ld wl ins fnl f: sn in command and r.o wl* **11/1**

1135 **2** 1 ½ **Zenon (IRE)**[26] 6421 3-9-0 94 (b1) RyanMoore 4 101+
(John Gosden) *midfield: rdn over 2f out: clsd to chse ldrs and nt clr run 1f out: squeezed through and chsd wnr wl ins fnl f: no imp: eased nr fin* **4/1**[2]

4533 **3** 1 ½ **William Hunter**[40] 5924 5-8-12 84 FergusSweeney 7 88
(Alan King) *hld up in last trio: hdwy to chse clr ldng pair over 2f out: rdn and clsd to press ldrs 1f out: drvn to ld ins fnl f: sn hdd and outpcd fnl 75yds* **7/1**

1254 **4** 1 ¾ **Star Of The East (IRE)**[5] 7163 3-8-4 84 JFEgan 3 85
(Mark Johnston) *chsd ldrs tl wnt 2nd 8f out: jnd ldr and kicked clr 4f out: rdn to ld over 2f out: hdd ins fnl f: no ex and wknd wl ins fnl f* **9/1**

-102 **5** 3 ¼ **Alqamar**[13] 6872 3-8-11 91 (b1) JamesDoyle 2 91
(Charlie Appleby) *led: wnt clr w rival 4f out: rdn and hdd over 1f out: kpt on and ev ch tl btn ins fnl f: eased wl ins fnl f* **9/4**[1]

1202 **6** 1 **Nadaitak**[22] 6580 3-8-7 87 (b1) StevieDonohoe 5 82
(Sir Michael Stoute) *s.i.s and rdn along in rr early: hdwy into midfield after 2f out: wnt 3rd 4f out tl lost pl qckly over 2f out: wl hld over 1f out* **6/1**[3]

5200 **7** nk **Cliff Face (IRE)**[19] 6675 4-9-4 90 LukeMorris 6 85
(Sir Mark Prescott Bt) *t.k.h: hld up in last trio: rdn and no imp over 2f out: 6th and wl hld over 1f out* **20/1**

1115 **8** 66 **Theydon Grey**[26] 6427 4-9-1 92 GeorgiaCox(5) 1
(William Haggas) *chsd ldr tl 8f out: chsd ldrs tl 4f out: dropped out and bhd 2f out: eased fnl f: t.o: burst blood vessel* **7/1**

3m 5.83s (-1.77) **Going Correction** +0.10s/f (Good)
**WFA** 3 from 4yo+ 8lb **8** Ran SP% **113.2**
Speed ratings (Par 109): **109,108,107,106,104 103,103,65**
CSF £53.42 CT £332.91 TOTE £12.20: £3.90, £1.50, £2.20; EX 36.00 Trifecta £290.40.
**Owner** M Quinn **Bred** Aston House Stud **Trained** Newmarket, Suffolk

**FOCUS**
A decent staying handicap, run to suit the closers. The winner has been rated back to his best.

## 7338 BRITISH EBF FILLIES' H'CAP 1m 3f 104y
**4:40** (4:42) (Class 4) (0-80,82) 3-Y-O+ **£5,983** (£1,780; £889; £444) **Stalls** Low

Form RPR

3211 **1** **So Sleek**[45] 5715 3-9-10 82 JamieSpencer 2 89
(Luca Cumani) *chsd ldr for 2f: chsd ldrs after: effrt 2f out: rdn to chse ldr over 1f out: drvn and styd on strly ins fnl f to ld towards fin* **6/4**[1]

2331 **2** ½ **Sea Tide**[23] 6548 3-9-9 81 (tp) RyanMoore 4 87
(Hugo Palmer) *t.k.h: hld up in tch in midfield: nt clrest of runs 2f out: followed wnr through jst over 1f out: chsd ldng pair ins fnl f: drvn and styd on wl to snatch 2nd last strides* **6/1**[3]

1100 **3** hd **Vernatti**[19] 6701 4-9-12 78 RobHornby 6 83
(Pam Sly) *stdd s: t.k.h: chsd ldrs: wnt 2nd after 2f tl led 8f out: clr 6f out: rdn 2f out: drvn over 1f out: kpt on wl u.p tl hdd and no ex towards fin: lost 2nd last strides* **10/1**

1240 **4** 2 ¼ **Jive Talking (IRE)**[18] 6722 3-9-6 78 JamesDoyle 5 79
(Michael Bell) *t.k.h: hld up in tch in midfield: effrt 2f out: sn drvn and chsd ldrs: 4th and outpcd ins fnl f* **13/2**

0455 **5** 2 ¼ **Pernickety**[42] 5822 4-9-0 66 (t1) FranBerry 7 63
(Lucy Wadham) *rn wout declared tongue tie (fell off in stalls): stdd s: hld up in tch in last pair: effrt 2f out: no imp u.p over 1f out: wl hld fnl f* **14/1**

1316 **6** ¾ **Bonnie Arlene (IRE)**[12] 6937 3-9-4 76 OisinMurphy 1 72
(Mark Johnston) *led tl 8f out: chsd ldr tl rdn and lost 2nd over 1f out: sn btn and wknd ins fnl f* **11/1**

424 **7** 10 **Fengate**[34] 6152 4-10-0 80 (t1) KieranShoemark 3 72
(Roger Charlton) *hld up in tch in last pair: effrt on inner but hanging lft fr 3f out: rdn and no hdwy over 1f out: eased fnl f* **7/2**[2]

2m 30.36s (1.66) **Going Correction** +0.10s/f (Good)
**WFA** 3 from 4yo 6lb **7** Ran SP% **113.9**
Speed ratings (Par 102): **97,96,96,94,93 92,85**
CSF £10.96 TOTE £2.20: £1.60, £2.80; EX 9.20 Trifecta £59.70.
**Owner** Lordship Stud **Bred** Fittocks Stud & Arrow Farm & Stud **Trained** Newmarket, Suffolk

**FOCUS**
Not a bad fillies' handicap. The winner continues to progress and a personal best from the runner-up.

## 7339 INTU CHAPELFIELD SHOPPING CENTRE NORWICH H'CAP 1m 3y
**5:15** (5:16) (Class 3) (0-90,90) 3-Y-O **£7,876** (£2,357; £1,178; £441; £441) **Stalls** Centre

Form RPR

4150 **1** **Mazyoun**[12] 6933 3-9-7 90 (b) JamesDoyle 6 95
(Hugo Palmer) *stdd s: t.k.h: hld up in tch in rr: swtchd lft jst over 2f out: rdn to chal 1f out: edgd rt and led ins fnl f: edging rt but hld on wl towards fin* **3/1**[2]

3412 **2** nse **Hugin (IRE)**[23] 6562 3-9-6 89 JamieSpencer 5 94
(David Simcock) *stdd s: hld up in tch in 4th: effrt over 1f out: str chal whn wnt lft u.p ins fnl f: kpt on wl: jst hld cl home* **13/8**[1]

3134 **3** 1 ½ **Whosyourhousemate**[35] 6110 3-8-10 79 StevieDonohoe 3 82
(Ed Vaughan) *t.k.h: led and set stdy gallop: rdn wl over 1f out: hdd ins fnl f: stl ev ch in 3rd but hld whn squeezed for room and eased nr fin* **5/1**

2510 **4** 3 ¾ **Maratha (IRE)**[27] 6389 3-8-13 82 SeanLevey 1 75
(Stuart Williams) *t.k.h: chsd ldr tl jst over 2f out: rdn over 1f out: sn outpcd and wl hld ins fnl f* **9/1**

3215 **4** dht **Working Class**[27] 6387 3-8-8 77 KieranShoemark 4 73
(Peter Chapple-Hyam) *t.k.h: trckd ldrs tl wnt 2nd jst over 2f out: drvn and ev ch over 1f out: jst getting outpcd whn squeezed for room and hmpd ins fnl f: wl hld after* **9/2**[3]

1m 41.69s (1.09) **Going Correction** +0.10s/f (Good) **5** Ran SP% **107.9**
Speed ratings (Par 105): **98,97,96,92,92**
CSF £7.97 TOTE £3.30: £1.50, £1.40; EX 7.10 Trifecta £20.00.
**Owner** Al Shaqab Racing **Bred** Cheveley Park Stud Ltd **Trained** Newmarket, Suffolk

**FOCUS**
A good-quality handicap and it's sound form.

## 7340 BOMBARDIER BEER H'CAP — 7f 3y
5:50 (5:50) (Class 3) (0-90,91) 3-Y-O+ £7,876 (£2,357; £1,178; £590; £293) **Stalls** Centre

Form | | | | RPR
1241 **1** **Big Tour (IRE)**[19] 6686 3-9-4 **90** ........ PatCosgrave 1 101+
(Saeed bin Suroor) *chsd ldr: clsd and travelling strly over 1f out: pushed into ld jst ins fnl f: sn rdn and qcknd clr: r.o strly: comf* **6/4**[1]
6210 **2** 2 1/4 **Mountain Rescue (IRE)**[33] 6192 5-9-8 **91** ........ JamesDoyle 2 96
(Chris Wall) *hld up in tch in 4th: effrt in 3rd and swtchd lft wl over 1f out: no ch w wnr ins fnl f: kpt on to go 2nd last strides* **5/2**[2]
6156 **3** nk **Theodorico (IRE)**[13] 6879 4-9-6 **89** ........ KieranShoemark 4 93
(David Loughnane) *led: set stdy gallop but allowed to go clr: rdn ent fnl 2f: drvn and hdd jst ins fnl f: sn outpcd and lost 2nd last strides* **9/1**
2261 **4** 1 **Pastoral Player**[77] 4524 10-9-6 **89** ........ OisinMurphy 5 90
(Hughie Morrison) *taken down early: stdd s: t.k.h: hld up in 3rd tl wl over 1f out: sn rdn: kpt on same pce and swtchd lft ins fnl f* **11/1**
3412 **5** 1 **Noble Masterpiece**[16] 6792 3-8-11 **83** ........ StevieDonohoe 3 81
(Sir Michael Stoute) *taken down early: stdd s: t.k.h: hld up in rr: swtchd rt and effrt over 1f out: rdn 1f out: kpt on same pce and no imp* **3/1**[3]

1m 27.31s (0.71) **Going Correction** +0.10s/f (Good)
**WFA** 3 from 4yo+ 3lb — **5** Ran SP% **111.9**
Speed ratings (Par 107): **99,96,96,94,93**
CSF £5.65 TOTE £1.90: £1.50, £1.60; EX 4.90 Trifecta £21.60.
**Owner** Godolphin **Bred** Rabbah Bloodstock Limited **Trained** Newmarket, Suffolk

**FOCUS**
This proved tactical, but it threw up a highly progressive winner. The winner has been rated close to form with the runner-up the benchmark.
T/Plt: £20.50 to a £1 stake. Pool: £86,473.81 - 3,073.22 winning units. T/Qpdt: £19.60 to a £1 stake. Pool: £5,413.53 - 203.84 winning units. **Steve Payne**

# 7068 SAINT-CLOUD (L-H)
Thursday, September 21

**OFFICIAL GOING: Turf: heavy**

## 7341a PRIX CORONATION (LISTED RACE) (3YO FILLIES) (TURF) — 1m
4:05 3-Y-O £23,504 (£9,401; £7,051; £4,700; £2,350)

RPR
**1** **Enlighted (IRE)**[37] 6054 3-8-11 0 ........ AurelienLemaitre 6 103+
(F Head, France) **143/10**
**2** 2 1/2 **Esquisse**[37] 6054 3-9-2 0 ........ MaximeGuyon 8 102
(A Fabre, France) **13/5**[1]
**3** 1 3/4 **Bijin (FR)**[30] 3-8-11 0 ........ Pierre-CharlesBoudot 4 93
(H-A Pantall, France) **179/10**
**4** 3/4 **La Poutanesca (IRE)**[44] 5777 3-8-11 0 ........ GregoryBenoist 1 92
(D Smaga, France) **122/10**
**5** shd **Rueing (USA)**[29] 3-8-11 0 ........ MickaelBarzalona 5 91
(A Fabre, France) *hld up towards rr: impr to take cl order over 2f out: sn pushed along: rdn over 1f out: wknd ins fnl f* **59/10**
**6** 1 3/4 **Limited Edition (FR)**[37] 6054 3-8-11 0 ........ TonyPiccone 7 87
(E Lellouche, France) **16/5**[2]
**7** nk **Silver Cape (FR)**[16] 6804 3-8-13 0 ow2 ........ ChristopheSoumillon 2 89
(T Clout, France) **172/10**
**8** nk **Body Sculpt (FR)**[33] 6227 3-8-11 0 ........ StephanePasquier 9 86
(S Kobayashi, France) **137/10**
**9** 6 **Mitigate**[23] 6562 3-8-11 0 ........ TheoBachelot 3 72
(Jane Chapple-Hyam) *hld up in midfield: rdn 2f out: little rspnse and eased ins fnl f* **50/1**
**10** 8 **Louversey**[23] 3-8-11 0 ........ CristianDemuro 10 54
(P Sogorb, France) **9/2**[3]

1m 44.95s (-2.55) — **10** Ran SP% **117.9**
PARI-MUTUEL (all including 1 euro stake): WIN 2.90; PLACE 2.60, 2.10, 3.50; DF 12.60; SF 22.90.
**Owner** Wertheimer & Frere **Bred** Wertheimer & Frere **Trained** France

**FOCUS**
The winner kept on well and won with a bit to spare.

## 7342a PRIX DE HOUDAN (CLAIMER) (4YO+) (TURF) — 1m
5:35 4-Y-O+ £6,837 (£2,735; £2,051; £1,367; £683)

RPR
**1** **Malaspina (ITY)**[24] 6541 5-9-3 0 ........ (b) ChristopheSoumillon 9 77
(Antonio Marcialis, Italy) **19/10**[1]
**2** 1 3/4 **Menardais (FR)**[22] 8-8-10 0 ........ KyllanBarbaud(8) 12 74
(N Caullery, France) **116/10**
**3** 3/4 **Intensical (IRE)**[43] 5788 6-8-10 0 ........ (b) HayleyTurner(5) 11 69
(Ivan Furtado) *sn trcking ldrs: hdwy over 2f out: drvn to chal over 1f out: styd on u.p fnl f* **144/10**
**4** 2 **King's Hollow (FR)**[133] 4-9-8 0 ........ (b) Pierre-CharlesBoudot 10 72
(Henk Grewe, Germany) **32/5**
**5** 2 1/2 **Royal Prize**[22] 7-9-4 0 ........ AlexisBadel 3 62
(Mme M Bollack-Badel, France) **9/2**[3]
**6** snk **Xedra**[24] 6541 5-8-4 0 ........ (p) MlleAlisonMassin(4) 2 52
(H De Nicolay, France) **75/1**
**7** 3 **Kencharova (FR)**[706] 7276 5-9-1 0 ........ (b) ThierryThulliez 4 52
(F Vermeulen, France) **10/1**
**8** 4 **Stemster**[234] 6-9-0 0 ........ MlleAnnaVanDenTroost(4) 7 45
(Ecurie Avant-Garde, Belgium) **31/1**
**9** 2 **Atreju (GER)**[382] 5-9-1 0 ........ ClementLecoeuvre(3) 1 41
(Waldemar Hickst, Germany) **22/5**[2]
**10** 2 1/2 **Mariele (IRE)**[300] 6-8-10 0 ........ DelphineSantiago(5) 5 32
(U Schwinn, Germany) **27/1**
**11** 2 **Rosecomb (IRE)**[400] 5548 4-8-7 0 ........ DanaZamecnikova(4) 6 24
(Frank Sheridan, Italy) **85/1**
**12** 1/2 **Shamar Love (IRE)**[11] 7-8-9 0 ........ (p) ThomasTrullier(6) 8 26
(Carina Fey, France) **70/1**

1m 45.08s (-2.42) — **12** Ran SP% **118.8**
PARI-MUTUEL (all including 1 euro stake): WIN 2.90; PLACE 1.70, 2.60, 3.40; DF 15.40; SF 23.70.
**Owner** Paolo Ferrario **Bred** Scuderia Fert Di Ferrario Paolo Et Al **Trained** Italy

# 5990 AYR (L-H)
Friday, September 22

**7343 Meeting Abandoned** - Waterlogged

# 6189 NEWBURY (L-H)
Friday, September 22

**OFFICIAL GOING: Good (good to firm in places) changing to good after race 2 (1.50)**
Wind: light, against Weather: sunny

## 7351 BRITISH STALLION STUDS EBF MAIDEN STKS (PLUS 10 RACE) (DIV I) — 6f
1:20 (1:23) (Class 4) 2-Y-O £6,469 (£1,925; £962; £481) **Stalls** Centre

Form | | | | RPR
**1** **Orange Suit (IRE)** 2-9-5 0 ........ SeanLevey 14 75+
(Richard Hannon) *str: lw: hld up in tch in midfield: clsd to trck ldrs and travelling wl 2f out: shkn up over 1f out: rdn and r.o wl ins fnl f to ld towards fin* **20/1**
2 **2** nk **Jack Crow**[30] 6319 2-9-5 0 ........ CharlesBishop 13 74
(Eve Johnson Houghton) *unf: swtg: t.k.h: w ldr tl led after 2f: shkn up ent fnl f: rdn jst ins fnl f: kpt on wl tl hdd and no ex towards fin* **14/1**
02 **3** 1/2 **Mr Top Hat**[102] 3668 2-9-5 0 ........ SilvestreDeSousa 11 72
(David Evans) *w'like: led for 2f: styd upsides ldr: rdn over 1f out: drvn 1f out: kpt on wl: unable qck and one pced towards fin* **7/1**
**4** 3/4 **Final Treat (IRE)** 2-9-0 0 ........ RyanMoore 7 65+
(William Haggas) *tall: athletic: lw: trckd ldrs: effrt over 1f out: rdn and styd on same pce ins fnl f* **5/2**[1]
4 **5** nk **Buffer Zone**[37] 6071 2-9-5 0 ........ KieranShoemark 10 69+
(Roger Charlton) *lw: stdd s: t.k.h: hld up in tch in midfield: swtchd lft: pushed along and clsd to chse ldrs ent fnl f: nt clrest of runs and kpt on same pce ins fnl f* **3/1**[2]
**6** 1 1/2 **Royal Residence** 2-9-5 0 ........ MartinHarley 15 64+
(James Tate) *unf: scope: dwlt: in tch in rr: shkn up 2f out: hdwy ins fnl f: styd on wl fnl 100yds: nvr trbld ldrs* **33/1**
06 **7** 1/2 **Quick Breath**[37] 6070 2-9-5 0 ........ RobHornby 16 63
(Jonathan Portman) *in tch in midfield: wnt rt 2f out: sn rdn: kpt on same pce ins fnl f* **66/1**
03 **8** hd **Blackheath**[28] 6394 2-9-5 0 ........ PatCosgrave 8 62
(Ed Walker) *dwlt: hld up in tch in midfield: swtchd lft and hdwy over 1f out: rdn and no imp jst ins fnl f: wknd fnl 100yds* **6/1**
60 **9** nse **Avon Green**[29] 6338 2-9-0 0 ........ OisinMurphy 9 57
(Joseph Tuite) *w'like: t.k.h: shkn up jst over 1f out: unable qck and sn outpcd: wknd ins fnl f* **80/1**
6 **10** 1 1/4 **Appenzeller (USA)**[36] 6093 2-9-5 0 ........ ShaneKelly 4 58
(Richard Hughes) *w'like: stdd and dropped in bhd after s: t.k.h: in tch in rr: swtchd rt 1f out: pushed along and kpt on ins fnl f: nvr trbld ldrs* **66/1**
0 **11** 1/2 **Goodbye Lulu (IRE)**[27] 6438 2-9-0 0 ........ (h[1]) TrevorWhelan 5 51
(George Baker) *taken down early: hld up in rr: shkn up ent fnl f: kpt on: nvr trbld ldrs* **100/1**
3 **12** 1 3/4 **Go Roo**[30] 6304 2-9-5 0 ........ AdamKirby 6 51
(Clive Cox) *unf: swtg: hld up in tch towards rr: effrt over 1f out: no imp: n.d* **11/2**[3]
0 **13** nk **Dracarys**[16] 6826 2-9-5 0 ........ OscarPereira 3 50
(Jose Santos) *w'like: in tch in midfield: rdn over 1f out: no imp and wknd ins fnl f* **125/1**
0 **14** 3 3/4 **Spirit Of Ishy**[65] 5026 2-9-0 0 ........ LiamKeniry 12 33
(Stuart Kittow) *unf: t.k.h: chsd ldrs tl lost pl over 2f out: bhd fnl f* **150/1**

1m 14.43s (1.43) **Going Correction** +0.125s/f (Good) — **14** Ran SP% **116.8**
Speed ratings (Par 97): **95,94,93,92,92 90,89,89,89,87 87,84,84,79**
CSF £261.01 TOTE £20.10: £4.20, £3.40, £1.90; EX 295.40 Trifecta £810.70.
**Owner** Martin Hughes & Michael Kerr-Dineen **Bred** Barronstown Stud **Trained** East Everleigh, Wilts

**FOCUS**
The inside rail on the 5f & 7f bend was 4yds from the inside line, so round course races were 14.5yds longer than advertised. There was 1mm of rain on Friday. After riding this opening race Adam Kirby said the ground was on the "easy side of good", Shane Kelly said they were "just kicking the top off" and Ryan Moore's view was it was "good". They raced up the middle in what looked an ordinary 2yo maiden and they didn't seem to go that quick - the time was 1.9sec slower than the second leg - but a promising winner.

## 7352 BRITISH STALLION STUDS EBF MAIDEN STKS (PLUS 10 RACE) (DIV II) — 6f
1:50 (1:54) (Class 4) 2-Y-O £6,469 (£1,925; £962; £481) **Stalls** Centre

Form | | | | RPR
2 **1** **Beshaayir**[35] 6138 2-9-0 0 ........ RyanMoore 14 82+
(William Haggas) *str: lw: hld up in tch in midfield: swtchd rt and effrt over 1f out: rdn to ld and edgd lft 1f out: r.o wl and in command fnl 100yds* **11/10**[1]
032 **2** 1 1/2 **Foxtrot Lady**[26] 6480 2-9-0 **80** ........ DavidProbert 9 77
(Andrew Balding) *lw: chsd ldrs: effrt to chal over 1f out: rdn to ld ent fnl f: sn hdd and carried sltly lft: styd on same pce ins fnl f* **13/2**
2430 **3** 1 **Prince Ahwahnee**[29] 6353 2-9-5 **77** ........ (p[1]) AdamKirby 12 81
(Clive Cox) *t.k.h: hld up in tch in midfield: clsd to trck ldrs over 1f out: effrt 1f out: pressing ldrs whn squeezed out jst ins fnl f: rallied u.p fnl 100yds: snatched 3rd last strides* **16/1**
**4** nk **George Of Hearts (FR)** 2-9-5 0 ........ ShaneKelly 6 78+
(Richard Hughes) *t.k.h early: swtchd lft and trckd ldrs after 1f: effrt to chal over 1f out: unable qck u.p 1f out: outpcd fnl 100yds: lost 3rd last strides* **6/1**[3]
**5** 1 3/4 **Haylah (IRE)** 2-9-0 0 ........ FrankieDettori 2 68
(Richard Hannon) *leggy: athletic: t.k.h early: led for 2f: styd chsng ldr: rdn and ev ch over 1f out tl no ex and btn ins fnl f: wknd fnl 100yds* **8/1**
**6** 3/4 **Foreseeable Future (FR)** 2-9-5 0 ........ MartinHarley 3 71
(James Tate) *w'like: leggy: dwlt: sn rcvrd to chse ldr: led after 2f: rdn and hdd ent fnl f: sltly squeezed for room and btn ins fnl f: wknd fnl 100yds* **14/1**
**7** 1 1/4 **Billycock Hill** 2-9-5 0 ........ RichardKingscote 8 67
(Tom Dascombe) *cmpt: hld up in tch in midfield: swtchd rt and pushed along over 1f out: styd on steadily ins fnl f: nvr trbld ldrs* **66/1**

0 **8** *1 1/4* **Philamundo (IRE)**[27] 6424 2-9-5 0 StevieDonohoe 10 63
(Richard Spencer) *w'like: t.k.h early: hld up in tch: nt clr run 2f out: effrt over 1f out: kpt on same pce and no imp ins fnl f* **150/1**

**9** *1 3/4* **Rewaayat** 2-9-5 0 JimCrowley 15 58
(Charles Hills) *athletic: lw: stdd s: t.k.h: hld up in tch in midfield: pushed along over 1f out: sn outpcd: wl hld and one pced fnl f* **11/2**[2]

**10** *1 1/4* **Rogue Hero (IRE)** 2-9-5 0 SilvestreDeSousa 4 54
(Paul Cole) *str: lw: chsd ldrs tl 2f out: sn rdn and lost pl: wknd fnl f* **40/1**

65 **11** *1/2* **Authentic Art**[18] 6761 2-9-5 0 PatDobbs 7 53
(Ralph Beckett) *cmpt: a towards rr: rdn 2f out: sn outpcd: wknd fnl f* **100/1**

0 **12** *1 1/4* **Stylish Grace (FR)**[7] 7126 2-9-0 0 LiamJones 5 44
(J S Moore) *in tch in last trio: pushed along over 2f out: wknd over 1f out* **200/1**

**13** *3/4* **Jazzy Girl (IRE)** 2-9-0 0 MartinDwyer 1 42
(Brendan Powell) *leggy: s.i.s: rn green and in rr thrght* **100/1**

1m 12.53s (-0.47) **Going Correction** +0.125s/f (Good) **13** Ran SP% **121.4**
Speed ratings (Par 97): **108,106,104,104,101 100,99,97,95,93 92,91,90**
CSF £8.96 TOTE £1.80: £1.10, £1.60, £3.60; EX 8.00 Trifecta £55.80.
**Owner** Sheikh Rashid Dalmook Al Maktoum **Bred** Exors Of The Late Sir Eric Parker **Trained** Newmarket, Suffolk

**FOCUS**
A useful maiden with the winning favourite looking a smart prospect.

## 7353 DUBAI DUTY FREE NURSERY H'CAP 7f (S)
**2:25** (2:25) (Class 3) (0-95,91) 2-Y-O

**£6,225** (£1,864; £932; £466; £233; £117) **Stalls** Centre

Form RPR
4441 **1** **Rogue**[37] 6071 2-8-9 **79** TomMarquand 4 81
(Richard Hannon) *mostly chsd ldr: rdn and ev ch 2f out: led and edgd rt ent fnl f: drvn and hrd pressed ins fnl f: kpt on wl u.p: all out* **15/2**

0015 **2** *shd* **Red Roman**[30] 6330 2-9-6 **90** JimCrowley 5 92
(Charles Hills) *lw: hld up in tch: clsd and swtchd rt over 1f out: rdn and str chal ins fnl f: kpt on wl: jst hld* **6/1**[3]

051 **3** *1 3/4* **Deadly Accurate**[25] 6510 2-8-5 **78** CharlieBennett(3) 1 75
(Hughie Morrison) *in tch in midfield tl dropped to rr over 4f out: outpcd and pushed along over 2f out: swtchd lft and hdwy 1f out: styd on wl ins fnl f to snatch 3rd last strides: no threat to ldng pair* **14/1**

232 **4** *nk* **Bombastic (IRE)**[28] 6394 2-8-11 **81** SilvestreDeSousa 6 77
(Ed de Giles) *lw: stdd s: t.k.h: hld up in tch: effrt over 2f out: hdwy to chse ldrs and drvn over 1f out: wnt 3rd but no imp ins fnl f: lost 3rd last strides* **9/4**[1]

153 **5** *1* **Running Cloud (IRE)**[67] 4973 2-8-13 **83** CharlesBishop 3 76
(Eve Johnson Houghton) *in tch in midfield: outpcd: dropped to rr and rdn over 1f out: swtchd lft and rallied ins fnl f: kpt on but no threat to ldrs* **7/1**

2423 **6** *1* **Dragons Tail (IRE)**[12] 6977 2-9-7 **91** RichardKingscote 2 82
(Tom Dascombe) *led tl 4f out: styd prom: rdn and ev ch 2f out tl no ex 1f out: wknd ins fnl f* **9/2**[2]

314 **7** *2* **Lethal Lunch**[20] 6699 2-8-13 **83** SamHitchcott 7 68
(Clive Cox) *wnt rt s: sn rcvrd to chse ldrs: hdwy to ld 4f out: rdn 2f out: hdd and nudged rt ent fnl f: no ex and wknd qckly ins fnl f* **9/2**[2]

1m 25.86s (0.16) **Going Correction** +0.125s/f (Good) **7** Ran SP% **112.3**
Speed ratings (Par 99): **104,103,101,101,100 99,96**
CSF £49.09 TOTE £7.50: £3.10, £2.60; EX 39.40 Trifecta £473.00.
**Owner** Michael Daniels & Norman Woodcock **Bred** Maywood Stud **Trained** East Everleigh, Wilts

**FOCUS**
An ordinary-looking nursery for the grade, and the action unfolded middle to stands' side.

## 7354 DUBAI DUTY FREE H'CAP 1m 4f
**2:55** (2:58) (Class 2) (0-110,103) 3-Y-O+**£16,172** (£4,812; £2,405; £1,202) **Stalls** Low

Form RPR
4424 **1** **Blakeney Point**[27] 6427 4-9-6 **97** (p) KieranShoemark 8 102
(Roger Charlton) *s.i.s: styd wd and rcvrd to chse ldr 9f out tl pushed into ld jst over 2f out: edgd lft u.p and 2 l clr 1f out: kpt on and a doing enough after: rdn out* **9/1**

3-14 **2** *3/4* **Danehill Kodiac (IRE)**[13] 6931 4-9-12 **103** RyanMoore 4 107
(Richard Hannon) *lw: got his hd under the rail, uns rdr and galloped bk to paddock exit bef s: in tch in midfield: effrt ent fnl 2f: drvn over 1f out: chsd wnr ins fnl f: styd on u.p: nvr quite getting on terms* **3/1**[2]

6503 **3** *1 1/2* **Wild Hacked (USA)**[13] 6931 4-9-9 **100** FrankieDettori 3 102
(Marco Botti) *hld up in tch in midfield: effrt to chse ldrs 2f out: drvn over 1f out: chsd wnr briefly 1f out: 3rd and kpt on same pce ins fnl f* **7/2**[3]

0124 **4** *1/2* **Gawdawpalin (IRE)**[14] 6872 4-9-5 **96** JimCrowley 5 97
(Sylvester Kirk) *led: hdd and rdn jst over 2f out: unable qck over 1f out: styd on same pce ins fnl f* **8/1**

3544 **5** *2* **Temple Church (IRE)**[62] 5157 3-8-13 **97** (t[1]) JamesDoyle 9 95+
(Hughie Morrison) *hld up in tch in last pair: clsd on outer over 2f out: effrt 2f out: no imp over 1f out: btn whn wnt lft u.p and hmpd jst ins fnl f: eased towards fin* **11/4**[1]

01-3 **6** *1 1/2* **Dance The Dream**[139] 2389 4-9-7 **98** MartinDwyer 6 93
(Marcus Tregoning) *lw: hld up in tch in last pair: effrt over 2f out: no imp and kpt on same pce fnl 2f* **8/1**

-046 **7** *3/4* **Eye Of The Storm (IRE)**[20] 6675 7-9-5 **96** RichardKingscote 2 90
(Amanda Perrett) *chsd ldrs tl 2f out: sn rdn and unable qck: lost pl over 1f out: bhd and one pced fnl f* **25/1**

2m 35.24s (-0.26) **Going Correction** +0.25s/f (Good)
**WFA** 3 from 4yo+ 7lb **7** Ran SP% **110.0**
Speed ratings (Par 109): **110,109,108,108,106 105,105**
CSF £33.35 CT £105.52 TOTE £11.40: £4.70, £1.90; EX 46.60 Trifecta £156.30.
**Owner** Axom LX **Bred** Mr & Mrs A E Pakenham **Trained** Beckhampton, Wilts

**FOCUS**
Add 14.5yds to race distance. A useful handicap, but little got into it from off the ordinary pace and the winner got first run on some of the closers who were well fancied.

## 7355 HAYNES, HANSON & CLARK CONDITIONS STKS (PLUS 10 RACE) (C&G) 1m (S)
**3:30** (3:32) (Class 2) 2-Y-O

**£9,960** (£2,982; £1,491; £745; £372; £187) **Stalls** Centre

Form RPR
12 **1** **White Mocha (USA)**[15] 6859 2-9-1 0 JamesDoyle 7 98
(Hugo Palmer) *str: hld up in tch: c towards stands' rail and clsd to ld over 1f out: rdn and qcknd 2 l clr 1f out: pressed and hung lft towards fin: jst hld on* **13/8**[1]

**2** *nse* **Knight To Behold (IRE)** 2-8-12 0 RichardKingscote 6 95+
(Harry Dunlop) *cmpt: stdd s: hld up in tch in rr: c towards stands rail and followed wnr through over 1f out: shkn up to chse wnr and swtchd lft ins fnl f: r.o strly fnl 75yds: jst failed* **33/1**

6102 **3** *3 3/4* **Sallab (IRE)**[25] 6505 2-8-12 81 FrankieDettori 5 86
(Richard Hannon) *chsd ldrs tl wnt 2nd 1/2-way: rdn and ev ch 2f out: unable qck w wnr jst over 1f out: 3rd and wknd ins fnl f* **9/1**

0212 **4** *1 1/4* **Macaque**[26] 6472 2-8-12 88 DavidProbert 1 83
(Andrew Balding) *t.k.h: trckd ldr tl 1/2-way: styd prom: effrt 2f out: unable qck and sligtly impeded over 1f out: wl hld and kpt on same pce ins fnl f* **3/1**[2]

1 **5** *hd* **Bon Scotte (IRE)**[28] 6374 2-9-1 0 RyanMoore 2 86
(Richard Hannon) *cmpt: lw: led: shkn up 2f out: rdn and hdd over 1f out: sn outpcd and edging lft: wknd ins fnl f* **4/1**[3]

**6** *3 1/2* **Khazaf** 2-8-12 0 JimCrowley 4 75
(Marcus Tregoning) *athletic: in tch in midfield: rdn 2f out: sn outpcd and wknd fnl f* **9/1**

**7** *18* **Candidate (IRE)** 2-8-12 0 RobertWinston 3 33
(Hughie Morrison) *str: bit bkwd: in tch towards rr: hdwy into midfield 3f out: rdn 2f out: sn outpcd and btn over 1f out: bhd and eased ins fnl f* **25/1**

1m 40.7s (1.00) **Going Correction** +0.125s/f (Good) **7** Ran SP% **109.9**
Speed ratings (Par 101): **100,99,96,94,94 91,73**
CSF £50.97 TOTE £2.20: £1.20, £11.30; EX 54.60 Trifecta £263.30.
**Owner** Dr Ali Ridha **Bred** Woodford Thoroughbreds **Trained** Newmarket, Suffolk

**FOCUS**
In truth this looked nothing more than a decent conditions race and the first two came clear late on towards the stands' side, but another step forward from the winner.

## 7356 DUBAI DUTY FREE TENNIS CHAMPIONSHIPS CUP STKS (LISTED RACE) 7f (S)
**4:00** (4:04) (Class 1) 3-Y-O+

**£20,982** (£7,955; £3,981; £1,983; £995; £499) **Stalls** Centre

Form RPR
1502 **1** **Tabarrak (IRE)**[36] 6105 4-9-5 110 JimCrowley 9 112
(Richard Hannon) *lw: trckd ldrs: effrt over 1f out: rdn to ld ins fnl f: r.o wl and a doing enough whn pressed wl ins fnl f: rdn out* **5/1**[3]

-501 **2** *nk* **Accidental Agent**[13] 6936 3-8-13 92 CharlesBishop 6 107
(Eve Johnson Houghton) *stdd s: hld up in tch in last trio: swtchd rt and effrt over 1f out: rdn and hdwy to press wnr wl ins fnl f: r.o wl but a hld* **16/1**

4200 **3** *1* **George William**[76] 4636 4-9-2 97 TomMarquand 11 105
(Richard Hannon) *taken down early: hld up in tch in midfield: swtchd rt and effrt over 1f out: rdn and hdwy to chse ldrs ins fnl f: kpt on but hld whn squeezed for room towards fin* **33/1**

0040 **4** *nse* **Urban Fox**[20] 6697 3-8-8 99 (v[1]) HarryBentley 7 99
(James Tate) *trckd ldrs: effrt to chal over 1f out: drvn out: no ex and outpcd fnl 100yds* **20/1**

-201 **5** *nk* **Dream Of Dreams (IRE)**[6] 7154 3-8-13 102 RyanMoore 2 103
(Sir Michael Stoute) *lw: t.k.h: pressed ldr tl rdn to ld over 1f out: drvn and hdd ins fnl f: no ex and outpcd fnl 100yds* **4/1**[2]

1112 **6** *1 1/4* **Second Thought (IRE)**[118] 3078 3-8-13 105 RobertWinston 4 100
(William Haggas) *lw: hld up in tch in midfield: effrt 2f out: sme hdwy but nt clrest of runs whn swtchd rt and jostling w rival jst ins fnl f: kpt on but no threat to ldrs* **11/4**[1]

6030 **7** *nk* **Tupi (IRE)**[27] 6428 5-9-5 109 SeanLevey 8 103
(Richard Hannon) *hld up in tch: nt clr run wl over 1f out: effrt whn nt clrest of runs and jostling w rival jst ins fnl f: kpt on but no threat to ldrs* **14/1**

1220 **8** *2* **Golden Stunner (IRE)**[56] 5352 4-8-11 105 PatDobbs 10 89
(Ralph Beckett) *led tl rdn and hdd over 1f out: wknd ins fnl f* **9/1**

1 **9** *nse* **Princess De Lune (IRE)**[154] 1948 3-8-8 90 KieranShoemark 12 88
(Roger Charlton) *stdd s: t.k.h: hld up in tch: effrt 2f out: no imp over 1f out tl kpt on ins fnl f: nvr trbld ldrs* **10/1**

0132 **10** *2 3/4* **Eartha Kitt**[33] 6234 3-8-8 97 (p) RichardKingscote 3 81
(Tom Dascombe) *t.k.h: hld up in tch in midfield: effrt to chse ldrs: unable qck over 1f out: wknd ins fnl f* **10/1**

2100 **11** *2* **Koropick (IRE)**[40] 5974 3-9-4 108 JamesDoyle 1 86
(Hugo Palmer) *in tch in midfield: effrt ent fnl 2f: unable qck over 1f out: wknd ins fnl f* **25/1**

1m 24.5s (-1.20) **Going Correction** +0.125s/f (Good)
**WFA** 3 from 4yo+ 3lb **11** Ran SP% **115.6**
Speed ratings (Par 111): **111,110,109,109,109 107,107,105,105,101 99**
CSF £77.82 TOTE £5.10: £1.60, £4.20, £9.10; EX 85.90 Trifecta £1726.00.
**Owner** Hamdan Al Maktoum **Bred** Rathbarry Stud & F & N Woods **Trained** East Everleigh, Wilts

**FOCUS**
They raced middle to stands' side, with the main action towards the near rail. This looked ordinary for the grade but there could be some more nice prizes in the winner, who has been rated close to form.

## 7357 DUBAI DUTY FREE FULL OF SURPRISES EBF STALLIONS FILLIES' CONDITIONS STKS (PLUS 10 RACE) 7f (S)
**4:35** (4:36) (Class 2) 2-Y-O

**£10,271** (£3,075; £1,537; £768; £384; £193) **Stalls** Centre

Form RPR
**1** **Magnolia Springs (IRE)** 2-8-12 0 CharlesBishop 5 90+
(Eve Johnson Houghton) *stdd s: hld up in tch in rr: swtchd lft and hdwy to ld 1f out: r.o strly and drew clr ins fnl f: v readily* **25/1**

4 **2** *3 1/2* **Melodies**[15] 6862 2-8-12 0 SilvestreDeSousa 2 81
(Ed Dunlop) *t.k.h: chsd ldr for 3f: rdn 2f out: outpcd whn sltly impeded over 1f out: rallied ins fnl f: styd on to go 2nd last strides: no ch w wnr* **9/2**

**3** *hd* **Veracious** 2-8-12 0 RyanMoore 8 80
(Sir Michael Stoute) *t.k.h early: hld up in tch: rdn hands and heels and ev ch over 1f out tl unable qck w wnr jst ins fnl f: wnt 2nd but wnr gng clr ins fnl f: lost 2nd last strides* **3/1**[1]

61 **4** *3/4* **Lamya (GER)**[27] 6438 2-8-12 0 TomMarquand 4 78
(Richard Hannon) *chsd ldrs: wnt 2nd 1/2-way tl rdn to ld wl over 1f out: hdd 1f out and sn outpcd by wnr: lost btn 2nd ins fnl f: wknd towards fin* **7/2**[3]

01 **5** *3/4* **Boreagh Lass (IRE)**[40] 5963 2-8-12 0 HarryBentley 3 76
(Henry Candy) *in tch in midfield: dropped to rr and rdn over 2f out: no ch w wnr but rallied and swtchd lft ins fnl f: kpt on* **5/1**

50 **6** *2* **Chillala (IRE)**[37] 6070 2-8-12 0 (h) StevieDonohoe 7 71
(Harry Dunlop) *led: rdn and hdd wl over 1f out: sn outpcd: wknd ins fnl f* **50/1**

6 **7** ¾ **Naqaawa (IRE)**[51] 5528 2-8-12 0........................................ JimCrowley 1 69
(Owen Burrows) *in tch: shkn up 2f out: rdn and lost pl over 1f out: bhd and kpt on same pce ins fnl f* **10/3**[2]

1m 25.99s (0.29) **Going Correction** +0.125s/f (Good) **7** Ran SP% **111.0**
Speed ratings (Par 98): **103,99,98,97,97 94,93**
CSF £124.50 TOTE £22.50: £8.00, £2.60; EX 144.30 Trifecta £802.50.
**Owner** Anthony Rogers **Bred** Airlie Stud **Trained** Blewbury, Oxon

**FOCUS**
A useful conditions event and hard not to be taken with the winning newcomer.

## 7358 SOUTH DOWNS WATER H'CAP 1m 2f
**5:05** (5:08) (Class 4) (0-85,86) 3-Y-0+ **£4,690** (£1,395; £697; £348) **Stalls** Low

Form RPR
66 **1** **Breden (IRE)**[14] 6887 7-9-9 **84**.................................(h) RobertWinston 16 89
(Linda Jewell) *t.k.h: hld up in tch in midfield: clsd to trck ldrs and travelling strly 2f out: rdn to ld over 1f out: drvn ins fnl f: kpt on: jst hld on: all out* **16/1**

1416 **2** *shd* **Bedouin (IRE)**[20] 6701 3-9-4 **84**...............................(p[1]) PatCosgrave 13 89
(Luca Cumani) *midfield and niggled along at times: rdn over 2f out: hdwy u.p 1f out: styd on wl ins fnl f to press wnr nr fin: jst hld* **13/2**[3]

3-66 **3** *nk* **Mia Tesoro (IRE)**[19] 6722 4-9-3 **78**.........................(h) StevieDonohoe 11 82
(Charlie Fellowes) *taken down early: hld up in tch in last quartet: hdwy on inner 2f out: swtchd lft 1f out: drvn and ev ch ins fnl f: kpt on* **10/1**

0203 **4** *nse* **Rumpole**[28] 6387 3-9-0 **80**.......................................... SilvestreDeSousa 15 84+
(Hughie Morrison) *stdd and dropped in after s: hld up in tch in last quartet: effrt on outer 2f out: hdwy u.p 1f out: styd on wl u.p ins fnl f: nt quite rch ldrs* **6/1**[2]

323 **5** 1 **Majboor (IRE)**[16] 6808 3-8-11 **77**.................................... LiamKeniry 14 79
(Dominic Ffrench Davis) *t.k.h: chsd ldr: drvn and ev ch over 1f out tl no ex ins fnl f: wknd towards fin* **25/1**

3431 **6** *nse* **Red Royalist**[17] 6775 3-8-11 **77**...................................(p) MartinDwyer 8 79
(Marcus Tregoning) *t.k.h: chsd ldrs: effrt ent fnl 2f: stl chsng ldrs and drvn 1f out: kpt on same pce ins fnl f* **8/1**

0455 **7** *shd* **Grapevine (IRE)**[25] 6515 4-9-8 **83**.................................... JimCrowley 12 85
(Charles Hills) *hld up in tch in last quartet: effrt on outer 2f out: hdwy 1f out: kpt on ins fnl f: nvr quite getting on terms w ldrs* **7/1**

0300 **8** 3 **Balmoral Castle**[27] 6422 8-9-1 **83**......................... Pierre-LouisJamin[(7)] 9 79
(Jonathan Portman) *in tch in midfield: rdn over 2f out: sn outpcd and lost pl: rallied 1f out and kpt on to pass btn horses ins fnl f: nvr threatened ldrs* **25/1**

10-3 **9** 1 ¾ **Nonios (IRE)**[211] 885 5-9-10 **85**.................................(h) MartinHarley 10 77
(David Simcock) *stdd s: hld up in tch in last quartet: clsd 2f out: rdn and no rspnse 1f out: wknd ins fnl f* **16/1**

2431 **10** 1 **Crushed (IRE)**[18] 6766 3-8-5 **76**.................................... GeorgiaCox[(5)] 7 66
(William Haggas) *t.k.h: led: rdn 2f out: hdd over 1f out: sn lost pl: wknd ins fnl f* **10/3**[1]

0314 **11** ¾ **Graceful James (IRE)**[15] 6848 4-9-0 **75**......................... KieranO'Neill 6 64
(Jimmy Fox) *chsd ldrs: rdn over 2f out: sn struggling: bhd ins fnl f* **9/1**

5200 **12** 1 ½ **Mikmak**[20] 6701 4-9-0 **75**.........................................(p) KieranShoemark 5 61
(William Muir) *in tch in midfield: rdn jst over 2f out: sn struggling: bhd ins fnl f* **25/1**

2m 8.9s (0.10) **Going Correction** +0.25s/f (Good)
**WFA** 3 from 4yo+ 5lb **12** Ran SP% **116.7**
Speed ratings (Par 105): **109,108,108,108,107 107,107,105,103,103 102,101**
CSF £112.16 CT £1095.80 TOTE £18.40: £4.80, £2.80, £4.00; EX 98.00 Trifecta £2014.40.
**Owner** The Breden Racing Partnership **Bred** Mrs C L Weld **Trained** Sutton Valence, Kent
■ Stewards' Enquiry : Pat Cosgrave seven-day ban; using his whip above the permitted level (6th-13th Oct)

**FOCUS**
Add 14.5yds to race distance. A fair handicap, but a bunched finish with little more than a length covering the first seven finishers.
T/Jkpt: £109,446.40 to a £1 stake. Pool: £164,169.69 - 1.50 winning units T/Plt: £1,238.90 to a £1 stake. Pool: £97,246.64 - 57.30 winning units T/Qpdt: £161.70 to a £1 stake. Pool: £11,055.86 - 50.58 winning units **Steve Payne**

# 7234 NEWCASTLE (A.W) (L-H)
Friday, September 22

**OFFICIAL GOING: Tapeta: standard**
Wind: Almost nil Weather: Overcast, raining

## 7359 FLAME BATHROOM SHOWROOM DURHAM H'CAP 2m 56y (Tp)
**5:45** (5:46) (Class 4) (0-85,84) 3-Y-0+ **£4,851** (£1,443; £721; £360) **Stalls** Low

Form RPR
254 **1** **Waiting For Richie**[43] 5832 4-8-12 **68**................................ AndrewMullen 2 76
(Tom Tate) *led 4f: cl up: regained ld over 2f out: rdn and edgd lft over 1f out: hld on wl fnl f* **25/1**

4232 **2** *nk* **On Fire**[21] 6661 4-9-5 **75**.........................................(p) JosephineGordon 9 82
(James Bethell) *hld up in tch: nt clr run over 2f out: effrt and rdn wl over 1f out: chsd wnr ins fnl f: kpt on fin* **10/1**

1202 **3** ½ **Dominating (GER)**[6] 7163 3-9-3 **83**................................... FrannyNorton 7 89
(Mark Johnston) *sn trcking ldr: led after 4f to over 2f out: rallied: lost pl ins fnl f: kpt on same pce* **9/2**[3]

1 **4** 1 **Mobbhij**[22] 6623 3-9-0 **83**.............................................. DavidEgan[(3)] 5 88+
(Saeed bin Suroor) *dwlt: t.k.h in midfield: rdn over 2f out: hdwy and edgd rt over 1f out: kpt on ins fnl f: nt pce to chal* **13/8**[1]

521 **5** 1 **Chocolate Box (IRE)**[15] 6849 3-9-0 **80**.......................(p) LukeMorris 8 84
(Luca Cumani) *prom: drvn over 2f out: outpcd over 1f out: rallied ins fnl f: no imp* **11/4**[2]

5214 **6** ¾ **Montanna**[46] 5706 3-8-11 **77**........................................... JackGarritty 4 80
(Jedd O'Keeffe) *cl up: rdn and outpcd over 2f out: rallied over 1f out: sn no imp* **14/1**

4506 **7** ½ **Carthage (IRE)**[14] 6901 6-8-9 **65** oh1.................................. BenCurtis 3 68
(Brian Ellison) *hld up on ins: rdn over 2f out: effrt over 1f out: nvr rchd ldrs* **100/1**

0144 **8** *nk* **Whitecliff Park (IRE)**[14] 6889 4-8-11 **72**..................(p) BenRobinson[(5)] 1 74
(Brian Ellison) *dwlt: hld up midfield on ins: rdn over 2f out: no imp fr over 1f out* **25/1**

3660 **9** ¾ **Tetradrachm**[15] 6849 4-9-5 **75**......................................(p) JoeyHaynes 6 76
(David Simcock) *hld up: rdn whn edgd lft over 2f out: sn no imp* **50/1**

32-0 **10** ½ **Rite To Reign**[20] 6680 6-9-11 **84**.......................... AdamMcNamara[(3)] 11 85
(Philip McBride) *hld up: drvn along whn hung lft over 2f out: sn no imp: btn over 1f out* **33/1**

4344 **11** 2 ¾ **Stoneham**[14] 6895 6-8-3 **66**....................................(h) JamieGormley[(7)] 10 63
(Iain Jardine) *hld up: drvn and outpcd over 2f out: sn btn* **33/1**

3520 **12** 4 **Wor Lass**[10] 7032 9-9-5 **75**............................................. DougieCostello 12 68
(Donald Whillans) *hld up on outside: stdy hdwy over 3f out: wknd fr 2f out* **50/1**

3m 38.7s (3.50) **Going Correction** +0.075s/f (Slow)
**WFA** 3 from 4yo+ 10lb **12** Ran SP% **117.2**
Speed ratings (Par 105): **94,93,93,93,92 92,91,91,91,91 89,87**
CSF £241.78 CT £1345.58 TOTE £26.00: £6.40, £2.20, £1.60; EX 225.90 Trifecta £613.30.
**Owner** The Ivy Syndicate **Bred** Juddmonte Farms Ltd **Trained** Tadcaster, N Yorks

**FOCUS**
A moderate Class 4 event run at a modest tempo and as usual round here it paid to race prominently. The winner has been rated back to his best with the 2nd to form.

## 7360 FLAME THE HEAT IS ON H'CAP 1m 4f 98y (Tp)
**6:15** (6:15) (Class 6) (0-60,60) 3-Y-0+ **£2,425** (£721; £360; £180) **Stalls** High

Form RPR
450/ **1** **British Art**[33] 6244 5-9-1 **51**.......................................(v[1]) KevinStott 10 59+
(R K Watson, Ire) *prom: hdwy to ld over 2f out: rdn clr fr over 1f out* **15/2**[3]

25U2 **2** 2 **Padleyourowncanoe**[14] 6901 3-9-2 **59**..............................(b) LukeMorris 6 65
(Daniel Mark Loughnane) *t.k.h: hld up: hdwy on outside and ev ch briefly over 2f out: sn chsng wnr: kpt on same pce fnl f* **4/1**[2]

625 **3** ¾ **Angel In The Snow**[45] 5740 4-8-7 **48**........................ BenRobinson[(5)] 2 52+
(Brian Ellison) *hld up in midfield: drvn over 2f out: hdwy wl over 1f out: kpt on fnl f: nt pce of first two* **4/1**[2]

3205 **4** 4 **Chauvelin**[26] 6471 6-9-1 **51**........................................(bt) TomEaves 14 48
(Nigel Tinkler) *hld up: stdy hdwy whn nt clr run over 2f out: sn rdn: kpt on fr over 1f out: no imp* **12/1**

-431 **5** ¾ **Chilli Jam**[22] 6622 4-9-3 **56**....................................(p) DavidEgan[(3)] 12 52
(Ed de Giles) *hld up in midfield on outside: hdwy and ev ch briefly over 2f out: rdn and outpcd over 1f out: btn fnl f* **15/8**[1]

0064 **6** 3 ¼ **Rock Island Line**[41] 5950 3-9-3 **60**..........................(p) DougieCostello 8 52
(Mark Walford) *t.k.h: chsd ldrs: effrt and ev ch briefly over 2f out: sn wknd* **22/1**

6066 **7** 3 ½ **Pennerley**[23] 6569 4-8-13 **49**........................................ FrannyNorton 13 34
(Micky Hammond) *dwlt and swtchd lft s: hld up: rdn along 3f out: kpt on fnl f: nvr able to chal* **80/1**

4503 **8** 1 ¼ **Flying Power**[43] 5850 9-8-10 **46**..................................(p) PaddyAspell 7 29
(John Norton) *t.k.h: prom: rdn over 2f out: sn wknd* **20/1**

0006 **9** 8 **Molten Lava (IRE)**[42] 5897 5-9-1 **51**................................ JimmyQuinn 11 21
(Philip Kirby) *t.k.h: led: clr after 2f: hdd over 2f out: sn wknd* **20/1**

2300 **10** *shd* **Desktop**[14] 6898 5-9-4 **54**.............................................. CamHardie 4 24
(Antony Brittain) *t.k.h: cl up in chsng gp tl rdn and wknd wl over 2f out* **40/1**

026- **11** 1 **Allfredandnobell (IRE)**[152] 6840 4-9-1 **51**..................... AndrewMullen 5 20
(Micky Hammond) *hld up: drvn and outpcd 3f out: sn btn* **80/1**

1641 **12** 28 **Adrakhan (FR)**[23] 6595 6-8-9 **48**................................ SammyJoBell[(3)] 1
(Wilf Storey) *hld up in midfield: drvn and outpcd 4f out: btn fnl 2f* **28/1**

2m 39.93s (-1.17) **Going Correction** +0.075s/f (Slow)
**WFA** 3 from 4yo+ 7lb **12** Ran SP% **116.5**
Speed ratings (Par 101): **106,104,104,101,101 98,96,95,90,90 89,70**
CSF £34.14 CT £138.15 TOTE £7.50: £2.80, £1.70, £1.70; EX 36.20 Trifecta £158.90.
**Owner** Cousins Plus One Syndicate **Bred** Rabbah Bloodstock Limited **Trained** Killylea, Co Armagh

**FOCUS**
A modest enough event enlivened by a well-punted Irish raider winning decisively. The 2nd/3rd/4th help to pin a straightforward level.

## 7361 BAXI MAIDEN AUCTION STKS 1m 5y (Tp)
**6:45** (6:46) (Class 5) 2-Y-O **£3,234** (£962; £481; £240) **Stalls** Centre

Form RPR
633 **1** **Champarisi**[10] 7033 2-9-0 ................................................ JackGarritty 1 69+
(Grant Tuer) *chsd ldrs: led over 2f out: drvn clr ins fnl f: r.o wl* **4/1**[3]

**2** 2 ¾ **Te Koop** 2-9-5 0..................................................................... JoeyHaynes 6 68
(David Simcock) *hld up: hdwy 3f out: chsd ldr over 2f out: no imp on wnr ins fnl f* **17/2**

**3** 1 ¼ **Sunhill Lad (IRE)** 2-9-5 0........................................................ ShaneGray 3 65
(Ann Duffield) *prom: rdn and outpcd 4f out: rallied over 1f out: hung lft and green ins fnl f: kpt on: nt pce of ldrs* **50/1**

**4** 2 ¾ **Cheeky Kiki (IRE)** 2-9-0 0...................................................... LukeMorris 4 54
(Giles Bravery) *s.s: in rr: rdn over 3f out: hdwy to chse ldrs over 2f out: one pce fr over 1f out* **10/1**

5 **5** 11 **Losingmyreligion (FR)**[44] 5808 2-9-2 0................... MarcMonaghan[(3)] 5 35
(Marco Botti) *prom: led 5f out: rdn and hdd over 2f out: wknd wl over 1f out* **6/4**[1]

6 **6** 1 ¾ **Snax**[15] 6861 2-9-0 0........................................................... FrannyNorton 2 26
(Mark Johnston) *led: hdd 5f out: remained prom: rdn over 2f out: wknd wl over 1f out: lame* **5/2**[2]

1m 41.32s (2.72) **Going Correction** +0.075s/f (Slow) **6** Ran SP% **110.1**
Speed ratings (Par 95): **89,86,85,82,71 69**
CSF £34.09 TOTE £5.20: £2.00, £3.10; EX 33.80 Trifecta £250.00.
**Owner** Allerton Racing & G Tuer **Bred** Faisal Meshrf Alqahtani **Trained** Birkby, N Yorks

**FOCUS**
A modest-looking juvenile mile maiden won in taking style, although the market principals ran below expectations.

## 7362 0800 REPAIR NURSERY H'CAP (DIV I) 6f (Tp)
**7:15** (7:20) (Class 5) (0-75,77) 2-Y-O **£3,234** (£962; £481; £240) **Stalls** Centre

Form RPR
3136 **1** **Armed Response**[63] 5127 2-9-10 **77**................................... JackGarritty 1 82
(Jedd O'Keeffe) *racd keenly: mde all: rdn over 1f out: kpt on gamely* **6/1**

2540 **2** 1 **Gangland**[12] 6977 2-9-0 **67**.........................................(h) DavidNolan 7 69
(Richard Fahey) *hld up: rdn and hdwy over 1f out: r.o ins fnl f: gng on at fin* **4/1**[1]

2330 **3** *hd* **Indian Warrior**[13] 6951 2-9-6 **73**..................................... FrannyNorton 8 74
(Ed Dunlop) *racd keenly: prom: rdn to chse wnr over 1f out: unable qck ins fnl f: lost 2nd nr fin* **11/2**[3]

0006 **4** 1 ½ **French Silk**[23] 6567 2-8-1 **54** oh5 ow1........................... DuranFentiman 10 51
(Chris Fairhurst) *prom: effrt over 2f out: kpt on u.p ins fnl f: nt quite pce of ldrs* **100/1**

042 **5** ½ **Geesala Brave (IRE)**[30] 6311 2-9-0 **70**........................ DavidEgan[(3)] 4 65
(John Quinn) *chsd ldrs: rdn over 1f out: styd on same pce ins fnl f* **4/1**[1]

4053 **6** 3 ½ **Revenge**[9] 7057 2-8-2 **55**..............................................(b) AndrewMullen 2 40
(Tim Easterby) *chsd ldrs: rdn 2f out: wknd fnl 150yds* **9/2**[2]

224 **7** ½ **Sosian**[54] 5453 2-9-4 **74**............................................. AdamMcNamara[(3)] 3 57
(Richard Fahey) *prom: rdn 2f out: wknd over 1f out* **6/1**

365 **8** 1 ½ **Duke Of Freedom**[58] 5278 2-8-11 **64**.............................. DougieCostello 5 43
(Ann Duffield) *towards rr: rdn over 2f out: outpcd after* **28/1**

353 **9** *8* **Onesarnieshort (FR)**[64] 5068 2-8-11 **67** ........................ JoshDoyle(3) 9 22
(David O'Meara) *towards rr: rdn and outpcd over 2f out: hung lft u.p whn btn over 1f out* **16/1**

050 **10** *4½* **Elusive Bird**[26] 6480 2-8-5 **58** ........................ LukeMorris 6
(Giles Bravery) *v keen to post: a in rr: lft bhd over 1f out: eased whn wl btn ins fnl f* **33/1**

1m 13.02s (0.52) **Going Correction** +0.075s/f (Slow) **10** Ran SP% **115.4**
Speed ratings (Par 95): **99,97,97,95,94 90,89,87,76,70**
CSF £29.57 CT £142.46 TOTE £6.40: £2.00, £1.60, £2.10; EX 35.10 Trifecta £186.10.
**Owner** Caron & Paul Chapman **Bred** Alvediston Stud **Trained** Middleham Moor, N Yorks

**FOCUS**
Division one of the 6f nursery was won under a well-judged front-running ride.

## 7363 0800 REPAIR NURSERY H'CAP (DIV II) 6f (Tp)
**7:45** (7:46) (Class 5) (0-75,74) 2-Y-O **£3,234** (£962; £481; £240) **Stalls** Centre

Form RPR

4323 **1** **Lina's Star (IRE)**[24] 6547 2-8-12 **65** ........................ PhillipMakin 5 67
(David O'Meara) *mde all: rdn and edgd rt over 1f out: pressed ins fnl f: kpt on gamely* **10/1**

2006 **2** *hd* **Onefootinparadise**[21] 6651 2-9-1 **68** ........................ JosephineGordon 9 69
(Philip McBride) *towards rr: hdwy 2f out: r.o to chal ins fnl f: hld fnl strides* **11/2**[3]

3635 **3** *½* **Another Day Of Sun (IRE)**[22] 6636 2-9-4 **74** ........................ DavidEgan(3) 2 74
(Mick Channon) *hld up in midfield: rdn and outpcd over 2f out: swtchd rt over 1f out: rallied ins fnl f: styd on towards fin* **9/1**

643 **4** *½* **Fink Hill (USA)**[27] 6432 2-9-3 **70** ........................ ConnorBeasley 4 68
(Richard Guest) *racd keenly: hld up: hdwy over 2f out: chsd ldrs over 1f out: tried to chal ins fnl f: nt quite pce of front three* **9/4**[1]

000 **5** *1* **El Bertie (IRE)**[43] 5834 2-8-5 **58** ........................ DuranFentiman 3 53
(Tim Easterby) *chsd ldrs: rdn over 2f out: styd on same pce ins fnl f* **40/1**

4160 **6** *1* **Leeshaan (IRE)**[42] 5875 2-9-6 **73** ........................ LukeMorris 7 65
(James Tate) *chsd ldrs: rdn over 2f out: lost pl over 1f out: kpt on again towards fin* **7/2**[2]

5525 **7** *hd* **Sinaloa (IRE)**[20] 6693 2-9-5 **72** ........................ DavidNolan 6 63
(Richard Fahey) *prom: rdn and lost pl over 2f out: kpt on same pce ins fnl f* **6/1**

000 **8** *hd* **Albarino**[32] 6264 2-8-0 **53** oh2 ........................ AndrewMullen 1 44
(Kevin Ryan) *s.i.s: in rr: rdn and outpcd over 1f out: kpt on ins fnl f: nvr able to trble ldrs* **33/1**

6536 **9** *nse* **Skyva**[9] 7041 2-8-10 **63** ........................ (h) CamHardie 8 54
(Brian Ellison) *prom: rdn and ch whn n.m.r and checked 1f out: sn lost pl: n.d after* **16/1**

1m 13.28s (0.78) **Going Correction** +0.075s/f (Slow) **9** Ran SP% **113.0**
Speed ratings (Par 95): **97,96,96,95,94 92,92,92,92**
CSF £62.59 CT £518.31 TOTE £6.70: £2.30, £1.90, £2.30; EX 36.40 Trifecta £319.70.
**Owner** Sheikh Abdullah Almalek Alsabah **Bred** Highbank Stud **Trained** Upper Helmsley, N Yorks

**FOCUS**
Division two of the sprint nursery was run 0.26 seconds slower than the first. The winner again received a good front-running ride.

## 7364 VIEGA FILLIES' H'CAP 1m 5y (Tp)
**8:15** (8:15) (Class 5) (0-75,75) 3-Y-O+ **£3,234** (£962; £481; £240) **Stalls** Centre

Form RPR

0025 **1** **Ibazz**[31] 6288 4-9-1 **71** ........................ (p1) ManuelFernandes(7) 7 77
(Ian Williams) *prom: rdn to ld over 2f out: kpt on gamely ins fnl f: a doing enough nr fin* **5/1**[2]

0100 **2** *½* **Table Manners**[10] 7034 5-8-11 **63** ........................ SammyJoBell(3) 3 68
(Wilf Storey) *towards rr: rdn and outpcd over 2f out: hdwy over 1f out: r.o ins fnl f: fin wl* **33/1**

-600 **3** *nk* **Vanity Queen**[35] 6134 3-9-7 **74** ........................ LukeMorris 5 78
(Luca Cumani) *hld up: rdn and hdwy over 2f out: chsd wnr over 1f out: styd on ins fnl f: lost 2nd nr fin: nt quite pce of wnr* **2/1**[1]

3205 **4** *3* **Alouja (IRE)**[39] 6015 3-9-7 **74** ........................ (t1) JosephineGordon 2 71
(Hugo Palmer) *chsd ldrs: rdn over 2f out: no ex fnl 100yds* **11/1**

362 **5** *hd* **Deleyla**[23] 6577 3-9-2 **72** ........................ DavidEgan(3) 1 68
(Roger Varian) *led: rdn and hdd over 2f out: kpt on same pce ins fnl f* **9/1**

4144 **6** *2¼* **Carol (IRE)**[16] 6818 3-9-8 **75** ........................ FrannyNorton 8 66
(Ed Dunlop) *hld up: rdn 2f out: nvr able to trble ldrs* **13/2**[3]

060 **7** *¾* **Hidden Charms (IRE)**[16] 6818 3-9-2 **69** ........................ (p1) DougieCostello 9 58
(David Simcock) *in rr: rdn and outpcd over 2f out: nvr able to get on terms* **14/1**

2040 **8** *3¼* **Full Of Promise**[24] 6549 4-8-9 **65** ........................ SebastianWoods(7) 6 46
(Richard Fahey) *prom tl rdn and wknd over 2f out* **20/1**

421 **9** *nk* **Rinaria (IRE)**[26] 6468 3-9-8 **75** ........................ (h) JoeyHaynes 4 56
(K R Burke) *racd keenly: prom: rdn 2f out: wknd over 1f out* **5/1**[2]

1m 39.18s (0.58) **Going Correction** +0.075s/f (Slow)
**WFA** 3 from 4yo+ 4lb **9** Ran SP% **112.7**
Speed ratings (Par 100): **100,99,99,96,96 93,93,89,89**
CSF £142.06 CT £433.83 TOTE £4.90: £1.80, £5.30, £1.30; EX 171.00 Trifecta £908.40.
**Owner** Randolph & Mortimer Racing **Bred** Trebles Holford Farm Thoroughbreds **Trained** Portway, Worcs

■ Stewards' Enquiry : Manuel Fernandes two-day ban; used whip above shoulder height (tba)

**FOCUS**
A bit muddling, but a small pb from the 2nd, and the 3rd to form.

## 7365 INTERGAS MAIDEN STKS 5f (Tp)
**8:45** (8:46) (Class 5) 3-Y-O+ **£3,234** (£962; £481; £240) **Stalls** Centre

Form RPR

02 **1** **Lady Of The Lamp (IRE)**[14] 6904 3-9-0 0 ........................ LukeMorris 6 65+
(Rae Guest) *chsd ldr: rdn over 1f out: led fnl 150yds: kpt on wl* **5/4**[1]

2000 **2** *½* **Raffle King (IRE)**[69] 4910 3-9-2 68 ........................ DavidEgan(3) 7 66
(Mick Channon) *led: rdn over 1f out: hdd fnl 150yds: kpt on for press towards fin* **4/1**[3]

3563 **3** *1½* **Eltanin (IRE)**[17] 6786 3-9-2 62 ........................ (v) AdamMcNamara(3) 5 61
(John Quinn) *chsd ldrs: rdn 2f out: unable qck ins fnl f: kpt on but no imp on front two* **2/1**[2]

0/0 **4** *3¼* **Encoded (IRE)**[41] 5946 4-9-1 0 ........................ BarryMcHugh 4 44
(Lynn Siddall) *midfield: rdn over 1f out: kpt on ins fnl f: nt pce to rch ldrs* **100/1**

65 **5** *nk* **High Anxiety**[14] 6904 3-9-0 0 ........................ JimmyQuinn 8 43
(John Weymes) *prom: rdn 2f out: one pce fnl f* **40/1**

50 **6** *3¾* **Roubles (USA)**[71] 4793 3-9-0 0 ........................ JoeDoyle 1 30
(Julie Camacho) *in tch: rdn whn chsng ldrs over 1f out: wknd fnl 150yds* **14/1**

60- **7** *2* **Spruce Lodge**[363] 6789 3-9-5 0 ........................ BenCurtis 2 28
(David Barron) *stdd s: hld up: rdn over 1f out: nvr a threat* **9/1**

40 **8** *3¼* **Kaylen's Mischief**[14] 6904 4-9-6 0 ........................ PaddyAspell 3 16
(Philip Kirby) *racd keenly: hld up: rdn and outpcd over 1f out: nvr a threat* **100/1**

59.8s (0.30) **Going Correction** +0.075s/f (Slow)
**WFA** 3 from 4yo 1lb **8** Ran SP% **118.9**
Speed ratings (Par 103): **100,99,96,91,91 85,81,76**
CSF £7.21 TOTE £2.10: £1.10, £1.80, £1.10; EX 6.80 Trifecta £16.40.
**Owner** Sonia M Rogers & Anthony Rogers **Bred** Airlie Stud **Trained** Newmarket, Suffolk

**FOCUS**
A weak maiden but a small pb from the winner.

## 7366 DSE H'CAP 5f (Tp)
**9:15** (9:17) (Class 6) (0-60,60) 3-Y-O+ **£2,425** (£721; £360; £180) **Stalls** Centre

Form RPR

0002 **1** **Young Tiger**[10] 7036 4-8-8 **47** ........................ (h) AndrewMullen 12 56
(Tom Tate) *hld up: hdwy 2f out: led jst over 1f out: edgd lft ins fnl f: r.o* **4/1**[1]

5500 **2** *1* **Windforpower (IRE)**[6] 7164 7-9-0 **53** ........................ (v) BarryMcHugh 1 58
(Tracy Waggott) *hld up: hdwy over 1f out: wnt 2nd wl ins fnl f: styd on: nt quite pce of wnr* **15/2**

1334 **3** *1* **Ambitious Icarus**[35] 6148 8-9-7 **60** ........................ (p) ConnorBeasley 5 62
(Richard Guest) *hld up: rdn and hdwsy over 1f out: r.o and edgd lft ins fnl f: nt quite rch front two* **7/1**[3]

003 **4** *½* **Thornaby Princess**[14] 6896 6-8-7 **46** oh1 ........................ (p) JoeDoyle 7 46
(Colin Teague) *chsd ldrs: rdn to chal 1f out: kpt on ins fnl f: nt pce of ldrs towards fin* **50/1**

4050 **5** *2* **Bond Bombshell**[20] 6670 4-8-11 **57** ........................ (p) PatrickVaughan(7) 2 50
(David O'Meara) *chsd ldrs: rdn to chal over 1f out: sn hung lft: styd on same pce fnl 100yds* **25/1**

0010 **6** *½* **See Vermont**[6] 7164 9-9-6 **59** ........................ (b) DuranFentiman 6 50
(Rebecca Bastiman) *s.i.s: bhd: outpcd 1/2-way: hdwy ins fnl f: fin wl* **25/1**

2312 **7** *hd* **Hadley**[22] 6631 4-9-7 **60** ........................ (p) BenCurtis 13 50
(Tracy Waggott) *led: rdn 2f out: hdd jst over 1f out: no ex fnl 100yds* **15/2**

4556 **8** *hd* **Mitchum**[10] 7020 8-8-7 **49** ........................ (p) PhilDennis(3) 14 39
(Ron Barr) *towards rr: styd on ins fnl f: nvr able to rch ldrs* **12/1**

5603 **9** *½* **Canford Bay (IRE)**[10] 7036 3-8-13 **53** ........................ CamHardie 9 41
(Antony Brittain) *w ldr: rdn over 1f out: fdd fnl 100yds* **10/1**

6645 **10** *shd* **Trick Of The Lyte (IRE)**[10] 7018 3-8-3 **46** oh1 ........................ (p1) DavidEgan(3) 8 33
(John Quinn) *chsd ldrs: rdn 1/2-way: one pce fnl f* **7/1**[3]

0-00 **11** *2* **Sunnyside Bob (IRE)**[22] 6631 4-8-10 **56** ........................ (p) FayeMcManoman(7) 3 36
(Neville Bycroft) *hld up: outpcd 2f out: nvr a threat* **33/1**

0053 **12** *shd* **La Haule Lady**[26] 6469 3-8-4 **47** ........................ (b1) SammyJoBell(3) 4 27
(Paul Midgley) *midfield: rdn over 1f out: wknd ins fnl f* **20/1**

5541 **13** *½* **Groundworker (IRE)**[10] 7036 6-9-0 **60** 6ex ........................ (t) ConnorMurtagh(7) 11 38
(Paul Midgley) *chsd ldrs tl rdn and wknd over 1f out* **11/2**[2]

59.08s (-0.42) **Going Correction** +0.075s/f (Slow)
**WFA** 3 from 4yo+ 1lb **13** Ran SP% **118.1**
Speed ratings (Par 101): **106,104,102,102,98 98,97,97,96,96 93,93,92**
CSF £30.97 CT £212.33 TOTE £4.70: £1.90, £2.60, £2.20; EX 33.90 Trifecta £295.50.
**Owner** T T Racing **Bred** Mrs J McMahon & Mickley Stud **Trained** Tadcaster, N Yorks

**FOCUS**
A competitive low-grade sprint which was run at a decent pace.
T/Plt: £321.20 to a £1 stake. Pool: £105,066.55 - 238.73 winning units T/Qpdt: £47.20 to a £1 stake. Pool: £11,847.60 - 185.71 winning units **Darren Owen**

# 7310 AYR (L-H)
Saturday, September 23
**7375 Meeting Abandoned** - Waterlogged

# 7013 CATTERICK (L-H)
Saturday, September 23

**OFFICIAL GOING: Good to soft (7.2)**
Wind: Moderate behind Weather: Overcast

## 7383 BRITISH STALLION STUDS EBF NOVICE STKS 5f 212y
**2:25** (2:27) (Class 5) 2-Y-O **£2,911** (£866; £432; £216) **Stalls** Low

Form RPR

61 **1** **Canford's Joy (IRE)**[31] 6312 2-9-9 0 ........................ ShaneGray 5 80+
(Ann Duffield) *mde all: rdn over 1f out: edgd rt ins fnl f: styd on* **10/1**

24 **2** *½* **Three Saints Bay (IRE)**[24] 6590 2-9-2 0 ........................ DanielTudhope 4 71
(David O'Meara) *trckd ldrs: hdwy over 2f out: chal over 1f out and sn rdn: drvn and ev ch ins fnl f: kpt on same pce* **6/4**[1]

0 **3** *2¼* **Emphatic (IRE)**[77] 4599 2-9-2 0 ........................ LukeMorris 6 64
(Robert Cowell) *trckd wnr: cl up 1/2-way: pushed along over 2f out: rdn wl over 1f out: kpt on same pce fnl f* **14/1**

6 **4** *½* **Dalawyna (FR)**[79] 4528 2-8-11 0 ........................ AndrewMullen 2 57
(Kevin Ryan) *trckd ldng pair: pushed along over 2f out: rdn wl over 1f out: sn drvn and kpt on same pce* **8/1**

**5** *2¾* **Dutch Academy** 2-9-2 0 ........................ JoeyHaynes 8 54
(K R Burke) *wnt rt s: hld up in tch: hdwy over 2f out: n.m.r and sn swtchd rt: rdn to chse ldrs wl over 1f out: sn no imp* **7/2**[2]

0 **6** *3½* **Swiss Marlin**[15] 6897 2-8-11 0 ........................ JasonHart 1 39
(John Quinn) *trckd ldrs whn n.m.r on inner and lost pl after 1 1/2f: in rr after* **20/1**

**7** *½* **Balmec (IRE)** 2-9-2 0 ........................ ConnorBeasley 3 42
(Ann Duffield) *a in rr* **40/1**

**8** *1½* **Altered Method (IRE)** 2-9-2 0 ........................ PJMcDonald 7 38
(Hugo Palmer) *chsd ldrs on outer: rdn along wl over 2f out: sn wknd* **9/2**[3]

1m 16.22s (2.62) **Going Correction** +0.40s/f (Good) **8** Ran SP% **114.5**
Speed ratings (Par 95): **98,97,94,93,90 85,84,82**
CSF £25.55 TOTE £7.10: £2.50, £1.10, £2.90; EX 23.20 Trifecta £140.90.
**Owner** J R Dwyer **Bred** Dr D Harron **Trained** Constable Burton, N Yorks

**FOCUS**
The ground was officially good to soft (GoingStick 7.2) with the clerk of the course saying: "We had 2mm of rain yesterday afternoon and it was dry overnight". Bend turning into the home straight and the parade ring bend both out 2yds, adding 6yds to races 1, 2, 6, 7 and 8 and 12yds to races 4 and 5. A routine novice event to start, but a decent performance from the winner. Luke Morris and Joey Haynes called the ground good to soft, PJ McDonald said it was soft while Jason Hart said it was very loose. The winning time was 5.42sec outside standard and while these may have been 2yos, that still suggests conditions were pretty testing.

## 7384 HAPPY 40TH BIRTHDAY VICKY WALPOLE NURSERY H'CAP 7f 6y
3:00 (3:02) (Class 4) (0-85,80) 2-Y-O £4,528 (£1,347; £673; £336) Stalls Low

Form RPR
3552 1 **El Chapo**[14] 6940 2-8-11 **70** PaulHanagan 5 75
(Richard Fahey) *t.k.h early: trckd ldrs: hdwy 2f out: rdn to chal jst over 1f out: drvn ins fnl f: led last 100 yds* **3/1**[1]

6525 2 ½ **Poet's Dawn**[15] 6900 2-8-11 **73** RachelRichardson(3) 6 77
(Tim Easterby) *prom: hdwy to chse ldr 1/2-way: rdn to ld wl over 1f out: drvn ins fnl f: hdd last 100 yds: no ex* **12/1**

1330 3 nk **Star Of Zaam (IRE)**[15] 6900 2-8-10 **72** (p) CliffordLee(3) 9 75
(K R Burke) *trckd ldrs: hdwy on outer over 2f out: rdn to chal over 1f out: drvn and ev ch ins fnl f: no ex towards fin* **8/1**

3430 4 2 **Austin Powers (IRE)**[13] 6977 2-9-0 **73** FrannyNorton 2 71
(Mark Johnston) *trckd ldr on inner: pushed along wl over 2f out: sn rdn: drvn over 1f out and kpt on same pce* **12/1**

4215 5 shd **Barford (IRE)**[21] 6699 2-9-7 **80** AndrewMullen 8 77+
(Pam Sly) *awkward s and rr: hdwy on outer 3f out: rdn over 2f out: kpt on u.p fnl f* **4/1**[2]

6325 6 1¾ **Tunes Of Glory**[14] 6932 2-9-6 **79** (p[1]) LukeMorris 4 72
(Sir Mark Prescott Bt) *led: rdn along over 2f out: hdd wl over 1f out: sn drvn and wknd* **5/1**[3]

0444 7 ¾ **Bibbidibobbidiboo (IRE)**[25] 6561 2-8-3 **62** CamHardie 3 53
(Ann Duffield) *dwlt: a in rr* **16/1**

2503 8 shd **Dontgiveuponbob**[14] 6940 2-8-13 **72** TonyHamilton 1 62
(Richard Fahey) *chsd ldrs on inner: rdn along 3f out: sn one pce* **14/1**

4361 9 ½ **Bungee Jump (IRE)**[10] 7045 2-9-5 **78** ShaneGray 7 67
(Kevin Ryan) *towards rr whn n.m.r after 1f: nvr a factor* **7/1**

1m 29.39s (2.39) **Going Correction** +0.40s/f (Good) 9 Ran SP% **113.2**
Speed ratings (Par 97): **102,101,101,98,98 96,95,95,95**
CSF £39.31 CT £261.09 TOTE £3.50: £1.60, £3.70, £2.50; EX 43.00 Trifecta £376.90.
**Owner** Merchant And Missionaries And Partner **Bred** Tibthorpe Stud **Trained** Musley Bank, N Yorks

**FOCUS**
Race distance increased by 6yds. A fair nursery. They went a respectable gallop and one of Richard Fahey's two runners justified favouritism. The 2nd/3rd help set the level.

## 7385 CHARLIE HARDY MEMORIAL, GREAT DAYS HAD NURSERY H'CAP 5f
3:35 (3:37) (Class 5) (0-75,73) 2-Y-O £3,234 (£962; £481; £240) Stalls Low

Form RPR
2005 1 **Bahuta Acha**[10] 7041 2-8-11 **63** LukeMorris 5 72
(David Loughnane) *dwlt and wnt rt s: sn chsng ldrs: cl up on outer over 2f out: rdn to ld ent fnl f: kpt on wl* **7/2**[3]

034 2 2¾ **Undercover Brother**[19] 6756 2-9-7 **73** DanielTudhope 2 72
(David O'Meara) *cl up on inner: pushed along 1/2-way: rdn to chal wl over 1f out: led briefly jst over 1f out: sn drvn and hdd ent fnl f: sn edgd rt and kpt on same pce* **85/40**[1]

5130 3 hd **Bow Belles**[27] 6466 2-9-3 **72** (h[1]) RachelRichardson(3) 6 70
(Tim Easterby) *trckd ldrs: hdwy 2f out: effrt whn n.m.r and swtchd lft ins fnl f: styd on wl on inner towards fin* **5/2**[2]

6301 4 1½ **Funkadelic**[40] 6011 2-9-1 **67** (p[1]) CamHardie 1 60
(Ben Haslam) *dwlt and rr: swtchd rt to outer and hdwy 1/2-way: cl up 2f out: sn rdn and wknd over 1f out* **12/1**

6366 5 3¾ **Mocead Cappall**[26] 6525 2-8-8 **60** (h) RoystonFfrench 4 39
(John Holt) *led: rdn along 2f out: drvn and hdd jst over 1f out: wknd* **14/1**

0050 6 5 **The Auld Hoose (IRE)**[10] 7041 2-8-3 **55** (b[1]) PaulHanagan 3 16
(Richard Fahey) *chsd ldrs: rdn along 1/2-way: sn lost pl and bhd* **11/2**

1m 1.38s (1.58) **Going Correction** +0.225s/f (Good) 6 Ran SP% **112.5**
Speed ratings (Par 95): **96,91,91,88,82 74**
CSF £11.45 TOTE £4.50: £2.10, £1.60; EX 12.90 Trifecta £22.70.
**Owner** Lancashire Lads Partnership **Bred** Mrs G S Rees **Trained** Market Drayton, Shropshire

**FOCUS**
An ordinary sprint nursery with three of the six runners sporting new headgear. The winning time suggested the ground wasn't quite as testing on the sprint track. This has been rated around the runner-up to his recent level.

## 7386 HAPPY 70TH BIRTHDAY JEAN WALPOLE H'CAP 1m 5f 192y
4:10 (4:12) (Class 4) (0-80,77) 3-Y-O+ £5,175 (£1,540; £769; £384) Stalls Low

Form RPR
0112 1 **Brandon Castle**[15] 6895 5-9-7 **74** (t) AndrewMullen 1 91
(Archie Watson) *sn led and clr: allowed an uncontested ld and 20 l ahd at 1/2-way: pushed along 3f out: rdn 2f out: kpt on strly: unchal* **6/5**[1]

-054 2 11 **First Quest (USA)**[42] 5932 3-8-12 **73** (bt) LukeMorris 5 76
(Ed Dunlop) *disp 2nd tl hdwy to chse wnr 5f out: tk clsr order over 3f out: rdn over 2f out: sn drvn and no imp* **11/1**

216 3 8 **Fulham (IRE)**[15] 6880 3-8-13 **77** LewisEdmunds(3) 4 67
(Robyn Brisland) *trckd ldrs: effrt and pushed along 4f out: rdn over 3f out: plodded on one pce* **10/3**[2]

0640 4 1 **Star Of Lombardy (IRE)**[26] 6513 4-9-3 **70** FrannyNorton 2 59
(Mark Johnston) *racd in 2nd: 20 l bhd wnr 1/2-way: pushed along 5f out: drvn along wl over 3f out: sn one pce* **20/1**

2154 5 4 **Sheriff Garrett (IRE)**[11] 7019 3-8-6 **70** (p) RachelRichardson(3) 6 53
(Tim Easterby) *hld up: a in rr* **5/1**[3]

000 6 7 **Up Ten Down Two (IRE)**[19] 6757 8-9-0 **67** (t) CamHardie 3 41
(Michael Easterby) *hld up: a in rr: bhd fr over 3f out* **33/1**

1100 7 2¾ **Mr Globetrotter (USA)**[43] 5896 4-9-1 **75** JamieGormley(7) 7 45
(Iain Jardine) *hld up: a in rr: bhd fr over 3f out* **11/1**

3m 6.03s (2.43) **Going Correction** +0.40s/f (Good)
**WFA** 3 from 4yo+ 8lb 7 Ran SP% **109.6**
Speed ratings (Par 105): **109,102,98,97,95 91,89**
CSF £14.52 TOTE £1.70: £1.30, £3.80; EX 13.90 Trifecta £41.70.
**Owner** C R Hirst **Bred** Barry Walters **Trained** Upper Lambourn, W Berks

**FOCUS**
Race distance increased by 12yds. A fair staying handicap. The heavily supported favourite proved thoroughly dominant and has been rated back to something like his best.

## 7387 LA FILLE ROUGE H'CAP (CATTERICK TWELVE FURLONG SERIES FINAL) 1m 4f 13y
4:45 (4:48) (Class 2) 3-Y-O+
£12,450 (£3,728; £1,864; £932; £466; £234) Stalls Centre

Form RPR
1312 1 **Mr Sundowner (USA)**[11] 7015 5-7-12 **69** oh9 ow1.(t) SammyJoBell(3) 1 75
(Wilf Storey) *trckd ldrs: hdwy over 2f out: swtchd rt wl over 1f out: sn rdn: chal ins fnl f: kpt on wl to ld towards fin* **16/1**

2051 2 ½ **Je Suis Charlie**[24] 6573 3-8-8 **83** ConnorBeasley 6 88
(Michael Bell) *hld up in tch: rapid hdwy on outer wl over 3f out: cl up over 2f out: sn led and rdn: drvn and jnd ins fnl f: hdd and no ex towards fin* **11/8**[1]

1500 3 3½ **Mukhayyam**[14] 6929 5-9-7 **92** (p) RachelRichardson(3) 4 91
(Tim Easterby) *led: pushed along 3f out: rdn and hdd 2f out: sn drvn and kpt on same pce* **17/2**

3525 4 1 **Sellingallthetime (IRE)**[19] 6757 6-8-3 **71** (p) LukeMorris 7 69
(Michael Appleby) *trckd ldr: hdwy over 3f out: rdn along wl over 2f out: sn drvn and kpt on one pce* **17/2**

103 5 ¾ **Airton**[34] 6232 4-8-5 **80** JamieGormley(7) 8 77
(James Bethell) *trckd ldrs: pushed along 4f out: rdn along 3f out: sn drvn and btn* **7/1**[3]

4354 6 1½ **Monaco Rose**[15] 6880 4-8-3 **71** (h) FrannyNorton 5 65
(Richard Fahey) *trckd ldng pair: pushed along over 4f out: rdn along over 3f out: sn drvn and wknd* **4/1**[2]

0501 7 2½ **Wotabreeze (IRE)**[11] 7015 4-8-0 **68** (p) CamHardie 2 58
(John Quinn) *hld up: a towards rr* **10/1**

1304 8 9 **Midnight Warrior**[36] 6126 7-7-9 **70** oh11 ow2....(t) RobertDodsworth(7) 3 46
(Ron Barr) *a in rr* **66/1**

2m 42.61s (3.71) **Going Correction** +0.40s/f (Good)
**WFA** 3 from 4yo+ 7lb 8 Ran SP% **112.1**
Speed ratings (Par 109): **103,102,100,99,99 98,96,90**
CSF £37.14 CT £207.78 TOTE £19.50: £4.00, £1.10, £2.50; EX 55.80 Trifecta £495.10.
**Owner** W Storey **Bred** Hunter Valley Farm Et Al **Trained** Muggleswick, Co Durham

**FOCUS**
Race distance increased by 12yds. The feature contest was a decent middle-distance handicap. They went a respectable gallop and the strong favourite got collared by an outsider in the closing stages. A pb from the winner.

## 7388 MARIE CURIE CARE AND SUPPORT MAIDEN STKS 7f 6y
5:20 (5:22) (Class 5) 3-4-Y-O £2,911 (£866; £432; £216) Stalls Low

Form RPR
6402 1 **Old China**[28] 6435 4-9-8 64 SamJames 7 72
(John Davies) *.trckd ldr: hdwy over 2f out: rdn over 1f out: led ins fnl f: drvn out* **10/3**[2]

2 ½ **Vive La Difference (IRE)**[161] 3-9-5 73 DuranFentiman 5 69
(Tim Easterby) *led: rdn and qcknd over 2f out: drvn jst over 1f out: hdd ins fnl f: kpt on wl* **10/1**

-222 3 8 **Ambrosia**[14] 6941 3-9-0 73 (p) LukeMorris 3 42
(Roger Varian) *trckd ldrs: hdwy 3f out: rdn along over 2f out: drvn wl over 1f out: sn btn* **8/11**[1]

5263 4 3¾ **Ember's Glow**[21] 6667 3-9-5 67 CamHardie 6 37
(Jason Ward) *in tch: rdn along 3f out: sn outpcd* **9/1**

4 5 2 **Guiding Passion (FR)**[142] 2345 3-9-0 0 RoystonFfrench 1 27
(K R Burke) *dwlt: green and a in rr* **8/1**[3]

5-00 6 15 **Kirkby's Phantom**[33] 6268 3-8-11 32 LewisEdmunds(3) 2
(Alan Berry) *chsd ldng pair on inner: rdn along 3f out: sn drvn and wknd* **250/1**

1m 28.94s (1.94) **Going Correction** +0.40s/f (Good)
**WFA** 3 from 4yo 3lb 6 Ran SP% **111.6**
Speed ratings (Par 103): **104,103,94,90,87 70**
CSF £33.41 TOTE £3.90: £2.50, £4.10; EX 29.60 Trifecta £72.70.
**Owner** The Maroon Stud **Bred** The Maroon Stud **Trained** Piercebridge, Durham

**FOCUS**
Race distance increased by 6yds. An ordinary maiden rated around the winner to a better view of his handicap latest.

## 7389 WE WILL MISS YOU BRIAN H'CAP (DIV I) 7f 6y
5:55 (5:55) (Class 6) (0-65,67) 3-Y-O+ £2,587 (£770; £384; £192) Stalls Low

Form RPR
1300 1 **Chickenfortea (IRE)**[21] 6679 3-9-7 **65** JasonHart 9 72
(Eric Alston) *mde all: rdn wl over 1f out: drvn ins fnl f: hld on wl towards fin* **12/1**

6604 2 ¾ **Tanawar (IRE)**[11] 7018 7-9-5 **60** (b) JamesSullivan 4 66
(Ruth Carr) *t.k.h early: trckd ldrs: hdwy 2f out: swtchd rt and rdn over 1f out: drvn to chal ins fnl f: ev ch tl no ex towards fin* **17/2**

3021 3 2 **Bold Spirit**[11] 7018 6-9-0 **58** (t) PhilDennis(3) 10 59
(Declan Carroll) *trckd ldrs: hdwy over 2f out: swtchd rt to outer and rdn over 1f out: drvn and kpt on same pce fnl f* **13/2**

31 4 2½ **Bernie's Boy**[59] 5280 4-9-5 **67** (p) JamieGormley(7) 7 61
(Iain Jardine) *trckd wnr: hdwy and cl up over 2f out: rdn wl over 1f out: drvn ent fnl f: grad wknd* **5/2**[1]

1352 5 nse **Carlovian**[18] 6783 4-8-12 **53** (p) CamHardie 12 47
(Mark Walford) *hld up in rr: hdwy on wd outside 2f out: rdn over 1f out: kpt on fnl f* **7/2**[2]

5045 6 1½ **Be Bold**[18] 6786 5-9-5 **60** (b) ConnorBeasley 3 50
(Rebecca Bastiman) *trckd ldng pair on inner: pushed along over 2f out: rdn wl over 1f out: sn drvn and kpt on same pce* **11/1**

2030 7 1¼ **Jack Nevison**[32] 6288 4-9-5 **60** AlistairRawlinson 5 46
(Michael Appleby) *trckd ldrs: rdn along 2f out: sn drvn and wknd* **6/1**[3]

6400 8 nk **Lukoutoldmakezebak**[24] 6571 4-8-7 **48** oh3 PaddyAspell 8 33
(David Thompson) *a towards rr* **100/1**

4350 9 nk **Regal Decree**[15] 6902 3-8-3 **54** (t[1]) HarrisonShaw(7) 11 38
(Jedd O'Keeffe) *a in rr* **10/1**

0-50 10 11 **Rebel Flame**[3] 7270 3-8-11 **55** AndrewMullen 6 9
(John Weymes) *dwlt: a in rr* **100/1**

1m 29.83s (2.83) **Going Correction** +0.40s/f (Good)
**WFA** 3 from 4yo+ 3lb 10 Ran SP% **116.0**
Speed ratings (Par 101): **99,98,95,93,92 91,89,89,89,76**
CSF £109.20 CT £743.24 TOTE £12.20: £2.70, £2.50, £2.10; EX 133.80 Trifecta £684.60.
**Owner** Brian Chambers **Bred** Seamus Finucane **Trained** Longton, Lancs


The Form Book Flat, Raceform Ltd, Newbury, RG14 5SJ

**FOCUS**
Race distance increased by 6yds. The first division of a modest handicap. The winner got a breather in whilst doing it bravely from the front and posted a minor pb.

## 7390 WE WILL MISS YOU BRIAN H'CAP (DIV II) 7f 6y
**6:25** (6:28) (Class 6) (0-65,65) 3-Y-O+ **£2,587** (£770; £384; £192) **Stalls** Low

Form RPR
6433 **1** **Someone Exciting**[28] 6437 4-8-5 **53**........................ JamieGormley(7) 12 62
(David Thompson) *towards rr: hdwy and in tch 1/2-way: chsd ldrs on outer over 2f out: rdn to ld over 1f out: edgd lft ins fnl f: kpt on* **9/2**[2]
40 **2** *2* **Donnelly's Rainbow (IRE)**[35] 6182 4-9-10 **65**............. DanielTudhope 2 69
(Rebecca Bastiman) *trckd ldrs: smooth hdwy on inner 3f out: cl up over 2f out: rdn to dispute ld over 1f out: ev ch tl drvn ins fnl f and kpt on same pce* **3/1**[1]
3020 **3** *1* **Redrosezorro**[25] 6549 3-8-10 **54**........................................(h) NeilFarley 7 54
(Eric Alston) *dwlt and towards rr: hdwy on inner over 2f out: rdn to chse ldrs over 1f out: kpt on same pce* **14/1**
4446 **4** *nk* **Mischief Managed (IRE)**[25] 6546 3-9-4 **62**................ DuranFentiman 5 61
(Tim Easterby) *rr: hdwy on wd outside 2f out: sn rdn and styd on wl fnl f* **8/1**
2225 **5** *2 1/4* **Danot (IRE)**[28] 6435 5-8-9 **57**.................................(p) HarrisonShaw(7) 10 51
(Jedd O'Keeffe) *trckd ldrs: cl up 1/2-way: led 2f out: sn rdn and hdd over 1f out: grad wknd* **7/1**
5R0 **6** *5* **Tellovoi (IRE)**[28] 6435 9-9-5 **60**..................................(v) ConnorBeasley 9 41
(Richard Guest) *cl up: led 4f out: rdn along and hdd 2f out: sn drvn and grad wknd* **12/1**
2122 **7** *4* **Melaniemillie**[18] 6785 3-8-11 **55**..................................... JamesSullivan 1 24
(Ruth Carr) *trckd ldrs: hdwy and cl up over 2f out: rdn wl over 1f out: sn drvn and wknd* **11/2**[3]
5060 **8** *2* **Iceaxe**[102] 3702 4-9-7 **62**............................................... RoystonFfrench 3 26
(John Holt) *led: hdd 4f out: cl up: rdn along 3f out: wknd fnl 2f* **66/1**
4000 **9** *nk* **Refuse Colette (IRE)**[53] 5512 8-8-6 **50**.............. RachelRichardson(3) 4 14
(Adrian Nicholls) *a towards rr* **14/1**
5-40 **10** *1 1/2* **Sugar Beach (FR)**[143] 2304 3-9-7 **65**...............................(p[1]) ShaneGray 8 23
(Ann Duffield) *chsd ldrs: rdn along wl 3f out: sn wknd* **33/1**
500 **11** *7* **My Angel**[33] 6268 3-8-4 **48** oh1........................................ AndrewMullen 11
(Ollie Pears) *a in rr: bhd fnl 2f* **33/1**

1m 29.34s (2.34) **Going Correction** +0.40s/f (Good)
**WFA** 3 from 4yo+ 3lb **11** Ran SP% **110.6**
Speed ratings (Par 101): **102,99,98,98,95 89,85,83,82,81 73**
CSF £16.27 CT £150.52 TOTE £5.40: £2.10, £1.60, £4.30; EX 21.00 Trifecta £365.00.
**Owner** Wayne Fleming **Bred** Trebles Holford Farm Thoroughbreds **Trained** Bolam, Co Durham
■ Blue Jacket was withdrawn. Price at time of withdrawal 14-1. Rule 4 applies to all bets - deduction 5p in the pound.

**FOCUS**
Race distance increased by 6yds. The second division of a modest handicap.
T/Plt: £209.10 to a £1 stake. Pool: £64,609.42 - 225.52 winning units. T/Qpdt: £53.10 to a £1 stake. Pool: £4,164.58 - 58 winning units. **Joe Rowntree**

# 7351 NEWBURY (L-H)
### Saturday, September 23

**OFFICIAL GOING: Good (6.8)**
Wind: mild breeze across Weather: sunny periods

## 7391 WEDGEWOOD ESTATES EBF NOVICE STKS (PLUS 10 RACE) (DIV I) 7f (S)
**1:15** (1:17) (Class 4) 2-Y-O **£5,175** (£1,540; £769; £384) **Stalls** Centre

Form RPR
5 **1** **Fennaan (IRE)**[15] 6884 2-9-2 0.....................................(t) JimmyFortune 11 88
(John Gosden) *trckd ldrs: led over 1f out: kpt on w enough in hand fnl f: rdn out* **7/1**
0 **2** *hd* **Sam Gold (IRE)**[22] 6653 2-9-2 0........................................ HarryBentley 7 87
(Roger Varian) *trckd ldrs: rdn 2f out: swtchd rt jst ins fnl f: str run fnl 100yds: clsng rapidly on wnr cl home* **7/2**[1]
**3** *3 1/4* **Alfarqad (USA)** 2-9-2 0.................................................... JimCrowley 13 78
(Owen Burrows) *led: rdn and hdd over 1f out: kpt on but no ex fnl 120yds* **9/2**[2]
023 **4** *1 1/4* **Cuban Heel**[41] 5960 2-9-2 77............................................. AdamKirby 10 75
(Clive Cox) *mid-div: rdn and stdy prog fr 2f out: kpt on fnl f but nt pce to threaten: snatched 4th cl home* **8/1**
**5** *hd* **Epaulement (IRE)** 2-9-2 0.......................................... RichardKingscote 5 74
(Tom Dascombe) *trckd ldrs: rdn over 2f out: kpt on same pce: lost 4th cl home* **40/1**
**6** *2 1/2* **Carp Kid (IRE)** 2-9-2 0.................................................... SeanLevey 15 68
(Richard Hannon) *mid-div: rdn over 2f out: no imp tl kpt on ins fnl f* **12/1**
**7** *1 1/4* **Gronkowski (USA)** 2-9-2 0............................................... RyanMoore 9 67+
(Jeremy Noseda) *s.i.s: towards rr: pushed along fr over 3f out: making hdwy whn nt clr run briefly ent fnl f: kpt on wout ever threatening* **5/1**[3]
**8** *shd* **Face Like Thunder** 2-9-2 0............................................ DavidProbert 12 64
(Andrew Balding) *s.i.s: towards rr: rdn over 2f out: no ch but kpt on ins fnl f* **16/1**
**9** *1/2* **Pact Of Steel** 2-9-2 0..................................................... DaneO'Neill 14 63
(Harry Dunlop) *a mid-div* **50/1**
**10** *nse* **Battle Lines** 2-9-2 0....................................................... MartinHarley 4 63
(James Tate) *s.i.s: sn pushed along towards rr: nvr any imp* **33/1**
4 **11** *hd* **Reshaan (IRE)**[15] 6884 2-9-2 0.......................................... FrankieDettori 3 62
(Richard Hannon) **13/2**
**12** *5* **Casa Comigo (IRE)** 2-9-2 0.................................... SilvestreDeSousa 16 49
(John Best) *hld up towards rr: pushed along over 2f out: little imp* **40/1**
0 **13** *3* **Boko Fittleworth (IRE)**[9] 7079 2-9-2 0............................. WilliamCarson 2 40
(Jonjo O'Neill) *mid-div: rdn over 2f out: nvr any imp: wknd ent fnl f* **200/1**
00 **14** *1* **Peggie Sue**[9] 7093 2-8-11 0.............................................. JimmyQuinn 8 33
(Adam West) *mid-div: rdn 2f out: sn wknd* **200/1**
**15** *8* **Macho Mover (IRE)** 2-9-2 0............................................ RobHornby 6 16
(Mick Channon) *in tch: rdn 3f out: sn wknd* **40/1**
**16** *5* **Arlecchino's Arc (IRE)** 2-9-2 0........................................ SteveDrowne 1 3
(Mark Usher) *sn struggling towards rr: bhd fnl 3f* **150/1**

1m 25.09s (-0.61) **Going Correction** -0.15s/f (Firm) **16** Ran SP% **121.5**
Speed ratings (Par 97): **97,96,93,91,91 88,87,87,86,86 86,80,77,75,66 61**
CSF £30.67 TOTE £7.90: £2.70, £1.90, £1.90; EX 33.30 Trifecta £243.00.
**Owner** M Al-Qatami & K M Al-Mudhaf **Bred** Minch Bloodstock And Castletown Stud **Trained** Newmarket, Suffolk

**FOCUS**
All race distances as advertised. Sean Levey and David Probert agreed it was good ground after the first while Martin Harley called it "beautiful" and Harry Bentley said it was "nice". Division one of a good novice event and the first two, both with previous experience, came clear. The field raced centre-to-stands' side.

## 7392 WEDGEWOOD ESTATES EBF NOVICE STKS (PLUS 10 RACE) (DIV II) 7f (S)
**1:45** (1:50) (Class 4) 2-Y-O **£5,175** (£1,540; £769; £384) **Stalls** Centre

Form RPR
4 **1** **Emaraaty**[22] 6653 2-9-2 0................................................... JimCrowley 10 94+
(John Gosden) *lw: mde all: travelling best and in command fnl 2f: comf* **4/9**[1]
642 **2** *2 1/4* **Magnificent**[47] 5710 2-9-2 79............................................... SeanLevey 4 85
(Richard Hannon) *trckd ldrs: rdn to chse wnr 2f out: kpt on wl to draw clr of remainder but nt pce of easy wnr* **7/1**[2]
**3** *6* **Epic Fantasy** 2-9-2 0.......................................................... FranBerry 6 69+
(Charles Hills) *leggy: hld up towards rr: hdwy fr 2f out: rdn into 3rd ins fnl f: kpt on but no threat to ldng pair* **50/1**
**4** *1 3/4* **Brother Ralph (IRE)** 2-9-2 0.................................. SilvestreDeSousa 16 64+
(Brian Meehan) *unf: hld up towards rr: swtchd lft over 2f out: hdwy over 1f out: running green but r.o nicely ins fnl f* **33/1**
**5** *1 1/4* **Baritone (IRE)** 2-9-2 0.................................................... RyanMoore 2 61+
(Sir Michael Stoute) *lengthy: lw: hld up towards rr: nt best of runs but hdwy over 1f out: no ch but kpt on fnl f* **16/1**
**6** *1/2* **Diocles Of Rome (IRE)** 2-9-2 0.......................................... PatDobbs 14 59
(Ralph Beckett) *str: mid-div tl outpcd over 2f out: kpt on fnl f* **50/1**
434 **7** *1 1/2* **Ateem (FR)**[21] 6674 2-9-2 80.......................................... FrankieDettori 11 55
(Richard Hannon) *trckd ldrs: rdn 2f out: sn outpcd by front pair: fdd ins fnl f* **8/1**[3]
30 **8** *1/2* **Capital Flight (IRE)**[29] 6403 2-9-2 0................................ JamieSpencer 5 54
(Paul Cole) *swtg: stdd s: in rr: swtchd lft over 2f out: hdwy into midfield over 1f out: no further imp fnl f* **9/1**
**9** *1 1/4* **Harry Callahan (IRE)** 2-9-2 0................................. RichardKingscote 8 51
(Tom Dascombe) *str: trckd wnr tl rdn over 2f out: wknd ent fnl f* **50/1**
0 **10** *2 1/2* **Sugar Plum Fairy**[28] 6417 2-8-11 0................................... SteveDrowne 9 39
(Tony Carroll) *in tch: rdn 2f out: wknd fnl f* **200/1**
**11** *1/2* **Icart Point** 2-9-2 0........................................................... AdamKirby 1 42
(Clive Cox) *w'like: in tch: rdn 3f out: wknd jst over 1f out* **50/1**
00 **12** *1* **Matewan (IRE)**[47] 5710 2-9-2 0......................................... DavidProbert 12 40
(Ian Williams) *mid-div: rdn over 2f out: sn outpcd* **100/1**
00 **13** *2 1/4* **Foxangel**[19] 6747 2-8-11 0...........................................(h) OscarPereira 15 29
(Jose Santos) *leggy: in tch: rdn over 2f out: wknd over 1f out* **150/1**
6 **14** *7* **Sapper**[16] 6853 2-9-2 0...................................................... DaneO'Neill 3 15
(Ed Walker) *w'like: mid-div: rdn over 2f out: wknd over 1f out* **100/1**
**15** *10* **Tour De Paris (IRE)** 2-9-2 0............................................ CharlesBishop 7
(Eve Johnson Houghton) *unf: dwlt: a in rr* **25/1**

1m 24.1s (-1.60) **Going Correction** -0.15s/f (Firm) **15** Ran SP% **126.5**
Speed ratings (Par 97): **103,100,93,91,90 89,87,87,85,83 82,81,78,70,59**
CSF £4.22 TOTE £1.40: £1.10, £2.10, £11.50; EX 6.10 Trifecta £203.70.
**Owner** Hamdan Al Maktoum **Bred** Meon Valley Stud **Trained** Newmarket, Suffolk

**FOCUS**
Crystal Ocean was a narrow second in a division of this last year while the 2015 winner, Tabarrak, has won two Listed races this season. The quicker division by a second, with an impressive odds-on scorer. The first two had it between them in the last couple of furlongs, drawing well clear before some of the others closed slightly, and they look to have improved.

## 7393 DUBAI DUTY FREE LEGACY CUP STKS (GROUP 3) (FORMERLY THE ARC TRIAL) 1m 3f
**2:15** (2:16) (Class 1) 3-Y-O+
**£34,026** (£12,900; £6,456; £3,216; £1,614; £810) **Stalls** Low

Form RPR
1236 **1** **Desert Encounter (IRE)**[56] 5394 5-9-3 114.....................(h) SeanLevey 8 112+
(David Simcock) *hld up towards rr: hdwy fr 2f out: swtchd lft jst over 1f out: str run to ld ins fnl f: styd on wl: rdn out* **13/2**[3]
1221 **2** *nk* **Second Step (IRE)**[28] 6440 6-9-3 110.............................. JamieSpencer 4 110
(Roger Charlton) *lw: broke wl: stdd bk bhd ldrs sn after: rdn 2f out: edging lft u.p but tk narrow advantage ent fnl f: sn bmpd and hdd: styd on* **9/2**[1]
00-1 **3** *3/4* **Secret Number**[20] 6744 7-9-8 114.................................... GeraldMosse 1 114
(Saeed bin Suroor) *trckd ldrs: chal 3f out: rdn 2f out: drifted rt over 1f out: ev ch whn bmpd jst ins fnl f: styd on but no ex* **10/1**
236- **4** *nse* **Architecture (IRE)**[343] 7351 4-9-0 111.............................. PatSmullen 5 106
(Hugo Palmer) *hld up: rdn and hdwy over 2f out: styd on ins fnl f but nt pce to threaten: nrly snatched 3rd fnl stride* **9/1**
4621 **5** *2* **Fabricate**[28] 6441 5-9-6 112............................................(p) JimCrowley 6 108
(Michael Bell) *led: rdn and narrowly hdd ent fnl f: sn hmpd: no ex fnl 120yds* **7/1**
2 **6** *hd* **Wingingit (IRE)**[65] 5088 3-8-8 92...................................... RobHornby 11 103
(Andrew Balding) *hld up: rdn 3f out: no imp tl styd on fnl f* **25/1**
5002 **7** *1* **Across The Stars (IRE)**[7] 7139 4-9-3 107......................... RyanMoore 10 103
(Sir Michael Stoute) *trckd ldrs: rdn w ch whn squeezed out and lost pl jst over 2f out: nt pce to get bk on terms* **12/1**
2400 **8** *3/4* **My Dream Boat (IRE)**[31] 6328 5-9-3 113..........................(p) AdamKirby 2 102
(Clive Cox) *mid-divsion: hdwy to chse ldrs 3f out: sn rdn: styd on same pce fnl f* **13/2**[3]
210 **9** *2* **What About Carlo (FR)**[53] 5500 6-9-3 108....................... JimmyFortune 9 99
(Eve Johnson Houghton) *trckd ldr tl rdn 2f out: losing pce whn hmpd over 2f out: outpcd after* **25/1**
0301 **10** *nk* **Dylan Mouth (IRE)**[77] 4614 6-9-3 110............................... HarryBentley 3 98
(Marco Botti) *hld up: rdn 3f out: nt pce to get involved* **10/1**
0302 **11** *shd* **Scarlet Dragon**[14] 6931 4-9-3 108................................. CharlesBishop 7 98
(Eve Johnson Houghton) *mid-div: hdwy 3f out: hung lft u.p jst over 2f out: ev ch sn after: wknd fnl f* **6/1**[2]

2m 17.91s (-3.29) **Going Correction** -0.075s/f (Good)
**WFA** 3 from 4yo+ 6lb **11** Ran SP% **115.2**
Speed ratings (Par 113): **108,107,107,107,105 105,104,104,102,102 102**
CSF £35.05 TOTE £6.00: £2.00, £1.80, £3.70; EX 20.10 Trifecta £353.80.
**Owner** Abdulla Al Mansoori **Bred** Tally-Ho Stud **Trained** Newmarket, Suffolk

**FOCUS**
A really competitive Group 3, with little between most of these, and that was reflected in the betting and the race itself, with plenty having their chance inside the last 2f. This has been rated around the penalised 3rd to his best.

## 7394 DUBAI DUTY FREE MILL REEF STKS (GROUP 2) 6f
**2:50** (2:51) (Class 1) 2-Y-O

**£42,532** (£16,125; £8,070; £4,020; £2,017; £1,012) **Stalls** Centre

Form RPR
3142 **1** **James Garfield (IRE)**[31] 6326 2-9-1 106........................ FrankieDettori 3 113
(George Scott) *cl up early: last pair after 2f: hdwy over 2f out: drifted rt chsng ldr ent fnl f: led fnl 160yds: r.o strly* **10/3**[2]
4221 **2** 3/4 **Invincible Army (IRE)**[14] 6935 2-9-1 109........................ MartinHarley 7 111+
(James Tate) *hld up but in tch: hdwy travelling strly whn nt clr run 2f out: shkn up whn clr jst over 1f out: swtchd lft fnl 160yds: r.o wl: hld towards fin* **5/2**[1]
0226 **3** 1/2 **Nebo (IRE)**[28] 6446 2-9-1 109........................ RyanMoore 1 109
(Charles Hills) *prom: rdn to ld 2f out: hdd fnl 160yds: kpt on but no ex towards fin* **15/2**
13 **4** 3 1/2 **Lansky (IRE)**[31] 6326 2-9-1 0........................ JamieSpencer 8 99
(Jeremy Noseda) *hld up: pushed along over 2f out: r.o ent fnl f: wnt 4th towards fin: nt pce of ldrs* **15/2**
10 **5** 3/4 **Grand Koonta (IRE)**[72] 4812 2-9-1 94........................ AdamKirby 2 97
(Clive Cox) *chsd ldrs: rdn and ev ch 2f out: kpt on same pce fnl f: no ex whn lost 4th towards fin* **9/1**
1215 **6** 1/2 **Staxton**[28] 6446 2-9-1 103........................ DavidAllan 9 95
(Tim Easterby) *trckd ldrs: ev ch 2f out: sn rdn: one pce fnl f* **14/1**
4223 **7** 3/4 **Rebel Streak**[35] 6199 2-9-1 81........................ DavidProbert 4 93
(Andrew Balding) *led: rdn and hdd 2f out: sn one pce* **50/1**
21 **8** 5 **No I'm Easy (IRE)**[33] 6264 2-9-1 0........................ RichardKingscote 6 78
(Tom Dascombe) *lw: chsd ldrs: rdn over 2f out: wknd over 1f out* **25/1**
0161 **9** nse **Enjazaat**[26] 6521 2-9-1 103........................ JimCrowley 10 78
(Owen Burrows) *lw: prom: rdn and ev ch briefly wl over 1f out: wknd ent fnl f: eased* **11/2**[3]

1m 10.64s (-2.36) **Going Correction** -0.15s/f (Firm) **9** Ran SP% **113.0**
Speed ratings (Par 107): **109,108,107,102,101 101,100,93,93**
CSF £11.78 TOTE £3.80: £1.40, £1.10, £2.20; EX 11.30 Trifecta £55.20.
**Owner** W J and T C O Gredley **Bred** Stetchworth & Middle Park Studs Ltd **Trained** Newmarket, Suffolk

**FOCUS**
The last two winners, Ribchester and Harry Angel, have both progressed into proven Group 1 performers. This was the joint-biggest field since 2005 and it looked a good edition, with some solid Group-race form represented. The first two came from the rear and the centre of the track appeared favoured. The time was a juvenile track record. This has been rated to race averages which sees the winner find a bit more.

## 7395 DUBAI DUTY FREE H'CAP 1m 2f
**3:25** (3:28) (Class 2) (0-105,108) 3-Y-O+

**£46,687** (£13,980; £6,990; £3,495; £1,747; £877) **Stalls** Low

Form RPR
0324 **1** **Brorocco**[28] 6449 4-8-9 **89**........................(h) DavidProbert 13 98
(Andrew Balding) *travelled wl: mid-div: smooth hdwy fr 2f out: led ent fnl f: drifted lft: styd on wl: comf* **8/1**[1]
1001 **2** 1 **Fidaawy**[29] 6399 4-9-9 **103** 5ex........................ JimCrowley 14 110+
(Sir Michael Stoute) *lw: mid-div: hdwy 2f out: sn rdn: squeezed up by wnr ent fnl f: styd on wl fnl 120yds: wnt 2nd cl home* **8/1**[1]
1320 **3** hd **Anythingtoday (IRE)**[14] 6920 3-8-12 **97**........................(p) PatSmullen 9 104
(Hugo Palmer) *in tch: hdwy 3f out: chal 2f out: sn rdn to dispute ld: hdd ent fnl f: styd on but no ex whn lost 2nd cl home* **17/2**[2]
1114 **4** nk **Silver Ghost (IRE)**[21] 6698 4-8-13 **93**........................ CharlesBishop 12 99
(Eve Johnson Houghton) *trckd ldrs: led 2f out: rdn whn jnd sn after: hdd ent fnl f: styd on but no ex towards fin* **8/1**[1]
-100 **5** 1 1/4 **Banksea**[15] 6873 4-9-10 **104**........................ JamieSpencer 5 108
(Luca Cumani) *lw: in tch: rdn jst over 2f out: styng on ins fnl f whn short of room briefly and swtchd rt fnl 120yds: kpt on towards fin* **12/1**
5401 **6** nk **Leshlaa (USA)**[21] 6717 3-9-9 **108** 5ex........................ JimmyQuinn 17 111
(Saeed bin Suroor) *lw: in tch: hung bdly rt on bnd leaving bk st: rdn in cl 3rd 2f out: styd on same pce fnl f* **20/1**
6041 **7** 1 1/4 **Eddystone Rock (IRE)**[28] 6449 5-9-8 **102** 5ex........................ PatDobbs 18 103
(John Best) *hld up towards rr: hdwy over 2f out: sn swtchd rt and rdn: styd on fnl f wout ever threatening* **16/1**
0013 **8** hd **Erik The Red (FR)**[29] 6399 5-9-6 **100**........................(p) KevinStott 15 100
(Kevin Ryan) *lw: mid-div: rdn 2f out: styd on but nt pce to get involved* **8/1**[1]
1040 **9** 1 1/2 **Snoano**[28] 6449 5-9-5 **104**........................ FinleyMarsh(5) 1 101
(Tim Easterby) *mid-div: rdn over 2f out: nvr any imp* **33/1**
2643 **10** 1 1/4 **Al Neksh**[9] 7091 4-8-11 **91**........................(p[1]) FrankieDettori 6 86
(William Haggas) *trckd ldrs: rdn over 2f out: wknd fnl f* **12/1**
3405 **11** nse **Reaver (IRE)**[14] 6933 4-8-2 **82**........................(v) KieranO'Neill 16 77
(Eve Johnson Houghton) *hld up towards rr: rdn 2f out: styd on fnl f: n.d* **33/1**
2612 **12** shd **Azari**[16] 6857 5-8-11 **96**........................(p) JennyPowell(5) 3 91
(Tom Dascombe) *hld up towards rr: sme late prog: nvr any threat* **25/1**
1055 **13** 1/2 **Curlew River**[14] 6924 3-8-10 **95**........................ HarryBentley 10 89
(Mark Johnston) *prom: rdn wl over 2f out: wknd ent fnl f* **40/1**
4-40 **14** 3/4 **Shabbah (IRE)**[21] 6698 4-8-7 **90**........................ HectorCrouch(3) 20 82
(Sir Michael Stoute) *hld up towards rr: rdn 2f out: sme late prog: nvr a factor* **33/1**
12- **15** 4 1/2 **Threat Assessed (IRE)**[448] 3887 4-8-6 **86**........................ SamHitchcott 8 69
(Clive Cox) *mid-div: effrt over 2f out: no imp whn swtchd rt over 1f out: wknd fnl f* **20/1**
2060 **16** shd **First Flight (IRE)**[13] 6978 6-9-3 **97**........................(b[1]) GeraldMosse 7 80
(Heather Main) *mid-div: rdn over 2f out: wknd over 1f out* **25/1**
4425 **17** 1 **Law And Order (IRE)**[14] 6931 3-9-1 **100**........................ MartinHarley 4 82
(James Tate) *mid-div: rdn over 2f out: wknd over 1f out* **12/1**
0111 **18** 1 1/2 **Teodoro (IRE)**[27] 6482 3-8-8 **93** 5ex........................(h) RichardKingscote 11 72
(Tom Dascombe) *led: rdn 3f out: hdd 2f out: sn wknd* **10/1**[3]
0000 **19** 5 **Baydar**[28] 6449 4-9-6 **100**........................(p) SilvestreDeSousa 19 68
(Ian Williams) *a bhd* **20/1**

2m 4.62s (-4.18) **Going Correction** -0.075s/f (Good)
**WFA** 3 from 4yo+ 5lb **19** Ran SP% **126.3**
Speed ratings (Par 109): **113,112,112,111,110 110,109,109,108,107 107,107,106,106,102 102,101,100,96**
CSF £60.82 CT £576.71 TOTE £8.30: £2.20, £2.10, £3.00, £2.70; EX 58.00 Trifecta £404.20.
**Owner** Kingsclere Racing Club **Bred** Kingsclere Stud **Trained** Kingsclere, Hants

**FOCUS**
A good-quality handicap, they got racing a fair way out and the form looks rock-solid. A length pb from the winner.

## 7396 DUBAI INTERNATIONAL AIRPORT WORLD TROPHY STKS (GROUP 3) 5f 34y
**4:00** (4:02) (Class 1) 3-Y-O+

**£34,026** (£12,900; £6,456; £3,216; £1,614; £810) **Stalls** Centre

Form RPR
1401 **1** **Take Cover**[21] 6668 10-9-1 111........................ DavidAllan 10 115
(David C Griffiths) *mde all: r.o gamely: rdn out* **8/1**
3435 **2** 3/4 **Cotai Glory**[13] 6973 5-9-1 112........................ SilvestreDeSousa 1 112
(Charles Hills) *lw: trckd ldrs: rdn for str chal over 1f out: kpt on ins fnl f: hld towards fin* **9/2**[1]
0144 **3** 3/4 **Muthmir (IRE)**[77] 4635 7-9-6 114........................(p) JimCrowley 6 115
(William Haggas) *s.i.s: towards rr: hdwy 2f out: nt best of runs briefly over 1f out: rdn ent fnl f: r.o but nt quite pce to chal* **5/1**[2]
-601 **4** nk **Waady (IRE)**[11] 7027 5-9-1 107........................(h) DaneO'Neill 2 109
(John Gosden) *mid-div: hdwy 2f out: sn rdn: kpt on wl w 3rd fnl f but nt pce to chal* **7/1**
5205 **5** 1/2 **Mirza**[21] 6668 10-9-1 105........................(p) MartinHarley 8 107
(Rae Guest) *chsd ldrs: rdn 2f out: kpt on same pce fnl f* **25/1**
1142 **6** 1 3/4 **Judicial (IRE)**[48] 5684 5-9-1 107........................(e) JoeDoyle 7 100
(Julie Camacho) *lw: mid-div: rdn to chse ldrs 2f out: kpt on same pce fnl f* **13/2**[3]
0000 **7** nk **Line Of Reason (IRE)**[7] 7144 7-9-1 100........................ PatDobbs 17 99
(Paul Midgley) *s.i.s: bhd: swtchd lft 2f out: rdn and hdwy ent fnl f: n.d to ldrs but r.o wl* **50/1**
1005 **8** hd **Priceless**[29] 6402 4-9-3 108........................ AdamKirby 16 101
(Clive Cox) *mid-div: swtchd lft 2f out: sn rdn: little imp* **9/1**
0301 **9** 1 **Encore D'Or**[10] 7051 5-9-1 106........................ RyanMoore 4 95
(Robert Cowell) *lw: hld up towards rr: rdn and hdwy over 2f out: nt pce to get on terms: fdd fnl 120yds* **14/1**
1414 **10** 1 1/4 **Caspian Prince (IRE)**[13] 6973 8-9-6 115........................(t) DeclanMcDonogh 13 96
(Tony Coyle) *chsd wnr: rdn over 2f out: fdd fnl f* **14/1**
0335 **11** shd **Thesme**[10] 7051 5-8-12 100........................ GeorgiaCox 9 87
(Nigel Tinkler) *swtg: chsd ldrs: rdn and ev ch 2f out: fdd ins fnl f* **33/1**
3630 **12** 1/2 **Goldream**[29] 6402 8-9-1 105........................(p) FranBerry 15 88
(Robert Cowell) *s.i.s: towards rr: sn pushed along: hdwy 2f out: nt clr run over 1f out: no ch after* **25/1**
0124 **13** nk **Hit The Bid**[70] 4927 3-9-0 107........................(t[1]) LeighRoche 14 87
(D J Bunyan, Ire) *s.i.s: a towards rr* **12/1**
0000 **14** shd **Just Glamorous (IRE)**[57] 5354 4-9-1 100........................ DavidProbert 3 87
(Ronald Harris) *prom: rdn and ev ch 2f out: wknd ent fnl f* **80/1**
1-03 **15** nk **Rosie Briar**[106] 3539 3-8-11 96........................ RobHornby 5 83
(Andrew Balding) *mid-div: rdn over 2f out: wknd ent fnl f* **50/1**
-003 **16** nk **Go On Go On Go On**[10] 7051 4-8-12 95........................ HectorCrouch 11 82
(Clive Cox) *mid-div: rdn 3f out: wknd ent fnl f* **50/1**
00-3 **17** 14 **Abstraction (IRE)**[56] 5445 7-9-1 92........................(b[1]) RonanWhelan 12 34
(J S Moore) *mid-div tl wknd over 1f out* **125/1**

58.79s (-2.61) **Going Correction** -0.15s/f (Firm)
**WFA** 3 from 4yo+ 1lb **17** Ran SP% **121.4**
Speed ratings (Par 113): **114,112,111,111,110 107,107,106,105,103 102,102,101,101,101 100,78**
CSF £40.91 TOTE £8.20: £2.70, £2.00, £2.10; EX 34.90 Trifecta £274.60.
**Owner** Norcroft Park Stud **Bred** Norcroft Park Stud **Trained** Bawtry, S Yorks

**FOCUS**
A competitive Group 3 sprint. The winner raced down the stands' side with the next three wider out on the track. The winner was as good as ever, and the runner-up has been rated to this year's form.

## 7397 DUBAI DUTY FREE FINEST SURPRISE H'CAP 1m 4f
**4:35** (4:36) (Class 3) (0-95,93) 3-Y-O+ **£7,439** (£2,213; £1,106; £553) **Stalls** Low

Form RPR
621- **1** **Daphne**[367] 6667 4-9-3 **84**........................ RyanMoore 9 97
(William Haggas) *mid-div: hdwy over 2f out: sn rdn: chal over 1f out: led fnl 130yds: styd on wl: rdn out* **8/1**[3]
-131 **2** 3/4 **Weekender**[92] 4048 3-9-4 **92**........................ FrankieDettori 8 103
(John Gosden) *lw: mid-div: pushed along over 3f out: rdn and hdwy over 2f out: led over 1f out: edgd lft: hdd fnl 130yds: styd on but no ex cl home* **13/8**[1]
121- **3** 4 **Withhold**[344] 7320 4-9-6 **87**........................ RobertWinston 7 92
(Roger Charlton) *trckd ldrs: rdn to ld wl over 1f out: sn hdd: kpt on same pce fnl f* **8/1**[3]
1432 **4** 1 1/2 **Okool (FR)**[35] 6202 3-8-11 **85**........................ JimCrowley 1 88
(Owen Burrows) *trckd ldrs: led 2f out: sn rdn and hdd: kpt on same pce fnl f* **5/1**[2]
3503 **5** 1/2 **Paris Protocol**[36] 6135 4-9-6 **87**........................(p) SeanLevey 4 89
(Richard Hannon) *lw: trckd ldr: rdn to ld briefly over 2f out: kpt on same pce fr over 1f out* **20/1**
2210 **6** 1 3/4 **Seafarer (IRE)**[14] 6920 3-9-5 **93**........................ PatDobbs 10 92
(Marcus Tregoning) *s.i.s: last pair: hdwy 2f out: sn rdn: styd on wout ever threatening to get on terms* **12/1**
1302 **7** 3/4 **Galactic Prince**[28] 6415 3-8-6 **80**........................ DavidProbert 6 78
(Andrew Balding) *hld up towards rr: rdn and stdy prog fr over 2f out: styd on same pce fnl f* **5/1**[2]
660 **8** 3 1/4 **Sea Fox (IRE)**[21] 6671 3-9-4 **92**........................(t) FranBerry 12 85
(David Evans) *mid-div: rdn wl over 2f out: nt pce to get involved* **40/1**
5560 **9** 1/2 **Barye**[161] 1798 6-9-2 **90**........................ StephenCummins(7) 3 82
(Richard Hughes) *swtg: trckd ldrs: rdn wl over 2f out: wknd over 1f out* **50/1**
2040 **10** 2 3/4 **Sunblazer (IRE)**[52] 5524 7-9-5 **86**........................(t) JamieSpencer 5 73
(Kim Bailey) *s.i.s: a towards rr* **40/1**
31-0 **11** 11 **You're Hired**[49] 5643 4-9-9 **90**........................ AdamKirby 11 60
(Amanda Perrett) *hld up towards rr: rdn over 2f out: nvr threatened: wknd over 1f out* **16/1**
4415 **12** 9 **Croquembouche (IRE)**[9] 7096 8-9-3 **84**........................(p) SilvestreDeSousa 2 39
(Ed de Giles) *led: rdn and hdd over 2f out: wknd over 1f out: eased fnl f* **33/1**

2m 31.94s (-3.56) **Going Correction** -0.075s/f (Good)
**WFA** 3 from 4yo+ 7lb **12** Ran SP% **121.8**
Speed ratings (Par 107): **108,107,104,103,103 102,101,99,99,97 90,84**
CSF £21.05 CT £115.10 TOTE £7.00: £2.40, £1.20, £2.70; EX 18.60 Trifecta £213.80.
**Owner** The Queen **Bred** The Queen **Trained** Newmarket, Suffolk


The Form Book Flat, Raceform Ltd, Newbury, RG14 5SJ

**FOCUS**
Strong handicap form for the level, with a decent gallop and the first two clear. The first three posted their best figures yet.

## 7398 HEATHERWOLD STUD H'CAP 7f (S)
**5:05** (5:10) (Class 4) (0-80,80) 3-Y-0 **£4,690** (£1,395; £697; £348) **Stalls** Centre

Form RPR
0101 **1** **Warsaw Road (IRE)**[32] 6297 3-9-7 **80** JamieSpencer 11 90
(Luca Cumani) *lw: mid-div: hdwy over 2f out: rdn to ld wl over 1f out: strly pressed fnl f: kpt on gamely: drvn rt out* **10/1**
4245 **2** ½ **Esprit De Corps**[24] 6576 3-9-6 **79** (p[1]) SilvestreDeSousa 10 87
(Roger Charlton) *hld up: hdwy over 1f out: rdn for str chal ins fnl f: edgd lft u.p: kpt on but no ex cl home* **6/1**[2]
221 **3** 1 **Killay**[37] 6103 3-9-7 **80** CharlesBishop 4 85+
(Eve Johnson Houghton) *lw: trckd ldrs: rdn and ev ch 2f out: kpt on but no ex ins fnl f* **7/2**[1]
2313 **4** ½ **Multicultural (IRE)**[32] 6297 3-9-6 **79** (v[1]) MartinHarley 8 83
(James Tate) *hld up: hdwy over 1f out: nt clr run bhd wnr sn after: swtchd lft: sn rdn: r.o but nt quite pce to get on terms* **10/1**
240 **5** 3 ¼ **Mr Tyrrell (IRE)**[36] 6134 3-8-10 **76** RossaRyan(7) 9 71
(Richard Hannon) *mid-div: rdn 2f out: nt best of runs ent fnl f: kpt on* **20/1**
6632 **6** 1 **Sfumato**[26] 6519 3-9-6 **79** DavidNolan 6 71
(Iain Jardine) *trckd ldr: rdn and ev ch over 1f out: no ex ins fnl f* **10/1**
-453 **7** *hd* **Ariena (IRE)**[28] 6426 3-9-6 **79** AdamKirby 5 71
(Clive Cox) *mid-div: hdwy 2f out: sn rdn: ch over 1f out: fdd fnl 120yds* **6/1**[2]
1110 **8** 1 ¼ **Pursuing Steed**[36] 6134 3-9-3 **79** CharlieBennett(3) 12 68
(Hughie Morrison) *hld up: hdwy 2f out: sn rdn: one pce fnl f* **11/1**
0441 **9** 1 **Katheefa (USA)**[17] 6808 3-9-4 **77** JimCrowley 2 63
(Charles Hills) *hld up towards rr: hdwy over 2f out: rdn over 1f out: nvr threatened: wknd fnl 120yds* **12/1**
-511 **10** ¾ **Dourado (IRE)**[25] 6558 3-9-5 **78** DavidProbert 1 62
(Patrick Chamings) *mid-div: rdn and hdwy over 1f out: wknd fnl f* **14/1**
1000 **11** 1 **Dark Destroyer (IRE)**[35] 6203 3-8-11 **70** (v[1]) JimmyQuinn 7 51
(Joseph Tuite) *mid-div: rdn 2f out: nt clr run over 1f out where snatched up: no ch after* **50/1**
2402 **12** *nse* **Inner Circle (IRE)**[35] 6203 3-9-6 **79** SeanLevey 13 60
(Richard Hannon) *lw: trckd ldr: rdn and ev ch 2f out: wknd ent fnl f* **9/1**[3]
5506 **13** 1 ½ **Awesome Allan (IRE)**[7] 7156 3-8-11 **70** FranBerry 3 47
(David Evans) *led: hdd over 1f out: sn wknd* **66/1**

1m 24.11s (-1.59) **Going Correction** -0.15s/f (Firm) **13 Ran SP% 119.0**
Speed ratings (Par 103): **103,102,101,100,97 95,95,94,93,92 91,91,89**
CSF £67.71 CT £264.54 TOTE £9.70: £3.10, £2.30, £1.70; EX 80.30 Trifecta £532.40.
**Owner** Mrs A Silver & Partner **Bred** Tally-Ho Stud **Trained** Newmarket, Suffolk

**FOCUS**
A fair handicap which saw many in with chances a furlong and a half out. They raced down the centre and the winner, second and fourth were positioned more towards the stands' side than the third home. The winner is progressive, and a pb from the second as well.
T/Jkpt: Not won. T/Plt: £11.60 to a £1 stake. Pool: £165,841.60 - 10,393.38 winning units.
T/Qpdt: £5.30 to a £1 stake. Pool: £16,214.49 - 2263.38 winning units. **Tim Mitchell**

# 6424 NEWMARKET (R-H)
## Saturday, September 23
**OFFICIAL GOING: Good (good to soft in places; 7.1)**
Wind: Light against Weather: Cloudy with sunny spells

## 7399 FAIRFAX & FAVOR EBF FILLIES' NOVICE STKS (PLUS 10 RACE) (DIV I) 1m
**1:25** (1:26) (Class 4) 2-Y-0 **£4,528** (£1,347; £673; £336) **Stalls** Low

Form RPR
04 **1** **Stream Song**[35] 6183 2-9-0 0 KieranShoemark 7 84
(John Gosden) *chsd ldrs: rdn to go 2nd over 1f out: r.o to ld nr fin* **11/2**[3]
2 **2** *nk* **Sheikha Reika (FR)**[14] 6917 2-9-0 0 AndreaAtzeni 8 83
(Roger Varian) *chsd ldr tl led over 2f out: shkn up over 1f out: rdn ins fnl f: edgd lft and hdd nr fin* **8/13**[1]
**3** 4 **Hadith (IRE)** 2-9-0 0 JamesDoyle 2 74+
(Charlie Appleby) *hld up in tch: rdn over 1f out: styd on same pce fnl f* **5/2**[2]
**4** *shd* **Must Be Magic (IRE)** 2-9-0 0 OisinMurphy 5 74+
(Andrew Balding) *hld up: hdwy over 2f out: shkn up and edgd rt over 1f out: styd on same pce fnl f* **16/1**
0 **5** 2 ½ **Gift Of Hera**[18] 6777 2-9-0 0 MartinDwyer 9 68
(Sylvester Kirk) *s.i.s: sn rcvrd to ld: hdd over 2f out: wknd ins fnl f* **33/1**
0 **6** 11 **Late Change**[42] 5938 2-9-0 0 StevieDonohoe 4 43
(David Simcock) *hld up: pushed along over 3f out: wknd over 1f out* **33/1**
**7** 2 ¼ **Boscastle (USA)** 2-9-0 0 LiamKeniry 3 37
(Hughie Morrison) *s.i.s: hld up: racd keenly: shkn up and wknd over 1f out* **33/1**
05 **8** 3 **Narodowa**[16] 6861 2-9-0 0 TedDurcan 1 30
(David Lanigan) *hld up: pushed along over 2f out: wknd over 1f out* **50/1**

1m 41.13s (2.53) **Going Correction** +0.325s/f (Good) **8 Ran SP% 122.5**
Speed ratings (Par 94): **100,99,95,95,93 82,79,76**
CSF £9.94 TOTE £7.70: £1.30, £1.02, £1.20; EX 11.60 Trifecta £30.10.
**Owner** George Strawbridge **Bred** George Strawbridge **Trained** Newmarket, Suffolk

**FOCUS**
A hot-looking novice event with the top two in the market both holding entries in next month's Group 1 Fillies' Mile.

## 7400 INTERNATIONAL STUD BOOK COMMITTEE H'CAP 1m 2f
**2:00** (2:00) (Class 3) (0-95,95) 3-Y-0 **£9,703** (£2,887; £1,443; £721) **Stalls** Low

Form RPR
6321 **1** **The Statesman**[3] 7277 3-8-6 **87** 6ex ManuelFernandes(7) 1 99
(Ian Williams) *chsd ldr towards far side tl gps merged over 3f out: led over 1f out: edgd lft ins fnl f: styd on wl: comf* **10/3**[3]
2245 **2** 2 ½ **First Nation**[14] 6920 3-9-7 **95** JamesDoyle 4 102
(Charlie Appleby) *racd centre: hld up: hdwy over 2f out: rdn and ev ch over 1f out: styd on same pce ins fnl f* **3/1**[2]
-100 **3** 1 **Crowned Eagle**[72] 4811 3-9-7 **95** AndreaAtzeni 5 100
(John Gosden) *overall ldr in centre: rdn and hdd over 1f out: no ex ins fnl f* **5/2**[1]
1005 **4** 3 ¼ **City Of Joy**[29] 6404 3-9-6 **94** TedDurcan 8 93
(Sir Michael Stoute) *racd centre: hld up: swtchd rt over 2f out: hdwy over 1f out: sn rdn: wknd ins fnl f* **9/1**
4-55 **5** 2 **Apex King (IRE)**[133] 2614 3-9-6 **94** JosephineGordon 6 89
(Ed Dunlop) *racd centre: chsd ldr tl rdn over 2f out: wknd over 1f out* **14/1**
1222 **6** ½ **Harbour Rock**[17] 6822 3-8-7 **81** OisinMurphy 7 75
(David Simcock) *racd centre: hld up: rdn over 2f out: nvr on terms* **10/1**
2000 **7** ½ **Monticello (IRE)**[25] 6563 3-8-11 **85** JoeFanning 3 78
(Mark Johnston) *led trio towards far side and up w the pce in centre: gps merged over 3f out: rdn over 2f out: wknd over 1f out* **16/1**
4655 **8** 2 ½ **Ay Ay (IRE)**[42] 5940 3-8-13 **87** TomQueally 2 75
(David Elsworth) *trckd ldrs towards far side tl gps merged over 3f out: rdn over 2f out: wknd over 1f out* **25/1**

2m 6.91s (1.11) **Going Correction** +0.325s/f (Good) **8 Ran SP% 112.1**
Speed ratings (Par 105): **108,106,105,102,101 100,100,98**
CSF £13.20 CT £27.52 TOTE £4.20: £1.40, £1.30, £1.30; EX 14.00 Trifecta £33.60.
**Owner** Randolph & Mortimer Racing **Bred** Barry Walters **Trained** Portway, Worcs

**FOCUS**
A decent 3yo handicap and a smooth performance from the progressive The Statesman, who improved again to gain his second win in the space of three days.

## 7401 EBFSTALLIONS.COM BENTLEY CAMBRIDGE FILLIES' H'CAP 1m 4f
**2:35** (2:35) (Class 3) (0-95,92) 3-Y-0+ **£9,703** (£2,887; £1,443; £721) **Stalls** Centre

Form RPR
5-21 **1** **Star Rock**[126] 2834 3-8-9 **80** JosephineGordon 3 88+
(Hughie Morrison) *plld hrd and a.p: led over 2f out: rdn over 1f out: styd on wl* **5/2**[1]
1101 **2** 1 ½ **Cribbs Causeway (IRE)**[37] 6104 3-9-3 **88** KieranShoemark 1 94
(Roger Charlton) *hld up: hdwy over 3f out: rdn and ev ch over 1f out: no ex towards fin* **7/1**
1131 **3** 1 **Lady Bergamot (FR)**[27] 6477 3-8-7 **81** GeorgeWood(3) 8 85
(James Fanshawe) *led: hdd over 10f out: chsd ldrs: rdn and ev ch over 2f out: edgd lft over 1f out: styd on same pce ins fnl f* **4/1**[2]
-250 **4** *nse* **Elysian Fields (GR)**[37] 6104 6-10-0 **92** JackMitchell 6 96
(Amanda Perrett) *hld up: hdwy over 3f out: rdn and edgd rt over 1f out: styd on* **25/1**
5312 **5** 3 **Tarte Tropezienne (IRE)**[31] 6307 3-8-13 **84** TomMarquand 9 83
(William Haggas) *hld up: rdn over 2f out: outpcd over 1f out: styd on towards fin* **9/2**[3]
6064 **6** 1 ¾ **Lucy The Painter (IRE)**[14] 6924 5-9-7 **85** (p) LiamKeniry 5 81
(Ed de Giles) *prom: chsd ldr 8f out: rdn over 2f out: wknd ins fnl f* **25/1**
-142 **7** 6 **Vuela**[41] 5957 4-9-5 **83** AndreaAtzeni 10 70
(Luca Cumani) *led over 10f out: rdn and hdd 2f out: wknd fnl f* **7/1**
5115 **8** 3 ½ **Langlauf (USA)**[16] 6865 4-9-4 **85** (p) DavidEgan(3) 2 66
(Rod Millman) *hld up: racd keenly: hdwy over 3f out: rdn: edgd rt and wknd over 1f out* **14/1**
330 **9** 2 **Sagely (IRE)**[46] 5745 4-9-10 **88** OisinMurphy 4 66
(Ed Dunlop) *hld up: shkn up over 1f out: wknd fnl f* **18/1**

2m 38.44s (6.44) **Going Correction** +0.325s/f (Good)
**WFA** 3 from 4yo+ 7lb **9 Ran SP% 111.4**
Speed ratings (Par 104): **91,90,89,89,87 86,82,79,78**
CSF £19.34 CT £64.60 TOTE £2.90: £1.20, £2.50, £1.70; EX 22.90 Trifecta £73.10.
**Owner** Ben & Sir Martyn Arbib **Bred** Arbib Bloodstock Partnership **Trained** East Ilsley, Berks

**FOCUS**
Race distance increased by 14yds. A good renewal of this fillies' handicap, victory going to the least-exposed runner in the field. The 4th helps set the level.

## 7402 BETFRED CESAREWITCH TRIAL H'CAP 2m 2f
**3:10** (3:15) (Class 2) (0-105,103) 3-Y-0+
**£31,125** (£9,320; £4,660; £2,330; £1,165; £585) **Stalls** Centre

Form RPR
-430 **1** **Who Dares Wins (IRE)**[21] 6675 5-9-0 **93** (p) TomMarquand 9 103
(Alan King) *chsd ldrs: rdn over 2f out: led over 1f out: hung lft ins fnl f: styd on* **7/1**[2]
32-1 **2** 1 ¾ **Coeur De Lion**[123] 2928 4-7-11 **79** HollieDoyle(3) 14 88+
(Alan King) *hld up: pushed along over 6f out: hdwy 5f out: led over 3f out: rdn and hdd over 1f out: edgd lft ins fnl f: styd on same pce* **9/2**[1]
0003 **3** 1 ¾ **Shrewd**[8] 7115 7-8-11 **95** CallumRodriguez(5) 11 102
(Iain Jardine) *hld up in tch: rdn and nt clr run over 4f out: edgd rt over 1f out: styd on* **9/1**[3]
1500 **4** 3 ¼ **Oriental Fox (GER)**[31] 6329 9-9-10 **103** JoeFanning 5 107
(Mark Johnston) *hld up: hdwy over 7f out: nt clr run and lost pl over 4f out: hdwy over 2f out: rdn and edgd rt over 1f out: styd on same pce ins fnl f* **16/1**
1214 **5** 2 **Graceful Lady**[13] 6968 4-7-7 **79** oh4 DarraghKeenan(7) 8 81
(Robert Eddery) *s.i.s: hld up: hdwy over 4f out: outpcd and swtchd lft over 2f out: styd on ins fnl f* **25/1**
0411 **6** *nk* **Taws**[26] 6508 6-8-7 **89** (p) DavidEgan(3) 10 91
(Rod Millman) *prom: rdn over 3f out: styd on same pce fr over 1f out* **12/1**
2042 **7** 2 **Medburn Cutler**[26] 6508 7-7-12 **80** oh1 ow1 (p) AaronJones(3) 17 80
(Paul Henderson) *hld up: hdwy over 4f out: rdn and ev ch over 3f out: wknd fnl f* **40/1**
5200 **8** *nk* **Oceane (FR)**[31] 6329 5-8-13 **92** (v) FergusSweeney 15 92
(Alan King) *hld up: hdwy over 3f out: rdn and edgd rt over 1f out: wknd ins fnl f* **20/1**
110- **9** 8 **The Graduate (IRE)**[89] 7123 4-8-11 **90** OisinMurphy 20 83
(A J Martin, Ire) *hld up: rdn over 2f out: nt trble ldrs* **16/1**
4110 **10** 1 ½ **Hawkerland (IRE)**[52] 5524 4-7-12 **80** oh1 ow1 GeorgeWood(3) 16 71
(Marcus Tregoning) *hld up: hdwy over 4f out: rdn and ev ch over 3f out: wknd over 1f out* **10/1**
0321 **11** 14 **Arthur Mc Bride (IRE)**[18] 6779 8-8-8 **87** ow1 (t) LiamKeniry 2 66
(Nigel Twiston-Davies) *chsd ldrs tl wknd over 2f out* **9/1**[3]
3231 **12** 10 **Sternrubin (GER)**[39] 6033 6-9-2 **95** TomQueally 13 65
(Philip Hobbs) *prom: led wl over 3f out: sn hdd: wknd over 1f out* **10/1**
3152 **13** 3 **Denmead**[31] 6323 4-8-2 **81** ow2 JosephineGordon 6 48
(John Butler) *led: hdd over 4f out: wknd over 2f out* **16/1**
-664 **14** 4 ½ **Agent Murphy**[16] 6857 6-9-7 **100** MartinLane 21 63
(Brian Meehan) *sn bhd: hdwy u.p on outer over 3f out: sn wknd* **25/1**
0206 **15** 3 ¼ **Mister Manduro (FR)**[18] 6779 3-7-11 **92** RichardOliver(5) 18 55
(Mark Johnston) *hld up in tch: lost pl over 7f out: hdwy over 4f out: wknd over 2f out* **16/1**
1525 **16** 5 **Great Fighter**[14] 6929 7-8-6 **85** (v) RyanTate 1 41
(Jim Goldie) *s.i.s: hld up: pushed along over 6f out: wknd over 2f out* **33/1**
5 **17** 35 **Percy Veer**[31] 6323 5-8-1 **80** (p) NickyMackay 4
(Sylvester Kirk) *hld up in tch: lost pl over 4f out: wknd over 3f out* **33/1**
2216 **18** 12 **Corpus Chorister (FR)**[31] 6323 4-8-6 **85** MartinDwyer 12
(David Menuisier) *chsd ldr 15f out tl led over 4f out: hdd wl over 3f out: sn wknd* **20/1**

26/0 **19** *19* **Seaport**[57] 5353 6-9-2 **95**......(t[1]) KieranShoemark 19
(Seamus Durack) *hld up: rdn over 4f out: wknd over 3f out* **100/1**

-000 **20** *14* **Havana Beat (IRE)**[83] 3091 7-8-7 **86**......(t) JFEgan 7
(Tony Carroll) *chsd ldr over 3f: lost pl 10f out: bhd fnl 8f* **50/1**

3m 52.27s (0.27) **Going Correction** +0.325s/f (Good)
**WFA** 3 from 4yo+ 11lb **20** Ran SP% **128.6**
Speed ratings (Par 109): **112,111,110,109,108 107,107,106,103,102 96,92,90,88,87 85,69,64,55,49**
CSF £35.10 CT £302.03 TOTE £7.20: £2.00, £1.80, £2.30, £3.50; EX 34.10 Trifecta £206.80.
**Owner** HP Racing Who Dares Wins **Bred** Mount Coote Stud **Trained** Barbury Castle, Wilts

**FOCUS**
Race distance increased by 14yds. An ultra-competitive trial for next month's Cesarewitch and a notable 1-2 for trainer Alan King. A small Flat pb from the winner.

## 7403 FAIRFAX & FAVOR EBF FILLIES' NOVICE STKS (PLUS 10 RACE) (DIV II) 1m
**3:45** (3:48) (Class 4) 2-Y-O **£4,528** (£1,347; £673; £336) **Stalls** Low

Form RPR

**1** **Magic Lily** 2-9-0 0......(t[1]) JamesDoyle 7 89+
(Charlie Appleby) *s.i.s: hdwy over 5f out: shkn up to ld over 1f out: rdn clr fnl f* **5/2**[1]

**2** *8* **Mystic Meg** 2-9-0 0......(h[1]) JackMitchell 1 71
(Hugo Palmer) *led: rdn and hdd over 1f out: edgd lft and wknd ins fnl f* **5/2**[1]

**3** *nse* **Heather Lark (IRE)** 2-9-0 0...... NickyMackay 8 70+
(John Gosden) *hld up: styd on to go 3rd nr fin: nt trble ldrs* **14/1**

20 **4** *hd* **Dance To Paris**[66] 5030 2-9-0 0...... JosephineGordon 5 70
(Lucy Wadham) *prom: chsd ldr over 2f out tl rdn and edgd lft over 1f out: no ex fnl f* **7/1**[3]

**5** *1/2* **Consolida** 2-8-7 0...... GabrieleMalune(7) 4 69
(Luca Cumani) *prom: lost pl over 6f out: styd on ins fnl f* **40/1**

**6** *6* **India** 2-9-0 0...... LouisSteward 3 55
(Michael Bell) *pushed along early in rr: wknd over 1f out* **25/1**

**7** *3/4* **Bob's Girl** 2-9-0 0......(h[1]) StevieDonohoe 9 53
(David Simcock) *s.i.s: hld up: pushed along over 2f out: n.d* **33/1**

5 **8** *nk* **Trump Alexander (IRE)**[14] 6917 2-9-0 0...... TomMarquand 6 53
(Richard Hannon) *plld hrd and prom: wnt 2nd over 5f out tl rdn over 2f out: wknd over 1f out* **11/4**[2]

0 **9** *10* **Speed Craft**[24] 6575 2-9-0 0......(p) RyanTate 2 30
(James Eustace) *chsd ldr tl over 5f out: remained handy tl wknd over 2f out* **50/1**

1m 40.86s (2.26) **Going Correction** +0.325s/f (Good) **9** Ran SP% **114.2**
Speed ratings (Par 94): **101,93,92,92,92 86,85,85,75**
CSF £8.59 TOTE £3.10: £1.10, £1.20, £3.50; EX 9.00 Trifecta £42.40.
**Owner** Godolphin **Bred** Godolphin **Trained** Newmarket, Suffolk

**FOCUS**
An informative novice event and a hugely impressive win from newcomer Magic Lily. It was run at a stronger pace than the first division and it was 0.27sec faster on the clock.

## 7404 ROA/RACING POST OWNERS JACKPOT H'CAP 7f
**4:20** (4:20) (Class 4) (0-85,86) 3-Y-O+ **£5,175** (£1,540; £769; £384) **Stalls** Low

Form RPR

0040 **1** **Medieval (IRE)**[15] 6870 3-9-5 **86**......(p[1]) RaulDaSilva 10 97
(Paul Cole) *hld up: hdwy: nt clr run and swtchd lft over 2f out: rdn to ld over 1f out: edgd rt: r.o* **11/2**[3]

41-3 **2** *1 3/4* **Noble Star (IRE)**[249] 277 4-8-13 **77**...... TomQueally 11 84+
(James Fanshawe) *s.i.s: pushed along in rr: rdn over 1f out: hung rt and r.o ins fnl f: nt rch wnr* **7/1**

3410 **3** *3/4* **Wannabe Friends**[15] 6882 4-9-2 **80**...... ShaneKelly 6 85
(Richard Hughes) *hld up: hdwy over 1f out: sn rdn: styd on same pce ins fnl f* **12/1**

402 **4** *3/4* **Easy Tiger**[11] 7025 5-9-7 **85**...... LiamKeniry 2 88
(Malcolm Saunders) *led: hdd over 5f out: remained w ldr tl led again over 2f out: rdn: hung lft and hdd over 1f out: no ex ins fnl f* **5/1**[2]

5264 **5** *1 3/4* **Noble Peace**[15] 6879 4-9-7 **85**...... KieranShoemark 1 83
(Henry Candy) *prom: racd keenly: rdn over 1f out: wknd wl ins fnl f* **5/1**[2]

-402 **6** *hd* **Prost (GER)**[47] 5719 3-9-5 **86**...... OisinMurphy 4 83
(Ed Vaughan) *hld up: rdn over 1f out: nt trble ldrs* **9/1**

16 **7** *3/4* **Robin Weathers (USA)**[22] 6655 3-9-3 **84**...... AndreaAtzeni 5 79
(William Haggas) *trckd ldrs: nt clr run over 2f out: rdn over 1f out: wknd ins fnl f* **4/1**[1]

135 **8** *1 1/4* **Bernardo O'Reilly**[28] 6426 3-9-0 **81**...... StevieDonohoe 3 72
(Richard Spencer) *racd keenly: w ldr tl led over 5f out: rdn and hdd over 2f out: wknd fnl f* **14/1**

1-00 **9** *1 1/2* **Daschas**[80] 4501 3-8-10 **80**......(t) AaronJones(3) 9 67
(Stuart Williams) *hld up: hung rt fr over 2f out: n.d* **40/1**

2303 **10** *1/2* **Shyron**[37] 6111 6-8-3 **72**...... JaneElliott(5) 8 59
(George Margarson) *chsd ldrs: shkn up over 2f out: wknd ins fnl f* **11/1**

1m 26.67s (1.27) **Going Correction** +0.325s/f (Good)
**WFA** 3 from 4yo+ 3lb **10** Ran SP% **116.3**
Speed ratings (Par 105): **105,103,102,101,99 99,98,96,95,94**
CSF £43.68 CT £445.22 TOTE £6.20: £2.10, £2.20, £3.60; EX 53.70 Trifecta £608.00.
**Owner** Mrs Fitri Hay **Bred** Patrick Cassidy **Trained** Whatcombe, Oxon

**FOCUS**
Quite a decent handicap, with the winner back to something like his best.

## 7405 WINGATE SIGNS WSG H'CAP 6f
**4:55** (4:55) (Class 4) (0-85,86) 3-Y-O+ **£6,469** (£1,925; £962; £481) **Stalls** Low

Form RPR

314 **1** **Glenamoy Lad**[42] 5936 3-8-13 **79**......(t) TomQueally 10 89
(Michael Wigham) *racd far side: s.i.s: hld up: hdwy over 1f out: rdn to ld overall and hung lft wl ins fnl f: r.o: 1st of 9 in gp* **14/1**

0014 **2** *3/4* **Mont Kiara (FR)**[14] 6923 4-9-7 **85**...... KieranShoemark 14 93
(Kevin Ryan) *racd stands' side: chsd ldr tl led that gp over 2f out: rdn to ld overall and hung rt fr over 1f out: hdd wl ins fnl f: 1st of 3 that side* **7/1**

051 **3** *1 1/4* **Ninjago**[28] 6429 7-9-2 **80**...... JoeFanning 5 84
(Paul Midgley) *racd far side: chsd ldrs: led that side over 1f out: hdd wl ins fnl f: 2nd of 9 in gp* **13/2**[3]

3004 **4** *3/4* **Moonraker**[26] 6506 5-9-4 **82**...... JFEgan 9 83
(Mick Channon) *racd far side: s.i.s: pushed along in rr early: hdwy u.p over 1f out: nt rch ldrs: 3rd of 9 in gp* **8/1**

1004 **5** *2 1/4* **Related**[9] 7086 7-9-6 **84**......(b) MartinLane 4 78
(Paul Midgley) *racd far side: chsd ldrs: rdn and ev ch over 1f out: no ex ins fnl f: 4th of 9 in gp* **17/2**

033 **6** *1 1/2* **Ancient Astronaut**[59] 5280 4-8-10 **77**......(v[1]) DavidEgan(3) 6 66
(John Quinn) *racd freely and sn led overall far side: rdn and hdd over 1f out: wknd wl ins fnl f: 5th of 9 in gp* **8/1**

2300 **7** *1 1/4* **Farleigh Mac**[21] 6695 3-8-12 **78**......(b) OisinMurphy 13 63
(Andrew Balding) *led stands' side trio over 3f: sn rdn: wknd over 1f out: 2nd of 3 in gp* **14/1**

1054 **8** *1 1/4* **Hart Stopper**[22] 6662 3-9-4 **84**...... LouisSteward 8 65
(Michael Bell) *racd far side: in rr: hdwy u.p over 1f out: wknd ins fnl f: 6th of 9 in gp* **11/2**[2]

2560 **9** *1* **Captain Lars (SAF)**[7] 7137 8-8-12 **76**......(v) KierenFox 2 54
(Derek Shaw) *racd far side: s.i.s: hld up: rdn and wknd over 1f out: 7th of 9 in gp* **25/1**

31- **10** *shd* **Gorgeous Noora (IRE)**[315] 7939 3-9-3 **83**...... AndreaAtzeni 3 61
(Luca Cumani) *racd far side: prom tl rdn and wknd over 1f out: 8th of 9 in gp* **5/1**[1]

6600 **11** *shd* **Majeste**[21] 6700 3-8-13 **79**......(b[1]) TomMarquand 12 56
(Richard Hannon) *racd stands' side: sn pushed along in rr: nvr on terms: last of 3 in gp* **14/1**

0234 **12** *nk* **Yorkee Mo Sabee (IRE)**[82] 4438 4-8-6 **73**......(t[1]) AaronJones(3) 7 49
(Stuart Williams) *racd freely on far side: prom tl rdn and wknd over 1f out: last of 9 in gp* **28/1**

1m 14.25s (2.05) **Going Correction** +0.325s/f (Good)
**WFA** 3 from 4yo+ 2lb **12** Ran SP% **117.9**
Speed ratings (Par 105): **99,98,96,95,92 90,88,87,85,85 85,85**
CSF £108.26 CT £718.85 TOTE £14.70: £4.70, £3.10, £2.00; EX 131.50 Trifecta £1332.60.
**Owner** V Healy **Bred** Mrs T A Foreman **Trained** Newmarket, Suffolk

**FOCUS**
A competitive sprint handicap. They raced in two distinct groups, the smaller group positioned against the stands' rail and contained only three runners.

## 7406 DISCOVERNEWMARKET.CO.UK FILLIES' H'CAP 1m
**5:30** (5:30) (Class 3) (0-95,96) 3-Y-O+ **£9,703** (£2,887; £1,443; £721) **Stalls** Low

Form RPR

3621 **1** **Shenanigans (IRE)**[53] 5506 3-9-6 **91**...... AndreaAtzeni 1 98
(Roger Varian) *led early: remained w ldr tl led again at stdy pce 6f out: qcknd over 2f out: rdn out* **9/4**[1]

5422 **2** *1 1/4* **Panova**[29] 6377 3-9-2 **90**......(p[1]) DavidEgan(3) 3 94
(Sir Michael Stoute) *trckd ldrs: racd keenly: rdn over 1f out: r.o to go 2nd nr fin: nt rch wnr* **11/4**[3]

3241 **3** *shd* **Dubara**[29] 6377 3-9-6 **91**...... KieranShoemark 5 95
(Luca Cumani) *trckd ldrs: plld hrd: chsd wnr over 1f out: sn rdn: styd on: lost 2nd nr fin* **5/2**[2]

0160 **4** *1/2* **Soul Silver (IRE)**[14] 6919 3-9-7 **92**...... OisinMurphy 4 95
(David Simcock) *hld up: pushed along over 2f out: r.o ins fnl f: nt rch ldrs* **7/1**

6-45 **5** *4 1/2* **Blending**[143] 2287 3-9-0 **85**...... NickyMackay 6 78
(John Gosden) *sn led at stdy pce: hdd 6f out: remained w wnr tl shkn up over 1f out: wknd ins fnl f* **7/1**

1m 45.75s (7.15) **Going Correction** +0.325s/f (Good) **5** Ran SP% **111.0**
Speed ratings (Par 104): **77,75,75,75,70**
CSF £8.82 TOTE £2.60: £1.40, £1.80; EX 9.00 Trifecta £11.10.
**Owner** Ann Black,M Al Qatami & K M Al Mudhaf **Bred** Ringfort Stud **Trained** Newmarket, Suffolk

**FOCUS**
A disappointing turnout for the prize on offer, especially as just five 3yos lined up for a race also open to older fillies and mares. They also went no pace, so suspect form, but the winner is progressive.
T/Plt: £14.10 to a £1 stake. Pool: £113,589.65 - 5864.02 winning units. T/Qpdt: £9.80 to a £1 stake. Pool: £8,889.71 - 669.38 winning units. **Colin Roberts**

# 6946 WOLVERHAMPTON (A.W) (L-H)
Saturday, September 23

**OFFICIAL GOING: Tapeta: standard**
Wind: almost nil Weather: fine

## 7407 BANKS'S AMBER BITTER H'CAP 5f 21y (Tp)
**5:40** (5:43) (Class 6) (0-55,55) 3-Y-O+ **£2,425** (£721; £360; £180) **Stalls** Low

Form RPR

0620 **1** **Staffa (IRE)**[35] 6174 4-9-1 **54**...... PaddyPilley(5) 8 64
(Denis Coakley) *hld up towards rr: hdwy over 2f out: swtchd lft appr fnl f: styd on to ld last 100yds* **9/1**

2500 **2** *2 1/4* **Tasaaboq**[143] 2319 6-8-12 **53**......(t) NicolaCurrie(7) 7 55
(Phil McEntee) *in rr: hdwy on ins 2f out: styd on fnl f: tk 2nd nr fin* **13/2**[3]

6553 **3** *nk* **Swendab (IRE)**[23] 6612 9-9-5 **53**......(b) TimmyMurphy 2 54
(John O'Shea) *chsd ldrs: hmpd over 3f out: kpt on same pce last 100yds* **9/1**

0465 **4** *hd* **Digital Revolution**[27] 6469 3-8-4 **46**...... WilliamCox(7) 4 46
(Antony Brittain) *mid-div: hdwy over 2f out: w ldrs over 1f out: kpt on same pce last 100yds* **5/1**[2]

0600 **5** *1 1/2* **Roy's Legacy**[26] 6531 8-9-5 **53**...... DannyBrock 5 48
(Shaun Harris) *led: hdd last 100yds: fdd* **20/1**

3214 **6** *nk* **David's Beauty (IRE)**[6] 7191 4-9-7 **55**......(b) WilliamCarson 1 49
(Brian Baugh) *w ldrs: hmpd over 3f out: fdd fnl 150yds* **11/4**[1]

3340 **7** *2 1/4* **Lady Joanna Vassa (IRE)**[23] 6631 4-8-6 **47**......(v) JackOsborn(7) 10 33
(Richard Guest) *chsd ldrs: one pce appr fnl f* **25/1**

5060 **8** *nse* **Kodiac Pearl (IRE)**[30] 6339 3-8-11 **46**......(h) AdamBeschizza 6 31
(Robert Cowell) *led to s: mid-div: hung rt over 1f out: nvr a factor* **22/1**

0310 **9** *3/4* **Toni's A Star**[47] 5695 5-8-9 **50**...... ManuelFernandes(7) 9 33
(Tony Carroll) *in rr: drvn and sme hdwy over 2f out: nvr on terms: eased nr fin* **15/2**

2600 **10** *1/2* **Elusivity (IRE)**[26] 6529 9-8-13 **54**......(b) KatherineGlenister(7) 3 35
(Conor Dore) *t.k.h: mid-div: hdwy over 3f out: chsng ldrs 2f out: hung rt and wknd appr fnl f* **9/1**

1m 1.54s (-0.36) **Going Correction** -0.15s/f (Stan)
**WFA** 3 from 4yo+ 1lb **10** Ran SP% **111.4**
Speed ratings (Par 101): **96,92,91,91,89 88,85,85,83,83**
CSF £61.28 CT £540.07 TOTE £10.50: £3.00, £2.20, £2.90; EX 70.20 Trifecta £752.90.
**Owner** The Good Mixers **Bred** Kildaragh Stud **Trained** West Ilsley, Berks
■ Stewards' Enquiry : Danny Brock three-day ban: careless riding (9-11 Oct)



The Form Book Flat, Raceform Ltd, Newbury, RG14 5SJ

**FOCUS**
Plenty of pace on here and it set up for the closers. A pb from the winner; 2nd/3rd/4th help pin base level.

## 7408 JENNINGS CUMBERLAND H'CAP (DIV I) 6f 20y (Tp)
6:10 (6:11) (Class 5) (0-75,75) 3-Y-0+ £3,234 (£962; £481; £240) Stalls Low

Form RPR
353 1 **Miracle Garden**[18] 6795 5-9-4 **72**..........(b[1]) RichardKingscote 6 81
(Ian Williams) *wnt lft s: chsd ldrs: edgd lft and kpt on to ld last 100yds* **7/2[1]**
5400 2 1 1/4 **Lord Cooper**[28] 6455 3-9-5 **75**..........(tp) OscarPereira 1 80
(Jose Santos) *in rr: hdwy over 2f out: kpt on fnl f: tk 2nd clsng stages* **14/1**
0124 3 nk **Liberatum**[15] 6891 3-8-10 **73**.......... NicolaCurrie(7) 2 77
(Ruth Carr) *trckd ldrs: led over 1f out: hdd and kpt on same pce last 100yds* **16/1**
0121 4 1 **Newstead Abbey**[16] 6850 7-9-1 **69**..........(p) DougieCostello 4 70
(Michael Herrington) *hmpd s: hdwy over 2f out: chsng ldrs over 1f out: kpt on same pce* **4/1[2]**
2332 5 shd **The Amber Fort (USA)**[34] 6237 3-8-11 **70**.......... JoshDoyle(3) 13 70
(David O'Meara) *rr-div: hdwy over 2f out: nt clr run appr fnl f: hung rt and kpt on same pce* **6/1[3]**
21 6 3 **Mr Strutter (IRE)**[22] 6660 3-8-4 **67**..........(h) ManuelFernandes(7) 10 58
(Ronald Thompson) *mid-div: effrt on outer over 1f out: nvr a factor* **33/1**
0606 7 hd **Rockley Point**[54] 5481 4-9-2 **70**.......... JoeyHaynes 7 60
(Paul D'Arcy) *w ldrs: wknd appr fnl f* **10/1**
6224 8 1/2 **Trotter**[162] 1761 3-8-10 **71**.......... GeorgeBuckell(5) 9 60
(Stuart Kittow) *mid-div: effrt on outer over 1f out: nvr nr ldrs* **40/1**
0155 9 1 1/4 **Cat Silver**[28] 6442 4-9-1 **69**..........(p) WilliamCarson 8 54
(Charlie Wallis) *mid-div: effrt whn n.m.r bnd 2f out: effrt on outer over 1f out: nvr trbld ldrs* **16/1**
1-20 10 1 3/4 **Don't Blame Me**[131] 2692 4-9-0 **75**.......... WilliamCox(7) 12 54
(Clive Cox) *hld up: a towards rr* **10/1**
2323 11 2 1/2 **Major Valentine**[24] 6586 5-9-1 **74**.......... BenRobinson(5) 3 45
(John O'Shea) *w ldrs: led over 3f out: hung rt: hdd and lost pl over 1f out: sn wknd* **15/2**
32-6 12 4 1/2 **Thankyou Stars**[19] 6759 4-9-2 **70**.......... DanielMuscutt 5 27
(Jonathan Portman) *hmpd s: led tl over 3f out: lost pl over 1f out: lame* **80/1**

1m 13.12s (-1.38) **Going Correction** -0.15s/f (Stan)
**WFA** 3 from 4yo+ 2lb 12 Ran SP% **111.5**
Speed ratings (Par 103): **103,101,100,99,99 95,95,94,92,90 87,81**
CSF £49.48 CT £679.72 TOTE £4.30: £1.60, £4.00, £5.00; EX 54.00 Trifecta £743.80.
**Owner** M A Geobey **Bred** W And R Barnett Ltd **Trained** Portway, Worcs

**FOCUS**
A fair sprint, and a good performance from the winner, who has been rated back to last winter's form.

## 7409 JENNINGS CUMBERLAND H'CAP (DIV II) 6f 20y (Tp)
6:40 (6:41) (Class 5) (0-75,75) 3-Y-0+ £3,234 (£962; £481; £240) Stalls Low

Form RPR
0444 1 **Qatari Riyals (IRE)**[29] 6373 3-9-1 **71**.......... KieranO'Neill 2 79
(Richard Hannon) *towards rr: hdwy over 2f out: led last 150yds: all out* **11/2[3]**
3326 2 shd **Logi (IRE)**[90] 4122 3-9-1 **71**..........(b) PhillipMakin 6 78
(Richard Guest) *chsd ldrs: kpt on fnl f: jst hld* **5/1[2]**
0506 3 1/2 **Born To Finish (IRE)**[26] 6503 4-9-6 **74**..........(p) DougieCostello 5 79
(Jamie Osborne) *s.i.s: hdwy 2f out: swtchd lft: styd on fnl f: n.m.r: no ex clsng stages* **7/1**
1551 4 1 1/2 **Magic Moments**[36] 6157 4-8-12 **66**.......... FergusSweeney 4 67+
(Alan King) *trckd ldrs: hmpd and c v wd wl over 1f out: edgd lft and kpt on wl fnl f* **9/2[1]**
5242 5 1 1/4 **Whitecrest**[5] 7214 9-9-2 **70**.......... WilliamCarson 3 67
(John Spearing) *sn trcking ldrs: led over 1f out: hdd last 150yds: fdd* **9/1**
1623 6 1/2 **Murdanova (IRE)**[23] 6620 4-9-5 **73**.......... DannyBrock 1 68
(Denis Quinn) *mid-div: hdwy over 2f out: sn chsng ldrs: fdd last 150yds* **7/1**
5460 7 3/4 **Big Lachie**[8] 7127 3-9-5 **75**..........(b[1]) SteveDrowne 9 68
(Daniel Mark Loughnane) *s.i.s: t.k.h toward rr: hdwy over 1f out: kpt on: nvr trbld ldrs* **20/1**
0432 8 1 1/4 **Higher Court (USA)**[164] 1728 9-8-10 **71**.......... KatherineGlenister(7) 11 60
(Emma Owen) *w ldrs: led ocver 2f out: hung rt: hdd over 1f out: fdd* **16/1**
1-00 9 2 **Four Dragons**[15] 6878 3-9-0 **70**..........(p[1]) RichardKingscote 8 52
(Tom Dascombe) *led: hdd over 2f out: wknd over 1f out: eased clsng stages* **8/1**
0106 10 1/2 **Joey's Destiny (IRE)**[14] 6949 7-9-7 **75**.......... RyanPowell 10 56
(Kevin Frost) *s.i.s: nvr a factor* **22/1**
22-0 11 10 **Vastly (USA)**[14] 6948 8-8-13 **67**..........(t[1]) SaleemGolam 7 16
(Sophie Leech) *trckd ldrs: lost pl over 2f out: sn bhd: eased fnl f* **40/1**

1m 13.42s (-1.08) **Going Correction** -0.15s/f (Stan)
**WFA** 3 from 4yo+ 2lb 11 Ran SP% **113.8**
Speed ratings (Par 103): **101,100,100,98,96 95,94,93,90,89 76**
CSF £31.13 CT £193.67 TOTE £6.70: £2.30, £2.10, £2.60; EX 41.20 Trifecta £380.40.
**Owner** Mubarak Al Naemi **Bred** Mubarak Al Naemi **Trained** East Everleigh, Wilts

**FOCUS**
The slower of the two divisions by 0.30sec, but still a length pb from the winner as rated.

## 7410 WAINWRIGHT GOLDEN BEER (S) STKS 6f 20y (Tp)
7:10 (7:11) (Class 6) 2-Y-0 £2,425 (£721; £360; £180) Stalls Low

Form RPR
1200 1 **Our Man In Havana**[13] 6977 2-9-6 72.......... RichardKingscote 9 76+
(Tom Dascombe) *mde all: pushed clr over 1f out: unchal* **6/4[1]**
2556 2 4 **The Love Doctor (IRE)**[19] 6762 2-9-0 67.......... ShaneKelly 10 58
(David Evans) *chsd ldrs: mod 2nd over 1f out: no ch w wnr* **15/2[3]**
0056 3 1/2 **Shesgotthelot**[24] 6608 2-8-9 65..........(p[1]) LiamJones 6 52
(J S Moore) *in rr: hdwy 2f out: kpt on one pce fnl f* **11/1**
0205 4 3/4 **Bodybuilder**[11] 7023 2-9-0 64.......... TimmyMurphy 3 54
(Richard Hannon) *rr-div: hdwy over 2f out: kpt on one pce fnl f* **14/1**
0606 5 1 1/2 **Mirek (IRE)**[96] 3918 2-8-7 49.......... WilliamCox(7) 7 50
(Patrick Chamings) *in tch: hdwy over 1f out: one pce* **50/1**
00 6 1 1/2 **Ruby Sound**[43] 5893 2-8-9 0.......... AdamBeschizza 4 40
(Steph Hollinshead) *in rr: sme hdwy over 1f out: kpt on: nvr a factor* **100/1**
2550 7 1/2 **Highland Mary**[17] 6806 2-8-9 68..........(v) KieranO'Neill 2 39
(Richard Hannon) *in rr: sme hdwy over 1f out: nvr nr ldrs* **9/1**
6444 8 nk **Auntie Pam (IRE)**[29] 6379 2-8-4 64..........(p) JaneElliott(5) 8 38
(Tom Dascombe) *chsd ldrs: effrt 2f out: fdd fnl f* **5/2[2]**
9 8 **Pauvre Moi (IRE)** 2-8-6 0.......... TimClark(3) 1 14
(John Butler) *s.s: a in rr* **33/1**
05 10 8 **Violet Beauregarde**[14] 6950 2-8-9 0..........(h) RyanPowell 12
(Harry Dunlop) *in tch: hung rt over 1f out: sn lost pl and bhd* **28/1**
00 11 3 **Western Dynamisme (FR)**[26] 6504 2-8-9 0.......... WilliamCarson 13
(Harry Dunlop) *s.s: racd wd: in rr: wl bhd fnl 2f* **100/1**

1m 13.77s (-0.73) **Going Correction** -0.15s/f (Stan) 11 Ran SP% **115.7**
Speed ratings (Par 93): **98,92,92,91,89 87,86,85,75,64 60**
CSF £13.03 TOTE £2.30: £1.30, £2.00, £2.50; EX 12.50 Trifecta £69.90.
**Owner** John Abbey & Mike Nolan **Bred** Alvediston Stud & Partners **Trained** Malpas, Cheshire

**FOCUS**
The favourite dominated this from the front.

## 7411 MARSTON'S PEDIGREE EBF NOVICE STKS (PLUS 10 RACE) 1m 142y (Tp)
7:40 (7:42) (Class 4) 2-Y-0 £4,592 (£1,366; £683; £341) Stalls Low

Form RPR
52 1 **Kind Act (USA)**[23] 6616 2-9-2 0.......... JamesDoyle 3 80+
(Charlie Appleby) *led: hdd 7f out: effrt over 2f out: styd on over 1f out: edgd lft and led last 100yds: readily* **4/9[1]**
20 2 2 1/4 **Miss Mumtaz (IRE)**[29] 6403 2-8-4 0.......... ManuelFernandes(7) 6 69
(Tony Carroll) *trckd ldr: t.k.h: led 7f out: hdd and no ex last 100yds* **10/1[3]**
2 3 1 **Staunch (USA)**[33] 6260 2-9-2 0.......... JamieSpencer 8 72
(Jeremy Noseda) *s.i.s: sn trcking ldrs: 2nd over 4f out: drvn over 2f out: one pce whn n.m.r 100yds out* **9/4[2]**
4 1 3/4 **Rusper (IRE)** 2-9-2 0.......... DougieCostello 5 68+
(Jamie Osborne) *in rr: shkn up and hdwy 5f out: outpcd over 2f out: styd on fnl f* **66/1**
0 5 9 **Society Secret (IRE)**[68] 4977 2-9-2 0.......... RichardKingscote 2 49
(Tom Dascombe) *sn chsng ldrs: outpcd over 3f out: lost pl over 2f out* **66/1**
6 2 **Seaborough (IRE)** 2-9-2 0.......... FergusSweeney 7 45
(Alan King) *t.k.h in rr: hdwy 5f out: lost pl over 2f out: sn bhd* **80/1**

1m 49.36s (-0.74) **Going Correction** -0.15s/f (Stan) 6 Ran SP% **113.3**
Speed ratings (Par 97): **97,95,94,92,84 82**
CSF £6.54 TOTE £1.30: £1.10, £4.30; EX 6.10 Trifecta £7.40.
**Owner** Godolphin **Bred** Godolphin **Trained** Newmarket, Suffolk

**FOCUS**
A fair maiden, but it's tricky to pin the level.

## 7412 RINGWOOD RAZORBACK H'CAP 2m 120y (Tp)
8:10 (8:11) (Class 4) (0-85,86) 3-Y-0+ £5,175 (£1,540; £769; £384) Stalls Low

Form RPR
0011 1 **Noble Behest**[22] 6661 3-8-3 **68**..........(p) MartinDwyer 8 78+
(Marcus Tregoning) *trckd ldrs: t.k.h: drvn to ld over 2f out: kpt on wl last 100yds* **11/4[1]**
104 2 1/2 **Opposition**[16] 6865 4-9-13 **82**.......... LukeMorris 7 90
(Ed Dunlop) *trckd ldrs: 2nd over 1f out: kpt on same pce last 100yds* **11/2**
0665 3 3 **Gavlar**[18] 6793 6-10-3 **86**.......... HarryBentley 2 90
(William Knight) *trckd ldrs: drvn over 4f out: one pce over 1f out* **3/1[2]**
515 4 1 1/4 **Wordiness**[26] 6508 9-9-1 **70**.......... ShaneKelly 9 73
(David Evans) *hld up in rr: effrt over 3f out: kpt on: nvr a threat* **22/1**
1253 5 nse **King Calypso**[18] 6793 6-9-12 **81**.......... DougieCostello 3 84
(Denis Coakley) *hld up in mid-div: pushed along 5f out: outpcd over 2f out: kpt on one pce* **11/1**
2434 6 1 1/4 **Fleeting Visit**[18] 6779 4-10-0 **83**..........(p) CharlesBishop 1 84
(Eve Johnson Houghton) *led: hdd after 3f: effrt over 3f out: lost pl over 1f out* **7/2[3]**
5530 7 12 **Duke Of Sonning**[11] 7015 5-8-9 **64** oh9..........(b) DannyBrock 5 51
(Shaun Harris) *t.k.h: trckd ldr: led after 3f: hdd over 2f out: sn lost pl and bhd* **125/1**
4341 8 3 **Mister Bob (GER)**[23] 6618 8-9-8 **77**..........(p) TedDurcan 6 60
(James Bethell) *hld up in rr: effrt over 4f out: outpcd over 2f out: bhd whn eased clsng stages* **10/1**

3m 38.84s (-4.86) **Going Correction** -0.15s/f (Stan)
**WFA** 3 from 4yo+ 10lb 8 Ran SP% **111.8**
Speed ratings (Par 105): **105,104,103,102,102 102,96,95**
CSF £17.46 CT £46.13 TOTE £3.30: £1.60, £1.80, £1.30; EX 17.60 Trifecta £57.80.
**Owner** The FOPS **Bred** Mr & Mrs A E Pakenham **Trained** Whitsbury, Hants

**FOCUS**
A steadily run staying handicap; a bit muddling.

## 7413 HOBGOBLIN H'CAP 1m 4f 51y (Tp)
8:40 (8:41) (Class 6) (0-65,65) 3-Y-0+ £2,425 (£721; £360; £180) Stalls Low

Form RPR
5210 1 **Frozon**[14] 6953 4-8-11 **57**..........(h) BenRobinson(5) 3 63
(Brian Ellison) *trckd ldrs: kpt on fnl f: led post* **10/1**
0420 2 nse **Mr Frankie**[37] 6095 6-9-4 **59**.......... LiamKeniry 5 65
(John Spearing) *led 1f: trckd ldrs: led 100yds out: hdd post* **20/1**
604- 3 1 **Singular Quest**[455] 3651 5-9-4 **59**.......... RichardKingscote 2 63
(Daniel Mark Loughnane) *trckd ldrs: t.k.h: keeping on whn n.m.r and struck over hd by rival rdr's whip 100yds out* **10/1**
0401 4 nse **Hussar Ballad (USA)**[14] 6953 8-9-3 **65**.......... WilliamCox(7) 1 70
(Antony Brittain) *dwlt: t.k.h in rr: hdwy over 3f out: n.m.r over 1f out: styd on wl clsng stages* **3/1[1]**
2343 5 nk **Captain Swift (IRE)**[147] 2162 6-9-9 **64**..........(p) LukeMorris 11 68
(John Mackie) *trckd ldrs: led over 1f out: hdd 100yds out: one pce* **9/1**
2350 6 1/2 **Life Of Luxury**[14] 6953 4-9-3 **58**.......... WilliamCarson 6 61
(Mark Brisbourne) *hld up in mid-div: hdwy 6f out: kpt on one pce fnl f* **25/1**
2000 7 shd **Gold Merlion (IRE)**[11] 7015 4-9-8 **63**.......... FrannyNorton 7 66
(Mark Johnston) *led after 1f: hdd over 1f out: one pce* **12/1**
6106 8 3/4 **Hayward Field (IRE)**[27] 6467 4-9-3 **65**.......... NatalieHambling(7) 9 67
(Noel Wilson) *hld up in rr: t.k.h: effrt over 2f out: kpt on fnl f* **17/2[3]**
-030 9 nk **Almutamarred (USA)**[43] 5872 5-9-10 **65**..........(p[1]) TimmyMurphy 12 66
(James Unett) *hld up in rr: hdwy on outer over 5f out: kpt on appr fnl f* **20/1**
0-03 10 1/2 **The Way You Dance (IRE)**[18] 6781 5-9-8 **63**..........(p) RobertWinston 8 64
(Neil Mulholland) *trckd ldrs: effrt 3f out: kpt on one pce fnl f* **7/2[2]**
4/2- 11 10 **Innish Man (IRE)**[607] 329 5-9-10 **65**.......... SteveDrowne 10 50
(John Mackie) *hld up in rr: drvn 3f out: bhd whn eased fnl 150yds* **17/2[3]**

2m 43.22s (2.42) **Going Correction** -0.15s/f (Stan) 11 Ran SP% **117.5**
Speed ratings (Par 101): **85,84,84,84,84 83,83,83,82,82 75**
CSF £194.59 CT £2048.05 TOTE £9.70: £2.50, £5.40, £3.80; EX 198.00 Trifecta £4190.60.
**Owner** A Barnes **Bred** Mrs Hugh Maitland-Jones **Trained** Norton, N Yorks

**FOCUS**
They went no pace and it developed into a sprint.

## 7414 LANCASTER BOMBER H'CAP — 7f 36y (Tp)
9:10 (9:11) (Class 6) (0-65,65) 3-Y-O — £2,587 (£770; £384; £192) Stalls High

Form / RPR

334 1 **Glenn Coco**[33] 6268 3-9-2 64 ........ AaronJones(3) 7 71
(Stuart Williams) *trckd ldrs: 2nd over 1f out: led last 75yds: drvn out* **5/1[2]**

0033 2 ½ **Showdance Kid**[28] 6435 3-9-5 64 ........ DougieCostello 6 70
(Neville Bycroft) *rr-div: hdwy over 2f out: n.m.r appr fnl f: edgd rt and kpt on wl to take 2nd last 50yds* **7/1**

3654 3 1¼ **Zilza (IRE)**[24] 6581 3-9-4 63 ........(bt) MartinDwyer 3 66
(Conrad Allen) *led after 1f: hdd and no ex last 75yds* **7/1**

0-53 4 ¾ **Mishari**[68] 4964 3-9-2 61 ........ TedDurcan 10 62
(David Lanigan) *trckd ldrs: hung lft over 1f out: one pce* **13/2**

3353 5 ½ **Challow (IRE)**[25] 6556 3-9-4 63 ........ LiamKeniry 2 63
(Sylvester Kirk) *trckd ldrs: t.k.h: kpt on one pce fnl f* **11/2[3]**

020 6 3½ **Miss Anticipation (IRE)**[45] 5797 3-9-6 65 ........(h) RichardKingscote 11 56
(Roger Charlton) *hld up in rr: effrt over 2f out: kpt on fnl f* **10/1**

0040 7 1¼ **Gala Celebration (IRE)**[8] 7122 3-9-5 64 ........(p[1]) ShaneKelly 8 52
(John Gallagher) *s.i.s: reluctant early: towards rr: sme late hdwy: nvr a factor* **18/1**

0032 8 ½ **Jumping Around (IRE)**[21] 6681 3-8-13 65 ........(p) ManuelFernandes(7) 1 52
(Ian Williams) *led 1f: trckd ldrs: wknd last 150yds* **11/4[1]**

000- 9 5 **Amherst Rock**[311] 7975 3-9-5 64 ........(t[1]) DannyBrock 5 39
(Luke McJannet) *stmbld s: rr-div: brief effrt on inner over 1f out: sn wknd and bhd* **50/1**

1m 27.06s (-1.74) **Going Correction** -0.15s/f (Stan) 9 Ran SP% **113.4**
Speed ratings (Par 99): **103,102,101,100,99 95,94,93,87**
CSF £38.97 CT £243.06 TOTE £5.30: £1.80, £2.50, £2.10; EX 47.80 Trifecta £443.60.
**Owner** Miss Emily Stevens Partnership **Bred** Old Mill Stud And S C Williams **Trained** Newmarket, Suffolk

**FOCUS**
A modest handicap run at a solid gallop; straightforward form around the 3rd/4th.
T/Plt: £101.40 to a £1 stake. Pool: £99,545.73 - 716.42 winning units. T/Qpdt: £7.80 to a £1 stake. Pool: £12,663.55 - 1186.65 winning units. **Walter Glynn**

# [6773] CRAON (R-H)
## Saturday, September 23
**OFFICIAL GOING: Turf: very soft**

## 7415a PRIX YVES LALLEMAN (MAIDEN) (2YO FILLIES) (TURF) — 1m 55y
1:20 2-Y-O — £7,692 (£3,076; £2,307; £1,538; £769)

RPR

1 **Connivence (FR)** 2-8-11 0 ........ Pierre-CharlesBoudot 12 72
(A Fabre, France) **76/10**

2 1½ **La Peregrina (FR)** 2-9-2 0 ........ HugoJourniac 3 74
(J-C Rouget, France) **19/5[2]**

3 nk **Star Of Vendome (FR)**[26] 6542 2-9-2 0 ........ EddyHardouin 2 73
(Harry Dunlop) **106/10**

4 1½ **Sistah (IRE)**[62] 2-9-2 0 ........ MaximeGuyon 11 70
(Y Durepaire, France) **17/10[1]**

5 2 **Melburnian (FR)** 2-9-2 0 ........ SoufianeSaadi 9 65
(H-A Pantall, France) **24/1**

6 2 **Siyougirl**[156] 1929 2-9-2 0 ........ AlexandreRoussel 7 61
(A Vetault, France) **35/1**

7 4 **Fabuleuse Bere (FR)** 2-8-11 0 ........ ChristopherGrosbois 10 47
(J Boisnard, France) **156/10**

8 4 **Riviera (FR)** 2-9-2 0 ........ JulienAuge 8 43
(E J O'Neill, France) **14/1**

9 nk **Neteb (FR)** 2-9-2 0 ........ AdrienFouassier 5 43
(J-L Guillochon, France) **97/1**

10 1½ **Filrine (FR)**[51] 5585 2-9-2 0 ........ MickaelBerto 13 39
(Jean-Raymond Breton, France) **84/1**

11 6 **For You (FR)** 2-8-11 0 ........ RichardJuteau 6 21
(P Chevillard, France) **60/1**

12 10 **Snowflake (FR)**[44] 5988 2-9-2 0 ........ WilliamsSaraiva 1
(M Nigge, France) **51/10[3]**

PARI-MUTUEL (all including 1 euro stake): WIN 8.60; PLACE 3.20, 2.00, 3.30; DF 16.20; SF 38.70.
**Owner** Baron Edouard De Rothschild **Bred** Sc Ecurie De Meautry **Trained** Chantilly, France

## 7416a PRIX DU POINT DU JOUR (LISTED RACE) (3YO+) (TURF) — 1m 55y
2:30 3-Y-O+ — £22,222 (£8,888; £6,666; £4,444; £2,222)

RPR

1 **Maximum Aurelius (FR)**[59] 5312 4-9-3 0 ........ Pierre-CharlesBoudot 1 104
(F-H Graffard, France) **2/1[1]**

2 ½ **Miracle Des Aigles (FR)**[13] 4-9-3 0 ........ ThierryThulliez 2 103
(Mme C Barande-Barbe, France) **6/1**

3 hd **Grand Vintage (FR)**[59] 5312 8-9-3 0 ........ AnthonyCrastus 3 102
(A Schutz, France) **32/1**

4 nk **Nordic Dream (IRE)**[27] 6498 4-9-3 0 ........ VincentCheminaud 5 102
(A Fabre, France) **5/1[3]**

5 ½ **Calvin (FR)**[433] 4-9-3 0 ........ JeromeCabre 6 101
(Y Durepaire, France) **105/10**

6 1 **Zafiro (FR)**[39] 6052 5-9-3 0 ........ HugoJourniac 8 98
(J-C Rouget, France) **76/10**

7 ½ **Chika Dream (FR)**[123] 7-9-3 0 ........ ArnaudBourgeais 4 97
(N Leenders, France) **228/10**

8 nk **Boomshackerlacker (IRE)**[36] 6173 7-9-3 0 ........(p) MaximeGuyon 7 96
(George Baker) **27/10[2]**

PARI-MUTUEL (all including 1 euro stake): WIN 3.00; PLACE 1.40, 2.20, 4.50; DF 10.80; SF 20.40.
**Owner** Craig Mather **Bred** Pontchartrain Stud **Trained** France

7417 - 7420a (Foreign Racing) - See Raceform Interactive

# [5305] NAAS (L-H)
## Sunday, September 24
**OFFICIAL GOING: Soft (soft to heavy in places on round course)**

## 7421a C.L. & M.F. WELD PARK STKS (GROUP 3) (FILLIES) — 7f
2:30 (2:32) 2-Y-O — £34,038 (£10,961; £5,192; £2,307; £1,153; £576)

RPR

1 **Ellthea (IRE)**[10] 7087 2-9-0 92 ........ ColmO'Donoghue 4 110
(K R Burke) *trckd ldrs in 3rd: clsr to press ldr in 2nd on far side under 2f out: led 1f out and sn rdn clr: styd on wl* **10/1**

2 2¾ **Sizzling (IRE)**[10] 7088 2-9-0 103 ........ RyanMoore 5 103
(A P O'Brien, Ire) *sn trckd ldr in 2nd: rdn 2f out: edgd rt appr fnl f in 3rd: kpt on again clsng stages into 2nd: nt trble wnr* **3/1[2]**

3 ½ **Ballet Shoes (IRE)**[14] 6974 2-9-0 102 ........ DonnachaO'Brien 8 102
(A P O'Brien, Ire) *led: hdd 1f out: no imp on wnr in 2nd fnl 100yds: dropped to 3rd cl home* **6/1[3]**

4 2 **Mary Tudor (IRE)**[35] 6242 2-9-0 0 ........ WJLee 3 97
(W McCreery, Ire) *racd in mid-div: clsr to chse ldrs in 4th 2f out: no imp ent fnl f: kpt on same pce* **15/8[1]**

5 nk **Juliet Foxtrot**[19] 6776 2-9-0 0 ........ JimCrowley 2 96
(Charles Hills) *racd towards rr: pushed along to take clsr order 2f out: wnt 5th appr fnl f: nvr on terms* **7/1**

6 4½ **Fille Du Septembre (IRE)**[84] 4418 2-9-0 89 ........ PatSmullen 1 85
(D K Weld, Ire) *racd in rr: pushed along in 8th under 2f out: kpt on into 7th ent fnl f: wnt 6th clsng stages: nvr on terms* **25/1**

7 ¾ **Athena (IRE)**[47] 5762 2-9-0 0 ........ SeamieHeffernan 9 83
(A P O'Brien, Ire) *chsd ldrs in 5th: rdn and nt qckn under 2f out: sn no imp* **33/1**

8 7 **New To Town (IRE)**[45] 5858 2-9-0 85 ........ KevinManning 6 65
(J S Bolger, Ire) *chsd ldrs in 4th: niggled along 3f out: nt qckn under 2f out: sn no ex: eased ins fnl f* **28/1**

9 9½ **Ball Girl (IRE)**[28] 6488 2-9-0 92 ........ ColinKeane 7 42
(G M Lyons, Ire) *racd in mid-div: towards rr at 1/2-way: sme prog on outer under 2f out: sn no imp: eased down ins fnl f* **7/1**

1m 30.23s (2.73) 9 Ran SP% **118.4**
CSF £40.52 TOTE £11.80: £3.30, £1.40, £2.20; DF 44.10 Trifecta £240.20.
**Owner** Mrs M Gittins **Bred** George Kent **Trained** Middleham Moor, N Yorks
■ Stewards' Enquiry : Colm O'Donoghue one-day ban: failing to give his mount time to respond to the whip

**FOCUS**
A first British success in this race since Mick Channon scored with Eva's Request in 2007. The winner has been rated up to the best winners of this.

## 7422a LOUGHBROWN STKS (GROUP 3) — 2m
3:00 (3:00) 3-Y-O+ — £30,256 (£9,743; £4,615; £2,051)

RPR

1 **Renneti (FR)**[15] 6956 8-9-8 109 ........ PatSmullen 3 111+
(W P Mullins, Ire) *trckd ldr in 2nd: travelled wl to ld over 2f out: styd on strly to go clr ins fnl f* **4/5[1]**

2 5 **Stars Over The Sea (USA)**[66] 5082 6-9-8 100 ........ WayneLordan 2 106
(Henry De Bromhead, Ire) *t.k.h to ld: hdd over 2f out: no imp on wnr in 2nd ent fnl f: kpt on same pce* **6/1[3]**

3 3 **Wild Irish Rose (IRE)**[10] 7089 3-8-10 102 ow1 ........ SeamieHeffernan 4 102
(A P O'Brien, Ire) *racd in rr: clsr 3f out: swtchd wd 2f out to centre of trck: no imp ent fnl f: sn one pce* **2/1[2]**

4 12 **Return Ace**[64] 5155 5-9-5 90 ........ ColmO'Donoghue 1 86
(James Fanshawe) *settled off ldrs in 3rd: briefly clsr 3f out: rdn and nt qckn in 4th 2f out: sn no imp* **16/1**

3m 49.95s
**WFA** 3 from 5yo+ 10lb 4 Ran SP% **109.1**
CSF £6.00 TOTE £1.40; DF 4.30 Trifecta £6.30.
**Owner** Mrs S Ricci **Bred** Pierre Julienne & Etienne Leenders **Trained** Muine Beag, Co Carlow

**FOCUS**
The 2nd/3rd set the standard in line with their latest, and a small pb from the winner.

## 7423a FORAN EQUINE IRISH EBF AUCTION RACE (PLUS 10 RACE) — 6f
3:30 (3:31) 2-Y-O — £13,141 (£4,059; £1,923; £854; £320)

RPR

1 **Powersville (IRE)**[4] 7289 2-8-11 73 ........ NGMcCullagh 11 80
(Thomas Mullins, Ire) *racd in mid-div: clsr to chse ldrs 2f out: wnt 2nd appr fnl f: styd on wl to ld fnl 100yds: kpt on wl* **16/1**

2 hd **Sunday Smart (IRE)**[42] 5970 2-8-8 0 ........ RonanWhelan 12 76
(P J Prendergast, Ire) *racd in mid-div: clsr on stands' side appr fnl f in 3rd where hung lft u.p: kpt on wl into 2nd clsng stages* **14/1**

3 1½ **The Broghie Man**[14] 6977 2-8-11 77 ........ KevinManning 8 75
(Brendan W Duke, Ire) *chsd ldrs: clsr to press ldr in 2nd at 1/2-way: led over 1f out: strly pressed ins fnl f and hdd fnl 100yds: dropped to 3rd cl home* **7/2[2]**

4 1¼ **Soffia** 2-9-0 0 ........ WayneLordan 13 74+
(Edward Lynam, Ire) *bit slowly away: sn mid-div: prog to chse ldrs appr fnl f: kpt on wl into 4th fnl 150yds: nvr nrr* **16/1**

5 3½ **Tuamhain**[177] 1476 2-8-6 0 ........ ChrisHayes 6 56
(Kevin Prendergast, Ire) *hld up: rdn and prog over 1f out: kpt on same pce into 5th cl home: nvr nrr* **25/1**

6 ½ **Face Off (CAN)** 2-8-12 0 ........ PatSmullen 2 60
(Charles O'Brien, Ire) *racd in rr of mid-div: prog whn forced rt over 1f out: kpt on wl on outer into 6th cl home: nvr nrr* **25/1**

7 nk **Stewardess (IRE)**[16] 6905 2-8-8 70 ........ ShaneFoley 14 55
(John James Feane, Ire) *trckd ldrs: 4th at 1/2-way: rdn in 3rd over 1f out where hmpd and swtchd rt: kpt on one pce* **25/1**

8 1 **Spiorad Saoirse**[13] 7010 2-9-6 84 ........ DeclanMcDonogh 1 64
(Andrew Slattery, Ire) *chsd ldrs towards far side: rdn in 5th over 1f out: wknd ins fnl f* **11/1**

9 nk **Apple Anni (IRE)**[4] 7266 2-8-13 0 ........ JFEgan 5 56
(Mick Channon) *racd in mid-div: pushed along 2f out: no imp appr fnl f* **5/1[3]**

10 2¾ **Swiss Cottage**[35] 6240 2-9-1 0 ........ GaryCarroll 4 50
(Joseph G Murphy, Ire) *bit keen and chsd ldrs on far side: rdn and no imp over 1f out* **6/1**

11 8 **Eadbhard (IRE)**[22] 6702 2-8-11 0 SeamieHeffernan 3 22
(M C Grassick, Ire) *t.k.h early to trck ldr in 2nd: 3rd at 1/2-way: nt qckn under 2f out: sn wknd* **50/1**
12 1 ½ **Rockafilly (FR)**[36] 6212 2-8-6 0 LeighRoche 7 13
(J A Nash, Ire) *a towards rr: rdn and no imp under 2f out* **66/1**
13 1 **Sea The Spray (IRE)**[13] 7007 2-8-6 0 KillianLeonard(5) 9 15
(Andrew Slattery, Ire) *hld up: pushed along towards rr at 1/2-way: no imp 2f out* **66/1**
P **Would You Believe (IRE)**[36] 6212 2-9-4 88 ColinKeane 10
(G M Lyons, Ire) *led tl hdd over 1f out: wknd qckly and p.u injured* **7/4**[1]

1m 15.39s (2.19) **14 Ran SP% 132.8**
CSF £230.91 TOTE £16.70: £5.10, £5.30, £1.40; DF 465.60 Trifecta £5698.40.
**Owner** Mrs Helen Mullins **Bred** Patrick Keane **Trained** Goresbridge, Co Kilkenny

**FOCUS**
An injury incurred by the well-fancied Would You Believe cast a shadow over a race won by a filly who was unplaced in a nursery earlier in the week.

## 7424a RENAISSANCE STKS (GROUP 3) 6f
**4:00** (4:00) 3-Y-O+

**£30,256** (£9,743; £4,615; £2,051; £1,025; £512)

RPR

1 **Quiet Reflection**[120] 3079 4-9-2 116 MartinHarley 5 118+
(K R Burke) *racd in mid-div: short of room 2f out: gd hdwy into 2nd ent fnl f: qcknd wl to ld fnl 150yds and sn clr: comf* **5/2**[1]
2 2 ¾ **Alphabet**[14] 6973 3-9-0 110 (t) RyanMoore 3 109
(A P O'Brien, Ire) *led: rdn to extend advantage appr fnl f: edgd rt ins fnl f and hdd fnl 150yds: nt match wnr in 2nd* **13/2**
3 2 ¾ **Ardhoomey (IRE)**[14] 6973 5-9-5 107 (t) ColinKeane 10 103+
(G M Lyons, Ire) *hld up towards rr: rdn in 9th ent fnl f: styd on strly into 3rd cl home: nrst fin* **14/1**
4 hd **Cougar Mountain (IRE)**[15] 6926 6-9-5 110 (tp) DonnachaO'Brien 11 103
(A P O'Brien, Ire) *hld up towards rr: rdn along in 8th ent fnl f: kpt on strly into 4th clsng stages: nvr nrr* **8/1**
5 ½ **Downforce (IRE)**[14] 6966 5-9-5 110 WJLee 9 101
(W McCreery, Ire) *racd in mid-div: 5th at 1/2-way: rdn and nt qckn appr fnl f: kpt on same pce* **3/1**[2]
6 hd **Gordon Lord Byron (IRE)**[30] 6401 9-9-10 111 WayneLordan 6 106
(T Hogan, Ire) *chsd ldrs in 3rd: rdn in 4th 2f out: swtchd lft ent fnl f: kpt on same pce tl no ex clsng stages* **14/1**
7 1 **Khukri (IRE)**[42] 5974 3-9-3 105 ColmO'Donoghue 2 97
(Mrs John Harrington, Ire) *chsd ldrs in 4th: rdn in 3rd 2f out: wknd ins fnl f* **25/1**
8 2 ½ **Flight Risk (IRE)**[38] 6119 6-9-8 111 KevinManning 4 92
(J S Bolger, Ire) *racd in rr: clsr on far side 2f out: nvr on terms* **16/1**
9 1 ¼ **Only Mine (IRE)**[60] 5308 4-9-2 104 GaryCarroll 7 82
(Joseph G Murphy, Ire) *pressed ldr in 2nd tl under 2f out: rdn and wknd appr fnl f* **9/2**[3]
10 4 ½ **Mr Scarlet**[22] 6703 3-9-3 103 PatSmullen 1 71
(Ms Sheila Lavery, Ire) *racd in mid-div: rdn and nt qckn under 2f out: wknd to rr appr fnl f: eased* **33/1**

1m 13.19s (-0.01)
**WFA** 3 from 4yo+ 2lb **10 Ran SP% 122.2**
CSF £20.53 TOTE £3.30: £1.20, £1.80, £4.00; DF 17.00 Trifecta £143.70.
**Owner** Ontoawinner, Strecker & Burke **Bred** Springcombe Park Stud **Trained** Middleham Moor, N Yorks

**FOCUS**
This revolved around dual Group 1 winner Quiet Reflection, and she was more than equal to the task on only her second run of the season. She is the first British-trained winner of this since Benbaun in 2007. The winner has been rated close to her best, with the 2nd confirming her recent improvement.

## 7425a JOE MCGRATH H'CAP (PREMIER HANDICAP) 5f
**4:30** (4:30) 3-Y-O+

**£25,213** (£8,119; £3,846; £1,709; £854; £427)

RPR

1 **Tylery Wonder (IRE)**[11] 7055 7-8-8 **80** (v) LeighRoche 1 92+
(Paul Midgley) *broke smartly and mde all on far side: rdn to extend advantage appr fnl f: styd on wl* **10/1**
2 1 ½ **Monsieur Joe (IRE)**[15] 6927 10-9-2 **88** PatSmullen 5 95
(Paul Midgley) *chsd ldrs in 3rd: rdn and nt qckn appr fnl f: wnt 2nd ins fnl f: kpt on wl: nt rch wnr* **5/1**[2]
3 ½ **Enter The Red (IRE)**[14] 6971 8-8-4 **76** (b) ChrisHayes 12 81
(Aidan Anthony Howard, Ire) *hld up on stands' side: gd prog over 1f out: wnt 4th ent fnl f: kpt on wl into 3rd fnl 150yds: nvr quite on terms* **8/1**
4 shd **Maarek**[14] 6971 10-9-5 **91** SeamieHeffernan 8 96
(Miss Evanna McCutcheon, Ire) *racd towards rr: rdn and prog over 1f out: styd on strly ins fnl f into 4th fnl 100yds: nvr nrr* **10/1**
5 1 ¾ **Tithonus (IRE)**[14] 6971 6-9-4 **95** (bt) KillianHennessy(5) 7 94
(Denis Gerard Hogan, Ire) *chsd ldrs in 4th: rdn 2f out: nt qckn appr fnl f: kpt on same pce in 5th fnl f* **5/1**[2]
6 1 ½ **Polly Douglas (IRE)**[28] 6489 4-7-11 **76** oh5 AndrewBreslin(7) 11 69
(Kieran P Cotter, Ire) *hld up: rdn to take clsr order over 1f out: no imp fnl 150yds* **12/1**
7 hd **Ducky Mallon (IRE)**[14] 6971 6-8-11 **83** NGMcCullagh 6 75
(Donal Kinsella, Ire) *racd in mid-div: clsr over 1f out to chse ldrs: no imp fnl 150yds* **12/1**
8 ¾ **Sahreej (IRE)**[24] 6640 4-8-4 **76** oh1 (b) RoryCleary 2 66
(Adrian Paul Keatley, Ire) *trckd ldr in 2nd on far side: rdn 2f out: nt qckn appr fnl f: wknd* **16/1**
9 nk **Magic Bear (IRE)**[24] 6640 4-9-2 **93** OisinOrr(5) 10 82
(Edward Lynam, Ire) *hld up towards rr: rdn and sme prog whn short of room and checked over 1f out: nvr on terms* **9/2**[1]
10 ½ **Imagine If (IRE)**[108] 3509 3-9-2 **89** ColinKeane 9 76
(G M Lyons, Ire) *racd in mid-div: travelled wl whn short of room over 1f out and again ins fnl f: nt hrd rdn afterwards* **7/1**[3]
11 2 ¼ **A Few Dollars More (IRE)**[105] 3631 5-7-13 **76** oh1 KillianLeonard(5) 13 55
(Andrew Slattery, Ire) *racd towards rr on stands' side: rdn over 2f out and sn detached: modest late hdwy wout threatening* **16/1**
12 ¾ **Spirit Quartz (IRE)**[14] 6973 9-9-10 **103** DylanHogan(7) 3 79
(Barry John Murphy, Ire) *racd in mid-div on far side: rdn and nt qckn over 1f out: sn no ex* **20/1**

1m 1.26s (-0.74)
**WFA** 3 from 4yo+ 1lb **12 Ran SP% 125.2**
CSF £62.84 CT £442.63 TOTE £9.50: £2.50, £2.20, £3.00; DF 60.80 Trifecta £631.40.
**Owner** Taylor's Bloodstock Ltd **Bred** Michael Kavanagh **Trained** Westow, N Yorks
■ Stewards' Enquiry : Seamie Heffernan one-day ban: used whip with excessive frequency

**FOCUS**
A fine training performance by Paul Midgley who supplied the winner and second, in reverse order to market signals. The winner was also successful in this race in 2015 when trained by Willie McCreery and has been rated back to that level.

## 7426a JUDDMONTE BERESFORD STKS (GROUP 2) 1m
**5:00** (5:00) 2-Y-O **£60,512** (£19,487; £9,230; £4,102; £2,051)

RPR

1 **Saxon Warrior (JPN)**[28] 6486 2-9-3 0 RyanMoore 1 111
(A P O'Brien, Ire) *chsd ldrs in 3rd: clsr in 2nd over 2f out: rdn to ld over 1f out and edgd lft to far rails: clr ins fnl f: kpt on wl* **5/6**[1]
2 2 ½ **Delano Roosevelt (IRE)**[15] 6955 2-9-3 0 SeamieHeffernan 2 105
(A P O'Brien, Ire) *t.k.h early in 2nd: reminders over 2f out: edgd rt u.p appr fnl f in 3rd: styd on wl fnl f into 2nd cl home* **3/1**[2]
3 hd **Warm The Voice (IRE)**[13] 7010 2-9-3 96 KevinManning 4 105
(Brendan W Duke, Ire) *hld up in 4th: prog on outer over 1f out whn sltly impeded: kpt on wl into 2nd fnl 150yds: dropped to 3rd cl home* **12/1**
4 hd **Kew Gardens (IRE)**[15] 6955 2-9-3 104 DonnachaO'Brien 3 104
(A P O'Brien, Ire) *led: rdn and hdd over 1f out: dropped to 3rd fnl 150yds: no ex in 4th clsng stages* **4/1**[3]
5 1 ¾ **Riyazan (IRE)**[15] 6955 2-9-3 0 PatSmullen 5 100
(M Halford, Ire) *racd in rr: clsr 2f out: sltly hmpd over 1f out: kpt on same pce fnl f: nvr on terms* **14/1**

1m 46.45s (6.45) **5 Ran SP% 113.9**
CSF £3.83 TOTE £1.60: £1.02, £2.30; DF 3.40 Trifecta £14.30.
**Owner** Derrick Smith & Mrs John Magnier & Michael Tabor **Bred** Orpendale, Chelston & Wynatt **Trained** Cashel, Co Tipperary

**FOCUS**
A 17th win in this event for Aidan O'Brien, and seventh in a row. The winner looks genuine Group 1 material.

7427 - (Foreign Racing) - See Raceform Interactive

# 3923 BRO PARK (L-H)
Sunday, September 24

**OFFICIAL GOING: Turf: good to soft; dirt: standard**

## 7428a STOCKHOLM CUP INTERNATIONAL (GROUP 3) (3YO+) (TURF) 1m 4f
4:17 3-Y-O+ **£70,921** (£26,595; £13,297; £8,865; £4,432)

RPR

1 **Dorcia** 3-8-8 0 Per-AndersGraberg 4 106
(Lennart Reuterskiold Jr, Sweden) *w.w in rr: tk clsr order 2 1/2f out: str run to ld 1 1/2f out: rdn clr fnl f* **11/2**[3]
2 5 **Bokan (FR)**[28] 6501 5-9-4 0 AlexandreDosSantos 2 100
(Wido Neuroth, Norway) *settled next to last: clsd 2 1/2f out: styd on fnl f: no ch w wnr* **201/10**
3 3 **Jubilance (IRE)**[28] 6501 8-9-4 0 ElioneChaves 1 95
(Bent Olsen, Denmark) *led: hdd after 2f: racd in midfield: outpcd and dropped to rr 3f out: styd on again fnl f: tk 3rd late on* **97/10**
4 ½ **Icecapada (IRE)**[57] 5-9-1 0 CarlosLopez 7 91
(Niels Petersen, Norway) *racd towards rr: gd hdwy to ld 2 1/2f out: sn rdn and hd more than 1 1/2f out: kpt on at one pce* **12/5**[2]
5 nse **Hurricane Red (IRE)**[28] 6501 7-9-4 0 JacobJohansen 3 94
(Lennart Reuterskiold Jr, Sweden) *settled cl up: chsd clr ldr 1/2-way: grad reeled in ldr to go on over 3f out: hdd 2f out: rallied briefly u.p: no ex fnl f* **6/5**[1]
6 2 **Pas De Secrets (IRE)**[28] 6501 4-9-4 0 (p) Jan-ErikNeuroth 6 91
(Wido Neuroth, Norway) *racd keenly: hld up in midfield: clsd to press ldng pair 2f out: grad dropped away ins fnl 1 1/2f* **149/10**
7 nk **Fields Of Athenry (IRE)**[50] 5676 5-9-4 0 FannyOlsson 5 91
(Flemming Velin, Denmark) *chsd ldrs: led after 2f and upped tempo: 5l clr 1/2-way: grad reeled in and hdd over 3f out: wl hld fnl 2f* **604/100**

**Owner** Stall Q C **Bred** Qatar Bloodstock Ltd **Trained** Sweden

# 4939 COLOGNE (R-H)
Sunday, September 24

**OFFICIAL GOING: Turf: soft**

## 7429a 55TH PREIS VON EUROPA (GROUP 1) (3YO+) (TURF) 1m 4f
2:55 3-Y-O+ **£85,470** (£25,641; £12,820; £5,982; £2,564)

RPR

1 **Windstoss (GER)**[21] 6727 3-9-0 0 AdriedeVries 3 118+
(Markus Klug, Germany) *w.w in fnl pair: moved to outside rail bk st and stl last overall: tk clsr order 4f out: c stands side st: drvn to ld 2f out: forged clr fnl f: eased cl home* **11/5**[3]
2 4 **Son Macia (GER)**[22] 6710 4-9-3 0 (b) GregoryBenoist 7 106
(Andreas Suborics, Germany) *cl up: dropped into fnl trio bef 1/2-way: moved to outside rail bk st chsd ldr 5f out: w ldrs stands' side and rdn over 2f out: chsd ldr wl over 1f out: no match for wnr fnl f: jst hld on for 2nd* **199/10**
3 hd **Colomano**[21] 6727 3-9-0 0 EduardoPedroza 2 110
(Markus Klug, Germany) *hld up in fnl pair: hdwy on stands' side over 2f out: styd on fnl f: nt pce to chal* **2/1**[2]
4 ¾ **Savoir Vivre (IRE)**[28] 6499 4-9-6 0 FilipMinarik 5 107
(Jean-Pierre Carvalho, Germany) *led after 1f: hdd 5f out: remained cl up: rdn to chal stands' side 2f out: sn one pce u.p* **19/10**[1]
5 1 ¾ **Parviz (IRE)**[56] 5464 3-9-0 0 MarcLerner 8 106
(Waldemar Hickst, Germany) *settled in fnl trio: moved up to chse ldr after 3f: moved to outside rail bk st and led 5f out: kicked for home in centre of trck 3f out: hdd 2f out: dropped away fr over 1f out* **191/10**
6 9 **Kasalla (GER)**[21] 4-9-3 0 MartinSeidl 1 87
(Markus Klug, Germany) *led early: hdd after 1f: remained cl up: lost pl 4f out: last and drvn 3 1/2f out: wl bhd fnl 1 1/2f* **128/10**
7 4 ½ **Real Value (FR)**[35] 6255 3-9-0 0 AlexanderPietsch 6 85
(Mario Hofer, Germany) *trckd ldng trio: lost pl 3 1/2f out: wl bhd fnl 1 1/2f* **31/5**

2m 32.4s (-0.50)
**WFA** 3 from 4yo 7lb **7 Ran SP% 130.0**
PARI-MUTUEL (all including 10 euro stake): WIN 32; PLACE: 20, 46; SF: 603.
**Owner** Gestut Rottgen **Bred** Gestut Rottgen **Trained** Germany

# NANCY

Sunday, September 24

**OFFICIAL GOING: Turf: soft**

## 7430a PRIX DE LUNEVILLE (CLAIMER) (4YO+) (TURF) 1m 4f

10:50 4-Y-O+ £5,982 (£2,393; £1,794; £1,196; £598)

RPR

1 **Just You And Me (FR)**[139] 4-9-6 0 AntoineHamelin 8 62
(Henk Grewe, Germany) 63/10[3]

2 1 **Polo (GER)**[8] 7-9-6 0 (b) EddyHardouin 2 60
(Carina Fey, France) 29/10[2]

3 2 ½ **Barwick**[42] 5987 9-8-2 0 MlleCoraliePacaut(9) 3 47
(George Baker) *pushed along early: sn rcvrd to chse ldr: led 3f out: drvn 1 1/2f fr home: hdd ins fnl f: wknd late on: jst hld 3rd* 8/5[1]

4 nse **Zawadi (GER)** 4-8-8 0 MlleAnnaVanDenTroost(5) 6 49
(Frau V Henkenjohann, Germany) 137/10

5 1 **Kalibur (GER)**[79] 5-9-2 0 (b) RaphaelMarchelli 1 50
(Mlle Y Vollmer, France) 76/10

6 4 **Red Ghost (GER)**[465] 8-8-11 0 (p) AntoineCoutier 7 39
(Waldemar Hickst, Germany) 7/1

7 ¾ **Manito (GER)** 4-8-11 0 JeromeClaudic 5 38
(Frau S Steinberg, Germany) 168/10

8 15 **Bluvida (FR)**[187] 6-8-13 0 (p) MlleZoePfeil(4) 4 20
(Pascal Vannereux, France) 27/1

2m 37.69s 8 Ran SP% 117.9
PARI-MUTUEL (all including 1 euro stake): WIN 7.30; PLACE 1.70, 1.30, 1.30; DF 7.00; SF 14.80.
**Owner** Green C R E A M Racing **Bred** Mlle K Morice & S.C.E.A. Ecurie De Montfort **Trained** Germany

7431-7440a (Foreign Racing) - See Raceform Interactive

# 7205 SAN SIRO (R-H)

Sunday, September 24

**OFFICIAL GOING: Turf: good**

## 7441a PREMIO ELENA E SERGIO CUMANI (GROUP 3) (3YO+ FILLIES & MARES) (TURF) 1m

2:35 3-Y-O+ £29,914 (£13,162; £7,179; £3,589)

RPR

1 **Candy Store (IRE)**[119] 3121 3-8-9 0 DarioVargiu 6 99
(Stefano Botti, Italy) *settled bhd ldrs: almost upsides front two under 2f out: drvn to ld 1 1/2f out: drvn clr ins fnl f:* 14/5[1]

2 1 ½ **Musa D'Oriente**[21] 6-9-0 0 LucaManiezzi 9 97
(M Gonnelli, Italy) *chsd ldr: chal ldr under 2f out: styd on fnl f: nt pce of wnr* 106/10

3 1 ¼ **Liwa Palace**[35] 6254 4-9-0 0 CristianDemuro 7 94+
(Rod Collet, France) *racd keenly: hld up next to last: hdwy on outer ins fnl 2f: drvn to stay on fnl f: tk 3rd cl home: nt rch front two* 63/20[2]

4 nk **Sporty Doll (ITY)**[21] 5-9-0 0 PierantonioConvertino 3 93
(Silvia Casati, Italy) *racd keenly: hld up towards rr: clsd to chse ldrs 2f out: styd on fnl f: run flattened out late on: lost 3rd cl home* 192/10

5 nk **Lorenzetta (IRE)**[21] 5-9-0 0 ClaudioColombi 8 92
(Riccardo Santini, Italy) *missed break: adrift in rr: in tch in rr 1/2-way: last whn began to cl 1 1/2f out: styd on u.p fnl f: nvr nrr* 79/10

6 ½ **Lady Ramon (ITY)**[119] 3-8-9 0 AntonioFresu 1 90
(A Di Dio, Italy) *racd keenly: hld up towards rr: rdn and no imp 2f out: styd on ins fnl f: nvr on terms* 604/100

7 2 ½ **Movees (IRE)**[146] 2244 3-8-9 0 CarloFiocchi 2 84
(Stefano Botti, Italy) *cl up: outpcd and drvn 2f out: grad lft bhd ins fnl f: wl hld whn eased late on* 145/10

8 3 **Stamp Collecting (IRE)**[119] 3121 3-8-9 0 FabioBranca 4 77
(R Biondi, Italy) *led: drvn 2f out: hdd 1 1/2f out: sn btn: eased ins fnl f* 13/4[3]

9 nk **Thanx For Nothing (FR)**[120] 3-8-9 0 MickaelBarzalona 5 77
(P Decouz, France) *racd in midfield: drvn and nt clr run 3f out: sn in open but rdn and no imp 2f out: wl hld fnl f* 18/5

1m 36.1s (-6.00)
**WFA** 3 from 4yo+ 4lb 9 Ran SP% 141.1
PARI-MUTUEL (all including 1 euro stake): WIN 3.80; PLACE 1.66, 2.92, 1.75; DF 48.93.
**Owner** Scuderia New Age Srl **Bred** Razza Del Velino **Trained** Italy

## 7442a PREMIO VITTORIO DI CAPUA (GROUP 2) (3YO+) (TURF) 1m

3:10 3-Y-O+ £100,000 (£44,000; £24,000; £12,000)

RPR

1 **Amore Hass (IRE)**[70] 4941 3-8-11 0 CristianDemuro 5 108+
(Stefano Botti, Italy) *settled 3rd: drvn to chse ldr over 2f out: rdn along and grad clsd on ldr fr 1 1/2f out: led 125yds out* 31/10[3]

2 nk **Greg Pass (IRE)**[119] 3120 5-9-2 0 DarioVargiu 2 108
(Nicolo Simondi, Italy) *led: kicked 3l clr over 2f out: styd on gamely u.p: hdd 125yds out: no ex* 2/5[1]

3 1 ¼ **Time To Choose**[98] 3884 4-9-2 0 FabioBranca 1 105
(Stefano Botti, Italy) *racd keenly: chsd ldr under restraint: shkn up and no imp 2f out: cl 3rd whn rdn and styd on over 1f out: nt pce to chal but clr of 3rd* 293/100[2]

4 4 ½ **Nice Name (IRE)**[490] 4-9-2 0 LucaManiezzi 3 95
(Marco Gasparini, Italy) *racd in fnl pair: drvn and effrt 1 1/2f out: kpt on at one pce fnl f* 26/1

5 3 ¼ **Pythius (IRE)**[146] 4-9-2 0 (b) ClaudioColombi 4 87
(Riccardo Santini, Italy) *racd keenly: hld up in rr: rdn and no imp fr 2f out: wl hld fnl f* 16/1

1m 37.4s (-4.70)
**WFA** 3 from 4yo+ 4lb 5 Ran SP% 130.9
PARI-MUTUEL (all including 1 euro stake): WIN 4.11; PLACE 1.19, 1.04; DF 6.97.
**Owner** Scuderia Rencati Srl **Bred** T Boylan **Trained** Italy

# 6782 HAMILTON (R-H)

Monday, September 25

**7443 Meeting Abandoned** - waterlogged

# 7056 KEMPTON (A.W) (R-H)

Monday, September 25

**OFFICIAL GOING: Polytrack: standard to slow**
Wind: Light, across Weather: Overcast

## 7450 BETTER ODDS WITH MATCHBOOK NOVICE AUCTION STKS 5f (P)

1:50 (1:50) (Class 5) 2-Y-O £3,234 (£962; £481; £240) Stalls Low

Form RPR

0246 1 **Knockout Blow**[86] 4335 2-9-1 77 SilvestreDeSousa 6 75
(Mark Johnston) *dwlt: sn rcvrd to chse ldng trio: wnt 3rd 2f out and clsd over 1f out: drvn to ld last 150yds: sn clr* 2/1[2]

3302 2 1 ½ **Iconic Knight (IRE)**[19] 6816 2-9-1 74 JamieSpencer 7 70+
(Ed Walker) *hanging lft in midfield: unable to make prog tl into st over 1f out: drvn and styd on to take 2nd last strides* 6/4[1]

1262 3 ½ **Deviate (IRE)**[8] 7193 2-8-13 77 PaddyPilley(5) 8 71
(Tom Dascombe) *spd fr wd draw and led 1f: trckd ldr: shkn up to chal whn wnr shot past 1f out: kpt on same pce after* 11/2[3]

4 ¾ **No More Commisery (IRE)** 2-8-11 0 FrannyNorton 4 61
(Mick Quinn) *t.k.h: led after 1f: rdn over 1f out: hdd and fdd last 150yds* 16/1

00 5 3 **Poppy Jag (IRE)**[16] 6950 2-8-10 0 RyanPowell 2 49
(Kevin Frost) *nvr beyond midfield: one pce and no imp on ldrs over 1f out* 100/1

05 6 nk **Shadow Seeker (IRE)**[18] 6844 2-8-11 0 JoeyHaynes 1 49
(Paul D'Arcy) *dwlt: mostly in last to 2f out: pushed along and kpt on steadily fr over 1f out* 25/1

4 7 ½ **Shamrock Emma (IRE)**[19] 6816 2-8-9 0 LukeMorris 9 45
(John Best) *chsd ldng pair to 2f out: wknd* 16/1

8 7 **Another Situation (USA)** 2-8-10 0 JFEgan 5 21
(Richard Guest) *hanging lft in rr: wd bnd 2f out: no ch after: eased last 100yds* 12/1

5 9 ¾ **Pretty Risky**[22] 6719 2-8-5 0 CharlieBennett(3) 3 17
(Patrick Chamings) *a towards rr: wknd 2f out* 25/1

59.87s (-0.63) **Going Correction** -0.225s/f (Stan) 9 Ran SP% 116.9
Speed ratings (Par 95): **96,93,92,91,86 86,85,74,73**
CSF £5.34 TOTE £2.50: £1.40, £1.10, £2.20; EX 6.50 Trifecta £16.40.
**Owner** A D Spence **Bred** Christopher & Annabelle Mason **Trained** Middleham Moor, N Yorks

**FOCUS**
A fair novice, with the right horses coming to the fore, and a minor pb from the winner.

## 7451 MATCHBOOK/BRITISH STALLION STUDS EBF NOVICE STKS (PLUS 10 RACE) 1m 1f 219y(P)

2:25 (2:25) (Class 4) 2-Y-O £4,528 (£1,347; £673; £336) Stalls Low

Form RPR

4 1 **Graffiti Master**[24] 6654 2-9-2 0 JamesDoyle 2 81+
(John Gosden) *sn trckd ldng pair: wnt 2nd over 2f out: chalng whn carried lft bnd sn after: led wl over 1f out: shkn up to assert fnl f* 2/7[1]

31 2 1 ¾ **Baileys Excelerate (FR)**[40] 6057 2-9-8 0 FrannyNorton 8 82
(Mark Johnston) *sn led: pressed whn hung lft bnd 2f out: hdd wl over 1f out: styd on and clr of rest but no match for wnr* 3/1[2]

3026 3 5 **Trogon (IRE)**[18] 6860 2-9-2 69 JFEgan 1 67
(Mick Channon) *hld up in tch: prog to chse ldng pair 2f out: sn outpcd* 8/1[3]

05 4 3 ¾ **Masters Apprentice (IRE)**[29] 6472 2-8-11 0 MitchGodwin(5) 6 59
(Sylvester Kirk) *hld up in last pair: rdn over 2f out: tk wl hld 4th wl over 1f out: no imp after* 33/1

5 2 ½ **Harbour Nights** 2-9-2 0 HarryBentley 3 55
(Hugo Palmer) *dwlt: hld up in last pair: outpcd over 2f out: pushed along and passed a few after* 8/1[3]

0 6 1 ½ **Spice War**[10] 7128 2-9-2 0 TomMarquand 5 52
(Brian Meehan) *pressed ldrs but pushed along at various times: rdn 4f out: wknd over 2f out* 20/1

0 7 7 **See The Tar (IRE)**[77] 4696 2-9-2 0 DougieCostello 4 38
(Jo Hughes) *t.k.h: chsd ldr after 2f to over 2f out: wknd rapidly* 66/1

0060 8 1 ½ **Duggary**[13] 7030 2-9-2 58 SilvestreDeSousa 7 36
(Kevin Frost) *dwlt: t.k.h and hld up towards rr: no prog over 2f out: sn eased* 33/1

2m 7.41s (-0.59) **Going Correction** -0.225s/f (Stan) 8 Ran SP% 137.1
Speed ratings (Par 97): **93,91,87,84,82 81,75,74**
CSF £2.26 TOTE £1.20: £1.02, £1.10, £1.80; EX 2.60 Trifecta £7.80.
**Owner** HH Sheikha Al Jalila Racing **Bred** Cliveden Stud Ltd **Trained** Newmarket, Suffolk

**FOCUS**
This went according to the market, the first three finishing in betting order.

## 7452 WINNERS ARE WELCOME AT MATCHBOOK H'CAP 1m 1f 219y(P)

2:55 (2:58) (Class 4) (0-80,81) 3-Y-O+ £5,175 (£1,540; £769; £384) Stalls Low

Form RPR

5053 1 **Ply**[31] 6389 3-8-11 75 HarryBentley 5 92+
(Roger Charlton) *s.i.s: no bttr than 9th for much of r tl rapid prog on inner 2f out: led over 1f out and shot clr: eased nr fin: impressive* 7/4[1]

1042 2 4 ½ **Exceeding Power**[23] 6700 6-9-3 79 GeorgeWood(3) 11 85
(Martin Bosley) *in tch: urged along wl over 2f out and no prog: styd on wl fr over 1f out to take 2nd last strides* 14/1

-214 3 hd **Asaas (USA)**[29] 6468 3-9-2 80 SilvestreDeSousa 1 86
(Roger Varian) *t.k.h: trckd ldng trio: rdn 2f out: chsd wnr 1f out but no ch: one pce and lost 2nd last strides* 5/1[2]

-504 4 ½ **Diamond Bear (USA)**[11] 7095 3-8-7 71 LukeMorris 2 76
(Sir Mark Prescott Bt) *wl in tch: trying to cl on ldrs whn nt clr run wl over 1f out: renewed effrt fnl f: kpt on* 20/1

51- 5 2 ¼ **Intermodal**[292] 8246 3-8-11 75 RichardKingscote 3 75
(Amanda Perrett) *trckd ldng pair: tried to chal on inner over 1f out but qckly outpcd: wknd ins fnl f* 7/1[3]

1330 6 ½ **Fast And Hot (IRE)**[10] 7132 4-9-6 79 (b) TomMarquand 4 78
(Richard Hannon) *hld up in midfield: effrt whn nt clr run over 1f out: kpt on fnl f but nvr any ch* 16/1

3004 **7** 1 1/4 **Tangramm**[16] 6937 5-9-6 **79**......(p) PatCosgrave 13 76
(Dean Ivory) *chsd ldrs: flat out fr 4f out: steadily outpcd* **33/1**
5010 **8** *nk* **Blushing Red (FR)**[23] 6701 3-8-12 **76**...... JimCrowley 10 72
(Ed Dunlop) *hld up wl in rr: pushed along over 2f out: kpt on fr over 1f out on outer: nvr involved* **12/1**
5600 **9** *hd* **Luv U Whatever**[6] 7234 7-9-5 **78**......(t[1]) JoeyHaynes 14 74
(Marjorie Fife) *s.s: hld up in last pair: shkn up and passed sme rivals fr over 1f out: nvr involved* **66/1**
3400 **10** 2 **Count Montecristo (FR)**[56] 5484 5-9-8 **81**...... JamieSpencer 8 73
(Kevin Ryan) *led at gd pce to over 1f out: wknd* **11/1**
0312 **11** *shd* **Dark Titan (IRE)**[195] 1195 3-8-9 **73**...... LiamKeniry 9 65
(Ed Walker) *a towards rr: rdn and no prog 3f out* **25/1**
2446 **12** 1 1/4 **Biotic**[29] 6475 6-8-13 **72**...... SteveDrowne 6 61
(Rod Millman) *s.s: mostly in last pair: pushed along in last 2f out: nvr in it* **16/1**
4050 **13** 1 **Oasis Spear**[39] 6110 5-9-2 **75**...... TedDurcan 12 67
(Chris Wall) *trckd ldr to wl over 1f out: hanging and wknd: heavily eased ins fnl f* **25/1**
0535 **14** 1 3/4 **Masterofdiscovery**[20] 6792 3-8-7 **71**......(b) SamHitchcott 7 55
(Clive Cox) *a towards rr: rdn 3f out and struggling after* **25/1**

2m 2.93s (-5.07) **Going Correction** -0.225s/f (Stan) course record
**WFA** 3 from 4yo+ 5lb **14** Ran SP% **120.7**
Speed ratings (Par 105): **111,107,107,106,105 104,103,103,103,101 101,100,99,98**
CSF £26.14 CT £111.26 TOTE £3.10: £1.60, £4.10, £2.10; EX 30.70 Trifecta £146.60.
**Owner** Lady Rothschild **Bred** Carwell Equities Ltd **Trained** Beckhampton, Wilts

**FOCUS**
There was a fair gallop on, and an impressive winner.

## 7453 MATCHBOOK/BRITISH STALLION STUDS EBF FILLIES' NOVICE STKS (PLUS 10 RACE) (DIV I) 7f (P)

**3:30** (3:32) (Class 4) 2-Y-O **£4,528** (£1,347; £673; £336) **Stalls** Low

Form RPR
1 **1** **Teppal (FR)**[26] 6584 2-9-3 0...... JamieSpencer 6 90+
(David Simcock) *trckd ldrs: clsd gng easily 2f out: pushed into the ld jst over 1f out and immediately stretched clr* **11/10[1]**
0 **2** 4 **Gather**[18] 6861 2-9-0 0...... SteveDrowne 8 72
(Amanda Perrett) *led 3f: trckd ldr: shkn up to ld again briefly over 1f out: styd on but totally outpcd by wnr* **20/1**
**3** 1 1/2 **Line House** 2-9-0 0...... TomMarquand 9 68
(Robyn Brisland) *chsd ldrs: shkn up wl over 2f out: styd on fr over 1f out to take 3rd ins fnl f* **66/1**
**4** 2 1/4 **Guns Drawn (IRE)** 2-9-0 0...... SeanLevey 3 62
(Richard Hannon) *pressed ldr: led after 3f to over 1f out: wknd fnl f* **20/1**
**5** 1 1/4 **Kavora** 2-9-0 0...... PatCosgrave 11 59
(George Baker) *dwlt: wl in rr: pushed along over 2f out: passed rivals to take 5th ins fnl f: nvr nrr* **66/1**
**6** 3 1/4 **Murasaki** 2-9-0 0...... JamesDoyle 12 50
(Charlie Appleby) *lost pl after 2f and then in midfield: shkn up and green 3f out: wl btn after but kpt on fnl f* **9/2[3]**
**7** *nk* **Flor De Seda (FR)** 2-9-0 0...... DougieCostello 14 49
(Jo Hughes) *racd wd towards rr: nvr beyond midfield: pushed along over 2f out: kpt on fr over 1f out* **100/1**
**8** 1 **Saffah (USA)** 2-9-0 0...... DaneO'Neill 1 46
(Charles Hills) *s.s: wl in rr: nvr a factor but plugged on fr over 1f out* **25/1**
**9** 1/2 **Savannah Dusk (IRE)** 2-9-0 0...... CharlesBishop 4 45
(Eve Johnson Houghton) *wl in rr: sme prog over 2f out: rchd 5th briefly jst over 1f out: fdd ins fnl f* **33/1**
**10** 1 3/4 **Spritzig** 2-8-11 0...... GeorgeWood(3) 7 40
(Chris Wall) *green preliminaries: dwlt: a in rr* **50/1**
**11** 1 **Shurooq** 2-9-0 0...... JimCrowley 5 38
(Owen Burrows) *chsd ldrs: wknd 2f out* **3/1[2]**
**12** 2 **Allante (IRE)** 2-9-0 0...... TedDurcan 2 32
(Sir Michael Stoute) *chsd ldng pair to 2f out: wknd qckly* **14/1**
0 **13** 15 **Kahlo (IRE)**[18] 6861 2-9-0 0...... RichardKingscote 13
(Jonathan Portman) *prom to 1/2-way: wknd rapidly over 2f out: t.o* **66/1**

1m 24.73s (-1.27) **Going Correction** -0.225s/f (Stan) **13** Ran SP% **121.2**
Speed ratings (Par 94): **98,93,91,89,87 84,83,82,81,79 78,76,59**
CSF £32.55 TOTE £2.10: £1.10, £6.50, £26.60; EX 25.00 Trifecta £1776.00.
**Owner** Never Say Die Partnership **Bred** Gestut Zur Kuste Ag **Trained** Newmarket, Suffolk

**FOCUS**
This probably took little winning, but the impressive winner confirmed the promise she showed on her debut.

## 7454 MATCHBOOK/BRITISH STALLION STUDS EBF FILLIES' NOVICE STKS (PLUS 10 RACE) (DIV II) 7f (P)

**4:05** (4:06) (Class 4) 2-Y-O **£4,528** (£1,347; £673; £336) **Stalls** Low

Form RPR
**1** **Homeopathic** 2-9-0 0...... TedDurcan 6 77+
(Sir Michael Stoute) *trckd ldrs: shkn up to cl 2f out: chal jst over 1f out: rdn to ld ins fnl f: styd on* **7/1[3]**
31 **2** *nk* **Odyssa (IRE)**[17] 6868 2-9-3 0...... ShaneKelly 2 79
(Richard Hughes) *led: shkn up over 1f out: hdd ins fnl f and edgd lft: styd on but jst hld nr fin* **9/4[1]**
42 **3** 3/4 **Power And Peace (IRE)**[98] 3908 2-9-0 0...... JamieSpencer 10 74
(David Simcock) *trckd ldr: rdn 2f out: edgd lft after: lost 2nd fnl f: styd on* **7/1[3]**
**4** *nk* **Heptathlete (IRE)** 2-9-0 0...... PatCosgrave 11 73
(George Baker) *dwlt: t.k.h and sn prom on outer: trying to mount a chal whn nudged by rival over 1f out: edgd lft after but styd on* **50/1**
**5** 1 1/2 **Poyle Charlotte** 2-9-0 0...... PatDobbs 7 69
(Ralph Beckett) *in tch: shkn up 2f out: no imp on ldrs fr over 1f out: styd on* **8/1**
**6** 2 **Black Lotus** 2-8-11 0...... GeorgeWood(3) 8 64+
(Chris Wall) *wl in rr: pushed along and prog jst over 2f out: rchd 6th fnl f: no imp on ldrs after* **50/1**
**7** 2 1/4 **Timpani (IRE)** 2-9-0 0...... NickyMackay 1 58+
(John Gosden) *slowly away: sn in midfield on inner: pushed along over 2f out: sn outpcd and btn* **9/1**
0 **8** *hd* **Grace's Secret**[13] 7021 2-9-0 0...... LiamKeniry 12 57
(Ed Walker) *dwlt and stdd s: hld up in last pair: pushed along and sme prog fr 2f out: no hdwy fnl f* **66/1**
**9** *hd* **Rahaaba (IRE)** 2-9-0 0...... JimCrowley 4 57
(Owen Burrows) *nvr beyond midfield: no prog 2f out: sn btn* **3/1[2]**
5 **10** *nk* **Isle Of Avalon (IRE)**[12] 7045 2-9-0 0...... LukeMorris 3 56
(Sir Mark Prescott Bt) *trckd ldng pair to over 2f out: sn btn* **33/1**

**11** 2 **Teenage Gal (IRE)** 2-9-0 0...... SilvestreDeSousa 9 50
(Ed Dunlop) *hld up in last pair: pushed along and no prog over 2f out: wl btn after* **16/1**
**12** 7 **Benger's Pursuit** 2-9-0 0...... DougieCostello 5 31
(Jo Hughes) *a in rr: wknd 2f out* **100/1**

1m 27.46s (1.46) **Going Correction** -0.225s/f (Stan) **12** Ran SP% **117.1**
Speed ratings (Par 94): **82,81,80,80,78 76,73,73,73,73 70,62**
CSF £22.42 TOTE £8.40: £2.30, £1.10, £2.30; EX 24.30 Trifecta £118.40.
**Owner** Cheveley Park Stud **Bred** Cheveley Park Stud Ltd **Trained** Newmarket, Suffolk

**FOCUS**
The slower of the two divisions by 2.73sec, and it didn't pay to be too far off the gallop.

## 7455 MATCHBOOK CASINO H'CAP 6f (P)

**4:35** (4:35) (Class 3) (0-95,95) 3-Y-O+
**£7,470** (£2,236; £1,118; £559; £210; £210) **Stalls** Low

Form RPR
4203 **1** **Jaywalker (IRE)**[49] 5705 6-9-1 **89**...... MartinHarley 2 97
(Rebecca Bastiman) *disp ld thrght: def advantage over 1f out: drvn and hrd pressed ins fnl f: hld on wl* **4/1[1]**
3014 **2** *hd* **Seeking Magic**[49] 5720 9-9-1 **89**......(t) RyanTate 1 96
(Clive Cox) *t.k.h early: prom: rdn 2f out: tk 2nd 1f out: str chal last 100yds: jst hld* **6/1[3]**
0500 **3** 1 3/4 **Stellarta**[18] 6864 6-9-3 **91**...... TomMarquand 3 92
(Michael Blanshard) *sn urged along in midfield: prog u.p 2f out: kpt on to take 3rd ins fnl f* **8/1**
0040 **4** *nse* **Gentlemen**[170] 1622 6-9-2 **90**......(h) DannyBrock 5 91+
(Phil McEntee) *towards rr: rdn over 2f out: prog over 1f out: styd on and nrly snatched 3rd* **20/1**
0-00 **5** 1/2 **Barracuda Boy (IRE)**[29] 6484 7-9-7 **95**...... RichardKingscote 6 95
(Marjorie Fife) *rdn in midfield at 1/2-way: rdn over 2f out: nvr pce to rch ldrs: kpt on* **25/1**
0266 **5** *dht* **Sign Of The Kodiac (IRE)**[30] 6412 4-9-4 **92**...... LukeMorris 4 92
(James Given) *chsd ldrs: rdn over 2f out: nt qckn u.p over 1f out: one pce after* **7/1**
0400 **7** 1 1/4 **Tropics (USA)**[10] 7118 9-9-1 **92**......(h) JackDuern(3) 8 88
(Dean Ivory) *w wnr after 1f to over 1f out: lost 2nd and wknd fnl f* **12/1**
0000 **8** *hd* **Naadirr (IRE)**[37] 6206 6-9-6 **94**......(v) JamieSpencer 7 89
(Kevin Ryan) *s.i.s and n.m.r s: off the pce in last pair: tried to make prog 2f out: swtchd rt ins fnl f: nvr a threat* **6/1[3]**
0340 **9** 1/2 **Barrington (IRE)**[16] 6922 3-9-3 **93**......(bt[1]) JamesDoyle 9 86
(Charles Hills) *towards rr: urged along 1/2-way and smeway off the pce: threatened to make prog on outer 2f out: kpt on same pce and n.d* **12/1**
1000 **10** 1 **Goodwood Crusader (IRE)**[44] 5916 3-8-11 **92**...... FinleyMarsh(5) 10 82
(Richard Hughes) *hld up in last pair and off the pce: shkn up over 2f out: plugged on and nvr in it* **20/1**
5100 **11** 2 3/4 **Lightning Charlie**[35] 6275 5-9-1 **89**...... JimCrowley 11 70
(Amanda Perrett) *chsd ldrs on outer: shkn up over 2f out and sn wknd* **11/2[2]**
0000 **12** *nse* **Blaine**[16] 6922 7-9-4 **92**...... NickyMackay 12 73
(Brian Barr) *a towards rr: struggling over 2f out* **50/1**

1m 10.66s (-2.44) **Going Correction** -0.225s/f (Stan)
**WFA** 3 from 4yo+ 2lb **12** Ran SP% **118.3**
Speed ratings (Par 107): **107,106,104,104,103 103,102,101,101,99 96,96**
CSF £25.96 CT £160.25 TOTE £5.00: £1.70, £2.00, £2.40; EX 26.10 Trifecta £160.90.
**Owner** Ms M Austerfield **Bred** Kilfrush Stud **Trained** Cowthorpe, N Yorks

**FOCUS**
With only one or two exceptions the whole field finished in draw order. The first four raced on the inside into the straight. A small pb from the solid winner.

## 7456 ROA/RACING POST OWNERS' JACKPOT H'CAP 1m (P)

**5:05** (5:08) (Class 4) (0-85,85) 3-Y-O+ **£5,175** (£1,540; £769; £384) **Stalls** Low

Form RPR
154 **1** **Moolazim**[41] 6026 3-9-3 **85**......(t[1]) DanielMuscutt 1 95
(Marco Botti) *wl in tch: prog on inner and rdn 2f out: chsd ldr fnl f: drvn and styd on wl to ld last strides* **7/1[3]**
4214 **2** *nk* **Ventura Blues (IRE)**[16] 6933 3-9-3 **85**......(p) SilvestreDeSousa 3 94
(Richard Hannon) *t.k.h: trckd ldrs: prog to ld over 1f out: more than a l in front ins fnl f: kpt on but hdd last strides* **4/1[2]**
1345 **3** 1 **Family Fortunes**[9] 7156 3-9-3 **85**...... DaneO'Neill 12 92
(Sylvester Kirk) *hld up in rr: prog on inner over 2f out: drvn to chse ldng pair fnl f: styd on but nvr quite cl enough to chal* **14/1**
3266 **4** 1 1/4 **Tom's Rock (IRE)**[51] 5663 4-9-3 **81**...... PatCosgrave 5 85
(John Butler) *dwlt sltly but sn in midfield: rdn over 2f out: kpt on u.p but nvr able to threaten* **12/1**
2112 **5** *nk* **Masarzain (IRE)**[11] 7098 4-9-5 **83**...... LukeMorris 8 86
(Archie Watson) *chsd ldrs: cl up 2f out but u.p: one pce jst over 1f out* **14/1**
300 **6** 3/4 **Wind In My Sails**[30] 6422 5-9-4 **82**......(h) LiamKeniry 10 84
(Ed de Giles) *stdd s and hld up in last trio: pushed along over 2f out: prog and shkn up over 1f out: styd on but nvr threatened ldrs* **50/1**
4411 **7** *shd* **Mudallel (IRE)**[26] 6576 3-9-2 **84**...... JamesDoyle 6 85+
(Ed Dunlop) *hld up in rr: plenty to do whn shkn up 2f out: styd on fnl f but too late to make an impact* **5/2[1]**
26 **8** 1 1/4 **Cherbourg (FR)**[222] 736 5-9-5 **83**...... PatDobbs 14 81
(Ralph Beckett) *stdd s and hld up in last trio: stl last over 2f out: pushed along and kpt on fr over 1f out but nvr involved* **25/1**
0243 **9** *shd* **Golden Wedding (IRE)**[16] 6933 5-9-5 **83**...... CharlesBishop 11 81
(Eve Johnson Houghton) *trckd ldng pair: shkn up and no rspnse over 2f out: wknd over 1f out* **9/1**
1-04 **10** *nk* **Finelcity (GER)**[16] 6936 4-9-7 **85**......(v) JimCrowley 4 83
(Harry Dunlop) *pressed ldr: rdn to ld over 2f out: hdd & wknd over 1f out* **7/1[3]**
0000 **11** 1/2 **Pearl Spectre (USA)**[101] 3777 6-9-7 **85**...... DannyBrock 7 81
(Phil McEntee) *led to over 2f out: steadily wknd* **100/1**
5000 **12** 1 **Presumido (IRE)**[16] 6933 7-9-2 **80**...... JFEgan 13 74
(Simon Dow) *in tch but out wd: prog over 3f out: no hdwy 2f out: sn wknd* **25/1**
0625 **13** 7 **Wink Oliver**[23] 6676 5-9-5 **83**......(p) DougieCostello 9 61
(Jo Hughes) *hld up in rr: pushed along and no prog 2f out: eased fnl f* **50/1**

1m 37.16s (-2.64) **Going Correction** -0.225s/f (Stan)
**WFA** 3 from 4yo+ 4lb **13** Ran SP% **117.2**
Speed ratings (Par 105): **104,103,102,101,101 100,100,99,98,98 98,97,90**
CSF £33.11 CT £397.33 TOTE £8.30: £3.10, £1.50, £4.10; EX 36.70 Trifecta £342.50.
**Owner** Sheikh Mohammed Bin Khalifa Al Maktoum **Bred** Essafinaat **Trained** Newmarket, Suffolk

**FOCUS**
Once again the first three hugged the rail into the straight. This has been rated positively.

## 7457 MATCHBOOK BETTING EXCHANGE H'CAP — 1m (P)
5:35 (5:36) (Class 5) (0-70,70) 3-Y-O — £3,234 (£962; £481; £240) Stalls Low

Form RPR
6240 1 **Evening Hill**[21] 6766 3-9-5 **68**..........(p) ShaneKelly 12 78
(Richard Hughes) *s.i.s: rapid prog fr rr to trck ldr after 3f: led over 2f out: rdn and edgd lft fr over 1f out: hrd pressed last 100yds: hld on wl* **9/1**
4010 2 ½ **Pinnata (IRE)**[67] 5067 3-9-5 **68**..........(t) PatCosgrave 7 77+
(Stuart Williams) *hld up in midfield: prog 2f out: drvn and r.o to take 2nd last 100yds: chal after but jst hld* **12/1**
-200 3 ½ **Peace And Plenty**[24] 6657 3-9-7 **70**.......... SilvestreDeSousa 11 78
(William Muir) *led after 1f: rdn and hdd over 2f out: edgd lft over 1f out: lost 2nd last 100yds but wl clr of rest* **13/2**[3]
4621 4 7 **Solent Meads (IRE)**[12] 7062 3-9-6 **69**..........(b) GeorgeDowning 8 61
(Daniel Kubler) *trckd ldrs: rdn and nt qckn over 2f out: readily lft bhd by ldng trio over 1f out* **5/1**[1]
005 5 1 **Chicago Star**[12] 7058 3-9-5 **68**.......... JFEgan 1 57
(Mick Channon) *led 1f: styd prom: rdn over 2f out: steadily wknd* **7/1**
0600 6 ¾ **Marilyn**[40] 6067 3-9-0 **63**.......... TedDurcan 10 51
(Chris Wall) *hld up in last trio: prog into midfield over 2f out: no ch w ldrs but plugged on* **25/1**
0000 7 1½ **Zoffany Bay (IRE)**[12] 7061 3-9-1 **64**..........(b) HarryBentley 2 48
(George Peckham) *chsd ldrs: hrd rdn over 2f out: sn lft wl bhd* **9/1**
066 8 ¾ **Discovered (IRE)**[37] 6182 3-9-2 **65**..........(t[1]) TrevorWhelan 4 47
(Roger Charlton) *nvr beyond midfield: shkn up and lft bhd fr 2f out* **12/1**
3500 9 1¼ **Quinteo (IRE)**[38] 6160 3-9-7 **70**..........(p[1]) DougieCostello 14 50
(Jo Hughes) *a towards rr: struggling over 2f out: sn no ch* **20/1**
106 10 ½ **Mont Royal (FR)**[28] 6518 3-9-6 **69**.......... MartinHarley 9 47
(Ollie Pears) *mostly in last pair: no ch over 2f out: nvr a factor* **9/1**
3060 11 ½ **Mulsanne Chase**[20] 6791 3-9-2 **65**.......... LukeMorris 13 42
(Brian Barr) *sn pushed along: a wl in rr and nvr figured* **66/1**
2460 12 4 **Tailor's Row (USA)**[13] 7034 3-9-7 **70**.......... JamesDoyle 5 38
(Mark Johnston) *hld up: shkn up and wknd over 2f out: eased fnl f* **6/1**[2]
3643 13 8 **Characterized**[23] 6681 3-8-9 **63**.......... GeorgiaCox[(5)] 3 13
(Geoffrey Deacon) *prom over 4f: wknd rapidly over 2f out: t.o* **12/1**

1m 37.25s (-2.55) **Going Correction** -0.225s/f (Stan) **13 Ran SP% 120.0**
Speed ratings (Par 101): **103,102,102,95,94 93,91,91,89,89 88,84,76**
CSF £110.70 CT £759.34 TOTE £7.90: £2.40, £5.90, £1.60; EX 138.10 Trifecta £1279.00.
**Owner** The Heffer Syndicate **Bred** Natton House Thoroughbreds **Trained** Upper Lambourn, Berks

**FOCUS**
The time was decent for the grade of race and the first three finished clear of the rest, so this is form to be positive about.
T/Plt: £4.80 to a £1 stake. Pool: £67,645.70 - 10,249.60 winning units T/Qpdt: £4.80 to a £1 stake. Pool: £6,597.60 - 1,012.46 winning units **Jonathan Neesom**

# 7021 LEICESTER (R-H)
## Monday, September 25

**OFFICIAL GOING: Heavy (5.5)**
Wind: Light across Weather: Overcast

## 7458 ASTON FLAMVILLE FILLIES' NURSERY H'CAP — 6f
2:00 (2:00) (Class 5) (0-75,75) 2-Y-O — £3,234 (£962; £481; £240) Stalls High

Form RPR
0540 1 **Titchy Digits**[20] 6778 2-8-13 **67**.......... AdamBeschizza 2 71
(Michael Attwater) *a.p: rdn to chse ldr over 2f out: led ins fnl f: styd on u.p* **20/1**
1652 2 1 **Queen Of Kalahari**[21] 6749 2-9-6 **74**.......... PJMcDonald 6 75
(Charles Hills) *led: rdn over 1f out: hdd ins fnl f: no ex nr fin* **7/2**[1]
445 3 ½ **Hippeia (IRE)**[26] 6590 2-9-3 **71**.......... PaulMulrennan 4 71
(Jedd O'Keeffe) *sn pushed along in rr: hdwy u.p over 1f out: edgd lft and styd on: nt rch ldrs* **13/2**
4221 4 1¾ **Felisa**[13] 7023 2-8-12 **66**.......... FranBerry 7 60
(David Evans) *sn pushed along in rr: hdwy u.p over 1f out: no ex ins fnl f* **4/1**[2]
045 5 8 **Hollywood Dream**[29] 6480 2-9-4 **72**.......... PhillipMakin 3 42
(William Muir) *hld up: rdn over 2f out: sn btn* **7/2**[1]
626 6 2¾ **Isabella Mayson**[19] 6824 2-8-13 **67**.......... MartinLane 11 29+
(Stuart Kittow) *chsd ldrs: rdn over 2f out: wknd over 1f out* **5/1**[3]
5530 7 1½ **Terri Rules (IRE)**[25] 6634 2-8-0 **57**.......... AaronJones[(3)] 13 15+
(Julia Feilden) *w ldrs to 1/2-way: sn rdn: wknd 2f out* **20/1**
2140 8 9 **Atalanta Queen**[11] 7082 2-7-13 **58**..........(b) JaneElliott[(5)] 14
(Michael Appleby) *w ldrs tl rdn 1/2-way: wknd over 2f out* **11/1**

1m 18.46s (5.46) **Going Correction** +0.725s/f (Yiel) **8 Ran SP% 112.3**
Speed ratings (Par 92): **92,90,90,87,77 73,71,59**
CSF £85.77 CT £514.17 TOTE £19.30: £4.20, £1.80, £1.70; EX 112.00 Trifecta £744.20.
**Owner** The Attwater Partnership **Bred** Derra Park Stud **Trained** Epsom, Surrey

**FOCUS**
The main action unfolded down the centre. Straightforward form with the front trio, all near, or just below in winner's case, their pre-race marks.

## 7459 GOLDEN HAND (S) STKS — 7f
2:35 (2:35) (Class 5) 3-Y-O — £3,234 (£962; £481; £240) Stalls High

Form RPR
2030 1 **Spirit Of Belle**[11] 7083 3-8-10 72..........(b[1]) FranBerry 2 70
(David Evans) *led 1f: remained w ldrs: led again over 2f out: rdn clr fnl f* **5/2**[1]
143 2 5 **Kings Academy**[12] 7056 3-9-0 67..........(p) PJMcDonald 9 62
(Paul Cole) *hld up: hdwy u.p over 2f out: edgd rt ins fnl f: styd on to go 2nd post* **5/1**[3]
3534 3 shd **Oakley Pride (IRE)**[14] 7005 3-8-11 53..........(v) DavidEgan[(3)] 3 61
(Gay Kelleway) *s.i.s: racd keenly and sn prom: hmpd over 5f out: rdn over 2f out: edgd rt and styd on same pce fnl f* **9/1**
0400 4 1½ **Undiscovered Angel (FR)**[12] 7052 3-8-5 66.......... JosephineGordon 11 49
(K R Burke) *racd keenly: led 6f out to 1/2-way: rdn over 1f out: hung rt and wknd ins fnl f* **9/2**[2]
0534 5 ¾ **Solitary Sister (IRE)**[7] 7213 3-8-5 50..........(v) KieranO'Neill 13 47
(Richard Spencer) *hld up: pushed along over 4f out: hdwy whn flashed tail over 1f out: sn hung rt: nt trble ldrs* **14/1**
0055 6 1¼ **Jet Setter (IRE)**[18] 6866 3-9-0 59.......... GeorgeDowning 6 53
(Tony Carroll) *hld up in tch: rdn over 2f out: wknd fnl f* **10/1**
5054 7 1½ **Hisar (IRE)**[28] 6507 3-8-10 58..........(p) DavidProbert 4 45
(Ronald Harris) *w ldrs: led 1/2-way: hdd over 2f out: sn rdn: wknd fnl f* **25/1**
0050 8 6 **Traveltalk (IRE)**[13] 7017 3-8-9 60..........(p) BenRobinson[(5)] 1 34
(Brian Ellison) *s.s: sn chsng ldrs: jinked lft over 5f out: rdn over 2f out: wknd over 1f out: eased* **12/1**
0062 9 7 **Queen Beatrice**[43] 5958 3-8-2 51.......... HollieDoyle[(3)] 12 7
(William Muir) *s.i.s: racd keenly and sn prom: pushed along 1/2-way: wknd over 2f out* **10/1**
10 1¾ **Broughtons Sport** 3-8-10 0.......... StevieDonohoe 10 8
(Andi Brown) *hld up: pushed along and wknd over 2f out* **50/1**
0 11 29 **Amber Mischief**[205] 1024 3-8-7 0 ow2.......... RobHornby 8
(Adam West) *hld up: pushed along over 4f out: lost tch 1/2-way* **100/1**

1m 30.37s (4.17) **Going Correction** +0.725s/f (Yiel) **11 Ran SP% 112.8**
Speed ratings (Par 101): **105,99,99,97,96 95,93,86,78,76 43**
CSF £13.66 TOTE £3.00: £1.40, £1.70, £2.50; EX 15.70 Trifecta £66.70.The winner waa sold to Mr Oliver Cole for 8000gns. Hisar was claimed by Mr Michael Appleby for £7000. Kings Academy was claimed by Mr David Penman for £7000.
**Owner** D E Edwards **Bred** W Hennessey **Trained** Pandy, Monmouths

**FOCUS**
They again headed down the centre in this seller and the favourite won with plenty in hand. He's been rated just below his best, with the 3rd the key to the level.

## 7460 BRITISH STALLION STUDS EBF KEGWORTH NOVICE STKS (PLUS 10 RACE) — 7f
3:05 (3:06) (Class 4) 2-Y-O — £6,469 (£1,925; £962; £481) Stalls High

Form RPR
4 1 **Alkhawaneej Boy (IRE)**[16] 6938 2-9-2 0.......... TomQueally 4 84+
(Kevin Ryan) *racd towards centre: led that gp tl overall ldr 1/2-way: shkn up and edgd lft over 1f out: c readily clr ins fnl f: 1st of 4 in gp* **7/2**[2]
320 2 6 **Porth Swtan (IRE)**[31] 6403 2-9-2 80.......... PJMcDonald 2 69
(Charles Hills) *racd towards centre: hld up: hdwy over 2f out: rdn to chse wnr over 1f out: no ex ins fnl f: 2nd of 4 in gp* **2/1**[1]
3 1½ **White Guard** 2-9-2 0.......... OisinMurphy 1 65
(Sir Mark Prescott Bt) *racd towards centre: hld up: pushed along over 2f out: styd on to go 3rd nr fin: 3rd of 4 in gp* **8/1**
0 4 ½ **Whitehall**[39] 6108 2-9-2 0.......... StevieDonohoe 3 64
(Sir Michael Stoute) *racd towards centre: chsd ldr: rdn over 2f out: no ex fnl f: last of 4 in gp* **6/1**
600 5 ¾ **Blacklooks (IRE)**[17] 6897 2-9-2 67.......... PhillipMakin 9 62
(Ivan Furtado) *overall ldr on stands' side to 1/2-way and hung rt: stl led his gp: rdn over 1f out: no ex fnl f* **28/1**
06 6 2 **Prince Consort (IRE)**[22] 6721 2-9-2 0.......... PaulMulrennan 8 57
(Brian Meehan) *racd stands' side: hld up: pushed along and outpcd over 2f out: 2nd of 4 in gp* **66/1**
7 2 **Beachcomber Bay (IRE)** 2-9-2 0.......... MartinLane 6 52
(Charlie Appleby) *racd stands' side: chsd ldr tl pushed along over 2f out: sn wknd: 3rd of 4 in gp* **11/2**[3]
00 8 1¼ **Bodie And Doyle**[17] 6869 2-9-2 0.......... DavidProbert 10 49
(Andrew Balding) *racd stands' side: chsd ldrs: rdn over 2f out: wknd over 1f out: last of 4 in gp* **10/1**

1m 31.31s (5.11) **Going Correction** +0.725s/f (Yiel) **8 Ran SP% 110.4**
Speed ratings (Par 97): **99,92,90,89,89 86,84,83**
CSF £10.09 TOTE £4.00: £1.80, £1.10, £2.30; EX 11.00 Trifecta £52.20.
**Owner** Ahmad Abdulla Al Shaikh **Bred** John R Jeffers **Trained** Hambleton, N Yorks

**FOCUS**
One-way traffic in this ordinary novice.

## 7461 RACING UK H'CAP — 5f
3:40 (3:40) (Class 3) (0-95,94) 3-Y-O+ — £7,561 (£2,263; £1,131; £566; £282) Stalls High

Form RPR
3002 1 **Soie D'Leau**[16] 6927 5-9-3 **90**.......... TonyHamilton 1 98
(Kristin Stubbs) *mde all: shkn up over 1f out: r.o wl* **2/1**[1]
0045 2 1½ **Smokey Lane (IRE)**[13] 7025 3-9-4 **92**.......... TimmyMurphy 8 94
(Christian Williams) *hld up: swtchd rt over 2f out: hdwy over 1f out: rdn to chse wnr fnl f: no imp* **12/1**
0062 3 nk **Iseemist (IRE)**[22] 6720 6-8-8 **84**..........(b[1]) DavidEgan[(3)] 7 85
(John Gallagher) *sn pushed along to chse ldrs: rdn over 1f out: styd on same pce ins fnl f* **9/2**[2]
6050 4 2¼ **Willytheconqueror (IRE)**[23] 6677 4-9-7 **94**.......... MartinDwyer 6 86
(William Muir) *racd keenly in 2nd pl tl pushed along 1/2-way: rdn and lost 2nd 1f out: no ex* **5/1**[3]
1404 5 ¾ **Union Rose**[38] 6137 5-8-13 **86**.......... OisinMurphy 3 76
(Ronald Harris) *hld up: pushed along 1/2-way: nt trble ldrs* **5/1**[3]
031 6 nse **Somewhere Secret**[12] 7055 3-8-3 **80** oh2..........(p) PhilDennis[(3)] 4 70
(Michael Mullineaux) *sn outpcd* **9/2**[2]

1m 3.73s (3.73) **Going Correction** +0.725s/f (Yiel)
**WFA** 3 from 4yo+ 1lb **6 Ran SP% 110.7**
Speed ratings (Par 107): **99,96,96,92,91 91**
CSF £25.71 CT £91.16 TOTE £2.80: £1.40, £5.30; EX 25.70 Trifecta £122.60.
**Owner** F A T J Partnership & Kristin Stubbs **Bred** Mrs M Lingwood **Trained** Norton, N Yorks

**FOCUS**
A decent little sprint, they came stands' side. The winner has been rated to this year's form.

## 7462 BREEDERS BACKING RACING EBF MAIDEN STKS — 1m 3f 179y
4:15 (4:16) (Class 5) 3-Y-O+ — £4,528 (£1,347; £673; £336) Stalls Low

Form RPR
1 **Golden Birthday (FR)**[23] 6-9-12 0..........(t) FranBerry 12 83+
(Harry Fry) *hld up: hdwy on bit over 3f out: led over 2f out: hung lft over 1f out: rdn out* **13/8**[1]
2320 2 1¼ **Lester Kris (IRE)**[12] 7063 3-8-12 75.......... RossaRyan[(7)] 1 82
(Richard Hannon) *chsd ldr tl nt clr run and hit rails 9f out: remained handy: rdn over 2f out: sn edgd lft: ev ch over 1f out: styd on same pce wl ins fnl f* **3/1**[2]
34 3 6 **Nelson's Touch**[25] 6623 4-9-12 0.......... TomQueally 7 71
(Denis Coakley) *hld up: hdwy over 2f out: styd on same pce fnl f* **4/1**[3]
04 4 ½ **Towie (IRE)**[21] 6765 3-9-5 0.......... OisinMurphy 11 72
(Hughie Morrison) *prom: pushed along over 3f out: styd on same pce fnl f* **7/1**
6523 5 12 **Ididitforyoooo (IRE)**[18] 6852 3-9-5 66.......... PaulMulrennan 10 52
(Brian Meehan) *chsd ldrs: wnt 2nd over 8f out tl led over 4f out: rdn and hdd over 2f out: wknd wl over 1f out* **7/1**
44 6 20 **Kai Tak And Back**[18] 6851 3-9-5 0.......... MartinDwyer 4 20
(William Muir) *led: pushed along and hdd over 4f out: rdn over 2f out: wknd wl over 1f out: eased* **50/1**


The Form Book Flat, Raceform Ltd, Newbury, RG14 5SJ

6 7 46 **Kwikstep**[12] 7059 3-9-0 0 MartinLane 8
(Andi Brown) *hld up: in rr and pushed along over 6f out: sn lost tch* **200/1**

2m 40.62s (6.72) **Going Correction** +0.725s/f (Yiel)
**WFA** 3 from 4yo+ 7lb 7 Ran SP% **110.6**
Speed ratings (Par 103): **106,105,101,100,92 79,48**
CSF £6.18 TOTE £2.40: £1.50, £2.00; EX 6.80 Trifecta £15.30.
**Owner** G C Stevens **Bred** E A R L La Croix Sonnet **Trained** Seaborough, Dorset

**FOCUS**
A decent little maiden.

## 7463 HIGHFIELDS FILLIES' H'CAP (DIV I) 1m 53y
**4:45** (4:45) (Class 5) (0-70,77) 3-Y-0+ **£2,518** (£2,518; £577; £288) **Stalls** Low

| Form | | | | RPR |
|---|---|---|---|---|
| 2231 | 1 | | **Fastnet Spin (IRE)**[8] 7199 3-10-1 77 6ex (vt) FranBerry 8 (David Evans) *hld up: hdwy 2f out: rdn to join wnr and edgd rt ins fnl f: styd on* **5/2**[1] | 80 |
| 4032 | 1 | dht | **Zaria**[13] 7028 6-8-1 52 (p) GabrieleMalune(7) 6 (Richard Price) *chsd ldrs: pushed along to go upsides over 3f out: rdn to ld over 1f out: jnd ins fnl f: styd on* **3/1**[2] | 55 |
| 5012 | 3 | 6 | **Royal Melody**[32] 6342 3-8-4 55 (p) DavidEgan(3) 10 (Heather Main) *prom: rdn to join ldrs over 3f out tl over 2f out: hung rt over 1f out: styd on same pce* **7/2**[3] | 44 |
| 0514 | 4 | ½ | **Duchess Of Fife**[19] 6822 3-9-4 66 (v) MartinLane 2 (William Knight) *chsd ldr tl led over 3f out: rdn and hdd over 1f out: wknd ins fnl f* **5/1** | 54 |
| 6030 | 5 | 10 | **Imperial Link**[8] 7199 5-8-2 51 oh6 (v) JaneElliott(5) 5 (John O'Shea) *led: racd freely: hdd over 3f out: wknd over 2f out* **14/1** | 16 |
| 2100 | 6 | 9 | **Accomplice**[20] 6792 3-9-4 66 DavidProbert 11 (Michael Blanshard) *hld up: rdn over 2f out: wkng whn hung rt over 1f out* **8/1** | 10 |

1m 50.72s (5.62) **Going Correction** +0.725s/f (Yiel)
**WFA** 3 from 4yo+ 4lb 6 Ran SP% **110.2**
Speed ratings (Par 100): **100,100,94,93,83 74**
WIN: ZA 1.90, FS 1.40 ; PL: ZA 1.90, FS 1.50; EX: FS/ZA 4.40, ZA/FS 4.70; CSF: FS/ZA 4.92, ZA/FS 5.25; TC: FS/ZA/RM 11.44, ZA/FS/RM 11.94; TF: FS/ZA/RM 13.20, ZA/FS/RM 13.50;.
**Owner** Dukes Head Racing **Bred** Rockhart Trading Ltd **Trained** Pandy, Monmouths
**Owner** Mrs K Oseman **Bred** Exors Of The Late J R Good **Trained** Ullingswick, H'fords

**FOCUS**
Run at a good gallop, the first two were inseparable as they hit the line.

## 7464 HIGHFIELDS FILLIES' H'CAP (DIV II) 1m 53y
**5:15** (5:15) (Class 5) (0-70,71) 3-Y-0+ **£3,881** (£1,155; £577; £288) **Stalls** Low

| Form | | | | RPR |
|---|---|---|---|---|
| 1361 | 1 | | **Love And Be Loved**[49] 5714 3-8-5 60 WilliamCox(7) 6 (John Flint) *racd keenly: w ldr tl led over 6f out: rdn over 1f out: styd on wl* **7/1** | 68 |
| 4020 | 2 | 1¼ | **Mama Africa (IRE)**[41] 6047 3-9-1 68 (p) JaneElliott(5) 7 (David Barron) *led: racd keenly: hdd over 6f out: chsd wnr: rdn over 1f out: styd on same pce towards fin* **9/1** | 73 |
| 0660 | 3 | 3¾ | **Harmonise**[19] 6818 3-9-6 71 HollieDoyle(3) 10 (Mick Channon) *hld up: pushed along over 4f out: styd on fr over 1f out: nt rch ldrs* **8/1** | 67 |
| 5603 | 4 | 4½ | **Waves (IRE)**[8] 7199 3-9-5 67 TomQueally 1 (Eve Johnson Houghton) *chsd ldrs: rdn over 2f out: wknd fnl f* **7/2**[2] | 53 |
| 4552 | 5 | 1½ | **Fire Palace**[12] 7052 3-9-5 70 DavidEgan(3) 5 (Robert Eddery) *s.s: hdwy over 3f out: rdn and wknd over 1f out* **9/4**[1] | 53 |
| 3402 | 6 | 10 | **Magic Mirror**[19] 6814 4-8-7 51 (v) JosephineGordon 4 (Mark Rimell) *hld up: shkn up over 2f out: rdn and wknd wl over 1f out* **6/1**[3] | 11 |
| 1056 | 7 | 1¼ | **Sea Tea Dea**[19] 6818 3-9-4 66 DavidProbert 2 (Anthony Carson) *hld up: pushed along over 3f out: wknd wl over 1f out* **12/1** | 23 |
| 5540 | 8 | 14 | **Navajo Storm (IRE)**[13] 7028 4-8-7 51 oh1 (p) MartinDwyer 9 (Michael Appleby) *chsd ldrs tl rdn and wknd over 2f out* **28/1** | |

1m 50.93s (5.83) **Going Correction** +0.725s/f (Yiel)
**WFA** 3 from 4yo 4lb 8 Ran SP% **112.0**
Speed ratings (Par 100): **99,97,94,89,88 78,76,62**
CSF £64.35 CT £510.17 TOTE £6.30: £2.40, £2.30, £2.60; EX 40.20 Trifecta £473.60.
**Owner** J L Flint **Bred** Sarah McNicholas **Trained** Kenfig Hill, Bridgend

**FOCUS**
Little got into this, with the pace holding up, and the first two had it to themselves from a fair way out. The winner is progressing.

## 7465 RACING EXCELLENCE "HANDS AND HEELS" APPRENTICE SERIES H'CAP 7f
**5:45** (5:45) (Class 6) (0-65,65) 3-Y-0+ **£3,234** (£962; £481; £240) **Stalls** High

| Form | | | | RPR |
|---|---|---|---|---|
| 056 | 1 | | **East Coast Lady (IRE)**[14] 7002 5-9-12 65 DavidEgan 7 (William Stone) *led: hdd over 4f out: remained handy: pushed along 1/2-way: styd on to ld nr fin* **8/1**[3] | 72 |
| 0412 | 2 | ¾ | **The Groove**[8] 7198 4-9-12 65 ManuelFernandes 1 (Fergal O'Brien) *chsd ldrs: led 2f out: sn pushed along: hdd nr fin* **9/4**[1] | 70 |
| 000 | 3 | 2¼ | **Dynamic Girl (IRE)**[9] 7158 4-9-0 56 NicolaCurrie(3) 10 (Brendan Powell) *mid-div: hdwy 1/2-way: pushed along over 1f out: styd on same pce ins fnl f* **22/1** | 56 |
| 0040 | 4 | nk | **Air Of York (IRE)**[28] 6502 5-9-7 60 (p) WilliamCox 11 (John Flint) *plld hrd and prom: pushed along over 1f out: edgd rt and styd on same pce ins fnl f* **33/1** | 59 |
| 2236 | 5 | 2¼ | **Coverham (IRE)**[12] 7062 3-9-8 64 RossaRyan 3 (James Eustace) *hld up: swtchd rt over 2f out: pushed along and hdwy over 1f out: no ex ins fnl f* **11/4**[2] | 56 |
| 4000 | 6 | hd | **Know The Truth**[12] 7058 3-9-1 62 KayleighStephens(5) 5 (Andrew Balding) *chsd ldrs: led over 4f out: pushed along and hdd 2f out: styd on same pce fr over 1f out* **10/1** | 54 |
| 3304 | 7 | 2½ | **Moi Aussie**[47] 5813 4-9-3 61 (p) KeelanBaker(5) 6 (Michael Appleby) *chsd ldrs: pushed along over 2f out: styd on same pce* **25/1** | 47 |
| 3566 | 8 | 2 | **Rafaaf (IRE)**[108] 3522 9-8-11 53 (p) BenSanderson(3) 2 (Peter Hiatt) *prom: pushed along over 2f out: wknd fnl f* **25/1** | 34 |
| 0025 | 9 | 3½ | **Champagne Bob**[12] 7046 5-9-8 64 GabrieleMalune(3) 15 (Richard Price) *towards rr: hdwy 1/2-way: pushed along over 2f out: wknd over 1f out* **14/1** | 37 |
| 0006 | 10 | 3 | **Gatillo**[124] 2974 4-9-9 62 MillyNaseb 9 (Julia Feilden) *s.i.s: hdwy over 2f out: pushed along and wknd over 1f out* **40/1** | 27 |
| 0401 | 11 | 2 | **Intimately**[14] 7006 4-9-1 59 Pierre-LouisJamin(5) 12 (Jonathan Portman) *s.s: nvr on terms* **10/1** | 19 |
| 0060 | 12 | 1 | **Poor Duke (IRE)**[12] 7052 7-8-11 55 TristanPrice(5) 13 (Michael Mullineaux) *prom: pushed along and lost pl over 4f out: wknd over 1f out* **25/1** | 13 |
| 0030 | 13 | 1½ | **Seebring (IRE)**[13] 7036 3-8-5 52 (p) JonathanFisher(5) 8 (Brian Ellison) *prom: pushed along over 2f out: wknd over 1f out* **20/1** | 5 |
| -000 | 14 | 10 | **Zebs Lad (IRE)**[8] 7198 5-8-9 51 JackOsborn(3) 4 (Nikki Evans) *s.i.s: outpcd* **66/1** | |

1m 30.3s (4.10) **Going Correction** +0.725s/f (Yiel)
**WFA** 3 from 4yo+ 3lb 14 Ran SP% **120.9**
Speed ratings (Par 101): **105,104,101,101,98 98,95,93,89,85 83,82,80,69**
CSF £23.73 CT £407.84 TOTE £9.00: £3.80, £1.60, £5.00; EX 32.60 Trifecta £892.90.
**Owner** Miss Caroline Scott **Bred** Mountarmstrong Stud **Trained** West Wickham, Cambs
■ Stewards' Enquiry : Tristan Price one-day ban: improper riding

**FOCUS**
A modest handicap in which they raced down the centre. It has been rated around the 2nd/3rd to recent form.
T/Jkpt: £10,000.00 to a £1 stake. Pool: £10,000.00 - 1.0 winning units T/Plt: £12.40 to a £1 stake. Pool: £87,357.01 - 5,136.12 winning units T/Qpdt: £5.70 to a £1 stake. Pool: £6,552.00 - 848.80 winning units **Colin Roberts**

7466 - 7469a (Foreign Racing) - See Raceform Interactive

# 7415 CRAON (R-H)
Monday, September 25

**OFFICIAL GOING: Turf: soft**

## 7470a PRIX GROUPAMA - PRIX DU VAL D'ATHEE (MAIDEN) (2YO) (TURF) 6f 165y
**1:20** 2-Y-0 **£7,692** (£3,076; £2,307; £1,538; £769)

| | | | RPR |
|---|---|---|---|
| 1 | | **Arrogant (IRE)**[14] 7012 2-9-2 0 TheoBachelot 8 (Jose Santos) *sn front rnk: settled 2nd: wd into the st and rdn: hdwy to take narrow ld over 1f out: u.str.p fnl f to hold advantage: all out* **66/10** | 80 |
| 2 | ½ | **Cristot (FR)**[111] 3445 2-9-2 0 (p) HugoJourniac 2 (J-C Rouget, France) **147/10** | 79 |
| 3 | nk | **Arguin (FR)** 2-9-2 0 EnzoCorallo 9 (C Ferland, France) **51/10**[3] | 78 |
| 4 | 5 | **Calaconta (FR)** 2-8-13 0 AlexandreRoussel 7 (F Foucher, France) **194/10** | 61 |
| 5 | ¾ | **Fauneta (FR)** 2-8-13 0 AnthonyCrastus 5 (P Sogorb, France) **23/10**[1] | 59 |
| 6 | snk | **Tadeem (IRE)**[46] 5989 2-9-2 0 VincentCheminaud 6 (J E Hammond, France) **47/10**[2] | 62 |
| 7 | 5 | **Pearl River Star**[28] 2-9-2 0 SoufianeSaadi 3 (H-A Pantall, France) **219/10** | 48 |
| 8 | 3 | **Ruby Flash (FR)**[44] 5952 2-8-11 0 MlleChloeHue(5) 10 (A Lamotte D'Argy, France) **35/1** | 40 |
| 9 | 4 | **Cooperate (IRE)**[24] 2-8-13 0 JulienAuge 4 (E J O'Neill, France) **58/10** | 27 |
| 10 | 1½ | **Baystone (FR)** 2-8-7 0 TristanBaron(6) 1 (H-A Pantall, France) **122/10** | 22 |

PARI-MUTUEL (all including 1 euro stake): WIN 7.60; PLACE 2.30, 3.70, 2.10; DF 53.40; SF 112.10.
**Owner** Jose Santos Racing Ltd **Bred** Miss Jill Finegan **Trained** Upper Lambourn, Berks

# 7304 MAISONS-LAFFITTE (R-H)
Monday, September 25

**OFFICIAL GOING: Turf: soft**

## 7471a PRIX HERBAGER (CONDITIONS) (3YO) (ROUND) (TURF) 1m
**1:05** 3-Y-0
**£14,059** (£5,683; £4,188; £2,692; £1,645; £1,047)

| | | | RPR |
|---|---|---|---|
| 1 | | **Archetype (FR)**[24] 6655 3-9-0 0 GregoryBenoist 4 (Simon Crisford) *disp ld early: led after 1f: pushed along to extend advantage over 2f out: rdn and qcknd over 1f out: clr and in command ins fnl f* **16/5**[2] | 104+ |
| 2 | 7 | **Westit**[52] 3-8-10 0 MaximeGuyon 3 (C Laffon-Parias, France) **39/10**[3] | 84 |
| 3 | ¾ | **Yuman (FR)**[25] 3-9-4 0 Pierre-CharlesBoudot 6 (H-A Pantall, France) **13/10**[1] | 90 |
| 4 | snk | **Spanish Fly (IRE)**[13] 3-8-10 0 MickaelBarzalona 1 (M Delcher Sanchez, France) **94/10** | 82 |
| 5 | 5 | **Mathix (FR)**[28] 3-9-0 0 StephanePasquier 7 (S Kobayashi, France) **83/10** | 74 |
| 6 | ¾ | **Nastenka**[105] 3656 3-8-10 0 AurelienLemaitre 8 (N Caullery, France) **31/1** | 69 |
| 7 | 1¼ | **Amaani (FR)**[114] 3-8-8 0 ow1 TonyPiccone 5 (G E Mikhalides, France) **29/1** | 64 |
| 8 | 3½ | **Kazaroza (FR)** 3-8-10 0 CristianDemuro 2 (V Luka Jr, Czech Republic) **31/1** | 58 |

1m 40.04s (-2.26) 8 Ran SP% **117.6**
PARI-MUTUEL (all including 1 euro stake): WIN 4.20; PLACE 1.20, 1.20, 1.10; DF 9.70; SF 17.70.
**Owner** Highclere Thoroughbred Racing-Wordsworth **Bred** E A R L Ecurie Du Grand Chene Haras **Trained** Newmarket, Suffolk

# [7264]BEVERLEY (R-H)

## Tuesday, September 26

**OFFICIAL GOING: Soft (6.2)**

Wind: Light behind Weather: Cloudy

### 7472 BEVERLEY ANNUAL BADGEHOLDERS NOVICE AUCTION STKS 5f

**2:10** (2:11) (Class 5) 2-Y-O **£3,881** (£1,155; £577; £288) **Stalls** Low

Form RPR

3044 **1** *nse* **Weeton (IRE)**[19] 6844 2-9-2 72........................ JoeDoyle 1 76
(Julie Camacho) *led: rdn and hung bdly lft ent fnl f: sn drvn: jnd last 50yds: sltly hmpd and hdd on line: fin 2nd: plcd 1st* **3/1**[2]

0620 **2** **Requinto Dawn (IRE)**[12] 7090 2-9-2 84................ SebastianWoods(7) 6 83
(Richard Fahey) *awkward s: trckd ldrs: n.m.r and swtchd rt over 1f out: sn rdn and hdwy to chal ent fnl f: drvn and ev ch whn edgd lft last 100yds: led on line: fin 1st: plcd 2nd* **15/8**[1]

3406 **3** *7* **Mr Greenlight**[10] 7138 2-9-2 71........................ DavidAllan 4 51
(Tim Easterby) *cl up: rdn along 2f out: drvn over 1f out: wknd ins fnl f* **4/1**[3]

24 **4** *½* **Tarnhelm**[24] 6682 2-8-11 0........................ JoeFanning 7 44
(Mark Johnston) *chsd ldng pair on outer: rdn along wl over 1f out: wknd appr fnl f* **9/2**

00 **5** *4 ½* **Little Red Berry (IRE)**[18] 6897 2-8-11 0........................ AndrewMullen 5 28
(James Given) *chsd ldrs: rdn along bef 1/2-way: sn outpcd* **50/1**

**6** *1 ½* **Joe Cable (IRE)** 2-9-2 0........................ TomEaves 3 27
(Nigel Tinkler) *sn outpcd and rdn along: a in rr* **20/1**

1m 6.71s (3.21) **Going Correction** +0.675s/f (Yiel) **6 Ran SP% 104.7**
Speed ratings (Par 95): **100,101,89,88,81 79**
CSF £7.82 TOTE £4.00: £1.60, £1.40; EX 8.90 Trifecta £21.20.
**Owner** David W Armstrong **Bred** Tally-Ho Stud **Trained** Norton, N Yorks
■ Scenic River was withdrawn. Price at time of withdrawal 9/1. Rule 4 applies to all bets - deduction 10p in the pound.
■ Stewards' Enquiry : Sebastian Woods caution: careless riding

**FOCUS**
A fair novice auction stakes for juveniles and the principals came clear in the last furlong. The jockeys reported the going was "bordering on heavy". Straightforward form with the front pair rated close to their respective bests.

### 7473 PONY RACING HERE ON 1 OCTOBER EBFSTALLIONS.COM NOVICE STKS 7f 96y

**2:45** (2:45) (Class 5) 2-Y-O **£3,881** (£1,155; £577; £288) **Stalls** Low

Form RPR

53 **1** **Buckstopper Kit (USA)**[16] 6967 2-9-2 0........................(b) PaulHanagan 3 78
(Richard Fahey) *trckd ldr: cl up whn n.m.r nr stands' rail and swtchd rt jst over 1f out: sn rdn: styd on wl fnl f to ld nr fin* **7/2**[2]

**2** *nk* **Big Kitten (USA)** 2-9-2 0........................ JoeFanning 4 77
(Mark Johnston) *dwlt and n.m.r s: hld up: smooth hdwy to trck ldrs over 2f out: edgd lft to stands' rail over 1f out: rdn to ld ins fnl f: green: hdd and no ex nr fin* **4/1**[3]

442 **3** *nk* **Mont Kinabalu (IRE)**[14] 7013 2-9-2 77........................ TomEaves 2 76
(Kevin Ryan) *trckd ldrs: hdwy over 2f out: rdn to ld wl over 1f out: drvn and hdd ins fnl f: kpt on* **7/2**[2]

0322 **4** *7* **Weellan**[18] 6900 2-9-2 76........................ PhillipMakin 6 59
(John Quinn) *trckd ldng pair: hdwy on outer 3f out: rdn along nr stands' rail to ld jst over 2f out: sn hdd and drvn: wknd appr fnl f* **11/8**[1]

03 **5** *4 ½* **Salire (IRE)**[17] 6938 2-8-11 0........................ JackGarritty 1 42
(Ann Duffield) *led: rdn along 3f out: wd st: hdd over 2f out: sn drvn and wknd* **20/1**

00 **6** *20* **Shef Wedsneigh (IRE)**[31] 6433 2-8-11 0........................ ConnorBeasley 5
(Roger Fell) *a in rr: rdn along over 3f out: sn outpcd and bhd* **100/1**

1m 40.3s (6.50) **Going Correction** +0.775s/f (Yiel) **6 Ran SP% 112.3**
Speed ratings (Par 95): **93,92,92,84,79 56**
CSF £17.67 TOTE £3.70: £2.00, £2.10; EX 20.70 Trifecta £82.10.
**Owner** Anthony F O'Callaghan **Bred** Kenneth L Ramsey And Sarah K Ramsey **Trained** Musley Bank, N Yorks

**FOCUS**
Some big northern stables represented in this run-of-the-mill juvenile contest and their runners dominated a close finish.

### 7474 COLIN MCGURRAN @ BEVERLEY RACECOURSE H'CAP 7f 96y

**3:15** (3:16) (Class 5) (0-75,77) 3-Y-O+ **£3,780** (£1,131; £565; £283; £141) **Stalls** Low

Form RPR

0602 **1** **Intense Style (IRE)**[10] 7156 5-9-3 77........................ FayeMcManoman(7) 6 84
(Les Eyre) *hld up towards rr: hdwy on inner 3f out: chsd ldrs wl over 1f out: rdn to chal ent fnl f: styd on wl to ld nr fin* **15/2**

2461 **2** *nk* **Kirkham**[25] 6663 4-9-3 70........................(p) JoeDoyle 1 76
(Julie Camacho) *trckd ldrs: smooth hdwy over 2f out: led 1 1/2f out: rdn ent fnl f: drvn last 100 yds: hdd and no ex nr fin* **7/1**

2133 **3** *hd* **Relight My Fire**[27] 6591 7-8-11 64........................(p) DavidAllan 2 69
(Tim Easterby) *dwlt and bhd: hdwy wl over 2f out: rdn along wl over 1f out: swtchd lft over 1f out: sn drvn and styd on to chal ins fnl f: ev ch tl no ex nr fin* **13/2**[3]

5500 **4** *3* **Beatbybeatbybeat**[47] 5835 4-8-8 61........................(v) CamHardie 10 59
(Antony Brittain) *hld up towards rr: hdwy 3f out: rdn wl over 1f out: drvn and kpt on fnl f* **50/1**

2400 **5** *½* **Navarone (IRE)**[18] 6879 3-9-6 76........................(t[1]) PaulHanagan 8 71
(Richard Fahey) *hld up towards rr: hdwy 3f out: rdn along wl over 1f out: kpt on fnl f* **10/1**

6300 **6** *½* **Hitman**[13] 7052 4-8-13 66........................(b[1]) ConnorBeasley 3 61
(Rebecca Bastiman) *trckd ldrs: hdwy on inner over 2f out: rdn to chal over 1f out: ev ch ent fnl f: sn drvn and wknd* **10/1**

3651 **7** *1 ¾* **Rose Eclair**[7] 7249 4-8-4 60 oh3........................(p) RachelRichardson(3) 12 51
(Tim Easterby) *sn disputing ld: cl up 1/2-way: rdn along and wd st towards stands rail: wknd over 1f out* **10/1**

4010 **8** *2 ¾* **Talent Scout (IRE)**[30] 6464 11-9-1 73........................(p) GemmaTutty(5) 5 56
(Karen Tutty) *nvr bttr than midfield* **33/1**

0300 **9** *½* **Chaplin Bay (IRE)**[16] 6964 5-8-12 65........................(p) JamesSullivan 13 47
(Ruth Carr) *in tch: trckd ldrs 1/2-way: rdn along towards stands rail 2f out: sn drvn and wknd over 1f out* **11/1**

6651 **10** *nk* **Glorious Poet**[10] 7158 4-9-9 76........................ WilliamCarson 9 57
(John Spearing) *trckd ldrs on outer: wd st towards stands rail: rdn along 2f out: sn wknd* **5/1**[1]

0164 **11** *8* **The Stalking Moon (IRE)**[26] 6627 3-9-6 76........................ DanielTudhope 7 36
(John Quinn) *a towards rr* **6/1**[2]

4431 **12** *5* **Equiano Springs**[24] 6667 3-9-4 74........................ TomEaves 4 21
(Tom Tate) *slt ld: wd st towards stands rail: rdn along over 2f out: drvn and hdd 1 1/2f out: sn wknd* **8/1**

0000 **13** *37* **Like No Other**[10] 7157 4-8-13 66........................(bt[1]) JoeFanning 11
(Les Eyre) *a bhd* **66/1**

1m 38.33s (4.53) **Going Correction** +0.775s/f (Yiel)
**WFA** 3 from 4yo+ 3lb **13 Ran SP% 121.7**
Speed ratings (Par 103): **105,104,104,101,100 99,97,94,94,93 84,78,36**
CSF £59.91 CT £368.23 TOTE £8.50: £2.60, £2.50, £2.70; EX 68.80 Trifecta £521.20.
**Owner** RP Racing Ltd **Bred** J S Bolger & John Corcoran **Trained** Catwick, N Yorks
■ Stewards' Enquiry : David Allan four-day ban: excessive use of whip (10-12, 15 Oct)
James Sullivan two-day ban: careless riding (10-11 Oct)

**FOCUS**
This competitive handicap was run at a good gallop and the time was nearly 2secs faster than the preceding juvenile contest. They again came stands' side in the straight. The winner has been rated to his best since early summer, with the runner-up to form.

### 7475 EDDIE AND VIOLET SMITH CONDITIONS STKS 5f

**3:50** (3:51) (Class 3) 3-Y-O+ **£12,450** (£3,728; £1,864; £932; £466) **Stalls** Low

Form RPR

0200 **1** **Alpha Delphini**[24] 6668 6-9-0 107........................(p) GrahamLee 3 97
(Bryan Smart) *cl up: rdn wl over 1f out: drvn to ld ins fnl f: hld on wl towards fin* **5/4**[1]

0000 **2** *nk* **Line Of Reason (IRE)**[3] 7396 7-9-10 100........................ JoeFanning 6 106
(Paul Midgley) *swityched rt s and hld up in rr: hdwy on inner whn nt clr run and hmpd over 1f out: swtchd lft and rdn ent fnl f: sn squeezed through to chal and ev ch: drvn and no ex towards fin* **11/1**

1144 **3** *2 ¼* **Ornate**[14] 7027 4-9-6 107........................(h) TomEaves 2 94
(Robert Cowell) *trckd ldng pair: hdwy to ld 2f out: rdn over 1f out: drvn and hdd ins fnl f: kpt on same pce* **4/1**[3]

0305 **4** *7* **Elysian Flyer (IRE)**[18] 6878 5-9-0 77........................ CamHardie 1 63
(Paul Midgley) *slt ld: rdn along 1/2-way: hdd 2f out and grad wknd* **20/1**

6002 **5** *14* **Edward Lewis**[34] 6325 4-9-6 100........................ DanielTudhope 5 18
(David O'Meara) *trckd ldrs: effrt 2f out: rdn and over 1f out: sn btn and eased fnl f* **2/1**[2]

1m 5.41s (1.91) **Going Correction** +0.675s/f (Yiel) **5 Ran SP% 110.9**
Speed ratings (Par 107): **111,110,106,95,73**
CSF £15.08 TOTE £2.00: £1.10, £3.60; EX 12.20 Trifecta £35.30.
**Owner** The Alpha Delphini Partnership **Bred** Mrs B A Matthews **Trained** Hambleton, N Yorks

**FOCUS**
The feature contest and a race that has been won by some smart sprinters in recent years, including Group 1 winners Tangerine Trees and Kingsgate Native. They stuck to the far side and the time was 1.3secs faster than the earlier juvenile contest. The runner-up is key, rated to this year's turf form.

### 7476 SEASON FINALE H'CAP 1m 100y

**4:25** (4:25) (Class 5) (0-70,70) 3-Y-O+ **£3,780** (£1,131; £565; £283; £141) **Stalls** Low

Form RPR

6201 **1** **Pioneering (IRE)**[30] 6471 3-9-0 66........................ DanielTudhope 4 81+
(David O'Meara) *hld up in midfield: hdwy on inner over 2f out: chsd ldrs and n.m.r over 1f out: squeezed through and rdn to ld ent fnl f: sn clr: kpt on* **15/2**[3]

45-3 **2** *2* **Doctor Cross (IRE)**[118] 3206 3-9-4 70........................ BarryMcHugh 7 79
(Richard Fahey) *hld up towards rr: hdwy over 2f out: rdn over 1f out: styd on to chse wnr ins fnl f: no imp towards fin* **16/1**

0030 **3** *2 ½* **Mustaqbal (IRE)**[13] 7052 5-8-13 66........................(p) CallumRodriguez(5) 3 70
(Michael Dods) *in tch: hdwy over 2f out: rdn to chse ldrs over 1f out: sn drvn and kpt on fnl f* **7/1**[2]

5442 **4** *½* **Mr Cool Cash**[5] 7327 5-9-2 64........................ ConnorBeasley 6 67
(Richard Guest) *trckd ldrs: hdwy 2f out: rdn over 1f out: drvn and kpt on same pce fnl f* **7/4**[1]

5336 **5** *1 ¼* **Infamous Lawman (IRE)**[55] 5540 3-8-12 67........................ JoshDoyle(3) 1 67
(David O'Meara) *prom on inner: pushed along wl over 1f out: sn rdn and kpt on same pce ent fnl f* **10/1**

6640 **6** *nse* **Make On Madam (IRE)**[42] 6049 5-9-7 69........................ DavidAllan 5 69
(Les Eyre) *trckd ldrs: rdn along 2f out: drvn over 1f out: kpt on same pce* **11/1**

4040 **7** *¾* **Ravenhoe (IRE)**[17] 6947 4-9-1 63........................ JoeFanning 10 61
(Mark Johnston) *sn led: pushed along over 2f out: rdn wl over 1f out: hdd ent fnl f: sn wknd* **16/1**

0135 **8** *1* **Beadlam (IRE)**[26] 6638 4-8-13 64........................ AdamMcNamara(3) 9 59
(Roger Fell) *prom: cl up over 3f out: rdn along 2f out: sn drvn and wknd* **20/1**

3230 **9** *½* **Chiswick Bey (IRE)**[16] 6964 9-9-3 65........................ PaulHanagan 8 59
(Richard Fahey) *hld up towards rr: sme hdwy 2f out: sn rdn and n.d* **12/1**

63-0 **10** *3* **Never A Word (USA)**[37] 6236 3-9-1 67........................(t) KevinStott 12 54
(Oliver Greenall) *dwlt and in rr: hdwy over 2f out: rdn wl over 1f out: sn hung lft and nvr a factor* **33/1**

1000 **11** *3 ¾* **Arcane Dancer (IRE)**[30] 6471 4-8-13 61........................(p) PaulMulrennan 2 40
(Lawrence Mullaney) *trckd ldrs: effrt over 2f out: rdn along wl over 1f out: sn wknd* **12/1**

4100 **12** *1* **Metronomic (IRE)**[18] 6901 3-8-11 63........................ AndrewMullen 11 40
(Peter Niven) *towards rr: wd towards stands rail in st: nvr a factor* **33/1**

4550 **13** *9* **Sooqaan**[40] 6092 6-8-8 56 oh8........................ CamHardie 15 12
(Antony Brittain) *trckd ldrs on outer: hdwy over 3f out: rdn along 2f out: sn drvn and wknd* **100/1**

4-40 **14** *8* **Miss Bates**[133] 2702 3-8-13 65........................ GrahamLee 14
(Ann Duffield) *a towards rr* **22/1**

0445 **15** *3 ¼* **Lil Sophella (IRE)**[18] 6893 8-9-3 65........................ JackGarritty 13
(Patrick Holmes) *towards rr: wd st to stands rail: sn rdn and nvr a factor* **16/1**

1m 52.65s (5.05) **Going Correction** +0.775s/f (Yiel)
**WFA** 3 from 4yo+ 4lb **15 Ran SP% 127.1**
Speed ratings (Par 103): **105,103,100,100,98 98,97,96,96,93 89,88,79,71,68**
CSF £120.91 CT £899.35 TOTE £6.90: £2.00, £6.50, £2.50; EX 158.70 Trifecta £948.10.
**Owner** Ebor Racing Club Vi **Bred** Miss Joan Murphy **Trained** Upper Helmsley, N Yorks

**FOCUS**
A big field for this modest handicap and they went a fair gallop, but the winner scored in taking fashion.

### 7477 BEVERLEY INTERACTIVE MAIDEN FILLIES' STKS 1m 4f 23y

**4:55** (5:03) (Class 5) 3-Y-O+ **£3,881** (£1,155; £577; £288) **Stalls** Low

Form RPR

3 **1** **River Icon**[11] 7109 5-9-2 0........................ CallumRodriguez(5) 4 78
(Iain Jardine) *trckd ldrs: wd st towards stands rail: hdwy over 2f out: rdn to chse ldr over 1f out: drvn ins fnl f: styd on wl to ld nr line* **3/1**[2]

23 **2** *shd* **Kohinur**[48] 5796 3-9-0 0 JackMitchell 5 79
(Hugo Palmer) *trckd ldr: hdwy and cl up over 2f out: led wl over 1f out: rdn clr ent fnl f: drvn and edgd lft towards fin: hdd nr line* **4/9**[1]

25 **3** *12* **Clemency**[11] 7109 6-9-7 0 PaulMulrennan 3 59
(Donald McCain) *led: pushed along 3f out: rdn over 2f out: hdd and drvn wl over 1f out: grad wknd appr fnl f* **28/1**

4535 **4** *7* **Princess Nearco (IRE)**[7] 7248 3-9-0 60 (v[1]) DanielTudhope 1 49
(Patrick Holmes) *hld up in rr: hdwy on outer 3f out: wd st towards stands rail: rdn over 2f out: sn one pce* **12/1**[3]

2-33 **5** *45* **Sea Dweller**[223] 747 4-9-7 67 DavidAllan 2
(Anthony Carson) *trckd ldng pair: pushed along over 3f out: rdn over 2f out. sn wknd* **16/1**

2m 48.27s (8.47) **Going Correction** +0.775s/f (Yiel)
**WFA** 3 from 4yo+ 7lb **5** Ran SP% **111.3**
Speed ratings (Par 100): **102,101,93,89,59**
CSF £4.80 TOTE £4.10: £1.70, £1.02; EX 5.30 Trifecta £22.60.
**Owner** M Friel, T Reid & K Wilson **Bred** Michael Dun **Trained** Carrutherstown, D'fries & G'way

**FOCUS**
A modest-looking fillies' maiden run at an ordinary gallop and a somewhat surprise result. The level is fluid.

## 7478 BRIAN AND JASON MERRINGTON MEMORIAL AMATEUR RIDERS' H'CAP (DIV I) 1m 1f 207y

**5:25** (5:30) (Class 6) (0-60,61) 3-Y-O+ **£2,495** (£774; £386; £193) **Stalls** Low

Form RPR

4035 **1** **Decima (IRE)**[36] 6269 3-10-9 60 MrPMillman 9 69
(Michael Easterby) *trckd ldrs: hdwy over 3f out: led over 2f out: rdn over 1f out: drvn clr ent fnl f: kpt on* **8/1**

6004 **2** *4 ½* **Inspector Norse**[8] 7220 6-10-1 50 (p) MissEEasterby(3) 7 50
(Tim Easterby) *trckd ldng pair on inner: hdwy and cl up 2f out: rdn over 1f out:. sn chsng wnr: kpt on same pce fnl f* **7/1**

4050 **3** *¾* **Almunther (IRE)**[67] 5131 4-10-11 57 (t[1]) MissBeckySmith 12 56
(Micky Hammond) *trckd ldrs: pushed along over 2f out: rdn wl over 1f out: kpt on u.p fnl f* **25/1**

-605 **4** *nk* **Bob's Boy**[33] 6153 4-10-2 55 (bt) MrHMyddelton(7) 6 53
(Oliver Greenall) *towards rr: hdwy over 3f out: rdn along on inner to chse ldrs over 1f out: drvn and kpt on same pce fnl f* **20/1**

1156 **5** *4* **My Renaissance**[19] 3400 7-10-8 59 PoppyBridgwater(5) 11 50
(Sam England) *towards rr: hdwy 3f out: rdn along on outer 2f out: drvn over 1f out: kpt on fnl f* **6/1**[2]

000 **6** *3* **Royal Holiday (IRE)**[29] 6529 10-10-6 57 (p) MrBillyGarritty(5) 10 42
(Marjorie Fife) *led: rdn along and hdd over 2f out: drvn over 1f out: grad wknd* **22/1**

606 **7** *nk* **I'm Super Too (IRE)**[24] 6673 10-10-2 48 (b) MissETodd 5 33
(Karen Tutty) *midfield: hdwy and in tch 4f out: rdn along wl over 2f out: n.d* **11/1**

5560 **8** *4 ½* **Aqua Libre**[14] 7015 4-11-1 61 (p[1]) MrSWalker 14 38
(Jennie Candlish) *trckd ldrs on outer: hdwy over 3f out: rdn along over 2f out: drvn wl over 1f out: grad wknd* **13/2**[3]

534 **9** *½* **Dragonite (IRE)**[7] 7253 3-9-9 46 MissSBrotherton 15 23
(Daniel Mark Loughnane) *chsd ldr: rdn along 3f out: wknd over 2f out* **5/1**[1]

0000 **10** *1 ½* **Swiss Lait**[21] 6788 6-9-7 46 oh1 (b[1]) MrJCummins(7) 4 19
(Patrick Holmes) *s.i.s and bhd: hdwy 4f out: chsd ldrs wl over 2f out: rdn along wl over 1f out: sn wknd* **50/1**

2000 **11** *12* **Etaad (USA)**[69] 5023 6-10-1 52 (bt) MrAAnderson(5) 13 4
(Lucinda Egerton) *dwlt: a in rr* **66/1**

/00- **12** *2 ½* **Kheskianto (IRE)**[315] 5522 11-9-7 46 oh1 MrKYeoman(7) 16
(Michael Chapman) *a in rr* **100/1**

0340 **13** *10* **Colour Contrast (IRE)**[8] 7219 4-10-4 53 (b) MrBLynn(3) 2
(Iain Jardine) *nvr bttr than midfield* **7/1**

2600 **14** *6* **Single Estate**[18] 6898 3-9-10 47 MissAWaugh 8
(Simon Waugh) *a in rr* **50/1**

0056 **15** *4 ½* **Fledermaus (IRE)**[29] 6523 7-9-7 46 oh1 (t) MissBJohnson(7) 3
(Tina Jackson) *a in rr* **33/1**

1250 **F** **Sakhalin Star (IRE)**[8] 7220 6-11-0 60 (p) MissJoannaMason 1
(Richard Guest) *hld up: hdwy and in tch whn clipped heels and fell 3f out* **7/1**

2m 17.35s (10.35) **Going Correction** +0.775s/f (Yiel)
**WFA** 3 from 4yo+ 5lb **16** Ran SP% **123.5**
Speed ratings (Par 101): **89,85,84,84,81 78,78,75,74,73 63,61,53,49,45**
CSF £59.22 CT £1368.94 TOTE £8.80: £2.20, £2.00, £5.20, £5.50; EX 73.80 Trifecta £780.00.
**Owner** B Padgett & Stittenham Racing **Bred** Mrs C Regalado-Gonzalez **Trained** Sheriff Hutton, N Yorks

**FOCUS**
The first division of a low-grade amateur riders' handicap and an open betting race, but a clear-cut winner.

## 7479 BRIAN AND JASON MERRINGTON MEMORIAL AMATEUR RIDERS' H'CAP (DIV II) 1m 1f 207y

**5:55** (6:00) (Class 6) (0-60,60) 3-Y-O+ **£2,495** (£774; £386; £193) **Stalls** Low

Form RPR

3201 **1** **John Caesar (IRE)**[6] 7270 6-10-7 53 (tp) MrPMillman 3 60
(Rebecca Bastiman) *trckd ldrs on inner: hdwy to chse ldr 2f out: rdn to ld over 1f out: drvn out* **5/1**[2]

3560 **2** *1 ½* **Royal Cosmic**[71] 4962 3-9-8 47 ow1 (b) MrBLynn(3) 6 53
(Richard Fahey) *in tch: hdwy over 2f out: rdn to chal and ev ch whn hung bdly lft jst over 1f out: hung rt ent fnl f: sn drvn and kpt on same pce* **16/1**

054 **3** *¾* **Palindrome (USA)**[41] 6058 4-10-0 46 oh1 MissJoannaMason 8 49
(Marjorie Fife) *towards rr: hdwy wl over 2f out: rdn wl over 1f out: styd on fnl f* **8/1**[3]

3615 **4** *½* **Bollin Ted**[5] 7325 3-10-6 60 MissEEasterby(3) 5 63
(Tim Easterby) *dwlt and towards rr: hdwy over 3f out: chsd ldrs on inner over 1f out: sn rdn and kpt on same pce* **7/2**[1]

5555 **5** *1 ¾* **Moojaned (IRE)**[14] 7028 6-10-11 57 MrJamesKing 9 56
(John Flint) *prom: chsd clr ldr 1/2-way: rdn along over 2f out: drvn wl over 1f out: kpt on same pce* **8/1**[3]

5025 **6** *¾* **Graceful Act**[31] 6431 9-10-5 51 (p) MissSBrotherton 2 48
(Ron Barr) *in tch: hdwy to chse ldrs 3f out: rdn along 2f out: sn drvn and no imp* **16/1**

600- **7** *1 ½* **L'Es Fremantle (FR)**[21] 6212 6-9-7 46 oh1 MrKYeoman(7) 7 41
(Michael Chapman) *prom: rdn along 3f out: drvn 2f out: grad wknd* **100/1**

0341 **8** *¾* **Ivors Involvement (IRE)**[24] 6673 5-10-3 49 (p) MissETodd 10 42
(Tina Jackson) *led: clr 1/2-way: rdn along over 2f out: drvn wl over 1f out: sn hdd & wknd* **9/1**

0064 **9** *shd* **The King's Steed**[56] 5074 4-10-0 46 oh1 MissBeckySmith 13 39
(Micky Hammond) *in tch on outer: rdn along wl over 2f out: sn wknd* **25/1**

5500 **10** *1 ¼* **Warfare**[7] 7236 8-10-9 60 (p) MissHDukes(5) 4 51
(Tim Fitzgerald) *dwlt: a towards rr* **12/1**

-142 **11** *2* **Life Knowledge (IRE)**[142] 2427 5-10-8 57 MissAMcCain(3) 1 44
(Patrick Holmes) *dwlt: a in rr* **12/1**

0324 **12** *6* **Outlaw Torn (IRE)**[5] 7324 8-10-1 54 MrSASmith(7) 12 30
(Richard Guest) *chsd ldrs on outer: rdn along 3f out: sn wknd* **14/1**

3130 **13** *1 ¼* **Diamond Runner (IRE)**[13] 7052 5-10-12 58 (b) MrSWalker 14 32
(Lawrence Mullaney) *in tch: hdwy to chse ldrs over 2f out: rdn along wl over 1f out: sn wknd* **12/1**

0042 **14** *11* **Lean On Pete (IRE)**[29] 6524 8-10-13 59 MissCWalton 11 13
(Ollie Pears) *chsd ;ldrs: rdn along and lost pl wl over 3f out: sn bhd* **20/1**

2m 18.63s (11.63) **Going Correction** +0.775s/f (Yiel)
**WFA** 3 from 4yo+ 5lb **14** Ran SP% **122.2**
Speed ratings (Par 101): **84,82,82,81,80 79,78,78,77,76 75,70,69,60**
CSF £82.56 CT £644.69 TOTE £6.20: £2.30, £4.70, £2.80; EX 108.10 Trifecta £876.70.
**Owner** Mrs K Hall & Mrs P Bastiman **Bred** Polish Belle Partnership **Trained** Cowthorpe, N Yorks
■ Shakabula was withdrawn. Price at time of withdrawal 25/1. Rule 4 does not apply.

**FOCUS**
This second leg of the amateurs' handicap was run 1.28secs slower than the first. Straightforward form around front quartet.
T/Plt: £104.00 to a £1 stake. Pool: £55,925.30 - 392.41 winning units T/Qpdt: £21.60 to a £1 stake. Pool: £5,451.63 - 186.71 winning units **Joe Rowntree**

# 7318 CHELMSFORD (A.W) (L-H)

Tuesday, September 26

**OFFICIAL GOING: Polytrack: standard**
Wind: virtually nil Weather: overcast

## 7480 BET TOTEPLACEPOT AT BETFRED.COM APPRENTICE H'CAP (DIV I) 7f (P)

**5:40** (5:41) (Class 6) (0-58,60) 3-Y-O+ **£3,234** (£962; £481; £240) **Stalls** Low

Form RPR

0300 **1** **Jack Nevison**[3] 7389 4-9-9 60 (v[1]) GabrieleMalune(3) 1 65
(Michael Appleby) *mde all: pushed along 2f out: edgd rt ins fnl f: hld on wl: rdn out* **4/1**[2]

4502 **2** *½* **Touch The Clouds**[19] 6847 6-8-12 46 ManuelFernandes 4 50
(William Stone) *chsd wnr: effrt over 2f out: styd on and ev ch 1f out: kpt on but hld fnl 100yds* **5/1**[3]

2336 **3** *½* **Justice Rock**[8] 7212 4-9-2 50 (t) RossaRyan 3 52
(Phil McEntee) *chsd ldrs: effrt in 5th over 2f out: kpt on u.p ins fnl f: wnt 3rd towards fin* **10/1**

404 **4** *½* **Good Business (IRE)**[22] 6751 3-9-2 53 (v[1]) FinleyMarsh 8 53
(Jeremy Noseda) *chsd ldrs: effrt over 1f out: kpt on same pce u.p ins fnl f: lost 3rd towards fin* **5/1**[3]

2025 **5** *nk* **Tallulah's Quest (IRE)**[33] 6345 3-9-8 59 MillyNaseb 13 58
(Julia Feilden) *dwlt: hld up off the pce in last trio: hdwy over 2f out: clsd on ldrs and hung lft over 1f out: kpt on ins fnl f: nvr quite getting on terms w ldrs* **7/1**

6421 **6** *¾* **Shyarch**[47] 5852 3-9-2 58 JacobMitchell(5) 9 55
(Christine Dunnett) *chsd ldrs: effrt in 4th ent fnl 2f: unable qck over 1f out: kpt on same pce and hld whn eased towards fin* **16/1**

432 **7** *2* **Dream Start**[6] 7282 3-9-5 59 (t) JackOsborn(3) 10 51
(John Ryan) *s.i.s and dropped in bhd after s: wl bhd in last: effrt on outer but stl plenty to do over 2f out: hdwy 1f out: styd on ins fnl f: nvr trbld ldrs* **3/1**[1]

6350 **8** *5* **Lesanti**[22] 6751 3-8-10 50 TylerSaunders(3) 11 28
(Ed de Giles) *bustled along early: chsd ldrs tl dropped to midfield 4f out: rdn and wknd over 1f out* **10/1**

0121 **9** *4 ½* **National Service (USA)**[29] 6544 6-8-12 46 oh1 (tp) CameronNoble 5 13
(Clare Ellam) *t.k.h: hld up in midfield: effrt over 2f out: wknd over 1f out* **25/1**

0000 **10** *3* **Back To Love (CAN)**[47] 5823 4-8-12 46 oh1 WilliamCox 12 5
(Mark Gillard) *a off the pce in rr: rdn and no hdwy over 1f out: wknd* **50/1**

00-P **11** *nse* **Katie Canford**[47] 5823 4-8-9 46 oh1 BenSanderson(3) 7 5
(Mark Hoad) *midfield: rdn over 2f out: sn dropped to rr: wknd over 1f out* **50/1**

004 **12** *8* **Compass Rose (IRE)**[14] 7035 3-9-4 55 (t[1]) NatalieHambling 6
(Scott Dixon) *midfield: lost pl and bhd 2f out: wl bhd fnl f* **50/1**

1m 26.06s (-1.14) **Going Correction** -0.175s/f (Stan)
**WFA** 3 from 4yo+ 3lb **12** Ran SP% **124.6**
Speed ratings (Par 101): **99,98,97,97,96 96,93,88,82,79 79,70**
CSF £25.27 CT £165.90 TOTE £5.40: £1.90, £1.80, £3.10; EX 30.10 Trifecta £201.60.
**Owner** New Kids On The Trot **Bred** Mr & Mrs A Archer **Trained** Oakham, Rutland

**FOCUS**
A moderate handicap in which the pace held up. The 2nd/3rd pin an ordinary, straightforward level.

## 7481 BET TOTEPLACEPOT AT BETFRED.COM APPRENTICE H'CAP (DIV II) 7f (P)

**6:10** (6:12) (Class 6) (0-58,57) 3-Y-O+ **£3,234** (£962; £481; £240) **Stalls** Low

Form RPR

0432 **1** **Prince Jai**[5] 7323 4-9-4 51 (b) ManuelFernandes 9 59
(Ian Williams) *pressed ldr tl pushed into ld 2f out: sustained duel w runner-up after: kpt on and forged ahd towards fin* **15/8**[1]

061 **2** *nk* **Frank's Legacy**[117] 3260 3-9-3 53 (p) JamieGormley 2 59
(Ivan Furtado) *led tl 2f out: sn hdd and sustained duel w wnr tl no ex and btn towards fin* **6/1**[3]

0304 **3** *3 ¼* **Latest Quest (IRE)**[8] 7212 3-8-6 49 ShariqMohd(7) 3 46+
(Sylvester Kirk) *midfield: rdn and hdwy towards inner over 1f out: nt clrest of runs ins fnl f: wnt between rivals to snatch 3rd nr fin: no threat to ldng pair* **6/1**[3]

5324 **4** *½* **Caledonian Gold**[40] 6112 4-8-9 49 (b) OliverDaykin(7) 12 46
(Paul D'Arcy) *taken down early: stdd s: t.k.h: in rr early: hdwy to chse ldrs 4f out: rdn over 1f out: 3rd and no imp ins fnl f: lost 3rd towards fin* **8/1**

0505 **5** *hd* **Percy Toplis**[14] 7027 3-8-4 45 (p) JacobMitchell(5) 7 40
(Christine Dunnett) *chsd ldrs: effrt in 3rd 2f out: unable qck over 1f out: kpt on same pce ins fnl f* **33/1**

1450 **6** *nk* **Mr Potter**[18] 6903 4-9-7 57 (v) JackOsborn(3) 1 53
(Richard Guest) *taken down early: stdd s: hld up in last trio: swtchd rt and effrt over 1f out: hdwy 1f out: styd on wl ins fnl f: nt rch ldrs* **8/1**

0600 **7** *1* **Encapsulated**[19] 6850 7-9-6 53 (p) RhiainIngram 8 46
(Roger Ingram) *led to post: t.k.h: hld up towards rr: lost cheek piece 5f out: swtchd rt after 2f out: effrt and hdwy u.p over 1f out: styd on ins fnl f: nt rch ldrs* **33/1**

6503 **8** 3¾ **Socrates**[34] 6324 3-9-0 **50**........(b) WilliamCox 5 32
(Daniel Kubler) *taken down early: s.i.s: sn in midfield: 6th and unable to wl over 1f out: wknd fnl f* **5/1**[2]

0310 **9** 2 **Zebelini (IRE)**[77] 4727 5-8-12 **48**........ BenSanderson(3) 11 25
(Roy Bowring) *chsd ldrs: rdn and outpcd over 2f out: lost pl and btn 1f out: wknd ins fnl f* **20/1**

3046 **10** 3 **Nonno Giulio (IRE)**[15] 7006 6-9-8 **55**........(b) KatherineGlenister 4 24
(Conor Dore) *midfield: lost pl and bhd whn hmpd 2f out: wknd over 1f out* **14/1**

005 **11** ¾ **Our Ruth**[27] 6577 4-8-12 **45**........ RossaRyan 6 12
(Jimmy Fox) *bhd whn hung rt and wd bnd 3f out: hung lft u.p over 1f out: swtchd rt and sn wknd* **50/1**

1m 26.86s (-0.34) **Going Correction** -0.175s/f (Stan)
**WFA** 3 from 4yo+ 3lb **11** Ran SP% **121.5**
Speed ratings (Par 101): **94,93,89,89,89 88,87,83,81,77 76**
CSF £13.27 CT £60.77 TOTE £2.70: £1.02, £2.70, £2.60; EX 14.40 Trifecta £78.90.
**Owner** Mr & Mrs H Parmar **Bred** Ellis Stud And Bellow Hill Stud **Trained** Portway, Worcs

**FOCUS**
As in the first division, the pace held up and the leaders fought it out up the straight. It was the slower of the two legs by 0.80sec. The winner has been rated back to near his best.

## 7482 BET TOTEJACKPOT AT BETFRED.COM NOVICE AUCTION STKS (PLUS 10 RACE) 6f (P)
6:40 (6:42) (Class 4) 2-Y-O £7,115 (£2,117; £1,058; £529) Stalls Centre

Form RPR

42 **1** **Episcia (IRE)**[23] 6719 2-8-8 0........ AaronJones(3) 9 69
(Stuart Williams) *squeezed for room s and dropped to rr: hld up in rr of main gp: clsd on inner and nt clr run over 1f out: gap opened and hdwy to chse ldr ins fnl f: rdr dropped reins but r.o wl to ld nr fin* **12/1**

201 **2** ½ **Ghepardo**[23] 6719 2-8-11 71........ RossaRyan(7) 3 74
(Richard Hannon) *t.k.h: pressed ldrs tl stdd into midfield after 2f: effrt over 1f out: rdn to ld ins fnl f: r.o wl but hdd towards fin* **9/2**[3]

13 **3** 3¼ **Equitant**[24] 6689 2-9-9 0........ TonyHamilton 6 69
(Richard Fahey) *midfield: effrt over 1f out: swtchd rt and kpt on ins fnl f: wnt 3rd cl home: no threat to ldng pair* **9/2**[3]

50 **4** ½ **Nampara**[131] 2750 2-8-11 0........ JoeyHaynes 5 56
(Paul D'Arcy) *chsd ldrs: wnt 2nd over 2f out: effrt to press ldr over 1f out: stl pressing ldr whn sltly impeded 1f out: wknd ins fnl f: lost 3rd cl home* **25/1**

**5** shd **Jackpot Royale** 2-9-2 0........ LukeMorris 4 60
(Michael Appleby) *dwlt: hld up in tch in rr of main gp: effrt 2f out: hdwy and swtchd lft ins fnl f: styd on same pce fnl 100yds* **33/1**

10 **6** shd **Marchingontogether**[98] 3929 2-9-4 0........ OisinMurphy 10 62
(Ivan Furtado) *in tch towards rr of main gp but stuck wd: effrt over 1f out: kpt on ins fnl f: no threat to ldrs* **6/4**[1]

2023 **7** ¾ **Oswald (IRE)**[18] 6890 2-8-13 71........(b[1]) GeorgeWood(3) 8 58
(Robyn Brisland) *bmpd and impeded leaving stalls: rcvrd and hdwy to ld over 4f out: rdn over 1f out: edgd rt 1f out: sn hdd & wknd ins fnl f* **3/1**[2]

5 **8** 2 **Harbour Storm**[36] 6262 2-9-2 0........ JohnFahy 2 52
(Laura Mongan) *led tl over 4f out: chsd ldr tl over 2f out: sn rdn and lost pl over 1f out: wknd ins fnl f* **50/1**

46 **9** 5 **Cristal Pallas Cat (IRE)**[20] 6827 2-8-11 0........ RhiainIngram(5) 7 37
(Roger Ingram) *wet rt and bmpd rival leaving stalls: in tch in midfield: hdwy to chse ldrs 4f out tl rdn and lost pl over 1f out: wknd ins fnl f* **16/1**

P0 **10** 24 **Tipi**[20] 6816 2-9-2 0........ BenCurtis 1
(Charlie Wallis) *s.i.s: rn green and all over the pl in rr: lost tch 3f out* **100/1**

1m 12.64s (-1.06) **Going Correction** -0.175s/f (Stan) **10** Ran SP% **124.7**
Speed ratings (Par 97): **100,99,95,94,94 94,93,90,83,51**
CSF £68.52 TOTE £11.60: £3.20, £1.80, £1.40; EX 69.20 Trifecta £490.40.
**Owner** T W Morley **Bred** Stockvale Bloodstock Ltd **Trained** Newmarket, Suffolk

**FOCUS**
This was run at a good gallop and set up for those ridden with a bit of patience.

## 7483 BET TOTEQUADPOT AT BETFRED.COM H'CAP 1m 5f 66y(P)
7:10 (7:10) (Class 6) (0-65,67) 3-Y-O+ £3,234 (£962; £481; £240) Stalls Low

Form RPR

0-01 **1** **Send Up (IRE)**[15] 7003 3-9-1 **63**........(p[1]) LukeMorris 3 69+
(Sir Mark Prescott Bt) *dwlt: t.k.h: hld up wl in tch in midfield: effrt 3f out: ev ch and squeezed for room over 1f out: led ent fnl f: styd on wl* **2/1**[1]

1030 **2** ½ **Avenue Des Champs**[18] 6889 5-9-10 **65**........(p) MartinHarley 1 68
(Jane Chapple-Hyam) *led tl 10f out: chsd ldr tl 8f out: styd trcking ldrs: nt clr run jst over 2f out: effrt to chal over 1f out: kpt on wl but a jst hld ins fnl f* **6/1**

2543 **3** ½ **Too Many Shots**[87] 4348 3-8-8 **56**........ JoeyHaynes 2 61
(John Best) *trckd ldrs: effrt over 2f out: edgd lft u.p and led over 1f out: sn hdd and kpt on same pce ins fnl f* **7/1**

6331 **4** hd **Iballisticvin**[40] 5652 4-9-10 **65**........ TomQueally 11 67
(Gary Moore) *hld up in tch in midfield: effrt over 1f out: drvn to press ldrs 1f out: styd on same pce u.p ins fnl f* **9/2**[2]

00 **5** 1¼ **Ballyfarsoon (IRE)**[20] 6820 6-8-13 **54**........(v) StevieDonohoe 8 54
(Ian Williams) *t.k.h: hld up in tch in midfield: hdwy on inner over 1f out: pressing ldrs and drvn whn squeezed for room ins fnl f: nt rcvr and one pced after* **8/1**

4322 **6** 1 **Best Example (USA)**[26] 6632 5-9-9 **67**........ ShelleyBirkett(3) 10 66
(Julia Feilden) *hld up in tch in last trio: clsd over 2f out: effrt to chse ldrs over 1f out: kpt on same pce and no imp ins fnl f* **5/1**[3]

6050 **7** 1½ **Royal Hall (FR)**[28] 6557 5-9-2 **57**........(p) ShaneKelly 4 54
(Gary Moore) *stdd s: t.k.h: hld up in last trio: rdn over 3f out: no imp over 1f out and hld whn swtchd rt 1f out:* **25/1**

25-0 **8** 1¾ **Atalanta Bay (IRE)**[7] 7232 7-9-0 **62**........(h) TylerSaunders(7) 5 57
(Marcus Tregoning) *stdd s: hld up in tch in rr: rdn over 3f out: no imp and hung lft over 1f out: nvr trbld ldrs* **14/1**

-000 **9** 3½ **Beaconsfield**[12] 7095 3-8-9 **57**........ SilvestreDeSousa 7 49
(Hughie Morrison) *chsd ldrs: wnt 2nd 8f out tl losing pl whn squeezed for room over 1f out: bhd ins fnl f* **10/1**

4320 **10** 3½ **Dream Serenade**[112] 3436 4-9-0 **55**........(h) AlistairRawlinson 9 39
(Michael Appleby) *t.k.h: pressed ldr tl led 10f out: rdn and hdd over 1f out: sn outpcd: wknd ins fnl f: eased towards fin* **50/1**

2m 53.04s (-0.56) **Going Correction** -0.175s/f (Stan)
**WFA** 3 from 4yo+ 7lb **10** Ran SP% **127.6**
Speed ratings (Par 101): **94,93,93,93,92 91,90,90,88,85**
CSF £16.18 CT £77.80 TOTE £3.90: £1.30, £2.50, £2.70; EX 20.30 Trifecta £137.50.
**Owner** Old Harrovian Racing Club **Bred** Barronstown Stud **Trained** Newmarket, Suffolk

**FOCUS**
They didn't go a great gallop and after sprinting up the straight they finished in a bit of a heap. The winner is open to significant improvement but didn't really need to progress to take this, with balance of 2nd/3rd suggesting this can't be much better.

## 7484 BET TOTEEXACTA AT BETFRED.COM FILLIES' H'CAP 1m (P)
7:40 (7:40) (Class 4) (0-85,85) 3-Y-O+ £8,086 (£2,406; £1,202; £601) Stalls Low

Form RPR

1122 **1** **Bumptious**[12] 7094 4-9-7 **80**........(p) SeanLevey 1 87
(Ismail Mohammed) *led for 2f: styd trcking ldrs: effrt u.p to chal ent fnl f: drvn to ld wl ins fnl f: styd on* **10/3**[1]

3252 **2** ½ **Stosur (IRE)**[35] 6294 6-8-10 **72**........(b) DavidEgan(3) 8 78
(Gay Kelleway) *jnd ldr after 2f: rdn and ev ch 2f out: led ent fnl f: kpt on u.p: hdd and styd on same pce ins fnl f* **25/1**

2-31 **3** ½ **Song Maker**[11] 7109 3-9-5 **82**........(b) JamesDoyle 9 87+
(Charlie Appleby) *hld up in tch in midfield: effrt whn forced wd and lost pl bnd 2f out: rallied 1f out: styd on wl u.p ins fnl f: nt quite rch ldrs* **9/2**[3]

6004 **4** 1½ **Queensbrydge**[27] 6576 3-9-0 **77**........ LukeMorris 2 78
(Robyn Brisland) *hld up in tch: rdn and hdwy to chse ldrs whn swtchd rt over 1f out: drifting rt u.str.p ins fnl f: styd on same pce fnl 100yds* **5/1**

4263 **5** ½ **Bint Dandy (IRE)**[36] 6261 6-9-12 **85**........(b) SilvestreDeSousa 7 85
(Chris Dwyer) *chsd ldr tl led 6f out: rdn ent fnl 2f: drvn over 1f out: hdd 1f out: wknd ins fnl f* **10/1**

-310 **6** 1½ **Roman Holiday (IRE)**[80] 4617 4-9-8 **81**........(p) HarryBentley 6 78
(Ed Vaughan) *s.i.s: hld up in tch in last pair: effrt over 1f out: styd on ins fnl f: nvr trbld ldrs* **12/1**

1112 **7** nk **Harba (IRE)**[36] 6261 3-9-6 **83**........ OisinMurphy 5 79
(William Haggas) *t.k.h: hld up in tch in midfield: effrt over 1f out: kpt on same pce ins fnl f* **7/1**

615 **8** nk **Simply Me**[34] 6321 4-9-8 **81**........(p) RichardKingscote 3 76
(Tom Dascombe) *hld up in last pair: effrt on inner and sme hdwy over 1f out: no imp ins fnl f* **12/1**

2140 **9** 5 **Ghadaayer (IRE)**[33] 6358 3-9-8 **85**........ DaneO'Neill 4 69
(Sir Michael Stoute) *in tch in midfield: effrt to chse ldrs ent fnl 2f: lost pl u.p over 1f out: wknd ins fnl f* **4/1**[2]

3301 **10** 9 **Andalusite**[8] 7216 4-8-9 **68** 6ex........(v) FergusSweeney 10 31
(John Gallagher) *dwlt: t.k.h: steadily rcvrd to chse ldrs 4f out: hung rt bnd 2f out and sn lost pl: bhd fnl f* **50/1**

1m 36.81s (-3.09) **Going Correction** -0.175s/f (Stan)
**WFA** 3 from 4yo+ 4lb **10** Ran SP% **120.7**
Speed ratings (Par 102): **108,107,107,105,105 103,103,102,97,88**
CSF £92.59 CT £396.64 TOTE £4.60: £1.70, £7.50, £2.30; EX 105.00 Trifecta £1442.90.
**Owner** Abdulla Al Mansoori **Bred** Swettenham Stud **Trained** Newmarket, Suffolk

**FOCUS**
A fair fillies' handicap rated around the runner-up to her recent form.

## 7485 BET TOTETRIFECTA AT BETFRED.COM MAIDEN FILLIES' STKS 1m (P)
8:10 (8:13) (Class 5) 3-Y-O+ £5,175 (£1,540; £769; £384) Stalls Low

Form RPR

2420 **1** **Kitty Boo**[23] 6722 3-9-0 77........(h) JamieSpencer 5 79+
(Luca Cumani) *mde all: rdn and drifted rt over 1f out: qcknd and in command ins fnl f: comf* **7/2**[3]

2- **2** 2 **Considered Opinion**[409] 5400 3-9-0 0........ PatDobbs 1 73
(Ralph Beckett) *hld up in tch in midfield: effrt and hdwy on inner over 1f out: chsd clr wnr jst ins fnl f: kpt on but nvr a threat* **5/2**[2]

2032 **3** 1¾ **Narjes**[20] 6818 3-9-0 76........(h) TomQueally 8 69
(James Fanshawe) *in tch in midfield: effrt on outer 2f out: swtchd lft and drvn over 1f out: wnt 3rd and edgd lft ins fnl f: kpt on but no threat to wnr* **7/2**[3]

6603 **4** 1½ **Junoesque**[55] 5545 3-8-9 58........(p) GeorgeBuckell(5) 6 65
(John Gallagher) *dwlt: hld up in tch in last pair: effrt 2f out: hdwy 1f out: styd on ins fnl f: nvr trbld ldrs* **66/1**

40 **5** ¾ **Isstoora (IRE)**[18] 6899 3-9-0 0........ DanielMuscutt 7 63
(Marco Botti) *in tch in midfield: effrt on inner whn squeezed for room over 1f out: sn drvn and no imp: wknd ins fnl f* **25/1**

**6** 1 **Wedding Photo (USA)** 3-9-0 0........ SilvestreDeSousa 4 61
(Saeed bin Suroor) *chsd ldrs tl wnt 2nd 3f out: unable qck u.p and edgd lft over 1f out: wkng whn sltly hmpd ins fnl f* **2/1**[1]

0 **7** nse **Tennessee Belle**[35] 6287 3-9-0 0........ LukeMorris 3 61
(James Tate) *t.k.h: chsd wnr tl 3f out: rdn and unable qck whn squeezed for room over 1f out: wknd ins fnl f* **33/1**

0 **8** 3¾ **Calm Charm (IRE)**[20] 6817 3-9-0 0........ TedDurcan 2 52
(Chris Wall) *s.i.s: hld up in tch in rr: pushed along over 1f out: no imp and swtchd rt 1f out: wknd* **33/1**

1m 37.93s (-1.97) **Going Correction** -0.175s/f (Stan) **8** Ran SP% **117.6**
Speed ratings (Par 100): **102,100,98,96,96 95,94,91**
CSF £12.76 TOTE £4.40: £1.20, £1.60, £1.40; EX 17.40 Trifecta £43.70.
**Owner** S Stuckey **Bred** Stuart Stuckey **Trained** Newmarket, Suffolk
■ Stewards' Enquiry : Tom Queally caution: careless riding

**FOCUS**
This looked quite a competitive little maiden, but the winner had the run of things and won easily, and the 4th limits the level.

## 7486 BET TOTEWIN AT BETFRED.COM H'CAP 5f (P)
8:40 (8:41) (Class 5) (0-70,72) 3-Y-O+ £5,175 (£1,540; £769; £384) Stalls Low

Form RPR

3624 **1** **You're Cool**[40] 6089 5-9-5 **71**........ LewisEdmunds(3) 4 81
(John Balding) *mde all: rdn over 1f out: clr w runner-up 1f out: styd on strly and asserted wl ins fnl f: rdn out* **7/1**

1225 **2** 1½ **Noah Amor (IRE)**[10] 7137 4-9-7 **70**........ DavidNolan 1 75
(David O'Meara) *trckd ldng pair: wnt 2nd over 1f out: effrt 1f out: drvn and pressing wnr ins fnl f: no ex and wknd towards fin* **3/1**[1]

6413 **3** 2½ **Annie Salts**[7] 7256 4-9-9 **72**........(h) SilvestreDeSousa 6 68
(Chris Dwyer) *taken down early: midfield: effrt over 1f out: kpt on ins fnl f to go 3rd 75yds out: no threat to wnr* **6/1**[3]

0200 **4** nk **Savannah Beau**[6] 7268 5-9-5 **68**........(v) TonyHamilton 5 63
(Derek Shaw) *stdd s: hld up off the pce in last trio: hdwy but stl plenty to do over 1f out: hdwy ins fnl f: styd on wl to go 4th cl home: nvr trbld ldrs* **16/1**

3605 **5** ¾ **Shackled N Drawn (USA)**[22] 6764 5-9-4 **67**........(p) TomMarquand 8 59
(Peter Hedger) *taken down early: chsd wnr tl over 1f out: 3rd and outpcd 1f out: wknd and lost 2 pls wl ins fnl f* **33/1**

1245 **6** 1 **Berryessa (IRE)**[81] 4574 3-9-7 **71**........ DavidProbert 3 59
(Rae Guest) *hld up off the pce in midfield: effrt and drvn over 1f out: kpt on same pce and no imp ins fnl f: nvr trbld ldrs* **6/1**[3]

6240 **7** *nk* **Red Stripes (USA)**[12] 7099 5-8-9 **58**....(b) BenCurtis 2 45
(Lisa Williamson) *awkward leaving stalls and s.i.s: sn bustled in rr: switching lft and sme hdwy ins fnl f: n.d* **7/2**[2]

1010 **8** *3/4* **Red Invader (IRE)**[50] 5723 7-9-6 **69**....(p) LiamKeniry 10 53
(John Butler) *awkward leaving stalls and s.i.s: hdwy into midfield 3f out: swtchd rt over 1f out: hung lft and no imp ins fnl f* **10/1**

0056 **9** *9* **Krystallite**[29] 6527 4-9-2 **65**....(p) LukeMorris 7 17
(Scott Dixon) *s.i.s: bhd and nvr travelling wl in rr: n.d* **25/1**

-313 **10** *6* **Absolutely Awesome**[96] 4005 3-9-4 **68**.... JFEgan 11
(John Butler) *sn pushed along in midfield and nvr travelling: lost pl over 1f out: bhd ins fnl f* **7/1**

58.76s (-1.44) **Going Correction** -0.175s/f (Stan)
**WFA** 3 from 4yo+ 1lb 10 Ran SP% **122.6**
Speed ratings (Par 103): **104,101,97,97,95 94,93,92,78,68**
CSF £29.85 CT £142.27 TOTE £9.50: £3.10, £1.10, £2.80; EX 35.60 Trifecta £195.90.
**Owner** D Bichan & The Late J Roberts **Bred** Tirnaskea Stud **Trained** Scrooby, S Yorks

**FOCUS**
This looked an open sprint but few got into it, with the pace holding up once again.

## 7487 BOOK YOUR CHRISTMAS PARTY HERE H'CAP 6f (P)
**9:10** (9:13) (Class 6) (0-55,55) 3-Y-0+ **£3,234** (£962; £481; £240) **Stalls** Centre

Form RPR
0004 **1** **Fikhaar**[18] 6903 3-9-4 **55**.... KevinStott 1 61
(Kevin Ryan) *mde all: rdn over 1f out: kpt on wl ins fnl f: rdn out* **5/2**[1]

0001 **2** *3/4* **Hurricane Rock**[26] 6635 4-9-3 **52**.... HarryBentley 10 56
(Simon Dow) *hld up in tch in midfield: effrt over 1f out: hdwy u.p ins fnl f: wnt 2nd wl ins fnl f: kpt on wl: nvr quite getting to wnr* **9/2**[2]

4105 **3** *1 1/4* **Firesnake (IRE)**[19] 6850 4-9-6 **55**....(v) LukeMorris 3 55
(Lisa Williamson) *chsd wnr: rdn over 1f out: drvn and kpt on same pce ins fnl f: lost 2nd wl ins fnl f* **8/1**

1533 **4** *hd* **State Residence (IRE)**[10] 7166 3-9-2 **53**....(vt) DavidNolan 11 52
(David O'Meara) *hld up in tch towards rr: effrt and swtchd rt over 1f out: styd on wl u.p fnl 100yds: nt rch ldrs* **10/1**

5002 **5** *hd* **Tasaaboq**[3] 7407 6-8-11 **53**....(t) NicolaCurrie(7) 4 52
(Phil McEntee) *hld up in tch in midfield: effrt over 1f out: chsd ldrs 1f out: kpt on same pce ins fnl f* **7/1**

5306 **6** *shd* **Doctor Parkes**[66] 5146 11-9-1 **55**.... PaddyPilley(5) 5 53
(Natalie Lloyd-Beavis) *chsd ldrs: effrt over 1f out: chsd ldrs 1f out: rdn and kpt on same pce ins fnl f* **25/1**

035 **7** *3 1/4* **Gaia Princess (IRE)**[62] 5297 3-9-4 **55**....(p[1]) SilvestreDeSousa 2 43
(Gary Moore) *t.k.h: chsd ldrs: drvn over 1f out: no ex jst ins fnl f: btn and eased wl ins fnl f* **6/1**[3]

0002 **8** *2* **Fever Few**[20] 6813 8-9-3 **55**.... SimonPearce(3) 8 37
(Chris Wall) *in tch towards rr: effrt over 1f out: sme hdwy 1f out: kpt on ins fnl f: nvr trbld ldrs* **9/1**

005- **9** *1 1/2* **Mellow**[307] 8066 3-9-4 **55**.... LiamKeniry 9 32
(Hughie Morrison) *taken down early: bhd and rdn over 1f out: sme hdwy u.p 1f out: nvr trbld ldrs* **20/1**

0220 **10** *nse* **Harlequin Rose (IRE)**[38] 6174 3-9-4 **55**....(v) DavidProbert 12 32
(Patrick Chamings) *hld up towards rr: effrt over 1f out: no imp: nvr trbld ldrs* **25/1**

4430 **11** *nk* **Manipura**[42] 6041 4-9-4 **53**....(p) RyanPowell 13 29
(Derek Shaw) *stuck wd: midfield: rdn over 2f out: wknd u.p fnl f* **33/1**

5600 **12** *1 1/2* **Jazz Legend (USA)**[8] 7218 4-9-2 **51**....(h) BenCurtis 7 22
(Mandy Rowland) *t.k.h: hld up in midfield: effrt over 1f out: no imp: wknd fnl f* **33/1**

-000 **13** *2* **Sandacres**[34] 6303 4-9-6 **55**....(p[1]) JohnFahy 6 19
(Laura Mongan) *chsd ldrs tl 2f: sn lost pl: bhd ins fnl f* **33/1**

1m 12.29s (-1.41) **Going Correction** -0.175s/f (Stan)
**WFA** 3 from 4yo+ 2lb 13 Ran SP% **125.0**
Speed ratings (Par 101): **102,101,99,99,98 98,94,91,89,89 89,87,84**
CSF £12.61 CT £82.13 TOTE £3.30: £1.50, £2.10, £1.60; EX 17.00 Trifecta £116.30.
**Owner** Hambleton Racing Ltd XVIII & CN Farm Ltd **Bred** Shadwell Estate Company Limited **Trained** Hambleton, N Yorks

**FOCUS**
A moderate sprint, and another winner from the front. A pb from the winner.
T/Jkpt: Not Won. T/Plt: £92.40 to a £1 stake. Pool: £86,106.71 - 679.85 winning units T/Qpdt: £15.90 to a £1 stake. Pool: £12,299.30 - 568.92 winning units **Steve Payne**

# 7151 LINGFIELD (L-H)
Tuesday, September 26

**OFFICIAL GOING: Polytrack: standard**
Wind: Virtually nil Weather: Fine, warm

## 7488 GET 1/4 ODDS AT 188BET MAIDEN AUCTION STKS (DIV I) 1m 1y(P)
**2:00** (2:05) (Class 5) 2-Y-0 **£2,911** (£866; £432; £216) **Stalls** High

Form RPR
00 **1** **Dream Mount (IRE)**[18] 6883 2-9-5 0.... HarryBentley 6 75
(Marco Botti) *trckd ldrs: shkn up and brought between rivals to ld jst over 1f out: rdn out: readily* **6/1**

0 **2** *1 1/4* **Blame Culture (USA)**[46] 5887 2-9-5 0.... DanielMuscutt 8 72
(George Margarson) *trckd ldrs: rdn to dispute 3rd over 2f out: tried to chal on outer over 1f out: drvn to take 2nd ins fnl f: no real threat to wnr* **7/2**[1]

**3** *1 1/4* **Exec Chef (IRE)** 2-9-5 0.... JamieSpencer 10 69+
(David Simcock) *trckd ldr after 2f: led 2f out: rdn and hdd jst over 1f out: one pce* **5/1**[3]

**4** *3/4* **Craving (IRE)** 2-9-5 0.... RyanPowell 4 67
(Simon Crisford) *trckd ldr 2f: styd cl up on inner: nt clr run over 1f out: swtchd rt and lost grnd: rdn and styd on ins fnl f* **15/2**

**5** *nk* **Mr Reckless (IRE)** 2-9-5 0.... DougieCostello 5 66
(Jamie Osborne) *in tch but pushed along in midfield bef 1/2-way: rdn 3f out: styd on wl fr over 1f out: nrst fin* **8/1**

**6** *4* **Pepper Street (IRE)** 2-9-0 0.... JamesDoyle 9 52
(Hugo Palmer) *difficult to load into stall: led: shkn up and hdd 2f out: wknd fnl f* **9/2**[2]

**7** *2 3/4* **Folies Bergeres** 2-9-0 0.... RobHornby 1 45
(Jonathan Portman) *s.i.s: wl in rr: outpcd fr 3f out: pushed along and one pce after: nt disgracd* **16/1**

**8** *8* **Demons And Wizards (IRE)** 2-9-0 0.... MitchGodwin(5) 3 31
(Sylvester Kirk) *in tch to 3f out: sn wknd and bhd* **25/1**

0 **9** *4 1/2* **Ede's A Winner**[50] 5717 2-9-0 0.... FergusSweeney 7 15
(Pat Phelan) *a in rr: lost tch over 3f out: t.o* **100/1**

**10** *nk* **Spring Ability (IRE)** 2-9-5 0.... JohnFahy 11 20
(Laura Mongan) *s.v.s: a in rr: wknd 3f out: t.o* **50/1**

1m 40.55s (2.35) **Going Correction** +0.225s/f (Slow) 10 Ran SP% **106.9**
Speed ratings (Par 95): **97,95,94,93,93 89,86,78,74,73**
CSF £22.57 TOTE £5.60: £1.90, £1.20, £1.90; EX 16.70 Trifecta £98.40.
**Owner** G Manfredini & J Allison **Bred** Oghill House, Limefield Stud & D Hyland **Trained** Newmarket, Suffolk

**FOCUS**
A weak maiden.

## 7489 GET 1/4 ODDS AT 188BET MAIDEN AUCTION STKS (DIV II) 1m 1y(P)
**2:35** (2:35) (Class 5) 2-Y-0 **£2,911** (£866; £432; £216) **Stalls** High

Form RPR
55 **1** **Connaught Ranger (IRE)**[18] 6885 2-9-5 0.... TomQueally 9 76
(Denis Coakley) *in tch: rdn and prog over 2f out: clsd on outer to ld jst over 1f out: sn clr: styd on* **6/1**

00 **2** *1 3/4* **Protected Guest**[7] 7250 2-9-5 0.... DanielMuscutt 7 74
(George Margarson) *in tch: shoved along in 6th over 2f out: nt clr run on inner over 1f out: swtchd rt and hanging briefly: drvn and r.o to take 2nd ins fnl f: nvr able to chal* **16/1**

0 **3** *1 3/4* **North Bay Sunrise (IRE)**[14] 7033 2-9-0 0.... AdamBeschizza 6 63
(Ed Vaughan) *trckd ldrs: shkn up over 2f out: nt qckn over 1f out: styd on fnl f to take 3rd last 75yds* **7/1**

4405 **4** *2* **Gossip Column (IRE)**[11] 7106 2-9-5 71.... SilvestreDeSousa 8 63
(Charles Hills) *sweating: pressed ldr: chal over 2f out: nt qckn and lost 2nd over 1f out: wknd* **2/1**[1]

4 **5** *1* **Gripper**[26] 6636 2-9-5 0.... PatDobbs 4 61
(Ralph Beckett) *trckd ldng pair on inner: rdn 3f out: stl cl up jst over 1f out: fdd* **3/1**[2]

564 **6** *1 1/4* **Montague (IRE)**[18] 6868 2-9-5 75.... DougieCostello 1 58
(Jamie Osborne) *mde most to jst over 1f out: wknd* **5/1**[3]

**7** *6* **Demurrer (USA)** 2-9-5 0.... LouisSteward 10 43
(Michael Bell) *s.i.s: pushed along in rr after 2f: nvr a factor* **12/1**

0 **8** *8* **Dorian Gray (IRE)**[18] 6885 2-9-5 0.... AdamKirby 5 24
(Hughie Morrison) *a in rr: bhd over 2f out* **25/1**

**9** *19* **Santiago Rock (IRE)** 2-9-5 0.... FergusSweeney 2
(Noel Williams) *s.i.s: v green and a struggling: t.o* **66/1**

1m 40.42s (2.22) **Going Correction** +0.225s/f (Slow) 9 Ran SP% **120.7**
Speed ratings (Par 95): **97,95,93,91,90 89,83,75,56**
CSF £99.50 TOTE £7.50: £2.00, £6.10, £2.10; EX 160.60 Trifecta £1108.90.
**Owner** A Killoran **Bred** Michael Ryan **Trained** West Ilsley, Berks

**FOCUS**
Another weak maiden and it set up for the closers.

## 7490 SOUTHERN TESTING 50TH ANNIVERSARY H'CAP 1m 7f 169y(P)
**3:05** (3:07) (Class 6) (0-65,65) 3-Y-0+ **£2,587** (£770; £384; £192) **Stalls** Low

Form RPR
0032 **1** **Alternate Route**[7] 7233 3-8-9 **56**....(p) LukeMorris 10 73+
(Sir Mark Prescott Bt) *w ldrs: led 7f out: rdn clr over 2f out: drvn 8 l ahd over 1f out: heavily eased last 100yds* **13/8**[1]

4250 **2** *3 3/4* **St Andrews (IRE)**[29] 6509 4-9-0 **51**....(p) StevieDonohoe 6 55
(Ian Williams) *pressed ldrs: racd awkwardly at times: chsd wnr over 6f out to 5f out: drvn and bdly outpcd in 4th over 2f out but stl wl clr of rest: styd on again over 1f out: tk 2nd last strides* **20/1**

0566 **3** *nk* **Archangel Raphael (IRE)**[21] 6781 5-10-0 **65**....(v) PatDobbs 1 68
(Amanda Perrett) *hld up in rr: stdy prog fr 6f out: chsd ldng pair 3f out: sn rdn and outpcd: drvn to chse clr wnr 1f out: no imp and lost 2nd last strides* **20/1**

1063 **4** *1 1/4* **Tojosimbre**[8] 7210 3-7-9 **49**....(tp) NicolaCurrie(7) 11 53
(Richard Hughes) *stdd s: hld up wl in rr: stl there and ldrs gng clr whn impeded 4f out: stdy prog over 3f out: shkn up to take remote 5th 2f out: styd on wl after: nrst fin but hopeless task* **16/1**

3561 **5** *1 3/4* **Macksville (IRE)**[5] 7319 4-9-8 **64** 6ex....(b) JoshuaBryan(5) 8 64
(James Eustace) *prom: chsd wnr 5f out: rdn and outpcd over 2f out: lost 2nd and wknd 1f out* **3/1**[2]

21-5 **6** *19* **Fearless Lad (IRE)**[36] 6258 7-9-13 **64**.... SilvestreDeSousa 2 41
(John Best) *dwlt: hld up in rr: already drvn whn hmpd 4f out: sme prog over 3f out but nvr remotely a threat* **7/1**[3]

06-0 **7** *8* **Magnus Romeo**[65] 3026 6-8-11 **48**....(t) JohnFahy 13 15
(Johnny Farrelly) *s.s: detached in last tl after 1/2-way: wl bhd 3f out: passed toiling rivals after* **66/1**

2123 **8** *1 1/4* **Night Generation (GER)**[96] 4000 5-9-13 **64**....(p) AdamKirby 7 30
(Chris Gordon) *pushed up to chse ldr after 3f but nvr looked that happy: lost 2nd sn after 1/2-way and lost pl steadily after: wl bhd 3f out* **10/1**

5066 **9** *3/4* **Crystal Secret**[30] 6473 3-8-0 **47** oh1....(b) KieranO'Neill 5 14
(John Bridger) *w ldrs to 1/2-way: sn lost pl u.p: wl bhd 3f out* **100/1**

0020 **10** *5* **Astroshadow**[29] 6530 3-8-3 **50** ow2.... JoeyHaynes 9 11
(Mark H Tompkins) *t.k.h early: hld up in tch: rdn and wknd over 5f out: sn wl bhd* **50/1**

4400 **11** *36* **See And Be Seen**[20] 6820 7-9-2 **58**....(p) MitchGodwin(5) 3
(Sylvester Kirk) *hld up: brief effrt 5f out: sn wknd rapidly: t.o* **14/1**

620 **12** *31* **Bumble Bay**[26] 6623 7-9-4 **55**....(t) LiamKeniry 4
(Robert Stephens) *dwlt: trckd ldrs: wnt 3rd over 5f out and looked to be gng wl: sn rdn and wknd v rapidly: t.o* **33/1**

5-05 **13** *34* **Meetings Man (IRE)**[21] 6796 10-9-6 **57**....(p) TomMarquand 12
(Ali Stronge) *led to over 7f out: wknd rapidly: t.o* **20/1**

3m 27.93s (2.23) **Going Correction** +0.225s/f (Slow)
**WFA** 3 from 4yo+ 10lb 13 Ran SP% **118.9**
Speed ratings (Par 101): **103,101,100,100,99 89,85,85,84,82 64,48,31**
CSF £42.94 CT £502.28 TOTE £2.30: £1.10, £6.40, £5.60; EX 38.20 Trifecta £572.40.
**Owner** P J McSwiney - Osborne House **Bred** Miss K Rausing & J S Bolger **Trained** Newmarket, Suffolk

**FOCUS**
A moderate staying handicap.

## 7491 EUROPEAN BREEDERS FUND NURSERY H'CAP 5f 6y(P)
**3:40** (3:42) (Class 5) (0-70,70) 2-Y-0 **£2,911** (£866; £432; £216) **Stalls** High

Form RPR
0342 **1** **Maygold**[9] 7194 2-9-1 **64**....(h) LiamKeniry 8 68+
(Ed Walker) *hld up towards rr: shkn up over 1f out: str run fnl f: edgd lft but led last strides* **4/1**[1]

064 **2** *1/2* **Three Little Birds**[23] 6719 2-9-4 **70**.... DavidEgan(3) 2 72
(Sylvester Kirk) *led but pressed: drvn over 1f out: looked like clinging on but hdd last strides* **8/1**

4233 **3** 3/4 **Spanish Star (IRE)**[9] 7193 2-9-6 **69**.............................. DavidProbert 3 68
(Patrick Chamings) *t.k.h: hld up towards rr: shkn up 2f out: prog to press ldrs ins fnl f: styd on same pce* **7/1**

6220 **4** 1/2 **Laura Knight (IRE)**[13] 7057 2-9-2 **65**..............................(p) AdamKirby 6 63
(Gary Moore) *pressed ldr: rdn to chal over 1f out: hanging and fnd nil: lost 2nd and already btn whn hmpd nr fin* **5/1**[3]

5036 **5** shd **Gaelic Spirit (IRE)**[11] 7126 2-9-4 **67**.............................. OisinMurphy 1 64
(Joseph Tuite) *trckd ldrs on inner: rdn to chal fnl f: nt qckn last 100yds* **10/1**

0530 **6** 1/2 **Adulate**[19] 6860 2-9-6 **69**..............................(v[1]) JamesDoyle 5 64
(Hugo Palmer) *trckd ldrs: shkn up wl over 1f out: nvr clrest of runs but nvr looked like finding much either* **9/2**[2]

404 **7** 1/2 **Blessed To Empress (IRE)**[22] 6749 2-9-1 **64**......... SilvestreDeSousa 4 63
(Amy Murphy) *dwlt: n.m.r after 100yds: last tl gd prog on inner over 1f out: nowhere to go fnl f and lost all ch* **9/2**[2]

2460 **8** 1 1/2 **Zain Flash**[20] 6825 2-9-1 **64**.............................. JFEgan 9 52
(David Evans) *chsd ldrs on outer: lost pl fr 2f out: no ch ins fnl f* **20/1**

4550 **9** hd **Catapult**[59] 5440 2-9-3 **66**.............................. PaoloSirigu 10 53
(Robert Eddery) *pressed ldrs on outer: wknd over 1f out* **20/1**

6246 **10** nse **Diamond Express (IRE)**[53] 5586 2-8-13 **67**.............. MitchGodwin(5) 7 54
(Roger Teal) *wl in rr: drvn in last over 1f out: no ch after: kpt on late* **50/1**

1m 1.4s (2.60) **Going Correction** +0.225s/f (Slow) **10** Ran SP% **117.2**
Speed ratings (Par 95): **88,87,86,85,85 84,83,81,80,80**
CSF £35.63 CT £224.89 TOTE £3.90: £1.60, £2.20, £2.40; EX 37.30 Trifecta £218.00.
**Owner** Farleigh Racing **Bred** Farleigh Court Racing Partnership **Trained** Upper Lambourn, Berks

**FOCUS**
A modest sprint nursery rated as straightforward form around 2/3/4.

## 7492 DAILY RACING SPECIALS AT 188BET MAIDEN FILLIES' STKS 1m 2f (P)
**4:15** (4:18) (Class 5) 3-Y-0+ **£2,911** (£866; £432; £216) **Stalls** Low

Form RPR

**1** **Part Exchange** 3-9-0 **0**.............................. JamesDoyle 13 91+
(Hugo Palmer) *dwlt: sn in midfield: shkn up over 3f out: gd prog on wd outside after: led 2f out: drvn clr over 1f out: styd on wl* **5/1**[3]

242 **2** 6 **Pretty Passe**[39] 6161 3-9-0 **75**.............................. MartinHarley 3 78
(William Haggas) *trckd ldrs: prog on outer to ld over 2f out: hdd 2f out: outpcd by wnr over 1f out* **4/1**[2]

**3** 4 **Valley Of Light** 3-9-0 **0**.............................. OisinMurphy 4 70+
(Saeed bin Suroor) *dwlt: sn wl in tch: shkn up and effrt to chse ldng pair 2f out: wl outpcd sn after* **5/6**[1]

303 **4** 3/4 **Jafetica**[20] 6817 3-9-0 **71**..............................(h) TomQueally 6 69+
(James Fanshawe) *trckd ldrs: outpcd 3f out: shkn up and kpt on fr over 1f out* **8/1**

-305 **5** 2 1/2 **Zafaranah (USA)**[35] 6287 3-9-0 **68**.............................. RobHornby 1 64
(Pam Sly) *trckd ldrs: gng strly 3f out: shkn up and fnd nil 2f out: wknd over 1f out* **25/1**

5423 **6** 1 1/4 **Saniyaat**[22] 6765 3-9-0 **74**..............................(v) HarryBentley 12 61
(George Peckham) *dwlt but led: hdd over 2f out: sn wknd* **9/1**

0005 **7** 11 **Shamonix (IRE)**[20] 6828 3-9-0 **40**.............................. DanielMuscutt 5 39
(Mark Usher) *in tch to over 4f out: sn wknd and bhd* **100/1**

**8** 9 **Hewouldwouldnthe** 3-9-0 **0**.............................. LukeMorris 8 21
(Jonathan Portman) *dwlt: a in rr: lost tch over 3f out: sn bhd* **66/1**

0-0 **9** 8 **Kath's Legend**[35] 6283 3-9-0 **0**.............................. RyanTate 2 5
(Ben De Haan) *t.k.h early: chsd ldr to 3f out: wknd rapidly* **66/1**

**10** 7 **Ali The Hunter (IRE)**[33] 4-9-5 **0**.............................. RobertWinston 11
(Johnny Farrelly) *hld up in last trio: lost tch over 3f out: eased 2f out* **66/1**

04 **11** 10 **The Lady Rules**[13] 7059 3-9-0 **0**.............................. AdamBeschizza 9
(Mrs Ilka Gansera-Leveque) *unruly bef s: swvd rt s: a wl in rr: t.o 3f out* **80/1**

**12** 2 1/4 **Bombay Rascal**[28] 4-9-0 **0**.............................. MitchGodwin(5) 10
(Robert Walford) *dwlt and impeded s: a in rr: t.o over 3f out* **100/1**

2m 6.47s (-0.13) **Going Correction** +0.225s/f (Slow)
**WFA** 3 from 4yo 5lb **12** Ran SP% **123.9**
Speed ratings (Par 100): **109,104,101,100,98 97,88,81,75,69 61,59**
CSF £26.25 TOTE £5.70: £2.10, £1.60, £1.10; EX 25.30 Trifecta £63.30.
**Owner** K Abdullah **Bred** Juddmonte Farms Ltd **Trained** Newmarket, Suffolk

**FOCUS**
An uncompetitive fillies' maiden but quite a good, promising performance from the winner. The form has been rated around the 2nd/4th.

## 7493 HAPPY 80TH BIRTHDAY EDDIE CHILDS H'CAP 1m 1y(P)
**4:45** (4:46) (Class 5) (0-75,75) 3-Y-0+ **£2,911** (£866; £432; £216) **Stalls** High

Form RPR

4133 **1** **Easy Code**[13] 7058 4-9-2 **69**.............................. JamesDoyle 9 78+
(William Haggas) *hld up but rchd midfield after 3f: prog on inner 2f out to chse clr ldng pair over 1f out: rdn and clsd qckly fnl f: led last 75yds: won gng away* **9/4**[1]

0015 **2** 1 **Bluff Crag**[21] 6795 4-8-13 **73**..............................(p[1]) StephenCummins(7) 3 79
(Richard Hughes) *disp ld 1f: trckd ldr after: rdn to ld over 1f out: styd on but hdd and outpcd last 75yds* **12/1**

0 **3** 1 1/4 **Spiritual Star (IRE)**[40] 6101 8-9-0 **72**.............................. PaddyBradley(5) 12 75
(Lee Carter) *dropped in fr wd draw and hld up in last: stl last over 2f out: rapid prog on inner over 1f out: drvn and r.o to take 3rd last 75yds: too late to threaten* **25/1**

4350 **4** 1 3/4 **First Experience**[11] 7130 6-9-3 **73**..............................(v) CharlieBennett(3) 11 72
(Lee Carter) *rousted on outer to ld after 1f: rdn 2f out: hdd over 1f out: fdd ins fnl f* **66/1**

0000 **5** 3/4 **Choral Clan (IRE)**[26] 6620 6-9-3 **70**.............................. DanielMuscutt 10 67
(Brendan Powell) *hld up towards rr: shkn up over 2f out: prog over 1f out: styd on fnl f: no ch to threaten* **33/1**

605U **6** 1 1/2 **Groor**[12] 7098 5-9-8 **75**.............................. DavidProbert 6 69
(Mohamed Moubarak) *hld up towards rr: shkn up over 2f out: sme prog over 1f out and kpt on: n.d* **10/1**

4600 **7** 1 1/2 **Braztime**[20] 6818 3-9-3 **74**.............................. TomMarquand 8 64
(Richard Hannon) *wl in rr and nt gng wl: nvr a factor but kpt on fr over 1f out* **33/1**

-300 **8** 3/4 **Manangatang (IRE)**[113] 3392 3-9-4 **75**.............................. JamieSpencer 4 64
(Luca Cumani) *trckd ldrs in 6th: shkn up 3f out: stl to make any prog whn trapped bhd wkng rivals over 1f out: no ch after* **5/2**[2]

0060 **9** 3/4 **Lacan (IRE)**[41] 6068 6-9-6 **73**.............................. SilvestreDeSousa 1 60
(Brett Johnson) *chsd ldrs: rdn over 2f out: wknd over 1f out* **12/1**

4606 **10** 1 3/4 **Warrior's Spirit (IRE)**[21] 6792 3-9-2 **73**.............................. SeanLevey 7 56
(Richard Hannon) *disp ld 1f: chsd ldrs: rdn on outer 3f out: wknd 2f out* **17/2**

2400 **11** 3/4 **Skidby Mill (IRE)**[20] 6818 7-9-5 **72**.............................. PatCosgrave 2 53
(Laura Mongan) *pressed ldrs: rdn over 2f out: wknd qckly over 1f out* **50/1**

2441 **12** 23 **Unified**[76] 4737 3-9-3 **74**.............................. AdamKirby 5 2
(Clive Cox) *in tch tl rdn and wknd qckly over 3f out: t.o* **7/1**[3]

1m 39.11s (0.91) **Going Correction** +0.225s/f (Slow)
**WFA** 3 from 4yo+ 4lb **12** Ran SP% **120.0**
Speed ratings (Par 103): **104,103,101,100,99 97,96,95,94,93 92,69**
CSF £29.59 CT £560.90 TOTE £3.50: £1.30, £2.40, £5.90; EX 30.20 Trifecta £479.90.
**Owner** A R Legal Partnership **Bred** Usk Valley Stud **Trained** Newmarket, Suffolk

**FOCUS**
A modest handicap. The winner has been rated back to his best, with the 2nd posting a length pb.

## 7494 A J HILLS H'CAP 5f 6y(P)
**5:15** (5:16) (Class 6) (0-60,60) 3-Y-0+ **£2,264** (£673; £336; £168) **Stalls** High

Form RPR

4360 **1** **Prominna**[9] 7195 7-9-3 **56**.............................. DavidProbert 1 61
(Tony Carroll) *hld up in midfield: prog on inner over 1f out: drvn to chal fnl f: led nr fin: hld on* **11/2**[3]

-400 **2** shd **Grand Myla (IRE)**[27] 6581 3-9-6 **60**..............................(p) AdamKirby 5 65
(Gary Moore) *mde most: rdn 2f out: jnd u.p ins fnl f: hdd nr fin: kpt on but jst failed* **6/1**

0041 **3** hd **Evening Starlight**[9] 7190 4-9-6 **59** 6ex.............................. SteveDrowne 2 63
(Ron Hodges) *pressed ldr: rdn 2f out: chal and upsides ins fnl f: nt qckn nr fin* **11/2**[3]

6532 **4** nk **Exquisite Ruby**[33] 6339 3-9-6 **60**.............................. HarryBentley 3 63
(Charles Hills) *taken down early: trckd ldng pair: rdn and nt qckn over 1f out: styd on ins fnl f but jst too late to rch ldrs* **4/1**[1]

5562 **5** 1 3/4 **Mercers**[23] 6724 3-9-6 **60**.............................. NickyMackay 9 57
(Peter Crate) *in tch in last trio: pushed along 1/2-way: styd on fr over 1f out: nvr nrr but n.d* **8/1**

402 **6** 3/4 **Miss Rosina (IRE)**[35] 6298 3-8-11 **56**..............................(p) JaneElliott(5) 10 50
(George Margarson) *chsd ldrs on outer: rdn 1/2-way: wknd fnl f* **18/1**

0552 **7** 1 **Fleeting Glimpse**[9] 7190 4-8-12 **54**.............................. CharlieBennett(3) 6 44
(Patrick Chamings) *taken down early: dwlt: mostly in last: effrt on inner over 1f out: sn no prog* **12/1**

110 **8** 3/4 **Ask The Guru**[30] 6478 7-9-2 **55**..............................(b) KierenFox 7 43
(Michael Attwater) *chsd ldng pair: rdn 1/2-way: wknd over 1f out* **10/1**

4455 **9** nse **Entertaining Ben**[26] 6615 4-9-6 **59**.............................. SilvestreDeSousa 4 46
(Amy Murphy) *t.k.h: hld up in tch: rdn and nt qckn wl over 1f out: wknd* **5/1**[2]

6100 **10** 1 3/4 **Snoozy Sioux (IRE)**[33] 6339 3-9-3 **60**.............................. NoelGarbutt(3) 8 41
(Martin Smith) *dwlt: a wl in rr* **40/1**

1m 0.07s (1.27) **Going Correction** +0.225s/f (Slow)
**WFA** 3 from 4yo+ 1lb **10** Ran SP% **117.3**
Speed ratings (Par 101): **98,97,97,97,94 93,91,90,90,87**
CSF £38.77 CT £191.85 TOTE £6.30: £2.30, £2.10, £1.70; EX 53.10 Trifecta £388.90.
**Owner** Mayden Stud **Bred** Mayden Stud, J A And D S Dewhurst **Trained** Cropthorne, Worcs

**FOCUS**
Moderate but competitive with little separating the first four.

## 7495 BEST ODDS GUARANTEED AT 188BET H'CAP 1m 2f (P)
**5:45** (5:45) (Class 6) (0-65,67) 3-Y-0+ **£2,911** (£866; £432; £216) **Stalls** Low

Form RPR

-054 **1** **Scoones**[41] 6067 3-9-2 **65**.............................. DanielMuscutt 5 77+
(James Fanshawe) *t.k.h: hld up in tch: clsd on ldrs fr 2f out: pushed into ld 1f out: v comf* **3/1**[1]

0314 **2** 1 1/4 **Ban Shoof**[27] 6588 4-9-4 **65**..............................(b) HectorCrouch(3) 4 70
(Gary Moore) *hld up towards rr: prog over 2f out: squeezed through jst over 1f out: drvn to chse wnr ins fnl f and edgd lft: styd on but no ch* **7/1**

365 **3** 1 **Bayston Hill**[28] 6557 3-9-2 **65**.............................. DavidProbert 7 69
(Mark Usher) *hld up towards rr: prog whn trapped bhd rivals over 1f out and swtchd rt: r.o to take 3rd nr fin* **14/1**

0251 **4** nk **My Brother Mike (IRE)**[7] 7235 3-9-4 **67** 6ex.............................. DavidNolan 11 70
(Kevin Frost) *t.k.h: pressed ldrs: rdn to ld briefly jst over 1f out: outpcd fnl f* **7/2**[2]

5522 **5** 1 1/2 **Silver Dixie (USA)**[27] 6588 7-9-3 **61**..............................(p) CharlesBishop 10 61
(Peter Hedger) *hld up in rr: shuffled along fr 2f out: styd on to take 5th ins fnl f: nvr nr to chal* **10/1**

3-01 **6** 1 **Barnaby Brook (CAN)**[17] 6948 7-9-7 **65**..............(b) RichardKingscote 9 63
(Tom Dascombe) *hld up in midfield: shkn up on outer 2f out: kpt on fnl f but nvr cl enough to threaten* **9/2**[3]

0445 **7** nk **Pink Ribbon (IRE)**[15] 7004 5-9-0 **63**..............................(p) MitchGodwin(5) 1 61
(Sylvester Kirk) *hld up in midfield: effrt on inner 2f out: cl up but hld whn n.m.r jst ins fnl f: fdd* **16/1**

5500 **8** 3/4 **St James's Park (IRE)**[13] 7061 4-9-4 **62**.............................. DannyBrock 3 58
(Luke McJannet) *led 1f: styd prom: rdn on inner 2f out: fdd fnl f* **33/1**

1054 **9** 1 1/4 **Berkeley Vale**[27] 5427 6-9-6 **64**..............................(v) RobertWinston 8 58
(Roger Teal) *s.i.s: rapid prog arnd rivals to go 2nd over 6f out: rdn to ld 2f out: hdd jst over 1f out: wkng whn hmpd jst ins fnl f* **20/1**

0013 **10** 1 1/4 **Cat Royale (IRE)**[46] 5895 4-9-0 **65**..............................(p) DarraghKeenan(7) 13 56
(John Butler) *prom on outer tl wknd wl over 1f out* **25/1**

0-60 **11** 2 1/2 **Top Diktat**[30] 6475 9-8-12 **61**.............................. JoshuaBryan(5) 2 47
(Gary Moore) *hld up in last: shkn up over 2f out: no significant prog* **33/1**

416 **12** 2 1/2 **Frantical**[17] 6370 5-8-13 **60**..............................(p) CharlieBennett(3) 6 41
(Tony Carroll) *t.k.h: hld up in last trio: shkn up and no prog over 2f out: wknd* **33/1**

0254 **13** nk **Longside**[81] 4572 5-9-5 **63**.............................. RyanTate 12 54
(James Eustace) *sweeping move on wd outside to ld after 1f: set mod pce: rdn and hdd 2f out: wkng whn hmpd ins fnl f: eased* **25/1**

2m 9.47s (2.87) **Going Correction** +0.225s/f (Slow)
**WFA** 3 from 4yo+ 5lb **13** Ran SP% **120.8**
Speed ratings (Par 101): **97,96,95,94,93 92,92,92,91,90 88,86,85**
CSF £22.29 CT £252.83 TOTE £3.60: £1.80, £2.40, £4.20; EX 28.70 Trifecta £286.20.
**Owner** T R G Vestey **Bred** T R G Vestey **Trained** Newmarket, Suffolk
■ Stewards' Enquiry : Hector Crouch two-day ban: careless riding (10-11 Oct)

**FOCUS**
A moderate handicap. The 3rd helps pin the level.
T/Plt: £215.60 to a £1 stake. Pool: £66,501.23 - 225.07 winning units T/Qpdt: £7.70 to a £1 stake. Pool: £6,957.20 - 663.45 winning units **Jonathan Neesom**

7496 - 7502a (Foreign Racing) - See Raceform Interactive

## 6775 GOODWOOD (R-H)

Wednesday, September 27

**OFFICIAL GOING: Soft (5.7)**

Wind: virtually nil Weather: overcast

### 7503 "GET 1/4 ODDS AT 188BET" FUTURE STAYERS' MAIDEN STKS (PLUS 10 RACE) 1m 1f 197y

**2:10** (2:12) (Class 3) 2-Y-O **£7,762** (£2,310; £1,154; £577) **Stalls** Low

Form RPR

2 **1** **Setting Sail**15 7026 2-9-5 0 JamesDoyle 11 82+
*(Charlie Appleby) str: lw: hld up in tch in midfield: hdwy to chse ldrs and swtchd rt 2f out: chal between rivals whn edgd rt: short of room and bmpd ldr ent fnl f: drvn to ld 100yds out: styd on* **1/1**1

46 **2** ½ **Mt Augustus**22 6777 2-9-5 0 DaneO'Neill 5 79
*(Henry Candy) chsd ldrs: ev ch ent fnl 2f: rdn to ld over 1f out: edging lft u.p and bmpd ent fnl f: drvn and hdd 100yds out: kpt on* **12/1**

03 **3** 3¾ **Knightly Spirit**22 6777 2-9-5 0 AndreaAtzeni 8 72
*(Roger Varian) t.k.h: hld up in tch in midfield: hdwy to chse ldr over 5f out tl led 2f out: sn rdn and hdd over 1f out: edgd sltly rt 1f out: 3rd and wknd ins fnl f* **7/2**2

54 **4** 2 **Nebuchadnezzar (FR)**20 6859 2-9-5 0 FergusSweeney 2 68
*(Alan King) lw: hld up in tch in midfield: effrt to chse ldrs and rdn 2f out: unable qck and btn 1f out: wknd ins fnl f* **12/1**

35 **5** hd **La La Land (IRE)**19 6883 2-9-5 0 JamieSpencer 4 68
*(Jamie Osborne) s.i.s: hld up towards rr: swtchd lft over 2f out: rdn and no imp over 1f out: wl hld and kpt on same pce ins fnl f* **10/1**3

65 **6** 2 **Berkshire Spirit**29 6553 2-9-5 0 RobHornby 7 64
*(Andrew Balding) wl in tch in midfield: rdn and lost pl over 2f out: trying to rally and swtchd rt 1f out: kpt on but no ch w ldrs* **12/1**

44 **7** 3½ **Voice Of The North**14 7043 2-9-5 0 TomQueally 9 58
*(Mark Johnston) angular: led: rdn over 2f out: hdd 2f out: losing pl whn sltly hmpd over 1f out: sn wknd* **20/1**

**8** 1½ **Clan McGregor (IRE)** 2-9-5 0 ShaneKelly 10 55
*(Seamus Durack) leggy: hld up in tch towards rr: effrt 2f out: edgd lft and no imp over 1f out: sn wknd* **66/1**

0 **9** 2 **French Kiss (IRE)**12 7120 2-9-5 0 SilvestreDeSousa 3 51+
*(Hughie Morrison) str: swtg: s.i.s: hld up in rr: effrt 2f out: no imp: wl hld and eased ins fnl f* **33/1**

**10** 9 **Billy Ray** 2-9-5 0 JFEgan 1 34
*(Mick Channon) tall: unf: s.i.s: hld up in rr: hdwy to chse ldrs 5f out: rdn and lost pl over 2f out: bhd over 1f out* **40/1**

00 **11** 27 **Amenhotepthethird**20 6859 2-9-5 0 TimmyMurphy 6
*(Mark Gillard) chsd ldr tl over 5f out: steadily lost pl: lost tch 2f out: t.o* **250/1**

2m 15.51s (7.41) **Going Correction** +0.70s/f (Yiel) 11 Ran SP% **116.4**
Speed ratings (Par 99): **98,97,94,93,92 91,88,87,85,78 56**
CSF £14.19 TOTE £1.70: £1.02, £3.80, £1.40; EX 16.50 Trifecta £51.50.
**Owner** Godolphin **Bred** Godolphin **Trained** Newmarket, Suffolk

**FOCUS**
Top and bottom bends dolled out. Straight dolled out to the 2f marker. Race distance increased by 7yds. A juvenile maiden that served up a proper test as it was run at a sound early pace on deep going. They came stands' side in the home straight.

### 7504 TBA SMALL BREEDERS' FILLIES' CONDITIONS STKS (PLUS 10 RACE) 7f

**2:40** (2:41) (Class 2) 2-Y-O

**£15,562** (£4,660; £2,330; £1,165; £582; £292) **Stalls** Low

Form RPR

646 **1** **Pastamakesufaster**28 6584 2-8-10 60 JFEgan 1 76
*(David Evans) leggy: mde all: rdn 2f out: fnd ex and clr 1f out: styd on strly: readily* **8/1**3

6 **2** 5 **Savaanah (IRE)**15 7022 2-8-8 0 SilvestreDeSousa 5 62
*(Roger Varian) str: lw: chsd wnr: rdn ent fnl 2f: outpcd by wnr and hung rt over 1f out: no ch w wnr and kpt on same pce ins fnl f* **5/4**1

5 **3** 1¼ **Giving Glances**43 6037 2-8-8 0 FergusSweeney 7 58
*(Alan King) unf: scope: hld up in tch in last trio: effrt jst over 2f out: no imp over 1f out: no ch w wnr but kpt on ins fnl f: wnt 3rd last strides* **2/1**2

**4** nk **Zahraa** 2-8-10 0 TomMarquand 6 60
*(Robyn Brisland) leggy: in tch in midfield: effrt ent fnl 2f: outpcd by wnr and hung rt over 1f out: kpt on same pce ins fnl f* **10/1**

**5** 2¼ **Sky Bandit** 2-8-10 0 HectorCrouch 3 54
*(Gary Moore) w'like: bit bkwd: dwlt: in tch in last trio: effrt ent fnl 2f: swtchd rt over 1f out: no imp: wknd ins fnl f* **16/1**

**6** 1 **Tigerfilly** 2-9-0 0 JackOsborn 2 56
*(John Ryan) w'like: dwlt: sn rcvrd to trck ldrs: swtchd lft jst over 2f out: rdn and outpcd by wnr over 1f out: wknd ins fnl f* **50/1**

**7** 10 **Maggie Jonks** 2-9-0 0 RobHornby 8 31
*(Andrew Balding) tall: rn green: sn dropped to rr: lost tch over 1f out* **12/1**

1m 32.04s (5.04) **Going Correction** +0.70s/f (Yiel) 7 Ran SP% **113.5**
Speed ratings (Par 98): **99,93,91,91,88 87,76**
CSF £18.26 TOTE £8.50: £3.10, £1.30; EX 21.10 Trifecta £48.90.
**Owner** R Kent **Bred** Nell Kent **Trained** Pandy, Monmouths

**FOCUS**
Race distance increased by 10yds. A 2yo fillies' event blown wide open by the non-runner. It was run at a fair pace and this time they kept far side.

### 7505 FULLER, SMITH & TURNER PLC H'CAP 1m 1f 197y

**3:10** (3:12) (Class 4) (0-85,86) 3-Y-O+ **£6,469** (£1,925; £962; £481) **Stalls** Low

Form RPR

2062 **1** **Lunar Jet**33 6389 3-8-6 71 JimmyQuinn 3 83
*(John Mackie) dwlt and pushed along leaving stalls: sn rcvrd and travelled wl in midfield: shkn up to ld over 1f out: readily qcknd clr fnl f: easily* **11/2**

6004 **2** 3¼ **Zamperini (IRE)**12 7132 5-9-1 75 JimmyFortune 7 80
*(Mike Murphy) stdd s: hld up in tch in rr: hdwy over 2f out: rdn to press ldrs 2f out: 2nd and outpcd by wnr 1f out: no ch w wnr but kpt on for 2nd* **12/1**

4142 **3** 1¼ **Me Too Nagasaki (IRE)**111 3504 3-9-7 86 JamesDoyle 4 89+
*(Jeremy Noseda) lw: hld up in tch in last trio: clsd to trck ldrs 2f out: sn swtchd lft and effrt to chse ldrs over 1f out: 3rd and outpcd whn hung lft and hmpd ins fnl f* **3/1**1

2454 **4** hd **Road To Dubai (IRE)**32 6423 3-8-12 77 SilvestreDeSousa 8 81+
*(George Scott) hld up in tch in last trio: short of room and hmpd over 1f out: sn swtchd rt and hdwy 1f out: styd on ins fnl f: no ch w wnr* **4/1**3

4611 **5** ¾ **Turnpike Trip**21 6822 3-9-3 82 DaneO'Neill 6 83
*(Henry Candy) lw: in tch in midfield: effrt whn carried lft and short of room over 1f out: squeezed through against rail but no ch w wnr 1f out: kpt on same pce after* **7/2**2

455 **6** 3¾ **Zzoro (IRE)**12 7132 4-9-12 86 PatDobbs 2 79
*(Amanda Perrett) led: rdn 2f out: edging lft and hdd over 1f out: sn outpcd and btn: wknd fnl f* **9/1**

5026 **7** 2¾ **Pendo**27 6617 6-9-3 77 LukeMorris 5 65
*(John Best) in tch in midfield: rdn 3f out: lost pl and bhd whn drifted rt over 1f out: wknd fnl f* **20/1**

3613 **8** ½ **Mr Red Clubs (IRE)**12 7111 8-9-3 77 (p) KierenFox 1 64
*(Henry Tett) chsd ldrs: rdn to chse ldr jst over 2f out: sn struggling and lost pl over 1f out: bhd ins fnl f* **25/1**

2361 **9** 3¼ **Lady Valdean**29 6566 3-9-0 79 OscarPereira 9 59
*(Jose Santos) swtg: chsd ldr tl jst over 2f out: sn lost pl: bhd fnl f* **25/1**

2m 13.37s (5.27) **Going Correction** +0.70s/f (Yiel)
**WFA** 3 from 4yo+ 5lb 9 Ran SP% **112.8**
Speed ratings (Par 105): **106,103,102,102,101 98,96,96,93**
CSF £64.13 CT £231.32 TOTE £5.40: £1.80, £3.40, £1.50; EX 75.10 Trifecta £853.10.
**Owner** Ladas **Bred** Ladas **Trained** Church Broughton , Derbys

■ Stewards' Enquiry : Pat Dobbs two day ban: careless riding (11/12 Oct)

**FOCUS**
Race distance increased by 7yds. A fair handicap, run at a sound pace, and another step forward from the winner. This time the runners kept to the middle before coming stands' side 2f out.

### 7506 EBF STALLIONS FOUNDATION STKS (LISTED RACE) 1m 1f 197y

**3:45** (3:46) (Class 1) 3-Y-O+

**£22,684** (£8,600; £4,304; £2,144; £1,076; £540) **Stalls** Low

Form RPR

1442 **1** **Monarchs Glen**25 6698 3-8-11 101 RobertTart 6 111
*(John Gosden) swtg: t.k.h: hld up in tch in midfield: hdwy to chse ldrs 4f out: rdn to ld over 1f out: sustained duel w runner up fnl f: hld on wl u.p: all out* **4/1**2

2100 **2** shd **What About Carlo (FR)**4 7393 6-9-5 108 CharlesBishop 1 113
*(Eve Johnson Houghton) swtg: hld up in tch: hdwy over 2f out: rdn and ev ch over 1f out: sustained duel w wnr fnl f: kpt on wl: jst hld cl home* **13/2**

2122 **3** 6 **Born To Be Alive (IRE)**40 6172 3-8-11 104 JimCrowley 2 98
*(K R Burke) lw: hld up in tch: effrt jst over 2f out: hdwy u.p to chse ldng pair jst over 1f out: wknd and edgd rt ins fnl f* **11/4**1

-130 **4** 4 **Promising Run (USA)**207 1046 4-8-11 107 (p) PatCosgrave 7 85
*(Saeed bin Suroor) chsd ldr: rdn and ev ch 2f out: lost pl and btn 4th 1f out: wknd fnl f* **5/1**

1211 **5** 1 **Billesdon Bess**42 6074 3-8-9 101 HollieDoyle 3 87
*(Richard Hannon) chsd ldrs: rdn over 2f out: lost pl and hung lft over 1f out: sn wknd* **6/1**

4215 **6** 2¼ **Frankuus (IRE)**32 6441 3-9-2 112 (b) JoeFanning 8 90
*(Mark Johnston) led: rdn ent fnl 2nd: edgd lft and hdd over 1f out: sn outpcd and wknd fnl f* **9/2**3

1-1 **7** 10 **Brittanic (IRE)**259 177 3-8-11 99 JamieSpencer 5 65
*(David Simcock) w'like: s.i.s: hld up in rr: effrt ent fnl 2f: sn btn and bhd* **18/1**

2m 12.23s (4.13) **Going Correction** +0.70s/f (Yiel)
**WFA** 3 from 4yo+ 5lb 7 Ran SP% **114.4**
Speed ratings (Par 111): **111,110,106,102,102 100,92**
CSF £29.65 TOTE £4.70: £2.50, £3.50; EX 28.20 Trifecta £128.90.
**Owner** K Abdullah **Bred** Juddmonte Farms Ltd **Trained** Newmarket, Suffolk

**FOCUS**
Race distance increased by 7yds. This was an open-looking Listed event. It was run at a solid enough pace and they kept down the middle off the home bend. Improved form from the first two.

### 7507 TBA CENTENARY FILLIES' H'CAP 1m 6f

**4:20** (4:20) (Class 3) (0-95,94) 3-Y-O+ **£16,172** (£4,812; £2,405; £1,202) **Stalls** Low

Form RPR

2126 **1** **Renfrew Street**13 7092 4-9-9 89 JoeFanning 8 96
*(Mark Johnston) led: hdd but stl travelling wl 2f out: rdn to ld again over 1f out: edgd lft and hld on wl u.p ins fnl f* **11/1**

4312 **2** nk **Melinoe**33 6391 3-8-7 81 LukeMorris 9 88
*(Sir Mark Prescott Bt) chsd ldng trio: effrt ent fnl 2f: drvn to chse ldrs over 1f out: pressing wnr 1f out: ev ch ins fnl f: kpt on u.p* **7/2**1

3224 **3** nk **Notice (IRE)**33 6391 4-9-4 84 JamieSpencer 6 90
*(David Simcock) lw: in tch in midfield: effrt 2f out: no imp and hung lft over 1f out: swtchd rt and rallied to chse ldng pair 100yds: styd on wl towards fin* **6/1**

2204 **4** 4 **Gallifrey**51 5715 3-8-6 83 (p) DavidEgan(3) 10 83
*(Lucy Wadham) pressed wnr tl rdn to ld 2f out: hdd over 1f out: lost 3rd and wknd fnl 100yds* **9/2**2

6212 **5** hd **St Mary's**11 7143 4-8-10 83 WilliamCox(7) 2 83
*(Andrew Balding) stdd after s: t.k.h: hld up in tch in midfield: hdwy to chse ldrs and rdn 2f out: unable qck over 1f out: wknd ins fnl f* **11/2**3

3401 **6** 7 **Fire Jet (IRE)**33 6391 4-9-7 87 JimmyQuinn 5 77
*(John Mackie) hld up in tch in midfield: effrt over 2f out: rdn and btn over 1f out: sn wknd* **12/1**

3324 **7** hd **Nathania**31 6477 3-8-9 83 ShaneKelly 1 73
*(Richard Hughes) hld up in tch in rr: effrt over 2f out: no imp u.p over 1f out: sn wknd* **8/1**

2302 **8** ½ **Graceland (FR)**18 6929 5-9-12 92 LouisSteward 3 81
*(Michael Bell) hld up in tch in last pair: effrt ent fnl 2f: sn drvn and no hdwy: wknd over 1f out* **7/1**

521 **9** 44 **Star Guide**21 6823 3-8-1 75 oh1 KieranO'Neill 7
*(Sylvester Kirk) lw: chsd ldrs: rdn and lost pl over 2f out: wl bhd and virtually p.u ins fnl f* **25/1**

3m 10.17s (6.57) **Going Correction** +0.70s/f (Yiel)
**WFA** 3 from 4yo+ 8lb 9 Ran SP% **113.6**
Speed ratings (Par 104): **109,108,108,106,106 102,102,101,76**
CSF £48.58 CT £255.79 TOTE £12.60: £3.50, £1.40, £2.30; EX 54.80 Trifecta £363.50.
**Owner** Douglas Livingston Racing **Bred** D Curran **Trained** Middleham Moor, N Yorks

**FOCUS**
Race distance increased by 7yds. A good-quality fillies' staying handicap. They went a routine pace and once more stuck to the middle of the home straight.

## 7508 188BET.CO.UK H'CAP 6f
4:50 (4:50) (Class 4) (0-80,79) 3-Y-O+ £6,469 (£1,925; £962; £481) Stalls High

Form RPR

3246 **1** **Showmethewayavrilo**[10] 7195 4-8-7 **68**.................. CharlieBennett(3) 4 75
(Malcolm Saunders) *dwlt and short of room leaving stalls: sn swtchd lft and in midfield: effrt against stands rail to ld over 1f out: drvn and hdd ins fnl f: battled bk wl to ld again towards fin* **14/1**

1424 **2** *nk* **Nezar (IRE)**[22] 6794 6-9-6 **78**.................................... RobertWinston 5 84
(Dean Ivory) *in tch in last pair: clsd to trck ldrs over 1f out: swtchd rt and pushed along to chal 1f out: rdn to ld ins fnl f: hdd and no ex towards fin* **8/1**

4421 **3** *5* **Abiento (IRE)**[32] 6442 3-9-1 **75**................................... JamieSpencer 3 65
(Ed Walker) *hld up in tch: swtchd rt and clsd jst over 2f out: rdn to chse ldrs but unable qck ent fnl f: wknd ins fnl f* **11/4**[2]

1101 **4** *3 ¾* **Ocean Temptress**[8] 7255 3-8-5 **72** 6ex......................(v) JackOsborn(7) 7 50
(John Ryan) *w ldr tl led after 2f: rdn and hdd ent fnl 2f: lost pl u.p over 1f out: wknd fnl f* **7/1**

0123 **5** *1 ¾* **Bahamian Sunrise**[25] 6695 5-9-4 **79**.....................(b) HectorCrouch(3) 6 51
(John Gallagher) *swtg: led for 2f: pressed ldr tl led again ent fnl 2f: rdn and hdd over 1f out: wknd qckly ins fnl f* **8/1**

4621 **6** *shd* **Zebulon (IRE)**[23] 6768 3-9-5 **79**.................................... SeanLevey 2 51
(Richard Hannon) *trckd ldrs: rdn over 2f out: rdn and lost pl ent fnl 2f: bhd over 1f out* **6/1**[3]

221 **7** *shd* **Island Cloud**[33] 6373 3-8-7 **70**................................... DavidEgan(3) 1 42
(Heather Main) *chsd ldrs: rdn to chal ent fnl 2f: no ex and lost pl over 1f out: sn wknd* **5/2**[1]

1m 13.77s (1.57) **Going Correction** +0.30s/f (Good)
**WFA** 3 from 4yo+ 2lb **7 Ran SP% 110.9**
Speed ratings (Par 105): **101,100,93,88,86 86,86**
CSF £109.80 TOTE £14.60: £6.10, £4.20; EX 104.20 Trifecta £729.40.
**Owner** Pat Hancock & Eric Jones **Bred** Eric Jones, Pat Hancock **Trained** Green Ore, Somerset

**FOCUS**
Not a bad sprint handicap, run to suit the closers. The first pair dominated the final furlong and the winner has been rated to this year's form.

## 7509 "DAILY RACING SPECIALS AT 188BET" APPRENTICE H'CAP 5f
5:25 (5:25) (Class 5) (0-75,76) 3-Y-O+ £4,528 (£1,347; £673; £336) Stalls High

Form RPR

2221 **1** **Jashma (IRE)**[12] 7127 3-9-4 **73**..................................(p) FinleyMarsh(3) 6 81
(Richard Hughes) *lw: hld up in tch: effrt against stands rail over 1f out: hdwy u.p to ld 100yds out: r.o wl: rdn out* **6/4**[1]

634 **2** *¾* **Flowing Clarets**[13] 7099 4-8-9 **60**................................ MitchGodwin 5 65
(John Bridger) *chsd ldr: rdn ent fnl 2f: drvn over 1f out: ev ch ins fnl f: kpt on: nt quite match pce of wnr towards fin* **5/1**

3324 **3** *½* **John Joiner**[21] 6810 5-8-5 **59** oh2.................. ManuelFernandes(3) 2 62
(Peter Hedger) *chsd ldng pair: effrt over 1f out: ev ch whn rdr dropped whip ins fnl f: styd on same pce towards fin* **4/1**[3]

1404 **4** *1 ¼* **Roundabout Magic (IRE)**[31] 6478 3-8-13 **65**............. PaddyBradley 4 64
(Simon Dow) *led: shkn up over 1f out: drvn 1f out: hdd 100yds out: no ex and wknd wl ins fnl f* **9/1**

5322 **5** *7* **The Big Short**[9] 7217 3-8-11 **66**......................... CameronNoble(3) 1 40
(Charles Hills) *wnt rt and v awkward leaving stalls: detached in rr: clsd and in tch 1/2-way: rdn and edgd rt over 1f out: sn wknd* **7/2**[2]

1m 0.78s (0.58) **Going Correction** +0.30s/f (Good)
**WFA** 3 from 4yo+ 1lb **5 Ran SP% 108.9**
Speed ratings (Par 103): **107,105,105,103,91**
CSF £9.04 TOTE £1.90: £1.10, £2.50; EX 9.00 Trifecta £23.70.
**Owner** M Clarke, S Geraghty, J Jeffries **Bred** Jonathan David Clague **Trained** Upper Lambourn, Berks

**FOCUS**
A modest sprint handicap, confined to apprentice riders, and the winner built on his recent form.
T/Plt: £330.90 to a £1 stake. Pool: £83,513.61. 184.19 winning units. T/Qpdt: £200.90 to a £1 stake. Pool: £6,439.74. 23.72 winning units. **Steve Payne**

# 7450 KEMPTON (A.W) (R-H)
## Wednesday, September 27

**OFFICIAL GOING: Polytrack: standard to slow**
Wind: Moderate, behind in home straight Weather: Becoming overcast, raining after race 4 (7.20) for rest of meeting

## 7510 RACINGUK.COM NURSERY H'CAP (JOCKEY CLUB GRASSROOTS NURSERY QUALIFIER) 7f (P)
5:40 (5:41) (Class 6) (0-65,65) 2-Y-O £2,587 (£770; £384; £192) Stalls Low

Form RPR

606 **1** **Letsbe Avenue (IRE)**[40] 6140 2-9-5 **63**............................ DaneO'Neill 11 73
(Richard Hannon) *hld up in midfield: prog on inner over 2f out: drvn to chse ldrs jst over 1f out: sustained chal to ld last 100yds* **6/1**[3]

4561 **2** *¾* **Roman Spinner**[22] 6790 2-8-13 **57**.......................(t) DavidProbert 5 65
(Rae Guest) *trckd ldrs: prog to take 2nd jst over 2f out: rdn to ld over 1f out: styd on but hdd and hld last 100yds* **4/1**[2]

0040 **3** *5* **Gold Eagle**[36] 6285 2-9-3 **61**................................ JosephineGordon 3 56
(Philip McBride) *trckd ldrs: led over 2f out to over 1f out: fdd fnl f but hld on for 3rd* **14/1**

5004 **4** *¾* **Rustang (FR)**[23] 6762 2-9-7 **65**...........................(h) JimmyFortune 7 57
(Richard Hughes) *t.k.h: hld up towards rr: rdn over 2f out: kpt on to take 4th ins fnl f: n.d* **8/1**

5155 **5** *1 ¼* **That's My Girl (IRE)**[20] 6845 2-9-6 **64**........................ TomMarquand 10 53
(Richard Hannon) *s.i.s: nt gng wl in last pair: rdn over 2f out: kpt on fr over 1f out: nvr nrr but n.d* **16/1**

000 **6** *hd* **Courteous Crown**[21] 6824 2-8-12 **63**............................ RossaRyan(7) 14 52
(Richard Hannon) *s.i.s: mostly in last pair: rdn over 2f out: kpt on fr over 1f out: nvr nrr but n.d* **33/1**

0543 **7** *3 ¾* **Tony Soprano (IRE)**[13] 7082 2-9-4 **62**.........................(b[1]) OisinMurphy 6 40
(Martyn Meade) *s.i.s: t.k.h in midfield: rdn and nt qckn over 2f out: disp wl btn 4th over 1f out: wknd fnl f* **3/1**[1]

0530 **8** *nk* **Giovanni Medici**[27] 6613 2-9-7 **65**................................ AdamKirby 13 43
(Seamus Durack) *dwlt: rapid prog on outer to press ldr after 1f: rdn and lost 2nd over 2f out: sn btn* **10/1**

400 **9** *2* **Mimram**[84] 4496 2-8-6 **53**......................................(t[1]) JackDuern(3) 1 25
(Dean Ivory) *led to over 2f out: wknd* **25/1**

0640 **10** *1 ½* **Silver Bullet (IRE)**[27] 6634 2-9-0 **58**......................(v) RichardKingscote 4 26
(Tom Dascombe) *chsd ldrs: rdn and wknd over 2f out* **6/1**[3]

406 **11** *1 ¼* **Prezzie**[44] 6010 2-9-1 **59**............................................. MartinDwyer 9 24
(William Muir) *chsd ldrs on outer 4f: wknd over 2f out* **16/1**

0000 **12** *½* **Alaskan Star (IRE)**[13] 7081 2-8-12 **56**.........................(p) SteveDrowne 8 19
(Amanda Perrett) *a towards rr: wl btn 2f out* **33/1**

6405 **13** *1 ¼* **Hastenplace**[10] 7193 2-9-1 **59**.................................(p) WilliamCarson 12 19
(Rod Millman) *a towards rr: rdn and no rspnse over 2f out: sn wknd* **25/1**

1m 24.91s (-1.09) **Going Correction** -0.225s/f (Stan) **13 Ran SP% 125.8**
Speed ratings (Par 93): **97,96,90,89,88 87,83,82,81,79 77,77,75**
CSF £30.73 CT £343.24 TOTE £7.40: £2.10, £2.60, £3.90; EX 31.90 Trifecta £752.90.
**Owner** Hitchcock, King, McFadden **Bred** Tinnakill Bloodstock **Trained** East Everleigh, Wilts

**FOCUS**
The Polytrack was officially riding slower than standard again, although the times didn't seem to back that up. The first two drew clear in this moderate nursery, showing improved form.

## 7511 32RED.COM NOVICE STKS (PLUS 10 RACE) (DIV I) 7f (P)
6:10 (6:11) (Class 4) 2-Y-O £4,528 (£1,347; £673; £336) Stalls Low

Form RPR

5 **1** **Corrosive (USA)**[33] 6403 2-9-2 0............................ JosephineGordon 2 84+
(Hugo Palmer) *mde all: pushed along firmly fr 2f out: styd on strly and nvr seriously under threat* **11/8**[1]

622 **2** *1 ¾* **Manthoor (IRE)**[21] 6827 2-9-2 78...................................... JimCrowley 11 79
(Owen Burrows) *in tch disputing 5th: sltly outpcd over 2f out: prog sn after: tk 2nd 1f out: wandered u.p but styd on: no threat to wnr* **11/4**[2]

6 **3** *2 ¼* **Georgian Manor (IRE)**[54] 5608 2-9-2 0............................ TedDurcan 4 73
(Sir Michael Stoute) *trckd ldng pair: rdn to chse wnr briefly jst over 1f out: one pce fnl f* **25/1**

**4** *1* **U S S Missouri (USA)** 2-9-2 0........................................ PatCosgrave 8 70+
(Ed Walker) *hld up in rr: shkn up and prog 2f out: styd on fr over 1f out: nrst fin: shaped w promise* **25/1**

6 **5** *nse* **Nicklaus**[90] 4266 2-9-2 0..................................... RichardKingscote 9 70
(William Haggas) *chsd wnr to over 1f out: one pce fnl f* **5/1**[3]

**6** *hd* **Court House (IRE)** 2-9-2 0.............................................. JamesDoyle 1 70+
(John Gosden) *s.v.s: detached in last early and rn green: prog on inner over 2f out: shkn up over 1f out: styd on fnl f: nrst fin* **6/1**

64 **7** *½* **Antagonist**[18] 6921 2-9-2 0.......................................... HarryBentley 7 68+
(Roger Charlton) *towards rr: pushed along over 2f out: kpt on steadily fr over 1f out: likely improver* **14/1**

0 **8** *5* **Roman Warrior**[19] 6884 2-9-2 0................................ StevieDonohoe 10 55
(Harry Dunlop) *a towards rr: shkn up and lft bhd over 2f out* **66/1**

45 **9** *3 ¼* **Queens Gallery**[24] 6721 2-9-2 0................................... TomMarquand 5 46
(Richard Hannon) *chsd ldrs: urged along 3f out: wknd over 2f out* **25/1**

**10** *shd* **Al Hareth (IRE)** 2-9-2 0...............................................(p[1]) LukeMorris 3 46
(George Peckham) *awkward s and then s.i.s: rn green and a in rr* **50/1**

**11** *8* **Percy Prosecco** 2-9-2 0............................................ FergusSweeney 12 24
(Noel Williams) *dwlt: rn green and a bhd: t.o* **66/1**

**12** *½* **Prince Rock (IRE)** 2-9-2 0................................................... JFEgan 6 23
(Simon Dow) *chsd ldng trio to over 2f out: wknd rapidly: t.o* **25/1**

1m 24.52s (-1.48) **Going Correction** -0.225s/f (Stan) **12 Ran SP% 126.7**
Speed ratings (Par 97): **99,97,94,93,93 93,92,86,83,82 73,73**
CSF £5.19 TOTE £2.70: £1.10, £1.60, £5.50; EX 7.00 Trifecta £82.90.
**Owner** V I Araci **Bred** Joemar Racing Stables, Llc **Trained** Newmarket, Suffolk

**FOCUS**
This was the quickest of the three C&D events, 0.34sec quicker than division two, and a step forward from the winner.

## 7512 32RED.COM NOVICE STKS (PLUS 10 RACE) (DIV II) 7f (P)
6:40 (6:43) (Class 4) 2-Y-O £4,528 (£1,347; £673; £336) Stalls Low

Form RPR

2 **1** **Barton Mills**[19] 6884 2-9-2 0........................................... MartinHarley 3 83
(William Haggas) *mde all: drew clr over 2f out: pushed out: v comf* **8/11**[1]

03 **2** *2 ½* **Exprompt (FR)**[19] 6884 2-9-2 0........................................ JamesDoyle 5 74+
(Hugo Palmer) *t.k.h: trckd ldrs: prog to chse wnr wl over 1f out: styd on but no hope of clsng* **7/2**[2]

5 **3** *¾* **Dazzle Gold (USA)**[82] 4567 2-9-2 0......................... SilvestreDeSousa 13 72+
(Robert Cowell) *in tch in midfield: pushed along over 2f out: prog over 1f out: shkn up and styd on to take 3rd ins fnl f* **14/1**

60 **4** *3* **Port Of Call**[13] 7093 2-9-2 0........................................... JackMitchell 6 64
(Amanda Perrett) *chsd ldng pair: rdn over 2f out: no ch w wnr and wknd fnl f* **14/1**

3 **5** *½* **Regular Income (IRE)**[12] 7105 2-9-2 0.....................(p[1]) SteveDrowne 11 63
(Adam West) *carried lft s: racd in 8th and last of those in tch: shkn up 2f out: nvr any ch but kpt on steadily* **20/1**

**6** *¾* **Jeopardy John** 2-9-2 0.......................................................... KierenFox 1 61
(Michael Attwater) *dwlt: sn chsd ldrs: shkn up and outpcd over 2f out: n.d after* **50/1**

**7** *3 ½* **Burlington (IRE)** 2-9-2 0.......................................(t[1]) NickyMackay 10 51
(John Gosden) *carried lft s: sn in tch in midfield: effrt on inner over 2f out: no hdwy over 1f out and sn wknd* **10/1**

00 **8** *shd* **Philamundo (IRE)**[5] 7352 2-9-2 0................................ StevieDonohoe 8 51
(Richard Spencer) *wnt lft s: detached in last quartet: wl bhd 3f out: nvr a factor but kpt on quite wl last 150yds* **50/1**

0 **9** *¾* **Matchmaking (GER)**[8] 7250 2-9-2 0................................... LukeMorris 9 49
(Sir Mark Prescott Bt) *wnt sharply lft s: detached in last quartet: nvr a factor but kpt on fnl f* **50/1**

**10** *½* **Mutajawel (USA)** 2-9-2 0.............................................. JimCrowley 12 47
(Charles Hills) *s.s: rn green and a detached in rr: kpt on fnl f* **9/1**[3]

60 **11** *7* **Swiss Psalm**[20] 6859 2-8-11 0........................................ RobHornby 2 29
(Mark Gillard) *chsd wnr to wl over 1f out: wknd rapidly: eased ins fnl f: t.o* **100/1**

**12** *3* **Jetpac** 2-9-2 0........................................................................ JohnFahy 7 20
(Laura Mongan) *a wl bhd: t.o* **50/1**

1m 24.86s (-1.14) **Going Correction** -0.225s/f (Stan) **12 Ran SP% 126.1**
Speed ratings (Par 97): **97,94,93,89,89 88,84,84,83,82 74,71**
CSF £3.48 TOTE £1.70: £1.10, £1.50, £3.60; EX 4.80 Trifecta £25.60.
**Owner** Abdulla Al Mansoori **Bred** Laundry Cottage Stud Farm **Trained** Newmarket, Suffolk

**FOCUS**
Not many got into this, the slower division by 0.34sec.

## 7513 100% PROFIT BOOST AT 32REDSPORT.COM NOVICE STKS 6f (P)
**7:10** (7:11) (Class 5) 2-Y-O **£3,234** (£962; £481; £240) **Stalls** Low

| Form | Pos | Dist | Horse / Details | RPR |
|---|---|---|---|---|
| 4 | 1 | | **Sarookh (USA)**[19] 6897 2-9-2 0 ... JimCrowley 4 (Roger Varian) *trckd ldr: pushed into ld over 2f out and sed to stretch rivals: romped clr jst over 1f out: v readily* **11/4**[1] | 85+ |
| | 2 | 3 | **Fakhoor (IRE)** 2-9-2 0 ... RichardKingscote 1 (Owen Burrows) *trckd ldrs: prog on inner over 2f out: chsd wnr wl over 1f out: pushed along and styd on but no ch* **14/1** | 75 |
| 01 | 3 | ¾ | **Sing Out Loud (IRE)**[37] 6262 2-9-3 0 ... HectorCrouch(3) 6 (Gary Moore) *trckd ldrs: shkn up and nt qckn jst over 2f out: styd on to take 3rd fnl f* **8/1** | 77 |
| | 4 | 1 ¼ | **Maghaweer (IRE)** 2-9-2 0 ... DaneO'Neill 2 (Richard Hannon) *slowly away: towards rr: shkn up and prog on inner 2f out: kpt on but nvr able to threaten* **8/1** | 69+ |
| 45 | 5 | nk | **It's Not Unusual**[32] 6424 2-8-11 0 ... HarryBentley 7 (Roger Charlton) *prom out wd: outpcd over 2f out: styd on same pce fr over 1f out* **7/1**[3] | 63 |
| | 6 | 1 | **Enzo's Lad (IRE)** 2-9-2 0 ... MartinHarley 9 (K R Burke) *in tch in midfield: outpcd over 2f out: kpt on same pce fr over 1f out* **16/1** | 65+ |
| 20 | 7 | ¾ | **Bowler Hat**[19] 6885 2-9-2 0 ... JamesDoyle 5 (Hugo Palmer) *wl in tch: pushed along and outpcd over 2f out: kpt on same pce after* **9/2**[2] | 63 |
| | 8 | ½ | **Nice Shot (IRE)** 2-9-2 0 ... FranBerry 10 (David Simcock) *dwlt: t.k.h: hld up in rr: shkn up and no prog over 2f out: kpt on fnl f* **15/2** | 61 |
| 34 | 9 | ¾ | **Storm Jazz (IRE)**[28] 6584 2-8-11 0 ... JimmyQuinn 8 (Ed Dunlop) *in tch towards rr: outpcd over 2f out: nudged along and one pce after* **25/1** | 54+ |
| | 10 | 2 ¼ | **Don't Cry About It (IRE)** 2-9-2 0 ... TomMarquand 11 (Ali Stronge) *struggling in last bef 1/2-way: nvr a factor* **66/1** | 52 |
| 45 | 11 | ¾ | **Bobby's Charm (USA)**[58] 5480 2-9-2 0 ... LukeMorris 3 (Robert Cowell) *led to over 2f out: wknd qckly* **14/1** | 50 |
| | 12 | 1 ½ | **Ace Of Spades (USA)** 2-9-2 0 ... SilvestreDeSousa 12 (George Scott) *trapped out wd in midfield: wknd over 2f out* **8/1** | 46 |

1m 12.7s (-0.40) **Going Correction** -0.225s/f (Stan) 12 Ran SP% **127.0**
Speed ratings (Par 95): **93,89,88,86,85 84,83,82,81,78 77,75**
CSF £48.56 TOTE £3.90: £1.80, £4.40, £2.30; EX 44.80 Trifecta £346.30.
**Owner** Hamdan Al Maktoum **Bred** Shadwell Farm LLC **Trained** Newmarket, Suffolk

**FOCUS**
It paid to be prominent in this fair event and the was quite impressive.

## 7514 32RED CASINO MEDIAN AUCTION MAIDEN STKS 1m (P)
**7:40** (7:43) (Class 5) 3-5-Y-O **£3,234** (£962; £481; £240) **Stalls** Low

| Form | Pos | Dist | Horse / Details | RPR |
|---|---|---|---|---|
| 55 | 1 | | **Psychotic**[22] 6775 4-9-9 0 ... JimCrowley 1 (David Menuisier) *s.i.s: pushed up to go prom then t.k.h: wnt 2nd wl over 1f out and sn rdn to chal: led ins fnl f: kpt on wl* **11/8**[1] | 76+ |
| 0224 | 2 | ½ | **Cape To Cuba**[18] 6941 3-8-11 76 ... GeorgeWood(3) 11 (James Fanshawe) *prom: led 2f out: drvn over 1f out: hdd ins fnl f: clr of rest but hld last 100yds* **2/1**[2] | 70 |
| 0250 | 3 | 5 | **My Illusionist**[22] 6792 3-9-5 69 ... (p[1]) LukeMorris 3 (Harry Dunlop) *chsd ldrs but urged along frequently: drvn over 2f out: wnt 3rd over 1f out: kpt on but no ch w ldng pair* **6/1**[3] | 63 |
| 0203 | 4 | 1 ½ | **Starboard Watch**[15] 7035 3-9-0 59 ... TomQueally 6 (James Given) *hld up but sn in midfield: prog on inner over 2f out: disp 3rd over 1f out but no ch w ldng pair* **16/1** | 54 |
| -000 | 5 | 4 | **Rivers Of Asia**[179] 1498 4-9-9 68 ... JohnFahy 10 (Martin Smith) *chsd ldrs but forced to r wd: outpcd fr over 2f out: no ch after* **14/1** | 50 |
| 0 | 6 | ¾ | **Peter Stuyvesant (IRE)**[21] 6817 3-9-5 0 ... OisinMurphy 8 (Denis Coakley) *chsd ldr to wl over 2f out: sn btn* **33/1** | 48 |
| 0-00 | 7 | 1 | **Compton Brave**[106] 3703 3-9-5 42 ... FergusSweeney 13 (J R Jenkins) *stdd s fr wd draw and hld up in last: t.k.h: prog on inner over 2f out: no hdwy over 1f out: fdd* **66/1** | 46 |
| 0 | 8 | ½ | **Fire Whirl**[20] 6851 3-9-2 0 ... CallumShepherd(3) 9 (William Knight) *dwlt: rchd midfield by 1/2-way: rdn over 2f out: sn lft bhd* **25/1** | 44 |
| 0 | 9 | 1 ¼ | **Captain Cockle**[49] 5794 4-9-4 0 ... MitchGodwin(5) 5 (Roger Teal) *hld up in rr: drvn over 2f out: plugging on but no ch whn nt clr run 1f out and lost pl* **66/1** | 41 |
| | 10 | shd | **Ladakhi** 3-9-0 0 ... WilliamCarson 12 (Rod Millman) *dwlt: t.k.h in rr: effrt and v wd over 3f out: wknd over 2f out* **20/1** | 36 |
| | 11 | 1 | **Saharan Star** 3-9-0 0 ... JimmyQuinn 7 (Patrick Chamings) *dwlt: a in rr: nvr a factor* **25/1** | 34 |
| 6-00 | 12 | 4 ½ | **Mette**[128] 2909 4-9-4 48 ... LiamKeniry 2 (Mark Usher) *led to 2f out: wkng qckly whn faltered over 1f out* **66/1** | 23 |
| 0 | 13 | 4 ½ | **Mini Moruga**[36] 6283 3-8-11 0 ... HectorCrouch(3) 4 (Gary Moore) *nvr bttr than midfield: wknd u.p 3f out* **25/1** | 12 |

1m 38.64s (-1.16) **Going Correction** -0.225s/f (Stan)
**WFA** 3 from 4yo 4lb 13 Ran SP% **126.0**
Speed ratings (Par 103): **96,95,90,89,85 84,83,82,81,81 80,75,71**
CSF £3.99 TOTE £2.50: £1.10, £1.50, £2.10; EX 6.80 Trifecta £17.20.
**Owner** Clive Washbourn **Bred** Cheveley Park Stud Ltd **Trained** Pulborough, W Sussex

**FOCUS**
Very little depth to this maiden, which was dominated by the two market leaders, but the winner progressed.

## 7515 32RED ON THE APP STORE H'CAP 1m 3f 219y(P)
**8:10** (8:15) (Class 4) (0-85,85) 3-Y-O+ **£4,690** (£1,395; £697; £348) **Stalls** Low

| Form | Pos | Dist | Horse / Details | RPR |
|---|---|---|---|---|
| 6404 | 1 | | **Banish (USA)**[8] 7234 4-9-6 81 ... (vt) JamesDoyle 12 (Hugo Palmer) *swtchd to inner after s: hld up in midfield: drvn and prog 2f out: chsd ldr over 1f out: led ins fnl f: styd on wl* **5/1**[3] | 88 |
| 1636 | 2 | 1 ¼ | **Sporting Times**[32] 6427 3-8-13 81 ... JimCrowley 1 (Ed Dunlop) *trckd ldrs: rdn and nt qckn over 2f out: styd on fr over 1f out to take 2nd last strides* **9/2**[2] | 86 |
| -111 | 3 | nk | **Pow Wow**[91] 4197 3-9-1 83 ... OisinMurphy 3 (Martyn Meade) *led: set mod pce but untrbld: tried to kick clr over 2f out but unable to do so: hdd and one pce ins fnl f: lost 2nd last strides* **8/1** | 88 |
| 0524 | 4 | 1 | **Batts Rock (IRE)**[18] 6952 4-9-10 85 ... (p) JamieSpencer 4 (Michael Bell) *dwlt but sn rcvrd and trckd ldr after 3f: rdn over 2f out: lost 2nd and one pce over 1f out* **10/3**[1] | 88 |
| 1260 | 5 | 1 ½ | **Regicide (IRE)**[12] 7132 4-9-9 84 ... TomQueally 9 (James Fanshawe) *hld up in last pair in modly run event: gng strly 3f out but lot to do: prog 2f out: hrd rdn and no imp over 1f out: styd on ins fnl f* **10/1** | 85 |
| 4253 | 6 | shd | **Saumur**[21] 6819 5-8-10 71 oh1 ... LukeMorris 8 (Denis Coakley) *hld up in midfield: rdn over 2f out: nt qckn then outpcd: n.d after but styd on ins fnl f* **20/1** | 71 |
| 66-4 | 7 | ½ | **Knight Music**[39] 6202 5-9-4 79 ... HarryBentley 2 (Michael Attwater) *disp 2nd pl to 2f out: fdd fnl f* **16/1** | 79 |
| 6060 | 8 | 1 ¾ | **Sennockian Star**[11] 7143 7-9-7 82 ... FrannyNorton 11 (Mark Johnston) *hld up in rr: effrt 3f out: outpcd over 2f out and no ch after* **16/1** | 79 |
| 1600 | 9 | 2 ½ | **Belabour**[39] 6196 4-9-3 78 ... JFEgan 5 (Mark Brisbourne) *t.k.h: trckd ldrs: rdn over 2f out: sn lost pl and btn* **33/1** | 71 |
| /20- | 10 | 1 ½ | **Cry Wolf**[128] 7280 4-9-0 75 ... TimmyMurphy 7 (James Evans) *hld up in last: shkn up and no prog over 2f out: nvr in it* **66/1** | 65 |
| -103 | 11 | 8 | **Elysian Prince**[122] 1289 6-9-6 81 ... TrevorWhelan 10 (Neil King) *racd wd: in tch: wknd over 3f out: t.o* **33/1** | 59 |

2m 32.94s (-1.56) **Going Correction** -0.225s/f (Stan)
**WFA** 3 from 4yo+ 7lb 11 Ran SP% **102.0**
Speed ratings (Par 105): **96,95,94,94,93 93,92,91,90,89 83**
CSF £18.92 CT £94.22 TOTE £5.40: £1.90, £1.60, £2.10; EX 21.90 Trifecta £207.20.
**Owner** HighclereThoroughbredRacing-Smart Strike **Bred** Nicole Gunther **Trained** Newmarket, Suffolk

■ Special Relation was withdrawn. Price at time of withdrawal 7-2. Rule 4 applies to all bets - deduction 20p in the pound.

**FOCUS**
Fair handicap form, but they didn't seem to go hard up front. The race was weakened when Special Relation refused to go into the stalls.

## 7516 32RED H'CAP (LONDON MIDDLE DISTANCE SERIES QUALIFIER) 2m 2f 219y(P)
**8:40** (8:45) (Class 3) (0-95,93) 3-Y-O
**£7,158** (£2,143; £1,071; £535; £267; £134) **Stalls** Low

| Form | Pos | Dist | Horse / Details | RPR |
|---|---|---|---|---|
| 1133 | 1 | | **Koeman**[18] 6937 3-8-8 83 ... DavidEgan(3) 2 (Mick Channon) *hld up in midfield: rdn and prog jst over 2f out: led over 1f out: hrd pressed after but kpt on wl fnl f* **20/1** | 91 |
| 5005 | 2 | ½ | **Al Hamdany (IRE)**[19] 6887 3-9-3 89 ... AdamKirby 3 (Marco Botti) *hld up in midfield: rdn 2f out: prog over 1f out: styd on u.p fnl f: tk 2nd last strides* **7/1** | 96 |
| 0103 | 3 | ½ | **Bush House (IRE)**[19] 6887 3-9-1 87 ... (b) JamesDoyle 5 (Hugo Palmer) *trckd ldrs: rdn and prog to ld jst over 2f out: hdd over 1f out: kpt on and stl w wnr 100yds out: no ex and lost 2nd last stride* **7/2**[2] | 93 |
| 1241 | 4 | ¾ | **Alfarris (FR)**[39] 6187 3-9-1 87 ... (b[1]) JimCrowley 8 (William Haggas) *hld up in last trio: rdn and prog on outer 2f out: disp 3rd ins fnl f: one pce last 75yds* **4/1**[3] | 92 |
| 2605 | 5 | nk | **Ray's The Money (IRE)**[29] 6563 3-8-5 80 ... (v) GeorgeWood(3) 4 (Michael Bell) *hld up in last trio: rdn 2f out: styd on after and nrst fin but nvr quite pce to threaten* **16/1** | 84 |
| 1226 | 6 | nk | **Stone The Crows**[39] 6202 3-9-0 86 ... (p) HarryBentley 6 (Roger Charlton) *led: urged along 3f out: rdn: hdd and nt qckn jst over 2f out: kpt on same pce after and steadily lost pls* **17/2** | 90 |
| 1-41 | 7 | 3 ½ | **Intrepidly (USA)**[86] 4443 3-9-6 92 ... JamieSpencer 10 (Jeremy Noseda) *restless stalls: s.v.s: detached in last most of way: tried to creep clsr 3f out: drvn and no prog 2f out: kpt on ins fnl f* **3/1**[1] | 92+ |
| 2303 | 8 | 2 | **Emenem**[31] 6474 3-9-5 91 ... JFEgan 9 (Simon Dow) *trapped out wd: prog fr midfield to press ldrs 4f out: wknd 2f out* **7/1** | 85 |
| 1-35 | 9 | nk | **Total Star**[124] 3042 3-9-7 93 ... LukeMorris 1 (Luca Cumani) *mostly trckd ldr to 5f out: rdn and wknd 2f out* **12/1** | 87 |
| 5256 | 10 | 2 | **X Rated (IRE)**[20] 6848 3-8-5 77 ... FrannyNorton 7 (Mark Johnston) *racd on outer: in tch: prog to chse ldr 5f out: drvn and lost 2nd over 2f out: wknd* **25/1** | 67 |

2m 17.44s (-4.46) **Going Correction** -0.225s/f (Stan) 10 Ran SP% **124.9**
Speed ratings (Par 105): **107,106,106,105,105 105,102,101,101,99**
CSF £163.94 CT £625.03 TOTE £18.80: £4.50, £2.60, £1.40; EX 144.90 Trifecta £704.90.
**Owner** Taplin & Bunney Partnership **Bred** B V Sangster **Trained** West Ilsley, Berks

**FOCUS**
This was a good 3yo handicap, but it wasn't truly run and the first six finished in a heap.

## 7517 RACING UK PROFITS RETURNED TO RACING H'CAP 6f (P)
**9:10** (9:11) (Class 6) (0-60,60) 3-Y-O+ **£2,264** (£673; £336; £168) **Stalls** Low

| Form | Pos | Dist | Horse / Details | RPR |
|---|---|---|---|---|
| 000 | 1 | | **Treacherous**[22] 6791 3-8-13 57 ... CallumShepherd(3) 6 (Ed de Giles) *dwlt: sn in midfield: smooth prog over 2f out: pushed into the ld over 1f out: styd on wl: readily* **5/1**[3] | 70 |
| 0031 | 2 | 2 | **Atlanta Belle (IRE)**[35] 6324 3-9-3 58 ... TedDurcan 1 (Chris Wall) *trckd ldr: shkn up to ld briefly wl over 1f out: chsd wnr after and drew clr of rest but safely hld* **7/4**[1] | 65 |
| 5200 | 3 | 4 ½ | **Triple Dream**[10] 7190 12-8-12 58 ... KerrieRaybould(7) 3 (Milton Bradley) *chsd ldng pair: pushed along and outpcd 2f out: hld on for 3rd ins fnl f* **25/1** | 52 |
| 1340 | 4 | ½ | **Whiteley (IRE)**[10] 7191 3-9-1 56 ... JFEgan 9 (Mick Channon) *hld up in last pair: prog on inner jst over 2f out: clsng on plcd horses whn nt clr run over 1f out: styd on again ins fnl f to take 4th last strides* **16/1** | 50 |
| 3066 | 5 | ½ | **Tigserin (IRE)**[49] 5813 4-9-7 60 ... PatCosgrave 2 (Giles Bravery) *chsd ldrs: rdn and outpcd 2f out: one pce after* **5/1**[3] | 51 |
| 050- | 6 | ½ | **Storm Lightning**[380] 6410 8-9-7 60 ... MartinHarley 4 (Mark Brisbourne) *hld up in rr: rdn and prog towards outer fr 2f out: clsd on 3rd horse ins fnl f: effrt petered out last 75yds* **33/1** | 49 |
| 00 | 7 | shd | **Something Lucky (IRE)**[9] 7217 5-8-12 56 ... (tp) PaddyBradley(5) 7 (Daniel Steele) *dwlt: hld up in rr: prog on inner over 2f out: pressed for a pl over 1f out: one pce fnl f* **25/1** | 45 |
| 0500 | 8 | 2 ¼ | **Rapid Rise (IRE)**[10] 7191 3-8-12 60 ... ManuelFernandes(7) 8 (Milton Bradley) *trapped out wd in midfield: lost grnd bnd 3f out: n.d after* **25/1** | 42 |
| 0450 | 9 | nk | **Monarch Maid**[31] 6485 6-8-12 58 ... WilliamCox(7) 12 (Peter Hiatt) *nudged s but gd spd fr wdst draw to ld: hdd wl over 1f out: sn wknd* **16/1** | 39 |
| 2106 | 10 | nk | **Krazy Paving**[154] 2091 5-9-4 57 ... (b) AdamKirby 10 (Anabel K Murphy) *chsd ldrs to 2f out: wknd* **25/1** | 37 |

0045 **11** *shd* **Who Told Jo Jo (IRE)**[28] 6581 3-9-5 **60**....................(b) OisinMurphy 11 40
(Joseph Tuite) *a in rr: rdn and no prog over 2f out* **16/1**
013 **12** *5* **Tifl**[9] 7212 4-8-13 **55**....................(bt) DavidEgan(3) 5 20
(Heather Main) *nvr beyond midfield: wknd qckly 2f out* **7/2**[2]
1m 11.56s (-1.54) **Going Correction** -0.225s/f (Stan)
**WFA** 3 from 4yo+ 2lb **12** Ran SP% **127.9**
Speed ratings (Par 101): **101,98,92,91,91 90,90,87,86,86 86,79**
CSF £14.40 CT £221.10 TOTE £6.90: £2.20, £1.40, £7.00; EX 19.30 Trifecta £327.40.
**Owner** Woodham Walter Partnership **Bred** P M Hicks **Trained** Ledbury, H'fords

**FOCUS**

The first two finished clear in this modest sprint, with the winner showing improved form.
T/Jkpt: £5,000 to a £1 stake. Pool: £10,000. 2 winning units. T/Plt: £23.30 to a £1 stake. Pool: £69,143.43. 2,160.13 winning units. T/Qpdt: £7.30 to a £1 stake. Pool: £11,901.03. 1,201.92 winning units. **Jonathan Neesom**

## 7242 REDCAR (L-H)

Wednesday, September 27

**OFFICIAL GOING: Good to soft (soft in places in back straight; 7.2)**
Wind: moderate behind Weather: overcast

## 7518 ALL NEW RACINGUK.COM NURSERY H'CAP 5f 217y

**2:00** (2:02) (Class 6) (0-60,59) 2-Y-O **£2,749** (£818; £408; £204) **Stalls** Centre

Form RPR
000 **1** **Crazy World**[50] 5755 2-8-5 **46**.................... PhilDennis(3) 14 51
(Declan Carroll) *chsd ldrs: pushed along to ld over 1f out: rdn and kpt on fnl f* **20/1**
0424 **2** *½* **Excellent Times**[14] 7041 2-9-7 **59**.................... DavidAllan 6 62
(Tim Easterby) *hld up in midfield: rdn over 2f out: hdwy appr fnl f: kpt on wl: wnt 2nd towards fin* **9/2**[2]
5405 **3** *½* **Istanbul Pasha (IRE)**[13] 7082 2-8-10 **48**....................(v1) TomEaves 2 50
(David Evans) *dwlt: sn trckd ldrs: rdn over 2f out: hdwy and ev ch appr fnl f: one pce fnl 110yds* **12/1**
P150 **4** *1¼* **Society's Dream (IRE)**[15] 7030 2-8-13 **51**.................... PJMcDonald 1 51
(K R Burke) *led: rdn 2f out: hdd over 1f out: one pce fnl f* **9/1**
2335 **5** *1* **Rock On Bertie (IRE)**[15] 7029 2-8-13 **54**.................... LewisEdmunds(3) 10 49
(Nigel Tinkler) *in tch: rdn over 2f out: one pce* **7/2**[1]
0500 **6** *nk* **Lady Sandy (IRE)**[14] 7041 2-9-3 **55**.................... BenCurtis 15 49
(David Barron) *midfield: rdn over 2f out: kpt on ins fnl f: nvr threatened* **16/1**
0005 **7** *shd* **Graphite Girl (IRE)**[8] 7243 2-8-12 **53**.................... RachelRichardson(3) 13 47
(Tim Easterby) *prom: rdn over 2f out: no ex fnl f* **28/1**
0430 **8** *3* **Angie B (IRE)**[15] 7029 2-8-7 **45**....................(p1) JamesSullivan 3 30
(John Wainwright) *midfield: rdn along over 3f out: nvr threatened* **25/1**
050 **9** *nse* **Marconi**[37] 6264 2-9-7 **59**.................... SamJames 9 44
(John Davies) *dwlt: hld up: pushed along 1/2-way: sme late hdwy: nvr threatened* **33/1**
0423 **10** *hd* **Ray Purchase**[21] 6815 2-8-12 **50**.................... ConnorBeasley 5 34
(Keith Dalgleish) *in tch: rdn over 2f out: wknd fnl f* **6/1**[3]
0060 **11** *nk* **Furni Factors**[28] 6567 2-9-4 **56**.................... GrahamLee 12 39
(Ronald Thompson) *chsd ldrs: rdn over 2f out: wknd over 1f out* **33/1**
0504 **12** *½* **Lord Of The Glen**[11] 7159 2-8-13 **51**....................(p) DanielTudhope 16 33
(Jim Goldie) *hld up in midfield: rdn over 2f out: sn btn* **14/1**
002 **13** *½* **Little Monkey**[46] 5945 2-8-8 **46**.................... CamHardie 8 26
(Antony Brittain) *midfield: sn rdn along: wknd over 1f out* **25/1**
044 **14** *¾* **Elements Quest (IRE)**[69] 5068 2-9-1 **56**.................... CliffordLee(3) 4 34
(K R Burke) *midfield: rdn over 2f out: wknd over 1f out* **14/1**
050 **15** *5* **Eyes Of Fire**[103] 3791 2-9-0 **52**.................... AndrewMullen 18 15
(Ollie Pears) *hld up: rdn along and bit clsr over 3f out: wknd over 1f out* **40/1**
006 **16** *1¼* **Magic Ship (IRE)**[38] 6231 2-9-6 **58**....................(h) PaulHanagan 11 17
(Ollie Pears) *hld up: sn pushed along: a towards rr* **20/1**
646 **17** *2¾* **Rema Al Kuwait (IRE)**[41] 6085 2-9-6 **58**.................... PhillipMakin 19 9
(David O'Meara) *midfield: rdn over 2f out: sn wknd and bhd* **20/1**
236 **18** *1¾* **Time For Treacle**[54] 5613 2-9-4 **56**.................... PaulMulrennan 7 2
(Ben Haslam) *hld up in midfield: rdn over 2f out: sn wknd* **33/1**
000 **19** *½* **The Gingerbreadman**[18] 6939 2-8-5 **50**.................... PaulaMuir(7) 20
(Chris Fairhurst) *dwlt: a towards rr* **66/1**
006 **20** *3* **Sir Walter (IRE)**[111] 3490 2-8-11 **49**.................... NeilFarley 17
(Eric Alston) *a towards rr* **50/1**
1m 11.46s (-0.34) **Going Correction** -0.075s/f (Good) **20** Ran SP% **131.7**
Speed ratings (Par 93): **99,98,97,96,94 94,94,90,90,89 89,88,88,87,80 78,75,72,72,68**
CSF £100.54 CT £1209.61 TOTE £36.40: £6.70, £1.50, £3.50, £2.40; EX 263.80 Trifecta £3402.30.
**Owner** John Blackburn & Andy Turton **Bred** D Carroll **Trained** Malton, N Yorks

**FOCUS**

The going was good to soft, soft in places in the back straight (GoingStick 7.2). A moderate nursery to start, containing just one previous winner. Almost half the field were making their handicap debut after the obligatory three outings, including the winner. They raced as one group up the centre and the jockeys described the ground as "nearly good", "a bit dead" or "good to soft". Much-improved form from the winner.

## 7519 WISE BETTING AT RACINGUK.COM NURSERY H'CAP 7f 219y

**2:30** (2:31) (Class 6) (0-65,66) 2-Y-O **£2,749** (£818; £408; £204) **Stalls** Centre

Form RPR
0050 **1** **Echo (IRE)**[8] 7239 2-8-11 **55**.................... JackGarritty 6 57
(Jedd O'Keeffe) *in tch centre: hdwy over 2f out: sn rdn and hung lft: drvn and edgd rt jst over 1f out: styd on wl u.p fnl f: led on line* **16/1**
4600 **2** *shd* **Ventura Crest (IRE)**[41] 6087 2-8-10 **54**.................... DavidAllan 1 56
(Tim Easterby) *racd alone nr far rail: chsd clr ldr: hdwy 3f out: cl up and rdn wl over 1f out: drvn to ld ent fnl f: hdd on line* **33/1**
0000 **3** *¾* **Progressive Jazz (IRE)**[18] 6940 2-7-12 **47**....................(v1) RhiainIngram(5) 3 47
(K R Burke) *racd centre: sn led and clr: rdn along and edgd rt 2f out: drvn and hung rt to stands rail jst over 1f out: hdd ent fnl f: ev ch tl no ex last 50 yds* **25/1**
4403 **4** *½* **Here In The Dark**[27] 6626 2-9-8 **66**....................(p) ConnorBeasley 8 65
(Keith Dalgleish) *chsd ldrs centre: hdwy 3f out: rdn along 2f out: drvn over 1f out: kpt on u.p fnl f* **16/1**
0000 **5** *¾* **Bee Machine (IRE)**[8] 7239 2-8-3 **47** ow2.................... PatrickMathers 16 45
(Declan Carroll) *towards rr: hdwy and swtchd lft over 2f out: rdn wl over 1f out: styd on wl appr fnl f* **20/1**
0046 **6** *2* **Ladycammyofclare (IRE)**[15] 7030 2-8-1 **45**.................... AndrewMullen 11 38
(Mark Johnston) *in tch: hdwy to chse ldrs over 2f out: sn rdn: drvn and no imp fr over 1f out* **22/1**
060 **7** *3* **Jaycols Star**[18] 6939 2-9-0 **58**.................... KevinStott 18 45
(Philip Kirby) *towards rr: hdwy over 2f out: sn rdn and no imp fnl f* **25/1**
600 **8** *½* **Makofitwhatyouwill**[32] 6432 2-8-4 **48**.................... JoeDoyle 9 34
(Nigel Tinkler) *towards rr tl sme late hdwy* **33/1**
0201 **9** *¾* **Milan Reef (IRE)**[13] 7082 2-9-1 **59**.................... PaulMulrennan 14 43
(David Loughnane) *racd towards stands rail: chsd ldrs: rdn along over 2f out: grad wknd* **15/2**[3]
5665 **10** *1* **Zoffinia (IRE)**[18] 6940 2-9-1 **59**.................... PaulHanagan 2 41
(Richard Fahey) *racd towards far side: towards rr: rdn along over 2f out: sme late hdwy* **8/1**
0645 **11** *¾* **Racing Radio (IRE)**[15] 7030 2-8-10 **54**.................... BenCurtis 4 34
(David Barron) *dwlt and a towards rr towards far side* **16/1**
0012 **12** *nk* **Dream Of Delphi (IRE)**[20] 6845 2-9-4 **62**....................(b) DanielTudhope 19 41
(William Haggas) *wnt rt s: bhd: hdwy 3f out: rdn along 2f out: n.d* **3/1**[1]
3416 **13** *2¼* **Faradays Spark (IRE)**[18] 6940 2-9-3 **61**.................... TonyHamilton 12 35
(Richard Fahey) *a towards rr* **9/1**
0344 **14** *3¼* **Emerald Rocket (IRE)**[8] 7243 2-9-4 **65**....................(v1) CliffordLee(3) 17 32
(K R Burke) *racd towards stands side: chsd ldrs: rdn along wl over 2f out: grad wknd* **11/2**[2]
055 **15** *¾* **Airplane (IRE)**[26] 6658 2-9-0 **61**.................... RachelRichardson(3) 5 27
(Tim Easterby) *racd towards far side: chsd ldrs: rdn along 3f out: sn outpcd* **28/1**
000 **16** *5* **Surrender**[43] 6042 2-9-0 **58**.................... DuranFentiman 13 13
(Tim Easterby) *.a towards rr* **40/1**
004 **17** *7* **Lucky's Dream**[43] 6029 2-9-5 **63**.................... TomEaves 15
(David Evans) *dwlt: a in rr* **20/1**
055 **18** *1¾* **Bertie Wallace (IRE)**[15] 7013 2-8-12 **56**....................(h1) GrahamLee 7
(Keith Dalgleish) *racd centre: chsd ldng pair: pushed along 1/2-way: rdn 3f out: sn wknd* **25/1**
040 **19** *6* **Situation**[27] 6625 2-9-3 **61**....................(p) DougieCostello 10
(Richard Guest) *dwlt: a in rr* **25/1**
1m 37.5s (0.90) **Going Correction** -0.075s/f (Good) **19** Ran SP% **131.9**
Speed ratings (Par 93): **92,91,91,90,89 87,84,84,83,82 81,81,79,76,75 70,63,61,55**
CSF £481.45 CT £6182.16 TOTE £21.30: £5.40, £6.40, £6.70, £4.30; EX 661.30.
**Owner** Paul & Dale Chapman Racing **Bred** Pat McCarthy **Trained** Middleham Moor, N Yorks
■ Stewards' Enquiry : Jack Garritty nine day ban: using his whip above the permitted level (11-19 Oct)

**FOCUS**

Another moderate nursery, this one more of a stamina test. This time they spread right across the track and not many got into it.

## 7520 BRITISH STALLION STUDS EBF MAIDEN STKS (PLUS 10 RACE) (DIV I) 7f

**3:00** (3:01) (Class 4) 2-Y-O **£6,469** (£1,925; £962; £481) **Stalls** Centre

Form RPR
24 **1** **Al Hajar (IRE)**[33] 6388 2-9-5 0.................... PhillipMakin 8 89+
(Charlie Appleby) *mde all: pushed clr over 1f out: v easily* **4/11**[1]
**2** *7* **Mametz Wood (IRE)** 2-8-12 0.................... PatrickO'Hanlon(7) 6 67+
(K R Burke) *midfield: rdn along and dropped to rr over 3f out: edgd lft but styd on fr over 1f out: wnt modest 2nd nr fin* **50/1**
5 **3** *nk* **Canadian George (FR)**[19] 6890 2-9-5 0.................... ConnorBeasley 1 66
(Keith Dalgleish) *in tch: rdn and outpcd over 2f out: plugged on fnl f* **20/1**
**4** *1* **Rare Groove (IRE)** 2-9-5 0.................... PJMcDonald 10 63
(Jedd O'Keeffe) *hld up: rdn 2f out: hdwy 2f out to chse clr ldr appr fnl f: hung persistently lft: no ex and lost 2 pls fnl 75yds* **20/1**
6 **5** *2* **Farhh Away**[19] 6897 2-9-5 0.................... PaulMulrennan 2 58
(Michael Dods) *sn trckd ldrs: rdn along over 2f out: sn one pce: no ex fnl 110yds* **6/1**[2]
06 **6** *3* **Railport Dolly**[15] 7021 2-9-0 0....................(h) AlistairRawlinson 7 45
(Michael Appleby) *prom: rdn along 3f out: wknd over 1f out* **33/1**
0 **7** *1½* **Echo Cove (IRE)**[26] 6654 2-9-5 0.................... PaulHanagan 9 47
(Jane Chapple-Hyam) *trckd ldrs: racd quite keenly: pushed along over 2f out: wknd over 1f out* **9/1**[3]
5 **8** *½* **Lineofintelligence**[52] 5680 2-9-5 0.................... TonyHamilton 5 45
(Richard Fahey) *a towards rr* **16/1**
**9** *8* **Recks (IRE)** 2-9-2 0.................... CliffordLee(3) 3 24
(K R Burke) *hld up: rdn along over 3f out: wknd and bhd fnl 2f* **16/1**
1m 23.2s (-1.30) **Going Correction** -0.075s/f (Good) **9** Ran SP% **123.8**
Speed ratings (Par 97): **104,96,95,94,92 88,87,86,77**
CSF £45.53 TOTE £1.30: £1.02, £12.50, £4.00; EX 37.10 Trifecta £279.30.
**Owner** Godolphin **Bred** Doc Bloodstock **Trained** Newmarket, Suffolk

**FOCUS**

A most uncompetitive maiden featuring a long odds-on favourite who won very much as he pleased, probably at least matching his pre-race form.

## 7521 BRITISH STALLION STUDS EBF MAIDEN STKS (PLUS 10 RACE) (DIV II) 7f

**3:35** (3:37) (Class 4) 2-Y-O **£6,469** (£1,925; £962; £481) **Stalls** Centre

Form RPR
053 **1** **Ventura Royal (IRE)**[26] 6659 2-9-0 67.................... DanielTudhope 3 68
(David O'Meara) *trckd ldrs: rdn 2f out: chal appr fnl f: led 75yds out: kpt on* **5/1**[3]
0 **2** *1¼* **Sunstorm**[37] 6260 2-9-5 0.................... PhillipMakin 5 70
(David Brown) *led: rdn over 2f out: strly pressed appr fnl f: hdd 75yds out: no ex* **33/1**
053 **3** *1½* **Calling Rio (IRE)**[14] 7045 2-9-0 68.................... PaulMulrennan 8 61
(David Loughnane) *midfield: rdn along over 2f out: styd on fnl f: wnt 3rd towards fin* **16/1**
3 **4** *nk* **Valdolobo (IRE)**[47] 5876 2-9-5 0.................... PJMcDonald 7 65
(K R Burke) *prom: rdn and upsides appr fnl f: wknd fnl 75yds* **8/11**[1]
**5** *7* **Muzaawel** 2-9-5 0.................... KevinStott 4 47
(Saeed bin Suroor) *trckd ldrs: pushed along over 2f out: edgd lft and sn wknd* **5/2**[2]
0 **6** *1¾* **Duffy**[20] 6854 2-9-5 0.................... PaulHanagan 6 42
(Richard Fahey) *midfield: sn pushed along: outpcd and dropped towards rr over 4f out: plugged on fnl f* **25/1**
00 **7** *½* **Lever Du Soleil (FR)**[104] 3742 2-9-5 0.................... DavidAllan 9 41
(Tim Easterby) *midfield: rdn along over 3f out: wknd fnl 2f* **50/1**
6 **8** *5* **Daffy Grey (IRE)**[18] 6939 2-8-12 0.................... HarrisonShaw(7) 2 28
(Michael Easterby) *dwlt: a rr* **66/1**
**9** *hd* **Angel Carlotta (IRE)** 2-9-0 0.................... TomEaves 1 23
(Nigel Tinkler) *dwlt: a rr* **33/1**
1m 25.02s (0.52) **Going Correction** -0.075s/f (Good) **9** Ran SP% **122.2**
Speed ratings (Par 97): **94,92,90,90,82 80,79,74,74**
CSF £148.63 TOTE £6.30: £1.60, £7.90, £3.80; EX 135.00 Trifecta £1254.00.
**Owner** Middleham Park Racing Cxvii **Bred** Rabbah Bloodstock Limited **Trained** Upper Helmsley, N Yorks

**FOCUS**
Another uncompetitive contest; weak form. The winning time was 1.82 sec slower than the first division.

## 7522 WATCH RACING UK IN HD H'CAP 5f
**4:10** (4:14) (Class 5) (0-70,70) 3-Y-O+ **£3,234** (£962; £481; £240) **Stalls** Centre

Form RPR
5302 **1** **Quatrieme Ami**[8] 7255 4-9-6 **69** ........ DanielTudhope 1 80
(Philip McBride) *racd towards far side: trckd ldrs: hdwy wl over 1f out: rdn to chal ins fnl f: kpt on to ld last 75 yds* **13/8**[1]

0000 **2** *hd* **See The Sun**[8] 7244 6-9-3 **66** ........ (b) DavidAllan 4 76
(Tim Easterby) *racd towards far side: led: rdn wl over 1f out: drvn ins fnl f: hdd and no ex last 75 yds* **11/1**[3]

6310 **3** *3* **Classic Pursuit**[25] 6670 6-9-5 **68** ........ (b) PhillipMakin 9 67
(Michael Appleby) *in tch: hdwy 2f out: rdn wl over 1f out: drvn and kpt on fnl f* **16/1**

5014 **4** *3/4* **Pavers Pride**[28] 6596 3-9-2 **66** ........ PatrickMathers 8 63
(Noel Wilson) *racd centre: cl up: rdn 2f out: ev ch tl drvn and wknd ent fnl f* **33/1**

5350 **5** *3/4* **Monte Cinq (IRE)**[32] 6411 3-9-6 **70** ........ (h) KevinStott 10 64+
(Jason Ward) *hld up towards rr: hdwy over 2f out: rdn over 1f out: kpt on fnl f* **16/1**

031 **6** *hd* **Jabbarockie**[30] 6526 4-9-4 **67** ........ NeilFarley 17 60+
(Eric Alston) *chsd ldrs on outer: cl up 2f out: sn rdn and edgd lft over 1f out: drvn and kpt on same pce fnl f* **18/1**

0524 **7** *3/4* **Racing Angel (IRE)**[45] 5962 5-9-0 **63** ........ AndrewMullen 18 53
(Adrian Nicholls) *midfield: hdwy wl over 1rf out: sn rdn and kpt on fnl f* **20/1**

-324 **8** *3/4* **Ayresome Angel**[47] 5877 4-9-4 **67** ........ DavidNolan 13 55
(John Mackie) *racd centre: prom: rdn along 2f out: grad wknd* **14/1**

6302 **9** *1/2* **Flash City (ITY)**[7] 7268 9-9-5 **68** ........ JamesSullivan 15 54
(Ruth Carr) *towards rr tl sme late hdwy* **16/1**

3510 **10** *nk* **Haworth**[35] 6313 3-9-5 **69** ........ (b) PJMcDonald 16 54
(James Bethell) *racd wd: a towards rr* **25/1**

1513 **11** *nse* **Perfect Words (IRE)**[33] 6384 7-8-13 **69** ........ (p) HarrisonShaw(7) 12 54
(Marjorie Fife) *nvr bttr than midfield* **25/1**

2000 **12** *hd* **Bronze Beau**[14] 7055 10-9-6 **69** ........ (tp) ShaneGray 3 53
(Kristin Stubbs) *racd towards far side: prom: rdn along wl over 1f out: sn drvn and wknd fnl f* **28/1**

0500 **13** *1/2* **Kibaar**[42] 6062 5-9-5 **68** ........ (p) JackGarritty 11 50
(Ruth Carr) *chsd ldrs centre: rdn along 2f out: sn wknd* **22/1**

51-5 **14** *nk* **Sky Gypsy**[30] 6526 3-9-1 **65** ........ TomEaves 2 46
(David Brown) *racd towards far side: chsd ldrs: rdn along wl over 1f out: sn wknd* **50/1**

2122 **15** *1 1/4* **Granny Roz**[47] 5877 3-9-4 **68** ........ (b[1]) BenCurtis 19 45
(David Barron) *racd centre: in tch: rdn along 2f out: sn wknd* **9/1**[2]

0503 **16** *hd* **Merdon Castle (IRE)**[12] 7127 5-9-5 **68** ........ TonyHamilton 6 44
(Jane Chapple-Hyam) *a in rr* **14/1**

4400 **17** *2 3/4* **Jack Luey**[49] 5804 10-9-3 **66** ........ PaulMulrennan 14 32
(Lawrence Mullaney) *a towards rr* **33/1**

3032 **18** *hd* **Compton River**[15] 7020 5-8-13 **65** ........ AdamMcNamara(3) 5 30
(Bryan Smart) *racd towards far side: in tch: rdn along 2f out: sn wknd* **14/1**

0120 **19** *3 1/2* **Hot Hannah**[15] 7014 3-8-11 **66** ........ CallumRodriguez(5) 7 19
(Michael Dods) *racd towards far side: a towards rr* **20/1**

57.89s (-0.71) **Going Correction** -0.075s/f (Good)
**WFA** 3 from 4yo+ 1lb **19** Ran SP% **132.2**
Speed ratings (Par 103): **102,101,96,95,94 94,92,91,90,90 90,90,89,88,86 86,82,81,76**
CSF £17.46 CT £252.00 TOTE £2.60: £1.10, £3.20, £3.80, £9.90; EX 30.60 Trifecta £480.30.
**Owner** Ten Fools & A Horse & Partner **Bred** Hall Of Fame Stud Ltd **Trained** Newmarket, Suffolk

**FOCUS**
A modest sprint handicap and a lopsided betting market as they bet 9-1 bar one, with the favourite going off surprisingly short for a race like this. He got the job done, but it was tight and the first two came clear. The one-two were both well in on old form; this level is fluid.

## 7523 BET AT RACINGUK.COM (S) STKS 7f 219y
**4:40** (4:46) (Class 5) 3-Y-O+ **£3,234** (£962; £481; £240) **Stalls** Centre

Form RPR
055 **1** **Candelisa (IRE)**[14] 7044 4-9-0 86 ........ (p) GrahamLee 6 75+
(Jedd O'Keeffe) *trckd ldrs: pushed along to ld over 2f out: rdn and kpt on fnl f* **11/10**[1]

4204 **2** *2 1/4* **Fort Bastion (IRE)**[30] 6520 8-9-0 85 ........ TomEaves 3 69+
(Brian Ellison) *s.i.s: hld up: hdwy over 3f out: rdn to chse ldr appr fnl f: kpt on same pce and a hld* **7/4**[2]

0200 **3** *nk* **Dandyleekie (IRE)**[6] 7327 5-9-0 74 ........ (v[1]) DanielTudhope 7 69+
(David O'Meara) *hld up in midfield: stdy hdwy 3f out: rdn to chse ldr appr fnl f: kpt on same pce* **7/1**[3]

1000 **4** *3/4* **Lady Lydia (IRE)**[151] 2138 6-9-0 74 ........ (t) PaulMulrennan 1 67
(Gay Kelleway) *stdd s: hld up in rr: pushed along over 2f out: swtchd lft and hdwy 2f out: rdn and kpt on same pce fnl f* **20/1**

0422 **5** *4 1/2* **Seaview**[111] 3496 3-8-7 69 ........ AaronJones(3) 9 57
(David Brown) *led: rdn whn hdd over 2f out: hung lft and wknd fnl f* **14/1**

6000 **6** *2 1/4* **Fidelma Moon (IRE)**[9] 7225 5-8-9 51 ........ (p[1]) BenCurtis 8 46
(Tracy Waggott) *prom: rdn over 2f out: wknd over 1f out* **40/1**

0-00 **7** *1 1/2* **Giveitsomeginger**[13] 7080 3-8-7 43 ow2 ........ (b[1]) ConnorBeasley 5 45?
(Jo Hughes) *trckd ldrs: rdn over 3f out: wknd over 1f out* **125/1**

4346 **8** *3 1/4* **Quadriga (IRE)**[147] 2312 7-8-7 45 ........ PaulaMuir(7) 2 41
(Chris Grant) *midfield: rdn over 3f out: wknd fnl 2f* **125/1**

0000 **9** *3 1/2* **Dark Illustrator**[9] 7220 4-8-9 44 ........ BarryMcHugh 4 27
(Lynn Siddall) *dwlt: a towards rr* **125/1**

6360 **10** *9* **Let's Twist**[29] 6550 5-9-0 65 ........ ShaneGray 11 12
(Kristin Stubbs) *hld up: rdn over 3f out: sn btn* **25/1**

0666 **11** *nk* **Tranquil Tracy**[33] 6381 3-8-5 44 ........ PaddyAspell 12
(John Norton) *a rr* **125/1**

5000 **12** *15* **Stolen Angel (IRE)**[8] 7235 3-8-10 59 ........ DavidAllan 10
(Antony Brittain) *prom: wknd over 2f out and eased* **50/1**

1m 36.92s (0.32) **Going Correction** -0.075s/f (Good)
**WFA** 3 from 4yo+ 4lb **12** Ran SP% **119.3**
Speed ratings (Par 103): **95,92,92,91,87 84,83,80,76,67 67,52**
CSF £2.98 TOTE £1.90: £1.10, £1.30, £1.90; EX 4.20 Trifecta £10.10.The winner was sold for £19,000 by Tony Coyle. Fort Bastion was claimed by Mr Claes Bjorling for £10,000.
**Owner** Paul & Dale Chapman Racing **Bred** Prostock Ltd **Trained** Middleham Moor, N Yorks

**FOCUS**
A wide range of abilities in this seller, with a couple rated in the 80s while four were rated in the 40s. The two highest-rated runners dominated the market and they finished 1-2.

## 7524 RACING UK PROFITS RETURNED TO RACING H'CAP 1m 2f 1y
**5:15** (5:16) (Class 5) (0-75,73) 3-Y-O+ **£3,234** (£962; £481; £240) **Stalls** Low

Form RPR
1020 **1** **Fire Leopard**[15] 7032 3-9-2 **73** ........ (h) DanielTudhope 12 83
(David O'Meara) *hld up: pushed along and hdwy on outer over 2f out: rdn and kpt on wl fnl f: led narrowly fnl 75yds* **14/1**

322 **2** *hd* **Desert Ruler**[69] 5072 4-9-7 **73** ........ JackGarritty 4 82
(Jedd O'Keeffe) *midfield: bit short of room over 2f out: angled rt and in clr 2f out: sn rdn and hdwy: chal strly fnl 110yds: kpt on but a jst hld* **9/2**[1]

0246 **3** *2 1/4* **Scottish Summit (IRE)**[44] 5993 4-9-2 **68** ........ KevinStott 10 73
(Geoffrey Harker) *prom: pushed along to ld 2f out: rdn ent fnl f: hdd 75yds out: wknd* **22/1**

4062 **4** *2 3/4* **House Of Commons (IRE)**[13] 7083 4-9-4 **70** ........ AlistairRawlinson 6 69
(Michael Appleby) *led: rdn whn hdd 2f out: grad wknd fnl f* **12/1**

63 **5** *3/4* **Polar Forest**[9] 7225 7-9-2 **68** ........ (e) PJMcDonald 5 66
(Richard Guest) *trckd ldrs: rdn along 3f out: wknd fnl f* **25/1**

2455 **6** *1/2* **Livella Fella (IRE)**[27] 6628 4-9-7 **73** ........ ConnorBeasley 2 70
(Keith Dalgleish) *prom: rdn along 3f out: wknd fnl f* **20/1**

00-6 **7** *hd* **Weather Front (USA)**[232] 611 4-9-2 **68** ........ (p) DougieCostello 14 64
(Karen McLintock) *dwlt: hld up: rdn over 2f out: nvr threatened* **40/1**

5260 **8** *1* **Maraakib (IRE)**[9] 7225 5-9-1 **70** ........ JoshDoyle(3) 8 64
(David O'Meara) *hld up in midfield: rdn over 2f out: no imp* **16/1**

5302 **9** *1 1/2* **Abushamah (IRE)**[9] 7225 6-9-5 **71** ........ JamesSullivan 15 62
(Ruth Carr) *hld up: nvr threatened* **9/1**

3603 **10** *hd* **Jabbaar**[11] 7142 4-9-7 **73** ........ PhillipMakin 3 64
(Iain Jardine) *s.i.s: sn midfield on outer: rdn along over 3f out: wknd over 1f out* **11/2**[3]

1123 **11** *nse* **Im Dapper Too**[14] 7042 6-9-5 **71** ........ SamJames 13 62
(John Davies) *midfield: rdn over 2f out: wknd over 1f out* **14/1**

0254 **12** *3* **Zealous (IRE)**[12] 7119 4-9-7 **73** ........ BenCurtis 7 58
(Sally Haynes) *trckd ldrs: rdn over 3f out: wknd fnl 2f* **5/1**[2]

5350 **13** *2 1/2* **Brother McGonagall**[11] 7162 3-9-2 **73** ........ DavidAllan 9 54
(Tim Easterby) *hld up: rdn over 3f out: sn btn* **12/1**

3240 **14** *3/4* **Azzir (IRE)**[6] 7328 5-9-4 **73** ........ (v[1]) CliffordLee(3) 1 51
(K R Burke) *in tch: rdn over 3f out: wknd over 1f out* **9/1**

2m 6.39s (-0.71) **Going Correction** -0.075s/f (Good)
**WFA** 3 from 4yo+ 5lb **14** Ran SP% **120.2**
Speed ratings (Par 103): **99,98,97,94,94 93,93,92,91,91 91,89,87,86**
CSF £72.39 CT £1412.72 TOTE £16.60: £4.30, £2.10, £7.90; EX 82.10 Trifecta £3093.20.
**Owner** Chris Napthine **Bred** Carwell Equities Ltd **Trained** Upper Helmsley, N Yorks
■ Stewards' Enquiry : Jack Garritty four day ban: using his whip above the permitted level (20/22-24 Oct)

**FOCUS**
A modest handicap, but a thrilling finish and the winner resumed her progress.

## 7525 WATCH RACE REPLAYS AT RACINGUK.COM H'CAP 5f 217y
**5:45** (5:46) (Class 6) (0-65,65) 3-Y-O+ **£2,749** (£818; £408; £204) **Stalls** Centre

Form RPR
2021 **1** **Nuns Walk**[19] 6904 3-9-4 **64** ........ DavidAllan 10 70
(Tim Easterby) *prom: rdn to chal strly fnl f: edgd ahd fnl 50yds* **9/1**

0202 **2** *nse* **Meandmyshadow**[15] 7017 9-9-2 **63** ........ (b) JoshDoyle(3) 14 69
(Alan Brown) *led: rdn over 2f out: edgd lft over 1f out: strly pressed fnl f: hdd narrowly 50yds out: kpt on* **14/1**

4432 **3** *shd* **Rapid Ranger**[15] 7018 3-9-0 **60** ........ (h) DanielTudhope 4 66
(David O'Meara) *midfield: pushed along and hdwy over 1f out: rdn to chal strly ins fnl f: kpt on* **4/1**[1]

5436 **4** *1 3/4* **Melrose Girl**[35] 6313 3-8-9 **58** ........ AdamMcNamara(3) 5 58
(Bryan Smart) *dwlt: hld up: rdn and hdwy over 1f out: kpt on wl fnl f: nrst fin* **25/1**

6243 **5** *1/2* **Semana Santa**[29] 6546 4-9-7 **65** ........ BenCurtis 6 64
(David Barron) *prom: rdn over 2f out: no ex ins fnl f* **7/1**[3]

2034 **6** *nse* **Point Of Woods**[8] 7244 4-8-12 **63** ........ (p) ConnorMurtagh(7) 2 62
(Tina Jackson) *midfield towards outer: smooth hdwy 2f out: rdn to chal ent fnl f: wknd fnl 110yds* **6/1**[2]

0034 **7** *nk* **Uncle Charlie (IRE)**[15] 7017 3-9-5 **65** ........ TomEaves 8 63
(Ann Duffield) *in tch: rdn over 2f out: kpt on same pce* **14/1**

1014 **8** *1 1/2* **Bogsnog (IRE)**[27] 6635 7-9-2 **60** ........ JackGarritty 13 53
(Ruth Carr) *trckd ldrs: rdn over 2f out: wknd ins fnl f* **25/1**

034 **9** *1 1/4* **Ypres**[29] 6546 8-9-3 **61** ........ (p) KevinStott 3 51
(Jason Ward) *hld up: rdn and sme hdwy appr fnl f: wknd fnl 50yds* **9/1**

6501 **10** *1 1/2* **Lucky Lodge**[48] 5836 7-9-6 **64** ........ (v) CamHardie 18 49
(Antony Brittain) *nvr bttr than midfield* **33/1**

4016 **11** *nk* **Cryptonite (IRE)**[32] 6437 3-8-8 **59** ........ JaneElliott(5) 16 43
(Michael Appleby) *nvr bttr than midfield* **25/1**

-000 **12** *3/4* **Barkston Ash**[15] 7018 9-8-13 **57** ........ (p) NeilFarley 7 39
(Eric Alston) *chsd ldrs: rdn over 2f out: wknd over 1f out* **28/1**

2400 **13** *hd* **Willsy**[29] 6546 4-8-11 **60** ........ (e[1]) GemmaTutty(5) 19 41
(Karen Tutty) *midfield on outer: rdn over 3f out: wknd over 1f out* **22/1**

3050 **14** *nk* **Market Choice (IRE)**[8] 7245 4-9-1 **64** ........ (p) CallumRodriguez(5) 17 44
(Tracy Waggott) *chsd ldrs: rdn over 2f out: wknd over 1f out* **25/1**

6000 **15** *1* **Big Amigo (IRE)**[46] 5930 4-9-2 **63** ........ LewisEdmunds(3) 11 40
(Daniel Mark Loughnane) *a towards rr* **20/1**

0213 **16** *1 1/4* **Spirit Of Zebedee (IRE)**[15] 7018 4-9-6 **64** ........ (p) PJMcDonald 1 38
(John Quinn) *chsd ldrs: rdn over 2f out: wknd over 1f out* **7/1**[3]

546 **17** *nk* **Bay Station**[15] 7014 3-8-8 **57** ........ (p) AaronJones(3) 12 30
(Jason Ward) *a rr* **33/1**

0500 **18** *5* **Funding Deficit (IRE)**[32] 6434 7-8-11 **58** ........ (h) PhilDennis(3) 20 16
(Jim Goldie) *a rr* **33/1**

1m 10.81s (-0.99) **Going Correction** -0.075s/f (Good)
**WFA** 3 from 4yo+ 2lb **18** Ran SP% **129.4**
Speed ratings (Par 101): **103,102,102,100,99 99,99,97,95,93 93,92,92,91,90 88,88,81**
CSF £117.55 CT £609.28 TOTE £8.00: £2.30, £3.30, £1.60, £6.40; EX 141.20 Trifecta £916.30.
**Owner** Ambrose Turnbull & Partner **Bred** Cockrill Emmerson & Woodley **Trained** Great Habton, N Yorks

**FOCUS**
A moderate sprint handicap, but another thriller with nothing to choose between the first three. The action unfolded centre to far side and the race went to the least-exposed runner in the field.
T/Plt: £913.00 to a £1 stake. Pool: £70,891.78. 56.68 winning units. T/Qpdt: £33.70 to a £1 stake. Pool: £6,203.39. 135.85 winning units. **Andrew Sheret & Joe Rowntree**

7526 - 7533a (Foreign Racing) - See Raceform Interactive

## 1070 GHLIN

Wednesday, September 27

**OFFICIAL GOING: Fibresand: standard**

### 7534a PRIX ZELLICK (CLAIMER) (3YO+) (FIBRESAND) 1m 3f 110y
7:55 3-Y-O+ £2,564 (£769; £384; £256; £128)

RPR
1 **Barwick**[3] 7430 9-9-8 0 StephaneBreux 1 58
(George Baker)
2 2 **Flers (GER)**[30] 6543 8-9-13 0 MlleZoePfeil 3 60
(Ecurie Fievez, Belgium)
3 3 ½ **Dabadiyan (IRE)**[432] 7-9-2 0 (b) JozefBojko 4 43
(C Von Der Recke, Germany)
4 1 **Doctor Kehoe**[263] 121 5-9-8 0 (b) KoenClijmans 6 48
(Mme A-M Verschueren, Belgium)
5 3 ½ **Kastini**[704] 7470 7-9-7 0 ow1 MichaelSultana 7 41
(Mme J Hendriks, Holland)
6 1 **Ariost (GER)** 3-8-10 0 StephenHellyn 5 37
(C Von Der Recke, Germany)
7 7 **Nimble Alpha (FR)**[391] 6-9-6 0 (b) JenteMarien 2 27
(R Roels, Germany)

**Owner** Michael H Watt **Bred** Dullingham Park **Trained** Manton, Wilts

## 7480 CHELMSFORD (A.W) (L-H)

Thursday, September 28

**OFFICIAL GOING: Polytrack: standard**
Wind: mild breeze across Weather: cloudy

### 7535 BET TOTEPLACEPOT AT BETFRED.COM NOVICE AUCTION STKS (PLUS 10 RACE) 7f (P)
5:45 (5:49) (Class 4) 2-Y-O £7,115 (£2,117; £1,058; £529) Stalls Low

Form RPR
36 1 **Harbour Vision**[44] 6042 2-8-13 0 KevinStott 1 73
(David Brown) *mde all: rdn whn strly chal 2f out: styd on wl to assert fnl f: rdn out* 25/1
452 2 1 ¼ **Merkava**[28] 6636 2-8-12 69 TomMarquand 3 69
(Robyn Brisland) *trckd ldrs: str chal 2f out: sn rdn: kpt on but no ex ins fnl f* 9/2[1]
0 3 ¾ **Laytown (IRE)**[28] 6636 2-8-9 0 DougieCostello 7 64
(Jamie Osborne) *in tch: hdwy to chse ldng pair wl over 1f out: sn rdn: kpt on ins fnl f but nt quite pce to threaten* 12/1[2]
64 4 6 **Dashing Dusty (IRE)**[38] 6262 2-9-0 0 ShaneKelly 5 53
(Jamie Osborne) *prom: rdn 3f out: one pce fr over 1f out* 14/1[3]
6 5 ½ **Midas Maggie**[23] 6776 2-8-8 0 CallumShepherd(3) 8 48
(Charles Hills) *trckd ldrs: rdn over 2f out: sn one pce* 12/1[2]
6 1 **Trick Shot Jenny** 2-8-9 0 FergusSweeney 6 44
(Jamie Osborne) *hld up last pair but in tch: rdn over 2f out: little imp* 33/1
7 nk **Kingofthesingers** 2-9-1 0 LukeMorris 9 49
(Sir Mark Prescott Bt) *hld up last pair but in tch: rdn over 2f out: nvr any imp* 16/1
0 8 nk **Baileys Rockstar**[45] 5998 2-8-9 0 ConnorBeasley 4 42
(James Given) *in tch: rdn over 2f out: nt pce to get involved* 33/1
1m 26.15s (-1.05) **Going Correction** -0.225s/f (Stan) 8 Ran SP% **55.8**
Speed ratings (Par 97): **97,95,94,87,87 86,85,85**
CSF £25.95 TOTE £14.30: £3.50, £1.10, £2.30; EX 44.70 Trifecta £518.30.
**Owner** New Vision Bloodstock **Bred** Newsells Park Stud **Trained** Averham Park, Notts
■ Wilson was withdrawn. Price at time of withdrawal 4-9f. Rule 4 applies to all bets - deduction 65p in the pound

**FOCUS**
With the odds-on favourite Wilson withdrawn after rearing up in the stalls and unshipping Pat Cosgrave, the complexion of the race changed. The runner-up has been rated to his mark in what looks an ordinary race.

### 7536 BET TOTEJACKPOT AT BETFRED.COM NURSERY H'CAP 6f (P)
6:15 (6:19) (Class 4) (0-85,85) 2-Y-O £7,115 (£2,117; £1,058; £529) Stalls Centre

Form RPR
4221 1 **Yafta**[36] 6304 2-9-4 82 DaneO'Neill 9 89
(Richard Hannon) *mde all: rdn clr over 1f out: in command fnl f: kpt on wl* 5/1[2]
1213 2 2 ¼ **Amazing Alice**[26] 6684 2-9-2 80 (p) LukeMorris 7 80
(Archie Watson) *chsd ldrs: rdn over 2f out: kpt on to go 2nd ins fnl f: a being hld by wnr* 9/1
166 3 ½ **Moseeb (IRE)**[48] 5891 2-8-9 76 (h) CallumShepherd(3) 10 75
(Saeed bin Suroor) *prom: rdn and ev ch 2f out: hld ent fnl f: kpt on same pce* 14/1
1440 4 1 ½ **Ghayadh**[36] 6330 2-9-1 79 JosephineGordon 2 73
(Hugo Palmer) *outpcd towards rr early: hdwy on inner turning in: kpt on wl fnl f: nvr trbld ldrs* 5/1[2]
1043 5 hd **Milton Road**[19] 6951 2-8-10 77 DavidEgan(3) 8 71
(Mick Channon) *s.i.s: towards rr: rdn whn swtchd rt over 1f out: kpt on but no threat fnl f* 12/1
1U32 6 ½ **Mraseel (IRE)**[32] 6481 2-9-1 79 (p) FranBerry 5 71
(James Tate) *s.i.s: towards rr: rdn in midfield over 2f out: kpt on same pce fnl f* 16/1
0200 7 hd **Declarationoflove (IRE)**[19] 6935 2-9-3 81 PatCosgrave 3 73
(Tom Clover) *mid-div: rdn over 2f out: kpt on ins fnl f but nt pce to get on terms* 20/1
4223 8 ½ **Jupiter**[22] 6827 2-9-0 78 FergusSweeney 12 68
(Henry Candy) *mid-div on outer: outpcd 2f out: kpt on but n.d fnl f* 8/1[3]
1504 9 hd **Guzman (IRE)**[15] 7050 2-9-0 78 (h) JackGarritty 11 67
(Richard Fahey) *mid-div: outpcd 2f out: kpt on fnl f but nvr any threat* 14/1
0341 10 ½ **Joe's Spirit (IRE)**[51] 5742 2-9-6 84 SilvestreDeSousa 1 72
(Michael Bell) *chsd ldrs: rdn 2f out: sn one pce* 3/1[1]
421 11 2 ¾ **Shaya (IRE)**[12] 7141 2-8-11 75 ConnorBeasley 4 55
(Roger Fell) *s.i.s: towards rr: hdwy after 2f: rdn to chse ldrs over 2f out: wknd ent fnl f* 11/1
260 12 10 **Faraasah (IRE)**[14] 7090 2-9-2 80 TomMarquand 14 30
(Brian Meehan) *prom: rdn over 2f out: sn wknd* 20/1
1m 11.91s (-1.79) **Going Correction** -0.225s/f (Stan) 12 Ran SP% **124.2**
Speed ratings (Par 97): **102,99,98,96,96 95,95,94,94,93 89,76**
CSF £52.30 CT £599.98 TOTE £5.70: £2.30, £3.20, £3.90; EX 48.80 Trifecta £1663.40.
**Owner** Hamdan Al Maktoum **Bred** Lordship Stud **Trained** East Everleigh, Wilts

**FOCUS**
A competitive nursery on paper, but once again getting to the front early on proved crucial. This rates another step forward from the winner, with the runner-up close to her mark again.

### 7537 BET TOTEQUADPOT AT BETFRED.COM H'CAP 1m 5f 66y(P)
6:45 (6:49) (Class 6) (0-65,64) 3-Y-O £3,234 (£962; £481; £240) Stalls Low

Form RPR
4320 1 **Snowy Winter (USA)**[12] 7152 3-9-3 60 (t) DanielTudhope 10 73+
(Archie Watson) *travelled strly: trckd ldrs: led over 1f out: qcknd clr: v easily* 10/1
3-03 2 7 **Glassalt**[37] 6293 3-9-6 63 SilvestreDeSousa 12 64
(Michael Bell) *mid-div: stdy prog fr 5f out: c wd turning in: sn rdn: styd on to go 2nd towards fin: no ch w wnr* 4/1[2]
000 3 ½ **Mr Davies**[37] 6293 3-9-0 57 TomQueally 8 57
(David Brown) *towards rr of midfield early: hdwy to ld after 5f: rdn and hdd over 1f out: sn outpcd by wnr: styd on but no ex fnl f* 25/1
0000 4 2 ½ **Navajo Star (IRE)**[68] 5142 3-7-13 45 (v) DavidEgan(3) 9 42
(Michael Appleby) *mid-div: hdwy over 2f out: c wd and rdn turning in: styd on same pce* 33/1
3535 5 1 ½ **Challow (IRE)**[5] 7414 3-9-6 63 LiamKeniry 3 58
(Sylvester Kirk) *mid-div: racd keenly: rdn over 2f out: styd on same pce fr over 1f out* 7/1[3]
2234 6 2 ½ **Starshell (IRE)**[15] 7047 3-9-7 64 (p[1]) LukeMorris 1 55
(Sir Mark Prescott Bt) *rn in snatches: s.i.s: towards rr: hdwy on outer 7f out to trck ldrs: rdn w ch over 2f out: one pce fr over 1f out* 6/4[1]
6655 7 5 **Artic Nel**[9] 7232 3-8-3 53 ManuelFernandes(7) 4 37
(Ian Williams) *mid-div: effrt 2f out: nvr threatened: wknd ent fnl f* 10/1
6000 8 2 ¼ **Lady Prima**[22] 6820 3-8-5 48 KieranO'Neill 2 29
(Mike Murphy) *mid-div: rn in snatches: rdn 3f out: wknd over 1f out* 66/1
26 9 1 ½ **Bermondsey Belle (IRE)**[71] 5024 3-9-7 64 (p[1]) JosephineGordon 11 43
(Lucy Wadham) *trckd ldrs tl lost pl after 5f: mid-div: rdn over 2f out: wknd over 1f out* 12/1
0040 10 4 ½ **Volturnus**[40] 6180 3-8-3 46 ow1 (b) MartinDwyer 5 19
(Jamie Osborne) *awkwardly away: nvr travelling: a towards rr* 16/1
6403 11 8 **Mungo Madness**[31] 6524 3-8-3 49 ShelleyBirkett(3) 14 10
(Julia Feilden) *trckd ldrs: rdn over 2f out: wknd over 1f out* 33/1
1253 12 5 **Ablaze**[17] 7003 3-8-13 56 (p[1]) PatCosgrave 7 10
(Laura Mongan) *prom: rdn 3f out: wknd over 2f out* 25/1
6314 13 7 **Tewafeedj**[45] 6002 3-9-5 62 (p[1]) KevinStott 13 7
(Kevin Ryan) *led for over 5f out: prom: rdn over 2f out: sn wknd* 11/1
0000 14 ¾ **Breeze Up**[14] 7085 3-7-11 45 (p) JaneElliott(5) 6
(Ed de Giles) *in tch: struggling 4f out: sn lost pl: wknd over 2f out* 66/1
2m 52.27s (-1.33) **Going Correction** -0.225s/f (Stan) 14 Ran SP% **129.1**
Speed ratings (Par 99): **95,90,90,88,87 86,83,81,81,78 73,70,65,65**
CSF £51.00 CT £1020.54 TOTE £11.10: £3.50, £2.00, £6.40; EX 66.60 Trifecta £1147.20.
**Owner** Boadicea Bloodstock **Bred** Darley **Trained** Upper Lambourn, W Berks

**FOCUS**
An ordinary handicap, but a runaway winner.

### 7538 BET TOTEEXACTA AT BETFRED.COM H'CAP 5f (P)
7:15 (7:18) (Class 4) (0-85,85) 3-Y-O+ £8,086 (£2,406; £1,202; £601) Stalls Low

Form RPR
2040 1 **Alsvinder**[20] 6891 4-9-3 81 DanielTudhope 4 94
(David O'Meara) *mde all: rdn whn strly pressed over 1f out: kpt on wl to assert towards fin: drvn out* 5/2[1]
4544 2 ½ **Rock Of America (USA)**[65] 5256 3-8-13 78 MartinHarley 2 89
(David O'Meara) *trckd ldrs: rdn for str chal over 1f out: ev ch ins fnl f: no ex towards fin* 4/1[2]
0266 3 4 **Royal Mezyan (IRE)**[33] 6411 6-8-8 79 JackOsborn(7) 1 76
(Henry Spiller) *towards rr: hdwy 2f out: sn rdn: r.o to go 3rd jst ins fnl f but nt pce to get on terms* 10/1
0650 4 ½ **Oh So Sassy**[33] 6430 7-9-5 83 TedDurcan 10 78+
(Chris Wall) *hld up last: hdwy over 1f out: r.o ins fnl f: wnt 4th cl home* 10/1
0530 5 1 ¼ **Majestic Hero (IRE)**[26] 6695 5-9-6 84 FranBerry 6 75
(Ronald Harris) *chsd wnr tl rdn 2f out: sn hung lft: kpt on same pce fnl f* 20/1
0225 6 hd **Monumental Man**[13] 7127 8-8-13 82 (p) PaddyBradley(5) 7 72
(Michael Attwater) *mid-div: rdn 2f out: kpt on same pce fnl f* 12/1
1010 7 ¾ **Normal Equilibrium**[8] 7307 7-9-5 83 StevieDonohoe 12 70
(Ivan Furtado) *mid-div: hdwy on outer over 2f out: sn rdn: one pce fnl f* 20/1
5202 8 1 **Diamond Lady**[33] 6430 6-9-4 85 HollieDoyle(3) 11 68
(William Stone) *sn pushed along on last pair: sme late prog but nvr gng pce to get involved* 8/1[3]
6600 9 3 ½ **Fast Act (IRE)**[15] 7055 5-8-11 75 KevinStott 8 46
(Kevin Ryan) *chsd ldrs: rdn over 2f out: wknd over 1f out* 8/1[3]
2050 10 ¾ **Merry Banter**[26] 6679 3-9-1 80 PatDobbs 5 48
(Paul Midgley) *mid-div: rdn 2f out: wknd fnl f* 8/1[3]
16 11 10 **Desert Sport (USA)**[96] 4104 3-8-12 77 LukeMorris 9 9
(Robert Cowell) *a towards rr* 20/1
58.5s (-1.70) **Going Correction** -0.225s/f (Stan)
**WFA** 3 from 4yo+ 1lb 11 Ran SP% **122.1**
Speed ratings (Par 105): **104,103,96,96,94 93,92,90,85,84 68**
CSF £12.11 CT £79.87 TOTE £3.20: £1.30, £2.20, £3.40; EX 14.90 Trifecta £120.20.
**Owner** F Gillespie **Bred** Northern Bloodstock Inc **Trained** Upper Helmsley, N Yorks

**FOCUS**
A one-two for David O'Meara, both improving, with the rest comfortably held. Few got into it, and the bottom three stalls filled the first three positions.

### 7539 BET TOTETRIFECTA AT BETFRED.COM H'CAP (DIV I) 7f (P)
7:45 (7:46) (Class 6) (0-62,63) 3-Y-O+ £3,234 (£962; £481; £240) Stalls Low

Form RPR
3065 1 **Art's Desire (IRE)**[12] 7157 3-9-4 62 LiamKeniry 12 68
(Ed Walker) *hld up wl off str pce: hdwy over 1f out: r.o strly fnl f: led cl home* 5/1[3]
1505 2 ½ **Viola Park**[50] 5783 3-8-12 56 (p) SamHitchcott 2 61+
(Ronald Harris) *chsd ldr: led 2f out: sn rdn: no ex whn hdd cl home: jst hld on for 2nd* 8/1

2530 **3** *nse* **Ronni Layne**[17] 7005 3-8-7 **51** oh4 MartinDwyer 8 56
(Conrad Allen) *mid-div: little imp u.p whn swtchd rt over 1f out: r.o strly w wnr fnl f: nrly snatched 2nd* **33/1**
612 **4** *2 ½* **Frank's Legacy**[2] 7481 3-8-9 **53** (p) ConnorBeasley 11 51+
(Ivan Furtado) *set str pce: hdd 2f out: no ex fnl f* **9/2**[2]
5-60 **5** *2 ½* **Zenovia (IRE)**[182] 1445 3-9-3 **61** LukeMorris 5 52
(Archie Watson) *chsd ldrs: rdn over 2f out: kpt on but nt pce to chal* **12/1**
0425 **6** *3 ½* **Tulip Dress**[24] 6753 4-9-8 **63** SilvestreDeSousa 4 46
(Anthony Carson) *towards rr of midfield: rdn 3f out: nt pce t get involved* **7/2**[1]
524 **7** *hd* **Agnethe (IRE)**[37] 6298 3-9-2 **60** TomMarquand 9 41
(Paul D'Arcy) *hld up towards rr: rdn over 2f out: little imp* **12/1**
63-0 **8** *2 ¾* **Touch Of Color**[10] 7213 4-8-13 **54** JackGarritty 3 29
(Richard Fahey) *chsd ldrs: rdn over 2f out: wknd fnl f* **10/1**
1053 **9** *2* **Miss Osier**[27] 6656 3-9-4 **62** (p) TomQueally 6 30
(Rae Guest) *towards rr of midfield: rdn 3f out: nvr threatened: wknd over 1f out* **5/1**[3]
3500 **10** *5* **Western Safari (IRE)**[12] 7157 3-9-3 **61** DanielTudhope 7 16
(Richard Hannon) *a last pair: wknd over 1f out* **12/1**

1m 25.83s (-1.37) **Going Correction** -0.225s/f (Stan)
**WFA** 3 from 4yo 3lb **10** Ran SP% **120.0**
Speed ratings (Par 101): **98,97,97,94,91 87,87,84,82,76**
CSF £46.14 CT £1234.54 TOTE £6.40: £2.40, £3.40, £9.30; EX 61.30 Trifecta £1963.60.
**Owner** Laurence Bellman & Billy Mills **Bred** Diomed Bloodstock Ltd **Trained** Upper Lambourn, Berks

**FOCUS**
There was a disputed gallop and the race set up nicely for a closer. Straightforward form, with the first two rated close to this year's best.

## 7540 BET TOTETRIFECTA AT BETFRED.COM H'CAP (DIV II) 7f (P)
**8:15** (8:16) (Class 6) (0-62,63) 3-Y-0+ **£3,234** (£962; £481; £240) **Stalls** Low

Form RPR
4321 **1** **Prince Jai**[2] 7481 4-8-3 **51** (b) ManuelFernandes(7) 3 57
(Ian Williams) *mde all: kpt on wl fnl f: rdn out* **13/8**[1]
0132 **2** *½* **La Isla Bonita**[21] 6846 3-9-4 **62** StevieDonohoe 6 66
(Richard Spencer) *chsd wnr: rdn 2f out: kpt on ins fnl f but a being hld* **5/1**[2]
0000 **3** *nk* **Beepeecee**[21] 6866 3-9-1 **59** (b) ShaneKelly 2 62+
(Richard Hughes) *mid-div: hdwy fr 2f out: rdn to chse ldng pair ent fnl f: kpt on wl towards fin* **16/1**
5403 **4** *1 ½* **Pass The Cristal (IRE)**[24] 6753 3-9-3 **61** DougieCostello 1 60
(William Muir) *trckd ldrs: rdn to dispute 2nd 2f out tl ent fnl f: kpt on same pce* **7/1**[3]
0212 **5** *¾* **My Girl Maisie (IRE)**[7] 7332 3-9-2 **60** ConnorBeasley 5 57
(Richard Guest) *hld up towards rr: hdwy over 1f out: nt clr run briefly whn swtchd lft ent fnl f: kpt on but nt pce to threaten* **5/1**[2]
6040 **6** *nk* **Lovely Acclamation (IRE)**[45] 6016 3-9-0 **61** (p[1]) HectorCrouch(3) 10 57
(Ismail Mohammed) *mid-div: rdn over 2f out: kpt on but nt pce to get involved fnl f* **20/1**
3043 **7** *2* **Latest Quest (IRE)**[2] 7481 3-8-7 **51** oh2 MartinDwyer 4 42
(Sylvester Kirk) *mid-div: hdwy over 2f out: sn rdn: wknd ent fnl f* **8/1**
6250 **8** *3 ¼* **Etienne Gerard**[44] 6046 5-8-13 **59** (p) GeorgiaCox(5) 8 42
(Nigel Tinkler) *mid-div: hdwy on outer over 2f out: sn rdn: wknd ent fnl f* **16/1**
6352 **9** *1* **Luduamf (IRE)**[29] 6587 3-8-4 **51** HollieDoyle(3) 12 30
(Richard Hannon) *chsd ldrs: rdn over 2f out: wknd over 1f out* **14/1**
3040 **10** *½* **Higgy's Heartbeat**[12] 7157 3-8-9 **56** JackDuern(3) 7 34
(Dean Ivory) *slowly away: a towards rr* **33/1**

1m 25.71s (-1.49) **Going Correction** -0.225s/f (Stan)
**WFA** 3 from 4yo+ 3lb **10** Ran SP% **121.2**
Speed ratings (Par 101): **99,98,98,96,95 95,92,89,88,87**
CSF £10.15 CT £100.58 TOTE £2.40: £1.50, £1.10, £4.80; EX 9.80 Trifecta £169.90.
**Owner** Mr & Mrs H Parmar **Bred** Ellis Stud And Bellow Hill Stud **Trained** Portway, Worcs

**FOCUS**
This was more steadily run early on than the first division, the pace held up, and the winning time was 0.12sec faster.

## 7541 BET TOTEWIN AT BETFRED.COM H'CAP 1m 2f (P)
**8:45** (8:45) (Class 5) (0-75,76) 3-Y-0+ **£5,175** (£1,540; £769; £384) **Stalls** Low

Form RPR
3061 **1** **Ourmullion**[21] 6848 3-9-6 **76** (p) PatDobbs 10 84
(John Best) *trckd ldr: rdn to ld ent fnl f: styd on wl* **9/2**[1]
033- **2** *nk* **Corked (IRE)**[429] 4743 4-9-7 **72** JosephineGordon 4 79
(Hugo Palmer) *led: rdn and hdd ent fnl f: styd on w ev ch: hld cl home* **9/2**[1]
1453 **3** *1* **Millie's Kiss**[8] 7279 3-8-6 **69** ow1 RossaRyan(7) 1 74
(Philip McBride) *trckd ldrs: rdn in cl 3rd over 1f out: styd on but no ex ins fnl f* **5/1**[2]
2214 **4** *1 ¼* **Hawridge Glory (IRE)**[14] 7097 3-9-1 **71** LiamKeniry 5 74
(Rod Millman) *mid-div: hdwy over 2f out: rdn to chse ldng trio over 1f out: styd on same pce fnl f* **8/1**[3]
6503 **5** *1 ¾* **Mighty Lady**[19] 6948 4-9-7 **72** MartinHarley 12 71
(Robyn Brisland) *hld up: hdwy 2f out: sn rdn: styd on fnl f but nt pce to get involved* **8/1**[3]
2110 **6** *1 ½* **Mutineer**[42] 6101 3-9-4 **74** GeorgeDowning 6 70
(Daniel Kubler) *mid-div: rdn 2f out: sn one pce* **10/1**
5306 **7** *¾* **The Gay Cavalier**[15] 7052 6-8-8 **66** (t) JackOsborn(7) 7 61
(John Ryan) *dwlt: adrift in last: drvn 2f out: styd on but nvr threatened to get on terms* **16/1**
2146 **8** *¾* **Scribner Creek (IRE)**[126] 2996 4-9-0 **68** CharlieBennett(3) 11 61
(Denis Quinn) *hld up towards rr: sme minor late prog but nvr threatened to get involved* **33/1**
3603 **9** *4* **True Colors**[15] 7062 3-8-8 **64** PatrickMathers 2 50
(Richard Fahey) *trckd ldrs: rdn over 2f out: wknd jst over 1f out* **9/2**[1]
3635 **10** *3* **Miss Mirabeau**[26] 6681 3-8-5 **61** (v) LukeMorris 3 41
(Sir Mark Prescott Bt) *mid-div: rdn over 2f out: wknd over 1f out* **8/1**[3]
3010 **11** *8* **Kicking The Can (IRE)**[20] 6893 6-8-8 **66** NatalieHambling(7) 13 29
(Noel Wilson) *towards rr of mid-div: rdn over 2f out: sn wknd* **33/1**

2m 4.88s (-3.72) **Going Correction** -0.225s/f (Stan)
**WFA** 3 from 4yo+ 5lb **11** Ran SP% **125.4**
Speed ratings (Par 103): **105,104,103,102,101 100,99,99,95,93 87**
CSF £26.36 CT £108.62 TOTE £6.10: £2.00, £1.20, £2.30; EX 34.40 Trifecta £177.40.
**Owner** David & Elaine Long **Bred** Best Breeding **Trained** Oad Street, Kent

**FOCUS**
The early gallop wasn't that fast and the pace held up well, the first three racing in the first four positions throughout.

## 7542 2018 MEMBERSHIP NOW AVAILABLE MAIDEN STKS 1m 2f (P)
**9:15** (9:15) (Class 5) 3-Y-0+ **£5,175** (£1,540; £769; £384) **Stalls** Low

Form RPR
22 **1** **Ennjaaz (IRE)**[21] 6851 3-9-5 0 (p[1]) PatCosgrave 3 84+
(Saeed bin Suroor) *trckd ldrs: rdn to chal jst over 1f out: drifted lft whn taking narrow advantage ins fnl f: styd on wl* **4/7**[1]
2526 **2** *hd* **Footman (GER)**[40] 6194 3-9-5 81 ShaneKelly 6 83
(Richard Hughes) *prom: rdn to ld over 1f out: sn strly chal: carried lft whn narrowly hdd ins fnl f: styd on wl* **4/1**[3]
0 **3** *6* **Timely Arrival**[55] 5611 3-9-5 0 SteveDrowne 4 71
(Amanda Perrett) *t.k.h early: trckd ldrs: rdn 2f out: kpt on to go 3rd towards fin but nt pce of front pair* **16/1**
2 **4** *¾* **Sacred Way**[38] 6268 3-9-5 0 KevinStott 2 70
(Kevin Ryan) *racd keenly: led: rdn and hdd over 1f out: no ex fnl f: lost 3rd towards fin* **7/2**[2]
0 **5** *7* **Lead A Dance (IRE)**[14] 7080 3-8-11 0 TimClark(3) 5 51
(John Butler) *hld up but in tch: effrt 2f out: drifted rt and fdd fnl f* **66/1**
4 **6** *7* **Wasted Sunsets (FR)**[29] 6577 3-9-0 0 (t) MartinHarley 7 37
(John Berry) *hld up but in tch: struggling 3f out: wknd over 1f out* **66/1**

2m 6.51s (-2.09) **Going Correction** -0.225s/f (Stan) **6** Ran SP% **114.7**
Speed ratings (Par 103): **99,98,94,93,87 82**
CSF £3.50 TOTE £1.50: £1.10, £2.50; EX 3.50 Trifecta £17.70.
**Owner** Godolphin **Bred** Darley **Trained** Newmarket, Suffolk
■ Stewards' Enquiry : Pat Cosgrave caution; careless riding

**FOCUS**
A fair maiden in which the first two finished clear. The winner has been rated as finding minor improvement, with the runner-up to form.
T/Plt: £220.50 to a £1 stake. Pool: £89,634.71 - 296.70 winning units T/Qpdt: £97.30 to a £1 stake. Pool: £10,941.04 - 83.15 winning units **Tim Mitchell**

# 7399 NEWMARKET (R-H)
Thursday, September 28

**OFFICIAL GOING: Good to soft (soft in places; stands' 6.4, centre 6.4, far 6.1)**
Wind: nil Weather: sunny; 20 degrees

## 7543 BRITISH STALLION STUDS EBF MAIDEN STKS (PLUS 10 RACE) 1m
**2:00** (2:01) (Class 4) 2-Y-O **£5,175** (£1,540; £769; £384) **Stalls** High

Form RPR
3 **1** **Ghaiyyath (IRE)**[13] 7117 2-9-0 0 (h[1]) JamesDoyle 8 90+
(Charlie Appleby) *str: lw: mde all towards outer: rdn clr over 1f out: styd on stoutly and easily in command after* **11/8**[1]
**2** *5* **Proschema (IRE)** 2-9-0 0 MartinHarley 3 79+
(Tom Dascombe) *athletic: towards rr: wnt fr outside over 2f out to ins and checked briefly 2f out: gd prog over 1f out: styd on gamely to go 2nd fnl 100yds and sn clr of rest: no ch w wnr* **40/1**
**3** *3 ¼* **Bombyx** 2-9-0 0 DanielMuscutt 15 71+
(James Fanshawe) *cmpt: towards rr: drvn over 2f out: styd on really wl ins fnl f to snatch wl hld 3rd* **25/1**
46 **4** *hd* **Sherzy Boy**[13] 7117 2-9-0 0 SeanLevey 14 71
(Richard Hannon) *prom and racd freely: rdn over 2f out: no ex 1f out: lost 3rd fnl strides* **22/1**
**5** *¾* **Mutanaqel** 2-9-0 0 JimCrowley 4 69
(Owen Burrows) *unf: chsd ldrs on outside: rdn 1/2-way: effrt over 2f out: nt qckn fnl f* **20/1**
0 **6** *1 ¾* **Baasha**[13] 7128 2-9-0 0 AntonioFresu 11 66
(Ed Dunlop) *t.k.h: trckd ldrs: rdn and wknd over 1f out* **100/1**
4 **7** *shd* **Tiffin Top**[13] 7117 2-9-0 0 FrankieDettori 18 65
(John Gosden) *athletic: plld hrd: pressed ldrs: rdn wl over 1f out: btn 1f out* **11/4**[2]
4 **8** *1* **Gododdin**[26] 6683 2-9-0 0 JosephineGordon 2 63
(Hugo Palmer) *unf: prom on outside: drvn 2f out: stl 2nd over 1f out: hung lft and lost several pls whn tiring after* **16/1**
4 **9** *1 ½* **Para Mio (IRE)**[20] 6869 2-9-0 0 ShaneKelly 9 60
(Seamus Durack) *pressed ldrs tl rdn and wknd wl over 1f out* **7/1**[3]
0 **10** *¾* **Nelson River**[20] 6869 2-9-0 0 AdamKirby 10 58
(Clive Cox) *midfield: rdn after 3f: btn over 2f out* **50/1**
0 **11** *shd* **Pippin**[21] 6859 2-9-0 0 OisinMurphy 13 58
(Hughie Morrison) *w'like: leggy: bhd fr 1/2-way: drvn over 2f out: no ch after* **40/1**
0 **12** *1* **Silver Crescent**[23] 6777 2-9-0 0 PatDobbs 12 56
(Ralph Beckett) *cl up: rdn over 3f out: edging lft and sn btn* **33/1**
**13** *¾* **Midi** 2-9-0 0 RyanMoore 6 54+
(Sir Michael Stoute) *str: gd-bodied: bit bkwd: missed break: rn green and rdn in rr: nvr rcvrd* **8/1**
0 **14** *1 ½* **Pentland Hills (IRE)**[21] 6854 2-9-0 0 TomQueally 16 51
(Chris Wall) *unf: on his toes and mounted outside paddock: plld hrd: chsd ldrs over 4f: btn over 2f out: eased cl home* **100/1**
**15** *12* **Highcastle (IRE)** 2-9-0 0 SilvestreDeSousa 17 24
(Ed Dunlop) *w'like: missed break: a bhd: t.o and eased fnl f* **66/1**
04 **16** *14* **Boniface (IRE)**[46] 5964 2-9-0 0 PaoloSirigu 7
(Robert Eddery) *racd freely: chsd ldrs 5f: t.o and eased fnl f* **100/1**

1m 39.41s (0.81) **Going Correction** +0.20s/f (Good) **16** Ran SP% **125.5**
Speed ratings (Par 97): **103,98,94,94,93 92,91,90,89,88 88,87,86,85,73 59**
CSF £84.58 TOTE £2.30: £1.20, £19.10, £7.50; EX 117.20 Trifecta £2535.30.
**Owner** Godolphin **Bred** Springbank Way Stud **Trained** Newmarket, Suffolk

**FOCUS**
Far side course. Stalls: stands' side, except 1m4f & 2m: centre. The ground was changed to Good to soft, soft in places after 5mm of rain overnight and just over 1mm more during the morning, with the ground described as being softer in the dip about 1f out. After riding the first winner James Doyle said: "The ground is not bad, just on the easy side. It has taken the rain well." Standout names on this race's role of honour are Telescope (2012) and Eminent (2016).

## 7544 NEWMARKETRACECOURSES.CO.UK NURSERY H'CAP 1m
**2:35** (2:35) (Class 2) 2-Y-O **£9,056** (£2,695; £1,346; £673) **Stalls** High

Form RPR
541 **1** **Rastrelli (FR)**[17] 7001 2-9-3 **85** JamesDoyle 4 90
(Charlie Appleby) *cl up: edging lft fr 1/2-way: drvn to chal and hung lft ins fnl f: styd on wl to ld fnl 75yds* **7/2**[3]
632 **2** *¾* **Global Conqueror**[21] 6854 2-9-0 **82** AndreaAtzeni 3 85+
(Simon Crisford) *led: drvn 2f out: hdd fnl 75yds and nt qckn* **10/3**[2]

0341 **3** ¾ **Paint**[28] 6613 2-8-4 **75**............ HollieDoyle[(3)] 1 76
(Richard Hannon) *bhd on outer: pushed along and outpcd on outer 3f out: clsd over 1f out: no imp fnl 100yds* **9/1**
3431 **4** 1½ **Blue Laureate**[13] 7117 2-9-6 **88**............ AdamKirby 5 86
(Clive Cox) *chsd ldrs: drvn and outpcd over 2f out: sme late prog ins fnl f to snatch 4th* **3/1**[1]
1014 **5** ½ **Maksab (IRE)**[12] 7148 2-9-3 **85**............ SilvestreDeSousa 2 82
(Mick Channon) *chsd ldrs: rdn to chal on outer 2f out: no ex over 1f out: lost 4th cl home* **13/2**
2115 **6** 5 **Rhosneigr (IRE)**[12] 7148 2-9-1 **83**............ SteveDrowne 6 69
(Charles Hills) *stdd to chse ldrs: rdn 2f out: floundering after* **16/1**
1221 **7** 6 **Tadleel**[19] 6934 2-9-7 **89**............ JimCrowley 7 62
(Ed Dunlop) *pressed ldr: drvn 2f out: wknd over 1f out: eased cl home* **7/1**

1m 39.63s (1.03) **Going Correction** +0.20s/f (Good) **7** Ran SP% **112.0**
Speed ratings (Par 101): **102,101,100,99,98 93,87**
CSF £14.90 TOTE £5.00: £2.60, £1.80; EX 17.90 Trifecta £131.00.
**Owner** Godolphin **Bred** T De La Heronniere Et Al **Trained** Newmarket, Suffolk

**FOCUS**
A decent nursery, they didn't go a great gallop and it paid to race handily.

## 7545 SWYNFORD MANOR WEDDING VENUE FILLIES' H'CAP 7f
**3:10** (3:10) (Class 3) (0-90,89) 3-Y-O+ **£9,056** (£2,695; £1,346; £673) **Stalls** High

Form RPR
0540 **1** **Toy Theatre**[28] 6620 3-8-4 **71** oh1............ SilvestreDeSousa 2 78
(Michael Appleby) *swtchd lft fr outer after s and sn led on stands side rail: rdn 2f out: drvn and hld on gamely cl home* **8/1**[3]
4340 **2** *nk* **Parlance (IRE)**[36] 6321 3-9-0 **81**............ RyanMoore 6 87
(Sir Michael Stoute) *wore ear plugs: sweating bdly and mounted ouside paddock: stdd to chse ldrs: rdn 2f out: wnt 2nd wl ins fnl f: tried to lunge late but jst hld* **11/2**[2]
6110 **3** 2 **Sayem**[58] 5506 3-9-1 **82**............ JamieSpencer 7 83
(Ed Walker) *pressed wnr: rdn 2f out: nt qckn ins fnl f and lost 2nd fnl 50yds* **11/2**[2]
4046 **4** 3½ **Rebel Surge (IRE)**[14] 7086 4-9-9 **87**............(p) StevieDonohoe 5 79
(Richard Spencer) *chsd ldrs: drvn over 2f out: hanging and racing v awkwardly after: no imp fnl f* **12/1**
6150 **5** 1¼ **Stellar Surprise**[11] 7204 3-9-2 **83**............(t) HarryBentley 4 71
(Stuart Williams) *pressed ldrs tl rdn and fdd over 1f out* **12/1**
2-01 **6** *nse* **First Dance (IRE)**[43] 6066 3-9-0 **81**............ JimCrowley 8 69
(James Tate) *racd freely: sn chsng ldrs: drvn 2f out: wl hld over 1f out* **11/2**[2]
0322 **7** 1½ **Summer Chorus**[26] 6686 4-9-10 **88**............ OisinMurphy 1 73
(Andrew Balding) *lw: taken down early: stdd and keen in last pl early: rdn 3f out: no rspnse and toiling after* **9/4**[1]
4215 **8** 3¾ **Peak Princess (IRE)**[26] 6686 3-9-8 **89**............(b) SeanLevey 3 62
(Richard Hannon) *t.k.h on outside: chsd ldrs: rdn and wknd 2f out: eased cl home* **11/1**

1m 26.17s (0.77) **Going Correction** +0.20s/f (Good)
**WFA** 3 from 4yo 3lb **8** Ran SP% **111.8**
Speed ratings (Par 104): **103,102,100,96,94 94,93,88**
CSF £48.87 CT £260.60 TOTE £8.70: £2.80, £1.40, £2.10; EX 47.40 Trifecta £316.00.
**Owner** L J Vaessen **Bred** Darley **Trained** Oakham, Rutland

**FOCUS**
A decent handicap for fillies in which they didn't go a strong gallop. The winner has been rated back to the level of her Wolverhampton win, with the runner-up close to form.

## 7546 TATTERSALLS STKS (GROUP 3) (C&G) (REGISTERED AS THE SOMERVILLE STAKES) 7f
**3:45** (3:45) (Class 1) 2-Y-O
**£28,355** (£10,750; £5,380; £2,680; £1,345; £675) **Stalls** High

Form RPR
1 **1** **Elarqam**[18] 6967 2-9-0 0............ JimCrowley 2 111+
(Mark Johnston) *str: swtg: led towards outside: drvn over 1f out: edgd lft briefly whn assuming command ins fnl f: styd on v resolutely: eased cl home* **11/8**[1]
1321 **2** 2¼ **Tip Two Win**[13] 7112 2-9-0 107............ AdamKirby 4 105
(Roger Teal) *medium-sized: w'like: towards rr: rdn to improve 2f out: wnt 2nd 1f out: no match for wnr but gamely clung on to 2nd pl* **9/2**[2]
4110 **3** *shd* **Tangled (IRE)**[14] 7090 2-9-0 102............ SeanLevey 8 105
(Richard Hannon) *hdwy on stands' rails to press wnr 2f out tl rdn 1f out: edgd rt and no ch w him after but kpt on wl cl home* **8/1**
1 **4** 1¾ **Fajjaj (IRE)**[19] 6916 2-9-0 0............ FrankieDettori 5 100+
(Hugo Palmer) *str: swtg: chsd ldrs: pushed along and no imp over 1f out: styd on nicely wout being asked too many questions cl home* **6/1**[3]
141 **5** ½ **Fortune's Pearl (IRE)**[34] 6388 2-9-0 88............ OisinMurphy 3 99
(Andrew Balding) *athletic: lw: awkward leaving stalls: sn prom: rdn wl over 1f out: no ex and edgd lft ins fnl f* **14/1**
122 **6** 6 **Albishr (IRE)**[34] 6396 2-9-0 102............ RyanMoore 9 84
(Richard Hannon) *str: prom tl rdn over 2f out: sn btn* **6/1**[3]
1 **7** 1½ **Morlock (IRE)**[20] 6884 2-9-0 0............ JamesDoyle 1 80
(Charlie Appleby) *cmpt: chsd ldrs on outer tl rdn and weakned 2f out* **12/1**
1102 **8** *nk* **Myboyhenry (IRE)**[25] 6721 2-9-0 87............ CliffordLee 7 80
(K R Burke) *chsd ldrs: drvn 3f out: btn over 2f out* **66/1**
1 **9** *hd* **Statuario**[14] 7079 2-9-0 0............ TomQueally 6 79
(Eve Johnson Houghton) *w'like: towards rr: rdn and btn over 2f out* **40/1**

1m 25.49s (0.09) **Going Correction** +0.20s/f (Good) **9** Ran SP% **118.3**
Speed ratings (Par 105): **107,104,104,102,101 94,93,92,92**
CSF £7.88 TOTE £2.30: £1.10, £1.50, £2.00; EX 8.40 Trifecta £29.40.
**Owner** Hamdan Al Maktoum **Bred** Floors Farming **Trained** Middleham Moor, N Yorks

**FOCUS**
Sound enough form for the level, taken at face value around the 2nd/3rd, and a winner on the up.

## 7547 JOCKEY CLUB ROSE BOWL STKS (LISTED RACE) 2m
**4:20** (4:24) (Class 1) 3-Y-O+
**£20,982** (£7,955; £3,981; £1,983; £995; £499) **Stalls** Centre

Form RPR
4062 **1** **Face The Facts (IRE)**[19] 6930 3-8-7 93............ TedDurcan 3 109
(John Gosden) *lw: v free gng to post and almost bolting: settled in last pair: stdy hdwy 4f out: rdn over 2f out: styd on wl to wear down ldr fnl 50yds* **9/2**[2]
0146 **2** 1 **Nearly Caught (IRE)**[18] 6984 7-9-6 109............ JamesDoyle 4 111
(Hughie Morrison) *prom: rdn 3f out: led 100yds out tl hdd and no ex fnl 50yds* **7/1**
1113 **3** 3 **UAE King**[33] 6421 3-8-7 99............ AndreaAtzeni 9 104
(Roger Varian) *lw: travelled wl in midfield: effrt 4f out: led wl over 2f out: rdn and hdd fnl 100yds and wknd* **5/2**[1]
3101 **4** 1½ **Jukebox Jive (FR)**[69] 5110 3-8-7 90............(t) DavidEgan 10 103
(Anthony Honeyball) *pressed ldrs on outside: led 5f out tl rdn and hdd over 2f out: wknd ins fnl f* **16/1**
5465 **5** 8 **Platitude**[36] 6329 4-9-3 103............ RyanMoore 6 93
(Sir Michael Stoute) *lw: mounted outside paddock: bhd: rdn 4f out: lost tch 3f out* **8/1**
3010 **6** 5 **Swashbuckle**[47] 5912 4-9-3 90............ OisinMurphy 8 87
(Andrew Balding) *sn chsng clr ldr: rdn 5f out: fdd 3f out: t.o* **40/1**
2100 **7** 9 **Higher Power**[34] 6400 5-9-3 110............(t[1]) TomQueally 7 76
(James Fanshawe) *a towards rr: lost tch 3f out: t.o* **12/1**
01-4 **8** 8 **Arch Villain (IRE)**[33] 6447 8-9-3 104............(b) JimCrowley 2 67
(Amanda Perrett) *chsd ldrs: rdn 3f out: no rspnse and sn btn: eased and t.o* **10/1**
5530 **9** 14 **Harlequeen**[14] 7089 4-8-12 101............(v) SilvestreDeSousa 5 45
(Mick Channon) *led early to post: led and racd freely and abt 5 l clr: rdn and hdd 5f out: hmpd over 3f out and dropped out rapidly: t.o and eased fnl f* **16/1**
1500 **P** **Winning Story**[33] 6447 4-9-3 107............(v) PatCosgrave 1
(Saeed bin Suroor) *v free gng to post: keen towards rr: effrt to chse ldrs 4f out: p.u and dismntd wl over 2f out: fatally injured* **6/1**[3]

3m 24.66s (-5.84) **Going Correction** +0.125s/f (Good)
**WFA** 3 from 4yo+ 10lb **10** Ran SP% **115.6**
Speed ratings (Par 111): **119,118,117,116,112 109,105,101,94,**
CSF £35.75 TOTE £5.40: £1.70, £2.20, £2.20; EX 36.40 Trifecta £124.70.
**Owner** George Strawbridge **Bred** George Strawbridge **Trained** Newmarket, Suffolk

**FOCUS**
A fair Listed race, which was run as the Fenwolf Stakes before 2011. Face The Facts is the first 3yo to win it. They went a decent gallop over the trip and only the first four saw it out. This has been rated around the runner-up to this year's form.

## 7548 WEATHERBYS GENERAL STUD BOOK ONLINE H'CAP 1m 4f
**4:55** (4:59) (Class 2) (0-100,95) 3-Y-O+ **£12,938** (£3,850; £1,924; £962) **Stalls** Centre

Form RPR
3116 **1** **Torcello (IRE)**[19] 6920 3-8-9 **85**............ OisinMurphy 1 99
(Andrew Balding) *lw: mde all: increased pce 3f out: 4 l clr 1f out: drvn along to maintain advantage after: readily* **5/4**[1]
0040 **2** 3 **Saunter (FR)**[41] 6151 4-9-10 **93**............ JamesDoyle 3 101
(Ian Williams) *settled towards rr: prog on far rails 4f out to chse wnr wl over 1f out: drvn and tried to get on terms and gng clr of rest 1f out but wl hld* **6/1**[3]
5533 **3** 5 **Jaameh (IRE)**[19] 6929 4-9-12 **95**............(b[1]) JimCrowley 5 95
(Mark Johnston) *swtg: pressed wnr tl rdn wl over 1f out: styd on same pce and wl hld fnl f* **12/1**
250/ **4** 1¾ **Ooty Hill**[719] 7118 5-9-12 **95**............(h[1]) StevieDonohoe 7 92
(Charlie Fellowes) *swtg: racd keenly and pressed ldrs: rdn and outpcd by ldrs 2f out: plugged on* **20/1**
1401 **5** ¾ **Marmajuke Bay**[21] 6857 4-9-8 **91**............(p) SteveDrowne 4 87
(Mark Usher) *midfield: rdn and outpcd 3f out: styd on wout threatening ins fnl f* **12/1**
6143 **6** 2 **Roar (IRE)**[20] 6872 3-8-5 **81**............ HarryBentley 2 75
(Brian Ellison) *swtg: prom: drvn over 3f out: sn btn: eased ins fnl f* **6/1**[3]
1405 **7** 6 **Afonso De Sousa (USA)**[19] 6952 7-9-2 **85**............ AlistairRawlinson 6 68
(Michael Appleby) *t.k.h in last pl: nt keen whn rdn 3f out: sn btn: t.o and eased* **50/1**
2042 **8** 7 **Amlad (IRE)**[16] 7031 3-8-11 **87**............ RyanMoore 8 60
(Ed Dunlop) *bhd: effrt on outside 3f out: rdn and fdd 2f out: t.o and eased* **9/2**[2]

2m 33.04s (1.04) **Going Correction** +0.125s/f (Good)
**WFA** 3 from 4yo+ 7lb **8** Ran SP% **113.3**
Speed ratings (Par 109): **101,99,95,94,94 92,88,84**
CSF £8.99 CT £59.93 TOTE £2.10: £1.10, £1.90, £3.00; EX 9.50 Trifecta £66.40.
**Owner** Mick and Janice Mariscotti **Bred** Rathasker Stud **Trained** Kingsclere, Hants

**FOCUS**
Little got into this useful handicap, the winner making all at his own tempo.

## 7549 MOLSON COORS H'CAP 1m
**5:30** (5:32) (Class 3) (0-95,96) 3-Y-O+ **£9,056** (£2,695; £1,346; £673) **Stalls** High

Form RPR
0624 **1** **Repercussion**[32] 6483 4-9-1 **88**............(t[1]) StevieDonohoe 3 101
(Charlie Fellowes) *racd keenly and prom on outside: led 2f out: clr 1f out: rdn and hung lft whn in command after* **14/1**
-300 **2** 5 **Knight Owl**[47] 5914 7-9-0 **90**............ GeorgeWood[(3)] 7 92
(James Fanshawe) *pressed ldrs: chsd wnr over wl over 1f out: sn drvn: wl hld fnl f* **16/1**
00-0 **3** ½ **Bronze Angel (IRE)**[12] 7149 8-9-9 **96**............(v) HayleyTurner 8 96
(Marcus Tregoning) *missed break and n.m.r sn after: bhd: outpcd 2f out: rdn and prog over 1f out: styd on gamely ins fnl f: too much to do* **14/1**
0442 **4** 2¼ **The Warrior (IRE)**[19] 6933 5-9-1 **88**............ RyanMoore 2 83
(Amanda Perrett) *lw: bhd: effrt on outside over 2f out: rdn over 1f out: nt qckn after* **10/1**
0063 **5** 1¼ **Via Serendipity**[44] 6026 3-8-9 **86**............(t) HarryBentley 5 78
(Stuart Williams) *chsd ldrs: n.m.r and pushed along over 1f out: no imp ins fnl f* **9/1**
5423 **6** ¾ **Night Circus (IRE)**[15] 7053 3-9-1 **92**............ JamesDoyle 6 83
(Charlie Appleby) *led: rdn 3f out: hdd 2f out: dropped out rapidly* **4/1**[3]
1431 **7** ½ **Rigoletto (SWI)**[22] 6809 3-9-3 **94**............ JamieSpencer 11 83
(Luca Cumani) *swtg: prom: w ldr 3f out: rdn and wknd 2f out: racing v awkwardly after* **11/4**[1]
5034 **8** 3¼ **Eltezam (IRE)**[8] 7285 4-8-7 **83**............(h) HollieDoyle[(3)] 10 65
(Amanda Perrett) *towards rr: drvn and struggling 3f out* **25/1**
1600 **9** 6 **Medburn Dream**[47] 5914 4-9-2 **89**............ SteveDrowne 9 57
(Paul Henderson) *cl up: rdn and wknd over 2f out: t.o and eased* **66/1**
5210 **10** 2½ **Intrude**[105] 3743 5-9-2 **89**............(t) MartinHarley 4 51
(Stuart Williams) *missed break: a bhd: t.o and eased* **40/1**
222 **11** 38 **Sun Lover**[33] 6414 4-9-2 **89**............ AndreaAtzeni 1
(Roger Varian) *lw: last early: struggling 1/2-way: eased 2f out: t.o and virtually p.u ins fnl f* **3/1**[2]

1m 38.72s (0.12) **Going Correction** +0.20s/f (Good)
**WFA** 3 from 4yo+ 4lb **11** Ran SP% **117.8**
Speed ratings (Par 107): **107,102,101,99,98 97,96,93,87,85 47**
CSF £214.05 CT £3230.98 TOTE £15.90: £3.20, £5.40, £3.90; EX 238.50 Trifecta £5149.20.
**Owner** Seventh Lap Racing & Partners **Bred** Darley **Trained** Newmarket, Suffolk

**FOCUS**
There was a late-season look to the form of this decent handicap, but an improved showing from the winner.

## 7550 NEWMARKET CHALLENGE WHIP H'CAP 1m 2f
**6:05** (6:05) (Class 4) (0-85,83) 3-Y-O+ £0Stalls High

Form RPR
4052 1 **Brief Visit**[34] 6369 4-9-3 **81** OisinMurphy 4 90
(Andrew Balding) *lw: mde all: set slow pce: rdn clr over 1f out: readily* **11/10**[1]
1100 2 *7* **Turning Gold**[13] 7119 3-8-10 **79** (v[1]) JamieSpencer 2 75
(Sir Mark Prescott Bt) *wnt 2nd 3f out: rdn over 2f out: nvr making any imp on easy wnr* **15/8**[2]
0602 3 *3 ½* **Shimmering Light**[8] 7279 3-7-11 **69** oh1 (v) AaronJones(3) 1 58
(Michael Bell) *chsd wnr for 7f: sn rdn: plodded on fr wl over 1f out* **3/1**[3]
2m 9.28s (3.48) **Going Correction** +0.20s/f (Good)
**WFA** 3 from 4yo 5lb 3 Ran SP% **107.4**
Speed ratings (Par 105): **94,88,85**
CSF £3.38 TOTE £2.00; EX 2.50 Trifecta £3.10.
**Owner** Cliveden Stud **Bred** Cliveden Stud Ltd **Trained** Kingsclere, Hants
**FOCUS**
Run at a steady gallop, this took little winning.
T/Jkpt: Part won. £10,000 to a £1 stake. Pool: £10,000 - 0.50 winning units. T/Plt: £30.90 to a £1 stake. Pool: £115,918.44 - 2,729.78 winning units T/Qpdt: £8.50 to a £1 stake. Pool: £7,660.43 - 659.76 winning units **Iain Mackenzie**

# 7326 PONTEFRACT (L-H)
Thursday, September 28

**OFFICIAL GOING: Heavy (6.5)**
Wind: Moderate behind Weather: Sunny

## 7551 PROCUREMENTSEMINARS.CO.UK NOVICE AUCTION STKS (PLUS 10 RACE) 6f
**2:20** (2:21) (Class 4) 2-Y-O £4,528 (£1,347; £673; £336) Stalls Low

Form RPR
5 1 **Dawn Breaking**[19] 6939 2-8-9 0 LewisEdmunds(3) 9 73
(Richard Whitaker) *mde all: rdn over 1f out: kpt on wl towards fin* **11/2**[3]
5 2 *½* **Se You**[30] 6545 2-9-2 0 DavidAllan 4 75
(Tim Easterby) *prom on inner: chsd wnr 1/2-way: rdn over 1f out: drvn to chal ins fnl f: kpt on* **9/4**[1]
25 3 *1 ¾* **Ormesher**[15] 7043 2-9-1 0 DavidNolan 10 69
(Donald McCain) *trckd wnr on outer: wd st: rdn wl over 1f out: edgd rt ent fnl f: kpt on* **7/2**[2]
4 *9* **Mercury Rising** 2-8-13 0 DavidProbert 2 40+
(Andrew Balding) *dwlt and n.m.r s: sn swtchd rt and towards rr: pushed along and green 1/2-way: styd on fnl 2f: nvr nr ldrs* **9/4**[1]
0 5 *5* **Watching Spirits**[162] 1873 2-9-1 0 GrahamLee 3 27
(Ann Duffield) *chsd ldrs: rdn along over 2f out: sn wknd* **16/1**
0 6 *10* **Blyton Lass**[16] 7013 2-8-8 0 JamesSullivan 1
(James Given) *sn outpcd and bhd fr 1/2-way* **20/1**
0 7 *3 ½* **Balmec (IRE)**[5] 7383 2-9-1 0 ShaneGray 7
(Ann Duffield) *a in rr: outpcd and bhd fr 1/2-way* **40/1**
0 8 *9* **Mayhem Maybe (IRE)**[22] 6824 2-8-6 0 JimmyQuinn 5
(Gay Kelleway) *chsd ldrs: rdn along 2f out: sn wknd* **40/1**
1m 21.79s (4.89) **Going Correction** +0.825s/f (Soft) 8 Ran SP% **114.7**
Speed ratings (Par 97): **100,99,97,85,78 65,60,48**
CSF £18.08 TOTE £5.70: £1.50, £1.10, £1.30; EX 22.20 Trifecta £70.00.
**Owner** D Gration, G Sutcliffe, N Farman, Jeaton **Bred** Mrs M J Blackburn **Trained** Scarcroft, W Yorks
**FOCUS**
The course passed an initial morning inspection and so it was obviously testing underfoot. After the first jockey David Nolan called the ground 'bottomless'. This was an ordinary novice event in which you had to be handy.

## 7552 IRISH STALLION FARMS EBF FILLIES' NURSERY H'CAP 1m 6y
**2:55** (2:55) (Class 4) (0-85,85) 2-Y-O £6,469 (£1,925; £962; £481) Stalls Low

Form RPR
1463 1 **Shazzab (IRE)**[24] 6762 2-8-7 **71** (p) PaulHanagan 8 78
(Richard Fahey) *hld up in tch: hdwy on outer 3f out: rdn to ld over 1f out: edgd lft ent fnl f: kpt on wl* **16/1**
0411 2 *2 ¼* **Dathanna (IRE)**[40] 6200 2-9-7 **85** (h) PhillipMakin 1 87
(Charlie Appleby) *hld up: hdwy on inner 3f out: chsd ldrs 2f out: rdn and ev ch over 1f out: drvn and kpt on same pce fnl f* **13/8**[1]
1023 3 *2 ¾* **Di Fede (IRE)**[19] 6934 2-9-4 **82** RichardKingscote 2 79+
(Ralph Beckett) *trckd ldrs on inner: hdwy 3f out: led 2f out: rdn and hdd over 1f out: sn drvn and kpt on same pce* **6/1**[2]
5031 4 *4* **Che Bella (IRE)**[19] 6940 2-9-0 **78** JoeFanning 9 66+
(Keith Dalgleish) *trckd ldrs on outer: hdwy and cl up over 2f out: rdn and ev ch wl over 1f out: sn drvn and one pce* **7/1**[3]
3453 5 *9* **Deadly Reel (IRE)**[34] 6395 2-8-7 **71** (p[1]) BenCurtis 6 40
(Archie Watson) *sn led: pushed along 3f out: rdn over 2f out: sn hdd and drvn: wknd wl over 1f out* **10/1**
4103 6 *1 ½* **Double Reflection**[31] 6504 2-8-10 **74** JoeyHaynes 7 40
(K R Burke) *chsd ldrs: rdn along 3f out: sn wknd* **25/1**
652 7 *¾* **Barefoot Baby (IRE)**[19] 6938 2-8-3 **67** PatrickMathers 5 31
(Richard Fahey) *towards rr whn n.m.r bnd after 1f: n.d after* **16/1**
431 8 *2* **Amazing Michele (FR)**[20] 6875 2-9-0 **78** TonyHamilton 3 38
(Richard Fahey) *towards rr: n.m.r bnd after 1f: bhd after* **6/1**[2]
051 9 *11* **Mahaarat**[29] 6575 2-9-6 **84** DavidProbert 11 21
(Sir Michael Stoute) *trckd ldrs: hdwy and cl up 3f out: rdn along over 2f out: sn wknd* **10/1**
200 10 *19* **Camomile Lawn (IRE)**[20] 6883 2-8-6 **70** PJMcDonald 10
(Ralph Beckett) *cl up: rdn along 3f out: sn wknd* **33/1**
1m 51.36s (5.46) **Going Correction** +0.825s/f (Soft) 10 Ran SP% **115.9**
Speed ratings (Par 94): **105,102,100,96,87 85,84,82,71,52**
CSF £42.10 CT £187.59 TOTE £20.40: £4.30, £1.10, £2.10; EX 61.10 Trifecta £277.80.
**Owner** Darren Barton **Bred** Pat Todd **Trained** Musley Bank, N Yorks
**FOCUS**
A fair fillies' nursery in which the front four came clear, and the first two have been rated as improving.

## 7553 VISIT THE ALL NEW RACINGUK.COM H'CAP (DIV I) 6f
**3:30** (3:36) (Class 4) (0-85,85) 3-Y-O+ £5,175 (£1,540; £769; £384) Stalls Low

Form RPR
6400 1 **Captain Dion**[27] 6662 4-9-7 **85** (p) TomEaves 8 95
(Kevin Ryan) *mde all: rdn over 1f out: drvn ins fnl f: kpt on strly towards fin* **14/1**
5365 2 *1 ½* **Johnny Cavagin**[29] 6570 8-9-1 **79** (t) GrahamLee 9 84
(Ronald Thompson) *dwlt and hld up towards rr: hdwy 3f out: trckd ldrs 2f out: rdn to chse wnr jst ins fnl f: sn drvn and no imp* **9/2**[2]
6015 3 *3 ½* **Hee Haw (IRE)**[18] 6970 3-9-4 **84** PaulMulrennan 4 78
(Paul Midgley) *trckd ldrs: smooth hdwy to trck wnr over 2f out: rdn over 1f out: drvn ent fnl f: kpt on same pce* **11/2**[3]
6-65 4 *4 ½* **Colonel Frank**[14] 7094 3-9-0 **80** RichardKingscote 1 59
(Ed Walker) *trckd ldrs: hdwy over 2f out: rdn and ev ch on outer 11/2f out: sn drvn and wknd* **2/1**[1]
6010 5 *4* **Suitcase 'N' Taxi**[31] 6519 3-8-9 **75** DavidAllan 2 42
(Tim Easterby) *trckd ldng pair on inner: chsd wnr halwfay: rdn along o ver 2f out: drvn wl over 1f out: sn wknd* **7/1**
-500 6 *1 ¼* **Tilly Trotter (IRE)**[15] 7055 3-8-12 **78** TonyHamilton 6 41
(Declan Carroll) *chsd ldrs: rdn along over 3f out: sn drvn and outpcd fnl 2f* **33/1**
4535 7 *3 ¼* **Courier**[23] 6787 5-9-3 **81** BarryMcHugh 7 33
(Marjorie Fife) *chsd wnr: rdn along over 3f out: sn wknd* **16/1**
0410 8 *2 ¾* **Khelman (IRE)**[14] 7086 7-9-6 **84** PaulHanagan 3 27
(Richard Fahey) *dwlt: a in rr* **8/1**
5354 9 *22* **Favourite Treat (USA)**[27] 6663 7-8-7 **71** oh1 (e) JamesSullivan 5
(Ruth Carr) *chsd ldrs. rdn along 1/2-way: sn lost pl and bhd* **10/1**
1m 20.17s (3.27) **Going Correction** +0.825s/f (Soft)
**WFA** 3 from 4yo+ 2lb 9 Ran SP% **115.1**
Speed ratings (Par 105): **111,109,104,98,93 91,87,83,54**
CSF £75.65 CT £397.26 TOTE £12.30: £3.70, £1.50, £1.60; EX 79.20 Trifecta £342.40.
**Owner** T A Rahman **Bred** Miss R J Dobson **Trained** Hambleton, N Yorks
**FOCUS**
The winner has been rated pretty much to his AW form.

## 7554 VISIT THE ALL NEW RACINGUK.COM H'CAP (DIV II) 6f
**4:05** (4:05) (Class 4) (0-85,84) 3-Y-O+ £5,175 (£1,540; £769; £384) Stalls Low

Form RPR
2040 1 **Inexes**[27] 6663 5-9-0 **77** (p) BarryMcHugh 2 84
(Marjorie Fife) *dwlt and towards rr: hdwy on inner 1/2-way: swtchd rt and effrt 2f out: sn chsng ldng pair: rdn to take slt ld ent fnl f: sn drvn and edgd rt: kpt on gamely towards fin* **6/1**
00-0 2 *nk* **Mujassam**[27] 6662 5-9-7 **84** (v) DavidNolan 3 90
(David O'Meara) *led: rdn along 2f out: drvn and hdd narrowly ent fnl f: rallied gamely on inner towards fin* **33/1**
033 3 *nk* **Letmestopyouthere (IRE)**[14] 7084 3-9-0 **82** LewisEdmunds(3) 10 87
(David Evans) *hld up: hdwy over 2f out: chal on outer over 1f out: rdn and ev ch ent fnl f: sn drvn: kpt on wl* **7/1**
4012 4 *5* **Kenny The Captain (IRE)**[14] 7086 6-9-1 **81** RachelRichardson(3) 9 70
(Tim Easterby) *in tch: hdwy over 2f out: rdn wl over 1f out: sn drvn and no imp fnl f* **9/2**[2]
2304 5 *3 ½* **Pomme De Terre (IRE)**[19] 6943 5-9-1 **78** (b) PaulMulrennan 6 56
(Michael Dods) *cl up: rdn along 2f out: sn drvn and wknd over 1f out* **10/1**
1305 6 *1 ¼* **Lexington Times (IRE)**[27] 6662 5-9-7 **84** (p) JamesSullivan 8 58
(Ruth Carr) *dwlt: a towards rr* **9/1**
1135 7 *2 ¼* **Mr Orange (IRE)**[39] 6238 4-8-11 **74** (p) CamHardie 7 41
(Paul Midgley) *chsd ldrs: rdn along over 2f out: wd st and sn outpcd* **16/1**
000 8 *hd* **Start Time (IRE)**[40] 6205 4-9-3 **80** (b[1]) JoeFanning 1 46
(Paul Midgley) *t.k.h: trckd ldrs on inner: rdn along over 2f out: sn wknd* **7/2**[1]
0642 9 *2 ¼* **Grandad's World (IRE)**[14] 7099 5-8-10 **73** PaulHanagan 4 32
(Richard Fahey) *chsd ldrs: pushed along over 3f out: sn rdn and wknd* **5/1**[3]
2605 10 *7* **Love Oasis**[23] 6780 3-8-10 **75** PJMcDonald 5 11
(Mark Johnston) *trckd ldrs: cl up 1/2-way: rdn along over 2f out: sn wknd* **25/1**
1m 22.25s (5.35) **Going Correction** +0.825s/f (Soft)
**WFA** 3 from 4yo+ 2lb 10 Ran SP% **115.6**
Speed ratings (Par 105): **97,96,96,89,84 83,80,79,76,67**
CSF £176.59 CT £1438.80 TOTE £7.40: £2.40, £7.90, £2.30; EX 195.20 Trifecta £1897.50.
**Owner** 21st Century Racing **Bred** Meon Valley Stud **Trained** Stillington, N Yorks
**FOCUS**
There was a tight three-way finish to this second division of the sprint handicap. It was 2.08secs slower than the preceding race. The winner has been rated to form.

## 7555 SIMON SCROPE DALBY SCREW-DRIVER H'CAP 1m 2f 5y
**4:40** (4:40) (Class 3) (0-95,90) 3-Y-O+
£12,450 (£3,728; £1,864; £932; £466; £234) Stalls Low

Form RPR
1064 1 **Dance King**[18] 6965 7-9-7 **85** (tp) DavidAllan 7 92+
(Tim Easterby) *hld up in rr: gd hdwy on inner 11/2f out: chsd ldrs ent fnl f: sn swtchd rt and rdn to chal: qcknd wl to ld last 50yds* **7/1**
3412 2 *½* **Empress Ali (IRE)**[19] 6924 6-9-12 **90** JamesSullivan 4 96
(Tom Tate) *led 2f: cl up: rdn to ld again over 1f out: drvn ins fnl f: hdd and no ex last 50yds* **3/1**[1]
5053 3 *1 ¼* **Andok (IRE)**[19] 6942 3-8-11 **80** TonyHamilton 3 85
(Richard Fahey) *cl up on inner: led after 2f at stdy pce: pushed along and qcknd 2f out: sn rdn and hdd over 1f out: drvn and kpt on fnl f* **9/1**
3351 4 *1 ¾* **Royal Shaheen (FR)**[7] 7328 4-9-5 **83** 6ex (v) GrahamLee 8 83
(Alistair Whillans) *trckd ldrs: effrt 2f out: rdn wl over 1f out: sn drvn and kpt on same pce* **7/1**
1041 5 *1 ¼* **Carnageo (FR)**[18] 6965 4-9-10 **88** (b) PaulHanagan 2 86
(Richard Fahey) *hld up in tch: hdwy to chse ldrs 2f out: sn rdn and no imp appr fnl f* **9/2**[3]
2213 6 *1 ½* **Indian Chief (IRE)**[18] 6965 7-9-6 **84** DavidProbert 6 79
(Rebecca Bastiman) *dwlt and hld up in rr: t.k.h: hdwy on inner to trck ldrs 1/2-way: effrt and nt clr run wl over 1f out and again appr fnl f: sn rdn and no imp* **7/1**
505R 7 *6* **La Casa Tarifa (IRE)**[26] 6687 3-8-11 **80** FrannyNorton 1 64
(Mark Johnston) *trckd ldrs: pushed along 3f out: rdn 2f out: sn drvn and wknd* **40/1**

4032 **8** *25* **Star Of Rory (IRE)**[20] 6881 3-9-6 **89**....................(b[1]) RichardKingscote 5 23
(Tom Dascombe) *t.k.h: hld up: a towards rr: outpcd and bhd fnl 2f* **4/1**[2]
2m 21.17s (7.47) **Going Correction** +0.825s/f (Soft)
**WFA** 3 from 4yo+ 5lb **8** Ran SP% **113.1**
Speed ratings (Par 107): **103,102,101,100,99 98,93,73**
CSF £27.69 CT £190.16 TOTE £9.90: £2.90, £1.40, £2.70; EX 36.10 Trifecta £318.70.
**Owner** Ambrose Turnbull & Partner **Bred** Meon Valley Stud **Trained** Great Habton, N Yorks
**FOCUS**
A good-quality handicap that was run at an average pace. The winner has been rated back to the level of his Cumberland Plate success.

## 7556 FRIER WOOD NOVICE AUCTION STKS (PLUS 10 RACE) 1m 6y
**5:15** (5:16) (Class 4) 2-Y-O **£4,528** (£1,347; £673; £336) **Stalls** Low

Form RPR
4 **1** **Unwritten**[34] 6380 2-9-2 0.................................................. PJMcDonald 8 85+
(K R Burke) *trckd ldrs: hdwy over 2f out: rdn to ld and hung lft ent fnl f: sn clr: readily* **4/1**[3]
3 **2** *9* **Sunhill Lad (IRE)**[6] 7361 2-8-12 0.......................................... ShaneGray 1 62
(Ann Duffield) *led: rdn along over 2f out: drvn over 1f out: hdd ent fnl f: kpt on: no ch w wnr* **8/1**
15 **3** *hd* **Austrian School (IRE)**[28] 6616 2-9-7 0......................... FrannyNorton 6 71
(Mark Johnston) *trckd ldrs on outer: pushed along and sltly outpcd 3f out: rdn 2f out: drvn and kpt on fnl f* **7/2**[2]
3 **4** *1 1/4* **Hyanna**[8] 7266 2-8-9 0........................................................... DavidAllan 7 56
(Tim Easterby) *towards rr: hdwy 3f out: chsd ldrs wl over 1f out: sn rdn and no imp* **10/3**[1]
6 **5** *2* **Sincerely Resdev**[27] 6658 2-8-12 0................................. PaddyAspell 2 55
(Philip Kirby) *trckd ldrs on inner: rdn along over 2f out: sn wknd* **33/1**
2 **6** *nse* **Great Shot Sam (USA)**[37] 6286 2-8-9 0......................... DavidProbert 5 52
(Andrew Balding) *cl up: chal 3f out: sn rdn: drvn over 1f out: wknd fnl f* **7/2**[2]
0 **7** *3/4* **The Fiddler**[16] 7026 2-9-0 0................................................ PaulMulrennan 4 55
(Chris Wall) *a in rr* **11/1**
05 **8** *1 3/4* **The Knot Is Tied (IRE)**[18] 6967 2-8-10 0........... RachelRichardson(3) 3 50
(Tim Easterby) *a in rr* **33/1**
1m 52.77s (6.87) **Going Correction** +0.825s/f (Soft) **8** Ran SP% **112.8**
Speed ratings (Par 97): **98,89,88,87,85 85,84,83**
CSF £34.61 TOTE £5.00: £1.70, £2.40, £1.60; EX 42.40 Trifecta £151.30.
**Owner** Titanium Racing Club **Bred** David & Nicola Leggate **Trained** Middleham Moor, N Yorks
**FOCUS**
They went a fair pace in this demanding novice event and it threw up an impressive winner.

## 7557 RACING UK HD ON SKY 432 H'CAP 5f 3y
**5:50** (5:53) (Class 4) (0-80,81) 3-Y-O+ **£5,175** (£1,540; £769; £384) **Stalls** Low

Form RPR
0503 **1** **Paddy Power (IRE)**[14] 7086 4-9-3 **76**.............................. PaulHanagan 5 85
(Richard Fahey) *towards rr: hdwy wl over 1f out: nt clr run and swtchd rt jst ins fnl f: nt clr run and swtchd again ins last 100yds: rdn and squeezed through to ld nr fin* **10/3**[1]
0005 **2** *nk* **Van Gerwen**[8] 7268 4-9-0 **73**........................................... PJMcDonald 14 81
(Les Eyre) *towards rr: hdwy 2f out: chsd ldrs on outer and rdn over 1f out: styng on wl and ev ch whn bmpd ins last 75yds: kpt on towards fin* **20/1**
4300 **3** *nk* **Oriental Splendour (IRE)**[29] 6574 5-8-9 **68**..............(p) JamesSullivan 7 75
(Ruth Carr) *trckd ldrs on inner: hdwy 2f out: swtchd rt and rdn over 1f out: led ins fnl f: sn drvn: hdd and no ex nr fin* **10/1**
3005 **4** *nk* **Gamesome (FR)**[29] 6593 6-9-6 **79**................................ PaulMulrennan 9 85
(Paul Midgley) *hld up towards rr: hdwy 2f out: chsd ldrs and nt clr run 1f out: sn rdn and styd on wl: n.m.r nr fin* **7/1**[3]
6145 **5** *2 1/2* **Musharrit**[33] 6430 5-9-7 **80**.................................................. TomEaves 3 77
(Declan Carroll) *hld up towards rr: hdwy on inner over 2f out: rdn to chse ldrs over 1f out: sn drvn and wknd* **10/1**
4320 **6** *3/4* **Quick Look**[18] 6964 4-9-4 **77**............................................. CamHardie 11 71
(Michael Easterby) *midfield and sn pushed along: lost pl and towards rr 1/2-way: hdwy 2f out: sn rdn: styd on fnl f* **11/1**
2123 **7** *nse* **Muatadel**[15] 7055 4-9-7 **80**................................................ TonyHamilton 16 77+
(Roger Fell) *in tch: hdwy on outer to chse ldrs over 1f out: rdn and styng on whn bmpd and hmpd ins last 100yds: kpt on same pce after* **7/1**[3]
6050 **8** *shd* **Impart**[12] 7137 3-8-9 **76**............................................ PatrickVaughan(7) 1 70
(David O'Meara) *led: rdn along wl over 1f out: drvn and hdd ins fnl f: wknd* **16/1**
4160 **9** *2 1/4* **Lexington Place**[24] 6758 7-8-7 **73**............................ JamieGormley(7) 10 59
(Ruth Carr) *cl up: chal 2f out: rdn and ev ch over 1f out sn drvn and wknd fnl f* **12/1**
3054 **10** *nk* **Elysian Flyer (IRE)**[2] 7475 5-9-4 **77**.............................. GrahamLee 8 62
(Paul Midgley) *nvr bttr than midfield* **5/1**[2]
0065 **11** *3* **Adam's Ale**[14] 7086 8-9-6 **79**....................................(e) BarryMcHugh 17 53
(Marjorie Fife) *in tch: rdn along over 2f out: sn wknd* **14/1**
-520 **12** *10* **Berlios (IRE)**[211] 971 4-9-0 **73**.................................... PhillipMakin 15 11
(Rebecca Bastiman) *a in rr* **25/1**
040 **13** *3* **Crosse Fire**[15] 7055 5-8-8 **67**.......................................(v) BenCurtis 12
(Scott Dixon) *prom: rdn along 2f out: wknd over 1f out* **25/1**
1m 7.41s (4.11) **Going Correction** +0.825s/f (Soft)
**WFA** 3 from 4yo+ 1lb **13** Ran SP% **124.0**
Speed ratings (Par 105): **100,99,99,98,94 93,93,93,89,89 84,68,63**
CSF £80.16 CT £638.68 TOTE £4.90: £2.10, £3.90, £3.20; EX 86.90 Trifecta £606.20.
**Owner** M Scaife & R A Fahey **Bred** Yeguada De Milagro Sa **Trained** Musley Bank, N Yorks
■ Stewards' Enquiry : Paul Hanagan two-day ban; careless riding (Oct 2, 15)
**FOCUS**
They went hard up front in this competitive sprint handicap and the winner has been rated to the level of his May success.

## 7558 FOLLOW @RACING_UK ON TWITTER NOW APPRENTICE H'CAP 1m 4f 5y
**6:20** (6:20) (Class 5) (0-75,77) 3-Y-O+ **£3,234** (£962; £481; £240) **Stalls** Low

Form RPR
4-26 **1** **Arrowtown**[89] 4380 5-9-8 **71**.....................................(h) HarrisonShaw(2) 5 78
(Michael Easterby) *hld up in rr: stdy hdwy over 3f out: rdn to chse ldrs over 1f out: drvn ent fnl f: styd on strly to ld nr fin* **11/1**
4012 **2** *1/2* **Mirimar (IRE)**[22] 6812 3-9-0 **68**....................................... CameronNoble 3 74+
(Ed Vaughan) *led: jnd and pushed along over 2f out: rdn wl over 1f out: drvn ins fnl f: hdd and no ex nr fin* **5/4**[1]
15 **3** *1 3/4* **Satisfy (IRE)**[36] 6307 3-9-4 **76**................................. PatrickO'Hanlon(4) 9 79+
(K R Burke) *prom: hdwy over 3f out: cl up over 2f out: rdn to chal wl over 1f out: ev ch tl drvn ins fnl f and kpt on same pce* **8/1**
600- **4** *nk* **Walsingham Grange (USA)**[166] 7060 4-9-12 **73**.............. WilliamCox 2 76
(Pam Sly) *hld up in tch: hdwy on inner over 4f out: chsd ldng pair 3f out: rdn wl over 1f out: drvn and styd on same pce fnl f* **13/2**[3]
2230 **5** *12* **Mambo Dancer**[16] 7019 3-9-0 **68**................................ JamieGormley 6 53
(Mark Johnston) *hld up towards rr: sme hdwy 3f out: rdn along 2f out: nvr nr ldrs* **14/1**
0306 **6** *20* **Parish Boy**[18] 6965 5-9-10 **75**.................................(t) LauraCoughlan(4) 1 27
(David Loughnane) *s.i.s and lost 8 l s: jnd field after 4f: hdwy on outer and cl up 1/2-way: rdn along over 3f out: sn wknd* **9/2**[2]
60-6 **7** *11* **Swift Cedar (IRE)**[13] 7111 7-9-9 **70**........................ KatherineGlenister 10 4
(David Evans) *t.k.h: trckd ldrs: hdwy on outer and cl up 7f out: rdn along over 3f out: sn wknd* **20/1**
0000 **8** *12* **Vettori Rules**[12] 7142 4-9-13 **74**....................................(h) ConnorMurtagh 4
(Gay Kelleway) *chsd ldrs: pushed along over 7f out: rdn and lost pl 1/2-way: bhd fnl 2f* **14/1**
2m 50.39s (9.59) **Going Correction** +0.825s/f (Soft)
**WFA** 3 from 4yo+ 7lb **8** Ran SP% **113.5**
Speed ratings (Par 103): **101,100,99,99,91 77,70,62**
CSF £24.90 CT £120.42 TOTE £8.60: £1.90, £1.30, £2.10; EX 27.70 Trifecta £222.50.
**Owner** S Hollings L Folwell S Hull M Bannister **Bred** Juddmonte Farms Ltd **Trained** Sheriff Hutton, N Yorks
**FOCUS**
This modest handicap for apprentice riders was run at a routine sort of pace.
T/Plt: £82.70 to a £1 stake. Pool: £69,386.00 - 612.30 winning units T/Qpdt: £45.30 to a £1 stake. Pool: £5,797.32 - 94.56 winning units **Joe Rowntree**

7559 - (Foreign Racing) - See Raceform Interactive

# 6924 HAYDOCK (L-H)
### Friday, September 29

**OFFICIAL GOING: Heavy**
Wind: breezy, across Weather: sunny, light cloud - shower after race 3

## 7560 JW LEES MPA H'CAP (DIV I) 1m 3f 175y
**1:40** (1:42) (Class 5) (0-70,72) 3-Y-O+ **£3,557** (£1,058; £529; £264) **Stalls** Centre

Form RPR
2433 **1** **Count Simon (IRE)**[21] 6871 3-9-7 **72**................................ DavidProbert 1 80+
(Andrew Balding) *mde all: 2 l clr gng wl over 2f out: pushed along over 1f out: rdn and 1 l clr ent fnl f: r.o wl* **3/1**[1]
5113 **2** *1 1/4* **Canny Style**[21] 6895 4-9-13 **71**........................................... TomEaves 7 77
(Kevin Ryan) *hld up in last: gd hdwy over 3f out: pushed along into 2nd 2f out: sn rdn: 1 l bhd wnr ent fnl f: kpt on but a hld* **11/1**
5224 **3** *1 1/2* **Paddy's Rock (IRE)**[11] 7219 6-9-1 **59**............................... JoeFanning 3 62
(Lynn Siddall) *hld up: pushed along and hdwy 4f out: 3rd 2f out: kpt on one pce fr over 1f out* **17/2**
5244 **4** *12* **Leapt**[10] 7232 3-9-2 **67**...................................................(h) ShaneKelly 8 51
(Richard Hughes) *trckd ldrs: drvn 4f out: rdn over 3f out: lost pl 2f out: no ex* **9/1**
2525 **5** *5* **Eyreborn (IRE)**[16] 7048 3-8-13 **64**.................................. PJMcDonald 2 40
(Keith Dalgleish) *racd in cl 2nd: pushed along 4f out: drvn 3f out: wknd over 2f out* **10/1**
3213 **6** *1 1/2* **Omotesando**[41] 6175 7-9-6 **67**...................................(p) CharlieBennett(3) 6 40
(Oliver Greenall) *trckd ldrs: rdn and wknd 3f out* **8/1**
4122 **7** *10* **Thorntoun Care**[22] 6858 6-9-5 **70**............................(p) JamieGormley(7) 9 27
(Iain Jardine) *t.k.h: hld up: effrt 4f out: drvn over 3f out: no imp* **15/2**[3]
1115 **8** *22* **Regal Mirage (IRE)**[44] 6061 3-9-3 **68**................................ DavidAllan 4
(Tim Easterby) *mid-div: pushed along 4f out: drvn and lost pl 3f out: eased whn btn* **4/1**[2]
603 **9** *32* **Golden Set**[23] 6823 3-9-2 **70**......................................... GeorgeWood(3) 5
(James Fanshawe) *mid-div: drvn over 4f out: wknd wl over 3f out: heavily eased: lost shoe* **20/1**
2m 43.35s (9.55) **Going Correction** +0.90s/f (Soft)
**WFA** 3 from 4yo+ 7lb **9** Ran SP% **110.6**
Speed ratings (Par 103): **104,103,102,94,90 89,83,68,47**
CSF £34.31 CT £237.14 TOTE £3.40: £1.70, £2.20, £2.10; EX 25.60 Trifecta £205.00.
**Owner** Philip Fox & I A Balding **Bred** Grange Stud **Trained** Kingsclere, Hants
**FOCUS**
The going was officially described as heavy. All races were run on the stands' side home straight. Rail movements added 8yds to races 1 & 2, 30yds to race 6 and reduced race 7 by 17yds and race 8 by 9yds. A moderate handicap and they came home at long intervals behind the principals. Joe Fanning, who finished third, said: "It's heavy, particularly down the back, but it's loose." The time was 14.35sec slower than standard, but 0.7sec faster than the following second division. The race has been rated around the placed horses.

## 7561 JW LEES MPA H'CAP (DIV II) 1m 3f 175y
**2:10** (2:11) (Class 5) (0-70,70) 3-Y-O+ **£3,557** (£1,058; £529; £264) **Stalls** Centre

Form RPR
0-02 **1** **Big Sigh (IRE)**[15] 7085 3-8-11 **65**.............................. HectorCrouch(3) 5 74
(Ismail Mohammed) *trckd ldrs: wnt 2nd 5f out: 1 l 2nd 4f out: hdwy to ease into ld 3f out: sn pushed along: 1 l clr whn rdn over 1f out: kpt on wl fnl f* **5/2**[1]
0040 **2** *1* **Buonarroti (IRE)**[41] 6188 6-9-4 **69**................................(t) GerO'Neill(7) 8 76
(Declan Carroll) *slowly away: in rr: last 4f out: hdwy 3f out: drvn over 2f out: rdn into 2nd over 1f out: tried to cl on ldr ent fnl f: hld last 100yds* **11/2**[3]
-544 **3** *2* **Clemento (IRE)**[14] 7125 3-9-5 **70**............................... KieranShoemark 6 74
(Roger Charlton) *hld up: rdn and hdwy on outer 2f out: wnt 3rd over 1f out: kpt on fnl f* **10/1**
553 **4** *3/4* **Hurricane Hollow**[49] 5872 7-9-7 **70**................................... JaneElliott(5) 7 73
(David Barron) *slowly away: in rr: hdwy 4f out: chsng ldrs 3f out: pushed along over 2f out: sn rdn and one pce* **11/2**[3]
-010 **5** *2* **King Of Scotland (FR)**[90] 4348 3-8-12 **66**............(p[1]) CharlieBennett(3) 4 66
(Hughie Morrison) *led: 1 l clr 4f out: pushed along and hdd 3f out: rdn over 2f out: grad wknd* **9/1**
5555 **6** *shd* **Moojaned (IRE)**[3] 7479 6-8-6 **57**.................................(p[1]) WilliamCox(7) 9 57
(John Flint) *mid-div: pushed along and lost pl 3f out: rdn 2f out: one pce* **8/1**
400 **7** *10* **Seinfeld**[41] 6194 3-9-2 **67**................................................. JoeFanning 3 52
(David Simcock) *trckd ldrs: pushed along 3f out: drvn over 2f out: wknd* **5/1**[2]
3204 **8** *6* **Ingleby Hollow**[30] 6569 5-9-8 **66**................................(p) MartinHarley 2 40
(David O'Meara) *trckd ldr: relegated to 3rd 5f out: hdwy and ev ch 3f out: rdn and wknd 2f out: eased* **16/1**
2m 44.05s (10.25) **Going Correction** +0.90s/f (Soft)
**WFA** 3 from 4yo+ 7lb **8** Ran SP% **112.1**
Speed ratings (Par 103): **101,100,99,98,97 97,90,86**
CSF £15.58 CT £113.30 TOTE £2.50: £1.10, £1.80, £2.70; EX 16.40 Trifecta £114.90.
**Owner** Sheikh Juma Dalmook Al Maktoum **Bred** Darley **Trained** Newmarket, Suffolk


The Form Book Flat, Raceform Ltd, Newbury, RG14 5SJ

**FOCUS**
This looked the weaker of the two divisions on paper. They went off quickly and they finished very tired. The winning time was 0.7sec slower than the earlier division.

## 7562 BRITISH STALLION STUDS EBF MAIDEN STKS (PLUS 10 RACE) (C&G) 6f
**2:45** (2:46) (Class 4) 2-Y-O **£4,528** (£1,347; £673; £336) **Stalls** Centre

Form RPR
03 **1** **Feebs**[30] 6567 2-8-7 0 HarrisonShaw(7) 4 74
(Michael Easterby) *mid-div: trckd ldrs gng wl 3f out: pushed along to ld over 1f out: reminders and drew 2 l clr 1f out: in command fnl f: pushed out* **7/2**[2]

**2** *2 ½* **Wrenthorpe** 2-8-11 0 AdamMcNamara(3) 3 66+
(Bryan Smart) *slowly away: sn pushed along in rr: last 1/2-way: drvn and hdwy over 2f out: rdn over 1f out: r.o wl fnl f: tk 2nd last 100yds* **7/1**

0 **3** *2* **Gullane One (IRE)**[20] 6939 2-9-0 0 DavidAllan 2 60
(Tim Easterby) *prom: led 2f out: pushed along and hdd over 1f out: sn rdn: lost 2nd last 100yds* **4/1**[3]

05 **4** *3* **Mutabaahy (IRE)**[23] 6826 2-9-0 0 (h) DavidProbert 5 51
(Ed Dunlop) *hld up: hdwy over 3f out: drvn into 3rd 2f out: rdn over 1f out: wknd ent fnl f* **9/4**[1]

6 **5** *12* **Kendergarten Kop (IRE)**[14] 7105 2-9-0 0 MartinHarley 7 15
(Tom Dascombe) *led: hdd 2f out: sn wknd and eased* **6/1**

40 **6** *2 ½* **Deecider**[13] 7141 2-9-0 0 (v[1]) TomEaves 8 8
(Tom Dascombe) *prom: relegated to 4th 1/2-way: drvn over 2f out: sn wknd: eased* **8/1**

1m 18.65s (4.85) **Going Correction** +0.65s/f (Yiel) **6 Ran SP% 110.9**
Speed ratings (Par 97): **93,89,87,83,67 63**
CSF £26.26 TOTE £4.30: £1.80, £2.70; EX 32.00 Trifecta £118.20.
**Owner** J Blackburn & S Winter **Bred** M W Easterby **Trained** Sheriff Hutton, N Yorks

**FOCUS**
A weak maiden, particularly for the track and not form to get excited about.

## 7563 EBF STALLIONS KENNY WASTE MANAGEMENT MAIDEN FILLIES' STKS (PLUS 10 RACE) 6f
**3:20** (3:24) (Class 5) 2-Y-O **£3,557** (£1,058; £529; £264) **Stalls** Centre

Form RPR
**1** **This Girl** 2-9-0 0 MartinHarley 8 84+
(Tom Dascombe) *mid-div: trckd ldrs gng wl 2f out: pushed along over 1f out: hdwy into 3rd 1f out: rdn and r.o strly fnl f: led last 100yds: sn clr: comf* **20/1**

205 **2** *1 ¾* **Maybride**[78] 4815 2-9-0 86 PaulHanagan 9 79
(Richard Fahey) *a.p: led 3f out: pushed along 2f out: 1 l clr whn rdn over 1f out: wandered ins fnl f: hdd last 100yds: sn lft trailing by wnr* **8/13**[1]

**3** *1* **Angel's Glory** 2-9-0 0 JackMitchell 7 76+
(Roger Varian) *mid-div: pushed along and hdwy 2f out: reminders in 4th 1f out: r.o wl fnl f: tk 3rd 150yds out* **7/1**[2]

53 **4** *4* **La Belle Mayson**[43] 6086 2-8-11 0 AdamMcNamara(3) 12 64
(Richard Fahey) *prom: 2nd and ev ch 2f out: rdn over 1f out: no ex fnl f: lost 3rd 150yds out* **12/1**

05 **5** *11* **Isabella Ruby**[13] 7141 2-8-7 0 (h) ConnorMurtagh(7) 6 31
(Lisa Williamson) *chsd ldrs: 5th 1/2-way: pushed along 2f out: sn rdn: no ex* **66/1**

4 **6** *¾* **Miss Wolverine**[43] 6085 2-9-0 0 TomEaves 1 29
(Michael Easterby) *slowly away: last and pushed along 1/2-way: hdwy past btn horses last 2 fs* **33/1**

00 **7** *1 ¼* **Agent Error (IRE)**[8] 7334 2-9-0 0 JoeFanning 5 25
(David Simcock) *mid-div: pushed along and ch 2f out: wknd over 1f out* **10/1**

6 **8** *hd* **Shakiah (IRE)**[16] 7045 2-9-0 0 PaddyAspell 11 24
(Sharon Watt) *trckd ldrs: pushed along 2f out: sn rdn and wknd* **100/1**

445 **9** *2* **Call Dawn**[25] 6755 2-8-7 58 HarrisonShaw(7) 13 18
(Michael Easterby) *hld up: drvn 2f out: wknd over 1f out* **40/1**

03 **10** *3 ¼* **Dusty**[88] 4440 2-9-0 0 RyanTate 10 9
(Mick Channon) *led: hdd and pushed along 3f out: sn drvn and lost pl* **9/1**[3]

**11** *nk* **Voguela (IRE)** 2-9-0 0 DavidAllan 2 8
(Tim Easterby) *mid-div: effrt 1/2-way: sn pushed along: lost pl 2f out: fdd* **25/1**

**12** *9* **Marcella** 2-9-0 0 ConnorBeasley 4
(David C Griffiths) *dwlt: a in rr* **50/1**

1m 17.63s (3.83) **Going Correction** +0.65s/f (Yiel) **12 Ran SP% 119.6**
Speed ratings (Par 92): **100,97,96,91,76 75,73,73,70,66 66,54**
CSF £32.15 TOTE £25.50: £4.40, £1.10, £2.40; EX 60.80 Trifecta £414.10.
**Owner** David Lowe & Russell Jones **Bred** Liam Sheridan **Trained** Malpas, Cheshire

**FOCUS**
A hugely promising start to the career of This Girl who readily ran down the odds-on favourite to win by a fast growing margin.

## 7564 J W LEES BITTER 1828 NURSERY H'CAP 5f
**3:55** (3:56) (Class 2) 2-Y-O **£9,056** (£2,695; £1,346; £673) **Stalls** Centre

Form RPR
0124 **1** **Diamond Dougal (IRE)**[10] 7228 2-7-13 70 DavidEgan(3) 7 77
(Mick Channon) *hld up: pushed along and hdwy on stands' rail 2f out: rdn and led over 1f out: 1 l clr 1f out: extended advantage under hand riding fnl f: comf* **11/2**

242 **2** *2 ½* **Up Sticks And Go**[27] 6689 2-8-10 78 ConnorBeasley 5 76
(Keith Dalgleish) *mid-div: pushed along 2f out: rdn over 1f out: hdwy ent fnl f: r.o wl: tk 2nd nr fin* **9/2**[3]

2423 **3** *shd* **Simmy's Copshop**[13] 7138 2-9-4 89 AdamMcNamara(3) 2 87
(Richard Fahey) *trckd ldrs: pushed along 2f out: rdn over 1f out: hdwy into 2nd ent fnl f: kpt on: lost 2nd nr fin* **9/2**[3]

612 **4** *3* **Mable Lee (IRE)**[13] 7138 2-8-3 71 JimmyQuinn 6 58
(Iain Jardine) *slowly away: pushed along 2f out: rdn over 1f out: r.o fnl f* **7/2**[2]

2151 **5** *nse* **Porchy Party (IRE)**[13] 7138 2-9-0 82 (p) MartinHarley 4 69+
(Tom Dascombe) *racd in cl 2nd: pushed along 2f out: drvn over 1f out: wknd ent fnl f* **3/1**[1]

056 **6** *2* **Rock Hill (IRE)**[55] 5665 2-7-13 70 ow1 AaronJones(3) 1 49
(Paul Midgley) *hld up: pushed along 2f out. wknd over 1f out* **18/1**

5010 **7** *nk* **Royal Diplomat (IRE)**[20] 6950 2-8-12 80 PaulHanagan 3 58+
(Richard Fahey) *led: pushed along 2f out: rdn and hdd over 1f out: fdd fnl f* **14/1**

1m 4.1s (3.30) **Going Correction** +0.65s/f (Yiel) **7 Ran SP% 110.9**
Speed ratings (Par 101): **99,95,94,90,89 86,86**
CSF £28.30 TOTE £6.10: £3.30, £2.20; EX 38.50 Trifecta £183.20.
**Owner** Insignia Racing (flag) **Bred** Con Marnane **Trained** West Ilsley, Berks

**FOCUS**
A competitive nursery handicap, despite the relatively small field. Three of the runners, who had dominated the finish of a similar event at Chester 13 days earlier, could finished only third, fourth and fifth on this occasion.

## 7565 WATCH RACING UK ON BT TV H'CAP 1m 6f
**4:30** (4:30) (Class 3) (0-95,94) 3-Y-O
**£8,715** (£2,609; £1,304; £652; £326; £163) **Stalls** Low

Form RPR
5113 **1** **Uber Cool (IRE)**[22] 6865 3-8-5 81 DavidEgan(3) 7 87
(Jane Chapple-Hyam) *trckd ldr: hdwy to ld 3f out: drvn 2f out: rdn over 1f out: narrow advantage ent fnl f: hdd 150yds out: rallied to regain ld fr reluctant runner-up last two strides: all out* **3/1**[2]

2001 **2** *shd* **Nordic Combined (IRE)**[21] 6880 3-8-2 75 oh2 KieranO'Neill 5 81
(Brian Ellison) *rn in snatches in rr: last 4f out: drvn 3f out: rdn and hdwy 2f out: clsd on ldrs over 1f out: led 150yds out: pricked ears and reluctant to go on: hdd last two strides: uns rdr sn after winning line* **16/1**

4315 **3** *1* **Orsino (IRE)**[20] 6930 3-8-2 75 oh1 JimmyQuinn 3 80+
(Andrew Balding) *hld up: hdwy to trck ldrs 3f out: pushed along in 3rd over 1f out: sn rdn: n.m.r bhd front two ins fnl f. kpt on* **10/1**

2101 **4** *2* **Tor**[13] 7163 3-8-9 89 JamieGormley(7) 1 90
(Iain Jardine) *led: pushed along and hdd 3f out: rdn 2f out: lost pl and no ex ent fnl f* **9/2**[3]

110 **5** *4* **Royal Associate**[47] 5982 3-9-7 94 (b[1]) MartinLane 2 90
(Charlie Appleby) *trckd ldrs: rdn 4f out: effrt in 3rd 3f out: wknd over 2f out* **13/2**

5111 **6** *7* **Taxmeifyoucan (IRE)**[20] 6930 3-9-2 89 (v) ConnorBeasley 6 75
(Keith Dalgleish) *hld up: hdwy on outer 4f out: pushed along and ev ch over 3f out: sn drvn and wknd* **9/4**[1]

5526 **7** *52* **Comrade Conrad (IRE)**[22] 6865 3-8-8 81 KieranShoemark 4
(Roger Charlton) *prom: pushed along and lost pl 4f out: rdn 3f out: fdd: heavily eased* **10/1**

3m 17.02s (15.02) **Going Correction** +0.90s/f (Soft) **7 Ran SP% 111.3**
Speed ratings (Par 105): **93,92,92,91,88 84,55**
CSF £44.23 TOTE £4.10: £1.90, £4.30; EX 44.80 Trifecta £516.30.
**Owner** Fiona and Ian Carmichael-Jennings **Bred** Albert Conneally **Trained** Dalham, Suffolk
■ Stewards' Enquiry : Kieran O'Neill four-day ban; using whip above the permitted level (15th-18th Oct)

**FOCUS**
Race run over an extra 30 yards. A strong renewal of this feature handicap and no shortage of drama as Nordic Combined idled badly and threw the race away. It was hard work in the conditions, the winning time over 20sec slower than standard.

## 7566 WATCH RACING UK ANYWHERE H'CAP 1m 37y
**5:05** (5:05) (Class 3) (0-90,89) 3-Y-O+
**£8,715** (£2,609; £1,304; £652; £326; £163) **Stalls** Low

Form RPR
1261 **1** **Fastar (IRE)**[14] 7131 3-8-11 83 CharlesBishop 8 95+
(Brian Meehan) *hld up: hdwy 3f out: swtchd to chal on outer 2f out: pushed along to ld 1f out: rdn and sn c clr: comf* **9/2**[1]

0465 **2** *1 ¾* **Silvery Moon (IRE)**[10] 7246 10-9-0 82 DavidAllan 6 88
(Tim Easterby) *disp ld early: sn settled in bhd ldrs: 4th 3f out: hdwy and ev ch in cl 3rd 2f out: disp ld over 1f out: passed by wnr 1f out: drvn ent fnl f: sn rdn into 2nd and kpt on: nt gng pce of winne* **6/1**[3]

4004 **3** *1 ¼* **Colibri (IRE)**[48] 5943 3-9-3 89 (p[1]) JackMitchell 3 92
(Hugo Palmer) *trckd ldrs: hdwy into 2nd over 2f out: disp ld over 1f out: passed by wnr 1f out: rdn ent fnl f: no ex* **9/2**[1]

3-05 **4** *3* **My Amigo**[21] 6879 4-9-1 83 PJMcDonald 2 79
(K R Burke) *trckd ldrs: hdwy on inner 3f out: drvn 2f out: sn rdn: one pce fnl f* **17/2**

0023 **5** *½* **Instant Attraction (IRE)**[13] 7140 6-9-0 85 (v[1]) AdamMcNamara(3) 12 80
(Jedd O'Keeffe) *dispiuted ld tl led on own after 1f: rdn and hdd over 1f out: no ex fnl f* **9/2**[1]

1165 **6** *½* **Magic City (IRE)**[55] 5643 8-8-10 85 HarrisonShaw(7) 14 79
(Michael Easterby) *in rr: pushed along 2f out: sn rdn: one pce fnl f* **25/1**

4300 **7** *2 ¾* **Spring Offensive (IRE)**[34] 6449 5-9-4 86 PaulHanagan 10 74
(Richard Fahey) *hld up: hdwy on outer 4f out: rdn 2f out: no imp* **11/2**[2]

2620 **8** *8* **Chosen Character (IRE)**[14] 7108 9-8-2 77 (vt) ElishaWhittington(7) 11 46
(Tom Dascombe) *prom: sn chsng ldr: pushed along 3f out: lost pl over 2f out* **33/1**

6200 **9** *6* **Finn Class (IRE)**[10] 7246 6-9-3 85 (p) TomEaves 7 40
(Michael Dods) *mid-div: pushed along 3f out: rdn 2f out: wknd* **25/1**

-061 **10** *1 ½* **Le Chat D'Or**[81] 4685 9-9-0 87 (bt) CallumRodriguez(5) 1 39
(Michael Dods) *hld up: hdwy on inner 4f out: drvn 3f out: wknd over 1f out* **20/1**

35-0 **11** *8* **Dwight D**[21] 6881 4-8-9 80 DavidEgan(3) 13 14
(Stuart Coltherd) *in rr: drvn and lost tch fr over 3f out* **66/1**

1m 48.57s (3.87) **Going Correction** +0.65s/f (Yiel)
**WFA** 3 from 4yo+ 4lb **11 Ran SP% 111.6**
Speed ratings (Par 107): **106,104,103,100,99 99,96,88,82,80 72**
CSF £27.60 CT £124.42 TOTE £4.60: £1.70, £2.60, £1.90; EX 34.60 Trifecta £133.40.
**Owner** Biddestone Racing Partnership XVIII **Bred** Ringfort Stud **Trained** Manton, Wilts

**FOCUS**
The race distance was reduced by 17 yards. They went hard up front early on here and a suspicion the race fell apart late on. The winner continues to progress and the second ran his best race this year.

## 7567 ROA/RACING POST JACKPOT APPRENTICE H'CAP (PART OF THE RACING EXCELLENCE INITIATIVE) 1m 2f 100y
**5:35** (5:35) (Class 5) (0-70,69) 3-Y-O+ **£4,851** (£1,443; £721; £360) **Stalls** Low

Form RPR
6054 **1** **Hajaam (IRE)**[16] 7063 3-9-0 62 PaddyBradley 12 75+
(Charlie Fellowes) *mid-div: hdwy on outer gng wl 4f out: led over 2f out: pushed along and sn 2 l clr: rdn 3 l clr 1f out: pushed out fnl f: comf* **8/1**

5504 **2** *3 ¾* **Stoneboat Bill**[17] 7028 5-9-2 62 GerO'Neill(3) 2 67
(Declan Carroll) *slowly away: qckly rcvrd to r in mid-div: pushed along and hdwy 3f out: swtchd to outer 2f out: drvn into 2nd over 1f out: kpt on fnl f: but no threat to wnr* **10/1**

2533 **3** *5* **Eben Dubai (IRE)**[8] 7336 5-8-12 55 oh5 (p) DavidEgan 10 52
(John Flint) *mid-div: pushed along and hdwy 3f out: drvn 2f out: styd on to take 3rd ent fnl f* **4/1**[2]

3151 **4** *3 ¾* **Beverley Bullet**[11] 7223 4-9-11 68 6ex (p) CallumRodriguez 3 58
(Lawrence Mullaney) *trckd ldrs: cl up and ev ch 3f out: 2nd whn rdn over 2f out: wknd and lost 3rd ent fnl f* **3/1**[1]

0565 **5** *shd* **Auxiliary**[9] 7267 4-9-9 **69**....(v[1]) PaulaMuir(3) 7 59
(Patrick Holmes) *hld up: rdn and mod hdwy 3f out: kpt on fnl 2 fs* **25/1**
1133 **6** *nk* **Inflexiball**[17] 7028 5-9-5 **62**.... JaneElliott 8 51
(John Mackie) *in rr: pushed along 4f out: drvn 2f out: one pce* **17/2**
0001 **7** *1 ¾* **Nazzaa (IRE)**[45] 6035 4-9-12 **69**.... JoshuaBryan 4 55
(Steve Flook) *led: pushed along 3f out: hdd over 2f out: sn rdn and no ex* **11/2**[3]
5230 **8** *2 ½* **Bollihope**[63] 5363 5-9-5 **67**.... JackOsborn(5) 9 49
(Richard Guest) *hld up: hdwy on inner 3f out: sn drvn and one pce* **33/1**
442 **9** *3 ¼* **Angelical (IRE)**[23] 6811 4-8-10 **58**.... TobyEley(5) 1 35
(Daniel Mark Loughnane) *trckd ldrs on inner: rdn 4f out: sn wknd* **12/1**
4650 **10** *nk* **Lord Franklin**[48] 5924 8-9-6 **66**.... JamieGormley(3) 6 42
(Eric Alston) *prom: pushed along in 2nd 4f out: drvn and lost pl 3f out* **8/1**
4504 **11** *6* **Peak Storm**[63] 5359 8-9-0 **62**.... GabrieleMalune(5) 5 28
(John O'Shea) *a in rr: lost tch 4f out* **50/1**

2m 24.58s (9.08) **Going Correction** +0.90s/f (Soft)
**WFA** 3 from 4yo+ 5lb **11** Ran SP% **118.7**
Speed ratings (Par 103): **99,96,92,89,88 88,87,85,82,82 77**
CSF £84.59 CT £371.73 TOTE £10.20: £1.90, £4.10, £2.30; EX 94.10 Trifecta £1508.00 Part won..
**Owner** Khalifa Bin Hamad Al Attiyah **Bred** Marston Stud **Trained** Newmarket, Suffolk
■ Stewards' Enquiry : Callum Rodriguez seven-day ban; use his whip contrary to the conditions of the race (13th-19th Oct)

**FOCUS**
The race distance was reduced by 9yds. An attritional test and they came home very slowly behind the unexposed Hajaam. He clearly has potential and can rate higher.
T/Plt: £221.30 to a £1 stake. Pool: £59,010.98 - 194.58 winning units T/Qpdt: £40.30 to a £1 stake. Pool: £4,216.60 - 77.31 winning units **Keith McHugh**

## 7359 NEWCASTLE (A.W) (L-H)

Friday, September 29

**OFFICIAL GOING: Tapeta: standard**
Wind: Breezy, half against in races on straight course and in over 3f of home straight on races on round c Weather: Cloudy, bright

### 7568 FUN88 H'CAP 1m 4f 98y (Tp)
**5:45** (5:48) (Class 5) (0-75,77) 3-Y-O **£3,234** (£962; £481; £240) **Stalls** High

Form RPR
4425 **1** **Pioneertown (IRE)**[13] 7163 3-9-6 **73**.... LukeMorris 7 83+
(Sir Mark Prescott Bt) *hld up in tch: smooth hdwy on outside over 2f out: rdn to ld over 1f out: edgd lft: kpt on wl fnl f* **3/1**[2]
2324 **2** *2 ½* **La Vie En Rose**[27] 6680 3-9-6 **73**.... FrannyNorton 3 78
(Mark Johnston) *led at ordinary gallop: rdn and hdd over 1f out: rallied: kpt on same pce ins fnl f* **14/1**
6114 **3** *nk* **Av A Word**[18] 7004 3-9-4 **71**....(p) TonyHamilton 10 75
(Daniel Kubler) *hld up: hdwy on outside over 2f out: rdn and kpt on ins fnl f: nvr able to chal* **25/1**
3356 **4** *¾* **Somnambulist**[13] 7163 3-8-10 **68**.... RowanScott(5) 8 71
(Keith Dalgleish) *dwlt: hld up: rdn over 2f out: hdwy over 1f out: kpt on ins fnl f: no imp* **13/2**
2212 **5** *½* **Astute Boy (IRE)**[21] 6880 3-9-7 **77**....(b[1]) CliffordLee(3) 9 79
(Ed Vaughan) *trckd ldr: rdn over 2f out: outpcd fr over 1f out* **5/2**[1]
2532 **6** *2 ¾* **Sir Gnet (IRE)**[20] 6948 3-8-13 **66**....(h) GrahamLee 6 64
(Ed Dunlop) *prom: drvn and outpcd over 2f out: rallied ins fnl f: sn no imp* **11/2**[3]
312 **7** *4 ½* **Clenymistra (IRE)**[34] 6436 3-9-1 **68**.... PhillipMakin 2 59
(David O'Meara) *t.k.h: trckd ldrs on ins: rdn over 2f out: wknd wl over 1f out* **20/1**
346 **8** *¾* **Ninepin Bowler**[152] 2185 3-9-7 **74**.... PaulMulrennan 1 63
(Michael Dods) *hld up in tch: nt clr run briefly over 2f out: sn rdn and outpcd: btn fnl f* **33/1**
5323 **9** *½* **Good Time Ahead (IRE)**[21] 6901 3-8-9 **62**.... AndrewMullen 11 51
(Philip Kirby) *t.k.h: prom on outside: rdn over 2f out: wknd wl over 1f out* **7/1**

2m 45.22s (4.12) **Going Correction** +0.375s/f (Slow) **9** Ran SP% **113.0**
Speed ratings (Par 101): **101,99,99,98,98 96,93,92,92**
CSF £41.19 CT £871.49 TOTE £3.70: £1.70, £2.30, £7.00; EX 38.80 Trifecta £383.90.
**Owner** Exors Of The Late J L C Pearce **Bred** Churchtown House Stud & Partners **Trained** Newmarket, Suffolk

**FOCUS**
They didn't go fast and those up with the pace were favoured. The winner looks to be getting his act together.

### 7569 125 PLATE H'CAP (DIV I) 1m 5y (Tp)
**6:15** (6:19) (Class 4) (0-80,82) 3-Y-O+ **£4,851** (£1,443; £721; £360) **Stalls** Centre

Form RPR
6145 **1** **Fayez (IRE)**[13] 7162 3-9-1 **81**.... ShelleyBirkett(3) 8 91
(David O'Meara) *hld up: pushed along over 2f out: hdwy over 1f out: led ins fnl f: rdn out* **12/1**
0254 **2** *1 ¼* **Rashford's Double (IRE)**[22] 6855 3-9-3 **80**....(p) TonyHamilton 12 87
(Richard Fahey) *cl up: led 2f out: rdn and hdd ins fnl f: kpt on same pce* **9/1**
3415 **3** *3 ¼* **Excel Again**[60] 5484 3-9-5 **82**.... LukeMorris 10 82
(James Tate) *hld up: stdy hdwy on nr side of gp over 3f out: rdn fr 2f out: kpt on ins fnl f: nt pce of first two* **5/2**[1]
0301 **4** *nk* **Auspicion**[17] 7034 3-9-5 **78**.... AndrewMullen 6 77
(Tom Tate) *dwlt: hld up: stdy hdwy over 2f out: rdn and outpcd over 1f out: kpt on ins fnl f* **5/1**[2]
5055 **5** *nse* **Archipeligo**[10] 7234 6-8-9 **71**....(p) LewisEdmunds(3) 9 70
(Iain Jardine) *hld up: effrt nr side of gp over 1f out: n.m.r briefly ins fnl f: kpt on: nvr rchd ldrs* **17/2**
5-44 **6** *1 ¾* **Dubai Elegance**[37] 6321 3-9-0 **80**....(p) CallumShepherd(3) 11 75
(Saeed bin Suroor) *dwlt: sn prom on nr side of gp: rdn and outpcd over 1f out: edgd lft and no imp ins fnl f* **7/1**[3]
250 **7** *½* **Torrid**[55] 5668 6-9-9 **82**.... CamHardie 5 76
(Michael Easterby) *t.k.h: in tch: rdn and outpcd 2f out: no imp fnl f* **14/1**
0040 **8** *nk* **Oud Metha Bridge (IRE)**[39] 6265 3-9-1 **78**.... FrannyNorton 2 71
(Ed Dunlop) *t.k.h: chsd ldrs: drvn and outpcd over 2f out: n.d after* **16/1**
2500 **9** *3* **Derek Duval (USA)**[14] 7131 3-9-0 **77**....(t) BenCurtis 1 63
(Stuart Williams) *taken early to post: cl up on outside of gp tl rdn and wknd fr 2f out* **9/1**
0000 **10** *1 ¾* **Alkashaaf (USA)**[29] 6637 3-9-1 **78**....(tp) PhillipMakin 3 60
(Archie Watson) *led at ordinary gallop: rdn and hdd 2f out: wknd fnl f* **33/1**

1m 40.0s (1.40) **Going Correction** +0.15s/f (Slow)
**WFA** 3 from 4yo+ 4lb **10** Ran SP% **111.4**
Speed ratings (Par 105): **99,97,94,94,94 92,91,91,88,86**
CSF £109.94 CT £350.69 TOTE £13.30: £3.20, £2.30, £1.10; EX 119.40 Trifecta £980.90.
**Owner** Northern Lads & Nawton Racing **Bred** Miss Siobhan Ryan **Trained** Upper Helmsley, N Yorks
■ Hidden Rebel was withdrawn. price at time of withdrawal 33-1. Rule 4 does not apply.

**FOCUS**
A competitive heat and they went a good pace down the middle. The first two came clear and the race has been rated around the runner-up.

### 7570 125 PLATE H'CAP (DIV II) 1m 5y (Tp)
**6:45** (6:48) (Class 4) (0-80,81) 3-Y-O+ **£4,851** (£1,443; £721; £360) **Stalls** Centre

Form RPR
3153 **1** **Cool Team (IRE)**[21] 6882 3-9-3 **79**....(tp) LouisSteward 5 87
(Hugo Palmer) *in tch: hdwy to ld over 2f out: rdn over 1f out: hrd pressed ins fnl f: kpt on gamely towards fin* **4/1**[1]
3000 **2** *½* **Newmarket Warrior (IRE)**[82] 4661 6-8-6 **67**....(p) LewisEdmunds(3) 12 74
(Iain Jardine) *hld up: angled lft over 3f out: effrt and pushed along over 1f out: disp ld ins fnl f: hld cl home* **14/1**
3243 **3** *½* **Gerry The Glover (IRE)**[17] 7034 5-9-5 **77**....(p) BenCurtis 1 83
(Brian Ellison) *hld up: pushed along over 2f out: effrt whn nt clr run briefly over 1f out: styd on u.p ins fnl f* **9/2**[2]
4432 **4** *nse* **Roll On Rory**[19] 6964 4-9-3 **78**....(v) CliffordLee(3) 7 84
(Jason Ward) *led to over 2f out: rallied: no ex ins fnl f* **5/1**[3]
0536 **5** *1 ¾* **Zamjar**[21] 6882 3-9-0 **76**.... GrahamLee 11 80+
(Ed Dunlop) *hld up: gng wl over 1f out: effrt whn nt clr run ins fnl f: r.o fin* **8/1**
245 **6** *shd* **Thello**[62] 5417 5-8-9 **70**.... PhilDennis(3) 9 71
(Jim Goldie) *t.k.h: hld up: rdn over 2f out: rallied over 1f out: no imp ins fnl f* **25/1**
5420 **7** *1 ¾* **Briyouni (FR)**[19] 6965 4-9-7 **79**....(p) KevinStott 4 76
(Kevin Ryan) *t.k.h early: hld up: hdwy and prom 2f out: wknd ins fnl f* **7/1**
0036 **8** *¾* **Zeshov (IRE)**[34] 6434 6-9-4 **76**.... LukeMorris 10 72
(Rebecca Bastiman) *hld up in tch: effrt and drvn along over 2f out: hung lft and wknd ins fnl f* **16/1**
4662 **9** *1 ½* **Rock N Rolla (IRE)**[13] 7162 3-8-10 **77**.... RowanScott(5) 6 69
(Keith Dalgleish) *pressed ldr: rdn over 2f out: wknd over 1f out* **7/1**
1-44 **10** *2 ¾* **Mamdood (IRE)**[17] 7016 3-9-2 **78**....(t) JoeyHaynes 8 64
(Susan Corbett) *dwlt: sn in tch: drvn along over 2f out: wknd over 1f out* **16/1**
5-05 **11** *3 ¾* **Jacquard (IRE)**[20] 6942 3-9-5 **81**.... FrannyNorton 3 58
(Mark Johnston) *cl up: ev ch briefly over 2f out: wknd over 1f out* **33/1**

1m 38.4s (-0.20) **Going Correction** +0.15s/f (Slow)
**WFA** 3 from 4yo+ 4lb **11** Ran SP% **116.2**
Speed ratings (Par 105): **107,106,106,105,104 104,102,101,100,97 93**
CSF £60.17 CT £267.67 TOTE £3.80: £1.80, £4.40, £2.00; EX 76.70 Trifecta £846.50.
**Owner** Lit Lung Lee **Bred** Ringfort Stud **Trained** Newmarket, Suffolk

**FOCUS**
They went a good gallop for the second division in which they recorded a 1.60s faster time. They ended up racing on the far side and the winner built on his latest run..

### 7571 GET FIT WITH SPEEDFLEX H'CAP 7f 14y (Tp)
**7:15** (7:18) (Class 5) (0-75,75) 3-Y-O+ **£3,234** (£962; £481; £240) **Stalls** Centre

Form RPR
05 **1** **Rock Warbler (IRE)**[17] 7034 4-9-5 **73**....(t) KevinStott 4 81
(Oliver Greenall) *hld up: smooth hdwy over 1f out: rdn and kpt on wl fnl f to ld cl home* **4/1**[1]
2145 **2** *nse* **Valentino Boy (IRE)**[56] 5604 3-9-0 **71**.... BenCurtis 1 78
(Brian Ellison) *led: rdn over 1f out: kpt on fnl f: hdd cl home* **10/1**
5160 **3** *1* **Mywayistheonlyway (IRE)**[19] 6964 4-9-4 **75**.... PhilDennis(3) 13 80
(Grant Tuer) *t.k.h: w ldr to ins fnl f: no ex towards fin* **11/1**
0206 **4** *shd* **Acrux**[17] 7034 4-9-4 **72**....(h) PhillipMakin 8 77+
(David O'Meara) *hld up: effrt whn no room fr over 1f out tl fnl 75yds: fin strly: unlucky* **13/2**[3]
041 **5** *½* **Deansgate (IRE)**[41] 6181 4-9-4 **72**.... JoeDoyle 3 79+
(Julie Camacho) *plld hrd in midfield: effrt and rdn over 1f out: chsng ldrs whn nt clr run last 75yds* **6/1**[2]
-330 **6** *¾* **Garter (IRE)**[19] 6964 4-8-10 **64**.... TonyHamilton 10 66
(Richard Fahey) *t.k.h: prom: effrt and rdn 2f out: no ex ins fnl f* **12/1**
4135 **7** *shd* **Whitkirk**[31] 6564 4-9-0 **68**.... JackGarritty 6 69
(Jedd O'Keeffe) *t.k.h: chsd ldrs: drvn along 2f out: no ex fnl f* **12/1**
1202 **8** *shd* **Hernando Torres**[31] 6564 9-8-8 **69**.... RyanTimby(7) 7 70
(Michael Easterby) *hld up: reminders and outpcd over 2f out: rallied ins fnl f: nvr able to chal* **20/1**
3034 **9** *½* **Portledge (IRE)**[21] 6899 3-9-2 **73**....(b) GrahamLee 9 72
(James Bethell) *hld up midfield: effrt on nr side of gp over 1f out: no imp fnl f* **6/1**[2]
1-56 **10** *¾* **Ferocity (IRE)**[216] 926 3-9-3 **74**.... LukeMorris 2 71
(Robyn Brisland) *in tch on far side of gp: rdn and hung lft over 1f out: wknd ins fnl f* **14/1**
0002 **11** *¾* **Red Tycoon (IRE)**[31] 6555 5-9-4 **72**.... PaulMulrennan 5 68
(Ken Cunningham-Brown) *t.k.h: prom on far side of gp: rdn and effrt over 1f out: wknd ins fnl f* **14/1**
0000 **12** *½* **Pickett's Charge**[150] 2267 4-8-13 **67**.... ShaneGray 11 61
(Richard Guest) *in tch on nr side of gp: effrt and rdn wl over 1f out: wknd fnl f* **33/1**
4500 **13** *¾* **Secret Missile**[16] 7052 7-9-2 **70**.... FrannyNorton 14 62
(David C Griffiths) *hld up: drvn and outpcd over 2f out: n.d after* **33/1**
0500 **14** *hd* **Caeser The Gaeser (IRE)**[8] 7332 5-8-7 **64**....(p) LewisEdmunds(3) 12 56
(Nigel Tinkler) *hld up midfield nr side of gp: drvn along over 2f out: wknd over 1f out* **20/1**

1m 27.01s (0.81) **Going Correction** +0.15s/f (Slow)
**WFA** 3 from 4yo+ 3lb **14** Ran SP% **123.5**
Speed ratings (Par 103): **101,100,99,99,99 98,98,98,97,96 95,95,94,94**
CSF £43.32 CT £427.69 TOTE £4.30: £1.60, £3.80, £4.30; EX 56.20 Trifecta £536.80.
**Owner** R A Royle & S Evason **Bred** Sir E J Loder **Trained** Oldcastle Heath, Cheshire

**FOCUS**
They didn't go much of a pace and finished bunched up, and there were a couple of hard-luck stories. The third helps set the standard.

## 7572 GALLOWGATE H'CAP — 6f (Tp)
**7:45** (7:48) (Class 5) (0-75,75) 3-Y-0+ **£3,234** (£962; £481; £240) **Stalls** Centre

Form RPR
4202 **1** **Athollblair Boy (IRE)**[41] 6181 4-9-3 **68** AndrewMullen 7 77
(Nigel Tinkler) *hld up: hdwy over 1f out: led ins fnl f: edgd lft: drvn out* **15/2**[3]
3006 **2** ½ **Major Crispies**[8] 7332 6-9-3 **68** (b) DavidNolan 3 75
(David O'Meara) *hld up: effrt and hdwy over 1f out: edgd lft and chsd wnr ins fnl f: kpt on: hld nr fin* **20/1**
0456 **3** 1¼ **Duke Cosimo**[10] 7244 7-9-5 **70** JoeDoyle 2 73
(Michael Herrington) *hld up: hdwy on far side of gp wl over 1f out: kpt on same pce ins fnl f* **6/1**[2]
4422 **4** nse **Mishaal (IRE)**[16] 7056 7-9-6 **71** PaulMulrennan 13 74
(Michael Herrington) *prom: rdn and outpcd over 2f out: rallied over 1f out: kpt on fnl f* **4/1**[1]
2005 **5** ½ **Perfect Symphony (IRE)**[10] 7245 3-9-6 **73** (p) KevinStott 8 77+
(Kevin Ryan) *hld up: nt clr run and swtchd rt over 1f out: kpt on ins fnl f: nvr able to chal* **6/1**[2]
5100 **6** 1¼ **Haworth**[2] 7522 3-9-2 **69** (b) CamHardie 9 67
(James Bethell) *s.i.s: hld up: rdn and hdwy over 1f out: no imp fnl f* **10/1**
4350 **7** ½ **Vallarta (IRE)**[82] 4663 7-9-7 **72** JackGarritty 6 68
(Ruth Carr) *cl up: rdn and ch over 1f out: no ex ins fnl f* **14/1**
0535 **8** ½ **The Nazca Lines (IRE)**[27] 6670 3-9-5 **72** (v) GrahamLee 10 66
(John Quinn) *prom: effrt and drvn along over 1f out: no ex ins fnl f* **25/1**
3050 **9** nk **Round The Island**[10] 7245 4-8-13 **67** LewisEdmunds[(3)] 11 60
(Richard Whitaker) *chsd ldrs: led over 1f out to ins fnl f: sn rdn and wknd* **9/1**
000 **10** nk **Salvatore Fury (IRE)**[30] 6571 7-8-12 **68** (p) RowanScott[(5)] 5 61
(Keith Dalgleish) *hld up midfield: effrt far side of gp over 1f out: sn no imp* **33/1**
00 **11** ¾ **Tavener**[15] 7086 5-9-2 **74** (p) RPWalsh[(7)] 14 64
(David C Griffiths) *led at decent gallop: rdn and hdd over 1f out: wknd fnl f* **33/1**
0003 **12** 3¼ **Treaty Of Rome (USA)**[32] 6527 5-9-10 **75** (v) TonyHamilton 12 55
(Derek Shaw) *hld up nr side of gp: drvn and outpcd over 2f out: n.d after* **20/1**
6034 **13** 1 **B Fifty Two (IRE)**[14] 7111 8-9-2 **67** BarryMcHugh 4 44
(Marjorie Fife) *in tch: rdn over 2f out: wknd over 1f out* **11/1**
53-1 **14** 12 **Shesthedream (IRE)**[154] 2124 4-9-4 **69** BenCurtis 1 7
(David Barron) *hld up on far side of gp: struggling over 2f out: sn wknd* **16/1**

1m 12.35s (-0.15) **Going Correction** +0.15s/f (Slow)
**WFA** 3 from 4yo+ 2lb **14** Ran SP% **119.6**
Speed ratings (Par 103): **107,106,104,104,103 102,101,100,100,100 99,94,93,77**
CSF £155.39 CT £960.27 TOTE £7.00: £2.50, £6.70, £2.30; EX 142.30 Trifecta £649.70.
**Owner** Leeds Plywood And Doors Ltd **Bred** Ms Ashley O'Leary **Trained** Langton, N Yorks

**FOCUS**
A good pace for this competitive sprint handicap.

## 7573 PLAY GOLF AT CLOSE HOUSE H'CAP — 7f 14y (Tp)
**8:15** (8:16) (Class 6) (0-60,60) 3-Y-0+ **£2,425** (£721; £360; £180) **Stalls** Centre

Form RPR
005 **1** **Intiwin (IRE)**[10] 7240 5-9-4 **57** DavidNolan 2 64
(Linda Perratt) *hld up: hdwy on far side of gp to ld wl over 1f out: sn qcknd over 2 l clr: edgd rt: hrd pressed wl ins fnl f: hld on wl* **16/1**
3540 **2** hd **Gun Case**[17] 7034 5-9-6 **59** (p) PhillipMakin 12 65
(Alistair Whillans) *hld up: gd hdwy on nr side of gp to chse wnr ent fnl f: kpt on: jst hld* **10/3**[1]
0650 **3** ¾ **Grey Destiny**[10] 7240 7-9-5 **58** (p) CamHardie 7 63
(Antony Brittain) *s.i.s: hld up: hdwy to chse ldrs whn nt clr run over 2f out: rdn over 1f out: kpt on ins fnl f* **16/1**
3400 **4** 2¼ **Ingleby Angel (IRE)**[27] 6673 8-9-3 **59** JoshDoyle[(3)] 4 58
(David O'Meara) *hld up: hdwy on far side over 1f out: kpt on same pce ins fnl f* **4/1**[2]
3251 **5** 2¼ **Masquerade Bling (IRE)**[21] 6902 3-9-4 **60** (p) AndrewMullen 11 52
(Daniel Mark Loughnane) *hld up: hdwy on nr side of gp over 2f out: rdn and no imp fr over 1f out* **9/2**[3]
0002 **6** ½ **Broughtons Fancy**[21] 6902 4-8-9 **53** GemmaTutty[(5)] 13 45
(Karen Tutty) *hld up midfield: drvn along over 2f out: effrt over 1f out: sn no imp* **22/1**
5461 **7** ¾ **Broctune Papa Gio**[21] 6903 10-9-2 **55** (p) PatrickMathers 10 45
(Gillian Boanas) *led 1f: cl up tl rdn and wknd over 1f out* **10/1**
6510 **8** 2¼ **Rose Eclair**[3] 7474 4-9-1 **57** (p) RachelRichardson[(3)] 5 41
(Tim Easterby) *dwlt: t.k.h and led after 1f: hdd wl over 1f out: sn wknd* **10/1**
2320 **9** 2½ **Jack Blane**[10] 7240 3-8-12 **59** (p) RowanScott[(5)] 6 36
(Keith Dalgleish) *chsd ldrs: effrt and ev ch briefly 2f out: wknd fnl f* **12/1**
5330 **10** 3¾ **Lady Volante (IRE)**[28] 6664 3-9-2 **58** GrahamLee 9 26
(Rebecca Menzies) *hld up: drvn along over 2f out: sn no imp* **50/1**
6500 **11** 13 **Stun Gun**[10] 7236 7-9-3 **56** (v) TonyHamilton 1
(Derek Shaw) *cl up on far side of gp: struggling wl over 2f out: sn btn* **80/1**
5006 **12** 3½ **Jacob Black**[13] 7166 6-9-2 **55** (tp) DougieCostello 14
(Kenny Johnson) *cl up on nr side of gp: rdn over 2f out: sn wknd* **16/1**
6042 **13** 44 **Tanawar (IRE)**[6] 7389 7-9-7 **60** (b) JackGarritty 3
(Ruth Carr) *in tch: lost pl over 3f out: lost tch fnl 2f* **10/1**

1m 26.8s (0.60) **Going Correction** +0.15s/f (Slow)
**WFA** 3 from 4yo+ 3lb **13** Ran SP% **121.4**
Speed ratings (Par 101): **102,101,100,98,95 95,94,91,88,84 69,65,15**
CSF £69.19 CT £928.88 TOTE £20.60: £3.90, £2.10, £4.30; EX 102.90 Trifecta £1237.70 Part won..
**Owner** John Murphy **Bred** Hugh O'Brien & Michael McCallan **Trained** East Kilbride, S Lanarks

**FOCUS**
A fair pace for those moderate handicap in which those coming from behind were favoured.

## 7574 BRITISH MASTERS 2017 MAIDEN STKS — 6f (Tp)
**8:45** (8:46) (Class 5) 3-Y-0+ **£3,234** (£962; £481; £240) **Stalls** Centre

Form RPR
6/64 **1** **Sexy Legs**[70] 5112 5-9-2 60 (t[1]) DougieCostello 10 65
(Rebecca Menzies) *in tch stands' side trio: hdwy over 1f out: led and edgd lft ins fnl f: hld on wl cl home* **10/1**
6320 **2** nk **Arnarson**[39] 6268 3-9-5 74 LukeMorris 6 69
(Ed Dunlop) *led stands' side trio and overall ldr: rdn over 1f out: hdd ins fnl f: rallied: hld cl home* **5/4**[1]
364- **3** hd **Pudding Chare (IRE)**[348] 7381 3-9-5 69 JackGarritty 8 68
(Richard Fahey) *t.k.h early: cl up in stands' side trio: rdn and outpcd over 1f out: rallied ins fnl f: hld cl home* **2/1**[2]
05 **4** 8 **Spring Beauty**[10] 7247 3-8-11 0 PhilDennis[(3)] 5 37
(John Weymes) *w ldrs in centre: drvn 2f out: tk modest 4th ins fnl f: no ch w stands' side ldrs* **66/1**
5636 **5** 1 **Poet's Time**[30] 6572 3-8-11 42 RachelRichardson[(3)] 7 34
(Tim Easterby) *hld up in tch centre: hdwy and ev ch over 2f out: sn drvn along: no ex fnl f* **20/1**
05 **6** 8 **Intoxikating**[17] 7035 3-9-5 0 (t) PaulMulrennan 1 14
(Gay Kelleway) *t.k.h: prom on far side of centre gp: struggling over 2f out: sn btn* **33/1**
04 **7** 2¼ **Coviglia (IRE)**[27] 6667 3-9-5 63 DavidNolan 3 6
(David O'Meara) *cl up centre: drvn and struggling over 2f out: sn wknd* **12/1**
**8** 2½ **Port Soif** 3-9-0 0 PhillipMakin 2
(David O'Meara) *s.i.s: hld up in centre: rdn and outpcd over 2f out: sn btn* **5/1**[3]

1m 13.34s (0.84) **Going Correction** +0.15s/f (Slow)
**WFA** 3 from 4yo+ 2lb **8** Ran SP% **120.4**
Speed ratings (Par 103): **100,99,99,88,87 76,73,70**
CSF £24.11 TOTE £12.10: £2.40, £1.10, £1.30; EX 34.50 Trifecta £115.40.
**Owner** EPDS Racing Partnership 21 **Bred** Gracelands Stud **Trained** Mordon, Durham

**FOCUS**
A three-way photo featuring a trio that raced alone on the stands' side, and they came well clear. The winner was formerly an 80+ horse in Ireland.

## 7575 ST JAMES' PARK APPRENTICE H'CAP — 5f (Tp)
**9:15** (9:21) (Class 6) (0-60,60) 3-Y-0+ **£2,425** (£721; £360; £180) **Stalls** Centre

Form RPR
6030 **1** **Canford Bay (IRE)**[7] 7366 3-9-2 **53** CliffordLee 9 66+
(Antony Brittain) *t.k.h in midfield: gd hdwy to ld over 1f out: edgd lft and qcknd clr ins fnl f: readily* **5/1**[2]
0505 **2** 3 **Bond Bombshell**[7] 7366 4-8-13 **57** (v[1]) PatrickVaughan[(8)] 7 59
(David O'Meara) *cajoled to s: prom: effrt and chsd wnr appr fnl f: kpt on: nt pce to chal* **12/1**
3343 **3** ½ **Ambitious Icarus**[7] 7366 8-9-3 **60** (p) BenSanderson[(7)] 3 60
(Richard Guest) *dwlt: hld up: rdn and hdwy over 1f out: kpt on ins fnl f: nrst fin* **4/1**[1]
0106 **4** shd **See Vermont**[7] 7366 9-9-9 **59** (b) CallumShepherd 13 59
(Rebecca Bastiman) *hld up on nr side of gp: hdwy and prom over 1f out: rdn and kpt on ins fnl f* **12/1**
5030 **5** 1¾ **Willbeme**[13] 7166 9-9-6 **56** (bt[1]) PhilDennis 5 50
(Simon West) *prom on far side of gp: drvn and outpcd over 1f out: edgd lft and rallied last 100yds: kpt on* **16/1**
5050 **6** shd **Little Miss Lola**[86] 4509 3-9-1 **55** CallumRodriguez[(3)] 14 48
(Lynn Siddall) *hld up: rdn and effrt on nr side of gp: hdwy over 1f out: kpt on fnl f: no imp* **12/1**
351 **7** shd **Dawoodi**[13] 7164 3-9-8 **59** (h) LewisEdmunds 12 52
(Linda Perratt) *dwlt: hld up: rdn and hdwy over 1f out: no imp fnl f* **11/2**[3]
034 **8** nk **Thornaby Princess**[7] 7366 6-8-5 **46** oh1 (p) ManuelFernandes[(5)] 6 38
(Colin Teague) *cl up: effrt and ev ch over 1f out: wknd ins fnl f* **12/1**
0454 **9** hd **Imperial Legend (IRE)**[17] 7036 8-9-7 **57** (p) JoshDoyle 1 48
(Alan Brown) *hld up: rdn and hdwy over 1f out: no ex ins fnl f* **7/1**
400 **10** ¾ **Archie Stevens**[21] 6896 7-9-1 **56** WilliamCox[(5)] 8 44
(Clare Ellam) *led to over 1f out: rdn and wknd fnl f* **25/1**
0602 **11** 1¼ **Lady Molly (IRE)**[13] 7164 3-8-3 **46** oh1 (v[1]) RowanScott[(6)] 4 30
(Keith Dalgleish) *cl up: drvn along over 2f out: wknd over 1f out* **12/1**
000 **12** 2¼ **Jorvik Prince**[84] 4559 3-8-13 **56** (b) GemmaTutty[(6)] 10 32
(Karen Tutty) *t.k.h: prom on nr side of gp: rdn and wknd over 1f out* **12/1**
-035 **13** 3 **Jebel Tara**[13] 7166 12-8-0 **46** oh1 (bt) RhonaPindar[(10)] 2 11
(Alistair Whillans) *racd against far rail: sn bhd: struggling fr 1/2-way: nvr on terms* **33/1**

59.79s (0.29) **Going Correction** +0.15s/f (Slow)
**WFA** 3 from 4yo+ 1lb **13** Ran SP% **123.4**
Speed ratings (Par 101): **103,98,97,97,94 94,94,93,93,92 90,86,81**
CSF £66.34 CT £278.04 TOTE £5.90: £2.10, £3.50, £2.10; EX 73.20 Trifecta £578.20.
**Owner** Ritchie Fiddes **Bred** R McCulloch **Trained** Warthill, N Yorks

**FOCUS**
A competitive little sprint turned into a procession by the winner.
T/Plt: £288.40 to a £1 stake. Pool: £86,907.82 - 219.93 winning units T/Qpdt: £51.90 to a £1 stake. Pool: £13,162.14 - 187.54 winning units **Richard Young**

# 7543 NEWMARKET (R-H)
Friday, September 29

**OFFICIAL GOING: Good to soft (soft in places; overall 6.6, stands' 6.7, centre 6.5, far 6.4)**
Wind: light, behind Weather: overcast

## 7576 MUHAARAR BRITISH EBF ROSEMARY STKS (LISTED RACE) (F&M) — 1m
**1:50** (1:53) (Class 1) 3-Y-0+
**£22,684** (£8,600; £4,304; £2,144; £1,076; £540) **Stalls** Low

Form RPR
3324 **1** **Muffri'Ha (IRE)**[145] 2432 5-9-2 107 PatCosgrave 5 105
(William Haggas) *taken down early: awkward leaving stalls: hld up in rr of main gp: hdwy to trck ldrs 5f out: rdn to chal over 1f out: led 1f out: styd on wl: rdn out* **5/1**[2]
-245 **2** 1 **Permission**[80] 4718 4-9-2 93 DanielMuscutt 1 102
(James Fanshawe) *s.i.s: detached in last pair early: clsd and in tch after 2f: hdwy into midfield 1/2-way: effrt u.p ent fnl 2f: styd on strly ins fnl f: wnt 2nd last stride* **20/1**
1323 **3** shd **Tisbutadream (IRE)**[27] 6697 3-9-1 103 SilvestreDeSousa 3 105
(David Elsworth) *taken down early: chsd ldrs: wnt 2nd after 2f tl rdn to ld 2f out: drvn and hdd 1f out: kpt on same pce ins fnl f: lost 2nd last stride* **11/2**[3]
2 **4** nk **La Figlia (IRE)**[24] 6791 3-8-12 0 FrankieDettori 4 101
(Jeremy Noseda) *leggy: athletic: lw: in tch in midfield: effrt to chse ldrs 2f out: kpt on u.p ins fnl f* **10/1**

2210 **5** 1 ¾ **Lincoln Rocks**[27] 6697 4-9-5 106................................ DanielTudhope 15 100
(David O'Meara) *led tl rdn and hdd 2f out: 4th and no ex u.p 1f out: wknd ins fnl f* **9/1**

1156 **6** 1 ¾ **Mittens**[48] 5927 3-8-12 99................................ RyanMoore 7 93
(Sir Michael Stoute) *t.k.h: hld up in tch in midfield: effrt 2f out: drvn and unable qck over 1f out: kpt on same pce fnl f* **10/1**

**7** *hd* **Ciaoadiosimdone (IRE)** 3-8-12 0................................ BrettDoyle 12 93
(John Ryan) *medium-sized: athletic: swtg: dwlt: sn rcvrd and in tch in midfield: rdn over 2f out: unable qck and outpcd 2f out: rallied 1f out: no threat to ldrs but styd on steadily ins fnl f* **200/1**

1 **8** 3 ¾ **Good Way Off (USA)**[29] 6614 4-9-2 83................................ JamieSpencer 14 84
(Luca Cumani) *str: chsd ldr for 2f: styd chsng ldrs: rdn 3f out: outpcd u.p ent fnl 2f out: no threat to ldrs after* **20/1**

-101 **9** 1 ¾ **Amabilis**[20] 6919 3-8-12 102................................ PatDobbs 9 80
(Ralph Beckett) *lw: s.i.s: detached in last and rdn along early: clsd and in tch after 2f: effrt ent fnl 2f: no imp over 1f out: wknd fnl f* **4/1**[1]

0315 **10** 3 **On Her Toes (IRE)**[14] 7113 3-9-1 102................................ JimCrowley 13 76
(William Haggas) *chsd ldrs tl jst over 2f out: sn u.p and lost pl over 1f out: wknd fnl f* **7/1**

-036 **11** 6 **Desert Haze**[86] 4679 4-9-2 98................................ HarryBentley 6 59
(Ralph Beckett) *hld up in tch in midfield: rdn jst over 2f out: sn struggling: wknd over 1f out* **12/1**

1 **12** 1 ¾ **Aquamarina**[198] 1199 3-8-12 77................................ TomMarquand 11 55
(Robyn Brisland) *unf: hld up in tch: rdn ent fnl 3f: unbalanced and dropped to rr wl over 1f out: bhd ins fnl f* **33/1**

000 **13** 56 **Somethingthrilling**[9] 7283 5-9-2 90................................ DaneO'Neill 10
(David Elsworth) *swtg: taken down early: hld up in tch: dropped to rr 3f out: eased wl over 1f out: t.o* **66/1**

1m 39.14s (0.54) **Going Correction** +0.40s/f (Good)
**WFA** 3 from 4yo+ 4lb **13** Ran SP% **114.9**
Speed ratings (Par 111): **113,112,111,111,109 108,107,104,102,99 93,91,35**
CSF £105.73 TOTE £5.20: £2.10, £5.70, £2.10; EX 105.70 Trifecta £697.90.
**Owner** Sheikh Juma Dalmook Al Maktoum **Bred** Lodge Park Stud **Trained** Newmarket, Suffolk
■ Stewards' Enquiry : Brett Doyle one-day ban; appeared to stop riding shortly before the winning post (Oct 15)

**FOCUS**
A couple of the fancied runners failed to give their running, but still sound form for the level.

## 7577 PRINCESS ROYAL NAYEF STKS (GROUP 3) (F&M) 1m 4f
2:25 (2:31) (Class 1) 3-Y-O+

**£34,026** (£12,900; £6,456; £3,216; £1,614; £810) **Stalls** Centre

Form RPR

5464 **1** **Apphia (IRE)**[27] 6675 3-8-10 98................................ JosephineGordon 1 107
(Hugo Palmer) *sn led and mde rest: rdn over 2f out: edgd lft 1f out: hrd pressed and hld on gamely u.p ins fnl f: all out* **20/1**

5122 **2** ½ **Pleasant Surprise (IRE)**[21] 6914 3-8-10 94.................. JamieSpencer 7 106
(Luca Cumani) *stdd s: hld up in rr: smooth hdwy jst over 2f out: trckd ldrs whn swtchd rt over 1f out: drvn to chal 1f out: kpt on u.p: a jst hld* **15/2**

2-10 **3** 1 ½ **To Eternity**[41] 6191 4-9-3 103................................ JamesDoyle 4 104
(John Gosden) *t.k.h: trckd ldrs: effrt 2f out: pressing ldrs u.p whn carried lft jst over 1f out: no ex and one pce ins fnl f* **5/1**[3]

1031 **4** 1 **Fleur Forsyte**[36] 6357 3-8-10 103................................(h) DanielMuscutt 9 102
(James Fanshawe) *t.k.h: hld up in tch in midfield: clsd to trck ldrs 3f out: wnt 2nd over 2f out tl jst over 1f out: sn swtchd rt and styd on same pce ins fnl f* **11/2**

0 **5** *hd* **Jet Streaming (IRE)**[19] 6978 3-8-10 86................(t[1]) SilvestreDeSousa 8 101
(Adrian Paul Keatley, Ire) *hld up in tch in last pair: rdn over 3f out: drvn 2f out: styd on u.p ins fnl f: nvr gng to rch ldrs* **33/1**

1120 **6** 2 ½ **Mori**[36] 6357 3-8-10 106................................ RyanMoore 10 97
(Sir Michael Stoute) *hld up in tch in midfield: rdn 3f out: no imp tl sme prog u.p over 1f out: one pce and hld fnl f* **9/2**[2]

4134 **7** 1 ¾ **Elas Ruby**[47] 5981 3-8-10 101................................ FrankieDettori 3 94
(John Gosden) *hld up in tch in last trio: effrt over 2f out: no imp u.p over 1f out: wl hld and one pce after* **7/2**[1]

2624 **8** *nk* **Isabel De Urbina (IRE)**[55] 5658 3-8-10 100................ PatDobbs 5 93
(Ralph Beckett) *chsd ldr tl over 2f out: lost pl u.p over 1f out: wl hld fnl f* **9/1**

4062 **9** 5 **Elbereth**[26] 6744 6-9-3 107................................ OisinMurphy 2 85
(Andrew Balding) *trckd ldrs: rdn over 2f out: sn btn and wknd over 1f out* **8/1**

2m 33.73s (1.73) **Going Correction** +0.40s/f (Good)
**WFA** 3 from 4yo+ 7lb **9** Ran SP% **113.0**
Speed ratings (Par 113): **110,109,108,108,107 106,105,104,101**
CSF £158.10 TOTE £28.00: £6.60, £2.20, £1.70; EX 221.60 Trifecta £3030.10.
**Owner** The Mixed Blessing Partnership **Bred** Lynch Bages, Camas Park & Brittas House **Trained** Newmarket, Suffolk

**FOCUS**
This former Listed contest carried Group 3 status for the first time, but was an ordinary race for the level. The winner has improved with the race rated around the third and fourth.

## 7578 SHADWELL ROCKFEL STKS (GROUP 2) (FILLIES) 7f
3:00 (3:04) (Class 1) 2-Y-O

**£61,813** (£23,435; £11,728; £5,842; £2,932; £1,471) **Stalls** Low

Form RPR

4312 **1** **Juliet Capulet (IRE)**[48] 5941 2-9-0 99................................ FrankieDettori 6 110
(John Gosden) *t.k.h: sn chsng ldr tl led 3f out: rdn and edgd lft over 1f out: kpt on u.p ins fnl f: a jst lasting home nr fin* **9/1**

2163 **2** *hd* **Nyaleti (IRE)**[15] 7088 2-9-0 110................................ JamesDoyle 1 109
(Mark Johnston) *trckd ldrs: effrt to chal and edgd lft over 1f out: ev ch fnl f but looked hld tl styd on u.p and clsng cl home* **2/1**[1]

11 **3** 1 ½ **Gavota**[30] 6583 2-9-0 95................................ JimCrowley 7 105+
(Roger Charlton) *leggy: athletic: t.k.h: hld up in tch towards rr: clsd and stuck bhd a wall of horses over 1f out: gap opened and effrt ent fnl f: styd on wl u.p to go 3rd towards fin: nt rch ldrs* **5/1**[3]

11 **4** ½ **Hikmaa (IRE)**[22] 6844 2-9-0 81................................ AdamBeschizza 3 104
(Ed Vaughan) *leggy: hld up in tch: effrt to chse ldrs and drifted rt over 1f out: hdwy u.p to chse ldng pair ins fnl f: kpt on but no imp fnl 100yds: lost 3rd towards fin* **25/1**

2 **5** 2 ¼ **Butterscotch (IRE)**[89] 4418 2-9-0 101................................(t) RyanMoore 10 98
(A P O'Brien, Ire) *cmpt: t.k.h: hld up in tch towards rr: clsd to trck ldrs 3f out: rdn and pressing wnr wl over 1f out: no ex 1f out: wknd ins fnl f* **5/1**[3]

1501 **6** 1 **Elizabeth Bennet (IRE)**[44] 6065 2-9-0 86................ SilvestreDeSousa 4 95
(Charles Hills) *t.k.h: sn led: hdd 3f out: styd chsng ldrs: unable qck u.p whn sltly impeded over 1f out: wknd ins fnl f* **33/1**

124 **7** *shd* **Capomento (IRE)**[41] 6228 2-9-0 0................................ RichardKingscote 2 95
(Tom Dascombe) *hld up in tch: shkn up over 1f out: sn rdn and no imp: styd on same pce fnl f* **16/1**

**8** 1 **Lightening Quick**[20] 6954 2-9-0 0................................ OisinMurphy 5 92
(G M Lyons, Ire) *athletic: lw: t.k.h: chsd ldrs tl 2f out: lost pl and edging rt over 1f out: wl hld and kpt on same pce ins fnl f* **4/1**[2]

63 **9** 1 ¼ **Club Tropicana**[21] 6886 2-9-0 0................................ StevieDonohoe 8 89
(Richard Spencer) *leggy: swtg: t.k.h: hld up in tch: dropped to rr and rdn wl over 1f out: n.d after* **100/1**

61 **10** ¾ **Roulette**[57] 5573 2-9-0 0................................ AndreaAtzeni 9 87
(Michael Bell) *lw: hld up in tch in rr: effrt ent fnl 2f: no imp u.p over 1f out: wknd ins fnl f* **33/1**

1m 27.23s (1.83) **Going Correction** +0.40s/f (Good) **10** Ran SP% **113.3**
Speed ratings (Par 104): **105,104,103,102,99 98,98,97,96,95**
CSF £25.94 TOTE £8.70: £2.30, £1.50, £1.50; EX 30.90 Trifecta £157.70.
**Owner** Cheveley Park Stud **Bred** Yeomanstown Stud **Trained** Newmarket, Suffolk

**FOCUS**
Traditionally a strong race, they went a steady gallop and the third looked unlucky not to go close. The winner took another big step forward.

## 7579 SHADWELL JOEL STKS (GROUP 2) 1m
3:35 (3:36) (Class 1) 3-Y-O+

**£56,710** (£21,500; £10,760; £5,360; £2,690; £1,350) **Stalls** Low

Form RPR

1011 **1** **Beat The Bank**[56] 5593 3-9-0 114................................ OisinMurphy 6 123
(Andrew Balding) *lw: t.k.h: sn prom in main gp: wnt 2nd and clsd over 2f out: rdn to ld wl over 1f out: styd on strly and drew clr fnl f: readily* **11/8**[1]

604 **2** 5 **Sir John Lavery (IRE)**[20] 6959 3-9-0 0................................ RyanMoore 9 112
(A P O'Brien, Ire) *swtg: hld up in rr: effrt ent fnl 2f: hdwy and hung lft over 1f out: wnt 2nd and hung rt 1f out: no ch w wnr but kpt on for clr 2nd ins fnl f* **3/1**[2]

3045 **3** 2 ¼ **Jallota**[26] 6729 6-9-4 110................................ JamieSpencer 1 106
(Charles Hills) *hld up in tch in midfield: clsd over 2f out: rdn to chse wnr over 1f out: no imp and lost 2nd 1f out: wl hld and kpt on same pce ins fnl f* **20/1**

1534 **4** 1 ¼ **Sovereign Debt (IRE)**[20] 6928 8-9-7 114................................ JamesSullivan 3 106
(Ruth Carr) *midfield: rdn 3f out: sn drvn: no ch w wnr and kpt on same pce fr over 1f out* **14/1**

0230 **5** 3 ½ **Custom Cut (IRE)**[20] 6959 8-9-4 107................................(p) DanielTudhope 7 95
(David O'Meara) *chsd ldr tl over 2f out: struggling and losing pl whn n.m.r over 1f out: wknd ins fnl f* **33/1**

**6** 2 **Whisky Baron (AUS)**[244] 5-9-4 0................................ GCheyne 5 91
(B Crawford, South Africa) *str: hld up in tch in last pair: effrt ent fnl 2f: no imp whn squeezed for room over 1f out: swtchd rt 1f out: sn wknd* **20/1**

-011 **7** 3 ½ **Mustashry**[34] 6444 4-9-4 112................................ JimCrowley 4 83
(Sir Michael Stoute) *dwlt: hld up towards rr: effrt 2f out: no hdwy u.p over 1f out: wknd fnl f* **7/2**[3]

1005 **7** *dht* **Whitecliffsofdover (USA)**[20] 6959 3-9-0 106................(bt) SeanLevey 8 83
(A P O'Brien, Ire) *led and sn clr: c bk to field over 2f out: hdd and edgd rt wl over 1f out: sn wknd* **20/1**

1m 38.67s (0.07) **Going Correction** +0.40s/f (Good)
**WFA** 3 from 4yo+ 4lb **8** Ran SP% **113.2**
Speed ratings (Par 115): **115,110,107,106,103 101,97,97**
CSF £5.12 TOTE £2.10: £1.10, £1.30, £4.70; EX 6.40 Trifecta £49.30.
**Owner** King Power Racing Co Ltd **Bred** A S Denniff **Trained** Kingsclere, Hants
■ Stewards' Enquiry : Jamie Spencer caution; careless riding

**FOCUS**
An impressive performance from the winner, who is a progressive miler now ready for the big time. The runner-up has been rated close to form.

## 7580 DERRINSTOWN BRITISH EBF MAIDEN STKS (PLUS 10 RACE) (C&G) 7f
4:10 (4:12) (Class 4) 2-Y-O **£5,175** (£1,540; £769; £384) **Stalls** Low

Form RPR

2 **1** **Thrave**[35] 6388 2-9-0 0................................ HarryBentley 12 89+
(Henry Candy) *str: trckd ldrs tl wnt 2nd 2f out: rdn to ld over 1f out: styd on wl and a in command ins fnl f: rdn out* **9/4**[2]

**2** 1 ¾ **Elwazir** 2-9-0 0................................ JimCrowley 14 84+
(Owen Burrows) *tall: scope: chsd ldng trio: rdn over 1f out: rn green: drifted but kpt on in fnl f: wnt 2nd last stride* **9/1**[3]

24 **3** *shd* **Coat Of Arms (IRE)**[19] 6975 2-9-0 0................................ RyanMoore 16 84
(A P O'Brien, Ire) *str: lw: hld up in tch: effrt over 1f out: drvn 1f out: chsd wnr ins fnl f: kpt on but a hld: lost 2nd last stride* **1/1**[1]

026 **4** 2 ¼ **Dark Spec**[28] 6653 2-9-0 78................................ RobHornby 8 78
(Pam Sly) *t.k.h: led: rdn and hdd over 1f out: no ex and lost 2 pls ins fnl f: eased cl home* **28/1**

**5** 4 **Recollect** 2-9-0 0................................ JamieSpencer 1 67+
(Luca Cumani) *athletic: midfield: shkn up over 1f out: no imp: wl hld 5th whn edgd rt and kpt on same pce ins fnl f* **50/1**

**5** *dht* **Tahreek** 2-9-0 0................................ DaneO'Neill 11 67+
(Sir Michael Stoute) *leggy: bit bkwd: rn green: t.k.h: hld up in midfield: no imp and struggling to handle dip over 1f out: styd on ins fnl f: nvr trbld ldrs* **28/1**

**7** 2 ½ **Dagian (IRE)** 2-9-0 0................................ MartinDwyer 13 60
(Amanda Perrett) *athletic: rn green: off the pce in midfield: rdn 3f out: no imp: wl hld and kpt on same pce fr over 1f out* **50/1**

**8** 1 ¼ **Burford Brown** 2-9-0 0................................ JamesDoyle 3 57
(Hugo Palmer) *str: chsd ldng quartet: effrt 2f out: no imp and btn 6th over 1f out: wknd ins fnl f* **33/1**

0 **9** 1 ¼ **Global Spirit**[34] 6424 2-9-0 0................................(h[1]) AntonioFresu 10 54
(Ed Dunlop) *w'like: swtg: s.i.s: t.k.h: hld up off the pce in last quintet: rdn over 2f out: sn outpcd: wl hld but plugged on to pass btn horses ins fnl f* **100/1**

06 **10** 1 **Vision Clear (GER)**[10] 7237 2-9-0 0................................ DanielTudhope 7 51
(Ed Dunlop) *unf: off the pce in midfield: pushed along ent fnl 2f: sn outpcd and wl hld over 1f out: wknd fnl f* **100/1**

0 **11** 2 **Tommy Boy**[35] 6388 2-9-0 0................................ JosephineGordon 15 46
(Tony Carroll) *leggy: t.k.h: chsd ldr tl 2f out: sn swtchd rt and rdn: 5th and btn over 1f out: fdd ins fnl f* **150/1**

**12** ¾ **Bacacarat (IRE)** 2-9-0 0................................ OisinMurphy 6 44
(Andrew Balding) *w'like: dwlt: hld up off the pce in last quintet: rdn over 2f out: sn struggling and wl btn over 1f out* **22/1**

**13** *nk* **Iconic Boy** 2-9-0 0................................ SilvestreDeSousa 2 43
(David Elsworth) *leggy: s.i.s: a off the pce in last quintet: rdn over 2f out: sn wl btn and wknd over 1f out* **50/1**

14 4 ½ **Cristal Spirit** 2-9-0 0........................ AndreaAtzeni 5 31
(William Haggas) *tall: lengthy: s.i.s: a off the pce in last pair: lost tch over 1f out* **16/1**

0 15 4 ½ **Thunderhooves**[14] 7117 2-9-0 0........................ StevieDonohoe 9 18
(John Ryan) *unf: a off the pce in rr: lost tch 2f out* **100/1**

1m 27.77s (2.37) **Going Correction** +0.40s/f (Good) 15 Ran SP% **120.4**
Speed ratings (Par 97): **102,100,99,97,92 92,89,88,87,85 83,82,82,77,72**
CSF £20.81 TOTE £3.10: £1.30, £2.70, £1.02; EX 23.70 Trifecta £46.60.
**Owner** Thomas Barr **Bred** Robert Allcock **Trained** Kingston Warren, Oxon

**FOCUS**
A good maiden, with two highly promising sorts accounting for a 101-rated favourite with Group 2-placed form in Ireland.

## 7581 MUKHADRAM GODOLPHIN STKS (LISTED RACE) 1m 4f
**4:45** (4:47) (Class 1) 3-Y-O+

**£20,982** (£7,955; £3,981; £1,983; £995; £499) **Stalls** Centre

Form RPR

2236 1 **Frontiersman**[33] 6499 4-9-5 117........................(b[1]) JamesDoyle 5 112+
(Charlie Appleby) *chsd ldr tl rdn to ld over 2f out: drvn and clr over 1f out: reduced advantage fnl 100yds but a holding on* **13/8**[1]

0022 2 ½ **Red Galileo**[35] 6399 6-9-5 105........................ DanielTudhope 3 111
(Saeed bin Suroor) *lw: led: c to centre 10f out: rdn and hdd over 2f out: kpt on u.p ins fnl f: nvr quite getting bck to wnr* **11/4**[2]

-034 3 ¾ **Best Of Days**[34] 6441 3-8-12 106........................(t[1]) JosephineGordon 2 110
(Hugo Palmer) *chsd ldrs: effrt in 3rd over 2f out: no imp over 1f out tl kpt on u.p ins fnl f: nvr getting to wnr* **8/1**

0-40 4 9 **Colonial Classic (FR)**[96] 4119 4-9-0 97........................ DanielMuscutt 6 90
(James Fanshawe) *stdd s: hld up in tch in last pair: effrt 3f out: sn rdn and no imp: wl btn over 1f out: plugged on to snatch 4th last strides* **66/1**

151/ 5 nk **Connecticut**[754] 6152 6-9-5 108........................ AndreaAtzeni 1 95
(Roger Varian) *t.k.h: hld up in last pair: effrt 3f out: 4th and swtchd lft over 1f out: sn struggling: wknd over 1f out* **7/1**

5042 6 17 **Red Verdon (USA)**[16] 7054 4-9-5 107........................ JimCrowley 7 68
(Ed Dunlop) *hld up in tch: effrt 3f out: sn drvn and btn: wl bhd over 1f out* **6/1**[3]

4041 7 21 **Uele River**[21] 6915 5-9-3 100........................ RyanMoore 4 32
(Henry Candy) *t.k.h: in tch in midfield: rdn and lost pl over 3f out: t.o and virtually p.u fnl f* **16/1**

2m 32.84s (0.84) **Going Correction** +0.40s/f (Good)
**WFA** 3 from 4yo+ 7lb 7 Ran SP% **110.0**
Speed ratings (Par 111): **113,112,112,106,105 94,80**
CSF £5.66 TOTE £2.40: £1.80, £1.40; EX 5.80 Trifecta £14.10.
**Owner** Godolphin **Bred** Stanley Estate And Stud Co **Trained** Newmarket, Suffolk

**FOCUS**
The first three finished well clear of the rest, although the winner didn't need to be at his best to collect. The time was 0.89sec faster than the fillies' Group 3 earlier on the card.

## 7582 SHADWELL FARM H'CAP (SILVER CAMBRIDGESHIRE) 1m 1f
**5:20** (5:23) (Class 2) 3-Y-O+

**£18,675** (£5,592; £2,796; £1,398; £699; £351) **Stalls** Low

Form RPR

4113 1 **Addeybb (IRE)**[57] 5568 3-9-9 **93**........................ RyanMoore 12 104
(William Haggas) *trckd ldrs: effrt to chse ldr 2f out: drvn and ev ch 1f out: kpt on wl u.p to ld towards fin: drvn out* **7/2**[1]

1044 2 ½ **Afaak**[21] 6873 3-9-8 **92**........................ JimCrowley 8 102
(Charles Hills) *lw: chsd ldr tl led 2f out: sn rdn and edgd lft over 1f out: hrd pressed 1f out: kpt on wl tl hdd and no ex towards fin* **6/1**[2]

5312 3 shd **Fire Brigade**[21] 6870 3-9-6 **90**........................ JamesDoyle 4 100
(Michael Bell) *hld up on tch in midfield: effrt and hdwy u.p over 1f out: nt clrest of runs briefly ent fnl f: sn drvn to chal jst ins fnl f: kpt on wl: unable qck cl home* **7/2**[1]

1340 4 2 ¼ **Chiefofchiefs**[20] 6933 4-9-9 **88**........................(p) StevieDonohoe 14 92
(Charlie Fellowes) *hld up wl in tch in midfield: effrt to chse ldrs over 1f out: nt clrest of runs and swtchd rt ent fnl f: styd on same pce fnl 100yds* **12/1**

2022 5 ½ **Mountain Angel (IRE)**[20] 6942 3-9-0 **84**........................ SilvestreDeSousa 9 88+
(Roger Varian) *t.k.h: hld up in tch in midfield: effrt u.p over 1f out: styd on ins fnl f: nvr getting to ldrs* **8/1**[3]

2020 6 1 ½ **Tyrsal (IRE)**[43] 6109 6-7-11 **65**........................(p) HollieDoyle[(3)] 6 65
(Clifford Lines) *stdd s: hld up in rr: rdn and hdwy over 1f out: kpt on ins fnl f: nvr trbld ldrs* **66/1**

0505 7 hd **One Word More (IRE)**[32] 6520 7-9-10 **89**........................(h) RobHornby 10 88
(Tim Easterby) *hld up wl in tch in midfield: effrt to chse ldrs 2f out: drvn and pressing ldrs over 1f out: no ex 1f out: wknd ins fnl f* **20/1**

1632 8 hd **Rotherwick (IRE)**[9] 7284 5-9-10 **89**........................(t) JFEgan 13 88+
(Paul Cole) *swtg: hld up in tch in last quartet: rdn over 2f out: swtchd lft over 1f out: hdwy ins fnl f: styd on: nvr trbld ldrs* **14/1**

1166 9 1 ½ **Wealth Tax**[9] 7285 4-9-4 **83**........................ OisinMurphy 15 79
(Ed Dunlop) *c to nr side after s: swtchd bk to r in rr of main gp after 1f: effrt over 1f out: squeezed through and hdwy jst ins fnl f: kpt on: nvr trbld ldrs* **66/1**

2141 10 nk **Daira Prince (IRE)**[71] 5077 3-9-2 **86**........................ AndreaAtzeni 16 82
(Roger Varian) *c to nr side after s: swtchd bk to main gp after 1f and hld up in main gp: effrt 2f out: no imp u.p over 1f out: kpt on same pce fnl f* **11/1**

3311 11 1 ¾ **Mon Beau Visage (IRE)**[34] 6434 4-9-9 **88**........................ DanielTudhope 2 80
(David O'Meara) *t.k.h: wl in tch in midfield: effrt 2f out: unable qck over 1f out: wknd ins fnl f* **25/1**

4350 12 nk **Boots And Spurs**[19] 6965 8-8-11 **81**........................(v) GeorgeBuckell[(5)] 1 72
(Scott Dixon) *led tl rdn and hdd 2f out: no ex u.p over 1f out: wknd ins fnl f* **50/1**

5005 13 nk **Archie (IRE)**[22] 6855 5-9-0 **79**........................ PatCosgrave 11 69
(Tom Clover) *lw: hld up in tch in last quartet: effrt wl over 1f out: no imp and wl hld fnl f* **14/1**

0152 14 shd **Lawmaking**[34] 6422 4-9-3 **82**........................(h) LiamKeniry 5 72
(Henry Spiller) *t.k.h: hld up wl in tch in midfield: effrt 2f out: rdn and unable qck over 1f out: sn btn and wknd ins fnl f* **25/1**

4134 15 8 **Captain Courageous (IRE)**[34] 6422 4-9-10 **89**.... RichardKingscote 17 62
(Ed Walker) *c towards stands side and racd alone after 1f: midfield: rdn over 2f out: lost pl and bhd over 1f out: wknd* **33/1**

100 16 27 **Fire Tree (IRE)**[27] 6700 4-9-2 **81**........................ JamieSpencer 3
(Charlie Fellowes) *lw: chsd ldrs: lost pl qckly and bhd over 1f out: bhd and heavily eased ins fnl f: t.o* **25/1**

1m 54.84s (3.14) **Going Correction** +0.40s/f (Good)
**WFA** 3 from 4yo+ 5lb 16 Ran SP% **123.4**
Speed ratings (Par 109): **102,101,101,99,99 97,97,97,96,95 94,93,93,93,86 62**
CSF £21.73 CT £84.43 TOTE £4.30: £1.30, £1.60, £1.50, £2.80; EX 25.30 Trifecta £57.30.
**Owner** Sheikh Ahmed Al Maktoum **Bred** Rabbah Bloodstock Limited **Trained** Newmarket, Suffolk

**FOCUS**
Strong handicap form with a trio of progressive 3yos dominating the closing stages and the winner continues to progress. They ended up stands' side having raced down the centre for much of it.
T/Jkpt: Not won. T/Plt: £30.00 to a £1 stake. Pool: £152,547.89 - 3,705.06 winning units T/Qpdt: £2.30 to a £1 stake. Pool: £13,243.49 - 4,223.50 winning units **Steve Payne**

7583 - 7587a (Foreign Racing) - See Raceform Interactive

# 7367 DUNDALK (A.W) (L-H)
Friday, September 29

**OFFICIAL GOING: Polytrack: standard**

## 7588a KOFFY DIAMOND STKS (GROUP 3) 1m 2f 150y(P)
**8:00** (8:01) 3-Y-O+

**£31,769** (£10,230; £4,846; £2,153; £1,076; £538)

RPR

1 **War Decree (USA)**[117] 3368 3-9-3 112........................ DonnachaO'Brien 10 114+
(A P O'Brien, Ire) *chsd ldrs in 4th: clsr in 3rd after 4f: travelled wl into 2nd over 1f out: sn led and readily wnt clr: easily* **7/2**[2]

2 2 ¼ **Absolute Blast (IRE)**[27] 6717 5-9-5 103........................ WJLee 6 103
(Archie Watson) *chsd ldrs in 5th: rdn into 3rd over 1f out: kpt on into 2nd ins fnl 100yds: nt trble wnr* **8/1**

3 1 **Abingdon (USA)**[36] 6356 4-9-5 108........................ PatSmullen 4 101
(Sir Michael Stoute) *sn led narrowly: extended advantage to 1l after 2f: hdd 1f out and sn no match for wnr: kpt on same pce and dropped to 3rd ins fnl 100yds* **7/4**[1]

4 1 ½ **Santa Monica**[19] 6972 4-9-5 99........................ DeclanMcDonogh 11 98
(Charles O'Brien, Ire) *bit slowly away and racd in rr: last 2f out: styd on wl towards inner ins fnl f into 4th cl home: nrst fin* **50/1**

5 ½ **Tennessee Wildcat (IRE)**[71] 5087 7-9-8 102........................ GaryCarroll 8 100
(G M Lyons, Ire) *hld up: 9th 2f out: styd on wl appr fnl f into 4th fnl 100yds: dropped to 5th cl home* **33/1**

6 ½ **Aneen (IRE)**[69] 5175 3-9-0 96........................ ChrisHayes 9 98
(Kevin Prendergast, Ire) *racd in mid-div: rdn to chse ldrs under 2f out: no imp ins fnl f: kpt on same pce* **22/1**

7 1 ¼ **De Coronado (USA)**[7] 7373 4-9-8 89........................(t) SeamieHeffernan 7 97
(A P O'Brien, Ire) *sn pressed ldr in 2nd: rdn and nt qckn in 4th ent fnl f: wknd* **9/1**

8 1 ¾ **Elusive Heights (IRE)**[78] 4822 4-9-8 100........................(t[1]) ColinKeane 5 93
(G M Lyons, Ire) *nvr bttr than mid-div: rdn and no imp ent fnl f: sn one pce* **8/1**

9 1 **Signe (IRE)**[33] 6490 4-9-5 85........................ ColmO'Donoghue 1 88
(Mrs John Harrington, Ire) *racd in mid-div on inner: rdn and nt qckn over 1f out: sn no ex* **66/1**

10 2 ¾ **Dilmun (USA)**[33] 6490 3-9-0 88........................(t) PBBeggy 3 85
(Joseph Patrick O'Brien, Ire) *a towards rr: rdn and no imp under 2f out* **50/1**

11 11 **Long Island Sound (USA)**[188] 1378 4-9-8 109........(vt) WayneLordan 2 65
(A P O'Brien, Ire) *t.k.h early to trck ldrs in 3rd: dropped to 4th after 4f: rdn and wknd qckly under 2f out: eased ins fnl f* **5/1**[3]

2m 12.66s (-2.84) **Going Correction** +0.075s/f (Slow)
**WFA** 3 from 4yo+ 6lb 11 Ran SP% **120.2**
Speed ratings: **113,111,110,109,109 108,107,106,105,103 95**
CSF £30.96 TOTE £4.20: £1.20, £2.00, £1.40; DF 28.80 Trifecta £136.60.
**Owner** Andrew Rosen, Mrs John Magnier, Michael Tabor, Der **Bred** Ar Enterprises Llc **Trained** Cashel, Co Tipperary

**FOCUS**
Little more than an exercise gallop for the winner, who looks capable of even better.

7589 - 7591a (Foreign Racing) - See Raceform Interactive

# 7341 SAINT-CLOUD (L-H)
Friday, September 29

**OFFICIAL GOING: Turf: good to soft**

## 7592a PRIX DES HALLES (CLAIMER) (2YO) (TURF) 1m
**3:10** 2-Y-O **£12,820** (£5,128; £3,846; £2,564; £1,282)

RPR

1 **Valle Inclan (IRE)** 2-9-1 0........................ MaximeGuyon 3 81
(Ana Imaz Ceca, Spain) **37/10**[2]

2 ¾ **Senoville (IRE)**[50] 5989 2-9-1 0........................ CristianDemuro 4 79
(C Ferland, France) **3/1**[1]

3 ¾ **Kabir (GER)**[26] 6726 2-9-4 0........................ AntoineHamelin 2 81
(A Wohler, Germany) **117/10**

4 2 **Rachael's Rocket (IRE)**[34] 6452 2-8-8 0........................ TonyPiccone 5 66
(J S Moore) **28/1**

5 shd **Controversial Lady (IRE)**[19] 6977 2-8-6 0........ MathieuPelletan[(5)] 9 69
(J S Moore) **83/10**

6 ¾ **Uchronique (FR)**[11] 2-8-8 0........................ AlexisBadel 6 64
(M Boutin, France) **105/10**

7 ½ **Calva D'Auge (FR)**[21] 6912 2-9-1 0........................ Francois-XavierBertras 1 70
(B De Montzey, France) **42/10**

8 3 **Babar (FR)** 2-8-11 0........................ Pierre-CharlesBoudot 8 59
(A Fabre, France) **4/1**[3]

9 20 **Assad Lawal (FR)**[24] 2-8-11 0........................ WilliamsSaraiva 7 13
(S Jeddari, France) **75/1**

1m 46.58s (-0.92) 9 Ran SP% **117.6**
PARI-MUTUEL (all including 1 euro stake): WIN 4.70; PLACE 1.90, 1.60, 3.40; DF 6.00; SF 12.50.
**Owner** Juan Peinado **Bred** D Eiffe **Trained** Spain

# 7137 CHESTER (L-H)

Saturday, September 30

**OFFICIAL GOING: Heavy (6.0)**

Wind: faint breeze Weather: light showers, overcast

## 7593 INSTARMAC NOVICE AUCTION STKS (PLUS 10 RACE) 7f 1y

2:30 (2:31) (Class 4) 2-Y-O

£6,225 (£1,864; £932; £466; £233; £117) Stalls Low

| Form | | | | RPR |
|---|---|---|---|---|
| 22 | 1 | | **Ayutthaya (IRE)**[20] 6967 2-9-2 0 .... TomEaves 3 (Kevin Ryan) *mde all: 2 l clr 2f out: pushed along over 1f out: 3 l clr 1f out: rdn and kpt on wl fnl f: comf* **10/11**[1] | 85 |
| | 2 | 2 ¼ | **Zatorius (GER)** 2-9-2 0 .... RobHornby 4 (Andrew Balding) *hld up: pushed along 2f out: hdwy into 4th over 1f out: reminder 1f out: urged along and r.o wl fnl f: tk 2nd last 50yds* **25/1** | 79 |
| 2 | 3 | ¾ | **Gabrial The Saint (IRE)**[14] 7141 2-9-2 0 .... JackGarritty 1 (Richard Fahey) *t.k.h: chsd ldr: drvn over 1f out: 3 l bhd wnr whn rdn 1f out: kpt on fnl f: lost 2nd last 50yds* **3/1**[2] | 78 |
| 122 | 4 | 2 ½ | **Book Of Dreams (IRE)**[12] 7221 2-9-8 86 .... FrannyNorton 2 (Mark Johnston) *mid-div: pushed along and hdwy into 3rd 2f out: rdn over 1f out: one pce and lost 3rd ins fnl f* **7/2**[3] | 78 |
| 0 | 5 | 4 ½ | **So Near So Farhh**[33] 6504 2-8-11 0 .... SeanLevey 9 (Mick Channon) *in rr: pushed along 3f out: drvn 2f out: kpt on fnl f* **66/1** | 55 |
| 4510 | 6 | 7 | **Dorcas**[35] 6433 2-9-0 70 .... LewisEdmunds(3) 10 (James Given) *in rr: drvn 3f out: no imp fr 2f out* **33/1** | 44 |
| 2445 | 7 | 3 ½ | **Zabaletaswansong (GER)**[20] 6986 2-8-9 71 .... RossaRyan(7) 6 (Richard Hannon) *prom: drvn over 2f out: wknd and lost pl wl over 1f out* **20/1** | 34 |
| 0 | 8 | 2 ¾ | **Nailed On Nina (IRE)**[20] 6977 2-8-11 0 .... MarkGallagher 5 (P M Mooney, Ire) *chsd ldrs: pushed along over 3f out: rdn and wknd over 2f out* **16/1** | 22 |
| 60 | 9 | 56 | **Cavalry Regiment**[23] 6853 2-9-2 0 .... AndrewMullen 8 (John Quinn) *hld up: tk false step and stmbld after 2 fs: sn dropped to last and qckly lost tch* **66/1** | |

1m 32.22s (5.72) **Going Correction** +1.00s/f (Soft) 9 Ran SP% **120.0**

Speed ratings (Par 97): **107,104,103,100,95 87,83,80,16**

CSF £35.59 TOTE £1.70: £1.02, £6.50, £1.40; EX 37.60 Trifecta £111.10.

**Owner** JCG Chua & CK Ong 1 **Bred** Pipe View Stud **Trained** Hambleton, N Yorks

**FOCUS**

Distances as advertised. The official description of the ground was changed to heavy before racing. \n\x\x The lowest four stalls were the first four home in this okay juvenile novice.

## 7594 #THEMBNATEAM H'CAP 7f 1y

3:05 (3:07) (Class 4) (0-85,91) 4-Y-O+

£6,225 (£1,864; £932; £466; £233; £117) Stalls Low

| Form | | | | RPR |
|---|---|---|---|---|
| 2005 | 1 | | **Gabrial The Tiger (IRE)**[15] 7108 5-8-3 74 .... ConnorMurtagh(7) 9 (Richard Fahey) *trckd ldr: pushed along 2f out: 1 l bhd in 2nd whn rdn over 1f out: led 100yds out: kpt on wl to repel several chalrs* **16/1** | 81 |
| 0631 | 2 | ½ | **Dark Devil (IRE)**[15] 7111 4-9-5 83 .... JackGarritty 5 (Richard Fahey) *mid-div: pushed along on outer 3f out: drvn 2f out: hdwy over 1f out: rdn ent fnl f: r.o strly: tk 2nd nr finih* **9/4**[1] | 88+ |
| 4302 | 3 | nk | **Worlds His Oyster**[28] 6672 4-9-3 81 .... (v) SeanLevey 2 (John Quinn) *mid-div: pushed along in 5th 1f out: nt clr run ins fnl f: sn swtchd: rdn and r.o strly: tk 3rd nr fin* **11/2**[2] | 85 |
| 1050 | 4 | shd | **Art Echo**[20] 6964 4-8-12 76 .... (t) AndrewMullen 4 (John Mackie) *mid-div: pushed along to trck ldrs 2f out: rdn over 1f out: chal ldrs ins fnl f: kpt on wl* **22/1** | 80 |
| 4001 | 5 | hd | **Captain Dion**[2] 7553 4-9-13 91 6ex .... (p) TomEaves 1 (Kevin Ryan) *led: 1 l ahd whn rdn over 1f out: hdd 100yds out: no ex* **13/2**[3] | 94 |
| 5252 | 6 | 2 | **Roaring Forties (IRE)**[22] 6894 4-8-10 77 .... CliffordLee(3) 3 (Rebecca Bastiman) *mid-div: pushed along and hdwy 3f out: wnt 3rd 2f out: pushed along over 1f out: ev ch ins fnl f: hld whn hmpd 100yds out* **20/1** | 78 |
| 1504 | 7 | 2 | **Showboating (IRE)**[11] 7246 9-9-1 82 .... LewisEdmunds(3) 11 (John Balding) *hld up in last: hdwy 1/2-way: pushed along 2f out: rdn over 1f out: kpt on fnl f* **40/1** | 75 |
| 1000 | 8 | 7 | **Meshardal (GER)**[22] 6877 7-8-12 76 .... (p) RobHornby 8 (Ruth Carr) *hld up: rdn over 1f out: no imp* **66/1** | 51 |
| 3641 | 9 | nse | **Dark Intention (IRE)**[20] 6964 4-8-9 80 .... WilliamCox(7) 6 (Lawrence Mullaney) *hld up: pushed along 2f out: rdn over 1f out: no imp* **11/2**[2] | 54 |
| 121 | 10 | 11 | **Here's Two**[29] 6656 4-8-10 74 .... KieranO'Neill 12 (Ron Hodges) *prom on outer: sn chsng ldr: drvn 3f out: wknd and lost pl over 2f out* **22/1** | 20 |
| 3642 | 11 | 1 ¾ | **Luis Vaz De Torres (IRE)**[15] 7108 5-9-6 84 .... (h) JackMitchell 7 (Richard Fahey) *mid-div: drvn on outer 3f out: rdn over 2f out: no imp* **10/1** | 25 |
| 4163 | 12 | 10 | **Be Kool (IRE)**[55] 5688 4-9-6 84 .... (v) FrannyNorton 10 (Brian Ellison) *prom: drvn and lost pl 3f out: wknd* **9/1** | |

1m 32.6s (6.10) **Going Correction** +1.05s/f (Soft) 12 Ran SP% **117.2**

Speed ratings (Par 105): **107,106,106,105,105 103,101,93,93,80 78,67**

CSF £48.67 CT £238.20 TOTE £12.60: £3.40, £1.10, £3.20; EX 38.50 Trifecta £94.90.

**Owner** Dr Marwan Koukash **Bred** Kenneth Heelan **Trained** Musley Bank, N Yorks

**FOCUS**

A desperate finish to this above-average handicap.

## 7595 SPORTINGBET.COM H'CAP 1m 2f 70y

3:40 (3:41) (Class 3) (0-90,90) 3-Y-O+

£12,450 (£3,728; £1,864; £932; £466; £234)

| Form | | | | RPR |
|---|---|---|---|---|
| 3141 | 1 | | **Alexander M (IRE)**[15] 7107 3-9-3 89 .... FrannyNorton 4 (Mark Johnston) *mde all: qcknd 3 l clr 2f out: extended advantage ent fnl f and sn in total command: heavily eased nr fin: v easily* **7/2**[2] | 102+ |
| 1236 | 2 | 1 ¾ | **Al Destoor**[22] 6881 7-9-9 90 .... (t) DavidNolan 2 (Jennie Candlish) *trckd ldrs: pushed along in 3rd over 1f out: drvn and tk 2nd ins fnl f: kpt on but no ch w wnr* **13/2** | 91 |
| 6030 | 3 | hd | **Jabbaar**[3] 7524 4-8-2 76 oh3 .... WilliamCox(7) 6 (Iain Jardine) *hld up: pushed along and hdwy 2f out: rdn over 1f out: r.o to take 3rd ins fnl f* **10/1** | 77 |
| 5236 | 4 | 3 ½ | **Itsakindamagic**[35] 6422 3-9-0 86 .... (t) RobHornby 9 (Andrew Balding) *ct flat footed at flip s and lost 15 l: sn rcvrd to join pack: t.k.h: last 2f out: drvn and hdwy over 1f out: rdn ent fnl f: r.o to take 4th nr fin* **4/1**[3] | 80+ |
| 3504 | 5 | 1 ¼ | **Gabrial's Kaka (IRE)**[14] 7142 7-8-2 76 oh2 .... ConnorMurtagh(7) 1 (Richard Fahey) *chsd ldr: drvn whn wnr qcknd 2f out: rdn over 1f out: 6 l 2nd ent fnl f: wknd: lost shoe* **7/1** | 68 |
| 3061 | 6 | 3 ¾ | **Bahama Moon (IRE)**[14] 7142 5-9-2 83 .... BenCurtis 3 (David Barron) *mid-div: pushed along in 4th 2f out: drvn over 1f out: wknd* **11/4**[1] | 68 |
| 1400 | 7 | hd | **Gulf Of Poets**[35] 6449 5-9-7 88 .... AndrewMullen 7 (Michael Easterby) *hld up: pushed along and effrt 2f out: sn drvn and no ex* **25/1** | 72 |
| 20P0 | 8 | 10 | **Pumaflor (IRE)**[23] 6855 5-8-11 78 .... (p) SeanLevey 8 (Philip Kirby) *chsd wnr: drvn and lost pl 2f out: fdd* **33/1** | 43 |
| 001 | 9 | 7 | **Mutamaded (IRE)**[32] 6563 4-9-6 87 .... TomEaves 5 (Ruth Carr) *hld up: pushed along and dropped to last 2f out: sn lost tch* **12/1** | 39 |

2m 23.11s (11.91) **Going Correction** +1.10s/f (Soft)

**WFA** 3 from 4yo+ 5lb 9 Ran SP% **118.3**

Speed ratings (Par 107): **96,94,94,91,90 87,87,79,73**

CSF £27.33 CT £210.72 TOTE £4.20: £1.40, £2.30, £3.30; EX 36.60 Trifecta £270.40.

**Owner** Christinee Budden, M Budden, Matthew Budden **Bred** Christine E Budden & Partners **Trained** Middleham Moor, N Yorks

**FOCUS**

This looked a good, close-knit handicap, but there was a problem with the stalls and a flag start was needed. This turned the start into something of a farce, the winner stole an early march and punters who backed the fourth placed finisher can rightly feel aggrieved.

## 7596 SPORTINGBET.COM NURSERY H'CAP 6f 17y

4:15 (4:17) (Class 2) 2-Y-O

£12,450 (£3,728; £1,864; £932; £466; £234) Stalls Low

| Form | | | | RPR |
|---|---|---|---|---|
| 2231 | 1 | | **Ginbar (IRE)**[23] 6853 2-8-2 80 .... NickyMackay 9 (Tom Dascombe) *led tl hdd after 3f: styd prom trcking ldr: pushed along and led again over 1f out: rdn ins fnl f and sn 2 l clr: kpt on wl to repel clsng runner-up* **4/1**[2] | 83 |
| 1506 | 2 | ¾ | **It Dont Come Easy (IRE)**[59] 5526 2-9-3 95 .... DavidNolan 7 (Richard Fahey) *trckd ldrs: pushed along in 3rd 2f out: swtchd to chal ent fnl f: rdn and r.o wl to cl on wnr: nvr a serious threat* **4/1**[2] | 96 |
| 3126 | 3 | 1 ½ | **Collingham Park (IRE)**[81] 4716 2-8-0 78 oh1 .... AndrewMullen 2 (Jedd O'Keeffe) *hld up: drvn over 2f out: rdn and hdwy over 1f out: styd on wl to take 3rd ins fnl f* **5/1**[3] | 75 |
| 0206 | 4 | hd | **Lady Anjorica (IRE)**[54] 5702 2-8-2 80 .... PaulQuinn 4 (Keith Dalgleish) *slowly away: in rr: rdn wl over 1f out: r.o wl fnl f: nvr nrr* **9/1** | 76 |
| 3465 | 5 | ¾ | **Zap**[16] 7090 2-9-1 93 .... JackGarritty 5 (Richard Fahey) *hld up: pushed along over 2f out: hdwy into 4th over 1f out: sn rdn and no ex* **9/4**[1] | 87 |
| 1005 | 6 | 2 ¾ | **Rufus King**[27] 6745 2-9-7 99 .... (b[1]) FrannyNorton 12 (Mark Johnston) *prom: led 3f out: 1 l clr 2f out: rdn and hdd over 1f out: fdd fnl f* **12/1** | 84 |
| 1040 | 7 | 6 | **June Dog**[74] 4991 2-8-1 78 ow1 .... KieranO'Neill 6 (Richard Hannon) *prom: pushed along in 3rd 1/2-way: drvn and wknd over 2f out: lost shoe* **14/1** | 46 |

1m 21.04s (7.24) **Going Correction** +1.15s/f (Soft) 7 Ran SP% **111.8**

Speed ratings (Par 101): **97,96,94,93,92 89,81**

CSF £19.33 CT £78.65 TOTE £5.00: £2.60, £2.20; EX 19.10 Trifecta £61.10.

**Owner** The BGW Partnership & Partner **Bred** Rockfield Farm **Trained** Malpas, Cheshire

**FOCUS**

A strange shape to this race with top-weight Rufus King allowing over half the field to run off 8-2 or less. Considering the conditions, the pace was good.

## 7597 BOODLES MAIDEN STKS 7f 127y

4:50 (4:52) (Class 4) 3-Y-O+

£6,225 (£1,864; £932; £466; £233; £117) Stalls Low

| Form | | | | RPR |
|---|---|---|---|---|
| 422 | 1 | | **Tamih (IRE)**[24] 6817 3-9-5 79 .... JackMitchell 2 (Roger Varian) *mde all: 2 l clr 2f out: pushed along in 3 f ld 1f out: rdn and r.o wl fnl f: readily* **1/2**[1] | 83+ |
| 0-4 | 2 | 1 ½ | **Ebqaa (IRE)**[15] 7109 3-9-0 0 .... AndrewMullen 1 (James Unett) *trckd ldrs: wnt 2nd 3f out: pushed along 2f out: 3 l bhd wnr 1f out: rdn and kpt on fnl f but no imp* **11/4**[2] | 73 |
| 06 | 3 | 12 | **Mr Slicker (FR)**[41] 6236 3-9-5 0 .... FrannyNorton 6 (Tom Dascombe) *hld up: pushed along into 3rd over 2f out: drvn over 1f out: one pce fnl f* **8/1**[3] | 56 |
| 2044 | 4 | 4 | **Jacksonfire**[12] 7218 5-9-9 48 .... (p) LiamJones 5 (Michael Mullineaux) *hld up in last: pushed along and hdwy 1/2-way: drvn 2f out: rdn over 1f out: wknd* **16/1** | 41 |
| 0400 | 5 | 22 | **Red Shanghai (IRE)**[91] 4332 3-8-11 42 .... LewisEdmunds(3) 3 (Charles Smith) *racd in 2nd: drvn and relegated to 3rd 3f out: wknd qckly fr wl over 2f out* **50/1** | |
| 0000 | 6 | 15 | **Just Heather (IRE)**[15] 7109 3-9-0 34 .... (h[1]) TomEaves 4 (John Wainwright) *hld up: pushed along 1/2-way: wknd and lost tch 3f out* **66/1** | |

1m 42.1s (8.30) **Going Correction** +1.20s/f (Soft)

**WFA** 3 from 5yo 4lb 6 Ran SP% **113.8**

Speed ratings (Par 105): **106,104,92,88,66 51**

CSF £2.22 TOTE £1.20: £1.10, £1.50; EX 2.20 Trifecta £5.40.

**Owner** M H Al Attiya **Bred** Philip Hore Jnr **Trained** Newmarket, Suffolk

**FOCUS**

A poor turnout for this maiden, so weak form and the odds-on favourite scored comfortably.

## 7598 MINSTRELL RECRUITMENT FILLIES' H'CAP 1m 2f 70y

5:25 (5:25) (Class 4) (0-80,80) 3-Y-O+

£6,225 (£1,864; £932; £466; £233; £117)

| Form | | | | RPR |
|---|---|---|---|---|
| 3662 | 1 | | **Marsh Pride**[14] 7142 5-9-12 80 .... PJMcDonald 9 (K R Burke) *trckd ldrs: pushed along in 4th 2f out: plenty to do whn drvn over 1f out: hdwy u.p ent fnl f: str run to ld last 50yds: on top at fin* **11/2**[3] | 86+ |
| 4145 | 2 | 1 | **Katebird (IRE)**[28] 6692 3-9-2 75 .... FrannyNorton 4 (Mark Johnston) *led: pushed along in narrow ld over 1f out: rdn ent fnl f: hdd 50yds out: kpt on* **14/1** | 79 |

0523 **3** ¾ **Rosemay (FR)**[22] 6892 3-8-6 **65** ........................ KieranO'Neill 6 68
(Iain Jardine) *racd in cl 2nd: rdn over 1f out: ev ch ins fnl f: no ex last 100yds* **10/1**

2261 **4** *hd* **Liquid Gold (IRE)**[45] 6060 3-8-13 **72** ........................ JackGarritty 10 74
(Richard Fahey) *hld up: hdwy over 2f out: drvn over 1f out: rdn and r.o ins fnl f: tk 4th nr fin* **13/2**

443 **5** ½ **Persistence (IRE)**[63] 5428 3-9-3 **76** ........................ JackMitchell 2 77+
(Ralph Beckett) *trckd ldrs: pushed along in 3rd 2f out: rdn over 1f out: one pce fnl f* **4/1**[2]

0450 **6** 1 ½ **Dellaguista (IRE)**[17] 7046 3-8-9 **68** ........................ AndrewMullen 3 66
(Tim Easterby) *mid-div: pushed along and hdwy 2f out: rdn over 1f out: no ex fnl f* **20/1**

321 **7** *4* **Caravela (IRE)**[21] 6941 3-9-2 **75** ........................ CharlesBishop 5 66
(Mick Channon) *mid-div: effrt on inner over 2f out: wknd over 1f out* **3/1**[1]

3546 **8** *nk* **Monaco Rose**[7] 7387 4-9-1 **69** ........................(h) DavidNolan 12 59
(Richard Fahey) *mid-div: pushed along 1/2-way: drvn and wknd 2f out* **10/1**

1303 **9** *12* **Mouille Point**[16] 7083 3-9-4 **77** ........................ SeanLevey 7 44
(Richard Hannon) *hld up: pushed along 2f out: rdn over 1f out: no imp* **7/1**

-500 **10** *21* **Italian Beauty (IRE)**[85] 4554 5-8-4 **61** oh1 ..............(p) NoelGarbutt(3) 11
(John Wainwright) *a last: pushed along 1/2-way: lost tch fr 3f out* **50/1**

2m 26.22s (15.02) **Going Correction** +1.25s/f (Soft)
**WFA** 3 from 4yo+ 5lb **10** Ran SP% **117.8**
Speed ratings (Par 102): **89,88,87,87,87 85,82,82,72,56**
CSF £80.13 CT £755.38 TOTE £6.00: £1.80, £4.20, £3.20; EX 90.50 Trifecta £1056.00.
**Owner** John Dance **Bred** Llety Farms **Trained** Middleham Moor, N Yorks

**FOCUS**
Flag start. A few unexposed fillies took their chance in this handicap and it looks to be fair form. It proved difficult to make up ground.

## 7599 ICOMPILE H'CAP 1m 6f 87y
**5:55** (6:00) (Class 4) (0-85,84) 3-Y-O+
**£6,225** (£1,864; £932; £466; £233; £117) **Stalls** Low

Form RPR

1121 **1** **Brandon Castle**[7] 7386 5-10-0 **84** ........................(t) AndrewMullen 5 100
(Archie Watson) *mde all: 4 l clr gng wl 3f out: pushed along and extended advantage 2f out: 5 l ahd whn drvn over 1f out: rdn and wnt further clr fnl f: unchal* **11/4**[2]

6104 **2** *15* **Plymouth Sound**[14] 7143 5-9-8 **78** ........................(v) CharlesBishop 4 74
(Bernard Llewellyn) *reluctant to load: hld up: pushed along and hdwy 4f out: drvn and wnt 3rd over 3f out: tk 2nd 2f out: sn rdn: one pce fnl f* **20/1**

2253 **3** *2* **Angel Gabrial (IRE)**[28] 6680 8-9-7 **84** ........................ ConnorMurtagh(7) 12 77
(Richard Fahey) *hld up in last: pushed along and hdwy 4f out: drvn in 4th 3f out: rdn in 3rd over 1f out: no ex* **15/2**

4065 **4** *4* **Gabrial's Star**[14] 7143 8-9-3 **73** ........................(b) JackGarritty 1 61
(Richard Fahey) *trckd ldrs: sn settled in mid-div: drvn and lost pl 4f out: plugged on past btn horses last 3 fs* **7/1**[3]

2221 **5** *13* **Kajaki (IRE)**[14] 7143 4-10-0 **84** ........................(p) TomEaves 6 55
(Kevin Ryan) *trckd ldrs: hdwy into 2nd 4f out: drvn 3f out: sn rdn and wknd* **2/1**[1]

6150 **6** *nk* **Earthly (USA)**[11] 7231 3-8-11 **75** ........................ KieranO'Neill 10 48
(Bernard Llewellyn) *reluctant to load: prom: drvn and lost pl 4f out: sn rdn and wknd* **40/1**

4330 **7** *23* **Amelia Dream**[14] 7163 3-8-7 **71** ........................ BenCurtis 2 14
(Mick Channon) *trckd ldrs: drvn in 2nd 4f out: sn rdn and wknd* **9/1**

500/ **8** *47* **Golden Bowl (FR)**[1242] 2073 7-9-12 **82** ........................ DougieCostello 7
(John Quinn) *hld up: pushed along and lost tch 6f out* **25/1**

3351 **9** *2* **Arty Campbell (IRE)**[15] 7110 7-9-6 **83** ........................(p) WilliamCox(7) 3
(Bernard Llewellyn) *mid-div: dropped to last 1/2-way: sn drvn: grad lost tch* **10/1**

3m 29.45s (22.45) **Going Correction** +1.30s/f (Soft)
**WFA** 3 from 4yo+ 8lb **9** Ran SP% **114.4**
Speed ratings (Par 105): **87,78,77,75,67 67,54,27,26**
CSF £57.20 CT £371.83 TOTE £4.10: £1.50, £5.40, £2.30; EX 39.30 Trifecta £348.30.
**Owner** C R Hirst **Bred** Barry Walters **Trained** Upper Lambourn, W Berks

**FOCUS**
No more than a fair handicap which was run at a good clip. It was hard work for most, but the winner handled conditions well.
T/Plt: £97.40 to a £1 stake. Pool: £61,250.51 - 458.61 winning units T/Qpdt: £48.50 to a £1 stake. Pool: £4,483.56 - 68.28 winning units **Keith McHugh**

# 7535 CHELMSFORD (A.W) (L-H)
Saturday, September 30

**OFFICIAL GOING: Polytrack: standard**
Wind: Light behind Weather: Overcast

## 7600 BET TOTEPLACEPOT AT BETFRED.COM MAIDEN STKS 1m (P)
**5:50** (5:53) (Class 5) 3-Y-O+ **£5,175** (£1,540; £769; £384) **Stalls** Low

Form RPR

22 **1** **Hyperloop**[67] 5243 3-9-5 77 ........................ RichardKingscote 4 83+
(William Haggas) *sn w ldr: led after 1f: rdn over 1f out: r.o wl* **4/6**[1]

5-3 **2** 3 ¼ **Ifubelieveindreams (IRE)**[176] 1609 3-8-11 0 ............ NathanAlison(3) 5 70+
(Ismail Mohammed) *hld up: hdwy over 2f out: r.o to go 2nd wl ins fnl f: no ch w wnr* **5/1**[3]

4 **3** ¾ **Colourful Career (USA)**[154] 2167 3-9-5 0 ........................ JimmyQuinn 6 73
(Ed Dunlop) *hld up in tch: shkn up over 1f out: styd on same pce ins fnl f* **14/1**

2 **4** 2 ¼ **Swiss Vinnare**[9] 7322 3-9-5 0 ........................ DannyBrock 1 68
(Phil McEntee) *s.i.s: sn prom: pushed along over 2f out: edgd rt over 1f out: styd on same pce* **6/1**

25 **5** *nk* **Manaahil**[163] 1905 3-9-0 0 ........................ DaneO'Neill 2 62
(Charles Hills) *racd keenly: led 1f: remained w wnr: rdn over 2f out: ev ch over 1f out: wknd ins fnl f* **3/1**[2]

56 **6** *8* **Freedom Fighter (IRE)**[24] 6817 7-9-9 67 ..................(t) TimmyMurphy 8 48
(Tim Pinfield) *s.i.s: sn pushed along in rr: wknd over 2f out* **50/1**

00 **7** 4 ½ **Lookintomyeyes**[77] 4911 3-9-0 0 ........................(t) AdamBeschizza 7 32
(Mrs Ilka Gansera-Leveque) *hld up in tch: lost pl over 4f out: rdn over 2f out: sn wknd* **50/1**

0/0 **8** *6* **Arrucian**[40] 6277 4-9-4 0 ........................ AntonioFresu 3 17
(Ms N M Hugo) *chsd ldrs: rdn over 3f out: wknd over 2f out* **66/1**

1m 38.62s (-1.28) **Going Correction** -0.175s/f (Stan)
**WFA** 3 from 4yo+ 4lb **8** Ran SP% **128.0**
Speed ratings (Par 103): **99,95,95,92,92 84,79,73**
CSF £5.75 TOTE £1.60: £1.02, £1.70, £3.20; EX 6.30 Trifecta £27.10.
**Owner** Messrs B Kantor & MJ Jooste **Bred** Northmore Stud **Trained** Newmarket, Suffolk

**FOCUS**
With the second favourite underperforming the winner didn't have to improve to win with something in hand. The gallop was reasonable.

## 7601 CAROL WHITWOOD MEMORIAL H'CAP 1m 2f (P)
**6:20** (6:23) (Class 5) (0-75,76) 4-Y-O+ **£5,175** (£1,540; £769; £384) **Stalls** Low

Form RPR

3612 **1** **Maestro Mac (IRE)**[25] 6781 4-8-13 **67** ........................ JosephineGordon 4 78+
(Tom Clover) *chsd ldrs: pushed along over 3f out: rdn to ld over 1f out: r.o wl: eased towards fin* **7/2**[1]

0440 **2** 2 ¾ **Archimento**[25] 6781 4-8-9 **66** ........................(t) HectorCrouch(3) 10 70
(Philip Hide) *s.i.s: hdwy over 8f out: rdn over 3f out: styd on same pce ins fnl f* **11/1**

3320 **3** ½ **Singapore Sling**[56] 5663 4-9-7 **75** ........................(h) TomQueally 3 78+
(James Fanshawe) *prom: lost pl after 1f: hrd rdn over 1f out: swtchd lft and r.o to go 3rd nr fin* **7/2**[1]

5425 **4** ¾ **Hard Toffee (IRE)**[25] 6781 6-9-1 **69** ........................ AdamBeschizza 11 71
(Conrad Allen) *chsd ldr over 8f out tl led over 4f out: rdn: hung rt and hdd over 1f out: no ex ins fnl f* **14/1**

1555 **5** *nk* **Tan Arabiq**[23] 6848 4-8-6 **67** ........................ KeelanBaker(7) 5 68
(Michael Appleby) *sn pushed along and prom: nt clr run and lost pl after 1f: hdwy on outer over 4f out: rdn and ev ch over 2f out: styng on same pce whn nt clr run ins fnl f* **9/2**[2]

60-0 **6** *nk* **Topamichi**[12] 7225 7-8-11 **65** ........................ TomMarquand 9 65
(Michael Appleby) *hld up: hmpd over 3f out: hung lft over 2f out: hdwy over 1f out: swtchd lft ins fnl f: styd on: nt rch ldrs* **8/1**

4555 **7** *1* **Pernickety**[9] 7338 4-8-11 **65** ........................(t) RichardKingscote 8 63
(Lucy Wadham) *prom: lost pl over 8f out: hdwy over 2f out: rdn over 1f out: styd on same pce* **7/1**[3]

0000 **8** ¾ **Accurate**[21] 6948 4-8-10 **64** ........................(p[1]) StevieDonohoe 1 61
(Ian Williams) *led 1f: chsd ldr: nt clr run and lost pl over 3f out: n.d after* **8/1**

5336 **9** 1 ¼ **Foie Gras**[53] 5747 7-8-6 **67** ........................(p) MillyNaseb(7) 7 61
(Chris Dwyer) *hld up: nt clr run over 2f out: nvr on terms* **20/1**

000 **10** *24* **Diana Lady (CHI)**[157] 2093 5-9-7 **75** ........................(h[1]) AntonioFresu 2 21
(Luke McJannet) *led after 1f: hdd over 4f out: sn rdn: wknd over 2f out* **50/1**

2m 5.9s (-2.70) **Going Correction** -0.175s/f (Stan) **10** Ran SP% **119.1**
Speed ratings (Par 103): **103,100,100,99,99 99,98,97,96,77**
CSF £44.56 CT £146.86 TOTE £3.90: £1.80, £2.90, £1.50; EX 48.00 Trifecta £176.60.
**Owner** B Keane & S Nugent **Bred** Tom McDonald **Trained** Newmarket, Suffolk

**FOCUS**
Mainly exposed performers in an ordinary handicap. The gallop was a reasonable one and the winner is getting closer to his old form.

## 7602 BET TOTEQUADPOT AT BETFRED.COM H'CAP 1m 2f (P)
**6:50** (6:52) (Class 2) (0-105,100) 4-Y-O+
**£18,675** (£5,592; £2,796; £1,398; £699; £351) **Stalls** Low

Form RPR

0020 **1** **Petite Jack**[49] 5913 4-9-5 **98** ........................(p) OisinMurphy 5 105
(Archie Watson) *chsd ldrs: rdn to ld over 1f out: hung lft ins fnl f: styd on* **4/1**[1]

4600 **2** ½ **Abdon**[28] 6698 4-9-2 **100** ........................ GeorgiaCox(5) 6 106
(Sir Michael Stoute) *s.s: hld up: rdn and r.o ins fnl f: wnt 2nd post: nt rch wnr* **10/1**[3]

4004 **3** *hd* **Pactolus (IRE)**[46] 6024 6-8-11 **93** ........................(t) AaronJones(3) 4 98
(Stuart Williams) *hld up: rdn over 1f out: hung lft and r.o ins fnl f* **14/1**

3050 **4** 3 ¾ **Noble Gift**[28] 6698 7-9-4 **97** ........................ SilvestreDeSousa 2 95
(William Knight) *sn led: pushed along over 3f out: rdn and hdd over 1f out: styd on same pce ins fnl f* **4/1**[1]

0132 **5** *1* **Ickymasho**[28] 6687 5-9-4 **97** ........................ RichardKingscote 7 93
(Jonathan Portman) *chsd ldr after 1f tl rdn to ld over 1f out: sn hdd: edgd lft and no ex ins fnl f* **6/1**[2]

3134 **6** *1* **Dark Red (IRE)**[16] 7091 5-9-3 **96** ........................ JamesDoyle 8 100+
(Ed Dunlop) *hld up: hdwy and nt clr run fr over 1f out: eased wl ins fnl f* **4/1**[1]

141- **7** *1* **Burcan (FR)**[273] 8594 5-9-1 **94** ........................ DanielMuscutt 1 86
(Marco Botti) *chsd ldrs: rdn over 1f out: wknd ins fnl f* **4/1**[1]

3000 **8** *4* **Brex Drago (ITY)**[133] 2828 5-9-2 **95** ........................ HarryBentley 3 79
(Marco Botti) *hld up: pushed along over 2f out: rdn over 1f out: wknd fnl f* **10/1**[3]

2m 3.44s (-5.16) **Going Correction** -0.175s/f (Stan) **8** Ran SP% **119.1**
Speed ratings (Par 109): **113,112,112,109,108 107,107,103**
CSF £47.25 CT £517.75 TOTE £4.70: £1.40, £2.70, £4.10; EX 52.50 Trifecta £722.10.
**Owner** W Burn **Bred** Mrs Liz Nelson Mbe **Trained** Upper Lambourn, W Berks
■ Stewards' Enquiry : Oisin Murphy two-day ban: used whip above permitted level (Oct 15-16)

**FOCUS**
A decent handicap run at a reasonable gallop. The first three deserve credit for pulling clear of the remainder. The winner continues to improve.

## 7603 BET TOTEEXACTA AT BETFRED.COM CONDITIONS STKS 7f (P)
**7:20** (7:23) (Class 2) 3-Y-O+ **£19,407** (£5,775; £2,886; £1,443) **Stalls** Low

Form RPR

2324 **1** **Steady Pace**[20] 6966 4-9-5 108 ........................ PatCosgrave 9 112
(Saeed bin Suroor) *chsd ldrs: rdn to ld wl ins fnl f: r.o* **3/1**[2]

6133 **2** *1* **Mazzini**[28] 6685 4-9-5 100 ........................(p) GeorgeWood 8 109
(James Fanshawe) *chsd ldr tl led over 1f out: rdn and hdd wl ins fnl f: styd on* **6/1**[3]

-400 **3** 2 ¼ **Certificate**[35] 6419 6-9-5 104 ........................ AndreaAtzeni 5 103
(Roger Varian) *hld up: rdn and r.o ins fnl f: wnt 3rd nr fin: nt rch ldrs* **6/1**[3]

0603 **4** ¾ **Intisaab**[35] 6428 6-9-9 108 ........................(p) DanielTudhope 2 105
(David O'Meara) *chsd ldrs: rdn over 1f out: styd on same pce ins fnl f* **6/1**[3]

-421 **5** ¾ **Aljuljalah (USA)**[30] 6619 4-9-4 98 ........................ HarryBentley 4 98
(Roger Varian) *hld up: hdwy u.p over 1f out: styd on same pce ins fnl f* **8/1**

0060 **6** 1 ½ **Magnus Maximus**[21] 6922 6-9-5 100 ........................ JosephineGordon 10 95
(Robyn Brisland) *led: rdn and hdd over 1f out: no ex ins fnl f* **40/1**

-050 **7** *7* **Richard Pankhurst**[10] 7275 5-9-5 107 ........................(v) JamesDoyle 7 76
(John Gosden) *hld up: rdn over 1f out: no rspnse* **11/1**

04-1 **P** **Afjaan (IRE)**[154] 2142 5-9-9 106 ........................ RichardKingscote 6
(William Haggas) *hld up: wnt wrong over 2f out: sn p.u* **5/2**[1]

1m 23.79s (-3.41) **Going Correction** -0.175s/f (Stan) **8** Ran SP% **118.3**
Speed ratings (Par 109): **112,110,108,107,106 104,96,**
CSF £22.27 TOTE £3.60: £1.40, £1.80, £2.30; EX 26.10 Trifecta £149.50.
**Owner** Godolphin **Bred** T G Roddick **Trained** Newmarket, Suffolk

**FOCUS**
A good-quality conditions event and a smart performance by the winner, through whom the race has been rated. The gallop was no more than fair.

## 7604 JOHN GOODE MEMORIAL H'CAP 5f (P)
7:50 (7:51) (Class 3) (0-95,95) 4-Y-0+ £10,350 (£3,080; £1,539; £769) Stalls Low

Form RPR
0013 1 **Udontdodou**[67] 5241 4-9-5 93 ConnorBeasley 7 106
(Richard Guest) *sn chsng ldrs: rdn to ld over 1f out: r.o* 7/2[2]
11 2 1¾ **Foxy Forever (IRE)**[35] 6430 7-8-13 87 (t) JamesDoyle 1 93
(Michael Wigham) *trckd ldrs: rdn and ev ch over 1f out: styd on same pce ins fnl f* 6/1
0000 3 hd **Show Stealer**[28] 6695 4-8-10 84 (p) DavidProbert 12 89
(Rae Guest) *sn pushed along in rr: rdn and hdwy over 1f out: r.o: nt rch ldrs* 16/1
1252 4 3 **Handytalk (IRE)**[32] 6554 4-8-12 86 OisinMurphy 11 80
(Rod Millman) *sn pushed along in rr: hdwy u.p and nt clr run over 1f out: swtchd rt and r.o ins fnl f: nt trble ldrs* 14/1
0122 5 nk **El Astronaute (IRE)**[28] 6677 4-9-7 95 RichardKingscote 5 88
(John Quinn) *sn led: rdn: hung lft and hdd over 1f out: no ex ins fnl f* 2/1[1]
4311 6 1¼ **Saved My Bacon (IRE)**[85] 4566 6-8-7 81 oh2 (h) SilvestreDeSousa 9 70
(Chris Dwyer) *hld up: rdn over 1f out: styd on ins fnl f: nvr nrr* 20/1
0054 7 nk **Stanghow**[26] 6758 5-8-9 83 JosephineGordon 2 71
(Antony Brittain) *w ldrs: rdn and ev ch over 1f out: wknd ins fnl f* 10/1
2-00 8 3¼ **Aleef (IRE)**[14] 7144 4-9-0 88 (h) DanielTudhope 6 64
(David O'Meara) *w ldrs: pushed along over 2f out: wknd fnl f* 9/2[3]
0-30 9 7 **Abstraction (IRE)**[7] 7396 7-9-4 92 PatCosgrave 8 43
(J S Moore) *prom: pushed along 1/2-way: wknd over 1f out* 40/1
060 10 1 **Lightscameraction (IRE)**[63] 5402 5-9-1 92 (b) DavidEgan(3) 4 39
(Gay Kelleway) *s.s: outpcd* 12/1

58.32s (-1.88) **Going Correction** -0.175s/f (Stan) 10 Ran SP% 124.6
Speed ratings (Par 107): **108,105,104,100,99 97,97,91,80,79**
CSF £26.96 CT £318.56 TOTE £4.40: £1.80, £2.70, £4.40; EX 34.90 Trifecta £303.70.
**Owner** Mrs Alison Guest **Bred** Times Of Wigan Ltd **Trained** Ingmanthorpe, W Yorks

**FOCUS**
A very useful handicap in which the gallop was sound throughout and the first three pulled clear in the closing stages.

## 7605 BET TOTEWIN AT BETFRED.COM H'CAP (DIV I) 7f (P)
8:20 (8:21) (Class 6) (0-55,57) 4-Y-0+ £3,234 (£962; £481; £240) Stalls Low

Form RPR
4506 1 **Mr Potter**[4] 7481 4-9-9 57 (v) ConnorBeasley 11 63
(Richard Guest) *hld up: plld hrd: hdwy: nt clr run and swtchd rt over 1f out: rdn to ld and edgd lft wl ins fnl f: r.o* 6/1[3]
0005 2 1 **Frangarry (IRE)**[24] 6814 5-8-11 50 (t[1]) JoshuaBryan(5) 6 53
(Alan Bailey) *hld up: racd keenly: hdwy over 2f out: rdn to ld over 1f out: hdd wl ins fnl f* 6/1[3]
3300 3 ¾ **Sakhee's Jem**[39] 6298 4-9-5 53 JosephineGordon 9 54
(Gay Kelleway) *racd keenly and prom: hung rt over 3f out: rdn over 2f out: styd on* 25/1
5260 4 ½ **Lily Ash (IRE)**[51] 5855 4-9-3 56 GeorgeBuckell(5) 2 56
(Mike Murphy) *hld up: rdn and r.o wl ins fnl f: nt rch ldrs* 12/1
/500 5 nk **Media World (IRE)**[42] 6182 4-9-2 50 DanielMuscutt 10 49
(Julie Camacho) *plld hrd and prom: rdn over 1f out: styd on same pce ins fnl f* 16/1
3363 6 ½ **Justice Rock**[4] 7480 4-8-8 49 (t) NicolaCurrie(7) 4 47
(Phil McEntee) *hld up: rdn over 1f out: r.o: nt rch ldrs* 7/2[2]
6054 7 ½ **Hot Mustard**[17] 7062 7-9-7 55 (h) MartinDwyer 1 51
(William Muir) *prom: sn pushed along: lost pl after 1f: hdwy u.p over 1f out: styd on same pce ins fnl f* 11/4[1]
3060 8 nk **Rosie Crowe (IRE)**[39] 6296 5-8-9 46 oh1 (v) CharlieBennett(3) 8 42
(Shaun Harris) *led: hdd over 5f out: led again 4f out: rdn and hdd over 1f out: no ex ins fnl f* 8/1
0530 9 1¾ **Kingfisher Girl**[66] 5285 4-8-12 46 oh1 (tp) TomMarquand 12 37
(Michael Appleby) *chsd ldrs: led over 5f out: hdd 4f out: rdn over 1f out: wknd ins fnl f* 25/1
000 10 4½ **Desi Daru (IRE)**[43] 6150 5-8-13 47 AdamBeschizza 7 26
(Conrad Allen) *hld up: rdn over 2f out: nvr on terms* 9/1
00 11 6 **Louis Vee (IRE)**[23] 6850 9-8-7 46 oh1 (p) GeorgiaCox(5) 3 9
(John O'Shea) *a in rr: rdn 1/2-way: bhd and eased over 1f out* 50/1
000- 12 2¾ **Cloak And Degas (IRE)**[273] 8595 5-9-7 55 (v) RyanTate 5 10
(Tim McCarthy) *chsd ldrs: rdn over 2f out: wknd over 1f out* 33/1

1m 27.33s (0.13) **Going Correction** -0.175s/f (Stan) 12 Ran SP% 124.7
Speed ratings (Par 101): **92,90,90,89,89 88,87,87,85,80 73,70**
CSF £42.78 CT £876.93 TOTE £8.10: £2.20, £2.90, £7.20; EX 64.90 Trifecta £525.20.
**Owner** A. Turton & Mrs Alison Guest **Bred** P Balding **Trained** Ingmanthorpe, W Yorks

**FOCUS**
Division one of a very moderate handicap. The gallop was reasonable throughout and the winner has been rated close to his better efforts.

## 7606 BET TOTEWIN AT BETFRED.COM H'CAP (DIV II) 7f (P)
8:50 (8:52) (Class 6) (0-55,56) 4-Y-0+ £3,234 (£962; £481; £240) Stalls Low

Form RPR
R-22 1 **Honey Badger**[11] 7240 6-9-5 56 (p) GeorgeWood(3) 2 67
(Michael Herrington) *a.p: nt clr run over 1f out: rdn to ld ins fnl f: r.o* 5/2[1]
1006 2 1¾ **Isntshesomething**[22] 6902 5-9-7 55 (v) ConnorBeasley 5 60
(Richard Guest) *hld up in tch: chsd ldr over 2f out: rdn to ld 1f out: hdd and unable qck ins fnl f* 5/1[3]
3505 3 ¾ **Binky Blue (IRE)**[33] 6502 5-9-2 53 (h) DavidEgan(3) 1 56
(Daniel Mark Loughnane) *hld up: pushed along and hdwy over 2f out: styd on* 5/1[3]
3244 4 ¾ **Caledonian Gold**[4] 7481 4-9-1 49 (b) JoeyHaynes 4 50
(Paul D'Arcy) *led: rdn and hdd 1f out: no ex ins fnl f* 3/1[2]
0025 5 2 **Tasaaboq**[4] 7487 6-9-5 53 (t) JosephineGordon 8 49
(Phil McEntee) *pushed along early in rr: hdwy and nt clr run over 1f out: styd on same pce ins fnl f* 8/1
500 6 ½ **Quick Monet (IRE)**[65] 5315 4-8-9 46 oh1 CharlieBennett(3) 6 40
(Shaun Harris) *hld up: plld hrd: hdwy over 1f out: styd* 33/1
/050 7 5 **Satellite Express (IRE)**[33] 6531 6-8-12 46 oh1 (t) MartinDwyer 10 27
(Tim Pinfield) *w ldr tl pushed along 4f out: rdn over 2f out: wknd fnl f* 50/1
0460 8 nk **Nonno Giulio (IRE)**[4] 7481 6-9-7 55 (b) OisinMurphy 12 35
(Conor Dore) *prom: racd keenly: rdn over 2f out: wknd over 1f out* 25/1
5350 9 4 **Upper Lambourn (IRE)**[23] 6850 9-8-12 46 oh1 (t) DannyBrock 11 15
(Denis Quinn) *chsd ldrs: rdn over 2f out: wknd over 1f out* 50/1
-304 10 1¾ **Royal Caper**[24] 6814 7-9-0 48 StevieDonohoe 9 12
(Miss Joey Ellis) *s.i.s: a in rr* 14/1

5643 11 5 **Monsieur Royale**[60] 5511 7-9-2 50 TomQueally 7
(Clive Drew) *hld up: rdn and wknd over 2f out* 14/1

1m 26.45s (-0.75) **Going Correction** -0.175s/f (Stan) 11 Ran SP% 122.1
Speed ratings (Par 101): **97,95,94,93,91 90,84,84,79,77 72**
CSF £15.62 CT £59.84 TOTE £3.50: £1.40, £2.10, £1.90; EX 19.50 Trifecta £69.50.
**Owner** Mrs Deborah Black **Bred** Mrs Deborah Black **Trained** Cold Kirby, N Yorks

**FOCUS**
Mainly exposed performers in division two. The gallop was fair, but those held up never figured.

## 7607 OKTOBERFEST HERE 13TH OCTOBER H'CAP 5f (P)
9:20 (9:21) (Class 6) (0-65,67) 4-Y-0+ £2,587 (£770; £384; £192) Stalls Low

Form RPR
2400 1 **Red Stripes (USA)**[4] 7486 5-9-0 58 (b) DavidProbert 7 67
(Lisa Williamson) *racd keenly in 2nd pl: rdn and ev ch fr over 1f out: styd on to ld post* 5/2[1]
5533 2 nse **Swendab (IRE)**[7] 7407 9-8-6 53 (b) DavidEgan(3) 1 62
(John O'Shea) *sn led: rdn over 1f out: hdd post* 3/1[2]
3334 3 4 **Frank The Barber (IRE)**[128] 2995 5-9-1 59 (t) AdamBeschizza 2 53
(Steph Hollinshead) *led early: settled to chse ldrs: rdn over 1f out: no ex ins fnl f* 10/1[3]
6201 4 ½ **Staffa (IRE)**[7] 7407 4-8-11 60 PaddyPilley(5) 5 53
(Denis Coakley) *hld up: racd keenly: rdn over 1f out: nt trble ldrs* 3/1[2]
2334 5 ½ **Pushkin Museum (IRE)**[51] 5827 6-9-4 67 CallumRodriguez(5) 6 58
(Patrick Morris) *awkward s: hld up: rdn over 1f out: styd on same pce* 3/1[2]

59.02s (-1.18) **Going Correction** -0.175s/f (Stan) 5 Ran SP% 112.7
Speed ratings (Par 101): **102,101,95,94,93**
CSF £10.53 TOTE £3.40: £2.00, £2.10; EX 11.50 Trifecta £59.50.
**Owner** E H Jones (paints) Ltd **Bred** Tim Ahearn **Trained** Saighton, Cheshire

**FOCUS**
An uncompetitive handicap in which the first two had the race to themselves from some way out.
T/Plt: £213.30 to a £1 stake. Pool: £88,341.00 - 302.29 winning units T/Qpdt: £57.80 to a £1 stake. Pool: £9,920.64 - 126.80 winning units **Colin Roberts**

# 7560 HAYDOCK (L-H)
## Saturday, September 30

**OFFICIAL GOING: Heavy (6.3)**
Wind: Virtually nil Weather: Rain - heavy at times

## 7608 32RED EBF FILLIES' NOVICE STKS (PLUS 10 RACE) 1m 37y
1:35 (1:38) (Class 5) 2-Y-O £3,557 (£1,058; £529; £264) Stalls Low

Form RPR
1 **Pioneer Spirit** 2-9-0 0 RobertTart 4 76+
(John Gosden) *hld up in rr: hdwy on inner 3f out: cl up wl over 1f out: rdn to ld ent fnl f: kpt on wl* 3/1[3]
0 2 1¾ **Endless Tangent (IRE)**[47] 5990 2-9-0 0 PJMcDonald 5 72
(Tom Dascombe) *trckd ldr: cl up 1/2-way: pushed along to ld over 2f out: rdn wl over 1f out: hdd ent fnl f: sn drvn and kpt on* 14/1
3 1¾ **Dramatic Queen (USA)** 2-9-0 0 DanielTudhope 1 68
(William Haggas) *hld up: hdwy on outer and wd st to stands rail: sn cl up: effrt over 2f out: sn rdn to chal and ev ch: kpt on same pce fnl f* 2/1[2]
60 4 3 **Pelice (IRE)**[10] 7266 2-9-0 0 PhillipMakin 3 62
(Mark Johnston) *led: pushed along 1/2-way: rdn over 3f out: hdd over 2f out: grad wknd* 16/1
31 5 1¾ **Hollydaze (IRE)**[16] 7093 2-9-4 0 ShaneKelly 2 62
(Richard Hughes) *trckd ldng pair: wd st: hdwy over 3f out and sn cl up: rdn over 2f out: drvn wl over 1f out: sn wknd* 6/4[1]

1m 54.75s (10.05) **Going Correction** +0.825s/f (Soft) 5 Ran SP% 110.9
Speed ratings (Par 92): **82,80,78,75,73**
CSF £35.67 TOTE £3.20: £1.90, £4.10; EX 24.50 Trifecta £52.80.
**Owner** Lady Bamford **Bred** Lady Bamford **Trained** Newmarket, Suffolk

**FOCUS**
Race distance reduced by 17yds. The going was heavy ahead of the opener, a small novice in which they headed towards the stands' side. The winner is bred and did this quite well, but it's hard to get excited over level of the bare form.

## 7609 32RED.COM H'CAP 1m 37y
2:05 (2:06) (Class 2) (0-105,99) 3-Y-O+
£12,450 (£3,728; £1,864; £932; £466; £234) Stalls Low

Form RPR
4116 1 **Century Dream (IRE)**[63] 5392 3-9-7 98 (t) GrahamLee 13 107
(Simon Crisford) *trckd ldrs on outer: hdwy over 2f out: chal over 1f out: rdn to ld jst ins fnl f: sn edgd lft: kpt on wl towards fin* 7/1[3]
6212 2 shd **Original Choice (IRE)**[63] 5400 3-9-1 92 DanielTudhope 10 101
(William Haggas) *trckd ldng pair: wd st: hdwy over 2f out: rdn to ld wl over 1f out: drvn and hdd jst ins fnl f: rallied gamely towards fin* 7/2[1]
65B6 3 ½ **Just Hiss**[14] 7149 4-9-2 89 (p) DavidAllan 1 97
(Tim Easterby) *dwlt and rr: hdwy on inner over 2f out: chsd ldrs and swtchd lft over 1f out: drvn ins fnl f: kpt on wl towards fin* 12/1
4012 4 nk **King's Pavilion (IRE)**[14] 7140 4-9-7 94 BenCurtis 2 101
(David Barron) *in tch: hdwy 3f out: chsd ldrs 2f out: rdn and ev ch over 1f out: drvn ins fnl f: kpt on* 4/1[2]
0012 5 3 **Muntadab (IRE)**[15] 7118 5-9-10 97 TonyHamilton 7 97
(Roger Fell) *cl up: led after 2f: pushed along wl over 2f out: rdn wl over 1f out: sn hdd and drvn: wknd appr fnl f* 10/1
2434 6 1½ **Calder Prince (IRE)**[15] 7108 4-9-3 90 AlistairRawlinson 3 87
(Tom Dascombe) *slt ld 2f: cl up: chal 3f out: rdn along over 2f out: drvn wl over 1f out: grad wknd* 12/1
1300 7 11 **Florenza**[10] 7283 4-8-12 90 RowanScott(5) 5 62
(Chris Fairhurst) *trckd ldrs on inner: pushed along 3f out: rdn over 2f out: sn wknd* 40/1
6-06 8 nk **Isomer (USA)**[44] 6105 3-9-8 99 PJMcDonald 9 70
(Andrew Balding) *chsd ldrs: wd st: rdn along wl over 2f out: sn wknd* 25/1
120 9 2½ **Hibou**[34] 6491 4-9-11 98 (b) DavidNolan 12 63
(Iain Jardine) *towards rr: wd st: sme hdwy 3f out: rdn along over 2f out: n.d* 10/1
3105 10 nk **Dream Walker (FR)**[17] 7066 8-9-5 95 (t) CallumShepherd(3) 4 60
(Brian Ellison) *towards rr: sme hdwy on inner 3f out: sn rdn along and n.d* 16/1
510 11 ¾ **Quixote (GER)**[37] 6355 7-9-8 95 (t[1]) CamHardie 11 58
(Michael Easterby) *a towards rr* 33/1
2105 12 1 **Constantino (IRE)**[28] 6685 4-9-6 93 (b) ShaneKelly 6 54
(Richard Fahey) *in tch: wd st: rdn along 3f out: sn wknd* 20/1

0-01 **13** *19* **Lord Of The Rock (IRE)**[64] 5382 5-9-7 **94**.................. PaulMulrennan 8 11
(Michael Dods) *chsd ldrs: rdn along 2 1/2f out: sn wknd* **15/2**

1m 50.21s (5.51) **Going Correction** +0.825s/f (Soft)
**WFA** 3 from 4yo+ 4lb **13** Ran SP% **119.9**
Speed ratings (Par 109): **105,104,104,104,101 99,88,88,85,85 84,83,64**
CSF £30.43 CT £306.74 TOTE £7.50: £2.60, £1.80, £3.80; EX 35.70 Trifecta £685.70.
**Owner** Abdullah Saeed **Bred** Rabbah Bloodstock Limited **Trained** Newmarket, Suffolk

**FOCUS**
Race distance reduced by 17yds. A good handicap dominated by 3yos in recent times, and it was that age-group who again provided the winner. There was a fair gallop and they came down the middle where the first four drew away in a bunched finish.

## 7610 NATIONWIDEVEHICLECONTRACTS.CO.UK H'CAP 5f
**2:40** (2:43) (Class 2) (0-105,99) 3-Y-O+

**£28,012** (£8,388; £4,194; £2,097; £1,048; £526) **Stalls** Centre

Form RPR
2121 **1** **Boundsy (IRE)**[28] 6679 3-8-8 **86**.............................. SammyJoBell(3) 10 93
(Richard Fahey) *in tch: hdwy to chse ldrs 2f out: rdn along over 1f out: drvn ins fnl f: styd on wl to ld nr line* **10/1**

3003 **2** *nse* **Rasheeq (IRE)**[22] 6878 4-8-11 **85**........................................ DavidAllan 3 92
(Tim Easterby) *chsd ldrs on inner: hdwy 2f out: rdn ent fnl f: ev ch last 75 yds: kpt on* **10/1**

1511 **3** *nk* **Tarboosh**[26] 6758 4-9-3 **91**.................................................. CamHardie 11 101+
(Paul Midgley) *trckd ldrs: hdwy 2f out: led over 1f out: rdn clr ent fnl f: drvn last 100 yds: hdd and no ex nr line* **12/1**

3303 **4** *nk* **Confessional**[21] 6927 10-8-12 **86**............................(be) ConnorBeasley 5 91
(Tim Easterby) *slt ld centre: rdn along 2f out: hdd jst over 1f out: sn drvn: kpt on wl* **9/1**[3]

0021 **5** *2* **Soie D'Leau**[5] 7461 5-9-8 **96** 6ex.............................. TonyHamilton 4 94
(Kristin Stubbs) *dwlt: sn cl up centre: rdn along wl over 1f out: wknd ins fnl f* **11/2**[2]

0251 **6** *2* **Mayleaf Shine (IRE)**[21] 6927 3-9-3 **92**..........................(h) GrahamLee 12 82
(Iain Jardine) *towards rr: pushed along over 2f out: rdn and hdwy to chse ldrs over 1f out: kpt on fnl f* **7/2**[1]

0241 **7** *nse* **Quench Dolly**[58] 5574 3-9-5 **99**................................ GeorgeBuckell(5) 8 89
(John Gallagher) *cl up centre: rdn along wl over 1f out: sn drvn and wknd fnl f* **11/2**[2]

2001 **8** *4* **Powerallied (IRE)**[28] 6677 4-8-12 **86**............................ PaulMulrennan 2 62
(Richard Fahey) *midfield: sme hdwy 2f out: sn rdn and n.d* **16/1**

0400 **9** *1 3/4* **Poyle Vinnie**[20] 6971 7-9-9 **97**................................(p) AlistairRawlinson 1 67
(Michael Appleby) *a towards rr* **20/1**

5200 **10** *1* **Coolfitch (IRE)**[35] 6450 3-9-2 **91**.................................. DanielTudhope 7 57
(David O'Meara) *dwlt: a towards rr* **20/1**

1426 **11** *1 1/2* **Kinglami**[36] 6371 8-8-5 **79**....................................................(p) JoeDoyle 6 40
(John O'Shea) *chsd ldrs centre: pushed along bef 1/2-way: sn lost pl and bhd* **25/1**

3001 **12** *5* **Poet's Society**[11] 7256 3-8-13 **88**.................................... PJMcDonald 14 31
(Mark Johnston) *racd towards stands side: chsd ldrs: rdn along bef 1/2-way: sn lost pl and bhd* **25/1**

0000 **13** *1* **Hoofalong**[16] 7086 7-9-0 **88**...........................................(v[1]) PhillipMakin 9 27
(Michael Easterby) *racd nr stands side: chsd ldrs: rdn along 1/2-way: sn wknd* **11/1**

0340 **14** *1 1/2* **Green Door (IRE)**[21] 6927 6-9-2 **97**.....................(v) JonathanFisher(7) 13 31
(Robert Cowell) *dwlt: a bhd* **25/1**

1m 3.75s (2.95) **Going Correction** +0.825s/f (Soft)
**WFA** 3 from 4yo+ 1lb **14** Ran SP% **124.1**
Speed ratings (Par 109): **109,108,108,107,104 101,101,95,92,90 88,80,78,76**
CSF £101.00 CT £1246.36 TOTE £10.50: £3.80, £3.50, £3.80; EX 142.00 Trifecta £2544.40 Partly Won..
**Owner** Kevin Mercer & Partner **Bred** Glenview House Stud **Trained** Musley Bank, N Yorks

**FOCUS**
A nice sprint handicap featuring a number of improving sorts and it was a progressive 3yo who came out on top. They initially split into two groups (middle and stands) and the form looks solid, with a step up from the winner and the fourth helping set the level.

## 7611 32RED GOLD CUP (HERITAGE H'CAP) 6f
**3:15** (3:18) (Class 2) 3-Y-O+

**£56,025** (£16,776; £8,388; £4,194; £2,097; £1,053) **Stalls** Centre

Form RPR
0301 **1** **Donjuan Triumphant (IRE)**[23] 6856 4-9-10 **109** 5ex...(h) PJMcDonald 4 118
(Andrew Balding) *dwlt and towards rr: stdy hdwy towards far side over 2f out: rdn to chse ldr ins fnl f: styd on wl to ld nr line* **13/2**[3]

0130 **2** *shd* **Stake Acclaim (IRE)**[14] 7144 5-8-13 **101**........................ JackDuern(3) 11 110
(Dean Ivory) *cl up centre: led wl over 1f out: rdn and wandered ent fnl f: drvn and edgd lft last 100 yds: hdd nr line* **20/1**

0111 **3** *3 3/4* **Ice Age (IRE)**[20] 6971 4-9-0 **99** 8ex.............................. CharlesBishop 2 96
(Eve Johnson Houghton) *racd towards far side: led to 1/2-way: cl up: rdn along wl over 1f out: drvn ent fnl f: kpt on same pce* **7/1**

0256 **4** *hd* **Mr Lupton (IRE)**[21] 6926 4-9-9 **108**.............................. TonyHamilton 14 104
(Richard Fahey) *trckd ldrs centre: pushed along 2f out: sn rdn and kpt on same pce fnl f* **16/1**

5143 **5** *1 1/4* **Get Knotted (IRE)**[21] 6922 5-9-0 **99**..........................(p) PaulMulrennan 15 91
(Michael Dods) *dwlt and towards rr: hdwy over 2f out: rdn to chse ldrs over 1f out: kpt on fnl f* **14/1**

4341 **6** *shd* **Johnny Barnes (IRE)**[35] 6419 5-9-7 **106** 5ex.................... RobertTart 17 98+
(John Gosden) *racd towards stands side: sn outpcd and bhd: hdwy 2f out: sn rdn and styd on fnl f* **5/1**[2]

0343 **7** *4 1/2* **Withernsea (IRE)**[21] 6961 6-8-11 **99**.......................... SammyJoBell(3) 9 76
(Richard Fahey) *towards rr: hdwy over 2f out: sn rdn along and kpt on: n.d* **10/1**

111P **8** *nk* **Glenrowan Rose (IRE)**[41] 6234 4-9-0 **99**.................... ConnorBeasley 8 75
(Keith Dalgleish) *cl up centre: led 1/2-way: rdn along over 2f out: sn hdd and drvn: grad wknd* **33/1**

0500 **9** *nk* **Perfect Pasture**[36] 6401 7-9-7 **106**..............................(v) PhillipMakin 13 81
(Michael Easterby) *nvr bttr than midfield* **66/1**

6400 **10** *2 1/2* **Growl**[21] 6926 5-9-10 **109**.....................................................(p) GrahamLee 5 76
(Richard Fahey) *midfield: effrt over 2f out: sn rdn along and n.d* **16/1**

-053 **11** *5* **Shanghai Glory (IRE)**[42] 6206 4-9-1 **103**........... CallumShepherd(3) 10 54
(Charles Hills) *chsd ldrs centre: rdn along over 2f out: sn wknd* **9/1**

-161 **12** *4* **Sainted**[51] 5828 4-9-0 **99**................................................ DanielTudhope 7 38
(William Haggas) *nvr bttr than midfield* **9/2**[1]

2420 **13** *3 3/4* **Aeolus**[36] 6401 6-9-4 **103**...................................................(p) PatCosgrave 12 30
(Ed Walker) *nvr bttr than midfield* **9/1**

0350 **14** *3 3/4* **Orion's Bow**[38] 6325 6-9-4 **103**............................................ DavidAllan 1 18
(Tim Easterby) *racd towards far side: chsd ldrs: rdn along over 2f out: sn wknd* **25/1**

060 **15** *1 1/2* **Doc Sportello (IRE)**[21] 6922 5-8-13 **98**...................(p) GeorgeDowning 6 8
(Tony Carroll) *chsd ldrs centre: rdn along wl over 2f out: sn wknd* **66/1**

00-1 **16** *9* **Kickboxer (IRE)**[133] 2839 6-9-1 **100**.............................. DougieCostello 3
(Michael Appleby) *midfield: rdn along 1/2-way: sn outpcd* **33/1**

0501 **17** *nk* **Rene Mathis (GER)**[161] 1974 7-9-1 **100**.................. KieranShoemark 16
(Richard Fahey) *a towards rr* **33/1**

1m 17.1s (3.30) **Going Correction** +0.825s/f (Soft) **17** Ran SP% **128.6**
Speed ratings (Par 109): **111,110,105,105,103 103,97,97,97,93 87,81,76,71,69 57,57**
CSF £140.96 CT £994.45 TOTE £8.50: £2.30, £4.90, £2.10, £4.80; EX 174.20 Trifecta £1609.30.
**Owner** King Power Racing Co Ltd **Bred** Patrick Cosgrove & Dream Ahead Syndicate **Trained** Kingsclere, Hants
■ Stewards' Enquiry : Jack Duern seven-day ban: used whip above permitted level (Oct 14-20)

**FOCUS**
A replacement for last weekend's abandoned Ayr Gold Cup, this cracking handicap may not have had 25 runners, but it still featured a host of improving sprinters and the winner looks back to his best. They headed down the middle and there was a close finish.

## 7612 ALAN MIRFIN 75TH BIRTHDAY H'CAP 6f
**3:50** (3:52) (Class 3) (0-90,90) 3-Y-O+ **£9,703** (£2,887; £1,443; £721) **Stalls** Centre

Form RPR
3461 **1** **Hyperfocus (IRE)**[22] 6877 3-9-5 **90**.............................. LouisSteward 15 104+
(Hugo Palmer) *sn cl up on outer: led over 3f out: qcknd clr 2f out: sn edgd lft towards far rail: kpt on strly: readily* **3/1**[1]

0333 **2** *2 1/4* **Letmestopyouthere (IRE)**[2] 7554 3-8-8 **82**.............. MattCosham(3) 11 88+
(David Evans) *hld up in rr: hdwy over 2f out: chsd ldrs and n.m.r over 1f out: swtchd rt and rdn jst ins fnl f: kpt on wl towards fin: no ch w wnr* **11/1**

0660 **3** *nk* **George Bowen (IRE)**[20] 6971 5-9-4 **90**................(p) SammyJoBell(3) 13 95
(Richard Fahey) *towards rr: hdwy over 2f out: rdn to chse ldrs over 1f out: hung lft ent fnl f: kpt on* **10/1**

1230 **4** *1 1/2* **Muatadel**[2] 7557 4-8-11 **80**................................................ TonyHamilton 4 80
(Roger Fell) *racd towards far side: chsd ldrs: rdn along 2f out: n.m.r ent fnl f: kpt on same pce* **20/1**

5001 **5** *hd* **Goring (GER)**[16] 7084 5-9-1 **84**.......................................(p) CharlesBishop 6 84
(Eve Johnson Houghton) *cl up centre: disp ld 4f out: rdn along wl over 2f out: sn drvn and grad wknd* **9/1**[3]

1453 **6** *3 3/4* **Sir Billy Wright (IRE)**[36] 6371 6-9-1 **84**........................ PJMcDonald 7 72
(David Evans) *cl up centre: rdn along 2f out: n.m.r and swtchd rt ent fnl f: sn drvn and kpt on same pce* **16/1**

6062 **7** *hd* **Toofi (FR)**[22] 6877 6-9-1 **84**.............................................(p) PaulMulrennan 14 71
(John Butler) *chsd ldrs centre: hdwy and prom over 2f out: sn rdn along and kpt on same pce* **12/1**

1255 **8** *shd* **Dark Defender**[21] 6923 4-9-0 **88**................................(v) RowanScott(5) 8 75
(Keith Dalgleish) *chsd ldrs towards far side: rdn along over 2f out: grad wknd* **25/1**

0415 **9** *1 3/4* **Russian Realm**[22] 6877 7-9-0 **83**...................................... GrahamLee 12 64
(Paul Midgley) *a towards rr* **14/1**

4026 **10** *2 1/2* **Eccleston**[71] 5093 6-9-3 **86**.................................................(v) JoeDoyle 3 59
(Julie Camacho) *rr tl sme late hdwy* **14/1**

5021 **11** *2 3/4* **Handsome Dude**[112] 3585 5-8-12 **86**..........................(b) JaneElliott(5) 1 50
(David Barron) *nvr bttr than midfield* **9/1**[3]

2005 **12** *1* **Fingal's Cave (IRE)**[14] 7140 5-8-13 **89**...................... JamieGormley(7) 2 50
(Philip Kirby) *racd towards far side: prom: rdn along wl over 2f out: sn drvn and wknd* **14/1**

0644 **13** *15* **Englishman**[22] 6877 7-8-8 **82**.............................. ManuelFernandes(5) 10
(Milton Bradley) *cl up centre: rdn along 1/2-way: sn wknd* **8/1**[2]

130 **14** *4 1/2* **Bouclier (IRE)**[35] 6414 7-9-0 **83**........................................ PhillipMakin 5
(Michael Easterby) *racd towards far side: prom: rdn along wl over 2f out: sn wknd* **25/1**

2010 **15** *3* **Major Pusey**[14] 7144 5-9-5 **88**...................................... FergusSweeney 9
(John Gallagher) *sn slt ld centre: hdd over 3f out and sn rdn along: drvn over 2f out and sn wknd* **10/1**

1m 17.86s (4.06) **Going Correction** +0.825s/f (Soft)
**WFA** 3 from 4yo+ 2lb **15** Ran SP% **128.7**
Speed ratings (Par 107): **105,102,101,99,99 94,94,93,91,88 84,83,63,57,53**
CSF £37.79 CT £254.75 TOTE £3.50: £1.80, £4.50, £4.70; EX 51.20 Trifecta £1423.60.
**Owner** MPH Racing - II **Bred** Stephanie Von Schilcher & Gavan Kinch **Trained** Newmarket, Suffolk

**FOCUS**
Another competitive sprint handicap in which three of the last four winners of the race triumphed during their next two outings, boding well for this year's winner, who ended up on the far rail. He is now 2-2 since being gelded, while the runner-up has been rated to his Pontefract figure from two days earlier.

## 7613 32RED CASINO EBF NOVICE STKS (PLUS 10 RACE) (C&G) 1m 37y
**4:25** (4:26) (Class 4) 2-Y-O **£4,528** (£1,347; £673; £336) **Stalls** Low

Form RPR
5 **1** **Real Gent**[45] 6057 2-9-0 0.................................................... GrahamLee 1 76
(Kevin Ryan) *.led: pushed along 2f out: hdd over 1f out: rdn to chal ins fnl f: sn edgd lft: kpt on wl to ld last 50 yds* **3/1**[2]

4 **2** *1/2* **Bold Reason (GER)**[66] 5301 2-9-0 0.................................. RobertTart 6 75
(John Gosden) *trckd ldrs: hdwy on inner over 3f out: cl up 2f out: rdn to ld over 1f out: drvn ins fnl f: hdd and no ex last 50 yds* **2/1**[1]

0 **3** *2 3/4* **Creel**[23] 6854 2-9-0 0.............................................................. PhillipMakin 5 69
(David Brown) *trckd ldrs on outer: hdwy 1/2-way: cl up 3f out: rdn over 2f out and ev ch: drvn over 1f out: kpt on same pce* **50/1**

**4** *8* **Spark Of War (IRE)** 2-9-0 0.......................................... ConnorBeasley 7 51
(Keith Dalgleish) *hld up in rr: hdwy over 3f out: rdn along to chse ldrs over 2f out: green and sn outpcd* **20/1**

65 **5** *1 1/4* **A Bit Of A Touch (IRE)**[21] 6938 2-8-11 0.................. SammyJoBell(3) 3 49
(Richard Fahey) *towards rr: pushed along 1/2-way: sn outpcd* **10/1**[3]

1 **6** *10* **Narcos (IRE)**[56] 5631 2-9-3 0........................................ TonyHamilton 4 30
(Richard Fahey) *trckd wnr: hdwy and cl up 3f out: rdn along over 2f out: sn wknd and eased* **2/1**[1]

33 **7** *9* **Skito Soldier**[34] 6465 2-8-9 0.......................................... RowanScott(5) 2 7
(K R Burke) *chsd ldrs on inner: rdn along 4f out: drvn 3f out: sn wknd* **14/1**

1m 52.91s (8.21) **Going Correction** +0.825s/f (Soft) **7** Ran SP% **114.1**
Speed ratings (Par 97): **91,90,87,79,78 68,59**
CSF £9.41 TOTE £3.90: £1.90, £1.30; EX 12.30 Trifecta £488.60.
**Owner** Mrs Jane Dwyer **Bred** R W Russell **Trained** Hambleton, N Yorks

**FOCUS**
Race distance reduced by 17yds. A moderate novice run at a sensible pace in testing conditions, and the first three came clear.

## 7614 32RED H'CAP 1m 6f
5:00 (5:00) (Class 2) (0-100,94) 3-Y-0+

£14,628 (£4,380; £2,190; £1,095; £547; £274) Stalls Low

Form RPR
2544 1 **Star Of The East (IRE)**[9] 7337 3-8-4 **83**.......................... JaneElliott(5) 2 91
(Mark Johnston) *led to 1/2-way: cl up on inner: led again 2f out and sn rdn: drvn ins fnl f: kpt on gamely* **6/1**[3]
1111 2 *1* **Sepal (USA)**[21] 6929 4-9-3 **90**.......................... JamieGormley(7) 4 96
(Iain Jardine) *trckd ldrs: hdwy over 3f out: rdn along 2f out: drvn to chse wnr ins fnl f: kpt on* **9/4**[1]
0005 3 *nk* **Suegioo (FR)**[15] 7110 8-9-9 **89**..........................(p) TonyHamilton 5 94
(Richard Fahey) *hld up in rr: hdwy on outer over 2f out: rdn wl over 1f out: styd on wl fnl f* **25/1**
0102 4 *2 1/2* **Amazing Red (IRE)**[14] 7150 4-9-9 **89**.......................... PaulMulrennan 6 91+
(Ed Dunlop) *t.k.h: hld up in rr: hdwy 3f out: rdn to chse ldrs over 2f out: drvn wl over 1f out: sn one pce* **7/2**[2]
5-00 5 *1/2* **Master Of Irony (IRE)**[105] 2774 5-9-4 **84**..........................(v) PhillipMakin 3 85
(John Quinn) *trckd ldrs: effrt over 3f out: rdn along over 2f out: sn drvn and one pce* **20/1**
5004 6 *3 3/4* **Cleonte (IRE)**[21] 6929 4-9-12 **92**..........................(v[1]) GrahamLee 1 88
(Andrew Balding) *trckd ldng pair: hdwy to ld over 3f out: rdn along and hdd 2f out: sn drvn and wknd over 1f out* **9/1**
2123 7 *20* **Getback In Paris (IRE)**[56] 5638 4-10-0 **94**.......................... ShaneKelly 7 62
(Richard Hughes) *hld up towards rr: rdn along over 3f out: outpcd and bhd fnl 2f* **7/2**[2]
0050 8 *1 1/4* **Intense Tango**[22] 6880 6-8-10 **79**..........................(t[1]) CallumShepherd(3) 9 45
(K R Burke) *cl up: racd wd bk st and led 1/2-way: pushed along over 4f out: rdn over 3f out: sn hdd & wknd: bhd and eased fnl 2f* **14/1**

3m 31.07s (29.07) **Going Correction** +1.725s/f (Heav)
**WFA** 3 from 4yo+ 8lb **8 Ran SP% 114.8**
Speed ratings (Par 109): **85,84,84,82,82 80,68,68**
CSF £20.02 CT £314.26 TOTE £6.00: £1.50, £1.20, £4.40; EX 22.40 Trifecta £495.50.
**Owner** Sheikh Hamdan bin Mohammed Al Maktoum **Bred** Darley **Trained** Middleham Moor, N Yorks

**FOCUS**
Race distance increased by 30yds. A fair staying handicap and they went a sensible gallop in the ground. A small personal best from the winner while the runner-up improved again in defeat.

## 7615 32RED CASINO H'CAP 1m 3f 175y
5:35 (5:35) (Class 3) (0-95,94) 3-Y-0+

£9,337 (£2,796; £1,398; £699; £349; £175) Stalls Centre

Form RPR
1 1 **Royal Line**[26] 6765 3-8-11 **88**.......................... RobertTart 4 103+
(John Gosden) *hld up in rr: pushed along briefly over 4f out: hdwy 3f out: rdn to ld wl over 1f out: sn hung bdly lft to far rail: clr ent fnl f: eased towards fin* **5/4**[1]
000 2 *2 1/4* **Night Of Glory**[35] 6445 3-9-1 **92**..........................(p) ShaneKelly 8 99
(Andrew Balding) *trckd ldng pair on outer: hdwy 4f out: cl up 3f out: rdn to take slt ld over 2f out: hdd wl over 1f out: sn drvn and kpt on: no ch w wnr* **7/2**[2]
-145 3 *2 1/4* **Archippos**[119] 3315 4-8-13 **83**.......................... PaulMulrennan 3 86
(Philip Kirby) *trckd ldrs: pushed along 4f out: rdn over 3f out: sn drvn and kpt on same pce* **10/1**
0543 4 *4* **Swaheen**[21] 6944 5-8-10 **80**..........................(p) JoeDoyle 1 77
(Julie Camacho) *trckd ldr: cl up over 3f out: rdn along over 2f out: sn drvn and outpcd fr wl over 1f out* **9/2**[3]
636 5 *12* **Tawdeea**[14] 7150 5-9-10 **94**..........................(p) GrahamLee 6 72
(David O'Meara) *hld up in tch: effrt on outer over 4f out: rdn along 3f out: sn drvn and outpcd* **7/1**
0-50 6 *2* **Trendsetter (IRE)**[20] 6965 6-8-10 **85**..........................(p) RowanScott(5) 7 59
(Micky Hammond) *led: pushed along 4f out: rdn over 3f out: drvn and hdd over 2f out: sn wknd* **33/1**
4006 7 *4* **Gabrial's King (IRE)**[14] 7143 8-8-10 **80**.......................... TonyHamilton 5 47
(Richard Fahey) *hld up: a rr: bhd fr over 2f out* **20/1**

2m 51.84s (18.04) **Going Correction** +1.725s/f (Heav)
**WFA** 3 from 4yo+ 7lb **7 Ran SP% 114.1**
Speed ratings (Par 107): **108,106,105,102,94 93,90**
CSF £5.76 CT £28.29 TOTE £2.00: £1.40, £2.50; EX 6.80 Trifecta £58.00.
**Owner** HH Sheikha Al Jalila Racing **Bred** Darley **Trained** Newmarket, Suffolk

**FOCUS**
Race distance increased by 8yds. An ordinary handicap turned into a procession by the impressive winner, while the runner-up has been rated back to his best.
T/Plt: £761.40 to a £1 stake. Pool: £111,865.00 - 107.24 winning units T/Qpdt: £126.20 to a £1 stake. Pool: £10,865.92 - 63.71 winning units **Joe Rowntree**

# 7576 NEWMARKET (R-H)
Saturday, September 30

**OFFICIAL GOING: Good to soft (overall 6.7, stands' 6.8, centre 6.6, far 6.5)**
Wind: light, across Weather: sunny, clouding over after race 4

## 7616 JUDDMONTE ROYAL LODGE STKS (GROUP 2) (C&G) 1m
1:50 (1:51) (Class 1) 2-Y-0 £56,710 (£21,500; £10,760; £5,360; £2,690) Stalls Low

Form RPR
11 1 **Roaring Lion (USA)**[22] 6883 2-9-0 91.......................... OisinMurphy 6 111
(John Gosden) *hld up wl in tch in last pair: pushed along to chal ent fnl 2f: rdn to ld over 1f out: wnt lft u.p ins fnl f: styd on wl: rdn out* **11/4**[2]
1 2 *nk* **Nelson (IRE)**[21] 6955 2-9-0 112.......................... RyanMoore 1 110
(A P O'Brien, Ire) *pressed ldr: rdn 3f out: drvn and ev ch over 1f out: kpt on wl u.p but a jst hld ins fnl f* **5/6**[1]
1131 3 *1 3/4* **Mildenberger**[36] 6396 2-9-0 104.......................... JamesDoyle 2 106
(Mark Johnston) *led: pushed along 3f out: rdn over 2f out: hdd and drvn over 1f out: no ex ins fnl f: wknd towards fin* **7/2**[3]
41 4 *2 1/4* **Petrus (IRE)**[85] 4583 2-9-0 0.......................... JamieSpencer 4 102
(Brian Meehan) *hld up wl in tch in last pair: effrt over 2f out: rdn and unable qck 2f out: wnt 4th over 1f out: kpt on but no imp ins fnl f: eased towards fin* **16/1**

1662 5 *6* **Midnight Wilde**[11] 7251 2-9-0 75..........................(b[1]) JosephineGordon 3 88
(John Ryan) *trckd ldng pair: rdn 3f out: outpcd u.p ent fnl 2f: dropped to last over 1f out: wknd fnl f* **100/1**

1m 39.56s (0.96) **Going Correction** +0.275s/f (Good) **5 Ran SP% 110.3**
Speed ratings (Par 107): **106,105,103,101,95**
CSF £5.48 TOTE £3.30: £1.80, £1.10; EX 5.40 Trifecta £8.00.
**Owner** Qatar Racing Limited **Bred** Ranjan Racing Inc **Trained** Newmarket, Suffolk

**FOCUS**
Stalls: far side course, all races far side. The going had dried out slightly, officially given as good to soft (from good to soft, soft in places the previous day). This has produced a few top-level winners in recent years including from the beaten runners, like the last running of the race at Ascot in 2010, when Frankel won and Treasure Beach was third. This has been rated as a par renewal.

## 7617 JUDDMONTE CHEVELEY PARK STKS (GROUP 1) (FILLIES) 6f
2:20 (2:22) (Class 1) 2-Y-O

£121,075 (£45,902; £22,972; £11,443; £5,743; £2,882) Stalls Low

Form RPR
011 1 **Clemmie (IRE)**[78] 4855 2-9-0 108..........................(t) RyanMoore 3 114
(A P O'Brien, Ire) *travelled strly: w ldrs tl led wl over 1f out: rdn and qcknd clr w runner up ent fnl f: styd on strly asserted fnl 100yds: gng away at fin* **15/8**[1]
13 2 *1 3/4* **Different League (FR)**[41] 6249 2-9-0 108.......................... AntoineHamelin 13 109
(Matthieu Palussiere, France) *sn w ldr and travelled strly: led 2f out: hdd wl over 1f out: rdn and qcknd clr w wnr ent fnl f: no ex 100yds: outpcd towards fin* **4/1**[3]
1512 3 *1 1/2* **Madeline (IRE)**[37] 6354 2-9-0 103.......................... AndreaAtzeni 2 105
(Roger Varian) *pressed ldrs: ev ch 3f out: unable to match pce of ldng pair jst over 1f out: kpt on same pce u.p ins fnl f* **8/1**
4 4 *hd* **Now You're Talking (IRE)**[86] 4680 2-9-0 99.......................... DonnachaO'Brien 4 104
(Joseph Patrick O'Brien, Ire) *squeezed for room leaving stalls: hld up in tch in last trio: hdwy and nt clrest of runs over 1f out: swtchd lft and rdn ent fnl f: battling for 3rd ins fnl f: kpt on* **50/1**
0025 5 *1/2* **Darkanna (IRE)**[37] 6353 2-9-0 95.......................... BarryMcHugh 9 102
(Richard Fahey) *pressed ldrs: rdn over 2f out: unable qck over 1f out: kpt on u.p but no imp ins fnl f* **66/1**
1212 6 *1 1/2* **Eirene**[23] 6863 2-9-0 99.......................... RobertWinston 7 98
(Dean Ivory) *t.k.h: hld up in tch in last trio: swtchd lft and effrt wl over 1f out: unbalanced on downhill run and no hdwy over 1f out: rallied ins fnl f: kpt on fnl 100yds: no threat to ldrs* **14/1**
11 7 *nk* **Threading (IRE)**[37] 6354 2-9-0 108.......................... JamesDoyle 11 97
(Mark Johnston) *hld up wl in tch in midfield: effrt over 2f out: unable qck u.p over 1f out: no threat to ldrs and kpt on same pce ins fnl f and no imp* **5/2**[2]
1 8 *1* **Betty F**[35] 6424 2-9-0 0.......................... PatSmullen 6 94
(Jeremy Noseda) *wnt rt s: hld up wl in tch in midfield: nt clrest of runs over 2f out: sn rdn and no imp whn unbalanced over 1f out: wl hld and kpt on same pce ins fnl f* **16/1**
01 9 *3 3/4* **Treasuring**[41] 6241 2-9-0 98.......................... ColinKeane 1 83
(G M Lyons, Ire) *led tl hdd and rdn 2f out: lost pl u.p jst over 1f out: wknd ins fnl f* **33/1**
16 10 *1 1/2* **Crossing The Line**[23] 6863 2-9-0 0.......................... JimCrowley 10 78
(Andrew Balding) *hld up in tch towards rr: rdn 3f out: no imp u.p over 2f out: bhd over 1f out* **28/1**
10 11 *10* **Chica La Habana (IRE)**[101] 3960 2-9-0 0.......................... SilvestreDeSousa 12 48
(Robert Cowell) *a towards rr: rdn wl over 2f out: bhd and lost tch over 1f out: hung lft and eased ins fnl f* **66/1**

1m 12.0s (-0.20) **Going Correction** +0.275s/f (Good) **11 Ran SP% 118.3**
Speed ratings (Par 106): **112,109,107,107,106 104,104,103,98,96 82**
CSF £9.42 CT £48.89 TOTE £2.40: £1.30, £1.60, £2.10; EX 11.50 Trifecta £50.10.
**Owner** Michael Tabor & Derrick Smith & Mrs John Magnier **Bred** Liberty Bloodstock **Trained** Cashel, Co Tipperary

**FOCUS**
They raced far side and not many got seriously involved from off the pace, but the time was 0.44sec quicker than the following Middle Park. The winner continues to progress.

## 7618 JUDDMONTE MIDDLE PARK STKS (GROUP 1) (COLTS) 6f
2:55 (2:56) (Class 1) 2-Y-O

£121,075 (£45,902; £22,972; £11,443; £5,743; £2,882) Stalls Low

Form RPR
0241 1 **U S Navy Flag (USA)**[34] 6488 2-9-0 111..........................(bt) SeamieHeffernan 11 117
(A P O'Brien, Ire) *pressed ldr tl rdn to ld and wnt rt over 1f out: styd on wl and a holding runner-up ins fnl f* **10/1**
0 2 *1/2* **Fleet Review (USA)**[38] 6326 2-9-0 102..........................(t) DonnachaO'Brien 12 116
(A P O'Brien, Ire) *pressed ldrs: effrt to chal over 1f out: ev ch and edgd rt 1f out: sustained chal u.p but a jst hld ins fnl f* **25/1**
3133 3 *2 1/4* **Cardsharp**[35] 6446 2-9-0 109.......................... JamesDoyle 3 109
(Mark Johnston) *chsd ldrs: ev ch 3f out: sn rdn and sustained chal tl no ex and outpcd by ldng pair ins fnl f: kpt on to go 3rd last strides* **14/1**
213 4 *hd* **Hey Jonesy (IRE)**[37] 6353 2-9-0 103.......................... KevinStott 5 108
(Kevin Ryan) *t.k.h: led: rdn ent fnl 2f: hdd over 1f out: drvn 1f out: outpcd by ldng pair ins fnl f: wknd towards fin and lost 3rd last strides* **8/1**
122 5 *1/2* **Beckford**[20] 6975 2-9-0 113.......................... PatSmullen 10 107
(Gordon Elliott, Ire) *hld up in tch in midfield: effrt 2f out: drvn over 1f out: kpt on u.p ins fnl f: nvr gng pce to rch ldng pair* **7/2**[1]
611 6 *hd* **Sioux Nation (USA)**[48] 5973 2-9-0 115.......................... RyanMoore 1 106
(A P O'Brien, Ire) *stdd s: t.k.h: hld up in tch in last pair: clsd and stuck bhd a wall of horses ent fnl 2f: swtchd lft wl over 1f out: hdwy u.p ins fnl f: kpt on but no threat to ldng pair* **11/2**[3]
00 7 *1/2* **Declarationofpeace (USA)**[48] 5973 2-9-0 107..........................(t) WayneLordan 4 105
(A P O'Brien, Ire) *hld up wl in tch in midfield: effrt to chse ldrs and swtchd lft over 1f out: drvn ent fnl f: keeping on same pce and hld whn nt clr run wl ins fnl f* **40/1**
3152 8 *nk* **Danzan (IRE)**[16] 7090 2-9-0 99.......................... DavidProbert 7 104
(Andrew Balding) *chsd ldrs: rdn jst over 2f out: unable qck over 1f out: kpt on same pce ins fnl f* **20/1**
2211 9 *1* **Unfortunately (IRE)**[41] 6249 2-9-0 117..........................(v) JimCrowley 6 101
(K R Burke) *s.i.s and pushed along in rr early: gd hdwy 3f out: rdn and ev ch 2f out: edgd lft u.p over 1f out: carried bk rt and unable qck over 1f out: wknd ins fnl f* **6/1**
4250 10 *nk* **Frozen Angel (IRE)**[35] 6446 2-9-0 108.......................... RichardKingscote 2 100
(Tom Dascombe) *chsd ldrs: rdn and pressing ldrs 2f out tl unable qck over 1f out: wknd ins fnl f* **40/1**
113 11 *1/2* **Rajasinghe (IRE)**[79] 4812 2-9-0 107.......................... StevieDonohoe 8 98
(Richard Spencer) *taken down early: sn dropped to last trio and rdn along: sme hdwy ins fnl f: nvr trbld ldrs* **10/1**



The Form Book Flat, Raceform Ltd, Newbury, RG14 5SJ

011 **12** *3 ¾* **Sands Of Mali (FR)**[35] 6446 2-9-0 116........................ PaulHanagan 9 87
(Richard Fahey) *taken down early: wl in tch in midfield: effrt ent fnl 2f: struggling whn intimidated and lost pl wl over 1f out: bhd after* **9/2**[2]

1m 12.44s (0.24) **Going Correction** +0.275s/f (Good) 12 Ran SP% **119.5**
Speed ratings (Par 109): **109,108,105,105,104 104,103,103,101,101 100,95**
CSF £242.42 CT £3506.62 TOTE £12.30: £3.20, £7.30, £4.30; EX 249.20 Trifecta £1661.30.
**Owner** Derrick Smith & Mrs John Magnier & Michael Tabor **Bred** Misty For Me Syndicate **Trained** Cashel, Co Tipperary

**FOCUS**
This year's Middle Park looked wide open and it threw up a messy finish, resulting in a slower time than the preceding Cheveley Park. The strength of the form is hard to assess.

## 7619 BETFRED CAMBRIDGESHIRE H'CAP (HERITAGE HANDICAP) 1m 1f
**3:35** (3:36) (Class 2) 3-Y-0+

**£99,600** (£29,824; £14,912; £7,456; £3,728; £1,872) **Stalls** Low

Form RPR
-506 **1** **Dolphin Vista (IRE)**[49] 5940 4-8-7 **96**........................ GeorgeWood(3) 29 107
(Martyn Meade) *racd stands' side: mid-div: hdwy 3f out: led gp 2f out: sn rdn: r.o strly to ld ins fnl 120yds: rdn out* **50/1**

5026 **2** *1 ½* **Sands Chorus**[32] 6563 5-8-6 **92** ow1........................ BarryMcHugh 22 100
(James Given) *led far side gp tl 2f out: sn rdn: kpt on gamely fnl f: regained 2nd towards fin* **100/1**

6060 **3** *nk* **Cote D'Azur**[71] 5130 4-8-7 **93**........................ PaulHanagan 13 100
(Les Eyre) *trckd ldr far side: led 2f out: sn rdn: no ex whn hdd ins fnl 120yds* **50/1**

P230 **4** *1* **Chelsea Lad (IRE)**[37] 6355 4-8-12 **98**........................ RichardKingscote 10 103
(Martyn Meade) *mid-div on far side: hdwy over 2f out: sn rdn: kpt on ins fnl f: wnt 4th towards fin* **16/1**

3241 **5** *hd* **Brorocco**[7] 7395 4-8-7 **93** 4ex........................(h) DavidProbert 33 98
(Andrew Balding) *racd stands' side: mid-div: hdwy 3f out: rdn and ev ch in gp 2f out: sn outpcd by wnr but kpt on fnl f* **17/2**[3]

1006 **6** *hd* **Examiner (IRE)**[49] 5914 6-8-5 **94**........................(t) AaronJones(3) 16 98
(Stuart Williams) *.racd far side: mid-div: hdwy over 2f out: sn rdn to chse ldrs: kpt on ins fnl f* **50/1**

3111 **7** *½* **Thundering Blue (USA)**[28] 6698 4-8-7 **93**........................ JimCrowley 20 96+
(David Menuisier) *towards rr of midfield on far side: rdn over 2f out: hdwy whn edgd lft over 1f out: kpt on ins fnl f: nt rch ldrs* **6/1**[1]

2-35 **8** *½* **Carry On Deryck**[27] 6746 5-9-7 **110**........................ DavidEgan(3) 6 112
(Saeed bin Suroor) *chsd ldrs on far side: rdn 2f out: kpt on same pce* **20/1**

6003 **9** *½* **You're Fired (IRE)**[14] 7149 6-8-12 **105**........................ PatrickO'Hanlon(7) 34 106+
(K R Burke) *racd stands' side: hld up towards rr: rdn over 2f out: no imp tl kpt on strly ins fnl f but no threat to ldrs* **25/1**

0020 **10** *½* **Gm Hopkins**[57] 5594 6-9-7 **107**........................ AdamKirby 19 107
(John Gosden) *hld up towards rr on far side: rdn and stdy prog fr 2f out: kpt on ent fnl f but nt gng pce to get involved* **25/1**

0410 **11** *½* **Eddystone Rock (IRE)**[7] 7395 5-9-1 **101**........................ PatDobbs 9 100+
(John Best) *hld up last pair on far side: rdn and stdy hdwy fr 2f out: styd on fnl f but no threat to ldrs* **28/1**

0246 **12** *½* **Red Tea**[34] 6483 4-8-5 **91**........................ RyanTate 2 89
(Peter Hiatt) *in tch on far side: rdn over 2f out: kpt on same pce fnl f* **66/1**

0000 **13** *½* **Bravery (IRE)**[35] 6449 4-8-11 **97**........................ ColinKeane 21 94
(David O'Meara) *hld up towards rr on far side: rdn and hdwy fr 2f out: styd on fnl f: nvr threatened ldrs* **33/1**

0014 **14** *hd* **Naval Warfare (IRE)**[10] 7275 3-8-7 **98**........................ OisinMurphy 3 96
(Andrew Balding) *trckd ldrs on far side: rdn over 2f out: wknd ins fnl f* **18/1**

0504 **15** *¾* **Battle Of Marathon (USA)**[14] 7149 5-8-4 **97**........................ JackOsborn(7) 23 92
(John Ryan) *sn racing stands' side: chsd ldr: led gp over 2f out tl rdn sn after: fdd ins fnl f* **40/1**

4102 **16** *¾* **Big Country (IRE)**[77] 4918 4-9-0 **100**........................ SilvestreDeSousa 17 94
(Michael Appleby) *racd far side: mid-div: rdn over 2f out: nvr any imp* **7/1**[2]

2160 **17** *nse* **Greenside**[57] 5594 6-8-12 **98**........................ HarryBentley 28 91
(Henry Candy) *racd stands' side: a mid-div* **14/1**

20-2 **18** *1 ¾* **Linguistic (IRE)**[182] 1500 4-9-3 **103**........................(p[1]) JamesDoyle 5 93
(John Gosden) *racd far side: hld up towards rr: hdwy into midfield 3f out: sn rdn: no further imp* **10/1**

5640 **19** *hd* **Captain Cat (IRE)**[22] 6873 8-8-4 **93**........................ HollieDoyle(3) 1 82
(Tony Carroll) *racd far side: nvr bttr than mid-div* **100/1**

1620 **20** *hd* **Sir Chauvelin**[56] 5638 5-8-10 **99**........................ PhilDennis(3) 11 88
(Jim Goldie) *racd far side: mid-div tl outpcd 3f out: n.d after* **80/1**

-512 **21** *3 ½* **Qassem (IRE)**[37] 6355 4-8-13 **99**........................ JosephineGordon 32 81
(Hugo Palmer) *prom stands' side: led gp 3f out tl rdn sn after: wknd over 1f out* **12/1**

4030 **22** *½* **Sinfonietta (FR)**[14] 7149 5-8-1 **90**........................ RosieJessop(3) 35 70
(David Menuisier) *trckd ldr on stands' side: rdn over 2f out: sn wknd* **40/1**

6210 **23** *½* **Weekend Offender (FR)**[35] 6449 4-8-12 **98**........................ KevinStott 30 77
(Kevin Ryan) *racd stands' side: rdn 3f out: nvr bttr than mid-div* **16/1**

-031 **24** *½* **Leader Writer (FR)**[22] 6873 5-8-10 **96** 4ex........................(p) FranBerry 8 74
(Henry Spiller) *racd far side: mid-div: rdn 3f out: nvr any imp: wknd over 1f out* **20/1**

0303 **25** *1 ½* **Kings Gift (IRE)**[36] 6404 3-8-5 **101** ow1........................ CallumRodriguez(5) 18 77
(Michael Dods) *racd far side: chsd ldr: rdn 3f out: wknd 2f out* **28/1**

3020 **26** *1 ¼* **Nicholas T**[35] 6449 5-8-6 **92**........................ JFEgan 7 65
(Jim Goldie) *in tch on far side: rdn over 2f out: wknd over 1f out: eased ins fnl f* **50/1**

/0-0 **27** *shd* **Tha'ir (IRE)**[60] 5500 7-9-0 **100**........................ RobertWinston 15 72
(Michael Appleby) *trckd ldrs on far side: rdn over 2f out: wknd over 1f out: eased ins fnl f* **33/1**

0611 **28** *4* **Novoman (IRE)**[34] 6474 3-8-3 **99**........................ GeorgiaCox(5) 26 64
(William Haggas) *racd stands' side: mid-div: outpcd 3f out: wknd over 1f out* **14/1**

015 **29** *4* **El Hayem (IRE)**[37] 6355 4-8-10 **96**........................ RyanMoore 4 52
(Sir Michael Stoute) *racd far side: a towards rr* **16/1**

1442 **30** *3* **Mulligatawny (IRE)**[32] 6563 4-8-4 **90**........................(p) JimmyQuinn 31 39
(Roger Fell) *led stands' side gp for over 4f: wknd 2f out* **40/1**

2144 **31** *1 ¼* **Master The World (IRE)**[35] 6444 6-9-8 **108**........................(p) JamieSpencer 25 55
(David Elsworth) *a towards rr on far side* **28/1**

0043 **32** *4 ½* **Central Square (IRE)**[41] 6243 5-9-5 **105**........................ AndreaAtzeni 27 42
(Roger Varian) *s.i.s: a towards rr on stands' side* **33/1**

5304 **33** *14* **Secret Art (IRE)**[15] 7129 7-8-6 **92**........................ MartinDwyer 24
(William Knight) *mid-div on stands' side tl rdn 3f out: sn in rr* **66/1**

2100 **34** *1* **Briardale (IRE)**[77] 4918 5-8-12 **98**........................ TedDurcan 14 4
(James Bethell) *chsd ldrs on far side tl outpcd over 3f out: sn bhd* **80/1**

1m 51.24s (-0.46) **Going Correction** +0.275s/f (Good)
**WFA** 3 from 4yo+ 5lb 34 Ran SP% **149.3**
Speed ratings (Par 109): **113,111,111,110,110 110,109,109,108,108 107,107,107,106,106 105,105,103,103,103 100,100,99,99,**
CSF £2485.98 CT £90344.98 TOTE £105.20: £13.10, £31.90, £21.10, £4.80; EX 18290.00 TRIFECTA Not Won..
**Owner** Y Nasib **Bred** Jim McDonald **Trained** Newmarket, Suffolk

**FOCUS**
A typically deep edition of the Cambridgeshire with the placed horses the key to the form. The majority tacked over to the far side and they went a proper pace, but the winner came up the stands' rail. The pace held up.

## 7620 BLANDFORD BLOODSTOCK MAIDEN FILLIES' STKS (PLUS 10 RACE) 7f
**4:10** (4:11) (Class 4) 2-Y-0 **£5,175** (£1,540; £769; £384) **Stalls** Low

Form RPR
4 **1** **Bye Bye Baby (IRE)**[21] 6954 2-9-0 0........................ RyanMoore 5 95+
(A P O'Brien, Ire) *mde all: rdn: qcknd and edgd lft over 1f out: r.o wl and in command ins fnl f* **11/10**[1]

2 **2** *2* **Altyn Orda (IRE)**[49] 5938 2-9-0 0........................ AndreaAtzeni 11 90+
(Roger Varian) *chsd wnr: clsd and upsides ent fnl 2f: rdn over 1f out: unable qck w wnr and swtchd rt 1f out: clr 2nd and kpt on same pce ins fnl f* **2/1**[2]

3 **3** *5* **Princess Harley (IRE)**[26] 6747 2-9-0 0........................ FranBerry 10 77
(Mick Quinn) *chsd ldrs: clsd to press ldng pair 2f out: rdn and unable qck over 1f out: wl hld 3rd and edgd rt u.p ins fnl f* **20/1**

00 **4** *4* **Faay (IRE)**[11] 7238 2-9-0 0........................ AntonioFresu 4 66
(Ed Dunlop) *flashing tail: chsd ldrs: effrt 2f out: 4th and outpcd over 1f out: wl btn ins fnl f* **50/1**

0 **5** *2 ¼* **Livvys Dream (IRE)**[14] 7153 2-9-0 0........................ HarryBentley 6 61+
(Charles Hills) *hld up in tch in midfield: shkn up 2f out: sn outpcd and wl btn 1f out* **40/1**

**6** *nk* **Umaimah (USA)** 2-9-0 0........................ JimCrowley 12 60+
(William Haggas) *rn green in midfield: pushed along ent fnl 2f: sn outpcd and wl btn over 1f out* **15/2**[3]

**7** *¾* **French Heroine** 2-9-0 0........................ JamesDoyle 3 58+
(William Haggas) *rn green pushed along off the pce in last quartet: nvr trbld ldrs* **16/1**

64 **8** *2 ¼* **Sigrid Nansen**[28] 6666 2-9-0 0........................ SilvestreDeSousa 7 52
(George Scott) *stdd s: hld up off the pce in last trio: shkn up over 2f out: sn btn and bhd* **33/1**

06 **9** *½* **Late Change**[7] 7399 2-9-0 0........................ JamieSpencer 8 51
(David Simcock) *stdd s: hld up off the pce in last trio: pushed along over 2f out: sn wl btn* **50/1**

**10** *8* **Glitterdust** 2-9-0 0........................ TedDurcan 9 30
(Sir Michael Stoute) *s.i.s: rn green and a bhd* **16/1**

00 **11** *20* **Miss Minding (IRE)**[9] 7334 2-9-0 0........................(h) OisinMurphy 1
(Ed Dunlop) *bolted 3f to post: stdd s: t.k.h: hld up in midfield: lost pl over 2f out: sn bhd: t.o* **100/1**

1m 27.21s (1.81) **Going Correction** +0.275s/f (Good) 11 Ran SP% **119.5**
Speed ratings (Par 94): **100,97,92,87,84 84,83,81,80,71 48**
CSF £3.20 TOTE £1.80: £1.10, £1.10, £4.00; EX 3.80 Trifecta £23.20.
**Owner** Michael Tabor & Derrick Smith & Mrs John Magnier **Bred** Remember When Syndicate **Trained** Cashel, Co Tipperary

**FOCUS**
They raced up the middle before edging stands' side. The winner had already shown a decent level of form, but this maiden lacked depth and they were strung out behind, with the first six barely changing positions.

## 7621 BRITISH EBF "JERSEY LILY" FILLIES' NURSERY H'CAP 7f
**4:45** (4:46) (Class 2) 2-Y-0

**£31,125** (£9,320; £4,660; £2,330; £1,165; £585) **Stalls** Low

Form RPR
462 **1** **Awesometank**[31] 6584 2-8-13 **80**........................ AndreaAtzeni 5 84
(William Haggas) *w ldr: rdn over 1f out: drvn to ld ins fnl f: jst hld on: all out: gamely* **7/1**[3]

2322 **2** *shd* **Clubbable**[16] 7087 2-8-9 **76**........................ PaulHanagan 11 80+
(Richard Fahey) *dwlt: hld up in tch in last quartet: hdwy and switching rt over 1f out: chsd ldrs jst ins fnl f: r.o strly fnl 100yds: jst failed* **10/3**[1]

3641 **3** *nk* **Dark Liberty (IRE)**[11] 7243 2-8-10 **77**........................ HarryBentley 6 80
(Simon Crisford) *t.k.h: hld up wl in tch in midfield: effrt over 1f out: carried rt and hdwy 1f out: ev ch and drvn ins fnl f: kpt on: unable qck nr fin* **7/1**[3]

3634 **4** *1 ¼* **Ziarah (IRE)**[18] 7021 2-8-12 **79**........................ OisinMurphy 10 79
(James Tate) *led: rdn over 1f out: hdd and drvn jst ins fnl f: no ex 100yds out: wknd towards fin* **12/1**

325 **5** *1* **Goodnight Girl (IRE)**[11] 7226 2-8-7 **77**........................ GeorgeWood(3) 13 74
(Jonathan Portman) *t.k.h: chsd ldrs: clsd to press ldrs 3f out: rdn and ev ch over 1f out tl ti no ex 100yds out: wknd wl ins fnl f* **16/1**

211 **6** *shd* **Exhort**[29] 6659 2-9-2 **83**........................ RyanMoore 4 80
(Richard Fahey) *hld up in tch in last quartet: swtchd rt over 4f out: rdn and hdwy into midfield over 2f out: no imp u.p over 1f out: kpt on same pce ins fnl f* **6/1**[2]

430 **7** *2 ¾* **Falcon's Vision**[52] 5795 2-8-2 **72**........................ DavidEgan(3) 14 62
(David Simcock) *tok t.k.h: chsd ldrs: effrt over 1f out: drifting rt 1f out: kpt on same pce ins fnl f* **16/1**

414 **8** *½* **Lady Alavesa**[11] 7239 2-7-9 **69** oh3 ow2........................ MillyNaseb(7) 7 58
(Gay Kelleway) *dwlt: t.k.h: hld up in tch in rr: rdn and hdwy over 1f out: edgd rt and nt clrest of runs 1f out: wknd wl ins fnl f* **33/1**

202 **9** *1 ¼* **Last Enchantment (IRE)**[22] 6868 2-8-3 **73**........................ HollieDoyle(3) 9 58
(Eve Johnson Houghton) *in tch in midfield: rdn over 2f out: lost pl and struggling in rr on downhill run over 1f out: rallied ins fnl f: no threat to ldrs* **12/1**

214 **10** *½* **Time Change**[36] 6396 2-9-1 **82**........................ PatDobbs 2 66
(Ralph Beckett) *hld up in tch in last quartet: effrt and swtchd rt over 1f out: kpt on but no imp ins fnl f* **11/1**

5031 **11** *7* **Bee Ina Bonnet**[10] 7265 2-8-8 **75**........................ MartinDwyer 1 41
(Tim Easterby) *chsd ldrs: rdn and losing pl whn hmpd over 1f out: wknd fnl f* **25/1**

0350 **12** *1 ¾* **Get Even**[48] 5978 2-9-7 **88**........................ JFEgan 12 49
(Jo Hughes) *t.k.h: chsd ldrs tl 3f out: lost pl over 1f out: wknd fnl f* **50/1**

0524 **13** 3/4 **Cosmopolitan Queen**[31] 6575 2-8-10 **77**............(p[1]) SilvestreDeSousa 3 39
(David Elsworth) *t.k.h: wl in tch in midfield: losing pl and unbalanced whn hmpd over 1f out: wknd fnl f* **8/1**

1m 27.72s (2.32) **Going Correction** +0.275s/f (Good) **13** Ran SP% **117.7**
Speed ratings (Par 98): **97,96,96,95,93 93,90,90,88,88 80,78,77**
CSF £29.48 CT £172.85 TOTE £6.70: £2.50, £1.70, £2.80; EX 38.00 Trifecta £317.40.
**Owner** Lee Yuk Lun Alan **Bred** Eminent Kind Ltd **Trained** Newmarket, Suffolk

**FOCUS**
This was a good-quality fillies' nursery and there was a compressed finish.

## 7622 ILIFFE MEDIA AND VELVET MAGAZINE H'CAP 7f
**5:20** (5:21) (Class 2) (0-105,100) 3-Y-O+ **£12,938** (£3,850; £1,924; £962) **Stalls** Low

Form RPR

0126 **1** **Makzeem**[63] 5393 4-9-9 **97**............ RyanMoore 17 111
(Roger Charlton) *racd stands side: hld up in rr: hdwy over 2f out: trcking ldrs over 1f out: rdn to ld 1f out r.o strly: readily: 1st of 11 in gp* **5/1**[1]

4031 **2** 3 1/4 **Ice Lord (IRE)**[21] 6922 5-9-4 **92**............ FranBerry 18 97
(Chris Wall) *racd stands side: hld up in rr: clsd and swtchd lft over 1f out: hdwy u.p ent fnl f: styd on wl to go 2nd nr fin: no ch w wnr: 2nd of 11 in gp* **10/1**

0100 **3** 1/2 **Bertiewhittle**[21] 6918 9-8-11 **92**............ GabrieleMalune[(7)] 10 96
(David Barron) *racd stands side: swtchd lft after s: hld up towards rr: hdwy and switching rt over 1f out: r.o strly ins fnl f: snatched 3rd on post: no ch w wnr: 3rd of 11 in gp* **25/1**

054 **4** nse **Highland Colori (IRE)**[17] 7044 9-8-11 **85**............(v) DavidProbert 4 89
(Andrew Balding) *racd far side: chsd ldrs: effrt and ev ch over 1f out: kpt on same pce ins fnl f: 1st of 7 in gp* **16/1**

61 **5** nk **Baron Bolt**[33] 6506 4-8-12 **89**............(p) DavidEgan[(3)] 14 92
(Paul Cole) *racd stands side: chsd ldrs and in tch in midfield overall: effrt over 2f out: ev ch over 1f out: kpt on same pce ins fnl f: 4th of 11 in gp* **14/1**

3350 **6** 1/2 **That Is The Spirit**[28] 6685 6-9-8 **96**............ ColinKeane 1 98
(David O'Meara) *racd far side: overall ldr: rdn 2f out: hdd 1f out: kpt on same pce after: lost 4 pls towards fin: 2nd of 7 in gp* **25/1**

0015 **7** nse **Hyde Park**[17] 7053 3-9-7 **98**............(t) AndreaAtzeni 3 99
(John Gosden) *racd far side: in tch in midfield overall: effrt 2f out: drvn and ev ch over 1f out: kpt on same pce ins fnl f: 3rd of 7 in gp* **7/1**[2]

4423 **8** 1/2 **Qeyaadah (IRE)**[18] 7025 4-8-11 **85**............ RyanTate 20 85
(Michael Appleby) *racd stands side: chsd ldrs overall: effrt 2f out: ev ch over 1f out: unable qck 1f out: kpt on same pce ins fnl f: 5th of 11 in gp* **14/1**

5150 **9** 1 1/4 **Robero**[42] 6206 5-9-7 **95**............ SilvestreDeSousa 6 92
(Michael Easterby) *racd far side: t.k.h: hld up in rr: swtchd lft and hdwy over 2f out: drvn and ev ch over 1f out: no ex ins fnl f: wkng whn short of room wl ins fnl f: 4th of 7 in gp* **12/1**

0321 **10** nk **Ower Fly**[14] 7156 4-9-0 **91**............(b) HollieDoyle[(3)] 7 87
(Richard Hannon) *racd far side: in tch in midfield overall: swtchd lft and effrt over 2f out: drvn to press ldrs over 1f out: no ex ins fnl f: wknd towards fin: 5th of 7 in gp* **12/1**

1563 **11** 3/4 **Theodorico (IRE)**[9] 7340 4-9-1 **89**............ JimCrowley 2 83
(David Loughnane) *racd far side: chsd ldr and prom overall: rdn ent fnl 2f: ev ch over 1f out tl ins fnl f: wknd fnl 75yds: 6th of 7 in gp* **20/1**

04P **12** 1 **Mount Tahan (IRE)**[35] 6419 5-9-5 **93**............ KevinStott 15 84
(Kevin Ryan) *taken down early: racd stands side: awkward leaving stalls: hld up in midfield overall: no imp u.p over 1f out: wl hld and one pced fnl f: 6th of 11 in gp* **12/1**

0016 **13** nk **Accession (IRE)**[23] 6856 8-9-12 **100**............ MartinLane 12 90
(Charlie Fellowes) *racd stands side: gp ldr and chsd ldrs overall: rdn and ev ch 2f out tl unable qck jst over 1f out: wknd ins fnl f: 7th of 11 in gp* **25/1**

0300 **14** 1 1/2 **Suzi's Connoisseur**[28] 6685 6-8-13 **87**............(vt) OisinMurphy 11 73
(Stuart Williams) *racd stands side: hld up in midfield overall: no imp over 1f out: wl hld fnl f: 8th of 11 in gp* **16/1**

3461 **15** hd **Scofflaw**[16] 7094 3-8-8 **85**............ PaulHanagan 16 70
(Richard Fahey) *racd stands side: hld up in midfield: rdn ent fnl f: sn struggling and lost pl over 1f out: wknd fnl f: 9th of 11 in gp* **8/1**[3]

5-04 **16** 5 **Fighting Temeraire (IRE)**[34] 6484 4-9-3 **91**............ RobertWinston 9 63
(Dean Ivory) *racd stands side: stdd s: swtchd lft after 1f: midfield: rdn over 2f out: sn struggling: bhd and hung rt over 1f out: 10th of 11 in gp* **20/1**

003 **17** 1 **Firmdecisions (IRE)**[39] 6289 7-9-0 **88**............ JamieSpencer 13 58
(Dean Ivory) *racd stands side: chsd gp ldr and prom overall tl 3f out: rdn and lost pl over 2f out: bhd over 1f out: 11th of 11 in gp* **25/1**

-160 **18** 7 **Ifwecan**[59] 5530 6-9-7 **95**............ JamesDoyle 5 46
(Martin Smith) *racd far side: hld up towards rr of gp: effrt ent fnl 2f: no imp over 1f out: btn and eased ins fnl f: 7th of 7 in gp* **25/1**

1m 25.7s (0.30) **Going Correction** +0.275s/f (Good)
**WFA** 3 from 4yo+ 3lb **18** Ran SP% **126.3**
Speed ratings (Par 109): **109,105,104,104,104 103,103,103,101,101 100,99,99,97,97 91,90,82**
CSF £48.38 CT £1147.20 TOTE £5.20: £1.70, £2.90, £5.60, £3.90; EX 50.90 Trifecta £1434.80.
**Owner** D J Deer **Bred** D J And Mrs Deer **Trained** Beckhampton, Wilts

**FOCUS**
The field split into two groups early on and the pace looked hot, with the first three emerging from the last three places in the stands' side bunch. The horses were spread all over the track in the closing stages and there wasn't much in it behind the runaway winner, who built on previous handicap form.
T/Jkpt: Not Won. T/Plt: £1,131.00 to a £1 stake. Pool: £184,806.25 - 119.28 winning units
T/Qpdt: £696.30 to a £1 stake. Pool: £11,875.91 - 12.62 winning units
**Steve Payne & Tim Mitchell**

# 6755 RIPON (R-H)
## Saturday, September 30

**OFFICIAL GOING: Soft (6.5)**
Wind: moderate half behind Weather: Fine

## 7623 THEAKSTON LEGENDARY ALES EBF NOVICE STKS 6f
**2:00** (2:01) (Class 5) 2-Y-O **£3,881** (£1,155; £577; £288) **Stalls** High

Form RPR

32 **1** **Showmethedough**[41] 6231 2-8-13 0............ AdamMcNamara[(3)] 11 83
(Richard Fahey) *trckd ldr: rdn over 1f out: led 110yds out: styd on wl* **10/3**[2]

41 **2** 2 1/4 **Rastacap**[22] 6897 2-9-4 0............ JoeFanning 8 78
(Mark Johnston) *led: pushed along over 1f out: rdn ins fnl f: hdd 110yds out: no ex* **7/2**[3]

51 **3** 2 1/2 **Elation (IRE)**[54] 5702 2-9-4 0............ LukeMorris 9 71
(Roger Varian) *midfield towards outer: rdn over 2f out: hdwy into 3rd over 1f out: edgd lft ins fnl f: kpt on same pce* **2/1**[1]

4 **4** 6 **Gleaming Sun**[11] 7242 2-8-9 0............ HarrisonShaw[(7)] 5 51
(Michael Easterby) *prom: rdn 2f out: wknd fnl f* **40/1**

3634 **5** 1 1/4 **Bustam (IRE)**[61] 5465 2-9-2 85............(h) MartinHarley 12 47
(John Quinn) *in tch: rdn over 2f out: wknd fnl f* **4/1**

**6** shd **Tashaaboh (IRE)** 2-9-2 0............ WilliamCarson 2 47
(Owen Burrows) *in tch: rdn along 2f out: wknd fnl f* **9/1**

**7** 6 **Whinmoor** 2-8-13 0............ RachelRichardson[(3)] 1 29
(Nigel Tinkler) *slowly away and in rr: minor hdwy over 1f out: nvr threatened* **50/1**

**8** 8 **The Hoppings** 2-8-11 0............ SamJames 6
(John Davies) *hld up: rdn over 2f out: wknd over 1f out* **100/1**

**9** 1 3/4 **Eddiethebung (IRE)** 2-8-9 0............ FayeMcManoman[(7)] 10
(Nigel Tinkler) *dwlt: a rr* **50/1**

1m 16.77s (3.77) **Going Correction** +0.70s/f (Yiel) **9** Ran SP% **116.0**
Speed ratings (Par 95): **102,99,95,87,86 85,77,67,64**
CSF £15.36 TOTE £3.90: £1.80, £1.10, £1.10; EX 15.10 Trifecta £39.10.
**Owner** R A Fahey **Bred** J P Coggan **Trained** Musley Bank, N Yorks

**FOCUS**
Rail on bend from back straight to home straight dolled out 3yds, adding 6yds to races 2, 5 & 7. The official going description was soft. A decent novice and solid form, with the winner improving.

## 7624 MICHAEL RABY MEMORIAL NURSERY H'CAP 1m
**2:35** (2:35) (Class 4) (0-85,79) 2-Y-O **£5,175** (£1,540; £769; £384) **Stalls** Low

Form RPR

2126 **1** **Indomeneo**[22] 6900 2-9-4 **79**............ AdamMcNamara[(3)] 1 83
(Richard Fahey) *trckd ldrs: rdn to ld over 1f out: sn strly pressed: kpt on wl* **7/2**[2]

5252 **2** nk **Poet's Dawn**[7] 7384 2-9-1 **76**............ RachelRichardson[(3)] 2 79
(Tim Easterby) *dwlt: hld up in tch: racd keenly: hdwy on inner over 2f out: rdn along to chal strly over 1f out: kpt on: hld towards fin* **7/2**[2]

424 **3** 10 **Knight In Armour (IRE)**[70] 5136 2-8-12 **70**............ JoeFanning 3 50
(Mark Johnston) *led: rdn over 2f out: hdd over 1f out: wknd fnl f* **11/4**[1]

11 **4** 2 1/2 **Trumps Up**[29] 6658 2-9-5 **77**............ LiamKeniry 8 51
(Mick Channon) *prom: rdn over 2f out: wknd over 1f out* **5/1**[3]

0362 **5** 1 **Panophobia**[17] 7057 2-8-10 **68**............ PatrickMathers 4 40
(Richard Fahey) *trckd ldrs: rdn over 2f out: wknd over 1f out* **11/1**

062 **6** nse **Normandy Blue**[35] 6410 2-8-9 **67**............ JamesSullivan 5 39
(Richard Fahey) *hld up: rdn along over 3f out: sn struggling* **10/1**

3660 **7** shd **Jack Regan**[22] 6867 2-9-1 **73**............(b[1]) MartinHarley 7 45
(Charles Hills) *hld up: racd quite keenly: rdn over 2f out: sn btn* **10/1**

1m 46.52s (5.12) **Going Correction** +0.70s/f (Yiel) **7** Ran SP% **114.3**
Speed ratings (Par 97): **102,101,91,89,88 88,88**
CSF £16.14 CT £37.38 TOTE £7.30: £2.50, £1.60; EX 19.70 Trifecta £80.70.
**Owner** Middleham Park Racing LX **Bred** Hungerford Park Stud **Trained** Musley Bank, N Yorks

**FOCUS**
Race distance increased by 6yds. A fair nursery, albeit not the strongest for the grade, and the first two pulled well clear of the field. They may have just handled conditions better than the rest.

## 7625 NOEL HETHERTON MEMORIAL H'CAP 5f
**3:10** (3:11) (Class 4) (0-85,87) 3-Y-O+ **£6,301** (£1,886; £943; £472; £235) **Stalls** High

Form RPR

1101 **1** **Show Palace**[14] 7137 4-9-6 **84**............ JoeFanning 10 92+
(Jennie Candlish) *trckd ldrs: racd keenly: short of room and shuffled bk a bit 2f out: swtchd rt and in clr over 1f out: rdn and sn hdwy: kpt on wl: led towards fin* **5/2**[1]

0324 **2** 1/2 **Ballesteros**[14] 7137 8-8-10 **74**............ PatrickMathers 3 80
(Richard Fahey) *prom: rdn to ld 2f out: drvn ins fnl f: one pce and hdd towards fin* **11/1**

066 **3** 3/4 **Venturous (IRE)**[17] 7055 4-9-4 **82**............ MartinHarley 6 85
(David Barron) *dwlt: hld up: pushed along and hdwy 2f out: rdn to chse ldr appr fnl f: kpt on* **4/1**[2]

3440 **4** 2 1/2 **Lathom**[49] 5929 4-9-2 **80**............ WilliamCarson 4 74+
(Julie Camacho) *hld up: stl in rr whn short of room over 1f out: kpt on fnl f: nrst fin* **7/1**[3]

1106 **5** 1 **Henley**[56] 5647 5-9-1 **82**............ AdamMcNamara[(3)] 5 73
(Tracy Waggott) *midfield: rdn 2f out: one pce and nvr threatened* **20/1**

5000 **6** 3/4 **Move In Time**[14] 7144 9-9-5 **86**............(v) JoshDoyle[(3)] 9 74
(David O'Meara) *prom: rdn over 2f out: wknd fnl f* **7/1**[3]

1442 **7** 1/2 **Royal Brave (IRE)**[31] 6593 6-9-9 **87**............ DuranFentiman 1 73
(Rebecca Bastiman) *hld up towards outer: rdn 1/2-way: nvr threatened* **16/1**

4444 **8** nk **Foxtrot Knight**[17] 7055 5-8-7 **71**............ JamesSullivan 7 56
(Ruth Carr) *midfield: rdn and outpcd 1/2-way: no threat after* **8/1**

2310 **9** 1 1/4 **Midnight Malibu (IRE)**[21] 6927 4-9-4 **85**............ RachelRichardson[(3)] 8 66
(Tim Easterby) *led: rdn whn hdd 2f out: wknd fnl f* **12/1**

6043 **10** 22 **Yorkshiredebut (IRE)**[21] 6945 3-8-11 **76**............ LukeMorris 2
(Paul Midgley) *chsd ldrs: rdn 1/2-way: wknd over 1f out and eased* **16/1**

1m 2.62s (2.62) **Going Correction** +0.70s/f (Yiel)
**WFA** 3 from 4yo+ 1lb **10** Ran SP% **117.2**
Speed ratings (Par 105): **107,106,105,101,99 98,97,96,94,59**
CSF £31.80 CT £111.27 TOTE £3.20: £1.20, £3.00, £1.90; EX 33.70 Trifecta £181.20.
**Owner** P and Mrs G A Clarke **Bred** M C Humby **Trained** Basford Green, Staffs

**FOCUS**
A competitive-looking sprint and they went a sensible pace.

## 7626 RIPON CATHEDRAL CITY OF THE DALES H'CAP 6f
**3:45** (3:47) (Class 2) (0-105,99) 3-Y-O+
**£15,562** (£4,660; £2,330; £1,165; £582; £292) **Stalls** High

Form RPR

1015 **1** **Flying Pursuit**[42] 6206 4-9-3 **96**............(p) RachelRichardson[(3)] 7 107
(Tim Easterby) *racd stands' side: mde all: rdn clr in gp over 1f out: edgd rt ins fnl f: kpt on* **15/2**

0000 **2** 1/2 **Nameitwhatyoulike**[42] 6206 8-9-4 **94**............ JoeFanning 3 103
(Bryan Smart) *led far side: hdd in gp over 2f out: sn rdn: rallied to ld gp again over 1f out: kpt on wl: 1st of 5 in gp* **16/1**

1401 **3** 2 **Golden Apollo**[49] 5916 3-9-4 **99**............ JoshDoyle[(3)] 1 102
(Tim Easterby) *chsd ldr far side: rdn over 2f out: kpt on same pce: 2nd of 5 in gp* **13/2**[3]

6600 **4** *nse* **Right Touch**[15] 7108 7-9-0 **90**........................................ PatrickMathers 4 93
(Richard Fahey) *chsd ldr far side: rdn over 2f out: kpt on same pce: 3rd of 5 in gp* **20/1**

1335 **5** *1 ¾* **Magical Effect (IRE)**[22] 6894 5-8-11 **87**........................ JamesSullivan 2 84
(Ruth Carr) *hld up far side: rdn 2f out: plugged on fnl f: nvr threatened: 4th of 5 in gp* **11/2**[1]

0423 **6** *¾* **Red Pike (IRE)**[29] 6662 6-9-0 **93**.......................... AdamMcNamara(3) 14 88
(Bryan Smart) *trckd ldr stands' side: rdn and outpcd by wnr 2f out: plugged on: 2nd of 8 in gp* **6/1**[2]

2000 **7** *1 ¼* **Big Time (IRE)**[63] 5393 6-9-6 **96**..................................(v) MartinHarley 11 87
(Kevin Ryan) *hld up stands' side: hdwy over 2f out: rdn to go 3rd in gp over 1f out: swtchd rt appr fnl f: plugged on* **20/1**

0250 **8** *4* **Bossipop**[14] 7144 4-8-12 **88**..................................................(b) NeilFarley 5 66
(Tim Easterby) *dwlt: sn in tch far side: hdwy to ld gp over 2f out: rdn and hdd in gp over 1f out: wknd: last of 5 in gp* **22/1**

5002 **9** *1* **Classic Seniority**[29] 6662 5-9-3 **93**.........................(p) WilliamCarson 12 68
(Marjorie Fife) *hld up stands' side: nvr threatened: 4th of 8 in gp* **18/1**

1200 **10** *2 ¼* **Naggers (IRE)**[71] 5094 6-9-7 **97**....................................... LukeMorris 13 65
(Paul Midgley) *midfield stands' side: rdn over 2f out: wknd over 1f out: 5th of 8 in gp* **6/1**[2]

5600 **11** *½* **Brian The Snail (IRE)**[56] 5640 3-9-6 **98**............................ ShaneGray 8 64
(Richard Fahey) *prom: rdn over 2f out: wknd over 1f out: 6th of 8 in gp* **16/1**

0021 **12** *¾* **Explain**[15] 7108 5-9-1 **91**.......................................................(b) SamJames 6 55
(Ruth Carr) *midfield stands' side: rdn over 2f out: wknd over 1f out: 7th of 8 in gp* **10/1**

5003 **13** *3 ½* **Mobsta (IRE)**[20] 6966 5-9-8 **98**........................................... LiamKeniry 10 50
(Mick Channon) *hld up stands' side: rdn over 2f out: wknd over 1f out* **12/1**

0R40 **R** **Snap Shots (IRE)**[20] 6971 5-9-2 **92**..........................(p) DuranFentiman 9
(Tony Coyle) *ref to r* **33/1**

1m 15.8s (2.80) **Going Correction** +0.70s/f (Yiel)
**WFA** 3 from 4yo+ 2lb **14** Ran SP% **119.7**
Speed ratings (Par 109): **109,108,105,105,103 102,100,95,93,90 90,89,84,**
CSF £114.05 CT £850.39 TOTE £8.90: £2.80, £7.00, £1.80; EX 187.00 Trifecta £759.90 Partly Won..
**Owner** Ontoawinner, M Hulin & Partner **Bred** Crossfields Bloodstock Ltd **Trained** Great Habton, N Yorks

**FOCUS**
A wide-open sprint handicap, although again not the strongest for the grade. They split into two groups, the winner coming up the stands' side and the next five home racing far side. The winner has been rated in line with his better form.

## 7627 CONSTANT SECURITY H'CAP 1m 4f 10y
**4:20** (4:20) (Class 4) (0-85,85) 3-Y-O+ **£6,301** (£1,886; £943; £472; £235) **Stalls** Centre

Form RPR

5123 **1** **Michael's Mount**[22] 6881 4-9-8 **81**.................................(b) LukeMorris 2 89+
(Ed Dunlop) *hld up: hdwy 3f out to trck ldrs gng wl 2f out: rdn to ld 1f out: edgd lft ins fnl f: drvn out* **7/2**[2]

116 **2** *½* **Indy (IRE)**[36] 6383 6-9-10 **83**............................................. MartinHarley 9 90
(John Quinn) *trckd ldrs: rdn over 2f out: chal over 1f out: kpt on* **5/1**[3]

0030 **3** *1 ¾* **Jacbequick**[20] 6965 6-9-6 **82**.......................................(p) JoshDoyle(3) 6 86
(David O'Meara) *led: rdn over 2f out: hdd 1f out: no ex* **14/1**

0-44 **4** *4* **Henry Smith**[21] 6944 5-9-6 **79**...................................(be) DuranFentiman 1 77
(John Weymes) *trckd ldrs: rdn over 2f out: wknd fnl f* **20/1**

4100 **5** *3 ¾* **Pumblechook**[21] 6929 4-9-12 **85**......................................... JoeFanning 3 77
(Mark Johnston) *hld up: rdn along 3f out: nvr threatened* **6/1**

5502 **6** *2 ¾* **Al Zaman (IRE)**[35] 6423 3-9-2 **82**................................(tp) WilliamCarson 5 70
(Simon Crisford) *hld up: rdn along 3f out: sn struggling* **5/2**[1]

2613 **7** *1 ¼* **Stormin Tom (IRE)**[29] 6661 5-8-11 **73**.................. RachelRichardson(3) 4 58
(Tim Easterby) *in tch: rdn 3f out: wknd over 1f out* **7/1**

6630 **8** *2 ½* **Albert's Back**[119] 3335 3-8-7 **73**.................................... JamesSullivan 10 55
(Michael Easterby) *in tch on outer: rdn over 3f out: wknd over 2f out* **12/1**

2m 50.09s (13.39) **Going Correction** +0.70s/f (Yiel)
**WFA** 3 from 4yo+ 7lb **8** Ran SP% **113.4**
Speed ratings (Par 105): **83,82,81,78,76 74,73,72**
CSF £20.96 CT £213.76 TOTE £3.90: £1.20, £2.30, £8.00; EX 24.10 Trifecta £201.00.
**Owner** Miltil Consortium **Bred** Southill Stud **Trained** Newmarket, Suffolk

**FOCUS**
Race distance increased by 6yds. A decent middle-distance handicap, but the pace was ordinary. The race has been rated around the third.

## 7628 LLOYD LAND ROVER RIPON APPRENTICE H'CAP 6f
**4:55** (4:55) (Class 5) (0-70,77) 3-Y-O+ **£3,881** (£1,155; £577; £288) **Stalls** High

Form RPR

0346 **1** **Point Of Woods**[3] 7525 4-9-0 **63**...........................(p) SophieRalston(3) 11 71
(Tina Jackson) *prom: led over 2f out: rdn and edgd rt over 1f out: idled ins fnl f and jnd fnl 25 yds: edgd rt again: did jst enough* **8/1**

0340 **2** *shd* **B Fifty Two (IRE)**[1] 7572 8-9-7 **67**.................................... HarrisonShaw 3 74
(Marjorie Fife) *prom: rdn over 2f out: kpt on: upsides fnl 25yds: jst failed* **7/1**

2311 **3** *2* **Penny Pot Lane**[9] 7332 4-10-0 **77**............................ JonathanFisher(3) 6 78
(Richard Whitaker) *prom: rdn over 2f out: no ex fnl 75yds* **9/2**[1]

5023 **4** *hd* **Royal Connoisseur (IRE)**[22] 6894 6-9-5 **71**....... SebastianWoods(6) 10 71+
(Richard Fahey) *hld up: rdn over 2f out: kpt on fnl f: nrst fin* **9/2**[1]

6263 **5** *hd* **Cliff (IRE)**[9] 7332 7-8-13 **67**.................................... FayeMcManoman(8) 4 66
(Nigel Tinkler) *in tch: rdn over 2f out: kpt on same pce* **5/1**[2]

5240 **6** *2 ¼* **Racing Angel (IRE)**[3] 7522 5-9-3 **63**........................... BenSanderson 12 55
(Adrian Nicholls) *chsd ldrs: rdn and ev ch 2f out: wknd fnl 110yds* **14/1**

2604 **7** *2 ½* **Burtonwood**[28] 6670 5-9-3 **63**..............................(p) SeamusCronin 13 47
(Julie Camacho) *hld up in tch: rdn along over 2f out: nvr threatened* **16/1**

2000 **8** *3* **Magical Molly Joe**[42] 6181 3-8-9 **57**............................. StephenCummins 7 32
(David Barron) *swtchd lft s and hld up in rr: rdn 2f out: nvr threatened* **25/1**

1344 **9** *1 ¼* **Danish Duke (IRE)**[11] 7245 6-9-5 **68**...............(b[1]) RobertDodsworth(3) 5 39
(Ruth Carr) *trckd ldrs: rdn over 2f out: wknd over 1f out* **28/1**

6211 **10** *3 ¼* **Dodgy Bob**[25] 6785 4-9-8 **68**............................................(v) AledBeech 1 28
(Michael Mullineaux) *in tch on outer: rdn over 2f out: wknd over 1f out* **12/1**

0053 **11** *1* **Honeysuckle Lil (IRE)**[11] 7245 5-8-12 **66**.............(p) HannahWorrall(8) 9 23
(Tim Easterby) *led: rdn whn hdd over 2f out: sn wknd* **6/1**[3]

5560 **12** *3 ¼* **Maldonado (FR)**[49] 5948 3-8-13 **69**.............................. RyanTimby(8) 2 16
(Michael Easterby) *hld up: rdn along 3f out: sn wknd* **40/1**

1m 18.55s (5.55) **Going Correction** +0.70s/f (Yiel)
**WFA** 3 from 4yo+ 2lb **12** Ran SP% **120.9**
Speed ratings (Par 103): **91,90,88,87,87 84,81,77,75,71 70,65**
CSF £63.22 CT £292.87 TOTE £14.40: £4.40, £2.50, £1.50; EX 107.50 Trifecta £929.70.
**Owner** H L Thompson **Bred** Bearstone Stud Ltd **Trained** Liverton, Cleveland

**FOCUS**
A fair handicap with the winner stepping up on this year's form.

## 7629 THANK YOU TO OUR GROUNDSTAFF MAIDEN STKS 1m 4f 10y
**5:30** (5:30) (Class 5) 3-Y-O+ **£3,881** (£1,155; £577; £288) **Stalls** Centre

Form RPR

**1** **Mixboy (FR)**[161] 7-9-12 0.......................................................... JoeFanning 9 78+
(Keith Dalgleish) *mde all: pushed along over 2f out: rdn over 1f out: kpt on pushed out fnl f* **13/8**[1]

60 **2** *3 ½* **Stylish Dancer**[108] 3720 3-9-0 0......................................... LukeMorris 1 68+
(Luca Cumani) *trckd ldrs: rdn 3f out: wnt 2nd over 1f out: styd on but a hld: eased nr fin* **2/1**[2]

**3** *6* **Lough Salt (IRE)**[158] 6-9-12 0............................................. ShaneGray 3 61
(Richard Guest) *s.i.s: hld up: rdn along over 3f out: plugged on to go modest 3rd ins fnl f* **9/1**

6404 **4** *2* **Silver Gleam (IRE)**[11] 7248 3-9-0 46........................... JamesSullivan 2 53
(Chris Fairhurst) *hld up: rdn along over 3f out: plugged on: nvr threatened* **14/1**

62 **5** *5* **Lazarus (IRE)**[26] 6765 3-9-5 0.........................................(t) MartinHarley 4 50
(Amy Murphy) *prom: rdn over 2f out: wknd over 1f out* **3/1**[3]

**6** *16* **Dollar And A Dream (IRE)**[29] 8-9-5 0............................. AledBeech(7) 8 23
(Michael Mullineaux) *in tch: rdn over 3f out: sn wknd* **40/1**

6 **7** *7* **Newgate Duchess**[46] 6044 3-9-0 0.................................... DuranFentiman 6 8
(Tony Coyle) *midfield: rdn over 3f out: sn wknd* **50/1**

0- **8** *33* **Le Pinchy (GER)**[351] 7318 3-9-5 0...................................... LiamKeniry 5
(Tom Dascombe) *s.i.s: hld up in rr: rdn along over 5f out: wknd and t.o fnl 3f* **28/1**

2m 47.8s (11.10) **Going Correction** +0.70s/f (Yiel)
**WFA** 3 from 6yo+ 7lb **8** Ran SP% **120.9**
Speed ratings (Par 103): **91,88,84,83,80 69,64,42**
CSF £5.47 TOTE £2.40: £1.10, £1.10, £2.00; EX 6.70 Trifecta £35.60.
**Owner** Paul & Clare Rooney **Bred** E A R L Jourdier **Trained** Carluke, S Lanarks

**FOCUS**
Race distance increased by 6yds. Ordinary maiden form in a race lacking depth.
T/Plt: £94.20 to a £1 stake. Pool: £62,594.15 - 484.76 winning units T/Qpdt: £26.50 to a £1 stake. Pool: £4,652.51 - 129.62 winning units **Andrew Sheret**

7630 - 7632a (Foreign Racing) - See Raceform Interactive

# 4648 BELMONT PARK (L-H)
Saturday, September 30

**OFFICIAL GOING: Dirt: standard; turf: firm**

## 7633a JOE HIRSCH TURF CLASSIC STKS (GRADE 1) (3YO+) (TURF) 1m 4f
**10:45** 3-Y-O+
**£243,902** (£81,300; £40,650; £20,325; £12,195; £1,355)

RPR

**1** **Beach Patrol (USA)**[48] 5977 4-9-0 0..............................(b) JoelRosario 5 117
(Chad C Brown, U.S.A) *cl up in chsng gp: wnt 2nd after 2f: led over 2f out: rdn clr fnl f: readily* **5/1**

**2** *5* **Fanciful Angel (IRE)**[48] 5977 5-9-0 0.................................. IradOrtizJr 9 109+
(Chad C Brown, U.S.A) *t.k.h: hld up in tch: effrt and rdn over 1f out: kpt on fnl f to take 2nd cl home: no ch w wnr* **84/10**

**3** *nse* **Oscar Performance (USA)**[49] 5953 3-8-9 0...................... JoseLOrtiz 3 112
(Brian A Lynch, Canada) *chsd clr ldr 2f: effrt and pressed wnr over 1f out: kpt on same pce fnl f: lost 2nd cl home* **19/5**[2]

**4** *1* **Sadler's Joy (USA)**[35] 6461 4-9-0 0.......................... JulienRLeparoux 4 107+
(Thomas Albertrani, U.S.A) *s.i.s: hld up: hdwy on outside over 1f out: kpt on fnl f: nvr able to chal* **7/2**[1]

**5** *1 ½* **Ascend (USA)**[48] 5977 5-9-0 0...............................................(b) JoeBravo 6 105
(H Graham Motion, U.S.A) *hld up in tch on outside: effrt and drvn along over 2f out: no imp appr fnl f* **102/10**

**6** *1 ¼* **Channel Maker (CAN)**[41] 3-8-9 0..............................(b) ManuelFranco 7 106
(William Mott, U.S.A) *hld up towards rr on outside: effrt and rdn 2f out: no imp appr fnl f* **59/1**

**7** *1 ¾* **Tricked Up (USA)**[40] 4-9-0 0............................................ LuisRReyes 11 100
(Naipaul Chatterpaul, U.S.A) *hld up: rdn and hdwy on ins over 1f out: no further imp fnl f* **168/1**

**8** *nse* **Money Multiplier (USA)**[35] 6461 5-9-0 0.................. JavierCastellano 1 100
(Chad C Brown, U.S.A) *prom: effrt and disp 2nd pl briefly over 1f out: wknd ins fnl f* **23/5**[3]

**9** *3* **The Grey Gatsby (IRE)**[21] 6960 6-9-0 0...............(p) JohnRVelazquez 10 95
(D K Weld, Ire) *hld up: rdn along over 2f out: no imp over 1f out: sn btn* **179/10**

**10** *¾* **Mekhtaal**[48] 5977 4-9-0 0................................................... JuniorAlvarado 8 94
(H Graham Motion, U.S.A) *dwlt: hld up: rdn along over 2f out: wknd over 1f out* **59/10**

**11** *20* **Converge (USA)**[13] 4-9-0 0................................................... EricCancel 2 62
(Naipaul Chatterpaul, U.S.A) *led and clr to over 3f out: hdd over 2f out: wknd over 1f out* **148/1**

2m 26.29s (-2.29)
**WFA** 3 from 4yo+ 7lb **11** Ran SP% **119.9**
PARI-MUTUEL (all including 2 usd stake): WIN 12.00; PLACE (1-2) 6.70, 9.00; SHOW (1-2-3) 4.70, 6.80, 4.50; SF 119.00.
**Owner** James Covello, Sheep Pond Partners & Head Of Plain **Bred** Nancy C Shuford **Trained** USA

**FOCUS**
The three home-trained winners of the Breeders' Cup Turf in the past ten years were also winners of this race, though one had already landed that race before success here. This year's winner looks a live prospect for the big one next month.

# 6979 CHANTILLY (R-H)

Saturday, September 30

**OFFICIAL GOING: Turf: good to soft changing to soft after race 1 (12.30); polytrack: standard**

## 7634a QATAR PRIX CHAUDENAY (GROUP 2) (3YO) (TURF) 1m 7f

12:30 3-Y-0 £97,435 (£37,606; £17,948; £11,965; £5,982)

RPR

1 **Ice Breeze**[20] 6980 3-9-2 0 ........ VincentCheminaud 2 109+
(P Bary, France) *racd a little keenly: a cl up: rdn to chse ldng pair fr 1 1/2f out: sustained run on ins rail fnl f: led cl home* **11/2[3]**

2 *snk* **Call To Mind**[35] 6421 3-9-2 0 ........ FrankieDettori 6 109
(William Haggas) *sn pressing ldr on outer: shkn up 3f out: sn drvn and responded to ld 2 1/2f out: rdn and hdd ent last 1 1/2f: rallied u.p to regain ld last 110yds: hdd cl home* **11/4[2]**

3 *1/2* **Darbuzan (FR)**[22] 6913 3-9-2 0 ........ ChristopheSoumillon 3 108
(M Delzangles, France) *settled in midfield: smooth prog 2 1/2f out: drvn to ld under 1 1/2f fr home: sn rdn and no ex: hdd last 110yds: kpt on same pce* **5/2[1]**

4 *1* **Lady Paname (FR)**[25] 6805 3-8-13 0 ........ TonyPiccone 7 104+
(E Lellouche, France) *settled towards rr: tk clsr order 2 1/2f out: drvn to go 4th 1 1/2f out: styd on fnl f: nvr able to get on terms* **16/1**

5 *1/2* **Soleil Marin (IRE)**[46] 6053 3-9-2 0 ........ MickaelBarzalona 5 106
(A Fabre, France) *a.p: pushed along to chse ldr 2f out: sn sltly outpcd by ldrs: styd on u.p ins fnl f* **8/1**

6 *5 1/2* **Casterton (IRE)**[22] 6913 3-9-2 0 ........ Pierre-CharlesBoudot 9 99
(A Fabre, France) *w.w in rr: prog fr 2f out: rdn and chsng ldng gp sn after: wknd fnl f* **8/1**

7 *4 1/2* **Monreal (IRE)**[22] 6913 3-9-2 0 ........ FabriceVeron 1 93
(Jean-Pierre Carvalho, Germany) *led: tried to raise tempo 3f out: hdd 2 1/2f out: wknd fnl 1 1/2f* **10/1**

8 *1/2* **Cap Verite (IRE)**[22] 6914 3-8-13 0 ........ StephanePasquier 4 90
(N Clement, France) *w.w in midfield: lost pl bef 1/2-way: last and rdn 3f out: short-lived effrt wl over 1 1/2f out: sn btn* **16/1**

9 *3 1/2* **Boy Royal (FR)**[31] 6607 3-9-2 0 ........ OlivierPeslier 8 88
(Alain Couetil, France) *settled in fnl pair: rdn and no imp 2 1/2f out: nvr in contention* **25/1**

3m 17.88s (1.78) **Going Correction** +0.50s/f (Yiel) **9** Ran SP% **117.5**
Speed ratings: **115,114,114,114,113 110,108,108,106**
PARI-MUTUEL (all including 1 euro stake): WIN 6.30; PLACE 1.70, 1.60, 1.30; DF 14.70; SF 27.10.
**Owner** K Abdullah **Bred** Juddmonte Farms **Trained** Chantilly, France

## 7635a QATAR PRIX DE ROYALLIEU (GROUP 2) (3YO+ FILLIES & MARES) (TURF) 1m 4f

1:35 3-Y-0+ £121,794 (£47,008; £22,435; £14,957; £7,478)

RPR

1 **The Juliet Rose (FR)**[55] 5691 4-9-1 0 ........ StephanePasquier 7 107+
(N Clement, France) *mde virtually all: pushed along to raise tempo 2 1/2f out: rdn wl over 1 1/2f out and hrd pressed: r.o gamely fnl f to hold off all chalrs* **2/1[1]**

2 *snk* **Listen In (IRE)**[37] 6364 3-8-8 0 ........ AurelienLemaitre 2 107
(F Head, France) *settled bhd ldng pair: hemmed in on inner fr 2 1/2f out: cl up whn gap c more than 1f out: styd on u.p fnl f: nvr quite gng to overhaul wnr* **3/1[2]**

3 *hd* **Kitesurf**[55] 5691 3-8-8 0 ........ MickaelBarzalona 8 106
(A Fabre, France) *trckd ldr on outer: shkn up and virtually alongside ldr 2f out: styd on u.p: nvr quite able to get hd in front: no ex late on* **8/1[3]**

4 *nk* **Bebe D'Amour (FR)**[11] 3-8-8 0 ........ EddyHardouin 5 106
(J-Y Artu, France) *w.w in tch on inner: angled out but nt clr run 1 1/2f out: sn in clr: styd on fnl f: nvr quite getting there* **14/1**

5 *1 1/4* **Baltic Duchess (IRE)**[27] 6732 3-8-8 0 ........ MaximeGuyon 1 104
(A Fabre, France) *settled in fnl pair: drvn to cl under 2f out: kpt on under driving fnl f: nt pce to chal* **14/1**

6 *1 1/2* **Furia Cruzada (CHI)**[14] 7177 6-9-7 0 ........ GregoryBenoist 6 107
(S Kobayashi, France) *w.w in rr: tk clsr order more than 1 1/2f fr home: kpt on ins fnl f: nvr nrr* **20/1**

7 *4 1/2* **Baiyouna (FR)**[20] 6981 3-8-9 0 ow1 ........ ChristopheSoumillon 3 95
(A De Royer-Dupre, France) *settled in tch on outer: 4th and drvn 2 1/2f out: no imp over 1 1/2f out: wknd fnl f* **8/1[3]**

2m 35.55s (4.55) **Going Correction** +0.50s/f (Yiel)
**WFA** 3 from 4yo+ 7lb **7** Ran SP% **98.7**
Speed ratings: **104,103,103,103,102 101,98**
PARI-MUTUEL (all including 1 euro stake): WIN 2.40; PLACE 1.10, 1.10, 1.20; DF 2.80; SF 5.10.
**Owner** Mayfair Speculators Sarl & Equifrance Holdings **Bred** Guy Heald **Trained** Chantilly, France

**FOCUS**
A tight finish with last year's winner following up, but she didn't need to match her 2016 figure in order to do so.

## 7636a QATAR GRAND H'CAP DES MILERS (4YO+) (POLYTRACK) 1m

2:15 4-Y-0+

£28,119 (£11,367; £8,376; £5,384; £3,290; £2,094)

RPR

1 **London Protocol (FR)**[30] 6648 4-9-3 0 ........ TonyPiccone 2 98
(K R Burke) *wl into stride: mde all: pushed along over 2f out: drvn to hold advantage over 1f out: kpt on strly ins fnl f* **97/10**

2 *1 3/4* **Sky Ship**[12] 4-8-8 0 ........(p) FabriceVeron 1 85
(Christos Kouvaras, France) **159/10**

3 *hd* **Arvios**[30] 6648 5-8-9 0 ........ StephanePasquier 4 86
(F-X Belvisi, France) **6/1[1]**

4 *snk* **Donuts Reyor (FR)**[20] 4-8-9 0 ........ EddyHardouin 11 85
(V Luka Jr, Czech Republic) **67/10[3]**

5 *1/2* **Beama (FR)**[116] 4-8-11 0 ........(p) Pierre-CharlesBoudot 7 86
(H-A Pantall, France) **205/10**

6 *nk* **Nice To See You (FR)**[14] 4-9-7 0 ........(b) VincentCheminaud 5 95
(Robert Collet, France) **213/10**

7 *nk* **Dylaban (IRE)**[35] 6454 5-8-7 0 ........ MathieuAndrouin 9 81
(Alain Couetil, France) **66/10[2]**

8 *snk* **Lucky Team (FR)**[31] 5-9-0 0 ........(p) ChristopheSoumillon 14 87
(J Boisnard, France) **125/10**

9 *hd* **Snaad**[48] 5979 5-9-8 0 ........(p) GregoryBenoist 6 95
(F-H Graffard, France) **99/10**

10 *1 3/4* **Zarose (FR)**[31] 4-9-2 0 ........ TheoBachelot 3 85
(H-A Pantall, France) **137/10**

11 *hd* **Vedeux (IRE)**[31] 6-8-6 0 ........(p) CristianDemuro 15 74
(C Lerner, France) **195/10**

12 *1 3/4* **Crepusculedesdieux (FR)**[22] 6-8-8 0 ........(p) AlexisBadel 8 72
(P Sobry, France) **33/1**

13 *2* **Aprilios (FR)**[30] 6648 5-8-11 0 ........ JeromeMoutard 17 71
(J-M Lefebvre, France) **244/10**

14 *1/2* **Dhevanafushi**[12] 4-9-7 0 ........ MickaelBarzalona 10 80
(H-A Pantall, France) **10/1**

15 *snk* **Alfieri (FR)**[14] 4-9-0 0 ........ MaximeGuyon 12 72
(T Castanheira, France) **156/10**

16 *3/4* **Extinguish (FR)**[136] 4-9-1 0 ........ OlivierPeslier 16 72
(P Sobry, France) **46/1**

PARI-MUTUEL (all including 1 euro stake): WIN 10.70; PLACE 3.70, 5.00, 2.70; DF 64.40; SF 111.10.
**Owner** Ontoawinner, R Mckeown & E Burke **Bred** Gerard Rollain **Trained** Middleham Moor, N Yorks

## 7637a HARAS DE BOUQUETOT - CRITERIUM DE LA VENTE D'OCTOBRE D'ARQANA (CONDITIONS) (2YO) (TURF) 1m

2:45 2-Y-0

£117,094 (£60,888; £32,786; £14,051; £2,341; £2,341)

RPR

1 **Dice Roll (FR)**[25] 2-9-0 0 ........ CristianDemuro 17 93
(F Chappet, France) **76/10[3]**

2 *1 3/4* **Lilac Fairy (FR)**[43] 6171 2-8-8 0 ........(p) VincentCheminaud 8 83
(F-H Graffard, France) **54/1**

3 *nse* **Louis D'Or (IRE)**[31] 6606 2-8-11 0 ........ MaximeGuyon 10 86
(T Castanheira, France) **116/10**

4 *nse* **Chipolata (FR)**[27] 6731 2-8-8 0 ........ TheoBachelot 12 83
(J Reynier, France) **144/10**

5 *1 1/4* **Feralia (FR)**[22] 6912 2-8-13 0 ........ Jean-BernardEyquem 1 85
(J-C Rouget, France) **5/2[1]**

6 *2* **Fatou (FR)**[5] 2-8-8 0 ........ EddyHardouin 13 75
(F Chappet, France) **40/1**

7 *1 1/4* **Samphire (FR)**[33] 6542 2-8-8 0 ........ AurelienLemaitre 9 72
(H-F Devin, France) **61/1**

8 *shd* **Crown Vallary (FR)**[25] 6803 2-8-8 0 ........ TonyPiccone 16 72
(K R Burke) *disp ld early: settled in 2nd: rdn over 2f out: drvn over 1f out: wknd fnl f* **98/10**

9 *shd* **Miss Sienna**[16] 2-8-8 0 ........ AlexisBadel 2 72
(H-F Devin, France) **96/10**

10 *nse* **Phoenix Rose (FR)**[10] 7304 2-8-8 0 ........ StephanePasquier 7 72
(N Clement, France) **40/1**

11 *1* **Jackfinbar (FR)**[15] 7120 2-8-11 0 ........ FranckBlondel 14 72
(Harry Dunlop) *settled in midfield: pushed along over 2f out: limited rspnse whn rdn over 1f out: no ex fnl f* **52/1**

12 *snk* **Urban Poete (FR)**[20] 2-8-8 0 ........ GregoryBenoist 3 69
(M Delzangles, France) **169/10**

13 *3/4* **Sweety Dream (FR)**[27] 2-8-9 0 ow1 ........ Pierre-CharlesBoudot 6 68
(P Bary, France) **17/5[2]**

14 *nk* **Ivirka (FR)**[62] 2-8-8 0 ........ ThierryThulliez 11 67
(C Laffon-Parias, France) **53/1**

15 *2 1/2* **Compainville (FR)**[28] 6713 2-8-8 0 ........ MickaelForest 18 61
(X Thomas-Demeaulte, France) **76/1**

16 *4* **Ahorita (FR)** 2-8-8 0 ........ JeromeMoutard 15 52
(J-M Lefebvre, France) **93/1**

17 *9* **Mafeking**[15] 7120 2-8-11 0 ........(p) FabriceVeron 4 34
(Harry Dunlop) *a towards rr: effrt 3f out: nvr a factor* **43/1**

1m 42.34s (4.34) **17** Ran SP% **118.3**
PARI-MUTUEL (all including 1 euro stake): WIN 8.60; PLACE 3.50, 12.40, 3.90; DF 192.20; SF 367.60.
**Owner** Giacomo Algranti **Bred** Gestut Zur Kuste Ag **Trained** France

## 7638a QATAR PRIX DOLLAR (GROUP 2) (3YO+) (TURF) 1m 2f

3:25 3-Y-0+ £97,435 (£37,606; £17,948; £11,965; £5,982)

RPR

1 **Garlingari (FR)**[14] 7177 6-9-2 0 ........(p) StephanePasquier 3 113
(Mme C Barande-Barbe, France) *chsd ldr: rdn 2 1/2f out: styd on to press ldr fr 1 1/2f out: led ins fnl f: drvn out* **4/1[3]**

2 *snk* **Subway Dancer (IRE)**[14] 7177 5-9-2 0 ........ VincentCheminaud 4 113
(Z Koplik, Czech Republic) *settled in midfield on inner: rdn to cl over 1 1/2f out: styd on ins fnl f: nvr quite on terms w wnr* **50/1**

3 *1 1/4* **Salouen (IRE)**[46] 6053 3-8-11 0 ........ MaximeGuyon 7 111+
(Sylvester Kirk) *settled towards rr on outer: outpcd and scrubbed along 3f out: styng on 5th whn sltly impeded 1 1/2f out: kpt on wl fnl f: nvr nrr* **6/1**

4 *snk* **Kourkan (FR)**[22] 6915 4-9-2 0 ........ ChristopheSoumillon 6 110
(J-M Beguigne, France) *w.w in rr: began to cl on outer appr 2f out: chsd ldng pair into fnl f: run flattened out last 100yds* **10/1**

5 *3/4* **Robin Of Navan (FR)**[20] 6982 4-9-2 0 ........ CristianDemuro 1 108+
(Harry Dunlop) *sn led: drvn 2f out: hrd rdn over 1f out: hdd ins fnl f: no ex* **3/1[1]**

6 *3* **Avilius**[20] 6980 3-8-11 0 ........ MickaelBarzalona 8 103
(A Fabre, France) *hld up in fnl pair: last and drvn 2f out but no imp: kpt on same pce fnl f: nvr in contention* **10/3[2]**

7 *snk* **Wild Chief (GER)**[62] 5464 6-9-2 0 ........ AdriedeVries 2 102
(J Hirschberger, Germany) *w.w bhd ldr on inner: angled out between horses 2f out: sn rdn and no imp: wl hld fnl f* **20/1**

8 *4* **First Sitting**[46] 6052 6-9-2 0 ........ FrankieDettori 5 94
(Chris Wall) *chsd ldrs on outer: pushed along 2 1/2f out: lost pl 2f out: bhd fnl f* **5/1**

2m 4.48s (-0.32) **Going Correction** +0.50s/f (Yiel)
**WFA** 3 from 4yo+ 5lb **8** Ran SP% **114.8**
Speed ratings: **121,120,119,119,119 116,116,113**
PARI-MUTUEL (all including 1 euro stake): WIN 5.30; PLACE 1.80, 6.30, 2.10; DF 85.00; SF 106.30.
**Owner** Mme Corine Barande-Barbe **Bred** Mme C Barande Barbe & Mme J J Massy **Trained** France

**FOCUS**
The winner, third and fourth all ran close to their recent form, but a big personal best from the second.

## 7639a QATAR PRIX DU CADRAN (GROUP 1) (4YO+) (TURF) 2m 4f 110y
4:12 4-Y-O+ £146,512 (£58,615; £29,307; £14,641; £7,333)

RPR

1 **Vazirabad (FR)**[20] 6984 5-9-2 0 ChristopheSoumillon 2 109+
(A De Royer-Dupre, France) *w.w in fnl pair: shkn up to cl on outer 2f fr home: lugged in bhd ldr appr fnl f: rdn and styd on to ld last 140yds: hld off runner-up's rally* **1/6**[1]

2 ½ **Mille Et Mille**[34] 6499 7-9-2 0 FranckBlondel 6 108
(C Lerner, France) *led: 2 l ld and rdn over 1 1/2f out: hdd fnl 140yds: rallied u.p but a hld by wnr* **12/1**[2]

3 7 **Trip To Rhodos (FR)**[20] 6984 8-9-2 0 TheoBachelot 1 101
(Pavel Tuma, Czech Republic) *cl up: outpcd and lost pl under 3f out: sn rdn: kpt on again to go 3rd ins fnl f: no ch w front two* **16/1**[3]

4 ¾ **High Jinx (IRE)**[15] 7116 9-9-2 0 (p) OlivierPeslier 4 100
(Tim Easterby) *trckd ldrs on inner: drvn to chse ldr 2 1/2f out: kpt on at same pce* **16/1**[3]

5 5 **Pearl Dragon (FR)**[18] 6-9-2 0 VincentCheminaud 3 95
(M Delzangles, France) *w.w in midfield on outer: tk clsr order 3 1/2f out: 3rd and pushed along 2 1/2f out: sn rdn and no imp: wknd more than 1f out* **28/1**

6 shd **Aussi Celebre (IRE)**[35] 8-9-2 0 DelphineSantiago 5 95
(C Martinon, France) *w.w in rr: detached bef 1/2-way: hdwy to latch on to main gp appr fnl bnd: no further imp* **66/1**

4m 34.6s 6 Ran SP% **110.1**
PARI-MUTUEL (all including 1 euro stake): WIN 1.20; PLACE 1.10, 1.10, SF 4.10.
**Owner** H H Aga Khan **Bred** Haras De Son Altesse L'Aga Khan Scea **Trained** Chantilly, France

**FOCUS**
After the withdrawal of Big Orange this year's Cadran was all about the winner. The placed horses help set the standard.

## 7640a QATAR PRIX DANIEL WILDENSTEIN (GROUP 2) (3YO+) (TURF) 1m
4:42 3-Y-O+ £97,435 (£37,606; £17,948; £11,965; £5,982)

RPR

1 **Taareef (USA)**[20] 6982 4-9-2 0 ChristopheSoumillon 9 117+
(J-C Rouget, France) *w.w in fnl trio on outer: began to cl 2f out: rdn and styd on to chal 1f out: r.o to ld last 120yds: drvn clr: wl on top fin* **8/13**[1]

2 1¼ **Buthela (FR)**[30] 3-8-13 0 GregoryBenoist 1 113+
(A Fabre, France) *chsd ldng pair: cl up but hemmed in 2f out: grad fnd room: rdn and styd on ins fnl f: no ch w wnr* **10/1**

3 ¾ **Noor Al Hawa (FR)**[62] 5464 4-9-2 0 EduardoPedroza 3 110+
(A Wohler, Germany) *w.w in midfield: drvn 2f out: tk clsr order but only 8th over 1f out: r.o u.p ins fnl f: nvr nrr* **25/1**

4 nse **Hathal (USA)**[35] 6420 5-9-2 0 (p) FrankieDettori 8 110
(William Haggas) *settled in midfield on outer: 3rd and pushed along over 2f out: ld appr fnl f: rdn and kpt on: hdd last 120yds: no ex* **11/2**[2]

5 1¼ **Wireless (FR)**[34] 6498 6-9-2 0 TheoBachelot 4 107
(V Luka Jr, Czech Republic) *w.w in fnl trio: rdn and hdwy 1 1/2f out: kpt on fnl 150yds: nvr on terms* **20/1**

6 shd **Royal Julius (IRE)**[27] 6729 4-9-2 0 VincentCheminaud 2 107
(J Reynier, France) *led: hrd pressed fr 2f out: hdd over 1f out: kpt on at one pce* **33/1**

7 snk **Gold Luck (FR)**[48] 5980 3-8-9 0 MaximeGuyon 7 104
(F Head, France) *chsd ldr on outer: drvn to chal fnl 2f: sn rdn and nt qckn: grad lft bhd fnl f* **8/1**[3]

8 ½ **Dicton**[34] 6498 4-9-2 0 OlivierPeslier 5 106
(Gianluca Bietolini, Italy) *racd keenly: hld up towards rr: pushed along 2f out: kpt on ins fnl f: could nvr muster pce to get involved* **16/1**

9 ¾ **Wonnemond (GER)**[27] 6746 4-9-4 0 BayarsaikhanGanbat 6 106
(S Smrczek, Germany) *hld up in rr: last and rdn over 2f out but no real imp: kpt on fnl 150yds but nvr in contention* **16/1**

1m 40.19s (2.19) **Going Correction** +0.50s/f (Yiel)
**WFA** 3 from 4yo+ 4lb 9 Ran SP% **120.8**
Speed ratings: **109,107,107,106,105 105,105,104,104**
PARI-MUTUEL (all including 1 euro stake): WIN 1.70; PLACE 1.10, 2.10, 2.10; DF 6.80; SF 8.30.
**Owner** Hamdan Al Maktoum **Bred** Dixiana Farms Llc **Trained** Pau, France

**FOCUS**
The winner did this cosily, while the progressive runner-up recorded a personal best.

7641 - 7646a (Foreign Racing) - See Raceform Interactive

# 7093 EPSOM (L-H)
Sunday, October 1

**OFFICIAL GOING: Heavy (soft in places; 5.2; straight: stands' 5.8, far 5.9)**
Wind: strong, across Weather: blustery, showers

## 7647 BET TOTEPLACEPOT AT BETFRED.COM NURSERY H'CAP 7f 3y
2:10 (2:12) (Class 4) (0-85,81) 2-Y-O £6,469 (£1,925; £962; £481) Stalls Low

Form RPR

5316 1 **Shrewd Approach (IRE)**[43] 6200 2-8-7 67 SilvestreDeSousa 6 72
(Simon Crisford) *mde all: rdn ent fnl 2f: edgd lft but styd on wl and drew clr wl ins fnl f* **9/2**[1]

3502 2 1¼ **George (IRE)**[46] 6065 2-9-2 81 MitchGodwin(5) 7 83
(Sylvester Kirk) *chsd wnr: effrt to chal 2f out: drvn over 1f out: no ex and btn wl ins fnl f: wknd towards fin* **8/1**

6540 3 nk **Reverberation**[24] 6860 2-8-4 67 DavidEgan(3) 5 68
(Sylvester Kirk) *chsd ldrs: rdn over 2f out: outpcd and swtchd rt 2f out: rallied to chse ldng pair again ins fnl f: styd on: nvr getting on terms w ldr* **22/1**

4422 4 1¾ **Kimifive (IRE)**[56] 5685 2-9-3 77 FranBerry 9 74
(Joseph Tuite) *chsd ldng trio: pushed along 3f out: drvn and hdwy to chse ldng pair over 1f out: no ex and lost 3rd ins fnl f: wknd towards fin* **7/1**[3]

2602 5 ¾ **Zalshah**[16] 7121 2-9-0 74 (p[1]) TomMarquand 1 69
(Richard Hannon) *t.k.h: hld up in midfield: hdwy to chse ldng quartet over 2f out: edgd lft but kpt on u.p ins fnl f: nvr getting on terms w ldrs* **9/1**

623 6 2 **Hateya (IRE)**[17] 7093 2-8-7 70 CharlieBennett(3) 2 60
(Jim Boyle) *s.i.s: sn rcvrd and in tch in midfield: rdn and outpcd over 2f out:swtchd lft over 1f out and rallied ent fnl f: styd on but nvr threatening ldrs* **20/1**

3253 7 3 **Paramount Love**[33] 6561 2-8-13 73 AndreaAtzeni 11 56
(Richard Fahey) *hld up in last trio: effrt over 2f out: stl plenty to do whn nt clr run over 1f out: modest hdwy and swtchd lft 1f out: nvr trbld ldrs* **5/1**[2]

3320 8 1¼ **Phoenix Lightning (IRE)**[21] 6977 2-9-0 74 (p) ShaneKelly 8 53
(Richard Fahey) *dwlt and pushed along early: sn rcvrd and in tch in midfield: rdn and outpcd over 2f out: hung rt and no imp over 1f out: wknd ins fnl f* **10/1**

0125 9 1½ **Make Good (IRE)**[34] 6510 2-9-6 80 KieranShoemark 10 56
(David Brown) *hld up in last trio: effrt jst over 2f out: no hdwy and wl btn over 1f out* **14/1**

524 10 7 **Sarstedt**[20] 7001 2-9-0 74 DaneO'Neill 12 32
(Henry Candy) *stdd and dropped in bhd after s: hld up in last trio: effrt over 2f out: no hdwy: wl bhd and eased ins fnl f* **9/1**

6303 11 3¾ **Alifax**[16] 7121 2-8-12 72 DougieCostello 4 21
(Jamie Osborne) *in tch in midfield: rdn over 2f out: sn struggling: wknd over 1f out: bhd ins fnl f* **8/1**

1m 26.15s (2.85) **Going Correction** +0.575s/f (Yiel) 11 Ran SP% **114.4**
Speed ratings (Par 97): **106,104,104,102,101 99,95,94,92,84 80**
CSF £39.10 CT £710.45 TOTE £4.70: £2.00, £2.60, £5.90; EX 40.00 Trifecta £721.60.
**Owner** Ali Saeed **Bred** Rabbah Bloodstock Limited **Trained** Newmarket, Suffolk

**FOCUS**
Following over 21mm of rain since Wednesday, the going was riding heavy, soft in places. The winning jockey said it was "hard work". A competitive-looking nursery, but a contest in which nothing got involved from behind.

## 7648 TOTEPOOL CONDITIONS STKS (PLUS 10 RACE) 1m 113y
2:40 (2:42) (Class 2) 2-Y-O
£12,450 (£3,728; £1,864; £932; £466; £234) Stalls Low

Form RPR

163 1 **Dee Ex Bee**[22] 6925 2-9-7 96 FrannyNorton 7 99
(Mark Johnston) *s.i.s: bhd: hdwy on outer to chse ldr over 6f out: rdn and ev ch over 2f out: sustained duel w runner-up after: edgd lft briefly ins fnl f: styd on to ld and forge ahd towards fin: gamely* **7/2**[3]

2114 2 ¾ **Move Over**[21] 6985 2-9-5 87 (b) SilvestreDeSousa 6 95
(Richard Hannon) *sn led: rdn over 2f out: sustained duel w wnr after: edgd lft u.p after: battled on gamely tl hdd and no ex towards fin* **20/1**

1 3 1¼ **The Revenant**[24] 6854 2-9-5 0 JosephineGordon 3 93
(Hugo Palmer) *hld up in tch: hdwy on stands' rail over 2f out: chsd ldrs and swtchd lft 2f out: pressing ldng pair and swtchd lft again 1f out: no ex wl ins fnl f: wknd towards fin* **6/4**[1]

1 4 nk **Lisheen Castle (IRE)**[37] 6380 2-9-2 0 AndreaAtzeni 1 89
(John Quinn) *hld up in tch in midfield: stuck on inner and shuffled bk on downhill run over 4f out: rdn and hdwy to chse ldrs 2f out: drifting rt and outpcd over 1f out: rallied ins fnl f: styd on wl towards fin* **3/1**[2]

54 5 7 **Bowditch (IRE)**[10] 7333 2-9-2 0 KieranShoemark 4 74
(John Gosden) *broke wl: sn hdd and chsd ldr tl over 6f out: chsd ldrs: rdn over 2f out: sn outpcd: 5th and btn over 1f out: wknd fnl f* **14/1**

1312 6 ½ **Regimented (IRE)**[15] 7148 2-9-5 91 TomMarquand 5 75
(Richard Hannon) *t.k.h: hld up in tch in midfield: rdn over 2f out: sn struggling: wl hld whn wandered over 1f out: wknd fnl f* **12/1**

0210 7 1½ **Veejay (IRE)**[22] 6925 2-9-5 89 DavidEgan 2 72
(Mick Channon) *hld up in tch in last pair: effrt over 2f out: sn struggling: wl hld whn wandered over 1f out: sn wknd* **20/1**

1m 49.97s (3.87) **Going Correction** +0.575s/f (Yiel) 7 Ran SP% **111.1**
Speed ratings (Par 101): **105,104,103,102,96 96,94**
CSF £60.51 TOTE £4.30: £2.20, £4.40; EX 33.40 Trifecta £101.80.
**Owner** Sheikh Hamdan bin Mohammed Al Maktoum **Bred** Godolphin **Trained** Middleham Moor, N Yorks

**FOCUS**
The feature race and a very decent juvenile contest, but another contest where it paid to be prominent, as the first two were in those positions throughout. The first four came clear. The winner has been rated to his previous Listed-placed form.

## 7649 BET TOTEQUADPOT AT BETFRED.COM H'CAP 1m 2f 17y
3:15 (3:15) (Class 3) (0-95,91) 3-Y-O+
£12,450 (£3,728; £1,864; £932; £466; £234) Stalls Low

Form RPR

4222 1 **Native Prospect**[16] 7107 3-8-10 81 DavidProbert 2 91
(Andrew Balding) *pushed along leaving stalls: sn chsng ldr: led and rdn 2f out: pressed 1f out: r.o wl and drew clr fnl 100yds* **6/4**[1]

0312 2 2¼ **Sparte Quercus (IRE)**[16] 7132 4-9-0 81 AndreaAtzeni 4 86
(Ed Dunlop) *in tch in midfield: effrt in 3rd over 3f out: clsd on ldrs and swtchd lft 2f out: wnt 2nd jst over 1f out and pressing wnr: sn drvn and no ex ins fnl f: wknd towards fin* **4/1**[2]

3030 3 ¾ **Emenem**[4] 7516 3-9-1 91 PaddyBradley(5) 5 94
(Simon Dow) *hld up in last pair: effrt over 2f out: clsd on ldrs and nt clrest of runs over 1f out: kpt on same pce u.p ins fnl f* **6/1**[3]

1024 4 nse **Fast Dancer (IRE)**[29] 6701 5-9-3 84 FranBerry 6 86
(Joseph Tuite) *stdd s: hld up in last pair: effrt over 2f out: clsd on ldrs and swtchd lft over 1f out: kpt on same pce ins fnl f* **13/2**

6003 5 6 **Kharbetation (IRE)**[10] 7328 4-9-4 85 HarryBentley 1 75
(David O'Meara) *taken down early: led: rdn and hdd 2f out: lost 2nd jst over 1f out and sn btn: wknd ins fnl f: eased towards fin* **6/1**[3]

630 6 9 **Oasis Fantasy (IRE)**[29] 6698 6-9-10 91 (p) SeanLevey 3 63
(David Simcock) *chsd ldng pair tl over 2f out: sn dropped to last: wknd over 1f out* **12/1**

2m 14.52s (4.82) **Going Correction** +0.575s/f (Yiel)
**WFA** 3 from 4yo+ 4lb 6 Ran SP% **109.6**
Speed ratings (Par 107): **103,101,100,100,95 88**
CSF £7.22 TOTE £2.10: £1.30, £2.20; EX 8.00 Trifecta £25.80.
**Owner** Mick and Janice Mariscotti **Bred** Overbury Stallions Ltd & Dukes Stud **Trained** Kingsclere, Hants

**FOCUS**
Despite the small field this looked a pretty competitive contest. Again they came stands' side and the winner was always in the first two. The winner has been rated to his better form.

## 7650 BET TOTEEXACTA AT BETFRED.COM H'CAP 1m 113y
3:45 (3:48) (Class 3) (0-90,90) 3-Y-O £9,337 (£2,796; £1,398; £699; £349) Stalls Low

Form RPR

1501 1 **Heatongrad (IRE)**[15] 7162 3-8-7 76 oh1 SilvestreDeSousa 1 89
(Richard Fahey) *mde all: rdn over 2f out: gng clr 2f out: r.o strly drew wl clr fnl f: easily* **3/1**[1]

3621 2 9 **Fujaira Bridge (IRE)**[34] 6516 3-9-2 85 AndreaAtzeni 6 79
(Roger Varian) *trckd ldrs tl wnt 2nd 6f out: effrt wl over 2f out: outpcd by wnr 2f out: wl hld after but plugged on for clr 2nd* **4/1**[3]

01-0 3 3¼ **Swiss Storm**[136] 2766 3-9-6 89 DaneO'Neill 2 76
(David Elsworth) *taken down early: hld up in tch: effrt in 3rd 3f out: sn outpcd: wl hld fnl 2f* **7/2**[2]

2436 **4** *1 ½* **Dr Julius No**[23] 6870 3-9-6 **89**..........................................(p) ShaneKelly 4 73
(Richard Hughes) *hld up in tch in rr: outpcd and effrt over 2f out: wl hld whn swtchd lft over 1f out* **16/1**

1120 **5** *2 ¼* **Lord Clenaghcastle (IRE)**[17] 7094 3-8-10 **82**........... HectorCrouch(3) 3 61
(Gary Moore) *chsd wnr tl 6f out: rdn and dropped to 4th 3f out: sn struggling: wl hld fnl 2f* **6/1**

1m 49.55s (3.45) **Going Correction** +0.575s/f (Yiel) **5** Ran SP% **87.4**
Speed ratings (Par 105): **107,99,96,94,92**
CSF £9.10 TOTE £2.60: £1.30, £1.80; EX 8.90 Trifecta £18.20.
**Owner** Middleham Park Racing XXXV & Partner **Bred** M Morgan **Trained** Musley Bank, N Yorks
■ Isabella was withdrawn. Price at time of withdrawal 3-1J. Rule 4 applies to all bets - deduction 25p in the pound

**FOCUS**
Another small field, but still a decent contest, although devalued by the withdrawal of Isabella who refused to enter the stalls, which resulted in a 25p in the pound deduction. The time was 0.42sec faster than the earlier juvenile contest over the trip and they finished well strung out.

## 7651 BET TOTETRIFECTA AT BETFRED.COM APPRENTICES' DERBY STKS (A H'CAP) 1m 4f 6y
**4:20** (4:24) (Class 4) (0-85,85) 3-Y-O+ **£6,469** (£1,925; £962; £481) **Stalls** Centre

Form RPR

2260 **1** **Whinging Willie (IRE)**[34] 6513 8-9-7 **78**......................(v) HectorCrouch 5 88
(Gary Moore) *in tch in midfield: clsd to trck ldrs 5f out: effrt to ld over 2f out: edging rt over 1f out: styd on wl ins fnl f: rdn out* **14/1**

2213 **2** *½* **Golden Wolf (IRE)**[30] 6657 3-8-12 **80**.............................. FinleyMarsh(5) 6 89
(Richard Hughes) *hld up in tch in midfield and travelled strly: clsd to trck ldrs over 3f out: effrt on stands rail to press wnr over 1f out: kpt on u.p but a hld ins fnl f* **3/1**[1]

-001 **3** *2 ¾* **Bazooka (IRE)**[14] 7202 6-9-0 **71** oh2.................................... HollieDoyle 4 76
(David Flood) *s.i.s: bhd and detached in last: clsd onto bk of field 8f out: rdn and hdwy over 2f out: swtchd lft and chsd ldng pair over 1f out: kpt on* **12/1**

3616 **4** *4* **Compton Mill**[22] 6929 5-9-11 **82**...................................... CharlieBennett 3 80
(Hughie Morrison) *chsd ldrs tl pushed along and lost pl 5f out: rdn and hdwy against stands rail over 2f out: 5th and no imp over 1f out: kpt on same pce* **8/1**

5410 **5** *1 ½* **Cordite (IRE)**[17] 7096 6-9-1 **72**..........................................(h) TimClark 7 68
(Jim Boyle) *taken down early: dwlt: sn in tch in midfield: hdwy on outer to trck ldrs 5f out: led over 3f out tl rdn and hdd over 2f out: lost 2nd and struggling over 1f out: wknd ins fnl f* **16/1**

1311 **6** *7* **C'Est No Mour (GER)**[17] 7096 4-10-0 **85**.................. KieranShoemark 8 70
(Peter Hedger) *hld up in last trio: clsd over 3f out: effrt over 2f out: 6th and no imp wl over 1f out: wknd fnl f* **4/1**[2]

4214 **7** *12* **State Sovereignty**[26] 6789 5-9-6 **77**................................. CliffordLee 13 43
(Michael Scudamore) *chsd ldr tl led 7f out: hdd over 3f out: lost pl u.p and btn 2f out: sn wknd* **5/1**[3]

-650 **8** *¾* **Hatsaway (IRE)**[95] 4222 6-8-13 **73**........................... PaddyBradley(3) 11 37
(Pat Phelan) *chsd ldrs: wnt 2nd 6f out: ev ch over 3f out tl outpcd u.p over 2f out: sn wknd* **16/1**

2400 **9** *6* **Inke (IRE)**[16] 7132 5-9-1 **72**............................................... GeorgeWood 12 27
(Jim Boyle) *a towards rr: rdn over 3f out: sn bhd* **40/1**

5100 **10** *8* **Star Maker**[18] 7063 3-8-10 **76**...................................... MitchGodwin(3) 9 19
(Sylvester Kirk) *in tch in midfield tl lost pl u.p 4f out: bhd over 2f out: t.o* **12/1**

656 **11** *6* **Panko (IRE)**[38] 6344 4-9-5 **79**.......................................... JaneElliott(3) 2 11
(Ed de Giles) *led tl 7f out: lost pl 6f out and bhd 3f out: sn lost tch: t.o* **12/1**

2m 47.88s (8.98) **Going Correction** +0.575s/f (Yiel)
**WFA** 3 from 4yo+ 6lb **11** Ran SP% **116.7**
Speed ratings (Par 105): **93,92,90,88,87 82,74,74,70,64 60**
CSF £55.42 CT £534.82 TOTE £12.00: £3.20, £1.70, £3.50; EX 45.80 Trifecta £600.00.
**Owner** P B Moorhead **Bred** Joe Rogers **Trained** Lower Beeding, W Sussex
■ Stewards' Enquiry : Hector Crouch two-day ban: careless riding (Oct 15-16)

**FOCUS**
This Apprentices' Derby looked a competitive handicap on paper and, despite an ordinary gallop, several didn't handle the conditions and they finished well strung out.

## 7652 TOTEPOOL BETTING AT BETFRED.COM MAIDEN STKS 1m 2f 17y
**4:55** (4:57) (Class 5) 3-Y-O **£3,881** (£1,155; £577; £288) **Stalls** Low

Form RPR

52-2 **1** **Ajman King (IRE)**[16] 7125 3-9-5 85.................................... AndreaAtzeni 1 85+
(Roger Varian) *led for 1f: styd trcking ldr tl led over 3f out: rdn and readily asserted over 1f out: r.o wl: comf* **2/5**[1]

4 **2** *2* **Dash Of Spice**[37] 6390 3-9-5 0................................... SilvestreDeSousa 4 81
(David Elsworth) *t.k.h: trckd ldrs after 2f: effrt to chse wnr 3f out: unable qck over 1f out: clr 2nd and kpt on same pce f* **9/1**[3]

6-4 **3** *5* **Wine List**[59] 5563 3-9-5 0............................................. DavidProbert 6 71
(Andrew Balding) *stdd s: t.k.h: hld up in tch in rr: clsd and swtchd lft 2f out: chsd clr ldng pair and rdn over 1f out: no imp* **14/1**

0-2 **4** *1 ¾* **Star Story**[64] 5428 3-9-0 0................................................ PatDobbs 5 63
(Ralph Beckett) *hld up wl in tch in midfield: wnt 3rd and rdn over 2f out: outpcd and lost 3rd over 1f out: wl hld and kpt on same pce fnl f* **9/2**[2]

**5** *5* **Nevalyashka** 3-9-0 0..................................................(p[1]) MartinDwyer 2 53
(Marcus Tregoning) *hld up wl in tch in midfield: effrt over 2f out: sn outpcd: wl btn 5th over 1f out* **40/1**

60 **6** *28* **Manners Maketh Man (IRE)**[25] 6817 3-9-2 0........... HectorCrouch(3) 3
(Ralph Beckett) *pushed along to ld after 1f out: drvn and hdd over 3f out: lost pl 2f out: wknd and eased ins fnl f* **50/1**

2m 16.39s (6.69) **Going Correction** +0.575s/f (Yiel) **6** Ran SP% **110.7**
Speed ratings (Par 101): **96,94,90,89,85 62**
CSF £4.78 TOTE £1.40: £1.10, £2.90; EX 4.90 Trifecta £19.80.
**Owner** Sheikh Mohammed Obaid Al Maktoum **Bred** Swordlestown Little **Trained** Newmarket, Suffolk
■ Stewards' Enquiry : David Probert caution: careless riding

**FOCUS**
An uncompetitive little maiden despite some well-bred sorts. The time was 1.87sec slower than the earlier handicap over the trip. The race has been rated around the winner.

## 7653 COLLECT TOTEPOOL WINNINGS AT BETFRED SHOPS H'CAP 7f 3y
**5:30** (5:30) (Class 4) (0-80,80) 3-Y-O+ **£6,469** (£1,925; £962; £481) **Stalls** Low

Form RPR

2102 **1** **London (FR)**[11] 7285 4-9-7 **80**.....................................(h) JosephineGordon 5 93
(Phil McEntee) *chsd clr ldr: rdn and clsd to ld over 1f out: r.o strly and drew clr fnl f: readily* **10/3**[1]

5312 **2** *3 ¼* **King Of Swing**[20] 7002 4-9-0 **73**.......................................(h) ShaneKelly 2 78
(Richard Hughes) *hld up in tch in 4th: effrt over 2f out: drvn to chse wnr 1f out: kpt on u.p but no imp on wnr* **5/1**[2]

6641 **3** *1 ¼* **Storm Cry**[20] 7000 3-9-5 **80**............................................. DavidProbert 8 81
(Mark Johnston) *chsd ldng pair: effrt over 2f out: swtchd lft and drvn over 1f out: kpt on same pce ins fnl f* **6/1**[3]

6534 **4** *½* **Munfallet (IRE)**[17] 7094 6-9-4 **77**..................................... SeanLevey 1 77
(David Brown) *led and sn clr: rdn 2f out: hdd over 1f out and unable qck: kpt on same pce ins fnl f* **5/1**[2]

4502 **5** *1* **Poetic Force (IRE)**[24] 6866 3-8-10 **71**.........................(t) WilliamCarson 9 68+
(Tony Carroll) *taken down early: hld up in tch in last trio: rdn and hdwy on outer over 3f out: nt clr run and shuffled bk to rr 3f out: nvr enough room after: swtchd lft and kpt on ins fnl f* **7/1**

044 **6** *1 ¼* **Duke Of North (IRE)**[15] 7157 5-8-0 **66**........................ IsobelFrancis(7) 4 61
(Jim Boyle) *s.i.s: hld up off the pce in rr: effrt over 2f out: no imp and kpt on same pce ins fnl f* **7/1**

2413 **7** *1 ¼* **Morache Music**[73] 5051 9-9-4 **77**......................................(p) LiamKeniry 7 68
(Patrick Chamings) *hld up in midfield: effrt over 2f out: n.m.r over 1f out: sn rdn and no hdwy: wknd ins fnl f* **16/1**

0151 **8** *1* **Good Luck Charm**[20] 7002 8-9-0 **76**........................(b) HectorCrouch(3) 3 65
(Gary Moore) *wnt rt s: in tch in midfield: effrt over 2f out: no imp u.p over 1f out: wknd ins fnl f* **8/1**

0400 **9** *½* **El Torito (IRE)**[17] 7094 3-8-6 **70**.................................. CharlieBennett(3) 6 56
(Jim Boyle) *s.i.s: off the pce in last pair: rdn and hdwy in centre 3f out: outpcd and btn over 1f out: wknd ins fnl f* **33/1**

1m 27.37s (4.07) **Going Correction** +0.575s/f (Yiel)
**WFA** 3 from 4yo+ 2lb **9** Ran SP% **115.6**
Speed ratings (Par 105): **99,95,93,93,92 90,89,88,87**
CSF £19.90 CT £96.13 TOTE £3.90: £1.70, £1.70, £2.30; EX 20.10 Trifecta £84.70.
**Owner** Trevor Johnson **Bred** Jean-Pierre Dubois **Trained** Newmarket, Suffolk

**FOCUS**
This fair handicap featured several in-form sorts and was run at what looked a sound gallop, but the time was 1.22sec slower than the opening nursery, indicating the ground had deteriorated. The winner built on his last run and the runner-up has been rated to his recent form.
T/Plt: £48.40 to a £1 stake. Pool: £90,429.78 - 1363.66 winning units T/Qpdt: £5.60 to a £1 stake. Pool: £7,053.02 - 928.76 winning units **Steve Payne**

# 7159 MUSSELBURGH (R-H)
Sunday, October 1

**OFFICIAL GOING: Soft (good to soft in places; 6.3)**
Wind: Fairly strong, 1/2 across sprint course & 4f of round course Weather: Dry, bright

## 7654 SAVE THE CHILDREN IRISH STALLION FARMS EBF NOVICE STKS (PLUS 10 RACE) 1m 208y
**2:00** (2:00) (Class 4) 2-Y-O **£4,528** (£1,347; £673; £336) **Stalls** Low

Form RPR

5 **1** **House Edge**[16] 7128 2-9-2 0.......................................... PaulMulrennan 5 87+
(Michael Bell) *in tch: hdwy on outside to ld over 2f out: rdn and edgd rt over 1f out: drew clr ins fnl f* **6/4**[2]

16 **2** *5* **Lynwood Gold (IRE)**[19] 7026 2-9-8 0................................ JoeFanning 6 80
(Mark Johnston) *led: rdn and hdd over 2f out: rallied: kpt on same pce fnl f* **6/5**[1]

66 **3** *4 ½* **French Resistance (IRE)**[24] 6854 2-9-2 0.................. TonyHamilton 4 64
(Roger Fell) *trckd ldr: rdn and ch over 2f out: outpcd fr over 1f out* **28/1**

6 **4** *½* **Handsome Bob (IRE)**[39] 6312 2-9-2 0........................ ConnorBeasley 3 63
(Keith Dalgleish) *chsd ldrs: rdn whn faltered sltly over 2f out: sn outpcd: n.d after* **9/1**[3]

**5** *¾* **Sienna Dream** 2-8-11 0.................................................... BarryMcHugh 8 56
(Alistair Whillans) *t.k.h: stdd in tch: effrt and rdn over 2f out: no imp fr over 1f out: btn fnl f* **66/1**

0 **6** *¾* **Making Miracles**[12] 7237 2-9-2 0.............................. RichardKingscote 2 59
(Mark Johnston) *hld up: rdn and outpcd over 4f out: shortlived effrt 2f out: sn n.d* **20/1**

**7** *10* **Wowsham (IRE)** 2-8-11 0................................................ RowanScott(5) 1 38
(Keith Dalgleish) *s.i.s: rn green in rr: struggling bef 1/2-way: nvr on terms* **22/1**

1m 57.67s (3.77) **Going Correction** +0.425s/f (Yiel) **7** Ran SP% **109.5**
Speed ratings (Par 97): **100,95,91,91,90 89,80**
CSF £3.21 TOTE £2.40: £1.60, £1.10; EX 4.30 Trifecta £26.10.
**Owner** Edward J Ware **Bred** Aston House Stud **Trained** Newmarket, Suffolk

**FOCUS**
Bottom bend moved out 3yds, adding 7yds to races 1, 3, 5 & 6. After 2mm of rain during the morning the going was changed to soft, good to soft in places. Little depth to the opening novice and the two market leaders were dominant, with the winner very much one to keep an eye on in the future.

## 7655 ROYAL SCOTS CLUB NURSERY H'CAP 5f 1y
**2:30** (2:31) (Class 6) (0-65,66) 2-Y-O **£2,587** (£770; £384; £192) **Stalls** High

Form RPR

5502 **1** **Savannah's Show**[15] 7159 2-9-0 **58**.............................. ConnorBeasley 6 64
(Richard Guest) *t.k.h: in tch: effrt whn nt clr run and swtchd rt over 1f out: led ins fnl f: kpt on wl* **5/1**[3]

6600 **2** *hd* **Where's Jeff**[47] 6043 2-8-6 **57**...................................... HarrisonShaw(7) 9 62+
(Michael Easterby) *hld up: hdwy whn n.m.r and swtchd rt over 1f out: kpt on wl fnl f: jst hld* **25/1**

6053 **3** *1 ½* **Eller Brook**[15] 7159 2-9-3 **61**........................................... PaulMulrennan 7 61
(Michael Dods) *dwlt: hld up: hdwy and cl up on outside 1/2-way: led over 1f out: edgd lft and hdd ins fnl f: no ex* **11/4**[2]

2361 **4** *2 ¼* **Seen The Lyte (IRE)**[11] 7264 2-9-3 **66**.................. CallumRodriguez(5) 8 59
(John Quinn) *in tch: effrt whn nt clr run over 1f out: sn swtchd lft: kpt on same pce fnl f* **2/1**[1]

00 **5** *1 ½* **Rocket Man Dan (IRE)**[15] 7159 2-9-3 **61**........................(t[1]) JoeFanning 2 47
(Keith Dalgleish) *cl up: effrt and ev ch over 1f out: wknd ins fnl f* **8/1**

0504 **6** *1 ¼* **Lady Lintera (IRE)**[11] 7264 2-8-8 **52**..................................(h) ShaneGray 4 34
(Ann Duffield) *w ldr: led 1/2-way to over 1f out: sn rdn and wknd* **25/1**

0300 **7** *2* **Alaskan Beauty (IRE)**[15] 7159 2-9-2 **60**............................ DavidAllan 10 34
(Tim Easterby) *led against stands' rail to 1/2-way: rdn and wknd over 1f out* **14/1**

6600 **8** *nk* **Our Kid (IRE)**[18] 7057 2-9-3 **61**......................................(b) TonyHamilton 5 34
(Richard Fahey) *hld up: rdn over 2f out: wknd over 1f out* **9/1**

1m 2.23s (1.83) **Going Correction** +0.425s/f (Yiel) **8** Ran SP% **112.1**
Speed ratings (Par 93): **102,101,99,95,93 91,88,87**
CSF £107.83 CT £406.21 TOTE £5.00: £1.80, £4.80, £1.60; EX 101.00 Trifecta £685.00.
**Owner** Mrs Alison Guest **Bred** Mrs Mary Taylor **Trained** Ingmanthorpe, W Yorks

**FOCUS**
A modest nursery run at a good pace with the winner confirming recent form with the third.

## 7656 ROYAL REGIMENT OF SCOTLAND H'CAP 7f 33y
**3:00** (3:01) (Class 4) (0-85,87) 3-Y-O **£6,469** (£1,925; £962; £481) **Stalls** Low

Form RPR
1015 **1** **Aimez La Vie (IRE)**[19] 7016 3-9-0 **81** AdamMcNamara(3) 3 90
(Richard Fahey) *in tch: rdn over 2f out: rallied over 1f out: led wl ins fnl f: kpt on* **9/1**
2551 **2** *hd* **Raselasad (IRE)**[31] 6627 3-9-7 **85** BarryMcHugh 8 93
(Tracy Waggott) *led: rdn over 1f out: hdd wl ins fnl f: kpt on* **5/1**[2]
0021 **3** *2 1/2* **Our Charlie Brown**[19] 7016 3-8-13 **77** JamesSullivan 6 79
(Tim Easterby) *t.k.h: trckd ldrs: effrt and drvn along over 1f out: kpt on same pce ins fnl f* **6/1**[3]
0204 **4** *nk* **Brogan**[16] 7130 3-9-1 **79** (p) RichardKingscote 1 80
(Tom Dascombe) *chsd ldr: rdn over 2f out: kpt on same pce ins fnl f* **14/1**
6220 **5** *3/4* **Areen Heart (FR)**[37] 6404 3-9-9 **87** (h) DavidNolan 7 86
(David O'Meara) *hld up: pushed along over 2f out: effrt and edgd lft over 1f out: sn no imp* **7/1**
-440 **6** *nk* **Mamdood (IRE)**[2] 7570 3-8-5 **76** (t) JamieGormley(7) 9 74
(Susan Corbett) *hld up: rdn over 2f out: effrt over 1f out: nvr able to chal* **25/1**
4014 **7** *1/2* **Chinese Spirit (IRE)**[29] 6692 3-8-3 **67** JoeFanning 2 64
(R Mike Smith) *hld up: drvn along and outpcd over 2f out: sme late hdwy: nvr rchd ldrs* **8/1**
1240 **8** *nk* **Saint Equiano**[18] 7044 3-9-6 **84** (h) GrahamLee 11 80
(Keith Dalgleish) *cl up on outside: rdn and outpcd over 2f out: wknd over 1f out* **16/1**
4-14 **9** *2 1/4* **Lomu (IRE)**[42] 6235 3-9-8 **86** PaulMulrennan 4 76
(Keith Dalgleish) *slowly away: plld hrd in rr: rdn and outpcd over 2f out: sn btn* **9/2**[1]
**10** *8* **At Your Service**[11] 7293 3-8-12 **76** (h[1]) JFEgan 5 45
(W P Browne, Ire) *bhd: drvn and struggling over 3f out: nvr on terms* **12/1**
2422 **P** **Heir Of Excitement (IRE)**[19] 7016 3-9-0 **78** (p) ShaneGray 10
(Kevin Ryan) *slowly away: nvr gng wl in last pl: p.u after 2f* **10/1**

1m 31.79s (2.79) **Going Correction** +0.425s/f (Yiel) **11** Ran SP% **115.9**
Speed ratings (Par 103): **101,100,97,97,96 96,95,95,92,83**
CSF £52.79 CT £300.54 TOTE £10.80: £2.80, £1.70, £2.20; EX 55.70 Trifecta £357.20.
**Owner** Mr & Mrs N Wrigley **Bred** Lynn Lodge Stud And Foxtale Farm **Trained** Musley Bank, N Yorks

**FOCUS**
Race distance increased by 7yds. A open-looking 3yo handicap and solid form for the grade., with the form rated around the placed horses.

## 7657 BRIAN FINDLAY MEMORIAL RESTRICTED H'CAP (FOR HORSES THAT HAVE NOT WON THIS YEAR) 5f 1y
**3:35** (3:35) (Class 5) (0-75,74) 3-Y-O+ **£3,234** (£962; £481; £240) **Stalls** High

Form RPR
4505 **1** **Economic Crisis (IRE)**[23] 6891 8-8-9 **65** LewisEdmunds(3) 3 71
(Alan Berry) *hld up on outside: hdwy over 1f out: led wl ins fnl f: hld on* **9/1**
0002 **2** *shd* **See The Sun**[4] 7522 6-8-9 **62** (b) DavidAllan 9 67
(Tim Easterby) *led against stands' rail: rdn and edgd rt over 1f out: pricked ears and hdd wl ins fnl f: jst hld* **5/4**[1]
0560 **3** *1 3/4* **Luv U Always**[19] 7036 3-8-0 **60** oh14 (p) JamieGormley(7) 5 60?
(Iain Jardine) *cl up: rdn along wl over 1f out: kpt on same pce ins fnl f* **50/1**
2022 **4** *1 1/2* **Vintage Dream (IRE)**[19] 7014 3-8-7 **60** (be) PatrickMathers 1 55
(Noel Wilson) *chsd ldrs: rdn over 1f out: outpcd ins fnl f* **6/1**[3]
4400 **5** *nk* **Olivia Fallow (IRE)**[27] 6758 5-9-7 **74** GrahamLee 7 67
(Paul Midgley) *dwlt: t.k.h: hld up in tch: effrt and rdn 2f out: no imp fnl f* **5/1**[2]
0500 **6** *nk* **Market Choice (IRE)**[4] 7525 4-8-8 **61** (v[1]) BarryMcHugh 2 52
(Tracy Waggott) *dwlt and blkd s: hld up: rdn and outpcd 2f out: sme late hdwy: nvr on terms* **11/1**
0400 **7** *1 3/4* **Apricot Sky**[29] 6670 7-9-7 **74** PaulMulrennan 4 59
(Michael Dods) *prom tl rdn and wknd over 1f out* **14/1**
2253 **8** *1 1/2* **Oriental Lilly**[23] 6891 3-8-3 **63** SeanMooney(7) 8 44
(Jim Goldie) *dwlt: bhd on ins: drvn and struggling 2f out: sn btn* **17/2**

1m 2.46s (2.06) **Going Correction** +0.425s/f (Yiel) **8** Ran SP% **112.9**
Speed ratings (Par 103): **100,99,97,94,94 93,90,88**
CSF £20.19 CT £543.79 TOTE £10.60: £2.50, £1.10, £7.20; EX 29.30 Trifecta £604.40.
**Owner** William Burns & Alan Berry **Bred** Philip Hore Jnr **Trained** Cockerham, Lancs

**FOCUS**
Just a fair handicap and not the most competitive for the grade.

## 7658 IRISH STALLIONS FARMS EBF SCOTTISH PREMIER SERIES FILLIES' H'CAP 1m 2y
**4:10** (4:10) (Class 3) (0-90,92) 3-Y-O+
**£12,450** (£3,728; £1,864; £932; £466; £234) **Stalls** Low

Form RPR
2000 **1** **Sophie P**[22] 6924 4-9-9 **92** CallumRodriguez(5) 2 101
(R Mike Smith) *in tch: hdwy over 2f out: sn pushed along: led ins fnl f: styd on strly* **11/1**
1120 **2** *2* **Peach Melba**[22] 6919 3-9-8 **89** JoeFanning 4 93
(Mark Johnston) *t.k.h early: prom: smooth hdwy on outside to ld over 2f out: shkn up and drifted lft over 1f out: hdd ins fnl f: no ex* **6/1**[3]
5444 **3** *3/4* **Forever A Lady (IRE)**[15] 7161 4-8-7 **71** oh4 AndrewMullen 6 73
(Keith Dalgleish) *hld up: rdn and effrt over 2f out: ev ch briefly ins fnl f: one pce towards fin* **25/1**
1110 **4** *2* **Whatsthemessage (IRE)**[16] 7113 3-9-10 **91** GrahamLee 1 89
(Keith Dalgleish) *prom: rdn and outpcd over 2f out: rallied ins fnl f: nt pce to chal* **6/1**[3]
060 **5** *7* **Alexandrakollontai (IRE)**[15] 7161 7-8-13 **77** (b) JamesSullivan 3 59
(Alistair Whillans) *s.i.s: hld up: rdn and outpcd over 2f out: n.d after* **40/1**
6111 **6** *1/2* **Set In Stone (IRE)**[15] 7161 3-9-6 **92** RowanScott(5) 7 72
(John Patrick Shanahan, Ire) *cl up: drvn and ev ch over 2f out: edgd lft and wknd over 1f out* **6/4**[1]
3542 **7** *3/4* **Invermere**[15] 7161 4-8-9 **73** TonyHamilton 8 52
(Richard Fahey) *led: rdn and hdd over 2f out: wknd over 1f out* **4/1**[2]
221- **8** *4 1/2* **Lucky Violet (IRE)**[422] 5115 5-8-9 **73** DavidAllan 5 41
(Iain Jardine) *dwlt: hld up: drvn along over 2f out: sn wknd* **10/1**

1m 42.84s (1.64) **Going Correction** +0.425s/f (Yiel)
**WFA** 3 from 4yo+ 3lb **8** Ran SP% **112.3**
Speed ratings (Par 104): **108,106,105,103,96 95,95,90**
CSF £72.16 CT £1615.53 TOTE £11.40: £2.90, £2.20, £5.90; EX 82.30 Trifecta £930.10.
**Owner** Smith, Matheson, Stewart **Bred** New Hall Stud **Trained** Galston, E Ayrshire

**FOCUS**
Race distance increased by 7yds. A useful handicap in which they went good pace throughout and a small personal best from the winner.

## 7659 ROBERT PURVIS PLANT HIRE H'CAP 1m 5f 216y
**4:45** (4:45) (Class 5) (0-70,69) 3-Y-O+ **£3,234** (£962; £481; £240) **Stalls** Low

Form RPR
1326 **1** **Jonny Delta**[23] 6895 10-9-4 **59** JamesSullivan 2 66+
(Jim Goldie) *hld up: stdy hdwy and prom whn n.m.r over 2f out and over 1f out: rdn to ld wl ins fnl f: kpt on wl* **20/1**
6601 **2** *nk* **London Glory**[26] 6788 4-9-6 **61** (b) JoeFanning 5 66
(David Thompson) *hld up: smooth hdwy over 2f out: led over 1f out: sn pushed along and hung lft: hdd wl ins fnl f: r.o* **5/1**[3]
3605 **3** *hd* **Schmooze (IRE)**[23] 6895 8-8-9 **50** oh3 AndrewMullen 12 55
(Linda Perratt) *hld up: pushed along over 5f out: gd hdwy 2f out: disp ld ins fnl f: no ex: hld towards fin* **33/1**
1545 **4** *1 1/4* **Sheriff Garrett (IRE)**[8] 7386 3-9-7 **69** DavidAllan 6 72
(Tim Easterby) *hld up: hdwy over 3f out: rdn and kpt on ins fnl f: nt pce to chal* **9/2**[2]
0263 **5** *3* **Traditional Dancer (IRE)**[23] 6898 5-8-4 **52** (b) JamieGormley(7) 4 50
(Iain Jardine) *awkward s: hld up: hdwy and cl up after 3f: led over 5f out to over 2f out: hung rt and no ex fr over 1f out* **4/1**[1]
0412 **6** *3/4* **Stanarley Pic**[12] 7248 6-9-7 **62** NeilFarley 7 59
(Sally Haynes) *cl up: effrt and ev ch over 2f out: no ex ins fnl f* **15/2**
5505 **7** *nse* **Falcon's Fire (IRE)**[12] 7236 4-9-1 **61** (b) RowanScott(5) 1 58
(Keith Dalgleish) *hld up: hdwy on outside to ld over 2f out: hdd over 1f out: sn wknd* **14/1**
4650 **8** *2 1/4* **Archibelle**[36] 6436 3-8-3 **58** ConnorMurtagh(7) 10 52
(R Mike Smith) *hld up: pushed along and effrt over 3f out: btn over 1f out* **33/1**
20-5 **9** *2 3/4* **Ghostly Arc (IRE)**[33] 6551 5-9-5 **60** PatrickMathers 13 50
(Noel Wilson) *led to over 5f out: cl up tl lost pl over 2f out: sn wknd* **20/1**
0 **10** *7* **Bibliotheca (JPN)**[25] 6835 4-9-13 **68** JFEgan 9 47
(W P Browne, Ire) *dwlt: sn prom: rdn over 4f out: wknd over 2f out* **9/2**[2]
4506 **11** *12* **Wee Bogus**[23] 6898 4-8-11 **52** (p) GrahamLee 8 13
(Alistair Whillans) *midfield: drvn and outpcd over 5f out: struggling fnl 3f: t.o* **50/1**
4300 **12** *20* **Torremar (FR)**[51] 5873 4-10-0 **69** (p) KevinStott 11
(Kevin Ryan) *in tch: rdn over 5f out: lost tch fr over 3f out: t.o* **14/1**
000 **13** *92* **Optima Petamus**[19] 7015 5-9-5 **60** (p) JackGarritty 3
(Patrick Holmes) *midfield: drvn and lost pl over 5f out: lost tch and eased fr over 3f out* **50/1**

3m 12.15s (6.85) **Going Correction** +0.425s/f (Yiel)
**WFA** 3 from 4yo+ 7lb **13** Ran SP% **117.5**
Speed ratings (Par 103): **97,96,96,96,94 93,93,92,90,86 80,68,16**
CSF £109.40 CT £3295.08 TOTE £15.30: £2.90, £2.30, £6.10; EX 92.10 Trifecta £1993.10.
**Owner** Johnnie Delta Racing **Bred** Miss Gill Quincey **Trained** Uplawmoor, E Renfrews
■ Stewards' Enquiry : Jamie Gormley two-day ban: careless riding (Oct 15-16)

**FOCUS**
Race distance increased by 7yds. A modest staying handicap and plenty were in with a chance at the 2f pole.

## 7660 UBS WEALTH MANAGEMENT APPRENTICE H'CAP 5f 1y
**5:20** (5:20) (Class 6) (0-60,60) 3-Y-O+ **£2,587** (£770; £384; £192) **Stalls** High

Form RPR
3400 **1** **Lady Joanna Vassa (IRE)**[8] 7407 4-8-3 **46** (v) SeanMooney(7) 2 52
(Richard Guest) *mde all: clr over 1f out: hld on wl cl home* **15/2**
4050 **2** *shd* **Kodimoor (IRE)**[19] 7018 4-9-5 **58** (bt) RobJFitzpatrick(3) 4 64
(Christopher Kellett) *dwlt: hld up in midfield on outside: hdwy and rdn over 1f out: chsd wnr ins fnl f: r.o: hld cl home* **14/1**
3510 **3** *nk* **Dawoodi**[2] 7575 3-9-9 **59** (h) LewisEdmunds 12 65
(Linda Perratt) *dwlt: hld up: swtchd lft and hdwy whn rdr dropped rein briefly and hung bdly rt appr fnl f: stened and kpt on wl fnl f: hld nr fin* **9/2**[1]
4660 **4** *1 1/4* **Goninodaethat**[13] 7218 9-9-2 **55** CallumRodriguez(3) 11 55
(Jim Goldie) *bhd: rdn along 1/2-way: gd hdwy fnl f: kpt on: nt rch first three* **16/1**
0034 **5** *3/4* **Twentysvnthlancers**[15] 7164 4-9-7 **57** AdamMcNamara 8 54
(Paul Midgley) *hld up: hdwy whn nt clr run briefly over 1f out: r.o ins fnl f: nvr able to chal* **9/2**[1]
6020 **6** *1/2* **Lady Molly (IRE)**[2] 7575 3-8-4 **46** oh1 (v) RowanScott(6) 13 43
(Keith Dalgleish) *prom: effrt and rdn whn carried rt appr fnl f: sn no ex* **11/2**[2]
6316 **7** *1* **Star Cracker (IRE)**[38] 6351 5-9-9 **59** (p) PhilDennis 6 51
(Jim Goldie) *in tch: drvn along 1/2-way: kpt on same pce fr over 1f out* **10/1**
0000 **8** *1* **Lackaday**[19] 7020 5-8-10 **54** (b) NatalieHambling(8) 5 42
(Noel Wilson) *sn prom: drvn along and outpcd whn carried rt over 1f out: sn btn* **12/1**
4203 **9** *nk* **Mighty Bond**[12] 7247 5-8-6 **47** (p) ConnorMurtagh(5) 9 34
(Tracy Waggott) *bhd and outpcd: plenty to do 1/2-way: hdwy fnl f: nvr on terms* **6/1**[3]
6050 **10** *1* **Roman Times (IRE)**[50] 5919 4-8-3 **46** oh1 FayeMcManoman(7) 7 30
(Alan Berry) *in tch: drvn and outpcd 1/2-way: n.d after* **28/1**
0620 **11** *1 1/2* **Bop It**[32] 6572 8-9-0 **60** HarrisonShaw(10) 3 38
(Michael Easterby) *chsd ldrs tl rdn and wknd over 1f out* **14/1**
0005 **12** *3 3/4* **Vecheka (IRE)**[15] 7164 6-8-6 **47** (p[1]) JamieGormley(5) 14 12
(Kenny Johnson) *prom tl rdn and wknd fr 2f out* **33/1**

1m 3.12s (2.72) **Going Correction** +0.425s/f (Yiel) **12** Ran SP% **120.2**
Speed ratings (Par 101): **95,94,94,92,91 90,88,87,86,85 82,76**
CSF £109.41 CT £542.01 TOTE £7.90: £3.40, £4.80, £1.50; EX 110.10 Trifecta £859.40.
**Owner** www.primelawns.co.uk **Bred** Tom Radley **Trained** Ingmanthorpe, W Yorks

**FOCUS**
Only a modest handicap, but it was competitive and there was a thrilling finish. The third looks the key to the form.

T/Jkpt: Not won. T/Plt: £319.40 to a £1 stake. Pool: £81,651.30 - 186.59 winning units T/Qpdt: £82.70 to a £1 stake. Pool: £6,461.29 - 57.80 winning units **Richard Young**

7661 - 7662a (Foreign Racing) - See Raceform Interactive

## 7496 TIPPERARY (L-H)

Sunday, October 1

**OFFICIAL GOING: Flat & chase courses - heavy; hurdle course - soft to heavy**

### 7663a COOLMORE STUD HOME OF CHAMPIONS CONCORDE STKS (GROUP 3) 7f 100y

2:50 (2:51) 3-Y-O+

£34,038 (£10,961; £5,192; £2,307; £1,153; £576)

RPR

1 **Psychedelic Funk**[22] 6959 3-9-3 108..............................(b) ColinKeane 7 109+
(G M Lyons, Ire) *trckd ldr in 2nd: 3rd at 1/2-way: travelled wl to join issue 2f out and sn rdn to ld: 2l clr ins fnl f: advantage reduced cl home: kpt on wl* **6/1**

2 ½ **Downforce (IRE)**[7] 7424 5-9-5 110.................................. WJLee 10 109+
(W McCreery, Ire) *racd in mid-div: clsr to chse ldrs under 2f out: wnt 4th ent fnl f: styd on strly into 2nd fnl 150yds: kpt on wl to cl on wnr at fin* **15/8**[1]

3 1 ¾ **Spanish Tenor (IRE)**[115] 3509 3-9-3 98.................. DeclanMcDonogh 9 103
(Timothy Doyle, Ire) *keen early to chse ldrs in 4th: clsr to press ldrs in 3rd under 2f out: wnt 2nd appr fnl f: no imp in 3rd fnl 150yds: kpt on same pce* **25/1**

4 1 **Flight Risk (IRE)**[7] 7424 6-9-8 109.............................. KevinManning 1 105+
(J S Bolger, Ire) *racd in mid-div: clsr to chse ldrs 2f out towards far rails: no imp appr fnl f in 7th: swtchd rt and styd on wl into 4th cl home* **16/1**

5 ½ **Onenightidreamed (IRE)**[173] 1710 6-9-5 103...............(p) ChrisHayes 5 101
(J A Stack, Ire) *bit slowly away: racd towards rr: pushed along 1/2-way: prog on far rails under 2f out: no imp in 6th ent fnl f: kpt on same pce* **11/2**[3]

6 ¾ **Gordon Lord Byron (IRE)**[7] 7424 9-9-10 111.............. RonanWhelan 3 104
(T Hogan, Ire) *led tl hdd under 2f out: 3rd ent fnl f: wknd fnl 100yds* **16/1**

7 1 ¾ **Tobacco Bay (IRE)**[35] 6489 3-9-0 85.......................... NGMcCullagh 4 90
(J P Murtagh, Ire) *racd in mid-div: keen: rdn and no imp under 2f out 8th: kpt on same pce fnl f* **66/1**

8 nk **I'm So Fancy (IRE)**[15] 7171 3-9-0 104....................... ColmO'Donoghue 2 90
(Mrs John Harrington, Ire) *trckd ldrs in 3rd: pressed ldr in 2nd at 1/2-way: pushed along in 4th under 2f out: wknd ins fnl f* **5/1**[2]

9 1 ½ **Silverkode (IRE)**[22] 6961 3-9-3 103.............................. GaryCarroll 6 89
(Joseph G Murphy, Ire) *racd in mid-div: pushed along 3f out: no imp over 1f out in 9th: kpt on same pce* **7/1**

10 1 ½ **Sruthan (IRE)**[115] 3510 7-9-5 104.................................(bt) ShaneFoley 11 86
(P D Deegan, Ire) *racd in rr thrght: detached 2f out: nvr a factor* **20/1**

1m 46.14s
**WFA** 3 from 5yo+ 2lb **10 Ran SP% 115.5**
CSF £17.10 TOTE £5.00: £1.70, £1.10, £5.20; DF 19.10 Trifecta £329.40.
**Owner** Sean Jones **Bred** Mrs J Imray **Trained** Dunsany, Co Meath

**FOCUS**
A typically competitive edition of this Group 3 event witnessed a good, tough display by the 3yo winner.

7664 - 7665a (Foreign Racing) - See Raceform Interactive

## 7634 CHANTILLY (R-H)

Sunday, October 1

**OFFICIAL GOING: Turf: soft**

### 7666a TOTAL PRIX MARCEL BOUSSAC - CRITERIUM DES POULICHES (GROUP 1) (2YO FILLIES) (TURF) 1m

1:10 2-Y-O

£146,512 (£58,615; £29,307; £14,641; £7,333)

RPR

1 **Wild Illusion**[28] 6731 2-8-11 0..........................................(p) JamesDoyle 6 115
(Charlie Appleby) *trckd ldr on outer: jnd ldr 2 1/2f out: drvn to ld w 2f to run: rdn whn pressed wl over 1f out: styd on strly fnl f* **25/1**

2 1 ½ **Polydream (IRE)**[43] 6228 2-8-11 0................................ MaximeGuyon 2 112
(F Head, France) *hld up in midfield on inner: outpcd and pushed along 2f out: hdwy u.p more than 1f out: styd on fnl f: tk 2nd cl home: nt rch wnr* **11/8**[1]

3 hd **Mission Impassible (IRE)**[29] 6713 2-8-11 0...... ChristopheSoumillon 4 111
(J-C Rouget, France) *racd in midfield on outer: clsd to chse ldng pair 2 1/2f out: rdn to press ldr wl over 1f out: styd on u.p but no match for wnr: lost 2nd cl home* **16/1**

4 shd **Magical (IRE)**[21] 6974 2-8-11 0.......................................... RyanMoore 3 111
(A P O'Brien, Ire) *chsd ldng pair on inner: cl up and drvn but n.m.r 2f out: angled out and then bk ins over 1f out: styd on fnl f: nt pce to reel in wnr* **6/4**[2]

5 3 ½ **Zonza (FR)**[42] 6249 2-8-11 0........................................... CristianDemuro 7 103
(D Guillemin, France) *w.w in rr: kpt on to pass btn horses ent fnl f: nvr trbld ldrs* **25/1**

6 1 ¾ **Soustraction (IRE)**[28] 6731 2-8-13 0 ow2........................ OlivierPeslier 1 101
(C Laffon-Parias, France) *led: jnd 2 1/2f out: hdd w 2f to run: wknd wl over 1f out* **12/1**[3]

7 shd **Narella (IRE)**[28] 6726 2-8-11 0.................. Christophe-PatriceLemaire 5 99
(Markus Klug, Germany) *settled next to last: rdn and short-lived effrt over 1 1/2f out: wl hld fnl f* **12/1**[3]

1m 37.47s (-0.53) **Going Correction** +0.325s/f (Good) **7 Ran SP% 111.1**
Speed ratings: **115,113,113,113,109 107,107**
PARI-MUTUEL (all including 1 euro stake): WIN 16.50; PLACE 5.00, 2.00, SF 42.30.
**Owner** Godolphin **Bred** Godolphin **Trained** Newmarket, Suffolk

**FOCUS**
The second successive year this meeting was run at Chantilly with Longchamp still undergoing renovations. The going was a lot softer this season. This was a deep edition of the Boussac with only two of the seven fillies not arriving with Group success already in the bag. It was run at an uneven pace and it definitely paid to race handily. The form makes sense.

### 7667a QATAR PRIX JEAN-LUC LAGARDERE (GRAND CRITERIUM) (GROUP 1) (2YO COLTS & FILLIES) (TURF) 1m

1:45 2-Y-O

£170,931 (£68,384; £34,192; £17,081; £8,555)

RPR

1 **Happily (IRE)**[21] 6974 2-8-10 0.......................................... RyanMoore 4 112
(A P O'Brien, Ire) *bmpd along early: sn settled in fnl pair: drvn to chse ldng pair more than 1 1/2f out: styd on u.p to chal outside two rivals 150yds out: led fnl 60yds: drvn out* **6/5**[1]

2 1 ¼ **Olmedo (FR)**[28] 6730 2-9-0 0....................................... CristianDemuro 1 113
(J-C Rouget, France) *hld up bhd ldrs on inner: travelled strly between two ldrs 2 1/2f out: rdn to chse ldr 1 1/2f out: chal ins two rivals fnl f: no ex fnl 60yds* **7/2**[2]

3 snk **Masar (IRE)**[29] 6696 2-9-0 0.......................................... JamesDoyle 5 113
(Charlie Appleby) *racd keenly early on: chsd ldr: disp ld 2 1/2f out: led wl over 2f out: sn rdn and styd on: chal on both sides ins fnl f: hdd 60yds out: no ex* **7/2**[2]

4 1 ¾ **Woodmax (GER)**[11] 7304 2-9-0 0............................ StephanePasquier 3 109
(N Clement, France) *settled in rr: hdwy appr 1 1/2f fr home: sn rdn: wnt 4th 1f out: kpt on fnl f but no real imp on ldrs* **33/1**

5 2 ½ **Mythical Magic (IRE)**[15] 7146 2-9-0 0........................ JamieSpencer 2 103
(Charlie Appleby) *led: jnd 2 1/2f out: hdd wl over 2f out: grad dropped away* **8/1**[3]

6 6 ½ **Francesco Bere (FR)**[43] 6229 2-9-0 0..................... AlexandreGavilan 6 89
(D Guillemin, France) *racd keenly: restrained bhd ldrs: drvn and no imp 1 1/2f out: sn btn: bhd fnl f* **14/1**

1m 38.51s (0.51) **Going Correction** +0.325s/f (Good) **6 Ran SP% 110.6**
Speed ratings: **110,108,108,106,104 97**
PARI-MUTUEL (all including 1 euro stake): WIN 2.40; PLACE 1.50, 1.50, SF 7.10.
**Owner** Derrick Smith & Mrs John Magnier & Michael Tabor **Bred** Orpendale And Chelston Ireland **Trained** Cashel, Co Tipperary

**FOCUS**
A fascinating affair largely thanks to the participation of the filly Happily, the sole previous Group 1 winner in the line-up. She has been rated to her Moyglare mark.

### 7668a QATAR PRIX DE L'ARC DE TRIOMPHE (GROUP 1) (3YO+ NO GELDINGS) (TURF) 1m 4f

3:05 3-Y-O+

£2,441,880 (£976,923; £488,461; £244,017; £122,222)

RPR

1 **Enable**[38] 6356 3-8-9 0........................................................ FrankieDettori 2 129+
(John Gosden) *a handy: angled out to chse ldng pair ins fnl 2 1/2f: qcknd to ld under 2f out: rdn clr 1 1/2f out: styd on strly* **10/11**[1]

2 2 ½ **Cloth Of Stars (IRE)**[21] 6983 4-9-5 0....................... MickaelBarzalona 3 126
(A Fabre, France) *settled in midfield: gd hdwy over 1 1/2f out: drvn and styd on to go 2nd 110yds fr home: no ch w wnr* **20/1**

3 1 ¼ **Ulysses (IRE)**[39] 6328 4-9-5 0............................................ JimCrowley 1 124
(Sir Michael Stoute) *racd a little freely early: a.p: trckd eventual wnr through 2f out: rdn to go 2nd appr fnl f but unable to keep tabs on wnr: kpt on fnl f: lost 2nd 110yds fr home: no ex* **9/1**[3]

4 1 ½ **Order Of St George (IRE)**[21] 6976 5-9-5 0............ DonnachaO'Brien 9 122
(A P O'Brien, Ire) *a cl up: 2nd and scrubbed along 2 1/2f out: chsd ldrs fr 2f out: styd on wout having pce to chal* **8/1**[2]

5 1 ¼ **Brametot (IRE)**[47] 6053 3-8-13 0...................................... CristianDemuro 4 121
(J-C Rouget, France) *cl up on inner: 4th and drvn 2 1/2f out: no imp wl over 1 1/2f out: kpt on u.p fnl f* **20/1**

6 ½ **Dschingis Secret (GER)**[21] 6983 4-9-5 0....................... AdriedeVries 10 119
(Markus Klug, Germany) *w.w in midfield on outer: 5th and travelling wl enough 3f out: scrubbed along in pursuit of ldrs 2f out: sn rdn and no imp: kpt on same pce fnl f* **14/1**

7 hd **Iquitos (GER)**[28] 6727 5-9-5 0...................................... AndraschStarke 6 118+
(H-J Groschel, Germany) *towards rr: hdwy 2f out: styd on u.p fnl 1 1/2f: nvr nrr* **100/1**

8 nse **Idaho (IRE)**[36] 6461 4-9-5 0........................................ SeamieHeffernan 7 118
(A P O'Brien, Ire) *led: drvn ins fnl 2 1/2f: hdd under 2f out: kpt on same pce u.p* **25/1**

9 nk **Winter (IRE)**[22] 6958 3-8-9 0................................................ RyanMoore 8 115
(A P O'Brien, Ire) *w.w in midfield on rail: drvn along but n.m.r over 1 1/2f out: no imp appr fnl f: nvr trbld ldrs* **9/1**[3]

10 ¾ **Zarak (FR)**[91] 4423 4-9-5 0.................................... ChristopheSoumillon 18 117+
(A De Royer-Dupre, France) *w.w towards rr: began to cl more than 2f out: effrt petered out fnl f: nvr beyond midfield* **28/1**

11 nk **One Foot In Heaven (IRE)**[15] 7177 5-9-5 0...................... JamesDoyle 11 116+
(A De Royer-Dupre, France) *racd towards rr: rdn along over 2f out: styd on fr 1 1/2f out: run flattened out fnl 100yds* **80/1**

12 nk **Doha Dream (FR)**[35] 6499 4-9-5 0................................ GregoryBenoist 12 116+
(A Fabre, France) *w.w in fnl trio: hdwy 1 1/2f out: kpt on past btn horses: nvr in contention* **200/1**

13 1 ½ **Plumatic**[15] 7176 3-8-13 0............................................... MaximeGuyon 14 114
(A Fabre, France) *settled in midfield: niggled along but n.m.r over 2f out: angled out and effrt u.p 1 1/2f out: wknd fnl f* **100/1**

14 ½ **Seventh Heaven (IRE)**[21] 6972 4-9-2 0.............................. PatSmullen 17 110+
(A P O'Brien, Ire) *racd towards rr: rdn and no prog 2 1/2f out: nvr able to get involved* **50/1**

15 hd **Satono Diamond (JPN)**[21] 6983 4-9-5 0. Christophe-PatriceLemaire 13 112
(Yasutoshi Ikee, Japan) *w.w in fnl 3rd on outer: rdn and brief effrt 2f out: sn btn* **40/1**

16 ½ **Satono Noblesse (JPN)**[21] 6983 7-9-5 0........................ YugaKawada 5 111
(Yasutoshi Ikee, Japan) *prom: outpcd and drvn 2f out: sn dropped away* **250/1**

17 1 **Capri (IRE)**[15] 7147 3-8-13 0........................................... WayneLordan 15 111
(A P O'Brien, Ire) *scrubbed along early: sn settled towards rr of midfield: rdn towards rr over 2f out but no imp: wl hld fnl f* **20/1**

18 20 **Silverwave (FR)**[21] 6983 5-9-5 0...........................(h) Pierre-CharlesBoudot 16 78+
(P Bary, France) *w.w in rr: lost tch fr 2f out: t.o* **150/1**

2m 28.69s (-2.31) **Going Correction** +0.325s/f (Good)
**WFA** 3 from 4yo+ 6lb **18 Ran SP% 120.9**
Speed ratings: **120,118,117,116,115 115,115,115,114,114 114,114,113,112,112 112,111,98**
PARI-MUTUEL (all including 1 euro stake): WIN 1.80; PLACE 1.30, 3.40, 2.80; DF 17.50; SF 24.50.
**Owner** K Abdullah **Bred** Juddmonte Farms Ltd **Trained** Newmarket, Suffolk

**FOCUS**
As the market suggested, the winner was the clear form horse - she had upwards of 4lb in hand on adjusted RPRs - and it was straightforward. A low draw proved helpful, with the first five coming from stalls 2-3-1-9-4, and not many got seriously involved. The Arc has now been won by a filly in seven of the last ten years. She has been rated to her King George mark, while the runner-up achieved a personal best and the fourth has been rated in line with last year's mark in this event.

## 7669a PRIX DE L'OPERA LONGINES (GROUP 1) (3YO+ FILLIES & MARES) (TURF) 1m 2f
3:50 3-Y-O+ £195,350 (£78,153; £39,076; £19,521; £9,777)

RPR

1 **Rhododendron (IRE)**[22] 6958 3-8-11 0 SeamieHeffernan 5 116+
(A P O'Brien, Ire) *a cl up: rdn to ld 1 1/2f out: pressed thrght fnl f by eventual runner-up: r.o gamely u.p* **7/1**[3]

2 *hd* **Hydrangea (IRE)**[22] 6958 3-8-11 0 (p) RyanMoore 9 115
(A P O'Brien, Ire) *nvr far away: drvn 2 1/2f out: styd on to chse ldr 1 1/2f out: sustained chal thrght fnl f: rn gamely u.p: nt quite get there* **11/2**[2]

3 *nk* **Lady Frankel**[21] 6982 3-8-11 0 Pierre-CharlesBoudot 4 114+
(A Fabre, France) *settled in midfield: scrubbed along to take clsr order 2f out: styd on wl fnl f: nrest at fin* **40/1**

4 *nk* **Wuheida**[22] 6958 3-8-11 0 JamesDoyle 3 114
(Charlie Appleby) *a.p: 5th and gng wl enough over 2f out: styd on fnl f: nt pce to chal* **12/1**

5 *hd* **Left Hand**[21] 6981 4-9-2 0 (p) MaximeGuyon 13 113
(C Laffon-Parias, France) *w.w in midfield on outer: 6th and styng on ins fnl f: could nvr quite reel in ldrs* **11/1**

6 *2½* **Ashiana (GER)**[29] 6710 3-8-11 0 AdriedeVries 8 108+
(P Schiergen, Germany) *in rr: hdwy u.p 1 1/2f out: styd on fnl f: unable to get on terms* **28/1**

7 *nk* **The Black Princess (FR)**[21] 6981 4-9-2 0 FrankieDettori 10 108
(John Gosden) *sn led: drvn along 2f out: hdd 1 1/2f out: lft bhd ins fnl f* **20/1**

8 *½* **Queen's Trust**[38] 6356 4-9-2 0 OlivierPeslier 2 107
(Sir Michael Stoute) *racd keenly: hld up bhd ldrs: 6th and settled 1/2-way: rdn but no imp wl over 1 1/2f out: sn btn* **9/1**

9 *nk* **Lacazar (GER)**[56] 5693 3-8-11 0 AndraschStarke 14 106
(P Schiergen, Germany) *towards rr: rdn and effrt 1 1/2f out: nvr able to get involved* **11/2**[2]

10 *¾* **Onthemoonagain (FR)**[43] 6227 3-8-11 0 ChristopheSoumillon 11 105
(J-C Rouget, France) *racd in midfield: drvn along 2f out but no hdwy: wl hld fnl f* **16/1**

11 *5½* **Senga (USA)**[43] 6227 3-8-11 0 StephanePasquier 1 94
(P Bary, France) *w.w towards rr on inner: outpcd and drvn 1 1/2f out: wknd fnl f* **11/1**

12 *3½* **Melesina (IRE)**[28] 6732 3-8-11 0 AlexisBadel 12 87
(Richard Fahey) *w.w towards rr: bhd fnl 1 1/2f* **80/1**

13 *6* **Shamreen (IRE)**[21] 6972 4-9-2 0 PatSmullen 7 75
(D K Weld, Ire) *prom: 4th and rdn over 2f out but nt qckn: wknd fnl 1 1/2f* **7/2**[1]

2m 3.6s (-1.20) **Going Correction** +0.325s/f (Good)
**WFA** 3 from 4yo 4lb **13** Ran SP% **117.6**
Speed ratings: **117,116,116,116,116 114,113,113,113,112 108,105,100**
PARI-MUTUEL (all including 1 euro stake): WIN 10.20; PLACE 3.90, 2.60, 8.60; DF 28.00; SF 37.10.
**Owner** Mrs John Magnier & Michael Tabor & Derrick Smith **Bred** Orpendale, Chelston & Wynatt **Trained** Cashel, Co Tipperary

**FOCUS**
This looked a competitive edition and it saw a tight finish.

## 7670a PRIX DE L'ABBAYE DE LONGCHAMP LONGINES (GROUP 1) (2YO+) (TURF) 5f
4:35 2-Y-O+ £170,931 (£68,384; £34,192; £17,081; £8,555)

RPR

1 **Battaash (IRE)**[37] 6402 3-9-11 0 JimCrowley 2 128
(Charles Hills) *mde virtually all towards stands' side: drvn 2 l clr 1 1/2f out: r.o strly fnl f: unchal* **9/4**[1]

2 *4* **Marsha (IRE)**[37] 6402 4-9-7 0 LukeMorris 4 109
(Sir Mark Prescott Bt) *w.w in fnl pair: drvn along and hdwy 2f out: chsd ldr over 1f out: kpt on but no match for wnr* **11/4**[2]

3 *nk* **Profitable (IRE)**[37] 6402 5-9-11 0 (p) JamesDoyle 12 112
(Clive Cox) *led gp of five towards centre: a cl up overall: chsd ldr appr fnl f: kpt on in battle for 2nd but no match for wnr* **8/1**

4 *1* **Duke Of Firenze**[15] 7144 8-9-11 0 OisinMurphy 10 108
(David C Griffiths) *settled last of five in gp towards centre: swtchd ins and scrubbed along to cl wl over 1 1/2f out: kpt on fnl f: nvr able to chal* **80/1**

5 *½* **Queen Kindly**[22] 6926 3-9-7 0 PaulHanagan 9 104
(Richard Fahey) *chsd ldrs in gp towards centre: lost pl bef 1/2-way: last and pushed along more than 1 1/2f out: hdwy on outer over 1f out: styd on u.p* **33/1**

6 *hd* **Rimini (FR)**[28] 6728 2-8-7 0 JulienAuge 13 101
(C Ferland, France) *chsd ldrs towards centre: outpcd and drvn along 2f out: kpt on at one pce* **28/1**

7 *2½* **Finsbury Square (IRE)**[35] 6497 5-9-11 0 (b) ChristopheSoumillon 8 97
(F Chappet, France) *dwlt: towards rr: drvn and effrt 2f out: no imp u.p wl over 1f out* **16/1**

8 *1* **Largent Du Bonheur (FR)**[21] 6979 4-9-11 0(b) Christophe-PatriceLemaire 7 93
(M Delzangles, France) *chsd ldrs: rdn and no imp 1 12f out: grad dropped away fnl f* **100/1**

9 *2½* **Fashion Queen**[21] 6979 3-9-7 0 DanielTudhope 6 81
(David O'Meara) *racd between the two gps much of the way: midfield overall: rdn and nt qckn 2f out: wl hld fnl f* **33/1**

10 *nse* **Alphabet**[7] 7424 3-9-7 0 RyanMoore 11 81
(A P O'Brien, Ire) *pressed ldr towards centre: outpcd and niggled along over 2f out: sn wknd* **14/1**

11 *2* **Son Cesio (FR)**[35] 6495 6-9-11 0 Pierre-CharlesBoudot 5 77
(H-A Pantall, France) *in rr: began to cl sn after 1/2-way: sn rdn and no further hdwy: bhd fnl f* **40/1**

12 *5* **Signs Of Blessing (IRE)**[35] 6497 6-9-11 0 StephanePasquier 3 59
(F Rohaut, France) *w.w towards rr: no prog whn asked over 1 1/2f out: eased whn hld over 1f out* **4/1**[3]

13 *2½* **Der Graue (IRE)**[42] 6-9-11 0 AntoineHamelin 1 50
(B Mohamed, France) *pressed ldr: outpcd and drvn over 2f out: sn btn: wknd fnl f* **150/1**

57.59s (-0.71) **Going Correction** +0.325s/f (Good) **13** Ran SP% **115.8**
Speed ratings: **118,111,111,109,108 108,104,102,98,98 95,87,83**
PARI-MUTUEL (all including 1 euro stake): WIN 4.30; PLACE 1.70, 1.50, 2.30; DF 6.10; SF 15.00.
**Owner** Hamdan Al Maktoum **Bred** Ballyphilip Stud **Trained** Lambourn, Berks

**FOCUS**
A top-class performance from the winner in a race where it paid to be handy.

## 7671a QATAR PRIX DE LA FORET (GROUP 1) (3YO+) (TURF) 7f
5:15 3-Y-O+ £146,512 (£58,615; £29,307; £14,641; £7,333)

RPR

1 **Aclaim (IRE)**[15] 7145 4-9-2 0 OisinMurphy 1 117
(Martyn Meade) *a cl up on inner: nt clr run and swtchd outside two rivals 1 1/2f fr home: str run fnl f: led 100yds fr home: drvn out* **5/2**[1]

2 *¾* **So Beloved**[24] 6856 7-9-2 0 DanielTudhope 2 115+
(David O'Meara) *w.w in midfield: 5th and pushed along 1 1/2f out: styd on wl ins fnl f: nvr quite on terms w wnr* **33/1**

3 *shd* **Karar**[28] 6729 5-9-2 0 Pierre-CharlesBoudot 3 115
(F-H Graffard, France) *led: rallied gamely whn pressed 2f out: styd on u.str.p: hdd fnl 100yds: no ex: lost 2nd fnl stride* **9/2**[3]

4 *hd* **Dame Du Roi (IRE)**[28] 6729 3-8-10 0 AurelienLemaitre 4 109+
(F Head, France) *settled towards rr: hdwy wl over 1f out: styd on wl fnl f: nrest at fin* **12/1**

5 *½* **Zalamea (IRE)**[28] 6729 4-9-2 0 EddyHardouin 5 113
(Carina Fey, France) *chsd ldr: drvn to chal 2f out: kpt on at same pce* **66/1**

6 *snk* **Zelzal (FR)**[60] 5527 4-9-2 0 GregoryBenoist 7 112
(J-C Rouget, France) *hld up towards rr: gd hdwy 1 1/2f out: 3rd and clsng 1f out: sn rdn and btn* **3/1**[2]

7 *1* **Brando**[22] 6926 5-9-2 0 TomEaves 6 110
(Kevin Ryan) *dwlt: w.w towards rr: hdwy on inner over 1 1/2f out: styd on u.p but nt pce to trble ldrs* **5/1**

8 *1¼* **Toscanini (IRE)**[37] 6401 5-9-2 0 JamesDoyle 9 106
(Richard Fahey) *hld up in rr: rdn and effrt over 1 1/2f out: nvr in contention* **14/1**

9 *2* **Attendu (FR)**[35] 6498 4-9-2 0 MaximeGuyon 8 101
(C Laffon-Parias, France) *settled towards rr of midfield: rdn and tried to cl 2f out: sn btn* **20/1**

10 *1* **Realtra (IRE)**[31] 6642 5-8-13 0 YugaKawada 10 95
(Roger Varian) *nvr far away on outer: drvn and lost pl 1 1/2f out: wl hld fnl f* **20/1**

1m 25.75s (-0.35) **Going Correction** +0.325s/f (Good)
**WFA** 3 from 4yo+ 2lb **10** Ran SP% **116.7**
Speed ratings: **115,114,114,113,113 113,111,110,108,107**
PARI-MUTUEL (all including 1 euro stake): WIN 4.20; PLACE 2.20, 6.90, 2.50; DF 68.20; SF 88.10.
**Owner** Canning Downs & Partner **Bred** D Farrington And Canning Downs **Trained** Newmarket, Suffolk

**FOCUS**
A weak Group 1.

# 6985 DUSSELDORF (R-H)
Sunday, October 1

**OFFICIAL GOING: Turf: good**

## 7672a 97TH GROSSER PREIS DER LANDESHAUPTSTADT DUSSELDORF (GROUP 3) (3YO+) (TURF) 1m 110y
3:50 3-Y-O+ £27,350 (£10,256; £5,128; £2,564; £1,709)

RPR

1 **Millowitsch (GER)**[21] 6987 4-9-4 0 AndreasHelfenbein 2 108
(Markus Klug, Germany) *led after 1f: mde rest: sn 3 l clr: 1 l ld 1 1/2f out: rdn clr fnl f: won easing down* **13/10**[1]

2 *2¾* **A Raving Beauty (GER)**[31] 6647 4-8-13 0 ow4.(b) ClementLecoeuvre 5 97
(Andreas Suborics, Germany) *led early: hdd after 1f: chsd ldr: 1 l 2nd and hrd rdn 1 1/2f out: sn no imp: no match for wnr fnl f* **51/10**

3 *4¼* **Felician (GER)**[8] 9-9-2 0 JozefBojko 1 91
(Ferdinand J Leve, Germany) *hld up in rr: drvn along but no immediate imp more than 2 1/2f out: styd on over 1f out: nvr trbld ldrs* **155/10**

4 *1* **Arazza (GER)**[21] 6987 3-8-9 0 LukasDelozier 6 86
(J Hirschberger, Germany) *w.w in fnl pair: sme late prog to take 4th cl home: nvr really in contention* **81/10**

5 *nk* **Silver Meadow (IRE)**[26] 6804 4-8-13 0 FilipMinarik 4 85
(F-H Graffard, France) *hld up in midfield: rdn and nt qckn wl over 1 1/2f out: kpt on at one pce* **12/5**[2]

6 *27* **Attica**[154] 3-8-9 0 MartinSeidl 7 26
(Markus Klug, Germany) *racd v keenly: hld up in tch: rdn and no imp over 2f out: wkng whn eased ins fnl 1 1/2f* **14/5**[3]

1m 47.59s (0.01)
**WFA** 3 from 4yo+ 3lb **6** Ran SP% **132.6**
PARI-MUTUEL (all including 10 euro stake): WIN 23; PLACE: 14, 27; SF: 240.
**Owner** Dr Alexandra Margarete Renz **Bred** Frau Dr Alexandra Margarete Renz **Trained** Germany

# 7204 HANOVER (L-H)
Sunday, October 1

**OFFICIAL GOING: Turf: good to soft**

## 7673a GROSSER PREIS DER BMW NIEDERLASSUNG HANNOVER (LISTED RACE) (3YO+ FILLIES & MARES) (TURF) 1m 3f
4:05 3-Y-O+ £11,965 (£5,555; £2,564; £1,282)

RPR

1 **Ostana (GER)**[15] 4-9-0 0 WladimirPanov 1 97
(Daniel Paulick, Germany) **154/10**

2 *nk* **Agathonia (USA)**[26] 6805 3-8-8 0 AndreBest 3 96
(H-A Pantall, France) *sn settled in midfield: hdwy u.p 2f out: styd on fnl f: nvr quite on terms w wnr* **115/10**

3 *1* **Titi Makfi**[11] 7283 3-8-8 0 PJMcDonald 2 94
(Mark Johnston) *cl up early: sn settled bhd ldng gp: drvn to go 3rd over 2 1/2f out: styd on to chal ins fnl f: no ex last 50yds* **48/10**[2]

4 *½* **Glade**[25] 4-9-0 0 HugoJourniac 12 93
(C Ferland, France) **13/1**

5 *½* **Fosun (GER)**[29] 6710 4-9-3 0 MaximPecheur 7 95
(Markus Klug, Germany) **147/10**

6 hd **Margie's Music (FR)**[28] 3-8-8 0 DanielePorcu 10 92
(P Schiergen, Germany) **115/10**
7 4 **Diana Storm (GER)**[29] 6710 3-8-11 0 MarcLerner 8 88
(Waldemar Hickst, Germany) **2/1**[1]
8 3 ³/₄ **Wild Comet (GER)**[69] 4-9-0 0 RenePiechulek 4 78
(J Hirschberger, Germany) **118/10**
9 13 **Greta (FR)**[69] 4-9-0 0 (b) EduardoPedroza 9 55
(Frau Erika Mader, Germany) **49/1**
10 2 **White Rosa (IRE)**[38] 6350 3-8-8 0 (h) JackMitchell 5 51
(Hugo Palmer) *prom early: sn settled in midfield: sltly impeded and scrubbed along after 3 1/2f: lost pl more than 2f out: wl hld fnl f* **74/10**
11 1 **Baby Love (GER)**[31] 4-9-0 0 AlexanderPietsch 13 49
(R Dzubasz, Germany) **32/1**
12 2 ¹/₄ **Erica (GER)**[29] 6710 4-9-3 0 StephenHellyn 6 48
(Lennart Hammer-Hansen, Germany) **61/10**[3]
13 18 **La Tanzania (GER)**[749] 4-9-0 0 BauyrzhanMurzabayev 14 13
(Eva Fabianova, Germany) **58/1**
14 nk **Vallante (GER)**[14] 7204 4-9-0 0 MichaelCadeddu 11 12
(J Hirschberger, Germany) **45/1**

PARI-MUTUEL (all including 10 euro stake): WIN 164 PLACE: 54, 39, 30 SF: 1241.
**Owner** Ralf Paulick **Bred** R Paulick **Trained** Germany

7674 - 7687a (Foreign Racing) - See Raceform Interactive

## 7190 BATH (L-H)

Monday, October 2

**OFFICIAL GOING: Soft (good to soft in places; 6.6)**
Wind: Strong against Weather: Overcast

## 7688 DRIBUILD GROUP FILLIES' NOVICE MEDIAN AUCTION STKS (PLUS 10 RACE) 5f 160y

**2:10** (2:11) (Class 5) 2-Y-O **£4,528** (£1,347; £673; £336) **Stalls** Centre

Form RPR
664 1 **Lady Marigold (IRE)**[33] 6583 2-9-0 65 CharlesBishop 7 70
(Eve Johnson Houghton) *trckd ldrs: rdn and edgd lft ins fnl f: r.o to ld post* **9/1**
5 2 hd **Haylah (IRE)**[10] 7352 2-9-0 0 SeanLevey 5 69
(Richard Hannon) *led: rdn and edgd lft ins fnl f: hdd post* **1/1**[1]
2223 3 shd **Time For Wine (IRE)**[17] 7126 2-9-0 72 FranBerry 2 69
(David Evans) *w ldr: rdn over 1f out: styd on* **5/2**[2]
4 6 **Fanfare Lady (IRE)** 2-9-0 0 MartinHarley 4 49
(William Knight) *s.i.s: hdwy over 1f out: nt trble ldrs* **33/1**
0 5 4 ¹/₂ **Rose Of Shiraz**[17] 7126 2-8-7 0 GeorgiaDobie(7) 6 34
(J S Moore) *broke wl enough: sn lost pl: hdwy on outer and hung rt over 2f out: wknd over 1f out* **66/1**
3 6 3 **Fashion Sense (IRE)**[24] 6868 2-9-0 0 SamHitchcott 8 24
(Clive Cox) *chsd ldrs: pushed along 3f out: wknd over 1f out* **4/1**[3]
1m 17.5s (6.30) **Going Correction** +0.80s/f (Soft) **6 Ran SP% 113.0**
Speed ratings (Par 92): **90,89,89,81,75 71**
CSF £18.95 TOTE £11.30: £3.60, £1.80; EX 24.90 Trifecta £80.40.
**Owner** The Ascot Revellers **Bred** Mrs R F Johnson Houghton **Trained** Blewbury, Oxon

**FOCUS**
A fair juvenile fillies' novice sprint. They went a contested gallop on ground officially described as soft, good to soft in places. It looked hard work and there is a reported headwind. The opening level is guided by the runner-up's debut.

## 7689 ISG FILLIES' H'CAP 5f 10y

**2:40** (2:40) (Class 5) (0-70,70) 3-Y-O+ **£3,881** (£1,155; £577; £288) **Stalls** Centre

Form RPR
365 1 **Spirit Of Rosanna**[52] 5877 5-8-10 59 (tp) AdamBeschizza 2 67
(Steph Hollinshead) *led 3f: sn rdn: rallied to ld nr fin* **6/1**[3]
3100 2 nk **Toni's A Star**[9] 7407 5-8-0 56 (b) SophieRalston(7) 5 63
(Tony Carroll) *trckd ldrs: plld hrd: led 2f out: edgd lft ins fnl f: shkn up and hdd nr fin* **8/1**
3200 3 2 ¹/₂ **Nuzha**[17] 7122 3-8-8 62 (p) RhiainIngram(5) 4 61
(Karen George) *s.i.s and hmpd s: sn outpcd: r.o to go 3rd wl ins fnl f: nt rch ldrs* **33/1**
400 4 1 ¹/₄ **Broadhaven Honey (IRE)**[32] 6612 3-9-0 63 (v[1]) SamHitchcott 1 58
(Ronald Harris) *hld up: rdn 2f out: nt trble ldrs* **25/1**
5-31 5 shd **Her Terms**[29] 6724 3-9-7 70 (p) AdamKirby 7 64
(Clive Cox) *s.i.s: sn rcvrd to dispute 2nd: hrd rdn over 1f out: no ex ins fnl f* **7/4**[2]
6210 6 1 ¹/₂ **Beau Mistral (IRE)**[163] 1979 8-9-6 69 GeorgeDowning 3 57
(Tony Carroll) *hld up: rdn over 2f out: outpcd fr over 1f out* **25/1**
2212 7 ³/₄ **Bellevarde (IRE)**[15] 7192 3-9-4 67 JosephineGordon 6 54
(Richard Price) *disp 2nd tl rdn over 2f out: wknd ins fnl f* **11/8**[1]
1m 6.12s (3.62) **Going Correction** +0.80s/f (Soft) **7 Ran SP% 114.5**
Speed ratings (Par 100): **103,102,98,96,96 93,92**
CSF £49.55 TOTE £5.00: £2.90, £4.50; EX 44.10 Trifecta £734.00.
**Owner** J Holcombe **Bred** Redmyre Bloodstock & Tweenhills Stud **Trained** Upper Longdon, Staffs

**FOCUS**
A modest fillies' sprint handicap. They went a strong gallop on the testing ground and the long-time leader rallied to victory in the final furlong. The winner has been rated to form.

## 7690 IESIS GROUP NURSERY H'CAP 5f 160y

**3:10** (3:10) (Class 5) (0-75,76) 2-Y-O **£3,881** (£1,155; £577; £288) **Stalls** Centre

Form RPR
2021 1 **Jim Rockford**[15] 7193 2-9-7 76 GeorgiaCox(5) 4 81
(Ralph Beckett) *sn outpcd: hdwy over 1f out: rdn to ld and edgd lft ins fnl f: styd on* **9/4**[1]
0400 2 ³/₄ **Diamond Pursuit**[34] 6552 2-9-2 66 TomMarquand 3 69
(Jo Hughes) *a.p: rdn over 1f out: styd on* **9/1**
4630 3 nk **Joegogo (IRE)**[16] 7138 2-9-3 67 FranBerry 6 69
(David Evans) *hld up: hdwy 1/2-way: led over 1f out: sn rdn and edgd lft: hdd ins fnl f: keeping on whn nt clr run nr fin* **5/1**[3]
2054 4 3 ³/₄ **Bodybuilder**[9] 7410 2-8-9 62 HollieDoyle(3) 7 52
(Richard Hannon) *chsd ldrs: rdn and ev ch over 1f out: wknd wl ins fnl f* **7/1**
0051 5 ³/₄ **Bahuta Acha**[9] 7385 2-9-7 71 LukeMorris 2 58
(David Loughnane) *led: rdn and hdd over 1f out: wknd wl ins fnl f* **3/1**[2]
0054 6 4 ¹/₂ **Madame Jo Jo**[18] 7081 2-8-10 60 JosephineGordon 1 32
(Sarah Hollinshead) *chsd ldrs: rdn over 2f out: wknd fnl f* **13/2**
5500 7 7 **Highland Mary**[9] 7410 2-9-1 65 SeanLevey 5 14
(Richard Hannon) *w ldr tl wknd and eased over 1f out* **20/1**
1m 15.53s (4.33) **Going Correction** +0.80s/f (Soft) **7 Ran SP% 113.0**
Speed ratings (Par 95): **103,102,101,96,95 89,80**
CSF £22.55 TOTE £3.50: £2.40, £4.80; EX 26.30 Trifecta £142.10.
**Owner** Chelsea Thoroughbreds-The Rockford Files **Bred** Mrs Fiona Denniff **Trained** Kimpton, Hants
■ Stewards' Enquiry : Georgia Cox caution: careless riding

**FOCUS**
A fair nursery sprint handicap. The favourite came through to win well after initially struggling to lay up behind another forceful gallop. The runner-up has been rated near her mark.

## 7691 CURTINS "HANDS AND HEELS" APPRENTICE H'CAP (PART OF THE RACING EXCELLENCE INITIATIVE) 5f 160y

**3:40** (3:41) (Class 5) (0-75,73) 3-Y-O+ **£3,428** (£1,020; £509; £254) **Stalls** Centre

Form RPR
1134 1 **Pastfact**[15] 7192 3-9-7 73 DavidEgan 3 81
(Malcolm Saunders) *prom: chsd ldr over 3f out: shkn up over 1f out: styd on to ld wl ins fnl f* **5/4**[1]
361 2 nk **Oeil De Tigre (FR)**[32] 6615 6-9-0 68 SophieRalston(3) 1 75
(Tony Carroll) *plld hrd in 2nd pl 2f: remained handy: pushed along over 1f out: chsd wnr wl ins fnl f: r.o* **5/1**[3]
2500 3 2 ³/₄ **Seamster**[15] 7195 10-9-5 73 (t) LauraCoughlan(3) 2 71
(David Loughnane) *sn led: pushed along over 1f out: hdd and no ex wl ins fnl f* **10/1**
30-3 4 3 ¹/₂ **Peter Park**[24] 6874 4-9-2 72 AmeliaGlass(5) 4 58
(Clive Cox) *hld up: pushed along over 2f out: nt trble ldrs* **5/2**[2]
1140 5 3 **Jaganory (IRE)**[15] 7195 5-8-12 63 (p) NicolaCurrie 5 39
(Christopher Mason) *hld up: pushed along over 2f out: nvr on terms* **8/1**
6 12 **Evanescent (IRE)**[114] 3572 8-9-6 71 AledBeech 6 8
(Tony Carroll) *hld up: bhd fnl 3f* **25/1**
1m 16.42s (5.22) **Going Correction** +0.80s/f (Soft)
**WFA** 3 from 4yo+ 1lb **6 Ran SP% 113.7**
Speed ratings (Par 103): **97,96,92,88,84 68**
CSF £8.26 TOTE £2.30: £1.40, £2.10; EX 7.20 Trifecta £27.80.
**Owner** Premier Conservatory Roofs **Bred** M S Saunders & D Collier **Trained** Green Ore, Somerset

**FOCUS**
An ordinary sprint handicap for apprentice riders. They went a respectable gallop on the testing ground. It's been rated around the runner-up to last year's C&D form on soft.

## 7692 CONSTRUCTING EXCELLENCE SOUTH WEST H'CAP 5f 10y

**4:10** (4:11) (Class 6) (0-60,59) 3-Y-O+ **£2,911** (£866; £432; £216) **Stalls** Centre

Form RPR
0133 1 **Everkyllachy (IRE)**[14] 7217 3-9-4 59 (b) HollieDoyle(3) 9 70
(J S Moore) *sn pushed along in rr: hdwy 1/2-way: rdn to ld ins fnl f: r.o* **7/1**[3]
4032 2 2 ¹/₄ **Time Medicean**[15] 7191 11-9-5 57 (t) GeorgeDowning 11 59
(Tony Carroll) *mid-div: hdwy 1/2-way: led over 1f: rdn: edgd lft and hdd ins fnl f: styd on same pce* **5/1**[2]
4001 3 2 ¹/₂ **Lady Joanna Vassa (IRE)**[1] 7660 4-8-8 46 (v) ConnorBeasley 7 39
(Richard Guest) *hood removed late: s.i.s and edgd lft s: sn rcvrd to ld: rdn and hdd over 1f out: wknd ins fnl f* **11/4**[1]
0060 4 nse **Silver Penny**[15] 7191 3-8-4 45 (p) DavidEgan(3) 10 39
(Jim Boyle) *w ldr: rdn and ev ch over 1f out: wknd ins fnl f* **8/1**
6030 5 1 ¹/₂ **Fivos**[90] 4458 3-9-1 53 SeanLevey 6 41
(David Bridgwater) *hmpd s: in rr tl r.o ins fnl f: nvr nrr* **66/1**
0000 6 nk **Harrison Stickle**[36] 6478 5-9-4 56 (p[1]) TomMarquand 3 42
(John Gallagher) *prom: rdn over 1f out: wknd fnl f* **9/1**
6 7 1 ¹/₄ **Malaysian Boleh**[67] 5340 7-8-12 50 (v) JosephineGordon 2 32
(Phil McEntee) *sn pushed along in rr: nvr on terms* **8/1**
5520 8 nk **Fleeting Glimpse**[6] 7494 4-9-2 57 CharlieBennett(3) 1 38
(Patrick Chamings) *mid-div: rdn 1/2-way: wknd over 1f out* **7/1**[3]
2100 9 1 ¹/₄ **Tea El Tee (IRE)**[20] 7036 3-9-3 55 (b[1]) LukeMorris 8 32
(Gay Kelleway) *chsd ldrs tl rdn and wknd over 1f out* **9/1**
000 10 3 ³/₄ **Emilene**[98] 4164 3-9-2 54 (h) FranBerry 4 18
(Mark Brisbourne) *mid-div: pushed along 3f out: sn lost pl* **33/1**
0051 11 1 ¹/₄ **Foxford**[114] 3569 6-9-1 53 RobHornby 5 11
(Patrick Chamings) *edgd rt and hmpd s: sn pushed along in rr: rdn: hung rt and wknd over 1f out* **15/2**
1m 5.71s (3.21) **Going Correction** +0.80s/f (Soft) **11 Ran SP% 126.8**
Speed ratings (Par 101): **106,102,98,98,95 95,93,92,90,84 82**
CSF £45.44 CT £124.86 TOTE £5.70: £2.70, £1.10, £1.90; EX 24.30 Trifecta £184.90.
**Owner** Ever Equine & J S Moore **Bred** Mrs T Mahon **Trained** Upper Lambourn, Berks

**FOCUS**
A moderate sprint handicap. Three of the first four home were drawn in the three highest stalls and they raced wider out on the track in this bigger field.

## 7693 BARTON WILLMORE H'CAP (DIV I) 5f 160y

**4:40** (4:40) (Class 6) (0-60,60) 3-Y-O+ **£2,911** (£866; £432; £216) **Stalls** Centre

Form RPR
0404 1 **Air Of York (IRE)**[7] 7465 5-9-0 60 (p) WilliamCox(7) 6 66
(John Flint) *hld up in tch: rdn over 1f out: r.o to ld wl ins fnl f: comf* **10/3**[2]
000 2 ¹/₂ **Nutini (IRE)**[18] 7083 4-9-7 60 (p) SteveDrowne 5 64
(Malcolm Saunders) *chsd ldrs: led 2f out: rdn and hdd wl ins fnl f* **5/2**[1]
06 3 ¹/₂ **Captain Scooby**[15] 7191 11-8-7 46 oh1 (b) ConnorBeasley 8 49
(Richard Guest) *hld up in tch: n.m.r and lost pl 4f out: hdwy to chse ldr over 1f out: sn rdn: styd on* **7/1**[3]
000 4 6 **Keene's Pointe**[34] 6546 7-8-8 47 (p) AdamBeschizza 7 30
(Steph Hollinshead) *s.s: hdwy 1/2-way: sn rdn: styd on same pce fr over 1f out: eased nr fin* **7/1**[3]
3255 5 1 ¹/₄ **Fantasy Justifier (IRE)**[15] 7190 6-9-6 59 (p) SamHitchcott 1 38
(Ronald Harris) *pushed along early then hld up and plld hrd: hdwy 1/2-way: rdn over 1f out: wknd ins fnl f* **15/2**
50 6 2 **Q Cee**[11] 7320 4-9-4 57 (b) FranBerry 2 29
(Eugene Stanford) *chsd ldr: ev ch 2f out: sn rdn: wknd fnl f* **11/1**
00 7 2 **Louis Vee (IRE)**[2] 7605 9-8-7 46 oh1 (p) EdwardGreatrex 4 12
(John O'Shea) *led: hdd 2f out: sn rdn and wknd* **33/1**
0000 8 1 **Tally's Song**[15] 7191 4-8-7 46 oh1 (p) JimmyQuinn 3 8
(Grace Harris) *chsd ldrs: rdn 1/2-way: wknd over 1f out* **33/1**
640 9 ³/₄ **Caius College Girl (IRE)**[39] 6341 5-8-9 51 (p) HollieDoyle(3) 10 11
(Adrian Wintle) *hld up: rdn over 2f out: wknd over 1f out* **7/1**[3]
540 10 11 **Kath's Boy (IRE)**[39] 6341 3-8-6 46 oh1 LukeMorris 9
(Tony Carroll) *s.i.s: hld up: rdn over 2f out: sn wknd* **14/1**
1m 16.1s (4.90) **Going Correction** +0.80s/f (Soft)
**WFA** 3 from 4yo+ 1lb **10 Ran SP% 121.8**
Speed ratings (Par 101): **99,98,97,89,88 85,82,81,80,65**
CSF £12.74 CT £55.28 TOTE £4.10: £1.50, £2.00, £2.80; EX 15.80 Trifecta £80.70.
**Owner** Mrs Lynn Cullimore **Bred** Hugh Ryan **Trained** Kenfig Hill, Bridgend

**FOCUS**
The first division of another moderate sprint handicap. They went a respectable gallop centrally. It's been rated around the winner and third.

## 7694 BARTON WILLMORE H'CAP (DIV II) 5f 160y
**5:10** (5:13) (Class 6) (0-60,60) 3-Y-0+ **£2,911** (£866; £432; £216) **Stalls** Centre

Form RPR
5000 **1** **Perfect Pastime**[18] 7099 9-8-13 **57**.........................(p) PaddyBradley(5) 6 64
(Jim Boyle) *chsd ldrs: rdn to ld ins fnl f: styd on* **10/1**
3020 **2** *nk* **Captain Ryan**[36] 6478 6-9-7 **60**........................................ TimmyMurphy 7 66
(Geoffrey Deacon) *hld up: hdwy over 1f out: r.o to go 2nd nr fin: nt rch wnr* **5/1**[3]
3433 **3** *½* **Ambitious Icarus**[3] 7575 8-9-7 **60**...........................(b) ConnorBeasley 3 64
(Richard Guest) *hld up in tch: racd keenly: rdn over 1f out: edgd lft ins fnl f: styd on* **7/4**[1]
-500 **4** *nk* **Coral Caye**[35] 6507 3-8-6 **46** oh1................................ AdamBeschizza 10 49
(Steph Hollinshead) *hld up: hdwy over 1f out: rdn and ev ch ins fnl f: no ex towards fin* **25/1**
6000 **5** *1 ¾* **Arizona Snow**[15] 7191 5-8-7 **46** oh1................................(p) LukeMorris 2 44
(Ronald Harris) *led: rdn over 1f out: hdd and no ex ins fnl f* **20/1**
6040 **6** *3 ½* **Ambitious Boy**[32] 6615 8-8-7 **46** oh1.........................(p) EdwardGreatrex 8 32
(John O'Shea) *hld up: rdn over 2f out: hdwy over 1f out: wknd ins fnl f* **16/1**
3000 **7** *3 ¼* **Royal Normandy**[35] 6507 5-8-7 **46** oh1.........................(b) JimmyQuinn 4 21
(Grace Harris) *chsd ldr: rdn over 2f out: wknd over 1f out* **25/1**
-556 **8** *2* **Delahay**[17] 7122 3-8-10 **50**................................................ TomMarquand 5 19
(Michael Blanshard) *prom: rdn over 2f out: wknd over 1f out* **7/1**
1140 **9** *1 ½* **Concur (IRE)**[72] 5146 4-8-11 **53**.....................................(tp) DavidEgan(3) 1 17
(Rod Millman) *prom tl rdn and wknd over 1f out* **3/1**[2]
/-00 **10** *nse* **Pound Note**[44] 6184 5-8-4 **46** oh1.................................(p[1]) PhilDennis(3) 9 10
(Michael Mullineaux) *prom: lost pl over 3f out: sn rdn: wknd over 1f out* **20/1**

1m 16.92s (5.72) **Going Correction** +0.80s/f (Soft)
**WFA** 3 from 4yo+ 1lb **10** Ran SP% **122.7**
Speed ratings (Par 101): **93,92,91,91,89 84,80,77,75,75**
CSF £59.19 CT £131.25 TOTE £12.40: £3.30, £1.40, £1.20; EX 91.70 Trifecta £152.60.
**Owner** The Paddock Space Partnership 2 **Bred** R G & T E Levin **Trained** Epsom, Surrey

**FOCUS**
The second division of another moderate sprint handicap. The winning time was nearly a second slower. The runner-up helps set a straightforward level.

## 7695 M J CHURCH NURSERY H'CAP 5f 10y
**5:40** (5:41) (Class 6) (0-60,64) 2-Y-0 **£2,911** (£866; £432; £216) **Stalls** Centre

Form RPR
0105 **1** **Just For The Craic (IRE)**[18] 7081 2-9-8 **61**....................... AdamKirby 1 68
(Neil Mulholland) *s.i.s: rcvrd to ld 4f out: rdn and edgd rt fr over 1f out: styd on u.p* **11/2**
303 **2** *2* **Jonnysimpson (IRE)**[32] 6609 2-9-7 **60**........................... MartinDwyer 7 60
(Brendan Powell) *hld up: rdn over 1f out: r.o to go 2nd towards fin: nt rch wnr* **5/1**[3]
0240 **3** *hd* **Zapateado**[18] 7081 2-9-4 **57**................................................ ShaneKelly 9 56
(Richard Hughes) *chsd ldrs: rdn over 1f out: styd on* **6/1**
4056 **4** *1 ½* **Red For Danger**[18] 7081 2-8-8 **47**.............................(h) EdwardGreatrex 2 41
(Eve Johnson Houghton) *chsd ldrs: rdn over 1f out: no ex ins fnl f* **9/2**[2]
601 **5** *¾* **Owen The Law**[18] 7081 2-9-3 **56**.........................................(v) FranBerry 8 47
(David Evans) *led 1f: remained handy: rdn over 1f out: no ex ins fnl f* **10/3**[1]
5300 **6** *1* **Terri Rules (IRE)**[7] 7458 2-9-4 **57**.................................... JimmyQuinn 6 44
(Julia Feilden) *plld hrd and prom: lost pl after 1f: n.d after* **11/1**
0000 **7** *2 ¼* **Bucks Frizz (IRE)**[27] 6790 2-8-6 **48**................................ DavidEgan(3) 5 27
(David Evans) *hld up: hdwy over 2f out: rdn over 1f out: wknd fnl f* **22/1**
003 **8** *2 ¾* **Cove Beach**[18] 7081 2-9-3 **61**......................................... MitchGodwin(5) 4 30
(Paul Cole) *trckd ldrs: rdn over 2f out: wknd over 1f out* **5/1**[3]

1m 6.97s (4.47) **Going Correction** +0.80s/f (Soft) **8** Ran SP% **116.9**
Speed ratings (Par 93): **96,92,92,90,88 87,83,79**
CSF £33.84 CT £172.58 TOTE £4.00: £1.80, £1.70, £1.90; EX 23.30 Trifecta £96.30.
**Owner** John J Maguire **Bred** Corrin Stud & Blackwater Bloodstock Ltd **Trained** Limpley Stoke, Wilts

**FOCUS**
A modest nursery sprint handicap. They went a respectable gallop and the top-weight won well. The winner has been rated only just above his early season form for Ruth Carr.
T/Plt: £131.50 to a £1 stake. Pool: £73,358.71 - 406.93 winning units T/Qpdt: £6.90 to a £1 stake. Pool: £7,753.17 831.03 winning units **Colin Roberts**

7696 - (Foreign Racing) - See Raceform Interactive

# 7471 MAISONS-LAFFITTE (R-H)
Monday, October 2

**OFFICIAL GOING: Turf: soft**

## 7697a PRIX DE BONNEVAL (LISTED RACE) (3YO+) (TURF) 5f 110y
**3:40** 3-Y-0+ **£22,222** (£8,888; £6,666; £4,444; £2,222)

RPR
**1** **Spiritfix**[36] 6497 4-8-10 0................................................ MaximeGuyon 3 101
(A Fabre, France) **49/10**[3]
**2** *hd* **Gold Vibe (IRE)**[22] 6979 4-9-0 0...........................(p) ChristopheSoumillon 1 104
(P Bary, France) **23/10**[1]
**3** *snk* **Moon Trouble (IRE)**[31] 4-9-0 0....................................... FabriceVeron 12 104
(E J O'Neill, France) **112/10**
**4** *hd* **Immediate**[21] 5-8-10 0.......................................................... AlexisBadel 2 99
(H-F Devin, France) **102/10**
**5** *snk* **Al Johrah**[376] 6694 3-8-10 0............................................. GregoryBenoist 5 99
(H-F Devin, France) **153/10**
**6** *snk* **Clem Fandango (FR)**[114] 3614 3-8-10 0............................ CristianDemuro 7 99
(Keith Dalgleish) *wl into stride: sn led: rdn over 1f out: drvn and ev ch fnl f: no ex cl home* **102/10**
**7** *3 ½* **Stunning Spirit**[36] 6497 3-9-0 0................................... AurelienLemaitre 11 91
(F Head, France) **41/10**[2]
**8** *snk* **Rayon Vert (FR)**[20] 3-9-0 0.................................. Pierre-CharlesBoudot 13 91
(H-A Pantall, France) **127/10**
**9** *2* **High Quality (IRE)**[27] 6804 4-8-10 0............................ MickaelBarzalona 6 79
(A Fabre, France) **184/10**
**10** *1 ¾* **Futoon (IRE)**[53] 5828 4-8-10 0........................................ AntoineHamelin 4 74
(Kevin Ryan) *sn trcking ldr: rdn 2f out: limited rspnse and no ex fnl f* **39/1**
**11** *1 ¼* **Love Spirit**[96] 4234 7-9-4 0............................................ AdrienFouassier 8 77
(Louis Baudron, France) **51/1**
**12** *6* **Evil Spell**[22] 6979 5-8-10 0............................................ TheoBachelot 10 50
(Robert Cowell) *dwlt: settled midfield: rdn over 2f out: sn btn and eased fnl f* **41/1**

1m 3.69s (-3.61) **12** Ran SP% **118.3**
PARI-MUTUEL (all including 1 euro stake): WIN 4.50; PLACE 2.00, 1.70, 3.40; DF 9.50; SF 22.70.
**Owner** Wertheimer & Frere **Bred** Wertheimer & Frere **Trained** Chantilly, France

# 5990 AYR (L-H)
Tuesday, October 3

**OFFICIAL GOING: Soft (heavy in places; 6.2)**
Wind: Fresh, half against Weather: Overcast

## 7698 WILLIAM HILL BET BOOST NURSERY H'CAP 1m
**2:20** (2:20) (Class 6) (0-65,66) 2-Y-0 **£2,587** (£770; £384; £192) **Stalls** Low

Form RPR
500 **1** **Burn Some Dust (IRE)**[73] 5162 2-8-13 **57**......................... JoeyHaynes 6 59+
(Brian Ellison) *hld up: rdn and hdwy wl over 1f out: led ins fnl f: edgd rt: hld on wl cl home* **7/1**[3]
4034 **2** *shd* **Here In The Dark**[6] 7519 2-9-8 **66**.............................(p) ConnorBeasley 4 68
(Keith Dalgleish) *led: rdn along 2f out: hdd ins fnl f: rallied: hld cl home* **2/1**[1]
0600 **3** *nse* **Saxonroad Boy (USA)**[14] 7239 2-8-0 **47**................(p) SammyJoBell(3) 9 49
(Richard Fahey) *hld up: rdn and hdwy whn nt clr run and swtchd rt over 1f out: kpt on wl fnl f: jst hld* **12/1**
0300 **4** *2* **Admiral Rooke (IRE)**[20] 7041 2-9-7 **65**......................... PaulMulrennan 3 62
(Michael Dods) *prom: effrt and rdn over 1f out: kpt on same pce ins fnl f* **5/1**[2]
0606 **5** *2 ¾* **Mountain Meadow**[21] 7029 2-8-5 **49**..........................(p) PatrickMathers 2 40
(Richard Fahey) *trckd ldrs: effrt and rdn over 2f out: wknd over 1f out* **17/2**
560 **6** *¾* **Retirement Beckons**[40] 6347 2-8-6 **50**......................... AndrewMullen 8 40
(Linda Perratt) *dwlt: hld up: effrt on outside over 2f out: wknd over 1f out* **22/1**
0430 **7** *2 ¼* **Cuillin Hills**[33] 6625 2-9-0 **63**....................................(p[1]) RowanScott(5) 10 48
(Keith Dalgleish) *prom on outside: rdn along over 2f out: wknd over 1f out* **8/1**
005 **8** *hd* **Barney George**[52] 5918 2-9-6 **64**...................................... TomEaves 5 48
(Iain Jardine) *pressed ldr: rdn over 2f out: wknd over 1f out* **12/1**
5000 **9** *1 ¼* **Lil Gem (IRE)**[15] 7222 2-8-2 **46**...................................... JoeFanning 7 28
(Keith Dalgleish) *hld up: drvn and struggling over 2f out: sn btn* **16/1**
000 **10** *2* **Chef United**[14] 7238 2-8-8 **52**........................................ JamesSullivan 1 29
(Roger Fell) *t.k.h: hld up towards rr: struggling over 2f out: sn wknd* **33/1**

1m 50.41s **10** Ran SP% **112.7**
CSF £20.55 CT £168.25 TOTE £8.60: £2.80, £1.10, £3.90; EX 23.10 Trifecta £206.10.
**Owner** Dan Gilbert **Bred** Dan Gilbert **Trained** Norton, N Yorks

**FOCUS**
Ayr was granted permission by the BHA to switch this fixture to the hurdles course following the cancellation of the previous week's three-day Western meeting due to a patch of waterlogged ground on the home straight on the Flat course. As a result, five races - over 6f, 7f and 1m2f - were abandoned and replaced by four contests over 1m, 1m1f and 1m5f. No speed figures have been generated for this meeting due to the course switch. There had been 1.5mm of rain in the previous 24 hours. A modest but competitive nursery to start, and they gradually edged stands' side in the straight. It's been rated around the second and third.

## 7699 WILLIAM HILL JOIN PLUS IN SHOP TODAY H'CAP 1m 1f
**2:55** (2:55) (Class 5) (0-75,73) 3-Y-0+ **£3,881** (£1,155; £577; £288) **Stalls** Low

Form RPR
6302 **1** **Rubis**[15] 7219 4-8-5 **60**...................................................... SammyJoBell(3) 6 67
(Richard Fahey) *s.i.s: hld up towards rr: rdn and chsd ldr over 1f out: led ins fnl f: kpt on* **11/4**[1]
1320 **2** *¾* **High Draw (FR)**[31] 6700 4-9-4 **73**...................................... CliffordLee(3) 5 78
(K R Burke) *led: clr after 2f: rdn over 1f out: hdd ins fnl f: kpt on* **5/1**[3]
0140 **3** *shd* **Wasm**[26] 6855 3-9-2 **72**................................................... TonyHamilton 4 78
(Roger Fell) *s.i.s: hld up: rdn and hung lft 2f out: rallied fnl f: kpt on wl nr fin* **8/1**
6114 **4** *2 ¾* **Edgar Allan Poe (IRE)**[25] 6893 3-8-10 **71**................... RowanScott(5) 2 71
(Rebecca Bastiman) *prom: effrt and rdn over 2f out: one pce fr over 1f out* **7/2**[2]
2200 **5** *nk* **Magistral**[64] 5469 7-8-10 **67**.................................(p) CallumRodriguez(5) 3 66
(R Mike Smith) *s.i.s: hld up: drvn and outpcd over 2f out: rallied fnl f: kpt on: nt pce to chal* **15/2**
2450 **6** *3 ½* **Crazy Tornado (IRE)**[20] 7042 4-9-3 **69**..............................(h) GrahamLee 1 60
(Keith Dalgleish) *chsd clr ldr: racd alone on far side ent st: lost 2nd over 1f out: sn wknd* **8/1**
6500 **7** *9* **Something Brewing (FR)**[43] 5400 3-8-11 **67**....................(b) TomEaves 7 40
(Iain Jardine) *cl up in chsng gp: rdn along over 2f out: wknd wl over 1f out* **8/1**

2m 3.32s
**WFA** 3 from 4yo+ 4lb **7** Ran SP% **110.7**
CSF £15.55 CT £90.15 TOTE £2.60: £1.70, £2.30; EX 13.50 Trifecta £72.20.
**Owner** Mr & Mrs P Ashton **Bred** Mr & Mrs P Ashton **Trained** Musley Bank, N Yorks

**FOCUS**
The main action was up the middle in this modest handicap. It's been rated around the first two.

## 7700 WILLIAM HILL GET THE APP ON GOOGLE PLAY H'CAP 1m 7f
**3:25** (3:28) (Class 5) (0-75,72) 3-Y-0+ **£3,881** (£1,155; £577; £288) **Stalls** Low

Form RPR
0211 **1** **Question Of Faith**[20] 7047 6-9-1 **64**....................... CallumRodriguez(5) 2 74+
(Martin Todhunter) *trckd ldng pair: smooth hdwy to ld over 2f out: rdn and drifted lft fr over 1f out: kpt on strly* **5/6**[1]
5200 **2** *2 ¼* **Wor Lass**[11] 7359 9-9-9 **72**............................................... RowanScott(5) 5 78
(Donald Whillans) *trckd ldr: effrt and ev ch over 1f out: kpt on same pce ins fnl f* **4/1**[2]
5043 **3** *8* **La Bacouetteuse (FR)**[34] 6595 12-8-11 **55**......................(b) DavidAllan 3 51
(Iain Jardine) *awkward s: hld up in tch: pushed along 1/2-way: rallied: outpcd over 2f out: plugged on fnl f: no ch w first two* **8/1**
0/03 **4** *½* **New Youmzain (FR)**[20] 7047 8-9-7 **65**.......................... AndrewMullen 1 61
(Lucy Normile) *t.k.h: led to over 2f out: rdn and wknd over 1f out* **8/1**

0300 **5** *6* **Archie's Advice**[40] 6349 6-9-11 **69**........................................ GrahamLee 7 58
(Keith Dalgleish) *hld up in last pl: rdn and outpcd over 2f out: sn wknd* **6/1**[3]

3m 36.98s
**WFA** 3 from 6yo+ 8lb **5** Ran **SP% 111.1**
CSF £4.54 TOTE £1.40: £1.10, £3.00; EX 4.70 Trifecta £13.90.
**Owner** K Fitzsimons & G Fell **Bred** Sir Robert Ogden **Trained** Orton, Cumbria

**FOCUS**
They were spread all over the place late on in this weak staying handicap. The runner-up has been rated close to this year's form.

## 7701 WILLIAM HILL BEST ODDS GUARANTEED H'CAP 1m 5f
**4:00** (4:00) (Class 4) (0-85,90) 3-Y-O+ **£5,822** (£1,732; £865; £432) **Stalls** Low

Form RPR
1211 **1** **Brandon Castle**[3] 7599 5-10-6 **90** 6ex..........................(t) AndrewMullen 5 100+
(Archie Watson) *mde all: qcknd clr over 2f out: pushed out: readily* **6/4**[1]
4121 **2** *6* **Vindicator (IRE)**[21] 7019 3-9-1 **82**.......................(p) CallumRodriguez(5) 1 86
(Michael Dods) *hld up: rdn and hdwy to chse (clr) wnr over 2f out: edgd lft over 1f out: kpt on fnl f: no imp* **4/1**[3]
0055 **3** *1 ¾* **Corton Lad**[39] 6383 7-9-12 **87**..................................(tp) RowanScott(5) 6 85
(Keith Dalgleish) *in tch: drvn and outpcd over 2f out: rallied ins fnl f: styd on: no imp* **50/1**
1320 **4** *hd* **Northwest Frontier (IRE)**[38] 6445 3-9-5 **81**................. TonyHamilton 9 81
(Richard Fahey) *chsd ldr 4f: cl up: wnt 2nd over 4f out to over 2f out: outpcd over 1f out* **3/1**[2]
5254 **5** *2 ½* **Braes Of Lochalsh**[32] 6661 6-8-12 **68**.......................(v) JamesSullivan 4 62
(Jim Goldie) *hld up: rdn over 3f out: hdwy over 1f out: sn no imp* **20/1**
2123 **6** *1 ¼* **Donnachies Girl (IRE)**[39] 6383 4-9-1 **71**......................... GrahamLee 3 63
(Alistair Whillans) *in tch: effrt and drvn along over 3f out: wknd wl over 1f out* **13/2**
2340 **7** *10* **Gworn**[39] 6383 7-9-2 **79**.................................................. RhonaPindar(7) 7 56
(R Mike Smith) *hld up: drvn and struggling over 3f out: btn fnl 2f* **50/1**
313 **8** *56* **Sebastian's Wish (IRE)**[53] 5882 4-9-13 **83**...................... JoeFanning 8
(Keith Dalgleish) *dwlt: sn chsng ldrs on outside: struggling over 3f out: sn lost tch: eased whn no ch fnl 2f* **14/1**

3m 1.14s
**WFA** 3 from 4yo+ 6lb **8** Ran **SP% 113.7**
CSF £7.60 CT £190.18 TOTE £1.70: £1.10, £1.70, £6.30; EX 8.10 Trifecta £225.60.
**Owner** C R Hirst **Bred** Barry Walters **Trained** Upper Lambourn, W Berks

**FOCUS**
A good race for the grade, and another relentless front-running display from the rapidly progressive winner. They raced up the centre in the straight. The runner-up has been rated to his latest form.

## 7702 WILLIAM HILL PROUD TO SUPPORT SCOTTISH SPORT H'CAP 1m
**4:30** (4:33) (Class 3) (0-90,98) 3-Y-O+ **£9,056** (£2,695; £1,346; £673) **Stalls** Low

Form RPR
4232 **1** **Jay Kay**[20] 7042 8-8-7 **71** oh1...........................................(h) JoeyHaynes 6 80
(K R Burke) *t.k.h: mde all: rdn and clr 2f out: styd on wl fnl f: unchal* **4/1**[2]
6-00 **2** *1 ¾* **Clef**[20] 7044 3-8-10 **77**................................................ TonyHamilton 7 82
(Richard Fahey) *chsd wnr thrght: rdn over 2f out: kpt on ins fnl f: nt pce of wnr* **20/1**
3332 **3** *¾* **Royal Regent**[50] 5996 5-9-3 **84**................................. SammyJoBell(3) 1 87+
(Lucy Normile) *hld up: rdn and hdwy wl over 1f out: kpt on ins fnl f: no imp* **5/2**[1]
-054 **4** *2 ¾* **Bamber Bridge (IRE)**[38] 6434 3-9-4 **85**......................... PaulMulrennan 5 82
(Michael Dods) *dwlt: sn prom: rdn along 2f out: sn one pce* **4/1**[2]
-004 **5** *3 ½* **Ce La Vie**[136] 2817 3-9-4 **85**........................................... ConnorBeasley 4 74
(Keith Dalgleish) *dwlt: t.k.h: hld up: rdn along over 2f out: sn outpcd: btn fnl f* **7/1**
2000 **6** *9* **Finn Class (IRE)**[4] 7566 6-9-1 **84**....................(bt[1]) CallumRodriguez(5) 3 52
(Michael Dods) *prom: rdn over 2f out: wknd wl over 1f out* **6/1**[3]
0140 **7** *7* **Strong Steps**[40] 6349 5-9-7 **85**....................................... JamesSullivan 2 37
(Jim Goldie) *hld up in tch: rdn over 2f out: wknd wl over 1f out* **8/1**

1m 45.7s
**WFA** 3 from 4yo+ 3lb **7** Ran **SP% 111.2**
CSF £68.57 CT £229.37 TOTE £5.50: £2.50, £6.80; EX 63.90 Trifecta £289.20.
**Owner** John Kenny & Partner **Bred** Miss S E Hall **Trained** Middleham Moor, N Yorks

**FOCUS**
The one-two filled those positions pretty much throughout, with the favourite coming from last to take third. The action was up the centre. The winner has been rated back to his best, and the third a bit below.

## 7703 WILLIAM HILL THIS IS MORE TRAINING SERIES APPRENTICE H'CAP (DIV I) 1m
**5:05** (5:05) (Class 6) (0-65,67) 3-Y-O+ **£2,587** (£770; £384; £192) **Stalls** Low

Form RPR
0303 **1** **Mustaqbal (IRE)**[7] 7476 5-9-12 **66**.......................(p) CallumRodriguez 3 72
(Michael Dods) *blindfold slow to remove and dwlt: hld up: hdwy over 1f out: rdn to ld ins fnl f: r.o wl* **6/1**
0325 **2** *½* **Green Howard**[28] 6783 9-9-3 **57**.............................................(p) GerO'Neill 7 62
(Rebecca Bastiman) *hld up: rdn over 2f out: hdwy over 1f out: led briefly ins fnl f: kpt on: hld cl home* **5/1**[3]
4004 **3** *1* **Ingleby Angel (IRE)**[4] 7573 8-9-5 **59**.......................... PatrickVaughan 10 62+
(David O'Meara) *hld up in tch: effrt and ev ch over 1f out: sn hung lft: no ex ins fnl f* **7/2**[1]
3525 **4** *shd* **Carlovian**[10] 7389 4-8-10 **53**........................................(p) SeamusCronin(3) 6 56
(Mark Walford) *cl up: led over 2f out to ins fnl f: kpt on same pce* **9/2**[2]
5405 **5** *¾* **Stardrifter**[31] 6690 5-8-5 **50** oh3.............................. LeanneFerguson(5) 8 51
(Linda Perratt) *hld up: rdn over 2f out: hdwy over 1f out: kpt on ins fnl f* **20/1**
4003 **6** *2 ½* **Restive (IRE)**[14] 7235 4-9-10 **64**.................................... JamieGormley 12 59
(Iain Jardine) *cl up: ev ch over 2f out: sn rdn: wknd ins fnl f* **12/1**
0000 **7** *1 ¼* **Swiss Lait**[7] 7478 6-8-10 **50** oh5............................................(b) PaulaMuir 1 43
(Patrick Holmes) *missed break: bhd: rdn over 2f out: hdwy fnl f: kpt on: nt pce to chal* **80/1**
0460 **8** *¾* **Red Shadow**[17] 7165 8-8-10 **50** oh5.............................(v) ConnorMurtagh 11 41
(Alistair Whillans) *hld up in tch: rdn over 2f out: wknd over 1f out* **66/1**
0-02 **9** *nk* **Granite City Doc**[31] 6690 4-8-7 **50** oh4...................... BenSanderson(3) 4 40
(Lucy Normile) *prom: rdn and outpcd over 2f out: btn over 1f out* **16/1**
5032 **10** *½* **Inglorious**[25] 6893 3-9-10 **67**...................................(p) JaneElliott 2 56
(Keith Dalgleish) *t.k.h led to over 2f out: wknd over 1f out* **8/1**
2001 **11** *1 ¾* **Billy Bond**[15] 7225 5-9-1 **60**.......................................(b) SebastianWoods(5) 5 45
(Richard Fahey) *missed break: hld up: rdn over 2f out: sn no imp: btn over 1f out* **5/1**[3]

1m 48.95s
**WFA** 3 from 4yo+ 3lb **11** Ran **SP% 120.2**
CSF £36.55 CT £126.22 TOTE £7.70: £2.90, £2.00, £1.40; EX 40.80 Trifecta £150.90.
**Owner** M J K Dods **Bred** Shadwell Estate Company Limited **Trained** Denton, Co Durham

**FOCUS**
A moderate handicap in which they raced middle to far side in the straight. Another small step forward from the third.

## 7704 WILLIAM HILL THIS IS MORE TRAINING SERIES APPRENTICE H'CAP (DIV II) 1m
**5:35** (5:38) (Class 6) (0-65,67) 3-Y-O+ **£2,587** (£770; £384; £192) **Stalls** Low

Form RPR
5543 **1** **Cliff Bay (IRE)**[28] 6783 3-9-7 **63**................................. PatrickVaughan 5 70
(Keith Dalgleish) *dwlt: hld up: hdwy on far side of gp over 2f out: led ins fnl f: r.o wl* **7/1**
0310 **2** *1 ½* **Rioja Day (IRE)**[31] 6690 7-8-12 **54**.................................(b) SeanMooney(3) 9 58
(Jim Goldie) *prom: drvn and outpcd over 2f out: rallied ins fnl f: kpt on to take 2nd nr fin* **11/1**
0000 **3** *½* **Twiggy**[24] 6946 3-9-5 **61**.................................................... JamieGormley 11 64
(Iain Jardine) *led: clr w one other 1/2-way: rdn and hdd ins fnl f: sn one pce* **9/1**
0603 **4** *shd* **Hellavashock**[28] 6788 4-8-10 **49** oh4..........................(b) ConnorMurtagh 8 51
(Alistair Whillans) *prom: stdy hdwy over 2f out: rdn and ev ch over 1f out: one pce ins fnl f* **8/1**
2011 **5** *1 ¾* **John Caesar (IRE)**[7] 7479 6-9-8 **61** 6ex..............................(tp) GerO'Neill 7 60
(Rebecca Bastiman) *hld up in midfield: drvn and outpcd over 2f out: rallied fnl f: kpt on: nt pce to chal* **7/2**[1]
3410 **6** *1 ½* **Ivors Involvement (IRE)**[7] 7479 5-8-7 **49**.............(p) BenSanderson(3) 1 44
(Tina Jackson) *chsd ldr: clr w one other 1/2-way: rdn over 2f out: outpcd over 1f out* **4/1**[2]
5000 **7** *hd* **Ingleby Spring (IRE)**[20] 7042 5-8-8 **52**................. SebastianWoods(5) 4 47
(Richard Fahey) *hld up: stdy hdwy over 2f out: rdn and no further imp over 1f out: btn ins fnl f* **13/2**[3]
4000 **8** *2 ½* **Let Right Be Done**[31] 6688 5-8-5 **49** oh4............(b) LeanneFerguson(5) 6 38
(Linda Perratt) *dwlt: plld hrd in rr: shortlived effrt over 2f out: sn wknd* **16/1**
556 **9** *5* **Dream Team**[48] 6058 3-9-11 **67**...............................(p) CallumRodriguez 10 45
(Michael Dods) *dwlt: hld up: rdn over 2f out: wknd over 1f out* **10/1**
-000 **10** *16* **Chookie Valentine**[15] 7219 4-8-10 **49** oh4.............................(p) JaneElliott 3
(Keith Dalgleish) *bhd: lost tch over 3f out: t.o* **40/1**

1m 48.79s
**WFA** 3 from 4yo+ 3lb **10** Ran **SP% 114.9**
CSF £79.90 CT £715.65 TOTE £9.30: £2.60, £2.60, £2.90; EX 43.60 Trifecta £595.90.
**Owner** David McKenzie **Bred** John Hutchinson **Trained** Carluke, S Lanarks

**FOCUS**
The second leg of a moderate race. They were all over the place in the closing stages, with the winner towards the far side. It's been rated around the balance of the likes of the second and fourth.
T/Plt: £72.10 to a £1 stake. Pool: £60,834.42 - 615.09 winning units. T/Qpdt: £26.60 to a £1 stake. Pool: £4,633.79 - 128.52 winning units. **Richard Young**

# 7510 KEMPTON (A.W) (R-H)
### Tuesday, October 3

**OFFICIAL GOING: Polytrack: standard to slow**
Wind: Moderate, across (away from stands) Weather: Fine

## 7705 WATCH RACING UK ON BT TV H'CAP 5f (P)
**5:40** (5:41) (Class 7) (0-50,50) 3-Y-O+ **£1,940** (£577; £288; £144) **Stalls** Low

Form RPR
5000 **1** **Deer Song**[27] 6813 4-9-4 **47**.......................................... JosephineGordon 5 54
(John Bridger) *mde all: rdn fnl f and sn hrd pressed: hld on wl* **7/1**
3406 **2** *nk* **Billy's Boots**[40] 6339 3-9-4 **47**.......................................(p) AdamKirby 4 54
(J R Jenkins) *racd on inner and chsd ldng pair over 3f out: rdn to take 2nd jst over 1f out: chal ins fnl f: jst hld* **5/1**[3]
3504 **3** *1* **Essaka (IRE)**[16] 7195 5-9-0 **50**.................................... SophieRalston(7) 1 53+
(Tony Carroll) *n.m.r on inner after s: dropped to last and t.k.h: gd prog over 1f out: tk 3rd 150yds out and threatened to chal: nt qckn after* **3/1**[1]
-600 **4** *1 ¾* **Joshlee (IRE)**[55] 5792 3-9-6 **49**....................................... TomQueally 2 46
(Emma Owen) *in tch in midfield: rdn and prog on inner over 1f out: one pce and no imp ins fnl f* **10/1**
400 **5** *nse* **Dalalah**[126] 3185 4-8-13 **45**................................................(v) DavidEgan(3) 3 41
(Richard Guest) *pushed along in last pair bef 1/2-way: no prog tl kpt on u.p fnl f: nrst fin* **4/1**[2]
065 **6** *¾* **Popsilca**[89] 4543 3-9-7 **50**.................................................. FranBerry 7 44
(Mick Quinn) *chsd wnr to jst over 1f out: fdd* **15/2**
0500 **7** *½* **Cherry Leyf**[30] 6724 3-8-10 **46**...................................(t[1]) MillyNaseb(7) 8 38
(Stuart Williams) *chsd ldrs: nt qckn over 1f out: sn fdd* **12/1**
-020 **8** *1* **Bubbly Bailey**[151] 2370 7-8-9 **45**..............................(v) GinaMangan(7) 10 33
(J R Jenkins) *wl away but trapped out wd and lost pl bnd over 3f out: hanging and no prog over 1f out* **50/1**
2000 **9** *1 ½* **Leonardo (GER)**[78] 4967 5-9-7 **50**.............................. KieranShoemark 6 32
(Mark Pitman) *nvr beyond midfield: no prog over 1f out: wknd fnl f* **12/1**
/4-0 **10** *½* **Special Code (IRE)**[59] 5657 5-9-5 **48**...........................(t) RobertWinston 9 29
(Paddy Butler) *hld up but stl trapped out wd and lost grnd bnds over 3f out and 2f out: eased whn no ch fnl f* **20/1**

1m 0.44s (-0.06) **Going Correction** -0.20s/f (Stan) **10** Ran **SP% 117.1**
Speed ratings (Par 97): **92,91,89,87,87 85,85,83,81,80**
CSF £42.14 CT £128.75 TOTE £9.40: £2.30, £1.50, £1.20; EX 47.90 Trifecta £161.00.
**Owner** The Deer's Hut **Bred** J Khan & P Wilson **Trained** Liphook, Hants

**FOCUS**
A low-grade handicap. The first four hugged the rail into the straight. The third has been rated to the balance of this year's form.

## 7706 32RED CASINO NURSERY H'CAP 5f (P)
**6:10** (6:11) (Class 5) (0-75,74) 2-Y-O **£3,234** (£962; £481; £240) **Stalls** Low

Form RPR
333 **1** **Big Time Maybe (IRE)**[16] 7194 2-9-6 **73**..............(t[1]) RichardKingscote 1 82
(Tom Dascombe) *mde all: pushed 2 l clr over 1f out: shkn up fnl f: readily* **10/1**
2056 **2** *1 ¼* **Bath And Tennis (IRE)**[40] 6338 2-9-4 **71**.........................(b[1]) LukeMorris 9 76
(Sir Mark Prescott Bt) *dwlt fr wdst draw: sn in tch as others rn wd: rdn and prog into 3rd over 1f out: drvn and styd on to take 2nd last strides* **16/1**
042 **3** *½* **City Gent**[27] 6826 2-9-7 **74**............................................... PatDobbs 3 77
(Ralph Beckett) *chsd wnr: rdn and nt qckn over 1f out: wl hld after: lost 2nd last strides* **5/1**[3]

302 **4** *3 ½* **Lady Dancealot (IRE)**[25] 6867 2-9-6 **73**.................. SilvestreDeSousa 6 63+
(David Elsworth) *dwlt: hanging lft in rr and then carried bdly lft bnd over 3f out: no ch after: rdn and kpt on fr over 1f out to take 4th nr fin* **13/8**[1]

044 **5** *¾* **Expelled**[27] 6826 2-9-4 **71**.................................................. DanielMuscutt 2 58
(James Fanshawe) *dwlt: sn chsd ldrs on inner: pushed along and no imp over 1f out: shkn up and wknd ins fnl f* **3/1**[2]

2231 **6** *3 ½* **Haveoneyerself (IRE)**[55] 5785 2-9-5 **72**.................................. JFEgan 4 47
(John Butler) *hung bdly lft bnd over 3f out and dropped to last pair: nvr on terms after* **9/1**

316 **7** *1 ¼* **Zain Smarts (IRE)**[16] 7194 2-8-13 **69**.............................. DavidEgan(3) 7 39
(David Evans) *chsd ldrs but hanging bnd over 3f out: wd bnd 2f out: sn wknd* **40/1**

342 **8** *1 ½* **Undercover Brother**[10] 7385 2-9-6 **73**....................(v[1]) DanielTudhope 5 38
(David O'Meara) *trapped out wd and also hanging bnd over 3f out: v wd bnd 2f out: wknd* **11/1**

59.51s (-0.99) **Going Correction** -0.20s/f (Stan) **8** Ran SP% **115.5**
Speed ratings (Par 95): **99,97,96,90,89 83,81,79**
CSF £152.01 CT £900.71 TOTE £9.40: £2.30, £3.70, £1.70; EX 141.10 Trifecta £638.80.
**Owner** Jones', Langfords' & Owens' **Bred** Joe Fogarty **Trained** Malpas, Cheshire

**FOCUS**
Once again early pace won the day.

## 7707 WATCH RACING UK ON TALKTALK TV NOVICE AUCTION STKS 7f (P)
**6:40** (6:41) (Class 6) 2-Y-O £2,587 (£770; £384; £192) **Stalls** Low

Form RPR

42 **1** **Lady Of Aran (IRE)**[17] 7153 2-8-11 0................................. JimCrowley 7 78+
(Charlie Fellowes) *hld up in 7th: prog on outer 2f out: pushed into the ld ins fnl f: comf* **5/4**[1]

2 **2** *1 ½* **Rotherhithe**[38] 6433 2-8-11 0........................................ TomMarquand 10 72
(Robyn Brisland) *t.k.h: led after 1f: rdn and pressed 2f out: kpt on wl but hdd and outpcd ins fnl f* **5/2**[2]

30 **3** *2 ½* **Coast Guard**[25] 6875 2-8-11 0..............................(p[1]) RichardKingscote 6 65
(Tom Dascombe) *led 1f: chsd ldr: shifted lft whn rdn 2f out: lost 2nd and one pce fnl f* **20/1**

0 **4** *1* **Crystal Casque**[120] 3390 2-8-11 0.................................... DavidProbert 2 63
(Rod Millman) *trckd ldng pair: cl up 2f out: rdn over 1f out: one pce after* **50/1**

**5** *shd* **Destinata** 2-8-11 0.......................................................... DanielMuscutt 12 62+
(James Fanshawe) *hld up in 8th fr wd draw: pushed along 2f out: kpt on encouraging fr over 1f out* **33/1**

61 **6** *½* **Claudine (IRE)**[27] 6824 2-9-4 0........................................... DaneO'Neill 8 68
(Henry Candy) *trckd ldng trio: effrt whn intimidated 2f out: nt qckn over 1f out: one pce after* **10/1**[3]

**7** *nk* **Brisk Tempo (FR)** 2-9-2 0................................................ PJMcDonald 5 65+
(Richard Fahey) *slowly away: mostly in last pair: stl there 2f out: pushed along and kpt on fr over 1f out: nt disgracd* **12/1**

60 **8** *1 ¾* **King Athelstan (IRE)**[19] 7093 2-9-2 0........................ JosephineGordon 4 60
(John Best) *chsd ldrs in 5th: rdn 2f out: no imp over 1f out: wknd ins fnl f* **40/1**

**9** *nk* **Duke Of Dorset** 2-9-2 0........................................................ FranBerry 14 60
(Harry Fry) *a in rr and pushed along fr an early stage: nvr able to make significant prog* **16/1**

335 **10** *¾* **Silvington**[61] 5561 2-9-2 **66**................................................ TomQueally 3 58
(Tony Carroll) *chsd ldrs in 6th: rdn 2f out: wknd jst over 1f out* **25/1**

60 **11** *1* **Sapper**[10] 7392 2-9-2 0........................................................... LukeMorris 9 55
(Ed Walker) *nvr bttr than 9th: rdn and no prog over 2f out* **50/1**

**12** *1 ¼* **Mom Said (IRE)** 2-9-2 0...................................................... LiamKeniry 11 51
(Ed Walker) *s.s: wl off the pce in last: brief effrt on inner over 2f out: sn no prog* **16/1**

0 **13** *nk* **Elegance (IRE)**[34] 6584 2-8-11 0........................................... JFEgan 1 46
(Martin Smith) *a towards rr: shkn up 2f out: wknd over 1f out* **100/1**

1m 26.9s (0.90) **Going Correction** -0.025s/f (Stan) **13** Ran SP% **120.5**
Speed ratings (Par 93): **93,91,88,87,87 86,86,84,83,83 81,80,80**
CSF £3.86 TOTE £2.20: £1.10, £1.30, £5.80; EX 5.70 Trifecta £68.70.
**Owner** O'Callaghan Bengough Horsford Capon **Bred** Mountarmstrong Stud **Trained** Newmarket, Suffolk

**FOCUS**
An ordinary novice. The opening level is slightly fluid.

## 7708 100% PROFIT BOOST AT 32REDSPORT.COM MAIDEN STKS 1m 3f 219y(P)
**7:10** (7:13) (Class 5) 3-Y-O+ £3,234 (£962; £481; £240) **Stalls** Low

Form RPR

**1** **Isaac Bell (IRE)**[258] 9-9-11 0.............................................(t) LukeMorris 2 82
(Alex Hales) *wl in tch: prog to trck ldng pair 4f out: rdn over 2f out: styd on wl fr over 1f out to ld nr fin: pushed out* **100/1**

32-3 **2** *nk* **Stanley**[33] 6623 4-9-11 77..................................................... ShaneKelly 4 81
(Richard Hughes) *mde most: briefly hdd 7f out: pressed 4f out: rdn over 2f out: fended off persistent chalr fnl f but then worn down last strides* **6/1**[3]

220 **3** *½* **Musaahim (USA)**[67] 5364 3-9-5 84..................................... JimCrowley 3 80
(Roger Varian) *cl up: prog to trck ldr 5f out: rdn to chal over 2f out: nt qckn and hld fnl f: sn lost 2nd but kpt on again nr fin* **13/8**[1]

0- **4** *4* **Soghan (IRE)**[314] 8063 3-9-5 0.......................................(t[1]) NickyMackay 7 74
(John Gosden) *mostly pressed ldr to 5f out: urged along 4f out: outpcd over 2f out: no threat to ldng trio over 1f out* **7/1**

033 **5** *2 ¼* **Tranquil Star (IRE)**[18] 7125 3-9-0 78.................................... JFEgan 12 65
(Jeremy Noseda) *wl in tch: rdn to try to make prog on wd outside bnd over 3f out: outpcd over 2f out: one pce after* **6/1**[3]

42 **6** *nse* **Symbol**[20] 7059 3-8-11 0.............................................. GeorgeWood(3) 8 65
(James Fanshawe) *t.k.h: cl up: lost pl 4f out: renewed effrt to dispute 4th 2f out but no ch: fdd fnl f* **7/2**[2]

**7** *4 ½* **Country'N'Western (FR)**[11] 5-9-11 0..................................... DaneO'Neill 5 63
(David Elsworth) *s.s: mostly in last pair: shkn up and passed toiling rivals fnl 2f but nvr a factor* **66/1**

04- **8** *8* **Dinsdale**[163] 7753 4-9-11 0................................................. DougieCostello 6 50
(Michael Scudamore) *hld up towards rr: rchd midfield 4f out and gng wl enough: no prog 2f out: wknd* **50/1**

00 **9** *3 ¼* **Lady Of Steel**[12] 7322 3-9-0 0.......................................... DanielMuscutt 10 40
(John Butler) *mostly in last and a bhd* **100/1**

**10** *1 ½* **Tinted (IRE)** 3-9-0 0.......................................................... HarryBentley 9 38
(John Gosden) *dwlt: rn green and a in rr: effrt 3f out: wknd over 2f out* **7/1**

6 **11** *5* **Triple First**[33] 6614 3-9-0 0............................................... SteveDrowne 1 30
(Seamus Mullins) *towards rr: pushed along over 3f out: wknd qckly over 2f out* **100/1**

6 **12** *26* **Nagamaat (IRE)**[102] 4042 3-9-0 0......................................... CharlesBishop 11
(Nikki Evans) *trapped out wd bnd 9f out: pushed along ldng pair: brief effrt for glory whn led for few strides 7f out: wknd rapidly over 4f out: t.o* **150/1**

2m 33.67s (-0.83) **Going Correction** -0.025s/f (Stan)
**WFA** 3 from 4yo+ 6lb **12** Ran SP% **121.0**
Speed ratings (Par 103): **101,100,100,97,96 96,93,87,85,84 81,64**
CSF £647.39 TOTE £37.80: £9.30, £1.80, £1.30; EX 805.80 Trifecta £1981.00.
**Owner** S Brown & D Raftery **Bred** M Kennelly **Trained** Edgcote, Northamptonshire

**FOCUS**
Quite a turn-up here. It's been rated around the runner-up.

## 7709 32RED.COM H'CAP 6f (P)
**7:40** (7:42) (Class 4) (0-80,80) 3-Y-O+ £4,690 (£1,395; £697; £348) **Stalls** Low

Form RPR

3235 **1** **Dark Side Dream**[12] 7321 5-9-1 **77**......................(p) LewisEdmunds(3) 12 85
(Chris Dwyer) *fast away fr wdst draw: mde all: rdn 2f out: hrd pressed on both sides fr over 1f out: hld on gamely* **12/1**

0125 **2** *hd* **Summerghand (IRE)**[14] 7244 3-9-2 **76**......................... DanielTudhope 4 83
(David O'Meara) *trckd ldrs: rdn 2f out: clsd over 1f out: tk 2nd ins fnl f: chal last 100yds: jst hld* **7/2**[2]

3151 **3** *1* **Seprani**[36] 6511 3-9-0 **74**..........................................(h) JosephineGordon 3 78
(Marco Botti) *trckd ldrs: rdn 2f out: clsd and looked a threat jst ins fnl f: nt qckn after* **8/1**

2211 **4** *½* **Buxted Dream (USA)**[42] 6282 3-9-6 **80**.............................. PatCosgrave 8 83
(Luca Cumani) *wl away but couldn't ld: chsd wnr 1f and again 2f out: drvn to chal over 1f out: lost 2nd and one pce ins fnl f* **5/1**[3]

10 **5** *1 ¼* **Cappananty Con**[38] 6442 3-9-5 **79**................................. RobertWinston 1 80+
(Dean Ivory) *hld up in midfield: shkn up over 2f out: kpt on same pce fr over 1f out and nvr able to threaten* **12/1**

123 **6** *nse* **Hackney Road**[42] 6290 4-9-1 **79**................................... JoshuaBryan(5) 7 77
(John Butler) *t.k.h: hld up in midfield: rdn 2f out: kpt on but nvr pce to threaten ldrs* **12/1**

-354 **7** *2 ½* **Fivetwoeight**[38] 6442 3-9-4 **78**................................ SilvestreDeSousa 6 68
(Peter Chapple-Hyam) *hld up towards rr: hanging bdly rt whn asked for effrt 2f out and no great prog after* **11/4**[1]

4002 **8** *hd* **Lord Cooper**[10] 7408 3-9-2 **76**..........................................(tp) OscarPereira 2 66
(Jose Santos) *hld up in rr: pushed along over 2f out: brief effrt and only one to stay against ins rail after: fdd fnl f* **16/1**

3000 **9** *1 ¾* **War Whisper (IRE)**[38] 6442 4-9-4 **77**............................ TomMarquand 9 61
(Richard Hannon) *mostly in last and a outpcd* **50/1**

2520 **10** *2 ¾* **Mulzim**[24] 6936 3-9-2 **76**.................................................(b[1]) JimCrowley 5 51
(Ed Dunlop) *chsd wnr after 1f to 2f out: wknd rapidly over 1f out* **12/1**

0505 **11** *2* **Dutiful Son (IRE)**[28] 6794 7-9-1 **74**...................................... JFEgan 11 43
(Simon Dow) *struggling to keep up in rr and trapped out wd: wknd 2f out* **33/1**

1m 11.73s (-1.37) **Going Correction** -0.025s/f (Stan)
**WFA** 3 from 4yo+ 1lb **11** Ran SP% **118.2**
Speed ratings (Par 105): **108,107,106,105,104 104,100,100,98,94 91**
CSF £54.07 CT £374.30 TOTE £15.30: £4.20, £2.00, £2.60; EX 76.70 Trifecta £507.80.
**Owner** M M Foulger & Mrs Shelley Dwyer **Bred** Newsells Park Stud **Trained** Newmarket, Suffolk

**FOCUS**
The winner dominated from the front. The third and fourth have been rated close to form.

## 7710 32RED FILLIES' H'CAP 1m (P)
**8:10** (8:12) (Class 4) (0-80,81) 3-Y-O+ £4,690 (£1,395; £697; £348) **Stalls** Low

Form RPR

0044 **1** **Queensbrydge**[7] 7484 3-9-3 **77**........................................... MartinHarley 4 86+
(Robyn Brisland) *hld up in midfield: prog on inner over 2f out: led wl over 1f out and sn clr: pushed out: comf* **5/2**[1]

4260 **2** *1 ½* **Medicean Ballet (IRE)**[19] 7083 3-8-13 **73**.......................... DaneO'Neill 10 77+
(Henry Candy) *s.i.s: wl in rr: stl in last pair whn wd bnd 3f out: gd prog on outer over 1f out: styd on wl fnl f to take 2nd last strides* **16/1**

5063 **3** *nk* **Hawatif (IRE)**[13] 7285 4-9-5 **76**........................................ DavidProbert 6 79
(Anthony Carson) *hld up and sn in last: rdn over 2f out: gd prog between rivals over 1f out: styd on to take 2nd briefly nr fin: no ch w wnr* **12/1**

000 **4** *½* **Assanilka (FR)**[13] 7276 3-9-4 **78**.........................................(p) AdamKirby 2 80
(Harry Dunlop) *trckd ldrs: prog to ld briefly 2f out: chsd wnr after but sn outpcd: lost 2 pls nr fin* **20/1**

5-52 **5** *¾* **Caledonia Duchess**[20] 7061 4-8-9 **66**.................... JosephineGordon 12 66
(Jo Hughes) *t.k.h: trckd ldrs on outer: rdn and nt qckn over 2f out: kpt on wl again fnl f* **8/1**[3]

3635 **6** *½* **Normandie Lady**[74] 5125 4-9-7 **81**......................... AdamMcNamara(3) 1 80
(Richard Fahey) *pushed along early and sn in last pair: effrt against rail 2f out: kpt on but nvr pce to threaten* **8/1**[3]

4145 **7** *hd* **The Yellow Bus**[27] 6818 4-8-11 **73**................................ PaddyBradley(5) 3 72
(Daniel Steele) *chsd ldrs: rdn over 2f out: pressed for 3rd 1f out: one pce after* **16/1**

6000 **8** *½* **Braztime**[7] 7493 3-9-0 **74**................................................ TomMarquand 9 71
(Richard Hannon) *nvr beyond midfield: urged along sn after 1/2-way: rdn and effrt over 2f out: no imp on ldrs fnl f* **33/1**

6-1 **9** *hd* **Influent (IRE)**[42] 6287 3-9-4 **78**........................................ LukeMorris 11 75
(James Tate) *t.k.h: trckd ldng pair: rdn and nt qckn 2f out: disp 3rd 1f out: wknd last 100yds* **9/2**[2]

6420 **10** *2 ¾* **Carducci**[43] 6274 3-9-3 **77**................................................... SeanLevey 5 67
(Richard Hannon) *in tch: rdn over 2f out: no imp on ldrs over 1f out: wknd fnl f* **14/1**

2530 **11** *3 ¼* **Patching**[20] 7052 3-8-7 **67**..................................................(b) JFEgan 8 49
(Giles Bravery) *led 1f: chsd ldr to 2f out: wknd: eased fnl f* **25/1**

5140 **12** *3 ½* **Distant (USA)**[55] 5798 3-9-4 **78**.............................(p) KieranShoemark 13 52
(Roger Charlton) *led after 1f and set str pce: hdd 2f out: wknd rapidly* **10/1**

553 **13** *2 ¼* **Teomaria**[24] 6941 3-8-7 **67**.............................................. PJMcDonald 7 36
(K R Burke) *chsd ldrs early: lost pl and shoved along by 1/2-way: wknd over 2f out* **16/1**

1m 38.35s (-1.45) **Going Correction** -0.025s/f (Stan)
**WFA** 3 from 4yo 3lb **13** Ran SP% **121.6**
Speed ratings (Par 102): **106,104,104,103,102 102,102,101,101,98 95,92,89**
CSF £46.27 CT £435.35 TOTE £3.50: £1.40, £5.30, £3.90; EX 48.90 Trifecta £600.90.
**Owner** Franconson Partners **Bred** D Curran **Trained** Newmarket, Suffolk

**FOCUS**
A fair fillies' handicap. The winner has been rated a little off her 2yo peak, but a small pb from the runner-up.

## 7711 32RED ON THE APP STORE H'CAP (DIV I) 1m 3f 219y(P)
8:40 (8:43) (Class 6) (0-65,69) 3-Y-O+ £2,264 (£673; £336; £168) Stalls Low

Form RPR
0541 1 **Hajaam (IRE)**[4] 7567 3-9-1 62 ........ JimCrowley 1 80+
(Charlie Fellowes) *led 1f: sn settled in 4th: pushed along over 2f out: clsd to ld over 1f out: sn drew rt away* 4/6[1]
3314 2 6 **Iballisticvin**[7] 7483 4-9-10 65 ........ AdamKirby 5 73
(Gary Moore) *trckd ldng pair after 2f: chal 2f out: upsides whn wnr shot past over 1f out: tk 2nd fnl f but no ch* 7/2[2]
4315 3 2 **Chilli Jam**[11] 7360 4-9-1 56 ........(p) LiamKeniry 7 60
(Ed de Giles) *trckd ldr after 2f: rdn to ld 2f out: hdd over 1f out: outpcd and lost 2nd fnl f* 8/1[3]
1266 4 2 **Rowlestonerendezvu**[27] 6811 4-9-3 58 ........ GeorgeDowning 14 59
(Tony Carroll) *wl in tch: outpcd fr 3f out: hung bdly lft 2f out: kpt on to take 4th ins fnl f* 40/1
4432 5 1 3/4 **Daily Trader**[46] 6139 3-8-12 66 ........ KatherineGlenister(7) 4 65
(David Evans) *plld hrd: hld up towards rr: outpcd wl over 2f out: no ch after: kpt on fnl f* 8/1[3]
6003 6 hd **Jersey Bull (IRE)**[28] 6796 5-9-4 59 ........(h) RobertWinston 13 57
(Michael Madgwick) *t.k.h: hld up wl in rr: pushed along and sme prog over 2f out but ldrs already gone: kpt on but nvr in it* 16/1
4040 7 nse **Magic Beans**[14] 7253 3-8-4 54 ........ CharlieBennett(3) 12 53
(Hughie Morrison) *led after 1f to 2f out: stl clr of rest in 4th over 1f out: sn wknd* 25/1
4-60 8 1 **Caracas**[33] 6623 3-9-5 66 ........ MartinHarley 3 63
(Harry Dunlop) *hld up in midfield: outpcd over 2f out: reminders and no hdwy after: fdd fnl f* 50/1
1000 9 3 **Victor's Bet (SPA)**[37] 6475 8-9-7 67 ........ MeganNicholls(5) 11 58
(Ralph J Smith) *hld up in last: lft bhd wl over 2f out: no ch after* 20/1
126- 10 14 **Gracesome (IRE)**[347] 7508 6-9-8 63 ........ DavidProbert 9 32
(Michael Blanshard) *t.k.h: trckd ldrs: wknd qckly over 2f out: t.o* 50/1
0-00 11 8 **Prosecute (FR)**[68] 5333 4-9-11 66 ........(t[1]) TomMarquand 2 22
(Ali Stronge) *awkward s: t.k.h: hld up in rr: rdn and wknd qckly over 2f out: t.o* 50/1
0000 12 2 3/4 **Back To Love (CAN)**[7] 7480 4-8-7 51 oh6........(b[1]) GeorgeWood(3) 6
(Mark Gillard) *t.k.h: hld up in rr: wknd 3f out: t.o* 100/1

2m 33.67s (-0.83) **Going Correction** -0.025s/f (Stan)
**WFA** 3 from 4yo+ 6lb 12 Ran SP% 128.2
Speed ratings (Par 101): **101,97,95,94,93 93,93,92,90,81 75,73**
CSF £3.32 CT £12.89 TOTE £1.60: £1.10, £1.90, £2.80; EX 4.30 Trifecta £18.50.
**Owner** Khalifa Bin Hamad Al Attiyah **Bred** Marston Stud **Trained** Newmarket, Suffolk

**FOCUS**
They went a modest gallop and the odds-on winner proved much too good. The third is a decent guide to the level.

## 7712 32RED ON THE APP STORE H'CAP (DIV II) 1m 3f 219y(P)
9:10 (9:12) (Class 6) (0-65,67) 3-Y-O+ £2,264 (£673; £336; £168) Stalls Low

Form RPR
3244 1 **Hepplewhite**[33] 6610 4-9-10 65 ........(p) MartinDwyer 3 71
(William Muir) *hld up towards rr: stdy prog fr 3f out: shkn up over 2f out: clsd over 1f out: drvn and kpt on to ld last 100yds* 9/1
3003 2 3/4 **Abel Tasman**[38] 6443 3-9-5 66 ........ RichardKingscote 12 72
(Ed Walker) *stdd s and dropped in fr wd draw: hld up in last pair: stl there over 3f out: prog and shkn up over 2f out: styd on wl after and tk 2nd last strides: too late to chal* 9/2[2]
1235 3 hd **Let's Be Happy (IRE)**[35] 6556 3-9-1 62 ........(p) ShaneKelly 11 67
(Richard Hughes) *led to 7f out: led again wl over 2f out and sent for home: edgd lft over 1f out: hdd and no ex last 100yds* 20/1
5333 4 nse **Time To Sea (IRE)**[29] 6767 3-9-3 64 ........ RobertWinston 7 69
(John Butler) *t.k.h: wl in tch: prog to dispute 2nd over 2f out: rdn to chal and edgd lft over 1f out: nt qckn ins fnl f* 10/1
4641 5 3 3/4 **Windsorlot (IRE)**[41] 6306 4-9-1 56 ........ GeorgeDowning 14 54
(Tony Carroll) *hld up towards rr: prog fr 4f out: disp 2nd over 2f out: nt qckn over 1f out: fdd fnl f* 20/1
0133 6 3/4 **Free Forum (IRE)**[20] 7063 3-9-6 67 ........ SeanLevey 4 65
(David Simcock) *t.k.h: w ldr 1f but sn restrained bhd ldrs: prog and cl up 2f out: wknd fnl f* 7/2[1]
063 7 1 1/4 **Dance Rock**[19] 7080 4-9-10 65 ........(v) AdamKirby 1 60
(Neil Mulholland) *s.s: mostly in last and nt gng wl: eventually kpt on fnl 2f but no ch* 12/1
4231 8 1/2 **Transmitting**[34] 6588 4-9-11 66 ........(e) HarryBentley 2 60
(Ed Vaughan) *t.k.h: hld up towards rr: prog over 3f out: no imp on ldrs 2f out: fdd over 1f out* 7/2[1]
-526 9 nk **Rock On Dandy (FR)**[38] 6443 3-8-8 62 ........(v[1]) WilliamCox(7) 6 57
(Harry Dunlop) *hld up towards rr: effrt on wd outside bnd over 3f out: no prog fnl 2f* 33/1
0 10 3 3/4 **Missguided (IRE)**[21] 7028 4-9-8 63 ........ LukeMorris 10 51
(Alex Hales) *hld up in rr: stl gng wl enough 3f out: shkn up over 2f out: no rspnse and sn btn* 20/1
0660 11 10 **Crystal Secret**[7] 7490 3-8-4 51 oh5........ KieranO'Neill 9 24
(John Bridger) *chsd ldrs tl wknd over 3f out* 100/1
3543 12 1 1/4 **Starlight Circus (IRE)**[38] 6436 3-9-0 61 ........ SilvestreDeSousa 13 32
(Marco Botti) *chsd ldr after 1f to 7f out: styd cl up tl wknd qckly over 2f out: eased* 8/1[3]
0505 13 8 **Elusive Cowboy (USA)**[34] 6588 4-9-5 60 ........(p) KieranShoemark 8 17
(Chris Gordon) *hld up in rr: sweeping move on wd outside bnd 4f out to 3f out: wknd qckly over 2f out* 25/1
-650 14 17 **Poet's Charm (IRE)**[36] 6503 3-8-3 53 ........ DavidEgan(3) 5
(Martin Hill) *t.k.h: prom: led 7f out to wl over 2f out: wknd rapidly: t.o* 50/1

2m 34.31s (-0.19) **Going Correction** -0.025s/f (Stan)
**WFA** 3 from 4yo 6lb 14 Ran SP% 124.5
Speed ratings (Par 101): **99,98,98,98,95 95,94,94,93,91 84,83,78,67**
CSF £47.13 CT £818.81 TOTE £11.10: £2.80, £2.10, £4.30; EX 57.50 Trifecta £1456.30.
**Owner** Foursome Thoroughbreds **Bred** Meon Valley Stud **Trained** Lambourn, Berks

**FOCUS**
The gallop was a bit stop-start and the final time 0.64sec slower than the first division. The third and fourth have been rated to their marks.
T/Jkpt: Not Won. T/Plt: £144.70 to a £1 stake. Pool: £73,311.12 - 369.66 winning units. T/Qpdt: £22.60 to a £1 stake. Pool: £11,027.72 - 359.81 winning units. **Jonathan Neesom**

7713 - 7720a (Foreign Racing) - See Raceform Interactive

# 5268 COMPIEGNE (L-H)
Tuesday, October 3

**OFFICIAL GOING: Turf: heavy**

## 7721a PRIX D'EMEVILLE (CLAIMER) (4YO+) (TURF) 1m 4f
4:55 4-Y-O+ £8,119 (£3,247; £2,435; £1,623; £811)

RPR
1 **Blue Diamond (FR)**[338] 5-9-1 0 ........ LukasDelozier 10 73
(J Hirschberger, Germany) 8/1
2 3 1/2 **Montesquieu (FR)**[20] 7070 7-8-13 0 ........(p) MlleCoraliePacaut(9) 6 74
(M Boutin, France) 83/10
3 1 1/4 **Cosmic City**[279] 5-9-6 0 ........ Pierre-CharlesBoudot 7 70
(J-P Gauvin, France) 11/5[1]
4 2 **Settler's Son (IRE)**[96] 6-9-4 0 ........ SebastienMaillot 4 65
(J Michal, France) 39/10[2]
5 1 1/2 **En Souplesse (FR)**[15] 4-8-9 0 ........ ClementLecoeuvre(6) 2 59
(E Lellouche, France) 43/5
6 3 **Rodyana (FR)**[20] 7070 4-8-11 0 ........(b) FabienLefebvre 9 51
(P Monfort, France) 25/1
7 6 **Zillion Dollar Cup (FR)**[17] 9-8-7 0 ........(b) MlleAlisonMassin(4) 3 41
(F Cheyer, France) 238/10
8 3 1/2 **Ejayteekay**[17] 7151 4-8-11 0 ........ MaximeGuyon 1 35
(Hughie Morrison) *wl into stride: settled bhd ldrs: pushed along 3f out: drvn over 1f out: sn btn and eased fnl f* 42/10[3]
9 10 **Trigger Flash (FR)**[20] 7070 6-8-11 0 ........ MarcNobili 5 19
(F Cheyer, France) 39/1
10 snk **Track Star (FR)**[92] 4457 5-9-1 0 ........ TheoBachelot 11 23
(Gerard Martin, Austria) 17/1

PARI-MUTUEL (all including 1 euro stake): WIN 9.00; PLACE 2.40, 2.30, 1.50; DF 33.70; SF 67.10.
**Owner** Manfred Anton Schmelzer **Bred** R Peters **Trained** Germany

# 5983 HOPPEGARTEN (R-H)
Tuesday, October 3

**OFFICIAL GOING: Turf: good**

## 7722a 27TH PREIS DER DEUTSCHEN EINHEIT (GROUP 3) (3YO+) (TURF) 1m 2f
3:55 3-Y-O+ £38,461 (£13,675; £5,982; £3,846; £2,136)

RPR
1 **Matchwinner (GER)**[38] 6451 6-9-4 0 ........ AndreasHelfenbein 8 110+
(A Kleinkorres, Germany) *hld up: rdn and hdwy on outer over 1f out: chal fnl f and sn led: styd on: asserted: readily* 13/2
2 2 1/2 **Navaro Girl (IRE)**[31] 6710 3-8-10 0 ........ AndraschStarke 5 102
(P Schiergen, Germany) *hld up: hdwy on outer early in st: rdn to chal over 1f out and led ent fnl f: hdd sn after: kpt on wout matching wnr* 6/1
3 3 **Amigo (GER)**[44] 6255 3-9-0 0 ........ BauyrzhanMurzabayev 9 100
(Eva Fabianova, Germany) *led: rdn into st: hdd ent fnl f: no ex and hld in 3rd sn after* 26/5[3]
4 3 **Potemkin (GER)**[38] 6451 6-9-4 0 ........ EduardoPedroza 7 93
(A Wohler, Germany) *midfield: rdn early st: outpcd by ldrs fnl 2f: plugged on for mod 4th* 6/4[1]
5 1/2 **Devastar (GER)**[25] 5-9-4 0 ........ AdriedeVries 6 92
(Markus Klug, Germany) *prom: rdn and outpcd in st: fdd* 3/1[2]
6 3/4 **Capitano (GER)**[23] 6987 4-9-4 0 ........ FilipMinarik 4 91
(J Hirschberger, Germany) *trckd ldr: rdn into st: no ex fnl 2f: wknd* 186/10
7 1 3/4 **Well Spoken (GER)**[58] 5693 3-8-10 0 ........ MaximPecheur 3 84
(Markus Klug, Germany) *in tch: shuffled bk on rail appr st: sn rdn: no ex and btn fnl 2f* 148/10
8 6 **Space Cowboy (GER)**[38] 6451 5-9-4 0 ........ AlexanderPietsch 2 75
(Markus Klug, Germany) *midfield: rdn into st: sn no ex and btn: wknd* 128/10
9 3 **Apoleon (GER)**[91] 4487 7-9-4 0 ........ BayarsaikhanGanbat 1 69
(Frau Anna Schleusner-Fruhriep, Germany) *dwlt sltly and a in rr: btn fnl 2f: no factor* 45/1

2m 9.72s (3.02)
**WFA** 3 from 4yo+ 4lb 9 Ran SP% 129.6
PARI-MUTUEL (all including 10 euro stake): WIN: 75; PLACE: 25, 23, 21; SF: 528.
**Owner** Jens Schwarma **Bred** Gestut Gorlsdorf **Trained** Germany

# 7705 KEMPTON (A.W) (R-H)
Wednesday, October 4

**OFFICIAL GOING: Polytrack: standard to slow**
Wind: 1/2 behind Weather: White cloud

## 7723 RACING UK PROFITS RETURNED TO RACING H'CAP 7f (P)
5:40 (5:40) (Class 6) (0-65,65) 3-Y-O+ £2,264 (£673; £336; £168) Stalls Low

Form RPR
-500 1 **Tuscany (IRE)**[21] 7063 3-9-5 65 ........ RaulDaSilva 4 71
(Paul Cole) *pressed ldr on outer: rdn 2f out and led: drifted sltly lft u.p: kpt on wl ins fnl f* 16/1
2005 2 1/2 **Waqt (IRE)**[15] 7254 3-9-4 64 ........ DaneO'Neill 10 69
(Marcus Tregoning) *hld up in mid-div: rdn over 2f out: kpt on and prog tl ct on heels ent fnl f: gap appeared over 150yds out: shuffled along and styd on best to cl on wnr fnl strides: nvr nrr* 16/1
0661 3 3/4 **Inlawed**[35] 6581 3-9-5 65 ........ PatCosgrave 8 68
(Ed Walker) *trckd ldrs: rdn over 2f out on outer: kpt on ins fnl f to take 3rd nr fin* 6/1[3]
2220 4 nk **Seyasah (IRE)**[14] 7282 3-9-5 65 ........ TomQueally 3 67
(Chris Wall) *hld up in rr-div: shkn up fr 2f out: kpt on wl over 1f out and gd prog: tk 2nd ins fnl f: no ex nr fin and lost two pls* 20/1
-266 5 nk **Connemera Queen**[15] 7249 4-9-7 65 ........ RobertWinston 14 67
(John Butler) *chsd ldrs: kpt on over 2f out: kpt on wl between horses ent fnl f: tk 3rd ins fnl f: no ex cl home and lost two pls* 22/1

3602 **6** ¾ **Ubla (IRE)**[29] 6795 4-9-5 **63** AdamBeschizza 5 63
(Jane Chapple-Hyam) *trckd ldrs on inner: rdn jst over 2f out: pressed wnr ent fnl f: no ex ins fnl f and fdd* **5/1**[2]

0001 **7** *hd* **Treacherous**[7] 7517 3-9-0 **63** 6ex CallumShepherd(3) 7 61
(Ed de Giles) *s.s: hld up in rr: shkn up and prog over 3f out on outer: rdn on outer over 2f out: sme prog tl no ex ins fnl f* **7/4**[1]

0000 **8** ½ **Fire Diamond**[22] 7034 4-9-5 **63** (p) RichardKingscote 1 61
(Tom Dascombe) *in rr-div on inner: rdn 2f out and stuck to inner: kpt on one pce tl no ex wl ins fnl f* **10/1**

6352 **9** ½ **Miss Icon**[30] 6753 3-9-5 **65** DavidProbert 11 61
(Patrick Chamings) *racd in mid-div: rdn over 2f out: plugged on one pce ins fnl f* **25/1**

5201 **10** ½ **Corporal Maddox**[37] 6503 10-9-4 **62** (p) AdamKirby 12 57
(Ronald Harris) *hld up in rr: shkn up on outer over 2f out: hanging fr over 1f out: pushed out fnl f* **25/1**

0034 **11** ¾ **Mezmaar**[21] 7058 8-9-7 **65** LiamKeniry 9 58
(Mark Usher) *wnt to post early: chsd ldrs: shkn up over 2f out: rdn and front rnk 2f out: one pce fr over 1f out and wknd* **6/1**[3]

-000 **12** *21* **Mossy's Lodge**[15] 7255 4-9-2 **60** RyanTate 6
(Anthony Carson) *a in rr: pushed along at 1/2-way: no prog and eased fr over 1f out: t.o* **33/1**

5060 **13** 1 ¼ **Awesome Allan (IRE)**[11] 7398 3-9-5 **65** SeanLevey 2
(David Evans) *marginal ldr on inner: rdn over 2f out: hdd 2f out: no more to give and eased over 1f out: t.o* **33/1**

1m 25.77s (-0.23) **Going Correction** -0.075s/f (Stan)
**WFA** 3 from 4yo+ 2lb 13 Ran SP% **125.1**
Speed ratings (Par 101): **98,97,96,96,95 95,94,94,93,93 92,68,66**
CSF £232.95 CT £1790.94 TOTE £17.60: £4.70, £6.00, £2.40; EX 177.40 Trifecta £2126.20.
**Owner** P F I Cole Ltd **Bred** Kildaragh Stud & M Downey **Trained** Whatcombe, Oxon

**FOCUS**
The surface was once again officially described as Standard to Slow. Despite the favourite blowing out this had the look of a fair Class 6 and winners should emerge from it.

## 7724 32RED.COM/BRITISH STALLION STUDS EBF MAIDEN FILLIES' STKS (PLUS 10 RACE) (DIV I) 6f (P)
**6:10** (6:13) (Class 5) 2-Y-O **£3,234** (£962; £481; £240) **Stalls** Low

Form RPR

206 **1** **Mushahadaat (IRE)**[28] 6806 2-9-0 75 (p[1]) DaneO'Neill 12 77
(Brian Meehan) *cl up and t.k.h: led after 2f: mde rest: rdn wl over 1f out and 3 l ldr ent fnl f: pushed out* **6/1**[2]

0 **2** 1 ¼ **Scandaleuse (USA)**[133] 2958 2-9-0 0 TedDurcan 5 73
(Sir Michael Stoute) *wl away and settled in mid-div on inner: shkn up and gd prog over 2f out: rdn 2f out: kpt on wl chsng clr ldr fr over 1f out: no ex nr fin* **3/1**[1]

**3** 3 ¾ **No More Thrills** 2-9-0 0 SeanLevey 8 62+
(Richard Hannon) *trckd ldr on outer: rdn over 2f out: outpcd wl over 1f out: kpt on ent fnl f* **12/1**

0 **4** 1 ¼ **Cwynar**[90] 4533 2-8-11 0 CallumShepherd(3) 7 58+
(Charles Hills) *mid-div on outer: rdn over 2f out: kpt on wl ins fnl f to take 4th cl home* **12/1**

06 **5** ½ **Obrigada**[18] 7153 2-9-0 0 JosephineGordon 9 57
(Tom Clover) *trckd ldrs on inner: rdn over 2f out: 3rd on inner over 1f out: kpt on tl no ex nr fin and lost two pls* **20/1**

5 **6** *1* **Chizz De Biz (IRE)**[39] 6417 2-9-0 0 GeorgeDowning 11 54
(Daniel Kubler) *led for 2f: chsd ldr after: rdn over 2f out: sn no ex and fdd over 1f out* **16/1**

00 **7** *1* **Goodbye Lulu (IRE)**[12] 7351 2-9-0 0 (h) PatCosgrave 6 51
(George Baker) *wnt lft s: racd in mid-div on outer: rdn over 2f out on outer: kpt on one pce* **20/1**

**8** 1 ½ **L'Explora (USA)** 2-9-0 0 KieranShoemark 10 46
(Roger Charlton) *edgy in paddock: in rr-div on outer: shkn up between horses over 2f out w plenty to do: hands and heels fr over 1f out* **10/1**

00 **9** *nk* **Salty Sugar**[68] 5371 2-9-0 0 RaulDaSilva 1 45
(Paul Cole) *settled in rr-div: rdn on inner over 2f out: no ex fr over 1f out* **25/1**

**10** 1 ½ **Silver Swift** 2-9-0 0 DavidProbert 2 41
(Andrew Balding) *a in rr: gng okay whn checked on inner over 2f out: nvr involved after* **7/1**[3]

0 **11** 3 ¼ **Gowing Gowing Gone (IRE)**[28] 6827 2-9-0 0 GrahamLee 4 31
(Richard Spencer) *wnt rt s and hmpd rival: a in rr: shkn up over 2f out on inner: no ex sn after* **33/1**

6 **12** *6* **Society Lilly (IRE)**[26] 6868 2-9-0 0 JamesDoyle 3 13
(Hugo Palmer) *hmpd s: a in rr* **3/1**[1]

1m 13.6s (0.50) **Going Correction** -0.075s/f (Stan) 12 Ran SP% **123.5**
Speed ratings (Par 92): **93,91,86,84,84 82,81,79,78,76 72,64**
CSF £24.11 TOTE £7.50: £2.00, £1.60, £3.90; EX 37.40 Trifecta £353.20.
**Owner** Hamdan Al Maktoum **Bred** Shadwell Estate Company Limited **Trained** Manton, Wilts

**FOCUS**
Up with the pace was the place to be in the first division of this fair fillies' maiden.

## 7725 32RED.COM/BRITISH STALLION STUDS EBF MAIDEN FILLIES' STKS (PLUS 10 RACE) (DIV II) 6f (P)
**6:40** (6:40) (Class 5) 2-Y-O **£3,234** (£962; £481; £240) **Stalls** Low

Form RPR

423 **1** **Tivoli (IRE)**[22] 7021 2-9-0 84 AndreaAtzeni 9 83
(John Gosden) *sn led and mde all: rdn 2f out and qcknd up: pressed by 3rd over 1f out: kpt on strly ins fnl f: rdn out* **6/4**[1]

3 **2** 1 ¼ **Left Alone**[13] 7334 2-9-0 0 JamesDoyle 10 79
(Hugo Palmer) *hld up on inner in rr-div: gng wl and hld together waiting for cutaway over 2f out: swtchd to inner and rdn 2f out: prog w a bit to do over 1f out: kpt on wl ins fnl f to take 2nd nr fin: nvr nrr* **15/8**[2]

**3** ½ **Modern Love (IRE)**[25] 6954 2-9-0 0 OisinMurphy 3 78+
(M D O'Callaghan, Ire) *chsd ldr on inner: rdn 2f out and pressed wnr tl ent fnl f: stuck on after: lost 2nd cl home* **5/2**[3]

4 **4** 2 ¾ **Guns Drawn (IRE)**[9] 7453 2-9-0 0 SeanLevey 6 70
(Richard Hannon) *t.k.h early: chsd ldr: rdn over 2f out: kpt on in 4th fr over 1f out: no ex ent fnl f* **33/1**

2 **5** *1* **Procedure**[101] 4116 2-9-0 0 TedDurcan 8 67+
(Sir Michael Stoute) *tk fierce hold for 1f: t.k.h after in rr on outer: shkn up over 2f out and kpt on wl fr over 1f out: likely improver* **7/1**

0 **6** ¾ **Glamorous Dream (IRE)**[20] 7079 2-9-0 0 SamHitchcott 2 64
(Ronald Harris) *trckd ldrs on inner: rdn over 2f out: one pce fr over 1f out* **100/1**

2334 **7** *1* **Kareva**[39] 6417 2-9-0 76 JimCrowley 7 61
(Charles Hills) *settled bhd ldrs: rdn over 2f out: no ex ent fnl f* **16/1**

60 **8** ¾ **Golden Deal (IRE)**[28] 6824 2-9-0 0 (h) TomQueally 1 59
(Richard Phillips) *hld up in rr-div on inner and racd freely taking a t.k.h at times: rdn over 2f out and sme prog tl no ex over 1f out and pushed out* **100/1**

**9** 1 ¼ **Serabrina (IRE)**[151] 2-9-0 0 KieranShoemark 5 55
(David Menuisier) *mid-div on outer: rdn 2f out: one pce after* **20/1**

0 **10** *4* **Jazzy Girl (IRE)**[12] 7352 2-9-0 0 MartinDwyer 4 43
(Brendan Powell) *squeezed up s: in rr on outer: rn green at times: rdn along wl over 2f out: no ex sn after* **66/1**

0 **11** 2 ¼ **Seaquinn**[28] 6826 2-8-7 0 LeviWilliams(7) 12 37
(John Best) *kpt st leaving stalls tl c to pack after 2f: sn mde rapid hdwy on bnd racing wd: cl up w ldrs 4f out: rdn over 2f out: spent force and wknd qckly sn after* **100/1**

1m 13.31s (0.21) **Going Correction** -0.075s/f (Stan) 11 Ran SP% **133.9**
Speed ratings (Par 92): **95,93,92,89,87 86,85,84,82,77 74**
CSF £5.34 TOTE £2.00: £1.10, £1.50, £1.20; EX 7.90 Trifecta £19.90.
**Owner** K Abdullah **Bred** Redpender Stud Ltd **Trained** Newmarket, Suffolk

**FOCUS**
Marginally quicker than the first division. Again, a fair fillies' maiden, which the market got spot on.

## 7726 32RED CASINO EBF NOVICE STKS (PLUS 10 RACE) 1m (P)
**7:10** (7:11) (Class 4) 2-Y-O **£4,592** (£1,366; £683; £341) **Stalls** Low

Form RPR

**1** **Kassar (IRE)** 2-9-2 0 KieranShoemark 14 77+
(Roger Charlton) *chsd ldrs on outer: shkn up wl over 2f out on outer: sn rdn and kpt on wl ent fnl f: led 110yds out: rdn out to hold on* **33/1**

**2** *nk* **Msayyan (IRE)** 2-9-2 0 RobertTart 6 76+
(John Gosden) *restrained between horses in mid-div: shkn up over 2f out and sltly hmpd: sn mde gd prog: rdn wl over 1f out: on heels and nt clr run ent fnl f: kpt on wl ins fnl f: pushed out nr fin* **6/1**

**3** *shd* **Bow Street** 2-9-2 0 JamesDoyle 13 76+
(Charlie Appleby) *pushed along leaving stalls: in rr-div on outer but racd lazily w jockey crouched low: rdn over 2f out on outer: kpt on wl fr over 1f out: pushed out fnl strides: fin 4th: plcd 3rd* **5/1**[3]

01 **4** ½ **Tansheet (IRE)**[15] 7237 2-9-8 0 JimCrowley 1 81
(William Haggas) *chsd ldr on inner: rdn 2f out on inner: kpt on one pce fr over 1f out: fin 5th: plcd 4th* **9/2**[2]

4 **5** *nk* **Neeraan (USA)**[54] 5876 2-9-2 0 DaneO'Neill 9 74
(Roger Varian) *chsd ldrs on outer: rdn 2f out: kpt on one pce fr over 1f out: fin 6th: plcd 5th* **9/2**[2]

**6** *2* **Metkaif** 2-9-2 0 SeanLevey 8 69
(Richard Hannon) *pressed ldr: rdn 2f out and ev ch over 1f out: one pce ent fnl f and fdd: fin 7th: plcd 6th* **8/1**

**7** 1 ¾ **Desert Path** 2-9-2 0 RichardKingscote 5 65+
(Amanda Perrett) *in rr: pushed along over 2f out w plenty to do: shuffled along but kpt on wl after: nvr nrr: fin 8th: plcd 7th* **40/1**

**8** *shd* **Accessor (IRE)** 2-9-2 0 AndreaAtzeni 11 65
(Richard Hannon) *in rr-div between horses: rdn over 2f out: no ex fr over 1f out: fin 9th: plcd 8th* **20/1**

**9** *1* **Rapier (USA)** 2-9-2 0 TedDurcan 10 62
(Sir Michael Stoute) *s.s and in rr: t.k.h early: swtchd to inner and shuffled along fr 2f out: fin 10th: plcd 9th* **33/1**

**10** *hd* **Future Score (IRE)** 2-9-2 0 PatCosgrave 2 62
(Saeed bin Suroor) *settled in mid-div chsng ldrs: shkn up wl over 2f out: sn struggling and no ex fr over 1f out: fin 11th: plcd 10th* **8/1**

6 **11** *shd* **Global Excel**[40] 6367 2-9-2 0 LiamKeniry 4 62
(Ed Walker) *in rr-div between horses and t.k.h: rdn 2f out: no ex sn after: fin 12th: plcd 11th* **33/1**

**12** *6* **Safarhi** 2-9-2 0 FergusSweeney 12 47
(Alan King) *s.s and in rr: rdn over 2f out: sn hld: fin 13th: plcd 12th* **66/1**

0 **13** *16* **Timoshenko**[14] 7280 2-9-2 0 LukeMorris 3 9
(Sir Mark Prescott Bt) *in rr on inner: shkn up over 2f out: eased fr over 1f out: fin 14th: plcd 13th* **100/1**

3 **D** ¾ **Dragon Mountain**[26] 6883 2-9-2 0 JosephineGordon 7 69
(Hugo Palmer) *sn led: kicked for home 2f out: drifted to inner rail over 1f out: no ex wl ins fnl f: hdd 110yds out and lost 2nd sn after: fin 3rd: disqualified and plcd last* **3/1**[1]

1m 39.57s (-0.23) **Going Correction** -0.075s/f (Stan) 14 Ran SP% **133.0**
Speed ratings (Par 97): **98,97,96,96,96 94,92,92,91,91 90,84,68,96**
CSF £234.92 TOTE £39.80: £13.50, £1.90, £2.20; EX 895.80.
**Owner** Al Shaqab Racing **Bred** Woodcote Stud Ltd **Trained** Beckhampton, Wilts

**FOCUS**
A host of well-bred sorts from powerful stables marks this down as a potentially strong novice event. However, there was a bit of a bunch finish, which resulted in an Al Shaqab one-two.

## 7727 32RED H'CAP 1m (P)
**7:40** (7:43) (Class 3) (0-95,95) 3-Y-O+
**£7,158** (£2,143; £1,071; £535; £267; £134) **Stalls** Low

Form RPR

2041 **1** **Brigliadoro (IRE)**[38] 6483 6-9-6 **94** DavidProbert 5 103
(Philip McBride) *s.s and hld up in rr: rdn over 2f out: kpt on strly fr over 1f out w plenty to do on outer: fin qckly wdst of all and got up post* **10/1**

005 **2** *hd* **Belgian Bill**[32] 6717 9-9-7 **95** PatCosgrave 12 103
(George Baker) *pressed ldr on outer: rdn over 1f out and led ent fnl f: kpt on wl tl ct post* **33/1**

1020 **3** *hd* **Eagle Creek (IRE)**[26] 6873 3-9-4 **95** AndreaAtzeni 8 103
(Simon Crisford) *hld up in rr: shkn up over 2f out and prog on rail over 1f out: switch out ent fnl f: kpt on strly between horses nr fin: gng on fnl strides* **5/1**[2]

4111 **4** 1 ½ **Brilliant Vanguard (IRE)**[25] 6933 4-9-5 **93** (p) KevinStott 14 97
(Kevin Ryan) *chsd ldr: rdn 2f out: kpt on ins fnl f but nt pl of plcd horses* **6/1**[3]

1210 **5** *hd* **Don't Give Up**[26] 6881 3-9-4 **95** (p[1]) OisinMurphy 2 98
(Saeed bin Suroor) *sluggish s: hld up bhd ldrs between horses: rdn 2f out: kpt on tl no ex ins fnl f* **3/1**[1]

0635 **6** ¾ **Big Baz (IRE)**[18] 7149 7-9-6 **94** KieranShoemark 13 96
(William Muir) *racd in rr: rdn out wd over 2f out: kpt on one pce tl styd on wl ins fnl f* **8/1**

6000 **7** ½ **Omran**[32] 6685 3-9-2 **93** DanielMuscutt 3 93
(Marco Botti) *hld up in mid-div between horses: rdn over 2f out: kpt on one pce fr over 1f out* **20/1**

0226 **8** ½ **Sultan Baybars**[38] 6484 3-8-11 **91** DavidEgan(3) 10 90
(Roger Varian) *racd in rr: rdn over 2f out: no ex over 1f out where one pce* **25/1**

0520 9 3/4 **Kentuckyconnection (USA)**[39] 6449 4-9-2 **90**................ GrahamLee 6 87
(Bryan Smart) *chsd ldrs on inner: rdn over 2f out: no ex and wknd ent fnl f* **25/1**

000 10 3/4 **Early Morning (IRE)**[25] 6918 6-9-6 **94**............................ AdamKirby 11 90
(Harry Dunlop) *sn led: rdn over 2f out: stuck on wl tl hdd ent fnl f and sn wknd* **25/1**

-360 11 1 3/4 **Replenish (FR)**[97] 4261 4-9-2 **93**.......................... GeorgeWood(3) 1 88
(James Fanshawe) *trckd ldrs for 2f: clipped heels w horse in front and lost action sn after: rcvrd and in rr: shuffled along fr over 2f out* **10/1**

000 12 4 **Mr Bossy Boots (IRE)**[19] 7129 6-9-6 **94**............ RichardKingscote 9 76
(Amanda Perrett) *in rr-div on outer: rdn over 2f out: sn hld* **33/1**

0000 13 9 **Gossiping**[25] 6933 5-9-6 **94**.....................................(p) ShaneKelly 4 68
(Gary Moore) *in rr-div: rdn over 2f out: no ex fr over 1f out* **12/1**

30 14 shd **Manson**[19] 7129 4-9-6 **94**............................................(p) JamesDoyle 7 75
(Dominic Ffrench Davis) *chsd ldrs: rdn over 2f out: wknd qckly fr over 1f out* **12/1**

1m 37.59s (-2.21) **Going Correction** -0.075s/f (Stan)
**WFA** 3 from 4yo+ 3lb 14 Ran SP% **122.8**
Speed ratings (Par 107): **108,107,107,106,105 105,104,104,103,102 100,96,87,87**
CSF £319.35 CT £1894.56 TOTE £11.00: £3.50, £7.10, £2.10; EX 328.80 Trifecta £3650.50.
**Owner** Serafinoagodino,C M Budgett,P J McBride **Bred** D Naughton, Zubieta & Javier Salmean **Trained** Newmarket, Suffolk

**FOCUS**
5lb covered these on official ratings, they went a solid pace and everything points to it being a good handicap.

## 7728 100% PROFIT BOOST AT 32REDSPORT.COM H'CAP (LONDON MIDDLE DISTANCE SERIES QUALIFIER) 1m 2f 219y(P)
8:10 (8:11) (Class 4) (0-80,81) 3-Y-O+ £4,690 (£1,395; £697; £348) Stalls Low

Form RPR

0531 1 **Ply**[9] 7452 3-9-6 **81** 6ex.................................... KieranShoemark 5 97+
(Roger Charlton) *hld up in mid-div on inner: shkn up 2f out and smooth prog between horses: gng wl over 1f out: chal between horses and led ent fnl f: sn clr* **4/7**[1]

222 2 3 **Desert Ruler**[7] 7524 4-9-3 **73**.................................... JackGarritty 4 80
(Jedd O'Keeffe) *chsd ldr: rdn over 1f out: ev ch ent fnl f: wnr sn wnt by: one pce after* **6/1**[2]

4551 3 2 1/4 **Romanor**[30] 6763 3-9-4 **79**.................................... PatCosgrave 8 82
(Ed Walker) *sltly rrd leavings stalls: in rr and t.k.h: rdn over 2f out: kpt on wl to take 3rd ent fnl f* **10/1**

6035 4 nk **Artful Rogue (IRE)**[28] 6819 6-9-8 **78**.................... RichardKingscote 13 80
(Amanda Perrett) *settled in mid-div: rdn over 2f out: kpt on one pce* **16/1**

4446 5 1/2 **Sonnetist**[98] 4224 3-9-1 **76**.................................... SeanLevey 14 78
(Richard Hannon) *hld up in rr: rdn over 2f out: kpt on wl fr over 1f out: nvr nrr* **50/1**

6000 6 3/4 **Luv U Whatever**[9] 7452 7-9-5 **75**..............................(tp) JoeyHaynes 3 75
(Marjorie Fife) *led: rdn 2f out: hdd ent fnl f: no ex and wknd sn after* **50/1**

1040 7 1 **Admiral's Sunset**[75] 5108 4-9-7 **80**........................ CharlieBennett(3) 1 79
(Hughie Morrison) *chsd ldrs: rdn over 2f out: no ex over 1f out and kpt on one pce* **33/1**

4325 8 2 1/2 **Election Day**[13] 7327 3-9-5 **80**.................................... JamesDoyle 6 74
(Mark Johnston) *pressed ldr: rdn 2f out: no ex fr over 1f out and wknd* **7/1**[3]

000 9 shd **Dolphin Village (IRE)**[27] 6848 7-9-3 **73**...............(h) JosephineGordon 2 68
(Shaun Harris) *chsd ldrs on inner: effrt on inner 2f out: n.m.r ent fnl f: pushed out sn after* **25/1**

1126 10 1 **Perfect Quest**[113] 3693 4-9-10 **80**.................................(t) AdamKirby 12 73
(Clive Cox) *a in rr: rdn wl over 2f out: wknd* **25/1**

1503 11 8 **Jufn**[27] 6848 4-9-9 **79**..............................................(h) LiamKeniry 10 58
(John Butler) *trckd ldrs on outer: rdn over 2f out: sn fnd nil u.p and wknd* **12/1**

1/50 12 dist **Sleep Easy**[27] 6865 5-9-10 **80**..............................(tp) RobertWinston 7
(Neil Mulholland) *mid-div on outer: lost pl at 1/2-way: eased fr over 3f out: t.o* **33/1**

2m 18.15s (-3.75) **Going Correction** -0.075s/f (Stan)
**WFA** 3 from 4yo+ 5lb 12 Ran SP% **130.6**
Speed ratings (Par 105): **110,107,106,105,105 105,104,102,102,101 95,**
CSF £4.81 CT £24.10 TOTE £1.30: £1.02, £1.50, £3.00; EX 5.20 Trifecta £29.90.
**Owner** Lady Rothschild **Bred** Carwell Equities Ltd **Trained** Beckhampton, Wilts

**FOCUS**
Straightforward form with the field going a good pace and the odds-on favourite winning easily.

## 7729 32RED ON THE APP STORE H'CAP 1m 2f 219y(P)
8:40 (8:40) (Class 6) (0-60,60) 3-Y-O+ £2,264 (£673; £336; £168) Stalls Low

Form RPR

5033 1 **Beatisa**[14] 7278 3-9-2 **58**.................................... RichardKingscote 4 70
(Ed Walker) *sn led: rdn 2f out and qcknd up: clr ld ent fnl f: kpt on wl* **5/2**[1]

2461 2 3 1/2 **Strictly Art (IRE)**[37] 6523 4-9-0 **56**........................ JoshuaBryan(5) 6 61
(Alan Bailey) *bhd ldr on inner: swtchd sharply off rail wl over 1f out and racd awkward: nt pick up instantly: kpt on wl ent fnl f: no ch w wnr wl ins fnl f* **5/1**[2]

004 3 3/4 **Bergholt (IRE)**[32] 6673 4-9-2 **58**..............................(p) MitchGodwin(5) 2 62
(Tim Vaughan) *settled in mid-div: rdn 2f out: kpt on one pce fr over 1f out* **8/1**[3]

006 4 1 1/4 **Kirkland Forever**[30] 6765 3-9-4 **60**.................................... TedDurcan 11 62
(Brendan Powell) *trckd ldrs: rdn over 2f out: kpt on one pce ent fnl f* **20/1**

0163 5 3 3/4 **Lyrica's Lion (IRE)**[31] 6723 3-8-13 **58**........................ DavidEgan(3) 9 54
(Michael Attwater) *mid-div on outer: rdn over 2f out: kpt on one pce: no ex fnl f* **5/1**[2]

3314 6 1 1/2 **Avocadeau (IRE)**[46] 6175 6-9-7 **58**..............................(tp) MartinDwyer 8 50
(Stuart Kittow) *settled in mid-div: rdn on inner over 2f out: no ex ins fnl f and wknd* **16/1**

206/ 7 3/4 **Reality Show (IRE)**[644] 8392 10-9-2 **56**................... CharlieBennett(3) 12 47
(Shaun Harris) *racd in rr-div: rdn 2f out: sme prog under hands and heels ins fnl f* **66/1**

500 8 2 3/4 **Corredordel Viento (USA)**[109] 3839 3-8-11 **58**....(e[1]) PaddyBradley(5) 7 45
(Simon Dow) *hld up in mid-div on inner: rdn over 2f out: no ex fr over 1f out* **10/1**

5060 9 nse **Arrowzone**[49] 6060 6-9-3 **54**.................................... RyanPowell 1 40
(Kevin Frost) *in rr: rdn along wl over 2f out: kpt on one pce fr over 1f out* **8/1**[3]

3003 10 1/2 **Live Dangerously**[18] 7158 7-9-4 **55**..............................(p) KieranO'Neill 10 40
(John Bridger) *t.k.h in mid-div: plld way to press ldr by 1/2-way: rdn over 2f out: wknd sn after* **33/1**

30 11 1 1/2 **Gunner Moyne**[37] 6524 5-9-3 **57**..............................(b) HectorCrouch(3) 13 39
(Gary Moore) *chsd ldrs on outer: rdn 2f out: sn hld and wknd* **10/1**

000 12 5 **Lopito De Vega (IRE)**[22] 7015 5-9-6 **57**........................ TomQueally 5 30
(David C Griffiths) *a in rr: shuffled along over 3f out: no prog* **16/1**

5206 R **Spirit Of The Vale (IRE)**[15] 7236 4-9-4 **55**......................(t) KevinStott 3
(Oliver Greenall) *stood stl in stalls: then tried to whip rnd: sn dismntd* **12/1**

2m 21.25s (-0.65) **Going Correction** -0.075s/f (Stan)
**WFA** 3 from 4yo+ 5lb 13 Ran SP% **131.0**
Speed ratings (Par 101): **99,96,95,95,92 91,90,88,88,88 87,83,**
CSF £15.66 CT £96.69 TOTE £3.20: £1.20, £2.10, £3.20; EX 19.70 Trifecta £196.50.
**Owner** Chasemore Farm **Bred** Chasemore Farm **Trained** Upper Lambourn, Berks

**FOCUS**
Low grade fare and it's just moderate form. They went three seconds slower than the preceding Class 4 event.

## 7730 DARREN WARD 50TH BIRTHDAY H'CAP 1m 7f 218y(P)
9:10 (9:12) (Class 6) (0-60,60) 3-Y-O+ £2,264 (£673; £252; £252) Stalls Low

Form RPR

2502 1 **St Andrews (IRE)**[8] 7490 4-9-3 **51**..............................(v[1]) AdamKirby 5 58
(Ian Williams) *bhd ldrs on inner: rdn along over 3f out and swtchd off rail over 2f out: led wl over 1f out: kpt on wl ins fnl f* **7/2**[2]

5522 2 3 **Paris Bound**[189] 1436 4-9-5 **60**..............................(p[1]) JasonWatson(7) 2 63
(Andrew Balding) *trckd ldrs on inner: rdn along wl over 2f out: gd prog fr over 1f out on inner: tk 2nd jst ins fnl f: kpt on but no ch w wnr* **10/1**[3]

6300 3 1 1/4 **Wintour Leap**[15] 7232 6-9-1 **56**..............................(p) WilliamCox(7) 9 58
(Robert Stephens) *hld up in rr: shkn up wl over 4f out: rdn over 2f out: swtchd to inner over 1f out and kpt on wl: tk 3rd ins fnl f: no ex fnl strides and ct for dead-heat 3rd* **33/1**

4134 3 dht **Ocean Gale**[21] 7048 4-8-13 **50**.................................... DavidEgan(3) 14 52
(Richard Price) *hld up in mid-div between horses: rdn over 3f out: kpt on fr over 1f out: stuck ins fnl f to dead-heat for 3rd* **16/1**

/00- 5 1 **Royal Battalion**[24] 3767 6-9-9 **60**..............................(p) HectorCrouch(3) 4 61
(Gary Moore) *led early: hdd after 4f but remained disputing: ldr wl over 4f out and increased pce: rdn 3f out: hdd wl over 1f out: stuck on tl lost 2nd jst ins fnl f: no ex after and wknd* **25/1**

0036 6 3/4 **Briac (FR)**[42] 6309 6-9-2 **50**.................................... DanielMuscutt 12 50
(Mark Pattinson) *hld up in rr-div and plld hrd: prog under restraint fr over 7f out and racd in 4th over 4f out: rdn along over 2f out: no ex and one pce fr over 1f out* **20/1**

7 hd **Mizen Master (IRE)**[14] 2353 4-9-7 **55**..............................(t) LukeMorris 3 55
(Olly Murphy) *restrained in rr-div on inner: swtchd to outer wl over 4f out: rdn over 3f out: hanging and nt picked up fr over 1f out: kpt on one pce* **11/8**[1]

4002 8 1 **Ivanhoe**[15] 7232 7-9-10 **58**.................................... SteveDrowne 8 56
(Michael Blanshard) *racd in mid-div on outer: shuffled along over 3f out w n.m.r: swtchd to inner over 1f out: shuffled along after* **25/1**

0653 9 1 1/4 **The Last Melon**[25] 6953 5-9-2 **55**........................ RachealKneller(5) 1 52
(James Bennett) *cl up bhd ldrs: rdn along over 3f out: kpt on tl no ex ent fnl f* **12/1**

05/5 10 1 1/4 **Island Authority**[35] 6578 5-9-5 **56**........................ AaronJones(3) 10 51
(Eugene Stanford) *in rr-div between horses: shkn up wl over 3f out and sme prog ent st: swtchd to out 2f out and rdn: kpt on one pce* **50/1**

-250 11 1 **Intimidator (IRE)**[28] 6820 6-9-4 **57**........................ PaddyBradley(5) 7 51
(Miss Joey Ellis) *racd in rr: shkn up over 3f out and kpt on inner: gd prog fr over 1f out tl no ex ent fnl f* **10/1**[3]

-030 12 3 1/4 **The Way You Dance (IRE)**[11] 7413 5-9-12 **60**......(v[1]) RobertWinston 6 50+
(Neil Mulholland) *bhd ldrs tl squeezed up and wnt bk to rr after 2f: rcvrd and hld up in rr: rdn over 2f out and no ex sn after* **14/1**

6050 13 3 3/4 **Treble Strike (USA)**[13] 7330 4-9-8 **56**..............................(b[1]) TomQueally 13 42
(David C Griffiths) *pressed ldr: narrow ldr after 4f: hdd wl over 4f out where shkn up to hold position: rdn along wl over 3f out: no imp in st* **33/1**

4000 14 34 **See And Be Seen**[8] 7490 7-9-5 **58**..............................(p) MitchGodwin(5) 11 3
(Sylvester Kirk) *racd in rr-div: rdn along wl over 4f out: hrd rdn and chsd ldrs over 3f out: wknd qckly in st: eased over 1f out: t.o* **33/1**

3m 31.77s (1.67) **Going Correction** -0.075s/f (Stan) 14 Ran SP% **126.0**
Speed ratings (Par 101): **92,90,89,89,89 89,88,88,87,87 86,85,83,66**
WIN: £4.50 PL: SA £1.80, PB £3.20, WL £3.90, OG £2.50; EX: £43.00; CSF: £37.28; TC: SA\PB\WL £518.34, SA\PB\OG £259.81; TF: SA\PB\WL £326.40, SA\PB\OG £161.70;.
**Owner** H Downs & R Bedford **Bred** S Rudolf **Trained** Portway, Worcs
■ Stewards' Enquiry : Jason Watson five day ban: careless riding as he maneuvered left-handed causing considerable interference (18-22 Oct)

**FOCUS**
Weak staying form.
T/Jkpt: Not won. T/Plt: £318.70 to a £1 stake. Pool: £90,691.50 - 207.73 winning units. T/Qpdt: £28.30 to a £1 stake. Pool: £16,086.14 - 419.80 winning units. **Cathal Gahan**

# 6146 NOTTINGHAM (L-H)
Wednesday, October 4

**OFFICIAL GOING: Good to soft (soft in places) changing to good to soft after race 4 (3.25)**
Wind: Strong against Weather: Overcast

## 7731 IRISH EBF PLAY COSTA BINGO SLIP ANCHOR MAIDEN STKS (PLUS 10 RACE) (DIV I) 5f 8y
1:50 (1:50) (Class 4) 2-Y-O £5,175 (£1,540; £769; £384) Stalls Centre

Form RPR

1 **All Out** 2-9-0 0.................................... TomMarquand 9 76+
(Richard Hannon) *trckd ldrs: hdwy 2f out: effrt and nt clr run whn swtchd rt over 1f out: sn rdn: chal ins fnl f: kpt on wl to ld last 75 yds* **11/1**

2 2 nk **Little Boy Blue**[70] 5270 2-9-5 0.................................... LukeMorris 3 80
(Bill Turner) *trckd ldng pair: hdwy 2f out: rdn to ld jst over 1f out: drvn ins fnl f: hdd and no ex last 75 yds* **9/2**[3]

004 3 2 3/4 **Rozanne (IRE)**[13] 7334 2-9-0 75.................................... JFEgan 6 65
(Jeremy Noseda) *trckd ldrs: hdwy 2f out: rdn over 1f out: kpt on same pce fnl f* **11/4**[2]

2403 4 1 1/4 **Charnock Richard**[22] 7013 2-9-5 80.................................... PaulMulrennan 2 66+
(David Brown) *led: pushed along 2f out: sn rdn: hdd jst over 1f out: wknd fnl f* **9/4**[1]

5 1 **Zouch** 2-9-5 0.................................... JohnFahy 7 62
(J S Moore) *half rrd and dwlt s: towards rr: hdwy wl over 1f out: kpt on fnl f* **66/1**

250 6 1 **Princess Keira (IRE)**[38] 6480 2-9-0 77.................................... FranBerry 4 53
(Mick Quinn) *cl up: rdn along 2f out: grad wknd* **11/2**

7 4 1/2 **Broughton Excels** 2-9-5 0.................................... TimmyMurphy 8 42
(Henry Spiller) *dwlt: a in rr* **50/1**

0 **8** ½ **Amazing Amaya**[26] 6876 2-8-11 0............................ LewisEdmunds(3) 1 35
(Derek Shaw) *dwlt and wnt lft s: a towards rr* **100/1**

5 **9** 1¾ **Littlelordconford (IRE)**[60] 5654 2-9-5 0......................... HarryBentley 5 34
(Richard Spencer) *chsd ldng pair: pushed along 1/2-way: sn rdn and wknd wl over 1f out* **11/1**

1m 2.42s (0.92) **Going Correction** +0.175s/f (Good) **9** Ran SP% **112.1**
Speed ratings (Par 97): **99,98,94,92,90 88,81,80,78**
CSF £57.49 TOTE £11.70: £4.20, £1.10, £1.20; EX 45.00 Trifecta £137.50.
**Owner** R Barnett **Bred** W & R Barnett Ltd **Trained** East Everleigh, Wilts

**FOCUS**
The outer course was used for the first time since August, opening up fresh ground. Clerk of the course Jane Hedley said: 'It will ride slightly sticky and there is quite a strong headwind so it will be quite hard work'. After winning the first Tom Marquand said: 'It is dead, good to soft, possibly a tad worse'. They kept to the centre in this modest 2yo maiden and the headwind played its part. The first two should be at least as good as rated, while the fourth was below form again.

## 7732 IRISH EBF PLAY COSTA BINGO SLIP ANCHOR MAIDEN STKS (PLUS 10 RACE) (DIV II) 5f 8y
**2:20** (2:20) (Class 4) 2-Y-O **£5,175** (£1,540; £769; £384) **Stalls** Centre

Form RPR

0422 **1** **Kodiac Express (IRE)**[28] 6825 2-8-9 71.................... GeorgeBuckell(5) 2 72
(Mike Murphy) *led: rdn along wl over 1f out: hdd briefly ent fnl f: sn drvn and rallied to ld again last 100 yds: hld on wl* **3/1**[1]

**2** *hd* **Cowboy Soldier (IRE)** 2-9-5 0......................................... LukeMorris 8 76+
(Robert Cowell) *cl up: effrt to chal over 1f out: rdn to ld briefly ent fnl f: sn edgd lft and hdd last 100 yds: kpt on wl towards fin* **3/1**[1]

4 **3** 1 **Alba Del Sole (IRE)**[126] 3215 2-9-0 0............................ NickyMackay 6 68
(John Gosden) *t.k.h early: trckd ldrs: pushed along and sltly outpcd wl over 1f out: rdn ent fnl f: sn edgd lft and kpt on towards fin* **7/2**[2]

**4** 1¼ **National Anthem** 2-9-5 0...................................................(h[1]) JFEgan 1 68
(John Butler) *trckd ldrs: hdwy 2f out: rdn over 1f out: kpt on same pce* **20/1**

**5** ½ **Spenny's Lass** 2-9-0 0.......................................................... BrettDoyle 4 61
(John Ryan) *in tch: hdwy 2f out: rdn over 1f out: kpt on fnl f: nrst fin* **33/1**

0 **6** ¾ **Kodi Beach**[60] 5665 2-9-5 0............................................ DavidAllan 5 64
(David Barron) *t.k.h: cl up: rdn along jst over 2f out: sn wknd* **9/2**[3]

P **7** 3½ **Rivendicato**[114] 3668 2-9-0 0........................................... PaulHanagan 3 46
(Joseph Tuite) *trckd ldrs: hdwy over 2f out: sn rdn and wknd over 1f out* **7/1**

6 **8** 1¾ **Prime Chief (IRE)**[106] 3936 2-9-5 0................................. TrevorWhelan 7 45
(George Baker) *rr: pushed along 1/2-way: nvr a factor* **50/1**

00 **9** 28 **Night Air**[54] 5891 2-9-0 0...........................................(v) PatrickMathers 9
(Derek Shaw) *dwlt: green and rdn along in rr: outpcd and bhd fr 1/2-way* **200/1**

1m 2.7s (1.20) **Going Correction** +0.175s/f (Good) **9** Ran SP% **113.1**
Speed ratings (Par 97): **97,96,95,93,92 91,85,82,37**
CSF £11.57 TOTE £3.10: £1.30, £1.20, £1.40; EX 12.90 Trifecta £31.70.
**Owner** The Kodi Bunch **Bred** Michael O'Mahony **Trained** Westoning, Beds

**FOCUS**
The middle was again favoured in this second division of the 2yo maiden. The winner sets the level.

## 7733 EBF COSTA BINGO OH SO SHARP MAIDEN FILLIES' STKS (PLUS 10 RACE) 1m 75y
**2:55** (2:57) (Class 4) 2-Y-O **£5,175** (£1,540; £769; £384) **Stalls** Centre

Form RPR

**1** **Fayrouz Rose (IRE)** 2-9-0 0........................................ CharlesBishop 2 76
(Mick Channon) *sn trckd ldrs: pushed along over 2f out: chal ins fnl f: kpt on: rdn to ld towards fin* **25/1**

24 **2** ½ **La Diva**[47] 6140 2-9-0 0....................................................... HarryBentley 8 75
(Roger Varian) *prom: pushed along over 2f out: rdn to chal strly ent fnl f: kpt on* **13/8**[1]

0533 **3** *shd* **Calling Rio (IRE)**[7] 7521 2-9-0 68................................. PaulMulrennan 6 75
(David Loughnane) *led: rdn over 2f out: strly pressed ent fnl f: hdd towards fin: lost 2nd post* **20/1**

**4** 1¼ **Sailing Home** 2-9-0 0...................................................... DanielTudhope 3 72+
(Michael Bell) *trckd ldrs: pushed along 2f out: kpt on* **10/1**

**5** *nk* **Expensive Liaison (IRE)** 2-8-11 0................................ DavidEgan(3) 13 71+
(Hugo Palmer) *hld up: pushed along and hdwy 2f out: kpt on ins fnl f* **10/1**

**6** 1½ **Royal Goldie (IRE)** 2-9-0 0............................................... JFEgan 11 68+
(Mick Channon) *slowly away: hld up in rr: pushed along and hdwy on inner 2f out: edgd rt and briefly short of room jst ins fnl f: kpt on wl fnl 75yds* **50/1**

5 **7** ½ **Girls Talk (IRE)**[40] 6385 2-9-0 0...................................... LouisSteward 1 67
(Michael Bell) *racd keenly in tch: pushed along over 2f out: one pce* **7/1**[2]

50 **8** *nk* **Isle Of Avalon (IRE)**[9] 7454 2-9-0 0................................... LukeMorris 12 66
(Sir Mark Prescott Bt) *trckd ldrs towards outer: rdn over 2f out: no ex fnl f* **100/1**

0 **9** 2 **Boscastle (USA)**[11] 7399 2-9-0 0................................... TomMarquand 10 62
(Hughie Morrison) *in tch: pushed along over 2f out: wknd fnl 110yds* **66/1**

00 **10** 1 **Bessie Warfield**[46] 6183 2-8-7 0.............................. GabrieleMalune(7) 4 60
(Luca Cumani) *a midfield* **33/1**

**11** ¾ **Navajo Squaw** 2-9-0 0...................................................(h[1]) PJMcDonald 9 58
(Ed Dunlop) *dwlt: hld up: pushed along over 3f out: minor late hdwy: nvr threatened* **66/1**

**12** 1¼ **Arendelle** 2-9-0 0................................................................ PaulHanagan 16 55+
(Ed Walker) *midfield towards outer: pushed along over 2f out: nvr threatened* **8/1**[3]

**13** 2¼ **Bossiney Bay (IRE)** 2-9-0 0............................................(h[1]) FranBerry 14 50
(Hughie Morrison) *v.s.a: a towards rr* **28/1**

**14** ½ **Sageness (IRE)** 2-9-0 0.............................................. SilvestreDeSousa 15 49
(Ed Dunlop) *slowly away: a towards rr* **12/1**

**15** 1 **Pescedora (IRE)** 2-8-9 0.................................................. PaddyPilley(5) 5 47
(Roger Charlton) *midfield: pushed along over 2f out: wknd over 1f out* **50/1**

5 **16** ½ **Come With Me**[43] 6292 2-9-0 0......................................... NickyMackay 7 46
(John Gosden) *midfield: pushed along over 3f out: wknd fnl 2f* **8/1**[3]

1m 52.54s (3.54) **Going Correction** +0.025s/f (Good) **16** Ran SP% **121.6**
Speed ratings (Par 94): **83,82,82,81,80 79,78,78,76,75 74,73,71,70,69 69**
CSF £62.59 TOTE £27.90: £6.10, £1.50, £3.50; EX 96.30 Trifecta £1982.00.
**Owner** Jaber Abdullah **Bred** James Waldron **Trained** West Ilsley, Berks

**FOCUS**
A 2yo fillies' maiden that often goes to a very useful prospect. It paid to be prominent. The runner-up anchors the form for the moment, being rated to a similar level to her debut effort.

## 7734 JOCKEY CLUB GRASSROOTS NURSERY H'CAP SERIES FINAL STKS 6f 18y
**3:25** (3:29) (Class 3) 2-Y-O **£12,938** (£3,850; £1,924; £962) **Stalls** Centre

Form RPR

3041 **1** **Daddies Girl (IRE)**[19] 7123 2-9-7 81.................................. SteveDrowne 8 92
(Rod Millman) *trckd ldrs: hdwy 2f out: rdn to chal ins fnl f: drvn to ld last 100 yds: styd on wl* **10/1**

5612 **2** 2 **Roman Spinner**[7] 7510 2-8-0 60 oh3..............................(t) JimmyQuinn 7 65
(Rae Guest) *rr: hdwy 2f out: rdn over 1f out: kpt on strly fnl f* **15/2**[2]

4242 **3** *shd* **Excellent Times**[7] 7518 2-8-0 63 oh1 ow3........... RachelRichardson(3) 3 68
(Tim Easterby) *trckd ldrs: hdwy to ld 11/2f out: rdn ent fnl f: hdd and no ex last 100 yds* **8/1**[3]

1241 **4** 5 **Diamond Dougal (IRE)**[5] 7564 2-8-13 76 6ex............... DavidEgan(3) 10 66
(Mick Channon) *trckd ldrs: rdn along on outer and edgd rt wl over 1f out: drvn and kpt on fnl f* **13/2**[1]

3051 **5** 1¼ **Life For Rent**[30] 6756 2-8-9 69............................................ DavidAllan 9 55
(Tim Easterby) *cl up: ev ch wl over 1f out: sn rdn and grad wknd* **8/1**[3]

0052 **6** ½ **Saria**[15] 7228 2-7-7 60 oh7............................................. SophieRalston(7) 2 44
(Tony Carroll) *chsd ldrs on inner: pushed along and outpcd 1/2-way: rdn 2f out: kpt on fnl f* **25/1**

0545 **7** *hd* **Hard Graft**[13] 7335 2-8-12 72............................................. FranBerry 6 56
(David Brown) *t.k.h early: trckd ldrs: pushed along over 2f out: rdn wl over 1f out:. kpt on same pce* **25/1**

3313 **8** 2½ **Shania Says (IRE)**[29] 6778 2-8-6 71.................. ManuelFernandes(5) 12 47
(Tony Carroll) *cl up on outer: led over 3f out: rdn along 2f out: sn hdd and grad wknd* **8/1**[3]

5143 **9** 1¾ **W G Grace (IRE)**[15] 7228 2-8-5 65................................ FrannyNorton 11 36
(Mark Johnston) *cl up: rdn along over 2f out: drvn wl over 1f out: grad wknd* **14/1**

0630 **10** ½ **Plansina**[16] 7222 2-8-0 60 oh9....................................... DuranFentiman 13 30
(Tim Easterby) *in tch on outer: rdn along over 2f out:. sn drvn and wknd* **100/1**

0104 **11** 1¼ **Cameo Star (IRE)**[49] 6065 2-9-0 74................................ PaulHanagan 14 40
(Richard Fahey) *in tch: rdn along over 2f out: sn wknd* **14/1**

0536 **12** 4½ **Revenge**[12] 7362 2-8-0 60 oh2.......................................(b) JamesSullivan 5 12
(Tim Easterby) *slt ld: hdd over 3f out: rdn along wl over 2f out: edgd lft and wknd wl over 1f out* **50/1**

4204 **13** 8 **Alaska (IRE)**[25] 6951 2-8-12 72............................................ LukeMorris 4
(Sylvester Kirk) *sn pushed along in rr: outpcd and bhd fr 1/2-way* **20/1**

4542 **14** 5 **Ce De Nullis (IRE)**[50] 6036 2-8-10 70 ow1........................ MartinLane 16
(Paul Midgley) *in tch on outer: rdn along 1/2-way: sn wknd* **16/1**

1m 15.97s (1.27) **Going Correction** +0.175s/f (Good) **14** Ran SP% **102.1**
Speed ratings (Par 99): **98,95,95,88,86 86,85,82,80,79 77,71,61,54**
CSF £59.56 CT £460.07 TOTE £9.40: £3.10, £2.50, £2.60; EX 68.70 Trifecta £457.90.
**Owner** Daddies Girl Partnership **Bred** William Blake **Trained** Kentisbeare, Devon
■ Global Exceed was withdrawn. Price at time of withdrawal 6-1. Rule 4 applies to all bets - deduction 10p in the pound.

**FOCUS**
The principals finished clear down the middle in this modest nursery. Sound form. It's been rated slightly cautiously.

## 7735 PLAY COSTA BINGO ON YOUR MOBILE H'CAP (THE JOCKEY CLUB GRASSROOTS MIDDLE DISTANCE SERIES FINAL) 1m 2f 50y
**4:00** (4:01) (Class 3) 3-Y-O+
**£15,562** (£4,660; £2,330; £1,165; £582; £292) **Stalls** Low

Form RPR

6164 **1** **Compton Mill**[3] 7651 5-8-12 82.......................................... PJMcDonald 6 89
(Hughie Morrison) *in tch: rdn along 3f out: hdwy over 1f out: led 1f out: strly pressed towards fin: all out* **5/1**[2]

2136 **2** *shd* **Indian Chief (IRE)**[6] 7555 7-9-0 84............................... DanielTudhope 8 90+
(Rebecca Bastiman) *hld up in midfield: smooth hdwy over 3f out: pushed along to chse ldrs over 1f out: briefly short of room ent fnl f: rdn and r.o wl: jst failed* **11/2**[3]

1144 **3** 2¼ **Silver Ghost (IRE)**[11] 7395 4-9-10 94............................ CharlesBishop 11 96
(Eve Johnson Houghton) *trckd ldrs: rdn over 2f out: chal over 1f out: edgd ahd appr fnl f: hdd 1f out: no ex fnl 110yds* **2/1**[1]

6603 **4** *shd* **Harmonise**[9] 7464 3-7-11 74 oh3...................................(h[1]) DavidEgan(3) 4 76
(Mick Channon) *midfield: rdn over 2f out: styd on fnl f* **20/1**

5050 **5** 1 **Tomahawk Kid**[51] 6007 4-8-7 77.................................. SilvestreDeSousa 9 76
(Ian Williams) *hld up in midfield: rdn and gd hdwy on outer over 2f out: ev ch appr fnl f: wknd fnl 110yds* **13/2**

0134 **6** 1 **Parole (IRE)**[16] 7225 5-8-0 73 oh3 ow3..............(t) RachelRichardson(3) 2 71+
(Tim Easterby) *trckd ldrs: rdn along over 2f out: short of room over 1f out tl ins fnl f: kpt on but no ch after* **12/1**

3045 **7** 1¾ **Miningrocks (FR)**[16] 7225 5-8-2 72.............................(b[1]) PatrickMathers 10 66
(Declan Carroll) *led at gd pce: rdn over 2f out: hdd appr fnl f: wknd ins fnl f* **25/1**

0050 **8** *nk* **Boycie**[27] 6848 4-8-7 77 ow1.......................................... TomMarquand 14 71
(Richard Hannon) *midfield on outer: rdn 3f out: no imp* **25/1**

635 **9** 1¾ **Polar Forest**[7] 7524 7-8-0 70 oh2....................................(p[1]) AndrewMullen 1 60
(Richard Guest) *in tch: rdn over 2f out: wknd ins fnl f* **25/1**

3166 **10** *nk* **Bonnie Arlene (IRE)**[13] 7338 3-8-1 75............................ FrannyNorton 5 66
(Mark Johnston) *hld up in rr: rdn along 3f out: minor late hdwy: nvr threatened* **25/1**

2250 **11** 2¼ **Sir Jack**[22] 7028 4-7-7 70 oh9...................................... SophieRalston(7) 13 55
(Tony Carroll) *hld up: nvr threatened* **33/1**

6500 **12** ½ **Lord Franklin**[5] 7567 8-8-0 70 oh4...........................(p) DuranFentiman 15 55
(Eric Alston) *prom: rdn 3f out: wknd over 1f out* **40/1**

3060 **13** 5 **The Gay Cavalier**[6] 7541 6-8-0 70 oh4............................(t) CamHardie 16 45
(John Ryan) *dwlt: a towards rr* **100/1**

3233 **14** ½ **Duck Egg Blue (IRE)**[32] 6692 3-8-0 74 oh4...............(p) JamesSullivan 3 49
(Patrick Holmes) *midfield: rdn over 3f out: wknd over 2f out* **25/1**

0021 **15** 4½ **Jack Of Diamonds (IRE)**[25] 6947 8-8-0 70 oh3............ JimmyQuinn 12 36
(Roger Teal) *a towards rr* **50/1**

2m 12.67s (-1.63) **Going Correction** +0.025s/f (Good)
**WFA** 3 from 4yo+ 4lb **15** Ran SP% **118.7**
Speed ratings (Par 107): **107,106,105,105,104 103,102,101,100,100 98,97,93,93,89**
CSF £27.83 CT £73.41 TOTE £5.10: £1.70, £2.00, £2.00; EX 34.50 Trifecta £98.80.
**Owner** M T Bevan,Rolyluard,M D W Morrison **Bred** M E Broughton **Trained** East Ilsley, Berks

**FOCUS**
The going was changed to good to soft prior to this feature handicap. They were soon strung out and the closers came to the fore. A small pb from the winner, while the runner-up has been rated to his easy Hamilton win.

## 7736 YOU CAN JOIN COSTA BINGO ONLINE TODAY H'CAP 1m 75y
4:30 (4:31) (Class 4) (0-85,85) 3-Y-O £5,175 (£1,540; £769; £384) **Stalls** Centre

Form RPR
4113 **1** **Salt Whistle Bay (IRE)**[15] 7229 3-9-0 78 ................ SilvestreDeSousa 6 86
(Rae Guest) *mde most: rdn along 2f out: drvn ins fnl f: hld on gamely towards fin* **5/1[2]**
613 **2** *hd* **Mooltazem (IRE)**[71] 5242 3-9-0 78 ................ NickyMackay 2 85
(John Gosden) *trckd ldng pair: hdwy 3f out: chsd wnr wl over 1f out: sn rdn: chal ent fnl f: sn drvn and ev ch tl no ex nr line* **9/2[1]**
5104 **3** *1 ½* **Maratha (IRE)**[13] 7339 3-9-2 80 ................(t[1]) DanielTudhope 4 84
(Stuart Williams) *trckd ldrs on inner: hdwy over 2f out: effrt and nt clr run over 1f out: swtchd rt and rdn ent fnl f: kpt on* **8/1**
146 **4** *¾* **Casimiro (IRE)**[57] 5744 3-9-7 85 ................ HarryBentley 7 87
(Roger Charlton) *hld up towards rr: hdwy on inner over 2f out: rdn wl over 1f out: kpt on u.p fnl f* **9/2[1]**
6141 **5** *nk* **Hedging (IRE)**[18] 7157 3-8-8 72 ................(p) JFEgan 8 73
(Eve Johnson Houghton) *t.k.h: trckd ldrs: hdwy over 3f out: rdn along over 2f out: drvn over 1f out: kpt on same pce* **7/1[3]**
4-31 **6** *½* **Heaven's Rock (IRE)**[27] 6855 3-8-8 72 ................ FrannyNorton 9 72
(Tom Dascombe) *t.k.h: chsd ldrs: pushed along over 2f out: rdn wl over 1f out. drvn and kpt on same pce fnl f* **9/1**
1636 **7** *14* **Music Seeker (IRE)**[14] 7277 3-9-5 83 ................(b[1]) PaulMulrennan 1 51
(James Eustace) *dwlt: t.k.h in rr: hdwy on outer 4f out: chsd wnr over 2f out: sn rdn and hung bdly rt over 1f out: sn wknd and eased* **8/1**
250 **8** *1 ½* **Trading Punches (IRE)**[14] 7277 3-9-7 85 ................(p[1]) FranBerry 5 49
(David Brown) *chsd wnr: pushed along 4f out: rdn over 3f out: sn wknd* **12/1**

1m 47.9s (-1.10) **Going Correction** +0.025s/f (Good) **8 Ran SP% 105.4**
Speed ratings (Par 103): **106,105,104,103,103 102,88,87**
CSF £23.40 CT £140.03 TOTE £4.50: £1.80, £1.80, £2.00; EX 17.10 Trifecta £126.40.
**Owner** The Hightailers & Rae Guest **Bred** Shortgrove Manor Stud **Trained** Newmarket, Suffolk
■ Stewards' Enquiry : Nicky Mackay two day ban: using his whip above the permitted level (18/19 Oct)

**FOCUS**
There was a sound pace on in this fair 3yo handicap. The third has been rated close to his C&D win.

## 7737 COSTA BINGO - YOUR FUNSHINE DESTINATION H'CAP (JOCKEY CLUB GRASSROOTS SPRINT DISTANCE SERIES) 6f 18y
5:05 (5:07) (Class 3) 3-Y-O+
£15,562 (£4,660; £2,330; £1,165; £582; £292) **Stalls** Centre

Form RPR
6654 **1** **Syrian Pearl**[39] 6429 6-9-5 79 ................ FranBerry 12 89
(Chris Wall) *dwlt and hld up in rr: hdwy wl over 1f out: rdn ent fnl f: styd on strly to ld nr fin* **10/1**
3200 **2** *½* **Fantasy Keeper**[14] 7287 3-8-8 69 ................ AndrewMullen 8 77
(Michael Appleby) *cl up: led 2f out: rdn over 1f out: drvn ins fnl f: hdd and no ex nr fin* **14/1**
513 **3** *1 ¼* **Ninjago**[11] 7405 7-9-6 80 ................ MartinLane 9 85
(Paul Midgley) *trckd ldrs: hdwy 2f out: rdn over 1f out: styd on to chal ins fnl f: sn drvn: hld whn n.m.r towards fin* **12/1**
0550 **4** *2* **Casterbridge**[18] 7137 5-8-8 68 ................(p) JasonHart 6 66
(Eric Alston) *led: hdd 2f out and sn rdn along: drvn ent fnl f: kpt on* **20/1**
112 **5** *nk* **Maid In India (IRE)**[47] 6149 3-9-2 77 ................ NeilFarley 2 74+
(Eric Alston) *trckd ldrs: smooth hdwy and cl up 1/2-way: rdn and ev ch over 1f out: grad wknd fnl f* **5/1[2]**
1355 **6** *¾* **Bahamian Dollar**[37] 6506 4-9-7 81 ................ JFEgan 14 75
(David Evans) *chsd ldrs on outer: rdn along wl over 1f out: drvn and no imp fnl f* **14/1**
0421 **7** *½* **Tricky Dicky**[37] 6527 4-9-1 75 ................ SamJames 15 68
(Olly Williams) *in tch: rdn along 2f out: drvn and no imp fr over 1f out* **12/1**
2461 **8** *1* **Showmethewayavrilo**[7] 7508 4-8-12 72 6ex ................ PJMcDonald 7 61
(Malcolm Saunders) *chsd ldrs: cl up 1/2-way: rdn along 2f out: grad wknd* **12/1**
2211 **9** *½* **Operative**[14] 7272 4-9-6 80 ................ SilvestreDeSousa 10 68
(Ed de Giles) *nvr bttr than midfield* **15/2[3]**
4225 **10** *2 ½* **Seaview**[7] 7523 3-8-5 69 ................(v[1]) AaronJones(3) 3 49
(David Brown) *dwlt: a towards rr* **33/1**
2142 **11** *3* **Ventura Blues (IRE)**[9] 7456 3-9-10 85 ................(p) TomMarquand 13 55
(Richard Hannon) *a towards rr* **14/1**
3021 **12** *2 ¼* **Quatrieme Ami**[7] 7522 4-9-2 76 6ex ................ DanielTudhope 4 39
(Philip McBride) *chsd ldrs on inner: rdn along 2f out: sn drvn and wknd* **9/2[1]**
3160 **13** *1 ½* **Specialv (IRE)**[16] 7223 4-8-9 69 ................(v[1]) DavidAllan 11 27
(Brian Ellison) *dwlt: a in rr* **20/1**
1503 **14** *3 ½* **Curious Fox**[18] 7155 4-9-8 82 ................ PaulHanagan 16 29
(Anthony Carson) *dwlt: a in rr* **20/1**

1m 15.83s (1.13) **Going Correction** +0.175s/f (Good)
**WFA** 3 from 4yo+ 1lb **14 Ran SP% 116.0**
Speed ratings (Par 107): **99,98,96,94,93 92,91,90,89,86 82,79,77,72**
CSF £129.20 CT £1694.98 TOTE £9.80: £4.20, £3.80, £4.50; EX 156.20 Trifecta £1461.60.
**Owner** The Clodhoppers **Bred** Jeremy Green And Sons **Trained** Newmarket, Suffolk

**FOCUS**
Most seemed to get found out by the tacky going in this fair sprint handicap. The runner-up has been rated to his earlier C&D form and the third to his recent form.

## 7738 COSTA BINGO FUN AND JACKPOTS H'CAP 5f 8y
5:35 (5:36) (Class 5) (0-75,76) 3-Y-O+ £3,881 (£1,155; £577; £288) **Stalls** Centre

Form RPR
3103 **1** **Classic Pursuit**[7] 7522 6-9-0 68 ................(b) SilvestreDeSousa 9 81
(Michael Appleby) *prom: led over 3f out: rdn clr wl over 1f out: kpt on strly* **7/2[1]**
1203 **2** *6* **Jacob's Pillow**[14] 7268 6-9-7 75 ................(p) DanielTudhope 12 66
(Rebecca Bastiman) *prom: chse wnr fr 1/2-way: rdn wl over 1f out: drvn and kpt on fnl f: no ch w wnr* **5/1[2]**
3130 **3** *½* **Mininggold**[14] 7268 4-9-8 76 ................(p) PaulMulrennan 4 66
(Michael Dods) *hld up: hdwy on inner 2f out: rdn to chse ldrs over 1f out: kpt on fnl f* **9/1**
3404 **4** *shd* **Appleberry (IRE)**[117] 3541 5-9-7 75 ................ AndrewMullen 5 64
(Michael Appleby) *prom: rdn along 2f out: drvn over 1f out:. kpt on same pce fnl f* **16/1**
4206 **5** *½* **Viva Verglas (IRE)**[20] 7099 6-8-9 70 ................ TobyEley(7) 13 57
(Daniel Mark Loughnane) *in tch: hdwy 2f out: rdn over 1f out: kpt on fnl f: nrst fin* **33/1**
3003 **6** *nse* **Oriental Splendour (IRE)**[6] 7557 5-9-0 68 ................(p) JamesSullivan 3 55
(Ruth Carr) *prom: rdn along wl over 1f out: sn drvn and grad wknd* **5/1[2]**
2324 **7** *shd* **Father McKenzie**[14] 7287 3-9-1 74 ................ PaddyPilley(5) 14 62
(James Eustace) *dwlt: sn chsng ldrs on outer: rdn along 2f out: sn drvn: edgd lft and wknd* **6/1[3]**
2406 **8** *1 ½* **Borough Boy (IRE)**[104] 4005 7-8-9 63 ................(v) PatrickMathers 6 45
(Derek Shaw) *prom: cl up 1/2-way: rdn along 2f out: sn wknd* **33/1**
5600 **9** *½* **Captain Lars (SAF)**[11] 7405 8-9-3 74 ................(v) AaronJones(3) 8 54
(Derek Shaw) *a towards rr* **12/1**
0600 **10** *3 ¼* **Lydia's Place**[14] 7268 4-9-3 74 ................ CliffordLee(3) 11 42
(Richard Guest) *blind removed after s and slowly away: a bhd* **16/1**
3664 **11** *hd* **Foxy Boy**[14] 7268 3-8-12 71 ................ CallumRodriguez(5) 7 39
(Michael Dods) *slt ld: hdd over 3f out: rdn along over 2f out: sn drvn and wknd* **9/1**

1m 1.8s (0.30) **Going Correction** +0.175s/f (Good) **11 Ran SP% 115.2**
Speed ratings (Par 103): **104,94,93,93,92 92,92,90,89,84 83**
CSF £19.88 CT £144.23 TOTE £4.10: £1.70, £2.00, £2.80; EX 24.00 Trifecta £97.10.
**Owner** From The Front Racing **Bred** B & B Equine Limited **Trained** Oakham, Rutland

**FOCUS**
They went hard early on in this modest sprint handicap but it was one-way traffic. The winner has been rated back to his old best.
T/Plt: £40.20 to a £1 stake. Pool: £67,031.13 - 1214.69 winning units. T/Qpdt: £15.10 to a £1 stake. Pool: £5,171.62 - 252.57 winning units. **Joe Rowntree & Andrew Sheret**

# [7120] SALISBURY (R-H)
Wednesday, October 4

**OFFICIAL GOING: Heavy (soft in places: 4.9)**
Wind: light against Weather: overcast with brighter periods

## 7739 PKF FRANCIS CLARK EBF NOVICE STKS (PLUS 10 RACE) 1m
2:00 (2:00) (Class 4) 2-Y-O £4,043 (£1,203; £601; £300) **Stalls** Low

Form RPR
5 **1** **Ace Ventura**[19] 7117 2-9-2 0 ................ AndreaAtzeni 10 77
(Roger Varian) *trckd ldrs: led over 3f out: rdn over 1f out: hld on* **8/11[1]**
**2** *hd* **Mandalayan (IRE)** 2-9-2 0 ................ RobHornby 6 77+
(Jonathan Portman) *mid-div: hdwy 3f out: disputing 2nd whn bmpd and briefly outpcd over 2f out: rdn over 1f out: kpt on wl ins fnl f: clsng on wnr nring fin* **40/1**
35 **3** *nk* **Regular Income (IRE)**[7] 7512 2-9-2 0 ................(p) AdamBeschizza 4 76
(Adam West) *mid-div: hdwy over 3f out: disp cl 2nd over 2f out: sn edgd lft and rdn: nt quite upsides ent fnl f: kpt on: no ex cl home* **12/1**
**4** *8* **Corgi** 2-9-2 0 ................ LiamKeniry 9 58
(Hughie Morrison) *little slowly away: sn mid-div: rdn over 2f out: kpt on ins fnl f but nt pce to get on terms w ldrs* **14/1**
6 **5** *½* **Carp Kid (IRE)**[11] 7391 2-9-2 0 ................ SeanLevey 3 57
(Richard Hannon) *trckd ldrs: disp 2nd 3f out tl rdn 2f out: wknd fnl f* **5/2[2]**
5 **6** *14* **Red Miracle**[27] 6859 2-8-11 0 ................ OisinMurphy 1 21
(Rod Millman) *prom: rdn 3f out: wknd over 1f out* **6/1[3]**
**7** *2 ¾* **Gozo Girl** 2-8-11 0 ................ EdwardGreatrex 2 15
(Joseph Tuite) *hld up last pair: rdn and sme prog over 2f out: wknd over 1f out* **33/1**
0 **8** *3* **Tour De Paris (IRE)**[11] 7392 2-9-2 0 ................ TomQueally 8 14
(Eve Johnson Houghton) *trckd ldrs: rdn over 2f out: wknd over 1f out* **40/1**
0 **9** *15* **Santiago Rock (IRE)**[8] 7489 2-9-2 0 ................(p[1]) FergusSweeney 7
(Noel Williams) *led tl over 3f out: sn rdn: wknd 2f out* **100/1**
0 **10** *10* **Masons Belle**[40] 6367 2-9-2 0 ................ SamHitchcott 5
(Ronald Harris) *sn pushed along in last pair: wknd over 2f out* **100/1**

1m 51.91s (8.41) **Going Correction** +0.925s/f (Soft) **10 Ran SP% 124.9**
Speed ratings (Par 97): **94,93,93,85,85 71,68,65,50,40**
CSF £53.80 TOTE £1.70: £1.10, £15.60, £3.50; EX 62.70 Trifecta £495.70.
**Owner** Sheikh Mohammed Obaid Al Maktoum **Bred** Meon Valley Stud **Trained** Newmarket, Suffolk

**FOCUS**
Hard work for these juveniles on this ground and the favourite scraped home. They headed stands' side in the straight and the first three finished clear. The opening level is fluid.

## 7740 BECOME A WILTSHIRE FREEMASON EBF NOVICE STKS (PLUS 10 RACE) 6f 213y
2:30 (2:30) (Class 4) 2-Y-O £4,043 (£1,203; £601; £300) **Stalls** Low

Form RPR
**1** **Jamil (IRE)** 2-9-2 0 ................ AndreaAtzeni 8 79+
(Roger Varian) *hld up: pushed along and hdwy over 2f out whn briefly short of room and swtchd rt: wnt 3rd sn after: rdn to ld ins fnl f: r.o strly* **4/1[2]**
05 **2** *2 ¼* **Dance Emperor (IRE)**[28] 6827 2-9-2 0 ................ LiamKeniry 2 73
(Ed Walker) *led: rdn 2f out: hdd over 1f out: kpt on ins fnl f to regain 2nd towards fin* **12/1**
6 **3** *¾* **Mr Gent (IRE)**[14] 7280 2-9-2 0 ................ JimCrowley 6 71
(Ed Dunlop) *trckd ldr: rdn to ld over 1f out: hdd ins fnl f: no ex towards fin* **5/4[1]**
**4** *2 ¼* **Consultant** 2-9-2 0 ................ OisinMurphy 7 65+
(Andrew Balding) *little slowly away: in tch: outpcd over 2f out: no threat but kpt on ins fnl f: wnt 4th towards fin* **5/1[3]**
0 **5** *¾* **Roundhead**[25] 6916 2-9-2 0 ................ PatDobbs 9 64
(Richard Hannon) *trckd ldrs: rdn over 1f out: kpt on same pce fnl f* **6/1**
0 **6** *12* **Rock Chic**[39] 6438 2-8-8 0 ................ GeorgeWood(3) 4 29
(Rod Millman) *trckd ldrs: rdn over 2f out: wknd over 1f out* **50/1**
**7** *5* **Sir Leonard Kitter (IRE)** 2-8-13 0 ................ HollieDoyle(3) 3 21
(Richard Hannon) *awkward s: in tch: struggling over 2f out: sn wknd* **10/1**

1m 35.93s (7.33) **Going Correction** +0.925s/f (Soft) **7 Ran SP% 114.1**
Speed ratings (Par 97): **95,92,91,89,88 74,68**
CSF £48.29 TOTE £4.20: £1.80, £5.10; EX 39.70 Trifecta £82.30.
**Owner** Abdullatif M Al-Abdulrazzaq **Bred** Mrs James Wigan & London TB Services Ltd **Trained** Newmarket, Suffolk



The Form Book Flat, Raceform Ltd, Newbury, RG14 5SJ

**FOCUS**
An ordinary novice but still a likeable performance from the winning newcomer. The opening level is fluid but perhaps the runner-up is key.

## 7741 BATHWICK TYRES CONDITIONS STKS (PLUS 10 RACE) 6f
**3:05** (3:05) (Class 2) 2-Y-O **£9,703** (£2,887; £1,443; £721) **Stalls** Low

Form RPR
023 **1** **Mr Top Hat**[12] 7351 2-8-12 80........................................ JimCrowley 1 85
(David Evans) *kpt apart fr main gp towards far rail for over 2f: led: steadily swtchd lft fr over 2f out to join gp jst over 1f out: hld on gamely: all out* **15/2**
2612 **2** *hd* **Algam (IRE)**[32] 6683 2-9-2 87........................................ SeanLevey 5 88
(Richard Hannon) *hld up: hdwy 2f out: sn rdn to chse ldrs: str chal fnl 120yds: kpt on: jst hld* **9/4[1]**
1 **3** *2 ¾* **Thechildren'strust (IRE)**[64] 5504 2-9-2 0..................... HectorCrouch 3 80
(Gary Moore) *prom: rdn and ev ch over 1f out: sltly short of room fnl 140yds: no ex fnl 75yds* **9/4[1]**
0400 **4** *1* **Helvetian**[20] 7090 2-9-0 91........................................ AndreaAtzeni 2 75
(Mick Channon) *trckd ldrs: rdn to chse wnr jst over 1f out tl sltly short of room fnl 140yds: sn no ex* **9/2[3]**
1100 **5** *43* **Nine Below Zero**[82] 4866 2-9-6 88..............................(b[1]) OisinMurphy 4
(Ralph Beckett) *trckd ldrs: rdn over 2f out: wknd over 1f out* **4/1[2]**
1m 19.6s (4.80) **Going Correction** +0.925s/f (Soft) **5** Ran SP% **111.5**
Speed ratings (Par 101): **105,104,101,99,42**
CSF £24.85 TOTE £7.80: £2.80, £1.50; EX 28.80 Trifecta £55.80.
**Owner** B McCabe & Mrs E Evans **Bred** Mrs S Field, R Field & A Turbitt **Trained** Pandy, Monmouths

**FOCUS**
Just a fair conditions race, it went to the only previous non-winner in the field. The first two have been rated as improving, and the third near his debut effort.

## 7742 CORINTECH RUBY ANNIVERSARY H'CAP 6f
**3:35** (3:36) (Class 4) (0-85,85) 3-Y-O+ **£5,175** (£1,540; £769; £384) **Stalls** Low

Form RPR
532 **1** **Clear Spring (IRE)**[20] 7084 9-9-7 **85**.............................. ShaneKelly 7 96
(John Spearing) *hld up: swtchd rt travelling strly whn nt clr run over 1f out: qcknd up wl to ld ins fnl f: sn clr: readily* **6/1**
5205 **2** *2 ¾* **Satchville Flyer**[40] 6371 6-8-6 **73**............................. MattCosham(3) 5 75
(David Evans) *squeezed up s: sn cl up: rdn over 1f out: kpt on to go 2nd ins fnl f: nt pce of wnr* **25/1**
000 **3** *½* **Poet's Princess**[27] 6864 3-8-12 **80**.......................... CharlieBennett(3) 4 81
(Hughie Morrison) *hld up but wl in tch: hdwy to hold ev ch over 1f out: kpt on same pce ins fnl f* **9/1**
4536 **4** *½* **Sir Billy Wright (IRE)**[4] 7612 6-9-6 **84**............................ JimCrowley 8 83
(David Evans) *trckd ldrs: rdn and ch over 1f out: kpt on same pce fnl f* **4/1[2]**
-203 **5** *2 ½* **Francisco**[29] 6780 5-9-1 **79**........................................... OisinMurphy 9 70
(Tony Carroll) *hld up wl in tch: rdn over 1f out: nt pce to get involved* **12/1**
1614 **6** *1 ¼* **The Daley Express (IRE)**[20] 7084 3-9-6 **85**.................. SamHitchcott 6 72
(Ronald Harris) *squeezed up s: sn cl up: rdn to ld over 1f out: hdd ins fnl f: no ex fnl 100yds* **16/1**
4233 **7** *1 ½* **Amood (IRE)**[20] 7099 6-8-7 **71** oh1..........................(p) EdwardGreatrex 1 53
(Archie Watson) *prom: rdn over 2f out: stl ev ch over 1f out: wknd ins fnl f* **5/2[1]**
115 **8** *½* **Dandy Flame (IRE)**[49] 6072 3-8-11 **81**.....................(p[1]) FinleyMarsh(5) 3 62
(Richard Hughes) *led: rdn and hdd over 1f out: wknd fnl f* **16/1**
1141 **9** *2 ¼* **Our Lord**[17] 7195 5-9-2 **85**........................................ PaddyBradley(5) 2 58
(Michael Attwater) *prom: rdn and ev ch over 1f out: wknd ent fnl f* **9/2[3]**
1m 19.45s (4.65) **Going Correction** +0.925s/f (Soft)
**WFA** 3 from 5yo+ 1lb **9** Ran SP% **114.3**
Speed ratings (Par 105): **106,102,101,101,97 96,94,93,90**
CSF £136.57 CT £1332.37 TOTE £6.70: £2.10, £7.10, £3.30; EX 134.20 Trifecta £1985.60.
**Owner** H James **Bred** Rocal Bloodstock **Trained** Kinnersley, Worcs

**FOCUS**
They came towards the stands' side but again the winner challenged more down the middle. The level is a bit fluid.

## 7743 WEATHERBYS GENERAL STUD BOOK ONLINE H'CAP 1m 1f 201y
**4:10** (4:10) (Class 2) (0-105,104) 3-Y-O+ **£12,450** (£3,728; £1,864; £932) **Stalls** Low

Form RPR
5504 **1** **Ayrad (IRE)**[37] 6514 6-9-12 **104**..............................(b) AndreaAtzeni 1 112
(Roger Charlton) *mde all: jnd briefly 2f out: sn rdn clr: styd on strly* **4/1[3]**
1213 **2** *4 ½* **Almoreb (IRE)**[19] 7129 3-8-10 **92**.................................. JimCrowley 5 92
(Richard Hannon) *travelled wl bhd wnr: chal 2f out: sn rdn and hld: styd on same pce fnl f* **5/4[1]**
040 **3** *¾* **Storm Rock**[26] 6881 5-8-4 **85** oh8.............................. HollieDoyle(3) 2 83
(Harry Dunlop) *trckd ldng pair: rdn and ev ch 2f out tl over 1f out: styd on same pce fnl f* **9/2**
0000 **4** *½* **Master Carpenter (IRE)**[18] 7149 6-9-3 **98**.................. GeorgeWood(3) 3 95
(Rod Millman) *trckd ldrs: swtchd lft for effrt over 2f out: sn rdn: styd on but nt pce to chal* **11/4[2]**
2m 18.66s (8.76) **Going Correction** +0.925s/f (Soft)
**WFA** 3 from 5yo+ 4lb **4** Ran SP% **109.3**
Speed ratings (Par 109): **102,98,97,97**
CSF £9.57 TOTE £5.40; EX 6.80 Trifecta £19.10.
**Owner** Saleh Al Homaizi & Imad Al Sagar **Bred** Gerrardstown House Stud **Trained** Beckhampton, Wilts

**FOCUS**
Just the four runners and with two of them entering the race out of form and the favourite looking a non-stayer, it's doubtful it took much winning. They raced centre-field in the straight. The winner has been rated to his best.

## 7744 BATHWICK TYRES H'CAP 1m 6f 44y
**4:40** (4:41) (Class 5) (0-75,75) 3-Y-O+ **£3,396** (£1,010; £505; £252) **Stalls** Far side

Form RPR
0205 **1** **Quothquan (FR)**[20] 7097 3-9-1 **72**.............................. GeorgeWood(3) 4 82
(Michael Madgwick) *hld up towards rr: hdwy 3f out: rdn into narrow advantage jst over 1f out: styd on strly to assert fnl 70yds* **14/1**
0654 **2** *1* **Fields Of Fortune**[35] 6580 3-8-6 **65**.............................. HollieDoyle(3) 10 74
(Alan King) *mid-div: hdwy 3f out: rdn to chal over 1f out: ev ch fnl f: no ex fnl 70yds* **7/1**
3202 **3** *5* **Lester Kris (IRE)**[9] 7462 3-9-0 **75**.............................. RossaRyan(7) 6 78+
(Richard Hannon) *racd keenly: travelled wl most of way: trckd ldr: chal 3f out: rdn to ld v briefly over 1f out: no ex fnl f* **3/1[1]**
2352 **4** *¾* **Perla Blanca (USA)**[18] 7152 3-8-8 **62**.......................... EdwardGreatrex 12 64
(Marcus Tregoning) *hld up towards rr: hdwy fr 3f out: rdn to chse ldrs 2f out: styd on same pce* **9/2[3]**
0231 **5** *2 ¾* **Incredible Dream (IRE)**[20] 7085 4-9-4 **68**....................(p) JackDuern(3) 5 64
(Dean Ivory) *hld up towards rr: hdwy over 4f out: led narrowly over 3f out: sn rdn: hdd jst over 1f out: no ex fnl f* **7/2[2]**
0556 **6** *2* **Cousin Khee**[24] 6968 10-9-4 **68**.................................. CharlieBennett(3) 1 61
(Hughie Morrison) *mid-div tl outpcd over 3f out: bhd: styd on fnl 2f but nvr any danger* **14/1**
5355 **7** *9* **Roy Rocket (FR)**[37] 6513 7-8-11 **65**............................ NicolaCurrie(7) 14 47
(John Berry) *mid-div: rdn 3f out: nvr any imp* **25/1**
0020 **8** *4 ½* **Onorina (IRE)**[83] 4809 5-9-0 **66**................................ PaddyBradley(5) 13 42
(Jim Boyle) *trckd ldrs: rdn 3f out: wknd over 1f out* **25/1**
2344 **9** *3* **Safira Menina**[37] 6513 5-9-8 **72**.................................. NoelGarbutt(3) 7 44
(Martin Smith) *led in and slowly away: bhd: hdwy 3f out: sn rdn: nvr threatened: wknd over 1f out* **33/1**
4453 **10** *1 ¾* **Southern States**[67] 5407 4-8-9 **59**............................ HectorCrouch(3) 8 29
(Lydia Richards) *trckd ldrs: rdn over 4f out: wknd over 2f out* **25/1**
0610 **11** *7* **I'm Running Late**[112] 3721 3-9-3 **71**.................................. PatDobbs 9 34
(Dean Ivory) *trckd ldrs: rdn 3f out: wknd over 2f out* **50/1**
0041 **12** *¾* **Murchison River**[37] 6509 3-9-1 **69**.............................. FergusSweeney 3 31
(Henry Candy) *mid-div: hdwy over 5f out: rdn over 3f out: wknd 2f out* **9/1**
6R06 **13** *1 ½* **Retrieve (AUS)**[46] 6176 10-9-9 **75**.............................. MeganNicholls(5) 2 33
(Carroll Gray) *mid-div tl wknd 2f out* **66/1**
1000 **14** *3 ¼* **Investigation**[46] 6202 3-9-4 **72**..................................(h) RobHornby 11 27
(Andrew Balding) *racd keenly: led tl over 3f out: sn wknd* **50/1**
3m 16.87s (9.47) **Going Correction** +0.925s/f (Soft)
**WFA** 3 from 4yo+ 7lb **14** Ran SP% **121.1**
Speed ratings (Par 103): **109,108,105,105,103 102,97,94,93,92 88,87,86,84**
CSF £103.32 CT £381.25 TOTE £15.00: £4.20, £2.50, £1.30; EX 134.10 Trifecta £748.00.
**Owner** Los Leader **Bred** Daniel Cherdo & Georges Boulard **Trained** Denmead, Hants

**FOCUS**
The front pair drew clear late in a race that was run at a slow tempo. The fourth has been rated close to form.
T/Plt: £586.00 to a £1 stake. Pool: £59,023.18 - 73.52 winning units. T/Qpdt: £106.00 to a £1 stake. Pool: £5,023.94 - 35.05 winning units. **Tim Mitchell**

7745 - 7752a (Foreign Racing) - See Raceform Interactive

# [7592] SAINT-CLOUD (L-H)
Wednesday, October 4

**OFFICIAL GOING: Turf: very soft**

## 7753a PRIX DAHLIA - FONDS EUROPEEN DE L'ELEVAGE (LISTED RACE) (4YO+ FILLIES & MARES) (TURF) 1m 2f
**1:35** 4-Y-O+ **£20,512** (£8,205; £6,153; £4,102; £2,051)

RPR
**1** **Rosental**[24] 6972 5-8-11 0........................................ JamieSpencer 8 106+
(Luca Cumani) *sn trcking ldrs: hdwy to take clsr order 2f out: rdn to ld over 1f out out: styd on strly fnl f* **13/5[2]**
**2** *2 ½* **Company Asset (IRE)**[25] 6924 4-8-11 0.............................. TomEaves 3 101
(Kevin Ryan) *w.w in rr: pushed along over 2f out: rdn over 1f out: hdwy u.p ins fnl f to take 2nd cl home* **59/10**
**3** *¾* **Happy Approach (FR)**[157] 2201 4-8-11 0...................... MaximeGuyon 5 100
(M Nigge, France) **54/10**
**4** *1 ¼* **Mint Julep (FR)**[91] 4679 4-8-11 0............................ DelphineSantiago 7 97
(J E Hammond, France) **222/10**
**5** *¾* **Meliora (IRE)**[33] 6665 5-9-2 0.................................. StephanePasquier 4 101
(N Clement, France) **5/2[1]**
**6** *½* **Ozeville (FR)**[84] 4-8-11 0........................................ CristianDemuro 6 95
(D Guillemin, France) **53/10[3]**
**7** *1 ¾* **Roche Rose (IRE)**[21] 4-8-11 0.................................. ClementLecoeuvre 1 91
(E Lellouche, France) **35/1**
**8** *4* **Mahati (FR)**[26] 6914 4-8-11 0.................................. Pierre-CharlesBoudot 2 83
(A Fabre, France) **96/10**
2m 14.68s (-1.32) **8** Ran SP% **118.9**
PARI-MUTUEL (all including 1 euro stake): WIN 3.60; PLACE 1.30, 2.00, 1.80; DF 8.40; SF 12.00.
**Owner** B W Neill **Bred** Darley **Trained** Newmarket, Suffolk

## 7754a PRIX THOMAS BRYON (GROUP 3) (2YO) (TURF) 7f
**2:05** 2-Y-O **£34,188** (£13,675; £10,256; £6,837; £3,418)

RPR
**1** **Sacred Life (FR)**[35] 6606 2-8-13 0.............................. TheoBachelot 6 113+
(S Wattel, France) *midfield: rdn to chal over 1f out: led fnl f: qcknd clr: pushed out: readily* **51/10[2]**
**2** *6* **Alba Power (IRE)**[20] 7090 2-8-13 0........................ JosephineGordon 2 98
(Hugo Palmer) *led: rdn 2f out: hdd fnl f: kpt on wout matching wnr after* **73/10**
**3** *1* **Julio (GER)**[31] 6726 2-8-13 0.................................. AlexanderPietsch 3 96
(Mario Hofer, Germany) *hld up: rdn over 1f out: kpt on for 3rd but nt pce to chal* **229/10**
**4** *1 ¼* **Aqabah (USA)**[19] 7112 2-8-13 0.................................. JamesDoyle 5 92
(Charlie Appleby) *trckd ldr: rdn to chal early st: sn outpcd: fdd* **32/5**
**5** *¾* **High Dream Milena (FR)**[45] 6249 2-8-10 0 ow1 Pierre-CharlesBoudot 8 88
(Mme C Head-Maarek, France) *in tch on outer: rdn and effrt to chal 2f out: no ex over 1f out: fdd and jst hld on for 5th* **16/5[1]**
**6** *nse* **Baillolet (FR)**[18] 7175 2-8-13 0.................................. CristianDemuro 7 90
(Mme Pia Brandt, France) *restrained and hld up: rdn and outpcd in st: plugged on: jst missed 5th but n.d* **87/10**
**7** *5* **Sonjeu (FR)**[23] 7011 2-8-9 0........................................ MaximeGuyon 4 74
(C Ferland, France) *in tch on inner: rdn and outpcd in st: wknd: eased nring fin* **16/5[1]**
**8** *3* **Cold Stare (IRE)**[64] 5501 2-8-13 0.................................. FabriceVeron 1 70
(E J O'Neill, France) *hld up: rdn into st: no imp and wl btn* **31/5[3]**
1m 29.82s (-2.38) **8** Ran SP% **118.0**
PARI-MUTUEL (all including 1 euro stake): WIN 6.10; PLACE 2.40, 2.50, 5.20; DF 27.10; SF 40.00.
**Owner** Ecurie Jean-Louis Bouchard **Bred** V Timoshenko & A Milovanov **Trained** France

**FOCUS**
The second has been rated as running a minor pb.

7755 - (Foreign Racing) - See Raceform Interactive

# [7600] CHELMSFORD (A.W) (L-H)

Thursday, October 5

**OFFICIAL GOING: Polytrack: standard**

Wind: fresh, across Weather: Cloudy

## 7756 BET TOTEPLACEPOT AT BETFRED.COM NURSERY H'CAP 6f (P)

**5:45** (5:45) (Class 6) (0-60,60) 2-Y-O **£3,234** (£962; £481; £240) **Stalls** Centre

Form RPR

0362 **1** **Vegas Boy (IRE)**[30] 6790 2-9-5 **58**.............................(t) DougieCostello 1 71+
(Jamie Osborne) *trckd ldrs: pushed along to ld 1f out: r.o strly to draw clr* **7/4**[1]

3030 **2** *5* **Hope And Glory (IRE)**[21] 7081 2-9-0 **53**................ RichardKingscote 4 51+
(Tom Dascombe) *led narrowly: rdn over 2f out: hdd 1f out: one pce and no ch wnr* **7/2**[2]

656 **3** *1* **Agent Of Fortune**[28] 6844 2-9-4 **57**..............................(h) SaleemGolam 13 52
(Christine Dunnett) *s.i.s: sn midfield: rdn over 2f out: kpt on fr over 1f out* **40/1**

304 **4** *nk* **Avenging Red (IRE)**[62] 5586 2-9-5 **58**........................... SteveDrowne 3 52
(Adam West) *in tch: rdn over 2f out: one pce and edgd lft ins fnl f* **12/1**

500 **5** *1* **Long Embrace**[14] 7334 2-9-7 **60**................................ SilvestreDeSousa 8 51
(Simon Crisford) *chsd ldrs: rdn over 2f out: edgd rt appr fnl f: plugged on* **6/1**[3]

2445 **6** *2* **Dyson's Girl**[19] 7159 2-9-4 **60**...........................(p) AdamMcNamara(3) 12 45
(Bryan Smart) *chsd ldrs towards outer: rdn over 2f out: wknd fnl 110yds* **10/1**

0500 **7** *½* **Elusive Bird**[13] 7362 2-9-2 **55**............................................ LiamJones 10 39
(Giles Bravery) *dwlt: hld up in rr: pushed along 3f out: kpt on ins fnl f: nrst fin* **66/1**

005 **8** *½* **Arachina (IRE)**[17] 7211 2-9-4 **57**..............................(v) KieranShoemark 7 39
(Harry Dunlop) *dwlt: hld up: pushed along 3f out: kpt on ins fnl f: nvr threatened* **20/1**

005 **9** *½* **Disapproval (IRE)**[29] 6816 2-9-4 **57**.......................(h) GeorgeDowning 11 38
(Daniel Kubler) *hld up in midfield: rdn over 2f out: no imp* **25/1**

005 **10** *½* **Swift Fox**[24] 7001 2-9-0 **56**............................................ HectorCrouch(3) 5 35
(Gary Moore) *nvr bttr than midfield* **16/1**

0200 **11** *1* **Red Snapper**[23] 7023 2-8-11 **53**................................... HollieDoyle(3) 14 29
(William Stone) *pressed ldrs: rdn over 2f out: wknd appr fnl f* **25/1**

060 **12** *1¾* **Wotamadam**[14] 7334 2-9-5 **58**...................................... RobertWinston 6 29
(Dean Ivory) *hld up: nvr threatened* **16/1**

305 **13** *8* **Lady Of Petra**[36] 6584 2-9-7 **60**................................ JosephineGordon 9 7
(Eve Johnson Houghton) *hld up: rdn over 2f out: wknd over 1f out* **7/1**

5060 **14** *¾* **Hollie's Dream**[21] 7081 2-9-0 **53**..................................(t[1]) FranBerry 2
(David Evans) *midfield: rdn over 2f out: wknd over 1f out* **20/1**

1m 12.25s (-1.45) **Going Correction** -0.275s/f (Stan) **14 Ran SP% 135.1**

Speed ratings (Par 93): **98,91,90,89,88 85,84,84,83,82 81,79,68,67**

CSF £7.86 CT £214.68 TOTE £2.30: £1.10, £1.80, £10.10; EX 9.50 Trifecta £429.40.

**Owner** The Fabulous Fifty Boys **Bred** Brian Miller **Trained** Upper Lambourn, Berks

**FOCUS**

A moderate nursery won easily by the well-backed favourite.

## 7757 BET TOTEJACKPOT AT BETFRED.COM FILLIES' NOVICE STKS (PLUS 10 RACE) 7f (P)

**6:15** (6:19) (Class 4) 2-Y-O **£5,822** (£1,732; £865; £432) **Stalls** Low

Form RPR

315 **1** **Expressly (FR)**[32] 6731 2-9-6 0.........................................(h) JamesDoyle 5 89+
(Charlie Appleby) *trckd ldrs: rdn and hung rt on bnd over 2f out: drvn to ld ins fnl f: continued to hang rt but kpt on wl* **9/4**[2]

423 **2** *2½* **Perfect Thought**[39] 6480 2-9-0 76...................................... JimCrowley 9 76
(William Haggas) *led: rdn over 2f out: hdd appr fnl f: kpt on* **10/1**

3 **3** *¾* **Beautiful Memory (IRE)**[23] 7022 2-9-0 0..................... OisinMurphy 10 74
(Saeed bin Suroor) *prom: rdn to ld appr fnl f: hdd ins fnl f: one pce* **3/1**[3]

3 **4** *1½* **Line House**[10] 7453 2-9-0 0........................................ MartinHarley 13 70
(Robyn Brisland) *trckd ldrs: keen early: rdn 2f out: no ex ins fnl f* **33/1**

3 **5** *3¾* **West Palm Beach (IRE)**[57] 5795 2-9-0 0....................... RyanMoore 2 60
(John Gosden) *slowly away: hld up: pushed along and no prog over 2f out: stl plenty to do over 1f out: kpt on ins fnl f: nvr involved* **2/1**[1]

3022 **6** *¾* **Frolic**[16] 7226 2-9-0 77.................................................(b[1]) LukeMorris 6 58
(Sir Mark Prescott Bt) *in tch: rdn over 2f out: hung lft over 1f out: wknd ins fnl f* **8/1**

5 **7** *4* **Bint Huwaar (USA)**[40] 6438 2-9-0 0..............................(b[1]) HarryBentley 4 47
(George Peckham) *dwlt: sn in tch: rdn over 2f out: wknd over 1f out* **16/1**

**8** *1¾* **Montana Dawn (USA)** 2-8-11 0...........................(t[1]) AdamMcNamara(3) 8 42
(Bryan Smart) *hld up: sn pushed along: sme late hdwy* **66/1**

0 **9** *2* **Connoisseur**[14] 7334 2-9-0 0........................................... RyanPowell 7 37
(Sir Mark Prescott Bt) *midfield: rdn 3f out: wknd over 1f out* **66/1**

**10** *3¼* **Dragonfly Dream** 2-9-0 0........................................... PatDobbs 11 28
(John Best) *wnt rt s: midfield on outer: rdn along over 3f out: wknd fnl 2f* **66/1**

00 **11** *shd* **Speed Craft**[12] 7403 2-9-0 0.........................................(p) RyanTate 3 28
(James Eustace) *a outpcd in rr* **66/1**

**12** *3* **Geetanjali (IRE)** 2-9-0 0.......................................... LouisSteward 12 20
(Michael Bell) *dwlt and carried rt s: sn pushed along and a rr* **100/1**

00 **13** *1¾* **Ms Tilly**[14] 7326 2-8-11 0......................................... AaronJones(3) 1 15
(David Brown) *midfield: sn pushed along: wknd over 2f out* **100/1**

1m 25.23s (-1.97) **Going Correction** -0.275s/f (Stan) **13 Ran SP% 126.1**

Speed ratings (Par 94): **100,97,96,94,90 89,84,82,80,76 76,73,71**

CSF £26.71 TOTE £3.20: £1.40, £3.20, £2.10; EX 27.30 Trifecta £86.00.

**Owner** Godolphin **Bred** Elevage De La Croix De Place **Trained** Newmarket, Suffolk

**FOCUS**

A good performance from the class-dropping winner, who gave weight all round. The runner-up helps set the opening level.

## 7758 WEATHERBYS GLOBAL STALLIONS APP MAIDEN STKS (PLUS 10 RACE) 1m 2f (P)

**6:45** (6:59) (Class 4) 2-Y-O **£5,822** (£1,732; £865; £432) **Stalls** Low

Form RPR

52 **1** **Deyaarna (USA)**[20] 7120 2-9-5 0.................................... JimCrowley 3 84
(Saeed bin Suroor) *led for 2f: remained prom: pushed along to ld again 2f out: rdn clr over 1f out: pushed out ins fnl f* **4/5**[1]

4 **2** *2¼* **Dalileo (IRE)**[19] 7160 2-9-5 0...................................... FrannyNorton 8 80
(Mark Johnston) *trckd ldrs: pushed along over 2f out: wandered but wnt 2nd ins fnl f: kpt on but no ch wnr* **10/1**

**3** *1½* **Jeremiah** 2-9-5 0.......................................................... OisinMurphy 5 77+
(Charlie Fellowes) *s.i.s: hld up: pushed along and hdwy over 1f out: kpt on ins fnl f: nrst fin* **20/1**

65 **4** *2½* **Falcon Eye (IRE)**[15] 7273 2-9-5 0.................................... JamesDoyle 1 72
(Charlie Appleby) *trckd ldrs: rdn over 2f out: outpcd over 1f out: kpt on same pce ins fnl f* **4/1**[3]

43 **5** *1¼* **Going Native**[16] 7237 2-9-0 0 ........................................ PatCosgrave 6 65
(Ed Walker) *led after 2f: rdn whn hdd 2f out: wknd ins fnl f* **16/1**

3 **6** *3¼* **Heather Lark (IRE)**[12] 7403 2-9-0 0................................ RobertHavlin 7 59
(John Gosden) *midfield: pushed along to chse ldrs on outer over 2f out: rdn along 2f out: wknd fnl f* **3/1**[2]

00 **7** *¾* **Global Angel**[15] 7273 2-9-5 0........................................ LukeMorris 2 62
(Ed Dunlop) *midfield: rdn along over 2f out: wknd fnl f* **100/1**

0 **8** *21* **Astrofire**[23] 7022 2-9-0 0............................................. TimmyMurphy 9 18
(Mark H Tompkins) *hld up: rdn over 2f out: wknd and bhd* **250/1**

2m 5.92s (-2.68) **Going Correction** -0.275s/f (Stan) **8 Ran SP% 121.7**

Speed ratings (Par 97): **99,97,96,94,93 90,89,73**

CSF £11.86 TOTE £1.60: £1.10, £3.20, £4.20; EX 14.30 Trifecta £105.30.

**Owner** Godolphin **Bred** Shadwell Farm LLC **Trained** Newmarket, Suffolk

**FOCUS**

A fair maiden. The level is a bit fluid, but the runner-up has been rated as taking a step forward.

## 7759 BET TOTEEXACTA AT BETFRED.COM H'CAP 1m (P)

**7:15** (7:27) (Class 4) (0-80,82) 3-Y-O+ **£6,469** (£1,925; £962; £481) **Stalls** Low

Form RPR

2341 **1** **Musical Terms**[38] 6522 3-9-3 **77**.......................................... RyanMoore 5 84+
(William Haggas) *hld up: pushed along over 2f out: angled rt to outer and hdwy over 1f out: drvn and r.o fnl f: led post* **3/1**[2]

433 **2** *shd* **Toga Tiger (IRE)**[56] 5849 10-9-7 **78**........................ RichardKingscote 8 84
(Daniel Mark Loughnane) *midfield: pushed along and hdwy to chse ldrs over 2f out: rdn to chal ins fnl f: edgd ahd towards fin: hdd post* **16/1**

2051 **3** *hd* **Tamayef (IRE)**[30] 6792 3-9-7 **81**........................................ JamesDoyle 3 87
(Hugo Palmer) *prom: rdn to ld over 1f out: edgd lft ins fnl f: rdr briefly dropped rein: no ex and hdd towards fin* **2/1**[1]

6150 **4** *1* **Wigan Warrior**[28] 6855 3-9-3 **77**....................................... TomQueally 1 80+
(David Brown) *awkward s and slowly away: hld up: pushed along and stl plenty to do whn briefly short of room over 1f out: rdn and hdwy appr fnl f: kpt on wl: nrst fin* **66/1**

6010 **5** *½* **Balestra**[41] 6404 3-9-8 **82**................................................. JimCrowley 4 84
(Charles Hills) *midfield: pushed along and in tch over 2f out: rdn over 1f out: briefly short of room 110yds out: one pce* **8/1**

3360 **6** *½* **Foie Gras**[5] 7601 7-8-3 **67**...........................................(p) NicolaCurrie(7) 11 68
(Chris Dwyer) *hld up in midfield: sn pushed along: hdwy on outer over 1f out: kpt on fnl f* **66/1**

001 **7** *½* **Casina Di Notte (IRE)**[65] 5510 3-9-1 **78**..............(p) MarcMonaghan(3) 6 78
(Marco Botti) *slowly away: hld up in rr: pushed along and angled rt to wd outside over 1f out: kpt on fnl f* **25/1**

5036 **8** *1¼* **Buckland Beau**[49] 6111 6-9-5 **76**...................................... OisinMurphy 13 73
(Charlie Fellowes) *hld up: rdn over 2f out: nvr threatened* **20/1**

0530 **9** *1¼* **Carnival King (IRE)**[45] 6273 5-9-7 **78**....................(b) SilvestreDeSousa 7 72
(Amy Murphy) *led: rdn over 2f out: hdd over 1f out: wknd* **20/1**

1362 **10** *9* **Badenscoth**[20] 7131 3-9-4 **81**.......................................(h) JackDuern(3) 10 62
(Dean Ivory) *midfield: rdn 3f out: hdwy to chse ldrs 2f out: wknd appr fnl f: eased* **6/1**[3]

6111 **11** *2½* **Chetan**[14] 7323 5-8-12 **74**...............................................(t) JoshuaBryan(5) 9 40
(Charlie Wallis) *chsd ldrs: rdn along over 3f out: wknd over 2f out* **12/1**

0020 **12** *8* **Kingsley Klarion (IRE)**[35] 6637 4-9-5 **76**.................... RobertWinston 12 23
(John Butler) *midfield on wd outside: rdn along 3f out: edgd lft and wknd over 1f out* **50/1**

500 **13** *¾* **Dream Of Summer (IRE)**[27] 6882 4-9-6 **77**.................... HarryBentley 2 22
(Jeremy Noseda) *trckd ldrs: rdn over 2f out: wknd over 1f out* **10/1**

1m 37.67s (-2.23) **Going Correction** -0.275s/f (Stan)

**WFA** 3 from 4yo+ 3lb **13 Ran SP% 124.7**

Speed ratings (Par 105): **100,99,99,98,98 97,97,95,94,85 83,75,74**

CSF £48.44 CT £121.81 TOTE £3.70: £1.50, £5.80, £1.50; EX 61.10 Trifecta £187.00.

**Owner** The Queen **Bred** Darley **Trained** Newmarket, Suffolk

**FOCUS**

This was run at a good gallop and suited those held up. The runner-up is the key to the form.

## 7760 BET TOTETRIFECTA AT BETFRED.COM H'CAP (DIV I) 1m 2f (P)

**7:45** (7:56) (Class 6) (0-60,62) 3-Y-O+ **£3,234** (£962; £481; £240) **Stalls** Low

Form RPR

500- **1** **Kohinoor Diamond (IRE)**[361] 7184 3-9-1 **55**..................... LukeMorris 9 69+
(Sir Mark Prescott Bt) *midfield: pushed along and hdwy over 2f out: led 1f out: edgd lft: styd on pushed out: comf* **7/2**[1]

0000 **2** *2½* **Gold Merlion (IRE)**[12] 7413 4-9-11 **61**.......................... FrannyNorton 4 67
(Mark Johnston) *trckd ldrs: rdn over 2f out: bmpd 110yds out: styd on: wnt 2nd towards fin: no ch wnr* **7/1**[3]

0650 **3** *½* **King Kevin**[15] 7270 3-8-8 **48**..................................(b[1]) SilvestreDeSousa 15 53
(Ed Dunlop) *led for 2f: remained prom: led again over 2f out: sn rdn: hdd 1f out: one pce* **11/1**

1305 **4** *nk* **Champagne Rules**[16] 7235 6-8-10 **51**.......................... BenRobinson(5) 10 58
(Sharon Watt) *s.i.s: hld up: stl plenty to do over 1f out: pushed along and gd hdwy whn hmpd 110yds out: kpt on wl: nrst fin* **10/1**

6543 **5** *nk* **Broughtons Knight**[31] 6766 3-9-6 **60**......................(t[1]) RobertWinston 12 64
(Henry Spiller) *hld up: hdwy on outer to trck ldrs 6f out: rdn to chal strly over 1f out: edgd rt 110yds out: no ex fnl 50yds* **9/2**[2]

5546 **6** *1¾* **Malt Teaser (FR)**[29] 6812 3-9-8 **62**.................................... PatDobbs 1 63
(John Best) *hld up in midfield on inner: pushed along over 2f out: briefly short of room over 1f out: kpt on fnl f: nvr involved* **7/2**[1]

3240 **7** *¾* **Outlaw Torn (IRE)**[9] 7479 8-9-4 **54**.........................(e) ConnorBeasley 11 52
(Richard Guest) *chsd ldrs: rdn over 2f out: grad wknd fnl f* **12/1**

0000 **8** *1* **Raashdy (IRE)**[42] 6342 4-8-4 **47**................................. WilliamCox(7) 14 44
(Peter Hiatt) *midfield on outer: rdn over 2f out: no imp* **25/1**

00 **9** *1¼* **Jungle George**[38] 6528 3-8-6 **46** oh1............................. KieranO'Neill 6 41
(Scott Dixon) *hld up in midfield: rdn over 2f out: nvr threatened* **66/1**

2220 **10** *nse* **Simply Clever**[169] 1893 4-9-7 **57**.................................... TomQueally 3 51
(David Brown) *midfield: rdn over 2f out: wknd over 1f out* **20/1**

0030 **11** *nk* **Jazri**[14] 7324 6-8-10 **46** oh1.......................................(p) JosephineGordon 2 39
(Milton Bradley) *slowly away: a towards rr* **20/1**

0006 **12** *28* **Rubheira**[202] 1237 5-8-10 **46** oh1..................................... FranBerry 13
(Neil Mulholland) *led after 2f: rdn whn hdd over 2f out: wknd* **50/1**

2m 6.87s (-1.73) **Going Correction** -0.275s/f (Stan)

**WFA** 3 from 4yo+ 4lb **12 Ran SP% 117.1**

Speed ratings (Par 101): **95,93,92,92,92 90,90,89,88,88 88,65**

CSF £24.97 CT £216.08 TOTE £4.50: £1.80, £2.40, £3.20; EX 30.90 Trifecta £205.80.

**Owner** Bluehills Racing Limited **Bred** Lisbunny Bloodstock **Trained** Newmarket, Suffolk

■ Struck By The Moon was withdrawn. Price at time of withdrawal 12-1. Rule 4 applies to all bets - deduction 5p in the pound.

**FOCUS**
An ordinary handicap, but the winner has the potential to rate higher. Those in behind the first two help set the opening level.

## 7761 BET TOTETRIFECTA AT BETFRED.COM H'CAP (DIV II) 1m 2f (P)
**8:15** (8:25) (Class 6) (0-60,62) 3-Y-O+ **£3,234** (£962; £481; £240) **Stalls** Low

Form RPR

3106 **1** **Luxford**[24] 7005 3-9-4 **56** ........ PatDobbs 2 63
(John Best) *midfield: pushed along and hdwy over 1f out: rdn to ld 110yds out: sn strly pressed: hld on wl* **16/1**

-000 **2** *hd* **Wootyhoot (FR)**[99] 4211 3-9-0 **55** ........ GeorgeWood(3) 8 62
(James Fanshawe) *hld up: pushed along and hdwy over 1f out: rdn to chal strly fnl 110yds: hld nr fin* **8/1[3]**

0-05 **3** *2 ¼* **Mach One**[50] 6067 3-9-10 **62** ........(p[1]) OisinMurphy 9 65
(Archie Watson) *midfield: hdwy and prom 7f out: led over 4f out: rdn over 2f out: hdd 110yds out: one pce* **9/4[2]**

3361 **4** *1 ¼* **Arcadian Sea (IRE)**[14] 7324 3-9-6 **58** ........ JosephineGordon 6 58
(William Jarvis) *hld up in midfield: rdn along over 2f out: hdwy over 1f out: kpt on same pce fnl f* **15/8[1]**

6600 **5** *½* **Bird For Life**[14] 7323 3-8-0 **45** ........ NicolaCurrie(7) 4 46
(Mark Usher) *hld up: rdn and n.m.r towards outer over 1f out: in clr appr fnl f: r.o wl* **33/1**

2040 **6** *1* **Adventureman**[16] 7235 5-9-6 **54** ........(b) JamesSullivan 14 51
(Ruth Carr) *trckd ldrs: rdn over 2f out: edgd lft and no ex fnl f* **25/1**

5044 **7** *1* **Just Fred (IRE)**[43] 6306 4-8-11 **45** ........(t) FranBerry 1 40
(Neil Mulholland) *hld up in midfield: forced way to outer over wl over 1f out: rdn and hung lft: kpt on same pce* **12/1**

04 **8** *shd* **Lord Of The Storm**[28] 6847 9-9-3 **54** ........ DavidEgan(3) 12 48
(Michael Attwater) *chsd ldrs: rdn over 2f out: chal over 1f out: wknd ins fnl f* **20/1**

2010 **9** *hd* **Hannington**[33] 6673 6-9-13 **61** ........(t) LukeMorris 11 55
(Michael Appleby) *hld up: rdn along whn c v wd on bnd 2f out: nvr threatened* **16/1**

0064 **10** *1 ½* **Yasir (USA)**[26] 6953 9-9-1 **49** ........ MartinHarley 7 40
(Conor Dore) *hld up: nvr threatened* **20/1**

5005 **11** *2 ½* **Dibloam (USA)**[166] 1985 4-8-8 **45** ........ MattCosham(3) 3 31
(David Evans) *midfield: rdn over 2f out: wknd over 1f out* **25/1**

0-00 **12** *7* **Somepink (IRE)**[223] 900 4-8-8 **45** ........ EoinWalsh(3) 10 18
(Daniel Mark Loughnane) *in tch: rdn along 3f out: wknd over 1f out* **100/1**

003 **13** *3* **Sonnet Rose (IRE)**[22] 7059 3-9-5 **57** ........(t[1]) SaleemGolam 5 25
(Conrad Allen) *midfield: short of room 3f out and dropped to rr: no ch after* **33/1**

0-00 **14** *nk* **Tilly Devine**[64] 5542 3-8-7 **45** ........ KieranO'Neill 13 13
(Scott Dixon) *led for 2f: trckd ldrs: rdn 3f out: wknd over 1f out* **80/1**

4206 **15** *4 ½* **Nouvelle Ere**[44] 6280 6-9-8 **56** ........(t) GeorgeDowning 15 14
(Tony Carroll) *led after 2f: hdd over 4f out: rdn over 3f out: wknd 2f out* **25/1**

2m 6.14s (-2.46) **Going Correction** -0.275s/f (Stan)
**WFA** 3 from 4yo+ 4lb **15** Ran SP% **125.3**
Speed ratings (Par 101): **98,97,96,95,94 93,93,92,92,91 89,84,81,81,77**
CSF £128.01 CT £408.98 TOTE £25.40: £5.70, £2.70, £1.50; EX 223.10 Trifecta £1501.40.
**Owner** Stuart Mair, Wendy Bush & Steve Summers **Bred** Best Breeding **Trained** Oad Street, Kent
■ Stewards' Enquiry : Nicola Currie caution: careless riding

**FOCUS**
The faster of the two divisions by 0.73sec. The runner-up has been rated close to his 2yo best.

## 7762 BET TOTEWIN AT BETFRED.COM FILLIES' H'CAP 1m 2f (P)
**8:45** (8:53) (Class 5) (0-75,76) 3-Y-O+ **£5,175** (£1,540; £769; £384) **Stalls** Low

Form RPR

352 **1** **Feint**[104] 4042 3-9-5 **73** ........(t[1]) RyanMoore 11 81
(William Haggas) *hld up on inner: pushed along and hdwy over 1f out: rdn to ld 110yds out: kpt on* **9/1**

6024 **2** *½* **Rayaa**[64] 5533 4-9-3 **67** ........(t) TomQueally 1 74
(Michael Appleby) *trckd ldrs on inner: rdn to chse ldr 2f out: chal strly appr fnl f: kpt on* **12/1**

2440 **3** *hd* **Light Of Joy (USA)**[28] 6848 3-9-8 **76** ........ FranBerry 10 83
(David Lanigan) *hld up: hdwy on outer 2f out: rdn to chse ldrs appr fnl f: edgd lft jst ins fnl f: kpt on* **16/1**

3000 **4** *1 ½* **Celestation**[19] 7142 3-9-4 **72** ........ FrannyNorton 2 76
(Mark Johnston) *prom: led 7f out: rdn over 2f out: strly pressed appr fnl f: hdd 110yds out: no ex* **16/1**

5035 **5** *½* **Mighty Lady**[7] 7541 4-9-8 **72** ........ MartinHarley 4 75
(Robyn Brisland) *midfield on inner: pushed along and brought towards centre over 1f out: rdn and hung lft ins fnl f: kpt on same pce* **6/1[2]**

22 **6** *hd* **Love Conquers (JPN)**[40] 6443 3-9-5 **73** ........ OisinMurphy 6 75
(Ralph Beckett) *dwlt: midfield: rdn along 2f out: kpt on ins fnl f: nvr threatened ldrs* **8/1**

3453 **7** *1 ¾* **Kath's Legacy**[32] 6722 4-9-2 **71** ........ FinleyMarsh(5) 5 70
(Ben De Haan) *trckd ldrs: rdn over 2f out: outpcd over 1f out* **10/1**

1440 **8** *1 ¾* **Estrella Eria (FR)**[48] 6144 4-9-5 **69** ........(h) HarryBentley 12 64
(George Peckham) *hld up: rdn and minor hdwy on outer over 1f out: nvr threatened* **7/1[3]**

**9** *nse* **Deduce (FR)**[185] 4-9-10 **74** ........ RyanTate 13 69
(James Eustace) *dwlt: hld up: nvr threatened* **50/1**

4060 **10** *3 ½* **Darkroom Angel**[15] 7276 3-9-1 **72** ........ HectorCrouch(3) 9 61
(Philip Hide) *midfield: rdn over 2f out: wknd over 1f out* **22/1**

5044 **11** *6* **Diamond Bear (USA)**[10] 7452 3-9-3 **71** ........(v[1]) LukeMorris 3 48
(Sir Mark Prescott Bt) *sn led: hdd 7f out: trckd ldrs: rdn over 2f out: wknd over 1f out* **5/1[1]**

1305 **12** *3 ¼* **Paradise Cove**[18] 7201 3-9-4 **72** ........ PatCosgrave 14 43
(Charlie Fellowes) *trckd ldrs on outside: rdn over 2f out: wknd over 1f out* **33/1**

2062 **13** *12* **Luminous**[15] 7278 3-9-2 **70** ........ SilvestreDeSousa 7 17
(Simon Crisford) *trckd ldrs: racd keenly: rdn over 2f out: sn wknd* **7/1[3]**

4202 **14** *10* **Music Lesson**[21] 7097 3-9-5 **73** ........ RobertWinston 8
(Hughie Morrison) *prom on outer: rdn over 2f out: sn wknd* **8/1**

2m 5.6s (-3.00) **Going Correction** -0.275s/f (Stan)
**WFA** 3 from 4yo 4lb **14** Ran SP% **126.0**
Speed ratings (Par 100): **101,100,100,99,98 98,97,95,95,93 88,85,76,68**
CSF £116.11 CT £1733.30 TOTE £7.90: £3.20, £4.40, £4.70; EX 140.40 Trifecta £2821.50.
**Owner** Hamer Hawkes Hellin & Whatton Manor Stud **Bred** Whatton Manor Stud **Trained** Newmarket, Suffolk

**FOCUS**
The early gallop wasn't that strong. The runner-up has been rated close to her best and the third to form.

## 7763 CHELMSFORDCITYRACECOURSE.COM H'CAP 6f (P)
**9:15** (9:18) (Class 7) (0-50,50) 3-Y-O+ **£2,587** (£770; £384; £192) **Stalls** Centre

Form RPR

3636 **1** **Justice Rock**[5] 7605 4-8-12 **49** ........(t) NicolaCurrie(7) 2 55
(Phil McEntee) *dwlt: hld up: pushed along 2f out: angled rt and hdwy over 1f out: rdn and on r.o fnl f: led 50yds out* **5/1[3]**

3-06 **2** *1 ¼* **Dream Revival**[15] 7270 4-9-5 **49** ........(p[1]) JamesSullivan 8 51
(Paul Collins) *trckd ldrs: racd keenly: rdn 2f out: led ins fnl f: hung bdly lft and hdd 50yds out: no ex* **12/1**

0000 **3** *1* **Banta Bay**[30] 6791 3-9-5 **50** ........ JosephineGordon 7 49
(John Best) *dwlt and in rr: rdn along 1/2-way: hdwy on outside over 1f out: kpt on fnl f: wnt 3rd nr fin* **5/1[3]**

006 **4** *hd* **Snow Excuse**[62] 5619 3-9-1 **49** ........(t) AdamMcNamara(3) 5 47
(Bryan Smart) *midfield on inner: rdn over 2f out: kpt on fnl f* **16/1**

-020 **5** *hd* **Miss Uppity**[23] 7020 4-9-2 **46** ........ SilvestreDeSousa 6 44
(Ivan Furtado) *chsd ldrs: rdn and ev ch 2f out: no ex fnl 110yds* **6/1**

4020 **6** *nk* **Goadby**[58] 5738 6-8-13 **46** ........(p) EoinWalsh(3) 9 43
(John Holt) *hld up: rdn over 2f out: kpt on fnl f: nvr threatened* **25/1**

6000 **7** *½* **Whaleweigh Station**[29] 6813 6-9-6 **50** ........(v) FrannyNorton 4 45
(J R Jenkins) *midfield: rdn over 2f out: one pce* **16/1**

0006 **8** *¾* **Jasmincita (IRE)**[29] 6814 3-9-3 **48** ........(p) PatCosgrave 13 41
(George Baker) *hld up: nvr threatened* **10/1**

0052 **9** *2 ½* **Frangarry (IRE)**[5] 7605 5-9-1 **50** ........(t) JoshuaBryan(5) 11 36
(Alan Bailey) *pressed ldr: drvn into narrow ld 2f out: hdd ins fnl f: wknd* **4/1[1]**

4026 **10** *11* **Gettin' Lucky**[194] 1371 4-9-3 **47** ........(p) BenCurtis 1
(John Balding) *led narrowly: rdn whn hdd 2f out: wknd* **9/2[2]**

0000 **11** *6* **Silver Springs (IRE)**[79] 4990 4-9-1 **50** ........ RhiainIngram(5) 14
(Roger Ingram) *in tch on outside: rdn over 2f out: wknd over 1f out* **50/1**

1m 12.61s (-1.09) **Going Correction** -0.275s/f (Stan)
**WFA** 3 from 4yo+ 1lb **11** Ran SP% **120.2**
Speed ratings (Par 97): **96,94,93,92,92 92,91,90,87,72 64**
CSF £65.22 CT £326.80 TOTE £6.50: £1.80, £3.10, £2.00; EX 68.90 Trifecta £415.10.
**Owner** Steve Jakes **Bred** Ashbrittle Stud **Trained** Newmarket, Suffolk

**FOCUS**
There was a decent pace on here and two of the first three went into the bend in the last three positions. The winner has been rated to this year's best.
T/Jkpt: Not won. T/Plt: £37.70 to a £1 stake. Pool: £95,193.50. 1,842.51 winning units. T/Qpdt: £14.60 to a £1 stake. Pool: £13,086.13. 659.48 winning units. **Andrew Sheret**

# 7488 LINGFIELD (L-H)
## Thursday, October 5

**OFFICIAL GOING: Polytrack: standard to slow**
Wind: medium, against Weather: bright spells, breezy

## 7764 RACING WELFARE NURSERY H'CAP 1m 1y(P)
**1:50** (1:52) (Class 4) (0-80,74) 2-Y-O **£3,946** (£1,174; £586; £293) **Stalls** High

Form RPR

0032 **1** **Motabassim (IRE)**[41] 6395 2-9-7 **74** ........(b) JimCrowley 1 77
(Brian Meehan) *dwlt: sn rcvrd and wl in tch in midfield: effrt and reminders over 1f out: hdwy under hands and heels riding ins fnl f: r.o wl to ld nr fin* **7/1[3]**

5334 **2** *½* **Fleeting Freedom**[27] 6875 2-9-2 **74** ........ JoshuaBryan(5) 2 76
(Alan Bailey) *led: rdn over 1f out: drvn and edgd rt ins fnl f: kpt on u.p tl hdd and no ex nr fin* **12/1**

32 **3** *1 ¼* **Simply Breathless**[41] 6375 2-9-5 **72** ........ AdamKirby 11 71
(Clive Cox) *chsd ldr: effrt u.p over 1f out: stl pressing ldr but unable qck whn drvn 1f out: carried sltly rt jst ins fnl f: lost 2nd wl ins fnl f: wknd towards fin* **4/1[1]**

0350 **4** *¾* **Levante Player (IRE)**[42] 6353 2-9-4 **71** ........(p) RichardKingscote 3 68
(Tom Dascombe) *chsd ldrs: effrt over 1f out: kpt on same pce u.p ins fnl f* **16/1**

0263 **5** *½* **Trogon (IRE)**[10] 7451 2-9-2 **69** ........ JFEgan 6 65
(Mick Channon) *hld up in tch in midfield: hdwy u.p over 1f out: chsd ldrs and kpt on same pce fnl 100yds* **8/1**

0540 **6** *shd* **Stormy Sand (IRE)**[29] 6825 2-9-1 **68** ........ AndreaAtzeni 9 64
(Marco Botti) *chsd ldrs: effrt to dispute 3rd over 2f out: no ex 1f out: wknd ins fnl f* **16/1**

563 **7** *nse* **Ashington**[24] 7001 2-9-4 **71** ........ JamieSpencer 7 67+
(Luca Cumani) *hld up towards rr: effrt and wd bnd 2f out: hdwy 1f out: styd on ins fnl f: nvr trbld ldrs* **14/1**

445 **8** *¾* **Bajan Gold (IRE)**[15] 7281 2-9-1 **68** ........ AdamBeschizza 5 62+
(Stuart Williams) *hld up in last pair: effrt towards inner over 1f out: styd on ins fnl f: nvr trbld ldrs* **11/2[2]**

6565 **9** *½* **Galactic (IRE)**[22] 7057 2-8-10 **66** ........ HollieDoyle(3) 10 59+
(Richard Hannon) *hld up in towards rr: effrt wl over 1f out: styd on ins fnl f: nvr trbld ldrs* **12/1**

2562 **10** *hd* **Collateral (IRE)**[26] 6932 2-9-7 **74** ........ OisinMurphy 8 66
(James Tate) *midfield: pushed along briefly 5f out: unable qck over 1f out: wknd ins fnl f* **7/1[3]**

4040 **11** *4* **Rainbow Jazz (IRE)**[28] 6860 2-9-2 **69** ........(p) SteveDrowne 4 52
(Mark Usher) *stdd after s: hld up towards rr: effrt u.p towards inner over 1f out: no hdwy: n.d* **33/1**

353 **12** *¾* **Viceroy Mac**[37] 6552 2-9-4 **71** ........ JosephineGordon 12 52
(David Loughnane) *s.i.s: a bhd* **9/1**

1m 39.0s (0.80) **Going Correction** +0.025s/f (Slow) **12** Ran SP% **118.3**
Speed ratings (Par 97): **97,96,95,94,94 93,93,93,92,92 88,87**
CSF £87.99 CT £390.70 TOTE £5.30: £2.10, £4.60, £1.60; EX 53.50 Trifecta £168.00.
**Owner** Hamdan Al Maktoum **Bred** Lynn Lodge Stud **Trained** Manton, Wilts
■ Stewards' Enquiry : Joshua Bryan caution: careless riding

**FOCUS**
The going was officially standard to slow and they were racing into a headwind up the straight. An ordinary, if open nursery with only one of these having scored before. It's been rated around the second and third.

## 7765 INJURED JOCKEYS FUND EBF NOVICE STKS 7f 1y(P)
2:25 (2:27) (Class 5) 2-Y-O £3,234 (£962; £481; £240) Stalls Low

Form RPR

14 **1** **Purser (USA)**[33] 6696 2-9-9 0 .......... RobertHavlin 6 99+
(John Gosden) *mde all: shkn up and readily qcknd clr over 1f out: r.o strly fnl f: v easily* **4/9**[1]

**2** *9* **Key Player** 2-9-2 0 .......... CharlesBishop 5 67
(Eve Johnson Houghton) *t.k.h: hld up in tch in midfield: shkn up over 1f out: hdwy 1f out: styd on to go 2nd wl ins fnl f: no ch w wnr* **66/1**

**3** *½* **Wajaaha (IRE)** 2-9-2 0 .......... JimCrowley 2 66
(Saeed bin Suroor) *hld up in tch in midfield: effrt 2f out: outpcd by wnr over 1f out: kpt on to chse clr wnr 100yds out: no imp: lost 2nd wl ins fnl f* **7/1**[3]

05 **4** *2¼* **Masked Defender (USA)**[34] 6653 2-9-2 0 .......... PatDobbs 1 60
(Amanda Perrett) *chsd ldng pair: effrt to chse wnr 2f out: sn rdn and outpcd by wnr: lost wl hld 2nd 100yds out and wknd towards fin* **14/1**

**5** *hd* **Valentino Dancer** 2-9-2 0 .......... JackMitchell 4 59
(Robyn Brisland) *hld up in last trio: shkn up wl over 1f out: swtchd lft and hdwy over 1f out: no ch w wnr but styd on wl ins fnl f* **50/1**

0 **6** *shd* **Beachwalk**[34] 6653 2-9-2 0 .......... AndreaAtzeni 8 59+
(Sir Michael Stoute) *in tch in midfield on outer: 7th and struggling over 2f out: no ch w wnr after: swtchd rt and styd on u.p ins fnl f* **5/1**[2]

0 **7** *nk* **Conversant (IRE)**[26] 6938 2-9-2 0 .......... JosephineGordon 9 58
(Hugo Palmer) *chsd ldrs: rdn 2f out: outpcd by wnr and wl btn over 1f out: plugged on same pce ins fnl f* **16/1**

0 **8** *1½* **Pact Of Steel**[12] 7391 2-9-2 0 .......... TomMarquand 7 54
(Harry Dunlop) *chsd wnr: rdn 4f out: lost 2nd 2f out and sn outpcd u.p: wl btn 1f out: wknd ins fnl f* **50/1**

6 **9** *5* **Grey Spirit (IRE)**[21] 7079 2-9-2 0 .......... LukeMorris 3 41
(Sir Mark Prescott Bt) *sn bustled along and dropped to rr: nvr on terms* **40/1**

0 **10** *3¾* **Danish Dancer (IRE)**[20] 7120 2-9-2 0 .......... (b) LiamKeniry 12 31
(Ed Walker) *dropped in bhd after s: t.k.h in rr: n.d: lost tch over 1f out* **66/1**

**11** *3¼* **Blue Candy** 2-9-2 0 .......... EdwardGreatrex 10 22
(Archie Watson) *a towards rr: pushed along 4f out: rdn and outpcd over 2f out: wl bhd over 1f out* **33/1**

5 **12** *5* **Fanan**[20] 7105 2-9-2 0 .......... SilvestreDeSousa 11 8
(Simon Crisford) *a towards rr: reminders 4f out: outpcd and bhd over 2f out: eased fr over 1f out* **16/1**

1m 23.79s (-1.01) **Going Correction** +0.025s/f (Slow) 12 Ran SP% 129.1
Speed ratings (Par 95): **106,95,95,92,92 92,91,90,84,80 76,70**
CSF £81.43 TOTE £1.20: £1.02, £22.10, £2.10; EX 77.40 Trifecta £499.90.
**Owner** K Abdullah **Bred** Juddmonte Farms Inc **Trained** Newmarket, Suffolk
■ Stewards' Enquiry : Liam Keniry £290 fine: use of mobile phone

**FOCUS**
An interesting novice event with several top stables represented, but this was all about one horse and one jockey, and the combination didn't disappoint.

## 7766 #TAKETHEREINS H'CAP 1m 7f 169y(P)
2:55 (2:56) (Class 5) (0-75,76) 3-Y-O+ £2,911 (£866; £432; £216) Stalls Low

Form RPR

2111 **1** **Imphal**[41] 6376 3-9-0 76 .......... (p) TylerSaunders(7) 2 86+
(Marcus Tregoning) *hld up in last trio: clsd and nt clr run over 2f out: swtchd rt and hdwy bnd 2f out: edgd lft and wnt 3rd jst ins fnl f: clsd to pressed ldrs whn squeezed for room and swtchd rt nr fin: led last strides* **2/1**[1]

2163 **2** *shd* **Fulham (IRE)**[12] 7386 3-9-7 76 .......... TomMarquand 7 83
(Robyn Brisland) *hld up in midfield: swtchd rt and hdwy over 2f out: chsd clr ldr over 1f out: kpt on wl and chalng whn bmpd towards fin: led nr fin: hdd last strides* **5/1**[2]

1365 **3** *hd* **Veiled Secret (IRE)**[22] 7060 3-9-4 73 .......... (p) LukeMorris 1 79
(Sir Mark Prescott Bt) *rousted along leaving stalls: led after 1f: rdn and kicked clr 3f out: drvn over 1f out: hung rt ins fnl f: hdd and no ex nr fin* **6/1**[3]

2551 **4** *8* **Ayr Of Elegance**[78] 5025 5-10-2 76 .......... RichardKingscote 13 72
(Philip Hide) *stdd s: hld up in last trio: clsd and nt clr run over 2f out: effrt ent fnl 2f: hdwy over 1f out: no threat to ldrs but kpt on ins fnl f* **14/1**

6210 **5** *1¼* **Fitzwilly**[27] 6889 7-9-6 69 .......... DavidEgan(3) 5 64
(Mick Channon) *midfield tl pushed along and hdwy to chse ldrs 10f out: outpcd u.p over 2f out: wl hld and plugged on same pce after* **14/1**

5424 **6** *hd* **Sputnik Planum (USA)**[14] 7319 3-9-2 71 .......... (t) TedDurcan 3 66
(David Lanigan) *trckd ldrs: hdwy on inner to chse ldr 4f out: rdn and unable qck over 2f out: lost wl hld 2nd and wknd fnl f* **5/1**[2]

3-20 **7** *2¾* **Yes Daddy (IRE)**[38] 6508 9-9-3 70 .......... (bt) WilliamCox(7) 8 61
(Robert Stephens) *in tch in midfield: clsd and trckd ldrs: 4f out: rdn and outpcd over 2f out: sn btn and wknd over 1f out* **28/1**

2444 **8** *shd* **Goldslinger (FR)**[16] 7233 5-9-0 63 .......... JackDuern(3) 10 54
(Dean Ivory) *hld up in midfield on outer: effrt over 2f out: sn struggling and n.d fnl 2f* **33/1**

311U **9** *2* **Golly Miss Molly**[27] 6889 6-9-8 68 .......... (b) MartinLane 9 57
(Martin Bosley) *stdd s: hld up in rr: effrt wl over 3f out: nvr getting on terms w ldrs and wl hld 2f out* **22/1**

4030 **10** *4* **Tapdancealltheway**[36] 6578 3-8-10 65 .......... SteveDrowne 6 49
(Amanda Perrett) *t.k.h: hld up in midfield: effrt wl over 3f out: no prog and wl btn 2f out* **50/1**

000- **11** *4½* **Kalann (IRE)**[68] 5446 10-9-2 62 .......... (bt) BenCurtis 4 41
(Denis Gerard Hogan, Ire) *hld up in tch in midfield: clsd to trck ldrs on outer over 4f out: rdn over 2f out: sn outpcd and lost pl: wknd wl over 1f out* **25/1**

464 **12** *15* **Sure To Explore (IRE)**[22] 7060 3-9-5 74 .......... (p[1]) MartinDwyer 11 37
(William Muir) *t.k.h: chsd ldrs after 2f tl rdn and lost pl over 4f out: wl bhd fnl 2f: t.o* **14/1**

2-20 **13** *4½* **Makkadangdang**[15] 7277 3-9-2 71 .......... DavidProbert 12 28
(Andrew Balding) *chsd ldr tl 4f out: sn dropped out: wl bhd fnl 2f: t.o* **25/1**

3m 22.63s (-3.07) **Going Correction** +0.025s/f (Slow)
**WFA** 3 from 5yo+ 9lb 13 Ran SP% 121.3
Speed ratings (Par 103): **108,107,107,103,103 103,101,101,100,98 96,88,86**
CSF £10.53 CT £53.72 TOTE £2.30: £1.10, £2.10, £2.10; EX 16.30 Trifecta £76.10.
**Owner** Mrs M E Slade **Bred** G S Bishop **Trained** Whitsbury, Hants

**FOCUS**
A modest staying handicap, but a thrilling finish after nearly 2m with little between the first three. Things got tight between the trio near the line, but the placings were left alone. The third has been rated back to his Yarmouth win.

## 7767 FIREWORKS NIGHT AT LINGFIELD PARK 4TH NOVEMBER H'CAP 5f 6y(P)
3:30 (3:30) (Class 6) (0-65,66) 3-Y-O+ £2,264 (£673; £336; £168) Stalls High

Form RPR

4550 **1** **Entertaining Ben**[9] 7494 4-9-1 59 .......... (p) KieranShoemark 5 66
(Amy Murphy) *mde all: rdn and kicked clr over 1f out: styd on wl and in command fnl f* **20/1**

0002 **2** *1½* **Raffle King (IRE)**[13] 7365 3-9-5 66 .......... DavidEgan(3) 6 69
(Mick Channon) *taken down early: chsd ldng trio: effrt over 1f out: hanging lft but kpt on ins fnl f: snatched 2nd on post: no threat to wnr* **9/2**[2]

3000 **3** *nse* **Kyllukey**[14] 7320 4-9-2 60 .......... (v[1]) LukeMorris 1 61
(Milton Bradley) *chsd ldng pair: effrt to go 2nd but wnr clr wl over 1f out: kpt on but nvr threatening wnr: lost 2nd on post* **9/1**

004 **4** *½* **Broadhaven Honey (IRE)**[3] 7689 3-9-5 63 .......... (v) SamHitchcott 2 64
(Ronald Harris) *midfield: effrt on inner over 1f out: kpt on same pce u.p ins fnl f* **25/1**

4044 **5** *¾* **Roundabout Magic (IRE)**[8] 7509 3-9-2 65 .......... PaddyBradley(5) 10 63
(Simon Dow) *t.k.h: hld up off the pce in midfield: effrt over 1f out: hdwy and swtchd rt 1f out: styd on: no threat to wnr* **11/2**[3]

335 **6** *½* **Zambezi Queen (IRE)**[51] 6028 3-9-8 66 .......... (p) RaulDaSilva 3 62
(Paul Cole) *taken down early: dwlt and impeded leaving stalls: racd in last trio: effrt and hdwy on inner over 1f out: kpt on ins fnl f: nvr trbld ldrs* **7/1**

2342 **7** *1½* **Picansort**[55] 5871 10-9-4 62 .......... (b) ShaneKelly 4 52+
(Peter Crate) *stmbld bdly leaving stalls: hld up off the pce in last trio: clsd and nt clr run 1f out: swtchd rt and rdn ins fnl f: kpt on: nvr trbld ldrs* **11/1**

4002 **8** *¾* **Grand Myla (IRE)**[9] 7494 3-9-2 60 .......... (p) AdamKirby 9 48
(Gary Moore) *chsd wnr tl drifted rt and lost 2nd wl over 1f out: sn outpcd u.p: wknd ins fnl f* **7/2**[1]

05 **9** *½* **Archimedes (IRE)**[35] 6612 4-9-6 64 .......... (tp) TomQueally 8 49
(David C Griffiths) *midfield: effrt whn wd and lost pl bnd 2f out: n.d after* **16/1**

5030 **10** *1¼* **Top Of The Bank**[14] 7320 4-9-6 64 .......... (p) TonyHamilton 7 45
(Kristin Stubbs) *sn dropped to last trio and pushed along: n.d* **6/1**

59.1s (0.30) **Going Correction** +0.025s/f (Slow) 10 Ran SP% 115.4
Speed ratings (Par 101): **98,95,95,94,93 92,90,89,88,86**
CSF £106.83 CT £904.09 TOTE £22.10: £5.50, £1.40, £3.10; EX 190.20 Trifecta £2227.60.
**Owner** Amy Murphy Racing Club **Bred** C J Mills **Trained** Newmarket, Suffolk

**FOCUS**
A moderate sprint handicap.

## 7768 AG MAIDEN STKS 1m 1y(P)
4:00 (4:01) (Class 5) 3-Y-O+ £2,911 (£866; £432; £216) Stalls High

Form RPR

5023 **1** **Dawaaleeb (USA)**[48] 6150 3-9-5 83 .......... (b[1]) JimCrowley 2 79
(Charles Hills) *led: rdn and hdd narrowly over 1f out: rallied u.p to ld again cl home* **11/8**[1]

2405 **2** *nk* **Mr Tyrrell (IRE)**[12] 7398 3-9-5 74 .......... SeanLevey 4 78
(Richard Hannon) *pressed wnr: drvn to ld narrowly over 1f out: kpt on u.p tl hdd and no ex cl home* **4/1**[3]

**3** *1* **Francis Xavier (IRE)** 3-9-5 0 .......... PatCosgrave 1 76
(Hugo Palmer) *s.i.s: sn rcvrd to trck ldrs after 2f and t.k.h: effrt and swtchd rt over 1f out: kpt on same pce ins fnl f* **11/4**[2]

3324 **4** *6* **Hats Off To Larry**[14] 7331 3-9-5 75 .......... JFEgan 10 61+
(Mick Channon) *midfield: outpcd over 2f out: rallied and kpt on ins fnl f to go 4th nr fin: nvr threatened ldrs* **15/2**

00 **5** *½* **What A Welcome**[45] 6277 3-9-5 0 .......... JoeyHaynes 7 60
(Patrick Chamings) *hld up in midfield: rdn and effrt on inner 2f out: chsd clr ldng trio 1f out: kpt on same pce and no imp: lost 4th nr fin* **100/1**

43 **6** *2¾* **Yogiyogiyogi (IRE)**[14] 7322 3-8-11 0 .......... DavidEgan(3) 9 48
(Denis Coakley) *wl in tch in midfield: 6th and struggling u.p 2f out: sn btn and wknd fnl f* **12/1**

3636 **7** *1¾* **Zamalight**[82] 4912 3-9-5 76 .......... PatDobbs 3 49
(Amanda Perrett) *chsd ldrs: 4th and struggling u.p 2f out: sn btn and wknd fnl f* **16/1**

00 **8** *8* **Tango Fire (USA)**[166] 1962 3-9-5 0 .......... TomMarquand 11 30
(Richard Hannon) *s.i.s: sn swtchd lft: nvr travelling wl in rr gp: lost tch 2f out* **25/1**

00 **9** *2¾* **Fire Whirl**[8] 7514 3-9-5 0 .......... MartinLane 8 23
(William Knight) *sn dropped to rr and nvr travelling wl: lost tch 2f out* **100/1**

0 **10** *21* **No Damage (IRE)**[44] 6283 3-9-0 0 .......... KierenFox 6
(Michael Attwater) *taken downe early: midfield: rdn 3f out: sn struggling and dropped out: wl bhd 2f out: t.o* **100/1**

1m 37.48s (-0.72) **Going Correction** +0.025s/f (Slow)
**WFA** 3 from 5yo 3lb 10 Ran SP% 120.9
Speed ratings (Par 103): **104,103,102,96,96 93,91,83,80,59**
CSF £7.53 TOTE £1.90: £1.10, £1.60, £1.50; EX 7.10 Trifecta £18.70.
**Owner** Hamdan Al Maktoum **Bred** Greenwood Lodge Farm Inc **Trained** Lambourn, Berks

**FOCUS**
A modest older-horse maiden and few got into it with the first two holding those positions throughout. The first three finished clear of the rest. The runner-up is the key to the level.

## 7769 RACING WELFARE 24 HOUR HELPLINE 08006300443 H'CAP (DIV I) 1m 1y(P)
4:35 (4:35) (Class 5) (0-70,75) 3-Y-O+ £2,911 (£866; £432; £216) Stalls High

Form RPR

2401 **1** **Evening Hill**[10] 7457 3-9-9 75 6ex ow1 .......... (p) ShaneKelly 3 84
(Richard Hughes) *led for 2f: mostly trckd ldrs after: effrt and reminder 2f out: swtchd rt and rdn over 1f out: hdwy u.p to ld 100yds out: styd on: rdn out* **9/4**[1]

2415 **2** *¾* **Sandy Shores**[31] 6766 3-9-3 69 .......... (b) TomMarquand 8 76
(Brian Meehan) *chsd ldrs on outer: rdn over 3f out: kpt on u.p ins fnl f: wnt 2nd last stride* **14/1**

2003 **3** *shd* **Peace And Plenty**[10] 7457 3-9-4 70 .......... MartinDwyer 4 77
(William Muir) *chsd ldrs tl wnt 2nd over 4f out: effrt and ev ch 2f out: drvn to ld jst over 1f out: hdd and one pced fnl 100yds: lost 2nd last stride* **9/4**[1]

2566 **4** *1½* **Cadeaux Boxer**[30] 6795 4-9-2 70 .......... (h) PaddyBradley(5) 9 73
(Lee Carter) *chsd ldrs tl led after 2f: jnd and rdn 2f out: hdd jst over 1f out: no ex ins fnl f: wknd wl ins fnl f* **20/1**

1331 **5** *1 3/4* **Easy Code**[9] 7493 4-9-7 **75** 6ex.......................... GeorgiaCox(5) 7 74+
(William Haggas) *hld up in last trio: effrt over 1f out: hdwy u.p 1f out: kpt on ins fnl f: nvr trbld ldrs* **11/4**[2]

5346 **6** *1 1/4* **Nuncio**[14] 7322 3-9-1 **67**.......................... TomQueally 10 63+
(Daniel Kubler) *stdd s: t.k.h: hld up in last trio: rdn and wd bnd 2f out: kpt on same pce and no imp after* **25/1**

3154 **7** *shd* **Fantasy Queen**[28] 6866 4-9-5 **68**.......................... CharlesBishop 6 64
(Eve Johnson Houghton) *midfield: effrt to chse clr ldng quartet ent fnl 2f: kpt on same pce and no imp over 1f out* **10/1**[3]

0-50 **8** *4* **German Whip**[31] 6753 4-9-6 **69**.......................... SeanLevey 1 55
(Gary Moore) *hld up in tch in midfield: effrt and outpcd 2f out: sn lost pl: wknd fnl f* **33/1**

3-00 **9** *4* **Expectation (IRE)**[152] 2395 3-8-7 **59** ow1.......................... RobHornby 2 36
(Michael Blanshard) *dwlt: sn pushed along and rcvrd to r in midfield: rdn 4f out: dropped to rr 2f out: sn bhd* **66/1**

1m 37.97s (-0.23) **Going Correction** +0.025s/f (Slow)
**WFA** 3 from 4yo 3lb **9** Ran SP% **117.0**
Speed ratings (Par 103): **102,101,101,99,97 96,96,92,88**
CSF £33.70 CT £80.14 TOTE £2.90: £1.10, £3.80, £1.30; EX 33.70 Trifecta £82.70.
**Owner** The Heffer Syndicate **Bred** Natton House Thoroughbreds **Trained** Upper Lambourn, Berks

**FOCUS**
The first division of an ordinary handicap with three dominating the market. The third has been rated close to form.

## 7770 RACING WELFARE 24 HOUR HELPLINE 08006300443 H'CAP (DIV II) 1m 1y(P)
**5:05** (5:11) (Class 5) (0-70,72) 3-Y-O+ **£2,911** (£866; £432; £216) **Stalls High**

Form RPR

1563 **1** **Dreaming Time**[34] 6664 3-9-5 **71**.......................... JoeFanning 5 80+
(James Tate) *trckd ldr after 1f tl led wl over 1f out: sn pushed along and kicked clr: rdn ins fnl f: kpt on and a doing enough* **3/1**[1]

0046 **2** *3/4* **Passing Star**[38] 6502 6-9-3 **66**..........................(tp) AdamKirby 1 72
(Daniel Kubler) *hld up in tch in midfield: effrt jst over 2f out: nt clr run and swtchd rt over 1f out: chsd wnr 150yds out: styd on but nvr getting on terms w wnr* **6/1**

2500 **3** *1* **Beyond Recall**[48] 6139 3-9-4 **70**..........................(v) JamieSpencer 3 74+
(Luca Cumani) *hld up in tch in last trio: clsd and nt clr run wl over 1f out: swtchd rt and hdwy 1f out: rdn and styd on wl ins fnl f: wnt 3rd nr fin: nt rch ldrs* **13/2**

3600 **4** *1/2* **Top Beak (IRE)**[20] 7131 4-9-9 **72**..........................(t) RobHornby 2 74
(Michael Attwater) *hld up in tch in midfield: effrt and lost pl on outer bnd 2f out: rallied 1f out: styd on wl u.p ins fnl f: nt rch ldrs* **11/2**[3]

203 **5** *nk* **Himalayan Queen**[40] 6439 4-9-4 **67**.......................... AndreaAtzeni 10 69
(William Jarvis) *hld up in tch in last trio: hdwy on inner over 1f out: chsd ldrs ins fnl f: kpt on but lost 2 pls nr fin* **12/1**

2530 **6** *1/2* **Shifting Star (IRE)**[21] 7098 12-9-2 **70**..........................(vt) MitchGodwin(5) 9 70
(John Bridger) *chsd ldrs: effrt to chse ldrs 2f out: drvn to chse clr wnr over 1f out: no imp and lost 2nd 150yds out: kpt on same pce after* **33/1**

400 **7** *1 3/4* **The Happy Hammer (IRE)**[14] 7323 11-8-7 **56** oh2.......... JoeyHaynes 7 52
(Eugene Stanford) *hld up in tch in rr: clsd and n.m.r over 1f out: kpt on same pce ins fnl f: nvr trbld ldrs* **66/1**

1440 **8** *1/2* **Paradwys (IRE)**[22] 7058 3-9-1 **67**..........................(p) EdwardGreatrex 4 62
(Archie Watson) *led for 1f: trckd ldrs after 1f tl rdn and unable qck over 1f out: wknd ins fnl f* **5/1**[2]

0024 **9** *2 1/4* **Carcharias (IRE)**[32] 6725 4-9-0 **63**.......................... LiamKeniry 6 53
(Ed de Giles) *led after 1f: rdn and hdd 2f out: lost 2nd over 1f out: wknd ins fnl f* **33/1**

6263 **10** *shd* **Character Onesie (IRE)**[22] 7052 5-9-6 **69**.......................... TonyHamilton 8 58
(Richard Fahey) *in tch in midfield: shkn up and clsd to chse ldrs 2f: unable qck and lost pl over 1f out: wknd ins fnl f* **5/1**[2]

1m 38.11s (-0.09) **Going Correction** +0.025s/f (Slow)
**WFA** 3 from 4yo+ 3lb **10** Ran SP% **116.4**
Speed ratings (Par 103): **101,100,99,98,98 97,96,95,93,93**
CSF £20.95 CT £109.21 TOTE £3.10: £1.30, £2.20, £2.50; EX 21.80 Trifecta £140.10.
**Owner** Saeed Manana **Bred** Rabbah Bloodstock Limited **Trained** Newmarket, Suffolk

**FOCUS**
A few of these proved awkward before the start, but it went to the least-exposed runner in the field. The winning time was fractionally slower than the first division.

## 7771 HAPPY 50TH BIRTHDAY TOM FILLIES' H'CAP 7f 1y(P)
**5:35** (5:38) (Class 5) (0-75,77) 3-Y-O+ **£2,911** (£866; £432; £216) **Stalls Low**

Form RPR

1546 **1** **Dealer's Choice (IRE)**[22] 7056 3-9-3 **70**.......................... AndreaAtzeni 12 78
(Roger Varian) *swtchd lft sn after s: t.k.h: chsd ldrs: effrt over 1f out: drvn to ld ins fnl f: kpt on wl u.p* **17/2**

6300 **2** *3/4* **Dashing Poet**[20] 7127 3-8-7 **63**.......................... DavidEgan(3) 3 68
(Heather Main) *t.k.h: hld up wl in tch in midfield: rdn and hdwy on inner over 1f out: wnt 2nd and pressing wnr wl ins fnl f: kpt on but a hld* **16/1**

2213 **3** *nse* **Lady In Question (IRE)**[16] 7241 3-9-6 **73**.......................... TonyHamilton 1 78+
(Richard Fahey) *t.k.h: hld up in tch in last quartet: effrt and gd hdwy on inner over 1f out: chsd ldrs and swtchd rt ins fnl f: r.o wl to press for 2nd cl home: nt rch wnr* **7/2**[1]

5142 **4** *1/2* **Monteamiata (IRE)**[24] 7000 3-9-8 **75**.......................... LiamKeniry 4 79
(Ed Walker) *tk hold: led: rdn over 1f out: hdd and kpt on same pce ins fnl f: lost 2 pls wl ins fnl f* **11/2**[2]

020 **5** *nk* **High On Love (IRE)**[36] 6576 3-9-10 **77**.......................... JamieSpencer 9 80
(Charlie Fellowes) *chsd ldrs: effrt over 1f out: drvn 1f out: styd on same pce ins fnl f* **14/1**

000 **6** *shd* **Mississippi Miss**[22] 7058 3-8-9 **65**.......................... GeorgeWood(3) 5 68
(Dr Jon Scargill) *hld up in tch in last trio: clsd and swtchd rt over 1f out: hdwy and swtchd lft jst ins fnl f: chsd ldrs and styd on same pce wl ins fnl f* **20/1**

5253 **7** *1 1/2* **One Big Surprise**[55] 5869 5-9-8 **73**..........................(t[1]) ShaneKelly 13 73
(Richard Hughes) *t.k.h: chsd ldr: effrt to cl and press ldr ent fnl 2f tl no ex 1f out: wknd wl ins fnl f* **33/1**

1-11 **8** *shd* **Burren View Lady (IRE)**[29] 6831 7-8-12 **63**..........................(bt) BenCurtis 7 63
(Denis Gerard Hogan, Ire) *hmpd sn after s: hld up in midfield: wd and lost pl bnd 2f out: rallied 1f out: kpt on wl u.p ins fnl f: nt rch ldrs* **9/1**

4345 **9** *nk* **Anastazia**[34] 6656 5-9-2 **67**.......................... JoeyHaynes 10 66
(Paul D'Arcy) *stdd s: hld up in tch in last quartet: effrt and hdwy ent fnl f: kpt on wout threatening ldrs* **16/1**

055 **10** *1 1/4* **Chicago Star**[10] 7457 3-9-1 **68**.......................... JFEgan 2 62
(Mick Channon) *hld up in midfield: shuffled bk on inner bnd 4f out: rdn and hdwy over 1f out: keeping on same pce whn squeezed for room ins fnl f: no imp after* **7/1**[3]

-400 **11** *nse* **Wild Dancer**[59] 5711 4-9-4 **69**.......................... DavidProbert 6 64
(Patrick Chamings) *hld up in tch in midfield: effrt over 1f out: unable qck and wknd ins fnl f* **16/1**

-404 **12** *5* **Mistime (IRE)**[31] 6759 3-9-10 **77**.......................... JoeFanning 8 58
(Mark Johnston) *dwlt: hld up in tch but stuck wd: effrt ent fnl 2f: no imp: wknd fnl f* **8/1**

5460 **13** *2 1/4* **Many A Tale**[29] 6818 3-8-13 **66**.......................... SeanLevey 11 41
(Ismail Mohammed) *hld up in midfield: effrt ent fnl 2f: sn struggling and lost pl over 1f out: wknd fnl f* **11/1**

1m 25.37s (0.57) **Going Correction** +0.025s/f (Slow)
**WFA** 3 from 4yo+ 2lb **13** Ran SP% **122.1**
Speed ratings (Par 100): **97,96,96,95,95 95,93,93,92,91 91,85,83**
CSF £140.18 CT £591.15 TOTE £8.30: £2.60, £6.10, £2.50; EX 170.10 Trifecta £1207.30.
**Owner** J Shack & G Barnard **Bred** Jc Bloodstock & Goodwill Bloodstock **Trained** Newmarket, Suffolk

■ Stewards' Enquiry : Andrea Atzeni three-day ban: careless riding (19, 20, 22 Oct)

**FOCUS**
A modest fillies' handicap and a messy race, with the early pace slow and it didn't pick up until the final bend. As a result it paid to be handy. Suspect form. The winner has been rated close to her best.
T/Plt: £42.90 to a £1 stake. Pool: £79,111.91. 1,344.31 winning units. T/Qpdt: £13.40 to a £1 stake. Pool: £6,953.37. 381.70 winning units. **Steve Payne**

7772 - 7779a (Foreign Racing) - See Raceform Interactive

# 6916 ASCOT (R-H)
Friday, October 6

**OFFICIAL GOING: Good to soft (soft in places on round course)**
Wind: Light, half against Weather: Fine

## 7780 VEOLIA H'CAP 7f
**2:00** (2:01) (Class 4) (0-85,87) 3-Y-O+ **£6,469** (£1,925; £962; £481) **Stalls High**

Form RPR

0000 **1** **Shady McCoy (USA)**[27] 6918 7-7-9 **85**.......................... RyanMoore 17 98
(Ian Williams) *hld up wl in rr: gd prog on outer of gp 2f out: wl-timed run to ld ins fnl f: sn clr* **13/2**[2]

4313 **2** *1 1/2* **Hajjam**[20] 7156 3-8-12 **78**..........................(h) PhillipMakin 1 86
(David O'Meara) *lw; hld up wl in rr: gd prog on outer of gp over 2f out: rdn to ld 1f out: hdd and outpcd ins fnl f* **16/1**

4130 **3** *1* **Another Boy**[17] 7229 4-8-9 **73**..........................(p) HarryBentley 14 79
(Ralph Beckett) *trckd ldrs: plld out nr side of gp 2f out: rdn to chal 1f out: styd on same pce* **33/1**

5022 **4** *hd* **Alaadel**[28] 6874 4-9-1 **79**..........................(bt) JimCrowley 4 85+
(William Haggas) *hld up in midfield: prog 3f out: chal and upsides 1f out: one pce* **9/2**[1]

2136 **5** *2* **Black Caesar (IRE)**[22] 7094 6-9-0 **78**.......................... JamieSpencer 2 78
(Philip Hide) *racd alone on far side and on terms: jnd main gp and overall ldr 3f out: stl gng wl 2f out: hdd and fdd 1f out* **25/1**

2112 **6** *1/2* **Custard The Dragon**[136] 2922 4-9-7 **85**..........................(p) JoeFanning 8 84
(John Mackie) *hld up in midfield: prog to chse ldrs over 1f out: rdn and no imp after* **25/1**

-054 **7** *1/2* **My Amigo**[7] 7566 4-9-5 **83**..........................(p[1]) PJMcDonald 16 81
(K R Burke) *w ldrs: upsides fr 3f out to over 2f out: fdd fnl f* **14/1**

5525 **8** *1 3/4* **Fire Palace**[11] 7464 3-8-5 **71** oh1..........................(p[1]) PaulHanagan 6 63
(Robert Eddery) *v s.i.s and lost many l: in tch in rr: rdn on outer of gp 2f out: kpt on but no ch* **33/1**

2101 **9** *hd* **Crafty Madam (IRE)**[21] 7130 3-8-13 **79**.......................... SamHitchcott 11 70
(Clive Cox) *t.k.h: hld up bhd ldrs: rdn 2f out: fdd fnl f* **16/1**

2452 **10** *hd* **Esprit De Corps**[13] 7398 3-9-1 **81**..........................(p) KieranShoemark 12 72
(Roger Charlton) *blindfold off sltly late and dwlt: in tch in midfield: prog nr side of gp and cl up over 1f out: no prog after* **8/1**[3]

3436 **11** *1/2* **High Acclaim (USA)**[23] 7053 3-9-5 **85**..........................(v[1]) SilvestreDeSousa 3 74
(Roger Teal) *taken down early: t.k.h: trckd ldrs: gng wl enough whn squeezed for room 2f out: rdn and nt clr run over 1f out: fdd* **10/1**

005 **12** *nk* **Gothic Empire (IRE)**[40] 6484 5-9-2 **83**.......................... GeorgeWood(3) 18 73
(James Fanshawe) *dwlt: in tch towards rr: effrt on nr side of gp 2f out: no prog 1f out: wknd* **10/1**

0044 **13** *hd* **Moonraker**[13] 7405 5-9-3 **81**.......................... GrahamLee 10 70
(Mick Channon) *lw; hld up in rr: gng wl 3f out: coaxed along 2f out: sn rdn and no real prog* **14/1**

142 **14** *nk* **Cricklewood Green (USA)**[49] 6134 6-8-10 **79**.......... MitchGodwin(5) 9 67
(Sylvester Kirk) *hld up and sn detached in last: effrt over 2f out but no great prog* **10/1**

1630 **15** *2 1/4* **Fox Trotter (IRE)**[21] 7129 5-9-7 **85**.......................... CharlesBishop 5 67
(Brian Meehan) *on toes; w ldr: stl rt there over 2f out: wknd qckly wl over 1f out* **16/1**

-000 **16** *4* **Daschas**[13] 7404 3-8-9 **78**..........................(t) AaronJones(3) 13 48
(Stuart Williams) *nvr bttr than midfield: rdn and wknd 2f out* **50/1**

5254 **17** *3/4* **Plant Pot Power (IRE)**[17] 7229 3-9-3 **83**.......................... TomMarquand 7 51
(Richard Hannon) *w ldr: upsides over 3f out: wknd rapidly 2f out* **16/1**

644 **18** *1 1/2* **Scottish Glen**[72] 5302 11-9-6 **87**.......................... HectorCrouch(3) 15 52
(Patrick Chamings) *mde most to 3f out: wknd rapidly 2f out* **20/1**

1m 30.06s (2.46) **Going Correction** +0.475s/f (Yiel)
**WFA** 3 from 4yo+ 2lb **18** Ran SP% **127.1**
Speed ratings (Par 105): **104,102,101,100,98 98,97,95,95,95 94,94,93,93,90 86,85,83**
CSF £100.87 CT £3323.95 TOTE £7.20: £2.10, £3.80, £11.90, £1.40; EX 117.80 Trifecta £5783.00.
**Owner** Allwins Stables **Bred** Bluegrass Hall Llc **Trained** Portway, Worcs

**FOCUS**
The straight course was divided into two with a rail in the middle from the 1m start to 2.5f from the winning line. The stands' side course was used at this meeting. The going was good to soft (soft in places on round course). A competitive handicap which included the last two winners of the race. It was run at an honest pace with the first two home coming with their challenge towards the centre. A small step up from the runner-up, with the third rated close to form.

## 7781 NEPTUNE INVESTMENT MANAGEMENT CLASSIFIED STKS 1m (S)
**2:35** (2:37) (Class 3) 3-Y-O+ **£9,703** (£2,887; £1,443; £721) **Stalls High**

Form RPR

1344 **1** **Zwayyan**[28] 6881 4-9-3 **90**..........................(b[1]) FrankieDettori 8 98+
(William Haggas) *trckd ldrs: prog over 2f out: led over 1f out: drvn a l clr ins fnl f: idled last 50yds but hld on* **11/4**[1]

5050 **2** *nk* **One Word More (IRE)**[7] 7582 7-9-0 **89**..........(h) RachelRichardson(3) 2 96
(Tim Easterby) *trckd ldr: rdn to ld 2f out to over 1f out: chsd wnr after: a hld after but clsd again nr fin* **8/1**

1300 **3** 1¼ **Sibilance**[21] [7113] 3-8-11 90 PatDobbs 11 90
(Ralph Beckett) *hld up bhd ldrs: effrt 2f out: rdn to chse ldng pair fnl f: styd on but nvr able to chal* **16/1**

0003 **4** 1¼ **Heaven's Guest (IRE)**[27] [6918] 7-9-3 90 PaulHanagan 9 90
(Richard Fahey) *hld up in midfield: prog 2f out: drvn to dispute 3rd fnl f: one pce last 100yds* **8/1**

5004 **5** 1¾ **Summer Icon**[20] [7154] 4-9-0 90 GrahamLee 3 83
(Mick Channon) *sltly on toes; stdd s: plld hrd and hld up in rr: prog over 2f out: no imp on ldrs fr jst over 1f out* **33/1**

2614 **6** ¾ **Pastoral Player**[15] [7340] 10-9-0 88 CharlieBennett(3) 12 85
(Hughie Morrison) *blindfold off late and slowly away: hld up in last pair: shkn up 2f out: styd on fr over 1f out: nvr able to threaten* **33/1**

4502 **7** *hd* **Storm Ahead (IRE)**[28] [6873] 4-9-3 90 (p) HayleyTurner 7 84
(Marcus Tregoning) *trckd ldr: upsides 3f out to 2f out: sn rdn and fdd* **9/2**[3]

1006 **8** 2 **Taurean Star (IRE)**[24] [7025] 4-9-3 89 JamieSpencer 4 81
(Michael Bell) *hld up in rr: trying to make prog whn nt clr run and swtchd lft over 1f out: no ch whn n.m.r 100yds out and eased* **12/1**

1161 **9** ½ **Golden Goal (IRE)**[36] [6617] 3-8-9 89 PaddyBradley(5) 6 78
(Saeed bin Suroor) *racd freely: led to 2f out: sn btn* **3/1**[2]

0140 **10** 3¼ **Native Soldier (IRE)**[22] [7083] 3-9-0 76 (p) DanielMuscutt 1 71
(John Flint) *hld up in last pair: rdn and wknd over 2f out* **66/1**

024 **11** 2¾ **Zain Star (IRE)**[30] [6817] 3-9-0 81 JFEgan 10 64
(John Butler) *sltly on toes; trckd ldr: rdn and wknd 2f out* **33/1**

1m 44.8s (4.00) **Going Correction** +0.475s/f (Yiel)
**WFA** 3 from 4yo+ 3lb **11** Ran SP% **116.0**
Speed ratings (Par 107): **99,98,97,96,94 93,93,91,91,87 85**
CSF £24.25 TOTE £3.10: £1.30, £2.70, £3.40; EX 29.00 Trifecta £306.20.
**Owner** Al Shaqab Racing **Bred** Newsells Park Stud & Cheveley Park Stud **Trained** Newmarket, Suffolk

**FOCUS**
A useful contest with nine of the 11 runners rated within 2lb of the ceiling. It was run at a steady pace with the field racing up the centre. The runner-up has been rated close to this year's form.

## 7782 ORIGINAL HARROGATE WATER H'CAP 6f
3:10 (3:15) (Class 2) (0-105,105) 3-Y-O
**£18,675** (£5,592; £2,796; £1,398; £699; £351) **Stalls** High

Form RPR

3446 **1** **Nobly Born**[27] [6922] 3-8-12 **96** (b[1]) FrankieDettori 10 107
(John Gosden) *mde all: shkn up 2f out: asserted and drvn over 1f out: clr fnl f: readily* **9/1**

1164 **2** 2 **Silent Echo**[48] [6198] 3-8-6 **90** (h) HarryBentley 8 94
(Roger Charlton) *lw; chsd wnr: cl up over 1f out: sn drvn: kpt on but nvr able to chal after* **10/1**

4-05 **3** *nse* **Waqaas**[56] [5890] 3-8-6 **90** TomMarquand 4 94+
(Charles Hills) *hld up in rr: rdn on outer of gp 2f out: styd on fr over 1f out: tk 3rd last strides* **50/1**

0531 **4** *hd* **Bacchus**[48] [6198] 3-9-7 **105** AdamKirby 11 108
(Brian Meehan) *trckd ldrs: shkn up 2f out: styd on fnl f to press for 2nd last 100yds: no threat to wnr* **8/1**[3]

2151 **5** ½ **Ekhtiyaar**[85] [4813] 3-9-2 **100** JimCrowley 2 101
(Roger Varian) *wl in tch: prog to dispute 2nd over 1f out: nvr able to chal wnr: one pce last 100yds* **9/4**[1]

30 **6** ¾ **Ultimate Avenue (IRE)**[41] [6419] 3-9-2 **100** (t) JamieSpencer 14 99
(Ed Walker) *lw; heavily restrained s: hld up in last: tried to make prog over 1f out: kpt on but no hope of rching ldrs* **8/1**[3]

5110 **7** *nk* **Dark Power (IRE)**[48] [6197] 3-8-6 **90** (t) DavidProbert 12 88
(Clive Cox) *pressed wnr: rdn wl over 1f out: hanging and nt qckn after: steadily lost pl* **12/1**

0001 **8** *nse* **Victory Angel (IRE)**[66] [5513] 3-9-1 **99** SilvestreDeSousa 1 101+
(Roger Varian) *hld up in rr: shkn up 2f out: kpt on one pce fr over 1f out and nvr able to rch ldrs* **16/1**

2331 **9** *nk* **The Feathered Nest (IRE)**[69] [5423] 3-8-2 **86** (p) PaulHanagan 9 83
(Richard Fahey) *chsd ldrs: rdn wl over 1f out: no prog and lost pl sn after* **7/1**[2]

-600 **10** ½ **Repton (IRE)**[27] [6922] 3-8-3 **90** HollieDoyle(3) 13 85
(Richard Hannon) *sweating; chsd ldrs: rdn and nt qckn 2f out: lost pl and wl btn in last pair over 1f out* **33/1**

0452 **11** *hd* **Smokey Lane (IRE)**[11] [7461] 3-8-8 **92** JoeFanning 6 87
(Christian Williams) *stdd s: hld up in rr: rdn 2f out: nvr able to make significant prog* **33/1**

2140 **12** *nk* **Parnassian (IRE)**[46] [6275] 3-8-3 **87** MartinDwyer 7 81
(Amanda Perrett) *chsd ldrs: rdn 2f out: lost pl u.p over 1f out and wl btn after* **33/1**

2130 **13** 1 **Merlin**[20] [7144] 3-8-11 **95** RyanMoore 3 86
(Michael Bell) *w ldrs: stl disputing 2nd over 1f out: sn wknd tamely* **8/1**[3]

1m 15.57s (1.07) **Going Correction** +0.475s/f (Yiel) **13** Ran SP% **120.1**
Speed ratings (Par 107): **111,108,108,108,107 106,105,105,105,104 104,104,102**
CSF £93.71 CT £4234.26 TOTE £10.40: £3.20, £3.80, £10.60; EX 136.90 Trifecta £9419.40.
**Owner** Cheveley Park Stud **Bred** Cheveley Park Stud Ltd **Trained** Newmarket, Suffolk

**FOCUS**
They went a fair pace for this decent handicap with the winner making all. It paid to race handy. The runner-up has been rated to form and the third to his 2yo best.

## 7783 LONDONMETRIC NOEL MURLESS STKS (LISTED RACE) 1m 6f 34y
3:45 (3:46) (Class 1) 3-Y-O
**£20,982** (£7,955; £3,981; £1,983; £995; £499) **Stalls** Low

Form RPR

3410 **1** *nse* **Raheen House (IRE)**[20] [7147] 3-9-6 110 JamieSpencer 1 111
(Brian Meehan) *hld up in last pair: clsd fr 2f out: hrd rdn to chal ins fnl f: jnd ldr whn bmpd 50yds out: jst failed: fin 2nd: awrdd the r* **9/2**

1312 **2** **Weekender**[13] [7397] 3-9-1 98 FrankieDettori 5 106
(John Gosden) *trckd ldng trio: pushed along 3f out: rdn to cl 2f out: narrow ld jst over 1f out: edgd lft u.p and bmpd rival 50yds out: jst hld on: fin 1st: disqualified and plcd 2nd* **4/1**[3]

2610 **3** ¾ **Hochfeld (IRE)**[27] [6930] 3-9-1 101 PJMcDonald 3 105
(Mark Johnston) *lw; racd quite freely: led: rdn 2f out: hdd jst over 1f out: kpt on wl but jst hld fnl 100yds* **16/1**

3241 **4** ¾ **On To Victory**[21] [7124] 3-9-1 103 TomMarquand 6 104
(Eve Johnson Houghton) *trckd ldr: rdn to chal fr 2f out: nt qckn over 1f out: lost pl but stl cl up ins fnl f: kpt on* **7/2**[2]

1133 **5** ½ **Mount Moriah**[26] [6976] 3-9-1 106 HarryBentley 2 103
(Ralph Beckett) *lw; trckd ldng pair: tried to chal on inner 2f out: nt qckn over 1f out: one pce fnl f* **9/4**[1]

1352 **6** 15 **Zenon (IRE)**[15] [7337] 3-9-1 96 (b) RyanMoore 4 87
(John Gosden) *hld up in last: clsd 4f out: rdn and no rspnse over 2f out: sn wknd* **15/2**

3m 9.76s **6** Ran SP% **108.8**
CSF £21.04 TOTE £5.50: £2.40, £2.10; EX 21.20 Trifecta £164.40.
**Owner** J L Day **Bred** Sunderland Holdings Inc **Trained** Manton, Wilts

**FOCUS**
Rail movement added 33yds to race distance. This Listed contest had been won by some nice types in recent years, including Big Orange in 2014 and Alyssa in 2016. It was run at a steady pace that turned into a sprint up the straight and produced a thrilling finish, with the placings of the first two home reversed in the stewards room. The third has been rated close to form.

## 7784 TROY ASSET MANAGEMENT H'CAP 7f
4:20 (4:20) (Class 3) (0-95,94) 3-Y-O
**£8,409** (£2,502; £1,250; £625) **Stalls** High

Form RPR

1244 **1** **Mukalal**[41] [6419] 3-9-6 **93** JimCrowley 4 100
(Marcus Tregoning) *taken down early: mde all: clr 1/2-way: shkn up over 1f out: drvn: edgd lft and all out fnl f: jnd last 50yds: clung on* **9/2**[3]

4110 **2** *nse* **Tribute Act**[66] [5506] 3-8-11 **87** GeorgeWood(3) 6 94+
(James Fanshawe) *lw; sltly impeded s: t.k.h and sn prom: tk 2nd 3f out: rdn 2f out: clsd fr over 1f out: edgd lft fnl f: jnd wnr last 50yds: jst pipped* **9/2**[3]

600 **3** ¾ **Sea Fox (IRE)**[13] [7397] 3-9-2 **89** (t) FranBerry 8 94
(David Evans) *wnt lft s: hld up and sn in last: rdn and prog fr 2f out: edgd lft fnl f but clsd on ldng pair: jst unable to chal* **25/1**

0036 **4** 5 **Medici Banchiere**[21] [7118] 3-8-12 **88** CliffordLee(3) 2 80
(K R Burke) *chsd wnr to 3f out: readily lft bhd fr 2f out* **16/1**

2112 **5** 2 **Bengal Lancer**[23] [7053] 3-8-8 **86** ManuelFernandes(5) 7 72
(Ian Williams) *sltly impeded s: sn chsd ldrs: urged along 3f out: steadily wknd fr 2f out* **7/2**[2]

0521 **6** 1¾ **Graphite Storm**[24] [7025] 3-9-7 **94** AdamKirby 5 75
(Clive Cox) *in tch: rdn and nt qckn over 2f out: sn btn* **3/1**[1]

4401 **7** 4½ **Berkshire Boy (IRE)**[17] [7229] 3-9-0 **87** (b) RobHornby 1 56
(Andrew Balding) *chsd ldrs: rdn sn after 1/2-way: wknd over 2f out* **5/1**

0344 **8** 1 **Maths Prize**[28] [6870] 3-8-13 **86** (p) KieranShoemark 3 53
(Roger Charlton) *hld up: rdn 3f out: no prog and sn wl btn* **20/1**

1m 29.79s (2.19) **Going Correction** +0.475s/f (Yiel) **8** Ran SP% **114.7**
Speed ratings (Par 105): **106,105,105,99,97 95,89,88**
CSF £25.13 CT £456.06 TOTE £4.90: £1.40, £2.00, £4.50; EX 27.20 Trifecta £309.00.
**Owner** Hamdan Al Maktoum **Bred** Shadwell Estate Company Limited **Trained** Whitsbury, Hants

**FOCUS**
A fair handicap run at a sound pace with the front three finishing a long way clear. A small pb from the winner.

## 7785 CANACCORD GENUITY GORDON CARTER H'CAP 1m 7f 209y
4:55 (4:55) (Class 3) (0-95,94) 3-Y-O+
**£8,409** (£2,502; £1,250; £625) **Stalls** High

Form RPR

2023 **1** **Dominating (GER)**[14] [7359] 3-8-11 **86** PJMcDonald 9 97+
(Mark Johnston) *trckd ldrs: led jst over 2f out: drvn for home and sn at least 2 l clr: hrd pressed ins fnl f: edgd lft to join chalr and fnd ex nr fin* **3/1**[1]

21/2 **2** *nk* **Altaayil (IRE)**[22] [7096] 6-9-2 **85** HectorCrouch(3) 10 94
(Gary Moore) *trapped out wd to 1/2-way: hld up in last trio: prog 3f out: rdn to chse wnr wl over 1f out: clsd to chal ins fnl f and upsides 100yds out: nt qckn nr fin* **9/2**[2]

002 **3** 4½ **Perfect Summer (IRE)**[21] [7110] 7-8-9 **75** (b) FranBerry 3 79
(Ian Williams) *pressed ldr: led 4f out: hdd jst over 2f out: racd awkwardly and sn outpcd: clung on for 3rd* **16/1**

0460 **4** *shd* **Eye Of The Storm (IRE)**[14] [7354] 7-9-10 **90** PatDobbs 2 93
(Amanda Perrett) *sn trckd ldng pair: shkn up to dispute 2nd briefly 2f out but sn outpcd by ldng pair: n.d after but pressed for 3rd after* **14/1**

6653 **5** 1¼ **Gavlar**[13] [7412] 6-9-5 **85** HarryBentley 4 87
(William Knight) *settled in 7th: rdn and no prog wl over 2f out: kpt on fr over 1f out but n.d* **12/1**

210/ **6** 1½ **Big Easy (GER)**[100] [6539] 10-9-5 **85** (p) AdamKirby 7 85
(Ian Williams) *lw; racd on and off the bridle in 6th: drvn 3f out: nt pce to cl on ldrs fnl 2f* **10/1**

3124 **7** ¾ **With Pleasure**[15] [7336] 4-8-6 **75** oh4 GeorgeWood(3) 8 74
(John Flint) *hld up in last pair: pushed along 3f out: rdn and passed a few fr 2f out but nvr in it* **8/1**

2-00 **8** 7 **Rite To Reign**[14] [7359] 6-9-2 **82** DavidProbert 5 73
(Philip McBride) *lw; chsd ldrs in 5th: rdn wl over 2f out: no prog and sn btn: wknd qckly fnl f* **14/1**

3100 **9** ½ **Master Singer (USA)**[41] [6445] 3-9-5 **94** (p) RobertHavlin 6 86
(John Gosden) *hld up in last pair: effrt on outer over 3f out: sn rdn and no prog: wl btn 2f out* **5/1**[3]

2060 **10** 54 **Mister Manduro (FR)**[13] [7402] 3-9-1 **90** (b[1]) JoeFanning 1 17
(Mark Johnston) *led to 4f out: wknd qckly 3f out: t.o whn virtually p.u nr fin* **7/1**

3m 36.38s (7.38) **Going Correction** +0.65s/f (Yiel)
**WFA** 3 from 4yo+ 9lb **10** Ran SP% **119.5**
Speed ratings (Par 107): **107,106,104,104,103 103,102,99,99,72**
CSF £16.59 CT £188.70 TOTE £3.50: £1.40, £1.80, £3.70; EX 16.40 Trifecta £92.50.
**Owner** A D Spence **Bred** Gestut Etzean **Trained** Middleham Moor, N Yorks
■ Stewards' Enquiry : Hector Crouch two-day ban; used whip above the permitted level (Oct 20-22)
Harry Bentley two-day ban; used whip above the permitted level (Oct 20-22)

**FOCUS**
Rail movement added 33yds to race distance. A competitive staying handicap run at a sound pace. It's been rated around the third.
T/Jkpt: Not won. T/Plt: £895.70 to a £1 stake. Pool: £157,149.30 - 128.07 winning units. T/Qpdt: £101.70 to a £1 stake. Pool: £12,860.28 - 93.50 winning units. **Jonathan Neesom**

# 7756 CHELMSFORD (A.W) (L-H)
Friday, October 6

**OFFICIAL GOING: Polytrack: standard**
Wind: virtually nil Weather: dry

## 7786 BET TOTEPLACEPOT AT BETFRED.COM NOVICE AUCTION STKS 1m (P)
5:45 (5:45) (Class 5) 2-Y-O
**£4,528** (£1,347; £673; £336) **Stalls** Low

Form RPR

4522 **1** **Merkava**[8] [7535] 2-8-13 69 MartinHarley 6 74
(Robyn Brisland) *mde all: rdn and qcknd to assert ent fnl f: in command and r.o wl ins fnl f: comf* **7/4**[2]

204 **2** 1 ¾ **Dance To Paris**[13] 7403 2-8-11 73 JosephineGordon 5 68
(Lucy Wadham) *trckd ldrs: effrt ent fnl 2f: chsd wnr over 1f out: kpt on same pce and no imp ins fnl f* **11/8**[1]

0 **3** *hd* **Sky Rocket**[21] 7120 2-8-9 0 MitchGodwin(5) 7 71
(Sylvester Kirk) *hld up in tch in midfield: swtchd rt and effrt over 1f out: hdwy 1f out: kpt on to press for 2nd nr fin: no threat to wnr* **33/1**

2350 **4** ¾ **Tranquil Soul**[23] 7057 2-8-9 66 TedDurcan 3 64
(David Lanigan) *in tch in midfield: effrt ent fnl 2f: styd on same pce ins fnl f* **10/3**[3]

00 **5** 4 ½ **Roof Garden**[16] 7281 2-9-0 0 JoeyHaynes 4 58
(Mark H Tompkins) *hld up in tch in last pair: effrt over 2f out: unable qck and outpcd over 1f out: wknd ins fnl f* **33/1**

5 **6** 3 ¼ **Hidden Dream (IRE)**[45] 6286 2-8-5 0 AaronJones(3) 2 44
(Christine Dunnett) *taken down early and led to post: trckd wnr: rdn ent fnl 2f: lost pl qckly jst over 1f out: wknd ins fnl f* **33/1**

**7** 1 ¾ **Pretty Pearl** 2-8-7 0 PaoloSirigu 1 39
(Robert Eddery) *hld up in tch in last pair: effrt u.p on inner over 1f out: sn btn and wknd fnl f* **25/1**

1m 39.65s (-0.25) **Going Correction** -0.20s/f (Stan) 7 Ran SP% **114.2**
Speed ratings (Par 95): **93,91,91,90,85 82,80**
CSF £4.42 TOTE £2.40: £1.40, £1.20; EX 5.00 Trifecta £49.60.
**Owner** Franconson Partners **Bred** Llety Farms **Trained** Newmarket, Suffolk

**FOCUS**
Modest novice form. The second, fifth and sixth offer perspective to the level of the form.

## 7787 BET TOTEJACKPOT AT BETFRED.COM NURSERY H'CAP 6f (P)
**6:15** (6:15) (Class 4) (0-85,84) 2-Y-O **£5,822** (£1,732; £865; £432) **Stalls** Centre

Form RPR

4321 **1** **Expecting**[27] 6950 2-9-1 78 RyanMoore 2 83
(Charles Hills) *pushed into ld sn after s: mde rest: rdn and qcknd clr over 1f out: in command and r.o wl ins fnl f* **15/8**[1]

0216 **2** 2 ¼ **Central City (IRE)**[15] 7335 2-9-4 81 JamesDoyle 4 79
(Hugo Palmer) *wl in tch in midfield: swtchd rt and effrt wl over 1f out: hdwy and edging lft ins fnl f: wnt 2nd wl ins fnl f: kpt on but nvr threatening wnr* **3/1**[2]

6434 **3** *nk* **Fink Hill (USA)**[14] 7363 2-8-7 70 (b[1]) ConnorBeasley 1 67
(Richard Guest) *taken down early: t.k.h: chsd ldrs: effrt on inner over 1f out: chsd clr wnr jst ins fnl f: kpt on same pce and lost 2nd wl ins fnl f* **9/2**

6353 **4** 1 ½ **Another Day Of Sun (IRE)**[14] 7363 2-8-11 74 TedDurcan 6 66
(Mick Channon) *stdd s: sn niggled along in last pair: hdwy on outer and travelling bttr over 2f out: effrt 2f out: unable qck ent fnl f: wknd ins fnl f* **8/1**

4336 **5** ¾ **Story Minister (IRE)**[52] 6036 2-8-6 69 (p) NickyMackay 3 59
(Tom Dascombe) *in tch in last pair: dropped to last and rdn over 2f out: sme hdwy and swtchd rt ins fnl f: kpt on: no threat to wnr* **20/1**

1002 **6** ¾ **Emilia James**[15] 7318 2-9-7 84 FrannyNorton 5 71
(Mark Johnston) *pressed wnr tl unable qck u.p over 1f out: outpcd and lost 2nd jst ins fnl f: sn wknd* **7/2**[3]

1m 11.88s (-1.82) **Going Correction** -0.20s/f (Stan) 6 Ran SP% **116.1**
Speed ratings (Par 97): **104,101,100,98,97 96**
CSF £8.17 TOTE £2.40: £1.20, £2.10; EX 5.70 Trifecta £23.30.
**Owner** Kangyu International Racing (HK) Limited **Bred** D J And Mrs Deer **Trained** Lambourn, Berks

**FOCUS**
A bit of a tactical affair, the winner dominating things from the front.

## 7788 BET TOTEQUADPOT AT BETFRED.COM NOVICE STKS 7f (P)
**6:45** (6:47) (Class 5) 2-Y-O **£4,528** (£1,347; £673; £336) **Stalls** Low

Form RPR

21 **1** **Society Power (IRE)**[30] 6827 2-9-9 0 JamesDoyle 3 84+
(William Haggas) *hld up wl in tch in midfield: ct on heels and hmpd 5f out: nt clr run and swtchd lft over 1f out: qcknd ins fnl f to ld wl ins fnl f: sn in command: comf* **4/5**[1]

23 **2** ¾ **Barig Al Thumama**[49] 6146 2-9-2 0 DanielMuscutt 2 74
(Marco Botti) *trckd ldrs: swtchd rt and effrt to press wnr over 1f out: drvn to ld ins fnl f: hdd and no ex* **10/1**

06 **3** 1 ¾ **Topapinion**[34] 6683 2-9-2 0 ShaneKelly 14 69
(Mark H Tompkins) *stdd s: clsd and in tch in midfield after 2f: effrt ent fnl 2f: swtchd rt over 1f out: styd on wl u.p ins fnl f: wnt 3rd last stride* **100/1**

**4** *shd* **On The Warpath** 2-9-2 0 LukeMorris 1 69
(Sir Mark Prescott Bt) *led: rdn over 1f out: hdd ins fnl f: no ex and outpcd wl ins fnl f: lost 3rd last stride* **33/1**

34 **5** *nk* **Zaajer**[21] 7128 2-9-2 0 DaneO'Neill 13 68
(Owen Burrows) *trckd ldrs: effrt over 1f out: pressing ldrs but unable qck 1f out: outpcd fnl 100yds* **4/1**[2]

00 **6** 3 ½ **Elsaakb (USA)**[46] 6260 2-9-2 0 (p[1]) RobertTart 10 59
(John Gosden) *dwlt and pushed along leaving early: clsd into midfield and t.k.h after 2f: swtchd rt and rdn wl over 1f out: sn outpcd: wknd ins fnl f* **16/1**

0 **7** *nk* **Macho Mover (IRE)**[13] 7391 2-9-2 0 CharlesBishop 6 58
(Mick Channon) *in tch in midfield after 2f: rdn and unable qck over 1f out: wl hld and kpt on same fnl f* **66/1**

0 **8** *hd* **Billycock Hill**[14] 7352 2-9-2 0 RichardKingscote 9 57
(Tom Dascombe) *w ldr tl unable qck and losing pl whn impeded over 1f out: wknd ins fnl f* **14/1**

0 **9** 1 ¾ **Al Hareth (IRE)**[9] 7511 2-9-2 0 (p) StevieDonohoe 8 53
(George Peckham) *hld up wl in tch in midfield: effrt u.p but unable qck over 1f out: wknd ins fnl f* **66/1**

**10** ½ **Nasee** 2-9-2 0 RyanMoore 15 51+
(Sir Michael Stoute) *wnt rt s and slowly away: rn green: pushed and clsd into midfield on outer after 2f: rdn over 2f out: lost pl and btn over 1f out: wknd fnl f* **5/1**[3]

**11** 13 **College King** 2-8-9 0 JacobMitchell(7) 7 16
(Christine Dunnett) *v.s.a: nvr on terms* **150/1**

0 **12** ½ **Saint Anthony**[16] 7280 2-9-2 0 JoeyHaynes 5 15
(Mark H Tompkins) *sn outpcd in last trio: n.d* **100/1**

**13** 1 **Feel The Wrath (IRE)** 2-8-13 0 CharlieBennett(3) 11 12
(Denis Quinn) *sn outpcd in last trio: n.d* **100/1**

1m 26.18s (-1.02) **Going Correction** -0.20s/f (Stan) 13 Ran SP% **123.4**
Speed ratings (Par 95): **97,96,94,94,93 89,89,89,87,86 71,71,69**
CSF £11.24 TOTE £1.60: £1.02, £2.70, £33.10; EX 9.20 Trifecta £828.00.
**Owner** Sheikh Rashid Dalmook Al Maktoum **Bred** Tally-Ho Stud **Trained** Newmarket, Suffolk

**FOCUS**
A fair novice, and a decent performance from the winner, who defied a penalty. The runner-up helps set the opening level.

## 7789 BET TOTEEXACTA AT BETFRED.COM H'CAP 7f (P)
**7:15** (7:21) (Class 4) (0-85,85) 3-Y-O+ **£6,469** (£1,925; £962; £481) **Stalls** Low

Form RPR

3134 **1** **Blue On Blue (USA)**[15] 7321 3-8-11 77 (h) RobertTart 2 85+
(John Gosden) *wnt rt s: in tch in midfield: effrt on inner to chse ldrs 1f out: styd on u.p to ld 75yds out: rdn out* **7/2**[1]

4024 **2** ¾ **Easy Tiger**[13] 7404 5-9-1 84 ManuelFernandes(5) 3 91
(Malcolm Saunders) *missed break and squeezed for room s: rcvrd and in tch in midfield: rdn over 3f out: swtchd rt and effrt wd wl over 1f out: pressed ldrs ins fnl f: styd on to go 2nd towards fin* **4/1**[2]

3531 **3** ½ **Miracle Garden**[13] 7408 5-8-12 76 (v) RichardKingscote 5 82
(Ian Williams) *trckd ldrs and travelled strly: swtchd rt and effrt over 1f out: rdn to chal 1f out: kpt on same pce u.p wl ins fnl f: lost 2nd towards fin* **7/1**

0000 **4** 1 ¼ **Pearl Spectre (USA)**[11] 7456 6-9-0 85 NicolaCurrie(7) 16 88
(Phil McEntee) *led: rdn wl over 1f out: kpt on wl u.p tl hdd 75yds out: no ex and wknd towards fin* **33/1**

2236 **5** 1 ¾ **Fieldsman (USA)**[15] 7321 5-9-1 79 SilvestreDeSousa 4 77
(David O'Meara) *chsd ldrs: effrt to chal u.p over 1f out: no ex ins fnl f: wknd fnl 75yds* **5/1**[3]

002 **6** 1 ¾ **Archer's Arrow (USA)**[28] 6882 3-8-10 79 LewisEdmunds(3) 10 71
(Saeed bin Suroor) *hld up in tch in midfield: effrt over 1f out: unable qck and styd on same pce ins fnl f* **6/1**

0412 **7** 1 ¼ **Rouge Nuage (IRE)**[15] 7321 7-8-13 77 JimmyQuinn 7 67
(Conrad Allen) *in tch in midfield: rdn 3f out: outpcd and lost pl over 1f out: kpt on same pce and no threat to ldrs fnl f* **20/1**

5025 **8** 1 **Procurator (IRE)**[83] 4910 3-8-12 78 RyanMoore 1 64
(Richard Hannon) *hld up in tch in midfield: shkn up over 1f out: nt clrest of runs jst over 1f out: wknd ins fnl f* **12/1**

6100 **9** *shd* **Groupie**[56] 5881 3-8-12 78 AndrewMullen 13 64
(Tom Tate) *stdd s: t.k.h: hld up in tch towards rr: hdwy on inner over 1f out: no imp ins fnl f* **50/1**

4400 **10** *nk* **Ice Royal (IRE)**[162] 2116 4-9-7 85 DougieCostello 12 71
(Jamie Osborne) *hld up in tch towards rr: effrt and swtchd rt over 1f out: no imp and wl hld fnl f* **20/1**

0540 **11** 3 **Athassel**[34] 6672 8-9-3 81 ShaneKelly 9 59
(David Evans) *a towards rr: effrt over 1f out: no imp: wknd fnl f* **25/1**

000 **12** ½ **Tavener**[7] 7572 5-8-10 74 (p) TomQueally 6 51
(David C Griffiths) *w ldr: rdn ent fnl 2f: lost pl and swtchd rt over 1f out: wknd fnl f* **50/1**

2406 **13** 1 ¼ **Red Touch (USA)**[36] 6637 5-8-9 73 (p) LukeMorris 11 46
(Michael Appleby) *sn drvn along in last trio: n.d* **50/1**

3431 **14** 6 **Gold Hunter (IRE)**[15] 7321 7-8-10 79 (p) PaddyPilley(5) 15 36
(Steve Flook) *hld up in tch in midfield on on outer: losing pl whn hmpd over 1f out: bhd and eased ins fnl f* **25/1**

1m 23.86s (-3.34) **Going Correction** -0.20s/f (Stan)
**WFA** 3 from 4yo+ 2lb 14 Ran SP% **119.4**
Speed ratings (Par 105): **111,110,109,108,106 104,102,101,101,101 97,97,95,88**
CSF £14.66 CT £79.21 TOTE £3.50: £1.60, £1.80, £2.40; EX 14.10 Trifecta £102.40.
**Owner** George Strawbridge **Bred** Alberta Davies **Trained** Newmarket, Suffolk
■ Favourite Treat and Siege Of Boston were withdrawn. Prices at time of withdrawal 50-1 and 10-1. Rule 4 applies to all bets - deduction 5p in the pound.

**FOCUS**
A competitive heat run at a sound gallop. It's been rated around the third to his latest form.

## 7790 BET TOTETRIFECTA AT BETFRED.COM H'CAP 2m (P)
**7:45** (7:50) (Class 6) (0-60,66) 3-Y-O **£3,234** (£962; £481; £240) **Stalls** Low

Form RPR

0303 **1** **Black Prince (FR)**[30] 6820 3-9-0 53 (t) JFEgan 10 59
(Anthony Honeyball) *chsd ldr for 4f: styd chsng ldrs tl rdn to chse ldr again over 3f out: led and hrd pressed ins fnl f: hld on gamely: dismntd after fin* **6/1**[3]

003 **2** ½ **Mr Davies**[8] 7537 3-9-4 57 TomQueally 2 62
(David Brown) *chsd ldrs: effrt over 2f out: ev ch fnl f: kpt on wl u.p but hld towards fin* **10/1**

3422 **3** *hd* **Broughtons Admiral**[17] 7253 3-9-7 60 (p) StevieDonohoe 5 65
(Henry Spiller) *hld up in tch in last quartet: hdwy over 2f out: pressing ldrs u.p 1f out: edging lft ins fnl f: styd on wl towards fin* **20/1**

-606 **4** 3 ¾ **Legalized**[17] 7248 3-8-7 46 FrannyNorton 4 47
(James Given) *hld up in tch in midfield: effrt over 2f out: edgd lft over 1f out: styd on ins fnl f: no threat to ldrs* **33/1**

3201 **5** ½ **Snowy Winter (USA)**[8] 7537 3-9-13 66 6ex (t) OisinMurphy 11 66
(Archie Watson) *stdd s: hld up wl in tch in midfield: effrt to chse ldrs over 2f out: no ex 1f out: wknd ins fnl f* **9/4**[2]

0321 **6** *shd* **Alternate Route**[10] 7490 3-9-13 66 6ex (p) LukeMorris 8 66
(Sir Mark Prescott Bt) *bustled along leaving stalls: hdwy to chse ldr after 4f: led 4f out: rdn ent fnl 2f: drvn over 1f out: hdd ins fnl f: sn wknd* **5/4**[1]

4400 **7** 3 ½ **Indian Red**[15] 7319 3-9-7 60 JoeyHaynes 9 56
(Mark H Tompkins) *stdd s: t.k.h: hld up in last pair: effrt and sme hdwy over 2f out: kpt on but no threat to ldrs fr over 1f out* **12/1**

0-53 **8** 2 **Fortia**[17] 7253 3-9-6 59 SilvestreDeSousa 6 52
(Dean Ivory) *midfield: effrt 3f out: no imp and wl hld over 1f out: plugged on* **14/1**

-000 **9** 13 **Street Jester**[36] 6611 3-8-7 46 oh1 RobHornby 12 24
(Robert Stephens) *hld up in last trio: reminder after 4f: effrt 3f out: sn struggling and wl btn whn hung lft over 1f out: wknd* **100/1**

0600 **10** 15 **Jump Around**[18] 7210 3-8-4 46 oh1 (t[1]) HollieDoyle(3) 7 6
(Ali Stronge) *t.k.h: hld up in last pair: rdn 4f out: lost tch 2f out: t.o: dismntd after fin (lame)* **66/1**

-000 **11** 5 **Lulu The Rocket**[36] 6621 3-8-9 51 (h) TimClark(3) 1 5
(John Butler) *t.k.h: led tl 4f out: lost pl u.p 3f out: wl bhd fnl f: t.o* **50/1**

06-0 **12** 30 **Myhorsewithnoname (IRE)**[17] 7230 3-8-4 46 oh1 (t[1]) AaronJones(3) 3
(Mark Hoad) *midfield: rdn 5f out: steadily lost pl: bhd and lost tch 2f out: eased fnl f: t.o* **100/1**

3m 28.56s (-1.44) **Going Correction** -0.20s/f (Stan) 12 Ran SP% **126.1**
Speed ratings (Par 99): **95,94,94,92,92 92,90,89,83,75 73,58**
CSF £65.36 CT £1158.14 TOTE £6.60: £1.80, £2.60, £3.50; EX 79.80 Trifecta £651.20.
**Owner** Owners For Owners: Black Prince **Bred** S A R L Haras Du Logis Saint Germain **Trained** Mosterton, Dorset

**FOCUS**
A moderate staying handicap run at a sound gallop. The third and fourth help set the opening level.

## 7791 BET TOTEWIN AT BETFRED.COM H'CAP (DIV I) 1m (P)
**8:15** (8:28) (Class 6) (0-65,67) 3-Y-O+ **£3,234** (£962; £481; £240) **Stalls** Low

Form RPR

4034 **1** **Pass The Cristal (IRE)**[8] 7540 3-9-1 **61**.................... DougieCostello 10 67
(William Muir) *hld up in tch in rr: stl last and nt clr run 2f: swtchd lft and hdwy towards inner over 1f out: str run ins fnl f to ld fnl 50yds: sn in command and eased* **16/1**

5156 **2** *1/2* **African Blessing**[23] 7058 4-9-9 **66**.................... BenCurtis 5 71
(Charlie Wallis) *chsd ldrs: wnt 2nd 4f out: rdn and ev ch over 1f out: drvn to ld jst ins fnl f: hdd and nt match pce of wnr fnl 50yds* **12/1**

5332 **3** *1 1/4* **Break The Silence**[18] 7216 3-8-6 **52**.................... KieranO'Neill 2 54
(Scott Dixon) *led: rdn over 1f out: hdd jst ins fnl f: no ex and outpcd wl ins fnl f* **6/1[3]**

5612 **4** *nse* **Fantasy Gladiator**[15] 7324 11-9-5 **62**....................(be) LukeMorris 4 64
(Michael Appleby) *dwlt and short of room sn after s: rousted along in midfield: swtchd rt and hdwy after 2f: chsd ldrs 4f out: drvn over 1f out: kpt on same pce ins fnl f* **5/1[2]**

0125 **5** *2 1/4* **Slow To Hand**[23] 7062 3-9-2 **62**....................(b) RichardKingscote 7 58
(William Jarvis) *hld up in last quartet: swtchd rt and effrt wd wl over 1f out: kpt on u.p ins fnl f: nvr trbld ldrs* **5/2[1]**

4-0 **6** *1/2* **Breathoffreshair**[140] 2790 3-8-9 **55**.................... ConnorBeasley 3 50
(Richard Guest) *t.k.h: chsd ldng trio: rdn over 2f out: unable qck over 1f out: styd on same pce ins fnl f* **16/1**

0040 **7** *3 3/4* **My Fantasea (IRE)**[27] 6946 4-9-5 **62**.................... ShaneKelly 8 48
(David Evans) *hld up in tch in midfield: effrt over 1f out: drvn and no imp 1f out: wknd ins fnl f* **12/1**

0640 **8** *5* **Widnes**[23] 7062 3-9-4 **64**....................(b) RobertTart 9 38
(Alan Bailey) *nvr travelling wl in last pair: no hdwy u.p over 1f out: wknd ins fnl f* **10/1**

-500 **9** *18* **Brasted (IRE)**[23] 7062 5-9-0 **62**....................(t) PaddyBradley(5) 1
(Lee Carter) *t.k.h: chsd ldr tl 1/2-way: rdn and lost pl ent fnl 2f: dropped out qckly over 1f out: eased fnl f* **6/1[3]**

3606 **10** *23* **Foie Gras**[1] 7759 7-9-10 **67**....................(p) SilvestreDeSousa 6
(Chris Dwyer) *in tch in last quartet: rdn over 2f out: dropped to last and losing tch over 1f out: sn eased: t.o (lame)* **7/1**

1m 38.7s (-1.20) **Going Correction** -0.20s/f (Stan)
**WFA** 3 from 4yo+ 3lb **10 Ran SP% 122.5**
Speed ratings (Par 101): **98,97,96,96,93 93,89,84,66,43**
CSF £202.23 CT £1326.86 TOTE £17.70: £4.20, £4.30, £2.40; EX 210.60 Trifecta £688.80.
**Owner** O'Mulloy, Schwartz **Bred** Grangecon Stud **Trained** Lambourn, Berks

**FOCUS**
A modest handicap. Straightforward form rated around the second and third.

## 7792 BET TOTEWIN AT BETFRED.COM H'CAP (DIV II) 1m (P)
**8:45** (8:54) (Class 6) (0-65,67) 3-Y-O+ **£3,234** (£962; £481; £240) **Stalls** Low

Form RPR

0003 **1** **Beepeecee**[8] 7540 3-9-0 **59**....................(b) ShaneKelly 1 66
(Richard Hughes) *hld up in tch in midfield: c to centre and effrt u.p over 1f out: styd on to ld 100yds out: rdn out* **4/1[2]**

0 **2** *3/4* **Paved With Gold (IRE)**[34] 6708 4-9-6 **62**....................(p[1]) BenCurtis 3 67
(John Joseph Murphy, Ire) *hld up in tch in last quartet: clsd and nt clr over 1f out: swtchd rt 1f out: hdwy to chse wnr wl ins fnl f: r.o* **3/1[1]**

640 **3** *2* **Celtic Artisan (IRE)**[27] 6946 6-9-7 **63**....................(bt) OisinMurphy 9 63
(Rebecca Menzies) *chsd ldr over 6f out: rdn and ev ch 2f out: drvn to ld 1f out: hdd 100yds out: no ex: sn lost 2nd and outpcd towards fin* **6/1**

3203 **4** *1/2* **Medici Moon**[32] 6760 3-8-9 **54**....................(p) LukeMorris 8 53
(Scott Dixon) *sn led: rdn and hrd pressed 2f out: hdd 1f out: no ex: edgd lft and outpcd fnl 100yds* **33/1**

1020 **5** *hd* **Ellaal**[28] 6893 8-9-6 **62**....................(p) JamesSullivan 4 61
(Ruth Carr) *broke wl: chsd ldr tl over 6f out: styd trcking ldrs: effrt but nt clr run over 1f out: swtchd rt ins fnl f: kpt on towards fin* **20/1**

6606 **6** *1* **Marbooh (IRE)**[46] 6263 4-9-11 **67**....................(t) RichardKingscote 2 63
(Amy Murphy) *chsd ldng trio: effrt over 1f out: unable qck and styd on same pce ins fnl f* **8/1**

3033 **7** *1 1/2* **Lord Kitten (USA)**[17] 7236 3-9-4 **63**....................(tp) TedDurcan 5 59
(David Lanigan) *hld up in tch in last quartet: effrt on inner over 1f out: drvn 1f out: no imp and btn whn nt clr run and eased towards fin* **5/1[3]**

0022 **8** *1/2* **Breaking Free**[39] 6528 3-8-4 **49** oh1.................... FrannyNorton 10 41
(John Quinn) *t.k.h: hld up in tch in last pair: effrt over 1f out: drvn 1f out: no imp* **14/1**

0441 **9** *2* **Kilbaha Lady (IRE)**[17] 7240 3-9-3 **62**....................(t) SilvestreDeSousa 6 49
(Nigel Tinkler) *t.k.h: hld up in tch in last pair: swtchd lft and effrt whn nt clr run over 1f out: no prog* **4/1[2]**

-600 **10** *8* **St Patrick's Day (IRE)**[23] 7062 5-9-5 **61**....................(v) DougieCostello 7 29
(J R Jenkins) *hld up in tch in midfield: shkn up over 1f out: sn btn and lost pl: bhd ins fnl f* **50/1**

1m 38.29s (-1.61) **Going Correction** -0.20s/f (Stan)
**WFA** 3 from 4yo+ 3lb **10 Ran SP% 123.4**
Speed ratings (Par 101): **100,99,97,96,96 95,94,93,91,83**
CSF £17.24 CT £76.35 TOTE £6.00: £2.00, £1.70, £2.30; EX 21.10 Trifecta £142.90.
**Owner** BPC Partnership **Bred** Equine Origin Ltd **Trained** Upper Lambourn, Berks

**FOCUS**
The faster of the two divisions by 0.41sec. The winner has been rated near this year's best.

## 7793 BOOK YOUR CHRISTMAS PARTY AT CCR MAIDEN STKS 7f (P)
**9:15** (9:21) (Class 5) 3-Y-O+ **£5,175** (£1,540; £769; £384) **Stalls** Low

Form RPR

2 **1** **Diagnostic**[17] 7227 3-9-0 0.................... RyanMoore 2 79+
(William Haggas) *taken down early: wnt rt leaving stalls: t.k.h: trckd ldrs: wnt 2nd 5f out tl jst over 2f out: sn rdn: ev ch over 1f out: led ins fnl f: styd on and drew clr towards fin* **30/100[1]**

352 **2** *2 3/4* **Perfect Sense**[17] 7254 3-9-5 72....................(v) OisinMurphy 1 76
(Saeed bin Suroor) *t.k.h: chsd ldr tl 5f out: styd trcking ldrs tl swtchd rt and effrt to press ldr jst over 2f out: hrd pressed over 1f out: edgd rt and hdd ins fnl f: outpcd fnl 100yds* **10/3[2]**

-030 **3** *7* **Ghaseedah**[46] 6265 3-9-0 70....................(b[1]) SilvestreDeSousa 4 56
(Simon Crisford) *led: rdn and hdd over 1f out: 3rd and btn 1f out: wknd fnl f* **14/1[3]**

00 **4** *5* **Subotal (IRE)**[17] 7247 4-9-7 0.................... ConnorBeasley 3 45
(Richard Guest) *bmpd s: a last: in tch: rdn over 3f out: outpcd 2f out: wl btn 1f out* **66/1**

1m 25.49s (-1.71) **Going Correction** -0.20s/f (Stan)
**WFA** 3 from 4yo 2lb **4 Ran SP% 108.2**
Speed ratings (Par 103): **101,97,89,84**
CSF £1.60 TOTE £1.10; EX 1.40 Trifecta £2.60.
**Owner** Cheveley Park Stud **Bred** Cheveley Park Stud Ltd **Trained** Newmarket, Suffolk

**FOCUS**
A straightforward task for the favourite. The runner-up has been rated to form.
T/Plt: £144.20 to a £1 stake. Pool: £95,287.07 - 482.06 winning units. T/Qpdt: £62.10 to a £1 stake. Pool: £11,046.83 - 131.49 winning units. **Steve Payne**

7794 - 7796a (Foreign Racing) - See Raceform Interactive

# 7713 DUNDALK (A.W) (L-H)
Friday, October 6

**OFFICIAL GOING: Polytrack: standard**

## 7797a IRISH STALLION FARMS EBF STAR APPEAL STKS (LISTED RACE) 7f (P)
**7:00** (7:01) 2-Y-O

**£27,735** (£8,931; £4,230; £1,880; £940; £470)

RPR

**1** **Riyazan (IRE)**[12] 7426 2-9-3 103.................... PatSmullen 5 100
(M Halford, Ire) *chsd ldrs in 4th: clsr in 3rd under 2f out: wnt 2nd ent fnl f: rdn to assert ins fnl 100yds: kpt on wl* **11/4[2]**

**2** *1/2* **Battle Of Jericho (USA)**[78] 5083 2-9-3 0....................(t) SeamieHeffernan 1 99
(A P O'Brien, Ire) *chsd ldrs in 3rd: clsr under 2f out: briefly 2nd appr fnl f: dropped to 3rd fnl 100yds: kpt on wl into 2nd cl home* **7/2[3]**

**3** *shd* **Lake Volta (IRE)**[27] 6935 2-9-3 97.................... KevinManning 2 98
(Mark Johnston) *led: rdn under 2f out: pressed ins fnl f: hdd ins fnl 100yds: dropped to 3rd cl home* **4/1**

**4** *1/2* **Lethal Steps**[26] 6975 2-9-3 95.................... ColinKeane 7 97
(G M Lyons, Ire) *sn trckd ldr in 2nd: rdn and nt qckn in 4th appr fnl f: no imp ins fnl f: kpt on again cl home* **9/4[1]**

**5** *6* **Grace Rafaela (IRE)**[49] 6167 2-8-12 0.................... WJLee 3 76
(M D O'Callaghan, Ire) *hld up in 6th: no imp under 2f out: kpt on one pce into 5th ins fnl f: nvr on terms* **8/1**

**6** *1 1/4* **Damselfly (IRE)**[16] 7290 2-8-12 83.................... WayneLordan 6 72
(Joseph Patrick O'Brien, Ire) *hld up in 5th: rdn and nt qckn appr fnl f: sn no ex* **50/1**

**7** *13* **Liberty Lass (USA)**[27] 6954 2-8-12 0.................... RonanWhelan 4 37
(Emmet Mullins, Ire) *bit slowly away and racd in rr thrght: pushed along 1/2-way: detached under 2f out* **100/1**

1m 24.52s (-0.58) **Going Correction** 0.0s/f (Stan) **7 Ran SP% 113.7**
Speed ratings: **102,101,101,100,93 92,77**
CSF £12.69 TOTE £3.30: £1.60, £1.80; DF 11.80 Trifecta £32.50.
**Owner** H H Aga Khan **Bred** His Highness The Aga Khan's Studs S C **Trained** Doneany, Co Kildare

**FOCUS**
A solid performance from a smart colt who appreciated this drop in grade, and potentially the drop in trip. An entertaining finish, with the front four well clear of the rest. The third and fourth help set the level.

7798 - 7803a (Foreign Racing) - See Raceform Interactive

# 7780 ASCOT (R-H)
Saturday, October 7

**OFFICIAL GOING: Good to soft**
Wind: Moderate, against Weather: Overcast

## 7804 HOPE AND HOMES FOR CHILDREN ROUS STKS (LISTED RACE) 5f
**1:50** (1:50) (Class 1) 3-Y-O+

**£25,519** (£9,675; £4,842; £2,412; £1,210; £607) **Stalls** High

Form RPR

0000 **1** **Just Glamorous (IRE)**[14] 7396 4-9-0 99.................... OisinMurphy 3 108
(Ronald Harris) *mde all: edgd rt 2f out: drvn and hung lft fnl f: hld on wl* **33/1**

1602 **2** *3/4* **Sir Robert Cheval**[56] 5911 6-9-0 103.................... PhillipMakin 2 106
(Robert Cowell) *hld up: prog to chse wnr over 1f out: carried sltly lft whn chalng ins fnl f: a hld* **7/1[3]**

6014 **3** *nk* **Waady (IRE)**[14] 7396 5-9-0 107....................(h) JimCrowley 8 105
(John Gosden) *sweating; pressed ldrs: rdn and nt qckn over 1f out: carried sltly lft ins fnl f: styd on* **10/11[1]**

2055 **4** *1* **Mirza**[14] 7396 10-9-0 106....................(p) MartinHarley 1 101
(Rae Guest) *chsd ldrs on outer: rdn and nt qckn over 1f out: one pce fnl f* **15/2**

3246 **5** *nk* **A Momentofmadness**[21] 7144 4-9-0 94.................... CallumShepherd 7 100
(Charles Hills) *t.k.h: pressed wnr to over 1f out: fdd* **11/1**

0624 **6** *2* **Kyllang Rock (IRE)**[27] 6979 3-9-0 105.................... LukeMorris 5 94
(James Tate) *hld up: effrt to chse ldrs whn nt clr run wl over 1f out: no prog whn in the clr and fdd last 150yds* **5/1[2]**

512 **7** *1 3/4* **Razzmatazz**[24] 7051 3-8-9 97.................... SamHitchcott 4 83
(Clive Cox) *rrd s: in tch: rdn 2f out: sn fdd* **16/1**

20-0 **8** *12* **Mister Trader**[139] 2863 3-9-0 102....................(t) LeighRoche 6 44
(D J Bunyan, Ire) *sltly s.i.s: sn chsd ldrs: wknd qckly 2f out: t.o* **16/1**

1m 2.96s (2.46) **Going Correction** +0.65s/f (Yiel) **8 Ran SP% 116.4**
Speed ratings (Par 111): **106,104,104,102,102 99,96,77**
CSF £248.79 TOTE £34.50: £5.20, £2.10, £1.10; EX 338.30 Trifecta £757.40.
**Owner** Robert & Nina Bailey **Bred** Glamorous Air Partnership **Trained** Earlswood, Monmouths
■ Stewards' Enquiry : Oisin Murphy caution: careless riding

**FOCUS**
The rail on the round course was 3yds out from its innermost position from the 1m4f start increasing to 14yds out at the home straight where the rail finished with a cutaway. The straight was divided in two with a rail in the middle from the 1m start to 2.5f out, and the stands' side was used for this meeting. The field gradually edged towards the stands' rail, and the form of this ordinary Listed sprint has an unreliable end-of-season look to it. It's been rated around the second and fifth.

## 7805 GIGASET CUMBERLAND LODGE STKS (GROUP 3) 1m 3f 211y
**2:25** (2:25) (Class 1) 3-Y-O+

**£34,026** (£12,900; £6,456; £3,216; £1,614; £810) **Stalls** Low

Form RPR
-142 **1** **Danehill Kodiac (IRE)**[15] 7354 4-9-2 105 SeanLevey 9 112
(Richard Hannon) *lw; mde all: pressed and rdn over 2f out: kpt on wl after: hrd pressed last 100yds: hld on gamely* **8/1**[3]
-224 **2** *nk* **Waldgeist**[98] 4387 3-8-10 117 VincentCheminaud 4 112+
(A Fabre, France) *hld up in 6th: pushed along and prog wl over 1f out: chsd wnr fnl f: rdn to chal 100yds out: styd on but nt get by nr fin* **4/7**[1]
0-13 **3** *1 ¾* **Secret Number**[14] 7393 7-9-7 114 GeraldMosse 5 114
(Saeed bin Suroor) *trckd wnr: rdn to chal fr over 2f out to over 1f out: lost 2nd and one pce fnl f* **5/1**[2]
3616 **4** *¾* **Midterm**[28] 6931 4-9-2 110 TedDurcan 1 108
(Sir Michael Stoute) *trckd ldng pair: rdn and tried to chal over 2f out: one pce u.p over 1f out* **12/1**
**5** *1 ¾* **Flying Tiger (IRE)**[184] 4-9-2 0 OisinMurphy 6 105
(Nick Williams) *dwlt: t.k.h: hld up in 7th: shkn up over 2f out and no prog: kpt on fr over 1f out: n.d but nt disgracd* **33/1**
6111 **6** *nk* **Great Hall**[16] 7337 7-9-2 105 FranBerry 2 104
(Mick Quinn) *chsd ldrs in 5th: rdn over 2f out: no imp after: fdd fnl f* **10/1**
0263 **7** *1* **Arthenus**[29] 6915 5-9-2 103 (p) TomQueally 3 103
(James Fanshawe) *trckd ldng trio: rdn over 2f out: nt qckn and no imp wl over 1f out: fdd fnl f* **25/1**
4250 **8** *hd* **Law And Order (IRE)**[14] 7395 3-8-10 102 JimCrowley 7 102
(James Tate) *blindfold off late and slowly away: hld up in last pair: shkn up and no prog over 2f out: no ch after but plugged on fnl f* **22/1**
0503 **9** *1 ¾* **Restorer**[21] 7150 5-9-2 98 MartinDwyer 8 100
(William Muir) *hld up in last pair: rdn over 2f out: no prog and sn btn* **40/1**
2m 40.02s (7.52) **Going Correction** +0.975s/f (Soft)
**WFA** 3 from 4yo+ 6lb **9** Ran SP% **121.8**
Speed ratings (Par 113): **113,112,111,111,109 109,109,108,107**
CSF £13.38 TOTE £9.70: £2.50, £1.02, £1.70; EX 15.30 Trifecta £55.30.
**Owner** Davies, Smith, Carr, Brown, Govier **Bred** Rathbarry Stud **Trained** East Everleigh, Wilts
**FOCUS**
Add 25yds. A muddling Group 3, the 1-2-3-4 raced 1-6-2-3 for much of the way. A length plus pb from the winner.

## 7806 JOHN GUEST BENGOUGH STKS (GROUP 3) 6f
**3:00** (3:01) (Class 1) 3-Y-O+

**£39,697** (£15,050; £7,532; £3,752; £1,883; £945) **Stalls** High

Form RPR
-134 **1** **Blue Point (IRE)**[28] 6926 3-9-4 116 WilliamBuick 7 119+
(Charlie Appleby) *sweating; mde all: drew clr over 2f out: 3 l ahd 1f out: edgd lft and rdn after: ld whittled down nr fin: hld on* **1/1**[1]
-630 **2** *½* **Projection**[63] 5640 4-9-2 105 KieranShoemark 1 113
(Roger Charlton) *lw; hld up in last pair: prog over 2f out: rdn to chse wnr fnl f and 3 l bhd: clsd qckly nr fin* **9/1**
1140 **3** *3 ¼* **Magical Memory (IRE)**[28] 6926 5-9-5 109 OisinMurphy 5 106
(Charles Hills) *hld up: prog over 2f out: rdn to chse wnr over 1f out: no imp and lost 2nd fnl f: one pce* **9/1**
6510 **4** *2* **Danzeno**[63] 5640 6-9-2 109 TomQueally 9 96
(Michael Appleby) *chsd wnr: rdn over 2f out: lost 2nd over 1f out: nt qckn and fdd* **9/2**[2]
1126 **5** *shd* **Second Thought (IRE)**[15] 7356 3-9-1 105 JimCrowley 3 96
(William Haggas) *in tch: rdn fr 1/2-way and struggling for pce: no prog tl styd on ins fnl f: nrly snatched 4th* **7/1**[3]
6034 **6** *1 ¼* **Intisaab**[7] 7603 6-9-2 108 (p) MartinHarley 8 92
(David O'Meara) *rrd bef stalls opened and dwlt: in tch: rdn and no prog over 2f out: fdd over 1f out* **16/1**
2001 **7** *hd* **Tommy Taylor (USA)**[27] 6966 3-9-1 107 TomEaves 2 91
(Kevin Ryan) *hld up in last pair: effrt 2f out: hanging rt over 1f out and racd awkwardly: no great prog* **14/1**
1-25 **8** *3* **Simmie (IRE)**[119] 3613 3-8-12 98 CliffordLee 6 79
(K R Burke) *prom to 2f out: sn wknd* **33/1**
-030 **9** *3 ¾* **Rosie Briar**[14] 7396 3-8-12 96 RobHornby 4 67
(Andrew Balding) *chsd ldrs to over 2f out: wknd wl over 1f out* **50/1**
2100 **10** *17* **Visionary (IRE)**[77] 5149 3-9-1 100 LukeMorris 10 15
(Robert Cowell) *prom to 1/2-way: wknd qckly u.p: t.o* **50/1**
1m 16.24s (1.74) **Going Correction** +0.65s/f (Yiel)
**WFA** 3 from 4yo+ 1lb **10** Ran SP% **120.1**
Speed ratings (Par 113): **114,113,109,106,106 104,104,100,95,72**
CSF £11.59 TOTE £1.80: £1.02, £3.10, £2.80; EX 10.80 Trifecta £78.70.
**Owner** Godolphin **Bred** Oak Lodge Bloodstock **Trained** Newmarket, Suffolk
**FOCUS**
Few got into this Group 3 sprint. The winner has been rated close to form, with the runner-up a length up on his top handicap form.

## 7807 TOTESCOOP6 CHALLENGE CUP (HERITAGE H'CAP) 7f
**3:35** (3:36) (Class 2) 3-Y-O+

**£112,050** (£33,552; £16,776; £8,388; £4,194; £2,106) **Stalls** High

Form RPR
5012 **1** **Accidental Agent**[15] 7356 3-9-3 **104** CharlesBishop 8 113
(Eve Johnson Houghton) *dwlt: hld up wl in rr: swtchd towards far side and prog over 2f out: rdn to chse ldr over 1f out: drvn ahd last 150yds: styd on* **16/1**
1 **2** *½* **Lord Glitters (FR)**[145] 4-9-3 **102** MartinHarley 14 111+
(David O'Meara) *dwlt: hld up in last: stl there jst over 2f out: gd prog wl over 1f out gng strly: rdn and r.o to take 2nd nr fin: too late to rch wnr* **20/1**
0614 **3** *¾* **Raising Sand**[28] 6918 5-8-13 **98** DougieCostello 1 105
(Jamie Osborne) *led far side quartet 3f: led again 2f out and overall ldr: sn clr: hdd and no ex last 150yds* **16/1**
1261 **4** *1 ½* **Makzeem**[7] 7622 4-9-4 **103** 6ex KieranShoemark 12 106
(Roger Charlton) *hld up towards rr: stylish prog over 2f out: disp 2nd over 1f out: drvn to chal 150yds out: one pce nr fin* **7/1**[3]
3416 **5** *¾* **Johnny Barnes (IRE)**[7] 7611 5-9-9 **108** RobertHavlin 5 109+
(John Gosden) *hld up towards rr: gng wl enough whn waiting for a gap over 2f out: prog over 1f out: styd on: nvr pce to threaten* **12/1**
1022 **6** *hd* **Mjjack (IRE)**[28] 6918 3-8-12 **102** ow2 CliffordLee(3) 13 102
(K R Burke) *pressed ldrs in centre: rdn 3f out: stl on terms over 1f out: one pce* **6/1**[2]
532/ **7** *1 ¾* **Speculative Bid (IRE)**[778] 5599 6-9-9 **108** SeanLevey 17 104
(David Elsworth) *sweating; hld up wl in rr: rdn over 2f out: prog towards nr side over 1f out: kpt on and nvr nrr* **33/1**
5535 **8** *2 ¾* **Firmament**[28] 6918 5-9-10 **109** PhillipMakin 7 98
(David O'Meara) *hld up in midfield: effrt over 2f out: cl enough wl over 1f out: steadily wknd* **16/1**
3053 **9** *2* **Straight Right (FR)**[42] 6419 3-9-2 **103** OisinMurphy 15 86
(Andrew Balding) *hld up in midfield: gng wl 3f out: effrt 2f out: sn rdn and no prog* **14/1**
6202 **10** *3 ½* **Mutawathea**[21] 7154 6-8-13 **101** (p) LewisEdmunds(3) 11 76
(Simon Crisford) *overall ldr in main gp in centre: hdd 3f out: wknd 2f out* **33/1**
3430 **11** *1 ¼* **Withernsea (IRE)**[7] 7611 6-9-0 **99** FranBerry 9 70
(Richard Fahey) *trckd ldrs: shkn up and cl enough over 2f out: wknd over 1f out* **16/1**
0415 **12** *4* **Mitchum Swagger**[28] 6928 5-9-6 **105** (p) TedDurcan 10 66
(David Lanigan) *nvr bttr than midfield: struggling over 2f out: wknd over 1f out* **16/1**
6030 **13** *1* **Birchwood (IRE)**[28] 6918 4-9-6 **105** GeraldMosse 4 63
(Richard Fahey) *racd in far side quartet: chsd ldrs: rdn and wknd 2f out* **14/1**
1010 **14** *nk* **Flaming Spear (IRE)**[28] 6928 5-9-8 **107** RobertWinston 3 65
(Kevin Ryan) *lw; racd in far side quartet: led gp after 3f: overall ldr 3f out gng strly: hdd 2f out and wknd v rapidly* **9/1**
3001 **15** *3 ¾* **Amazour (IRE)**[22] 7118 5-9-0 **99** (p) StevieDonohoe 2 47
(Ismail Mohammed) *racd in far side quartet: in tch: wknd u.p over 2f out* **40/1**
0221 **16** *½* **Burnt Sugar (IRE)**[28] 6961 5-9-4 **103** DeclanMcDonogh 6 50
(Roger Fell) *chsd ldrs over 4f: wknd qckly 2f out* **14/1**
20 **17** *10* **Arcanada (IRE)**[34] 6746 4-9-1 **105** PaddyPilley(5) 16 26
(Tom Dascombe) *prom in centre 4f: wknd qckly: t.o* **20/1**
3111 **18** *1 ¼* **Mojito (IRE)**[43] 6404 3-9-3 **104** JimCrowley 18 20
(William Haggas) *wl there towards nr side of centre gp tl wknd qckly over 2f out: t.o* **4/1**[1]
1m 30.51s (2.91) **Going Correction** +0.65s/f (Yiel)
**WFA** 3 from 4yo+ 2lb **18** Ran SP% **131.7**
Speed ratings (Par 109): **109,108,107,105,105 104,102,99,97,93 91,87,86,85,81 81,69,68**
CSF £325.35 CT £5301.78 TOTE £19.70: £4.10, £3.40, £4.40, £2.10; EX 480.90 Trifecta £13609.30.
**Owner** Mrs R F Johnson Houghton **Bred** Mrs R F Johnson Houghton **Trained** Blewbury, Oxon
**FOCUS**
They were spread out in the early stages, but the main action was up the middle, and it set up for the late runners.

## 7808 TOTEPOOL BRITISH EBF OCTOBER STKS (LISTED RACE) (F&M) 7f
**4:10** (4:12) (Class 1) 3-Y-O+

**£22,684** (£8,600; £4,304; £2,144; £1,076; £540) **Stalls** High

Form RPR
31 **1** **One Master**[18] 7254 3-8-12 75 MartinHarley 7 108+
(William Haggas) *athletic; hld up in rr: prog jst over 2f out: sustained hdwy to ld 1f out: styd on wl* **20/1**
-120 **2** *1 ¼* **Bletchley**[64] 5597 3-8-12 99 OisinMurphy 6 104
(Ralph Beckett) *hld up wl in rr: prog 2f out: rdn and styd on fnl f to take 2nd last 75yds: too late to chal and no imp on wnr after* **10/1**[3]
1-22 **3** *¾* **Eternally**[22] 7113 4-9-0 106 RobertHavlin 4 104
(John Gosden) *lw; mde most: rdn jst over 2f out: hdd and no ex 1f out* **10/11**[1]
0404 **4** *2 ½* **Urban Fox**[15] 7356 3-8-12 98 (v) JimCrowley 9 96
(James Tate) *prom: rdn over 2f out: 3rd and in tch over 1f out: fdd ins fnl f* **12/1**
3216 **5** *1 ¼* **Pirouette**[22] 7113 4-9-3 107 (b) RobertWinston 11 97
(Hughie Morrison) *racd centre early: prom: chsd wnr over 3f out to over 1f out: wknd fnl f* **8/1**[2]
3-50 **6** *nk* **Belle Meade (IRE)**[37] 6619 3-8-12 89 RobHornby 8 92
(Andrew Balding) *in tch: nt pce to chal fr 2f out but kpt on same pce* **66/1**
10 **7** *¾* **Princess De Lune (IRE)**[15] 7356 3-8-12 90 KieranShoemark 5 90
(Roger Charlton) *slowly away: hld up in rr: prog 2f out: drvn and no imp on ldrs over 1f out* **12/1**
**8** *3* **Xenobia (IRE)**[49] 6215 3-8-12 92 FranBerry 13 82
(W T Farrell, Ire) *racd centre early: hld up: rdn over 2f out: no great prog over 1f out* **8/1**[2]
1146 **9** *1* **Hells Babe**[38] 6605 4-9-0 98 AlistairRawlinson 12 81
(Michael Appleby) *racd centre: led quartet there 3f: wknd 2f out* **40/1**
1221 **10** *1 ½* **Bumptious**[11] 7484 4-9-0 84 (p) SeanLevey 2 77
(Ismail Mohammed) *t.k.h: hld up bhd ldrs: rdn and no rspnse 2f out: wknd* **33/1**
44 **11** *2 ½* **Orangey Red (IRE)**[41] 6476 4-9-0 94 LeighRoche 3 70
(W T Farrell, Ire) *chsd ldrs: u.p by 1/2-way: lost pl over 2f out: sn wl btn* **50/1**
0202 **12** *½* **Havre De Paix (FR)**[28] 6919 5-9-0 91 TedDurcan 1 69
(David Menuisier) *in tch: shkn up and no prog over 2f out: wknd and eased* **20/1**
2413 **13** *12* **Dubara**[14] 7406 3-8-12 91 (h[1]) LukeMorris 10 37
(Luca Cumani) *dwlt: racd centre early: in tch tl wknd qckly jst over 2f out: t.o* **33/1**
1m 30.77s (3.17) **Going Correction** +0.65s/f (Yiel)
**WFA** 3 from 4yo+ 2lb **13** Ran SP% **120.4**
Speed ratings (Par 111): **107,105,104,101,100 100,99,95,94,92 90,89,75**
CSF £197.90 TOTE £16.90: £5.10, £2.90, £1.10; EX 127.90 Trifecta £340.20.
**Owner** Lael Stable **Bred** Lael Stables **Trained** Newmarket, Suffolk
**FOCUS**
An interesting-enough fillies' Listed race, and it unfolded up the middle. The runner-up has been rated back to her best.

## 7809 MCGEE LIGHTHOUSE CLUB H'CAP 5f
**4:45** (4:46) (Class 3) (0-95,95) 3-Y-O+ **£12,938** (£3,850; £1,924; £962) **Stalls** High

Form RPR
2121 **1** **Erissimus Maximus (FR)**[28] 6945 3-8-8 **85** (b) LewisEdmunds(3) 4 93
(Chris Dwyer) *racd towards far side: mde all: rdn 2f out: hrd pressed fnl f: hld on wl* **11/1**

530 **2** ½ **Evergate**[21] 7144 3-9-4 **92** GeraldMosse 5 98
(Robert Cowell) *trckd ldrs towards far side: wnt 2nd 2f out: rdn to chal 1f out: nrly upsides after but nt qckn nr fin* **13/2**[2]

030 **3** 1 **Lincoln (IRE)**[97] 4411 6-9-5 **93** RobHornby 3 94+
(Mick Channon) *dwlt: racd towards far side: hld up in last: stl in last pair jst over 1f out: gd prog fnl f: tk 3rd last 100yds: unable to rch ldng pair* **8/1**

0001 **4** ¾ **Equimou**[17] 7286 3-9-7 **95** MartinHarley 1 95
(Robert Eddery) *trckd ldrs towards far side: rdn to chse ldng pair over 1f out: no imp and lost 3rd last 100yds* **10/1**

4110 **5** nk **Vimy Ridge**[23] 7086 5-8-10 **84** (t) StevieDonohoe 7 82
(Alan Bailey) *in tch towards far side: rdn over 1f out: one pce and nvr much imp* **25/1**

6040 **6** hd **Shamshon (IRE)**[28] 6923 6-8-13 **87** (t) OisinMurphy 8 84
(Stuart Williams) *hld up towards far side: stl wl in rr 1f out: styd on after but no ch to chal* **8/1**

4045 **7** 1¾ **Union Rose**[12] 7461 5-8-11 **85** FranBerry 6 76
(Ronald Harris) *chsd wnr towards far side to 2f out: steadily wknd* **20/1**

111 **8** ½ **Delagate This Lord**[20] 7192 3-8-8 **82** oh1 ow1 TedDurcan 11 72
(Michael Attwater) *racd towards centre: struggling and nt on terms fr 1/2-way: no ch over 1f out* **7/1**[3]

310 **9** nk **Escalating**[99] 4306 5-8-13 **87** (t) LukeMorris 12 75
(Michael Appleby) *racd centre early: nt on terms sn after 1/2-way and struggling: no ch over 1f out* **16/1**

406 **10** nk **Signore Piccolo**[23] 7084 6-8-8 **82** (h) JohnFahy 13 69
(David Loughnane) *racd centre: nt on terms fr 1/2-way and struggling: no ch over 1f out* **25/1**

0504 **11** nk **Willytheconqueror (IRE)**[12] 7461 4-9-3 **91** (p1) MartinDwyer 9 77
(William Muir) *led gp of five that racd in centre early: on terms 1/2-way: sn rdn: wknd over 1f out* **10/1**

1441 **12** hd **Justice Lady (IRE)**[35] 6695 4-8-11 **85** JimCrowley 10 70+
(David Elsworth) *t.k.h: hld up in tch and racd centre early: rdn and no prog over 1f out: wknd* **4/1**[1]

6001 **13** hd **Pettochside**[28] 6923 8-8-7 **86** MitchGodwin(5) 2 70
(John Bridger) *prom towards far side: on terms w ldng pair 2f out: wknd qckly over 1f out* **12/1**

1m 2.69s (2.19) **Going Correction** +0.65s/f (Yiel) **13** Ran SP% **120.6**
Speed ratings (Par 107): **108,107,105,104,103 103,100,100,99,99 98,98,97**
CSF £79.55 CT £451.34 TOTE £10.70: £3.50, £2.50, £2.70; EX 85.00 Trifecta £951.20.
**Owner** P Venner **Bred** Derek Clee **Trained** Newmarket, Suffolk

**FOCUS**
This didn't look that strong a race for the grade and towards the far side proved the place to be, with the first seven drawn eight or lower. A pb from the winner, with the runner-up rated to the better view of his form.
T/Jkpt: Not Won. T/Plt: £32.20 to a £1 stake. Pool: £181,931.71 - 4,116.33 winning units. T/Qpdt: £22.00 to a £1 stake. Pool: £11,905.34 - 400.11 winning units. **Jonathan Neesom**

# 7616 NEWMARKET (R-H)
## Saturday, October 7

**OFFICIAL GOING: Good (8.1)**
Wind: medium to strong, behind Weather: overcast, rain from race 4

## 7810 1ST SECURITY SOLUTIONS EBF STALLIONS NOVICE STKS (PLUS 10 RACE) (DIV I) 1m
**1:30** (1:31) (Class 4) 2-Y-O
**£4,528** (£1,347; £673; £336) **Stalls** High

Form RPR

31 **1** **Old Persian**[35] 6683 2-9-8 0 AdamKirby 8 97+
(Charlie Appleby) *led for 1f: styd upsides ldr tl rdn to ld 2f out: qcknd clr and in command 1f out: r.o strly: easily* **8/11**[1]

0 **2** 4½ **Gronkowski (USA)**[14] 7391 2-9-2 0 RyanMoore 6 79
(Jeremy Noseda) *t.k.h: trckd ldrs: effrt ent fnl 2f: outpcd u.p over 1f out: kpt on ins fnl f to chse clr wnr 100yds out: no ch w wnr* **11/4**[2]

06 **3** 1½ **Arthenia (IRE)**[28] 6917 2-8-11 0 SteveDrowne 3 70
(Charles Hills) *dwlt and bustled along leaving stalls: hdwy to ld after 1f: rdn and hdd 2f out: edgd rt and nt match pce of wnr over 1f out: wl hld 1f out: lost 2nd ins fnl f* **40/1**

00 **4** 1 **Echo Cove (IRE)**[10] 7520 2-8-13 0 DavidEgan(3) 4 73
(Jane Chapple-Hyam) *t.k.h early: trckd ldrs: rdn in 5th and outpcd 2f out: no ch w wnr but kpt on ins fnl f* **50/1**

**5** ½ **Courtside (FR)** 2-9-2 0 JamieSpencer 5 72
(David Simcock) *v.s.a: off the pce in last pair: clsd over 2f out: shkn up 2f out: no ch w wnr but kpt on ins fnl f* **20/1**

**6** 1¼ **Hazarfan** 2-9-2 0 DavidProbert 10 69
(Ed Dunlop) *dwlt: off the pce in last pair: effrt wl over 2f out: no ch w wnr and kpt on same pce fr over 1f out* **16/1**

4 **7** ½ **Balletomane**[42] 6424 2-9-2 0 TomMarquand 2 68
(Richard Hannon) *chsd ldrs: over 2f out: outpcd u.p over 1f out: wknd fnl f* **14/1**

**8** 16 **Wilfred Owen** 2-9-2 0 FrankieDettori 9 31
(John Gosden) *midfield: rdn over 3f out: bhd over 1f out* **8/1**[3]

1m 36.9s (-1.70) **Going Correction** -0.075s/f (Good) **8** Ran SP% **117.4**
Speed ratings (Par 97): **105,100,99,98,97 96,95,79**
CSF £2.91 TOTE £1.50: £1.10, £1.30, £8.50; EX 3.60 Trifecta £57.10.
**Owner** Godolphin **Bred** Godolphin **Trained** Newmarket, Suffolk

**FOCUS**
Far side course used. Stalls: 1m4f centre; remainder stands' side. The first division of a decent juvenile novice contest. They went a respectable gallop on good ground. The odds-on favourite had far too much know how for this field.

## 7811 BRITISH EBF BREEDERS' FILLIES SERIES SPRINT H'CAP 6f
**2:05** (2:06) (Class 2) 3-Y-O+
**£31,125** (£9,320; £4,660; £2,330; £1,165; £585) **Stalls** High

Form RPR

1053 **1** **Pixeleen**[20] 7195 5-9-1 **89** AdamKirby 5 97
(Malcolm Saunders) *led: rdn over 2f out: drvn over 1f out: hdd ins fnl f: battled bk wl to ld again last strides: gamely* **12/1**

4222 **2** hd **Magical Dreamer (IRE)**[18] 7256 3-8-4 **82** GeorgeWood(3) 3 89
(James Fanshawe) *trckd ldrs: effrt to chal over 1f out: drvn to ld ins fnl f: kpt on u.p: hdd in last strides* **8/1**

1320 **3** shd **Eartha Kitt**[15] 7356 3-9-6 **95** (p) RichardKingscote 4 102+
(Tom Dascombe) *hld up in tch: hdwy u.p over 1f out: chsd ldng trio 1f out: swtchd lft ins fnl f: r.o strly towards fin: nt quite get to ldrs* **7/1**[3]

06 **4** 1 **Madame Bounty (IRE)**[50] 6137 3-7-13 **77** HollieDoyle(3) 2 81
(Ed Walker) *chsd ldrs: effrt over 1f out: ev ch and drvn 1f out: no ex wl ins fnl f: wknd towards fin* **16/1**

4052 **5** 1½ **Kassia (IRE)**[30] 6864 4-9-10 **98** FrannyNorton 1 97+
(Mick Channon) *sn off the pce in last pair: swtchd rt and hdwy wl over 1f out: styd on ins fnl f: nvr getting on terms w ldrs* **13/2**[2]

4053 **6** 2¼ **Rose Berry**[17] 7287 3-8-4 **82** (h) DavidEgan(3) 6 74
(Chris Dwyer) *taken down early: short of room leaving stalls: in tch in midfield: effrt and n.m.r briefly over 1f out: kpt on same pce and no imp ins fnl f* **20/1**

-100 **7** ½ **Tundra**[48] 6234 3-8-10 **85** MickaelBarzalona 8 75
(Roger Varian) *t.k.h: wl in tch in midfield: chsd ldng trio and rdn over 1f out: unable qck and wknd ins fnl f* **20/1**

436 **8** ½ **Turanga Leela**[28] 6923 3-8-2 **82** (v) ManuelFernandes(5) 10 71
(Ian Williams) *hld up in midfield: shuffled bk towards rr and shkn up 2f out: kpt on ins fnl f: no threat to ldrs* **14/1**

1160 **9** 1 **Under The Covers**[21] 7144 4-9-2 **90** ShaneKelly 13 75
(Ronald Harris) *taken down early: chsd ldr tl over 1f out: unable qck u.p and wknd ins fnl f* **40/1**

0204 **10** 1 **Clear Water (IRE)**[30] 6864 4-8-12 **86** JamieSpencer 14 68
(Michael Wigham) *sn in rr: swtchd rt 2f out: sme prog ins fnl f: nvr trbld ldrs* **12/1**

2513 **11** ½ **Rely On Me (IRE)**[30] 6864 3-8-10 **85** (p) DavidProbert 9 66
(Andrew Balding) *chsd ldrs: rdn ent fnl 2f: unable qck and lost pl over 1f out: wknd ins fnl f* **9/1**

-000 **12** ½ **Gravity Flow (IRE)**[53] 6025 4-9-4 **92** JoeFanning 12 71
(William Haggas) *t.k.h: hld up in tch towards rr: effrt whn nt clr run and hmpd over 1f out: n.d after* **11/1**

6401 **13** 1½ **Rosabelle**[21] 7155 3-8-7 **87** ow2 (b) JoshuaBryan(5) 11 61
(Alan Bailey) *chsd ldrs: unable qck u.p and lost pl over 1f out: wknd ins fnl f* **12/1**

3011 **14** hd **Marie Of Lyon**[16] 7329 3-9-4 **93** RyanMoore 7 67+
(Richard Fahey) *short of room and squeezed out sn after s: racd in last trio: effrt whn nt clr run and hmpd over 1f out: nvr enough room to make hdwy after* **11/2**[1]

1m 10.2s (-2.00) **Going Correction** -0.075s/f (Good)
**WFA** 3 from 4yo+ 1lb **14** Ran SP% **118.3**
Speed ratings (Par 109): **110,109,109,108,106 103,102,101,100,99 98,97,95,95**
CSF £100.43 CT £527.30 TOTE £15.60: £3.70, £3.10, £2.80; EX 143.00 Trifecta £1088.70.
**Owner** M S Saunders **Bred** Glebe Farm Stud **Trained** Green Ore, Somerset

**FOCUS**
A good quality, competitive fillies' sprint handicap. The market didn't really know what to make of it and three horses from awkward, low draws came to the fore in a time only marginally above standard. It paid to race prominently. The winner has been rated back to her best, and the second as running a pb.

## 7812 KINGDOM OF BAHRAIN SUN CHARIOT STKS (GROUP 1) (BRITISH CHAMPIONS SERIES) 1m
**2:40** (2:45) (Class 1) 3-Y-O+
**£141,775** (£53,750; £26,900; £13,400; £6,725; £3,375) **Stalls** High

Form RPR

2116 **1** **Roly Poly (USA)**[28] 6958 3-9-0 114 (p) RyanMoore 1 116
(A P O'Brien, Ire) *broke wl to ld and crossed towards stands' rail: rdn and hdd 2f out: styd upsides ldrs and drvn to ld again ins fnl f: styd on strly and gng away at fin* **4/1**[2]

2-53 **2** 1¼ **Persuasive (IRE)**[28] 6958 4-9-3 112 FrankieDettori 10 113
(John Gosden) *trckd ldrs: effrt and swtchd rt 2f out: chsd ldrs and drvn 1f out: wnt 2nd and pressing wnr ins fnl f: styd on same pce towards fin* **9/4**[1]

6322 **3** 1¼ **Nathra (IRE)**[21] 7145 4-9-3 111 JimmyFortune 13 110
(John Gosden) *hld up in tch in midfield: effrt ent fnl 2f: hdwy u.p 1f out: styd on wl ins fnl f to go 3rd last strides: no threat to ldng pair* **20/1**

3361 **4** hd **Usherette (IRE)**[32] 6804 5-9-3 111 MickaelBarzalona 9 110+
(A Fabre, France) *hld up in tch in midfield: shuffled bk over 2f out: towards rr and effrt 2f out: hdwy ent fnl f: squeezed between rivals ins fnl f: r.o wl to snatch 4th last stride: no threat to ldng pair* **9/1**

0235 **5** shd **Dawn Of Hope (IRE)**[17] 7305 4-9-3 105 ColmO'Donoghue 12 110
(Roger Varian) *pressed wnr: rdn to ld narrowly 2f out: drvn over 1f out: hdd ins fnl f: no ex: wknd towards fin and lost 2 pls last strides* **66/1**

2145 **6** ¾ **Qemah (IRE)**[28] 6958 4-9-3 114 GregoryBenoist 8 108+
(J-C Rouget, France) *stdd s: hld up in tch in rr: effrt wl over 2f out: switching rt and hdwy over 1f out: styd on ins fnl f: nvr trbld ldrs* **5/1**[3]

3241 **7** ½ **Muffri'Ha (IRE)**[8] 7576 5-9-3 107 JoeFanning 4 107
(William Haggas) *taken down early: ponied to s: awkward leaving stalls and s.i.s: steadily rcvrd to chse ldrs 5f out: effrt ent fnl 2f: unable qck and outpcd 1f out: wknd ins fnl f* **18/1**

1505 **8** 1 **Alluringly (USA)**[21] 7171 3-9-0 102 SeamieHeffernan 3 105+
(A P O'Brien, Ire) *chsd ldrs early: impeded sn after s and hld up in midfield after: effrt to chse ldrs and rdn 2f out: unable qck ent fnl f: wkng whn short of room wl ins fnl f* **50/1**

1521 **9** nk **Aljazzi**[35] 6697 4-9-3 112 (h) AdamKirby 6 105+
(Marco Botti) *hld up in tch towards rr: effrt over 2f out: hdwy to chse ldrs u.p 2f out: no ex 1f out: wkng whn short of room ins fnl f* **8/1**

0332 **10** 2 **Siyoushake (IRE)**[48] 6248 5-9-3 112 StephanePasquier 5 99
(F Head, France) *hld up wl in tch in midfield: effrt over 2f out: unable qck and outpcd over 1f out: wknd ins fnl f* **9/1**

1633 **11** 1¾ **Tomyris**[22] 7113 3-9-0 105 JamieSpencer 7 95
(Roger Varian) *midfield tl bdly hmpd and snatched up sn after s: dropped to rr: shkn up over 1f out: no hdwy: wknd ins fnl f* **50/1**

11-0 **12** 4 **Spangled**[43] 6401 5-9-3 107 HarryBentley 11 86
(Roger Varian) *t.k.h: hld up in tch towards rr: rdn 3f out: sn struggling: bhd whn hung rt over 1f out: wknd fnl f* **66/1**

1301 **13** 1¼ **Arabian Hope (USA)**[35] 6718 3-9-0 110 (h) JimmyQuinn 2 83
(Saeed bin Suroor) *chsd ldrs: hmpd sn after s: styd chsng ldrs: shkn up and losing pl whn nt clr run and hmpd ent fnl 2f: hmpd again and dropped to rr over 1f out: wknd* **50/1**

1m 34.88s (-3.72) **Going Correction** -0.075s/f (Good)
**WFA** 3 from 4yo+ 3lb **13** Ran SP% **117.4**
Speed ratings (Par 117): **115,113,112,112,112 111,110,109,109,107 105,101,100**
CSF £12.53 CT £163.90 TOTE £4.40: £1.70, £1.20, £5.10; EX 15.70 Trifecta £190.10.
**Owner** Michael Tabor & Derrick Smith & Mrs John Magnier **Bred** Misty For Me Syndicate **Trained** Cashel, Co Tipperary

■ Stewards' Enquiry : Ryan Moore two-day ban: careless riding (Oct 22-23)

**FOCUS**
An intriguingly competitive renewal of this all-aged Group 1 prize for fillies and mares. The second favourite proved too strong for the favourite in the closing stages in a time which dipped under standard. Once again it proved hard to get into contention from off the pace. A length pb from the winner, with the runner-up to form and the third close to her 1m best.

## 7813 1ST SECURITY SOLUTIONS EBF STALLIONS NOVICE STKS (PLUS 10 RACE) (DIV II) 1m

**3:15** (3:21) (Class 4) 2-Y-O **£4,528** (£1,347; £673; £336) **Stalls** High

Form RPR

**1** **Just Brilliant (IRE)** 2-9-2 0 RyanMoore 4 78
(Peter Chapple-Hyam) *mde virtually all: rdn ent fnl 2f: hdd narrowly 1f out: rallied to ld again ins fnl f: styd on wl* **10/3[2]**

**2** *1* **Silver Quartz** 2-9-2 0 (t[1]) HarryBentley 5 76
(Hugo Palmer) *hld up in tch in midfield: hdwy over 2f out: rdn to chal 2f out: led narrowly and edgd lft 1f out: hdd ins fnl f: no ex and outpcd towards fin* **11/4[1]**

**3** *3/4* **Coolongolook** 2-8-13 0 GeorgeWood(3) 7 74+
(Luca Cumani) *t.k.h: hld up in tch in midfield: effrt 2f out: swtchd rt ent fnl f: styd on wl to go 3rd towards fin: nt rch ldrs* **14/1**

65 **4** *1/2* **Soldiers Bay (IRE)**[28] 6916 2-9-2 0 (p[1]) TomMarquand 2 73
(Brian Meehan) *chsd ldrs: rdn 2f out: 3rd and sltly outpcd 1f out: styd on same pce ins fnl f: lost 3rd towards fin* **8/1**

**5** *nse* **Supernova** 2-9-2 0 JamieSpencer 6 73
(David Simcock) *hld up in last pair: effrt and switching rt 2f out: rdn and hdwy over 1f out: styd on wl ins fnl f: no threat to ldrs* **13/2**

0 **6** *3/4* **Diocletian (IRE)**[22] 7128 2-9-2 0 DavidProbert 9 71+
(Andrew Balding) *t.k.h: hld up in tch in midfield: effrt over 2f out: nt clr run and swtchd rt over 1f out: hdwy and swtchd bk lft ins fnl f: styd on: no threat to ldrs* **7/2[3]**

0 **7** *3 3/4* **Institution (IRE)**[22] 7128 2-9-2 0 SteveDrowne 8 62
(Charles Hills) *w wnr tl unable qck u.p 2f out: lost pl over 1f out: wknd ins fnl f* **20/1**

**8** *3/4* **Astrologist (IRE)** 2-9-2 0 AdamKirby 1 61
(Clive Cox) *rn green: s.i.s: in tch in last pair: hdwy over 2f out: rn green and no imp over 1f out: wknd ins fnl f* **7/1**

0 **9** *45* **Banjo's Voice**[43] 6388 2-9-2 0 NickyMackay 3
(Jane Chapple-Hyam) *in tch in midfield: rdn 3f out: dropped to rr 2f out and sn lost tch: virtually p.u ins fnl f: t.o* **80/1**

1m 38.95s (0.35) **Going Correction** -0.075s/f (Good) 9 Ran SP% **121.6**
Speed ratings (Par 97): **95,94,93,92,92 91,88,87,42**
CSF £13.77 TOTE £3.00: £1.40, £1.40, £4.00; EX 11.40 Trifecta £95.20.
**Owner** P Makin **Bred** David Hyland **Trained** Newmarket, Suffolk

**FOCUS**
The second division of the juvenile novice contest was the weaker of the two in terms of prior form and the winning time was about two seconds slower.

## 7814 £150,000 TATTERSALLS OCTOBER AUCTION STKS 6f

**3:50** (3:54) (Class 2) 2-Y-O

**£81,165** (£33,210; £14,775; £7,365; £3,690; £1,470) **Stalls** High

Form RPR

0436 **1** **Elysium Dream**[23] 7090 2-8-6 83 TomMarquand 4 84
(Richard Hannon) *racd far side: chsd ldrs: effrt to chse gp ldr and edgd rt over 1f out: styd on u.p to ld wl ins fnl f: 1st of 11 in gp* **11/2[3]**

2211 **2** *nk* **Arcavallo (IRE)**[52] 6055 2-8-7 83 AndrewMullen 29 84
(Michael Dods) *racd stands' side: chsd gp and prom overall: rdn to ld gp over 1f out: ev ch ins fnl f: styd on: 1st of 17 in gp* **16/1**

2100 **3** *3/4* **Misty Spirit**[30] 6863 2-8-4 75 DavidEgan 2 79
(David Elsworth) *racd far side: overall ldr: rdn ent fnl 2f: hdd wl ins fnl f: no ex: 2nd of 11 in gp* **33/1**

4421 **4** *1* **Escape The City**[42] 6433 2-8-2 75 CharlieBennett 7 74
(Hughie Morrison) *racd far side: midfield overall: effrt wl over 1f out: styd on strly ins fnl f: nt rch ldrs: 3rd of 11 in gp* **14/1**

3313 **5** *nk* **Yaafour**[30] 6859 2-8-11 85 RyanMoore 27 82
(Richard Hannon) *racd stands' side: gp ldr and chsd ldr overall tl over 1f out: unable qck 1f out: styd on same pce ins fnl f: 2nd of 17 in gp* **9/2[1]**

2341 **6** *1* **Wahoo**[53] 6042 2-8-9 77 CallumRodriguez 30 77
(Michael Dods) *racd stands' side: in tch in midfield: effrt 2f out: hdwy 1f out: styd on ins fnl f: no threat to ldrs: 3rd of 17 in gp* **25/1**

116 **7** *1/2* **She Believes (IRE)**[23] 7088 2-8-8 95 LiamKeniry 17 74
(Sylvester Kirk) *racd stands' side: in tch in midfield: effrt ent fnl 2f: unable qck over 1f out: kpt on but no threat to ldrs ins fnl f: 4th of 17 in gp* **5/1[2]**

650 **8** *nse* **Aquadabra (IRE)**[21] 7159 2-8-4 68 HollieDoyle 3 70
(Mick Channon) *racd far side: in tch in midfield: effrt to chse ldrs whn swtchd lft over 1f out: kpt on same pce ins fnl f: 4th of 11 in gp* **66/1**

01 **9** *1* **Fake News**[39] 6545 2-8-7 0 BenCurtis 15 70
(David Barron) *racd stands' side: in tch in midfield: effrt 2f out: kpt on ins fnl f: no threat to ldrs: 5th of 17 in gp* **12/1**

43 **10** *nk* **Priscilla's Dream**[30] 6844 2-8-2 0 RaulDaSilva 14 67
(Philip McBride) *racd stands' side: stdd and swtchd lft after s: t.k.h: hld up towards rr: nt clr run and swtchd rt jst over 1f out: kpt on ins fnl f: nvr trbld ldrs: 6th of 17 in gp* **50/1**

6144 **11** *nk* **Holy Tiber (IRE)**[41] 6481 2-8-4 78 JimmyQuinn 22 69
(George Scott) *racd stands' side: hld up in tch in midfield: nt clr run 2f out: effrt over 1f out: kpt on ins fnl f: no threat to ldrs: 7th of 17 in gp* **22/1**

1500 **12** *1* **Connery (IRE)**[28] 6935 2-8-9 81 ow2 ShaneKelly 16 68
(Sylvester Kirk) *racd stands' side: hld up in tch in midfield: effrt ent fnl 2f: no imp over 1f out: kpt on same pce ins fnl f: 8th of 17 in gp* **66/1**

0062 **13** *1 3/4* **Onefootinparadise**[15] 7363 2-8-3 69 ow1 DannyBrock 20 56
(Philip McBride) *racd stands' side: hld up in tch in midfield: shkn up 2f out: no imp u.p over 1f out: wl hld and kpt on same pce ins fnl f: 9th of 17 in gp* **50/1**

4510 **14** *shd* **Just For Fun**[28] 6951 2-8-2 64 (b) AaronJones 28 55
(Richard Fahey) *racd stands' side: trckd gp ldrs: effrt and unable qck over 1f out: wknd ins fnl f: 10th of 17 in gp* **100/1**

43 **15** *hd* **Scenery**[29] 6867 2-8-7 0 HarryBentley 12 59
(Eve Johnson Houghton) *racd far side: swtchd rt after s: in tch in midfield: effrt 2f out: no imp over 1f out: wknd ins fnl f: 5th of 11 in gp* **20/1**

504 **16** *nk* **Nampara**[11] 7482 2-8-2 62 JoeyHaynes 21 53
(Paul D'Arcy) *racd stands' side: pressed gp ldr: rdn 2f out: drvn and no ex over 1f out: wknd ins fnl f: 11th of 17 in gp* **100/1**

2134 **17** *nk* **Wensley**[35] 6693 2-8-11 79 MickaelBarzalona 23 62
(James Bethell) *racd stands' side: hld up towards rr: effrt 3f out: no imp u.p over 1f out: btn whn squeezed for room 1f out: kpt on same pce after: 12th of 17 in gp* **25/1**

031 **18** *hd* **Arden Pearl (IRE)**[61] 5717 2-8-4 75 (h) EdwardGreatrex 5 54
(Archie Watson) *racd far side: taken down early: hld up in midfield: effrt to chse gp ldrs 2f out: no imp u.p over 1f out: wknd ins fnl f: 6th of 11 in gp* **28/1**

0066 **19** *1/2* **Starlight Mystery (IRE)**[34] 6726 2-8-2 85 FrannyNorton 25 50
(Mark Johnston) *racd stands' side: dwlt: bhd: sme hdwy ins fnl f: n.d: 13th of 17 in gp* **10/1**

263 **20** *1/2* **Tember**[81] 4995 2-8-10 71 ow1 (b[1]) JamieSpencer 19 57
(David Barron) *racd stands' side: hld up in rr: switching rt 2f out: effrt u.p over 1f out: nvr getting on terms and pushed rt jst over 1f out: wknd ins fnl f: 14th of 17 in gp* **33/1**

2132 **21** *nse* **Amazing Alice**[9] 7536 2-8-4 81 (p) GeorgeWood 9 51
(Archie Watson) *racd far side: chsd gp ldrs: rdn ent fnl 2f: unable qck u.p over 1f out: wknd ins fnl f: 7th of 11 in gp* **14/1**

622 **22** *1 1/4* **Sweet Vixen**[75] 5216 2-8-2 72 NickyMackay 18 45
(Tom Clover) *racd stands' side: towards rr: effrt 2f out: no imp and btn whn pushed rt jst over 1f out: wknd ins fnl f: 15th of 17 in gp* **33/1**

503 **23** *1 3/4* **Queen Adelaide**[46] 6286 2-8-2 67 JackOsborn 8 40
(John Ryan) *racd far side: chsd ldrs tl over 2f out: sn u.p: lost pl over 1f out: wknd fnl f: 8th of 11 in gp* **100/1**

0 **24** *1/2* **Ipsilante**[21] 7153 2-8-2 0 ManuelFernandes 24 38
(Jonathan Portman) *racd stands' side: s.i.s: a towards rr: n.d: 16th of 17 in gp* **66/1**

1406 **25** *hd* **Royal Liberty**[28] 6932 2-8-7 70 JoeFanning 26 43
(Mark Johnston) *racd stands' side: bmpd s: in tch in midfield: rdn over 2f out: losing pl and sltly impeded over 1f out: wknd fnl f: 17th of 17 in gp* **66/1**

1005 **26** *1 3/4* **Poetic Steps (FR)**[23] 7087 2-8-4 77 JFEgan 11 34
(Mark Johnston) *racd far side: chsd gp ldrs tl struggling u.p jst over 2f out: sn lost pl: wknd fnl f: 9th of 11 in gp* **50/1**

5401 **27** *nk* **Titchy Digits**[12] 7458 2-8-5 71 ow3 KierenFox 1 35
(Michael Attwater) *racd far side: a towards rr: rdn over 2f out: wknd over 1f out: 10th of 11 in gp* **66/1**

52 **28** *3/4* **Se You**[9] 7551 2-8-9 0 DavidProbert 6 36
(Tim Easterby) *racd far side: a bhd: rdn 3f out: no imp over 1f out: wl btn and eased ins fnl f: 11th of 11 in gp* **28/1**

1m 11.76s (-0.44) **Going Correction** -0.075s/f (Good) 28 Ran SP% **135.1**
Speed ratings (Par 101): **99,98,97,96,95 94,93,93,92,92 91,90,88,87,87 87,86,86,85,85 85,83,81,80,80 77,77,76**
CSF £78.68 TOTE £6.00: £2.70, £5.40, £10.70; EX 135.80 Trifecta £2784.30.
**Owner** The Racing Cricketers & Partner **Bred** Bolton Grange **Trained** East Everleigh, Wilts

**FOCUS**
A valuable, good quality juvenile sales' contest. They went a decent gallop in two distinct groups, far and stands' side. There didn't appear to be any particular bias. The principals have been rated near their pre-race levels.

## 7815 BRITISH STALLION STUDS EBF BREEDERS' FILLIES SERIES H'CAP 1m

**4:25** (4:28) (Class 2) 3-Y-O+

**£31,125** (£9,320; £4,660; £2,330; £1,165; £585) **Stalls** High

Form RPR

1202 **1** **Peach Melba**[6] 7658 3-8-12 **89** FrannyNorton 5 99
(Mark Johnston) *w ldr tl led and crossed to stands' rail over 4f out: rdn 2f out: forged ahd 1f out: styd on wl* **8/1**

6211 **2** *1 1/2* **Shenanigans (IRE)**[14] 7406 3-9-4 **95** FrankieDettori 9 102
(Roger Varian) *t.k.h: trckd ldrs tl wnt 2nd over 3f out: rdn and ev ch 2f out: no ex 1f out: chsd wnr and kpt on same pce ins fnl f* **10/3[1]**

2123 **3** *1 1/2* **Dowayla (IRE)**[35] 6687 3-8-11 **91** DavidEgan(3) 6 95
(Saeed bin Suroor) *chsd ldrs: effrt in cl 4th 2f out: kpt on same pce fr over 1f out: wnt 3rd towards fin* **13/2[3]**

0001 **4** *1/2* **Lady Perignon**[23] 7098 4-8-3 **77** RaulDaSilva 8 79
(Andrew Balding) *t.k.h: led tl hdd and impeded over 4f out: effrt and ev ch 2f out tl no ex 1f out: wknd ins fnl f* **12/1**

013 **5** *3/4* **Clearly**[17] 7276 3-8-5 **82** NickyMackay 1 83
(John Gosden) *pushed rt s: sn rcvrd and in tch in midfield: effrt wl over 1f out: styd on same pce and no imp ins fnl f* **9/2[2]**

1134 **6** *1 1/4* **Seduce Me**[28] 6919 3-8-13 **90** (p) JoeyHaynes 3 88
(K R Burke) *s.i.s: sn in tch in midfield: effrt over 2f out: drvn and no imp over 1f out: kpt on same pce fnl f* **20/1**

4222 **7** *hd* **Panova**[14] 7406 3-8-13 **90** (p) RyanMoore 12 87
(Sir Michael Stoute) *hld up in tch in midfield: rdn 2f out: unable qck u.p over 1f out: wl hld and kpt on same pce after* **8/1**

0010 **8** *hd* **Favourite Royal (IRE)**[23] 7094 3-8-2 **79** JoeFanning 13 76
(Eve Johnson Houghton) *t.k.h: hld up in tch in midfield: shkn up and flashed tail over 2f out: rdn and no imp over 1f out: nvr trbld ldrs* **20/1**

440 **9** *3/4* **Indian Blessing**[52] 6074 3-9-5 **96** LiamKeniry 2 91
(Ed Walker) *stmbld bdly leaving stalls: hld up in last pair: swtchd rt and effrt 2f out: no imp u.p over 1f out: kpt on same pce fnl f* **16/1**

51-6 **10** *1 1/4* **Daisy Bere (FR)**[274] 99 4-8-7 **81** (p) BenCurtis 7 73
(K R Burke) *hld up in tch in midfield: effrt over 2f out: unable qck u.p and wl hld over 1f out* **50/1**

1604 **11** *1/2* **Soul Silver (IRE)**[14] 7406 3-9-0 **91** JamieSpencer 10 82
(David Simcock) *rrd as stalls opened and slowly away: a bhd* **16/1**

51 **12** *hd* **Crowning Glory (FR)**[78] 5130 4-9-7 **98** GeorgiaCox(3) 4 89
(Ralph Beckett) *in tch in midfield: effrt over 2f out: lost pl u.p over 1f out: wknd ins fnl f* **11/1**

1014 **13** *2* **Jalela**[17] 7276 3-8-11 **88** TomMarquand 11 74
(Richard Hannon) *t.k.h: hld up in tch: effrt 2f out: no hdwy u.p over 1f out: wknd fnl f* **12/1**

1m 36.52s (-2.08) **Going Correction** -0.075s/f (Good)
**WFA** 3 from 4yo 3lb 13 Ran SP% **123.8**
Speed ratings (Par 109): **107,105,104,103,102 101,101,101,100,99 98,98,96**
CSF £35.24 CT £192.57 TOTE £11.00: £3.30, £1.30, £2.10; EX 52.50 Trifecta £360.20.
**Owner** Lowther Racing & Partner **Bred** Lowther Racing **Trained** Middleham Moor, N Yorks

**FOCUS**
A good quality fillies' handicap. They went a decent gallop and once again it paid to race prominently. A pb from the winner, with the third rated to form.

## 7816 BRITISH EBF BREEDERS' FILLIES SERIES MIDDLE DISTANCE H'CAP 1m 2f
**5:00** (5:01) (Class 2) 3-Y-0+

**£31,125** (£9,320; £4,660; £2,330; £1,165; £585) **Stalls High**

Form RPR
013 **1** **Neshmeya**[50] 6152 3-8-13 **81** HarryBentley 10 92+
(Charles Hills) *t.k.h: hld up in tch in midfield: clsd to trck ldrs 7f out: swtchd rt and rdn to ld 1f out: r.o wl* **5/1**[2]

4311 **2** 1 1/2 **Blushing Rose**[35] 6687 3-9-6 **88** RyanMoore 11 95
(Sir Michael Stoute) *t.k.h: w ldrs tl led 7f out: rdn 2f out: hdd 1f out: styd on same pce u.p ins fnl f* **9/2**[1]

5412 **3** 1 3/4 **Ice Dancing (IRE)**[30] 6848 3-7-13 **74** (h) TristanPrice(7) 1 78
(Michael Bell) *taken down early: hld up in tch in midfield: hdwy over 2f out: rdn and ev ch over 1f out: unable qck 1f out: kpt on same pce ins fnl f* **10/1**

251 **4** nk **Twenty Times (IRE)**[43] 6369 3-9-3 **85** (p) ShaneKelly 9 88
(Richard Hughes) *w ldrs: rdn and ev ch 2f out tl unable qck 1f out: styd on same pce ins fnl f* **12/1**

5312 **5** 1 1/2 **Great Court (IRE)**[34] 6722 3-8-10 **81** DavidEgan(3) 2 81
(Roger Varian) *trckd ldrs: clsd 3f out: rdn and ev ch 2f out tl no ex ent fnl f: wknd ins fnl f* **7/1**[3]

0162 **6** 1 **Voi**[51] 6110 3-8-4 **72** (t) JimmyQuinn 3 70
(Conrad Allen) *s.i.s and niggled along early: in tch in rr: effrt 2f out: kpt on u.p ins fnl f: no threat to ldrs* **33/1**

3312 **7** 1 **Sea Tide**[16] 7338 3-9-1 **83** (tp) BenCurtis 6 79
(Hugo Palmer) *s.i.s: in tch in rr and t.k.h after 2f: effrt ent fnl 2f: drvn over 1f out: styd on same pce* **7/1**[3]

221 **8** nse **Lorelina**[20] 7201 4-9-2 **80** DavidProbert 7 75
(Andrew Balding) *t.k.h: w ldrs tl rdn and unable qck over 2f out: outpcd and btn over 1f out: wknd fnl f* **5/1**[2]

4166 **9** shd **Euro Nightmare (IRE)**[35] 6671 3-9-10 **92** JoeFanning 8 88
(Keith Dalgleish) *in tch in rr: rdn and ent fnl 2f: no prog and wl hld over 1f out* **12/1**

5216 **10** hd **Keeper's Choice (IRE)**[36] 6657 3-8-2 **73** GeorgeWood(3) 5 68
(Denis Coakley) *hld up in tch in last trio: effrt 2f out: no imp whn drvn over 1f out: wknd ins fnl f* **25/1**

5036 **11** 1 1/2 **Appointed**[28] 6924 3-9-8 **90** AndrewMullen 4 82
(Tim Easterby) *t.k.h: hld up in tch in midfield: rdn 2f out: drvn and lost pl over 1f out: wknd fnl f* **14/1**

2m 4.21s (-1.59) **Going Correction** -0.075s/f (Good)
**WFA** 3 from 4yo 4lb **11 Ran SP% 114.4**
Speed ratings (Par 109): **103,101,100,100,98 98,97,97,97,97 95**
CSF £26.94 CT £215.54 TOTE £5.70: £1.80, £1.70, £4.20; EX 19.70 Trifecta £413.90.
**Owner** Hamdan Al Maktoum **Bred** J Wigan & G Strawbridge **Trained** Lambourn, Berks

**FOCUS**
A decent fillies' handicap. There had been rain ahead of this contest, and the time was modest, but they didn't go much of a gallop initially. It's been rated around the runner-up to her latest AW form.

## 7817 EBF BREEDERS' FILLIES' SERIES #THISFILLYCAN H'CAP 1m 4f
**5:35** (5:35) (Class 2) 3-Y-0+

**£31,125** (£9,320; £4,660; £2,330; £1,165; £585) **Stalls Centre**

Form RPR
1012 **1** **Cribbs Causeway (IRE)**[14] 7401 3-9-0 **90** (p[1]) FrankieDettori 3 100+
(Roger Charlton) *trckd ldrs and travelled strly: clsd and upsides ldrs over 2f out: rdn to ld and rdr dropped whip over 1f out: clr ins fnl f: kpt on: pushed out* **5/2**[1]

5-50 **2** 1 **Teofonic (IRE)**[98] 4376 3-8-12 **88** FrannyNorton 1 95
(Mark Johnston) *t.k.h: hld up in tch in midfield: effrt ent fnl 2f: nt clr run over 1f out: hdwy u.p to chse wnr ins fnl f: kpt on but nvr getting to wnr* **10/1**

5350 **3** 1 3/4 **Jelly Monger (IRE)**[17] 7283 5-8-12 **85** GeorgeWood(3) 9 88
(Dominic Ffrench Davis) *t.k.h: chsd ldr tl 9f out: effrt and switching lft over 1f out: wnt 3rd ins fnl f: kpt on but no threat to wnr* **16/1**

2536 **4** 3/4 **Saumur**[10] 7515 5-8-0 **70** oh1 NickyMackay 2 72
(Denis Coakley) *chsd ldrs: wnt 2nd 9f out tl led 6f out: jnd over 2f out: rdn and hdd over 1f out: wknd ins fnl f* **33/1**

0550 **5** 1 3/4 **Curlew River**[14] 7395 3-9-2 **92** JoeFanning 7 92
(Mark Johnston) *led tl 6f out: chsd ldr: clsd and upsides over 2f out: sn rdn and unable qck over 1f out: wknd ins fnl f* **13/2**

2404 **6** 3/4 **Jive Talking (IRE)**[16] 7338 3-7-8 **77** (h[1]) DarraghKeenan(7) 8 76
(Michael Bell) *t.k.h: hld up in tch towards rr: effrt 2f out: kpt on same pce and no imp ins fnl f* **16/1**

2424 **7** 3/4 **White Chocolate (IRE)**[34] 6722 3-8-11 **87** JamieSpencer 4 85
(David Simcock) *stdd s: hld up in tch: shkn up 2f out: sn rdn and no imp: wl hld and kpt on same pce ins fnl f* **4/1**[2]

2504 **8** 4 **Elysian Fields (GR)**[14] 7401 6-9-8 **92** HarryBentley 6 82
(Amanda Perrett) *hld up in tch in midfield: effrt ent fnl 2f: no hdwy u.p over 1f out: wknd ins fnl f* **9/1**

5120 **9** 1/2 **Ebbesbourne (IRE)**[63] 5658 3-9-2 **92** (h) RyanMoore 10 83
(Sir Michael Stoute) *t.k.h: hld up in tch towards rr: effrt 3f out: sn drvn and no hdwy: wknd over 1f out* **9/2**[3]

-530 **10** 2 1/2 **Groovejet**[23] 7089 6-9-10 **94** AdamKirby 5 80
(Richard Spencer) *stdd s: hld up in rr: short-lived effrt over 2f out: sn btn* **20/1**

2m 33.03s (1.03) **Going Correction** -0.075s/f (Good)
**WFA** 3 from 5yo+ 6lb **10 Ran SP% 118.6**
Speed ratings (Par 96): **93,92,91,90,89 89,88,85,85,83**
CSF £29.69 CT £338.73 TOTE £2.30: £1.10, £3.80, £5.20; EX 30.90 Trifecta £426.00.
**Owner** Nick Bradley Racing 13 **Bred** N Bradley **Trained** Beckhampton, Wilts

**FOCUS**
A decent middle-distance fillies' handicap. There had been some heavy rain and once again the winning time was modest. They went a steady gallop. The third has been rated not far off this year's turf form.

T/Plt: £75.60 to a £1 stake. Pool: £124,139.12 - 1,198.01 winning units. T/Qpdt: £18.90 to a £1 stake. Pool: £8,978.61 - 351.08 winning units. **Steve Payne**

# 7518 REDCAR (L-H)
Saturday, October 7

**OFFICIAL GOING: Good to soft (7.8)**
Wind: Fairly strong half against Weather: Overcast

## 7818 JACK'S COACHES EBF STALLIONS NOVICE STKS (DIV I) 7f
**1:40** (1:40) (Class 5) 2-Y-0 **£3,234** (£962; £481; £240) **Stalls Centre**

Form RPR
0 **1** **Shuhood (IRE)**[86] 4792 2-9-2 0 DaneO'Neill 1 75
(Richard Hannon) *trckd ldrs: racd quite keenly: rdn over 1f out: wandered lft and rt appr fnl f: chal strly ins fnl f: edgd ahd fnl 75yds: kpt on* **25/1**

441 **2** hd **Poets Dream (IRE)**[28] 6938 2-9-9 80 JosephineGordon 7 81
(Mohamed Moubarak) *prom: rdn to ld over 1f out: strly pressed fnl f: hdd 75yds out: kpt on* **5/1**[2]

2 **3** hd **Rich Identity**[17] 7281 2-9-2 0 SilvestreDeSousa 11 73
(Roger Varian) *dwlt: midfield: pushed along and hdwy over 2f out: rdn over 1f out: edgd rt appr fnl f: ev ch ins fnl f: kpt on* **4/7**[1]

44 **4** 4 1/2 **How Bizarre**[17] 7266 2-9-2 0 ShaneGray 10 61
(Kevin Ryan) *led: rdn whn hdd over 1f out: wknd fnl f* **33/1**

**5** nse **Sioux Frontier (IRE)** 2-9-2 0 TonyHamilton 6 61
(Richard Fahey) *dwlt: hld up: pushed along and hdwy over 1f out: kpt on fnl f* **25/1**

**6** 1 1/2 **Tigershark (IRE)** 2-9-2 0 GrahamLee 5 57
(Bryan Smart) *trckd ldrs: rdn over 2f out: wknd fnl f* **50/1**

526 **7** 2 **Lifeboat (IRE)**[23] 7093 2-9-2 77 PaulHanagan 9 52
(Charles Hills) *trckd ldrs: racd keenly: rdn over 2f out: wknd fnl f* **8/1**

4 **8** 2 1/4 **Chantresse (IRE)**[29] 6876 2-8-11 0 KevinStott 12 41
(K R Burke) *midfield: rdn along 3f out: wknd over 1f out* **6/1**[3]

00 **9** 1 **Eeh Bah Gum (IRE)**[16] 7326 2-9-2 0 DavidNolan 8 43
(David O'Meara) *hld up: nvr threatened* **100/1**

46 **10** 3 **Miss Wolverine**[8] 7563 2-8-11 0 CamHardie 13 30
(Michael Easterby) *a outpcd in rr* **100/1**

6 **11** 1 1/4 **Joe Cable (IRE)**[11] 7472 2-8-9 0 FayeMcManoman(7) 2 31
(Nigel Tinkler) *hld up: rdn over 3f out: sn wknd* **100/1**

**12** 4 **Jiro Boy** 2-9-2 0 DuranFentiman 3 21
(Rebecca Bastiman) *midfield: rdn over 3f out: sn wknd* **100/1**

1m 24.9s (0.40) **Going Correction** +0.025s/f (Good) **12 Ran SP% 122.3**
Speed ratings (Par 95): **98,97,97,92,92 90,88,85,84,81 79,75**
CSF £146.27 TOTE £27.60: £5.20, £1.60, £1.10; EX 181.90 Trifecta £536.70.
**Owner** Hamdan Al Maktoum **Bred** Shadwell Estate Company Limited **Trained** East Everleigh, Wilts
■ Stewards' Enquiry : Dane O'Neill four-day ban: excessive use of whip (Oct 22-25)

**FOCUS**
The ground had dried out slightly and was now good to soft all over (from good to soft, soft in places). GoingStick 7.8. Not a bad novice event to start, with a few of these having already shown a decent level of promise and the first three pulled clear. The winning time was 2.9sec outside standard, but they were racing into quite a headwind. Paul Hanagan said the ground was "just on the slow side of good", Cam Hardie said: "It's on the easy side, but not all that soft" while Duran Fentiman said: "It's good to soft, but not that bad - it's drying up".

## 7819 JACK'S COACHES EBF STALLIONS NOVICE STKS (DIV II) 7f
**2:10** (2:10) (Class 5) 2-Y-0 **£3,234** (£962; £481; £240) **Stalls Centre**

Form RPR
242 **1** **Three Saints Bay (IRE)**[14] 7383 2-9-2 72 DavidNolan 10 77
(David O'Meara) *trckd ldrs: rdn to ld over 1f out: kpt on* **12/1**

5 **2** 1 1/4 **Tamkeen**[17] 7280 2-9-2 0 DaneO'Neill 5 74
(Owen Burrows) *prom: rdn 2f out: kpt on same pce fnl f* **7/2**[2]

0 **3** shd **Launceston Place (FR)**[17] 7281 2-9-2 0 JosephineGordon 3 73
(Henry Spiller) *trckd ldrs: rdn over 2f out: kpt on fnl f* **16/1**

0 **4** 1/2 **Commander Han (FR)**[43] 6403 2-9-2 0 KevinStott 8 72
(Kevin Ryan) *awkward s: sn in midfield racing keenly: drvn and no prog 2f out: edgd rt to outer over 1f out: styd on fnl f* **1/1**[1]

444 **5** nk **Picture No Sound (IRE)**[45] 6312 2-9-2 72 PaulHanagan 7 71
(Richard Fahey) *midfield: rdn over 2f out: kpt on ins fnl f* **7/1**[3]

05 **6** nse **Bertog**[30] 6854 2-9-2 0 PaulMulrennan 2 71
(John Mackie) *hld up: racd keenly: pushed along and hdwy over 1f out: kpt on* **22/1**

62 **7** 1 1/4 **The Cliff Horse (IRE)**[24] 7045 2-8-11 0 JackGarritty 4 63
(Donald McCain) *led: rdn whn hdd over 1f out: wknd ins fnl f* **20/1**

**8** 7 **Red Seeker** 2-9-2 0 NeilFarley 12 49
(Andrew Crook) *midfield: rdn over 2f out: wknd over 1f out* **100/1**

44 **9** 2 1/4 **Gleaming Sun**[7] 7623 2-9-2 0 CamHardie 1 43
(Michael Easterby) *a towards rr* **66/1**

0 **10** 3 1/2 **Kenmare River**[19] 7221 2-9-2 0 PJMcDonald 11 33
(Jedd O'Keeffe) *hld up: rdn over 2f out: sn wknd* **66/1**

0 **11** 10 **Comporta**[17] 7281 2-9-2 0 SilvestreDeSousa 6
(Ismail Mohammed) *dwlt: hld up: rdn over 2f out: wknd and bhd fnl 2f* **11/1**

1m 25.03s (0.53) **Going Correction** +0.025s/f (Good) **11 Ran SP% 119.7**
Speed ratings (Par 95): **98,96,96,95,95 95,94,86,83,79 68**
CSF £53.04 TOTE £10.10: £3.80, £1.10, £5.60; EX 48.50 Trifecta £461.90.
**Owner** York Thoroughbred Racing **Bred** Epona Bloodstock Ltd **Trained** Upper Helmsley, N Yorks

**FOCUS**
Probably not quite as deep a race as the first division and the winning time was 0.13sec slower. The winner already had an official mark of 72, suggesting the form is nothing special, and it was another race where favourite backers got their fingers burnt. Straightforward form, with the runner-up and a few in behind all rated near their pre-race marks.

## 7820 VISIT THE ALL NEW RACINGUK.COM (S) STKS 1m 2f 1y
**2:45** (2:47) (Class 5) 3-5-Y-0 **£3,234** (£962; £481; £240) **Stalls Low**

Form RPR
0450 **1** **Miningrocks (FR)**[3] 7735 5-9-1 72 (v) GerO'Neill(7) 3 64+
(Declan Carroll) *mde all: 4 l clr on bit 3f out: rdn 2f out: drvn and reduced advantage 1f out: idled and pressed fnl 110yds: fnd ex* **1/1**[1]

2600 **2** 1 **Maraakib (IRE)**[10] 7524 5-9-3 67 DavidNolan 2 58+
(David O'Meara) *midfield on inner: rdn and hdwy over 2f out: chsd ldr 1f out: ev ch 100yds out: one pce* **5/2**[2]

6000 **3** 1 **Rita's Man (IRE)**[28] 6937 3-9-4 67 (p[1]) SilvestreDeSousa 10 62
(Richard Hannon) *prom: rdn along over 3f out: one pce in 3rd ins fnl f* **7/1**[3]

4605 **4** 3 1/2 **Urban Spirit (IRE)**[16] 7331 3-8-13 51 TonyHamilton 1 50
(Roger Fell) *hld up: rdn over 2f out: kpt on fr over 1f out: nvr threatened* **33/1**

3406 **5** *nk* **Siyahamba (IRE)**[17] 7271 3-8-6 48 HarryRussell(7) 9 49
(Bryan Smart) *midfield: rdn over 2f out: plugged on fnl f* **100/1**

3300 **6** *½* **Lady Volante (IRE)**[8] 7573 3-8-3 53 RowanScott(5) 8 43
(Rebecca Menzies) *hld up: nvr threatened* **20/1**

33-0 **7** *8* **Ritasun (FR)**[36] 6475 4-9-3 70 (p) DaneO'Neill 6 32
(Harry Whittington) *chsd ldrs: rdn over 3f out: wknd over 2f out* **14/1**

6003 **8** *4½* **Leopard (IRE)**[19] 7220 3-8-13 55 (p[1]) BarryMcHugh 4 25
(Tony Coyle) *chsd ldrs: rdn over 3f out: sn wknd* **14/1**

0660 **9** *1¼* **Kitsey (IRE)**[19] 7210 3-8-8 48 KieranO'Neill 7 17
(Richard Hannon) *a in rr* **50/1**

6000 **10** *1½* **Whip Up A Frenzy (IRE)**[21] 7165 5-9-0 44 ShelleyBirkett(3) 5 19
(David O'Meara) *in tch: rdn over 3f out: sn wknd* **50/1**

2m 6.66s (-0.44) **Going Correction** +0.025s/f (Good)
**WFA** 3 from 4yo+ 4lb 10 Ran SP% **117.0**
Speed ratings (Par 103): **102,101,100,97,97 96,90,86,85,84**
CSF £3.34 TOTE £2.00: £1.10, £1.30, £2.00; EX 4.20 Trifecta £14.50.Winner bought in for £6,500.
**Owner** Mrs Sarah Bryan **Bred** M Daguzan-Garros & Rolling Hills Farm **Trained** Malton, N Yorks

**FOCUS**
An uncompetitive seller and few ever got into it. The third and fourth set the level.

## 7821 TOTEPOOL TWO-YEAR-OLD TROPHY (LISTED RACE) 5f 217y
**3:20** (3:21) (Class 1) 2-Y-O

**£99,242** (£37,625; £18,830; £9,380; £4,707; £2,362) **Stalls** Centre

Form RPR

0255 **1** **Darkanna (IRE)**[7] 7617 2-8-11 104 BarryMcHugh 12 95
(Richard Fahey) *racd centre: cl up: led over 2f out: rdn ent fnl f: sn edgd lft: kpt on wl towards fin* **4/1**[1]

12 **2** *½* **Flying Sparkle (IRE)**[16] 7334 2-8-4 0 HayleyTurner 15 87
(Michael Bell) *racd centre: in tch: hdwy over 2f out: n.m.r and swtchd rt over 1f out: rdn and styd on to chse wnr ins fnl f: kpt on wl towards fin* **11/1**

0322 **3** *1¾* **Foxtrot Lady**[15] 7352 2-8-4 80 CamHardie 1 81
(Andrew Balding) *racd far side: in tch: hdwy 2f out: rdn over 1f out: kpt on wl fnl f* **12/1**

0152 **4** *¾* **Red Roman**[15] 7353 2-9-2 94 PJMcDonald 9 91
(Charles Hills) *racd centre: trckd ldrs: hdwy over 2f out and sn cl up: rdn over 1f out: wknd ins fnl f* **10/1**

2052 **5** *nse* **Maybride**[8] 7563 2-8-9 83 TonyHamilton 14 83
(Richard Fahey) *towards rr centre: hdwy over 2f out: rdn along wl over 1f out: kpt on wl fnl f* **16/1**

21 **6** *¾* **Never Back Down (IRE)**[161] 2148 2-9-2 0 JosephineGordon 10 88
(Hugo Palmer) *racd centre: led: rdn along 1/2-way: hdd over 2f out: drvn wl over 1f out and grad wknd* **10/1**

2125 **7** *hd* **Regulator (IRE)**[40] 6521 2-9-2 86 DavidNolan 7 87
(Richard Fahey) *towards rr: hdwy over 2f out: rdn wl over 1f out: styd on wl fnl f* **22/1**

1000 **8** *1* **De Bruyne Horse**[22] 7112 2-9-5 98 (b) RachelRichardson 17 87
(Richard Hannon) *racd towards stands' side: hld up and mde hdwy 2f out: swtchd rt and rdn over 1f out: kpt on fnl f* **33/1**

6201 **9** *nk* **Requinto Dawn (IRE)**[11] 7472 2-8-9 84 PatrickMathers 5 76
(Richard Fahey) *racd towards far side: chsd ldrs: hdwy over 2f out: sn cl up: and rdn: drvn and kpt on same pce fnl f* **16/1**

0521 **10** *½* **Hunni**[63] 5659 2-8-0 77 KieranO'Neill 21 66
(Tom Clover) *racd towards stands' side: chsd ldrs: rdn along 2f out: grad wknd* **25/1**

2212 **11** *shd* **Crownthorpe**[24] 7050 2-8-3 87 PaulHanagan 19 68
(Richard Fahey) *racd towards stands' side: in rr: pushed along and hdwy over 2f out: rdn wl over 1f out: kpt on fnl f* **9/1**[3]

2064 **12** *¾* **Lady Anjorica (IRE)**[7] 7596 2-8-7 79 JamesSullivan 8 70
(Keith Dalgleish) *in rr centre and rdn along 1/2-way: hdwy 2f out: swtchd lft wl over 1f out: kpt on u.p fnl f* **66/1**

3105 **13** *nk* **Green Fortune**[28] 6935 2-8-6 89 (b) LiamJones 4 68
(William Haggas) *trckd ldrs far side: pushed along over 2f out: sn rdn and wknd* **16/1**

1264 **14** *½* **Silver Starlight**[23] 7087 2-8-11 80 DavidAllan 3 71
(Tim Easterby) *racd towards far side: prom: rdn along over 2f out: sn drvn and wknd* **33/1**

0132 **15** *1* **Billy Dylan (IRE)**[35] 6682 2-9-0 87 DaneO'Neill 13 71
(Richard Hannon) *cl up centre: rdn along over 2f out: sn drvn and wknd* **33/1**

4233 **16** *shd* **Simmy's Copshop**[8] 7564 2-9-0 88 SilvestreDeSousa 20 71
(Richard Fahey) *racd towards stands' side: in tch: rdn along wl over 2f out: sn wknd* **20/1**

0500 **17** *1* **Inviolable Spirit (IRE)**[24] 7050 2-8-6 77 DuranFentiman 18 60
(Richard Fahey) *cl up: rdn along over 2f out: sn wknd* **80/1**

106 **18** *hd* **Pilkington**[85] 4862 2-9-0 79 GrahamLee 16 67
(David O'Meara) *dwlt: a towards rr* **100/1**

3323 **19** *½* **Move It Move It**[85] 4836 2-9-2 76 KevinStott 11 67
(Keith Dalgleish) *s.i.s: a bhd* **80/1**

5460 **20** *1½* **Jedi Master (IRE)**[23] 7090 2-8-9 83 AdamMcNamara 23 56
(Richard Fahey) *racd towards stands' rail: in tch: hdwy on wd outside 1/2-way: sn rdn along and wknd fnl 2f* **33/1**

2142 **21** *nse* **John Kirkup**[24] 7049 2-8-9 92 PaulMulrennan 2 55
(Michael Dods) *racd towards far side: in tch: effrt over 2f out: sn rdn along and nvr a factor* **6/1**[2]

1305 **22** *¾* **Chatburn (IRE)**[16] 7318 2-9-0 82 JasonHart 6 58
(David O'Meara) *a towards rr* **50/1**

1220 **23** *4* **Rumshak (IRE)**[41] 6466 2-8-6 83 ConnorBeasley 22 37
(Michael Dods) *a towards rr* **28/1**

1m 10.49s (-1.31) **Going Correction** +0.025s/f (Good) 23 Ran SP% **131.2**
Speed ratings (Par 103): **109,108,106,105,104 103,103,102,101,101 101,100,99,99,97 97,96,96,95,93 93,92,86**
CSF £42.82 TOTE £4.60: £2.00, £3.80, £4.20; EX 59.60 Trifecta £1071.60.
**Owner** The Cool Silk Partnership **Bred** Mountarmstrong Stud **Trained** Musley Bank, N Yorks

**FOCUS**
The annual Cleveland cavalry charge which has been won by some top-class performers over the years, such as Pipalong, Somnus and Limato. This year Richard Fahey saddled eight of the 23 runners, having never won the race before, and he hit the target this time. Despite the size of the field only a handful had a realistic chance on these terms and the highest-rated runner landed the prize. The main action unfolded up the middle and fillies filled the first three places. An improved run from the runner-up, while the third and those close up fit.

## 7822 TOTESCOOP6 EBF STALLIONS GUISBOROUGH STKS (LISTED RACE) 7f
**3:55** (3:56) (Class 1) 3-Y-O+

**£22,684** (£8,600; £4,304; £2,144; £1,076; £540) **Stalls** Centre

Form RPR

0453 **1** **Jallota**[8] 7579 6-9-0 110 DaneO'Neill 2 112
(Charles Hills) *trckd ldrs: pushed along to chal over 1f out: rdn to ld jst ins fnl f: r.o wl* **11/4**[2]

0630 **2** *4½* **Von Blucher (IRE)**[28] 6918 4-9-0 95 (p[1]) PJMcDonald 3 100
(Rebecca Menzies) *hld up: hdwy and in tch over 2f out: rdn and hung lft over 1f out: kpt on* **33/1**

1151 **3** *nse* **Lahore (USA)**[24] 7053 3-8-12 99 SilvestreDeSousa 6 99
(Roger Varian) *stdd s: hld up: pushed along and hdwy over 2f out: rdn to chse ldr over 1f out: one pce fnl f* **2/1**[1]

14 **4** *¾* **Jordan Sport**[28] 6922 4-9-0 98 (h) HayleyTurner 8 98
(David Simcock) *led: rdn over 2f out: hdd jst ins fnl f: no ex* **12/1**[3]

50-2 **5** *hd* **Yattwee (USA)**[30] 6856 4-9-0 102 JosephineGordon 4 97
(Saeed bin Suroor) *trckd ldrs: rdn along over 2f out: one pce* **11/4**[2]

2006 **6** *¾* **Don't Touch**[27] 6966 5-9-0 105 (b[1]) TonyHamilton 7 95
(Richard Fahey) *trckd ldrs: rdn over 2f out: outpcd over 1f out* **12/1**[3]

001 **7** *1* **Stamp Hill (IRE)**[70] 5393 4-9-0 98 (b) PaulHanagan 5 92
(Richard Fahey) *hld up: rdn along over 2f out: nvr threatened* **14/1**

3124 **8** *3* **Rutherford (IRE)**[32] 6787 3-8-7 83 BarryMcHugh 1 78
(Kevin Ryan) *a towards rr* **50/1**

4156 **9** *12* **Caridade (USA)**[22] 7130 3-8-7 80 JamesSullivan 9 46
(Kevin Ryan) *midfield: rdn along over 3f out: sn wknd and bhd* **100/1**

1m 23.11s (-1.39) **Going Correction** +0.025s/f (Good)
**WFA** 3 from 4yo+ 2lb 9 Ran SP% **114.6**
Speed ratings (Par 111): **108,102,102,101,101 100,99,96,82**
CSF £85.30 TOTE £3.80: £1.40, £7.90, £1.10; EX 105.00 Trifecta £313.20.
**Owner** Mrs Fitri Hay **Bred** Barry Walters **Trained** Lambourn, Berks

**FOCUS**
An interesting Listed event, but once again class told with the highest-rated runner in the race successful. The winner has been rated back to something like his best, and the runner-up to this year's handicap form.

## 7823 RACING UK STRAIGHT-MILE SERIES FINAL H'CAP 7f 219y
**4:30** (4:31) (Class 2) 3-Y-O+

**£12,450** (£3,728; £1,864; £932; £466; £234) **Stalls** Centre

Form RPR

5164 **1** **Khamaary (IRE)**[35] 6676 3-9-10 **95** DaneO'Neill 7 105
(Mark Johnston) *mde all: rdn over 2f out: edgd rt 1f out: kpt on wl* **11/2**[2]

0360 **2** *¾* **Zeshov (IRE)**[8] 7570 6-8-6 **74** (p) DuranFentiman 9 82
(Rebecca Bastiman) *hld up: swtchd rt to outer and rdn and hdwy over 1f out: chsd ldr whn edgd lft and bmpd into 4th jst ins fnl f: continued to edge lft but kpt on* **33/1**

5631 **3** *1¾* **Off Art**[24] 7052 7-8-1 **72** ow1 (p) RachelRichardson(3) 4 76
(Tim Easterby) *hld up: pushed along and hdwy 2f out: rdn to chse ldr 1f out: kpt on* **8/1**

1031 **4** *½* **Ventura Secret (IRE)**[24] 7042 3-8-1 **72** JamesSullivan 5 75
(Tim Easterby) *trckd ldrs: rdn 2f out: edgd rt and bmpd into 2nd jst ins fnl f: one pce* **8/1**

3110 **5** *2½* **Mon Beau Visage (IRE)**[8] 7582 4-9-6 **88** (p) DavidNolan 6 85
(David O'Meara) *hld up: rdn and sme hdwy over 1f out: one oace and nvr threatened ldrs* **14/1**

1510 **6** *1¾* **Zodiakos (IRE)**[24] 7044 4-9-4 **86** (p) TonyHamilton 3 78
(Roger Fell) *trckd ldrs: rdn over 2f out: wknd ins fnl f* **7/1**[3]

4652 **7** *nk* **Silvery Moon (IRE)**[8] 7566 10-9-1 **83** JasonHart 8 75
(Tim Easterby) *trckd ldrs: rdn over 2f out: wknd ins fnl f* **12/1**

0603 **8** *4* **Woody Bay**[18] 7246 7-7-12 **73** JamieGormley(7) 1 55
(Mark Walford) *in tch: rdn along 3f out: wknd* **9/1**

05 **9** *4* **Palmerston**[42] 6434 4-8-11 **79** GrahamLee 2 51
(Michael Appleby) *hld up: rdn over 2f out: wknd* **12/1**

2542 **10** *1¼* **Rashford's Double (IRE)**[8] 7569 3-8-10 **81** (p) SilvestreDeSousa 10 50
(Richard Fahey) *in tch on outside: rdn over 2f out: wknd over 1f out* **7/2**[1]

6066 **11** *5* **Father Bertie**[18] 7246 5-9-0 **82** (tp) DavidAllan 11 48
(Tim Easterby) *trckd ldrs: rdn over 2f out: wknd and eased* **8/1**

1m 36.82s (0.22) **Going Correction** +0.025s/f (Good)
**WFA** 3 from 4yo+ 3lb 11 Ran SP% **118.4**
Speed ratings (Par 109): **99,98,96,96,93 91,91,87,83,82 77**
CSF £169.06 CT £1478.57 TOTE £4.50: £2.00, £11.60, £3.60; EX 188.00 Trifecta £977.30.
**Owner** Hamdan Al Maktoum **Bred** Shadwell Estate Company Limited **Trained** Middleham Moor, N Yorks

**FOCUS**
A decent final of this series, but they didn't seem to go a great pace early and that probably helped the winner. Tim Easterby had trained the winner of the race four times in the past nine years and saddled four this time, but had to be content with third and fourth. The runner-up has been rated to his best and the third to his recent form.

## 7824 MARKET CROSS JEWELLERS H'CAP 1m 2f 1y
**5:05** (5:05) (Class 4) (0-80,80) 3-Y-O+ **£6,469** (£1,925; £962; £481) **Stalls** Low

Form RPR

4544 **1** **Road To Dubai (IRE)**[10] 7505 3-9-3 **77** HayleyTurner 5 86
(George Scott) *midfield: pushed along and hdwy 2f out: rdn to ld narrowly 1f out: kpt on wl* **7/1**[2]

2100 **2** *nk* **Armandihan (IRE)**[37] 6617 3-9-5 **79** KevinStott 9 88
(Kevin Ryan) *hld up: hdwy fr over 2f out: rdn to chal strly 1f out: kpt on but a jst hld* **10/1**[3]

2231 **3** *3¼* **Dream Machine (IRE)**[23] 7097 3-9-6 **80** SilvestreDeSousa 6 82
(Michael Bell) *hld up: hdwy on outer over 2f out: rdn and hung lft over 1f out: kpt on ins fnl f: wnt 3rd fnl 50yds: no threat to ldng pair* **15/8**[1]

325 **4** *¾* **Meccabah (FR)**[61] 5721 3-9-3 **77** PaulMulrennan 10 78
(Andrew Balding) *trckd ldrs: rdn over 2f out: led narrowly over 1f out: hdd 1f out: no ex* **7/1**[2]

4400 **5** *¾* **Chancery (USA)**[18] 7234 9-9-6 **76** (b[1]) DavidNolan 1 74
(David O'Meara) *midfield: rdn over 2f out: one pce* **12/1**

1150 **6** ¾ **Regal Mirage (IRE)**[8] 7560 3-8-8 68 ...... DavidAllan 13 66
(Tim Easterby) *trckd ldr: led 7f out: rdn over 3f out: hdd over 1f out: grad wknd* **20/1**

1204 **7** ¾ **Breanski**[40] 6518 3-8-13 73 ......(v[1]) PaulHanagan 14 69
(David O'Meara) *trckd ldrs: rdn and ev ch 2f out: wknd ins fnl f* **18/1**

6116 **8** 1½ **Maulesden May (IRE)**[25] 7032 4-9-6 76 ...... GrahamLee 4 68
(Keith Dalgleish) *in tch: rdn over 2f out: wknd fnl f* **18/1**

0005 **9** ¾ **Throckley**[21] 7142 6-9-6 76 ......(t) SamJames 8 67
(John Davies) *midfield: pushed along over 2f out: rdn and edgd lft over 1f out: short of room appr fnl f: nvr threatened* **16/1**

6460 **10** 2½ **Town Charter (USA)**[56] 5949 3-9-2 76 ......(t[1]) BarryMcHugh 3 63
(Tony Coyle) *dwlt: hld up: nvr threatened* **50/1**

1452 **11** 5 **Katebird (IRE)**[7] 7598 3-9-2 76 ...... PJMcDonald 11 53
(Mark Johnston) *led: hdd 7f out: trckd ldrs: rdn over 3f out: wknd over 1f out* **16/1**

5601 **12** 2¾ **Big Time Dancer (IRE)**[25] 7028 4-8-5 66 oh3......(p) BenRobinson(5) 2 36
(Brian Ellison) *hld up: rdn along over 4f out: sn btn* **10/1**[3]

3644 **13** 29 **Dubai's Secret**[40] 6516 4-9-9 79 ......(h) JosephineGordon 12
(David Brown) *midfield: rdn over 3f out: sn wknd: eased* **28/1**

-000 **14** 3 **Maifalki (FR)**[30] 6855 4-9-9 79 ...... JasonHart 7
(Mark Walford) *trckd ldrs: racd keenly: rdn over 2f out: wknd and eased* **16/1**

2m 6.21s (-0.89) **Going Correction** +0.025s/f (Good)
**WFA** 3 from 4yo+ 4lb **14** Ran SP% **124.0**
Speed ratings (Par 105): **104,103,101,100,99 99,98,97,96,94 90,88,65,63**
CSF £76.26 CT £187.77 TOTE £6.90: £1.80, £4.80, £1.70; EX 114.70 Trifecta £435.70.
**Owner** Mohammed Al Nabouda **Bred** Rabbah Bloodstock Limited **Trained** Newmarket, Suffolk

**FOCUS**
A fair handicap which had gone to a 3yo in each of the past three seasons and that age group dominated again, providing the first four home.

## 7825 WATCH RACE REPLAYS AT RACINGUK.COM H'CAP 5f
**5:40** (5:43) (Class 5) (0-70,71) 3-Y-0+ **£3,234** (£962; £481; £240) **Stalls** Centre

Form RPR

5311 **1** **Lydiate Lady**[25] 7020 5-8-7 56 oh1 ...... NeilFarley 2 70
(Eric Alston) *mde all: rdn 2f out: kpt on wl: easily* **9/1**

2260 **2** 4 **Astrophysics**[17] 7268 5-9-3 66 ...... PJMcDonald 1 66
(Lynn Siddall) *hld up: rdn and hdwy over 1f out: kpt on to go 2nd ins fnl f: no ch w wnr* **5/1**[2]

0000 **3** 1 **Bronze Beau**[10] 7522 10-9-4 67 ......(tp) TonyHamilton 6 63
(Kristin Stubbs) *prom: rdn 2f out: one pce* **33/1**

3505 **4** nk **Monte Cinq (IRE)**[10] 7522 3-9-5 68 ......(h) KevinStott 10 64+
(Jason Ward) *hld up: rdn 2f out: kpt on fnl f: nrst fin* **7/1**[3]

0211 **5** nk **Nuns Walk**[10] 7525 3-9-3 66 ...... DavidAllan 15 61
(Tim Easterby) *midfield: rdn and sme hdwy over 1f out: kpt on same pce* **3/1**[1]

0600 **6** nse **Tan**[17] 7268 3-9-7 70 ......(t) BarryMcHugh 7 65
(Tony Coyle) *hld up: pushed along over 1f out: swtchd lft appr fnl f: kpt on: nrst fin* **33/1**

4540 **7** ½ **Imperial Legend (IRE)**[8] 7575 8-8-7 56 oh1......(p) DuranFentiman 5 48
(Alan Brown) *chsd ldrs: rdn 1/2-way: no ex fnl 110yds* **11/1**

4440 **8** nk **Foxtrot Knight**[7] 7625 5-9-7 70 ...... JamesSullivan 16 61
(Ruth Carr) *hld up: rdn and sme hdwy over 1f out: nvr threatened* **10/1**

6640 **9** ½ **Foxy Boy**[3] 7738 3-9-3 71 ...... BenRobinson(5) 13 61
(Michael Dods) *dwlt: hld up: sme late hdwy: nvr threatened* **22/1**

1300 **10** hd **Racquet**[18] 7244 4-9-2 65 ...... PaulHanagan 11 53
(Ruth Carr) *midfield: rdn 2f out: no imp* **16/1**

5130 **11** 1¼ **Perfect Words (IRE)**[10] 7522 7-8-12 68......(p) HarrisonShaw(7) 14 52
(Marjorie Fife) *hld up: rdn 1/2-way: nvr threatened* **40/1**

5000 **12** hd **Kibaar**[10] 7522 5-9-2 65 ......(p) JackGarritty 12 48
(Ruth Carr) *chsd ldrs: rdn 1/2-way: wknd fnl f* **14/1**

0000 **13** ½ **Tinsill**[43] 6384 6-8-4 56 oh11 ...... PhilDennis(3) 9 37
(Nigel Tinkler) *chsd ldrs: rdn 1/2-way: wknd fnl f* **66/1**

0005 **14** ½ **Coiste Bodhar (IRE)**[25] 7020 6-8-8 62 ow1...... GeorgeBuckell(5) 8 41
(Scott Dixon) *hld up: nvr threatened* **16/1**

4000 **15** 1¼ **Jack Luey**[10] 7522 10-9-2 65 ......(b) DavidNolan 4 40
(Lawrence Mullaney) *prom: rdn 1/2-way: wknd over 1f out* **25/1**

0660 **16** 4½ **Sir Domino (FR)**[19] 7218 5-8-4 56 oh9......(b) RachelRichardson(3) 17 15
(Patrick Holmes) *midfield: rdn 1/2-way: wknd over 1f out* **66/1**

5052 **17** 4 **Bond Bombshell**[8] 7575 4-8-4 56......(v) ShelleyBirkett(3) 3
(David O'Meara) *midfield: rdn and hung lft 2f out: wknd and eased* **12/1**

58.27s (-0.33) **Going Correction** +0.025s/f (Good) **17** Ran SP% **127.2**
Speed ratings (Par 103): **103,96,95,94,94 93,93,92,91,91 89,89,88,87,85 78,72**
CSF £52.40 CT £1004.69 TOTE £9.80: £1.60, £1.90, £6.50, £1.90; EX 84.40 Trifecta £2167.10.
**Owner** The Scotch Piper Racing **Bred** Catridge Farm Stud **Trained** Longton, Lancs
■ Stewards' Enquiry : Kevin Stott caution: careless riding

**FOCUS**
A modest sprint handicap, taken apart by the winner. The front pair came from the two lowest stalls, though the winner raced more up the centre. A pb from the winner.
T/Plt: £33.30 to a £1 stake. Pool: £75,299.53 - 1,649.62 winning units. T/Qpdt: £10.40 to a £1 stake. Pool: £4,411.81 - 312.25 winning units. **Andrew Sheret & Joe Rowntree**

# 7407 WOLVERHAMPTON (A.W) (L-H)
Saturday, October 7

**OFFICIAL GOING: Tapeta: standard**
Wind: Light half behind Weather: Overcast

## 7826 BET365 MAIDEN FILLIES' STKS 7f 36y (Tp)
**5:45** (5:47) (Class 5) 3-Y-0+ **£3,234** (£962; £481; £240) **Stalls** High

Form RPR

2-2 **1** **Considered Opinion**[11] 7485 3-8-11 0 ...... HectorCrouch(3) 6 68
(Ralph Beckett) *chsd ldrs: pushed along over 2f out: rdn: edgd rt and r.o to ld wl ins fnl f* **4/9**[1]

**2** nk **Secret Return (IRE)** 4-8-11 0 ...... RhiainIngram(5) 4 68
(Karen George) *hld up: hdwy over 1f out: bmpd ins fnl f: r.o* **100/1**

0-03 **3** ¾ **Jazaalah (USA)**[46] 6287 3-9-0 71 ......(h) TimmyMurphy 5 65
(Owen Burrows) *prom: chsd ldr 1/2-way: led over 1f out: rdn: hung rt and hdd wl ins fnl f* **7/1**[3]

23 **4** 3½ **Natheer (USA)**[18] 7227 3-9-0 0 ...... JackMitchell 1 56
(Roger Varian) *w ldr: led 6f out tl 5f out: remained handy: rdn over 2f out: no ex fnl f* **11/4**[2]

0060 **5** 1¾ **Toolatetodelegate**[44] 6341 3-8-9 43 ...... JoshuaBryan(5) 2 51?
(Brian Barr) *led 1f: led again 5f out: rdn and hdd over 1f out: wknd ins fnl f* **150/1**

0000 **6** 3¼ **May Mist**[25] 7028 5-8-13 47 ......(b[1]) EoinWalsh(3) 3 43?
(Trevor Wall) *chsd ldrs: pushed along 3f out: wknd over 1f out* **80/1**

2663 **7** ½ **Hazell Berry (IRE)**[219] 987 3-9-0 45 ......(b) AdamBeschizza 7 41?
(Karen George) *sn pushed along in rr: outpcd fr over 2f out* **100/1**

1m 28.3s (-0.50) **Going Correction** -0.05s/f (Stan)
**WFA** 3 from 4yo+ 2lb **7** Ran SP% **112.3**
Speed ratings (Par 100): **100,99,98,94,92 89,88**
CSF £57.20 TOTE £1.30: £1.10, £38.20; EX 59.10 Trifecta £142.40.
**Owner** The Eclipse Partnership **Bred** Car Colston Hall Stud **Trained** Kimpton, Hants

**FOCUS**
The odds-on favourite made her backers sweat here.

## 7827 BET365 (S) STKS 7f 36y (Tp)
**6:15** (6:16) (Class 6) 2-Y-0 **£2,587** (£770; £384; £192) **Stalls** High

Form RPR

0203 **1** **Grimeford Lane (IRE)**[25] 7023 2-8-11 65 ......(p) TomEaves 1 63
(Michael Dods) *chsd ldrs: led over 1f out: sn rdn and hung rt: styd on* **11/4**[1]

65 **2** ½ **Kendergarten Kop (IRE)**[8] 7562 2-8-11 0 ...... RichardKingscote 3 62
(Tom Dascombe) *led: hung rt fr over 2f out: rdn and hdd over 1f out: styd on* **5/1**

0563 **3** 1¼ **Shesgotthelot**[14] 7410 2-7-13 63 ......(p) NicolaCurrie(7) 8 53
(J S Moore) *chsd ldrs: rdn over 1f out: edgd rt ins fnl f: styd on* **3/1**[2]

1166 **4** 1¾ **Princess Lyla (IRE)**[18] 7228 2-8-9 66 ...... StephenCummins(7) 4 59
(Richard Hughes) *plld hrd in 2nd pl: rdn and ev ch over 1f out: no ex wl ins fnl f* **7/2**[3]

0640 **5** ½ **Miss Mazzie**[53] 6022 2-8-6 47 ...... JoeDoyle 10 47
(Michael Easterby) *sn pushed along in rr: drvn 1/2-way: r.o ins fnl f: nvr nrr* **25/1**

006 **6** ½ **Miss Perception**[29] 6875 2-8-1 58 ......(p[1]) JaneElliott(5) 11 46
(Tom Dascombe) *s.i.s: pushed along in rr: r.o towards fin: nvr nrr* **12/1**

4006 **7** nk **Blazing Beryl (IRE)**[23] 7082 2-8-6 55 ......(p[1]) RyanTate 9 45
(Brian Meehan) *sn pushed along to chse ldr: rdn over 2f out: no ex fr over 1f out* **10/1**

0 **8** 9 **Pauvre Moi (IRE)**[14] 7410 2-8-6 0 ow3...... TimClark(3) 5 24
(John Butler) *hld up in tch: racd keenly: rdn over 1f out: wknd fnl f* **100/1**

060 **9** 7 **Paulamey**[30] 6861 2-8-3 34 ...... MattCosham(3) 2 2
(David Evans) *sn outpcd* **80/1**

1m 29.58s (0.78) **Going Correction** -0.05s/f (Stan) **9** Ran SP% **113.4**
Speed ratings (Par 93): **93,92,91,89,88 87,87,77,69**
CSF £16.45 TOTE £3.60: £1.90, £2.10, £1.50; EX 17.60 Trifecta £67.20.There was no bid for the winner. Kendergarten Kop was claimed by Mr D J Flood for £6000.
**Owner** D W Armstrong & M J K Dods **Bred** Mrs Helen Keaveney **Trained** Denton, Co Durham

**FOCUS**
A moderate seller. The winner has been rated near her best, with the third and fifth fitting.

## 7828 BET365 H'CAP 6f 20y (Tp)
**6:45** (6:48) (Class 3) (0-95,95) 3-Y-O-**£7,561** (£2,263; £1,131; £566; £282) **Stalls** Low

Form RPR

2062 **1** **Gulliver**[28] 6922 3-9-2 91 ......(t[1]) JackMitchell 7 101+
(Hugo Palmer) *prom: lost pl over 4f out: hdwy over 1f out: rdn and hung lft ins fnl f: r.o to ld post* **5/2**[1]

2665 **2** nk **Sign Of The Kodiac (IRE)**[12] 7455 4-9-3 91 ...... JoeDoyle 12 100
(James Given) *chsd ldrs: led over 4f out: rdn over 1f out: hdd post* **12/1**

-005 **3** 2¼ **Barracuda Boy (IRE)**[12] 7455 7-9-6 94 ...... RichardKingscote 2 96
(Marjorie Fife) *hld up: rdn and r.o to go 3rd wl ins fnl f: nt rch ldrs* **16/1**

3460 **4** 1¼ **Watchable**[45] 6325 7-8-10 91 ......(v) PatrickVaughan(7) 8 89
(David O'Meara) *chsd ldrs: wnt 2nd over 2f out: rdn over 1f out: no ex wl ins fnl f* **22/1**

0142 **5** nk **Seeking Magic**[12] 7455 9-9-4 92 ......(t) RyanTate 3 89
(Clive Cox) *chsd ldrs: rdn over 2f out: styd on same pce fnl f* **17/2**

20 **6** nk **Hakam (USA)**[21] 7144 5-9-7 95 ......(p) CharlesBishop 5 91+
(Michael Appleby) *hood removed late: s.i.s: hld up: nt clr run wl over 1f out: sn swtchd lft: r.o ins fnl f: nt rch ldrs* **9/2**[2]

0306 **7** hd **King Robert**[49] 6205 4-9-5 93 ......(p[1]) TomEaves 10 88
(Bryan Smart) *prom: rdn over 2f out: edgd rt and no ex ins fnl f* **8/1**[3]

0010 **8** nk **Poet's Society**[7] 7610 3-9-1 90 ...... JFEgan 4 84
(Mark Johnston) *sn pushed along to ld: hdd over 4f out: chsd ldr tl rdn over 2f out: no ex fnl f* **16/1**

5000 **9** hd **George Dryden (IRE)**[49] 6206 5-9-3 91 ...... ShaneGray 1 85+
(Ann Duffield) *hld up: gng wl whn hmpd over 1f out: nvr trbld ldrs* **33/1**

-400 **10** hd **Sir Ottoman (FR)**[126] 3324 4-9-2 90......(p) AdamBeschizza 13 83
(Ivan Furtado) *hld up: rdn over 1f out: nvr on terms* **50/1**

6002 **11** 3¼ **Go Far**[43] 6371 7-9-2 95 ......(v) JoshuaBryan(5) 6 78
(Alan Bailey) *chsd ldrs: lost pl over 3f out: sn drvn along: hung rt over 1f out: wknd ins fnl f* **8/1**[3]

0404 **12** 1½ **Gentlemen**[12] 7455 6-8-9 90 ......(h) NicolaCurrie(7) 11 68
(Phil McEntee) *sn outpcd* **12/1**

1501 **13** 3¼ **Highland Acclaim (IRE)**[39] 6554 6-9-0 91......(h) JoshDoyle(3) 9 58
(David O'Meara) *mid-div: nt clr run over 4f out: rdn over 2f out: wknd over 1f out* **50/1**

1m 12.59s (-1.91) **Going Correction** -0.05s/f (Stan)
**WFA** 3 from 4yo+ 1lb **13** Ran SP% **117.9**
Speed ratings (Par 107): **110,109,106,104,104 104,103,103,103,102 98,96,92**
CSF £32.72 CT £414.70 TOTE £3.80: £1.50, £3.80, £4.60; EX 40.90 Trifecta £448.80.
**Owner** Saleh Al Homaizi & Imad Al Sagar **Bred** S A Douch **Trained** Newmarket, Suffolk

**FOCUS**
A decent sprint handicap run at a good gallop.

## 7829 BET365 NURSERY H'CAP 1m 142y (Tp)
**7:15** (7:16) (Class 6) (0-65,65) 2-Y-0 **£2,587** (£770; £384; £192) **Stalls** Low

Form RPR

4555 **1** **Tiny Tempest (IRE)**[30] 6860 2-9-7 65 ...... CharlesBishop 5 69
(Eve Johnson Houghton) *a.p: chsd ldr over 2f out: led over 1f out: sn rdn: jst hld on* **13/2**[3]

0403 **2** hd **Gold Eagle**[10] 7510 2-8-10 61 ...... RossaRyan(7) 7 65
(Philip McBride) *hld up: hmpd over 2f out: hdwy over 1f out: r.o wl* **14/1**

3032 **3** 1¼ **Far Dawn**[18] 7239 2-9-7 65 ......(v[1]) MartinLane 13 66
(Simon Crisford) *sn chsng ldr: led over 2f out: rdn and hdd over 1f out: styd on same pce towards fin* **5/1**[2]

6520 **4** 3 **Barefoot Baby (IRE)**[9] 7552 2-9-4 65 ...... AdamMcNamara(3) 10 60
(Richard Fahey) *hld up: rdn and r.o ins fnl f: nt rch ldrs* **16/1**

0020 **5** ½ **Mouchee (IRE)**[31] 6815 2-9-1 62 ...... MattCosham(3) 12 56
(David Evans) *hld up: rdn over 1f out: r.o towards fin: nt rch ldrs* **20/1**

560 **6** ½ **Amazing Rock (SWI)**[18] 7237 2-9-4 **62** JFEgan 11 55
(Mark Johnston) *hld up: rdn over 2f out: swtchd rt ins fnl f: r.o towards fin* **25/1**

0500 **7** ½ **Sotomayor**[30] 6860 2-9-6 **64** (t[1]) TimmyMurphy 8 56
(Richard Hannon) *mid-div: rdn over 2f out: hung lft and wknd ins fnl f* **14/1**

0006 **8** ½ **Courteous Crown**[10] 7510 2-9-0 **61** HollieDoyle(3) 6 51
(Richard Hannon) *mid-div: rdn over 2f out: wknd ins fnl f* **20/1**

6612 **9** ¾ **Data Protection**[31] 6815 2-9-3 **64** HectorCrouch(3) 1 53
(William Muir) *chsd ldrs: rdn over 2f out: wknd ins fnl f* **3/1**[1]

540 **10** *nk* **Affluence (IRE)**[28] 6916 2-9-7 **65** DanielMuscutt 4 53
(Martin Smith) *hld up in tch: rdn over 1f out: wknd fnl f* **8/1**

050 **11** 1¾ **The Night King**[30] 6859 2-9-7 **65** GeorgeDowning 9 50
(Mick Channon) *hld up: nt clr run over 2f out: rdn over 1f out: wknd ins fnl f* **22/1**

4505 **12** *15* **Shootingthe Breeze**[28] 6951 2-9-6 **64** (p) RichardKingscote 2 17
(Tom Dascombe) *led: hdd over 2f out: nt clr run sn after: wknd over 1f out* **13/2**[3]

650 **13** *6* **The Fettler (IRE)**[55] 5960 2-9-2 **60** (p[1]) DougieCostello 3
(Kevin Frost) *sn pushed along in rr: wknd over 2f out* **66/1**

1m 49.15s (-0.95) **Going Correction** -0.05s/f (Stan) **13** Ran SP% **117.9**
Speed ratings (Par 93): **102,101,100,98,97 97,96,96,95,95 93,80,75**
CSF £84.94 CT £510.68 TOTE £7.00: £2.20, £5.20, £1.90; EX 105.50 Trifecta £570.30.
**Owner** P Twomey **Bred** Mrs J Norris **Trained** Blewbury, Oxon

**FOCUS**
An open-looking nursery, but the first three pulled clear.

## 7830 BET365 FILLIES' H'CAP 1m 142y (Tp)
**7:45** (7:47) (Class 4) (0-85,85) 3-Y-0+ **£5,175** (£1,540; £769; £384) **Stalls** Low

Form RPR

4210 **1** **Rinaria (IRE)**[15] 7364 3-8-9 **74** (h) JoeyHaynes 8 81
(K R Burke) *hld up: hdwy over 1f out: rdn and r.o to ld post* **20/1**

-313 **2** *nse* **Song Maker**[11] 7484 3-9-5 **84** (b) MartinLane 5 91
(Charlie Appleby) *hld up: hdwy over 2f out: rdn to ld wl ins fnl f: hdd post* **2/1**[1]

45 **3** 1½ **Sunchisetagioo**[47] 6261 3-9-6 **85** (h) DanielMuscutt 1 88
(Marco Botti) *a.p: chsd ldr over 2f out: hrd rdn fr over 1f out: ev ch wl ins fnl f: no ex towards fin* **22/1**

1141 **4** 2¾ **Alnasl (IRE)**[23] 7095 3-9-2 **81** (h) EdwardGreatrex 10 78
(Archie Watson) *chsd ldr over 7f out: led over 2f out: rdn over 1f out: hdd and no ex wl ins fnl f* **8/1**[3]

4530 **5** 2¾ **Ariena (IRE)**[14] 7398 3-8-6 **78** WilliamCox(7) 6 69
(Clive Cox) *s.i.s: hld up: pushed along over 2f out: rdn: hung lft and nt clr run over 1f out: hung rt ins fnl f: nvr trble ldrs* **5/1**[2]

4533 **6** *nk* **Millie's Kiss**[9] 7541 3-8-1 **71** oh2 JaneElliott(5) 2 61
(Philip McBride) *led 1f: chsd ldrs: rdn over 2f out: wknd ins fnl f* **10/1**

2522 **7** *5* **Stosur (IRE)**[11] 7484 6-8-10 **74** (b) DavidEgan(3) 3 51
(Gay Kelleway) *drvn along to ld over 7f out: rdn and hdd over 2f out: wknd fnl f* **12/1**

3114 **8** *1* **Cheerfilly (IRE)**[72] 5324 3-9-6 **85** (p) RichardKingscote 9 61
(Tom Dascombe) *hld up: pushed along 1/2-way: wknd over 1f out* **12/1**

0004 **9** *10* **Lady Lydia (IRE)**[10] 7523 6-9-2 **77** (t) LukeMorris 7 29
(Gay Kelleway) *s.s: a bhd* **40/1**

1m 47.41s (-2.69) **Going Correction** -0.05s/f (Stan)
**WFA** 3 from 6yo 4lb **9** Ran SP% **97.1**
Speed ratings (Par 102): **109,108,107,105,102 102,98,97,88**
CSF £43.34 CT £545.67 TOTE £18.80: £6.00, £1.02, £5.30; EX 64.60 Trifecta £1517.90.
**Owner** The Mount Racing Club & A Kavanagh **Bred** Rathdown Stud Ltd **Trained** Middleham Moor, N Yorks

■ Al Nafoorah was withdrawn. Price at time of withdrawal 5-1. Rule 4 applies to all bets. Deduction - 15p in the pound.

**FOCUS**
A fair fillies' handicap.

## 7831 BET365.COM H'CAP (DIV I) 1m 4f 51y (Tp)
**8:15** (8:16) (Class 5) (0-70,72) 3-Y-0+ **£3,234** (£962; £481; £240) **Stalls** Low

Form RPR

6404 **1** **Star Of Lombardy (IRE)**[14] 7386 4-9-8 **68** JFEgan 1 75+
(Mark Johnston) *chsd ldrs: nt clr run over 1f out: sn swtchd rt: r.o to ld wl ins fnl f* **9/1**

2136 **2** *nk* **Omotesando**[8] 7560 7-9-3 **66** (p) CharlieBennett(3) 7 71
(Oliver Greenall) *hld up in tch: effrt on outer over 2f out: rdn and ev ch wl ins fnl f: r.o* **6/1**

04-3 **3** *hd* **Singular Quest**[14] 7413 5-8-13 **59** LukeMorris 8 64
(Daniel Mark Loughnane) *hld up: rdn over 2f out: hdwy u.p and hung lft fr over 1f out: r.o* **8/1**

565- **4** ½ **Enriching (USA)**[590] 708 9-9-2 **62** TomMarquand 6 66
(Robyn Brisland) *chsd ldr: rdn over 1f out: ev ch wl ins fnl f: unable qck towards fin* **40/1**

5326 **5** 1¾ **Sir Gnet (IRE)**[8] 7568 3-9-0 **66** (h) KieranShoemark 4 67
(Ed Dunlop) *led at stdy pce tl qcknd over 2f out: rdn over 1f out: hdd and no ex wl ins fnl f* **7/2**[2]

2332 **6** *nk* **Ode To Glory**[39] 6556 3-9-1 **67** DavidProbert 2 68
(Rae Guest) *hld up: hdwy over 5f out: rdn over 1f out: styd on same pce ins fnl f* **3/1**[1]

0-06 **7** 3¾ **Mayasa (IRE)**[37] 6610 4-9-12 **72** (b) DanielMuscutt 3 67
(John Flint) *sn pushed along to chse ldrs: rdn over 3f out: wknd ins fnl f* **50/1**

0555 **8** ½ **Archipeligo**[8] 7569 6-9-3 **70** JamieGormley(7) 10 64
(Iain Jardine) *plld hrd and prom: stdd and lost pl over 8f out: shkn up over 2f out: styd on same pce fr over 1f out* **9/2**[3]

/2-0 **9** *shd* **Innish Man (IRE)**[14] 7413 5-9-2 **62** JoeyHaynes 5 56
(John Mackie) *hld up: shkn up over 2f out: nvr on terms* **40/1**

5455 **10** 2½ **Kaisan**[31] 6821 4-8-10 **56** oh1 (vt[1]) AdamBeschizza 12 46
(Bernard Llewellyn) *s.i.s: hld up: rdn over 2f out: a in rr* **33/1**

6055 **11** ¾ **Voski (USA)**[25] 7031 3-9-3 **69** RichardKingscote 11 57
(Mark Johnston) *s.i.s: hld up: rdn over 2f out: sme hdwy over 1f out: wknd fnl f* **9/1**

2m 41.42s (0.62) **Going Correction** -0.05s/f (Stan)
**WFA** 3 from 4yo+ 6lb **11** Ran SP% **120.6**
Speed ratings (Par 103): **95,94,94,94,93 92,90,90,90,88 87**
CSF £62.36 CT £460.49 TOTE £10.10: £3.00, £2.60, £1.50; EX 72.80 Trifecta £663.50.
**Owner** Paul Dean **Bred** Tom Darcy And Vincent McCarthy **Trained** Middleham Moor, N Yorks

**FOCUS**
A messy race that was steadily run and turned into a sprint from the turn in.

## 7832 BET365.COM H'CAP (DIV II) 1m 4f 51y (Tp)
**8:45** (8:45) (Class 5) (0-70,70) 3-Y-0+ **£3,234** (£962; £481; £240) **Stalls** Low

Form RPR

2350 **1** **Deep Challenger (IRE)**[88] 4730 5-9-10 **70** DougieCostello 5 78
(Jamie Osborne) *chsd ldr tl over 10f out: remained handy: shkn up to ld ins fnl f: r.o* **9/1**[3]

1535 **2** 1¼ **Stepney**[50] 6144 3-9-2 **68** TomMarquand 10 74
(Robyn Brisland) *prom: chsd ldr 9f out tl over 4f out: remained handy: rdn 3f out: r.o* **7/1**[2]

2305 **3** ½ **Mambo Dancer**[9] 7558 3-9-0 **66** RichardKingscote 11 71+
(Mark Johnston) *hld up: rdn over 1f out: r.o ins fnl f: nt rch ldrs* **7/1**[2]

-011 **4** *nse* **Send Up (IRE)**[11] 7483 3-9-0 **66** (p) LukeMorris 9 71
(Sir Mark Prescott Bt) *prom: chsd ldr over 10f out tl 9f out: remained handy: rdn 3f out: styd on u.p* **6/4**[1]

52/0 **5** *hd* **Pershing**[23] 7085 6-8-10 **56** oh2 (h) RyanPowell 4 61
(Kevin Frost) *hld up in tch: plld hrd: led over 4f out: rdn and hdd over 2f out: stl ev ch tl styd on same pce wl ins fnl f* **66/1**

3045 **6** ½ **Norab (GER)**[20] 7200 6-9-10 **70** (b) CharlesBishop 1 74
(Bernard Llewellyn) *prom: rdn over 3f out: hung lft and nt clr run ins fnl f: styd on* **9/1**[3]

3326 **7** *nk* **Epitaph (IRE)**[49] 6210 3-9-1 **67** (p) RyanTate 6 70
(Michael Appleby) *led at stdy pce tl hdd over 4f out: led again over 2f out: sn rdn: hdd and no ex ins fnl f* **7/1**[2]

4440 **8** 3¾ **Royal Headley (IRE)**[18] 7248 3-8-13 **65** ShaneGray 12 62
(David O'Meara) *s.i.s: hld up: rdn over 2f out: nvr nrr* **50/1**

0602 **9** *nk* **Berlusca (IRE)**[42] 6416 8-9-8 **68** (h) BenCurtis 3 65
(David Loughnane) *hld up: rdn over 1f out: sn hung lft: wknd ins fnl f* **9/1**[3]

0300 **10** 1¼ **Almutamarred (USA)**[14] 7413 5-9-2 **62** (p) TimmyMurphy 8 57
(James Unett) *hld up: shkn up over 2f out: nvr on terms* **28/1**

6460 **11** *6* **King's Coinage (IRE)**[18] 7234 3-9-4 **70** (h) JoeDoyle 2 55
(Ruth Carr) *hld up: plld hrd: wknd over 1f out* **25/1**

2m 41.63s (0.83) **Going Correction** -0.05s/f (Stan)
**WFA** 3 from 5yo+ 6lb **11** Ran SP% **118.2**
Speed ratings (Par 103): **95,94,93,93,93 93,93,90,90,89 85**
CSF £68.96 CT £473.46 TOTE £12.20: £3.40, £2.20, £2.30; EX 81.10 Trifecta £980.90.
**Owner** D Margolis **Bred** Healing Music Partnership **Trained** Upper Lambourn, Berks

**FOCUS**
This was another steadily run race, the time being 0.21sec slower than the first division.

## 7833 CASINO AT BET365 H'CAP 1m 1f 104y (Tp)
**9:15** (9:16) (Class 6) (0-55,55) 3-Y-0 **£2,587** (£770; £384; £192) **Stalls** Low

Form RPR

0300 **1** **Born To Reason (IRE)**[16] 7323 3-9-3 **52** (b[1]) DougieCostello 5 58
(Kevin Frost) *stdd s: hld up: nt clr run over 2f out: hdwy over 1f out: rdn and r.o to ld towards fin* **7/2**[1]

6004 **2** *1* **Dixon**[16] 7325 3-9-6 **55** JoeyHaynes 11 59
(Mark H Tompkins) *plld hrd and prom: rdn to ld ins fnl f: hdd towards fin* **9/1**[3]

3140 **3** *shd* **Mr C (IRE)**[41] 6471 3-9-6 **55** JoeDoyle 2 59
(Ollie Pears) *hld up: hdwy and nt clr run over 1f out: sn rdn: r.o* **6/1**[2]

4030 **4** 1½ **Equal Rights**[21] 7158 3-9-6 **55** (p) CharlesBishop 9 56
(Eve Johnson Houghton) *led 8f out: rdn over 1f out: hdd and no ex ins fnl f* **6/1**[2]

0003 **5** *nk* **London Grammar (IRE)**[18] 7230 3-9-5 **54** RyanTate 3 54
(Ralph J Smith) *mid-div: drvn along 1/2-way: hung lft and r.o ins fnl f: nt rch ldrs* **10/1**

0006 **6** *nk* **Follow Me (IRE)**[19] 7210 3-8-13 **51** CharlieBennett(3) 7 51
(Lee Carter) *chsd ldr after 1f: rdn and ev ch over 1f out: styd on same pce wl ins fnl f* **20/1**

6000 **7** 1¾ **Mistress Viz (IRE)**[20] 7199 3-8-12 **54** JamieGormley(7) 6 51
(Sarah Hollinshead) *hld up: rdn over 3f out: n.d* **22/1**

0000 **8** *hd* **Babette (IRE)**[51] 6112 3-8-13 **53** JoshuaBryan(5) 8 49
(Alan Bailey) *hld up: rdn over 1f out: nt trble ldrs* **7/2**[1]

6660 **9** *2* **Super Ruby**[63] 5666 3-9-2 **51** BenCurtis 1 43
(K R Burke) *prom: rdn over 2f out: wknd fnl f* **16/1**

0300 **10** *5* **Masterfilly (IRE)**[37] 6611 3-9-5 **54** (v[1]) LukeMorris 4 37
(Ed Walker) *led: hdd 8f out: chsd ldrs: rdn over 2f out: wknd over 1f out* **9/1**[3]

000- **11** 3¼ **Alligator**[322] 8025 3-9-6 **55** GeorgeDowning 10 32
(Tony Carroll) *hld up: rdn over 3f out: n.d* **50/1**

2m 1.54s (0.74) **Going Correction** -0.05s/f (Stan) **11** Ran SP% **119.1**
Speed ratings (Par 99): **94,93,93,91,91 91,89,89,87,83 80**
CSF £35.89 CT £186.74 TOTE £5.10: £1.10, £3.40, £2.40; EX 34.20 Trifecta £360.80.
**Owner** Ryan Carroll **Bred** Christopher Glynn **Trained** Market Drayton, Shropshire

**FOCUS**
A moderate contest but the winner landed quite a punt.

T/Plt: £42.40 to a £1 stake. Pool: £88,410.37 - 1,518.71 winning units. T/Qpdt: £24.80 to a £1 stake. Pool: £9,982.44 - 296.96 winning units. **Colin Roberts**

7834 - 7836a (Foreign Racing) - See Raceform Interactive

# 4061 LIMERICK (R-H)
Saturday, October 7

**OFFICIAL GOING: Heavy**

## 7837a MARTIN MOLONY STKS (LISTED RACE) 1m 4f 110y
**3:10** (3:11) 3-Y-0+
**£22,692** (£7,307; £3,461; £1,538; £769; £384)

RPR

**1** **Detailed (IRE)**[23] 7089 3-8-10 101 WayneLordan 6 97
(Joseph Patrick O'Brien, Ire) *settled in 4th: clsr on outer 3f out to trck ldrs: wnt 2nd appr fnl f: styd on wl to assert cl home* **7/2**[3]

**2** ½ **Cannonball (IRE)**[28] 6957 3-9-1 105 ColinKeane 1 101
(G M Lyons, Ire) *hld up in 5th: clsr on inner 3f out: led 2f out: strly pressed ins fnl f: hdd cl home* **3/1**[2]

**3** 1¾ **Red Stars (IRE)**[18] 7261 4-9-2 97 (h) NGMcCullagh 5 91
(John M Oxx, Ire) *trckd ldr in 2nd: on terms at 1/2-way: hdd 2f out: dropped to 3rd appr fnl f: kpt on same pce: jst hld on for 3rd* **16/1**

**4** *hd* **Daybreak Boy (IRE)**[28] 6956 4-9-7 89 ChrisHayes 4 96
(Henry De Bromhead, Ire) *led: jnd at 1/2-way: hdd 2f out: nt qckn in 4th appr fnl f: kpt on again cl home* **14/1**

5 5 ½ **Rashaan (IRE)**36 5488 5-9-7 87 WJLee 3 87
(Colin Kidd, Ire) *chsd ldrs in 3rd: pushed along in 5th over 3f out: nt qckn under 2f out: sn one pce* **14/1**

6 4 ½ **Glamorous Approach (IRE)**21 7171 4-9-5 102 (p) KevinManning 7 78
(J S Bolger, Ire) *bit slowly away: hld up in rr: rdn and nt qckn 2f out: sn one pce* **12/1**

7 11 **Zawraq (IRE)**24 7066 5-9-7 105 PatSmullen 2 62
(D K Weld, Ire) *hld up in rr: rdn and nt qckn under 2f out: dropped to rr appr fnl f: sn eased: lame* **5/4**1

3m 2.28s
**WFA** 3 from 4yo+ 6lb **7 Ran SP% 118.6**
CSF £15.28 TOTE £4.90: £1.90, £1.40; DF 12.50 Trifecta £117.90.
**Owner** Annus Mirabilis Syndicate **Bred** Whisperview Trading Ltd **Trained** Owning Hill, Co Kilkenny

**FOCUS**
A tremendous finish to the feature and the winner has continued her rapid improvement. The fourth, who has been rated as running a pb, limits the form.

7838 - 7843a (Foreign Racing) - See Raceform Interactive

## 7666 CHANTILLY (R-H)
Saturday, October 7

**OFFICIAL GOING: Turf: very soft; polytrack; standard**

### 7844a PRIX VAUBLANC (MAIDEN) (2YO COLTS & GELDINGS) (TURF) 7f
1:05 2-Y-O **£11,538** (£4,615; £3,461; £2,307; £1,153)

RPR

1 **Dream Warrior**17 7281 2-9-2 0 JamesDoyle 5 85
(Charlie Appleby) *away wl and settled in 3rd: pushed along 3f out: rdn over 1f out and gd hdwy to lay down chal: led 150yds out: sn u.p and battled on wl: jst hld on* **2/5**1

2 nse **Corsen**34 2-9-2 0 Pierre-CharlesBoudot 4 85
(A Fabre, France) *slowest away and in rr early: moved into 4th after 2f: pushed along 3f out: slowly clsd on ldrs: rdn 1f out to go 2nd: sn chal: jst hld* **57/10**3

3 2 **Manchester City (GER)**132 2-8-6 0 MlleCoraliePacaut(10) 1 80
(S Smrczek, Germany) **33/1**

4 2 **Drummore (IRE)**83 2-8-10 0 NicolasBarzalona(6) 6 74
(A Fabre, France) *upsides ldr early: settled in 2nd after 2f: pushed along to ld over 2f out: rdn appr fnl f: hdd 150yds out: wknd and eased late on* **27/10**2

5 10 **Siglo De Oro (IRE)**70 2-9-2 0 CristianDemuro 2 47
(F Chappet, France) **41/1**

6 6 **Crystal Dolois (FR)**106 2-9-2 0 CesarPasserat 3 31
(A Bonin, France) **84/1**

1m 28.51s (2.41) **6 Ran SP% 119.9**
PARI-MUTUEL (all including 1 euro stake): PLACE 1.70, 1.70 DF; SF 5.90.
**Owner** Godolphin **Bred** St Albans Bloodstock Llp **Trained** Newmarket, Suffolk

### 7845a PRIX LE FABULEUX (LISTED RACE) (3YO) (TURF) 1m 1f
1:35 3-Y-O **£23,504** (£9,401; £7,051; £4,700; £2,350)

RPR

1 **Glen Shiel**50 6172 3-9-0 0 MaximeGuyon 3 106
(A Fabre, France) *sn settled in 2nd: pushed along over 2f out: hdwy and moved into ld over 1 1/2f out: rdn over 1f out: u.str.p fnl 100yds: jst hld on* **112/10**

2 hd **Liwanu (FR)**73 3-9-0 0 Pierre-CharlesBoudot 2 105
(A Fabre, France) **16/5**3

3 1 ¼ **Cape Byron**29 6870 3-9-0 0 AndreaAtzeni 4 103
(Roger Varian) *away wl and upsides ldr early: sn settled in 3rd: drvn along and c w a run ent fnl f: little short of room ins fnl f: unable to rch ldng pair* **12/5**2

4 nk **Heuristique (IRE)**17 7305 3-8-10 0 AlexisBadel 1 98
(F-H Graffard, France) **9/5**1

5 2 ½ **D'bai (IRE)**17 7275 3-9-0 0 (b) JamesDoyle 6 97
(Charlie Appleby) *led: qcknd pce 3f out: u.p and rdn ins 2f out: hdd over 1 1/2f out: wknd fnl f* **9/2**

6 6 **Tikitiki (FR)**46 6299 3-8-10 0 CristianDemuro 5 80
(Mlle J Soudan, France) **30/1**

1m 51.39s (0.29) **6 Ran SP% 118.5**
PARI-MUTUEL (all including 1 euro stake): WIN 3.80 (coupled with D'bai); PLACE 3.40, 2.50; SF 30.60.
**Owner** Godolphin SNC **Bred** Darley **Trained** Chantilly, France

### 7846a CRITERIUM DE VITESSE (LISTED RACE) (2YO) (TURF) 5f
2:55 2-Y-O **£25,641** (£10,256; £7,692; £5,128; £2,564)

RPR

1 **Beau Ideal**26 7011 2-8-13 0 Pierre-CharlesBoudot 11 97
(A Fabre, France) **2/1**1

2 nse **Absolute City (FR)** 2-8-9 0 NicolasPerret 9 93
(J-P Gauvin, France) **53/10**3

3 1 ¼ **Looks A Million**42 6448 2-8-9 0 AlexisBadel 4 88
(Joseph Tuite) **57/1**

4 nk **Rioticism (FR)**34 6728 2-8-13 0 AntoineHamelin 7 91
(Matthieu Palussiere, France) **89/10**

5 hd **River Cannes (FR)**17 7306 2-8-9 0 MaximeGuyon 2 87
(T Castanheira, France) **152/10**

6 ¾ **Rebel Assault (IRE)**70 5391 2-8-9 0 TheoBachelot 1 84
(Mark Johnston) **231/10**

7 ½ **Shaya (IRE)**9 7536 2-8-9 0 EddyHardouin 10 82
(Roger Fell) **40/1**

8 hd **Over Reacted (FR)**34 6728 2-8-9 0 TonyPiccone 3 81
(F Chappet, France) **63/10**

9 snk **May Girl**22 7114 2-8-13 0 JamesDoyle 8 85
(Robert Cowell) **51/10**2

10 12 **Consequences (IRE)**107 3993 2-8-13 0 AndreaAtzeni 6 42
(David O'Meara) **43/5**

11 2 ½ **Kentish Waltz (IRE)**67 5694 2-8-9 0 FabriceVeron 5 29
(E J O'Neill, France) **28/1**

59.34s (1.04) **11 Ran SP% 117.7**
PARI-MUTUEL (all including 1 euro stake): WIN 3.00; PLACE 1.60, 2.30, 8.50; DF 8.60; SF 17.30.
**Owner** Godolphin SNC **Bred** W & R Barnett Ltd **Trained** Chantilly, France

**FOCUS**
The form has been rated around the third's form in Britain.

### 7847a PRIX DE CONDE (GROUP 3) (2YO) (TURF) 1m 1f
3:30 2-Y-O **£34,188** (£13,675; £10,256; £6,837; £3,418)

RPR

1 **Luminate (IRE)**46 2-8-9 0 AurelienLemaitre 4 106+
(F Head, France) *midfield early: moved into 2nd after 2f: pushed along 2f out and sn clsd on ldr: led over 1 1/2f out: pushed along to stretch clr: rdn late on but a in control fnl f* **71/10**3

2 3 **Kingstar (FR)**34 2-8-13 0 MaximeGuyon 3 104
(Mme Pia Brandt, France) *little s.i.s: sn settled midfield: pushed along 3f out: rdn over 1f out and sn wnt 2nd: 3 l bhd and chsd ldr fnl f but unable to cl* **26/5**2

3 6 **King Of Camelot (FR)**30 2-8-13 0 Pierre-CharlesBoudot 1 92
(A Fabre, France) *racd in 5th: dropped to last turning in: passed btn horses late on: nvr on terms* **8/1**

4 nk **Parabak (FR)**27 2-8-13 0 ChristopheSoumillon 5 91
(M Delzangles, France) *settled in last early: wnt 5th turning in: pushed along 2f out: kpt on same pce: nvr on terms w ldrs* **71/10**3

5 shd **Korevsky (IRE)**22 2-8-13 0 Jean-BernardEyquem 2 91
(Simone Brogi, France) *racd in 2nd early: settled in midfield after 2f: pushed along 3f out: nt qckn: kpt on same pce* **227/10**

6 4 **Stage Magic (IRE)**34 6730 2-9-2 0 JamesDoyle 6 86
(Charlie Appleby) *away wl and led: 3 l clr turning in: stl clr whn pushed along 2f out: sn rdn and hdd over 1 1/2f out: qckly wknd* **3/5**1

1m 51.16s (0.06) **6 Ran SP% 118.7**
PARI-MUTUEL (all including 1 euro stake): WIN 8.10; PLACE 4.80, 3.90; SF 33.70.
**Owner** Highclere Thoroughbred Racing **Bred** Philip & Mrs Jane Myerscough **Trained** France

7848 - 7850a (Foreign Racing) - See Raceform Interactive

## 7802 KEENELAND (L-H)
Saturday, October 7

**OFFICIAL GOING: Dirt: fast; turf: firm**

### 7851a SHADWELL TURF MILE STKS (GRADE 1) (3YO+) (TURF) 1m
10:45 3-Y-O+
**£487,804** (£162,601; £81,300; £40,650; £24,390; £1,807)

RPR

1 **Suedois (FR)**28 6959 6-9-0 0 DanielTudhope 3 117
(David O'Meara) **97/10**

2 ½ **Heart To Heart (CAN)**33 6-9-0 0 FlorentGeroux 10 116
(Brian A Lynch, Canada) **11/5**1

3 hd **Ballagh Rocks (USA)**56 5955 4-9-0 0 (b) JoseLezcano 6 115
(William Mott, U.S.A) **61/10**

4 1 ¾ **Divisidero (USA)**55 5977 5-9-0 0 JulienRLeparoux 2 111
(William Bradley, U.S.A) **47/10**2

5 nse **Mondialiste (IRE)**21 7179 7-9-0 0 FergalLynch 7 111
(David O'Meara) **44/5**

6 hd **Miss Temple City (USA)**28 5-8-11 0 EdgarSPrado 8 108
(H Graham Motion, U.S.A) **26/5**3

7 2 ¼ **Offering Plan (USA)**43 5-9-0 0 JavierCastellano 12 106
(Chad C Brown, U.S.A) **117/10**

8 1 ¾ **Le Ken (ARG)**47 4-9-0 0 CoreyJLanerie 4 102
(Ignacio Correas IV, U.S.A) **27/1**

9 ½ **Flatlined (USA)**31 5-9-0 0 JosephRoccoJr 9 100
(Charles L Dickey, U.S.A) **39/1**

10 ½ **American Patriot (USA)**56 5955 4-9-0 0 (b) JoeBravo 14 99
(Todd Pletcher, U.S.A) **157/10**

11 nk **Christian C (USA)**33 4-9-0 0 (b) JoseValdiviaJr 11 99
(Wayne Catalano, U.S.A) **111/1**

12 nse **Applicator (USA)**14 4-9-0 0 ShaunBridgmohan 13 98
(Mikhail Yanakov, U.S.A) **145/1**

13 nk **Tyler U (USA)**27 3-8-11 0 (b) RobbyAlbarado 1 98
(Troy S Wismer, U.S.A) **77/1**

14 1 ¼ **Dimension**28 9-9-0 0 ChrisLanderos 5 95
(Conor Murphy, U.S.A) **144/1**

1m 35.94s
**WFA** 3 from 4yo+ 3lb **14 Ran SP% 122.0**
PARI-MUTUEL (all including 2 usd stake): WIN 21.40; PLACE (1-2) 8.60, 4.00; SHOW (1-2-3) 6.40, 3.40, 4.40; SF 102.40.
**Owner** George Turner & Clipper Logistics **Bred** Mme Elisabeth Vidal **Trained** Upper Helmsley, N Yorks

**FOCUS**
The first two have been rated to their best, with a small pb from the third.

7852 - 7854a (Foreign Racing) - See Raceform Interactive

## 6702 NAVAN (L-H)
Sunday, October 8

**OFFICIAL GOING: Yielding to soft changing to soft after race 1 (2.00)**

### 7855a LEGACY STKS (LISTED RACE) 5f 182y
2:35 (2:39) 2-Y-O
**£22,692** (£7,307; £3,461; £1,538; £769; £384)

RPR

1 **Gobi Desert**18 7290 2-9-3 0 ColinKeane 11 102
(G M Lyons, Ire) *hld up towards rr: prog nr side to chse ldrs in 4th over 1f out where rdn: r.o wl ins fnl f to ld cl home* **3/1**2

2 ½ **Golden Spell**18 7290 2-8-12 92 NGMcCullagh 9 95
(J P Murtagh, Ire) *wnt rt s and sltly bmpd rival: cl up bhd ldr: rdn over 1f out and clsd u.p to ld narrowly briefly wl ins fnl f tl hdd cl home* **14/1**

3 1 **Brick By Brick (IRE)**18 7290 2-9-6 101 ChrisHayes 7 100
(Mrs John Harrington, Ire) *sn led: stl gng wl after 1/2-way: rdn over 1f out and hdd u.p wl ins fnl f: no ex in 3rd clsng stages* **5/1**3

4 1 ½ **Dali (USA)**62 5726 2-9-3 91 (t1) DonnachaO'Brien 2 92
(A P O'Brien, Ire) *hld up towards rr: sltly impeded early: tk clsr order 2f out where pushed along: rdn bhd ldrs over 1f out and u.p in 5th ins fnl f: kpt on clsng stages: nvr trbld ldrs* **12/1**

5 ½ **Aurora Eclipse (IRE)**[4] 7746 2-8-12 0 ................................ LeighRoche 8 86
(M D O'Callaghan, Ire) *chsd ldrs: 6th 1/2-way: rdn into 3rd after 1/2-way: no ex u.p in 4th wl ins fnl f and one pce clsng stages* **10/1**

6 4 **Verhoyen**[4] 7746 2-9-3 85 ........................................................ FranBerry 5 78
(M C Grassick, Ire) *settled towards rr: rdn 2f out and no imp u.p in 8th ent fnl f: kpt on one pce into nvr nrr 6th on line* **33/1**

7 nse **Brother Bear (IRE)**[28] 6975 2-9-6 104 ........................(p¹) ShaneFoley 10 81
(Mrs John Harrington, Ire) *bmpd sltly and forced sltly rt s: chsd ldrs: pushed along after 1/2-way: rdn disputing 6th 1 1/2f out and no ex ins fnl f: eased in 6th cl home: lost pl on line* **9/4**[1]

8 8 ½ **Blue Uluru (IRE)**[36] 6705 2-8-12 93 .................................... GaryCarroll 4 45
(G M Lyons, Ire) *chsd ldrs: rn freely and sltly impeded early: 4th 1/2-way: rdn 2f out and sn no ex: no imp over 1f out and one pce after: eased ins fnl f* **7/1**

9 1 ½ **Flamin Audi (GER)**[38] 6643 2-8-12 0 ............................. WayneLordan 1 47
(Lee Smyth, Ire) *chsd ldrs early: 2nd 1/2-way: sn pushed along and wknd bhd ldrs under 2f out* **100/1**

10 nk **Abamanova (IRE)**[39] 6601 2-8-12 91 ........................................ WJLee 6 40
(W McCreery, Ire) *chsd ldrs: rn freely and wnt sltly lft early: 5th 1/2-way: pushed along 2f out and sn wknd: eased ins fnl f* **9/1**

1m 16.81s (2.21) **10** Ran SP% **122.3**
CSF £47.31 TOTE £4.50: £1.40, £3.70, £1.60; DF 42.50 Trifecta £263.10.
**Owner** Mrs Annette O'Callaghan **Bred** Countess De La Warr **Trained** Dunsany, Co Meath

**FOCUS**
An exciting finish, with Colin Keane poking his nose back in front in the jockeys' championship through this success. He truly pulled this victory out of the fire but had a talented and willing partner, whose stamina on the dam's side kicked in late-on.

## 7856a WATERFORD TESTIMONIAL STKS (LISTED RACE) 5f 182y
3:05 (3:09) 3-Y-0+

**£22,692** (£7,307; £3,461; £1,538; £769; £384)

RPR

1 **Texas Rock (IRE)**[29] 6961 6-9-8 103 ................................(p) FranBerry 12 110
(M C Grassick, Ire) *wnt sltly lft s: led and disp: cl 2nd bef 1/2-way: rdn 2f out and kpt on wl u.p bhd ldrs to ld wl ins fnl f: all out* **16/1**

2 nk **Son Of Rest**[28] 6973 3-9-5 110 ........................................... ChrisHayes 3 107
(J A Stack, Ire) *dwlt sltly: sn chsd ldrs: rdn in 3rd 2f out and wnt 2nd over 1f out: kpt on wl ins fnl f: jst hld* **3/1**[1]

3 ½ **Maarek**[14] 7425 10-9-5 91 .............................................. KillianHennessy 11 104
(Miss Evanna McCutcheon, Ire) *dwlt and sltly impeded s: sn settled towards rr and pushed along after 1f: rdn after 1/2-way and sme hdwy over 1f out: clsd u.p nr side ins fnl f into 3rd cl home: hld* **25/1**

4 hd **G Force (IRE)**[50] 6215 6-9-5 92 ...................................(b¹) GaryCarroll 10 104+
(Adrian Paul Keatley, Ire) *hld up towards rr: rdn over 1f out and r.o wl ins fnl f: nrst fin* **33/1**

5 nk **Alphabet**[7] 7670 3-9-0 110 ................................................(t) WayneLordan 2 99+
(A P O'Brien, Ire) *led and disp: narrow advantage bef 1/2-way: extended advantage after 1/2-way gng wl: rdn over 1f out and sn pressed clly: hdd wl ins fnl f and no ex clsng stages where dropped to 5th* **4/1**[3]

6 ½ **Ardhoomey (IRE)**[14] 7424 5-9-5 107 ..................................(t) ColinKeane 9 101
(G M Lyons, Ire) *hooded to load: w.w towards rr: sme hdwy far side to chse ldrs over 1f out: kpt on same pce ins fnl f* **7/2**[2]

7 4 **Magic Bear (IRE)**[14] 7425 4-9-0 92 ...................................... RobbieDowney 14 83
(Edward Lynam, Ire) *wnt rt s: in tch: 6th 1/2-way: rdn 2f out and no imp on ldrs ins fnl f: one clsng stages* **16/1**

8 1 **Cougar Mountain (IRE)**[14] 7424 6-9-5 110 .........(tp) DonnachaO'Brien 4 85
(A P O'Brien, Ire) *mid-div and pushed along early: tk clsr order after 1/2-way: sn rdn in 6th and no ex over 1f out: one pce after* **9/2**

9 shd **Peticoatgovernment (IRE)**[49] 6234 4-9-0 94 ................... LeighRoche 6 80
(W McCreery, Ire) *chsd ldrs: 5th 1/2-way: rdn 2f out and sn no ex: wknd* **16/1**

10 1 ¾ **Duchess Of France (IRE)**[29] 6961 4-9-0 90 ..............(t) DannySheehy 7 74
(Adrian Paul Keatley, Ire) *cl up: pushed along in 3rd fr 1/2-way and sn lost pl: no ex and wknd fr over 1f out* **50/1**

11 2 ½ **Snowstar (IRE)**[38] 6640 3-9-0 97 ................................................ WJLee 8 67
(W McCreery, Ire) *sn settled in mid-div: rdn and no imp 2f out: wknd ins fnl f* **12/1**

12 38 **Rattling Jewel**[28] 6971 5-9-5 89 ...................................(p) KevinManning 1
(Miss Nicole McKenna, Ire) *dwlt and wnt sltly lft s: in rr of mid-div early: rdn and wknd to rr after 1/2-way: sn eased* **33/1**

1m 15.5s (0.90)
**WFA** 3 from 4yo+ 1lb **12** Ran SP% **122.4**
CSF £64.18 TOTE £15.20: £3.70, £1.40, £6.80; DF 76.70 Trifecta £1940.00.
**Owner** Joseph E Keeling **Bred** M C Grassick **Trained** Curragh, Co. Kildare
■ Stewards' Enquiry : Killian Hennessy caution; concerning his use of the whip in the latter stages of this race

**FOCUS**
A good renewal of this Listed Waterford Testimonial stakes, normally staged at the Curragh, with three of the thirteen strong field rated 110, and the front four in the market trading at single figure odds. A pb from the winner, with the third and fourth helping to set the standard.

7857 - 7858a (Foreign Racing) - See Raceform Interactive

## 7859a STAFFORDSTOWN STUD STKS (LISTED RACE) 1m
4:45 (4:45) 2-Y-0 **£23,700** (£7,632; £3,615; £1,606; £803; £401)

RPR

1 **Bye Bye Baby (IRE)**[8] 7620 2-9-0 93 ........................ DonnachaO'Brien 7 100+
(A P O'Brien, Ire) *sn led and tacked over to nr side: stl gng wl under 3f out: pushed along under 2f out: rdn over 1f out and kpt on wl ins fnl f: comf* **5/4**[1]

2 2 ¼ **Coeur D'Amour (IRE)**[19] 7260 2-9-0 88 ...................................... WJLee 3 95
(Madeleine Tylicki, Ire) *prom tl sn settled bhd ldr: disp 2nd fr bef 1/2-way: rdn in 2nd 1 1/2f out and no imp on wnr ins fnl f: kpt on same pce* **10/1**

3 1 ½ **Ballet Shoes (IRE)**[14] 7421 2-9-3 102 ........................................ PBBeggy 5 95
(A P O'Brien, Ire) *chsd ldrs: bmpd sltly after 1f: 6th 1/2-way: sme hdwy on outer under 2f out: sn rdn in 4th and disp 2nd briefly ins fnl f: no imp on wnr and kpt on same pce in 3rd clsng stages* **5/1**[3]

4 hd **Sizzling (IRE)**[14] 7421 2-9-0 103 ........................................ WayneLordan 1 91
(A P O'Brien, Ire) *chsd ldrs: disp 2nd fr bef 1/2-way: pushed along in 3rd 2f out: sn rdn and no imp on wnr u.p in 4th ins fnl f: kpt on same pce* **2/1**[2]

5 nk **Gasta (IRE)**[28] 6974 2-9-0 93 ........................................(p¹) RonanWhelan 6 91
(J S Bolger, Ire) *s.i.s and settled in rr: last at 1/2-way: stl gng wl under 3f out: pushed along into 6th ins fnl f and no imp on wnr in 5th wl ins fnl f: kpt on* **25/1**

6 1 ¼ **Solar Wave (IRE)**[18] 7289 2-9-0 86 ..............................(e) KevinManning 4 90
(J S Bolger, Ire) *w.w: 5th 1/2-way: pushed along fr 2f out and n.m.r ins fnl f where checked briefly: no imp after and one pce in 6th clsng stages* **20/1**

7 1 ½ **Lady Camelot (IRE)**[23] 7133 2-9-0 81 ................................. ShaneFoley 2 85
(Gavin Cromwell, Ire) *chsd ldrs: racd keenly early: 4th 1/2-way: pushed along in 4th under 3f out and no imp on wnr u.p in 4th under 2f out: wknd fr over 1f out* **25/1**

1m 53.01s (6.71) **7** Ran SP% **116.0**
CSF £14.85 TOTE £2.20: £1.70, £2.00; DF 14.60 Trifecta £48.10.
**Owner** Michael Tabor & Derrick Smith & Mrs John Magnier **Bred** Remember When Syndicate **Trained** Cashel, Co Tipperary

**FOCUS**
A straightforward victory for the winner, who really has begun to put it all together of late. The pace wasn't overly strong by any means, with the Donnacha O'Brien dictating the tempo from the front.

## 7860a IRISH CESAREWITCH (PREMIER H'CAP) 2m
5:15 (5:15) 3-Y-0+

**£50,427** (£16,239; £7,692; £3,418; £1,709; £854)

RPR

1 **Lord Erskine (IRE)**[23] 7135 4-8-5 **77** ...................................... ConorHoban 87+
(H Rogers, Ire) *chsd ldrs: 5th 5f out: gng wl between horses into st: effrt 2f out: rdn to ld 1 1/2f out and sn clr: styd on wl ins fnl f* **25/1**

2 2 ½ **Snow Falcon (IRE)**[29] 6956 7-9-11 **97** ................................... ColinKeane 104+
(Noel Meade, Ire) *mid-div early: clsr in 8th bef 1/2-way: 7th 5f out: gng wl into st and impr on outer to chse ldrs: rdn into 2nd 1f out and sn no imp on wnr: kpt on same pce* **5/1**[2]

3 5 **Ted Veale (IRE)**[23] 7136 10-9-6 **97** ............................ DonaghO'Connor(5) 99+
(A J Martin, Ire) *hld up in rr of mid-div: hdwy gng wl 3f out: rdn in 10th over 2f out and clsd u.p into nvr threatening 3rd wl ins fnl f: nvr trbld ldrs* **16/1**

4 ½ **Miles To Memphis (IRE)**[39] 6603 8-8-13 **85** ............................(t) WJLee 86
(Mrs Denise Foster, Ire) *chsd ldrs: 6th 5f out: rdn on outer over 2f out and tk clsr order in 4th: no imp on wnr u.p in 3rd ins fnl f: denied 3rd wl ins fnl f* **14/1**

5 1 **Neverushacon (IRE)**[30] 6911 6-7-11 **79** ...............(p) ScottMcCullagh(10) 79
(Mrs John Harrington, Ire) *chsd ldrs: 6th 1/2-way: 8th 5f out: tk clsr order under 3f out: sn rdn and u.p in 6th 1 1/2f out: kpt on same pce in 5th wl ins fnl f: nvr trbld ldrs* **20/1**

6 1 ¾ **Wonder Laish**[25] 5488 5-9-0 **86** .....................................(p¹) NGMcCullagh 84
(C Byrnes, Ire) *in tch and rn freely early: 9th 1/2-way: impr to chse ldrs 3f out: wnt 3rd over 2f out and rdn: no ex over 1f out and one pce after* **16/1**

7 ¾ **Grand Partner (IRE)**[23] 7136 9-8-1 **80** ................................ NathanCrosse(7) 77
(Thomas Mullins, Ire) *hld up towards rr: prog 3f out: rdn into 8th 1f out and kpt on same pce: nvr trbld ldrs* **33/1**

8 1 ¾ **Artful Artist (IRE)**[29] 6956 8-8-9 **84** ......................................(t) OisinOrr(3) 79
(A J Martin, Ire) *in tch: rdn in 8th over 2f out and no imp on ldrs u.p in 7th over 1f out: one pce after* **8/1**[3]

9 nk **Lucca (IRE)**[36] 6706 5-8-4 **76** oh2 ............................................ RoryCleary 71
(Jarlath P Fahey, Ire) *led tl hdd after 3f: 3rd 1/2-way: regained advantage fr 3f out: sn rdn and hdd u.p 1 1/2f out: wknd fnl f* **20/1**

10 2 **Benkei (IRE)**[28] 6976 7-9-8 **94** ......................................(b¹) JonathanBurke 87
(H Rogers, Ire) *chsd ldrs and racd keenly early: 2nd 1/2-way: rdn bhd ldrs over 2f out and sn no ex: wknd 1 1/2f out* **33/1**

11 8 **Ibsen (IRE)**[23] 7136 8-7-12 **77** .................................................(tp) SeanDavis(7) 61
(Gordon Elliott, Ire) *mid-div: rdn 2f out and no imp u.p in 11th over 1f out: one pce after* **12/1**

12 1 **Here For The Craic (IRE)**[18] 7295 10-8-3 **80** ...........(p) DannySheehy(5) 63
(David Kenneth Budds, Ire) *hld up towards rr: prog over 3f out: sn rdn in 11th and no ex 1 1/2f out: one pce after* **33/1**

13 5 ½ **Gustavus Vassa**[90] 4706 3-8-5 **86** ................................................. ChrisHayes 65
(W P Mullins, Ire) *hld up in rr of mid-div: racd keenly: rdn over 2f out and no imp in 15th 1 1/2f out: kpt on one pce* **9/2**[1]

14 nk **Mr Everest (IRE)**[24] 7103 4-8-10 **82** ........................................ WayneLordan 58
(Joseph Patrick O'Brien, Ire) *hld up towards rr: rdn and no imp 3f out: kpt on one pce fnl 2f* **33/1**

15 1 ¾ **Nietzsche**[22] 7150 4-8-9 **86** ...............................................(h) BenRobinson(5) 60
(Brian Ellison) *in rr of mid-div best: 14th under 5f out: rdn over 2f out and no imp: one pce fnl 2f* **11/1**

16 4 **San Remo (IRE)**[53] 6079 3-8-10 **91** ...................................... MichaelHussey 63
(A P O'Brien, Ire) *towards rr: rdn and no imp over 2f out: kpt on one pce* **22/1**

17 nk **Western Boy (IRE)**[24] 6361 8-9-1 **87** ............................................ FranBerry 57
(P A Fahy, Ire) *hld up in rr: last at 1/2-way: tk clsr order briefly over 3f out where hmpd and nt clr run: rdn over 2f out and sme hdwy into mod 14th over 1f out: eased ins fnl f* **12/1**

18 17 **St Stephens Green (IRE)**[29] 6956 6-8-12 **84** ........................ ShaneFoley 35
(Emmet Mullins, Ire) *mid-div: short of room after 1/2-way and pushed along briefly: rdn and no imp under 3f out: wknd in 14th over 1f out: sn eased* **16/1**

19 ¾ **Tara Dylan (IRE)**[19] 7261 5-8-11 **86** ........................(bt¹) RobbieDowney(3) 36
(Thomas Mullins, Ire) *hld up in tch: gng wl in 8th into st: sn lost pl and rdn under 3f out: wknd* **50/1**

20 12 **Sir Ector (USA)**[37] 5488 10-8-7 **84** ................................ KillianLeonard(5) 21
(Miss Nicole McKenna, Ire) *mid-div best: rdn and wknd fr over 3f out: eased over 1f out* **33/1**

21 2 ¼ **Felix Mendelssohn (IRE)**[9] 7589 6-9-4 **93** ...................(t) SeanCorby(3) 28
(Joseph Patrick O'Brien, Ire) *mid-div: rdn over 3f out and sn wknd* **40/1**

22 2 ¼ **Travertine (IRE)**[38] 7708 7-9-7 **98** ...............................(v¹) TomMadden(5) 30
(Niall Madden, Ire) *in rr of mid-div best: pushed along over 4f out and wknd u.p towards rr over 3f out where bmpd rival: eased fnl f* **66/1**

23 1 ¾ **Sea The Lion (IRE)**[29] 6956 6-9-0 **86** ..............................(p¹) RonanWhelan 16
(Jarlath P Fahey, Ire) *chsd ldrs: pushed along disputing 3rd 5f out: no ex u.p 3f out: wknd: eased fr over 2f out* **18/1**

24 14 **Bhutan (IRE)**[46] 6337 4-9-1 **87** ...................................... DonnachaO'Brien
(Joseph Patrick O'Brien, Ire) *chsd ldrs tl led after 3f: hdd fr 3f out and wknd qckly: eased under 2f out* **14/1**

3m 51.8s (6.80)
**WFA** 3 from 4yo+ 9lb **24** Ran SP% **144.2**
CSF £147.82 CT £2185.67 TOTE £38.40: £6.80, £2.20, £4.30, £3.70; DF 268.60 Trifecta £5490.70.
**Owner** Jeremiah Nolan **Bred** Northern Bloodstock Agency Ltd **Trained** Ardee, Co. Louth
■ Stewards' Enquiry : Donagh O'Connor caution; excessive use of whip

**FOCUS**
No stalls here, with the race getting underway via flag start. An impressive performance from the winner who loves getting his toe in and is obviously progressing. The standard is set around the third, fourth, fifth and seventh.

7861 - 7874a (Foreign Racing) - See Raceform Interactive

# 7723 KEMPTON (A.W) (R-H)

Monday, October 9

**OFFICIAL GOING: Polytrack: standard to slow**

Wind: virtually nil Weather: dry

## 7875 WATCH RACING UK ON THE GO FILLIES' NOVICE AUCTION STKS 7f (P)

4:55 (4:57) (Class 6) 2-Y-O £2,587 (£770; £384; £192) Stalls Low

Form RPR

1 **Augenblick (IRE)** 2-9-0 0 AndreaAtzeni 7 76
(Roger Varian) *trckd ldrs: waiting for gap to open 2f out: effrt and hdwy to chse ldr over 1f out: rdn and r.o wl to ld ins fnl f: a doing enough after* 5/1[2]

51 2 hd **Ortiz**[33] 6816 2-9-4 0 HollieDoyle(3) 1 83
(Henry Candy) *t.k.h: trckd ldrs: swtchd ins and effrt 2f out: rdn and qcknd to ld over 1f out: hdd ins fnl f: kpt on wl but a hld* 8/13[1]

3 2 **Lady Al Thumama** 2-9-0 0 StevieDonohoe 11 70
(Charlie Fellowes) *hld up wl in tch: effrt and hdwy wl over 1f out: clr in ldng trio and pressing ldrs 1f out: kpt on same pce ins fnl f* 25/1

03 4 6 **Laytown (IRE)**[11] 7535 2-9-0 0 DougieCostello 2 54+
(Jamie Osborne) *t.k.h: led: rdn and edgd lft wl over 1f out: 4th and outpcd ent fnl f: wknd ins fnl f* 5/1[2]

06 5 1 1/4 **Free Talkin**[43] 6472 2-9-0 0 KierenFox 13 51
(Michael Attwater) *dropped in after s: hdwy into midfield 1/2-way: effrt over 2f out: outpcd wl over 1f out: rallied and edgd rt ins fnl f: kpt on but no ch* 66/1

6 1/2 **Mrs Benson (IRE)** 2-9-0 0 RobHornby 4 49
(Michael Blanshard) *pushed rt s and slowly away: in tch in last trio: effrt and swtchd rt ent fnl 2f: midfield and no imp over 1f out: wknd fnl f* 50/1

7 2 **Trouble And Strife (IRE)** 2-9-0 0 LukeMorris 12 44+
(Sir Mark Prescott Bt) *sn bustled in last trio: rdn and sme hdwy on outer over 3f out: outpcd 2f out: n.d after* 25/1

0 8 1/2 **Dolydaydream**[77] 5216 2-9-0 0 JFEgan 3 43
(Pat Phelan) *chsd ldr tl 2f out: sn rdn: outpcd and lost pl: wknd fnl f* 66/1

6 9 nk **Dragon Tattoo (IRE)**[19] 7266 2-9-0 0 JosephineGordon 5 42
(Hugo Palmer) *wnt rt s: rn green in rr: swtchd lft and effrt over 2f out: no imp and outpcd over 1f out: wknd fnl f* 9/1[3]

5 10 1/2 **Ainne**[42] 6504 2-8-9 0 MitchGodwin(5) 9 40
(Sylvester Kirk) *trckd ldng pair on outer: rdn 2f out: sn outpcd and btn: wknd fnl f* 25/1

11 30 **Jonathans Girl** 2-8-7 0 JacobMitchell(7) 10
(Christine Dunnett) *midfield tl rdn and dropped to rr 1/2-way: lost tch over 2f out: t.o* 100/1

1m 25.86s (-0.14) **Going Correction** -0.15s/f (Stan) 11 Ran SP% 122.7
Speed ratings (Par 90): **94,93,91,84,83 82,80,79,79,78 44**
CSF £8.51 TOTE £6.50: £2.00, £1.02, £4.90; EX 12.80 Trifecta £141.20.
**Owner** Ajay Anne & Partner **Bred** Michael O'Mahony **Trained** Newmarket, Suffolk

**FOCUS**
An ordinary-looking fillies' novice with a nice enough start from the winner.

## 7876 MATCHBOOK CASINO NOVICE STKS (DIV I) 6f (P)

5:25 (5:26) (Class 5) 2-Y-O £3,234 (£962; £481; £240) Stalls Low

Form RPR

62 1 **Sergio Leone (IRE)**[35] 6761 2-9-2 0 AndreaAtzeni 6 74
(Richard Hannon) *bustled along leaving stalls: sn w ldr: rdn ent fnl 2f: sustained duel w ldr: led ins fnl f: styd on: rdn out* 2/1[1]

30 2 nk **Go Roo**[17] 7351 2-9-2 0 AdamKirby 4 73
(Clive Cox) *led: rdn wl over 1f out: drvn and sustained duel w wnr after: hdd ins fnl f: kpt on wl but a jst hld* 12/1

4 3 1 1/2 **Society Prince (IRE)**[20] 7250 2-9-2 0 TomQueally 10 68
(James Fanshawe) *hld up in tch: effrt and hdwy on inner over 1f out: chsd ldng pair ins fnl f: kpt on but no imp fnl 100yds* 7/1

6 4 nk **Walk On Walter (IRE)**[30] 6921 2-9-2 0 JamieSpencer 5 74+
(David Simcock) *s.i.s: hld up in last trio: hung bdly lft fr over 4f out: v wd bnd ent st 3f out: stl hanging and racing nr stands rail over 1f out but remarkably clsd to chse ldrs ins fnl f: eased towards fin* 8/1

0 5 1 1/4 **Ace Of Spades (USA)**[12] 7513 2-9-2 0 RobertHavlin 1 63
(George Scott) *chsd ldrs: rdn 2f out: unable qck u.p and lost 3rd ins fnl f: wknd towards fin* 25/1

2461 6 1 **Knockout Blow**[14] 7450 2-9-6 78 SilvestreDeSousa 3 64
(Mark Johnston) *t.k.h: chsd ldrs: unable qck u.p over 1f out: wknd ins fnl f* 9/4[2]

460 7 1 **Cardaw Lily (IRE)**[24] 7126 2-8-11 76 ShaneKelly 7 52
(Richard Hughes) *hld up in tch in midfield: effrt over 1f out: kpt on same pce ins fnl f: nvr trbld ldrs* 25/1

8 1 1/4 **Fleeting Steps (IRE)** 2-9-2 0 LukeMorris 2 53
(Sir Mark Prescott Bt) *s.i.s and short of room leaving stalls: rousted along in tch in last trio: outpcd wl over 1f out: wl hld and kpt on same pce after* 33/1

63 9 nk **Bakht Khan (IRE)**[30] 6950 2-9-2 0 KevinStott 9 52
(Kevin Ryan) *in tch: effrt but unable qck u.p over 1f out: wknd ins fnl f* 6/1[3]

0 10 7 **Prince Rock (IRE)**[12] 7511 2-8-11 0 PaddyBradley(5) 8 29
(Simon Dow) *s.i.s: a bhd* 50/1

1m 13.05s (-0.05) **Going Correction** -0.15s/f (Stan) 10 Ran SP% 122.3
Speed ratings (Par 95): **94,93,91,91,89 88,86,85,84,75**
CSF £27.77 TOTE £3.10: £1.90, £2.70, £2.90; EX 31.90 Trifecta £216.60.
**Owner** Chelsea Thoroughbreds-A Few Dollars More **Bred** Barnane Stud **Trained** East Everleigh, Wilts

**FOCUS**
This looks ordinary juvenile form and it's hard to justify higher figures.

## 7877 MATCHBOOK CASINO NOVICE STKS (DIV II) 6f (P)

5:55 (5:57) (Class 5) 2-Y-O £3,234 (£962; £481; £240) Stalls Low

Form RPR

45 1 **Buffer Zone**[17] 7351 2-9-2 0 KieranShoemark 1 83+
(Roger Charlton) *hld up in tch in last trio: clsd and nt clr run over 2f out: smooth hdwy to press ldrs over 1f out: rdn to ld 1f out: r.o wl: comf* 8/11[1]

50 2 1 1/4 **Perfect Hustler (USA)**[65] 5631 2-9-2 0 JFEgan 3 77
(Jeremy Noseda) *chsd ldng trio: effrt and clsd over 2f out: rdn and ev ch over 1f out: clr 2nd but nt match pce of wnr fnl f: kpt on* 12/1

10 3 1 3/4 **Villa Savina (IRE)**[29] 6977 2-9-1 0 AdamKirby 2 70
(Clive Cox) *led and sn clr: rdn wl over 1f out: hdd 1f out: 3rd and outpcd ins fnl f* 3/1[2]

604 4 2 **By Royal Approval (IRE)**[24] 7126 2-9-2 75 DougieCostello 4 65
(Michael Appleby) *chsd ldr tl 2f out: 4th and outpcd over 1f out: kpt on same pce ins fnl f* 12/1

5 5 1 3/4 **Mzoon (IRE)**[31] 6876 2-8-11 0 StevieDonohoe 7 54
(Charlie Fellowes) *hld up in tch: effrt 2f out: no imp and drifted rt over 1f out: wl hld and kpt on same pce ins fnl f* 8/1[3]

0 6 nk **Don't Cry About It (IRE)**[12] 7513 2-8-13 0 HollieDoyle(3) 8 58
(Ali Stronge) *t.k.h: hld up in rr: swtchd rt and hdwy on inner ent fnl 2f: no imp and one pced fr over 1f out* 66/1

7 hd **Sporting Bill (IRE)** 2-9-2 0 TomQueally 5 58+
(James Fanshawe) *hld up in tch: nt clrest of runs and swtchd lft bnd 3f out: effrt and nt clr run over 1f out: nvr trbld ldrs* 25/1

00 8 4 1/2 **Arigato**[19] 7280 2-9-2 0 MartinLane 9 43
(William Jarvis) *dwlt: hdwy on outer into midfield after 2f: rdn over 2f out: sn struggling and lost pl: bhd fnl f* 66/1

9 3 3/4 **Master Poet** 2-9-2 0 LukeMorris 6 31
(Robert Cowell) *chsd ldng pair: rdn over 2f out: sn struggling and lost pl: bhd fnl f* 25/1

1m 12.64s (-0.46) **Going Correction** -0.15s/f (Stan) 9 Ran SP% 120.1
Speed ratings (Par 95): **97,95,93,90,88 87,87,81,76**
CSF £11.97 TOTE £1.70: £1.02, £3.50, £1.40; EX 11.00 Trifecta £31.50.
**Owner** K Abdullah **Bred** Juddmonte Farms Ltd **Trained** Beckhampton, Wilts

**FOCUS**
The time was 0.41sec quicker than the first division. The winner is likely to rate higher from here.

## 7878 MATCHBOOK BETTING PODCAST H'CAP 1m (P)

6:25 (6:27) (Class 5) (0-70,70) 3-Y-O+ £3,234 (£962; £481; £240) Stalls Low

Form RPR

1520 1 **Golden Guest**[38] 6664 3-8-12 69 JaneElliott(5) 13 76
(George Margarson) *hld up in midfield on outer: effrt 2f out: hdwy over 1f out: str chal ins fnl f: r.o wl to ld last strides* 10/1

0005 2 hd **Choral Clan (IRE)**[13] 7493 6-9-5 68 JackMitchell 5 75
(Brendan Powell) *trckd ldrs: swtchd rt and effrt 2f out: chsd ldr over 1f out: drvn to ld ins fnl f: kpt on u.p: hdd last strides* 8/1

0440 3 1/2 **Luang Prabang (IRE)**[23] 7158 4-9-1 67 HollieDoyle(3) 10 73
(Chris Wall) *hld up in tch towards rr: nt clr run over 2f out: swtchd rt and hdwy wl over 1f out: chsd ldrs ins fnl f: kpt on wl* 10/1

1562 4 nk **African Blessing**[3] 7791 4-8-12 66 JoshuaBryan(5) 1 71
(Charlie Wallis) *led: rdn and fnd ex 2f out: hdd ins fnl f: no ex and one pced towards fin* 5/1[2]

0600 5 hd **Lacan (IRE)**[13] 7493 6-8-13 69 RossaRyan(7) 12 74+
(Brett Johnson) *awkward s and slowly away: hld up: hdwy into midfield 1/2-way: effrt 2f out: gd hdwy between rivals 1f out: chsng ldrs and running on whn nt clr run and eased nr fin* 16/1

405 6 3 1/4 **Isstoora (IRE)**[13] 7485 3-9-2 68 DanielMuscutt 9 65
(Marco Botti) *hld up in tch in midfield: effrt 2f out: sme hdwy u.p over 1f out: no imp 1f out: wknd ins fnl f* 8/1

1460 7 1/2 **Scribner Creek (IRE)**[11] 7541 4-9-1 67 CharlieBennett(3) 3 63
(Denis Quinn) *t.k.h early: hld up in last trio: hdwy on inner ent fnl 2f: drvn and no imp over 1f out: wknd ins fnl f* 20/1

4400 8 1/2 **South Sea Belle (IRE)**[33] 6818 3-9-1 67 KieranShoemark 4 62
(David Menuisier) *chsd ldrs: effrt to chse ldr 2f out tl edgd lft and lost 2nd over 1f out: sltly impeded and wknd ins fnl f* 33/1

1560 9 1/2 **Music Major**[24] 7131 4-9-6 69 AdamBeschizza 6 63
(Michael Attwater) *chsd ldrs: unable qck u.p and btn over 1f out: wknd ins fnl f* 20/1

3254 10 hd **Precious Angel (IRE)**[19] 7278 3-9-2 68 TomMarquand 7 61
(Richard Hannon) *midfield: rdn 5f out: drvn over 2f out: no imp over 1f out: wknd ins fnl f* 9/2[1]

/440 11 1 3/4 **Ogbourne Downs**[24] 7131 7-9-7 70 AdamKirby 2 59
(Ben Pauling) *s.i.s: hld up in rr: swtchd lft and effrt ent fnl 2f: no hdwy: nvr trbld ldrs* 6/1[3]

603- 12 1 3/4 **Fullon Clarets**[348] 7606 5-9-2 70 PaddyBradley(5) 14 55
(Laura Mongan) *chsd ldr tl 2f out: sn lost pl: wknd fnl f* 66/1

5140 13 13 **Muthraab Aldaar (IRE)**[95] 4523 4-9-1 64 TomQueally 11 19
(Jim Boyle) *a towards rr: lost tch over 1f out* 20/1

0406 14 14 **Squire**[41] 6557 6-9-6 69 (t) RobertHavlin 8
(Michael Attwater) *chsd ldrs tl lost pl qckly over 1f out: bhd over 1f out: t.o* 6/1[3]

1m 38.5s (-1.30) **Going Correction** -0.15s/f (Stan)
**WFA** 3 from 4yo+ 3lb 14 Ran SP% 128.4
Speed ratings (Par 103): **100,99,99,99,98 95,95,94,94,93 92,90,77,63**
CSF £87.89 CT £871.82 TOTE £11.80: £3.60, £3.20, £4.10; EX 144.20 Trifecta £1427.20.
**Owner** John Guest Racing **Bred** P A & M J Reditt & Catridge Stud **Trained** Newmarket, Suffolk

**FOCUS**
A modest but competitive handicap, rated around the fourth. A pb from the winner.

## 7879 SMARTER BETS WITH MATCHBOOK H'CAP 1m 3f 219y(P)

6:55 (6:56) (Class 6) (0-65,65) 3-Y-O £2,587 (£770; £384; £192) Stalls Low

Form RPR

6534 1 **Katabatika**[33] 6812 3-8-10 54 PJMcDonald 14 63+
(Hughie Morrison) *s.i.s: hld up in last trio: swtchd lft and effrt over 1f out: gd hdwy to ld over 1f out: sn clr and in n.d ins fnl f: eased cl home* 14/1

5466 2 3 3/4 **Malt Teaser (FR)**[4] 7760 3-9-4 62 RobertHavlin 12 67
(John Best) *hld up in tch in midfield: clsd to trck ldrs and gng wl whn nt clr run and snatched up over 1f out: eventually enough room and hdwy to chse clr wnr ins fnl f: kpt on but no ch w wnr* 10/1

033 3 1 1/2 **Secret Soul**[84] 4971 3-9-5 63 (v) HarryBentley 6 64
(Ralph Beckett) *in tch in midfield: effrt to chse ldrs 2f out: wnt 2nd but wnr gng clr 1f out: one pced and lost 2nd ins fnl f* 9/2[2]

2100 4 1 1/2 **Epsom Secret**[41] 6557 3-8-13 57 JFEgan 8 55
(Pat Phelan) *hld up in last quartet: effrt ent fnl 2f: hdwy u.p over 1f out: kpt on same pce ins fnl f: no threat to wnr* 20/1

0024 5 1 1/2 **Kings City (IRE)**[48] 6281 3-9-4 62 (v[1]) JamieSpencer 2 58
(Luca Cumani) *s.i.s and rousted along early: bhd: rdn and no immediate rspnse over 2f out: hdwy u.p over 1f out: styd on to pass btn horses ins fnl f: nvr trbld ldrs* 5/1[3]

0000 6 1 1/4 **Spiritofedinburgh (IRE)**[26] 7056 3-8-13 57 (t[1]) ShaneKelly 5 51
(Brendan Powell) *hld up in last trio: effrt over 2f out: styd on u.p ins fnl f: nvr trbld ldrs* 33/1

0601 7 1/2 **Delirium (IRE)**[19] 7279 3-8-9 56 (p) DavidEgan(3) 4 49
(Ed de Giles) *in tch in midfield: effrt to chse ldrs but unable qck over 1f out: wknd ins fnl f* 14/1

2444 8 hd **Leapt**[10] 7560 3-9-0 65 (h) NicolaCurrie(7) 10 58
(Richard Hughes) *in tch in midfield on outer: rdn 3f out: no imp and btn over 1f out: wknd fnl f* 6/1

4460 **9** *nk* **Helf (IRE)**[33] 6812 3-9-7 **65**....(t[1]) TomMarquand 9 57
(Richard Hannon) *t.k.h: chsd ldrs pushed along 4f out: led over 2f out tl over 1f out: wknd fnl f* **20/1**

-032 **10** *½* **Glassalt**[11] 7537 3-9-5 **63**.... SilvestreDeSousa 7 54
(Michael Bell) *hld up in midfield: effrt over 2f out: swtchd lft and no hdwy 2f out: n.d after* **3/1**[1]

501 **11** *4 ½* **Moonlight Silver**[40] 6578 3-9-4 **62**.... AdamKirby 3 46
(William Muir) *led early: sn hdd and chsd ldrs: effrt and ev ch jst over 2f out tl over 1f out: wknd qckly fnl f* **8/1**

0000 **12** *45* **Beaconsfield**[13] 7483 3-8-9 **53**.... JosephineGordon 11
(Hughie Morrison) *led after 1f tl 9f out: chsd ldr tl led again over 3f out tl over 2f out: dropped out and eased over 1f out: t.o* **33/1**

00 **13** *½* **Kingwilliamstown**[21] 7215 3-8-7 **51** oh6....(p[1]) OscarPereira 1
(Jose Santos) *w ldrs tl led 9f out: hdd 3f out and sn dropped out: t.o fnl 2f* **66/1**

2m 31.35s (-3.15) **Going Correction** -0.15s/f (Stan) **13** Ran SP% **124.6**
Speed ratings (Par 99): **104,101,100,99,98 97,97,97,97,96 93,63,63**
CSF £144.35 CT £747.74 TOTE £18.90: £4.90, £3.70, £2.00; EX 237.20 Trifecta £3363.30.
**Owner** Lady Blyth **Bred** Lemington Grange Stud **Trained** East Ilsley, Berks

**FOCUS**
A moderate handicap. The winner found a bit and the second ran his best race to date.

## 7880 MATCHBOOK VIP H'CAP 1m 3f 219y(P)
**7:25** (7:29) (Class 4) (0-85,85) 3-Y-O+ **£4,690** (£1,395; £697; £348) **Stalls** Low

Form RPR

1 **1** **Golden Birthday (FR)**[14] 7462 6-9-4 **79**....(t) FranBerry 6 87+
(Harry Fry) *trckd ldrs and travelled wl: effrt and rdn to chse ldr over 1f out: led ins fnl f: r.o wl* **7/4**[1]

-620 **2** *¾* **St Malo (USA)**[72] 5421 4-9-9 **84**.... AndreaAtzeni 9 91
(Roger Varian) *hld up in last trio: clsd and nt clrest of runs 2f out: rdn and gd hdwy to chse ldrs 1f out: styd on wl to go 2nd towards fin* **7/1**

4346 **3** *½* **Fleeting Visit**[16] 7412 4-9-6 **81**....(p) EdwardGreatrex 5 87
(Eve Johnson Houghton) *led tl 7f out: chsd ldr tl rdn to ld again wl over 1f out: hdd and one pced ins fnl f: lost 2nd towards fin* **10/1**

0506 **4** *nse* **Captain Peacock**[25] 7096 4-9-3 **78**....(v) RichardKingscote 1 84
(William Knight) *hld up in midfield: rdn and hdwy over 1f out: chsd ldrs 1f out: kpt on* **20/1**

4041 **5** *2* **Banish (USA)**[12] 7515 4-9-9 **84**....(vt) JamesDoyle 13 87
(Hugo Palmer) *dwlt: swtchd rt and rousted along early: hld up in midfield: rdn and hdwy on inner 2f out: no imp 1f out: wknd ins fnl f* **5/1**[3]

560 **6** *1* **Panko (IRE)**[8] 7651 4-9-4 **79**....(p[1]) LiamKeniry 2 80
(Ed de Giles) *chsd ldrs: unable qck u.p over 1f out: wknd ins fnl f* **50/1**

0600 **7** *½* **Sennockian Star**[12] 7515 7-9-4 **79**.... PJMcDonald 7 79
(Mark Johnston) *in tch in midfield: rdn 3f out: unable qck u.p and styd on same pce fr over 1f out* **25/1**

3203 **8** *¾* **Faithful Creek (IRE)**[19] 7284 5-9-8 **83**....(p) SilvestreDeSousa 11 82
(Michael Appleby) *t.k.h: chsd ldrs tl led 7f out: rdn and hdd wl over 1f out: no ex over 1f out: wknd ins fnl f* **14/1**

1103 **9** *shd* **Fair Power (IRE)**[24] 7132 3-8-10 **82**.... MitchGodwin(5) 12 82
(Sylvester Kirk) *hld up in tch towards rr: effrt and hdwy u.p over 1f out: styd on same pce and no imp fnl f* **16/1**

5664 **10** *shd* **Murgan**[20] 7231 5-9-3 **78**....(t[1]) AdamKirby 3 77
(Stuart Kittow) *in tch in midfield: rdn and no imp over 1f out: kpt on same pce fnl f* **25/1**

14 **11** *nk* **Mobbhij**[17] 7359 3-9-1 **85**.... DavidEgan(3) 4 84+
(Saeed bin Suroor) *hld up in tch in midfield: stuck bhd wkng rival: hmpd and shuffled bk towards rr over 2f out: tried to rally over 1f out: kpt on but no ch* **7/2**[2]

6000 **12** *1 ½* **Belabour**[12] 7515 4-8-12 **73**.... JFEgan 8 69
(Mark Brisbourne) *hld up towards rr: hdwy on outer over 3f out: no hdwy u.p over 2f out: lost pl and btn over 1f out* **66/1**

0510 **13** *10* **Viking Hoard (IRE)**[38] 6657 3-8-10 **77**....(p[1]) LukeMorris 10 58
(Harry Dunlop) *stdd s: hld up in rr: no hdwy u.p over 1f out: wknd fnl f* **50/1**

0000 **14** *10* **Samtu (IRE)**[43] 6467 6-9-8 **83**.... JoeyHaynes 14 47
(Marjorie Fife) *chsd ldrs tl lost pl rapidly over 2f out: bhd over 1f out* **66/1**

2m 31.97s (-2.53) **Going Correction** -0.15s/f (Stan)
**WFA** 3 from 4yo+ 6lb **14** Ran SP% **128.8**
Speed ratings (Par 105): **102,101,101,101,99 99,98,98,98,98 97,96,90,83**
CSF £15.03 CT £106.44 TOTE £2.80: £1.50, £2.60, £3.60; EX 22.20 Trifecta £144.90.
**Owner** G C Stevens **Bred** E A R L La Croix Sonnet **Trained** Seaborough, Dorset
■ Stewards' Enquiry : Edward Greatrex two day ban: using his whip above the permitted level (23/24 Oct)

**FOCUS**
A useful handicap. The winner was on a good mark compared with his Flat form and the second posted a pb.

## 7881 BETTER ODDS WITH MATCHBOOK H'CAP 7f (P)
**7:55** (7:56) (Class 5) (0-70,70) 3-Y-O+ **£3,234** (£962; £481; £240) **Stalls** Low

Form RPR

262 **1** **Bounty Pursuit**[42] 6502 5-8-13 **68**.... MitchGodwin(5) 9 76
(Michael Blake) *chsd ldng pair: clsd to ld 1f out: hld on wl u.p ins fnl f: drvn out* **16/1**

5161 **2** *hd* **Daring Guest (IRE)**[26] 7058 3-8-13 **70**.... JaneElliott(5) 3 76
(George Margarson) *hld up in midfield: rdn and clsd over 1f out: str chal ins fnl f: r.o but a jst hld* **4/1**[1]

5002 **3** *nk* **Balgair**[26] 7062 3-9-2 **68**.... TomMarquand 12 73
(Tom Clover) *stdd and dropped in bhd after s: hld up towards rr: hdwy over 1f out: styd on wl ins fnl f: nt quite rch ldrs* **9/2**[2]

5646 **4** *¾* **Tigerwolf (IRE)**[23] 7157 4-9-5 **69**.... SilvestreDeSousa 13 73
(Mick Channon) *in tch in midfield: effrt over 1f out: swtchd rt and hdwy ent fnl f: styd on wl u.p ins fnl f* **7/1**

313/ **5** *hd* **Exit Europe**[688] 7939 5-9-2 **66**.... LukeMorris 5 70
(Sir Mark Prescott Bt) *chsd ldrs: rdn over 1f out: pressed ldrs and hrd drvn 1f out: kpt on same pce ins fnl f* **5/1**[3]

6340 **6** *nk* **Otomo**[31] 6888 3-9-3 **69**....(h) LiamKeniry 6 71
(Philip Hide) *w ldr tl rdn to ld over 1f out: hdd 1f out: styd on same pce ins fnl f* **50/1**

1214 **7** *½* **Newstead Abbey**[16] 7408 7-9-5 **69**....(p) PJMcDonald 7 70
(Michael Herrington) *chsd ldrs: effrt over 1f out: kpt on same pce ins fnl f* **8/1**

2220 **8** *3* **Fine Example**[20] 7249 4-8-13 **70**....(b) SeamusCronin(7) 11 63
(Kevin Ryan) *led and sn clr w rival: rdn and hdd over 1f out: wknd ins fnl f* **12/1**

5610 **9** *3 ¼* **Iftitah (IRE)**[26] 7058 3-9-2 **68**....(bt) HarryBentley 4 52
(George Peckham) *in tch in midfield: swtchd lft and effrt over 2f out: no hdwy u.p: wknd fnl f* **16/1**

0506 **10** *2 ½* **Fareeq**[31] 6888 3-8-12 **69**....(t[1]) JoshuaBryan(5) 2 46
(Charlie Wallis) *a towards rr: no hdwy u.p over 2f out: wknd over 1f out* **25/1**

5250 **11** *hd* **Fire Palace**[3] 7780 3-9-4 **70**.... AndreaAtzeni 1 46
(Robert Eddery) *v.s.a: n.d* **11/2**

1100 **12** *1* **Prince Of Time**[55] 6049 5-8-12 **69**.... FayeMcManoman(7) 8 44
(Richard Ford) *a towards rr: bhd whn bdly hmpd and swtchd lft wl over 1f out: no ch after* **50/1**

0004 **13** *3* **Sophisticated Heir (IRE)**[18] 7332 7-9-5 **69**.... DougieCostello 10 36
(Kevin Frost) *chsd ldrs tl lost pl qckly over 2f out: bhd over 1f out* **50/1**

1m 24.79s (-1.21) **Going Correction** -0.15s/f (Stan)
**WFA** 3 from 4yo+ 2lb **13** Ran SP% **123.0**
Speed ratings (Par 103): **100,99,99,98,98 98,97,94,90,87 87,86,82**
CSF £79.95 CT £356.78 TOTE £22.80: £5.30, £1.90, £1.40; EX 90.80 Trifecta £1051.50.
**Owner** Racing For A Cause **Bred** Cecil And Miss Alison Wiggins **Trained** Trowbridge, Wilts

**FOCUS**
Another modest yet competitive handicap, run at a good pace. A small pb from the winner.

## 7882 MATCHBOOK TRADERS CONFERENCE H'CAP 6f (P)
**8:25** (8:26) (Class 5) (0-75,74) 3-Y-O+ **£3,234** (£962; £481; £240) **Stalls** Low

Form RPR

4320 **1** **Higher Court (USA)**[16] 7409 9-8-13 **70**.... DavidEgan(3) 6 76
(Emma Owen) *mde all: rdn and fnd ex 2f out: hrd pressed wl ins fnl f: hld on: all out* **16/1**

4266 **2** *nk* **Maazel (IRE)**[49] 6276 3-9-5 **74**.... AndreaAtzeni 2 79
(Roger Varian) *hld up in midfield: effrt on inner over 1f out: chsd ldrs 1f out: wnt 2nd ins fnl f: str chal fnl 100yds: jst hld* **8/1**

104 **3** *nk* **Debonaire David**[66] 5606 3-9-3 **72**....(t) ShaneKelly 10 76
(Richard Hughes) *stdd and dropped in after s: t.k.h: hld up in last trio: clsd and swtchd lft 1f out: squeezed through between rivals and r.o strly fnl 100yds: nt quite rch ldrs* **12/1**

4224 **4** *nk* **Mishaal (IRE)**[10] 7572 7-9-2 **70**.... KieranShoemark 5 73
(Michael Herrington) *led to s: midfield: effrt over 1f out: hdwy u.p 1f out: styd on wl ins fnl f* **11/4**[1]

0345 **5** *shd* **Very Honest (IRE)**[38] 6652 4-8-11 **72**.... RossaRyan(7) 3 75
(Brett Johnson) *chsd ldrs: effrt over 1f out: kpt on u.p ins fnl f: lost 2 pls cl home* **16/1**

002 **6** *½* **Himself**[44] 6442 3-9-5 **74**.... TomMarquand 8 75
(Richard Hannon) *off the pce towards rr: swtchd lft 2f out: hdwy u.p 1f out: styd on ins fnl f: nt rch ldrs* **7/1**[3]

5063 **7** *nk* **Born To Finish (IRE)**[16] 7409 4-9-6 **74**....(p) DougieCostello 1 74
(Jamie Osborne) *hld up in midfield: hdwy u.p on inner over 1f out: n.m.r 1f out: kpt on ins fnl f* **7/2**[2]

633 **8** *½* **Red Alert**[22] 7192 3-9-5 **74**....(p[1]) SilvestreDeSousa 12 73
(William Muir) *t.k.h: sn chsng wnr: unable qck u.p over 1f out: kpt on same pce ins fnl f* **12/1**

4600 **9** *nse* **Big Lachie**[16] 7409 3-9-3 **72**.... LukeMorris 11 70
(Daniel Mark Loughnane) *dropped in bhd after s: racd in last pair: effrt over 2f out: hdwy over 1f out: kpt on ins fnl f: n.m.r towards fin* **50/1**

1004 **10** *2 ¼* **Highly Sprung (IRE)**[21] 7214 4-9-5 **73**.... PJMcDonald 7 64
(Mark Johnston) *sn bustled along in last trio: swtchd rt 1f out: kpt on but nvr trbld ldrs* **20/1**

-251 **11** *2 ½* **Kowaiyess (IRE)**[25] 7099 3-9-3 **72**.... AdamBeschizza 9 55
(Mohamed Moubarak) *t.k.h: midfield: hdwy to chse ldrs on outer after 2f: unable qck over 1f out: wknd ins fnl f* **10/1**

-200 **12** *2* **Don't Blame Me**[16] 7408 4-9-5 **73**.... AdamKirby 4 50
(Clive Cox) *midfield tl lost pl u.p over 1f out: wknd ins fnl f* **8/1**

1m 11.57s (-1.53) **Going Correction** -0.15s/f (Stan)
**WFA** 3 from 4yo+ 1lb **12** Ran SP% **126.6**
Speed ratings (Par 103): **104,103,103,102,102 102,101,100,100,97 94,91**
CSF £147.73 CT £1651.07 TOTE £23.60: £5.30, £2.80, £3.80; EX 217.70 Trifecta £4466.90.
**Owner** Miss Emma L Owen **Bred** Darley **Trained** Nether Winchendon, Bucks

**FOCUS**
More ordinary but competitive stuff. A congested finish and a small pb from the winner.
T/Jkpt: Not Won. T/Plt: £130.80 to a £1 stake. Pool: £66,586.45 - 371.49 winning units T/Qpdt: £38.70 to a £1 stake. Pool: £9,426.71 - 180.21 winning units **Steve Payne**

# 7654 MUSSELBURGH (R-H)
Monday, October 9

**OFFICIAL GOING: Good to soft (good in places; 6.1)**
Wind: Breezy, half against in races over 5f and in over 3f of home straight in races on the round course Weather: Overcast

## 7883 ALL-NEW RACINGUK.COM NOVICE AUCTION STKS 7f 33y
**3:10** (3:11) (Class 6) 2-Y-O **£2,264** (£673; £336; £168) **Stalls** Low

Form RPR

314 **1** **Han Solo Berger (IRE)**[41] 6545 2-9-7 79.... PaulMulrennan 4 80+
(Keith Dalgleish) *mde virtually all: rdn and clr over 1f out: kpt on wl fnl f: eased nr fin* **2/1**[1]

03 **2** *3 ¼* **Southpark**[21] 7221 2-9-2 0.... PaulHanagan 2 66
(Richard Fahey) *t.k.h: prom: effrt and rdn over 1f out: chsng wnr whn veered lft ins fnl f: stened and kpt on: no ch w wnr* **3/1**[2]

500 **3** *nse* **Tommy Shelby (FR)**[20] 7237 2-8-13 0.... AdamMcNamara(3) 6 66+
(Richard Fahey) *s.i.s: hld up in tch: effrt and hdwy over 1f out: kpt on fnl f: nvr able to chal* **20/1**

53 **4** *hd* **Canadian George (FR)**[12] 7520 2-9-2 0.... ConnorBeasley 1 66
(Keith Dalgleish) *disp ld early: pressed wnr: rdn over 2f out: edgd lft over 1f out: one pce ins fnl f* **10/3**[3]

106 **5** *1 ¼* **Marchingontogether**[13] 7482 2-9-0 77.... TomEaves 5 60
(Ivan Furtado) *cl up on outside: effrt and rdn 2f out: outpcd ins fnl f* **4/1**

**6** *7* **Wynfaul The Wizard (USA)** 2-9-2 0.... ShaneGray 7 43
(Richard Guest) *noisy and colty in paddock: missed break: rcvrd to join pack after 1f: rdn and outpcd over 2f out: btn over 1f out* **20/1**

1m 32.99s (3.99) **Going Correction** +0.425s/f (Yiel) **6** Ran SP% **110.9**
Speed ratings (Par 93): **94,90,90,90,88 80**
CSF £8.05 TOTE £3.60: £2.30, £1.10; EX 11.00 Trifecta £87.30.
**Owner** Thats My Boys **Bred** Irish National Stud **Trained** Carluke, S Lanarks

**FOCUS**
This fixture was only introduced the previous week following a few recent abandonments in Scotland, including the Ayr Great Western meeting. The ground had dried out slightly and was now good to soft, good in places (from good to soft). However, even though these were 2yos a winning time 6.89sec outside standard suggests the ground was still testing. The rail was out 3yds on the bottom bend, adding 7yds to the distance of all races on the round course. An ordinary novice auction event to start with the six runners representing just four stables. Ordinary form, the second and third setting the level.

## 7884 WISE BETTING AT RACINGUK.COM H'CAP — 5f 1y
**3:40** (3:40) (Class 6) (0-65,71) 3-Y-O+ **£2,264** (£673; £336; £168) **Stalls** High

Form / RPR

1200 **1** **Knockamany Bends (IRE)**[21] 7218 7-8-4 **48**..........(h) JamesSullivan 10 — 54
(John Wainwright) *disp ld: wnt on over 1f out: kpt on gamely fnl f* **25/1**

5051 **2** ¾ **Economic Crisis (IRE)**[8] 7657 8-9-6 **71** 6ex.......... ConnorMurtagh(7) 2 — 74
(Alan Berry) *in tch on outside: effrt and chsd wnr fnl f: kpt on: hld nr fin* **11/2**[1]

3115 **3** nk **Our Place In Loule**[47] 6318 4-8-11 **55**........................ PatrickMathers 6 — 57
(Noel Wilson) *bhd and sn pushed along: angled rt and hdwy over 1f out: kpt on ins fnl f: nt pce to chal* **6/1**[2]

5103 **4** hd **Dawoodi**[8] 7660 3-9-1 **59**..............................................(h) DavidNolan 1 — 62
(Linda Perratt) *hld up on outside: effrt and hdwy over 1f out: kpt on ins fnl f: no ex towards fin* **6/1**[2]

5603 **5** 1 **Luv U Always**[8] 7657 3-7-9 **46**..............................(p) JamieGormley(7) 5 — 45
(Iain Jardine) *disp ld to over 1f out: rdn and one pce ins fnl f* **7/1**[3]

3160 **6** ¾ **Star Cracker (IRE)**[8] 7660 5-8-8 **59**........................(p) SeanMooney(7) 8 — 54
(Jim Goldie) *in tch: drvn along over 3f out: rallied over 1f out: kpt on fnl f: no imp* **12/1**

0320 **7** ¾ **Compton River**[12] 7522 5-9-4 **65**........................... AdamMcNamara(3) 7 — 58
(Bryan Smart) *rrd s: in tch: rdn along over 2f out: rallied over 1f out: sn no imp* **8/1**

6666 **8** nk **Reckless Serenade (IRE)**[34] 6785 3-9-8 **66**.............. ConnorBeasley 3 — 58
(Keith Dalgleish) *awkward s: bhd and sn outpcd: rdn and kpt on fnl f: nvr able to chal* **18/1**

0144 **9** ¾ **Pavers Pride**[12] 7522 3-9-7 **65**.............................................. JasonHart 11 — 55
(Noel Wilson) *disp ld against stands' rail to over 1f out: wknd ins fnl f* **6/1**[2]

0206 **10** shd **Lady Molly (IRE)**[8] 7660 3-8-2 **46** oh1..............................(b) AndrewMullen 9 — 35
(Keith Dalgleish) *in tch against stands' rail: drvn over 3f out: wknd over 1f out* **16/1**

5410 **11** ½ **Groundworker (IRE)**[17] 7366 6-9-0 **58**......................(t) PaulMulrennan 4 — 45
(Paul Midgley) *in tch: rdn along 1/2-way: wknd over 1f out* **8/1**

1m 1.84s (1.44) **Going Correction** +0.20s/f (Good) **11** Ran SP% **115.6**
Speed ratings (Par 101): **96,94,94,94,92 91,90,89,88,88 87**
CSF £154.91 CT £967.88 TOTE £34.30: £4.30, £2.30, £2.90; EX 255.30 Trifecta £1303.00.
**Owner** D R & E E Brown **Bred** Mike Hyde **Trained** Kennythorpe, N Yorks

**FOCUS**
A modest sprint handicap full of horses who find it hard to win. The winner raced towards the nearside, but the next three came up the middle so no great bias. The winner and third set a straightforward level.

## 7885 BET AT RACINGUK.COM H'CAP — 1m 4f 104y
**4:10** (4:10) (Class 6) (0-60,60) 3-Y-O+ **£2,264** (£673; £336; £168) **Stalls** Low

Form / RPR

5602 **1** **Royal Cosmic**[13] 7479 3-8-7 **49**........................................ PaulHanagan 1 — 60
(Richard Fahey) *hld up in tch on ins: smooth hdwy to chse wnr 2f out: sn pushed along and edgd rt: led ins fnl f: styd on wl* **8/1**

0042 **2** 1½ **Inspector Norse**[13] 7478 6-8-13 **49**.................................... DavidAllan 3 — 57
(Tim Easterby) *led 2f: chsd ldr: regained ld over 3f out: rdn 2f out: hdd ins fnl f: kpt on same pce* **9/2**[2]

056 **3** 13 **Good Man (IRE)**[18] 7331 4-8-11 **47**..............................(p) JoeDoyle 5 — 35
(Karen McLintock) *hld up in tch: effrt and rdn 3f out: chsd clr ldng pair over 1f out: no imp fnl f* **7/1**

250F **4** ¾ **Sakhalin Star (IRE)**[13] 7478 6-9-9 **59**......................(p) ConnorBeasley 12 — 46
(Richard Guest) *hld up: drvn along over 3f out: kpt on fr 2f out: nvr able to chal* **20/1**

0002 **5** 4½ **Royal Icon**[21] 7220 3-9-1 **57**.................................................. TomEaves 11 — 38
(Kevin Ryan) *hld up midfield: stdy hdwy whn swtchd lft 2f out: sn rdn and no imp* **5/1**[3]

0-26 **6** shd **Dirty Randy (IRE)**[132] 3180 3-8-13 **60**....................(p) RowanScott(5) 2 — 41
(Keith Dalgleish) *chsd ldrs: drvn along over 3f out: wknd over 1f out* **7/2**[1]

053 **7** 2 **Schmooze (IRE)**[8] 7659 8-8-11 **47**........................................ ShaneGray 10 — 24
(Linda Perratt) *bhd: outpcd and rdn over 5f out: rallied over 2f out: kpt on fnl f: nvr able to chal* **11/1**

/030 **8** 2½ **Ferngrove (USA)**[31] 6898 6-8-10 **46**.................................(t) JasonHart 7 — 19
(Susan Corbett) *hld up: hdwy to chse ldrs over 5f out: drvn and ev ch briefly over 3f out: wknd fr 2f out* **50/1**

0360 **9** 3¾ **Fillydelphia (IRE)**[75] 5284 6-8-11 **50**................... RachelRichardson(3) 9 — 18
(Patrick Holmes) *slowly away and wnt lft s: hld up: drvn along over 4f out: no imp fr over 2f out* **40/1**

1440 **10** 8 **Dyna Might**[66] 5617 3-9-3 **59**........................................(p) AndrewMullen 13 — 16
(Ollie Pears) *midfield: drvn and outpcd wl over 3f out: btn fnl 2f* **10/1**

421/ **11** 14 **Titus Bolt (IRE)**[727] 7185 8-9-9 **59**.................................. JamesSullivan 14
(Jim Goldie) *t.k.h: cl up: led after 2f to over 3f out: rdn and wknd fr 2f out* **33/1**

545 **12** 2 **Biba**[41] 6548 3-8-4 **46**..................................................................(p) JoeFanning 6
(Keith Dalgleish) *prom: drvn along over 3f out: wknd over 2f out* **22/1**

0000 **13** 33 **Galilee Chapel (IRE)**[20] 7236 8-9-8 **58**....................(b) PaulMulrennan 4
(Alistair Whillans) *hld up on ins: rdn and outpcd over 3f out: sn wknd: t.o* **50/1**

405- **14** 33 **Togetherwecan (IRE)**[406] 5980 5-8-6 **49**..............(p[1]) JamieGormley(7) 8
(Iain Jardine) *t.k.h: hld up: struggling over 5f out: sn lost tch: t.o* **33/1**

2m 45.78s (3.78) **Going Correction** +0.425s/f (Yiel)
**WFA** 3 from 4yo+ 6lb **14** Ran SP% **119.5**
Speed ratings (Par 101): **104,103,94,93,90 90,89,87,85,79 70,69,47,25**
CSF £40.54 CT £268.89 TOTE £9.30: £3.20, £2.60, £3.10; EX 48.20 Trifecta £379.90.
**Owner** The Cosmic Cases **Bred** The Cosmic Cases **Trained** Musley Bank, N Yorks

**FOCUS**
Add 7yds to race distance. A moderate middle-distance handicap, but they went a decent pace and the first two pulled miles clear of the rest. The pair had both finished second in different divisions of the 1m2f amateur riders' handicap at Beverley 13 days earlier. The winner is rated back to his best but this could underplay the first two's level.

## 7886 ISN'T IT WISER TO BET AT RACINGUK.COM H'CAP — 7f 33y
**4:40** (4:41) (Class 3) (0-95,98) 3-Y-O+ **£7,439** (£2,213; £1,106; £553) **Stalls** Low

Form / RPR

0001 **1** **Sophie P**[8] 7658 4-9-7 **98** 6ex................................ ConnorMurtagh(7) 2 — 108+
(R Mike Smith) *hld up in tch: hdwy whn nt clr run briefly over 1f out: chsd ldr ins fnl f: styd on wl to ld towards fin* **5/1**[2]

311 **2** ½ **Rousayan (IRE)**[37] 6672 6-8-12 **89**...................(h) PatrickVaughan(7) 12 — 97
(David O'Meara) *hld up: hdwy over 2f out: rdn to chse ldr over 1f out: led ins fnl f: kpt on: hdd and no ex towards fin* **14/1**

3506 **3** 2¾ **That Is The Spirit**[9] 7622 6-9-10 **94**.................................... DavidNolan 1 — 95
(David O'Meara) *led at decent gallop: rdn along 2f out: hdd ins fnl f: kpt on same pce* **9/2**[1]

0140 **4** 1¾ **Sakhee's Return**[18] 7321 5-8-9 **79**..................................(t) DavidAllan 11 — 75
(Tim Easterby) *hld up: rdn and hdwy over 2f out: kpt on ins fnl f: nvr able to chal* **9/1**

6413 **5** 1¾ **Storm Cry**[8] 7653 3-8-8 **80**.................................................. JoeFanning 4 — 71
(Mark Johnston) *prom: effrt and wnt 2nd briefly over 1f out: outpcd ins fnl f* **13/2**

5025 **6** 1¼ **Al Khan (IRE)**[30] 6949 8-8-11 **81**......................................(t[1]) JoeDoyle 10 — 70
(Kevin Ryan) *hld up: rdn over 2f out: kpt on ins fnl f: nvr able to chal* **22/1**

0513 **7** 1½ **Penwortham (IRE)**[24] 7108 4-9-5 **89**...........................(h) PaulHanagan 9 — 74
(Richard Fahey) *hld up midfield: drvn along wl over 2f out: no imp over 1f out* **8/1**

1306 **8** ½ **Gurkha Friend**[42] 6520 5-9-9 **93**.............................................. TomEaves 7 — 76
(Karen McLintock) *in tch: drvn along and effrt over 2f out: wknd over 1f out* **11/1**

6620 **9** ¾ **Rock N Rolla (IRE)**[10] 7570 3-8-5 **77**.............................. AndrewMullen 8 — 57
(Keith Dalgleish) *bhd: drvn and struggling over 3f out: sme late hdwy: nvr on terms* **14/1**

0210 **10** 1½ **Explain**[9] 7626 5-9-7 **91**..................................................(b) JamesSullivan 6 — 68
(Ruth Carr) *s.i.s: sn midfield on ins: drvn over 2f out: wknd wl over 1f out* **18/1**

0161 **11** 38 **Dark Profit (IRE)**[31] 6894 5-9-5 **89**.....................(p) ConnorBeasley 3
(Keith Dalgleish) *chsd ldr: drvn over 2f out: wknd over 1f out: sn eased: t.o* **6/1**[3]

1m 30.63s (1.63) **Going Correction** +0.425s/f (Yiel)
**WFA** 3 from 4yo+ 2lb **11** Ran SP% **114.9**
Speed ratings (Par 107): **107,106,103,101,99 97,96,95,94,93 49**
CSF £71.08 CT £341.90 TOTE £9.40: £2.70, £3.50, £1.70; EX 83.20 Trifecta £362.10.
**Owner** Smith, Matheson, Stewart **Bred** New Hall Stud **Trained** Galston, E Ayrshire

**FOCUS**
Add 7yds to race distance. A decent and open handicap, but the leaders may have done a bit too much early. The first two both posted pbs, helped by their riders' claims.

## 7887 EBF MUSSELBURGH FILLIES' SPRINT STKS (LISTED RACE) (REGISTERED AS THE ARRAN STAKES) — 5f 1y
**5:10** (5:11) (Class 1) 3-Y-O+ **£17,244** (£6,543; £3,273; £1,635; £816) **Stalls** High

Form / RPR

3111 **1** **Mabs Cross**[107] 4081 3-9-0 **90**....................................... PaulMulrennan 8 — 105+
(Michael Dods) *dwlt: hld up: rdn and hdwy on outside over 1f out: led ins fnl f: rdn out* **5/1**[2]

46 **2** ¾ **Clem Fandango (FR)**[7] 7697 3-9-0 **100**............................. JoeFanning 3 — 102
(Keith Dalgleish) *trckd ldrs: effrt and rdn over 1f out: led briefly ins fnl f: kpt on: hld cl home* **9/4**[1]

11P0 **3** ½ **Glenrowan Rose (IRE)**[9] 7611 4-9-0 **98**..................... ConnorBeasley 2 — 99
(Keith Dalgleish) *cl up: led over 1f out: rdn and hdd ins fnl f: kpt on same pce towards fin* **11/2**[3]

3100 **4** 1¾ **Midnight Malibu (IRE)**[9] 7625 4-9-0 **84**............................. DavidAllan 9 — 93
(Tim Easterby) *prom: drvn along wl over 1f out: kpt on same pce ins fnl f* **40/1**

-155 **5** 1¾ **Cosmopolitan Girl (IRE)**[73] 5355 4-9-0 **86**................ JamesSullivan 5 — 86
(Robert Cowell) *in tch: checked sn after s: effrt and drvn along 2f out: no imp ins fnl f* **16/1**

1003 **6** shd **The Wagon Wheel (IRE)**[37] 6668 3-9-0 **100**..........(b) PaulHanagan 1 — 87
(Richard Fahey) *hld up: effrt on outside 1/2-way: drvn and no imp fr over 1f out* **6/1**

2000 **7** 3 **Coolfitch (IRE)**[9] 7610 3-9-0 **89**.......................................(v[1]) DavidNolan 7 — 76
(David O'Meara) *hld up: nt clr run over 2f out to over 1f out: sn rdn and no imp: btn fnl f* **25/1**

2141 **8** 3 **Intense Romance (IRE)**[44] 6450 3-9-0 **91**....................... AndrewMullen 6 — 65
(Michael Dods) *hld up in tch: rdn over 2f out: wknd over 1f out* **8/1**

3350 **9** 3½ **Thesme**[16] 7396 5-9-0 **99**........................................................... TomEaves 4 — 52
(Nigel Tinkler) *led and sn crossed to stands' rail: rdn and hdd over 1f out: wknd fnl f* **13/2**

59.7s (-0.70) **Going Correction** +0.20s/f (Good) **9** Ran SP% **113.7**
Speed ratings (Par 108): **113,111,111,108,105 105,100,95,90**
CSF £16.36 TOTE £6.20: £1.70, £1.20, £2.10; EX 22.10 Trifecta £122.60.
**Owner** David W Armstrong **Bred** Highfield Farm Llp **Trained** Denton, Co Durham
■ Stewards' Enquiry : Connor Beasley three day ban: careless riding (23-25 Oct)

**FOCUS**
This race was originally due to be run at the abandoned Ayr Western Meeting last month. A fascinating Listed contest and there was no hanging about. The placed horses pressed the pace from the start and hung in there, which makes the winner's performance all the more commendable. She continues to progress, while the fourth would seem to limit the form.

## 7888 GET DAILY TIPS AT RACINGUK.COM H'CAP (DIV I) — 7f 33y
**5:40** (5:41) (Class 6) (0-60,62) 3-Y-O+ **£2,264** (£673; £336; £168) **Stalls** Low

Form / RPR

0000 **1** **Let Right Be Done**[6] 7704 5-8-7 **45**...........................(b) AndrewMullen 12 — 51
(Linda Perratt) *t.k.h: pressed ldr: led over 4f out: clr over 2f out: hrd pressed ins fnl f: hld on gamely* **18/1**

1220 **2** shd **Melaniemillie**[16] 7390 3-9-1 **55**........................................ JamesSullivan 8 — 60
(Ruth Carr) *hld up in tch: hdwy to chse (clr) wnr 2f out: rdn to dispute ld ins fnl f: kpt on: jst hld* **8/1**

6562 **3** 1½ **Quiet Moment (IRE)**[23] 7165 3-8-10 **50**..........................(h) JoeFanning 3 — 51
(Keith Dalgleish) *s.i.s: hld up: hdwy over 2f out: rdn and kpt on ins fnl f: nt rch first two* **5/1**[1]

3003 **4** ½ **Bonnie Gals**[34] 6784 3-8-12 **57**....................................... RowanScott(5) 10 — 56
(Keith Dalgleish) *s.i.s: hld up: hdwy on outside over 2f out: rdn and kpt on fnl f: nrst fin* **8/1**

405 **5** *2 ¾* **Swiftee (IRE)**[53] 6112 4-8-12 **50**.................(v) DavidAllan 9 43
(Ivan Furtado) *hld up: effrt whn hung rt over 2f out: rdn and no imp fr over 1f out* **8/1**

3006 **6** *½* **Hitman**[13] 7474 4-9-10 **62**.................(b) DuranFentiman 4 54
(Rebecca Bastiman) *s.i.s: hld up: hdwy on ins whn nt clr run over 2f out to over 1f out: rdn and no imp fnl f* **5/1**[1]

0040 **7** *½* **Pipe Dreamer**[56] 5992 3-8-5 **45**.................(v[1]) ShaneGray 6 34
(Kevin Ryan) *s.i.s: hld up: drvn and effrt over 2f out: no imp fr over 1f out* **10/1**

4364 **8** *1* **Melrose Girl**[12] 7525 3-9-0 **57**................. AdamMcNamara(3) 7 44
(Bryan Smart) *s.i.s: hld up: rdn along 3f out: no imp fr 2f out* **6/1**[3]

0036 **9** *3 ¾* **Reflation**[21] 7218 5-8-4 **45**................. RachelRichardson(3) 2 22
(Patrick Holmes) *trckd ldrs: rdn over 2f out: wknd wl over 1f out* **33/1**

R06 **10** *2 ¼* **Tellovoi (IRE)**[16] 7390 9-9-6 **58**.................(v) ConnorBeasley 5 29
(Richard Guest) *t.k.h: led at decent gallop: hdd over 4f out: rdn and wknd fr 2f out* **11/2**[2]

6604 **11** *hd* **Goninodaethat**[8] 7660 9-8-10 **55**................. SeanMooney(7) 1 26
(Jim Goldie) *t.k.h: trckd ldrs: rdn over 3f out: wknd over 2f out* **20/1**

1m 32.38s (3.38) **Going Correction** +0.425s/f (Yiel)
**WFA** 3 from 4yo+ 2lb **11 Ran SP% 118.4**
Speed ratings (Par 101): **97,96,95,94,91 90,90,89,84,82 82**
CSF £156.10 CT £857.45 TOTE £17.70: £4.20, £2.00, £2.70; EX 160.70 Trifecta £748.60.
**Owner** Ken McGarrity & Linda Perratt Racing Club **Bred** LAM Partnership **Trained** East Kilbride, S Lanarks
■ Stewards' Enquiry : Andrew Mullen two day ban: using his whip above the permitted level (23/24 Oct)

**FOCUS**
Add 7yds to race distance.The first division of a moderate handicap in which there was a mad dash to the first bend and two soon went well clear, but whilst one of them dropped out the other one kept on to win. The finish was fought out between two greys. Not much to be positive about.

## 7889 GET DAILY TIPS AT RACINGUK.COM H'CAP (DIV II) 7f 33y
**6:10** (6:11) (Class 6) (0-60,62) 3-Y-O+ **£2,264** (£673; £336; £168) **Stalls** Low

Form RPR

2125 **1** **My Girl Maisie (IRE)**[11] 7540 3-9-9 **61**................. ConnorBeasley 6 69
(Richard Guest) *in tch: effrt over 2f out: chsd ldr over 1f out: led ins fnl f: hld on wl cl home* **5/2**[1]

2255 **2** *hd* **Danot (IRE)**[16] 7390 5-9-3 **56**.................(p) AdamMcNamara(3) 2 64
(Jedd O'Keeffe) *led at ordinary gallop: rdn 2f out: hdd ins fnl f: rallied: hld cl home* **10/3**[2]

0660 **3** *4* **Peny Arcade**[31] 6903 3-8-10 **48**................. JoeDoyle 11 45
(Alistair Whillans) *hld up: effrt on outside over 2f out: chsd clr ldng pair ins fnl f: kpt on: nt pce to chal* **25/1**

3200 **4** *nk* **Jack Blane**[10] 7573 3-9-5 **57**.................(v[1]) JoeFanning 8 53
(Keith Dalgleish) *prom: stdy hdwy gng wl over 2f out: rdn over 1f out: one pce ins fnl f* **13/2**[3]

3404 **5** *nk* **Harbour Patrol (IRE)**[23] 7165 5-9-1 **51**.................(b) DuranFentiman 3 47
(Rebecca Bastiman) *hld up: hdwy and prom 2f out: drvn and no ex ins fnl f* **10/1**

0420 **6** *2* **Tanawar (IRE)**[10] 7573 7-9-12 **62**.................(b) JamesSullivan 1 53
(Ruth Carr) *t.k.h: led 1f: chsd ldrs: effrt and rdn over 2f out: wknd fnl f* **14/1**

5366 **7** *shd* **Coral Princess (IRE)**[58] 5922 3-8-8 **46**................. AndrewMullen 7 35
(Keith Dalgleish) *hld up: rdn and edgd rt fr over 2f out: no imp over 1f out* **11/1**

6220 **8** *5* **Boogie Babe**[27] 7036 3-9-3 **55**................. PaulHanagan 5 31
(Richard Fahey) *s.i.s: hld up: drvn and outpcd over 2f out: n.d after* **15/2**

6365 **9** *3 ¾* **Circuitous**[41] 6550 9-9-5 **55**.................(v) TomEaves 9 22
(Keith Dalgleish) *cl up: drvn over 2f out: wknd over 1f out: eased* **16/1**

0603 **10** *¾* **Irvine Lady (IRE)**[34] 6782 4-8-9 **45**................. DavidAllan 4 10
(R Mike Smith) *hld up in tch: drvn and outpcd over 2f out: sn wknd* **33/1**

46 **11** *½* **Thorntoun Lady (USA)**[31] 6896 7-8-10 **53**................. SeanMooney(7) 10 16
(Jim Goldie) *s.i.s: hld up: drvn and struggling over 2f out: sn btn* **20/1**

1m 32.03s (3.03) **Going Correction** +0.425s/f (Yiel)
**WFA** 3 from 4yo+ 2lb **11 Ran SP% 118.3**
Speed ratings (Par 101): **99,98,94,93,93 91,91,85,81,80 79**
CSF £10.30 CT £171.91 TOTE £4.10: £1.40, £1.40, £7.00; EX 12.30 Trifecta £187.50.
**Owner** Alfa Site Services Ltd/Mrs Alison Guest **Bred** Patrick M Ryan **Trained** Ingmanthorpe, W Yorks

**FOCUS**
Add 7yds to race distance. A few of these pulled their chance away early, but it produced another cracking finish. The winning time was 0.35 sec quicker than the first division and the winner has a generally progressive profile.
T/Plt: £102.80 to a £1 stake. Pool: £44,942.41 - 319.0 winning units T/Qpdt: £19.90 to a £1 stake. Pool: £4,505.64 - 167.30 winning units **Richard Young**

# 7551 PONTEFRACT (L-H)
Monday, October 9

**OFFICIAL GOING: Soft (good to soft in places; 7.2)**
Wind: Moderate half behind Weather: Cloudy

## 7890 RACINGUK.COM/BRITISH STALLION STUDS EBF NOVICE STKS (PLUS 10 RACE) 1m 2f 5y
**1:55** (1:56) (Class 4) 2-Y-O **£5,175** (£1,540; £769; £384) **Stalls** Low

Form RPR

153 **1** **Austrian School (IRE)**[11] 7556 2-9-5 79................. FrannyNorton 8 77
(Mark Johnston) *mde all: jnd and rdn wl over 1f out: drvn ins fnl f: kpt on gamely towards fin* **10/3**[2]

06 **2** *¾* **Making Miracles**[8] 7654 2-9-2 0................. PhillipMakin 9 72+
(Mark Johnston) *dwlt and towards rr: hdwy 3f out: chsd ldrs wl over 1f out: sn rdn and edgd lft: styd on wl fnl f* **33/1**

5030 **3** *½* **Dontgiveuponbob**[16] 7384 2-9-2 70................. JackGarritty 1 71
(Richard Fahey) *trckd ldng pair on inner: hdwy over 2f out: chal wl over 1f out: sn rdn and ev ch: drvn ins fnl f: kpt on same pce towards fin* **5/1**[3]

36 **4** *2 ¾* **Eyecatcher (IRE)**[31] 6883 2-9-2 0................. GrahamLee 3 66
(Simon Crisford) *trckd ldrs: hdwy 3f out: rdn along wl over 1f out: drvn and no imp fnl f* **6/4**[1]

0600 **5** *3* **Duggary**[14] 7451 2-9-2 58.................(b[1]) TonyHamilton 2 61
(Kevin Frost) *trckd ldrs: hdwy 3f out: pushed along 2f out: sn rdn and no imp* **50/1**

20 **6** *¾* **Kannapolis (IRE)**[45] 6403 2-8-9 0................. HarrisonShaw(7) 4 60
(Michael Easterby) *hld up in rr: hdwy on inner 3f out: rdn along wl over 1f out: kpt on fnl f* **8/1**

6014 **7** *¾* **Hemingford (IRE)**[20] 7251 2-9-8 70................. RobertTart 7 64
(Charlie Fellowes) *in tch: pushed along 1/2-way: rdn along to chse ldrs 3f out: drvn 2f out: sn one pce* **8/1**

**8** *29* **East Wind** 2-8-11 0................. BarryMcHugh 5
(Tony Coyle) *a towards rr* **50/1**

6425 **9** *13* **Bombshell Bay**[35] 6762 2-9-2 64.................(p[1]) SeanLevey 10
(Richard Hannon) *trckd wnr: cl up on outer 1/2-way: rdn along over 3f out: sn wknd* **20/1**

00 **10** *16* **Charming Power (IRE)**[69] 5492 2-9-2 0................. DanielTudhope 11
(Ann Duffield) *chsd ldrs on outer: rdn along over 4f out: sn wknd* **100/1**

2m 20.69s (6.99) **Going Correction** +0.675s/f (Yiel) **10 Ran SP% 114.6**
Speed ratings (Par 97): **99,98,98,95,93 92,92,69,58,45**
CSF £110.23 TOTE £3.40: £1.30, £6.90, £1.70; EX 82.20 Trifecta £756.80.
**Owner** Dr J Walker **Bred** G O'Brien **Trained** Middleham Moor, N Yorks

**FOCUS**
Rail dolled out up to 3yds between the 2f and 4f markers, adding approximately 5yds to all races. A demanding test for these juveniles and it paid to be handy. Straightforward form.

## 7891 DEM WINDOW SOLUTIONS EBF NURSERY H'CAP 6f
**2:25** (2:26) (Class 4) (0-85,84) 2-Y-O **£6,469** (£1,925; £962; £481) **Stalls** Low

Form RPR

433 **1** **Big Les (IRE)**[87] 4862 2-8-10 **73**................. GrahamLee 4 77+
(Karen McLintock) *trckd ldr: cl up 2f out: rdn to ld over 1f out: drvn ins fnl f and kpt on wl towards fin* **6/1**

1135 **2** *1* **Camacho Chief (IRE)**[29] 6977 2-9-4 **84**.................(p[1]) CallumRodriguez(3) 3 85
(Michael Dods) *trckd ldng pair on inner: hdwy 2f out: rdn and nt clr run over 1f out: sn swtchd rt: swtchd lft and drvn to chal ins fnl f: kpt on same pce towards fin* **6/4**[1]

412 **3** *2 ¾* **Rastacap**[9] 7623 2-9-3 **80**................. FrannyNorton 2 73
(Mark Johnston) *led: rdn along 2f out: drvn over 1f out: hdd over 1f out: kpt on same pce* **11/4**[2]

1003 **4** *1 ½* **Danehill Desert (IRE)**[19] 7264 2-8-4 **70**................. SammyJoBell(3) 6 58
(Richard Fahey) *trckd ldrs: niggled along bef 1/2-way: rdn 2f out: kpt on u.p fnl f* **9/1**

540 **5** *1* **Finnion Fox**[23] 7141 2-8-3 **66**................. CamHardie 5 51
(Tim Easterby) *a in rr* **33/1**

031 **6** *1* **Feebs**[10] 7562 2-8-5 **75**................. HarrisonShaw(7) 1 57
(Michael Easterby) *dwlt: t.k.h and chsd ldrs on inner: rdn along and sltly outpcd over 2f out: swtchd rt to outer and drvn wl over 1f out: no imp* **5/1**[3]

1m 20.86s (3.96) **Going Correction** +0.675s/f (Yiel) **6 Ran SP% 110.6**
Speed ratings (Par 97): **100,98,95,93,91 90**
CSF £15.05 TOTE £4.60: £1.40, £1.30; EX 14.30 Trifecta £47.30.
**Owner** Roger Stockdale **Bred** Corrin Stud **Trained** Ingoe, Northumberland

**FOCUS**
Add 5yds to race distance. Not a bad nursery, rated around the runner-up. The winner was fairly treated on his latest York form.

## 7892 LESLIE BURTON (FISHER) H'CAP 1m 6y
**2:55** (2:57) (Class 3) (0-95,97) 3-Y-O **£11,205** (£3,355; £1,677; £838; £419; £210) **Stalls** Low

Form RPR

3201 **1** **The Grape Escape (IRE)**[24] 7129 3-10-3 **97**................. SeanLevey 2 110
(Richard Hannon) *trckd ldr: hdwy and cl up over 2f out: led wl over 1f out: rdn ent fnl f: kpt on strly* **9/4**[1]

1423 **2** *2 ¼* **Me Too Nagasaki (IRE)**[12] 7505 3-9-6 **86**................. FrannyNorton 1 94
(Jeremy Noseda) *trckd ldrs on inner: hdwy 3f out: chsd wnr over 1f out: sn rdn: drvn ins fnl f: kpt on same pce* **9/4**[1]

-041 **3** *¾* **Mushaireb**[18] 7327 3-9-5 **85**................. JackGarritty 8 82+
(Richard Fahey) *t.k.h early: hld up in rr: hdwy on outer wl over 1f out: sn rdn and kpt on wl fnl f* **8/1**[3]

5011 **4** *¾* **Heatongrad (IRE)**[8] 7650 3-9-1 **81** 6ex................. TonyHamilton 4 77
(Richard Fahey) *led: rdn along over 2f out: hdd wl over 1f out: sn drvn and grad wknd* **5/1**[2]

0213 **5** *¾* **Our Charlie Brown**[8] 7656 3-8-8 **77**................. SammyJoBell(3) 7 71
(Tim Easterby) *chsd ldrs on outer: rdn along over 2f out: sn drvn and one pce* **12/1**

6060 **6** *½* **Shamrokh (IRE)**[58] 5924 3-8-5 **74**.................(t) LewisEdmunds(3) 5 67
(Michael Appleby) *a towards rr* **16/1**

2310 **7** *5* **Made Of Honour (IRE)**[34] 6787 3-8-11 **77**................. BenCurtis 6 58
(K R Burke) *a towards rr* **50/1**

2205 **8** *3 ¾* **Areen Heart (FR)**[8] 7656 3-9-7 **87**.................(h) PhillipMakin 3 84
(David O'Meara) *trckd ldng pair on outer: effrt over 2f out: rdn along wl over 1f out: sn drvn and no imp* **10/1**

1m 49.38s (3.48) **Going Correction** +0.675s/f (Yiel) **8 Ran SP% 113.9**
Speed ratings (Par 105): **109,106,102,101,100 100,95,103**
CSF £6.93 CT £32.18 TOTE £3.20: £1.30, £1.30, £2.20; EX 8.50 Trifecta £41.00.
**Owner** John Manley **Bred** John Manley **Trained** East Everleigh, Wilts
■ Stewards' Enquiry : Phillip Makin two day ban: failure to draw the weight (23/24 Oct)

**FOCUS**
Add 5yds to race distance. A good-quality 3yo handicap, run at a fair enough pace. Solid form, with a smart effort from the winner.

## 7893 RACING UK HD BLUFF COVE H'CAP (ROUND 7 OF THE PONTEFRACT STAYERS 2017) 2m 2f 2y
**3:25** (3:30) (Class 5) (0-75,75) 3-Y-O+ **£3,881** (£1,155; £577; £288) **Stalls** Low

Form RPR

0045 **1** **Madam Lilibet (IRE)**[18] 7330 8-8-6 **56** oh2................. PhilDennis(3) 5 63
(Sharon Watt) *reluctant in preliminaries: midfield: hdwy 5f out: chsd ldng pair and n.m.r over 2f out: rdn to chal over 1f out: led ins fnl f: sn drvn and flashed tail: hld on wl towards fin* **12/1**

0504 **2** *hd* **Tuscan Gold**[18] 7330 10-8-13 **60**.................(p) FrannyNorton 2 66
(Micky Hammond) *hld up in rr: stdy hdwy over 5f out: chsd ldrs 3f out: rdn wl over 1f out: styd on strly fnl f: jst hld* **7/1**

4631 **3** *1 ¾* **La Fritillaire**[18] 7330 5-9-6 **67**.................(p) GrahamLee 9 71
(James Given) *chsd clr ldr: hdwy over 4f out: led 2f out: rdn over 1f out: drvn and hdd ins fnl f: kpt on same pce* **9/2**[2]

004/ **4** *7* **Raktiman (IRE)**[191] 8149 10-9-4 **65**.................(t) SeanLevey 6 63
(Sam England) *trckd ldrs: hdwy 4f out: rdn 2f out: chsd ldng pair over 1f out: sn drvn and kpt on same pce* **20/1**

0060 **5** *¾* **Rock On Bollinski**[106] 4120 7-9-5 **66**.................(p) BenCurtis 8 63
(Brian Ellison) *hld up towards rr: hdwy over 3f out: sn rdn and plugged on fnl 2f: nvr nr ldrs* **33/1**

0032 **6** *9* **Riptide**[46] 6343 11-8-13 **60**................. PhillipMakin 10 49
(Michael Scudamore) *towards rr: styd on fnl 3f: nvr a factor* **11/1**

3-65 **7** *5* **Lady Of Yue**[133] 3148 7-9-1 **62**........................................(p) RobertTart 7 47
(Eugene Stanford) *prom: rdn along 4f out: wknd 3f out* **16/1**

4232 **8** *4 ½* **Transpennine Star**[18] 7330 4-9-11 **75**..................(p) CallumRodriguez(3) 4 56
(Michael Dods) *led and sn clr: pushed along over 3f out: sn jnd: rdn and hdd 2f out: sn drvn and wknd* **9/4**[1]

0/04 **9** *67* **Dan Emmett (USA)**[139] 2928 7-9-3 **64**.................. DanielTudhope 3
(Michael Scudamore) *midfield: pushed along and lost pl over 7f out: sn bhd* **5/1**[3]

233/ **10** *19* **Gran Maestro (USA)**[66] 6049 8-9-1 **67**...................... BenRobinson(5) 1
(Peter Winks) *chsd ldng pair: rdn along over 6f out: wknd over 3f out* **11/1**

4m 11.98s (15.78) **Going Correction** +0.675s/f (Yiel) **10** Ran SP% **116.1**
Speed ratings (Par 103): **91,90,90,87,86 82,80,78,48,40**
CSF £92.94 CT £440.41 TOTE £14.20: £3.20, £2.20, £1.80; EX 110.10 Trifecta £1468.50.
**Owner** D H & E Montgomerie **Bred** Mrs Clodagh McStay **Trained** Brompton-on-Swale, N Yorks

**FOCUS**
Add 5yds to race distance. This modest marathon handicap served up a real test due to a decent gallop.The winner is only rated to this year's form.

## 7894 NAPOLEONS CASINO BRADFORD H'CAP 1m 6y
**3:55** (3:58) (Class 5) (0-75,76) 3-Y-0+ **£3,881** (£1,155; £577; £288) **Stalls** Low

Form RPR

2011 **1** **Pioneering (IRE)**[13] 7476 3-9-4 **75**.................................... DanielTudhope 2 89+
(David O'Meara) *trckd ldrs on inner: hdwy and swtchd rt to outer 2f out: led wl over 1f out: rdn and kpt on strly fnl f* **4/1**[1]

364 **2** *1 ½* **Trinity Star (IRE)**[18] 7327 6-8-6 **63**................(b) CallumRodriguez(3) 4 71
(Michael Dods) *hld up in rr: hdwy on outer 2f out: rdn over 1f out: chsd wnr ins fnl f: sn drvn and no imp* **7/1**

3500 **3** *6* **Dutch Artist (IRE)**[23] 7142 5-8-12 **66**.................(b) PhillipMakin 3 60
(Alan Brown) *towards rr: effrt and nt clr run 2f out: sn swtchd rt and rdn: styd on wl fnl f* **16/1**

3204 **4** *3 ¼* **The Eagle's Nest (IRE)**[83] 5009 3-8-13 **70**.................. TonyHamilton 17 57+
(Richard Fahey) *towards rr: sme hdwy whn nt clr run and hmpd 2f out: rdn over 1f out: styd on strly fnl f* **20/1**

6533 **5** *¾* **Keepup Kevin**[57] 5961 3-8-11 **71**........................... CallumShepherd(3) 10 56
(Pam Sly) *prom: hdwy to ld 2f out: sn rdn and hdd over 1f out: drvn and wknd fnl f* **13/2**[3]

1514 **6** *2 ¼* **Beverley Bullet**[10] 7567 4-8-13 **67**..........................(p) GrahamLee 12 47
(Lawrence Mullaney) *chsd ldrs: rdn along wl over 1f out: sn drvn and kpt on same pce* **12/1**

2416 **7** *½* **Kiwi Bay**[63] 5698 12-9-0 **68**......................................... BarryMcHugh 13 47
(Michael Dods) *towards rr: gd hdwy 2f out: rdn over 1f out: kpt on same pce fnl f* **33/1**

000 **8** *nk* **Something Brewing (FR)**[6] 7699 3-8-7 **67**.............. SammyJoBell(3) 6 45
(Iain Jardine) *towards rr: styd on fnl 2f: nvr nrr* **50/1**

2045 **9** *¾* **Totally Magic (IRE)**[20] 7241 5-8-7 **64**................. LewisEdmunds(3) 14 40
(Richard Whitaker) *chsd ldrs: rdn along 2f out: sn drvn and grad wknd* **16/1**

0202 **10** *5* **Mama Africa (IRE)**[14] 7464 3-8-6 **70**......................(p) HarrisonShaw(7) 5 35
(David Barron) *led: rdn along 3f out: hdd 2f out and sn wknd* **12/1**

5604 **11** *5* **Detachment**[26] 7052 4-9-1 **69**......................................... DaneO'Neill 9 22
(Les Eyre) *chsd ldrs: rdn along over 2f out: sn wknd* **11/2**[2]

1303 **12** *8* **Roman De Brut (IRE)**[76] 5265 5-9-5 **76**........................... CliffordLee(3) 8 11
(Denis Quinn) *cl up: pushed along 3f out: rdn 2f out: sn drvn and wknd* **25/1**

0400 **13** *9* **Ravenhoe (IRE)**[13] 7476 4-8-7 **61**......................................... FrannyNorton 7
(Mark Johnston) *a in rr* **20/1**

2154 **14** *1 ¼* **Working Class**[18] 7339 3-9-5 **76**......................................... SeanLevey 16
(Peter Chapple-Hyam) *chsd ldrs on outer: rdn along over 2f out: sn drvn and wknd over 1f out* **20/1**

2003 **15** *1 ½* **Dandyleekie (IRE)**[12] 7523 5-9-0 **71**.............................(b) JoshDoyle(3) 1
(David O'Meara) *hld up towards rr: effrt and sme hdwy on inner 3f out: rdn over 2f out: sn wknd* **16/1**

4424 **16** *½* **Mr Cool Cash**[13] 7476 5-8-12 **66**......................................... BenCurtis 11
(Richard Guest) *midfield: rdn along over 2f out: sn wknd* **11/1**

1m 49.2s (3.30) **Going Correction** +0.675s/f (Yiel)
**WFA** 3 from 4yo+ 3lb **16** Ran SP% **125.6**
Speed ratings (Par 103): **110,108,102,99,98 96,95,95,94,89 84,76,67,66,64 64**
CSF £28.67 CT £329.75 TOTE £4.90: £1.60, £2.10, £4.40, £4.30; EX 45.80 Trifecta £788.10.
**Owner** Ebor Racing Club Vi **Bred** Miss Joan Murphy **Trained** Upper Helmsley, N Yorks

**FOCUS**
Add 5yds to race distance. They went a fair pace in this competitive handicap. The progressive winner was much the best to race prominently.

## 7895 RACING UK CLUB DAY 23RD OCTOBER H'CAP 1m 4f 5y
**4:25** (4:25) (Class 5) (0-70,70) 3-Y-0 **£3,881** (£1,155; £577; £288) **Stalls** Low

Form RPR

2305 **1** **Cornerstone Lad**[27] 7019 3-8-13 **62**.................................... PhillipMakin 8 70
(Micky Hammond) *trckd ldrs: hdwy 3f out: cl up wl over 1f out: sn rdn: led ent fnl f: drvn out* **10/1**

2543 **2** *2* **Duke's Girl**[27] 7019 3-9-3 **66**............................................... LouisSteward 5 71
(Michael Bell) *led: rdn along over 2f out: drvn and hdd ent fnl f: kpt on u.p* **11/2**[2]

5061 **3** *2 ¼* **Costa Percy**[31] 6892 3-9-1 **64**............................................... GrahamLee 11 66
(Jennie Candlish) *in tch: hdwy 3f out: rdn along on inner 2f out: drvn over 1f out: kpt on fnl f* **7/1**[3]

0122 **4** *¾* **Mirimar (IRE)**[11] 7558 3-9-7 **70**............................................... DaneO'Neill 7 70
(Ed Vaughan) *prom: effrt and cl up over 2f out: sn rdn along: drvn over 1f out and sn one pce* **11/8**[1]

4000 **5** *1 ½* **See The City (IRE)**[26] 7063 3-9-4 **67**...................................(b) RyanTate 3 65
(James Eustace) *trckd ldr: cl up 3f out: rdn along over 2f out: sn drvn and grad wknd* **12/1**

3103 **6** *2* **Snookered (IRE)**[25] 7097 3-9-5 **68**......................................... TonyHamilton 6 63
(Richard Fahey) *t.k.h: hld up in tch: hdwy 3f out: rdn along 2f out: sn no imp* **7/1**[3]

4036 **7** *1 ¾* **Little Jo**[26] 7047 3-8-4 **56** oh4.................................... SammyJoBell(3) 9 48
(Chris Grant) *a towards rr* **50/1**

3404 **8** *4* **Tristram**[103] 4197 3-9-7 **70**............................................... BenCurtis 10 56
(John Mackie) *a towards rr* **33/1**

0360 **9** *8* **Tread Lightly**[42] 6518 3-9-0 **63**............................................... JackGarritty 2
(Tim Easterby) *trckd ldng pair on inner: pushed along 3f out: rdn over 2f out: sn wknd* **16/1**

-600 **10** *35* **Miss Danby (IRE)**[42] 6518 3-8-9 **58**.............................(b[1]) FrannyNorton 4
(Mark Johnston) *a towards rr* **25/1**

2m 49.82s (9.02) **Going Correction** +0.675s/f (Yiel) **10** Ran SP% **113.9**
Speed ratings (Par 101): **96,94,93,92,91 90,89,86,57,57**
CSF £61.59 CT £412.59 TOTE £10.10: £3.10, £2.50, £3.20; EX 75.40 Trifecta £522.70.
**Owner** Mrs B M Lofthouse **Bred** Cranford Bloodstock & Overbury Stallions **Trained** Middleham, N Yorks

**FOCUS**
Add 5yds to race distance. This modest 3yo handicap was another race where it paid to race prominently. The winner reversed Catterick form with the runner-up.

## 7896 BUY YOUR 2018 ANNUAL BADGE TODAY MAIDEN STKS 1m 6y
**5:00** (5:01) (Class 5) 3-Y-0+ **£3,881** (£1,155; £577; £288) **Stalls** Low

Form RPR

0052 **1** **Frankster (FR)**[18] 7331 4-9-8 **60**..................................(tp) FrannyNorton 3 72
(Micky Hammond) *hld up in rr: hdwy over 2f out: rdn over 1f out: chsd ldr ins fnl f: led last 100yds: drvn out* **8/1**

340 **2** *nk* **Graphite (IRE)**[65] 5632 3-9-5 **72**......................................... TonyHamilton 2 71
(David Simcock) *trckd ldrs: hdwy on inner to chal wl over 1f out: rdn to ld appr fnl f: drvn and hdd last 100yds: kpt on* **7/2**[3]

22 **3** *8* **Bombay (IRE)**[34] 6782 3-9-5 0.......................................... DanielTudhope 6 53
(David O'Meara) *sn led: rdn along over 2f out: hdd briefly 2f out: sn led again: drvn and hdd appr fnl f: sn one pce* **10/3**[2]

4533 **4** *2 ¼* **Munthany (USA)**[32] 6851 3-9-5 **73**.......................................... DaneO'Neill 4 47
(Charles Hills) *trckd ldrs: effrt 3f out: rdn along over 2f out: sn drvn and outpcd fr wl over 1f out* **7/2**[3]

**5** *2 ½* **Bittersweet (IRE)** 3-9-0 0............................................... CamHardie 5 37
(Jason Ward) *hld up in tch: hdwy 3f out: rdn along over 2f out: sn wknd* **40/1**

0630 **6** *26* **Soldier Blue (FR)**[26] 7052 3-9-0 **68**.............................. BenRobinson(5) 1
(Brian Ellison) *trckd ldr: cl up 3f out: rdn to ld briefly 2f out: sn hdd & wknd* **2/1**[1]

45 **7** *6* **Guiding Passion (FR)**[16] 7388 3-8-11 0...................(p[1]) CliffordLee(3) 7
(K R Burke) *chsd ldrs on outer: rdn along 3f out: sn outpcd* **25/1**

1m 51.46s (5.56) **Going Correction** +0.675s/f (Yiel)
**WFA** 3 from 4yo 3lb **7** Ran SP% **118.3**
Speed ratings (Par 103): **99,98,90,88,85 59,53**
CSF £37.73 TOTE £6.70: £3.80, £2.10; EX 37.90 Trifecta £159.00.
**Owner** The Cobb Family **Bred** Thierry De La Heronniere & Jedburgh Stud **Trained** Middleham, N Yorks

**FOCUS**
Add 5yds to race distance. An ordinary maiden and another slow-motion finish. Two came clear and the winner is rated to last year's mark when fourth in this race.
T/Plt: £159.70 to a £1 stake. Pool: £60,103.47 - 274.68 winning units T/Qpdt: £32.40 to a £1 stake. Pool: £5,408.89 - 123.40 winning units **Joe Rowntree**

# 7739 SALISBURY (R-H)
## Monday, October 9

**OFFICIAL GOING: Soft (good to soft in places; 6.2)**
Wind: virtually nil Weather: overcast

## 7897 BATHWICK CAR & VAN HIRE NOVICE AUCTION STKS 6f 213y
**2:05** (2:05) (Class 5) 2-Y-0 **£4,043** (£1,203; £601; £300) **Stalls** Low

Form RPR

**1** **N Over J** 2-9-1 0................................................ AdamBeschizza 4 75
(William Knight) *hld up but in tch: hdwy over 2f out: rdn over 1f out: led fnl 100yds: r.o wl* **12/1**

**2** *1* **Bodes Well (IRE)** 2-9-1 0.......................................... EdwardGreatrex 5 73
(Warren Greatrex) *hld up but in tch: hdwy fr 3f out: led over 1f out: sn rdn: hdd fnl 100yds: kpt on but no ex* **12/1**

003 **3** *nk* **Lamb Chop**[20] 7226 2-8-9 **74**......................................(p) OisinMurphy 1 66
(Rod Millman) *led: hdd after 1f and sn short of room: rdn over 2f out whn sltly outpcd: swtchd lft over 1 out: kpt on ins fnl f:* **1/1**[1]

0 **4** *4* **Demons And Wizards (IRE)**[13] 7488 2-8-11 0.......... MitchGodwin(5) 6 63
(Sylvester Kirk) *racd keenly: trckd ldrs: rdn over 2f out: sn one pce* **25/1**

060 **5** *4* **Hurricane Lil (IRE)**[20] 7226 2-8-11 **64**.............................. LiamKeniry 7 47
(George Baker) *hld up but in tch: rdn over 2f out: nvr any imp* **9/1**[3]

02 **6** *1 ¾* **Beyond Equal**[25] 7079 2-9-1 0.......................................... MartinDwyer 8 47+
(Stuart Kittow) *stmbld leaving stalls and nrly uns jockey: t.k.h: led after 1f: rdn and hdd over 1f out: wknd ins fnl f* **2/1**[2]

0 **7** *2 ½* **Ragstone Sand (IRE)**[33] 6816 2-9-0 0.......................................... ShaneKelly 2 39
(Murty McGrath) *trckd ldrs: rdn over 2f out: wknd over 1f out* **80/1**

1m 32.82s (4.22) **Going Correction** +0.55s/f (Yiel) **7** Ran SP% **113.8**
Speed ratings (Par 95): **97,95,95,90,86 84,81**
CSF £136.07 TOTE £12.10: £4.40, £2.50; EX 66.70 Trifecta £641.70.
**Owner** A Hetherton **Bred** New Hall Stud **Trained** Patching, W Sussex

**FOCUS**
A weak novice and the two newcomers came to the fore. A late=season feel to the form, which is taken at face value.

## 7898 BYERLEY STUD EBF FILLIES' NOVICE STKS (PLUS 10 RACE) 6f 213y
**2:35** (2:36) (Class 5) 2-Y-0 **£4,043** (£1,203; £601; £300) **Stalls** Low

Form RPR

**1** **Caiya** 2-8-12 0.......................................................... CharlesBishop 7 72
(Eve Johnson Houghton) *mid-div: hdwy over 2f out: shkn up ent fnl f: kpt on wl to ld cl home: pushed out (b.b.v)* **12/1**

0 **2** *nk* **Teenage Gal (IRE)**[14] 7454 2-8-12 0.......................................... FranBerry 10 71
(Ed Dunlop) *racd keenly: trckd ldrs: rdn to chal over 1f out: led ins fnl f: edgd sltly rt: kpt on but no ex whn hdd cl home* **33/1**

**3** *1 ¾* **Dream Of Camelot (IRE)** 2-8-12 0.......................................... ShaneKelly 3 69+
(Gary Moore) *s.i.s: in last pair: hdwy over 2f out: wnt 4th entl fnl f: running on w ev ch whn short of room and snatched up fnl 100yds: hld after: unlucky* **20/1**

6 **4** *½* **High Seas (IRE)**[20] 7238 2-8-12 0.......................................... JosephineGordon 6 67+
(Hugo Palmer) *rrd leaving stalls: mid-div: outpcd over 2f out: hdwy ent fnl f: fin strly: wnt 4th cl home* **5/2**[1]

05 **5** *½* **Gift Of Hera**[16] 7399 2-8-12 0.......................................... MartinDwyer 4 66
(Sylvester Kirk) *led: rdn over 1f out whn strly chal: hdd ins fnl f: keeping on at same pce disputing cl 3rd whn edgd lft and squeezed up fnl 100yds: lost 4th nring fin* **7/2**[2]

**6** *1 ½* **Red Starlight** 2-8-12 0.......................................... TomMarquand 2 60+
(Richard Hannon) *chsd ldrs: sn pushed along: rdn over 2f out: kpt on same pce fnl f* **5/2**[1]

4 **7** *hd* **River Cafe (IRE)**[23] 7153 2-8-12 0.......................................... OisinMurphy 8 60
(Sylvester Kirk) *trckd ldr: rdn over 2f out: wknd ent fnl f* **7/1**[3]

60 **8** *3 ¼* **Be Mindful (IRE)**[96] 4496 2-8-8 0 ow3.................... SophieScardifield(7) 5 56
(Charles Hills) *racd keen early: trckd ldrs: pushed along whn nt clr run over 2f out and again over 1f out: sn swtchd lft: wknd fnl f* **50/1**

9 6 **Birthday Girl (IRE)** 2-8-12 0 SteveDrowne 9 36
(Amanda Perrett) *mid-div: pushed along over 3f out: rdn over 2f out: nvr threatened: wknd ent fnl f* **20/1**

10 12 **Molliana** 2-8-12 0 LiamKeniry 1 4
(Neil Mulholland) *s.i.s: in last pair: rdn 2f out: no imp: wknd over 1f out* **40/1**

1m 33.25s (4.65) **Going Correction** +0.55s/f (Yiel) **10** Ran SP% **116.4**
Speed ratings (Par 92): **95,94,92,92,91 89,89,85,79,65**
CSF £343.38 TOTE £13.10: £3.50, £7.20, £4.90; EX 284.40 Trifecta £6619.90.
**Owner** MrsJamesBlythCurrie&BissettDownRacing **Bred** Saxtead Livestock, M Coleman & S Hoskins **Trained** Blewbury, Oxon

**FOCUS**
Little got into this, with it an advantage to race handily. The pace was steady and the form is just ordinary.

## 7899 BATHWICK TYRES H'CAP (DIV I) 6f 213y
**3:05** (3:06) (Class 6) (0-60,64) 3-Y-O+ **£3,234** (£962; £481; £240) **Stalls** Low

Form RPR
5042 1 **Vixen (IRE)**[24] 7122 3-9-2 **57** (h) EdwardGreatrex 5 63
(Eve Johnson Houghton) *mid-div: pushed along over 3f out: hdwy 2f out: rdn to ld narrowly fnl 140yds: kpt on gamely: all out* **9/4**[1]

4411 2 *nk* **Topmeup**[22] 7198 3-9-4 **59** (v) FranBerry 10 64
(David Evans) *in tch: rdn 2f out: hdwy ent fnl f: r.o w ev ch fnl 120yds: kpt on* **11/2**[2]

-454 3 *nk* **Swot**[22] 7198 5-8-11 **57** (p) RossaRyan(7) 8 62
(Roger Teal) *trckd ldrs: rdn 2f out: tk narrow advantage ent fnl f: hdd fnl 140yds: kpt on but hld cl home* **9/1**

4041 4 *nk* **Air Of York (IRE)**[7] 7693 5-9-4 **64** 6ex (p) WilliamCox(7) 3 68
(John Flint) *trckd ldrs: rdn 2f out: ev ch fnl f: kpt on but hld cl home* **8/1**

0600 5 *4 ½* **Mulsanne Chase**[14] 7457 3-9-4 **59** (b[1]) SteveDrowne 7 51
(Brian Barr) *prom: led over 3f out: rdn 2f out: narrowly hdd jst over 1f out: fdd ins fnl f* **33/1**

543 6 *1* **Mooroverthebridge**[40] 6577 3-9-5 **60** OisinMurphy 4 49
(Grace Harris) *led for over 3f: pressed ldr: rdn over 2f out: regained ld briefly jst over 1f out: fdd ins fnl f* **33/1**

0003 7 *1* **Dynamic Girl (IRE)**[14] 7465 4-8-8 **54** NicolaCurrie(7) 6 42
(Brendan Powell) *mid-div: hdwy to chse ldrs 2f out: sn rdn w nt clrest of runs: fdd ins fnl f* **13/2**

6203 8 *2* **Bella's Venture**[21] 7213 4-8-13 **52** ShaneKelly 1 34
(John Gallagher) *stmbld leaving stalls: sn in tch: rdn to chse ldrs 2f out: wknd fnl f* **10/1**

321 9 *1* **Robbie Roo Roo**[31] 6888 4-9-3 **56** (vt) AdamBeschizza 9 36
(Mrs Ilka Gansera-Leveque) *racd keenly: trckd ldrs: rdn 2f out: wknd ent fnl f* **6/1**[3]

4010 10 *2 ½* **Intimately**[14] 7465 4-9-3 **59** GeorgeWood(3) 2 32+
(Jonathan Portman) *dwlt bdly: a bhd* **14/1**

1m 33.11s (4.51) **Going Correction** +0.55s/f (Yiel)
**WFA** 3 from 4yo+ 2lb **10** Ran SP% **116.5**
Speed ratings (Par 101): **96,95,95,94,89 88,87,85,84,81**
CSF £14.27 CT £94.11 TOTE £2.90: £1.10, £2.10, £2.40; EX 16.20 Trifecta £118.40.
**Owner** Mrs Jennifer Simpson Racing **Bred** Rossenarra Bloodstock Limited **Trained** Blewbury, Oxon

**FOCUS**
A moderate handicap with a tight finish, but sound enough form for the level. There was little between the first four at the line and it set up for the closers.

## 7900 BATHWICK TYRES H'CAP (DIV II) 6f 213y
**3:35** (3:38) (Class 6) (0-60,60) 3-Y-O+ **£3,234** (£962; £481; £240) **Stalls** Low

Form RPR
3212 1 **Edge (IRE)**[21] 7210 6-9-3 **56** (b) DavidProbert 6 61
(Bernard Llewellyn) *s.i.s: towards rr: hdwy 3f out: led gng best jst over 1f out: sn rdn: a holding on w enough in hand: rdn out* **7/2**[2]

0105 2 *½* **Misu Pete**[22] 7198 5-8-11 **57** (p) NicolaCurrie(7) 9 61
(Mark Usher) *mid-div: rdn and hdwy 2f out: kpt on to chse wnr ins fnl f but a being hld* **13/2**

065 3 *3 ¼* **Topology**[25] 7099 4-9-7 **60** (v) OisinMurphy 8 55
(Joseph Tuite) *trckd ldrs: rdn and ev ch over 1f out: kpt on same pce fnl f* **5/2**[1]

0053 4 *1* **Rolling Dice**[22] 7198 6-9-6 **59** (b) LiamKeniry 5 52
(Dominic Ffrench Davis) *trckd ldrs: nt best of runs and swtchd rt over 1f out: sn rdn: kpt on but nt pce to get on terms* **11/2**[3]

0030 5 *¾* **Live Dangerously**[5] 7729 7-9-2 **55** (p) KieranO'Neill 4 46
(John Bridger) *trckd ldr: rdn and ev ch over 2f out tl over 1f out: kpt on same pce* **6/1**

0600 6 *½* **Iceaxe**[16] 7390 4-9-1 **57** EoinWalsh(3) 7 46
(John Holt) *sn led: rdn and hdd jst over 1f out: wknd ins fnl f* **12/1**

000- 7 *5* **Sixth Of June**[376] 6880 3-9-3 **58** SteveDrowne 3 33
(Rod Millman) *in tch: rdn over 3f out: nvr threatened: wknd over 1f out* **33/1**

6030 8 *4 ½* **Head Space (IRE)**[22] 7190 9-8-8 **52** (v) JoshuaBryan(5) 10 17
(Brian Barr) *a towards rr* **50/1**

0010 9 *5* **Kaaber (USA)**[22] 7191 6-8-13 **52** TomMarquand 1 4
(Michael Blake) *chsd ldrs tl wknd 2f out* **12/1**

1m 31.99s (3.39) **Going Correction** +0.55s/f (Yiel)
**WFA** 3 from 4yo+ 2lb **9** Ran SP% **114.1**
Speed ratings (Par 101): **102,101,97,96,95 95,89,84,78**
CSF £26.19 CT £65.46 TOTE £4.20: £1.60, £2.50, £1.20; EX 30.00 Trifecta £104.60.
**Owner** D Maddocks & Partner **Bred** Swordlestown Stud **Trained** Fochriw, Caerphilly

**FOCUS**
A similarly moderate race to the first division and again it set up for the closers, with the front pair pulling away late. The winner is rated to his recent best and the runner-up fits.

## 7901 BRITISH STALLION STUDS EBF BATHWICK TYRES CONDITIONS STKS 6f 213y
**4:05** (4:07) (Class 3) 3-Y-O+ **£9,056** (£2,695; £1,346; £673) **Stalls** Low

Form RPR
2003 1 **George William**[17] 7356 4-9-2 102 TomMarquand 2 100
(Richard Hannon) *trckd ldr: rdn to chal 2f out: led ent fnl f: kpt on wl to assert fnl 100yds* **11/8**[1]

3136 2 *1 ¼* **Black Bess**[30] 6919 4-8-8 90 CharlieBennett(3) 4 92
(Jim Boyle) *led: rdn and hdd ent fnl f: kpt on but no ex fnl 100yds* **9/2**[3]

6000 3 *¾* **Repton (IRE)**[3] 7782 3-9-0 90 OisinMurphy 1 94
(Richard Hannon) *hld up last pair wl in tch: hdwy 2f out: sn rdn to chse ldng pair: kpt on but nt pce to get on terms* **8/1**

0045 4 *2 ½* **Summer Icon**[3] 7781 4-8-8 90 DavidEgan(3) 3 84
(Mick Channon) *pushed along briefly leaving stalls: last pair: rdn 2f out: kpt on to go 4th ins fnl f but nt gng pce to get involved* **5/1**

03-3 5 *¾* **Global Applause**[65] 5633 3-9-0 103 FranBerry 5 86
(Ed Dunlop) *trckd ldng pair tl rdn wl over 1f out: fdd into 5th ins fnl f* **7/2**[2]

1m 31.47s (2.87) **Going Correction** +0.55s/f (Yiel)
**WFA** 3 from 4yo 2lb **5** Ran SP% **110.3**
Speed ratings (Par 107): **105,103,102,99,99**
CSF £7.88 TOTE £1.90: £1.10, £2.40; EX 5.80 Trifecta £31.90.
**Owner** Lady Coventry & Partners **Bred** Rachel Countess Of Coventry **Trained** East Everleigh, Wilts

**FOCUS**
A decent conditions race, they went just a steady gallop and the favourite won with something to spare. The form is rated a bit cautiously.

## 7902 BATHWICKCARANDVANHIRE.CO.UK H'CAP 1m 1f 201y
**4:35** (4:36) (Class 5) (0-70,72) 3-Y-O **£3,396** (£1,010; £505; £252) **Stalls** Low

Form RPR
-652 1 **Poseidon (IRE)**[35] 6767 3-9-6 **69** LiamKeniry 3 78+
(Ed Walker) *mid-div: hdwy fr 4f out: rdn to chal 2f out: led ent fnl f: jst hld on: all out* **9/2**[1]

33 2 *hd* **Haulani (USA)**[28] 7004 3-9-9 **72** (bt) JohnFahy 6 80
(Philip Hide) *hld up towards rr: hdwy over 2f out: nt clr run and swtchd lft sn after: str run ent fnl f: clsng rapidly on wnr at fin: jst failed* **12/1**

4325 3 *2* **Daily Trader**[6] 7711 3-9-3 **66** FranBerry 2 70
(David Evans) *trckd ldrs: led over 2f out: sn rdn: hdd ent fnl f: kpt on but no ex fnl 100yds* **11/2**[2]

3603 4 *¾* **Unit Of Assessment (IRE)**[25] 7095 3-9-5 **68** (t) SteveDrowne 9 71
(William Knight) *mid-div: rdn and hdwy over 2f out: kpt on fnl f but nt pce to get on terms: wnt 4th towards fin* **25/1**

1614 5 *½* **Take A Turn (IRE)**[40] 6594 3-9-4 **67** MartinDwyer 12 71+
(David Lanigan) *hld up towards rr: hdwy over 2f out: swtchd to far rails over 1f out: sn rdn: attempted to mount chal but tight for room ins fnl f: no ex fnl 100yds* **12/1**

6516 6 *1 ½* **Swaffham Bulbeck (IRE)**[25] 7097 3-9-5 **68** (p[1]) AdamBeschizza 14 67
(Ed Vaughan) *hld up towards rr: rdn over 2f out: no imp tl styd on wl fnl f: nvr threatened to get on terms* **8/1**

4026 7 *nk* **It's How We Roll (IRE)**[48] 6291 3-8-13 **62** (b) DavidProbert 8 60
(John Spearing) *mid-div: hdwy to trck ldrs over 2f out but nt best of runs tl rdn over 1f out: kpt on same pce fnl f* **17/2**

6343 8 *1 ¼* **Cotinga**[22] 7201 3-9-8 **71** (p[1]) OisinMurphy 1 66
(Ralph Beckett) *trckd ldrs: rdn whn short of room and hmpd over 1f out: no threat after* **13/2**

1341 9 *¾* **Flood Defence (IRE)**[19] 7278 3-9-4 **70** GeorgeWood(3) 7 64
(Chris Wall) *mid-div: rdn over 2f out: little imp* **6/1**[3]

2242 10 *1* **Greenview Paradise (IRE)**[34] 6784 3-8-8 **64** JackOsborn(7) 13 56
(Brian Barr) *hld up towards rr: hdwy 4f out: rdn in midfield over 2f out: no further imp* **33/1**

0-60 11 *7* **Lucky Esteem**[35] 6766 3-8-11 **63** DavidEgan(3) 11 41
(Neil Mulholland) *racd keenly: mid-div: hdwy over 4f out: rdn and ev ch briefly over 2f out: sn wknd* **50/1**

6034 12 *¾* **Junoesque**[13] 7485 3-8-8 **60** (p) GeorgeBuckell(3) 10 36
(John Gallagher) *hld up towards rr: hdwy over 3f out: rdn over 2f out: wknd over 1f out* **25/1**

323 13 *1 ½* **Funky Footsteps (IRE)**[54] 6075 3-9-8 **71** (p) EdwardGreatrex 4 44
(Eve Johnson Houghton) *trckd ldr: led over 6f out: rdn and hdd over 2f out: wkng whn short of room and snatched up over 1f out* **10/1**

0000 14 *52* **Moorea**[35] 6767 3-8-7 **56** oh11 (t[1]) KieranO'Neill 5
(John Bridger) *led tl over 6f out: trckd ldr: rdn 4f out: sn wknd: t.o* **100/1**

2m 13.56s (3.66) **Going Correction** +0.375s/f (Good) **14** Ran SP% **120.9**
Speed ratings (Par 101): **100,99,98,97,97 96,95,94,94,93 87,87,86,44**
CSF £57.19 CT £309.95 TOTE £5.60: £1.80, £4.20, £2.40; EX 68.00 Trifecta £442.40.
**Owner** P K Siu **Bred** Epona Bloodstock Ltd And P A Byrne **Trained** Upper Lambourn, Berks

**FOCUS**
Modest handicap form and the runner-up looked unfortunate. The winner might have more to offer.

## 7903 BYERLEY STUD "SEASON FINALE" H'CAP 1m 6f 44y
**5:05** (5:05) (Class 3) (0-95,95) 3-Y-O+ **£7,762** (£2,310; £1,154; £577) **Stalls** Far side

Form RPR
512 1 **Moabit (GER)**[55] 6033 5-8-5 **77** (t) MeganNicholls(5) 5 89
(Paul Nicholls) *racd keenly: hld up: hdwy to ld over 6f out: sn clr: drifted lft fr 2f out: styd on wl: rdn out* **9/5**[1]

0352 2 *4 ½* **Champagne Champ**[22] 7200 5-9-7 **88** SteveDrowne 6 93
(Rod Millman) *trckd ldrs: rdn 3f out: styd on fnl 2f but nt pce to get on terms w wnr: snatched 2nd cl home* **5/1**[3]

2540 3 *nk* **Rydan (IRE)**[52] 6135 6-9-0 **81** (p[1]) LiamKeniry 4 85
(Gary Moore) *hld up: hdwy over 2f out: rdn to chse wnr wl over 1f out: nt quite pce to mount chal: no ex whn lost 2nd cl home* **9/1**

3225 4 *4 ½* **Waterville Dancer (IRE)**[40] 6580 3-8-3 **77** (p[1]) KieranO'Neill 3 77
(Richard Hughes) *trckd ldrs: rdn 3f out: styd on same pce fnl 2f* **11/2**

5035 5 *½* **Paris Protocol**[16] 7397 4-9-5 **86** (p) FranBerry 8 83
(Richard Hannon) *trckd ldrs: rdn to chse wnr 3f out tl jst over 2f out: one pce after* **6/1**

1244 6 *6* **Gawdawpalin (IRE)**[17] 7354 4-9-12 **93** MartinDwyer 1 82
(Sylvester Kirk) *racd keenly: hld up: rdn 3f out: nvr any imp: wknd fnl f* **9/2**[2]

0-04 7 *13* **Treasure The Ridge (IRE)**[48] 2021 8-8-9 **76** (b) DavidProbert 2 47
(Martin Hill) *led tl over 6f out: trckd wnr: rdn wl over 2f out: wknd over 1f out* **33/1**

3m 9.85s (2.45) **Going Correction** +0.375s/f (Good)
**WFA** 3 from 4yo+ 7lb **7** Ran SP% **113.2**
Speed ratings (Par 107): **108,105,105,102,102 98,91**
CSF £10.86 CT £61.76 TOTE £2.40: £1.20, £3.50; EX 7.00 Trifecta £70.80.
**Owner** Owners Group 014 **Bred** Gestut Am Schlossgarten Gbr **Trained** Ditcheat, Somerset

**FOCUS**
A fair staying handicap, they went a steady gallop and the winner was given a fine ride, being enterprisingly ridden into a clear lead after halfway and never looking in any danger of being caught. Not the most conclusive of form.

T/Plt: £4,743.90 to a £1 stake. Pool: £52,508.45 - 8.08 winning units T/Qpdt: £9.20 to a £1 stake. Pool: £5,439.90 - 434.36 winning units **Tim Mitchell**

# [6761]WINDSOR (R-H)

Monday, October 9

**OFFICIAL GOING: Good to soft (good in places; 7.4)**

Wind: Moderate, half behind Weather: Overcast

## 7904 WINDSOR VEHICLE LEASING NURSERY H'CAP 1m 31y
**2:15** (2:15) (Class 4) (0-85,80) 2-Y-O **£3,946** (£1,174; £586; £293) **Stalls** Low

Form RPR

0541 **1** **Motown Mick (IRE)**[20] 7228 2-9-2 **75**.......................... TimmyMurphy 1 81+
(Richard Hannon) *trckd ldng pair: gap appeared on inner and clsd to ld jst over 1f out: drvn and edgd lft fnl f: hld on* **7/1**

503 **2** *nk* **Shaherezada (IRE)**[32] 6862 2-9-0 **73**.......................... AndreaAtzeni 8 78
(Clive Cox) *racd sltly awkwardly early: in tch disputing 5th: rdn and prog on outer over 2f out: chal over 1f out: w wnr ins fnl f: jst hld last strides* **7/2**[2]

3513 **3** *1 1/4* **Simpson (IRE)**[20] 7251 2-9-7 **80**.......................... JamieSpencer 2 84
(Ed Walker) *hld up in last: stl there over 2f out but gng easily: prog but nt clr run bhd ldng gp jst over 1f out: prog and nt clr run ins fnl f: styd on to take 3rd nr fin but a too much to do* **2/1**[1]

1126 **4** *1/2* **Go Now Go Now (IRE)**[24] 7121 2-9-0 **73**.......................... PJMcDonald 7 74
(Mark Johnston) *trckd ldr: rdn to chal over 2f out: upsides after tl one pce ins fnl f* **10/1**

065 **5** *1/2* **Berkshire Royal**[34] 6777 2-8-7 **66**.......................... RobHornby 5 66
(Andrew Balding) *trckd ldng pair: rdn to chal over 2f out: upsides after tl fnl f: one pce after* **10/1**

3413 **6** *3/4* **Paint**[11] 7544 2-9-2 **78**.......................... HollieDoyle(3) 4 76
(Richard Hannon) *t.k.h early: hld up disputing 5th: pushed along over 3f out: dropped to last over 2f out and struggling: swtchd out wd and kpt on again last 150yds* **4/1**[3]

0210 **7** *2 1/4* **Livingstones Quest (IRE)**[37] 6699 2-9-1 **74**.......................... WilliamCarson 6 67
(Rod Millman) *t.k.h: led: rdn and jnd over 2f out: hdd jst over 1f out: wknd fnl f* **16/1**

1m 46.36s (1.66) **Going Correction** -0.025s/f (Good) **7 Ran SP% 112.1**

Speed ratings (Par 97): **90,89,88,87,87 86,84**

CSF £30.32 CT £66.23 TOTE £6.30: £3.60, £2.80; EX 25.20 Trifecta £79.30.

**Owner** N Woodcock & M Daniels **Bred** Top Row Partnership **Trained** East Everleigh, Wilts

**FOCUS**

There was a suggestion that the ground was riding slightly quicker nearer to the stands' rail. A fair nursery in which the pace slowed right down when they reached the first bend. The time was 5.76sec outside standard. Motown Mick built on his first win.

## 7905 FIREWORKS SPECTACULAR HERE ON 4TH NOVEMBER CLAIMING STKS 1m 2f
**2:45** (2:45) (Class 6) 3-4-Y-O **£2,264** (£673; £336; £168) **Stalls** Centre

Form RPR

3-00 **1** **Unsuspected Girl (IRE)**[18] 7319 4-8-5 64.......................(t) LukeMorris 6 57
(Graeme McPherson) *cl up: trckd ldr 1/2-way: stl gng easily whn led 2f out: drvn clr over 1f out* **11/1**

2532 **2** *3 1/2* **Prerogative (IRE)**[28] 7004 3-9-0 73..........................(p) HollieDoyle(3) 5 68
(Richard Hannon) *trckd ldr to 1/2-way: styd cl up: shkn up over 2f out: wnt 2nd jst over 1f out: one pce and no imp on wnr* **11/10**[1]

3406 **3** *1 1/4* **Outback Blue**[23] 7142 4-9-2 71..........................(t) JFEgan 7 59
(David Evans) *reluctant to get gng and lost several l: in tch in last pair: urged along 4f out: prog on outer 2f out: one pce in 3rd pl fnl f* **11/4**[2]

3550 **4** *nk* **Betsalottie**[53] 6101 4-8-12 52.......................... WilliamCarson 8 55
(John Bridger) *led: rdn and hdd 2f out: lost 2nd and one pce jst over 1f out* **16/1**

5235 **5** *3/4* **Ididitforyoooo (IRE)**[14] 7462 3-9-6 66.......................... JamesDoyle 4 67
(Brian Meehan) *cl up: rdn over 2f out: fdd jst over 1f out* **9/2**[3]

-000 **6** *13* **Giveitsomeginger**[12] 7523 3-7-12 44..........................(b) NoelGarbutt(3) 2 24
(Jo Hughes) *in tch to 2f out: wknd qckly* **100/1**

600- **7** *15* **Persaverance**[220] 6654 4-9-2 59..........................(b) AdamKirby 3 7
(Gary Moore) *a in last pair: struggling 4f out: t.o* **50/1**

2m 9.98s (1.28) **Going Correction** -0.025s/f (Good)

**WFA** 3 from 4yo 4lb **7 Ran SP% 109.6**

Speed ratings (Par 101): **93,90,89,88,88 77,65**

CSF £21.77 TOTE £8.30: £3.20, £1.30; EX 24.70 Trifecta £43.80.The winner was claimed by Mr J. M. Bradley for £4,000. Prerogative was claimed by Mr A. W. Carroll for £15,000.

**Owner** Good Evans Racing Partnership **Bred** Mrs E Henry **Trained** Upper Oddington, Gloucs

**FOCUS**

They went what looked a reasonable gallop in this modest claimer. The fourth and fifth give an insight into the form's true worth.

## 7906 BRITISH STALLION STUDS EBF NOVICE STKS 1m 31y
**3:15** (3:15) (Class 5) 2-Y-O **£2,911** (£866; £432; £216) **Stalls** Low

Form RPR

03 **1** **Delsheer (FR)**[19] 7273 2-9-2 0.......................... JamesDoyle 8 76
(Hugo Palmer) *led 1f: pressed ldr: led again 3f out: sn jnd: drvn and gd battle w runner-up after: jst prevailed* **15/8**[1]

2 **2** *shd* **Celestin's**[19] 7265 2-8-11 0.......................... MartinHarley 7 71
(William Haggas) *trckd ldng pair: chal and w wnr over 2f out: gd battle after and upsides thrght fnl f: jst pipped* **5/2**[2]

**3** *1 1/2* **Come On Tier (FR)** 2-9-2 0.......................... JamieSpencer 4 73+
(David Simcock) *dwlt: rn green in last and wl off the pce by 1/2-way: prog on outer over 2f out: styd on wl after to take 3rd nr fin: shaped wl* **20/1**

0 **4** *nk* **Candidate (IRE)**[17] 7355 2-9-2 0.......................... RobertWinston 6 72
(Hughie Morrison) *racd in 4th: off the pce sn after 1/2-way: shoved along and kpt on steadily over 2f out: tk 3rd briefly ins fnl f: should improve* **40/1**

3253 **5** *1 1/2* **White Feather**[75] 5270 2-9-2 0.......................... DougieCostello 9 68+
(Jo Hughes) *t.k.h: led after 1f: rdn and hdd 3f out: kpt on in 3rd pl tl fdd ins fnl f* **20/1**

**6** *1 1/4* **Low Profile** 2-9-2 0.......................... KieranShoemark 2 66
(Roger Charlton) *dwlt: off the pce in rr gp: pushed along over 3f out: nvr on terms but plugged on fr over 1f out* **9/1**

**7** *1 3/4* **Profound (IRE)** 2-9-2 0.......................... AndreaAtzeni 3 62
(Roger Varian) *slowly away: mostly in last trio: carried lft bnd over 5f out: shkn up and no great prog fr 3f out* **11/2**[3]

6 **8** *3 1/4* **Enforcement (IRE)**[29] 6967 2-9-2 0.......................... TimmyMurphy 1 54
(Martin Keighley) *racd in 5th but wl off the pce fr 1/2-way: wknd 2f out* **66/1**

**9** *3/4* **Mythological (IRE)** 2-9-2 0.......................... RobertHavlin 5 52
(John Gosden) *dwlt: rn green in rr: hung lft bnd over 5f out: shkn up and no prog 3f out* **7/1**

1m 45.34s (0.64) **Going Correction** -0.025s/f (Good) **9 Ran SP% 114.7**

Speed ratings (Par 95): **95,94,93,93,91 90,88,85,84**

CSF £6.27 TOTE £3.50: £1.60, £1.10, £4.80; EX 8.50 Trifecta £114.70.

**Owner** Al Shaqab Racing **Bred** S A R L Ecurie Des Charmes **Trained** Newmarket, Suffolk

**FOCUS**

Not a strong novice event, the second and fifth offering perspective, but one or two winners should come out of it.

## 7907 KALTENBERG MAIDEN STKS 6f 12y
**3:45** (3:47) (Class 5) 3-Y-O+ **£2,911** (£866; £432; £216) **Stalls** Low

Form RPR

**1** **Our Oystercatcher** 3-9-5 0..........................(h[1]) AdamKirby 12 73
(Henry Candy) *taken down early: racd wd early: w ldrs: wnt 2nd over 3f out: chal 2f out: narrow ld fnl f and sn jnd: jst hld on* **9/1**

32 **2** *shd* **Holiday Girl (IRE)**[25] 7080 3-9-0 75.......................... TomQueally 10 68
(Eve Johnson Houghton) *pressed ldrs: rdn 2f out: clsd to chal fnl f: w wnr after: jst pipped* **7/4**[1]

6543 **3** *1/2* **Zilza (IRE)**[16] 7414 3-9-0 65..........................(bt) RobertHavlin 6 66
(Conrad Allen) *fast away: led against nr side rail: rdn and pressed 2f out: hdd fnl f: styd on* **9/2**[2]

0006 **4** *1/2* **Know The Truth**[14] 7465 3-8-7 59.......................... KayleighStephens(7) 5 64+
(Andrew Balding) *hld up off the pce in midfield: stdy prog fr 1/2-way: pushed along and clsd on ldrs over 1f out: nvr quite rchd them* **11/2**[3]

0 **5** *1/2* **Ladakhi**[12] 7514 3-9-0 0.......................... WilliamCarson 13 63
(Rod Millman) *chsd ldrs: shkn up and effrt on outer 2f out: kpt on but nvr quite able to chal* **100/1**

5326 **6** *5* **Cherished (IRE)**[20] 7227 3-9-0 68.......................... TimmyMurphy 1 47
(Geoffrey Deacon) *wl in rr early: pushed along and prog against nr side rail fr 2f out: nvr a threat but kpt on* **13/2**

066 **7** *1 1/4* **Bleu Et Noir**[25] 7080 6-9-6 0..........................(h) RobHornby 4 48
(Tim Vaughan) *outpcd in 12th and long way adrift bef 1/2-way: pushed along and kpt on fnl 2f: nvr nrr* **16/1**

0 **8** *3/4* **Dilinger**[25] 7080 3-9-5 0.......................... KieranShoemark 8 45
(Stuart Kittow) *awkward s: wl in rr: effrt on outer and rdn over 2f out: sme prog into midfield over 1f out: no hdwy after* **10/1**

0 **9** *6* **Linda Doris (IRE)**[121] 3595 3-9-0 0..........................(t[1]) LukeMorris 7 21
(Gay Kelleway) *nvr beyond midfield: struggling u.p 1/2-way: wknd* **40/1**

06 **10** *2 1/4* **Spitfire Limited**[56] 6009 3-9-0 0..........................(h) FergusSweeney 9 14
(George Baker) *taken down early: spd to press ldr over 2f: wknd qckly over 2f out* **28/1**

00 **11** *8* **Val's Magic Touch**[34] 6791 3-9-0 0.......................... RobertWinston 3
(John O'Shea) *chsd ldrs to 1/2-way: wknd qckly* **250/1**

0 **12** *2* **Eye Burner**[20] 7254 3-8-12 0.......................... GinaMangan(7) 2
(J R Jenkins) *a struggling in rr: bhd fnl 2f* **100/1**

4000 **13** *17* **Rockalater**[53] 6097 3-9-0 43.......................... SamHitchcott 11
(John Spearing) *outpcd and sn t.o* **150/1**

0500 **U** **Akuna Mattatta (IRE)**[18] 7322 3-9-0 45.......................... PaddyBradley(5) 14
(Ralph J Smith) *ducked lft s and uns rdr* **100/1**

1m 11.89s (-1.11) **Going Correction** +0.025s/f (Good)

**WFA** 3 from 6yo 1lb **14 Ran SP% 118.2**

Speed ratings (Par 103): **108,107,107,106,105 99,97,96,88,85 74,72,49,**

CSF £24.41 TOTE £8.40: £3.10, £1.20, £1.70; EX 29.90 Trifecta £129.70.

**Owner** Mrs F A Veasey & G B Partnership **Bred** Mrs F A Veasey **Trained** Kingston Warren, Oxon

■ Stewards' Enquiry : Tom Queally two day ban: using his whip above the permitted level (23/24 Oct)

**FOCUS**

A modest late-season maiden in which the first five finished clear. It's rated around the third.

## 7908 KONIG LUDWIG H'CAP 1m 3f 99y
**4:15** (4:16) (Class 3) (0-90,90) 3-Y-O **£7,246** (£2,168; £1,084; £542; £270) **Stalls** Centre

Form RPR

4145 **1** **Solar Cross**[51] 6187 3-8-8 **79**.......................... HarryBentley 6 88
(Roger Charlton) *mde virtually all: kicked for home 3f out and spread field out: drvn over 1f out against nr side rail: hld on wl* **7/2**[1]

0042 **2** *3/4* **Zamperini (IRE)**[12] 7505 5-8-10 **76** oh1.......................... KieranShoemark 8 82
(Mike Murphy) *slowly away: hld up in last pair: plenty to do once wnr kicked on 3f out: prog on outer over 2f out: rdn and styd on to take 2nd ins fnl f: a jst hld* **10/1**

12 **3** *1 1/2* **Lawless Secret**[24] 7119 3-9-0 **85**..........................(h) RyanPowell 3 89
(Simon Crisford) *trckd ldrs: rdn in 3rd pl whn wnr kicked for home 3f out: kpt on after but nvr quite able to chal* **7/2**[1]

3311 **4** *nse* **Take Two**[32] 6858 8-8-10 **76** oh1.......................... WilliamCarson 5 79
(Alex Hales) *in tch: outpcd by ldng trio 3f out: sn rdn: kpt on fr over 1f out but nvr able to chal* **12/1**

4403 **5** *1* **Desert God (IND)**[22] 7200 5-9-1 **88**.......................... StephenCummins(7) 9 89
(Richard Hughes) *cl up: chsd wnr 4f out: rdn 3f out: hld over 1f out: one pce and lost pls ins fnl f* **12/1**

0-51 **6** *9* **Giveaway Glance**[140] 2893 4-9-1 **81**..........................(h[1]) FergusSweeney 7 64
(Alan King) *dwlt: hld up in last pair: outpcd 3f out and nt clr run briefly after: nvr a factor* **25/1**

0205 **7** *2* **Zambeasy**[37] 6701 6-8-13 **79**.......................... RichardKingscote 1 58
(Philip Hide) *hld up bhd ldrs: gng strly 5f out: rdn whn pce lifted 3f out and fnd nil: wl btn after* **8/1**

-024 **8** *16* **Rising (IRE)**[38] 6657 3-8-10 **81** ow1.......................... JamieSpencer 4 29
(Brian Meehan) *w wnr to 1/2-way: rdn and wknd qckly 3f out* **15/2**[3]

1P **9** *47* **Zamfir**[149] 2614 3-9-5 **90**..........................(b[1]) WilliamBuick 2
(Charlie Appleby) *prom: pressed wnr 6f out to 4f out: wknd v rapidly: t.o* **9/2**[2]

2m 26.61s (-2.89) **Going Correction** -0.025s/f (Good)

**WFA** 3 from 4yo+ 5lb **9 Ran SP% 113.8**

Speed ratings (Par 107): **109,108,107,107,106 100,98,86,52**

CSF £38.72 CT £129.90 TOTE £4.60: £1.40, £3.60, £1.60; EX 45.60 Trifecta £294.30.

**Owner** De Zoete, Inglett, Mercer And Smartt **Bred** Usk Valley Stud **Trained** Beckhampton, Wilts

**FOCUS**

Decent handicap form, with the first five clear. The form is rated around the second and fourth who were both a pound out of the handicap.

## 7909 MARSTON'S H'CAP 1m 31y
**4:45** (4:46) (Class 4) (0-85,87) 3-Y-O+ **£4,690** (£1,395; £697; £348) **Stalls** Low

Form RPR

100 **1** **Dragons Voice**[37] 6700 3-8-8 **75**.......................... HarryBentley 6 84+
(Philip Hide) *trckd ldrs: rdn 3f out: tk 2nd 2f out: drvn to ld over 1f out: in command fnl f* **9/2**[2]

060 **2** 1 1/4 **Ghalib (IRE)**[30] 6936 5-9-7 **85**................................(bt) RichardKingscote 8 90
(Amy Murphy) *led at decent pce: kicked on 3f out against nr side rail: hdd over 1f out: safely hld by wnr after but kpt on wl* **20/1**

4050 **3** 1 1/4 **Reaver (IRE)**[16] 7395 4-9-1 **79**..................................(p[1]) CharlesBishop 10 81
(Eve Johnson Houghton) *hld up in midfield: no immediate rspnse whn ldrs kicked on 3f out: styd on fr 2f out to take 3rd nr fin* **4/1**[1]

0600 **4** nk **Dutch Uncle**[23] 7156 5-8-11 **75**.................................... FergusSweeney 4 76
(Robert Cowell) *chsd ldr: rdn 3f out: lost 2nd 2f out: one pce after* **50/1**

61 **5** 2 3/4 **Breden (IRE)**[17] 7358 7-9-9 **87**..................................(h) RobertWinston 1 82
(Linda Jewell) *hld up in last pair: lft bhd fr 3f out: shkn up 2f out: passed rivals to take modest 5th ins fnl f: nvr really in it* **7/1**

5100 **6** 1/2 **Sir Plato (IRE)**[24] 7131 3-8-13 **80**.................................... WilliamCarson 7 74
(Rod Millman) *chsd ldng pair: rdn 3f out: steadily fdd fnl 2f* **14/1**

041 **7** hd **Whip Nae Nae (IRE)**[45] 6387 3-9-2 **83**....................(p[1]) TimmyMurphy 3 77
(Richard Hannon) *nvr beyond midfield: outpcd whn ldrs kicked 3f out: no prog after* **11/2**[3]

4341 **8** 1 3/4 **Alemaratalyoum (IRE)**[25] 7083 3-8-11 **78**......................... JimmyQuinn 9 67
(Ed Dunlop) *hld up in last pair: lft bhd fr 3f out: shkn up and no prog 2f out: nvr in it* **9/1**

-100 **9** 1 1/2 **Manchego**[79] 5157 3-9-3 **84**............................................(t[1]) JamesDoyle 2 70
(Hugo Palmer) *hld up in rr: lft bhd by ldrs fr 3f out: pushed along and no prog: nvr in it* **7/1**

3236 **10** 11 **Black Trilby (IRE)**[54] 6073 3-9-1 **82**...........................(h) SamHitchcott 5 43
(Clive Cox) *chsd ldrs to 1/2-way: sn lost pl u.p: bhd fnl 2f* **15/2**

1m 42.06s (-2.64) **Going Correction** -0.025s/f (Good)
**WFA** 3 from 4yo+ 3lb **10** Ran SP% **113.7**
Speed ratings (Par 105): **112,110,109,109,106 105,105,104,102,91**
CSF £86.92 CT £386.75 TOTE £5.60: £1.80, £3.90, £1.80; EX 93.10 Trifecta £420.30.
**Owner** Heart Of The South Racing **Bred** Parry, Stratton, Steele-Mortimer **Trained** Findon, W Sussex

**FOCUS**
Ordinary handicap form. Nothing got into it from off the pace. The second looks the best guide.

## 7910 PRINCE LUITPOLD AMATEUR RIDERS' H'CAP (DIV I) 6f 12y
**5:15** (5:20) (Class 6) (0-65,66) 3-Y-0+ **£2,183** (£677; £338; £169) **Stalls** Low

Form RPR

0002 **1** **Nutini (IRE)**[7] 7693 4-11-4 **60**............................................(p) MrSWalker 10 68+
(Malcolm Saunders) *prom: trckd ldr 1/2-way: rdn to ld jst over 1f out: urged along and drew clr* **11/10**[1]

000 **2** 2 1/4 **Louis Vee (IRE)**[7] 7693 9-10-7 **49** oh4..............(b) MissBrodieHampson 7 50
(John O'Shea) *led: rdn 2f out: hdd jst over 1f out: no ex* **80/1**

1002 **3** 1 **Toni's A Star**[7] 7689 5-10-7 **56**...............................(b) MrGGilbertson[(7)] 1 54
(Tony Carroll) *hld up in rr: prog over 2f out: pushed along and kpt on to take 3rd ins fnl f: unable to threaten* **12/1**

3564 **4** 1 1/2 **Princess Way (IRE)**[46] 6345 3-10-4 **52**............................(v) MrJFlook[(5)] 6 46
(David Evans) *chsd ldrs: rdn over 2f out: disp 3rd over 1f out: one pce fnl f* **8/1**[3]

5630 **5** 3 3/4 **Flying Sakhee**[25] 7099 4-10-8 **50**........................................(b) MrRBirkett 2 32
(John Bridger) *slowly away: prog fr rr to chse ldrs on outer 1/2-way: no imp over 1f out: wknd fnl f* **14/1**

0305 **6** 1 1/4 **Fivos**[7] 7692 3-10-5 **53**.............................................(p) PoppyBridgwater[(5)] 5 32
(David Bridgwater) *chsd ldrs: lost pl 1/2-way: n.d fnl 2f* **25/1**

1130 **7** 1/2 **Sweet Pursuit**[33] 6807 3-11-9 **66**........................................ MrPMillman 8 43+
(Rod Millman) *rrng as stalls opened and v.s.a: nvr able to rcvr* **3/1**[2]

0505 **8** 1/2 **The Hooded Claw (IRE)**[58] 5930 6-11-4 **63**...........(p) MissAMcCain[(3)] 3 39
(Patrick Morris) *in tch towards rr: no prog over 2f out: sn btn* **8/1**[3]

4044 **9** nk **All Or Nothin (IRE)**[65] 5657 8-10-2 **49** oh2.................. MissMBryant[(5)] 4 24
(Paddy Butler) *chsd ldr to 1/2-way: sn wknd* **40/1**

1m 12.98s (-0.02) **Going Correction** +0.025s/f (Good)
**WFA** 3 from 4yo+ 1lb **9** Ran SP% **116.7**
Speed ratings (Par 101): **101,98,96,94,89 88,87,86,86**
CSF £137.60 CT £763.01 TOTE £2.30: £1.30, £11.60, £2.30; EX 54.80 Trifecta £439.50.
**Owner** Mrs L F Wei **Bred** Colm McEvoy **Trained** Green Ore, Somerset
■ Doctor Parkes was withdrawn. Price at time of withdrawal 22/1. Rule 4 does not apply.

**FOCUS**
Very moderate sprint form. It was the quicker division by 0.14sec and the form could be rated higher.

## 7911 PRINCE LUITPOLD AMATEUR RIDERS' H'CAP (DIV II) 6f 12y
**5:45** (5:48) (Class 6) (0-65,63) 3-Y-0+ **£2,183** (£677; £338; £169) **Stalls** Low

Form RPR

0234 **1** **Arcanista (IRE)**[19] 7282 4-10-3 **52**..............................(p) MrMSHarris[(7)] 1 62
(Chris Dwyer) *chsd ldr: clr of rest fr 1/2-way: shkn up to ld over 1f out: pushed along and drew away fnl f* **6/1**[3]

203 **2** 3 3/4 **Cruise Tothelimit (IRE)**[27] 7020 9-11-7 **63**.....................(b) MrSWalker 6 62
(Patrick Morris) *led against nr side rail: clr w wnr 1/2-way: hdd over 1f out: one pce* **11/2**[2]

0220 **3** 1 **Whatalove**[89] 4754 3-9-13 **49** oh2......................................... MrAHark[(7)] 8 45
(Martin Keighley) *racd wdst of all: chsd ldrs: outpcd fr 1/2-way: kpt on fnl 2f and won battle for 3rd* **8/1**

5660 **4** 1 **Rafaaf (IRE)**[14] 7465 9-10-1 **50**...................................... MissHTLees[(7)] 5 43
(Peter Hiatt) *racd on outer: chsd ldrs: outpcd fr 1/2-way: disp 3rd fr 2f out to fnl f: n.d* **10/1**

2000 **5** 3/4 **Lucky Di**[35] 6748 7-10-0 **49** oh1...................................... MissKEvans[(7)] 3 40
(Peter Hedger) *sn in rr: pushed along and effrt against nr side rail over 2f out: plugged on but nvr on terms* **22/1**

0304 **6** 1 3/4 **Multi Quest**[55] 6041 5-10-2 **49** oh4...................(b) MissEMacKenzie[(5)] 2 34
(John E Long) *chsd ldrs: outpcd fr 1/2-way: nt on terms after* **14/1**

0322 **7** 1/2 **Time Medicean**[7] 7692 11-10-8 **57**................................ MissSAColl[(7)] 7 41
(Tony Carroll) *racd on outer: chsd ldrs: outpcd fr 1/2-way: nt on terms after* **11/4**[1]

0000 **8** nk **Herm (IRE)**[42] 6502 3-10-7 **55**...............................................(t) MrJFlook[(5)] 9 38
(David Evans) *chsd ldrs and racd on outer: outpcd fr 1/2-way: no ch fnl 2f* **13/2**

1400 **9** 20 **Concur (IRE)**[7] 7694 4-10-11 **53**...........................................(tp) MrPMillman 10
(Rod Millman) *sn outpcd: nvr on terms: wknd 2f out: t.o* **11/1**

3-00 **10** 6 **Captain Sue (IRE)**[86] 4892 3-10-12 **62**...............(t[1]) MrJamesMorley[(7)] 4 +
(Ian Williams) *v s.i.s: a t.o* **22/1**

1m 13.12s (0.12) **Going Correction** +0.025s/f (Good)
**WFA** 3 from 4yo+ 1lb **10** Ran SP% **113.6**
Speed ratings (Par 101): **100,95,93,92,91 89,88,87,61,53**
CSF £37.89 CT £268.66 TOTE £6.70: £2.10, £2.20, £2.80; EX 35.10 Trifecta £473.50.
**Owner** Mr & Mrs J Harris **Bred** Cattiva Generosa Partnership **Trained** Newmarket, Suffolk

**FOCUS**
Very ordinary form indeed, and the slower division by 0.14sec. Only the first two really got into it. The winner is rated to her form of a year ago.
T/Plt: £33.60 to a £1 stake. Pool: £68,239.49 - 1,480.50 winning units T/Qpdt: £5.10 to a £1 stake. Pool: £6,370.00 - 912.18 winning units **Jonathan Neesom**

# 7210 BRIGHTON (L-H)
Tuesday, October 10

**OFFICIAL GOING: Good to soft (7.0)**
Wind: light to medium, half against Weather: overcast, light rain and gloomy from race 4

## 7912 GARY ATKINS 40TH BIRTHDAY H'CAP 5f 60y
**2:10** (2:10) (Class 6) (0-65,67) 3-Y-0+ **£2,587** (£770; £384; £192) **Stalls** Centre

Form RPR

5144 **1** **Wotadoll**[25] 7122 3-9-0 **56**................................................ RobertWinston 4 67+
(Dean Ivory) *t.k.h: hld up in tch in rr: swtchd lft and hdwy nrest inner over 1f out: rdn to ld ent fnl f: r.o strly and drew clr fnl f: readily* **9/2**[3]

6342 **2** 4 **Flowing Clarets**[13] 7509 4-8-13 **60**.................................. MitchGodwin[(5)] 7 56
(John Bridger) *w ldr tl led after 1f: rdn over 1f out: hdd ent fnl f: sn hung lft and outpcd by wnr: no ch w but kpt on for clr 2nd ins fnl f* **10/3**[1]

4340 **3** 1 1/2 **Pride Of Angels**[73] 5429 4-9-4 **63**.............................. HectorCrouch[(3)] 9 53
(Gary Moore) *chsd ldrs: c towards stands' side over 2f out: 4th and outpcd u.p whn hung lft 1f out: no ch w wnr but kpt on same pce to go 3rd nr fin* **8/1**

6423 **4** 1/2 **Taajub (IRE)**[20] 7272 10-9-11 **67**.................................. FergusSweeney 3 55
(Peter Crate) *taken down early and led to post: led for 1f: styd pressing ldr: rdn and ev ch over 1f out unable outpcd by wnr 1f out: wknd wl ins fnl f and lost 3rd nr fin* **8/1**

000 **5** 1 3/4 **Something Lucky (IRE)**[13] 7517 5-8-6 **51**..................(tp) DavidEgan[(3)] 5 33
(Daniel Steele) *chsd ldrs: rdn over 2f out: 5th and outpcd whn carried lft 1f out: wl hld and kpt on same pce ins fnl f* **16/1**

5236 **6** 3/4 **Zavikon**[36] 6753 3-9-10 **66**..................................................(b[1]) ShaneKelly 10 46
(Richard Hughes) *dwlt: hdwy into midfield on outer over 3f out: c towards stands' side and effrt ent fnl 2f: no imp over 1f out: hung lft and plugged on same pce fnl f* **6/1**

64 **7** 1 **Shelneverwalkalone**[54] 6114 3-8-13 **55**........................(b[1]) LukeMorris 2 32
(Ivan Furtado) *t.k.h: hld up in tch in midfield: shkn up 3f out: rdn and no hdwy ent fnl 2f: wl hld and plugged on same pce fr over 1f out* **20/1**

3320 **8** 1/2 **Little Miss Daisy**[20] 7272 3-9-4 **63**.............................. GeorgeWood[(3)] 6 38
(William Muir) *restless in stalls: s.i.s: hld up in tch: effrt ent fnl 2f: no imp and wl hld over 1f out* **12/1**

1331 **9** 1/2 **Everkyllachy (IRE)**[8] 7692 3-9-6 **65** 6ex......................(b) HollieDoyle[(3)] 8 38
(J S Moore) *in tch towards rr: no hdwy u.p over 1f out: wl hld fnl f* **4/1**[2]

006 **10** 12 **Steady (IRE)**[41] 6577 3-8-7 **49** oh4..............................(t[1]) EdwardGreatrex 1
(Dan Skelton) *s.i.s: a in rr: no hdwy u.p over 1f out: wknd fnl f* **50/1**

1m 3.78s (1.48) **Going Correction** +0.375s/f (Good) **10** Ran SP% **118.1**
Speed ratings (Par 101): **103,96,94,93,90 89,87,86,86,67**
CSF £20.18 CT £120.22 TOTE £6.10: £1.90, £2.00, £2.40; EX 26.80 Trifecta £266.30.
**Owner** David C Mead **Bred** David C Mead **Trained** Radlett, Herts

**FOCUS**
Distance increased by 7yds. A moderate sprint, the winner drew away late on challenging more towards the inside of the track. A personal best from her with the form taken at face value.

## 7913 NORTH ROAD TIMBER COMPANY NOVICE AUCTION STKS 6f 210y
**2:45** (2:45) (Class 5) 2-Y-O **£2,911** (£866; £432; £216) **Stalls** Centre

Form RPR

4451 **1** **Move To The Front (IRE)**[33] 6860 2-9-5 73....................(v) AdamKirby 7 76
(Clive Cox) *mde all: rdn and edgd lft over 1f out: hld on u.p ins fnl f: drvn out* **2/1**[2]

013 **2** nk **Sing Out Loud (IRE)**[13] 7513 2-9-4 78........................ HectorCrouch[(3)] 4 78+
(Gary Moore) *t.k.h: hld up in tch: effrt on inner to press wnr ent fnl f: ev ch and n.m.r on rail: rdr unbalanced briefly ins fnl f: kpt on towards fin: sddle slipped* **13/8**[1]

4201 **3** 2 1/4 **Groundnut**[22] 7211 2-9-0 75............................................(p) GeorgeWood[(3)] 2 67
(Jonathan Portman) *dwlt: sn rcvrd to chse wnr: lost 2nd and sltly outpcd whn swtchd rt over 1f out: kpt on same pce ins fnl f* **5/2**[3]

00 **4** 2 **Gas Monkey**[70] 5507 2-8-7 0.......................................... ShelleyBirkett[(3)] 6 55
(Julia Feilden) *t.k.h: chsd ldrs: 4th and outpcd over 1f out: kpt on same pce ins fnl f* **50/1**

00 **5** nse **Rupert's Lass**[19] 7334 2-8-7 0.......................................... DavidProbert 8 52
(Michael Bell) *in tch: effrt ent fnl 2f: outpcd and btn over 1f out: kpt on same pce ins fnl f* **12/1**

60 **6** 5 **Mirror Magic**[54] 6100 2-8-7 0.......................................... EdwardGreatrex 5 38
(Geoffrey Deacon) *in tch in rr: pushed along over 4f out: rdn over 3f out: wknd over 1f out* **33/1**

1m 26.66s (3.56) **Going Correction** +0.375s/f (Good) **6** Ran SP% **112.6**
Speed ratings (Par 95): **94,93,91,88,88 83**
CSF £5.69 TOTE £2.60: £1.40, £1.50; EX 5.40 Trifecta £9.20.
**Owner** Paul & Clare Rooney **Bred** Redpender Stud Ltd **Trained** Lambourn, Berks

**FOCUS**
Distance increased by 7yds. The market leaders dominated, with the main action again unfolding far side. There wasn't much room for the favourite late on, but he had enough chance to get past. The winner seems to be progressing.

## 7914 BEATTIE-FARRANCE NURSERY H'CAP 6f 210y
**3:15** (3:17) (Class 5) (0-75,76) 2-Y-O **£2,911** (£866; £432; £216) **Stalls** Centre

Form RPR

0055 **1** **Starboy (IRE)**[21] 7239 2-8-13 **66**........................................ MartinHarley 10 69
(George Scott) *sn off the pce in last pair: rdn and gd hdwy over 1f out: led jst ins fnl f: styd on wl: rdn out* **12/1**

30 **2** 1/2 **Jo's Girl (IRE)**[63] 5752 2-9-0 **67**.................................... DougieCostello 5 69
(Jamie Osborne) *awkward leaving stalls and slowly away: in rr: effrt 2f out: swtchd rt to stands' rail over 1f out: hdwy ins fnl f: r.o strly ins fnl f: wnt 2nd towards fin: nvr quite getting to wnr* **33/1**

011 **3** 1 **Lexington Grace (IRE)**[42] 6552 2-9-7 **74**..................(p) TomMarquand 8 75
(Richard Hannon) *in tch in midfield: pushed rt and hmpd ent fnl 2f: rallied u.p to chal and hung lft 1f out: chsd wnr wl ins fnl f: kpt on but lost 2nd towards fin* **7/1**

4002 **4** 1/2 **Diamond Pursuit**[8] 7690 2-8-10 **66**.................................. DavidEgan[(3)] 9 64
(Jo Hughes) *in tch in midfield: effrt 2f out: drvn to ld over 1f out: hdd jst ins fnl f: kpt on same pce and lost 2 pls wl ins fnl f* **10/1**

236 **5** nk **Warsaan**[32] 6884 2-9-6 **73**.................................................. DaneO'Neill 2 70
(Owen Burrows) *sn pushed up to chse ldr: rdn to ld 2f out: hdd over 1f out: kpt on same pce ins fnl f* **9/2**[2]

1663 **6** 3/4 **Moseeb (IRE)**[12] 7536 2-9-6 **76**..........................(h) CallumShepherd[(3)] 11 71
(Saeed bin Suroor) *in tch in midfield: effrt nr stands' rail 2f out: ev ch and hrd drvn over 1f out: unable qck 1f out: kpt on same pce ins fnl f* **6/1**[3]

0233 **7** *7* **Tiepolo (IRE)**[37] 6721 2-9-7 **74**............................................ AdamKirby 6 50
(Gary Moore) *chsd ldrs: rdn ent fnl 2f: hrd drvn and ev ch over 1f out tl no ex and btn 1f out: wknd qckly ins fnl f* **13/2**

0531 **8** *1* **Chai Chai (IRE)**[25] 7106 2-9-9 **76**....................................... DavidProbert 4 50
(Andrew Balding) *hld up in tch in midfield: swtchd lft and effrt u.p jst over 2f out: no imp u.p over 1f out: wknd qckly fnl f* **11/4**[1]

064 **9** *2* **Lady Godiva (IRE)**[36] 6747 2-9-5 **72**....................................... SeanLevey 7 40
(Richard Hannon) *chsd ldng trio: effrt and pushed rt ent fnl 2f: tried to rally and pressing ldrs whn edgd lft ent fnl f: sn struggling: wknd qckly ins fnl f* **16/1**

6653 **10** *2 ½* **General Marius (IRE)**[36] 6749 2-9-0 **67**.......................(p[1]) HarryBentley 3 28
(Roger Varian) *midfield tl short of room and room and dropped to rr over 4f out: n.d after: wl btn over 1f out* **9/1**

6065 **11** *14* **Mirek (IRE)**[17] 7410 2-7-11 **53** oh2.................................. HollieDoyle(3) 1 +
(Patrick Chamings) *taken down early and led part of way to post: led: jinked rt jst over 2f out: sn hdd and lost pl over 1f out: bhd and eased ins fnl f* **50/1**

1m 25.33s (2.23) **Going Correction** +0.375s/f (Good) 11 Ran SP% **122.5**
Speed ratings (Par 95): **102,101,100,99,99 98,90,89,87,84 68**
CSF £355.66 CT £3022.82 TOTE £10.20: £3.30, £8.60, £2.50; EX 252.10 Trifecta £5624.10.
**Owner** Excel Racing VI **Bred** Kevin Lyons **Trained** Newmarket, Suffolk

**FOCUS**
Distance increased by 7yds. Spread centre-to-stands' side in the finish, it was those racing towards the near side that came out on top. The race set up for the closers. Modest-looking form.

## 7915 IRISH STALLION FARMS EBF NOVICE STKS 7f 211y
**3:45** (3:46) (Class 5) 2-Y-O £3,881 (£1,155; £577; £288) **Stalls** Centre

Form RPR

016 **1** **Enzo (IRE)**[33] 6859 2-9-9 73..........................................(t) LiamKeniry 8 74
(Ed Walker) *uns rdr and galloped loose briefly bef s: stdd s: t.k.h: hld up in tch in rr: hdwy nrest stands' rail 2f out: rdn to ld 1f out: hung lft wl ins fnl f: styd on* **7/1**

5 **2** *hd* **Dukeofwallingford**[26] 7093 2-9-2 0.............................. CharlesBishop 3 67
(Eve Johnson Houghton) *w ldr: rdn to ld wl over 1f out: hdd 1f out: maintained effrt and ev ch after: nudged and hld nr fin* **4/1**[3]

06 **3** *nk* **Baasha**[12] 7543 2-9-2 0............................................ AntonioFresu 6 66
(Ed Dunlop) *t.k.h: hld up in tch: effrt 2f out: hdwy and ev ch u.p ent fnl f: kpt on: hld nr fin* **8/1**

03 **4** *shd* **Blooriedotcom (IRE)**[19] 7333 2-9-2 0............................ MartinHarley 5 66
(Peter Chapple-Hyam) *in tch: effrt and ev ch over 1f out: kpt on ins fnl f: unable qck towards fin* **3/1**[2]

0 **5** *9* **Unbridled Spirit**[20] 7273 2-9-2 0................................. DavidProbert 1 45
(Andrew Balding) *dwlt: sn rcvrd to ld: hdd wl over 1f out: sn rdn and outpcd: wknd qckly fnl f* **4/1**[3]

**6** *4 ½* **Astrobreeze** 2-8-8 0.............................................. GeorgeWood(3) 7 32
(Mark H Tompkins) *hld up in tch in last pair: clsd and swtchd lft ent fnl 2f: sn rdn and outpcd over 1f out: wknd qckly fnl f* **40/1**

000 **7** *8* **Peggie Sue**[17] 7391 2-8-11 0..................................... SteveDrowne 10 19
(Adam West) *t.k.h: hld up in tch: rdn whn bdly hmpd 2f out: nt rcvr and wknd over 1f out* **100/1**

000 **8** *46* **Amenhotepthethird**[13] 7503 2-9-2 16................................ JohnFahy 4
(Mark Gillard) *t.k.h: chsd ldrs tl dropped to rr over 4f out: lost tch over 3f out: t.o* **150/1**

03 **F** **Westbrook Bertie**[25] 7120 2-8-13 0............................. DavidEgan(3) 9
(Mick Channon) *trckd ldrs: pushed along whn short of room: clipped heels and fell 2f out* **11/4**[1]

1m 40.19s (4.19) **Going Correction** +0.375s/f (Good) 9 Ran SP% **119.4**
Speed ratings (Par 95): **94,93,93,93,84 79,71,25,**
CSF £36.37 TOTE £7.50: £2.80, £1.60, £2.90; EX 33.90 Trifecta £272.40.
**Owner** P K Siu **Bred** Rabbah Bloodstock Limited **Trained** Upper Lambourn, Berks
■ Stewards' Enquiry : Liam Keniry caution: careless riding

**FOCUS**
Distance increased by 7yds. The first four finished clear and little separated them in what was an ordinary novice contest. The action unfolded stands' side and the form is rated as straightforward.

## 7916 MERTON GROUP UK LOO ROLL MANUFACTURERS H'CAP 7f 211y
**4:20** (4:20) (Class 6) (0-65,66) 3-Y-O+ £2,587 (£770; £384; £192) **Stalls** Centre

Form RPR

6066 **1** **Wordismybond**[46] 6393 8-9-3 **61**..............................(p) AdamKirby 14 71
(Amanda Perrett) *hld up in tch in rr: pushed along and gd hdwy over 1f out: led ins fnl f: r.o wl and sn clr: readily* **7/1**

5420 **2** *2 ¼* **Pick A Little**[54] 6101 9-8-13 **62**................................ MitchGodwin(5) 7 67
(Michael Blake) *hld up in tch in midfield: swtchd rt and hdwy 1f out: led and hung lft jst ins fnl f: sn hdd: outpcd by wnr but kpt on for clr 2nd fnl 100yds* **10/1**

0400 **3** *2 ½* **Gala Celebration (IRE)**[17] 7414 3-8-8 **58**..............(p) HectorCrouch(3) 3 57
(John Gallagher) *t.k.h: led: sn hdd and chsd ldrs: rdn 2f out: led again and edgd lft over 1f out: hdd jst ins fnl f: wknd fnl 100yds* **14/1**

1161 **4** *nk* **The Special One (IRE)**[22] 7213 4-9-1 **59**...............(t) TomMarquand 10 57
(Ali Stronge) *hld up in tch: clsd to chse ldrs whn swtchd lft and rt over 1f out: kpt on same pce ins fnl f* **10/1**

1210 **5** *1 ½* **Buzz Lightyere**[26] 7098 4-8-12 **63**........................ SebastianWoods(7) 2 58
(Philip Hide) *stdd s: hld up in tch: effrt and nt clrest of runs over 1f out: swtchd lft and kpt on ins fnl f: no threat to ldrs* **11/2**[2]

6400 **6** *hd* **Welsh Inlet (IRE)**[34] 6814 9-8-6 **53**.............................. HollieDoyle(3) 4 47
(John Bridger) *chsd ldrs: c nrest stands' rail and rdn 2f out: sn unable qck: wl hld and kpt on same pce ins fnl f* **20/1**

0406 **7** *1* **Lovely Acclamation (IRE)**[12] 7540 3-8-12 **59**.............(p) SeanLevey 11 51
(Ismail Mohammed) *sn led: hdd over 6f out: chsd ldrs tl swtchd rt and rdn to ld again wl over 1f out: sn hdd & wknd ins fnl f* **9/1**

0000 **8** *½* **Mr Andros**[22] 7212 4-8-0 **51** oh3...........................(vt[1]) NicolaCurrie(7) 13 42
(Brendan Powell) *t.k.h: chsd ldrs tl led over 6f out: rdn and hdd wl over 1f out: no ex u.p over 1f out: wknd ins fnl f* **33/1**

6430 **9** *hd* **Characterized**[15] 7457 3-9-1 **62**.................................. TimmyMurphy 6 53
(Geoffrey Deacon) *hld up wl in tch: rdn and unable qck whn short of room over 1f out: wknd fnl f* **25/1**

-001 **10** *1 ¾* **Buskin River (IRE)**[29] 7005 3-9-4 **65**............................... RyanTate 5 52
(James Eustace) *hld up in tch: hung lft u.p and no hdwy over 1f out: wknd ins fnl f* **7/2**[1]

0446 **11** *2 ½* **Duke Of North (IRE)**[9] 7653 5-9-5 **66**...................(p) CharlieBennett(3) 1 47
(Jim Boyle) *in tch in midfield: rdn and lost pl over 1f out: wknd ins fnl f* **6/1**[3]

336- **12** *1 ¼* **African Showgirl**[284] 8587 4-9-4 **62**............................ SteveDrowne 12 40
(Ivan Furtado) *stdd s: hld up in midfield: effrt 2f out: no hdwy and btn over 1f out: wknd fnl f* **33/1**

6300 **13** *1* **Altiko Tommy (IRE)**[55] 6076 3-9-3 **64**............................ LiamKeniry 8 40
(George Baker) *taken down early: stdd s: hld up in tch: lost pl and dropped to rr 2f out: sn wknd* **20/1**

0413 **14** *72* **With Approval (IRE)**[22] 7216 5-9-0 **58**..................(p) EdwardGreatrex 9 +
(Laura Mongan) *lunged forward as stalls opened and rdr unable to remove hood: lost all ch and a t.o* **10/1**

1m 38.47s (2.47) **Going Correction** +0.375s/f (Good)
**WFA** 3 from 4yo+ 3lb 14 Ran SP% **127.6**
Speed ratings (Par 101): **102,99,97,96,95 95,94,93,93,91 89,88,87,15**
CSF £74.46 CT £998.87 TOTE £6.90: £2.50, £3.80, £4.20; EX 106.30 Trifecta £3667.00.
**Owner** Bond Racing **Bred** Henry And Mrs Rosemary Moszkowicz **Trained** Pulborough, W Sussex

**FOCUS**
Distance increased by 7yds. A moderate handicap, the action unfolded centre-to-stands' side. The second and third fit.

## 7917 BRIGHTON LIONS FIREWORK NIGHT 5 NOVEMBER H'CAP 1m 1f 207y
**4:50** (4:51) (Class 6) (0-65,66) 3-Y-O+ £2,587 (£770; £384; £192) **Stalls** High

Form RPR

000 **1** **Fort Jefferson**[33] 6866 4-9-6 **66**.................................. JoshuaBryan(5) 3 72
(Andrew Balding) *chsd ldrs: effrt to chal u.p over 1f out: led ins fnl f: r.o wl: rdn out* **8/1**

5245 **2** *½* **Rocksette**[40] 6622 3-8-6 **51** oh4.......................................... LukeMorris 5 57
(Philip Hide) *chsd ldr tl led wl over 1f out: sn rdn: hdd and kpt on same pce ins fnl f* **8/1**

4060 **3** *2 ¼* **Sussex Girl**[19] 7324 3-8-5 **57**................................. NicolaCurrie(7) 11 59
(John Berry) *t.k.h: early: in tch in midfield: rdn wl over 2f out: edgd lft and bmpd over 1f out: chsd ldrs and kpt on same pce ins fnl f* **12/1**

6204 **4** *nse* **Getgo**[21] 7235 3-9-5 **64**...............................................(b) ShaneKelly 7 66
(David Lanigan) *chsd ldrs: rdn 2f out: unable qck and edgd rt 1f out: kpt on same pce ins fnl f* **7/1**[3]

2001 **5** *nk* **Broughtons Story**[20] 7271 3-8-9 **54**.......................... StevieDonohoe 12 55
(Henry Spiller) *hld up in tch in midfield: effrt over 2f out: nt clrest of runs over 1f out: hdwy u.p 1f out: kpt on same pce ins fnl f* **14/1**

132 **6** *1 ¾* **Fanfair**[57] 6006 3-9-7 **66**............................................... SeanLevey 4 64
(Richard Hannon) *hld up in last pair: clsd and nt clr run 2f out: gap eventually opened and hdwy jst ins fnl f: styd on but nvr any ch of getting to ldrs* **8/1**

653 **7** *1* **Bayston Hill**[14] 7495 3-9-6 **65**.......................................... DavidProbert 1 61
(Mark Usher) *hld up in tch in midfield: effrt 2f out: chsng ldrs whn edgd rt and bmpd over 1f out: wknd ins fnl f* **7/1**[3]

005 **8** *1* **Crystal Sunstone**[25] 7125 3-9-3 **62**.......................... CharlesBishop 10 56
(Eve Johnson Houghton) *s.i.s: hld up in last trio: shkn up and sme hdwy over 1f out: no hdwy u.p over 1f out: wknd ins fnl f* **10/1**

3142 **9** *1* **Ban Shoof**[14] 7495 4-9-8 **66**..............................(b) HectorCrouch(3) 9 57
(Gary Moore) *t.k.h: rdn ent fnl 2f: unable qck over 1f out: wknd ins fnl f* **4/1**[1]

3521 **10** *4* **Oceanus (IRE)**[22] 7210 3-9-2 **64**........................... ShelleyBirkett(3) 13 56
(Julia Feilden) *hld up in tch in midfield: nt clrest of runs 2f out: dropped to rr and swtchd rt and hmpd 1f out: no ch and nt given a hrd time after* **6/1**[2]

2414 **11** *1 ¾* **Bradfield Magic (IRE)**[20] 7279 3-8-13 **61**.............. CallumShepherd(3) 8 42
(Charles Hills) *stdd after s: hld up towards rr: nt clr run and hmpd over 1f out: sn swtchd lft and no hdwy: bhd and eased ins fnl f* **10/1**

0000 **12** *1* **Zoffany Bay (IRE)**[15] 7457 3-9-3 **62**....................(b) HarryBentley 6 41
(George Peckham) *t.k.h: sn led: rdn and hdd wl over 1f out: dropped out u.p and bhd 1f out: eased ins fnl f* **14/1**

2m 7.71s (4.11) **Going Correction** +0.375s/f (Good)
**WFA** 3 from 4yo+ 4lb 12 Ran SP% **131.8**
Speed ratings (Par 101): **98,97,95,95,95 94,93,92,91,88 87,86**
CSF £78.91 CT £798.44 TOTE £9.90: £3.00, £3.10, £5.30; EX 85.70 Trifecta £1828.30.
**Owner** Kingsclere Racing Club **Bred** Kingsclere Stud **Trained** Kingsclere, Hants

**FOCUS**
Distance increased by 7yds. Modest handicap form, rated around the balance of the younger placed horses.

## 7918 SANTA FUN RUN 25 NOV "HANDS AND HEELS" APPRENTICE H'CAP (PART OF RACING EXCELLENCE INITIATIVE) 1m 3f 198y
**5:20** (5:22) (Class 6) (0-55,56) 3-Y-O+ £2,587 (£770; £384; £192) **Stalls** High

Form RPR

2031 **1** **Esspeegee**[22] 7215 4-8-11 **50**..................................(p) PaulHainey(5) 2 59
(Alan Bailey) *chsd ldr tl led 2f out: sn rdn and hld on wl ins fnl f* **5/1**[2]

6012 **2** *shd* **Kilim**[22] 7215 4-9-6 **54**...................................................(t) NicolaCurrie 9 62
(John Berry) *t.k.h: hld up in tch in midfield: hdwy to chse ldrs 4f out: ev ch 2f out: drifted rt to stands' rail over 1f out: kpt on: jst hld* **7/1**

0401 **3** *nk* **Seventii**[21] 7253 3-9-0 **54**........................................ DarraghKeenan 5 63
(Robert Eddery) *hld up in tch in midfield: hdwy over 3f out: swtchd lft and rdn to chal ent fnl f: kpt on: unable qck cl home* **15/2**

4136 **4** *9* **Affair**[19] 7336 3-8-11 **54**...................................... TheodoreLadd(3) 11 49
(Hughie Morrison) *hld up towards rr: hdwy into midfield over 3f out: rdn and no imp over 1f out: wnt modest 4th ins fnl f* **8/1**

3450 **5** *½* **Lemon Drop**[49] 6291 3-8-4 **47**.........................(p) IsobelFrancis(3) 4 41
(Jim Boyle) *hld up off the pce towards rr: pushed along and hdwy over 1f out: styd on ins fnl f: no ch w ldrs* **25/1**

5333 **6** *2 ½* **Eben Dubai (IRE)**[11] 7567 5-9-2 **50**..............................(p) DavidEgan 8 39
(John Flint) *chsd ldrs: rdn and ev ch 2f out: 4th and outpcd jst over 1f out: wknd fnl f* **11/4**[1]

0000 **7** *¾* **Clearance**[21] 7253 3-8-6 **46**.......................................... AledBeech 14 35
(Mark H Tompkins) *s.i.s: off the pce in last trio: rdn 3f out: no ch whn swtchd rt over 1f out: plugged on to pass btn rivals fnl f* **50/1**

0220 **8** *1* **Rianna Star**[35] 6796 4-9-4 **55**.................................. JasonWatson(3) 10 41
(Gary Moore) *chsd ldrs: rdn 3f out: struggling and btn 2f out: sn wknd* **10/1**

4054 **9** *10* **Performance Art (IRE)**[21] 7230 3-8-6 **46** oh1..............(p) MillyNaseb 1 17
(Seamus Mullins) *led tl 2f out: sn btn and wknd over 1f out* **50/1**

045 **10** *4* **Melanna (IRE)**[22] 7220 6-9-5 **56**.....................(p) FayeMcManoman(3) 6 20
(Richard Ford) *hld up in tch in midfield: lost pl and struggling towards rr 4f out: wknd over 2f out* **20/1**

0445 **11** *nk* **Iley Boy**[26] 7085 3-8-7 **50**.................................... SebastianWoods(3) 3 14
(John Gallagher) *midfield but nvr on terms: struggling over 3f out: bhd fnl 2f* **10/1**

0323 **12** *10* **Ravenswood**[24] 7152 4-9-6 **54**...............................(p) WilliamCox 13
(Patrick Chamings) *s.i.s and nvr gng wl in rr: t.o fnl 2f* **6/1**[3]

0-00 **13** 1 ¼ **Maysonri**[22] 7210 3-8-9 **49** oh1 ow3.................................(p) FinleyMarsh 7
(Mark Hoad) *sn up to chse ldrs: rdn and lost pl over 3f out: t.o and eased ins fnl f* **50/1**

2m 38.09s (5.39) **Going Correction** +0.375s/f (Good)
**WFA** 3 from 4yo+ 6lb **13** Ran SP% **125.7**
Speed ratings (Par 101): **97,96,96,90,90 88,88,87,80,78 78,71,70**
CSF £40.32 CT £267.49 TOTE £5.50: £2.10, £2.70, £2.70; EX 43.50 Trifecta £301.40.
**Owner** The Skills People Group Ltd **Bred** Trinity Park Stud **Trained** Newmarket, Suffolk

**FOCUS**
Distance increased by 7yds. A lowly handicap, three in-form runners came clear and the form isn't bad for the level. The winner just confirmed C&D form with the second.
T/Plt: £10,067.00 to a £1 stake. Pool: £71,020.69 - 5.15 winning units. T/Qpdt: £1,673.00 to a £1 stake. Pool: £7,008.89 - 3.10 winning units. **Steve Payne**

# 7383 CATTERICK (L-H)
## Tuesday, October 10

**OFFICIAL GOING: Good to soft (7.2)**
Wind: Moderate behind Weather: Cloudy

## 7919 EBF NOVICE STKS 5f
**1:30** (1:34) (Class 5) 2-Y-O **£2,911** (£866; £432; £216) **Stalls** Low

Form RPR
4 **1** **Fool For You (IRE)**[30] 6969 2-8-11 0................................ PJMcDonald 6 75
(Richard Fahey) *dwlt: sn trcking ldrs: cl up 1/2-way: chal wl over 1f out: rdn to ld ent fnl f: kpt on wl* **7/2**[2]

20 **2** 1 ½ **Paco Escostar**[20] 7269 2-8-11 0.......................................... CamHardie 3 70
(Paul Midgley) *hld up: hdwy over 2f out: chsd ldrs over 1f out: rdn ins fnl f: kpt on* **20/1**

6100 **3** ¾ **Wirral Girl (IRE)**[38] 6678 2-9-4 75..................................... PaulHanagan 4 74
(Richard Fahey) *led: rdn along and jnd wl over 1f out: drvn and hdd ent fnl f: kpt on same pce* **11/1**

1300 **4** 1 ½ **Gift In Time (IRE)**[19] 7318 2-9-9 80.................................(b[1]) JoeDoyle 1 74
(James Given) *trckd ldrs on inner: effrt over 1f out: rdn and n.m.r ins fnl f: swtchd rt and kpt on same pce* **11/4**[1]

4034 **5** ¾ **Charnock Richard**[6] 7731 2-9-2 80.................................(v[1]) TomEaves 8 64
(David Brown) *cl up: rdn along over 2f out: wknd over 1f out* **13/2**[3]

40 **6** nk **Swiss Chocolate (IRE)**[21] 7238 2-8-11 0........................... BenCurtis 10 58+
(William Haggas) *towards rr: styd on appr fnl f* **14/1**

2332 **7** 1 ¼ **Palmer (IRE)**[20] 7269 2-9-2 74........................................... GrahamLee 9 58
(Bryan Smart) *v keen to post: prom on outer: pushed along 1/2-way: rdn along wl over 1f out: sn wknd* **7/2**[2]

1504 **8** 2 ¼ **Society's Dream (IRE)**[13] 7518 2-8-11 51......................... JoeyHaynes 5 51
(K R Burke) *towards rr: rdn along 1/2-way: n.d* **16/1**

0060 **9** 10 **Sir Walter (IRE)**[13] 7518 2-9-2 47....................................(bt[1]) JasonHart 7 14
(Eric Alston) *a in rr* **100/1**

1m 1.37s (1.57) **Going Correction** +0.325s/f (Good) **9** Ran SP% **111.1**
Speed ratings (Par 95): **100,97,96,94,92 92,90,86,70**
CSF £65.29 TOTE £4.20: £1.70, £4.80, £3.10; EX 78.40 Trifecta £896.60.
**Owner** John Dance **Bred** Serdal Adali **Trained** Musley Bank, N Yorks

**FOCUS**
There was 2mm of rain overnight and the going was given as good to soft (GoingStick: 7.2). A fairly ordinary novice in which the third sets the level.

## 7920 ALL NEW RACINGUK.COM NURSERY H'CAP 5f 212y
**2:00** (2:00) (Class 6) (0-65,65) 2-Y-O **£2,587** (£770; £384; £192) **Stalls** Low

Form RPR
443 **1** **Fortunate Vision**[50] 6262 2-9-6 **64**.................................(v[1]) TomEaves 4 68
(David Brown) *towards rr: hdwy over 2f out: rdn over 1f out: chsd ldng pair ins fnl f: drvn and styd on wl to ld nr fin* **14/1**

0 **2** ¾ **Zizum**[21] 7250 2-9-5 **63**..........................................(t) SilvestreDeSousa 10 65
(George Scott) *cl up: led over 2f out: sn rdn: drvn ins fnl f: hdd and no ex towards fin* **7/2**[1]

054 **3** 1 ½ **Gorse (IRE)**[36] 6755 2-9-5 **63**........................................ FrannyNorton 2 60
(Ann Duffield) *cl up on inner: effrt 2f out and ev ch tl drvn ent fnl f and kpt on same pce towards fin* **8/1**

006 **4** 1 ½ **Forest Dragon**[46] 6386 2-9-3 **61**.............................(p[1]) JosephineGordon 1 54+
(Hugo Palmer) *in tch on inner: n.m.r and lost pl 1/2-way: effrt and n.m.r over 2f out: swtchd rt to outer over 1f out: sn rdn and styd on wl fnl f* **10/1**

5240 **5** 1 ¼ **Llamrei**[40] 6634 2-8-11 **55**................................................ JasonHart 3 44
(Jo Hughes) *chsd ldrs on inner: rdn along over 2f out: drvn wl over 1f out: kpt on same pce* **12/1**

0005 **6** ½ **El Bertie (IRE)**[18] 7363 2-8-13 **57**................................ DuranFentiman 11 44
(Tim Easterby) *towards rr: rdn along over 2f out: styd on u.p appr fnl f* **18/1**

4644 **7** nk **Poppy Walton (IRE)**[44] 6465 2-9-7 **65**............................ AndrewMullen 9 51
(Ollie Pears) *chsd ldrs: rdn along 2f out: drvn over 1f out: wknd appr fnl f* **16/1**

1430 **8** hd **W G Grace (IRE)**[6] 7734 2-9-7 **65**................................... PJMcDonald 6 51
(Mark Johnston) *towards rr: rdn along wl over 2f out: sme late hdwy* **5/1**[2]

3536 **9** 2 ¼ **Sienna Says**[40] 6634 2-8-13 **64**................................ JamieGormley[(7)] 5 43
(Tony Carroll) *led: rdn along and hdd over 2f out: sn drvn and wknd wl over 1f out* **15/2**[3]

450 **10** 1 **Ben My Chree**[70] 5494 2-9-4 **62**........................................ GrahamLee 8 40
(Bryan Smart) *in tch: rdn along over 2f out: hld whn hmpd 1 1/2f out* **66/1**

3650 **11** ¾ **Duke Of Freedom**[18] 7362 2-9-3 **61**...............................(b[1]) BenCurtis 12 35
(Ann Duffield) *chsd ldrs on outer: rdn along 3f out: sn wknd* **16/1**

040 **12** 15 **Peter Leonard**[88] 4862 2-8-13 **57**..............................(b[1]) PaulHanagan 7
(Richard Fahey) *squeezed out and hmpd shortly after s: a in rr* **8/1**

1m 16.22s (2.62) **Going Correction** +0.325s/f (Good) **12** Ran SP% **114.8**
Speed ratings (Par 93): **95,94,92,90,88 87,87,87,84,82 81,61**
CSF £60.53 CT £433.79 TOTE £11.20: £4.10, £1.40, £2.80; EX 79.90 Trifecta £621.70.
**Owner** New Vision Bloodstock **Bred** Rosyground Stud **Trained** Averham Park, Notts

**FOCUS**
Race distance increased by 6yds. A modest nursery in which the first four had all had the minimum three runs.

## 7921 BET AT RACINGUK.COM NURSERY H'CAP 7f 6y
**2:35** (2:35) (Class 3) (0-95,93) 2-Y-O **£7,470** (£2,236; £1,118; £559; £279) **Stalls** Low

Form RPR
5521 **1** **El Chapo**[17] 7384 2-8-3 **75**................................................ PaulHanagan 5 79
(Richard Fahey) *hld up: hdwy over 2f out: rdn to chal jst over 1f out: drvn and edgd lft ins fnl f: styd on to ld last 50yds* **9/4**[1]

0314 **2** ½ **Che Bella (IRE)**[12] 7552 2-8-8 **80**................................ ConnorBeasley 4 83
(Keith Dalgleish) *trckd ldng pair: hdwy to ld wl over 1f out and sn rdn: drvn ent fnl f: n.m.r and hdd last 60yds: kpt on* **4/1**[3]

3303 **3** 1 ¼ **Star Of Zaam (IRE)**[17] 7384 2-8-3 **75**...........................(p) JoeyHaynes 2 75
(K R Burke) *chsd ldrs: rdn along 2f out: drvn ent fnl f: kpt on* **6/1**

2522 **4** 1 ¼ **Poet's Dawn**[10] 7624 2-8-5 **80**................................ RachelRichardson[(3)] 3 76
(Tim Easterby) *sn led: rdn along and hdd wl over 1f out: drvn and wknd fnl f* **7/2**[2]

053 **5** 8 **Ventura Knight (IRE)**[24] 7148 2-9-7 **93**................... SilvestreDeSousa 1 68
(Mark Johnston) *towards rr and sn pushed along: rdn along 1/2-way: sn outpcd and bhd* **7/2**[2]

1m 28.15s (1.15) **Going Correction** +0.325s/f (Good) **5** Ran SP% **109.5**
Speed ratings (Par 99): **106,105,104,102,93**
CSF £11.23 TOTE £2.50: £1.20, £2.40; EX 10.50 Trifecta £46.70.
**Owner** Merchant And Missionaries And Partner **Bred** Tibthorpe Stud **Trained** Musley Bank, N Yorks

**FOCUS**
Race distance increased by 6yds. Not a bad nursery. Richard Fahey has dominated this race in recent years, and he sent out the winner once again, for the sixth time in ten years. The winner reversed Thirsk form with the second.

## 7922 SKYRAM H'CAP 1m 7f 189y
**3:05** (3:07) (Class 6) (0-60,60) 3-Y-O+ **£2,587** (£770; £384; £192) **Stalls** Low

Form RPR
2423 **1** **General Allenby**[21] 7233 3-8-8 **51**................................(be) KierenFox 8 58
(Henry Tett) *hld up in midfield: stdy hdwy 4f out: rdn to chse ldr ent fnl f: led last 100yds* **2/1**[1]

0202 **2** ¾ **In Focus (IRE)**[27] 7047 6-8-13 **54**...........................(h) JamieGormley[(7)] 5 58
(Dianne Sayer) *led: clr and rdn along 2f out: drvn and jnd ent fnl f: hdd and no ex last 100yds* **7/1**[3]

6410 **3** ¾ **Adrakhan (FR)**[18] 7360 6-8-11 **48**................................ SammyJoBell[(3)] 3 51
(Wilf Storey) *hld up: hdwy 1/2-way: chsd ldrs 2f out: rdn over 1f out: drvn and kpt on fnl f* **17/2**

0166 **4** 4 **Adherence**[35] 6788 4-9-7 **55**...........................................(p) BarryMcHugh 7 53
(Tony Coyle) *in rr: hdwy over 4f out: rdn to chse ldrs 2f out: sn drvn and no imp fnl f* **18/1**

26-0 **5** ½ **Allfredandnobell (IRE)**[18] 7360 4-9-0 **48**................ SilvestreDeSousa 2 46
(Micky Hammond) *trckd ldrs: hdwy over 4f out: chsd ldr 3f out: rdn along 2f out: sn drvn and grad wknd appr fnl f* **11/1**

5024 **6** 1 ¼ **Jan Smuts (IRE)**[32] 6898 9-9-0 **55**.......................(tp) ConnorMurtagh[(7)] 6 51
(Wilf Storey) *hld up: hdwy 4f out: rdn along 3f out: kpt on fnl 2f: n.d* **10/1**

0433 **7** 10 **La Bacouetteuse (FR)**[7] 7700 12-9-7 **55**...................(b) AndrewMullen 4 39
(Iain Jardine) *dwlt: a in rr* **33/1**

0063 **8** 1 ¾ **Patent**[21] 7248 4-8-12 **46**..............................................(b) JasonHart 10 28
(Peter Niven) *a in rr* **15/2**

-000 **9** 15 **Oracle Boy**[43] 6530 6-8-12 **46** oh1...............................(bt[1]) GrahamLee 12 10
(Michael Chapman) *prom: rdn along 6f out: sn lost pl and bhd* **150/1**

042/ **10** 3 ¾ **Anne's Valentino**[798] 4962 7-9-1 **49**................................ PaulMulrennan 9 9
(Rebecca Menzies) *chsd ldr: rdn along over 3f out: drvn over 2f out: sn wknd* **28/1**

630- **11** 99 **Becky The Thatcher**[216] 7045 4-9-10 **58**........................ PJMcDonald 1
(Micky Hammond) *in tch: pushed along on inner over 7f out: lost pl over 5f out: sn bhd and eased* **13/2**[2]

3m 38.5s (6.50) **Going Correction** +0.325s/f (Good)
**WFA** 3 from 4yo+ 9lb **11** Ran SP% **111.2**
Speed ratings (Par 101): **96,95,95,93,93 92,87,86,79,77 27**
CSF £14.52 CT £91.82 TOTE £2.80: £1.10, £2.50, £3.70; EX 20.10 Trifecta £106.70.
**Owner** David Cohen **Bred** David Cohen **Trained** Lambourn, Berks

**FOCUS**
Race distance increased by 21yds. Moderate staying form, but straightforward enough.

## 7923 GET DAILY TIPS AT RACINGUK.COM H'CAP 5f 212y
**3:35** (3:36) (Class 5) (0-75,75) 3-Y-O+ **£2,911** (£866; £432; £216) **Stalls** Low

Form RPR
4131 **1** **Short Work**[21] 7245 4-9-7 **75**.........................................(b) DanielTudhope 4 85
(David O'Meara) *prom: wd st to centre: rdn to ld wl over 1f out: kpt on wl u.p fnl f* **7/4**[1]

1243 **2** 1 ¾ **Liberatum**[17] 7408 3-8-11 **73**................................ JamieGormley[(7)] 8 77+
(Ruth Carr) *towards rr: hdwy 2f out: rdn over 1f out: styd on wl fnl f* **11/1**

4000 **3** nk **Apricot Sky**[9] 7657 7-9-6 **74**....................................(p) PaulMulrennan 2 77
(Michael Dods) *led: rdn along and styd on far rail st: hdd wl over 1f out: sn drvn and kpt on fnl f* **33/1**

0153 **4** nk **Geoff Potts (IRE)**[21] 7244 4-9-2 **70**................................ PaulHanagan 7 72
(Richard Fahey) *trckd ldrs on inner: hdwy over 2f out: rdn wl over 1f out: drvn and kpt on same pce fnl f* **3/1**[2]

3500 **5** 1 ¾ **Vallarta (IRE)**[11] 7572 7-9-4 **72**........................................ JackGarritty 10 68
(Ruth Carr) *chsd ldrs: wd st to centre: rdn wl over 1f out: drvn and kpt on same pce fnl f* **16/1**

6050 **6** shd **Love Oasis**[12] 7554 3-9-3 **72**........................................... PJMcDonald 3 68
(Mark Johnston) *prom: rdn along and ev ch 2f out: drvn over 1f out: grad wknd* **25/1**

1600 **7** ½ **Cosmic Chatter**[21] 7244 7-9-7 **75**..................................(p) KevinStott 5 70
(Ruth Carr) *hmpd s and bhd: styd on fnl 2f* **15/2**[3]

0105 **8** 1 ¾ **Suitcase 'N' Taxi**[12] 7553 3-9-2 **74**.................... RachelRichardson[(3)] 12 63
(Tim Easterby) *in tch on outer: rdn along over 2f out: sn drvn and no imp* **25/1**

3066 **9** 1 ¾ **Gilmer (IRE)**[22] 7223 6-9-0 **75**................................ DanielleMooney[(7)] 1 58
(James Ewart) *a towards rr* **14/1**

5003 **10** 1 ¼ **Seamster**[8] 7691 10-8-12 **73**..................................(t) LauraCoughlan[(7)] 6 52
(David Loughnane) *nvr bttr than midfield* **20/1**

5200 **11** 5 **Berlios (IRE)**[12] 7557 4-9-3 **71**........................................ PhillipMakin 9 34
(Rebecca Bastiman) *a towards rr* **50/1**

415 **U** **Fujin**[23] 7192 6-9-7 **75**...................................................(v) TomEaves 11
(Shaun Harris) *sprawled bdly: wnt bdly rt s and uns rdr* **40/1**

1m 14.6s (1.00) **Going Correction** +0.325s/f (Good)
**WFA** 3 from 4yo+ 1lb **12** Ran SP% **113.8**
Speed ratings (Par 103): **106,103,103,102,100 100,99,97,95,93 86,**
CSF £19.11 CT £470.39 TOTE £2.60: £1.10, £3.60, £10.50; EX 20.70 Trifecta £935.60.
**Owner** N D Crummack Ltd & Arthur Rhodes **Bred** Downfield Cottage Stud **Trained** Upper Helmsley, N Yorks

**FOCUS**
Race distance increased by 6yds. The winner and third had this between them from the turn in, with the winner rated back to his 3yo form.

## 7924 WISE BETTING AT RACINGUK.COM H'CAP (DIV I) — 1m 4f 13y
4:10 (4:10) (Class 5) (0-75,76) 3-Y-O+ — £2,911 (£866; £432; £216) Stalls Centre

Form — RPR
6006 1 — **Riviere Argentee (FR)**[28] 7019 3-8-6 61 oh1 .....(v) JoeyHaynes 5 — 70
(K R Burke) *trckd ldrs: smooth hdwy 3f out: cl up 2f out: rdn to ld ent fnl f: styd on wl* — 25/1

5254 2 2 1/4 **Sellingallthetime (IRE)**[17] 7387 6-9-6 69 .....(p) BenCurtis 6 — 74
(Michael Appleby) *trckd ldrs: hdwy to ld 3f out: jnd 2f out and sn rdn along: hdd and drvn ent fnl f: kpt on same pce* — 4/1[2]

2154 3 1/2 **The New Pharaoh (IRE)**[28] 7024 6-9-12 75 ..... PaulMulrennan 10 — 79
(Chris Wall) *hld up and bhd: hdwy 3f out: chsd ldrs wl over 1f out: sn rdn: kpt on fnl f: nrst fin* — 4/1[2]

0542 4 1 **First Quest (USA)**[17] 7386 3-9-4 73 .....(bt) SilvestreDeSousa 9 — 76
(Ed Dunlop) *t.k.h: hld up towards rr: effrt and hdwy over 2f out: rdn to chse ldrs and hung bdly lft to inner rail over 1f out: drvn and kpt on fnl f* — 7/4[1]

120 5 1 1/4 **Clenymistra (IRE)**[11] 7568 3-8-12 67 ..... PhillipMakin 7 — 68
(David O'Meara) *hld up: hdwy 4f out: chsd ldrs 3f out: rdn 2f out and ev ch tl drvn appr fnl f and grad wknd* — 8/1[3]

020- 6 9 **Only Orsenfoolsies**[248] 7321 8-9-7 70 ..... FrannyNorton 1 — 56
(Micky Hammond) *in tch: pushed along on inner 4f out: sn rdn and outpcd 3f out* — 12/1

006 7 1 **Up Ten Down Two (IRE)**[17] 7386 8-8-13 65 ..... RachelRichardson(3) 8 — 50
(Michael Easterby) *trckd ldr: pushed along over 3f out: rdn along over 2f out: sn wknd* — 66/1

0406 8 13 **Toboggan's Fire**[22] 7225 4-9-9 72 ..... ShaneGray 2 — 36
(Ann Duffield) *trckd ldng pair: rdn along over 3f out: sn wknd* — 16/1

-363 9 6 **Burning Heat (IRE)**[90] 4762 4-9-6 69 .....(v[1]) TomEaves 4 — 23
(Mohamed Moubarak) *awkward s: sn led: rdn along and hdd 3f out: sn wknd* — 18/1

2m 41.97s (3.07) **Going Correction** +0.325s/f (Good)
**WFA** 3 from 4yo+ 6lb — 9 Ran SP% 111.7
Speed ratings (Par 103): **102,100,100,99,98 92,92,83,79**
CSF £117.25 CT £488.16 TOTE £22.60: £4.40, £1.40, £1.80; EX 158.70 Trifecta £575.60.
**Owner** Global Racing Club & Mrs E Burke **Bred** San Gabriel Inv Inc & R Geringer **Trained** Middleham Moor, N Yorks

**FOCUS**
Race distance increased by 18yds. The faster of the two divisions by 1.20sec, and the winner did it cosily. The runner-up is a fair guide.

## 7925 WISE BETTING AT RACINGUK.COM H'CAP (DIV II) — 1m 4f 13y
4:40 (4:42) (Class 5) (0-75,77) 3-Y-O+ — £2,911 (£866; £432; £216) Stalls Centre

Form — RPR
2400 1 — **All My Love (IRE)**[28] 7024 5-9-9 74 ..... SammyJoBell(3) 5 — 85
(Pam Sly) *hld up in tch: smooth hdwy 3f out: cl up 2f out: rdn to ld ent fnl f: sn clr and kpt on strly* — 17/2

3310 2 4 1/2 **Desert Cross**[19] 7336 4-9-5 67 ..... JoeFanning 4 — 71
(Jonjo O'Neill) *trckd ldrs: hdwy over 3f out: cl up over 2f out: rdn and ev ch over 1f out: kpt on same pce fnl f* — 6/1

4310 3 1 1/4 **Crushed (IRE)**[18] 7358 3-9-8 76 ..... BenCurtis 6 — 79
(William Haggas) *t.k.h early: trckd ldr: hdwy over 3f out: cl up 2f out: sn rdn and ev ch tl drvn ent fnl f and kpt on same pce* — 5/2[1]

0201 4 nk **Fire Leopard**[13] 7524 3-9-9 77 .....(h) DanielTudhope 3 — 79
(David O'Meara) *hld up: gd hdwy on outer over 3f out: chsd ldrs over 2f out: rdn and edgd lft over 1f out: sn drvn and kpt on same pce* — 3/1[2]

3101 5 1 1/2 **Percys Princess**[50] 6270 6-9-4 71 ..... JaneElliott(5) 7 — 70
(Michael Appleby) *trckd ldr: hdwy 3f out: cl up over 2f out: rdn to ld narrowly wl over 1f out: drvn and hdd ent fnl f: grad wknd* — 20/1

0054 6 1 **Modernism**[33] 6858 8-9-7 69 .....(b[1]) SilvestreDeSousa 1 — 66
(Ian Williams) *led: rdn along 3f out: hdd wl over 1f out: sn drvn and grad wknd* — 5/1[3]

-006 7 3 3/4 **The Resdev Way**[55] 6061 4-9-3 65 ..... PaulMulrennan 8 — 56
(Philip Kirby) *a towards rr* — 66/1

5655 8 7 **Auxiliary**[11] 7567 4-9-4 66 .....(p) AndrewMullen 2 — 46
(Patrick Holmes) *a towards rr* — 28/1

6224 9 8 **Correggio**[50] 6269 7-8-12 60 ..... FrannyNorton 9 — 27
(Micky Hammond) *trckd ldrs: pushed along 4f out: rdn over 3f out: sn wknd* — 16/1

2m 43.17s (4.27) **Going Correction** +0.325s/f (Good)
**WFA** 3 from 4yo+ 6lb — 9 Ran SP% 110.6
Speed ratings (Par 103): **98,95,94,93,92 92,89,85,79**
CSF £54.38 CT £157.40 TOTE £10.10: £2.90, £2.40, £1.10; EX 61.80 Trifecta £218.70.
**Owner** David L Bayliss **Bred** Irish National Stud **Trained** Thorney, Cambs

**FOCUS**
Race distance increased by 18yds. Another easy winner, but this was the slower of the two divisions. The winner is rated to his best, taking into account the rider's claim.

## 7926 RACING AGAIN SATURDAY 21ST OCTOBER AMATEUR RIDERS' H'CAP — 5f
5:10 (5:13) (Class 6) (0-55,55) 3-Y-O+ — £2,183 (£677; £338; £169) Stalls Low

Form — RPR
0240 1 — **Mr Enthusiastic**[41] 6596 3-10-0 46 oh1 ..... MissKLAdams(5) 6 — 53
(Noel Wilson) *trckd ldng pair: hdwy to chse ldr wl over 1f out: rdn and styd on ins fnl f to ld last 50yds* — 28/1

0013 2 1/2 **Lady Joanna Vassa (IRE)**[8] 7692 4-10-5 46 .....(v) MissJoannaMason 9 — 50
(Richard Guest) *cl up: led over 2f out: rdn and hung bdly lft to far rail over 1f out: hdd and no ex last 50yds* — 7/2[1]

5400 3 nk **Imperial Legend (IRE)**[3] 7825 8-10-11 55 ..... MissAMcCain(3) 12 — 58
(Alan Brown) *dwlt and swtchd lft towards inner: in rr: hdwy 2f out: rdn over 1f out: styd on wl fnl f* — 9/2[2]

5560 4 3/4 **Mitchum**[18] 7366 8-10-6 47 .....(p) MissBeckySmith 2 — 47
(Ron Barr) *chsd ldrs: rdn wl over 1f out: kpt on u.p fnl f* — 8/1[3]

255 5 1 3/4 **Minty Jones**[74] 5360 8-10-0 46 .....(v) MrLewisStones(5) 11 — 40
(Michael Mullineaux) *chsd ldrs: rdn wl over 1f out: kpt on same pce fnl f* — 12/1

0050 6 nk **Vecheka (IRE)**[9] 7660 6-9-13 47 ..... MrKYeoman(7) 5 — 40
(Kenny Johnson) *chsd ldrs: rdn along wl over 1f out: kpt on same pce* — 33/1

00-0 7 hd **Miss Mayson**[95] 4559 3-11-0 55 ..... MissETodd 3 — 48
(Karen Tutty) *chsd ldrs: rdn over 1f out: wknd fnl f* — 66/1

2033 8 1 **Red Forever**[24] 7164 6-10-2 46 .....(h) MissHelenCuthbert(3) 13 — 35+
(Thomas Cuthbert) *dwlt: a towards rr* — 11/1

0530 9 hd **La Haule Lady**[18] 7366 3-10-6 47 ..... MrSWalker 7 — 36
(Paul Midgley) *a towards rr* — 10/1

63 10 nk **Captain Scooby**[8] 7693 11-9-13 47 oh1 ow1 .....(b) MrSASmith(7) 15 — 34
(Richard Guest) *dwlt: a towards rr* — 16/1

1400 11 nk **Whipphound**[22] 7218 9-10-5 51 .....(b) MissEmilyBullock(5) 1 — 37
(Ruth Carr) *a towards rr* — 8/1[3]

5006 12 nk **Permanent**[42] 6560 3-10-11 52 ..... MissCWalton 10 — 38
(Eric Alston) *a towards rr* — 16/1

0002 13 1 3/4 **Men United (FR)**[43] 6531 4-10-0 46 .....(b) MissJCooley(5) 4 — 24
(Roy Bowring) *led: rdn along and hdd over 2f out: sltly hmpd over 1f out: sn wknd* — 12/1

6005 14 3 1/2 **Roy's Legacy**[17] 7407 8-10-10 51 ..... MrsCBartley 8 — 17
(Shaun Harris) *chsd ldrs: rdn along 1/2-way: grad wknd* — 18/1

1m 2.97s (3.17) **Going Correction** +0.325s/f (Good) — 14 Ran SP% 120.3
Speed ratings (Par 101): **87,86,85,84,81 81,80,79,79,78 78,77,74,69**
CSF £122.85 CT £561.91 TOTE £45.00: £11.60, £1.60, £1.70; EX 261.30 Trifecta £1091.00.
**Owner** Ian & Debbie Paver **Bred** P Balding **Trained** Marwood, Co Durham

**FOCUS**
The race developed towards the far side and few got seriously involved, the first two racing in the first three throughout. Pretty weak sprinting form, but straightforward enough. The pace held up.
T/Plt: £98.00 to a £1 stake. Pool: £51,555.30 - 383.95 winning units T/Qpdt: £12.40 to a £1 stake. Pool: £4,570.26 - 271.48 winning units **Joe Rowntree**

# 7458 LEICESTER (R-H)
Tuesday, October 10

**OFFICIAL GOING: Soft (4.9)**
Wind: Fresh half behind Weather: Overcast

## 7927 BROCK HILL BADGER H'CAP — 1m 3f 179y
1:50 (1:53) (Class 4) (0-85,86) 3-Y-O — £6,469 (£1,925; £962; £481) Stalls Low

Form — RPR
-211 1 — **Just In Time**[27] 7063 3-8-10 73 ..... MartinDwyer 6 — 85+
(Alan King) *hld up: pushed along over 4f out: hdwy over 2f out: led over 1f out: sn rdn: styd on gamely* — 5/4[1]

60 2 nk **Reshoun (FR)**[45] 6427 3-9-3 80 ..... FranBerry 7 — 91
(Ian Williams) *hld up: hdwy 2f out: chsd wnr over 1f out: sn rdn and ev ch: edgd rt ins fnl f: styd on* — 6/1

5006 3 7 **Aardwolf (USA)**[21] 7234 3-9-9 86 ..... JamesDoyle 3 — 86
(Mark Johnston) *led: rdn and hdd over 1f out: wknd ins fnl f* — 16/1

3251 4 3/4 **Fibonacci**[33] 6852 3-9-7 84 ..... AndreaAtzeni 4 — 83
(Hugo Palmer) *prom: rdn over 2f out: wknd fnl f* — 4/1[2]

6362 5 5 **Sporting Times**[13] 7515 3-9-5 82 ..... JimCrowley 5 — 73
(Ed Dunlop) *sn pushed along and prom: chsd ldr over 6f out: rdn over 3f out: wknd over 1f out* — 5/1[3]

6104 6 6 **Lightly Squeeze**[20] 7277 3-9-0 77 .....(p) KieranShoemark 2 — 58
(Philip Hide) *s.i.s: hld up: racd keenly: rdn over 2f out: wknd wl over 1f out* — 16/1

2516 7 3/4 **American History (USA)**[27] 7063 3-8-9 72 .....(p) RobHornby 1 — 52
(William Muir) *chsd ldr over 5f: remained handy: rdn over 3f out: wknd wl over 1f out* — 25/1

2m 37.99s (4.09) **Going Correction** +0.45s/f (Yiel) — 7 Ran SP% 111.0
Speed ratings (Par 103): **104,103,99,98,95 91,90**
CSF £8.66 TOTE £1.90: £1.40, £3.90; EX 9.60 Trifecta £71.20.
**Owner** HP Racing Just In Time **Bred** Overbury Stallions Ltd And D Boocock **Trained** Barbury Castle, Wilts

**FOCUS**
There was a false rail from the top of the hill on the back straight all the way to the winning line, thus increasing all distances on the round course by approx 9yds. This was a fair opening handicap for 3yos. It was run at a brisk early pace and the first pair came well clear. The winner continues on the upgrade.

## 7928 STOAT (S) STKS — 1m 2f
2:20 (2:20) (Class 6) 3-Y-O — £2,587 (£770; £384; £192) Stalls Low

Form — RPR
0003 1 — **Rita's Man (IRE)**[3] 7820 3-9-6 67 ..... KieranO'Neill 7 — 67+
(Richard Hannon) *mde all: set stdy pce tl qcknd over 3f out: rdn over 1f out: edgd lft ins fnl f: jst hld on* — 4/5[1]

-066 2 hd **Four Kingdoms (IRE)**[31] 6946 3-8-12 47 ..... JimCrowley 4 — 59
(K R Burke) *hld up: pushed along over 3f out: hdwy over 2f out: rdn to chse wnr ins fnl f: styd on* — 7/1[3]

0500 3 2 **Traveltalk (IRE)**[15] 7459 3-8-7 56 ..... BenRobinson(5) 5 — 55
(Brian Ellison) *sn prom: chsd wnr 8f out: rdn over 2f out: lost 2nd ins fnl f: styd on same pce* — 7/1[3]

0556 4 1 1/2 **Jet Setter (IRE)**[15] 7459 3-9-2 59 ..... GeorgeDowning 3 — 56
(Tony Carroll) *hld up: hdwy u.p over 1f out: no imp ins fnl f* — 9/2[2]

5540 5 3 1/4 **Hidden Stash**[19] 7325 3-8-7 49 ..... ManuelFernandes(5) 1 — 46
(William Stone) *chsd wnr 2f: remained handy: rdn over 3f out: wknd fnl f* — 9/1

2m 14.9s (7.00) **Going Correction** +0.45s/f (Yiel) — 5 Ran SP% 108.7
Speed ratings (Par 99): **90,89,88,87,84**
CSF £6.70 TOTE £1.50: £1.10, £2.80; EX 5.70 Trifecta £20.40.There was no bid for the winner.
**Owner** Middleham Park Racing XX **Bred** L White & D McGregor **Trained** East Everleigh, Wilts

**FOCUS**
Add 9yds to race distance. A typically weak 3yo seller, run at a steady pace. Not form to dwell on.

## 7929 TBA SMALL BREEDERS' CONDITIONS STKS (PLUS 10 RACE) (C&G) — 7f
2:55 (2:55) (Class 2) 2-Y-O
£15,562 (£4,660; £2,330; £1,165; £582; £292) Stalls High

Form — RPR
1261 1 — **Indomeneo**[10] 7624 2-9-2 84 ..... AdamMcNamara 9 — 81
(Richard Fahey) *sn w ldr: led 4f out: rdn over 1f out: styd on* — 5/2[1]

0234 2 1 **Cuban Heel**[17] 7391 2-9-0 77 .....(p[1]) JimCrowley 8 — 77
(Clive Cox) *prom: pushed along 1/2-way: rdn to chse wnr and hung rt ins fnl f: styd on* — 6/1[3]

0 3 nk **Face Like Thunder**[17] 7391 2-8-8 0 ..... RobHornby 1 — 70
(Andrew Balding) *prom: pushed along and lost pl 5f out: hdwy over 1f out: styd on* — 3/1[2]

2 4 1/2 **Glacier Fox**[79] 5180 2-8-12 0 ..... JamesSullivan 3 — 73
(Tom Tate) *s.i.s: hld up: hdwy over 1f out: styd on* — 9/1

440 5 2 3/4 **Homerton**[20] 7273 2-8-10 75 ..... KieranShoemark 4 — 64
(Robyn Brisland) *chsd ldrs: pushed along 1/2-way: rdn over 1f out: no ex fnl f* — 11/1

5 **6** *1* **Jackpot Royale**[14] 7482 2-9-0 0 MartinDwyer 2 65
(Michael Appleby) *chsd ldrs: rdn over 2f out: ev ch over 1f out: wknd wl ins fnl f* **50/1**

10 **7** *3½* **Statuario**[12] 7546 2-9-3 0 TomQueally 6 59
(Eve Johnson Houghton) *led 3f: remained w wnr: ev ch 2f out: rdn and wknd over 1f out* **7/1**

**8** *½* **Noble Expression** 2-8-12 0 AndreaAtzeni 5 53
(Roger Varian) *dwlt: outpcd* **15/2**

1m 27.5s (1.30) **Going Correction** +0.375s/f (Good) **8** Ran SP% **112.4**
Speed ratings (Par 101): **107,105,105,104,101 100,96,96**
CSF £17.28 TOTE £3.90: £1.60, £2.20, £1.20; EX 14.50 Trifecta £76.50.
**Owner** Middleham Park Racing LX **Bred** Hungerford Park Stud **Trained** Musley Bank, N Yorks

**FOCUS**
A fair 2yo conditions event. They raced down the middle and experience counted for plenty. The winner was probably just below his best in success.

## 7930 BREEDERS BACKING RACING EBF DORMOUSE MAIDEN STKS 7f
**3:25** (3:26) (Class 5) 3-Y-O+ **£4,528** (£1,347; £673; £336) **Stalls** High

Form RPR

2323 **1** **Ptarmigan Ridge**[35] 6791 3-9-5 74 DanielMuscutt 4 82+
(James Fanshawe) *trckd ldrs: led on bit over 1f out: shkn up ins fnl f: r.o: comf* **15/8**[2]

4262 **2** *1¼* **Mohsen**[21] 7229 3-9-5 73 JimCrowley 7 77
(Marcus Tregoning) *w ldr tl led 1/2-way: rdn and hdd over 1f out: styd on same pce ins fnl f* **13/8**[1]

**3** *16* **Hi Ho Silver** 3-9-5 0 TedDurcan 1 35
(Chris Wall) *s.s: hld up: hung rt over 4f out: wknd over 2f out: wnt 3rd over 1f out* **33/1**

**4** *2¾* **Divine Messenger** 3-9-5 0 MartinDwyer 3 28
(Emma Owen) *s.s: in rr: pushed along 1/2-way: wknd over 2f out* **66/1**

5 **5** *nk* **Gorham's Cave**[75] 5315 3-9-5 0 AndreaAtzeni 5 27
(Roger Varian) *led to 1/2-way: shkn up over 2f out: sn wknd* **5/2**[3]

**6** *12* **Ritas Legacy** 3-9-5 0 TrevorWhelan 6
(Roy Brotherton) *s.i.s: sn prom: pushed along and lost pl over 5f out: bhd fnl 4f: hung rt 2f out* **100/1**

1m 28.25s (2.05) **Going Correction** +0.375s/f (Good) **6** Ran SP% **106.9**
Speed ratings (Par 103): **103,101,83,80,79 66**
CSF £4.73 TOTE £2.30: £1.30, £1.50; EX 4.30 Trifecta £29.10.
**Owner** Fred Archer Racing - Energy **Bred** Widgham Stud **Trained** Newmarket, Suffolk

**FOCUS**
A modest 3yo maiden in which only the first pair mattered from 2f out. The winner improved a little on his previous form.

## 7931 SQUIRREL H'CAP 1m 3f 179y
**3:55** (3:59) (Class 2) (0-110,108) 3-Y-O+ **£16,762** (£4,715; £2,357; £1,180; £587) **Stalls** Low

Form RPR

4241 **1** **Blakeney Point**[18] 7354 4-9-2 100 (p) KieranShoemark 4 108+
(Roger Charlton) *hld up: hdwy 3f out: nt clr run 2f out: swtchd lft over 1f out: rdn to ld and edgd rt wl ins fnl f: r.o* **10/3**[2]

1-36 **2** *½* **Dance The Dream**[18] 7354 4-8-12 96 MartinDwyer 6 103
(Marcus Tregoning) *plld hrd and prom: wnt 2nd 10f out: rdn to ld over 1f out: hdd wl ins fnl f* **13/2**

4214 **3** *2¼* **My Reward**[24] 7139 5-9-2 100 JimCrowley 1 103
(Tim Easterby) *led at stdy pce: qcknd over 3f out: rdn and hdd over 1f out: no ex towards fin* **13/2**

3/2- **4** *2½* **Minotaur (IRE)**[116] 6203 5-9-5 103 FranBerry 3 102
(Jonjo O'Neill) *hld up: shkn up over 2f out: styd on to go 4th towards fin: nvr nr to chal* **25/1**

0002 **5** *nk* **Night Of Glory**[10] 7615 3-8-6 96 RobHornby 2 96
(Andrew Balding) *chsd ldrs: pushed along over 3f out: rdn over 1f out: no ex* **5/2**[1]

3105 **6** *1¾* **Soldier In Action (FR)**[24] 7139 4-9-10 108 JamesDoyle 5 104
(Mark Johnston) *chsd ldr 2f: remained handy: rdn over 3f out: sn lost pl: nt clr run wl over 2f out: n.d after* **10/1**

64-3 **7** *1* **Sumbal (IRE)**[27] 7054 5-9-8 106 AndreaAtzeni 7 100
(David Simcock) *hld up: racd keenly: hdwy 3f out: rdn and wknd over 1f out* **9/2**[3]

2m 38.28s (4.38) **Going Correction** +0.45s/f (Yiel)
**WFA** 3 from 4yo+ 6lb **7** Ran SP% **109.4**
Speed ratings (Par 109): **103,102,101,99,99 98,97**
CSF £22.66 TOTE £3.90: £1.80, £3.30; EX 25.20 Trifecta £149.40.
**Owner** Axom LX **Bred** Mr & Mrs A E Pakenham **Trained** Beckhampton, Wilts

**FOCUS**
Add 9yds to race distance.This classy handicap suited those racing handily. It's rated around the third.

## 7932 RED DEER H'CAP (DIV I) 6f
**4:30** (4:31) (Class 5) (0-70,72) 3-Y-O+ **£3,881** (£1,155; £577; £288) **Stalls** High

Form RPR

1014 **1** **Ocean Temptress**[13] 7508 3-8-13 68 (v) JackOsborn(7) 6 77
(John Ryan) *chsd ldrs: led over 2f out: rdn over 1f out: styd on* **7/1**[3]

0213 **2** *½* **Bold Spirit**[17] 7389 6-8-8 58 (t) PhilDennis(3) 12 65
(Declan Carroll) *chsd ldrs: rdn over 1f out: r.o* **12/1**

4122 **3** *1½* **The Groove**[15] 7465 4-9-1 67 ManuelFernandes(5) 1 69
(Fergal O'Brien) *prom: rdn to chse wnr and hung lft over 1f out: no ex wl ins fnl f* **13/8**[1]

6404 **4** *2½* **Mad Endeavour**[20] 7272 6-8-12 59 (b) MartinLane 3 53
(Stuart Kittow) *led over 3f: sn rdn: edgd lft over 1f out: nt clr run and no ex ins fnl f* **14/1**

1303 **5** *1¼* **Cupid's Arrow (IRE)**[28] 7017 3-9-0 62 JamesSullivan 8 52
(Ruth Carr) *wnt lft s: hld up: hdwy u.p over 1f out: nt trble ldrs* **17/2**

2110 **6** *1¾* **Dodgy Bob**[10] 7628 4-9-7 68 (v) LiamJones 4 53
(Michael Mullineaux) *prom: pushed along over 4f out: outpcd over 2f out: rallied over 1f out: wknd ins fnl f* **20/1**

3614 **7** *½* **Hindsight**[24] 7155 3-9-9 71 (h[1]) AlistairRawlinson 10 54
(Michael Appleby) *hmpd s: hld up: rdn and hung rt fr over 1f out: n.d* **16/1**

4452 **8** *shd* **Storm Melody**[23] 7195 4-9-11 72 FranBerry 11 55
(Jonjo O'Neill) *s.i.s: hld up: rdn over 2f out: nvr on terms* **6/1**[2]

1060 **9** *1½* **Joey's Destiny (IRE)**[17] 7409 7-9-11 72 DavidNolan 7 50
(Kevin Frost) *sn pushed along in rr: n.d* **20/1**

5055 **10** *2½* **Percy Toplis**[14] 7481 3-8-6 54 oh9 (p) RyanPowell 2 24
(Christine Dunnett) *prom: rdn over 2f out: wknd fnl f* **100/1**

504 **11** *3½* **Fintech (IRE)**[21] 7254 3-9-5 67 (t) AdamBeschizza 5 26
(Mrs Ilka Gansera-Leveque) *prom: pushed along 1/2-way: rdn and wknd over 1f out* **12/1**

04-0 **12** *shd* **Faulkwood**[43] 6526 3-8-10 65 (v[1]) PatrickO'Hanlon(7) 9 23
(K R Burke) *hmpd s: hld up: rdn over 2f out: wknd over 1f out* **25/1**

1m 14.92s (1.92) **Going Correction** +0.375s/f (Good)
**WFA** 3 from 4yo+ 1lb **12** Ran SP% **117.7**
Speed ratings (Par 103): **102,101,99,96,94 92,91,91,89,85 81,81**
CSF £83.01 CT £204.66 TOTE £7.40: £2.70, £3.90, £1.10; EX 91.70 Trifecta £389.50.
**Owner** The Temptations **Bred** Old Mill Stud Ltd And Oomswell Ltd **Trained** Newmarket, Suffolk
■ Stewards' Enquiry : Manuel Fernandes two-day ban: careless riding (Oct 24-25)

**FOCUS**
A modest sprint handicap. Again the middle was favoured. The first four were always prominent and the winner is rated back to form.

## 7933 RED DEER H'CAP (DIV II) 6f
**5:00** (5:00) (Class 5) (0-70,72) 3-Y-O+ **£3,881** (£1,155; £577; £288) **Stalls** High

Form RPR

4323 **1** **Rapid Ranger**[13] 7525 3-8-11 61 (h) KieranShoemark 1 70
(David O'Meara) *s.i.s: hld up: hdwy to chse ldr over 1f out: r.o u.p to ld nr fin* **3/1**[2]

0020 **2** *nk* **General Alexander (IRE)**[38] 6672 4-9-4 72 (p) BenRobinson(5) 10 80
(Brian Ellison) *w ldr tl led over 3f out: rdn over 2f out: hdd nr fin* **8/1**[3]

3452 **3** *2* **Metisian**[21] 7245 3-9-4 68 (p) DavidNolan 3 70
(Jedd O'Keeffe) *hld up: hdwy over 2f out: rdn over 1f out: styd on same pce ins fnl f* **15/8**[1]

0140 **4** *4½* **Bogsnog (IRE)**[13] 7525 7-8-8 57 JamesSullivan 4 44
(Ruth Carr) *sn led: hdd over 3f out: rdn over 1f out: hung lft and wknd ins fnl f* **8/1**[3]

4060 **5** *hd* **Borough Boy (IRE)**[6] 7738 7-9-0 63 (v) PatrickMathers 7 50
(Derek Shaw) *s.i.s: hld up: plld hrd: hdwy over 1f out: sn rdn: wknd ins fnl f* **16/1**

2425 **6** *¾* **Whitecrest**[17] 7409 9-9-7 70 WilliamCarson 5 54
(John Spearing) *prom: rdn over 2f out: wknd fnl f* **10/1**

0600 **7** *¾* **Drop Kick Murphi (IRE)**[21] 7255 3-9-3 67 RobertHavlin 2 49
(Christine Dunnett) *chsd ldrs: rdn over 1f out: wknd ins fnl f* **50/1**

5360 **8** *nk* **Commanche**[19] 7320 8-8-2 56 (b) ManuelFernandes(5) 8 37
(Chris Dwyer) *prom: lost pl 5f out: swtchd lft and pushed along over 4f out: hdwy 1/2-way: rdn over 1f out: wknd ins fnl f* **11/1**

1506 **9** *1* **Peachey Carnehan**[32] 6878 3-9-3 70 (v) PhilDennis(3) 11 48
(Michael Mullineaux) *prom: rdn over 2f out: wknd over 1f out* **16/1**

5000 **10** *12* **Secret Missile**[11] 7571 7-9-2 65 (b) MartinDwyer 9 4
(David C Griffiths) *racd alone on stands' side rail tl over 3f out: up w the pce: rdn 1/2-way: wknd 2f out: eased* **33/1**

1m 15.22s (2.22) **Going Correction** +0.375s/f (Good)
**WFA** 3 from 4yo+ 1lb **10** Ran SP% **116.1**
Speed ratings (Par 103): **100,99,96,90,90 89,88,88,86,70**
CSF £27.32 CT £57.14 TOTE £3.80: £1.40, £3.10, £1.10; EX 31.80 Trifecta £76.10.
**Owner** Kristen McEwen & Caroline Head **Bred** Clive Dennett **Trained** Upper Helmsley, N Yorks
■ Stewards' Enquiry : Kieran Shoemark two-day ban: excessive use of whip (Oct 24-25)

**FOCUS**
This second division of the 6f handicap saw the principals finish clear more towards the near side. It was 0.30secs slower than the first. The runner-up looks the best guide.

## 7934 LEVERET APPRENTICE H'CAP 7f
**5:30** (5:31) (Class 6) (0-65,67) 3-Y-O+ **£3,234** (£962; £481; £240) **Stalls** High

Form RPR

4315 **1** **Wahaab (IRE)**[26] 7083 6-9-12 67 (t) JackOsborn(5) 1 79
(Sophie Leech) *hld up: hdwy to ld over 1f out: sn rdn and edgd lft: styd on wl* **10/1**

0332 **2** *3¼* **Showdance Kid**[17] 7414 3-9-12 67 CameronNoble(3) 4 70
(Neville Bycroft) *prom: rdn and ev ch over 1f out: styd on same pce ins fnl f* **7/1**

402 **3** *1½* **Donnelly's Rainbow (IRE)**[17] 7390 4-10-3 67 BenRobinson 8 67
(Rebecca Bastiman) *mid-div: pushed along 1/2-way: r.o to go 3rd nr fin* **5/1**[3]

5022 **4** *¾* **Reinforced**[27] 7046 4-10-2 66 (tp) CallumRodriguez 15 64
(Michael Dods) *led: rdn and hdd over 2f out: styd on same pce fr over 1f out* **4/1**[1]

4315 **5** *hd* **Size Matters**[43] 6529 3-9-2 59 SeamusCronin(5) 12 56
(Mark Walford) *chsd ldrs: rdn over 2f out: styd on same pce fr over 1f out* **9/2**[2]

0250 **6** *hd* **Champagne Bob**[15] 7465 5-9-7 62 (p) GabrieleMalune(5) 3 59
(Richard Price) *w ldrs: led over 2f out: rdn and hdd over 1f out: no ex ins fnl f* **14/1**

0140 **7** *nse* **Samphire Coast**[138] 2996 4-9-9 62 (v) PatrickVaughan(3) 5 59
(Derek Shaw) *w ldrs: rdn and ev ch over 1f out: no ex ins fnl f* **40/1**

2001 **8** *nse* **Monsieur Jimmy**[43] 6528 5-9-2 55 GerO'Neill(3) 10 52
(Declan Carroll) *hld up: pushed along 1/2-way: styd on fr over 1f out: nt trble ldrs* **14/1**

3266 **9** *1¾* **Dragon Dream (IRE)**[42] 6558 3-9-7 62 RhiainIngram(3) 2 54
(Roger Ingram) *mid-div: drvn along 1/2-way: styd on fr over 1f out: nvr on terms* **20/1**

0442 **10** *½* **Joys Delight**[28] 7035 3-9-4 61 TobyEley(5) 7 52
(Daniel Mark Loughnane) *s.s: sn pushed along in rr: nvr nrr* **20/1**

5600 **11** *6* **Aqua Libre**[14] 7478 4-9-5 58 (t[1]) RossaRyan(3) 11 35
(Jennie Candlish) *prom: rdn over 2f out: sn wknd* **16/1**

0444 **12** *23* **Jacksonfire**[10] 7597 5-8-12 48 (p) MeganNicholls 13
(Michael Mullineaux) *sn pushed along and a in rr* **14/1**

0004 **13** *1¼* **Keene's Pointe**[8] 7693 7-8-12 48 oh1 (p) GeorgiaCox 9
(Steph Hollinshead) *sn pushed along and in rr fnl 4f* **25/1**

/00R **14** *43* **Dylan's Centenary**[19] 7323 6-8-9 48 oh3 (h[1]) KatherineGlenister(3) 14
(Phil McEntee) *rel to r: a wl bhd* **66/1**

1m 28.65s (2.45) **Going Correction** +0.375s/f (Good)
**WFA** 3 from 4yo+ 2lb **14** Ran SP% **119.6**
Speed ratings (Par 101): **101,97,95,94,94 94,94,94,92,91 84,58,57,7**
CSF £73.11 CT £409.15 TOTE £8.30: £3.10, £2.50, £2.40; EX 58.80 Trifecta £255.20.
**Owner** Out Of Bounds & Mike Harris Racing Club **Bred** Shadwell Estate Company Limited **Trained** Elton, Gloucs

**FOCUS**
This moderate handicap for apprentice riders looked wide open, but the winner dotted up. The form looks solid enough at this level.

T/Plt: £12.50 to a £1 stake. Pool: £50,984.59 - 2,967.25 winning units. T/Qpdt: £7.90 to a £1 stake. Pool: £3,844.35 - 359.96 winning units. **Colin Roberts**

# 7568 NEWCASTLE (A.W) (L-H)

Tuesday, October 10

**OFFICIAL GOING: Tapeta: standard**

Wind: Breezy, half against in races on straight course and in over 3f of home straight in races on the rou Weather: Dry

## 7935 LEATHERS THE ACCOUNTANTS MAIDEN STKS 1m 4f 98y (Tp)

5:25 (5:26) (Class 5) 3-Y-O+ £2,911 (£866; £432; £216) Stalls High

Form RPR

606 **1** **Magellan**[124] 3506 3-9-5 77 ........ GrahamLee 9 80+
(Roger Charlton) *hld up in tch on outside: smooth hdwy over 2f out: drvn along over 1f out: styd on wl to ld nr fin* **10/3**[2]

**2** *nk* **Darksideoftarnside (IRE)** 3-9-5 0 ........ ConnorBeasley 8 79+
(Sally Haynes) *bhd and green: sn pushed along: drvn along over 3f out: hdwy over 1f out: styd on wl to take 2nd cl home* **80/1**

6542 **3** *nse* **Nurse Nightingale**[19] 7319 3-8-7 73 ........ (h) TristanPrice(7) 4 74
(Michael Bell) *led: rdn and edgd rt wl over 1f out: edgd lft ins fnl f: kpt on: hdd nr fin* **6/1**

33 **4** *1 1/4* **Mahabba (IRE)**[81] 5124 3-9-0 0 ........ JamieSpencer 3 72
(Luca Cumani) *chsd ldr: rdn over 2f out: rallied: kpt on same pce last 100yds* **2/1**[1]

**5** *1/2* **Loud And Clear**[96] 6-9-6 0 ........ PaddyPilley(5) 2 75
(Iain Jardine) *dwlt: sn prom: effrt and cl up over 2f out: sn rdn: no ex ins fnl f* **8/1**

225 **6** *2 3/4* **Balashakh (USA)**[46] 6389 3-9-5 74 ........ (h) TonyHamilton 5 72
(David Simcock) *blkd s: hld up: effrt and rdn 2f out: wknd ins fnl f* **4/1**[3]

23 **7** *16* **Military Parade**[40] 6633 3-9-5 0 ........ JosephineGordon 1 46
(Saeed bin Suroor) *trckd ldrs: rdn over 2f out: wknd over 1f out* **8/1**

**8** *14* **Disturb**[203] 5-9-11 0 ........ NeilFarley 7 23
(Andrew Crook) *bhd and sn pushed along: drvn and effrt 3f out: wknd wl over 1f out* **100/1**

**9** *4* **Maggie The Third M** 3-9-0 0 ........ SamJames 6 12
(John Davies) *blkd s: bhd: rdn and struggling over 3f out: sn lost tch* **100/1**

2m 41.04s (-0.06) **Going Correction** +0.025s/f (Slow)
**WFA** 3 from 5yo+ 6lb **9** Ran SP% **116.1**
Speed ratings (Par 103): **101,100,100,99,99 97,87,77,75**
CSF £202.83 TOTE £6.80: £1.40, £12.10, £2.00; EX 238.80 Trifecta £475.90.
**Owner** Mrs Doreen M Swinburn **Bred** Genesis Green, Scott, Sunderland Holding **Trained** Beckhampton, Wilts

**FOCUS**

A fair middle-distance maiden. They went an initially steady gallop on standard Tapeta and finished in a bit of a heap, but the form seems sound. It's rated around the third.

## 7936 RYDER ARCHITECTURE H'CAP 1m 4f 98y (Tp)

5:55 (5:56) (Class 6) (0-65,65) 3-Y-O+ £2,264 (£673; £336; £168) Stalls High

Form RPR

3230 **1** **Good Time Ahead (IRE)**[11] 7568 3-9-1 62 ........ KevinStott 11 70
(Philip Kirby) *hld up: hdwy on outside over 2f out: rdn to ld over 1f out: kpt on wl fnl f* **9/1**

0036 **2** *1 3/4* **Restive (IRE)**[7] 7703 4-9-6 64 ........ LewisEdmunds(3) 5 68
(Iain Jardine) *hld up in midfield: effrt and hdwy over 2f out: kpt on fnl f to take 2nd cl home: nt rch wnr* **7/1**

5050 **3** *shd* **Falcon's Fire (IRE)**[9] 7659 4-9-1 61 ........ (b) RowanScott(5) 13 65
(Keith Dalgleish) *hld up: smooth hdwy over 2f out: rdn whn hung lft and ev ch briefly over 1f out: kpt on same pce ins fnl f: lost 2nd cl home* **16/1**

4014 **4** *2* **Hussar Ballad (USA)**[17] 7413 8-9-10 65 ........ CamHardie 14 66
(Antony Brittain) *hld up: rdn and hdwy on outside 2f out: kpt on ins fnl f: nt pce to chal* **12/1**

4542 **5** *1 1/2* **Champagne Pink (FR)**[21] 7235 3-8-12 62 ........ (h) CliffordLee(3) 9 61+
(K R Burke) *t.k.h: cl up: rdn to ld over 2f out: hdd over 1f out: wknd ins fnl f* **13/2**[3]

066 **6** *3 1/4* **Spin Point (IRE)**[42] 6556 5-9-8 63 ........ (b[1]) RichardKingscote 8 56+
(Ian Williams) *pressed ldr: led over 3f out to over 2f out: rallied: wknd fnl f* **5/1**[2]

0423 **7** *hd* **Steccando (IRE)**[28] 7015 4-9-1 56 ........ TonyHamilton 3 49
(Sally Haynes) *hld up in tch: effrt over 2f out: wknd fnl f* **20/1**

0301 **8** *1 1/4* **Sir Runs A Lot**[32] 6901 5-9-1 56 ........ (b) SamJames 12 47
(David Barron) *midfield: stdy hdwy over 2f out: sn rdn and hung lft: btn over 1f out* **7/2**[1]

0063 **9** *1 3/4* **Marmion**[20] 7267 5-9-10 65 ........ (h) PJMcDonald 2 53
(Les Eyre) *hld up in midfield: drvn and outpcd over 2f out: btn over 1f out* **28/1**

4054 **10** *1* **Major Rowan**[32] 6901 6-9-8 63 ........ PhillipMakin 1 50
(John Davies) *hld up: rdn and hdwy over 2f out: wknd over 1f out* **12/1**

2101 **11** *6* **Frozon**[17] 7413 4-9-3 58 ........ (h) JasonHart 10 35
(Brian Ellison) *hld up: struggling over 2f out: sn btn* **14/1**

-460 **12** *6* **Page Of Wands**[22] 7225 4-8-5 53 ........ ConnorMurtagh(7) 7 20
(George Bewley) *t.k.h: prom: rdn over 2f out: sn wknd* **80/1**

0243 **13** *51* **Kerry Icon**[43] 6523 4-8-3 51 oh4 ........ (h) JamieGormley(7) 6
(Iain Jardine) *t.k.h: led to over 3f out: wknd over 2f out: t.o* **40/1**

0050 **14** *28* **Afterburner**[36] 6767 3-9-2 63 ........ (v[1]) JosephineGordon 4
(Hugo Palmer) *trckd ldrs: drvn and outpcd over 3f out: lost tch fnl 2f: t.o* **25/1**

2m 40.35s (-0.75) **Going Correction** +0.025s/f (Slow)
**WFA** 3 from 4yo+ 6lb **14** Ran SP% **118.4**
Speed ratings (Par 101): **103,101,101,100,99 97,97,96,95,94 90,86,52,33**
CSF £65.75 CT £1003.92 TOTE £10.40: £2.90, £3.40, £5.40; EX 70.70 Trifecta £859.90.
**Owner** Greenbank, Fairhurst & Fletcher **Bred** Mrs M Dowdall Blake **Trained** East Appleton, N Yorks

**FOCUS**

A modest middle-distance handicap. They went a respectable gallop and it paid to be played late. The winner is rated to this year's best.

## 7937 LYCETTS FILLIES' NOVICE AUCTION STKS (PLUS 10 RACE) 1m 5y (Tp)

6:25 (6:28) (Class 5) 2-Y-O £2,911 (£866; £432; £216) Stalls Centre

Form RPR

5 **1** **Consolida**[17] 7403 2-9-0 0 ........ JamieSpencer 6 79+
(Luca Cumani) *hld up: swtchd rt and hdwy to ld over 1f out: pushed out fnl f: comf* **5/2**[1]

**2** *2* **Broken Wings (IRE)** 2-8-13 0 ........ ConnorBeasley 9 73+
(Keith Dalgleish) *dwlt: hld up: nt clr run over 2f out: hdwy nr side of gp and chsd wnr appr fnl f: kpt on: nt pce to chal* **25/1**

4 **3** *3 1/4* **Sassie (IRE)**[43] 6504 2-8-9 0 ........ JosephineGordon 7 61
(Sylvester Kirk) *dwlt: hld up in tch: rdn and outpcd over 1f out: rallied fnl f: nt rch first two* **12/1**

422 **4** *hd* **Vera Drake (FR)**[20] 7266 2-8-12 73 ........ TonyHamilton 8 64
(Richard Fahey) *in tch: effrt and hdwy over 2f out: outpcd appr fnl f* **11/4**[2]

6331 **5** *1 1/4* **Champarisi**[18] 7361 2-9-3 71 ........ JackGarritty 10 66
(Grant Tuer) *cl up: led over 2f out to over 1f out: rdn and outpcd fnl f* **11/4**[2]

0 **6** *shd* **She's Royal**[31] 6938 2-8-9 0 ........ GrahamLee 4 58
(Bryan Smart) *hld up: rdn and effrt over 2f out: no imp over 1f out* **25/1**

**7** *2* **Time To Perfection (IRE)** 2-9-0 0 ........ RichardKingscote 5 59
(Sylvester Kirk) *hld up in tch: drvn and outpcd 2f out: btn fnl f* **50/1**

03 **8** *5* **Havana Mariposa**[42] 6545 2-8-11 0 ........ CliffordLee(3) 3 48
(K R Burke) *t.k.h: cl up: rdn and wknd wl over 1f out* **8/1**[3]

**9** *13* **Santa Anna (IRE)** 2-8-9 0 ........ SamJames 1 14
(Mrs Caroline McCaldin, Ire) *dwlt and wnt lft s: prom on outside: rdn and lost pl over 2f out: wknd qckly* **50/1**

4 **10** *3/4* **Cheeky Kiki (IRE)**[18] 7361 2-8-10 0 ........ KevinStott 2 13
(Giles Bravery) *t.k.h: led to over 2f out: rdn and wknd wl over 1f out* **25/1**

1m 40.24s (1.64) **Going Correction** -0.025s/f (Stan) **10** Ran SP% **116.2**
Speed ratings (Par 92): **90,88,84,84,83 83,81,76,63,62**
CSF £70.83 TOTE £3.30: £1.40, £4.90, £3.10; EX 52.60 Trifecta £455.30.
**Owner** Jonathan Shack & Friends **Bred** J A Khan **Trained** Newmarket, Suffolk

**FOCUS**

An ordinary juvenile fillies' novice auction contest. They went an, at best, respectable gallop but the strong late market support for the favourite proved entirely accurate. Questionable depth to the race.

## 7938 HAY AND KILNER NURSERY H'CAP 7f 14y (Tp)

6:55 (6:56) (Class 6) (0-65,65) 2-Y-O £2,264 (£673; £336; £168) Stalls Centre

Form RPR

3440 **1** **Emerald Rocket (IRE)**[13] 7519 2-9-4 62 ........ BenCurtis 11 75+
(K R Burke) *prom on nr side of gp: hdwy to ld over 1f out: rdn and r.o wl fnl f* **9/1**

0043 **2** *3 3/4* **Admiral Spice (IRE)**[21] 7239 2-9-5 63 ........ (p) RichardKingscote 9 65
(Tom Dascombe) *cl up on nr side of gp: effrt and chsd wnr over 1f out: kpt on fnl f: nt pce to chal* **9/2**[1]

5463 **3** *2 1/2* **Contribute**[56] 6036 2-9-7 65 ........ JosephineGordon 13 60
(Martyn Meade) *led against stands' rail: rdn and hdd over 1f out: sn outpcd* **5/1**[2]

455 **4** *nk* **Firby (IRE)**[20] 7266 2-9-6 64 ........ DanielTudhope 6 58
(James Bethell) *hld up: hdwy in centre over 1f out: rdn and r.o ins fnl f: nt pce to chal* **9/2**[1]

500 **5** *hd* **Arctic Treasure (IRE)**[21] 7242 2-9-5 63 ........ PaulHanagan 5 57
(Richard Fahey) *hld up in centre: rdn over 2f out: hdwy and edgd lft over 1f out: no imp ins fnl f* **9/1**

4042 **6** *3/4* **Foxy Lady**[28] 7030 2-9-6 64 ........ TomEaves 3 56
(Kevin Ryan) *hld up towards stands' side: rdn along and hdwy over 1f out: sn no imp* **8/1**[3]

6500 **7** *2 1/4* **Stopwatch**[60] 5878 2-8-10 54 ........ (p) KevinStott 14 40
(Karen McLintock) *trckd ldrs nr stands' rail: drvn along over 2f out: wknd over 1f out* **40/1**

654 **8** *2 1/4* **Mecca's Spirit (IRE)**[62] 5801 2-9-3 61 ........ (p[1]) PaulMulrennan 7 41
(Michael Dods) *prom in centre: drvn and outpcd over 2f out: btn over 1f out* **20/1**

0060 **9** *1* **Magic Ship (IRE)**[13] 7518 2-8-12 56 ........ AndrewMullen 4 33
(Ollie Pears) *in tch on far side: rdn over 2f out: wknd over 1f out* **50/1**

0040 **10** *1 1/2* **Marsh Storm (IRE)**[21] 7239 2-8-12 56 ........ PJMcDonald 2 29
(K R Burke) *cl up on far side of gp tl rdn and wknd over 1f out* **40/1**

2334 **11** *3 3/4* **Elysee Star**[22] 7222 2-9-5 63 ........ (p[1]) GrahamLee 1 26
(Ben Haslam) *hld up on far side of gp: shkn up over 1f out: sn btn* **14/1**

005 **12** *3 1/2* **Rocket Man Dan (IRE)**[9] 7655 2-9-3 61 ........ (t) ConnorBeasley 10 18
(Keith Dalgleish) *dwlt: hld up in centre: nt clr run over 3f out to over 2f out: sn rdn: wknd over 1f out* **25/1**

3563 **13** *2 1/2* **Peace Prevails**[34] 6825 2-9-7 65 ........ (p) TonyHamilton 8 12
(Richard Fahey) *prom in centre: drvn and outpcd over 2f out: sn wknd* **20/1**

0202 **P** **Claramara (IRE)**[22] 7222 2-9-6 64 ........ SilvestreDeSousa 12
(Mark Johnston) *prom in centre: lost pl qckly over 3f out: lost tch and p.u over 1f out: b.b.v* **8/1**[3]

1m 26.8s (0.60) **Going Correction** -0.025s/f (Stan) **14** Ran SP% **122.1**
Speed ratings (Par 93): **95,90,87,87,87 86,83,81,80,78 74,70,67,**
CSF £46.17 CT £232.86 TOTE £10.60: £3.20, £2.20, £2.30; EX 51.20 Trifecta £585.30.
**Owner** Hambleton Racing Ltd III & E Burke **Bred** Elton Lodge Stud **Trained** Middleham Moor, N Yorks

**FOCUS**

A modest nursery handicap. They went a respectable gallop. The race developed towards the near rail and the first three home were drawn that side. It was all about the winner.

## 7939 ROA/RACING POST OWNERS JACKPOT H'CAP (DIV I) 5f (Tp)

7:30 (7:31) (Class 4) (0-80,80) 3-Y-O+ £4,690 (£1,395; £697; £348) Stalls Centre

Form RPR

6126 **1** **Sandra's Secret (IRE)**[19] 7329 4-8-13 77 ........ JaneElliott(5) 9 85
(Les Eyre) *led centre: rdn and hdd over 1f out: rallied to regain ld ins fnl f: carried lft: kpt on gamely* **22/1**

1040 **2** *shd* **Liquid (IRE)**[32] 6891 3-8-12 71 ........ BenCurtis 11 79
(David Barron) *hld up: gd hdwy in centre and led over 1f out: hung lft and hdd ins fnl f: rallied: hld cl home* **16/1**

2304 **3** *1* **Muatadel**[10] 7612 4-9-6 79 ........ TonyHamilton 7 82
(Roger Fell) *bhd and outpcd centre: hdwy over 1f out: kpt on ins fnl f: nrst fin* **5/1**[2]

5006 **4** *1* **Tilly Trotter (IRE)**[12] 7553 3-9-7 80 ........ TomEaves 10 80
(Declan Carroll) *in tch centre: effrt and rdn 2f out: kpt on ins fnl f: nt pce to chal* **14/1**

0054 **5** *nk* **Gamesome (FR)**[12] 7557 6-9-6 79 ........ PaulMulrennan 4 77
(Paul Midgley) *hld up in tch on far side of gp: effrt and rdn 2f out: kpt on same pce ins fnl f* **7/1**

6250 **6** *hd* **Fruit Salad**[50] 6267 4-9-2 75 ........ (p) JosephineGordon 6 73
(James Bethell) *bhd and outpcd centre: swtchd rt and hdwy fnl f: kpt on: nvr able to chal* **10/1**

3120 **7** *nk* **Suwaan (IRE)**[20] 7268 3-9-2 75 ........ JackGarritty 12 73
(Ruth Carr) *cl up on nr side of gp: effrt and rdn over 1f out: wknd ins fnl f* **6/1**[3]

0334 **8** *hd* **Twizzell**[48] 6314 3-9-5 78 ........ PJMcDonald 5 75
(K R Burke) *bhd and sn outpcd in centre: rdn 1/2-way: hdwy fnl f: no imp* **7/1**

-040 **9** *hd* **Sumner Beach**[126] 3434 3-9-7 **80** JasonHart 14 76
(Brian Ellison) *bhd and outpcd in centre: rdn and kpt on fnl f: nvr able to chal* **25/1**

210 **10** *1 ¼* **Bahango (IRE)**[176] 1836 5-8-12 **74** (p) LewisEdmunds(3) 3 65
(Patrick Morris) *hung lft thrght: bhd on far side of gp: sme hdwy over 1f out: sn no imp* **28/1**

400 **11** *2 ¼* **Crosse Fire**[12] 7557 5-8-13 **77** (p) PaddyPilley(5) 1 60
(Scott Dixon) *prom on far side of gp: sn rdn along: wknd wl over 1f out* **80/1**

2252 **12** *nk* **Noah Amor (IRE)**[14] 7486 4-8-11 **70** SilvestreDeSousa 2 51
(David O'Meara) *cl up on far side of gp tl rdn and wknd wl over 1f out* **4/1**[1]

500 **13** *¾* **First Bombardment**[54] 6089 4-8-9 **68** ShaneGray 13 47
(David O'Meara) *cl up on nr side of gp tl rdn and wknd over 1f out* **14/1**

-514 **14** *6* **Wadood (IRE)**[83] 5020 3-9-4 **77** PhillipMakin 8 35
(Robert Cowell) *midfield in centre: drvn and outpcd over 2f out: sn wknd* **25/1**

58.93s (-0.57) **Going Correction** -0.025s/f (Stan) 14 Ran SP% **121.0**
Speed ratings (Par 105): **103,102,101,99,99 98,98,98,97,95 92,91,90,80**
CSF £324.32 CT £2050.47 TOTE £16.90: £4.40, £5.90, £1.90; EX 456.70 Trifecta £4497.00.
**Owner** Sunpak Potatoes **Bred** Tally-Ho Stud **Trained** Catwick, N Yorks

**FOCUS**
The first division of a fair sprint handicap. It was a messy race with the pace spread right across the track. The first two home were drawn near side but went past the post together far side, having drifted left. A small pb from the winner.

## 7940 ROA/RACING POST OWNERS JACKPOT H'CAP (DIV II) 5f (Tp)
**8:00** (8:02) (Class 4) (0-80,80) 3-Y-O+ **£4,690** (£1,395; £697; £348) **Stalls** Centre

Form RPR

0216 **1** **Landing Night (IRE)**[24] 7137 5-9-4 **77** (tp) PJMcDonald 10 87+
(Rebecca Menzies) *hld up centre of gp: cruised through to ld appr fnl f: rdn and r.o wl fnl f* **10/1**

4563 **2** *¾* **Duke Cosimo**[11] 7572 7-8-10 **69** (p) JoeDoyle 12 75
(Michael Herrington) *hld up in centre of gp: effrt and weaved though over 1f out: rdn and kpt on fnl f: tk 2nd cl home: no ch w wnr* **9/2**[2]

1455 **3** *shd* **Musharrif**[12] 7557 5-9-6 **79** TomEaves 8 85
(Declan Carroll) *cl up in centre of gp: led on bit briefly over 1f out: sn rdn: chsd wnr tl no ex and lost 2nd nr fin* **14/1**

30-0 **4** *1* **Bondi Beach Boy**[24] 7137 8-8-10 **72** ow1 CliffordLee(3) 4 74
(Antony Brittain) *hld up on far side of gp: stdy hdwy gng wl over 2f out: rdn over 1f out: kpt on ins fnl f: nrst fin* **33/1**

450 **5** *nk* **Singeur (IRE)**[27] 7055 10-9-6 **79** PhillipMakin 7 80
(Rebecca Bastiman) *bhd centre: rdn and hdwy over 1f out: kpt on ins fnl f: nt pce to chal* **14/1**

2500 **6** *½* **Aprovado (IRE)**[31] 6943 5-9-7 **80** (p) ConnorBeasley 1 79
(Michael Dods) *cl up on far side of gp: rdn over 1f out: outpcd ins fnl f* **12/1**

1200 **7** *1 ½* **Dundunah (USA)**[38] 6669 3-9-1 **74** (t) DanielTudhope 13 69
(David O'Meara) *prom on nr side of gp: drvn along 1/2-way: outpcd over 1f out* **33/1**

1260 **7** *dht* **Scuzeme**[138] 2992 3-9-5 **78** BenCurtis 3 73
(David Barron) *hld up on far side of gp: effrt and hdwy over 1f out: no imp fnl f* **4/1**[1]

6633 **9** *¾* **Straightothepoint**[83] 5018 5-9-2 **75** GrahamLee 14 66
(Bryan Smart) *hld up on nr side of gp: rdn along 1/2-way: no imp fr over 1f out* **9/1**[3]

5533 **10** *½* **Tallinski (IRE)**[38] 6670 3-9-4 **77** SilvestreDeSousa 2 67
(Brian Ellison) *prom on far side of gp: rdn along 1/2-way: wknd over 1f out* **9/2**[2]

1065 **11** *½* **Henley**[10] 7625 5-9-7 **80** BarryMcHugh 5 67
(Tracy Waggott) *cl up in centre of gp tl rdn and wknd appr fnl f* **9/1**[3]

1040 **12** *hd* **Lady Cristal (IRE)**[91] 4717 3-8-9 **68** (p) JosephineGordon 11 56
(K R Burke) *prom on nr side of gp tl rdn and wknd over 1f out* **22/1**

0336 **13** *2 ¼* **Ancient Astronaut**[17] 7405 4-9-2 **75** (v) JasonHart 6 54
(John Quinn) *in tch centre: rdn 1/2-way: wknd over 1f out* **14/1**

4410 **14** *2* **Penny Dreadful**[27] 7055 5-8-9 **73** (p) PaddyPilley(5) 9 44
(Scott Dixon) *cl up on far side of gp tl rdn and wknd over 1f out* **33/1**

58.6s (-0.90) **Going Correction** -0.025s/f (Stan) 14 Ran SP% **126.3**
Speed ratings (Par 105): **106,104,104,103,102 101,99,99,98,97 96,96,92,89**
CSF £55.38 CT £647.19 TOTE £11.10: £4.30, £2.30, £4.00; EX 70.80 Trifecta £860.10.
**Owner** John Dance **Bred** Mrs Claire Doyle **Trained** Mordon, Durham
■ Stewards' Enquiry : P J McDonald caution: careless riding
Paddy Pilley one-day ban: weighed in overweight (Oct 24)

**FOCUS**
The second division of a fair sprint handicap. The pace was spread, but this race developed more near side, and the winner clocked the quickest comparative time on the night. The first three home were drawn high to middle. The winner looks back to his best at least.

## 7941 GEORGE F WHITE H'CAP 1m 5y (Tp)
**8:30** (8:32) (Class 4) (0-85,85) 3-Y-O+ **£4,690** (£1,395; £697; £348) **Stalls** Centre

Form RPR

4026 **1** **Prost (GER)**[17] 7404 3-9-3 **84** PaulMulrennan 1 91
(Ed Vaughan) *hld up on far side of gp: effrt and hdwy over 1f out: led ins fnl f: kpt on wl* **16/1**

**2** *1* **Waarif (IRE)**[455] 4243 4-9-1 **79** DanielTudhope 2 84
(David O'Meara) *cl up on far side of gp: effrt and chsd wnr ins fnl f: kpt on fin* **10/1**

164 **3** *nse* **Zymyran**[34] 6809 3-9-2 **83** (h) JamieSpencer 5 88+
(David Simcock) *hld up in centre: rdn and hdwy over 1f out: kpt on wl fnl f: nrst fin* **11/1**

1300 **4** *½* **Harlow**[80] 5153 3-9-3 **84** (h) JosephineGordon 10 87
(Hugo Palmer) *hld up towards nr side of gp: effrt and rdn over 1f out: kpt on fnl f: nt pce to chal* **7/1**[2]

0605 **5** *hd* **Alexandrakollontai (IRE)**[9] 7658 7-8-13 **82** (b) RowanScott(5) 9 85
(Alistair Whillans) *prom in centre: led over 2f out: edgd lft and hdd ins fnl f: sn no ex* **33/1**

4062 **6** *1 ½* **Testa Rossa (IRE)**[45] 6434 7-8-9 **80** (b) SeanMooney(7) 7 80
(Jim Goldie) *hld up: rdn and hdwy in centre over 1f out: kpt on fnl f: no imp* **25/1**

511- **7** *shd* **Tiercel**[372] 7017 4-9-6 **84** SilvestreDeSousa 12 83
(Roger Varian) *t.k.h: in tch in centre: effrt and hdwy over 1f out: wknd ins fnl f* **2/1**[1]

0666 **8** *½* **Thomas Cranmer (USA)**[21] 7229 3-9-0 **81** JoeFanning 3 79
(Mark Johnston) *cl up far side of gp: drvn and outpcd over 2f out: n.d after* **66/1**

5420 **9** *nk* **Rashford's Double (IRE)**[3] 7823 3-9-0 **81** (p) TonyHamilton 4 78
(Richard Fahey) *prom in centre: drvn and outpcd over 2f out: sn no imp* **12/1**

3010 **10** *hd* **Timeless Art (IRE)**[31] 6933 4-9-4 **85** (e) CliffordLee(3) 11 82
(K R Burke) *hld up in tch towards nr side of gp: rdn over 2f out: wknd over 1f out* **16/1**

21-0 **11** *1 ¼* **Poet's Beauty (IRE)**[21] 7246 4-9-7 **85** (p) BenCurtis 14 79
(Ismail Mohammed) *cl up on nr side of gp: led over 2f out to over 1f out: sn wknd* **25/1**

3014 **12** *1 ¼* **Auspicion**[11] 7569 5-9-0 **78** AndrewMullen 8 69
(Tom Tate) *prom in centre of gp: rdn and outpcd over 2f out: btn over 1f out* **11/1**

0334 **13** *nk* **Madroos**[53] 6158 4-8-7 **78** HarrisonShaw(7) 6 69
(Michael Easterby) *hld up in centre of gp: drvn along over 2f out: sn wknd* **22/1**

5530 **14** *2 ¾* **Omeros**[21] 7246 3-9-1 **82** JackMitchell 13 66
(Hugo Palmer) *led against stands' rail: rdn and hdd over 2f out: wknd over 1f out* **17/2**[3]

1m 39.71s (1.11) **Going Correction** -0.025s/f (Stan)
**WFA** 3 from 4yo+ 3lb 14 Ran SP% **118.0**
Speed ratings (Par 105): **93,92,91,91,91 89,89,89,88,88 87,86,85,83**
CSF £155.06 CT £1181.84 TOTE £18.30: £5.70, £2.90, £3.30; EX 254.00 Trifecta £2891.30.
**Owner** Hawkes Anzac Partnership **Bred** Lord W Huntingdon U L Norris **Trained** Newmarket, Suffolk

**FOCUS**
A decent handicap. Any draw advantage seems to switch towards the far side over further than 7f on this straight track. They went a modest gallop and the first three home were drawn low. The winner is rated back to his best.

## 7942 MY NAME'5 DODDIE FOUNDATION H'CAP 7f 14y (Tp)
**9:00** (9:04) (Class 5) (0-75,77) 3-Y-O **£2,911** (£866; £432; £216) **Stalls** Centre

Form RPR

0340 **1** **Portledge (IRE)**[11] 7571 3-9-3 **71** DanielTudhope 10 79
(James Bethell) *dwlt: hld up: hdwy over 2f out: rdn to ld appr fnl f: hld on wl cl home* **4/1**[2]

0440 **2** *hd* **Kreb's Cycle (IRE)**[46] 6387 3-9-4 **72** (p) JosephineGordon 4 79
(Ian Williams) *trckd ldrs: led over 2f out to appr fnl f: rallied: kpt on wl fin: jst hld* **5/1**[3]

21 **3** *1 ¼* **Clock Chimes**[209] 1205 3-9-6 **74** PJMcDonald 3 78
(David Brown) *trckd ldrs: effrt on far side of gp and ev ch over 2f out to over 1f out: kpt on same pce ins fnl f* **14/1**

5365 **4** *2 ½* **Zamjar**[11] 7570 3-9-8 **76** SilvestreDeSousa 12 73
(Ed Dunlop) *hld up: hdwy on nr side of gp over 2f out: rdn wl over 1f out: kpt on same pce fnl f* **15/8**[1]

0634 **5** *1 ½* **Used To Be**[42] 6562 3-8-12 **66** BenCurtis 7 59
(K R Burke) *hld up in tch: effrt and rdn nr side of gp wl over 1f out: sn one pce* **33/1**

6005 **6** *nk* **Red Gunner**[27] 7056 3-8-12 **66** PhillipMakin 6 58
(David O'Meara) *hld up in tch: effrt in centre over 2f out: no imp fr over 1f out* **12/1**

6160 **7** *½* **Alfie's Angel (IRE)**[21] 7245 3-9-6 **74** GrahamLee 8 65
(Bryan Smart) *hld up: rdn and outpcd in centre of gp over 2f out: n.d after* **20/1**

305 **8** *2* **Hemingway (IRE)**[88] 4835 3-9-9 **77** (p) TomEaves 2 63
(Kevin Ryan) *t.k.h: in tch: effrt on far side of gp over 2f out: wknd over 1f out* **18/1**

1260 **9** *2* **Miss Sheridan (IRE)**[56] 6026 3-8-9 **70** HarrisonShaw(7) 5 50
(Michael Easterby) *led in centre of gp: rdn and hdd over 2f out: wknd over 1f out* **28/1**

4005 **10** *¾* **Navarone (IRE)**[14] 7474 3-9-7 **75** (t) JackGarritty 1 53
(Richard Fahey) *cl up in centre of gp: effrt and ev ch over 2f out: sn rdn and wknd* **16/1**

3042 **11** *nse* **Champion Harbour (IRE)**[24] 7166 3-8-7 **61** PaulHanagan 11 39
(Richard Fahey) *hld up nr side of gp: drvn and outpcd over 2f out: btn over 1f out* **14/1**

1m 25.32s (-0.88) **Going Correction** -0.025s/f (Stan) 11 Ran SP% **114.8**
Speed ratings (Par 101): **104,103,102,99,97 97,96,94,92,91 91**
CSF £23.08 CT £256.15 TOTE £5.60: £2.10, £2.40, £2.60; EX 33.80 Trifecta £309.00.
**Owner** Tony Buckingham **Bred** S P Hussain **Trained** Middleham Moor, N Yorks

**FOCUS**
A fair 3yo handicap. They went a decent gallop centrally and a well-backed horse showed a likeable attitude to prevail. A small pb from the winner and the second's best form this year.
T/Jkpt: Not won. T/Plt: £2,958.50 to a £1 stake. Pool: £85,880.19 - 21.19 winning units. T/Qpdt: £123.50 to a £1 stake. Pool: £14,992.78 - 89.78 winning units. **Richard Young**

# 6962 BORDEAUX LE BOUSCAT (R-H)
Tuesday, October 10

**OFFICIAL GOING: Turf: good to soft**

## 7943a PRIX ANDRE BABOIN - GRAND PRIX DES PROVINCES (GROUP 3) (3YO+) (TURF) 1m 1f 110y
**12:25** 3-Y-O+ **£34,188** (£13,675; £10,256; £6,837; £3,418)

RPR

**1** **Zafiro (FR)**[17] 7416 5-9-3 0 Jean-BernardEyquem 4 110+
(J-C Rouget, France) *w.w in rr: pushed along to take clsr order over 2f out: rdn to chal 1f out: drvn into ld fnl 100yds* **61/10**

**2** *1* **Morando (FR)**[31] 6928 4-9-3 0 ChristopheSoumillon 2 108
(Roger Varian) *trckd ldr: pushed into ld over 1f out: drvn whn chal ins fnl f: styd on but no ex fnl 100yds* **9/10**[1]

**3** *3* **Miracle Des Aigles (FR)**[17] 7416 4-9-0 0 RonanThomas 1 99
(Mme C Barande-Barbe, France) *sn led: 5 l clr 4f out: rdn along and hdd over 2f out: sn drvn and styd on same pce fnl f* **9/2**[3]

**4** *hd* **Heaven On Earth (FR)**[34] 6-9-0 0 Roberto-CarlosMontenegro 3 99
(C Gourdain, France) *wl into stride: led early: settled in 2nd: tk clsr order 3f out: briefly led over 2f out: sn hdd and styd on same pce fnl f* **109/10**

**5** *2 ½* **Qurbaan (USA)**[38] 6717 4-9-3 0 (p) Francois-XavierBertras 5 96
(F Rohaut, France) *settled bhd ldrs: pushed along over 2f out: sn drvn and limited rspnse: no ex fnl f* **29/10**[2]

2m 4.79s 5 Ran SP% **118.9**
PARI-MUTUEL (all including 1 euro stake): WIN 7.10; PLACE 2.20, 1.40; SF 15.80.
**Owner** Ecurie Antonio Caro **Bred** Earl Haras De Nonant Le Pin & P Tholly **Trained** Pau, France

7944 - (Foreign Racing) - See Raceform Interactive

7875 **KEMPTON (A.W)** (R-H)

Wednesday, October 11

**OFFICIAL GOING: Polytrack: standard to slow**

Wind: Fresh, across (away from stands) Weather: Overcast

## 7945 CLOSE BROTHERS BUSINESS FINANCE H'CAP (DIV I) 7f (P)

**5:20** (5:21) (Class 6) (0-55,55) 3-Y-0+ **£2,587** (£770; £384; £192) **Stalls** Low

Form RPR

0062 **1** **Isntshesomething**[11] 7606 5-9-7 **55**..........(v) ConnorBeasley 2 61
(Richard Guest) *hld up in midfield: prog over 2f out: clsd on ldrs and squeezed through fnl f: rdn to ld last 100yds* **7/1**

4460 **2** ¾ **Treagus**[44] 6529 3-9-2 **52**.......... RyanTate 10 55
(Anthony Carson) *led 1f: styd prom: rdn over 2f out: kpt on fr over 1f out to chal fnl f: tk 2nd nr fin* **20/1**

5053 **3** ½ **Binky Blue (IRE)**[11] 7606 5-9-4 **52**..........(h) ShaneKelly 11 55
(Daniel Mark Loughnane) *chsd ldrs: prog 2f out: chsd ldr over 1f out: rdn to ld jst ins fnl f: hdd and no ex last 100yds* **12/1**

2052 **4** 2 **Satchville Flyer**[7] 7742 6-9-7 **55**.......... FranBerry 13 52
(David Evans) *t.k.h: hld up in rr and racd wd: rdn and prog 2f out: kpt on to take 4th fnl f: no imp ldrs after* **5/1[2]**

0630 **5** *shd* **Belgravian (FR)**[20] 7323 3-9-5 **55**..........(tp) OisinMurphy 4 51
(Archie Watson) *v awkward s and slowly away: plld hrd and hld up in last trio: prog 2f out: styd on wl fnl f and nrly snatched 4th* **3/1[1]**

0003 **6** 1¾ **Banta Bay**[6] 7763 3-9-0 **50**.......... JosephineGordon 8 41
(John Best) *nt gng wl in last after 3f: rdn over 2f out: kpt on fr over 1f out but nvr able to threaten* **8/1**

0406 **7** ½ **Never Folding (IRE)**[20] 7323 3-9-3 **53**.......... RobertWinston 5 43
(Seamus Durack) *taken down early: restless stalls: led after 6f out to 5f out: chsd ldr to over 1f out: wknd qckly* **6/1[3]**

050 **8** 1¾ **Freddy With A Y (IRE)**[44] 6528 7-9-6 **54**.......... KierenFox 14 40
(J R Jenkins) *led after 2f: kicked on 3f out: styd on inner after: hdd & wknd rapidly jst ins fnl f* **14/1**

045 **9** ½ **Thechampagnesonice**[27] 7080 4-9-6 **54**.......... SteveDrowne 9 39
(Malcolm Saunders) *hld up in midfield: shkn up and no prog over 2f out: one pce and no hdwy after* **33/1**

6000 **10** *nk* **Encapsulated**[15] 7481 7-8-12 **51**.......... RhiainIngram(5) 6 35
(Roger Ingram) *taken down early: t.k.h: trckd ldrs: effrt over 2f out: in tch over 1f out: sn wknd* **33/1**

500 **11** 3¼ **Pulsating (IRE)**[23] 7212 3-9-4 **54**..........(p[1]) LiamKeniry 3 28
(Daniel Steele) *a wl in rr: shkn up and no prog over 2f out* **25/1**

0060 **12** 4½ **Bearag**[62] 5836 3-9-4 **54**.......... DanielTudhope 1 43+
(David O'Meara) *chsd ldrs on inner: hmpd over 4f out and dropped to rr: nvr able to rcvr: eased whn no ch fnl f* **10/1**

6-00 **13** 18 **Ede's E Rider**[128] 3412 3-8-10 **51**.......... PaddyBradley(5) 12
(Pat Phelan) *dwlt: racd wd and wnt prom after 2f: wknd rapidly 3f out: t.o* **50/1**

1m 26.71s (0.71) **Going Correction** -0.125s/f (Stan)
**WFA** 3 from 4yo+ 2lb **13** Ran SP% **119.5**
Speed ratings (Par 101): **90,89,88,86,86 84,83,81,81,80 76,71,51**
CSF £145.50 CT £1707.38 TOTE £5.50: £1.80, £6.90, £3.20; EX 169.70 Trifecta £2737.40.
**Owner** Chris Penney **Bred** P Balding **Trained** Ingmanthorpe, W Yorks

**FOCUS**
Just an ordinary handicap, and quite a messy race. Typically modest form.

## 7946 32RED/BRITISH STALLION STUDS EBF NOVICE STKS 7f (P)

**5:55** (5:58) (Class 5) 2-Y-0 **£3,234** (£962; £481; £240) **Stalls** Low

Form RPR

2 **1** **Glendevon (USA)**[33] 6885 2-9-2 0.......... JamieSpencer 4 95+
(Richard Hughes) *mde all: shkn up and qckly drew clr wl over 1f out: pushed out: v comf* **8/11[1]**

3 **2** 5 **Moqarrar (USA)**[46] 6424 2-9-2 0.......... TedDurcan 12 78
(Sir Michael Stoute) *chsd wnr 2f: rdn to go 2nd again 2f out: sn outpcd: kpt on but no ch* **8/1[3]**

**3** 1½ **Kawasir (USA)** 2-9-2 0.......... JimCrowley 5 74+
(Roger Varian) *in tch in midfield: rdn and prog jst over 2f out: tk 3rd fnl f: kpt on but no ch* **10/1**

**4** *nk* **Laieth** 2-9-2 0.......... TomMarquand 6 73+
(Saeed bin Suroor) *hld up in 8th: shkn up and prog 2f out: disp 3rd fnl f and kpt on* **11/2[2]**

0 **5** 2½ **Dagian (IRE)**[12] 7580 2-9-2 0.......... MartinDwyer 3 66
(Amanda Perrett) *hld up in rr: prog on inner 2f out: no hdwy over 1f out: wknd fnl f* **20/1**

032 **6** *hd* **Exprompt (FR)**[14] 7512 2-9-2 77.......... JamesDoyle 11 66
(Hugo Palmer) *t.k.h: racd v wd early: chsd wnr after 2f to 2f out: steadily wknd* **9/1**

0 **7** *shd* **Burlington (IRE)**[14] 7512 2-9-2 0..........(t) NickyMackay 2 66
(John Gosden) *chsd ldrs: pushed along over 2f out: sn outpcd but plugged on* **40/1**

440 **8** 1 **Metatrons Cube (IRE)**[54] 6133 2-9-2 76.......... OisinMurphy 9 63
(Charles Hills) *chsd ldrs: pushed along and outpcd 2f out: one pce after* **50/1**

00 **9** 8 **Matchmaking (GER)**[14] 7512 2-9-2 0.......... LukeMorris 10 41
(Sir Mark Prescott Bt) *a in rr: urged along and lft bhd over 2f out* **100/1**

1 **10** 1¾ **Cheeseandpickle**[180] 1776 2-9-4 0.......... RobertWinston 7 39
(Keith Dalgleish) *chsd ldrs over 4f: wknd* **20/1**

00 **11** *hd* **Dracarys**[19] 7351 2-9-2 0.......... SteveDrowne 13 36
(Jose Santos) *sn struggling in last pair: a bhd* **100/1**

**12** 3½ **Dreamdancer (IRE)** 2-8-11 0.......... LiamKeniry 8 22
(Joseph Tuite) *s.i.s: rn green and a in last pair* **100/1**

1m 25.12s (-0.88) **Going Correction** -0.125s/f (Stan) **12** Ran SP% **120.4**
Speed ratings (Par 95): **100,94,92,92,89 89,89,87,78,76 76,72**
CSF £6.95 TOTE £1.50: £1.10, £2.50, £3.00; EX 9.20 Trifecta £41.80.
**Owner** D Campbell, D Waters & Partners **Bred** Justin Carthy **Trained** Upper Lambourn, Berks

**FOCUS**
A decent novice, and an impressive performance from the winner, who could be smart. He'll post bigger figures.

## 7947 32RED.COM H'CAP 7f (P)

**6:25** (6:25) (Class 4) (0-80,80) 3-Y-0+ **£4,690** (£1,395; £697; £348) **Stalls** Low

Form RPR

1623 **1** **Cainhoe Star**[20] 7321 4-8-12 **71**.......... LukeMorris 3 84
(Anthony Carson) *trckd ldng pair: wnt 2nd 3f out: rdn to ld over 1f out: styd on wl and drew clr last 100yds* **16/1**

0001 **2** 3 **Monteverdi (FR)**[36] 6802 4-9-7 **80**.......... DanielTudhope 2 85
(Jamie Osborne) *led: rdn and pressed 2f out: hdd over 1f out but clr w wnr: wknd last 100yds but hld on for 2nd* **9/2[3]**

5110 **3** *nk* **Dourado (IRE)**[18] 7398 3-9-3 **78**.......... DavidProbert 1 81+
(Patrick Chamings) *hld up in last quartet: rdn and prog jst over 2f out: r.o to take 3rd ins fnl f: clsd on runner-up nr fin* **33/1**

1-32 **4** 1 **Noble Star (IRE)**[18] 7404 4-9-6 **79**.......... TomQueally 8 80
(James Fanshawe) *in tch in midfield: rdn over 2f out: kpt on one pce and nvr able to threaten* **3/1[1]**

1312 **5** *nk* **Sheikspear**[47] 6378 3-9-3 **78**.......... JFEgan 6 78
(Ed de Giles) *chsd ldrs: urged along by 1/2-way: rdn over 2f out: wnt 3rd sn after to ins fnl f: no ex* **8/1**

3134 **6** 3 **Multicultural (IRE)**[18] 7398 3-9-4 **79**..........(v) JimCrowley 5 71
(James Tate) *hld up in last quartet: pushed along over 2f out: sme prog over 1f out but nvr threatened to be involved* **7/2[2]**

0000 **7** *nk* **Dark Destroyer (IRE)**[18] 7398 3-9-3 **78**..........(v) OisinMurphy 11 69
(Joseph Tuite) *nvr beyond midfield: shkn up over 2f out: no real prog* **14/1**

4610 **8** *nk* **Showmethewayavrilo**[7] 7737 4-8-9 **71**.......... CharlieBennett(3) 14 62
(Malcolm Saunders) *chsd wnr to 3f out: shkn up and steadily wknd fnl 2f* **33/1**

5003 **9** 1¼ **Tai Sing Yeh (IRE)**[29] 7016 3-9-3 **78**..........(t) JamesDoyle 9 65
(Charles Hills) *chsd ldrs: rdn and no imp 2f out: eased whn btn fnl f* **8/1**

0300 **10** ½ **Steal The Scene (IRE)**[20] 7321 5-9-4 **77**.......... RyanPowell 7 63
(Kevin Frost) *dwlt: a wl in rr: nvr a factor* **80/1**

0-03 **11** 2¾ **Marylebone**[32] 6936 4-9-7 **80**..........(t) RichardKingscote 13 59
(Ed Walker) *t.k.h: racd wd: chsd ldrs to 3f out: sn btn* **5/1**

0346 **12** 1¼ **Papou Tony**[23] 7213 4-9-1 **74**.......... LiamKeniry 4 49
(George Baker) *a in last pair: nvr a factor* **28/1**

1m 24.21s (-1.79) **Going Correction** -0.125s/f (Stan)
**WFA** 3 from 4yo+ 2lb **12** Ran SP% **127.4**
Speed ratings (Par 105): **105,101,101,100,99 96,95,95,94,93 90,89**
CSF £91.29 CT £1676.00 TOTE £10.80: £2.90, £2.20, £5.00; EX 113.30 Trifecta £1555.70.
**Owner** Hugh & Mindi Byrne & W H Carson **Bred** Cheveley Park Stud Ltd **Trained** Newmarket, Suffolk

**FOCUS**
Few got into this fair handicap.

## 7948 CLOSE BROTHERS BUSINESS FINANCE MEDIAN AUCTION MAIDEN STKS 1m 2f 219y(P)

**6:55** (6:55) (Class 5) 3-5-Y-0 **£3,234** (£962; £481; £240) **Stalls** Low

Form RPR

6-43 **1** **Wine List**[10] 7652 3-9-5 0.......... OisinMurphy 5 75+
(Andrew Balding) *sn trckd ldr: rdn to ld jst over 2f out: edgd lft fr over 1f out: drvn and kpt on* **6/4[1]**

2503 **2** 2¼ **My Illusionist**[14] 7514 3-9-5 69.......... LukeMorris 2 70
(Harry Dunlop) *chsd ldng pair: drvn over 2f out: chsd wnr over 1f out: kpt on but nvr pce to chal* **16/1**

0223 **3** 1¾ **Rainbow Rising (FR)**[25] 7151 3-9-0 71.......... KieranShoemark 3 62
(David Menuisier) *hld up towards rr: stdy prog over 3f out: rdn to go 3rd jst over 1f out: kpt on but nvr nr enough to chal* **3/1[2]**

3366 **4** 1¼ **Second Page**[41] 6623 3-9-5 72.......... KieranO'Neill 7 65
(Richard Hannon) *in tch: drvn wl over 2f out: plugged on to take 4th ins fnl f: no ch* **6/1**

0455 **5** 2¼ **D'Waterside**[28] 7061 3-9-5 57.......... JosephineGordon 6 61
(David Loughnane) *pressed ldrs but urged along at various stages: steadily lft bhd fr over 2f out* **25/1**

3-35 **6** 4½ **Deliberator**[20] 7322 3-9-5 75..........(h[1]) SilvestreDeSousa 1 55
(William Knight) *led at decent pce: rdn and hdd jst over 2f out: wknd over 1f out* **4/1[3]**

0540 **7** 4½ **Cloud Nine (FR)**[34] 6847 4-9-5 47.......... TomMarquand 10 38
(Tony Carroll) *a towards rr: no real prog over 2f out* **80/1**

3 **8** 4 **Tiar Na Nog (IRE)**[49] 6320 5-9-5 0.......... TomQueally 8 31
(Denis Coakley) *in tch: pushed along and stl looked green over 2f out: sn wknd and eased* **20/1**

54 **9** 2¼ **Cthulhu (USA)**[100] 4449 3-9-0 0.......... MartinDwyer 4 28
(William Muir) *dwlt: mostly detached in last pair: nvr a factor* **50/1**

**10** 6 **Paco Filly** 3-9-0 0.......... DanielMuscutt 9 17
(Nikki Evans) *hld up: pushed along 3f out: sn wknd* **100/1**

3-00 **11** 10 **Trust The Man (IRE)**[23] 7215 4-9-5 48..........(bt[1]) RhiainIngram(5) 11 3
(Adam West) *a in last pair: t.o over 3f out* **100/1**

2m 18.61s (-3.29) **Going Correction** -0.125s/f (Stan)
**WFA** 3 from 4yo+ 5lb **11** Ran SP% **119.0**
Speed ratings (Par 103): **106,104,103,102,100 97,94,91,89,85 77**
CSF £28.22 TOTE £2.50: £1.10, £5.90, £1.20; EX 28.90 Trifecta £75.90.
**Owner** Another Bottle Racing 2 **Bred** David Taylor **Trained** Kingsclere, Hants

**FOCUS**
Modest maiden form.

## 7949 32RED ON THE APP STORE H'CAP (LONDON MIDDLE DISTANCE SERIES QUALIFIER) 1m 2f 219y(P)

**7:25** (7:26) (Class 4) (0-85,85) 3-Y-0+ **£4,690** (£1,395; £697; £348) **Stalls** Low

Form RPR

-053 **1** **Seniority**[58] 6007 3-9-2 **85**.......... JamesDoyle 5 94
(William Haggas) *hld up in midfield: sltly impeded after 2f: lost pl 4f out and towards rr 3f out: gd prog on inner over 2f out: dashed into the ld wl over 1f but then hung lft: drvn and hrd pressed fnl f: jnd nr fin: won on the nod* **7/2[1]**

221 **2** *nse* **Ennjaaz (IRE)**[13] 7542 3-8-10 **82**..........(p) DavidEgan(3) 12 91
(Saeed bin Suroor) *chsd ldrs: rdn over 2f out: wnt 2nd over 1f out: sn chalng: sustained effrt to join wnr nr fin: jst pipped* **15/2**

0400 **3** 2 **Sunblazer (IRE)**[18] 7397 7-8-13 **82**..........(t) JoshuaBryan(5) 2 87
(Kim Bailey) *in tch: prog on inner 2f out: nt clr run briefly jst over 2f out: drvn over 1f out: chsd ldng pair last 100yds: jst hld on for 3rd* **33/1**

1-15 **4** *shd* **Eldritch (IRE)**[139] 3005 3-9-2 **85**.......... RobertHavlin 8 90
(John Gosden) *hld up in midfield: lost pl sltly over 2f out then swtchd lft and racd sltly awkwardly: styd on fr jst over 1f out: nrly snatched 3rd* **7/2[1]**

2034 **5** *hd* **Rumpole**[19] 7358 3-8-12 **81**.......... RobertWinston 9 85
(Hughie Morrison) *hld up towards rr: effrt whn nt clr run briefly 2f out: shkn up and styd on fr over 1f out to press for a pl nr fin* **14/1**

2635 **6** *hd* **Eskendash (USA)**[32] 6937 4-8-13 **77**.......... OisinMurphy 14 81
(Pam Sly) *hld up in last trio: prog on outer 2f out: rdn to press for a pl ins fnl f: one pce nr fin* **16/1**

2664 **7** ¾ **Tom's Rock (IRE)**[16] 7456 4-9-3 **81**.......... DanielMuscutt 7 84
(John Butler) *trckd ldr: chal over 2f out to wl over 1f out: stl disputing 3rd ins fnl f: fdd nr fin* **16/1**

5221 **8** 1/2 **Royal Reserve**[35] 6819 4-9-6 **84**.......... DanielTudhope 4 86
(David O'Meara) *hld up in last trio: nt clr run briefly over 2f out: shkn up and styd on fr over 1f out: no imp ldrs nr fin* **9/2**[2]

31 **9** 2 3/4 **Airway**[34] 6851 3-8-11 **83**.......... GeorgeWood(3) 6 80
(James Fanshawe) *t.k.h: trckd ldrs: rdn over 2f out: wknd over 1f out* **6/1**[3]

3140 **10** shd **Graceful James (IRE)**[19] 7358 4-9-3 **81**.......... KieranO'Neill 11 78
(Jimmy Fox) *hld up in last trio: pushed along over 3f out: no great prog after* **25/1**

3430 **11** 5 **Ravenous**[32] 6929 6-9-1 **79**.......... SilvestreDeSousa 1 67
(Luke Dace) *pressed ldng pair: rdn to ld jst over 2f out to wl over 1f out: sn wknd* **20/1**

**12** 16 **Herminio (FR)**[52] 5-9-7 **85**.......... KieranShoemark 3 44
(Gary Moore) *led to jst over 2f out: wknd rapidly: t.o* **50/1**

2m 18.36s (-3.54) **Going Correction** -0.125s/f (Stan)
**WFA** 3 from 4yo+ 5lb 12 Ran SP% **120.6**
Speed ratings (Par 105): **107,106,105,105,105 105,104,104,102,102 98,86**
CSF £29.57 CT £759.55 TOTE £4.60: £1.70, £2.20, £5.90; EX 40.30 Trifecta £1238.40.
**Owner** The Queen **Bred** Darley **Trained** Newmarket, Suffolk
■ Artful Rogue was withdrawn. Price at time of withdrawal 14/1. Rule 4 applies to board prices prior to withdrawal - deduction 5p in the pound. New market formed.
■ Stewards' Enquiry : Robert Havlin caution: careless riding

**FOCUS**
They finished in a heap behind the first two, who are both unexposed.

## 7950 EBFSTALLIONS.COM CONDITIONS STKS 6f (P)
7:55 (7:56) (Class 3) 3-Y-0+
**£9,648** (£2,889; £1,444; £722; £361; £181) **Stalls** Low

Form RPR

1043 **1** **Solomon's Bay (IRE)**[34] 6856 3-9-8 105.......... (b) SilvestreDeSousa 4 109
(Roger Varian) *chsd ldrs: rdn to cl fr over 1f out: chal ins fnl f: drvn ahd last 50yds* **9/4**[1]

2-36 **2** nk **Blue De Vega (GER)**[137] 3099 4-9-2 105.......... OisinMurphy 2 101
(Robert Cowell) *trckd ldrs: wnt 2nd over 1f out: rdn to chal on inner fnl f: led briefly 75yds out: jst outpcd* **4/1**[2]

4014 **3** 1/2 **Coronation Day**[43] 6554 4-8-11 88.......... LukeMorris 5 94
(James Tate) *led: rdn and hrd pressed fr over 1f out: clung on wl but hdd last 75yds and dropped to 3rd* **20/1**

6000 **4** 1 **Top Score**[32] 6918 3-9-12 103.......... (v) KevinStott 8 107
(Saeed bin Suroor) *trapped out wd: chsd ldrs: rdn 2f out: nt qckn over 1f out: kpt on ins fnl f: tk 4th last strides* **13/2**

100 **5** shd **Out Do**[53] 6206 8-9-6 104.......... (v) DanielTudhope 1 100
(David O'Meara) *hld up: prog on inner 2f out: rdn over 1f out: clsng on ldng trio but no ch whn nowhere to go nr fin and lost 4th* **11/2**

0040 **6** 4 1/2 **Verne Castle**[39] 6677 4-9-2 97.......... (h) DavidProbert 7 82
(Andrew Balding) *t.k.h: mostly chsd ldr to over 1f out: wknd* **20/1**

4330 **7** 3/4 **Calvados Spirit**[26] 7129 4-9-2 89.......... MartinDwyer 3 79
(William Muir) *awkward s: a in rr: shkn up and no prog 2f out* **14/1**

503 **8** nk **Dougan**[26] 7118 5-9-2 97.......... FranBerry 6 78
(David Evans) *dwlt: a in rr: rdn and no prog over 2f out* **5/1**[3]

1m 11.23s (-1.87) **Going Correction** -0.125s/f (Stan)
**WFA** 3 from 4yo+ 1lb 8 Ran SP% **112.3**
Speed ratings (Par 107): **107,106,105,104,104 98,97,97**
CSF £10.78 TOTE £3.30: £1.20, £1.40, £3.40; EX 8.70 Trifecta £90.30.
**Owner** Prince A A Faisal **Bred** Nawara Stud Company Ltd S A **Trained** Newmarket, Suffolk

**FOCUS**
A decent contest, although the form can't be rated too highly with the 88-rated third finishing close up.

## 7951 32RED CASINO H'CAP 6f (P)
8:25 (8:25) (Class 6) (0-60,60) 3-Y-0+ **£2,587** (£770; £384; £192) **Stalls** Low

Form RPR

06-0 **1** **Run With Pride (IRE)**[76] 5318 7-9-1 **60**.......... LewisEdmunds(3) 6 71+
(Derek Shaw) *hld up: prog on inner over 2f out: rdn to ld jst over 1f out: drvn clr fnl f* **5/1**[3]

0003 **2** 2 **Kyllukey**[6] 7767 4-9-4 **60**.......... (v) LukeMorris 3 65
(Milton Bradley) *trckd ldng pair gng wl: rdn to ld wl over 1f out to jst over 1f out: outpcd by wnr fnl f* **9/1**

0545 **3** 1 **Fairway To Heaven (IRE)**[20] 7320 8-8-13 **60**.......... PaddyBradley(5) 4 63
(Lee Carter) *hld up in midfield: gng easily over 2f out: nt clr run briefly over 1f out: rdn and styd on to take 3rd last 100yds: too late to chal* **5/1**[3]

2023 **4** 1/2 **Frank Cool**[24] 7190 4-9-2 **58**.......... TomMarquand 9 59
(Tony Carroll) *t.k.h: hld up in rr: prog over 2f out: chsd ldng pair over 1f out: no imp and lost 3rd fnl 100yds* **8/1**

5324 **5** 1/2 **Exquisite Ruby**[15] 7494 3-9-3 **60**.......... SilvestreDeSousa 1 59+
(Charles Hills) *t.k.h: pressed ldr to 2f out: grad fdd u.p* **10/3**[1]

3063 **6** nk **Billyoakes (IRE)**[20] 7320 5-8-13 **60**.......... (p) JoshuaBryan(5) 5 58
(Charlie Wallis) *pushed along in midfield by 1/2-way: u.p and no hdwy 2f out: plugged on* **10/1**

0124 **7** nk **Lucky Clover**[63] 5778 6-9-2 **58**.......... (p) JosephineGordon 2 55
(Malcolm Saunders) *chsd ldrs urged along bef 1/2-way: lost pl and fdd 2f out* **16/1**

0300 **8** 1 **Noble Deed**[63] 5791 7-9-4 **60**.......... (p) KierenFox 8 54
(Michael Attwater) *slowly away: a in rr: shkn up and no prog 2f out* **20/1**

0041 **9** 2 **Fikhaar**[15] 7487 3-9-2 **59**.......... KevinStott 7 47+
(Kevin Ryan) *led but pressed: hdd wl over 1f out: wknd qckly* **4/1**[2]

440 **10** 7 **Mags Well (IRE)**[24] 7190 3-9-2 **59**.......... LiamKeniry 10 26
(Geoffrey Deacon) *trapped out wd in midfield: dropped to last over 2f out: sn bhd* **50/1**

1m 12.54s (-0.56) **Going Correction** -0.125s/f (Stan)
**WFA** 3 from 4yo+ 1lb 10 Ran SP% **119.2**
Speed ratings (Par 101): **98,95,94,93,92 92,91,90,87,78**
CSF £50.66 CT £240.18 TOTE £5.80: £2.10, £2.70, £2.60; EX 51.80 Trifecta £312.90.
**Owner** The Whiteman Partnership **Bred** Barouche Stud Ireland Ltd **Trained** Sproxton, Leics

**FOCUS**
Moderate sprinting form. The pace was pretty strong and the second, third and fourth help with the level.

## 7952 CLOSE BROTHERS BUSINESS FINANCE H'CAP (DIV II) 7f (P)
8:55 (8:55) (Class 6) (0-55,55) 3-Y-0+ **£2,587** (£770; £384; £192) **Stalls** Low

Form RPR

6220 **1** **Chough**[20] 7323 3-9-4 **54**.......... RobertWinston 2 65+
(Hughie Morrison) *chsd ldng pair: rousted along 2f out: clsd over 1f out: led last 150yds: sn clr* **3/1**[2]

4026 **2** 3 1/2 **Magic Mirror**[16] 7464 4-9-7 **55**.......... (v) JosephineGordon 7 58
(Mark Rimell) *hld up wl in rr: prog on outer over 2f out: tk 3rd fnl f: r.o to take 2nd last stride: too late to chal* **4/1**[3]

0000 **3** shd **Whaleweigh Station**[6] 7763 6-9-2 **50**.......... (v) DanielTudhope 11 53
(J R Jenkins) *pressed ldr at str pce: drvn ahd over 1f out: hdd and btn 150yds out: lost 2nd last stride* **25/1**

0355 **4** 1/2 **New Rich**[121] 3660 7-9-6 **54**.......... (b) CharlesBishop 1 55
(Eve Johnson Houghton) *hld up in last trio: nt clr run over 2f out to over 1f out and no ch after: fin strly* **8/1**

0456 **5** 2 3/4 **Stringybark Creek**[23] 7217 3-8-12 **53**.......... PaddyBradley(5) 3 46
(Daniel Steele) *stdd after s: hld up in last: stl in last pair 2f out: swtchd towards inner and passed rivals over 1f out: reminders fnl f: kpt on to take 5th nr fin: nvr in it* **33/1**

5345 **6** 1/2 **Solitary Sister (IRE)**[16] 7459 3-8-7 **50**.......... (v) NicolaCurrie(7) 5 42
(Richard Spencer) *wl in rr: nt gng wl fr 1/2-way: kpt on passed tiring rivals over 1f out: n.d* **12/1**

3211 **7** shd **Prince Jai**[13] 7540 4-9-2 **55**.......... (v[1]) ManuelFernandes(5) 8 48
(Ian Williams) *led at str pce but pressed: hdd over 1f out: wknd qckly fnl f* **9/4**[1]

4000 **8** nk **Stragar**[41] 6622 3-9-0 **50**.......... LukeMorris 9 41
(Michael Appleby) *chsd ldrs: wnt 4th 2f out but nt on terms: no hdwy after: wknd ins fnl f* **33/1**

6/0- **9** 1 3/4 **Ambuscade**[482] 3319 4-9-2 **50**.......... LiamKeniry 13 37
(Neil Mulholland) *nvr beyond midfield: shkn up and no prog over 2f out* **66/1**

5030 **10** 3/4 **Locommotion**[25] 7157 5-8-11 **52**.......... (t) MillyNaseb(7) 6 37
(Matthew Salaman) *slowly away: t.k.h and prog on outer into midfield by 1/2-way: racd awkwardly and btn 2f out* **10/1**

000 **11** 11 **Harbour Town**[65] 5714 3-9-1 **51**.......... (p) DavidProbert 4 7
(Harry Dunlop) *hld up in tch: shkn up over 2f out: wknd qckly over 1f out: t.o* **25/1**

6046 **12** 2 1/2 **Knight Of The Air**[37] 6754 5-9-4 **52**.......... (t) OisinMurphy 10
(Joseph Tuite) *t.k.h: prom: urged along over 3f out: wknd rapidly 2f out: t.o* **14/1**

1m 25.81s (-0.19) **Going Correction** -0.125s/f (Stan)
**WFA** 3 from 4yo+ 2lb 12 Ran SP% **125.4**
Speed ratings (Par 101): **96,92,91,91,88 87,87,87,85,84 71,68**
CSF £15.73 CT £271.23 TOTE £3.90: £1.30, £1.50, £5.20; EX 17.90 Trifecta £316.10.
**Owner** Lord Margadale **Bred** Lord Margadale **Trained** East Ilsley, Berks

**FOCUS**
This was the quicker of the two divisions by 0.90sec. The third and fourth help with the form.
T/Jkpt: Not Won. T/Plt: £383.60 to a £1 stake. Pool: £89,895.83 - 171.07 winning units T/Qpdt: £39.50 to a £1 stake. Pool: £15,177.43 - 284.19 winning units **Jonathan Neesom**

# 7731 NOTTINGHAM (L-H)
### Wednesday, October 11
**OFFICIAL GOING: Good to soft (6.7)**
Wind: Strong against Weather: Cloudy

## 7953 32RED.COM EBF NOVICE STKS 6f 18y
1:45 (1:46) (Class 5) 2-Y-O **£3,234** (£962; £481; £240) **Stalls** Centre

Form RPR

4 **1** **Alwasmiya**[22] 7238 2-8-11 0.......... SilvestreDeSousa 6 80+
(Simon Crisford) *trckd ldrs: hdwy 1/2-way: cl up over 2f out: led wl over 1f out: rdn and kpt on wl fnl f* **11/4**[1]

**2** 1 1/2 **Ocala** 2-8-11 0.......... DavidProbert 10 76+
(Andrew Balding) *dwlt and towards rr: hdwy over 2f out: chsd ldrs: rdn and green jst over 1f out: kpt on wl towards fin* **10/1**

**3** 1/2 **Al Asef** 2-9-2 0.......... AndreaAtzeni 7 79
(Marco Botti) *in tch: hdwy to trck ldr 1/2-way: rdn over 1f out: chsd wnr ins fnl f: kpt on same pce* **6/1**[3]

542 **4** 1/2 **Wafeer (IRE)**[26] 7126 2-9-2 78.......... DaneO'Neill 9 78
(Richard Hannon) *cl up: narrow ld over 2f out: sn rdn and hdd wl over 1f out: wknd fnl f* **3/1**[2]

2 **5** 1 1/2 **Knighted (IRE)**[34] 6853 2-9-2 0.......... TomEaves 4 73
(Kevin Ryan) *trckd ldrs on outer: pushed along wl over 2f out: rdn and sltly outpcd over 1f out: kpt on ins fnl f* **3/1**[2]

**6** 2 **Royal Prospect (IRE)** 2-9-2 0.......... PaulMulrennan 8 67
(Julie Camacho) *trckd ldrs: hdwy over 2f out: rdn over 1f out: green and sn edgd lft: kpt on same pce* **66/1**

**7** 1 3/4 **I Know How (IRE)** 2-9-2 0.......... JoeDoyle 11 62
(Julie Camacho) *wnt rt s: green and rr tl sme late hdwy* **66/1**

00 **8** 3 **Kylie Style**[20] 7326 2-8-11 0.......... AdamBeschizza 3 48
(Steph Hollinshead) *in tch on outer: rdn along over 2f out: sn wknd* **100/1**

**9** 3 1/4 **Cocktail (IRE)** 2-9-2 0.......... GrahamLee 12 43
(Jedd O'Keeffe) *a in rr* **33/1**

0 **10** 3 **My Rock (IRE)**[55] 6093 2-9-2 0.......... (t[1]) DougieCostello 5 34
(David Dennis) *dwlt: a in rr* **100/1**

03 **11** 3/4 **Flere Imsaho (IRE)**[25] 7141 2-9-2 0.......... RichardKingscote 2 32
(Tom Dascombe) *led: rdn along 1/2-way: sn hdd & wknd* **25/1**

1m 16.85s (2.15) **Going Correction** +0.25s/f (Good) 11 Ran SP% **111.8**
Speed ratings (Par 95): **95,93,92,91,89 87,84,80,76,72 71**
CSF £27.82 TOTE £3.50: £1.20, £2.90, £2.10; EX 33.60 Trifecta £229.80.
**Owner** Shaikh Duaij Al Khalifa **Bred** Bumble Bloodstock Ltd **Trained** Newmarket, Suffolk

**FOCUS**
Races run on outer track. An ordinary novice but the first two put up promising efforts. The form is taken at something like face value.

## 7954 32RED CASINO NURSERY H'CAP 5f 8y
2:15 (2:16) (Class 4) (0-85,87) 2-Y-O **£5,175** (£1,540; £769; £384) **Stalls** Centre

Form RPR

162 **1** **Kick On Kick On**[56] 6070 2-10-1 **87**.......... AdamKirby 6 89
(Clive Cox) *trckd ldrs: hdwy to chse ldr 2f out: rdn over 1f out: drvn to chal ins fnl f: kpt on wl to ld nr fin* **9/4**[1]

1303 **2** hd **Bow Belles**[18] 7385 2-8-11 **72**.......... (h) RachelRichardson(3) 5 74
(Tim Easterby) *hld up in rr: stdy hdwy 1/2-way: chsd ldrs whn n.m.r and hmpd over 1f out: swtchd lft and rdn jst ins fnl f: fin strly* **7/1**

4023 **3** hd **Brandy Station (IRE)**[20] 7318 2-9-4 **76**.......... RobertTart 3 77
(Lisa Williamson) *led: rdn and edgd lft over 1f out: drvn ins fnl f: hdd and no ex nr fin* **10/1**

1105 **4** 2 1/4 **Time Trail**[68] 5614 2-9-7 **79**.......... PaulMulrennan 4 71
(Michael Dods) *awkward s: t.k.h in rr: hdwy over 2f out: chsd ldrs and rdn over 1f out: kpt on same pce* **16/1**

041 **5** 3 1/4 **Wear It Well**[37] 6747 2-9-5 **77**.......... DaneO'Neill 7 58
(Henry Candy) *prom: rdn along 2f out: grad wknd* **6/1**[3]

040 **6** 1 3/4 **Billiebrookedit (IRE)**[43] 6547 2-8-7 **65**.......... FrannyNorton 8 39
(Steph Hollinshead) *chsd ldrs: rdn along 2f out: sn wknd* **25/1**

5310 **7** ¾ **The Golden Cue**[40] 6651 2-8-12 **70** AdamBeschizza 2 42
(Steph Hollinshead) *chsd ldrs: rdn along over 2f out: sn wknd* **10/1**

003 **8** 2 **Floss The Hoss (IRE)**[102] 4335 2-8-9 **67** JFEgan 9 32
(David Evans) *towards rr: rdn along over 2f out: nvr nr ldrs* **14/1**

1014 **9** ¾ **Viscount Loftus (IRE)**[25] 7138 2-10-1 **87** PJMcDonald 1 49
(Mark Johnston) *trckd ldrs: pushed along bef 1/2-way: rdn wl over 2f out: sn drvn and wknd* **4/1**[2]

1m 3.01s (1.51) **Going Correction** +0.25s/f (Good) **9** Ran SP% **112.1**
Speed ratings (Par 97): **97,96,96,92,87 84,83,80,79**
CSF £17.60 CT £127.39 TOTE £2.50: £1.40, £1.90, £3.00; EX 17.10 Trifecta £90.60.
**Owner** Paul & Clare Rooney **Bred** Fifehead Farms M C Denning **Trained** Lambourn, Berks

**FOCUS**
A tight nursery and a useful effort by the top weight. Straightforward form.

## 7955 EBF STALLIONS OATH RESTRICTED MAIDEN STKS (PLUS 10 RACE) (SIRE OR DAM RESTRICTED RACE) 1m 75y
**2:50** (2:53) (Class 4) 2-Y-O £**6,469** (£1,925; £962; £481) **Stalls** Centre

Form RPR

325 **1** **Merlin Magic**[33] 6869 2-9-5 84 SilvestreDeSousa 7 86
(David Elsworth) *qckly away and mde all: clr over 4f out and stdd pce over 3f out: rdn along and qcknd over 2f out: drvn over 1f out: kpt on wl towards fin* **8/1**

02 **2** ¾ **Sam Gold (IRE)**[18] 7391 2-9-5 0 AndreaAtzeni 8 84
(Roger Varian) *trckd ldrs: hdwy to chse ldng pair 5f out: rdn over 2f out: drvn over 1f out: kpt on u.p fnl f* **9/4**[2]

2 **3** *shd* **Sevenna Star (IRE)**[21] 7273 2-9-5 0 RobertHavlin 3 84
(John Gosden) *chsd wnr: tk clsr order over 3f out: rdn 2f out: drvn over 1f out: edgd lft ins fnl f: kpt on* **7/4**[1]

63 **4** 3 ¼ **Danceteria (FR)**[32] 6916 2-9-5 0 KieranShoemark 2 77+
(David Menuisier) *chsd ldrs: rdn along on outer over 2f out: drvn and edgd rt wl over 1f out: kpt on same pce* **14/1**

4 **5** 2 ¾ **Regal Director (IRE)**[29] 7026 2-9-5 0 HarryBentley 10 71
(Simon Crisford) *in tch: hdwy over 3f out: chsd ldrs over 2f out: rdn and green over 1f out: sn one pce* **14/1**

0 **6** 4 ½ **First Eleven**[21] 7273 2-9-5 0 RyanMoore 9 61+
(John Gosden) *s.i.s: a towards rr* **4/1**[3]

00 **7** 4 **Nelson River**[13] 7543 2-9-5 0 AdamKirby 5 52
(Clive Cox) *a towards rr* **66/1**

**8** *nk* **Artarmon (IRE)** 2-9-5 0 LouisSteward 1 52
(Michael Bell) *in tch: hdwy on inner over 3f out: sn rdn along and outpcd* **50/1**

0 **9** 5 **Twisted Logic (IRE)**[34] 6854 2-9-5 0 PJMcDonald 6 41
(Keith Dalgleish) *a in rr* **100/1**

1m 48.37s (-0.63) **Going Correction** 0.0s/f (Good) **9** Ran SP% **116.0**
Speed ratings (Par 97): **103,102,102,98,96 91,87,87,82**
CSF £26.54 TOTE £9.50: £2.50, £1.30, £1.10; EX 34.00 Trifecta £44.20.
**Owner** J C Smith **Bred** Littleton Stud **Trained** Newmarket, Suffolk

**FOCUS**
Distance increased by 6yds. Run at a decent pace, it paid to race handily and the winner maintained the gallop, always looking to be doing enough inside the last furlong or so. The winner at least matched his pre-race form.

## 7956 BREEDERS BACKING RACING EBF NURSERY H'CAP 1m 1f
**3:20** (3:21) (Class 3) (0-90,87) 2-Y-O £**9,703** (£2,887; £1,443; £721) **Stalls** Low

Form RPR

352 **1** **Ship Of The Fen**[36] 6777 2-8-9 **75** SilvestreDeSousa 1 78+
(Martyn Meade) *trckd ldng pair on inner: swtchd rt and hdwy 2f out: sn chal: rdn to ld ent fnl f: kpt on strly* **15/8**[1]

312 **2** 2 **Baileys Excelerate (FR)**[16] 7451 2-9-5 **85** JoeFanning 7 84
(Mark Johnston) *led: rdn along 3f out: hdd briefly over 2f out: led again wl over 1f out: drvn and hdd ent fnl f: kpt on* **6/1**[3]

5106 **3** 2 ¾ **Ventura Dragon (IRE)**[25] 7148 2-8-12 **78** TonyHamilton 6 72
(Richard Fahey) *trckd ldrs: hdwy 3f out: rdn along 2f out: sn drvn and kpt on same pce* **20/1**

334 **4** 1 **Adams Park**[21] 7273 2-9-1 **81** AndreaAtzeni 3 73
(Roger Varian) *dwlt and towards rr: hdwy wl over 2f out: rdn wl over 1f out: no imp fnl f* **2/1**[2]

0431 **5** 2 ¼ **Powerful Society (IRE)**[23] 7222 2-8-7 **73** PaulHanagan 5 60
(Richard Fahey) *dwlt: a in rr* **7/1**

4243 **6** 1 ¼ **Knight In Armour (IRE)**[11] 7624 2-8-0 **69** DavidEgan(3) 2 54
(Mark Johnston) *t.k.h: chsd ldr: hdwy 3f out: rdn and slt ld over 2f out: hdd wl over 1f out and sn wknd* **10/1**

1m 57.97s (0.37) **Going Correction** 0.0s/f (Good) **6** Ran SP% **108.8**
Speed ratings (Par 99): **98,96,93,92,90 89**
CSF £12.52 TOTE £2.50: £1.30, £2.70; EX 12.70 Trifecta £42.30.
**Owner** C J Murfitt **Bred** Pantile Stud **Trained** Newmarket, Suffolk

**FOCUS**
Distance increased by 6yds. A good nursery run at a steady gallop. The winner built on his novice promise.

## 7957 32REDSPORT.COM H'CAP (DIV I) 1m 75y
**3:50** (3:54) (Class 5) (0-75,81) 3-Y-O+ £**3,234** (£962; £481; £240) **Stalls** Centre

Form RPR

46P5 **1** **Rosarno (IRE)**[21] 7277 3-9-5 **76** (bt) HarryBentley 5 82
(Charles Hills) *dwlt and towards rr: hdwy over 2f out: effrt and n.m.r over 1f out: rdn and squeezed through ent fnl f: drvn to ld last 100yds: kpt on* **3/1**[2]

2000 **2** *nk* **Mikmak**[19] 7358 4-9-4 **72** (p) DougieCostello 1 79+
(William Muir) *s.i.s and in rr: tk clsr order over 5f out: in tch on inner over 3f out: effrt and nt clr run wl over 1f out: swtchd markedly rt to outer ins fnl f: rdn and fin wl: jst hld* **5/1**[3]

1136 **3** *hd* **Pacific Salt (IRE)**[27] 7098 4-9-3 **74** CallumShepherd(3) 3 79
(Pam Sly) *t.k.h: trckd ldrs: hdwy over 2f out: swtchd rt and rdn to ld jst over 1f out: sn drvn: hdd last 100yds: kpt on* **5/2**[1]

0606 **4** ½ **Lord Commander**[27] 7095 3-8-11 **68** PaulHanagan 10 72
(Richard Fahey) *hld up in rr: hdwy on outer 2 1/2f out: rdn to chalr over 1f out: drvn and ev ch ins fnl f: no ex towards fin* **14/1**

5060 **5** 4 ½ **Thaqaffa (IRE)**[20] 7327 4-9-9 **77** AdamKirby 4 71
(Amy Murphy) *led: pushed along 3f out: rdn over 2f out: hdd appr 1f out: hmpd jst ins fnl f: sn wknd* **7/1**

5600 **6** 3 ¼ **Maldonado (FR)**[11] 7628 3-8-2 **66** HarrisonShaw(7) 6 52
(Michael Easterby) *trckd ldrs: pushed along wl over 2f out: rdn wl over 1f out: sn wknd* **33/1**

0053 **7** 1 ½ **Tadaany (IRE)**[22] 7249 5-9-1 **69** TomEaves 8 52
(Ruth Carr) *trckd ldr: cl up over 3f out: rdn along over 2f out: hld whn n.m.r over 1f out: wknd* **7/1**

455 **8** 4 ½ **Gold Dust**[65] 5712 3-8-7 **64** SamHitchcott 7 36
(Clive Cox) *chsd ldrs on outer: rdn along 3f out: drvn 2f out: sn wknd* **12/1**

1m 47.61s (-1.39) **Going Correction** 0.0s/f (Good)
**WFA** 3 from 4yo+ 3lb **8** Ran SP% **112.5**
Speed ratings (Par 103): **106,105,105,105,100 97,95,91**
CSF £17.79 CT £41.14 TOTE £3.50: £1.10, £1.50, £1.40; EX 18.30 Trifecta £55.90.
**Owner** Abdulla Al Khalifa **Bred** Wilgerbosdrift (uk) Ltd **Trained** Lambourn, Berks

**FOCUS**
Distance increased by 6yds. The first leg of a modest handicap, several had their chance and there was little between the first four at the line. The form is rated around the third.

## 7958 32REDSPORT.COM H'CAP (DIV II) 1m 75y
**4:20** (4:20) (Class 5) (0-75,75) 3-Y-O+ £**3,234** (£962; £481; £240) **Stalls** Centre

Form RPR

4400 **1** **Harlequin Striker (IRE)**[27] 7098 5-9-4 **72** (p[1]) CharlesBishop 9 80
(Dean Ivory) *mde all: rdn wl over 1f out: drvn ins fnl f: kpt on wl towards fin* **9/2**[3]

5004 **2** ½ **Beatbybeatbybeat**[15] 7474 4-8-7 **61** oh2 (v) CamHardie 7 68
(Antony Brittain) *hld up in rr: hdwy 3f out: swtchd lft towards inner over 2f out: sn nt clr run: swtchd markedly rt to outer jst over 1f out: rdn and edgd lft ins fnl f: styd on strly towards fin: jst hld* **12/1**

-430 **3** 2 ¾ **William Booth (IRE)**[95] 4633 3-8-11 **68** FrannyNorton 8 69
(Ivan Furtado) *trckd ldrs: hdwy over 3f out: cl up 2f out: rdn over 1f out: drvn ins fnl f and kpt on same pce* **7/1**

2602 **4** 2 **Medicean Ballet (IRE)**[8] 7710 3-9-2 **73** DaneO'Neill 5 69
(Henry Candy) *hld up in tch: hdwy 3f out: rdn to chse ldrs 2f out: drvn over 1f out: kpt on same pce* **3/1**[1]

2131 **5** 1 ¼ **El Principe**[65] 5699 4-9-2 **75** (h) JaneElliott(5) 6 68
(Les Eyre) *t.k.h: chsd wnr: rdn along on outer wl over 2f out: drvn over 1f out: hld whn n.m.r ent fnl f* **10/3**[2]

1144 **6** *hd* **Edgar Allan Poe (IRE)**[8] 7699 3-9-0 **71** MartinHarley 4 64
(Rebecca Bastiman) *hld up towards rr: hdwy over 3f out: chsd ldrs 2f out: rdn over 1f out: wknd fnl f* **6/1**

0-50 **7** 1 ¼ **Cornelious (IRE)**[251] 517 5-8-8 **62** AdamBeschizza 3 52
(Clifford Lines) *trckd ldrs: hdwy 3f out: rdn along 2f out: drvn over 1f out: wknd* **16/1**

6054 **8** 16 **Hanseatic**[65] 5698 8-8-12 **73** RyanTimby(7) 1 26
(Michael Easterby) *trckd ldrs: hdwy to chse ldng pair over 3f out: rdn along over 2f out: sn wknd and eased fnl f* **10/1**

1m 47.27s (-1.73) **Going Correction** 0.0s/f (Good)
**WFA** 3 from 4yo+ 3lb **8** Ran SP% **115.7**
Speed ratings (Par 103): **108,107,104,102,101 101,100,84**
CSF £56.53 CT £304.26 TOTE £5.90: £1.70, £4.00, £2.40; EX 50.00 Trifecta £436.90.
**Owner** Harlequin Direct Ltd & D Bloy **Bred** John Doyle **Trained** Radlett, Herts

**FOCUS**
Distance increased by 6yds. They appeared to go steady and the winner made all. The second was close to this year's form.

## 7959 32RED ON THE APP STORE H'CAP 1m 2f 50y
**4:55** (4:56) (Class 4) (0-85,84) 3-Y-O+ £**5,175** (£1,540; £769; £384) **Stalls** Low

Form RPR

6550 **1** **Ay Ay (IRE)**[18] 7400 3-9-6 **84** RyanMoore 7 92
(David Elsworth) *hld up: hdwy over 3f out: trckd ldrs 2f out: rdn ent fnl f: sn chal: drvn last 100yds: led nr line* **7/1**

3306 **2** *hd* **Fast And Hot (IRE)**[16] 7452 4-8-11 **78** (b) RossaRyan(7) 5 85
(Richard Hannon) *trckd ldrs: hdwy 3f out: cl up 2f out: rdn to ld over 1f out: drvn ins fnl f: hdd and no ex nr line* **7/1**

0403 **3** ½ **Storm Rock**[7] 7743 5-9-0 **77** HollieDoyle(3) 4 83
(Harry Dunlop) *prom: cl up over 2f out: rdn wl over 1f out: drvn ent fnl f: ev ch tl no ex towards fin* **13/2**

0334 **4** ½ **Grand Inquisitor**[26] 7131 5-9-5 **79** (p) StevieDonohoe 10 84
(Ian Williams) *hld up in rr: hdwy 3f out: trckd ldrs 2f out: sn swtchd lft and nt clr run over 1f out: swtchd rt and rdn ins fnl f: kpt on wl towards fin* **9/1**

1362 **5** 1 ¼ **Indian Chief (IRE)**[7] 7735 7-9-10 **84** MartinHarley 2 87+
(Rebecca Bastiman) *hld up in rr travelling strly: smooth hdwy on inner 3f out: nowhere to go fr 2f out: barely c off the bridle* **7/2**[1]

5201 **6** 1 ¼ **Italian Heiress**[26] 7125 3-9-3 **81** AdamKirby 12 81
(Clive Cox) *chsd ldrs on outer: hdwy and cl up over 2f out: rdn along wl over 1f out: drvn and wknd ent fnl f* **6/1**[3]

-156 **7** *hd* **Angrywhitepyjamas (IRE)**[32] 6952 4-9-8 **82** DougieCostello 6 82
(William Muir) *slt ld: rdn along wl over 2f out: hdd 1 1/2f out: sn drvn and wknd* **16/1**

1656 **8** 1 **Magic City (IRE)**[12] 7566 8-9-3 **84** RyanTimby(7) 3 82
(Michael Easterby) *dwlt and towards rr: effrt and sme hdwy over 2f out: sn rdn and n.d* **50/1**

1033 **9** ¾ **Hadeeqa (IRE)**[47] 6369 3-9-5 **83** (h) DaneO'Neill 11 79
(Simon Crisford) *t.k.h: hld up: a towards rr* **16/1**

01 **10** 10 **William Sayle**[197] 1410 3-8-13 **77** WilliamBuick 9 67
(John Gosden) *cl up: disp ld 1/2-way: rdn along 3f out: wknd 2f out* **9/2**[2]

2m 14.8s (0.50) **Going Correction** 0.0s/f (Good)
**WFA** 3 from 4yo+ 4lb **10** Ran SP% **116.7**
Speed ratings (Par 105): **98,97,97,97,96 95,94,94,93,85**
CSF £55.37 CT £336.38 TOTE £8.30: £2.80, £2.80, £2.50; EX 56.50 Trifecta £601.10.
**Owner** Mrs Doreen Tabor **Bred** Eyrefield Lodge Stud **Trained** Newmarket, Suffolk

**FOCUS**
Distance increased by 6yds. No great gallop on here and a couple of them found trouble, so not sure how strong the form is. The winner was close to his best with the second helping with the standard.

## 7960 32RED APPRENTICE H'CAP 1m 2f 50y
**5:25** (5:25) (Class 5) (0-70,70) 3-Y-O+ £**3,234** (£962; £481; £240) **Stalls** Low

Form RPR

0013 **1** **Essenaitch (IRE)**[37] 6763 4-9-9 **70** KatherineGlenister(3) 1 77
(David Evans) *t.k.h: trckd ldrs: hdwy over 2f out: chal over 1f out: rdn to ld ent fnl f: sn edgd rt: styd on* **6/1**[2]

3260 **2** ½ **Epitaph (IRE)**[4] 7832 3-9-5 **67** (p) MitchGodwin 6 73
(Michael Appleby) *trckd ldrs: hdwy 3f out: effrt 2f out: rdn over 1f out: styd on to chal wl ins fnl f: kpt on* **7/1**[3]

0115 **3** 2 **John Caesar (IRE)**[8] 7704 6-8-13 **57** (tp) BenRobinson 14 59
(Rebecca Bastiman) *t.k.h: prom: cl up over 2f out: rdn to ld briefly appr fnl f: sn hdd and drvn: kpt on same pce* **11/1**

15-0 **4** 1 ¼ **Tower Power**[56] 6075 6-9-11 **69** HollieDoyle 8 69
(Phil McEntee) *led: rdn along and hdd 3f out: cl up: rallied and ev ch over 1f out: kpt on same pce fnl f* **50/1**

0246 **5** *1 ¼* **Quoteline Direct**[23] 7219 4-9-2 **60**................................(h) RowanScott 16 57
(Micky Hammond) *in tch: hdwy on outer 4f out: led 3f out: rdn along and hdd jst over 1f out: wknd fnl f* **8/1**

**6** *nse* **Quids In (IRE)**[165] 7521 4-9-3 **66**..................(t) SeamusCronin(5) 5 63
(Oliver Greenall) *hld up in rr: effrt on wd outside fr 3f out: sn rdn along: edgd lft and drvn over 1f out: styd on* **4/1**[1]

2-16 **7** *nk* **Dubaitwentytwenty**[21] 7279 3-9-5 **67**..............................(t) GeorgiaCox 2 63
(Hugo Palmer) *prom: rdn along 3f out: drvn wl over 1f out: grad wknd appr fnl f* **9/1**

0-0 **8** *nk* **Unblinking**[144] 2841 4-9-2 **60**.................................... JoshDoyle 15 56
(Nigel Twiston-Davies) *towards rr tl styd on fnl 2f* **33/1**

6350 **9** *1* **Polar Forest**[7] 7735 7-9-4 **67**.......................................(p) JackOsborn(5) 3 61
(Richard Guest) *in tch on inner: hdwy to chse ldrs wl over 2f out: rdn wl over 1f out: wknd appr fnl f* **8/1**

0351 **10** *½* **Decima (IRE)**[15] 7478 3-8-13 **66**.......................... HarrisonShaw(5) 10 60
(Michael Easterby) *t.k.h: hld up: hdwy over 2f out: sn rdn and no imp* **7/1**[3]

0000 **11** *hd* **Rock'n Gold**[29] 7028 4-8-13 **60**.................................... FinleyMarsh(3) 7 52
(Adrian Wintle) *a towards rr* **50/1**

6402 **12** *1 ½* **Perceived**[22] 7236 5-9-4 **65**.......................................... WilliamCox(3) 4 54
(Antony Brittain) *towards rr: hdwy on outer 3f out: rdn along and in tch wl over 1f out: sn drvn and wknd* **8/1**

0045 **13** *3* **Sir Lancelott**[32] 6947 5-8-13 **57**...................................... PhilDennis 13 40
(Adrian Nicholls) *chsd ldrs: cl up over 3f out: sn rdn and wknd fnl 2f* **25/1**

2m 16.92s (2.62) **Going Correction** 0.0s/f (Good)
**WFA** 3 from 4yo+ 4lb **13** Ran SP% **121.7**
Speed ratings (Par 103): **89,88,87,86,85 84,84,84,83,83 83,81,79**
CSF £47.33 CT £458.48 TOTE £7.10: £2.60, £2.90, £3.20; EX 49.10 Trifecta £394.40.
**Owner** Spiers & Hartwell Ltd & Mrs E Evans **Bred** Charel Park Stud **Trained** Pandy, Monmouths

**FOCUS**
Distance increased by 6yds. Another race run at a steady enough gallop where it paid to race handily. Ordinary form.
T/Plt: £85.90 to a £1 stake. Pool: £61,521.69 - 522.69 winning units T/Qpdt: £21.90 to a £1 stake. Pool: £6,306.38 - 212.30 winning units **Joe Rowntree**

7961 - 7968a (Foreign Racing) - See Raceform Interactive

## 7844 CHANTILLY (R-H)
### Wednesday, October 11
**OFFICIAL GOING: Polytrack: standard; turf: very soft**

## 7969a PRIX DE LA GRANDE RAILLE (MAIDEN) (2YO FILLIES) (TURF) 1m 1f
**1:35** 2-Y-O **£11,538** (£4,615; £3,461; £2,307; £1,153)

RPR

**1** **Tempel (FR)**[38] 2-9-2 0.............................. MaximeGuyon 9 78
(A Fabre, France) **16/5**[2]

**2** *½* **Lypharty Ka (FR)**[44] 6542 2-9-2 0.......................... StephanePasquier 6 77
(Y Gourraud, France) **14/1**

**3** *1* **Estijlaa**[36] 6803 2-9-2 0.............................. AurelienLemaitre 11 75
(F Head, France) **9/5**[1]

**4** *2* **Liberty Belle (FR)**[20] 2-8-10 0.......................... ClementLecoeuvre(6) 3 71
(E Lellouche, France) **11/1**

**5** *nk* **Lots Of Tea (FR)**[38] 2-9-2 0.............................. Pierre-CharlesBoudot 13 70
(Mme C Head-Maarek, France) **20/1**

**6** *snk* **Save The Date (FR)**[21] 7304 2-8-6 0.................. MlleCoraliePacaut(10) 7 70
(T Castanheira, France) **11/1**

**7** *1 ¼* **Zillione Sun (FR)**[12] 2-9-2 0.............................. GregoryBenoist 2 68
(Mme P Butel & J-L Beaunez, France) **20/1**

**8** *1 ¾* **Petrosinella (FR)** 2-8-8 0.............................. ThomasTrullier(8) 4 64
(N Clement, France) **83/1**

**9** *nk* **Pyramid First (FR)** 2-9-2 0.............................. CristianDemuro 8 64
(L Gadbin, France) **19/1**

**10** *1* **Luna Riska (FR)** 2-8-11 0.............................. DelphineSantiago(5) 1 62
(J-P Gallorini, France) **49/1**

**11** *¾* **Etoile Du Ficheaux (FR)** 2-9-2 0.......................... VincentCheminaud 12 60
(J-P Gallorini, France) **43/1**

**12** *3* **Star Of Vendome (FR)**[18] 7415 2-9-2 0.......................... EddyHardouin 10 54
(Harry Dunlop) *led: rdn 2f out and hdd sn after: no ex: wknd* **5/1**[3]

1m 53.07s (1.97) **12** Ran SP% **119.5**
PARI-MUTUEL (all including 1 euro stake): WIN 4.20; PLACE 1.80, 2.80, 1.50; DF 25.20; SF 40.00.
**Owner** Wertheimer & Frere **Bred** Wertheimer & Frere **Trained** Chantilly, France

7970 - 7977a (Foreign Racing) - See Raceform Interactive

## 7698 AYR (L-H)
### Thursday, October 12
**OFFICIAL GOING: Heavy**
Wind: Fresh, half against in over 3f of home straight Weather: Overcast

## 7978 BEN EBF NOVICE STKS (PLUS 10 RACE) 1m
**2:00** (2:00) (Class 4) 2-Y-O **£6,469** (£1,925; £962; £481) **Stalls** Low

Form RPR

61 **1** **Wax And Wane**[29] 7043 2-9-9 0.............................. BenCurtis 1 86
(K R Burke) *mde all: rdn along 2f out: styd on gamely fnl f* **8/11**[1]

162 **2** *1 ¾* **Lynwood Gold (IRE)**[11] 7654 2-9-9 0.......................... JoeFanning 2 82
(Mark Johnston) *dwlt: sn w wnr: rdn over 1f out: kpt on same pce ins fnl f* **11/4**[2]

4 **3** *4 ½* **Spark Of War (IRE)**[12] 7613 2-9-2 0.......................... GrahamLee 6 65
(Keith Dalgleish) *hld up in tch: effrt and shkn up over 2f out: hdwy over 1f out: no imp fnl f* **9/2**[3]

65 **4** *9* **Sincerely Resdev**[14] 7556 2-9-2 0.............................. PaddyAspell 3 45
(Philip Kirby) *prom: rdn and hung lft over 2f out: wknd wl over 1f out* **40/1**

0 **5** *10* **Dicktation**[33] 6938 2-8-13 0.............................. LewisEdmunds(3) 4 23
(Richard Whitaker) *trckd ldrs: rdn and hung lft over 2f out: sn wknd* **50/1**

1m 48.53s **5** Ran SP% **107.2**
CSF £2.77 TOTE £1.50: £1.10, £1.30; EX 2.80 Trifecta £5.10.
**Owner** Tim Dykes **Bred** Stowell Hill Partners **Trained** Middleham Moor, N Yorks

**FOCUS**
After recent rain the meeting had to pass a morning inspection and, as at the last fixture here, they used the hurdles track, meaning that comparisons to standard times and speed figures aren't possible. Not surprisingly the going was heavy and the top bend was moved out, adding 3yds to all race distances. An uncompetitive novice event to start, despite being the most valuable race on the card, and weakened further by the absence of the likely favourite Soldier's Minute. They came up the centre in the straight and finished in market order. The runner-up is the best guide.

## 7979 TENNENT'S H'CAP (DIV I) 1m
**2:30** (2:32) (Class 6) (0-60,60) 3-Y-O+ **£2,587** (£770; £384; £192) **Stalls** Low

Form RPR

5623 **1** **Quiet Moment (IRE)**[3] 7888 3-8-8 **50**.......................... ConnorBeasley 10 57
(Keith Dalgleish) *hld up midfield on outside: smooth hdwy to ld over 2f out: rdn and hrd pressed fr over 1f out: hld on gamely nr fin* **8/1**

2003 **2** *nk* **Catastrophe**[22] 7271 4-9-0 **53**.............................. JasonHart 14 59
(John Quinn) *t.k.h: in tch: hdwy to chal over 2f out: kpt on u.p fnl f: hld nr fin* **9/1**

0455 **3** *hd* **Little Pippin**[22] 7270 4-8-7 **46** oh1..............................(p[1]) BarryMcHugh 7 52
(Tony Coyle) *hld up: hdwy to chse ldrs over 1f out: rdn and kpt on fnl f: hld cl home* **20/1**

3402 **4** *5* **Jessie Allan (IRE)**[59] 5991 6-8-2 **48**.......................... SeanMooney(7) 9 43
(Jim Goldie) *hld up: hdwy and prom over 1f out: drvn and wknd ins fnl f* **16/1**

6034 **5** *2 ¼* **Hellavashock**[9] 7704 4-8-7 **46** oh1..............................(b) JoeDoyle 8 36
(Alistair Whillans) *hld up midfield: drvn and outpcd over 2f out: rallied fnl f: sn no imp* **7/1**[2]

3354 **6** *1 ½* **Highway Robber**[37] 6788 4-8-12 **51**.......................... PaulMulrennan 13 38
(Wilf Storey) *in tch: drvn and outpcd over 2f out: rallied ins fnl f: no imp* **12/1**

0456 **7** *1 ¼* **Be Bold**[19] 7389 5-9-0 **58**..............................(p[1]) RowanScott(5) 6 42
(Rebecca Bastiman) *chsd ldrs: rdn over 2f out: wknd over 1f out* **20/1**

0006 **8** *1* **Royal Holiday (IRE)**[16] 7478 10-9-2 **55**.......................(p) JoeyHaynes 1 37
(Marjorie Fife) *led to over 2f out: rdn and wknd over 1f out* **16/1**

4464 **9** *1* **Mischief Managed (IRE)**[19] 7390 3-9-4 **60**................ DuranFentiman 3 40
(Tim Easterby) *midfield: drvn and outpcd over 2f out: n.d after* **15/2**[3]

0043 **10** *hd* **Ingleby Angel (IRE)**[9] 7703 8-9-4 **57**.......................... DanielTudhope 5 36
(David O'Meara) *s.i.s: hld up: rdn over 2f out: sn no imp* **3/1**[1]

0042 **11** *2 ¼* **Cosmic Dust**[22] 7270 4-8-10 **52**.......................... LewisEdmunds(3) 2 26
(Richard Whitaker) *t.k.h: cl up: effrt and ev ch over 2f out: wknd over 1f out* **10/1**

4055 **12** *nse* **Stardrifter**[9] 7703 5-8-8 **47**.............................. AndrewMullen 11 21
(Linda Perratt) *s.i.s: hld up: rdn along over 2f out: sn n.d: btn over 1f out* **16/1**

6030 **13** *9* **Irvine Lady (IRE)**[3] 7889 4-8-7 **46** oh1....................(h[1]) JamesSullivan 12
(R Mike Smith) *prom: rdn and lost pl over 2f out: sn wknd* **100/1**

0-00 **14** *31* **Daleelak (IRE)**[250] 579 4-9-7 **60**.............................. JoeFanning 4
(Mark Johnston) *bhd: lost tch wl over 2f out: t.o* **50/1**

1m 48.6s
**WFA** 3 from 4yo+ 3lb **14** Ran SP% **117.3**
CSF £73.32 CT £1428.37 TOTE £7.90: £2.40, £2.80, £7.70; EX 71.50 Trifecta £1861.90.
**Owner** We'Re Electric **Bred** Messrs D & J Fitzgerald **Trained** Carluke, S Lanarks
■ Stewards' Enquiry : Jason Hart two day ban: using his whip above the permitted level (26/27 Oct)

**FOCUS**
Add 3yds to race distance. The first division of a moderate handicap in which a few of these ran at the last meeting here nine days earlier. The runners again came towards the centre of the track turning in, but then tended to edge more towards the stands' rail and that is where the main action unfolded, with a thrilling finish between the front trio. The leaders paid for doing too much early in the conditions and the winning time was fractionally slower than the 2yos in the opener. Ordinary form.

## 7980 TENNENT'S H'CAP (DIV II) 1m
**3:05** (3:05) (Class 6) (0-60,60) 3-Y-O+ **£2,587** (£770; £384; £192) **Stalls** Low

Form RPR

0640 **1** **The King's Steed**[16] 7479 4-8-7 **46** oh1......................(t[1]) BarryMcHugh 5 52
(Micky Hammond) *trckd ldrs gng wl: rdn to ld over 1f out: sn hrd pressed: hld on gamely cl home* **25/1**

3252 **2** *shd* **Green Howard**[9] 7703 9-9-4 **57**..............................(p) DanielTudhope 10 63
(Rebecca Bastiman) *hld up: smooth hdwy over 2f out: effrt and disp ld fr over 1f out: hld cl home* **10/3**[1]

0000 **3** *1 ¼* **Magical Molly Joe**[12] 7628 3-8-11 **53**.......................... BenCurtis 8 56
(David Barron) *hld up: effrt whn nt clr run over 2f out to wl over 1f out: rdn and r.o ins fnl f: nt rch first two* **33/1**

4331 **4** *¾* **Someone Exciting**[19] 7390 4-8-12 **58**.......................... JamieGormley(7) 7 61
(David Thompson) *t.k.h early: hld up: effrt whn nt clr run and swtchd lft over 1f out: rdn and r.o fnl f: nt pce to chal* **5/1**[2]

3660 **5** *½* **Coral Princess (IRE)**[3] 7889 3-8-4 **46**.......................... JoeFanning 4 47
(Keith Dalgleish) *t.k.h: hld up: hdwy and prom over 1f out: rdn and no ex ins fnl f* **10/1**

0010 **6** *3 ½* **Billy Bond**[9] 7703 5-9-4 **60**..............................(b) AdamMcNamara(3) 2 53
(Richard Fahey) *s.i.s: hld up: smooth hdwy on outside over 2f out: rdn and wknd fnl f* **10/1**

5254 **7** *1* **Carlovian**[9] 7703 4-9-0 **53**..............................(p) GrahamLee 6 44
(Mark Walford) *t.k.h: trckd ldrs: rdn over 2f out: wknd over 1f out* **11/2**[3]

0006 **8** *1 ½* **Niqnaaqpaadiwaaq**[29] 7046 5-8-9 **48**.......................... NeilFarley 12 35
(Eric Alston) *in tch: effrt over 2f out: rdn and wknd over 1f out* **10/1**

3102 **9** *6* **Rioja Day (IRE)**[9] 7704 7-8-8 **54**..............................(b) SeanMooney(7) 14 28
(Jim Goldie) *s.i.s: bhd: struggling over 3f out: sme late hdwy: nvr on terms* **10/1**

3003 **10** *2 ½* **Orientelle**[64] 5802 3-8-5 **50**..............................(b) LewisEdmunds(3) 13 19
(Richard Whitaker) *t.k.h: pressed ldr: rdn over 2f out: wknd over 1f out* **8/1**

6-60 **11** *1 ¾* **Arabela Dawn (IRE)**[92] 4743 3-8-7 **49**.......................... JasonHart 3 14
(John Quinn) *t.k.h: hld up in tch: drvn along 3f out: wknd wl over 1f out* **50/1**

0001 **12** *6* **Let Right Be Done**[3] 7888 5-8-12 **51** 6ex...................(b) AndrewMullen 9 3
(Linda Perratt) *t.k.h: led to over 1f out: sn wknd* **18/1**

060 **13** *4 ½* **Delegation**[85] 5019 3-8-6 **48**.............................. DuranFentiman 11
(Tim Easterby) *in tch: drvn along over 2f out: wknd wl over 1f out* **50/1**

400 **14** *2 ½* **Kaylen's Mischief**[20] 7365 4-9-3 **56**..............................(h[1]) PaddyAspell 1
(Philip Kirby) *slowly away: bhd and detached: nvr on terms* **66/1**

1m 49.59s
**WFA** 3 from 4yo+ 3lb **14** Ran SP% **120.1**
CSF £104.44 CT £2839.67 TOTE £30.40: £8.80, £1.50, £7.40; EX 160.10 Trifecta £3434.40 Part Won..
**Owner** The Charlie Partners **Bred** Littleton Stud **Trained** Middleham, N Yorks

**FOCUS**
Add 3yds to race distance. Again a few of these ran over C&D nine days earlier and again the runners were inclined to come more over towards the stands' rail up the straight. The winning time was almost exactly a second slower than the first division and, as with the first leg, it went to a maiden. The winner was hard to find but has back form.

## 7981 WILLIAM HILL BET BOOST H'CAP 1m
**3:35** (3:36) (Class 4) (0-85,87) 3-Y-0+ £5,822 (£1,732; £865; £432) **Stalls** Low

Form RPR
2321 **1** **Jay Kay**[9] 7702 8-8-12 **76** 6ex.........................................(h) JoeyHaynes 10 84
(K R Burke) *mde all: clr over 2f out: rdn and r.o wl fnl f: unchal* **11/4**[2]
0610 **2** *3* **Le Chat D'Or**[13] 7566 9-9-9 **87**.........................(bt) PaulMulrennan 6 88
(Michael Dods) *hld up in rr: hdwy to chse (clr) wnr over 1f out: sn rdn and drifted lft: kpt on same pce ins fnl f* **22/1**
4506 **3** *2 ½* **Crazy Tornado (IRE)**[9] 7699 4-8-7 **71** oh2.................(h) AndrewMullen 3 66
(Keith Dalgleish) *trckd ldrs: rdn over 2f out: kpt on ins fnl f: nt rch first two* **25/1**
0002 **4** *hd* **Newmarket Warrior (IRE)**[13] 7570 6-8-0 **71** oh3..(p) JamieGormley(7) 7 66
(Iain Jardine) *s.i.s: hld up: pushed along over 2f out: kpt on fnl f: nvr able to chal* **16/1**
2662 **5** *2* **Prying Pandora (FR)**[62] 5889 4-9-0 **81**................. AdamMcNamara(3) 1 71
(Richard Fahey) *dwlt: t.k.h and sn prom: rdn over 2f out: wknd over 1f out* **15/2**
6200 **6** *½* **Rock N Rolla (IRE)**[3] 7886 3-8-10 **77**.......................... ConnorBeasley 2 66
(Keith Dalgleish) *chsd wnr: rdn over 2f out: edgd lft and outpcd whn checked over 1f out: sn btn* **13/2**[3]
5434 **7** *2* **Royal Duchess**[61] 5922 7-8-7 **71** oh4.................................... JoeDoyle 4 55
(Lucy Normile) *in tch: drvn along over 2f out: wknd over 1f out* **12/1**
551 **8** *3* **Candelisa (IRE)**[15] 7523 4-9-8 **86**................................(p) BarryMcHugh 5 64
(Tony Coyle) *hld up towards rr: rdn and outpcd over 2f out: sn btn* **8/1**
6312 **9** *2* **Dark Devil (IRE)**[12] 7594 4-9-6 **84**.................................. PaulHanagan 8 57
(Richard Fahey) *hld up midfield: effrt and c alone to stands' rail over 3f out: rdn and wknd 2f out* **5/2**[1]

1m 47.97s
**WFA** 3 from 4yo+ 3lb **9** Ran SP% **113.2**
CSF £58.82 CT £1243.85 TOTE £3.50: £1.10, £4.20, £6.20; EX 72.60 Trifecta £1133.90.
**Owner** John Kenny & Partner **Bred** Miss S E Hall **Trained** Middleham Moor, N Yorks

**FOCUS**
Add 3yds to race distance. A decent handicap for the grade, despite three of the nine runners racing from out of the handicap, as two of the other six were rated above the race ceiling. Unsurprisingly the winning time was the fastest of the four races over the trip, but the perceived track bias was turned on it head with the main players coming up the centre in the straight. This rates a pb from the winner although there are doubts given the conditions.

## 7982 WILLIAM HILL JOIN PLUS IN SHOP TODAY H'CAP 1m 5f
**4:05** (4:05) (Class 6) (0-65,66) 3-Y-0+ £2,587 (£770; £384; £192) **Stalls** Low

Form RPR
1664 **1** **Adherence**[2] 7922 4-9-0 **55**..........................................(p) BarryMcHugh 11 61
(Tony Coyle) *hld up in tch: rdn along over 2f out: edgd lft: rallied and led over 1f out: styd on wl fnl f* **9/1**
5255 **2** *1 ½* **Eyreborn (IRE)**[13] 7560 3-8-9 **61**.................................. RowanScott(5) 2 67
(Keith Dalgleish) *hld up: rdn and outpcd over 2f out: rallied over 1f out: kpt on wl to take 2nd nr fin: nt rch wnr* **5/1**[2]
000 **3** *½* **Main Fact (USA)**[9] 1716 4-9-5 **60**...............................(h) PaulMulrennan 7 63
(Dianne Sayer) *cl up: led over 3f out: edgd lft and hdd over 1f out: kpt on same pce fnl f* **40/1**
6600 **4** *1 ¾* **Red Star Dancer (IRE)**[24] 7220 3-8-4 **51**.......................... JoeFanning 6 53
(David Barron) *hld up: hdwy over 2f out: rdn and kpt on ins fnl f: nvr able to chal* **6/1**[3]
0060 **5** *3 ¼* **Glance My Way (IRE)**[50] 6316 4-9-5 **60**..................(b) AndrewMullen 10 56
(Tim Easterby) *trckd ldrs: rdn along over 2f out: hung lft: wknd appr fnl f* **40/1**
5050 **6** *hd* **Rob's Legacy**[23] 7233 4-8-10 **51** oh6......................... DuranFentiman 8 46
(Shaun Harris) *led 2f: cl up: drvn and outpcd over 2f out: no imp fr over 1f out* **66/1**
4126 **7** *hd* **Druid's Diamond**[28] 6153 4-8-12 **53**................................(p) JasonHart 5 48
(Mark Walford) *prom: drvn along over 2f out: edgd lft and wknd over 1f out* **7/1**
4650 **8** *12* **Celtic Power**[23] 7248 5-8-10 **51** oh6...........................(b) JamesSullivan 1 28
(Jim Goldie) *hld up: rdn and outpcd over 2f out: sn btn* **25/1**
0105 **9** *4 ½* **King Of Scotland (FR)**[13] 7561 3-9-4 **65**...................... DanielTudhope 9 45
(Hughie Morrison) *t.k.h: cl up: led after 2f to over 3f out: rdn and wknd 2f out: eased whn btn fnl f* **15/8**[1]
3053 **10** *1 ¼* **Mambo Dancer**[5] 7832 3-9-5 **66**........................................ PJMcDonald 3 36
(Mark Johnston) *towards rr: nvr gng wl: shortlived effrt over 4f out: struggling fr over 3f out* **13/2**

3m 11.29s
**WFA** 3 from 4yo+ 6lb **10** Ran SP% **111.8**
CSF £49.86 CT £1683.96 TOTE £8.80: £2.40, £1.70, £6.40; EX 57.00 Trifecta £1602.10.
**Owner** M A Scaife **Bred** Wrottesley Limited **Trained** Norton, N Yorks

**FOCUS**
Add 3yds to race distance. A moderate middle-distance handicap, but they went a fair pace. The field stayed centre to far side up the straight this time. The third and fourth emphasise the form's limitations.

## 7983 WILLIAM HILL GET THE APP ON GOOGLEPLAY H'CAP 1m 7f
**4:40** (4:40) (Class 4) (0-80,78) 3-Y-0+ £5,822 (£1,732; £865; £432) **Stalls** Low

Form RPR
0402 **1** **Buonarroti (IRE)**[13] 7561 6-9-6 **70**...............................(t) DanielTudhope 3 79+
(Declan Carroll) *hld up: smooth hdwy to ld over 1f out: shkn up and qcknd ins fnl f: readily* **11/2**
534 **2** *2* **Hurricane Hollow**[13] 7561 7-9-5 **69**...................................... BenCurtis 1 74
(David Barron) *hld up: hdwy on outside over 2f out: rdn over 1f out: kpt to chse wnr wl ins fnl f: r.o* **10/1**
0654 **3** *nse* **Gabrial's Star**[12] 7599 8-9-7 **71**.....................................(p) PaulHanagan 4 76
(Richard Fahey) *hld up in tch: stdy hdwy 1/2-way: rdn and outpcd over 2f out: rallied over 1f out: kpt on fin* **22/1**
5122 **4** *½* **Bodacious Name (IRE)**[15] 7048 3-8-7 **65**.......................... JasonHart 9 69
(John Quinn) *hld up: hdwy and disp ld over 2f out to over 1f out: no ex and lost two pls wl ins fnl f* **5/1**[3]
1 **5** *2 ¾* **Mixboy (FR)**[12] 7629 7-10-0 **78**.......................................... JoeFanning 6 79
(Keith Dalgleish) *chsd ldr: led gng wl over 2f out: rdn and hdd over 1f out: outpcd fnl f* **11/4**[1]
2545 **6** *9* **Braes Of Lochalsh**[9] 7701 6-9-4 **68**............................(v) JamesSullivan 7 58
(Jim Goldie) *chsd ldrs: rdn and outpcd over 2f out: btn over 1f out* **20/1**
3435 **7** *1* **Captain Swift (IRE)**[19] 7413 6-8-13 **63**............................(p) GrahamLee 2 52
(John Mackie) *prom: rdn along over 2f out: wknd over 1f out* **22/1**
/034 **8** *1 ½* **New Youmzain (FR)**[9] 7700 8-9-1 **65**.......................... AndrewMullen 10 52
(Lucy Normile) *dwlt: bhd: rdn and struggling over 3f out: nvr on terms* **50/1**
6012 **9** *1 ¾* **London Glory**[11] 7659 4-8-11 **61**.................................(b) PJMcDonald 5 46
(David Thompson) *hld up: rdn and outpcd over 2f out: sn btn* **10/1**
4414 **10** *11* **Golden Jeffrey (SWI)**[14] 5923 4-9-0 **71**....................... JamieGormley(7) 8 43
(Iain Jardine) *sn pushed into ld and set str pce: stdd over 5f out: hdd over 2f out: sn wknd* **10/3**[2]

3m 36.21s
**WFA** 3 from 4yo+ 8lb **10** Ran SP% **115.4**
CSF £54.71 CT £1117.52 TOTE £6.30: £1.80, £3.20, £4.50; EX 66.40 Trifecta £777.30.
**Owner** Denis Hardy **Bred** Beauty Is Truth Syndicate **Trained** Malton, N Yorks

**FOCUS**
Add 3yds to race distance. A fair staying handicap and quite a test in the conditions, but the leaders went off far too quick and the first two were dropped right out early. They came centre to nearside up the straight. The winner gave the second a slightly bigger beating than at Haydock.

## 7984 WILLIAM HILL BEST ODDS GUARANTEED H'CAP 1m 1f
**5:10** (5:11) (Class 5) (0-75,77) 3-Y-0+ £3,881 (£1,155; £577; £288) **Stalls** Low

Form RPR
0140 **1** **Chinese Spirit (IRE)**[11] 7656 3-8-13 **67**........................... PJMcDonald 5 74
(R Mike Smith) *prom: led over 2f out: rdn over 1f out: edgd rt and kpt on wl fnl f* **6/1**[3]
4506 **2** *1 ¼* **Dellaguista (IRE)**[12] 7598 3-8-11 **65**............................ AndrewMullen 8 69
(Tim Easterby) *prom: effrt and chsd wnr over 1f out: kpt on ins fnl f: hld nr fin* **9/1**
5431 **3** *hd* **Cliff Bay (IRE)**[9] 7704 3-8-9 **63**........................................... JoeFanning 2 67
(Keith Dalgleish) *s.i.s: t.k.h: hld up: stdy hdwy over 2f out: effrt and disp 2nd pl ins fnl f: no ex towards fin* **7/2**[1]
3365 **4** *½* **Infamous Lawman (IRE)**[16] 7476 3-8-13 **67**............. DanielTudhope 10 70
(David O'Meara) *cl up: rdn and outpcd over 1f out: rallied ins fnl f: kpt on* **4/1**[2]
3031 **5** *1 ¼* **Mustaqbal (IRE)**[9] 7703 5-8-12 **65**.....................(p) CallumRodriguez(3) 9 65
(Michael Dods) *hld up: hdwy and prom over 1f out: outpcd ins fnl f* **7/2**[1]
5-00 **6** *6* **Dwight D**[13] 7566 4-9-13 **77**............................................ PatrickMathers 7 65
(Stuart Coltherd) *s.i.s: hld up: pushed along over 2f out: sn outpcd: n.d after* **50/1**
0000 **7** *2 ¼* **Spes Nostra**[37] 6789 9-8-10 **60**.....................................(b) PaulHanagan 3 43
(Iain Jardine) *led tl hung lft and hdd over 2f out: wknd over 1f out* **22/1**
050/ **8** *11* **Bo Bridget (IRE)**[26] 7170 4-8-7 **57**................................ JamesSullivan 6 18
(Adrian Murray, Ire) *cl up: drvn and outpcd over 2f out: wknd wl over 1f out* **7/2**[1]

2m 7.66s
**WFA** 3 from 4yo+ 4lb **8** Ran SP% **117.3**
CSF £59.39 CT £220.43 TOTE £6.60: £1.80, £2.40, £1.50; EX 51.40 Trifecta £327.50.
**Owner** Y C Luk **Bred** J Murphy **Trained** Galston, E Ayrshire
■ She's Pukka was withdrawn. Price at time of withdrawal 9/1. Rule 4 applies to bets struck at board prices prior to withdrawal but not to SP bets - deduction 10p in the pound. New market formed

**FOCUS**
Add 3yds to race distance. A modest handicap, though made more interesting by the presence of two horses who were both well in having won different divisions of the apprentice handicap over 1m here nine days earlier. The early pace wasn't strong, causing a couple to race keenly, and again they came centre to nearside up the straight. A small pb from the winner.
T/Plt: £2,323.30 to a £1 stake. Pool: £65,784.56 - 20.67 winning units T/Qpdt: £235.50 to a £1 stake. Pool: £6,398.19 - 20.10 winning units **Richard Young**

# 7786 CHELMSFORD (A.W) (L-H)
Thursday, October 12

**OFFICIAL GOING: Polytrack: standard**
Wind: virtually nil Weather: dry

## 7985 BET TOTEPLACEPOT AT BETFRED.COM CLAIMING STKS 7f (P)
**5:45** (5:46) (Class 5) 2-Y-O £4,528 (£1,347; £673; £336) **Stalls** Low

Form RPR
5646 **1** **Montague (IRE)**[16] 7489 2-9-7 72.................................. DougieCostello 2 75
(Jamie Osborne) *mde all: shkn up 2f out: rdn over 1f out: styd on wl and a doing ins fnl f* **8/1**
0520 **2** *½* **Fusion Central (IRE)**[23] 7226 2-8-2 66.......................... HollieDoyle(3) 4 58
(Richard Hannon) *chsd wnr: effrt ent fnl 2f: rdn over 1f out: edging lft ins fnl f: kpt on same pce* **5/1**[3]
00 **3** *1 ¼* **One For June (IRE)**[54] 6200 2-8-4 70....................... SilvestreDeSousa 6 53+
(William Haggas) *short of room sn after s: sn swtchd lft and keen in last pair: rdn 1/2-way: 4th and drvn wl over 1f out: chsd clr ldng pair jst ins fnl f: styd on wl: nvr getting to ldrs* **11/10**[1]
004 **4** *1 ¼* **Smugglers Top**[28] 7079 2-8-13 67............................(p[1]) RichardKingscote 1 59
(Tom Dascombe) *dwlt: hld up in last pair: nt clrest of runs over 2f out: swtchd rt and hdwy over 1f out: styd on ins fnl f: nvr trbld ldrs* **9/2**[2]
36 **5** *1* **Little Poem**[30] 7023 2-8-3 0........................................(h) LukeMorris 5 46
(Marco Botti) *chsd ldng pair: rdn ent fnl 2f: 3rd and outpcd u.p over 1f out: lost 3rd and wknd jst ins fnl f* **16/1**
0 **6** *5* **Archibald Leitch**[22] 7280 2-8-8 0............................................ JFEgan 3 38
(David Evans) *rn in snatches in midfield: struggling over 2f out: 6th and wl hld 1f out: wknd* **8/1**
000 **7** *16* **Koin**[30] 7023 2-8-0 33.................................................(b[1]) DavidEgan(3) 7
(Mark H Tompkins) *midfield: rdn 3f out: dropped to rr over 1f out: sn wknd* **100/1**

1m 26.21s (-0.99) **Going Correction** -0.25s/f (Stan) **7** Ran SP% **111.6**
Speed ratings (Par 95): **95,94,93,91,90 84,66**
CSF £44.73 TOTE £8.10: £3.60, £2.90; EX 45.50 Trifecta £113.90.No claims for this race
**Owner** Mrs A G Kavanagh **Bred** Kildaragh Stud **Trained** Upper Lambourn, Berks

**FOCUS**
A typically weak 2yo claimer and the first pair dominated.

## 7986 BET TOTEJACKPOT AT BETFRED.COM FILLIES' NOVICE STKS (PLUS 10 RACE) 6f (P)
**6:15** (6:16) (Class 5) 2-Y-O £4,528 (£1,347; £673; £336) **Stalls** Centre

Form RPR
2 **1** **Pretty Baby (IRE)**[32] 6969 2-9-0 0..................................... RyanMoore 3 82+
(William Haggas) *mde all: rdn and qcknd over 1f out: clr and in command 1f out: r.o wl: comf* **1/5**[1]

6 **2** 3 ½ **Musical Theatre**[38] 6747 2-9-0 0.................................(h[1]) OisinMurphy 1 70
(David Simcock) *stdd s: trckd ldrs: effrt to go 2nd over 1f out but unable to match pce on wnr 1f out: wl hld but clr in 2nd ins fnl f: kpt on* **14/1**

06 **3** 1 ½ **Image**[21] 7334 2-9-0 0.......................................... DavidProbert 6 65
(Philip McBride) *dwlt: sn rcvrd to chse ldng pair: rdn and outpcd over 1f out: wl hld 3rd and kpt on same pce ins fnl f* **25/1**

20 **4** 1 ¼ **Angel's Whisper (IRE)**[22] 7269 2-9-0 0........................... JamesDoyle 5 61
(Jeremy Noseda) *awkward leaving stalls and dwlt: hld up in tch: shkn up over 1f out: sn outpcd: rdn and no hdwy ent fnl f: wl hld and kpt on same pce ins fnl f* **7/1**[2]

025 **5** 2 ½ **Havana Heart**[38] 6747 2-9-0 69.................................. SilvestreDeSousa 4 53
(Ismail Mohammed) *pressed wnr tl rdn: lost 2nd and unable qck over 1f out: wknd ins fnl f* **10/1**[3]

04 **6** 3 ¾ **Rock On Baileys**[103] 4349 2-9-0 0.........................(h[1]) AdamBeschizza 2 41
(Chris Dwyer) *in tch: rdn and outpcd over 1f out: sn wknd* **66/1**

**7** 1 ¾ **Denham** 2-9-0 0.......................................... LukeMorris 7 35+
(Michael Appleby) *wnt rt s and v.s.a: clsd onto bk of field over 3f out: shkn up ent fnl 2f: rdn and outpcd over 1f out: sn bhd* **50/1**

1m 12.96s (-0.74) **Going Correction** -0.25s/f (Stan) 7 Ran SP% **118.9**
Speed ratings (Par 92): **94,89,87,85,82 77,75**
CSF £5.37 TOTE £1.10: £1.10, £4.20; EX 5.10 Trifecta £25.10.
**Owner** Sheikh Rashid Dalmook Al Maktoum **Bred** Dayton Investments Ltd **Trained** Newmarket, Suffolk

**FOCUS**
An uncompetitive fillies' novice. The winner made all on a pace-favouring card.

## 7987 BET TOTEQUADPOT AT BETFRED.COM NOVICE STKS 1m (P)
**6:45** (6:46) (Class 5) 2-Y-O **£4,528** (£1,347; £673; £336) **Stalls** Low

Form RPR

5 **1** **Main Street**[110] 4094 2-9-2 0.......................................... RobertHavlin 3 85+
(John Gosden) *s.i.s and rousted along early: hld up in tch in rr: swtchd rt and shkn up over 1f out: str to run ins fnl f to ld 50yds out: gng away at fin* **8/1**

23 **2** 1 ¾ **Rua Augusta (USA)**[42] 6616 2-9-2 0.......................................... TomEaves 2 78
(Kevin Ryan) *led: rdn over 1f out: drvn and forged ahd 1f out: hdd and nt match pce of wnr fnl 50yds* **3/1**[2]

10 **3** 1 **Morlock (IRE)**[14] 7546 2-9-9 0.......................................... WilliamBuick 6 83
(Charlie Appleby) *pressed ldr: pushed along and ev ch ent fnl 2f: edgd rt and unable qck 1f out: kpt on same pce ins fnl f* **11/4**[1]

**4** 1 **Welsh Lord** 2-9-2 0.......................................... SilvestreDeSousa 4 75+
(Saeed bin Suroor) *trckd ldrs: nt clrest of runs 2f out: swtchd rt and effrt over 1f out: rn green and wanting to hang lft after: styd on same pce ins fnl f* **4/1**

0 **5** 1 **Revolutionary Man (IRE)**[48] 6388 2-9-2 0.................... AndreaAtzeni 1 71
(Simon Crisford) *dwlt: rcvrd to trck ldrs after 2f out: effrt over 1f out: unable qck u.p 1f out: outpcd ins fnl f* **33/1**

**6** 3 **Red Striker (IRE)** 2-9-2 0.......................................... RyanMoore 8 65
(Sir Michael Stoute) *dropped in after s: hld up in tch: pushed along and effrt over 1f out: sn no imp: wknd ins fnl f* **10/3**[3]

**7** 1 ½ **Ready To Impress (USA)** 2-9-2 0.............................. FrannyNorton 7 61
(Mark Johnston) *in tch in midfield on outer: effrt over 1f out: unable qck and outpcd whn swtchd lft jst over 1f out: wknd ins fnl f* **11/1**

0 **8** ¾ **Kingofthesingers**[14] 7535 2-9-2 0.......................................... LukeMorris 5 59
(Sir Mark Prescott Bt) *dwlt: in tch towards rr: rdn 2f out: unable qck and outpcd whn hmpd and swtchd lft 1f out: wknd ins fnl f* **100/1**

1m 39.05s (-0.85) **Going Correction** -0.25s/f (Stan) 8 Ran SP% **118.1**
Speed ratings (Par 95): **94,92,91,90,89 86,84,84**
CSF £33.42 TOTE £9.70: £2.10, £1.40, £1.50; EX 33.10 Trifecta £129.60.
**Owner** Newsells Park Stud **Bred** Newsells Park Stud **Trained** Newmarket, Suffolk

**FOCUS**
A good-quality novice event which saw changing fortunes inside the final furlong. The winner impressed and the form is taken at face value.

## 7988 BET TOTEEXACTA AT BETFRED.COM CONDITIONS STKS 1m 2f (P)
**7:15** (7:17) (Class 3) 3-Y-O+ **£9,703** (£2,887; £1,443; £721) **Stalls** Low

Form RPR

0400 **1** **Victory Bond**[33] 6928 4-9-3 105.......................................... RyanMoore 6 110
(William Haggas) *in tch in 4th: rdn over 2f out: swtchd rt over 1f out: styd on and rdn to ld wl ins fnl f: r.o wl* **3/1**[2]

113- **2** ½ **Boynton (USA)**[443] 4732 3-8-13 113.............................. WilliamBuick 2 109
(Charlie Appleby) *dwlt: sn rcvrd to chse ldr and t.k.h: effrt to chal 1f out: drvn and ev ch fr over 1f out: nt quite match pce of wnr wl ins fnl f* **4/6**[1]

0426 **3** ½ **Red Verdon (USA)**[13] 7581 4-9-3 107...........................(p) OisinMurphy 1 108
(Ed Dunlop) *trckd ldrs: swtchd rt and chal between rivals over 1f out: rdn to ld 1f out: hdd and no ex wl ins fnl f* **8/1**[3]

1325 **4** 2 ½ **Ickymasho**[12] 7602 5-9-2 97.......................................... RichardKingscote 3 102
(Jonathan Portman) *led: shkn up ent fnl 2f: rdn over 1f out: hdd 1f out: wknd ins fnl f* **12/1**

1000 **5** 2 ¼ **Murad Khan (FR)**[22] 7275 4-9-7 100..............................(h) JamesDoyle 5 103
(Hugo Palmer) *hld up in tch: swtchd rt and effrt over 1f out: no hdwy and hung bdly lft 1f out: wknd ins fnl f* **12/1**

2m 4.25s (-4.35) **Going Correction** -0.25s/f (Stan)
**WFA** 3 from 4yo+ 4lb 5 Ran SP% **111.5**
Speed ratings (Par 107): **107,106,106,104,102**
CSF £5.52 TOTE £4.00: £1.80, £1.10; EX 7.20 Trifecta £19.10.
**Owner** Bloomsbury Stud **Bred** Bloomsbury Stud **Trained** Newmarket, Suffolk

**FOCUS**
There was a fair pace on in this decent conditions event. The third sets the standard.

## 7989 BET TOTETRIFECTA AT BETFRED.COM MAIDEN STKS 1m 2f (P)
**7:45** (7:47) (Class 5) 3-4-Y-O **£5,175** (£1,540; £769; £384) **Stalls** Low

Form RPR

**1** **Spinning Melody (USA)** 3-9-0 0.............................. SilvestreDeSousa 1 82
(Simon Crisford) *mde all: rdn and hrd pressed over 1f out: sustained battle w runner up after: styd on wl and forged narrowly ahd towards fin: gamely* **12/1**

5262 **2** nk **Footman (GER)**[14] 7542 3-9-0 81..............................(p[1]) FinleyMarsh(5) 2 86
(Richard Hughes) *hld up in tch in midfield: swtchd rt jst over 2f out: rdn to chal over 1f out: sustained battle w wnr after: flashed tail u.p 1f out: jst outpcd towards fin* **7/4**[1]

2422 **3** 5 **Pretty Passe**[16] 7492 3-9-0 78.......................................... RyanMoore 5 71
(William Haggas) *chsd ldng pair: rdn 3f out: unable qck and swtchd rt 1f out: kpt on same pce fnl f* **5/2**[3]

643 **4** ¾ **Abaad (IRE)**[121] 3682 3-9-5 76.......................................... StevieDonohoe 6 74
(Mohamed Moubarak) *stdd and dropped in bhd after s: hld up in last pair: clsd over 2f out: effrt and swtchd rt over 1f out: hung lft and one pced ins fnl f* **33/1**

3 **5** 9 **Valley Of Light**[16] 7492 3-9-0 0.......................................... OisinMurphy 7 51
(Saeed bin Suroor) *chsd ldr tl wl over 1f out: 5th and btn over 1f out: wknd fnl f* **9/4**[2]

**6** 12 **Kerre (IRE)** 3-9-0 0.......................................... MartinLane 4 27
(William Jarvis) *wnt lft leaving stalls: hld up in last pair: rdn 3f out: lost tch over 1f out* **50/1**

**7** 3 ¾ **Choose** 3-9-0 0.......................................... RichardKingscote 3 20
(Ralph Beckett) *rn green: bmpd s: t.k.h in midfield: rdn over 2f out: drifted rt and lost pl bnd 2f out: sn dropped to rr and lost tch* **8/1**

2m 5.31s (-3.29) **Going Correction** -0.25s/f (Stan) 7 Ran SP% **119.4**
Speed ratings (Par 103): **103,102,98,98,90 81,78**
CSF £35.53 TOTE £10.50: £3.80, £1.30; EX 27.60 Trifecta £93.90.
**Owner** Saif Ali & Saeed H Al Tayer **Bred** Rabbah Bloodstock Llc **Trained** Newmarket, Suffolk

**FOCUS**
They went an uneven pace in this modest 3yo maiden and the first two dominated the finish. The runner-up rates a small best for a claim.

## 7990 BET TOTEWIN AT BETFRED.COM H'CAP (DIV I) 1m 2f (P)
**8:15** (8:17) (Class 6) (0-55,61) 3-Y-O+ **£3,234** (£962; £481; £240) **Stalls** Low

Form RPR

006 **1** **Miss M (IRE)**[38] 6766 3-9-2 **54**.......................................... MartinDwyer 9 61
(William Muir) *t.k.h: hld up in tch in midfield: effrt and rdn to chse ldrs over 1f out: led ins fnl f: r.o wl* **14/1**

4064 **2** 1 **Haldaw**[24] 7215 3-8-9 **50**.......................................... DavidEgan(3) 12 55
(Mick Channon) *chsd ldrs tl wnt 2nd 3f out: rdn and ev ch 2f out: hung lft but led 1f out: hdd and one pced ins fnl f* **16/1**

0353 **3** 1 ¾ **Master Of Heaven**[21] 7324 4-8-10 **49**....................(p) PaddyBradley(5) 15 50
(Jim Boyle) *w ldrs on outer tl led after 2f: drvn and hrd pressed 2f out: hdd 1f out: no ex and styd on same pce ins fnl f* **14/1**

6023 **4** shd **Tommy's Secret**[21] 7325 7-8-11 **48**..............................(p) HollieDoyle(3) 2 49
(Jane Chapple-Hyam) *hld up in midfield: rdn and hdwy over 1f out: styd ion strly ins fnl f: nt rch ldrs* **3/1**[2]

5355 **5** ½ **Sexy Secret**[23] 7253 6-8-10 **47**..............................(p) SimonPearce(3) 3 47
(Lydia Pearce) *led for 2f: chsd ldr tl 3f out: drvn over 1f out: styd on same pce u.p ins fnl f* **20/1**

00-1 **6** 1 **Kohinoor Diamond (IRE)**[7] 7760 3-9-9 **61** 6ex.............. LukeMorris 13 60+
(Sir Mark Prescott Bt) *awkward leaving stalls and s.i.s: off the pce in midfield: rdn over 2f out: hdwy 1f out: keeping on whn n.m.r ins fnl f: styd on: nvr trbld ldrs* **11/10**[1]

0044 **7** ½ **Understory (USA)**[42] 6621 10-8-12 **46** oh1.......................... RyanTate 1 43
(Tim McCarthy) *chsd ldrs: effrt 2f out: unable qck over 1f out: kpt on same pce ins fnl f* **33/1**

6054 **8** 3 ½ **Bob's Boy**[16] 7478 4-9-5 **53**..............................(bt) KevinStott 16 43
(Oliver Greenall) *s.i.s: off the pce in rr: nt clr run over 2f out: c wd wl over 1f out: sme hdwy and edgd lft ins fnl f: nvr trbld ldrs* **14/1**

000 **9** 2 ¼ **Bed Of Diamonds**[24] 7212 3-8-3 **46** oh1.............. ManuelFernandes(5) 8 33
(Adam West) *stdd s: hld up in rr: hdwy on outer 5f out: 5th and rdn over 2f out: wnt rt and wknd over 1f out* **50/1**

0465 **10** 2 ¼ **The Dukkerer (IRE)**[42] 6621 6-9-7 **55**.......................... TomQueally 10 37
(James Given) *midfield: rdn over 2f out: lost pl and btn over 1f out: wknd fnl f* **25/1**

05-0 **11** ½ **Dance With Kate**[153] 2581 6-8-5 **46** oh1............(p[1]) DarraghKeenan(7) 11 27
(Olly Murphy) *a towards rr: effrt on inner over 1f out: rdn and no hdwy 1f out: nvr on terms* **33/1**

0365 **12** nk **False Id**[24] 7216 4-9-4 **52**..............................(t) StevieDonohoe 7 32
(Daniel Steele) *stdd s: t.k.h: hld up in rr: hdwy into midfield on outer over 2f out: lost pl and btn over 1f out: wknd fnl f* **12/1**[3]

0562 **13** 16 **Dawn Goddess**[31] 7005 3-8-9 **47**.......................................... DavidProbert 14
(Gary Moore) *s.i.s: a towards rr: lost tch over 1f out: eased ins fnl f* **16/1**

060P **14** 84 **Race Time (USA)**[141] 2964 4-8-12 **46** oh1....................(t[1]) KieranO'Neill 4
(Zoe Davison) *chsd ldrs: rdn 3f out: sn lost pl and bhd 2f out: virtually p.u over 1f out* **100/1**

2m 6.34s (-2.26) **Going Correction** -0.25s/f (Stan)
**WFA** 3 from 4yo+ 4lb 14 Ran SP% **129.5**
Speed ratings (Par 101): **99,98,96,96,96 95,95,92,90,88 88,88,75,8**
CSF £220.44 CT £3218.43 TOTE £16.50: £4.30, £5.10, £3.60; EX 286.70 Trifecta £6038.90 Part Won..
**Owner** Brian Willis **Bred** J & J Waldron **Trained** Lambourn, Berks

**FOCUS**
A solid pace in this weak handicap took plenty out of their comfort zone. Reliable form for the grade.

## 7991 BET TOTEWIN AT BETFRED.COM H'CAP (DIV II) 1m 2f (P)
**8:45** (8:46) (Class 6) (0-55,56) 3-Y-O+ **£3,234** (£962; £481; £240) **Stalls** Low

Form RPR

0000 **1** **Raashdy (IRE)**[7] 7760 4-9-0 **47**.......................................... LukeMorris 15 55
(Peter Hiatt) *hld up in midfield: effrt u.p over 1f out: chsd ldng pair 1f out: styd on to ld wl ins fnl f: rdn out* **16/1**

0521 **2** 1 **The Juggler**[42] 6621 4-9-7 **54**..............................(v) MartinLane 7 60
(William Knight) *awkward leaving stalls and s.i.s: racd off the pce in last quintet: rdn and hdwy into midfield 3f out: hdwy and hung lft jst ins fnl f: styd on to go 2nd towards fin: nvr getting to wnr* **2/1**[1]

3153 **3** ¾ **Chilli Jam**[9] 7711 4-9-9 **56**..............................(p) LiamKeniry 3 61
(Ed de Giles) *chsd ldrs: wnt 2nd and rdn 2f out: styd on u.p to ld ins fnl f: hdd and lost 2 pls wl ins fnl f* **11/4**[2]

0050 **4** ¾ **Dibloam (USA)**[7] 7761 4-8-9 **45**..............................(h[1]) MattCosham(3) 6 48
(David Evans) *off the pce towards rr: effrt to cl whn nt clr run and swtchd rt over 1f out: hdwy u.p 1f out: styd on u.p: nt rch ldrs* **50/1**

0600 **5** 1 ¾ **Arrowzone**[8] 7729 6-9-7 **54**..............................(b) RyanPowell 9 54+
(Kevin Frost) *t.k.h: pressed ldrs tl led after 2f: rdn 2f out: drvn over 1f out: hdd ins fnl f: no ex and wknd fnl 100yds* **7/1**[3]

02-0 **6** 1 ¼ **Moon Arrow (IRE)**[164] 2219 4-8-12 **50**....................(h) MitchGodwin(5) 4 47
(Michael Blake) *in rr: reminders over 4f out: swtchd rt and effrt jst over 2f out: hdwy and hung lft ins fnl f: nvr trbld ldrs* **12/1**

5454 **7** ½ **Hellomoto**[22] 7270 3-9-1 **52**..............................(p) TomEaves 8 50
(Kevin Ryan) *hld up towards rr: clsd but nt clr run on inner over 2f out: swtchd rt 2f out: nt clr run and swtchd lft over 1f out: drvn 1f out: styd on same pce and no imp ins fnl f* **14/1**

5125 **8** 2 **Captain Sedgwick (IRE)**[31] 7005 3-9-2 **53**.......................... JimmyQuinn 11 47
(John Spearing) *hld up towards rr: rdn and hdwy over 1f out: kpt on same pce and no imp ins fnl f: nvr trbld ldrs* **25/1**

2400 **9** *2* **Outlaw Torn (IRE)**[7] 7760 8-9-6 53................(e) DougieCostello 1 42
(Richard Guest) *taken down early: chsd ldrs tl wnt 2nd 7f out tl 2f out: unable qck over 1f out: wknd ins fnl f* **14/1**

0036 **10** *nse* **Avocet (USA)**[21] 7324 4-8-5 45........................ MillyNaseb(7) 12 34
(Julia Feilden) *hld up in tch in midfield: hdwy to chse ldrs 4f out: unable qck and losing pl whn short of room over 1f out: wknd ins fnl f* **16/1**

0066 **11** *5* **Seeing Things (IRE)**[107] 4177 3-8-6 50................(t) RossaRyan(7) 10 30
(Philip McBride) *in tch in midfield: unable qck u.p and btn over 1f out: wknd fnl f* **40/1**

6434 **12** *8* **African Quest**[31] 7003 3-8-5 45........................ NoelGarbutt(3) 13 10
(Gary Moore) *s.i.s: hld up in rr: no hdwy over 1f out: sn wknd* **33/1**

6542 **13** *8* **California Cliffs (IRE)**[21] 7325 3-8-13 50........................ DavidProbert 5
(Rae Guest) *t.k.h: hld up in tch in midfield: struggling over 2f out: wknd over 1f out: bhd and eased ins fnl f* **8/1**

0350 **14** *75* **Moving Robe (IRE)**[51] 6296 4-8-12 45................(t) MartinDwyer 2
(Conrad Allen) *led for 2f: chsd ldrs tl lost pl qckly 4f out: wl bhd and virtually p.u fnl 2f: t.o* **33/1**

2m 5.35s (-3.25) **Going Correction** -0.25s/f (Stan)
**WFA** 3 from 4yo+ 4lb **14** Ran SP% **130.5**
Speed ratings (Par 101): **103,102,101,101,99 98,98,96,95,94 90,84,78,18**
CSF £50.43 CT £127.71 TOTE £13.60: £4.50, £1.10, £1.50; EX 72.60 Trifecta £337.70.
**Owner** P W Hiatt **Bred** Shadwell Estate Company Limited **Trained** Hook Norton, Oxon

**FOCUS**
This second division of the weak 1m2f handicap was another strongly run affair. The placed horses set the level. Straightforward form.

## 7992 BOOK YOUR CHRISTMAS PARTY HERE H'CAP 2m (P)
**9:15** (9:18) (Class 6) (0-65,67) 3-Y-0+ **£3,234** (£962; £481; £240) **Stalls Low**

Form RPR

0004 **1** **Navajo Star (IRE)**[14] 7537 3-7-12 45................(v) DavidEgan(3) 3 56
(Michael Appleby) *trckd ldrs: wnt 2nd and effrt jst over 3f out: rdn to ld ent fnl 2f: clr whn hung rt 1f out: in command but continued to hang ins fnl f: styd on* **8/1**[3]

005 **2** *5* **Ballyfarsoon (IRE)**[16] 7483 6-9-5 54................(v) StevieDonohoe 6 57
(Ian Williams) *in tch in midfield: effrt to chse clr ldng pair over 2f out: chsd clr wnr 1f out: kpt on same pce and no imp ins fnl f* **9/2**[2]

565- **3** *½* **Knight Commander**[18] 7421 4-9-7 63........................ DarraghKeenan(7) 11 65
(Olly Murphy) *sn dropped to rr and niggled along early: stuck bhd a wall of horses over 2f out: swtchd rt and hdwy wl over 1f out: 5th 1f out: styd on wl ins fnl f: no threat to wnr* **8/1**[3]

0300 **4** *hd* **The Way You Dance (IRE)**[8] 7730 5-9-11 60................(v) JFEgan 7 62
(Neil Mulholland) *in tch in midfield: effrt over 2f out: 4th over 1f out: styd on same pce ins fnl f* **12/1**

2346 **5** *4* **Starshell (IRE)**[14] 7537 3-9-5 63................(b[1]) LukeMorris 1 62
(Sir Mark Prescott Bt) *sn led: rdn and hdd ent fnl 2f: outpcd and btn over 1f out: hung lft and wknd ins fnl f* **15/8**[1]

0630 **6** *5* **Scarlet Thrush (IRE)**[26] 7157 3-8-12 56........................ DannyBrock 9 49
(Luke McJannet) *s.i.s: sn in tch in midfield: rdn over 2f out: no imp u.p over 1f out: wknd fnl f* **50/1**

0-42 **7** *2¾* **Gold Class**[41] 5866 6-8-10 45................(bt) KieranShoemark 8 33
(Olly Murphy) *hld up in last trio: effrt over 1f out: no imp and wl hld over 1f out: wknd fnl f* **9/1**

200 **8** *5* **Wassail**[21] 7336 4-8-12 50........................ CallumShepherd(3) 10 32
(Ed de Giles) *hld up in last trio: effrt u.p over 2f out: no hdwy: wknd over 1f out* **25/1**

603 **9** *4* **Midnight Mood**[24] 7215 4-9-2 51........................ LiamKeniry 5 28
(Dominic Ffrench Davis) *hld up in midfield: struggling u.p over 2f out: bhd over 1f out: wknd* **16/1**

5360 **10** *½* **Gee Sixty Six**[29] 7060 3-9-4 62........................ JoeyHaynes 2 41
(Mark H Tompkins) *t.k.h: chsd ldrs tl lost pl u.p over 2f out: wknd over 1f out: bhd ins fnl f* **14/1**

-045 **11** *10* **Nepeta (USA)**[30] 7032 3-9-9 67........................ FrannyNorton 4 34
(Mark Johnston) *chsd ldr tl jst over 3f out: sn dropped out and bhd 2f out: wknd: t.o* **8/1**[3]

3m 29.46s (-0.54) **Going Correction** -0.25s/f (Stan)
**WFA** 3 from 4yo+ 9lb **11** Ran SP% **122.3**
Speed ratings (Par 101): **91,88,88,88,86 83,82,79,77,77 72**
CSF £45.78 CT £307.67 TOTE £8.80: £2.40, £1.60, £4.00; EX 59.90 Trifecta £649.00.
**Owner** Ferrybank Properties Limited **Bred** Robert Dunne **Trained** Oakham, Rutland

**FOCUS**
An ordinary staying handicap, run at an uneven pace. It didn't appear to be a fluke.
T/Plt: £311.40 to a £1 stake. Pool: £88,939.01 - 208.43 winning units T/Qpdt: £43.30 to a £1 stake. Pool: £14,359.03 - 245.38 winning units **Steve Payne**

# 7945 KEMPTON (A.W) (R-H)
Friday, October 13

**OFFICIAL GOING: Polytrack: standard to slow**
Wind: Fresh, across (away from stands) Weather: Cloudy, mild

## 7993 RACINGUK.COM H'CAP 5f (P)
**5:45** (5:49) (Class 7) (0-50,55) 3-Y-0+ **£1,940** (£577; £288; £144) **Stalls Low**

Form RPR

0132 **1** **Lady Joanna Vassa (IRE)**[3] 7926 4-8-10 46................(v) JackOsborn(7) 1 52
(Richard Guest) *chsd ldng pair: outpcd 2f out: drvn to cl fr over 1f out: styd on to ld last 50yds* **11/4**[1]

0604 **2** *¾* **Silver Penny**[11] 7692 3-8-11 45................(p) PaddyBradley(5) 10 49
(Jim Boyle) *pressed ldr: chal and upsides fr 2f out tl narrow ld 100yds out: sn hdd and outpcd nr fin* **6/1**

656 **3** *nk* **Popsilca**[10] 7705 3-9-7 50........................ FranBerry 5 53
(Mick Quinn) *led: hrd pressed fr 2f out: kpt on but hdd last 100yds* **11/1**

005 **4** *1¼* **Dalalah**[10] 7705 4-9-2 45................(v) DougieCostello 7 42
(Richard Guest) *chsd ldrs: pushed along 1/2-way and sn outpcd: kpt on fr over 1f out: nt pce to chal* **20/1**

5043 **5** *nk* **Essaka (IRE)**[10] 7705 5-9-7 50........................ DavidProbert 8 46
(Tony Carroll) *t.k.h: trapped out wd and hld up in 6th: rdn over 1f out: kpt on but nt rch ldrs* **10/3**[2]

6361 **6** *1½* **Justice Rock**[8] 7763 4-9-5 55 6ex................(t) NicolaCurrie(7) 2 46
(Phil McEntee) *a in rr: pushed along on inner 2f out and no prog* **4/1**[3]

060 **7** *½* **Molly Jones**[47] 6478 8-9-2 45........................ JohnFahy 4 35
(Matthew Salaman) *t.k.h: prom early but hanging lft and restrained into last trio: brief effrt jst over 1f out: no great prog* **50/1**

6004 **8** *nk* **Joshlee (IRE)**[10] 7705 3-9-1 49........................ JoshuaBryan(5) 6 38
(Emma Owen) *chsd ldrs to 1/2-way: wknd over 1f out* **11/1**

0200 **9** *5* **Bubbly Bailey**[10] 7705 7-9-2 45................(v) FergusSweeney 3 15
(J R Jenkins) *s.i.s: a in last pair: wknd over 1f out* **33/1**

1m 0.5s **Going Correction** -0.125s/f (Stan) **9** Ran SP% **110.4**
Speed ratings (Par 97): **95,93,93,91,90 88,87,87,79**
CSF £18.02 CT £144.22 TOTE £3.30: £1.10, £2.00, £3.50; EX 17.70 Trifecta £124.50.
**Owner** www.primelawns.co.uk **Bred** Tom Radley **Trained** Ingmanthorpe, W Yorks

**FOCUS**
A low-grade handicap run at a reasonable gallop but one in which those held up were at a disadvantage. The winner has been rated as replicating her recent turf form.

## 7994 32RED H'CAP 5f (P)
**6:15** (6:15) (Class 4) (0-85,87) 3-Y-0+ **£4,690** (£1,395; £697; £348) **Stalls Low**

Form RPR

3036 **1** **Orvar (IRE)**[34] 6927 4-9-10 87........................ MartinHarley 1 96
(Robert Cowell) *chsd ldr: rdn over 1f out: clsd to ld 150yds out: drvn out and hld on* **10/3**[1]

11-0 **2** *nk* **Thammin**[154] 2579 3-9-7 84........................ DaneO'Neill 2 93
(Owen Burrows) *dwlt: pushed up to chse ldng pair: rdn 2f out: clsd on inner 1f out: tk 2nd last 75yds: jst unable to rch wnr* **4/1**[2]

1203 **3** *1¼* **Come On Dave (IRE)**[27] 7137 8-9-0 77................(v) LiamKeniry 4 80
(John Butler) *bowled along in front: rdn over 1f out: hdd and no ex last 150yds* **11/1**

12 **4** *1* **Foxy Forever (IRE)**[13] 7604 7-9-10 87................(t) DavidProbert 7 87+
(Michael Wigham) *n.m.r s: sn in 6th: rdn to take 4th over 1f out: kpt on but nt pce to chal* **9/2**[3]

4133 **5** *nk* **Annie Salts**[17] 7486 4-8-0 70................(h) NicolaCurrie(7) 9 69
(Chris Dwyer) *sn off the pce in 8th: prog on inner over 1f out: kpt on and nrst fin* **20/1**

6504 **6** *1* **Oh So Sassy**[15] 7538 7-9-4 81........................ TomQueally 8 76+
(Chris Wall) *mostly in 7th: rdn on outer and no prog wl over 1f out: kpt on ins fnl f: nrst fin* **7/1**

3116 **7** *nk* **Saved My Bacon (IRE)**[13] 7604 6-8-13 79..........(h) LewisEdmunds(3) 5 73
(Chris Dwyer) *dwlt: hld up in last and sn wl off the pce: brought wdst in st: drvn over 1f out: kpt on but no ch* **12/1**

5305 **8** *1* **Majestic Hero (IRE)**[15] 7538 5-9-5 82........................ LukeMorris 6 72
(Ronald Harris) *in tch tl rdn and fdd over 1f out* **20/1**

5421 **9** *1* **Midnightly**[56] 6155 3-8-10 73................(t) MartinDwyer 3 61
(Rae Guest) *disp 3rd pl to 2f out: wknd over 1f out* **13/2**

58.91s (-1.59) **Going Correction** -0.125s/f (Stan) **9** Ran SP% **112.6**
Speed ratings (Par 105): **107,106,104,102,102 100,100,98,97**
CSF £16.06 CT £126.98 TOTE £3.50: £1.10, £1.40, £4.90; EX 14.40 Trifecta £151.00.
**Owner** Saleh Al Homaizi & Imad Al Sagar **Bred** David Harrison **Trained** Six Mile Bottom, Cambs
■ Stewards' Enquiry : Dane O'Neill ban tba; used his whip above permitted level

**FOCUS**
A useful handicap but, as with the first race, the pace wasn't overly strong and it disadvantaged those held up.

## 7995 32RED ON THE APP STORE FILLIES' NOVICE STKS (PLUS 10 RACE) 7f (P)
**6:45** (6:46) (Class 5) 2-Y-0 **£3,234** (£962; £481; £240) **Stalls Low**

Form RPR

43 **1** **Cavatina**[35] 6875 2-9-0 0........................ MartinHarley 4 76
(William Haggas) *trckd ldng pair tl chsd ldr over 2f out: rdn to chal over 1f out: kpt on wl to ld last 75yds* **4/1**[2]

02 **2** *nk* **Scandaleuse (USA)**[9] 7724 2-9-0 0........................ TedDurcan 5 75
(Sir Michael Stoute) *led: rdn over 1f out: kpt on u.p but hdd last 75yds and jst hld after* **9/2**[3]

41 **3** *2½* **Clairette (IRE)**[36] 6862 2-9-7 0........................ KieranShoemark 10 75
(Roger Charlton) *t.k.h and sn hld up in 4th: outpcd 2f out: kpt on to take 3rd fnl f: no imp ldng pair* **6/4**[1]

**4** *½* **Ghanimah** 2-9-0 0........................ DaneO'Neill 11 67+
(William Haggas) *dwlt: sn in midfield: shkn up and outpcd 2f out: kpt on wl to chal for 3rd fnl f:* **14/1**

4 **5** *½* **Zahraa**[16] 7504 2-9-0 0........................ TomQueally 7 66
(Robyn Brisland) *t.k.h: hld up in midfield: rn green and reminder over 2f out: sn outpcd: kpt on wl fr jst over 1f out* **20/1**

00 **6** *shd* **Grace's Secret**[18] 7454 2-9-0 0........................ LiamKeniry 1 65
(Ed Walker) *stdd after s and hld up in last: pushed along and promising prog 2f out: swtchd to inner and ch of a pl 1f out: no ex* **100/1**

**7** *½* **American Endeavour (USA)** 2-8-11 0........................ MarcMonaghan(3) 2 64+
(Marco Botti) *hld up towards rr: outpcd 2f out: kpt on quite wl fnl f though n.d* **25/1**

0 **8** *hd* **Saffah (USA)**[18] 7453 2-8-11 0........................ CallumShepherd(3) 3 63
(Charles Hills) *chsd ldrs in 5th: shkn up over 2f out: sn in 4th: chsd ldng pair briefly jst over 1f out: fdd ins fnl f* **40/1**

**9** *nse* **Ruffina (USA)** 2-9-0 0........................ NickyMackay 6 63+
(John Gosden) *in tch in midfield: outpcd 2f out: kpt on fnl f but n.d* **12/1**

**10** *1* **Brexitmeansbrexit** 2-9-0 0........................ TomMarquand 8 61
(Richard Hannon) *mostly in last trio: bdly outpcd over 2f out and lost tch: no ch after but styd on last 150yds* **25/1**

630 **11** *1½* **Club Tropicana**[14] 7578 2-9-0 87........................ FranBerry 12 57
(Richard Spencer) *trapped out wd early: chsd ldr: lost 2nd u.p over 2f out: lost 3rd jst over 1f out and wknd* **8/1**

**12** *8* **Altra Vita** 2-9-0 0........................ LukeMorris 9 35
(Sir Mark Prescott Bt) *s.s: rn green and a in last pair: t.o* **66/1**

1m 25.49s (-0.51) **Going Correction** -0.125s/f (Stan) **12** Ran SP% **121.0**
Speed ratings (Par 92): **97,96,93,93,92 92,91,91,91,90 88,79**
CSF £21.40 TOTE £4.70: £1.80, £1.40, £1.30; EX 24.80 Trifecta £57.90.
**Owner** Cheveley Park Stud **Bred** Cheveley Park Stud Ltd **Trained** Newmarket, Suffolk

**FOCUS**
A fair maiden in which the first two pulled a few lengths clear of the rest (who finished in a heap) in the last quarter mile. The gallop was an ordinary one.

## 7996 "EL NINO 'ORSES FOR COURSES" NURSERY H'CAP 7f (P)
**7:15** (7:15) (Class 6) (0-60,59) 2-Y-0 **£2,587** (£770; £384; £192) **Stalls Low**

Form RPR

4022 **1** **Dark Blue (IRE)**[29] 7082 2-9-7 59........................ RaulDaSilva 8 61
(Mick Channon) *in tch: urged along over 2f out: prog over 1f out: pushed into the ld 150yds out: jst hld on* **2/1**[1]

0004 **2** *hd* **Puramente**[29] 7082 2-9-6 58........................ DougieCostello 9 59
(Jo Hughes) *in tch: rdn and prog 2f out: hrd drvn and styd on fnl f to take 2nd last 50yds: jst failed* **9/2**[2]

0050 **3** *¾* **Arachina (IRE)**[8] 7756 2-9-5 57................(v) DaneO'Neill 11 56
(Harry Dunlop) *t.k.h early: trckd ldrs: prog 2f out: rdn to ld over 1f out: hdd last 150yds: kpt on* **33/1**

052 4 ¾ **Secratario (FR)**[64] 5819 2-9-6 **58** (p1) ShaneKelly 3 55
(Richard Hughes) *trckd ldrs: effrt on inner and cl up over 1f out: nt qckn fnl f* **6/1[3]**

566 5 nk **Kalakchee**[32] 7001 2-9-0 **52** (p1) KieranShoemark 6 48
(Amy Murphy) *restless stalls: s.i.s: wl in rr: rdn over 2f out: prog over 1f out: kpt on fnl f: nvr able to chal* **20/1**

3040 6 3 ¾ **Roses In June (IRE)**[29] 7081 2-8-7 **45** JohnFahy 7 31
(J S Moore) *dwlt: tk fierce hold early in rr: effrt but wd 3f out: tried to cl on ldrs over 1f out: wknd ins fnl f* **20/1**

0550 7 1 **Deauville Society (IRE)**[44] 6585 2-9-3 **55** (p1) LukeMorris 14 38
(Sir Mark Prescott Bt) *racd wd early: led after 1f and t.k.h: hdd & wknd over 1f out* **15/2**

5000 8 2 ¼ **Elusive Bird**[8] 7756 2-9-3 **55** LiamJones 10 32
(Giles Bravery) *t.k.h: trckd ldr after 1f to 2f out: hanging and wknd over 1f out* **50/1**

0050 9 1 ¼ **Disapproval (IRE)**[8] 7756 2-9-5 **57** (h) GeorgeDowning 4 31
(Daniel Kubler) *led 1f: trckd ldrs: effrt on inner 2f out: hanging rt and hit rail over 1f out: wknd* **14/1**

006 10 ½ **Harbour Seal**[27] 7141 2-8-10 **55** (p1) JackOsborn(7) 5 28
(Henry Spiller) *dwlt: a struggling in rr* **10/1**

0000 11 3 ¾ **Rue Cambon (IRE)**[52] 6285 2-8-9 **47** (b1) SamHitchcott 1 9
(George Peckham) *uns rdr bef ent stalls: hld up in rr: pushed along and no prog over 2f out: sn wknd* **20/1**

1m 27.19s (1.19) **Going Correction** -0.125s/f (Stan) 11 Ran SP% **112.5**
Speed ratings (Par 93): **88,87,86,86,85 81,80,77,76,75 71**
CSF £8.94 CT £213.90 TOTE £2.80: £1.10, £1.90, £6.00; EX 13.00 Trifecta £100.40.
**Owner** Mrs Ann C Black **Bred** Cavalier Bloodstock **Trained** West Ilsley, Berks
■ Stewards' Enquiry : Dougie Costello two-day ban; using his whip above the permitted level (Oct 27, 30)

**FOCUS**
A low-grade nursery in which a modest gallop picked up around the intersection.

## 7997 32REDSPORT.COM MAIDEN FILLIES' STKS (PLUS 10 RACE) 1m (P)
**7:45** (7:45) (Class 5) 2-Y-O **£3,234** (£962; £481; £240) **Stalls** Low

Form RPR

0 1 **Preening**[31] 7021 2-8-11 0 GeorgeWood(3) 5 76+
(James Fanshawe) *hld up in midfield: gd prog fr 2f out: shkn up over 1f out: chsd ldr ins fnl f: styd on wl to ld last strides* **10/1**

2 2 ½ **Beckton**[35] 6875 2-9-0 0 MartinHarley 11 75
(Robyn Brisland) *fast away: led: kicked for home over 2f out: 3 l clr over 1f out: wilted last 100yds: hdd fnl strides* **7/1**

02 3 nk **Gather**[18] 7453 2-9-0 0 PatDobbs 9 74
(Amanda Perrett) *chsd ldr 2f and again over 2f out: sn outpcd and shkn up: lost 2nd ins fnl f but styd on* **6/1[3]**

4 1 ½ **Mrs Sippy (USA)** 2-9-0 0 SeanLevey 3 71+
(David Simcock) *hld up in rr: pushed along and prog fr 2f out: styd on steadily to take 4th ins fnl f: shaped w promise* **12/1**

42 5 nk **Melodies**[21] 7357 2-9-0 0 DavidProbert 8 70
(Ed Dunlop) *trckd ldrs: outpcd and shkn up 2f out: one pce and nvr able to chal after* **3/1[2]**

0 6 7 **Timpani (IRE)**[18] 7454 2-9-0 0 NickyMackay 12 53
(John Gosden) *chsd ldr after 2f to over 2f out: wknd over 1f out* **16/1**

6 7 hd **Murasaki**[18] 7453 2-9-0 0 WilliamBuick 2 53
(Charlie Appleby) *nvr beyond midfield: outpcd over 2f out: no ch after* **5/2[1]**

8 ½ **Maid Up** 2-9-0 0 LiamKeniry 13 51
(Andrew Balding) *dwlt: racd wd: hld up in rr: pushed along and no real prog over 2f out* **50/1**

0 9 ¾ **Arabian Sea (USA)**[34] 6917 2-8-9 0 PaddyPilley(5) 10 50
(Roger Charlton) *racd wd in midfield: rdn over 2f out: sn wknd* **66/1**

06 10 ½ **Casima**[44] 6575 2-9-0 0 (h) SamHitchcott 4 48
(Clive Cox) *pushed along in rr: nvr on terms* **25/1**

11 1 **Secret Eye (IRE)** 2-9-0 0 (b1) JFEgan 7 46
(Paul Cole) *t.k.h early: chsd ldrs: rdn 3f out: wknd qckly wl over 1f out* **66/1**

0 12 1 ¼ **Sister Celine (IRE)**[49] 6386 2-9-0 0 KieranShoemark 6 43
(Roger Charlton) *dwlt: a in last trio: no prog over 2f out* **33/1**

0 13 4 ½ **Spritzig**[18] 7453 2-9-0 0 TomQueally 1 32
(Chris Wall) *dwlt: a in last pair: bhd over 2f out* **100/1**

1m 39.05s (-0.75) **Going Correction** -0.125s/f (Stan) 13 Ran SP% **115.7**
Speed ratings (Par 92): **98,97,97,95,95 88,88,87,86,86 85,84,79**
CSF £72.99 TOTE £11.30: £3.80, £2.20, £2.30; EX 74.20 Trifecta £684.80.
**Owner** Cheveley Park Stud **Bred** Cheveley Park Stud Ltd **Trained** Newmarket, Suffolk

**FOCUS**
A fair maiden in which the first five, who finished in a bit of a heap, pulled clear of the remainder. The runner-up has been rated close to her debut effort.

## 7998 32RED.COM H'CAP (DIV I) 1m (P)
**8:15** (8:16) (Class 4) (0-80,80) 3-Y-O+ **£4,690** (£1,395; £697; £348) **Stalls** Low

Form RPR

412 1 **Azaly (IRE)**[69] 5664 3-9-2 **78** DaneO'Neill 12 86
(Owen Burrows) *trckd ldng pair: rdn 2f out: clsd grad fr over 1f out: drvn ahd last 100yds: jst hld on* **5/1[2]**

0340 2 shd **Eltezam (IRE)**[15] 7549 4-9-5 **78** (b1) PatDobbs 8 85
(Amanda Perrett) *trckd ldrs disputing 5th: pushed along over 2f out: rdn and prog over 1f out: tk 2nd last 50yds and nrly jnd wnr: nt qckn fnl strides* **10/1**

0450 3 ½ **Sidewinder (IRE)**[53] 6266 3-9-1 **77** AlistairRawlinson 4 83
(Tom Dascombe) *trckd ldng pair: rdn to ld 2f out but hrd pressed: hdd 100yds out: kpt on* **16/1**

343 4 ½ **Ahlan Bil Zain (FR)**[51] 6322 3-9-3 **79** TomQueally 5 84
(David Simcock) *trckd ldrs disputing 5th: prog on inner to chal 2f out: w ldr after to 100yds out: one pce after* **9/2[1]**

6236 5 1 **Murdanova (IRE)**[20] 7409 4-9-0 **73** JFEgan 3 75
(Denis Quinn) *hld up disputing 7th: lost pl sltly over 2f out: shkn up and prog on outer over 1f out: styd on ins fnl f but too late to chal* **20/1**

051 6 nk **Rock Warbler (IRE)**[14] 7571 4-9-0 **76** (t) LewisEdmunds(3) 6 78
(Oliver Greenall) *hld up disputing 9th: rdn over 2f out: kpt on fr over 1f out: nrst fin but no threat* **11/2[3]**

1100 7 nk **Pursuing Steed**[20] 7398 3-9-0 **79** CharlieBennett(3) 7 80
(Hughie Morrison) *hld up disputing 9th and bhd early: urged along 3f out: no prog tl kpt on fr over 1f out: nrst fin* **14/1**

0050 8 nk **Archie (IRE)**[14] 7582 5-9-4 **77** MartinHarley 11 77+
(Tom Clover) *stdd s fr wd draw: hld up in 11th and wl off the pce: pushed along over 2f out: nt clr run over 1f out: rdn and kpt on fnl f: nvr really in it* **6/1**

4400 9 1 ½ **Ogbourne Downs**[4] 7878 7-8-11 **70** (b1) ShaneKelly 2 67
(Ben Pauling) *slowly away: hld up disputing 7th: gng strly whn effrt over 2f out: rdn over 1f out: wknd tamely fnl f* **25/1**

0000 10 ¾ **Presumido (IRE)**[18] 7456 7-9-0 **78** PaddyBradley(5) 9 73
(Simon Dow) *t.k.h: hld up in last and wl off the pce: urged along on inner 2f out: sme prog over 1f out: no hdwy after* **12/1**

551 11 3 **Psychotic**[16] 7514 4-9-7 **80** KieranShoemark 10 68
(David Menuisier) *walked to post early: led 2f: pressed ldr: upsides jst over 2f out: wknd qckly over 1f out* **15/2**

5100 12 2 ¼ **War Of Succession**[23] 7277 3-8-10 **75** EoinWalsh(3) 1 58
(Tony Newcombe) *led after 2f: racd awkwardly and hdd 2f out: sn wknd qckly* **66/1**

1m 38.16s (-1.64) **Going Correction** -0.125s/f (Stan)
**WFA** 3 from 4yo+ 3lb 12 Ran SP% **115.7**
Speed ratings (Par 105): **103,102,102,101,100 100,100,100,98,97 94,92**
CSF £51.76 CT £755.98 TOTE £5.60: £1.90, £3.30, £5.30; EX 59.40 Trifecta £1036.60.
**Owner** Hamdan Al Maktoum **Bred** Rabbah Bloodstock Limited **Trained** Lambourn, Berks

**FOCUS**
A fair handicap but one in which the gallop was no more than fair.

## 7999 32RED.COM H'CAP (DIV II) 1m (P)
**8:45** (8:45) (Class 4) (0-80,81) 3-Y-O+ **£4,690** (£1,395; £697; £348) **Stalls** Low

Form RPR

1531 1 **Cool Team (IRE)**[14] 7570 3-9-6 **81** (tp) JamesDoyle 1 89
(Hugo Palmer) *trckd ldrs: prog jst over 2f out: drvn to ld over 1f out: hrd pressed after: kpt on wl* **13/8[1]**

4432 2 ½ **Traveller (FR)**[29] 7095 3-9-0 **75** (t) DavidProbert 8 82
(Charles Hills) *hld up in rr: gd prog 2f out: drvn to chal over 1f out: pressed wnr after but a hld* **8/1[3]**

1-30 3 hd **Under Control (IRE)**[27] 7162 3-9-2 **77** (b1) MartinHarley 2 83
(William Haggas) *hld up in midfield: gng strly over 2f out: coaxed along to cl over 1f out and racd awkwardly: rdn fnl f: styd on nr fin but nvr enough resolution to chal properly* **7/2[2]**

3000 4 1 ½ **Manangatang (IRE)**[17] 7493 3-8-12 **73** LukeMorris 9 76
(Luca Cumani) *hld up in last trio: rdn in last over 2f out and no prog: styd on u.p fnl f: nrst fin* **12/1**

-560 5 1 ¼ **Kitten's Johnstown (USA)**[69] 5664 3-8-11 **72** JFEgan 5 72
(Kevin Ryan) *prom: led over 2f out: rdn and hdd over 1f out: wknd fnl f* **20/1**

0152 6 3 ¼ **Bluff Crag**[17] 7493 4-8-10 **75** (p) StephenCummins(7) 10 68
(Richard Hughes) *t.k.h: sn led: hdd and fnd nil over 2f out: sn btn* **9/1**

2-05 7 ½ **Rebel Cause (IRE)**[28] 7119 4-9-6 **78** (p1) KieranShoemark 6 70
(Richard Spencer) *trckd ldrs: urged along over 3f out: nt qckn over 2f out and sn btn* **8/1[3]**

0414 8 1 **Tee It Up Tommo (IRE)**[134] 3235 8-9-4 **76** (t) TomMarquand 4 65
(Daniel Steele) *dwlt: hld up in last: rdn over 2f out: no real prog* **33/1**

6000 9 2 ¼ **Gambit**[43] 6617 4-9-4 **76** FergusSweeney 12 60
(Robert Cowell) *t.k.h: sn pressed ldr: rdn over 2f out: fnd nil and sn btn* **14/1**

3130 10 2 ¼ **Fit For The Job (IRE)**[29] 7083 5-9-3 **75** (p) FranBerry 7 54
(Jonjo O'Neill) *hld up in rr: in tch and rdn 2f out: wknd over 1f out: eased* **40/1**

1m 38.2s (-1.60) **Going Correction** -0.125s/f (Stan)
**WFA** 3 from 4yo+ 3lb 10 Ran SP% **117.0**
Speed ratings (Par 105): **103,102,102,100,99 96,95,94,92,90**
CSF £15.20 CT £42.39 TOTE £2.40: £1.10, £2.40, £1.50; EX 17.40 Trifecta £61.10.
**Owner** Lit Lung Lee **Bred** Ringfort Stud **Trained** Newmarket, Suffolk

**FOCUS**
A reasonable handicap in which the gallop was no more than fair.

## 8000 100% PROFIT BOOST AT 32REDSPORT.COM H'CAP 1m 3f 219y(P)
**9:15** (9:15) (Class 5) (0-70,72) 3-Y-O+ **£3,234** (£962; £481; £240) **Stalls** Low

Form RPR

3424 1 **Pastoral Music**[26] 7202 4-9-6 **69** (p) CharlieBennett(3) 2 76
(Hughie Morrison) *trckd ldr 4f: styd cl up: rdn to chal over 1f out: drvn ahd 100yds out: jst hld on* **11/2[3]**

-006 2 shd **So Celebre (GER)**[28] 7132 4-9-10 **70** FranBerry 5 76
(Ian Williams) *trckd ldr after 4f: rdn to ld wl over 1f out: hdd last 100yds: rallied nr fin* **5/2[1]**

1060 3 ½ **Hayward Field (IRE)**[20] 7413 4-9-3 **63** LiamKeniry 6 68
(Noel Wilson) *hld up towards rr: prog on inner over 2f out: drvn to chal over 1f out: kpt on but a jst hld* **16/1**

4305 4 1 ½ **Bridge Of Sighs**[29] 7098 5-9-5 **70** PaddyBradley(5) 4 73+
(Lee Carter) *hld up in midfield: prog over 1f out to chal fnl f: nt qckn last 100yds* **12/1**

400 5 ½ **Rum Swizzle**[23] 7278 5-9-9 **69** LukeMorris 10 71
(Harry Dunlop) *chsd ldrs: rdn and cl enough 2f out: kpt on same pce fr over 1f out* **25/1**

5536 6 1 ½ **Broad Appeal**[39] 6767 3-9-2 **68** RyanTate 7 67
(Jonathan Portman) *hld up in last pair: rdn over 2f out: sme prog over 1f out but nvr on terms w ldrs* **12/1**

5505 7 nk **Mullarkey**[64] 5820 3-9-4 **70** JoeyHaynes 9 69
(John Best) *hld up in last trio: rdn and no prog over 2f out: kpt on one pce fr over 1f out: n.d* **9/1**

3224 8 nk **Prosecution**[39] 6767 3-9-3 **69** RobertWinston 11 67
(Hughie Morrison) *racd on outer: hld up in tch: gng wl enough 2f out: shkn up and fnd nil over 1f out: wknd fnl f* **4/1[2]**

3300 9 2 ½ **Amelia Dream**[13] 7599 3-9-3 **69** JFEgan 8 63
(Mick Channon) *hld up in last: rdn over 2f out: no prog* **12/1**

562 10 2 ¼ **Sula Island**[37] 6823 3-9-6 **72** FergusSweeney 1 63
(Alan King) *hld up in midfield: shkn up over 2f out: no prog and btn over 1f out* **10/1**

050 11 2 **Foresee (GER)**[35] 6880 4-9-5 **65** DavidProbert 3 53
(Tony Carroll) *led: rdn and hdd wl over 1f out: wknd rapidly* **33/1**

2m 33.04s (-1.46) **Going Correction** -0.125s/f (Stan)
**WFA** 3 from 4yo+ 6lb 11 Ran SP% **118.8**
Speed ratings (Par 103): **99,98,98,97,97 96,96,95,94,92 91**
CSF £19.78 CT £211.94 TOTE £5.30: £2.00, £1.60, £5.20; EX 20.50 Trifecta £299.90.
**Owner** MNC Racing **Bred** Melksham Craic **Trained** East Ilsley, Berks
■ Stewards' Enquiry : Charlie Bennett two-day ban; used whip above the permitted level (Oct 27, 30)

**FOCUS**
A modest handicap in which the gallop to the home turn was a moderate one and this bare form may not be entirely reliable.
T/Plt: £177.50 to a £1 stake. Pool: £75,250.48 - 309.45 winning units T/Qpdt: £25.50 to a £1 stake. Pool: £9,900.42 - 286.62 winning units **Jonathan Neesom**

# 7810 NEWMARKET (R-H)

Friday, October 13

**OFFICIAL GOING: Good (7.8)**

Wind: medium, across Weather: dry, breezy

## 8001 NEWMARKET ACADEMY GODOLPHIN BEACON PROJECT CORNWALLIS STKS (GROUP 3) 5f

**1:50** (1:50) (Class 1) 2-Y-O

**£34,026** (£12,900; £6,456; £3,216; £1,614; £810) **Stalls** High

Form RPR

1212 **1** **Abel Handy (IRE)**[48] 6448 2-9-1 100 JamesDoyle 3 104
(Declan Carroll) *sn led: rdn and hdd narrowly over 1f out: battled bk wl u.p to ld again wl ins fnl f: gamely* **9/2**[2]

0121 **2** *nk* **Sound And Silence**[23] 7306 2-9-4 107 (tp) WilliamBuick 8 106
(Charlie Appleby) *t.k.h: w wnr tl rdn to ld narrowly over 1f out: hdd wl ins fnl f: kpt on but hld cl home* **5/2**[1]

2421 **3** *½* **Mokaatil**[39] 6755 2-9-1 96 JimCrowley 6 101
(Owen Burrows) *in tch in midfield: effrt over 1f out: hdwy ins fnl f: styd on wl to go 3rd last strides: nt quite rch ldrs* **8/1**

**4** *nk* **Yolo Star (IRE)**[9] 7747 2-8-12 85 ColmO'Donoghue 1 97
(J P Murtagh, Ire) *compact; pressed ldrs: rdn and ev ch over 1f out: kpt on wl and stl ev ch ins fnl f: unable qck towards fin* **20/1**

5110 **5** *shd* **Spoof**[28] 7114 2-9-1 80 (h) CallumShepherd 12 100
(Charles Hills) *taken down early: in tch in midfield: effrt over 1f out: drvn and swtchd rt 1f out: kpt wl on ins fnl f: nvr quite enough pce to get to ldrs* **100/1**

2336 **6** *½* **To Wafij (IRE)**[48] 6448 2-9-1 103 AndreaAtzeni 2 98
(Roger Varian) *sltly on toes; stmbld leaving stalls: in tch in midfield: effrt over 1f out: kpt on ins fnl f: nvr quite enough pce to get on terms* **15/2**

2 **7** *1¼* **Battle Of Jericho (USA)**[7] 7797 2-9-1 100 (t) RyanMoore 9 99+
(A P O'Brien, Ire) *str; lw; hld up wl in tch in last pair: clsd and swtchd lft over 1f out: sn rdn: nt clr run and trying to switch rt jst ins fnl f: nt given a hrd time but kpt on same pce after: nvr trbld ldrs* **5/1**[3]

4514 **8** *shd* **Pursuing The Dream (IRE)**[28] 7114 2-8-12 100 DougieCostello 7 90
(Jamie Osborne) *stdd after s: hld up in tch in last pair: clsd over 1f out: nt clr run 1f out: swtchd rt and hdwy ins fnl f: styd on: nt rch ldrs* **20/1**

0130 **9** *½* **Mrs Gallagher**[36] 6863 2-8-12 91 JosephineGordon 5 88
(William Jarvis) *wnt rt s: t.k.h: hld up in tch in midfield: effrt over 1f out: kpt on same pce and no imp ins fnl f* **16/1**

6010 **10** *¾* **Neola**[29] 7090 2-8-12 95 JFEgan 4 86
(Mick Channon) *sltly on toes; bmpd s: hld up in tch in last trio: effrt over 1f out: no imp and kpt on same pce ins fnl f* **20/1**

24 **11** *½* **Sankari Royale (IRE)**[47] 6488 2-8-12 93 FrankieDettori 10 84
(J P Murtagh, Ire) *w'like; in tch in midfield: pushed along 1/2-way: rdn and unable qck over 1f out: btn whn squeezed for room jst ins fnl f: bhd and one pce after* **12/1**

1255 **12** *1½* **Angel Force (IRE)**[27] 7138 2-8-12 84 (h) OisinMurphy 11 78
(David C Griffiths) *pressed ldrs: rdn and unable qck over 1f out: nudged rt and impeded jst ins fnl f: bhd after* **100/1**

58.65s (-0.45) **Going Correction** -0.125s/f (Firm) 2y crse rec **12 Ran SP% 116.1**

Speed ratings (Par 105): **98,97,96,96,96 95,93,93,92,91 90,87**

CSF £14.77 TOTE £4.80: £1.60, £1.30, £2.70; EX 17.90 Trifecta £89.10.

**Owner** F Gillespie **Bred** Mr & Mrs G Middlebrook **Trained** Malton, N Yorks

**FOCUS**

Stands' side course used. Stalls Stands' side except 1m4f, centre. After the first William Buick said: "It's lovely ground." Fillies had won the three previous runnings since the Cornwallis was transferred from Ascot in 2014. One of them was Quiet Reflection who went on to win twice at the top level, while Battaash was third last year. The 1-2 were always prominent and both raced near the stands' rail in the closing stages. Reasonable form for the grade, and a new record time for 2yos, breaking that set by Mrs Danvers in this race last year by 0.04sec.

## 8002 GODOLPHIN LIFETIME CARE OH SO SHARP STKS (GROUP 3) (FILLIES) 7f

**2:25** (2:27) (Class 1) 2-Y-O

**£34,026** (£12,900; £6,456; £3,216; £1,614; £810) **Stalls** High

Form RPR

22 **1** **Altyn Orda (IRE)**[13] 7620 2-9-0 0 AndreaAtzeni 9 106
(Roger Varian) *athletic; uns rdr on way to s and got loose: racd stands' side: chsd ldrs: clsd to ld gp and veered rt 2f out: pressing ldrs and rdn over 1f out: styd on wl against stands' rail to ld cl home: 1st of 7 in gp* **25/1**

113 **2** *nk* **Gavota**[14] 7578 2-9-0 102 JamesDoyle 2 105
(Roger Charlton) *racd in centre: chsd ldrs overall: clsd and upsides 2f out: rdn to ld over 1f out: hdd briefly ins fnl f: sn led again: kpt on u.p: hdd last strides: 1st of 7 in gp* **7/2**[2]

**3** *1* **I Can Fly**[14] 7585 2-9-0 0 RyanMoore 3 102+
(A P O'Brien, Ire) *str; lw; racd in centre: hld up in rr: hdwy 1/2-way: clsd and rdn to chse ldrs 2f out: ev ch over 1f out: led ins fnl f: sn hdd & wknd towards fin: 2nd of 7 in gp* **2/1**[1]

25 **4** *1¼* **Butterscotch (IRE)**[14] 7578 2-9-0 98 (t) SeamieHeffernan 1 99
(A P O'Brien, Ire) *compact; racd in centre: overall ldr: rdn and hdd over 1f out: no ex ins fnl f: wknd wl ins fnl f: 3rd of 7 in gp* **14/1**

114 **5** *2½* **Hikmaa (IRE)**[14] 7578 2-9-0 101 AdamBeschizza 6 92
(Ed Vaughan) *racd in centre: hld up towards rr: hdwy 1/2-way: rdn to chse ldrs 2f out: unable qck over 1f out: wknd ins fnl f: 4th of 7 in gp* **16/1**

3151 **6** *¾* **Expressiy (FR)**[8] 7757 2-9-0 0 (h) WilliamBuick 8 90
(Charlie Appleby) *w'like; racd stands' side: hld up in midfield: effrt ent fnl 2f: unable qck over 1f out: wl hld and kpt on same pce ins fnl f: 2nd of 7 in gp* **14/1**

1 **7** *¾* **Herecomesthesun (IRE)**[36] 6861 2-9-0 0 EdwardGreatrex 11 88
(Archie Watson) *str; racd stands' side: hld up in rr: hdwy 1/2-way: swtchd rt and rdn to chse ldrs whn pushed rt 2f out: unable qck over 1f out: wknd ins fnl f: 3rd of 7 in gp* **25/1**

5016 **8** *1¾* **Elizabeth Bennet (IRE)**[14] 7578 2-9-0 93 PJMcDonald 14 83
(Charles Hills) *sltly on toes; racd stands' side: chsd ldr: rdn ent fnl 2f: unable qck and outpcd over 1f out: wknd ins fnl f: 4th of 7 in gp* **66/1**

6311 **9** *1¾* **Anna Nerium**[36] 6863 2-9-3 100 TomMarquand 7 82
(Richard Hannon) *racd in centre: midfield: rdn 1/2-way: struggling to qckn and losing pl whn sltly impeded 2f out: wknd over 1f out: 5th of 7 in gp* **25/1**

1153 **10** *nse* **Special Purpose (IRE)**[36] 6863 2-9-0 99 OisinMurphy 13 79
(William Haggas) *lw; racd stands' side: pushed along and lost pl over 2f out: n.d after: 5th of 7 in gp* **14/1**

232 **11** *hd* **Blanchefleur (IRE)**[36] 6861 2-9-0 79 SeanLevey 12 78
(Richard Hannon) *unf; racd stands' side: hld up in rr: effrt over 2f out: no imp: wl btn over 1f out: 6th of 7 in gp* **100/1**

512 **12** *½* **Dark Rose Angel (IRE)**[29] 7088 2-9-0 104 FrankieDettori 10 77
(Simon Crisford) *athletic; racd stands' side: led gp and chsd ldrs overall: lost gp ld and rdn 2f out: sn btn and wknd over 1f out: 7th of 7 in gp* **11/2**[3]

4102 **13** *1* **Jousi**[35] 6886 2-9-0 85 JosephineGordon 4 74
(Hugo Palmer) *racd in centre: hld up in tch in midfield: rdn ent fnl 2f: sn struggling and wkng whn drifted rt over 1f out: 6th of 7 in gp* **80/1**

2104 **14** *1* **One Minute (IRE)**[36] 6863 2-9-0 96 JimCrowley 5 71
(William Haggas) *racd in centre: chsd ldr tl over 2f out: pushed rt 2f out: sn dropped out and bhd ins fnl f: 7th of 7 in gp* **22/1**

1m 23.71s (-1.69) **Going Correction** -0.125s/f (Firm) **14 Ran SP% 116.4**

Speed ratings (Par 102): **104,103,102,101,98 97,96,94,92,92 92,91,90,89**

CSF £103.31 TOTE £24.40: £5.30, £1.30, £1.20; EX 102.00 Trifecta £668.80.

**Owner** Nurlan Bizakov **Bred** Hesmonds Stud Ltd **Trained** Newmarket, Suffolk

**FOCUS**

A competitive Group 3 and a race that can throw up a high-class filly, with Miss France winning this four years ago before going on to take the following year's 1,000 Guineas. A few of these had met each other before including the third, fourth, fifth and sixth from the Rockfel over C&D a fortnight earlier and the winner, third and fourth from the Dick Poole Stakes at Salisbury last month. They split into two equal groups of seven with one group racing up the centre and the other up the stands' rail. Although the winner came up the nearside, the next four home all raced up the middle. Straightforward form, with the runner-up replicating her recent C&D form.

## 8003 GODOLPHIN STUD AND STABLE STAFF AWARDS CHALLENGE STKS (GROUP 2) 7f

**3:00** (3:04) (Class 1) 3-Y-O+

**£68,052** (£25,800; £12,912; £6,432; £3,228; £1,620) **Stalls** High

Form RPR

0324 **1** **Limato (IRE)**[73] 5502 5-9-3 115 HarryBentley 9 123
(Henry Candy) *racd stands' side: hld up in midfield overall: clsd and jnd overall ldr travelling wl 2f out: rdn to ld over 1f out: r.o strly and drew clr ins fnl f: 1st of 5 in gp* **6/4**[1]

0-13 **2** *3½* **Massaat (IRE)**[33] 6982 4-9-6 116 JimCrowley 8 116
(Owen Burrows) *sweating; racd stands' side: led gp but midfield overall: rdn and clsd to ld overall 2f out: hdd over 1f out: edging rt and outpcd by wnr ins fnl f: kpt on for 2nd: 2nd of 5 in gp* **11/2**[2]

3066 **3** *1½* **Gordon Lord Byron (IRE)**[12] 7663 9-9-6 111 AndreaAtzeni 1 112
(T Hogan, Ire) *racd in centre: chsd ldrs overall: effrt wl over 1f out: outpcd by wnr and kpt on same pce ins fnl f: 1st of 5 in gp* **66/1**

3153 **4** *1¼* **Rehana (IRE)**[79] 5308 3-8-12 104 ColmO'Donoghue 4 101
(M Halford, Ire) *athletic; racd in centre: chsd clr ldr: clsd over 2f out: effrt 2f out: led gp and chsd ldng pair over 1f out: unable qck and wknd ins fnl f: 2nd of 5 in gp* **33/1**

2540 **5** *hd* **Cougar Mountain (IRE)**[5] 7856 6-9-3 110 (tp) RyanMoore 10 105
(A P O'Brien, Ire) *racd stands' side: midfield tl dropped to rr and outpcd over 4f out: rdn and effrt over 2f out: hdwy and hung rt 1f out: kpt on same pce ins fnl f: 3rd of 5 in gp* **16/1**

100 **6** *¾* **Mix And Mingle (IRE)**[49] 6401 4-9-0 110 TedDurcan 6 100
(Chris Wall) *lw; racd in centre: hmpd leaving stalls: hld up in midfield: effrt 2f out: rdn to chse ldrs over 1f out: unable qck and wknd ins fnl f: 3rd of 5 in gp* **25/1**

0102 **7** *½* **True Valour (IRE)**[34] 6959 3-9-1 109 OisinMurphy 2 100
(J P Murtagh, Ire) *racd in centre: hld up in midfield: clsd over 2f out: no imp over 1f out and hld whn nt clrest of runs ins fnl f: 4th of 5 in gp* **25/1**

0011 **8** *10* **Gifted Master (IRE)**[48] 6428 4-9-3 109 (b) WilliamBuick 3 74
(Hugo Palmer) *racd in centre: overall ldr and sn clr: hdd and rdn 2f out: lost pl jst over 1f out: sn wknd: 5th of 5 in gp* **9/1**

0421 **9** *10* **Absolutely So (IRE)**[125] 3587 7-9-3 108 DavidProbert 5 47
(Andrew Balding) *racd stands' side: t.k.h early: swtchd lft sn after s: hld up in midfield: effrt over 2f out: sn struggling: wknd over 1f out: 4th of 5 in gp* **33/1**

3-14 **10** *7* **Dabyah (IRE)**[112] 4031 3-8-12 112 FrankieDettori 7 24
(John Gosden) *lw; racd stands' side: midfield: rdn 3f out: sn struggling: wl bhd and eased ins fnl f: 5th of 5 in gp* **6/1**[3]

6616 **P** **Dutch Connection**[27] 7179 5-9-3 112 JamesDoyle 11
(Charles Hills) *sweating; racd stands' side: stmbld leaving stalls: bhd: eased 5f out: p.u and dismntd 3f out: lame* **15/2**

1m 22.24s (-3.16) **Going Correction** -0.125s/f (Firm)

**WFA** 3 from 4yo+ 2lb **11 Ran SP% 112.4**

Speed ratings (Par 115): **113,109,107,105,105 104,104,92,81,73**

CSF £8.34 TOTE £2.20: £1.10, £1.90, £13.20; EX 10.50 Trifecta £283.90.

**Owner** Paul G Jacobs **Bred** Seamus Phelan **Trained** Kingston Warren, Oxon

**FOCUS**

A good edition of this Group 2. They split into two groups with five racing down the centre and half a dozen, including the winner and second, on the stands' side. The time beat the standard by 0.26sec. The runner-up has been rated close to form.

## 8004 BET365 FILLIES' MILE (GROUP 1) 1m

**3:35** (3:37) (Class 1) 2-Y-O

**£321,829** (£122,012; £61,063; £30,418; £15,265; £7,661) **Stalls** High

Form RPR

121 **1** **Laurens (FR)**[29] 7088 2-9-0 0 PJMcDonald 10 113
(K R Burke) *ly; lw; led after 1f: mde rest: shkn up wl over 1f out: rdn over 1f out: kpt on gamely u.p ins fnl f: jst hld on: all out* **10/1**

143 **2** *nse* **September (IRE)**[33] 6974 2-9-0 104 SeamieHeffernan 7 113+
(A P O'Brien, Ire) *hld up in tch in midfield: n.m.r over 1f out: switching rt but stl nowhere to go ent fnl f: swtchd lft and in the clr but 2 l down ins fnl f: r.o strly wl ins fnl f: jst failed* **9/2**[2]

1 **3** *¾* **Magic Lily**[20] 7403 2-9-0 0 (t) WilliamBuick 12 111
(Charlie Appleby) *str; lw; hld up wl in tch in midfield: n.m.r wl over 1f out: swtchd rt and effrt between horses 1f out: ev ch ins fnl f: edgd rt and kpt on same pce wl ins fnl f* **8/1**

124 **4** *3* **Magical (IRE)**[12] 7666 2-9-0 111 RyanMoore 2 104+
(A P O'Brien, Ire) *w'like; in tch in midfield: clsd to press ldrs over 3f out: rdn and ev ch over 1f out tl ins fnl f: no ex and wknd wl ins fnl f* **15/8**[1]

6011 **5** *¾* **Ellthea (IRE)**[19] 7421 2-9-0 109 ColmO'Donoghue 8 103
(K R Burke) *w ldrs: rdn and ev ch 2f out tl unable qck jst ins fnl f: wknd wl ins fnl f* **20/1**

23 **6** *1 3/4* **Lubinka (IRE)**[34] 6917 2-9-0 0 JackMitchell 9 99
(Peter Chapple-Hyam) *stdd s: hld up in tch in last pair: effrt ent fnl 2f: no imp tl passed btn horses 1f out: kpt on but no threat to ldrs* **150/1**

136 **7** *1 1/2* **Musical Art (IRE)**[55] 6228 2-9-0 0 (t[1]) JimCrowley 11 95
(Paul Cole) *lw; in tch in last pair: nt clrest of runs ent fnl 2f: outpcd on downhill run over 1f out: n.d but kpt on to pass btn horses ins fnl f: nvr trbld ldrs* **33/1**

2 **8** *1* **Efaadah (IRE)**[40] 6731 2-9-0 103 AurelienLemaitre 3 93+
(F Head, France) *athletic; w ldrs: rdn 2f out: unable qck and outpcd over 1f out: wknd ins fnl f* **11/2[3]**

1632 **9** *2 1/4* **Nyaleti (IRE)**[14] 7578 2-9-0 108 JamesDoyle 6 88
(Mark Johnston) *led for 1f: styd upsides ldrs: rdn 2f out: sn struggling: outpcd and losing pl whn impeded over 1f out: wknd fnl f* **8/1**

4 **10** *4 1/2* **Muirin (IRE)**[33] 6974 2-9-0 100 DeclanMcDonogh 1 77
(Edward Lynam, Ire) *w'like; sweating; hld up in tch: effrt ent fnl 2f: sn struggling and lost pl over 1f out: bhd ins fnl f* **20/1**

114 **11** *12* **Quivery (USA)**[48] 6418 2-9-0 95 FrankieDettori 5 50
(Jeremy Noseda) *hld up in tch in midfield: rdn 2f out: sn lost pl and btn: bhd ins fnl f* **50/1**

1m 36.15s (-2.45) **Going Correction** -0.125s/f (Firm) **11** Ran SP% **114.8**
Speed ratings (Par 106): **107,106,106,103,102 100,99,98,95,91 79**
CSF £50.57 CT £388.67 TOTE £9.40: £2.70, £1.80, £2.60; EX 54.60 Trifecta £443.80.

**Owner** John Dance **Bred** Bloodstock Agency Ltd **Trained** Middleham Moor, N Yorks

■ Stewards' Enquiry : William Buick four-day ban; misuse of whip (Oct 27, 30-31, Nov 1)

**FOCUS**
A race with a rich tradition, having been won by the likes of Bosra Sham, Reams Of Verse, Soviet Song and Minding in the past 25 years, and the seventh running of the Fillies' Mile since the race was moved permanently to Newmarket. This year's contest lost a key participant when the likely warm favourite Happily was ruled out with a temperature during the morning, but despite her absence this still looked a competitive renewal featuring the second, third and fourth from the Moyglare and the first and third from the May Hill. They raced as one group up the stands' side and the early pace didn't look strong, but getting as close to the rail as possible was again shown to be an advantage. It's hard to be dogmatic about the level, but a nice step forward from the winner in a weaker race than recent renewals of this Group 1.

## 8005 BET365 OLD ROWLEY CUP H'CAP (HERITAGE HANDICAP) 1m 4f
**4:10** (4:14) (Class 2) 3-Y-O

**£74,700** (£22,368; £11,184; £5,592; £2,796; £1,404) **Stalls** Centre

Form RPR

2452 **1** **First Nation**[20] 7400 3-9-0 **95** WilliamBuick 15 106
(Charlie Appleby) *hld up towards rr: hdwy over 1f out: rdn to chal jst over 1f out: led 1f out: styd on wl ins fnl f* **12/1**

1243 **2** *3/4* **Eynhallow**[24] 7252 3-8-10 **91** SeanLevey 13 100
(Roger Charlton) *lw; hld up in midfield: clsd over 2f out: rdn to ld and hung lft jst over 1f out: bmpd wnr and hdd 1f out: kpt on same pce u.p ins fnl f* **9/1**

141 **3** *nk* **Duke Of Bronte**[34] 6920 3-8-5 **89** GeorgeWood(3) 8 97
(Rod Millman) *lw; hld up in midfield: dropped towards rr 1/2-way: hdwy over 2f out: rdn and pressed ldng pair ent fnl f: kpt on same pce u.p ins fnl f* **9/1**

1003 **4** *2 1/2* **Crowned Eagle**[20] 7400 3-9-0 **95** (p) TedDurcan 10 99
(John Gosden) *t.k.h: hld up in last quartet: hdwy into midfield 4f out: rdn to chse ldrs over 1f out: kpt on same pce ins fnl f* **16/1**

6103 **5** *2 1/2* **Hochfeld (IRE)**[7] 7783 3-9-6 **101** PJMcDonald 12 101
(Mark Johnston) *chsd ldrs: wnt 2nd 10f out: rdn 2f out: ev ch briefly over 1f out: outpcd and btn 1f out: wknd ins fnl f* **16/1**

1126 **6** *1 3/4* **Medalla De Oro**[23] 7267 3-7-11 **81** oh1 (h) NoelGarbutt(3) 11 79
(Peter Chapple-Hyam) *led: styd on far rail and racing alone in clr ld 9f out: hung bdly lft over 1f out: sn hdd: pushed along and wknd ins fnl f* **50/1**

3000 **7** *3/4* **Bear Valley (IRE)**[34] 6920 3-7-12 **84** JaneElliott(5) 9 80
(Mark Johnston) *chsd ldng trio: unable qck u.p over 1f out and btn 1f out: wknd ins fnl f* **50/1**

1331 **8** *shd* **Koeman**[16] 7516 3-8-8 **89** 6ex JFEgan 7 85
(Mick Channon) *midfield: effrt over 2f out: no imp u.p over 1f out: wl hld and plugged on same pce ins fnl f* **50/1**

1161 **9** *hd* **Torcello (IRE)**[15] 7548 3-8-10 **91** 6ex OisinMurphy 1 87
(Andrew Balding) *chsd ldr for 2f: styd chsng ldrs: rdn ent fnl 2f: unable qck and outpcd over 1f out: wknd ins fnl f* **7/2[1]**

2622 **10** *2 1/4* **Melting Dew**[34] 6920 3-8-10 **91** RyanMoore 3 83
(Sir Michael Stoute) *in tch in midfield: effrt ent fnl 2f: unable qck and lost pl over 1f out: wknd fnl f* **8/1[3]**

1312 **11** *hd* **Arab Moon**[35] 6887 3-8-11 **92** AdamBeschizza 16 84
(William Knight) *sltly on toes; hld up in tch in last pair: effrt ent fnl 2f: no imp and btn over 1f out: wknd fnl f* **33/1**

1423 **12** *1 1/4* **Here And Now**[48] 6445 3-8-10 **91** PatDobbs 4 81
(Ralph Beckett) *hld up in midfield: rdn 2f out: sn struggling and lost pl over 1f out: wknd fnl f* **12/1**

1364 **13** *1 3/4* **Winston C (IRE)**[34] 6930 3-8-7 **88** HarryBentley 14 75
(Michael Bell) *sweating; in tch in midfield: rdn 3f out: lost pl over 1f out: wl hld whn sltly impeded and swtchd rt 1f out: wknd fnl f* **14/1**

1112 **14** *2 1/2* **High End**[24] 7252 3-9-7 **102** (p[1]) JimCrowley 5 85
(Saeed bin Suroor) *lw; sltly on toes; restless in stalls: hld up in midfield: pushed along jst over 2f out: lost pl on downhill run over 1f out: sn wl btn and wknd fnl f* **6/1[2]**

2141 **15** *1 1/4* **Humble Hero (IRE)**[31] 7031 3-8-8 **89** AndreaAtzeni 2 70
(William Haggas) *lw; stdd s: hld up towards rr: shkn up and effrt jst over 2f out: sn btn and wknd over 1f out* **10/1**

-410 **16** *36* **Intrepidly (USA)**[16] 7516 3-8-11 **92** FrankieDettori 6 16
(Jeremy Noseda) *hld up in last quartet: rdn 3f out: sn struggling: bhd over 1f out: eased: t.o* **20/1**

2m 29.13s (-2.87) **Going Correction** -0.125s/f (Firm) **16** Ran SP% **124.1**
Speed ratings (Par 107): **104,103,103,101,99 98,98,98,98,96 96,95,94,92,91 67**
CSF £113.38 CT £1032.73 TOTE £13.30: £2.70, £2.50, £2.10, £3.30; EX 148.70 Trifecta £3431.70.

**Owner** Godolphin **Bred** Darley **Trained** Newmarket, Suffolk

**FOCUS**
Race distance increased 15yds. The fourth running of this very valuable handicap, the third under the Old Rowley Cup name. It brought together formlines from a number of similar events. The field gradually tacked over and the first four home ended up nearest the stands' rail. It's been rated around the race averages.

## 8006 GODOLPHIN UNDER STARTERS ORDERS MAIDEN FILLIES' STKS (PLUS 10 RACE) 7f
**4:45** (4:51) (Class 4) 2-Y-O

**£6,469** (£1,925; £962; £481) **Stalls** High

Form RPR

3 **1** **Veracious**[21] 7357 2-9-0 0 RyanMoore 1 94
(Sir Michael Stoute) *lw; pressed ldr tl pushed into ld over 1f out: rdn and r.o strly to draw clr ins fnl f: easily* **3/1[2]**

**2** *4* **Winter Lightning (IRE)** 2-9-0 0 OisinMurphy 13 83+
(Saeed bin Suroor) *quite str; led: rdn and hdd over 1f out: outpcd whn rn green and hung rt jst ins fnl f: outpcd by wnr but kpt on for clr 2nd ins fnl f* **11/4[1]**

4 **3** *1 1/2* **Final Treat (IRE)**[21] 7351 2-9-0 0 JamesDoyle 6 79+
(William Haggas) *lw; hld up wl in tch in midfield: effrt to chse ldrs 2f out: disputing 3rd and unable qck over 1f out: wl hld 3rd and kpt on same pce ins fnl f* **6/1[3]**

3 **4** *1 3/4* **Angel's Glory**[14] 7563 2-9-0 0 AndreaAtzeni 10 74
(Roger Varian) *compact; lw; t.k.h: trckd ldrs: shkn up 2f out: disputing 3rd and unable qck over 1f out: wknd ins fnl f* **11/4[1]**

00 **5** *1/2* **Wild Impala (FR)**[47] 6480 2-9-0 0 FrankieDettori 9 73
(John Gosden) *hld up in tch in midfield: swtchd lft and effrt 2f out: unable qck and edgd rt over 1f out: no ch w wnr and kpt on same pce ins fnl f* **14/1**

**6** *1 1/4* **Canimar** 2-9-0 0 PJMcDonald 8 69
(Ed Dunlop) *athletic; bit on the leg; hld up in tch in midfield: rdn and reminders 2f out: sn outpcd and unbalanced on downhill run over 1f out: wl hld and plugged on same pce fnl f* **100/1**

**7** *nk* **Gumriyah** 2-9-0 0 HarryBentley 5 68+
(John Gosden) *str; dwlt: hld up in last pair: shkn up and effrt ent fnl 2f: sme hdwy but no threat ti ldrs whn rn green and edgd rt on downhill run over 1f out: wl hld and kpt on same pce after* **14/1**

640 **8** *1* **Sigrid Nansen**[13] 7620 2-8-11 0 GeorgeWood(3) 12 66
(George Scott) *hld up in tch in rr of midfield: pushed along and nt clrest of runs 2f out: no hdwy and wl btn over 1f out* **100/1**

**9** *nse* **Colourfield (IRE)** 2-9-0 0 AdamBeschizza 2 66
(Ed Vaughan) *compact; on toes; s.i.s: hld up in rr: effrt 2f out: sn struggling and outpcd: wl hld over 1f out* **100/1**

**10** *5* **Mirror Mirror (IRE)** 2-9-0 0 JackMitchell 11 52+
(Peter Chapple-Hyam) *quite str; dwlt: hld up in tch: effrt 2f out: no imp whn nt clr run over 1f out: no ch after* **33/1**

**11** *5* **Star Of Assisi (USA)** 2-9-0 0 GeraldMosse 4 39
(John Ryan) *compact; bit bkwd; chsd ldrs tl 2f out: sn outpcd and lost pl: wknd fnl f* **66/1**

**12** *3 1/2* **Esme Kate (IRE)** 2-9-0 0 LouisSteward 3 29
(Michael Bell) *w'like; bit on the leg; on toes; dwlt: in tch towards rr: rdn 2f out: sn bhd* **66/1**

1m 25.28s (-0.12) **Going Correction** -0.125s/f (Firm) **12** Ran SP% **114.8**
Speed ratings (Par 94): **95,90,88,86,86 84,84,83,83,77 71,67**
CSF £11.12 TOTE £3.60: £1.50, £1.50, £1.80; EX 14.50 Trifecta £41.50.

**Owner** Cheveley Park Stud **Bred** Cheveley Park Stud Ltd **Trained** Newmarket, Suffolk

**FOCUS**
An interesting fillies' maiden featuring a couple that had already shown promise and some choicely bred newcomers. Again they stayed against the nearside rail and went only steadily early, so that those who raced up with the pace were at an advantage, but it was still hard not to have been impressed by the winner.

## 8007 JOIN CLUB GODOLPHIN PRIDE STKS (LISTED RACE) (F&M) 1m 2f
**5:20** (5:23) (Class 1) 3-Y-O+

**£22,684** (£8,600; £4,304; £2,144; £1,076; £540) **Stalls** High

Form RPR

-623 **1** **Chain Of Daisies**[48] 6441 5-9-3 106 HarryBentley 1 111
(Henry Candy) *mde all: gng best and asserting whn rdn 2f out: sn clr and in command over 1f out: styd on wl: rdn out* **7/2[2]**

2452 **2** *2 1/4* **Permission**[14] 7576 4-9-3 100 DanielMuscutt 5 106
(James Fanshawe) *stdd and swtchd lft after s: hld up in rr: gd hdwy 3f out: swtchd lft and chsd clr wnr 2f out: wandered u.p 1f out: styd on wl for clr 2nd but nvr threatening wnr* **10/1**

36-4 **3** *7* **Architecture (IRE)**[20] 7393 4-9-3 111 JamesDoyle 10 92
(Hugo Palmer) *lw; hld up in midfield: effrt to chse ldrs 3f out: no imp on wnr over 1f out: wl hld 3rd and kpt on same pce fnl f* **7/4[1]**

1204 **4** *2 1/4* **Coconut Creme**[58] 6074 3-8-13 97 GeraldMosse 9 88
(William Haggas) *lw; chsd ldr: effrt and chsd wnr jst over 3f out: sn drvn and unable qck and lost 2nd 1f out: outpcd and wl hld over 1f out: wknd ins fnl f* **20/1**

1203 **5** *1/2* **Wilamina (IRE)**[27] 7171 4-9-3 105 OisinMurphy 3 86
(Martyn Meade) *s.i.s: hld up in last trio: effrt 3f out: drvn and no imp whn wandered over 1f out: wknd fnl f* **10/1**

4140 **6** *3* **Ouja**[23] 7283 3-8-13 95 (b[1]) FrankieDettori 6 81
(John Gosden) *t.k.h: chsd ldrs: rdn 3f out: unable qck u.p 2f out: btn and drifted rt over 1f out: wknd fnl f* **25/1**

210 **7** *nk* **Natavia**[133] 3301 3-8-13 102 (t[1]) RyanMoore 11 80
(Roger Charlton) *hld up in midfield: effrt against stands' rail over 2f out: no hdwy u.p and btn over 1f out: wknd* **6/1[3]**

-663 **8** *2 1/4* **Mia Tesoro (IRE)**[21] 7358 4-9-3 79 (h) StevieDonohoe 7 75
(Charlie Fellowes) *taken down early: hld up in midfield: rdn over 2f out: sn struggling to qckn and btn over 1f out: wknd* **100/1**

3503 **9** *1 3/4* **Jelly Monger (IRE)**[6] 7817 5-9-3 85 RobertWinston 2 71
(Dominic Ffrench Davis) *hld up in tch in midfield: clsd to chse ldrs and rdn 3f out: sn struggling and outpcd 2f out: wknd over 1f out* **100/1**

1- **10** *8* **Crimson Rock (USA)**[356] 7543 3-8-13 84 PatDobbs 8 56
(Ralph Beckett) *hld up in last trio: effrt 3f out: no imp and struggling u.p over 2f out: wl bhd over 1f out* **12/1**

1023 **11** *6* **High Hopes**[23] 7283 4-9-3 99 JimCrowley 4 43
(David Simcock) *hld up in midfield: short-lived effrt 3f out: no hdwy over 2f out: wl bhd over 1f out* **20/1**

-150 **12** *26* **Al Mayda (USA)**[23] 7283 3-8-13 78 (t) LouisSteward 12
(Hugo Palmer) *w ldr tl lost pl qckly over 3f out: bhd fnl 2f: eased fnl f: t.o* **100/1**

0121 **13** 1 ¾ **UAE Queen**[23] 7276 3-8-13 82.................................. AndreaAtzeni 13
(Roger Varian) *midfield: rdn 3f out: sn struggling and dropped to rr 2f: sn lost tch and eased fnl f: t.o* **33/1**

2m 2.02s (-3.78) **Going Correction** -0.125s/f (Firm)
**WFA** 3 from 4yo+ 4lb **13** Ran SP% **118.0**
Speed ratings (Par 111): **110,108,102,100,100 98,97,95,94,88 83,62,61**
CSF £35.24 TOTE £3.90: £1.50, £3.20, £1.20; EX 38.20 Trifecta £131.50.
**Owner** Girsonfield Ltd **Bred** Girsonfield Ltd **Trained** Kingston Warren, Oxon

**FOCUS**
They split into three groups with last home UAE Queen on her own against the rail, seven positioned a little further out, and a group of five containing the winner more up the centre. They finished well stretched out behind the dominant winner. A pb from the runner-up.
T/Jkpt: Not won. T/Plt: £34.30 to a £1 stake. Pool: £151,570.48 - 3,218.87 winning units T/Qpdt: £19.10 to a £1 stake. Pool: £11,185.10 - 432.48 winning units **Steve Payne**

## 6964 YORK (L-H)
### Friday, October 13

**OFFICIAL GOING: Good (good to soft in places; 6.2)**
Wind: Strong half behind Weather: Overcast & breezy

## 8008 TSG PAUL BEIOLEY MEMORIAL NURSERY H'CAP 6f
**2:10** (2:11) (Class 3) (0-95,92) 2-Y-O **£9,703** (£2,887; £1,443; £721) **Stalls** Centre

Form RPR

2103 **1** **Beatbox Rhythm (IRE)**[30] 7049 2-9-1 **89**.................. CliffordLee(3) 14 99
(K R Burke) *racd centre: prom: cl up 1/2-way: rdn to ld wl over 1f out: drvn and edgd rt ins fnl f: kpt on wl towards fin* **12/1**

623 **2** nk **Kyllachy Dragon (IRE)**[24] 7242 2-7-8 **72** oh2 ow1... JamieGormley(7) 7 81+
(Iain Jardine) *wnt rt s: in tch centre: chsd ldrs over 2f out: rdn to chal ent fnl f: sn swtchd lft and drvn: ev ch tl nio ex towards fin* **12/1**

331 **3** 3 **Captain Jameson (IRE)**[31] 7013 2-8-10 **81**.................. JasonHart 4 81
(John Quinn) *racd towards far side: prom: rdn along and ev ch over 1f out: kpt on same pce* **12/1**

3130 **4** 2 **Alkhalifa (IRE)**[41] 6699 2-8-10 **81**..................(p[1]) PaulMulrennan 2 75
(Brian Meehan) *racd towards far side: led: rdn along 2f out: sn drvn and hdd: wknd fnl f* **20/1**

5040 **5** shd **Guzman (IRE)**[15] 7536 2-8-5 **76**..................(h) PaulHanagan 10 70
(Richard Fahey) *midfield centre: rdn along over 2f out: kpt on u.p fnl f* **11/1**

4655 **6** nk **Zap**[13] 7596 2-9-7 **92**.................................. TonyHamilton 6 85
(Richard Fahey) *racd towards far side: pushed along and rr 1/2-way: swtchd rt and rdn over 2f out: styd on appr fnl f* **12/1**

3105 **7** ¾ **Savalas (IRE)**[33] 6969 2-8-10 **81**.................................. TomEaves 13 72
(Kevin Ryan) *racd towards stands side: towards rr: hdwy 4f out: chsd ldrs over 2f out: sn rdn and no imp fnl f* **20/1**

3300 **8** 1 ¼ **Astraea**[34] 6940 2-8-0 **71** oh3.................................. JamesSullivan 1 58
(Michael Easterby) *in tch towards far side: pushed along 2f out: rdn over 1f out: kpt on one pce* **50/1**

3131 **9** ½ **Tulip Fever**[47] 6481 2-8-11 **82**.................................. DavidAllan 5 67
(William Haggas) *racd towards far side: prom: rdn along over 2f out: grad wknd* **7/1[3]**

2131 **10** 1 ½ **Roundhay Park**[26] 7194 2-8-10 **81**.................. SilvestreDeSousa 9 62
(Nigel Tinkler) *hld up towards rr in centre: hdwy 2f out: sn rdn along and nvr nr ldrs* **5/1[1]**

432 **11** nk **Black Friday**[22] 7326 2-8-9 **80**.................................. GrahamLee 17 60
(Karen McLintock) *racd towards stands side: midfield: hdwy wl over 2f out: sn rdn along and edgd lft 2f out: sn wknd* **16/1**

1263 **12** hd **Collingham Park (IRE)**[13] 7596 2-8-6 **77**.................. AndrewMullen 3 56
(Jedd O'Keeffe) *prom towards far side: rdn along over 2f out: sn wknd* **20/1**

535 **13** ½ **Our Little Pony**[47] 6466 2-8-0 **71** oh5.................. CamHardie 15 49
(Lawrence Mullaney) *racd towards stands side: chsd ldrs: rdn along wl over 2f out: sn wknd* **66/1**

3320 **14** ¾ **Havana Star (IRE)**[30] 7041 2-8-3 **74**.................................. JoeDoyle 8 50
(Kevin Ryan) *towards rr: rdn along and sme hdwy centre 2f out: sn wknd* **14/1**

1420 **15** 1 ¼ **International Man**[29] 7090 2-8-11 **82**.................. BarryMcHugh 11 54
(Richard Fahey) *a towards rr* **14/1**

2311 **16** 3 ¾ **Ginbar (IRE)**[13] 7596 2-8-13 **84**.................. RichardKingscote 16 45+
(Tom Dascombe) *racd towards stands side: chsd ldrs: rdn along 1/2-way: sn wknd* **6/1[2]**

611 **17** hd **Canford's Joy (IRE)**[20] 7383 2-8-11 **82**.................. ShaneGray 12 42
(Ann Duffield) *a in rr* **25/1**

1m 11.49s (-0.41) **Going Correction** +0.10s/f (Good) **17** Ran SP% **123.4**
Speed ratings (Par 99): **106,105,101,98,98 98,97,95,95,93 92,92,91,90,89 84,83**
CSF £136.75 CT £1848.00 TOTE £13.70: £3.00, £3.60, £3.40, £4.60; EX 226.80 Trifecta £4584.30.
**Owner** John Dance **Bred** Martyn J McEnery **Trained** Middleham Moor, N Yorks

**FOCUS**
Distance increased by 17yds. The going was good, good to soft in places, with a brisk tail-wind helping the runners up the straight. An open handicap run at a strong pace with the front two pulling clear. The race could be rated a little higher.

## 8009 UNIBET.CO.UK H'CAP 7f 192y
**2:45** (2:47) (Class 2) (0-100,96) 4-Y-0+
**£18,675** (£5,592; £2,796; £1,398; £699; £351) **Stalls** Low

Form RPR

2-11 **1** **Zabeel Prince (IRE)**[23] 7285 4-9-7 **96**.................. SilvestreDeSousa 4 109+
(Roger Varian) *t.k.h: hld up in tch: smooth hdwy to ld over 2f out: rdn clr fr over 1f out: readily* **15/8[1]**

0000 **2** 2 ¾ **Bravery (IRE)**[13] 7619 4-9-6 **95**.................................. DanielTudhope 9 102
(David O'Meara) *hld up: hdwy over 2f out: sn rdn: chsd (clr) wnr ins fnl f: kpt on: nt pce to chal* **11/1**

0422 **3** ¾ **Home Cummins (IRE)**[46] 6520 5-9-3 **92**..................(p) PaulHanagan 6 97
(Richard Fahey) *sn pushed along in tch: effrt and rdn over 2f out: kpt on ins fnl f: nrst fin* **9/1[2]**

3441 **4** nk **Zwayyan**[7] 7781 4-9-7 **96** 6ex..................(b) AdamKirby 16 101
(William Haggas) *hld up: stdy hdwy on far side of gp over 2f out: effrt and rdn over 1f out: kpt on fnl f: nvr able to chal* **10/1[3]**

5B63 **5** nse **Just Hiss**[13] 7609 4-9-1 **90**..................(p) DavidAllan 15 94
(Tim Easterby) *hld up: hdwy on far side of gp over 2f out: rdn and kpt on fnl f: nrst fin* **10/1[3]**

2440 **6** ½ **Baraweez (IRE)**[34] 6961 7-8-12 **92**.................. BenRobinson(5) 20 95
(Brian Ellison) *hld up midfield: stdy hdwy over 2f out: sn rdn along: kpt on same pce fnl f* **20/1**

0200 **7** ¾ **Nicholas T**[13] 7619 5-9-1 **90**.................................. JamesSullivan 7 92
(Jim Goldie) *t.k.h: hld up midfield: rdn over 2f out: kpt on fnl f: nvr rchd ldrs* **25/1**

5100 **8** 1 ½ **Quixote (GER)**[13] 7609 7-9-4 **93**..................(t) CamHardie 3 91
(Michael Easterby) *prom: hdwy and ev ch over 2f out to over 1f out: chsd wnr to ins fnl f: sn no ex* **50/1**

0103 **9** ½ **Mohab**[30] 7044 4-8-11 **86**.................................. TomEaves 5 83
(Kevin Ryan) *hld up midfield: pushed along over 4f out: effrt on far side of gp over 2f out: wknd ins fnl f* **33/1**

3500 **10** ¾ **Boots And Spurs**[14] 7582 8-8-0 **82** oh5..................(v) JamieGormley(7) 2 77
(Scott Dixon) *prom: rdn and outpcd 2f out: kpt on ins fnl f: no imp* **66/1**

0603 **11** ½ **Cote D'Azur**[13] 7619 4-9-7 **96**.................................. JoeFanning 1 90
(Les Eyre) *led to over 2f out: rdn and wknd over 1f out* **9/1[2]**

544 **12** hd **Highland Colori (IRE)**[13] 7622 9-8-10 **85**..................(b) FrannyNorton 10 79
(Andrew Balding) *trckd ldr: rdn on nr side of gp over 2f out: edgd lft and wknd wl over 1f out* **10/1[3]**

0502 **13** nk **One Word More (IRE)**[7] 7781 7-8-9 **87**..........(h) RachelRichardson(3) 8 80
(Tim Easterby) *hld up: stdy hdwy over 3f out: rdn over 2f out: no imp fr over 1f out* **10/1[3]**

0020 **14** 4 **Classic Seniority**[13] 7626 5-9-4 **93**.................................. BarryMcHugh 18 77
(Marjorie Fife) *s.i.s: hld up: rdn along and outpcd over 2f out: sme late hdwy: nvr on terms* **66/1**

4300 **15** 1 **Two For Two (IRE)**[46] 6520 9-8-13 **88**..................(p) TonyHamilton 19 69
(Roger Fell) *hld up: drvn and outpcd over 2f out: n.d after* **66/1**

0000 **16** ½ **Steel Train (FR)**[153] 2606 6-9-3 **95**.................. ShelleyBirkett(3) 17 75
(David O'Meara) *t.k.h: hld up: effrt whn nt clr run briefly 2f out: sn wknd* **50/1**

1105 **17** 1 ¼ **Mon Beau Visage (IRE)**[6] 7823 4-8-13 **88**..................(p) ShaneGray 13 65
(David O'Meara) *hld up: effrt and drvn over 2f out: sn wknd* **33/1**

5106 **18** ½ **Zodiakos (IRE)**[6] 7823 4-8-4 **86**..................(p) BenSanderson(7) 12 62
(Roger Fell) *prom: drvn along on nr side of gp over 2f out: sn wknd* **50/1**

2105 **19** 1 ½ **Truth Or Dare**[35] 6873 6-9-1 **90**.................................. KevinStott 11 63
(James Bethell) *in tch: rdn and lost pl over 2f out: sn btn* **20/1**

0-00 **20** 17 **Tha'ir (IRE)**[13] 7619 7-9-6 **95**..................(p) BenCurtis 14 29
(Michael Appleby) *hld up: drvn on nr side of gp over 3f out: wknd over 2f out* **33/1**

1m 37.46s (-1.54) **Going Correction** +0.10s/f (Good) **20** Ran SP% **132.0**
Speed ratings (Par 109): **111,108,107,107,107 106,105,104,103,103 102,102,102,98,97 96,95,94,93,76**
CSF £21.45 CT £167.71 TOTE £2.60: £1.10, £3.10, £2.20, £2.90; EX 29.00 Trifecta £301.20.
**Owner** Sheikh Mohammed Obaid Al Maktoum **Bred** Roundhill Stud **Trained** Newmarket, Suffolk

**FOCUS**
Rail movement increased race distance by 17yds. They went a sound pace for this competitive handicap with the winning scoring impressively. It's been rated around the third.

## 8010 BRITISH STALLION STUDS EBF NOVICE STKS (PLUS 10 RACE) 5f 89y
**3:20** (3:22) (Class 3) 2-Y-O **£7,762** (£2,310; £1,154; £577) **Stalls** Centre

Form RPR

0241 **1** **Awesome**[37] 6806 2-9-3 75.................................. AdamKirby 4 79
(Clive Cox) *mde all: rdn wl over 1f out: drvn and edgd rt ins fnl f: kpt on strly* **4/1[2]**

4226 **2** 1 **Midsummer Knight**[28] 7114 2-9-2 77.................................. BenCurtis 3 75
(K R Burke) *trckd ldrs: hdwy and cl up 2f out: rdn over 1f out: chal ent fnl f: sn drvn and ev ch whn swtchd lft ins fnl f: kpt on same pce towards fin* **6/1**

34 **3** nk **Militia**[22] 7326 2-9-2 0.................................. PaulHanagan 8 73
(Richard Fahey) *prom on outer: cl up 2f out: rdn to chal ent fnl f: sn drvn and kpt on same pce* **5/1[3]**

3 **4** 1 **Machree (IRE)**[45] 6559 2-8-11 0.................................. TomEaves 5 72+
(Declan Carroll) *cl up: ev ch whn j. path and lost 2 l wl over 1f out: sn rdn and kpt on* **6/1**

325 **5** 1 **Makanah**[107] 4213 2-9-2 75.................................. JoeDoyle 11 66
(Julie Camacho) *in tch: hdwy over 2f out: rdn along wl over 1f out: kpt on fnl f: nrst fin* **10/1**

133 **6** ½ **Equitant**[17] 7482 2-9-5 78.................................. AdamMcNamara(3) 12 71
(Richard Fahey) *dwlt and towards rr: hdwy wl over 2f out: sn rdn along and kpt on fnl f: nrst fin* **14/1**

03 **7** 1 ¼ **Gullane One (IRE)**[14] 7562 2-9-2 0.................................. DavidAllan 2 60
(Tim Easterby) *chsd ldrs: rdn along 2f out: sn drvn and grad wknd* **14/1**

0 **8** 3 ½ **Whinmoor**[13] 7623 2-9-2 0.................................. AndrewMullen 6 48
(Nigel Tinkler) *dwlt: a in rr* **50/1**

**9** shd **I'm Yer Man** 2-9-2 0.................................. ShaneGray 9 48
(Ann Duffield) *dwlt: a in rr* **50/1**

0223 **10** nk **Harrogate (IRE)**[22] 7326 2-9-2 78.................................. DanielTudhope 7 47
(James Bethell) *chsd ldrs: rdn along over 2f out: sn drvn and wknd* **3/1[1]**

0 **11** 7 **Voguela (IRE)**[14] 7563 2-8-8 0.................. RachelRichardson(3) 1 17
(Tim Easterby) *a towards rr: outpcd and bhd fnl 2f* **50/1**

1m 5.18s (1.08) **Going Correction** +0.10s/f (Good) **11** Ran SP% **118.5**
Speed ratings (Par 99): **95,93,92,91,89 88,86,81,81,80 69**
CSF £28.39 TOTE £4.10: £1.70, £2.20, £1.80; EX 28.10 Trifecta £151.10.
**Owner** Carmel Stud **Bred** Carmel Stud **Trained** Lambourn, Berks

**FOCUS**
Not a bad contest for the grade. It was run at an honest pace with the prominent runners in control throughout. It's been rated around those close up.

## 8011 UNIBET H'CAP 1m 5f 188y
**3:55** (3:58) (Class 2) 3-Y-O
**£62,250** (£18,640; £9,320; £4,660; £2,330; £1,170) **Stalls** Low

Form RPR

4102 **1** **Brimham Rocks**[49] 6383 3-8-8 **91**.................. RichardKingscote 6 101+
(Ralph Beckett) *hld up in tch: hdwy on inner over 3f out: led 2f out: rdn clr appr fnl f: drvn out* **16/1**

5131 **2** 1 ¼ **Fools And Kings**[24] 7231 3-7-11 **83**.................. HollieDoyle(3) 1 89
(Robyn Brisland) *dwlt and hld up in rr: hdwy 3f out: rdn to chse ldrs on inner over 1f out: drvn and chsd wnr ins fnl f: kpt on* **20/1**

-211 **3** 1 ¼ **Star Rock**[20] 7401 3-8-2 **85**.................................. KieranO'Neill 2 89+
(Hughie Morrison) *trckd ldng pair: hdwy to chse ldr over 4f out: led 3f out: rdn and hdd 2f out: sn drvn: kpt on wl u.p fnl f* **11/2[3]**

5441 **4** nk **Star Of The East (IRE)**[13] 7614 3-8-3 **86**.................. JoeFanning 4 90
(Mark Johnston) *hld up: hdwy on outer 3f out: rdn along 2f out: styd on wl fnl f: nrst fin* **20/1**

0512 **5** hd **Je Suis Charlie**[20] 7387 3-8-1 **84**.................................. PaulHanagan 11 87
(Michael Bell) *hld up in rr: hdwy 3f out: rdn along wl over 1f out: drvn to chse ldrs ent fnl f: kpt on* **20/1**

1-31 **6** *nk* **Percy's Word**[44] 6580 3-8-6 **89** ... RyanPowell 7 92
(Simon Crisford) *chsd ldrs: rdn along over 2f out: sltly outpcd wl over 1f out: sn drvn and kpt on fnl f* **25/1**

4331 **7** *2 1/4* **Count Simon (IRE)**[14] 7560 3-8-0 **83** oh7 ... JimmyQuinn 12 83
(Andrew Balding) *prom: cl up over 3f out: rdn along 2f out: sn drvn: wknd fnl f* **25/1**

6415 **8** *2 1/4* **The Grand Visir**[48] 6445 3-8-8 **91** ... (p) SilvestreDeSousa 10 88
(William Haggas) *led 2f: prom: disp ld 3f out and sn rdn: drvn wl over 1f out: sn wknd* **10/3**[1]

0231 **9** *1* **Dominating (GER)**[7] 7785 3-8-9 **92** 6ex ... FrannyNorton 8 87
(Mark Johnston) *a towards rr* **12/1**

0621 **10** *3/4* **Face The Facts (IRE)**[15] 7547 3-9-7 **104** ... RobertHavlin 13 98
(John Gosden) *a towards rr* **8/1**

3411 **11** *1* **Bolder Bob (IRE)**[23] 7267 3-8-1 **84** ... AndrewMullen 9 77
(David Barron) *hld up towards rr: hdwy on outer 5f out: chsd ldrs 4f out: cl up 3f out: rdn along over 2f out: sn drvn and wknd* **20/1**

3110 **12** *24* **Joshua Reynolds**[34] 6930 3-8-10 **93** ... (b) RobertTart 5 52
(John Gosden) *cl up: led after 2f and sn clr: pushed along over 4f out: rdn over 3f out: sn hdd & wknd* **10/1**

311 **13** *14* **Gold Star**[34] 6952 3-9-1 **101** ... DavidEgan(3) 3 41
(Saeed bin Suroor) *hld up: hdwy into midfield 1/2-way: chsd ldrs 5f out: rdn along over 3f out: drvn and wknd over 2f out* **4/1**[2]

3m 1.02s (0.82) **Going Correction** +0.10s/f (Good) **13** Ran SP% **119.0**
Speed ratings (Par 107): **101,100,99,99,99 99,97,96,95,95 94,81,73**
CSF £304.65 CT £1980.73 TOTE £18.00: £5.10, £6.70, £2.20; EX 357.20 Trifecta £5852.60.
**Owner** Mr and Mrs David Aykroyd **Bred** Mr & Mrs David Aykroyd **Trained** Kimpton, Hants

**FOCUS**
Rail movement increased race distance by 22yds. A decent renewal of this staying handicap which had nine last-time-out winners in a field. It was run at a sound pace and the winner did it well. The third has been rated to her Newmarket win.

## 8012 PARSONAGE HOTEL AND CLOISTERS SPA H'CAP 5f
**4:30** (4:32) (Class 3) (0-95,93) 3-Y-0+
**£12,450** (£3,728; £1,864; £932; £466; £234) **Stalls** Centre

Form RPR

0064 **1** **East Street Revue**[41] 6677 4-9-3 **89** ... (b) DuranFentiman 6 99
(Tim Easterby) *prom in far side gp: led as gps merged over 1f out: kpt on strly fnl f* **12/1**

514 **2** *1 1/4* **Memories Galore (IRE)**[35] 6878 5-8-11 **83** ... (p) TonyHamilton 11 89
(Roger Fell) *in tch stands' side gp: effrt and angled rt as gps merged over 1f out: kpt on wl fnl f to take 2nd cl home* **16/1**

0043 **3** *shd* **Justanotherbottle (IRE)**[27] 7144 3-9-0 **93** ... GerO'Neill(7) 16 99
(Declan Carroll) *prom stands' side gp: effrt and ev ch briefly as gps merged wl over 1f out: sn chsng wnr: kpt on fnl f: lost 2nd cl home* **8/1**

0001 **4** *1 1/4* **Tylery Wonder (IRE)**[19] 7425 7-9-0 **86** ... (v) MartinLane 9 87
(Paul Midgley) *led in far side gp: rdn: edgd rt and hdd as gps merged wl over 1f out: rallied ins fnl f* **16/1**

663 **5** *shd* **Venturous (IRE)**[13] 7625 4-8-10 **82** ... BenCurtis 7 82
(David Barron) *prom far side gp: effrt and rdn as gps merged wl over 1f out: kpt on same pce ins fnl f* **10/1**

4420 **6** *3/4* **Royal Brave (IRE)**[13] 7625 6-9-1 **87** ... DanielTudhope 13 85
(Rebecca Bastiman) *hld up midfield stands' side gp: rdn over 2f out: hdwy as gps merged over 1f out: kpt on fnl f: nrst fin* **20/1**

0032 **7** *1 1/2* **Rasheeq (IRE)**[13] 7610 4-9-1 **87** ... DavidAllan 2 79
(Tim Easterby) *cl up far side gp: rdn as gps merged over 1f out: no ex ins fnl f* **6/1**[2]

5150 **8** *nk* **Atletico (IRE)**[53] 6275 5-9-6 **92** ... SilvestreDeSousa 8 83
(Roger Varian) *hld up on outside of stands' side gp: effrt and drifted lft as gps merged over 1f out: sn no imp* **5/1**[1]

2260 **9** *nk* **Bogart**[30] 7055 8-8-9 **81** ... (tp) TomEaves 10 71
(Kevin Ryan) *led stands' side gp to 2f out: sn rdn and outpcd as gps merged: btn fnl f* **25/1**

330 **10** *1 1/2* **Bashiba (IRE)**[55] 6185 6-8-7 **84** ... (t) RowanScott(5) 3 69
(Nigel Tinkler) *bhd far side gp: rdn along over 2f out: no imp as gps merged over 1f out* **16/1**

3445 **11** *hd* **Fumbo Jumbo (IRE)**[30] 7055 4-8-7 **82** ... CallumRodriguez(3) 4 66
(Michael Dods) *dwlt: hld up in tch far side gp: drvn along over 2f out: sn no imp: btn as gps merged over 1f out* **7/1**[3]

5052 **12** *1 1/2* **Monsieur Joe (IRE)**[19] 7425 10-9-3 **89** ... AdamKirby 17 68
(Paul Midgley) *cl up stands' side gp: rdn and outpcd 2f out: n.d after* **16/1**

1000 **13** *nk* **Carlton Frankie**[48] 6450 3-9-0 **86** ... PhillipMakin 1 64
(Michael Easterby) *cl up far side gp: rdn as gps merged over 1f out: outpcd whn checked ins fnl f* **25/1**

6250 **14** *1/2* **Top Boy**[35] 6878 7-8-8 **80** ... (v) PatrickMathers 14 56
(Derek Shaw) *bhd and sn pushed along stands' side gp: sme late hdwy: nvr on terms* **50/1**

1011 **15** *hd* **Show Palace**[13] 7625 4-9-2 **88** ... JoeFanning 20 63
(Jennie Candlish) *hld up stands' side gp: rdn and hung lft over 2f out: btn as gps merged over 1f out* **18/1**

3100 **16** *nk* **Escalating**[6] 7809 5-8-12 **87** ... (t) DavidEgan(3) 18 61
(Michael Appleby) *dwlt: bhd and pushed along stands' side: struggling 1/2-way: nvr on terms* **33/1**

0100 **17** *hd* **Normal Equilibrium**[15] 7538 7-8-10 **82** ... FrannyNorton 12 55
(Ivan Furtado) *hld up in stands' side gp: rdn and edgd lft 2f out: sn outpcd: btn fnl f* **40/1**

0000 **18** *nk* **Lucky Beggar (IRE)**[41] 6677 7-8-9 **81** ... GrahamLee 5 53
(David C Griffiths) *bhd far side gp: rdn and outpcd over 2f out: sn btn* **25/1**

2500 **19** *8* **Bossipop**[13] 7626 4-9-0 **86** ... (b) PaulMulrennan 19 29
(Tim Easterby) *restless in stalls: cl up on nr side of stands' side gp tl rdn and wknd over 2f out* **28/1**

1100 **20** *1 1/2* **Rich Again (IRE)**[55] 6185 8-8-9 **81** ... (b) PaulHanagan 15 19
(James Bethell) *dwlt: bhd and outpcd stands' side gp: drvn and struggling 1/2-way: sn btn* **50/1**

57.98s (-1.32) **Going Correction** +0.10s/f (Good) **20** Ran SP% **129.2**
Speed ratings (Par 107): **114,112,111,109,109 108,106,105,105,102 102,100,99,98,98 97,97,97,84,81**
CSF £177.08 CT £1686.30 TOTE £15.40: £3.00, £4.30, £2.70, £5.20; EX 322.50 Trifecta £4258.40.
**Owner** S A Heley & Partner **Bred** Habton Farms & Mr A Heley **Trained** Great Habton, N Yorks

**FOCUS**
Distance increased by 17yds. A typically warm race of its type run at a strong pace. The winner has been rated back to his best, the runner-up to his turf best and the third to a small pb.

## 8013 ELEVATOR COMPANY NOVICE AUCTION STKS (PLUS 10 RACE) 7f 192y
**5:05** (5:06) (Class 3) 2-Y-O **£7,762** (£2,310; £1,154; £577) **Stalls** Low

Form RPR

2155 **1** **Barford (IRE)**[20] 7384 2-9-6 79 ... AdamKirby 11 89+
(Pam Sly) *trckd ldrs: hdwy to ld jst over 2f out: rdn clr over 1f out: kpt on strly* **7/1**

232 **2** *2 3/4* **Qianlong**[34] 6939 2-9-2 80 ... SilvestreDeSousa 12 79
(Roger Varian) *trckd ldrs: hdwy 3f out: cl up over 2f out: rdn to chse wnr appr fnl f: sn drvn and no imp* **4/1**[2]

2230 **3** *nse* **Cosa Nostra (IRE)**[29] 7090 2-9-0 81 ... PaulHanagan 8 77
(Richard Fahey) *hld up towards rr: hdwy 3f out: rdn along 2f out: styd on u.p fnl f: nrst fin* **8/1**

2 **4** *5* **Zatorius (GER)**[13] 7593 2-8-12 0 ... RobHornby 7 63
(Andrew Balding) *trckd ldng pair: hdwy and cl up 3f out: rdn along over 2f out: drvn wl over 1f out: kpt on one pce* **9/4**[1]

1 **5** *1 3/4* **Salazar (IRE)**[62] 5918 2-9-6 0 ... KevinStott 10 67
(Kevin Ryan) *led: pushed along over 3f out: sn rdn and hdd jst over 2f out: drvn and wknd over 1f out* **7/1**

0 **6** *shd* **Contrebasse**[30] 7043 2-8-12 0 ... DavidAllan 16 59
(Tim Easterby) *stdd and swtchd lft s: hld up in rr: hdwy wl over 2f out: rdn wl over 1f out: kpt on wl fnl f: nrst fin* **50/1**

34 **7** *1/2* **Hyanna**[15] 7556 2-8-4 0 ... RachelRichardson(3) 5 53
(Tim Easterby) *towards rr: hdwy 3f out: rdn along 2f out: kpt on appr fnl f* **33/1**

0 **8** *nse* **Power Sail**[34] 6939 2-8-12 0 ... (b[1]) DuranFentiman 2 58
(Tim Easterby) *chsd ldrs: rdn along over 2f out: drvn wl over 1f out: grad wknd* **80/1**

066 **9** *2* **Prince Consort (IRE)**[18] 7460 2-9-0 63 ... CharlesBishop 15 55
(Brian Meehan) *in tch: effrt and sme hdwy 3f out: rdn over 2f out: sn one pce* **66/1**

6 **10** *2* **Aphaea**[34] 6938 2-8-7 0 ... CamHardie 9 43
(Michael Easterby) *towards rr and rdn along 1/2-way: n.d* **33/1**

2 **11** *1/2* **Photonics (IRE)**[24] 7237 2-9-2 0 ... RichardKingscote 14 51
(Hugo Palmer) *cl up: pushed along over 3f out: rdn wl over 2f out: sn wknd* **6/1**[3]

000 **12** *10* **Caviar Royale**[35] 6867 2-9-2 66 ... (p[1]) PaulMulrennan 6 28
(Brian Meehan) *t.k.h early: hld up towards rr: sme hdwy 3f out: rdn along 2f out: n.d* **66/1**

5204 **13** *1 3/4* **Barefoot Baby (IRE)**[6] 7829 2-8-9 65 ... TonyHamilton 1 17
(Richard Fahey) *nvr bttr than midfield* **20/1**

05 **14** *9* **So Near So Farhh**[13] 7593 2-8-7 0 ... BenCurtis 13
(Mick Channon) *a in rr* **33/1**

60 **15** *6* **Joe Cable (IRE)**[6] 7818 2-8-5 0 ... FayeMcManoman(7) 3
(Nigel Tinkler) *a in rr* **100/1**

0 **16** *2 3/4* **Eddiethebung (IRE)**[13] 7623 2-9-2 0 ... TomEaves 4
(Nigel Tinkler) *a in rr* **100/1**

1m 39.78s (0.78) **Going Correction** +0.10s/f (Good) **16** Ran SP% **122.9**
Speed ratings (Par 99): **100,97,97,92,90 90,89,89,87,85 85,75,73,64,58 55**
CSF £33.44 TOTE £7.80: £2.60, £1.60, £2.50; EX 38.30 Trifecta £239.80.
**Owner** G Libson & P M Sly **Bred** L Lynch & R Sherrard **Trained** Thorney, Cambs

**FOCUS**
Rail movement increased race distance by 17yds. This was competitive enough for the grade with the winner doing it nicely. The second and third have been rated near their pre-race figures.

## 8014 IRISH THOROUGHBRED MARKETING H'CAP 7f
**5:35** (5:38) (Class 4) (0-85,91) 3-Y-O+ **£7,762** (£2,310; £1,154; £577) **Stalls** Low

Form RPR

0001 **1** **Shady McCoy (USA)**[7] 7780 7-9-13 **91** 6ex ... RichardKingscote 12 102
(Ian Williams) *hld up in rr: stdy hdwy on inner 3f out: trckd ldrs over 1f out: rdn to chal ins fnl f: led last 100 yds: sn clr* **5/1**[1]

1003 **2** *2* **Echo Of Lightning**[22] 7327 7-8-9 **80** ... (p) BenSanderson(7) 6 86
(Roger Fell) *led: pushed along over 2f out: sn jnd and rdn: drvn ent fnl f: hdd and no ex last 100 yds* **25/1**

1311 **3** *2 1/4* **Short Work**[3] 7923 4-9-3 **81** 6ex ... (b) DanielTudhope 11 81
(David O'Meara) *prom: cl up 3f out: chal 2f out: rdn and ev ch over 1f out: drvn ins fnl f: kpt on same pce last 100 yds* **5/1**[1]

1060 **4** *shd* **The Commendatore**[48] 6429 4-9-2 **83** ... DavidEgan(3) 5 83
(David Barron) *chsd ldrs: hdwy and cl up over 2f out: rdn wl over 1f out: sn drvn and kpt on same pce fnl f* **25/1**

6410 **5** *nk* **Dark Intention (IRE)**[13] 7594 4-8-13 **80** ... CallumRodriguez(3) 16 82+
(Lawrence Mullaney) *rr: pushed along and hdwy 3f out: rdn 2f out: styd on wl fnl f: nrst fin* **8/1**[3]

6420 **6** *nk* **Luis Vaz De Torres (IRE)**[13] 7594 5-9-5 **83** ... (h) TonyHamilton 14 81
(Richard Fahey) *hld up in rr: hdwy over 2f out: rdn wl over 1f out: styd on wl fnl f: nrst fin* **25/1**

3056 **7** *1 1/2* **Lexington Times (IRE)**[15] 7554 5-9-4 **82** ... (p) JamesSullivan 13 76
(Ruth Carr) *dwlt and rr: hdwy on inner over 2f out: sn rdn and styd on fnl f: nrst fin* **14/1**

4060 **8** *1/2* **Twin Appeal (IRE)**[35] 6879 6-9-7 **85** ... (b) BenCurtis 7 78
(David Barron) *midfield: hdwy 3f out: chsd ldrs 2f out: sn rdn and wknd appr fnl f* **10/1**

0235 **9** *nk* **Instant Attraction (IRE)**[14] 7566 6-9-6 **84** ... (v) PaulMulrennan 18 76
(Jedd O'Keeffe) *chsd ldrs on wd outside:. rdn along over 2f out: drvn wl over 1f out: kpt on same pce* **16/1**

4230 **10** *1 1/2* **Qeyaadah (IRE)**[13] 7622 4-9-6 **84** ... (p[1]) SilvestreDeSousa 10 72
(Michael Appleby) *midfield: pushed along and hdwy 3f out: rdn to chse ldrs 2f out: sn drvn and no imp* **11/2**[2]

3000 **11** *3/4* **Shouranour (IRE)**[27] 7140 7-9-2 **83** ... (b) JoshDoyle(3) 8 69
(Alan Brown) *chsd ldrs: pushed along 3f out: rdn over 2f out: grad wknd* **33/1**

1126 **12** *3/4* **Custard The Dragon**[7] 7780 4-9-7 **85** ... (p) JoeFanning 9 69
(John Mackie) *rr and pushed along early: hdwy 3f out: styng on whn n.m.r and hmpd 2f out: n.d after* **16/1**

0124 **13** *hd* **Kenny The Captain (IRE)**[15] 7554 6-8-13 **80** ... RachelRichardson(3) 15 63
(Tim Easterby) *in tch towards outer: rdn along over 2f out: sn wknd* **25/1**

1300 **14** *nk* **Bouclier (IRE)**[13] 7612 7-9-2 **80** ... CamHardie 19 62
(Michael Easterby) *racd wd: in tch: rdn along over 2f out: sn wknd* **50/1**

4000 **15** *3* **Heir To A Throne (FR)**[27] 7140 4-9-1 **79** ... (p) ShaneGray 3 53
(Kevin Ryan) *towards rr: hdwy 3f out: rdn along and keeping on whn n.m.r and hmpd 2f out: n.d* **33/1**

0-02 **16** *6* **Mujassam**[15] 7554 5-9-7 **85** ... (v) DavidNolan 4 43
(David O'Meara) *prom: rdn along over 3f out: wknd over 2f out* **14/1**

4100 **17** *4 ½* **Khelman (IRE)**[15] 7553 7-9-5 **83**.................................... PaulHanagan 2 29
(Richard Fahey) *chsd ldrs on inner: rdn along 3f out: sn wknd* **33/1**
0624 **18** *5* **Lagenda**[33] 6964 4-9-2 **80**.......................................(p) KevinStott 17 12
(Kevin Ryan) *a towards rr* **10/1**
2-16 **19** *1 ¼* **Glorious Politics**[205] 1311 3-9-3 **83**.................................... AdamKirby 1 11
(David Barron) *chsd ldrs on inner: rdn along wl over 2f out: sn wknd* **20/1**

1m 25.68s (0.38) **Going Correction** +0.10s/f (Good)
**WFA** 3 from 4yo+ 2lb **19** Ran SP% **134.0**
Speed ratings (Par 105): **101,98,96,96,95 95,93,93,92,91 90,89,89,88,85 78,73,67,66**
CSF £142.44 CT £691.86 TOTE £5.50: £1.70, £5.90, £2.20, £5.80; EX 164.30 Trifecta £3059.10.

**Owner** Allwins Stables **Bred** Bluegrass Hall Llc **Trained** Portway, Worcs

**FOCUS**
A competitive race for the grade. They went a strong pace which suited the winner. The runner-up has been rated to form.
T/Plt: £1,312.20 to a £1 stake. Pool: £134,568.24 - 74.86 winning units T/Qpdt: £95.40 to a £1 stake. Pool: £9,865.50 - 76.45 winning units **Joe Rowntree & Richard Young**

8015 - 8023a (Foreign Racing) - See Raceform Interactive

7696 **MAISONS-LAFFITTE** (R-H)
Friday, October 13

**OFFICIAL GOING: Turf: soft**

## 8024a CRITERIUM DE MAISONS-LAFFITTE (GROUP 2) (2YO) (TURF) 6f
**1:10** 2-Y-O **£92,564** (£35,726; £17,051)

RPR
**1** **Fighting Irish (IRE)**[22] 7335 2-9-2 0.......................... CristianDemuro 5 106
(Harry Dunlop) **5/2**[2]
**2** *hd* **Nebo (IRE)**[20] 7394 2-9-2 0................................................ OlivierPeslier 2 105
(Charles Hills) **1/2**[1]
**3** *3* **French Pegasus (FR)**[23] 7306 2-9-2 0............. Pierre-CharlesBoudot 3 96
(Y Barberot, France) **27/10**[3]

1m 11.59s (-1.81) **3** Ran SP% **122.3**
PARI-MUTUEL (all including 1 euro stake): WIN 3.50; SF 6.00.
**Owner** Daniel Macauliffe & Anoj Don **Bred** Kilcarn Stud **Trained** Lambourn, Berks

**FOCUS**
A weal race for the level with two of the declared runners absentees. It's been rated around the balance of the second and third.

## 8025a PRIX DE VAUREAL (CLAIMER) (3YO) (ROUND) (TURF) 7f
**1:40** 3-Y-O **£9,829** (£3,931; £2,948; £1,965; £982)

RPR
**1** **King Of Spades (FR)**[23] 7308 3-8-11 0................(b) StephanePasquier 3 75
(Gianluca Bietolini, Italy) **92/10**
**2** *nse* **Norwegian Highness (FR)**[43] 6650 3-8-8 0.............. GregoryBenoist 2 72
(H-A Pantall, France) **26/1**
**3** *½* **Epileptic (FR)**[18] 3-8-11 0................................................ AdriedeVries 6 74
(Henk Grewe, Germany) **188/10**
**4** *1* **Chatoyer (FR)**[23] 7308 3-8-11 0........................................... AlexisBadel 5 71
(J S Moore) *chsd ldrs under a tight hold: swtchd outside and led appr 1/2-way: 2l clr and drvn wl over 1 1/2f out: rdn ent fnl f: hdd last 50yds and wknd* **231/10**
**5** *snk* **Larno (FR)**[30] 3-9-1 0.......................................... AdrienMoreau(3) 4 78
(M Boutin, France) **41/5**
**6** *nk* **Ettu**[63] 5910 3-8-8 0..............................................(b) TheoBachelot 8 67
(S Wattel, France) **47/10**[3]
**7** *nk* **Rebecca (FR)**[30] 3-8-5 0................................... MlleLauraGrosso(8) 1 71
(C Lerner, France) **68/10**
**8** *1 ¼* **Andalouse Eria (FR)**[84] 3-8-11 0.............................(b) MaximeGuyon 10 66
(C Escuder, France) **5/2**[1]
**9** *4* **Alliance Secrete (FR)**[30] 3-9-2 0...........................(p) JeromeMoutard(3) 9 63
(T Castanheira, France) **29/10**[2]

1m 28.91s (0.91) **9** Ran SP% **118.2**
PARI-MUTUEL (all including 1 euro stake): WIN 10.20; PLACE 3.90, 7.30, 6.60; DF 54.60; SF 98.70.
**Owner** Ecurie Faroan **Bred** E A R L Elevage Des Loges Et Al **Trained** Italy

8026 - (Foreign Racing) - See Raceform Interactive

7993 **KEMPTON (A.W)** (R-H)
Saturday, October 14

**OFFICIAL GOING: Polytrack: standard to slow (racing abandoned after race 6 (8.15))**
Wind: Light breeze Weather: Cloudy, mild

## 8027 32RED ON THE APP STORE NURSERY H'CAP 6f (P)
**5:45** (5:46) (Class 6) (0-60,71) 2-Y-O **£2,587** (£770; £384; £192) **Stalls** Low

Form RPR
5644 **1** **Inuk (IRE)**[27] 7196 2-8-7 **53**.......................................(p) NicolaCurrie(7) 5 56
(Richard Hughes) *trckd ldr: urged along to ld over 1f out: hrd pressed ins fnl f: hld on wl* **10/3**[2]
0346 **2** *nk* **Super Florence (IRE)**[38] 6815 2-9-7 **60**......................... CharlesBishop 2 64
(Eve Johnson Houghton) *squeezed out s and dropped to last pair: prog over 2f out: swtchd to inner and chsd wnr jst over 1f out: str chal ins fnl f: jst hld* **9/4**[1]
3044 **3** *3* **Avenging Red (IRE)**[9] 7756 2-9-4 **57**..................................(p[1]) RobHornby 7 50
(Adam West) *chsd ldng pair: rdn 2f out: cl enough over 1f out: one pce after* **11/2**[3]
0050 **4** *1 ¾* **Swift Fox**[9] 7756 2-9-0 **53**.......................................(b[1]) KieranShoemark 6 41
(Gary Moore) *led: rdn over 2f out: hdd over 1f out: wknd fnl f* **12/1**
0526 **5** *nk* **Saria**[10] 7734 2-9-0 **53**................................................... DavidProbert 9 40
(Tony Carroll) *trapped out wd in midfield: rdn and outpcd over 2f out: nvr on terms after* **15/2**
4050 **6** *½* **Hastenplace**[17] 7510 2-9-1 **54**........................................(p) WilliamCarson 1 39
(Rod Millman) *wnt lft s then hanging lft: in tch: outpcd over 2f out: nvr on terms after* **12/1**
005 **7** *½* **Poppy Jag (IRE)**[19] 7450 2-9-1 **54**........................................... RyanPowell 3 38
(Kevin Frost) *squeezed and bmpd s: rdn in last bef 1/2-way: nvr on terms: plugged on* **25/1**
6500 **8** *4* **Catch The Pigeon**[31] 7057 2-8-9 **51**......................... CallumShepherd(3) 4 23
(Ed de Giles) *bdly bmpd s: chsd ldrs: wknd over 2f out* **8/1**

1m 12.59s (-0.51) **Going Correction** -0.175s/f (Stan) **8** Ran SP% **111.3**
Speed ratings (Par 93): **96,95,91,89,88 88,87,82**
CSF £10.62 CT £37.15 TOTE £3.20: £1.10, £1.30, £1.80; EX 12.70 Trifecta £53.40.
**Owner** Mrs Fiona Young **Bred** Tally-Ho Stud **Trained** Upper Lambourn, Berks

**FOCUS**
A modest nursery handicap. They went a decent gallop after a significantly messy start on standard to slow Polytrack.

## 8028 32RED/BRITISH STALLION STUDS EBF NOVICE STKS 6f (P)
**6:15** (6:16) (Class 5) 2-Y-O **£3,234** (£962; £481; £240) **Stalls** Low

Form RPR
134 **1** **Lansky (IRE)**[21] 7394 2-9-9 102..............................(b[1]) KieranShoemark 6 81+
(Jeremy Noseda) *restless bef ent stall: dwlt: hld up in last trio: hanging rt whn asked to make prog 2f out: gap appeared and qckly clsd to ld jst ins fnl f: pushed out: comf* **2/9**[1]
40 **2** *¾* **Balletomane**[7] 7810 2-9-2 0.............................................. SeanLevey 7 68
(Richard Hannon) *chsd ldng pair: rdn to chal jst over 1f out: styd on to win battle for 2nd but no ch w wnr* **7/1**[3]
**3** *nk* **Etisalat** 2-9-2 0................................................................ DavidProbert 5 67+
(Owen Burrows) *in tch but rn green: prog 2f out: clsd on ldrs and swtchd to inner 1f out: styd on to take 3rd nr fin* **5/1**[2]
6 **4** *¾* **Jeopardy John**[17] 7512 2-9-2 0.......................................... KierenFox 4 65
(Michael Attwater) *chsd ldr: rdn to chal jst over 1f out: one pce fnl f* **25/1**
0 **5** *½* **United Kingdom**[36] 6868 2-9-2 0...................................... RaulDaSilva 2 63
(Paul Cole) *chsd ldng trio: swtchd lft over 1f out and clsd to chal sn after: fdd last 100yds* **10/1**
60 **6** *2* **Prime Chief (IRE)**[10] 7732 2-8-13 0.............................. HectorCrouch(3) 1 57
(George Baker) *nvr bttr than midfield: shkn up and no prog 2f out* **33/1**
50 **7** *2* **Littlelordconford (IRE)**[10] 7731 2-9-2 0............................ CharlesBishop 8 50
(Richard Spencer) *sweating: led: clr 1/2-way: hdd & wknd qckly jst ins fnl f* **33/1**
0 **8** *nk* **Fitzrovia**[77] 5437 2-9-2 0................................................... LiamKeniry 9 49
(Ed de Giles) *c out of stall slowly: hld up in last: nudged along over 2f out: reminders over 1f out: nvr in it* **33/1**
00 **9** *4 ½* **Gowing Gowing Gone (IRE)**[10] 7724 2-8-4 0........... NicolaCurrie(7) 3 30
(Richard Spencer) *a in rr: struggling over 2f out* **33/1**

1m 12.38s (-0.72) **Going Correction** -0.175s/f (Stan) **9** Ran SP% **135.7**
Speed ratings (Par 95): **97,96,95,94,93 91,88,88,82**
CSF £3.77 TOTE £1.10: £1.02, £1.50, £1.50; EX 3.60 Trifecta £7.90.
**Owner** Phoenix Thoroughbred Limited **Bred** Mrs S M Rogers & Sir Thomas Pilkington **Trained** Newmarket, Suffolk

**FOCUS**
The long-odds favourite brought a useful level of form to the table in this juvenile novice contest. He started poorly but was able to show his class edge off the decent gallop.

## 8029 32RED CASINO NOVICE MEDIAN AUCTION STKS (DIV I) 1m (P)
**6:45** (6:47) (Class 6) 2-Y-O **£2,587** (£770; £384; £192) **Stalls** Low

Form RPR
0 **1** **Indiscretion (IRE)**[28] 7153 2-8-11 0................................ DanielMuscutt 9 71
(Jonathan Portman) *trckd ldrs: wnt 2nd over 2f out: pushed up to chal over 1f out: rdn to ld last 100yds: styd on wl* **100/1**
3102 **2** *¾* **Jazeel (IRE)**[35] 6934 2-9-9 87......................................... CharlesBishop 5 81
(Mick Channon) *disp ld at modest pce tl increased the tempo over 4f out and stretched field: rdn 2f out: kpt on but hdd and hld last 100yds* **15/8**[1]
20 **3** *1 ¼* **Nuits St Georges (IRE)**[37] 6859 2-9-2 0................. KieranShoemark 8 71
(David Menuisier) *dwlt: swift prog on outer to join dispute ld after 2f to over 4f out: rdn and nt qckn over 2f out and sn dropped to 3rd: kpt on again fnl f* **10/1**[2]
00 **4** *½* **Universal Command**[57] 6132 2-8-11 0........................ PaddyPilley(5) 10 70
(Roger Charlton) *hld up in midfield: 7th 1/2-way: shkn up and prog 2f out: pushed along and kpt on steadily to take 4th last stride* **25/1**
33 **5** *shd* **Dragon Mountain**[10] 7726 2-9-2 0...................................... JackMitchell 11 70
(Hugo Palmer) *disp ld at modest pce for 2f: styd cl up: rdn 2f out: no imp ldrs over 1f out: fdd* **15/8**[1]
6 **6** *1 ½* **India**[21] 7403 2-8-11 0..................................................... DavidProbert 3 61
(Michael Bell) *in tch bhd ldrs: tried to cl on inner 2f out: fdd fnl f* **16/1**
**7** *2 ¼* **Doctor Jazz (IRE)** 2-9-2 0............................................. SeanLevey 12 61
(Richard Hannon) *dwlt but sn trckd ldrs: rn green whn pushed along over 3f out: outpcd over 2f out: tried to rally over 1f out: fdd fnl f* **14/1**[3]
**8** *1 ½* **Point In Time (IRE)** 2-8-11 0........................................ StevieDonohoe 1 53+
(Mark Usher) *difficult to load into stall: dwlt then snatched up sn after s: mostly in last pair: bhd over 3f out: kpt on steadily fnl 2f* **40/1**
0 **9** *hd* **Munstead Gold**[29] 7120 2-9-2 0......................................... RobHornby 2 57
(Andrew Balding) *dwlt: rn green in rr: outpcd over 3f out: nvr on terms after: plugged on* **10/1**[2]
**10** *7* **Praeceps (IRE)** 2-9-2 0...................................................... LukeMorris 6 41
(Sir Mark Prescott Bt) *rn green in midfield: struggling 3f out: sn bhd* **33/1**
**11** *5* **Davina** 2-8-11 0............................................................. RobertHavlin 4 25
(Jeremy Scott) *a in rr: bhd 3f out* **50/1**
00 **12** *9* **Blackwood**[30] 7079 2-9-2 0................................................ LiamKeniry 7 9
(Michael Blanshard) *dwlt and s.i.s: a in rr: t.o* **100/1**

1m 39.91s (0.11) **Going Correction** -0.175s/f (Stan) **12** Ran SP% **113.5**
Speed ratings (Par 93): **92,91,90,89,89 87,85,84,83,76 71,62**
CSF £268.58 TOTE £58.60: £12.30, £1.10, £1.90; EX 701.70 Trifecta £7068.40.
**Owner** Turf Club 2016 **Bred** J Kenny **Trained** Upper Lambourn, Berks

**FOCUS**
The first division of a fair juvenile novice contest. They went an initially sedate, and then contested gallop, which produced a shock outcome. The second, third and fifth have been rated near their pre-race marks.

## 8030 32RED CASINO NOVICE MEDIAN AUCTION STKS (DIV II) 1m (P)
**7:15** (7:17) (Class 6) 2-Y-O **£2,587** (£770; £384; £192) **Stalls** Low

Form RPR
**1** **Blue Mist** 2-9-2 0.......................................................... KieranShoemark 5 81+
(Roger Charlton) *chsd ldng quartet: rn green whn shkn up over 2f out but sn mde quick prog: pushed into the ld over 1f out: rdn clr: taking debut* **9/4**[2]
**2** *3* **Communique (IRE)** 2-9-2 0................................................ PJMcDonald 2 74+
(Mark Johnston) *led after 2f: struck for home over 2f out: rdn and hdd over 1f out: styd on but no match for wnr* **5/1**
551 **3** *2 ¼* **Connaught Ranger (IRE)**[18] 7489 2-9-9 77.................. TomQueally 11 76
(Denis Coakley) *prog to press ldr after 2f: outpcd and dropped to 3rd 2f out: no ch w ldng pair after but clr of rest* **3/1**[3]
6 **4** *2* **Pepper Street (IRE)**[18] 7488 2-8-11 0...........................(h[1]) JackMitchell 7 59
(Hugo Palmer) *settled in 7th: outpcd over 2f out: shkn up and kpt on to take modest 4th ins fnl f* **12/1**
4 **5** *nk* **Tullyallen (IRE)**[56] 6199 2-9-2 0....................................... SeanLevey 8 64
(Richard Hannon) *hld up in 8th: shkn up and no prog over 2f out: plugged on u.p to press for modest 4th fnl f* **2/1**[1]

0 **6** *1* **Billy Ray**[17] 7503 2-9-2 0 CharlesBishop 3 61
(Mick Channon) *s.i.s: hld up in last: outpcd whn pushed along and sme prog 2f out: nvr any ch and no hdwy fnl f* **25/1**

000 **7** *1 3/4* **Say About It**[49] 6456 2-9-2 0 JohnFahy 1 57
(J S Moore) *led 2f: chsd ldng pair after: wknd over 2f out* **50/1**

0 **8** *shd* **Demurrer (USA)**[18] 7489 2-9-2 0 DavidProbert 4 57
(Michael Bell) *broke on terms but stdd into rr: pushed along over 2f out: hanging lft and sn btn* **20/1**

0 **9** *6* **Arlecchino's Arc (IRE)**[21] 7391 2-9-2 0 (p[1]) LiamKeniry 10 43
(Mark Usher) *chsd ldrs to 3f out: sn wknd* **100/1**

1m 39.51s (-0.29) **Going Correction** -0.175s/f (Stan) **9** Ran SP% **125.0**
Speed ratings (Par 93): **94,91,88,86,86 85,83,83,77**
CSF £14.99 TOTE £3.70: £1.30, £1.70, £1.50; EX 23.30 Trifecta £66.50.
**Owner** K Abdullah **Bred** Juddmonte Farms (east) Ltd **Trained** Beckhampton, Wilts

**FOCUS**
The second division of a fair juvenile novice contest. The winning time was marginally quicker and the second favourite won in taking style off another muddling gallop. The level is set around the third.

## 8031 WATCH RACING UK ON BT TV H'CAP 1m (P)
7:45 (7:46) (Class 6) (0-60,60) 3-Y-O+ £2,587 (£770; £384; £192) Stalls Low

Form RPR

5435 **1** **Broughtons Knight**[9] 7760 3-9-3 59 (t) StevieDonohoe 6 66
(Henry Spiller) *wl in tch: rdn over 2f out and no immediate rspnse: prog over 1f out: styd on to ld last 75yds: won gng away* **9/4**[1]

0150 **2** *1 1/4* **Doctor Bong**[27] 7198 5-9-1 54 (b) EdwardGreatrex 5 58
(Grace Harris) *led: urged along 3f out: hrd rdn and pressed 2f out: edgd rt and lft after but kpt on wl u.p: hdd and outpcd last 75yds* **33/1**

00-0 **3** *1* **Peak Hill**[38] 6811 4-9-0 56 HollieDoyle(3) 12 58
(Adrian Wintle) *t.k.h: trckd ldr 2f and again 2f out whn trying to chal on inner: nt qckn over 1f out: hld on for 3rd* **50/1**

653 **4** *shd* **Topology**[5] 7900 4-9-0 60 StephenCummins(7) 11 62
(Joseph Tuite) *wl in tch: rdn and prog fr 2f out: nt qckn 1f out: kpt on same pce* **8/1**[3]

4060 **5** *1/2* **Moonstone Rock**[26] 7216 3-8-12 57 (p) CharlieBennett(3) 1 57+
(Jim Boyle) *dwlt: hld up in last: rdn over 2f out: prog over 1f out: styd on wl fnl f: nrst fin* **40/1**

0006 **6** *3/4* **Caribbean Spring (IRE)**[37] 6847 4-8-12 56 JaneElliott(5) 9 55
(George Margarson) *trapped out wd in midfield: rdn over 2f out: kpt on same pce and nvr able to chal* **12/1**

410 **7** *shd* **Garth Rockett**[33] 7005 3-9-2 58 (p) MartinDwyer 14 56
(Brendan Powell) *trckd ldr after 2f to 2f out: stl on terms over 1f out: fdd fnl f* **33/1**

0450 **8** *nse* **Russian Ranger (IRE)**[26] 7210 4-9-3 56 (p) RichardKingscote 8 54
(Jonathan Portman) *chsd ldrs: rdn over 2f out: tried to cl over 1f out: fdd fnl f* **16/1**

6636 **9** *1 1/4* **Famous Dynasty (IRE)**[26] 7216 3-9-3 59 RobHornby 3 57
(Michael Blanshard) *pushed along in rr early: rdn over 2f out: sme prog over 1f out: nvr able to rch ldrs and eased nr fin* **8/1**[3]

-400 **10** *nk* **Miss Bates**[18] 7476 3-9-1 60 (h[1]) DavidEgan(3) 4 55
(Ann Duffield) *chsd ldrs: rdn over 2f out: wknd jst over 1f out* **20/1**

3230 **11** *2* **Loveatfirstsight**[61] 6015 4-9-4 57 LukeMorris 7 47
(Jane Chapple-Hyam) *rn in snatches: mostly in rr: no prog fnl 2f* **9/2**[2]

0560 **12** *1 1/4* **Candesta (USA)**[31] 7062 7-9-7 60 (v[1]) DanielMuscutt 13 47
(Julia Feilden) *dropped in fr wd draw and hld up in last trio: no prog over 2f out* **12/1**

6400 **13** *2* **Bois D'Ebene (IRE)**[27] 7199 3-9-2 58 (p[1]) TimmyMurphy 2 41
(John O'Shea) *hld up towards rr: effrt over 2f out: sn no prog: wknd over 1f out* **33/1**

40-4 **14** *3* **Tazmania (IRE)**[25] 7227 3-9-0 59 HectorCrouch(3) 10 35
(Clive Cox) *trapped out wd towards rr: u.p 3f out: sn wknd* **9/1**

1m 38.35s (-1.45) **Going Correction** -0.175s/f (Stan)
**WFA** 3 from 4yo+ 3lb **14** Ran SP% **120.4**
Speed ratings (Par 101): **100,98,97,97,97 96,96,96,95,94 92,91,89,86**
CSF £100.33 CT £3077.36 TOTE £3.50: £1.80, £5.60, £8.20; EX 88.80 Trifecta £2394.30.
**Owner** Broughton Thermal Insulation **Bred** Broughton Bloodstock **Trained** Newmarket, Suffolk
■ Stewards' Enquiry : Edward Greatrex tba: excessive use of whip
Stephen Cummins four-day ban: excessive use of whip (Oct 30 - Nov 2)
Timmy Murphy tba: enquiry into use of whip

**FOCUS**
A moderate handicap. They went a decent gallop and the heavily backed favourite won well.

## 8032 32RED H'CAP 1m (P)
8:15 (8:16) (Class 2) (0-105,102) 3-Y-O+ £11,827 (£3,541; £1,770; £885; £442; £222) Stalls Low

Form RPR

21- **1** **Reach High**[525] 2023 3-8-10 91 PatCosgrave 3 99
(Saeed bin Suroor) *trckd ldng quartet: prog to chse ldr over 1f out: drvn to ld 150yds out: hld on wl* **5/2**[1]

4424 **2** *hd* **The Warrior (IRE)**[16] 7549 5-8-10 88 RobertHavlin 2 95
(Amanda Perrett) *dwlt: hld up in 9th: coaxed along and gd prog over 1f out: clsd to take 2nd last 50yds and tried to chal: fended off last strides* **7/1**

1114 **3** *3/4* **Brilliant Vanguard (IRE)**[10] 7727 4-9-1 93 (p) KevinStott 13 98
(Kevin Ryan) *trckd ldrs in 6th: rdn 2f out: prog on outer 1f out: drvn and styd on to take 3rd last strides: jst unable to chal* **11/2**[3]

1-00 **4** *hd* **Chester Street**[231] 918 4-8-9 87 KieranShoemark 5 92
(Roger Charlton) *racd freely: led: rdn over 2f out: kpt on wl but hdd 150yds and lost 2 more pls nr fin* **14/1**

0000 **5** *3/4* **Mr Bossy Boots (IRE)**[10] 7727 6-8-13 91 (p[1]) RichardKingscote 7 94
(Amanda Perrett) *hld up in 8th: rdn 2f out: prog over 1f out: kpt on to take 5th ins fnl f: nvr able to chal* **33/1**

5613 **6** *3/4* **Plutonian (IRE)**[63] 5943 3-8-10 91 PJMcDonald 11 92
(Charles Hills) *hld up in rr: rdn and no prog over 2f out: styd on fr jst over 1f out: nrst fin* **16/1**

0-03 **7** *1/2* **Bronze Angel (IRE)**[16] 7549 8-9-4 96 (v) HayleyTurner 6 96
(Marcus Tregoning) *awkward s: hld up in last trio: rdn and no prog over 2f out: styd on fr jst over 1f out: nrst fin* **4/1**[2]

0036 **8** *1/2* **Kyllachy Gala**[142] 2999 4-9-10 102 DanielMuscutt 1 101
(Marco Botti) *in tch in 7th: rdn and effrt on inner 2f out: nt rch ldrs 1f out: lost pls last 100yds* **20/1**

0500 **9** *1/2* **Escobar (IRE)**[24] 7275 3-9-5 100 (tp) JackMitchell 10 98
(Hugo Palmer) *t.k.h: trckd ldr after 2f to over 1f out: wknd fnl f* **8/1**

3600 **10** *hd* **Replenish (FR)**[10] 7727 4-8-13 91 TomQueally 12 88
(James Fanshawe) *mostly in last trio and nvr gng wl: last and struggling over 2f out: fnlly picked up last 150yds and fin w a flourish* **16/1**

3210 **11** *3/4* **Kenstone (FR)**[28] 7140 4-8-6 87 (p) HollieDoyle(3) 9 82
(Adrian Wintle) *t.k.h: trckd ldng trio: wknd over 1f out* **25/1**

3040 **12** *1/2* **Secret Art (IRE)**[14] 7619 7-8-10 88 MartinDwyer 4 82
(William Knight) *chsd ldr 2f: styd prom: rdn over 2f out: wknd jst over 1f out* **12/1**

0000 **13** *3/4* **Emell**[36] 6873 7-8-8 86 (v) KieranO'Neill 8 79
(Tim Vaughan) *stdd s and hld up in last: rdn and no prog over 2f out* **66/1**

1m 36.68s (-3.12) **Going Correction** -0.175s/f (Stan)
**WFA** 3 from 4yo+ 3lb **13** Ran SP% **126.7**
Speed ratings (Par 109): **108,107,107,106,106 105,104,104,103,103 102,102,101**
CSF £20.91 CT £97.99 TOTE £3.40: £1.60, £2.70, £1.80; EX 19.30 Trifecta £90.00.
**Owner** Godolphin **Bred** Darley **Trained** Newmarket, Suffolk

**FOCUS**
The feature contest was a good quality handicap. The favourite came through to win in a time only marginally above standard. The fourth has been rated to form.

## 8033 32RED.COM H'CAP 6f (P)
(8:45) (Class 4) (0-85,) 3-Y-O+ £

## 8034 100% PROFIT BOOST AT 32REDSPORT.COM H'CAP 1m 2f 219y(P)
(9:15) (Class 6) (0-65,) 3-Y-O+ £

T/Plt: £11.00 to a £1 stake. Pool: £72,986.90 - 4,830.04 winning units T/Qpdt: £5.20 to a £1 stake. Pool: £9,888.51 - 1,403.36 winning units **Jonathan Neesom**

# 8001 NEWMARKET (R-H)
Saturday, October 14

**OFFICIAL GOING: Good (good to firm in places; 7.8)**
Wind: light to medium, half behind Weather: fine, bright spells

## 8035 GODOLPHIN FLYING START ZETLAND STKS (LISTED RACE) 1m 2f
1:50 (1:54) (Class 1) 2-Y-O £22,684 (£8,600; £4,304; £2,144; £1,076; £540) Stalls High

Form RPR

24 **1** **Kew Gardens (IRE)**[20] 7426 2-9-2 106 RyanMoore 7 106+
(A P O'Brien, Ire) *quite str; racd stands' side: mde virtually all: rdn jst over 2f out: styd on strly and drew clr ins fnl f: readily* **13/8**[1]

1631 **2** *3 1/2* **Dee Ex Bee**[13] 7648 2-9-2 96 PJMcDonald 3 99
(Mark Johnston) *lw; racd stands' side: chsd ldrs overall: effrt over 1f out: drvn over 1f out: stl cl enough in 3rd 1f out: outpcd by wnr but kpt on to go 2nd wl ins fnl f* **7/2**[2]

41 **3** *1/2* **Graffiti Master**[19] 7451 2-9-2 0 JamesDoyle 4 98
(John Gosden) *lw; stdd after s and swtchd lft to r stands' side: hld up in last pair: hdwy over 2f out: sn rdn: chsd wnr over 1f out: outpcd ins fnl f: kpt on but lost 2nd wl ins fnl f* **6/1**[3]

5411 **4** *4* **Rastrelli (FR)**[16] 7544 2-9-2 92 WilliamBuick 6 91
(Charlie Appleby) *racd stands' side: trckd ldrs: effrt and nt clrest of runs ent fnl f: rdn over 1f out: sn outpcd and wknd ins fnl f* **13/2**

0221 **5** *3/4* **Westerland**[28] 7148 2-9-2 94 (p) FrankieDettori 2 89+
(John Gosden) *racd in centre: hdwy over 2f out: rdn 2f out: unable qck u.p over 1f out: wknd ins fnl f* **7/1**

541 **6** *5* **Dubai Empire (FR)**[28] 7160 2-9-2 81 TomQueally 1 80+
(John Quinn) *racd in centre: t.k.h: hld up in tch: rdn over 2f out: sn outpcd and dropped to rr 2f: wknd over 1f out* **50/1**

1226 **7** *hd* **Albishr (IRE)**[16] 7546 2-9-2 102 SeanLevey 5 79+
(Richard Hannon) *racd in centre: w wnr tl rdn and unable qck jst over 2f out: lost pl over 1f out: wknd* **16/1**

2m 2.76s (-3.04) **Going Correction** -0.15s/f (Firm) 2y crse rec **7** Ran SP% **108.3**
Speed ratings (Par 103): **106,103,102,99,99 95,94**
CSF £6.48 TOTE £2.10: £1.50, £2.00; EX 6.90 Trifecta £35.10.
**Owner** Derrick Smith & Mrs John Magnier & Michael Tabor **Bred** Barronstown Stud **Trained** Cashel, Co Tipperary

**FOCUS**
Stands' side course used. Stalls Stands' side except 1m6f, centre. Following another dry night and sunny morning the going was officially upgraded to good, good firm in places. This year's Zetland saw something of a mixed bunch. Three went down the middle and unsurprisingly, remembering the recent track bias, the main action was on the stands' side. The runner-up sets the level.

## 8036 MASAR GODOLPHIN AUTUMN STKS (GROUP 3) 1m
2:25 (2:27) (Class 1) 2-Y-O £34,026 (£12,900; £6,456; £3,216; £1,614; £810) Stalls High

Form RPR

31 **1** **Ghaiyyath (IRE)**[16] 7543 2-9-1 0 (h) WilliamBuick 9 111
(Charlie Appleby) *lw; hld up wl in tch in midfield: nt clr run ent fnl 2f: gap opened and rdn to chal over 1f out: led jst ins fnl f: styd on strly: rdn out* **11/4**[2]

15 **2** *1 3/4* **Dream Today (IRE)**[28] 7146 2-9-1 0 PJMcDonald 6 107
(Mark Johnston) *led: pushed along 2f out: rdn and hrd pressed over 1f out: hdd 1f out: nt match pce of wnr but kpt on for clr 2nd ins fnl f* **10/1**

141 **3** *2 1/2* **Purser (USA)**[9] 7765 2-9-1 100 FrankieDettori 4 101+
(John Gosden) *hld up in tch in midfield: effrt ent fnl 2f: unable qck u.p over 1f out: wnt 3rd ins fnl f: kpt on but no threat to ldrs* **9/4**[1]

414 **4** *nk* **Petrus (IRE)**[14] 7616 2-9-1 100 TomMarquand 1 101
(Brian Meehan) *lw; hld up in tch in last pair: effrt over 2f out: sme hdwy ent fnl f: kpt on and battling for 3rd ins fnl f: no threat to ldrs* **25/1**

**5** *2* **Flag Of Honour (IRE)**[10] 7751 2-9-1 0 SeamieHeffernan 2 96
(A P O'Brien, Ire) *compact; lw; stdd s: hld up in last pair and grad moving across to stands' rail: nt clr run and swtchd rt over 2f out: no imp over 1f out: switching lft and kpt on same pce ins fnl f* **15/2**

2213 **6** *nse* **Arbalet (IRE)**[42] 6696 2-9-1 99 JamesDoyle 7 96
(Hugo Palmer) *lw; on toes; trckd ldrs: clsd to press ldr 3f out: rdn 2f out: 3rd and outpcd whn swtchd rt over 1f out: wknd and lost 2 pls ins fnl f* **10/1**

01 **7** *2* **Wafy (IRE)**[24] 7274 2-9-1 0 JimCrowley 8 91
(Charles Hills) *hld up wl in tch in midfield: effrt ent fnl 2f: sn squeezed for room and shuffled bk to rr: stl nt clr run and lost any ch over 1f out: pushed along and kpt on same pce fnl f* **7/1**[3]

**8** *nk* **Zabriskie (IRE)**[18] 7498 2-9-1 0 RyanMoore 5 91
(A P O'Brien, Ire) *compact; pressed ldr: rdn over 2f out: edgd rt and outpcd 2f out: lost pl over 1f out: bhd ins fnl f* **8/1**

1m 35.92s (-2.68) **Going Correction** -0.15s/f (Firm) **8** Ran SP% **114.8**
Speed ratings (Par 105): **107,105,102,102,100 100,98,98**
CSF £30.28 TOTE £3.30: £1.30, £2.50, £1.40; EX 33.80 Trifecta £62.90.
**Owner** Godolphin **Bred** Springbank Way Stud **Trained** Newmarket, Suffolk

**FOCUS**
The Autumn Stakes usually throws up a high-class winner. The runners predictably wanted to be stands' side and it was another event where being prominent there was a must. It's been rated around the recent averages for the race, and the pre-race figures of the third.

## 8037 DARLEY DEWHURST STKS (GROUP 1) (C&F) 7f
3:00 (3:01) (Class 1) 2-Y-O

£283,550 (£107,500; £53,800; £26,800; £13,450; £6,750) Stalls High

Form RPR
2411 1 **U S Navy Flag (USA)**[14] 7618 2-9-1 117........................(bt) RyanMoore 1 122
(A P O'Brien, Ire) *broke wl and crossed to r on stands' rail: mde all: rdn 2f out: kicked clr over 1f out: in command and styd on strly fnl f: rdn out* 5/1[2]

0 2 2 ½ **Mendelssohn (USA)**[28] 7146 2-9-1 0..........................(b[1]) WayneLordan 7 115
(A P O'Brien, Ire) *quite tall; trckd ldrs: effrt to chse wnr wl over 1f out but wnr sn kicking clr: no imp but kpt on for clr 2nd ins fnl f* 50/1

51 3 2 ½ **Seahenge (USA)**[28] 7146 2-9-1 112.......................... DonnachaO'Brien 9 109+
(A P O'Brien, Ire) *stdd and bmpd s: hld up in rr: switching rt 4f out: effrt ent fnl 2f: jostling w rival and unbalanced wl over 1f out: no ch w ldng pair but kpt on ins fnl f to go 3rd last strides* 9/1

4 hd **Threeandfourpence (USA)**[24] 7288 2-9-1 0.......... SeamieHeffernan 6 108
(A P O'Brien, Ire) *quite tall; str; lw; hld up in tch: effrt ent fnl 2f but nt clrest of runs tl gap opened and hdwy 1f out: chsd clr ldng pair jst ins fnl f: no imp and lost 3rd last strides* 20/1

1333 5 1 ½ **Cardsharp**[14] 7618 2-9-1 110.............................. JamesDoyle 4 104+
(Mark Johnston) *chsd ldr over 1f out: sn jostled and lost pl: in tch in last trio: effrt ent fnl 2f: no imp u.p over 1f out: wknd ins fnl f* 20/1

1324 6 ¾ **Great Prospector (IRE)**[30] 7090 2-9-1 104.................... PaulHanagan 3 102
(Richard Fahey) *taken down early: hld up wl in tch in midfield: effrt ent fnl 2f: outpcd u.p over 1f out: wknd ins fnl f* 50/1

220 7 2 **Theobald (IRE)**[35] 6955 2-9-1 0................................(p[1]) KevinManning 8 96
(J S Bolger, Ire) *compact; wnt lft s: hld up in last pair: switching rt and effrt over 2f out: unbalanced on downhill run and jostling w rival wl over 1f out: no imp and wl hld whn short of room and hmpd 1f out* 33/1

41 8 shd **Emaraaty**[21] 7392 2-9-1 0.......................................... JimCrowley 2 96
(John Gosden) *wl in tch in midfield: effrt to chse ldrs ent fnl 2f: unable qck over 1f out: wknd ins fnl f* 6/1[3]

11 9 1 **Expert Eye**[74] 5501 2-9-1 118.............................. AndreaAtzeni 5 94
(Sir Michael Stoute) *lw; t.k.h: hdwy to trck ldr after 1f: rdn over 2f out: unable qck and outpcd over 1f out: wknd ins fnl f: lame after r* 4/7[1]

1m 22.37s (-3.03) **Going Correction** -0.15s/f (Firm) 2y crse rec 9 Ran SP% 121.0
Speed ratings (Par 109): **111,108,105,105,103 102,100,100,98**
CSF £225.28 CT £2219.05 TOTE £5.30: £1.70, £11.70, £2.60; EX 188.20 Trifecta £1204.90.
**Owner** Derrick Smith & Mrs John Magnier & Michael Tabor **Bred** Misty For Me Syndicate **Trained** Cashel, Co Tipperary

**FOCUS**
Another brilliant training performance from the great Aidan O'Brien, responsible for the first four home, but this doesn't look form to buy into. The winner had the run of the race in front against the near rail, while the next two shaped better than the bare result, and the odds-on favourite flopped. Plus, National Stakes winner Verbal Dexterity was missing.

## 8038 BETFRED CESAREWITCH H'CAP (HERITAGE HANDICAP) 2m 2f
3:40 (3:46) (Class 2) 3-Y-O+

£155,625 (£46,600; £23,300; £11,650; £5,825; £2,925) Stalls Centre

Form RPR
21-3 1 **Withhold**[21] 7397 4-8-8 87.................................(p) SilvestreDeSousa 24 102+
(Roger Charlton) *lw; sn prom: led 8f out: rdn over 2f out: drifted lft over 1f out: styd on strly to draw clr ins fnl f* 5/1[1]

-211 2 3 ¾ **London Prize**[105] 4355 6-9-2 95.............................. JamesDoyle 28 105
(Ian Williams) *trckd ldr: swtchd to nr side rails over 8f out: rdn to chse wnr 2f out: sn hmpd and swtchd rt: styd on fnl f but nt pce of wnr* 16/1

0-3 3 5 **Lagostovegas (IRE)**[30] 5488 5-8-12 91........................... RyanMoore 5 96
(W P Mullins, Ire) *mid-div: hdwy 3f out: sn rdn: chsd ldng pair 2f out: styd on same pce fnl f* 10/1[3]

4-11 4 2 ¼ **Dubawi Fifty**[57] 6151 4-8-11 90.............................. GrahamLee 19 92+
(Karen McLintock) *hld up towards rr: rdn and hdwy fr 3f out: wnt 4th ins fnl f: styd on wl but nt pce to get on terms* 14/1

1230 5 ¾ **Getback In Paris (IRE)**[14] 7614 4-9-1 94........................ ShaneKelly 18 95+
(Richard Hughes) *mid-div tl lost pl and dropped towards rr over 3f out: sn swtchd to centre and gd hdwy fr over 2f out: styd on fnl f but nvr threatened to get on terms* 66/1

30-2 6 hd **Swamp Fox (IRE)**[30] 5488 5-8-11 90.......................(b) GaryCarroll 17 91
(Joseph G Murphy, Ire) *mid-div: nt clrest of runs 3f out: rdn and hdwy over 2f out: hmpd over 1f out: styd on to go 4th briefly ins fnl f: no ex towards fin* 14/1

2222 7 1 ¼ **Byron Flyer**[29] 7115 6-9-0 93.......................................(p) FranBerry 4 93
(Ian Williams) *trckd ldrs: rdn to chse ldng pair over 3f out tl 2f out: styd on but no ex fnl f* 16/1

/3-1 8 ½ **Duke Street (IRE)**[26] 759 5-8-6 88.......................(p) HectorCrouch(3) 11 87
(Dr Richard Newland) *mid-div: hdwy u.p but nt best of runs over 1f out: n.d but styd on wl fnl f* 33/1

132/ 9 ½ **Cape Caster (IRE)**[26] 7410 6-8-9 88........................ SamHitchcott 10 87
(Evan Williams) *hld up towards rr: rdn and hdwy fr over 2f out: styd on but nvr any threat* 100/1

4301 10 nk **Who Dares Wins (IRE)**[21] 7402 5-9-4 97 4ex..........(p) TomMarquand 8 95
(Alan King) *trckd ldrs: rdn wl over 3f out: styd on but nt pce to mount chal: no ex fnl f* 7/1[2]

4116 11 ¾ **Taws**[21] 7402 6-8-7 89....................................................(p) DavidEgan(3) 33 86
(Rod Millman) *towards rr of mid-div: styd on fnl 2f wout ever threatening* 50/1

3210 12 1 ¾ **Arthur Mc Bride (IRE)**[21] 7402 8-8-9 88 4ex..................(t) LiamKeniry 25 83
(Nigel Twiston-Davies) *trckd ldrs: rdn over 3f out: nt pce to mount chal: wknd ent fnl f* 80/1

5015 13 2 ¼ **Magic Circle (IRE)**[49] 6447 5-9-6 102................ CallumRodriguez(3) 30 95
(Ralph Beckett) *lw; rdn over 3f out: nvr bttr than mid-div* 25/1

5-02 14 1 **Snow Falcon (IRE)**[6] 7860 7-9-4 97.............................. PaulHanagan 29 89
(Noel Meade, Ire) *lw; mid-div: rdn over 3f out: nvr threatened* 12/1

2000 15 ½ **Oceane (FR)**[21] 7402 5-8-10 92....................................(v) GeorgiaCox(3) 32 83
(Alan King) *hld up towards rr: rdn over 3f out: styd on fnl 2f but nvr any danger* 40/1

1114 16 ¾ **Rolling Maul (IRE)**[27] 7200 9-8-4 88 ow3...............(b) JoshuaBryan(5) 27 78
(Peter Bowen) *mid-div: drvn along 4f out: nvr any imp* 50/1

1531 17 1 **Time To Study (FR)**[29] 7115 3-8-13 102 4ex.................. PJMcDonald 12 94
(Mark Johnston) *mid-div: hdwy over 3f out: sn rdn: wknd over 1f out* 11/1

1013 18 1 ¾ **Euchen Glen**[52] 6329 4-8-12 91............................... PaulMulrennan 20 78
(Jim Goldie) *racd keenly: hld up towards rr: rdn and sme prog 3f out: wknd over 1f out* 20/1

300- 19 1 **Mirsaale**[24] 3913 7-8-13 97.................................... RowanScott(5) 23 83
(Keith Dalgleish) *hld up towards rr: rdn and no imp over 3f out: styng on but no ch whn nt clr run wl over 1f out* 66/1

3222 20 nk **Aurora Gray**[39] 6779 4-8-3 85.............................. CharlieBennett(3) 21 71
(Hughie Morrison) *sweating; mid-div: rdn over 3f out: wknd over 1f out* 33/1

21 1 **John Constable (IRE)**[84] 5737 6-8-9 88..........................(t) JimCrowley 7 73
(Evan Williams) *hld up towards rr: rdn over 3f out: nvr threatened to get involved* 10/1[3]

1146 22 1 ¾ **Frederic**[11] 5524 6-8-5 89 ow1.............................. FinleyMarsh(5) 35 72
(Keith Dalgleish) *in tch tl wknd u.p over 2f out* 50/1

6600 23 1 ¼ **Star Rider**[52] 6329 5-8-11 90...............................(t[1]) RichardKingscote 36 72
(Hughie Morrison) *mid-div: swtchd to nr side rails w runner-up over 8f out: rdn over 3f out: wknd over 2f out* 33/1

0033 24 1 ½ **Shrewd**[21] 7402 7-8-10 96.................................... JamieGormley(7) 9 76
(Iain Jardine) *nvr bttr than mid-div* 20/1

0106 25 9 **Swashbuckle**[16] 7547 4-8-11 90..............................(p) OisinMurphy 2 60
(Andrew Balding) *led tl over 8f out: chsd wnr: drvn 3f out: sn wknd* 40/1

26 shd **Friday Night Light (FR)**[353] 4-8-7 86...........................(t[1]) TedDurcan 26 56
(David Pipe) *a towards rr* 66/1

00/4 27 ½ **Digeanta (IRE)**[51] 6361 10-8-13 92..............................(t) KevinManning 1 61
(W P Mullins, Ire) *mid-div: rdn and hdwy over 3f out: tight for room briefly over 2f out: sn wknd* 50/1

5410 28 ¾ **Fun Mac (GER)**[29] 7116 6-9-10 103...................................(t) AdamKirby 14 72
(Hughie Morrison) *towards rr of midfield: rdn 4f out: wknd over 2f out* 50/1

1000 29 1 ¾ **First Mohican**[112] 4073 9-9-1 97...................................(h) HollieDoyle(3) 6 64
(Alan King) *hld up towards rr: u.p and no imp 4f out: n.d* 28/1

365 30 7 **Tawdeea**[14] 7615 5-9-5 98.......................................... PatDobbs 16 57
(David O'Meara) *a bhd* 100/1

1126 31 1 **Watersmeet**[157] 2525 6-9-8 101.................................. JoeFanning 22 59
(Mark Johnston) *sweating; mid-div: hdwy 6f out: effrt 3f out: wknd 2f out: eased* 40/1

1-1 32 2 **Laws Of Spin (IRE)**[35] 6956 4-9-8 101 4ex................(t) AndreaAtzeni 15 57
(W P Mullins, Ire) *mid-div tl wknd 2f out* 25/1

0-06 33 43 **Poyle Thomas**[36] 6872 8-8-6 88................................(p) GeorgeWood(3) 13
(Michael Madgwick) *sweating; mid-div tl wknd 3f out: sn eased* 50/1

1322 P **Endless Acres (IRE)**[116] 3928 4-9-5 98.....................(v) StevieDonohoe 31
(Charlie Fellowes) *trckd ldrs: rdn whn lost action and eased 4f out: p.u and dismntd over 1f out* 20/1

3m 45.59s (-6.41) **Going Correction** -0.15s/f (Firm) course record
**WFA** 3 from 4yo+ 10lb 34 Ran SP% 149.5
Speed ratings (Par 109): **108,106,104,103,102 102,102,101,101,101 101,100,99,99,98 98,98,97,96,96 96,95,94,94,90 90,89,**
CSF £75.82 CT £840.69 TOTE £6.60: £2.50, £4.10, £2.90, £4.60; EX 121.10 Trifecta £1224.70.
**Owner** Tony Bloom **Bred** Millsec Limited **Trained** Beckhampton, Wilts

**FOCUS**
Although only three came into it officially rated over 100, this was a deep Cesarewitch. Just two came stands' side entering the home straight before the majority tacked over half a mile out. Strong form and another course record lowered. The re-positioning of the rail between the 1m6f start & the bend into the home straight increased the distance 17yds. The third has been rated in line with his improved jumps form. The fourth and fifth have not been rated far below form despite racing further back than ideal.

## 8039 DARLEY NURSERY H'CAP 7f
4:15 (4:22) (Class 2) 2-Y-O

£18,675 (£5,592; £2,796; £1,398; £699; £351) Stalls High

Form RPR
0056 1 **Rufus King**[14] 7596 2-9-7 97.......................................... PJMcDonald 4 102
(Mark Johnston) *lw; mde all: travelling best 2f out: rdn over 1f out: sustained duel w runner-up after: kpt on gamely and a jst holding rival: rdn out* 16/1

3202 2 ½ **Porth Swtan (IRE)**[19] 7460 2-8-3 79.................................... JoeFanning 2 83
(Charles Hills) *chsd ldng trio: effrt 2f out: rdn to chal over 1f out: sustained duel w wnr after: kpt on wl: hld towards fin* 14/1

011 3 2 ¼ **Prestbury Park (USA)**[69] 5681 2-9-0 90.......................... JamesDoyle 6 88
(Mark Johnston) *quite tall; ly; chsd ldrs: nt clr run 2f out tl swtchd sharply rt and chsd ldng pair 1f out: styd on same pce and no imp ins fnl f* 4/1[3]

0145 4 hd **Maksab (IRE)**[16] 7544 2-8-8 84.......................................... OisinMurphy 1 81
(Mick Channon) *chsd wnr tl unable qck over 1f out: getting outpcd whn short of room and swtchd rt 1f out: kpt on same pce after* 9/1

643 5 1 **Character Witness (IRE)**[65] 5834 2-8-1 80...................... DavidEgan(3) 8 74
(Roger Varian) *sltly on toes; sweating; t.k.h: hld up in tch in midfield: effrt 2f out: unable qck u.p over 1f out: kpt on same pce ins fnl f* 8/1

3222 6 ½ **Clubbable**[14] 7621 2-8-5 81.......................................... PaulHanagan 3 74
(Richard Fahey) *sltly on toes; hld up in tch in midfield: unable qck u.p over 1f out: styd on same pce ins fnl f* 3/1[2]

2101 7 7 **Nobleman's Nest**[31] 7050 2-9-6 96.............................. SilvestreDeSousa 7 70+
(Simon Crisford) *str; lw; in tch in last pair: swtchd rt 4f out: rdn ent fnl 2f: no hdwy u.p over 1f out: wknd fnl f* 5/2[1]

1040 8 1 **Etefaaq (IRE)**[52] 6330 2-9-7 97.......................................... FrankieDettori 9 68+
(Richard Hannon) *taken down early: stdd s: hld up in tch in rr: effrt 2f out: sn struggling and bhd over 1f out* 25/1

1m 23.91s (-1.49) **Going Correction** -0.15s/f (Firm) 8 Ran SP% 111.1
Speed ratings (Par 101): **102,101,98,98,97 96,88,87**
CSF £200.28 CT £1040.52 TOTE £20.10: £4.20, £3.50, £1.90; EX 161.50 Trifecta £1733.10.
**Owner** Garrett J Freyne Racing **Bred** Newsells Park Stud **Trained** Middleham Moor, N Yorks

**FOCUS**
Another winner from the front against the near rail. The winner has been rated in line with his Ascot win.

## 8040 DARLEY EBF STALLIONS BOADICEA STKS (LISTED RACE) (F&M) 6f
4:50 (4:56) (Class 1) 3-Y-O+

£22,684 (£8,600; £4,304; £2,144; £1,076; £540) Stalls High

Form RPR
3203 1 **Eartha Kitt**[7] 7811 3-9-0 97.......................................(p) RichardKingscote 6 102
(Tom Dascombe) *chsd ldrs: effrt over 1f out: drvn and styd on to ld wl ins fnl f: pushed out towards fin* 5/1[3]

0110 2 ¾ **Marie Of Lyon**[7] 7811 3-9-0 93.............................. PaulMulrennan 8 99
(Richard Fahey) *lw; hld up in midfield: rdn and hdwy over 1f out: nt clr run and swtchd rt 1f out: styd on strly u.p to snatch 2nd on post: nt rch wnr* 40/1

0531 **3** *nse* **Pixeleen**[7] 7811 5-9-1 92 AdamKirby 3 99
(Malcolm Saunders) *led for 2f: rdn ent fnl 2f: drvn to ld again over 1f out: hdd and kpt on same pce wl ins fnl f: lost 2nd on post* **12/1**

2105 **4** *nk* **Queen Kindly**[13] 7670 3-9-3 103 PaulHanagan 10 101
(Richard Fahey) *lw; t.k.h: trckd ldrs: effrt between horses to chal ent fnl f: styd on same pce wl ins fnl f* **9/2**[2]

2412 **5** *¾* **Tirania**[23] 7329 3-9-0 88 AndreaAtzeni 2 96+
(William Haggas) *swtchd lft after s: hld up in rr of main gp: nt clr run 2f out: switching rt over 1f out: hdwy 1f out: r.o strly ins fnl f: nt rch ldrs* **16/1**

2020 **6** *1¾* **Gymnaste (IRE)**[77] 5422 3-9-0 94 FrankieDettori 7 90
(John Gosden) *t.k.h: hld up in tch in midfield: swtchd rt over 2f out: hdwy u.p to chse ldrs and edgd lft over 1f out: no ex 1f out: wknd ins fnl f* **9/1**

4530 **7** *2* **Classical Times**[29] 7113 3-9-0 95 JamesDoyle 1 84
(Peter Chapple-Hyam) *v reluctant to post: swtchd lft after s: hld up in rr of main gp: effrt 2f out: no imp u.p over 1f out: nvr trbld ldrs* **16/1**

11-0 **8** *1¾* **Spiritual Lady**[34] 6966 3-9-0 105 RyanMoore 11 78
(Philip McBride) *in tch in midfield: effrt wl over 1f out: keeping on same pce and no imp whn short of room and hmpd 1f out: wl hld and one pce after* **15/2**

2410 **9** *½* **Quench Dolly**[14] 7610 3-9-0 99 ShaneKelly 12 76
(John Gallagher) *w ldr tl led after 2f: rdn and hdd over 1f out: wknd ins fnl f* **16/1**

0036 **9** *dht* **The Wagon Wheel (IRE)**[5] 7887 3-9-0 100 (b) TonyHamilton 9 76
(Richard Fahey) *restless in stalls: hld up in midfield: effrt 2f out: no imp u.p and btn whn nt clr run: hmpd and swtchd rt 1f out: wknd ins fnl f* **20/1**

4111 **11** *4* **Thafeera (USA)**[37] 6864 3-9-0 97 JimCrowley 5 64
(Charles Hills) *taken down early: hld up in tch in midfield: clsd to chse ldrs 1/2-way: struggling to qckn u.p whn squeezed for room and hmpd over 1f out: no ch after and wknd ins fnl f* **3/1**[1]

3034 **12** *¾* **Savannah Slew**[23] 7329 3-9-0 85 (b) SilvestreDeSousa 13 61
(James Given) *taken down early: v.s.a: a bhd* **66/1**

1m 10.52s (-1.68) **Going Correction** -0.15s/f (Firm)
**WFA** 3 from 5yo 1lb **12** Ran SP% **115.6**
Speed ratings (Par 111): **105,104,103,103,102 100,97,95,94,94 89,88**
CSF £192.13 TOTE £5.80: £2.10, £8.00, £3.50; EX 177.10 Trifecta £1264.30.
**Owner** Chasemore Farm **Bred** Chasemore Farm **Trained** Malpas, Cheshire

**FOCUS**
This time the rail didn't prove crucial, and this looked just an ordinary fillies' Listed race. It's been rated a bit cautiously around the third. The winner has been rated to form.

## 8041 DARLEY CLUB STKS (GROUP 3) 1m 1f
**5:25** (5:26) (Class 1) 3-Y-O+

**£34,026** (£12,900; £6,456; £3,216; £1,614; £810) **Stalls** High

Form RPR

4421 **1** **Monarchs Glen**[17] 7506 3-8-13 106 FrankieDettori 12 117+
(John Gosden) *t.k.h: hld up in tch in last trio: switching rt and hdwy over 2f out: rdn to chse ldrs and edgd lft over 1f out: led ins fnl f: r.o wl: gng away at fin* **7/2**[1]

1045 **2** *1¼* **Robin Of Navan (FR)**[14] 7638 4-9-6 114 JamesDoyle 11 115
(Harry Dunlop) *hld up in tch in midfield: clsd to trck ldrs and nt clr run over 2f out: swtchd rt and hdwy between rivals to chse ldr 2f out: drvn to ld 1f out: hdd and one pce ins fnl f* **10/1**

12 **3** *1* **Spark Plug (IRE)**[49] 6441 6-9-3 110 (p) TomMarquand 2 110
(Brian Meehan) *swtchd lft after s and niggled along early: in tch in rr: swtchd rt and effrt over 1f out: hdwy u.p and edgd lft over 1f out: kpt on same pce ins fnl f: wnt 3rd nr fin* **5/1**[3]

5344 **4** *nk* **Sovereign Debt (IRE)**[15] 7579 8-9-8 114 JamesSullivan 8 114
(Ruth Carr) *chsd ldrs: rdn over 2f out: drvn and stl cl enough over 1f out: unable qck 1f out and one pce ins fnl f: lost 3rd nr fin* **22/1**

2410 **5** *1¾* **Muffri'Ha (IRE)**[7] 7812 5-9-0 107 JoeFanning 4 102
(William Haggas) *lw; ponied to s: w ldr and travelled strly tl led 4f out: rdn wl over 1f out: hdd 1f out: no ex and wknd ins fnl f: eased towards fin* **4/1**[2]

-225 **6** *3¼* **Intimation**[42] 6697 5-9-0 104 RyanMoore 3 95
(Sir Michael Stoute) *hld up in tch in last trio: effrt whn carried rt and swtchd lft over 2f out: no imp over 1f out: no threat to ldrs but kpt on to pass btn horses fnl f* **7/1**

1310 **7** *1¼* **First Sitting**[14] 7638 6-9-6 114 GeraldMosse 7 98
(Chris Wall) *stmbld leaving stalls: t.k.h: hld up in tch in midfield: rdn over 1f out: sn outpcd and btn: wknd ins fnl f* **14/1**

5232 **8** *1¼* **Forest Ranger (IRE)**[49] 6444 3-8-13 110 TonyHamilton 9 94
(Richard Fahey) *led tl 4f out: chsd ldr tl lost 2nd 2f out and nt clr run wl over 1f out: wknd fnl f* **7/1**

0012 **9** *2* **Fidaawy**[21] 7395 4-9-3 105 JimCrowley 6 88
(Sir Michael Stoute) *hmpd leaving stalls: sn rcvrd to chse ldrs: unable qck u.p and struggling whn sltly impeded over 1f out: sn btn and wknd fnl f* **15/2**

1m 48.54s (-3.16) **Going Correction** -0.15s/f (Firm)
**WFA** 3 from 4yo+ 4lb **9** Ran SP% **115.8**
Speed ratings (Par 113): **108,106,106,105,104 101,100,99,97**
CSF £39.12 TOTE £3.50: £1.50, £3.20, £2.00; EX 39.90 Trifecta £153.00.
**Owner** K Abdullah **Bred** Juddmonte Farms Ltd **Trained** Newmarket, Suffolk

**FOCUS**
The first two came from the top two stalls but even so, a solid-looking Group 3 and an impressive winner. The runner-up has been rated to his best, and the fourth to his recent form.
T/Jkpt: Not Won. T/Plt: £1,001.70 to a £1 stake. Pool: £177,805.36 - 129.57 winning units
T/Qpdt: £257.10 to a £1 stake. Pool: £12,941.04 - 37.24 winning units
**Steve Payne & Tim Mitchell**

# 8008 YORK (L-H)
Saturday, October 14

**OFFICIAL GOING: Good (6.8)**
Wind: Strong half behind Weather: Cloudy

## 8042 DOWNLOAD THE CORAL APP H'CAP 1m 2f 56y
**2:05** (2:05) (Class 2) (0-110,103) 3-Y-O+

**£21,787** (£6,524; £3,262; £1,631; £815; £409) **Stalls** Low

Form RPR

1346 **1** **Dark Red (IRE)**[14] 7602 5-9-4 96 (b[1]) FrannyNorton 8 106
(Ed Dunlop) *hld up in rr: smooth hdwy over 3f out: trckd ldrs 2f out: sn chal: rdn to ld ent fnl f: sn edgd lft and kpt on strly* **10/1**

2000 **2** *2¼* **Syphax (USA)**[50] 6404 3-9-2 98 (p[1]) KevinStott 4 104
(Kevin Ryan) *in tch: hdwy over 4f out: cl up over 2f out: rdn to ld wl over 1f out: hdd and drvn ent fnl f: kpt on* **8/1**[3]

0-20 **3** *¾* **Linguistic (IRE)**[14] 7619 4-9-11 103 (p) RobertHavlin 12 107
(John Gosden) *in tch: hdwy 4f out:: chsd ldrs over 2f out: rdn over 1f out: kpt on fnl f* **10/1**

0004 **4** *hd* **Master Carpenter (IRE)**[10] 7743 6-9-5 97 PhillipMakin 3 101
(Rod Millman) *trckd ldrs: hdwy on inner 4f out: cl up over 2f out: rdn and ev ch over 1f out: drvn and kpt on same pce fnl f* **12/1**

1020 **5** *hd* **Big Country (IRE)**[14] 7619 4-9-5 100 LewisEdmunds[(3)] 13 103
(Michael Appleby) *trckd ldrs on outer: hdwy and cl up 3f out: effrt to chal 2f out: sn rdn and ev ch: drvn and kpt on same pce fnl f* **4/1**[1]

2304 **6** *hd* **Chelsea Lad (IRE)**[14] 7619 4-9-7 99 DanielTudhope 5 102
(Martyn Meade) *trckd ldng pair: hdwy over 3f out: led 3f out: rdn along and hdd 2f out: sn drvn and grad wknd appr fnl f* **4/1**[1]

200 **7** *1* **Hibou**[14] 7609 4-9-5 97 (b) DavidNolan 1 98
(Iain Jardine) *hld up in rr: hdwy 3f out: chsd ldrs and rdn along 2f out: sn drvn and no imp* **20/1**

6120 **8** *1¼* **Azari**[21] 7395 5-8-13 96 (p) JennyPowell[(5)] 14 95
(Tom Dascombe) *dwlt and swtchd lft s: hld up in rr: sme hdwy 3f out: rdn along 2f out: n.d* **25/1**

3203 **9** *1½* **Anythingtoday (IRE)**[21] 7395 3-9-3 99 (p) LouisSteward 7 96
(Hugo Palmer) *hld up: a towards rr* **5/1**[2]

2500 **10** *½* **Law And Order (IRE)**[7] 7805 3-9-6 102 DavidAllan 11 98
(James Tate) *chsd ldrs: pushed along 3f out: rdn 2f out: sn wknd* **25/1**

2100 **11** *2½* **Weekend Offender (FR)**[14] 7619 4-9-6 98 TomEaves 9 88
(Kevin Ryan) *sn trcking ldr: cl up 1/2-way: rdn along 3f out: sn wknd* **20/1**

1505 **12** *14* **Speed Company (IRE)**[49] 6449 4-9-7 99 (h) JasonHart 10 62
(John Quinn) *sn led: rdn along over 3f out: sn hdd & wknd* **14/1**

2m 8.36s (-4.14) **Going Correction** 0.0s/f (Good)
**WFA** 3 from 4yo+ 4lb **12** Ran SP% **117.5**
Speed ratings (Par 109): **116,114,113,113,113 113,112,111,110,109 107,96**
CSF £81.88 CT £821.03 TOTE £10.10: £3.00, £3.50, £3.00; EX 108.50 Trifecta £789.60.
**Owner** The Hon R J Arculli **Bred** T Jones **Trained** Newmarket, Suffolk

**FOCUS**
The going was good, GoingStick: 6.8 overall. Home straight, far side 6.9; centre 6.7; stands' side 6.8. Rails: Innermost line providing fresh ground from 9f to entrance to home straight. Race distances as advertised. Stalls: 5f, 5½f & 6f - centre. Remainder - inside.\n\x\x After riding in the opener, jockey Kevin Stott said: "The ground is drying up." Robert Havlin said: "It is good ground, loose on top," and Philip Makin remarked: "It is good, a bit easier down the back.\n\x\x The opener was won in a time just 1.36sec over Racing Post standard, which showed the ground was certainly no softer than good\n\x\x A competitive handicap which saw the winner score decisively in first-time blinkers. The third has been rated to his best.

## 8043 CORAL.CO.UK ROCKINGHAM STKS (LISTED RACE) 6f
**2:40** (2:41) (Class 1) 2-Y-O

**£28,355** (£10,750; £5,380; £2,680; £1,345; £675) **Stalls** Centre

Form RPR

1056 **1** **Rebel Assault (IRE)**[7] 7846 2-8-10 93 FrannyNorton 9 96
(Mark Johnston) *slt ld: pushed along and hdd 2f out: cl up and rdn over 1f out: drvn and edgd lft ins fnl f: kpt on wl to ld last 50 yds* **25/1**

5062 **2** *1¼* **It Dont Come Easy (IRE)**[14] 7596 2-9-1 96 DavidNolan 6 97
(Richard Fahey) *cl up: led 2f out: sn rdn: drvn ent fnl f: sn edgd lft: hdd and no ex last 50 yds* **12/1**

2156 **3** *¾* **Staxton**[21] 7394 2-9-1 103 DavidAllan 7 95
(Tim Easterby) *in tch: gd hdwy over 2f out: trckd ldrs over 1f out: swtchd lft and rdn to chal ent fnl f: ev ch tl drvn and kpt on same pce last 100 yds* **11/2**[2]

311 **4** *¾* **Shabaaby**[31] 7049 2-9-1 109 DaneO'Neill 1 93
(Owen Burrows) *trckd ldrs on inner: hdwy and cl up 2f out: sn rdn: drvn ent fnl f: kpt on same pce* **1/1**[1]

031 **5** *½* **Pulitzer**[36] 6876 2-8-10 75 HarryBentley 8 86
(Hugo Palmer) *trckd ldrs: hdwy over 2f out: rdn along and sltly outpcd 11/2f out: kpt on u.p fnl f* **33/1**

0411 **6** *2* **Daddies Girl (IRE)**[10] 7734 2-8-10 89 SteveDrowne 11 80
(Rod Millman) *rr tl styd on fnl 2f: n.d* **14/1**

1120 **7** *1* **Dance Diva**[63] 5941 2-8-13 99 TomEaves 10 80
(Richard Fahey) *chsd ldrs: rdn along 2f out: sn drvn and one pce* **10/1**

5021 **8** *2½* **Savannah's Show**[13] 7655 2-8-10 63 ConnorBeasley 5 70
(Richard Guest) *dwlt: a towards rr* **100/1**

21 **9** *2* **Barton Mills**[17] 7512 2-9-1 0 MartinHarley 12 69
(William Haggas) *racd wd: chsd ldrs: rdn along wl over 2f out: sn wknd* **7/1**[3]

14 **10** *nk* **Island Drive (IRE)**[72] 5576 2-8-10 0 AndrewMullen 2 63
(William Haggas) *dwlt: a in rr* **33/1**

511 **11** *2½* **Peggy's Angel**[42] 6678 2-8-10 87 JFEgan 4 55
(Jo Hughes) *cl up: rdn along wl over 2f out: sn wknd* **16/1**

1m 11.72s (-0.18) **Going Correction** 0.0s/f (Good) **11** Ran SP% **117.9**
Speed ratings (Par 103): **101,99,98,97,96 94,92,89,86,86 82**
CSF £290.59 TOTE £29.40: £6.90, £3.70, £2.20; EX 484.20 Trifecta £1876.50.
**Owner** Mrs Christine E Budden & Partners **Bred** Christine E Budden & Partners **Trained** Middleham Moor, N Yorks

**FOCUS**
A decent Listed contest which saw the hot favourite disappoint, leaving the way clear for the winner to prove her worth over this trip. The third and fourth have been rated below form.

## 8044 CORAL SPRINT TROPHY H'CAP 6f
**3:15** (3:15) (Class 2) (0-105,105) 3-Y-O+

**£62,250** (£18,640; £9,320; £4,660; £2,330; £1,170) **Stalls** Centre

Form RPR

-041 **1** **Teruntum Star (FR)**[56] 6205 5-9-3 98 (p) KevinStott 2 109
(Kevin Ryan) *prom: led over 2f out: rdn 2f out: edgd rt and bmpd into chalr appr fnl f: kpt on wl* **10/1**

2531 **2** *1¾* **Spring Loaded (IRE)**[28] 7144 5-9-6 101 JoeyHaynes 13 106
(Paul D'Arcy) *hld up: pushed along 2f out: stl plenty to do appr fnl f: rdn and r.o wl: edgd lft fnl 50yds: wnt 2nd nr fin* **10/1**

0151 **3** *nk* **Flying Pursuit**[14] 7626 4-9-3 101 (p) RachelRichardson[(3)] 15 105
(Tim Easterby) *prom: rdn 2f out: kpt on* **12/1**

0000 **4** *nk* **Eastern Impact (IRE)**[28] 7144 6-8-13 97 (p) AdamMcNamara[(3)] 5 100
(Richard Fahey) *chsd ldrs: rdn 2f out: slty hmpd ent fnl f: kpt on* **16/1**

0000 **5** *nk* **Outback Traveller (IRE)**[35] 6922 6-9-2 97 (p[1]) HarryBentley 10 99
(Robert Cowell) *hld up in midfield: rdn along over 3f out: r.o ins fnl f: nrst fin* **33/1**

150 **6** *nk* **Eqtiraan (IRE)**[56] 6198 3-9-8 104 DaneO'Neill 9 105
(Richard Hannon) *hld up: rdn 3f out: kpt on fnl f: nrst fin* **25/1**

2132 **7** hd **Upstaging**[54] 6275 5-9-5 **100**......(p) JFEgan 20 101
(Paul Cole) *hld up in midfield: rdn over 2f out: kpt on fnl f: bit short of room nr fin* **16/1**

2564 **8** nk **Mr Lupton (IRE)**[14] 7611 4-9-3 **105**...... SebastianWoods(7) 7 105+
(Richard Fahey) *midfield: rdn 2f out: sltly hmpd over 1f out: kpt on fnl f* **11/2**[1]

4013 **9** nk **Golden Apollo**[14] 7626 3-9-3 **99**...... DavidAllan 19 98+
(Tim Easterby) *s.i.s: outpcd in rr tl kpt on fnl f: nvr threatened* **12/1**

2002 **10** hd **Al Qahwa (IRE)**[34] 6971 4-9-3 **98**......(v[1]) DanielTudhope 12 96
(David O'Meara) *prom: rdn over 2f out: sltly hmpd ent fnl f: no ex* **17/2**[3]

4000 **11** 1 ¼ **Growl**[14] 7611 5-9-5 **105**......(b) ConnorMurtagh(5) 16 99
(Richard Fahey) *trckd ldrs: rdn along to chal over 1f out: edging lft whn bmpd by wnr appr fnl f: wknd fnl 110yds* **16/1**

-066 **12** shd **Hoof It**[52] 6325 10-8-9 **97**...... HarrisonShaw(7) 6 91
(Michael Easterby) *hld up in midfield: rdn 2f out: one pce and nvr threatened* **16/1**

5000 **13** ¾ **Perfect Pasture**[14] 7611 7-9-5 **100**......(v) PhillipMakin 11 91
(Michael Easterby) *nvr bttr than midfield: sltly hmpd ent fnl f* **50/1**

0025 **14** 1 **Edward Lewis**[18] 7475 4-9-2 **100**...... JoshDoyle(3) 17 88
(David O'Meara) *in tch towards outer: rdn to chse ldrs over 1f out: wknd ins fnl f* **33/1**

1302 **15** ¾ **Stake Acclaim (IRE)**[14] 7611 5-9-10 **105**...... RobertWinston 1 91
(Dean Ivory) *trckd ldrs: rdn over 2f out: wknd ins fnl f: eased fnl 50yds* **10/1**

4000 **16** 1 **Raucous**[34] 6971 4-9-2 **97**...... MartinHarley 3 79
(William Haggas) *midfield: rdn over 2f out: wknd ins fnl f* **8/1**[2]

4205 **17** 2 ½ **Pipers Note**[28] 7144 7-9-2 **100**...... LewisEdmunds(3) 14 74
(Ruth Carr) *dwlt: sn in tch: rdn over 2f out: wknd ins fnl f* **20/1**

3500 **18** ½ **Orion's Bow**[14] 7611 6-9-4 **99**...... BarryMcHugh 8 72
(Tim Easterby) *prom: rdn over 2f out: wknd ins fnl f* **33/1**

0002 **19** 1 ½ **Nameitwhatyoulike**[14] 7626 8-9-2 **97**...... TomEaves 4 65
(Bryan Smart) *led narrowly: rdn whn hdd over 2f out: wknd over 1f out* **14/1**

0-10 **20** 6 **Kickboxer (IRE)**[14] 7611 6-9-3 **98**...... BenCurtis 18 47
(Michael Appleby) *swtchd lft s: a in rr* **40/1**

1m 11.02s (-0.88) **Going Correction** 0.0s/f (Good)
**WFA** 3 from 4yo+ 1lb **20** Ran SP% **131.7**
Speed ratings (Par 109): **105,102,102,101,101 101,100,100,100,99 98,97,96,95,94 93,89,89,87,79**
CSF £104.79 CT £1277.22 TOTE £9.90: £3.00, £3.20, £3.10, £4.30; EX 137.50 Trifecta £1949.30.
**Owner** T A Rahman **Bred** Petra Bloodstock Agency **Trained** Hambleton, N Yorks
■ Stewards' Enquiry : Joey Haynes two-day ban: careless riding (Oct 30-31)

**FOCUS**
A valuable sprint handicap which looked wide-open beforehand, but produced a decisive winner. The winner has been rated back to his best, the runner-up as matching his Portland win and the third close to his Ripon latest.

## 8045 CORAL NURSERY H'CAP 7f 192y
3:50 (3:53) (Class 2) 2-Y-O
**£21,787** (£6,524; £3,262; £1,631; £815; £409) **Stalls** Low

Form RPR

4621 **1** **Awesometank**[14] 7621 2-9-5 **86**...... DanielTudhope 3 90
(William Haggas) *trckd ldng pair on inner: hdwy 3f out: led jst over 2f out: sn jnd and rdn: drvn ent fnl f: kpt on wl u.p* **3/1**[3]

6413 **2** nk **Dark Liberty (IRE)**[14] 7621 2-9-0 **81**...... HarryBentley 7 84
(Simon Crisford) *dwlt and towards rr: hdwy 1/2-way: trckd ldrs 3f out: chsd wnr wl over 1f out and sn rdn to chal: drvn and ev ch ins fnl f: kpt on* **9/2**[2]

2100 **3** 1 ¼ **Veejay (IRE)**[13] 7648 2-9-7 **88**...... JFEgan 5 88
(Mick Channon) *hld up towards rr: hdwy over 3f out: chsd ldrs 2f out: rdn over 1f out: kpt on fnl f* **7/1**

4260 **4** 1 **Reinbeau Prince**[25] 7243 2-8-0 **67**...... PatrickMathers 8 65
(Richard Fahey) *trckd ldr: cl up 1/2-way: rdn along on outer over 2f out: drvn and edgd lft over 1f out: kpt on same pce fnl f* **20/1**

531 **5** ½ **Buckstopper Kit (USA)**[18] 7473 2-8-12 **79**......(b) BarryMcHugh 6 76
(Richard Fahey) *trckd ldrs: hdwy 3f out: cl up 2f out and sn rdn: drvn appr fnl f and kpt on same pce* **6/1**[3]

1224 **6** 7 **Book Of Dreams (IRE)**[14] 7593 2-9-4 **85**...... FrannyNorton 9 66
(Mark Johnston) *chsd ldrs: rdn along wl over 2f out: grad wknd* **8/1**

4631 **7** 4 ½ **Shazzab (IRE)**[16] 7552 2-8-9 **79**......(p) AdamMcNamara(3) 2 50
(Richard Fahey) *a towards rr* **13/2**

0640 **8** hd **Lady Anjorica (IRE)**[7] 7821 2-8-11 **78**...... ConnorBeasley 4 48
(Keith Dalgleish) *a in rr* **14/1**

3511 **9** 15 **Sunbreak (IRE)**[31] 7057 2-8-8 **75**...... JasonHart 1 11
(Mark Johnston) *led: rdn along 3f out: hdd over 2f out: sn wknd* **8/1**

1m 36.92s (-2.08) **Going Correction** 0.0s/f (Good) 2y crse rec **9** Ran SP% **117.0**
Speed ratings (Par 101): **110,109,108,107,106 99,95,95,80**
CSF £16.55 CT £87.69 TOTE £2.90: £1.50, £1.80, £2.70; EX 17.40 Trifecta £117.10.
**Owner** Lee Yuk Lun Alan **Bred** Eminent Kind Ltd **Trained** Newmarket, Suffolk

**FOCUS**
A competitive nursery which produced a good duel between the determined winner and persistent runner-up. The third has been rated to his mark.

## 8046 CORAL.CO.UK EBFSTALLIONS.COM NOVICE STKS (PLUS 10 RACE) 7f
4:25 (4:26) (Class 3) 2-Y-O
**£9,703** (£2,887; £1,443; £721) **Stalls** Low

Form RPR

4423 **1** **Mont Kinabalu (IRE)**[18] 7473 2-9-2 77...... TomEaves 3 79
(Kevin Ryan) *trckd ldrs on inner: hdwy to ld jst 2f out: rdn and edgd rt jst over 1f out: drvn fnl f and hld on wl towards fin* **6/1**

2R2 **2** ½ **Chief Justice**[36] 6897 2-8-13 0...... AdamMcNamara(3) 7 78
(Richard Fahey) *dwlt and towards rr: hdwy over 2f out: rdn to chse ldrs whn nt clr run and swtchd lft jst over 1f out: drvn fnl f: kpt on wl towards fin* **11/2**[3]

4 **3** ¾ **Maghaweer (IRE)**[17] 7513 2-9-2 0...... DaneO'Neill 12 76
(Richard Hannon) *in tch on outer: hdwy over 2f out: rdn to chal and ev ch whn hmpd jst over 1f out: sn drvn and kpt on same pce ins fnl f* **11/2**[3]

1 **4** 3 ¼ **Air Raid**[35] 6939 2-9-8 0...... DavidNolan 10 73
(Jedd O'Keeffe) *trckd ldrs: hdwy 3f out: cl up over 2f out: rdn to chal whn hmpd jst over 1f out: sn drvn and kpt on same pce* **4/1**[2]

02 **5** ½ **Agar's Plough**[35] 6921 2-9-2 0...... DanielTudhope 11 67
(Ed Dunlop) *prom: cl up 3f out: rdn along and ch whn hmpd jst over 1f out: one pce after* **7/2**[1]

51 **6** 6 **Dawn Breaking**[16] 7551 2-9-5 0...... LewisEdmunds(3) 2 55
(Richard Whitaker) *led: rdn along and hdd over 2f out: drvn and hld whn n.m.r and edgd rt jst over 1f out: sn wknd* **14/1**

0 **7** nk **Cristal Spirit**[15] 7580 2-9-2 0...... MartinHarley 9 48
(William Haggas) *dwlt: a towards rr* **14/1**

44 **8** nk **Sempre Presto (IRE)**[24] 7265 2-8-11 0...... BarryMcHugh 4 43
(Richard Fahey) *a towards rr* **28/1**

10 **9** 5 **Highest Rank (IRE)**[35] 6938 2-9-5 0......(v[1]) CliffordLee(3) 5 40
(K R Burke) *chsd ldrs to 1/2-way: sn wknd* **20/1**

0 **10** 5 **Angel Carlotta (IRE)**[17] 7521 2-8-11 0...... AndrewMullen 1 16
(Nigel Tinkler) *a towards rr* **66/1**

02 **11** 1 ¾ **Sunstorm**[17] 7521 2-9-2 0...... PhillipMakin 8 16
(David Brown) *trckd ldng pair: pushed along 1/2-way: sn rdn and wknd* **16/1**

0 **12** 42 **Marcella**[15] 7563 2-8-11 0...... DavidAllan 6
(David C Griffiths) *a towards rr* **66/1**

1m 26.31s (1.01) **Going Correction** 0.0s/f (Good) **12** Ran SP% **117.7**
Speed ratings (Par 99): **94,93,92,88,88 81,81,80,75,69 67,19**
CSF £37.51 TOTE £6.80: £2.10, £2.10, £2.40; EX 37.20 Trifecta £545.90.
**Owner** JCG Chua & CK Ong 1 **Bred** Tally-Ho Stud **Trained** Hambleton, N Yorks

**FOCUS**
Quite an exciting finish to a fair juvenile contest. The first three may well pay to follow. The fourth has been rated below his debut effort.

## 8047 CORAL STAYERS H'CAP 2m 56y
5:00 (5:01) (Class 3) (0-90,88) 4-Y-O+ **£9,703** (£2,887; £1,443; £721) **Stalls** Low

Form RPR

0000 **1** **October Storm**[52] 6323 4-8-6 **73**...... JFEgan 17 81
(Mick Channon) *hld up in rr: brought to outer and hdwy into midfield over 5f out: pushed along and further hdwy over 2f out: rdn to ld over 1f out: edgd rt: styd on: all out* **12/1**[3]

-261 **2** shd **Arrowtown**[16] 7558 5-8-7 **74**......(h) CamHardie 7 83+
(Michael Easterby) *hld up in midfield on inner: n.m.r and stl plenty to do 2f out: pushed along and hdwy over 1f out: briefly had to wait bef squeezing through gap 110yds out: r.o strly: jst failed* **33/1**

2-12 **3** 2 ½ **Coeur De Lion**[21] 7402 4-9-2 **83**...... FergusSweeney 12 88
(Alan King) *trckd ldrs: led over 2f out: sn rdn: hdd over 1f out and outpcd: styd on ins fnl f* **5/4**[1]

1042 **4** nse **Opposition**[21] 7412 4-9-0 **84**...... AdamMcNamara(3) 13 89
(Ed Dunlop) *hld up: pushed along and hdwy on outside 3f out: rdn to chal over 1f out: no ex fnl 75yds* **12/1**[3]

1453 **5** 1 ¾ **Archippos**[14] 7615 4-9-1 **82**...... PaddyAspell 15 85
(Philip Kirby) *hld up: rdn and hdwy 3f out: kpt on same pce* **33/1**

6130 **6** ½ **Stormin Tom (IRE)**[14] 7627 5-8-3 **73**...... RachelRichardson(3) 10 75
(Tim Easterby) *led: rdn whn hdd over 2f out: no ex fnl f* **25/1**

/1-0 **7** hd **Captain Navarre**[32] 7024 5-8-9 **76**...... HarryBentley 5 78
(Charlie Fellowes) *in tch: rdn and outpcd 3f out: styd on fnl f* **7/1**[2]

2533 **8** nk **Angel Gabrial (IRE)**[14] 7599 8-8-11 **83**...... ConnorMurtagh(5) 8 85
(Richard Fahey) *midfield: rdn over 2f out: one pce and nvr threatened ldrs* **12/1**[3]

0-31 **9** shd **Blue Hussar (IRE)**[34] 6968 6-9-3 **84**...... PhillipMakin 16 85
(Micky Hammond) *in tch: rdn to chse ldrs over 2f out: ev ch over 1f out: wknd fnl 110yds* **7/1**[2]

31 **10** 2 **River Icon**[18] 7477 5-9-1 **85**...... LewisEdmunds(3) 4 84
(Iain Jardine) *midfield: rdn and outpcd 3f out: no threat after* **16/1**

0-43 **11** 3 ¼ **Always Resolute**[36] 6880 6-8-6 **78**...... BenRobinson(5) 11 73
(Brian Ellison) *hld up in midfield: shuffled bk towards rr over 5f out: rdn along 3f out: nvr threatened* **14/1**

2322 **12** 2 ¼ **On Fire**[22] 7359 4-8-11 **78**......(p) TomEaves 2 70
(James Bethell) *midfield: pushed along 3f out: wknd fnl f* **16/1**

2P46 **13** 1 ¾ **Lost The Moon**[37] 6849 4-8-10 **77**...... JoeyHaynes 9 67
(Mark H Tompkins) *hld up in midfield: rdn 4f out: sn btn* **66/1**

5500 **14** 2 **Icefall (IRE)**[25] 7234 4-8-12 **79**...... DavidAllan 3 67
(Tim Easterby) *in tch: rdn over 2f out: wknd over 1f out* **33/1**

0-26 **15** 2 ¾ **Slunovrat (FR)**[63] 5944 6-9-5 **86**...... DavidNolan 1 71
(David Menuisier) *trckd ldrs: quite keen early: rdn over 3f out: wknd appr fnl f: eased fnl 100yds* **25/1**

5- **16** 31 **Dalshand (FR)**[146] 4-9-7 **88**...... DanielTudhope 14 35
(David O'Meara) *prom: rdn and lost pce qckly 3f out: wknd and eased* **20/1**

3m 36.73s (2.23) **Going Correction** 0.0s/f (Good) **16** Ran SP% **133.7**
Speed ratings (Par 107): **94,93,92,92,91 91,91,91,91,90 88,87,86,85,84 68**
CSF £385.86 CT £859.84 TOTE £14.00: £2.90, £8.70, £1.10, £2.80; EX 900.80 Trifecta £3458.60.
**Owner** Jon and Julia Aisbitt **Bred** Meon Valley Stud **Trained** West Ilsley, Berks
■ Stewards' Enquiry : J F Egan two-day ban: excessive use of whip (30-31 Oct)

**FOCUS**
They did not go much of a gallop, which was probably against the hot favourite, but the winner travelled best and deserved to hang on. The winner has been rated to his handicap best, while the fourth, fifth and sixth help set the standard.

## 8048 COLDSTREAM GUARDS ASSOCIATION CUP H'CAP 1m 2f 56y
5:30 (5:32) (Class 3) (0-90,89) 3-Y-O+ **£9,703** (£2,887; £1,443; £721) **Stalls** Low

Form RPR

3344 **1** **Grand Inquisitor**[3] 7959 5-9-0 **79**......(p) PhillipMakin 12 95+
(Ian Williams) *hld up in rr: smooth hdwy over 3f out: trckd ldrs 2f out: shkn up to ld 11/2f out: sn clr: readily* **5/1**[1]

3000 **2** 5 **Swift Emperor (IRE)**[107] 4261 5-9-9 **88**...... BenCurtis 17 93
(David Barron) *dwlt and hld up in rr: hdwy 3f out: rdn along wl over 1f out: styd on to chse wnr ins fnl f: sn no imp* **20/1**

1045 **3** 1 ¼ **Alwahsh (IRE)**[42] 6671 3-9-0 **83**...... DaneO'Neill 16 86
(William Haggas) *hld up towards rr: hdwy over 3f out: rdn along 2f out: drvn over 1f out: kpt on fnl f* **11/2**[2]

0641 **4** 1 **Dance King**[16] 7555 7-9-9 **88**......(tp) DavidAllan 1 88
(Tim Easterby) *hld up in rr: hdwy 3f out: nt clr run and hmpd 2f out: sn swtchd lft and rdn: styd on wl u.p fnl f* **7/1**[3]

4162 **5** nk **Bedouin (IRE)**[22] 7358 3-9-3 **86**......(v[1]) FrannyNorton 19 87
(Luca Cumani) *hld up and bhd: hdwy 3f out: rdn along 2f out: drvn over 1f out: kpt on fnl f* **8/1**

3323 **6** 1 ¾ **Royal Regent**[11] 7702 5-9-5 **84**...... JoeDoyle 2 80
(Lucy Normile) *chsd ldrs:. rdn along over 2f out: drvn over 1f out: kpt on same pce* **14/1**

6520 **7** hd **Silvery Moon (IRE)**[7] 7823 10-9-0 **82**...... RachelRichardson(3) 13 78
(Tim Easterby) *t.k.h early: hld up towards rr: hdwy on wd outside 3f out: rdn along 2f out: kpt on fnl f* **25/1**

4000 **8** ½ **Gulf Of Poets**[14] 7595 5-9-8 **87** ........ CamHardie 11 82
(Michael Easterby) *midfield: hdwy on outer 1/2-way and sn trcking ldrs: rdn to ld 2f out: sn hdd and drvn: wknd ent fnl f* **50/1**

0415 **9** ¾ **Carnageo (FR)**[16] 7555 4-9-4 **88** ........ (b) ConnorMurtagh(5) 14 82
(Richard Fahey) *hld up in rr: hdwy on outer 3f out: rdn along 2f out: in tch and drvn over 1f out: wknd* **16/1**

0001 **10** 2 ¼ **Society Red**[42] 6671 3-8-10 **82** ........ AdamMcNamara(3) 15 72
(Richard Fahey) *prom: effrt and cl up over 3f out: rdn along over 2f out: sn wknd* **8/1**

1024 **11** ¾ **Save The Bees**[23] 7328 9-9-0 **86** ........ GerO'Neill(7) 18 74
(Declan Carroll) *sn led: rdn along 3f out: hdd 2f out and sn wknd* **14/1**

-506 **12** 1 **Trendsetter (IRE)**[14] 7615 6-8-13 **81** ........ (p) AaronJones(3) 10 67
(Micky Hammond) *midfield: hdwy on outer over 3f out: rdn to chse ldrs 2f out: sn drvn and wknd appr fnl f* **50/1**

6560 **13** nk **Magic City (IRE)**[3] 7959 8-9-5 **84** ........ TomEaves 20 69
(Michael Easterby) *stdd s and hld up towards rr: hdwy 1/2-way and sn in tch: effrt to chse ldrs 3f out: rdn along over 2f out: sn drvn and wknd* **25/1**

1- **14** nk **Coroberee (IRE)**[96] 1483 4-9-6 **85** ........ BarryMcHugh 8 70
(Tony Coyle) *in tch: rdn along over 3f out: sn wknd* **33/1**

0160 **15** 3 **Mutadaffeq (IRE)**[36] 6872 4-9-9 **88** ........ DavidNolan 9 67
(David O'Meara) *trckd ldrs: pushed along over 4f out: rdn 3f out and sn wknd* **33/1**

0035 **16** 14 **Kharbetation (IRE)**[13] 7649 4-9-3 **82** ........ DanielTudhope 3 35
(David O'Meara) *trckd ldng pair: effrt to chse ldr over 4f out: rdn along over 3f out: sn wknd* **9/1**

0320 **17** 2 **Star Of Rory (IRE)**[16] 7555 3-9-6 **89** ........ (p[1]) MartinHarley 7 39
(Tom Dascombe) *in tch on inner: rdn along over 3f out: sn wknd* **20/1**

0303 **18** 4 ½ **Jacbequick**[14] 7627 6-8-13 **81** ........ (p) JoshDoyle(3) 5 21
(David O'Meara) *disp ld early: cl up: rdn along over 4f out: sn wknd* **16/1**

2m 9.16s (-3.34) **Going Correction** 0.0s/f (Good)
**WFA** 3 from 4yo+ 4lb **18** Ran SP% **128.9**
Speed ratings (Par 107): **113,109,108,107,106 105,105,105,104,102 102,101,100,100,98 87,85,81**
CSF £112.28 CT £589.78 TOTE £6.10: £2.00, £5.60, £1.90, £1.90; EX 172.10 Trifecta £962.80.
**Owner** Sir Alex Ferguson & Peter Done **Bred** Floors Farming And Dominic Burke **Trained** Portway, Worcs

**FOCUS**
What looked to be a competitive finale was blown apart by the easy winner who would be of serious interest if turned out under a penalty. The second has been rated close to his best, and the third and fourth close to form.
T/Plt: £510.80 to a £1 stake. Pool: £160,103.95 - 228.78 winning units T/Qpdt: £14.70 to a £1 stake. Pool: £13,731.31 - 690.45 winning units **Joe Rowntree & Andrew Sheret**

## 7664 CAULFIELD (R-H)

Saturday, October 14

**OFFICIAL GOING: Turf: good**

### 8056a LADBROKES HERBERT POWER STKS (GROUP 2 H'CAP) (3YO+) (TURF) 1m 4f

**4:05** 3-Y-O+

**£140,935** (£42,105; £21,052; £10,526; £5,847; £4,678)

RPR

**1** **Lord Fandango (GER)**[15] 4-8-5 **0** ........ BenAllen 2 103
(Archie Alexander, Australia) **11/1**

**2** 1 **Wall Of Fire (IRE)**[56] 6191 4-9-2 **0** ........ (b) MarkZahra 9 112
(Hugo Palmer) *in fnl pair early: settled in last after 2f: pushed along 2 1/12f out and gd hdwy on outside turning in: drvn along and continued to cl down st: wnt 2nd 50yds out: nt able to rch ldr: clst fin* **8/1**

**3** ½ **Gallic Chieftain (FR)**[15] 4-8-5 **0** ........ DeanYendall 7 101
(Darren Weir, Australia) **18/5**[2]

**4** 1 **Boom Time (AUS)**[15] 6-8-13 **0** ........ (b) CoryParish 6 107
(David A & B Hayes & Tom Dabernig, Australia) **15/2**

**5** 2 **Annus Mirabilis (IRE)**[15] 6-8-10 **0** ........ (b) LukeCurrie 3 101
(Stuart Webb, Australia) **50/1**

**6** ½ **Fanatic (NZ)**[15] 5-8-5 **0** ........ (b) BeauMertens 4 95
(David A & B Hayes & Tom Dabernig, Australia) **30/1**

**7** 6 **Harlow Gold (NZ)**[21] 4-8-5 **0** ........ (p) ChrisParnham 1 85
(David A & B Hayes & Tom Dabernig, Australia) **19/1**

**8** 3 ¼ **Kidmenever (IRE)**[99] 4584 4-8-10 **0** ........ (p) GlynSchofield 8 85
(Charlie Appleby) *little slowly away and nudged along early to settle in 3rd: wnt 2nd after 3f: led ins fnl 3f: sn pressed and hdd 2f out: wknd over 1f out: eased fnl f* **6/1**[3]

**9** 17 **Aloft (IRE)**[28] 5-8-10 **0** ........ BenMelham 10 58
(Robert Hickmott, Australia) **16/5**[1]

**10** 1 ½ **Foundry (IRE)**[14] 7643 7-8-11 **0** ........ (t) MichaelDee 5 57
(Robert Hickmott, Australia) **13/2**

2m 27.67s **10** Ran SP% **114.6**

**Owner** Oti Racing, Anglo Australian Racing Et Al **Bred** Gestut Etzean **Trained** Australia

**FOCUS**
It's been rated around the balance of the second, fourth, fifth and sixth.

### 8057a KENO WEEKEND HUSSLER STKS (LISTED H'CAP) (2YO+) (TURF) 7f

**4:40** 2-Y-O+

**£42,397** (£12,631; £6,315; £3,157; £1,754; £1,403)

RPR

**1** **Fast 'N' Rocking (AUS)**[21] 7-9-0 **0** ........ LukeNolen 2 101
(David A & B Hayes & Tom Dabernig, Australia) **9/1**

**2** shd **Religify (AUS)**[112] 7-9-7 **0** ........ DwayneDunn 6 108
(Chris Waller, Australia) **4/1**[2]

**3** 1 ¼ **Dibayani (IRE)**[28] 7-9-1 **0** ........ CoryParish 12 98
(David A & B Hayes & Tom Dabernig, Australia) **18/1**

**4** shd **Coldstone (FR)**[91] 5-8-7 **0** ........ BeauMertens 3 90
(Michael Kent, Australia) **30/1**

**5** ½ **Oregon's Day (AUS)**[28] 4-8-8 **0** ow1 ........ MarkZahra 13 90
(Mick Price, Australia) **5/1**[3]

**6** ¾ **Mubakkir (AUS)**[15] 7-8-7 **0** ........ (t) StephenBaster 8 87
(Bill Papazaharoudakis, Australia) **40/1**

**7** shd **Orient Line (AUS)**[15] 6-8-7 **0** ........ (p) CraigNewitt 4 86
(John Moloney, Australia) **40/1**

**8** hd **Fastnet Tempest (IRE)**[42] 6685 4-8-7 **0** ........ (p) DeanYendall 1 86
(William Haggas) **9/1**

**9** shd **Attention (AUS)**[13] 7665 4-8-8 **0** ow1 ........ (bt) BenMelham 9 87
(Peter & Paul Snowden, Australia) **19/5**[1]

**10** shd **Mighty Like (AUS)**[21] 8-8-7 **0** ........ NoelCallow 10 85
(Mick Price, Australia) **25/1**

**11** ½ **Lucky Hussler (AUS)**[13] 7665 8-9-10 **0** ........ (t) BradRawiller 7 101
(Darren Weir, Australia) **16/1**

**12** hd **Duke Of Brunswick (AUS)**[21] 6-8-7 **0** ........ (t) DamienOliver 11 83
(Mick Price, Australia) **7/1**

**13** 5 **Mongolian Wolf (AUS)**[126] 4-8-7 **0** ........ (bt) BenAllen 70
(Darren Weir, Australia) **20/1**

1m 23.94s
**WFA** 3 from 4yo+ 2lb **13** Ran SP% **117.9**
.
**Owner** P B Devitt, C A Gordon Et Al **Bred** P B Devitt **Trained** Australia

### 8058a LADBROKES STKS (GROUP 1) (3YO+) (TURF) 1m 2f

**5:50** 3-Y-O+

**£352,485** (£105,263; £52,631; £26,315; £14,619; £11,695)

RPR

**1** **Gailo Chop (FR)**[13] 7664 6-9-4 0 ........ MarkZahra 5 114
(Darren Weir, Australia) **9/2**[3]

**2** hd **Johannes Vermeer (IRE)**[65] 5862 4-9-4 0 ........ (t) KatelynMallyon 6 114+
(A P O'Brien, Ire) **30/1**

**3** 2 ½ **Jon Snow (NZ)**[15] 4-9-2 0 ........ (v) StephenBaster 9 107
(Murray Baker & Andrew Forsman, New Zealand) **15/2**

**4** shd **Single Gaze (AUS)**[13] 7664 5-9-0 0 ........ KathyO'Hara 1 105
(Nick Olive, Australia) **20/1**

**5** 1 ¼ **Inference (AUS)**[13] 7664 4-9-2 0 ........ (tp) DwayneDunn 3 104
(Michael, Wayne & John Hawkes, Australia) **20/1**

**6** shd **Bonneval (NZ)**[13] 7664 4-8-11 0 ........ DamianLane 11 99
(Murray Baker & Andrew Forsman, New Zealand) **27/10**[1]

**7** ½ **Riven Light (IRE)**[31] 7066 5-9-4 0 ........ GlenBoss 4 105
(W P Mullins, Ire) **20/1**

**8** shd **Abbey Marie (AUS)**[21] 5-9-0 0 ........ BeauMertens 10 101
(Michael Kent, Australia) **25/1**

**9** 1 ¼ **Hartnell**[13] 7664 6-9-4 0 ........ GlynSchofield 7 102
(James Cummings, Australia) **16/5**[2]

**10** 2 **The Taj Mahal (IRE)**[35] 6960 3-8-13 0 ........ DamienOliver 2 98
(A P O'Brien, Ire) **9/1**

**11** 3 **Calderon (IRE)**[105] 4371 4-9-4 0 ........ LukeCurrie 8 98
(Tony McEvoy, Australia) **50/1**

2m 2.17s
**WFA** 3 from 4yo+ 4lb **11** Ran SP% **114.1**
**Owner** OTI Racing, J Higgins Et Al **Bred** Alain Chopard **Trained** Australia

**FOCUS**
The first two have been rated in line with their best.

### 8059a UNITED PETROLEUM TOORAK (GROUP 1 H'CAP) (2YO+) (TURF) 1m

**7:10** 2-Y-O+

**£177,046** (£52,631; £26,315; £13,157; £7,309; £5,847)

RPR

**1** **Tosen Stardom (JPN)**[13] 7665 6-9-1 **0** ........ (bt) DamianLane 16 113
(Darren Weir, Australia) **9/1**

**2** 1 **Sovereign Nation (AUS)**[13] 7665 5-8-3 **0** ........ BeauMertens 17 99
(David A & B Hayes & Tom Dabernig, Australia) **20/1**

**3** 1 **Petrology (AUS)**[13] 6-8-3 **0** ........ (v) ChrisParnham 13 97
(David A & B Hayes & Tom Dabernig, Australia) **100/1**

**4** hd **Mask Of Time (IRE)**[60] 6053 3-8-3 **0** ........ DanielMoor 1 99
(Hugo Palmer) **90/1**

**5** shd **Seaburge (AUS)**[28] 7174 4-8-9 **0** ........ (p) MarkZahra 12 102
(David A & B Hayes & Tom Dabernig, Australia) **80/1**

**6** nk **Tom Melbourne (IRE)**[14] 7642 6-8-9 **0** ........ GlenBoss 15 101+
(Chris Waller, Australia) **15/2**

**7** ½ **Egg Tart (AUS)**[35] 4-8-6 **0** ........ DamienOliver 9 97
(Chris Waller, Australia) **9/2**[1]

**8** hd **Turnitaround (AUS)**[13] 7-8-8 **0** ........ (tp) BenEThompson 2 99
(Matthew Williams, Australia) **50/1**

**9** shd **Jacquinot Bay (AUS)**[13] 10-8-3 **0** ........ (v) BenAllen 11 93
(David A & B Hayes & Tom Dabernig, Australia) **40/1**

**10** 1 **Wyndspelle (NZ)**[7] 4-8-3 **0** ........ NikitaBeriman 7 91
(Michael Kent, Australia) **25/1**

**11** shd **Omei Sword (AUS)**[21] 4-8-3 **0** ........ StephenBaster 5 91
(Chris Waller, Australia) **13/1**

**12** nk **Mr Sneaky (AUS)**[13] 7665 4-8-4 **0** ........ (bt) DeanYendall 8 91
(Anthony Freedman, Australia) **5/1**[2]

**13** hd **He Or She (AUS)**[21] 7-8-8 **0** ........ (b) DwayneDunn 18 95
(David A & B Hayes & Tom Dabernig, Australia) **100/1**

**14** shd **Snitzson (AUS)**[14] 7642 4-8-3 **0** ........ (t) CoryParish 10 90
(David A & B Hayes & Tom Dabernig, Australia) **30/1**

**15** 2 ¾ **Comin' Through (AUS)**[14] 7642 4-8-6 **0** ........ (vt) MichaelWalker 4 86
(Chris Waller, Australia) **8/1**

**16** shd **Kaspersky (IRE)**[35] 6928 6-8-11 **0** ........ LukeNolen 3 91+
(Jane Chapple-Hyam) **30/1**

**17** 3 ¼ **Theanswermyfriend (AUS)**[13] 7665 4-8-3 **0** ........ (t) MichaelDee 6 76
(Robert Smerdon, Australia) **6/1**[3]

**18** 1 ¼ **I Am A Star (NZ)**[15] 4-8-8 **0** ........ BenMelham 14 78+
(Shane Nichols, Australia) **19/1**

1m 35.86s
**WFA** 3 from 4yo+ 3lb **18** Ran SP% **117.9**
**Owner** Australian Bloodstock No 2 Syndicate, Doonaree Rac **Bred** Northern Racing **Trained** Australia

**FOCUS**
The winner has been rated to his best.

8060 - 8070a (Foreign Racing) - See Raceform Interactive

## 7864 KEENELAND (L-H)

Saturday, October 14

**OFFICIAL GOING: Turf: firm**

### 8071a QUEEN ELIZABETH II CHALLENGE CUP STKS PRESENTED BY LANE'S END (GRADE 1) (3YO FILLIES) (TURF) — 1m 1f (T)

**10:30** 3-Y-O

**£243,902** (£81,300; £40,650; £20,325; £12,195; £1,626)

RPR

1 **La Coronel (USA)**[28] 3-8-9 0 ........ JoseLezcano 6 110
(Mark Casse, Canada) **51/10**[3]

2 ½ **Daddys Lil Darling (USA)**[34] 3-8-9 0 ........ RobbyAlbarado 3 109
(Kenneth McPeek, U.S.A) **19/2**

3 3 ½ **Madam Dancealot (IRE)**[55] 6253 3-8-9 0 ........ JamieTheriot 7 102
(Richard Baltas, U.S.A) **207/10**

4 1 ½ **Uni**[28] 3-8-9 0 ........ IradOrtizJr 9 98
(Chad C Brown, U.S.A) **56/10**

5 nse **Beau Recall (IRE)**[55] 6253 3-8-9 0 ........ JosephTalamo 8 98
(Simon Callaghan, U.S.A) **149/10**

6 1 **New Money Honey (USA)**[56] 6230 3-8-9 0 ........ JavierCastellano 10 96
(Chad C Brown, U.S.A) **13/5**[1]

7 nse **Dream Dancing (USA)**[55] 6253 3-8-9 0 ........ JulienRLeparoux 4 96
(Mark Casse, Canada) **109/10**

8 1 ¾ **Proctor's Ledge (USA)**[56] 3-8-9 0 ........ CoreyJLanerie 2 92
(Brendan P Walsh, U.S.A) **18/5**[2]

9 2 **Con Te Partiro (USA)**[55] 6253 3-8-9 0 ........ MikeESmith 1 88
(Wesley A Ward, U.S.A) **93/10**

10 1 ½ **Unforgetable Filly**[29] 7113 3-8-9 0 ........ JosephineGordon 5 85
(Hugo Palmer) **34/1**

1m 48.99s (-0.81) **10 Ran SP% 122.5**
PARI-MUTUEL (all including 2 usd stake): WIN 12.20; PLACE (1-2) 7.00, 10.40; SHOW (1-2-3) 4.80, 6.80, 8.60; SF 121.00.
**Owner** John C Oxley **Bred** Kim Nardelli, Rodney Nardelli Et Al **Trained** Canada

**FOCUS**
The first two have been rated to their best.

## 7503 GOODWOOD (R-H)

Sunday, October 15

**OFFICIAL GOING: Soft (good to soft in places; 5.9)**
Wind: mild, half-across Weather: cloudy with sunny periods

### 8072 "BEST ODDS GUARANTEED AT 188BET" ALDERBROOK H'CAP — 2m

**2:00** (2:00) (Class 4) (0-80,80) 4-Y-0+ **£6,469** (£1,925; £962; £481) **Stalls** Low

Form RPR

/03- 1 **Song Light**[155] 7625 7-11-4 72 ........ KevinJones 8 86
(Seamus Mullins) *hld up bhd: smooth hdwy 3f out: shkn up to ld over 1f out: sn clr: readily* **10/1**

2223 2 8 **Taper Tantrum (IRE)**[45] 6618 5-11-11 79 ........(p) TrevorWhelan 3 83
(Michael Bell) *led: rdn and hdd over 1f out: kpt on gamely but sn hld by wnr* **8/1**[3]

0420 3 ¾ **Medburn Cutler**[22] 7402 7-11-10 78 ........(p) JamesBest 11 81
(Paul Henderson) *trckd ldrs: rdn to chse ldr 3f out tl over 1f out: styd on same pce* **11/2**[1]

20-5 4 1 ½ **Harry Hunt**[141] 3086 10-11-12 80 ........ KielanWoods 9 81
(Graeme McPherson) *lw; trckd ldrs: disp 2nd over 4f out tl rdn over 3f out: sn one pce* **15/2**[2]

50-6 5 nk **Jack Bear**[37] 6889 6-11-7 75 ........ HarryBannister 5 76
(Harry Whittington) *mid-div: rdn 3f out: no imp tl styd on fnl f: nrly snatched 4th cl home* **11/2**[1]

-500 6 1 ¾ **Wind Place And Sho**[35] 6968 5-11-12 80 ........(p) JackQuinlan 4 79
(James Eustace) *hld up towards rr: rdn 3f out: little imp tl styd on ent fnl f* **16/1**

2105 7 3 ¼ **Fitzwilly**[10] 7766 7-11-0 68 ........ DaveCrosse 7 63
(Mick Channon) *trckd ldr: rdn over 3f out: wknd jst over 1f out* **8/1**[3]

1230 8 6 **Night Generation (GER)**[19] 7490 5-10-8 62 ........(p) DavidNoonan 12 50
(Chris Gordon) *mid-div tl over 3f out* **25/1**

3003 9 10 **Age Of Wisdom (IRE)**[37] 6889 4-11-2 70 ........(p) JamieMoore 2 46
(Gary Moore) *mid-div: hdwy u.p over 3f out: sn chsng ldrs: wknd over 1f out* **11/2**[1]

4463 10 5 **Bamako Du Chatelet (FR)**[31] 7096 6-11-0 68 ........ RobertDunne 6 38
(Ian Williams) *trckd ldrs: rdn over 3f out: wknd over 1f out* **10/1**

-430 11 1 ¼ **Spice Fair**[37] 6889 10-10-13 67 ........ JeremiahMcGrath 13 35
(Mark Usher) *a towards rr: wknd 3f out* **11/1**

3m 43.66s (14.66) **Going Correction** +0.775s/f (Yiel) **11 Ran SP% 116.4**
Speed ratings (Par 105): **94,90,89,88,88 87,86,83,78,75 75**
CSF £86.72 CT £489.29 TOTE £9.60: £3.30, £2.70, £1.60; EX 87.50 Trifecta £530.10.
**Owner** Phoenix Bloodstock & A A Goodman **Bred** D & C Bloodstock **Trained** Wilsford-Cum-Lake, Wilts

**FOCUS**
This fair staying handicap confined to jump jockeys was run at an ordinary gallop that picked up down the hill from the home turn. The winner scored a runaway success. The runner-up has been rated close to form, with the third to his May/June C&D form.

### 8073 HILDON NOVICE AUCTION STKS — 6f

**2:35** (2:35) (Class 5) 2-Y-O **£4,528** (£1,347; £673; £336) **Stalls** High

Form RPR

024 1 **Lady Dancealot (IRE)**[12] 7706 2-8-9 73 ........ SilvestreDeSousa 5 73
(David Elsworth) *mde all: edgd lft 2f out and again over 1f out: kpt on wl and in command fnl f: rdn out* **11/8**[1]

2 2 ¾ **Is It Off (IRE)** 2-9-0 0 ........ KieranShoemark 2 70+
(Gary Moore) *str; s.i.s: in last but in tch: pushed along and hdwy whn swtchd to centre over 2f out: kpt on ins fnl f: wnt 2nd nring fin: no threat to wnr* **14/1**

4224 3 nk **Kimifive (IRE)**[14] 7647 2-9-2 77 ........ EdwardGreatrex 3 71
(Joseph Tuite) *racd keenly: trckd ldrs: rdn to chse wnr wl over 1f out: nt pce to mount chal: no ex whn lost 2nd nring fin* **7/2**[2]

4 nk **Maypole** 2-8-12 0 ........ SeanLevey 6 66
(Richard Hannon) *quite str; ly; lw; trckd wnr tl rdn 2f out: kpt on same pce fnl f* **4/1**[3]

5 5 2 ¼ **Dutch Academy**[22] 7383 2-9-0 0 ........ PJMcDonald 7 61
(K R Burke) *compact; cl up tl outpcd 2f out: kpt on again fnl f but n.d* **8/1**

6 1 ¾ **Jack Taylor (IRE)** 2-9-2 0 ........ ShaneKelly 1 58
(Richard Hughes) *w'like; nt over-big; sltly on toes; hld up but in tch: rdn 2f out: nt pce to get involved* **25/1**

65 7 1 ¼ **Section Onesixsix (IRE)**[30] 7126 2-8-5 0 ........ DavidEgan(3) 4 46
(Mick Channon) *trckd wnr tl rdn over 2f out: wknd over 1f out* **10/1**

1m 15.74s (3.54) **Going Correction** +0.475s/f (Yiel) **7 Ran SP% 115.0**
Speed ratings (Par 95): **95,91,90,90,87 85,83**
CSF £23.43 TOTE £2.20: £1.20, £6.20; EX 25.70 Trifecta £82.20.
**Owner** Kevin Quinn **Bred** P J B O'Callaghan **Trained** Newmarket, Suffolk

**FOCUS**
Those with the most experience set a reasonable standard in this juvenile novice auction and they dominated from the start and set the level. It's been rated around the balance of the winner and third.

### 8074 GOODWOOD RACEHORSE OWNERS GROUP IRISH EBF NURSERY H'CAP — 7f

**3:10** (3:10) (Class 4) (0-85,78) 2-Y-O **£6,469** (£1,925; £962; £481) **Stalls** Low

Form RPR

0401 1 **Zoraya (FR)**[26] 7226 2-9-7 78 ........ RaulDaSilva 7 81
(Paul Cole) *sweating; last pair: hdwy over 2f out: rdn to take narrow advantage ent fnl f: kpt on wl to assert towards fin* **8/1**

1233 2 ¾ **Travelcard (USA)**[30] 7123 2-9-5 76 ........ PJMcDonald 1 77
(Mark Johnston) *led for 1f: trckd ldr: rdn to ld jst ins 2f out: hdd narrowly ent fnl f: kpt on gamely tl no ex towards fin* **11/4**[2]

0400 3 ¾ **Rainbow Jazz (IRE)**[10] 7764 2-8-2 66 ........(v[1]) NicolaCurrie(7) 4 65
(Mark Usher) *plld hrd: sn trcking ldrs: bmpd ins 1st f: swtchd to centre over 3f out: rdn 2f out: kpt on ins fnl f: clsng on 2nd nring fin* **14/1**

000 4 3 ¼ **Ocean Side**[30] 7128 2-8-11 68 ........ TomMarquand 2 59
(Richard Hannon) *sn pushed along in tch: rdn over 2f out: nt pce to get on terms but kpt on ins fnl f: wnt 4th cl home* **10/1**

4042 5 ½ **Royal Household**[24] 7335 2-9-2 76 ........ HollieDoyle(3) 6 65
(Richard Hannon) *on toes; racd keenly: bmpd ins 1st f: led after 1f out: rdn and hdd jst ins fnl 2f: wknd ins fnl f: lost 4th cl home* **5/2**[1]

3564 6 4 ½ **Ann Without An E**[32] 7045 2-9-6 77 ........ SilvestreDeSousa 5 55
(Mick Channon) *s.i.s: in last pair: rdn over 2f out: nvr threatened: wknd fnl f* **10/1**

0513 7 1 **Deadly Accurate**[23] 7353 2-9-7 78 ........ RobertWinston 3 53
(Hughie Morrison) *lw; trckd ldrs: edgd lft ins 1st f and bmpd: rdn over 2f out: wknd ent fnl f* **7/2**[3]

1m 31.87s (4.87) **Going Correction** +0.775s/f (Yiel) **7 Ran SP% 113.4**
Speed ratings (Par 97): **103,102,101,97,97 91,90**
CSF £29.77 TOTE £9.60: £3.80, £1.60; EX 31.40 Trifecta £197.40.
**Owner** The Fairy Story Partnership **Bred** Jedburgh Stud & Deepwood Farm Stud **Trained** Whatcombe, Oxon

**FOCUS**
An ordinary nursery which has been dominated by the Hannon and Channon yards in recent seasons but their runners disappointed here. It's been rated as ordinary form for the level.

### 8075 NICK BROOKS EBF NOVICE STKS (PLUS 10 RACE) — 1m 1f 11y

**3:45** (3:45) (Class 4) 2-Y-O **£4,197** (£4,197; £962; £481) **Stalls** Low

Form RPR

52 1 **Istanbul Sultan (IRE)**[24] 7333 2-9-2 0 ........ JimCrowley 5 76
(William Haggas) *athletic; lw; trckd ldrs: rdn 2f out: led jst ins fnl f: edgd lft: r.o: jnd cl home* **3/1**[2]

1 dht **Loxley (IRE)** 2-9-2 0 ........ WilliamBuick 2 79+
(Charlie Appleby) *leggy; scope; sltly on toes; s.i.s: in last pair tl tk clsr order after 2f: nt clr run bhd ldrs over 2f out tl swtchd lft ent fnl f: rdn and r.o strly: jnd ldr cl home* **5/4**[1]

3 3 1 ½ **Starcaster**[33] 7026 2-9-2 0 ........ RobertWinston 6 76
(Hughie Morrison) *compact; lw; s.i.s: racd keenly in last pair: hdwy 3f out: nt clr run on rails over 2f out tl swtchd lft ent fnl f: kpt on ins fnl f* **9/2**[3]

6 4 1 ¼ **We Know (IRE)**[47] 6553 2-9-2 0 ........(t) SilvestreDeSousa 3 71
(Simon Crisford) *compact; led: rdn over 2f out: hdd jst ins fnl f: no ex* **20/1**

5 ¾ **Racing Country (IRE)** 2-9-2 0 ........ PatCosgrave 1 69
(Saeed bin Suroor) *quite str; lw; trckd ldr: chal over 2f out: sn rdn: wknd jst ins fnl f* **9/1**

6 9 **Perfect Blue (IRE)** 2-9-2 0 ........ PJMcDonald 4 51
(Mark Johnston) *athletic; bit on the leg; trckd ldrs: rdn over 2f out: wknd over 1f out* **9/1**

2m 4.56s (8.26) **Going Correction** +0.775s/f (Yiel) **6 Ran SP% 112.4**
Speed ratings (Par 97): **94,94,92,91,90 82**
WIN: .90 Loxley, 1.90 Istanbul Sultan; PL: 1.10 Loxley, 1.70 Istanbul Sultan; EX: IS&L: 4.50, L&IS: 2.40; CSF: IS&L: 3.59, L&IS 2.60; TF: IS&L&S 13.00, L&IS&S 6.80;.
**Owner** Godolphin **Bred** Godolphin **Trained** Newmarket, Suffolk
**Owner** Simon Munir & Isaac Souede **Bred** B Minde **Trained** Newmarket, Suffolk

**FOCUS**
Some major yards represented in this interesting juvenile novice stakes and it produced a terrific finish and a dead-heat. The runner-up has been rated similar to his pre-race form.

### 8076 "DOWNLOAD THE APP AT 188BET" H'CAP — 1m 3f 218y

**4:20** (4:22) (Class 2) (0-100,100) 3-Y-O+ **£16,172** (£4,812; £2,405; £1,202) **Stalls** High

Form RPR

-502 1 **Teofonic (IRE)**[8] 7817 3-8-8 90 ........ PJMcDonald 5 103
(Mark Johnston) *lw; trckd ldr: led 3f out: rdn clr fnl f: comf* **3/1**[1]

-400 2 7 **Shabbah (IRE)**[22] 7395 4-8-11 87 ........ TedDurcan 3 89
(Sir Michael Stoute) *sweating; led tl over 3f out: rdn to chse ldrs 2f out: sn chsng wnr: drifted rt ent fnl f: styd on same pce and no threat to comfortable wnr* **6/1**

1231 3 3 **Michael's Mount**[15] 7627 4-8-10 86 oh1 ........(b) LukeMorris 1 83
(Ed Dunlop) *trckd ldrs: trckd wnr gng wl 3f out: rdn 2f out: lost 2nd ent fnl f: no ex* **5/1**[3]

4340 4 nk **Tartini (USA)**[115] 3998 3-8-13 95 ........ RobertHavlin 8 92
(John Gosden) *sweating; trckd ldr tl over 3f out: rdn chalng for 2nd sn after: styd on same pce fnl 2f* **9/2**[2]

P543 5 3 ½ **Plutocracy (IRE)**[36] 6952 7-8-11 87 ........(p) KieranShoemark 6 78
(Gary Moore) *mid-div: hdwy 3f out: sn rdn to chse ldrs: hung lft over 1f out: one pce after* **14/1**

0033 6 hd **Jacob Cats**[40] 6779 8-8-10 86 ........(v) SilvestreDeSousa 2 77
(William Knight) *steadily away: in last pair: rdn over 2f out: nvr threatened* **8/1**

1242 7 nk **Machine Learner**[36] 6956 4-9-1 91 ........(v) EdwardGreatrex 7 81
(Joseph Tuite) *hld up last tl 3f out: sn rdn: nvr threatened: wknd over 1f out* **9/2**[2]

00/6 **8** *27* **Aussie Reigns (IRE)**[57] 6214 7-9-10 **100**...................... TimmyMurphy 4 47
(Gary Moore) *hld up: rdn over 2f out: sn wknd: t.o* **33/1**
2m 45.45s (7.05) **Going Correction** +0.775s/f (Yiel)
**WFA** 3 from 4yo+ 6lb **8** Ran SP% **113.0**
Speed ratings (Par 109): **107,102,100,100,97 97,97,79**
CSF £20.81 CT £85.35 TOTE £3.60: £1.50, £1.80, £1.80; EX 21.30 Trifecta £118.90.
**Owner** Kingsley Park 5 **Bred** Floors Farming And Dominic Burke **Trained** Middleham Moor, N Yorks
**FOCUS**
The feature race and a strong middle-distance handicap, but won in emphatic style by the only filly in the race. She looks an improver with more to come. The second has been rated to this year's form.

## 8077 188BET.CO.UK H'CAP 6f
**4:55** (4:57) (Class 3) (0-95,91) 3-Y-O+ **£9,703** (£2,887; £1,443; £721) **Stalls** High

Form RPR
0010 **1** **Pettochside**[8] 7809 8-8-12 **85**.......................................... HollieDoyle(3) 12 93
(John Bridger) *sltly on toes; racd keenly: trckd ldrs: led jst ins fnl f: r.o gamely* **14/1**
615 **2** *nk* **Baron Bolt**[15] 7622 4-9-5 **89**..........................................(p) PJMcDonald 9 96
(Paul Cole) *lw; hld up towards rr: hdwy over 1f out: rdn to press wnr fnl 120yds: kpt on: hld cl home* **5/1**[2]
0623 **3** *1 1/4* **Iseemist (IRE)**[20] 7461 6-8-11 **84**................................(b) DavidEgan(3) 10 87
(John Gallagher) *led: rdn over 1f out: drifted rt and hdd jst ins fnl f: no ex* **8/1**
0003 **4** *1 1/2* **Poet's Princess**[11] 7742 3-8-5 **79**................................ CharlieBennett(3) 3 77
(Hughie Morrison) *lw; prom: rdn 2f out: ch ent fnl f: no ex fnl 120yds* **11/2**[3]
0620 **5** *nk* **Toofi (FR)**[15] 7612 6-8-13 **83**..........................................(p) DanielMuscutt 1 80
(John Butler) *trckd ldrs: rdn 2f out: kpt on same pce fnl f* **13/2**
5321 **6** *1/2* **Clear Spring (IRE)**[11] 7742 9-9-6 **90**.................................... ShaneKelly 2 86
(John Spearing) *mid-div: rdn 2f out: kpt on same pce fnl f* **9/2**[1]
3332 **7** *1 1/2* **Letmestopyouthere (IRE)**[15] 7612 3-8-9 **83**............ MattCosham(3) 11 74
(David Evans) *towards rr: effrt 2f out: nvr threatened to get involved* **8/1**
5003 **8** *1 1/2* **Stellarta**[20] 7455 6-9-2 **86**.................................................... DavidProbert 4 72
(Michael Blanshard) *hld up towards rr: sme prog 2f out: sn rdn: nvr threatened to get involved* **8/1**
0000 **9** *3/4* **Goodwood Crusader (IRE)**[20] 7455 3-9-0 **90**............. FinleyMarsh(5) 8 74
(Richard Hughes) *hung lft u.p over 1f out: a towards rr* **20/1**
6440 **10** *9* **Englishman**[15] 7612 7-8-11 **81**............................................... LukeMorris 5 36
(Milton Bradley) *lw; chsd ldrs: rdn 2f out: sn wknd* **16/1**
0540 **11** *25* **Golden Amber (IRE)**[158] 2518 6-9-6 **90**........................ RobertWinston 6
(Dean Ivory) *outpcd over 2f out: a in rr* **33/1**
1m 13.91s (1.71) **Going Correction** +0.475s/f (Yiel)
**WFA** 3 from 4yo+ 1lb **11** Ran SP% **117.2**
Speed ratings (Par 107): **107,106,104,102,102 101,99,97,96,84 51**
CSF £82.32 CT £466.75 TOTE £17.00: £3.80, £2.00, £3.10; EX 119.10 Trifecta £1057.30.
**Owner** P Cook **Bred** New Hall Stud **Trained** Liphook, Hants
**FOCUS**
A good, competitive sprint handicap but it paid to race close to the pace, as only one got involved from behind. The time was 1.85 secs faster than the earlier juvenile contest. A pb from the winner, with the runner-up rated back to his best.

## 8078 "BET £10 GET £20 AT 188BET" H'CAP 1m
**5:25** (5:27) (Class 4) (0-85,87) 3-Y-O+ **£6,469** (£1,925; £962; £481) **Stalls** Low

Form RPR
2645 **1** **Noble Peace**[22] 7404 4-9-7 **84**............................................ HarryBentley 4 93
(Henry Candy) *trckd ldrs: rdn to ld wl over 1f out: styd on strly and wl in command fnl f* **11/4**[2]
0310 **2** *2 1/2* **Casement (IRE)**[30] 7132 3-9-1 **81**................................ KieranShoemark 3 84
(Roger Charlton) *lw; hld up: hdwy over 2f out: rdn to chse wnr over 1f out: kpt on but nvr threatened to get on terms* **2/1**[1]
4316 **3** *6* **Red Royalist**[23] 7358 3-8-10 **76**.........................................(p) MartinDwyer 8 65
(Marcus Tregoning) *trckd ldrs: rdn over 2f out: styd on wout pce to get on terms: wnt 3rd ins fnl f* **9/2**[3]
0566 **4** *1 3/4* **Ice Slice (IRE)**[29] 7140 6-9-10 **87**............................................ RyanTate 9 72
(James Eustace) *pressed ldr: rdn to ld briefly 2f out: sn hld: no ex whn lost 3rd fnl f* **8/1**
6000 **5** *2 1/2* **Medburn Dream**[17] 7549 4-9-9 **86**..................................... SteveDrowne 2 66
(Paul Henderson) *led at decent pce: rdn and hdd 2f out: sn wknd* **20/1**
4103 **6** *5* **Wannabe Friends**[22] 7404 4-9-3 **80**..................................... ShaneKelly 5 48
(Richard Hughes) *hld up: effrt 2f out: nvr threatened: wknd fnl f* **7/1**
0-30 **7** *9* **Nonios (IRE)**[23] 7358 5-9-7 **84**..........................................(h) SeanLevey 1 31
(David Simcock) *hld up: rdn 2f out: nvr threatened: wknd fnl f* **10/1**
1m 43.17s (3.27) **Going Correction** +0.775s/f (Yiel)
**WFA** 3 from 4yo+ 3lb **7** Ran SP% **115.6**
Speed ratings (Par 105): **114,111,105,103,101 96,87**
CSF £8.92 CT £22.91 TOTE £3.30: £2.10, £2.10; EX 10.90 Trifecta £47.60.
**Owner** One Too Many & Candy **Bred** The Pocock Family **Trained** Kingston Warren, Oxon
**FOCUS**
Another decent handicap although weakened by the late withdrawal of one of the market leaders. They finished well strung out behind the clear-cut winner. The winner has been rated to his best.
T/Plt: £138.90 to a £1 stake. Pool: £97,869.64 - 514.36 winning units T/Qpdt: £17.80 to a £1 stake. Pool: £8,349.95 - 346.97 winning units **Tim Mitchell**

8079 - 8081a (Foreign Racing) - See Raceform Interactive

# [7745]NAAS (L-H)
Sunday, October 15

**OFFICIAL GOING: Soft**

## 8082a FORAN EQUINE IRISH EBF AUCTION RACE FINAL (PLUS 10 RACE) 7f
**3:00** (3:03) 2-Y-O
**£60,512** (£19,487; £9,230; £4,102; £2,051; £1,025)

RPR
**1** **Yulong Gold Fairy**[70] 5687 2-8-10 0.................................... PatSmullen 8 102+
(D K Weld, Ire) *chsd ldrs: 5th 1/2-way: edgd rt over 2f out and sn wnt 2nd gng best: rdn to ld over 1f out and extended advantage ins fnl f: styd on wl: easily* **9/4**[1]
**2** *6* **Quizical (IRE)**[34] 7010 2-9-1 90........................................ RonanWhelan 1 91
(Ms Sheila Lavery, Ire) *led and disp: narrow advantage fr 3f out: rdn and hdd over 1f out: sn no imp on easy wnr and kpt on same pce ins fnl f* **5/1**[2]
**3** *2 3/4* **Red Persian (IRE)**[11] 7747 2-9-1 87................................(v) ChrisHayes 5 83
(P J Prendergast, Ire) *hld up: mid-div bef 1/2-way: rdn into 4th over 1f out where no imp on ldrs: kpt on same pce in 3rd wl ins fnl f: nt trble easy wnr* **22/1**
**4** *2 1/4* **Apple Anni (IRE)**[21] 7423 2-8-12 77........................................ JFEgan 3 74
(Mick Channon) *chsd ldrs: 4th 1/2-way: rdn under 3f out and no imp on ldrs u.p disputing 5th 1 1/2f out: kpt on one pce in 4th wl ins fnl f* **20/1**
**5** *1/2* **Powersville (IRE)**[21] 7423 2-8-10 82............................... NGMcCullagh 6 71
(Thomas Mullins, Ire) *mid-div: rdn over 2f out and sme hdwy u.p ins fnl f to snatch 5th fnl stridesn: nvr trbld ldrs* **20/1**
**6** *hd* **The Broghie Man**[21] 7423 2-8-11 77........................(b[1]) KevinManning 16 71
(Brendan W Duke, Ire) *mid-div: rdn over 2f out and sme hdwy u.p into 5th wl ins fnl f: denied 5th fnl strides: nvr trbld ldrs* **11/1**
**7** *hd* **Captain Vancouver (FR)**[58] 6163 2-8-11 0...............(p[1]) LeighRoche 12 71
(M D O'Callaghan, Ire) *chsd ldrs early: 6th 1/2-way: rdn under 3f out and no imp on ldrs in 9th 1f out: kpt on one pce ins fnl f* **8/1**
**7** *dht* **Lisard Lady (IRE)**[79] 5386 2-8-10 0.............................. WayneLordan 11 70
(Thomas Cooper, Ire) *hld up towards rr: rdn under 2f out where short of room briefly: r.o u.p ins fnl f: nvr nrr* **12/1**
**9** *1 1/4* **Vocal Music (IRE)**[37] 6907 2-8-13 73................................ RoryCleary 9 69
(J S Bolger, Ire) *chsd ldrs: 3rd 1/2-way: rdn under 3f out and no imp on ldrs under 2f out: sn wknd* **33/1**
**10** *nk* **Beach Wedding (IRE)**[37] 6907 2-8-12 74................ ColmO'Donoghue 7 68
(J P Murtagh, Ire) *hld up towards rr: racd keenly early: sme hdwy after 1/2-way: rdn in 6th 2f out and no ex over 1f out: one pce after* **12/1**
**11** *1/2* **Burmese Blazer (IRE)**[25] 7288 2-8-11 0........................... GaryCarroll 14 65
(G M Lyons, Ire) *dwlt: settled in rr: pushed along and sme hdwy fr 2f out: nt clr run ins fnl f and sn eased* **33/1**
**12** *2 3/4* **Verhoyen**[7] 7855 2-8-11 82..........................................................(p[1]) WJLee 4 58
(M C Grassick, Ire) *mid-div best: pushed along and no imp 2f out: wknd fnl f* **16/1**
**13** *nk* **Sollertia (IRE)**[25] 7290 2-9-2 0.................................... SeamieHeffernan 2 62
(Tracey Collins, Ire) *led and disp: pushed along in cl 2nd fr 3f out and no ex under 2f out: sn wknd* **33/1**
**14** *11* **Cocohulababy (IRE)**[16] 7586 2-8-10 85.....................(h[1]) ShaneFoley 15 26
(Noel Meade, Ire) *mid-div best: rdn and no imp towards rr after 1/2-way: eased ins fnl f* **16/1**
**15** *2 1/4* **Spiorad Saoirse**[21] 7423 2-9-5 83.......................... DeclanMcDonogh 10 29
(Andrew Slattery, Ire) *chsd ldrs early tl sn settled in rr of mid-div after 1f where checked sltly: pushed along and no imp over 2f out: eased towards rr ins fnl f* **33/1**
**16** *7 1/2* **Ball Girl (IRE)**[21] 7421 2-8-10 92........................................ ColinKeane 13
(G M Lyons, Ire) *disp early tl settled settled bhd ldrs: 5th 1/2-way: pushed along over 2f out and sn wknd: eased ins fnl f* **6/1**[3]
1m 31.18s (3.68) **16** Ran SP% **134.0**
CSF £12.60 TOTE £3.50: £1.70, £1.90, £7.10; DF 17.10 Trifecta £294.10.
**Owner** Zhang Yuesheng **Bred** Lady Fairhaven **Trained** Curragh, Co Kildare
**FOCUS**
An emphatic winner in what had looked a competitive affair. Pat Smullen answered Colin Keane's victory in the previous race, taking the deficit back to five winners in the jockeys' championship. The form makes sense in behind the winner.

## 8083a CLODOVIL IRISH EBF GARNET STKS (LISTED RACE) (F&M) 1m
**3:35** (3:36) 3-Y-O+
**£28,995** (£9,337; £4,423; £1,965; £982; £491)

RPR
**1** **Elegant Pose (IRE)**[60] 6080 3-9-0 99................................ ColinKeane 7 104+
(G M Lyons, Ire) *mid-div: hdwy to chse ldrs over 1f out: rdn and r.o wl in 5th ins fnl f to ld fnl stride* **9/4**[1]
**2** *shd* **Making Light (IRE)**[49] 6490 3-9-0 101.............................. PatSmullen 9 104
(D K Weld, Ire) *chsd ldrs: 4th 1/2-way: gd hdwy over 2f out to chal in 2nd: led 1 1/2f out: sn rdn and extended advantage: all out nr fin where strly pressed and hdd fnl stride: jst denied* **3/1**[2]
**3** *3/4* **I'm So Fancy (IRE)**[14] 7663 3-9-0 104..................... ColmO'Donoghue 3 102
(Mrs John Harrington, Ire) *chsd ldrs: 6th 1/2-way: rdn under 2f out and tk clsr order in 3rd over 1f out: r.o to press ldr in 2nd nr fin: dropped to 3rd cl home* **13/2**[3]
**4** *3 1/2* **Panstarr**[25] 7295 3-9-0 92.................................................. KevinManning 2 94
(J S Bolger, Ire) *sn led: rdn over 2f out and hdd u.p 1 1/2f out: sn no imp on ldr and wknd into 4th wl ins fnl f* **8/1**
**5** *2 1/2* **Pavlenko (JPN)**[26] 7261 3-9-0 93............................ DonnachaO'Brien 14 89
(A P O'Brien, Ire) *mid-div: sme hdwy to chse ldrs in 5th wl ins fnl f: kpt on clsng stages: nvr trbld ldrs* **20/1**
**6** *1 1/2* **Perle De La Mer (IRE)**[14] 7662 3-9-0 89................................(h) WJLee 8 85
(W McCreery, Ire) *disp early tl sn settled bhd ldr: 2nd 1/2-way: rdn bhd ldrs 2f out and no ex over 1f out: wknd* **40/1**
**7** *1 1/4* **Petticoat**[90] 4986 3-9-0 91................................................... ConorHoban 4 82
(M Halford, Ire) *in tch: pushed along and no imp under 2f out: one pce after* **12/1**
**8** *nk* **Sister Blandina (IRE)**[14] 7662 4-9-3 94........................(v) ShaneFoley 11 81
(J P Murtagh, Ire) *sn chsd ldrs: 5th 1/2-way: rdn 2f out and no imp on ldrs over 1f out: one pce after* **16/1**
**9** *2* **Stormy Belle (IRE)**[36] 6961 3-9-0 91................................ LeighRoche 6 77
(P A Fahy, Ire) *settled towards rr: 13th 1/2-way: pushed along over 2f out and kpt on one pce* **33/1**
**10** *1* **Pocketfullofdreams (FR)**[29] 7171 3-9-0 94.........(t[1]) SeamieHeffernan 1 75
(A P O'Brien, Ire) *chsd ldrs: 3rd 1/2-way: rdn over 2f out and sn wknd* **16/1**
**11** *1/2* **Tobacco Bay (IRE)**[14] 7663 3-9-0 91.......................... NGMcCullagh 13 73
(J P Murtagh, Ire) *hld up: 11th 1/2-way: rdn and no imp 2f out* **50/1**
**12** *3 1/2* **Secret Existence (IRE)**[25] 7295 4-9-3 87........................ GaryHalpin 12 65
(John James Feane, Ire) *hld up in rr: last at 1/2-way: rdn and no imp over 2f out* **40/1**
**13** *2* **Smoulder**[30] 7113 3-9-0 93..........................................(h) WayneLordan 10 61
(A P O'Brien, Ire) *towards rr: 12th 1/2-way: rdn and no imp over 2f out* **16/1**
**14** *27* **Old Time Waltz (USA)**[81] 5308 3-9-0 84..........................(bt) PBBeggy 5
(A P O'Brien, Ire) *settled in mid-div: pushed along in 7th fr 1/2-way and sn no ex u.p: wknd over 2f out* **50/1**
1m 45.17s (5.17)
**WFA** 3 from 4yo 3lb **14** Ran SP% **122.1**
CSF £8.17 TOTE £2.90: £1.10, £1.30, £2.30; DF 10.80 Trifecta £33.30.
**Owner** Anamoine Limited **Bred** Windflower Overseas Holdings Inc **Trained** Dunsany, Co Meath

**FOCUS**
The first three in the market (three highest-rated runners) drew well clear of the remainder in a contest which culminated in a thrilling duel between Colin Keane and Pat Smullen. The standard is set around the second, third and fourth.

8084 - 8085a (Foreign Racing) - See Raceform Interactive

## 8086a ANJAAL IRISH EBF BLUEBELL STKS (LISTED RACE) 1m 4f
5:20 (5:23) 3-Y-0+

**£28,995** (£9,337; £4,423; £1,474; £1,471; £491)

RPR

1 **Red Stars (IRE)**[8] 7837 4-9-6 97..........................(h) DeclanMcDonogh 2 91
(John M Oxx, Ire) *sn led tl jnd after 1/2-way: hdd narrowly appr st: rdn 2f out and u.p in 2nd ent fnl f: rallied and r.o again to ld clsng stages* **9/1**

2 ½ **Tilly's Chilli (IRE)**[36] 6956 3-9-0 87.......................... ColmO'Donoghue 1 91
(Mrs John Harrington, Ire) *prom tl sn settled bhd ldr for most: disp ld after 1/2-way: narrow ld bef st: rdn 2f out and over 1 l clr ins fnl f: reduced advantage and hdd clsng stages: jst hld on for 2nd* **20/1**

3 shd **Dew Line (IRE)**[26] 7261 5-9-6 94.......................... GaryCarroll 10 90+
(Michael Mulvany, Ire) *chsd ldrs tl wnt 2nd briefly: 3rd 1/2-way: rdn over 2f out and no imp on ldr ent fnl f: kpt on u.p wl ins fnl f: jst failed for 2nd* **28/1**

4 shd **Detailed (IRE)**[8] 7837 3-9-3 101.......................... DonnachaO'Brien 9 94+
(Joseph Patrick O'Brien, Ire) *mid-div: sme hdwy on outer over 3f out: rdn into 4th 1 1/2f out and no imp on ldr ent fnl f: kpt on u.p wl ins fnl f: nrst fin and jnd for 4th* **2/1**[1]

4 dht **Bound (IRE)**[26] 7263 3-9-0 92.......................... WayneLordan 11 91+
(A P O'Brien, Ire) *hld up towards rr: sme hdwy under 3f out: no imp on ldrs in 7th 1 1/2f out: kpt on u.p wl ins fnl f to dead heat for 4th: nrst fin* **7/1**[3]

6 shd **Jeremys Joy (IRE)**[26] 7261 5-9-6 87.......................... RobbieDowney 12 90+
(Keith Henry Clarke, Ire) *hld up in mid-div: rdn 2f out and u.p in 8th 1 1/2f out: r.o wl ins fnl f: nrst fin* **50/1**

7 1½ **High Language (IRE)**[51] 6407 3-9-0 81.......................... MichaelHussey 6 88
(Joseph Patrick O'Brien, Ire) *mid-div: hdwy to chse ldrs 2f out: sn rdn in 5th and no imp on ldrs ins fnl f where hmpd between horses: no imp after and wknd into 7th* **33/1**

8 2½ **Lovemenot (IRE)**[102] 4515 3-9-0 79.......................... WJLee 5 84
(W McCreery, Ire) *chsd ldrs: 4th 1/2-way: pushed along bhd ldrs 3f out and no ex u.p under 2f out: sn wknd* **33/1**

9 13 **Longing (IRE)**[19] 7501 3-9-0 88.......................... SeamieHeffernan 14 64
(A P O'Brien, Ire) *in tch: pushed along disputing 7th under 4f out and no imp on ldrs into st: mod 9th 1 1/2f out* **9/4**[2]

10 ¾ **Tara Dylan (IRE)**[7] 7860 5-9-6 85..........................(t) NGMcCullagh 13 61
(Thomas Mullins, Ire) *dwlt and settled in rr: sme hdwy into mod 11th under 2f out: nvr involved* **50/1**

11 2 **Jet Streaming (IRE)**[16] 7577 3-9-0 92..........................(t) ColinKeane 15 59
(Adrian Paul Keatley, Ire) *chsd ldrs: 5th 1/2-way: pushed along in 5th over 3f out and sn wknd* **7/1**[3]

12 39 **Cirin Toinne (IRE)**[63] 5976 4-9-6 90..........................(t) KevinManning 8
(J S Bolger, Ire) *chsd ldrs: rdn in 6th under 4f out and sn wknd: eased over 1f out* **33/1**

13 1 **Remarkable Lady (IRE)**[26] 7261 4-9-6 97..........................(tp) PatSmullen 7
(H Rogers, Ire) *w.w: rdn in 9th under 4f out and sn wknd: eased over 1f out* **12/1**

14 39 **Love Potion (IRE)**[154] 2658 4-9-6 88..........................(t[1]) PBBeggy 3
(A P O'Brien, Ire) *hld up in tch: disp 6th at 1/2-way: pushed along over 4f out and sn wknd: eased over 1f out* **25/1**

2m 47.6s
**WFA** 3 from 4yo+ 6lb **14** Ran SP% **131.6**
Tote Aggregate: 2017: 314,407.00 - 2016: 411,905.00 CSF £185.86 TOTE £9.20: £2.00, £5.50, £9.50; DF 195.00 Trifecta £3333.30.
**Owner** Newtown Anner Stud Farm Ltd **Bred** Mr Maurice Regan **Trained** Currabeg, Co Kildare
■ Stewards' Enquiry : Robbie Downey one day ban: using his whip with excessive frequency
Gary Carroll two-day ban; excessive use of whip (tba)
Declan McDonogh caution; use of whip
Colm O'Donoghue two-day ban; excessive use of whip (tba)

**FOCUS**
Not a strong Listed race on paper, and they finished in a heap behind a 97-rated filly winning for the second time at this level. The standard is set around the second to the eighth.
T/Jkpt: @492.43. Pool: @703.46 T/Plt: @78.40. Pool: @25,568.78 **Brian Fleming**

# 7969 CHANTILLY (R-H)
Sunday, October 15

**OFFICIAL GOING: Polytrack: standard; turf: soft**

## 8087a PRIX DU CONSEIL DE PARIS (GROUP 2) (3YO+) (TURF) 1m 4f
1:35 3-Y-0+ **£63,333** (£24,444; £11,666; £7,777)

RPR

1 **Traffic Jam (IRE)**[35] 6981 4-8-13 0.......................... StephanePasquier 2 110+
(N Clement, France) *mde all: rdn 2 1/2f out: drvn 1 1/2f out: kpt on strly* **31/10**[3]

2 1 **Akihiro (JPN)**[32] 7068 3-8-9 0.......................... MaximeGuyon 1 111+
(A Fabre, France) *in tch in 3rd: chsd ldr under 5f out: rdn 2f out: kpt on wl: nt pce to chal wnr fnl f* **8/5**[2]

3 2½ **One Foot In Heaven (IRE)**[14] 7668 5-9-2 0....... ChristopheSoumillon 3 107+
(A De Royer-Dupre, France) *bmpd leaving stalls: hld up in rr: rdn and effrt 2f out: no ex ins fnl f* **6/5**[1]

4 1¼ **Soleil Marin (IRE)**[15] 7634 3-8-11 0.......................... MickaelBarzalona 4 107+
(A Fabre, France) *chsd ldr: dropped to 3rd under 5f out: rdn 2 1/2f out: wknd steadily fr over 1f out* **71/10**

2m 32.13s (1.13)
**WFA** 3 from 4yo+ 6lb **4** Ran SP% **120.7**
PARI-MUTUEL (all including 1 euro stake): WIN 4.10; PLACE 1.60, 1.20, 2.90; DF 9.50;.
**Owner** Alexis Adamian **Bred** Lynch Bages Ltd **Trained** Chantilly, France

## 8088a PRIX CASIMIR DELAMARRE - FONDS EUROPEEN DE L'ELEVAGE (LISTED RACE) (3YO+ FILLIES & MARES) (TURF) 1m 1f
2:45 3-Y-0+ **£22,222** (£8,888; £6,666; £4,444; £2,222)

RPR

1 **Crystal River**[40] 6782 3-8-11 0.......................... MaximeGuyon 7 106+
(William Haggas) *wl into stride: keen early: settled bhd ldrs: hdwy over 2f out: jnd ldrs over 1f out: rdn to ld and styd on wl ins fnl f* **68/10**

2 1½ **Garance (FR)**[36] 6962 3-8-11 0.......................... ChristopheSoumillon 5 102
(J-C Rouget, France) **26/5**

3 1½ **Folie De Louise (FR)**[26] 3-8-11 0.......................... TonyPiccone 1 99
(Carmen Bocskai, Germany) **41/10**[1]

4 shd **Thank You Bye Bye (FR)**[44] 6665 5-9-1 0.......................... MickaelForest 11 98
(J-P Gauvin, France) **7/1**

5 ¾ **Penny Lane (GER)**[36] 6962 3-8-11 0.......................... Pierre-CharlesBoudot 6 97
(F-H Graffard, France) **23/5**[3]

6 hd **Maimara (FR)**[84] 5197 5-9-1 0..........................(b) GregoryBenoist 3 96
(M Delzangles, France) **189/10**

7 1¼ **Terre (FR)**[36] 6962 3-8-11 0.......................... AurelienLemaitre 10 94
(F Head, France) **138/10**

8 6 **Diamond Daisy (GER)**[28] 7204 4-9-1 0.......................... EddyHardouin 4 80
(Ferdinand J Leve, Germany) **39/1**

9 2½ **Innevera (FR)**[53] 3-8-11 0.......................... OlivierPeslier 9 76
(C Laffon-Parias, France) **9/2**[2]

10 1 **Guiliana (FR)**[42] 3-8-11 0..........................(p) AlexisBadel 8 74
(Waldemar Hickst, Germany) **39/1**

11 dist **Kanji (GER)**[148] 3-8-11 0.......................... VincentCheminaud 2
(Waldemar Hickst, Germany) **231/10**

1m 48.42s (-2.68)
**WFA** 3 from 4yo+ 4lb **11** Ran SP% **118.0**
PARI-MUTUEL (all including 1 euro stake): WIN 7.80; PLACE 2.80, 2.00, 1.70; DF 26.20 SF 41.60.
**Owner** Somerville Lodge Limited **Bred** Darley **Trained** Newmarket, Suffolk

**FOCUS**
The second, fourth and sixth help set the standard.

## 8089a PRIX DU RANELAGH (LISTED RACE) (3YO+) (TURF) 1m
3:25 3-Y-0+ **£22,222** (£8,888; £6,666; £4,444; £2,222)

RPR

1 **Stormy Antarctic**[75] 5502 4-9-7 0.......................... ChristopheSoumillon 2 115+
(Ed Walker) *settled 3rd: hdwy to join ldr over 1f out: rdn to ld: styd on strly ins fnl f: comf* **6/4**[1]

2 4 **Blessed Silence (FR)**[63] 5979 4-8-13 0.......................... MickaelBarzalona 6 98
(J-M Beguigne, France) **5/2**[2]

3 2 **Skalleto (FR)**[16] 3-8-13 0.......................... AnthonyCrastus 3 96
(P Sogorb, France) **118/10**

4 snk **Instant De Reve (FR)**[10] 4-9-2 0.......................... ThierryThulliez 4 96
(Mme C Barande-Barbe, France) **49/10**[3]

5 ½ **Grand Vintage (FR)**[22] 7416 8-9-2 0.......................... StephanePasquier 8 95
(A Schutz, France) **162/10**

6 6 **Lbretha (FR)**[43] 6697 4-9-2 0.......................... GregoryBenoist 5 81
(F-H Graffard, France) **7/1**

7 snk **Flemish Duchesse (FR)**[28] 7204 4-9-2 0.......................... OlivierPeslier 1 81
(Andreas Suborics, Germany) **171/10**

8 5½ **Intendantin (GER)**[56] 6254 4-8-13 0.......................... EddyHardouin 7 65
(Ferdinand J Leve, Germany) **71/1**

1m 36.39s (-1.61)
**WFA** 3 from 4yo+ 3lb **8** Ran SP% **118.6**
PARI-MUTUEL (all including 1 euro stake): WIN 2.50; PLACE 1.40, 1.40, 2.30; DF 3.70 SF 6.90.
**Owner** P K Siu **Bred** East Bloodstock Ltd **Trained** Upper Lambourn, Berks

# 7429 COLOGNE (R-H)
Sunday, October 15

**OFFICIAL GOING: Turf: soft**

## 8090a KOLNER STEHER CUP DER PFERDEKLINIK BURG (LISTED RACE) (3YO+) (TURF) 1m 7f
1:35 3-Y-0+ **£11,965** (£5,555; £2,564; £1,282)

RPR

1 **Renfrew Street**[18] 7507 4-8-13 0.......................... JoeFanning 1 99
(Mark Johnston) *wl into stride: sn led: hdd after 4f: remained cl up: regained ld over 3f out: qckn over 2f out: rdn 1f out: styd on u.p ins fnl f* **3/1**[2]

2 ¾ **Adler (GER)**[184] 3-8-8 0.......................... MartinSeidl 3 103
(Markus Klug, Germany) **148/10**

3 1¼ **Moonshiner (GER)**[28] 7203 4-9-4 0..........................(b) FilipMinarik 10 102
(Jean-Pierre Carvalho, Germany) **9/10**[1]

4 3¾ **Iraklion (GER)**[93] 4879 5-9-2 0.......................... BauyrzhanMurzabayev 2 95
(Christian Sprengel, Germany) **109/10**

5 ¾ **Par Coeur (GER)** 3-8-8 0.......................... LukasDelozier 6 96
(W Mongil, Germany) **243/10**

6 10 **Kashmar (GER)**[14] 7687 4-9-1 0.......................... JackMitchell 9 81
(Werner Glanz, Germany) **39/1**

7 21 **Golden Gazelle (IRE)**[43] 4-8-13 0.......................... DennisSchiergen 5 54
(P Schiergen, Germany) **179/10**

8 7 **Sexy Juke (GER)** 3-8-5 0.......................... AndreBest 7 48
(P Schiergen, Germany) **168/10**

9 7½ **Shadow Sadness (GER)**[21] 5-9-2 0.......................... AdriedeVries 4 40
(C Von Der Recke, Germany) **59/10**[3]

10 2½ **Super Ridge (FR)**[402] 4-9-2 0..........................(b) JozefBojko 8 37
(J D Hillis, Germany) **37/1**

11 25 **Greta (FR)**[14] 7673 4-8-13 0..........................(b) MaximPecheur 11 4
(Frau Erika Mader, Germany) **38/1**

PARI-MUTUEL (all including 10 euro stake): WIN 40 PLACE: 14, 22, 11 SF: 497.
**Owner** Douglas Livingston Racing **Bred** D Curran **Trained** Middleham Moor, N Yorks

## 8091a PREIS DES WINTERFAVORITEN (GROUP 3) (2YO) (TURF) 1m
3:10 2-Y-0 **£72,649** (£26,495; £17,521; £8,803; £4,700; £2,307)

RPR

1 **Erasmus (GER)** 2-9-2 0.......................... AdriedeVries 2
(Markus Klug, Germany) *w ldr: led 3f out: rdn 2f out: sn drew wl clr: pushed out* **19/10**[2]

2 8 **Salve Del Rio (IRE)** 2-9-2 0.......................... MichaelCadeddu 6
(Jean-Pierre Carvalho, Germany) *in tch in midfield: rdn under 3f out: drvn under 2f out: kpt on to go 2nd 100yds out: no ch w clr wnr* **186/10**

3 1 1/4 **Wild Max (GER)** 2-9-2 0 EduardoPedroza 7
(A Wohler, Germany) *led: rdn and hdd 3f out: outpcd by clr wnr 2f out: lost 2nd 100yds out: no ex clsng stages* **8/5**[1]

4 3 1/2 **Pathfinder (GER)** 2-9-2 0 MaximPecheur 9
(K Demme, Germany) *chsd ldrs: rdn 2 1/2f out: outpcd under 2f out: kpt on steadily* **138/10**

5 3 1/2 **Ancient Spirit (GER)** 2-9-2 0 FilipMinarik 8
(Jean-Pierre Carvalho, Germany) *t.k.h: towards rr: rdn 3f out: plugged on fr 1 1/2f out: n.d* **36/5**

6 1/2 **Tenger (IRE)** 2-9-2 0 AndreasHelfenbein 5
(M G Mintchev, Germany) *hld up towards rr: wd into st: rdn and outpcd 3f out: sme late hdwy: nvr a factor* **66/10**[3]

7 1/2 **Theo (GER)**[35] 6986 2-9-2 0 MarcLerner 4
(Waldemar Hickst, Germany) *hld up towards rr: slipped 3f out: sn rdn and no imp* **208/10**

8 9 **Ernesto (GER)**[35] 6986 2-9-2 0 MartinSeidl 1
(Markus Klug, Germany) *midfield: rdn 3f out: wknd under 2f out* **103/10**

9 3 1/4 **Zargun (GER)** 2-9-2 0 JackMitchell 3
(A Wohler, Germany) *midfield: rdn 3f out: wknd over 1f out* **154/10**

1m 39.37s (0.98) **9** Ran SP% **129.7**
PARI-MUTUEL (all including 10 euro stake): WIN 29 PLACE: 13, 26, 14 SF: 659.
**Owner** Gestut Rottgen **Bred** Gestut Rottgen **Trained** Germany

8092 - 8093a (Foreign Racing) - See Raceform Interactive

## 7441 SAN SIRO (R-H)
Sunday, October 15

**OFFICIAL GOING: Turf: good**

### 8094a PRIX DORMELLO (GROUP 3) (2YO FILLIES) (TURF) 1m
**2:50** 2-Y-O **£58,974** (£25,948; £14,153; £7,076)

RPR

1 **Sweet Gentle Kiss (IRE)**[21] 2-8-11 0 DarioVargiu 4
(Stefano Botti, Italy) *mde all: rdn 1 1/2f out: drvn whn pressed last 100yds: hld on wl* **29/20**[2]

2 1/2 **Binti Al Nar (GER)**[49] 6494 2-8-11 0 FabioBranca 3
(P Schiergen, Germany) *chsd ldr: rdn over 2f out: drvn over 1f out: kpt on wl to press wnr last 100yds: a hld* **10/11**[1]

3 2 3/4 **Dancer Cross**[21] 2-8-11 0 CarloFiocchi 5
(Stefano Botti, Italy) *in tch in midfield: rdn 2 1/2f out: kpt on fnl f: no imp on front pair* **87/20**[3]

4 3/4 **Isole Canarie (IRE)**[28] 2-8-11 0 SamueleDiana 2
(Melania Cascione, Italy) *hld up towards rr: rdn and gd hdwy appr 2f out: wknd steadily ins fnl f* **97/10**

5 2 1/2 **Key Master (IRE)** 2-8-11 0 SilvanoMulas 1
(R Biondi, Italy) *hld up towards rr of midfield: tk clsr order appr 2f out: sn rdn: wknd over 1f out* **198/10**

6 1 3/4 **Intello Kiss**[28] 2-8-11 0 CristianDemuro 6
(Stefano Botti, Italy) *hld up towards rr: hdwy on outer fr under 3f out rdn and effrt 2f out: wknd fnl f* **87/20**[3]

7 18 **Briateke (FR)**[34] 2-8-11 0 PierantonioConvertino 7
(Antonio Marcialis, Italy) *trckd ldrs: rdn and lost pl under 3f out: sn struggling: eased under 2f out* **197/10**

1m 37.1s (-5.00) **7** Ran SP% **149.6**
PARI-MUTUEL (all including 1 euro stake): WIN 2.47 PLACE 1.29, 2.16 DF 2.17.
**Owner** Scuderia New Age Srl **Bred** Allevamento Deni Srl **Trained** Italy

### 8095a PREMIO DEL PIAZZALE M ENRICO CAMICI (GROUP 3) (3YO+) (TURF) 1m 1f
**4:00** 3-Y-O+ **£27,777** (£12,222; £6,666; £3,333)

RPR

1 **Anda Muchacho (IRE)**[22] 3-8-11 0 DarioVargiu 4 110
(Nicolo Simondi, Italy) *chsd ldr: pushed along over 2f out: rdn to ld narrowly over 1f out: drvn to assert last 100yds: comf* **4/6**[1]

2 1 1/4 **Voice Of Love (IRE)**[119] 4-9-1 0 CristianDemuro 1 106
(Stefano Botti, Italy) *led: rdn under 2f out: hdd over 1f out: pressed ldr tl no ex last 100yds* **49/20**[2]

3 2 **Red Label (IRE)**[68] 5775 3-8-9 0 FabioBranca 2 101
(Marco Botti) *midfield: rdn to go 3rd 2f out: kpt on: nt pce of front pair* **19/4**[3]

4 4 **Together Again**[22] 3-8-9 0 SilvanoMulas 3 93
(Stefano Botti, Italy) *towards rr of midfield: rdn and kpt on same pce fr over 2f out* **49/20**[2]

5 1 3/4 **Father Frost (IRE)**[81] 5312 5-8-13 0 PierantonioConvertino 7 88
(Josef Vana, Czech Republic) *t.k.h in rr: rdn 2 1/2f out: kpt on steadily fr 1 1/2f out: n.d* **147/10**

6 4 **Dulciboy**[167] 2245 3-8-9 0 CarloFiocchi 5 81
(Stefano Botti, Italy) *trckd ldrs: rdn and wknd qckly under 2f out: eased ins fnl f* **156/10**

7 1 **Diplomat (GER)**[42] 6746 6-8-13 0 AlexanderPietsch 6 78
(Mario Hofer, Germany) *a towards rr* **8/1**

1m 50.1s (-7.80)
**WFA** 3 from 4yo+ 4lb **7** Ran SP% **158.9**
PARI-MUTUEL (all including 1 euro stake): WIN 1.66 PLACE 1.18, 1.39 DF 2.29.
**Owner** Scuderia Incolinx & Diego Romeo **Bred** Thomas Hassett **Trained** Italy

### 8096a PREMIO VERZIERE MEMORIAL ALDO CIRLA (GROUP 3) (3YO+ FILLIES & MARES) (TURF) 1m 2f
**4:40** 3-Y-O+ **£29,914** (£13,162; £7,179; £3,589)

RPR

1 **Distain**[43] 6710 5-9-0 0 CristianDemuro 5 97+
(Frau S Steinberg, Germany) *chsd clr ldr: rdn under 3f out: styd on fr 1 1/2f out: reeled in tired ldr 100yds out: sn in command* **87/100**[1]

2 2 1/2 **Alambra (IRE)**[14] 3-8-9 0 PierantonioConvertino 3 92+
(Stefano Botti, Italy) *dwlt: rcvrd qckly and led: sn wl clr: pushed along 2f out: rdn and began to tire appr fnl f: hdd 100yds out: plugged on gamely* **19/1**

3 1 1/4 **Lorenzetta (IRE)**[21] 7441 5-9-0 0 ClaudioColombi 1 90
(Riccardo Santini, Italy) *hld up in rr gp: rdn 3f out: kpt on fr 1 1/2f out: nrst fin* **59/10**[3]

4 2 1/2 **Zattera (IRE)**[119] 4-9-0 0 LucaManiezzi 2 85
(Marco Gasparini, Italy) *hld up in rr gp: rdn under 3f out: kpt on steadily ins fnl f: n.d* **168/10**

5 hd **Folega**[140] 3121 3-9-0 0 DarioVargiu 7 89
(Stefano Botti, Italy) *racd in 3rd bhd clr ldr: rdn over 3f out: wknd steadily ins fnl f* **15/8**[2]

6 3 1/2 **Aury Touch (ITY)**[154] 5-9-0 0 CarloFiocchi 4 77
(Stefano Botti, Italy) *hld up in rr gp: rdn and no imp fr under 2f out* **104/10**

7 3 1/2 **Extremely Vintage (IRE)**[14] 4-9-0 0 SilvanoMulas 6 70
(Endo Botti, Italy) *a towards rr* **123/10**

2m 4.2s (-2.50)
**WFA** 3 from 4yo+ 4lb **7** Ran SP% **129.7**
PARI-MUTUEL (all including 1 euro stake): WIN 1.86 PLACE 1.54, 4.27 DF 23.96.
**Owner** Stall Salzburg **Bred** Juddmonte Farms Ltd **Trained** Germany

## 7206 WOODBINE (L-H)
Sunday, October 15

**OFFICIAL GOING: Turf: soft; tapeta: fast**

### 8097a NEARCTIC STKS (GRADE 2) (3YO+) (TURF) 6f
**8:48** 3-Y-O+ **£108,433** (£30,120; £15,060; £7,530; £3,614; £1,506)

RPR

1 **Field Of Courage (CAN)**[45] 5-8-5 0 (b) LuisContreras 8 110
(Mark Casse, Canada) **40/1**

2 1 3/4 **Cotai Glory**[22] 7396 5-8-5 0 OisinMurphy 7 104
(Charles Hills) *hld up early and swtchd towards ins: sn tucked in bhd ldng pair: pushed along 2f out: hdwy between horses to go 2nd: rdn fnl f: nt pce of wnr fnl 100yds* **51/20**[2]

3 1 1/4 **White Flag (USA)**[35] 3-8-6 0 ow2 JoelRosario 2 102
(Christophe Clement, U.S.A) **37/20**[1]

4 1 3/4 **Ikerrin Road (IRE)**[29] 4-8-7 0 DJMoran 4 96
(Vito Armata, Canada) **11/1**

5 5 3/4 **Conquest Tsunami (CAN)**[42] 5-8-6 0 ow1 PatrickHusbands 5 77
(Mark Casse, Canada) **89/10**

6 hd **Dowse's Beach (USA)**[44] 6-8-5 0 JoseLOrtiz 1 75
(Brad H Cox, U.S.A) **27/10**[3]

7 1/2 **Yorkton (CAN)**[41] 3-8-6 0 ow2 JesseMCampbell 6 76
(Stuart C Simon, Canada) **213/10**

8 13 1/4 **Circle Of Friends (CAN)**[29] 3-8-4 0 (b[1]) EuricoRosaDaSilva 3 31
(Robert Tiller, Canada) **40/1**

1m 12.07s
**WFA** 3 from 4yo+ 1lb **8** Ran SP% **118.1**

**Owner** Quintessential Racing Florida LLC **Bred** Cavendish Investing Ltd **Trained** Canada

**FOCUS**
The winner has been rated back to the best view of his 2015 form.

### 8098a E. P. TAYLOR STKS (GRADE 1) (3YO+ FILLIES & MARES) (TURF) 1m 2f (T)
**10:28** 3-Y-O+ **£180,722** (£60,240; £33,132; £15,060; £6,024; £3,012)

RPR

1 **Blond Me (IRE)**[35] 6981 5-8-12 0 OisinMurphy 7 113+
(Andrew Balding) *settled towards rr: pushed along and hdwy 3f out: moved into 2nd and chsd ldr 2f out: rdn along to ld 1f out: rdn out* **17/2**

2 1 **Kitten's Roar (USA)**[31] 5-8-12 0 JoseLOrtiz 1 111
(Michael J Maker, U.S.A) *prom early: sn settled 3rd: wnt 2nd 1/2-way: upsides ldr 3f out: led over 2f out: sn u.p: hdd ent fnl f: no ex* **54/10**

3 1 1/2 **Fourstar Crook (USA)**[21] 5-8-12 0 JavierCastellano 2 108+
(Chad C Brown, U.S.A) *midfield: pushed along 3f out: lost grnd top of st bef styng on again f: wnt 3rd 100yds out: r.o wl* **107/20**[3]

4 3 3/4 **Rainha Da Bateria (USA)**[64] 5954 5-8-12 0 (b) JulienRLeparoux 4 101
(Chad C Brown, U.S.A) *midfield early: moved into ld after 2f: hdd over 2f out: wknd fnl f* **17/2**

5 3 **Nezwaah**[52] 6356 4-8-12 0 AndreaAtzeni 5 95
(Roger Varian) *midfield: pushed along and hdwy up ins turning in: outpcd over 1f out: wknd* **27/10**[1]

6 1 1/2 **Quidura**[29] 4-8-12 0 JuniorAlvarado 3 92
(H Graham Motion, U.S.A) *led early: hdd after 2f: trckd ldr: 3rd 1/2-way: pushed along over 2f out: sn lost position: wknd fnl f* **14/5**[2]

7 13 1/4 **Rain Goddess (IRE)**[35] 6972 3-8-7 0 RyanMoore 6 65
(A P O'Brien, Ire) *a in rr* **143/20**

2m 8.08s (4.06)
**WFA** 3 from 4yo+ 4lb **7** Ran SP% **118.0**
PARI-MUTUEL (all including 2 cad stake): WIN 18.90; PLACE (1-2) 8.30, 6.40; SHOW (1-2-3) 5.70, 4.00, 4.00; SF 137.90.
**Owner** Mrs Barbara M Keller **Bred** Wardstown Stud Ltd **Trained** Kingsclere, Hants

### 8099a PATTISON CANADIAN INTERNATIONAL STKS (GRADE 1) (3YO+) (TURF) 1m 4f (T)
**11:10** 3-Y-O+ **£289,156** (£96,385; £48,192; £24,096; £9,638; £4,819)

RPR

1 **Bullards Alley (USA)**[36] 5-9-0 0 (b) EuricoRosaDaSilva 7 116
(Tim Glyshaw, U.S.A) *settled in 4th: nudged along and hdwy fr half m out: moved into ld 3f out: rdn along fnl 2f and stretched clr: comf* **43/1**

2 10 3/4 **Oscar Nominated (USA)**[36] 4-9-0 0 (b) JulienRLeparoux 1 99
(Michael J Maker, U.S.A) *midfield: tk clsr order turning in: rdn along in 2nd over 1f out: kpt on wl for 2nd but no ch w wnr* **33/4**

3 1/2 **Flamboyant (FR)**[56] 6-9-0 0 JoelRosario 2 98
(Patrick Gallagher, U.S.A) *in rr of midfield: pushed along and hdwy between runners fr 2f out: chal for 2nd fnl f: jst hld at bay* **11/1**

4 1/2 **Idaho (IRE)**[14] 7668 4-9-0 0 RyanMoore 4 97+
(A P O'Brien, Ire) *towards rr: pushed along over 3f out: stl towards rr and plenty to do 2f out: rdn and styd on past btn horses fnl 1 1/2f: nvr on terms* **23/10**[1]

5 1 **Erupt (IRE)**[50] 6461 5-9-0 0 JuniorAlvarado 9 96
(H Graham Motion, U.S.A) *towards rr early: hdwy fr 1/2-way: midfield turning in: rdn along fnl 2f: no further imp* **89/20**[2]

6 5 **Chemical Charge (IRE)**36 6931 5-9-0 0 OisinMurphy 10 88
(Ralph Beckett) *last: rdn along and passed a few fnl 2f: nvr involved* **19/4**3

7 1 1/4 **Enterprising (USA)**36 6-9-0 0 (b) RafaelManuelHernandez 3 86
(Michael J Maker, U.S.A) *in rr of midfield: dropped to last 2f out: passed a few late* **56/1**

8 1 1/4 **Postulation (USA)**36 5-9-0 0 (b) JorgeAVargasJr 6 84
(Edward Graham, U.S.A) *disp ld early: settled in 2nd: pushed along in 3rd 3f out: wknd fnl 2f* **14/1**

9 1 1/2 **Messi (GER)**29 7178 7-9-0 0 JoseLOrtiz 8 81
(H Graham Motion, U.S.A) *sn led: hdd 3f out: rdn along in 2nd 2f out: wknd fnl 1 1/2f* **8/1**

10 22 1/2 **Johnny Bear (CAN)**29 7178 6-9-0 0 (b) LuisContreras 5 81
(Ashlee Brnjas, Canada) *away wl and disp ld early: settled in 3rd: outpcd turning in: eased fnl f* **41/5**

2m 34.37s (4.77) **10** Ran SP% **117.9**
PARI-MUTUEL (all including 2 cad stake): WIN 87.90; PLACE (1-2) 29.50, 9.40; SHOW (1-2-3) 10.90, 5.80, 8.40; SF 685.80.
**Owner** Wayne Spalding & Faron McCubbins **Bred** Eugene Melnyk **Trained** North America
**FOCUS**
The winner has been rated in line with the best recent winners of this race.

# CRANBOURNE
Sunday, October 15

**OFFICIAL GOING: Turf: good**

## 8100a TAB CRANBOURNE CUP (LISTED H'CAP) (3YO+) (TURF) 1m 2f 28y
6:35 3-Y-0+
**£105,263** (£31,578; £15,789; £7,894; £4,385; £3,508)

RPR

1 **Folkswood**134 3320 4-9-4 0 (p) KerrinMcEvoy 16 114
(Charlie Appleby) *settled midfield: impr to go 2nd over 2f out: rdn to ld over 1f out: styd on strly ins fnl f* **17/5**1

2 2 3/4 **Berisha (AUS)**16 6-8-10 0 (v) RyanMaloney 9 100
(Robert Smerdon, Australia) **17/1**

3 hd **Grey Lion (IRE)**16 5-8-7 0 (b) DeanYendall 5 97
(Matt Cumani, Australia) **30/1**

4 1 1/4 **Our Century (IRE)**14 6-8-7 0 BeauMertens 6 94
(Robert Hickmott, Australia) **9/1**

5 1 **Nozomi (AUS)**14 6-8-7 0 CraigAWilliams 7 92
(Anthony Freedman, Australia) *w.w in rr: hdwy whn nt clr run over 2f out: effrt over 1f out: no ex ins fnl f* **11/2**3

6 1 **Cool Chap (AUS)**14 5-8-9 0 (p) ReganBayliss 2 92
(David A & B Hayes & Tom Dabernig, Australia) **9/2**2

7 2 1/2 **Moonovermanhattan (AUS)**16 6-8-7 0 (bt) DamianLane 12 85
(Darren Weir, Australia) **13/2**

8 1 1/4 **Red Alto (AUS)**14 5-8-7 0 (b) MichaelWalker 10 83
(Brent Stanley, Australia) **50/1**

9 3/4 **Spanish Reef (AUS)**16 4-8-7 0 BenEThompson 15 81
(Ken Keys, Australia) **15/1**

10 1 1/4 **Lizzie L'Amour (NZ)**16 5-9-0 0 (b) DamienOliver 14 86
(Murray Baker & Andrew Forsman, New Zealand) **6/1**

11 3/4 **Magnapal (AUS)**22 8-8-7 0 (b) NikitaBeriman 11 77
(Daniel Bowman, Australia) **70/1**

12 4 1/4 **Guardini (FR)**14 6-9-3 0 BradRawiller 17 79
(Darren Weir, Australia) **25/1**

2m 3.3s **12** Ran SP% **116.2**

**Owner** Godolphin **Bred** Hascombe & Valiant Studs **Trained** Newmarket, Suffolk
**FOCUS**
The form makes sense rated around the second, fifth and sixth.

8101a (Foreign Racing) - See Raceform Interactive

# 7883 MUSSELBURGH (R-H)
Monday, October 16

**OFFICIAL GOING: Soft (good to soft in places on round course; 5.9)**
Wind: Breezy, half against in sprints and in nearly 4f of home straight on round course. Weather: Overcast

## 8102 RACING UK PROFITS RETURNED TO RACING NOVICE STKS 5f 1y
1:50 (1:51) (Class 5) 2-Y-0 **£3,314** (£1,042; £561) **Stalls** High

Form RPR

6010 1 **Marnie James**53 6353 2-9-4 82 (t) RowanScott(5) 2 81
(Iain Jardine) *trckd ldrs: shkn up to ld over 1f out: drvn clr fnl f* **8/11**1

05 2 3 1/2 **Ace Of Spades (USA)**7 7876 2-9-2 0 DanielTudhope 3 61
(George Scott) *pressed ldr: rdn and ev ch briefly over 1f out: sn chsng wnr: kpt on same pce fnl f* **5/1**3

20 3 2 1/4 **Eva Docc (IRE)**53 6347 2-8-11 0 JoeFanning 4 48
(Keith Dalgleish) *led to over 1f out: rdn and wknd fnl f* **10/1**

1054 R **Time Trail**5 7954 2-9-8 79 PaulMulrennan 1
(Michael Dods) *reluctant to enter stalls: ref to r* **3/1**2

1m 4.0s (3.60) **Going Correction** +0.525s/f (Yiel) **4** Ran SP% **108.7**
Speed ratings (Par 95): **92,86,82,**
CSF £4.73 TOTE £1.50; EX 4.60 Trifecta £14.20.
**Owner** James Property Ltd **Bred** Newsells Park Stud **Trained** Carrutherstown, D'fries & G'way
**FOCUS**
A fair little juvenile novice contest. They went a sensible gallop on ground officially described as soft, good to soft in places on the round course.

## 8103 STANLEY GUTHRIE LOVED RACING AT MUSSELBURGH H'CAP 1m 4f 104y
2:20 (2:20) (Class 5) (0-70,70) 3-Y-0+ **£3,234** (£962; £481; £240) **Stalls** Low

Form RPR

6021 1 **Royal Cosmic**7 7885 3-8-2 55 6ex ConnorMurtagh(5) 2 64
(Richard Fahey) *trckd ldrs: pushed along over 3f out: hdwy to ld over 1f out: edgd lft and sn hrd pressed: hld on gamely fnl f* **13/8**1

1236 2 hd **Donnachies Girl (IRE)**13 7701 4-9-9 70 RowanScott(5) 8 78
(Alistair Whillans) *hld up in last pl: hdwy on outside over 2f out: rdn to dispute ld over 1f out: kpt on fnl f: jst hld* **3/1**2

5001 3 6 **Al Hawraa**44 6690 4-9-4 60 KevinStott 5 58
(Kevin Ryan) *stdd in tch: effrt and drvn along over 2f out: edgd rt: hdwy to chse clr ldng pair ins fnl f: no imp* **6/1**

2320 4 1/2 **Theglasgowwarrior**48 6565 3-9-1 63 JamesSullivan 4 60
(Jim Goldie) *hld up in tch: drvn along over 2f out: no imp fr over 1f out* **10/1**

5233 5 3/4 **Rosemay (FR)**16 7598 3-9-3 65 GrahamLee 1 61
(Iain Jardine) *led: rdn over 2f out: hdd over 1f out: btn fnl f* **9/2**3

2005 6 nse **Magistral**13 7699 7-9-9 65 (p) PJMcDonald 3 61
(R Mike Smith) *chsd ldr: rdn and edgd rt over 2f out: wknd over 1f out* **18/1**

2m 53.21s (11.21) **Going Correction** +0.65s/f (Yiel)
**WFA** 3 from 4yo+ 6lb **6** Ran SP% **109.9**
Speed ratings (Par 103): **88,87,83,83,83 83**
CSF £6.35 CT £19.34 TOTE £2.30: £1.30, £1.60; EX 6.40 Trifecta £32.40.
**Owner** The Cosmic Cases **Bred** The Cosmic Cases **Trained** Musley Bank, N Yorks
**FOCUS**
A modest middle-distance handicap. The front two in the market fought out an engaging battle in the final furlong off another sensible gallop on the soft ground.

## 8104 100% RACING UK PROFITS BACK TO RACING H'CAP 7f 33y
2:50 (2:51) (Class 2) (0-100,99) 3-Y-0+ **£12,938** (£3,850; £1,924; £962) **Stalls** Low

Form RPR

0125 1 **Muntadab (IRE)**16 7609 5-9-5 97 TonyHamilton 4 105
(Roger Fell) *mde all: rdn over 1f out: kpt on wl ins fnl f* **8/1**

6004 2 1 1/4 **Right Touch**16 7626 7-8-6 89 ConnorMurtagh(5) 3 94
(Richard Fahey) *hld up: hdwy over 2f out: rdn to chse wnr ins fnl f: kpt on: nt pce to chal* **16/1**

1500 3 2 1/4 **Robero**16 7622 5-9-2 94 JamesSullivan 10 93
(Michael Easterby) *cl up on outside: wnt 2nd after 3f: effrt and rdn 2f out: lost 2nd and one pce fnl f* **20/1**

5630 4 1 3/4 **Theodorico (IRE)**16 7622 4-8-11 89 BenCurtis 1 83
(David Loughnane) *bhd: rdn over 2f out: swtchd lft and hdwy over 1f out: kpt on fnl f: nvr able to chal* **25/1**

0510 5 1/2 **Masham Star (IRE)**37 6918 3-9-3 97 JoeFanning 6 89
(Mark Johnston) *t.k.h early: in tch: effrt and drvn along over 2f out: outpcd fnl f* **14/1**

1435 6 1/2 **Get Knotted (IRE)**16 7611 5-9-5 97 (p) PaulMulrennan 8 89
(Michael Dods) *s.i.s: t.k.h: hld up: effrt on outside over 2f out: no imp fr over 1f out* **7/1**3

-330 7 1 **Fawaareq (IRE)**79 5393 4-9-0 92 GrahamLee 12 81
(Owen Burrows) *hld up: rdn along over 2f out: no imp over 1f out* **9/1**

0034 8 hd **Heaven's Guest (IRE)**10 7781 7-8-9 90 ow1 AdamMcNamara(3) 7 79
(Richard Fahey) *in tch: effrt and rdn over 2f out: wknd ins fnl f* **9/1**

6302 9 5 **Von Blucher (IRE)**9 7822 4-9-7 99 (p) PJMcDonald 2 75
(Rebecca Menzies) *s.i.s: hld up: rdn over 2f out: sn n.d: btn over 1f out* **11/1**

2411 10 nse **Big Tour (IRE)**25 7340 3-9-2 96 DanielTudhope 11 71
(Saeed bin Suroor) *hld up midfield on outside: effrt and rdn over 2f out: wknd over 1f out* **3/1**1

1126 11 2 **Lualiwa**37 6918 3-9-0 94 KevinStott 9 63
(Kevin Ryan) *chsd wnr 3f: cl up tl rdn and wknd over 2f out* **6/1**2

0500 12 3 1/4 **Lat Hawill (IRE)**104 4475 6-8-9 87 (v) ConnorBeasley 5 49
(Keith Dalgleish) *hld up: drvn and struggling wl over 2f out: sn btn* **33/1**

1m 30.76s (1.76) **Going Correction** +0.65s/f (Yiel)
**WFA** 3 from 4yo+ 2lb **12** Ran SP% **115.3**
Speed ratings (Par 109): **115,113,111,109,108 107,106,106,100,100 98,94**
CSF £121.72 CT £2478.83 TOTE £8.10: £2.30, £6.50, £5.80; EX 157.10 Trifecta £5391.90.
**Owner** Fell & High Hopes Partnership **Bred** Mrs James Wigan **Trained** Nawton, N Yorks
**FOCUS**
A good handicap. The winner has been rated back to his best.

## 8105 BREEDERS BACKING RACING EBF FLYING SCOTSMAN CONDITIONS STKS 5f 1y
3:20 (3:20) (Class 3) 3-Y-0+ **£12,938** (£3,850; £1,924; £962) **Stalls** High

Form RPR

2001 1 **Alpha Delphini**20 7475 6-9-2 107 (p) GrahamLee 3 106
(Bryan Smart) *w ldr: led 1/2-way: rdn over 1f out: kpt on wl fnl f* **6/5**1

1443 2 1 **Ornate**20 7475 4-9-2 105 (h) DanielTudhope 1 102
(Robert Cowell) *led to 1/2-way: styd w wnr: rdn over 1f out: kpt on same pce wl ins fnl f* **6/4**2

2516 3 3 3/4 **Mayleaf Shine (IRE)**16 7610 3-9-0 92 (h) JamesSullivan 5 88
(Iain Jardine) *dwlt: bhd: rdn and hdwy to chse clr ldng pair appr fnl f: kpt on: nt pce to chal* **4/1**3

4600 4 2 3/4 **Zapper Cass (FR)**46 6637 4-9-2 77 (b) BarryMcHugh 4 79
(Tony Coyle) *hung rt thrght: in tch: rdn along 1/2-way: wknd over 1f out* **66/1**

00-3 5 19 **I'll Be Good**284 71 8-9-2 83 PatrickMathers 2 11
(Alan Berry) *t.k.h: trckd ldrs to 1/2-way: sn rdn and wknd* **80/1**

1m 1.93s (1.53) **Going Correction** +0.525s/f (Yiel) **5** Ran SP% **108.2**
Speed ratings (Par 107): **108,106,100,96,65**
CSF £3.15 TOTE £1.90: £1.10, £1.10; EX 3.20 Trifecta £4.50.
**Owner** The Alpha Delphini Partnership **Bred** Mrs B A Matthews **Trained** Hambleton, N Yorks
**FOCUS**
A good-quality conditions sprint. They went a respectable gallop and the form horses dominated.

## 8106 NEVER MISS A RACE ON RACING UK H'CAP 5f 1y
3:50 (3:50) (Class 5) (0-75,75) 3-Y-0+ **£3,234** (£962; £481; £240) **Stalls** High

Form RPR

0512 1 **Economic Crisis (IRE)**7 7884 8-9-2 70 JamesSullivan 4 79
(Alan Berry) *in tch: effrt on outside over 1f out: led ins fnl f: r.o wl* **7/1**2

2032 2 hd **Jacob's Pillow**12 7738 6-9-7 75 (p) DanielTudhope 1 83
(Rebecca Bastiman) *led on outside: rdn over 1f out: hdd ins fnl f: rallied: hld cl home* **5/1**1

3242 3 1 1/2 **Ballesteros**16 7625 8-9-2 75 ConnorMurtagh(5) 8 78
(Richard Fahey) *hld up in tch: effrt and swtchd rt over 1f out: kpt on ins fnl f: nt pce to chal* **5/1**1

3402 4 1 1/4 **B Fifty Two (IRE)**16 7628 8-8-8 69 (bt) HarrisonShaw(7) 3 67
(Marjorie Fife) *cl up: chal 1/2-way: rdn over 1f out: one pce ins fnl f* **5/1**1

6000 5 1 **Fast Act (IRE)**18 7538 5-9-4 72 KevinStott 10 67
(Kevin Ryan) *chsd ldrs: rdn along 1/2-way: effrt and edgd rt over 1f out: sn one pce* **8/1**

0-50 6 1/2 **Naples Bay**109 4250 3-9-2 70 JasonHart 6 64
(John Quinn) *hld up: drvn along over 2f out: edgd rt over 1f out: kpt on ins fnl f: nvr able to chal* **22/1**

6006 7 nse **Tan**9 7825 3-9-1 69 (t) BarryMcHugh 12 63
(Tony Coyle) *hld up: pushed along over 1f out: sme late hdwy: nvr rchd ldrs* **14/1**

000 **8** *shd* **Tavener**[10] 7789 5-9-3 **71** (p) DavidAllan 2 63
(David C Griffiths) *cl up: rdn over 2f out: wknd over 1f out* **14/1**

0500 **9** *1¾* **Laughton**[38] 6877 4-9-7 **75** (t) TomEaves 9 61
(Kevin Ryan) *dwlt: hld up: drvn along 1/2-way: sn no imp: btn over 1f out* **8/1**

0101 **10** *3¾* **One Boy (IRE)**[26] 7268 6-9-7 **75** GrahamLee 11 47
(Paul Midgley) *in tch: rdn and outpcd 1/2-way: btn over 1f out* **15/2**[3]

1m 2.55s (2.15) **Going Correction** +0.525s/f (Yiel) 10 Ran SP% **114.2**
Speed ratings (Par 103): **103,102,100,98,96 95,95,95,92,86**
CSF £41.00 CT £195.13 TOTE £7.60: £2.30, £1.90, £1.80; EX 45.20 Trifecta £188.80.
**Owner** William Burns & Alan Berry **Bred** Philip Hore Jnr **Trained** Cockerham, Lancs

**FOCUS**
A fair sprint handicap and it is sound form, with the winner back close to her old best.

## 8107 FINEST COLLECTION OF RACING ON RACING UK H'CAP (DIV I) 7f 33y
**4:20** (4:20) (Class 5) (0-75,77) 3-Y-0+ **£3,234** (£962; £481; £240) **Stalls** Low

Form RPR

2526 **1** **Roaring Forties (IRE)**[16] 7594 4-9-13 **77** (p[1]) DanielTudhope 7 90+
(Rebecca Bastiman) *hld up: smooth hdwy over 2f out: led over 1f out: sn rdn clr: eased last 75yds: readily* **5/2**[2]

005 **2** *3¾* **So It's War (FR)**[44] 6673 6-8-11 **61** (p) ConnorBeasley 8 63
(Keith Dalgleish) *t.k.h: hld up: rdn over 3f out: hdwy wl over 1f out: chsd (clr) wnr ins fnl f: kpt on: nt pce to chal* **7/1**

0051 **3** *1* **Gabrial The Tiger (IRE)**[16] 7594 5-9-7 **76** ConnorMurtagh(5) 4 76
(Richard Fahey) *trckd ldrs: rdn over 2f out: edgd lft over 1f out: kpt on same pce ins fnl f* **2/1**[1]

2250 **4** *1¾* **Seaview**[12] 7737 3-9-1 **67** TomEaves 5 61
(David Brown) *prom: drvn along over 2f out: kpt on same pce fr over 1f out* **12/1**

3650 **5** *shd* **Circuitous**[7] 7889 9-8-7 **57** oh2 (v) JoeDoyle 1 52
(Keith Dalgleish) *led: rdn and hdd over 1f out: wknd ins fnl f* **25/1**

5600 **6** *¾* **Lexington Sky (IRE)**[27] 7244 3-9-5 **71** TonyHamilton 6 63
(Roger Fell) *hld up: rdn along over 2f out: sn no imp* **18/1**

0010 **7** *1¾* **Let Right Be Done**[4] 7980 5-8-7 **51** 6ex (b) AndrewMullen 9 45
(Linda Perratt) *t.k.h: hld up: drvn along over 2f out: sn n.d* **33/1**

3440 **8** *2* **Danish Duke (IRE)**[16] 7628 6-9-2 **66** (b) JamesSullivan 2 49
(Ruth Carr) *dwlt: hld up: drvn along over 2f out: edgd rt: wknd over 1f out* **16/1**

2200 **9** *9* **Fine Example**[7] 7881 4-9-6 **70** (b) KevinStott 3 30
(Kevin Ryan) *pressed ldr: rdn and ev ch over 2f out: wknd over 1f out* **6/1**[3]

5412 **10** *3½* **Mimic's Memory**[150] 2790 3-8-12 **64** JoeFanning 10 14
(Ann Duffield) *t.k.h: hld up on outsie: rdn and edgd rt over 2f out: sn wknd* **20/1**

1m 33.54s (4.54) **Going Correction** +0.65s/f (Yiel)
**WFA** 3 from 4yo+ 2lb 10 Ran SP% **119.1**
Speed ratings (Par 103): **100,95,94,92,92 91,89,87,77,73**
CSF £20.53 CT £41.82 TOTE £3.30: £1.10, £3.00, £1.50; EX 21.70 Trifecta £64.20.
**Owner** Mrs K Hall & Partner **Bred** Agricola Del Parco **Trained** Cowthorpe, N Yorks

**FOCUS**
The first division of a fair handicap. They went a respectable gallop and one of the best-backed horses on this card ran out an easy winner. He looks back to his 2yo best.

## 8108 FINEST COLLECTION OF RACING ON RACING UK H'CAP (DIV II) 7f 33y
**4:55** (4:55) (Class 5) (0-75,76) 3-Y-0+ **£3,234** (£962; £481; £240) **Stalls** Low

Form RPR

0320 **1** **Inglorious**[13] 7703 3-8-12 **66** (p) ConnorBeasley 4 73
(Keith Dalgleish) *mde virtually all: hrd pressed fr over 2f out: hld on gamely u.p ins fnl f* **14/1**

0504 **2** *shd* **Art Echo**[16] 7594 4-9-10 **76** (p[1]) BenCurtis 6 84
(John Mackie) *t.k.h early: hld up in tch: stdy hdwy over 2f out: drvn over 1f out: disp ld ins fnl f: kpt on: jst hld* **11/4**[2]

4023 **3** *1¼* **Donnelly's Rainbow (IRE)**[6] 7934 4-9-1 **67** (t[1]) DanielTudhope 5 72
(Rebecca Bastiman) *s.i.s: t.k.h in rr: effrt over 2f out: rdn and kpt on ins fnl f* **5/2**[1]

0021 **4** *1¾* **Tagur (IRE)**[33] 7046 3-8-10 **64** TomEaves 9 63
(Kevin Ryan) *pressed ldr: disp ld over 2f out to ins fnl f: sn one pce* **7/1**[3]

21-0 **5** *nk* **Lucky Violet (IRE)**[15] 7658 5-9-7 **73** (h) DavidAllan 3 72
(Iain Jardine) *trckd ldrs: drvn along over 2f out: kpt on same pce fr over 1f out* **16/1**

3306 **6** *1¾* **Garter (IRE)**[17] 7571 4-8-11 **63** TonyHamilton 1 58
(Richard Fahey) *t.k.h: hld up in tch: rdn along and outpcd over 2f out: no imp fr over 1f out* **12/1**

4443 **7** *2¼* **Forever A Lady (IRE)**[15] 7658 4-9-5 **71** GrahamLee 2 60
(Keith Dalgleish) *hld up: rdn along over 3f out: no imp fr 2f out* **15/2**

/641 **8** *6* **Sexy Legs**[17] 7574 5-8-9 **66** (t) RowanScott(5) 7 39
(Rebecca Menzies) *awkward s: hld up: drvn along and outpcd over 2f out: sn btn* **10/1**

0440 **9** *6* **Tafteesh (IRE)**[34] 7034 4-8-7 **59** CamHardie 10 17
(Michael Easterby) *t.k.h: in tch: drvn and outpcd 3f out: sn btn* **33/1**

4000 **10** *4½* **Geophony (IRE)**[11] 3243 3-8-10 **64** PJMcDonald 8 9
(Mark Johnston) *bhd: struggling 1/2-way: sn btn* **50/1**

1m 33.34s (4.34) **Going Correction** +0.65s/f (Yiel)
**WFA** 3 from 4yo+ 2lb 10 Ran SP% **113.7**
Speed ratings (Par 103): **101,100,99,97,97 95,92,85,78,73**
CSF £51.22 CT £130.97 TOTE £15.20: £4.10, £1.60, £1.20; EX 64.00 Trifecta £205.00.
**Owner** Weldspec Glasgow Limited **Bred** Kassala Limited **Trained** Carluke, S Lanarks
■ Stewards' Enquiry : Ben Curtis two day ban: using his whip above the permitted level (30/31 Oct)

**FOCUS**
The second division of a fair handicap. The winning time was marginally quicker and a small personal best from the winner.

## 8109 RACING UK NOW IN HD! AMATEUR RIDERS' H'CAP 1m 7f 217y
**5:25** (5:25) (Class 5) (0-75,73) 3-Y-0+ **£3,119** (£967; £483; £242) **Stalls** Low

Form RPR

5-01 **1** **Tawseef (IRE)**[19] 5700 9-9-7 **57** MissEllaMcCain(5) 8 72
(Donald McCain) *mde all: drew clr fr 3f out: v easily* **2/1**[1]

4330 **2** *15* **La Bacouetteuse (FR)**[6] 7922 12-9-9 **54** oh2 (p) MissSBrotherton 5 51
(Iain Jardine) *hld up in tch: hdwy on outside over 3f out: chsd (clr) wnr over 1f out: no imp* **8/1**

6110 **3** *3* **Chebsey Beau**[25] 7330 7-10-11 **73** MissAMcCain(3) 7 66
(John Quinn) *t.k.h: chsd wnr 6f: cl up: effrt and rdn 3f out: outpcd fr over 1f out* **7/2**[2]

3261 **4** *9* **Jonny Delta**[15] 7659 10-10-2 **61** MissCWalton 6 44
(Jim Goldie) *in tch: hdwy to chse wnr after 6f to over 2f out: rdn and wknd wl over 1f out* **4/1**[3]

2002 **5** *1½* **Wor Lass**[13] 7700 9-10-13 **72** MissAnnaHesketh 2 53
(Donald Whillans) *trckd ldrs: wnt 2nd over 2f out to over 1f out: wknd fnl f* **5/1**

133- **6** *7* **Down Time (USA)**[146] 1296 7-9-13 **65** MrTomMidgley(7) 4 37
(Paul Midgley) *hld up in tch: dropped to last pl after 4f: detached and pushed along over 6f out: wknd fr 3f out* **25/1**

320 **7** *19* **Tectonic (IRE)**[8] 6895 8-10-3 **62** (p) MrsCBartley 3 12
(Keith Dalgleish) *hld up: rdn and struggling over 3f out: sn btn* **20/1**

3m 46.26s (12.76) **Going Correction** +0.65s/f (Yiel) 7 Ran SP% **111.9**
Speed ratings (Par 103): **94,86,85,80,79 76,66**
CSF £18.06 CT £51.36 TOTE £2.70: £1.60, £3.80; EX 20.90 Trifecta £72.30.
**Owner** D McCain Jnr **Bred** Shadwell Estate Company Limited **Trained** Cholmondeley, Cheshire

**FOCUS**
A modest staying handicap for apprentice riders. The market leader routed this opposition from the front at his own increasing tempo.
T/Plt: £82.40 to a £1 stake. Pool: £55,861.28 - 494.81 winning units T/Qpdt: £25.50 to a £1 stake. Pool: £4,699.78 - 136.15 winning units **Richard Young**

# 7904 WINDSOR (R-H)
## Monday, October 16

**OFFICIAL GOING: Good (7.0)**
Wind: Strong, mostly behind in home straight Weather: Overcast, threatening becoming bright warm

## 8110 BARRY GOULD MEMORIAL NURSERY H'CAP 5f 21y
**2:00** (2:00) (Class 5) (0-70,70) 2-Y-0 **£2,911** (£866; £432; £216) **Stalls** Low

Form RPR

2612 **1** **Global Exceed**[32] 7081 2-9-7 **70** (b) AdamKirby 7 74
(Ed Dunlop) *rdn thrght: mostly in last tl prog on outer 2f out: drvn to chal ins fnl f: led last 75yds: kpt on* **3/1**[1]

500 **2** *½* **Aquadabra (IRE)**[9] 7814 2-9-5 **68** CharlesBishop 6 70
(Mick Channon) *hld up in tch: smooth prog on outer over 2f out: shkn up to ld fnl f: rdn and hdd last 75yds: nt qckn* **5/1**[3]

2405 **3** *nk* **Llamrei**[6] 7920 2-8-6 **55** MartinDwyer 9 56
(Jo Hughes) *racd on outer: in tch: shkn up and prog 2f out: rdn to chal fnl f: nt qckn last 100yds* **11/1**

54 **4** *¾* **Fab (IRE)**[29] 7193 2-9-7 **70** DougieCostello 8 68+
(Jamie Osborne) *taken down early: led and r against nr side rail: rdn and edgd lft over 1f out: hdd and one pce fnl f* **12/1**

534 **5** *1¾* **La Belle Mayson**[17] 7563 2-9-3 **66** PaulHanagan 5 59
(Richard Fahey) *wl in tch: cl up bhd ldrs over 1f out: fdd fnl f* **9/2**[2]

2205 **6** *1¾* **Tonkolili (IRE)**[29] 7194 2-9-6 **69** (h[1]) KieranShoemark 10 55
(William Muir) *mostly pressed ldr to over 1f out: fdd fnl f* **7/1**

3160 **7** *½* **Zain Smarts (IRE)**[13] 7706 2-9-1 **67** DavidEgan(3) 3 51
(David Evans) *trckd ldrs: rdn and hanging over 1f out: wknd* **12/1**

0062 **8** *2½* **Following Breeze (IRE)**[46] 6609 2-7-7 **49** oh4 IsobelFrancis(7) 4 24
(Jim Boyle) *a in rr: rdn and no prog over 2f out* **25/1**

5306 **9** *1¾* **Adulate**[20] 7491 2-9-4 **67** (v) AndreaAtzeni 1 36
(Hugo Palmer) *racd against nr side rail: trckd ldrs: pushed along and dropped away fr 2f out* **13/2**

4600 **10** *1½* **Comselle**[27] 7228 2-8-12 **61** (t[1]) PatDobbs 2 24
(Stuart Kittow) *racd towards nr side rail: hld up: rdn 2f out: wknd* **40/1**

59.54s (-0.76) **Going Correction** -0.275s/f (Firm) 10 Ran SP% **115.7**
Speed ratings (Par 95): **95,94,93,92,89 86,86,82,79,76**
CSF £17.60 CT £144.38 TOTE £3.00: £1.10, £3.30, £4.00; EX 16.40 Trifecta £166.50.
**Owner** Dr Johnny Hon **Bred** The Blue Maiden Partnership **Trained** Newmarket, Suffolk

**FOCUS**
Modest nursery form, they came stands' side but the main action unfolded more down the centre late on.

## 8111 PRIDE OF BIFFA H'CAP 1m 2f
**2:30** (2:30) (Class 4) (0-85,85) 3-Y-0+ **£4,690** (£1,395; £697; £174; £174) **Stalls** Centre

Form RPR

021 **1** **Jus Pires (USA)**[68] 5794 3-9-3 **82** (t) SeanLevey 12 90+
(Jeremy Noseda) *trckd ldr: rdn over 2f out: led over 1f out towards outer: hrd pressed fnl f: jst hld on* **8/1**

-532 **2** *nse* **Lime And Lemon (IRE)**[140] 3158 4-9-1 **76** AdamKirby 11 83
(Clive Cox) *trckd ldrs: rdn over 2f out: chal on outer jst over 1f out: jnd wnr 75yds out: jst pipped* **10/1**

3122 **3** *nk* **Sparte Quercus (IRE)**[15] 7649 4-9-6 **81** AndreaAtzeni 8 87
(Ed Dunlop) *trckd ldrs: rdn 3f out: clsd u.p on outer over 1f out: chal ins fnl f: nt qckn nr fin* **7/1**[3]

0533 **4** *1* **Andok (IRE)**[18] 7555 3-9-1 **80** PaulHanagan 5 84+
(Richard Fahey) *hld up: outpcd whn pce lifted 3f out: styd on fr 2f out on outer: nvr quite able to rch ldrs* **13/2**[2]

10 **4** *dht* **Good Way Off (USA)**[17] 7576 4-9-8 **83** JamieSpencer 2 87
(Luca Cumani) *in tch in midfield: 6th whn pce lifted 3f out: rdn and tried to cl fr 2f out: kpt on but nvr able to chal* **13/2**[2]

550 **6** *nk* **Grapevine (IRE)**[24] 7358 4-9-4 **82** CallumShepherd(3) 6 85
(Charles Hills) *led: kicked on 3f out: edgd away fr nr side rail fr 2f out: hdd over 1f out: one pce* **9/1**

1 **7** *1¼* **Garrick**[254] 580 3-9-6 **85** RobertHavlin 9 87+
(John Gosden) *hld up in midfield: sltly outpcd whn pce lifted 3f out: shkn up and no imp ldrs fnl 2f: one pce* **3/1**[1]

310- **8** *½* **Genetics (FR)**[373] 7151 3-9-6 **85** RobHornby 4 85
(Andrew Balding) *in tch in midfield: rdn whn pce lifted 3f out: no prog fnl 2f* **14/1**

0060 **9** *nse* **Island Brave (IRE)**[51] 6455 3-8-6 **74** DavidEgan(3) 10 74
(Heather Main) *hld up in last trio: outpcd whn pce lifted 3f out: nvr on terms w ldrs after* **100/1**

1520 **10** *½* **Lawmaking**[17] 7582 4-9-7 **82** (h) LiamKeniry 7 81
(Henry Spiller) *awkward to post: t.k.h and hld up in last pair: outpcd whn pce lifted 3f out: nvr on terms after* **16/1**

51-5 **11** *1½* **Intermodal**[21] 7452 3-8-10 **75** RichardKingscote 3 72
(Amanda Perrett) *trckd ldrs: wl plcd whn pce lifted 3f out: hanging lft and fnd nil after: wknd 2f out* **12/1**

6360 **12** 2 ¾ **Zamalight**[11] 7768 3-8-11 **76** ow3............................................. PatDobbs 1 67
(Amanda Perrett) *t.k.h: hld up in last trio: outpcd whn pce lifted 3f out: nvr on terms after* **100/1**

2m 9.51s (0.81) **Going Correction** -0.075s/f (Good)
**WFA** 3 from 4yo+ 4lb **12** Ran SP% **116.6**
Speed ratings (Par 105): **93,92,92,91,91 91,90,90,90,89 88,86**
CSF £84.14 CT £589.33 TOTE £7.80: £3.00, £2.80, £1.90; EX 61.40 Trifecta £330.90.
**Owner** Nigel O'Sullivan **Bred** Adrian Regan & Fergus Galvin **Trained** Newmarket, Suffolk

**FOCUS**
Distance increased by 20yds. They went pretty steady and, as in the first race, the finish was fought out down the centre.

## 8112 STARSPORTSBET.CO.UK EBF NOVICE STKS 6f 12y
3:00 (3:00) (Class 5) 2-Y-O £2,911 (£866; £432; £216) Stalls Low

Form RPR

1 **1** **All Out**[12] 7731 2-9-4 0............................................. TomMarquand 11 83
(Richard Hannon) *trckd ldng pair: 4 l bhd them 1/2-way: clsd fr 2f out: shkn up to chal fnl f: led last 75yds: won narrowly but decisively* **11/10**[1]

46 **2** nk **Global Tango (IRE)**[151] 2769 2-9-2 0............................. DavidProbert 9 80
(Charles Hills) *mde most: clr w one rival 1/2-way: rdn over 1f out: hdd last 75yds: kpt on wl but a hld* **11/1**

5 **3** 5 **Spenny's Lass**[12] 7732 2-8-11 0............................................. BrettDoyle 4 60
(John Ryan) *rdr nrly off s: w ldr: clr of rest 1/2-way: rdn 2f out: lost 2nd over 1f out and sn wl hld but clr of rest* **13/2**[3]

**4** 4 ½ **Heavenly Guest** 2-9-2 0............................................. DougieCostello 8 52
(George Margarson) *mostly in 4th: outpcd fr 1/2-way: one pce and no imp after* **20/1**

60 **5** ½ **Appenzeller (USA)**[24] 7351 2-9-2 0..............................(h[1]) ShaneKelly 10 50
(Richard Hughes) *hld up: outpcd in 5th plcd 1/2-way: pushed along and nvr on terms after: kpt on: should do bttr* **50/1**

**6** hd **Conflagration** 2-9-2 0............................................. RichardKingscote 6 49+
(Ed Dunlop) *nvr beyond midfield: outpcd fr 1/2-way: nt on terms after* **11/4**[2]

**7** nk **Haverland (IRE)** 2-9-2 0............................................. StevieDonohoe 2 49+
(Charlie Fellowes) *nvr beyond midfield: outpcd 1/2-way: pushed along against nr side rail over 2f out: nvr on terms but styd on last 100yds* **33/1**

**8** ½ **Desert Trip (FR)** 2-9-2 0............................................. KieranShoemark 3 47+
(David Menuisier) *dwlt: towards rr: pushed along over 2f out: kpt on fnl f but nvr in it* **20/1**

55 **9** 4 ½ **Kingfast (IRE)**[64] 5964 2-9-2 0............................................. TimmyMurphy 7 34
(David Dennis) *hld up wl in rr: pushed along over 2f out: nvr in it* **100/1**

54 **10** 1 ½ **Rosedale Topping (IRE)**[32] 7093 2-8-11 0............................. FranBerry 5 24
(Ed Vaughan) *hld up in last pair: nvr on terms* **14/1**

00 **11** 3 ¼ **Spirit Of Ishy**[24] 7351 2-8-11 0............................................. LiamKeniry 12 14
(Stuart Kittow) *wnt lft s: a wl in rr* **150/1**

1m 12.07s (-0.93) **Going Correction** -0.275s/f (Firm) **11** Ran SP% **118.7**
Speed ratings (Par 95): **95,94,87,81,81 81,80,79,73,71 67**
CSF £14.37 TOTE £2.00: £1.10, £2.60, £2.00; EX 15.60 Trifecta £50.50.
**Owner** R Barnett **Bred** W & R Barnett Ltd **Trained** East Everleigh, Wilts

**FOCUS**
Run at a good gallop, the first two finished clear down the centre with little getting into it.

## 8113 CALL STAR SPORTS ON 08000 521 321 FILLIES' H'CAP 1m 31y
3:30 (3:30) (Class 4) (0-80,82) 3-Y-O+ £4,690 (£1,395; £697; £348) Stalls Low

Form RPR

-655 **1** **Hidden Steps**[100] 4618 3-9-6 **82**..............................(h) DavidProbert 3 89+
(Andrew Balding) *mde all: hung lft bnd over 5f out: styd on nr side rail in st: rdn and kpt on wl fnl 2f: hung lft nr fin* **16/1**

-002 **2** 1 ½ **Clef**[13] 7702 3-8-13 **75**............................................. PaulHanagan 8 79
(Richard Fahey) *t.k.h: hld up in 5th: prog on outer over 2f out: rdn to chse wnr over 1f out: nt qckn and hld ins fnl f* **9/2**[2]

2213 **3** nk **Killay**[23] 7398 3-9-4 **80**............................................. CharlesBishop 5 83
(Eve Johnson Houghton) *dwlt: t.k.h and hld up in rr: prog on outer over 2f out: tried to cl and looked a threat over 1f out: kpt on same pce after* **15/8**[1]

4152 **4** ¾ **Sandy Shores**[11] 7769 3-8-9 **71**..............................(b) TomMarquand 7 73
(Brian Meehan) *trckd ldrs: rdn over 2f out: kpt on same pce fr over 1f out: nvr able to chal* **10/1**

1142 **5** ¾ **Finale**[26] 7276 3-9-3 **79**............................................. AdamKirby 10 79
(Hughie Morrison) *plld hrd: hld up in last pair: prog on wd outside over 2f out: looked a threat over 1f out: wknd last 100yds* **9/2**[2]

2311 **6** 1 ¼ **Fastnet Spin (IRE)**[21] 7463 3-9-4 **80**..............................(bt) FranBerry 4 77
(David Evans) *hld up in last trio: shkn up and no prog over 2f out: n.d after* **14/1**

4201 **7** nk **Kitty Boo**[20] 7485 3-9-5 **81**..............................(h) JamieSpencer 1 77
(Luca Cumani) *chsd ldng trio: rdn and no prog over 2f out: fdd over 1f out* **5/1**[3]

4555 **8** 2 **La Celebs Ville (IRE)**[31] 7130 4-9-2 **75**..............(p) RichardKingscote 2 68
(Tom Dascombe) *hld up in midfield: shkn up and no prog over 2f out: wl hld fr over 1f out* **25/1**

1160 **9** 4 **Arctic Flower (IRE)**[30] 7157 4-8-2 **66** oh4............ ManuelFernandes(5) 9 50
(John Bridger) *t.k.h: trckd wnr to over 1f out: wknd rapidly* **50/1**

1m 43.24s (-1.46) **Going Correction** -0.075s/f (Good)
**WFA** 3 from 4yo 3lb **9** Ran SP% **115.3**
Speed ratings (Par 102): **104,102,102,101,100 99,99,97,93**
CSF £86.36 CT £203.23 TOTE £18.80: £4.60, £1.80, £1.30; EX 112.00 Trifecta £423.50.
**Owner** Kingsclere Racing Club **Bred** Kingsclere Stud **Trained** Kingsclere, Hants

**FOCUS**
Distance increased by 20yds. A decent little handicap and a tough front-running effort from the winner.

## 8114 FOLLOW US ON TWITTER @STARSPORTS_BET H'CAP 1m 3f 99y
4:00 (4:02) (Class 5) (0-70,70) 3-Y-O £2,911 (£866; £432; £216) Stalls Centre

Form RPR

0-35 **1** **Zeelander**[58] 6194 3-9-5 **68**............................................. AndreaAtzeni 10 77+
(Roger Varian) *hld up towards rr: urged along 3f out and no great prog: rdn and hdwy on outer to chse ldng pair wl over 1f out: fnlly clsd to ld last 75yds and suddenly looked in full command* **10/11**[1]

4336 **2** 1 **Orin Swift (IRE)**[55] 6293 3-9-5 **68**............................................. PatCosgrave 8 75
(Jonathan Portman) *led 2f: trckd ldng pair: led again 3f out and racd on outer: rdn and pressed 2f out: hdd and outpcd last 75yds: kpt on* **14/1**

2144 **3** 1 ¼ **Hawridge Glory (IRE)**[18] 7541 3-9-7 **70**............................. LiamKeniry 7 75
(Rod Millman) *hld up in 5th: smooth prog on outer to trck ldr over 2f out: rdn to chal over 1f out: nt qckn and dropped to 3rd ins fnl f* **9/1**[3]

66-6 **4** 1 ¼ **Leonidas (IRE)**[129] 3531 3-9-3 **66**............................................. MartinDwyer 5 69+
(Marcus Tregoning) *s.i.s: hld up in last pair: shkn up and prog jst over 2f out: kpt on same pce fr over 1f out to take 4th ins fnl f* **11/1**

5060 **5** 1 **Outofthequestion**[32] 7097 3-8-12 **61**............................. FergusSweeney 4 62
(Alan King) *t.k.h early: hld up in tch: rdn over 2f out: chsd ldng trio wl over 1f out: no imp and lost 4th ins fnl f* **25/1**

6253 **6** 3 **Uptown Funk (IRE)**[25] 7319 3-9-5 **68**..............................(bt[1]) RobertHavlin 2 64
(John Gosden) *trckd ldng trio: rdn over 2f out: sn lost pl and btn* **9/2**[2]

0064 **7** 1 ¾ **Kirkland Forever**[12] 7729 3-8-10 **59**............................................. FranBerry 6 52
(Brendan Powell) *t.k.h early: hld up in last pair: rdn wl over 2f out: no great prog* **33/1**

-200 **8** shd **Makkadangdang**[11] 7766 3-8-12 **68**............................. JasonWatson(7) 11 61
(Andrew Balding) *led after 2f to 3f out: racd on inner and steadily wknd over 2f out* **33/1**

5355 **9** 9 **Challow (IRE)**[18] 7537 3-8-9 **61**............................................. MitchGodwin(3) 3 39
(Sylvester Kirk) *fractious bef gng in stall: pressed ldr after 2f to over 3f out: wknd 2f out: bhd fnl f* **11/1**

4000 **10** 8 **South Sea Belle (IRE)**[7] 7878 3-9-4 **67**............................. KieranShoemark 9 32
(David Menuisier) *t.k.h early: hld up in tch: rdn wl over 2f out: wknd qckly wl over 1f out: t.o* **33/1**

2m 27.1s (-2.40) **Going Correction** -0.075s/f (Good) **10** Ran SP% **116.6**
Speed ratings (Par 101): **105,104,103,102,101 99,98,98,91,85**
CSF £15.09 CT £72.06 TOTE £1.70: £1.10, £3.90, £2.40; EX 15.30 Trifecta £78.00.
**Owner** Sheikh Mohammed Obaid Al Maktoum **Bred** Darley **Trained** Newmarket, Suffolk

**FOCUS**
Distance increased by 20yds. A modest handicap, but a winner capable of rating a good bit higher.

## 8115 BEN WOOLLACOTT MEMORIAL H'CAP 6f 12y
4:30 (4:31) (Class 4) (0-80,80) 3-Y-O+ £4,690 (£1,395; £697; £348) Stalls Low

Form RPR

5031 **1** **Paddy Power (IRE)**[18] 7557 4-9-6 **79**............................................. PaulHanagan 8 87
(Richard Fahey) *hld up in midfield: prog 2f out: rdn and clsd to ld ins fnl f: styd on* **8/1**

2041 **2** ¾ **Buccaneers Vault (IRE)**[32] 7086 5-9-4 **77**............................. PatDobbs 9 84+
(Paul Midgley) *pressed ldrs: trying to chal whn squeezed for room over 1f out: rallied fnl f: tk 2nd last strides* **11/1**

3556 **3** nk **Bahamian Dollar**[12] 7737 4-9-0 **80**............................. KatherineGlenister(7) 16 85
(David Evans) *in tch on wd outside: prog over 2f out: rdn to ld 1f out and edgd rt: hdd and no ex ins fnl f* **7/1**[3]

1341 **4** 1 ½ **Pastfact**[14] 7691 3-8-13 **76**............................................. DavidEgan(3) 10 76
(Malcolm Saunders) *chsd ldrs: rdn over 2f out: kpt on same pce fr over 1f out* **8/1**

1350 **5** 1 **Bernardo O'Reilly**[23] 7404 3-9-5 **79**..............................(h) KieranShoemark 4 76
(Richard Spencer) *wl in rr and rdn bef 1/2-way: effrt on outer over 2f out: kpt on: nrst fin* **14/1**

4213 **6** nse **Abiento (IRE)**[19] 7508 3-9-1 **75**............................................. PatCosgrave 7 72
(Ed Walker) *pressed ldr: led over 1f out to 1f out: short of room briefly sn after and fdd* **6/1**[2]

2114 **7** shd **Buxted Dream (USA)**[13] 7709 3-9-6 **80**............................. JamieSpencer 5 77
(Luca Cumani) *pressed ldrs: rdn 2f out: cl up but hld whn impeded jst ins fnl f: one pce* **7/2**[1]

34 **8** hd **Caesar's Comet (IRE)**[70] 5708 3-8-6 **66** oh1............(h[1]) MartinDwyer 15 62
(Paul Midgley) *wl in rr: rdn over 2f out: kpt on fr over 1f out on outer: nt pce to threaten* **25/1**

4014 **9** 2 **Waseem Faris (IRE)**[42] 6764 8-9-4 **80**............................. HectorCrouch(3) 12 69
(Ken Cunningham-Brown) *hld up in rr: shkn up sn after 1/2-way: kpt on fnl f but nvr a factor* **40/1**

6340 **10** 3 **Coastal Cyclone**[26] 7272 3-8-10 **70**............................. RichardKingscote 2 50
(Harry Dunlop) *trckd ldrs on inner: wknd 2f out* **20/1**

0530 **11** shd **Anfaass (IRE)**[55] 6297 3-9-3 **77**............................................. FranBerry 3 57
(George Margarson) *struggling in rr by 1/2-way: nvr a factor* **28/1**

05 **12** nk **Cappananty Con**[13] 7709 3-9-4 **78**............................................. RobertWinston 6 57
(Dean Ivory) *t.k.h: hld up in midfield: pushed along towards inner whn nt clr run over 1f out: no ch after and nvr in it* **16/1**

6510 **13** 1 ¼ **Malcolm The Pug (IRE)**[34] 7016 3-8-4 **67**............................. AaronJones(3) 1 42
(David Brown) *led to over 1f out: wknd rapidly* **28/1**

6300 **14** 17 **Ballymore Castle (IRE)**[109] 4270 5-9-4 **77**............................. StevieDonohoe 13
(Richard Fahey) *scratchy to post: s.v.s: a t.o* **14/1**

1m 10.62s (-2.38) **Going Correction** -0.275s/f (Firm)
**WFA** 3 from 4yo+ 1lb **14** Ran SP% **116.7**
Speed ratings (Par 105): **104,103,102,100,99 99,99,98,96,92 92,91,89,67**
CSF £83.74 CT £667.51 TOTE £8.80: £2.40, £3.60, £2.80; EX 51.40 Trifecta £268.30.
**Owner** M Scaife & R A Fahey **Bred** Yeguada De Milagro Sa **Trained** Musley Bank, N Yorks

**FOCUS**
A useful sprint and plenty had their chance spread centre-to-stands' side. The winner is pretty much back to his best.

## 8116 MPM FLOORING LTD MAIDEN STKS (DIV I) 1m 31y
5:00 (5:03) (Class 5) 3-Y-O+ £2,911 (£866; £432; £216) Stalls Low

Form RPR

6-2 **1** **Spanish History (USA)**[52] 6368 3-9-5 0............................................. ShaneKelly 10 76
(Seamus Durack) *racd freely early: mde all: rdn over 1f out: kpt on wl whn pressed fnl f* **4/1**[3]

6-36 **2** nk **Paradise Lake (IRE)**[144] 3005 3-9-5 76............................................. TedDurcan 8 75
(Sir Michael Stoute) *hld up in tch: prog over 2f out: rdn to cl over 1f out: tk 2nd ins fnl f and tried to chal: nt qckn last strides* **13/8**[1]

43 **3** 1 ¼ **Colourful Career (USA)**[16] 7600 3-9-5 0............................. AndreaAtzeni 4 72
(Ed Dunlop) *trckd wnr after 3f: rdn to try to chal over 1f out: no imp and dropped to 3rd ins fnl f* **9/4**[2]

0 **4** 7 **Saharan Star**[19] 7514 3-9-0 0............................................. JimmyQuinn 2 51
(Patrick Chamings) *hld up: nudged along and lost tch w ldng gp 3f out: no ch after but kpt on w sme encouragement fnl 2f* **100/1**

00 **5** hd **Calm Charm (IRE)**[20] 7485 3-9-0 0............................................. FranBerry 7 50
(Chris Wall) *hld up: effrt 3f out: outpcd 2f out: no ch after* **20/1**

**6** ¾ **Deauville Diva (IRE)** 3-8-7 0............................................. TylerSaunders(7) 3 49
(Marcus Tregoning) *v s.i.s: mostly in last pair: lost tch 3f out: no ch after but kpt on steadily fnl 2f* **8/1**

06 **7** 1 ¼ **Peter Stuyvesant (IRE)**[19] 7514 3-9-5 0............................................. PatCosgrave 5 51
(Denis Coakley) *t.k.h: trckd ldr 3f: shkn up over 2f out: steadily wknd* **50/1**

00 **8** 1 ¼ **Captain Cockle**[19] 7514 4-9-5 0............................................. MitchGodwin(3) 1 49
(Roger Teal) *chsd ldrs: urged along 3f out: wknd 2f out* **100/1**

**9** 15 **Amajari (FR)** 3-9-2 0............................................. HectorCrouch(3) 9 13
(Gary Moore) *dwlt: a in rr: shkn up 1/2-way: t.o* **20/1**

1m 44.01s (-0.69) **Going Correction** -0.075s/f (Good)
**WFA** 3 from 4yo 3lb **9** Ran SP% **113.4**
Speed ratings (Par 103): **100,99,98,91,91 90,89,88,73**
CSF £10.31 TOTE £4.30: £1.50, £1.10, £1.80; EX 12.60 Trifecta £20.10.

**Owner** Andrew Wyke & Ownaracehorse **Bred** Darley **Trained** Upper Lambourn, Berkshire

**FOCUS**

Distance increased by 20yds. The first leg of an ordinary maiden, the front three pulled clear. The placed horses set the standard.

## 8117 MPM FLOORING LTD MAIDEN STKS (DIV II) 1m 31y

**5:30** (5:30) (Class 5) 3-Y-O+ **£2,911** (£866; £432; £216) **Stalls** Low

Form RPR

0-35 **1** **Crimson Rosette (IRE)**[142] 3094 3-9-0 78..............(h[1]) StevieDonohoe 4 79
(Charlie Fellowes) *trckd ldng pair: shkn up over 2f out: rdn to chse ldr over 1f out: led ins fnl f: styd on wl* **7/4**[2]

3235 **2** *1 1/4* **Majboor (IRE)**[24] 7358 3-9-5 76........................................ LiamKeniry 9 81
(Dominic Ffrench Davis) *sn trckd ldr: rdn to ld 2f out: kpt on wl but hdd and outpcd ins fnl f* **4/1**[3]

24 **3** *6* **Sacred Way**[18] 7542 3-9-5 0........................................ JamieSpencer 10 67
(Kevin Ryan) *sn led: rdn and hdd 2f out: no ch w ldng pair over 1f out: clung on for 3rd* **6/1**

**4** *shd* **My Brunette (IRE)** 3-9-0 0........................................ TimmyMurphy 5 62
(Geoffrey Deacon) *s.v.s: mostly in last: pushed along and sme prog over 2f out: styd on fnl f and nrly snatched 3rd* **33/1**

0 **5** *1* **Ciaoadiosimdone (IRE)**[17] 7576 3-9-0 0........................... BrettDoyle 7 60
(John Ryan) *chsd ldrs: rdn 3f out: nvr able to mount a chal: wknd over 1f out* **6/4**[1]

0 **6** *1/2* **Broughtons Sport**[21] 7459 3-9-5 0........................................ MartinLane 3 63
(Andi Brown) *s.s: wl in rr: pushed along on wd outside over 2f out: kpt on same pce: nt disgracd* **100/1**

0 **7** *6* **Sunset Bounty**[166] 2316 3-8-11 0................................ HectorCrouch[(3)] 6 44
(Julia Feilden) *in tch in 6th: pushed along 3f out: wknd wl over 1f out* **125/1**

6500 **8** *5* **Bingo George (IRE)**[29] 7190 4-9-8 42............................(t) RobHornby 2 39
(Mark Rimell) *chsd ldrs in 5th: tried to cl over 2f out: wknd qckly wl over 1f out* **100/1**

065 **9** *14* **Nitro**[27] 7230 3-9-5 29........................................ KieranShoemark 8 5
(Roy Brotherton) *a in rr: wknd 3f out: t.o* **200/1**

0 **R** **Shanghai Shane (IRE)**[46] 6633 3-9-0 0........................ JoshuaBryan[(5)] 1
(Brian Barr) *rn off the crse sn after s* **250/1**

1m 43.17s (-1.53) **Going Correction** -0.075s/f (Good)
**WFA** 3 from 4yo 3lb **10** Ran SP% **117.3**
Speed ratings (Par 103): **104,102,96,96,95 95,89,84,70,**
CSF £9.40 TOTE £2.90: £1.10, £1.50, £2.00; EX 10.00 Trifecta £34.80.
**Owner** A E Oppenheimer **Bred** Hascombe & Valiant Studs **Trained** Newmarket, Suffolk

**FOCUS**

Distance increased by 20yds. Probably the lesser of the two divisions with the race rated around the first two.

T/Jkpt: Not Won. T/Plt: £44.70 to a £1 stake. Pool: £79,884.86 - 1,303.67 winning units T/Qpdt: £7.70 to a £1 stake. Pool: £8,557.13 - 821.89 winning units **Jonathan Neesom**

# 7333 YARMOUTH (L-H)

Monday, October 16

**OFFICIAL GOING: Good (good to firm in places; watered; 7.3)**

Wind: light, across Weather: sunny, overcast from race 4

## 8118 BRITISH EBF NOVICE STKS (PLUS 10 RACE) 6f 3y

**1:40** (1:41) (Class 4) 2-Y-O **£4,528** (£1,347; £673; £336) **Stalls** Centre

Form RPR

6 **1** **Foreseeable Future (FR)**[24] 7352 2-9-2 0........................ LukeMorris 5 77
(James Tate) *sn led and mde rest: rdn over 1f out: sn asserted and in command whn edgd lft ins fnl f: comf* **5/2**[1]

**2** *2 1/4* **Elite Shadow** 2-9-2 0........................................ MartinHarley 1 70
(Gay Kelleway) *hld up in tch in midfield: effrt to chse wnr over 1f out: kpt on same pce ins fnl f* **66/1**

64 **3** *3/4* **Pranceaboottheetoon (IRE)**[66] 5865 2-8-12 74........... JackOsborn[(7)] 4 71
(John Ryan) *stdd after s: trckd ldrs: rdn and unable qck over 1f out: wnt 3rd and kpt on same pce ins fnl f* **20/1**[3]

6 **4** *3* **Tigerfilly**[19] 7504 2-8-11 0........................................ GeraldMosse 6 54
(John Ryan) *chsd wnr: rdn ent fnl 2f: lost 2nd and struggling over 1f out: wknd ins fnl f* **16/1**[2]

0 **5** *15* **Equo**[26] 7280 2-9-2 0........................................ AdamBeschizza 7 14
(Chris Wall) *s.i.s: in tch in last pair: rdn over 2f out: sn outpcd and btn over 1f out: eased wl ins fnl f* **66/1**

**6** *1/2* **Patienceisavirtue** 2-8-4 0..............................(h[1]) JacobMitchell[(7)] 2 8
(Christine Dunnett) *s.i.s: sn clsd and in tch in last pair: struggling and pushed along over 2f out: sn lost tch* **200/1**

1m 16.29s (1.89) **Going Correction** +0.225s/f (Good) **6** Ran SP% **42.7**
Speed ratings (Par 97): **96,93,92,88,68 67**
CSF £15.60 TOTE £1.40: £1.02, £11.30; EX 10.10 Trifecta £43.80.
**Owner** Saeed Manana **Bred** Derek Price **Trained** Newmarket, Suffolk
■ Fakhoor was withdrawn. Price at time of withdrawal 2/5. Rule 4 applies to all bets - deduction 70p in the pound.

**FOCUS**

A warm day and the ground had been watered. The odds-on favourite was withdrawn at the start, leaving a straightforward task for the winner in what was a weak novice.

## 8119 BRITISH STALLION STUDS EBF NOVICE STKS (PLUS 10 RACE) 7f 3y

**2:10** (2:12) (Class 4) 2-Y-O **£4,657** (£1,386; £692; £346) **Stalls** Centre

Form RPR

**1** **Willie John** 2-9-2 0........................................ GeraldMosse 15 83+
(William Haggas) *s.i.s: hld up in tch in last quartet: shkn up and gd hdwy to ld over 1f out: r.o strly to go clr ins fnl f: readily* **15/2**[3]

**2** *2 1/2* **Humbolt Current** 2-9-2 0........................................ WilliamBuick 2 79+
(William Haggas) *s.i.s: rn green in detached last tl clsd onto bk of field 3f out: swtchd rt and hdwy over 1f out: styd on wl ins fnl f: wnt 2nd wl ins fnl f: nvr threatening wnr* **12/1**

**3** *3/4* **Amplification (USA)** 2-9-2 0........................................ AntonioFresu 14 74
(Ed Dunlop) *chsd ldrs: swtchd lft over 2f out: effrt over 1f out: swtchd lft 1f out: kpt on u.p ins fnl f: no threat to wnr* **10/1**

3 **4** *1/2* **Alfarqad (USA)**[23] 7391 2-9-2 0........................................ JimCrowley 9 73
(Owen Burrows) *t.k.h: led for 2f out: styd prom: ev ch 2f out: rdn and pressing wnr over 1f out: outpcd by wnr ins fnl f: wknd and lost 2 pls wl ins fnl f* **10/11**[1]

4 **5** *2* **Herdwick**[26] 7280 2-9-2 0........................................ RyanMoore 7 70
(Sir Michael Stoute) *s.i.s: hld up in tch in last quartet: clsd and nt clr run 2f out: swtchd rt over 1f out: hdwy ent fnl f: keeping on but no threat to wnr whn nt clr run and eased wl towards fin* **5/1**[2]

6 **6** *1* **Black Lotus**[21] 7454 2-8-8 0........................................ GeorgeWood[(3)] 6 60+
(Chris Wall) *in tch in midfield: effrt over 1f out: kpt on same pce ins fnl f* **25/1**

**7** *hd* **Dark Side Jazz (IRE)** 2-8-9 0........................................ JackOsborn[(7)] 12 64
(John Ryan) *hld up in tch in midfield: nt clr run over 1f out: hdwy and edging lft 1f out: kpt on ins fnl f: no threat to wnr* **200/1**

00 **8** *1 3/4* **Conversant (IRE)**[11] 7765 2-9-2 0........................ JosephineGordon 4 60
(Hugo Palmer) *t.k.h: w ldr tl led 5f out: rdn and hdd over 1f out: no ex 1f out and wknd ins fnl f* **50/1**

**9** *2* **Pass Mark** 2-9-2 0........................................ AdamBeschizza 1 54
(Mrs Ilka Gansera-Leveque) *dwlt: t.k.h and sn rcvrd to r in tch in midfield: effrt over 1f out: unable qck and short of room 1f out: wknd ins fnl f* **100/1**

**10** *shd* **Jawan** 2-8-9 0........................................ TristanPrice[(7)] 3 54
(Michael Bell) *chsd ldrs: wnt 2nd 1/2-way tl 2f out: no ex u.p over 1f out: wknd ins fnl f* **100/1**

00 **11** *1 1/4* **Timoshenko**[12] 7726 2-9-2 0........................................ LukeMorris 13 51
(Sir Mark Prescott Bt) *chsd ldrs tl shkn up and lost pl qckly over 2f out: sme modest hdwy to pass btn horses ins fnl f: no threat to ldrs* **250/1**

0 **12** *2 1/2* **Go Fox**[26] 7281 2-9-2 0........................................ HarryBentley 10 44
(Tom Clover) *hld up in tch in midfield: nt clr run over 1f out: wknd fnl f* **100/1**

6 **13** *3/4* **Sheriff**[26] 7281 2-9-2 0........................................ LouisSteward 8 42
(Michael Bell) *chsd ldrs: rdn over 1f out: no ex and struggling ent fnl f: fdd ins fnl f* **14/1**

**14** *3 1/4* **Spring Praise (IRE)** 2-9-2 0........................................ DanielMuscutt 11 33
(Marco Botti) *hld up in tch in last quartet: rdn over 1f out: sn btn and bhd ins fnl f* **66/1**

**15** *1/2* **Vantasy** 2-9-2 0........................................ JackMitchell 5 32
(Chris Wall) *dwlt: hld up in tch in last quartet: effrt over 1f out: sn btn and bhd ins fnl f* **66/1**

1m 28.74s (2.14) **Going Correction** +0.225s/f (Good) **15** Ran SP% **116.9**
Speed ratings (Par 97): **96,93,92,91,89 88,88,86,83,83 82,79,78,74,74**
CSF £88.16 TOTE £9.50: £3.10, £3.50, £4.30; EX 94.90 Trifecta £780.50.
**Owner** M J Jooste & China Horse Club **Bred** Meon Valley Stud **Trained** Newmarket, Suffolk

**FOCUS**

This looked a good novice, although stands' side proved the place to be in the closing stages, with those up the middle struggling. The first two created good impressions.

## 8120 PAUL GILL 70TH BIRTHDAY NURSERY H'CAP 7f 3y

**2:40** (2:43) (Class 5) (0-70,72) 2-Y-O **£2,911** (£866; £432; £216) **Stalls** Centre

Form RPR

045 **1** **Mutafarrid (IRE)**[67] 5844 2-9-6 69........................................ JimCrowley 4 80+
(Owen Burrows) *hld up in midfield: hdwy and rdn to chal 2f out: led 1f out: styd on wl and drew clr ins fnl f: rdn out* **9/2**[1]

5500 **2** *3 3/4* **Catapult**[20] 7491 2-8-11 63........................................ HollieDoyle[(3)] 12 64
(Clifford Lines) *racd in stands side trio: hld up in rr overall: swtchd lft over 2f out: rdn and hdwy to chal 2f out: led over 1f out: hdd 1f out: outpcd by wnr but hld onto 2nd ins fnl f* **25/1**

0003 **3** *1/2* **Progressive Jazz (IRE)**[19] 7519 2-7-10 50...........(v) RhiainIngram[(5)] 10 50
(K R Burke) *racd in stands trio: led gp but only midfield overall: effrt over 1f out: edgd lft ins fnl f: kpt on to go 3rd ins fnl f: no threat to wnr* **12/1**

2214 **4** *2* **Felisa**[21] 7458 2-9-2 65........................................ JFEgan 8 59
(David Evans) *chsd ldng trio: unable qck u.p over 1f out: wknd ins fnl f* **12/1**

6530 **5** *3/4* **General Marius (IRE)**[6] 7914 2-9-4 67..........................(b) JackMitchell 2 59
(Roger Varian) *s.i.s: hld up in last trio: rdn and hdwy over 2f out: drvn to press ldrs 2f out: no ex and hung rt 1f out: wknd ins fnl f* **12/1**

5420 **6** *1 1/2* **Ventura Gold (IRE)**[36] 6977 2-9-9 72........................................ DavidNolan 11 60
(Richard Fahey) *midfield: rdn over 2f out: hdwy u.p to chse ldrs and swtchd lft over 1f out: no imp and plugged on same pce ins fnl f* **10/1**

060 **7** *1/2* **Quick Breath**[24] 7351 2-9-6 69........................................ LukeMorris 13 56
(Jonathan Portman) *racd in stands side trio: midfield overall: effrt 2f out: hdwy and drvn to chse ldrs over 1f out: wknd ins fnl f* **20/1**

600 **8** *1 1/2* **Gembari**[38] 6897 2-8-13 62..............................(p[1]) SilvestreDeSousa 9 45
(Ivan Furtado) *bhd: rdn 4f out: edging rt over 2f out: sme hdwy but nt on terms w ldrs over 1f out: no imp ins fnl f* **16/1**

6563 **9** *hd* **Agent Of Fortune**[11] 7756 2-8-2 56..........................(h) JaneElliott[(5)] 5 38
(Christine Dunnett) *midfield: effrt over 2f out: no imp u.p over 1f out: wl hld and plugged on same pce fnl f* **20/1**

634 **10** *nk* **Divine Intuition (IRE)**[28] 7221 2-9-8 71........................ TomQueally 1 52
(Kevin Ryan) *chsd ldr tl 2f out: unable qck over 1f out: wknd ins fnl f* **11/1**

4343 **11** *4 1/2* **Fink Hill (USA)**[10] 7787 2-9-7 70..................................(b) FrannyNorton 7 39
(Richard Guest) *taken down early: led tl hdd and hung lft over 1f out: wl hld and eased ins fnl f* **6/1**[3]

5406 **12** *4* **Stormy Sand (IRE)**[11] 7764 2-9-4 67..........................(t) HarryBentley 6 25
(Marco Botti) *chsd ldrs: rdn 1/2-way: lost pl and btn over 1f out: bhd and eased ins fnl f* **11/2**[2]

005 **13** *11* **Mandarin Princess**[27] 7250 2-8-12 61........................ MartinHarley 3
(Philip McBride) *midfield: rdn over 3f out: bhd over 1f out* **10/1**

1m 28.03s (1.43) **Going Correction** +0.225s/f (Good) **13** Ran SP% **116.7**
Speed ratings (Par 95): **100,95,95,92,92 90,89,88,87,87 82,77,65**
CSF £122.77 CT £1311.01 TOTE £3.70: £1.70, £6.50, £3.40; EX 104.50 Trifecta £1565.00.
**Owner** Hamdan Al Maktoum **Bred** Deer Forest Stud **Trained** Lambourn, Berks

**FOCUS**

Only three of these stayed stands' side (which looked favoured in the previous race), including the second and third, and the remainder were more middle to far side. A decisive winner.

## 8121 BRITISH STALLION STUDS EBF BECKFORD STKS (LISTED RACE) (F&M) 1m 6f 17y

**3:10** (3:10) (Class 1) 3-Y-O+

**£22,684** (£8,600; £4,304; £2,144; £1,076; £540) **Stalls** High

Form RPR

-332 **1** **Aljezeera**[32] 7089 3-8-11 102........................................ FrankieDettori 5 104+
(Luca Cumani) *travelled strly: trckd ldr tl rdn to ld 2f out: qcknd and in command 1f out: r.o wl: eased towards fin* **15/8**[1]

2506 **2** *1 3/4* **Capricious Cantor (IRE)**[45] 6665 4-9-4 93........... SilvestreDeSousa 8 99
(Ed Dunlop) *stdd and swtchd sharply lft after s: hld up in tch in last pair: clsd and nt clr run on inner 2f out: sn swtchd rt and hdwy over 1f out: swtchd lft 1f out: styd on wl to go 2nd wl ins fnl f: no threat* **25/1**

1132 **3** *1* **Pacharana**[32] 7092 4-9-4 94........................................ LukeMorris 3 98
(Luca Cumani) *hld up in tch in midfield effrt over 2f out: drvn to chse clr wnr over 1f out: kpt on same pce and lost 2nd ins fnl f* **16/1**

21-1 **4** *3/4* **Daphne**[23] 7397 4-9-4 91........................................ JimCrowley 7 97
(William Haggas) *stdd s: t.k.h early: hld up in last pair: effrt on outer over 2f out: wnt 4th and edging lft ins fnl f: kpt on but no threat to wnr* **4/1**[2]

-404 **5** 3 ¾ **Colonial Classic (FR)**[17] 7581 4-9-4 **94** ........................ DanielMuscutt 1 92
(James Fanshawe) *led early: sn hdd and trckd ldrs: nt clrest of runs over 2f out: unable qck over 1f out: wknd ins fnl f* **33/1**

0206 **6** ½ **Dubka**[32] 7089 4-9-4 **102** ........................ RyanMoore 2 91
(Sir Michael Stoute) *awkward leaving stalls and sn swtchd lft: led after 1f: rdn 3f out: hdd 2f out: lost 2nd and unable qck over 1f out: wknd ins fnl f* **9/2**[3]

2243 **7** 1 ¼ **Notice (IRE)**[19] 7507 4-9-4 **85** ........................ MartinHarley 6 89
(David Simcock) *in tch in midfield: effrt to chse ldrs 3f out: struggling and dropped to rr 2f out: wknd ins fnl f* **16/1**

26 **8** 2 ¼ **Wingingit (IRE)**[23] 7393 3-8-11 **103** ........................ WilliamBuick 4 91
(Andrew Balding) *t.k.h: hld up in tch in midfield: effrt over 2f out: struggling and lost pl over 1f out and btn whn sltly impeded jst ins fnl f: bhd and eased towards fin* **4/1**[2]

3m 6.7s (-0.90) **Going Correction** -0.125s/f (Firm)
**WFA** 3 from 4yo 7lb **8** Ran SP% **111.5**
Speed ratings (Par 111): **97,96,95,95,92 92,91,90**
CSF £51.35 TOTE £2.50: £1.10, £4.40, £4.00; EX 53.60 Trifecta £276.20.
**Owner** Al Shaqab Racing **Bred** Newsells Park Stud **Trained** Newmarket, Suffolk

**FOCUS**
An ordinary-looking fillies' Listed race, with the form rated around the second, third and fourth.

## 8122 OPTIMIST DESIGN LTD H'CAP 1m 3f 104y
**3:40** (3:40) (Class 6) (0-55,55) 3-Y-O+ **£2,264** (£673; £336; £168) **Stalls** Low

Form RPR

0662 **1** **Four Kingdoms (IRE)**[6] 7928 3-8-8 **47** ........................ JoeyHaynes 1 63+
(K R Burke) *hld up in tch: clsd to press ldr and travelling strly 3f out: led over 2f out: sn gng clr: rdn and wl clr over 1f out: styd on wl: easily* **4/1**[1]

3555 **2** 8 **Sexy Secret**[4] 7990 6-8-10 **47** ........................(p) SimonPearce(3) 3 49
(Lydia Pearce) *t.k.h early: chsd ldrs: rdn and swtchd rt over 2f out: battling for 2nd but no ch w wnr fnl 2f: kpt on to go 2nd nr fin* **8/1**

4030 **3** ½ **Mungo Madness**[18] 7537 3-8-1 **47** ........................ MillyNaseb(7) 2 49
(Julia Feilden) *t.k.h: chsd ldrs: effrt to chse wnr over 2f out: sn outpcd and no ch w wnr: kpt on but lost wl hld 2nd nr fin* **20/1**

-036 **4** 4 **Hint Of Grey (IRE)**[112] 3575 4-9-4 **55** ........................ GeorgeWood(3) 12 50
(Don Cantillon) *keen early: hld up in tch in midfield:: effrt over 2f out: wl hld 4th and plugged on same pce fnl f* **5/1**[2]

2054 **5** 2 ½ **Chauvelin**[24] 7360 6-8-13 **50** ........................(v) LewisEdmunds(3) 8 41
(Nigel Tinkler) *hld up in tch in midfield: rdn 3f out: no imp whn sltly hmpd over 2f out: no ch and plugged on same pce fnl 2f* **7/1**

4540 **6** ¾ **Hellomoto**[4] 7991 3-8-13 **52** ........................(p) ShaneGray 4 43
(Kevin Ryan) *trckd ldng trio: rdn 3f out: sn outpcd: no ch and plugged on same pce fnl 2f* **11/2**[3]

2636 **7** 2 ¼ **Bizet (IRE)**[11] 7253 3-8-3 **49** ........................ JackOsborn(7) 7 36
(John Ryan) *s.i.s and rousted along early: hld up in last trio: modest hdwy u.p into midfield over 2f out: no prog after and wl btn fnl 2f* **16/1**

2200 **8** 2 ¾ **Simply Clever**[11] 7760 4-9-7 **55** ........................ TomQueally 5 37
(David Brown) *stdd s: t.k.h: hld up in rr: stl and nt clr of runs over 2f out: sn wl btn* **33/1**

1660 **9** 1 ¼ **The Lock Master (IRE)**[111] 4187 10-9-7 **55** ..........(p) AlistairRawlinson 9 35
(Michael Appleby) *rousted along early: in tch in midfield on outer: rdn 4f out: struggling over 2f out: bhd over 1f out* **50/1**

0204 **10** ¾ **Annoushka**[34] 7015 4-9-0 **48** ........................(vt[1]) AdamBeschizza 10 27
(Mrs Ilka Gansera-Leveque) *taken down early: t.k.h: led: rdn and hdd over 2f out: sn outpcd by wnr and btn: wknd over 1f out* **10/1**

3340 **11** 6 **Saga Sprint (IRE)**[59] 6153 4-9-5 **53** ........................(v[1]) FrannyNorton 6 22
(J R Jenkins) *t.k.h: hld up in last trio: effrt over 3f out: swtchd rt and no hdwy over 2f out: sn wknd and wl bhd ins fnl f* **12/1**

3006 **12** 8 **Lady Volante (IRE)**[9] 7820 3-8-12 **51** ow1 ........................ MartinHarley 11 8
(Rebecca Menzies) *chsd ldr tl 3f out: sn struggling: wl bhd and eased ins fnl f: t.o* **11/1**

2m 26.69s (-2.01) **Going Correction** -0.125s/f (Firm)
**WFA** 3 from 4yo+ 5lb **12** Ran SP% **116.3**
Speed ratings (Par 101): **102,96,95,92,91 90,88,86,86,85 81,75**
CSF £34.50 CT £571.92 TOTE £4.70: £2.00, £2.80, £5.70; EX 41.30 Trifecta £600.50.
**Owner** D Simpson & Mrs E Burke **Bred** Camogue Stud Ltd **Trained** Middleham Moor, N Yorks

**FOCUS**
A moderate handicap and the form looks straightforward.

## 8123 HAVEN SEASHORE HOLIDAY PARK H'CAP 1m 2f 23y
**4:10** (4:11) (Class 6) (0-60,60) 3-Y-O **£2,264** (£673; £336; £168) **Stalls** Low

Form RPR

0015 **1** **Broughtons Story**[6] 7917 3-8-8 **54** ........................ JackOsborn(7) 2 62
(Henry Spiller) *dwlt: hld up in tch in midfield: clsd to trck ldrs and swtchd rt 2f out: chal over 1f out: led ins fnl f: styd on wl: rdn out* **11/4**[1]

5260 **2** 2 **Rock On Dandy (FR)**[13] 7712 3-9-7 **60** ........................(v) LukeMorris 9 64
(Harry Dunlop) *pressed ldr tl led 2f out: sn drvn and hrd pressed: hdd and one pced ins fnl f* **13/2**[3]

6503 **3** 1 **King Kevin**[11] 7760 3-8-9 **48** ........................(b) SilvestreDeSousa 4 50
(Ed Dunlop) *stdd s: t.k.h: hld up in tch in last pair: swtchd lft and hdwy on inner 2f out: nt clr run and swtchd rt over 1f out: hdwy and styd on wl ins fnl f to go 3rd fnl 50yds: nvr getting to ldrs* **3/1**[2]

6300 **4** 1 ¼ **Ripper Street (IRE)**[39] 6851 3-8-2 **46** ........................(h) JaneElliott(5) 1 46
(Christine Dunnett) *stdd s: t.k.h: hld up in tch in last pair: effrt and hdwy over 2f out: rdn to chse clr ldng pair over 1f out: kpt on same pce and lost 3rd fnl 50yds* **33/1**

0042 **5** 3 ¼ **Dixon**[9] 7833 3-9-2 **55** ........................ JoeyHaynes 3 49
(Mark H Tompkins) *chsd ldng pair: effrt ent fnl 2f: unable qck u.p and btn 4th 1f out: wknd ins fnl f* **13/2**[3]

650 **6** 2 ¼ **My Name Is Jeff**[56] 6277 3-9-4 **57** ........................ AdamBeschizza 5 46
(Julia Feilden) *hld up in tch in midfield: effrt over 2f out: no imp u.p whn nt clr run and swtchd rt over 1f out: wknd fnl f* **8/1**

0030 **7** 2 ½ **Sonnet Rose (IRE)**[11] 7761 3-9-2 **55** ........................ GeraldMosse 6 40
(Conrad Allen) *led tl 2f out: sn rdn and outpcd: wknd and eased wl ins fnl f* **18/1**

3532 **8** 3 ¾ **Kulgri**[26] 7271 3-8-11 **53** ........................ LewisEdmunds(3) 7 31
(Kevin Ryan) *wl in tch in midfield: effrt 3f out: no imp u.p and btn whn wnt rt over 1f out: wknd fnl f* **13/2**[3]

2034 **9** 5 **Starboard Watch**[19] 7514 3-9-6 **59** ........................ TomQueally 8 27
(James Given) *hld up in midfield on outer: effrt over 2f out: sn dropped to rr: bhd and eased ins fnl f* **25/1**

2m 9.36s (-1.14) **Going Correction** -0.125s/f (Firm) **9** Ran SP% **114.8**
Speed ratings (Par 99): **99,97,96,95,93 91,89,86,82**
CSF £20.99 CT £56.28 TOTE £3.50: £1.40, £2.00, £1.60; EX 22.90 Trifecta £89.60.
**Owner** Broughton Thermal Insulation **Bred** M E Broughton **Trained** Newmarket, Suffolk

**FOCUS**
A weak race rated around the firs three.

## 8124 GREAT YARMOUTH & CAISTER GOLF CLUB MECHANTS GALLOP H'CAP (DIV I) 1m 3y
**4:40** (4:43) (Class 6) (0-65,66) 3-Y-O+ **£2,264** (£673; £336; £168) **Stalls** Centre

Form RPR

0400 **1** **Harlequin Rock**[42] 6751 4-8-8 **52** ........................(p[1]) FrannyNorton 7 59
(Mick Quinn) *trckd ldrs: swtchd lft and trckd ldr 2f out: rdn over 1f out: pushed along hands and heels ins fnl f: doing little in front but in command after: pushed out* **11/1**

5050 **2** ¾ **Harry Beau**[87] 5111 3-9-2 **63** ........................ JFEgan 9 67
(David Evans) *t.k.h: led: rdn over 1f out: hdd and styd on same pce ins fnl f* **16/1**

2365 **3** ½ **Coverham (IRE)**[21] 7465 3-9-1 **62** ........................ RyanTate 1 65
(James Eustace) *in tch in midfield: effrt u.p to chse ldrs over 1f out: kpt on same pce u.p ins fnl f* **7/2**[2]

0060 **4** 1 ¼ **Gatillo**[21] 7465 4-8-12 **56** ........................ AdamBeschizza 2 57
(Julia Feilden) *stdd after s: hld up in tch in rr: clsd and swtchd rt 2f out: 4th and kpt on same pce ins fnl f* **25/1**

2300 **5** 2 ¾ **Chiswick Bey (IRE)**[20] 7476 9-9-4 **62** ........................ DavidNolan 6 57
(Richard Fahey) *hld up in tch: rdn over 2f out: sn outpcd: rallied ent fnl f: kpt on but no threat to ldrs* **5/1**

6006 **6** 4 **Marilyn**[21] 7457 3-8-11 **61** ........................(p[1]) GeorgeWood(3) 5 46
(Chris Wall) *t.k.h: chsd ldr tl over 2f out: sn u.p and unable qck: wknd fnl f* **3/1**[1]

3450 **7** 1 ¼ **Anastazia**[11] 7771 5-9-7 **65** ........................ JoeyHaynes 8 48
(Paul D'Arcy) *chsd ldrs: wnt 2nd over 2f out tl 2f out: lost pl u.p over 1f out: wknd fnl f* **7/1**

5555 **8** 2 ¼ **Tan Arabiq**[16] 7601 4-9-8 **66** ........................ LukeMorris 3 44
(Michael Appleby) *impeded leaving stalls: hld up in tch: rdn 1/2-way: dropped to rr and btn 2f out: bhd fnl f* **9/2**[3]

/0-0 **9** 1 **Birikyno**[29] 7198 6-8-4 **51** oh6 ........................ NathanAlison(3) 4 26
(Matthew Salaman) *stdd and wnt lft leaving stalls: hld up in tch: rdn over 2f out: no imp and dropped to rr over 1f out: wknd fnl f* **66/1**

1m 42.03s (1.43) **Going Correction** +0.225s/f (Good)
**WFA** 3 from 4yo+ 3lb **9** Ran SP% **114.1**
Speed ratings (Par 101): **101,100,99,98,95 91,90,88,87**
CSF £167.25 CT £747.75 TOTE £11.80: £3.10, £3.30, £1.80; EX 159.90 Trifecta £762.00.
**Owner** Andy Viner & M Quinn **Bred** Woodcote Stud Ltd **Trained** Newmarket, Suffolk

**FOCUS**
They raced towards the middle in this modest handicap. The placed horses set the level.

## 8125 GREAT YARMOUTH & CAISTER GOLF CLUB MECHANTS GALLOP H'CAP (DIV II) 1m 3y
**5:10** (5:10) (Class 6) (0-65,65) 3-Y-O+ **£2,264** (£673; £336; £168) **Stalls** Centre

Form RPR

4410 **1** **Kilbaha Lady (IRE)**[10] 7792 3-8-12 **62** ........................(t) LewisEdmunds(3) 9 68
(Nigel Tinkler) *stdd s: hld up in tch in rr: swtchd rt and effrt jst over 1f out: rdn and hdwy to ld 100yds out: edgd lft and sn hrd pressed: hld on: all out* **5/1**[3]

5003 **2** *nse* **Titan Goddess**[43] 6725 5-9-7 **65** ........................ AntonioFresu 7 71
(Mike Murphy) *stdd s: t.k.h: hld up in tch: shkn up and effrt over 1f out: rdn and hdwy to chal wl ins fnl f: styd on: jst hld* **7/2**[1]

4560 **3** 2 **Dor's Law**[25] 7324 4-8-7 **51** oh2 ........................(p[1]) LukeMorris 6 52
(Dean Ivory) *a.p: rdn to ld over 1f out: edgd lft 1f out: hdd 100yds out: sn squeezed for room and one pce* **6/1**

0530 **4** ½ **Miss Osier**[18] 7539 3-9-1 **62** ........................(p) MartinHarley 1 61
(Rae Guest) *racd away fr main body of the field towards far side: led tl over 6f out: styd chsng ldr: rdn and ev ch 2f out tl no ex ins fnl f: styd on same pce fnl 75yds* **11/2**

4440 **5** *hd* **Luna Magic**[26] 7278 3-9-4 **65** ........................(h) TomQueally 2 64
(Lydia Pearce) *nt that wl away: steadily rcvrd to ld over 6f out: rdn and hdd over 1f out: stl ev ch tl no ex and squeezed for room wl ins fnl f: one pce after* **20/1**

0000 **6** *nk* **Pickett's Charge**[17] 7571 4-9-7 **65** ........................(b[1]) ShaneGray 5 64
(Richard Guest) *t.k.h: hld up in tch: effrt ent fnl 2f: rdn and unable qck over 1f out: kpt on same pce ins fnl f* **9/1**

0000 **7** 1 **Tawfeer**[25] 7325 3-7-11 **51** oh5 ........................(p) NicolaCurrie(7) 8 47
(Phil McEntee) *hld up wl in tch in midfield: hdwy u.p to chse ldrs over 1f out: no ex 1f out: kpt on same pce ins fnl f* **50/1**

0321 **8** 2 **Zaria**[21] 7463 6-8-4 **55** ........................(p) GabrieleMalune(7) 3 47
(Richard Price) *trckd ldrs: rdn over 2f out: unable qck u.p and dropped to rr over 1f out: wknd ins fnl f* **4/1**[2]

0050 **9** 1 ¼ **Gabrielle**[30] 7158 4-8-10 **57** ........................(h) GeorgeWood(3) 4 46
(Dr Jon Scargill) *wl in tch in midfield: shkn up 3f out: unable qck u.p and dropped to rr over 1f out: wknd ins fnl f* **11/1**

1m 41.6s (1.00) **Going Correction** +0.225s/f (Good)
**WFA** 3 from 4yo+ 3lb **9** Ran SP% **113.6**
Speed ratings (Par 101): **104,103,101,101,101 100,99,97,96**
CSF £22.45 CT £106.04 TOTE £4.80: £1.50, £1.40, £2.50; EX 21.70 Trifecta £63.80.
**Owner** The Dapper Partnership **Bred** Helen Lyons **Trained** Langton, N Yorks

**FOCUS**
The time was 0.42sec faster than the first division. A minor personal best by the winner.

## 8126 RACING WELFARE H'CAP 1m 3y
**5:40** (5:40) (Class 5) (0-75,77) 3-Y-O+ **£2,911** (£866; £432; £216) **Stalls** Centre

Form RPR

6610 **1** **Blaze Of Hearts (IRE)**[31] 7131 4-9-6 **74** ........................ JFEgan 9 82
(Dean Ivory) *mde all: shkn up over 1f out: rdn and hung lft 1f out: stl gng lft but styd on wl ins fnl f* **8/1**

1 **2** 1 ¼ **Monaadhil (IRE)**[133] 3394 3-9-5 **76** ........................ JimCrowley 3 80
(Marcus Tregoning) *stdd s: t.k.h: hld up in tch: rdn and hdwy over 1f out: ev ch 1f out: keeping on same pce and hld whn carried lft wl ins fnl f* **15/8**[1]

3602 **3** ½ **Zeshov (IRE)**[9] 7823 6-9-9 **77** ........................(p) MartinHarley 4 81
(Rebecca Bastiman) *chsd wnr: rdn and ev ch over 1f out: 3rd and jst getting outpcd whn carried lft and squeezed fro room jst ins fnl f: kpt on same pce fnl 100yds* **7/2**[3]

3114 **4** ½ **Lunar Deity**[102] 4541 8-8-7 **68** ........................(t) MillyNaseb(7) 7 71
(Stuart Williams) *stdd and awkward leaving stalls: t.k.h: hld up wl in tch: shkn up over 1f out: unable qck 1f out: hdwy ins fnl f: styd on towards fin: nt rch ldrs* **10/1**

6003 **5** 1 ¼ **Vanity Queen**[24] 7364 3-9-4 **75** ........................ LukeMorris 2 74
(Luca Cumani) *wl in tch in midfield: shkn up over 1f out: sn rdn: styd on same pce ins fnl f* **3/1**[2]

0040 **6** 3 ½ **Lady Lydia (IRE)**[9] 7830 6-9-3 71 ........................(tp) DanielMuscutt 1 63
(Gay Kelleway) *stdd s: t.k.h: hld up in tch in rr: clsd 2f out: effrt u.p over 1f out: sn btn and wknd ins fnl f* **40/1**

1504 **7** 8 **Wigan Warrior**[11] 7759 3-9-5 76 ........................ TomQueally 5 49
(David Brown) *s.i.s: bhd: hdwy to chse ldrs after 1f: shkn up 2f out: lost pl u.p and btn over 1f out: bhd and eased ins fnl f* **16/1**

1m 42.4s (1.80) **Going Correction** +0.225s/f (Good)
**WFA** 3 from 4yo+ 3lb 7 Ran SP% **110.5**
Speed ratings (Par 103): **100,98,98,97,96 93,85**
CSF £21.89 CT £58.86 TOTE £9.50: £3.90, £1.50; EX 34.40 Trifecta £100.00.
**Owner** Miss N Yarrow **Bred** Camogue Stud Ltd **Trained** Radlett, Herts

**FOCUS**
The winner dominated up the middle of the track. The winner has earned his best three figures here now.
T/Plt: £266.20 to a £1 stake. Pool: £65,119.41 - 178.57 winning units T/Qpdt: £12.80 to a £1 stake. Pool: £8,510.51 - 491.76 winning units **Steve Payne**

## 6566 CLAIREFONTAINE (R-H)
Monday, October 16

**OFFICIAL GOING: Turf: very soft**

### 8127a PRIX DES LAIS DE MER (CONDITIONS) (4YO+) (TURF) 1m
12:25 4-Y-0+ £11,965 (£4,786; £3,589; £2,393; £1,196)

RPR

**1** **Jasnin (FR)**[351] 5-8-11 0 ........................ EddyHardouin 6 93
(Waldemar Hickst, Germany) **51/10**

**2** 1 ¼ **Kiwi Green Suite (BRZ)**[33] 4-9-0 0 ........................ GregoryBenoist 7 93
(D Smaga, France) **74/10**

**3** ¾ **Blue Soave (FR)**[43] 6729 9-9-11 0 ........................ TonyPiccone 2 102
(F Chappet, France) **39/10**[3]

**4** 9 **Kendemai (FR)**[508] 6-9-4 0 ........................ ChristopheSoumillon 1 75
(J-C Rouget, France) **37/10**[2]

**5** 10 **Light Of The World (IRE)**[991] 327 5-8-4 0 .....(p) DelphineSantiago(4) 5 42
(Georgios Alimpinisis, Greece) **222/10**

**6** 15 **Veronica's Napkin (IRE)**[36] 5-8-8 0 ........................ WilliamsSaraiva 3 7
(J Moon, Jersey) **56/1**

**P** **Boomshackerlacker (IRE)**[23] 7416 7-9-2 0 ..........(p) MaximeGuyon 4
(George Baker) *Well into stride: settled 2nd: beginning to chal ldr over 2f out whn wnt bdly wrong and p.u* **7/5**[1]

1m 40.3s 7 Ran SP% **117.7**
PARI-MUTUEL (all including 1 euro stake): WIN 6.10; PLACE 3.20, 3.90, SF 40.00.
**Owner** Guido Werner Hermann Schmitt **Bred** Mme A De La Motte Saint-Pierre Et Al **Trained** Germany

## 8027 KEMPTON (A.W) (R-H)
Tuesday, October 17

**OFFICIAL GOING: Polytrack: standard to slow**
Wind: Light, across Weather: Overcast

### 8128 100% PROFIT BOOST AT 32REDSPORT.COM H'CAP 5f (P)
5:15 (5:17) (Class 6) (0-60,60) 3-Y-0+ £2,587 (£770; £384; £192) Stalls Low

Form RPR

1240 **1** **Lucky Clover**[6] 7951 6-9-5 58 ........................ AdamKirby 4 64
(Malcolm Saunders) *led 100yds: chsd ldr: shkn up 2f out: clsd u.p fnl f to ld last 75yds* **7/1**

0032 **2** ¾ **Kyllukey**[6] 7951 4-9-7 60 ........................(v) LukeMorris 5 63
(Milton Bradley) *led after 100yds: kicked for home bnd 2f out: kpt on but hdd last 75yds* **9/2**[2]

5625 **3** 1 ¼ **Mercers**[21] 7494 3-9-6 59 ........................ ShaneKelly 7 59
(Peter Crate) *hld up in tch: shkn up on outer over 1f out: styd on ins fnl f to take 3rd last strides* **8/1**

3601 **4** nk **Prominna**[21] 7494 7-9-4 57 ........................ DavidProbert 2 55
(Tony Carroll) *t.k.h: trckd ldrs: chsd ldng pair 2f out: no imp 1f out: one pce and lost 3rd last strides* **11/2**[3]

2014 **5** shd **Staffa (IRE)**[17] 7607 4-9-2 60 ........................ PaddyPilley(5) 10 57
(Denis Coakley) *trapped out wd in last trio: shkn up over 1f out: styd on ins fnl f to press for 3rd nr fin* **20/1**

0312 **6** ¾ **Atlanta Belle (IRE)**[20] 7517 3-9-7 60 ........................ TedDurcan 6 56
(Chris Wall) *trapped out wd: chsd ldng pair to 2f out: pushed along and one pce after: lost pls last 100yds* **7/4**[1]

630 **7** ½ **Captain Scooby**[7] 7926 11-8-7 46 oh1 ........................(b) FrannyNorton 1 39
(Richard Guest) *struggling to go the pce early in last trio: effrt 2f out: no prog on inner 1f out: fdd* **8/1**

000- **8** 7 **Aegean Boy**[378] 7048 4-8-13 52 ........................ WilliamCarson 9 20
(John Bridger) *plld hrd: hld up: last fr 1/2-way: wknd 2f out: t.o* **66/1**

59.44s (-1.06) **Going Correction** -0.175s/f (Stan) 8 Ran SP% **110.9**
Speed ratings (Par 101): **101,99,97,97,97 95,95,83**
CSF £36.05 CT £246.58 TOTE £6.20: £2.60, £1.40, £2.60; EX 26.10 Trifecta £159.00.
**Owner** Paul Nicholas & M S Saunders **Bred** Cobhall Court Stud **Trained** Green Ore, Somerset

**FOCUS**
Few got into this.

### 8129 32RED H'CAP 5f (P)
5:45 (5:47) (Class 3) (0-90,89) 3-Y-0+
£7,158 (£2,143; £1,071; £535; £267; £134) Stalls Low

Form RPR

124 **1** **Foxy Forever (IRE)**[4] 7994 7-9-5 87 ........................(t) FrannyNorton 1 96
(Michael Wigham) *trckd ldng pair: tk 2nd on inner over 1f out: rdn to ld jst ins fnl f: kpt on wl* **7/2**[2]

0401 **2** ¾ **Alsvinder**[19] 7538 4-9-5 87 ........................ DanielTudhope 4 93
(David O'Meara) *t.k.h: led after 1f: steered away fr rail in st: rdn over 1f out: hdd jst ins fnl f: kpt on but a hld after* **3/1**[1]

0406 **3** 1 ¼ **Shamshon (IRE)**[10] 7809 6-9-4 86 ........................(t) AdamBeschizza 5 88
(Stuart Williams) *mostly in last pair: rdn over 2f out: no prog tl styd on fnl f to take 3rd last strides* **5/1**[3]

31-0 **4** nse **Gorgeous Noora (IRE)**[24] 7405 3-8-13 81 ........................ JamieSpencer 7 83
(Luca Cumani) *t.k.h: trckd ldng trio: rdn and fnd nil over 1f out: styd on ins fnl f to press for 3rd nr fin* **12/1**

-605 **5** hd **Kodiline (IRE)**[53] 6392 3-9-5 87 ........................(v) AdamKirby 3 89
(Clive Cox) *in tch in 5th: rdn and no prog over 1f out: kpt on ins fnl f to press for 3rd nr fin* **5/1**[3]

2234 **6** 1 **Arzaak (IRE)**[27] 7286 3-9-0 85 ........................(b) LewisEdmunds(3) 6 83
(Chris Dwyer) *wl away fr wd draw: led 1f: pressed ldr to over 1f out: wl hld after: wknd last 100yds* **6/1**

4040 **7** 3 **Gentlemen**[10] 7828 6-9-0 89 ........................(h) NicolaCurrie(7) 2 75
(Phil McEntee) *pushed along in last bef 1/2-way: a struggling* **14/1**

58.26s (-2.24) **Going Correction** -0.175s/f (Stan) course record 7 Ran SP% **109.2**
Speed ratings (Par 107): **110,108,106,106,106 104,100**
CSF £13.05 TOTE £4.90: £2.10, £1.70; EX 14.20 Trifecta £65.60.
**Owner** D Hassan, J Cullinan **Bred** Tally-Ho Stud **Trained** Newmarket, Suffolk

**FOCUS**
Once again few were able to get involved over this sharp 5f. The winner is getting close to his old best.

### 8130 32RED/BRITISH STALLIONS STUDS EBF FILLIES' NOVICE STKS (PLUS 10 RACE) 6f (P)
6:15 (6:15) (Class 5) 2-Y-O £3,234 (£962; £481; £240) Stalls Low

Form RPR

44 **1** **Guns Drawn (IRE)**[13] 7725 2-9-0 0 ........................ DanielTudhope 5 73
(Richard Hannon) *chsd ldrs: plld out and rdn in 5th 2f out: styd on strly fnl f to ld last 50yds* **6/1**[2]

**2** ½ **Gilded Hour (IRE)** 2-9-0 0 ........................ OisinMurphy 1 72
(Ralph Beckett) *trckd ldng pair: rdn to ld on inner over 1f out: styd on but hdd last 50yds* **6/1**[2]

43 **3** ½ **Alba Del Sole (IRE)**[13] 7732 2-9-0 0 ........................ NickyMackay 6 70
(John Gosden) *chsd ldrs on outer: shkn up over 2f out: clsd over 1f out: styd on but nvr quite pce to chal* **8/1**[3]

**4** 1 **Hit The Beat** 2-9-0 0 ........................ SamHitchcott 3 67
(Clive Cox) *mde most to over 1f out: one pce fnl f* **20/1**

04 **5** 2 ½ **Crystal Casque**[14] 7707 2-9-0 0 ........................ DavidProbert 4 60
(Rod Millman) *pressed ldr: stl upsides 2f out: lost 2nd sn after and wknd fnl f* **25/1**

145 **6** 3 ¼ **Spring Cosmos (IRE)**[59] 6228 2-9-7 0 ........................ WilliamBuick 8 57
(Charlie Appleby) *racd on outer in 6th: nt gng wl bef 1/2-way: rdn and no rspnse over 2f out: wl btn after* **2/7**[1]

**7** shd **Praxedis** 2-9-0 0 ........................ TomQueally 7 49
(James Fanshawe) *slowly away: rn green in rr and sn t.k.h: in tch on inner over 2f out: pushed along and fdd over 1f out* **20/1**

0 **8** 2 ¾ **Poorauldjosephine**[117] 3993 2-9-0 0 ........................ FrannyNorton 2 41
(J R Jenkins) *sn outpcd: nvr a factor* **50/1**

1m 12.02s (-1.08) **Going Correction** -0.175s/f (Stan) 8 Ran SP% **132.8**
Speed ratings (Par 92): **100,99,98,97,94 89,89,85**
CSF £44.98 TOTE £8.50: £1.50, £1.70, £2.10; EX 56.90 Trifecta £247.30.
**Owner** Clipper Logistics **Bred** Michael Rogers **Trained** East Everleigh, Wilts

**FOCUS**
The odds-on favourite disappointed so this is just fair novice form.

### 8131 32RED ON THE APP STORE NURSERY H'CAP 6f (P)
6:45 (6:46) (Class 5) (0-75,75) 2-Y-O £3,234 (£962; £481; £240) Stalls Low

Form RPR

0562 **1** **Bath And Tennis (IRE)**[14] 7706 2-9-4 72 ........................(b) LukeMorris 12 77
(Sir Mark Prescott Bt) *t.k.h early: trckd ldrs on outer: rdn and no immediate rspnse 2f out: picked up really strly fnl f: edgd lft but led last 75yds: gng away qckly at fin* **11/2**[2]

6522 **2** 1 ¾ **Queen Of Kalahari**[22] 7458 2-9-4 75 ........................ CallumShepherd(3) 3 75
(Charles Hills) *trckd ldrs on inner: shkn up 2f out: prog fnl f: fin wl to take 2nd last strides* **8/1**

2263 **3** nk **Airshow**[63] 6030 2-9-2 70 ........................ AdamBeschizza 2 69
(Rod Millman) *t.k.h early: led 100yds: cl up: rdn to ld on inner over 1f out: drvn fnl f: hdd last 75yds: lost 2nd fnl strides* **10/1**

5224 **4** hd **Forever In Love**[26] 7335 2-9-1 69 ........................ WilliamBuick 5 67
(Sir Michael Stoute) *rousted fr stalls to ld after 100yds: drvn over 2f out: hdd over 1f out: chsd ldr to 100yds out: one pce* **13/2**

0011 **5** nse **Mountain Peak**[41] 6815 2-9-2 70 ........................ LiamKeniry 4 68
(Ed Walker) *chsd ldr after 1f to over 2f out: drvn and stl disputing 2nd fnl f: one pce last 100yds* **3/1**[1]

2330 **6** 1 ¼ **Tiepolo (IRE)**[7] 7914 2-9-6 74 ........................ AdamKirby 6 68
(Gary Moore) *hld up towards rr: shkn up over 2f out: trying to make prog but u.p whn nt clr run briefly ins fnl f: no hdwy after* **8/1**

030 **7** ¾ **Little Miss Lilly**[103] 4533 2-9-0 68 ........................ SamHitchcott 7 60
(Clive Cox) *chsd ldrs but trapped out wd: rdn wl over 2f out: no prog* **25/1**

541 **8** hd **Straight Ash (IRE)**[129] 3570 2-9-1 72 ........................ HollieDoyle(3) 10 64
(Richard Hannon) *dropped in fr wd draw and hld up in last pair: rdn and no prog over 2f out* **10/1**

000 **9** 2 ¼ **Bodie And Doyle**[22] 7460 2-8-7 61 ........................ DavidProbert 1 46
(Andrew Balding) *hld up in rr: shkn up and no prog over 2f out: wl btn over 1f out* **6/1**[3]

2316 **10** 4 **Haveoneyerself (IRE)**[14] 7706 2-9-3 71 ........................ JFEgan 11 44
(John Butler) *hld up in last pair: shkn up 2f out: wknd over 1f out* **33/1**

1m 12.08s (-1.02) **Going Correction** -0.175s/f (Stan) 10 Ran SP% **115.2**
Speed ratings (Par 95): **99,96,96,96,95 94,93,93,90,84**
CSF £48.36 CT £438.60 TOTE £5.80: £2.20, £2.40, £3.00; EX 50.70 Trifecta £285.40.
**Owner** Timothy J Rooney **Bred** Kildaragh Stud **Trained** Newmarket, Suffolk

**FOCUS**
The early pace wasn't that strong and they finished in a bit of a heap behind the winner. The first five were in the first five positions heading into the turn. The second sets the level.

### 8132 32RED CASINO H'CAP 1m (P)
7:15 (7:17) (Class 5) (0-70,70) 3-Y-0+ £3,234 (£962; £481; £240) Stalls Low

Form RPR

-362 **1** **Medicean El Diablo**[34] 7058 4-9-6 69 ........................ TomMarquand 2 78+
(Jimmy Fox) *s.i.s but sn in 8th: stdy prog jst over 2f out: pushed into the ld jst ins fnl f: shkn up to make sure nr fin but won w authority* **7/2**[1]

2665 **2** ¾ **Connemera Queen**[13] 7723 4-9-1 64 ........................ RobertWinston 3 69
(John Butler) *trckd ldrs in 6th: shkn up and effrt 2f out: prog over 1f out: styd on wl to take 2nd last 75yds: nvr really able to chal wnr* **16/1**

5003 **3** shd **Beyond Recall**[12] 7770 3-9-4 70 ........................(v) JamieSpencer 10 74
(Luca Cumani) *hld up in 9th: prog and shifted lft wl over 1f out: drvn and r.o fnl f: tk 2nd last 75yds and pressed runner-up after* **15/2**

5624 **4** ¾ **African Blessing**[8] 7878 4-9-3 69 ........................ DavidEgan(3) 14 72
(Charlie Wallis) *chsd ldr: rdn 2f out: cl enough 1f out: sn outpcd: kpt on but lost pls nr fin* **14/1**

1223 **5** *nk* **The Groove**[7] 7932 4-9-4 **67** TrevorWhelan 4 69
(Fergal O'Brien) *chsd ldng trio: rdn over 2f out: cl enough jst over 1f out: one pce u.p after* **10/1**

6214 **6** *nk* **Solent Meads (IRE)**[22] 7457 3-9-3 **69** (b) GeorgeDowning 8 70
(Daniel Kubler) *led at gd pce and stretched field: rdn over 2f out: hdd and fdd jst ins fnl f* **16/1**

4600 **7** *hd* **Tailor's Row (USA)**[22] 7457 3-9-1 **67** FrannyNorton 6 67
(Mark Johnston) *hld up in 7th: rdn and nt qckn over 2f out and lost pl: hdwy again jst over 1f out: fin wl but too late to threaten* **16/1**

4460 **8** *1 ¼* **Biotic**[22] 7452 6-9-6 **69** OisinMurphy 5 67
(Rod Millman) *s.i.s: hld up in 10th: sme prog 2f out: one pce fr over 1f out* **6/1**

-002 **9** *hd* **Spun Gold**[31] 7157 3-9-0 **66** StevieDonohoe 13 63
(Charlie Fellowes) *hld up in last trio fr wd draw: pushed along over 2f out and no prog: rdn ins fnl f and kpt on: nvr in it* **9/2**[3]

0052 **10** *½* **Waqt (IRE)**[13] 7723 3-9-0 **66** JimCrowley 9 62
(Marcus Tregoning) *chsd ldng pair: rdn over 2f out: wknd over 1f out* **4/1**[2]

0240 **11** *3 ½* **Dream Magic (IRE)**[38] 6947 3-8-10 **65** EoinWalsh(3) 11 53
(Daniel Mark Loughnane) *stdd s fr wd draw: hld up in last pair: nvr a factor* **40/1**

000 **12** *7* **Prosecute (FR)**[14] 7711 4-8-13 **62** (t[1]) LiamKeniry 1 35
(Ali Stronge) *s.v.s: a in last pair: t.o* **66/1**

4306 **13** *2 ¼* **World Of Good**[180] 1898 4-9-2 **65** (b) LukeMorris 12 32
(Anabel K Murphy) *chsd ldrs in 5th: sing to lost pl whn impeded wl over 1f out: wknd rapidly: t.o* **50/1**

1m 38.13s (-1.67) **Going Correction** -0.175s/f (Stan)
**WFA** 3 from 4yo+ 3lb **13** Ran SP% **125.8**
Speed ratings (Par 103): **101,100,100,99,99 98,98,97,97,96 93,86,83**
CSF £65.29 CT £427.88 TOTE £4.60: £1.90, £5.00, £2.40; EX 69.00 Trifecta £717.80.
**Owner** Sugar Syndicate **Bred** Pantile Stud **Trained** Collingbourne Ducis, Wilts

**FOCUS**
They were well strung out early on and the gallop was a sound one. The form looks straightforward.

## 8133 TALKSPORT H'CAP (DIV I) 7f (P)
7:45 (7:45) (Class 6) (0-55,55) 3-Y-0+ **£2,587** (£770; £384; £192) **Stalls** Low

Form RPR

0500 **1** **Freddy With A Y (IRE)**[6] 7945 7-9-6 **54** (b) KierenFox 9 63
(J R Jenkins) *prom in chsng gp: rdn over 2f out: clsd qckly to ld over 1f out: sn clr: drvn out* **8/1**[3]

0533 **2** *2* **Binky Blue (IRE)**[6] 7945 5-9-4 **52** (h) ShaneKelly 12 56
(Daniel Mark Loughnane) *hld up in rr: prog 2f out: rdn and r.o to take 2nd last 100yds: too late to threaten wnr* **7/2**[2]

0005 **3** *½* **Lucky Di**[8] 7911 7-9-0 **48** CharlesBishop 13 51
(Peter Hedger) *hld up wl in rr: shkn up over 2f out: prog jst over 1f out: styd on to take 3rd nr fin: nvr nrr* **12/1**

0060 **4** *½* **Jasmincita (IRE)**[12] 7763 3-8-10 **46** (p) LiamKeniry 8 46
(George Baker) *dwlt: in tch in chsng gp: rdn and nt qckn over 2f out: n.d after but styd on again fnl f* **16/1**

5303 **5** *½* **Ronni Layne**[19] 7539 3-9-2 **52** MartinDwyer 1 51
(Conrad Allen) *prom in chsng gp: wnt 2nd briefly over 1f out: fdd ins fnl f* **7/2**[2]

3040 **6** *¾* **Royal Caper**[17] 7606 7-9-0 **48** StevieDonohoe 2 46
(Miss Joey Ellis) *in tch in chsng gp: rdn and no prog over 2f out: one pce and no imp ldrs after* **8/1**[3]

006 **7** *1 ½* **Spirit Of Gondree (IRE)**[106] 4451 9-8-12 **46** oh1...(b) RobertWinston 11 40
(Milton Bradley) *dwlt: hld up in last pair: pushed along over 2f out: passed a few rivals fnl f but nvr in it and eased last 75yds* **40/1**

0054 **8** *hd* **Dalalah**[4] 7993 4-8-12 **46** oh1 (b) DougieCostello 4 39
(Richard Guest) *nvr bttr than midfield: rdn over 2f out: wknd jst over 1f out* **16/1**

004 **9** *nse* **Instigator**[55] 6324 3-8-12 **48** DavidProbert 5 40
(Ralph J Smith) *dwlt: hld up in last pair: effrt over 2f out: one pce and no significant hdwy over 1f out* **3/1**[1]

0/ **10** *¾* **Pegi Browne (IRE)**[93] 4703 4-9-5 **53** MartinLane 6 44
(Paul Midgley) *s.s: mostly in last quartet: shkn up and sme prog wl over 1f out: sn no hdwy* **16/1**

0305 **11** *¾* **Live Dangerously**[8] 7900 7-9-7 **55** WilliamCarson 3 44
(John Bridger) *wl away: led 1f: chsd clr ldr to over 1f out: wknd rapidly* **14/1**

6400 **12** *4 ½* **Caius College Girl (IRE)**[15] 7693 5-8-10 **47** (b) HollieDoyle(3) 10 24
(Adrian Wintle) *plld hrd: led after 1f and tore off into clr ld: hung to nr side rail in st: wknd qckly and hdd over 1f out* **25/1**

0006 **13** *13* **Tink**[113] 4161 3-8-7 **46** oh1 CharlieBennett(3) 7
(Mark Brisbourne) *prom in chsng gp to 1/2-way: hung lft bnd sn after and wknd qckly: t.o* **66/1**

1m 25.16s (-0.84) **Going Correction** -0.175s/f (Stan)
**WFA** 3 from 4yo+ 2lb **13** Ran SP% **131.5**
Speed ratings (Par 101): **97,94,94,93,93 92,90,90,90,89 88,83,68**
CSF £39.47 CT £293.76 TOTE £10.50: £3.20, £1.70, £3.70; EX 51.30 Trifecta £373.00.
**Owner** Andy Taylor **Bred** David McGuinness **Trained** Royston, Herts

**FOCUS**
A moderate handicap. The field largely ignored the runaway leader Caius College Girl. The form looks straightforward rated around the second, third and fourth.

## 8134 TALKSPORT H'CAP (DIV II) 7f (P)
8:15 (8:15) (Class 6) (0-55,55) 3-Y-0+ **£2,587** (£770; £384; £192) **Stalls** Low

Form RPR

0262 **1** **Magic Mirror**[6] 7952 4-9-7 **55** (p) TomMarquand 1 66
(Mark Rimell) *dwlt: towards rr: gd prog on inner over 2f out: rdn to ld over 1f out: styd on wl and clr fnl f* **5/2**[1]

46 **2** *2 ¼* **Kafeel (USA)**[138] 3263 6-9-2 **53** (b[1]) HectorCrouch(3) 4 58
(Gary Moore) *hld up in midfield: shkn up and no prog over 2f out: hdwy and drvn over 1f out: styd on wl to take 2nd last 100yds: no threat to wnr* **4/1**[2]

4404 **3** *1 ½* **Black Truffle (FR)**[41] 6813 7-8-8 **49** (v) NicolaCurrie(7) 5 50
(Mark Usher) *hld up towards rr: prog on inner over 2f out and followed wnr through: rdn to take 2nd 1f out to last 100yds: one pce* **12/1**

0000 **4** *4 ½* **Twistsandturns (IRE)**[52] 6437 6-8-10 **47** PhilDennis(3) 13 36
(Declan Carroll) *chsd ldr to wl over 1f out: sn btn but clung on for modest 4th* **10/1**

-600 **5** *shd* **Angelical Eve (IRE)**[43] 6748 3-8-12 **48** (p[1]) LiamKeniry 10 35
(George Baker) *dwlt: wl in rr: sme prog 2f out: no hdwy 1f out: kpt on last 100yds and nrly snatched modest 4th* **50/1**

0003 **6** *¾* **Whaleweigh Station**[6] 7952 6-9-0 **48** (v) FrannyNorton 9 34
(J R Jenkins) *led at gd pce: hdd over 1f out: wknd qckly fnl f* **15/2**[3]

5000 **7** *½* **Rapid Rise (IRE)**[20] 7517 3-9-5 **55** LukeMorris 3 39
(Milton Bradley) *chsd ldrs: drvn wl over 2f out: wknd over 1f out* **16/1**

05-0 **8** *½* **Mellow**[21] 7487 3-8-13 **52** (h) CharlieBennett(3) 2 35
(Hughie Morrison) *chsd ldng pair 2f and again wl over 2f out: wknd over 1f out* **16/1**

0142 **9** *1* **Lutine Charlie (IRE)**[29] 7213 10-8-12 **46** MartinDwyer 6 27
(Emma Owen) *wl in rr: shkn up and brief effrt over 2f out: no great prog and eased fnl f* **10/1**

430 **10** *¾* **Latest Quest (IRE)**[19] 7540 3-8-8 **47** MitchGodwin(3) 7 25
(Sylvester Kirk) *chsd ldrs: rdn wl over 2f out: wknd wl over 1f out* **10/1**

5000 **11** *nk* **Cherry Leyf**[14] 7705 3-8-10 **46** oh1 (p[1]) OisinMurphy 12 23
(Stuart Williams) *dwlt: t.k.h: hld up wl in rr: rdn and no prog over 2f out* **33/1**

130 **12** *5* **Tifl**[20] 7517 4-9-4 **55** (bt) DavidEgan(3) 11 20
(Heather Main) *sweeping move on wd outside to chse ldng pair after 2f: wknd qckly wl over 2f out* **20/1**

4600 **13** *nk* **Rising Sunshine (IRE)**[50] 6503 4-8-12 **46** oh1 RobertWinston 14 10
(Milton Bradley) *chsd ldrs: rdn and wknd qckly 3f out: bhd over 1f out* **40/1**

040 **14** *7* **Danica Ashton**[26] 7322 3-8-11 **47** oh1 ow1 StevieDonohoe 8
(Miss Joey Ellis) *t.k.h early: in tch to 1/2-way: sn wknd and bhd* **66/1**

1m 24.58s (-1.42) **Going Correction** -0.175s/f (Stan)
**WFA** 3 from 4yo+ 2lb **14** Ran SP% **120.7**
Speed ratings (Par 101): **101,98,96,91,91 90,90,89,88,87 87,81,81,73**
CSF £11.07 CT £99.90 TOTE £3.30: £1.50, £2.40, £3.00; EX 14.50 Trifecta £98.80.
**Owner** William Wood **Bred** Hesmonds Stud Ltd **Trained** Leafield, Oxon

**FOCUS**
The faster of the two divisions by 0.58sec. The form looks quite strong for the grade.

## 8135 RACINGUK.COM H'CAP 1m 3f 219y(P)
8:45 (8:46) (Class 6) (0-60,60) 3-Y-0+ **£2,587** (£770; £384; £192) **Stalls** Low

Form RPR

1635 **1** **Lyrica's Lion (IRE)**[13] 7729 3-9-0 **57** DavidEgan(3) 14 63
(Michael Attwater) *mde all: set stdy pce tl kicked on over 2f out: edgd lft over 1f out but kpt on wl to fend off chals* **16/1**

5433 **2** *1* **Too Many Shots**[21] 7483 3-9-2 **56** JoeyHaynes 2 60
(John Best) *trckd ldrs: rdn 2f out: rchd 3rd fnl f but hld: styd on to take 2nd nr fin* **5/1**[2]

0406 **3** *hd* **Honourable Knight (IRE)**[84] 5267 9-8-11 **45** SteveDrowne 12 48
(Mark Usher) *trckd wnr: rdn to chal 2f out: stl pressing ins fnl f: no ex last 100yds and lost 2nd nr fin* **33/1**

6005 **4** *½* **Bird For Life**[12] 7761 3-7-12 **45** NicolaCurrie(7) 3 48
(Mark Usher) *t.k.h: trckd ldrs: rdn and nt qckn 2f out: kpt on again ins fnl f and gaining at fin* **16/1**

5341 **5** *hd* **Katabatika**[8] 7879 3-9-6 **60** 6ex AdamKirby 10 63+
(Hughie Morrison) *s.i.s: hld up in rr in modly run r: prog over 2f out: rchd 4th ins fnl f but nvr able to threaten* **5/6**[1]

0504 **6** *½* **Garcon De Soleil**[42] 6796 4-8-11 **45** RobHornby 4 46
(Michael Blanshard) *trckd ldng pair: rdn to chal 2f out: btn and fdd ins fnl f* **12/1**

4550 **7** *1 ½* **Kaisan**[10] 7831 4-9-4 **52** (t) DavidProbert 9 51+
(Bernard Llewellyn) *hld up in last trio in modly run r: prog on inner and drvn 2f out: kpt on but no hope of threatening* **16/1**

3506 **8** *shd* **Life Of Luxury**[24] 7413 4-9-8 **56** WilliamCarson 7 55
(Mark Brisbourne) *hld up in midfield: rdn over 2f out: no imp on ldrs* **20/1**

4560 **9** *nk* **Vexillum (IRE)**[26] 7336 8-8-11 **45** (t) LukeMorris 1 43
(Neil Mulholland) *t.k.h: hld up in midfield: rdn over 2f out: one pce and no imp* **25/1**

2500 **10** *½* **Sir Jack**[13] 7735 4-9-0 **51** HollieDoyle(3) 11 48+
(Tony Carroll) *s.i.s: hld up in last in modly run r: effrt over 2f out: passed sme rivals over 1f out: no ch and fdd fnl f* **8/1**[3]

0036 **11** *1 ¼* **Jersey Bull (IRE)**[14] 7711 5-9-10 **58** (h) JFEgan 6 53
(Michael Madgwick) *t.k.h: hld up in midfield: rdn and nt qckn over 2f out: fdd fnl f* **8/1**[3]

06/0 **12** *1 ½* **Reality Show (IRE)**[13] 7729 10-9-2 **53** CharlieBennett(3) 8 46+
(Shaun Harris) *a in last trio: rdn and no prog over 2f out* **50/1**

20-0 **13** *7* **Zarliman (IRE)**[42] 6796 7-9-2 **55** RhiainIngram(5) 13 37
(Roger Ingram) *pressed ldrs on outer tl wknd qckly over 2f out* **50/1**

2m 37.9s (3.40) **Going Correction** -0.175s/f (Stan)
**WFA** 3 from 4yo+ 6lb **13** Ran SP% **134.3**
Speed ratings (Par 101): **81,80,80,79,79 79,78,78,78,77 76,75,71**
CSF £101.67 CT £2709.15 TOTE £15.30: £4.40, £1.90, £15.40; EX 107.80 Trifecta £1688.10.
**Owner** Ricki Vaughan **Bred** Schneider Adolf **Trained** Epsom, Surrey
■ Stewards' Enquiry : Steve Drowne six-day ban: weighed in 2lbs overweight (Oct 31 - Nov 6)

**FOCUS**
They went no pace and it was an advantage to be handy. The four 3yos in the line-up finished 1-2-4-5, but not form to place too much faith in.
T/Plt: £322.60 to a £1 stake. Pool: £65,604.33 - 148.45 winning units T/Qpdt: £72.20 to a £1 stake. Pool: £12,465.80 - 127.73 winning units **Jonathan Neesom**

# 7927 LEICESTER (R-H)
Tuesday, October 17

**OFFICIAL GOING: Good to soft (5.8)**
Wind: Light half behind Weather: Fine

## 8136 BRITISH STALLION STUDS EBF NOVICE STKS (PLUS 10 RACE) 1m 53y
2:00 (2:02) (Class 4) 2-Y-O **£5,175** (£1,540; £769; £384) **Stalls** Low

Form RPR

3 **1** **Bombyx**[19] 7543 2-9-2 0 DanielMuscutt 9 82+
(James Fanshawe) *prom: lost pl 6f out: hdwy over 3f out: led over 1f out: edgd rt: styd on wl: comf* **15/8**[2]

**2** *1 ¾* **Sea Youmzain (IRE)** 2-8-11 0 JoeFanning 6 71
(Mark Johnston) *chsd ldrs: led 2f out: rdn and hdd over 1f out: styd on same pce ins fnl f* **20/1**

**3** *1 ¼* **Natural History** 2-9-2 0 OisinMurphy 10 73
(Andrew Balding) *chsd ldr: rdn over 2f out: ev ch over 1f out: nt clr run sn after: no ex ins fnl f* **12/1**

42 **4** *1 ¼* **Bold Reason (GER)**[17] 7613 2-9-2 0 RobertHavlin 3 70
(John Gosden) *chsd ldrs: rdn over 1f out: edgd lft: styd on same pce* **7/4**[1]

**5** *nk* **Escalator** 2-9-2 0 TomQueally 8 71+
(Charlie Fellowes) *s.s: hld up: pushed along over 2f out: swtchd lft over 1f out: r.o ins fnl f: nvr nrr* **50/1**

| | 6 | 1 1/4 | **Nibras Galaxy (IRE)** 2-9-2 0 ... SeanLevey 4 | 66+ |
|---|---|---|---|---|
| | | | (Ismail Mohammed) *prom: pushed along over 3f out: styd on same pce fr over 1f out* **33/1** | |
| 6 | 7 | 1 | **Faadhel (GER)**[73] 5631 2-9-2 0 ... AndreaAtzeni 1 | 64 |
| | | | (Roger Varian) *sn led: rdn and hdd 2f out: wknd ins fnl f* **7/1[3]** | |
| 04 | 8 | 4 | **Whitehall**[22] 7460 2-9-2 0 ... RyanMoore 5 | 55 |
| | | | (Sir Michael Stoute) *unruly to post: prom: stdd and lost pl after 1f: hdwy over 2f out: wknd over 1f out* **8/1** | |
| 0 | 9 | shd | **Quantatmental (IRE)**[32] 7117 2-9-2 0 ... PJMcDonald 2 | 55 |
| | | | (Tom Dascombe) *sn pushed along in rr: nvr on terms* **33/1** | |
| | 10 | 3 1/4 | **Dawn Dash** 2-8-11 0 ... HarryBentley 7 | 42 |
| | | | (Ralph Beckett) *s.i.s: hld up: pushed along over 3f out: wknd over 2f out* **20/1** | |

1m 44.77s (-0.33) **Going Correction** +0.025s/f (Good) **10** Ran SP% **119.8**
Speed ratings (Par 97): **102,100,99,97,97 96,95,91,91,87**
CSF £45.67 TOTE £2.50: £1.10, £6.90, £4.00; EX 57.30 Trifecta £324.30.
**Owner** Mr And Mrs A E Pakenham **Bred** Mr & Mrs A E Pakenham **Trained** Newmarket, Suffolk

**FOCUS**
The going was good to soft (Goingstick 5.8). False rail from the top of the hill on the back straight to the winning line, increasing distances for races on the round course, including the opener, by around 9yds. A fascinating novice event to start, with some choicely bred debutants taking on a couple that had already shown plenty of promise. The winner came from the latter group and a time 2.77sec outside standard suggests the official going description was about right. Andrea Atzeni thought it was "good", PJ McDonald thought it was on the "easy side of good" and Oisin Murphy called it "good to soft".

## 8137 WHISSENDINE (S) STKS 7f
**2:30** (2:34) (Class 6) 3-4-Y-O **£3,234** (£962; £481; £240) **Stalls** High

| Form | | | | RPR |
|---|---|---|---|---|
| 0200 | 1 | | **Sans Souci Bay**[31] 7156 3-9-3 83 ... (b) HollieDoyle(3) 6 | 78+ |
| | | | (Richard Hannon) *chsd ldrs: led over 1f out: sn rdn and edgd rt: styd on wl* **6/4[1]** | |
| 6566 | 2 | 2 3/4 | **Many Dreams (IRE)**[31] 7158 4-8-9 64 ... KieranShoemark 8 | 55 |
| | | | (Gary Moore) *hld up: hdwy 2f out: rdn and swtchd rt over 1f out: styd on* **3/1[2]** | |
| 5644 | 3 | nse | **Princess Way (IRE)**[8] 7910 3-8-4 52 ... (b[1]) MattCosham(3) 1 | 54 |
| | | | (David Evans) *led after 1f: rdn: edgd lft and hdd over 1f out: styd on same pce ins fnl f* **6/1** | |
| 5343 | 4 | 8 | **Oakley Pride (IRE)**[22] 7459 3-9-2 59 ... (p) JosephineGordon 4 | 41 |
| | | | (Gay Kelleway) *s.s: pushed along in rr: hdwy over 2f out: wknd fnl f* **5/1[3]** | |
| 000- | 5 | 1 | **Echoism (IRE)**[330] 8046 3-8-7 53 ... (h[1]) RobHornby 3 | 30 |
| | | | (Peter Hiatt) *led 1f: chsd ldr tl rdn over 2f out: wknd over 1f out* **14/1** | |
| 4660 | 6 | 1/2 | **Bushwise (IRE)**[59] 6174 4-8-9 45 ... (p) JoeFanning 12 | 29 |
| | | | (Milton Bradley) *hld up: rdn over 2f out: n.d* **33/1** | |
| P-56 | 7 | 3 3/4 | **Maddys Dream**[77] 5511 4-8-11 58 ... SimonPearce(3) 2 | 24 |
| | | | (Lydia Pearce) *chsd ldrs: rdn over 2f out: wknd over 1f out* **12/1** | |
| | 8 | 2 3/4 | **Moana** 4-8-6 0 ... GeorgeWood(3) 11 | 12 |
| | | | (Dr Jon Scargill) *s.s: a in rr: bhd fr 1/2-way* **50/1** | |
| 0000 | 9 | 3 3/4 | **The Perfect Show**[80] 5429 4-9-0 44 ... (v) BenCurtis 5 | 7 |
| | | | (Milton Bradley) *hld up: hdwy 1/2-way: rdn over 2f out: sn wknd* **100/1** | |
| 0/5- | 10 | 16 | **Pericles (IRE)**[540] 1710 4-8-9 57 ... JaneElliott(5) 10 | |
| | | | (Denis Quinn) *hld up: rdn 1/2-way: sn wknd* **50/1** | |

1m 24.07s (-2.13) **Going Correction** -0.25s/f (Firm)
**WFA** 3 from 4yo 2lb **10** Ran SP% **118.2**
Speed ratings (Par 101): **102,98,98,89,88 87,83,80,76,57**
CSF £6.00 TOTE £2.20: £1.10, £1.40, £2.00; EX 6.40 Trifecta £21.20.No bid for the winner
**Owner** J R Shannon **Bred** J R Shannon **Trained** East Everleigh, Wilts
■ Dusty Bin was withdrawn. Price at time of withdrawal 20/1. Rule 4 does not apply

**FOCUS**
A moderate seller and they finished well spread out.

## 8138 WREAKE H'CAP 7f
**3:00** (3:01) (Class 2) (0-110,109) 3£16,762 (£4,715; £2,357; £1,180; £587) **Stalls** High

| Form | | | | RPR |
|---|---|---|---|---|
| 14- | 1 | | **Emmaus (IRE)**[362] 7491 3-8-9 99 ... AndreaAtzeni 10 | 105+ |
| | | | (Roger Varian) *hld up: hdwy over 1f out: n.m.r wl ins fnl f: shkn up and qcknd to ld post* **10/1** | |
| 2056 | 2 | nse | **Sir Dancealot (IRE)**[31] 7145 3-9-5 109 ... RyanMoore 6 | 114 |
| | | | (David Elsworth) *hld up: racd keenly: hdwy over 1f out: rdn to ld wl ins fnl f: hdd post* **2/1[1]** | |
| 0150 | 3 | 1 1/2 | **Hyde Park**[17] 7622 3-8-7 97 ... (t) KieranShoemark 4 | 98 |
| | | | (John Gosden) *hld up: hdwy over 2f out: rdn to ld and hung lft fr over 1f out: hdd and unable qck wl ins fnl f* **7/2[2]** | |
| 31-1 | 4 | 1/2 | **Via Via (IRE)**[222] 1105 5-8-8 96 ... OisinMurphy 7 | 97 |
| | | | (James Tate) *s.i.s: hld up: hdwy over 1f out: hung lft ins fnl f: nt clr run and swtchd rt sn after: styd on* **7/1[3]** | |
| 5010 | 5 | 1 3/4 | **Rene Mathis (GER)**[17] 7611 7-8-9 97 ... PaulHanagan 9 | 93 |
| | | | (Richard Fahey) *hld up: rdn over 2f out: hdwy 1f out: styd on: nt trble ldrs* **16/1** | |
| 0000 | 6 | nse | **Captain Colby (USA)**[31] 7144 5-8-8 96 ... (b) SilvestreDeSousa 2 | 92 |
| | | | (Ed Walker) *sn led: rdn and hdd over 1f out: wknd towards fin* **8/1** | |
| 0160 | 7 | 1 | **Georgian Bay (IRE)**[38] 6933 7-8-8 96 ... (v) BenCurtis 3 | 89 |
| | | | (K R Burke) *sn pushed along in rr: rdn over 1f out: nt trble ldrs* **25/1** | |
| 3224 | 8 | 1 1/4 | **War Glory (IRE)**[35] 7025 4-8-8 96 ... SeanLevey 8 | 86 |
| | | | (Richard Hannon) *prom: rdn over 2f out: wknd ins fnl f* **10/1** | |
| 1021 | 9 | 3 1/4 | **London (FR)**[16] 7653 4-8-8 96 ... (h) JosephineGordon 11 | 77 |
| | | | (Phil McEntee) *chsd ldr 3f: rdn over 2f out: wknd over 1f out* **14/1** | |
| 2305 | 10 | 1 1/4 | **Custom Cut (IRE)**[18] 7579 8-9-5 107 ... (v[1]) DavidNolan 5 | 85 |
| | | | (David O'Meara) *prom: chsd ldr 4f out: rdn over 2f out: wknd over 1f out* **16/1** | |

1m 22.63s (-3.57) **Going Correction** -0.25s/f (Firm)
**WFA** 3 from 4yo+ 2lb **10** Ran SP% **119.6**
Speed ratings (Par 109): **110,109,108,107,105 105,104,103,99,97**
CSF £31.13 CT £91.11 TOTE £8.40: £2.90, £1.50, £1.30; EX 29.70 Trifecta £105.30.
**Owner** China Horse Club International Limited **Bred** Kilcarn Stud **Trained** Newmarket, Suffolk

**FOCUS**
A warm handicap, if a little top heavy with half the field out of the weights. They went a decent pace, the winning time dipping under standard, and the three 3yos filled the first three places. Strong form rated through the runner-up.

## 8139 RACING UK AUTUMN SPRINT H'CAP 5f
**3:30** (3:30) (Class 2) (0-110,106) 3-Y-O+
**£15,562** (£4,660; £2,330; £1,165; £582; £292) **Stalls** High

| Form | | | | RPR |
|---|---|---|---|---|
| 0635 | 1 | | **Gracious John (IRE)**[27] 7286 4-8-11 96 ... JFEgan 5 | 103 |
| | | | (David Evans) *a.p: rdn to ld over 1f out: edgd rt: r.o* **10/1[3]** | |
| 0001 | 2 | 1/2 | **Just Glamorous (IRE)**[10] 7804 4-9-7 106 ... OisinMurphy 4 | 111 |
| | | | (Ronald Harris) *led: rdn and hdd over 1f out: r.o* **10/1[3]** | |
| 3400 | 3 | 1/2 | **Green Door (IRE)**[17] 7610 6-8-8 96 ... (v) EoinWalsh(3) 1 | 99 |
| | | | (Robert Cowell) *prom: jnd ldr over 3f out: rdn and ev ch over 1f out: styd on* **33/1** | |
| 6300 | 4 | nk | **Goldream**[24] 7396 8-9-6 105 ... (p) GeraldMosse 7 | 107+ |
| | | | (Robert Cowell) *s.i.s: in rr and swtchd rt over 3f out: hdwy over 1f out: styd on* **14/1** | |
| 0554 | 5 | 3/4 | **Mirza**[10] 7804 10-9-6 105 ... (p) MartinHarley 10 | 104 |
| | | | (Rae Guest) *chsd ldrs: rdn over 1f out: styd on* **14/1** | |
| 0645 | 6 | nk | **Taexali (IRE)**[9] 7858 4-8-6 96 ... RowanScott(5) 8 | 94 |
| | | | (John Patrick Shanahan, Ire) *hld up: rdn 1/2-way: r.o ins fnl f: nt rch ldrs* **10/1[3]** | |
| 2050 | 7 | hd | **Pipers Note**[3] 8044 7-9-1 100 ... JamesSullivan 6 | 98 |
| | | | (Ruth Carr) *hld up: rdn over 1f out: r.o ins fnl f: nvr nrr* **14/1** | |
| 3202 | 8 | 1 1/4 | **Jumira Bridge**[27] 7286 3-8-12 97 ... AndreaAtzeni 3 | 91 |
| | | | (Roger Varian) *hld up: hdwy 1/2-way: nt clr run over 1f out: styd on same pce ins fnl f* **5/1[2]** | |
| 2022 | 9 | 3 1/2 | **Vibrant Chords**[31] 7144 4-8-13 98 ... RyanMoore 2 | 79 |
| | | | (Henry Candy) *trckd ldrs: shkn up over 1f out: wknd ins fnl f* **5/4[1]** | |
| 0215 | 10 | 4 1/2 | **Soie D'Leau**[17] 7610 5-8-11 96 ... TonyHamilton 9 | 60 |
| | | | (Kristin Stubbs) *chsd ldrs: rdn 1/2-way: wknd over 1f out* **10/1[3]** | |

58.85s (-1.15) **Going Correction** -0.25s/f (Firm) **10** Ran SP% **120.4**
Speed ratings (Par 109): **99,98,97,96,95 95,94,92,87,80**
CSF £108.90 CT £3178.18 TOTE £11.70: £2.90, £3.00, £9.70; EX 120.60 Trifecta £6869.30 Part Won..
**Owner** Terry Reffell **Bred** Skeaghmore Hill **Trained** Pandy, Monmouths

**FOCUS**
Another decent handicap, this time for sprinters, with four of the ten runners out of the weights. Again they dipped under standard time.

## 8140 EBFSTALLIONS.COM REFERENCE POINT MAIDEN STKS (PLUS 10 RACE) (C&G) 7f
**4:00** (4:00) (Class 4) 2-Y-O **£6,469** (£1,925; £962; £481) **Stalls** High

| Form | | | | RPR |
|---|---|---|---|---|
| 0 | 1 | | **Accessor (IRE)**[13] 7726 2-9-0 0 ... SeanLevey 1 | 80+ |
| | | | (Richard Hannon) *plld hrd and a.p: rdn to ld and edgd lft ins fnl f: r.o* **7/1** | |
| | 2 | 1/2 | **Ostilio** 2-9-0 0 ... AndreaAtzeni 4 | 79+ |
| | | | (Simon Crisford) *hld up: plld hrd: hdwy over 1f out: rdn and edgd lft ins fnl f: r.o* **6/1[3]** | |
| 4 | 3 | 1 | **Rare Groove (IRE)**[20] 7520 2-9-0 0 ... PJMcDonald 2 | 76 |
| | | | (Jedd O'Keeffe) *led: rdn over 1f out: hdd and unable qck ins fnl f* **10/1** | |
| 3 | 4 | 2 1/4 | **George Villiers (IRE)**[123] 3783 2-9-0 0 ... RobertHavlin 10 | 70 |
| | | | (John Gosden) *hld up: hdwy over 2f out: rdn and ev ch over 1f out: edgd lft and styd on same pce fnl f* **6/4[1]** | |
| 2 | 5 | nk | **Prime Minister (IRE)**[27] 7280 2-9-0 0 ... HarryBentley 5 | 69 |
| | | | (Ed Vaughan) *trckd ldr: shkn up: wnt upsides 1/2-way: rdn and ev ch whn edgd lft over 1f styd on same pce fnl f* **3/1[2]** | |
| 0 | 6 | 1 1/4 | **Mom Said (IRE)**[14] 7707 2-9-0 0 ... SilvestreDeSousa 3 | 66 |
| | | | (Ed Walker) *prom: racd keenly: shkn up over 1f out: styd on same pce* **50/1** | |
| 0 | 7 | 2 | **Compulsive (IRE)**[39] 6884 2-9-0 0 ... JackMitchell 11 | 61 |
| | | | (Roger Varian) *hld up: hdwy over 2f out: wknd over 1f out* **8/1** | |
| | 8 | 1 1/4 | **Chikoko Trail** 2-9-0 0 ... CharlesBishop 7 | 57 |
| | | | (Mick Channon) *hld up: shkn up over 2f out: wknd over 1f out* **50/1** | |
| 0 | 9 | 3/4 | **Percy Prosecco**[20] 7511 2-9-0 0 ... FergusSweeney 6 | 55 |
| | | | (Noel Williams) *chsd ldrs: wnt upsides 1/2-way tl shkn up over 2f out: wkng whn nt clr run over 1f out* **100/1** | |

1m 25.14s (-1.06) **Going Correction** -0.25s/f (Firm) **9** Ran SP% **116.9**
Speed ratings (Par 97): **96,95,94,91,91 89,87,86,85**
CSF £48.76 TOTE £8.70: £2.10, £2.30, £2.50; EX 49.80 Trifecta £435.60.
**Owner** M J Jooste **Bred** Gestut Schlenderhan **Trained** East Everleigh, Wilts

**FOCUS**
A fair maiden, but the low draws had the advantage with the main action unfolding up the middle.

## 8141 FOSSE WAY NURSERY H'CAP 1m 53y
**4:30** (4:31) (Class 6) (0-60,60) 2-Y-O **£3,234** (£962; £481; £240) **Stalls** Low

| Form | | | | RPR |
|---|---|---|---|---|
| 0000 | 1 | | **Galloping Hogan (IRE)**[33] 7082 2-9-3 57 ... SilvestreDeSousa 5 | 63 |
| | | | (Sylvester Kirk) *led 1f: chsd ldrs: wnt 2nd over 4f out: rdn over 2f out: led over 1f out: edgd rt ins fnl f: styd on wl: eased nr fin* **5/1[2]** | |
| 0600 | 2 | 2 | **Daffrah**[41] 6815 2-8-9 56 ... PaulHainey(7) 3 | 56 |
| | | | (James Tate) *chsd ldrs: wnt 2nd over 6f out tl over 4f out: rdn over 2f out: swtchd lft over 1f out: styd on to go 2nd again wl ins fnl f* **14/1** | |
| 0540 | 3 | 3/4 | **Couldn't Could She**[30] 7196 2-9-5 59 ... SteveDrowne 4 | 57 |
| | | | (Adam West) *prom: rdn over 3f out: styd on* **20/1** | |
| 5606 | 4 | hd | **Amazing Rock (SWI)**[10] 7829 2-9-6 60 ... JoeFanning 9 | 58 |
| | | | (Mark Johnston) *led 7f out: rdn and hdd over 1f out: no ex wl ins fnl f* **5/1[2]** | |
| 0042 | 5 | shd | **Puramente**[4] 7996 2-9-4 58 ... DougieCostello 10 | 56+ |
| | | | (Jo Hughes) *hld up: hdwy u.p over 1f out: styd on: nt rch ldrs* **3/1[1]** | |
| 0600 | 6 | 6 | **Jaycols Star**[20] 7519 2-9-2 56 ... KevinStott 8 | 40 |
| | | | (Philip Kirby) *hld up: pushed along over 5f out: rdn over 3f out: sn outpcd* **8/1[3]** | |
| 2230 | 7 | nse | **Mr Carbonator**[38] 6940 2-9-4 58 ... JimmyQuinn 6 | 42 |
| | | | (Philip Kirby) *prom: rdn over 3f out: wknd over 1f out* **5/1[2]** | |
| 606 | 8 | 3 | **Pearl's Calling (IRE)**[83] 5277 2-9-3 57 ... BenCurtis 2 | 34 |
| | | | (David Barron) *hld up: pushed along over 3f out: a in rr* **25/1** | |
| 0120 | 9 | 2 1/2 | **Dream Of Delphi (IRE)**[20] 7519 2-9-3 60 ... (v[1]) GeorgiaCox(3) 7 | 31 |
| | | | (William Haggas) *dwlt: hld up: pushed along over 3f out: a in rr* **5/1[2]** | |

1m 46.78s (1.68) **Going Correction** +0.025s/f (Good) **9** Ran SP% **118.1**
Speed ratings (Par 93): **92,90,89,89,88 82,82,79,77**
CSF £73.18 CT £1294.76 TOTE £5.90: £1.90, £4.30, £4.50; EX 86.10 Trifecta £1012.20.
**Owner** The Goring Society **Bred** Ciaran Mac Ferran **Trained** Upper Lambourn, Berks

**FOCUS**
Add 9yds to race distance. A moderate nursery containing just one previous winner and a race where you had to be handy. Straightforward form.

## 8142 STEWARDS H'CAP (DIV I) 1m 2f
**5:00** (5:00) (Class 5) (0-75,76) 3-Y-O+ **£3,881** (£1,155; £577; £288) **Stalls** Low

| Form | | | | RPR |
|---|---|---|---|---|
| 5411 | 1 | | **Hajaam (IRE)**[14] 7711 3-9-5 74 ... SilvestreDeSousa 5 | 85+ |
| | | | (Charlie Fellowes) *chsd ldr after 1f: led 2f out: shkn up over 1f out: edgd rt: styd on wl: comf* **2/1[1]** | |
| 0422 | 2 | 1 3/4 | **Zamperini (IRE)**[8] 7908 5-9-10 75 ... KieranShoemark 8 | 81+ |
| | | | (Mike Murphy) *s.i.s: hld up racd keenly: swtchd lft over 2f out: hdwy over 1f out: hung rt and r.o ins fnl f: no ch w wnr* **9/2[2]** | |

0131 **3** *hd* **Essenaitch (IRE)**[6] 7960 4-8-12 **70**...................... KatherineGlenister(7) 3 76
(David Evans) *a.p: rdn over 2f out: chsd wnr over 1f out: edgd rt: styd on same pce ins fnl f* **8/1**

0513 **4** *1* **What Wonders Weave (IRE)**[31] 7162 3-8-13 **73**......... RowanScott(5) 2 77
(John Patrick Shanahan, Ire) *chsd ldrs: rdn and swtchd lft over 1f out: styd on same pce ins fnl f* **5/1**[3]

**5** *1 3/4* **Aiguille Rouge (FR)**[195] 3-9-3 **75**............................... HectorCrouch(3) 1 76
(Gary Moore) *s.i.s: hdwy over 6f out: pushed along and outpcd over 2f out: rallied over 1f out: styd on same pce ins fnl f* **33/1**

4520 **6** *1* **Katebird (IRE)**[10] 7824 3-9-7 **76**........................................ JoeFanning 4 76
(Mark Johnston) *sn led: rdn and hdd 2f out: wknd ins fnl f* **20/1**

305- **7** *1/2* **Booborowie (IRE)**[377] 7063 4-8-13 **67**........................... GeorgeWood(3) 12 65
(Ali Stronge) *hld up in tch: hmpd and lost pl over 8f out: rdn over 2f out: styd on ins fnl f* **33/1**

2626 **8** *1 1/4* **Bartholomew J (IRE)**[60] 6144 3-8-10 **68**.................... SimonPearce(3) 6 64
(Lydia Pearce) *hld up: effrt over 1f out: nvr on terms* **25/1**

4465 **9** *nse* **Sonnetist**[13] 7728 3-9-6 **75**................................................ SeanLevey 9 71
(Richard Hannon) *plld hrd and prom: rdn over 2f out: wknd fnl f* **14/1**

2025 **10** *nk* **Ghinia (IRE)**[27] 7279 6-9-6 **71**............................................ RobHornby 7 65
(Pam Sly) *hld up: hdwy over 3f out: rdn and wknd over 1f out* **14/1**

3066 **11** *5* **Parish Boy**[19] 7558 5-9-9 **74**.................................(t) JosephineGordon 11 58
(David Loughnane) *s.s: pushed along and sme hdwy over 2f out: wknd over 1f out* **25/1**

0541 **12** *4 1/2* **Scoones**[21] 7495 3-9-2 **71**............................................. DanielMuscutt 13 47
(James Fanshawe) *prom: lost pl over 7f out: hdwy over 2f out: wknd over 1f out* **7/1**

2m 8.21s (0.31) **Going Correction** +0.025s/f (Good)
**WFA** 3 from 4yo+ 4lb **12 Ran SP% 123.5**
Speed ratings (Par 103): **99,97,97,96,95 94,94,93,93,92 88,85**
CSF £10.27 CT £61.50 TOTE £2.80: £1.40, £2.40, £2.50; EX 11.90 Trifecta £57.00.
**Owner** Khalifa Bin Hamad Al Attiyah **Bred** Marston Stud **Trained** Newmarket, Suffolk

**FOCUS**
Add 9yds to race distance. The first division of an ordinary handicap and another race where it paid to be handy. The winner continues to progress.

## 8143 STEWARDS H'CAP (DIV II) 1m 2f
**5:30** (5:31) (Class 5) (0-75,77) 3-Y-O+ **£3,881** (£1,155; £577; £288) **Stalls** Low

Form RPR

160 **1** **Villette (IRE)**[145] 2998 3-9-6 **75**........................................... RobHornby 8 85
(Dean Ivory) *hld up: rdn over 3f out: hdwy over 1f out: hmpd ins fnl f: led sn after: jnd on line: awrdd r* **50/1**

3021 **2** *dht* **Entangling (IRE)**[68] 5853 3-9-6 **75**.......................... SilvestreDeSousa 9 85
(Chris Wall) *pushed along towards rr: rdn over 3f out: hdwy u.p to ld and hung rt fr over 1f out: hdd ins fnl f: rallied to dead heat on line: disqualified and pl 2nd* **4/1**[1]

0-60 **3** *3* **Swift Cedar (IRE)**[19] 7558 7-8-13 **67**........................ MattCosham(3) 2 71
(David Evans) *hld up: pushed along over 3f out: hdwy and hung rt over 1f out: styd on: nt rch ldrs* **20/1**

0242 **4** *1 3/4* **Rayaa**[12] 7762 4-9-4 **69**..................................(t) JosephineGordon 10 70
(Michael Appleby) *chsd ldr tl over 8f out: remained handy: wnt 2nd again over 3f out: rdn over 2f out: ev ch over 1f out: no ex ins fnl f* **6/1**[3]

1660 **5** *1* **Bonnie Arlene (IRE)**[13] 7735 3-9-5 **74**.......................... JoeFanning 7 73
(Mark Johnston) *s.i.s: in rr and pushed along over 3f out: hdwy and hung rt fr over 1f out: nt rch ldrs* **16/1**

6203 **6** *2* **Squiggley**[33] 7098 4-9-9 **74**.................................................. DaneO'Neill 5 69
(Henry Candy) *hld up in tch: rdn over 2f out: wknd ins fnl f* **4/1**[1]

-260 **7** *nk* **Dora's Field (IRE)**[83] 5290 4-9-4 **69**....................... KieranShoemark 6 63
(Stuart Kittow) *s.i.s: in rr: rdn over 2f out: n.d* **50/1**

6244 **8** *1/2* **Flight Of Fantasy**[76] 5550 3-9-8 **77**............................ GeraldMosse 11 70
(Harry Dunlop) *unruly in stalls: chsd ldrs: rdn over 3f out: wknd and eased fnl f* **6/1**[3]

4501 **9** *1 1/2* **Miningrocks (FR)**[10] 7820 5-8-13 **71**............................ GerO'Neill(7) 4 61
(Declan Carroll) *led: rdn over 2f out: hdd over 1f out: wknd ins fnl f* **5/1**[2]

0206 **10** *1/2* **Tyrsal (IRE)**[18] 7582 6-8-6 **64**..............................(p) DarraghKeenan(7) 3 53
(Clifford Lines) *s.i.s: rdn over 3f out: nvr on terms* **12/1**

0100 **11** *2 3/4* **Blushing Red (FR)**[22] 7452 3-9-6 **75**............................ PJMcDonald 1 58
(Ed Dunlop) *hld up in tch: rdn over 3f out: wknd over 1f out* **8/1**

60-6 **12** *11* **Austerity (IRE)**[162] 2467 4-9-0 **65**.................................. BenCurtis 12 26
(Sally Haynes) *chsd ldr over 8f out tl over 3f out: sn rdn: wknd wl over 1f out* **33/1**

2m 7.07s (-0.83) **Going Correction** +0.025s/f (Good)
**WFA** 3 from 4yo+ 4lb **12 Ran SP% 121.5**
Speed ratings (Par 103): **104,104,101,100,99 97,97,97,95,95 93,84**
CSF £243.19 CT £4215.77 TOTE £39.80: £15.10, £1.70, £5.70; EX 371.60 Trifecta £3960.30.
**Owner** Dean Ivory **Bred** S Roy **Trained** Radlett, Herts

**FOCUS**
Add 9yds to race distance. Quite a dramatic conclusion to the second division of this handicap, with some serious interference late on between the two dead-heaters and the result was deemed to have been affected. The pace was strong and the winning time was 1.14sec quicker than the first division. The first two are both improving.
T/Jkpt: Not Won. T/Plt: £1,202.40 to a £1 stake. Pool: £68,851.01 - 41.80 winning units T/Qpdt: £500.80 to a £1 stake. Pool: £6,598.54 - 9.75 winning units **Colin Roberts**

8144 - (Foreign Racing) - See Raceform Interactive

# 8128 KEMPTON (A.W) (R-H)
Wednesday, October 18

**OFFICIAL GOING: Polytrack: standard to slow**
Wind: Nil Weather: Misty

## 8145 RACING UK NURSERY H'CAP 5f (P)
**5:45** (5:46) (Class 6) (0-60,60) 2-Y-O **£2,587** (£770; £384; £192) **Stalls** Low

Form RPR

032 **1** **Jonnysimpson (IRE)**[16] 7695 2-9-6 **60**.................... SilvestreDeSousa 5 70+
(Brendan Powell) *mde all: rdn over 1f out: qcknd clr ent fnl f: pushed out wl ins fnl f: readily* **9/4**[1]

004 **2** *2 1/2* **Magic Pulse (IRE)**[28] 7269 2-9-3 **57**................................ TomQueally 3 60+
(Ann Duffield) *wnt lft s: n.m.r on inner and taken bk to rr: swtchd to outer: carried v wd off bnd and dropped to last: smooth prog fr 2f out: rdn between horses 1f out: no ch w wnr but shuffled along to take 2nd cl home* **12/1**

030 **3** *1/2* **Cove Beach**[16] 7695 2-9-6 **60**......................................(b) RaulDaSilva 2 56+
(Paul Cole) *short of room s: hld up in mid-div on inner: travelling wl on heels over 1f out: sn rdn: no ch w wnr ent fnl f: pushed along for 150ys out: lost 2nd cl home* **6/1**[3]

2403 **4** *3/4* **Zapateado**[16] 7695 2-8-10 **57**........................................ NicolaCurrie(7) 9 51
(Richard Hughes) *rdn along early: settled in rr: gd prog over 2f out: shuffled along fr over 1f out: pushed out fnl f* **7/1**

000 **5** *1 1/4* **Mossketeer**[93] 4972 2-9-6 **60**.................................... JosephineGordon 8 49
(John Best) *missed break and in rr: rdn wl over 1f out: plugged on one pce fr over 1f out* **12/1**

0443 **6** *1* **Avenging Red (IRE)**[4] 8027 2-9-3 **57**..........................(b[1]) SteveDrowne 4 42+
(Adam West) *checked sn after s: t.k.h in mid-div early where tight for room: rdn 2f out: no ex ent fnl f* **6/1**[3]

050 **7** *3* **Devil Or Angel**[98] 4740 2-9-6 **60**...................................... WilliamCarson 1 35
(Bill Turner) *chsd ldrs on inner: rdn over 1f out: no ex ent fnl f* **25/1**

0544 **8** *hd* **Bodybuilder**[16] 7690 2-9-2 **59**........................................ HollieDoyle(3) 10 33+
(Richard Hannon) *wnt rt s and hmpd rival: chsd ldr on outer: rdn wl over 2f out to hold pl: one pce fr over 1f out* **5/1**[2]

3665 **9** *3* **Mocead Cappall**[25] 7385 2-8-13 **56**................................... EoinWalsh(3) 7 19+
(John Holt) *hmpd s: chsd ldr: rdn 2f out: one pce fr over 1f out* **33/1**

0400 **10** *1/2* **Acromatic (IRE)**[35] 7041 2-9-3 **57**.....................................(b) JasonHart 6 18
(John Quinn) *t.k.h early being squeezed up between horses for 1f: wnt v wd bnd and carried rival: in rr-div and rdn over 1f out: sn fdd* **16/1**

59.65s (-0.85) **Going Correction** -0.225s/f (Stan) **10 Ran SP% 116.6**
Speed ratings (Par 93): **97,93,92,91,89 87,82,82,77,76**
CSF £31.82 CT £145.78 TOTE £2.70: £1.10, £4.00, £2.40; EX 32.50 Trifecta £192.00.
**Owner** Sterling Racing **Bred** Tiger Bloodstock **Trained** Upper Lambourn, Berks
■ Stewards' Enquiry : Hollie Doyle four-day ban: careless riding (Nov 1-4)

**FOCUS**
A moderate nursery which proved plain sailing for the favourite.

## 8146 32RED CASINO H'CAP 5f (P)
**6:15** (6:16) (Class 6) (0-55,55) 3-Y-O+ **£2,587** (£770; £384; £192) **Stalls** Low

Form RPR

100 **1** **Ask The Guru**[22] 7494 7-9-4 **54**.......................................(b) KierenFox 3 59
(Michael Attwater) *broke wl but snatched up by ldr shortly after s: t.k.h racing in 3rd on inner: rdn between horses over 1f out: pressed ldr ent fnl f: stuck on and led 110yds out: kpt on* **4/1**[2]

600 **2** *nk* **Dontforgettocall**[33] 7122 3-9-4 **54**.............................(v[1]) OisinMurphy 8 59
(Joseph Tuite) *hld up in rr: shkn up over 1f out and effrt between horses ent fnl f: sn switch lft and kpt on strly to take 2nd nr fin: nvr nrr* **8/1**

000 **3** *3/4* **Archie Stevens**[19] 7575 7-8-11 **52**................................ PaddyPilley(5) 4 53
(Clare Ellam) *sn led and c across to rail: rdn over 1f out: kpt on wl tl hdd 110yds out and lost 2nd cl home* **16/1**

026 **4** *1/2* **Miss Rosina (IRE)**[22] 7494 3-9-0 **55**.........................(p) JaneElliott(5) 7 55
(George Margarson) *chsd ldr on outer: rdn over 1f out: ev ch ent fnl f: no ex sn after and plugged on one pce* **6/1**

5332 **5** *hd* **Swendab (IRE)**[18] 7607 9-9-2 **55**.................................(b) DavidEgan(3) 2 54+
(John O'Shea) *sluggish leaving stalls and rdn along for 50yds: t.k.h in last trio: swtchd to outer and rdn 2f out: kpt on one pce fr over 1f out* **2/1**[1]

040 **6** *1 3/4* **Emilysbutterscotch**[43] 6791 3-9-2 **52**............................ AdamBeschizza 1 45
(Rae Guest) *hld up in last trio on rail: rdn over 2f out: sme prog tl no ex fnl f* **8/1**

3404 **7** *2 1/4* **Whiteley (IRE)**[21] 7517 3-9-5 **55**.............................................. JFEgan 5 40+
(Mick Channon) *between horses bhd ldr and t.k.h hold appr bnd: rdn sn after to hold pl: no ex fr over 1f out* **5/1**[3]

59.54s (-0.96) **Going Correction** -0.225s/f (Stan) **7 Ran SP% 112.4**
Speed ratings (Par 101): **98,97,96,95,95 92,88**
CSF £33.74 CT £454.01 TOTE £4.80: £2.50, £3.30; EX 44.30 Trifecta £636.70.
**Owner** Canisbay Bloodstock **Bred** Redmyre Bloodstock & Tweenhills Stud **Trained** Epsom, Surrey
■ Stewards' Enquiry : Paddy Pilley two-day ban: careless riding (Nov 1-2)

**FOCUS**
An ordinary sprint handicap.

## 8147 32RED ON THE APP STORE FILLIES' NOVICE STKS (PLUS 10 RACE) (DIV I) 7f (P)
**6:45** (6:46) (Class 5) 2-Y-O **£3,234** (£962; £481; £240) **Stalls** Low

Form RPR

23 **1** **Fille De Reve**[41] 6861 2-9-0 0............................................ PatCosgrave 8 76+
(Ed Walker) *bhd ldrs on outer and tk fierce hold early and over 4f out: settled bttr by over 3f out: shkn up and smooth prog to sit on quarters of ldr wl over 1f out: rdn jst ins fnl f: led 150yds out: gng on at fin: snug* **8/11**[1]

6 **2** *1 1/4* **Light Relief**[54] 6385 2-9-0 0.................................. SilvestreDeSousa 10 73
(James Tate) *broke v qckly and sn led: rdn 2f out: pressed by wnr fr over 1f out: no ex and hdd 150yds out: stuck on* **6/1**[3]

**3** *3 1/2* **Junderstand** 2-8-11 0............................................... HollieDoyle(3) 7 64+
(Alan King) *hld up in rr-div and rr in snatches: rdn over 2f out on outer w a bit to do: kpt on wl under hands and heels and tk 3rd nr fin: likely improver* **25/1**

**4** *1/2* **Private View** 2-9-0 0.......................................................... TedDurcan 6 62
(Sir Michael Stoute) *slty hmpd s: settled in mid-div on inner: rdn over 2f out: kpt on tl no ex ins fnl f and lost 3rd nr fin* **4/1**[2]

**5** *1 1/4* **Fire Orchid** 2-9-0 0.......................................................... SeanLevey 9 59
(Richard Hannon) *settled in rr-div on outer: rdn over 2f out: kpt on wl and chalng for 3rd ent fnl f: no ex wl ins fnl f* **16/1**

**6** *3 1/4* **Thistimelastyear** 2-9-0 0.................................................. ShaneKelly 2 50
(Philip Hide) *chsd ldr on inner: rdn over 2f out: sn one pce* **33/1**

00 **7** *1 3/4* **Alacritas**[36] 7033 2-9-0 0............................................... StevieDonohoe 1 45
(David Simcock) *t.k.h in rr-div on inner: hld together and travelling strly w plenty to do ent fnl f whn snatched up and clipped heels: nudged out after: nvr involved: likely improver* **20/1**

**8** *3/4* **Queen Maureen (USA)** 2-9-0 0...............................(t[1]) JosephineGordon 4 43
(Hugo Palmer) *a in rr and pushed along fr 1/2-way: no ex wl over 3f out* **7/1**

00 **9** *2 1/4* **Happy Ending (IRE)**[44] 6747 2-9-0 0...................................... JFEgan 3 37
(Seamus Mullins) *hmpd s: a in rr: effrt over 2f out: nt qckn* **66/1**

1m 26.47s (0.47) **Going Correction** -0.225s/f (Stan) **9 Ran SP% 123.6**
Speed ratings (Par 92): **88,86,82,82,80 76,74,74,71**
CSF £6.13 TOTE £1.90: £1.10, £1.80, £5.20; EX 7.10 Trifecta £71.80.
**Owner** Bjorn Nielsen & Lord Lloyd Webber **Bred** Watership Down Stud **Trained** Upper Lambourn, Berks

**FOCUS**
The first two finished clear in this fair fillies' novice.

## 8148 32RED ON THE APP STORE FILLIES' NOVICE STKS (PLUS 10 RACE) (DIV II) 7f (P)
**7:15** (7:16) (Class 5) 2-Y-O **£3,234** (£962; £481; £240) **Stalls** Low

Form RPR

0 **1** **Revalue**[36] 7022 2-9-0 0 WilliamBuick 6 76
(Charles Hills) *t.k.h in mid-div on inner: rdn wl over 1f out where swtchd to inner and gd prog: led jst ins fnl f: kpt on wl* **9/1**

**2** 1 1/4 **Bubble And Squeak** 2-8-11 0 MitchGodwin(3) 8 73
(Sylvester Kirk) *carried lft s: settled in rr-div on inner: prog over 2f out whn swtchd to inner: w wnr over 1f out: kpt on wl ins fnl f: tk 2nd 150yds out: plugged on* **33/1**

04 **3** 3/4 **Admired**[41] 6861 2-9-0 0 OisinMurphy 2 71
(Sir Michael Stoute) *chsd ldrs on inner: rdn 2f out: kpt on one pce ins fnl f tl lost 2nd 150yds out* **9/2**[2]

220 **4** 1/2 **Your Choice**[53] 6418 2-9-0 82 JohnFahy 1 69+
(Laura Mongan) *sn led: rdn 2f out: kpt on tl hdd jst ins fnl f: plugged on tl no ex and wknd wl ins fnl f* **7/2**[1]

**5** 1 1/4 **Watheeqa (USA)** 2-9-0 0 JimCrowley 9 68+
(Roger Varian) *carried wd lft s: hld up in rr: plenty to do over 2f out whn shkn up: shuffled along and kpt on nicely past btn horses fr over 1f out: nvr nrr* **5/1**[3]

**6** 1/2 **Beautiful Artist (USA)** 2-9-0 0 RobertHavlin 4 65+
(John Gosden) *mid-div on outer: switch to outer over 2f out: sn after for effrt: kpt on one pce fr over 1f out* **6/1**

**7** 3/4 **Fondest** 2-8-11 0 GeorgeWood(3) 5 63
(James Fanshawe) *in rr-div on outer: rdn over 2f out: plugged on fr over 1f out* **12/1**

0545 **8** 1/2 **Toomer**[35] 7050 2-9-0 67 SeanLevey 3 61
(Richard Hannon) *bhd ldr on outer and racd keenly: rdn 2f out: no ex and one pce fr over 1f out* **8/1**

**9** 1 1/4 **Kismat** 2-9-0 0 MartinHarley 10 58
(Alan King) *in rr: shkn up over 2f out and swtchd to outer: kpt on after being pushed out* **50/1**

6 **10** 1 **Showdancing**[181] 1909 2-9-0 0 SilvestreDeSousa 7 55+
(James Tate) *sltly rrd s and wnt lft: slow away: racd wd in mid-div early: rapid prog over 4f out to press ldr: rdn over 2f out: sn wknd* **8/1**

1m 25.05s (-0.95) **Going Correction** -0.225s/f (Stan) **10** Ran SP% **116.2**
Speed ratings (Par 92): **96,94,93,93,91 91,90,89,88,87**
CSF £257.46 TOTE £8.30: £2.50, £8.20, £1.70; EX 387.60 Trifecta £2329.10.
**Owner** K Abdullah **Bred** Juddmonte Farms Ltd **Trained** Lambourn, Berks

**FOCUS**
This was the quicker of the two divisions by 1.42sec.

## 8149 32RED.COM NOVICE STKS 7f (P)
**7:45** (7:46) (Class 5) 2-Y-O **£3,234** (£962; £481; £240) **Stalls** Low

Form RPR

33 **1** **Archie McKellar**[40] 6869 2-9-2 0 PatDobbs 3 83
(Ralph Beckett) *racd in mid-div on inner: prog over 2f out: rdn 2f out: kpt on wl and led ent fnl f: stuck on wl and asserted nr fin* **11/4**[2]

5 **2** 1 1/4 **Recollect**[19] 7580 2-9-2 0 JamieSpencer 5 80
(Luca Cumani) *racd between horses bhd ldr: rdn 2f out: kpt on wl between horses to take 2nd ins fnl f* **9/2**[3]

4 **3** shd **U S S Missouri (USA)**[21] 7511 2-9-2 0 PatCosgrave 9 79
(Ed Walker) *cl up w ldrs: shkn up 2f out and travelling sweetly: rdn over 1f out: nt qckn and stuck on ins fnl f: jst hld for 3rd* **8/1**

13 **4** nse **Last Voyage (USA)**[28] 7274 2-9-9 0 (h[1]) WilliamBuick 13 86
(Charlie Appleby) *chsd ldrs on outer: rdn 2f out: kpt on wl ent fnl f: plugged on on outer and jst hld for 3rd* **7/1**

**5** 3 1/4 **Haader (FR)** 2-9-2 0 JimCrowley 12 70+
(Owen Burrows) *in rr: rdn 2f out: kpt on fr over 1f out: no match for front four* **25/1**

0 **6** 1 1/4 **Metkaif**[14] 7726 2-9-2 0 SeanLevey 10 67+
(Richard Hannon) *hld up in mid-div between horses: shkn up over 2f out: no immediate rspnse tl ent fnl f whn kpt on promisingly under hands and heels* **14/1**

65 **7** 3/4 **Carp Kid (IRE)**[14] 7739 2-8-13 0 HollieDoyle(3) 11 65+
(Richard Hannon) *sluggish s and pushed along leaving stalls: in rr: passed btn horses fr over 1f out under hands and heels* **25/1**

0 **8** 3 **Tiger Lyon (USA)**[96] 4862 2-9-2 0 (h[1]) JFEgan 6 57
(John Butler) *sn led: rdn along whn hdd ent fnl f: wknd qckly after* **66/1**

5 **9** nk **Comrade In Arms (USA)**[66] 5960 2-9-2 0 TedDurcan 1 56
(Sir Michael Stoute) *in rr-div on inner: shkn up and tk clsr order over 2f out: sn swtchd to inner and rdn: briefly threatened tl no ex ent fnl f* **14/1**

60 **10** 1/2 **Grey Spirit (IRE)**[13] 7765 2-9-2 0 LukeMorris 14 55
(Sir Mark Prescott Bt) *racd wd early in mid-div: rdn 2f out: kpt on one pce* **100/1**

6 **11** nse **Al Mustashar (IRE)**[58] 6264 2-9-2 0 OisinMurphy 2 55
(Saeed bin Suroor) *chsd ldr on inner: rdn 2f out: sn wknd and lost pl fr over 1f out* **5/2**[1]

06 **12** 3/4 **Don't Cry About It (IRE)**[9] 7877 2-9-2 0 TomMarquand 4 53
(Ali Stronge) *in rr-div: rdn over 2f out: one pce fr over 1f out* **100/1**

**13** 5 **Ezz (IRE)** 2-9-2 0 AdamBeschizza 8 39
(Mrs Ilka Gansera-Leveque) *in rr: rdn over 2f out: no ex fr over 1f out* **100/1**

1m 24.7s (-1.30) **Going Correction** -0.225s/f (Stan) **13** Ran SP% **122.5**
Speed ratings (Par 95): **98,96,96,96,92 91,90,86,86,86 86,85,79**
CSF £15.60 TOTE £4.10: £1.40, £2.30, £3.00; EX 16.30 Trifecta £103.40.
**Owner** Quantum Leap Racing II **Bred** Strawberry Fields Stud **Trained** Kimpton, Hants

**FOCUS**
This looked a decent novice, and the first four finished nicely clear. The race has been rated around the winner.

## 8150 32RED/STALLIONS BREEDING WINNERS EBF FILLIES' H'CAP 7f (P)
**8:15** (8:24) (Class 4) (0-85,87) 3-Y-O+ **£6,469** (£1,925; £962; £481) **Stalls** Low

Form RPR

41-1 **1** **Yellowhammer**[82] 5369 3-9-0 79 KieranShoemark 3 86+
(Roger Charlton) *reluctant to load: between horses chsng ldrs: rdn on outer over 2f out and no immediate rspnse: picked up wl ent fnl f: c home best and got up post* **5/2**[1]

2150 **2** nse **Peak Princess (IRE)**[20] 7545 3-9-8 87 (b) SeanLevey 11 94
(Richard Hannon) *hld up in rr: shkn up over 2f out and gd prog fr over 1f out: sn rdn and kpt on wl between horses to ld briefly nr fin: hdd post* **12/1**

1010 **3** nk **Crafty Madam (IRE)**[12] 7780 3-9-0 79 PatCosgrave 2 85
(Clive Cox) *hld up in rr: rdn along over 2f out w plenty to do: picked up wl over 1f out and gd prog: r.o to take 3rd fnl strides* **5/1**[2]

1241 **4** nk **Castle Hill Cassie (IRE)**[29] 7241 3-8-12 77 OisinMurphy 6 82
(Ben Haslam) *chsd ldr: rdn 2f out: led 1f out: hdd nr fin and wknd qckly fnl strides* **14/1**

2443 **5** 1 **Snow Squaw**[33] 7130 3-8-4 72 (p) DavidEgan(3) 14 74
(David Elsworth) *v reluctant to go to post: pressed ldr: led 2f out: rdn wl over 1f out: hdd 1f out: wknd qckly after* **25/1**

0323 **6** 1/2 **Narjes**[22] 7485 3-8-11 76 (h) TomQueally 7 77
(James Fanshawe) *hld up in rr on outer: rdn 2f out and c wdst: kpt on one pce fr over 1f out* **8/1**[3]

3402 **7** 1 **Parlance (IRE)**[20] 7545 3-9-2 84 GeorgiaCox(3) 4 82
(Sir Michael Stoute) *mid-div on outer: rdn over 2f out: kpt on one pce* **8/1**[3]

10 **8** nk **Aquamarina**[19] 7576 3-8-12 77 MartinHarley 9 74
(Robyn Brisland) *bhd ldrs: shkn up over 2f out: plugged on after tl wknd fnl f* **8/1**[3]

-016 **9** nk **First Dance (IRE)**[20] 7545 3-9-2 81 LukeMorris 1 78
(James Tate) *in rr-div on inner: rdn over 2f out: plugged on one pce* **10/1**

0464 **10** nk **Rebel Surge (IRE)**[20] 7545 4-9-3 87 (p) NicolaCurrie(7) 8 84
(Richard Spencer) *mid-div on outer: t.k.h at 1/2-way: rdn over 2f out: kpt on one pce* **20/1**

2044 **11** 2 1/2 **Brogan**[17] 7656 3-8-12 77 (p) RichardKingscote 12 66
(Tom Dascombe) *c across fr wd draw and sn led: hdd ent 2f out: sn no ex and wknd qckly ent fnl f* **16/1**

1120 **12** 1/2 **Harba (IRE)**[22] 7484 3-9-3 82 WilliamBuick 5 70
(William Haggas) *settled in rr-div: rdn over 2f out: kpt on one pce* **10/1**

005 **13** 1 1/4 **Jersey Breeze (IRE)**[49] 6586 4-8-12 75 JFEgan 10 60
(Mick Channon) *settled in rr-div on outer: shkn up on outer over 2f out: nt picked up and plugged on under hands and heels* **66/1**

1m 23.88s (-2.12) **Going Correction** -0.225s/f (Stan)
**WFA** 3 from 4yo 2lb **13** Ran SP% **127.1**
Speed ratings (Par 102): **103,102,102,102,101 100,99,99,98,98 95,94,93**
CSF £36.78 CT £155.40 TOTE £4.00: £1.70, £4.60, £2.30; EX 67.00 Trifecta £372.40.
**Owner** Lady Rothschild **Bred** Kincorth Investments Inc **Trained** Beckhampton, Wilts

**FOCUS**
There was a tight finish to this fillies' handicap, which was run at a decent clip. The fourth and fifth horses set the standard.

## 8151 SHIPTON WEALTH MAIDEN STKS 1m 3f 219y(P)
**8:45** (8:52) (Class 5) 3-5-Y-O **£3,234** (£962; £481; £240) **Stalls** Low

Form RPR

2-32 **1** **Stanley**[15] 7708 4-9-11 79 ShaneKelly 12 77
(Richard Hughes) *chsd ldr tl led after 4f: hdd sn after tl regained ld 6f out: shkn up over 2f out and wnt clr: rdn wl over 1f out: ld diminishing ins fnl f: plld out more whn pressed cl home* **15/8**[1]

6 **2** 1/2 **Warm Oasis**[90] 5075 3-9-5 0 TomQueally 5 76
(James Fanshawe) *chsd ldr: rdn over 2f out: chsd clr ldr over 1f out: kpt on wl ins fnl f: no ex nr fin and jst hld on for 2nd* **16/1**

333 **3** shd **Fearsome**[43] 6775 3-9-5 73 OisinMurphy 9 76
(Ralph Beckett) *sluggish s: chsd ldr: rdn over 2f out: kpt on wl fr over 1f out: clsng on ldr ins fnl f: jst hld for 2nd* **11/2**[3]

0-4 **4** shd **Soghan (IRE)**[15] 7708 3-9-5 0 (t) RobertHavlin 10 76
(John Gosden) *hld up in mid-div: shkn up over 2f out w a bit to do: rdn wl over 1f out and picked up wl on outer: keeping on wl tl run flattened out nr fin* **4/1**[2]

4334 **5** 1 1/2 **War At Sea (IRE)**[42] 6823 3-9-5 76 (h) SeanLevey 2 73
(David Simcock) *bhd ldrs on inner: sltly checked 7f out: rdn over 2f out: kpt on wl and clsng nr fin* **8/1**

5 **6** 7 **Nevalyashka**[17] 7652 3-9-0 0 MartinDwyer 11 57
(Marcus Tregoning) *settled in mid-div: rdn wl over 2f out: plugged on one pce fr over 1f out* **20/1**

0240 **7** 1 **Rising (IRE)**[9] 7908 3-9-5 80 (t[1]) TomMarquand 7 61
(Brian Meehan) *racd in mid-divsion: rdn over 2f out: nt picked up and plugged on one fr over 1f out* **10/1**

**8** 1 3/4 **Hadfield (IRE)**[200] 5-9-11 0 (tp) RobertWinston 8 58
(Neil Mulholland) *a in rr: shkn up fr over 2f out: no ex sn after* **8/1**

**9** 3/4 **Mr Boycie Quest** 3-9-2 0 HectorCrouch(3) 3 57
(Gary Moore) *hld up in rr and t.k.h: ct on heels over 4f out: shkn up over 2f out: plugged on after: can do bttr* **50/1**

**10** 16 **Rosie Lea (FR)**[16] 4-9-6 0 LiamKeniry 1 25
(Stuart Kittow) *a in rr* **50/1**

**11** 8 **I Should Coco**[39] 4-9-1 0 RhiainIngram(5) 13 12
(Karen George) *a in rr on outer: no ex fr wl over 2f out* **100/1**

0 **12** 4 **Bombay Rascal**[22] 7492 4-9-3 0 (p[1]) MitchGodwin(3) 6 6
(Robert Walford) *a in rr: btn fr over 3f out* **100/1**

0 **13** 8 **Perfect Art**[42] 6817 3-9-0 0 PatDobbs 4
(Ralph Beckett) *sn led: hdd after 4f: led again sn after: hdd 6f out: bhd ldr and pushed along to hold pl wl over 3f out: wknd qckly after* **33/1**

2m 31.41s (-3.09) **Going Correction** -0.225s/f (Stan)
**WFA** 3 from 4yo+ 6lb **13** Ran SP% **121.0**
Speed ratings (Par 103): **101,100,100,100,99 94,94,93,92,81 76,73,68**
CSF £35.84 TOTE £2.90: £1.20, £3.90, £2.80; EX 43.00 Trifecta £210.20.
**Owner** Normandie Stud Ltd **Bred** Normandie Stud Ltd **Trained** Upper Lambourn, Berks
■ Stewards' Enquiry : Oisin Murphy two-day ban: used whip above the permitted level (Nov 1-2)

**FOCUS**
No more than fair maiden form.

## 8152 100% PROFIT BOOST AT 32REDSPORT.COM CLASSIFIED STKS 1m (P)
**9:15** (9:23) (Class 6) 3-Y-O+ **£2,587** (£770; £384; £192) **Stalls** Low

Form RPR

-000 **1** **Lady Kaviar (IRE)**[68] 5867 3-8-11 55 JaneElliott(5) 2 61
(George Margarson) *settled bhd ldrs on inner: shkn up 2f out and travelling wl: rdn and led ent fnl f: in n.d and pushed out cl home* **12/1**

5000 **2** 2 **Tarseekh**[107] 4446 4-9-5 51 (v[1]) KieranShoemark 1 57
(Chris Gordon) *led: kicked for home over 3f out: kpt on wl tl hdd ent fnl f: plugged on wl ins fnl f* **9/1**[3]

2201 **3** 3 **Chough**[7] 7952 3-9-8 54 RobertWinston 8 56
(Hughie Morrison) *early pce: sn hld up between horses chsng ldrs: rdn over 2f out: kpt on one pce tl no ex ins fnl f* **10/11**[1]

0325 **4** 1 1/2 **Just Fab (IRE)**[27] 7323 4-9-2 52 (b) CharlieBennett(3) 7 47
(Lee Carter) *tk hold early in mid-divsion: gd prog over 3f out and racd in 3rd on inner 2f out: sn rdn and kpt on wl tl no ex and wknd ins fnl f* **10/1**

5504 **5** *1 3/4* **Betsalottie**[9] 7905 4-9-5 52 WilliamCarson 5 43+
(John Bridger) *hld up in rr and t.k.h for much of way: stl in rr whn rdn over 2f out: kpt on wl fr over 1f out to taken 5th ins fnl f* **8/1**[2]
3102 **6** *1/2* **Born To Please**[31] 7199 3-8-9 53 NicolaCurrie(7) 12 41
(Mark Usher) *hld up in rr-div on outer: rdn along along wl over 1f out: kpt on one pce tl no ex ins fnl f* **14/1**
0505 **7** *1 1/2* **Everdina**[31] 7199 3-9-2 55 LiamKeniry 9 37
(Ed Walker) *racd in rr-div on inner: rdn wl over 2f out: kpt one one pce fr over 1f out tl no ex nr ins fnl f* **12/1**
5/00 **8** *1* **I'mwaitingforyou**[54] 6368 8-9-0 20 (t1) JoshuaBryan(5) 6 36
(Peter Bowen) *s.s and in rr: c wd bnd and rdn over 2f out: plugged on at one pce* **33/1**
0000 **9** *1* **Sandacres**[22] 7487 4-9-5 48 (p) OisinMurphy 11 34+
(Laura Mongan) *in rr: rdn over 2f out w plenty to do: kpt on one pce fr over 1f out* **16/1**
0006 **10** *hd* **Gog Elles (IRE)**[39] 6947 3-9-2 49 ShaneKelly 10 32
(J S Moore) *pressed ldr: rdn over 3f out: no ex 2f out and wknd* **20/1**
0-00 **11** *11* **Designamento (IRE)**[30] 7216 3-8-13 43 DavidEgan(3) 13 7
(Ed de Giles) *hld up in rr-div and racd keenly at times: shkn up over 3f out and no rspnse: wknd sn after* **20/1**
00/ **12** *50* **Flaming Fynn**[677] 8177 4-9-5 42 JimmyQuinn 3
(Paul Burgoyne) *in mid-div on outer and plld v hrd early: shkn up wl over 3f out: no ex and eased fr over 2f out: t.o* **50/1**

1m 38.0s (-1.80) **Going Correction** -0.225s/f (Stan)
**WFA** 3 from 4yo+ 3lb **12 Ran SP% 124.9**
Speed ratings (Par 101): **100,98,95,93,91 91,89,88,87,87 76,26**
CSF £116.75 TOTE £12.40: £2.80, £2.60, £1.30; EX 163.90 Trifecta £715.00.
**Owner** Graham Lodge Partnership **Bred** Thomas Hassett **Trained** Newmarket, Suffolk

**FOCUS**
A moderate heat run at a muddling pace. The winner has been rated back to his best.
T/Jkpt: £4,687.80 to a £1 stake. Pool: £60,942.49. 13.00 winning units. T/Plt: £96.90 to a £1 stake. Pool: £81,436.26. 613.50 winning units. T/Qpdt: £11.80 to a £1 stake. Pool: £10,808.67. 674.40 winning units. **Cathal Gahan**

# 7764 LINGFIELD (L-H)

## Wednesday, October 18

**OFFICIAL GOING: Polytrack: standard to slow**
Wind: light, half-across Weather: overcast

## 8153 LINGFIELD PARK MARRIOTT FILLIES' NURSERY H'CAP 7f 1y(P)
**1:50** (1:52) (Class 5) (0-70,70) 2-Y-O **£3,234** (£962; £481; £240) **Stalls Low**

Form RPR
2330 **1** **Sardenya (IRE)**[54] 6395 2-9-7 **70** (b) KieranShoemark 10 78
(Roger Charlton) *mde all at decent pce: rdn clr over 1f out: in command fnl f: kpt on strly* **7/1**
320 **2** *1 3/4* **Not After Midnight (IRE)**[43] 6776 2-9-6 **69** GeorgeDowning 2 72
(Daniel Kubler) *in tch: rdn into 3rd over 2f out: chsd wnr over 1f out: kpt on but a being hld* **33/1**
6126 **3** *3 1/4* **Song Of Summer**[42] 6825 2-9-5 **68** EdwardGreatrex 3 62+
(Archie Watson) *mid-div: rdn and no imp fr over 2f out: hdwy over 1f out: r.o fnl f: wnt 3rd cl home* **10/1**
435 **4** *nk* **Going Native**[13] 7758 2-9-0 **68** JennyPowell(5) 6 61+
(Ed Walker) *mid-div: rdn wl over 2f out: no imp tl r.o wl fnl f: snatched 4th fnl stride* **6/1**[3]
0024 **5** *hd* **Diamond Pursuit**[8] 7914 2-9-3 **66** JFEgan 7 59
(Jo Hughes) *chsd wnr: rdn to chal over 2f out: outpcd over 1f out: no ex whn losing 2 pls towards fin* **9/1**
0032 **6** *nk* **Puchita (IRE)**[46] 6699 2-9-1 **67** HollieDoyle(3) 8 59+
(Richard Hannon) *wnt rt and bmpd leaving stalls: towards rr: rdn and no imp fr over 2f out: kpt on but no ch fnl f* **4/1**[1]
5541 **7** *2 1/4* **Sulafaat (IRE)**[36] 7029 2-9-7 **70** JimCrowley 12 56
(Mark Johnston) *mid-div: sn pushed along: drvn 3f out: nvr any imp* **5/1**[2]
3304 **8** *nse* **Retained (FR)**[39] 6932 2-9-3 **66** JosephineGordon 1 52
(John Best) *chsd ldrs: rdn wl over 2f out: wknd jst ins fnl f* **13/2**
6324 **9** *nse* **Dandiesque (IRE)**[33] 7121 2-9-5 **68** SeanLevey 14 53
(Richard Hannon) *a towards rr* **16/1**
400 **10** *2 1/2* **Supersymmetry (IRE)**[46] 6678 2-9-7 **70** RichardKingscote 9 49
(Tom Dascombe) *hmpd leaving stalls: a in rr* **28/1**
303 **11** *3/4* **Coast Guard**[15] 7707 2-9-2 **65** (p) AlistairRawlinson 4 42
(Tom Dascombe) *trckd ldrs: rdn wl over 2f out: wknd ent fnl f* **20/1**
0455 **12** *6* **Hollywood Dream**[23] 7458 2-9-7 **70** FranBerry 11 31
(William Muir) *mid-div: rdn wl over 2f out: wknd over 1f out* **20/1**

1m 24.44s (-0.36) **Going Correction** -0.05s/f (Stan) **12 Ran SP% 117.7**
Speed ratings (Par 92): **100,98,94,93,93 93,90,90,90,87 86,80**
CSF £225.15 CT £2333.14 TOTE £6.70: £2.30, £8.80, £2.90; EX 220.70 Trifecta £2468.80.
**Owner** Sheikh Rashid Dalmook Al Maktoum **Bred** Patrick F Kelly **Trained** Beckhampton, Wilts

**FOCUS**
The Polytrack was officially on the slow side at this fixture, which was transferred from Bath. They went a decent clip in the first and the time was 2.24sec outside the standard. Not many got into this modest nursery for fillies, the winner making all, and the first two finished clear.

## 8154 EBF STALLIONS NOVICE STKS 5f 6y(P)
**2:20** (2:21) (Class 5) 2-Y-O **£3,881** (£1,155; £577; £288) **Stalls High**

Form RPR
642 **1** **Three Little Birds**[22] 7491 2-8-11 71 RenatoSouza 10 73
(Sylvester Kirk) *pressed ldr: rdn into narrow advantage ent fnl f: kpt on wl to assert cl home* **20/1**
4222 **2** *1/2* **Gold Filigree (IRE)**[41] 6844 2-8-11 75 ShaneKelly 4 71
(Richard Hughes) *led: drvn and narrowly hdd ent fnl f: edgd lft: kpt on w ev ch: hld nring fin* **5/6**[1]
**3** *1 1/4* **Drakefell (IRE)** 2-9-2 0 SeanLevey 6 72
(Richard Hannon) *trckd ldrs: rdn 2f out: r.o to go 3rd ins fnl f* **9/1**
5002 **4** *1* **Aquadabra (IRE)**[2] 8110 2-9-1 68 DavidEgan(3) 8 70
(Mick Channon) *awkwardly away: last pair: rdn 2f out: kpt on ins fnl f: wnt 4th towards fin* **12/1**
0233 **5** *1/2* **Brandy Station (IRE)**[7] 7954 2-9-9 76 RobertTart 3 73
(Lisa Williamson) *trckd ldng pair: rdn 2f out: one pce fnl f* **5/1**[2]
**6** *3/4* **Baileys Excel** 2-9-2 0 SilvestreDeSousa 2 64
(Chris Dwyer) *last trio but in tch: sn pushed along: nvr gng pce to get on terms* **15/2**[3]
0460 **7** *3/4* **Debutante's Ball (IRE)**[60] 6228 2-9-1 91 (p) LiamKeniry 1 60
(J S Moore) *hld up: drvn 2f out: nt pce to get involved* **9/1**

59.11s (0.31) **Going Correction** -0.05s/f (Stan) **7 Ran SP% 115.4**
Speed ratings (Par 95): **95,94,92,90,89 88,87**
CSF £38.38 TOTE £18.60: £8.10, £1.10; EX 39.60 Trifecta £268.60.
**Owner** Miss Amanda Rawding **Bred** T J Cooper **Trained** Upper Lambourn, Berks

**FOCUS**
A fair novice stakes contested by five exposed juveniles and a couple of newcomers. Again the pace held up.

## 8155 LINGFIELD PARK EBF STALLIONS NOVICE STKS 1m 2f (P)
**2:55** (2:55) (Class 5) 2-Y-O **£3,881** (£1,155; £577; £288) **Stalls Low**

Form RPR
545 **1** **Bowditch (IRE)**[17] 7648 2-9-2 76 KieranShoemark 3 81
(John Gosden) *mde all: kicked clr 2f out: in command after: readily* **3/1**[3]
16 **2** *2* **Yabass (IRE)**[39] 6925 2-9-6 0 EdwardGreatrex 6 81
(Archie Watson) *trckd ldrs: rdn 2f out: chsd wnr jst over 1f out but a being hld: kpt on same pce* **5/2**[2]
**3** *nk* **Elegiac** 2-9-2 0 FrannyNorton 8 77+
(Mark Johnston) *rn green: sn pushed along in last trio: hdwy 2f out: r.o nicely fnl f: improve* **14/1**
6 **4** *3 1/2* **Extraction (USA)**[116] 4094 2-9-2 0 PatCosgrave 5 70
(Martyn Meade) *mid-div: rdn into cl enough 4th 2f out: kpt on same pce fnl f* **12/1**
5 **5** *3/4* **Imminent Approach**[49] 6575 2-8-11 0 SilvestreDeSousa 2 64
(James Tate) *trckd wnr: drvn over 2f out: sn outpcd: no ex fnl f* **2/1**[1]
3504 **6** *4 1/2* **Levante Player (IRE)**[13] 7764 2-9-2 71 (p) RichardKingscote 7 60
(Tom Dascombe) *rrd leaving stalls: last trio: rdn over 2f out: little imp* **12/1**
5 **7** *5* **Harbour Nights**[23] 7451 2-9-2 0 (v1) JosephineGordon 4 51
(Hugo Palmer) *struggling over 3f out: a towards rr* **20/1**
00 **8** *hd* **See The Tar (IRE)**[23] 7451 2-9-2 0 DougieCostello 1 50
(Jo Hughes) *mid-div: disputing 5th u.p whn briefly tight for room on rails over 2f out: sn btn* **100/1**
0 **9** *21* **Sir Leonard Kitter (IRE)**[14] 7740 2-9-2 0 SeanLevey 9 10
(Richard Hannon) *chsd ldng pair: struggling over 4f out: wknd over 3f out* **33/1**

2m 5.09s (-1.51) **Going Correction** -0.05s/f (Stan) **9 Ran SP% 117.6**
Speed ratings (Par 95): **104,102,102,99,98 95,91,91,74**
CSF £11.02 TOTE £4.60: £1.40, £1.40, £3.60; EX 12.50 Trifecta £82.20.
**Owner** HRH Princess Haya Of Jordan **Bred** Airlie Stud **Trained** Newmarket, Suffolk

**FOCUS**
Quite a stamina test for these juveniles, and another race won from the front.

## 8156 LINGFIELDPARK.CO.UK FILLIES' H'CAP 1m 1y(P)
**3:25** (3:26) (Class 5) (0-70,70) 3-Y-O+ **£4,204** (£1,251; £625; £312) **Stalls High**

Form RPR
3002 **1** **Dashing Poet**[13] 7771 3-8-12 **64** SilvestreDeSousa 2 71
(Heather Main) *in tch: swtchd rt to mount chal jst over 1f out: led ins fnl f: kpt on wl and a holding on* **9/2**[1]
3055 **2** *1/2* **Zafaranah (USA)**[22] 7492 3-8-12 **67** CallumShepherd(3) 1 73
(Pam Sly) *s.i.s: sn mid-div: hdwy over 1f out: swtchd rt sn after: rdn and r.o strly fnl f: nt quite rch wnr* **8/1**
5230 **3** *1/2* **Miss Pacific**[33] 7131 3-9-2 **68** KieranShoemark 11 73
(William Jarvis) *sn pushed along towards rr: gd hdwy over 1f out: sn rdn: ev ch fnl 100yds: no ex cl home* **12/1**
3530 **4** *1/2* **Ashazuri**[41] 6866 3-8-12 **64** (h) RichardKingscote 3 68
(Jonathan Portman) *mid-div: nt clr run 2f out tl ent fnl f: r.o wl but nvr threatening to get on terms* **7/1**[3]
4112 **5** *nse* **Topmeup**[9] 7899 3-8-7 **59** (v) JFEgan 7 63
(David Evans) *hld up towards rr: c wd on bnd turning in: r.o wl fnl f but nvr looking a threat to ldrs* **6/1**[2]
0/4- **6** *1 1/2* **Miss Blondell**[322] 8163 4-8-11 **67** TylerSaunders(7) 10 68
(Marcus Tregoning) *mid-div: c wd on bnd turning in: kpt on nicely fnl f wout ever threatening* **14/1**
3010 **7** *1/2* **Andalusite**[22] 7484 4-9-0 **66** (v) HectorCrouch(3) 4 66
(John Gallagher) *trckd ldr: rdn 2f out: one pce fnl f* **25/1**
0006 **8** *1 3/4* **Auntie Barber (IRE)**[49] 6578 4-9-7 **70** (t) SeanLevey 5 66
(Stuart Williams) *in tch: rdn over 2f out: fading whn rdr lost whip ent fnl f* **10/1**
4320 **9** *nk* **Halinka (IRE)**[29] 7241 3-8-13 **68** DavidEgan(3) 9 62
(Roger Varian) *led: rdn and hdd ins fnl f: wknd* **9/1**
1664 **10** *1* **Orithia (USA)**[35] 7061 3-8-12 **64** (bt) ShaneKelly 8 56
(Seamus Durack) *in tch: rdn over 2f out: wknd over 1f out* **6/1**[2]
4000 **11** *1/2* **Skidby Mill (IRE)**[22] 7493 7-9-2 **70** PaddyBradley(5) 6 62
(Laura Mongan) *trckd ldr: rdn 2f out: sn wknd* **33/1**
0605 **12** *12* **Moonstone Rock**[4] 8031 3-8-5 **57** (p) FrannyNorton 12 20
(Jim Boyle) *dwlt bdly: nvr rcvrd: a wl bhd* **14/1**

1m 37.23s (-0.97) **Going Correction** -0.05s/f (Stan)
**WFA** 3 from 4yo+ 3lb **12 Ran SP% 117.3**
Speed ratings (Par 100): **102,101,101,100,100 98,98,96,96,95 94,82**
CSF £39.53 CT £412.94 TOTE £4.00: £1.90, £2.80, £4.00; EX 43.90 Trifecta £698.50.
**Owner** Malcolm Moss **Bred** Qatar Bloodstock Ltd **Trained** Kingston Lisle, Oxon

**FOCUS**
This was run at what looked an ordinary gallop. Straightforward fillies' form.

## 8157 LINGFIELD PARK GOLF CLUB H'CAP 1m 7f 169y(P)
**3:55** (3:56) (Class 5) (0-70,69) 3-Y-O+ **£4,528** (£1,347; £673; £336) **Stalls Low**

Form RPR
0611 **1** **Dovils Date**[42] 3775 8-10-0 **69** DavidProbert 12 75
(Tim Vaughan) *trckd ldrs: rdn for str chal form over 2f out: tk narrow advantage fnl 120yds: styd on gamely* **14/1**
602 **2** *1/2* **Stylish Dancer**[18] 7629 3-9-4 **67** PatCosgrave 2 73
(Luca Cumani) *trckd ldrs: rdn over 2f out: styd on fnl f: wnt 2nd towards fin* **6/4**[1]
3000 **3** *1 1/4* **Everlasting Sea**[28] 7278 3-8-5 **54** MartinDwyer 5 58
(Stuart Kittow) *mid-div: hdwy over 2f out: swtchd rt over 1f out: immediately hung lft and rdn: styd on: wnt 3rd towards fin* **33/1**
-600 **4** *nk* **Caracas**[15] 7711 3-8-13 **62** StevieDonohoe 9 66
(Harry Dunlop) *mid-div: rdn over 2f out: no imp tl styd on fnl f: wnt 4th towards fin* **20/1**
0302 **5** *1 3/4* **Avenue Des Champs**[22] 7483 5-9-11 **66** (p) MartinHarley 7 70
(Jane Chapple-Hyam) *trckd ldr: led over 8f out: rdn whn strly chal fr over 2f out: hdd fnl 120yds: kpt battling tl lost action and heavily eased towards fin (dismntd)* **5/1**[2]
60 **6** *1/2* **Bermondsey Belle (IRE)**[20] 7537 3-8-13 **62** (t1) KieranShoemark 11 63
(Lucy Wadham) *led for over 7f: trckd ldrs: rdn over 2f out: one pce fnl f* **12/1**
5-00 **7** *shd* **Atalanta Bay (IRE)**[22] 7483 7-9-3 **58** (h) ShaneKelly 4 59
(Marcus Tregoning) *racd keenly in midfield: hmpd and lost pl over 8f out: towards rr: rdn and hdwy over 1f out: styng on wl but hld whn hmpd cl home* **17/2**

1300 **8** *shd* **Danglydontask**[55] 6343 6-9-8 **63**..........................(p[1]) RichardKingscote 1 64
(David Arbuthnot) *hld up towards rr: rdn over 2f out: styd on fnl f wout ever threatening to get involved* **12/1**

5154 **9** *shd* **Wordiness**[25] 7412 9-9-7 **69**.......................... KatherineGlenister(7) 6 70
(David Evans) *hld up towards rr: c wd on bnd turning in: styd on wout ever threatening to get involved fnl f* **7/1**[3]

0000 **10** *nk* **Victor's Bet (SPA)**[15] 7711 8-9-5 **65**.......................... PaddyBradley(5) 8 66
(Ralph J Smith) *s.i.s: last: rdn over 2f out: c wd on bnd turning in: styd on wout ever threatening to get involved fnl f* **25/1**

0020 **11** *hd* **Ivanhoe**[14] 7730 7-9-1 **56**.......................... SteveDrowne 13 56
(Michael Blanshard) *mid-div: rdn over 3f out: nvr any imp* **16/1**

-060 **12** *9* **Mayasa (IRE)**[11] 7831 4-9-10 **68**..........................(b) HectorCrouch(3) 10 58
(John Flint) *in tch: rdn 3f out: wknd over 1f out* **33/1**

0000 **13** *10* **Breeze Up**[20] 7537 3-7-12 **50** oh5..........................(b[1]) DavidEgan(3) 3 28
(Ed de Giles) *s.i.s: last pair: hdwy into midfield over 8f out: rdn over 3f out: wknd over 2f out* **50/1**

3m 27.29s (1.59) **Going Correction** -0.05s/f (Stan)
**WFA** 3 from 4yo+ 8lb **13** Ran SP% **124.1**
Speed ratings (Par 103): **94,93,93,92,92 91,91,91,91,91 91,86,81**
CSF £34.89 CT £750.62 TOTE £9.70: £3.10, £1.30, £9.00; EX 40.00 Trifecta £796.00.
**Owner** Itsfuninit **Bred** Cranford Stud **Trained** Aberthin, Vale of Glamorgan

**FOCUS**
They went rather a sedate gallop in this ordinary staying handicap and it developed into a dash for home. The winner is getting closer to his old form.

## 8158 ARENA RACING COMPANY H'CAP (DIV I) 6f 1y(P)
**4:30** (4:31) (Class 5) (0-75,77) 3-Y-O+ **£4,204** (£1,251; £625; £312) **Stalls** Low

Form RPR

2105 **1** **Danecase**[111] 4251 4-9-6 **74**.......................... DougieCostello 1 79
(David Dennis) *mid-div: hdwy in inner turning in: sn rdn: str run ins fnl f: led towards fin* **16/1**

0000 **2** *nk* **Alkashaaf (USA)**[19] 7569 3-9-5 **74**..........................(bt[1]) EdwardGreatrex 2 78
(Archie Watson) *trckd ldrs: rdn 2f out: ev ch ins fnl f: kpt on* **9/1**

6660 **3** *nk* **Swanton Blue (IRE)**[35] 7058 4-8-9 **66**.......................... CallumShepherd(3) 4 69
(Ed de Giles) *led: rdn over 1f out: no ex whn hdd towards fin* **12/1**

0006 **4** *hd* **Juan Horsepower**[79] 5473 3-9-1 **77**.......................... RossaRyan(7) 9 79
(Richard Hannon) *trckd ldrs: outpcd 2f out: kpt on again fnl f: clsng on ldrs at fin* **7/1**

3240 **5** *1 ½* **Father McKenzie**[14] 7738 3-9-3 **72**.......................... RyanTate 11 70
(James Eustace) *trckd ldrs: rdn over 2f out: kpt on tl no ex ins fnl f* **16/1**

1424 **6** *1* **Monteamiata (IRE)**[13] 7771 3-9-6 **75**..........................(p[1]) LiamKeniry 6 69+
(Ed Walker) *s.i.s: in rr: sme late prog: n.d* **11/2**[3]

0-34 **7** *nk* **Peter Park**[16] 7691 4-8-13 **70**.......................... HectorCrouch(3) 3 63
(Clive Cox) *mid-div: rdn over 2f out: no imp* **4/1**[1]

-560 **8** *shd* **Ferocity (IRE)**[19] 7571 3-9-3 **72**..........................(p[1]) MartinHarley 8 65
(Robyn Brisland) *hld up towards rr: rdn 2f out: kpt on fnl f: n.d* **13/2**

0320 **9** *½* **Jumping Around (IRE)**[25] 7414 3-8-3 **63**..........(b[1]) ManuelFernandes(5) 5 55
(Ian Williams) *towards rr: hdwy 3f out: wknd fnl f* **5/1**[2]

3066 **10** *8* **Soaring Spirits (IRE)**[41] 6850 7-8-7 **61** oh1..............(v) FrannyNorton 10 27
(Dean Ivory) *nvr bttr than mid-div on outer: last and btn whn c wd turning in* **14/1**

1550 **11** *¾* **Cat Silver**[25] 7408 4-8-10 **67**..........................(p) DavidEgan(3) 7 31
(Charlie Wallis) *trckd ldrs: rdn over 2f out: wknd over 1f out* **20/1**

1m 11.7s (-0.20) **Going Correction** -0.05s/f (Stan)
**WFA** 3 from 4yo+ 1lb **11** Ran SP% **118.8**
Speed ratings (Par 103): **99,98,98,97,95 94,94,94,93,82 81**
CSF £154.11 CT £1199.47 TOTE £20.00: £4.90, £2.60, £4.60; EX 135.10 Trifecta £4236.60.
**Owner** Professor L P Hardwick & Partner **Bred** D D & Mrs J P Clee **Trained** Hanley Swan, Worcestershire

**FOCUS**
Just a modest sprint, but the quicker division by 0.31sec. The winner apart, the principals raced up with the pace and the first two came out of stalls 1 and 2.

## 8159 ARENA RACING COMPANY H'CAP (DIV II) 6f 1y(P)
**5:05** (5:05) (Class 5) (0-75,75) 3-Y-O+ **£4,204** (£1,251; £625; £312) **Stalls** Low

Form RPR

6330 **1** **Red Alert**[9] 7882 3-9-5 **74**.......................... FranBerry 1 81
(William Muir) *trckd ldrs: outpcd by front pair 2f out: r.o ins fnl f: led fnl stride* **5/2**[1]

0-00 **2** *hd* **Desert Grey (IRE)**[43] 6792 3-8-12 **67**..........................(bt) KieranShoemark 7 73
(Roger Charlton) *trckd ldr: chal over 2f out: tk narrow advantage ins fnl f: hdd fnl stride* **7/1**

0630 **3** *½* **Born To Finish (IRE)**[9] 7882 4-9-6 **74**..........................(p) DougieCostello 10 78+
(Jamie Osborne) *hld up last pair: hdwy over 1f out: sn hrd drvn: kpt on wl fnl f* **9/2**[2]

5566 **4** *½* **Bahamian Heights**[78] 5514 6-8-9 **70**.......................... JonathanFisher(7) 8 73
(Robert Cowell) *in tch: rdn and hdwy over 1f out: kpt on ins fnl f* **25/1**

4001 **5** *nk* **Red Stripes (USA)**[18] 7607 5-8-7 **61**..........................(b) DavidProbert 5 63
(Lisa Williamson) *led: rdn 2f out: narrowly hdd ins fnl f: no ex cl home* **13/2**[3]

4114 **6** *2 ½* **Hamidans Girl (IRE)**[36] 7014 3-9-6 **75**.......................... FrannyNorton 4 69
(Keith Dalgleish) *chsd ldrs: rdn 3f out: nt pce to get on terms* **15/2**

6615 **7** *hd* **Coronation Cottage**[31] 7195 3-9-0 **72**.......................... CharlieBennett(3) 9 65
(Malcolm Saunders) *rrd leaving stalls: last: rdn over 2f out: nvr threatened to get on terms* **12/1**

0301 **8** *nk* **Langley Vale**[31] 7191 8-8-11 **65**.......................... JackMitchell 6 57
(Roger Teal) *hld up last trio: rdn 2f out: nvr any imp* **9/2**[2]

1m 12.01s (0.11) **Going Correction** -0.05s/f (Stan)
**WFA** 3 from 4yo+ 1lb **8** Ran SP% **114.1**
Speed ratings (Par 103): **97,96,96,95,95 91,91,91**
CSF £20.49 CT £74.43 TOTE £3.30: £1.10, £2.10, £1.80; EX 23.30 Trifecta £99.10.
**Owner** A A Byrne **Bred** Miss Jacqueline Goodearl **Trained** Lambourn, Berks

**FOCUS**
Very modest form, and the slower division by 0.31sec. A small personal best from the winner.

## 8160 RACING PARTNERSHIP H'CAP 1m 4f (P)
**5:35** (5:35) (Class 5) (0-70,72) 3-Y-O+ **£3,557** (£1,058; £396; £396) **Stalls** Low

Form RPR

4041 **1** **Star Of Lombardy (IRE)**[11] 7831 4-9-10 **70**.......................... JoeFanning 2 78
(Mark Johnston) *travelled wl most of way: led for 1f: trckd ldrs: swtchd out and shkn up over 1f out: drifted lft ins fnl f: led fnl 70yds: styd on wl* **10/1**

0062 **2** *½* **So Celebre (GER)**[5] 8000 4-9-10 **70**..........................(p[1]) FranBerry 6 77
(Ian Williams) *hld up: hdwy fr 5f out to chal 4f out: rdn to take narrow advantage over 1f out: styd on but no ex whn hdd fnl 70yds* **15/8**[1]

5443 **3** *1 ¼* **Clemento (IRE)**[19] 7561 3-9-3 **69**.......................... KieranShoemark 3 74
(Roger Charlton) *mid-div tl dropped to last trio 4f out: hdwy over 1f out where briefly hung lft: styd on wl fnl f: jnd 3rd on line* **4/1**[2]

5352 **3** *dht* **Stepney**[11] 7832 3-9-2 **68**.......................... MartinHarley 7 73
(Robyn Brisland) *trckd ldrs: chal over 2f out: rdn and ev ch over 1f out: no ex ins fnl f* **8/1**

6100 **5** *1 ½* **I'm Running Late**[14] 7744 3-9-2 **68**.......................... LiamKeniry 1 71
(Dean Ivory) *mid-div: rdn over 2f out: styd on fnl f but nt pce to get involved* **33/1**

3226 **6** *½* **Best Example (USA)**[22] 7483 5-9-3 **66**.......................... ShelleyBirkett(3) 5 68
(Julia Feilden) *hld up: nt clr run turning in: styd on fnl f but nvr any ch* **16/1**

4662 **7** *2 ¼* **Malt Teaser (FR)**[9] 7879 3-8-10 **62**.......................... FrannyNorton 4 60
(John Best) *s.i.s: towards rr: rdn over 2f out: sme prog over 1f out: no further imp fnl f* **9/2**[3]

4402 **8** *5* **Archimento**[18] 7601 4-9-3 **66**..........................(t) HectorCrouch(3) 9 56
(Philip Hide) *s.i.s: mid-div: pushed along over 3f out: nvr any imp* **12/1**

4000 **9** *2 ¾* **Inke (IRE)**[17] 7651 5-9-6 **69**..........................(v[1]) CharlieBennett(3) 12 55
(Jim Boyle) *led after 1f: rdn and hdd over 2f out: wknd over 1f out* **50/1**

5400 **10** *1* **Sakurajima (IRE)**[42] 6812 3-8-7 **62**..........................(t) CallumShepherd(3) 10 47
(Charles Hills) *s.i.s: sn mid-div: drvn over 3f out: wknd over 1f out* **33/1**

0200 **11** *40* **Onorina (IRE)**[14] 7744 5-8-13 **64**.......................... PaddyBradley(5) 11
(Jim Boyle) *trckd ldr tl over 4f out: sn dropped to rr: eased over 2f out* **33/1**

2m 32.06s (-0.94) **Going Correction** -0.05s/f (Stan)
**WFA** 3 from 4yo+ 6lb **11** Ran SP% **117.5**
Speed ratings (Par 103): **101,100,99,99,98 98,97,93,91,91 64**
WIN: £6.80; PL: SOL £3.00, SC £1.10, S £1.40, C £1.00; EX: £26.60; CSF: £28.39; TC: SOL-SC-C £45.70, SOL-SC-S £82.24; TF: SOL-SC-C £47.50, SOL-SC-S £33.40;.
**Owner** Paul Dean **Bred** Tom Darcy And Vincent McCarthy **Trained** Middleham Moor, N Yorks

**FOCUS**
A moderate handicap run at what looked an ordinary gallop.
T/Plt: £913.70 to a £1 stake. Pool: £63,021.62. 50.35 winning units. T/Qpdt: £132.50 to a £1 stake. Pool: £7,187.10. 40.12 winning units. **Tim Mitchell**

# 7953 NOTTINGHAM (L-H)
Wednesday, October 18

**OFFICIAL GOING: Good to soft (good in places; 7.1)**
Wind: moderate, behind Weather: Overcast

## 8161 KIER CONSTRUCTION EBF MAIDEN STKS (DIV I) 1m 75y
**1:30** (1:31) (Class 5) 2-Y-O **£3,234** (£962; £481; £240) **Stalls** Centre

Form RPR

2 **1** **Msayyan (IRE)**[14] 7726 2-9-5 0.......................... FrankieDettori 10 75+
(John Gosden) *sn led: pushed along over 2f out: green and rdn over 1f out: kpt on wl fnl f* **4/6**[1]

4 **2** *1* **Corgi**[14] 7739 2-9-5 0.......................... OisinMurphy 5 73+
(Hughie Morrison) *trckd ldrs: hdwy over 3f out and sn chsng ldng pair: rdn 2f out: sn drvn and edgd lft: kpt on wl towards fin* **14/1**

05 **3** *½* **Ghazan (IRE)**[36] 7026 2-9-5 0.......................... AdamKirby 9 72
(Clive Cox) *prom: cl up 1/2-way: chal over 2f out: sn rdn: drvn and ev ch ent fnl f: kpt on same pce last 100 yds* **12/1**

50 **4** *nk* **Baghdad (FR)**[78] 5504 2-9-5 0.......................... PJMcDonald 4 71+
(Mark Johnston) *dwlt and towards rr: hdwy over 3f out: chsd ldrs and rdn along over 2f out: drvn over 1f out: kpt on fnl f* **16/1**

**5** *1 ¼* **Victory Chime (IRE)** 2-9-5 0.......................... PatDobbs 2 68+
(Ralph Beckett) *hld up towards rr: hdwy 1/2-way: in tch and rdn along 2f out: kpt on fnl f* **25/1**

**6** *¾* **My Lord And Master (IRE)** 2-9-5 0.......................... DanielTudhope 1 66
(William Haggas) *in tch on inner: pushed along 3f out: rdn 2f out: no imp fnl f* **9/1**[3]

**7** *2 ½* **Strongarm Chaser (IRE)** 2-9-5 0.......................... TomMarquand 8 60+
(Richard Hannon) *towards rr: pushed along and hdwy 3f out: rdn 2f out: sn no imp* **6/1**[2]

00 **8** *½* **Pippin**[20] 7543 2-9-5 0.......................... RobertWinston 3 59
(Hughie Morrison) *chsd ldrs: rdn along over 2f out: wknd appr fnl f* **33/1**

0 **9** *12* **Feragust**[40] 6883 2-9-5 0.......................... HarryBentley 7 30
(Marco Botti) *plld hrd: prom: rdn along over 3f out: sn wknd* **33/1**

0 **10** *11* **College King**[12] 7788 2-8-12 0.......................... JacobMitchell(7) 6 4+
(Christine Dunnett) *a in rr: stmbld 5f out: bhd after* **100/1**

1m 48.58s (-0.42) **Going Correction** -0.175s/f (Firm) **10** Ran SP% **115.2**
Speed ratings (Par 95): **95,94,93,93,91 91,88,88,76,65**
CSF £11.13 TOTE £1.40: £1.02, £3.50, £2.90; EX 11.50 Trifecta £57.70.
**Owner** Al Shaqab Racing **Bred** Corrin Stud & Sean O'Keeffe **Trained** Newmarket, Suffolk

**FOCUS**
Outer track used. A nice group of horses, but a muddling race. Distance increased by 12yds.

## 8162 KIER CONSTRUCTION EBF MAIDEN STKS (DIV II) 1m 75y
**2:00** (2:00) (Class 5) 2-Y-O **£3,234** (£962; £481; £240) **Stalls** Centre

Form RPR

**1** **Blazing Tunder (IRE)** 2-9-5 0.......................... DaneO'Neill 2 76+
(Henry Candy) *mde most: rdn wl over 1f out: drvn ins fnl f: kpt on gamely towards fin* **9/4**[1]

0 **2** *nk* **Astrologist (IRE)**[11] 7813 2-9-5 0.......................... AdamKirby 1 75+
(Clive Cox) *chsd ldrs: pushed along over 3f out: rdn wl over 2f out: drvn to chal over 1f out: ev ch ins fnl f: no ex towards fin* **3/1**[2]

0 **3** *1* **Gendarme (IRE)**[33] 7120 2-9-5 0.......................... TomMarquand 3 73
(Richard Hannon) *trckd ldng pair: pushed along over 3f out: rdn wl over 1f out: kpt on fnl f* **8/1**

**4** *3* **Imaginative (IRE)** 2-9-5 0.......................... AndreaAtzeni 4 66+
(Roger Varian) *in tch: green and pushed along over 3f out: hdwy to chse ldrs over 2f out: rdn wl over 1f out: no imp fnl f* **7/2**[3]

**5** *3 ¼* **Hilborough** 2-9-5 0.......................... CharlesBishop 9 61+
(Mick Channon) *s.i.s and lost several l s: bhd: hdwy over 4f out: chsd ldrs 2f out: sn rdn and wknd over 1f out* **16/1**

00 **6** *2* **Boko Fittleworth (IRE)**[25] 7391 2-9-5 0.......................... WilliamCarson 8 54+
(Jonjo O'Neill) *a towards rr* **100/1**

00 **7** *shd* **French Kiss (IRE)**[21] 7503 2-9-5 0.......................... OisinMurphy 7 54
(Hughie Morrison) *cl up: disp ld 1/2-way: rdn along over 2f out: sn drvn and wknd wl over 1f out* **20/1**

0 **8** *6* **Wilfred Owen**[11] 7810 2-9-5 0.......................... RobertHavlin 6 40
(John Gosden) *chsd ldrs: pushed along over 4f out: rdn along wl over 3f out: sn wknd* **16/1**

0 **9** 3/4 **Safarhi**[14] 7726 2-9-5 0 ........ FergusSweeney 5 38+
(Alan King) *.a in rr* **25/1**

1m 47.89s (-1.11) **Going Correction** -0.175s/f (Firm) **9** Ran SP% **110.5**
Speed ratings (Par 95): **98,97,96,93,90 88,88,82,81**
CSF £8.27 TOTE £3.00: £1.10, £1.50, £2.30; EX 10.10 Trifecta £67.70.

**Owner** B McNeill **Bred** Northern Bloodstock Agency Ltd **Trained** Kingston Warren, Oxon

**FOCUS**
Distance increased by 12yds. The weaker of the two divisions, although it was run at a fair gallop and went to a promising newcomer.

## 8163 KIER CONSTRUCTION CENTRAL EBF MAIDEN FILLIES' STKS (PLUS 10 RACE) 1m 75y

**2:30** (2:37) (Class 5) 2-Y-O £3,234 (£962; £481; £240) **Stalls** Centre

Form RPR

3 **1** **Hadith (IRE)**[25] 7399 2-9-0 0 ........ WilliamBuick 7 88
(Charlie Appleby) *mde all: clr 3f out: rdn and hung rt appr fnl f: kpt on strly* **11/4**[2]

22 **2** 2 1/2 **Sheikha Reika (FR)**[25] 7399 2-9-0 0 ........ AndreaAtzeni 5 82
(Roger Varian) *trckd ldrs: hdwy over 3f out: rdn to chse wnr wl over 1f out: swtchd lft and drvn ent fnl f: kpt on same pce* **4/6**[1]

60 **3** 3 3/4 **Naqaawa (IRE)**[26] 7357 2-9-0 0 ........ DaneO'Neill 2 74
(Owen Burrows) *in tch: hdwy over 3f out: rdn along over 2f out: kpt on fnl f* **16/1**[3]

5333 **4** 1 3/4 **Calling Rio (IRE)**[14] 7733 2-9-0 74 ........ PaulMulrennan 9 70
(David Loughnane) *prom: cl up 4f out: rdn along wl over 2f out: drvn and wknd wl over 1f out* **25/1**

**5** 3/4 **Espadrille** 2-9-0 0 ........ MartinLane 14 70+
(Charlie Appleby) *green and sn outpcd in rr: hdwy 3f out: styd on wl appr fnl f: nrst fin* **20/1**

**6** 3/4 **Crystal Hope** 2-9-0 0 ........ PatDobbs 8 67+
(Sir Michael Stoute) *dwlt and rr: hdwy over 3f out: rdn along 2f out: kpt on fnl f* **20/1**

0 **7** 3/4 **Pescedora (IRE)**[14] 7733 2-9-0 0 ........ DanielTudhope 6 65
(Roger Charlton) *trckd wnr: rdn along 4f out: sn wknd* **100/1**

**8** 3/4 **Saving Grace** 2-9-0 0 ........ JamieSpencer 13 65+
(Luca Cumani) *dwlt and rr: hdwy 3f out: rdn along 2f out: kpt on fnl f* **33/1**

56 **9** 2 3/4 **Red Miracle**[14] 7739 2-9-0 0 ........ WilliamCarson 1 57
(Rod Millman) *chsd ldrs on inner: rdn along 4f out: sn wknd* **66/1**

**10** 2 1/2 **Voluminous** 2-8-11 0 ........ GeorgeWood(3) 12 52+
(James Fanshawe) *a towards rr* **16/1**[3]

**11** 3 1/4 **Hot Off The Press (IRE)** 2-9-0 0 ........ LouisSteward 3 45+
(Michael Bell) *a towards rr* **100/1**

56 **12** 3/4 **Hidden Dream (IRE)**[12] 7786 2-9-0 0 ........ TimmyMurphy 11 43
(Christine Dunnett) *in tch on outer: rdn along over 4f out: sn wknd* **100/1**

**13** 1/2 **Eden Rose** 2-9-0 0 ........ CharlesBishop 4 42
(Mick Channon) *midfield: rdn along wl over 3f out: sn wknd* **50/1**

**14** 9 **Fen Caroline** 2-9-0 0 ........ LukeMorris 10 22
(Robert Cowell) *in tch on outer: hdwy to chse ldrs 4f out: rdn along over 3f out: sn wknd* **100/1**

1m 47.64s (-1.36) **Going Correction** -0.175s/f (Firm) **14** Ran SP% **122.1**
Speed ratings (Par 92): **99,96,92,91,90 89,88,88,85,82 79,78,78,69**
CSF £4.56 TOTE £4.10: £1.40, £1.02, £3.40; EX 6.20 Trifecta £38.20.

**Owner** Godolphin **Bred** Godolphin **Trained** Newmarket, Suffolk

■ Traumatised was withdrawn. Price at time of withdrawal 100-1. Rule 4 does not apply.

**FOCUS**
Distance increased by 12yds. The big two in the market dominated this decent-looking maiden, with the winner coming more down the centre in the straight. The runner-up has been rated near her mark.

## 8164 KIER GROUP NURSERY H'CAP 1m 75y

**3:05** (3:06) (Class 5) (0-70,71) 2-Y-O £3,234 (£962; £481; £240) **Stalls** Centre

Form RPR

3655 **1** **Ruysch (IRE)**[28] 7265 2-9-7 70 ........ JimmyQuinn 6 74
(Ed Dunlop) *dwlt and sn pushed along in rr: rdn along bef 1/2-way: hdwy on outer 3f out: rdn to chse ldrs over 1f out: drvn to chal and and edgd lft ins fnl f: kpt on u.p to ld last 50 yds* **10/1**

0500 **2** nk **Colorado Dream**[50] 6553 2-9-0 63 ........ (b[1]) DaneO'Neill 7 66
(George Baker) *sn led: rdn along over 2f out: drvn ent fnl f: hdd and no ex last 50 yds* **25/1**

2635 **3** 2 1/2 **Trogon (IRE)**[13] 7764 2-9-6 69 ........ CharlesBishop 5 66
(Mick Channon) *trckd ldrs: hdwy over 3f out: rdn and chsd wnr over 1f out: drvn and ev ch ent fnl f: kpt on same pce* **3/1**[1]

550 **4** 2 1/4 **Onefootinfront**[36] 7026 2-9-0 63 ........ LukeMorris 3 55
(Daniel Mark Loughnane) *dwlt and towards rr: gd hdwy on outer over 4f out: chsd ldrs 3f out: rdn along 2f out: sn drvn and kpt on same pce* **10/1**

4021 **5** 3/4 **Show Of Force**[51] 6504 2-9-5 68 ........ RobHornby 9 58
(Jonathan Portman) *cl up: rdn along over 3f out: drvn over 2f out: grad wknd* **8/1**

0640 **6** hd **Polar Light**[64] 6036 2-9-8 71 ........ PatDobbs 4 61
(David Elsworth) *.in tch on inner: hdwy 3f out: rdn to chse ldrs over 2f out: drvn wl over 1f out: sn wknd* **8/1**

5650 **7** nk **Galactic (IRE)**[13] 7764 2-9-2 65 ........ TomMarquand 1 54
(Richard Hannon) *trckd ldrs: hdwy over 3f out: sn chsng ldng pair: rdn along 2f out: sn drvn and wknd* **7/1**[3]

663 **8** nse **French Resistance (IRE)**[17] 7654 2-9-2 65 ........ TonyHamilton 2 54
(Roger Fell) *dwlt: a in rr* **6/1**[2]

4043 **9** 1 **Show Princess**[30] 7222 2-9-0 63 ........ GrahamLee 8 50
(Michael Appleby) *trckd ldrs on outer: hdwy and cl up 5f out: rdn along 3f out: sn wknd* **12/1**

604 **10** 11 **Pelice (IRE)**[18] 7608 2-9-5 68 ........ PJMcDonald 10 29
(Mark Johnston) *chsd ldrs: rdn along wl over 3f out: sn wknd* **8/1**

1m 48.78s (-0.22) **Going Correction** -0.175s/f (Firm) **10** Ran SP% **114.8**
Speed ratings (Par 95): **94,93,91,88,88 88,87,87,86,75**
CSF £224.43 CT £931.42 TOTE £12.90: £3.70, £7.60, £1.70; EX 301.10 Trifecta £727.10.

**Owner** St Albans Bloodstock Limited **Bred** St Albans Bloodstock Llp **Trained** Newmarket, Suffolk

**FOCUS**
Distance increased by 12yds. They went a fair gallop, no more, and the winner did really well to come from off the pace having never been travelling, possibly benefiting from challenging down the outside.

## 8165 KIER PROPERTY H'CAP 1m 2f 50y

**3:35** (3:36) (Class 3) (0-95,94) 3-Y-O+

**£9,337** (£2,796; £1,398; £699; £349; £175) **Stalls** Low

Form RPR

0152 **1** shd **Jupiter Light**[28] 7277 3-9-3 91 ........ FrankieDettori 1 101
(John Gosden) *trckd ldrs: hdwy over 2f out: rdn to chse ldr over 1f out: drvn to chal ins fnl f: carried lft and ev ch last 100 yds: jst hld. Finished 2nd plcd 1st* **7/1**[1]

0211 **2** **Capton**[33] 7132 4-9-3 87 ........ DaneO'Neill 15 96
(Henry Candy) *mde all: rdn over 2f out: drvn over 1f out: edgd lft ins fnl f: hld on wl nr fin. Finished 1st plcd 2nd* **8/1**[2]

3145 **3** 2 3/4 **In First Place**[40] 6881 3-8-6 80 ........ (b[1]) PaulHanagan 13 84
(Richard Fahey) *towards rr: hdwy over 2f out and sn rdn: drvn and kpt on wl fnl f* **20/1**

1045 **4** nk **Toulson**[65] 6007 4-9-5 89 ........ (p) CharlesBishop 11 92
(Eve Johnson Houghton) *prom: cl up 3f out: chal over 2f out: sn rdn and ev ch tl drvn and kpt on same pce fnl f* **10/1**

4122 **5** 2 **Empress Ali (IRE)**[20] 7555 6-9-7 91 ........ JamesSullivan 16 91
(Tom Tate) *trckd ldrs: hdwy over 3f out: rdn along 2f out: sn drvn and kpt on same pce* **10/1**

3300 **6** shd **Mutarakez (IRE)**[46] 6698 5-9-1 85 ........ JamieSpencer 14 84
(Brian Meehan) *stdd s and hld up in rr: hdwy 3f out: rdn along 2f out: styd on fnl f* **12/1**

3625 **7** 3/4 **Indian Chief (IRE)**[7] 7959 7-9-3 87 ........ DanielTudhope 12 85
(Rebecca Bastiman) *hld up in rr: hdwy 3f out: chsd ldrs 2f out: sn rdn and one pce fnl f* **8/1**[2]

1641 **8** 1/2 **Compton Mill**[14] 7735 5-9-2 86 ........ PJMcDonald 7 83
(Hughie Morrison) *trckd ldrs: hdwy over 3f out: rdn along 2f out: drvn over 1f out: no imp* **8/1**[2]

100 **9** 3 3/4 **Nayel (IRE)**[53] 6422 5-9-5 89 ........ (p) TomMarquand 2 79
(Richard Hannon) *trckd ldrs on inner: pushed along 3f out: rdn over 2f out: grad wknd* **33/1**

6320 **10** 1/2 **Rotherwick (IRE)**[19] 7582 5-9-5 89 ........ (t) LukeMorris 4 78
(Paul Cole) *towards rr: sme hdwy over 3f out: sn rdn along and n.d* **14/1**

2-0 **11** shd **Threat Assessed (IRE)**[25] 7395 4-9-2 86 ........ AdamKirby 8 75
(Clive Cox) *hld up: hdwy on inner 3f out: chsd ldrs 2f out: sn rdn and wknd appr fnl f* **8/1**[2]

-025 **12** nk **Zumurudee (USA)**[151] 2829 3-9-4 92 ........ DanielMuscutt 5 80
(Marco Botti) *nvr bttr than midfield* **14/1**

4556 **13** 3 1/4 **Zzoro (IRE)**[21] 7505 4-9-0 84 ........ PatDobbs 3 66
(Amanda Perrett) *nvr bttr than midfield* **18/1**

001 **14** 4 **Awake My Soul (IRE)**[40] 6881 8-9-4 88 ........ AndrewMullen 6 62
(Tom Tate) *chsd ldr: rdn along 3f out: snd riven and grad wknd* **9/1**[3]

2m 11.0s (-3.30) **Going Correction** -0.175s/f (Firm)
**WFA** 3 from 4yo+ 4lb **14** Ran SP% **119.1**
Speed ratings (Par 107): **105,106,103,103,101 101,101,100,97,97 97,97,94,91**
CSF £60.13 CT £1079.77 TOTE £6.00: £2.30, £3.50, £7.70; EX 24.00.

**Owner** George Strawbridge **Bred** George Strawbridge **Trained** Newmarket, Suffolk

■ Stewards' Enquiry : Dane O'Neill two-day ban: careless riding (Nov 1-2)

**FOCUS**
Distance increased by 12yds. A good handicap, the main action unfolded down the centre and the first two fought out a tough finish, with first past the post Capton being demoted to second having been judged to cost Jupiter Light the race.

## 8166 TBA CENTENARY FILLIES' H'CAP 1m 6f

**4:05** (4:05) (Class 3) (0-95,91) 3-Y-O+

**£15,562** (£4,660; £2,330; £1,165; £582; £292) **Stalls** Low

Form RPR

4016 **1** **Fire Jet (IRE)**[21] 7507 4-9-10 87 ........ JimmyQuinn 4 94
(John Mackie) *trckd ldrs: smooth hdwy on inner over 2f out: chal wl over 1f out: rdn and edgd rt ent fnl f: drvn to ld last 100 yds: styd on* **16/1**

2125 **2** nk **St Mary's**[21] 7507 4-8-12 82 ........ WilliamCox(7) 7 88
(Andrew Balding) *trckd ldrs: hdwy over 2f out: cl up 2f out: rdn to ld briefly over 1f out: hdd ent fnl f: cl up and ev ch whn n.m.r ins fnl f: drvn and kpt on wl towards fin* **6/1**

3122 **3** nk **Melinoe**[21] 7507 3-8-13 83 ........ LukeMorris 8 89
(Sir Mark Prescott Bt) *hld up in rr: stdy hdwy on wd outside 3f out: cl up 2f out: rdn to chal over 1f out: led and hung bdly lft ent fnl f: sn drvn: hdd and no ex last 100 yds* **11/4**[1]

2-22 **4** 2 3/4 **Silver Link (IRE)**[84] 5273 3-8-6 76 ........ HarryBentley 2 78
(Marcus Tregoning) *trckd ldng pair: hdwy over 3f out and sn cl up: rdn to ld over 2f out: hdd over 1f out: drvn and hld whn n.m.r and swtchd lft ins fnl f: kpt on one one pce* **9/2**[2]

1523 **5** 3 3/4 **Stoney Broke**[34] 7092 4-9-8 85 ........ DanielMuscutt 9 81
(James Fanshawe) *hld up: hdwy over 3f out: chsd ldrs and rdn along 2f out: sn drvn and no imp* **8/1**

1112 **6** 1/2 **Sepal (USA)**[18] 7614 4-9-7 91 ........ JamieGormley(7) 3 87
(Iain Jardine) *led: pushed along over 3f out: rdn and hdd over 2f out: grad wknd* **5/1**[3]

153 **7** 2 3/4 **Satisfy (IRE)**[20] 7558 3-8-5 75 ........ JoeyHaynes 6 67
(K R Burke) *chsd ldrs: rdn along over 2f out: sn drvn and grad wknd* **8/1**

1150 **8** 39 **Langlauf (USA)**[25] 7401 4-9-4 81 ........ (p) RobertWinston 5 18
(Rod Millman) *chsd ldrs: rdn along 3f out: sn drvn and wknd* **33/1**

-504 **9** 99 **Return Ace**[24] 7422 5-9-10 87 ........ AdamKirby 1
(James Fanshawe) *hld up: pushed along 4f out: rdn over 3f out: sn outpcd and bhd* **12/1**

3m 6.47s (-0.53) **Going Correction** -0.175s/f (Firm)
**WFA** 3 from 4yo+ 7lb **9** Ran SP% **114.5**
Speed ratings (Par 104): **94,93,93,92,89 89,88,65,9**
CSF £107.70 CT £348.38 TOTE £24.30: £4.40, £2.10, £1.10; EX 188.50 Trifecta £640.00.

**Owner** Ladas **Bred** Ladas **Trained** Church Broughton , Derbys

**FOCUS**
Distance increased by 12yds. A decent staying handicap for fillies, they went a pretty steady gallop and, spread across the track, there was little between the first three at the line.

## 8167 KIER CENTRAL SUPPORTING CASY H'CAP 5f 8y
4:40 (4:41) (Class 4) (0-85,85) 3-Y-O+ £5,175 (£1,540; £769; £384) Stalls High

| Form | | | | RPR |
|---|---|---|---|---|
| 140 | 1 | | **Tahoo (IRE)**[53] 6450 3-9-5 **83** ... BenCurtis 15<br>(K R Burke) *racd towards stands side: prom: led wl over 1f out: : drvn and edgd lft ins fnl f: hld on wl towards fin* **20/1** | 92+ |
| 1235 | 2 | nk | **Bahamian Sunrise**[21] 7508 5-9-1 **79** ... (b) PJMcDonald 3<br>(John Gallagher) *racd centre: chsd ldr: led 1/2-way: rdn and hdd wl over 1f out: drvn ent fnl f: kpt on wl towards fin* **7/1**[3] | 86 |
| 4060 | 3 | nk | **Signore Piccolo**[11] 7809 6-9-1 **79** ... (h) PaulHanagan 6<br>(David Loughnane) *dwlt: sn chsng ldrs centre: hdwy wl over 1f out: sn rdn: drvn and styd on wl fnl f* **7/1**[3] | 85 |
| 1160 | 4 | 2 | **Ocelot**[39] 6923 3-9-2 **80** ... DanielTudhope 2<br>(Robert Cowell) *racd centre: chsd ldrs: hdwy 2f out: sn rdn and kpt on fnl f* **12/1** | 80 |
| 4404 | 5 | ½ | **Lathom**[18] 7625 4-9-1 **79** ... JoeDoyle 8<br>(Julie Camacho) *racd towards centre: in tch: pushed along and hdwy wl over 1f out: rdn and styd on wl fnl f: nrst fin* **11/2**[2] | 76 |
| 0006 | 6 | ¾ | **Move In Time**[18] 7625 9-9-5 **83** ... PaulMulrennan 17<br>(Paul Midgley) *racd towards stands side: prom: rdn along over 2f out: drvn over 1f out: kpt on fnl f* **8/1** | 77 |
| 6500 | 7 | ½ | **Invincible Ridge (IRE)**[40] 6878 9-8-9 **73** ... NeilFarley 10<br>(Eric Alston) *racd towards centre: in tch: hdwy to chse ldrs wl over 1f out: sn rdn and kpt on same pce* **20/1** | 65 |
| 2020 | 8 | nk | **Diamond Lady**[20] 7538 6-9-7 **85** ... AdamKirby 9<br>(William Stone) *racd towards centre: chsd ldrs: rdn along wl over 1f out: wknd fnl f* **20/1** | 76 |
| 6146 | 9 | shd | **The Daley Express (IRE)**[14] 7742 3-9-6 **84** ... GrahamLee 16<br>(Ronald Harris) *racd nr stands rail: bhd: rdn along 1/2-way: styd on wl appr fnl f* **12/1** | 76 |
| 0450 | 10 | nk | **Union Rose**[11] 7809 5-9-5 **83** ... (p) SamHitchcott 1<br>(Ronald Harris) *racd centre: led: hdd 1/2-way: sn rdn along and wknd over 1f out* **16/1** | 73 |
| 4044 | 11 | 1½ | **Appleberry (IRE)**[14] 7738 5-8-10 **74** ... AndrewMullen 13<br>(Michael Appleby) *racd towards stands rail: a towards rr* **12/1** | 58 |
| 2663 | 12 | ¾ | **Royal Mezyan (IRE)**[20] 7538 6-8-7 **78** ... JackOsborn(7) 7<br>(Henry Spiller) *a towards rr* **25/1** | 60 |
| 1302 | 13 | 5 | **African Friend (IRE)**[28] 7272 4-9-0 **78** ... DaneO'Neill 14<br>(Henry Candy) *dwlt: a in rr* **9/2**[1] | 42 |
| 0-30 | 14 | 5 | **Mysterious Look**[223] 1110 4-8-9 **73** ... RobHornby 12<br>(Sarah Hollinshead) *.a towards rr* **50/1** | 19 |
| 316 | 15 | 1½ | **Somewhere Secret**[23] 7461 3-8-10 **77** ... (p) PhilDennis(3) 11<br>(Michael Mullineaux) *dwlt: rr and swtchd lft towards far side after 1f: sn outpcd and bhd* **20/1** | 18 |

58.88s (-2.62) **Going Correction** -0.375s/f (Firm) 15 Ran SP% **123.5**
Speed ratings (Par 105): **105,104,104,100,100 98,98,97,97,96 94,93,85,77,74**
CSF £145.03 CT £1126.59 TOTE £20.40: £4.90, £3.30, £2.10; EX 232.60 Trifecta £1534.80.
**Owner** Nick Bradley Racing 19 **Bred** Tally-Ho Stud **Trained** Middleham Moor, N Yorks

**FOCUS**
A fair little sprint, they raced centre-to-stands' side and the pace held up.

## 8168 KIER CONSTRUCTION CENTRAL NOTTINGHAM H'CAP 5f 8y
5:15 (5:17) (Class 6) (0-65,65) 3-Y-O+ £2,587 (£770; £384; £192) Stalls High

| Form | | | | RPR |
|---|---|---|---|---|
| 0316 | 1 | | **Jabbarockie**[21] 7522 4-9-7 **65** ... NeilFarley 1<br>(Eric Alston) *racd centre: cl up: led 1/2-way: rdn clr appr fnl f: eased towards fin* **5/1**[2] | 77+ |
| 0600 | 2 | ½ | **Awesome Allan (IRE)**[14] 7723 3-8-13 **60** ... (t) MattCosham(3) 8<br>(David Evans) *trckd ldrs towards centre: hdwy 2f out: rdn over 1f out: chsd wnr ins fnl f: kpt on wl towards fin* **6/1**[3] | 67 |
| 1441 | 3 | ¾ | **Wotadoll**[8] 7912 3-9-4 **62** 6ex ... RobertWinston 2<br>(Dean Ivory) *racd centre: trckd ldrs: hdwy on outer wl over 1f out: rdn ent fnl f: kpt on wl towards fin* **5/2**[1] | 66 |
| 333 | 4 | 1 | **Ambitious Icarus**[16] 7694 8-9-1 **59** ... (p[1]) ConnorBeasley 12<br>(Richard Guest) *dwlt and rr centre: hdwy over 2f out: rdn over 1f out: swtchd rt ent fnl f: kpt on wl towards fin* **12/1** | 59 |
| 0311 | 5 | 1¼ | **Teepee Time**[68] 5877 4-8-11 **58** ... (b) PhilDennis(3) 5<br>(Michael Mullineaux) *cl up: centre: chsd wnr 2f out: rdn over 1f out: edgd lft ins fnl f: sn wknd* **16/1** | 53 |
| 3000 | 6 | ¾ | **Racquet**[11] 7825 4-9-6 **64** ... JamesSullivan 17<br>(Ruth Carr) *racd nr stands rail: prom: rdn wl over v1f out: sn drvn and kpt on same pce fnl f* **20/1** | 57+ |
| 1115 | 7 | 1½ | **Culloden**[64] 6040 5-9-0 **65** ... TobyEley(7) 11<br>(Shaun Harris) *racd centre: led: pushed along and hdd 1/2-way: rdn wl over 1f out: grad wknd* **33/1** | 52 |
| 0345 | 8 | ½ | **Twentysvnthlancers**[17] 7660 4-8-12 **56** ... GrahamLee 6<br>(Paul Midgley) *cl up centre: rdn along over 2f out: grad wknd* **14/1** | 41 |
| 0605 | 9 | hd | **Borough Boy (IRE)**[8] 7933 7-9-3 **61** ... (v) PatrickMathers 7<br>(Derek Shaw) *chsd ldrs centre: rdn along 2f out: sn drvn and wknd* **20/1** | 46 |
| 2406 | 10 | ½ | **Racing Angel (IRE)**[18] 7628 5-9-0 **58** ... AndrewMullen 9<br>(Adrian Nicholls) *chsd ldrs centre: rdn along bef 1/2-way: sn wknd* **7/1** | 41 |
| 044 | 11 | nk | **Broadhaven Honey (IRE)**[13] 7767 3-9-4 **62** ... (v) SamHitchcott 15<br>(Ronald Harris) *racd nr stands rail: prom: rdn along over 2f out: sn wknd* **25/1** | 45+ |
| 2001 | 12 | 1¾ | **Knockamany Bends (IRE)**[9] 7884 7-8-10 **54** 6ex ... (h) BarryMcHugh 13<br>(John Wainwright) *racd towards stands side: in tch: rdn along 1/2-way: sn wknd* **25/1** | 29+ |
| 4446 | 13 | 1½ | **Primanora**[85] 5263 4-9-4 **62** ... (p[1]) AdamKirby 3<br>(Michael Appleby) *a in rr centre* **16/1** | 32 |
| 3343 | 14 | 1¼ | **Frank The Barber (IRE)**[18] 7607 5-8-9 **53** ... (t) JimmyQuinn 16<br>(Steph Hollinshead) *a bhd nr stands rail* **33/1** | 19+ |
| 050 | 15 | 2½ | **Archimedes (IRE)**[13] 7767 4-9-4 **62** ... (bt) PaulHanagan 10<br>(David C Griffiths) *racd towards stands side: chsd ldrs: rdn along over 2f out: sn wknd* **33/1** | 19+ |

59.34s (-2.16) **Going Correction** -0.375s/f (Firm) 15 Ran SP% **124.2**
Speed ratings (Par 101): **102,101,100,98,96 95,92,92,91,90 90,87,85,83,79**
CSF £32.59 CT £95.06 TOTE £6.90: £2.30, £2.70, £1.70; EX 44.80 Trifecta £159.10.
**Owner** M Balmer, K Sheedy, P Copple, C Dingwall **Bred** Paul Green **Trained** Longton, Lancs

**FOCUS**
A modest sprint and those down the centre triumphed this time. The winner is value for further.
T/Plt: £25.80 to a £1 stake. Pool: £50,701.19. 1,429.81 winning units. T/Qpdt: £17.10 to a £1 stake. Pool: £4,820.92. 207.66 winning units. **Joe Rowntree**

# 8144 DEAUVILLE (R-H)
Wednesday, October 18

**OFFICIAL GOING: Polytrack: fast; turf: very soft changing to soft after race 5 (1.05)**

## 8169a PRIX DE MONTALOUVEAU (CLAIMER) (2YO) (POLYTRACK) 7f 110y
11:55 2-Y-O £11,538 (£4,615; £3,461; £2,307; £1,153)

| | | | RPR |
|---|---|---|---|
| 1 | | **Supergirl (FR)**[86] 5232 2-8-10 0 ... (p) StefanieHofer(5) 9<br>(Mario Hofer, Germany) **47/1** | 79 |
| 2 | 2 | **Senoville (IRE)**[19] 7592 2-9-4 0 ... CristianDemuro 8<br>(C Ferland, France) **23/10**[1] | 77 |
| 3 | 1¾ | **Money Sister**[75] 5629 2-8-11 0 ... ChristopheSoumillon 10<br>(Francesco Santella, Italy) **6/1**[3] | 66 |
| 4 | ¾ | **Hurricane Light (FR)** 2-9-0 0 ... HayleyTurner(4) 11<br>(S Wattel, France) **5/2**[2] | 71 |
| 5 | hd | **Zone Regard (IRE)**[28] 7304 2-9-2 0 ... StephanePasquier 7<br>(M Delcher Sanchez, France) **12/1** | 69 |
| 6 | 2½ | **Palya (FR)**[12] 2-8-11 0 ... (b) ClementLecoeuvre(4) 5<br>(B Legros, France) **26/1** | 62 |
| 7 | nk | **Controversial Lady (IRE)**[19] 7592 2-8-7 0 ... MathieuPelletan(6) 6<br>(J S Moore) *broke wl and led: rdn 2f out: hdd over 1f out: no ex fnl f: wknd* **19/1** | 59 |
| 8 | ½ | **Belgrano (FR)**[30] 2-8-11 0 ... RonanThomas 1<br>(C Lerner, France) **21/1** | 56 |
| 9 | snk | **Valhala (FR)**[23] 2-8-2 0 ... (p) MlleCoraliePacaut(9) 3<br>(T Castanheira, France) **63/10** | 55 |
| 10 | snk | **Aria Laforlongeuse (FR)**[32] 2-8-10 0 ... MlleAlisonMassin(5) 2<br>(S Wattel, France) **17/1** | 59 |
| 11 | 3 | **Hoquilebo (FR)**[30] 2-8-11 0 ... MaximeGuyon 4<br>(T Castanheira, France) **28/1** | 48 |

PARI-MUTUEL (all including 1 euro stake): WIN 48.40; PLACE 6.40, 1.50, 2.40; DF 71.30; SF 246.80.
**Owner** LMGW Bloodstock **Bred** Mme P Lemarie, R-Y Simon Et Al **Trained** Germany

## 8170a PRIX DES RESERVOIRS - ETALON KENDARGENT (GROUP 3) (2YO FILLIES) (ROUND) (TURF) 1m (R)
12:25 2-Y-O £34,188 (£13,675; £10,256; £6,837; £3,418)

| | | | RPR |
|---|---|---|---|
| 1 | | **With You**[27] 2-8-10 0 ... AurelienLemaitre 2<br>(F Head, France) *sn led: mde rest: shkn up and qcknd 2f out: kpt on wl under mostly hand ride and a in full control: v readily* **7/10**[1] | 103+ |
| 2 | 2½ | **Altea (FR)**[46] 6713 2-8-10 0 ... AnthonyCrastus 7<br>(P Sogorb, France) *hld up in rr: clsd gng wl over 1f out: rdn fnl f: kpt on and wnt 2nd towards fin but too much to do w wnr: nvr nrr* **78/10** | 97 |
| 3 | 1 | **Prontamente**[19] 2-8-10 0 ... ChristopheSoumillon 1<br>(F Chappet, France) *cl up on inner: rdn and outpcd by wnr fnl f: lost 2nd towards fin* **63/10**[3] | 95 |
| 4 | ½ | **Connivence (FR)**[25] 7415 2-8-10 0 ... Pierre-CharlesBoudot 6<br>(A Fabre, France) *trckd wnr: rdn to chal 2f out: outpcd fnl f: fdd into 4th* **53/10**[2] | 94 |
| 5 | 1½ | **Tosen Gift (IRE)**[27] 2-8-10 0 ... FabriceVeron 5<br>(S Kobayashi, France) *restrained and hld up: rdn 2f out: sn outpcd: plugged on wout threatening fnl f* **25/1** | 90 |
| 6 | nk | **Miss Sienna**[18] 7637 2-8-10 0 ... AlexisBadel 3<br>(H-F Devin, France) *midfield: rdn and effrt 2f out: sn outpcd: fdd* **16/1** | 89 |
| 7 | 1 | **Auenperle (GER)**[45] 6726 2-8-10 0 ... NicolasGuilbert 4<br>(Christina Bucher, Switzerland) *hld up: rdn 2f out: awkward u.p and sn dropped to last: n.d fnl f* **9/1** | 87 |

1m 44.76s (3.96) 7 Ran SP% **119.5**
PARI-MUTUEL (all including 1 euro stake): WIN 1.70; PLACE 1.30, 2.20; SF 7.20.
**Owner** George Strawbridge **Bred** George Strawbridge **Trained** France

8171 - 8178a (Foreign Racing) - See Raceform Interactive

# 7912 BRIGHTON (L-H)
Thursday, October 19

**OFFICIAL GOING: Good to soft (soft in places) changing to soft (good to soft in places) after race 2 (2.30)**
Wind: medium, half against Weather: cloudy

## 8179 BRITISH STALLION STUDS EBF NOVICE STKS 5f 215y
2:00 (2:00) (Class 5) 2-Y-O £3,234 (£962; £481; £240) Stalls Low

| Form | | | | RPR |
|---|---|---|---|---|
| 0132 | 1 | | **Sing Out Loud (IRE)**[9] 7913 2-9-6 78 ... AdamKirby 1<br>(Gary Moore) *broke wl: sn stdd to trck ldrs: effrt on inner over 2f out: rdn to ld 2f out: over 2 l clr 1f out: a doing enough ins fnl f: rdn out* **5/4**[1] | 80 |
| 22 | 2 | ½ | **Rotherhithe**[16] 7707 2-8-12 0 ow1 ... MartinHarley 2<br>(Robyn Brisland) *sn led: rdn over 2f out: hdd 2f out: 3rd and outpcd jst over 1f out: rallied to chse clr wnr 150yds out: styd on wl: nvr quite getting to wnr* **5/2**[3] | 71 |
| 63 | 3 | 4 | **Mr Gent (IRE)**[15] 7740 2-9-2 0 ... SilvestreDeSousa 7<br>(Ed Dunlop) *sn trcking ldr: effrt and ev ch jst over 2f out: wanting to hang lft and unable qck over 1f out: lost 2nd 150yds out: sn wknd* **9/4**[2] | 63 |
| 2460 | 4 | 3½ | **Diamond Express (IRE)**[23] 7491 2-8-8 64 ... MitchGodwin(3) 5<br>(Roger Teal) *hld up in tch: rdn ent fnl 2f: outpcd and btn 4th whn hung rt 1f out: wknd fnl f* **33/1** | 47 |
| 00 | 5 | 5 | **Miss Recycled**[33] 7153 2-8-11 0 ... DanielMuscutt 3<br>(Michael Madgwick) *dwlt: hld up wl in tch: rdn ent fnl 2f: sn struggling and btn over 1f out: wknd fnl f* **150/1** | 32 |
| 050 | 6 | 3¾ | **Spix's Macaw**[50] 6583 2-8-11 49 ... CharlesBishop 6<br>(Bill Turner) *in tch in midfield tl dropped to rr over 4f out: no ch terms after: pushed along and no hdwy over 2f out: wknd over 1f out* **150/1** | 21 |

1m 12.63s (2.43) **Going Correction** +0.25s/f (Good) 6 Ran SP% **108.1**
Speed ratings (Par 95): **93,92,87,82,75 70**
CSF £4.32 TOTE £2.10: £1.10, £1.40; EX 4.10 Trifecta £6.10.
**Owner** Mrs Susan Neville & Mike George **Bred** J S Bolger **Trained** Lower Beeding, W Sussex

**FOCUS**

Rain had eased the ground to good to soft, soft in places (from good) resulting in a few non-runners (GoingStick 6.2). Running rail on inside line. An ordinary novice event to start and, with no false rail this time, the runners tended to stick towards the inside. The runner-up has been rated close to form.

## 8180 IRISH STALLION FARMS EBF NOVICE MEDIAN AUCTION STKS 7f 211y

**2:30** (2:30) (Class 5) 2-Y-O **£4,204** (£1,251; £625; £312) **Stalls** Centre

Form RPR

32 **1** **King Of The Sand (IRE)**[35] 7093 2-9-2 0 AdamKirby 10 86
(Gary Moore) *mde all: sn clr: styd on inner rail and rdn ent fnl 2f: styd on wl u.p over 1f out and in n.d after: unchal* **4/1**[2]

5022 **2** 4½ **George (IRE)**[18] 7647 2-8-13 84 MitchGodwin(3) 8 76
(Sylvester Kirk) *chsd ldng trio: effrt over 2f out: wnt 2nd and hung lft over 1f out: kpt on for clr 2nd but no imp on wnr* **3/1**[1]

6 **3** 1¾ **Royal Goldie (IRE)**[15] 7733 2-8-11 0 SilvestreDeSousa 7 67
(Mick Channon) *stdd after s: off the pce in last quartet: sme hdwy in centre over 2f out: modest 6th 2f out: rdn over 1f out: styd on wl ins fnl f to go 3rd cl home: nvr trbld ldrs* **7/1**

01 **4** ¾ **Wilson (IRE)**[46] 6721 2-9-9 0 JamieSpencer 4 77
(Luca Cumani) *hld up in midfield: effrt in centre over 2f out: disputing 2nd but no imp on clr wnr over 1f out: 3rd and btn whn edgd lft ins fnl f: lost 3rd cl home* **3/1**[1]

2 **5** 3½ **Key Player**[14] 7765 2-9-2 0 CharlesBishop 3 62
(Eve Johnson Houghton) *chsd wnr: rdn over 2f out: no imp and wl hld whn lost 2nd and carried lft over 1f out: wknd fnl f* **8/1**

**6** 11 **Qadiriyyah**[104] 4588 2-9-2 0 StevieDonohoe 2 37
(Mohamed Moubarak) *chsd ldng pair tl ent fnl 2f: sn struggling and wknd over 1f out* **33/1**

0 **7** ¾ **Clan McGregor (IRE)**[22] 7503 2-9-2 0 ShaneKelly 9 35
(Seamus Durack) *midfield: c centre and rdn over 2f out: no prog and sn struggling: wl btn over 1f out* **50/1**

00 **8** ½ **The Fiddler**[21] 7556 2-8-13 0 GeorgeWood(3) 6 34
(Chris Wall) *sn dropped towards rr: rdn 4f out: struggling and wl btn whn swtchd rt over 2f out: lost tch 2f out* **80/1**

464 **9** 6 **Sherzy Boy**[21] 7543 2-9-2 74 TomMarquand 5 20
(Richard Hannon) *midfield but sn pushed along: dropped to rr and rdn 4f out: lost tch over 2f out* **6/1**[3]

0 **10** 4 **Folies Bergeres**[23] 7488 2-8-4 0 Pierre-LouisJamin(7) 1 6
(Jonathan Portman) *s.i.s: a in rr: rdn 4f out: lost tch over 2f out* **66/1**

1m 38.41s (2.41) **Going Correction** +0.25s/f (Good) **10** Ran SP% **115.5**
Speed ratings (Par 95): **97,92,90,90,86 75,74,74,68,64**
CSF £16.06 TOTE £5.60: £1.90, £1.70, £3.50; EX 17.40 Trifecta £89.10.
**Owner** Jacobs Construction & J Harley **Bred** R Coffey **Trained** Lower Beeding, W Sussex

**FOCUS**

Another novice event, but probably not a bad race of its type with some promising types taking part. Few ever got into it and the winner was impressive. The runner-up has been rated a few lengths off, and the winner has been credited with improvement for now.

## 8181 BRIGHTON LIONS FIREWORK NIGHT 5 NOVEMBER H'CAP (DIV I) 7f 211y

**3:05** (3:11) (Class 6) (0-60,67) 3-Y-O+ **£2,587** (£770; £384; £192) **Stalls** Centre

Form RPR

3323 **1** **Break The Silence**[13] 7791 3-8-11 52 (p[1]) KieranO'Neill 6 58
(Scott Dixon) *mde all: edgd rt u.p over 1f out: styd on wl ins fnl f: rdn out* **8/1**

0050 **2** ¾ **Crystal Sunstone**[9] 7917 3-9-7 62 CharlesBishop 7 66
(Eve Johnson Houghton) *hld up in midfield: effrt to chse ldrs 2f out: pressing wnr jst ins fnl f: styd on same pce u.p ins fnl f* **7/1**[3]

2022 **3** nk **World Record (IRE)**[38] 7006 7-9-5 57 WilliamCarson 10 62
(Mick Quinn) *t.k.h: chsd wnr: rdn ent fnl 2f: carried rt over 1f out: lost 2nd jst ins fnl f and kpt on same pce after* **7/2**[2]

0661 **4** 6 **Wordismybond**[9] 7916 8-10-1 67 6ex (p) AdamKirby 9 58
(Amanda Perrett) *hld up in tch in rr of main gp: effrt over 2f out: swtchd lft and hdwy u.p over 1f out: 4th and no imp fnl f: nvr threatened ldrs* **11/8**[1]

6005 **5** 1¾ **Mulsanne Chase**[10] 7899 3-9-4 59 (b) SteveDrowne 2 45
(Brian Barr) *dwlt: sn rcvrd to chse ldrs: rdn over 2f out: sn outpcd and wl hld over 1f out: plugged on* **18/1**

0000 **6** 2¾ **Kafoo**[40] 6946 4-9-2 54 SilvestreDeSousa 8 34
(Michael Appleby) *in tch in midfield: rdn over 2f out: sn outpcd and wl hld whn wnt lft u.p over 1f out: wknd fnl f* **9/1**

6330 **7** 1¾ **Assertor**[32] 7199 3-8-12 53 TomMarquand 11 28
(Tony Carroll) *taken down early: hld up in midfield: rdn over 3f out: sn struggling and wl btn 2f out* **33/1**

-000 **8** ½ **Maysonri**[9] 7918 3-8-1 45 (p) AaronJones(3) 5 19
(Mark Hoad) *in rr of main gp: reminder over 4f out: struggling over 2f out: wknd 2f out* **66/1**

033 **9** 2½ **Bloodsweatandtears**[209] 1338 9-9-9 61 KierenFox 1 31
(William Knight) *sn dropped to rr and nvr travelling: n.d* **12/1**

365 **10** 10 **Blackadder**[31] 7213 5-8-7 45 RobHornby 3
(Mark Gillard) *chsd ldrs tl 1/2-way: steadily lost pl: wl bhd and eased ins fnl f* **20/1**

1m 39.88s (3.88) **Going Correction** +0.575s/f (Yiel)
**WFA** 3 from 4yo+ 3lb **10** Ran SP% **120.1**
Speed ratings (Par 101): **103,102,101,95,94 91,89,89,86,76**
CSF £63.67 CT £236.01 TOTE £7.60: £2.30, £2.70, £1.90; EX 59.70 Trifecta £280.20.
**Owner** Winning Connections Racing **Bred** Richard Moses Bloodstock **Trained** Babworth, Notts

**FOCUS**

The ground was changed to soft, good to soft in places before this race. The first division of a modest handicap and another race where few got into it. Most of the runners moved out towards the centre of the track turning for home this time and the conditions really seemed to be taking their toll by now. The winner has been rated to his best, with the fourth below his recent win here.

## 8182 BRIGHTON LIONS FIREWORK NIGHT 5 NOVEMBER H'CAP (DIV II) 7f 211y

**3:35** (3:36) (Class 6) (0-60,62) 3-Y-O+ **£2,587** (£770; £384; £192) **Stalls** Centre

Form RPR

4202 **1** **Pick A Little**[9] 7916 9-9-7 62 MitchGodwin(3) 7 68
(Michael Blake) *trckd ldrs: effrt over 1f out: drvn to chal 1f out: sustained duel w ldr after: kpt on wl u.p to ld last stride* **85/40**[1]

0000 **2** shd **Tawfeer**[3] 8125 3-7-12 46 (p) NicolaCurrie(7) 3 51
(Phil McEntee) *sn led: rdn over 1f out: sustained duel w wnr and kpt on wl u.p ins fnl f: hdd on post* **16/1**

6534 **3** 1¾ **Indiana Dawn**[31] 7210 4-8-13 51 (p) LiamKeniry 10 54
(Robert Stephens) *in tch: pushed along briefly 1/2-way: swtchd lft over 2f out: trcking ldrs and nt clr run over 1f out: swtchd and flashed tail u.p ins fnl f: kpt on same pce after* **5/1**

0030 **4** 1¾ **Port Lairge**[31] 7210 7-8-0 45 (b) GabrieleMalune(7) 6 43
(Michael Chapman) *v.s.a: wl detached in last nt travelling wl: clsd u.p 2f out: styd on to pass btn horses ins fnl f: nvr trbld ldrs* **8/1**

0534 **5** 3 **Rolling Dice**[10] 7900 6-9-4 59 (b) CallumShepherd(3) 2 50
(Dominic Ffrench Davis) *pressed ldr tl unable qck u.p and edgd lft jst over 1f out: wknd ins fnl f* **9/2**[3]

4130 **5** dht **With Approval (IRE)**[9] 7916 5-9-6 58 (p) PatCosgrave 9 49
(Laura Mongan) *chsd ldrs: effrt to press ldrs 3f out tl no ex 1f out: wknd ins fnl f* **4/1**[2]

6010 **7** 7 **Altaira**[31] 7215 6-9-1 53 (b) WilliamCarson 8 28
(Tony Carroll) *t.k.h: chsd ldrs tl lost pl u.p over 1f out: bhd 1f out: wknd ins fnl f* **8/1**

1m 41.02s (5.02) **Going Correction** +0.575s/f (Yiel)
**WFA** 3 from 4yo+ 3lb **7** Ran SP% **115.0**
Speed ratings (Par 101): **97,96,95,93,90 90,83**
CSF £38.09 CT £154.14 TOTE £2.80: £1.70, £7.70; EX 36.50 Trifecta £244.30.
**Owner** Mrs J M Haines **Bred** D R Tucker **Trained** Trowbridge, Wilts

■ Stewards' Enquiry : Mitch Godwin ban: used his whip above the permitted level (TBA)

**FOCUS**

The fourth horse completely blew the start, but the other six raced almost in a line across the track for much of the way. They came nearside up the straight this time and the winning time was 1.14sec slower than the first division. The second has been rated to his best.

## 8183 LOUD SHIRT BREWING CO BRIGHTON H'CAP 1m 1f 207y

**4:05** (4:05) (Class 6) (0-60,62) 3-Y-O+ **£2,815** (£837; £418; £209) **Stalls** High

Form RPR

0603 **1** **Sussex Girl**[9] 7917 3-8-10 57 NicolaCurrie(7) 7 64
(John Berry) *hld up in midfield: clsd to press ldrs 4f out: rdn to chse ldr ent fnl 2f: kpt on wl ins fnl f to ld last strides* **6/1**[2]

2452 **2** nk **Rocksette**[9] 7917 3-8-7 47 SilvestreDeSousa 4 53
(Philip Hide) *t.k.h: hld up in midfield: clsd to press ldr 4f out tl led 3f out: rdn and kicked clr 2f out: drvn ins fnl f: hdd last strides* **10/11**[1]

-111 **3** 1 **Hermosa Vaquera (IRE)**[33] 7151 7-9-7 60 (p) HectorCrouch(3) 5 64
(Gary Moore) *t.k.h: chsd ldrs: clsd to trck ldrs 4f out: rdn and edgd lft over 1f out: pressed wnr ins fnl f: no ex and one pce fnl 100yds* **7/1**[3]

0330 **4** nse **Zoffanist (IRE)**[38] 7005 3-8-12 52 (be) PatDobbs 6 56
(Amanda Perrett) *off the pce in last pair: clsd and in tch 4f out: effrt jst over 2f out: chsd ldrs u.p over 1f out: styd on steadily ins fnl f: nvr quite getting to ldrs* **16/1**

0010 **5** nse **About Glory**[92] 5023 3-9-3 57 (b) TomMarquand 3 61
(Richard Hannon) *dwlt: hld up in midfield: effrt over 2f out: chsd ldrs and drvn over 1f out: styd on steadily ins fnl f: nvr quite getting to ldrs* **14/1**

122- **6** 6 **Monday Club**[268] 7628 4-9-10 60 JFEgan 9 52
(Dominic Ffrench Davis) *off the pce in last pair: clsd and in tch 4f out: swtchd rt and effrt over 2f out: 6th and no imp over 1f out: wl hld and plugged on same pce fnl f* **12/1**

00 **7** 15 **Jungle George**[14] 7760 3-8-6 46 oh1 KieranO'Neill 12 10
(Scott Dixon) *led tl hdd and rdn 3f out: dropped out qckly over 1f out: wknd fnl f* **80/1**

040 **8** 15 **Lord Of The Storm**[14] 7761 9-9-1 51 KierenFox 2
(Michael Attwater) *chsd ldrs: rdn and lost pl jst over 2f out: wl btn and eased over 1f out: t.o* **16/1**

6625 **9** 5 **Saint Helena (IRE)**[31] 7210 9-9-10 60 (b) RobHornby 13
(Mark Gillard) *t.k.h: chsd ldr tl 4f out: sn lost pl: wl bhd over 1f out: eased ins fnl f: t.o* **20/1**

0-00 **10** 6 **Lazizah**[42] 6846 4-9-0 50 (t[1]) MartinDwyer 11
(Marcus Tregoning) *a towards rr: pushed along 6f out: rdn 3f out: sn bhd: eased over 1f out: t.o* **50/1**

3522 **11** 6 **Tommys Geal**[141] 3208 5-9-7 57 DanielMuscutt 1
(Michael Madgwick) *midfield: rdn and struggling 3f out: wl bhd and eased over 1f out: t.o* **14/1**

2m 8.88s (5.28) **Going Correction** +0.575s/f (Yiel)
**WFA** 3 from 4yo+ 4lb **11** Ran SP% **119.9**
Speed ratings (Par 101): **101,100,99,99,99 95,83,71,67,62 57**
CSF £11.84 CT £41.81 TOTE £7.20: £2.00, £1.10, £2.80; EX 17.50 Trifecta £97.00.
**Owner** D Tunmore & John Berry **Bred** Elusive Bloodstock **Trained** Newmarket, Suffolk

■ Stewards' Enquiry : Nicola Currie two day ban: using her whip above the permitted level (2/3 Nov)

**FOCUS**

Another moderate handicap, in which they bet 6-1 bar one, and two fillies and a mare filled the first three places. This time the field stayed more towards the inside rail, but again they looked to finish wearily with something of a slow-motion finish.

## 8184 LOVE FAIRS ANTIQUE FAIR 22 OCTOBER H'CAP 6f 210y

**4:40** (4:40) (Class 5) (0-75,76) 3-Y-O+ **£3,234** (£962; £481; £240) **Stalls** Centre

Form RPR

0250 **1** **Procurator (IRE)**[13] 7789 3-9-3 76 HollieDoyle(3) 7 83
(Richard Hannon) *hld up in tch: chsng ldrs whn nt clr run and swtchd lft jst over 1f out: chsd ldrs jst ins fnl f: styd on wl u.p to ld last strides* **9/1**

1365 **2** hd **Black Caesar (IRE)**[13] 7780 6-9-1 76 SebastianWoods(7) 1 83
(Philip Hide) *chsd ldrs: effrt to chal and rdn over 1f out: led ins fnl f: kpt on: hdd last strides* **4/1**[3]

0660 **3** 1¾ **Soaring Spirits (IRE)**[1] 8158 7-9-0 68 (p) RobHornby 2 71
(Dean Ivory) *sn led: rdn 2f out: drvn and hdd ins fnl f: no ex and one pce fnl 100yds* **20/1**

3151 **4** 1¾ **Wahaab (IRE)**[9] 7934 6-8-6 67 (t) JackOsborn(7) 9 65
(Sophie Leech) *in tch in midfield: effrt nrest stands' rail 2f out: hung lft u.p and kpt on same pce ins fnl f* **5/2**[2]

2231 **5** 1¾ **Spinnaka (IRE)**[30] 7227 3-9-5 75 (v) JamieSpencer 3 68
(Luca Cumani) *hld up in tch in last trio: clsd over 1f out: effrt ent fnl f: fnd nil for press ins fnl f: wknd fnl 100yds* **9/4**[1]

6-41 **6** nk **Mister Freeze (IRE)**[266] 418 3-9-1 71 (vt[1]) DavidProbert 5 63
(Patrick Chamings) *chsd ldrs: clsd to press ldrs 4f out tl unable qck over 1f out and outpcd whn sltly impeded 1f out: wknd ins fnl f* **33/1**

0200 **7** 1 **Pour La Victoire (IRE)**[53] 6478 7-8-12 66 (p) TomMarquand 4 56
(Tony Carroll) *bhd: pushed and clsd over 1f out: kpt on ins fnl f: nvr trbld ldrs* **25/1**

1510 **8** 1 **Good Luck Charm**[18] 7653 8-9-5 76 (b) HectorCrouch(3) 6 64
(Gary Moore) *hld up in tch in last trio: effrt 2f out: no hdwy u.p over 1f out: wknd ins fnl f* **12/1**

0061 **9** ¾ **Baltic Prince (IRE)**[31] 7212 7-8-12 66 GeorgeDowning 10 52
(Tony Carroll) *w ldr tl 4f out: unable qck u.p and lost pl over 1f out: wknd ins fnl f* **16/1**

4000 **10** 2 ½ **El Torito (IRE)**[18] 7653 3-8-12 **68** ........................ PatCosgrave 8 46
(Jim Boyle) *t.k.h: hld up in midfield: nt clr run and swtchd lft over 1f out: no imp whn hmpd and snatched up 1f out: nt rcvr and sn dropped to rr: eased towards fin* **33/1**

1m 26.13s (3.03) **Going Correction** +0.575s/f (Yiel)
**WFA** 3 from 6yo+ 2lb **10** Ran SP% **117.4**
Speed ratings (Par 103): **105,104,102,100,98 98,97,96,95,92**
CSF £43.34 CT £717.80 TOTE £9.40: £2.70, £1.70, £6.90; EX 56.10 Trifecta £795.40.
**Owner** J Palmer-Brown & R Hannon **Bred** Lisieux Stud **Trained** East Everleigh, Wilts

**FOCUS**
An ordinary handicap, though seven of the ten runners had already won at least once around here. Again they came centre-to-nearside inside the last 3f, but eventually the main action unfolded up the centre of the track. The winner has been rated back to his best.

## 8185 SANTA FUN RUN 25 NOVEMBER H'CAP 5f 215y
**5:10** (5:10) (Class 6) (0-55,55) 3-Y-0+ **£2,587** (£770; £384; £192) **Stalls** Low

Form RPR
4040 **1** **Rebel Heart**[34] 7122 3-9-1 **50** ........................(v) WilliamCarson 2 58
(Bill Turner) *broke fast and mde all: clr and rdn over 1f out: kpt on: eased nr fin: unchal* **11/2[3]**

4602 **2** 1 ¾ **Treagus**[8] 7945 3-9-3 **52** ........................ RyanTate 15 55
(Anthony Carson) *off the pce in last quartet: rdn 1/2-way: hdwy 1f out: styd on strly ins fnl f to go 2nd towards fin: no threat to wnr* **4/1[1]**

1420 **3** 1 **Lutine Charlie (IRE)**[2] 8134 10-8-12 **46** ........................ MartinDwyer 11 46
(Emma Owen) *wl in tch in midfield: effrt to chse ldrs 2f out: chsd clr wnr ins fnl f: kpt on but nvr getting on terms: lost 2nd towards fin* **13/2**

5004 **4** 1 **Coral Caye**[17] 7694 3-8-11 **46** oh1 ........................ AdamBeschizza 3 43
(Steph Hollinshead) *midfield: rdn 3f out: clsd to chse ldrs over 1f out: squeezed through on inner ins fnl f: kpt on but no threat to wnr* **12/1**

0066 **5** ½ **General Gerrard**[46] 6724 3-8-4 **46** oh1 ........................(vt) WilliamCox(7) 14 41
(Michael Madgwick) *hld up in tch in midfield and travelled strly: effrt 2f out: unable qck over 1f out: kpt on same pce and no threat to wnr ins fnl f* **25/1**

0600 **6** 1 ¼ **Kodiac Pearl (IRE)**[26] 7407 3-8-11 **46** oh1 ........................(h) JFEgan 16 38
(Robert Cowell) *chsd ldrs: rdn over 2f out: unable qck and outpcd over 1f out: wl hld and kpt on same pce ins fnl f* **25/1**

3320 **7** ¾ **Wedgewood Estates**[63] 6112 6-9-7 **55** ........................ TomMarquand 1 44
(Tony Carroll) *off the pce in last quartet: swtchd rt and rdn over 2f out: kpt on ins fnl f: nvr trbld ldrs* **8/1**

5300 **8** ½ **Kingfisher Girl**[19] 7605 4-8-12 **46** oh1 ........................(tp) SilvestreDeSousa 12 34
(Michael Appleby) *s.i.s: sn rcvrd and in tch in midfield: effrt ent fnl 2f: no imp whn hung lft and n.m.r over 1f out: kpt on same pce fnl f* **13/2**

350 **9** ¾ **Gaia Princess (IRE)**[23] 7487 3-8-13 **51** ........................(p) HectorCrouch(3) 9 37
(Gary Moore) *in tch in midfield: clsd to chse ldrs 3f out: rdn to chse wnr and swtchd rt 2f out: no imp and hung lft 1f out: lost 2nd and wknd ins fnl f* **8/1**

0060 **10** 3 **Blistering Dancer (IRE)**[32] 7190 7-8-9 **46** oh1 ........................ MitchGodwin(3) 5 23
(Tony Carroll) *chsd wnr tl 2f out: sn struggling and lost pl over 1f out: wknd ins fnl f* **20/1**

0500 **11** hd **Golden Cannon**[31] 7212 6-9-6 **54** ........................ StevieDonohoe 7 30
(Sheena West) *a off the pce in last quartet: n.d* **33/1**

1210 **12** 2 ¼ **National Service (USA)**[23] 7480 6-8-9 **46** oh1 ........................(tp) HollieDoyle(3) 4 15
(Clare Ellam) *sn dropped to rr: n.d* **33/1**

2030 **13** 3 ¼ **Bella's Venture**[10] 7899 4-9-4 **52** ........................ FergusSweeney 8 17
(John Gallagher) *hld up in midfield: rdn ande no hdwy whn hung lft over 1f out: bhd and eased ins fnl f* **5/1[2]**

1m 13.56s (3.36) **Going Correction** +0.575s/f (Yiel)
**WFA** 3 from 4yo+ 1lb **13** Ran SP% **127.0**
Speed ratings (Par 101): **100,97,96,95,94 92,91,91,90,86 85,82,78**
CSF £27.77 CT £157.16 TOTE £6.60: £1.90, £2.10, £2.60; EX 34.30 Trifecta £188.90.
**Owner** Mascalls Stud **Bred** Mascalls Stud **Trained** Sigwells, Somerset

**FOCUS**
A particularly moderate sprint handicap with the winner making all. The runners stayed towards the inside this time.

## 8186 WILDSTRAWBERRYEVENTS.COM CHRISTMAS FAIR 2 DECEMBER H'CAP 5f 60y
**5:40** (5:40) (Class 5) (0-75,75) 3-Y-0+ **£3,234** (£962; £481; £240) **Stalls** Low

Form RPR
3651 **1** **Spirit Of Rosanna**[17] 7689 5-8-8 **62** ........................(tp) AdamBeschizza 3 68
(Steph Hollinshead) *mde virtually all: rdn ent fnl 2f: forged ahd over 1f out: hld on gamely u.p ins fnl f: all out* **11/2[3]**

161 **2** ½ **Bella Alissa**[31] 7217 3-9-7 **75** ........................(p) PatCosgrave 1 80
(Robert Cowell) *midfield: clsd to chse ldrs and swtchd rt jst over 2f out: chsd wnr jst over 1f out: kpt on u.p but hld wl ins fnl f* **6/1**

2210 **3** 1 ½ **Case Key**[35] 7086 4-9-7 **75** ........................(p) SilvestreDeSousa 4 74+
(Michael Appleby) *racd in last pair: rdn and outpcd whn edgd rt 3f out: rallied u.p 1f out: wnt 3rd ins fnl f: nvr getting to ldrs and eased cl home* **3/1[1]**

2124 **4** 2 ¾ **Glacier Point**[63] 6098 3-9-7 **75** ........................(v[1]) AdamKirby 2 65
(Clive Cox) *dwlt: sn rcvrd to chse ldrs: rdn ent fnl 2f: 3rd and no ex 1f out: wknd ins fnl f* **4/1[2]**

5030 **5** 1 ¼ **Merdon Castle (IRE)**[22] 7522 5-8-13 **67** ........................ MartinHarley 5 52
(Jane Chapple-Hyam) *dwlt: sn outpcd in rr and pushed along: rdn over 2f out: hung lft over 1f out: nvr trbld ldrs* **13/2**

5663 **6** 2 **Diable D'Or (IRE)**[41] 6888 3-9-1 **69** ........................(v) CharlesBishop 6 48
(Eve Johnson Houghton) *w wnr: rdn ent fnl 2f: lost 2nd and btn jst over 1f out: wknd ins fnl f* **3/1[1]**

1m 4.61s (2.31) **Going Correction** +0.575s/f (Yiel) **6** Ran SP% **113.0**
Speed ratings (Par 103): **104,103,100,96,94 91**
CSF £37.31 TOTE £5.90: £2.30, £2.10; EX 35.40 Trifecta £101.80.
**Owner** J Holcombe **Bred** Redmyre Bloodstock & Tweenhills Stud **Trained** Upper Longdon, Staffs

**FOCUS**
An ordinary sprint handicap to end. Again they stayed on the inside and another all-the-way winner. A small pb from the winner, with the second rated as building slightly on her previous C&D win.

T/Plt: £50.90 to a £1 stake. Pool: £74,739.16 - 1,069.93 winning units. T/Qpdt: £20.10 to a £1 stake. Pool: £6,499.03 - 239.25 winning units. **Steve Payne**

# [7935]NEWCASTLE (A.W) (L-H)
Thursday, October 19

**OFFICIAL GOING: Tapeta: standard**
Wind: Almost nil Weather: Raining

## 8187 FOUNDATION OF LIGHT H'CAP 2m 56y (Tp)
**5:15** (5:16) (Class 6) (0-65,64) 3-Y-0+ **£2,587** (£770; £384; £192) **Stalls** Low

Form RPR
0041 **1** **Navajo Star (IRE)**[7] 7992 3-8-4 **51** 6ex ........................(v) DavidEgan(3) 7 59
(Michael Appleby) *t.k.h: trckd ldrs: hdwy to ld over 2f out: pushed along and drifted rt fr over 1f out: styd on wl fnl f* **9/4[1]**

040- **2** 1 ½ **Thankyou Very Much**[16] 3706 7-9-5 **55** ........................(bt) DanielTudhope 13 59
(James Bethell) *stdd s: hld up on outside: hdwy to press wnr over 2f out: rdn and carried rt ent fnl f: kpt on same pce last 100yds* **12/1**

2651 **3** ½ **Hallstatt (IRE)**[41] 6898 11-10-0 **64** ........................(t) LukeMorris 12 67
(John Mackie) *sn chsng ldr: rdn and ev ch briefly over 2f out: kpt on ins fnl f* **15/2**

5 **4** nk **Im Waiting (IRE)**[16] 7720 4-9-2 **57** ........................(vt) ConorMcGovern(5) 8 60+
(Anthony McCann, Ire) *hld up: rdn over 2f out: hdwy over 1f out: kpt on: nt pce to chal* **40/1**

032 **5** hd **Mr Davies**[13] 7790 3-9-1 **59** ........................ TomQueally 11 64
(David Brown) *led at ordinary gallop: rdn and hdd over 2f out: one pce fr over 1f out* **7/2[2]**

550/ **6** 1 ¼ **Mitcd (IRE)**[168] 6000 6-8-8 **49** ........................ ConnorMurtagh(5) 3 50
(George Bewley) *hld up towards rr: rdn and effrt over 2f out: no imp fr over 1f out* **40/1**

0246 **7** 1 ¾ **Jan Smuts (IRE)**[9] 7922 9-9-0 **50** ........................(tp) PaulMulrennan 5 49
(Wilf Storey) *plld hrd in midfield: drvn and outpcd over 2f out: no imp fr over 1f out* **14/1**

0350 **8** 1 ¼ **Cavalieri (IRE)**[30] 7248 7-10-0 **64** ........................(tp) KevinStott 6 62
(Philip Kirby) *hld up towards rr: rdn along over 2f out: sn n.d* **22/1**

2635 **9** ½ **Traditional Dancer (IRE)**[18] 7659 5-9-1 **51** ........................ DavidNolan 1 48
(Iain Jardine) *hld up in midfield on ins: rdn and drifted rt over 2f out: sn n.d: btn fnl f* **11/2[3]**

-600 **10** 5 **Kisumu**[41] 6898 5-9-4 **54** ........................(p) PJMcDonald 9 45
(Micky Hammond) *hld up in midfield on outside: rdn and outpcd over 2f out: sn btn* **40/1**

6064 **11** shd **Legalized**[13] 7790 3-8-2 **46** ........................ FrannyNorton 2 39
(James Given) *trckd ldrs: rdn over 3f out: wknd over 2f out* **12/1**

3000 **12** 6 **Desktop**[27] 7360 5-9-1 **51** ........................ CamHardie 10 35
(Antony Brittain) *hld up: drvn and struggling 3f out: btn fnl 2f* **40/1**

3m 37.86s (2.66) **Going Correction** +0.10s/f (Slow)
**WFA** 3 from 4yo+ 8lb **12** Ran SP% **116.3**
Speed ratings (Par 101): **97,96,96,95,95 95,94,93,93,90 90,87**
CSF £28.93 CT £170.93 TOTE £3.40: £1.40, £3.20, £1.80; EX 29.70 Trifecta £138.40.
**Owner** Ferrybank Properties Limited **Bred** Robert Dunne **Trained** Oakham, Rutland
■ Stewards' Enquiry : David Egan three day ban: careless riding (2-4 Nov)

**FOCUS**
An ordinary staying handicap, run at an average pace. The first pair had it to themselves from 2f out. The third has been rated to his recent best.

## 8188 BOWBURN HOTEL H'CAP 1m 4f 98y (Tp)
**5:45** (5:47) (Class 4) (0-85,86) 3-Y-0+ **£5,175** (£1,540; £769; £384) **Stalls** High

Form RPR
4251 **1** **Pioneertown (IRE)**[20] 7568 3-8-10 **77** ........................ LukeMorris 4 86+
(Sir Mark Prescott Bt) *t.k.h: hld up in tch: hdwy on outside 3f out: led over 1f out: styd on wl fnl f* **15/2**

-154 **2** ½ **Eldritch (IRE)**[8] 7949 3-9-4 **85** ........................ RobertHavlin 6 93
(John Gosden) *hld up towards rr: rdn and hdwy 2f out: edgd lft: chsd wnr ins fnl f: kpt on fin* **5/2[1]**

602 **3** 1 ¼ **Reshoun (FR)**[9] 7927 3-8-13 **80** ........................ KieranShoemark 5 87+
(Ian Williams) *dwlt: hld up: rdn and hdwy over 2f out: kpt on ins fnl f: nvr able to chal* **7/2[2]**

5026 **4** 1 **Al Zaman (IRE)**[19] 7627 3-9-1 **82** ........................(vt[1]) GrahamLee 8 86+
(Simon Crisford) *hld up: rdn over 2f out: hdwy over 1f out: r.o ins fnl f: nrst fin* **7/1**

0553 **5** ¾ **Corton Lad**[16] 7701 7-9-6 **86** ........................(tp) RowanScott(5) 14 88
(Keith Dalgleish) *pressed ldr: rdn over 2f out: wknd over 1f out* **50/1**

6403 **6** shd **Redicean**[45] 6757 3-9-0 **81** ........................ DanielTudhope 10 83
(David O'Meara) *led: rdn and over 2 l clr over 2f out: hdd over 1f out: wknd ins fnl f* **10/1**

1040 **7** 3 ½ **Maghfoor**[42] 6849 3-9-3 **84** ........................(v[1]) KevinStott 1 79
(Saeed bin Suroor) *hld up in tch: effrt and pushed along 3f out: wknd over 1f out* **16/1**

035 **8** 1 ¾ **Airton**[26] 7387 4-9-5 **80** ........................ PJMcDonald 13 71
(James Bethell) *hld up: outpcd over 3f out: rallied ins fnl f: kpt on: nt pce to chal* **12/1**

4021 **9** 1 ¼ **Lopes Dancer (IRE)**[30] 7234 5-9-5 **80** ........................ JoeFanning 12 69
(Sally Haynes) *chsd ldrs: rdn along over 2f out: wknd over 1f out* **6/1[3]**

2015 **10** nse **Globetrotter (IRE)**[129] 3665 3-9-0 **81** ........................ DavidAllan 3 70
(James Tate) *chsd ldrs: rdn along 3f out: wknd 2f out* **50/1**

4005 **11** 2 **Chancery (USA)**[12] 7824 9-8-13 **74** ........................(b) DavidNolan 7 59
(David O'Meara) *hld up: rdn and hung lft over 2f out: sn wknd* **50/1**

0415 **12** 7 **Banish (USA)**[10] 7880 4-9-9 **84** ........................(vt) LouisSteward 11 55
(Hugo Palmer) *hld up in tch on outside: struggling over 2f out: sn wknd* **20/1**

0000 **13** hd **Samtu (IRE)**[10] 7880 6-9-8 **83** ........................ JamesSullivan 2 53
(Marjorie Fife) *hld up towards rr: struggling 3f out: btn fnl 2f* **125/1**

2m 39.17s (-1.93) **Going Correction** +0.10s/f (Slow)
**WFA** 3 from 4yo+ 6lb **13** Ran SP% **123.4**
Speed ratings (Par 105): **110,109,108,108,107 107,105,104,103,103 101,97,97**
CSF £26.74 CT £81.52 TOTE £6.70: £2.30, £1.70, £1.80; EX 33.20 Trifecta £78.20.
**Owner** Exors Of The Late J L C Pearce **Bred** Churchtown House Stud & Partners **Trained** Newmarket, Suffolk

**FOCUS**
This good-quality handicap was run at a decent early pace and it's solid form for the class. It's been rated around the fifth and sixth.

## 8189 NEW SPA AT RAMSIDE HALL/BRITISH EBF NOVICE STKS 6f (Tp)
6:15 (6:17) (Class 5) 2-Y-O £3,234 (£962; £481; £240) Stalls Centre

Form RPR
3 **1** **Mountain Breath**[30] 7238 2-8-11 0 JasonHart 11 72
(Chris Fairhurst) *cl up: rdn to ld wl over 1f out: hrd pressed and hung lft ins fnl f: stened and r.o wl towards fin* **4/1**[3]

6 **2** ¾ **Royal Residence**[27] 7351 2-9-2 0 LukeMorris 9 75
(James Tate) *s.i.s: hld up: stdy hdwy over 2f out: effrt and chsd wnr over 1f out: disp ld ins fnl f: kpt on: hld cl home* **13/8**[1]

6 **3** ¾ **Enzo's Lad (IRE)**[22] 7513 2-9-2 0 PJMcDonald 10 73+
(K R Burke) *plld hrd: trckd ldrs: effrt and rdn over 1f out: carried lft ins fnl f: one pce last 75yds* **2/1**[2]

**4** 4 **Riverside Walk** 2-8-11 0 DanielTudhope 5 56
(Keith Dalgleish) *in tch: drvn and outpcd over 1f out: kpt on ins fnl f: no ch w first three* **20/1**

0 **5** 1 **Mystical Mac (IRE)**[28] 7326 2-9-2 0 GrahamLee 1 58
(Iain Jardine) *hld up: hdwy on far side of gp over 2f out: sn rdn: no imp fr over 1f out* **50/1**

0 **6** hd **The Hoppings**[19] 7623 2-8-11 0 SamJames 3 52
(John Davies) *led: rdn over 2f out: hdd wl over 1f out: wknd ins fnl f* **100/1**

0 **7** ½ **La Cabana**[30] 7238 2-8-11 0 TonyHamilton 7 50
(Richard Fahey) *hld up: shkn up and hdwy 2f out: no imp fnl f* **25/1**

**8** 2¾ **Bucklow Brook** 2-8-11 0 TomEaves 8 42
(David Brown) *s.i.s: hld up: effrt on nr side of gp over 2f out: wknd over 1f out* **50/1**

**9** ½ **Amadeus (IRE)** 2-9-2 0 PaulHanagan 6 46
(Richard Fahey) *bhd and sn drvn along: no imp fr 2f out* **10/1**

0 **10** 2¾ **Working Together**[112] 4258 2-8-11 0 CamHardie 2 32
(Antony Brittain) *cl up: drvn along over 2f out: wknd over 1f out* **100/1**

00 **11** 19 **My Rock (IRE)**[8] 7953 2-9-2 0 (t) DougieCostello 4
(David Dennis) *hld up: rdn and struggling 1/2-way: lost tch fnl 2f* **100/1**

1m 12.72s (0.22) **Going Correction** -0.125s/f (Stan) 11 Ran SP% **116.0**
Speed ratings (Par 95): **93,92,91,85,84 84,83,79,79,75 50**
CSF £10.35 TOTE £4.70: £1.60, £1.10, £1.90; EX 15.00 Trifecta £33.40.
**Owner** Mrs R D Peacock **Bred** Mrs R D Peacock **Trained** Middleham, N Yorks

**FOCUS**
A modest novice event dominated by the market principals.

## 8190 RAMSIDE EVENT CATERING NURSERY H'CAP (DIV I) 6f (Tp)
6:45 (6:45) (Class 6) (0-65,66) 2-Y-O £2,587 (£770; £384; £192) Stalls Centre

Form RPR
6601 **1** **Crown Of Cortez**[37] 7030 2-9-6 **64** (b) PaulHanagan 12 70
(Richard Fahey) *in tch: drvn along over 2f out: rallied over 1f out: led ins fnl f: styd on strly* **11/4**[2]

5624 **2** ¾ **Gabrial The Devil (IRE)**[34] 7106 2-9-7 **65** DanielTudhope 14 69
(David O'Meara) *mde most tl rdn and hdd ins fnl f: edgd both ways and kpt on same pce* **2/1**[1]

4440 **3** 1¼ **Bibbidibobbidiboo (IRE)**[26] 7384 2-9-1 **59** GrahamLee 13 59
(Ann Duffield) *hld up in tch: hdwy nr side of gp and prom over 1f out: kpt on same pce ins fnl f* **11/1**

6000 **4** 1¾ **Swissal (IRE)**[30] 7228 2-9-3 **61** DougieCostello 11 56
(David Dennis) *hld up: hdwy nr side of gp 2f out: rdn and kpt on ins fnl f: nt pce to chal* **20/1**

0536 **5** shd **Leaderofthepack**[40] 6951 2-9-5 **66** (p[1]) AdamMcNamara(3) 3 60
(Bryan Smart) *disp ld to 2f out: sn rdn: outpcd fnl f* **14/1**

5040 **6** ½ **Lord Of The Glen**[22] 7518 2-8-5 **49** (p) JamesSullivan 4 42
(Jim Goldie) *hld up: rdn over 2f out: hdwy over 1f out: kpt on fnl f: nvr able to chal* **28/1**

0000 **7** 1¾ **Partry Flyer (IRE)**[37] 7030 2-7-9 **46** ow1 (v) JamieGormley(7) 7 34
(Oliver Greenall) *hld up: rdn over 2f out: kpt on fnl f: nvr rchd ldrs* **50/1**

2206 **8** 1¼ **Christmas Night**[29] 7264 2-9-3 **61** AndrewMullen 8 45
(Ollie Pears) *prom: drvn over 2f out: wknd over 1f out* **10/1**

3064 **9** ½ **Medici Oro**[52] 6525 2-9-4 **62** TomEaves 2 44
(David Brown) *cl up on far side of gp tl rdn and wknd over 1f out* **20/1**

055 **10** ½ **Isabella Ruby**[20] 7563 2-8-7 **56** (h) ConnorMurtagh(5) 9 37
(Lisa Williamson) *bhd: drvn along over 2f out: sme late hdwy: nvr on terms* **33/1**

0064 **11** 1½ **Forest Dragon**[9] 7920 2-9-3 **61** (p) LouisSteward 5 37
(Hugo Palmer) *prom: drvn and outpcd over 2f out: wknd over 1f out* **9/1**[3]

5426 **12** 1 **Hypnotic Dancer (IRE)**[33] 7159 2-8-9 **53** ConnorBeasley 1 26
(Keith Dalgleish) *in tch on far side of gp: rdn and hung lft over 2f out: sn wknd* **14/1**

0000 **13** 2 **Chef United**[16] 7698 2-8-4 **48** JoeDoyle 10 15
(Roger Fell) *in tch: lost pl 1/2-way: struggling fnl 2f* **66/1**

1m 11.68s (-0.82) **Going Correction** -0.125s/f (Stan) 13 Ran SP% **120.1**
Speed ratings (Par 93): **100,99,97,95,94 94,91,90,89,88 86,85,82**
CSF £7.91 CT £52.56 TOTE £4.30: £1.50, £1.50, £3.10; EX 9.70 Trifecta £73.70.
**Owner** Cheveley Park Stud **Bred** Cheveley Park Stud Ltd **Trained** Musley Bank, N Yorks

**FOCUS**
A moderate nursery.

## 8191 RAMSIDE EVENT CATERING NURSERY H'CAP (DIV II) 6f (Tp)
7:15 (7:16) (Class 6) (0-65,65) 2-Y-O £2,587 (£770; £384; £192) Stalls Centre

Form RPR
005 **1** **Cuppacoco**[29] 7269 2-8-4 **48** ow2 ShaneGray 2 51
(Ann Duffield) *racd on far side of gp: mde all: rdn clr 2f out: kpt on wl fnl f* **33/1**

5100 **2** 1 **Just For Fun**[12] 7814 2-9-6 **64** (b) PaulHanagan 13 64
(Richard Fahey) *hld up: hdwy nr side of gp to chse (clr) wnr over 1f out: kpt on ins fnl f: nt pce to chal* **6/1**[3]

460 **3** 1 **Arty But Poor**[105] 4526 2-9-0 **58** KevinStott 14 55
(Oliver Greenall) *bhd: hdwy nr side of gp over 1f out: kpt on ins fnl f: nrst fin* **5/1**[2]

600 **4** shd **Avon Green**[27] 7351 2-9-5 **63** LukeMorris 7 60
(Joseph Tuite) *prom: effrt on far side of gp and disp 2nd pl over 1f out to ins fnl f: kpt on same pce* **22/1**

4600 **5** 1¾ **Zain Flash**[23] 7491 2-9-0 **61** DavidEgan(3) 11 52
(David Evans) *in tch: effrt on nr side of gp 2f out: no ex ins fnl f* **11/1**

4456 **6** shd **Dyson's Girl**[14] 7756 2-8-13 **57** (p) GrahamLee 5 48
(Bryan Smart) *w wnr to over 2f out: rdn and outpcd fnl f* **16/1**

4300 **7** nk **W G Grace (IRE)**[9] 7920 2-9-7 **65** FrannyNorton 3 55
(Mark Johnston) *bhd: rdn along 1/2-way: hdwy over 1f out: no imp fnl f* **5/1**[2]

0000 **8** 2 **Albarino**[27] 7363 2-8-6 **50** JoeDoyle 4 34
(Kevin Ryan) *in tch on far side of gp: rdn and outpcd over 2f out: btn over 1f out* **14/1**

0600 **9** 1¼ **Magic Ship (IRE)**[9] 7938 2-8-12 **56** AndrewMullen 12 37
(Ollie Pears) *towards rr: drvn and outpcd over 2f out: n.d after* **33/1**

6500 **10** 1 **Duke Of Freedom**[9] 7920 2-9-3 **61** (h[1]) DougieCostello 1 39
(Ann Duffield) *hld up on far side of gp: rdn over 2f out: sn no imp: btn over 1f out* **66/1**

0020 **11** 4½ **Little Monkey**[22] 7518 2-8-1 **45** CamHardie 6 9
(Antony Brittain) *trckd ldrs: drvn along over 2f out: wknd over 1f out* **33/1**

4230 **12** 1½ **Ray Purchase**[22] 7518 2-8-5 **49** (p[1]) JoeFanning 9 9
(Keith Dalgleish) *in tch: rdn over 2f out: wknd wl over 1f out* **9/2**[1]

5540 **13** ½ **Plundered (IRE)**[65] 6043 2-9-2 **60** BenCurtis 8 18
(David Brown) *bhd: drvn and outpcd wl over 2f out: sn wknd* **12/1**

0003 **14** 13 **Mabo**[36] 7041 2-9-3 **61** TonyHamilton 10
(Richard Fahey) *bhd and nvr gng wl: struggling 1/2-way: sn btn* **10/1**

1m 12.03s (-0.47) **Going Correction** -0.125s/f (Stan) 14 Ran SP% **118.1**
Speed ratings (Par 93): **98,96,95,95,92 92,92,89,88,86 80,78,78,60**
CSF £210.81 CT £1213.78 TOTE £84.60: £11.70, £2.30, £2.40; EX 1029.70 Trifecta £5104.00.
**Owner** C A Gledhill & Partner **Bred** Llety Farms **Trained** Constable Burton, N Yorks

**FOCUS**
The raced in two groups and the time was 0.35secs slower than the preceding division.

## 8192 RAMSIDE HALL HOTEL FILLIES' H'CAP 1m 5y (Tp)
7:45 (7:46) (Class 5) (0-75,76) 3-Y-O+ £3,234 (£962; £481; £240) Stalls Centre

Form RPR
6303 **1** **Doria Road (USA)**[36] 7061 3-8-5 **62** ShaneGray 3 69
(Kevin Ryan) *cl up: rdn over 1f out: led ins fnl f: drvn out* **16/1**

33-2 **2** 1 **Corked (IRE)**[21] 7541 4-9-6 **74** LouisSteward 4 80
(Hugo Palmer) *led at stdy pce: rdn over 1f out: hdd ins fnl f: kpt on* **9/4**[1]

3034 **3** nk **Jafetica**[23] 7492 3-9-0 **71** (h) TomQueally 1 75
(James Fanshawe) *hld up in tch: hdwy on far side of gp over 1f out: rdn and ch ins fnl f: one pce last 75yds* **6/1**[3]

5-32 **4** 1¼ **Ifubelieveindreams (IRE)**[19] 7600 3-9-1 **75** NathanAlison(3) 9 77
(Ismail Mohammed) *hld up: rdn over 2f out: kpt on ins fnl f: nt pce to chal* **11/2**[2]

0042 **5** 2 **Beatbybeatbybeat**[8] 7958 4-8-7 **61** oh2 (v) CamHardie 11 59
(Antony Brittain) *hld up in tch on nr side of gp: rdn over 2f out: no imp over 1f out* **7/1**

1 **6** 2¼ **She's Pukka**[31] 7224 3-9-0 **71** GrahamLee 5 63
(Iain Jardine) *prom: rdn over 2f out: outpcd fr over 1f out* **12/1**

/050 **7** 1¾ **Belle De Lawers**[80] 5469 6-9-8 **76** DanielTudhope 2 65
(James Bethell) *hld up: rdn and outpcd over 2f out: no imp fr over 1f out* **17/2**

6406 **8** ½ **Make On Madam (IRE)**[23] 7476 5-8-8 **67** JaneElliott(5) 6 54
(Les Eyre) *cl up: drvn and outpcd over 2f out: btn over 1f out* **10/1**

1640 **9** 5 **The Stalking Moon (IRE)**[23] 7474 3-9-4 **75** JasonHart 8 50
(John Quinn) *hld up: rdn and outpcd over 2f out: sn btn* **14/1**

1m 38.01s (-0.59) **Going Correction** -0.125s/f (Stan)
**WFA** 3 from 4yo+ 3lb 9 Ran SP% **112.8**
Speed ratings (Par 100): **97,96,95,94,92 90,88,87,82**
CSF £50.95 CT £247.28 TOTE £18.50: £3.80, £1.40, £2.00; EX 64.70 Trifecta £458.00.
**Owner** Mrs Clodagh McStay **Bred** Mr & Mrs Broussard Hundley **Trained** Hambleton, N Yorks

**FOCUS**
This modest fillies' handicap was another race on the straight track where it paid to be handy. It's been rated around the runner-up.

## 8193 HARDWICK HALL HOTEL MEDIAN AUCTION MAIDEN STKS 1m 5y (Tp)
8:15 (8:15) (Class 5) 3-5-Y-O £3,234 (£962; £481; £240) Stalls Centre

Form RPR
6064 **1** **Lord Commander**[8] 7957 3-9-5 68 PaulHanagan 7 70
(Richard Fahey) *hld up: smooth hdwy on nr side of gp to ld over 1f out: pushed out fnl f: comf* **15/8**[1]

444 **2** 3 **Lewinsky (IRE)**[28] 7322 3-9-0 68 LouisSteward 1 57
(Hugo Palmer) *trckd ldrs: rdn and ev ch briefly over 1f out: sn chsng wnr: kpt on ins fnl f* **7/2**[2]

6003 **3** 1 **American Hustle (IRE)**[30] 7240 5-8-12 54 BenRobinson(5) 4 56
(Brian Ellison) *hld up in tch: hdwy on far side of gp and disp 2nd pl over 1f out to ins fnl f: kpt on same pce fnl f* **4/1**[3]

0060 **4** ¾ **Diamond Avalanche (IRE)**[85] 5283 4-9-8 44 TonyHamilton 3 59?
(Kristin Stubbs) *plld hrd: led after 2f: rdn and hdd over 1f out: outpcd fnl f* **25/1**

5233 **5** 3 **Eddiebet**[150] 2901 3-9-5 70 DanielTudhope 2 51
(David O'Meara) *t.k.h: in tch: effrt and rdn over 1f out: wknd fnl f* **11/2**

-000 **6** 2¼ **Trois Bon Amis (IRE)**[28] 7331 3-9-5 53 (t) PaddyAspell 6 46
(Mark Campion) *led 2f: cl up tl rdn and wknd over 1f out* **100/1**

00 **P** **Saradani Bay**[28] 7322 3-9-5 0 DavidAllan 5
(Rae Guest) *in tch tl broke down and p.u at 1/2-way* **6/1**

1m 40.6s (2.00) **Going Correction** -0.125s/f (Stan)
**WFA** 3 from 4yo+ 3lb 7 Ran SP% **111.5**
Speed ratings (Par 103): **85,82,81,80,77 75,**
CSF £8.16 TOTE £3.40: £1.60, £2.20; EX 9.00 Trifecta £31.20.
**Owner** Nick Bradley Racing 23 **Bred** Shadwell Estate Company Limited **Trained** Musley Bank, N Yorks

**FOCUS**
A weak maiden, run at an early crawl. The third has been rated close to her C&D latest.

## 8194 COLONEL PORTERS EMPORIUM APPRENTICE H'CAP 6f (Tp)
8:45 (8:47) (Class 6) (0-60,60) 3-Y-O+ £2,587 (£770; £384; £192) Stalls Centre

Form RPR
5030 **1** **Kroy**[85] 5283 3-9-4 **57** (p) AdamMcNamara 8 63
(Ollie Pears) *hld up in midfield: hdwy 2f out: rdn and kpt on wl fnl f to ld towards fin* **10/1**

0000 **2** hd **Kommander Kirkup**[30] 7249 6-9-1 **58** ConnorMurtagh(5) 1 63
(Michael Herrington) *t.k.h: cl up on far side of gp: rdn and led 1f out: kpt on fnl f: hdd towards fin* **7/1**[2]

0301 **3** nk **Canford Bay (IRE)**[20] 7575 3-9-7 **60** CliffordLee 11 64
(Antony Brittain) *in tch: drvn and outpcd over 2f out: rallied on nr side of gp over 1f out: kpt on fnl f: hld cl home* **5/2**[1]

025- **4** 1¾ **Andys Girl (IRE)**[302] 8482 4-9-5 **60** BenRobinson(3) 7 59
(Brian Ellison) *hld up: rdn and effrt over 2f out: hdwy and drifted lft over 1f out: kpt on fnl f: nt rch first three* **20/1**

1500 **5** *nse* **Termsnconditions (IRE)**32 7191 3-9-1 **59**..........(v) PatrickVaughan(5) 9 58
(Tim Vaughan) *cl up: rdn along over 2f out: kpt on same pce fnl f* **16/1**
0305 **6** *1 1/4* **Willbeme**20 7575 9-9-2 **54**..........(bt) LouisSteward 10 49
(Simon West) *bhd: rdn along over 2f out: hdwy fnl f: kpt on: nvr able to chal* **20/1**
1043 **7** *1/2* **Searanger (USA)**50 6571 4-9-2 **57**.......... RowanScott(3) 4 50
(Rebecca Menzies) *prom: rdn and outpcd 2f out: no imp fnl f* **7/1**2
0000 **8** *1* **Arcane Dancer (IRE)**23 7476 4-9-8 **60**..........(b1) KieranShoemark 12 50
(Lawrence Mullaney) *hld up: drvn and outpcd over 2f out: drifted lft and kpt on ins fnl f: no imp* **8/1**3
1200 **9** *hd* **Kyllach Me (IRE)**37 7018 5-8-12 **57**..........(v) HarryRussell(7) 14 47
(Bryan Smart) *cl up on nr side of gp: rdn over 2f out: no ex fr over 1f out* **40/1**
/30- **10** *nse* **Chicago School (IRE)**209 1352 4-9-3 **58**..........(vt) ConorMcGovern(3) 3 48
(Anthony McCann, Ire) *led 1f: cl up: rdn to ld 2f out: hdd 1f out: sn wknd* **7/1**2
0224 **11** *nse* **Vintage Dream (IRE)**18 7657 3-9-7 **60**..........(b) PhilDennis 2 50
(Noel Wilson) *dwlt and wnt lft s: t.k.h and led after 1f: rdn and hdd over 2f out: wknd over 1f out* **12/1**
0500 **12** *9* **Compton Park**70 5836 10-9-5 **60**..........(t) JaneElliott(3) 6 23
(Les Eyre) *missed break: bhd on far side of gp: struggling 1/2-way: sn wknd* **14/1**

1m 11.67s (-0.83) **Going Correction** -0.125s/f (Stan)
**WFA** 3 from 4yo+ 1lb 12 Ran SP% **118.5**
Speed ratings (Par 101): **100,99,99,97,96 95,94,93,93,92 92,80**
CSF £76.37 CT £235.01 TOTE £8.80: £2.70, £3.50, £1.30; EX 103.20 Trifecta £704.40.
**Owner** Mrs Sheila Elsey **Bred** T Elsey **Trained** Norton, N Yorks

**FOCUS**
An ordinary sprint handicap, confined to apprentices. It's rated around the third.
T/Jkpt: Not Won. T/Plt: £18.90 to a £1 stake. Pool: £80,726.70 - 3,106.49 winning units. T/Qpdt: £6.00 to a £1 stake. Pool: £12,560.67 - 1,523.85 winning units. **Richard Young**

8188 - 8194a (Foreign Racing) - See Raceform Interactive

## 8169 DEAUVILLE (R-H)

Thursday, October 19

**OFFICIAL GOING: Polytrack: standard; turf: very soft**

### 8195a PRIX ARAZI (CONDITIONS) (2YO) (POLYTRACK) 7f 110y
**11:40** 2-Y-O **£17,675** (£7,145; £5,264; £3,384; £2,068; £1,316)

RPR
**1** **Louis D'Or (IRE)**19 7637 2-8-9 0.......... MaximeGuyon 4 86
(T Castanheira, France) **12/5**2
**2** *1/2* **Denaar (IRE)**54 6452 2-9-3 0.......... Pierre-CharlesBoudot 6 93
(Antonio Marcialis, Italy) **23/10**1
**3** *snk* **Taglioni**20 2-8-9 0.......... MickaelBarzalona 8 85
(A Fabre, France) **53/10**3
**4** *2 1/2* **Massina (FR)**33 2-8-9 0.......... GregoryBenoist 1 79
(S Wattel, France) **73/10**
**5** *3/4* **Salt Lake City (FR)**38 7011 2-8-13 0.......... SebastienMaillot 7 81
(Robert Collet, France) **87/10**
**6** *1/2* **Uther Pendragon (IRE)**54 6453 2-8-9 0..........(p) TonyPiccone 5 75
(J S Moore) **156/10**
**7** *nk* **Saint Roch (FR)**62 6170 2-8-9 0.......... CristianDemuro 2 75
(Mme Pia Brandt, France) **36/5**
**8** *12* **Boss For A Day** 2-8-7 0.......... JosephineGordon 3 43
(J S Moore) **40/1**

1m 30.84s 8 Ran SP% **118.6**
PARI-MUTUEL (all including 1 euro stake): WIN 3.40; PLACE 1.20, 1.40, 1.50; DF 3.60; SF 9.40.
**Owner** Camille Garnier **Bred** Dayton Investments Ltd **Trained** France

### 8196a PRIX ISONOMY (LISTED RACE) (2YO) (ROUND) (TURF) 1m (R)
**12:10** 2-Y-O **£25,641** (£10,256; £7,692; £5,128; £2,564)

RPR
**1** **Wootton (FR)**58 2-8-13 0.......... MickaelBarzalona 7 105
(H-A Pantall, France) **2/1**1
**2** *5* **Alternative Fact**34 7120 2-8-13 0.......... CristianDemuro 5 94
(Ed Dunlop) **42/10**3
**3** *nk* **African Sky**44 2-8-13 0.......... Pierre-CharlesBoudot 2 93
(A Fabre, France) **16/5**2
**4** *2* **Alba Power (IRE)**15 7754 2-8-13 0.......... JosephineGordon 4 89
(Hugo Palmer) **16/5**2
**5** *3* **Five Ice Cubes (FR)**20 2-8-13 0.......... GregoryBenoist 6 82
(D Smaga, France) **12/1**
**6** *1* **Blue Link (FR)**8 2-8-13 0.......... MaximeGuyon 1 80
(T Castanheira, France) **174/10**
**7** *12* **Pastamakesufaster**22 7504 2-8-9 0.......... TonyPiccone 3 50
(David Evans) **161/10**

1m 41.97s (1.17) 7 Ran SP% **119.2**
PARI-MUTUEL (all including 1 euro stake): WIN 3.00; PLACE 2.10, 2.60; SF 12.50.
**Owner** Godolphin SNC **Bred** Ecurie Haras De Quetieville **Trained** France

## 7608 HAYDOCK (L-H)

**8197 ABANDONED WATERLOGGED**

## 8187 NEWCASTLE (A.W) (L-H)

Friday, October 20

**OFFICIAL GOING: Tapeta: standard**
Wind: Almost nil Weather: Dry

### 8204 GLOBAL'S MAKE SOME NOISE FILLIES' H'CAP 1m 4f 98y (Tp)
**4:40** (4:41) (Class 5) (0-70,72) 3-Y-O+ **£3,234** (£962; £481; £240) **Stalls** High

Form RPR
2015 **1** **Snowy Winter (USA)**14 7790 3-9-7 **72**..........(t) AndrewMullen 4 82+
(Archie Watson) *in tch: effrt and chsd ldr over 1f out: rdn to ld ins fnl f: kpt on wl* **5/1**2
4243 **2** *1 1/2* **Alfa Queen (IRE)**38 7032 3-9-4 **69**.......... DavidNolan 5 76
(Iain Jardine) *cl up: led after 2f: rdn over 2f out: hdd ins fnl f: kpt on same pce* **9/1**
6030 **3** *6* **Golden Set**21 7560 3-9-4 **69**.......... JoeFanning 1 66
(James Fanshawe) *t.k.h: cl up: rdn over 2f out: kpt on same pce fr over 1f out* **8/1**
0031 **4** *1* **Bianca Minola (FR)**66 6032 3-9-2 **67**..........(p) KieranShoemark 7 63
(David Menuisier) *hld up: rdn and outpcd whn hung lft wl over 1f out: kpt on ins fnl f: nt pce to chal* **9/1**
3523 **5** *3/4* **Stepney**2 8160 3-9-0 **68**.......... DavidEgan(3) 8 63
(Robyn Brisland) *t.k.h: led 2f: cl up: rdn over 2f out: wknd over 1f out* **5/4**1
0465 **6** *nse* **Island Flame (IRE)**54 6467 4-8-12 **62**.......... ConnorMurtagh(5) 6 56
(Richard Fahey) *hld up: effrt on outside over 2f out: drvn and hung lft over 1f out: sn no imp* **11/2**3
0025 **7** *3 1/2* **Royal Icon**11 7885 3-8-6 **57**.......... ShaneGray 2 46
(Kevin Ryan) *hld up on ins: drvn and outpcd over 2f out: sn wknd* **28/1**

2m 42.61s (1.51) **Going Correction** +0.20s/f (Slow)
**WFA** 3 from 4yo 6lb 7 Ran SP% **111.1**
Speed ratings (Par 100): **103,102,98,97,96 96,94**
CSF £44.77 CT £339.58 TOTE £6.20: £3.10, £2.60; EX 39.20 Trifecta £292.10.
**Owner** Boadicea Bloodstock **Bred** Darley **Trained** Upper Lambourn, W Berks

**FOCUS**
A fair fillies handicap. They went an ordinary gallop, the pace picking up once in the home straight, and the first two pulled clear of the rest. Muddling form, but the runner-up has been rated as improving in line with the better view of her C&D latest.

### 8205 CAPITAL NORTH EAST H'CAP (DIV I) 1m 2f 42y (Tp)
**5:10** (5:15) (Class 5) (0-70,72) 3-Y-O+ **£3,234** (£962; £481; £240) **Stalls** High

Form RPR
0004 **1** **Celestation**15 7762 3-9-5 **71**.......... PJMcDonald 9 78
(Mark Johnston) *led at ordinary gallop: rdn and hdd over 2f out: rallied gamely fnl f: regained ld last stride* **15/2**
2514 **2** *nse* **My Brother Mike (IRE)**24 7495 3-9-2 **68**.......... DavidNolan 4 75
(Kevin Frost) *cl up: rdn to ld over 2f out: kpt on wl fnl f: hdd last stride* **7/2**1
455 **3** *3/4* **Chartbuster (IRE)**76 5632 3-9-3 **69**.......... JoeDoyle 12 75
(Julie Camacho) *prom: effrt and rdn over 2f out: kpt on ins fnl f* **9/2**2
3654 **4** *3/4* **Infamous Lawman (IRE)**8 7984 3-9-1 **67**.......... DanielTudhope 2 71
(David O'Meara) *prom: drvn along over 2f out: kpt on same pce ins fnl f* **9/1**
5550 **5** *1 1/2* **Archipeligo**13 7831 6-9-4 **69**..........(p) RowanScott(3) 5 69
(Iain Jardine) *hld up midfield: effrt and pushed along over 2f out: kpt on fr over 1f out: nvr able to chal* **11/2**3
0144 **6** *3/4* **Hussar Ballad (USA)**10 7936 8-9-3 **65**.......... CamHardie 1 64
(Antony Brittain) *hld up in tch: rdn over 2f out: no imp fr over 1f out* **16/1**
0006 **7** *1 1/2* **Bahamian C**91 5097 6-8-3 **56**..........(t) ConnorMurtagh(5) 11 52
(Richard Fahey) *hld up: rdn over 2f out: hdwy and hung lft over 1f out: kpt on fnl f: nrst fin* **22/1**
5206 **8** *nk* **Beauden Barrett**45 6784 4-9-10 **72**..........(t) AndrewMullen 10 67
(John Quinn) *hld up: rdn and outpcd over 2f out: kpt on fnl f: nvr able to chal* **28/1**
-116 **9** *3/4* **Exclusive Waters (IRE)**101 4722 7-9-1 **66**.......... AdamMcNamara(3) 3 59
(Tina Jackson) *dwlt: hld up: rdn and outpcd over 2f out: sme late hdwy: nvr on terms* **16/1**
005- **10** *3* **Hediddodinthe (IRE)**350 7792 3-8-4 **56** ow1.......... ShaneGray 14 44
(Richard Guest) *missed break: bhd: rdn over 2f out: sn outpcd: n.d after* **50/1**
6203 **11** *3/4* **New Abbey Angel (IRE)**48 6690 4-8-7 **55** oh3.......... JoeFanning 13 41
(Keith Dalgleish) *hld up midfield on outside: rdn and hung lft over 2f out: wknd over 1f out* **10/1**
1300 **12** *1 1/2* **Diamond Runner (IRE)**24 7479 5-8-6 **57**..........(b) DavidEgan(3) 8 40
(Lawrence Mullaney) *hld up: rdn along 3f out: wknd wl over 1f out* **16/1**
0100 **13** *1/2* **Kicking The Can (IRE)**22 7541 6-9-2 **64**.......... KieranShoemark 7 46
(Noel Wilson) *hld up on ins: drvn and struggling over 2f out: sn wknd* **33/1**

2m 14.13s (3.73) **Going Correction** +0.20s/f (Slow)
**WFA** 3 from 4yo+ 4lb 13 Ran SP% **117.0**
Speed ratings (Par 103): **93,92,92,91,90 89,88,88,87,85 84,83,83**
CSF £31.87 CT £134.19 TOTE £7.70: £2.70, £2.10, £2.10; EX 33.20 Trifecta £198.50.
**Owner** Kingsley Park 5 **Bred** The Lavington Stud **Trained** Middleham Moor, N Yorks

**FOCUS**
A fair handicap in which the pace was ordinary and it developed into a 2f sprint. Very few got into it and the first four were were always in a prominent position. The winner has been rated to her summer best.

### 8206 CAPITAL NORTH EAST H'CAP (DIV II) 1m 2f 42y (Tp)
**5:40** (5:44) (Class 5) (0-70,71) 3-Y-O+ **£3,234** (£962; £481; £240) **Stalls** High

Form RPR
2044 **1** **The Eagle's Nest (IRE)**11 7894 3-9-3 **70**.......... TonyHamilton 8 78
(Richard Fahey) *prom: rdn to ld over 1f out: hrd pressed fnl f: hld on gamely towards fin* **7/2**1
6002 **2** *nse* **Maraakib (IRE)**13 7820 5-9-1 **64**.......... DavidNolan 13 71
(David O'Meara) *hld up midfield: nt clr run briefly over 2f out: smooth hdwy wl over 1f out: rdn to chal ins fnl f: kpt on: jst hld* **8/1**2
5003 **3** *3/4* **Traveltalk (IRE)**10 7928 3-8-3 **56**.......... CamHardie 2 61
(Brian Ellison) *trckd ldrs: effrt and rdn wl over 1f out: kpt on ins fnl f* **50/1**
2300 **4** *2* **Bollihope**21 7567 5-9-2 **65**.......... ConnorBeasley 1 66
(Richard Guest) *t.k.h: hld up midfield on ins: rdn and hdwy over 1f out: kpt on fnl f: nt pce to chal* **8/1**2
1403 **5** *hd* **Mr C (IRE)**13 7833 3-8-3 **56**.......... AndrewMullen 9 56
(Ollie Pears) *t.k.h: hld up in tch: effrt over 2f out: rdn and ev ch over 1f out: no ex ins fnl f* **12/1**3
4230 **6** *1/2* **Steccando (IRE)**10 7936 4-8-7 **56**.......... BenCurtis 3 55
(Sally Haynes) *trckd ldrs: nt clr run briefly over 2f out: effrt and rdn over 1f out: kpt on same pce fnl f* **12/1**3
4450 **7** *1/2* **Lil Sophella (IRE)**24 7476 8-8-13 **62**.......... DanielTudhope 7 60
(Patrick Holmes) *missed break: hld up: rdn and hdwy over 1f out: kpt on fnl f: nt pce to chal* **20/1**
4254 **8** *1* **Knightsbridge Liam (IRE)**31 7236 3-8-0 **56** oh1.......... DavidEgan(3) 4 52
(Michael Easterby) *hld up: effrt whn nt clr run briefly over 2f out: hdwy over 1f out: no imp fnl f* **8/1**2
4600 **9** *1 3/4* **King's Coinage (IRE)**13 7832 3-9-2 **69**..........(h) JamesSullivan 12 61
(Ruth Carr) *hld up: rdn and hdwy wl over 1f out: no further imp ins fnl f* **33/1**
0000 **10** *1 1/4* **Etaad (USA)**24 7478 6-9-5 **68**.......... NeilFarley 5 57
(Lucinda Egerton) *hld up: rdn over 2f out: no imp fr wl over 1f out* **80/1**
-400 **11** *1/2* **Sugar Beach (FR)**27 7390 3-8-9 **62**..........(t1) ShaneGray 11 51
(Ann Duffield) *trckd ldr: led over 2f out to over 1f out: sn rdn and wknd* **66/1**
1006 **12** *1 3/4* **Valley Of Rocks (IRE)**64 6110 3-9-1 **68**.......... PJMcDonald 6 53
(Mark Johnston) *t.k.h: hld up midfield: drvn and outpcd 2f out: sn btn* **14/1**

3564 **13** 1¾ **Somnambulist**[21] 7568 3-9-0 **67**....................(h) JoeFanning 14 48
(Keith Dalgleish) *s.i.s: hld up on outside: rdn and outpcd over 2f out: hung bdly lft and sn wknd* **7/2**[1]

4556 **14** 2¾ **Livella Fella (IRE)**[23] 7524 4-9-8 **71**.................... KieranShoemark 10 44
(Keith Dalgleish) *led to over 2f out: rdn and wknd over 1f out* **25/1**

2m 11.54s (1.14) **Going Correction** +0.20s/f (Slow)
**WFA** 3 from 4yo+ 4lb **14** Ran SP% **116.1**
Speed ratings (Par 103): **103,102,102,100,100 100,99,99,97,96 96,94,93,91**
CSF £28.54 CT £1184.72 TOTE £5.20: £1.80, £2.60, £15.40; EX 37.10 Trifecta £2629.80.
**Owner** D O'Callaghan **Bred** Kevin & Meta Cullen **Trained** Musley Bank, N Yorks

**FOCUS**
The second division of a fair handicap, and another thrilling finish.

## 8207 CAPITAL BREAKFAST WITH BODG, MATT & HANNAH NURSERY H'CAP 1m 5y (Tp)
**6:15** (6:15) (Class 4) (0-85,83) 2-Y-O **£5,175** (£1,540; £769; £384) **Stalls** Centre

Form RPR

4401 **1** **Emerald Rocket (IRE)**[10] 7938 2-8-6 **68** 6ex.................... BenCurtis 3 75+
(K R Burke) *trckd ldrs: rdn and outpcd wl over 2f out: rallied and led over 1f out: drifted lft ins fnl f: styd on strly* **6/5**[1]

1234 **2** 2½ **Kit Marlowe**[42] 6900 2-9-7 **83**.................... PJMcDonald 1 83
(Mark Johnston) *chsd ldr: rdn and ev ch over 1f out: sn chsng wnr: one pce fnl f* **7/2**[3]

4405 **3** 4½ **Homerton**[10] 7929 2-8-13 **75**.................... KieranShoemark 4 65
(Robyn Brisland) *prom: rdn and outpcd over 2f out: no imp fr over 1f out* **5/1**

3224 **4** *nk* **Weellan**[24] 7473 2-9-0 **76**....................(p) PhillipMakin 2 65
(John Quinn) *led: rdn and hdd over 1f out: sn wknd* **3/1**[2]

1m 38.88s (0.28) **Going Correction** 0.0s/f (Stan) **4** Ran SP% **109.3**
Speed ratings (Par 97): **98,95,91,90**
CSF £5.68 TOTE £1.60; EX 3.70 Trifecta £12.30.
**Owner** Hambleton Racing Ltd III & E Burke **Bred** Elton Lodge Stud **Trained** Middleham Moor, N Yorks

**FOCUS**
A small-field nursery that predictably turned into a tactical affair.

## 8208 NIGHTMARE AT THE RACECOURSE NOVICE AUCTION STKS 7f 14y (Tp)
**6:45** (6:46) (Class 6) 2-Y-O **£2,425** (£721; £360; £180) **Stalls** Centre

Form RPR

34 **1** **Line House**[15] 7757 2-8-11 0.................... KieranShoemark 4 75
(Robyn Brisland) *mde all: set modest pce: qcknd clr over 2f out: drifted rt over 1f out: kpt on wl fnl f: unchal* **2/1**[1]

0 **2** 2 **Brisk Tempo (FR)**[17] 7707 2-9-2 0.................... PJMcDonald 5 75
(Richard Fahey) *in tch: hdwy to chse (clr) wnr over 2f out: clsd over 1f out: one pce ins fnl f* **13/2**

2 **3** ¾ **Mametz Wood (IRE)**[23] 7520 2-8-13 0.................... CliffordLee(3) 6 73
(K R Burke) *hld up on nr side of gp: rdn and hdwy whn nt clr run briefly over 1f out: kpt on same pce ins fnl f* **3/1**[2]

5 **4** 3½ **Sienna Dream**[19] 7654 2-8-11 0.................... BarryMcHugh 10 59
(Alistair Whillans) *t.k.h: chsd wnr to over 2f out: rdn and outpcd fnl f* **12/1**

**5** 2½ **Strawberryandcream** 2-8-11 0.................... KevinStott 8 52
(James Bethell) *s.s: hld up: effrt and rn green over 2f out: wknd over 1f out* **25/1**

3534 **6** ½ **Another Day Of Sun (IRE)**[14] 7787 2-9-6 74.................... DavidEgan(3) 7 63
(Mick Channon) *t.k.h: hld up towards rr: rdn and outpcd over 2f out: btn over 1f out* **6/1**[3]

06 **7** 3 **Blyton Lass**[22] 7551 2-8-11 0.................... JamesSullivan 3 43
(James Given) *hld up: rdn and struggling over 3f out: rallied over 1f out: nvr able to chal* **66/1**

55 **8** ¾ **Dutch Academy**[5] 8073 2-9-2 0.................... BenCurtis 9 46
(K R Burke) *prom on nr side of gp: rdn and effrt over 2f out: wknd over 1f out* **7/1**

**9** 12 **Amity Island** 2-9-2 0.................... AndrewMullen 1 15
(Ollie Pears) *s.i.s: t.k.h and sn prom: rdn and outpcd over 2f out: sn wknd* **66/1**

00 **10** 61 **Baileys Rockstar**[22] 7535 2-8-11 0.................... JoeDoyle 2
(James Given) *chsd ldrs: lost pl over 3f out: sn lost tch: t.o* **66/1**

1m 25.95s (-0.25) **Going Correction** 0.0s/f (Stan) **10** Ran SP% **114.5**
Speed ratings (Par 93): **101,98,97,93,91 90,87,86,72,2**
CSF £15.03 TOTE £2.60: £1.10, £1.90, £1.40; EX 14.20 Trifecta £35.20.
**Owner** Franconson Partners **Bred** Worksop Manor Stud **Trained** Newmarket, Suffolk

**FOCUS**
An ordinary novice and an all-the-way winner.

## 8209 HEART NORTH EAST H'CAP 1m 5y (Tp)
**7:15** (7:16) (Class 5) (0-75,74) 3-Y-O+ **£3,234** (£962; £481; £240) **Stalls** Centre

Form RPR

0024 **1** **Newmarket Warrior (IRE)**[8] 7981 6-9-1 **68**..........(p) KieranShoemark 2 77
(Iain Jardine) *hld up: smooth hdwy over 1f out: shkn up and qcknd between horses to ld ins fnl f: readily* **7/1**[3]

456 **2** 1¾ **Thello**[21] 7570 5-8-12 **68**.................... PhilDennis(3) 10 73+
(Jim Goldie) *hld up: hdwy whn nt clr run over 2f out tl swtchd rt appr fnl f: kpt on wl to take 2nd cl home: nt rch wnr* **12/1**

2064 **3** ¾ **Acrux**[21] 7571 4-9-5 **72**....................(h) DanielTudhope 9 75
(David O'Meara) *hld up: smooth hdwy to chse ldr over 2f out: rdn to chal ins fnl f: no ex last 50yds* **3/1**[2]

00 **4** *shd* **Majdool (IRE)**[41] 6943 4-9-3 **70**....................(h) PatrickMathers 5 73
(Noel Wilson) *led on far side of gp: rdn over 2f out: hdd ins fnl f: sn no ex* **50/1**

0006 **5** 1 **Pickett's Charge**[4] 8125 4-8-12 **65**....................(b) PhillipMakin 12 66
(Richard Guest) *hld up: hdwy nr side of gp whn hung lft over 1f out: kpt on same pce ins fnl f* **16/1**

1403 **6** ½ **Wasm**[17] 7699 3-9-2 **72**....................(t) TonyHamilton 6 71
(Roger Fell) *hld up: hdwy centre 2f out: chsng ldrs ins fnl f: one pce towards fin* **14/1**

2020 **7** 2¼ **Hernando Torres**[21] 7571 9-8-9 **69**....................(t) HarrisonShaw(7) 11 63
(Michael Easterby) *hld up: rdn over 2f out: hdwy nr side of gp over 1f out: no imp fnl f* **25/1**

1600 **8** ¾ **Alfie's Angel (IRE)**[10] 7942 3-9-4 **74**.................... GrahamLee 8 66
(Bryan Smart) *hld up: effrt nr side of gp over 2f out: rdn and one pce fnl f* **33/1**

3-00 **9** ¾ **Never A Word (USA)**[24] 7476 3-9-2 **72**....................(t[1]) KevinStott 3 62
(Oliver Greenall) *cl up on far side of gp: rdn over 2f out: wknd over 1f out* **28/1**

4402 **10** 4 **Kreb's Cycle (IRE)**[10] 7942 3-9-2 **72**....................(p) JosephineGordon 14 58
(Ian Williams) *prom on nr side of gp: rdn over 2f out: outpcd whn hmpd over 1f out: sn btn and eased* **5/2**[1]

4021 **11** 3¼ **Old China**[27] 7388 4-9-4 **71**.................... SamJames 13 45
(John Davies) *prom: rdn over 2f out: wknd over 1f out* **12/1**

0-60 **12** *nk* **Weather Front (USA)**[23] 7524 4-8-13 **66**....................(p) DougieCostello 4 40
(Karen McLintock) *dwlt: hld up: rdn and struggling 3f out: sn btn* **18/1**

1401 **13** 6 **Chinese Spirit (IRE)**[8] 7984 3-9-3 **73** 6ex.................... PJMcDonald 1 32
(R Mike Smith) *cl up on far side of gp tl rdn and wknd qckly over 2f out* **14/1**

1m 38.96s (0.36) **Going Correction** 0.0s/f (Stan)
**WFA** 3 from 4yo+ 3lb **13** Ran SP% **118.1**
Speed ratings (Par 103): **98,96,95,95,94 93,91,90,90,86 82,82,76**
CSF £83.94 CT £318.60 TOTE £7.70: £2.00, £3.00, £1.50; EX 54.00 Trifecta £371.90.
**Owner** Ms S A Booth & Partner **Bred** Newtown Stud And T J Pabst **Trained** Carrutherstown, D'fries & G'way

**FOCUS**
Another fair handicap run at an ordinary pace. The winner has been rated to his best since his 2yo days.

## 8210 HEART BREAKFAST WITH JUSTIN AND KELLY H'CAP 7f 14y (Tp)
**7:45** (7:46) (Class 6) (0-60,60) 3-Y-O+ **£2,425** (£721; £360; £180) **Stalls** Centre

Form RPR

4004 **1** **Captain Hawk**[29] 7323 3-9-4 **60**....................(v[1]) JosephineGordon 4 67
(Ian Williams) *cl up on far side of gp: led over 2f out to over 1f out: rallied gamely fnl f to regain ld last stride* **13/2**[3]

4522 **2** *nse* **See You Mush**[51] 6581 3-9-3 **59**....................(b) AdamBeschizza 6 66
(Mrs Ilka Gansera-Leveque) *prom on far side of gp: effrt over 2f out: led and edgd lft over 1f out: kpt on fnl f: hdd last stride* **7/1**

051 **3** 2 **Intiwin (IRE)**[21] 7573 5-9-5 **59**.................... DavidNolan 2 62
(Linda Perratt) *hld up: rdn and hdwy to chse ldrs over 1f out: rdn and kpt on same pce ins fnl f* **7/1**

5402 **4** 2½ **Gun Case**[21] 7573 5-9-3 **60**....................(p) RowanScott(3) 1 56
(Alistair Whillans) *hld up on far side of gp: hdwy over 2f out: rdn and one pce fnl f* **7/2**[1]

4000 **5** ½ **Willsy**[23] 7525 4-9-4 **58**.................... KevinStott 9 53
(Karen Tutty) *hld up in centre: drvn along over 2f out: effrt over 1f out: no imp fnl f* **16/1**

454 **6** 2¼ **Pepys**[77] 5601 3-9-3 **59**.................... GrahamLee 7 47
(Bryan Smart) *hld up centre: effrt and swtchd rt over 1f out: nvr able to chal* **16/1**

4400 **7** 3 **Tafteesh (IRE)**[4] 8108 4-8-12 **59**.................... RyanTimby(7) 3 40
(Michael Easterby) *cl up on far side of gp tl rdn and wknd over 1f out* **66/1**

-605 **8** 3 **Zenovia (IRE)**[22] 7539 3-9-2 **58**.................... DanielTudhope 12 30
(Archie Watson) *in tch on nr side of gp: effrt over 2f out: rdn and wknd fnl f* **11/2**[2]

6503 **9** 1¼ **Grey Destiny**[21] 7573 7-9-3 **57**....................(p) CamHardie 10 27+
(Antony Brittain) *s.s: hld up: shortlived effrt nr side of gp over 2f out: btn over 1f out* **8/1**

0646 **10** 3¼ **Luath**[31] 7240 4-9-5 **59**.................... NickyMackay 5 21
(Suzzanne France) *midfield in centre: drvn over 2f out: wknd over 1f out* **12/1**

2300 **11** ½ **Sulafah (IRE)**[58] 6313 3-9-4 **60**....................(tp[1]) JasonHart 13 19
(Simon West) *hld up on nr side of gp: struggling over 2f out: sn btn* **66/1**

5644 **12** ½ **Sunnua (IRE)**[31] 7249 4-9-3 **57**.................... TonyHamilton 11 16
(Richard Fahey) *prom: lost pl 3f out: n.d after* **18/1**

0630 **13** ¾ **Tilly Tinker**[114] 4209 3-8-9 **58**....................(b[1]) HarrisonShaw(7) 8 14
(Michael Easterby) *led to over 2f out: rdn and wknd over 1f out* **66/1**

1m 26.43s (0.23) **Going Correction** 0.0s/f (Stan)
**WFA** 3 from 4yo+ 2lb **13** Ran SP% **116.2**
Speed ratings (Par 101): **98,97,95,92,92 89,86,82,81,77 77,76,75**
Pick Six. Not Won. Pool of 2,572.72 carried forward to today. Tote Aggregate: 2017: 215,723 - 2016: 112,486 CSF £49.91 CT £326.50 TOTE £6.90: £2.60, £2.40, £2.10; EX 49.50 Trifecta £392.10.
**Owner** A L R Morton **Bred** P And Mrs A G Venner **Trained** Portway, Worcs
■ Stewards' Enquiry : Adam Beschizza two-day ban; used whip above permitted level (Nov 3-4); caution; careless riding

**FOCUS**
A modest handicap.

## 8211 GLOBAL NORTH EAST TRICK OR TREAT H'CAP 6f (Tp)
**8:15** (8:17) (Class 5) (0-75,75) 3-Y-O+ **£2,911** (£866; £432; £216) **Stalls** Centre

Form RPR

0062 **1** **Major Crispies**[21] 7572 6-9-2 **70**....................(b) DavidNolan 5 79
(David O'Meara) *hld up: smooth hdwy on far side of gp over 1f out: led ins fnl f: pushed out* **11/1**

2000 **2** *nk* **Samarmadi**[31] 7244 3-9-3 **72**....................(p[1]) JackMitchell 10 80
(Hugo Palmer) *hld up on nr side of gp: hdwy to ld over 1f out: rdn and hdd ins fnl f: kpt on: hld nr fin* **7/1**

2021 **3** *nk* **Atholblair Boy (IRE)**[21] 7572 4-9-4 **72**.................... AndrewMullen 13 79
(Nigel Tinkler) *hld up: hdwy nr side of gp over 1f out: effrt and ch ins fnl f: kpt on: hld cl home* **4/1**[1]

0055 **4** 1¾ **Perfect Symphony (IRE)**[21] 7572 3-9-2 **71**....................(p) KevinStott 7 72+
(Kevin Ryan) *hld up in centre of gp: hdwy over 1f out: swtchd lft ins fnl f: kpt on same pce last 75yds* **11/2**[3]

0420 **5** 1¼ **Avenue Of Stars**[38] 7017 4-8-11 **65**....................(p) PJMcDonald 12 62
(Karen McLintock) *hld up in tch on nr side of gp: rdn and edgd lft over 2f out: rallied over 1f out: no imp fnl f* **18/1**

3325 **6** *shd* **The Amber Fort (USA)**[27] 7408 3-8-12 **70**.................... JoshDoyle(3) 8 67
(David O'Meara) *hld up in centre of gp: effrt and rdn over 2f out: kpt on same pce fnl f* **7/1**

1350 **7** 2¾ **Mr Orange (IRE)**[22] 7554 4-9-4 **72**....................(p) DougieCostello 11 60
(Paul Midgley) *prom on nr side of gp: drvn along over 2f out: outpcd fnl f* **28/1**

3200 **8** ½ **My Dad Syd (USA)**[49] 6663 5-9-6 **74**....................(b) JosephineGordon 1 61
(Ian Williams) *cl up on far side of gp: rdn over 2f out: wknd over 1f out* **9/2**[2]

4310 **9** *nk* **Manatee Bay**[31] 7245 7-9-0 **75**....................(p) NatalieHambling(7) 3 61
(Noel Wilson) *t.k.h: cl up on far side of gp: effrt and ev ch over 2f out: wknd fnl f* **33/1**

4315 **10** *hd* **Hamish McGonagain**[59] 6298 4-9-2 **70**....................(p) DanielTudhope 9 55
(David O'Meara) *led in centre of gp to over 2f out: rdn and wknd over 1f out* **12/1**

6304 **11** ½ **Control Centre (IRE)**[74] 5697 3-9-2 **71**....................(p) BarryMcHugh 4 54
(Marjorie Fife) *chsd ldrs in centre of gp: effrt and rdn over 2f out: outpcd whn hmpd ins fnl f: sn btn* **40/1**

0250 **12** *3 1/4* **Benjamin Thomas (IRE)**[49] 6663 3-9-1 **70**.......................(v) JasonHart 6 43
(John Quinn) *s.i.s: hld up: rdn and struggling over 2f out: sn btn* **16/1**
1m 11.81s (-0.69) **Going Correction** 0.0s/f (Stan)
**WFA** 3 from 4yo+ 1lb **12** Ran SP% **114.6**
Speed ratings (Par 103): **104,103,103,100,99 99,95,94,94,94 93,89**
CSF £81.72 CT £368.96 TOTE £11.70: £3.40, £2.40, £1.80; EX 100.70 Trifecta £422.90.
**Owner** The Roses Partnership II **Bred** Lowther Racing **Trained** Upper Helmsley, N Yorks

**FOCUS**
A competitive sprint handicap, in which they went a good pace, and this suited the closers. The second has been rated back to the level of his AW handicap debut.
T/Plt: £85.70 to a £1 stake. Pool: £51,553.65 - 601.43 winning units. T/Qpdt: £13.30 to a £1 stake. Pool: £7,463.43 - 558.80 winning units. **Richard Young**

# 7818 REDCAR (L-H)
## Friday, October 20

**OFFICIAL GOING: Good to soft (7.7)**
Wind: Virtually nil Weather: Overcast

## 8212 ALL NEW RACINGUK.COM BRITISH EBF NOVICE STKS 5f 217y
**1:30** (1:30) (Class 5) 2-Y-O **£3,396** (£1,010; £505; £252) **Stalls** Centre

Form RPR
65 **1** **Nicklaus**[23] 7511 2-9-2 0.................................................. DanielTudhope 8 73
(William Haggas) *wnt rt s: sn trckd ldrs: pushed along to chal over 1f out: rdn and kpt on fnl f: led post* **11/10**[1]
2 **2** *hd* **Wrenthorpe**[21] 7562 2-8-13 0.................................. AdamMcNamara(3) 5 72
(Bryan Smart) *led narrowly: rdn appr fnl f: hung persistently lft ins fnl f: hdd post* **9/2**[3]
50 **3** *1* **Enrolment**[30] 7269 2-8-11 0.............................................. TonyHamilton 6 64
(Richard Fahey) *pressed ldr: rdn 2f out: one pce ins fnl f* **9/1**
553 **4** *1 1/4* **Saisons D'Or (IRE)**[42] 6897 2-9-2 74.................................. GrahamLee 4 65
(Jedd O'Keeffe) *prom: rdn 2f out: no ex fnl f* **2/1**[2]
60 **5** *2 1/2* **Shakiah (IRE)**[21] 7563 2-8-11 0.......................................... PaddyAspell 2 53
(Sharon Watt) *chsd ldrs: rdn over 2f out: wknd over 1f out* **66/1**
**6** *5* **Becker** 2-9-2 0.................................................................. PaulMulrennan 3 43
(James Given) *hld up: rdn over 2f out: wknd over 1f out* **25/1**
05 **7** *10* **Watching Spirits**[22] 7551 2-9-2 0.................................. DougieCostello 7 13
(Ann Duffield) *trckd ldrs. rdn over 2f out: sn wknd and bhd* **33/1**
1m 12.7s (0.90) **Going Correction** +0.175s/f (Good) **7** Ran SP% **117.4**
Speed ratings (Par 95): **101,100,99,97,94 87,74**
CSF £6.95 TOTE £1.80: £1.10, £3.20; EX 7.50 Trifecta £35.20.
**Owner** M J Jooste **Bred** Stiftung Gestut Fahrhof **Trained** Newmarket, Suffolk
■ National Anthem was withdrawn. Price at time of withdrawal 9-2. Rule 4 applies to bets placed prior to withdrawal but no to SP bets - deduction 15p in the pound. New market formed.

**FOCUS**
The going was given as good to soft (GoingStick: 7.7). No more than a fair novice.

## 8213 RACING UK PROFITS RETURNED TO RACING CLAIMING STKS 7f
**2:00** (2:00) (Class 6) 2-Y-O **£3,234** (£962; £481; £240) **Stalls** Centre

Form RPR
03 **1** **One For June (IRE)**[8] 7985 2-8-7 70.............................(p[1]) JoeFanning 8 60
(William Haggas) *trckd ldrs: rdn over 2f out: chal strly fnl f: kpt on: led post* **11/4**[1]
2031 **2** *nse* **Grimeford Lane (IRE)**[13] 7827 2-8-13 65.................(p) PaulMulrennan 1 66
(Michael Dods) *trckd ldrs: rdn over 2f out: chal strly fnl f: kpt on* **4/1**[3]
6461 **3** *shd* **Montague (IRE)**[8] 7985 2-9-7 72.................................. DougieCostello 2 74
(Jamie Osborne) *led: taken to far rail 4f out: pushed along 2f out: drvn appr fnl f: sn strly pressed: kpt on: lost 2 pls post* **7/2**[2]
0426 **4** *8* **Foxy Lady**[10] 7938 2-8-10 64.................................................. TomEaves 6 41
(Kevin Ryan) *prom: rdn over 2f out: wknd over 1f out* **6/1**
0300 **5** *1/2* **Hamba Moyo (IRE)**[41] 6940 2-8-6 52.......................(p) DuranFentiman 7 36
(Tim Easterby) *prom: rdn over 2f out: wknd over 1f out* **50/1**
3625 **6** *1* **Panophobia**[20] 7624 2-8-12 66.......................................... TonyHamilton 5 39
(Richard Fahey) *midfield: rdn over 2f out: sn no imp and btn* **4/1**[3]
30 **7** *nk* **Fabella Bere (FR)**[106] 4528 2-8-13 0.............................. JoeyHaynes 9 39
(K R Burke) *hld up: nvr threatened* **20/1**
6405 **8** *6* **Miss Mazzie**[13] 7827 2-8-3 47............................................ CamHardie 10 13
(Michael Easterby) *midfield: rdn over 3f out: sn btn* **66/1**
**9** *9* **Bobbie Green (IRE)** 2-9-0 0............................................ JasonHart 4
(Tim Easterby) *s.i.s: a rr* **33/1**
1m 25.15s (0.65) **Going Correction** +0.175s/f (Good) **9** Ran SP% **114.3**
Speed ratings (Par 93): **103,102,102,93,93 91,91,84,74**
CSF £13.41 TOTE £3.30: £1.20, £1.30, £1.30; EX 15.60 Trifecta £41.80.
**Owner** Scotney/Symonds/Fisher Partnership **Bred** N O'Callaghan **Trained** Newmarket, Suffolk
■ Stewards' Enquiry : Joe Fanning two-day ban; using his whip above the permitted level (Nov 3rd-4th)
Paul Mulrennan four-day ban; using his whip above the permitted level (Nov 3rd-4th, 6th-7th)

**FOCUS**
A tight finish between the first three in this ordinary claimer.

## 8214 SAM HALL MEMORIAL H'CAP 1m 5f 218y
**2:35** (2:36) (Class 5) (0-75,76) 3-Y-O+ **£3,396** (£1,010; £505; £252) **Stalls** Low

Form RPR
2040 **1** **Ingleby Hollow**[21] 7561 5-9-4 **63**................................(t[1]) DanielTudhope 11 71+
(David O'Meara) *stdd s: hld up in rr: smooth hdwy over 3f out: led 2f out: rdn and in command over 1f out: drvn out ins fnl f* **8/1**
5454 **2** *1* **Sheriff Garrett (IRE)**[19] 7659 3-9-3 **69**............................(p) JasonHart 10 74
(Tim Easterby) *hld up: rdn and hdwy on outer over 3f out: chsd ldr 2f out: styd on but a hld* **11/2**[3]
2000 **3** *1 1/2* **Saved By The Bell (IRE)**[29] 7330 7-9-4 **70**.............. HarrisonShaw(7) 8 73
(Lawrence Mullaney) *prom: rdn over 3f out: led wl over 2f out: hdd 2f out: plugged on* **25/1**
/0-6 **4** *nse* **Caged Lightning (IRE)**[29] 7319 7-9-6 **70**..................(p) FinleyMarsh(5) 3 73
(Steve Gollings) *midfield: rdn over 3f out: styd on same pce* **5/1**[2]
6010 **5** *2 1/4* **Big Time Dancer (IRE)**[13] 7824 4-9-4 **63**....................(p) JoeyHaynes 1 63
(Brian Ellison) *trckd ldrs: rdn over 2f out: no ex fnl f* **11/1**
2146 **6** *1 1/2* **Montanna**[28] 7359 3-9-10 **76**............................................... GrahamLee 4 74
(Jedd O'Keeffe) *hld up: drvn in rr over 4f out: bhd tl styd on fnl f* **3/1**[1]
1000 **7** *4 1/2* **Mr Globetrotter (USA)**[17] 7386 4-9-7 **73**.............(p[1]) JamieGormley(7) 7 64
(Iain Jardine) *midfield: rdn over 3f out: wknd over 2f out* **14/1**
4126 **8** *4 1/2* **Stanarley Pic**[19] 7659 6-9-3 **62**............................................ NeilFarley 9 47
(Sally Haynes) *led: rdn whn hdd wl over 2f out: wknd over 1f out* **15/2**
3040 **9** *5* **Midnight Warrior**[27] 7387 7-8-9 **57**...........................(t) RowanScott(3) 12 35
(Ron Barr) *prom: rdn over 3f out: wknd over 2f out* **33/1**
3501 **10** *dist* **Deep Challenger (IRE)**[13] 7832 5-10-0 **73**.................. DougieCostello 6
(Jamie Osborne) *hld up in midfield: rdn and wknd over 3f out: eased and t.o* **6/1**
3m 8.15s (3.45) **Going Correction** +0.325s/f (Good)
**WFA** 3 from 4yo+ 7lb **10** Ran SP% **116.0**
Speed ratings (Par 103): **103,102,101,101,100 99,96,94,91,**
CSF £51.32 CT £1056.37 TOTE £8.20: £3.20, £2.30, £8.00; EX 63.40 Trifecta £1247.40.
**Owner** Dave Scott & The Fallen Angels **Bred** Dave Scott **Trained** Upper Helmsley, N Yorks

**FOCUS**
A modest handicap in which the first two came from the back of the field. The winner has been rated to this year's form.

## 8215 MARKET CROSS JEWELLERS BRITISH EBF NOVICE STKS (PLUS 10 RACE) 7f 219y
**3:10** (3:12) (Class 4) 2-Y-O **£6,469** (£1,925; £962; £481) **Stalls** Centre

Form RPR
2 **1** **Stephensons Rocket (IRE)**[35] 7128 2-9-2 0................. PatCosgrave 9 82+
(Ed Walker) *trckd ldrs: racd keenly: led gng wl over 1f out: pushed clr fnl f: easily* **2/5**[1]
6 **2** *3 1/2* **Hazarfan**[13] 7810 2-9-2 0.................................................... TomEaves 10 70
(Ed Dunlop) *led: rdn over 2f out: hdd over 1f out: one pce and no ch wnr* **5/1**[2]
**3** *1* **The Navigator** 2-9-2 0................................................ TonyHamilton 2 68
(Richard Fahey) *midfield: pushed along and hdwy over 1f out: rdn and hung lft jst ins fnl f: kpt on* **14/1**
00 **4** *3 3/4* **Power Sail**[7] 8013 2-9-2 0............................................. DuranFentiman 8 59
(Tim Easterby) *trckd ldrs: rdn 2f out: wknd ins fnl f* **80/1**
5 **5** *1 1/2* **Mafdet**[84] 5372 2-8-11 0...................................................... GrahamLee 1 51
(Bryan Smart) *hld up: pushed along over 2f out: rdn over 1f out: nvr threatened* **25/1**
520 **6** *3 3/4* **Se You**[13] 7814 2-9-2 74...................................................... JasonHart 7 47
(Tim Easterby) *prom: rdn 2f out: wknd appr fnl f* **8/1**[3]
0 **7** *1 1/2* **Encryption (IRE)**[31] 7237 2-9-2 0.................................. JamieSpencer 6 44
(George Scott) *dwlt: hld up: pushed along 3f out: nvr threatened* **8/1**[3]
**8** *7* **Teatro (IRE)** 2-9-2 0.................................................... PaulMulrennan 3 27
(James Given) *rn green and a rr* **33/1**
1m 39.36s (2.76) **Going Correction** +0.175s/f (Good) **8** Ran SP% **125.0**
Speed ratings (Par 97): **93,89,88,84,83 79,78,71**
CSF £3.49 TOTE £1.20: £1.02, £1.50, £3.30; EX 3.70 Trifecta £13.70.
**Owner** B E Nielsen **Bred** Team Hogdala Ab **Trained** Upper Lambourn, Berks

**FOCUS**
This proved straightforward enough for the odds-on favourite.

## 8216 RACING UK IN GLORIOUS HD H'CAP 7f
**3:45** (3:47) (Class 5) (0-70,70) 3-Y-O+ **£3,396** (£1,010; £505; £252) **Stalls** Centre

Form RPR
0066 **1** **Hitman**[11] 7888 4-8-13 **62**............................................................ JFEgan 19 70
(Rebecca Bastiman) *hld up: pushed along and gd hdwy on outer over 2f out: rdn to ld ins fnl f: kpt on wl* **11/1**
0662 **2** *3/4* **Grinty (IRE)**[31] 7249 3-8-13 **64**..................................... PaulMulrennan 17 69
(Michael Dods) *trckd ldrs: rdn over 2f out: ev ch ent fnl f: kpt on* **10/1**
2000 **3** *3/4* **Call Out Loud**[35] 7108 5-9-7 **70**...............................(v) AlistairRawlinson 10 74
(Michael Appleby) *prom: rdn to ld over 2f out: hdd ins fnl f: one pce* **16/1**
6155 **4** *1/2* **Stubytuesday**[49] 6664 3-9-3 **68**............................................ PhillipMakin 20 70
(Michael Easterby) *midfield: rdn over 2f out: kpt on fnl f* **16/1**
-040 **5** *1 1/4* **Lanjano**[53] 6519 3-9-5 **70**........................................................ KevinStott 3 69
(Kevin Ryan) *chsd ldrs: rdn over 2f out: no ex fnl 110yds* **11/1**
1333 **6** *shd* **Relight My Fire**[24] 7474 7-9-2 **65**...........................(p) DuranFentiman 11 64
(Tim Easterby) *chsd ldrs: rdn over 2f out: no ex fnl 110yds* **16/1**
5100 **7** *3/4* **Rose Eclair**[21] 7573 4-8-7 **63**................................(p) RobertDodsworth(7) 18 60
(Tim Easterby) *s.i.s: hld up in midfield: rdn over 2f out: one pce and nvr threatened* **20/1**
5530 **8** *nk* **Teomaria**[17] 7710 3-8-11 **65**............................................ CliffordLee(3) 16 61
(K R Burke) *a midfield* **25/1**
1350 **9** *hd* **Whitkirk**[21] 7571 4-9-5 **68**.................................................. GrahamLee 2 64
(Jedd O'Keeffe) *a midfield* **7/1**[2]
5003 **10** *nk* **Dutch Artist (IRE)**[11] 7894 5-9-0 **66**.........................(b) JoshDoyle(3) 5 61
(Alan Brown) *slowly away: hld up in rr: minor late hdwy: nvr threatened* **10/1**
3322 **11** *1/2* **Showdance Kid**[10] 7934 3-9-2 **67**..........................(b[1]) DougieCostello 15 60
(Neville Bycroft) *midfield: hdwy and in tch gng wl over 2f out: rdn over 1f out: wknd ins fnl f* **8/1**[3]
532 **12** *3/4* **Essential**[31] 7247 3-9-2 **67**.......................................(p[1]) JamieSpencer 7 58
(George Scott) *hld up: rdn over 2f out: minor late hdwy whn short of room nr fin* **11/1**
221 **13** *1/2* **Van Velde (IRE)**[31] 7247 3-9-3 **68**..............................(p) JasonHart 8 58
(John Quinn) *hld up in midfield: rdn over 3f out: sn btn* **7/1**[2]
1101 **14** *1* **Rosy Ryan (IRE)**[52] 6564 7-8-11 **67**......................... SeamusCronin(7) 6 55
(Tina Jackson) *hld up in midfield: rdn over 3f out: sn btn* **6/1**[1]
0000 **15** *3/4* **Secret Missile**[10] 7933 7-8-9 **65**............................ HarrisonShaw(7) 1 51
(David C Griffiths) *a towards rr* **40/1**
0205 **16** *3* **Ellaal**[14] 7792 8-8-13 **62**........................................(p) JamesSullivan 4 40
(Ruth Carr) *led: rdn whn hdd over 2f out: sn wknd* **14/1**
1m 25.44s (0.94) **Going Correction** +0.175s/f (Good)
**WFA** 3 from 4yo+ 2lb **16** Ran SP% **128.9**
Speed ratings (Par 103): **101,100,99,98,97 97,96,95,95,95 94,93,93,92,91 87**
CSF £120.85 CT £1798.09 TOTE £12.30: £2.60, £3.60, £4.50, £4.90; EX 208.60 Trifecta £5657.60.
**Owner** Ms M Austerfield **Bred** Carmel Stud **Trained** Cowthorpe, N Yorks
■ Stewards' Enquiry : J F Egan two-day ban; using his whip above the permitted level (Nov 3rd-4th)

**FOCUS**
A modest handicap which saw the principals race centre to stands' side. It's been rated as ordinary form.

## 8217 WATCH RACING UK ANYWHERE MAIDEN STKS 5f 217y
**4:20** (4:24) (Class 5) 3-Y-O+ **£3,396** (£1,010; £505; £252) **Stalls** Centre

Form RPR
54 **1** **Give It Some Teddy**[173] 2185 3-9-5 0.................................. JasonHart 7 63+
(Tim Easterby) *dwlt: hld up: pushed along and outpcd 1/2-way: stl plenty to do over 1f out: r.o strly fnl f: led fnl 30yds* **7/2**[2]
5004 **2** *1 3/4* **Henrietta's Dream**[48] 6694 3-9-0 44.................................(b) TomEaves 2 52
(John Wainwright) *chsd ldr: rdn to ld appr fnl f: one pce and hdd 30yds out* **100/1**
2 **3** *1/2* **Vive La Difference (IRE)**[27] 7388 3-9-5 70................. DuranFentiman 1 55
(Tim Easterby) *led: rdn over 2f out: hdd appr fnl f* **11/8**[1]

2030 **4** 4½ **Mighty Bond**[19] 7660 5-9-6 47............(p) BarryMcHugh 11 41
(Tracy Waggott) *chsd ldr: rdn over 2f out: wknd fnl f* **40/1**

022 **5** ¾ **Dandys Denouement**[93] 5019 3-9-0 79............ BenRobinson(5) 12 39
(Brian Ellison) *chsd ldr: rdn over 2f out: hing lft over 1f out: wknd ins fnl f* **11/2**[3]

4 **6** 1 **Captain Bond**[239] 878 3-9-2 0............ JoshDoyle(3) 8 35
(David O'Meara) *trckd ldr: rdn over 2f out: wknd fnl f* **11/1**

**7** hd **Limoncino (IRE)** 3-9-0 0............(h[1]) PaulMulrennan 10 30
(Michael Dods) *slowly away: sn pushed along: bhd tl minor late hdwy* **8/1**

0-6P **8** 5 **Ninedarter**[116] 4164 3-8-12 0............ WilliamCox(7) 6 19
(Antony Brittain) *midfield: rdn 1/2-way: wknd over 1f out* **100/1**

**9** 1¾ **Wind Turbine (IRE)** 3-9-5 0............ PaulQuinn 3 13
(Tim Easterby) *a towards rr* **25/1**

4-00 **10** ¾ **Faulkwood**[10] 7932 3-9-2 65............(v) CliffordLee(3) 5 11
(K R Burke) *chsd ldrs: rdn over 2f out: wknd over 1f out* **11/1**

253- **11** 10 **Lucata (IRE)**[541] 1776 3-9-2 67............ LewisEdmunds(3) 9
(Alan Berry) *a rr* **25/1**

1m 13.05s (1.25) **Going Correction** +0.175s/f (Good)
**WFA** 3 from 5yo 1lb **11** Ran SP% **119.6**
Speed ratings (Par 103): **98,95,95,89,88 86,86,79,77,76 63**
CSF £338.05 TOTE £4.30: £1.70, £11.90, £1.10; EX 213.40 Trifecta £595.90.
**Owner** Lee Bond **Bred** Usk Valley Stud **Trained** Great Habton, N Yorks

**FOCUS**
This turned out to be a pretty weak maiden. It's been rated cautiously.

## 8218 WATCH RACE REPLAYS AT RACINGUK.COM H'CAP (FOR LADY AMATEUR RIDERS) (DIV I) 1m 2f 1y
**4:55** (4:58) (Class 6) (0-65,67) 3-Y-0+ **£3,293** (£1,013; £506) **Stalls** Low

Form RPR

0362 **1** **Restive (IRE)**[10] 7936 4-10-7 **62**............ MissSBrotherton 10 69
(Iain Jardine) *hld up: pushed along and stdy hdwy fr 3f out: styd on wl fnl f: led fnl 75yds* **10/3**[1]

0503 **2** 1 **Almunther (IRE)**[24] 7478 4-10-0 **55**............(t) MissBeckySmith 4 60
(Micky Hammond) *dwlt: sn trckd ldrs: rdn to ld wl over 1f out: edgd rt fnl f: hdd 75yds: one pce* **8/1**

0116 **3** 2¼ **Bigbadboy (IRE)**[57] 6346 4-9-8 **54**............ MissEllaMcCain(5) 5 55
(Clive Mulhall) *trckd ldrs: rdn over 2f out: one pce in 3rd ins fnl f* **9/1**

5140 **4** 3¾ **Akamanto (IRE)**[34] 7162 3-10-6 **65**............ MissCWalton 9 60
(R Mike Smith) *midfield: rdn over 2f out: plugged on fnl f: nvr threatened ldrs* **25/1**

3442 **5** hd **Relevant (IRE)**[32] 7224 3-10-8 **67**............ MsKWalsh 6 62
(K R Burke) *hld up: rdn along 4f out: styd on fnl f: nvr threatened* **7/2**[2]

0646 **6** nk **Rock Island Line**[28] 7360 3-9-13 **58**............ MissETodd 2 53
(Mark Walford) *midfield: rdn over 2f out: bit short of room and swtchd rt over 1f out: kpt on fnl f* **6/1**

3500 **7** 2¾ **Polar Forest**[9] 7960 7-10-12 **67**............(p) MissJoannaMason 14 56
(Richard Guest) *prom: rdn to ld over 2f out: hdd wl over 1f out: wknd fnl f* **11/1**

6154 **8** 1 **Bollin Ted**[24] 7479 3-9-12 **60**............ MissEEasterby(3) 8 48
(Tim Easterby) *led: rdn whn hdd over 2f out: wknd over 1f out* **11/2**[3]

6030 **9** 4½ **True Colors**[22] 7541 3-10-5 **64**............ MissAnnaHesketh 3 44
(Richard Fahey) *midfield: rdn over 3f out: wknd fnl over 1f out* **11/1**

-550 **10** 6 **Highwayman**[203] 1469 4-9-13 **57**............ MissAMcCain(3) 7 25
(David Thompson) *hld up: rdn over 3f out: sn wknd* **25/1**

-000 **11** 2¾ **Southview Lady**[79] 5544 5-9-0 **48** oh3............ MissMDabrowski(7) 11 11
(Sean Regan) *chsd ldrs: lost pl over 5f out: rdn over 3f out: sn wknd* **100/1**

/0-0 **12** 3½ **Jordaura**[286] 123 11-9-3 **49**............ MissEmilyBullock(5) 1 6
(Alan Berry) *a towards rr* **66/1**

0256 **13** 2 **Graceful Act**[24] 7479 9-9-8 **49**............(p) MrsCBartley 13 2
(Ron Barr) *midfield on outer: rdn over 3f out: sn wknd* **20/1**

2m 10.04s (2.94) **Going Correction** +0.325s/f (Good)
**WFA** 3 from 4yo+ 4lb **13** Ran SP% **127.7**
Speed ratings (Par 101): **101,100,98,95,95 95,92,92,88,83 81,78,77**
CSF £31.35 CT £233.73 TOTE £3.90: £1.50, £2.30, £2.90; EX 35.70 Trifecta £368.50.
**Owner** I J Jardine **Bred** Epona Bloodstock Ltd **Trained** Carrutherstown, D'fries & G'way

**FOCUS**
An ordinary handicap.

## 8219 WATCH RACE REPLAYS AT RACINGUK.COM H'CAP (FOR LADY AMATEUR RIDERS) (DIV II) 1m 2f 1y
**5:25** (5:26) (Class 6) (0-65,66) 3-Y-0+ **£3,293** (£1,013; £506) **Stalls** Low

Form RPR

0000 **1** **Ingleby Spring (IRE)**[17] 7704 5-9-3 **50**............ MissEllaMcCain(5) 6 56
(Richard Fahey) *midfield: hdwy over 3f out: led narrowly over 2f out: sn rdn: styd on: all out* **11/2**[3]

5000 **2** shd **Pindaric**[30] 7270 3-8-12 **49** oh1............(p) MissEmilyBullock(5) 13 56
(Alan Lockwood) *prom towards outer: rdn to ld over 3f out: hdd over 2f out: remained cl up: styd on: jst failed* **20/1**

3510 **3** 2½ **Decima (IRE)**[9] 7960 3-10-6 **66**............ MissJoannaMason 7 68
(Michael Easterby) *hld up in midfield: rdn over 3f out: styd on fr over 1f out: wnt 3rd fnl 110yds: no threat ldng pair* **5/1**[2]

0300 **4** 2½ **Dream Free**[31] 7236 4-9-13 **55**............(p) MissETodd 12 52
(Mark Walford) *chsd ldrs: rdn over 3f out: no ex fnl f* **14/1**

-600 **5** ½ **Indian Vision (IRE)**[52] 6564 3-9-6 **52**............ MissBeckySmith 11 49
(Micky Hammond) *dwlt: hld up in rr: rdn 3f out: styd on fr over 1f out: nrst fin* **16/1**

0100 **6** 1¼ **Hannington**[15] 7761 6-10-4 **60**............(t) MissSBrotherton 2 54
(Michael Appleby) *hld up: rdn over 3f out: plugged on nvr threatened* **3/1**[1]

1303 **7** 1¾ **Haymarket**[55] 6431 8-10-7 **63**............ MrsCBartley 10 54
(R Mike Smith) *prom: rdn over 3f out: wknd over 1f out* **11/1**

5425 **8** 1¾ **Champagne Pink (FR)**[10] 7936 3-10-2 **62**............(h) MissAnnaHesketh 8 50
(K R Burke) *midfield: rdn 3f out: wknd over 1f out* **5/1**[2]

5506 **9** 10 **Duke Of Yorkshire**[63] 6126 7-10-4 **63**............(p) MissEEasterby(3) 3 32
(Tim Easterby) *a towards rr* **15/2**

0300 **10** 1 **Ferngrove (USA)**[11] 7885 6-9-7 **49** oh3............(t) MissCWalton 1 17
(Susan Corbett) *led: rdn whn hdd 3f out: wknd qckly* **33/1**

000 **11** 1½ **Optima Petamus**[19] 7659 5-9-11 **56**............(p) MissAMcCain(3) 9 21
(Patrick Holmes) *chsd ldrs: rdn over 3f out: wknd* **20/1**

2m 11.88s (4.78) **Going Correction** +0.325s/f (Good)
**WFA** 3 from 4yo+ 4lb **11** Ran SP% **118.8**
Speed ratings (Par 101): **93,92,90,88,88 87,86,84,76,75 74**
CSF £113.16 CT £590.66 TOTE £6.20: £2.00, £9.10, £1.50; EX 172.20 Trifecta £1248.00.
**Owner** Percy Green Racing 3 **Bred** Stephanie Von Schilcher & Gavan Kinch **Trained** Musley Bank, N Yorks

**FOCUS**
The slower of the two divisions by 1.84sec.

T/Jkpt: Not won. T/Plt: £50.50 to a £1 stake. Pool: £68,320.39 - 986.01 winning units. T/Qpdt: £28.10 to a £1 stake. Pool: £6,847.15 - 179.76 winning units. **Andrew Sheret**

8220 - 8221a (Foreign Racing) - See Raceform Interactive

# 8015 DUNDALK (A.W) (L-H)
Friday, October 20

**OFFICIAL GOING: Polytrack: standard**

## 8222a BOOK YOUR CHRISTMAS PARTY AT DUNDALK H'CAP 7f (P)
**6:30** (6:31) (70-100,96) 3-Y-0+ **£13,666** (£4,222; £2,000; £888; £333)

RPR

**1** **Katiymann (IRE)**[7] 8018 5-9-7 **87**............(t) PatSmullen 9 94+
(M Halford, Ire) *hld up towards rr: hdwy nr side fr under 2f out to chse ldrs ins fnl f: r.o wl to ld cl home* **5/2**[1]

**2** nk **Fuwairt (IRE)**[13] 7839 5-9-7 **87**............(t) RonanWhelan 4 93
(Gavin Cromwell, Ire) *hld up in rr of mid-div: swtchd lft 2f out and prog to chse ldrs in 3rd over 1f out: sn rdn in 2nd and impr to ld briefly wl ins fnl f tl hdd cl home* **10/1**

**3** ¾ **Cenotaph (USA)**[79] 5530 5-9-9 **89**............ DonnachaO'Brien 11 93
(A P O'Brien, Ire) *mid-div: pushed along 2f out and prog nr side 1f out where rdn: disp 3rd u.p ins fnl f: kpt on same pce clsng stages: hld* **5/1**[2]

**4** nse **Grey Danube (IRE)**[189] 1769 8-9-13 **93**............(bt) ChrisHayes 5 97
(D J Bunyan, Ire) *cl up tl sn led: stl gng wl 2f out: rdn far side 1 1/2f out and hdd u.p wl ins fnl f: no ex clsng stages where dropped to 4th* **20/1**

**5** ½ **Atlas (IRE)**[7] 8018 4-9-6 **86**............(b) LeighRoche 6 88
(Denis Gerard Hogan, Ire) *in rr of mid-div: gng wl 2f out: nt clr run over 1f out: sn swtchd lft and sme late hdwy between horses into 5th wl ins fnl f: nvr trbld ldrs* **5/1**[2]

**6** hd **Have A Nice Day**[21] 7587 7-9-5 **90**............(p) KillianLeonard(5) 7 92
(John James Feane, Ire) *chsd ldrs: rdn 2f out and no imp on ldrs ins fnl f: kpt on same pce* **10/1**

**7** ¾ **Time To Reason (IRE)**[21] 7587 4-9-7 **87**............ ShaneFoley 1 87
(J P Murtagh, Ire) *chsd ldrs: rdn far side under 2f out and no ex ins fnl f: one pce clsng stages* **20/1**

**8** ½ **Rapid Applause**[40] 6971 5-9-6 **86**............ SeamieHeffernan 3 85
(M D O'Callaghan, Ire) *hld up in rr of mid-div: nt clr run under 2f out: swtchd rt and rdn towards rr 1 1/2f out: kpt on u.p nr side ins fnl f: nvr nrr* **33/1**

**9** nk **Red Avenger (USA)**[7] 8018 7-9-4 **84**............ RoryCleary 13 82
(Damian Joseph English, Ire) *hooded to load: towards rr: rdn 2f out and kpt on u.p fr over 1f out: nvr nrr* **33/1**

**10** 1 **Aventinus (IRE)**[35] 7118 3-9-7 **89**............(p[1]) WJLee 10 83
(Hugo Palmer) *chsd ldrs tl impr into 2nd after 2f: pushed along over 2f out: sn rdn in 3rd and no ex 1f out: wknd* **8/1**[3]

**11** ¾ **Tribal Path (IRE)**[6] 8050 7-9-2 **82**............(t) DeclanMcDonogh 14 75
(Damian Joseph English, Ire) *chsd ldrs: 4th 1/2-way: pushed along 2f out and sn no ex u.p: wknd fnl f* **22/1**

**12** ¾ **Geological (IRE)**[7] 8018 5-9-8 **93**............ DonaghO'Connor(5) 8 84
(Damian Joseph English, Ire) *chsd ldrs: 3rd 1/2-way: rdn 2f out and sn no imp on ldrs: wknd* **14/1**

**13** 2½ **St Brelades Bay (IRE)**[54] 6489 5-9-9 **89**............ ColmO'Donoghue 2 73
(Mrs John Harrington, Ire) *broke wl to ld tl sn hdd and settled bhd ldrs: 5th 1/2-way: short of room briefly under 2f out and dropped to mid-div: swtchd lft over 1f out and sn eased* **14/1**

**14** 3¼ **Lightening Fast**[79] 5552 3-10-0 **96**............(b[1]) ColinKeane 12 70
(G M Lyons, Ire) *in rr thrght: pushed along 2f out and no imp over 1f out: eased ins fnl f* **14/1**

1m 24.93s (-0.17) **Going Correction** 0.0s/f (Stan)
**WFA** 3 from 4yo+ 2lb **14** Ran SP% **131.0**
Speed ratings: **100,99,98,98,98 97,97,96,96,95 94,93,90,86**
CSF £29.54 CT £130.26 TOTE £3.50: £1.30, £3.50, £1.90; DF 37.20 Trifecta £232.70. **Owner** Paul Rooney **Bred** His Highness The Aga Khan's Studs S C **Trained** Doneany, Co Kildare

**FOCUS**
A race of contrasting fortunes as hold-up horses proved at an advantage. The standard is set by the second down to the sixth.

8223 - 8224a (Foreign Racing) - See Raceform Interactive

## 8225a AL BASTI EQUIWORLD MERCURY STKS (LISTED) 5f (P)
**8:00** (8:01) 2-Y-0+ **£23,952** (£7,713; £3,653; £1,623; £811; £405)

RPR

**1** **Take Cover**[27] 7396 10-10-2 113............ DavidAllan 1 109
(David C Griffiths) *broke wl to ld: stl gng wl fr 1/2-way: edgd rt under 2f out and brought to nr side where sn jnd: rdn and hdd narrowly ins fnl f: kpt on wl u.p to regain advantage cl home* **8/11**[1]

**2** nk **Hit The Bid**[27] 7396 3-10-2 107............(t) LeighRoche 8 109
(D J Bunyan, Ire) *trckd ldrs: prog nr side to chal 1 1/2f out: rdn to ld narrowly ins fnl f: all out wl ins fnl f and hdd cl home* **16/1**

**3** 1½ **Declarationofpeace (USA)**[14] 7794 2-8-9 107............(t) WayneLordan 11 94
(A P O'Brien, Ire) *hld up in mid-div: gng wl after 1/2-way and hdwy nr side to chse ldrs over 1f out where swtchd lft: no imp on ldrs in 3rd wl ins fnl f: kpt on same pce* **9/2**[2]

**4** ¾ **Moviesta (USA)**[21] 7587 7-9-13 112............(v) RobbieDowney 14 97
(Edward Lynam, Ire) *hld up: rdn in 11th under 2f out and hdwy nr side to chse ldrs in 4th wl ins fnl f: kpt on clsng stages: nvr trbld ldrs* **8/1**

**5** 1¼ **Ardhoomey (IRE)**[12] 7856 5-9-13 106............(t) ColinKeane 12 92+
(G M Lyons, Ire) *w.w towards rr: pushed along after 1/2-way and sme hdwy down centre over 1f out: rdn and no imp on ldrs ins fnl f: kpt on same pce* **6/1**[3]

**6** 1¼ **Love On The Rocks (IRE)**[53] 6512 4-9-8 90............(h) ColmO'Donoghue 7 83+
(Charles Hills) *trckd ldrs: racd keenly in 3rd bef 1/2-way: pushed along fr 2f out and no ex u.p ins fnl f: one pce in 6th clsng stages* **16/1**

**7** ¾ **Duplication (IRE)**[21] 7587 3-9-13 88............(b) DonnachaO'Brien 2 86+
(Joseph Patrick O'Brien, Ire) *trckd ldrs: gng wl bhd ldrs fr 1/2-way and impr down centre to dispute ld briefly 1 1/2f out: sn hdd & wknd ins fnl f* **22/1**

**8** 2¾ **Blue Uluru (IRE)**[12] 7855 2-8-4 93............ ChrisHayes 6 64+
(G M Lyons, Ire) *mid-div: sme hdwy down centre to chse ldrs 1 1/2f out: no ex and one pce ins fnl f* **20/1**

**9** 1¾ **Confrontational (IRE)**[63] 6164 3-9-13 90............ ShaneFoley 4 70+
(John Joseph Murphy, Ire) *chsd ldrs: pushed along 2f out and sn no ex: wknd ins fnl f* **50/1**

**10** 1¼ **Intense Starlet (IRE)**[13] 7840 6-9-8 45............(bt[1]) GearoidBrouder 5 60?
(Thomas P O'Connor, Ire) *trckd ldr: 2nd 1/2-way: sltly hmpd under 2f out: sn wknd* **100/1**

11 5 ½ **Mrs Hitchcock (IRE)**[14] 7794 2-8-4 56 NGMcCullagh 13 34+
(Miss Katy Brown, Ire) *a bhd: rdn and no imp in rr nr side 2f out: kpt on one pce ins fnl f* **100/1**

12 ½ **Annie Fior (IRE)**[14] 7798 3-9-8 76 SeamieHeffernan 10 39+
(Thomas P O'Connor, Ire) *towards rr: pushed along and no imp far side fr 2f out* **80/1**

13 2 **Optionality** 3-9-8 0 MarkGallagher 3 32+
(D J Bunyan, Ire) *towards rr: rdn and no imp far side 2f out* **100/1**

58.55s (-0.85) **Going Correction** 0.0s/f (Stan) **13** Ran SP% **128.5**
Speed ratings: **104,103,101,99,97 95,94,90,87,85 76,75,72**
CSF £17.59 TOTE £1.60: £1.02, £4.40, £1.70; DF 18.10 Trifecta £78.90.
**Owner** Norcroft Park Stud **Bred** Norcroft Park Stud **Trained** Bawtry, S Yorks

**FOCUS**
A terrific battling performance from this admirable sprinter, arguably better than ever at the age of 10. The runner-up looks the best guide to the form, with the fourth rated in line with his course latest.

8226 - 8227a (Foreign Racing) - See Raceform Interactive

## 8127 CLAIREFONTAINE (R-H)
Friday, October 20

**OFFICIAL GOING: Heavy**

## 8228a PRIX DES IMPATIENCES (CLAIMER) (2YO FILLIES) (TURF) 1m
**2:10** 2-Y-0 **£7,264** (£2,905; £2,179; £1,452; £726)

RPR

1 **Tosen Hardi**[18] 2-8-7 0 (p) MlleAlisonMassin(4) 3 72
(S Kobayashi, France) **26/1**

2 3 **Rachael's Rocket (IRE)**[21] 7592 2-9-1 0 ChristopheSoumillon 1 69
(J S Moore) *sn settled front of midfield on inner: tk clsr order 3f out: pushed along to ld ins 2f out: rdn and hdd ent fnl f: kpt on to hold 2nd* **3/1**[2]

3 nk **So She Thinks (IRE)** 2-9-1 0 TonyPiccone 6 69
(J S Moore) *pushed along in last early: sn detached: run checked by jockey on grnd 1/2-way: appeared to have no ch: stdy hdwy between horses fr 3f out: rdn fnl f: stormed home fnl 100yds to take 3rd fnl strides* **131/10**

4 snk **Coral Slipper (FR)**[50] 2-8-11 0 (b) EddyHardouin 8 64
(Matthieu Palussiere, France) **158/10**

5 2 **La Cataleya (FR)**[63] 6171 2-9-1 0 (b) GregoryBenoist 10 64
(R Le Dren Doleuze, France) **26/1**

6 ¾ **Martha Jane (FR)**[75] 2-8-13 0 MlleAdelineMerou(9) 11 69
(B De Montzey, France) **2/1**[1]

7 nk **Trust In You (FR)**[53] 6542 2-9-1 0 ClementLecoeuvre(3) 13 65
(Alex Fracas, France) **18/1**

8 snk **Charming Ka (FR)**[10] 2-8-7 0 MlleAudeDuporte(4) 7 57
(H Fortineau, France) **151/1**

9 ¾ **First Pond (FR)**[50] 2-9-1 0 (b) ThierryThulliez 9 60
(Y Gourraud, France) **147/10**

10 10 **Powerful (GER)** 2-8-13 0 AlexandreChesneau(5) 15 41
(B Recher, France) **125/1**

11 1 ¼ **Shinyanga (FR)**[10] 2-8-4 0 TomLefranc(7) 2 31
(C Boutin, France) **96/1**

12 nse **Broadchurch (FR)**[129] 2-8-11 0 PierreBazire 16 31
(D Allard, France) **130/1**

13 12 **Via Appia (FR)**[9] 2-9-4 0 (b) AntoineHamelin 4 11
(Matthieu Palussiere, France) **48/10**[3]

14 12 **Benger's Pursuit**[25] 7454 2-8-6 0 GuillaumeTrolleyDePrevaux(5) 5
(Jo Hughes) *midfield: keen early: dropped towards rr 4f out: pushed along but continued to weaken: eased fnl f* **125/1**

U **Filrine (FR)**[10] 2-8-11 0 (p) MickaelBerto 12
(Jean-Raymond Breton, France) **164/10**

1m 45.3s **15** Ran SP% **117.4**
PARI-MUTUEL (all including 1 euro stake): WIN 26.80; PLACE 5.60,1.60, 4.20; DF 36.80; SF89.70.
**Owner** Japan Health Summit Inc **Bred** Japan Health Summit Inc **Trained** France

## 7804 ASCOT (R-H)
Saturday, October 21

**OFFICIAL GOING: Soft (heavy down the hill into swinley bottom)**
Wind: Gale force, half against in home straight Weather: bright becoming overcast

## 8229 QIPCO BRITISH CHAMPIONS LONG DISTANCE CUP (GROUP 2) 1m 7f 209y
**1:25** (1:25) (Class 1) 3-Y-0+
**£263,417** (£99,867; £49,980; £24,897; £12,495; £6,270) **Stalls** Low

Form RPR

2114 1 **Order Of St George (IRE)**[20] 7668 5-9-7 122 RyanMoore 12 117+
(A P O'Brien, Ire) *hld up in midfield: prog 7f out: chsd ldrs 4f out: rdn and outpcd wl over 2f out: wandered u.p wl over 1f out: clsd on ldng pair after: kpt on v gamely to ld last 75yds* **4/5**[1]

-152 2 ½ **Torcedor (IRE)**[41] 6976 5-9-7 111 (p) ColmO'Donoghue 7 116
(Mrs John Harrington, Ire) *racd wd: wl in tch: trckd ldr over 6f out: drvn to ld 2f out: more than 2 l clr 1f out but out on his feet: hdd last 75yds* **25/1**

2113 3 ½ **Stradivarius (IRE)**[35] 7147 3-8-13 118 FrankieDettori 5 115+
(John Gosden) *hld up in midfield: effrt 5f out: rdn over 3f out and outpcd wl over 2f out: kpt on fr over 1f out to cl on ldr but nt quite as qckly as wnr* **4/1**[2]

1335 4 1 ½ **Mount Moriah**[15] 7783 3-8-13 106 HarryBentley 13 113
(Ralph Beckett) *trckd ldr after 6f: led 7f out: kicked for home 3f out: drvn and hdd 2f out where clr of rest: no ex and lost 2 pls ins fnl f* **66/1**

1-31 5 4 **Duretto**[35] 7139 5-9-7 112 GrahamLee 11 109
(Andrew Balding) *lw; stdd s: hld up in rr: prog over 6f out: latched on to ldrs over 3f out: rdn and nt qckn 2f out: sltly impeded over 1f out and wknd* **16/1**

0364 6 8 **Clever Cookie**[36] 7116 9-9-7 109 (p) JamieSpencer 1 99
(Peter Niven) *hld up wl in rr: sme hdwy and rchd 7th over 3f out: sn lft bhd by ldrs and no ch* **33/1**

6043 7 ½ **Sheikhzayedroad**[36] 7116 8-9-7 112 (h) MartinHarley 8 99
(David Simcock) *cl up: chsd ldng pair 6f out: drvn over 3f out: wknd over 2f out* **25/1**

1462 8 24 **Nearly Caught (IRE)**[23] 7547 7-9-7 109 AdamKirby 10 70
(Hughie Morrison) *sn labouring in last pair: passed a few fr 6f out but nvr any hope: t.o and eased fnl f* **66/1**

2321 9 14 **Desert Skyline (IRE)**[36] 7116 3-8-13 112 (p) SilvestreDeSousa 9 55
(David Elsworth) *sltly on toes; t.k.h: trckd ldrs: rdn 6f out: sn btn: t.o* **9/1**[3]

1420 10 2 ¾ **Dartmouth**[41] 6976 5-9-7 115 JimCrowley 4 50
(Sir Michael Stoute) *hld up wl in rr: shkn up and no rspnse 4f out: t.o* **20/1**

4112 11 ½ **Big Orange**[81] 5503 6-9-7 121 (p) JamesDoyle 6 49
(Michael Bell) *lw; led after 1f to 7f out: sn lost pl: t.o* **10/1**

4-42 12 shd **Stars Over The Sea (USA)**[27] 7422 6-9-7 102 FranBerry 2 49
(Henry De Bromhead, Ire) *led 1f: pushed up to press ldr 11f out: sn lost pl: wknd 6f out: t.o* **100/1**

13 dist **Cap'N (IRE)** 6-9-7 0 MitchGodwin 3
(Brendan Powell) *s.s: in tch in last to 1/2-way: sn t.o: all but p.u 5f out and allowed to hack home* **150/1**

3m 37.84s (8.84) **Going Correction** +0.95s/f (Soft)
**WFA** 3 from 5yo+ 8lb **13** Ran SP% **120.6**
Speed ratings (Par 115): **115,114,114,113,111 107,107,95,88,87 86,86,**
CSF £33.83 CT £64.00 TOTE £1.80: £1.10, £4.60, £1.60; EX 17.00 Trifecta £75.80.
**Owner** M Tabor/D Smith/Mrs Magnier/L J Williams **Bred** Paget Bloodstock **Trained** Cashel, Co Tipperary

■ Stewards' Enquiry : James Doyle seven-day ban: careless riding (TBA)
Ryan Moore two-day ban: used whip above the permitted level (Nov 4-6)
Colm O'Donoghue seven-day ban: used whip above the permitted level (Nov 4-11) £800 fine: used whip above the permitted level

**FOCUS**
The straight course was divided in two with a rail in the middle from 1m to 3f where it ended in a cutaway. Far side track was used for this meeting. A strong edition of the race and the form looks good. They didn't go overly fast and several had their chance. The second and fourth are the keys to the level.

## 8230 QIPCO BRITISH CHAMPIONS SPRINT STKS (GROUP 1) 6f
**2:00** (2:03) (Class 1) 3-Y-0+
**£340,260** (£129,000; £64,560; £32,160; £16,140; £8,100) **Stalls** Centre

Form RPR

-402 1 **Librisa Breeze**[63] 6193 5-9-2 112 RobertWinston 3 121
(Dean Ivory) *hld up disputing 8th: smooth prog 2f out: delivered to ld 150yds: edgd sltly rt but kpt on stoutly u.p* **10/1**

1202 2 1 ¼ **Tasleet**[42] 6926 4-9-2 116 (p) JimCrowley 5 117
(William Haggas) *trckd ldrs: prog 2f out: rdn to ld 1f out: sn hdd and kpt on same pce after* **10/1**

1461 3 ¾ **Caravaggio (USA)**[41] 6973 3-9-1 121 RyanMoore 12 115
(A P O'Brien, Ire) *sltly awkward s: hld up in midfield: shkn up over 2f out and no prog: styd on fr over 1f out to take 3rd last strides* **9/2**[2]

1211 4 nk **Harry Angel (IRE)**[42] 6926 3-9-1 125 AdamKirby 9 114
(Clive Cox) *taken down early: rrd s: t.k.h: trckd ldng pair: prog to ld over 2f out: rdn and hdd 1f out: hld whn edgd sltly lft and impeded 100yds out: lost 3rd last strides* **5/4**[1]

5103 5 1 ¼ **The Tin Man**[42] 6926 5-9-2 117 TomQueally 7 110
(James Fanshawe) *racd in 9th and sn pushed along: kpt on wl fr over 1f out but nvr a serious threat* **9/1**

3100 6 1 **Brando**[20] 7671 5-9-2 115 TomEaves 2 106
(Kevin Ryan) *hld up in last trio: trying to make prog whn bmpd over 1f out: kpt on fnl f: nvr gng pce to threaten* **20/1**

0510 7 1 **Washington DC (IRE)**[57] 6402 4-9-2 110 (bt) DonnachaO'Brien 4 103
(A P O'Brien, Ire) *lw; hld up in last trio: effrt but plenty to do whn swtchd lft and bdly bmpd over 1f out: kpt on fnl f: no ch* **50/1**

3011 8 ¾ **Donjuan Triumphant (IRE)**[21] 7611 4-9-2 114 (h) PJMcDonald 11 101
(Andrew Balding) *led after 1f to over 2f out: sn wknd* **20/1**

0-01 9 nk **Quiet Reflection**[27] 7424 4-8-13 116 MartinHarley 1 97
(K R Burke) *broke wl but stdd bhd ldrs: shkn up and effrt over 2f out: wknd over 1f out* **6/1**[3]

5104 10 2 **Danzeno**[14] 7806 6-9-2 109 FrankieDettori 6 93
(Michael Appleby) *lw; dwlt: mostly in last and sn pushed along: nvr a factor* **33/1**

2205 11 9 **Alphabet**[13] 7856 3-8-12 110 (t) WayneLordan 8 62
(A P O'Brien, Ire) *pressed ldrs to 2f out: wkng rapidly whn bmpd over 1f out: t.o* **66/1**

0506 12 1 ¼ **Intelligence Cross (USA)**[49] 6703 3-9-1 110 (bt) SeamieHeffernan 13 61
(A P O'Brien, Ire) *led 1f: pressed ldr to over 2f out: wknd rapidly: t.o* **100/1**

1m 16.78s (2.28) **Going Correction** +0.875s/f (Soft)
**WFA** 3 from 4yo+ 1lb **12** Ran SP% **122.0**
Speed ratings (Par 117): **119,117,116,115,114 112,111,110,110,107 95,93**
CSF £100.88 CT £528.67 TOTE £9.90: £3.00, £3.00, £1.60; EX 101.00 Trifecta £493.30.
**Owner** Tony Bloom **Bred** Newsells Park Stud **Trained** Radlett, Herts

**FOCUS**
A top-class and fascinating sprint, featuring last year's winner and a dual Group 1-winning filly, while the market leaders were first and second in the Commonwealth Cup. They went a strong pace throughout, which suited the closers, and it was hard work at the finish, the winner seeing it out best and causing a minor upset. The runner-up helps set the standard.

## 8231 QIPCO BRITISH CHAMPIONS FILLIES & MARES STKS (GROUP 1) 1m 3f 211y
**2:40** (2:40) (Class 1) 3-Y-0+
**£355,855** (£134,912; £67,519; £33,634; £16,879; £8,471) **Stalls** Low

Form RPR

3412 1 **Hydrangea (IRE)**[20] 7669 3-8-13 114 (p) RyanMoore 8 119
(A P O'Brien, Ire) *wl in tch: pushed along jst over 3f out: prog to ld over 2f out: jnd over 1f out: urged along and kpt on wl to assert ins fnl f* **4/1**[3]

2111 2 2 **Bateel (IRE)**[41] 6981 5-9-5 119 (h) Pierre-CharlesBoudot 4 117
(F-H Graffard, France) *lw; hld up in midfield: swift prog to chse wnr 2f out and sn upsides: hrd rdn and nt qckn 1f out: readily hld ins fnl f* **7/4**[1]

1425 3 1 ¾ **Coronet**[35] 7147 3-8-13 113 OlivierPeslier 9 113
(John Gosden) *hld up in last pair: rdn and prog over 2f out: chsd clr ldng pair over 1f out: styd on but unable to land a blow* **11/2**

1-41 4 5 **The Juliet Rose (FR)**[21] 7635 4-9-5 108 (h[1]) StephanePasquier 1 104
(N Clement, France) *trckd ldr: upsides over 2f out: sn outpcd and btn: fdd over 1f out* **16/1**

2100 5 1 ½ **The Black Princess (FR)**[20] 7669 4-9-5 110 RobertHavlin 10 102
(John Gosden) *stdd s and dropped in fr wd draw: hld up in last: effrt and sme prog over 2f out: no hdwy and wl btn over 1f out* **40/1**

-502 6 2 ¼ **Journey**[41] 6981 5-9-5 118 (h) FrankieDettori 5 98
(John Gosden) *lw; t.k.h: pressed ldrs: chal and upsides over 2f out: wknd tamely over 1f out* **7/2**[2]

-031 7 3 ½ **Alyssa**[37] 7089 4-9-5 103 PatDobbs 7 92
(Ralph Beckett) *sltly on toes; led to over 2f out: sn wknd* **28/1**

-144 **8** *1 1/2* **Horseplay**[111] 4424 3-8-13 100........................................ DavidProbert 3 91
(Andrew Balding) *hld up in last trio: shkn up and no prog 3f out: sn btn*
**20/1**

5335 **9** *3 3/4* **Left Hand**[20] 7669 4-9-5 112........................................(b[1]) MaximeGuyon 2 84
(C Laffon-Parias, France) *trckd ldrs: rdn wl over 2f out: wknd wl over 1f out*
**16/1**

5353 **10** *106* **Wild Irish Rose (IRE)**[27] 7422 3-8-13 102............... SeamieHeffernan 6
(A P O'Brien, Ire) *in tch to 4f out: sn wknd: t.o whn virtually p.u ins fnl f*
**66/1**

2m 40.82s (8.32) **Going Correction** +0.95s/f (Soft)
**WFA** 3 from 4yo+ 6lb 10 Ran SP% **117.9**
Speed ratings (Par 117): **110,108,107,104,103 101,99,98,95,**
CSF £11.16 CT £38.72 TOTE £4.50: £1.60, £1.20, £1.90; EX 13.60 Trifecta £53.00.
**Owner** Derrick Smith & Mrs John Magnier & Michael Tabor **Bred** Beauty Is Truth Syndicate **Trained** Cashel, Co Tipperary

**FOCUS**
Strong Group 1 form, with three top performers pulling clear. It's been rated at face value, with the runner-up to form.

## 8232 QUEEN ELIZABETH II STKS (GROUP 1) (SPONSORED BY QIPCO) (BRITISH CHAMPIONS MILE) 1m (S)

**3:15** (3:23) (Class 1) 3-Y-O+

**£623,810** (£236,500; £118,360; £58,960; £29,590; £14,850) **Stalls** Centre

Form RPR

-532 **1** **Persuasive (IRE)**[14] 7812 4-9-1 113........................ FrankieDettori 6 121+
(John Gosden) *lw; hld up towards rr: prog fr 3f out: swtchd lft 2f out and clsd on ldrs: shkn up to ld jst over 1f out: sn in command: rdn out* **8/1**

1121 **2** *1* **Ribchester (IRE)**[41] 6982 4-9-4 125........................ WilliamBuick 13 120
(Richard Fahey) *t.k.h: trckd ldrs: led wl over 2f out: sn rdn and edgd rt after: hdd jst over 1f out: kpt on wl but wnr in command* **2/1**[1]

1420 **3** *1/2* **Churchill (IRE)**[42] 6960 3-9-1 123........................ RyanMoore 1 118
(A P O'Brien, Ire) *trckd ldrs: rdn to dispute 2nd fr 2f out: tried to chal but a hld: kpt on fnl f* **9/2**[3]

3223 **4** *nk* **Nathra (IRE)**[14] 7812 4-9-1 111........................ RobertHavlin 9 115
(John Gosden) *hld up in midfield: prog 3f out: chsd ldr over 2f out: drvn and stl disputing 2nd over 1f out: one pce after* **50/1**

2414 **5** *4 1/2* **Sea Of Grace (IRE)**[41] 6972 3-8-12 109........................ DanielTudhope 2 104
(William Haggas) *sltly on toes; dwlt: hld up in rr: prog over 2f out: rchd 6th over 1f out but nt on terms w ldrs: drvn into 5th last strides* **33/1**

0316 **6** *1/2* **Lightning Spear**[41] 6982 6-9-4 115........................ OisinMurphy 14 107
(David Simcock) *wl in tch: clsd to chse ldr over 2f out: stl disputing 2nd over 1f out: wknd fnl f* **40/1**

1321 **7** *3/4* **Al Wukair (IRE)**[69] 5980 3-9-1 119........................(p[1]) GregoryBenoist 11 104
(A Fabre, France) *lw; t.k.h: hld up in midfield: shkn up and yet to make prog whn short of room 2f out: no threat after* **7/1**

12-2 **8** *2 3/4* **Zonderland**[56] 6420 4-9-4 113........................ AdamKirby 8 98
(Clive Cox) *hld up towards rr: trying to make prog whn squeezed for room 2f out: no hdwy after* **66/1**

131 **9** *shd* **Here Comes When (IRE)**[80] 5527 7-9-4 116............(h) JamieSpencer 7 98
(Andrew Balding) *stdd s: hld up in last: coaxed along 3f out and no real prog: rdn and no great hdwy 2f out* **20/1**

0111 **10** *1* **Beat The Bank**[22] 7579 3-9-1 118........................ JimCrowley 12 95
(Andrew Balding) *t.k.h: hld up towards rr: rdn and no prog over 2f out* **4/1**[2]

6042 **11** *6* **Sir John Lavery (IRE)**[22] 7579 3-9-1 111........................ SeamieHeffernan 5 81
(A P O'Brien, Ire) *pressed ldr at str pce to 3f out: wkng whn short of room 2f out: sn bhd* **33/1**

3145 **12** *3 3/4* **Breton Rock (IRE)**[35] 7145 7-9-4 113........................ AndreaAtzeni 10 73
(David Simcock) *hld up in last pair: rdn and no real prog over 2f out* **66/1**

0520 **13** *9* **Toscanini (IRE)**[20] 7671 5-9-4 111........................ JamesDoyle 4 53
(Richard Fahey) *led at str pce to wl over 2f out: wknd qckly: t.o* **100/1**

5262 **14** *1/2* **Lancaster Bomber (USA)**[35] 7179 3-9-1 118........................ DonnachaO'Brien 3 51
(A P O'Brien, Ire) *pressed ldr at str pce to 3f out: sn wknd: t.o* **40/1**

2313 **15** *2 1/4* **Thunder Snow (IRE)**[69] 5980 3-9-1 118.......(v[1]) ChristopheSoumillon 15 45
(Saeed bin Suroor) *hld up in last pair: wknd over 2f out: t.o* **16/1**

1m 46.13s (5.33) **Going Correction** +0.875s/f (Soft)
**WFA** 3 from 4yo+ 3lb 15 Ran SP% **122.5**
Speed ratings (Par 117): **108,107,106,106,101 101,100,97,97,96 90,86,77,77,75**
CSF £23.05 CT £87.49 TOTE £8.60: £2.70, £1.20, £1.90; EX 31.20 Trifecta £152.80.
**Owner** Cheveley Park Stud **Bred** J F Tuthill **Trained** Newmarket, Suffolk

**FOCUS**
A high quality Group 1 event, in which five of the runners had been successful at the top level, and it was talked up of a clash between the best older miler in training against several strong 3yo challengers. They split into two groups, the majority racing far side, before merging after halfway, and a well backed 4yo filly spoiled the party for the favourite. The runner-up has been rated below his best.

## 8233 QIPCO CHAMPION STKS (BRITISH CHAMPIONS MIDDLE DISTANCE) (GROUP 1) 1m 1f 212y

**3:50** (4:01) (Class 1) 3-Y-O+

**£737,230** (£279,500; £139,880; £69,680; £34,970; £17,550) **Stalls** Low

Form RPR

3211 **1** **Cracksman**[41] 6980 3-9-1 122........................ FrankieDettori 4 131
(John Gosden) *lw; trckd ldng trio: led wl over 2f out: rdn and powered clr sn after: styd on strly: impressive* **13/8**[1]

1212 **2** *7* **Poet's Word (IRE)**[42] 6960 4-9-5 119........................ AndreaAtzeni 7 117
(Sir Michael Stoute) *lw; hld up in tch: prog to chse wnr over 2f out: sn lft bhd: dropped to 3rd over 1f out: kpt on to take 2nd again ins fnl f: no ch* **7/1**

0114 **3** *nk* **Highland Reel (IRE)**[84] 5394 5-9-5 123........................ RyanMoore 9 116
(A P O'Brien, Ire) *trckd ldr: mde move to far side rail 6f out where racd alone: jnd ldrs appr st: rdn and edgd rt whn umable to qckn 2f out: styd on to take 3rd towards fin* **17/2**

1301 **4** *1* **Recoletos (FR)**[35] 7176 3-9-1 114........................ OlivierPeslier 6 114
(C Laffon-Parias, France) *str; sltly on toes; dwlt: hld up towards rr: prog over 2f out: rdn to chse clr wnr over 1f out: no imp: lost 2nd and fdd ins fnl f* **14/1**

2361 **5** *1 1/2* **Desert Encounter (IRE)**[28] 7393 5-9-5 114........................(h) SeanLevey 8 111
(David Simcock) *hld up in last: rdn and prog over 2f out: rchd 5th and tried to press for a pl 1f out: wknd ins fnl f* **33/1**

1155 **6** *5* **Brametot (IRE)**[20] 7668 3-9-1 121........................ CristianDemuro 3 102
(J-C Rouget, France) *str; sltly on toes; hld up: effrt on inner wl over 2f out: sn no prog and wknd* **11/2**[3]

2446 **7** *shd* **Cliffs Of Moher (IRE)**[42] 6960 3-9-1 118................(t) SeamieHeffernan 1 102
(A P O'Brien, Ire) *hld up in tch: rdn wl over 2f out: sn wknd* **10/1**

0-40 **8** *1* **Maverick Wave (USA)**[84] 5394 6-9-5 101........................ RobertHavlin 5 99
(John Gosden) *pressed ldng pair: cl 2nd 3f out: sn wknd rapidly* **100/1**

2123 **9** *1* **Barney Roy**[59] 6328 3-9-1 122........................ JamesDoyle 2 98
(Richard Hannon) *sltly on toes; hld up in last trio: shkn up and floundering wl over 2f out: sn wknd* **9/2**[2]

4210 **10** *25* **Success Days (IRE)**[42] 6960 5-9-5 114........................(t) ShaneFoley 10 47
(K J Condon, Ire) *racd wd early: mde most to wl over 2f out: wknd qckly: t.o* **40/1**

2m 11.75s (4.35) **Going Correction** +0.95s/f (Soft)
**WFA** 3 from 4yo+ 4lb 10 Ran SP% **116.8**
Speed ratings (Par 117): **120,114,114,113,112 108,108,107,106,86**
CSF £13.53 CT £76.20 TOTE £2.50: £1.20, £2.10, £2.50; EX 12.80 Trifecta £55.90.
**Owner** A E Oppenheimer **Bred** Hascombe And Valiant Studs **Trained** Newmarket, Suffolk

**FOCUS**
This may not have been the deepest edition of the race and a couple of the supposed main threats to the favourite ran disappointingly, but none the less hard not to be taken with the winners 7l romp. The pace was a brisk one. The winner has been rated as putting up the best performance in Europe this year, up there with the best winners of this race apart from Frankel. The third has been rated similar to his King George figure.

## 8234 BALMORAL H'CAP (SPONSORED BY QIPCO) 1m (S)

**4:30** (4:39) (Class 2) 3-Y-O+

**£155,625** (£46,600; £23,300; £11,650; £5,825; £2,925) **Stalls** Centre

Form RPR

12 **1** **Lord Glitters (FR)**[14] 7807 4-9-3 **102**........................ DanielTudhope 3 113+
(David O'Meara) *tall; ly; hld up wl in rr: stl in last pair 2f out: nt clr run and swtchd lft wl over 1f out: rapid prog fnl f: str run to ld last strides* **3/1**[1]

0200 **2** *nk* **Gm Hopkins**[21] 7619 6-9-5 **104**........................ RobertHavlin 18 113
(John Gosden) *dwlt: hld up wl in rr: prog and shkn up 2f out: clsd on ldrs 1f out: drvn to ld 75yds out: r.o but hdd last strides* **20/1**

3461 **3** *1 1/4* **Dark Red (IRE)**[7] 8042 5-9-3 **102** 6ex........................(b) FrannyNorton 17 108
(Ed Dunlop) *trckd ldrs: clsd 2f out: rdn to ld jst ins fnl f: hdd and outpcd last 75yds* **25/1**

0121 **4** *3/4* **Accidental Agent**[14] 7807 3-9-8 **110** 6ex........................ CharlesBishop 15 113+
(Eve Johnson Houghton) *lw; hld up wl in rr: nt clr run 2f out: prog over 1f out: styd on wl fnl f but nt as qckly as wnr* **12/1**

3550 **5** *shd* **Gabrial (IRE)**[49] 6676 8-9-6 **105**........................ JamieSpencer 23 109
(Richard Fahey) *stdd and v awkward s: hld up wl in rr: prog 2f out: rdn and styd on wl fnl f but wnr sn overtk him* **28/1**

66-0 **6** *1 1/4* **White Lake**[156] 2767 5-9-2 **101**........................ JackMitchell 14 102
(Roger Varian) *lw; bowled along in untrbld ld: rdn 2f out: hdd & wknd jst ins fnl f* **33/1**

0043 **7** *hd* **Oh This Is Us (IRE)**[35] 7154 4-9-8 **107**........................ RyanMoore 11 108
(Richard Hannon) *hld up in midfield: lost pl 2f out and in rr: prog over 1f out: styd on wl fnl f but nvr quite pce to chal* **25/1**

5350 **8** *1 1/4* **Firmament**[14] 7807 5-9-10 **109**........................ JamesDoyle 5 107
(David O'Meara) *hld up wl in rr: effrt on far side of gp 2f out: styd on same pce fnl f and nvr able to threaten* **33/1**

1600 **9** *nk* **Greenside**[21] 7619 6-8-13 **98**........................ HarryBentley 4 95
(Henry Candy) *trckd ldrs: rdn and stl wl there over 1f out: fdd fnl f* **16/1**

32/0 **10** *3/4* **Speculative Bid (IRE)**[14] 7807 6-9-9 **108**........................ JimCrowley 6 104
(David Elsworth) *hld up in rr: prog wl over 1f out: chsd ldrs fnl f: fdd last 100yds* **8/1**

-111 **11** *2* **Zabeel Prince (IRE)**[8] 8009 4-9-3 **102** 6ex........................ AndreaAtzeni 16 93
(Roger Varian) *trckd ldr: rdn over 2f out: lost pl and wknd over 1f out* **4/1**[2]

1440 **12** *1/2* **Master The World (IRE)**[21] 7619 6-9-4 **108**..............(p) JoshuaBryan(5) 7 98
(David Elsworth) *hld up towards rr: lost pl and in last pair whn nt clr run 2f out: plugged on again over 1f out* **28/1**

4100 **13** *nk* **Eddystone Rock (IRE)**[21] 7619 5-9-2 **101**........... JosephineGordon 20 90
(John Best) *nvr bttr than midfield: rdn over 2f out: steadily wknd* **33/1**

5120 **14** *1* **Qassem (IRE)**[21] 7619 4-9-0 **99**........................(p[1]) FrankieDettori 19 86
(Hugo Palmer) *trckd ldr: rdn 2f out: wknd jst over 1f out* **16/1**

0042 **15** *1 1/2* **Hors De Combat**[31] 7275 6-9-2 **101**........................ TomQueally 8 84
(Denis Coakley) *wl plcd bhd ldrs: rdn and wknd 2f out* **50/1**

0031 **16** *hd* **George William**[12] 7901 4-9-6 **108** 6ex........................ HollieDoyle(3) 2 91
(Richard Hannon) *heavily restrained s: hld up wl in rr: effrt on far side of gp over 2f out: sn rdn and no prog* **25/1**

-203 **17** *1 1/2* **Linguistic (IRE)**[7] 8042 4-9-4 **103**........................(p) WilliamBuick 1 82
(John Gosden) *in tch: effrt on far side of gp 2f out: no prog over 1f out: wknd* **12/1**

0411 **18** *10* **Brigliadoro (IRE)**[17] 7727 6-9-1 **100** 6ex........................ DavidProbert 21 56
(Philip McBride) *nvr bttr than midfield: wknd u.p over 2f out: t.o* **33/1**

4300 **19** *1 3/4* **Withernsea (IRE)**[14] 7807 6-9-0 **99**........................ PaulHanagan 10 51
(Richard Fahey) *prom tl wknd qckly jst over 2f out: t.o* **25/1**

2011 **20** *7* **The Grape Escape (IRE)**[12] 7892 3-9-1 **103** 6ex............ SeanLevey 12 38
(Richard Hannon) *t.k.h: trckd ldrs: lost pl 2f out: wknd and eased over 1f out: t.o* **13/2**[3]

1m 45.91s (5.11) **Going Correction** +0.875s/f (Soft)
**WFA** 3 from 4yo+ 3lb 20 Ran SP% **137.4**
Speed ratings (Par 109): **109,108,107,106,106 105,105,103,103,102 100,100,100,99,97 97,95,85,84,77**
CSF £73.62 CT £1415.19 TOTE £3.40: £1.20, £5.30, £5.90, £3.30; EX 80.70 Trifecta £3032.50.
**Owner** Geoff & Sandra Turnbull **Bred** S C A Elevage De Tourgeville Et Al **Trained** Upper Helmsley, N Yorks

**FOCUS**
An ultra-competitive event, as is befitting a contest that is the most valuable of its type in Europe, and this fourth running was the strongest renewal so far. They went a good pace, the winning time being marginally quicker than the QEII earlier on the card, and this is serious handicap form. The fourth has been rated close to his latest form.

T/Jkpt: Not Won. T/Plt: £37.10 to a £1 stake. Pool: £359,314.09 - 7,066.69 winning units. T/Qpdt: £7.50 to a £1 stake. Pool: £27,167.92 - 2,652.61 winning units. **Jonathan Neesom**

# 7919 CATTERICK (L-H)

## Saturday, October 21

**OFFICIAL GOING: Soft (6.6)**

Wind: Strong behind Weather: Overcast and windy, heavy rain from mid-afternoon

## 8235 TOTEPLACEPOT NOVICE MEDIAN AUCTION STKS 5f 212y

**1:50** (1:50) (Class 6) 2-Y-O **£3,234** (£962; £481; £240) **Stalls** Low

Form RPR

5232 **1** **Biddy Brady (USA)**[32] 7242 2-8-11 68........................(h[1]) JasonHart 1 69
(Tim Easterby) *slt ld: rdn along 2f out: drvn and hdd ent fnl f: rallied gamely u.p to ld last 100yds* **7/4**[1]

03 **2** *1 1/4* **Emphatic (IRE)**[28] 7383 2-9-2 0 LukeMorris 9 70
(Robert Cowell) *cl up: chal 2f out and sn rdn: slt ld ent fnl f: sn drvn: hdd last 100yds: no ex towards fin* **9/1**

305 **3** *1 1/4* **Immortal Romance (IRE)**[43] 6867 2-9-2 76 (v[1]) KieranShoemark 3 67
(Michael Bell) *trckd ldrs: hdwy over 2f out: rdn over 1f out: ev ch whn drvn and hung bdly rt ins fnl f: one pce after* **7/2**[3]

**4** *1/2* **I Was Only Joking (IRE)** 2-8-11 0 TonyHamilton 2 60
(Richard Fahey) *dwlt and in rr: hdwy over 2f out: rdn along wl over 1f out: kpt on fnl f* **15/2**

26 **5** *1* **Mearing**[115] 4213 2-9-2 0 PhillipMakin 4 65+
(Iain Jardine) *trckd ldng pair on inner: pushed along over 2f out: rdn wl over 1f out: sn drvn and kpt on same pce* **3/1**[2]

0 **6** *8* **Blue Harmony**[43] 6876 2-8-11 0 JoeyHaynes 8 33
(K R Burke) *chsd ldrs: rdn along wl over 2f out: grad wknd* **40/1**

00 **7** *18* **Sovereign Katie (IRE)**[101] 4740 2-8-11 0 AndrewMullen 7
(Ollie Pears) *chsd ldrs: rdn along 3f out: sn outpcd and bhd* **125/1**

1m 17.49s (3.89) **Going Correction** +0.525s/f (Yiel) **7 Ran SP% 108.6**
Speed ratings (Par 93): **95,93,91,91,89 79,55**
CSF £16.65 TOTE £2.20: £1.70, £3.50; EX 16.20 Trifecta £33.40.
**Owner** F Gillespie **Bred** Brandywine Farm (Jim & Pam Robinson) **Trained** Great Habton, N Yorks
■ Stewards' Enquiry : Kieran Shoemark two-day ban: used whip above the permitted level (Nov 4-6)

**FOCUS**
Following 14mm of rain on Thursday and another 2.5mm of rain overnight, the ground was officially soft (GoingStick 6.6). All race distances as advertised. A classy meeting for Catterick was given extra spice with the battle for the apprentice title between David Egan (53) and Kieran Shoemark (52) going right down to the wire, and both riders were here. The handful of non-runners due to the softening ground included two due to be ridden by Egan, and one by Shoemark. A routine median auction novice event to start and the first two dominated from the off. Despite the ground, the runners stayed against the inside rail and the time was 6.69sec outside standard. Luke Morris said the ground was "'soft", but winning rider Jason Hart said: "it's not too bad".

## 8236 TOTESCOOP6 PLAY TODAY EBF FILLIES' NOVICE STKS (PLUS 10 RACE) 7f 6y
**2:25** (2:25) (Class 4) 2-Y-O **£5,175** (£1,540; £769; £384) **Stalls** Low

Form RPR

6400 **1** **Lady Anjorica (IRE)**[7] 8045 2-8-12 76 (b[1]) PaulMulrennan 3 76
(Keith Dalgleish) *towards rr early: hdwy over 4f out and sn in tch: effrt to chse ldrs 2f out: rdn over 1f out: drvn fnl f: styd on wl to ld nr fin* **17/2**[3]

045 **2** *3/4* **Lady Willpower**[39] 7022 2-8-9 69 DavidEgan(3) 2 74
(John Quinn) *trckd ldng pair: hdwy over 2f out: chal wl over 1f out: led ent fnl f: sn drvn: hdd and no ex nr fin* **16/1**

45 **3** *2 1/4* **Zahraa**[8] 7995 2-8-12 0 KieranShoemark 4 68
(Robyn Brisland) *led: pushed along over 2f out: jnd and rdn wl over 1f out: hdd and drvn ent fnl f: kpt on same pce* **12/1**

4232 **4** *1 1/2* **Perfect Thought**[16] 7757 2-8-12 77 JoeFanning 5 64
(William Haggas) *trckd ldr: pushed along over 2f out: rdn wl over 1f out: sn drvn and one pce* **5/4**[1]

40 **5** *1 1/4* **Chantresse (IRE)**[14] 7818 2-8-12 0 JoeyHaynes 8 61
(K R Burke) *towards rr: hdwy wl over 2f out: rdn along wl over 1f out: kpt on fnl f* **33/1**

223 **6** *1/2* **Kirbec (IRE)**[58] 6347 2-8-12 70 ConnorBeasley 7 60
(Keith Dalgleish) *dwlt and in rr: hdwy over 2f out: sn rdn along and kpt on fnl f: nrst fin* **10/1**

60 **7** *5* **Aphaea**[8] 8013 2-8-12 0 CamHardie 1 47
(Michael Easterby) *midfield: pushed along 1/2-way: rdn wl over 2f out: n.d* **100/1**

035 **8** *1/2* **Salire (IRE)**[25] 7473 2-8-12 64 JackGarritty 6 45
(Ann Duffield) *chsd ldrs: rdn along 3f out: wknd 2f out* **50/1**

**9** *1/2* **Ayton (IRE)** 2-8-12 0 AndrewMullen 12 44
(Ollie Pears) *green a towards rr* **66/1**

1 **10** *3 3/4* **Crotchet**[79] 5575 2-9-4 0 TonyHamilton 11 40
(Richard Fahey) *trckd ldrs: pushed along over 3f out: sn rdn and lost pl wl over 2f out* **3/1**[2]

0 **11** *2 3/4* **Military Madame (IRE)**[39] 7033 2-8-12 0 JasonHart 9 27
(John Quinn) *a towards rr* **25/1**

**12** *3/4* **Symphonic** 2-8-12 0 ShaneGray 10 25
(Ann Duffield) *a in rr* **66/1**

1m 31.74s (4.74) **Going Correction** +0.525s/f (Yiel) **12 Ran SP% 115.4**
Speed ratings (Par 94): **93,92,89,87,86 85,80,79,79,74 71,70**
CSF £122.41 TOTE £9.60: £2.70, £4.90, £2.80; EX 129.30 Trifecta £1233.00.
**Owner** Middleham Park Racing LXXIII **Bred** Mrs E Fitzsimons **Trained** Carluke, S Lanarks

**FOCUS**
A fair novice fillies' event and for a long time it looked as though the finish would be fought out between the pair going for the apprentice title, but a more established rider had other ideas.

## 8237 TOTEQUADPOT CLAIMING STKS 5f
**2:55** (2:58) (Class 6) 3-Y-O+ **£3,234** (£962; £481; £240) **Stalls** Low

Form RPR

0003 **1** **Apricot Sky**[11] 7923 7-9-3 73 (p) PaulMulrennan 2 78
(Michael Dods) *cl up: led jst over 2f out: rdn wl over 1f out: drvn ins fnl f: kpt on wl towards fin* **5/2**[2]

2222 **2** *1 3/4* **Desert Ace (IRE)**[35] 7137 6-9-4 79 LukeMorris 1 73
(Paul Midgley) *slt ld: pushed along and hdd jst over 2f out: sn rdn: drvn and ev ch ent fnl f tl no ex last 100yds* **4/9**[1]

3200 **3** *8 3/4* **Compton River**[12] 7884 5-9-1 64 AdamMcNamara(3) 5 41
(Bryan Smart) *chsd ldng pair: rdn along over 2f out: sn one pce* **14/1**[3]

4060 **4** *1 1/4* **Oriental Relation (IRE)**[49] 6670 6-9-10 72 (b) JamesSullivan 4 43
(James Given) *rdn along s: sn outpcd and bhd* **20/1**

1m 2.58s (2.78) **Going Correction** +0.60s/f (Yiel) **4 Ran SP% 109.3**
Speed ratings (Par 101): **101,98,84,82**
CSF £4.10 TOTE £3.20; EX 5.90 Trifecta £10.20.
**Owner** The Wayward Lads **Bred** Mrs James Bethell **Trained** Denton, Co Durham

**FOCUS**
A modest claimer with just the four remaining runners, but all of them often like to force it or be up there. The big two in the market dominated, but still a bit of a turn up. They raced centre to far side.

## 8238 TOTESCOOP6 CATTERICK DASH H'CAP 5f
**3:30** (3:31) (Class 2) (0-100,97) 3-Y-O+
**£18,675** (£5,592; £2,796; £1,398; £699; £351) **Stalls** Low

Form RPR

135 **1** **Storm Over (IRE)**[42] 6945 3-8-10 86 LukeMorris 15 97
(Robert Cowell) *racd towards stands' rail: prom: chal wl over 1f out: rdn to ld appr fnl f: drvn out* **9/1**

5142 **2** *3/4* **Memories Galore (IRE)**[8] 8012 5-8-5 84 (p) DavidEgan(3) 4 91
(Roger Fell) *racd towards centre: in tch: hdwy to chse ldrs 2f out: rdn wl over 1f out: swtchd rt and drvn ins fnl f: kpt on* **4/1**[1]

3034 **3** *1* **Confessional**[21] 7610 10-8-7 86 (be) LewisEdmunds(3) 1 89
(Tim Easterby) *racd towards centre: midfield: hdwy 2f out: rdn over 1f out: styd on strly fnl f* **9/2**[2]

0014 **4** *nk* **Equimou**[14] 7809 3-9-5 95 KieranShoemark 11 98
(Robert Eddery) *cl up centre: rdn along 2f out: ev ch over 1f out: drvn and kpt on same pce fnl f* **9/1**

000 **5** *3 1/4* **Aleef (IRE)**[21] 7604 4-8-9 85 (h) EdwardGreatrex 10 75
(David O'Meara) *racd nr stands' rail: cl up: led over 2f out: rdn wl over 1f out: drvn and hdd appr fnl f: grad wknd* **10/1**

4003 **6** *1/2* **Green Door (IRE)**[4] 8139 6-9-2 95 (v) EoinWalsh(3) 13 83
(Robert Cowell) *dwlt and in rr towards stands' side: hdwy over 2f out: chsd ldrs and rdn over 1f out: kpt on fnl f* **8/1**[3]

5000 **7** *1 1/2* **Orion's Bow**[7] 8044 6-9-5 95 JamesSullivan 7 78
(Tim Easterby) *dwlt and towards rr centre: hdwy and grad swtchd rt over 2f out: in tch and rdn along on stands' rail over 1f out: sn drvn and no imp* **9/1**

1004 **8** *3/4* **Midnight Malibu (IRE)**[12] 7887 4-8-8 87 RachelRichardson(3) 3 67
(Tim Easterby) *racd towards centre: a towards rr* **16/1**

0014 **9** *1/2* **Tylery Wonder (IRE)**[8] 8012 7-8-10 86 (v) MartinLane 12 65
(Paul Midgley) *cl up towards stands' side: rdn along over 2f out: grad wknd* **12/1**

2200 **10** *nk* **Bowson Fred**[126] 3829 5-9-0 97 HarrisonShaw(7) 5 74
(Michael Easterby) *chsd ldrs centre: rdn along over 2f out: sn wknd* **28/1**

120 **11** *1/2* **Longroom**[56] 6412 5-8-4 83 oh1 PhilDennis(3) 8 59
(Noel Wilson) *racd centre: led: rdn along 1/2-way: sn hdd and drvn: wknd over 1f out* **20/1**

-100 **12** *2* **Kickboxer (IRE)**[7] 8044 6-9-6 96 (p) DougieCostello 2 64
(Michael Appleby) *racd centre: towards rr: hdwy on outer and in tch 2f out: sn rdn and wknd* **28/1**

000 **13** *3 3/4* **Zanetto**[94] 5018 7-8-8 84 JasonHart 14 39
(John Quinn) *racd stands' side: a towards rr* **100/1**

0100 **14** *3 1/2* **Poet's Society**[14] 7828 3-8-12 88 JoeFanning 9 31
(Mark Johnston) *prom centre: rdn along 1/2-way: sn wknd* **40/1**

1m 1.23s (1.43) **Going Correction** +0.60s/f (Yiel) **14 Ran SP% 117.0**
Speed ratings (Par 109): **112,110,109,108,103 102,100,99,98,97 97,93,87,82**
CSF £41.32 CT £191.47 TOTE £9.50: £3.80, £1.90, £2.00; EX 40.40 Trifecta £221.40.
**Owner** Abdulla Al Mansoori **Bred** J Dorrian **Trained** Six Mile Bottom, Cambs
■ Stewards' Enquiry : David Egan two-day ban: used whip above the permitted level (Nov 4-6)

**FOCUS**
A really decent sprint handicap. They raced centre to nearside this time and this was a race where you had to be handy. Those drawn high had an advantage and the race went to the least-exposed runner in the field. The third has been rated close to his recent form.

## 8239 TOTEEXACTA H'CAP 1m 4f 13y
**4:05** (4:10) (Class 4) (0-80,80) 3-Y-O+
**£7,470** (£2,236; £1,118; £559; £279; £140) **Stalls** Centre

Form RPR

0303 **1** **Jabbaar**[21] 7595 4-9-2 72 PhillipMakin 7 80
(Iain Jardine) *hld up in rr: gd hdwy over 4f out: chsd ldrs 2f out: swtchd rt to stands' rail and rdn: led ent fnl f: sn drvn and hld on wl* **7/1**[3]

20-6 **2** *nk* **Only Orsenfoolsies**[11] 7924 8-8-8 67 RowanScott(3) 12 74
(Micky Hammond) *towards rr: pushed along 4f out: hdwy 3f out: rdn to chse ldrs in centre wl over 1f out: sn drvn and kpt on wl fnl f* **20/1**

-444 **3** *3/4* **Henry Smith**[21] 7627 5-9-6 76 (be) AndrewMullen 2 82
(John Weymes) *trckd ldng pair: hdwy and cl up 3f out: led over 2f out: rdn wl over 1f out: hdd and drvn ent fnl f: kpt on* **14/1**

6000 **4** *nk* **Sennockian Star**[12] 7880 7-9-6 76 JoeFanning 1 81
(Mark Johnston) *led 4f: trckd ldr tl led again briefly over 2f out: sn rdn and hdd: drvn and ch ent fnl f: kpt on* **14/1**

230 **5** *2 1/2* **Tamayuz Magic (IRE)**[47] 6757 6-9-1 78 (b) HarrisonShaw(7) 6 79
(Michael Easterby) *hld up towards rr: hdwy over 4f out: wd st to stands' rail and sn chsng ldrs: rdn along wl over 1f out: drvn ent fnl f and no imp* **10/1**

3121 **6** *7* **Mr Sundowner (USA)**[28] 7387 5-9-0 73 (t) RachelRichardson(3) 13 63
(Wilf Storey) *trckd ldrs: hdwy over 3f out: rdn along over 2f out: sn drvn and one pce* **14/1**

4532 **7** *2 3/4* **Peterhouse (USA)**[30] 7328 5-9-1 71 (p) KieranShoemark 15 57
(Jason Ward) *a towards rr* **12/1**

1003 **8** *shd* **Vernatti**[30] 7338 4-9-10 80 RobHornby 8 66
(Pam Sly) *cl up: led over 7f out: rdn along over 3f out: hdd over 2f out and sn wknd* **13/2**[2]

1362 **9** *5* **Omotesando**[14] 7831 7-8-8 67 (p) CharlieBennett(3) 10 45
(Oliver Greenall) *trckd ldrs: pushed along over 3f out: rdn wl over 2f out: sn drvn and wknd* **20/1**

3204 **10** *4 1/2* **Northwest Frontier (IRE)**[18] 7701 3-9-4 80 TonyHamilton 4 51
(Richard Fahey) *trckd ldrs: pushed along 4f out: rdn over 3f out: sn wknd* **9/4**[1]

6055 **11** *13* **Ray's The Money (IRE)**[24] 7516 3-8-10 79 (v) TristanPrice(7) 14 30
(Michael Bell) *a in rr* **12/1**

00/0 **P** **Golden Bowl (FR)**[21] 7599 7-9-7 77 JasonHart 5
(John Quinn) *in tch: pushed along 1/2-way: rdn over 4f out: sn lost pl and bhd whn p.u over 3f out* **66/1**

2m 49.93s (11.03) **Going Correction** +1.05s/f (Soft)
**WFA** 3 from 4yo+ 6lb **12 Ran SP% 112.1**
Speed ratings (Par 105): **105,104,104,104,102 97,95,95,92,89 80,**
CSF £135.41 CT £1878.51 TOTE £7.00: £2.60, £6.00, £3.90; EX 160.80 Trifecta £2545.80.
**Owner** Let's Be Lucky Racing 12 **Bred** Cheveley Park Stud Ltd **Trained** Carrutherstown, D'fries & G'way
■ Albert's Back was withdrawn. Price at time of withdrawal 22-1. Rule 4 does not apply.

**FOCUS**
A competitive middle-distance handicap and a thrilling finish. Again they came towards the nearside up the straight and the pace was good in the conditions, the first two coming from well back. A small pb from the winner, with the third rated to this year's form.

## 8240 TOTETRIFECTA H'CAP 7f 6y
**4:40** (4:43) (Class 4) (0-80,83) 3-Y-O+
**£7,470** (£2,236; £1,118; £559; £279; £140) **Stalls** Low

Form RPR

5000 **1** **Boots And Spurs**[8] 8009 8-8-11 77 (v) JamieGormley(7) 11 86
(Scott Dixon) *trckd ldrs: cl up over 2f out: rdn to ld ent fnl f: drvn and kpt on wl towards fin* **12/1**

2133 **2** 1 **Lady In Question (IRE)**[16] 7771 3-8-13 **74** ...................... JackGarritty 3 79+
(Richard Fahey) *trckd ldrs on inner: hdwy 3f out: cl up over 2f out: rdn to ld 1 1/2f out: hdd ent fnl f: sn drvn and kpt on same pce towards fin* **10/1**

0254 **3** 1 ¼ **God Willing**[33] 7223 6-9-0 **76** ........................ PhilDennis(3) 8 79
(Declan Carroll) *in tch: hdwy 3f out: chsd ldrs 2f out: sn rdn: drvn and kpt on fnl f* **11/2**[2]

113 **4** 1 **Penny Pot Lane**[21] 7628 4-9-1 **77** ........................ LewisEdmunds(3) 7 78
(Richard Whitaker) *towards rr: hdwy over 2f out: rdn to chse ldrs over 1f out: kpt on u.p fnl f* **10/1**

5261 **5** nk **Roaring Forties (IRE)**[5] 8107 4-9-9 **82** 6ex..................(p) PhillipMakin 15 82
(Rebecca Bastiman) *towards rr: hdwy and wd st: effrt on stands' rail to chse ldrs wl over 1f out and sn rdn: drvn ent fnl f: kpt on* **9/2**[1]

5040 **6** hd **Showboating (IRE)**[21] 7594 9-9-7 **80** ........................ JasonHart 1 79
(John Balding) *in tch on inner: hdwy 2f out: rdn over 1f out: kpt on same pce fnl f* **16/1**

2365 **7** 2 **Fieldsman (USA)**[15] 7789 5-9-5 **78** ..............................(h¹) ShaneGray 13 72
(David O'Meara) *in rr: wd st: hdwy towards stands' rail 2f out: sn rdn and kpt on fnl f* **20/1**

2136 **8** ½ **Our Charlie Brown**[12] 7892 3-9-2 **77** ........................ JamesSullivan 12 69
(Tim Easterby) *towards rr: hdwy over 2f out: rdn wl over 1f out: n.d* **10/1**

3000 **9** 2 **Bouclier (IRE)**[8] 8014 7-8-11 **77** ........................ RyanTimby(7) 5 65
(Michael Easterby) *a towards rr* **66/1**

3340 **10** nk **Madroos**[11] 7941 4-8-10 **76** ........................ HarrisonShaw(7) 2 63
(Michael Easterby) *a in rr* **20/1**

6021 **11** nk **Intense Style (IRE)**[25] 7474 5-9-0 **80** ................... FayeMcManoman(7) 9 66
(Les Eyre) *prom: rdn along wl over 2f out: sn wknd* **11/1**

6202 **12** 2 ¾ **Flyboy (IRE)**[33] 7223 4-9-5 **78** ........................(b) DavidNolan 4 57
(Richard Fahey) *cl up: chal 3f out: rdn to ld briefly jst over 2f out: hdd and drvn in centre wl over 1f out: grad wknd* **7/1**[3]

3010 **13** 1 ½ **Proud Archi (IRE)**[49] 6672 3-9-5 **80** ........................ PaulMulrennan 6 54
(Michael Dods) *a in rr* **16/1**

0032 **14** ¾ **Echo Of Lightning**[8] 8014 7-9-3 **83** ..............(p) BenSanderson(7) 10 56
(Roger Fell) *led: rdn along 3f out: hdd over 2f out: sn wknd* **12/1**

1m 33.02s (6.02) **Going Correction** +1.05s/f (Soft)
**WFA** 3 from 4yo+ 2lb **14** Ran SP% **119.8**
Speed ratings (Par 105): **107,105,104,103,102 102,100,99,97,97 96,93,92,91**
CSF £123.64 CT £765.31 TOTE £12.30: £4.00, £3.10, £1.20; EX 158.40 Trifecta £1198.90.
**Owner** S Chappell **Bred** Miss G Abbey **Trained** Babworth, Notts

**FOCUS**
Another competitive handicap and again they came nearside up the straight. This was a race where those who raced prominently were at an advantage. The third has been rated close to his recent form.

## 8241 COLLECT TOTEPOOL WINNINGS AT BETFRED SHOPS APPRENTICE H'CAP (GO RACING IN YORKSHIRE FUTURE STARS) 1m 5f 192y
**5:10** (5:11) (Class 6) (0-60,59) 3-Y-O+ **£3,234** (£962; £481; £240) **Stalls** Low

Form RPR

3300 **1** **Tonto's Spirit**[64] 6126 5-9-9 **59** ..................(h) SeamusCronin(5) 6 76
(Kenneth Slack) *mde all and sn clr: rdn wl over 1f out and styd on strly: unchal* **11/4**[1]

4061 **2** 14 **Jan De Heem**[32] 7248 7-9-11 **59** ..................(p) ConnorMurtagh(3) 10 55
(Tina Jackson) *hld up in rr: stdy hdwy over 5f out: chsd ldng pair 3f out: sn rdn and chsd wnr fr over 1f out: sn drvn and kpt on: no ch w wnr* **8/1**[3]

0422 **3** 1 ¾ **Inspector Norse**[12] 7885 6-9-4 **54** ..................(b¹) RobertDodsworth(5) 3 47
(Tim Easterby) *chsd wnr: hdwy and tk clsr order 4f out: rdn along 3f out: drvn 2f out and sn one pce* **9/1**

6-05 **4** 7 **Allfredandnobell (IRE)**[11] 7922 4-9-1 **46** ........................ RowanScott 7 29
(Micky Hammond) *hld up: rdn along and hdwy 3f out: plugged on fnl 2f: nvr a factor* **14/1**

4103 **5** 4 ½ **Adrakhan (FR)**[11] 7922 6-9-1 **49** ........................ NicolaCurrie(3) 9 25
(Wilf Storey) *in tch: hdwy to chse ldrs over 4f out: rdn along over 3f out: sn one pce* **9/1**

6004 **6** ¾ **Red Star Dancer (IRE)**[9] 7982 3-8-6 **49** ........................ BenSanderson(5) 13 26
(David Barron) *a towards rr* **8/1**[3]

0-36 **7** 2 ¾ **Aneedh**[106] 4558 7-9-0 **50** ..................(p) SebastianWoods(5) 4 21
(Clive Mulhall) *chsd ldrs: rdn along over 4f out: sn wknd* **40/1**

4131 **8** 2 ¼ **Our Cilla**[35] 7152 3-9-4 **59** ..................(b) MillyNaseb(3) 14 29
(Julia Feilden) *chsd ldrs: rdn along over 4f out: sn wknd* **7/2**[2]

0660 **9** 9 **Pennerley**[29] 7360 4-8-8 **46** ........................ LaurenSteade(7) 5
(Micky Hammond) *in tch: rdn along over 5f out: a bhd* **100/1**

0563 **10** 33 **Good Man (IRE)**[12] 7885 4-8-13 **47** ..................(p) JamieGormley(3) 1
(Karen McLintock) *in tch: pushed along 1/2-way: rdn over 5f out: sn wknd* **8/1**[3]

3600 **11** 16 **Fillydelphia (IRE)**[12] 7885 6-9-0 **48** ........................ PaulaMuir(3) 11
(Patrick Holmes) *a in rr* **40/1**

030/ **12** 6 **Missy Wells**[1143] 6062 7-9-2 **52** ..................(h¹) HarrisonShaw(5) 12
(Marjorie Fife) *a in rr* **50/1**

3m 19.95s (16.35) **Going Correction** +1.05s/f (Soft)
**WFA** 3 from 4yo+ 7lb **12** Ran SP% **116.7**
Speed ratings (Par 101): **95,87,86,82,79 79,77,76,71,52 43,39**
CSF £24.50 CT £176.00 TOTE £4.30: £1.40, £3.00, £2.60; EX 26.00 Trifecta £158.40.
**Owner** A Slack **Bred** Mrs J M Quy **Trained** Hilton, Cumbria

**FOCUS**
A moderate staying apprentice handicap and the way they finished so spread out was more like a 3m chase than a Flat race. The winner bolted up.
T/Plt: £8,507.80 to a £1 stake. Pool: £60,604.12 - 5.20 winning units. T/Qpdt: £154.80 to a £1 stake. Pool: £5,085.40 - 24.30 winning units. **Joe Rowntree**

# 7826 WOLVERHAMPTON (A.W) (L-H)
Saturday, October 21

**OFFICIAL GOING: Tapeta: standard**
Wind: Windy Weather: Rain

## 8242 FCL GLOBAL FORWARDING MAIDEN STKS 5f 21y (Tp)
**5:40** (5:40) (Class 5) 3-Y-O+ **£3,557** (£1,058; £529; £264) **Stalls** Low

Form RPR

3 **1** **Ahundrednotout**[101] 4770 3-9-5 50 ........................ StevieDonohoe 5 63
(John James Feane, Ire) *mde all: narrow ld tl kicked 1 l clr over 1f out: rdn ent fnl f: hld on wl* **8/1**[3]

0256 **2** ½ **Blazed (IRE)**[32] 7255 3-9-0 69 ..................(t) PaddyPilley(5) 7 61+
(Roger Charlton) *slowly away: t.k.h in rr: hdwy to trck ldrs over 1f out: n.m.r ent fnl f: sn in clr: rdn and r.o wl: nrst fin* **13/8**[1]

0022 **3** 1 **Raffle King (IRE)**[16] 7767 3-9-2 66 ........................ CallumShepherd(3) 2 58
(Mick Channon) *hld up: hdwy over 1f out: sn drvn: kpt on to take 3rd ins fnl f* **5/2**[2]

0-50 **4** 1 **Noneedtotellme (IRE)**[47] 6748 4-8-7 40 ..................(v) WilliamCox(7) 6 48?
(James Unett) *in rr: pushed along over 2f out: racd wd and hdwy over 1f out: rdn and briefly wnt lft 1f out: sn stened: kpt on wl fnl f* **66/1**

5433 **5** nk **Zilza (IRE)**[12] 7907 3-9-0 63 ..................(bt) JimmyQuinn 8 48
(Conrad Allen) *cl up in 2nd tl wnr kicked 1 l clr over 1f out: rdn fnl f: no ex* **5/2**[2]

600- **6** 3 ¼ **Like Minds**[334] 8046 3-9-0 41 ........................ KevinStott 4 36
(David Brown) *trckd ldrs: pushed along into 3rd over 1f out: sn rdn and no ex* **66/1**

60-0 **7** 2 ½ **Singula**[127] 3784 3-9-5 61 ........................ WilliamCarson 3 32
(Alan King) *trckd ldrs: pushed along in 3rd 2f out: sn rdn and wknd over 1f out* **22/1**

0060 **8** hd **Chillililli**[157] 2734 3-9-0 42 ........................ AlistairRawlinson 9 27
(Michael Appleby) *prom: pushed along 2f out: rdn and lost pl over 1f out* **100/1**

00 **9** 4 **Eye Burner**[12] 7907 3-9-5 0 ........................ KierenFox 1 17
(J R Jenkins) *slowly away: a in rr* **100/1**

1m 1.93s (0.03) **Going Correction** -0.125s/f (Stan) **9** Ran SP% **115.7**
Speed ratings (Par 103): **94,93,91,90,89 84,80,80,73**
CSF £21.43 TOTE £8.20: £2.60, £1.10, £1.40; EX 34.70 Trifecta £68.60.
**Owner** D A Lynch **Bred** Churchill Bloodstock Investments Ltd **Trained** Curragh, Co Kildare

**FOCUS**
Rainy conditions ahead of this eight-race evening fixture, which commenced with an already moderate maiden weakened further by the absence of 82-rated Connacht Girl. A clear pb from the winner, but the fourth and sixth highlight the limitations of the form.

## 8243 FCL GLOBAL FORWARDING FILLIES' H'CAP 6f 20y (Tp)
**6:15** (6:15) (Class 5) (0-70,69) 3-Y-O+ **£3,881** (£1,155; £577; £288) **Stalls** Low

Form RPR

0506 **1** **Love Oasis**[11] 7923 3-9-3 **66** ........................ PJMcDonald 5 73
(Mark Johnston) *trckd ldrs: rdn over 1f out: hdwy to ld 100yds out: r.o wl to assert nr fin* **7/1**

-000 **2** ½ **Four Dragons**[28] 7409 3-9-4 **67** ..................(p) RichardKingscote 6 72
(Tom Dascombe) *trckd ldrs: hdwy to chal over 1f out: sn ev ch: r.o to take 2nd wl ins fnl f: hld by wnr nr fin* **9/1**

4432 **3** nk **Kodicat (IRE)**[47] 6768 3-9-6 **69** ........................ KevinStott 3 73
(Kevin Ryan) *trckd ldrs: pushed along and hdwy over 1f out: rdn and led 1f out: hdd 100yds out: no ex* **9/2**[3]

45 **4** ¾ **Roys Dream**[30] 7332 3-8-10 **66** ........................ GabrieleMalune(7) 12 68
(Paul Collins) *hld up: pushed along and hdwy over 1f out: reminders and kpt on wl fnl f* **11/1**

0146 **5** nk **Look Surprised**[31] 7272 4-9-1 **66** ........................ MitchGodwin(3) 11 67
(Roger Teal) *hld up: drvn and hdwy over 1f out: rdn fnl f: kpt on* **33/1**

5514 **6** 1 **Magic Moments**[28] 7409 4-9-4 **66** ........................ TomMarquand 4 63
(Alan King) *mid-div: pushed along and hdwy on outer 2f out: ch 1f out: one pce fnl f* **7/2**[2]

4256 **7** ¾ **Whitecrest**[11] 7933 9-9-6 **68** ........................ WilliamCarson 2 63
(John Spearing) *mid-div: pushed along 2f out: rdn and hdwy over 1f out: no ex fnl f* **20/1**

5500 **8** 1 **Kachess**[91] 5134 3-9-3 **66** ........................ PatCosgrave 8 58
(David Loughnane) *cl 2nd: drvn to ld wl over 1f out: rdn and hdd 1f out: wknd* **16/1**

3210 **9** 2 ¼ **Robbie Roo Roo**[12] 7899 4-9-2 **64** ..................(vt) AdamBeschizza 10 49
(Mrs Ilka Gansera-Leveque) *mid-div: racd wd 2f out: drvn over 1f out: no imp* **9/4**[1]

3-10 **10** nk **Shesthedream (IRE)**[22] 7572 4-9-7 **69** ........................ BenCurtis 13 53
(David Barron) *slowly away: drvn 2f out: rdn over 1f out: no imp* **40/1**

1-00 **11** 2 ¼ **Mysterious Glance**[61] 6267 4-9-4 **66** ........................ CamHardie 9 43
(Sarah Hollinshead) *in rr: pushed along 2f out: rdn over 1f out: no imp* **100/1**

2106 **12** 1 ¼ **Beau Mistral (IRE)**[19] 7689 8-9-5 **67** ........................ GeorgeDowning 1 40
(Tony Carroll) *led tl hdd wl over 1f out: fdd* **50/1**

1m 13.45s (-1.05) **Going Correction** -0.125s/f (Stan)
**WFA** 3 from 4yo+ 1lb **12** Ran SP% **121.0**
Speed ratings (Par 100): **102,101,100,99,99 98,97,95,92,92 89,87**
CSF £66.88 CT £320.75 TOTE £7.30: £2.20, £2.80, £2.10; EX 85.00 Trifecta £469.40.
**Owner** Crone Stud Farms Ltd **Bred** New England, Mount Coote & P Barrett **Trained** Middleham Moor, N Yorks

**FOCUS**
The pace appeared to steady leaving the back straight in this modest fillies' handicap, and as many as seven horses held chances with just over a furlong to travel. The third has been rated to form.

## 8244 FCL GLOBAL FORWARDING MAKING LOGISTICS PERSONAL H'CAP 1m 4f 51y (Tp)
**6:45** (6:45) (Class 3) (0-95,95) 3-Y-O- **£7,561** (£2,263; £1,131; £566; £282) **Stalls** Low

Form RPR

1000 **1** **Master Singer (USA)**[15] 7785 3-9-0 **91** ..................(b¹) RobertTart 2 102+
(John Gosden) *trckd ldr: led 2f out: pushed 2 l clr over 1f out: reminders ent fnl f: r.o wl: readily* **2/1**[1]

-060 **2** 1 **Goldmember**[56] 6427 4-9-5 **90** ........................ PatCosgrave 3 98
(David Simcock) *trckd ldrs: pushed along into 2nd over 1f out: rdn ent fnl f: kpt on wl but hld by wnr* **11/1**

2160 **3** 1 ½ **Kasperenko**[43] 6887 3-9-3 **94** ..................(b) TedDurcan 5 100+
(David Lanigan) *hld up: drvn and hdwy over 1f out: rdn fnl f: styd on to take 3rd last 50yds* **3/1**[2]

2063 **4** ½ **Fierce Impact (JPN)**[54] 6514 3-9-4 **95** ..................(p) StevieDonohoe 4 100
(David Simcock) *mid-div: drvn into 4th 2f out: hdwy and rdn into 3rd 1f out: no ex ins fnl f: lost 3rd last 50yds* **10/1**

4006 **5** 1 **Start Seven**[57] 6398 5-9-3 **88** ........................ DougieCostello 7 91
(Jamie Osborne) *hld up: effrt and c wd over 1f out: rdn fnl f: styd on wl: nvr nrr* **40/1**

5600 **6** nk **Barye**[28] 7397 6-9-3 **95** ........................ StephenCummins(7) 10 98
(Richard Hughes) *mid-div: rdn ent fnl f: kpt on* **16/1**

0004 **7** ½ **Isharah (USA)**[36] 7110 4-9-2 **87** ........................ PJMcDonald 9 89
(Mark Johnston) *trckd ldrs: pushed along 2f out: 3rd whn rdn over 1f out: sn lost pl: fdd fnl f* **12/1**

0000 **8** ½ **Bear Valley (IRE)**[8] 8005 3-8-0 **82** ........................ JaneElliott(5) 12 83
(Mark Johnston) *hld up: rdn over 1f out: no imp* **9/1**[3]

2000 **9** ¾ **Cliff Face (IRE)**[30] 7337 4-9-2 **87** ..................(p) LukeMorris 11 87
(Sir Mark Prescott Bt) *hld up in last: rdn and mod late hdwy fr over 1f out* **12/1**

000- **10** 3 1/4 **Forgotten Hero (IRE)**[59] 7538 8-9-5 **90**......................(t) TimmyMurphy 6 85
(Kim Bailey) *trckd ldrs: pushed along and lost pl 2f out: sn drvn and wknd* **66/1**

666 **11** 1 3/4 **Coillte Cailin (IRE)**[49] 6687 7-9-2 **90**................................ JoshDoyle(3) 8 82
(David O'Meara) *hld up: pushed along 2f out: rdn fnl f: no imp* **40/1**

4604 **12** 3 1/2 **Eye Of The Storm (IRE)**[15] 7785 7-9-4 **89**............. RichardKingscote 1 76
(Amanda Perrett) *led: drvn and hdd 2f out: wknd qckly* **10/1**

2m 37.23s (-3.57) **Going Correction** -0.125s/f (Stan)
**WFA** 3 from 4yo+ 6lb 12 Ran SP% **122.5**
Speed ratings (Par 107): **106,105,104,104,103 103,102,102,101,99 98,96**
CSF £26.69 CT £69.14 TOTE £3.00: £1.60, £3.70, £1.70; EX 34.20 Trifecta £139.60.
**Owner** Teneri Farms Inc **Bred** Teneri Farm Inc & Bernardo A Calderon **Trained** Newmarket, Suffolk

**FOCUS**
A well-stocked feature on paper, but very few got into it off a routine gallop. It's been rated positively.

## 8245 FCL GLOBAL FORWARDING NOVICE STKS 1m 142y (Tp)
**7:15** (7:17) (Class 5) 2-Y-O £3,881 (£1,155; £577; £288) **Stalls** Low

Form RPR

**1** **Wissahickon (USA)** 2-9-2 0........................................ NickyMackay 12 76+
(John Gosden) *mid-div: effrt on outer 2f out: pushed along over 1f out: hdwy to chal ent fnl f: clsd on runner-up last 50yds: led last stride* **7/2**[2]

4 **2** *nse* **Craving (IRE)**[25] 7488 2-9-2 0.................................. RichardKingscote 3 75
(Simon Crisford) *led: pushed along 2f out: 1 l ahd whn rdn over 1f out: hrd pressed fnl f: ct last stride* **9/4**[1]

0 **3** *1* **Ready To Impress (USA)**[9] 7987 2-9-2 0.................... PJMcDonald 11 73
(Mark Johnston) *trckd ldrs: pushed along 2f out: drvn into 2nd over 1f out: rdn and clsd on ldr ent fnl f: sn ev ch: no ex and lost 2nd wl ins fnl f* **9/1**

1 **4** *1* **Ocean Voyage (IRE)**[33] 7221 2-9-1 0............................ BarryMcHugh 2 70
(Richard Fahey) *hld up: rdn and hdwy on inner over 1f out: kpt on to take 4th ins fnl f* **12/1**

3135 **5** *2* **Yaafour**[14] 7814 2-9-9 85................................................ TomMarquand 7 74
(Richard Hannon) *chsd ldr: drvn 2f out: lost pl over 1f out: sn rdn and wknd* **7/2**[2]

310 **6** *hd* **The Throstles**[36] 7106 2-9-1 71............................ ManuelFernandes(5) 1 71
(Kevin Frost) *trckd ldrs: pushed along 2f out: rdn over 1f out: wknd fnl f* **12/1**

0 **7** 1 1/2 **Battle Lines**[28] 7391 2-9-2 0............................................. PatCosgrave 5 63
(James Tate) *mid-div: drvn 2f out: rdn over 1f out: no imp* **11/2**[3]

0 **8** *hd* **Twister (IRE)**[31] 7281 2-9-2 0........................................ LukeMorris 8 63
(Sir Mark Prescott Bt) *mid-div: pushed along over 1f out: one pce* **66/1**

6 **9** *nk* **Seaborough (IRE)**[28] 7411 2-9-2 0.............................. WilliamCarson 6 62
(Alan King) *hld up: pushed along 2f out: one pce under hand riding fnl f* **100/1**

0 **10** *11* **Isle Of Man**[50] 6654 2-9-2 0.......................................... SamHitchcott 13 39
(Clive Cox) *hld up: bmpd along 3f out: racd wd 2f out: fdd* **40/1**

**11** *29* **Lisnamoyle Lady (IRE)** 2-8-11 0....................................... KierenFox 4
(Martin Smith) *v.s.a: a wl bhd* **100/1**

1m 48.53s (-1.57) **Going Correction** -0.125s/f (Stan) 11 Ran SP% **121.9**
Speed ratings (Par 95): **101,100,100,99,97 97,95,95,95,85 59**
CSF £12.26 TOTE £4.90: £1.90, £1.60, £2.70; EX 18.00 Trifecta £123.20.
**Owner** George Strawbridge **Bred** Augustin Stable **Trained** Newmarket, Suffolk

**FOCUS**
In all likelihood a fair novice event, and a nail-biting finish. The likes of the sixth help govern the level.

## 8246 CONTACT US AT FCLGF.COM H'CAP 2m 120y (Tp)
**7:45** (7:46) (Class 6) (0-60,60) 3-Y-O+ £2,587 (£770; £384; £192) **Stalls** Low

Form RPR

0052 **1** **Ballyfarsoon (IRE)**[9] 7992 6-9-7 **55**.........................(v) StevieDonohoe 7 63
(Ian Williams) *trckd ldrs: hmpd and lost pl 4f out: pushed along and hdwy 3f out: wnt 3rd 2f out: rdn over 1f out: clsd on ldr ent fnl f: led 150yds out: r.o wl: comf* **9/2**[3]

-520 **2** 2 1/2 **Hermarna (IRE)**[58] 6343 4-9-6 **57**............................ GeorgiaCox(3) 3 61
(Neil King) *led: drvn into 2 l ld 2f out: rdn over 1f out: clsd down by wnr ent fnl f: hdd 150yds out: no ex* **18/1**

1343 **3** 3/4 **Ocean Gale**[17] 7730 4-9-1 **49**............................................ LukeMorris 1 52
(Richard Price) *trckd ldrs: rdn and hdwy on inner over 1f out: styd on to go 3rd ins fnl f* **13/2**

0411 **4** 3/4 **Navajo Star (IRE)**[2] 8187 3-8-12 **59** 6ex.....................(v) JaneElliott(5) 12 63
(Michael Appleby) *hld up: effrt on outer 2f out: rdn and hdwy into 5th over 1f out: kpt on into 4th fnl f* **10/3**[1]

**5** *nse* **Molly Kaye**[8] 8022 4-9-5 **53**.......................................... RobertWinston 2 55
(S M Duffy, Ire) *trckd ldrs: drvn into 2nd 2f out: rdn and lost pl over 1f out: fdd ins fnl f* **15/2**

-550 **6** 3/4 **Medieval Bishop (IRE)**[72] 5850 8-8-8 **49**.....................(p) TobyEley(7) 4 50
(Tony Forbes) *mid-div: lost pl 2f out: sn rdn: kpt on fnl f* **50/1**

0640 **7** 1 3/4 **Yasir (USA)**[16] 7761 9-8-13 **47**...................................... WilliamCarson 6 46
(Conor Dore) *hld up: drvn 3f out: n.m.r 2f out: racd wd over 1f out: sn rdn and no imp* **12/1**

6200 **8** 1 1/4 **Bumble Bay**[25] 7490 7-9-2 **53**..............................(t) CallumShepherd(3) 8 51
(Robert Stephens) *hld up: drvn 2f out: effrt and rdn over 1f out: one pce* **28/1**

6004 **9** *3* **Gabrial The Duke (IRE)**[51] 6632 7-9-7 **55**................(p) FrannyNorton 10 49
(Patrick Morris) *hld up: drvn 2f out: no imp* **16/1**

3000 **10** 2 1/2 **Almutamarred (USA)**[14] 7832 5-9-12 **60**....................(p) TimmyMurphy 5 51
(James Unett) *slowly away: in rr: hdwy 4f out: drvn 2f out: rdn over 1f out: no imp* **20/1**

000 **11** *1* **Storming Harry**[66] 6069 5-8-7 **48**.................................. WilliamCox(7) 13 38
(Robin Dickin) *hld up: pushed along 2f out: rdn and racd wd over 1f out: wknd* **33/1**

6530 **12** 1 1/2 **The Last Melon**[17] 7730 5-9-5 **53**...................................... RyanPowell 11 41+
(James Bennett) *slowly away: sn rcvrd to go prom: 2nd after 5f: drvn and lost pl 3f out: fdd* **14/1**

03-3 **13** *7* **Asian Wing (IRE)**[49] 6709 8-8-9 **59**.................................(t) DavidEgan(3) 9 39
(John James Feane, Ire) *hld up: hdwy on outer 4f out: pushed along into 3rd 2f out: sn drvn and wknd* **4/1**[2]

3m 40.4s (-3.30) **Going Correction** -0.125s/f (Stan)
**WFA** 3 from 4yo+ 8lb 13 Ran SP% **125.0**
Speed ratings (Par 101): **102,100,100,100,100 99,98,98,96,95 95,94,91**
CSF £83.26 CT £542.78 TOTE £5.10: £1.70, £5.80, £2.70; EX 129.50 Trifecta £572.10.
**Owner** Patrick Kelly **Bred** A O'Sullivan **Trained** Portway, Worcs
■ Stewards' Enquiry : Robert Winston caution: careless riding

**FOCUS**
An ordinary marathon handicap run at a slow tempo until well past halfway. The winner has been rated close to the best of last year's form.

## 8247 FCL PERSONALISED GLOBAL FREIGHT SOLUTIONS H'CAP (DIV I) 1m 142y (Tp)
**8:15** (8:21) (Class 6) (0-55,55) 3-Y-O+ £2,587 (£770; £384; £192) **Stalls** Low

Form RPR

3001 **1** **Born To Reason (IRE)**[14] 7833 3-9-3 **55**...................(b) DougieCostello 1 60+
(Kevin Frost) *hld up: hdwy gng wl over 1f out: plld wd to chal 1f out: drvn ent fnl f: rdn to ld on fining line* **11/8**[1]

6-42 **2** *hd* **Stamp Duty (IRE)**[175] 2166 9-8-12 **46** oh1........................ LukeMorris 8 51
(Suzzanne France) *mid-div: pushed along and hdwy 2f out: led ent fnl f: rdn and r.o wl: ct on fining line* **11/1**

3646 **3** *hd* **Henry Did It (IRE)**[51] 6611 3-8-9 **47**............................. TomMarquand 4 52
(Tony Carroll) *mid-div: pushed along and hdwy to go 3rd 2f out: rdn and ev ch 1f out: kpt on wl towards fin* **12/1**

3250 **4** *hd* **Top Offer**[42] 6947 8-9-7 **55**.......................................(b[1]) FrannyNorton 7 59
(Patrick Morris) *hld up: hdwy over 1f out: rdn ent fnl f: r.o strly: fin wl* **5/1**[2]

0060 **5** 1/2 **Gog Elles (IRE)**[3] 8152 3-8-11 **49**.................................(b) BenCurtis 10 52
(J S Moore) *chsd ldr: led 2f out: rdn over 1f out: hdd ent fnl f: no ex* **10/1**

000 **6** 2 1/2 **Bed Of Diamonds**[9] 7990 3-8-3 **46** oh1........................ RhiainIngram(5) 6 44
(Adam West) *prom: drvn on outer 2f out: rdn fnl f: no ex* **33/1**

000 **7** 1 1/2 **Sunnyside Bob (IRE)**[29] 7366 4-9-4 **52**........................ RobertWinston 3 47
(Neville Bycroft) *trckd ldrs: drvn over 1f out: one pce* **16/1**

4000 **8** 1/2 **Kensington Palace (IRE)**[32] 7240 4-9-2 **50**...............(p) BarryMcHugh 5 44
(Marjorie Fife) *trckd ldrs: cl up whn rdn over 1f out: no ex fnl f* **20/1**

4200 **9** *hd* **Devil's Guard (IRE)**[52] 6594 3-8-13 **51**...................... ConnorBeasley 11 44
(Keith Dalgleish) *led: pushed along and hdd 2f out: sn rdn and wknd* **13/2**[3]

0600 **10** *5* **Bearag**[10] 7945 3-8-11 **52**............................................ ShelleyBirkett(3) 12 35
(David O'Meara) *hld up in last: pushed along 2f out: rdn over 1f out: no imp* **33/1**

6660 **11** *nk* **Tranquil Tracy**[24] 7523 3-8-8 **46** oh1............................ AdamBeschizza 2 28
(John Norton) *in rr: drvn and relegated to last 2f out: fdd* **50/1**

1m 50.15s (0.05) **Going Correction** -0.125s/f (Stan)
**WFA** 3 from 4yo+ 4lb 11 Ran SP% **115.7**
Speed ratings (Par 101): **94,93,93,93,93 90,89,89,88,84 84**
CSF £16.26 CT £120.65 TOTE £2.20: £1.10, £2.70, £3.10; EX 16.10 Trifecta £72.90.
**Owner** Ryan Carroll **Bred** Christopher Glynn **Trained** Market Drayton, Shropshire
■ Three Majors was withdrawn. Price at time of withdrawal 14/1. Rule 4 applies to all bets. Deduction - 5p in the pound.

**FOCUS**
Only a moderate handicap and a bit of a messy race, but a very tight finish and a winning effort to mark up a touch. The second and third are fair guides to the level.

## 8248 FCL PERSONALISED GLOBAL FREIGHT SOLUTIONS H'CAP (DIV II) 1m 142y (Tp)
**8:45** (8:47) (Class 6) (0-55,55) 3-Y-O+ £2,587 (£770; £384; £192) **Stalls** Low

Form RPR

0540 **1** **Hot Mustard**[21] 7605 7-9-4 **53**......................................(h) DavidEgan(3) 8 61
(William Muir) *trckd ldrs: pushed along and hdwy 2f out: drvn over 1f out: sn rdn: led ent fnl f: r.o wl to assert last 100yds* **5/1**[1]

6401 **2** 3/4 **The King's Steed**[9] 7980 4-9-2 **48**........................(t[1]) BarryMcHugh 3 54
(Micky Hammond) *trckd ldrs: hdwy to ld 2f out: rdn over 1f out: hdd ent fnl f: kpt on but hld last 100yds* **8/1**

6603 **3** *3* **Peny Arcade**[12] 7889 3-8-10 **46**......................................... PJMcDonald 2 46
(Alistair Whillans) *mid-div: pushed along into 4th 2f out: drvn into 3rd over 1f out: rdn and kpt on ins fnl f* **11/2**[2]

004 **4** 3/4 **Subotal (IRE)**[15] 7793 4-9-0 **46**.................................... ConnorBeasley 4 44
(Richard Guest) *mid-div: rdn and hdwy on outer over 1f out: r.o fnl f* **16/1**

0000 **5** *nse* **Whip Up A Frenzy (IRE)**[14] 7820 5-8-10 **45**.........(p) ShelleyBirkett(3) 10 43
(David O'Meara) *mid-div: hdwy 2f out: rdn over 1f out: kpt on fnl f* **16/1**

5043 **6** 1 3/4 **Dukes Meadow**[30] 7323 6-8-13 **50**........................... RhiainIngram(5) 11 44
(Roger Ingram) *in rr: hdwy over 1f out: kpt on fnl f* **6/1**[3]

0000 **7** 3 3/4 **Cookie Ring (IRE)**[51] 6621 6-8-6 **45**........................(vt) PaulaMuir(7) 12 31
(Kristin Stubbs) *slowly away: rdn over 1f out: one pce* **17/2**

3500 **8** 3/4 **Lesanti**[25] 7480 3-8-9 **48**........................................... CallumShepherd(3) 1 33
(Ed de Giles) *hld up: drvn 2f out: rdn over 1f out: no imp* **10/1**

0062 **9** 1 3/4 **Eium Mac**[42] 6947 8-9-0 **51**.........................................(b) JaneElliott(5) 7 32
(Neville Bycroft) *led: drvn and hdd 2f out: sn rdn and wknd* **6/1**[3]

0450 **10** 1 3/4 **Sir Lancelott**[10] 7960 5-9-4 **55**.................................(p) BenRobinson(5) 9 33
(Adrian Nicholls) *chsd ldr: drvn and lost pl 2f out: sn rdn: fdd* **6/1**[3]

6630 **11** *27* **Hazell Berry (IRE)**[14] 7826 3-8-9 **45**.......................(b) AdamBeschizza 6
(Karen George) *in rr: drvn 3f out: lost tch 2f out: eased* **33/1**

0000 **12** *7* **Maid In Brittain**[95] 5007 3-8-9 **45**................................... CamHardie 5
(Antony Brittain) *trckd ldrs: drvn and lost pl qckly 3f out: wknd and eased* **50/1**

1m 48.17s (-1.93) **Going Correction** -0.125s/f (Stan)
**WFA** 3 from 4yo+ 4lb 12 Ran SP% **122.3**
Speed ratings (Par 101): **103,102,99,99,98 97,94,93,91,90 66,60**
CSF £46.42 CT £236.99 TOTE £5.30: £2.80, £3.00, £3.00; EX 49.50 Trifecta £146.20.
**Owner** Mrs G Rowland-Clark **Bred** Mrs F A Veasey **Trained** Lambourn, Berks
■ Stewards' Enquiry : Callum Shepherd two day ban: careless riding (4/6 Nov)

**FOCUS**
A good clip on from the outset, and the quicker of the two divisions by 1.98 seconds. The winner has been rated near the best of this year's form.

## 8249 FCLGF.COM H'CAP 1m 1f 104y (Tp)
**9:15** (9:16) (Class 6) (0-55,54) 3-Y-O+ £2,587 (£770; £384; £192) **Stalls** Low

Form RPR

6005 **1** **Arrowzone**[9] 7991 6-9-4 **51**.......................................(b) DougieCostello 5 62
(Kevin Frost) *t.k.h: trckd ldrs: wnt 2nd gng wl 3f out: drvn to ld over 1f out: rdn and drew clr ins fnl f: comf* **11/4**[1]

0000 **2** 2 1/2 **Cockney Boy**[54] 6524 4-9-1 **48**...........................(v[1]) AlistairRawlinson 10 54
(Michael Appleby) *led: wnt 3 l clr 3f out: drvn and ld reduced 2f out: rdn and hdd over 1f out: kpt on fnl f* **25/1**

1200 **3** 1/2 **Filament Of Gold (USA)**[42] 6953 6-9-2 **54**...............(p) FinleyMarsh(5) 3 59
(Roy Brotherton) *hld up: drvn and hdwy on inner over 2f out: rdn over 1f out: r.o to take 3rd ins fnl f* **15/2**

5500 **4** 3/4 **Sooqaan**[25] 7476 6-9-6 **53**.................................................... CamHardie 8 57
(Antony Brittain) *hld up: effrt on outer 2f out: rdn and hdwy over 1f out: r.o wl ins fnl f: nrst fin* **50/1**

2430 **5** 3/4 **Kerry Icon**[11] 7936 4-9-0 **47**.........................................(h) BenCurtis 1 49
(Iain Jardine) *mid-div: hdwy into 4th 2f out: rdn in 3rd over 1f out: no ex and lost two pls ins fnl f* **16/1**

4005 **6** 1 1/4 **Huddersfilly Town**[155] 2790 3-9-1 **52**.............................. FrannyNorton 6 52
(Ivan Furtado) *hld up: rdn and hdwy 2f out: kpt on under hand riding ins fnl f* **16/1**

6020 **7** 1 **Pensax Lady (IRE)**[114] 4262 4-9-7 **54**.............................. LukeMorris 4 52
(Daniel Mark Loughnane) *mid-div: drvn over 1f out: rdn ins fnl f: one pce* **14/1**

4000 **8** 3 1/4 **Outlaw Torn (IRE)**[9] 7991 8-9-4 **51**.............................. (e) ConnorBeasley 11 42
(Richard Guest) *chsd ldr: drvn 3f out: rdn and lost pl over 2f out: wknd* **14/1**

/ **9** 3 **Multiviz**[18] 7720 4-9-5 **52**.............................. RobertWinston 7 37
(S M Duffy, Ire) *mid-div: drvn 2f out: rdn over 1f out: no imp* **7/2**[2]

0642 **10** 3/4 **Haldaw**[9] 7990 3-8-12 **52**.............................. DavidEgan(3) 2 36
(Mick Channon) *trckd ldrs: rdn and lost pl 3f out: fdd* **9/2**[3]

-000 **11** 3/4 **Daleelak (IRE)**[9] 7979 4-9-3 **50**.............................. (b[1]) PJMcDonald 12 32
(Mark Johnston) *in rr: drvn over 2f out: no rspnse* **25/1**

0060 **12** 2 1/2 **Molten Lava (IRE)**[29] 7360 5-9-1 **48**.............................. (h[1]) JimmyQuinn 9 25
(Philip Kirby) *mid-div: rdn 3f out: wknd* **10/1**

0006 **13** 6 **May Mist**[14] 7826 5-8-7 **47**.............................. (b) DarraghKeenan(7) 13 12
(Trevor Wall) *mid-div: lost pl 1/2-way: sn drvn and wknd* **66/1**

1m 58.94s (-1.86) **Going Correction** -0.125s/f (Stan)
**WFA** 3 from 4yo+ 4lb **13** Ran SP% **124.2**
Speed ratings (Par 101): **103,100,100,99,99 97,97,94,91,90 90,87,82**
CSF £84.55 CT £489.87 TOTE £3.60: £1.80, £6.70, £2.90; EX 74.40 Trifecta £537.60.
**Owner** C & D Racing **Bred** J K Beckitt & Son **Trained** Market Drayton, Shropshire

**FOCUS**
Very few got into a race in which recent winning form was in relatively limited supply. The second and third help set a straightforward level.
T/Plt: £30.70 to a £1 stake. Pool: £91,538.93 - 2,170.71 winning units. T/Qpdt: £11.00 to a £1 stake. Pool: £10,727.53 - 715.31 winning units. **Keith McHugh**

# 8056 CAULFIELD (R-H)
Saturday, October 21

**OFFICIAL GOING: Turf: good**

## 8250a BMW CAULFIELD CUP (GROUP 1 H'CAP) (3YO+) (TURF) 1m 4f
6:30 3-Y-O+
**£1,111,111** (£248,538; £131,578; £73,099; £58,479; £43,859)

RPR

**1** **Boom Time (AUS)**[7] 8056 6-8-3 **0**.............................. (b) CoryParish 3 111
(David A & B Hayes & Tom Dabernig, Australia) *in tch in midfield: trckd ldrs over 2f out: rdn 2f out: nt clr run 1 1/2f out: styd on wl to ld 100yds out: drvn out* **50/1**

**2** 1 1/4 **Single Gaze (AUS)**[7] 8058 5-8-5 **0**.............................. KathyO'Hara 12 111
(Nick Olive, Australia) *led after 1 1/2f: hdd after 3f: chsd clr ldr: rdn and led over 2f out: hdd 100yds out: no ex clsng stages* **30/1**

**3** hd **Johannes Vermeer (IRE)**[7] 8058 4-8-8 **0**.............................. (t) BenMelham 2 114+
(A P O'Brien, Ire) *hld up towards rr of midfield: stdy hdwy fr 2 1/2f out: rdn 2f out: short of room under 2f out: nt clr run under 1f out: kpt on wl last 150yds: nrst fin* **4/1**[1]

**4** 1/2 **Lord Fandango (GER)**[7] 8056 4-7-12 **0**.............................. BenAllen 9 103
(Archie Alexander, Australia) *midfield on outer: rdn 2 1/2f out: drvn and kpt on fr 1 1/2f out: nt quite able to chal* **20/1**

**5** 3/4 **Humidor (NZ)**[14] 7848 5-8-11 **0**.............................. (t) DamianLane 7 115
(Darren Weir, Australia) *trckd ldrs: rdn 3f out: ev ch 1 1/2f out: drvn and wknd steadily fr over 1f out* **11/2**[2]

**6** shd **Abbey Marie (AUS)**[7] 8058 5-8-2 **0**.............................. BeauMertens 5 106
(Michael Kent, Australia) *hld up towards rr of midfield on outer: rdn 2f out: kpt on ins fnl f* **30/1**

**6** dht **Marmelo**[62] 6250 4-8-9 **0**.............................. HughBowman 10 113
(Hughie Morrison) *dwlt: towards rr: rdn 2 1/2f out: styd on fnl f: nrst fin* **15/1**

**8** 3/4 **Harlem**[14] 5-8-2 **0**.............................. (b[1]) ChadSchofield 1 105
(David A & B Hayes & Tom Dabernig, Australia) *midfield: rdn and kpt on same pce fr 2f out* **8/1**

**9** 1 1/4 **Jon Snow (NZ)**[7] 8058 4-8-8 **0**.............................. (v) StephenBaster 6 109
(Murray Baker & Andrew Forsman, New Zealand) *in tch in midfield on outer: rdn under 3f: keeping on at same pce whn hmpd under 1f out: no ch after* **12/1**

**10** 1/2 **Hardham (AUS)**[20] 4-8-4 **0**.............................. CraigNewitt 8 104
(David Brideoake, Australia) *hld up towards rr: rdn and kpt on steadily fr over 2f out: n.d* **80/1**

**11** shd **Amelie's Star (AUS)**[14] 6-8-0 **0**.............................. CraigAWilliams 13 100
(Darren Weir, Australia) *led: hdd after 1 1/2f: remained in tch: rdn over 3f out: ev ch 1 1/2f out: wknd ins fnl f* **17/2**

**12** shd **Wicklow Brave**[41] 6976 8-8-7 **0**.............................. JoaoMoreira 16 107
(W P Mullins, Ire) *s.s: towards rr of midfield: rdn and kpt on steadily fr 1 1/2f out: n.d* **70/1**

**13** 1 **Ventura Storm (IRE)**[14] 7848 4-8-7 **0**.............................. DamienOliver 4 105
(David A & B Hayes & Tom Dabernig, Australia) *midfield: rdn over 2f out: bmpd 2f out: wknd steadily fr 1 1/2f out* **11/1**

**14** 1 3/4 **Bonneval (NZ)**[7] 8058 4-8-4 **0**.............................. KerrinMcEvoy 14 99
(Murray Baker & Andrew Forsman, New Zealand) *a towards rr* **7/1**[3]

**15** 1/2 **Inference (AUS)**[7] 8058 4-8-6 **0**.............................. (bt[1]) DwayneDunn 11 100
(Michael, Wayne & John Hawkes, Australia) *a towards rr* **25/1**

**16** 7 **He's Our Rokkii (NZ)**[7] 5-8-7 **0**.............................. LukeNolen 15 90
(David A & B Hayes & Tom Dabernig, Australia) *a towards rr* **100/1**

**17** 4 1/2 **Sir Isaac Newton**[14] 7848 5-8-7 **0**.............................. KatelynMallyon 17 83+
(Robert Hickmott, Australia) *led after 3f: sn wl clr: rdn and qckly c bk to field under 3f out: hdd over 2f out: sn lost pl and eased* **70/1**

2m 27.66s **17** Ran SP% **113.9**

**Owner** D A Hayes **Bred** I K Loxton **Trained** Australia

**FOCUS**
This had looked a competitive event beforehand, but there was still a surprise winner. The first two home were in the first four passing the winning post with a circuit remaining, and the free-running Sir Isaac Newton made sure the pace was decent. Only two of the first ten emerged from a double-digit draw.

# 8087 CHANTILLY (R-H)
Saturday, October 21

**OFFICIAL GOING: Turf: good to soft; polytrack: standard**

## 8251a PRIX TILBURY (CONDITIONS) (4YO+) (POLYTRACK) 6f 110y
2:30 4-Y-O+ **£14,102** (£5,641; £4,230; £2,820; £1,410)

RPR

**1** **Lucky Team (FR)**[21] 7636 5-9-0 0.............................. (p) HugoJourniac 6 90
(J Boisnard, France) **113/10**

**2** 1 **King Malpic (FR)**[33] 4-9-0 0.............................. AntoineWerle 11 87
(T Lemer, France) **9/5**[1]

**3** 3 1/2 **Mc Queen (FR)**[18] 5-9-6 0.............................. EddyHardouin 10 83
(Yasmin Almenrader, Germany) **229/10**

**4** 1 1/4 **Snaad**[21] 7636 5-9-0 0.............................. AlexisBadel 7 73
(F-H Graffard, France) **49/10**[3]

**5** hd **For Ever (FR)**[35] 6-9-3 0.............................. (b) AntoineCoutier 3 76
(Carina Fey, France) **9/2**[2]

**6** nk **Borsakov (IRE)**[14] 5-9-0 0.............................. TheoBachelot 8 72
(V Luka Jr, Czech Republic) **118/10**

**7** snk **High Quality (IRE)**[19] 7697 4-8-10 0.............................. (b) MickaelBarzalona 12 67
(A Fabre, France) **54/10**

**8** 3/4 **Art Collection (FR)**[50] 6662 4-9-3 0.............................. PierreBazire 2 72
(Ruth Carr) *settled midfield: pushed along over 2f out: rdn over 1f out: no ex ins fnl f* **132/1**

**9** 5 1/2 **Galantes Ivresses (FR)**[74] 4-8-10 0.............................. AntoineHamelin 1 49
(J-P Gauvin, France) **116/10**

**10** 6 **Eshaan (IRE)**[568] 1188 4-9-0 0.............................. (b) VincentCheminaud 4 36
(Georgios Alimpinisis, Greece) **57/1**

**11** 1/2 **Monocle**[452] 4749 4-8-9 0.............................. DelphineSantiago(5) 9 34
(Georgios Alimpinisis, Greece) **90/1**

PARI-MUTUEL (all including 1 euro stake): WIN 12.30; PLACE 2.90, 1.40, 5.10; DF 14.10; SF 40.10.
**Owner** Mme S Boulin Redouly & Haras Du Hoguenet **Bred** Mme S Boulin Redouly & Haras Du Hoguenet **Trained** France

# 4196 LE CROISE-LAROCHE
Saturday, October 21

**OFFICIAL GOING: Turf: soft**

## 8252a PRIX MIGUEL CLEMENT (MAIDEN) (2YO) (TURF) 5f 110y
5:50 2-Y-O **£6,837** (£2,735; £2,051; £1,367; £683)

RPR

**1** **Historia (FR)**[111] 2-8-13 0.............................. (b) IoritzMendizabal 3 74
(F Chappet, France) **22/5**[3]

**2** 3/4 **Silver Stripes (IRE)**[40] 2-8-8 0.............................. DelphineSantiago(5) 2 71
(P Vovcenko, Germany) **11/1**

**3** nse **Ma Petite Toscane (FR)**[19] 2-8-3 0.............................. (p) MlleCoraliePacaut(10) 1 71
(T Castanheira, France) **66/10**

**4** 1 1/4 **Zouch**[17] 7731 2-9-2 0.............................. TonyPiccone 5 70
(J S Moore) *midfield: rdn into st: hung lft: kpt on: nt pce to chal* **5/1**

**5** 1 1/2 **Haddaj (FR)** 2-8-8 0.............................. (p) ValentinGambart(3) 6 60
(A Fabre, France) **4/1**[2]

**6** 2 1/2 **East Of The Nile**[46] 2-8-13 0.............................. FabriceVeron 8 54
(E J O'Neill, France) **13/1**

**7** 1 1/4 **Kallikrates (FR)**[10] 2-8-5 0.............................. ClementGuitraud(8) 7 50
(Y Barberot, France) **9/1**

**8** 3 **Saphirrouge (FR)**[19] 2-8-13 0.............................. BayarsaikhanGanbat 4 40
(M Figge, Germany) **37/1**

**9** 10 **Linngaria (FR)** 2-8-13 0.............................. AntoineHamelin 9 7
(Mario Hofer, Germany) **7/2**[1]

PARI-MUTUEL (all including 1 euro stake): WIN 5.40; PLACE 2.00, 3.20, 2.30; DF 40.00; SF 45.60.
**Owner** A Gilibert, Ecurie Biraben & B Chalmel **Bred** J-C Coude **Trained** France

## 8253a PRIX DU PEVELE (CLAIMER) (2YO) (TURF) 5f 110y
7:20 2-Y-O **£6,410** (£2,564; £1,923; £1,282; £641)

RPR

**1** **The Pantry (IRE)**[101] 2-8-13 0.............................. TonyPiccone 4 69+
(A Giorgi, Italy) **11/5**[2]

**2** 1 1/2 **Big Words (GER)**[6] 2-9-3 0.............................. RonanThomas 1 68
(J Phelippon, France) **13/10**[1]

**3** 1/2 **Anotherfortheroad**[19] 2-8-11 0.............................. (bp) AntoineHamelin 2 60
(Matthieu Palussiere, France) **11/2**[3]

**4** 3/4 **Jurisprudance (FR)**[11] 2-8-3 0.............................. MlleMickaelleMichel(10) 5 60
(M Boutin, France) **15/1**

**5** 2 1/2 **Rose Of Shiraz**[19] 7688 2-8-8 0.............................. MickaelBerto 7 47
(J S Moore) **13/1**

**6** 2 **Timeless Gift (IRE)**[26] 2-8-9 0.............................. (b) ClementLecoeuvre(4) 6 45
(Matthieu Palussiere, France) **15/1**

**7** 1 **Belobog (FR)**[6] 2-8-2 0.............................. (p) MlleCoraliePacaut(9) 3 40
(M Boutin, France) **11/1**

PARI-MUTUEL (all including 1 euro stake): WIN 3.20; PLACE 1.30, 1.20; SF 6.60.
**Owner** Attilio Giorgi **Bred** Eamonn McEvoy **Trained** Italy

# 6524 SOUTHWELL (L-H)

Sunday, October 22

**OFFICIAL GOING: Fibresand: standard**

Wind: Strong behind Weather: Cloudy and breezy

## 8254 BRAMLEY APPLE H'CAP — 1m 13y(F)

1:30 (1:31) (Class 5) (0-75,77) 4-Y-0+ £2,911 (£866; £432; £216) Stalls Low

Form RPR

2000 1 **Muqarred (USA)**[76] 5698 5-9-4 71 (p) TonyHamilton 7 79
(Roger Fell) *trckd ldrs: hdwy and cl up 2f out: rdn to chal over 1f out: drvn ins fnl f: kpt on wl to ld last 75 yds* **8/1**

0010 2 ½ **Monsieur Jimmy**[12] 7934 5-8-11 **64** StevieDonohoe 6 71
(Declan Carroll) *dwlt and in rr: hdwy 1/2-way: wd st to stands' side and sn chsng ldrs: rdn along wl over 1f out: kpt on wl fnl f* **6/1**[3]

0624 3 1¼ **House Of Commons (IRE)**[25] 7524 4-9-3 **70** LukeMorris 9 74
(Michael Appleby) *dwlt: sn w ldrs: cl up on outer over 4f out: led wl over 2f out: rdn along over 1f out: drvn ins fnl f: hdd last 75 yds: kpt on same pce* **6/4**[1]

3005 4 1 **Majestic Moon (IRE)**[34] 7214 7-9-7 **77** ShelleyBirkett(3) 2 79
(Julia Feilden) *trckd ldrs: cl up 3f out: rdn along 2f out: drvn over 1f out: kpt on same pce* **25/1**

36-0 5 7 **African Showgirl**[12] 7916 4-8-0 **60** MillyNaseb(7) 5 46
(Ivan Furtado) *a towards rr* **16/1**

0000 6 hd **Shearian**[50] 6673 7-8-12 **68** PhilDennis(3) 1 53
(Declan Carroll) *trckd ldrs on inner: pushed along over 3f out: rdn wl over 2f out: sn outpcd* **16/1**

0030 7 7 **Dandyleekie (IRE)**[13] 7894 5-9-2 **69** (b) JoeFanning 3 38
(David O'Meara) *slt ld: hdd wl over 2f out and sn rdn: wknd over 1f out* **25/1**

3211 8 11 **Jay Kay**[10] 7981 8-9-7 **74** (h) JoeyHaynes 8 18
(K R Burke) *cl up: pushed along 3f out: rdn wl over 2f out: sn drvn and wknd* **5/2**[2]

1m 43.91s (0.21) **Going Correction** +0.15s/f (Slow) 8 Ran SP% **113.4**

Speed ratings (Par 103): **104,103,102,101,94 94,87,76**

CSF £54.00 CT £109.68 TOTE £8.80: £2.30, £1.80, £1.10; EX 54.50 Trifecta £146.80.

**Owner** R G Fell **Bred** Shadwell Farm LLC **Trained** Nawton, N Yorks

**FOCUS**

A fair handicap run at a good pace.

## 8255 BOOKIES.COM FREE BETS H'CAP — 1m 13y(F)

2:00 (2:01) (Class 6) (0-55,55) 3-Y-O £2,587 (£770; £384; £192) Stalls Low

Form RPR

2034 1 **Medici Moon**[16] 7792 3-8-13 **52** (p) PaddyPilley(5) 10 62
(Scott Dixon) *mde all: rdn clr over 2f out: kpt on strly* **3/1**[2]

6231 2 3¾ **Quiet Moment (IRE)**[10] 7979 3-9-5 **53** ConnorBeasley 12 54
(Keith Dalgleish) *dwlt: hdwy and in tch after 2f: trckd ldrs over 3f out: rdn along over 2f: sn chsng wnr: kpt on but no imp* **5/2**[1]

0445 3 5 **Queen Moon (IRE)**[48] 6767 3-9-7 **55** DavidProbert 9 45
(Andrew Balding) *hld up in tch: pushed along and outpcd over 3f out: swtchd rt to outer and rdn over 2f out: styd on appr fnl f* **5/1**[3]

06 4 5 **Breathoffreshair**[16] 7791 3-9-5 **53** (t[1]) JoeFanning 14 31
(Richard Guest) *dwlt: hdwy to trck ldrs after 2f: prom on outer 1/2-way: chsd wnr 3f out: rdn along over 2f out: drvn and wkng whn hung lft over 1f out* **6/1**

00-4 5 3½ **Harvest Ranger**[254] 667 3-8-11 **48** EoinWalsh(3) 1 18
(Michael Appleby) *towards rr and rdn along early: in tch on inner 1/2-way: pushed along whn n.m.r bnd 3f out: swtchd rt and rdn over 2f out: n.d* **8/1**

6600 6 1¼ **Super Ruby**[15] 7833 3-8-13 **47** BenCurtis 13 14
(K R Burke) *prom: chsd wnr over 4f out: rdn along 3f out: sn drvn and wknd* **12/1**

0046 7 6 **Ejabah (IRE)**[37] 7109 3-9-0 **48** JoeyHaynes 6 1
(Charles Smith) *chsd ldrs: rdn along 3f out: sn wknd* **22/1**

00-0 8 4 **Highland Clearance (FR)**[60] 6324 3-8-12 **46** oh1 KevinStott 3
(Giles Bravery) *trckd ldrs on inner: rdn along 3f out: drvn and wknd over 2f out* **66/1**

500- 9 1½ **Take This Waltz**[318] 8276 3-8-9 **46** oh1 PhilDennis(3) 7
(Bill Turner) *a towards rr* **100/1**

0030 10 1 **Orientelle**[10] 7980 3-8-11 **48** (h[1]) LewisEdmunds(3) 4
(Richard Whitaker) *a towards rr* **16/1**

6-00 11 20 **Ten In The Hat (IRE)**[110] 4473 3-8-12 **46** oh1 (p[1]) StevieDonohoe 5
(Tom Gretton) *sn outpcd and bhd fr 1/2-way* **50/1**

0040 12 21 **Compass Rose (IRE)**[26] 7480 3-9-2 **50** (t) LukeMorris 11
(Scott Dixon) *cl up: rdn along over 4f out: sn lost pl and bhd* **50/1**

1m 44.82s (1.12) **Going Correction** +0.15s/f (Slow) 12 Ran SP% **120.0**

Speed ratings (Par 99): **100,96,91,86,82 81,75,71,70,69 49,28**

CSF £10.76 CT £36.80 TOTE £3.90: £1.20, £1.30, £1.60; EX 11.60 Trifecta £39.50.

**Owner** D Sharp and Partners **Bred** G E Amey **Trained** Babworth, Notts

**FOCUS**

A moderate handicap and they finished well strung out. The runner-up has been rated close to the level of his Ayr win.

## 8256 COMPARE HORSE RACING ODDS @ BOOKIES.COM MAIDEN STKS — 7f 14y(F)

2:30 (2:30) (Class 5) 3-Y-0+ £2,911 (£866; £432; £216) Stalls Low

Form RPR

2020 1 **Mama Africa (IRE)**[13] 7894 3-8-9 69 JaneElliott(5) 7 76
(David Barron) *mde most: rdn clr over 2f out: kpt on strly fnl f* **3/1**[1]

2032 2 7 **Nellie's Dancer**[45] 6850 3-8-9 56 (p) PaddyPilley(5) 8 58
(Scott Dixon) *trckd ldrs: hdwy 3f out: rdn along over 2f out: drvn over 1f out: kpt on fnl f* **15/2**

2463 3 ½ **Eponina (IRE)**[53] 6568 3-9-0 60 LukeMorris 5 57
(Ben Haslam) *chsd ldrs: rdn along over 2f out: drvn wl over 1f out: kpt on fnl f* **11/2**

0064 4 ½ **Know The Truth**[13] 7907 3-8-7 59 WilliamCox(7) 4 55
(Andrew Balding) *trckd ldrs: hdwy wl over 2f out: rdn wl over 1f out: kpt on same pce* **7/2**[2]

5 3 **Subjectivity (USA)** 3-9-5 0 AlistairRawlinson 2 52
(Michael Appleby) *prom: cl up 1/2-way: rdn along over 2f out: drvn on inner over 1f out: grad wknd* **4/1**[3]

0302 6 1 **Bo Selecta (IRE)**[55] 6529 3-9-5 60 (p) StevieDonohoe 3 50
(Richard Spencer) *towards rr and sn pushed along: rdn over 3f out: wd st and drvn 2f out: plugged on* **11/2**

7 12 **Born For Champagne (IRE)** 3-9-0 0 (h[1]) PatrickMathers 9 14
(Derek Shaw) *s.i.s and a in rr* **66/1**

4005 8 4½ **Red Shanghai (IRE)**[22] 7597 3-8-11 42 NoelGarbutt(3) 1 2
(Charles Smith) *prom on inner: rdn along wl over 3f out: sn wknd* **100/1**

9 4½ **Got My Mojo** 7-9-7 0 CamHardie 6
(Gary Sanderson) *s.i.s and a in rr* **100/1**

1m 31.38s (1.08) **Going Correction** +0.15s/f (Slow)

**WFA** 3 from 7yo 2lb 9 Ran SP% **113.2**

Speed ratings (Par 103): **99,91,90,89,86 85,71,66,61**

CSF £25.62 TOTE £3.10: £1.10, £2.40, £1.60; EX 21.50 Trifecta £85.40.

**Owner** M Rozenbroek & Harrowgate Bloodstock Ltd **Bred** G J King **Trained** Maunby, N Yorks

**FOCUS**

An ordinary maiden.

## 8257 RICHARD GIBSON MEMORIAL H'CAP — 7f 14y(F)

3:05 (3:06) (Class 3) (0-95,97) 4-Y-O+ £7,762 (£2,310; £1,154; £577) Stalls Low

Form RPR

6503 1 **Florencio**[52] 6637 4-8-9 **80** (p) BenCurtis 1 90
(Roger Fell) *trckd ldrs on inner: hdwy 3f out: cl up wl over 1f out: rdn to chal ent fnl f: sn drvn and kpt on wl to ld nr fin* **12/1**

0004 2 nk **Pearl Spectre (USA)**[16] 7789 6-8-4 **82** NicolaCurrie(7) 11 91
(Phil McEntee) *cl up: slt ld after 2f: rdn along wl over 1f out: edgd lft ent fnl f: sn drvn: hdd and no ex nr fin* **5/1**[2]

0014 3 2¾ **Lady Perignon**[15] 7815 4-8-7 **78** oh1 DavidProbert 3 80
(Andrew Balding) *led 2f: cl up on inner: rdn along 2f out: drvn and n.m.r ent fnl f: sn swtchd rt: kpt on same pce* **9/1**

0400 4 ½ **Hammer Gun (USA)**[107] 4563 4-8-10 **81** (v) PatrickMathers 12 82
(Derek Shaw) *prom on outer: hdwy 3f out: cl up 2f out and sn rdn: drvn appr fnl f: kpt on same pce* **5/1**[2]

5130 5 2¼ **Penwortham (IRE)**[13] 7886 4-9-4 **89** (h) TonyHamilton 6 84
(Richard Fahey) *t.k.h: hld up in rr: hdwy over 2f out: rdn to chse ldrs over 1f out: drvn ins fnl f: no imp* **12/1**

1260 6 ½ **Custard The Dragon**[9] 8014 4-9-0 **85** (p) JoeFanning 2 78
(John Mackie) *hld up: hdwy on inner over 2f out: rdn to chse ldrs over 1f out: drvn and kpt on same pce fnl f* **9/2**[1]

4000 7 2½ **Supersta**[50] 6685 6-9-11 **96** (p) LukeMorris 5 83
(Michael Appleby) *trckd ldrs: pushed along over 3f out: rdn wl over 2f out: sn drvn and wknd* **5/1**[2]

100 8 1 **War Department (IRE)**[68] 6024 4-9-7 **92** (v) ConnorBeasley 9 76
(Keith Dalgleish) *towards rr: hdwy 1/2-way: chsd ldrs 2f out: sn rdn and wknd* **8/1**[3]

6650 9 shd **Holiday Magic (IRE)**[99] 4905 6-9-5 **97** HarrisonShaw(7) 7 81
(Michael Easterby) *in rr: wd st: sn rdn and nvr a factor* **16/1**

3100 10 3¼ **Alpha Tauri (USA)**[102] 4766 11-8-5 **81** BenRobinson(5) 10 57
(Charles Smith) *prom: cl up and rdn wl over 3f out: sn wknd* **50/1**

0320 11 2½ **Echo Of Lightning**[1] 8240 7-8-5 **83** (p) BenSanderson(7) 4 52
(Roger Fell) *chsd ldrs: rdn along over 3f out: sn wknd* **20/1**

1m 29.43s (-0.87) **Going Correction** +0.15s/f (Slow) 11 Ran SP% **117.3**

Speed ratings (Par 107): **110,109,106,105,103 102,99,98,98,94 92**

CSF £70.85 CT £585.83 TOTE £11.60: £3.40, £2.40, £3.50; EX 101.50 Trifecta £1040.80.

**Owner** Colne Valley Racing & Partner **Bred** Newsells Park Stud **Trained** Nawton, N Yorks

**FOCUS**

A competitive, open-looking handicap, which featured several Fibresand specialists and solid form for the track.

## 8258 BOOKMAKERS.CO.UK FREE BETS H'CAP (DIV I) — 6f 16y(F)

3:40 (3:41) (Class 6) (0-55,57) 4-Y-O+ £2,264 (£673; £336; £168) Stalls Low

Form RPR

0100 1 **Kaaber (USA)**[13] 7900 6-9-2 **52** (bt) MitchGodwin(3) 8 62+
(Michael Blake) *hld up towards rr: hdwy 3f out: swtchd lft to chse ldrs 2f out: n.m.r and swtchd rt over 1f out: drvn to chal ent fnl f: kpt on wl to ld last 100 yds* **7/1**[3]

0440 2 3¼ **All Or Nothin (IRE)**[13] 7910 8-8-9 **45** CallumShepherd(3) 9 45
(Paddy Butler) *trckd ldrs: hdwy and cl up over 2f out: rdn to chal over 1f out: drvn to ld ent fnl f: hdd and no ex last 100 yds* **7/1**[3]

5-00 3 2¼ **Master Of Song**[31] 7324 10-8-12 **45** (b) AlistairRawlinson 1 37+
(Roy Bowring) *v.s.a and bhd: wd st and hdwy over 2f out: rdn over 1f out: fin wl* **10/1**

650 4 1 **Sarabi**[40] 7017 4-9-10 **57** (p) LukeMorris 6 46
(Scott Dixon) *trckd ldrs on inner: cl up 3f out: led 2f out: sn rdn: drvn and hdd ent fnl f: sn wknd* **4/1**[1]

000- 5 2 **Interchoice Star**[441] 5194 12-8-12 **45** (p) TonyHamilton 5 28
(Ray Peacock) *towards rr: rdn along and hdwy wl over 2f out: sn drvn and kpt on same pce* **66/1**

00-0 6 3 **Clouded Gold**[40] 7017 5-8-12 **45** (p[1]) TomMarquand 12 18
(Michael Appleby) *prom on outer: cl up 1/2-way: rdn wl over 2f out: sn drvn and wknd* **22/1**

6604 7 ½ **Rafaaf (IRE)**[13] 7911 9-9-0 **47** LiamKeniry 2 19
(Peter Hiatt) *hld up: hdwy on inner over 3f out: chsd ldrs and rdn wl over 2f out: sn wknd* **8/1**

0500 8 ½ **George Bailey (IRE)**[68] 6046 5-8-12 **45** (h[1]) JamesSullivan 11 15
(Suzzanne France) *a towards rr* **20/1**

4000 9 ½ **Lukoutoldmakezebak**[29] 7389 4-8-5 **45** (p[1]) JamieGormley(7) 4 13
(David Thompson) *a in rr* **16/1**

0050 10 1¼ **Coiste Bodhar (IRE)**[15] 7825 6-9-2 **54** PaddyPilley(5) 10 18
(Scott Dixon) *led: rdn along 3f out: sn hdd and drvn: wknd over 2f out* **5/1**[2]

5000 11 5 **Autumn Tonic (IRE)**[117] 4179 5-9-5 **52** (b) BenCurtis 7
(Charlie Wallis) *chsd ldrs: rdn along wl over 2f out: sn wknd* **14/1**

0000 12 5 **Very First Blade**[62] 6271 8-8-9 **45** (be) PhilDennis(3) 3
(Michael Mullineaux) *t.k.h: in tch: pushed along 3f out: sn wknd* **8/1**

1m 17.25s (0.75) **Going Correction** +0.15s/f (Slow) 12 Ran SP% **116.1**

Speed ratings (Par 101): **101,96,93,92,89 85,85,84,83,82 75,68**

CSF £52.97 CT £498.97 TOTE £7.60: £2.30, £2.70, £3.70; EX 65.60 Trifecta £569.10.

**Owner** Jeremy Holt **Bred** Shadwell Farm LLC **Trained** Trowbridge, Wilts

**FOCUS**

A moderate handicap and a decisive winner.

## 8259 BOOKMAKERS.CO.UK FREE BETS H'CAP (DIV II) — 6f 16y(F)

4:10 (4:11) (Class 6) (0-55,54) 4-Y-O+ £2,264 (£673; £336; £168) Stalls Low

Form RPR

5000 1 **Bingo George (IRE)**[6] 8117 4-8-12 **45** (t) TomMarquand 3 57
(Mark Rimell) *trckd ldrs on inner: hdwy over 2f out: rdn to ld over 1f out: clr ins fnl f* **15/2**

0255 **2** 3 1/4 **Tasaaboq**[22] 7606 6-8-12 **52**....................(t) NicolaCurrie(7) 9 54
(Phil McEntee) *dwlt and rr: hdwy wl over 2f out: rdn wl over 1f out: styd on to chse wnr ins fnl f: no imp towards fin* **9/2**[1]
3460 **3** 1 1/4 **Quadriga (IRE)**[25] 7523 7-8-5 **45**....................(b) PaulaMuir(7) 1 43
(Chris Grant) *trckd ldrs: hdwy wl over 2f out: rdn wl over 1f out: n.m.r and drvn appr fnl f: kpt on same pce* **12/1**
4640 **4** nk **Excellent World (IRE)**[40] 7020 4-9-0 **47**....................(p[1]) BarryMcHugh 8 44
(Tony Coyle) *cl up: rdn to ld 2f out: hdd and drvn over 1f out: kpt on same pce fnl f* **5/1**[2]
0004 **5** nk **Le Laitier (FR)**[53] 6572 6-8-12 **45**....................(v) KieranO'Neill 6 41
(Scott Dixon) *slt ld: rdn along over 2f out: sn hdd and drvn: grad wknd fr over 1f out* **8/1**
0606 **6** 1 1/2 **Prisom (IRE)**[173] 2285 4-9-3 **53**....................(p) LewisEdmunds(3) 7 44
(Gay Kelleway) *towards rr: hdwy over 2f out: swtchd lft and rdn wl over 1f out: kpt on fnl f* **6/1**[3]
5006 **7** shd **Quick Monet (IRE)**[22] 7606 4-8-9 **45**.................... CharlieBennett(3) 4 36
(Shaun Harris) *dwlt: a towards rr* **14/1**
4560 **8** 3 **Be Bold**[10] 7979 5-9-7 **54**.................... LukeMorris 11 35
(Rebecca Bastiman) *chsd ldrs on outer: rdn along wl over 2f out: drvn and wknd over 1f out* **5/1**[2]
0002 **9** 1 1/2 **Louis Vee (IRE)**[13] 7910 9-8-8 **46**....................(b) BenRobinson(5) 10 22
(John O'Shea) *chsd ldng pair: cl up 1/2-way: rdn along over 2f out: sn drvn and wknd* **16/1**
5605 **10** 11 **Nellie Deen (IRE)**[55] 6528 4-8-12 **45**....................(b) JasonHart 5
(Simon West) *a towards rr* **16/1**
-000 **11** 20 **Pound Note**[20] 7694 5-8-9 **45**....................(be[1]) PhilDennis(3) 2 +
(Michael Mullineaux) *chsd ldrs whn n.m.r bnd after 2f: sn lost pl and bhd* **66/1**

1m 18.03s (1.53) **Going Correction** +0.15s/f (Slow) **11** Ran SP% **116.3**
Speed ratings (Par 101): **95,90,89,88,88 86,86,82,80,65 38**
CSF £40.72 CT £412.00 TOTE £7.80: £2.40, £1.40, £3.40; EX 49.10 Trifecta £536.20.
**Owner** Jack Henley **Bred** G A E & J Smith Bloodstock Ltd **Trained** Leafield, Oxon

**FOCUS**
The second division of moderate handicap and, similar to the first leg, a comfortable winner. The second and third help set the level.

## 8260 JIGSAW SPORTS BRANDING H'CAP 4f 214y(F)
**4:40** (4:40) (Class 4) (0-80,80) 4-Y-0+ **£5,175** (£1,540; £769; £384) **Stalls** Centre

Form RPR
2115 **1** **Piazon**[32] 7272 6-8-11 **77**....................(be) DarraghKeenan(7) 8 86
(John Butler) *hld up towards rr: hdwy 3f out: sn swtchd rt towards stands' side and chsd ldrs: rdn to chal over 1f out and sn edgd lft: led ins fnl f: hung bdly lft last 100 yds: hld on* **13/2**[3]
0030 **2** 1/2 **Treaty Of Rome (USA)**[23] 7572 5-9-0 **73**....................(v) TonyHamilton 2 80
(Derek Shaw) *towards rr: hdwy 2f out: rdn over 1f out: styd on strly ins fnl f: n.m.r and sltly hmpd nr line* **4/1**[1]
4100 **3** 1 **Penny Dreadful**[12] 7940 5-8-8 **72**....................(b) PaddyPilley(5) 11 76
(Scott Dixon) *sn led towards stands' side: rdn along 2f out: drvn and edgd lft over 1f out: hdd ins fnl f: sn carried lft and hmpd towards fin: kpt on* **33/1**
2520 **4** shd **Noah Amor (IRE)**[12] 7939 4-8-10 **69**.................... LukeMorris 12 74+
(David O'Meara) *prom towards stands' side: swtchd lft and rdn over 1f out: drvn and carried lft ins fnl f: hld whn hmpd and snatched up nr fin* **16/1**
4553 **5** shd **Musharrif**[12] 7940 5-9-0 **80**.................... GerO'Neill(7) 13 83
(Declan Carroll) *racd towards stands' side: chsd ldrs: rdn along over 1f out: drvn and kpt on fnl f* **7/1**
4000 **6** 2 3/4 **Crosse Fire**[12] 7939 5-9-2 **75**....................(p) KieranO'Neill 10 69
(Scott Dixon) *cl up: rdn along wl over 1f out: drvn and wknd fnl f* **11/1**
6630 **7** 1/2 **Royal Mezyan (IRE)**[4] 8167 6-8-12 **78**....................(e) JackOsborn(7) 6 71
(Henry Spiller) *towards rr: hdwy nr stands side 2f out: sn rdn and kpt on fnl f* **12/1**
0550 **8** nk **Ace Master**[50] 6669 9-8-7 **69**....................(b) EoinWalsh(3) 7 61
(Roy Bowring) *towards rr: sme hdwy 2f out: kpt on fnl f: n.d* **20/1**
6000 **9** nk **Captain Lars (SAF)**[18] 7738 8-9-1 **77**....................(v) AaronJones(3) 4 68
(Derek Shaw) *racd towards far side: chsd ldrs: rdn along 2f out: grad wknd* **10/1**
0000 **10** nk **Lucky Beggar (IRE)**[9] 8012 7-9-6 **79**.................... ConnorBeasley 3 69
(David C Griffiths) *racd far side: chsd ldrs: rdn along 2f out: grad wknd appr fnl f wknd* **8/1**
0440 **11** 5 **Appleberry (IRE)**[4] 8167 5-8-13 **72**....................(h) TomMarquand 9 46
(Michael Appleby) *a towards rr* **14/1**
3240 **12** 3/4 **Ayresome Angel**[25] 7522 4-8-7 **66** oh1....................(p) JoeFanning 1 37
(John Mackie) *racd towards far side: prom: rdn along over 2f out: sn wknd* **11/2**[2]

58.39s (-1.31) **Going Correction** -0.125s/f (Stan) **12** Ran SP% **117.7**
Speed ratings (Par 105): **105,104,102,102,102 97,97,96,96,95 87,86**
CSF £32.36 CT £817.84 TOTE £6.70: £1.70, £1.40, £8.10; EX 36.10 Trifecta £583.60.
**Owner** Royale Racing Syndicate **Bred** Peter Baldwin **Trained** Newmarket, Suffolk
■ Stewards' Enquiry : Darragh Keenan seven-day ban: careless riding (Nov 6-11, 13)

**FOCUS**
A competitive handicap and there was late drama, the winner failing to keep a straight course and causing interference, but the result stood after an enquiry.

## 8261 COMPARE BOOKMAKERS @ BOOKMAKERS.CO.UK H'CAP 1m 4f 14y(F)
**5:10** (5:10) (Class 6) (0-65,66) 4-Y-0+ **£2,264** (£673; £336; £168) **Stalls** Low

Form RPR
262- **1** **Mister Showman**[92] 6367 4-9-2 **60**....................(p[1]) ConnorBeasley 6 68
(Keith Dalgleish) *in tch: hdwy to trck ldrs over 4f out: chsd ldr 3f out: rdn to ld 11/2f out: drvn out* **8/1**
4230 **2** 1 1/4 **Eugenic**[60] 6305 6-8-0 **51** oh1.................... DarraghKeenan(7) 7 57
(Tracey Barfoot-Saunt) *hld up: hdwy 5f out: chsd ldrs 3f out: ruidden along 2f out: styd on to chse wnr ins fnl furlong: kpt on* **66/1**
0-06 **3** 4 **Topamichi**[22] 7601 7-9-5 **63**.................... LukeMorris 12 63
(Michael Appleby) *cl up: led 5f out: rdn along 3f out: drvn 2f out: hdd 11/2f out and kpt on same pce* **3/1**[1]
0004 **4** 1 1/4 **Serenity Now (IRE)**[32] 7267 9-9-3 **66**.................... BenRobinson(5) 8 64
(Brian Ellison) *hld up in rr: swtchd wd 1/2-way: hdwy and wd st: sn rdn to chse ldrs: drvn wl over 1f out: kpt on fnl f* **9/2**[2]
0645 **5** 1/2 **Star Ascending (IRE)**[43] 6953 5-8-7 **51** oh1....................(p) CamHardie 13 48
(Jennie Candlish) *in tch: hdwy 4f out: rdn along to chse ldrs 3f out: drvn 2f out: kpt on one pce* **8/1**
5525 **6** 4 **Aumerle**[82] 5508 5-9-0 **61**.................... CallumShepherd(3) 5 51
(Shaun Lycett) *in tch: hdwy 4f out: rdn along on inner over 2f out: drvn wl over 1f out: grad wknd* **33/1**

1565 **7** 6 **My Renaissance**[26] 7478 7-9-2 **65**.................... JaneElliott(5) 11 46
(Sam England) *chsd ldrs on outer: rdn along over 3f out: drvn wl over 2f out and sn wknd* **6/1**[3]
0500 **8** 6 **Treble Strike (USA)**[18] 7730 4-8-1 **52**.................... JackOsborn(7) 9 23
(David C Griffiths) *a in rr* **14/1**
5000 **9** 1 1/4 **Lord Franklin**[18] 7735 8-9-4 **62**.................... JasonHart 14 31
(Eric Alston) *cl up: lked after 2f: hdd 1/2-way: rdn along 34f out: wknd 3f out* **20/1**
550 **10** 4 **Rupert Boy (IRE)**[66] 6092 4-8-0 **51** oh4.................... NicolaCurrie(7) 4 14
(Scott Dixon) *a in rr* **50/1**
0002 **11** 10 **Gold Merlion (IRE)**[17] 7760 4-9-4 **62**.................... JoeFanning 1 9
(Mark Johnston) *led 2f: trckd ldrs: pushed along over 5f out: rdn along and lost pl over 4f: sn bhd* **12/1**
0540 **12** hd **Bob's Boy**[10] 7990 4-8-9 **53**....................(bt) KevinStott 2
(Oliver Greenall) *a in rr* **16/1**
0120 **13** 4 **London Glory**[10] 7983 4-8-11 **62**....................(b) JamieGormley(7) 3 2
(David Thompson) *a in rr* **12/1**
4-10 **14** 9 **Stand Guard**[249] 738 13-9-4 **62**.................... LiamKeniry 10
(John Butler) *chsd ldrs: rdn along over 4f out: sn wknd* **28/1**

2m 40.76s (-0.24) **Going Correction** +0.15s/f (Slow) **14** Ran SP% **122.2**
Speed ratings (Par 101): **106,105,102,101,101 98,94,90,89,87 80,80,77,71**
CSF £483.11 CT £1950.40 TOTE £9.50: £3.10, £12.70, £1.70; EX 352.60 Trifecta £7025.70.
**Owner** Richard & Katherine Gilbert **Bred** Mrs A Plummer **Trained** Carluke, S Lanarks

**FOCUS**
A modest handicap and not many got into it. The winner has been rated to a minor pb, with the runner-up to the best of this year's form.
T/Jkpt: Not Won. T/Plt: £104.90 to a £1 stake. Pool: £10,2274.61 - 711.35 winning units T/Qpdt: £46.90 to a £1 stake. Pool: £8,595.37 - 135.40 winning units **Joe Rowntree**

8262 - 8264a (Foreign Racing) - See Raceform Interactive

# 6954 LEOPARDSTOWN (L-H)
Sunday, October 22

**OFFICIAL GOING: Soft**

## 8265a KILLAVULLAN STKS (GROUP 3) 7f
**3:30** (3:31) 2-Y-0

**£30,256** (£9,743; £4,615; £2,051; £1,025; £512)

RPR
**1** **Kenya (IRE)**[8] 8049 2-9-3 0....................(t) DonnachaO'Brien 4 107
(A P O'Brien, Ire) *cl up tl sn led and mde rest: 1 l clr at 1/2-way: rdn and extended advantage 1 1/2f out where edgd sltly rt briefly: kpt on wl u.p ins fnl f* **7/4**[1]
**2** 1 **Mcmunigal (IRE)**[28] 7420 2-9-3 0.................... ColinKeane 7 104
(G M Lyons, Ire) *chsd ldrs: 5th 1/2-way: pushed along after 1/2-way and outpcd briefly 2f out where rdn in 6th: r.o u.p on outer into 2nd wl ins fnl f: a hld* **4/1**[3]
**3** 1/2 **Bye Bye Baby (IRE)**[14] 7859 2-9-0 105.................... SeamieHeffernan 5 100
(A P O'Brien, Ire) *broke wl to ld briefly tl sn hdd and settled bhd ldr: 2nd 1/2-way lost pl 2f out and sn rdn in 3rd: no imp on wnr ins fnl f: kpt on same pce* **2/1**[2]
**4** 1 1/2 **Guessthebill (IRE)**[7] 8081 2-9-3 93.................... PatSmullen 1 99
(J P Murtagh, Ire) *chsd ldrs: 4th 1/2-way: pushed along and impr on inner into 2nd 2f out: sn rdn and no imp on wnr u.p in 2nd ins fnl f: wknd into 4th clsng stages* **9/1**
**5** hd **Dramatically (USA)**[7] 8080 2-9-0 0....................(t) WayneLordan 3 96
(A P O'Brien, Ire) *hld up towards rr: 6th 1/2-way: pushed along after 1/2-way and sme hdwy u.p to chse ldrs ent fnl f: no imp on wnr in 5th wl ins fnl f* **14/1**
**6** 3 1/2 **Quizical (IRE)**[7] 8082 2-9-3 90.................... RonanWhelan 6 89
(Ms Sheila Lavery, Ire) *chsd ldrs: 3rd 1/2-way: lost pl into st: pushed along in 4th 1 1/2f out and no imp on wnr: wknd ins fnl f* **20/1**
**7** 1 3/4 **Gasta (IRE)**[7] 8081 2-9-0 91....................(p) KevinManning 8 82
(J S Bolger, Ire) *dwlt and pushed along in rr early: last at 1/2-way: rdn and no imp under 2f out: one pce* **66/1**

1m 35.28s (6.58) **7** Ran SP% **112.6**
CSF £8.93 TOTE £2.50: £1.10, £2.40; DF 8.50 Trifecta £18.60.
**Owner** Mrs John Magnier & Michael Tabor & Derrick Smith **Bred** Lynch-Bages & Rhinestone Bloodstock **Trained** Cashel, Co Tipperary

**FOCUS**
A good staying performance from the winner, a horse that seems to revel on soft ground and one to look forward to next year. It's been rated a par renewal, with the winner taking a nice step forward and the third, sixth and seventh suggesting this level is sensible.

8266 - 8268a (Foreign Racing) - See Raceform Interactive

# 6726 BADEN-BADEN (L-H)
Sunday, October 22

**OFFICIAL GOING: Turf: soft**

## 8269a ITTLINGEN - PREIS DER WINTERKONIGIN (GROUP 3) (2YO FILLIES) (TURF) 1m
**3:10** 2-Y-0

**£51,282** (£19,658; £9,401; £5,128; £2,564; £1,709)

RPR
**1** **Rock My Love (GER)**[29] 2-9-2 0.................... AdriedeVries 7 104
(Markus Klug, Germany) *mde all: rdn over 2f out: drvn fnl f: kpt on wl* **9/10**[1]
**2** 3/4 **Suada (GER)** 2-9-2 0.................... MaximPecheur 9 102
(Markus Klug, Germany) *trckd ldrs: rdn to chse ldr 2 1/2f out: kpt on wl: no imp on wnr fnl f* **31/5**[3]
**3** 1 1/4 **Angelita (GER)** 2-9-2 0.................... DanielePorcu 10 99
(P Schiergen, Germany) *dwlt: in rr: rdn and kpt on fr 2 1/2f out: wnt 3rd appr fnl f: nrst fin* **161/10**
**4** 3 3/4 **Dina (GER)**[42] 6985 2-9-2 0.................... MartinSeidl 4 91
(Markus Klug, Germany) *hld up towards rr: rdn and kpt on steadily fr 3f out: tk 4th 1f out: no imp on front three ins fnl f* **94/10**
**5** 2 3/4 **Cabarita (GER)**[29] 2-9-2 0.................... FilipMinarik 1 84
(H-J Groschel, Germany) *towards rr of midfield: rdn and plugged on same pce fr over 3f out: n.d* **13/2**
**6** 14 **Butzje (GER)** 2-9-2 0.................... AndreasHelfenbein 2 52
(Markus Klug, Germany) *chsd ldr: rdn 2 1/2f out: outpcd 2f out: wkng whn hmpd over 1f out: sn btn and eased* **117/10**

7 2½ **Barista (GER)**[29] 2-9-2 0 LukasDelozier 3 47
(J Hirschberger, Germany) *midfield: rdn over 3f out: lost pl 2 1/2f out: sn btn* **155/10**
8 ¾ **Sword Peinture (GER)** 2-9-2 0 JozefBojko 8 45
(A Wohler, Germany) *trckd ldrs: rdn and lost pl over 3f out: sn wl btn* **51/10**[2]
9 3¾ **I Am What I Am (GER)** 2-9-2 0 RobertHavlin 6 36
(Lennart Hammer-Hansen, Germany) *midfield: rdn and lost pl 4f out: sn struggling* **28/1**

1m 51.88s (12.77) **9** Ran SP% **129.1**
PARI-MUTUEL (all including 10 euro stake): WIN 19 PLACE:13, 18; 20 SF: 72.
**Owner** Gunter Merkel **Bred** Ralf Kredel **Trained** Germany

## 8270a BADEN-WURTTEMBERG-TROPHY - DEFI DU GALOP (GROUP 3) (3YO+) (TURF) 1m 2f
**4:20** 3-Y-0+ **£27,350** (£10,256; £5,128; £2,564; £1,709)

RPR
1 **Navaro Girl (IRE)**[19] 7722 3-8-6 0 DanielePorcu 1 103
(P Schiergen, Germany) *t.k.h in 4th: tk clsr order 3f out: rdn to chal over 2f out: led 1 1/2f out: kpt on wl fnl f* **13/5**[3]
2 1½ **Devastar (GER)**[19] 7722 5-9-0 0 AdriedeVries 3 103
(Markus Klug, Germany) *led: hdd after 3f: trckd ldrs: led 3f out: sn rdn: chal over 2f out: hdd 1 1/2f out: no ex clsng stages* **54/10**
3 ½ **Matchwinner (GER)**[19] 7722 6-9-2 0 AndreasHelfenbein 6 104
(A Kleinkorres, Germany) *hld up in rr: rdn and hdwy fr 2 1/2f out: chsd ldrs appr fnl f: kpt on same pce ins fnl f* **19/10**[2]
4 5 **Palace Prince (GER)**[52] 6647 5-9-4 0 (p) FilipMinarik 5 97
(Jean-Pierre Carvalho, Germany) *t.k.h: chsd ldr: led under 4f out: rdn and hdd 3f out: wknd 2f out* **8/5**[1]
5 14 **Promise Of Peace (JPN)**[112] 4422 3-8-9 0 (p) JozefBojko 2 66
(A Wohler, Germany) *chsd ldr: led after 3f: hdd under 4f out: sn rdn: wknd over 2f out* **66/10**

2m 20.18s (15.19)
**WFA** 3 from 5yo+ 4lb **5** Ran SP% **129.5**
PARI-MUTUEL (all including 10 euro stake): WIN 36 PLACE:21, 26; SF: 169.
**Owner** Stall Nizza **Bred** Jurgen Imm **Trained** Germany

# CHOLET (R-H)
Sunday, October 22
**OFFICIAL GOING: Turf: very soft**

## 8271a PRIX AXA MERLET TISON (CONDITIONS) (2YO) (TURF) 6f 165y
**1:12** 2-Y-0 **£8,547** (£3,418; £2,564; £1,709; £854)

RPR
1 **Tawahid**[27] 2-9-4 0 (p) HugoJourniac 3 76
(E J O'Neill, France) **113/10**
2 shd **Arrogant (IRE)**[27] 7470 2-9-4 0 ThomasHuet 4 76
(Jose Santos) *wl into stride: trckd ldr: pushed along to chal 2f out: rdn 1f out: drvn and ev ch ins fnl f: jst hld* **1/5**[1]
3 1½ **Heads Together**[41] 2-8-8 0 ow1 CyrilleStefan 2 62
(S Kobayashi, France) **213/10**
4 ½ **Motym (FR)** 2-8-9 0 TristanBaron(6) 1 67
(H-A Pantall, France) **73/10**[3]
5 8 **Qatar Sunshine**[77] 2-8-13 0 SoufianeSaadi 5 43
(H-A Pantall, France) **69/10**[2]

PARI-MUTUEL (all including 1 euro stake): WIN 12.30; PLACE 2.60, 1.20; SF 17.90.
**Owner** Jaber Abdullah **Bred** Rabbah Bloodstock Limited **Trained** France

8272 - (Foreign Racing) - See Raceform Interactive

# 8101 SAINT-CLOUD (L-H)
Sunday, October 22
**OFFICIAL GOING: Turf: good to soft**

## 8273a PRIX DE FLORE (GROUP 3) (3YO+ FILLIES & MARES) (TURF) 1m 2f 110y
**2:45** 3-Y-0+ **£34,188** (£13,675; £10,256; £6,837; £3,418)

RPR
1 **Intimation**[8] 8041 5-9-0 0 MickaelBarzalona 2 109
(Sir Michael Stoute) *trckd ldrs: rdn over 2f out: led under 1f out: kpt on strly: drvn out* **97/10**
2 ½ **Son Macia (GER)**[28] 7429 4-9-0 0 (b) GregoryBenoist 8 108
(Andreas Suborics, Germany) *chsd ldr: rdn to chal over 2f out: drvn and led narrowly 1f out: hdd under 1f out: kpt on wl* **152/10**
3 1¼ **Listen In (IRE)**[22] 7635 3-8-9 0 AurelienLemaitre 1 107
(F Head, France) *led: chal over 2f out: rdn 2f out: hdd 1f out: kpt on same pce fnl f* **7/5**[1]
4 ¾ **Bebe D'Amour (FR)**[22] 7635 3-8-10 0 ow1 ChristopheSoumillon 6 107
(J-Y Artu, France) *in tch in midfield: gd hdwy under 2f out: rdn and ev ch appr fnl f: no ex last 100yds* **36/5**[3]
5 hd **Normandel (FR)**[49] 6732 3-8-9 0 CristianDemuro 3 105
(Mme Pia Brandt, France) *in tch in midfield: rdn and kpt on fr over 2f out: nt gng pce to chal* **269/10**
6 ½ **Golden Legend (FR)**[32] 7305 3-8-13 0 AlexisBadel 11 108
(H-F Devin, France) *t.k.h towards rr: rdn and kpt on fr 2f out: nrst fin* **49/10**[2]
7 2 **Happy Approach (FR)**[18] 7753 4-9-0 0 MaximeGuyon 4 100
(M Nigge, France) *in tch: rdn and effrt 2 1/2f out: hmpd under 2f out: wknd steadily fr over 1f out* **99/10**
8 1¼ **Furia Cruzada (CHI)**[22] 7635 6-9-6 0 FabriceVeron 5 103
(S Kobayashi, France) *midfield on outer: rdn and no imp fr 2 1/2f out* **47/1**
9 ¾ **Pleasant Surprise (IRE)**[23] 7577 3-8-9 0 JamieSpencer 9 97
(Luca Cumani) *hld up towards rr of midfield: rdn and effrt 2f out: wknd 100yds out: eased clsng stages* **122/10**
10 ¾ **Ma Cherie**[20] 7696 3-8-9 0 VincentCheminaud 10 96
(A Fabre, France) *a towards rr* **196/10**
11 nk **Company Asset (IRE)**[18] 7753 4-9-0 0 TomEaves 7 94
(Kevin Ryan) *a towards rr* **242/10**

2m 17.69s (-1.91)
**WFA** 3 from 4yo+ 4lb **11** Ran SP% **117.6**
PARI-MUTUEL (all including 1 euro stake): WIN 10.70; PLACE 2.80, 2.90, 1.30; DF 66.80; SF 147.20.
**Owner** Cheveley Park Stud **Bred** Cheveley Park Stud Ltd **Trained** Newmarket, Suffolk

**FOCUS**
The runner-up has been rated as improving 7lb, but her latest run could easily be rated 5lb-8lb better.

## 8274a PRIX ROYAL-OAK (GROUP 1) (3YO+) (TURF) 1m 7f 110y
**3:25** 3-Y-0+ **£170,931** (£68,384; £34,192; £17,081; £8,555)

RPR
1 **Ice Breeze**[22] 7634 3-8-10 0 VincentCheminaud 4 118
(P Bary, France) *hld up in midfield: trckd ldrs 4f out: rdn to ld 2 1/2f out: drvn whn pressed over 1f out: rallied whn chal by different rival ins fnl f: styd on gamely to assert clsng stages* **6/1**[3]
2 1¼ **Vazirabad (FR)**[22] 7639 5-9-4 0 ChristopheSoumillon 5 115+
(A De Royer-Dupre, France) *hld up towards rr: gd hdwy fr 2 1/2f out: rdn 2f out: drvn to chal ins fnl f: no ex and hld clsng stages* **8/15**[1]
3 2 **Holdthasigreen (FR)**[42] 6984 5-9-4 0 (p) TonyPiccone 3 112
(C Le Lay, France) *chsd clr ldrs: led 5f out: rdn and hdd 2 1/2f out: rallied to press ldr appr fnl f: wknd 100yds out: eased clsng stages* **5/1**[2]
4 8 **Renneti (FR)**[28] 7422 8-9-4 0 Pierre-CharlesBoudot 8 102
(W P Mullins, Ire) *hld up towards rr: hmpd under 3f out: sn rdn: kpt on steadily fr 2 1/2f out: snatched mod 4th cl home* **16/1**
5 snk **Kitesurf**[22] 7635 3-8-7 0 MickaelBarzalona 6 101
(A Fabre, France) *towards rr of midfield: tk clsr order 4f out: rdn under 3f out: outpcd under 2f out: lost mod 4th cl home* **10/1**
6 4 **Oriental Eagle (GER)**[35] 7203 3-8-10 0 JackMitchell 1 99
(J Hirschberger, Germany) *chsd ldr: rdn 3f out: wknd steadily fr over 2f out* **50/1**
7 1¾ **Montaly**[37] 7116 6-9-4 0 OisinMurphy 9 95
(Andrew Balding) *hld up towards rr: rdn and no imp fr 4f out* **22/1**
8 dist **Mille Et Mille**[22] 7639 7-9-4 0 FranckBlondel 2
(C Lerner, France) *midfield: rdn 3 1/2f out: lost pl 2 1/2f out: sn wl btn and eased* **12/1**
9 10 **Brandon Castle**[19] 7701 5-9-4 0 AndrewMullen 7
(Archie Watson) *led: 5 l clr at 1/2-way: hdd 5f out: grad dropped towards rr: lost tch 2 1/2f out* **22/1**

3m 25.4s (-13.30)
**WFA** 3 from 5yo+ 7lb **9** Ran SP% **129.5**
PARI-MUTUEL (all including 1 euro stake): WIN 6.10; PLACE 1.10, 1.10, 1.10; DF 4.30; SF 10.90.
**Owner** K Abdullah **Bred** Juddmonte Farms **Trained** Chantilly, France

**FOCUS**
The form looks believable, with the runner-up rated to the level of his win in this race last year, and the third rated to form.

# 8094 SAN SIRO (R-H)
Sunday, October 22
**OFFICIAL GOING: Turf: good**

## 8275a GRAN PREMIO DEL JOCKEY CLUB (GROUP 2) (3YO+) (TURF) 1m 4f
**3:35** 3-Y-0+ **£100,000** (£44,000; £24,000; £12,000)

RPR
1 **Full Drago (ITY)**[35] 7205 4-9-4 0 DarioVargiu 1 114
(Stefano Botti, Italy) *mde all: rdn 2 1/2f out: kpt on strly: unchal* **51/100**[1]
2 3 **Savoir Vivre (IRE)**[28] 7429 4-9-4 0 EduardoPedroza 3 109
(Jean-Pierre Carvalho, Germany) *chsd ldr: rdn and kpt on fr under 3f out: no imp on wnr* **9/5**[2]
3 6 **Way To Paris**[35] 7205 4-9-4 0 PierantonioConvertino 4 101
(Antonio Marcialis, Italy) *hld up in tch: rdn and outpcd over 2f out: sn no imp* **71/20**[3]
4 10 **Aethos (IRE)**[21] 3-8-13 0 SilvanoMulas 2 88
(Stefano Botti, Italy) *hld up in tch: rdn 3f out: wknd 2f out* **143/10**

2m 31.2s (-0.30)
**WFA** 3 from 4yo 6lb **4** Ran SP% **130.5**
PARI-MUTUEL (all including 1 euro stake): WIN 1.51; PLACE 1.01, 1.07, DF 3.49.
**Owner** Dioscuri Srl **Bred** Massimo Dragoni **Trained** Italy

## 8276a GRAN CRITERIUM (GROUP 2) (2YO COLTS & FILLIES) (TURF) 7f 110y
**4:45** 2-Y-0 **£111,111** (£48,888; £26,666; £13,333)

RPR
1 **Royal Youmzain (FR)**[42] 6985 2-8-11 0 EduardoPedroza 7 105
(A Wohler, Germany) *in tch: rdn 2 1/2f out: led over 1f out: styd on wl fnl f* **85/40**[1]
2 1½ **Sopran Roccia (ITY)** 2-8-11 0 SilvanoMulas 2 102
(Il Cavallo In Testa, Italy) *hld up towards rr: rdn 3f out: styd on fr over 1f out: nrst fin* **217/10**
3 ½ **Beautiful Vintage (IRE)** 2-8-11 0 DarioVargiu 5 101
(Stefano Botti, Italy) *broke wl and led: rdn 2f out: hdd over 1f out: wknd clsng stages* **13/4**[3]
4 1½ **Move Over**[21] 7648 2-8-11 0 (b) PierantonioConvertino 1 97
(Richard Hannon) *t.k.h: trckd ldrs: rdn 2 1/2f out: drvn and wknd steadily fr over 1f out* **17/5**
5 1 **Met Spectrum**[29] 2-8-11 0 CarloFiocchi 8 95
(Stefano Botti, Italy) *chsd ldr: rdn over 2f out: wknd steadily fr over 1f out* **27/10**[2]
6 3 **Bakchich Game (FR)**[24] 7559 2-8-11 0 (b[1]) PierreBazire 3 88
(G Botti, France) *t.k.h in midfield: rdn under 3f out: wknd steadily fr 1 1/2f out* **27/4**
7 3 **De Bruyne Horse**[15] 7821 2-8-11 0 (b) LucaManiezzi 6 81
(Richard Hannon) *hld up towards rr: rdn and stdy hdwy fr under 3f out: making no further imp whn sltly hmpd ins fnl f: sn eased* **17/5**
8 14 **Iframe (IRE)**[119] 4131 2-8-11 0 FabioBranca 4 48
(Il Cavallo In Testa, Italy) *midfield: rdn 2 1/2f out: wknd 1 1/2f out: sn wl btn and eased* **121/10**

1m 34.0s (-1.50) **8** Ran SP% **153.0**
PARI-MUTUEL (all including 1 euro stake): WIN 3.13; PLACE 1.57, 3.30, 1.72 DF 47.14.
**Owner** Jaber Abdullah **Bred** Rabbah Bloodstock Limited **Trained** Germany

8277- 8286a (Foreign Racing) - See Raceform Interactive

## 7890 PONTEFRACT (L-H)
Monday, October 23

**OFFICIAL GOING: Soft (good to soft in places) changing to soft after race 1 (2.20)**
Wind: Light across Weather: Cloudy

### 8287 TOTEPLACEPOT EBF NURSERY H'CAP — 1m 6y
2:20 (2:21) (Class 5) (0-75,74) 2-Y-O — £3,234 (£962; £481; £240) Stalls Low

Form — RPR

446 **1** **Iconic Code**[40] 7043 2-8-11 **64** ........ JFEgan 8 — 69
(Mick Channon) *hld up towards rr: stdy hdwy over 3f out: trckd ldrs over 2f out: rdn to chse ldr and edgd lft over 1f out: styd on to chal ins fnl f: led last 75yds* **16/1**

2010 **2** *1* **Milan Reef (IRE)**[26] 7519 2-8-6 **59** ........ JamesSullivan 4 — 62
(David Loughnane) *cl up: led 1/2-way: pushed clr 2f out: rdn over 1f out: jnd and drvn ins fnl f: hdd and no ex last 75yds* **8/1**

0626 **3** *1* **Normandy Blue**[23] 7624 2-8-12 **65** ........ PJMcDonald 7 — 66
(Richard Fahey) *hld up in rr: hdwy on outer 3f out: rdn along to chse ldrs 11/2f out: styd on fnl f: nrst fin* **10/1**

5022 **4** *9* **Gamesters Icon**[37] 7160 2-9-6 **73** ........ GrahamLee 14 — 54
(Bryan Smart) *in tch: hdwy to chse ldrs 3f out: rdn along wl over 1f out: drvn appr fnl f: kpt on same pce* **20/1**

340 **5** *1* **Hyanna**[10] 8013 2-9-0 **67** ........ DavidAllan 2 — 46
(Tim Easterby) *towards rr: pushed along over 2f out: rdn wl over 1f out: styd on appr fnl f* **9/2**[1]

0005 **6** *nk* **Bee Machine (IRE)**[26] 7519 2-8-0 **53** oh5 ........ CamHardie 9 — 31
(Declan Carroll) *hld up towards rr: hdwy over 3f out: chsd ldrs 2f out: sn rdn and kpt on one pce* **12/1**

5250 **7** *4* **Sinaloa (IRE)**[31] 7363 2-9-3 **70** ........ DavidNolan 11 — 40
(Richard Fahey) *in tch: effrt and sme hdwy 3f out: rdn along 2f out: sn drvn and wknd* **14/1**

0140 **8** *2* **Hemingford (IRE)**[14] 7890 2-9-1 **68** ........ PaulMulrennan 5 — 33
(Charlie Fellowes) *chsd ldrs: rdn along over 3f out: sn wknd* **7/1**[3]

6002 **9** *4 ½* **Ventura Crest (IRE)**[26] 7519 2-8-2 **58** ........ RachelRichardson(3) 3 — 13
(Tim Easterby) *led to 1/2-way: cl up: rdn along 3f out: sn wknd* **5/1**[2]

6630 **10** *5* **French Resistance (IRE)**[5] 8164 2-8-12 **65** ........ TonyHamilton 13 — 9
(Roger Fell) *chsd ldrs: rdn along over 3f out: wknd over 2f out* **16/1**

0050 **11** *6* **Barney George**[20] 7698 2-8-5 **61** ........ LewisEdmunds(3) 1
(Iain Jardine) *dwlt: sn trcking ldrs on inner: rdn along over 3f out: sn wknd* **10/1**

440 **12** *1 ¾* **Voice Of The North**[26] 7503 2-9-3 **70** ........ JoeFanning 10
(Mark Johnston) *chsd ldrs: pushed along bef 1/2-way: sn rdn and wknd over 3f out* **10/1**

0056 **13** *15* **El Bertie (IRE)**[13] 7920 2-8-2 **55** ........ DuranFentiman 6
(Tim Easterby) *a in rr* **28/1**

1m 51.81s (5.91) **Going Correction** +0.875s/f (Soft) — 13 Ran SP% **120.1**
Speed ratings (Par 95): **105,104,103,94,93 92,88,86,82,77 71,69,54**
CSF £139.37 CT £1365.20 TOTE £21.40: £6.00, £3.10, £3.30; EX 135.30 Trifecta £2930.70 Part won..
**Owner** Norman Court Stud **Bred** Norman Court Stud **Trained** West Ilsley, Berks

**FOCUS**
The rail was out up to 3yds between the 2f and 4f markers, adding approximately 5yds to all races. After this opening race the going was changed to soft (from soft, good to soft in places). A modest nursery and it proved hard work.

### 8288 TOTEEXACTA NOVICE AUCTION STKS — 6f
2:50 (2:50) (Class 5) 2-Y-O — £3,234 (£962; £481; £240) Stalls Low

Form — RPR

516 **1** **Dawn Breaking**[9] 8046 2-9-1 72 ........ LewisEdmunds(3) 7 — 73
(Richard Whitaker) *sltly hmpd s: hld up in tch: hdwy 1/2-way: chsd ldrs wl over 1f out and sn chsng ldr: drvn ins fnl f: styd on wl to ld towards fin* **7/2**[1]

4431 **2** *hd* **Fortunate Vision**[13] 7920 2-9-3 70 ........ (v) TomEaves 3 — 71
(David Brown) *trckd ldrs on inner: hdwy 2f out: rdn over 1f out: drvn ins fnl f: chal last 100yds: sn drvn and ev ch: jst hld* **5/1**[3]

**3** *nk* **Brigand** 2-8-13 0 ........ DanielTudhope 10 — 67+
(William Haggas) *hld up towards rr: pushed along and green on outer 1/2-way: hdwy 2f out: rdn to chse ldrs over 1f out: styd on strly fnl f: jst hld* **7/1**

**4** *¾* **Rizzle Dizzle** 2-8-8 0 ........ PJMcDonald 8 — 59+
(K R Burke) *trckd ldr: led wl over 2f out: rdn clr wl over 1f out: drvn ins fnl f: hdd and no ex last 40yds* **10/1**

0425 **5** *2 ¾* **Geesala Brave (IRE)**[31] 7362 2-9-0 67 ........ JasonHart 4 — 57
(John Quinn) *chsd ldrs: hdwy over 2f out: rdn wl over 1f out: swtchd lft and drvn appr fnl f: kpt on same pce* **9/1**

0 **6** *3* **Scenic River**[45] 6876 2-8-9 0 ........ DavidAllan 1 — 43
(Tim Easterby) *in tch on inner: pushed along and sltly outpcd over 2f out: sn rdn and kpt on appr fnl f* **7/1**

5 **7** *nse* **Sioux Frontier (IRE)**[16] 7818 2-8-12 0 ........ TonyHamilton 6 — 46+
(Richard Fahey) *wnt rt and bmpd s: in rr tl sme late hdwy* **4/1**[2]

00 **8** *3 ¼* **Aislin Moon (IRE)**[83] 5494 2-8-5 0 ........ JoeFanning 2 — 29
(Les Eyre) *led: pushed along and hdd wl over 2f out: rdn 2f out: grad wknd* **25/1**

00 **9** *1 ¼* **Voguela (IRE)**[10] 8010 2-8-5 0 ........ RachelRichardson(3) 5 — 28
(Tim Easterby) *towards rr: rdn along wl over 2f out: n.d* **100/1**

**10** *4 ½* **Lady Sophiebella** 2-8-5 0 ........ ShaneGray 9 — 12
(Bryan Smart) *sn outpcd and bhd* **25/1**

5420 **11** *19* **Ce De Nullis (IRE)**[19] 7734 2-8-11 69 ........ PaulMulrennan 11
(Paul Midgley) *chsd ldrs: rdn along over 2f out: wknd qckly* **12/1**

1m 22.25s (5.35) **Going Correction** +0.875s/f (Soft) — 11 Ran SP% **119.4**
Speed ratings (Par 95): **99,98,98,97,93 89,89,85,83,77 52**
CSF £21.02 TOTE £4.80: £1.50, £2.30, £2.30; EX 22.40 Trifecta £94.70.
**Owner** D Gration, G Sutcliffe, N Farman, Jeaton **Bred** Mrs M J Blackburn **Trained** Scarcroft, W Yorks

■ Stewards' Enquiry : Tom Eaves six-day ban: excessive use of whip (Nov 6-11)

**FOCUS**
Add 5yds to race distance. A modest-looking novice race.

### 8289 TOTEQUADPOT H'CAP — 1m 2f 5y
3:20 (3:21) (Class 4) (0-85,85) 3-Y-O+ — £5,175 (£1,540; £769; £384) Stalls Low

Form — RPR

5200 **1** **Silvery Moon (IRE)**[9] 8048 10-9-2 **80** ........ DavidAllan 3 — 88
(Tim Easterby) *hld up in tch: hdwy 1/2-way: trckd ldrs 3f out: cl up 2f out: rdn to ld 11/2f out: drvn and kpt on wl fnl f* **9/2**[1]

4102 **2** *1 ¼* **Tuff Rock (USA)**[54] 6579 3-9-3 **85** ........ JamieSpencer 7 — 91
(Ed Walker) *hld up: hdwy and wd st to strnds' rail: sn prom and rdn: cl up jst ins fnl f: sn drvn and kpt on same pce* **11/2**[3]

4200 **3** *½* **Rashford's Double (IRE)**[13] 7941 3-8-11 **79** ........ (p) TonyHamilton 2 — 84
(Richard Fahey) *hld up in midfield: hdwy 3f out: chsd ldrs wl over 1f out and sn rdn: styd on fnl f* **10/1**

2030 **4** *shd* **Faithful Creek (IRE)**[14] 7880 5-9-4 **82** ........ (p) AdamKirby 1 — 86
(Michael Appleby) *trckd ldrs on inner: hdwy 3f out: cl up 2f out and sn rdn: drvn over 1f out: kpt on u.p fnl f* **5/1**[2]

0063 **5** *¾* **Aardwolf (USA)**[13] 7927 3-9-2 **84** ........ JoeFanning 9 — 87
(Mark Johnston) *led: pushed along 3f out: rdn over 2f out: drvn and hdd 11/2f out: grad wknd fnl f* **16/1**

0064 **6** *1 ¼* **Purple Rock (IRE)**[79] 5667 5-8-7 **78** ........ (t) HarrisonShaw(7) 4 — 77
(Michael Easterby) *hld up: hdwy over 4f out: chsd ldrs over 2f out: rdn wl over 1f out: kpt on same pce* **16/1**

3514 **7** *2 ¾* **Royal Shaheen (FR)**[25] 7555 4-9-4 **82** ........ (v) GrahamLee 12 — 75
(Alistair Whillans) *trckd ldrs: pushed along over 2f out: sn rdn and wknd approaching fnl f* **10/1**

4233 **8** *½* **Pirate Look (IRE)**[47] 6822 3-8-10 **78** ........ (p) DanielMuscutt 11 — 71
(Marco Botti) *trckd ldng pair: pushed along 3f out: rdn over 2f out: sn drvn and wknd ent fnl f* **11/1**

5060 **9** *4* **Trendsetter (IRE)**[9] 8048 6-9-0 **78** ........ (p) PJMcDonald 6 — 60
(Micky Hammond) *hld up: a towards rr* **16/1**

0544 **10** *1 ¼* **Bamber Bridge (IRE)**[20] 7702 3-9-2 **84** ........ PaulMulrennan 8 — 65
(Michael Dods) *a towards rr* **14/1**

-006 **11** *1 ½* **Dwight D**[11] 7984 4-8-10 **74** ........ PatrickMathers 5 — 50
(Stuart Coltherd) *a in rr* **66/1**

31 **12** *1 ¼* **Misscarlett (IRE)**[32] 7331 3-8-5 **73** ........ JoeyHaynes 10 — 47
(Sally Haynes) *hld up in rr: hdwy on outer over 3f out: cl up and rdn over 2f out: wd st to centre: sn drvn and wknd* **13/2**

0240 **13** *7* **Save The Bees**[9] 8048 9-9-0 **85** ........ GerO'Neill(7) 13 — 42
(Declan Carroll) *trckd ldrs: pushed along over 3f out: rdn and wknd wl over 2f out* **20/1**

2m 21.81s (8.11) **Going Correction** +0.875s/f (Soft)
**WFA** 3 from 4yo+ 4lb — 13 Ran SP% **120.6**
Speed ratings (Par 105): **102,101,100,100,99 98,96,96,93,92 90,89,84**
CSF £28.88 CT £240.84 TOTE £5.40: £2.00, £1.80, £2.50; EX 37.60 Trifecta £373.90.
**Owner** Mrs D Stevens & Partner **Bred** Colin Kennedy **Trained** Great Habton, N Yorks

**FOCUS**
Add 5yds to race distance. A useful, competitive handicap and the runner-up was the only horse to come stands' side in the straight - the others stayed far side. The third, fourth and fifth have been rated close to form.

### 8290 TOTEPOOL EBFSTALLIONS.COM SILVER TANKARD STKS (LISTED RACE) — 1m 6y
3:50 (3:56) (Class 1) 2-Y-O
£19,848 (£7,525; £3,766; £1,876; £941; £472) Stalls Low

Form — RPR

416 **1** **Connect**[51] 6696 2-9-3 91 ........ AdamKirby 2 — 100+
(Clive Cox) *trckd ldrs: hdwy to ld wl over 1f out: sn rdn and qcknd clr: rdr dropped rein ent fnl f: kpt on strly* **9/1**

14 **2** *2 ¾* **Lisheen Castle (IRE)**[22] 7648 2-9-3 0 ........ JasonHart 7 — 94
(John Quinn) *hld up in rr: hdwy on inner over 2f out: rdn along wl over 1f out: kpt on wl fnl f* **14/1**

414 **3** *hd* **Dark Acclaim (IRE)**[44] 6925 2-9-3 95 ........ DanielMuscutt 4 — 94
(Marco Botti) *trckd ldr on inner: effrt and cl up over 2f out: rdn wl over 1f out: kpt on u.p fnl f* **7/1**[3]

3142 **4** *2* **Learn By Heart**[44] 6925 2-9-3 99 ........ DanielTudhope 5 — 89
(William Haggas) *trckd ldrs: hdwy on outer 3f out: cl up over 2f out: rdn wl over 1f out: kpt on same pce fnl f* **3/1**[2]

41 **5** *3 ½* **Unwritten**[25] 7556 2-9-3 0 ........ PJMcDonald 10 — 81
(K R Burke) *hld up in rr: hdwy 3f out: chsd ldrs wl over 1f out: sn rdn and no imp fnl f* **14/1**

1003 **6** *2 ¼* **Veejay (IRE)**[9] 8045 2-9-3 90 ........ JFEgan 1 — 77
(Mick Channon) *hld up: a in rr* **16/1**

311 **7** *nk* **Old Persian**[16] 7810 2-9-3 94 ........ WilliamBuick 9 — 76
(Charlie Appleby) *trckd ldng pair: hdwy and cl up 1/2-way: effrt over 2f out: sn rdn and wknd wl over 1f out* **6/5**[1]

4412 **8** *4 ½* **Poets Dream (IRE)**[16] 7818 2-9-3 85 ........ GeraldMosse 11 — 66
(Mohamed Moubarak) *led: rdn along wl over 2f out: drvn and hdd wl over 1f out: sn wknd* **33/1**

1m 51.87s (5.97) **Going Correction** +0.875s/f (Soft) — 8 Ran SP% **115.1**
Speed ratings (Par 103): **105,102,102,100,96 94,94,89**
CSF £123.22 TOTE £9.80: £2.30, £3.60, £2.20; EX 131.00 Trifecta £812.20.
**Owner** A D Spence **Bred** D J Weston **Trained** Lambourn, Berks

**FOCUS**
Add 5yds to race distance. A weak Listed race, with the favourite below form. The runners avoided the inside rail pretty much throughout, racing up the middle in the straight. It's been rated as a par race for the grade.

### 8291 TOTETRIFECTA MAIDEN STKS — 1m 4f 5y
4:20 (4:22) (Class 5) 3-Y-O+ — £3,234 (£962; £481; £240) Stalls Low

Form — RPR

2 **1** **Darksideoftarnside (IRE)**[13] 7935 3-9-5 0 ........ BenCurtis 3 — 86
(Sally Haynes) *trckd ldr: pushed along over 2f out: rdn wl over 1f out: drvn ent fnl f: sn swtchd lft and styd on wl to ld nr line* **13/2**

0335 **2** *hd* **Tranquil Star (IRE)**[20] 7708 3-9-0 77 ........ JFEgan 6 — 80
(Jeremy Noseda) *led: rdn clr wl over 1f out: drvn and edgd lft ent fnl f: kpt on: hdd nr line* **7/2**[2]

2222 **3** *5* **Know Your Limit (IRE)**[52] 6657 3-9-5 80 ........ JamieSpencer 2 — 80+
(Ed Walker) *trckd ldrs: smooth hdwy over 3f out: cl up 2f out: rdn to chse ldr 2f out: drvn over 1f out: sn one pce* **6/5**[1]

P024 **4** *7* **War Brigade (FR)**[45] 6871 3-9-5 70 ........ (h) AdamKirby 7 — 66
(David Simcock) *hld up: hdwy 4f out: rdn along to chse ldrs over 2f out: sn drvn and no imp* **8/1**

| | | | | |
|---|---|---|---|---|
| - | 5 | hd | **Aristo Du Plessis (FR)**261 7-9-4 0 JamieGormley(7) 1 (James Ewart) *dwlt and towards rr: rdn along over 3f out: plugged on one pce* **9/2**3 | 64 |
| | 6 | 10 | **Pandinus Imperator (IRE)**78 4-9-11 0 GrahamLee 8 (Martin Smith) *dwlt: a towards rr* **100/1** | 48 |
| 0000 | 7 | 3 3/4 | **Grey Mist**34 7248 3-9-5 59 (b) DavidAllan 5 (Tim Easterby) *trckd ldrs: hdwy on outer and cl up 4f out: rdn along over 3f out: wknd over 2f out* **50/1** | 43 |
| 040 | 8 | 9 | **Pontecarlo Boy**33 7271 3-9-5 43 (p) CamHardie 9 (Richard Whitaker) *prom: rdn along 4f out: wknd 3f out* **100/1** | 29 |

2m 51.49s (10.69) **Going Correction** +0.875s/f (Soft)
**WFA** 3 from 4yo+ 6lb 8 Ran SP% **114.2**
Speed ratings (Par 103): **99,98,95,90,90 84,81,75**
CSF £29.35 TOTE £8.30: £2.00, £1.20, £1.02; EX 29.60 Trifecta £90.70.
**Owner** Bluegrass Thoroughbreds 4 **Bred** Ballycrighaun Stud **Trained** Melsonby, N Yorks

**FOCUS**
Add 5yds to race distance. An ordinary maiden in which they raced middle to near side in the straight. It's been rated around the runner-up.

## 8292 TOTEPOOL LIVE INFO DOWNLOAD THE APP PHIL BULL TROPHY CONDITIONS STKS 2m 2f 2y

4:50 (4:50) (Class 2) 3-Y-O+ £12,450 (£3,728; £1,864; £932; £466) Stalls Low

| Form | | | | RPR |
|---|---|---|---|---|
| 2310 | 1 | | **Dominating (GER)**10 8011 3-8-7 91 PJMcDonald 1 (Mark Johnston) *trckd clr ldr: tk clsr order 3f out: led 2f out and sn rdn: drvn ins fnl f: kpt on wl towards fin* **6/4**2 | 84+ |
| 0053 | 2 | 3/4 | **Suegioo (FR)**23 7614 8-9-2 89 (p) TonyHamilton 2 (Richard Fahey) *hld up in rr: hdwy wl over 2f out: rdn wl over 1f out: kpt on u.p fnl f* **6/1**3 | 80+ |
| 6313 | 3 | 2 3/4 | **La Fritillaire**14 7893 5-8-11 67 (p) GrahamLee 5 (James Given) *led and sn wl clr: pushed along and hdd 2f out: c wd st to stands' rail and rdn: drvn and rallied ent fnl f: sn no ex* **14/1** | 73 |
| /2-4 | 4 | 9 | **Minotaur (IRE)**13 7931 5-9-2 102 FranBerry 4 (Jonjo O'Neill) *trckd ldrs: hdwy over 3f out: rdn along over 2f out: sn btn* **6/5**1 | 70 |
| 5042 | 5 | 41 | **Tuscan Gold**14 7893 10-9-2 62 (v1) PaulMulrennan 3 (Micky Hammond) *a in rr* **40/1** | 33 |

4m 19.06s (22.86) **Going Correction** +0.875s/f (Soft)
**WFA** 3 from 5yo+ 9lb 5 Ran SP% **108.8**
Speed ratings (Par 109): **84,83,82,78,60**
CSF £10.27 TOTE £1.90: £1.10, £3.00; EX 7.60 Trifecta £26.50.
**Owner** A D Spence **Bred** Gestut Etzean **Trained** Middleham Moor, N Yorks

**FOCUS**
Add 5yds to race distance. A disappointingly small field and a muddling race with the third, who had a tough task at the weights, opening up a big lead, and the favourite failed to fire. They came stands' side in the straight. It's been rated around the third.

## 8293 COLLECT TOTEPOOL WINNINGS FROM BETFRED SHOPS H'CAP 5f 3y

5:20 (5:24) (Class 4) (0-85,89) 3-Y-O+ £5,175 (£1,540; £769; £384) Stalls Low

| Form | | | | RPR |
|---|---|---|---|---|
| 0052 | 1 | | **Van Gerwen**25 7557 4-8-11 75 JoeFanning 6 (Les Eyre) *trckd ldr: hdwy to chal over 1f out: rdn to ld jst ins fnl f: drvn out* **4/1**2 | 85 |
| 0650 | 2 | 1 1/4 | **Henley**13 7940 5-9-0 78 BarryMcHugh 12 (Tracy Waggott) *led: rdn along 2f out: sn jnd: drvn and hdd jst ins fnl f: kpt on u.p towards fin* **28/1** | 84 |
| 0260 | 3 | 1 1/2 | **Eccleston**23 7612 6-9-6 84 (v) JoeDoyle 13 (Julie Camacho) *towards rr: hdwy wl over 1f out: sn rdn and stdy on fnl f* **14/1** | 84 |
| 6000 | 4 | nk | **Cosmic Chatter**13 7923 7-8-9 73 (p) JamesSullivan 11 (Ruth Carr) *chsd ldrs: rdn along 2f out: drvn over 1f out: edgd lft and kpt on fnl f* **10/1** | 72 |
| 3043 | 5 | nk | **Muatadel**13 7939 4-9-1 79 TonyHamilton 10 (Roger Fell) *anticipated s and stmbld bdly s: bhd: hdwy over 2f out: rdn over 1f out: chsd ldrs ent fnl f: kpt on* **7/1**3 | 77 |
| 4206 | 6 | nk | **Royal Brave (IRE)**10 8012 6-9-8 86 DanielTudhope 2 (Rebecca Bastiman) *chsd ldrs: rdn along 2f out: drvn over 1f out: kpt on same pce fnl f* **7/2**1 | 83 |
| 6050 | 7 | 2 3/4 | **My Name Is Rio (IRE)**61 6314 7-9-6 84 PaulMulrennan 1 (Michael Dods) *chsd ldrs on inner: hdwy 2f out: rdn over 1f out: wknd ins fnl f* **12/1** | 71 |
| 0545 | 8 | 3/4 | **Gamesome (FR)**13 7939 6-9-0 78 DougieCostello 15 (Paul Midgley) *in tch on outer: rdn along and wd st: sn bhd* **16/1** | 62 |
| 1000 | 9 | nk | **Escalating**10 8012 5-9-4 85 (tp) LewisEdmunds(3) 7 (Michael Appleby) *chsd ldrs: rdn along 2f out: drvn and wknd over 1f out* **11/1** | 68 |
| 6330 | 10 | 1 1/4 | **Straightothepoint**13 7940 5-9-0 78 GrahamLee 14 (Bryan Smart) *chsd ldrs: wd st: sn rdn and wknd* **28/1** | 57 |

1m 7.08s (3.78) **Going Correction** +0.875s/f (Soft) 10 Ran SP% **99.3**
Speed ratings (Par 105): **104,102,99,99,98 98,93,92,92,90**
CSF £74.06 CT £735.34 TOTE £3.90: £1.10, £5.10, £4.20; EX 87.70 Trifecta £3872.40 Part won..
**Owner** Sunpak Potatoes **Bred** Broughton Bloodstock **Trained** Catwick, N Yorks
■ Hoofalong (8/1) and Aleef (7/1) were withdrawn. Rule 4 applies to all bets - deduction 20p in the pound

**FOCUS**
Add 5yds to race distance. The 1-2 were positioned 2-1 for much of the way, and the action was up the middle in the straight. The runner-up has been rated close to his June peak.
T/Plt: £785.60 to a £1 stake. Pool: £75,606.87 - 70.25 winning units T/Qpdt: £49.00 to a £1 stake. Pool: £8,386.89 - 126.56 winning units **Joe Rowntree**

# 8110 WINDSOR (R-H)

Monday, October 23

**OFFICIAL GOING: Soft (good to soft in places) changing to soft after race 2 (2.10)**
Wind: Light, half behind Weather: Overcast, drizzly

## 8294 HAPPY 70TH BIRTHDAY PETER GILES NOVICE MEDIAN AUCTION STKS 5f 21y

1:40 (1:40) (Class 5) 2-Y-O £2,911 (£866; £432; £216) Stalls Low

| Form | | | | RPR |
|---|---|---|---|---|
| 3022 | 1 | | **Iconic Knight (IRE)**28 7450 2-9-2 74 LiamKeniry 2 (Ed Walker) *trckd ldrs: prog to go 2nd over 1f out: shkn up to ld jst ins fnl f: styd on wl* **9/2**3 | 74 |
| | 2 | 2 1/4 | **Big Brave Bob** 2-9-2 0 ShaneKelly 10 (Richard Hughes) *dwlt: hld up in rr but wl in tch: prog 2f out towards far rail: pushed along over 1f out: styd on fnl f to take 2nd nr fin* **25/1** | 67+ |
| 0 | 3 | nk | **Axe Cap (IRE)**150 3023 2-8-11 0 RichardKingscote 9 (Archie Watson) *taken down early: mde most in narrow ld to 2f out: nt qckn and lost pl sn after: styd on again fnl f to take 3rd last strides* **7/2**2 | 60+ |
| 21 | 4 | 1/2 | **Lord Riddiford (IRE)**160 2698 2-9-9 0 PatCosgrave 6 (John Quinn) *pressed ldr: led 2f out: rdn over 1f out: hdd & wknd jst ins fnl f: lost 2 pls nr fin* **7/4**1 | 70 |
| 530 | 5 | 1 | **Sovereign State**32 7326 2-9-2 65 OisinMurphy 3 (Robert Cowell) *trckd ldrs: pushed along 2f out: nvr landed a blow but kpt on steadily fnl f* **16/1** | 59 |
| 04 | 6 | 1/2 | **Cool Baby**54 6567 2-8-8 0 EoinWalsh(3) 13 (Robert Cowell) *dwlt: sn w ldrs: lost pl and shkn up 2f out: one pce after* **40/1** | 53 |
| 0303 | 7 | 3/4 | **Ivy Leaguer**52 6651 2-9-2 68 (p1) TomMarquand 12 (Brian Meehan) *wl in tch: shkn up 2f out: one pce and no imp on ldrs after* **9/1** | 55 |
| 2 | 8 | 1 | **Elite Shadow**7 8118 2-8-13 0 GeorgiaCox(3) 4 (Gay Kelleway) *wl in tch: rdn 2f out: no prog over 1f out: fdd* **8/1** | 51 |
| 00 | 9 | 1/2 | **Jazzy Girl (IRE)**19 7725 2-8-11 0 MartinDwyer 1 (Brendan Powell) *sn pushed along in last: nvr a factor but plugged on fr over 1f out* **100/1** | 45 |
| 00 | 10 | hd | **Choral Music**94 5107 2-8-11 0 RobHornby 11 (Jonathan Portman) *in tch: pushed along fr 1/2-way: steadily fdd over 1f out* **66/1** | 44 |
| 40 | 11 | 2 1/4 | **Shamrock Emma (IRE)**28 7450 2-8-11 0 JosephineGordon 7 (John Best) *w ldrs 2f: sn lost pl: wl in rr and struggling 2f out* **50/1** | 36 |

1m 1.41s (1.11) **Going Correction** +0.225s/f (Good) 11 Ran SP% **114.5**
Speed ratings (Par 95): **100,96,95,95,93 92,91,89,89,88 85**
CSF £112.44 TOTE £4.50: £1.50, £5.60, £1.30; EX 88.90 Trifecta £580.50.
**Owner** J Nicholls, J Moorhouse & J Kinning **Bred** Tally-Ho Stud **Trained** Upper Lambourn, Berks
■ Stewards' Enquiry : Pat Cosgrave caution: careless riding

**FOCUS**
Rail from 1m start and around bottom bend was moved in on to fresher ground for Windsor's final meeting of 2017. Stand-side rail also moved in 2-6 yards to keep off worn ground. No surprise to see them head far side in this modest novice event. The winner has been rated to the balance of his recent efforts.

## 8295 SKY BET EXTRA PLACES EVERY DAY H'CAP 1m 2f

2:10 (2:14) (Class 4) (0-80,82) 3-Y-O+ £4,690 (£1,395; £697; £348) Stalls Centre

| Form | | | | RPR |
|---|---|---|---|---|
| 5441 | 1 | | **Road To Dubai (IRE)**16 7824 3-9-5 82 HayleyTurner 5 (George Scott) *hld up in rr: stdy prog fr 3f out: led over 1f out: pushed out: readily* **15/2** | 91 |
| 0013 | 2 | 3/4 | **Bazooka (IRE)**22 7651 6-8-6 70 HollieDoyle(3) 15 (David Flood) *s.s: hld up in last: prog over 2f out: rdn to chse wnr fnl f: styd on and clsd but nvr able to chal* **10/1** | 77 |
| 332 | 3 | 1 1/2 | **Haulani (USA)**14 7902 3-8-10 76 (bt) HectorCrouch(3) 13 (Philip Hide) *w ldrs: disp fr 1/2-way tl rdn to ld 2f out: hdd and one pce over 1f out* **8/1** | 80 |
| 0621 | 4 | 3/4 | **Lunar Jet**26 7505 3-9-1 78 JimmyQuinn 6 (John Mackie) *t.k.h: hld up towards rr: gng wl whn making prog 3f out: shkn up and nt qckn wl over 1f out: disp 2nd briefly fnl f: one pce* **7/2**1 | 81 |
| 6521 | 5 | 2 | **Poseidon (IRE)**14 7902 3-8-11 74 LiamKeniry 10 (Ed Walker) *got loose in paddock: hld up in rr: pushed along over 2f out: kpt on fr over 1f out: nvr nrr* **7/1**3 | 73 |
| 1313 | 6 | 2 | **Essenaitch (IRE)**6 8142 4-8-8 74 KatherineGlenister(7) 3 (David Evans) *hld up in midfield: rdn 3f out: in tch u.p 2f out: steadily fdd* **16/1** | 69 |
| 2614 | 7 | 3/4 | **Liquid Gold (IRE)**23 7598 3-8-9 72 PaulHanagan 12 (Richard Fahey) *in rr: dropped to last pair and urged along 1/2-way: nvr on terms after but rallied to pass sme rivals fr 2f out* **8/1** | 65 |
| 000 | 8 | 1/2 | **Mansfield**123 4017 4-8-10 69 DavidProbert 1 (Michael Wigham) *trckd ldrs: led after 4f: jnd 1/2-way: hdd 2f out: wknd over 1f out* **50/1** | 61 |
| 3062 | 9 | 6 | **Fast And Hot (IRE)**12 7959 4-8-13 79 (b) RossaRyan(7) 7 (Richard Hannon) *trckd ldrs: rdn to dispute 3rd 3f out: wknd 2f out* **13/2**2 | 59 |
| 0611 | 10 | 5 | **Ourmullion**25 7541 3-8-10 73 (p) JosephineGordon 11 (John Best) *chsd ldrs tl wknd u.p over 2f out* **12/1** | 44 |
| 4360 | 11 | 1 | **Paddy A (IRE)**116 4267 3-8-9 72 GeorgeDowning 4 (Ian Williams) *hld up in midfield: urged along and struggling sn after 1/2-way: sn no threat* **66/1** | 41 |
| 1560 | 12 | shd | **Angrywhitepyjamas (IRE)**12 7959 4-9-7 80 MartinDwyer 2 (William Muir) *chsd ldrs: rdn and in tch 3f out: lost pl and wknd 2f out* **16/1** | 48 |
| 1450 | 13 | 2 | **The Yellow Bus**20 7710 4-8-13 72 KieranO'Neill 9 (Daniel Steele) *hld up wl in rr: rdn and no prog over 3f out: wl btn after* **66/1** | 36 |
| 0040 | 14 | 11 | **Tangramm**28 7452 5-9-5 78 (p) RobHornby 14 (Dean Ivory) *mde most 4f: lost pl rapidly fr 1/2-way: t.o* **33/1** | 20 |

2m 10.48s (1.78) **Going Correction** +0.225s/f (Good)
**WFA** 3 from 4yo+ 4lb 14 Ran SP% **118.5**
Speed ratings (Par 105): **101,100,99,98,97 95,94,94,89,85 84,84,83,74**
CSF £77.98 CT £620.30 TOTE £7.40: £2.40, £3.40, £3.00; EX 83.10 Trifecta £840.50.
**Owner** Mohammed Al Nabouda **Bred** Rabbah Bloodstock Limited **Trained** Newmarket, Suffolk

**FOCUS**
A fair handicap, run at an average pace. It's been rated as ordinary late season form.

## 8296 SKY BET TOP PRICE PROMISE CLASSIFIED CLAIMING STKS 6f 12y
**2:40** (2:45) (Class 5) 3-Y-0+ **£2,911** (£866; £432; £216) **Stalls** Low

Form RPR

2423 **1** **Ballesteros**[7] 8106 8-8-9 75 PaulHanagan 5 76
(Richard Fahey) *hld up bhd ldrs: prog fr 1/2-way: urged along to ld over 1f out: rdn out and in command fnl f* **10/11**[1]

6300 **2** 1 3/4 **The Big Lad**[40] 7056 5-8-11 69 (e) ShaneKelly 2 72
(Richard Hughes) *pressed ldrs: rdn to chal 2f out: nt qckn and wnr sn overtk: kpt on and jst hld on for 2nd* **12/1**

4130 **3** shd **Morache Music**[22] 7653 9-8-11 75 (p) LiamKeniry 1 72
(Patrick Chamings) *reluctant to go to post: slowly away: off the pce in last: prog fr 1/2-way: rdn 2f out: styd on to take 3rd ins fnl f and jst failed to snatch 2nd* **5/1**[3]

0660 **4** 1 **Gilmer (IRE)**[13] 7923 6-8-2 72 (b[1]) DavidEgan(3) 8 62
(James Ewart) *nt that wl away but sn w ldrs: led over 3f out to over 1f out: one pce u.p* **11/4**[2]

0000 **5** 3 **El Torito (IRE)**[4] 8184 3-9-0 68 (p) PatCosgrave 7 63
(Jim Boyle) *wl in tch: rdn to chse ldng pair over 3f out to 2f out: fdd over 1f out* **20/1**

0500 **6** 14 **Vroom (IRE)**[56] 6541 4-8-10 73 (p) RhiainIngram(5) 6 18
(Gay Kelleway) *w ldrs to 1/2-way: sn wknd: t.o* **20/1**

03-0 **7** 3/4 **Fullon Clarets**[14] 7878 5-8-9 67 (p) GeorgeDowning 3 10
(Laura Mongan) *led to over 3f out: sn wknd: t.o* **25/1**

0300 **8** 4 **Head Space (IRE)**[14] 7900 9-7-12 48 (t[1]) HollieDoyle(3) 4
(Brian Barr) *struggling in last pair after 2f: t.o* **100/1**

1m 13.21s (0.21) **Going Correction** +0.225s/f (Good)
**WFA** 3 from 4yo+ 1lb **8 Ran SP% 117.8**
Speed ratings (Par 103): **107,104,104,103,99 80,79,74**
CSF £13.60 TOTE £1.60: £1.02, £3.10, £2.00; EX 12.80 Trifecta £34.40.The winner was claimed by Mr Roger Ingram for £7000.
**Owner** Dr Marwan Koukash **Bred** Exors Of The Late J R Good **Trained** Musley Bank, N Yorks

**FOCUS**
Not a bad claimer. Again they went far side off the home turn. It's been rated cautiously, with the fourth and fifth not in much form recently.

## 8297 SKY BET BEST ODDS GUARANTEED H'CAP 1m 31y
**3:10** (3:10) (Class 4) (0-85,87) 3-Y-0+ **£4,690** (£1,395; £697; £348) **Stalls** Low

Form RPR

602 **1** **Ghalib (IRE)**[14] 7909 5-9-7 **85** (bt) RichardKingscote 11 93
(Amy Murphy) *rousted after s: pressed ldr: led 3f out: rdn over 2f out: clr over 1f out: kpt on wl and unchal after* **8/1**

3120 **2** 1 1/4 **Dark Devil (IRE)**[11] 7981 4-9-6 **84** PaulHanagan 10 89+
(Richard Fahey) *hld up in last trio: rdn in last 3f out: stl there over 1f out: threaded through rivals fnl f and styd on wl to take 2nd nr fin* **13/2**[2]

6510 **3** nk **Glorious Poet**[27] 7474 4-8-12 **76** WilliamCarson 6 80
(John Spearing) *led at gd pce: steered towards nr side in st initially then bk to join rest: hdd 3f out: chsd wnr after: no imp fnl 2f: kpt on but lost 2nd nr fin* **16/1**

1103 **4** nk **Sayem**[25] 7545 3-9-2 **83** LiamKeniry 8 85
(Ed Walker) *hld up in midfield: effrt and swtchd to far rail 2f out: disp 2nd over 1f out: kpt on same pce fnl f* **12/1**

1660 **5** nk **Wealth Tax**[24] 7582 4-9-2 **80** ShaneKelly 12 83
(Ed Dunlop) *hld up towards rr: shkn up over 2f out: no prog tl kpt on fnl f: nvr able to threaten* **12/1**

4001 **6** shd **Harlequin Striker (IRE)**[12] 7958 5-8-13 **77** (p) RobHornby 7 79
(Dean Ivory) *chsd ldng pair: rdn 3f out: nt qckn 2f out and wl hld after: kpt on fnl f* **7/1**[3]

2430 **7** 1 **Golden Wedding (IRE)**[28] 7456 5-9-4 **82** (p) CharlesBishop 2 82
(Eve Johnson Houghton) *chsd ldrs: rdn 3f out: no imp 2f out: wl hld after* **7/1**[3]

1210 **8** nk **Kyllachys Tale (IRE)**[33] 7276 3-9-1 **82** JackMitchell 5 80
(Roger Teal) *chsd ldrs: rdn 3f out: styd chsng but no imp after: wknd fnl f* **12/1**

0002 **9** 1 1/2 **Mikmak**[12] 7957 4-8-10 **74** (p) MartinDwyer 3 70
(William Muir) *s.i.s: hld up in last: shkn up 3f out: no real prog* **13/2**[2]

0300 **10** 1 1/4 **Sir Roderic (IRE)**[38] 7129 4-9-5 **83** RobertHavlin 9 76
(Rod Millman) *hld up in 8th: rdn and no prog over 2f out* **5/1**[1]

6004 **11** nk **Dutch Uncle**[14] 7909 5-8-9 **73** OisinMurphy 1 65
(Robert Cowell) *hld up in 6th: lost pl 2f out: shkn up briefly jst over 1f out: steadily fdd* **16/1**

150- **12** nse **Wimpole Hall**[396] 6710 4-9-9 **87** DavidProbert 4 79
(William Jarvis) *hld up in last trio: shkn up and no prog wl over 2f out* **50/1**

1m 44.99s (0.29) **Going Correction** +0.225s/f (Good)
**WFA** 3 from 4yo+ 3lb **12 Ran SP% 116.2**
Speed ratings (Par 105): **107,105,105,105,104 104,103,103,101,100 100,100**
CSF £58.05 CT £827.34 TOTE £6.40: £2.70, £2.90, £5.30; EX 39.40 Trifecta £2439.70.
**Owner** Saleh Al Homaizi & Imad Al Sagar **Bred** T Molan **Trained** Newmarket, Suffolk

**FOCUS**
This good-quality handicap looked wide open. As is often the case around here it paid to be handy. The winner has been rated to this year's best.

## 8298 ANCASTER NISSAN SLOUGH H'CAP 5f 21y
**3:40** (3:40) (Class 6) (0-60,62) 3-Y-0+ **£2,264** (£673; £336; £168) **Stalls** Low

Form RPR

3422 **1** **Flowing Clarets**[13] 7912 4-9-4 **60** MitchGodwin(3) 13 68
(John Bridger) *trckd ldr: rdn to chal over 1f out: hanging and racd awkwardly after but drvn ahd last 100yds and sn in command* **4/1**[2]

6002 **2** 1 1/4 **Awesome Allan (IRE)**[5] 8168 3-9-4 **60** (t) MattCosham(3) 5 65
(David Evans) *sn chsd ldrs: rdn 2f out: prog on outer of gp over 1f out: styd on ins fnl f to take 2nd last strides* **7/4**[1]

6042 **3** shd **Silver Penny**[10] 7993 3-8-4 **46** (p) CharlieBennett(3) 11 50
(Jim Boyle) *chsd ldr: rdn 2f out: nt qckn over 1f out: kpt on again nr fin* **12/1**

6253 **4** nse **Mercers**[6] 8128 3-9-6 **59** (b[1]) ShaneKelly 15 63
(Peter Crate) *led: taken to far rail 1/2-way: rdn over 1f out: hdd last 100yds: lost 2 pls last strides* **12/1**

0145 **5** nk **Staffa (IRE)**[6] 8128 4-9-7 **60** OisinMurphy 4 62
(Denis Coakley) *hld up in rr: prog 1/2-way: rdn to chse ldrs over 1f out: kpt on but nvr able to chal* **16/1**

3056 **6** 2 1/4 **Fivos**[14] 7910 3-8-7 **49** GeorgeWood(3) 14 44
(David Bridgwater) *chsd ldrs: rdn 2f out: no imp over 1f out: one pce and no threat after* **40/1**

060 **7** 1/2 **Dollywaggon Pike**[56] 6526 3-8-5 **47** HollieDoyle(3) 1 40
(J R Jenkins) *chsd ldng trio: rdn over 2f out: no imp 1f out: wknd ins fnl f* **100/1**

0202 **8** 1 1/4 **Captain Ryan**[21] 7694 6-9-4 **60** GeorgiaCox(3) 6 47
(Geoffrey Deacon) *nvr bttr than midfield: rdn and no prog 2f out* **10/1**

3243 **9** 3/4 **John Joiner**[26] 7509 5-9-4 **57** JosephineGordon 8 42
(Peter Hedger) *dwlt: sn in midfield: rdn over 2f out: no prog and wl btn over 1f out* **6/1**[3]

2003 **10** 2 1/4 **Nuzha**[21] 7689 3-9-4 **60** EoinWalsh(3) 7 38
(Tony Newcombe) *hld up in rr: shkn up and no prog jst over 2f out: no ch after* **16/1**

0036 **11** nk **Naralsaif (IRE)**[71] 5956 3-8-11 **50** (v) PaulHanagan 3 27
(Derek Shaw) *sn struggling in rr: nvr a factor* **25/1**

6300 **12** 2 1/4 **Captain Scooby**[6] 8128 11-8-8 **47** oh1 ow1 (b) TomMarquand 9 15
(Richard Guest) *s.v.s: nvr able to rcvr and a bhd* **16/1**

4-00 **13** 11 **Special Code (IRE)**[20] 7705 5-8-9 **48** (t) DannyBrock 12
(Paddy Butler) *s.i.s: sn struggling in rr: t.o* **100/1**

1m 1.22s (0.92) **Going Correction** +0.225s/f (Good) **13 Ran SP% 121.0**
Speed ratings (Par 101): **101,99,98,98,98 94,93,91,90,87 86,83,65**
CSF £11.29 CT £81.45 TOTE £4.60: £1.50, £1.30, £3.10; EX 12.60 Trifecta £123.20.
**Owner** Wood Marshall Bridger **Bred** R A Fahey **Trained** Liphook, Hants
■ Stewards' Enquiry : Matt Cosham two-day ban: excessive use of whip (Nov 6-7)

**FOCUS**
A moderate sprint handicap in which those racing prominently dominated. It's been rated around the first two.

## 8299 SKY BET RACING CASH OUT H'CAP (DIV I) 1m 31y
**4:10** (4:10) (Class 5) (0-70,72) 3-Y-0+ **£2,911** (£866; £432; £216) **Stalls** Low

Form RPR

3611 **1** **Love And Be Loved**[28] 7464 3-8-7 **66** WilliamCox(7) 2 75
(John Flint) *mde all: shkn up and 2 l clr 2f out: rdn and styd on fnl f: unchal* **10/3**[1]

1446 **2** 2 **Edgar Allan Poe (IRE)**[12] 7958 3-9-3 **69** MartinHarley 6 73
(Rebecca Bastiman) *hld up: 9th whn styd alone against nr side fr 3f out: prog after: tk 2nd fnl f and styd on but nvr able to threaten wnr* **8/1**

1026 **3** 1 **Born To Please**[5] 8152 3-7-11 **56** oh3 NicolaCurrie(7) 8 58
(Mark Usher) *chsd ldrs: shkn up and prog over 2f out: disp 2nd fnl f: kpt on but nvr able to chal* **8/1**

4003 **4** nk **Gala Celebration (IRE)**[13] 7916 3-8-5 **57** (p) JimmyQuinn 1 58
(John Gallagher) *plld hrd: trckd ldng pair: rdn and nt qckn 2f out: one pce after* **11/1**

0260 **5** 1 1/4 **It's How We Roll (IRE)**[14] 7902 3-8-8 **60** (b) TomMarquand 3 58
(John Spearing) *chsd ldrs: rdn over 2f out: tried to cl over 1f out: no imp ins fnl f* **4/1**[3]

1415 **6** 3/4 **Hedging (IRE)**[19] 7736 3-9-6 **72** (p) CharlesBishop 11 69
(Eve Johnson Houghton) *chsd wnr: rdn over 2f out: lost 2nd and fdd over 1f out* **7/2**[2]

030 **7** 4 1/2 **Mitigate**[32] 7341 3-9-1 **70** HollieDoyle(3) 7 56
(Jane Chapple-Hyam) *hld up in midfield: shkn up and no prog over 2f out: n.d after* **10/1**

5040 **8** 1 1/2 **Peak Storm**[24] 7567 8-8-4 **58** (p) BenRobinson(5) 4 42
(John O'Shea) *chsd ldrs: rdn over 2f out: sn wknd* **33/1**

004 **9** 4 **Sky Marshal (IRE)**[39] 7080 3-8-13 **65** LiamKeniry 5 39
(Ed Walker) *mostly in rr: shkn up 5f out: effrt and sme prog 3f out: wknd 2f out* **16/1**

5533 **10** 7 **Dana's Present**[171] 2365 8-9-2 **68** EoinWalsh(3) 9 27
(Tony Newcombe) *slowly away: a in last pair: t.o* **50/1**

1400 **11** shd **Muthraab Aldaar (IRE)**[14] 7878 4-8-13 **62** JackMitchell 10 20
(Jim Boyle) *a in rr: rdn and wknd 4f out: t.o* **66/1**

1m 45.78s (1.08) **Going Correction** +0.225s/f (Good)
**WFA** 3 from 4yo+ 3lb **11 Ran SP% 117.2**
Speed ratings (Par 103): **103,101,100,99,98 97,93,91,87,80 80**
CSF £30.11 CT £202.73 TOTE £4.30: £1.80, £2.50, £2.50; EX 36.50 Trifecta £200.30.
**Owner** J L Flint **Bred** Sarah McNicholas **Trained** Kenfig Hill, Bridgend

**FOCUS**
An ordinary handicap. This time the main action came away from the far side. The third and fourth help set the standard.

## 8300 SKY BET RACING CASH OUT H'CAP (DIV II) 1m 31y
**4:40** (4:41) (Class 5) (0-70,71) 3-Y-0+ **£1,888** (£1,888; £432; £216) **Stalls** Low

Form RPR

0500 **1** **International Law**[86] 5404 3-9-4 **69** (p) TomMarquand 6 75
(Brian Meehan) *hld up in midfield: urged along over 3f out: drvn and prog against nr side rail over 1f out: styd on fnl f to force dead-heat last stride* **9/1**

0561 **1** dht **East Coast Lady (IRE)**[28] 7465 5-9-4 **69** DavidEgan(3) 1 76
(William Stone) *led: kicked on 3f out: drvn 2f out: hdd over 1f out: rallied fnl f to force dead-heat last stride* **13/2**[3]

525 **3** shd **Caledonia Duchess**[20] 7710 4-8-8 **56** JosephineGordon 8 63
(Jo Hughes) *hld up in midfield: hanging lft bnd over 5f out: prog over 2f out: rdn to ld over 1f out: hrd pressed last 100yds: hdd fnl stride* **6/1**[2]

4303 **4** 1 1/4 **William Booth (IRE)**[12] 7958 3-9-2 **67** KieranShoemark 4 71
(Ivan Furtado) *trckd ldrs: pushed along over 3f out: clsd over 1f out: trying to chal ins fnl f whn squeezed out: nt rcvr* **6/1**[2]

1052 **5** 3/4 **Misu Pete**[14] 7900 5-8-4 **59** (p) NicolaCurrie(7) 7 61
(Mark Usher) *hld up in midfield: effrt on outer over 2f out: rdn to chse ldrs over 1f out: one pce after* **6/1**[2]

2522 **6** 1/2 **Green Howard**[11] 7980 9-8-10 **58** (p) DavidProbert 2 59
(Rebecca Bastiman) *hld up wl in rr: clsd on ldrs 2f out: rdn and nt qckn over 1f out: one pce after* **7/2**[1]

003 **7** 2 **Highway One (USA)**[37] 7157 3-9-6 **71** PatCosgrave 3 67
(George Baker) *prom: rdn 3f out: lost pl 2f out: sn btn* **8/1**

4460 **8** 1/2 **Duke Of North (IRE)**[13] 7916 5-8-12 **63** (p) CharlieBennett(3) 5 58
(Jim Boyle) *slowly away: hld up wl in rr: effrt on outer over 2f out: no prog over 1f out: fdd* **14/1**

5306 **9** 1 **Shifting Star (IRE)**[18] 7770 12-9-6 **68** (vt) WilliamCarson 10 61
(John Bridger) *chsd ldr to 2f out: steadily wknd* **16/1**

4565 **10** hd **Stringybark Creek**[12] 7952 3-8-4 **55** oh5 KieranO'Neill 12 47
(Daniel Steele) *hld up in rr: prog on outer bnd over 5f out: rdn 3f out: wknd 2f out* **66/1**

0-00 **11** 3/4 **Kath's Legend**[27] 7492 3-8-5 **56** JimmyQuinn 9 46
(Ben De Haan) *chsd ldng pair to jst over 2f out: sn wknd steadily* **50/1**

5144 **12** *6* **Duchess Of Fife**[28] 7463 3-9-0 **65**...(v) MartinLane 11 41
(William Knight) *fractious bef gng bhd stalls: s.i.s: mostly in last: bhd fnl 2f* **16/1**

1m 46.44s (1.74) **Going Correction** +0.225s/f (Good)
**WFA** 3 from 4yo+ 3lb **12** Ran SP% **121.4**
Speed ratings (Par 103): **100,100,99,98,97 97,95,94,93,93 92,86**
WIN: 4.50 International Law, 3.40 East Coast Lady; PL: IL 2.30, ECL 2.30, CD 1.70; EX: IL/ECL 41.30, ECL/IL 36.60; CSF: ECL/IL 32.80, IL/ECL 34.07; TC: ECL/IL/CD 191.12, IL/ECL/CD 197.00; TF: IL/ECL/CD 536.00, ECL/IL/CD 351.80.
**Owner** Miss Caroline Scott **Bred** Mountarmstrong Stud **Trained** West Wickham, Cambs
**Owner** The Pony Club **Bred** Ed's Stud Ltd **Trained** Manton, Wilts

**FOCUS**
This second division of the ordinary 1m handicap saw a tight three-way finish on the near side. The third has been rated close to her recent AW figures.

## 8301 IVOR LAWS MEMORIAL H'CAP (FOR GENTLEMAN AMATEUR RIDERS ) 1m 3f 99y
**5:10** (5:11) (Class 6) (0-65,67) 3-Y-O+ **£2,183** (£677; £338; £169) **Stalls** Centre

Form RPR
5045 **1** **Betsalottie**[5] 8152 4-10-3 **52**... MrBJames(5) 11 59
(John Bridger) *chsd ldrs: urged along over 3f out: rdr in a tangle 2f out: hrd rdn to chal over 1f out: led 100yds out: hld on* **6/1**[3]
4013 **2** *shd* **Seventii**[13] 7918 3-10-8 **57**... MrRBirkett 2 65+
(Robert Eddery) *hld up in midfield: prog 3f out: clsng on ldrs whn nt clr run wl over 1f out: rallied fnl f: chal last 100yds: jst failed* **7/2**[2]
4634 **3** *1* **Dakota City**[138] 3470 6-11-3 **61**...(b) MrJJCodd 10 66
(Olly Murphy) *s.s and detached in last pair early: prog fr 5f out: clsd on ldrs fr 2f out: drvn and stydd on to take 3rd last 50yds: too late to chal* **7/1**
3643 **4** *3/4* **Turnbury**[39] 7085 6-10-10 **54**...(p) MrJordanWilliams 5 58
(Nikki Evans) *trckd ldrs: prog to go 2nd 3f out: rdn to ld over 1f out: hdd and no ex last 100yds* **11/1**
3150 **5** *1 1/4* **Party Royal**[88] 5320 7-11-4 **62**...(p) MrDHDunsdon 7 64
(Nick Gifford) *hld up wl in rr: stdy prog fr 3f out: chsd ldrs over 1f out but nt on terms: shkn up and kpt on: nvr rchd chalng position* **40/1**
5556 **6** *3* **Moojaned (IRE)**[24] 7561 6-10-6 **55**...(b[1]) MrCPrice(5) 8 52
(John Flint) *led: kicked on 4f out: drvn and hdd over 1f out: wknd* **5/2**[1]
1153 **7** *1 1/4* **John Caesar (IRE)**[12] 7960 6-10-12 **56**...(tp) MrPMillman 9 51
(Rebecca Bastiman) *prom: chsd ldr 4f out to 3f out: wknd u.p 2f out* **6/1**[3]
600- **8** *4 1/2* **Mr Fickle (IRE)**[201] 7183 8-11-4 **67**... MrSRoche(5) 6 55
(Gary Moore) *hld up and sn detached in last pair: bhd 5f out: passed a few late after but nvr any ch* **20/1**
-264 **9** *3* **Chestnut Storm (IRE)**[240] 741 4-10-8 **59**... MrCJTodd(7) 4 42
(Brian Barr) *in tch: rdn over 3f out: sn lft bhd* **50/1**
013- **10** *13* **Madame Claud**[375] 7309 4-11-2 **60**... MrAlexFerguson 3 22
(Mark Gillard) *in tch to 4f out: sn bhd: t.o* **66/1**
350- **11** *4* **Argyle (IRE)**[202] 6730 4-11-7 **65**... MrSWalker 1 21
(Gary Moore) *chsd ldr after 4f to 4f out: wknd qckly: t.o* **17/2**
5060 **12** *4 1/2* **Megalala (IRE)**[42] 7006 16-10-7 **51** oh6... MrHHunt 12
(John Bridger) *chsd ldr 4f: wknd qckly 4f out: t.o* **100/1**

2m 35.83s (6.33) **Going Correction** +0.225s/f (Good)
**WFA** 3 from 4yo+ 5lb **12** Ran SP% **122.4**
Speed ratings (Par 101): **86,85,85,84,83 81,80,77,75,65 62,59**
CSF £27.46 CT £156.09 TOTE £6.90: £1.80, £1.30, £2.10; EX 33.50 Trifecta £258.30.
**Owner** J J Bridger **Bred** P A & M J Reditt & Catridge Stud **Trained** Liphook, Hants
■ Stewards' Enquiry : Mr J J Codd two-day ban: didn't give horse time to respond to whip (Nov 7-8)

**FOCUS**
A moderate handicap, confined to gentleman amateurs. The winner has been rated near the best of this year's form.
T/Jkpt: £17,820.60 to a £1 stake. Pool: £17,820.60 - 1 winning unit T/Plt: £116.70 to a £1 stake. Pool: £86,983.28 - 544.02 winning units T/Qpdt: £13.40 to a £1 stake. Pool: £8,859.92 - 487.86 winning units **Jonathan Neesom**

# 8251 CHANTILLY (R-H)
Monday, October 23
**OFFICIAL GOING: Polytrack: standard**

## 8302a PRIX DU BUISSON CREUX (MAIDEN) (2YO COLTS & GELDINGS) (POLYTRACK) 6f 110y
**11:25** 2-Y-O **£11,538** (£4,615; £3,461; £2,307; £1,153)

RPR
**1** **Drummore (IRE)**[16] 7844 2-9-2 0... MickaelBarzalona 5 80
(A Fabre, France) *sn trcking ldr: pushed along 2f out: rdn to chal over 1f out: drvn into ld and styd on wl fnl f* **7/10**[1]
**2** *1 3/4* **The Gates Of Dawn (FR)**[37] 7175 2-9-2 0... AurelienLemaitre 4 75
(F Head, France) **7/1**
**3** *nk* **The Lamplighter (FR)**[42] 7012 2-9-2 0... TheoBachelot 1 74
(George Baker) *led: pushed along to hold advantage 2f out: rdn and led 1f out: lost 2nd cl home* **26/5**[3]
**4** *1 1/2* **Taxman (USA)** 2-8-11 0... AlexisBadel 2 65
(H-F Devin, France) **74/10**
**5** *1* **Out Of System**[12] 2-9-2 0... ChristopheSoumillon 3 67
(F Chappet, France) **4/1**[2]

1m 18.54s **5** Ran SP% **119.4**
PARI-MUTUEL (all including 1 euro stake): WIN 1.70; PLACE 1.10, 1.90; SF 7.50.
**Owner** Godolphin SNC **Bred** Godolphin **Trained** Chantilly, France

## 8303a PRIX DES ALLEES CAVALIERES (CLAIMER) (4YO+) (AMATEUR RIDERS) (POLYTRACK) 1m 5f 110y
**11:55** 4-Y-O+ **£6,837** (£2,735; £2,051; £1,367; £683)

RPR
**1** **Al Murqab (IRE)**[103] 7-10-3 0...(p) MlleMarionBas(9) 4 80
(J Phelippon, France) **54/10**[3]
**2** *3/4* **Ball Lightning (FR)**[580] 7-10-3 0...(p) MrThibaudMace 6 70
(E Libaud, France) **31/10**[1]
**3** *2 1/2* **Balsa Baie (FR)** 6-10-4 0 ow1... MrRomainBoisnard 1 67
(D Meslin, France) **203/10**
**4** *3* **Rodyana (FR)**[20] 7721 4-10-2 0...(b) JulienDelaunay(5) 3 66
(P Monfort, France) **141/10**
**5** *1 1/2* **Barwick**[26] 7534 9-10-2 0... MlleLaraLeGeay(5) 10 64
(George Baker) *settled bhd ldrs: hdwy to join front rnk over 2f out: briefly led over 1f out: sn hdd & wknd fnl f* **78/10**
**6** *5* **Book Of Days (FR)**[13] 6-10-4 0...(p) MrFlorentGuy 8 54
(N Caullery, France) **49/10**[2]
**7** *7* **Oratory Davis (FR)**[518] 7-10-2 0... MissMartinaLukova(5) 7 47
(V Luka Jr, Czech Republic) **92/10**
**8** *3* **Give Love (FR)**[19] 7-10-3 0... MlleMarieArtu(5) 11 44
(J-Y Artu, France) **116/10**
**9** *3* **Big Mec (FR)**[733] 7409 6-10-6 0... MrCharles-AntoinePrunault(4) 9 42
(Mlle B Renk, France) **57/10**
**10** *nk* **Anakin Skywalker (GER)**[494] 8-9-8 0..(p) MlleAlexandraCambalova(9) 5 35
(W Mongil, Germany) **204/10**
**11** *dist* **Blond Magicien (FR)** 4-9-8 0... MlleLucieLenglart(9) 2
(F Lenglart, France) **97/1**

PARI-MUTUEL (all including 1 euro stake): WIN 6.40; PLACE 2.10, 1.60, 4.60; DF 12.60; SF 23.80.
**Owner** Suc J-F Vignion & J Phelippon **Bred** Barronstown Stud **Trained** France

## 8304a PRIX DU BOIS DU TRIANGLE (CLAIMER) (3YO FILLIES) (POLYTRACK) 6f 110y
**1:35** 3-Y-O **£8,119** (£3,247; £2,435; £1,623; £811)

RPR
**1** **Made Of Honour (IRE)**[14] 7892 3-9-4 0...(b) TonyPiccone 3 74
(K R Burke) *rdn early: settled bhd ldr: rdn along to chal over 1f out: drvn to ld ins fnl f: hrd pressed towards fin: all out* **78/10**
**2** *hd* **Qatar Divine (FR)**[187] 3-9-1 0... OlivierPeslier 4 70
(H-A Pantall, France) **18/5**[2]
**3** *1 1/2* **Rajeline (FR)**[4] 3-8-13 0... KyllanBarbaud(5) 12 69
(M Boutin, France) **191/10**
**4** *nk* **Sweeticon**[33] 7308 3-9-3 0... MlleCoraliePacaut(10) 1 77
(Antonio Marcialis, Italy) **11/5**[1]
**5** *1/2* **Tamarama (FR)**[80] 3-9-1 0... GregoryBenoist 7 64
(D Smaga, France) **119/10**
**6** *1 1/2* **La Dame En Rouge (FR)**[90] 3-9-2 0... StephanePasquier 10 60
(J Phelippon, France) **211/10**
**7** *3/4* **Hurry (IRE)**[29] 3-9-2 0... AnthonyCrastus 2 58
(P Sogorb, France) **54/10**[3]
**8** *nk* **Elusiva (FR)**[71] 3-9-1 0... MickaelBarzalona 8 56
(H-A Pantall, France) **44/5**
**9** *2 1/2* **Sunderia (FR)**[24] 3-8-4 0...(b) MlleLauraGrosso(7) 6 45
(Mme S Allouche, France) **69/1**
**10** *3 1/2* **Rancheria (FR)**[85] 3-8-11 0...(p) TheoBachelot 5 35
(S Wattel, France) **151/10**
**11** *3/4* **Stuhna (FR)** 3-8-7 0... DelphineSantiago(4) 9 33
(V Luka Jr, Czech Republic) **30/1**

PARI-MUTUEL (all including 1 euro stake): WIN 8.80; PLACE 3.20 2.10, 4.10; DF 18.70; SF 45.00.
**Owner** Ontoawinner, D Mackay & Mrs E Burke **Bred** Limetree Stud **Trained** Middleham Moor, N Yorks

## 8305a PRIX DU BOIS DU LIEUTENANT (CLAIMER) (3YO COLTS & GELDINGS) (POLYTRACK) 6f 110y
**2:40** 3-Y-O **£8,119** (£3,247; £2,435; £1,623; £811)

RPR
**1** **Cavaprun (FR)**[91] 5231 3-9-5 0... AlexandreGavilan 9 87
(D Guillemin, France) **9/5**[1]
**2** *2 1/2* **Dibazari (FR)**[24] 3-8-4 0... AlexandreChesneau(7) 10 72
(G Botti, France) **159/10**
**3** *1/2* **Dolokhov**[12] 3-8-11 0...(p) StephanePasquier 8 70
(J Phelippon, France) **29/10**[2]
**4** *nk* **Bay Of Biscaine (FR)**[12] 3-9-0 0...(p) StefanieHofer(4) 6 76
(Mario Hofer, Germany) **92/10**
**5** *6* **Soho Universe (FR)**[64] 3-9-5 0... JulienAuge 3 60
(C Ferland, France) **57/10**[3]
**6** *1 3/4* **Happy Dream (ITY)**[33] 7308 3-9-1 0... AntoineHamelin 11 51
(J Parize, France) **77/10**
**7** *1* **Killing Joke (FR)**[4] 3-8-9 0...(b) KyllanBarbaud(6) 12 48
(M Boutin, France) **80/1**
**8** *nk* **Dubai Knights (IRE)**[71] 3-8-9 0...(p) TristanBaron(6) 7 47
(P Monfort, France) **43/1**
**9** *3/4* **Gerrard's Return**[12] 3-8-11 0... KoenClijmans 1 41
(Joeri Goossens, Belgium) **66/1**
**10** *nk* **Chatoyer (FR)**[10] 8025 3-9-1 0... AlexisBadel 5 44
(J S Moore) *settled in midfield: tk clsr order 3f out: rdn over 2f out: drvn over 1f out: limited rspnse and eased ins fnl f* **43/5**

PARI-MUTUEL (all including 1 euro stake): WIN 2.80; PLACE 1.40, 2.70, 1.60; DF 14.40; SF 26.10.
**Owner** Ecurie Jarlan **Bred** Ecurie Jarlan **Trained** France

# 8145 KEMPTON (A.W) (R-H)
Tuesday, October 24
**OFFICIAL GOING: Polytrack: standard to slow**
Wind: light, across Weather: dry

## 8306 RACINGUK.COM/JOIN NURSERY H'CAP 1m (P)
**5:45** (5:48) (Class 6) (0-60,60) 2-Y-O **£2,587** (£770; £384; £192) **Stalls** Low

Form RPR
556 **1** **Sauchiehall Street (IRE)**[75] 5847 2-8-9 **51**... MitchGodwin(3) 4 56+
(Sylvester Kirk) *hld up in last quartet: nt clr run jst over 2f out and again 2f out: hdwy u.p but stl plenty to do over 1f out: str run ins fnl f to ld 50yds out* **8/1**
0033 **2** *1/2* **Progressive Jazz (IRE)**[8] 8120 2-8-6 **50**...(v) RhiainIngram(5) 6 52
(K R Burke) *chsd ldrs: chsd ldr over 2f out tl 2f out: 3rd and unable qck over 1f out: kpt on ins fnl f: ev ch fnl 50yds: kpt on* **5/2**[1]
0524 **3** *1/2* **Secratario (FR)**[11] 7996 2-9-3 **56**...(b[1]) ShaneKelly 13 57
(Richard Hughes) *sn led: rdn and hung lft 2f out: hdd 1f out: kpt on same pce u.p ins fnl f* **11/4**[2]
0466 **4** *shd* **Ladycammyofclare (IRE)**[27] 7519 2-8-6 **45**... JFEgan 9 46
(Mark Johnston) *chsd ldrs tl effrt to chse ldr 2f out: styd on u.p to ld 1f out: wknd and hdd 50yds out: lost 2 pls towards fin* **7/1**[3]

5665 **5** ¾ **Kalakchee**[11] 7996 2-8-12 **51** (p) OisinMurphy 10 51
(Amy Murphy) *stdd bk to rr after s: hld up in last pair: hdwy and nt clr run over 2f out: clsd u.p over 1f out: kpt on ins fnl f* **8/1**

600 **6** 1 ¾ **Sapper**[21] 7707 2-9-7 **60** LiamKeniry 12 55
(Ed Walker) *hld up in last pair: effrt on inner over 2f out: swtchd rt and hdwy 2f out: chsng ldrs but bhd a wall of horses whn swtchd lft wl ins fnl f: nvr trbld ldrs* **16/1**

005 **7** 1 **Roof Garden**[18] 7786 2-9-6 **59** JoeyHaynes 2 51
(Mark H Tompkins) *dwlt and bustled along early: towards rr: rdn and hdwy over 1f out: kpt on ins fnl f: nvr enough pce to chal* **7/1**[3]

0000 **8** 5 **Elusive Bird**[11] 7996 2-8-12 **51** WilliamCarson 3 31
(Giles Bravery) *taken down early: in tch in midfield: rdn over 3f out: no imp u.p over 1f out: wknd fnl f* **50/1**

0406 **9** 1 ½ **Roses In June (IRE)**[11] 7996 2-7-13 **45** MillyNaseb(7) 11 22
(J S Moore) *midfield: wd and rdn bnd 3f out: no threat to ldrs fnl 2f* **25/1**

050 **10** 6 **Changing (IRE)**[57] 6517 2-8-11 **50** GeorgeDowning 8 12
(Daniel Kubler) *dwlt: in tch in midfield: lost pl u.p and dropped to rr over 2f out: wknd over 1f out* **33/1**

6200 **11** 3 **Cranworth Phoenix**[40] 7081 2-8-7 **46** RobHornby 14
(Brian Barr) *led early: sn hdd and chsd ldr tl over 2f out: sn dropped out: wknd over 1f out* **50/1**

060 **P** **Sunset Flyer**[111] 4504 2-8-1 **45** ManuelFernandes(5) 5
(Amy Murphy) *midfield tl lost action and plld 5f out (dismntd)* **50/1**

1m 41.21s (1.41) **Going Correction** -0.05s/f (Stan) 12 Ran SP% **121.0**
Speed ratings (Par 93): **90,89,89,88,88 86,85,80,78,72 69,**
CSF £27.99 CT £71.79 TOTE £8.50: £3.20, £1.40, £1.30; EX 39.50 Trifecta £153.80.
**Owner** The Quiet Men Partnership **Bred** Top Trail Syndicate **Trained** Upper Lambourn, Berks
■ Stewards' Enquiry : J F Egan four-day ban: excessive use of whip (Nov 7-10)

**FOCUS**
A moderate nursery.

## 8307 32RED CASINO H'CAP 1m (P)
**6:15** (6:17) (Class 6) (0-55,58) 3-Y-O+ **£2,587** (£770; £384; £192) **Stalls** Low

Form RPR

462 **1** **Kafeel (USA)**[7] 8134 6-9-2 **53** (b) HectorCrouch(3) 3 62
(Gary Moore) *trckd ldrs tl led 2f out: rdn and kicked clr wl over 1f out: a holding on ins fnl f: rdn out* **15/8**[1]

5603 **2** ½ **Dor's Law**[8] 8125 4-9-1 **49** (p) RobHornby 1 57
(Dean Ivory) *hld up in tch in midfield: effrt to go between rivals and edgd lft over 1f out: chsd clr wnr jst over 1f out: styd on wl: nvr quite getting to wnr* **16/1**

2000 **3** 3 ¾ **Ixelles Diamond (IRE)**[36] 7213 6-9-5 **53** OisinMurphy 10 52
(Lee Carter) *awkward leaving stalls and s.i.s: bhd: swtchd rt and hdwy on inner over 1f out: wnt 3rd ins fnl f: no threat to ldng pair* **50/1**

0066 **4** 1 ¾ **Caribbean Spring (IRE)**[10] 8031 4-9-1 **54** JaneElliott(5) 13 49
(George Margarson) *broke wl: stdd bk into midfield on outer: effrt 2f out: kpt on same pce to go 4th wl ins fnl f: no threat to ldrs* **16/1**

5001 **5** ¾ **Freddy With A Y (IRE)**[7] 8133 7-9-10 **58** 6ex (b) KierenFox 7 51
(J R Jenkins) *t.k.h: trckd ldrs and travelled strly: effrt 2f out: rdn whn edgd rt and bmpd wl over 1f out: no imp and wl hld after* **7/1**[3]

0300 **6** ½ **Sonnet Rose (IRE)**[8] 8123 3-9-4 **55** (t) MartinDwyer 6 46
(Conrad Allen) *sn led: rdn and hdd 2f out: unable qck and outpcd over 1f out: wknd and lost 3 pls ins fnl f* **50/1**

**7** hd **Reason To Believe (FR)**[91] 3-9-0 **54** GeorgeWood(3) 12 44
(David Bridgwater) *t.k.h: hld up towards rr: effrt on outer over 2f out: kpt on same pce and no imp fr over 1f out* **66/1**

050 **8** ¾ **Living Leader**[60] 6393 8-8-13 **52** BenRobinson(5) 11 42
(Grace Harris) *midfield: drvn briefly 4f out: no hdwy u.p over 1f out: wl hld and plugged on same pce fnl f* **33/1**

5332 **9** 1 **Binky Blue (IRE)**[7] 8133 5-9-4 **52** ShaneKelly 4 39
(Daniel Mark Loughnane) *short of room leaving stalls: hld up in midfield: nt clr run over 2f out tl over 1f out: sme late hdwy but nvr any ch* **7/1**[3]

4055 **10** 1 ¾ **Swiftee (IRE)**[15] 7888 4-8-13 **47** (v) DavidProbert 2 30
(Ivan Furtado) *bustled along in last trio early: hdwy on inner over 2f out: no imp over 1f out: wknd ins fnl f* **12/1**

4006 **11** ½ **Welsh Inlet (IRE)**[14] 7916 9-9-0 **48** WilliamCarson 5 30
(John Bridger) *hld up in midfield: n.m.r over 2f out: no hdwy over 1f out: wl btn fnl f* **40/1**

0002 **12** 2 ½ **Tarseekh**[6] 8152 4-9-3 **51** (v) AdamKirby 8 31
(Chris Gordon) *hld up in tch in midfield: rdn over 2f out: unable qck and swtchd lft wl over 1f out: n.d after: bhd ins fnl f* **11/2**[2]

1502 **13** 8 **Doctor Bong**[10] 8031 5-9-7 **55** (b) LukeMorris 14 12
(Grace Harris) *led briefly: chsd ldr tl jst over 2f out: struggling to qckn whn edgd rt and bmpd wl over 1f out: sn dropped out: bhd and eased ins fnl f* **16/1**

00 **14** 32 **Freight Train (IRE)**[202] 1553 5-9-6 **54** (p) TomMarquand 9
(Adrian Wintle) *chsd ldrs tl lost pl u.p 3f out: bhd 2f out: eased: t.o: burst blood vessel* **10/1**

1m 39.67s (-0.13) **Going Correction** -0.05s/f (Stan)
**WFA** 3 from 4yo+ 3lb 14 Ran SP% **120.4**
Speed ratings (Par 101): **98,97,93,92,91 90,90,89,88,87 86,84,76,44**
CSF £35.48 CT £1199.30 TOTE £2.30: £1.30, £4.10, £8.00; EX 34.00 Trifecta £3294.30.
**Owner** K Johnson & K Jessup **Bred** Shadwell Farm LLC **Trained** Lower Beeding, W Sussex

**FOCUS**
The first two finished clear of the rest in this ordinary handicap. The second has been rated as running as well as she has this year.

## 8308 32RED.COM NOVICE STKS (DIV I) 6f (P)
**6:45** (6:47) (Class 5) 2-Y-O **£3,234** (£962; £481; £240) **Stalls** Low

Form RPR

502 **1** **Perfect Hustler (USA)**[15] 7877 2-9-2 **77** JFEgan 3 80+
(Jeremy Noseda) *hld up in tch in midfield: swtchd lft and effrt 2f out: hdwy to chal and wnt clr w ldr 1f out: led ins fnl f: r.o wl: rdn out* **4/1**[3]

25 **2** ¾ **Procedure**[20] 7725 2-8-11 **0** RyanMoore 2 73
(Sir Michael Stoute) *t.k.h: chsd ldng trio: effrt ent fnl 2f: hdwy u.p to ld over 1f out: strly pressed and wnt clr w wnr 1f out: hdd and one pce ins fnl f* **6/4**[1]

00 **3** 6 **Global Spirit**[25] 7580 2-8-9 **0** HarryBurns(7) 1 58
(Ed Dunlop) *chsd ldrs: effrt ent fnl 2f: unable qck and outpcd over 1f out: wnt wl hld 3rd ins fnl f: no imp and hung lft nr fin* **50/1**

1003 **4** 1 ¼ **Misty Spirit**[17] 7814 2-8-12 **78** DavidEgan(3) 5 53
(David Elsworth) *led: rdn 2f out: hdd over 1f out: no ex and btn 3rd 1f out: wknd ins fnl f* **2/1**[2]

**5** ¾ **Eraad (IRE)** 2-8-13 **0** CallumShepherd(3) 7 52
(Charles Hills) *s.i.s: hld up off the pce in last pair: swtchd lft and pushed along 2f out: wl hld 5th and kpt on same pce fr over 1f out* **8/1**

02 **6** 3 ½ **Frostbite**[136] 3570 2-9-2 **0** CharlesBishop 8 41
(Eve Johnson Houghton) *t.k.h: chsd ldr: rdn ent fnl 2f: sn lost 2nd and dropped out qckly over 1f out: wknd fnl f* **16/1**

000 **7** 4 **Philamundo (IRE)**[27] 7512 2-9-2 **0** AdamKirby 4 28
(Richard Spencer) *s.i.s: t.k.h: hld up in rr: n.d* **50/1**

**8** ½ **Felstead Knight (IRE)** 2-9-2 **0** OisinMurphy 6 26
(Joseph Tuite) *hld up off the pce in last quartet: pushed along over 2f out: n.d* **66/1**

**9** 21 **Ocean Spray** 2-8-11 **0** KieranO'Neill 9
(Richard Hannon) *wnt lft s and pushed along: a off the pce in last quartet: bhd and lost tch over 2f out: t.o* **40/1**

1m 12.1s (-1.00) **Going Correction** -0.05s/f (Stan) 9 Ran SP% **118.2**
Speed ratings (Par 95): **104,103,95,93,92 87,82,81,53**
CSF £10.61 TOTE £5.60: £1.50, £1.10, £8.40; EX 13.30 Trifecta £296.70.
**Owner** N M Watts **Bred** Highclere Inc **Trained** Newmarket, Suffolk

**FOCUS**
A fair novice. The runner-up has been rated just below form.

## 8309 32RED.COM NOVICE STKS (DIV II) 6f (P)
**7:15** (7:15) (Class 5) 2-Y-O **£3,234** (£962; £481; £240) **Stalls** Low

Form RPR

6 **1** **Tashaaboh (IRE)**[24] 7623 2-9-2 **0** DavidProbert 1 74
(Owen Burrows) *led: rdn 2f out: drvn and hdd 1f out: battled bk u.p to ld again last strides* **5/2**[2]

054 **2** nk **Masked Defender (USA)**[19] 7765 2-9-2 **72** RobertHavlin 5 73
(Amanda Perrett) *trckd ldrs: effrt on inner to chal wl over 1f out: rdn to ld 1f out: drvn ins fnl f: hdd and no ex lat strides* **7/2**[3]

402 **3** 2 **Balletomane**[10] 8028 2-9-2 **72** TomMarquand 2 67
(Richard Hannon) *chsd ldr tl wl over 1f out: 3rd and styd on same pce u.p fr over 1f out* **9/4**[1]

6004 **4** 2 ¼ **Avon Green**[5] 8191 2-8-11 **65** OisinMurphy 9 54
(Joseph Tuite) *chsd ldrs: effrt ent fnl 2f: 4th and outpcd over 1f out: kpt on same pce and wl hld after* **16/1**

00 **5** 7 **Fitzrovia**[10] 8028 2-9-2 **0** LiamKeniry 7 37+
(Ed de Giles) *stdd s: t.k.h: hld up in midfield: outpcd 2f out: wl hld 5th and no imp whn rdn over 1f out* **66/1**

0 **6** ¾ **Fleeting Steps (IRE)**[15] 7876 2-9-2 **0** (h[1]) LukeMorris 4 35+
(Sir Mark Prescott Bt) *hld up in midfield: outpcd and shkn up 2f out: wl btn over 1f out* **25/1**

6 **7** shd **Conflagration**[8] 8112 2-9-2 **0** RichardKingscote 8 34+
(Ed Dunlop) *stdd s: hld up in last trio: shkn and edgd rt ent fnl 2f: sn outpcd and no ch over 1f out* **9/2**

60 **8** 1 ¼ **Enforcement (IRE)**[15] 7906 2-9-2 **0** (h[1]) TimmyMurphy 3 30+
(Martin Keighley) *hld up in last trio: outpcd and shkn up 2f out: no ch whn nt clr run and swtchd lft ins fnl f* **66/1**

65 **9** ½ **Global Wonder (IRE)**[73] 5934 2-9-2 **0** AdamKirby 6 29+
(Ed Dunlop) *s.i.s and impeded leaving stalls: a towards rr: n.d* **11/1**

1m 13.88s (0.78) **Going Correction** -0.05s/f (Stan) 9 Ran SP% **120.8**
Speed ratings (Par 95): **92,91,88,85,76 75,75,73,73**
CSF £12.33 TOTE £3.20: £1.60, £1.40, £1.10; EX 16.20 Trifecta £50.20.
**Owner** Hamdan Al Maktoum **Bred** Miss Vivien Cullen **Trained** Lambourn, Berks

**FOCUS**
The slower of the two divisions by 1.78sec and it paid to race handily. It's been rated as straightforward form around the third.

## 8310 32RED H'CAP 6f (P)
**7:45** (7:47) (Class 4) (0-85,85) 3-Y-O+ **£4,690** (£1,395; £697; £348) **Stalls** Low

Form RPR

0045 **1** **Related**[31] 7405 7-9-5 **83** (b) LukeMorris 11 91
(Paul Midgley) *wnt rt s: sn led and mde rest: rdn wl over 1f out: clr 1f out: drvn ins fnl f: a holding on: rdn out* **16/1**

0003 **2** ¾ **Show Stealer**[24] 7604 4-9-6 **84** (p) DavidProbert 4 90+
(Rae Guest) *bustled along leaving stalls: in tch in midfield: effrt 2f out: hdwy over 1f out: chsd clr wnr 150yds out: styd on and clsd but nvr quite getting to wnr* **4/1**[2]

1-05 **3** ½ **Tropical Rock**[101] 4903 3-9-4 **83** RichardKingscote 2 87
(Ralph Beckett) *wl in tch in midfield: effrt 2f out: styd on to go 3rd ins fnl f: kpt on but nvr getting to wnr* **5/1**

1400 **4** ¾ **Parnassian (IRE)**[18] 7782 3-9-6 **85** MartinDwyer 8 87
(Amanda Perrett) *s.i.s and swtchd rt after s: pushed along off the pce in last pair: clsd and swtchd rt 2f out: hdwy u.p over 1f out: kpt on: nt rch ldrs* **8/1**

2351 **5** nk **Dark Side Dream**[21] 7709 5-8-13 **80** (p) LewisEdmunds(3) 1 81
(Chris Dwyer) *chsd ldrs: wnt 2nd 3f out: rdn and unable qck over 1f out: lost 2nd ins fnl f: kpt on same pce* **7/2**[1]

0015 **6** ¾ **Goring (GER)**[24] 7612 5-9-6 **84** (v[1]) CharlesBishop 3 83
(Eve Johnson Houghton) *hld in tch in midfield: effrt 2f out: unable qck over 1f out and kpt on same pce ins fnl f* **9/2**[3]

0502 **7** 2 **Secondo (FR)**[49] 6794 7-9-6 **84** OisinMurphy 6 76
(Joseph Tuite) *t.k.h: hld up in tch in midfield: rdn over 1f out: no imp and kpt on same pce fnl f* **8/1**

2020 **8** 2 ¾ **Patchwork**[37] 7192 3-9-3 **82** (p[1]) TomMarquand 9 65
(Richard Hughes) *chsd wnr tl 3f out: unable qck and lost pl u.p over 1f out: wknd ins fnl f* **16/1**

2264 **9** 1 **Mr Pocket (IRE)**[85] 5473 3-9-2 **81** RaulDaSilva 10 61
(Paul Cole) *impeded and swtchd rt after s: hld up off the pce in last pair: swtchd lft and effrt over 2f out: no hdwy u.p and wl hld over 1f out* **25/1**

620/ **10** 4 ½ **Absolute Champion (USA)**[179] 5-9-1 **82** HectorCrouch(3) 7 48
(George Peckham) *a towards rr: swtchd lft over 2f out: no hdwy and sn wl btn* **50/1**

0430 **11** 14 **Just An Idea (IRE)**[87] 5396 3-9-5 **84** (v) AdamKirby 12 5
(Harry Dunlop) *pushed along early: midfield on outer tl lost pl qckly over 2f out: bhd and eased ins fnl f* **50/1**

1m 11.44s (-1.66) **Going Correction** -0.05s/f (Stan)
**WFA** 3 from 4yo+ 1lb 11 Ran SP% **118.8**
Speed ratings (Par 105): **109,108,107,106,105 104,102,98,97,91 72**
CSF £79.11 CT £382.26 TOTE £17.60: £5.60, £1.50, £2.10; EX 129.40 Trifecta £1130.40.
**Owner** Taylor's Bloodstock Ltd **Bred** Laundry Cottage Stud Farm **Trained** Westow, N Yorks
■ Whirl Me Round was withdrawn. Price at the time of withdrawal 50-1. Rule 4 does not apply.

**FOCUS**
Although the winner made most of the running, this was a well-run handicap. The winner has been rated back to his summer turf form.

## 8311 100% PROFIT BOOST AT 32REDSPORT.COM H'CAP 6f (P)
8:15 (8:16) (Class 5) (0-70,70) 3-Y-O+ £3,234 (£962; £481; £240) Stalls Low

Form RPR
6613 1 **Inlawed**[20] 7723 3-9-1 **65** RichardKingscote 3 74
(Ed Walker) *chsd ldr: effrt over 1f out: hdwy to ld 1f out: r.o wl and a holding chalr ins fnl f: rdn out* **5/2**[1]

2240 2 *nk* **Trotter**[31] 7408 3-9-4 **68** (b[1]) OisinMurphy 2 76
(Stuart Kittow) *hld up in tch in midfield: effrt 2f out: hdwy u.p to chal ins fnl f: r.o wl but a jst hld* **12/1**

2560 3 *2* **Whitecrest**[3] 8243 9-9-5 **68** WilliamCarson 7 70
(John Spearing) *t.k.h: hld up in tch in midfield: hdwy u.p 1f out: chsd ldng pair wl ins fnl f: kpt on but nvr getting on terms* **25/1**

6000 4 *½* **Big Lachie**[15] 7882 3-9-6 **70** LukeMorris 8 70
(Daniel Mark Loughnane) *t.k.h: hld up in tch in last trio: swtchd rt and gd hdwy 2f out: kpt on same pce u.p ins fnl f* **10/1**

3660 5 *nk* **Artscape**[34] 7272 5-9-5 **68** RobHornby 1 67
(Dean Ivory) *t.k.h: trckd ldrs: unable qck over 1f out: kpt on same pce ins fnl f* **9/1**

2000 6 *¾* **Don't Blame Me**[15] 7882 4-9-7 **70** AdamKirby 12 67
(Clive Cox) *led and crossed over fr wd draw: rdn wl over 1f out: hdd 1f out: no ex and wknd ins fnl f* **14/1**

0000 7 *½* **Picture Dealer**[41] 7056 8-9-3 **69** SimonPearce(3) 6 64
(Lydia Pearce) *hld up in tch: effrt on inner over 1f out: no imp and kpt on same pce ins fnl f* **25/1**

4431 8 *nk* **Harlequin Storm (IRE)**[33] 7320 3-9-6 **70** CharlesBishop 5 64
(Dean Ivory) *t.k.h: hld up wl in tch in midfield: effrt 2f out: sn swtchd lft and no imp u.p: wl hld and kpt on same pce fnl f* **7/2**[2]

0100 9 *1 ½* **Red Invader (IRE)**[28] 7486 7-9-2 **68** TimClark(3) 9 58
(John Butler) *stdd and awkward leaving stalls: hld up in rr: pushed along over 1f out: nvr getting on terms* **50/1**

-002 10 *2 ½* **Desert Grey (IRE)**[6] 8159 3-9-3 **67** (bt) DavidProbert 11 49
(Roger Charlton) *t.k.h: hld up in tch in last trio: effrt and swtchd lft over 2f out: sn rdn and no hdwy: wl hld over 1f out* **4/1**[3]

5000 11 *10* **Bridge Builder**[40] 7099 7-9-7 **70** (p) TomMarquand 10 20
(Peter Hedger) *chsd ldrs on outer: lost pl u.p over 1f out: bhd ins fnl f* **50/1**

1m 12.38s (-0.72) **Going Correction** -0.05s/f (Stan)
**WFA** 3 from 4yo+ 1lb 11 Ran SP% **115.9**
Speed ratings (Par 103): **102,101,98,98,97 96,96,95,93,90 77**
CSF £32.60 CT £602.73 TOTE £2.80: £1.50, £2.80, £4.60; EX 32.40 Trifecta £196.50.
**Owner** Laurence Bellman **Bred** Snailwell Stud Co Ltd **Trained** Upper Lambourn, Berks

**FOCUS**
A modest sprint handicap. The winner is progressing and the form makes sense rated around the third and fourth.

## 8312 RACING UK HD H'CAP 1m 3f 219y(P)
8:45 (8:46) (Class 6) (0-65,65) 3-Y-O £2,587 (£770; £384; £192) Stalls Low

Form RPR
6621 1 **Four Kingdoms (IRE)**[8] 8122 3-9-1 **59** 6ex JoeyHaynes 4 65
(K R Burke) *hld up in midfield: effrt and swtchd lft over 2f out: stl plenty to do over 1f out: styd on strly ins fnl f: led on post* **11/4**[1]

034 2 *nse* **Sky Eagle (IRE)**[47] 6852 3-9-3 **61** LiamKeniry 8 67
(Ed Walker) *dwlt and pushed along early: hld up in midfield: clsd and swtchd rt 2f out: gd hdwy on inner to ld 1f out: kpt on wl u.p: hdd on post* **8/1**[3]

0105 3 *hd* **About Glory**[5] 8183 3-8-13 **57** (b) TomMarquand 9 63
(Richard Hannon) *wl in tch in midfield: effrt 2f out: drvn and ev ch ins fnl f: kpt on wl: no ex cl home* **25/1**

2353 4 *3 ½* **Let's Be Happy (IRE)**[21] 7712 3-9-4 **62** (p) ShaneKelly 5 62
(Richard Hughes) *led: rdn ent fnl 2f: drvn and hdd 1f out: no ex and wknd ins fnl f* **6/1**[2]

2356 5 *½* **Percy Thrower (IRE)**[38] 7152 3-8-8 **55** (b[1]) CallumShepherd(3) 2 55
(Charles Hills) *hld up in tch in midfield: effrt u.p over 1f out: no imp and kpt on same pce ins fnl f* **10/1**

3524 6 *½* **Perla Blanca (USA)**[20] 7744 3-9-4 **62** OisinMurphy 14 61
(Marcus Tregoning) *stdd s: hld up towards rr: hdwy u.p over 1f out: no imp and kpt on same pce ins fnl f* **6/1**[2]

0425 7 *1 ¾* **Dixon**[8] 8123 3-8-11 **55** DavidProbert 6 51+
(Mark H Tompkins) *hld up in tch in midfield: unable qck u.p ent fnl 2f: kpt on same pce and no imp fr over 1f out: sddle slipped* **20/1**

43 8 *1 ¼* **Mister Chow**[82] 5565 3-9-7 **65** (v[1]) TimmyMurphy 12 59
(Gary Moore) *stdd s and dropped in bhd: hld up in last pair: sme hdwy on inner over 1f out: nvr trbld ldrs* **20/1**

0245 9 *¾* **Kings City (IRE)**[15] 7879 3-9-3 **61** (p) AdamKirby 11 54
(Luca Cumani) *sn chsng ldr: rdn over 3f out: styd pressing ldrs tl no ex and outpcd ent fnl f: wknd ins fnl f* **10/1**

0530 10 *1 ¼* **Mambo Dancer**[12] 7982 3-9-7 **65** RichardKingscote 3 56
(Mark Johnston) *sn dropped to rr and nvr travelling: n.d* **20/1**

4555 11 *shd* **D'Waterside**[13] 7948 3-9-1 **59** LukeMorris 1 50
(David Loughnane) *chsd ldrs: drvn and chal briefly over 1f out: sn outpcd and lost pl: wknd ins fnl f* **20/1**

5366 12 *¾* **Broad Appeal**[11] 8000 3-9-7 **65** RobHornby 13 54
(Jonathan Portman) *hld up in midfield on outer: rdn 3f out: sn struggling: wknd wl over 1f out* **16/1**

4332 13 *20* **Too Many Shots**[7] 8135 3-8-12 **56** RobertHavlin 10 13
(John Best) *hld up in tch in midfield: hdwy to chse ldrs 8f out tl lost pl over 2f out: bhd and eased ins fnl f* **9/1**

5000 14 *12* **Corredordel Viento (USA)**[20] 7729 3-8-11 **55** (h) JFEgan 7
(Simon Dow) *short of room leaving stalls: hld up towards rr: rdn over 3f out: dropped to rr over 2f out: wl bhd and eased fnl f: t.o* **40/1**

2m 32.42s (-2.08) **Going Correction** -0.05s/f (Stan) 14 Ran SP% **125.7**
Speed ratings (Par 99): **104,103,103,101,101 100,99,98,98,97 97,96,83,75**
CSF £22.85 CT £482.71 TOTE £2.60: £1.10, £3.30, £6.20; EX 30.60 Trifecta £759.20.
**Owner** D Simpson & Mrs E Burke **Bred** Camogue Stud Ltd **Trained** Middleham Moor, N Yorks

**FOCUS**
Sound form for the grade. The form could easily be better than rated.

## 8313 32RED ON THE APP STORE H'CAP 1m 2f 219y(P)
9:15 (9:15) (Class 5) (0-70,70) 3-Y-O+ £3,234 (£962; £481; £240) Stalls Low

Form RPR
3142 1 **Iballisticvin**[21] 7711 4-9-5 **65** AdamKirby 1 75
(Gary Moore) *led for 1f: trckd ldrs after tl effrt to chal 2f out: led over 1f out: in command and r.o wl ins fnl f* **4/1**[2]

0032 2 *1 ¾* **Abel Tasman**[21] 7712 3-9-2 **67** RichardKingscote 5 74
(Ed Walker) *mostly chsd ldr tl rdn to ld 2f out: hdd and unable to match pce of wnr over 1f out: kpt on same pce ins fnl f* **7/4**[1]

0052 3 *1* **Choral Clan (IRE)**[15] 7878 6-9-6 **69** HectorCrouch(3) 6 74
(Brendan Powell) *hld up in midfield: nt clr run and swtchd rt 2f out: hdwy to chse ldrs over 1f out: kpt on ins fnl f but nvr threatening wnr* **14/1**

0440 4 *2 ¼* **Diamond Bear (USA)**[19] 7762 3-9-5 **70** LukeMorris 7 72
(Sir Mark Prescott Bt) *stdd after s: hld up in midfield: swtchd rt and effrt towards inner 2f out: 4th and kpt on same pce u.p ins fnl f* **10/1**

2000 5 *1 ¾* **Makkadangdang**[8] 8114 3-9-3 **68** OisinMurphy 11 67
(Andrew Balding) *stdd after s: t.k.h: hld up in last quartet: effrt whn carried lft ent fnl 2f: swtchd rt and hdwy jst ins fnl f: styd on wl: nvr trbld ldrs* **25/1**

0000 6 *hd* **Belabour**[15] 7880 4-9-10 **70** JFEgan 3 68
(Mark Brisbourne) *hld up towards rr: rdn and hdwy on outer 3f out: no imp over 1f out: wl hld and kpt on same pce ins fnl f* **12/1**

0000 7 *1 ¼* **Threediamondrings**[55] 6588 4-8-13 **62** (t) MitchGodwin(3) 8 58
(Mark Usher) *v.s.a: t.k.h: hld up in last quartet: swtchd lft and hdwy ent fnl 2f: wandering arnd and no imp over 1f out: nvr trbld ldrs* **66/1**

3054 8 *nk* **Bridge Of Sighs**[11] 8000 5-9-9 **69** TomMarquand 2 65
(Lee Carter) *hld up in tch in midfield: clsd to chse ldrs 2f out: unable qck u.p over 1f out: wknd ins fnl f* **9/1**[3]

4400 9 *1 ¾* **Estrella Eria (FR)**[19] 7762 4-9-8 **68** (h) LiamKeniry 12 61
(George Peckham) *stdd after s: t.k.h: hld up in rr: clsd and swtchd rt 2f out: no imp u.p over 1f out: wknd ins fnl f* **25/1**

-504 10 *shd* **Mesophere**[40] 7083 3-9-2 **67** ShaneKelly 4 59
(Harry Fry) *wl in tch in midfield: effrt over 2f out: unable qck and lost pl over 1f out: wknd fnl f* **9/1**[3]

550 11 *6* **Gracious George (IRE)**[132] 3718 7-9-1 **61** KieranO'Neill 14 43
(Jimmy Fox) *swtchd rt after s: hld up in last quartet: short-lived effrt over 2f out: wknd over 1f out* **25/1**

-001 12 *nk* **Unsuspected Girl (IRE)**[15] 7905 4-9-4 **64** (t) DavidProbert 13 46
(Milton Bradley) *hdwy to ld and crossed to inner after 1f: rdn and hdd 2f out: sn outpcd: fdd fnl f* **33/1**

0550 13 *4* **Voski (USA)**[17] 7831 3-8-12 **66** DavidEgan(3) 9 42
(Mark Johnston) *chsd ldrs: pushed along 4f out: drvn over 2f out: sn struggling and lost pl: wknd over 1f out* **33/1**

0540 14 *1 ¼* **Berkeley Vale**[28] 7495 6-8-10 **63** (v) RossaRyan(7) 10 36
(Roger Teal) *midfield: rdn over 3f out: sn struggling: bhd over 1f out* **50/1**

2m 20.47s (-1.43) **Going Correction** -0.05s/f (Stan)
**WFA** 3 from 4yo+ 5lb 14 Ran SP% **120.7**
Speed ratings (Par 103): **103,101,101,99,98 97,97,96,95,95 91,90,87,87**
CSF £10.53 CT £91.69 TOTE £5.00: £1.90, £1.20, £3.60; EX 15.60 Trifecta £85.20.
**Owner** Scuderia Vita Bella **Bred** Houghton-Barrons Partnership **Trained** Lower Beeding, W Sussex

**FOCUS**
Few got into this, the front two in the market dominating after taking over from the leader at the cutaway. The third has been rated to his recent form.
T/Plt: £28.00 to a £1 stake. Pool: £84,522.48 - 2,202.14 winning units T/Qpdt: £8.50 to a £1 stake. Pool: £9,504.85 - 821.50 winning units **Steve Payne**

# 8204 NEWCASTLE (A.W) (L-H)
Tuesday, October 24

**OFFICIAL GOING: Tapeta : standard**
Wind: fresh against Weather: overcast

## 8314 BETWAY APPRENTICE H'CAP 1m 4f 98y (Tp)
1:40 (1:40) (Class 6) (0-60,60) 3-Y-O+ £2,587 (£770; £384; £192) Stalls High

Form RPR
3054 1 **Champagne Rules**[19] 7760 6-9-4 **52** ConnorMurtagh 11 63
(Sharon Watt) *trckd ldrs: smooth hdwy over 3f out: pushed along to ld wl over 1f out: edgd rt but kpt on wl and sn clr: easily* **17/2**

253 2 *7* **Angel In The Snow**[32] 7360 4-8-9 **48** SebastianWoods(5) 9 48
(Brian Ellison) *midfield: rdn and hdwy 2f out: wnt 2nd ins fnl f: kpt on but no ch wnr* **15/8**[1]

3546 3 *2* **Highway Robber**[12] 7979 4-9-2 **50** PaulaMuir 7 47
(Wilf Storey) *prom: led 8f out: rdn whn hdd wl over 1f out: no ex: lost 2nd ins fnl f* **12/1**

0005 4 *½* **Naupaka**[96] 5076 3-8-6 **46** oh1 JamieGormley 1 43+
(Brian Ellison) *hld up: rdn along 3f out: styd on fnl f: nrst fin* **25/1**

5060 5 *1* **Wee Bogus**[23] 7659 4-8-7 **48** (p) RhonaPindar(7) 13 42
(Alistair Whillans) *prom: rdn 3f out: grad wknd fnl f* **66/1**

0260 6 *nk* **Lozah**[35] 7240 4-9-4 **55** BenSanderson(3) 8 49
(Roger Fell) *hld up: rdn and hdwy on outer over 2f out: one pce fnl f* **12/1**

0543 7 *½* **Palindrome (USA)**[28] 7479 4-8-9 **46** HarrisonShaw(3) 2 39
(Marjorie Fife) *in tch: rdn over 2f out: no imp* **4/1**[2]

0046 8 *¾* **Red Star Dancer (IRE)**[3] 8241 3-8-6 **49** (b[1]) GabrieleMalune(3) 5 42
(David Barron) *hld up in rr: rdn over 2f out: kpt on ins fnl f* **8/1**[3]

0-50 9 *½* **Ghostly Arc (IRE)**[23] 7659 5-9-9 **57** NatalieHambling 4 48
(Noel Wilson) *led: hdd 8f out: remained prom: rdn over 2f out: wknd ins fnl f* **14/1**

21/0 10 *1 ¼* **Titus Bolt (IRE)**[15] 7885 8-9-6 **57** SeanMooney(3) 12 46
(Jim Goldie) *in tch: rdn 3f out: wknd fnl f* **40/1**

0-30 11 *¾* **Toola Boola**[36] 7220 7-9-0 **53** (v) PatrickO'Hanlon(5) 10 41
(Jedd O'Keeffe) *midfield: rdn over 2f out: wknd fnl f* **33/1**

4400 12 *3* **Dyna Might**[15] 7885 3-9-0 **57** (p) SeamusCronin(3) 6 41
(Ollie Pears) *hld up in midfield: rdn over 2f out: sn wknd* **12/1**

10-0 13 *11* **Pertuis (IRE)**[177] 2183 11-9-9 **60** RossTurner(3) 14 25
(Micky Hammond) *a towards rr* **66/1**

-000 14 *½* **Bilko's Back (IRE)**[207] 1469 5-8-7 **46** oh1 (t) RussellHarris(5) 3 11
(Susan Corbett) *a towards rr* **150/1**

2m 42.14s (1.04) **Going Correction** +0.075s/f (Slow)
**WFA** 3 from 4yo+ 6lb 14 Ran SP% **119.0**
Speed ratings (Par 101): **99,94,93,92,92 91,91,90,90,89 89,87,79,79**
CSF £23.60 CT £200.34 TOTE £9.40: £2.50, £1.10, £3.30; EX 29.30 Trifecta £356.70.
**Owner** Rosey Hill Partnership **Bred** Heather Raw **Trained** Brompton-on-Swale, N Yorks

**FOCUS**
This moderate handicap was confined to apprentices who had ridden not more than 25 winners.

## 8315 BETWAY SUPER CLAIMING STKS — 1m 2f 42y (Tp)
2:10 (2:11) (Class 3) 3-Y-O+ — £12,938 (£3,850; £1,924; £962) Stalls High

Form — RPR

05R0 **1** **La Casa Tarifa (IRE)**[26] 7555 3-8-0 78 ... JoeFanning 4 — 78
(Mark Johnston) *trckd ldrs: rdn to chal wl over 1f out: led ins fnl f: kpt on* — **50/1**

41-0 **2** ½ **Burcan (FR)**[24] 7602 5-8-9 94 ... PaulHanagan 8 — 81
(Marco Botti) *in tch: pushed along and hdwy over 2f out: led narrowly wl over 1f out: rdn whn hdd ins fnl f: kpt on but hld* — **1/1**[1]

1451 **3** 4 **Fayez (IRE)**[25] 7569 3-9-10 86 ... DanielTudhope 12 — 93
(David O'Meara) *s.i.s: hld up: pushed along and hdwy on inner over 2f out: briefly n.m.r 2f out: wnt 3rd appr fnl f: kpt on but no ch ldng pair* **4/1**[2]

2433 **4** 2¼ **Gerry The Glover (IRE)**[25] 7570 5-8-9 77 ... (p) JasonHart 2 — 68
(Brian Ellison) *midfield: hdwy and sltly hmpd 2f out: rdn and kpt on* **7/1**[3]

-000 **5** hd **Tha'ir (IRE)**[11] 8009 7-9-4 89 ... (h[1]) RobertWinston 1 — 77
(Michael Appleby) *in tch: rdn over 2f out: bit outpcd over 1f: plugged on fnl f* — **33/1**

3621 **6** 1 **Restive (IRE)**[4] 8218 4-8-9 64 ... JamieGormley 5 — 66
(Iain Jardine) *midfield: rdn over 2f out: kpt on* — **20/1**

3001 **7** 1½ **Zabeel Star (IRE)**[188] 1891 5-8-9 74 ... PJMcDonald 14 — 63
(Karen McLintock) *slowly away: hld up in rr: rdn over 2f out: kpt on fnl f: nvr threatened* — **22/1**

5000 **8** nk **Lat Hawill (IRE)**[8] 8104 6-9-9 87 ... (v) PaulMulrennan 7 — 76
(Keith Dalgleish) *hld up in midfield: rdn over 2f out: nvr threatened* **40/1**

0006 **9** nk **Luv U Whatever**[20] 7728 7-8-10 73 ... (tp) BarryMcHugh 3 — 63
(Marjorie Fife) *trckd ldrs: rdn over 2f out: grad wknd over 1f out* **80/1**

2314 **10** 1¼ **Every Chance (IRE)**[178] 2165 4-9-0 92 ... DougieCostello 9 — 64
(Jamie Osborne) *midfield on outside: rdn over 2f out: wknd fnl f* **10/1**

4060 **11** ½ **Toboggan's Fire**[14] 7924 4-8-4 80 ... JamesSullivan 6 — 53
(Ann Duffield) *led: rdn whn hdd wl over 1f out: wknd* **100/1**

000- **12** 2¼ **Balty Boys (IRE)**[444] 5146 8-8-13 92 ... TomEaves 11 — 58
(Brian Ellison) *hld up: nvr threatened* **33/1**

552- **13** ¾ **Dance Of Fire**[16] 3855 5-8-13 85 ... GrahamLee 10 — 56
(N W Alexander) *hld up in midfield: rdn over 2f out: wknd over 1f out* **40/1**

0001 **14** 3¼ **Muqarred (USA)**[2] 8254 5-8-9 71 ... (p) TonyHamilton 13 — 46
(Roger Fell) *tracjked ldrs: rdn over 2f out: wknd over 1f out* **33/1**

2m 8.46s (-1.94) **Going Correction** +0.075s/f (Slow)
**WFA** 3 from 4yo+ 4lb — **14** Ran SP% **118.6**
Speed ratings (Par 107): **110,109,106,104,104 103,102,102,101,100 100,98,98,95**
CSF £94.57 TOTE £22.60: £7.10, £1.10, £2.10; EX 128.30 Trifecta £520.50.
**Owner** Kingsley Park 5 **Bred** Tony Kilduff **Trained** Middleham Moor, N Yorks

**FOCUS**
A valuable and competitive race of its type. The first two came clear. The likes of the sixth help set the standard.

## 8316 32RED.COM EBF NOVICE STKS (PLUS 10 RACE) — 7f 14y (Tp)
2:40 (2:41) (Class 4) 2-Y-O — £6,469 (£1,925; £962; £481) Stalls Centre

Form — RPR

32 **1** **Moqarrar (USA)**[13] 7946 2-9-2 0 ... DanielTudhope 7 — 84
(Sir Michael Stoute) *trckd ldrs: pushed along to chal 2f out: led over 1f out: rdn and kpt on fnl f* — **7/4**[2]

2 **2** 1¾ **Big Kitten (USA)**[28] 7473 2-9-2 0 ... JoeFanning 6 — 79
(Mark Johnston) *prom: pushed along to ld over 2f out: rdn whn hdd over 1f out: kpt on but a hld* — **13/8**[1]

2322 **3** 3 **Qianlong**[11] 8013 2-9-2 81 ... JackMitchell 3 — 71
(Roger Varian) *trckd ldrs: rdn over 2f out: one pce in 3rd fr appr fnl f* **3/1**[3]

**4** 1 **Windsor Cross (IRE)** 2-9-2 0 ... TonyHamilton 2 — 68+
(Richard Fahey) *midfield: outpcd and rn green 2f out: kpt on ins fnl f: improve for run* — **33/1**

**5** 1 **Gowanbuster** 2-9-2 0 ... (t[1]) PaulMulrennan 11 — 66+
(Susan Corbett) *hld up: pushed along and hdwy 2f out: wknd fnl f 110yds* — **100/1**

43 **6** 2 **Spark Of War (IRE)**[12] 7978 2-9-2 0 ... GrahamLee 4 — 60
(Keith Dalgleish) *led: rdn whn hdd over 2f out: wknd fnl f* **33/1**

330 **7** nse **Skito Soldier**[24] 7613 2-8-13 72 ... CliffordLee[(3)] 5 — 60
(K R Burke) *trckd ldrs: rdn along 3f out: grad wknd over 1f out* **33/1**

**8** ¾ **Howbaar (USA)** 2-9-2 0 ... KevinStott 12 — 58
(James Bethell) *dwlt: hld up: nvr threatened* **33/1**

0 **9** 1¼ **Altered Method (IRE)**[31] 7383 2-9-2 0 ... PJMcDonald 1 — 55
(Hugo Palmer) *midfield: rdn over 2f out: wknd fnl f* **33/1**

0 **10** 5 **Wowsham (IRE)**[23] 7654 2-8-13 0 ... RowanScott[(3)] 8 — 41
(Keith Dalgleish) *sn outpcd in rr* **100/1**

**11** 12 **Leahcar** 2-8-11 0 ... TomEaves 9 — 4
(James Ewart) *hld up in midfield: rdn over 2f out: wknd and bhd* **100/1**

1m 28.07s (1.87) **Going Correction** +0.225s/f (Slow) **11** Ran SP% **117.1**
Speed ratings (Par 97): **98,96,92,91,90 88,87,87,85,79 66**
CSF £4.66 TOTE £2.30: £1.10, £1.10, £1.50; EX 5.70 Trifecta £10.90.
**Owner** Hamdan Al Maktoum **Bred** Exchange Rate Syndicate Et Al **Trained** Newmarket, Suffolk

**FOCUS**
There was a fresh headwind at this stage. Fair novice form. The runner-up has been rated to his debut form.

## 8317 32RED CASINO CONDITIONS STKS (PLUS 10 RACE) (ALL-WEATHER FAST-TRACK QUALIFIER) — 6f (Tp)
3:10 (3:11) (Class 2) 2-Y-O — £16,172 (£4,812; £2,405; £1,202) Stalls Centre

Form — RPR

1031 **1** **Beatbox Rhythm (IRE)**[11] 8008 2-9-9 98 ... PJMcDonald 7 — 100
(K R Burke) *mde all: rdn 2f out: hung lft fr appr fnl f but kpt on wl* **9/2**

**2** 2¼ **River Boyne (IRE)**[11] 8015 2-9-2 0 ... RobertWinston 8 — 86
(Gordon Elliott, Ire) *dwlt: hld up: pushed along and sme hdwy over 2f out: rdn and kpt on fr over 1f out: wnt 2nd towards fin* — **20/1**

0622 **3** 1 **It Dont Come Easy (IRE)**[10] 8043 2-9-6 101 ... PaulHanagan 6 — 87
(Richard Fahey) *trckd ldr: pushed along 2f out: rdn appr fnl f: no ex fnl 75yds and lost 2nd towards fin* — **11/4**[1]

2421 **4** 1¼ **Three Saints Bay (IRE)**[17] 7819 2-9-6 77 ... DanielTudhope 4 — 84
(David O'Meara) *hld up in tch: rdn over 2f out: kpt on same pce fnl f* **20/1**

41 **5** 1 **Sarookh (USA)**[27] 7513 2-9-6 0 ... JackMitchell 9 — 81
(Roger Varian) *in tch: rdn along over 2f out: no ex ins fnl f* — **7/2**[3]

1333 **6** 6 **Lake Volta (IRE)**[18] 7797 2-9-9 100 ... JoeFanning 2 — 66
(Mark Johnston) *trckd ldr: rdn over 2f out: wknd over 1f out* **10/3**[2]

2100 **7** 1 **Shaya (IRE)**[17] 7846 2-9-1 85 ... TonyHamilton 5 — 55
(Roger Fell) *hld up in tch: rdn over 2f out: sn btn* — **50/1**

1430 **8** 8 **Yogi's Girl (IRE)**[39] 7114 2-9-4 88 ... TomEaves 3 — 34
(David Evans) *hld up: rdn 3f out: wknd and bhd* **50/1**

3001 **9** 12 **Encrypted**[33] 7318 2-9-9 89 ... JosephineGordon 1
(Hugo Palmer) *trckd ldr: racd keenly: rdn over 2f out: sn wknd and bhd* — **10/1**

1m 13.35s (0.85) **Going Correction** +0.225s/f (Slow) **9** Ran SP% **112.7**
Speed ratings (Par 101): **103,100,98,97,95 87,86,75,59**
CSF £87.45 TOTE £5.70: £1.70, £4.30, £1.50; EX 80.80 Trifecta £396.30.
**Owner** John Dance **Bred** Martyn J McEnery **Trained** Middleham Moor, N Yorks

**FOCUS**
The first Fast-Track qualifier of the new All-Weather Championships, and a suitably classy line-up.

## 8318 SUNBETS.CO.UK CLASSIFIED STKS — 1m 5y (Tp)
3:40 (3:40) (Class 5) 3-Y-O+ — £4,722 (£1,405; £702; £351) Stalls Centre

Form — RPR

2442 **1** **Subhaan**[46] 6899 3-9-2 75 ... JackMitchell 8 — 84
(Roger Varian) *s.i.s: hld up: smooth hdwy over 2f out: pushed along to ld 2f out: strly pressed appr fnl f: drvn and kpt on to a maintain narrow advantage* — **4/5**[1]

2040 **2** nk **Breanski**[17] 7824 3-9-2 72 ... (v) DanielTudhope 6 — 83
(David O'Meara) *in tch: pushed along and hdwy over 2f out: rdn to chal strly appr fnl f: kpt on but a jst hld* — **4/1**[2]

0230 **3** 3¼ **Bahamian Bird**[55] 6570 4-9-5 75 ... PaulHanagan 4 — 77
(Richard Fahey) *hld up: rdn over 2f out: hdwy to go 3rd over 1f out: kpt on but a hld* — **12/1**

-050 **4** 8 **Jacquard (IRE)**[25] 7570 3-9-2 75 ... PJMcDonald 5 — 58
(Mark Johnston) *led: rdn whn hdd 2f out: wknd over 1f out* **25/1**

1-05 **5** ½ **Lucky Violet (IRE)**[8] 8108 5-9-5 73 ... (h) DavidAllan 7 — 57
(Iain Jardine) *trckd ldr: rdn over 2f out: sn wknd* **14/1**

5016 **6** ½ **Born To Boom (IRE)**[38] 7162 3-8-13 73 ... CliffordLee[(3)] 1 — 55
(K R Burke) *in tch: racd centre and wd of main gp stands' side: rdn over 2f out: wknd over 1f out* — **14/1**

0646 **7** 24 **Palawan**[49] 6801 4-9-5 75 ... DougieCostello 3
(Jamie Osborne) *trckd ldrs: rdn 3f out: hung lft and sn wknd: eased and t.o* — **20/1**

0314 **8** 2½ **Ventura Secret (IRE)**[17] 7823 3-8-13 72 ... RachelRichardson[(3)] 2
(Tim Easterby) *prom: racd cente and wd of main gp stands' side: rdn along 3f out: sn wknd: t.o* — **9/1**[3]

1m 39.99s (1.39) **Going Correction** +0.225s/f (Slow)
**WFA** 3 from 4yo+ 3lb — **8** Ran SP% **115.2**
Speed ratings (Par 103): **102,101,98,90,89 89,65,62**
CSF £4.17 TOTE £2.10: £1.20, £1.30, £1.90; EX 4.90 Trifecta £26.80.
**Owner** Hamdan Al Maktoum **Bred** R J Cornelius **Trained** Newmarket, Suffolk
■ Stewards' Enquiry : Daniel Tudhope caution: careless riding

**FOCUS**
They went 9/1 bar two in this modest classified stakes. Two of the runners raced alone more towards the far side than the other group of six, which produced the first five home. The first three were all held up. The first two have been rated to the better view of their maiden form.

## 8319 BETWAY SPRINT H'CAP — 6f (Tp)
4:10 (4:12) (Class 4) (0-80,86) 3-Y-O+ — £8,086 (£2,406; £1,202; £601) Stalls Centre

Form — RPR

364 **1** **Boy In The Bar**[52] 6686 6-9-4 **79** ... (b) JosephineGordon 2 — 88
(Ian Williams) *chsd ldr: rdn over 2f out: chal appr fnl f: drvn into narrow ld 110yds out: all out* — **4/1**[2]

1240 **2** nse **Kenny The Captain (IRE)**[11] 8014 6-9-1 **79** ... RachelRichardson[(3)] 6 — 88
(Tim Easterby) *led: rdn over 2f out: strly pressed appr fnl f: hdd narrowly 110yds: kpt on: jst failed* — **8/1**

4210 **3** 1¼ **Tricky Dicky**[20] 7737 4-9-5 **80** ... SamJames 5 — 85
(Olly Williams) *chsd ldrs: rdn over 2f out: kpt on same pce* **16/1**

5031 **4** ¾ **Florencio**[2] 8257 4-9-11 **86** 6ex ... (p) TonyHamilton 3 — 89
(Roger Fell) *midfield: rdn 2f out: chsd ldrs appr fnl f: drvn and one pce* — **14/1**

0401 **5** shd **Inexes**[26] 7554 5-9-4 **79** ... (p) BarryMcHugh 4 — 81+
(Marjorie Fife) *dwlt: sn hld up in midfield racing keenly: short of room appr fnl f: rdn and kpt on* — **20/1**

3652 **6** ½ **Johnny Cavagin**[26] 7553 8-9-5 **80** ... (t) GrahamLee 11 — 81
(Ronald Thompson) *in tch: rdn appr fnl f: one pce* — **28/1**

1252 **7** nk **Summerghand (IRE)**[21] 7709 3-9-2 **78** ... DanielTudhope 13 — 78
(David O'Meara) *dwlt: sn midfield: rdn over 2f out: one pce* — **3/1**[1]

3200 **8** 1½ **Tommy G**[61] 6348 4-8-13 **77** ... PhilDennis[(3)] 10 — 72+
(Jim Goldie) *dwlt: hld up: stl plenty to do whn short of room appr fnl f: kpt on ins fnl f* — **28/1**

6326 **9** shd **Sfumato**[31] 7398 3-9-2 **78** ... TomEaves 12 — 73
(Iain Jardine) *hld up: rdn 2f out: nvr threatened* **17/2**

1000 **10** nk **Art Obsession (IRE)**[44] 6971 6-9-5 **80** ... DougieCostello 9 — 74
(Paul Midgley) *hld up: rdn 2f out: nvr threatened* **33/1**

4242 **11** 1¼ **Nezar (IRE)**[27] 7508 6-9-5 **80** ... RobertWinston 7 — 70
(Dean Ivory) *hld up: rdn 2f out: hdwy and bit clsr appr fnl f: wknd fnl 110yds* — **7/1**[3]

5563 **12** 3¼ **Bahamian Dollar**[8] 8115 4-8-12 **80** ... KatherineGlenister[(7)] 14 — 59
(David Evans) *chsd ldrs: rdn over 2f out: wknd fnl f* **9/1**

0000 **13** 3 **Start Time (IRE)**[26] 7554 4-9-2 **77** ... (v) PaulMulrennan 8 — 47
(Paul Midgley) *prom: rdn over 2f out: wknd over 1f out* **33/1**

0400 **14** 1¾ **Sumner Beach**[14] 7939 3-9-2 **78** ... JasonHart 1 — 42
(Brian Ellison) *midfield: rdn along 3f out: sn dropped to rr and btn* **50/1**

1m 13.2s (0.70) **Going Correction** +0.225s/f (Slow)
**WFA** 3 from 4yo+ 1lb — **14** Ran SP% **121.2**
Speed ratings (Par 105): **104,103,102,101,101 100,100,98,97,97 95,91,87,85**
CSF £33.35 CT £473.82 TOTE £4.80: £1.70, £3.10, £3.90; EX 44.70 Trifecta £430.40.
**Owner** Sovereign Racing **Bred** Brinkley Stud S R L **Trained** Portway, Worcs

**FOCUS**
A competitive race of its type. They raced centre-to-far-side before the principals drifted across the track towards the stands' rail in the latter stages. Prominent racers dominated, as did low numbers. The winner has been rated 10lb off this year's turf form.

## 8320 BETWAY DASH H'CAP (DIV I) — 5f (Tp)
4:40 (4:41) (Class 5) (0-75,77) 3-Y-O+ — £5,175 (£1,540; £769; £384) Stalls Centre

Form — RPR

2506 **1** **Fruit Salad**[14] 7939 4-9-7 **74** ... (p) JosephineGordon 2 — 80+
(James Bethell) *dwlt: hld up: sn rdn along: swtchd lft to outside and hdwy over 1f out: r.o fnl f: edgd rt fnl 50yds but led nr fin* — **7/1**[2]

0500 **2** nk **Impart**[26] 7557 3-9-7 **74** ... DanielTudhope 7 — 80
(David O'Meara) *prom: pushed along to ld appr fnl f: sn rdn: drvn and one pce fnl 110yds: hdd nr fin* — **7/2**[1]

0402 **3** *hd* **Liquid (IRE)**[14] 7939 3-9-6 **73** ........ BenCurtis 9 78
(David Barron) *midfield: hdwy to trck ldrs gng wl over 1f out: rdn and kpt on fnl f* **7/2**[1]

5632 **4** *1 ¼* **Duke Cosimo**[14] 7940 7-9-3 **70** ........ (p) TomEaves 1 70
(Michael Herrington) *hld up: rdn over 2f out: kpt on fnl f: nrst fin* **7/2**[1]

3460 **5** *½* **Fredricka**[41] 7055 6-9-10 **77** ........ (p) RenatoSouza 8 75
(Ivan Furtado) *midfield: pushed along and bit outpcd whn short of room appr fnl f: rdn and kpt on ins fnl f* **25/1**

2004 **6** *hd* **Savannah Beau**[28] 7486 5-8-13 **66** ........ (v) PaulHanagan 5 63
(Derek Shaw) *slowly away: hld up: rdn and sme hdwy over 1f out: one pce fnl f* **20/1**

0-04 **7** *1* **Bondi Beach Boy**[14] 7940 8-9-1 **71** ........ CliffordLee(3) 6 64
(Antony Brittain) *led for 1f: prom: rdn and outpcd 2f out: one pce fnl f* **17/2**[3]

3225 **8** *1 ¼* **The Big Short**[27] 7509 3-9-3 **70** ........ PJMcDonald 10 60
(Charles Hills) *led after 1f: rdn 2f out: hdd appr fnl f: wknd ins fnl f* **14/1**

0036 **9** *1 ¼* **Oriental Splendour (IRE)**[20] 7738 5-9-2 **69** ........ (p) JamesSullivan 4 53
(Ruth Carr) *midfield: rdn over 2f out: sn btn* **20/1**

5011 **10** *3 ¼* **Indian Pursuit (IRE)**[42] 7017 4-9-0 **67** ........ JasonHart 3 40
(John Quinn) *midfield: rdn over 2f out: already wknd whn sltly hmpd ins fnl f* **16/1**

1m 0.44s (0.94) **Going Correction** +0.225s/f (Slow) **10** Ran SP% **115.6**
Speed ratings (Par 103): **101,100,100,98,97 97,95,93,91,86**
CSF £30.51 CT £103.10 TOTE £7.50: £2.40, £1.40, £2.00; EX 30.20 Trifecta £144.60.
**Owner** Clarendon Thoroughbred Racing **Bred** Mrs James Bethell **Trained** Middleham Moor, N Yorks

**FOCUS**
The first leg of a moderate sprint handicap, and the slower by 1.46sec. The third has been rated to his C&D latest.

## 8321 BETWAY DASH H'CAP (DIV II) 5f (Tp)
**5:10** (5:11) (Class 5) (0-75,76) 3-Y-0+ **£5,175** (£1,540; £769; £384) **Stalls** Centre

Form RPR

4005 **1** **Hilary J**[52] 6669 4-9-7 **74** ........ ShaneGray 3 86
(Ann Duffield) *prom: pushed along to ld over 1f out: edgd rt but kpt on wl: shade comf* **12/1**

5504 **2** *1 ¾* **Casterbridge**[20] 7737 5-9-0 **67** ........ (p) JasonHart 10 72
(Eric Alston) *led: racd towards stands' rail: rdn over 2f out: hdd over 1f out: kpt on same pce* **6/1**

0022 **3** *½* **See The Sun**[23] 7657 6-9-3 **70** ........ (b) DavidAllan 5 73
(Tim Easterby) *prom: pushed along 2f out: rdn and ev ch over 1f out: one pce fnl f* **7/2**[1]

3013 **4** *½* **Canford Bay (IRE)**[5] 8194 3-8-7 **60** ........ PJMcDonald 2 62
(Antony Brittain) *in tch: rdn and hung lft to far rail over 1f out: kpt on fnl f* **4/1**[2]

2432 **5** *hd* **Liberatum**[14] 7923 3-8-13 **73** ........ JamieGormley(7) 6 74
(Ruth Carr) *midfield: rdn along 2f out: kpt on same pce* **13/2**

6240 **6** *¾* **Poppy In The Wind**[129] 3847 5-9-2 **72** ........ (v) JoshDoyle(3) 8 70
(Alan Brown) *hld up: rdn along over 2f out: hdwy and in tch over 1f out: no ex fnl 110yds* **20/1**

2000 **7** *1 ½* **Berlios (IRE)**[14] 7923 4-9-3 **70** ........ DanielTudhope 4 62
(Rebecca Bastiman) *dwlt: hld up: pushed along over 2f out: minor late hdwy: nvr threatened* **20/1**

0400 **8** *1* **Lady Cristal (IRE)**[14] 7940 3-8-13 **66** ........ (p) BenCurtis 7 56
(K R Burke) *chsd ldrs: rdn over 2f out: wknd over 1f out* **16/1**

5005 **9** *¾* **Vallarta (IRE)**[14] 7923 7-9-3 **70** ........ JamesSullivan 9 56
(Ruth Carr) *midfield: rdn over 2f out: sn btn* **5/1**[3]

3045 **10** *1 ¼* **Pomme De Terre (IRE)**[26] 7554 5-9-9 **76** ........ (p) PaulMulrennan 1 58
(Michael Dods) *midfield: rdn over 2f out: sn btn* **10/1**

59.08s (-0.42) **Going Correction** +0.225s/f (Slow) **10** Ran SP% **118.7**
Speed ratings (Par 103): **112,109,108,107,107 106,103,102,100,98**
CSF £83.77 CT £315.85 TOTE £16.50: £4.40, £2.40, £1.40; EX 113.00 Trifecta £1074.90.
**Owner** E & R Stott **Bred** Bumble Bloodstock Ltd **Trained** Constable Burton, N Yorks

**FOCUS**
The quicker of the two divisions by 1.46sec. The third has been rated close to his recent form.
T/Jkpt: Not won. T/Plt: £9.40 to a £1 stake. Pool: £63,318.90 - 4,891.72 winning units T/Qpdt: £5.40 to a £1 stake. Pool: £5,804.18 - 785.34 winning units **Andrew Sheret**

# 8118 YARMOUTH (L-H)
## Tuesday, October 24
**OFFICIAL GOING: Good to soft (good in places; 7.0)**

## 8322 BREEDERS BACKING RACING EBF FILLIES' NOVICE STKS (PLUS 10 RACE) (DIV I) 1m 3y
**1:30** (1:31) (Class 4) 2-Y-0 **£4,528** (£1,347; £673; £336) **Stalls** Centre

Form RPR

3 **1** **Dramatic Queen (USA)**[24] 7608 2-9-0 0 ........ JamesDoyle 3 75+
(William Haggas) *mde all: rdn over 1f out: hld on gamely ins fnl f* **11/4**[2]

36 **2** *1 ¼* **Heather Lark (IRE)**[19] 7758 2-9-0 0 ........ NickyMackay 6 72
(John Gosden) *a pressing wnr: rdn 3f out: ev ch 1f out: kpt trying but hld fnl 100yds* **16/1**

**3** *¾* **Qazyna (IRE)** 2-9-0 0 ........ AndreaAtzeni 10 70+
(Roger Varian) *towards rr: effrt over 3f out: fait bit to do do and running green 2f out: pushed along and swtchd rt and then hanging rt whn chsng ldng pair fr 1f out: kpt on wl cl home: will do bttr* **15/8**[1]

4 **4** *2 ½* **Orchid Lily**[63] 6292 2-9-0 0 ........ RobertHavlin 8 65
(John Gosden) *racd keenly: cl up: rdn 2f out: 4th and hld whn crossed by eventual 3rd ins fnl f* **7/2**[3]

**5** *3 ¼* **Anaakeed** 2-9-0 0 ........ JimCrowley 11 57+
(Owen Burrows) *dwlt: rdn 1/2-way: prog over 2f out: no ch w ldng trio fnl f but kpt on steadily despite hanging lft fnl f* **7/1**

0 **6** *¾* **Navajo Squaw**[20] 7733 2-9-0 0 ........ JimmyQuinn 7 55
(Ed Dunlop) *plld hrd early: towards rr: rdn and btn 2f out* **66/1**

0 **7** *shd* **Bob's Girl**[31] 7403 2-9-0 0 ........ (h) StevieDonohoe 1 55
(David Simcock) *stdd s: towards rr: rdn over 2f out: little rspnse and sn btn* **50/1**

0 **8** *1 ¾* **Trouble And Strife (IRE)**[15] 7875 2-9-0 0 ........ RyanPowell 5 51
(Sir Mark Prescott Bt) *chsd ldrs 5f : rdn and sn btn* **100/1**

50 **9** *½* **Girls Talk (IRE)**[20] 7733 2-9-0 0 ........ LouisSteward 2 50
(Michael Bell) *t.k.h: pressed ldrs: rdn 3f out: fdd over 2f out* **33/1**

53 **10** *3* **Giving Glances**[27] 7504 2-9-0 0 ........ MartinHarley 9 43
(Alan King) *prom over 5f: rdn and lost pl tamely over 2f out* **14/1**

1m 41.54s (0.94) **Going Correction** -0.05s/f (Good) **10** Ran SP% **116.1**
Speed ratings (Par 94): **93,91,91,88,85 84,84,82,82,79**
CSF £44.09 TOTE £3.50: £1.10, £3.60, £1.10; EX 40.50 Trifecta £137.20.
**Owner** Sheikh Juma Dalmook Al Maktoum **Bred** Gary Chervenell **Trained** Newmarket, Suffolk

**FOCUS**
It was dry overnight and a mainly dry, overcast day. Some promising-looking types in this fillies' novice, but nothing made up significant ground and the time was 0.97sec slower than the second leg. The action was middle to stands' side.

## 8323 BREEDERS BACKING RACING EBF FILLIES' NOVICE STKS (PLUS 10 RACE) (DIV II) 1m 3y
**2:00** (2:00) (Class 4) 2-Y-0 **£4,528** (£1,347; £673; £336) **Stalls** Centre

Form RPR

**1** **Lady Of Shalott** 2-9-0 0 ........ JamieSpencer 9 79+
(David Simcock) *hld up: hdwy over 2f out: led over 1f out: r.o wl* **12/1**

50 **2** *2 ¾* **Come With Me**[20] 7733 2-9-0 0 ........ (t[1]) RobertHavlin 6 71
(John Gosden) *mid-div: hdwy over 2f out: rdn and ev ch over 1f out: styd on same pce wl ins fnl f* **20/1**

0 **3** *1 ¾* **Glitterdust**[24] 7620 2-9-0 0 ........ TedDurcan 7 67
(Sir Michael Stoute) *chsd ldrs: rdn and ev ch over 1f out: styd on same pce ins fnl f pce* **16/1**

22 **4** *½* **Celestin's**[15] 7906 2-9-0 0 ........ MartinHarley 8 66
(William Haggas) *chsd ldr who wnt clr over 6f out: clsd to ld over 1f out: sn rdn and hdd: no ex ins fnl f* **7/4**[2]

**5** *½* **Hameem** 2-9-0 0 ........ JimCrowley 5 65
(John Gosden) *s.i.s: sn pushed along in rr: hdwy over 1f out: nt rch ldrs* **6/4**[1]

**6** *1* **Hourglass (IRE)** 2-9-0 0 ........ AndreaAtzeni 10 62+
(Marco Botti) *s.i.s: rn green in rr: r.o ins fnl f: nvr nrr* **7/1**[3]

**7** *¾* **Goldspun** 2-9-0 0 ........ FranBerry 1 61
(Ed Dunlop) *chsd ldrs: rdn over 2f out: wknd fnl f* **28/1**

0 **8** *2 ¾* **Star Of Siena**[138] 3502 2-9-0 0 ........ (h[1]) GeraldMosse 11 54
(John Ryan) *led: racd keenly: wnt clr over 6f out: j. path over 5f out: rdn and hdd over 1f out: wknd ins fnl f* **100/1**

0 **9** *8* **Aldbury Lass (IRE)**[159] 2750 2-9-0 0 ........ AdamBeschizza 3 36
(Robert Eddery) *mid-div: rdn and wknd over 2f out* **100/1**

**10** *3 ½* **Fata Morgana** 2-8-7 0 ........ JacobMitchell(7) 2 28
(Christine Dunnett) *s.i.s: hld up: rdn and wknd over 2f out* **250/1**

0 **11** *1 ¾* **Esme Kate (IRE)**[11] 8006 2-9-0 0 ........ LouisSteward 4 24
(Michael Bell) *hld up: rdn and wknd over 2f out* **66/1**

1m 40.57s (-0.03) **Going Correction** -0.05s/f (Good) **11** Ran SP% **114.5**
Speed ratings (Par 94): **98,95,93,93,92 91,90,88,80,76 74**
CSF £212.36 TOTE £12.90: £3.80, £5.20, £4.80; EX 232.20 Trifecta £4407.90.
**Owner** Khalifa Dasmal **Bred** Mr & Mrs R & P Scott **Trained** Newmarket, Suffolk
■ Stewards' Enquiry : Jacob Mitchell £270 fine: use of mobile phone out of designated area

**FOCUS**
This looked a truer test than the first division - the time was 0.97sec faster - and another interesting race. The action unfolded to middle to stands' side. The opening level is fluid.

## 8324 BRITISH STALLION STUDS EBF FILLIES' NOVICE STKS (PLUS 10 RACE) 6f 3y
**2:30** (2:31) (Class 4) 2-Y-0 **£4,657** (£1,386; £692; £346) **Stalls** Centre

Form RPR

**1** **Talaaqy (IRE)** 2-9-0 0 ........ JimCrowley 6 74+
(William Haggas) *settled in midfield: pushed along over 2f out: rn green: wnt 2nd over 1f out: rdn to ld ins fnl f: in command fnl 100yds* **2/5**[1]

0 **2** *1 ½* **Puds**[116] 4296 2-9-0 0 ........ SteveDrowne 7 69+
(Charles Hills) *cl up: led 3f out: rdn and hdd and no match for wnr ins fnl f* **20/1**

53 **3** *2* **Spenny's Lass**[8] 8112 2-8-7 0 ........ JackOsborn(7) 4 63
(John Ryan) *chsd ldrs: effrt on outside and drvn over 2f out: ev ch over 1f out: nt qckn ins fnl f* **9/2**[2]

**4** *5* **Tropical Waters (IRE)** 2-9-0 0 ........ (h[1]) GeraldMosse 9 48
(Robert Cowell) *missed break and rdn and swished tail: hdwy to join ldr 3f out tl rdn and no rspnse over 1f out: sn btn* **10/1**[3]

**5** *1 ¼* **Poppy Line** 2-8-11 0 ........ AaronJones(3) 1 44
(Derek Shaw) *missed break: a bhd* **40/1**

**6** *shd* **Political Slot** 2-9-0 0 ........ (h[1]) PatrickMathers 8 44
(Derek Shaw) *slowly away: v green and drvn and racing awkwardly: a outpcd* **50/1**

0 **7** *2 ½* **Sandkissed (IRE)**[165] 2583 2-8-9 0 ........ (h[1]) FinleyMarsh(5) 2 36
(Amy Murphy) *led tl rdn and hdd 3f out: sn dropped out* **25/1**

1m 15.64s (1.24) **Going Correction** -0.05s/f (Good) **7** Ran SP% **111.7**
Speed ratings (Par 94): **89,87,84,77,76 75,72**
CSF £13.17 TOTE £1.20: £1.10, £5.30; EX 8.50 Trifecta £20.60.
**Owner** Hamdan Al Maktoum **Bred** Shadwell Estate Company Limited **Trained** Newmarket, Suffolk

**FOCUS**
They raced stands' side in a fillies' novice that lacked depth. It's been given a token rating around the third.

## 8325 DENNIS THE SAILOR BARRETT NURSERY H'CAP 6f 3y
**3:00** (3:01) (Class 5) (0-70,70) 2-Y-0 **£2,911** (£866; £432; £216) **Stalls** Centre

Form RPR

5402 **1** **Gangland**[32] 7362 2-9-5 **68** ........ (h) DavidNolan 9 73
(Richard Fahey) *hld up: racd keenly: hdwy over 1f out: r.o to ld towards fin* **6/1**[3]

4450 **2** *½* **Zabaletaswansong (GER)**[24] 7593 2-9-6 **69** ........ GeraldMosse 3 72
(Richard Hannon) *w ldr: rdn over 1f out: led wl ins fnl f: hdd towards fin* **9/1**

030 **3** *hd* **Havana Mariposa**[14] 7937 2-9-3 **66** ........ MartinLane 14 68
(K R Burke) *led: rdn over 1f out: hdd wl ins fnl f: r.o* **9/1**

0640 **4** *¾* **Lady Godiva (IRE)**[14] 7914 2-9-6 **69** ........ SeanLevey 11 69
(Richard Hannon) *hld up: hdwy over 1f out: r.o: nt rch ldrs* **20/1**

054 **5** *¾* **Mutabaahy (IRE)**[25] 7562 2-8-12 **61** ........ (h) AndreaAtzeni 6 59
(Ed Dunlop) *hld up: pushed along and hdwy over 2f out: rdn over 1f out: styd on same pce ins fnl f* **10/1**

505 **6** *¾* **Surfa Rosa**[60] 6394 2-9-0 **66** ........ HollieDoyle(3) 1 62
(Richard Hannon) *chsd ldrs: rdn over 1f out: edgd rt and no ex ins fnl f* **12/1**

046 **7** *1* **Rock On Baileys**[12] 7986 2-7-10 **52** ........ (p[1]) DarraghKeenan(7) 2 45+
(Chris Dwyer) *plld hrd and prom: rdn over 1f out: no ex whn nt clr run ins fnl f* **50/1**

2630 **8** 1 ¼ **Tember**[17] 7814 2-9-7 **70** ........ FranBerry 13 59
(David Barron) *prom: racd keenly: rdn over 2f out: styd on same pce fnl f* **12/1**

02 **9** ½ **Zizum**[14] 7920 2-9-3 **66** ........ (t) JamesDoyle 10 53
(George Scott) *hld up: nt clr run and swtchd lft over 1f out: nt trble ldrs* **4/1**[2]

2400 **10** 3 **Bomad**[41] 7050 2-9-6 **69** ........ PatrickMathers 7 47
(Derek Shaw) *s.s: pushed along over 2f out: nvr on terms* **50/1**

033 **11** 3 **Laubali**[34] 7269 2-9-6 **69** ........ JimCrowley 5 38
(Owen Burrows) *trckd ldrs: nt clr run and wknd over 1f out* **7/2**[1]

650 **12** 4 ½ **Roseau City**[38] 7153 2-8-13 **62** ........ TomQueally 15 18
(David Elsworth) *s.s: a in rr* **22/1**

324 **13** 12 **Johni Boxit**[87] 5398 2-9-2 **65** ........ MartinHarley 8
(Gay Kelleway) *hld up: rdn over 2f out: wknd and eased over 1f out* **18/1**

1m 13.98s (-0.42) **Going Correction** -0.05s/f (Good) 13 Ran SP% **119.3**
Speed ratings (Par 95): **100,99,99,98,97 96,94,93,92,88 84,78,62**
CSF £56.71 CT £501.13 TOTE £6.00: £2.40, £2.80, £4.20; EX 64.20 Trifecta £548.40.
**Owner** Merchants and Missionaries **Bred** Mrs J E Laws **Trained** Musley Bank, N Yorks

**FOCUS**
They raced stands' side in this modest nursery. The runner-up has been rated close to his best.

## 8326 PHILIP SOUTHGATE SOCKS & SANDALS H'CAP 1m 3f 104y
**3:30** (3:30) (Class 5) (0-75,80) 3-Y-0+ **£2,911** (£866; £432; £216) **Stalls** Low

Form RPR

4111 **1** **Hajaam (IRE)**[7] 8142 3-9-10 **80** 6ex ........ StevieDonohoe 1 92+
(Charlie Fellowes) *mde all: rdn over 1f out: qcknd clr fnl f: impressive* **9/4**[1]

5424 **2** 2 ¼ **First Quest (USA)**[14] 7924 3-9-1 **71** ........ (bt) MartinHarley 9 75
(Ed Dunlop) *midfield: effrt on outside gng wl 3f out: rdn 2f out: sn edgd lft u.p but wnt 2nd 1f out where wnr already dashing clr* **12/1**

3102 **3** ¾ **Desert Cross**[14] 7925 4-9-2 **67** ........ FranBerry 12 70
(Jonjo O'Neill) *towards rr early: hrd drvn 3f out: effrt over 2f out: 4th 1f out: no imp fnl 100yds* **20/1**

6-40 **4** ¾ **Knight Music**[27] 7515 5-9-11 **76** ........ AdamBeschizza 13 78
(Michael Attwater) *prom 2f: sn in midfield: rdn and outpcd 3f out: n.m.r 2f out: stl 8th and nt clr run ent fnl f: fin v strly fnl 75yds* **18/1**

-021 **5** hd **Big Sigh (IRE)**[25] 7561 3-9-0 **70** ........ SeanLevey 2 71
(Ismail Mohammed) *pressed wnr: rdn 3f out: stl 2nd 1f out but swamped late by three str finers* **3/1**[2]

2060 **6** ½ **Tyrsal (IRE)**[7] 8143 6-8-10 **64** ........ HollieDoyle(3) 8 65
(Clifford Lines) *bhd: rdn over 3f out: edgd lft wl over 1f out: styd on wout threatening ins fnl f* **33/1**

5615 **7** nse **Macksville (IRE)**[28] 7490 4-8-13 **64** ........ (b) RyanTate 10 65
(James Eustace) *cl up on outside: rdn over 4f out: keeping on same pce whn n.m.r over 1f out* **20/1**

0000 **8** ½ **Dolphin Village (IRE)**[20] 7728 7-9-2 **70** ........ CharlieBennett(3) 7 70
(Shaun Harris) *midfield: rdn over 2f out: n.m.r bhd bunching rivals and no imp on ldrs after* **25/1**

4105 **9** ½ **Cordite (IRE)**[23] 7651 6-9-1 **71** ........ (h) PaddyBradley(5) 6 70
(Jim Boyle) *taken down early: nvr bttr than midfield: rdn and effrt over 2f out: nvr got a clr run and bdly hmpd over 1f out: kpt on wout threatening ins fnl f* **22/1**

6121 **10** 1 ¼ **Maestro Mac (IRE)**[24] 7601 4-9-8 **73** ........ PatCosgrave 4 70
(Tom Clover) *t.k.h: prom: rdn 3f out: lost plae over 1f out: eased fnl 100yds* **14/1**

0512 **11** nk **Mystikana**[225] 1175 4-9-1 **73** ........ (bt) TylerSaunders(7) 5 69
(Marcus Tregoning) *a bhd: short-lived effrt on outer 3f out* **50/1**

625 **12** 12 **Lazarus (IRE)**[24] 7629 3-9-7 **77** ........ (t[1]) AndreaAtzeni 14 54
(Amy Murphy) *sn prom: rdn and lost pl and n.m.r wl over 1f out: eased and t.o* **33/1**

2315 **13** 5 **Incredible Dream (IRE)**[20] 7744 4-9-3 **68** ........ (p) JimCrowley 3 36
(Dean Ivory) *s.v.s: a lagging bdly and rel to r* **4/1**[3]

2m 28.45s (-0.25) **Going Correction** +0.05s/f (Good)
**WFA** 3 from 4yo+ 5lb 13 Ran SP% **121.0**
Speed ratings (Par 103): **102,100,99,99,99 98,98,98,98,97 96,88,84**
CSF £28.39 CT £450.39 TOTE £2.80: £1.40, £2.90, £6.30; EX 30.70 Trifecta £422.30.
**Owner** Khalifa Bin Hamad Al Attiyah **Bred** Marston Stud **Trained** Newmarket, Suffolk

**FOCUS**
A fair handicap. It's been rated around the second and third, with the sixth and seventh also close to their recent marks.

## 8327 INJURED JOCKEYS FUND H'CAP 1m 2f 23y
**4:00** (4:01) (Class 6) (0-65,65) 3-Y-0+ **£2,264** (£673; £336; £168) **Stalls** Low

Form RPR

6031 **1** **Sussex Girl**[5] 8183 3-8-7 **62** 6ex ........ NicolaCurrie(7) 2 68
(John Berry) *chsd ldr 1f: remained handy: rdn over 1f out: led ins fnl f: r.o* **5/1**[1]

1006 **2** 1 **Hannington**[4] 8219 6-9-2 **60** ........ (t) DanielMuscutt 5 63
(Michael Appleby) *hld up in tch: rdn and ev ch fr over 1f out: styd on same pce towards fin* **16/1**

5210 **3** hd **Oceanus (IRE)**[14] 7917 3-8-13 **64** ........ ShelleyBirkett(3) 7 68
(Julia Feilden) *a.p: rdn to ld over 1f out: hdd ins fnl f: styd on same pce towards fin* **14/1**

6400 **4** ¾ **Widnes**[18] 7791 3-9-0 **62** ........ (b) FranBerry 4 64
(Alan Bailey) *s.i.s: hld up: pushed along and hdwy over 3f out: rdn and edgd rt over 1f out: swtchd rt and styd on u.p ins fnl f* **33/1**

3021 **5** nk **Rubis**[21] 7699 4-9-4 **62** ........ DavidNolan 16 63
(Richard Fahey) *hld up in tch: rdn over 2f out: styd on* **8/1**[3]

4226 **6** nk **Castle Talbot (IRE)**[42] 7028 5-9-6 **64** ........ (p) PatCosgrave 12 64
(Tom Clover) *racd wd 2f: prom: swtchd lft and chsd ldr 8f out: rdn to ld wl over 1f out: sn hdd: no ex wl ins fnl f* **10/1**

1255 **7** 1 ½ **Slow To Hand**[18] 7791 3-8-13 **61** ........ (b) MartinLane 11 60
(William Jarvis) *hld up: rdn and swtchd rt over 1f out: styd on ins fnl f: nvr nrr* **10/1**

5000 **8** ½ **Polar Forest**[4] 8218 7-9-6 **64** ........ PhillipMakin 9 61
(Richard Guest) *sn led: rdn and hdd wl over 1f out: no ex ins fnl f* **10/1**

4202 **9** 2 **Mr Frankie**[31] 7413 6-9-1 **59** ........ JimCrowley 15 52
(John Spearing) *hld up: rdn over 2f out: nt trble ldrs* **6/1**[2]

0530 **10** ¾ **Thecornishbarron (IRE)**[41] 7061 5-8-11 **62** ........ JackOsborn(7) 10 54
(John Ryan) *plld hrd and prom: wnt 2nd after 1f tl 8f out: remained handy: rdn over 1f out: wknd ins fnl f* **20/1**

2206 **11** 3 ¾ **Captain Pugwash (IRE)**[41] 7061 3-9-2 **64** ........ JamieSpencer 3 52
(Henry Spiller) *hld up: shkn up and hung lft fr over 1f out: eased ins fnl f* **5/1**[1]

04-5 **12** 1 ¼ **Rockshine**[35] 7227 3-9-3 **65** ........ SeanLevey 1 49
(Richard Hannon) *hld up: rdn over 2f out: wknd over 1f out* **16/1**

2664 **13** ¾ **Rowlestonerendezvu**[21] 7711 4-8-12 **56** ........ TomQueally 8 37
(Tony Carroll) *hld up: pushed along over 3f out: nvr on terms* **25/1**

060 **14** 2 ½ **Rockley Point**[31] 7408 4-9-4 **62** ........ MartinHarley 14 39
(Paul D'Arcy) *hld up: hung lft over 3f out: wknd over 1f out* **25/1**

2m 10.5s **Going Correction** +0.05s/f (Good)
**WFA** 3 from 4yo+ 4lb 14 Ran SP% **119.8**
Speed ratings (Par 101): **102,101,101,100,100 99,98,98,96,96 93,92,91,89**
CSF £81.70 CT £1064.18 TOTE £4.30: £1.30, £5.60, £4.80; EX 83.80 Trifecta £1172.30.
**Owner** D Tunmore & John Berry **Bred** Elusive Bloodstock **Trained** Newmarket, Suffolk

**FOCUS**
A moderate handicap. The third has been rated near his Brighton win.

## 8328 GROSVENOR CASINO OF GREAT YARMOUTH H'CAP 7f 3y
**4:30** (4:32) (Class 6) (0-65,66) 3-Y-0+ **£2,264** (£673; £336; £168) **Stalls** Centre

Form RPR

360 **1** **Our Greta (IRE)**[53] 6664 3-9-2 **62** ........ RyanTate 15 68
(Michael Appleby) *led stand's side duo: rdn over 2f out: chal 1f out: kpt on to ld wl ins fnl f despite rdr dropping far side rein* **18/1**

0500 **2** ½ **Gabrielle**[8] 8125 4-8-10 **57** ........ HollieDoyle(3) 3 63
(Dr Jon Scargill) *plld hrd: chsd ldrs: chal 1f out: ev ch tl no ex fnl 50yds* **20/1**

6026 **3** 1 ¼ **Ubla (IRE)**[20] 7723 4-8-5 **56** ........ (p) PaulHainey(7) 4 58
(Gay Kelleway) *cl up in centre: led 2f out: pushed along and hdd wl ins fnl f* **10/1**

1400 **4** nse **Samphire Coast**[14] 7934 4-9-1 **59** ........ (h[1]) PatrickMathers 2 61
(Derek Shaw) *dwlt: racd far side: effrt 1/2-way: tried to chal 1f out: nt qckn ins fnl f* **6/1**[2]

0502 **5** 1 ¼ **Harry Beau**[8] 8124 3-9-3 **63** ........ JimCrowley 5 61
(David Evans) *led or disp ld in centre tl 2f out: sn rdn: no ex fnl 120yds* **4/1**[1]

226 **6** 2 **Still Waiting**[58] 6485 3-9-5 **65** ........ MartinLane 11 58
(William Jarvis) *s.s: effrt to chse ldrs 2f out: rdn and no imp ins fnl f* **14/1**

6345 **7** ½ **Used To Be**[14] 7942 3-9-4 **64** ........ (p[1]) MartinHarley 8 56
(K R Burke) *nvr bttr than midfield: rdn and btn over 2f out* **15/2**

441 **8** ½ **Twilight Spirit**[39] 7122 3-9-2 **62** ........ (b) TomQueally 14 55
(Tony Carroll) *dwlt: 2nd of pair racing stand's side: rdn and btn over 2f out* **7/1**[3]

5061 **9** 1 ½ **Mr Potter**[24] 7605 4-9-3 **61** ........ (v) PhillipMakin 1 48
(Richard Guest) *taken down early: racd v awkwardly: nvr on terms* **22/1**

-001 **10** ¾ **Noble Ballad**[57] 6529 3-9-1 **61** ........ (b) SeanLevey 7 45
(Ralph Beckett) *led centre gp to 1/2-way: sn drvn: btn 2f out* **10/1**

0640 **11** 2 **Claire's Secret**[123] 4050 3-8-12 **63** ........ FinleyMarsh(5) 6 42
(Philip McBride) *pressed ldrs: rdn 1/2-way: btn 2f out* **14/1**

2052 **12** 2 **Bahamian Paradise**[33] 7320 3-8-12 **61** ........ CharlieBennett(3) 13 35
(Hughie Morrison) *cl up over 4f: rdn 2f out: wknd fnl f* **8/1**

-650 **13** 9 **Love Me Again**[59] 6439 3-9-2 **62** ........ StevieDonohoe 16 13
(Charlie Fellowes) *rdn and struggling after 3f: t.o* **22/1**

6000 **14** 3 ¾ **Drop Kick Murphi (IRE)**[14] 7933 3-9-2 **62** ........ (p[1]) SteveDrowne 9 3
(Christine Dunnett) *spd to 1/2-way: t.o* **40/1**

1m 26.87s (0.27) **Going Correction** -0.05s/f (Good)
**WFA** 3 from 4yo+ 2lb 14 Ran SP% **122.3**
Speed ratings (Par 101): **96,95,94,93,92 90,89,89,87,86 84,81,71,67**
CSF £346.95 CT £3871.37 TOTE £20.00: £7.00, £7.80, £3.80; EX 557.90 Trifecta £3865.60.
**Owner** Alan Gray **Bred** Rathbarry Stud **Trained** Oakham, Rutland

**FOCUS**
The winner and eighth were the only two to race stands' side throughout, with the others towards the middle. A moderate handicap. The winner has been rated back towards her 2yo form, with the third just below his turf level.

## 8329 JOHN KEMP 4 X 4 CENTRE OF NORWICH H'CAP 6f 3y
**5:00** (5:01) (Class 6) (0-60,59) 3-Y-0+ **£2,264** (£673; £336; £168) **Stalls** Centre

Form RPR

-255 **1** **Sentinel**[38] 7158 3-9-6 **59** ........ StevieDonohoe 10 69
(Charlie Fellowes) *chsd ldrs: rdn to ld 1f out: r.o* **4/1**[1]

320 **2** 1 ¼ **Dream Start**[28] 7480 3-9-6 **59** ........ (t) GeraldMosse 6 65
(John Ryan) *s.i.s: hld up: hdwy over 2f out: led over 1f out: sn rdn and hdd: styd on same pce ins fnl f* **5/1**[2]

0160 **3** ¾ **Le Manege Enchante (IRE)**[42] 7017 4-9-4 **56** ........ (v) PatrickMathers 14 60
(Derek Shaw) *hld up: rdn over 2f out: hdwy over 1f out: r.o* **11/1**

3616 **4** ¾ **Justice Rock**[11] 7993 4-8-8 **53** ........ (t) NicolaCurrie(7) 2 55
(Phil McEntee) *hld up: pushed along and hdwy over 1f out: r.o: nt rch ldrs* **16/1**

3600 **5** shd **Commanche**[14] 7933 8-8-9 **54** ........ (b) DarraghKeenan(7) 4 55
(Chris Dwyer) *chsd ldrs: rdn and ev ch over 1f out: styd on same pce ins fnl f* **25/1**

3000 **6** ½ **Captain Scooby**[1] 8298 11-8-0 **45** ........ (b) JackOsborn(7) 11 45
(Richard Guest) *s.i.s: sn pushed along in rr: hdwy over 1f out: nt trble ldrs* **16/1**

6354 **7** ¾ **Robbian**[35] 7255 6-8-9 **50** ........ NoelGarbutt(3) 3 48
(Charles Smith) *prom: pushed along and lost pl over 3f out: styd on fr over 1f out: edgd rt ins fnl f* **10/1**

2030 **8** ½ **Scotch Myst**[153] 2949 3-9-5 **58** ........ DavidNolan 5 54
(Richard Fahey) *led early: chsd ldrs: rdn over 1f out: styd on same pce* **33/1**

060 **9** 1 **Tellovoi (IRE)**[15] 7888 9-9-3 **55** ........ (p) PhillipMakin 9 48
(Richard Guest) *sn led: hdd over 4f out: remained handy: rdn over 1f out: wknd ins fnl f* **16/1**

1000 **10** shd **Strictly Carter**[50] 6748 4-9-6 **58** ........ (b) FranBerry 7 51
(Alan Bailey) *hld up: hdwy over 1f out: sn rdn: nt clr run and eased wl ins fnl f* **14/1**

3003 **11** 4 ½ **Sakhee's Jem**[24] 7605 4-9-1 **53** ........ AdamBeschizza 8 32
(Gay Kelleway) *mid-div: pushed along over 3f out: wknd over 1f out* **16/1**

40-5 **12** ¾ **Oh So Dandy (IRE)**[293] 41 3-9-0 **56** ........ (v) AaronJones(3) 13 33
(Derek Shaw) *plld hrd and prom: led over 4f out: rdn and hdd over 1f out: sn wknd* **50/1**

0 **13** 1 ½ **Malaysian Boleh**[22] 7692 7-8-7 **48** ........ (v) HollieDoyle(3) 16 21
(Phil McEntee) *hld up: pushed along 1/2-way: n.d* **20/1**

4060 **14** 1 ½ **Lovely Acclamation (IRE)**[14] 7916 3-9-4 **57** ........ SeanLevey 15 25
(Ismail Mohammed) *chsd ldrs tl rdn and wknd over 1f out* **6/1**[3]

4504 **15** ½ **Nicky Baby (IRE)**[89] 5339 3-9-5 **58** ........ (b) SteveDrowne 12 25
(Dean Ivory) *s.s: a bhd* **8/1**

1m 13.56s (-0.84) **Going Correction** -0.05s/f (Good)
**WFA** 3 from 4yo+ 1lb 15 Ran SP% **123.2**
Speed ratings (Par 101): **103,101,100,99,99 98,97,96,95,95 89,88,86,84,83**
CSF £22.20 CT £216.08 TOTE £4.60: £1.80, £2.10, £4.20; EX 29.60 Trifecta £280.50.
**Owner** Elite Racing Club **Bred** Elite Racing Club **Trained** Newmarket, Suffolk
■ Stewards' Enquiry : Darragh Keenan caution: careless riding

**FOCUS**
A moderate handicap in which the runners were spread from the stands' side to the middle in the closing stages. The likes of the third and sixth testify to the form's limitations.
T/Plt: £1,019.30 to a £1 stake. Pool: £62,975.56 - 45.10 winning units T/Qpdt: £30.70 to a £1 stake. Pool: £7,143.62 - 172.16 winning units **Iain Mackenzie & C Roberts**

8330 - 8337a (Foreign Racing) - See Raceform Interactive

## 7721 COMPIEGNE (L-H)
Tuesday, October 24

**OFFICIAL GOING: Turf: heavy**

### 8338a PRIX DE LONGUEIL ANNEL (CLAIMER) (4YO+) (TURF) 1m 2f
10:55 4-Y-0+ £9,829 (£3,931; £2,948; £1,965; £982)

RPR
1 **Palang (USA)**66 5-8-10 0 HayleyTurner(5) 3 82
(Andreas Suborics, Germany) 9/5[2]
2 2 **High Draw (FR)**21 7699 4-8-11 0 TonyPiccone 1 74
(K R Burke) *wl into stride: led: pushed along over 2f out and styd alone against far side rail: rdn over 1f out: hdd ins fnl f and styd on same pce* 7/5[1]
3 4 **Swiss Man (IRE)**7 6-9-4 0 Pierre-CharlesBoudot 2 73
(M Boutin, France) 33/10[3]
4 ½ **Iceberg (IRE)**373 5-8-7 0 ErwannLebreton(8) 5 69
(C Laffon-Parias, France) 43/10
5 9 **Grey Magic Night (FR)**107 4-7-12 0 MlleMickaelleMichel(10) 4 44
(L Rovisse, France) 168/10
2m 16.22s 5 Ran SP% **125.1**
PARI-MUTUEL (all including 1 euro stake): WIN 2.80; PLACE 1.30, 1.50; SF 6.80.
**Owner** Guido Werner Hermann Schmitt **Bred** Paradise Productions LLC **Trained** Germany

## 8306 KEMPTON (A.W) (R-H)
Wednesday, October 25

**OFFICIAL GOING: Polytrack: standard to slow**
Wind: Almost nil Weather: Fine, mild

### 8339 32RED/BRITISH STALLION STUDS EBF NOVICE STKS (DIV I) 1m (P)
5:50 (5:50) (Class 5) 2-Y-O £3,234 (£962; £481; £240) Stalls Low

Form RPR
1 **King And Empire (IRE)** 2-9-2 0 OisinMurphy 6 78+
(Andrew Balding) *wl plcd: shkn up over 2f out: prog to chse ldr over 1f out: led last 150yds: readily* 12/1
3 2 1 **Coolongolook**18 7813 2-9-2 0 PatCosgrave 8 76
(Luca Cumani) *mde most: shkn up and tried to go for home over 2f out: kpt on fr over 1f out but hdd and outpcd last 150yds* 10/11[1]
45 3 2½ **Tullyallen (IRE)**11 8030 2-8-9 0 RossaRyan(7) 4 70
(Richard Hannon) *hld up in midfield: prog 2f out: rdn to chse ldng pair 1f out: no imp and jst hld on for 3rd* 10/1
0 4 hd **Desert Path**21 7726 2-9-2 0 RobertHavlin 11 70+
(Amanda Perrett) *wl in rr: t.k.h after 2f: sme prog 2f out: shkn up and styd on wl last 150yds: nrly snatched 3rd* 6/1[2]
0 5 2¼ **Blue Candy**20 7765 2-9-2 0 EdwardGreatrex 9 64
(Archie Watson) *chsd ldr to over 1f out: wknd fnl f* 33/1
0 6 hd **Brexitmeansbrexit**12 7995 2-8-11 0 LukeMorris 7 59
(Richard Hannon) *t.k.h: hld up in midfield: prog 2f out: no imp ldrs 1f out: fdd* 20/1
7 1 **King Tut (USA)** 2-9-2 0 JosephineGordon 5 61+
(Roger Charlton) *v s.i.s: detached in last early and rn green: pushed along over 2f out: styd on to pass a few rivals fnl f: nt disgracd* 8/1[3]
0 8 1½ **The Emperor Within (FR)**75 5887 2-9-2 0 DanielMuscutt 10 58
(Martin Smith) *trapped out wd: chsd ldrs to 2f out: steadily wknd* 66/1
00 9 2¾ **Newborough**35 7273 2-9-2 0 SteveDrowne 3 51
(Charles Hills) *chsd ldrs: shkn up over 2f out: wknd wl over 1f out* 50/1
10 ¾ **Reveleon** 2-9-2 0 TedDurcan 1 49
(Sir Michael Stoute) *hld up in rr: pushed along over 2f out: no prog and wknd over 1f out* 8/1[3]
00 11 3¾ **Safarhi**7 8162 2-9-2 0 DougieCostello 2 40
(Alan King) *trapped out wd: effrt fr rr over 3f out: wknd over 2f out* 100/1
1m 39.37s (-0.43) **Going Correction** -0.10s/f (Stan) 11 Ran SP% **117.8**
Speed ratings (Par 95): **98,97,94,94,92 91,90,89,86,85 82**
CSF £22.85 TOTE £13.40: £2.40, £1.10, £2.90; EX 30.50 Trifecta £185.60.
**Owner** Qatar Racing Limited **Bred** Paddy Burns **Trained** Kingsclere, Hants
**FOCUS**
This wasn't a bad novice event. It paid to be handy and the main action came down the middle.

### 8340 32RED/BRITISH STALLION STUDS EBF NOVICE STKS (DIV II) 1m (P)
6:20 (6:24) (Class 5) 2-Y-O £3,234 (£962; £481; £240) Stalls Low

Form RPR
1 **Tenedos** 2-9-2 0 (t¹) JosephineGordon 8 80+
(Hugo Palmer) *dwlt: sn in tch: pushed along over 3f out: prog on outer over 2f out: shkn up to ld 1f out: sn wl in command: quite promising* 10/1
2 2 **Maaward (IRE)** 2-9-2 0 TomMarquand 4 75
(Richard Hannon) *t.k.h: trckd ldrs: lft in 2nd pl over 3f out: shkn up to ld 2f out: styd on but hdd and outpcd 1f out* 9/2[3]
3 4½ **Passing Clouds** 2-9-2 0 KierenFox 2 64
(Michael Attwater) *in tch: pushed along over 3f out: prog over 2f out: tk 3rd over 1f out: outpcd by ldng pair but kpt on* 100/1
4 3½ **Urbino** 2-9-2 0 TedDurcan 11 56
(Sir Michael Stoute) *s.s: wl bhd in 10th early: jst in tch over 3f out: outpcd fr 2f out but pushed along on inner and kpt on to take 4th fnl f* 12/1
0 5 2½ **Praeceps (IRE)**11 8029 2-9-2 0 LukeMorris 10 54+
(Sir Mark Prescott Bt) *sn outpcd and detached in 8th: ct up and in tch 3f out: sme prog over 2f out but sn outpcd* 100/1
6 1 **Magojiro (USA)** 2-9-2 0 (b¹) JFEgan 7 48
(Jeremy Noseda) *s.s: rn green and t.o in last early: ct up sn after 1/2-way: shkn up and outpcd over 2f out: no ch after but plugged on* 12/1
53 7 hd **Dazzle Gold (USA)**28 7512 2-9-2 0 PatCosgrave 9 47
(Robert Cowell) *t.k.h: trckd ldrs: cl 3rd 3f out: wknd 2f out* 10/3[1]
0 8 1½ **Parisian (IRE)**103 4859 2-9-2 0 OisinMurphy 6 44+
(Ralph Beckett) *sn pressed ldr: carried v wd bnd fr 4f out to 3f out and lost all ch* 7/2[2]
2320 9 1½ **Blanchefleur (IRE)**12 8002 2-8-11 81 SeanLevey 1 35
(Richard Hannon) *trckd ldrs: lft in ld over 3f out: rdn and hdd 2f out: wknd qckly over 1f out* 7/2[2]
10 3 **Balgowlah (IRE)** 2-9-2 0 MartinLane 5 33
(David Lanigan) *dwlt: urged along and detached in 9th early: ct up over 3f out: wknd over 2f out* 50/1
055 11 15 **Snaffled (IRE)**34 7333 2-9-2 0 RobertWinston 3 +
(David Brown) *led: hung bdly lft bnd fr 4f out: sn hdd and no ch: t.o* 50/1
1m 38.53s (-1.27) **Going Correction** -0.10s/f (Stan) 11 Ran SP% **116.1**
Speed ratings (Par 95): **102,100,95,92,89 88,88,86,85,82 67**
CSF £53.73 TOTE £9.10: £3.20, £2.00, £12.60; EX 63.80 Trifecta £7464.90 Part won..
**Owner** V I Araci **Bred** Aston Mullins Stud **Trained** Newmarket, Suffolk
**FOCUS**
The second division of the novice event was 0.84secs quicker than the opener. The opening level is fluid.

### 8341 100% PROFIT BOOST AT 32REDSPORT.COM H'CAP 1m (P)
6:50 (6:54) (Class 5) (0-75,75) 3-Y-O+ £3,234 (£962; £481; £240) Stalls Low

Form RPR
322 1 **Glendun (USA)**109 4632 3-9-4 75 (p¹) RyanTate 14 83
(James Eustace) *led after 2f: mde rest: drvn over 2f out: all out fnl f but clung on wl* 14/1
0500 2 nk **Archie (IRE)**12 7998 5-9-7 75 PatCosgrave 2 83
(Tom Clover) *hld up and last early: gd prog 2f out: chsd wnr fnl f and swtchd lft: clsd u.p but a hld* 6/1[2]
2242 3 ½ **Cape To Cuba**28 7514 3-9-4 75 OisinMurphy 5 81
(James Fanshawe) *hld up towards rr: shkn up over 2f out: gd prog over 1f out: clsd ins fnl f: too late to chal* 5/1[1]
4360 4 1¼ **Sterling Silva (IRE)**56 6576 3-9-3 74 (p) TomMarquand 4 77
(Richard Hannon) *prom: rdn over 2f out: disp 2nd briefly 1f out: no ex* 25/1
5000 5 ¾ **Derek Duval (USA)**26 7569 3-9-3 74 (t) DanielMuscutt 7 75
(Stuart Williams) *hld up in rr: pushed along over 2f out: stl only 10th jst over 1f out: pushed along and fin quite strly: no ch to threaten* 12/1
6464 6 nse **Tigerwolf (IRE)**16 7881 4-9-0 68 RobertHavlin 3 70
(Mick Channon) *t.k.h: hld up bhd ldrs: 5th over 2f out: nt clr run over 1f out and sn lost pl: kpt on again nr fin* 6/1[2]
1106 7 hd **Mutineer**27 7541 3-9-2 73 GeorgeDowning 11 74
(Daniel Kubler) *prom: chsd ldr over 4f out: drvn over 2f out: lost 2nd 1f out and nudged sn after: fdd* 25/1
213 8 ½ **Clock Chimes**15 7942 3-9-4 75 SeanLevey 13 75
(David Brown) *led 2f: chsd ldr to over 4f out: drvn in 4th pl over 2f out: no imp 1f out: nudged sn after and fdd* 10/1[3]
4322 9 1½ **Traveller (FR)**12 7999 3-9-1 75 (t) CallumShepherd(3) 6 71
(Charles Hills) *a in midfield: rdn over 2f out: one pce and no prog* 5/1[1]
0355 10 ¾ **Mighty Lady**20 7762 4-9-2 70 (p¹) LukeMorris 1 65
(Robyn Brisland) *hld up towards rr: promising prog on inner over 2f out: wknd fnl f* 10/1[3]
6024 11 nk **Medicean Ballet (IRE)**14 7958 3-8-13 73 GeorgiaCox(3) 8 67
(Henry Candy) *nvr beyond midfield: dropped to rr over 2f out u.p: no ch after: plugged on fnl f* 11/1
1110 12 hd **Chetan**20 7759 5-9-1 74 (t) JoshuaBryan(5) 10 68
(Charlie Wallis) *chsd ldrs: rdn and lost pl fr 3f out: hrd drvn and in last trio 2f out: plugged on* 25/1
2312 13 3½ **Lucymai**149 3139 4-9-3 71 RobertWinston 9 57
(Dean Ivory) *broke on terms but restrained into last: stl racd wd: lost tch and shkn up over 2f out: nvr in it* 20/1
1m 38.92s (-0.88) **Going Correction** -0.10s/f (Stan)
**WFA** 3 from 4yo+ 3lb 13 Ran SP% **119.1**
Speed ratings (Par 103): **100,99,99,97,97 97,96,96,94,94 93,93,90**
CSF £90.75 CT £496.85 TOTE £13.00: £4.40, £2.50, £2.30; EX 102.20 Trifecta £366.10.
**Owner** The MacDougall Two **Bred** Timothy Wickes & Jeffry Morris **Trained** Newmarket, Suffolk
**FOCUS**
A tight handicap. The third has been rated close to her early maiden best.

### 8342 32RED CASINO MEDIAN AUCTION MAIDEN STKS 6f (P)
7:20 (7:20) (Class 5) 3-4-Y-O £3,234 (£962; £481; £240) Stalls Low

Form RPR
4335 1 **Zilza (IRE)**4 8242 3-9-0 63 (bt) RobertHavlin 2 66
(Conrad Allen) *mde all: rdn clr over 1f out: in n.d after: pushed out* 5/4[1]
0605 2 2¾ **Toolatetodelegate**18 7826 3-8-9 48 (t¹) JoshuaBryan(5) 4 57
(Brian Barr) *t.k.h: chsd wnr: rdn 2f out: nt qckn over 1f out: n.d after: jst hld on for 2nd* 25/1
55 3 hd **Gorham's Cave**15 7930 3-9-5 0 JackMitchell 3 62
(Roger Varian) *hld up in rr: prog on inner 2f out: hrd rdn over 1f out: tk 3rd fnl f: kpt on and nrly snatched 2nd* 15/8[2]
00 4 2¼ **Linda Doris (IRE)**16 7907 3-9-0 0 (t) DanielMuscutt 1 49
(Gay Kelleway) *pressed ldrs: rdn over 2f out disputing 2nd: wknd jst over 1f out* 25/1
5240 5 1½ **Agnethe (IRE)**27 7539 3-9-0 58 JoeyHaynes 8 45
(Paul D'Arcy) *chsd ldrs: rdn and nt qckn over 2f out: outpcd over 1f out: no ch after* 7/2[3]
0000 6 1¾ **Harbour Town**14 7952 3-9-5 45 (p) LukeMorris 6 44
(Harry Dunlop) *t.k.h: hld up in tch: rdn and fnd nil over 2f out: sn outpcd and btn* 25/1
0000 7 ½ **Moorea**16 7902 3-9-2 25 (t) MitchGodwin(3) 5 42
(John Bridger) *a in rr: urged along in last 1/2-way: passed two rivals fnl f* 100/1
4 8 1½ **Divine Messenger**15 7930 3-9-5 0 RobertWinston 9 38
(Emma Owen) *hld up in last pair: shkn up and no prog over 2f out: wl btn after* 25/1
0006 9 nk **Secret Willow**88 5409 3-9-5 44 (b¹) RyanPowell 7 37
(John E Long) *sn rdn in rr: nvr a factor: wknd over 1f out* 33/1
1m 12.51s (-0.59) **Going Correction** -0.10s/f (Stan) 9 Ran SP% **120.8**
Speed ratings (Par 103): **99,95,95,92,90 87,87,85,84**
CSF £40.57 TOTE £2.50: £1.10, £4.60, £1.20; EX 27.60 Trifecta £67.50.
**Owner** Sheikh Ahmad Jassim Al Thani **Bred** Ahmed Jassim Al-Thani **Trained** Newmarket, Suffolk
**FOCUS**
A weak 3yo maiden. The winner has been rated to his mark.

### 8343 32RED ON THE APP STORE NURSERY H'CAP 7f (P)
7:50 (7:50) (Class 4) (0-85,82) 2-Y-O £4,528 (£1,347; £673; £336) Stalls Low

Form RPR
0233 1 **Di Fede (IRE)**27 7552 2-9-7 82 OisinMurphy 7 91
(Ralph Beckett) *dwlt: sn in tch: gd prog over 1f out: pushed into the ld jst ins fnl f and sn at least half a l up: rdn nr fin and jst hld on* 3/1[1]

5411 **2** *nse* **Motown Mick (IRE)**[16] 7904 2-9-5 **80**.......................... TimmyMurphy 3 89
(Richard Hannon) *hld up: prog on inner over 2f out: led over 1f out: hdd jst ins fnl f and looked hld: rallied wl nr fin: needed one more stride* **7/2**[2]

232 **3** *5* **Barig Al Thumama**[19] 7788 2-9-2 **77**.......................... DanielMuscutt 4 72
(Marco Botti) *chsd ldng pair: rdn to chal wl over 1f out: readily outpcd fnl f* **7/2**[2]

4404 **4** *6* **Ghayadh**[27] 7536 2-9-3 **78**.......................... JosephineGordon 6 57
(Hugo Palmer) *t.k.h: hld up: shkn up and lft bhd fr 2f out* **7/2**[2]

0330 **5** *1* **Finsbury Park**[46] 6934 2-9-4 **79**.......................... FranBerry 1 55+
(Robyn Brisland) *pushed up to dispute ld at str pce: def advantage over 2f out: hdd & wknd over 1f out* **6/1**[3]

3260 **6** *4* **Sorority**[36] 7243 2-8-6 **67**.......................... JoeFanning 2 32
(Mark Johnston) *hld up in tch: effrt and cl up over 2f out: wknd rapidly over 1f out* **33/1**

0016 **7** *nk* **The Mums**[41] 7087 2-9-7 **82**..........................(p[1]) RobertHavlin 5 46+
(John Gosden) *disp ld at str pce to over 2f out: wknd qckly* **10/1**

1m 24.37s (-1.63) **Going Correction** -0.10s/f (Stan) **7** Ran SP% **118.0**
Speed ratings (Par 97): **105,104,99,92,91 86,86**
CSF £14.52 TOTE £3.10: £1.40, £2.60; EX 13.00 Trifecta £53.20.
**Owner** Robert Ng **Bred** Robert Ng **Trained** Kimpton, Hants
■ Stewards' Enquiry : Timmy Murphy two-day ban: using his whip above the permitted level (8-9 Nov)

**FOCUS**
They went a strong pace in this fair nursery. The winner has been rated as building on her latest promise.

## 8344 32RED.COM H'CAP 7f (P)

**8:20** (8:20) (Class 4) (0-85,85) 3-Y-O+ **£4,690** (£1,395; £697; £348) **Stalls** Low

Form RPR

21- **1** **Cliffs Of Capri**[348] 7906 3-9-4 **84**.......................... RobertHavlin 2 95+
(Simon Crisford) *trckd ldrs: prog over 2f out to ld over 1f out: rdn and edgd lft but clr fnl f: decisively* **7/2**[1]

5140 **2** *3* **Human Nature (IRE)**[64] 6289 4-8-11 **82**..........................(t) MillyNaseb[(7)] 10 86
(Stuart Williams) *led: rdn over 2f out: hdd over 1f out: no ch w wnr after but kpt on wl to hold on for 2nd* **33/1**

311 **3** *nk* **Siege Of Boston (IRE)**[50] 6795 4-9-6 **84**..........................(t) RobertWinston 6 87
(John Butler) *pressed ldrs: rdn over 2f out: nt qckn wl over 1f out: styd on again ins fnl f to take 3rd nr fin* **9/1**

0050 **4** *nse* **Gothic Empire (IRE)**[19] 7780 5-9-3 **81**.......................... DanielMuscutt 1 84
(James Fanshawe) *slowly away: sn in midfield on inner: rdn and prog jst over 2f out: kpt on fnl f to press for a pl nr fin* **9/1**

1-55 **5** *½* **Mandarin (GER)**[146] 3232 3-9-1 **84**.......................... MarcMonaghan[(3)] 9 85+
(Marco Botti) *rn wout declared tongue-strap: slowly away: hld up in last: shkn up and detached over 2f out: gd prog on wd outside jst over 1f out: fin wl* **14/1**

4065 **6** *1 ¾* **North Creek**[36] 7255 4-9-0 **81**.......................... GeorgeWood[(3)] 11 78
(Chris Wall) *pressed ldr to 2f out: steadily wknd over 1f out* **20/1**

5532 **7** *½* **Rebel De Lope**[61] 6397 3-9-1 **84**.......................... CallumShepherd[(3)] 3 79
(Charles Hills) *chsd ldr to 2f out: styd pressing for a pl tl wknd ins fnl f* **12/1**

0660 **8** *1 ½* **Outer Space**[41] 7094 6-9-7 **85**.......................... DougieCostello 14 77
(Jamie Osborne) *hld up in last trio fr wdst draw: shkn up and passed a few over 1f out: no great hdwy after* **33/1**

1-00 **9** *shd* **Poet's Beauty (IRE)**[15] 7941 4-9-5 **83**..........................(p) SeanLevey 12 74
(Ismail Mohammed) *chsd ldrs tl over 2f out: steadily wknd* **33/1**

3453 **10** *nse* **Family Fortunes**[30] 7456 3-9-5 **85**.......................... TomMarquand 8 75+
(Sylvester Kirk) *dwlt: t.k.h early and hld up: pushed along fr 1/2-way: no prog whn rdn over 2f out: wl btn after* **6/1**[3]

60 **11** *1* **Arlecchino's Leap**[34] 7321 5-9-1 **79**..........................(p) LiamKeniry 5 67
(Mark Usher) *hld up wl in rr: stl gng strly over 2f out: nudged along and no great prog: nvr in it* **66/1**

2105 **12** *½* **Honiara**[35] 7285 4-9-6 **84**..........................(b) LukeMorris 13 71
(Paul Cole) *slowly away: hld up in rr: prog on inner over 2f out: no hdwy over 1f out: wknd* **33/1**

4360 **13** *½* **High Acclaim (USA)**[19] 7780 3-8-10 **83**..........................(v) RossaRyan[(7)] 7 68
(Roger Teal) *pressed ldrs: rdn over 2f out: wknd wl over 1f out* **7/1**

352 **14** *1* **Noble Conquest (FR)**[81] 5670 3-9-3 **83**.......................... OisinMurphy 4 65
(Sir Michael Stoute) *hld up in midfield: shkn up and no prog jst over 2f out: wknd over 1f out* **5/1**[2]

1m 24.31s (-1.69) **Going Correction** -0.10s/f (Stan)
**WFA** 3 from 4yo+ 2lb **14** Ran SP% **118.1**
Speed ratings (Par 105): **105,101,101,101,100 98,98,96,96,96 95,94,93,92**
CSF £137.64 CT £1000.50 TOTE £4.50: £1.80, £8.70, £2.80; EX 150.90 Trifecta £742.30.
**Owner** Mrs Doreen Tabor **Bred** Glebe Farm Stud **Trained** Newmarket, Suffolk

**FOCUS**
This looked competitive and they went a fair pace, but the gambled-on winner was far too good. It's been rated around the runner-up, with the third to his C&D latest.

## 8345 WATCH RACING UK ON BT TV CLASSIFIED STKS 7f (P)

**8:50** (8:51) (Class 6) 3-Y-O+ **£2,587** (£770; £384; £192) **Stalls** Low

Form RPR

6305 **1** **Belgravian (FR)**[14] 7945 3-9-2 54..........................(tp[1]) OisinMurphy 4 61
(Archie Watson) *mde all: rdn clr 2f out: in n.d after: styd on* **13/8**[1]

-000 **2** *2* **Warba (IRE)**[223] 1220 3-9-2 54..........................(t) SeanLevey 2 56
(Mohamed Moubarak) *prom: chsd wnr wl over 2f out: drvn and no imp over 1f out: kpt on fnl f and hld on for 2nd* **14/1**

506 **3** *nk* **Q Cee**[23] 7693 4-9-4 55.......................... FranBerry 10 56+
(Eugene Stanford) *awkward s: hld up in last trio: gd prog over 2f out: tk 3rd bhd clr ldng pair jst over 1f out: styd on and nrly snatched 2nd* **7/1**[3]

-000 **4** *3 ¼* **Compton Brave**[28] 7514 3-9-2 42.......................... AdamBeschizza 12 46
(J R Jenkins) *stdd s: hld up in rr: rdn and prog 2f out: kpt on to take 4th fnl f:n.d* **40/1**

0060 **5** *¾* **Quick Monet (IRE)**[3] 8259 4-9-1 43.......................... CharlieBennett[(3)] 3 45
(Shaun Harris) *slowly away: sn in midfield: pushed along and outpcd over 2f out: n.d after but kpt on steadily* **33/1**

00-0 **6** *2* **Sixth Of June**[16] 7900 3-9-2 50.......................... LukeMorris 5 39
(Rod Millman) *chsd ldrs: outpcd in 4th over 2f out: fdd over 1f out* **20/1**

0000 **7** *1* **Slipalongtrevaskis**[170] 2472 4-9-4 36.......................... TimmyMurphy 11 37
(J R Jenkins) *stdd s: hld up in detached last: passed sme rival on inner fr over 2f out: nvr involved* **100/1**

0001 **8** *nse* **Lady Kaviar (IRE)**[7] 8152 3-9-3 55.......................... JaneElliott[(5)] 14 42
(George Margarson) *spd fr wdst draw to chse wnr: lost 2nd wl over 2f out: and steadily wknd* **15/8**[2]

0000 **9** *4 ½* **Stragar**[14] 7952 3-9-2 45..........................(p[1]) AlistairRawlinson 8 24
(Michael Appleby) *chsd ldrs to over 2f out: wknd* **20/1**

0060 **10** *6* **Arquus (IRE)**[37] 7212 4-9-4 45.......................... LiamKeniry 6 8
(Ed de Giles) *slowly away: a in rr: no ch fnl 2f* **25/1**

6005 **11** *13* **Angelical Eve (IRE)**[8] 8134 3-9-2 48..........................(p) PatCosgrave 13
(George Baker) *trapped out wd in midfield: wknd qckly over 2f out: t.o* **12/1**

-000 **12** *¾* **Paco Lady**[43] 7018 3-8-13 42.......................... MitchGodwin[(3)] 7
(Ivan Furtado) *a in rr and sn rdn: t.o* **80/1**

0050 **13** *14* **Our Ruth**[29] 7481 4-9-4 32..........................(p[1]) KieranO'Neill 9
(Jimmy Fox) *rdn in midfield after 3f: sn wknd: t.o* **150/1**

1m 25.31s (-0.69) **Going Correction** -0.10s/f (Stan)
**WFA** 3 from 4yo 2lb **13** Ran SP% **121.4**
Speed ratings (Par 101): **99,96,96,92,91 89,88,88,83,76 61,60,44**
CSF £24.50 TOTE £2.60: £1.10, £4.60, £2.20; EX 29.20 Trifecta £144.00.
**Owner** Greenfield Racing I **Bred** Al Asayl Bloodstock **Trained** Upper Lambourn, W Berks

**FOCUS**
Few landed a blow in this weak classified event. The fourth and fifth testify to the limitations of the form.

## 8346 WATCH RACING UK ON TALKTALK TV H'CAP 1m 2f 219y(P)

**9:20** (9:20) (Class 6) (0-55,55) 3-Y-O+ **£2,587** (£770; £384; £192) **Stalls** Low

Form RPR

0001 **1** **Raashdy (IRE)**[13] 7991 4-9-2 **50**.......................... LukeMorris 4 57+
(Peter Hiatt) *chsd ldrs: rdn wl over 2f out: prog to press ldr over 1f out: persistent chal fnl f to ld last 75yds* **11/4**[1]

0600 **2** *nk* **Desert Song**[84] 5545 3-8-10 **54**.......................... PaddyBradley[(5)] 1 61
(Pat Phelan) *led to over 9f out: sn in 3rd: led again wl over 1f out gng strly: drvn and hrd pressed sn after: hdd last 75yds* **20/1**

0006 **3** *1 ¼* **Spiritofedinburgh (IRE)**[16] 7879 3-9-1 **54**..........................(t) ShaneKelly 8 59
(Brendan Powell) *hld up off the pce disputing 8th: rdn over 2f out: prog to take 3rd fnl f: styd on but unable to chal* **8/1**

3430 **4** *½* **McDelta**[42] 7062 7-9-4 **52**.......................... JosephineGordon 3 55
(Geoffrey Deacon) *hld up off the pce disputing 8th: rdn wl over 2f out: prog to take 4th fnl f: nrst fin* **8/1**

030 **5** *hd* **Midnight Mood**[13] 7992 4-9-3 **51**..........................(t[1]) LiamKeniry 10 54
(Dominic Ffrench Davis) *n.m.r s: wl in rr: rdn and prog on outer over 2f out: kpt on to take 5th ins fnl f: nrst fin* **16/1**

3400 **6** *3* **Saga Sprint (IRE)**[9] 8122 4-9-5 **53**..........................(p[1]) AdamBeschizza 7 51
(J R Jenkins) *hmpd over 9f out: mostly in midfield: lost pl and struggling in rr 2f out: plugged on fnl f* **25/1**

2/05 **7** *hd* **Pershing**[4] 7832 6-9-6 **54**..........................(h) DougieCostello 6 53+
(Kevin Frost) *urged along early: towards rr whn hmpd over 9f out: rapid prog to ld over 7f out: hdd & wknd wl over 1f out* **6/1**[3]

5212 **8** *nk* **The Juggler**[13] 7991 4-9-7 **55**..........................(v) MartinLane 14 52
(William Knight) *pressed ldr fr wd draw: chsd new ldr over 7f out: upsides 2f out: wknd jst over 1f out* **3/1**[2]

60-5 **9** *nk* **Storm Runner (IRE)**[113] 4461 9-9-1 **54**.......................... JaneElliott[(5)] 11 50
(George Margarson) *hld up wl in rr: shkn up over 2f out: brief prog sn after but no hdwy over 1f out* **25/1**

6/00 **10** *½* **Reality Show (IRE)**[8] 8135 10-9-2 **53**.......................... CharlieBennett[(3)] 12 48
(Shaun Harris) *in tch: prog on inner over 2f out: cl enough and rdn over 1f out: sn wknd* **50/1**

046P **11** *2 ½* **L'Ami De Rouge**[105] 4756 4-8-13 **50**..........................(h) HollieDoyle[(3)] 9 41
(Ralph J Smith) *hld up in last and sn wl detached: jst in tch 4f out: no great prog over 2f out* **25/1**

000 **12** *nk* **Fire Whirl**[20] 7768 3-8-11 **53**.......................... CallumShepherd[(3)] 5 44
(William Knight) *a wl in rr: no prog over 2f out* **25/1**

2060 **13** *7* **Nouvelle Ere**[20] 7761 6-9-5 **53**..........................(t) GeorgeDowning 13 31
(Tony Carroll) *chsd ldrs to 3f out: wknd qckly* **20/1**

-000 **U** **Exspectation (IRE)**[20] 7769 3-9-1 **54**.......................... RobHornby 2
(Michael Blanshard) *t.k.h: 5th whn stmbld and uns rdr over 9f out* **66/1**

2m 21.41s (-0.49) **Going Correction** -0.10s/f (Stan)
**WFA** 3 from 4yo+ 5lb **14** Ran SP% **122.4**
Speed ratings (Par 101): **97,96,95,95,95 93,93,92,92,92 90,90,85,**
CSF £64.95 CT £411.36 TOTE £3.00: £1.60, £4.30, £3.20; EX 54.00 Trifecta £731.60.
**Owner** P W Hiatt **Bred** Shadwell Estate Company Limited **Trained** Hook Norton, Oxon

**FOCUS**
This moderate handicap was a messy affair. The runner-up has been rated as posting a pb.
T/Plt: £164.80 to a £1 stake. Pool: £86,277.98 - 382.02 winning units T/Qpdt: £12.30 to a £1 stake. Pool: £11,514.42 - 688.41 winning units **Jonathan Neesom**

# 8035 NEWMARKET (R-H)

Wednesday, October 25

**OFFICIAL GOING: Good to firm (good in places; 8.1)**
Wind: light, behind Weather: sunny, mild

## 8347 REWARDS4RACING FILLIES' NOVICE MEDIAN AUCTION STKS (PLUS 10 RACE) (DIV I) 7f

**1:15** (1:18) (Class 5) 2-Y-O **£3,881** (£1,155; £577; £288) **Stalls** High

Form RPR

005 **1** **Wild Impala (FR)**[12] 8006 2-9-0 75.......................... FrankieDettori 2 84+
(John Gosden) *w ldr tl led 3f out: rdn 2f out and readily kicked clr over 1f out: in command fnl f: eased towards fin: easily* **7/2**[3]

64 **2** *3 ¼* **High Seas (IRE)**[16] 7898 2-9-0 0.......................... JamesDoyle 10 73
(Hugo Palmer) *str; t.k.h: hld up in tch: swtchd rt and effrt over 2f out: chsd ldrs and drvn over 1f out chsd clr wnr ent fnl f: no imp* **3/1**[2]

0 **3** *1* **Colourfield (IRE)**[12] 8006 2-9-0 0.......................... AdamBeschizza 4 70
(Ed Vaughan) *w'like; bit on the leg; t.k.h: hld up in tch in midfield: effrt over 2f out: chsd ldng trio wl over 1f out: wnt 3rd ins fnl f: kpt on but no ch w wnr* **7/1**

3 **4** *5* **Lady Al Thumama**[16] 7875 2-9-0 0.......................... StevieDonohoe 8 57
(Charlie Fellowes) *str; led and crossed to r against stands' rail: hdd 3f out: sn rdn: outpcd and lost 2nd ent fnl f: wknd fnl f* **5/2**[1]

60 **5** *5* **River Rule**[49] 6827 2-9-0 0.......................... DanielMuscutt 3 43
(Stuart Williams) *w'like; stdd s: hld up in tch in rr: effrt over 2f out: sn outpcd and no ch w ldrs whn struggling on downhill run over 1f out: plugged on same pce after* **100/1**

**6** *hd* **Goldfox Girl** 2-9-0 0.......................... AndrewMullen 12 43
(Michael Appleby) *str; bit bkwd; in tch in midfield: rdn 3f out: sn outpcd u.p: no ch w ldrs and edgd rt over 1f out: plugged on same pce after* **25/1**

**7** *1* **Gemini** 2-9-0 0.......................... JimCrowley 1 40
(Charles Hills) *leggy; s.i.s: rn green in rr: pushed along 3f out: sn outpcd and no ch 2f out: plugged on to pass btn horses ins fnl f* **8/1**

8 1 3/4 **Queen Of Dreams (IRE)** 2-9-0 0 ........ MartinHarley 11 35
(William Knight) *neat; in tch in midfield: rdn over 2f out: sn outpcd and no ch w ldrs over 1f out: wknd ins fnl f* **14/1**

0 9 1 3/4 **Pretty Pearl**[19] 7786 2-9-0 0 ........ LukeMorris 9 31
(Robert Eddery) *leggy; on toes; chsd ldrs: rdn over 2f out: sn outpcd and struggling: wknd over 1f out* **100/1**

65 10 1/2 **Asheena**[176] 2258 2-9-0 0 ........ JoeyHaynes 7 29
(Paul D'Arcy) *w'like; trckd ldrs: rdn 3f out: sn struggling and outpcd ent fnl 2f: struggling to handle downhill run and lost pl over 1f out: wknd fnl f* **66/1**

11 hd **Carolyn's Voice** 2-9-0 0 ........ OisinMurphy 6 29
(Stuart Williams) *ly; in tch: rdn and rn green 3f out: sn outpcd and struggling: wl btn fnl 2f* **40/1**

12 25 **Astroblaze** 2-9-0 0 ........ ShaneKelly 5
(Mark H Tompkins) *str; bit bkwd; rn green: dropped to rr after 2f: lost tch over 2f out: eased fnl f* **100/1**

1m 24.1s (-1.30) **Going Correction** -0.20s/f (Firm) **12** Ran SP% **116.8**
Speed ratings (Par 92): **99,95,94,88,82 82,81,79,77,76 76,47**
CSF £13.86 TOTE £4.30: £1.70, £1.80, £2.40; EX 17.80 Trifecta £93.50.
**Owner** Sheikh Juma Dalmook Al Maktoum **Bred** Stratford Place Stud **Trained** Newmarket, Suffolk

**FOCUS**
Stands side course used. The first leg of a fair novice. A step forward from the winner, with the second and third rated as finding a fraction on their pre-race form.

## 8348 REWARDS4RACING FILLIES' NOVICE MEDIAN AUCTION STKS (PLUS 10 RACE) (DIV II) 7f

**1:45** (1:47) (Class 5) 2-Y-O **£3,881** (£1,155; £577; £288) **Stalls** High

Form RPR

06 1 **Timpani (IRE)**[12] 7997 2-9-0 0 ........ FrankieDettori 3 77
(John Gosden) *tall; pressed ldr: rdn over 1f out: sustained effrt and styd on u.p ins fnl f to ld last strides* **12/1**

32 2 nse **Left Alone**[21] 7725 2-9-0 0 ........ JamesDoyle 4 77
(Hugo Palmer) *tall; athletic; lw; t.k.h: led: rdn over 1f out: kpt on and sustained duel w wnr after: hdd last strides* **5/6**[1]

242 3 1 **La Diva**[21] 7733 2-9-0 79 ........ AndreaAtzeni 6 76
(Roger Varian) *pressed ldng pair: rdn over 2f out: styd on same pce ins fnl f* **3/1**[2]

6 4 1/2 **Canimar**[12] 8006 2-9-0 0 ........ PJMcDonald 2 73
(Ed Dunlop) *hld up wl in tch in midfield: effrt and drifting rt over 1f out: styd on wl ins fnl f: nt rch ldrs* **16/1**

5 1/2 **Forward Thinker** 2-9-0 0 ........ JamieSpencer 5 72+
(David Simcock) *tall; stdd after s: hld up in tch in last trio: pushed along and hdwy over 1f out: kpt on wl ins fnl f: nt rch ldrs* **20/1**

6 2 1/2 **Lethal Angel** 2-9-0 0 ........ OisinMurphy 7 65+
(Stuart Williams) *str; in tch in midfield: rdn 2f out: unable qck and struggling to handle downhill run over 1f out: edging lft and kpt on same pce ins fnl f* **100/1**

7 2 3/4 **Dance On The Day (IRE)** 2-9-0 0 ........ RichardKingscote 9 57+
(Tom Dascombe) *ly; str; s.i.s: in tch in last trio: effrt over 2f out: rn green: drifting rt and no imp over 1f out: nvr trbld ldrs* **8/1**[3]

8 1 1/4 **Rhigolter Rose (IRE)** 2-9-0 0 ........ GeraldMosse 11 56
(William Haggas) *w'like; cl-cpld; s.i.s: in tch in last trio: effrt ent fnl 2f: no hdwy over 1f out: wl hld and eased ins fnl f* **16/1**

0 9 1/2 **Maggie Jonks**[28] 7504 2-9-0 0 ........ RobHornby 10 53
(Andrew Balding) *in tch in midfield: swtchd rt and effrt ent fnl 2f: no imp and struggling to handle downhill run over 1f out: wknd ins fnl f* **80/1**

10 3/4 **Willingforshilling (IRE)** 2-9-0 0 ........(h[1]) MartinHarley 8 51
(Harry Dunlop) *leggy; in tch: dropped to rr and pushed along 3f out: no threat to ldrs after: wknd fnl f* **66/1**

1m 25.07s (-0.33) **Going Correction** -0.20s/f (Firm) **10** Ran SP% **118.6**
Speed ratings (Par 92): **93,92,91,91,90 87,84,83,82,81**
CSF £22.70 TOTE £11.30: £3.10, £1.10, £1.10; EX 28.60 Trifecta £67.90.
**Owner** Highclere T'Bred Racing-Steve Redgrave **Bred** Herbertstown House Stud **Trained** Newmarket, Suffolk

**FOCUS**
This looked the stronger of the two divisions, although the time was nearly a second slower. It's been rated around the balance of the first three.

## 8349 NEWMARKET EQUINE SECURITY NURSERY H'CAP 7f

**2:20** (2:22) (Class 5) (0-75,76) 2-Y-O **£3,881** (£1,155; £577; £288) **Stalls** High

Form RPR

113 1 **Lexington Grace (IRE)**[15] 7914 2-9-6 74 ........(p) SeanLevey 6 79
(Richard Hannon) *racd far side: chsd ldrs tl led 2f out: rdn over 1f out: styd on wl ins fnl f: rdn out: 1st of 12 in gp* **15/2**[2]

0230 2 1 1/4 **Oswald (IRE)**[29] 7482 2-9-2 70 ........ MartinHarley 14 72
(Robyn Brisland) *racd stands' side: hld up in rr: squeezed through against stands' rail to ld gp and chse ldrs over 1f out: styd on u.p to go 2nd last strides: 1st of 8 in gp* **25/1**

056 3 hd **Bertog**[18] 7819 2-9-4 72 ........ PaulMulrennan 7 73
(John Mackie) *compact; noisy in prelims; racd far side: chsd ldrs: rdn to chse wnr over 1f out: kpt on same pce u.p ins fnl f: lost 2nd last strides: 2nd of 12 in gp* **12/1**

006 4 nk **Elsaakb (USA)**[19] 7788 2-8-11 65 ........(b[1]) JimCrowley 8 65
(John Gosden) *str; lw; in tch in midfield: effrt to chse ldrs and drvn over 1f out: kpt on same pce ins fnl f: 3rd of 12 in gp* **10/1**[3]

0405 5 1 1/4 **Guzman (IRE)**[12] 8008 2-9-6 74 ........(h) PaulHanagan 13 71
(Richard Fahey) *lw; racd stands' side: hld up in midfield overall: effrt and hdwy 2f out: styd on same pce ins fnl f: 2nd of 8 in gp* **5/1**[1]

2604 6 1/2 **Reinbeau Prince**[11] 8045 2-8-13 67 ........ PatrickMathers 15 63
(Richard Fahey) *sltly on toes; racd stands' side: hld up towards rr: hdwy and bumping w rival over 2f out: no hdwy u.p over 1f out: kpt on same pce ins fnl f: 3rd of 8 in gp* **12/1**

5410 7 shd **Straight Ash (IRE)**[8] 8131 2-9-1 72 ........ HollieDoyle(3) 10 67
(Richard Hannon) *racd far side: hld up in midfield: effrt 2f out: sme hdwy over 1f out: kpt on ins fnl f: nvr getting to ldrs: 4th of 12 in gp* **20/1**

4054 8 3/4 **Gossip Column (IRE)**[29] 7489 2-9-2 70 ........ PJMcDonald 11 63
(Charles Hills) *lw; racd far side: chsd ldrs: rdn 3f out: unable qck u.p over 1f out: wknd ins fnl f: 5th of 12 in gp* **16/1**

6500 9 nk **Galactic (IRE)**[7] 8164 2-8-11 65 ........(b[1]) TomMarquand 16 57
(Richard Hannon) *racd stands' side: hld up in midfield: effrt 2f out: kpt on same pce and no imp ins fnl f: 4th of 8 in gp* **25/1**

5300 10 hd **Giovanni Medici**[28] 7510 2-8-9 63 ........ LukeMorris 12 55
(Seamus Durack) *racd far side: bhd: clsd and swtchd lft ent fnl 2f: hdwy over 1f out: keeping on but nt threatening ldrs whn nt clr run ins fnl f: 6th of 12 in gp* **33/1**

6044 11 nk **By Royal Approval (IRE)**[16] 7877 2-9-0 75 ........ GabrieleMalune(7) 20 66
(Michael Appleby) *sltly on toes; racd stands' side: led gp and chsd ldrs overall: rdn over 2f out: lost gp ld and btn over 1f out: wknd ins fnl f: 5th of 8 in gp* **33/1**

4633 12 hd **Contribute**[15] 7938 2-8-10 64 ........ OisinMurphy 3 55
(Martyn Meade) *racd far side: in tch in midfield: effrt 2f out: swtchd rt over 1f out: no imp and one pce ins fnl f: 7th of 12 in gp* **12/1**

0660 13 1/2 **Prince Consort (IRE)**[12] 8013 2-8-9 63 ........ RyanTate 1 52
(Brian Meehan) *leggy; racd far side: hld up in tch: effrt 2f out: sme hdwy on far rail over 1f out: kpt on same pce ins fnl f: 8th of 12 in gp* **50/1**

421 14 1/2 **Episcia (IRE)**[29] 7482 2-9-2 73 ........ AaronJones(3) 9 61
(Stuart Williams) *racd far side: chsd ldrs: rdn 3f out: unable qck over 1f out: wknd ins fnl f: 9th of 12 in gp* **20/1**

4511 15 1/2 **Move To The Front (IRE)**[15] 7913 2-9-8 76 ........(v) AdamKirby 4 63
(Clive Cox) *racd far side: chsd ldr tl over 2f out: lost pl u.p over 1f out: wknd ins fnl f: 10th of 12 in gp* **12/1**

063 16 3/4 **Image**[13] 7986 2-9-1 69 ........ DavidProbert 17 53
(Philip McBride) *str; lw; racd stands' side: in tch in midfield: effrt and bumping w rival over 2f out: no hdwy u.p over 1f out: wknd ins fnl f: 6th of 8 in gp* **20/1**

6061 17 5 **Letsbe Avenue (IRE)**[28] 7510 2-9-5 73 ........ RyanMoore 18 44
(Richard Hannon) *lw; on toes; racd stands' side: t.k.h: pressed gp ldr and chsd ldrs overall: rdn 2f out: lost pl and btn over 1f out: wknd fnl f: 7th of 8 in gp* **5/1**[1]

0044 18 1/2 **Smugglers Top**[13] 7985 2-8-12 66 ........(p) RichardKingscote 2 36
(Tom Dascombe) *w'like; sltly on the leg; racd far side: overall ldr tl 2f out: lost pl u.p over 1f out: wknd ins fnl f: 11th of 12 in gp* **33/1**

4600 19 1 1/4 **Cardaw Lily (IRE)**[16] 7876 2-9-4 72 ........ ShaneKelly 5 38
(Richard Hughes) *racd far side: hld up in midfield: shkn up 2f out: sn lost pl: wknd fnl f: 12th of 12 in gp* **50/1**

5450 20 78 **Hard Graft**[21] 7734 2-9-1 69 ........(h[1]) JamieSpencer 19
(David Brown) *bhd: lost tch 4f out: sn eased and t.o: 8th of 8 in gp* **16/1**

1m 24.57s (-0.83) **Going Correction** -0.20s/f (Firm) **20** Ran SP% **131.4**
Speed ratings (Par 95): **96,94,94,94,92 92,91,91,90,90 90,89,89,88,88 87,81,81,79,**
CSF £194.07 CT £2312.79 TOTE £7.30: £2.30, £7.40, £1.80, £2.90; EX 231.80 Trifecta £2320.40.
**Owner** Middleham Park Racing XII & A E Denham **Bred** Tally-Ho Stud **Trained** East Everleigh, Wilts

**FOCUS**
A wide-open nursery, they split into two but ended up spread across the track, with the main action unfolding centre-to-stands' side. It's been rated around the first two.

## 8350 32RED.COM NOVICE STKS (PLUS 10 RACE) (C&G) 7f

**2:55** (2:56) (Class 4) 2-Y-O **£4,528** (£1,347; £673; £336) **Stalls** High

Form RPR

1 **Key Victory (IRE)** 2-9-0 0 ........ WilliamBuick 8 91+
(Charlie Appleby) *compact; lw; hld up in tch in midfield: stuck bhd horses and forced to switch rt 2f out: effrt towards centre of crse ent fnl f: str run to ld wl ins fnl f: sn in command: eased nr fin* **10/3**[2]

2 1 **Qaysar (FR)** 2-9-0 0 ........ SeanLevey 5 85+
(Richard Hannon) *compact; hld up in tch in midfield: clsd to chse ldr 2f out: rn green and hung lft but chalng 1f out: led ins fnl f: hdd and nt match pce of wnr wl ins fnl f* **14/1**[3]

3 1/2 **Masaarr (USA)** 2-9-0 0 ........ AndreaAtzeni 4 84+
(Roger Varian) *athletic; lw; noisy in prelims; chsd ldrs: effrt to chse ldng pair over 1f out: carried lft 1f out: kpt on tl outpcd by wnr wl ins fnl f: swtchd lft towards fin* **33/1**

2 4 3/4 **Elwazir**[26] 7580 2-9-0 0 ........ JimCrowley 15 82
(Owen Burrows) *lw; led: rdn 2f out: struggling to handle downhill run over 1f out: hdd ins fnl f: no ex and wknd towards fin* **4/7**[1]

5 5 1 3/4 **Crack On Crack On**[72] 6005 2-9-0 0 ........ MartinHarley 14 77
(Clive Cox) *str; hld up in tch in midfield: effrt 2f out: unable qck and kpt on same pce ins fnl f* **33/1**

4 6 4 **Maypole**[10] 8073 2-9-0 0 ........ RyanMoore 7 66
(Richard Hannon) *chsd ldrs: rdn 2f out: unable qck and outpcd whn edgd rt over 1f out: wknd ins fnl f* **16/1**

7 1 1/4 **Bedouin's Story** 2-9-0 0 ........ PatCosgrave 9 63
(Saeed bin Suroor) *compact; lw; dwlt: sn rcvrd and t.k.h in midfield: effrt ent fnl 2f: unable qck and lost pl over 1f out: wknd ins fnl f* **33/1**

65 8 2 1/2 **Marble Bar**[79] 5709 2-8-11 0 ........ HectorCrouch(3) 13 56
(Henry Candy) *hld up in tch in rr: effrt over 2f out: no imp over 1f out: wknd ins fnl f* **66/1**

00 9 2 **Burlington (IRE)**[14] 7946 2-9-0 0 ........(t) FrankieDettori 11 51
(John Gosden) *w'like; chsd ldrs: rdn 3f out: unable qck and lost pl over 1f out: wknd ins fnl f* **16/1**

10 shd **Bond Street Beau** 2-9-0 0 ........ DavidProbert 3 51
(Philip McBride) *str; restless in stalls: in tch: effrt over 2f out: unable qck and lost pl over 1f out: wknd ins fnl f* **150/1**

0 11 nk **Dark Side Jazz (IRE)**[9] 8119 2-8-7 0 ........ JackOsborn(7) 1 50
(John Ryan) *w'like; noisy in prelims; s.i.s: a towards rr and nvr travelling wl: wknd u.p over 1f out* **125/1**

0 12 12 **Feel The Wrath (IRE)**[19] 7788 2-8-11 0 ........ CharlieBennett(3) 2 17
(Denis Quinn) *w'like; w ldr tl over 2f out: losing pl whn edgd lft wl over 1f out: sn dropped to rr: wl bhd ins fnl f* **200/1**

13 nk **Dubai Frame** 2-9-0 0 ........ PJMcDonald 12 17
(Ed Dunlop) *str; bit bkwd; a in rr: lost tch ent fnl 2f: wl bhd over 1f out* **125/1**

14 1/2 **Stylehunter** 2-9-0 0 ........ JamesDoyle 6 15
(John Gosden) *athletic; hld up in tch in midfield: pushed along whn hmpd and stmbld over 1f out: nt rcvr and sn bhd and eased* **16/1**

1m 23.59s (-1.81) **Going Correction** -0.20s/f (Firm) **14** Ran SP% **124.1**
Speed ratings (Par 97): **102,100,100,99,97 92,91,88,86,86 85,72,71,71**
CSF £49.51 TOTE £4.30: £1.50, £3.50, £7.10; EX 65.10 Trifecta £951.70.
**Owner** Godolphin **Bred** Godolphin **Trained** Newmarket, Suffolk
■ Stewards' Enquiry : Charlie Bennett five-day ban: interference & careless riding (8-11/13 Nov)

**FOCUS**
A good novice, they raced stands' side and the well-bred newcomers upstaged the hot favourite. The fourth has been rated as running a similar race to his debut.

## 8351 AR LEGAL FILLIES' H'CAP 1m

**3:30** (3:35) (Class 2) (0-100,95) 3-Y-O+ **£12,938** (£3,850; £1,924; £962) **Stalls** High

Form RPR

3-15 1 **Dynamic**[35] 7276 3-8-6 80 ........ TomMarquand 2 88+
(William Haggas) *ly; lw; in tch in midfield: niggled along: rdn and hdwy ent fnl 2f: led 1f out: hld on wl u.p ins fnl f* **4/1**[2]

1016 **2** *nk* **Al Nafoorah**[35] 7276 3-8-8 **82** ........................ PJMcDonald 4 89+
(Ed Dunlop) *short of room leaving stalls: hld up in tch in last pair: effrt over 2f out: hdwy over 1f out: drvn and ev ch ins fnl f: kpt on but hld towards fin* **12/1**

6055 **3** ½ **Alexandrakollontai (IRE)**[15] 7941 7-8-2 **76** oh2........(b) RowanScott(3) 1 83
(Alistair Whillans) *hld up in tch: effrt over 2f out: hdwy u.p to chse ldrs over 1f out: ev ch ins fnl f: kpt on same pce towards fin* **33/1**

004 **4** 2 **Assanilka (FR)**[22] 7710 3-8-3 **77** ........................(p) KieranO'Neill 10 78
(Harry Dunlop) *led: rdn and hrd pressed over 1f out: hdd 1f out: no ex and wknd ins fnl f* **50/1**

6551 **5** 1 **Hidden Steps**[9] 8113 3-9-0 **88** 6ex........................(h) DavidProbert 12 87
(Andrew Balding) *chsd ldr: effrt ev ch over 1f out tl unable qck 1f out: wknd ins fnl f* **7/1**

3132 **6** 1 ¼ **Song Maker**[18] 7830 3-8-13 **87** ........................(b) WilliamBuick 5 83
(Charlie Appleby) *lw; wnt rt s: hld up in tch in midfield: effrt ent fnl 2f: unable qck u.p over 1f out: kpt on same pce ins fnl f* **5/1[3]**

2635 **7** 1 ¼ **Bint Dandy (IRE)**[29] 7484 6-8-8 **82** ........................(p) LewisEdmunds(3) 3 76
(Chris Dwyer) *wl in tch in midfield: effrt over 2f out: chsng ldrs but unable qck u.p over 1f out: wknd ins fnl f* **25/1**

4140 **8** *nse* **Tai Hang Dragon (IRE)**[94] 5196 3-9-1 **89** ........................ RyanMoore 11 82
(Richard Hannon) *on toes; trckd ldrs: effrt over 2f out: unable qck u.p and no hdwy over 1f out: wknd ins fnl f* **10/1**

0151 **9** 3 ½ **Aimez La Vie (IRE)**[24] 7656 3-8-11 **85** ........................ PaulHanagan 9 70
(Richard Fahey) *hld up in tch towards rr: nt clr run over 2f out: no hdwy u.p over 1f out: wknd ins fnl f* **12/1**

0135 **10** 3 ¼ **Clearly**[18] 7815 3-8-8 **82** ........................(b[1]) AndreaAtzeni 7 59
(John Gosden) *stdd s and sn swtchd lft: plld hrd: hld up in tch towards rr: effrt over 2f out: no hdwy u.p over 1f out: wknd fnl f* **10/3[1]**

-310 **11** 4 ½ **Lady Freyja**[126] 3964 3-8-10 **84** ........................ GeraldMosse 8 51
(John Ryan) *lw; chsd ldrs tl over 2f out: lost pl and bhd over 1f out: wknd fnl f* **11/1**

1m 36.09s (-2.51) **Going Correction** -0.20s/f (Firm)
**WFA** 3 from 4yo+ 3lb **11** Ran SP% **113.8**
Speed ratings (Par 96): **104,103,103,101,100 98,97,97,94,90 86**
CSF £48.48 CT £1000.21 TOTE £4.40: £1.80, £3.40, £8.40; EX 46.90 Trifecta £758.40.
**Owner** Michael & Mrs Michelle Morris **Bred** W And R Barnett Ltd **Trained** Newmarket, Suffolk

**FOCUS**
A useful fillies' handicap, they raced stands' side but the winner challenged well away from the rail. The third has been rated close to this year's form.

## 8352 BRITISH EBF RACING UK NOVICE STKS (PLUS 10 RACE) (SIRE/DAM-RESTRICTED RACE) 1m
**4:05** (4:06) (Class 4) 2-Y-O **£6,469** (£1,925; £962; £481) **Stalls** High

Form RPR

2 **1** **Knight To Behold (IRE)**[33] 7355 2-9-2 0 ........................ RichardKingscote 6 93+
(Harry Dunlop) *lw; pressed wnr: rdn and wnt clr of field w wnr over 2f out: styd on u.p ins fnl f to ld fnl 50yds: rdn out* **11/8[1]**

4 **2** *nk* **Bow Street**[21] 7726 2-9-2 0 ........................ WilliamBuick 8 92
(Charlie Appleby) *str; lw; led: rdn and kicked clr w wnr over 2f out drvn ins fnl f: kpt on tl hdd and no ex fnl 50yds* **7/4[2]**

**3** 2 ¾ **Al Muffrih (IRE)** 2-9-2 0 ........................ GeraldMosse 3 85+
(William Haggas) *ly; athletic; lw; t.k.h: hld in tch in 4th: effrt to chse clr ldng pair 3f out: kpt on but nvr able to get on terms: eased towards fin* **9/2[3]**

**4** 9 **Talas (IRE)** 2-9-2 0 ........................ AndreaAtzeni 2 64
(Roger Varian) *compact; s.i.s and swtchd lft after s: t.k.h: hld up in tch: rdn over 2f out: sn outpcd: wl btn 4th and kpt on same pce fr over 1f out* **14/1**

00 **5** 7 **Pentland Hills (IRE)**[27] 7543 2-8-13 0 ........................ GeorgeWood(3) 1 47
(Chris Wall) *stdd s: t.k.h: hld up in rr: effrt over 2f out: sn outpcd and no ch fnl 2f* **100/1**

**6** 1 ¼ **Wild West Hero** 2-9-2 0 ........................ RyanMoore 4 44
(Sir Michael Stoute) *str; bit bkwd; in tch: rdn 4f out: struggling and outpcd 3f out: no ch fnl 2f* **20/1**

**7** 7 **Ttmab** 2-9-2 0 ........................ ShaneKelly 5 27
(Mark H Tompkins) *tall; chsd ldng pair tl 3f: sn rdn and outpcd: wl btn 2f out: wknd over 1f out* **150/1**

1m 38.15s (-0.45) **Going Correction** -0.20s/f (Firm) **7** Ran SP% **109.7**
Speed ratings (Par 97): **94,93,90,81,74 73,66**
CSF £3.62 TOTE £2.20: £1.10, £1.30; EX 4.00 Trifecta £7.30.
**Owner** Neil Jones **Bred** Abergwaun Farms **Trained** Lambourn, Berks

**FOCUS**
The market leaders dominated this useful novice, with the first three clear. The form has been rated at face value for now.

## 8353 DISCOVER NEWMARKET MAIDEN STKS (PLUS 10 RACE) 1m 2f
**4:40** (4:44) (Class 3) 2-Y-O **£6,469** (£1,925; £962; £481) **Stalls** High

Form RPR

**1** **Brundtland (IRE)** 2-9-5 0 ........................ WilliamBuick 6 82+
(Charlie Appleby) *athletic; lw; hld up in tch in midfield: effrt over 2f out: hdwy to press ldrs and racing against stands' rail 1f out: styd on to ld wl ins fnl f: gng away at fin* **6/1**

062 **2** 1 **Making Miracles**[16] 7890 2-9-5 76 ........................ PJMcDonald 4 79
(Mark Johnston) *tall; str; lw; dwlt: in rr and niggled along: swtchd and rdn over 3f out: drvn and ev ch ent fnl f: led and edgd lft ins fnl f: hdd and no ex wl ins fnl f* **7/1**

3 **3** *nk* **Jeremiah**[20] 7758 2-9-5 0 ........................ StevieDonohoe 3 78
(Charlie Fellowes) *str; lw; hld up in tch in midfield: effrt over 2f out: pressing ldrs u.p ent fnl f: kpt on ins fnl f* **8/1**

46 **4** 1 ½ **Neeraan (USA)**[21] 7726 2-9-5 0 ........................ JimCrowley 5 76
(Roger Varian) *w'like; str; pressed ldrs tl led 3f out: rdn ent fnl 2f: drvn over 1f out: hdd ins fnl f: no ex and btn whn carried lft and sltly impeded wl ins fnl f* **4/1[2]**

06 **5** 2 **Diocletian (IRE)**[18] 7813 2-9-5 0 ........................ DavidProbert 12 72
(Andrew Balding) *taken down early: mde most tl 3f: sn rdn: syill ev ch whn wandered on downhill run over 1f out: wknd ins fnl f* **5/1[3]**

5 **6** 9 **Courtside (FR)**[7] 7810 2-9-5 0 ........................ JamieSpencer 10 55
(David Simcock) *dwlt: hld up in tch in midfield: clsd to trck ldrs 5f out: rdn to chal 3f out tl outpcd 2f out: wknd over 1f out* **7/2[1]**

0 **7** 3 ¼ **Strongarm Chaser (IRE)**[7] 8161 2-9-5 0 ........................ AndreaAtzeni 11 49
(Richard Hannon) *athletic; in tch: rdn 3f out: sn struggling and outpcd 2f out: wl btn over 1f out* **10/1**

0 **8** 6 **Mythological (IRE)**[16] 7906 2-9-5 0 ........................ RyanMoore 8 37
(John Gosden) *sturdy; w ldr: ev ch and rdn 3f out: lost pl u.p jst over 2f out: wknd over 1f out* **16/1**

0 **9** 1 ¼ **Highcastle (IRE)**[27] 7543 2-9-5 0 ........................ RichardKingscote 7 35
(Ed Dunlop) *in tch: reminder after 2f: rdn over 2f out: sn outpcd and wl btn over 1f out* **100/1**

**10** 1 ¾ **Seinesational** 2-9-5 0 ........................ MartinHarley 9 31
(William Knight) *compact; bit bkwd; s.i.s and rn green early: in tch in rr: rdn 3f out: sn struggling and wknd 2f out* **50/1**

04 **11** 3 ½ **Candidate (IRE)**[16] 7906 2-9-5 0 ........................ AdamKirby 2 25
(Hughie Morrison) *in tch in midfield: effrt 3f out: unable qck and no imp 2f out: sn wknd* **16/1**

2m 5.04s (-0.76) **Going Correction** -0.20s/f (Firm) **11** Ran SP% **117.2**
Speed ratings (Par 99): **95,94,93,92,91 83,81,76,75,74 71**
CSF £64.49 TOTE £6.80: £3.00, £2.70, £2.80; EX 50.00 Trifecta £265.90.
**Owner** Godolphin **Bred** J Hanly **Trained** Newmarket, Suffolk
■ M C Muldoon was withdrawn. Price at time of withdrawal 66/1. Rule 4 does not apply.

**FOCUS**
A decent maiden that went to one of the two newcomers. The third and fourth have been rated close to their pre-race form.

## 8354 CAMBRIDGE ART FAIR NURSERY H'CAP 1m 1f
**5:15** (5:17) (Class 4) (0-85,85) 2-Y-O **£4,528** (£1,347; £673; £336) **Stalls** High

Form RPR

1622 **1** **Lynwood Gold (IRE)**[13] 7978 2-9-7 **85** ........................ PJMcDonald 4 96
(Mark Johnston) *ly; chsd ldrs: wnt 6 l 2nd 3f out: pushed and clsd to ld over 1f out: edgd lft 1f out: styd on wl and a doing enough ins fnl f: comf* **6/1[2]**

5133 **2** 2 ½ **Simpson (IRE)**[16] 7904 2-9-5 **83** ........................ JamieSpencer 9 89
(Ed Walker) *hld up in midfield: wnt 4th 3f out: grad clsd and effrt to chse wnr ent fnl f: kpt on but no imp on wnr* **7/1[3]**

5032 **3** 1 ¼ **Shaherezada (IRE)**[16] 7904 2-8-13 **77** ........................ AndreaAtzeni 8 81
(Clive Cox) *s.i.s and carried lft leaving stalls: sn swtchd rt and hld up in last quartet: rdn and hdwy over 1f out: wnt 3rd ins fnl f: kpt on wl: no threat to wnr* **10/1**

353 **4** 2 ¾ **Regular Income (IRE)**[21] 7739 2-8-10 **74** ........................(p) JimCrowley 5 72
(Adam West) *led and racd keenly: clr 6f out: 6 l clr 3f out: rdn 2f out: hdd over 1f out: no ex and wknd ins fnl f* **12/1**

055 **5** 1 ¼ **Gift Of Hera**[16] 7898 2-8-5 **69** ........................ MartinDwyer 2 65
(Sylvester Kirk) *stdd s: t.k.h: hld up in last quartet: effrt 3f out: drvn 2f out: kpt on same pce fr over 1f out: nvr trbld ldrs* **16/1**

3521 **6** *shd* **Ship Of The Fen**[14] 7956 2-9-3 **81** ........................ RyanMoore 6 76
(Martyn Meade) *hld up in midfield: rdn over 3f out: no imp u.p over 1f out: wl hld and kpt on same pce ins fnl f* **5/4[1]**

4032 **7** ½ **Gold Eagle**[18] 7829 2-8-1 **68** ........................ GeorgeWood(3) 7 62
(Philip McBride) *stdd s and wnt lft s: t.k.h: hld up in midfield: effrt over 2f out: unable qck and no hdwy over 1f out: wl btn fnl f* **25/1**

034 **8** 3 ¼ **Blooriedotcom (IRE)**[15] 7915 2-8-12 **76** ........................ MartinHarley 3 64
(Peter Chapple-Hyam) *tall; hld up in rr rdn wl over 2f out: no hdwy: nvr trbld ldrs* **16/1**

4450 **9** 2 **Bajan Gold (IRE)**[20] 7764 2-8-3 **67** ........................(t[1]) JimmyQuinn 1 51
(Stuart Williams) *stdd s: t.k.h: hld up in last quartet: effrt wl over 2f out: no hdwy u.p over 1f out: wknd fnl f* **20/1**

3523 **10** 14 **Cheeky Rascal (IRE)**[53] 6699 2-8-11 **75** ........................ KieranO'Neill 10 31
(Richard Hannon) *chsd ldr tl 3f out: lost pl u.p and dropped to rr 2f out: wl bhd ins fnl f* **12/1**

1m 51.44s (-0.26) **Going Correction** -0.20s/f (Firm) **10** Ran SP% **116.1**
Speed ratings (Par 97): **93,90,89,87,86 86,85,82,80,68**
CSF £47.39 CT £428.30 TOTE £6.00: £1.60, £3.20, £2.60; EX 32.70 Trifecta £128.70.
**Owner** J Barson **Bred** Epona Bloodstock Ltd **Trained** Middleham Moor, N Yorks

**FOCUS**
A useful nursery that went to the top weight. The second and third give some strength to the form and the race has been rated slightly positively.
T/Jkpt: Not Won. T/Plt: £127.10 to a £1 stake. Pool: £76,067.05 - 436.88 winning units T/Qpdt: £82.00 to a £1 stake. Pool: £6,363.72 - 57.38 winning units **Steve Payne**

8355 - 8370a (Foreign Racing) - See Raceform Interactive

# 7985 CHELMSFORD (A.W) (L-H)
Thursday, October 26

**OFFICIAL GOING: Polytrack: standard**
Wind: virtually nil Weather: light rain

## 8371 BET TOTEPLACEPOT AT BETFRED.COM NURSERY H'CAP 1m 2f (P)
**5:45** (5:46) (Class 6) (0-65,65) 2-Y-O **£3,234** (£962; £481; £240) **Stalls** Low

Form RPR

0044 **1** **Rustang (FR)**[29] 7510 2-9-5 **63** ........................(h) ShaneKelly 3 70+
(Richard Hughes) *hld up in tch in midfield and travelled strly: clsd on inner over 1f out: pushed along to ld jst ins fnl f: sn qcknd clr: pushed out: easily* **11/4[1]**

054 **2** 2 **Masters Apprentice (IRE)**[31] 7451 2-9-3 **64** ........... MitchGodwin(3) 14 65
(Sylvester Kirk) *s.i.s and bustled along early: racd in tch in last quartet: effrt and switching rt over 1f out: styd on wl ins fnl f to snatch 2nd last strides: no ch w wnr* **8/1**

3504 **3** *nk* **Tranquil Soul**[20] 7786 2-9-7 **65** ........................(b[1]) TedDurcan 12 65
(David Lanigan) *trckd ldrs on outer and travelled strly: clsd to press ldrs 2f out: rdn to ld and edgd lft 1f out: sn hdd and nt match pce on wnr: lost 2nd last strides* **8/1**

6002 **4** ½ **Daffrah**[9] 8141 2-8-5 **56** ........................ PaulHainey(7) 8 55
(James Tate) *led: rdn ent fnl 2f: hdd 1f out: kpt on same pce ins fnl f* **7/1**

000 **5** *hd* **Global Angel**[21] 7758 2-9-6 **64** ........................(b[1]) LukeMorris 9 63
(Ed Dunlop) *bmpd s: in tch in midfield: j. path over 4f out: effrt over 1f out: kpt on u.p ins fnl f: no ch w wnr* **12/1**

5403 **6** ¾ **Couldn't Could She**[9] 8141 2-9-1 **59** ........................(e[1]) SteveDrowne 11 56
(Adam West) *bmpd s: chsd ldr for 2f: styd prom: rdn over 1f out: styd on same pce ins fnl f* **14/1**

4160 **7** ¾ **Faradays Spark (IRE)**[29] 7519 2-9-1 **59** ........................ JackGarritty 2 56
(Richard Fahey) *mounted on crse: trckd ldrs and travelled wl: nt clr run wl over 1f out tl swtchd lft jst over 1f out: kpt on but no ch w wnr* **4/1[2]**

0205 **8** *hd* **Mouchee (IRE)**[19] 7829 2-9-2 **60** ........................ AdamKirby 13 55
(David Evans) *stdd and dropped in bhd after s: hld up in tch in last quartet: stuck bhd a wall of horses over 1f out: pushed along and kpt on ins fnl f: nvr trbld ldrs* **5/1[3]**

6050 **9** ½ **Misty Breese (IRE)**[43] 7057 2-8-2 **46** ........................(h[1]) JoeyHaynes 7 40
(Paul D'Arcy) *in tch in last quartet: effrt wl over 1f out: no imp u.p 1f out: wknd ins fnl f* **50/1**

6060 **10** 1 ¾ **Pearl's Calling (IRE)**[9] 8141 2-8-13 **57** ........................ BenCurtis 4 48
(David Barron) *in tch in midfield: swtchd rt over 4f out: effrt on outer over 2f out: no imp u.p over 1f out: wl hld and kpt on same pce ins fnl f* **33/1**


The Form Book Flat, Raceform Ltd, Newbury, RG14 5SJ

6000 11 *nk* **Gembari**[10] 8120 2-9-4 **62**...............(p) DavidProbert 15 53
(Ivan Furtado) *styd wd early: hdwy to press ldr after 2f: rdn and ev ch 2f out tl outpcd jst over 1f out: wknd ins fnl f* **33/1**

000 12 *1 1/4* **Speed Craft**[21] 7757 2-8-13 **57**...............(p) RyanTate 5 45
(James Eustace) *pushed along in rr early: a in rr: effrt on inner over 1f out: no imp and wknd ins fnl f* **20/1**

2m 7.93s (-0.67) **Going Correction** -0.25s/f (Stan) 12 Ran SP% **125.0**
Speed ratings (Par 93): **92,90,90,89,89 89,88,88,87,86 86,85**
CSF £26.23 CT £166.65 TOTE £3.90: £1.50, £4.30, £3.50; EX 31.00 Trifecta £262.40.
**Owner** White Beech Farm **Bred** Suc Michel Henochsberg & M Hassan **Trained** Upper Lambourn, Berks

**FOCUS**
A modest nursery, won comfortably by the favourite. The runner-up has been rated as improving on his nursery debut, with the third running her race.

## 8372 BET TOTEJACKPOT AT BETFRED.COM EBF NOVICE STKS (PLUS 10 RACE) 1m (P)
6:15 (6:19) (Class 4) 2-Y-O £6,469 (£1,925; £962; £481) Stalls Low

Form RPR

24 1 **Dukhan**[104] 4859 2-9-2 0............... JamesDoyle 1 85+
(Hugo Palmer) *trckd ldrs: effrt and swtchd rt over 2f out: swtchd lft and rdn to chal over 1f out: sn clr w ldr: drvn to ld 100yds out: styd on wl* **7/4**[1]

2 2 *1* **Communique (IRE)**[12] 8030 2-9-2 0............... PJMcDonald 3 83+
(Mark Johnston) *rdr had two goes at removing hood: sn w ldr: rdn to ld ent fnl 2f: hrd pressed and drew clr w wnr over 1f out: drvn and hdd 100yds out: no ex: hld and eased cl home* **6/1**

5 3 *4 1/2* **Mutanaqel**[28] 7543 2-9-2 0............... JimCrowley 4 72+
(Owen Burrows) *awkward leaving stalls: t.k.h: hld up in tch in rr: hdwy over 2f out: 4th over 1f out: no ch w ldng pair: kpt on into 3rd ins fnl f* **3/1**[2]

6 4 *nk* **Mekong**[41] 7128 2-9-2 0............... TedDurcan 2 71
(Sir Michael Stoute) *sn led: rdn and hdd 2f out: 3rd and outpcd over 1f out: wl hld and kpt on same pce after: lost 3rd ins fnl f* **6/1**

4 5 *8* **Cracker Factory**[70] 6108 2-9-2 0............... RyanMoore 6 52
(William Haggas) *in tch in midfield: rdn over 3f out: 5th and outpcd 2f out: sn wknd* **7/2**[3]

0 6 *1/2* **Dagueneau (IRE)**[41] 7117 2-9-2 0............... AdamKirby 7 51
(Ed Dunlop) *in tch in rr: rdn over 3f out: outpcd over 2f out and n.d after* **50/1**

00 7 *3/4* **Kingofthesingers**[14] 7987 2-9-2 0............... LukeMorris 8 49
(Sir Mark Prescott Bt) *t.k.h: hld up in last trio: rdn over 2f out: sn outpcd and n.d fnl 2f* **100/1**

8 *3/4* **Twickenham (IRE)**[18] 7854 2-9-2 0............... BenCurtis 5 47
(John Joseph Murphy, Ire) *chsd ldrs on outer: rdn over 2f out: sn struggling and outpcd: wknd over 1f out* **33/1**

1m 38.92s (-0.98) **Going Correction** -0.25s/f (Stan) 8 Ran SP% **118.0**
Speed ratings (Par 97): **94,93,88,88,80 79,78,78**
CSF £13.60 TOTE £2.30: £1.10, £1.90, £1.40; EX 12.40 Trifecta £31.50.
**Owner** Al Shaqab Racing **Bred** Ecurie Des Charmes & Skymarc Farm **Trained** Newmarket, Suffolk

**FOCUS**
Useful form from the first two, who pulled nicely clear of the rest. It's been rated around the winner.

## 8373 BET TOTEQUADPOT AT BETFRED.COM FILLIES' NOVICE STKS (PLUS 10 RACE) 7f (P)
6:45 (6:50) (Class 4) 2-Y-O £6,469 (£1,925; £962; £481) Stalls Low

Form RPR

5621 1 **Bath And Tennis (IRE)**[9] 8131 2-9-6 72...............(b) LukeMorris 13 79
(Sir Mark Prescott Bt) *t.k.h: led after 1f: clr 4f out: rdn 2f out: drvn fnl f: kpt on and a holding on: rdn out* **5/1**[2]

04 2 *1* **Cwynar**[22] 7724 2-9-0 0............... DavidProbert 5 70
(Charles Hills) *led for 1f: chsd wnr after: rdn ent fnl 2f: drvn over 1f out: hung lft but kpt on and steadily clsd ins fnl f: nvr quite getting to wnr* **16/1**

3 *nk* **Jamaican Jill** 2-9-0 0............... MartinDwyer 1 69
(William Muir) *hld up in midfield: effrt and swtchd rt over 1f out: styd on wl ins fnl f: wnt 3rd last strides: nvr quite getting to wnr* **33/1**

3 4 *nk* **Dance Me (USA)**[119] 4253 2-8-11 0............... MitchGodwin(3) 2 69
(Sylvester Kirk) *in tch in midfield: clsd to chse ldng pair over 2f out: rdn over 1f out: drvn and styd on ins fnl f: nvr quite getting on terms w wnr: lost 3rd last strides* **7/1**[3]

5 *3/4* **Sweet Symphony** 2-9-0 0............... RyanTate 3 67
(Marco Botti) *hld up in rr of main gp: gd hdwy on inner over 1f out: swtchd rt jst over 1f out: kpt on wl ins fnl f: nt rch ldrs* **50/1**

6 *2 1/4* **Flora Sandes (USA)** 2-9-0 0...............(h[1]) WilliamBuick 8 61+
(Charlie Appleby) *t.k.h: hld up in tch in midfield: effrt over 1f out: unable qck and kpt on same pce ins fnl f* **5/1**[2]

1 7 *1* **Dotted Swiss (IRE)**[149] 3174 2-9-6 0............... TomMarquand 4 64
(Richard Hannon) *t.k.h: early: in tch in midfield: wnt 4th over 2f out: no imp u.p over 1f out: styd on same pce and lost 3 pls ins fnl f* **9/2**[1]

8 *1 1/2* **Desert Diamond** 2-9-0 0............... RyanMoore 6 54
(Sir Michael Stoute) *hld up in tch in midfield: swtchd lft and effrt over 1f out: no hdwy: nvr trbld ldrs* **8/1**

9 *2 3/4* **Mesquite** 2-9-0 0............... RichardKingscote 7 46
(Ralph Beckett) *dwlt: rn green in rr of main gp: outpcd and edgd lft over 1f out: wknd ins fnl f* **10/1**

10 *1 3/4* **Spring Waterfall (IRE)** 2-9-0 0............... OisinMurphy 12 42
(Saeed bin Suroor) *squeezed for room leaving stalls: t.k.h and hdwy to chse ldrs on outer over 6f out: lost pl over 1f out: wknd over 1f out* **14/1**

11 *3/4* **Collegiate (IRE)** 2-9-0 0............... TedDurcan 14 40
(Sir Michael Stoute) *s.i.s: rn green in rr: pushed along on inner over 1f out: nvr trbld ldrs* **33/1**

6 12 *5* **Umaimah (USA)**[26] 7620 2-9-0 0............... JimCrowley 10 26
(William Haggas) *t.k.h: hld up in tch in midfield: rdn and btn over 1f out: bhd and eased ins fnl f* **9/2**[1]

0 13 *16* **Bucklow Brook**[7] 8189 2-9-0 0............... RobertWinston 11
(David Brown) *midfield: wd bnd 3f out: sn lost pl: bhd and eased fnl f: t.o* **100/1**

1m 25.42s (-1.78) **Going Correction** -0.25s/f (Stan) 13 Ran SP% **123.8**
Speed ratings (Par 94): **100,98,98,98,97 94,93,91,88,86 85,80,61**
CSF £83.69 TOTE £7.50: £2.30, £6.20, £9.50; EX 120.60 Trifecta £2431.30.
**Owner** Timothy J Rooney **Bred** Kildaragh Stud **Trained** Newmarket, Suffolk

**FOCUS**
On paper there were some interesting newcomers here, but the market wasn't keen on any of them and the race was dominated by the most exposed runner in the line-up. The winner was confirming her recent good effort at Kempton.

## 8374 BET TOTEEXACTA AT BETFRED.COM FILLIES' H'CAP 7f (P)
7:15 (7:18) (Class 5) (0-75,77) 3-Y-O+ £5,175 (£1,540; £769; £384) Stalls Low

Form RPR

21 1 **Diagnostic**[20] 7793 3-9-5 **75**............... RyanMoore 4 92+
(William Haggas) *t.k.h: trckd ldrs tl wnt 2nd over 2f out: rdn to ld over 1f out: r.o wl and in command ins fnl f: readily* **4/5**[1]

4056 2 *3* **Isstoora (IRE)**[17] 7878 3-8-7 **66**...............(h[1]) DavidEgan(3) 1 71
(Marco Botti) *hld up in tch in rr of main gp: rdn and hdwy on inner ent fnl 2f: chsd wnr 1f out: no threat to wnr but kpt on for clr 2nd ins fnl f* **12/1**

5305 3 *2 1/4* **Ariena (IRE)**[19] 7830 3-9-6 **76**............... AdamKirby 9 75
(Clive Cox) *t.k.h: hld up in tch in rr of main gp: effrt and wd bnd 2f out: hdwy 1f out: styd on ins fnl f to go 3rd 50yds out: no ch w wnr* **8/1**[3]

3656 4 *1 1/4* **Pretty Bubbles**[36] 7282 8-9-4 **72**...............(v) AdamBeschizza 8 69
(J R Jenkins) *stdd s: t.k.h: hld up in tch in midfield: effrt over 1f out: 3rd and no imp ins fnl f: kpt on same pce and lost 3rd 50yds out* **25/1**

0251 5 *hd* **Ibazz**[34] 7364 4-9-2 **75**...............(v[1]) ManuelFernandes(5) 2 71
(Ian Williams) *s.i.s: in rr and nvr travelling: swtchd rt 4f out: swtchd rt again and v wd bnd 2f out: hdwy 1f out: kpt on ins fnl f: nvr trbld ldrs* **9/2**[2]

0000 6 *3 1/2* **Maggie Pink**[41] 7111 8-8-12 **66**............... AlistairRawlinson 11 53
(Michael Appleby) *taken down early: hdwy to ld after 1f: rdn ent fnl 2f: hdd over 1f out sn outpcd and lost 2nd 1f out: wknd ins fnl f* **50/1**

0406 7 *1 3/4* **Lady Lydia (IRE)**[10] 8126 6-9-9 **77**...............(tp) MartinHarley 7 59
(Gay Kelleway) *s.i.s: bhd and styd wd early: clsd on to bk of field 1/2-way: effrt on inner over 1f out: nvr on terms* **66/1**

102 8 *1* **Always Thankful**[41] 7130 3-9-6 **76**...............(p) SeanLevey 10 54
(Ismail Mohammed) *t.k.h: led for 1f: chsd ldrs tl unable qck and lost pl u.p over 1f out: wknd ins fnl f* **16/1**

205 9 *1 1/2* **High On Love (IRE)**[21] 7771 3-9-6 **76**............... StevieDonohoe 3 50
(Charlie Fellowes) *chsd ldrs: rdn 3f out: struggling and btn over 1f out: wknd fnl f* **14/1**

2035 10 *9* **Himalayan Queen**[21] 7770 4-8-5 **66**............... MillyNaseb(7) 6 17
(William Jarvis) *t.k.h: hld up in tch in rr of main gp: effrt and nt clr run over 1f out: no ch after: bhd and eased ins fnl f* **25/1**

100 11 *8* **Aquamarina**[8] 8150 3-9-7 **77**............... TomMarquand 5 5
(Robyn Brisland) *chsd ldr after 1f tl over 2f out: lost pl qckly and dropped to rr over 1f out: wl bhd and eased ins fnl f* **14/1**

1m 24.36s (-2.84) **Going Correction** -0.25s/f (Stan)
**WFA** 3 from 4yo+ 2lb 11 Ran SP% **122.9**
Speed ratings (Par 100): **106,102,100,98,98 94,92,91,89,79 70**
CSF £12.74 CT £56.87 TOTE £1.60: £1.10, £4.10, £2.90; EX 14.20 Trifecta £58.10.
**Owner** Cheveley Park Stud **Bred** Cheveley Park Stud Ltd **Trained** Newmarket, Suffolk

**FOCUS**
This proved straightforward for the odds-on favourite.

## 8375 BET TOTETRIFECTA AT BETFRED.COM H'CAP 1m (P)
7:45 (7:48) (Class 4) (0-80,82) 3-Y-O+ £7,762 (£2,310; £1,154; £577) Stalls Low

Form RPR

1343 1 **Whosyourhousemate**[35] 7339 3-9-3 **79**...............(b[1]) AdamBeschizza 1 86+
(Ed Vaughan) *hld up wl in tch on inner: rdn and hdwy over 1f out: drvn to chse ldr 1f out: styd on wl u.p to ld fnl 50yds: drvn out* **6/1**[3]

036 2 *1/2* **Midnight Macchiato (IRE)**[130] 3857 4-9-3 **76**............... AdamKirby 3 83
(David Brown) *led: rdn and drifted to centre wl over 1f out: kpt on wl u.p tl hdd and no ex 50yds out* **20/1**

0530 3 *3/4* **Tadaany (IRE)**[15] 7957 5-9-1 **74**............... JamesSullivan 2 79
(Ruth Carr) *chsd ldrs: wnt 2nd ent fnl 2f: pressing ldr and swtchd rt over 1f out: kpt on wl: unable qck towards fin* **50/1**

231 4 *hd* **Dhalam (USA)**[149] 3188 3-9-4 **80**...............(t) RobertHavlin 9 86+
(John Gosden) *hld up in tch towards rr: hdwy on inner over 1f out: chsd ldrs 1f out: keeping on and pressing ldrs whn short of room and hmpd wl ins fnl f* **6/1**[3]

3411 5 *2 1/2* **Musical Terms**[21] 7759 3-9-4 **80**............... RyanMoore 10 78+
(William Haggas) *bmpd sn after s: t.k.h: hld up in midfield: effrt over 1f out: hung lft and no imp 1f out: kpt on same pce ins fnl f* **2/1**[1]

3250 6 *3/4* **Election Day**[22] 7728 3-9-2 **78**............... PJMcDonald 5 74
(Mark Johnston) *hld up in midfield: effrt u.p over 1f out: kpt on ins fnl f: no threat to ldrs* **7/1**

6440 7 *nk* **Dubai's Secret**[19] 7824 4-9-4 **77**............... RobertWinston 7 74
(David Brown) *chsd ldng trio: carried rt and wd bnd 2f out: lost pl: rallied and kpt on ins fnl f: nvr threatening ldrs* **33/1**

6231 8 *1 1/4* **Cainhoe Star**[15] 7947 4-9-5 **78**............... LukeMorris 6 72
(Anthony Carson) *hld up towards rr: effrt towards inner over 1f out: kpt on but no imp ins fnl f* **5/1**[2]

0403 9 *1* **Devil's Bridge (IRE)**[69] 6158 3-9-4 **80**...............(p) TomMarquand 11 70
(Richard Hannon) *bmpd sn after s: hld up in rr: effrt u.p and n.m.r on inner over 1f out: nvr trbld ldrs* **25/1**

2226 10 *nk* **Harbour Rock**[33] 7400 3-9-4 **80**............... OisinMurphy 13 70
(David Simcock) *hld up in rr: nt clr run and swtchd rt over 1f out: drvn and no hdwy ins fnl f: nvr trbld ldrs* **10/1**

34-0 11 *1/2* **Muhajjal**[119] 4269 3-9-2 **78**............... StevieDonohoe 4 67
(George Peckham) *t.k.h: hld up in tch in midfield: effrt over 1f out: no imp and wl hld ins fnl f* **33/1**

/00- 12 *1 1/4* **Markhan (USA)**[13] 8018 4-9-7 **80**...............(bt[1]) MartinHarley 15 67
(David Marnane, Ire) *t.k.h: chsd ldr tl over 2f out: sn drifted rt and lost pl: wknd over 1f out* **25/1**

50 13 *2 1/2* **Palmerston**[19] 7823 4-9-5 **78**............... TomQueally 12 59
(Michael Appleby) *hld up in midfield: lost pl and dropped towards rr whn nt clr run over 1f out: wknd fnl f* **40/1**

5040 14 *32* **Wigan Warrior**[10] 8126 3-9-0 **76**............... JosephineGordon 8
(David Brown) *taken down early: v.s.a and plunging whn leaving stalls: lost many l and nvr any ch of rcvring: eased over 1f out: t.o* **33/1**

1m 37.66s (-2.24) **Going Correction** -0.25s/f (Stan)
**WFA** 3 from 4yo+ 3lb 14 Ran SP% **125.8**
Speed ratings (Par 105): **101,100,99,99,97 96,96,94,93,93 92,91,89,57**
CSF £126.95 CT £3384.77 TOTE £6.00: £2.30, £5.80, £11.40; EX 126.10 Trifecta £4918.10.
**Owner** Ballymore Downunder Syndicate **Bred** Heather Raw **Trained** Newmarket, Suffolk
■ Stewards' Enquiry : Adam Beschizza three-day ban: careless riding (9-11 Nov)

**FOCUS**
A fair handicap.

## 8376 BET TOTEWIN AT BETFRED.COM H'CAP — 1m (P)
**8:15** (8:19) (Class 6) (0-65,66) 3-Y-O+ — **£3,234** (£962; £481; £240) **Stalls** Low

Form — RPR

0032 **1** **Titan Goddess**[10] 8125 5-9-7 **65**........ JimCrowley 2 — 72
(Mike Murphy) *hld up in tch in midfield on inner: swtchd rt and effrt over 1f out: rdn to chse ldr 1f out: drvn and chalng 100yds out: styd on to ld last strides* **3/1**[1]

-053 **2** *hd* **Mach One**[21] 7761 3-9-1 **62**........(p) OisinMurphy 3 — 68
(Archie Watson) *led: rdn and qcknd over 1f out: drvn ins fnl f: hrd pressed 100yds out: kpt on: hdd last strides* **3/1**[1]

6350 **3** *¾* **Miss Mirabeau**[28] 7541 3-8-12 **59**........(b) LukeMorris 10 — 63
(Sir Mark Prescott Bt) *stdd after s: hld up in rr: swtchd lft to inner after 1f: hdwy over 2f out: rdn to chse ldrs 1f out: kpt on same pce u.p fnl 100yds* **25/1**

0031 **4** *3* **Beepeecee**[20] 7792 3-9-3 **64**........(b) ShaneKelly 5 — 61
(Richard Hughes) *hld up in rr: pushed along 2f out: rdn and hdwy over 1f out: chsd ldng trio ins fnl f: kpt on but no threat to ldrs* **7/1**[3]

3001 **5** *3* **Jack Nevison**[30] 7480 4-8-11 **62**........(v) GabrieleMalune(7) 9 — 53
(Michael Appleby) *taken down early: chsd ldr: rdn and unable qck over 1f out: lost 2nd 1f out: wknd ins fnl f* **25/1**

0651 **6** *1* **Art's Desire (IRE)**[28] 7539 3-9-4 **65**........ LiamKeniry 4 — 52
(Ed Walker) *hld up towards rr: nt clr run ent fnl 2f tl swtchd rt ent fnl f: styd on ins fnl f: nvr trbld ldrs* **5/1**[2]

4000 **7** *½* **Ravenhoe (IRE)**[17] 7894 4-9-0 **58**........ PJMcDonald 1 — 45
(Mark Johnston) *chsd ldrs: 3rd and drvn ent fnl 2f: unable qck over 1f out: wknd ins fnl f* **10/1**

-221 **8** *2* **Honey Badger**[26] 7606 6-9-0 **61**........(p) GeorgeWood(3) 12 — 43
(Michael Herrington) *chsd ldrs: effrt ent fnl 2f: unable qck u.p over 1f out: wknd ins fnl f* **10/1**

3466 **9** *½* **Nuncio**[21] 7769 3-9-3 **64**........ TomQueally 6 — 44
(Daniel Kubler) *hld up in tch in midfield: effrt over 1f out: drvn 1f out: no imp and kpt on same pce after: nvr trbld ldrs* **33/1**

0005 **10** *2* **Rivers Of Asia**[29] 7514 4-9-6 **64**........ JohnFahy 14 — 40
(Martin Smith) *wd: midfield tl dropped to last quartet after 3f out: effrt over 1f out: no hdwy and wknd fnl f* **50/1**

4233 **11** *3* **The Bear Can Fly**[39] 7199 3-9-2 **63**........(p1) KieranShoemark 8 — 31
(David Menuisier) *squeezed out and hmpd leaving stalls: rcvrd to r in midfield and t.k.h after 1f out: rdn over 1f out: sn btn: wknd fnl f* **20/1**

2300 **12** *¾* **Loveatfirstsight**[12] 8031 4-8-11 **55**........(p) DanielMuscutt 7 — 22
(Jane Chapple-Hyam) *t.k.h: hld up in rr: nt clr run and swtchd rt over 1f out: effrt u.p 1f out: no imp: wknd fnl f* **20/1**

0004 **13** *19* **Masonic (IRE)**[47] 6946 3-9-1 **62**........(h) MartinHarley 13
(Robyn Brisland) *chsd ldrs on outer: rdn and lost pl ent fnl 2f out: bhd and eased ins fnl f: t.o* **20/1**

1m 37.68s (-2.22) **Going Correction** -0.25s/f (Stan)
**WFA** 3 from 4yo+ 3lb — **13** Ran SP% **124.2**
Speed ratings (Par 101): **101,100,100,97,94 93,92,90,90,88 85,84,65**
CSF £10.48 CT £203.64 TOTE £3.90: £1.80, £1.50, £4.20; EX 16.30 Trifecta £277.30.
**Owner** Phoebe's Friends **Bred** Mrs A D Bourne **Trained** Westoning, Beds

**FOCUS**
Modest form. The third has been rated back to this year's turf form.

## 8377 2018 MEMBERSHIP NOW AVAILABLE MAIDEN STKS — 1m 5f 66y(P)
**8:45** (8:47) (Class 5) 3-Y-O+ — **£5,175** (£1,540; £769; £384) **Stalls** Low

Form — RPR

2435 **1** **Steaming (IRE)**[52] 6765 3-9-5 75........(p1) RichardKingscote 1 — 76
(Ralph Beckett) *hld up in tch in midfield on inner: swtchd rt 2f out: effrt over 1f out: r.o to ld 100yds out: gng away at fin* **8/1**

5432 **2** *1½* **Marine One**[118] 4307 3-9-5 75........ OisinMurphy 2 — 73
(David Simcock) *t.k.h: hld up in tch in last pair: clsd over 2f out: effrt u.p over 1f out: pressed ldrs and hung lft ins fnl f: 2nd and styd on same pce fnl 75yds* **9/4**[1]

4- **3** *½* **Ocean Of Love**[358] 7761 3-8-11 0........ DavidEgan(3) 4 — 67
(Saeed bin Suroor) *sn led and t.k.h: hdd after 2f and chsd ldrs: swtchd rt and rdn ent fnl 2f: swtchd rt again and drvn to press ldrs 1f out: kpt on same pce fnl 75yds* **4/1**[3]

2203 **4** *1* **Musaahim (USA)**[23] 7708 3-9-5 81........ JimCrowley 6 — 71
(Roger Varian) *chsd ldrs tl wnt 2nd 10f out tl led over 2f out: sn pushed along: rdn over 1f out: hdd 100yds out: wknd towards fin* **5/2**[2]

0460 **5** *4½* **Two Dollars (IRE)**[65] 6293 3-9-5 59........ DavidProbert 5 — 64
(William Jarvis) *stdd s: pushed along early: hld up in rr: effrt over 2f out: sn outpcd and wl hld over 1f out: plugged on* **66/1**

334 **6** *nk* **Mahabba (IRE)**[16] 7935 3-9-0 75........ LukeMorris 3 — 58
(Luca Cumani) *trckd ldrs and travelled wl: wnt 2nd 2f out: sn hung lft and unable qck: outpcd and btn 1f out: wknd ins fnl f* **7/1**

42 **7** *15* **Assiduous**[122] 4146 3-9-5 0........ PJMcDonald 7 — 41
(Mark Johnston) *chsd ldrs: hdwy to ld after 2f: rdn and hdd over 2f out: lost pl and bhd 1f out: fdd* **10/1**

2m 50.9s (-2.70) **Going Correction** -0.25s/f (Stan) — **7** Ran SP% **113.5**
Speed ratings (Par 103): **98,97,96,96,93 93,83**
CSF £26.03 TOTE £10.30: £3.50, £1.80; EX 42.90 Trifecta £149.10.
**Owner** Gc Hartigan, Adg Oldrey & Ghc Wakefield **Bred** Mrs Brid Cosgrove **Trained** Kimpton, Hants

**FOCUS**
This was fairly steadily run and developed into a bit of a dash up the straight.
T/Jkpt: £7,246.66 to a £1 stake. 0.5 winning units. T/Plt: £241.80 to a £1 stake. Pool: £109,001.15 - 329.05 winning units T/Qpdt: £80.90 to a £1 stake. Pool: £12,523.50 - 114.45 winning units **Steve Payne**

8378 - (Foreign Racing) - See Raceform Interactive

# 7144 DONCASTER (L-H)
Friday, October 27

**OFFICIAL GOING: Good (good to soft in places on round course) changing to good to soft after race 1 (1.20)**
Wind: Virtually nil Weather: Fine and dry

## 8379 OWLERTON GREYHOUND STADIUM NURSERY H'CAP — 1m (S)
**1:20** (1:22) (Class 3) (0-95,92) 2-Y-O
**£6,847** (£1,537; £1,537; £512; £256; £128) **Stalls** High

Form — RPR

535 **1** **Ventura Knight (IRE)**[17] 7921 2-9-7 **92**........ PJMcDonald 4 — 95
(Mark Johnston) *mde all: rdn along and qcknd over 2f out: drvn and edgd rt ins fnl f: kpt on wl towards fin* **20/1**

3126 **2** *nk* **Regimented (IRE)**[26] 7648 2-9-6 **91**........ RyanMoore 1 — 93
(Richard Hannon) *hld up in tch: hdwy 1/2-way: trckd ldrs over 2f out: rdn over 1f out: drvn to chal ins fnl f: ev ch tl no ex nr line* **5/1**[3]

3142 **2** *dht* **Che Bella (IRE)**[17] 7921 2-8-12 **83**........ JoeFanning 5 — 85
(Keith Dalgleish) *trckd ldrs: hdwy 3f out: rdn to chal over 1f out: drvn and ev ch ins fnl f: no ex nr fin* **8/1**

6122 **4** *1¼* **Algam (IRE)**[23] 7741 2-9-3 **88**........(b1) SeanLevey 2 — 87
(Richard Hannon) *hld up in rr: hdwy 3f out: chsd ldrs over 1f out: sn rdn: drvn and kpt on fnl f* **6/1**

415 **5** *hd* **Dubhe**[48] 6925 2-9-5 **90**........ JamesDoyle 8 — 89
(Charlie Appleby) *dwlt and hld up in rr: hdwy over 3f out: rdn along 2f out: drvn over 1f out: styd on fnl f: nrst fin* **2/1**[1]

6435 **6** *1½* **Character Witness (IRE)**[13] 8039 2-8-8 **79**........ AndreaAtzeni 6 — 75
(Roger Varian) *trckd wnr: cl up over 3f out: rdn along 2f out: sn drvn and grad wknd* **9/2**[2]

4310 **7** *1* **Amazing Michele (FR)**[29] 7552 2-8-6 **77**........ BarryMcHugh 7 — 70
(Richard Fahey) *chsd ldrs: pushed along and lost pl 1/2-way: sn rdn and n.d* **16/1**

4200 **8** *1* **International Man**[14] 8008 2-8-8 **79**........ PaulHanagan 3 — 70
(Richard Fahey) *trckd ldng pair: pushed along 3f out: rdn over 2f pout: sn drvn and wknd* **14/1**

1m 41.82s (2.52) **Going Correction** +0.225s/f (Good) — **8** Ran SP% **110.9**
Speed ratings (Par 99): **96,95,95,94,94 92,91,90**
PL: 2.40 Che Bella, 1.90 Regimented; EX: 48.70, 57.80; CSF: VK&R 54.74, VK&CB 79.21; TC:VK&R&CB 425.75, VK&CB&R 452.09; TF: VK&R&CB 666.00, VK&CB&R 822.20 TOTE £17.60: £3.50.
**Owner** Middleham Park Racing XXXVII **Bred** L K I Bloodstock Ltd **Trained** Middleham Moor, N Yorks

**FOCUS**
All race distances as advertised. The official going was good, with some good to soft patches on the round course (GoingStick 7.5), though the riders in the opener felt it was a bit softer than that on the straight course. A decent little nursery to start in which they raced centre to nearside. This was a victory for enterprise with the winner repeating the best of this year's form.

## 8380 RACING POST TROPHY BETTING AT 188BET EBF MAIDEN FILLIES' STKS (PLUS 10 RACE) — 1m (S)
**1:50** (1:53) (Class 5) 2-Y-O — **£3,234** (£962; £481; £240) **Stalls** High

Form — RPR

4 **1** **Mrs Sippy (USA)**[14] 7997 2-9-0 0........ JamieSpencer 6 — 86
(David Simcock) *hld up towards rr: smooth hdwy over 3f out: cl up on bit 2f out: shkn up to ld over 1f out: rdn ins fnl f and kpt on* **2/1**[1]

**2** *1¼* **Ficanas** 2-9-0 0........ DanielMuscutt 3 — 83+
(Marco Botti) *dwlt and towards rr: hdwy over 3f out: rdn along to chse ldrs 2f out: styd on wl to chse wnr ins fnl f: no imp towards fin* **50/1**

0 **3** *1¼* **Gumriyah**[14] 8006 2-9-0 0........ RobertHavlin 13 — 80
(John Gosden) *trckd ldrs: hdwy 3f out and cl up: rdn to take slt ld 2f out: sn jnd and rdn: drvn and hdd over 1f out: kpt on same pce* **4/1**[2]

4 **4** *4* **Sailing Home**[23] 7733 2-9-0 0........ DanielTudhope 11 — 71
(Michael Bell) *trckd ldr: hdwy 3f out: cl up and rdn 2f out: sn drvn and wknd appr fnl f* **6/1**[3]

**5** *2½* **Nassya** 2-9-0 0........ NickyMackay 15 — 65
(John Gosden) *trckd ldrs: pushed along over 2f out: sn rdn and wknd over 1f out* **11/1**

40 **6** *nk* **Birdette (IRE)**[98] 5127 2-9-0 0........ PJMcDonald 7 — 65
(Mark Johnston) *led: rdn along over 2f out: sn hdd and drvn: grad wknd* **33/1**

**7** *½* **Pilaster** 2-9-0 0........ AndreaAtzeni 2 — 63+
(Roger Varian) *towards rr: hdwy 3f out: pushed along and edgd lft 2f out: sn rdn and kpt on fnl f* **10/1**

**8** *hd* **Lunar Corona** 2-9-0 0........ RyanMoore 4 — 63
(Sir Michael Stoute) *in tch: pushed along 3f out: rdn over 2f out: sn wknd* **7/1**

65 **9** *¾* **Midas Maggie**[29] 7535 2-8-11 0........ CallumShepherd(3) 12 — 61
(Charles Hills) *a towards rr* **80/1**

**10** *1* **Qaswarah (IRE)** 2-9-0 0........ DavidProbert 10 — 59
(Ed Dunlop) *chsd ldrs: rdn along wl over 2f out: sn wknd* **50/1**

0 **11** *hd* **Sageness (IRE)**[23] 7733 2-9-0 0........ FranBerry 9 — 59
(Ed Dunlop) *dwlt: a in rr* **66/1**

4 **12** *nk* **Golden Guide**[56] 6658 2-9-0 0........ JoeyHaynes 8 — 58
(K R Burke) *trckd ldrs: pushed along over 3f out: rdn wl over 2f out and sn wknd* **28/1**

**13** *¾* **Roystonia (IRE)** 2-9-0 0........ JamesDoyle 5 — 56
(Hugo Palmer) *a towards rr* **12/1**

**14** *12* **Fair Island** 2-9-0 0........ CharlesBishop 14 — 29
(Sarah Hollinshead) *in tch: rdn along 3f out: sn wknd* **150/1**

**15** *2¾* **Harbour Sunrise** 2-8-11 0........ CharlieBennett(3) 1 — 22
(Shaun Harris) *a towards rr* **150/1**

1m 41.02s (1.72) **Going Correction** +0.225s/f (Good) — **15** Ran SP% **119.6**
Speed ratings (Par 92): **100,98,97,93,91 90,90,90,89,88 88,87,87,75,72**
CSF £137.51 TOTE £2.70: £1.30, £13.40, £1.60; EX 170.20 Trifecta £789.80.
**Owner** St Albans Bloodstock Limited **Bred** Andrew Stone **Trained** Newmarket, Suffolk

FOCUS
The official going was changed to good to soft before this race. Several big stables were represented in this maiden, which has been won by some high-class fillies in recent years including the French Oaks winner Star Of Seville. They raced as one group up the middle and the first three pulled nicely clear of the rest. The winning time was 0.8sec quicker than the opening nursery, so solid form.

## 8381 BET £10 GET £20 AT 188BET EBF MAIDEN STKS (DIV I) 7f 6y
**2:25** (2:26) (Class 5) 2-Y-O £3,234 (£962; £481; £240) Stalls High

Form RPR
02 **1** **Breath Caught**[56] 6654 2-9-5 0 RyanMoore 3 86+
(Ralph Beckett) *mde all: rdn clr wl over 1f out: readily* **1/1**[1]

0 **2** 3 ¾ **Flavius Titus**[134] 3754 2-9-5 0 AndreaAtzeni 9 74
(Roger Varian) *prom: trckd wnr 3f out: rdn along 2f out: drvn over 1f out: kpt on same pce u.p fnl f* **8/1**

**3** *hd* **Kripke (IRE)** 2-9-5 0 BenCurtis 6 74
(David Barron) *in rr: hdwy 3f out: chsd ldrs on outer wl over 1f out: sn rdn: drvn and edgd rt ins fnl f: kpt on* **8/1**

4 **4** ½ **Grandscape**[37] 7281 2-9-5 0 PJMcDonald 1 72
(Ed Dunlop) *dwlt and wnt lft s: towards rr: hdwy 4f out: rdn to chse ldrs 2f out: drvn and edgd rt ins fnl f: kpt on* **5/1**[2]

**5** 1 **Mukhaater** 2-9-5 0 JamesDoyle 10 70
(Charles Hills) *trckd ldrs: pushed along over 2f out: rdn wl over 1f out: kpt on same pce* **14/1**

60 **6** *hd* **Technological**[56] 6653 2-9-5 0 TomQueally 7 71
(George Margarson) *hld up towards rr: hdwy at 1/2-way: rdn to chse ldrs over 2f out: styng on whn n.m.r and hmpd jst ins fnl f: one pce after* **33/1**

3 **7** 2 **Taghee**[37] 7280 2-9-2 0 MarcMonaghan(3) 2 66
(Marco Botti) *trckd ldrs: hdwy over 2f out: rdn along wl over 1f out: drvn and hld whn n.m.r and hmpd jst ins fnl f: one pce after* **6/1**[3]

00 **8** 9 **Lady Jayne (IRE)**[56] 6653 2-9-0 0 GeorgeDowning 8 36
(Ian Williams) *a in rr* **200/1**

05 **9** 3 **Society Secret (IRE)**[34] 7411 2-9-5 0 AlistairRawlinson 5 33
(Tom Dascombe) *prom: rdn along over 3f out: sn wknd* **66/1**

0 **10** 1 ¾ **Jiro Boy**[20] 7818 2-9-2 0 PhilDennis(3) 4 28
(Rebecca Bastiman) *chsd ldrs: rdn along 1/2-way: sn wknd* **200/1**

1m 29.09s (2.79) **Going Correction** +0.225s/f (Good) **10** Ran SP% **115.3**
Speed ratings (Par 95): **93,88,88,87,86 86,84,73,70,68**
CSF £9.80 TOTE £1.70: £1.10, £2.30, £3.10; EX 9.50 Trifecta £50.70.
**Owner** K Abdullah **Bred** Juddmonte Farms Ltd **Trained** Kimpton, Hants

FOCUS
The first division of an ordinary maiden lacking depth and the favourite bolted up with few getting into it. They raced closer to the stands' rail this time.

## 8382 BET £10 GET £20 AT 188BET EBF MAIDEN STKS (DIV II) 7f 6y
**3:00** (3:01) (Class 5) 2-Y-O £3,234 (£962; £481; £240) Stalls High

Form RPR
3 **1** **Amplification (USA)**[11] 8119 2-9-5 0 RyanMoore 2 77
(Ed Dunlop) *trckd ldng pair: hdwy over 2f out: led 11/2f out and sn rdn: jnd ent fnl f and sn drvn: hdd narrowly last 75 yds: rallied wl to ld on line* **7/4**[1]

3 **2** *shd* **Epic Fantasy**[34] 7392 2-9-5 0 AndreaAtzeni 4 77
(Charles Hills) *t.k.h early: trckd ldrs: hdwy 2f out: rdn to chal ent fnl f: drvn and slt ld last 75 yds: hdd and no ex on line* **15/8**[2]

30 **3** 2 **Moxy Mares**[57] 6636 2-9-5 0 GeorgeDowning 5 71
(Daniel Mark Loughnane) *dwlt and hld up towards rr: hdwy over 2f out: rdn wl over 1f out: styd on fnl f* **20/1**

4 **4** 2 ¼ **Consultant**[23] 7740 2-9-5 0 DavidProbert 6 66
(Andrew Balding) *cl up on inner: rdn to take slt ld 2f out: hdd 11/2f out: sn drvn and grad wknd fnl f* **7/1**[3]

4 **5** 1 ¼ **Elusif (IRE)**[48] 6916 2-9-5 0 JamesDoyle 7 62
(Marco Botti) *trckd ldrs: pushed along wl over 2f out: rdn wl over 1f out: kpt on same pce* **8/1**

05 **6** ½ **Mister Maestro**[43] 7079 2-9-5 0 SeanLevey 3 61
(Richard Hannon) *led: rdn along and hdd 2f out: sn drvn and wknd over 1f out* **16/1**

0 **7** 1 ¼ **Harry Callahan (IRE)**[34] 7392 2-9-5 0 BenCurtis 1 58
(Tom Dascombe) *in tch on outer: rdn along wl over 2f out: sn one pce* **22/1**

4 **8** 2 **Heavenly Guest**[11] 8112 2-9-5 0 TomQueally 8 53
(George Margarson) *a in rr* **40/1**

0 **9** 1 **Spring Praise (IRE)**[11] 8119 2-9-5 0 (t[1]) GrahamLee 9 50
(Marco Botti) *dwlt: a in rr* **66/1**

1m 29.38s (3.08) **Going Correction** +0.225s/f (Good) **9** Ran SP% **113.7**
Speed ratings (Par 95): **91,90,88,86,84 84,82,80,79**
CSF £4.90 TOTE £2.40: £1.10, £1.10, £6.40; EX 6.00 Trifecta £48.10.
**Owner** S F Hui **Bred** Don Alberto Corporation **Trained** Newmarket, Suffolk

FOCUS
Unlike in the first division, all of these had run before. Two dominated the market and there was precious between them at the line as well. Again they raced nearside and the winning time was 0.29sec slower than the first leg.

## 8383 RACING POST/SIS BETTING SHOP MANAGER H'CAP 6f 2y
**3:35** (3:39) (Class 2) (0-105,102) 3-Y-O+
£12,450 (£3,728; £1,864; £932; £466; £234) Stalls High

Form RPR
0000 **1** **Perfect Pasture**[13] 8044 7-9-5 97 (v) DavidAllan 13 106
(Michael Easterby) *prom centre: cl up 1/2-way: rdn to ld over 1f out: drvn ins fnl f: kpt on wl towards fin* **28/1**

1513 **2** *nk* **Flying Pursuit**[13] 8044 4-9-6 101 (p) RachelRichardson(3) 14 109
(Tim Easterby) *overall ldr centre: rdn along 2f out: hdd over 1f out: sn drvn and ev ch tl no ex nr fin* **8/1**[2]

0000 **3** *nk* **Naadirr (IRE)**[32] 7455 6-9-0 92 (v) GrahamLee 7 99
(Kevin Ryan) *racd towards far side: in tch: smooth hdwy 2f out: chsd ldrs over 1f out: rdn and ev ch ent fnl f: sn drvn and kpt on* **16/1**

0660 **4** ¾ **Hoof It**[13] 8044 10-8-10 95 HarrisonShaw(7) 16 100
(Michael Easterby) *racd towards stands rail: prom: cl up 2f out: sn rdn and ev ch: drvn ins fnl f: one pce towards fin* **33/1**

4200 **5** *nse* **Aeolus**[27] 7611 6-9-9 101 PatCosgrave 8 107
(Ed Walker) *racd towards far side: hld up: hdwy over 2f out: rdn to chse ldrs over 1f out: drvn and kpt on fnl f* **11/1**[3]

641 **6** 1 ¼ **Boy In The Bar**[3] 8319 6-9-0 97 6ex (b) ManuelFernandes(5) 5 97
(Ian Williams) *prom centre: cl up over 2f out and sn rdn: drvn over 1f out: grad wknd* **12/1**

0000 **7** 1 ¼ **Big Time (IRE)**[27] 7626 6-9-2 94 (v) KevinStott 12 90
(Kevin Ryan) *chsd ldrs centre: rdn along 2f out: drvn over 1f out: kpt on same pce* **40/1**

2000 **8** ¾ **Naggers (IRE)**[27] 7626 6-9-3 95 PaulMulrennan 9 89
(Paul Midgley) *towards rr: hdwy centre 2f out: rdn along wl over 1f out: n.m.r ent fnl f: kpt on* **20/1**

0530 **9** *nk* **Shanghai Glory (IRE)**[27] 7611 4-9-10 102 FranBerry 11 95
(Charles Hills) *towards rr: hdwy centre 2f out: rdn over 1f out: n.m.r ent fnl f: kpt on* **12/1**

0020 **10** ¾ **Al Qahwa (IRE)**[13] 8044 4-9-6 98 (b[1]) DanielTudhope 17 89
(David O'Meara) *rr: hdwy centre 2f out: sn swtchd lft and rdn: styd on fnl f* **12/1**

0006 **11** *nk* **Captain Colby (USA)**[10] 8138 5-8-12 90 SeanLevey 6 80
(Ed Walker) *dwlt and rr towards far side: rdn along and hdwy over 2f out: kpt on u.p fnl f* **8/1**[2]

4236 **12** *nk* **Red Pike (IRE)**[27] 7626 6-9-0 92 TomEaves 15 81
(Bryan Smart) *chsd ldrs centre: rdn along over 2f out: sn drvn and wknd* **20/1**

0030 **13** 1 ¼ **Mobsta (IRE)**[27] 7626 5-9-3 95 CharlesBishop 21 80
(Mick Channon) *a towards rr nr stands side* **33/1**

5003 **14** ½ **Robero**[11] 8104 5-9-2 94 BenCurtis 1 77
(Michael Easterby) *racd towards far side: chsd ldrs: rdn along over 2f out: sn wknd* **25/1**

6603 **15** ¾ **George Bowen (IRE)**[27] 7612 5-8-12 90 (p) TonyHamilton 10 71
(Richard Fahey) *chsd ldrs centre: rdn along 2f out: sn wknd* **14/1**

5030 **16** 2 ¼ **Dougan**[16] 7950 5-8-9 90 DavidEgan(3) 3 64
(David Evans) *racd towards far side: in tch on outer: rdn along over 2f out: sn drvn and wknd* **14/1**

0020 **17** ½ **Go Far**[20] 7828 7-8-10 93 (v) JoshuaBryan(5) 18 65
(Alan Bailey) *racd nr stands rail: chsd ldrs: rdn along over 2f out: sn drvn and wknd over 1f out* **50/1**

4611 **18** *nk* **Hyperfocus (IRE)**[27] 7612 3-9-5 98 JamesDoyle 4 69
(Hugo Palmer) *prom centre: rdn along over 2f out: sn drvn and wknd over 1f out* **6/1**[1]

5010 **19** *nk* **Highland Acclaim (IRE)**[20] 7828 6-8-12 90 (h) DavidProbert 2 60
(David O'Meara) *racd towards far side: dwlt: a towards rr* **80/1**

0600 **20** ½ **Gunmetal (IRE)**[105] 4854 4-8-13 91 AndreaAtzeni 20 59
(Charles Hills) *racd towards stands side: a in rr* **25/1**

1000 **21** 1 ¾ **Kickboxer (IRE)**[6] 8238 6-9-4 96 (v[1]) TomQueally 19 59
(Michael Appleby) *racd towards stands side: a towards rr* **80/1**

0005 **22** *nk* **Outback Traveller (IRE)**[13] 8044 6-9-5 97 (p) JamieSpencer 22 59
(Robert Cowell) *racd towards stands side: a towards rr* **12/1**

1m 12.8s (-0.80) **Going Correction** +0.225s/f (Good)
**WFA** 3 from 4yo+ 1lb **22** Ran SP% **128.2**
Speed ratings (Par 109): **114,113,113,112,112 110,108,107,107,106 106,105,103,103,102 99,98,98,97,97 94,94**
CSF £221.21 CT £3798.11 TOTE £33.70: £6.70, £2.30, £4.10, £6.70; EX 371.10 Trifecta £4097.60 Part won..
**Owner** S Hull & S Hollings **Bred** Mrs Jean Turpin **Trained** Sheriff Hutton, N Yorks
■ Stewards' Enquiry : David Allan four-day ban; using his whip above the permitted level (Nov 10-11, 13, 15)

FOCUS
A hot sprint handicap with the field racing centre to nearside and those that raced more towards the middle had the advantage. Not many got into it considering the type of race and it resulted in a 1-2-4 for the Easterbys.

## 8384 FREE BETS AT 188BET CASINO H'CAP 1m 6f 115y
**4:10** (4:11) (Class 3) (0-95,91) 3-Y-O-£7,561 (£2,263; £1,131; £566; £282) Stalls Low

Form RPR
11 **1** **Golden Birthday (FR)**[18] 7880 6-9-7 84 (t) FranBerry 2 96+
(Harry Fry) *trckd ldrs on inner: smooth hdwy over 3f out: led wl over 2f out: rdn over 1f out: kpt on strly fnl f* **11/8**[1]

04/0 **2** 2 ½ **Zaidiyn (FR)**[90] 5397 7-8-12 80 BenRobinson(5) 3 84
(Brian Ellison) *dwlt: hld up in rr: hdwy over 4f out: chsd ldrs over 2f out and sn rdn: drvn over 1f out: styd on fnl f* **22/1**

4650 **3** ¾ **Kensington Star**[63] 6383 4-9-7 84 (p) PaulMulrennan 5 87
(Keith Dalgleish) *trckd ldrs: hdwy over 3f out: rdn to chse wnr wl over 1f out: sn drvn and kpt on same pce* **10/1**[3]

1103 **4** 3 **Berrahri (IRE)**[41] 7143 6-9-8 85 JoeyHaynes 7 84
(John Best) *prom: trckd ldr after 4f: pushed along over 3f out: rdn over 2f out: drvn wl over 1f out: grad wknd* **14/1**

1316 **5** 1 ¼ **Great Sound (IRE)**[48] 6930 3-9-7 91 (p[1]) RobertHavlin 8 90
(John Gosden) *dwlt: hld up in rr: hdwy over 3f out: rdn along over 2f out: styd on u.p fr over 1f out: nvr nr ldrs* **7/2**[2]

002- **6** 16 **Continuum**[441] 5358 8-10-0 91 (p) CharlesBishop 9 67
(Peter Hedger) *dwlt: hld up in rr: effrt and sme hdwy 4f out: sn rdn and nvr a factor* **33/1**

3513 **7** 4 ½ **Key Bid**[42] 7110 3-9-4 88 (b) JamesDoyle 6 60
(Charlie Appleby) *trckd ldr 4f: prom: rdn along over 3f out: sn drvn and wknd* **7/2**[2]

-004 **8** 10 **Multellie**[118] 4380 5-9-2 82 RachelRichardson(3) 4 38
(Tim Easterby) *hld up in tch on inner: pushed along 4f out: rdn 3f out: sn btn* **33/1**

5000 **9** *shd* **Icefall (IRE)**[13] 8047 4-8-13 76 (t[1]) DavidAllan 1 32
(Tim Easterby) *led: rdn along 4f out: drvn 3f out: sn hdd & wknd* **33/1**

3m 12.2s (4.80) **Going Correction** +0.55s/f (Yiel)
**WFA** 3 from 4yo+ 7lb **9** Ran SP% **115.5**
Speed ratings (Par 107): **109,107,107,105,105 96,94,88,88**
CSF £40.14 CT £219.32 TOTE £2.10: £1.10, £5.60, £2.70; EX 33.00 Trifecta £211.50.
**Owner** G C Stevens **Bred** E A R L La Croix Sonnet **Trained** Seaborough, Dorset

FOCUS
A decent staying handicap which had gone to a 3yo nine times in the last ten years, but this time it went to a rather unusual older horse with the first two better known as hurdlers. They made for the centre of the track after turning for home, but gradually edged back to the inside rail.

## 8385 ROA/RACING POST OWNERS JACKPOT H'CAP 1m 2f 43y
**4:45** (4:46) (Class 3) (0-95,90) 3-Y-O £7,762 (£2,310; £1,154; £577) Stalls Low

Form RPR
2-21 **1** **Ajman King (IRE)**[26] 7652 3-9-2 85 AndreaAtzeni 8 99+
(Roger Varian) *sn trcking ldr: hdwy 3f out and sn cl up: rdn to ld wl over 1f out: styd on strly fnl f* **13/8**[1]

0010 **2** 3 ¼ **Society Red**[13] 8048 3-8-13 82 PaulHanagan 7 87
(Richard Fahey) *led: pushed along and jnd 3f out: rdn over 2f out: hdd wl over 1f out and sn drvn: kpt on: no ch w wnr* **16/1**

2611 **3** ½ **Canberra Cliffs (IRE)**[69] 6176 3-9-5 **88**............................... FranBerry 5 92
(Don Cantillon) *trckd ldrs: hdwy 3f out: effrt 2f out: sn chsng ldng pair and rdn: drvn and kpt on fnl f* **10/1**

1002 **4** 1¾ **Armandihan (IRE)**[20] 7824 3-9-0 **83**.......................... KevinStott 9 84
(Kevin Ryan) *hld up towards rr: hdwy over 3f out: rdn to chse ldrs wl over 1f out: drvn and kpt on fnl f* **6/1**[3]

0052 **5** ½ **Al Hamdany (IRE)**[30] 7516 3-9-7 **90**........................ GrahamLee 6 90
(Marco Botti) *in tch: hdwy over 3f out: rdn along to chse ldrs over 2f out: sn drvn and kpt on same pce* **20/1**

2100 **6** 1 **Glenys The Menace (FR)**[48] 6920 3-9-1 **84**.................. JoeyHaynes 3 82
(John Best) *trckd ldrs: hdwy over 3f out: rdn along over 2f out: sn drvn and no imp* **12/1**

314 **7** 3½ **Pouvoir Magique (FR)**[91] 5368 3-9-5 **88**................. JamesDoyle 10 79
(John Gosden) *dwlt: hld up: a towards rr* **4/1**[2]

0045 **8** 1½ **Ce La Vie**[24] 7702 3-8-12 **81**........................................ JamieSpencer 1 69
(Keith Dalgleish) *stdd s: hld up: a in rr* **33/1**

2260 **9** 2¾ **Sultan Baybars**[23] 7727 3-9-3 **89**.................................. DavidEgan(3) 4 71
(Roger Varian) *rrd s: a towards rr* **16/1**

5334 **10** ½ **Andok (IRE)**[11] 8111 3-8-11 **80**.................................... TonyHamilton 2 61
(Richard Fahey) *prom: pushed along 4f out: rdn 3f out: sn wknd* **14/1**

2m 14.57s (5.17) **Going Correction** +0.55s/f (Yiel) **10** Ran SP% **115.3**
Speed ratings (Par 105): **101,98,98,96,96 95,92,91,89,88**
CSF £31.20 CT £203.19 TOTE £2.40: £1.10, £3.80, £3.00; EX 26.00 Trifecta £139.50.

**Owner** Sheikh Mohammed Obaid Al Maktoum **Bred** Swordlestown Little **Trained** Newmarket, Suffolk

**FOCUS**
A useful 3yo handicap and an impressive winner, with the race rated around the runner-up. They stayed against the inside rail throughout this time.

## 8386 BEST ODDS GUARANTEED AT 188BET AMATEUR JOCKEYS ASSOCIATION AMATEUR RIDERS' H'CAP 1m 2f 43y

**5:20** (5:21) (Class 5) (0-75,76) 3-Y-O+ **£3,119** (£967; £483; £242) **Stalls** Low

Form RPR

0505 **1** **Tomahawk Kid**[23] 7735 4-10-11 **75**.............................. MissAMcCain(3) 4 85+
(Ian Williams) *hld up: hdwy wl over 2f out: chsd ldrs and swtchd lft to inner over 1f out: rdn and squeezed through ent fnl f: sn led and kpt on strly* **5/1**[1]

0253 **2** 3½ **England Expects**[78] 5838 3-9-5 **61** oh3..........................(h) MrJBrace(5) 3 65
(K R Burke) *hld up in tch: hdwy 3f out: swtchd rt to outer and effrt to chal 2f out: sn rdn and ev ch: drvn ins fnl f: kpt on* **14/1**

550 **3** 1¼ **Itlaaq**[53] 6757 11-10-1 **69**.......................................(t) MissJoannaMason 11 63
(Michael Easterby) *hld up towards rr: hdwy over 3f out: chsd ldrs 2f out: rdn over 1f out: styd on wl fnl f* **25/1**

3042 **4** *nse* **Deeley's Double (FR)**[209] 1498 4-10-0 **66**................. MissJCooley(5) 2 66
(Daniel Mark Loughnane) *trckd ldrs on inner: hdwy and swtchd rt wl over 1f out: sn rdn: kpt on fnl f* **9/1**

4254 **5** ½ **Hard Toffee (IRE)**[27] 7601 6-10-7 **68**....................... MissSBrotherton 17 67
(Conrad Allen) *trckd ;ldr: cl up 3f out: rdn along 2f out and ev ch: kpt on same pce fnl f* **12/1**

1443 **6** ½ **Hawridge Glory (IRE)**[11] 8114 3-10-5 **70**..................... MrPMillman 20 69+
(Rod Millman) *hld up: hdwy wl over 2f out: rdn wl over 1f out: kpt on fnl f* **11/2**[2]

0022 **7** ¾ **Maraakib (IRE)**[7] 8206 5-10-3 **64**............................. MrAlexFerguson 18 61
(David O'Meara) *towards rr: hdwy 3f out: rdn along wl over 1f out: styd on fnl f* **9/1**

-050 **8** *nk* **Rebel Cause (IRE)**[14] 7999 4-11-0 **75**............................(p) MrSWalker 1 71
(Richard Spencer) *hekld up in tch: hdwy over 3f out: chal over 2f out: sn rdn to ld: hdd ent fnl f: grad wknd* **10/1**

0630 **9** ½ **Marmion**[17] 7936 5-10-2 **63**.......................................(h) MissBeckySmith 7 58
(Les Eyre) *t.k.h: trckd ldng pair: hdwy and cl up 3f out: rdn along 2f out: grad wknd over 1f out* **28/1**

-002 **10** *nse* **Match My Fire (IRE)**[135] 3708 4-9-8 **62**..................(p) MissCADods(7) 19 57
(Michael Dods) *towards rr: hdwy on outer over 3f out: rdn along to chse ldrs 2f out: sn no imp* **25/1**

0206 **11** *shd* **Sir Reginald Brown**[50] 6855 3-10-4 **74**................... MissEllaMcCain(5) 8 70
(Richard Fahey) *rrd s and towards rr: hdwy on inner over 2f out: in tch and styng on whn n.m.r and hmpd on inner ent fnl f: one pce after* **13/2**

5225 **12** 1¾ **Silver Dixie (USA)**[31] 7495 7-9-7 **61**........................(p) MissKEvans(7) 16 53
(Peter Hedger) *dwlt: a towards rr* **33/1**

0600 **13** *nk* **The Gay Cavalier**[23] 7735 6-10-2 **63**..............................(t) MrHHunt 14 54
(John Ryan) *a towards rr* **33/1**

330- **14** 6 **Four Mile Beach**[176] 2687 4-10-2 **70**.................. MrKieranRundell(7) 9 49
(Malcolm Jefferson) *a in rr* **40/1**

33-6 **15** ¾ **Down Time (USA)**[11] 8109 7-9-11 **65**....................(v) MrTomMidgley(7) 10 42
(Paul Midgley) *a towards rr* **50/1**

6005 **16** 1 **Jackhammer (IRE)**[63] 6397 3-10-11 **76**...............(h) MissEmmaSayer 13 52
(Dianne Sayer) *led: rdn along 3f out: hdd 2f out: sn drvn and wknd* **40/1**

4123 **17** 5 **Ice Dancing (IRE)**[20] 7816 3-10-6 **74**.............................(h) MrBJames(3) 6 40
(Michael Bell) *chsd ldrs: rdn along 3f out: sn wknd* **6/1**[3]

300 **18** 2 **Captain Revelation**[59] 6564 5-10-2 **68**.................. MrLewisStones(5) 12 29
(Michael Mullineaux) *chsd ldrs: hdwy over 3f out: rdn along 2f out: sn wknd* **33/1**

3500 **19** 15 **Moving Robe (IRE)**[15] 7991 4-9-7 **61** oh16......(t) MissJMartensson(7) 15
(Conrad Allen) *midfield: hdwy on outer and in tch 1/2-way: rdn along over 3f out: sn wknd* **100/1**

2m 14.02s (4.62) **Going Correction** +0.55s/f (Yiel)
**WFA** 3 from 4yo+ 4lb **19** Ran SP% **130.9**
Speed ratings (Par 103): **103,100,99,99,98 98,97,97,97,97 97,95,95,90,89 89,85,83,71**
CSF £72.66 CT £1663.64 TOTE £5.70: £2.00, £3.50, £5.30, £3.40; EX 94.60 Trifecta £2007.90 Part won..

**Owner** Phil Mousley **Bred** Phil Mousley **Trained** Portway, Worcs

**FOCUS**
A modest amateur riders' handicap, but competitive enough. The winner has been rated back to something like his spring form.

T/Jkpt: Not won. T/Plt: £126.00 to a £1 stake. Pool: £85,632.95 - 496.12 winning units T/Qpdt: £12.90 to a £1 stake. Pool: £9,734.00 - 556.04 winning units **Joe Rowntree**

# 7391 NEWBURY (L-H)

Friday, October 27

**OFFICIAL GOING: Soft (5.4)**
Wind: virtually nil Weather: sunny

## 8387 JOIN HOT TO TROT FOR 2018 NOVICE STKS (PLUS 10 RACE) (DIV I) 1m (S)

**1:10** (1:12) (Class 4) 2-Y-O **£5,175** (£1,540; £769; £384) **Stalls** Centre

Form RPR

0 **1** **Military Law**[42] 7117 2-9-2 0........................................ OisinMurphy 12 82
(John Gosden) *hld up wl in tch in midfield: effrt and hdwy to chse ldr 2f out: rdn and ev ch over 1f out: led 1f out: hdd ins fnl f: sn battled bk to ld again: styd on wl* **6/1**[3]

1 **2** ½ **Blue Mist**[13] 8030 2-9-5 0........................................ KieranShoemark 10 84
(Roger Charlton) *hld up wl in tch in midfield: swtchd rt and clsd 2f out: pushed along to press ldrs 1f out: led and hung lft ins fnl f: sn hdd and unable qck towards fin* **7/4**[1]

2 **3** 2¾ **Proschema (IRE)**[29] 7543 2-9-2 0.......................... RichardKingscote 5 75+
(Tom Dascombe) *hld up in tch in midfield: effrt 2f out: sn outpcd: swtchd lft and rallied 1f out: wnt 3rd ins fnl f: styd on wout threatening ldng pair* **2/1**[2]

0 **4** 1 **Bacacarat (IRE)**[28] 7580 2-9-2 0........................................ LiamKeniry 15 72
(Andrew Balding) *trckd ldng pair tl led 2f out: rdn and hrd pressed over 1f out: hdd 1f out: wknd and lost 3rd ins fnl f* **40/1**

0 **5** 1½ **Profound (IRE)**[18] 7906 2-9-2 0........................................ JackMitchell 3 69
(Roger Varian) *trckd ldrs: effrt 2f out: 4th and outpcd ent fnl f: wknd ins fnl f* **25/1**

**6** 1¾ **Faraway Fields (USA)** 2-9-2 0........................................ SteveDrowne 1 65+
(Charles Hills) *s.i.s and swtchd rt after s: sn in tch in midfield: rdn and outpcd over 1f out: no threat to ldrs but kpt on steadily ins fnl f* **40/1**

03 **7** 1¼ **Creel**[27] 7613 2-9-2 0........................................ PhillipMakin 6 62
(David Brown) *w ldr: rdn 2f out: sn outpcd and lost pl over 1f out: wknd ins fnl f* **50/1**

6025 **8** 2¾ **Zalshah**[26] 7647 2-9-2 74........................................(p) TomMarquand 11 56
(Richard Hannon) *t.k.h: trckd ldrs: rdn over 1f out: sn drvn and btn: wknd ins fnl f* **33/1**

**9** ½ **Acquirer (IRE)** 2-9-2 0........................................ ShaneKelly 4 55
(Richard Hughes) *in tch in midfield: rdn and lost pl over 2f out: wl btn over 1f out* **50/1**

**10** 1¼ **Martinengo (IRE)** 2-9-2 0........................................ AdamKirby 7 52
(Peter Chapple-Hyam) *rn green in midfield: reminder over 4f out: effrt over 2f out: sn outpcd and wl btn over 1f out* **66/1**

4 **11** 1¾ **Brother Ralph (IRE)**[34] 7392 2-9-2 0........................................ JimCrowley 13 48
(Brian Meehan) *in tch in midfield but nvr really travelling wl: rdn over 2f out: sn btn and no ch over 1f out* **15/2**

**12** *hd* **Thunderbolt Rocks** 2-9-2 0........................................ JosephineGordon 8 47
(Hugo Palmer) *rn green in midfield: rdn over 2f out: sn struggling and wl btn over 1f out* **33/1**

00 **13** *hd* **Macho Mover (IRE)**[21] 7788 2-9-2 0........................................ TedDurcan 16 47
(Mick Channon) *hld up in tch in rr: effrt over 2f out: sn outpcd and wl btn over 1f out* **100/1**

00 **14** ½ **Arlecchino's Arc (IRE)**[13] 8030 2-9-2 0..................(p) DougieCostello 14 46
(Mark Usher) *led tl 2f out: sn lost pl and wknd ent fnl f* **100/1**

**15** 13 **Kenny George** 2-9-2 0........................................ FrannyNorton 9 16
(Mick Channon) *sn in last pair and rn green: flashed tail u.p 3f out: lost tch 2f out* **50/1**

**16** 13 **Forricherforpoorer (IRE)** 2-9-2 0........................................ AdamBeschizza 2
(William Knight) *swtchd rt after s: sn bhd and rn green: lost tch 3f out: t.o* **66/1**

1m 42.81s (3.11) **Going Correction** +0.35s/f (Good) **16** Ran SP% **121.2**
Speed ratings (Par 97): **98,97,94,93,92 90,89,86,86,84 83,82,82,82,69 56**
CSF £15.57 TOTE £5.60: £1.90, £1.10, £1.30; EX 22.20 Trifecta £50.90.

**Owner** Qatar Racing Limited **Bred** Qatar Bloodstock Ltd **Trained** Newmarket, Suffolk

**FOCUS**
The going was given as soft (GoingStick: 5.4) and all distances were as advertised. After riding in the first Adam Kirby, Steve Drowne and Liam Keniry all agreed with the official description of soft going. The first two had this between them inside the last and it proved an expensive start to the day for in-running money buyers. The race has been rated around the runner-up.

## 8388 ROBIN CRADDOCK MEMORIAL EBF MAIDEN STKS (PLUS 10 RACE) 6f 110y

**1:40** (1:44) (Class 4) 2-Y-O **£4,269** (£1,270; £634; £317) **Stalls** Centre

Form RPR

4445 **1** **Picture No Sound (IRE)**[20] 7819 2-9-2 75........... AdamMcNamara(3) 7 85
(Richard Fahey) *t.k.h: trckd ldrs: effrt to chal and hung rt ent fnl f: led ins fnl f: r.o strly and drew clr fnl 100yds* **12/1**

4 **2** 2¾ **George Of Hearts (FR)**[35] 7352 2-9-5 0........................ ShaneKelly 15 77
(Richard Hughes) *trckd ldrs: clsd to ld 2f out: sn pushed along and edgd lft: hdd ins fnl f: outpcd by wnr fnl 100yds: kpt on and hld on to 2nd towards fin* **11/10**[1]

**3** *hd* **Salute The Soldier (GER)** 2-9-5 0........................................ AdamKirby 10 77
(Clive Cox) *chsd ldrs: effrt to press ldrs 2f out: ev ch 1f out tl outpcd by wnr fnl 100yds: battling for 2nd after: kpt on* **3/1**[2]

**4** 1½ **Ballyquin (IRE)** 2-9-5 0........................................ OisinMurphy 4 73
(Andrew Balding) *in tch in midfield: pushed along over 2f out: swtchd lft over 1f out: hdwy 1f out: styd on wl ins fnl f to go 4th towards fin: no threat to ldrs* **33/1**

3 **5** ¾ **Drakefell (IRE)**[9] 8154 2-9-2 0........................................ HollieDoyle(3) 12 70
(Richard Hannon) *wnt rt s: racd keenly and sn led: hdd and rdn 2f out: no ex u.p 1f out: wknd ins fnl f* **8/1**[3]

3 **6** 2 **No More Thrills**[23] 7724 2-9-0 0........................................ TomMarquand 1 60
(Richard Hannon) *hld up in tch in midfield: effrt over 2f out: drvn and no imp over 1f out: wl hld and plugged on same pce ins fnl f* **14/1**

2 **7** ½ **Is It Off (IRE)**[12] 8073 2-9-5 0........................................ AdamBeschizza 13 63
(Gary Moore) *in tch in midfield: effrt 2f out: hanging lft: swtchd rt and unable qck over 1f out: no threat to ldrs and kpt on same pce ins fnl f* **8/1**[3]

**8** *nk* **Why We Dream (IRE)** 2-9-0 0........................................ TedDurcan 5 58+
(Mick Channon) *towards rr: switching rt over 2f out: racing nrest to stands rail whn pushed along and sme hdwy over 1f out: kpt on: nvr trbld ldrs* **50/1**

0 **9** *1 ¾* **Desert Trip (FR)**[11] 8112 2-9-5 0................................ KieranShoemark 9 58
(David Menuisier) *stdd s: hld up in tch in midfield: effrt 2f out: sn outpcd u.p and btn: wknd over 1f out* **66/1**

00 **10** *2 ½* **Percy Prosecco**[10] 8140 2-9-5 0................................ DougieCostello 11 51
(Noel Williams) *chsd ldr tl 2f out: sn lost pl and btn: wknd fnl f* **100/1**

**11** *½* **Rose Tinted Spirit** 2-9-5 0................................ RichardKingscote 3 49
(Ralph Beckett) *s.i.s: outpcd and rn green in rr: pushed along over 2f out: no ch but styd on ins fnl f* **40/1**

0 **12** *1 ¾* **Miniature Daffodil (IRE)**[43] 7079 2-9-5 0................................ TimmyMurphy 2 44
(Christian Williams) *rn green and a towards rr: n.d* **100/1**

**13** *¾* **Telltale** 2-9-5 0................................ JosephineGordon 6 42
(Mick Channon) *sn outpcd in rr: nvr on terms* **66/1**

**14** *¾* **Financial Crime (IRE)** 2-9-5 0................................ FrannyNorton 8 40
(Mick Channon) *sn outpcd in last trio: nvr on terms* **66/1**

1m 21.09s (1.79) **Going Correction** +0.35s/f (Good) **14** Ran SP% **123.0**
Speed ratings (Par 97): **103,99,99,97,97 94,94,93,91,89 88,86,85,84**
CSF £25.78 TOTE £12.70: £3.30, £1.10, £1.70; EX 29.40 Trifecta £147.90.
**Owner** Peter O'Callaghan **Bred** Little Audio Partnership **Trained** Musley Bank, N Yorks

**FOCUS**
Just an ordinary maiden for the track with plenty of projects for next year in here.

## 8389 JOIN HOT TO TROT FOR 2018 NOVICE STKS (PLUS 10 RACE) (DIV II) 1m (S)

**2:15** (2:18) (Class 4) 2-Y-O **£5,175** (£1,540; £769; £384) **Stalls** Centre

Form RPR

**1** **Extra Elusive** 2-9-2 0................................ KieranShoemark 11 82+
(Roger Charlton) *hld up in tch towards rr: clsd over 2f out: shkn up to ld 1f out:pushed along and r.o wl to draw clr ins fnl f: comf* **7/1**[3]

06 **2** *2 ¾* **First Eleven**[16] 7955 2-9-2 0................................ JosephineGordon 12 73
(John Gosden) *hld up wl in tch in midfield: effrt and swtchd lft over 1f out: hdwy to chse wnr ins fnl f: kpt on but no imp* **10/3**[1]

**3** *nk* **Mapped (USA)** 2-9-2 0................................ SteveDrowne 10 73+
(Charles Hills) *t.k.h: hld up in tch: effrt over 1f out: hdwy to chse ldrs ins fnl f: styd on to go 3rd towards fin: no threat to wnr* **33/1**

**4** *1* **Kasbaan** 2-9-2 0................................ JimCrowley 1 70+
(Owen Burrows) *wnt lft s and slowly away: hld up in tch in rr: clsd ent fnl 2f: rdn to chse ldrs 1f out: kpt on same pce and no imp ins fnl f* **6/1**[2]

**5** *¾* **Sharja Silk** 2-9-2 0................................ JackMitchell 6 68+
(Roger Varian) *in tch in rr: swtchd rt 2f out: pushed along and hdwy over 1f out: kpt on ins fnl f: nvr trbld ldrs* **8/1**

6 **6** *¾* **Airmax (GER)**[49] 6869 2-9-2 0................................ RichardKingscote 7 67
(Ralph Beckett) *trckd ldr tl led 2f out: rdn and hdd 1f out: unable qck and sn lost 2nd: wknd fnl 100yds* **10/3**[1]

**7** *¾* **Imperial Red (IRE)** 2-8-13 0................................ GeorgiaCox(3) 15 65
(William Haggas) *chsd ldng pair: rdn and unable qck over 1f out: wknd ins fnl f* **11/1**

**8** *nk* **Fenisa's Hook** 2-9-2 0................................ EdwardGreatrex 5 64
(Warren Greatrex) *hld up in tch towards rr: effrt over 1f out: swtchd lft and sme hdwy ins fnl f: nvr trbld ldrs* **33/1**

**9** *nk* **Oskemen** 2-9-2 0................................ AdamKirby 3 63
(Clive Cox) *chsd ldrs: rdn 2f out: unable qck u.p over 1f out: wknd ins fnl f* **16/1**

05 **10** *hd* **Unbridled Spirit**[17] 7915 2-9-2 0................................ OisinMurphy 4 63
(Andrew Balding) *stdd s: t.k.h: hld up in tch towards rr: effrt and clsd over 1f out: swtchd lft 1f out: kpt on wout threatening ldrs ins fnl f* **14/1**

**11** *nk* **Rocky Shores (IRE)** 2-9-2 0................................ ShaneKelly 9 62
(Mick Channon) *in tch in midfield: rdn ent fnl 2f: unable qck and lost pl over 1f out: wknd ins fnl f* **40/1**

**12** *1* **Phoenician Star (IRE)** 2-9-2 0................................ TomMarquand 8 60
(Brian Meehan) *in tch in midfield: rdn over 2f out: lost pl over 1f out: wl hld ins fnl f* **33/1**

0 **13** *¾* **Chaparral Prince (IRE)**[105] 4859 2-9-2 0................................ RobertWinston 2 58
(Charles Hills) *led tl over 1f out: sn struggling and lost pl 1f out: wknd ins fnl f* **40/1**

**14** *½* **Allied** 2-9-2 0................................ TedDurcan 14 57
(Sir Michael Stoute) *sn pushed along and early reminder: midfield: lost pl u.p and dropped to rr over 1f out: wknd ins fnl f* **20/1**

1m 44.04s (4.34) **Going Correction** +0.35s/f (Good) **14** Ran SP% **123.4**
Speed ratings (Par 97): **92,89,88,87,87 86,85,85,85,84 84,83,82,82**
CSF £29.26 TOTE £7.70: £2.70, £1.70, £7.40; EX 36.60 Trifecta £981.10.
**Owner** Saleh Al Homaizi & Imad Al Sagar **Bred** Saleh Al Homaizi & Imad Al Sagar **Trained** Beckhampton, Wilts

■ Mandalayan was withdrawn. Price at time of withdrawal 11-2. Rule 4 applies to bets placed prior to withdrawal, but not to SP bets. Deduction 15p in the pound. New market formed

**FOCUS**
There wasn't much pace on early and this was the slower of the two divisions by 1.23sec, but there was still plenty to like about the way the winner got the job done.

## 8390 ANDRESA SKIN CLINIC FILLIES' H'CAP 1m 2f

**2:50** (2:52) (Class 4) (0-85,82) 3-Y-O+ **£4,851** (£1,443; £721; £360) **Stalls** Centre

Form RPR

1- **1** **Precious Ramotswe**[311] 8465 3-9-2 **81**................................ FrankieDettori 7 92+
(John Gosden) *t.k.h: chsd clr ldng trio: clsd over 2f out: rdn to chse ldr jst over 1f out: c clr w ldr ins fnl f: pushed along fnl 100yds: styd on to ld last strides* **11/8**[1]

2210 **2** *hd* **Lorelina**[20] 7816 4-8-12 **80**................................ WilliamCox(7) 1 90
(Andrew Balding) *prom in main gp: effrt and clsd on ldrs over 2f out: rdn to ld over 1f out: c clr w wnr u.p ins fnl f: kpt on: hdd last strides* **5/1**[2]

4435 **3** *4 ½* **Persistence (IRE)**[27] 7598 3-8-10 **75**................................ OisinMurphy 13 76
(Ralph Beckett) *stdd s and sn swtchd lft: hld up in rr: effrt over 2f out: hdwy u.p over 1f out: styd on ins fnl f to go 3rd fnl 75yds: no ch w ldng pair* **12/1**

5364 **4** *1 ½* **Saumur**[20] 7817 5-8-7 **68**................................ JosephineGordon 2 66
(Denis Coakley) *chsd ldrs and clr in ldng trio: rdn to ld ent fnl 2f: hdd over 1f out: 3rd and outpcd 1f out: wknd ins fnl f* **11/1**

0646 **5** *½* **Lucy The Painter (IRE)**[34] 7401 5-9-7 **82**................................(p) LiamKeniry 5 79
(Ed de Giles) *hld up in midfield: effrt 3f out: no imp u.p over 1f out: kpt on same pce ins fnl f* **18/1**

3104 **6** *1 ¾* **Drumochter**[42] 7107 3-8-7 **72**................................ FrannyNorton 11 66
(Charles Hills) *stdd and swtchd lft after s: hld up in midfield: effrt 3f out: no imp u.p over 1f out: nvr trbld ldrs* **50/1**

6034 **7** *1 ½* **Harmonise**[23] 7735 3-8-5 **73**................................(h) HollieDoyle(3) 4 64
(Mick Channon) *stdd s: hld up in rr: effrt over 3f out: swtchd rt and drvn 2f out: nvr trbld ldrs* **14/1**

5322 **8** *nse* **Lime And Lemon (IRE)**[11] 8111 4-9-1 **76**................................ AdamKirby 6 66
(Clive Cox) *hld up in last quartet: effrt over 3f out: no real imp: nvr threatened ldrs* **11/2**[3]

3610 **9** *shd* **Lady Valdean**[30] 7505 3-8-12 **77**................................(h[1]) OscarPereira 10 67
(Jose Santos) *led and crossed to inner rail: rdn and hdd ent fnl 2f: lost pl and btn over 1f out: wknd fnl f* **100/1**

1000 **10** *¾* **Zain Arion (IRE)**[52] 6793 4-9-7 **82**................................ PhillipMakin 12 71
(John Butler) *sn w ldr tl unable qck u.p over 2f out: lost pl over 1f out: wknd fnl f* **40/1**

6625 **11** *4* **Prying Pandora (FR)**[15] 7981 4-9-2 **80**................................ AdamMcNamara(3) 3 61
(Richard Fahey) *hld up in midfield: rdn wl over 2f out: no imp u.p: wknd over 1f out* **33/1**

2120 **12** *3* **Lightening Dance**[81] 5715 3-8-13 **78**................................ JimCrowley 9 54
(Amanda Perrett) *hld up towards rr: effrt wl over 3f out: no imp: bhd over 1f out* **16/1**

4530 **P** **Kath's Legacy**[22] 7762 4-8-9 **70**................................ EdwardGreatrex 8
(Ben De Haan) *hld up in midfield tl wnt rt and v wd 5f out: sn eased: p.u and dismntd 4f out: sddle slipped* **40/1**

2m 11.44s (2.64) **Going Correction** +0.60s/f (Yiel)
**WFA** 3 from 4yo+ 4lb **13** Ran SP% **118.8**
Speed ratings (Par 102): **113,112,109,108,107 106,105,105,104,104 101,98,**
CSF £7.49 CT £60.39 TOTE £2.20: £1.30, £2.10, £3.30; EX 10.50 Trifecta £60.60.
**Owner** A E Oppenheimer **Bred** Hascombe And Valiant Studs **Trained** Newmarket, Suffolk
■ Stewards' Enquiry : William Cox two-day ban; misuse of whip (Nov 10th-11th)

**FOCUS**
Three went off in front, building up a bit of an advantage on the rest, but they'd gone too quick and were pulled back inside the final 2f. The first two drew nicely clear, but there wasn't much depth to this.

## 8391 BRITISH STALLION STUDS EBF CONDITIONS STKS (PLUS 10 RACE) 1m 5f 61y

**3:25** (3:25) (Class 2) 3-Y-O **£12,291** (£3,657; £1,827) **Stalls** Centre

Form RPR

5310 **1** **Time To Study (FR)**[13] 8038 3-9-5 **102**................................ FrannyNorton 3 101
(Mark Johnston) *mde all: jnd over 3f out: rdn 2f out: qcknd and forged ahd 1f out: r.o wl and in command ins fnl f* **15/8**[2]

413 **2** *2 ¼* **Duke Of Bronte**[14] 8005 3-9-5 **93**................................ JimCrowley 1 97
(Rod Millman) *hld up in 3rd: effrt over 2f out: swtchd rt and clsd u.p over 1f out: chsd wnr ins fnl f: kpt on but no imp* **4/1**[3]

11 **3** *¾* **Royal Line**[27] 7615 3-9-2 **96**................................ FrankieDettori 2 93
(John Gosden) *trckd wnr: clsd and upsides over 3f out: rdn 2f out: unable to match pce of wnr 1f out: lost 2nd and kpt on same pce fnl 150yds* **10/11**[1]

3m 3.77s (11.77) **Going Correction** +0.60s/f (Yiel) **3** Ran SP% **107.2**
Speed ratings (Par 107): **87,85,85**
CSF £7.54 TOTE £2.60; EX 7.70 Trifecta £6.70.
**Owner** Abdulla Al Mansoori **Bred** E A R L Haras Du Quesnay **Trained** Middleham Moor, N Yorks

**FOCUS**
Despite the small field, this was an interesting conditions event. The race has been rated around the runner-up.

## 8392 EQUINE PRODUCTIONS H'CAP 1m

**4:00** (4:01) (Class 4) (0-85,85) 3-Y-O **£4,851** (£1,443; £721; £360) **Stalls** Centre

Form RPR

-654 **1** **Colonel Frank**[29] 7553 3-9-0 **78**................................ LiamKeniry 6 86
(Ed Walker) *t.k.h: trckd ldrs: swtchd lft and effrt over 1f out: rdn and qcknd to ld 100yds out: r.o wl* **16/1**

2025 **2** *¾* **Redgrave (IRE)**[38] 7229 3-9-0 **78**................................(h) ShaneKelly 2 84
(Charles Hills) *hld up wl in tch in midfield: effrt over 1f out: rdn and ev ch 1f out: kpt on but unable to quite match pce of wnr fnl 100yds* **8/1**[3]

2540 **3** *nk* **Plant Pot Power (IRE)**[21] 7780 3-9-0 **81**................................ HollieDoyle(3) 3 86
(Richard Hannon) *stdd s: t.k.h: hld up in tch in rr: hdwy into midfield 1/2-way: clsd to chse ldrs 2f out: rdn to ld ent fnl f: hdd 100yds out: kpt on same pce after: lost 2nd wl ins fnl f* **10/1**

4055 **4** *nk* **Executive Force**[55] 6672 3-9-4 **82**................................(p[1]) OisinMurphy 11 87
(William Haggas) *stdd s: hld up in tch in rr: hmpd bnd over 4f out: rdn and hdwy over 1f out: chsd ldrs ins fnl f: kpt on* **11/2**[1]

2165 **5** *1 ¼* **Highland Pass**[111] 4617 3-8-4 **75**................................ WilliamCox(7) 9 77
(Andrew Balding) *stdd s: t.k.h: hld up in tch in last trio: swtchd rt and effrt 2f out: kpt on u.p ins fnl f: nvr trbld ldrs* **12/1**

3116 **6** *¾* **Fastnet Spin (IRE)**[11] 8113 3-8-13 **80**................................(vt) HectorCrouch(3) 5 80
(David Evans) *in tch in midfield: rdn over 2f out: chsd ldrs and drvn 1f out: no ex ins fnl f: wknd fnl 75yds* **12/1**

2053 **7** *1 ½* **Areen Heart (FR)**[18] 7892 3-9-7 **85**................................(h) JimCrowley 1 82
(David O'Meara) *t.k.h: led: rdn wl over 1f out: hdd ent fnl f: no ex and wknd fnl 150yds* **9/1**

-316 **8** *2 ½* **Heaven's Rock (IRE)**[23] 7736 3-8-8 **72**................................(p) FrannyNorton 7 63
(Tom Dascombe) *t.k.h: chsd ldr: rdn and ev ch ent fnl 2f: unable qck and lost pl over 1f out: wknd ins fnl f* **8/1**[3]

2500 **9** *2* **Trading Punches (IRE)**[23] 7736 3-9-5 **83**................................ KieranShoemark 4 69
(David Brown) *chsd ldrs: rdn jst over 2f out: unable qck and lost pl over 1f out: wknd ins fnl f* **16/1**

2602 **10** *4* **Makaarim**[112] 4564 3-9-6 **84**................................ AdamKirby 10 61
(Hughie Morrison) *t.k.h: hld up wl in tch in midfield: effrt 2f out: sn btn and lost pl: bhd and eased ins fnl f* **15/2**[2]

0513 **11** *1* **Tamayef (IRE)**[22] 7759 3-9-4 **82**................................ JosephineGordon 12 57
(Hugo Palmer) *stdd after s: t.k.h: hld up in last quartet: effrt ent fnl 2f: sn btn: bhd and eased ins fnl f* **8/1**[3]

21-0 **12** *nk* **Trading Point (FR)**[47] 6965 3-9-4 **82**................................ PhillipMakin 8 56
(John Quinn) *hld up in tch in midfield: swtchd rt 3f out: rdn over 1f out: sn btn: bhd and eased ins fnl f* **11/2**[1]

1m 41.86s (3.16) **Going Correction** +0.60s/f (Yiel) **12** Ran SP% **122.1**
Speed ratings (Par 103): **108,107,106,106,105 104,103,100,98,94 93,93**
CSF £142.65 CT £1369.92 TOTE £23.00: £5.40, £3.10, £3.70; EX 169.20 Trifecta £3621.60.
**Owner** Mrs Fitri Hay **Bred** Eliza Park International Pty Ltd **Trained** Upper Lambourn, Berks

**FOCUS**
This was steadily run in the early stages and a few raced keenly. A small personal best from the winner.

## 8393 THATCHAM BUTCHERS H'CAP 6f

**4:35** (4:39) (Class 3) (0-90,91) 3-Y-O+ **£7,439** (£2,213; £1,106; £553) **Stalls** Centre

Form RPR

0224 **1** **Alaadel**[21] 7780 4-8-10 **79**................................(bt) JimCrowley 7 88+
(William Haggas) *stdd s: hld up in tch in rr: clsd over 1f out: trckd ldrs 1f out: rdn ins fnl f: fnd enough and r.o to ld cl home* **9/4**[1]

6152 2 ½ **Baron Bolt**[12] 8077 4-9-6 89 (p) RaulDaSilva 5 96
(Paul Cole) awkward leaving stalls: sn rcvrd and in tch in midfield: swtchd lft and effrt 2f out: chsd ldr over 1f out: drvn to ld 150yds out: styd on: hdd and no ex cl home 7/2[2]
0101 3 1¼ **Pettochside**[12] 8077 8-9-5 91 6ex HollieDoyle(3) 3 94
(John Bridger) led: rdn over 1f out: hdd 150yds out: no ex and outpcd fnl 100yds 12/1
0003 4 3½ **Repton (IRE)**[18] 7901 3-9-3 87 OisinMurphy 14 79
(Richard Hannon) stdd s: hld up in rr: nt clr run 2f out: swtchd lft and effrt over 1f out: hdwy to go 4th ins fnl f: styd on: no threat to ldrs 20/1
3216 5 2 **Clear Spring (IRE)**[12] 8077 9-9-7 90 AdamKirby 11 75
(John Spearing) hld up in tch in midfield: n.m.r and swtchd lft over 1f out: kpt on ins fnl f: no threat to ldrs 7/1[3]
4-10 6 ½ **Dalton**[154] 3038 3-8-11 81 KieranShoemark 10 65
(David O'Meara) stdd s: hld up towards rr: clsd and nt clr run 2f out: swtchd lft and effrt over 1f out: kpt on ins fnl f: no threat to ldrs 40/1
-040 7 ½ **Finelcity (GER)**[32] 7456 4-8-12 84 (v) HectorCrouch(3) 9 66
(Harry Dunlop) chsd ldr tl 2f out: sn u.p and unable qck: wknd ins fnl f 16/1
0235 8 ½ **Huntsmans Close**[59] 6554 7-9-4 87 (h) PhillipMakin 12 68
(Robert Cowell) stdd s: t.k.h: hld up in tch towards rr: effrt and no imp over 1f out: wl hld and kpt on same pce ins fnl f 40/1
4520 9 ½ **Smokey Lane (IRE)**[21] 7782 3-9-6 90 TimmyMurphy 4 69
(Christian Williams) midfield: swtchd lft after 1f and racd away fr rivals: effrt to chse ldrs 2f out: unable qck over 1f out: wknd fnl f 25/1
0206 10 ½ **Gin In The Inn (IRE)**[47] 6971 4-9-4 90 AdamMcNamara(3) 1 67
(Richard Fahey) t.k.h: trckd ldrs: wnt 2nd and stl travelling wl 2f out: sn rdn and fnd little: wknd fnl f 12/1
0440 11 2¼ **Moonraker**[21] 7780 5-8-11 80 (v[1]) ShaneKelly 8 50
(Mick Channon) taken down early: in tch in midfield: lost pl and towards rr whn n.m.r over 1f out: sn wknd 20/1
2035 11 dht **Francisco**[23] 7742 5-8-1 77 AledBeech(7) 6 47
(Tony Carroll) chsd ldrs: rdn 1/2-way: struggling 2f out and sn lost pl: wknd fnl f 50/1
4135 13 1 **Storm Cry**[18] 7886 3-8-9 79 FrannyNorton 13 46
(Mark Johnston) chsd ldrs: rdn over 2f out: outpcd and lost pl over 1f out: bhd ins fnl f 25/1
51 14 5 **Dark Magic**[97] 5158 3-8-11 81 RobertWinston 2 32
(Dean Ivory) chsd ldrs tl 2f out: sn lost pl: bhd and eased ins fnl f 10/1

1m 13.17s (0.17) **Going Correction** +0.35s/f (Good)
**WFA** 3 from 4yo+ 1lb **14 Ran SP% 119.9**
Speed ratings (Par 107): **112,111,109,105,102 101,101,100,99,99 96,96,94,88**
CSF £8.43 CT £78.85 TOTE £2.80: £1.30, £1.80, £3.20; EX 12.70 Trifecta £90.20.
**Owner** Hamdan Al Maktoum **Bred** Cheveley Park Stud Ltd **Trained** Newmarket, Suffolk

**FOCUS**
The first three finished clear and it was a good ride on the winner.

## 8394 RAYNER BOSCH CAR SERVICE "HANDS AND HEELS" APPRENTICE H'CAP (FINAL) (RACING EXCELLENCE) 2m
5:10 (5:10) (Class 5) (0-75,76) 4-Y-0+ £2,911 (£866; £432; £216) Stalls Centre

Form RPR
2015 1 **Incus**[49] 6880 4-8-13 64 WilliamCox 11 72
(Ed de Giles) mde all: wnt clr 12f out: 8 l clr 6f out: rdn over 1f out: 3 l clr 1f out: kpt on: unchal: eased nr fin 6/1
1543 2 2½ **The New Pharaoh (IRE)**[17] 7924 6-9-9 74 FinleyMarsh 1 79
(Chris Wall) hld up off the pce in last trio: clsd 3f out: effrt to chse clr wnr over 1f out: kpt on same pce ins fnl f 9/2[2]
1050 3 ¾ **Fitzwilly**[12] 8072 7-8-12 68 PaulStJohn-Dennis(5) 8 72
(Mick Channon) chsd ldrs: effrt 2f out: kpt on same pce fnl f 12/1
6543 4 nse **Gabrial's Star**[15] 7983 8-9-6 71 (b) ConnorMurtagh 5 75
(Richard Fahey) hld up in midfield: clsd 3f out: rdn to chse clr wnr 2f out tl over 1f out: kpt on same pce ins fnl f 5/1[3]
2145 5 ¾ **Graceful Lady**[23] 7402 4-9-10 75 DarraghKeenan 12 78
(Robert Eddery) t.k.h: styd wd early and hld up in rr: clsd on inner 3f out: effrt 2f out: chsd ldrs over 1f out: kpt on same pce ins fnl f 11/4[1]
3550 6 5 **Roy Rocket (FR)**[23] 7744 7-8-12 63 MillyNaseb 9 60
(John Berry) chsd ldrs: clsd and effrt to chse ldr over 2f out tl 2f out: sn struggling and lost pl: wknd fnl f 20/1
/500 7 nk **Sleep Easy**[23] 7728 5-9-11 76 (p) TylerSaunders 10 73
(Neil Mulholland) bustled along leaving stalls: sn chsng wnr tl rdn and lost 2nd over 2f out: lost pl and bhd over 1f out: wknd fnl f 8/1
0555 8 1 **Spiritoftomintoul**[36] 7336 8-8-11 62 (p[1]) AledBeech 2 58
(Tony Carroll) s.i.s: hld up off the pce in last trio: effrt ent fnl 2f: sn btn and wknd over 1f out 10/1
0326 9 36 **Riptide**[18] 7893 11-8-4 58 JonathanFisher(3) 7 10
(Michael Scudamore) s.i.s: off the pce in midfield: rdn and dropped to rr 3f out: bhd and virtually p.u fnl f: t.o 16/1

3m 42.34s (10.34) **Going Correction** +0.60s/f (Yiel) **9 Ran SP% 114.3**
Speed ratings (Par 103): **98,96,96,96,95 93,93,92,74**
CSF £32.79 CT £313.24 TOTE £6.60: £2.30, £1.70, £3.60; EX 32.20 Trifecta £293.60.
**Owner** Mange Tout II **Bred** Lilly Hall Farm **Trained** Ledbury, H'fords
■ Stewards' Enquiry : Finley Marsh seven-day ban; use whip down the shoulder (Nov 10th,11th,13th,15th-18th)

**FOCUS**
An ordinary staying handicap with the third horse setting the level.
T/Plt: £74.50 to a £1 stake. Pool: £61,193.78 - 599.08 winning units T/Qpdt: £66.50 to a £1 stake. Pool: £4,461.27 - 49.60 winning units **Steve Payne**

# 8242 WOLVERHAMPTON (A.W) (L-H)
Friday, October 27

**OFFICIAL GOING: Tapeta: standard**
Wind: Nil Weather: Fine

## 8395 BETWAY SPRINT CLASSIFIED STKS 6f 20y (Tp)
5:45 (5:45) (Class 6) 3-Y-0+ £2,264 (£673; £336; £168) Stalls Low

Form RPR
0300 1 **Seebring (IRE)**[32] 7465 3-9-0 48 StevieDonohoe 3 56
(Brian Ellison) a.p: rdn to ld ins fnl f: r.o 10/1
0000 2 nk **Jorvik Prince**[28] 7575 3-9-0 53 SamJames 12 55
(Karen Tutty) chsd ldr: rdn to ld over 1f out: hdd ins fnl f: r.o 28/1
6022 3 1 **Treagus**[8] 8185 3-9-0 53 RyanTate 1 52
(Anthony Carson) mid-div: hdwy over 2f out: swtchd lft ins fnl f: r.o u.p 7/2[3]
6443 4 shd **Princess Way (IRE)**[10] 8137 3-8-11 50 (b) MattCosham(3) 4 52
(David Evans) mid-div: hdwy over 2f out: rdn over 1f out: r.o 10/1
0012 5 ½ **Hurricane Rock**[31] 7487 4-9-1 54 LukeMorris 7 50
(Simon Dow) s.i.s: hld up: hdwy over 1f out: sn rdn: styd on 5/2[2]
0540 6 1¼ **Hisar (IRE)**[32] 7459 3-9-0 55 (h) AlistairRawlinson 5 47
(Michael Appleby) s.i.s: sn pushed along in rr: hdwy over 1f out: nt clr run and swtchd rt ins fnl f: nt rch ldrs 9/4[1]
0000 7 1½ **Rapid Rise (IRE)**[10] 8134 3-8-9 55 (v[1]) JaneElliott(5) 13 42
(Milton Bradley) sn outpcd: r.o ins fnl f: nvr nrr 28/1
0000 8 1 **Emilene**[25] 7692 3-9-0 50 WilliamCarson 6 39
(Mark Brisbourne) led: rdn and hdd over 1f out: wknd ins fnl f 100/1
00-6 9 2¼ **Like Minds**[6] 8242 3-9-0 41 AndrewMullen 2 32
(David Brown) prom: rdn over 2f out: wknd fnl f 66/1
0060 10 1¾ **Permanent**[17] 7926 3-9-0 50 JasonHart 8 27
(Eric Alston) hld up: plld hrd: nt clr run and lost pl over 3f out: n.d after 28/1
2-00 11 ½ **La Fortuna**[77] 5892 4-8-12 54 LewisEdmunds(3) 11 26
(Charlie Wallis) hld up: wknd over 2f out 33/1
0566 12 13 **Fivos**[4] 8298 3-8-11 49 (v[1]) GeorgeWood(3) 10
(David Bridgwater) chsd ldrs: rdn over 3f out: hung rt over 2f out: sn wknd 33/1
5030 13 6 **New Tale**[116] 4447 3-8-11 50 (p[1]) CallumShepherd(3) 9
(Olly Williams) prom: rdn over 3f out: wknd over 2f out 80/1

1m 13.94s (-0.56) **Going Correction** -0.15s/f (Stan)
**WFA** 3 from 4yo 1lb **13 Ran SP% 119.7**
Speed ratings (Par 101): **97,96,95,95,94 92,90,89,86,84 83,66,58**
CSF £258.36 TOTE £11.40: £3.20, £5.70, £1.10; EX 341.30 Trifecta £2974.60.
**Owner** John James & Brian Ellison **Bred** Brian Williamson **Trained** Norton, N Yorks

**FOCUS**
A moderate classified contest. They went a decent gallop on standard Tapeta.

## 8396 BETWAY LIVE CASINO H'CAP 1m 5f 219y (Tp)
6:15 (6:15) (Class 6) (0-65,65) 3-Y-0+ £2,264 (£673; £336; £168) Stalls Low

Form RPR
1446 1 **Hussar Ballad (USA)**[7] 8205 8-9-13 64 CamHardie 11 72
(Antony Brittain) hld up: hdwy over 1f out: rdn and r.o to ld nr fin 14/1
4612 2 1 **Strictly Art (IRE)**[23] 7729 4-9-0 56 JoshuaBryan(5) 2 64
(Alan Bailey) led 1f: chsd ldrs: rdn and nt clr run over 1f out: swtchd rt: led wl ins fnl f: hdd nr fin 16/1
4-33 3 1 **Singular Quest**[20] 7831 5-9-8 59 PJMcDonald 1 64
(Daniel Mark Loughnane) hld up in tch: rdn and nt clr run over 1f out: swtchd rt: r.o 4/1[2]
1053 4 ¾ **About Glory**[3] 8312 3-8-13 57 (b) TomMarquand 8 63
(Richard Hannon) led after 1f: hdd over 8f out: chsd ldr: rdn over 2f out: ev ch ins fnl f: styd on same pce 9/4[1]
0613 5 ¾ **Costa Percy**[18] 7895 3-9-6 64 JoeFanning 10 69
(Jennie Candlish) chsd ldr after 1f: led over 8f out: rdn and edgd lft over 1f out: hdd and no ex wl ins fnl f 4/1[2]
5300 6 1¼ **The Last Melon**[6] 8246 5-8-11 53 RachealKneller(5) 3 54
(James Bennett) hld up in tch: shkn up over 2f out: styd on same pce ins fnl f 40/1
4350 7 ½ **Captain Swift (IRE)**[15] 7983 6-9-10 61 (p) LukeMorris 4 61
(John Mackie) hld up: rdn over 2f out: hdwy over 1f out: styd on same pce ins fnl f 14/1
6405 8 hd **Surround Sound**[49] 6901 7-9-4 55 (tp) JasonHart 7 55
(Tim Easterby) s.i.s: bhd: swtchd rt 3f out: hdwy and hung lft over 1f out: rdn and swtchd rt ins fnl f: r.o: nt trble ldrs 12/1
3200 9 ¾ **Dream Serenade**[31] 7483 4-9-3 54 (h) RyanTate 5 53
(Michael Appleby) prom: racd keenly: rdn over 1f out: no ex ins fnl f 80/1
0606 10 6 **Infiniti (IRE)**[48] 6953 4-8-12 54 JaneElliott(5) 12 44
(Barry Leavy) hld up: rdn over 1f out: nvr on terms 25/1
2-00 11 1¼ **Innish Man (IRE)**[20] 7831 5-9-7 58 (p[1]) BenCurtis 13 46
(John Mackie) hld up: rdn over 2f out: n.d 28/1
/600 12 13 **Rocky Elsom (USA)**[64] 6343 10-9-1 55 (p) GeorgeWood(3) 6 25
(Adrian Wintle) hld up: pushed along over 5f out: rdn and wknd over 2f out 100/1
6023 13 25 **Tyrolean**[19] 7048 4-9-7 65 (p) NicolaCurrie(7) 9
(Seamus Durack) prom: rdn over 3f out: wknd over 2f out 17/2[3]

3m 1.3s (-6.70) **Going Correction** -0.15s/f (Stan)
**WFA** 3 from 4yo+ 7lb **13 Ran SP% 120.2**
Speed ratings (Par 101): **113,112,111,111,111 110,110,109,109,106 105,97,83**
CSF £211.53 CT £1073.42 TOTE £15.00: £3.50, £3.50, £1.60; EX 229.80 Trifecta £3066.50.
**Owner** Antony Brittain **Bred** Darley **Trained** Warthill, N Yorks

**FOCUS**
A modest staying handicap. They went a respectable gallop and a particularly patient ride bore fruit. The form is straightforward around the principals.

## 8397 32RED CASINO (S) STKS 6f 20y (Tp)
6:45 (6:45) (Class 5) 2-Y-O £2,911 (£866; £432; £216) Stalls Low

Form RPR
3365 1 **Story Minister (IRE)**[21] 7787 2-8-12 67 (vp[1]) PJMcDonald 12 60
(Tom Dascombe) mde all: clr 5f out: rdn over 1f out: all out 15/8[1]
5046 2 1¼ **Lady Lintera (IRE)**[26] 7655 2-8-7 50 (h) JoeFanning 10 51
(Ann Duffield) hld up: hdwy over 1f out: r.o to go 2nd wl ins fnl f: nt rch wnr 18/1
0302 3 ½ **Hope And Glory (IRE)**[22] 7756 2-8-7 53 KieranO'Neill 9 50
(Tom Dascombe) chsd wnr who wnt clr 5f out: rdn over 2f out: styd on 11/2[2]
0564 4 ¾ **Red For Danger**[25] 7695 2-8-7 46 (h) LukeMorris 1 47
(Eve Johnson Houghton) chsd ldrs: rdn over 2f out: kpt on 16/1
004 5 ½ **Counterfeit**[54] 6721 2-8-0 63 (p[1]) NicolaCurrie(7) 5 46
(Richard Hughes) s.i.s: sn pushed along in rr: nt clr run over 2f out: rdn over 1f out: r.o towards fin 15/8[1]
5000 6 2¼ **Duke Of Freedom**[8] 8191 2-8-9 58 (h) LewisEdmunds(3) 7 44
(Ann Duffield) sn pushed along towards rr: rdn over 2f out: nvr on terms 12/1
0030 7 7 **Floss The Hoss (IRE)**[16] 7954 2-8-4 64 MattCosham(3) 8 18
(David Evans) chsd ldrs: hung rt almost thrght: wknd over 2f out 8/1[3]
0 8 1½ **Leanda J**[89] 5453 2-8-7 0 ShaneGray 6 14
(Ann Duffield) hld up: rdn over 2f out: hung lft and wknd over 1f out 80/1
9 15 **Eesha Says (IRE)** 2-8-8 0 ow1 BenCurtis 3
(Tony Carroll) s.s: outpcd 66/1

1m 14.29s (-0.21) **Going Correction** -0.15s/f (Stan) **9 Ran SP% 117.6**
Speed ratings (Par 95): **95,93,92,91,91 88,78,76,56**
CSF £44.43 TOTE £3.20: £1.10, £3.10, £1.40; EX 40.50 Trifecta £191.80.
**Owner** John Dance **Bred** Yeomanstown Stud **Trained** Malpas, Cheshire

**FOCUS**
A modest juvenile seller. The all-the-way winner and joint-favourite got tired in the final 150 yards, but he'd already done enough. Those behind the winner highlight the form's limitations.

## 8398 BETWAY H'CAP 1m 4f 51y (Tp)
**7:15** (7:15) (Class 4) (0-85,85) 3-Y-0+ **£4,690** (£1,395; £697; £348) **Stalls** Low

Form RPR
3125 **1** **Great Court (IRE)**[20] 7816 3-9-0 **81** JackMitchell 10 92
(Roger Varian) *s.i.s: hld up: hdwy over 1f out: shkn up to ld and hung lft ins fnl f: r.o* **14/1**
1542 **2** *1 ¾* **Eldritch (IRE)**[8] 8188 3-9-4 **85** (p[1]) RobertHavlin 12 94
(John Gosden) *hld up: hdwy over 2f out: led and hung lft fr over 1f out: rdn and hdd ins fnl f: styd on same pce* **5/4**[1]
5215 **3** *2 ¼* **Chocolate Box (IRE)**[35] 7359 3-8-13 **80** (p) LukeMorris 1 85
(Luca Cumani) *prom: drvn along over 3f out: ev ch over 1f out: edgd lft and styd on same pce fnl f* **11/2**[2]
0355 **4** *1 ¼* **Paris Protocol**[18] 7903 4-9-9 **84** (p) TomMarquand 6 87
(Richard Hannon) *chsd ldr 2f: remained handy: rdn over 2f out: ev ch over 1f out: nt clr run sn after: no ex ins fnl f* **14/1**
1223 **5** *1* **Sparte Quercus (IRE)**[11] 8111 4-9-6 **81** PJMcDonald 7 82
(Ed Dunlop) *prom: rdn and nt clr run over 1f out: no ex fnl f* **11/1**
5030 **6** *hd* **Jufn**[23] 7728 4-9-3 **78** (h) BenCurtis 8 79
(John Butler) *led: hdd over 8f out: chsd ldr tl led again wl over 1f out: sn rdn and hdd: wknd ins fnl f* **33/1**
5513 **7** *½* **Romanor**[23] 7728 3-8-12 **79** (h) PatCosgrave 3 79+
(Ed Walker) *s.i.s: hld up: plld hrd: nt clr run fr over 2f out: nvr able to chal* **8/1**[3]
-000 **8** *nk* **Rite To Reign**[21] 7785 6-9-4 **79** (v[1]) DavidProbert 2 79
(Philip McBride) *hld up: hdwy over 6f out: rdn and ev ch over 1f out: wknd ins fnl f* **40/1**
0004 **9** *6* **Sennockian Star**[6] 8239 7-9-1 **76** JoeFanning 5 66
(Mark Johnston) *hld up: rdn over 1f out: nvr on terms* **8/1**[3]
0000 **10** *4 ½* **Spes Nostra**[15] 7984 9-9-2 **77** (b) DougieCostello 11 60
(Iain Jardine) *hld up: shkn up over 2f out: sn wknd* **80/1**
1000 **11** *6* **Manchego**[18] 7909 3-9-1 **82** (t[1]) RichardKingscote 4 56
(Hugo Palmer) *chsd ldr 10f out tl led over 8f out: hdd wl over 1f out: wknd fnl f* **14/1**

2m 36.22s (-4.58) **Going Correction** -0.15s/f (Stan)
**WFA** 3 from 4yo+ 6lb **11** Ran SP% **117.0**
Speed ratings (Par 105): **109,107,106,105,104 104,104,104,100,97 93**
CSF £31.48 CT £116.47 TOTE £17.10: £3.10, £1.10, £2.10; EX 53.50 Trifecta £406.40.
**Owner** J Shack & G Barnard **Bred** James Waldron **Trained** Newmarket, Suffolk

**FOCUS**
The feature contest was a decent middle-distance handicap and it produced the quickest comparative winning time on the night. The race has been rated around the placed horses.

## 8399 32RED.COM EBF NOVICE STKS 1m 1f 104y (Tp)
**7:45** (7:45) (Class 5) 2-Y-0 **£2,911** (£866; £432; £216) **Stalls** Low

Form RPR
521 **1** **Deyaarna (USA)**[22] 7758 2-9-9 89 TomMarquand 6 83
(Saeed bin Suroor) *led: hdd over 6f out: chsd ldr tl over 4f out: remained handy: shkn up over 2f out: led over 1f out: drvn out* **1/4**[1]
43 **2** *1* **Sassie (IRE)**[17] 7937 2-8-8 0 MitchGodwin(3) 7 69
(Sylvester Kirk) *hld up: hdwy over 2f out: rdn and ev ch over 1f out: styd on* **10/1**[3]
6 **3** *2 ¾* **Perfect Blue (IRE)**[12] 8075 2-9-2 0 JoeFanning 8 69
(Mark Johnston) *w wnr 2f: remained handy: chsd ldr over 4f out: rdn over 2f out: styd on same pce ins fnl f* **14/1**
0 **4** *½* **Time To Perfection (IRE)**[17] 7937 2-8-11 0 CamHardie 11 63
(Sylvester Kirk) *s.i.s: hld up: hdwy over 1f out: r.o* **25/1**
00 **5** *1 ¾* **Quantatmental (IRE)**[10] 8136 2-9-2 0 PJMcDonald 1 65
(Tom Dascombe) *chsd ldrs: rdn and hung lft fr over 1f out: styd on same pce* **20/1**
6 **6** *1 ¼* **Qadiriyyah**[8] 8180 2-9-2 0 StevieDonohoe 10 62
(Mohamed Moubarak) *chsd ldrs: led over 6f out: rdn and hdd over 1f out: wknd ins fnl f* **33/1**
04 **7** *¾* **Parmenter**[38] 7226 2-8-11 0 WilliamCarson 5 56
(Alan King) *trckd ldrs: shkn up and hung lft over 1f out: wknd fnl f* **9/2**[2]
**8** *nse* **Four Champs** 2-9-2 0 RichardKingscote 2 61
(Tom Dascombe) *s.i.s: rn green in rr: pushed along and hung lft fr over 1f out: nvr on terms* **20/1**
000 **9** *18* **Timoshenko**[11] 8119 2-9-2 0 LukeMorris 9 27
(Sir Mark Prescott Bt) *s.i.s: hld up: pushed along over 4f out: rdn and wknd over 2f out* **50/1**
00 **10** *4 ½* **Masons Belle**[23] 7739 2-9-2 0 DavidProbert 3 18
(Ronald Harris) *s.i.s: a in rr: wknd over 3f out* **100/1**

2m 1.08s (0.28) **Going Correction** -0.15s/f (Stan) **10** Ran SP% **133.2**
Speed ratings (Par 95): **92,91,88,88,86 85,84,84,68,64**
CSF £5.03 TOTE £1.10: £1.02, £2.70, £3.70; EX 6.50 Trifecta £55.80.
**Owner** Godolphin **Bred** Shadwell Farm LLC **Trained** Newmarket, Suffolk

**FOCUS**
A decent juvenile novice contest. They went a muddling gallop, but the favourite managed to follow up his recent Chelmsford win.

## 8400 BET & WATCH AT SUNBETS.CO.UK H'CAP 1m 142y (Tp)
**8:15** (8:15) (Class 5) (0-70,72) 3-Y-0+ **£2,911** (£866; £432; £216) **Stalls** Low

Form RPR
4403 **1** **Luang Prabang (IRE)**[18] 7878 4-9-1 **67** HollieDoyle(3) 6 75+
(Chris Wall) *hld up: hdwy over 2f out: led over 1f out: sn hung lft: r.o* **3/1**[1]
0325 **2** *1 ¼* **Haraz (IRE)**[44] 7052 4-9-5 **68** (p) DougieCostello 3 73
(Jamie Osborne) *hld up: nt clr run: swtchd rt and hdwy over 1f out: shkn up to go 2nd wl ins fnl f: nt rch wnr* **6/1**[3]
5336 **3** *¾* **Millie's Kiss**[20] 7830 3-9-2 **69** DavidProbert 7 72
(Philip McBride) *chsd ldrs: nt clr run over 1f out: sn rdn: styd on* **10/1**
2146 **4** *½* **Solent Meads (IRE)**[10] 8132 3-9-2 **69** (b) GeorgeDowning 10 71
(Daniel Kubler) *chsd ldrs: rdn over 2f out: led over 1f out: sn hdd: styd on same pce ins fnl f* **7/1**
4600 **5** *½* **Scribner Creek (IRE)**[18] 7878 4-8-13 **65** CharlieBennett(3) 13 66
(Denis Quinn) *s.i.s: hld up: hdwy u.p over 1f out: r.o* **18/1**
4060 **6** *shd* **Red Touch (USA)**[21] 7789 5-9-7 **70** (p) AlistairRawlinson 11 71
(Michael Appleby) *s.i.s: in rr and pushed along over 4f out: rdn over 2f out: r.o ins fnl f: nvr nrr* **20/1**
0462 **7** *2* **Passing Star**[22] 7770 6-9-4 **67** (tp) LukeMorris 5 63
(Daniel Kubler) *prom: rdn and nt clr run over 1f out: no ex fnl f* **8/1**
5605 **8** *2* **Kitten's Johnstown (USA)**[14] 7999 3-9-2 **69** ShaneGray 8 61
(Kevin Ryan) *pushed along in rr: hdwy over 1f out: nvr on terms* **9/1**
5300 **9** *3* **Dubai Waves**[144] 3412 3-9-0 **70** EoinWalsh(3) 2 55
(Tony Newcombe) *w ldr: rdn over 2f out: ev ch over 1f out: wknd fnl f* **100/1**
0000 **10** *1 ¾* **Idol Deputy (FR)**[48] 6948 11-8-12 **66** (p) RachealKneller(5) 12 47
(James Bennett) *hld up: edgd lft over 7f out: pushed along over 2f out: n.d* **40/1**
6266 **11** *7* **Spinart**[36] 7327 4-9-0 **66** (b[1]) CallumShepherd(3) 1 31
(Pam Sly) *led: rdn and hdd over 1f out: wknd fnl f* **4/1**[2]
0425 **U** **Beatbybeatbybeat**[8] 8192 4-9-2 **65** (v) CamHardie 9
(Antony Brittain) *hld up: clipped heels and uns rdr over 7f out* **22/1**

1m 47.51s (-2.59) **Going Correction** -0.15s/f (Stan)
**WFA** 3 from 4yo+ 4lb **12** Ran SP% **119.8**
Speed ratings (Par 103): **105,103,103,102,102 102,100,98,96,94 88,**
CSF £20.43 CT £163.70 TOTE £3.80: £1.80, £2.20, £3.20; EX 23.20 Trifecta £229.00.
**Owner** Des Thurlby **Bred** Deerfield Farm **Trained** Newmarket, Suffolk
■ Stewards' Enquiry : Racheal Kneller five-day ban; careless riding (Nov 10,11,13,15,16)

**FOCUS**
A modest handicap. They went a decent gallop and the favourite came through in a rough race to win well. She can still do better.

## 8401 SUNBETS.CO.UK H'CAP (DIV I) 7f 36y (Tp)
**8:45** (8:45) (Class 6) (0-60,66) 3-Y-0+ **£2,264** (£673; £336; £168) **Stalls** High

Form RPR
0000 **1** **Fire Diamond**[23] 7723 4-9-7 **60** (p) RichardKingscote 3 70+
(Tom Dascombe) *hld up: hdwy over 1f out: hung lft: nt clr run and swtchd rt ins fnl f: r.o to ld wl ins fnl f: comf* **11/4**[2]
0621 **2** *2 ¼* **Isntshesomething**[16] 7945 5-9-5 **58** (v) DougieCostello 5 62
(Richard Guest) *hld up: hdwy over 1f out: nt clr run sn after: swtchd rt ins fnl f: r.o* **11/1**
5-40 **3** *nk* **Al's Memory (IRE)**[50] 6866 8-9-5 **58** PJMcDonald 10 62
(David Evans) *w ldr tl over 5f out: remained handy: rdn over 2f out: styd on* **12/1**
0006 **4** *hd* **Kafoo**[8] 8181 4-9-7 **60** (vt[1]) AlistairRawlinson 8 63
(Michael Appleby) *s.i.s: and hmpd s: hdwy to ld over 5f out: clr 1/2-way: rdn over 1f out: hdd and no ex wl ins fnl f* **33/1**
2000 **5** *½* **Little Choosey**[36] 7323 7-9-2 **58** (bt) EoinWalsh(3) 6 60
(Roy Bowring) *chsd ldrs: rdn over 2f out: sn outpcd: styd on ins fnl f* **14/1**
5052 **6** *¾* **Viola Park**[29] 7539 3-9-2 **57** (p) LukeMorris 2 56
(Ronald Harris) *led: hdd over 5f out: chsd ldr: rdn over 2f out: hung lft over 1f out: hmpd ins fnl f: no ex* **11/2**[3]
0041 **7** *hd* **Captain Hawk**[7] 8210 3-9-11 **66** 6ex (v) JosephineGordon 7 65
(Ian Williams) *s.i.s and hmpd s: in rr: pushed along over 2f out: r.o ins fnl f: nvr nrr* **2/1**[1]
5564 **8** *1 ¾* **Jet Setter (IRE)**[17] 7928 3-9-1 **56** (p) GeorgeDowning 1 50
(Tony Carroll) *prom: rdn over 1f out: no ex ins fnl f* **25/1**
2004 **9** *hd* **Jack Blane**[18] 7889 3-9-0 **55** (p) AndrewMullen 9 54
(Keith Dalgleish) *plld hrd and prom: lost pl over 4f out: hdwy and nt clr run fr over 1f out: hmpd and eased ins fnl f* **10/1**
060 **10** *12* **Quiet Warrior (IRE)**[91] 5377 6-8-12 **58** ow1 RyanTimby(7) 4 24
(Michael Easterby) *s.i.s: a in rr: wknd over 2f out* **66/1**

1m 28.03s (-0.77) **Going Correction** -0.15s/f (Stan)
**WFA** 3 from 4yo+ 2lb **10** Ran SP% **115.4**
Speed ratings (Par 101): **98,95,95,94,94 93,93,91,90,77**
CSF £32.16 CT £319.42 TOTE £3.50: £1.50, £3.10, £3.40; EX 36.90 Trifecta £180.90.
**Owner** John Brown **Bred** John Brown **Trained** Malpas, Cheshire
■ Stewards' Enquiry : Richard Kingscote two-day ban; careless riding (Oct 30, Nov 10)

**FOCUS**
The first division of a modest handicap. They went a respectable gallop and the second-favourite won easily. He was on a good mark.

## 8402 SUNBETS.CO.UK H'CAP (DIV II) 7f 36y (Tp)
**9:15** (9:15) (Class 6) (0-60,65) 3-Y-0+ **£2,264** (£673; £336; £168) **Stalls** High

Form RPR
2551 **1** **Sentinel**[3] 8329 3-9-10 **65** 6ex StevieDonohoe 7 70
(Charlie Fellowes) *s.i.s: hld up: swtchd rt and hdwy over 1f out: r.o u.p to ld post* **5/4**[1]
5030 **2** *shd* **Grey Destiny**[7] 8210 7-9-4 **57** CamHardie 9 63
(Antony Brittain) *s.i.s: hld up: rdn and r.o wl ins fnl f: jst failed* **20/1**
0-03 **3** *nse* **Peak Hill**[13] 8031 4-9-0 **56** HollieDoyle(3) 5 62
(Adrian Wintle) *a.p: rdn over 1f out: r.o* **20/1**
0026 **4** *shd* **Broughtons Fancy**[28] 7573 4-9-0 **53** SamJames 3 59
(Karen Tutty) *chsd ldrs: led over 1f out: rdn and edgd lft ins fnl f: hdd post* **25/1**
3000 **5** *1* **Caledonia Laird**[36] 7323 6-9-5 **58** (v[1]) JosephineGordon 2 61
(Jo Hughes) *hld up: hdwy over 2f out: nt clr run and swtchd rt over 1f out: sn rdn: r.o* **11/1**
063 **6** *1 ¼* **Mr Slicker (FR)**[27] 7597 3-9-2 **57** (p[1]) RichardKingscote 6 56
(Tom Dascombe) *hld up: pushed along over 4f out: r.o ins fnl f: nvr nrr* **7/2**[2]
460 **7** *nk* **Thorntoun Lady (USA)**[18] 7889 7-8-12 **51** PJMcDonald 10 50
(Jim Goldie) *s.i.s: hld up: rdn and r.o ins fnl f: nt trble ldrs* **50/1**
4000 **8** *nk* **Tafteesh (IRE)**[7] 8210 4-8-13 **59** HarrisonShaw(7) 4 58
(Michael Easterby) *s.i.s: plld hrd and hdwy over 5f out: rdn: hung lft and n.m.r over 1f out: no ex ins fnl f* **50/1**
2552 **9** *1 ¼* **Danot (IRE)**[18] 7889 5-9-2 **58** (p) AdamMcNamara(3) 1 54
(Jedd O'Keeffe) *led: hdd over 5f out: w ldr tl led again over 2f out: rdn and hdd over 1f out: no ex ins fnl f* **8/1**[3]
0000 **10** *shd* **Secret Missile**[7] 8216 7-9-7 **60** (v) DavidAllan 12 55
(David C Griffiths) *hld up: shkn up over 2f out: r.o ins fnl f: nt rch ldrs* **33/1**
4341 **11** *1 ½* **Queens Royale**[51] 6814 3-9-3 **58** LukeMorris 8 49
(Michael Appleby) *prom: led over 5f out: hdd over 2f out: wknd ins fnl f* **9/1**

1m 27.34s (-1.46) **Going Correction** -0.15s/f (Stan)
**WFA** 3 from 4yo+ 2lb **11** Ran SP% **116.3**
Speed ratings (Par 101): **102,101,101,101,100 99,98,98,97,96 95**
CSF £35.63 CT £345.35 TOTE £2.20: £1.10, £4.40, £5.00; EX 20.30 Trifecta £201.80.
**Owner** Elite Racing Club **Bred** Elite Racing Club **Trained** Newmarket, Suffolk

**FOCUS**
The second division of a modest handicap. The winning time was marginally quicker off another decent gallop which produced an enthralling four-way photo-finish.
T/Plt: £62.80 to a £1 stake. Pool: £94,360.53 - 1,096.37 winning units T/Qpdt: £3.90 to a £1 stake. Pool: £1,3541.68 - 2,566.14 winning units **Colin Roberts**

8402 - 8406a (Foreign Racing) - See Raceform Interactive

8220
# DUNDALK (A.W) (L-H)
Friday, October 27

**OFFICIAL GOING: Polytrack: standard**

## 8407a IRISH STALLION FARMS EBF COOLEY FILLIES STKS (LISTED RACE) 1m (P)
7:30 (7:33) 3-Y-O+ £27,735 (£8,931; £4,230; £1,880; £940; £470)

RPR
1 **Goldrush (IRE)**[14] 8020 3-9-3 95 KevinManning 12 99+
(J S Bolger, Ire) *settled bhd ldr in 2nd early: 3rd 1/2-way: rdn in 2nd under 2f out and disp ld ins fnl f: r.o wl u.p to ld wl ins fnl f: hld on wl* **9/4**[1]

2 ½ **Aneen (IRE)**[28] 7588 3-9-0 98 ChrisHayes 11 95+
(Kevin Prendergast, Ire) *bmpd s: hld up towards rr: rdn nr side under 2f out and r.o wl ins fnl f to snatch 2nd fnl strides: nrst fin* **12/1**

3 nk **Belle Boyd**[21] 7798 3-9-0 93 WJLee 4 94
(W McCreery, Ire) *mid-div early: clsr in 4th bef 1/2-way: rdn in 3rd under 2f out and clsd u.p to chal far side ins fnl f: hld by wnr clsng stages: denied 2 fnl strides* **9/1**

4 shd **Surrounding (IRE)**[21] 7798 4-9-3 87 ColmO'Donoghue 2 95
(M Halford, Ire) *w ldrs and sn disp ld: racd keenly: led after 3f: 1 l clr appr st: rdn and pressed clly over 1f out: sn jnd and hdd wl ins fnl f: no ex cl home where dropped to 4th* **14/1**

5 ½ **Love Potion (IRE)**[12] 8086 4-9-3 87 (t) SeamieHeffernan 8 94+
(A P O'Brien, Ire) *mid-div: rdn 2f out and sme hdwy u.p ins fnl f: kpt on in 5th clsng stages: nvr nrr* **25/1**

6 ½ **Crowning Glory (FR)**[20] 7815 4-9-3 97 ColinKeane 9 93+
(Ralph Beckett) *w.w: rdn in rr 2f out and sme late hdwy u.p ins fnl f: nrst fin* **7/1**

7 ½ **Peak Princess (IRE)**[9] 8150 3-9-0 89 (b) DeclanMcDonogh 1 90
(Richard Hannon) *dwlt: settled towards rr: hdwy under 2f out to chse ldrs over 1f out where swtchd lft: no ex far side in 4th briefly ins fnl f: one pce clsng stages* **14/1**

8 shd **Pavlenko (JPN)**[12] 8083 3-9-0 93 (p) DonnachaO'Brien 6 90
(A P O'Brien, Ire) *chsd ldrs: pushed along 2f out: rdn over 1f out and no imp on ldrs: one pce clsng stages* **16/1**

9 nk **Pocketfullofdreams (FR)**[12] 8083 3-9-0 92 (t) MichaelHussey 10 90
(A P O'Brien, Ire) *dwlt sltly: in rr of mid-div and pushed along early: rdn and sme hdwy to chse ldrs over 1f out: no ex and one pce ins fnl f* **33/1**

10 1 **Hunaina (IRE)**[21] 7798 3-9-0 100 (t) PatSmullen 7 87
(M Halford, Ire) *chsd ldrs: rdn under 2f out and no ex ent fnl f: wknd* **3/1**[2]

11 hd **Smoulder**[12] 8083 3-9-0 92 (h) WayneLordan 3 87
(A P O'Brien, Ire) *dwlt and pushed along in rr early: tk clsr order under 2f out where n.m.r briefly bhd horses: swtchd rt over 1f out and rdn: kpt on one pce* **13/2**[3]

12 2¼ **Dilmun (USA)**[28] 7588 3-9-0 88 (t) PBBeggy 5 82
(Joseph Patrick O'Brien, Ire) *hld up in mid-div: rdn 2f out and no ex over 1f out: wknd* **40/1**

13 ½ **Swish (IRE)**[21] 7798 3-9-0 85 GaryHalpin 13 80
(John James Feane, Ire) *broke wl to ld briefly tl sn jnd: hdd after 3f: rdn bhd ldrs into st and no ex u.p 1 1/2f out: wknd* **66/1**

14 3¾ **Stormy Belle (IRE)**[12] 8083 3-9-0 90 LeighRoche 14 72
(P A Fahy, Ire) *chsd ldrs: 5th 1/2-way: rdn over 2f out and sn wknd: eased in rr ins fnl f* **66/1**

1m 37.59s (-1.21) **Going Correction** 0.0s/f (Stan)
**WFA** 3 from 4yo+ 3lb **14 Ran SP% 130.7**
Speed ratings: **106,105,105,105,104 104,103,103,103,102 102,99,99,95**
CSF £33.70 TOTE £2.70: £1.40, £4.40, £2.80; DF 37.40 Trifecta £210.10.
**Owner** China Horse Club International Ltd **Bred** Noel O'Callaghan **Trained** Coolcullen, Co Carlow

**FOCUS**
A teak-tough display from the winner, who may not be overly big but undoubtedly has heart. The fourth limits the form.

8408 - 8411a (Foreign Racing) - See Raceform Interactive

8379
# DONCASTER (L-H)
Saturday, October 28

**OFFICIAL GOING: Good to soft (good in places; 7.5)**
Wind: Strong against Weather: Cloudy with sunny periods

## 8412 BET THROUGH THE RACING POST APP DONCASTER STKS (LISTED RACE) 6f 2y
1:45 (1:45) (Class 1) 2-Y-O
£17,013 (£6,450; £3,228; £1,608; £807; £405) **Stalls** Centre

Form RPR
31 1 **Speak In Colours**[50] 6867 2-9-1 0 AndreaAtzeni 8 101
(Marco Botti) *t.k.h early and hld up in rr: hdwy 1/2-way: effrt on inner to chal wl over 1f out: led appr fnl f: sn rdn and kpt on wl* **6/1**[2]

1 2 ½ **Mutaaqeb**[39] 7250 2-9-1 0 JimCrowley 2 99
(Owen Burrows) *dwlt and towards rr: hdwy and in tch 1/2-way: n.m.r over 2f out: rdn and hdwy wl over 1f out: styd on strly fnl f* **9/2**[1]

1563 3 1 **Staxton**[14] 8043 2-9-1 102 DavidAllan 4 96
(Tim Easterby) *trckd ldr: hdwy and cl up over 2f out: rdn to ld briefly 11/2f out: hdd appr fnl f: sn drvn and kpt on same pce* **9/2**[1]

0561 4 2½ **Rebel Assault (IRE)**[14] 8043 2-8-13 100 FrannyNorton 5 87
(Mark Johnston) *led: pushed along over 2f out: sn rdn and hdd 11/2f out: grad wknd* **6/1**[2]

216 5 2¾ **Never Back Down (IRE)**[21] 7821 2-9-1 95 RyanMoore 10 80
(Hugo Palmer) *dwlt and rr: hdwy on inner over 2f out: sn rdn: kpt on fnl f* **6/1**[2]

4130 6 1 **Ulshaw Bridge (IRE)**[66] 6326 2-9-1 90 OisinMurphy 1 77
(James Bethell) *chsd ldrs: rdn along wl over 2f out: sn wknd* **11/1**

0100 7 1 **Neola**[15] 8001 2-8-10 93 RonanWhelan 7 69
(Mick Channon) *hld up towards rr: hdwy on outer 1/2-way: rdn along to chse ldrs 2f out: sn drvn and kpt on one pce* **18/1**

1524 8 nk **Red Roman**[21] 7821 2-9-1 94 WilliamBuick 6 73
(Charles Hills) *prom: rdn along wl over 2f out: sn wknd* **13/2**[3]

240 9 ¾ **Sankari Royale (IRE)**[15] 8001 2-8-10 0 (p[1]) BenCurtis 9 66
(J P Murtagh, Ire) *in tch: hdwy to chse ldrs 1/2-way:. rdn along over 2f out: sn wknd* **14/1**

1m 14.09s (0.49) **Going Correction** +0.30s/f (Good) **9 Ran SP% 112.8**
Speed ratings (Par 103): **108,107,106,102,99 97,96,95,94**
CSF £32.27 TOTE £6.90: £2.30, £1.60, £1.50; EX 31.50 Trifecta £148.30.
**Owner** Scuderia Archi Romani **Bred** Scuderia Archi Romani **Trained** Newmarket, Suffolk

**FOCUS**
A decent little Listed race for juveniles, it looked an open race and was run at a good gallop down the centre. The first two are improving and the runner-up looked a little unfortunate.

## 8413 SCOTT DOBSON MEMORIAL NURSERY H'CAP 7f 6y
2:20 (2:20) (Class 3) (0-95,90) 2-Y-O £7,115 (£2,117; £1,058; £529) **Stalls** Centre

Form RPR
241 1 **Al Hajar (IRE)**[31] 7520 2-9-5 88 (p[1]) WilliamBuick 1 97+
(Charlie Appleby) *hld up: smooth hdwy on inner over 3f out: led wl over 1f out: sn rdn clr: readily* **10/11**[1]

6556 2 3½ **Zap**[15] 8008 2-9-4 90 AdamMcNamara(3) 8 89
(Richard Fahey) *hld up in rr: hdwy 2f out: rdn and hung lft ent fnl f: sn drvn and kpt on: no ch w wnr* **9/1**

4001 3 1 **Lady Anjorica (IRE)**[7] 8236 2-8-7 76 (b) AndrewMullen 7 72
(Keith Dalgleish) *hld up towards rr: swtchd lft and effrt wl over 2f out: rdn wl over 1f out: kpt on fnl f* **20/1**

4411 4 ½ **Rogue**[36] 7353 2-9-1 84 RyanMoore 6 79
(Richard Hannon) *trckd ldr: hdwy 3f out: rdn to ld briefly 2f out: sn hdd and drvn: kpt on same pce* **5/1**[2]

1340 5 1½ **Wensley**[21] 7814 2-8-5 77 GeorgeWood(3) 5 68
(James Bethell) *in tch: pushed along 3f out: rdn to chse ldrs 2f out: sn wknd* **25/1**

4331 6 1¾ **Big Les (IRE)**[19] 7891 2-8-10 79 GrahamLee 3 66
(Karen McLintock) *trckd ldrs: pushed along 3f out: rdn over 2f out: wknd wl over 1f out* **8/1**

4231 7 1½ **Mont Kinabalu (IRE)**[14] 8046 2-8-12 81 TomEaves 4 64
(Kevin Ryan) *led: rdn along 3f out: hdd 2f out: wknd and hld whn hmpd ent fnl f* **7/1**[3]

0310 8 1¼ **Bee Ina Bonnet**[28] 7621 2-8-1 73 (p[1]) RachelRichardson(3) 2 53
(Tim Easterby) *trckd ldrs: hdwy and cl up 3f out: sn rdn and wknd fnl 2f* **33/1**

1m 28.84s (2.54) **Going Correction** +0.30s/f (Good) **8 Ran SP% 114.2**
Speed ratings (Par 99): **97,93,91,91,89 87,85,84**
CSF £9.73 CT £99.07 TOTE £1.70: £1.02, £2.70, £5.20; EX 10.40 Trifecta £63.90.
**Owner** Godolphin **Bred** Doc Bloodstock **Trained** Newmarket, Suffolk
■ Stewards' Enquiry : Adam McNamara two-day ban; careless riding (11th,13th Nov)

**FOCUS**
Racing centre-field, it proved a very one-sided event with the favourite bolting up and the form looks straightforward.

## 8414 CROWNHOTEL-BAWTRY.COM H'CAP 1m 3f 197y
2:55 (2:55) (Class 2) (0-100,95) 3-Y-O+ £12,938 (£3,850; £1,924; £962) **Stalls** Low

Form RPR
6023 1 **Reshoun (FR)**[9] 8188 3-8-11 86 JimCrowley 7 98+
(Ian Williams) *hld up in rr: smooth hdwy over 3f out: chsd ldr wl over 1f out: rdn to ld appr fnl f: kpt on strly* **3/1**[2]

123 2 3¾ **Lawless Secret**[19] 7908 3-8-10 85 (h) AndreaAtzeni 9 90
(Simon Crisford) *hld up towards rr: rapid hdwy 3f out: led over 2f out: jnd and rdn wl over 1f out: hdd and drvn appr fnl f: kpt on same pce* **2/1**[1]

2255 3 1¼ **Rainbow Rebel (IRE)**[126] 4076 4-9-5 88 FrannyNorton 8 91
(Mark Johnston) *prom: sn trcking ldr: hdwy over 3f out: rdn and cl up 2f out: sn drvn and kpt on same pce* **25/1**

0600 4 8 **First Flight (IRE)**[35] 7395 6-9-9 92 GeraldMosse 6 82
(Heather Main) *hld up towards rr: hdwy on inner over 3f out: rdn along to chse ldrs 2f out: sn drvn and no imp* **16/1**

1220 5 3¼ **Burguillos**[105] 4882 4-9-12 95 RyanMoore 4 80
(Alan King) *in tch: sme hdwy 3f out: rdn along wl over 2f out: n.d* **13/2**[3]

0033 6 nk **Lustrous Light (IRE)**[43] 7124 4-9-12 95 (p[1]) OisinMurphy 5 80
(Ralph Beckett) *trckd ldrs: pushed along and hdwy 4f out: rdn 3f out: sn drvn and wknd* **8/1**

5030 7 2 **Jelly Monger (IRE)**[15] 8007 5-8-12 84 GeorgeWood(3) 3 65
(Dominic Ffrench Davis) *chsd ldrs: rdn along over 3f out: sn drvn and wknd* **20/1**

5003 8 3½ **Mukhayyam**[35] 7387 5-9-8 91 (p) DavidAllan 1 67
(Tim Easterby) *led: clr over 5f out: rdn along 3f out: hdd 2f out and sn wknd* **16/1**

50/4 9 28 **Ooty Hill**[30] 7548 5-9-11 94 (h) StevieDonohoe 2 25
(Charlie Fellowes) *trckd ldr 2f: prom: rdn along over 4f out: wknd over 3f out* **13/2**[3]

2m 34.9s **Going Correction** +0.225s/f (Good)
**WFA** 3 from 4yo+ 6lb **9 Ran SP% 116.5**
Speed ratings (Par 109): **109,106,105,100,98 97,96,94,75**
CSF £9.50 CT £122.29 TOTE £4.20: £1.70, £1.10, £3.90; EX 13.20 Trifecta £227.60.
**Owner** Michael Watt & Roy David **Bred** S C E A Haras De Son Altesse L'Aga Khan **Trained** Portway, Worcs

**FOCUS**
A decent handicap run at a good gallop and it set up for the closers, the two 3yos coming to the fore.

## 8415 RACING POST TROPHY STKS (GROUP 1) (ENTIRE COLTS & FILLIES) 1m (S)
3:25 (3:30) (Class 1) 2-Y-O
£122,210 (£46,332; £23,187; £11,550; £5,796; £2,909) **Stalls** Centre

Form RPR
1 1 **Saxon Warrior (JPN)**[34] 7426 2-9-1 110 RyanMoore 9 119
(A P O'Brien, Ire) *trckd ldrs: smooth hdwy to ld jst over 2f out: jnd and rdn over 1f out: hdd ins fnl f: drvn whn carried sltly lft and sltly hmpd last 100 yds: rallied gamely to ld towards fin* **13/8**[1]

111 2 nk **Roaring Lion (USA)**[28] 7616 2-9-1 112 OisinMurphy 12 118
(John Gosden) *hld up in rr: smooth hdwy on outer wl over 2f out: chal over 1f out and sn hung lft: rdn to ld ins fnl f: hung lft again last 100 yds: hdd and no ex towards fin* **8/1**[3]

1 3 2½ **The Pentagon (IRE)**[93] 5345 2-9-1 108 SeamieHeffernan 4 112
(A P O'Brien, Ire) *midfield: n.m.r and swtchd lft 3f out: hdwy over 2f out: sn chsng ldrs: rdn wl over 1f out: kpt on fnl f* **10/1**

21 **4** ¾ **Verbal Dexterity (IRE)**[48] 6975 2-9-1 117...................... KevinManning 1 111
(J S Bolger, Ire) *dwlt and wnt lft s: sn rdn along in rr: hdwy on inner and in tch 1/2-way: styd on u.p and cl up 2f out: drvn over 1f out: grad wknd* **5/2**[2]

221 **5** 1 ¾ **Gabr**[37] 7333 2-9-1 91.......................................................... JimCrowley 10 107
(Sir Michael Stoute) *trckd ldrs: hdwy and rdn along over 2f out: drvn wl over 1f out: kpt on same pce* **33/1**

411 **6** ¾ **Chilean**[49] 6925 2-9-1 106.................................................. AndreaAtzeni 3 105
(Martyn Meade) *hld up towards rr: hdwy on inner over 2f out: rdn wl over 1f out: no imp fnl f* **12/1**

1 **7** 2 ¼ **Loxley (IRE)**[13] 8075 2-9-1 0............................................. WilliamBuick 7 100
(Charlie Appleby) *hld up towards rr: hdwy wl over 2f out: sn rdn along and n.d* **25/1**

513 **8** 1 ¾ **Seahenge (USA)**[14] 8037 2-9-1 112......................... DonnachaO'Brien 11 96
(A P O'Brien, Ire) *hld up towards rr: hdwy 3f out: rdn along 2f out: n.d* **9/1**

3251 **9** 8 **Merlin Magic**[17] 7955 2-9-1 88........................................ PaulMulrennan 8 77
(David Elsworth) *chsd ldrs on wd outside: rdn along over 2f out: grad wknd* **66/1**

1310 **10** 3 ¾ **Alfa McGuire (IRE)**[44] 7090 2-9-1 88................................ GrahamLee 5 69
(Bryan Smart) *chsd ldrs: rdn along and wandered 3f out: sn lost pl and bhd* **100/1**

243 **11** 3 **Coat Of Arms (IRE)**[29] 7580 2-9-1 101........................... WayneLordan 2 62
(A P O'Brien, Ire) *led: rdn along 3f out: hdd over 2f out: sn wknd* **66/1**

2200 **12** ¾ **Theobald (IRE)**[14] 8037 2-9-1 103................................(p) RonanWhelan 6 60
(J S Bolger, Ire) *cl up: rdn along 3f out: sn wknd* **100/1**

1m 40.12s (0.82) **Going Correction** +0.30s/f (Good) **12** Ran SP% **116.3**
Speed ratings (Par 109): **107,106,104,103,101 100,98,96,88,85 82,81**
CSF £14.77 CT £100.60 TOTE £2.30: £1.20, £2.20, £3.10; EX 14.40 Trifecta £78.70.
**Owner** Derrick Smith & Mrs John Magnier & Michael Tabor **Bred** Orpendale, Chelston & Wynatt **Trained** Cashel, Co Tipperary
■ Stewards' Enquiry : Ryan Moore caution; careless riding

**FOCUS**
A strong edition of the race, they raced centre-field and the pacemakers did their job, ensuring a good gallop. Two came clear, with the favourite wrestling it back off the runner-up, who had looked certain for victory racing inside the last furlong. The winner improved again, whilst the runner-up travelled like the best horse on the day.

## 8416 SUN BETS RESPONSIBLE BETTING H'CAP 5f 3y
**4:00** (4:07) (Class 2) 3-Y-O+
**£28,012** (£8,388; £4,194; £2,097; £1,048; £526) **Stalls** Centre

Form RPR

4450 **1** **Tomily (IRE)**[68] 6275 3-8-5 **91**......................................... HollieDoyle(3) 17 100
(Richard Hannon) *hld up in rr: gd hdwy on wd outside 2f out: chsd ldrs ent fnl f: sn rdn: styd on wl to ld nr fin* **28/1**

2150 **2** ½ **Soie D'Leau**[11] 8139 5-8-10 **93**......................................... TonyHamilton 5 99
(Kristin Stubbs) *racd centre: qckly away and led: rdn along and jnd wl over 1f out: drvn ins fnl f: hdd and no ex nr fin* **25/1**

1211 **3** ¾ **Boundsy (IRE)**[28] 7610 3-8-6 **89**....................................... PaulHanagan 8 93
(Richard Fahey) *racd centre: in tch: hdwy 2f out: rdn over 1f out: styd on wl u.p fnl f* **7/1**[2]

0343 **4** nse **Confessional**[7] 8238 10-8-0 **88** ow2...................(be) JamieGormley(5) 14 91
(Tim Easterby) *chsd ldrs on outer: rdn along wl over 1f out: ev ch ent fnl f: sn drvn and kpt on same pce towards fin* **20/1**

3-35 **5** ½ **Global Applause**[19] 7901 3-9-1 **98**.................................... RyanMoore 15 103+
(Ed Dunlop) *hld up in rr: pushed along over 2f out: rdn and hdwy over 1f out: styd on wl fnl f* **16/1**

1500 **6** ½ **Atletico (IRE)**[15] 8012 5-8-8 **91**....................................... AndreaAtzeni 3 91
(Roger Varian) *dwlt and in rr: sn pushed along: rdn over 2f out: hdwy wl over 1f out: styd on u.p fnl f* **15/2**[3]

0012 **7** shd **Just Glamorous (IRE)**[11] 8139 4-9-10 **107**......................... OisinMurphy 2 106
(Ronald Harris) *racd towards far side: cl up: chal 2f out: sn rdn and ev ch: drvn and appr fnl f and grad wknd* **12/1**

0311 **8** 1 ½ **Paddy Power (IRE)**[12] 8115 4-8-0 **83**.............................. PatrickMathers 1 77
(Richard Fahey) *racd towards far side: in tch: rdn along and outpcd wl over 1f out: kpt on u.p fnl f* **9/1**

1211 **9** nse **Erissimus Maximus (FR)**[21] 7809 3-8-4 **90**.........(b) LewisEdmunds(3) 9 85
(Chris Dwyer) *chsd ldrs centre: rdn along 2f out: drvn and wknd over 1f out* **10/1**

5312 **10** nse **Spring Loaded (IRE)**[14] 8044 5-9-5 **102**.............................. JoeyHaynes 6 95
(Paul D'Arcy) *racd towards far side: in tch: rdn along and hdwy over 2f out: drvn and wknd over 1f out* **7/2**[1]

0320 **11** shd **Rasheeq (IRE)**[15] 8012 4-8-1 **87**......................... RachelRichardson(3) 12 80
(Tim Easterby) *mid-div: rdn 2f out: hmpd appr fnl f: kpt on* **14/1**

1241 **12** 3 ¾ **Foxy Forever (IRE)**[11] 8129 7-8-9 **92**..............................(t) FrannyNorton 7 72
(Michael Wigham) *chsd ldrs towards far side: rdn along 2f out: sn wknd* **20/1**

0641 **13** nk **East Street Revue**[15] 8012 4-8-11 **94**........................(b) DuranFentiman 16 72
(Tim Easterby) *chsd ldrs on wd outside: rdn along 2f out: wknd over 1f out* **10/1**

0000 **14** 1 ½ **Orion's Bow**[7] 8238 6-8-9 **92**................................................ DavidAllan 11 65
(Tim Easterby) *dwlt: a towards rr* **9/1**

0000 **15** ½ **Coolfitch (IRE)**[19] 7887 3-8-5 **88**........................................(v) ShaneGray 4 60
(David O'Meara) *dwlt: a towards rr* **66/1**

1m 0.44s (-0.06) **Going Correction** +0.30s/f (Good) **15** Ran SP% **123.2**
Speed ratings (Par 109): **112,111,110,109,109 108,108,105,105,105 105,99,98,96,95**
CSF £591.94 CT £5489.37 TOTE £36.50: £8.60, £5.10, £2.30; EX 894.40 Trifecta £5645.40 Part won..
**Owner** Des Anderson **Bred** D J Anderson **Trained** East Everleigh, Wilts

**FOCUS**
An open sprint, two of the outsiders came to the fore with the winner challenging wide and late. A small personal best from the winner with the fourth helping set the standard.

## 8417 JOIN RACING POST MEMBERS' CLUB CONDITIONS STKS 7f 6y
**4:35** (4:36) (Class 3) 3-Y-O+
**£9,337** (£2,796; £1,398; £699; £349; £175) **Stalls** Centre

Form RPR

0562 **1** **Sir Dancealot (IRE)**[11] 8138 3-8-12 111............................. RyanMoore 3 108+
(David Elsworth) *dwlt and hld up in rr: swtchd lft and hdwy 2f out: rdn over 1f out: qcknd to ld ins fnl f* **10/11**[1]

4531 **2** 1 ¾ **Jallota**[21] 7822 6-9-5 110...................................................... JimCrowley 4 109
(Charles Hills) *trckd ldrs: hdwy to take slt ld 2f out: sn rdn: drvn and hdd ins fnl f: kpt on same pce* **9/4**[2]

1-00 **3** ¾ **Mr Owen (USA)**[247] 892 5-9-0 107......................................... OisinMurphy 1 102
(David Simcock) *trckd ldrs: hdwy over 2f out: sn cl up: rdn and ev ch over 1f out: drvn and kpt on same pce fnl f* **7/1**[3]

0346 **4** ½ **Intisaab**[21] 7806 6-9-0 107...........................................(p) ShelleyBirkett(3) 7 104
(David O'Meara) *hld up in tch: hdwy over 2f out: rdn over 1f out: sn drvn and kpt on same pce* **14/1**

5040 **5** 1 ¼ **Battle Of Marathon (USA)**[28] 7619 5-9-0 92................. GeraldMosse 6 97
(John Ryan) *trckd ldr: cl up 1/2-way: led 3f out: rdn over 2f out: sn hdd: drvn and wknd* **10/1**

20 **6** 8 **Lavetta**[65] 6358 5-8-9 84........................................................ BenCurtis 2 71
(Sally Haynes) *led: pushed along 1/2-way: rdn and hdd 3f out: sn wknd* **40/1**

1m 28.44s (2.14) **Going Correction** +0.30s/f (Good)
**WFA** 3 from 5yo+ 2lb **6** Ran SP% **113.8**
Speed ratings (Par 107): **99,97,96,95,94 85**
CSF £3.24 TOTE £1.70: £1.10, £1.70; EX 3.90 Trifecta £7.40.
**Owner** C Benham/ D Whitford/ L Quinn/ K Quinn **Bred** Vincent Duignan **Trained** Newmarket, Suffolk

**FOCUS**
A good little conditions race that played out as the market suggested it would. They went just a steady gallop and raced down the centre. The race has been rated around the fifth.

## 8418 ALAN WOOD PLUMBING & HEATING APPRENTICE JOCKEYS' TRAINING SERIES FINAL H'CAP 7f 6y
**5:10** (5:10) (Class 4) (0-85,86) 3-Y-O
**£5,175** (£1,540; £769; £384) **Stalls** Centre

Form RPR

5401 **1** **Toy Theatre**[30] 7545 3-8-11 **75**.................................. GabrieleMalune(3) 4 84
(Michael Appleby) *hld up towards rr: hdwy over 2f out: chsd ldrs over 1f out: rdn to chal ent fnl f: edgd rt and kpt on wl to ld nr fin* **10/1**

1132 **2** nk **Pastime**[92] 5369 3-9-9 **84**....................................... CameronNoble 5 92
(Gay Kelleway) *hld up towards rr: hdwy over 2f out: rdn over 1f out: led appr fnl f: drvn and edgd lft last 100 yds: hdd and no ex nr fin* **9/1**

3132 **3** 1 ¼ **Hajjam**[22] 7780 3-9-5 **80**.....................................(h) PatrickVaughan 7 86+
(David O'Meara) *dwlt and rr: hdwy 2f out: rdn over 1f out: styd on wl fnl f* **5/1**[2]

0022 **4** 1 **Clef**[12] 8113 3-9-1 **76**........................................................ ConnorMurtagh 2 78
(Richard Fahey) *led 2f: trckd ldrs: effrt and hdwy wl over 1f out: rdn and n.m.r ent fnl: kpt on same pce* **7/2**[1]

0536 **5** hd **Rose Berry**[21] 7811 3-9-6 **81**.............................................(h) NicolaCurrie 3 83
(Chris Dwyer) *hld up in tch: : hdwy 2f out: rdn to chse ldrs over 1f out: kpt on same pce fnl f* **16/1**

1-10 **6** 2 ¼ **Ocean Air (FR)**[163] 2755 3-9-1 **81**....................................... PaulHainey(5) 11 77
(James Tate) *hld up: hdwy over 2f out: rdn wl over 1f out: kpt on fnl f* **13/2**[3]

0364 **7** ¾ **Medici Banchiere**[22] 7784 3-9-6 **86**...................(v[1]) PatrickO'Hanlon(5) 10 80
(K R Burke) *trckd ldrs: hdwy over 2f out: rdn to ld wl over 1f out: sn edgd lft and hdd: sn wknd* **11/1**

4610 **8** 5 **Scofflaw**[28] 7622 3-9-5 **85**............................................ SebastianWoods(5) 9 65
(Richard Fahey) *prom: rdn along 2f out: sn wknd* **8/1**

160 **9** shd **Robin Weathers (USA)**[35] 7404 3-9-3 **81**.............. DarraghKeenan(3) 1 61
(William Haggas) *trckd ldrs: led after 2f and sn clr: rdn over 2f out: drvn and hdd wl over 1f out: sn wknd* **7/1**

6660 **10** 9 **Thomas Cranmer (USA)**[18] 7941 3-9-4 **79**.................... JamieGormley 6 35
(Mark Johnston) *a towards rr* **20/1**

-400 **11** 1 **Dandyman Port (IRE)**[21] 7839 3-9-3 **81**..............(b[1]) SeamusCronin(3) 8 34
(Des Donovan, Ire) *t.k.h: chsd ldrs: rdn along wl over 2f out: sn wknd* **20/1**

1m 27.88s (1.58) **Going Correction** +0.30s/f (Good) **11** Ran SP% **118.7**
Speed ratings (Par 103): **103,102,101,100,99 97,96,90,90,80 79**
CSF £97.73 CT £504.53 TOTE £11.10: £3.40, £2.60, £1.80; EX 117.90 Trifecta £428.40.
**Owner** L J Vaessen **Bred** Darley **Trained** Oakham, Rutland

**FOCUS**
A fair handicap that saw the closers come to the fore, with the pace having increased significantly after a couple of furlongs.
T/Jkpt: Partly Won. £10,000.00 to a £1 stake. Pool: £8,438.68 - 0.5 winning unit. T/Plt: £28.60 to a £1 stake. Pool: £142,345.27 - 3,628.15 winning units T/Qpdt: £10.40 to a £1 stake. Pool: £8,538.79 - 607.05 winning units **Joe Rowntree**

# 8387 NEWBURY (L-H)
Saturday, October 28

**OFFICIAL GOING: Soft (5.5)**
Wind: light, against Weather: sunny spells, light cloud

## 8419 CONUNDRUM EBF FILLIES' NOVICE STKS (PLUS 10 RACE) (DIV I) 1m (S)
**1:10** (1:10) (Class 4) 2-Y-O
**£5,175** (£1,540; £769; £384) **Stalls** Centre

Form RPR

6 **1** **Red Starlight**[19] 7898 2-9-0 0.............................................. SeanLevey 3 76
(Richard Hannon) *trckd ldr tl pushed into ld wl over 1f out: styd on wl ins fnl f: rdn out* **6/1**[3]

5 **2** 1 **Expensive Liaison (IRE)**[24] 7733 2-9-0 0...................... JamesDoyle 14 74
(Hugo Palmer) *hld up wl in tch in midfield: effrt to press ldrs over 1f out: chsd wnr 1f out: kpt on but a hld ins fnl f* **2/1**[1]

**3** 2 ¼ **Hazarfiya** 2-9-0 0.................................................................. TedDurcan 4 69
(Sir Michael Stoute) *hld up wl in tch in midfield: effrt over 2f out: hdwy and switching rt 1f out: wnt 3rd ins fnl f: kpt on: no threat to ldrs* **11/1**

**4** ½ **Birch Grove (IRE)** 2-9-0 0............................................. JamieSpencer 12 68
(David Simcock) *hld up wl in tch in midfield: effrt wl over 1f out: hdwy whn rn green and hung lft 1f out: wnt 4th and kpt on ins fnl f: no threat to ldrs* **5/1**[2]

0 **5** 1 **Arendelle**[24] 7733 2-9-0 0........................................... RichardKingscote 1 66
(Ed Walker) *wl in tch in midfield: effrt and hdwy to chse ldrs over 1f out: chsd clr ldng pair 150yds: one pced and no imp: lost 2 pls wl ins fnl f* **7/1**

**6** 2 ¾ **Dawn Of Reckoning** 2-9-0 0................................................ RyanTate 2 60
(Jonathan Portman) *in tch in midfield: effrt over 2f out: unable qck and outpcd over 1f out: rallied and styd on ins fnl f: no threat to ldrs* **66/1**

0 **7** 1 ½ **Kiss Me Daily (FR)**[84] 5655 2-9-0 0.................................. DavidProbert 6 56
(Ralph Beckett) *wnt rt s: t.k.h: hld up in tch: effrt and swtchd lft over 1f out: no imp 1f out: wl hld and kpt on same pce ins fnl f* **33/1**

0 **8** ¾ **Mirror Mirror (IRE)**[15] 8006 2-9-0 0.................................. JackMitchell 5 55
(Peter Chapple-Hyam) *led tl rdn and hdd wl over 1f out: outpcd and lost 2nd 1f out: wknd ins fnl f* **16/1**

00 **9** ½ **Sister Celine (IRE)**[15] 7997 2-9-0 0............................ KieranShoemark 10 54
(Roger Charlton) *stdd s: t.k.h: hld up in tch in midfield: effrt over 1f out: sn struggling and outpcd: wknd ins fnl f* **66/1**

10 hd **Thresholdofadream (IRE)** 2-9-0 0 PJMcDonald 9 53
(Amanda Perrett) *s.i.s: hld up in tch towards rr: effrt 2f out: sn outpcd and btn over 1f out: wknd ins fnl f* **40/1**

11 hd **Snatty Dancer** 2-9-0 0 JosephineGordon 8 53
(Hughie Morrison) *chsd ldrs: rdn jst over 2f out: sn struggling and lost pl over 1f out: wknd fnl f* **12/1**

0033 12 1 **Lamb Chop**[19] 7897 2-9-0 74 (p) WilliamCarson 11 51
(Rod Millman) *chsd ldrs: rdn over 2f out: lost pl over 1f out: wknd and bhd ins fnl f* **14/1**

13 3 **Mille Tank** 2-9-0 0 MartinDwyer 13 44
(William Muir) *s.i.s: hld up in tch in rr: sme hdwy 3f out: dropped to rr again and rdn 2f out: sn struggling: wknd fnl f* **28/1**

1m 46.03s (6.33) **Going Correction** +0.475s/f (Yiel) **13** Ran SP% **117.2**
Speed ratings (Par 94): **87,86,83,83,82 79,78,77,76,76 76,75,72**
CSF £17.32 TOTE £7.00: £2.40, £1.20, £3.70; EX 26.00 Trifecta £75.80.
**Owner** Cheveley Park Stud **Bred** Cheveley Park Stud Ltd **Trained** East Everleigh, Wilts

**FOCUS**
The going was given as soft (GoingStick: 5.5) but after riding in the first Kieran Shoemark said that while it was soft, it was more holding than the previous day and Ted Durcan agreed that it was holding and sticky. Sean Levey agreed with the official description. The 7f and 5f bends had been moved out overnight to give fresh ground, so add 27yds to all round course races. The early pace wasn't that strong, but it still proved a test in the conditions.

## 8420 SIR GERALD WHENT MEMORIAL NURSERY H'CAP 6f
**1:40** (1:41) (Class 3) (0-95,90) 2-Y-O **£6,469** (£1,925; £962; £481) **Stalls** Centre

Form RPR

2633 1 **Airshow**[11] 8131 2-8-1 **70** KieranO'Neill 1 74
(Rod Millman) *stdd s: t.k.h: chsd ldrs: rdn 2f out: chsd ldr over 1f out: kpt on u.p to ld 75yds out: sn in command: rdn out* **11/1**

0231 2 1 ½ **Mr Top Hat**[24] 7741 2-9-2 **85** AdamKirby 8 85
(David Evans) *swtchd rt s: racd away fr field in midfield: drifted bk to join rivals 1/2-way: edgd rt 2f out: 3rd and unable qck 1f out: swtchd lft ins fnl f: kpt on to go 2nd towards fin: no threat to wnr* **9/2**[3]

0310 3 ½ **Tathmeen (IRE)**[66] 6330 2-9-2 **85** SeanLevey 7 83
(Richard Hannon) *in tch towards rr: hdwy to chse ldrs 1/2-way: nt clrest of runs and edging rt over 1f out: rallied ins fnl f: kpt on to snatch 3rd last strides: no threat to wnr* **4/1**[2]

0113 4 nk **Prestbury Park (USA)**[14] 8039 2-9-7 **90** JamesDoyle 2 87
(Mark Johnston) *led: wnt 2 l clr and sed edging rt 2f out: hung rt over 1f out: drvn 1f out: hdd 75yds out: wknd and lost 2 pls towards fin* **7/2**[1]

2414 5 ½ **Diamond Dougal (IRE)**[24] 7734 2-8-6 **78** DavidEgan(3) 5 74
(Mick Channon) *stdd s: hld up in last pair: effrt whn nt clr run and carried rt over 1f out: swtchd lft and kpt on ins fnl f: no threat to wnr* **5/1**

0425 6 3 ½ **Royal Household**[13] 8074 2-8-6 **75** TomMarquand 3 60
(Richard Hannon) *t.k.h: wl in tch in midfield: effrt wl over 1f out: unable qck and sn struggling: wknd ins fnl f* **7/2**[1]

0023 7 4 ½ **New Empire**[37] 7335 2-8-7 **79** (b) NoelGarbutt(3) 6 51
(Peter Chapple-Hyam) *t.k.h: pressed ldr tl 2f out: sn lost 2nd and dropped to rr: bhd and wknd ins fnl f* **20/1**

1m 15.48s (2.48) **Going Correction** +0.475s/f (Yiel) **7** Ran SP% **112.4**
Speed ratings (Par 99): **102,100,99,98,98 93,87**
CSF £57.17 CT £233.27 TOTE £12.10: £4.40, £2.20; EX 64.80 Trifecta £327.30.
**Owner** Mrs M E Slade **Bred** Mrs M E Slade **Trained** Kentisbeare, Devon

**FOCUS**
A few of these raced keenly early on, but they included the winner who overcame that to break his maiden at the eighth attempt and recorded a small personal best.

## 8421 WORTHINGTON'S "INDIGO LEISURE" STKS (REGISTERED AS THE ST SIMON STAKES) (GROUP 3) 1m 4f
**2:15** (2:15) (Class 1) 3-Y-O+
**£34,026** (£12,900; £6,456; £3,216; £1,614; £810) **Stalls** Centre

Form RPR

0025 1 **Best Solution (IRE)**[55] 6727 3-8-12 115 PatCosgrave 10 114
(Saeed bin Suroor) *trckd ldrs tl wnt 2nd 10f out: clsd to join ldr and travelling strly over 2f out: rdn and qcknd to ld over 1f out: edgd lft to rail but in command 1f out: r.o wl* **6/1**[3]

4102 2 1 ¾ **Raheen House (IRE)**[22] 7783 3-9-1 110 JamieSpencer 3 113
(Brian Meehan) *hld up in tch in midfield: effrt u.p to chse wnr over 1f out: kpt on u.p ins fnl f: nvr threatening wnr* **5/1**[2]

1421 3 1 ½ **Danehill Kodiac (IRE)**[21] 7805 4-9-7 112 SeanLevey 6 111
(Richard Hannon) *t.k.h: chsd ldr for 2f: chsd ldng pair after: effrt ent fnl 2f: drvn over 1f out: 3rd and kpt on same pce ins fnl f* **11/1**

312- 4 1 **Mountain Bell**[371] 7545 4-9-1 107 MartinHarley 7 103
(Ralph Beckett) *hld up in tch in rr: hdwy on outer and edging lft over 1f out: kpt on to go 4th ins fnl f: no threat to wnr* **7/1**

1002 5 nse **What About Carlo (FR)**[31] 7506 6-9-4 108 CharlesBishop 1 106
(Eve Johnson Houghton) *hld up in tch in midfield: shkn up 2f out: effrt over 1f out: kpt on u.p ins fnl f: no threat to wnr* **8/1**

2361 6 2 ½ **Frontiersman**[29] 7581 4-9-4 117 (b) JamesDoyle 4 102
(Charlie Appleby) *led: jnd and rdn over 2f out: lost 2nd and getting outpcd whn sltly impeded and nudged rail over 1f out: wknd ins fnl f* **9/2**[1]

0020 7 shd **Across The Stars (IRE)**[35] 7393 4-9-4 105 TedDurcan 8 102
(Sir Michael Stoute) *stdd s and dropped in bhd: hld up in tch in last quartet: nt clr run 2f out: swtchd rt and effrt over 1f out: styd on same pac ins fnl f: nvr trbld ldrs* **33/1**

2100 8 2 ½ **Natavia**[15] 8007 3-8-9 102 (t) KieranShoemark 2 96
(Roger Charlton) *stdd bk into last quartet after 1f: nt clr run on inner over 2f out: effrt over 1f out: sn no imp: wknd ins fnl f* **12/1**

5041 9 1 ½ **Ayrad (IRE)**[24] 7743 6-9-4 109 (b) RichardKingscote 9 95
(Roger Charlton) *chsd ldng trio: nt clr run and edgd out rt 2f out: sn u.p and no imp: wknd ins fnl f* **25/1**

1040 10 6 **Western Hymn**[48] 6976 6-9-7 108 (b[1]) FrankieDettori 5 89
(John Gosden) *hld up in tch in last quartet: clipped heels and stmbld after 2f: nt clr run ent fnl 2f: sn rdn and no hdwy: bhd and eased wl ins fnl f* **12/1**

6-43 11 ½ **Architecture (IRE)**[15] 8007 4-9-1 107 JosephineGordon 11 82
(Hugo Palmer) *in tch in midfield: rdn and lost pl 2f out: bhd and eased wl ins fnl f* **8/1**

2m 40.68s (5.18) **Going Correction** +0.775s/f (Yiel)
**WFA** 3 from 4yo+ 6lb **11** Ran SP% **114.4**
Speed ratings (Par 113): **113,111,110,110,110 108,108,106,105,101 101**
CSF £35.00 TOTE £6.40: £2.20, £1.80, £2.90; EX 33.00 Trifecta £201.40.
**Owner** Godolphin **Bred** Cecil & Martin McCracken **Trained** Newmarket, Suffolk

**FOCUS**
Race distance increased by 27yds. They went steady early on and the winner was always well placed just off the leader. He has been rated back to his best.

## 8422 BATHWICK TYRES STKS (REGISTERED AS THE HORRIS HILL STAKES) (GROUP 3) (C&G) 7f (S)
**2:50** (2:50) (Class 1) 2-Y-O
**£22,684** (£8,600; £4,304; £2,144; £1,076; £540) **Stalls** Centre

Form RPR

2632 1 **Nebo (IRE)**[15] 8024 2-9-0 108 FrankieDettori 4 107
(Charles Hills) *trckd ldrs: effrt over 1f out: ev ch 1f out: led 100yds out: styd on wl* **4/1**[3]

1103 2 ½ **Tangled (IRE)**[30] 7546 2-9-0 106 SeanLevey 2 106
(Richard Hannon) *stdd s: hld up in tch in last pair: effrt and clsd but hanging lft over 1f out: led briefly ins fnl f: hdd 100yds out: kpt on but a hld after* **15/2**

1135 3 ¾ **Mythical Magic (IRE)**[27] 7667 2-9-0 0 JamesDoyle 1 104
(Charlie Appleby) *led: rdn over 1f out: hrd pressed 1f out: sn hdd and styd on same pce ins fnl f* **2/1**[1]

331 4 ½ **Archie McKellar**[10] 8149 2-9-0 84 RichardKingscote 7 102
(Ralph Beckett) *stdd s: hld up in last pair: shkn up and effrt over 1f out: hdwy and rdn to chal 1f out: unable qck and outpcd fnl 100yds* **10/1**

15 5 1 ½ **Vintager**[56] 6696 2-9-0 0 KieranShoemark 5 99
(David Menuisier) *trckd ldrs: shkn up over 2f out: rdn fnd little and dropped to rr over 1f out: swtchd rt ent fnl f: kpt on same pce ins fnl f* **7/2**[2]

152 6 1 **Dream Today (IRE)**[14] 8036 2-9-0 107 PJMcDonald 6 96
(Mark Johnston) *chsd ldr: rdn ent fnl 2f: drvn and ev ch 1f out: sn no ex and wknd fnl 100yds* **5/1**

1m 27.87s (2.17) **Going Correction** +0.475s/f (Yiel) **6** Ran SP% **113.1**
Speed ratings (Par 105): **106,105,104,104,102 101**
CSF £32.68 TOTE £3.90: £2.70, £2.70; EX 28.60 Trifecta £47.10.
**Owner** Mrs Julie Martin And David R Martin **Bred** Select Bloodstock & Melchior Bloodstock **Trained** Lambourn, Berks

**FOCUS**
This looked an ordinary renewal. They slightly split into two groups of three, and the first three came from the lot that raced more towards the far side.

## 8423 WORTHINGTON'S ALZHEIMER'S SOCIETY H'CAP 1m 2f
**3:20** (3:20) (Class 2) (0-105,102) 3-Y-O+ **£12,938** (£3,850; £1,924; £962) **Stalls** Centre

Form RPR

1161 1 **Century Dream (IRE)**[28] 7609 3-9-7 **101** (t) FrankieDettori 11 111+
(Simon Crisford) *hld up in last trio: rdn and hdwy ent fnl 2f: styd on to ld 1f out: styd on wl ins fnl f* **13/8**[1]

6002 2 1 ¼ **Abdon**[28] 7602 4-9-9 **102** GeorgiaCox(3) 8 109
(Sir Michael Stoute) *chsd ldr tl clsd to ld over 3f out: rdn over 2f out: hdd 1f out: kpt on same pce ins fnl f* **12/1**

1/1- 3 ¾ **Towerlands Park (IRE)**[325] 8249 4-9-1 **91** JamesDoyle 5 96+
(Michael Bell) *hld up in midfield: clsd over 2f out: rdn and hdwy over 1f out: chsd ldrs 1f out: kpt on same pce ins fnl f* **9/1**

010 4 1 ½ **Awake My Soul (IRE)**[10] 8165 8-8-12 **88** JamesSullivan 1 90
(Tom Tate) *t.k.h: led: wnt clr 8f out tl hdd over 3f out: sn rdn: rallied to chse ldrs over 1f out: hung rt and kpt on same pce ins fnl f* **16/1**

6003 5 3 **Sea Fox (IRE)**[22] 7784 3-8-10 **90** (t) FranBerry 6 87
(David Evans) *stdd after s: t.k.h: hld up in rr: swtchd rt and hdwy but edging lft over 1f out: kpt on ins fnl f: nvr trbld ldrs* **16/1**

3006 6 ¾ **Mutarakez (IRE)**[10] 8165 5-8-7 **83** TomMarquand 7 78
(Brian Meehan) *t.k.h: hld up in rr: swtchd lft and hdwy over 2f out: drvn and ev ch wl over 1f out tl no ex 1f out: wknd ins fnl f* **9/2**[2]

1000 7 nk **Weekend Offender (FR)**[14] 8042 4-9-6 **96** KevinStott 3 90
(Kevin Ryan) *s.i.s: hld up in last trio: effrt over 2f out: hdwy ent fnl f: kpt on but nvr threatened ldrs* **16/1**

4033 8 3 ½ **Storm Rock**[17] 7959 5-8-7 **83** oh6 DavidProbert 9 70
(Harry Dunlop) *chsd ldrs: clsd to press ldr 3f out: sn rdn and ev ch tl outpcd wl over 1f out: wknd fnl f* **25/1**

10-0 9 7 **Genetics (FR)**[12] 8111 3-8-3 **83** JosephineGordon 10 57
(Andrew Balding) *midfield: rdn over 2f out: sn struggling and lost pl wl over 1f out: bhd and eased wl ins fnl f* **8/1**[3]

5030 10 1 ½ **Restorer**[21] 7805 5-9-8 **98** MartinDwyer 4 68
(William Muir) *dwlt: sn rcvrd and in tch in midfield: rdn and lost pl over 2f out: bhd and eased wl ins fnl f* **25/1**

0044 11 6 **Master Carpenter (IRE)**[14] 8042 6-9-7 **97** PhillipMakin 2 55
(Rod Millman) *chsd ldrs: rdn 3f out: sn struggling and lost pl 2f out: bhd and eased ins fnl f* **12/1**

2m 13.79s (4.99) **Going Correction** +0.775s/f (Yiel)
**WFA** 3 from 4yo+ 4lb **11** Ran SP% **118.1**
Speed ratings (Par 109): **111,110,109,108,105 105,104,102,96,95 90**
CSF £23.28 CT £136.27 TOTE £2.20: £1.10, £2.90, £2.90; EX 14.20 Trifecta £37.10.
**Owner** Abdullah Saeed **Bred** Rabbah Bloodstock Limited **Trained** Newmarket, Suffolk

**FOCUS**
Race distance increased by 27yds. Not a bad handicap and it was won by a progressive sort. The race has been rated around the runner-up.

## 8424 BATHWICK TYRES STKS (REGISTERED AS THE RADLEY STAKES) (LISTED RACE) 7f (S)
**3:55** (3:55) (Class 1) 2-Y-O
**£17,013** (£6,450; £3,228; £1,207; £1,207; £405) **Stalls** Centre

Form RPR

1145 1 **Hikmaa (IRE)**[15] 8002 2-9-0 101 AdamBeschizza 5 98
(Ed Vaughan) *wl in tch in midfield: effrt and hdwy to chse ldr wl over 1f out: led ins fnl f: styd on wl: rdn out* **7/2**[2]

412 2 ¾ **Shepherd Market (IRE)**[46] 7021 2-9-0 87 AdamKirby 8 96
(Clive Cox) *led: rdn and qcknd wl over 1f out: hung lft 1f out: hdd ins fnl f: tl hanging and kpt on same pce after* **10/1**

1516 3 ½ **Expressiy (FR)**[15] 8002 2-9-0 92 (h) JamesDoyle 10 95
(Charlie Appleby) *t.k.h: chsd ldrs: effrt wl over 2f out: 3rd and kpt on same pce ins fnl f* **6/1**

4116 4 1 ½ **Daddies Girl (IRE)**[14] 8043 2-9-0 89 SteveDrowne 6 91
(Rod Millman) *in tch in rr: pushed along 4f out: rdn 3f out: hdwy u.p jst over 1f out: kpt on ins fnl f: nvr threatened ldrs* **16/1**

5130 4 dht **Miss Bar Beach (IRE)**[44] 7088 2-9-0 96 ShaneKelly 4 91
(Keith Dalgleish) *t.k.h: hld up in tch towards rr: rdn and hdwy over 1f out: chsd laders 1f out: kpt on same pce and no imp ins fnl f* **25/1**

1 **6** 3/4 **Magnolia Springs (IRE)**[36] 7357 2-9-0 0 CharlesBishop 1 89
(Eve Johnson Houghton) *in tch in midfield: shkn up 2f out: nt clr run and trying to switch rt over 1f out: swtchd rt ins fnl f: kpt on fnl 100yds: no threat to ldrs* **10/3**[1]

4361 **7** *nk* **Elysium Dream**[21] 7814 2-9-0 85 TomMarquand 7 88
(Richard Hannon) *wnt rt s: hld up in tch: effrt and hdwy u.p 2f out: no imp 1f out: kpt on same pce ins fnl f* **16/1**

2 **8** *nse* **Sunday Smart (IRE)**[21] 7834 2-9-0 0 TedDurcan 13 88
(P J Prendergast, Ire) *stdd s: hld up in tch in rr: swtchd rt and hdwy u.p over 1f out: no imp ins fnl f: hld and hung lft towards fin* **28/1**

4 **9** 1 1/2 **Moonlight Bay**[13] 8081 2-9-0 95 JamieSpencer 11 86
(G M Lyons, Ire) *stdd and short of room leaving stalls: hld up in tch in rr: clsd and nt clr run 2f out: effrt and sme hdwy u.p over 1f out: no imp ins fnl f* **5/1**[3]

4214 **10** 1/2 **Escape The City**[21] 7814 2-9-0 76 CharlieBennett 2 83
(Hughie Morrison) *trckd ldr tl wl over 1f out: sn rdn and unable qck: wknd ins fnl f* **33/1**

120 **11** 1 1/2 **Model (FR)**[70] 6228 2-9-0 0 SeanLevey 9 79
(Richard Hannon) *trckd ldrs: unable qck u.p and lost pl over 1f out: wknd ins fnl f* **33/1**

1360 **12** 1 1/4 **Musical Art (IRE)**[15] 8004 2-9-0 97 PJMcDonald 14 76
(Paul Cole) *t.k.h: trckd ldrs: rdn 2f out: sn struggling and lost pl over 1f out: bhd ins fnl f* **12/1**

0315 **13** 1 **Pulitzer**[14] 8043 2-9-0 90 JosephineGordon 12 73
(Hugo Palmer) *t.k.h: hld up in tch in midfield: rdn 2f out: unable qck and lost pl over 1f out: bhd ins fnl f* **20/1**

1m 28.84s (3.14) **Going Correction** +0.475s/f (Yiel) **13** Ran SP% **122.7**
Speed ratings (Par 103): **101,100,99,97,97 97,96,96,94,94 92,91,90**
CSF £36.92 TOTE £4.40: £1.60, £3.00, £2.00; EX 37.80 Trifecta £230.00.
**Owner** Sheikh Hamed Dalmook Al Maktoum **Bred** L Wright **Trained** Newmarket, Suffolk

**FOCUS**
An average running of this Listed contest with the winner the pick on her best form.

## 8425 CONUNDRUM EBF FILLIES' NOVICE STKS (PLUS 10 RACE) (DIV II) 1m (S)

**4:30** (4:30) (Class 4) 2-Y-O **£5,175** (£1,540; £769; £384) **Stalls** Centre

Form RPR

**1** **Highgarden** 2-9-0 0 FrankieDettori 5 81+
(John Gosden) *hld up wl in tch in midfield and travelled strly: clsd 2f out: pushed into ld over 1f out: r.o wl and clr ins fnl f: pushed out: comf* **13/8**[1]

**2** 2 1/4 **Spirit Of Appin** 2-9-0 0 JamieSpencer 13 76
(Brian Meehan) *stdd s and hld up wl in tch in rr: hdwy and switching lft 2f out: chsd clr wnr 150yds out: styd on but no threat to wnr* **16/1**

**3** 1 1/4 **Arcadian Cat (USA)** 2-9-0 0 PhillipMakin 12 73
(Ralph Beckett) *hld up in tch towards rr: swtchd rt 2f out: hdwy to chse ldrs and edgd lft over 1f out: battling for 3rd and kpt on same pce ins fnl f* **14/1**

3 **4** *hd* **Dream Of Camelot (IRE)**[19] 7898 2-9-0 0 ShaneKelly 11 73
(Gary Moore) *t.k.h: hld up in tch: nt clr run 2f out: rdn and hdwy but edgd rt over 1f out: battling for 3rd and kpt on same pce ins fnl f* **11/2**[3]

02 **5** 4 **Endless Tangent (IRE)**[28] 7608 2-9-0 0 PJMcDonald 10 64
(Tom Dascombe) *led: rdn and hung lft over 1f out: sn hdd and unable qck: wknd ins fnl f* **9/1**

**6** 1 3/4 **Tuscan Pearl** 2-9-0 0 MartinHarley 8 60
(William Knight) *hld up in tch towards rr: n.m.r ent fnl 2f: sme hdwy to pass btn horses 1f out: keeping on but no ch w wnr whn nt clr run and swtchd rt towards fin* **66/1**

**7** 1/2 **Pink Phantom** 2-9-0 0 SeanLevey 9 59
(Paul Cole) *chsd ldrs: rdn and unable qck over 1f out: wknd ins fnl f* **33/1**

**8** 1/2 **Sudona** 2-9-0 0 JamesDoyle 7 58
(Hugo Palmer) *w ldr: ev ch and rdn whn carried lft and unable qck over 1f out: lost pl qckly and btn 1f out: wknd ins fnl f* **5/1**[2]

**9** 2 1/4 **Can Can Sixty Two** 2-8-11 0 DavidEgan(3) 3 53
(Mick Channon) *pushed along early: in tch: rdn 1/2-way: struggling 2f out and sn outpcd: wknd fnl f* **50/1**

0 **10** 3/4 **Maid Up**[15] 7997 2-9-0 0 DavidProbert 14 52
(Andrew Balding) *hld up in tch in midfield: clsd to trck ldrs 1/2-way: effrt 2f out: unable qck and losing pl whn squeezed for room over 1f out: sn wknd* **10/1**

**11** 3 1/4 **Physical Power (IRE)** 2-9-0 0 TomMarquand 1 44
(Richard Hannon) *in tch in rr: rdn over 2f out: sn outpcd and struggling: wl hld fnl 2f* **16/1**

**12** 9 **Homing Star** 2-9-0 0 RyanTate 4 25
(Jonathan Portman) *t.k.h: chsd ldrs tl over 2f out: sn struggling and lost pl: bhd and eased wl ins fnl f* **66/1**

00 **13** 1 1/4 **Pescedora (IRE)**[10] 8163 2-9-0 0 KieranShoemark 6 22
(Roger Charlton) *t.k.h: chsd ldrs tl over 2f out: sn rdn and lost pl 2f out: wl bhd and eased wl ins fnl f* **20/1**

00 **14** 12 **Boscastle (USA)**[24] 7733 2-9-0 0 JosephineGordon 2
(Hughie Morrison) *in tch in midfield: rdn 2f out: sn struggling and lost pl qckly over 1f out: lost action and eased ins fnl f* **40/1**

1m 45.24s (5.54) **Going Correction** +0.475s/f (Yiel) **14** Ran SP% **122.8**
Speed ratings (Par 94): **91,88,87,87,83 81,81,80,78,77 74,65,64,52**
CSF £31.33 TOTE £2.50: £1.30, £5.00, £4.10; EX 25.20 Trifecta £248.10.
**Owner** Mrs C R Philipson & Mrs H Lascelles **Bred** Mrs C R Philipson & Lofts Hall Stud **Trained** Newmarket, Suffolk

**FOCUS**
The quicker of the two divisions by 0.79sec and the winner did it well having been well backed to do so.

## 8426 WORTHINGTON'S "VICTORIA CLUB" LADY JOCKEYS' H'CAP (FOR LADY AMATEUR RIDERS) 1m 4f

**5:05** (5:05) (Class 5) (0-75,75) 4-Y-O+ **£2,807** (£870; £435; £217) **Stalls** Centre

Form RPR

-532 **1** **Bybrook**[41] 7201 4-10-0 71 (p) MissEEasterby(3) 5 78+
(David Simcock) *hld up off the pce in rr of main gp: clsd to chse ldrs whn nt clr run and swtchd rt 2f out: styd on to chal 1f out: led ins fnl f: kpt on* **5/1**

3114 **2** 1/2 **Take Two**[19] 7908 8-10-7 75 MissSBrotherton 8 81+
(Alex Hales) *v.s.a: detached in last: swtchd rt 9f out: pushed along and prog into midfield but stl plenty to do over 1f out: steadily clsd: reminders wl ins fnl f to go 2nd towards fin: nvr quite getting to wnr* **3/1**[2]

-603 **3** 3/4 **Togetherness (IRE)**[155] 3027 4-10-2 70 MissJoannaMason 6 75
(Patrick Chamings) *hld up off the pce in midfield: clsd to chse ldrs 4f out: rdn and ev ch 3f out: led over 1f out: hdd and styd on same pce ins fnl f: lost 2nd towards fin* **33/1**

-011 **4** *hd* **Tawseef (IRE)**[12] 8109 9-9-6 65 MissEllaMcCain(5) 2 69
(Donald McCain) *chsd ldr: clsd to ld over 3f out: rdn over 2f out: hdd over 1f out: kpt on same pce and lost 2 pls towards fin* **5/2**[1]

4241 **5** 2 1/2 **Pastoral Music**[15] 8000 4-9-11 72 (p) MissGDucker(7) 1 72
(Hughie Morrison) *chsd ldrs: clsd and wl in tch over 3f out: nudged along over 2f out: kpt on same pce fr over 1f out* **12/1**

00-4 **6** 2 1/2 **Walsingham Grange (USA)**[30] 7558 4-10-4 72 MissGAndrews 3 68
(Pam Sly) *hld up off the pce in midfield: clsd qckly to chse ldrs 4f out: rdn 3f out: sn drvn and unable qck: 6th and hld 1f out: plugged on* **7/2**[3]

4-05 **7** 5 **Mister Fizz**[7] 603 9-9-12 71 (p) MissJCooley(5) 9 59
(Miss Imogen Pickard) *hld up off the pce in midfield: rdn 4f out: nvr getting on terms and wl hld 7th over 1f out* **14/1**

500- **8** 9 **Tindaro (FR)**[116] 8558 10-10-0 75 (t) MissSophieSmith(7) 7 49
(Paul Webber) *s.i.s: hld up off the pce in rr of main gp: short lived effrt over 2f out: sn wknd* **50/1**

5663 **9** 3/4 **Archangel Raphael (IRE)**[32] 7490 5-9-6 67 ow2(v) MissDanielleSmith(7) 4 40
(Amanda Perrett) *off the pce in midfield: effrt over 3f out: no imp and sn wl btn* **25/1**

3145 **10** 7 **Glens Wobbly**[71] 6139 9-10-0 73 MissLMPinchin(5) 10 35
(Jonathan Geake) *led: wnt clr after 2f tl rdn and hdd over 3f out: sn dropped out and bhd* **40/1**

2m 47.05s (11.55) **Going Correction** +0.775s/f (Yiel) **10** Ran SP% **118.0**
Speed ratings (Par 103): **92,91,91,91,89 87,84,78,77,73**
CSF £20.10 CT £452.57 TOTE £5.80: £1.90, £1.30, £7.40; EX 20.70 Trifecta £567.50.
**Owner** Qatar Racing Limited **Bred** Qatar Bloodstock Ltd **Trained** Newmarket, Suffolk

**FOCUS**
Race distance increased by 27yds. This was run at a strong gallop and suited those ridden with patience.
T/Plt: £142.40 to a £1 stake. Pool: £83,550.69 - 428.05 winning units T/Qpdt: £25.70 to a £1 stake. Pool: £6,526.66 - 187.38 winning units **Steve Payne**

# 8395 WOLVERHAMPTON (A.W) (L-H)

Saturday, October 28

**OFFICIAL GOING: Tapeta: standard**
Wind: Fresh behind Weather: Cloudy

## 8427 BETWAY APPRENTICE H'CAP 6f 20y (Tp)

**5:45** (5:45) (Class 6) (0-65,65) 3-Y-O+ **£2,425** (£721; £360; £180) **Stalls** Low

Form RPR

030 **1** **Maureb (IRE)**[59] 6570 5-9-3 64 (p) CallumShepherd 3 71
(Tony Coyle) *prom: lost pl over 3f out: hdwy over 1f out: rdn to ld ins fnl f: hung lft: styd on* **25/1**

5220 **2** 1/2 **Indian Affair**[58] 6635 7-8-11 65 (bt) KerrieRaybould(7) 8 71
(Milton Bradley) *chsd ldrs: rdn and ev ch ins fnl f: styd on* **22/1**

0021 **3** 1/2 **Nutini (IRE)**[19] 7910 4-8-13 63 JoshuaBryan(3) 1 68
(Malcolm Saunders) *hld up: hdwy: nt clr run and swtchd rt over 1f out: rdn adn edgd lft ins fnl f: r.o* **7/4**[1]

2366 **4** *nk* **Zavikon**[18] 7912 3-8-12 65 FinleyMarsh(5) 4 68
(Richard Hughes) *pushed along early in rr: wnt prom: 5f out: nt clr run over 1f out: r.o* **10/1**

0000 **5** 1 1/2 **Big Amigo (IRE)**[31] 7525 4-9-2 63 EoinWalsh 6 62
(Daniel Mark Loughnane) *sn pushed along in rr: rdn over 2f out: r.o ins fnl f: nt rch ldrs* **22/1**

0040 **6** 1 **First Excel**[135] 3758 5-9-2 63 (b) HectorCrouch 7 59
(Roy Bowring) *sn led: hdd over 4f out: chsd ldr: rdn and ev ch 1f out: no ex ins fnl f* **22/1**

-055 **7** *nk* **Santafiora**[106] 4845 3-9-0 65 PaddyPilley(3) 9 60
(Roger Charlton) *s.i.s: hdwy 4f out: led over 2f out: rdn over 1f out: hdd and no ex ins fnl f* **11/1**

5420 **8** *hd* **Conqueress (IRE)**[39] 7241 3-9-0 65 (p) JaneElliott(3) 10 59
(Tom Dascombe) *chsd ldrs: pushed along over 2f out: nt clr run over 1f out: styd on same pce ins fnl f* **20/1**

0040 **9** *hd* **Sophisticated Heir (IRE)**[19] 7881 7-9-4 65 CliffordLee 13 59
(Kevin Frost) *hld up: carried rt wl over 1f out: r.o ins fnl f: nvr nrr* **16/1**

0500 **10** 1 **Round The Island**[29] 7572 4-8-13 65 (p) WilliamCox(5) 5 56
(Richard Whitaker) *hld up in tch: plld hrd: lost pl after 1f: hung rt over 2f out: styd on ins fnl f* **8/1**[3]

5100 **11** 1/2 **Malcolm The Pug (IRE)**[12] 8115 3-9-2 64 AaronJones 12 53
(David Brown) *chsd ldrs: led over 4f out: hdd over 2f out: rdn and ev ch over 1f out: no ex ins fnl f* **33/1**

3231 **12** 5 **Rapid Ranger**[18] 7933 3-9-3 65 (h) JoshDoyle 2 39
(David O'Meara) *s.i.s: hld up: hdwy and nt clr run over 1f out: cl up whn bdly hmpd and nrly fell ins fnl f: eased* **9/2**[2]

1010 **13** 12 **Castlerea Tess**[106] 4844 4-8-13 63 (p) BenRobinson(3) 11 1
(Sarah Hollinshead) *prom: pushed along over 3f out: wknd over 2f out* **33/1**

1m 13.2s (-1.30) **Going Correction** -0.25s/f (Stan)
**WFA** 3 from 4yo+ 1lb **13** Ran SP% **116.5**
Speed ratings (Par 101): **98,97,96,96,94 92,92,92,92,90 90,83,67**
CSF £446.86 CT £1508.98 TOTE £29.70: £8.10, £5.10, £1.20; EX 340.50 Trifecta £2176.00.
**Owner** Gap Personnel & Tony Coyle **Bred** Lynn Lodge Stud **Trained** Norton, N Yorks

**FOCUS**
A modest apprentice riders' handicap. They went a decent gallop on standard Tapeta, but the two horses at the head of the market didn't make use of their low draws.

## 8428 BETWAY SPRINT CLASSIFIED STKS 5f 21y (Tp)

**6:15** (6:15) (Class 6) 3-Y-O+ **£2,425** (£721; £360; £180) **Stalls** Low

Form RPR

6052 **1** **Toolatetodelegate**[3] 8342 3-8-11 48 (t[1]) JoshuaBryan(5) 4 60
(Brian Barr) *hld up in tch: led over 1f out: rdn out* **4/1**[2]

060 **2** 3 **Spitfire Limited**[19] 7907 3-8-13 50 (h) HectorCrouch(3) 6 49
(George Baker) *hld up: hdwy and nt clr run over 1f out: r.o to go 2nd wl ins fnl f: nt rch wnr* **16/1**

6002 **3** 1 1/4 **Dontforgettocall**[10] 8146 3-9-2 55 LukeMorris 11 45
(Joseph Tuite) *hld up: pushed along 1/2-way: hdwy to chse wnr over 1f out: sn rdn and hung lft: styd on same pce ins fnl f* **7/2**[1]

6404 **4** 3 1/4 **Excellent World (IRE)**[6] 8259 4-9-2 47 (p) BarryMcHugh 7 32
(Tony Coyle) *hld up: rdn 1/2-way: r.o ins fnl f: nvr nrr* **6/1**[3]

0264 **5** 3/4 **Miss Rosina (IRE)**[10] 8146 3-8-11 54 (p) JaneElliott(3) 9 30
(George Margarson) *chsd ldrs: pushed along and hung rt fr over 3f out: outpcd fnl 2f* **7/2**[1]

2401 **6** *nk* **Mr Enthusiastic**[18] 7926 3-8-13 49 PhilDennis(3) 2 29
(Noel Wilson) *s.i.s and hmpd s: plld hrd and sn prom: rdn over 1f out: wknd fnl f* **10/1**

0406 **7** *nk* **Emilysbutterscotch**[10] 8146 3-9-2 50 TomQueally 3 28
(Rae Guest) *hmpd s: outpcd: rdn over 1f out: n.d* **12/1**

0020 **8** *3* **Men United (FR)**[18] 7926 4-9-2 51 (b) RobertWinston 10 16
(Roy Bowring) *led 4f out: rdn and hdd over 1f out: wknd fnl f* **9/1**

6066 **9** *8* **Tartufo Classico**[173] 2472 4-9-2 37 TomEaves 1
(Derek Shaw) *wnt rt s and hung rt thrght: chsd ldrs: wknd over 1f out* **100/1**

0600 **10** *2 3/4* **Chillililli**[7] 8242 3-9-2 42 (p) AlistairRawlinson 8
(Michael Appleby) *led 1f: chsd ldrs: rdn 1/2-way: wknd over 1f out* **66/1**

500U **R** **Akuna Mattatta (IRE)**[19] 7907 3-9-2 45 AndrewMullen 5
(Ralph J Smith) *ref to r* **100/1**

1m 0.88s (-1.02) **Going Correction** -0.25s/f (Stan) 11 Ran SP% **114.9**
Speed ratings (Par 101): **98,93,91,86,84 84,83,79,66,61**
CSF £64.17 TOTE £5.00: £1.40, £6.00, £1.60; EX 77.80 Trifecta £266.50.
**Owner** Mike Sheridan **Bred** D R Tucker **Trained** Longburton, Dorset

**FOCUS**
A moderate classified contest. They went a decent gallop and a strong mover in the morning markets won readily. The race has been rated around the runner-up.

## 8429 BETWAY CASINO H'CAP 1m 1f 104y (Tp)
**6:45** (6:45) (Class 6) (0-65,65) 3-Y-O+ **£2,425** (£721; £360; £180) **Stalls** Low

Form RPR

6000 **1** **Tailor's Row (USA)**[11] 8132 3-9-3 65 AndrewMullen 9 73
(Mark Johnston) *prom: shkn up over 2f out: rdn to ld and edgd lft ins fnl f: styd on* **4/1**[1]

-016 **2** *1* **Barnaby Brook (CAN)**[32] 7495 7-9-7 65 (b) RichardKingscote 13 71
(Tom Dascombe) *s.i.s: hdwy to go prom over 7f out: chsd ldr over 6f out tl led over 1f out: rdn and hdd ins fnl f: styd on* **6/1**[2]

6530 **3** *1/2* **Bayston Hill**[18] 7917 3-9-2 64 DanielMuscutt 11 69
(Mark Usher) *hld up in tch: rdn over 1f out: ev ch sn after: styd on same pce wl ins fnl f* **8/1**

0130 **4** *hd* **Cat Royale (IRE)**[32] 7495 4-9-6 64 (p) DannyBrock 6 69
(John Butler) *pushed along to ld: hdd after 1f: remained handy: rdn over 1f out: styd on same pce wl ins fnl f* **11/1**

3-06 **5** *1 3/4* **Oregon Gift**[45] 7042 5-8-13 62 BenRobinson(5) 12 63
(Brian Ellison) *jnd ldr over 7f out: led over 6f out: rdn and hdd over 1f out: no ex ins fnl f* **12/1**

6200 **6** *2 1/2* **Chelwood Gate (IRE)**[49] 6946 7-9-7 65 (v) DavidNolan 7 62
(Conor Dore) *pushed along early and in tch whn hmpd and lost pl after 1f: hld up: shkn up and styd on fr over 1f out: nt trble ldrs* **50/1**

5040 **7** *1 3/4* **Fintech (IRE)**[18] 7932 3-9-3 65 (t) AdamBeschizza 3 58
(Mrs Ilka Gansera-Leveque) *s.i.s: hmpd after 1f: hld up: hdwy over 1f out: nt trble ldrs* **18/1**

4656 **8** *shd* **Island Flame (IRE)**[8] 8204 4-9-2 60 (p[1]) RobertWinston 5 53
(Richard Fahey) *hld up: hdwy over 1f out: no ex fnl f* **7/1**[3]

3346 **9** *2 1/2* **Perfect Spy**[42] 7151 3-9-3 65 LukeMorris 8 53
(Luca Cumani) *pushed along early to go prom ten plld hrd: stdd and lost pl over 7f out: hdwy over 1f out: sn rdn and hung lft: wknd fnl f* **11/1**

4500 **10** *4* **Lil Sophella (IRE)**[8] 8206 8-9-2 60 JackGarritty 1 41
(Patrick Holmes) *s.i.s: hmpd after 1f: hld up: nvr on terms* **20/1**

6066 **11** *7* **Marbooh (IRE)**[22] 7792 4-9-6 64 (t) TomQueally 2 32
(Amy Murphy) *hld up: hmpd over 2f out: n.d* **14/1**

5030 **12** *hd* **Know Your Name**[43] 7111 6-9-5 63 TomEaves 10 30
(Donald McCain) *led after 1f: hdd over 6f out: chsd ldrs: rdn over 2f out: wknd over 1f out* **25/1**

220 **13** *3 3/4* **Makhfar (IRE)**[67] 6288 6-9-4 65 (p) CallumShepherd(3) 4 25
(Mark Usher) *pushed along early in rr: nvr on terms* **9/1**

1m 57.89s (-2.91) **Going Correction** -0.25s/f (Stan)
**WFA** 3 from 4yo+ 4lb 13 Ran SP% **114.8**
Speed ratings (Par 101): **102,101,100,100,98 96,95,95,92,89 83,82,79**
CSF £24.64 CT £182.27 TOTE £4.70: £1.40, £2.30, £3.10; EX 33.20 Trifecta £306.80.
**Owner** Sheikh Hamdan bin Mohammed Al Maktoum **Bred** Darley **Trained** Middleham Moor, N Yorks

**FOCUS**
A modest handicap and straightforward form around the principals. They went a decent gallop and the favourite asserted in the final furlong.

## 8430 BETWAY MIDDLE H'CAP 1m 4f 51y (Tp)
**7:15** (7:15) (Class 7) (0-50,56) 3-Y-O+ **£2,264** (£673; £336; £168) **Stalls** Low

Form RPR

0011 **1** **Raashdy (IRE)**[3] 8346 4-9-12 56 6ex (p[1]) LukeMorris 7 63
(Peter Hiatt) *a.p: rdn to ld over 1f out: r.o* **5/2**[1]

5500 **2** *1 1/2* **Kaisan**[11] 8135 4-9-6 50 (t) DavidProbert 6 55
(Bernard Llewellyn) *hld up: hdwy over 1f out: rdn and hung lft ins fnl f: r.o to go 2nd nr fin: nt rch wnr* **12/1**

2532 **3** *nk* **Angel In The Snow**[4] 8314 4-8-13 48 BenRobinson(5) 1 52
(Brian Ellison) *chsd ldrs: rdn to chse wnr ins fnl f: styd on: lost 2nd nr fin* **5/2**[1]

6455 **4** *2* **Star Ascending (IRE)**[6] 8261 5-9-6 50 (p) TomQueally 8 51
(Jennie Candlish) *s.i.s: hdwy 10f out: shkn up to ld 2f out: rdn and hdd over 1f out: styd on same pce* **9/2**[2]

5030 **5** *nse* **Flying Power**[36] 7360 9-9-2 46 (p) AdamBeschizza 12 47
(John Norton) *led 1f: chsd ldr tl 8f out: remained handy: rdn and ev ch over 1f out: no ex wl ins fnl f* **10/1**[3]

2006 **6** *3/4* **Sir Dylan**[8] 6589 8-9-4 48 (h) RobertWinston 5 48
(Polly Gundry) *plld hrd and prom: nt clr run and lost pl after 1f: hdwy over 1f out: nt clr run sn after: no ex ins fnl f* **16/1**

0000 **7** *7* **Benissimo (IRE)**[74] 6038 7-8-13 50 (p) TobyEley(7) 4 38
(Tony Forbes) *s.i.s: hld up: plld hrd: hdwy on outer 4f out: led wl over 2f out: sn rdn and hung rt: hdd 2f out: wknd fnl f* **40/1**

5566 **8** *6* **Moojaned (IRE)**[5] 8301 6-8-13 50 (p) WilliamCox(7) 9 29
(John Flint) *prom: chsd ldr 8f out tl led 4f out: hdd over 2f out: sn rdn: wknd over 1f out* **10/1**[3]

355/ **9** *17* **Akula (IRE)**[211] 3189 10-8-13 48 JaneElliott(5) 2
(Barry Leavy) *hld up: rdn over 4f out: wknd over 2f out* **50/1**

0050 **10** *3/4* **Callaghan (GER)**[34] 6953 4-9-2 46 (bt[1]) DougieCostello 11
(Tom Gretton) *led after 1f: hdd 4f out: wknd over 2f out* **33/1**

0225 **11** *1 1/2* **Ted's Brother (IRE)**[112] 4627 9-9-5 49 ShaneKelly 3
(Laura Morgan) *hld up: wknd over 2f out* **20/1**

00-5 **12** *1/2* **Madrasa (IRE)**[58] 6632 9-8-13 46 (t) CallumShepherd(3) 10
(Ken Wingrove) *hld up: bhd fnl 6f* **150/1**

2m 37.74s (-3.06) **Going Correction** -0.25s/f (Stan) 12 Ran SP% **119.8**
Speed ratings (Par 97): **100,99,98,97,97 96,92,88,76,76 75,75**
CSF £35.10 CT £84.57 TOTE £3.10: £1.30, £3.40, £1.30; EX 40.00 Trifecta £180.40.
**Owner** P W Hiatt **Bred** Shadwell Estate Company Limited **Trained** Hook Norton, Oxon

**FOCUS**
A moderate middle-distance handicap. They went a respectable gallop and a slightly uneasy joint-favourite won well. The placed horses set the level.

## 8431 32RED.COM NURSERY H'CAP 5f 21y (Tp)
**7:45** (7:45) (Class 4) (0-85,86) 2-Y-O **£4,204** (£1,251; £625; £312) **Stalls** Low

Form RPR

331 **1** **Big Time Maybe (IRE)**[25] 7706 2-9-2 79 (tp) RichardKingscote 8 90
(Tom Dascombe) *mde all: shkn up and qcknd over 1f out: r.o: comf* **3/1**[1]

2001 **2** *2 3/4* **Our Man In Havana**[35] 7410 2-8-9 77 JoshuaBryan(5) 3 78
(Richard Price) *prom: rdn to go 2nd 1f out: r.o: no ch w wnr* **8/1**

5221 **3** *3/4* **Swing Out Sister (IRE)**[43] 7126 2-8-12 75 LukeMorris 7 73
(Clive Cox) *sn pushed along to chse ldrs: drvn along 1/2-way: styd on* **3/1**[1]

2215 **4** *1* **May Remain**[87] 5526 2-9-9 86 DavidProbert 6 81
(Paul Cole) *hld up: pushed along 1/2-way: r.o ins fnl f: nvr nrr* **7/2**[2]

0435 **5** *1 1/4* **Milton Road**[30] 7536 2-8-10 76 CallumShepherd(3) 10 69
(Mick Channon) *s.i.s: hld up: hdwy and nt clr run over 1f out: nt trble ldrs* **15/2**[3]

0500 **6** *1* **Wiff Waff**[74] 6021 2-8-0 63 (t) JimmyQuinn 2 50
(Stuart Williams) *hld up: plld hrd: hmpd 4f out: rdn over 1f out: nvr on terms* **14/1**

0050 **7** *1 3/4* **Rocket Man Dan (IRE)**[18] 7938 2-8-1 64 oh6 ow1.(bt[1]) AndrewMullen 5 44
(Keith Dalgleish) *s.i.s: a in rr* **50/1**

0400 **8** *1/2* **Wings Of The Rock (IRE)**[43] 7114 2-9-1 81 (p[1]) PaddyPilley(3) 4 60
(Scott Dixon) *plld hrd and prom: wnt 2nd over 3f out: rdn and hung lft over 1f out: wknd fnl f* **20/1**

124 **9** *1 3/4* **Jasi (IRE)**[105] 4888 2-8-13 76 PhillipMakin 1 48
(David O'Meara) *plld hrd in 2nd tl over 3f out: remained handy: pushed along 1/2-way: rdn whn nt clr run over 1f out: wknd fnl f* **9/1**

1m 0.1s (-1.80) **Going Correction** -0.25s/f (Stan) 9 Ran SP% **118.5**
Speed ratings (Par 97): **104,99,98,96,94 93,90,89,86**
CSF £28.67 CT £79.32 TOTE £3.70: £1.10, £3.00, £1.50; EX 32.10 Trifecta £126.70.
**Owner** Jones', Langfords' & Owens' **Bred** Joe Fogarty **Trained** Malpas, Cheshire
■ Stewards' Enquiry : Richard Kingscote three-day ban; careless riding (Nov 13th, 15th, 16th)

**FOCUS**
The feature contest was a decent sprint handicap. Another surprisingly uneasy joint-favourite produced the performance of the night from the front in the best comparative winning time on the card. Another significant personal best by him.

## 8432 32RED CASINO NOVICE MEDIAN AUCTION STKS 6f 20y (Tp)
**8:15** (8:15) (Class 5) 2-Y-O **£2,911** (£866; £432; £216) **Stalls** Low

Form RPR

U326 **1** **Mraseel (IRE)**[30] 7536 2-9-4 77 (p) LukeMorris 7 77
(James Tate) *chsd ldrs: rdn over 2f out: styd on u.p to ld nr fin* **4/1**[3]

2262 **2** *1/2* **Midsummer Knight**[15] 8010 2-9-2 78 BenCurtis 6 73
(K R Burke) *led: rdn over 1f out: hdd nr fin* **9/4**[2]

050 **3** *6* **Watching Spirits**[8] 8212 2-9-2 46 DougieCostello 2 54
(Ann Duffield) *prom: rdn over 2f out: no ex fnl f* **100/1**

64 **4** *3/4* **Walk On Walter (IRE)**[19] 7876 2-9-2 0 (h[1]) JamieSpencer 5 52
(David Simcock) *hld up: shkn up over 2f out: hung lft ins fnl f: nvr nr to chal* **7/4**[1]

43 **5** *1 1/4* **Society Prince (IRE)**[19] 7876 2-9-2 0 TomQueally 9 48
(James Fanshawe) *hld up: racd keenly: pushed along over 2f out: nvr on terms* **4/1**[3]

56 **6** *nk* **Chizz De Biz (IRE)**[24] 7724 2-8-11 0 GeorgeDowning 1 42
(Daniel Kubler) *chsd ldrs: rdn over 2f out: wknd fnl f* **33/1**

**7** *2 1/4* **Samovar** 2-9-2 0 KieranO'Neill 3 40
(Scott Dixon) *s.s: hdwy 4f out: rdn 1/2-way: wknd 2f out* **50/1**

4 **8** *1 3/4* **Fanfare Lady (IRE)**[26] 7688 2-8-11 0 MartinHarley 8 29
(William Knight) *hld up: shkn up and hung rt over 2f out: a in rr* **20/1**

1m 13.42s (-1.08) **Going Correction** -0.25s/f (Stan) 8 Ran SP% **117.8**
Speed ratings (Par 95): **97,96,88,87,85 85,82,79**
CSF £13.60 TOTE £4.80: £1.40, £1.30, £7.30; EX 15.90 Trifecta £432.10.
**Owner** Sheikh Hamed Dalmook Al Maktoum **Bred** Tally-Ho Stud **Trained** Newmarket, Suffolk

**FOCUS**
An ordinary juvenile novice contest. They went a decent gallop and the favourite failed to build on his wayward Kempton debut. The form looks straightforward around the first two.

## 8433 SUNBETS.CO.UK H'CAP (DIV I) 7f 36y (Tp)
**8:45** (8:45) (Class 5) (0-75,75) 3-Y-O+ **£2,911** (£866; £432; £216) **Stalls** High

Form RPR

5631 **1** **Dreaming Time**[23] 7770 3-9-5 75 LukeMorris 3 81+
(James Tate) *chsd ldrs: rdn over 2f out: edgd lft ins fnl f: r.o u.p to ld post* **4/1**[2]

0000 **2** *shd* **Tavener**[12] 8106 5-9-0 68 (p) DavidAllan 2 74
(David C Griffiths) *chsd ldr to 1/2-way: rdn to ld over 1f out: hdd post* **22/1**

0040 **3** *nse* **Highly Sprung (IRE)**[19] 7882 4-9-3 71 PJMcDonald 6 77+
(Mark Johnston) *s.i.s: hld up: rdn 2f out: edgd lft and r.o wl ins fnl f: jst failed* **16/1**

043 **4** *1/2* **Debonaire David**[19] 7882 3-9-2 72 (t) ShaneKelly 1 76
(Richard Hughes) *s.i.s: hdwy over 5f out: rdn over 1f out: r.o* **5/1**[3]

2006 **5** *shd* **Rock N Rolla (IRE)**[16] 7981 3-9-4 74 (v[1]) AndrewMullen 4 79+
(Keith Dalgleish) *s.i.s: hld up: hdwy 2f out: nt clr run and hmpd over 1f out: swtchd lft: rdn and r.o wl* **12/1**

5600 **6** *1 1/4* **Ferocity (IRE)**[10] 8158 3-8-13 69 (p) MartinHarley 9 70+
(Robyn Brisland) *hld up: hdwy and nt clr run fr over 1f out tl ins fnl f: r.o: nt rch ldrs* **9/1**

-000 **7** *nk* **Mr Christopher (IRE)**[143] 3471 5-9-6 74 (p) RichardKingscote 12 75
(Tom Dascombe) *hld up: hdwy over 1f out: edgd lft ins fnl f: r.o* **40/1**

2000 **8** *1 1/4* **Fine Example**[12] 8107 4-9-0 68 (v[1]) TomEaves 10 65
(Kevin Ryan) *prom: chsd ldr 1/2-way: rdn: edgd lft and ev ch over 1f out: no ex ins fnl f* **40/1**

5201 **9** *shd* **Golden Guest**[19] 7878 3-8-10 71 JaneElliott(5) 8 67
(George Margarson) *hld up: hdwy whn hmpd ins fnl f: nvr able to chal* **3/1**[1]

0605 **10** *2* **Thaqaffa (IRE)**[17] 7957 4-9-7 75 (p) DanielMuscutt 5 67
(Amy Murphy) *led: rdn: edgd rt and hdd over 1f out: no ex whn nt clr run ins fnl f* **14/1**

2065 **11** *1 1/4* **Viva Verglas (IRE)**[24] 7738 6-9-0 68 BenCurtis 11 56
(Daniel Mark Loughnane) *s.i.s: hld up: nvr on terms* **40/1**

2244 12 1 **Mishaal (IRE)**[19] 7882 7-9-2 70 PhillipMakin 7 55
(Michael Herrington) *hld up in tch: rdn over 2f out: wknd over 1f out* 5/1[3]
1m 27.06s (-1.74) **Going Correction** -0.25s/f (Stan)
**WFA** 3 from 4yo+ 2lb 12 Ran SP% **120.2**
Speed ratings (Par 103): **99,98,98,98,98 96,96,94,94,92 91,89**
CSF £95.50 CT £1268.10 TOTE £4.20: £1.60, £5.70, £4.70; EX 99.70 Trifecta £1197.30.
**Owner** Saeed Manana **Bred** Rabbah Bloodstock Limited **Trained** Newmarket, Suffolk
■ Stewards' Enquiry : Andrew Mullen two-day ban; careless riding (Nov 11th, 13th)

**FOCUS**
The first division of a fair handicap. They went a decent gallop and the morning favourite defied a slight drift to snatch the spoils in an exciting, three-way photo-finish. The fourth helps set the standard.

## 8434 SUNBETS.CO.UK H'CAP (DIV II) 7f 36y (Tp)
**9:15** (9:15) (Class 5) (0-75,75) 3-Y-0+ **£2,911** (£866; £432; £216) **Stalls** High

Form RPR
1600 1 **Ebbisham (IRE)**[115] 4501 4-9-0 68 JimmyQuinn 12 75
(John Mackie) *hld up: hdwy over 1f out: rdn and r.o to ld towards fin* **20/1**
2315 2 ½ **Spinnaka (IRE)**[9] 8184 3-9-5 75 (v) LukeMorris 5 80
(Luca Cumani) *chsd ldrs: rdn to ld wl ins fnl f: hdd towards fin* **4/1**[3]
2365 3 hd **Murdanova (IRE)**[15] 7998 4-9-1 72 CharlieBennett(3) 2 77
(Denis Quinn) *chsd ldrs: rdn over 1f out: styd on* **17/2**
1612 4 1½ **Daring Guest (IRE)**[19] 7881 3-8-11 72 JaneElliott(5) 1 72
(George Margarson) *chsd ldr tl led over 2f out: rdn and hdd wl ins fnl f: styd on same pce* **7/2**[2]
3256 5 2 **The Amber Fort (USA)**[8] 8211 3-8-10 69 ShelleyBirkett(3) 11 64
(David O'Meara) *hld up: hdwy over 2f out: rdn over 1f out: edgd lft and styd on same pce wl ins fnl f* **9/1**
3402 6 shd **Graphite (IRE)**[19] 7896 3-9-1 71 (p[1]) JamieSpencer 8 66+
(David Simcock) *s.i.s: hld up: shkn up and rn wd bnd over 2f out: styd on u.p ins fnl f: nvr nrr* **11/4**[1]
0414 7 shd **Air Of York (IRE)**[19] 7899 5-8-7 68 (p) WilliamCox(7) 10 63
(John Flint) *hld up: hdwy over 2f out: rdn over 1f out: styd on same pce fnl f* **20/1**
3000 8 1½ **Steal The Scene (IRE)**[17] 7947 5-9-4 72 DougieCostello 3 63
(Kevin Frost) *s.i.s: hld up: rdn over 2f out: nvr on terms* **28/1**
5300 9 1¼ **Carnival King (IRE)**[23] 7759 5-9-7 75 (v) MartinHarley 6 63
(Amy Murphy) *led: clr over 5f out tl rdn and hdd over 2f out: wknd fnl f* **9/1**
2140 10 1¾ **Newstead Abbey**[19] 7881 7-9-0 68 (p) TomEaves 7 51
(Michael Herrington) *hld up: rdn and hung lft over 1f out: n.d* **10/1**
1m 27.04s (-1.76) **Going Correction** -0.25s/f (Stan)
**WFA** 3 from 4yo+ 2lb 10 Ran SP% **121.5**
Speed ratings (Par 103): **100,99,99,97,95 95,94,93,91,89**
CSF £100.28 CT £775.33 TOTE £20.90: £5.00, £1.70, £3.10; EX 131.20 Trifecta £1834.10.
**Owner** P Riley **Bred** John Quigley **Trained** Church Broughton , Derbys

**FOCUS**
The second division of a fair handicap. The winning time was virtually identical off another decent gallop. The third helps set the standard.
T/Plt: £27.70 to a £1 stake. Pool: £99,286.90 - 2,607.75 winning units T/Qpdt: £7.30 to a £1 stake. Pool: £10,816.33 - 1,087.50 winning units **Colin Roberts**

8435 - 8437a (Foreign Racing) - See Raceform Interactive

# 8262 LEOPARDSTOWN (L-H)
Saturday, October 28

**OFFICIAL GOING: Yielding**

## 8438a THETOTE.COM KNOCKAIRE STKS (LISTED RACE) 7f
**3:05** (3:06) 3-Y-0+ **£23,700** (£7,632; £3,615; £1,606; £803; £401)

RPR
1 nse **Making Light (IRE)**[13] 8083 3-9-0 101 LeighRoche 15 104+
(D K Weld, Ire) *chsd ldrs early tl sn settled in mid-div: hdwy over 2f out to chse ldrs: rdn in 3rd 1 1/2f out and r.o wl to strly press wnr clsng stages where impeded: jst failed: fin 2nd: awrdd r* **6/1**[3]
2 **Larchmont Lad (IRE)**[38] 7275 3-9-5 103 DeclanMcDonogh 3 109
(David O'Meara) *sn led narrowly: jnd briefly bef 1/2-way: narrow advantage at 1/2-way: drvn clr 2f out: reduced advantage wl ins fnl f and strly pressed clsng stages where wnt rt: jst hld on: fin 1st: plcd 2nd* **8/1**
3 2 **Spanish Tenor (IRE)**[14] 8051 3-9-5 105 OisinOrr 5 104
(Timothy Doyle, Ire) *chsd ldrs early tl sn settled in mid-div: hdwy over 2f out to chse ldrs: rdn in 3rd 1 1/2f out and disp 2nd briefly ent fnl f: no imp on ldrs in 3rd ins fnl f: kpt on same pce* **14/1**
4 nk **So Beloved**[27] 7671 7-9-7 112 DanielTudhope 14 104
(David O'Meara) *mid-div: n.m.r stl gng wl 2f out: sn pushed along and hdwy over 1f out: wnt 4th ins fnl f where hung sltly: rdn and kpt on same pce clsng stages: nvr trbld ldrs* **9/4**[1]
5 ¾ **Flight Risk (IRE)**[27] 7663 6-9-12 108 RoryCleary 9 110+
(J S Bolger, Ire) *dwlt sltly and pushed along in rr early: 15th 1/2-way: prog 2f out: sn rdn and clsd u.p into 4th briefly ins fnl f where no imp on ldrs: kpt on same pce in 5th clsng stages* **16/1**
6 1¼ **Onenightidreamed (IRE)**[14] 8051 6-9-7 104 (b) ChrisHayes 2 98
(J A Stack, Ire) *mid-div: pushed along under 2f out where n.m.r briefly: sn swtchd rt in 10th and sme hdwy ins fnl f: nvr nrr* **7/1**
7 ½ **Hit The Silk (IRE)**[21] 7839 4-9-7 93 DonaghO'Connor 4 97
(P J F Murphy, Ire) *hld up: last at 1/2-way: tk clsr order under 2f out: sn rdn in 13th and r.o u.p ins fnl f: nvr nrr* **25/1**
8 3 **Mjjack (IRE)**[21] 7807 3-9-5 100 ShaneFoley 8 88
(K R Burke) *chsd ldrs: pushed along and disp 4th appr st: sn no ex u.p and wknd under 2f out* **5/1**[2]
9 nk **Silverkode (IRE)**[27] 7663 3-9-5 103 (p[1]) GaryCarroll 6 87
(Joseph G Murphy, Ire) *chsd ldrs: impr into 2nd 2f out: sn rdn and no imp on ldr: wknd fr over 1f out* **9/1**
10 2¼ **Dasheen**[14] 8050 4-9-7 82 (p) EmmetMcNamara 13 82
(Adrian McAllister, Ire) *w.w towards rr: rdn 2f out and no imp: kpt on one pce ins fnl f* **66/1**
11 ½ **No Education**[14] 8050 4-9-7 97 GaryHalpin 1 81
(John James Feane, Ire) *towards rr: sme hdwy far side 2f out: sn rdn and no ex 1 1/2f out: one pce after* **25/1**
12 ½ **Gymkhana**[14] 8051 4-9-7 97 ColmO'Donoghue 16 79
(Mrs John Harrington, Ire) *mid-div: gd hdwy on outer over 2f out to chse ldrs: rdn in 4th 1 1/2f out and sn wknd* **33/1**
13 1¾ **Perle De La Mer (IRE)**[13] 8083 3-9-0 87 (h) WJLee 10 69
(W McCreery, Ire) *mid-div best: rdn and no imp towards rr 2f out* **50/1**
14 ¾ **Geological (IRE)**[8] 8222 5-9-7 92 MichaelHussey 11 73
(Damian Joseph English, Ire) *w ldrs: sn settled in cl 2nd and disp ld briefly bef 1/2-way: cl 2nd at 1/2-way: sn pushed along and wknd in 3rd under 2f out* **50/1**
15 2¼ **Texas Rock (IRE)**[20] 7856 6-9-10 103 (p) NGMcCullagh 12 70
(M C Grassick, Ire) *chsd ldrs: pushed along in cl 3rd appr st and sn no ex u.p: wknd under 2f out* **16/1**
1m 32.83s (4.13)
**WFA** 3 from 4yo+ 2lb 15 Ran SP% **129.8**
CSF £54.64 TOTE £6.00: £2.10, £2.80, £4.70; DF 56.30 Trifecta £1755.50.
**Owner** Moyglare Stud Farm **Bred** Moyglare Stud Farm Ltd **Trained** Curragh, Co Kildare

**FOCUS**
A controversial finish here, but not the greatest of surprises that the places were reversed considering how close it was. The first three and fifth have been rated to their marks.

## 8440a THETOTE.COM EYREFIELD STKS (GROUP 3) 1m 1f
**4:15** (4:16) 2-Y-0 **£31,769** (£10,230; £4,846; £2,153; £1,076; £538)

RPR
1 **Flag Of Honour (IRE)**[14] 8036 2-9-3 98 PBBeggy 6 101
(A P O'Brien, Ire) *cl up and led narrowly after 1f tl sn jnd and hdd: 3rd after 2f: disp ld over 3f out and sn led narrowly: rdn clr 1 1/2f out and kpt on wl ins fnl f* **2/1**[1]
2 1½ **Giuseppe Garibaldi (IRE)**[17] 7961 2-9-3 0 (t) MichaelHussey 3 98
(A P O'Brien, Ire) *w.w: gng wl in 7th under 3f out: sn pushed along and prog far side under 2f out: sn rdn in 4th and clsd u.p into 2nd ins fnl f: kpt on wl wout matching wnr* **14/1**
3 2¼ **Hazapour (IRE)**[39] 7257 2-9-3 0 LeighRoche 9 93
(D K Weld, Ire) *hld up in tch: racd keenly early: cl 4th over 3f out: impr into 2nd on outer 1 1/2f out: no imp on wnr u.p ins fnl f where dropped to 3rd: kpt on same pce* **3/1**[2]
4 ¾ **Burgundy Boy (IRE)**[93] 5345 2-9-3 100 GaryCarroll 4 91
(Ms Sheila Lavery, Ire) *disp early tl sn settled bhd ldrs after 1f: gng wl in 5th over 3f out: pushed along into st and sn no imp on ldrs u.p in 5th 1 1/2f out: kpt on into 4th wl ins fnl f: nvr trbld ldrs* **5/1**[3]
5 1¼ **Saracen Knight (IRE)**[17] 7961 2-9-3 0 EmmetMcNamara 5 89
(A P O'Brien, Ire) *hld up in tch tl hdwy after 1f to sn ld: jnd over 4f out: hdd under 3f out: rdn in 2nd under 2f out and no imp on wnr u.p in 4th ins fnl f: one pce clsng stages* **7/1**
6 1¼ **Nibiru (IRE)**[13] 8079 2-9-3 0 OisinOrr 8 86
(A J Martin, Ire) *w.w towards rr: tk clsr order 3f out: rdn into st and no imp on ldrs u.p in 6th over 1f out: kpt on same pce* **14/1**
7 hd **Apple Anni (IRE)**[13] 8082 2-9-0 77 WJLee 1 83
(Mick Channon) *settled in rr: pushed along under 3f out and no imp into st: rdn into 7th 1f out and kpt on same pce* **25/1**
8 9½ **Sandaryann (IRE)**[100] 5084 2-9-3 0 DerekMcCormack 7 66
(D K Weld, Ire) *disp early tl settled bhd ldr after 1f: disp ld over 4f out tl hdd under 3f out: rdn and wknd into st* **66/1**
9 2½ **Cimeara (IRE)**[17] 7962 2-9-0 81 RoryCleary 2 58
(J S Bolger, Ire) *pushed along early: sn chsd ldrs: pushed along under 4f out and struggling u.p in 6th under 3f out: wknd into st* **10/1**
2m 4.79s (10.69) 9 Ran SP% **115.3**
CSF £32.46 TOTE £2.40: £1.02, £4.50, £1.50; DF 31.80 Trifecta £330.70.
**Owner** Mrs John Magnier & Michael Tabor & Derrick Smith **Bred** Barronstown Stud **Trained** Cashel, Co Tipperary

**FOCUS**
On first glance, probably not a bad renewal of this race, the runner-up may well be the one to take out of it long term.

8439 - 8442a (Foreign Racing) - See Raceform Interactive

# 4653 NANTES (R-H)
Saturday, October 28

**OFFICIAL GOING: Turf: soft**

## 8443a PRIX DES SABLONNETS (LISTED RACE) (2YO) (TURF) 1m
**12:20** 2-Y-0 **£25,641** (£10,256; £7,692; £5,128; £2,564)

RPR
1 **Lilac Fairy (FR)**[28] 7637 2-8-13 0 (p) Pierre-CharlesBoudot 9 92
(F-H Graffard, France) **9/5**[1]
2 ½ **Mon Amie Chop (FR)**[39] 2-8-13 0 AntoineHamelin 3 91
(F Vermeulen, France) **108/10**
3 nse **Shenoya (FR)**[40] 2-8-13 0 EddyHardouin 4 91
(N Leenders, France) **145/10**
4 5½ **Uther Pendragon (IRE)**[9] 8195 2-9-2 0 (p) TonyPiccone 1 81
(J S Moore) *racd 3rd: pushed along 2f out: rdn and outpcd fnl f: plugged on for 4th* **119/10**
5 1¼ **Seven Treffles (FR)** 2-8-13 0 JeromeCabre 6 75
(Y Barberot, France) **18/5**[2]
6 ¾ **Hello Princess (FR)**[22] 2-8-13 0 AdrienFouassier 8 73
(Louis Baudron, France) **74/10**
7 5 **Los Altos (FR)** 2-9-2 0 FabriceVeron 7 65
(E J O'Neill, France) **161/10**
8 14 **The Lamplighter (FR)**[5] 8302 2-9-2 0 TheoBachelot 2 33
(George Baker) *awkward leaving stalls: settled in midfield: pushed along over 2f out: btn and eased fnl f* **126/10**
9 3 **Bermonville (FR)**[21] 2-8-13 0 Roberto-CarlosMontenegro 5 23
(W Walton, France) **66/10**[3]
1m 40.15s 9 Ran SP% **118.4**
PARI-MUTUEL (all including 1 euro stake): WIN 2.80; PLACE 1.50, 3.00, 3.40; DF 16.10; SF 32.90.
**Owner** Golden East Horse **Bred** G Heald **Trained** France

## 8444a GRAND PRIX DE NANTES (LISTED RACE) (3YO+) (TURF) 1m 4f
**1:20** 3-Y-0+ **£25,641** (£10,256; £7,692; £5,128; £2,564)

RPR
1 **Smart Whip (FR)**[54] 6773 6-9-10 0 EddyHardouin 9 112+
(C Lotoux, France) **12/5**[2]
2 nk **Royalickly (FR)**[65] 6364 3-8-8 0 ChristopherGrosbois 8 102
(S Gouvaze, France) **144/10**
3 ¾ **Mint Julep (FR)**[24] 7753 4-8-11 0 DelphineSantiago 6 97
(J E Hammond, France) **174/10**
4 2 **Racing Bay (FR)**[52] 6-9-1 0 DavidBreux 5 98
(M Lelievre, France) **91/10**

5 *snk* **Teofonic (IRE)**13 8076 3-8-5 0............................ JoeFanning 10 94
(Mark Johnston) **11/5**1
6 *5 ½* **Black Night (IRE)**48 5-9-1 0............................ WilliamsSaraiva 4 89
(J Moon, Jersey) **37/1**
7 *2* **Satanicjim (IRE)**72 6123 8-9-1 0............................(p) MlleMarylineEon 1 85
(Alain Couetil, France) **19/1**
8 *3* **Astral Merit (FR)**28 7-8-11 0............................ FabriceVeron 3 77
(F Monnier, France) **216/10**
9 *1* **Baz (FR)**343 8042 7-9-1 0............................(p) Pierre-CharlesBoudot 7 79
(F-H Graffard, France) **109/10**
10 *¾* **Luire (IRE)**24 7755 3-8-5 0............................ DavidMichaux 2 75
(D De Watrigant, France) **11/2**3

2m 37.23s (2.23)
**WFA** 3 from 4yo+ 6lb **10** Ran SP% **118.3**
PARI-MUTUEL (all including 1 euro stake): WIN 3.40; PLACE 1.80, 3.40, 3.70; DF 17.40; SF 28.00.
**Owner** Mme Ernest Le Clezio **Bred** Ronchalon Racing (uk) Ltd **Trained** France

8445 - (Foreign Racing) - See Raceform Interactive

## 8411 MOONEE VALLEY (L-H)
Saturday, October 28

**OFFICIAL GOING: Turf: good**

### 8446a LADBROKES COX PLATE (GROUP 1) (3YO+) (TURF) 1m 2f 44y
**7:00** 3-Y-0+
**£1,081,871** (£257,309; £128,654; £76,023; £64,327; £58,479)

RPR
1 **Winx (AUS)**21 7848 6-9-0 0............................ HughBowman 5 119
(Chris Waller, Australia) **2/11**1
2 *½* **Humidor (NZ)**7 8250 5-9-4 0............................(bt) BlakeShinn 7 122
(Darren Weir, Australia) **30/1**
3 *4 ¼* **Folkswood**13 8100 4-9-4 0............................(p) KerrinMcEvoy 4 114
(Charlie Appleby) **25/1**
4 *1 ½* **Royal Symphony (AUS)**14 3-7-11 0............................(p) DeanYendall 6 106
(Tony McEvoy, Australia) **18/1**2
5 *shd* **Gailo Chop (FR)**14 8058 6-9-4 0............................ MarkZahra 3 110+
(Darren Weir, Australia) **20/1**3
6 *nk* **Happy Clapper (AUS)**14 7-9-4 0............................(b) DamienOliver 8 110
(Patrick Webster, Australia) **30/1**
7 *7* **Seaburge (AUS)**14 8059 4-9-1 0............................(p) ReganBayliss 1 93
(David A & B Hayes & Tom Dabernig, Australia) **100/1**
8 *1 ¼* **Hardham (AUS)**7 8250 4-9-1 0............................(b) LukeNolen 2 90
(David Brideoake, Australia) **100/1**

2m 2.94s
**WFA** 3 from 4yo+ 4lb **8** Ran SP% **106.9**
.
**Owner** Magic Bloodstock Racing, R G Treweeke & Mrs D N Ke **Bred** Fairway Thoroughbreds **Trained** Australia

**FOCUS**
The majority of Australia in addition to horse racing fans around the world had their eyes fixed on this race. It promised to add to the history of the sport, and no matter whether you are an ardent supporter of the superstar mare or have reservations about what she is beating, coming into such an established contest with 21 wins in a row, is something very few are likely to see again. The leader went off at a good pace and a new course record was set, beating the time Winx achieved in the 2015 running. The form has been rated around the second, third and fourth.

8447a - (Foreign Racing) - See Raceform Interactive

## 2866 CAPANNELLE (R-H)
Sunday, October 29

**OFFICIAL GOING: Turf: good**

### 8448a PREMIO RIBOT MEMORIAL LORETO LUCIANI (GROUP 3) (3YO+) (TURF) 1m
**1:20** 3-Y-0+ **£31,196** (£13,726; £7,487; £3,743)

RPR
1 **Time To Choose**35 7442 4-9-6 0............................ FabioBranca 2 109
(Stefano Botti, Italy) *hld up in midfield: rdn and hdwy fr 2f out: tk share of ld 1f out: kpt on strly fnl f: jst prevailed in bobbing fin* **13/2**
2 *shd* **Royal Julius (IRE)**29 7640 4-9-4 0............................ GuillaumeMillet 4 107
(J Reynier, France) *trckd ldrs: rdn 2 1/2f out: tk share of ld 1f out: kpt on strly fnl f: jst hld in bobbing fin* **10/3**3
3 *2 ½* **Aspettatemi (ITY)**181 2245 3-9-1 0............................ SalvatoreBasile 6 100
(D Grilli, Italy) *led: rdn over 2f out: hdd 1f out: kpt on same pce* **63/1**
4 *1 ½* **Jalapeno (IRE)**203 4-9-4 0............................ CarloFiocchi 7 98
(Agostino Affe', Italy) *hld up in 5th: rdn and kpt on same pce fr over 2f out* **42/1**
5 *hd* **Greg Pass (IRE)**35 7442 5-9-4 0............................ DarioVargiu 5 97
(Nicolo Simondi, Italy) *chsd ldr: rdn over 2f out: wknd steadily fnl f* **3/1**2
6 *shd* **Discursus**42 7204 3-8-11 0............................ AndreaAtzeni 1 92
(H-A Pantall, France) *hld up in rr: outpcd 3f out: kpt on fnl f: n.d* **7/5**1
7 *shd* **Amore Hass (IRE)**35 7442 3-9-3 0............................ NicolaPinna 3 98
(Stefano Botti, Italy) *hld up towards rr: rdn and no imp fr 2 1/2f out* **67/20**

1m 36.1s (-3.70)
**WFA** 3 from 4yo+ 3lb **7** Ran SP% **130.0**
PARI-MUTUEL (all including 1 euro stake): WIN: 7.54; PLACE: 3.35, 2.76; DF: 15.06.
**Owner** Scuderia Effevi SRL **Bred** Razza Del Velino Srl **Trained** Italy

### 8449a PREMIO CARLO & FRANCESCO ALOISI (GROUP 3) (2YO+) (TURF) 6f
**2:35** 2-Y-0+ **£27,777** (£12,222; £6,666; £3,333)

RPR
1 **My Lea (IRE)**14 3-9-1 0............................ CarloFiocchi 6 100
(V Fazio, Italy) *hld up towards rr of midfield: nt clr run whn gng wl appr fnl f: swtchd to outer and rdn under 1f out: qckly to ld narrowly 100yds out: kpt on strly: jst prevailed* **885/100**
2 *shd* **Zapel**140 4-9-5 0............................ DarioVargiu 1 103+
(Stefano Botti, Italy) *trckd ldrs: rdn over 1f out: kpt on wl fnl f: ev ch clsng stages: jst hld* **153/10**
3 *¾* **Imperial Tango (FR)**105 3-9-1 0............................ FabioBranca 5 98
(Stefano Botti, Italy) *chsd ldr: led over 1f out: rdn 1f out: hdd 100yds out: kpt on* **123/20**
4 *1* **Trust You**14 5-9-5 0............................(b) SilvanoMulas 7 97
(Endo Botti, Italy) *in tch in midfield: rdn and effrt 1 1/2f out: no ex last 100yds* **63/20**3
5 *½* **Plusquemavie (IRE)**147 3370 6-9-5 0............................(b) SalvatoreBasile 4 96
(V Fazio, Italy) *hld up towards rr: rdn and kpt on fr 2f out: nvr gng pce to chal* **10/9**1
6 *3 ¾* **Intense Life (IRE)**106 5-9-5 0............................ PierantonioConvertino 2 84
(Endo Botti, Italy) *led: rdn over 2f out: hdd over 1f out: wknd ins fnl f: eased last 100yds* **63/20**3
7 *dist* **Wild Bud (USA)**21 3-9-1 0............................ AndreaAtzeni 3
(H-A Pantall, France) *a in rr: eased ins fnl f* **5/2**2

1m 7.2s (-3.10)
**WFA** 3 from 4yo+ 1lb **7** Ran SP% **154.4**
PARI-MUTUEL (all including 1 euro stake): WIN: 9.83; PLACE: 4.50, 6.59; DF: 38.38.
**Owner** Marco Caracciolo **Bred** Clara Eglington **Trained** Italy

### 8450a PREMIO LYDIA TESIO (GROUP 1) (3YO+ FILLIES & MARES) (TURF) 1m 2f
**3:20** 3-Y-0+ **£115,384** (£50,769; £27,692; £13,846)

RPR
1 **Laganore (IRE)**43 7171 5-9-1 0............................ ColinKeane 9 108+
(A J Martin, Ire) *hld up towards rr: smooth hdwy fr 4f out: rdn 2f out: styd on wl to ld 100yds out: readily* **39/20**2
2 *2* **A Raving Beauty (GER)**28 7672 4-9-1 0..........(b) ClementLecoeuvre 10 104
(Andreas Suborics, Germany) *chsd ldr: rdn to ld 2f out: hdd 100yds out: no ex clsng stages* **117/10**
3 *5* **Absolute Blast (IRE)**30 7588 5-9-1 0............................ LukeMorris 4 94
(Archie Watson) *in tch in midfield: trckd ldrs 4f out: rdn over 3f out: wknd steadily fr 1 1/2f out* **114/10**
4 *2* **Candy Store (IRE)**35 7441 3-8-10 0............................ DarioVargiu 2 90
(Stefano Botti, Italy) *midfield: rdn and kpt on same pce fr 3f out* **77/10**
5 *4* **Alambra (IRE)**14 8096 3-8-10 0............................ PierantonioConvertino 5 82
(Stefano Botti, Italy) *led: rdn and hdd 3f out: wknd 2 1/2f out* **269/10**
6 *8* **Sky Full Of Stars (GER)**35 3-8-10 0............................ JackMitchell 3 66
(Henk Grewe, Germany) *dwlt: towards rr: rdn along fr 5f out: nvr in contention* **117/10**
7 *½* **Folega**14 8096 3-8-10 0............................ NicolaPinna 8 65
(Stefano Botti, Italy) *in rr: rdn and sme stdy hdwy fr 4f out: nvr in contention: eased appr 2f out* **13/1**
8 *1 ¼* **Ashiana (GER)**28 7669 3-8-10 0............................ FabioBranca 6 63
(P Schiergen, Germany) *midfield: rdn over 3f out: wknd 2 1/2f out: sn eased* **97/100**1
9 *4* **Paiardina (IRE)**28 3-8-10 0............................ CarloFiocchi 1 55
(Stefano Botti, Italy) *trckd ldrs: rdn over 4f out: lost pl over 3f out: sn wl btn and eased* **138/10**
10 *dist* **Distain**14 8096 5-9-1 0............................(b) AndreaAtzeni 7
(Frau S Steinberg, Germany) *a towards rr: lost tch 3f out* **76/10**3

1m 58.8s (-4.50)
**WFA** 3 from 4yo+ 4lb **10** Ran SP% **149.1**
PARI-MUTUEL (all including 1 euro stake): WIN: 2.97; PLACE: 1.62, 3.73, 2.97; DF: 47.26.
**Owner** Newtown Anner Stud Farm Ltd **Bred** Newtown Anner Stud Farm Ltd **Trained** Summerhill, Co. Meath

8451 - 8460a (Foreign Racing) - See Raceform Interactive

## 7673 HANOVER (L-H)
Sunday, October 29

**OFFICIAL GOING: Turf: soft**

### 8461a GROSSER SOLDIER HOLLOW PREIS (LISTED RACE) (2YO FILLIES) (TURF) 7f
**12:20** 2-Y-0 **£11,965** (£5,555; £2,564; £1,282)

RPR
1 **Dark Liberty (IRE)**15 8045 2-8-11 0............................ MaximPecheur 4 96
(Simon Crisford) *in tch: trckd ldrs over 3f out: rdn under 3f out: led narrowly over 1f out: kpt on wl: rdn out* **11/5**1
2 *½* **Wonderful Gorl (GER)**63 6494 2-8-11 0............................ FilipMinarik 3 95
(Gerald Geisler, Germany) **58/10**
3 *5* **Sojourn (GER)**36 2-8-11 0............................ MichaelCadeddu 1 82
(Jean-Pierre Carvalho, Germany) **7/1**
4 *5* **Fire For Goga** 2-8-11 0............................ DanielePorcu 6 69
(Gabor Maronka, Hungary) **194/10**
5 *4 ¾* **Queens Care (IRE)** 2-8-11 0............................ JozefBojko 10 56
(A Wohler, Germany) **5/1**3
6 *1 ½* **Mail Order**43 7160 2-8-11 0............................ FrannyNorton 9 52
(Mark Johnston) *pushed along towards rr: rdn 3f out: outpcd 2f out: wknd fnl f* **103/10**
7 *4 ¼* **Marinka (FR)**120 2-9-0 0............................ BauyrzhanMurzabayev 5 44
(R Rohne, Germany) **141/10**
8 *14* **Namara (GER)** 2-8-11 0............................ MartinSeidl 7
(Waldemar Hickst, Germany) **89/10**
9 *2 ½* **Tia Maria (GER)** 2-8-11 0............................ EduardoPedroza 8
(A Wohler, Germany) **31/10**2

PARI-MUTUEL (all including 10 euro stake): WIN: 32; PLACE: 14 17, 20; SF: 177.
**Owner** Sheikh Rashid Dalmook Al Maktoum **Bred** Yeomanstown Stud **Trained** Newmarket, Suffolk

### 8462a GROSSER PREIS DER MEHL-MULHENS-STIFTUNG GESTUT ROTTGEN (GROUP 3) (3YO+ FILLIES & MARES) (TURF) 1m 3f
**1:30** 3-Y-0+ **£27,350** (£10,256; £5,128; £2,564; £1,709)

RPR
1 **Ostana (GER)**28 7673 4-9-4 0............................ WladimirPanov 3 97
(Daniel Paulick, Germany) *hld up towards rr: stdy hdwy fr 1m out: w ldr 5f out: led 4f out: rdn and pressed fr 2 1/2f out: kpt on wl: drvn out* **47/10**3
2 *nk* **Agathonia (USA)**28 7673 3-9-0 0............................ DanielePorcu 6 98
(H-A Pantall, France) *midfield: rdn and hdwy to chse ldrs 2 1/2f out: kpt on wl fnl f: pressed wnr clsng stages* **5/2**1

3 ¾ **Fosun (GER)**[28] 7673 4-9-4 0 ........................................ MartinSeidl 12 95
(Markus Klug, Germany) *trckd ldrs: rdn and pressed ldr 2 1/2f out: kpt on wl tl no ex clsng stages* **109/10**

4 3 **Diana Storm (GER)**[28] 7673 3-9-0 0 ........................................ JozefBojko 4 91
(Waldemar Hickst, Germany) *trckd ldrs: rdn and ev ch 2 1/2f out: wknd steadily fr over 1f out* **17/5**[2]

5 4 ½ **Nacida (GER)**[77] 5981 3-9-0 0 ........................................ MichaelCadeddu 1 83
(Yasmin Almenrader, Germany) *midfield: rdn and effrt 2 1/2f out: wknd appr fnl f* **199/10**

6 ¾ **Litaara (GER)**[35] 3-9-0 0 ........................................ MrVinzenzSchiergen 10 82
(P Schiergen, Germany) *towards rr of midfield: sme hdwy 3f out: rdn and outpcd 2 1/2f out: plugged on same pce* **143/10**

7 dist **Alicante (GER)**[42] 7203 3-9-0 0 ........................................ MaximPecheur 7
(Markus Klug, Germany) *led: rdn and hdd 4f out: wknd qckly under 3f out: eased 2f out* **175/10**

8 hd **Arazza (GER)**[28] 7672 3-9-0 0 ........................................ LukasDelozier 11
(J Hirschberger, Germany) *midfield: lost pl over 4f out: rdn and struggling fr under 3f out: eased over 1f out* **59/10**

9 ½ **Margie's Music (FR)**[28] 7673 3-9-0 0 ........................................ FilipMinarik 9
(P Schiergen, Germany) *a towards rr: lost tch over 2f out: eased over 1f out* **128/10**

10 hd **Tres Belle (IRE)**[27] 7696 3-9-0 0 ........................................ SebastienMaillot 8
(N Clement, France) *a towards rr: rdn and struggling fr 3f out: eased appr fnl f* **32/5**

2m 33.79s
**WFA** 3 from 4yo 5lb **10** Ran SP% **129.2**
PARI-MUTUEL (all including 10 euro stake): WIN: 57; PLACE: 15 14, 25; SF: 138.
**Owner** Ralf Paulick **Bred** R Paulick **Trained** Germany

## 8463a GROSSER PREIS DES GESTUT HAUS ZOPPENBROICH (LISTED RACE) (3YO+) (TURF) 1m
**2:30** 3-Y-O+ **£11,965** (£5,555; £2,564; £1,282)

RPR

1 **Peach Melba**[22] 7815 3-8-7 0 ........................................ FrannyNorton 7 100
(Mark Johnston) *mde all: rdn and kpt on wl fr 2 1/2f out* **6/4**[1]

2 1 ½ **Vive Marie (GER)**[35] 3-8-8 0 ow1 ........................................ (b) LukasDelozier 3 98
(J Hirschberger, Germany) **31/5**[3]

3 ¾ **Jasnin (FR)**[13] 8127 5-9-0 0 ........................................ MartinSeidl 10 100
(Waldemar Hickst, Germany) **42/10**[2]

4 10 **Apoleon (GER)**[26] 7722 7-9-0 0 ........................................ BauyrzhanMurzabayev 9 77
(Frau Anna Schleusner-Fruhriep, Germany) **125/10**

5 nse **Night Queen (GER)**[26] 5-8-10 0 ........................................ MaximPecheur 4 73
(Frau Erika Mader, Germany) **197/10**

6 1 ½ **Seewolf (GER)**[171] 7-9-0 0 ........................................ AlexanderPietsch 8 74
(S Smrczek, Germany) **127/10**

7 15 **Pemina (GER)**[56] 3-8-7 0 ........................................ FilipMinarik 1 34
(J Hirschberger, Germany) **99/10**

8 5 **Cassilero (GER)**[598] 6-9-0 0 ........................................ BayarsaikhanGanbat 6 28
(K Demme, Germany) **94/10**

9 3 ½ **Dalila (GER)**[42] 7204 3-8-7 0 ........................................ MichaelCadeddu 11 15
(P Schiergen, Germany) **154/10**

10 22 **Cashman (FR)**[49] 6987 4-9-3 0 ........................................ JozefBojko 12
(A Wohler, Germany) **15/2**

PARI-MUTUEL (all including 10 euro stake): WIN: 25; PLACE: 13, 15, 15; SF: 129.
**Owner** Lowther Racing & Partner **Bred** Lowther Racing **Trained** Middleham Moor, N Yorks

# 8273 SAINT-CLOUD (L-H)
Sunday, October 29

**OFFICIAL GOING: Turf: good to soft (abandoned after race 1 due to owners' protest)**

## 8464a PRIX DE LA HUME (CLAIMER) (3YO) (TURF) 1m 4f
**12:35** 3-Y-O **£12,820** (£5,128; £3,846; £2,564; £1,282)

RPR

1 **Pangolin (FR)**[19] 3-8-8 0 ........................................ GregoryBenoist 1 74
(M Delzangles, France) **3/1**[3]

2 1 ½ **Hard Talk (FR)**[7] 3-8-11 0 ........................................ (b) MaximeGuyon 4 75
(Y Barberot, France) **12/5**[2]

3 snk **Rita's Man (IRE)**[19] 7928 3-8-11 0 ........................................ MickaelBarzalona 2 75
(Richard Hannon) *settled bhd ldrs: pushed up to chal 2f out: rdn and briefly led over 1f out: hdd ins fnl f and lost 2nd cl home* **138/10**

4 nk **Lester Kris (IRE)**[25] 7744 3-9-1 0 ........................................ ChristopheSoumillon 3 78
(Richard Hannon) *sn led: pushed along over 2f out: rdn over 1f out: hdd and styd on one pce fnl f* **21/10**[1]

5 2 **Love Money (FR)**[23] 3-8-11 0 ........................................ TheoBachelot 7 71
(Y Barberot, France) **76/10**

6 nk **Riviere Argentee (FR)**[19] 7924 3-8-9 0 ow1 ........................................ (b) TonyPiccone 6 69
(K R Burke) *hld up in midfield: rdn and effrt early st: no ex fnl f: wknd* **184/10**

7 18 **Parin**[15] 3-8-8 0 ........................................ (p) AntoineHamelin 5 39
(Henk Grewe, Germany) **112/10**

2m 42.5s (2.10) **7** Ran SP% **118.4**
PARI-MUTUEL (all including 1 euro stake): WIN: 4.00; PLACE: 1.80 2.00, SF: 13.90.
**Owner** A Black **Bred** Chasemore Farm **Trained** France

8465 - (Foreign Racing) - See Raceform Interactive

# 8136 LEICESTER (R-H)
Monday, October 30

**OFFICIAL GOING: Good to soft**
Wind: Almost nil Weather: Fine

## 8466 BRITISH STALLION STUDS EBF NOVICE STKS (PLUS 10 RACE) 6f
**12:15** (12:15) (Class 4) 2-Y-O **£6,469** (£1,925; £962; £481) **Stalls High**

Form RPR

5 1 **Zumurud (IRE)**[96] 5270 2-9-2 0 ........................................ JimCrowley 4 74
(Charles Hills) *w ldr 1f: remained handy: shkn up to ld over 1f out: sn rdn and hung lft: styd on* **8/1**

0 2 1 ¼ **Sporting Bill (IRE)**[21] 7877 2-9-2 0 ........................................ TomQueally 6 70
(James Fanshawe) *chsd ldrs: rdn over 1f out: edgd lft ins fnl f: styd on* **7/2**[2]

3 ½ **Red Cymbal** 2-9-2 0 ........................................ DanielTudhope 7 69+
(William Haggas) *hld up: swtchd rt and hdwy over 1f out: shkn up and edgd lft ins fnl f: styd on same pce nr fin* **7/4**[1]

4 3 ¼ **Takeonefortheteam** 2-9-2 0 ........................................ GeorgeDowning 5 59
(Daniel Mark Loughnane) *hld up: pushed along over 2f out: running on whn hung lft wl ins fnl f: nt rch ldrs* **50/1**

5240 5 1 ¼ **Sarstedt**[29] 7647 2-9-2 72 ........................................ FranBerry 3 55
(Henry Candy) *led: rdn and hdd over 1f out: wknd ins fnl f* **9/2**[3]

6 nk **Towelrads Boy (IRE)** 2-9-2 0 ........................................ PJMcDonald 9 55
(Paul Cole) *chsd ldr after 1f: rdn over 1f out: wkng whn hmpd wl ins fnl f* **16/1**

00 7 2 **Good Impression**[75] 6070 2-8-13 0 ........................................ GeorgeWood(3) 10 48
(Ali Stronge) *hld up: rdn over 1f out: wknd fnl f* **200/1**

06 8 1 ½ **Daddys Poppit (USA)**[48] 7033 2-8-8 0 ........................................ GeorgiaCox(3) 1 39
(William Haggas) *wnt rt s: sn pushed along in rr: wknd over 1f out* **7/1**

9 4 ½ **Scots Snap (IRE)** 2-8-11 0 ........................................ MartinDwyer 2 25
(Marcus Tregoning) *prom tl wknd over 1f out* **22/1**

1m 13.46s (0.46) **Going Correction** 0.0s/f (Good) **9** Ran SP% **113.1**
Speed ratings (Par 97): **96,94,93,89,87 87,84,82,76**
CSF £35.05 TOTE £7.70: £2.80, £1.30, £1.10; EX 41.50 Trifecta £137.60.
**Owner** Hamdan Al Maktoum **Bred** Miss Sinead Looney **Trained** Lambourn, Berks

**FOCUS**
Race times suggested that the ground was just on the soft side of good. Ordinary late-season novice form, but the first two are improvers.

## 8467 HAYMARKET NURSERY H'CAP 7f
**12:45** (12:47) (Class 5) (0-70,72) 2-Y-O **£3,234** (£962; £481; £240) **Stalls High**

Form RPR

6005 1 **Blacklooks (IRE)**[35] 7460 2-9-4 67 ........................................ DavidNolan 8 70
(Ivan Furtado) *trckd ldrs: rdn and hung lft over 1f out: hung rt ins fnl f: r.o to ld towards fin* **20/1**

4003 2 ½ **Rainbow Jazz (IRE)**[15] 8074 2-8-11 67 ........................................ (v) NicolaCurrie(7) 7 69
(Mark Usher) *plld hrd: w ldrs: led wl over 1f out: sn rdn: hdd towards fin* **8/1**[3]

236 3 nk **Kirbec (IRE)**[9] 8236 2-9-7 70 ........................................ (p[1]) AndrewMullen 5 71
(Keith Dalgleish) *chsd ldrs: rdn and ev ch fr wl over 1f out: styd on* **12/1**

2144 4 1 ¼ **Felisa**[14] 8120 2-9-1 64 ........................................ FranBerry 14 61
(David Evans) *chsd ldrs: rdn over 1f out: hung rt ins fnl f: kpt on* **12/1**

566 5 ½ **Robinson Crusoe (IRE)**[51] 6916 2-9-6 72 ........................................ HollieDoyle(3) 3 68+
(Richard Hannon) *s.i.s: in rr: swtchd lft over 2f out: hdwy over 1f out: edgd rt and styd on ins fnl f* **5/1**[1]

554 6 nse **Gabrials Centurion (IRE)**[44] 7141 2-9-8 71 ........................................ DanielTudhope 6 67
(David O'Meara) *hld up in tch: rdn over 2f out: styd on same pce ins fnl f* **7/1**[2]

0221 7 2 ½ **Dark Blue (IRE)**[17] 7996 2-8-13 62 ........................................ RaulDaSilva 12 51
(Mick Channon) *hld up: swtchd rt over 2f out: styd on fr over 1f out: nvr nrr* **12/1**

0530 8 nse **Strategic (IRE)**[66] 6395 2-9-6 69 ........................................ SeanLevey 1 58
(Richard Hannon) *mid-div: pushed along 1/2-way: hdwy u.p over 1f out: no ex ins fnl f* **10/1**

356 9 ¾ **He's Our Star (IRE)**[70] 6260 2-9-2 68 ........................................ (p[1]) GeorgeWood(3) 15 55
(Ali Stronge) *prom: rdn over 2f out: styd on same pce fr over 1f out* **20/1**

4060 10 1 **Royal Liberty**[23] 7814 2-9-6 69 ........................................ PJMcDonald 10 53
(Mark Johnston) *hld up: pushed along over 2f out: hdwy over 1f out: no ex fnl f* **25/1**

0233 11 4 **Foxrush Take Time (FR)**[66] 6366 2-8-13 62 ........................................ MartinDwyer 16 36
(Richard Guest) *hld up: rdn over 2f out: nvr on terms* **12/1**

030 12 ½ **Tulane (IRE)**[45] 7120 2-9-6 69 ........................................ TomQueally 11 41
(Richard Phillips) *hld up: rdn over 2f out: n.d* **50/1**

6065 13 ½ **Mountain Meadow**[27] 7698 2-8-0 49 oh2 ........................................ (p) PatrickMathers 17 20
(Richard Fahey) *sn pushed along and a in rr* **50/1**

340 14 ¾ **Storm Jazz (IRE)**[33] 7513 2-9-6 69 ........................................ JimCrowley 2 38
(Ed Dunlop) *chsd ldrs tl rdn and wknd over 1f out* **17/2**

540 15 ½ **Rosedale Topping (IRE)**[14] 8112 2-9-2 65 ........................................ (b[1]) AdamBeschizza 9 32
(Ed Vaughan) *hld up: rdn over 2f out: a in rr* **33/1**

5400 16 2 ¾ **Affluence (IRE)**[23] 7829 2-8-13 62 ........................................ DanielMuscutt 4 22
(Martin Smith) *hld up in tch: rdn over 2f out: wknd over 1f out* **10/1**

56 17 hd **Shadow Seeker (IRE)**[35] 7450 2-8-11 60 ........................................ PaulHanagan 13 20
(Paul D'Arcy) *led: hung rt 1/2-way: hdd & wknd wl over 1f out* **33/1**

1m 26.48s (0.28) **Going Correction** 0.0s/f (Good) **17** Ran SP% **122.9**
Speed ratings (Par 95): **98,97,97,95,95 95,92,92,91,90 85,84,84,83,82 79,79**
CSF £163.31 CT £2030.30 TOTE £27.70: £6.00, £2.30, £2.40, £2.80; EX 201.60 Trifecta £1752.10.
**Owner** John L Marriott **Bred** Premier Bloodstock **Trained** Wiseton, Nottinghamshire

**FOCUS**
Plenty were unexposed in this big-field nursery, with only three winners in the line-up. The pace held up with the principals always towards the fore. The time was quicker than the two Class 5 races for older horses over the trip.

## 8468 SIR GORDON RICHARDS H'CAP 1m 3f 179y
**1:20** (1:20) (Class 2) (0-110,107) 3-Y-O+ **£18,903** (£5,658; £2,829; £1,416; £705) **Stalls Low**

Form RPR

-362 1 **Dance The Dream**[20] 7931 4-8-10 98 ........................................ TylerSaunders(7) 7 106+
(Marcus Tregoning) *chsd ldrs: led over 1f out: sn rdn and edgd rt: styd on* **5/2**[1]

2140 2 1 ½ **Top Tug (IRE)**[65] 6447 6-9-10 105 ........................................ MartinDwyer 1 110
(Alan King) *hld up: hdwy over 2f out: rdn to chse wnr and edgd rt ins fnl f: styd on* **6/1**[3]

0504 3 2 ½ **Noble Gift**[30] 7602 7-8-13 97 ........................................ CallumShepherd(3) 9 98
(William Knight) *racd wd 2f: prom: jnd the rest and led 10f out: rdn and hdd over 1f out: no ex ins fnl f* **25/1**

2446 4 1 ½ **Gawdawpalin (IRE)**[21] 7903 4-8-12 96 ........................................ MitchGodwin(3) 8 95
(Sylvester Kirk) *led 2f: chsd ldr: rdn over 2f out: ev ch wl over 1f out: edgd rt and no ex fnl f* **8/1**

2630 5 2 **Arthenus**[23] 7805 5-9-5 103 ........................................ (p) GeorgeWood(3) 5 98
(James Fanshawe) *chsd ldrs: rdn over 2f out: wknd fnl f* **7/2**[2]

4400 6 nse **Master The World (IRE)**[9] 8234 6-9-12 107 ........................................ (p) JimCrowley 3 102
(David Elsworth) *s.i.s: hld up: shkn up over 2f out: nt clr run and swtchd lft over 1f out: nt trble ldrs* **8/1**

4015 7 ¾ **Marmajuke Bay**[32] 7548 4-8-8 96 ........................................ (p) NicolaCurrie(7) 4 90
(Mark Usher) *chsd ldrs: pushed along over 4f out: wknd and eased ins fnl f* **7/1**

2-25 **8** 1 3/4 **Rock Steady (IRE)**[256] 767 4-9-4 **99**........................ KieranShoemark 2 90
(Roger Charlton) *hld up: rdn over 2f out: hung rt over 1f out: wknd fnl f* **9/1**
053- **9** 2 1/2 **Captain Morley**[48] 6884 6-9-4 **99**........................ FranBerry 6 86
(David Simcock) *hld up: hdwy over 2f out: rdn and wknd over 1f out* **50/1**
2m 34.07s (0.17) **Going Correction** +0.275s/f (Good) 9 Ran SP% **115.6**
Speed ratings (Par 109): **110,109,107,106,105 104,104,103,101**
CSF £17.92 CT £301.48 TOTE £4.20: £1.90, £1.50, £4.40; EX 16.90 Trifecta £207.80.
**Owner** Mrs Hugh Dalgety **Bred** Minster Stud And Mrs H Dalgety **Trained** Whitsbury, Hants
**FOCUS**
Race distance increased by 9yds. A valuable handicap, but they didn't go a great gallop and it paid to be up with the pace.

## 8469 HOBY H'CAP 1m 53y
**1:55** (1:55) (Class 2) (0-105,102) 3-Y-O+ **£12,938** (£3,850; £1,924; £962) **Stalls** Low

Form RPR
3123 **1** **Fire Brigade**[31] 7582 3-9-1 **94**........................ JamieSpencer 3 99+
(Michael Bell) *hld up: hdwy over 4f out: nt clr run over 1f out: shkn up and qcknd to ld wl ins fnl f* **5/2**[1]
301/ **2** 1/2 **Chatez (IRE)**[947] 1078 6-9-7 **97**........................ FergusSweeney 6 101
(Alan King) *s.i.s: hld up: hdwy over 1f out: edgd rt ins fnl f: r.o* **20/1**
-030 **3** 1/2 **Bronze Angel (IRE)**[16] 8032 8-8-12 **95**........................(v) TylerSaunders(7) 2 98
(Marcus Tregoning) *hld up: nt clr run over 3f out: swtchd lft over 2f out: hdwy u.p over 1f out: r.o to go 3rd post: nt rch ldrs* **10/1**
1501 **4** *nse* **Mazyoun**[39] 7339 3-9-0 **93**........................(b) JosephineGordon 7 95
(Hugo Palmer) *trckd ldrs: racd keenly: nt clr run over 1f out: sn rdn: r.o* **17/2**
4223 **5** *nse* **Home Cummins (IRE)**[17] 8009 5-9-2 **92**........................(p) PaulHanagan 5 95
(Richard Fahey) *chsd ldrs: led over 1f out: sn rdn: hdd wl ins fnl f* **13/2**[3]
0002 **6** 1 **Bravery (IRE)**[17] 8009 4-9-7 **97**........................ DanielTudhope 4 98
(David O'Meara) *hld up: rdn over 1f out: edgd rt: r.o towards fin: nt rch ldrs* **9/2**[2]
B635 **7** *hd* **Just Hiss**[17] 8009 4-8-11 **90**........................(p) RachelRichardson(3) 1 91
(Tim Easterby) *s.i.s: hld up: racd keenly: hdwy and nt clr run over 1f out: r.o: nt rch ldrs* **7/1**
1041 **8** 1/2 **London Protocol (FR)**[30] 7636 4-9-9 **102**........................ CliffordLee(3) 8 101
(K R Burke) *chsd ldr tl led 2f out: rdn and hdd over 1f out: no ex wl ins fnl f* **16/1**
0124 **9** *hd* **King's Pavilion (IRE)**[30] 7609 4-9-4 **94**........................ FranBerry 9 93
(David Barron) *hld up in tch: rdn over 1f out: edgd lft ins fnl f: styd on same pce* **7/1**
3060 **10** 6 **Gurkha Friend**[21] 7886 5-9-1 **91**........................ DavidNolan 10 76
(Karen McLintock) *led: rdn and hdd 2f out: wknd fnl f* **25/1**
1m 45.65s (0.55) **Going Correction** +0.275s/f (Good)
**WFA** 3 from 4yo+ 3lb 10 Ran SP% **119.2**
Speed ratings (Par 109): **108,107,107,106,106 105,105,105,105,99**
CSF £59.84 CT £442.04 TOTE £4.40: £1.60, £4.40, £2.60; EX 41.00 Trifecta £818.10.
**Owner** The Fitzrovians **Bred** Stowell Hill Ltd **Trained** Newmarket, Suffolk
**FOCUS**
Race distance increased by 9yds. A decent handicap, but the pace wasn't great and the first nine were covered by around 3l at the line.

## 8470 GUMLEY CLAIMING STKS 7f
**2:30** (2:31) (Class 5) 3-4-Y-O **£3,234** (£962; £481; £240) **Stalls** High

Form RPR
1125 **1** **Topmeup**[12] 8156 3-8-1 60........................(v) MattCosham(3) 2 57
(David Evans) *hld up in tch: led ins fnl f: edgd rt towards fin: r.o* **3/1**[2]
2001 **2** 1 1/4 **Sans Souci Bay**[13] 8137 3-9-4 83........................(b) HollieDoyle(3) 7 71
(Scott Dixon) *s.s: in tch w the field 4f out: hdwy over 2f out: led over 1f out: rdn and hdd ins fnl f: styd on same pce* **11/4**[1]
300 **3** *nk* **Tifl**[13] 8134 4-8-4 54........................(bt) GeorgeWood(3) 1 55
(Heather Main) *stdd s: hld up: rdn over 1f out: r.o to go 3rd nr fin* **20/1**
0002 **4** 1 **Tawfeer**[11] 8182 3-7-12 47........................(p) NicolaCurrie(7) 5 51
(Phil McEntee) *chsd ldr: rdn and ev ch over 1f out: styd on same pce ins fnl f* **20/1**
6006 **5** 1 1/2 **Lexington Sky (IRE)**[14] 8107 3-8-10 69........................(p[1]) PJMcDonald 3 52
(Roger Fell) *hld up in tch: rdn over 1f out: no ex ins fnl f* **11/4**[1]
0215 **6** 2 1/2 **Vibes (IRE)**[78] 5961 3-9-7 80........................ JamieSpencer 8 56
(Jamie Osborne) *led: rdn and hdd over 1f out: wknd wl ins fnl f* **7/1**[3]
3434 **7** 1 1/4 **Oakley Pride (IRE)**[13] 8137 3-8-0 57........................(p) PaulHainey(7) 4 39
(Gay Kelleway) *s.i.s: pushed along in rr: rdn over 2f out: n.d* **12/1**
0600 **8** 2 1/2 **Majestic Girl (IRE)**[19] 5817 4-8-2 39........................ KieranO'Neill 6 26
(Steve Flook) *chsd ldrs: rdn 1/2-way: wknd 2f out* **200/1**
1m 26.52s (0.32) **Going Correction** 0.0s/f (Good)
**WFA** 3 from 4yo 2lb 8 Ran SP% **108.5**
Speed ratings (Par 103): **98,96,96,95,93 90,89,86**
CSF £10.33 TOTE £3.80: £1.20, £1.30, £4.10; EX 12.00 Trifecta £120.30.
**Owner** M W Lawrence **Bred** Whitwell Bloodstock **Trained** Pandy, Monmouths
**FOCUS**
Just a modest claimer rated around the third and fourth.

## 8471 COSSINGTON EBF FILLIES' NOVICE MEDIAN AUCTION STKS (PLUS 10 RACE) (DIV I) 6f
**3:05** (3:06) (Class 4) 2-Y-O **£6,469** (£1,925; £962; £481) **Stalls** High

Form RPR
2226 **1** **Clubbable**[16] 8039 2-8-12 81........................ PaulHanagan 1 75
(Richard Fahey) *prom: racd keenly: shkn up to chse ldr and hung lft fr over 1f out: rdn to ld ins fnl f: styd on* **4/11**[1]
0452 **2** 1/2 **Lady Willpower**[9] 8236 2-8-9 74 ow2........................ JoshuaBryan(5) 10 75
(John Quinn) *chsd ldr tl led over 3f out: rdn and hdd ins fnl f: kpt on* **4/1**[2]
**3** 5 **Moretti (IRE)** 2-8-12 0........................ DanielTudhope 3 58+
(David O'Meara) *plld hrd and sn prom: shkn up over 1f out: no ex fnl f* **5/1**[3]
**4** 1 1/2 **Star Attraction (FR)** 2-8-12 0........................ KieranShoemark 9 54
(David Menuisier) *s.i.s: hdwy over 1f out: no imp fnl f* **9/1**
0255 **5** 7 **Havana Heart**[18] 7986 2-8-12 67........................ StevieDonohoe 5 33
(Ismail Mohammed) *led: hdd over 3f out: rdn whn hmpd over 1f out: sn wknd* **12/1**
00 **6** 3 1/4 **Chloellie**[64] 6480 2-8-12 0........................ AdamBeschizza 8 23
(J R Jenkins) *prom: pushed along 1/2-way: wknd over 1f out* **100/1**
0 **7** 4 1/2 **Madam Pomfrey**[189] 2037 2-8-9 0........................ GeorgeWood(3) 6 9
(Jonathan Portman) *slowly into stride: hld up: racd keenly: wknd wl over 1f out* **50/1**
0 **8** 1 **Windsor Whirlybird (IRE)**[84] 5717 2-8-12 0........................ KieranO'Neill 7 6
(Ali Stronge) *plld hrd and prom: lost pl after 1f: wkng whn edgd rt over 1f out* **100/1**
1m 13.19s (0.19) **Going Correction** 0.0s/f (Good) 8 Ran SP% **131.6**
Speed ratings (Par 94): **98,97,90,88,79 75,69,67**
CSF £3.20 TOTE £1.30: £1.02, £1.60, £1.70; EX 3.10 Trifecta £7.80.
**Owner** Cheveley Park Stud **Bred** Cheveley Park Stud Ltd **Trained** Musley Bank, N Yorks
**FOCUS**
Pretty ordinary form, and the slower division by 0.19sec. The first two finished clear.

## 8472 COSSINGTON EBF FILLIES' NOVICE MEDIAN AUCTION STKS (PLUS 10 RACE) (DIV II) 6f
**3:40** (3:43) (Class 4) 2-Y-O **£6,469** (£1,925; £962; £481) **Stalls** High

Form RPR
0525 **1** **Maybride**[23] 7821 2-8-12 86........................ PaulHanagan 6 85
(Richard Fahey) *trckd ldrs: shkn up to ld and hung lft over 1f out: styd on wl* **8/13**[1]
2204 **2** 4 **Your Choice**[12] 8148 2-8-9 80........................ GeorgeWood(3) 3 73
(Laura Mongan) *led 1f: chsd ldr: rdn and ev ch whn hung lft over 1f out: no ex ins fnl f* **11/4**[2]
506 **3** 3 **Chillala (IRE)**[38] 7357 2-8-12 69........................(h) StevieDonohoe 1 64
(Harry Dunlop) *led 5f out: rdn and hdd over 1f out: nt clr run sn after: wknd ins fnl f* **9/1**
36 **4** *shd* **Katie Lee (IRE)**[54] 6826 2-8-12 0........................ FranBerry 8 64+
(Henry Candy) *s.s: bhd: swtchd rt over 1f out: r.o ins fnl f: nvr nrr* **20/1**
**5** 1 **Fyxenna** 2-8-9 0........................ HectorCrouch(3) 5 61
(Clive Cox) *prom: pushed along and lost pl 1/2-way: styd on ins fnl f* **8/1**[3]
00 **6** 3/4 **La Cabana**[11] 8189 2-8-12 0........................ PatrickMathers 7 58
(Richard Fahey) *hld up: hdwy over 3f out: rdn: hung lft and wknd over 1f out* **40/1**
**7** 4 1/2 **Pas De Blanc** 2-8-12 0........................ MartinLane 4 45
(Brian Barr) *hld up: pushed along 1/2-way: nvr on terms* **66/1**
6 **8** 3 3/4 **Patienceisavirtue**[14] 8118 2-8-5 0........................(h) NicolaCurrie(7) 2 34
(Christine Dunnett) *prom: pushed along over 2f out: sn wknd* **250/1**
0 **9** 4 **Magic Buddy**[63] 6525 2-8-12 0........................ AdamBeschizza 10 22
(J R Jenkins) *s.i.s: plld hrd and hdwy over 4f out: rdn and wknd wl over 1f out* **150/1**
**10** 11 **French Sparkle** 2-8-5 0........................ JonathanFisher(7) 9
(Robert Cowell) *s.i.s: sn pushed along in rr: wknd over 2f out* **33/1**
1m 13.0s **Going Correction** 0.0s/f (Good) 10 Ran SP% **122.4**
Speed ratings (Par 94): **100,94,90,90,89 88,82,77,71,57**
CSF £2.60 TOTE £1.50: £1.02, £1.30, £2.60; EX 2.60 Trifecta £10.60.
**Owner** Cheveley Park Stud **Bred** Cheveley Park Stud Ltd **Trained** Musley Bank, N Yorks
**FOCUS**
The quicker division by 0.19sec, and the fastest of the three C&D races.

## 8473 FOSSE WAY H'CAP (FOR GENTLEMAN AMATEUR RIDERS) 7f
**4:10** (4:13) (Class 5) (0-70,67) 3-Y-O+ **£3,743** (£1,161; £580; £290) **Stalls** High

Form RPR
2506 **1** **Champagne Bob**[20] 7934 5-10-12 **61**........................(p) MrBJames(3) 10 71
(Richard Price) *hld up: hdwy over 2f out: rdn: edgd rt and styd on to ld wl ins fnl f* **12/1**
1251 **2** 2 1/2 **My Girl Maisie (IRE)**[21] 7889 3-11-2 **64**........................ MrSWalker 4 67
(Richard Guest) *a.p: led over 1f out: rdn and hdd wl ins fnl f* **9/4**[1]
6614 **3** 3/4 **Wordismybond**[11] 8181 8-11-2 **67**........................(p) MrJamiePerrett(5) 3 69
(Amanda Perrett) *chsd ldrs: pushed along over 2f out: sn edgd rt: styd on* **12/1**
0604 **4** *hd* **Gatillo**[14] 8124 4-10-9 **55**........................ MrRBirkett 8 56
(Julia Feilden) *s.i.s: hdwy 1/2-way: rdn over 1f out: styd on* **16/1**
0- **5** 1/2 **True Companion (IRE)**[6] 8334 4-11-0 **60**........................(b) MrJamesKing 6 60
(Adrian Brendan Joyce, Ire) *s.i.s: hld up: swtchd rt over 2f out: hdwy u.p and swtchd lft over 1f out: sn hung lft: styd on: nt rch ldrs* **7/2**[2]
4546 **6** *nk* **Baron Run**[58] 6688 7-10-0 **53** oh1........................ MrJCummins(7) 1 52
(K R Burke) *prom: rdn over 2f out: no ex wl ins fnl f* **14/1**
2121 **7** 1 **Edge (IRE)**[21] 7900 6-11-0 **60**........................(b) MrJordanWilliams 13 56
(Bernard Llewellyn) *hld up: pushed along over 2f out: styd on ins fnl f: nvr trbld ldrs* **14/1**
/0-0 **8** *nk* **Sailors Warn (IRE)**[19] 3547 10-10-12 **65**........................(p) MrJamesMorley(7) 11 61
(Ian Williams) *s.i.s: sn pushed along in rr: styd on ins fnl f: nvr nrr* **50/1**
0610 **9** *hd* **Baltic Prince (IRE)**[11] 8184 7-10-13 **66**........................ MrGGilbertson(7) 5 61
(Tony Carroll) *led: hdd over 4f out: remained handy: rdn and hung lft over 1f out: no ex* **25/1**
2341 **10** 2 **Arcanista (IRE)**[21] 7911 4-10-7 **58**........................(p) MrMSHarris(5) 7 48
(Chris Dwyer) *chsd ldrs: led over 4f out: rdn and hdd over 1f out: wknd ins fnl f* **8/1**[3]
5025 **11** 2 **Harry Beau**[6] 8328 3-11-2 **64**........................(t[1]) MrPMillman 9 48
(David Evans) *chsd ldrs: rdn over 2f out: wknd over 1f out* **9/1**
-400 **12** 15 **Captain Kendall (IRE)**[250] 860 8-10-0 **53** oh8........................(p) MrAHark(7) 12
(Harry Chisman) *chsd ldrs: pushed along 1/2-way: wknd over 2f out* **100/1**
00-0 **13** 9 **No Refund (IRE)**[278] 398 6-10-3 **56**........................ MrDannyKerr(7) 2
(Martin Smith) *s.s: a bhd* **50/1**
1m 27.35s (1.15) **Going Correction** 0.0s/f (Good)
**WFA** 3 from 4yo+ 2lb 13 Ran SP% **117.5**
Speed ratings (Par 103): **93,90,89,89,88 88,87,86,86,84 81,64,54**
CSF £37.80 CT £357.12 TOTE £11.50: £3.50, £1.60, £3.30; EX 52.40 Trifecta £698.90.
**Owner** M F Oseman **Bred** London Thoroughbred Services Ltd **Trained** Ullingswick, H'fords
**FOCUS**
Very modest form with the winner earning his best figure since taking this race two years ago.
T/Plt: £25.30 to a £1 stake. Pool: £49763.42 - 1430.41 winning units T/Qpdt: £3.90 to a £1 stake. Pool: £5798.97 - 1097.00 winning units **Colin Roberts**

# 8212 REDCAR (L-H)
Monday, October 30

**OFFICIAL GOING: Soft (good to soft in places; 7.0)**
Wind: light half against Weather: overcast

## 8474 BRITISH STALLION STUDS EBF NOVICE STKS 5f 217y
**12:00** (12:01) (Class 5) 2-Y-O **£3,396** (£1,010; £505; £252) **Stalls** Centre

Form RPR
**1** **Aljady (FR)** 2-8-13 0........................ AdamMcNamara(3) 7 77+
(Richard Fahey) *trckd ldrs: pushed along 2f out: rdn and kpt on wl fnl f: led 50yds out* **8/1**



The Form Book Flat, Raceform Ltd, Newbury, RG14 5SJ

06 **2** 1/2 **Scenic River**[7] 8288 2-8-11 0 ........ DavidAllan 3 69
(Tim Easterby) *led after 1f: rdn 2f out: pressed over 1f out: kpt on but hdd 50yds out* **25/1**

22 **3** 1 1/4 **Wrenthorpe**[10] 8212 2-9-2 0 ........ GrahamLee 10 70
(Bryan Smart) *prom: rdn to chal strly over 1f out: one pce fnl 110yds* **7/4[1]**

6 **4** nse **Royal Prospect (IRE)**[19] 7953 2-9-2 0 ........ PaulMulrennan 9 70+
(Julie Camacho) *chsd ldrs: rdn along 2f out: edgd lft fr appr fnl f: kpt on same pce* **20/1**

**5** 1/2 **Tallow (IRE)** 2-8-11 0 ........ JoeFanning 12 63+
(William Haggas) *hld up in midfield: pushed along over 2f out: swtchd lft and hdwy appr fnl f: kpt on* **9/2[3]**

0 **6** 1 1/4 **I Know How (IRE)**[19] 7953 2-9-2 0 ........ JoeDoyle 8 65
(Julie Camacho) *led for 1f: trckd ldr racing keenly: rdn 2f out: no ex fnl f* **22/1**

**7** 3 1/4 **Rux Ruxx (IRE)** 2-8-11 0 ........ OisinMurphy 4 50
(Andrew Balding) *trckd ldrs: rdn over 2f out: wknd fnl f* **4/1[2]**

**8** 1 **Spanish Mane (IRE)** 2-8-11 0 ........ BarryMcHugh 2 47+
(Richard Fahey) *dwlt and wnt rt s: hld up: pushed along over 2f out: minor late hdwy: nvr threatened* **11/1**

0 **9** 1 1/2 **Symphonic**[9] 8236 2-8-11 0 ........ ShaneGray 5 42
(Ann Duffield) *midfield: rdn over 2f out: wknd over 1f out* **125/1**

**10** nk **Mayalee** 2-8-11 0 ........ JackGarritty 6 41+
(Richard Fahey) *hld up in midfield: rdn over 2f out: nvr threatened* **22/1**

**11** nse **Whatwouldyouknow (IRE)** 2-9-2 0 ........ PhillipMakin 14 46
(Richard Guest) *midfield: rdn over 2f out: wknd over 1f out* **33/1**

0 **12** 1 3/4 **Lady Sophiebella**[7] 8288 2-8-11 0 ........ DuranFentiman 1 36
(Bryan Smart) *s.i.s: sn rcvrd to chse ldrs: rdn over 2f out: wknd over 1f out* **100/1**

**13** 8 **Swissie** 2-9-2 0 ........ TomEaves 11 17
(Ivan Furtado) *slowly away: a towards rr* **66/1**

0 **14** 10 **Laharna (IRE)**[77] 5998 2-8-8 0 ........ PhilDennis(3) 13
(Noel Wilson) *a towards rr* **125/1**

1m 12.92s (1.12) **Going Correction** +0.175s/f (Good) **14** Ran SP% **118.3**
Speed ratings (Par 95): **99,98,96,96,95 94,89,88,86,86 86,83,73,59**
CSF £192.96 TOTE £6.90: £2.20, £5.70, £1.20; EX 186.60 Trifecta £751.70.
**Owner** Al Shaqab Racing **Bred** Al Shaqab Racing **Trained** Musley Bank, N Yorks

**FOCUS**
The going was given as soft, good to soft in places (GoingStick: 7.0). Modest novice form, but winner may have more to offer.

## 8475 ALL NEW RACINGUK.COM NURSERY H'CAP 5f 217y
**12:30** (12:32) (Class 6) (0-65,67) 2-Y-O **£3,234** (£962; £481; £240) **Stalls** Centre

Form RPR

2423 **1** **Excellent Times**[26] 7734 2-9-8 **66** ........ DavidAllan 1 74+
(Tim Easterby) *in tch: trckd ldr gng wl over 2f out: pushed along to ld over 1f out: kpt on wl: comf* **3/1[1]**

4053 **2** 2 3/4 **Istanbul Pasha (IRE)**[33] 7518 2-8-9 **51** ow2 ........(v) TomEaves 4 51
(David Evans) *dwlt: sn in tch: rdn and hdwy 2f out: chsd ldr appr fnl f: kpt on but a hld* **4/1[2]**

2300 **3** 1 3/4 **Mr Carbonator**[13] 8141 2-8-12 **56** ........ JimmyQuinn 6 49
(Philip Kirby) *hld up: rdn along 1/2-way: styd on fr over 1f out: wnt 3rd 110yds out* **16/1**

3530 **4** 3/4 **Onesarnieshort (FR)**[38] 7362 2-9-6 **64** ........ ShaneGray 11 54
(David O'Meara) *midfield: rdn over 2f out: styd on fnl f* **66/1**

005 **5** 2 1/2 **Honey Gg**[40] 7264 2-8-1 **45** ow3 ........ PhilDennis(3) 12 31
(Declan Carroll) *trckd ldrs: rdn over 2f out: ev ch over 1f out: edgd lft and wknd ins fnl f* **22/1**

2561 **6** nk **Give Em A Clump (IRE)**[43] 7196 2-9-7 **65** ........ CharlesBishop 13 47
(David Evans) *nvr bttr than midfield* **6/1[3]**

3050 **7** 1/2 **Corton Lass**[58] 6693 2-8-13 **60** ........(p[1]) RowanScott(3) 5 40
(Keith Dalgleish) *chsd ldrs: rdn over 2f out: wknd over 1f out* **14/1**

3000 **8** 1 3/4 **W G Grace (IRE)**[11] 8191 2-9-5 **63** ........ FrannyNorton 10 38
(Mark Johnston) *hld up: rdn along over 2f out: nvr threatened* **12/1**

0566 **9** 1/2 **Rock Hill (IRE)**[31] 7564 2-9-9 **67** ........ OisinMurphy 14 41
(Paul Midgley) *hld up: rdn 3f out: nvr threatened* **14/1**

0600 **10** 1 1/2 **Sir Walter (IRE)**[20] 7919 2-8-3 **47** ........(p[1]) DuranFentiman 2 16
(Eric Alston) *led: rdn and edgd lft over 2f out: hdd over 1f out: wknd* **40/1**

406 **11** 1 3/4 **Swiss Chocolate (IRE)**[20] 7919 2-9-6 **64** ........ PaulMulrennan 7 28
(William Haggas) *chsd ldrs: rdn over 2f out: wknd over 1f out* **10/1**

0543 **12** nk **Gorse (IRE)**[20] 7920 2-9-5 **63** ........(p[1]) GrahamLee 3 26
(Ann Duffield) *chsd ldrs: rdn over 2f out: wknd over 1f out* **8/1**

003 **13** 4 **Moremoneymoreparty (IRE)**[88] 5561 2-9-1 **59** ........ PhillipMakin 15 10
(Richard Guest) *dwlt: a towards rr* **20/1**

600 **14** 11 **Joe Cable (IRE)**[17] 8013 2-8-4 **46** ow2 ........(v[1]) JoeDoyle 8
(Nigel Tinkler) *sn pushed along: a in rr: eased and t.o fnl 2f* **40/1**

1m 12.77s (0.97) **Going Correction** +0.175s/f (Good) **14** Ran SP% **121.9**
Speed ratings (Par 93): **100,96,94,93,89 89,88,86,85,83 81,80,75,60**
CSF £13.62 CT £170.37 TOTE £4.20: £1.60, £2.10, £4.20; EX 17.40 Trifecta £109.70.
**Owner** Times Of Wigan **Bred** Times Of Wigan Ltd **Trained** Great Habton, N Yorks

**FOCUS**
A modest nursery run at a good pace and won in emphatic style.

## 8476 EUROPEAN BREEDERS' FUND EBF DOUBLE TRIGGER NOVICE STKS 1m 1f
**1:05** (1:10) (Class 5) 2-Y-O **£3,396** (£1,010; £505; £252) **Stalls** Low

Form RPR

33 **1** **I'm Improving (IRE)**[66] 6380 2-9-2 0 ........ GrahamLee 5 86+
(Keith Dalgleish) *sn trckd ldrs: hdwy to chal gng wl over 2f out: pushed along to ld wl over 1f out: rdn and styd on wl to draw clr* **5/2[2]**

2 **2** 6 **Sea Youmzain (IRE)**[13] 8136 2-8-11 0 ........ JoeFanning 3 69
(Mark Johnston) *trckd ldrs: rdn along 3f out: wnt 2nd 1f out: one pce and no ch w wnr* **8/11[1]**

**3** 1 1/4 **Lucky Deal** 2-9-2 0 ........ FrannyNorton 7 72
(Mark Johnston) *trckd ldrs on outer: pushed along over 5f out: rn green and dropped to rr: styd on fnl 2f* **12/1**

64 **4** 4 1/2 **We Know (IRE)**[15] 8075 2-9-2 0 ........(t) PaulMulrennan 2 63
(Simon Crisford) *led: rdn and strly pressed over 2f out: hdd wl over 1f out: wknd fnl f* **13/2[3]**

00 **5** 5 **Munstead Gold**[16] 8029 2-9-2 0 ........ OisinMurphy 6 53
(Andrew Balding) *prom: rdn along 4f out: wknd 2f out* **28/1**

000 **6** 22 **Renton**[121] 4335 2-9-2 45 ........(p[1]) DuranFentiman 1 9
(Tony Coyle) *stdd s: hld up: rdn 4f out: wknd over 2f out* **250/1**

1m 55.49s (2.49) **Going Correction** +0.25s/f (Good) **6** Ran SP% **111.3**
Speed ratings (Par 95): **98,92,91,87,83 63**
CSF £4.57 TOTE £3.50: £1.90, £1.10; EX 4.80 Trifecta £16.60.
**Owner** Paul & Clare Rooney **Bred** Minch Bloodstock **Trained** Carluke, S Lanarks
■ Red Seeker was withdrawn. Price at time of withdrawal 200-1. Rule 4 does not apply.

**FOCUS**
The impressive winner's Hamilton form has worked out well and this looked a useful performance.

## 8477 RACING UK ANYWHERE AVAILABLE NOW (S) STKS 1m 2f 1y
**1:40** (1:41) (Class 6) 3-5-Y-O **£3,408** (£1,006; £503) **Stalls** Low

Form RPR

0033 **1** **Traveltalk (IRE)**[10] 8206 3-8-8 57 ........ BenRobinson(5) 1 63
(Brian Ellison) *chsd ldrs: rdn to go 2nd over 2f out: sn clsd on ldr: led ent fnl f: styd on* **11/4[2]**

5010 **2** 2 3/4 **Miningrocks (FR)**[13] 8143 5-9-6 70 ........(v) GerO'Neill(7) 6 67
(Declan Carroll) *led: clr 3f out: rdn and reduced advantage over 1f out: hdd ent fnl f: sn no ex* **10/11[1]**

4553 **3** 3 3/4 **Little Pippin**[18] 7979 4-8-12 48 ........(p) BarryMcHugh 7 45
(Tony Coyle) *hld up in tch: rdn over 3f out: plugged on to go poor 3rd 2f out* **5/1[3]**

6450 **4** 7 **Scent Of Power**[48] 7028 5-8-7 45 ........ JaneElliott(5) 8 33
(Barry Leavy) *midfield: rdn over 3f out: no imp* **12/1**

0200 **5** 7 **Steel Helmet (IRE)**[12] 6902 3-8-13 59 ........(p[1]) TomEaves 3 26
(Brian Ellison) *midfield: rdn over 3f out: sn btn* **14/1**

60 **6** 3/4 **Newgate Duchess**[30] 7629 3-8-8 0 ........ DuranFentiman 5 20
(Tony Coyle) *hld up: rdn over 3f out: sn btn* **80/1**

0000 **7** 1 **Dark Illustrator**[33] 7523 4-8-9 39 ........ LewisEdmunds(3) 9 17
(Lynn Siddall) *hld up: rdn over 4f out: sn btn* **66/1**

5006 **8** 5 **Panther In Pink (IRE)**[89] 5539 3-8-8 45 ........ ShaneGray 2 9
(Ann Duffield) *prom: rdn over 3f out: wknd fnl 2f* **50/1**

6600 **9** 16 **Pennerley**[9] 8241 4-8-12 44 ........(p[1]) FrannyNorton 4
(Micky Hammond) *s.i.s: sn pushed along in rr: eased and t.o fnl 2f* **33/1**

2m 10.12s (3.02) **Going Correction** +0.25s/f (Good)
**WFA** 3 from 4yo+ 4lb **9** Ran SP% **117.7**
Speed ratings (Par 101): **97,94,91,86,80 80,79,75,62**
CSF £5.66 TOTE £3.50: £1.20, £1.10, £2.10; EX 6.90 Trifecta £17.90.There was no bid for the winner. Miningrocks was claimed by Mr Conor Dore for £6000.
**Owner** John James & Brian Ellison **Bred** Denis Noonan **Trained** Norton, N Yorks

**FOCUS**
With the favourite operating below his best in recent weeks and the winner rated 57, this is modest form.

## 8478 MARKET CROSS JEWELLERS H'CAP 1m 5f 218y
**2:15** (2:16) (Class 4) (0-80,80) 3-Y-O **£6,469** (£1,925; £962; £481) **Stalls** Low

Form RPR

4036 **1** **Redicean**[11] 8188 3-9-7 **80** ........ PhillipMakin 3 89
(David O'Meara) *hld up in rr: smooth hdwy over 2f out: rdn to ld 1f out: styd on wl* **6/1[2]**

4542 **2** 2 1/2 **Sheriff Garrett (IRE)**[10] 8214 3-8-12 **71** ........(p) DavidAllan 2 76
(Tim Easterby) *racd keenly: led: hdd 11f out: remained prom: rdn to ld again wl over 1f out: sn hdd: one pce and no ch w wnr* **9/2[1]**

3051 **3** 1 1/4 **Cornerstone Lad**[21] 7895 3-8-8 **67** ........ FrannyNorton 8 70
(Micky Hammond) *midfield: rdn over 2f out: chsd ldrs whn briefly short of room appr fnl f: wnt 3rd ins fnl f: styd on* **17/2**

2552 **4** nk **Eyreborn (IRE)**[18] 7982 3-8-3 **62** ........ JoeFanning 9 65
(Keith Dalgleish) *hld up: rdn over 2f out: styd on fr over 1f out* **7/1[3]**

3204 **5** 3 **Theglasgowwarrior**[14] 8103 3-8-2 **61** ........ JamesSullivan 1 59
(Jim Goldie) *trckd ldrs: rdn over 2f out: edgd lft and wknd ins fnl f* **12/1**

-224 **6** 1 3/4 **Silver Link (IRE)**[12] 8166 3-9-3 **76** ........ ShaneKelly 4 72
(Marcus Tregoning) *prom: led 11f out: rdn 3f out: hdd wl over 1f out: wknd ins fnl f* **9/2[1]**

1224 **7** 3/4 **Bodacious Name (IRE)**[18] 7983 3-8-6 **65** ........ JasonHart 7 60
(John Quinn) *in tch on outer: rdn 3f out: bit short of room and lost pl over 1f out: wknd ins fnl f* **9/2[1]**

0012 **8** 6 **Nordic Combined (IRE)**[31] 7565 3-9-4 **77** ........(p) TomEaves 5 63
(Brian Ellison) *midfield: rdn along 4f out: sn wknd* **15/2**

2301 **9** 3/4 **Good Time Ahead (IRE)**[20] 7936 3-8-6 **65** ........ JimmyQuinn 6 50
(Philip Kirby) *hld up: rdn 3f out: sn btn* **28/1**

3m 7.03s (2.33) **Going Correction** +0.25s/f (Good) **9** Ran SP% **114.8**
Speed ratings (Par 103): **103,101,100,100,98 97,97,94,93**
CSF £32.92 CT £229.44 TOTE £6.90: £2.30, £1.50, £3.40; EX 37.50 Trifecta £341.80.
**Owner** Dreaming Victory **Bred** Cheveley Park Stud Ltd **Trained** Upper Helmsley, N Yorks

**FOCUS**
A fair handicap and a nice performance from the winner.

## 8479 WATCH RACING UK ANYWHERE MAIDEN STKS 7f
**2:50** (2:54) (Class 5) 3-Y-O+ **£3,396** (£1,010; £505; £252) **Stalls** Centre

Form RPR

**1** **Straight Away** 3-9-0 0 ........ OisinMurphy 9 69
(Andrew Balding) *trckd ldrs: led on bit over 1f out: rdn fnl f: hung lft and pressed fnl 110yds: kpt on* **6/4[1]**

23 **2** nk **Vive La Difference (IRE)**[10] 8217 3-9-5 66 ........ DavidAllan 5 73
(Tim Easterby) *chsd ldrs: rdn 2f out: ev ch ins fnl f: hld towards fin* **4/1[3]**

322 **3** 3 1/4 **Holiday Girl (IRE)**[21] 7907 3-9-0 70 ........ CharlesBishop 2 60
(Eve Johnson Houghton) *prom: rdn 2f out: no ex fnl f* **11/4[2]**

0003 **4** 1 3/4 **Twiggy**[27] 7704 3-8-9 61 ........ JamieGormley(5) 4 55
(Iain Jardine) *prom: led 5f out: rdn over 2f out: wknd ins fnl f* **8/1**

**5** 4 1/2 **Flying Raconteur** 3-9-5 0 ........ TomEaves 11 48
(Nigel Tinkler) *slowly away: hld up: sme late hdwy: nvr threatened* **50/1**

2240 **6** 1 1/4 **Vintage Dream (IRE)**[11] 8194 3-9-5 58 ........ GrahamLee 8 45
(Noel Wilson) *led: hdd 5f out: rdn over 2f out: wknd over 1f out* **40/1**

0304 **7** 1 1/2 **Mighty Bond**[10] 8217 5-9-7 47 ........(p) BarryMcHugh 1 42
(Tracy Waggott) *in tch: rdn 3f out: wknd over 1f out* **40/1**

64-3 **8** nk **Pudding Chare (IRE)**[31] 7574 3-9-5 69 ........ JackGarritty 7 40
(Richard Fahey) *midfield: rdn over 2f out: wknd over 1f out* **10/1**

3202 **9** 2 1/4 **Arnarson**[31] 7574 3-9-5 70 ........ JimmyQuinn 12 35
(Ed Dunlop) *hld up: rdn over 2f out: wknd over 1f out* **25/1**

0 **10** 13 **Wind Turbine (IRE)**[10] 8217 3-9-5 0 ........ DuranFentiman 6
(Tim Easterby) *a towards rr* **100/1**

0 **11** 20 **Got My Mojo**[8] 8256 7-9-0 0 ........ JasonWatson(7) 10
(Gary Sanderson) *a towards rr* **250/1**

400 **12** 12 **Swing Time (IRE)**[52] 6904 3-9-5 35 ........ JasonHart 3
(Eric Alston) *a towards rr* **200/1**

1m 25.38s (0.88) **Going Correction** +0.175s/f (Good)
**WFA** 3 from 5yo+ 2lb **12** Ran SP% **119.4**
Speed ratings (Par 103): **102,101,97,95,90 89,87,87,84,69 47,33**
CSF £7.66 TOTE £2.70: £1.40, £1.60, £1.40; EX 9.40 Trifecta £21.20.
**Owner** J C Smith **Bred** Darley **Trained** Kingsclere, Hants

**FOCUS**
A modest maiden. The winner is likely to do better, while the runner-up has been rated back to his French form.

## 8480 RACING UK PROFITS RETURNED TO RACING APPRENTICE H'CAP (DIV I) 5f 217y
**3:25** (3:28) (Class 6) (0-65,67) 3-Y-O+ **£3,234** (£962; £481; £240) **Stalls** Centre

Form | | | | RPR
3155 **1** **Yes You (IRE)**[42] 7218 3-9-5 **64** ........ JamieGormley(3) 6 72
(Iain Jardine) *hld up: rdn and hdwy over 1f out: r.o wl: edgd lft: led 30yds out* **10/3**[1]
3461 **2** *1 1/4* **Point Of Woods**[30] 7628 4-9-8 **66** ........(p) RhiainIngram(3) 2 70
(Tina Jackson) *w ldr: led 4f out: rdn 2f out: strly pressed fnl f: one pce and hdd fnl 30yds* **4/1**[2]
3200 **3** *hd* **Ticks The Boxes (IRE)**[39] 7332 5-9-9 **67** ........(p) GerO'Neill(3) 10 71
(John Wainwright) *hld up: rdn and hdwy 2f out: chal strly 1f out: kpt on same pce* **7/1**
0000 **4** *1* **Tafteesh (IRE)**[3] 8402 4-8-8 **54** ........ HarrisonShaw(5) 7 55
(Michael Easterby) *led: hdd 4f out: remained prom: rdn over 2f out: one pce fnl f* **5/1**[3]
4000 **5** *2 1/2* **Gaelic Wizard (IRE)**[44] 7165 9-8-11 **52** ........(v) GemmaTutty 1 45
(Karen Tutty) *dwlt: hld up in tch: rdn over 2f out: one pce and nvr threatened* **9/1**
4120 **6** *2* **Mimic's Memory**[14] 8107 3-9-6 **62** ........(t[1]) JaneElliott 3 49
(Ann Duffield) *chsd ldrs: rdn and outpcd 2f out: plugged on ins fnl f* **33/1**
5604 **7** *2* **Mitchum**[20] 7926 8-8-7 **51** oh5 ........(v) ConnorMurtagh(3) 5 32
(Ron Barr) *prom: rdn over 2f out: wknd over 1f out* **13/2**
1606 **8** *1 3/4* **Star Cracker (IRE)**[21] 7884 5-8-11 **57** ........(p) SeanMooney(5) 4 33
(Jim Goldie) *hld up: rdn over 2f out: wknd over 1f out* **12/1**
0300 **9** *2 1/2* **Mad Rose (IRE)**[114] 4619 3-8-13 **62** ........(p) JasonWatson(7) 8 30
(Denis Quinn) *chsd ldrs: rdn over 2f out: wknd over 1f out* **66/1**
4206 **10** *3* **Tanawar (IRE)**[21] 7889 7-9-0 **60** ........(b) SeamusCronin(5) 9 19
(Ruth Carr) *hld up in tch: rdn over 2f out: sn wknd* **8/1**

1m 13.51s (1.71) **Going Correction** +0.175s/f (Good)
**WFA** 3 from 4yo+ 1lb **10** Ran SP% **118.8**
Speed ratings (Par 101): **95,93,93,91,88 85,83,80,77,73**
CSF £16.93 CT £91.34 TOTE £4.30: £1.70, £1.90, £2.30; EX 14.20 Trifecta £39.60.
**Owner** Taco Partners **Bred** Tower Place Bloodstock **Trained** Carrutherstown, D'fries & G'way

**FOCUS**
A modest sprint handicap, but the winner has steadily progressed this year.

## 8481 RACING UK PROFITS RETURNED TO RACING APPRENTICE H'CAP (DIV II) 5f 217y
**4:00** (4:00) (Class 6) (0-65,67) 3-Y-O+ **£3,234** (£962; £481; £240) **Stalls** Centre

Form | | | | RPR
0022 **1** **Awesome Allan (IRE)**[7] 8298 3-9-3 **62** ........(t) KatherineGlenister(3) 10 70
(David Evans) *trckd ldr: rdn 2f out: kpt on fnl f: led towards fin* **10/3**[1]
4400 **2** *3/4* **Danish Duke (IRE)**[14] 8107 6-9-4 **64** ........(b) SeamusCronin(5) 8 70
(Ruth Carr) *led: rdn 2f out: drvn fnl f: one pce and hdd towards fin* **13/2**
4046 **3** *1 3/4* **Cool Strutter (IRE)**[52] 6903 5-8-10 **51** ........(b) GemmaTutty 6 52
(Karen Tutty) *in tch: rdn 2f out: one pce in 3rd fr over 1f out* **13/2**
0340 **4** *3* **Uncle Charlie (IRE)**[33] 7525 3-9-8 **64** ........(t[1]) JaneElliott 7 56
(Ann Duffield) *in tch: rdn over 2f out: wknd fnl f* **4/1**[2]
2200 **5** *1 1/4* **Boogie Babe**[21] 7889 3-8-8 **53** ........(h) ConnorMurtagh(3) 1 41
(Richard Fahey) *hld up: rdn along over 3f out: nvr threatened* **13/2**
40 **6** *2 1/2* **Mr Michael (IRE)**[22] 7857 4-9-4 **59** ........ PaddyBradley 2 39
(Adrian Brendan Joyce, Ire) *slowly away: hld up: rdn and hdwy 2f out: wknd ins fnl f* **9/2**[3]
4005 **7** *shd* **Wilde Extravagance (IRE)**[89] 5543 4-9-2 **57** ........(h[1]) BenRobinson 4 37
(Julie Camacho) *slowly away: a towards rr* **8/1**
0050 **8** *6* **Red Shanghai (IRE)**[8] 8256 3-8-6 **51** oh6 ow2 ........ BenSanderson(5) 11 15
(Charles Smith) *chsd ldrs: rdn over 2f out: wknd and bhd* **125/1**

1m 13.07s (1.27) **Going Correction** +0.175s/f (Good)
**WFA** 3 from 4yo+ 1lb **8** Ran SP% **113.2**
Speed ratings (Par 101): **98,97,94,90,89 85,85,77**
CSF £24.81 CT £131.56 TOTE £4.70: £1.50, £1.60, £2.50; EX 32.60 Trifecta £177.40.
**Owner** A Cooke & K McCabe **Bred** D G Iceton **Trained** Pandy, Monmouths

**FOCUS**
The faster of the two divisions by 0.44sec. Few got involved, the leader enjoying the run of things out in front and the winner being the only one who could get near him.
T/Jkpt: Not won. T/Plt: £10.10 to a £1 stake. Pool: £46,927.52 - 3,360.45 winning units T/Qpdt: £3.00 to a £1 stake. Pool: £4,839.98 - 1,185.78 winning units **Andrew Sheret**

# 8302 CHANTILLY (R-H)
Monday, October 30

**OFFICIAL GOING: Polytrack: standard**

## 8482a PRIX DE L'ALLEE CAMELIA (CLAIMER) (2YO) (YOUNG JOCKEYS & APPRENTICES) (POLYTRACK) 6f 110y
**12:25** 2-Y-O **£8,119** (£3,247; £2,435; £1,623; £811)

RPR
**1** **Seqania** 2-8-11 0 ........(b[1]) NicolasBarzalona(4) 5 73
(Mario Hofer, Germany) *a* **9/1**
**2** *2 1/2* **La Farfallina**[9] 2-8-6 0 ........ JeremieMonteiro(5) 4 62
(Frank Sheridan, Italy) **153/10**
**3** *1/2* **Summer Dress**[20] 2-8-6 0 ........ ThomasTrullier(5) 15 61
(Louis Baudron, France) **9/2**[1]
**4** *nk* **Potioka (FR)**[16] 2-8-8 0 ........(b) ClementLecoeuvre(3) 2 60
(Matthieu Palussiere, France) **235/10**
**5** *1 1/4* **Le Tronquay (FR)** 2-8-5 0 ........ SebastienPrugnaud(6) 14 56
(P Sogorb, France) **58/10**[2]
**6** *4 1/2* **Formiga (IRE)**[48] 7033 2-8-9 0 ........ GuillaumeTrolleyDePrevaux(6) 1 48
(Jose Santos) *in rr of midfield on inner: plenty to do and shkn up 3f out: styd on fnl 2f: n.d* **15/2**
**7** *1 1/4* **Chante Blu (FR)**[9] 2-8-13 0 ........(b) AlexandreChesneau(5) 6 47
(A Giorgi, Italy) **66/10**[3]
**8** *nk* **Valhala (FR)**[12] 8169 2-9-2 0 ........(b) JeromeMoutard(3) 16 47
(T Castanheira, France) **7/1**
**9** *3/4* **Amiral Chop (FR)**[129] 2-8-6 0 ........(b) FlorentGavilan(5) 7 37
(A Chopard, France) **115/10**
**9** *dht* **Marina Palace (FR)**[15] 2-8-9 0 ........ ErwannLebreton(6) 10 41
(A Junk, France) **51/1**
**11** *1* **Mcklaya (FR)**[41] 2-8-11 0 ........ AdrienMoreau(4) 11 38
(D Zarroli, Italy) **81/1**
**12** *8* **Henry Brulard (FR)**[28] 2-8-2 0 ........ MlleLeaBails(9) 12 12
(C Boutin, France) **43/1**
**13** *3* **El Divo (FR)**[28] 2-8-5 0 ow1 ........(b[1]) KyllanBarbaud(7) 9
(N Caullery, France) **269/10**
**14** *5* **No Surrender (FR)** 2-8-4 0 ........(p) MlleLauraGrosso(7) 3
(Ferdy Murphy, France) **212/10**
**15** *15* **Chopemoi (FR)**[137] 2-8-5 0 ........(b) ClaraCornet(10) 8
(Mlle A Pelletant, France) **24/1**
**16** *15* **Timeless Gift (IRE)**[9] 8253 2-7-12 0 ........(b) MlleMickaelleMichel(10) 13
(Matthieu Palussiere, France) **57/1**

PARI-MUTUEL (all including 1 euro stake): WIN 10.00; PLACE 3.10, 4.70, 2.20; DF 81.10; SF 139.10.
**Owner** Stiftung Gestut Fahrhof **Bred** Stiftung Gestut Fahrhof **Trained** Germany

8482a - (Foreign Racing) - See Raceform Interactive

# 8235 CATTERICK (L-H)
Tuesday, October 31

**OFFICIAL GOING: Soft (good to soft in places; 6.6)**
Wind: Fresh half against Weather: Overcast and breezy

## 8483 HALLOWEEN EBF NOVICE STKS 5f
**12:35** (12:35) (Class 5) 2-Y-O **£3,557** (£1,058; £529; £264) **Stalls** Low

Form | | | | RPR
34 **1** **Machree (IRE)**[18] 8010 2-8-11 0 ........ TomEaves 3 66+
(Declan Carroll) *mde all centre: swtchd rt to stands' rail over 2f out: rdn over 1f out: kpt on* **4/6**[1]
0515 **2** *1 1/2* **Bahuta Acha**[29] 7690 2-9-9 70 ........ BenCurtis 5 73
(David Loughnane) *dwlt and towards rr: hdwy 3f out: rdn to chse wnr wl over 1f out: drvn and kpt on fnl f* **4/1**[2]
**3** *4 1/2* **Crikeyitswhykie** 2-9-2 0 ........ PatrickMathers 2 49
(Derek Shaw) *dwlt: green and sn outpcd in rr: hdwy in centre over 2f out: rdn along wl over 1f out: styd on fnl f* **100/1**
0 **4** *1* **Serabrina (IRE)**[27] 7725 2-8-11 0 ........ KieranShoemark 6 41
(David Menuisier) *chsd ldng pair: rdn along 2f out: drvn wl over 1f out: grad wknd* **4/1**[2]
**5** *1/2* **Liamba** 2-8-11 0 ........ ShaneGray 8 39
(David O'Meara) *dwlt and towards rr: pushed along 1/2-way: rdn and hdwy wl over 1f out: kpt on fnl f* **33/1**
56 **6** *1 1/2* **Loulin**[41] 7269 2-9-2 0 ........ DanielTudhope 9 39
(David O'Meara) *chsd ldrs: rdn along 2f out: sn wknd* **7/1**[3]
00 **7** *3* **Cathie's Dream (USA)**[136] 3846 2-8-11 0 ........ GrahamLee 7 23
(Noel Wilson) *a towards rr* **100/1**
0 **8** *1* **Warrior's Valley**[42] 7242 2-9-2 0 ........ DavidAllan 4 24
(David C Griffiths) *chsd wnr: rdn along over 2f out: drvn wl over 1f out: sn wknd* **28/1**
0000 **9** *3* **Dark Hedges**[41] 7264 2-8-11 46 ........ SamJames 1 8
(Olly Williams) *racd towards centre: chsd ldrs: rdn along 1/2-way: sn wknd* **100/1**

1m 3.6s (3.80) **Going Correction** +0.725s/f (Yiel) **9** Ran SP% **121.8**
Speed ratings (Par 95): **98,95,88,86,86 83,78,77,72**
CSF £4.06 TOTE £1.60: £1.02, £1.30, £31.20; EX 4.30 Trifecta £147.20.
**Owner** Yenilecas Syndicate **Bred** Camogue Stud Ltd **Trained** Malton, N Yorks

**FOCUS**
The going was officially soft, good to soft in places (GoingStick 6.6). Bend turning into the home straight out 4yds, adding 12yds to the distances of races 3, 4, 6, 7 and 8 and 24yds to race 5. An uncompetitive novice event to start, won by the smart 2yo Brian The Snail last year. The runners gradually made their way over to the stands' rail and few ever got into this. A winning time 5.6sec outside standard suggested conditions were testing and the jockeys said the ground was "soft", though they also had to contend with a strong crosswind. The winner has been rated below her pre-race mark.

## 8484 GO RACING IN YORKSHIRE H'CAP 5f
**1:05** (1:05) (Class 6) (0-65,67) 3-Y-O+ **£2,264** (£673; £336; £168) **Stalls** Low

Form | | | | RPR
1161 **1** **Ebitda**[49] 7014 3-9-5 **67** ........ JamieGormley(5) 12 81
(Scott Dixon) *trckd ldrs: smooth hdwy towards stands' side to ld wl over 1f out: rdn clr appr fnl f: readily* **4/1**[1]
0006 **2** *6* **Racquet**[13] 8168 4-9-5 **62** ........ JamesSullivan 9 53
(Ruth Carr) *prom: pushed along and outpcd 1/2-way: swtchd rt to stands' rail and mde hdwy wl over 1f out: sn rdn and kpt on fnl f* **9/2**[2]
0500 **3** *1/2* **Coiste Bodhar (IRE)**[9] 8258 6-8-13 **59** ........(p) PaddyPilley(3) 7 49
(Scott Dixon) *led early: cl up: rdn to ld again briefly towards stands' side 2f out: sn hdd and drvn: kpt on same pce fnl f* **11/1**
4003 **4** *1 3/4* **Imperial Legend (IRE)**[21] 7926 8-8-9 **55** ........(p) RachelRichardson(3) 4 38
(Alan Brown) *towards rr: hdwy 2f out: rdn to chse ldrs over 1f out: n.m.r ent fnl f: sn drvn and kpt on* **8/1**
2003 **5** *1 3/4* **Compton River**[10] 8237 5-8-12 **62** ........ HarryRussell(7) 3 39
(Bryan Smart) *racd towards centre: cl up: led 3f out: rdn along and hdd 2f out: sn drvn and grad wknd* **25/1**
6504 **6** *3/4* **Sarabi**[9] 8258 4-9-0 **57** ........(p) DavidAllan 2 31
(Scott Dixon) *racd centre: chsd ldrs: rdn along 2f out: sn drvn and wknd* **7/1**[3]
0060 **7** *2* **Tan**[15] 8106 3-9-10 **67** ........(t) BarryMcHugh 11 35
(Tony Coyle) *a towards rr* **9/1**
6660 **8** *2 3/4* **Reckless Serenade (IRE)**[22] 7884 3-9-5 **62** ........(v[1]) AndrewMullen 5 20
(Keith Dalgleish) *a towards rr* **20/1**
0-00 **9** *1 1/4* **Miss Mayson**[21] 7926 3-8-9 **52** ........ SamJames 1 6
(Karen Tutty) *racd towards centre: cl up: rdn along over 2f out: sn wknd* **16/1**
1150 **10** *1 3/4* **Culloden**[13] 8168 5-9-2 **64** ........(v) ManuelFernandes(5) 6 10
(Shaun Harris) *cl up: led after 1f: hdd 3f out and sn pushed along: rdn over 2f out: sn wknd* **4/1**[1]

1m 2.54s (2.74) **Going Correction** +0.725s/f (Yiel) **10** Ran SP% **114.6**
Speed ratings (Par 101): **107,97,96,93,91 89,86,82,80,77**
CSF £21.42 CT £159.52 TOTE £3.20: £1.40, £2.70, £3.20; EX 23.90 Trifecta £255.50.
**Owner** Chesterfield Estates **Bred** Selwood, Hoskins & Trickledown **Trained** Babworth, Notts

**FOCUS**
A moderate sprint handicap which the winner took apart. Again they came nearside.

## 8485 EAT DRINK SLEEP NAGS HEAD PICKHILL H'CAP — 1m 4f 13y
**1:35** (1:36) (Class 4) (0-85,85) 3-Y-O+ **£6,469** (£1,925; £962; £481) **Stalls** Centre

Form — RPR

15 **1** **Mixboy (FR)**[19] 7983 7-9-5 **78** JoeFanning 1 — 91
(Keith Dalgleish) *trckd ldr: cl up 5f out: led over 2f out: rdn clr over 1f out: kpt on strly* **15/8**[1]

4443 **2** *6* **Henry Smith**[10] 8239 5-9-4 **77** (be) AndrewMullen 4 — 80
(John Weymes) *trckd ldrs: hdwy 3f out: c wd st towards stands' side: rdn along to chse wnr jst over 1f out: sn drvn and no imp* **9/1**

1216 **3** *1* **Mr Sundowner (USA)**[10] 8239 5-8-7 **73** (t) NicolaCurrie(7) 5 — 74
(Wilf Storey) *in tch: hdwy over 3f out: sn chsng ldrs: rdn along over 2f out: drvn over 1f out: kpt on same pce* **9/1**

5423 **4** *½* **Nurse Nightingale**[21] 7935 3-8-0 **72** (h) TristanPrice(7) 10 — 74
(Michael Bell) *led: jnd 5f out: rdn along 3f out: hdd over 2f out: drvn wl over 1f out: kpt on same pce* **7/1**[3]

3031 **5** *¾* **Jabbaar**[10] 8239 4-9-2 **75** PhillipMakin 8 — 74
(Iain Jardine) *hld up in rr: hdwy over 3f out: c wd towards stands' side st: chsd ldrs wl over 1f out: sn rdn and no imp* **7/2**[2]

0000 **6** *11* **Dolphin Village (IRE)**[7] 8326 7-8-7 **71** oh1 ManuelFernandes(5) 6 — 53
(Shaun Harris) *trckd ldrs: hdwy over 4f out: chsd ldng pair 3f out: rdn along over 2f out: sn drvn and wknd* **16/1**

**7** *2¾* **Chocolat Noir (IRE)**[126] 4194 4-8-11 **73** ow1 CallumRodriguez(3) 9 — 50
(Martin Todhunter) *a towards rr* **20/1**

5-0 **8** *3½* **Dalshand (FR)**[17] 8047 4-9-12 **85** DanielTudhope 11 — 57
(David O'Meara) *hld up: stdy hdwy over 4f out: chsd ldrs wl over 2f out: sn rdn along and wknd* **33/1**

/20- **9** *11* **Weld Al Emarat**[480] 4104 5-9-2 **82** HarrisonShaw(7) 2 — 36
(Michael Easterby) *hld up: a in rr* **33/1**

5422 **10** *nk* **Henpecked**[49] 7032 7-8-12 **71** oh3 (p) PaulHanagan 3 — 25
(Alistair Whillans) *in tch on inner: pushed along 4f out: rdn 3f out: sn wknd* **10/1**

0600 **11** *2* **Trendsetter (IRE)**[8] 8289 6-9-5 **78** (p) FrannyNorton 7 — 29
(Micky Hammond) *hld up: a towards rr* **33/1**

2m 45.53s (6.63) **Going Correction** +0.725s/f (Yiel)
**WFA** 3 from 4yo+ 6lb — **11** Ran SP% **118.1**
Speed ratings (Par 105): **106,102,101,101,100 93,91,89,81,81 80**
CSF £19.01 CT £119.13 TOTE £2.40: £1.10, £2.70, £3.10; EX 18.60 Trifecta £81.50.
**Owner** Paul & Clare Rooney **Bred** E A R L Jourdier **Trained** Carluke, S Lanarks

**FOCUS**
Add 12yds to race distance. A fair middle-distance handicap and another easy winner. They came up the centre of the track this time and this was a race where those who raced close to the pace were favoured. The runner-up has been rated close to this year's form.

## 8486 DINE AND VIEW AT CATTERICK RACES H'CAP — 7f 6y
**2:10** (2:10) (Class 4) (0-85,87) 3-Y-O+ **£5,175** (£1,540; £769; £384) **Stalls** Low

Form — RPR

1360 **1** **Our Charlie Brown**[10] 8240 3-8-10 **75** JamesSullivan 1 — 83+
(Tim Easterby) *trckd ldrs: hdwy on inner 3f out: cl up 2f out: rdn to ld 1 1/2f out: kpt on wl* **7/1**

0001 **2** *½* **Boots And Spurs**[10] 8240 8-8-13 **81** (v) JamieGormley(5) 8 — 88
(Scott Dixon) *trckd ldrs: hdwy 3f out: rdn to chse wnr over 1f out: drvn and kpt on wl fnl f* **9/2**[1]

3023 **3** *1¾* **Worlds His Oyster**[31] 7594 4-9-4 **81** (v) JasonHart 14 — 83
(John Quinn) *hld up: hdwy and wd st: effrt on stands' rail 2f out: rdn to chse ldrs over 1f out: drvn and kpt on fnl f* **5/1**[2]

2615 **4** *½* **Roaring Forties (IRE)**[10] 8240 4-9-10 **87** (p) PhillipMakin 7 — 88
(Rebecca Bastiman) *hld up towards rr: hdwy and wd st: chsd ldrs 2f out: rdn whn n.m.r jst over 1f out: styd on towards fin* **10/1**

0234 **5** *nk* **Royal Connoisseur (IRE)**[31] 7628 6-8-7 **70** oh1 PaulHanagan 4 — 70
(Richard Fahey) *hld up: hdwy on inner over 2f out: rdn to chse ldrs over 1f out: sn drvn and kpt on same pce fnl f* **7/1**

-020 **6** *½* **Mujassam**[18] 8014 5-9-7 **84** (b) DanielTudhope 13 — 83
(David O'Meara) *sn led: rdn along over 2f out: hdd 1 1/2f out: sn drvn and kpt on same pce* **16/1**

0100 **7** *2* **Proud Archi (IRE)**[10] 8240 3-8-11 **79** CallumRodriguez(3) 11 — 72
(Michael Dods) *dwlt and in rr: hdwy over 2f out: rdn wl over 1f out: n.d* **28/1**

0000 **8** *1½* **Shouranour (IRE)**[18] 8014 7-9-1 **81** (b) JoshDoyle(3) 10 — 71
(Alan Brown) *cl up: wd st towards stands' rail: rdn along 2f out: drvn over 1f out: grad wknd* **11/1**

0050 **9** *nk* **Fingal's Cave (IRE)**[31] 7612 5-9-10 **87** GrahamLee 5 — 76
(Philip Kirby) *trckd ldrs: effrt over 2f out: rdn along wl over 1f out: sn drvn and btn* **13/2**[3]

4004 **10** *2¾* **Hammer Gun (USA)**[9] 8257 4-8-13 **76** (v) PatrickMathers 6 — 58
(Derek Shaw) *nvr bttr than midfield* **33/1**

2362 **11** *1½* **Tatlisu (IRE)**[52] 6949 7-9-0 **82** ConnorMurtagh(5) 15 — 60
(Richard Fahey) *dwlt: a towards rr* **16/1**

0256 **12** *¾* **Al Khan (IRE)**[22] 7886 8-9-1 **78** (v1) KevinStott 12 — 54
(Kevin Ryan) *a towards rr* **16/1**

2600 **13** *¾* **Miss Sheridan (IRE)**[21] 7942 3-8-3 **75** HarrisonShaw(7) 3 — 48
(Michael Easterby) *cl up on inner: rdn along 3f out: drvn and wknd 2f out* **100/1**

1m 30.57s (3.57) **Going Correction** +0.725s/f (Yiel)
**WFA** 3 from 4yo+ 2lb — **13** Ran SP% **115.6**
Speed ratings (Par 105): **108,107,105,104,104 103,101,99,99,96 94,93,93**
CSF £36.68 CT £178.98 TOTE £8.30: £3.30, £1.90, £2.30; EX 39.00 Trifecta £245.90.
**Owner** Ontoawinner, SDH Project Services Ltd 2 **Bred** North Bradon Stud & D R Tucker **Trained** Great Habton, N Yorks

**FOCUS**
Add 12yds to race distance. Another fair handicap and they came centre to nearside up the straight. The runner-up has been rated to his best over the past two years.

## 8487 BOOK NOW FOR NEW YEAR'S DAY H'CAP — 1m 7f 189y
**2:40** (2:40) (Class 5) (0-70,70) 3-Y-O+ **£2,911** (£866; £432; £216) **Stalls** Low

Form — RPR

3001 **1** **Tonto's Spirit**[10] 8241 5-9-5 **68** (h) SeamusCronin(7) 5 — 82
(Kenneth Slack) *trckd ldr: led 5f out: pushed clr home turn and styd on inner rail in st: kpt on strly* **11/10**[1]

4110 **2** *6* **Attention Seaker**[51] 6968 7-10-0 **70** (t) DavidAllan 4 — 77
(Tim Easterby) *trckd ldng pair: hdwy to chse wnr over 4f out: c wd home turn to r centre: rdn over 2f out: drvn wl over 1f out: kpt on: no ch w wnr* **8/1**[3]

5342 **3** *6* **Hurricane Hollow**[19] 7983 7-9-13 **69** BenCurtis 14 — 69
(David Barron) *dwlt and hld up in rr: racd wd and hdwy over 5f out: chsd ldng pair and c wd home turn to stands' rail: sn rdn: drvn wl over 1f out: no imp* **15/2**[2]

0-62 **4** *15* **Only Orsenfoolsies**[10] 8239 8-9-13 **69** FrannyNorton 8 — 51
(Micky Hammond) *chsd ldrs: rdn along and outpcd over 4f out: plugged on u.p fr wl over 2f out* **17/2**

2460 **5** *1½* **Jan Smuts (IRE)**[12] 8187 9-8-3 **52** (tp) NicolaCurrie(7) 6 — 32
(Wilf Storey) *in tch: pushed along over 4f out: rdn along and wd st to stands' rail: sn drvn and plugged on* **33/1**

0401 **6** *1* **Ingleby Hollow**[11] 8214 5-9-11 **67** (t) DanielTudhope 11 — 46
(David O'Meara) *hld up in rr: racd wd and hdwy over 4f out: chsd ldrs and wd st: rdn along over 2f out: sn wknd* **12/1**

0314 **7** *4½* **Bianca Minola (FR)**[11] 8204 3-9-3 **67** (p) KieranShoemark 10 — 42
(David Menuisier) *a towards rr* **14/1**

2022 **8** *34* **In Focus (IRE)**[21] 7922 6-8-9 **56** (h) JamieGormley(5) 7
(Dianne Sayer) *led: pushed along over 5f out: sn hdd and rdn: wknd 4f out* **16/1**

0132 **9** *2¼* **Newt**[51] 4790 3-9-3 **67** PhillipMakin 3
(Chris Wall) *trckd ldrs: hdwy over 5f out: rdn along to chse ldng pair over 3f out: wknd wl over 2f out* **16/1**

3302 **10** *9* **La Bacouetteuse (FR)**[15] 8109 12-8-10 **52** (p) JoeFanning 9
(Iain Jardine) *a in rr* **50/1**

0605 **11** *10* **Rock On Bollinski**[22] 7893 7-9-7 **63** TomEaves 12
(Brian Ellison) *slowly away: a in rr* **33/1**

3420 **12** *7* **Tred Softly (IRE)**[53] 6901 4-9-1 **57** (b) JasonHart 13
(John Quinn) *a towards rr* **33/1**

3m 43.22s (11.22) **Going Correction** +0.725s/f (Yiel)
**WFA** 3 from 4yo+ 8lb — **12** Ran SP% **117.9**
Speed ratings (Par 103): **100,97,94,86,85 85,83,66,64,60 55,51**
CSF £9.66 CT £48.08 TOTE £2.30: £1.10, £2.80, £2.60; EX 12.50 Trifecta £50.60.
**Owner** A Slack **Bred** Mrs J M Quy **Trained** Hilton, Cumbria
■ Stewards' Enquiry : Nicola Currie two-day ban: misuse of the whip (Nov 15-16)

**FOCUS**
Add 24yds to race distance. An ordinary staying handicap and a one-horse market, which proved to be correct. The winner came up the far rail, the second up the centre and the third up the stands' rail, while the field finished spread out all over North Yorkshire. A small pb from the runner-up.

## 8488 RACING UK.COM H'CAP (DIV I) — 5f 212y
**3:15** (3:15) (Class 4) (0-80,82) 3-Y-O+ **£5,175** (£1,540; £769; £384) **Stalls** Low

Form — RPR

3206 **1** **Quick Look**[33] 7557 4-9-2 **75** DavidAllan 1 — 89
(Michael Easterby) *dwlt and in rr: hdwy on inner to trck ldrs over 3f out: cl up over 2f out: rdn to ld wl over 1f out: kpt on strly* **15/8**[1]

5121 **2** *6* **Economic Crisis (IRE)**[15] 8106 8-8-11 **73** LewisEdmunds(3) 6 — 68
(Alan Berry) *dwlt: sn trcking ldrs: hdwy over 2f out: rdn wl over 1f out: kpt on u.p fnl f* **11/1**

0006 **3** *½* **Crosse Fire**[9] 8260 5-8-7 **66** oh1 (p) JamesSullivan 5 — 59
(Scott Dixon) *cl up: led over 3f out: rdn along over 2f out: hdd wl over 1f out: sn drvn and kpt on same pce* **22/1**

60 **4** *1* **Turanga Leela**[24] 7811 3-9-6 **80** (v) PhillipMakin 3 — 70
(Ian Williams) *towards rr: pushed along 1/2-way: rdn over 2f out: kpt on appr fnl f* **9/2**[3]

0322 **5** *1¾* **Jacob's Pillow**[15] 8106 6-9-4 **77** (p) DanielTudhope 9 — 61
(Rebecca Bastiman) *chsd ldng pair: rdn along over 2f out: drvn wl over 1f out: grad wknd* **11/2**

3001 **6** *½* **Chickenfortea (IRE)**[38] 7389 3-8-9 **69** JasonHart 4 — 52
(Eric Alston) *slt ld: hdd over 3f out and sn pushed along: cl up and rdn 2f out: sn wknd* **7/2**[2]

1000 **7** *¾* **Khelman (IRE)**[18] 8014 7-9-6 **82** (p) AdamMcNamara(3) 7 — 62
(Richard Fahey) *sn rdn along and a in rr* **16/1**

1m 17.12s (3.52) **Going Correction** +0.725s/f (Yiel)
**WFA** 3 from 4yo+ 1lb — **7** Ran SP% **109.1**
Speed ratings (Par 105): **105,97,96,95,92 92,91**
CSF £21.41 CT £302.27 TOTE £2.60: £1.70, £4.50; EX 18.40 Trifecta £170.80.
**Owner** Golden Ratio, Hull, Hollings & Winter **Bred** Susanna Ballinger **Trained** Sheriff Hutton, N Yorks

**FOCUS**
Add 12yds to race distance. The first division of a fair sprint handicap, but another race taken apart by a well-backed favourite. They came up the centre in the straight and the winner has been rated back to his best.

## 8489 RACING UK.COM H'CAP (DIV II) — 5f 212y
**3:45** (3:45) (Class 4) (0-80,80) 3-Y-O+ **£5,175** (£1,540; £769; £384) **Stalls** Low

Form — RPR

3113 **1** **Short Work**[18] 8014 4-9-7 **80** (b) DanielTudhope 1 — 87+
(David O'Meara) *trckd ldrs: hdwy 3f out: cl up over 2f out: rdn to ld over 1f out: drvn out* **11/8**[1]

0650 **2** *¾* **Adam's Ale**[33] 7557 8-9-4 **77** (p) BarryMcHugh 3 — 81
(Marjorie Fife) *in tch: hdwy on inner over 2f out: rdn wl over 1f out: styd on wl fnl f* **10/1**

2130 **3** *hd* **Spirit Of Zebedee (IRE)**[34] 7525 4-8-7 **66** oh2 (p) JasonHart 5 — 69
(John Quinn) *cl up: led 1/2-way: rdn along over 2f out: hdd over 1f out: sn drvn and kpt on same pce* **20/1**

0000 **4** *¾* **Lucky Beggar (IRE)**[9] 8260 7-9-6 **79** GrahamLee 6 — 80
(David C Griffiths) *trckd ldrs: hdwy wl over 2f out: rdn wl over 1f out: drvn and kpt on fnl f* **25/1**

2103 **5** *½* **Tricky Dicky**[7] 8319 4-9-1 **74** SamJames 7 — 73
(Olly Williams) *trckd ldng pair on outer: edgd rt and lost pl on home turn: rdn wl over 1f out: kpt on fnl f* **3/1**[2]

5060 **6** *3½* **Peachey Carnehan**[21] 7933 3-8-5 **68** (v) RachelRichardson(3) 2 — 56
(Michael Mullineaux) *a towards rr* **33/1**

0223 **7** *½* **See The Sun**[7] 8321 6-8-11 **70** (p) DavidAllan 4 — 56
(Tim Easterby) *slt ld: pushed along and hdd 1/2-way: sn rdn and wknd 2f out* **5/1**[3]

3000 **8** *2* **Ballymore Castle (IRE)**[15] 8115 5-9-2 **75** PaulHanagan 9 — 55
(Richard Fahey) *dwlt: sn outpcd and a in rr* **12/1**

5000 **9** *nk* **Laughton**[15] 8106 4-8-13 **72** TomEaves 8 — 51
(Kevin Ryan) *dwlt: sn in tch: hdwy to chse ldrs 3f out: rdn and wknd over 2f out* **33/1**

1m 17.8s (4.20) **Going Correction** +0.725s/f (Yiel)
**WFA** 3 from 4yo+ 1lb — **9** Ran SP% **115.0**
Speed ratings (Par 105): **101,100,99,98,98 93,92,90,89**
CSF £15.60 CT £186.79 TOTE £1.90: £1.10, £3.30, £4.40; EX 14.60 Trifecta £183.70.
**Owner** N D Crummack Ltd & Arthur Rhodes **Bred** Downfield Cottage Stud **Trained** Upper Helmsley, N Yorks

**FOCUS**
Add 12yds to race distance. They came centre-to-stands' side up the straight this time and another win for a warm favourite, though this was harder work. The winning time was 0.68sec slower than the first division, but a small personal best from the winner.

## 8490 JUMP SEASON NEXT H'CAP 5f 212y
4:20 (4:20) (Class 6) (0-55,55) 3-Y-0+ £2,264 (£673; £336; £168) Stalls Low

Form RPR
0203 1 **Redrosezorro**[38] 7390 3-9-5 54 (h) NeilFarley 6 60
(Eric Alston) *hld up: hdwy 2f out: swtchd rt towards stands' rail and rdn over 1f out: styd on wl fnl f: led nr line* 9/2[1]
0463 2 hd **Cool Strutter (IRE)**[1] 8481 5-8-12 51 (b) GemmaTutty(5) 9 56
(Karen Tutty) *chsd ldng pair: hdwy over 2f out: rdn to ld wl over 1f out: drvn clr ins fnl f: hdd nr line* 5/1[2]
3540 3 1 ½ **Robbian**[7] 8329 6-8-13 50 NoelGarbutt(3) 5 51
(Charles Smith) *hld up: hdwy over 2f out: rdn wl over 1f out: chsd ldr ins fnl f: kpt on* 9/2[1]
0002 4 3 **Jorvik Prince**[4] 8395 3-9-4 53 SamJames 11 45
(Karen Tutty) *chsd ldr: hdwy and cl up over 2f out: rdn wl over 1f out and ev ch tl drvn and wknd fnl f* 9/1[3]
600 5 nk **Tellovoi (IRE)**[7] 8329 9-9-7 55 (v) PhillipMakin 3 46
(Richard Guest) *hmpd s and towards rr: hdwy on inner 2f out: sn rdn and kpt on fnl f* 12/1
6005 6 1 ¾ **Commanche**[7] 8329 8-9-6 54 (b) DavidAllan 12 39
(Chris Dwyer) *chsd ldrs: wd st: sn rdn along and kpt on same pce* 9/1[3]
0000 7 ½ **Lackaday**[30] 7660 5-9-4 52 (p) JasonHart 1 36
(Noel Wilson) *led: rdn along over 2f out: drvn and hdd wl over 1f out: wknd ent fnl f* 14/1
0045 8 1 ½ **Le Laitier (FR)**[9] 8259 6-8-8 47 (b[1]) JamieGormley(5) 4 26
(Scott Dixon) *hmpd s: a bhd* 12/1
1053 9 nk **Firesnake (IRE)**[35] 7487 4-9-3 54 (b[1]) CallumRodriguez(3) 8 32
(Lisa Williamson) *in tch: hdwy to chse ldrs 1/2-way: rdn over 2f out: drvn wl over 1f out: sn wknd* 12/1
4000 10 2 **Whipphound**[21] 7926 9-9-1 49 (b) JamesSullivan 7 21
(Ruth Carr) *towards rr: effrt and sme hdwy 2f out: sn rdn and n.d* 25/1
4044 11 ½ **Excellent World (IRE)**[3] 8428 4-8-13 47 (t[1]) BarryMcHugh 2 18
(Tony Coyle) *chsd ldrs: hdwy on inner 1/2-way: rdn along and cl up 2f out: drvn over 1f out: wknd fnl f* 16/1
0064 P **Snow Excuse**[26] 7763 3-8-13 48 (t) GrahamLee 10
(Bryan Smart) *towards rr: lost action and p.u 2f out* 16/1

1m 18.53s (4.93) **Going Correction** +0.725s/f (Yiel)
**WFA** 3 from 4yo+ 1lb 12 Ran SP% 118.4
Speed ratings (Par 101): **96,95,93,89,89 87,86,84,83,81 80,**
CSF £26.35 CT £108.36 TOTE £4.60: £1.80, £1.90, £2.30; EX 22.80 Trifecta £129.40.
**Owner** Red Rose Partnership **Bred** Whitsbury Manor Stud & Jointsense Ltd **Trained** Longton, Lancs

**FOCUS**
Add 12yds to race distance. A particularly moderate handicap in which they again came centre-to-stands' side in the straight. The pace was decent.
T/Jkpt: £3,424.70 to a £1 stake. Pool: £10,274.23 - 3.0 winning units. T/Plt: £26.50 to a £1 stake. Pool: £62,449.92 - 1,720.26 winning units. T/Qpdt: £14.00 to a £1 stake. Pool: £6,351.85 - 335.62 winning units. **Joe Rowntree**

# [8427] WOLVERHAMPTON (A.W) (L-H)
Tuesday, October 31

**OFFICIAL GOING: Tapeta: standard**
Wind: Light behind Weather: Fine

## 8491 32RED.COM NURSERY H'CAP 1m 142y (Tp)
4:40 (4:40) (Class 4) (0-80,76) 2-Y-0 £3,946 (£1,174; £586; £293) Stalls Low

Form RPR
003 1 **Dr Richard Kimble (IRE)**[48] 7043 2-9-2 71 PJMcDonald 3 73
(Mark Johnston) *chsd ldr: pushed along over 3f out: led over 1f out: sn rdn: styd on* 12/1
355 2 hd **La La Land (IRE)**[34] 7503 2-9-4 73 (p[1]) DougieCostello 2 75
(Jamie Osborne) *sn pushed along to chse ldrs: rdn over 2f out: ev ch ins fnl f: styd on* 5/2[2]
2201 3 ¾ **Iconic Sunset**[69] 6319 2-9-5 74 RichardKingscote 6 74
(James Tate) *prom: lost pl over 7f out: pushed along: hung rt and outpcd over 2f out: r.o towards fin* 4/1[3]
3334 4 shd **Calling Rio (IRE)**[13] 8163 2-9-4 73 PaulMulrennan 1 73
(David Loughnane) *led at stdy pce tl qcknd over 2f out: rdn and hdd over 1f out: ev ch ins fnl f: no ex nr fin* 22/1
001 5 ½ **Dream Mount (IRE)**[35] 7488 2-9-7 76 TomQueally 4 75
(Marco Botti) *prom: rdn over 1f out: styd on* 11/8[1]
0450 6 ¾ **Ruby's Gem**[55] 6824 2-8-13 68 (t[1]) DavidProbert 5 65
(Philip McBride) *hld up: rdn over 1f out: nt rch ldrs* 40/1
6542 7 nk **Still Got It**[49] 7023 2-8-10 65 JosephineGordon 7 61
(Daniel Mark Loughnane) *hld up: racd keenly: rdn over 1f out: nt pce to chal* 22/1

1m 51.49s (1.39) **Going Correction** -0.125s/f (Stan) 7 Ran SP% 109.5
Speed ratings (Par 97): **88,87,87,87,86 85,85**
CSF £38.53 TOTE £11.10: £3.40, £1.90; EX 45.60 Trifecta £132.60.
**Owner** Garrett J Freyne Racing **Bred** Deer Forest Stud **Trained** Middleham Moor, N Yorks

**FOCUS**
A fair nursery, but a slow gallop and a bunched finish means this bare form isn't reliable.

## 8492 32RED CASINO NOVICE STKS 1m 142y (Tp)
5:10 (5:10) (Class 5) 2-Y-0 £2,911 (£866; £432; £216) Stalls Low

Form RPR
4 1 **Laieth**[20] 7946 2-9-2 0 PatCosgrave 4 79
(Saeed bin Suroor) *chsd ldr tl led wl over 1f out: sn pushed along: edgd lft and qcknd clr: eased towards fin* 8/15[1]
5 2 2 ¼ **Escalator**[14] 8136 2-9-2 0 TomQueally 1 71
(Charlie Fellowes) *chsd ldrs: rdn and outpcd over 1f out: styd on to go 2nd wl ins fnl f* 4/1[2]
3 nse **Grecian Spirit** 2-9-2 0 RichardKingscote 5 71
(James Tate) *s.i.s: hld up: hdwy over 1f out: styd on* 22/1
3 4 2 **Arch Gold (USA)**[124] 4245 2-9-2 0 PJMcDonald 3 67
(Mark Johnston) *led: rdn over 2f out: hdd over 1f out: no ex fnl f* 10/1
00 5 1 ¼ **Feragust**[13] 8161 2-8-13 0 MarcMonaghan(3) 2 64
(Marco Botti) *prom: rdn and edgd rt over 1f out: no ex* 100/1
6 1 **Alpine Peak (USA)** 2-9-2 0 JackMitchell 6 62
(Roger Varian) *s.i.s: rn green in rr: rdn and hung rt over 1f out: nvr on terms* 9/1[3]

1m 50.79s (0.69) **Going Correction** -0.125s/f (Stan) 6 Ran SP% 109.7
Speed ratings (Par 95): **91,89,88,87,86 85**
CSF £2.77 TOTE £1.60: £1.10, £2.20; EX 3.40 Trifecta £19.80.
**Owner** Godolphin **Bred** Rabbah Bloodstock Limited **Trained** Newmarket, Suffolk

**FOCUS**
Not the most competitive of novice events, but a useful performance from the winner who won with plenty in hand. The gallop was an ordinary one to the home straight.

## 8493 £10 FREE AT 32RED.COM NOVICE STKS 7f 36y (Tp)
5:40 (5:40) (Class 5) 2-Y-0 £2,911 (£866; £432; £216) Stalls High

Form RPR
4613 1 **Montague (IRE)**[11] 8213 2-9-2 77 DougieCostello 4 74
(Jamie Osborne) *mde all: set stdy pce tl qcknd 1/2-way: rdn over 1f out: all out* 7/2[2]
50 2 ½ **Comrade In Arms (USA)**[13] 8149 2-9-2 0 TedDurcan 3 73
(Sir Michael Stoute) *chsd ldrs: shkn up over 2f out: r.o to go 2nd wl ins fnl f: nt quite rch wnr* 9/1[3]
64 3 nk **Handsome Bob (IRE)**[30] 7654 2-8-13 0 (p[1]) RowanScott(3) 8 72
(Keith Dalgleish) *sn pushed along and prom: rdn 1/2-way: hung lft fr over 2f out: r.o* 14/1
06 4 nse **Beachwalk**[26] 7765 2-9-2 0 DavidProbert 5 72
(Sir Michael Stoute) *hld up: shkn up over 2f out: rdn and nt clr run over 1f out: r.o* 5/2[1]
6 5 ½ **Becker**[11] 8212 2-9-2 0 PaulMulrennan 7 70
(James Given) *chsd wnr: rdn over 2f out: styd on same pce wl ins fnl f* 80/1
000 6 22 **Ms Tilly**[26] 7757 2-8-12 38 ow1 TomQueally 1 7
(David Brown) *s.i.s: sn pushed along in rr: lost tch 1/2-way* 200/1
7 12 **Alright Dave** 2-9-2 0 KieranO'Neill 6
(Ronald Harris) *s.i.s: pushed along in rr: lost tch 1/2-way: hung rt over 2f out* 80/1

1m 28.68s (-0.12) **Going Correction** -0.125s/f (Stan) 7 Ran SP% 70.4
Speed ratings (Par 95): **95,94,94,94,93 68,54**
CSF £10.78 TOTE £2.30: £1.20, £3.10; EX 8.10 Trifecta £24.90.
**Owner** Mrs A G Kavanagh **Bred** Kildaragh Stud **Trained** Upper Lambourn, Berks
■ Jellmood was withdrawn. Price at time of withdrawal Evs. Rule 4 applies to all bets. Deduction - 45p in the pound.

**FOCUS**
A race that lost a lot of its interest when short-priced market leader Jellmood gave plenty of problems and was withdrawn at the start. The gallop was reasonable, but the first five finished in a heap and the form behind the winner is modest.

## 8494 BETWAY DASH H'CAP 5f 21y (Tp)
6:10 (6:10) (Class 6) (0-58,58) 3-Y-0+ £2,264 (£673; £336; £168) Stalls Low

Form RPR
325 1 **Swendab (IRE)**[13] 8146 9-8-13 55 (b) BenRobinson(5) 9 62
(John O'Shea) *mde all: edgd lft sn after s: rdn clr over 1f out: hld on* 16/1
2234 2 ½ **Tidal's Baby**[23] 7857 8-9-6 57 (b[1]) FranBerry 4 62
(Adrian Brendan Joyce, Ire) *n.m.r sn after s: hld up: pushed along on outer over 2f out: hdwy over 1f out: rdn to chse wnr and hung lft ins fnl f: r.o* 11/8[1]
3430 3 1 ¾ **Frank The Barber (IRE)**[13] 8168 5-9-4 55 (t) AdamBeschizza 2 54
(Steph Hollinshead) *hld up in tch: racd keenly: rdn over 1f out: styd on same pce ins fnl f* 13/2[3]
2145 4 nk **Cool Breeze (IRE)**[83] 5812 3-9-5 56 PatCosgrave 1 55
(David Simcock) *hld up: hdwy and nt clr run fr over 1f out: hmpd ins fnl f: swtchd rt: r.o: nvr able to chal* 9/2[2]
16 5 ½ **Your Gifted (IRE)**[81] 5877 10-9-6 57 (v) RobertTart 5 53
(Lisa Williamson) *hmpd sn after s: in rr: rdn and r.o ins fnl f: nvr nrr* 33/1
003 6 1 ¾ **Archie Stevens**[13] 8146 7-8-12 52 PaddyPilley(3) 7 42
(Clare Ellam) *chsd ldrs: rdn over 1f out: no ex ins fnl f* 14/1
3115 7 ½ **Teepee Time**[13] 8168 4-9-4 58 (b) PhilDennis(3) 11 46
(Michael Mullineaux) *chsd ldrs: rdn over 1f out: hung lft and no ex fnl f* 18/1
506 8 hd **Roubles (USA)**[39] 7365 3-9-6 57 JoeDoyle 3 45
(Julie Camacho) *hld up: plld hrd: hdwy and nt clr run over 1f out: nt trble ldrs* 22/1
0041 9 nk **Chip Or Pellet**[94] 5419 4-9-5 56 DannyBrock 10 42
(Mark Pattinson) *prom: rdn 1/2-way: hung lft over 1f out: nt clr run and no ex sn after* 12/1
-520 10 nk **Regal Miss**[81] 5871 5-9-5 56 DavidProbert 6 41
(Patrick Chamings) *hld up: plld hrd: hdwy and nt clr run over 1f out: wknd fnl f* 25/1
321 11 ½ **Lady Joanna Vassa (IRE)**[18] 7993 4-8-5 49 (v) JackOsborn(7) 8 32
(Richard Guest) *chsd wnr tl rdn over 1f out: wknd ins fnl f* 16/1

1m 1.03s (-0.87) **Going Correction** -0.125s/f (Stan) 11 Ran SP% 116.1
Speed ratings (Par 101): **101,100,97,96,96 93,92,92,91,91 90**
CSF £37.10 CT £171.10 TOTE £13.10: £3.10, £1.40, £2.20; EX 44.90 Trifecta £282.10.
**Owner** E&G Racing: Swendab **Bred** P Brady **Trained** Elton, Gloucs

**FOCUS**
A moderate handicap, but a fair gallop in which the fourth caught the eye.

## 8495 BETWAY H'CAP (DIV I) 6f 20y (Tp)
6:40 (6:40) (Class 6) (0-60,60) 3-Y-0+ £2,264 (£673; £336; £168) Stalls Low

Form RPR
4600 1 **Thorntoun Lady (USA)**[4] 8402 7-8-12 51 (p[1]) TomQueally 2 58
(Jim Goldie) *hmpd sn after s: in rr: hdwy over 1f out: rdn and r.o to ld wl ins fnl f* 8/1
5453 2 ¾ **Fairway To Heaven (IRE)**[20] 7951 8-9-4 60 CharlieBennett(3) 7 65
(Lee Carter) *hld up in tch: rdn and ev ch wl ins fnl f: styd on* 10/3[2]
3166 3 1 **Wild Flower (IRE)**[44] 7190 5-9-1 57 HollieDoyle(3) 9 59
(Jimmy Fox) *w ldr tl led 2f out: rdn and hdd wl ins fnl f* 9/1
5406 4 ½ **Hisar (IRE)**[4] 8395 3-9-1 55 AlistairRawlinson 4 55
(Michael Appleby) *pushed along to chse ldrs: nt clr run over 1f out: sn rdn: styd on* 9/4[1]
2003 5 1 **Triple Dream**[34] 7517 12-8-10 56 KerrieRaybould(7) 8 53
(Milton Bradley) *prom: rdn over 1f out: no ex wl ins fnl f* 40/1
0406 6 ¾ **Ambitious Boy**[29] 7694 8-8-7 46 oh1 (p) FrannyNorton 1 41
(John O'Shea) *in rr: hdwy and nt clr run fr over 1f out: nvr able to chal* 25/1
4440 7 nk **Jacksonfire**[21] 7934 5-8-4 46 oh1 (p) PhilDennis(3) 3 40
(Michael Mullineaux) *hld up in tch: rdn over 1f out: no ex ins fnl f* 66/1

6504 **8** 2 1/4 **Quite A Story**[54] 6850 5-9-4 **57** EdwardGreatrex 12 44
(Archie Watson) *hld up in tch: rdn over 2f out: hung lft ins fnl f* **5/1**[3]
6164 **9** shd **Justice Rock**[7] 8329 4-9-0 **53** (t) JosephineGordon 13 40
(Phil McEntee) *in rr: rdn over 2f out: nvr on terms* **20/1**
0440 **10** nk **Broadhaven Honey (IRE)**[13] 8168 3-9-6 **60** (h) DavidProbert 6 46
(Ronald Harris) *led 4f: wknd ins fnl f* **16/1**
0540 **11** 5 **Dalalah**[14] 8133 4-8-0 **46** oh1 (v) JackOsborn(7) 5 17
(Richard Guest) *s.i.s: a in rr* **33/1**
1m 13.34s (-1.16) **Going Correction** -0.125s/f (Stan)
**WFA** 3 from 4yo+ 1lb **11** Ran SP% **113.0**
Speed ratings (Par 101): **102,101,99,99,97 96,96,93,93,92 86**
CSF £31.63 CT £249.52 TOTE £8.70: £2.90, £1.50, £2.80; EX 42.80.
**Owner** Mrs M Craig & J S Goldie **Bred** Airlie Stud **Trained** Uplawmoor, E Renfrews
■ Stewards' Enquiry : Alistair Rawlinson caution: careless riding
**FOCUS**
Mainly exposed sorts in a low-grade handicap. The gallop was sound throughout.

## 8496 BETWAY H'CAP (DIV II) 6f 20y (Tp)
**7:10** (7:10) (Class 6) (0-60,60) 3-Y-O+ **£2,264** (£673; £336; £168) **Stalls** Low

Form RPR
6050 **1** **Zenovia (IRE)**[11] 8210 3-9-1 **55** (t[1]) EdwardGreatrex 3 63
(Archie Watson) *hld up: racd keenly: hdwy 1/2-way: rdn to ld wl ins fnl f: r.o* **9/2**[3]
2555 **2** 1 1/4 **Fantasy Justifier (IRE)**[29] 7693 6-9-4 **57** (p) DavidProbert 12 61
(Ronald Harris) *s.i.s: hld up: hdwy over 1f out: swtchd lft ins fnl f: r.o* **11/1**
0000 **3** 3/4 **Tally's Song**[29] 7693 4-8-7 **46** oh1 (p) JimmyQuinn 4 48
(Grace Harris) *a.p: chsd ldr over 2f out: rdn and ev ch wl ins fnl f: styd on same pce* **100/1**
4500 **4** nk **Monarch Maid**[34] 7517 6-8-10 **56** WilliamCox(7) 6 57
(Peter Hiatt) *sn led: rdn over 1f out: hdd wl ins fnl f: styd on same pce* **8/1**
3046 **5** 1/2 **Multi Quest**[22] 7911 5-8-4 **46** oh1 (b) HollieDoyle(3) 2 46
(John E Long) *chsd ldr 5f out tl over 2f out: sn rdn: no ex ins fnl f* **10/1**
2552 **6** 3 1/2 **Tasaaboq**[9] 8259 6-8-13 **52** (t) JosephineGordon 8 41
(Phil McEntee) *prom: lost pl after 1f: shkn up over 1f out: n.d after* **5/2**[1]
50-6 **7** nk **Storm Lightning**[34] 7517 8-9-7 **60** FrannyNorton 1 48
(Mark Brisbourne) *hld up in tch: rdn over 1f out: no ex ins fnl f* **10/1**
0225 **8** 1 1/4 **Mistry**[250] 874 4-8-2 **48** (p[1]) NicolaCurrie(7) 10 32
(Mark Usher) *chsd ldr 1f: remained handy: rdn over 2f out: wknd over 1f out* **33/1**
5505 **9** hd **Lotara**[49] 7036 5-8-2 **48** (v) SeanMooney(7) 5 32
(Jim Goldie) *mid-div: losing pl whn hmpd over 3f out: n.d after* **4/1**[2]
0206 **10** 1/2 **Goadby**[26] 7763 6-8-7 **46** oh1 (p) PatrickMathers 9 28
(John Holt) *prom: pushed along and lost pl over 3f out: n.d after* **22/1**
1m 13.82s (-0.68) **Going Correction** -0.125s/f (Stan)
**WFA** 3 from 4yo+ 1lb **10** Ran SP% **112.7**
Speed ratings (Par 101): **99,97,96,95,95 90,90,88,88,87**
CSF £49.96 CT £4309.24 TOTE £5.80: £2.10, £2.90, £17.70; EX 41.10 Trifecta £5517.00.
**Owner** Boadicea Bloodstock **Bred** Al Asayl Bloodstock Ltd **Trained** Upper Lambourn, W Berks
**FOCUS**
Division two of a moderate handicap. The early pace was less frenetic than the first division.

## 8497 BETWAY LIVE CASINO H'CAP 1m 1f 104y (Tp)
**7:40** (7:40) (Class 5) (0-75,74) 3-Y-O+ **£2,911** (£866; £432; £216) **Stalls** Low

Form RPR
0600 **1** **Island Brave (IRE)**[15] 8111 3-9-1 **72** PJMcDonald 10 79+
(Heather Main) *hld up: pushed along over 2f out: rdn and hung lft over 1f out: str run ins fnl f to ld nr fin* **22/1**
0033 **2** 1 **Peace And Plenty**[26] 7769 3-9-1 **72** FrannyNorton 7 76
(William Muir) *led: rdn over 1f out: hdd nr fin* **7/4**[1]
2602 **3** nk **Epitaph (IRE)**[20] 7960 3-8-12 **69** (p) TomQueally 12 72
(Michael Appleby) *jnd ldr after 1f tl settle into 2nd over 6f out: rdn over 2f out: styd on u.p* **12/1**
-000 **4** nk **Never A Word (USA)**[11] 8209 3-8-10 **67** (bt[1]) KevinStott 4 70
(Oliver Greenall) *chsd ldrs: rdn over 2f out: styd on u.p* **25/1**
620 **5** shd **Omotesando**[10] 8239 7-8-10 **66** (p) CharlieBennett(3) 6 69
(Oliver Greenall) *hld up in tch: rdn over 1f out: styd on* **9/1**[3]
6023 **6** 1 **Shimmering Light**[33] 7550 3-9-0 **71** (v) DavidProbert 8 71
(Michael Bell) *chsd ldrs: rdn over 1f out: edgd lft and no ex wl ins fnl f* **25/1**
6020 **7** 3/4 **Berlusca (IRE)**[24] 7832 8-9-0 **67** (h) PatCosgrave 5 66
(David Loughnane) *stdd s: hld up: hdwy over 1f out: styd on same pce ins fnl f* **9/1**[3]
**8** 3/4 **Gealach Ghorm (IRE)**[129] 4114 3-9-1 **72** DougieCostello 13 69
(Sarah Hollinshead) *hld up: hdwy over 1f out: sn rdn: keeping on whn nt clr run and eased wl ins fnl f*
4063 **9** 1 **Outback Blue**[22] 7905 4-9-2 **69** (t) FranBerry 2 64
(David Evans) *s.i.s: in rr: rdn over 1f out: nvr nrr* **12/1**
5142 **10** 1 **My Brother Mike (IRE)**[11] 8205 3-8-13 **70** PaulMulrennan 9 63
(Kevin Frost) *chsd ldrs: rdn over 2f out: no ex fnl f* **10/3**[2]
6-0 **11** 1 1/4 **Chelsea Corsage (IRE)**[40] 7321 3-9-3 **74** EdwardGreatrex 1 64
(Paul D'Arcy) *hld up in tch: rdn over 1f out: wknd ins fnl f* **50/1**
0360 **12** 1/2 **Buckland Beau**[26] 7759 6-9-7 **74** ShaneKelly 11 63
(Charlie Fellowes) *hld up: rdn over 1f out: nvr on terms* **14/1**
0600 **13** 3 **Ready (IRE)**[46] 7131 7-9-6 **73** DannyBrock 3 56
(Mark Pattinson) *hld up: rdn over 2f out: n.d* **40/1**
1m 58.53s (-2.27) **Going Correction** -0.125s/f (Stan)
**WFA** 3 from 4yo+ 4lb **13** Ran SP% **118.9**
Speed ratings (Par 103): **105,104,103,103,103 102,101,101,100,99 98,97,95**
CSF £57.99 CT £520.04 TOTE £21.00: £5.00, £1.20, £3.50; EX 91.00 Trifecta £965.40.
**Owner** Donald M Kerr **Bred** Tally-Ho Stud **Trained** Kingston Lisle, Oxon
**FOCUS**
A reasonable handicap in which the gallop was no more than fair. The race has been rated around the placed horses.

## 8498 BETWAY CASINO CLASSIFIED STKS 1m 1f 104y (Tp)
**8:10** (8:10) (Class 6) 3-Y-O+ **£2,264** (£673; £336; £168) **Stalls** Low

Form RPR
-536 **1** **Power Home (IRE)**[131] 4012 3-8-12 55 TomQueally 2 63
(Denis Coakley) *led 1f: chsd ldrs: rdn to go 2nd over 2f out: led ins fnl f: styd on wl* **6/1**[3]
0341 **2** 3 1/2 **Medici Moon**[9] 8255 3-9-1 52 (p) PaddyPilley(3) 7 62
(Scott Dixon) *led after 1f: rdn over 2f out: hdd ins fnl f: styd on same pce* **11/4**[1]
4505 **3** 3/4 **Joyful Dream (IRE)**[180] 2331 3-8-12 53 BenCurtis 1 55
(John Butler) *s.i.s: hld up: hdwy 1/2-way: rdn over 2f out: hung lft fnl f: styd on same pce* **11/1**
3004 **4** 1 1/4 **Dream Free**[11] 8219 4-9-2 53 (p) DougieCostello 4 53
(Mark Walford) *hld up: hdwy over 1f out: sn rdn: styd on same pce ins fnl f* **11/2**[2]
6420 **5** 3/4 **Haldaw**[10] 8249 3-8-9 52 CallumShepherd(3) 6 51
(Mick Channon) *hld up: hdwy over 1f out: rdn and hung lft ins fnl f: styd on same pce* **12/1**
3 **6** 2 **Lucky Ellen (IRE)**[41] 7270 3-8-12 50 FrannyNorton 12 47
(Jennie Candlish) *s.i.s: hld up: hdwy over 1f out: sn rdn: no imp fnl f* **6/1**[3]
1030 **7** nk **Vivre La Reve**[81] 5898 5-8-9 54 (h) WilliamCox(7) 9 47
(James Unett) *prom: rdn over 2f out: hung lft over 1f out: wknd ins fnl f* **25/1**
2000 **8** 10 **Simply Clever**[15] 8122 4-9-2 53 TomEaves 10 28
(David Brown) *chsd ldrs: rdn over 2f out: wknd over 1f out* **16/1**
0044 **9** 1 **Subotal (IRE)**[10] 8248 4-8-9 45 JackOsborn(7) 13 26
(Richard Guest) *plld hrd and prom: wnt 2nd over 7f out tl rdn over 2f out: hung rt and wknd over 1f out* **22/1**
0123 **10** 2 3/4 **Royal Melody**[36] 7463 3-8-12 54 (p) PJMcDonald 5 21
(Heather Main) *s.i.s: a in rr: wknd over 2f out* **11/2**[2]
1m 58.29s (-2.51) **Going Correction** -0.125s/f (Stan)
**WFA** 3 from 4yo+ 4lb **10** Ran SP% **116.1**
Speed ratings (Par 101): **106,102,102,101,100 98,98,89,88,86**
CSF £22.73 TOTE £7.40: £2.40, £1.80, £3.20; EX 27.40 Trifecta £305.00.
**Owner** Count Calypso Racing **Bred** C Farrell **Trained** West Ilsley, Berks
**FOCUS**
A low-grade classified event in which the gallop was fair.
T/Plt: £174.90 to a £1 stake. £88,490.42 - 369.33 winning units. T/Qpdt: £68.00 to a £1 stake. £15,236.98 - 165.62 winning units. **Colin Roberts**

8499a - (Foreign Racing) - See Raceform Interactive

# [8339] KEMPTON (A.W) (R-H)
Wednesday, November 1
**OFFICIAL GOING: Polytrack: standard to slow**
Wind: virtually nil Weather: clear

## 8500 RACING UK HD NURSERY H'CAP 6f (P)
**4:25** (4:27) (Class 6) (0-60,60) 2-Y-O **£2,587** (£770; £384; £192) **Stalls** Low

Form RPR
050 **1** **Hic Bibi**[70] 6312 2-9-3 **56** JosephineGordon 3 60
(David Brown) *pushed along leaving stalls and sn led: mde all: rdn 2f out: kpt on strly ins fnl f* **10/1**
0004 **2** 1/2 **Swissal (IRE)**[13] 8190 2-9-7 **60** BenCurtis 10 62
(David Dennis) *hld up in rr: shkn up on outer over 2f out: rdn 2f out and no immediate prog: prog over 1f out and kpt on strly on outer ins fnl f to take 2nd nr fin: nrst fin* **7/2**[1]
0000 **3** 3/4 **Peggie Sue**[22] 7915 2-9-3 **56** JimmyQuinn 9 56
(Adam West) *hld up in rr: travelling wl and hld together for cutaway 2f out: sn rdn and darted to inner: gd prog and tk 2nd ent fnl f: unable to sustain run fnl 100yds and lost 2nd nr fin* **50/1**
000 **4** nk **Salty Sugar**[28] 7724 2-9-3 **56** JFEgan 12 55
(Paul Cole) *hld up in rr: rdn 2f out: kpt on wl between horses fr over 1f out: stuck on wl ins fnl f but too much to do* **16/1**
4034 **5** nk **Zapateado**[14] 8145 2-9-3 **56** ShaneKelly 1 54
(Richard Hughes) *between horses chsng ldrs: rdn 2f out: 3rd ent fnl f: no ex nr fin and wknd* **7/2**[1]
000 **6** 1 1/2 **Jazz Affair (IRE)**[105] 5030 2-9-3 **56** DougieCostello 7 49
(Jamie Osborne) *t.k.h between horses in mid-div: plugged on over 1f out: one pce fnl f* **9/1**
0303 **7** 1/2 **Cove Beach**[14] 8145 2-9-6 **59** (b) RaulDaSilva 2 51
(Paul Cole) *settled bhd ldr on rail: gng wl and rdn 2f out: ev ch chsng ldrs ent fnl f: no ex wl ins fnl f* **9/2**[2]
0050 **8** 1/2 **Poppy Jag (IRE)**[18] 8027 2-8-8 **52** ManuelFernandes(5) 4 42
(Kevin Frost) *bhd ldr on outer: rdn on outer over 2f out: nt picked up and plugged on ins fnl f* **14/1**
000 **9** 3/4 **Blackwood**[18] 8029 2-8-13 **52** CharlesBishop 5 40
(Michael Blanshard) *racd in mid-div on inner: rdn 2f out: plugged on one pce* **33/1**
0503 **10** 1 1/4 **Arachina (IRE)**[19] 7996 2-9-4 **57** (v) DavidProbert 8 41
(Harry Dunlop) *racd in rr-div on outer: shkn up over 2f out: sn hrd rdn: no ex ent fnl f* **10/1**
4053 **11** 3/4 **Llamrei**[16] 8110 2-9-2 **55** LiamKeniry 6 37
(Jo Hughes) *early pce: sn restrained bhd ldrs and t.k.h: lost a couple of pl ent st: shkn up over 2f out: rdn over 1f out: sn hld* **6/1**[3]
1m 13.04s (-0.06) **Going Correction** -0.15s/f (Stan) **11** Ran SP% **122.5**
Speed ratings (Par 94): **94,93,92,91,91 89,88,88,87,85 84**
CSF £46.92 CT £1752.50 TOTE £9.60: £3.10, £1.80, £11.80; EX 60.20 Trifecta £3497.20.
**Owner** Mrs Sandra Brown & Mrs Ann Harrison **Bred** Peter Onslow **Trained** Averham Park, Notts
**FOCUS**
A moderate nursery.

## 8501 RACINGUK.COM/JOIN NOVICE AUCTION STKS (DIV I) 1m (P)
**4:55** (4:57) (Class 6) 2-Y-O **£2,587** (£770; £384; £192) **Stalls** Low

Form RPR
55 **1** **Losingmyreligion (FR)**[40] 7361 2-8-13 0 MarcMonaghan(3) 10 70
(Marco Botti) *hld up in rr and t.k.h at times: shkn up between horses wl over 1f out: sn rdn and kpt on wl to ld nr fin* **12/1**
3 **2** shd **Exec Chef (IRE)**[36] 7488 2-9-2 0 JamieSpencer 6 70
(David Simcock) *a handy on outer bhd ldrs: shkn up and swtchd to centre ent 2f out: led wl over 1f out and hrd rdn: plugged on ins fnl f tl hdd nr fin* **4/9**[1]
0 **3** nk **Icart Point**[39] 7392 2-9-1 0 DavidProbert 5 68
(Clive Cox) *t.k.h at times between horses in rr-div: shkn up wl over 2f out and prog into mid-div: rdn wl over 1f out: kpt on ins fnl f on outer and late flourish dying strides to take 3rd nr fin* **9/2**[2]
00 **4** nse **Tour De Paris (IRE)**[28] 7739 2-9-1 0 CharlesBishop 2 68
(Eve Johnson Houghton) *racd in mid-div: rdn 2f out: kpt on ins fnl f and ev ch between horses fnl 110yds: plugged on and jst lost 3rd fnl strides* **25/1**
00 **5** 4 **Trouble And Strife (IRE)**[8] 8322 2-8-10 0 RyanPowell 9 54
(Sir Mark Prescott Bt) *sn led: hdd wl over 1f out: plugged on tl no ex ins fnl f* **20/1**
0 **6** 1 1/4 **Boss For A Day**[13] 8195 2-9-0 0 JosephineGordon 3 55
(J S Moore) *early pce: bhd ldrs: rdn over 2f out: no ex fr over 1f out* **25/1**
0 **7** 4 1/2 **Duke Of Dorset**[29] 7707 2-9-1 0 ShaneKelly 8 46
(Harry Fry) *in rr-div on outer: pushed along to hold pl on bnd over 3f out: n.d* **8/1**[3]

0 **8** 3/4 **Balgowlah (IRE)**[7] 8340 2-9-0 0 .......... MartinLane 7 43
(David Lanigan) *racd in rr: rdn over 2f out: plugged on one pce but nvr really involved* **20/1**

**9** 2 **Hackbridge** 2-8-13 0 .......... (p[1]) JFEgan 11 37
(Pat Phelan) *pressed ldr on outer: rdn 2f out: no ex and wknd qckly ent fnl f* **33/1**

0 **10** 1 1/4 **Molliana**[23] 7898 2-8-8 0 .......... JimmyQuinn 4 29
(Neil Mulholland) *t.k.h early in rr on inner: rdn 2f out: sn no imp* **66/1**

1m 39.47s (-0.33) **Going Correction** -0.15s/f (Stan) **10 Ran SP% 127.9**
Speed ratings (Par 94): **95,94,94,94,90 89,84,84,82,80**
CSF £18.66 TOTE £15.30: £2.80, £1.10, £1.70; EX 32.60 Trifecta £141.20.

**Owner** Jonny Allison & Mrs L Botti **Bred** Gerard L Ferron Et Al **Trained** Newmarket, Suffolk

■ Stewards' Enquiry : Ryan Powell three-day ban: careless riding and failed to ride to draw (Nov 15-17)

**FOCUS**
Just a modest novice and there was a bunched finish.

## 8502 RACINGUK.COM/JOIN NOVICE AUCTION STKS (DIV II) 1m (P)
5:25 (5:28) (Class 6) 2-Y-O £2,587 (£770; £384; £192) Stalls Low

Form RPR

52 **1** **Pompey Chimes (IRE)**[44] 7211 2-8-12 0 .......... HectorCrouch(3) 9 78
(Gary Moore) *t.k.h bhd ldrs tl led after 3f: set sedate pce tl shkn up over 3f out and increased tempo: rdn 2f out and qcknd up wl: clr ins fnl f and kpt on strly: easily* **4/1**[3]

03 **2** 3 1/4 **Sky Rocket**[26] 7786 2-8-11 0 .......... MitchGodwin(3) 3 70
(Sylvester Kirk) *hld up in mid-div: rdn 2f out and swtchd to inner: plenty to do w ldr clr fr over 1f out: stuck on wl to hold 2nd ins fnl f: no ch w wnr* **2/1**[1]

00 **3** 1/2 **Go Fox**[16] 8119 2-9-0 0 .......... PatCosgrave 7 68+
(Tom Clover) *t.k.h early in mid-div on outer: rdn 2f out in centre: kpt on wl ins fnl f to take 3rd* **16/1**

0 **4** 1 1/2 **Spring Ability (IRE)**[36] 7488 2-9-1 0 .......... GeorgeDowning 8 66+
(Laura Mongan) *hld up in rr-div: rdn 2f out w plenty to do: kpt on wl fr over 1f out and snatched 4th post: nvr nrr* **66/1**

2 **5** nse **Te Koop**[40] 7361 2-9-1 0 .......... JamieSpencer 11 66
(David Simcock) *pressed ldr on outer: rdn 2f out: kpt on one pce ins fnl f tl lost 4th post* **11/4**[2]

3 **6** 2 **Ipcress File**[44] 7211 2-8-13 0 .......... KieranO'Neill 6 59
(Scott Dixon) *led for 3f taking a t.k.h: bhd ldr after: rdn over 2f out: no ex fr over 1f out* **16/1**

6 **7** 1 3/4 **Trick Shot Jenny**[34] 7535 2-8-10 0 .......... DougieCostello 1 52
(Jamie Osborne) *mid-div on inner: rdn over 2f out and edgd lft: no ex fr over 1f out* **25/1**

0 **8** 3 1/4 **Epsom Bounty**[111] 4805 2-8-10 0 .......... (t[1]) CharlieBennett(3) 5 48
(Pat Phelan) *in rr-div on inner: rdn along over 2f out: no imp after* **80/1**

00 **9** 1 3/4 **Ipsilante**[25] 7814 2-8-6 0 .......... GeorgeWood(3) 4 40
(Jonathan Portman) *plld hrd bhd ldrs: rdn over 2f out: sn struggling and wknd fr over 1f out* **25/1**

00 **10** 2 1/2 **Dolydaydream**[23] 7875 2-8-8 0 .......... JFEgan 10 33
(Pat Phelan) *a in rr: shkn up over 2f out: nt pick up* **66/1**

**11** 3 **Waiting Room** 2-9-2 0 .......... JosephineGordon 2 34
(James Tate) *missed break and a in rr* **9/2**

1m 39.36s (-0.44) **Going Correction** -0.15s/f (Stan) **11 Ran SP% 121.9**
Speed ratings (Par 94): **96,92,92,90,90 88,86,83,81,79 76**
CSF £12.55 TOTE £4.50: £1.50, £1.20, £5.10; EX 15.80 Trifecta £162.30.

**Owner** Mrs S Neville, M George & G Moore **Bred** Tinnakill Bloodstock & P Grimes **Trained** Lower Beeding, W Sussex

**FOCUS**
This was steadily run early on and the winner was always best placed. The time was 0.11sec faster than the first division.

## 8503 32RED CASINO H'CAP 1m (P)
5:55 (5:56) (Class 5) (0-70,69) 3-Y-O+ £3,234 (£962; £481; £240) Stalls Low

Form RPR

6005 **1** **Lacan (IRE)**[23] 7878 6-9-4 **69** .......... CallumShepherd(3) 5 78
(Brett Johnson) *hld up in rr-div on inner: shkn up and smooth prog past horses 2f out: rdn to ld 1f out: kpt on wl ins fnl f: snug* **9/2**[3]

0023 **2** 1 3/4 **Balgair**[23] 7881 3-9-5 **69** .......... PatCosgrave 1 74
(Tom Clover) *hld up in rr: shkn up and swtchd to outer over 2f out: rdn along fr over 1f out: nt pce of wnr fnl 100yds* **5/4**[1]

540 **3** 2 1/4 **Mio Ragazzo**[117] 4562 3-8-13 **63** .......... RyanTate 4 63
(Marco Botti) *t.k.h early: racd in mid-div: rdn 2f out and kpt on wl ins fnl f: no ch w front two* **12/1**

3000 **4** 1 **Altiko Tommy (IRE)**[22] 7916 3-9-1 **65** .......... (b[1]) LiamKeniry 9 63
(George Baker) *led and set decent clip: t.k.h: rdn 2f out: wknd qckly ins fnl f* **25/1**

0020 **5** 1/2 **Spun Gold**[15] 8132 3-9-2 **66** .......... ShaneKelly 10 62
(Charlie Fellowes) *bhd ldr on inner: rdn 2f out: ev ch enterin fnl f: no ex sn after and wknd qckly* **7/2**[2]

0606 **6** 1/2 **Runaiocht (IRE)**[140] 3718 7-8-12 **60** .......... JimmyQuinn 3 55
(Paul Burgoyne) *hld up in rr: rdn over 1f out: plugged on at one pce: keeping on wl ins fnl f* **50/1**

0021 **7** 1 3/4 **Dashing Poet**[14] 8156 3-9-2 **66** .......... DavidProbert 11 57
(Heather Main) *hld up in mid-div: rdn and prog fr over 1f out: n.m.r on inner 1f out: wknd qckly fnl 110yds* **8/1**

5600 **8** 5 **Music Major**[23] 7878 4-9-5 **67** .......... AdamBeschizza 7 47
(Michael Attwater) *in rr: rdn over 2f out: no ex* **14/1**

46-0 **9** 6 **Shee's Lucky**[261] 718 3-9-1 **65** .......... DougieCostello 6 31
(Neil Mulholland) *mid-div on inner and niggled along at times to hold pl: rdn over 2f out: sn hld* **33/1**

0000 **10** 4 1/2 **Red Cossack (CAN)**[161] 2974 6-8-10 **61** .......... (t) GeorgiaCox(3) 8 17
(Paul Webber) *half rrd s and missed break: rushed up after 2f to chse ldr on outer: rdn over 2f out: wknd sn after* **33/1**

1m 37.34s (-2.46) **Going Correction** -0.15s/f (Stan)
**WFA** 3 from 4yo+ 2lb **10 Ran SP% 122.0**
Speed ratings (Par 103): **106,104,102,101,100 100,98,93,87,82**
CSF £10.75 CT £66.62 TOTE £5.90: £1.90, £1.10, £3.60; EX 17.20 Trifecta £167.20.

**Owner** Colin Westley **Bred** Sheikh Sultan Bin Khalifa Al Nahyan **Trained** Epsom, Surrey

■ Stewards' Enquiry : Callum Shepherd caution: careless riding

**FOCUS**
There pace was wound up from a fair way out here and the first two came from behind, but there was a lack of depth to this.

## 8504 32RED ON THE APP STORE MAIDEN STKS 7f (P)
6:25 (6:27) (Class 5) 3-Y-O+ £3,234 (£962; £481; £240) Stalls Low

Form RPR

44 **1** **Damocles (GER)**[184] 2231 3-9-5 0 .......... (t) RobertHavlin 7 85+
(John Gosden) *chsd ldrs: travelling best over 2f out: shkn up on outer over 1f out and smooth prog: upsides whn pushed into ld ent fnl f: nudged out fnl f: cosy* **13/8**[1]

4 **2** 1 **Domitilla**[194] 1948 3-9-0 0 .......... RyanTate 8 73
(Marco Botti) *tk fierce hold early bhd ldr: upsides and rdn between horses over 1f out: kpt on wl but no ch w wnr ins fnl f* **2/1**[2]

**3** 3 1/4 **Peace Terms (IRE)** 3-9-0 0 .......... DavidProbert 14 64
(Ralph Beckett) *led: rdn 2f out: kpt on wl tl hdd ent fnl f: no ch w ldng pce but stuck on to hold 3rd* **6/1**[3]

40 **4** 1 1/2 **Wannabe Like You**[89] 5611 3-9-5 0 .......... EdwardGreatrex 5 65
(Archie Watson) *bhd ldrs on inner: rdn over 2f out: kpt on wl tl no ex ent fnl f: nudged out fnl 100yds: jst hld 4th* **8/1**

3 **5** 1/2 **Hi Ho Silver**[22] 7930 3-9-5 0 .......... ShaneKelly 11 64
(Chris Wall) *mid-div between horses: rdn over 2f out: outpcd and plugged on fr over 1f out* **33/1**

56 **6** 1 3/4 **Wardy (IRE)**[112] 4759 3-9-5 0 .......... JosephineGordon 12 59
(Peter Chapple-Hyam) *hld up in rr-div: rdn along w plenty to do fr wl over 2f out: no immediate imp: keeping on at fin: nvr nrr* **12/1**

05 **7** nk **Ladakhi**[23] 7907 3-9-0 0 .......... WilliamCarson 9 53
(Rod Millman) *bhd ldr on inner: rdn 2f out: no ex and wknd 1f out* **14/1**

60 **8** 5 **Musical Fire**[56] 6828 3-9-0 0 .......... (p[1]) CharlesBishop 3 40
(Peter Hedger) *racd in mid-div on outer: rdn along over 2f out: lft bhd over 1f out: no ex after* **100/1**

00 **9** 3 1/2 **Sunset Bounty**[16] 8117 3-9-0 0 .......... AdamBeschizza 2 30
(Julia Feilden) *in rr-div on outer: rdn wl over 2f out on inner: no imp and pushed out fr over 1f out* **100/1**

0 **10** 9 **Stockhill Star**[43] 7227 3-9-0 0 .......... (h[1]) LiamKeniry 13 6
(Brendan Powell) *tk fierce hold s: a in rr: plenty to do wl over 3f out: niggled along and no prog after* **100/1**

**11** 1 1/2 **Lady Carduros (IRE)** 3-9-0 0 .......... DougieCostello 1 2
(Neil Mulholland) *missed break and in rr: plenty to do fr over 3f out: nvr involved* **33/1**

**12** 8 **Catheadans Fury** 3-8-11 0 .......... (t[1]) GeorgeWood(3) 6
(Martin Bosley) *wnt lft ss: in rr tl kpt darting lft and racd v wd after 2f: remained racing wdst of all and c v wd into st: no ch after and pushed out* **40/1**

00 **13** 5 **Shanghai Shane (IRE)**[16] 8117 3-9-0 0 .......... JoshuaBryan(5) 10
(Brian Barr) *racd in mid-div on outer: pushed along and racing wd wl over 3f out: c wd into st and pushed along fr wl over 2f out* **200/1**

**14** 10 **Aegean Bounty (IRE)** 3-8-11 0 .......... MitchGodwin(3) 4
(John Bridger) *a in rr-div: shkn up over 3f out and struggling: no ex and eased over 1f out* **66/1**

1m 24.95s (-1.05) **Going Correction** -0.15s/f (Stan) **14 Ran SP% 124.5**
Speed ratings (Par 103): **100,98,95,93,92 90,90,84,80,70 68,59,53,42**
CSF £5.01 TOTE £2.40: £1.10, £1.50, £2.60; EX 5.70 Trifecta £18.60.

**Owner** Emma Capon, A Lloyd Webber & Rachel Hood **Bred** Gestut Hofgut Heymann **Trained** Newmarket, Suffolk

**FOCUS**
Just an ordinary maiden and the betting got it right, the first four finishing in market order. Another race with no depth. The runner-up has been rated to her debut effort.

## 8505 32RED.COM H'CAP 1m 7f 218y(P)
6:55 (6:55) (Class 4) (0-80,82) 3-Y-O+ £4,690 (£1,395; £697; £348) Stalls Low

Form RPR

1-00 **1** **Captain Navarre**[18] 8047 5-9-9 **75** .......... (v[1]) ShaneKelly 3 85
(Charlie Fellowes) *hld up in mid-div on inner: swtchd out and prog over 4f out: rdn and emerged fr pack to chse clr ldr over 3f out: kpt on wl and led over 1f out: fnd plenty ins fnl f* **10/11**[1]

232 **2** 4 1/2 **Innoko (FR)**[41] 7336 7-8-13 **65** .......... (p) PatCosgrave 4 69
(Robert Stephens) *racd in mid-div: rdn over 3f out and chsd wnr fr over 2f out in centre: kpt on wl tl over 1f out: no ex wl ins fnl f* **7/1**[3]

6600 **3** 4 **Tetradrachm**[40] 7359 4-9-7 **73** .......... (p) AdamBeschizza 5 72
(David Simcock) *hld up in rr: rdn wl over 3f and gd prog fr pack over 3f out: keeping on wl fr over 1f but too late to catch front pair* **12/1**

-060 **4** 3/4 **Poyle Thomas**[18] 8038 8-9-13 **82** .......... GeorgeWood(3) 9 80
(Michael Madgwick) *hld up in rr: rdn wl over 3f out: kpt on one pce past btn horses* **7/1**[3]

11U0 **5** 1 3/4 **Golly Miss Molly**[27] 7766 6-9-1 **67** .......... (b) MartinLane 1 63
(Martin Bosley) *hld up in rr: rdn over 3f out: plugged on wl fr over 1f out* **20/1**

2535 **6** 6 **King Calypso**[39] 7412 6-10-0 **80** .......... TomQueally 7 69
(Denis Coakley) *hld up in rr-div: rdn over 3f out: kpt on one pce* **6/1**[2]

4300 **7** 1 1/2 **Ravenous**[21] 7949 6-9-10 **76** .......... KieranO'Neill 10 63
(Luke Dace) *sn led and set a str pce: sn clr ldr: 10 l ld 4f out: hrd rdn fr over 3f out: kpt on wl tl hdd wl over 1f out: wknd sn after* **16/1**

1455 **8** 23 **Bracken Brae**[62] 6618 5-9-6 **72** .......... JoeyHaynes 8 32
(Mark H Tompkins) *racd between horses in mid-div: shkn up over 3f out: no rspnse and eased fr over 2f out: t.o* **33/1**

0-66 **9** 11 **Shades Of Silver**[45] 7200 7-10-0 **80** .......... LiamKeniry 12 26
(Ed de Giles) *chsd ldr ldr: rdn wl over 3f out: sn no ex and eased in st: t.o* **12/1**

0005 **10** 4 1/4 **Calvinist**[68] 6398 4-9-4 **70** .......... (p) JamesSullivan 2 11
(Ruth Carr) *plld hrd chsng clr ldr on rail: nudged along wl over 3f out but no ex and wknd qckly after: t.o* **20/1**

3000 **11** 25 **Danglydontask**[14] 8157 6-8-10 **62** .......... (p) JosephineGordon 11
(David Arbuthnot) *a in rr-div: struggling fr wl over 3f out: no ex and eased in st: t.o* **33/1**

3m 24.13s (-5.97) **Going Correction** -0.15s/f (Stan) **11 Ran SP% 128.3**
Speed ratings (Par 105): **108,105,103,103,102 99,98,87,81,79 67**
CSF £8.42 CT £55.79 TOTE £2.20: £1.10, £1.90, £3.80; EX 7.70 Trifecta £67.50.

**Owner** The Johnson'S **Bred** Shortgrove Manor Stud **Trained** Newmarket, Suffolk

**FOCUS**
This was soundly run. The winner has been rated back to his best.

## 8506 32RED H'CAP 1m 3f 219y(P)
**7:25** (7:26) (Class 3) (0-90,90) 3-Y-O
**£7,158** (£2,143; £1,071; £535; £267; £134) **Stalls** Low

Form RPR
0525 **1** **Al Hamdany (IRE)**[5] 8385 3-9-7 **90** JFEgan 1 97
(Marco Botti) *hld up bhd ldrs on inner: rdn wl over 1f out: led 1f out: hrd pressed by runner-up ins fnl f: hld on post* **2/1**[2]
2440 **2** *shd* **Flight Of Fantasy**[15] 8143 3-8-6 **75** (h[1]) KieranO'Neill 6 81
(Harry Dunlop) *bhd ldr on outer: pressed ldr wl over 2f out: sn rdn: briefly led ent fnl f: stuck to task wl pressing wnr all the way ins fnl f: jst failed post* **16/1**
2051 **3** *1 ¼* **Quothquan (FR)**[28] 7744 3-8-7 **79** GeorgeWood(3) 2 83
(Michael Madgwick) *bhd ldrs on outer: rdn over 2f out: kpt on wl ins fnl f but nt get to ldng pair* **9/1**
163 **4** *2 ½* **Yamarhaba Malayeen (IRE)**[151] 3336 3-8-13 **82** TomQueally 5 82
(Michael Bell) *s.s and t.k.h in rr: niggled along to hold pl over 3f out: kpt on one pce fnl f* **5/1**[3]
1111 **5** *3 ¼* **Hajaam (IRE)**[8] 8326 3-9-5 **88** 6ex ShaneKelly 7 83
(Charlie Fellowes) *sn led: shkn up wl over 2f out: pressed and rdn 2f out: hdd ent fnl f and sn no ex between horses: wknd qckly* **5/4**[1]
1506 **6** *5* **Earthly (USA)**[32] 7599 3-8-4 **73** (p[1]) JimmyQuinn 4 60
(Bernard Llewellyn) *bhd ldr on inner: rdn along over 3f out and losing pl: lft bhd fr over 1f out: no ex fnl f* **16/1**

2m 31.62s (-2.88) **Going Correction** -0.15s/f (Stan) **6** Ran SP% **116.2**
Speed ratings (Par 106): **103,102,102,100,98 94**
CSF £31.95 TOTE £3.90: £1.70, £4.80; EX 34.50 Trifecta £145.70.
**Owner** AlMohamediya Racing **Bred** Miss Debbie Kitchin **Trained** Newmarket, Suffolk

**FOCUS**
Not a bad handicap, but the early gallop wasn't strong and it developed into a bit of a sprint. The second, third and fourth have been rated close to form.

## 8507 100% PROFIT BOOST AT 32REDSPORT.COM H'CAP 1m 3f 219y(P)
**7:55** (7:56) (Class 6) (0-60,60) 3-Y-0+ **£2,587** (£770; £384; £192) **Stalls** Low

Form RPR
0541 **1** **Champagne Rules**[8] 8314 6-8-8 **52** ConnorMurtagh(5) 8 62+
(Sharon Watt) *hld up between horses in rr-div: sltly ct on heels ent first bnd and t.k.h: sn settled: shkn up w plenty to do over 2f out: sn rdn and qcknd up wl on outer to ld ent fnl f: drew clr: easily* **10/11**[1]
1004 **2** *2 ¾* **Epsom Secret**[23] 7879 3-8-12 **56** JFEgan 1 60
(Pat Phelan) *racd in mid-div: prog 2f out and w wnr over 1f out whn rdn: wnt to inner and kpt on ins fnl f but no threat to easy wnr* **8/1**[3]
000 **3** *¾* **Hong Kong Joe**[98] 5299 7-8-7 **46** (e) EdwardGreatrex 11 48
(Lydia Richards) *hld up in rr: shkn up and prog wl over 3f out: rdn and swtchd to inner 2f out: in firing line and ev ch over 1f out: kpt on one pce ins fnl f* **66/1**
0000 **4** *1* **Babette (IRE)**[25] 7833 3-8-0 **51** ow2 (v[1]) PaulHainey(7) 2 52
(Alan Bailey) *racd bhd ldrs on inner: rdn 2f out: plugging over 1f out between horses: tk 4th jst ins fnl f and kpt on one pce* **7/1**[2]
0305 **5** *1 ¼* **Midnight Mood**[7] 8346 4-8-12 **51** (t) LiamKeniry 9 49
(Dominic Ffrench Davis) *hld up bhd ldrs between horses: shkn up over 2f out: rdn 2f out: kpt on wl tl one pce ent fnl f* **12/1**
5060 **6** *hd* **Life Of Luxury**[15] 8135 4-9-1 **54** WilliamCarson 5 52
(Mark Brisbourne) *chsd ldr on outer: rdn to ld 2f out: swamped ent fnl f and plugged on one pce* **25/1**
1020 **7** *1 ¾* **Howardian Hills (IRE)**[48] 7085 4-9-7 **60** (h[1]) KieranShoemark 10 55
(Victor Dartnall) *slow s and in rr: shkn up on inner wl over 2f out and sme prog: rdn 2f out: no immediate imp: but picked up fr over 1f out and nudged out ins fnl f* **11/1**
4250 **8** *8* **Dixon**[8] 8312 3-8-11 **55** JoeyHaynes 14 38
(Mark H Tompkins) *racd in mid-divsion between horses: shkn up and rdn over 2f out: no imp wl over 1f out and nudged out after* **14/1**
2530 **9** *2* **Ablaze**[34] 7537 3-8-10 **54** (p) GeorgeDowning 7 34
(Laura Mongan) *in rr-div and racd a bit wd: pushed along to hold pl wl over 3f out: in rr wl over 2f out and hrd rdn: sn no ex* **33/1**
3230 **10** *½* **Ravenswood**[22] 7918 4-8-13 **52** DavidProbert 12 30
(Patrick Chamings) *bhd ldrs on outer: pushed along wl over 3f out to hold pl: no ex by over 2f out and pushed out* **14/1**
06 **11** *1* **Bermondsey Belle (IRE)**[14] 8157 3-9-2 **60** (tp) JosephineGordon 4 38
(Lucy Wadham) *narrow ldr: rdn along wl over 2f out and hanging onto ld: hdd 2f out and bk peddled through pack: eased fr 1f out* **7/1**[2]

2m 33.39s (-1.11) **Going Correction** -0.15s/f (Stan)
**WFA** 3 from 4yo+ 5lb **11** Ran SP% **126.1**
Speed ratings (Par 101): **97,95,94,94,93 93,91,86,85,84 84**
CSF £9.79 CT £333.94 TOTE £1.90: £1.02, £3.00, £11.50; EX 10.20 Trifecta £369.10.
**Owner** Rosey Hill Partnership **Bred** Heather Raw **Trained** Brompton-on-Swale, N Yorks
■ Stewards' Enquiry : J F Egan caution: careless riding

**FOCUS**
Despite what appeared to be a steady enough gallop, the first three came from off the pace. The winner was well in and won as he liked.
T/Jkpt: Not won. T/Plt: £9.00 to a £1 stake. Pool: £72,024.25. 5,790.24 winning units. T/Qpdt: £3.60 to a £1 stake. Pool: £10,794.95. 2,161.98 winning units. **Cathal Gahan**

# 8161 NOTTINGHAM (L-H)
Wednesday, November 1

**OFFICIAL GOING: Good (good to soft in places; 7.3)**
Wind: Virtually nil Weather: Cloudy

## 8508 EBF STALLIONS GOLDEN HORN MAIDEN STKS (PLUS 10 RACE) (C&G) (DIV I) 1m 75y
**12:30** (12:30) (Class 4) 2-Y-O **£6,469** (£1,925; £962; £481) **Stalls** Centre

Form RPR
5 **1** **King's Proctor (IRE)**[130] 4083 2-9-0 0 FrannyNorton 10 83+
(Mark Johnston) *trckd ldrs: hdwy over 2f out: swtchd rt and effrt over 1f out: rdn to chal ins fnl f: led last 100 yds* **5/2**[2]
52 **2** *1 ¼* **Tamkeen**[25] 7819 2-9-0 0 JimCrowley 7 80
(Owen Burrows) *le: pushed along over 2f out: rdn over 1f out: drvn ins fnl f: hdd last 100 yds* **15/8**[1]
0 **3** *5* **Artarmon (IRE)**[21] 7955 2-9-0 0 DanielTudhope 9 69+
(Michael Bell) *hld up in rr: hdwy 3f out: rdn to chse ldrs wl over 1f out: styd on wl fnl f* **25/1**
03F **4** *1 ¼* **Westbrook Bertie**[22] 7915 2-9-0 0 CharlesBishop 5 66
(Mick Channon) *in tch: hdwy 4f out: chsd ldrs over 2f out: sn rdn and kpt on same pce* **11/2**[3]
0 **5** *1 ¾* **Dubai Frame**[7] 8350 2-9-0 0 TomEaves 6 62
(Ed Dunlop) *midfield: hdwy on outer over 3f out: rdn along 2f out: kpt on one pce* **80/1**
60 **6** *1 ½* **Global Excel**[28] 7726 2-9-0 0 RichardKingscote 8 58
(Ed Walker) *cl up: rdn along* **8/1**
**7** *¾* **Change Maker** 2-9-0 0 DavidProbert 2 56
(Andrew Balding) *dwlt: green and a towards rr* **16/1**
00 **8** *3 ¼* **Twister (IRE)**[11] 8245 2-9-0 0 RyanPowell 4 49
(Sir Mark Prescott Bt) *chsd ldng pair on inner: rdn along over 3f out: sn drvn and wknd* **125/1**
0 **9** *4* **Teatro (IRE)**[12] 8215 2-9-0 0 JoeDoyle 3 40
(James Given) *a in rr* **125/1**
**10** *4 ½* **UAE Soldier (USA)** 2-9-0 0 JackMitchell 1 29
(Roger Varian) *in tch: hdwy 4f out: rdn along 3f out: green and wknd fnl 2f* **15/2**

1m 45.78s (-3.22) **Going Correction** -0.275s/f (Firm) **10** Ran SP% **114.2**
Speed ratings (Par 98): **105,103,98,97,95 94,93,90,86,81**
CSF £7.31 TOTE £3.20: £1.40, £1.10, £6.80; EX 8.80 Trifecta £122.70.
**Owner** Sheikh Hamdan bin Mohammed Al Maktoum **Bred** Airlie Stud **Trained** Middleham Moor, N Yorks

**FOCUS**
Inner track used and distances as advertised. The first division of the mile maiden was marginally quicker than the second. After riding in the opener Jim Crowley said: "The ground is slow, good to soft" and Danny Tudhope said: "It's not too bad, just on the slow side of good".

## 8509 EBF STALLIONS GOLDEN HORN MAIDEN STKS (PLUS 10 RACE) (C&G) (DIV II) 1m 75y
**1:00** (1:01) (Class 4) 2-Y-O **£6,469** (£1,925; £962; £481) **Stalls** Centre

Form RPR
3 **1** **Come On Tier (FR)**[23] 7906 2-9-0 0 JimCrowley 6 81
(David Simcock) *.trckd ldrs: smooth hdwy on outer over 2f out: led 1 1/2f out: rdn clr ent fnl f: styd on wl* **5/1**[3]
23 **2** *3 ¾* **Rich Identity**[25] 7818 2-9-0 0 JackMitchell 3 72
(Roger Varian) *trckd ldr: hdwy and cl up over 2f out: rdn to chal and ev ch 1 1/2f out: drvn ent fnl f: kpt on same pce* **3/1**[2]
**3** *hd* **The Lincoln Lawyer** 2-9-0 0 FrannyNorton 8 72
(Mark Johnston) *trckd ldrs on outer: hdwy 3f out: rdn along 2f out: styd on u.p fnl f* **40/1**
**4** *shd* **Ispolini** 2-9-0 0 (t[1]) JamesDoyle 4 74+
(Charlie Appleby) *rrd s and slowly away: rr: hdwy on outer 3f out: rdn along wl over 1f out: styd on wl fnl f* **8/11**[1]
025 **5** *3* **Agar's Plough**[18] 8046 2-9-0 79 DanielTudhope 2 65
(Ed Dunlop) *trckd ldng pair on inner: hdwy wl over 2f out: rdn along wl over 1f out: n.m.r and wknd ent fnl f* **10/1**
**6** *2 ½* **Petit Palais** 2-9-0 0 RobertHavlin 10 59
(John Gosden) *hld up in rr: pushed along and green 3f out: styd on fr wl over 1f out* **14/1**
0 **7** *½* **Chikoko Trail**[15] 8140 2-9-0 0 CharlesBishop 1 58
(Mick Channon) *led: rdn along wl over 2f out: drvn and hdd 1 1/2f out: grad wknd* **100/1**
**8** *1 ½* **Trevithick** 2-9-0 0 GrahamLee 7 54
(Bryan Smart) *a towards rr* **100/1**
**9** *nk* **Dawn Dancer** 2-9-0 0 DavidProbert 9 54
(Andrew Balding) *green and a in rr* **40/1**
60 **10** *2 ¾* **Seaborough (IRE)**[11] 8245 2-9-0 0 FergusSweeney 5 47
(Alan King) *chsd ldrs: rdn along 3f out: wknd over 2f out* **100/1**

1m 45.94s (-3.06) **Going Correction** -0.275s/f (Firm) **10** Ran SP% **123.2**
Speed ratings (Par 98): **104,100,100,99,96 94,93,92,92,89**
CSF £21.59 TOTE £7.80: £1.70, £1.10, £6.90; EX 28.00 Trifecta £354.30.
**Owner** Genting Casinos Uk Limited **Bred** T De La Heronniere Et Al **Trained** Newmarket, Suffolk

**FOCUS**
The second division of the 1m maiden in which the well-backed market leader got away slowly and couldn't get involved.

## 8510 ROA/RACING POST OWNERS JACKPOT H'CAP 1m 75y
**1:30** (1:31) (Class 4) (0-85,82) 3-Y-O+ **£5,175** (£1,540; £769; £384) **Stalls** Centre

Form RPR
12 **1** **Monaadhil (IRE)**[16] 8126 3-9-0 **77** JimCrowley 1 89+
(Marcus Tregoning) *trckd ldrs on inner: swtchd rt and hdwy over 2f out: rdn to ld ent fnl f: kpt on wl* **9/2**[1]
6P51 **2** *2* **Rosarno (IRE)**[21] 7957 3-9-1 **78** (bt) DavidProbert 4 82
(Charles Hills) *hld up: hdwy 3f out: sn trcking ldrs: effrt wl over 1f out: rdn to chse wnr ins fnl f: kpt on same pce* **7/1**[3]
5600 **3** *nse* **Magic City (IRE)**[18] 8048 8-9-0 **82** HarrisonShaw(7) 5 86
(Michael Easterby) *trckd ldrs on inner: hdwy 3f out: effrt and n.m.r over 1f out: sn swtchd rt and rdn. styd on wl towards fin* **20/1**
**4** *¾* **Pure Action (IRE)**[40] 7368 4-9-1 **76** (p) DavidNolan 8 78
(John James Feane, Ire) *led: rdn along over 2f out: drvn over 1f out: hdd ent fnl f: kpt on same pce* **15/2**
6023 **5** *1* **Zeshov (IRE)**[16] 8126 6-9-2 **77** (p) DanielTudhope 6 77
(Rebecca Bastiman) *hld up in rr: hdwy wl over 2f out: rdn to chse ldrs over 1f out: drvn and no imp fnl f* **8/1**
6313 **6** *½* **Off Art**[25] 7823 7-8-10 **71** (p) DavidAllan 2 70
(Tim Easterby) *trckd ldr: cl up on inner 3f out: rdn along 2f out: sn ev ch tl drvn appr fnl f and sn wknd* **5/1**[2]
2350 **7** *1 ½* **Instant Attraction (IRE)**[19] 8014 6-9-7 **82** (v) JackGarritty 3 77
(Jedd O'Keeffe) *trckd ldrs: pushed along over 3f out: rdn wl over 2f out: sn wknd* **17/2**
4036 **8** *½* **Wasm**[12] 8209 3-8-9 **72** JoeFanning 10 66
(Roger Fell) *dwlt: a in rr* **25/1**
1043 **9** *5* **Maratha (IRE)**[28] 7736 3-9-2 **79** (t) JamesDoyle 9 70
(Stuart Williams) *prom: cl up on outer 4f out: rdn along 3f out: sn drvn and wknd* **9/2**[1]
4406 **10** *nk* **Mamdood (IRE)**[31] 7656 3-8-10 **73** (t) JoeyHaynes 7 55
(Susan Corbett) *midfield: effrt and sme hdwy on outer 1/2-way: rdn along 3f out: sn wknd* **28/1**

1m 45.3s (-3.70) **Going Correction** -0.275s/f (Firm)
**WFA** 3 from 4yo+ 2lb **10** Ran SP% **111.0**
Speed ratings (Par 105): **107,105,104,104,103 102,101,100,95,95**
CSF £33.00 CT £542.91 TOTE £2.10: £1.80, £2.40, £6.20; EX 27.50 Trifecta £536.80.
**Owner** Hamdan Al Maktoum **Bred** Oak Hill Stud **Trained** Whitsbury, Hants

**FOCUS**
A competitive handicap run at just an ordinary gallop. The race has been rated around the second.

## 8511 WATCH RACING UK ON BT TV H'CAP 1m 6f
**2:00** (2:00) (Class 4) (0-85,85) 3-Y-0+ **£5,175** (£1,540; £769; £384) **Stalls** Low

Form RPR
1252 **1** **St Mary's**[14] 8166 4-9-7 **85**.................................. WilliamCox(7) 8 91
(Andrew Balding) *hmpd after 1f and in rr: nt clr run on inner 3f out and sn swtchd markedly rt to outer: rdn over 2f out: chsd ldrs over 1f out: styd on wl fnl f to ld towards fin* **10/3**[2]
4222 **2** ½ **Master Archer (IRE)**[49] 7060 3-8-12 **78**.................(p) GeorgeWood(3) 10 83
(James Fanshawe) *hld up in tch: hdwy on outer 3f out: cl up over 2f out: rdn to ld 1 1/2f out: drvn ins fnl f: hdd and no ex towards fin* **5/2**[1]
1306 **3** ¾ **Stormin Tom (IRE)**[18] 8047 5-8-12 **72**................ RachelRichardson(3) 3 76
(Tim Easterby) *sn led: pushed along 3f out: rdn over 2f out: hdd 1 1/2f out: sn drvn and kpt on wl u.p ins fnl f* **12/1**
0003 **4** shd **Saved By The Bell (IRE)**[12] 8214 7-8-6 **70**............. HarrisonShaw(7) 5 74
(Lawrence Mullaney) *hld up in rr: hdwy 3f out: rdn to chse ldrs wl over 1f out: sn nt clr run: styd on fnl f* **25/1**
5403 **5** hd **Rydan (IRE)**[23] 7903 6-9-9 **80**....................................(p) TomQueally 1 84+
(Gary Moore) *hld up in midfield: gng wl 3f out: nt clr run fr jst over 2f out tl ent fnl f: sn swtchd rt and rdn: styd on wl towards fin* **5/1**[3]
2601 **6** ½ **Whinging Willie (IRE)**[31] 7651 8-9-9 **83**.................(v) HectorCrouch(3) 7 86
(Gary Moore) *hld up towards rr: hdwy 3f out: chsd ldrs on inner over 1f out: sn rdn and kpt on fnl f* **7/1**
6400 **7** 3 ¾ **Bertie Moon**[82] 5873 7-9-2 **73**........................................ AlistairRawlinson 2 71
(Michael Appleby) *trckd ldr: hdwy and cl up over 3f out: chal over 2f out and sn rdn: drvn wl over 1f out: wknd* **10/1**
5434 **8** 1 ½ **Swaheen**[32] 7615 5-9-8 **79**..........................................(p) JoeDoyle 4 75
(Julie Camacho) *trckd ldng pair: rdn along 3f out: sn wknd* **12/1**
2313 **9** 1 ½ **Eurato (FR)**[211] 1548 7-8-12 **74**....................................(p) FinleyMarsh(5) 6 67
(Steve Gollings) *trckd ldng pair: hdwy 4f out: rdn along 3f out: sn drvn and wknd* **20/1**

3m 5.39s (-1.61) **Going Correction** -0.275s/f (Firm)
**WFA** 3 from 4yo+ 6lb **9** Ran SP% **113.9**
Speed ratings (Par 105): **93,92,92,92,92 91,89,88,87**
CSF £11.89 CT £85.91 TOTE £4.10: £1.60, £1.10, £3.30; EX 12.50 Trifecta £114.80.
**Owner** Kingsclere Racing Club **Bred** Kingsclere Stud **Trained** Kingsclere, Hants
■ Stewards' Enquiry : William Cox three-day ban: careless riding (Nov 15-17)

**FOCUS**
A decent enough staying event. The pace seemed even early, but plenty finished close up. The third helps set the standard.

## 8512 WATCH RACING UK ON VIRGIN 536 H'CAP 5f 8y
**2:30** (2:31) (Class 5) (0-75,77) 3-Y-0+ **£3,234** (£962; £481; £240) **Stalls** High

Form RPR
0030 **1** **Seamster**[22] 7923 10-8-9 **70**..........................................(t) LauraCoughlan(7) 4 78
(David Loughnane) *mde most: rdn over 1f out: kpt on wl fnl f* **10/1**
3111 **2** ¾ **Lydiate Lady**[25] 7825 5-8-12 **66**........................................ NeilFarley 12 71
(Eric Alston) *cl up on stands rail: rdn along over 1f out: drvn and kpt on fnl f* **4/1**[2]
0000 **3** 2 ¼ **Start Time (IRE)**[8] 8319 4-9-9 **77**........................................ PhillipMakin 7 74+
(Paul Midgley) *towards rr: hdwy wl over 1f out: sn rdn and kpt on fnl f* **6/1**[3]
3243 **4** 2 ¾ **Angel Palanas**[44] 7218 3-8-7 **61** oh3................................(p) JoeyHaynes 8 48
(K R Burke) *chsd ldrs: rdn along 2f out: drvn over 1f out: sn one pce* **10/1**
1244 **5** 3 **Glacier Point**[13] 8186 3-8-13 **74**......................................(p) WilliamCox(7) 9 51
(Clive Cox) *racd nr stands rail: in tch: pushed along over 2f out: rdn wl over 1f out: no hdwy* **13/2**
1303 **6** hd **Miningold**[28] 7738 4-9-7 **75**..........................................(p) TomEaves 1 51
(Michael Dods) *racd towards centre: in tch: pushed along 1/2-way: rdn wl over 1f out: n.d* **10/1**
0031 **7** shd **Apricot Sky**[11] 8237 7-9-4 **75**.....................................(p) CallumRodriguez(3) 3 50
(Michael Dods) *racd centre: cl up: rdn along 2f out: grad wknd* **7/2**[1]
**8** ¾ **Twist Of Magic (IRE)**[25] 7840 3-9-0 **68** ow1.................. DavidNolan 11 41
(John James Feane, Ire) *chsd ldrs on stands rail: rdn along over 2f out: sn drvn and wknd* **8/1**
3310 **9** 1 ½ **Everkyllachy (IRE)**[22] 7912 3-8-4 **65**...........................(b) GeorgiaDobie(7) 2 32
(J S Moore) *dwlt and rr centre: swtchd rt to stands rail bef 1/2-way: nvr a factor* **33/1**
3160 **10** 12 **Somewhere Secret**[14] 8167 3-9-8 **76**...............................(p) TomQueally 6
(Michael Mullineaux) *sn outpcd in rr: detached fr 1/2-way* **25/1**

59.62s (-1.88) **Going Correction** -0.275s/f (Firm) **10** Ran SP% **115.0**
Speed ratings (Par 103): **104,102,99,94,90 89,89,88,85,66**
CSF £49.13 CT £270.27 TOTE £11.70: £3.10, £1.90, £2.60; EX 62.50 Trifecta £664.20.
**Owner** Miss Sarah Hoyland **Bred** D G Hardisty Bloodstock **Trained** Market Drayton, Shropshire

**FOCUS**
It proved crucial to show early speed in this, as the first two were the front two throughout. The winner has been rated to the balance of his form since the spring.

## 8513 WATCH RACING UK ON SKY 432 H'CAP (DIV I) 1m 75y
**3:00** (3:01) (Class 6) (0-65,67) 3-Y-0+ **£2,587** (£770; £384; £192) **Stalls** Centre

Form RPR
6440 **1** **Sunnua (IRE)**[12] 8210 4-8-6 **54**.................................. SebastianWoods(7) 6 65
(Richard Fahey) *midfield: hdwy and in tch over 3f out: trckd ldrs 2f out: rdn over 1f out: styd on to ld last 150 yds* **17/2**
3231 **2** 2 ½ **Break The Silence**[13] 8181 3-8-12 **55**...............................(p) DavidAllan 12 60
(Scott Dixon) *trckd ldrs: hdwy 1/2-way: led 3f out: rdn along and hdd wl over 1f out: drvn and kpt on fnl f* **9/2**[2]
5062 **3** ½ **Dellaguista (IRE)**[20] 7984 3-9-8 **65**........................................ AndrewMullen 1 69
(Tim Easterby) *trckd ldrs: hdwy and cl up 3f out: rdn to take slt ld wl over 1f out: drvn ent fnl f: hdd and no ex last 150 yds* **7/2**[1]
5400 **4** 5 **Berkeley Vale**[8] 8313 6-9-8 **63**........................................ FergusSweeney 9 56
(Roger Teal) *in tch early: rdn along and lost pl after 11/2f and towards rr: hdwy u.p wl over 2f out: kpt on appr fnl f: nvr nr ldrs* **18/1**
0005 **5** 2 ¼ **Willsy**[12] 8210 4-9-1 **56**........................................ ShaneGray 11 43
(Karen Tutty) *towards rr: hdwy over 3f out: rdn along to chse ldrs over 2f out: sn wknd wl over 1f out* **40/1**
0223 **6** ¾ **World Record (IRE)**[13] 8181 7-9-2 **57**........................................ FrannyNorton 4 43
(Mick Quinn) *trckd ldng pair: hdwy and cl up 4f out: rdn along wl over 2f out: drvn and wknd over 1f out* **7/2**[1]
0000 **7** 2 ¼ **Diana Lady (CHI)**[32] 7601 5-9-7 **67**...............................(h) BenRobinson(5) 13 48
(Luke McJannet) *a towards rr* **100/1**
4650 **8** 4 **Tally's Son**[45] 7198 3-7-12 **48**........................................ RPWalsh(7) 7 19
(Grace Harris) *midfield: hdwy and in tch over 3f out: rdn along wl over 2f out: sn wknd* **33/1**

-600 **9** 6 **Lucky Esteem**[23] 7902 3-9-2 **59**........................................ KieranShoemark 2 17
(Neil Mulholland) *a towards rr* **12/1**
5500 **10** 2 ¾ **Ace Master**[10] 8260 9-9-4 **62**........................................(b) PaddyPilley(3) 5 13
(Roy Bowring) *sn led: rdn along 4f out: hdd 3f out: sn drvn and wknd 2f out* **28/1**
0101 **11** hd **Riponian**[46] 7166 7-9-4 **59**........................................(t) JoeyHaynes 10 10
(Susan Corbett) *cl up: rdn along 3f out: sn drvn and wknd* **14/1**
6030 **12** 12 **Unonothinjonsnow**[41] 7325 3-8-3 **46** oh1........................ JoeFanning 3
(Richard Guest) *dwlt: a in rr* **7/1**[3]
4460 **13** 17 **Primanora**[14] 8168 4-9-4 **59**........................................(p) TomQueally 8
(Michael Appleby) *v unruly in stalls: dwlt: plld hrd: a in rr* **33/1**

1m 45.57s (-3.43) **Going Correction** -0.275s/f (Firm)
**WFA** 3 from 4yo+ 2lb **13** Ran SP% **118.0**
Speed ratings (Par 101): **106,103,103,98,95 95,92,88,82,80 79,67,50**
CSF £44.30 CT £166.66 TOTE £12.30: £2.80, £2.10, £1.70; EX 57.90 Trifecta £203.70.
**Owner** Richard Fahey Ebor Racing Club Ltd **Bred** J Waldron & W R Muir **Trained** Musley Bank, N Yorks

**FOCUS**
This didn't look a strong race for the level, but it was run at a solid gallop. That said, those who got behind didn't really feature, more those in midfield picking up the pieces.

## 8514 WATCH RACING UK ON SKY 432 H'CAP (DIV II) 1m 75y
**3:30** (3:30) (Class 6) (0-65,65) 3-Y-0+ **£2,587** (£770; £384; £192) **Stalls** Centre

Form RPR
5300 **1** **Teomaria**[12] 8216 3-9-3 **63**........................................ CliffordLee(3) 8 69
(K R Burke) *trckd ldrs: hdwy 3f out: cl up 2f out: rdn to chal jst over 1f out: drvn and n.m.r ins fnl f: kpt on gamely to ld nr line* **12/1**
0001 **2** shd **Hitchcock**[46] 7165 3-9-8 **65**........................................(b) KevinStott 7 71
(Kevin Ryan) *led: pushed along over 2f out: rdn over 1f out: drvn ins fnl f: edgd rt last 100 yds: hdd no line* **11/2**[3]
0430 **3** ¾ **Ingleby Angel (IRE)**[20] 7979 8-9-2 **57**........................ DanielTudhope 13 61
(David O'Meara) *hld up in rr: stdy hdwy on outer over 3f out: chsd ldrs wl over 1f out: rdn to chal ent fnl f: sn drvn and ev ch: edgd lft last 100 yds: no ex* **11/4**[1]
0065 **4** 2 ¾ **Pickett's Charge**[12] 8209 4-9-8 **63**...............................(p[1]) PhillipMakin 10 61
(Richard Guest) *dwlt and rr: hdwy 3f out: rdn along 2f out: styd on wl appr fnl f: nrst fin* **11/1**
4001 **5** 1 **Harlequin Rock**[16] 8124 4-9-0 **55**...............................(p) FrannyNorton 6 50
(Mick Quinn) *hld up in tch: hdwy 3f out: rdn along 2f out: drvn over 1f out: kpt on same pce* **15/2**
600 **6** ½ **Big Bad Lol (IRE)**[68] 6368 3-8-13 **56**........................ RichardKingscote 9 50
(Ed Walker) *prom: cl up 6f out: rdn along wl over 2f out: ev ch tl drvn wl over 1f out and grad wknd* **4/1**[2]
5226 **7** 1 ¾ **Green Howard**[9] 8300 9-9-0 **58**...............................(p) PhilDennis(3) 11 48
(Rebecca Bastiman) *towards rr: sme hdwy and in tch 3f out: sn rdn along and n.d* **8/1**
0030 **8** ½ **Dynamic Girl (IRE)**[23] 7899 4-8-4 **52**...............................(t[1]) NicolaCurrie(7) 2 41
(Brendan Powell) *dwlt and towards rr: hdwy and in tch over 3f out: rdn along wl over 2f out: n.d* **16/1**
3600 **9** 3 ¾ **Tread Lightly**[14] 7895 3-9-2 **59**........................................ DavidAllan 12 39
(Tim Easterby) . *a towards rr* **20/1**
-000 **10** 12 **Designamento (IRE)**[14] 8152 3-7-12 **46** oh1........................ JaneElliott(5) 1
(Ed de Giles) *prom: rdn along on inner 4f out: wknd 3f out* **100/1**
5000 **11** 2 ¼ **St James's Park (IRE)**[36] 7495 4-8-13 **59**..............(p[1]) BenRobinson(5) 4 7
(Luke McJannet) *trckd ldng pair: rdn along 3f out: wknd over 2f out* **33/1**

1m 46.61s (-2.39) **Going Correction** -0.275s/f (Firm)
**WFA** 3 from 4yo+ 2lb **11** Ran SP% **115.5**
Speed ratings (Par 101): **100,99,99,96,95 94,93,92,88,76 74**
CSF £74.22 CT £241.31 TOTE £14.30: £3.50, £1.90, £1.50; EX 122.10 Trifecta £1255.80.
**Owner** David & Yvonne Blunt **Bred** W A Tinkler **Trained** Middleham Moor, N Yorks

**FOCUS**
This was the stronger of the two divisions and it produced a thrilling finish. Three came clear.

## 8515 AJA AMATEUR RIDERS' H'CAP 1m 2f 50y
**4:00** (4:02) (Class 6) (0-60,60) 3-Y-0+ **£2,495** (£774; £386; £193) **Stalls** Low

Form RPR
2465 **1** **Quoteline Direct**[21] 7960 4-10-12 **58**...............................(h) MissBeckySmith 9 66
(Micky Hammond) *midfield: hdwy 3f out: chsd ldrs 2f out: cl up and sltly hmpd over 1f out: rdn to ld jst ins fnl f: drvn and hld on wl towards fin* **16/1**
2532 **2** shd **England Expects**[5] 8386 3-10-4 **58**...............................(h) MrJBrace(5) 7 67
(K R Burke) *hld up in rr: hdwy and nt clr run over 3f out: swtchd rt towards outer over 2f out: rdn to chse ldrs over 1f out: chal ins fnl f: sn drvn and ev ch: kpt on wl towards fin: jst failed* **7/2**[1]
0211 **3** 1 ¼ **Royal Cosmic**[16] 8103 3-10-4 **58**........................................ MissEllaMcCain(5) 10 64
(Richard Fahey) *hld up: hdwy on inner over 3f out: chsd ldrs 2f out: rdn over 1f out: ev ch ent fnl f: sn drvn and kpt on same pce* **5/1**[2]
1163 **4** 2 ¾ **Bigbadboy (IRE)**[12] 8218 4-10-5 **54**........................................ MissAMcCain(3) 3 54
(Clive Mulhall) *chsd ldrs: rdn along over 2f out: drvn over 1f out: kpt on same pce fnl f* **13/2**[3]
0000 **5** ½ **Different Journey**[43] 7235 4-11-0 **60**...............................(b[1]) MissJoannaMason 5 59
(Michael Easterby) *t.k.h: sn led and clr: rdn along 2f out: drvn and hdd jst ins fnl f: grad wknd* **10/1**
0001 **6** 1 ¾ **Ingleby Spring (IRE)**[12] 8219 5-10-7 **53**........................ MissGAndrews 14 49
(Richard Fahey) *midfield: hdwy on outer 4f out: chsd ldrs over 2f out: rdn along wl over 1f out: edgd lft appr fnl f: sn one pce* **14/1**
4010 **7** ½ **Tingo In The Tale (IRE)**[53] 6953 8-10-6 **57**..........(p) MissJCooley(5) 16 52
(Tony Forbes) *prom: rdn along 3f out: drvn wl over 1f out: grad wknd* **18/1**
22-6 **8** 1 **Monday Club**[13] 8183 4-10-12 **58**........................................ MrPMillman 12 51
(Dominic Ffrench Davis) *chsd ldrs: rdn along 3f out: sn wknd* **12/1**
3-60 **9** 4 ½ **Down Time (USA)**[5] 8386 7-10-7 **60**...............................(v) MrTomMidgley(7) 4 45
(Paul Midgley) *chsd ldrs: rdn along 3f out: sn drvn and wknd* **66/1**
-600 **10** 1 ¼ **Top Diktat**[36] 7495 9-10-9 **58**........................................ MrBJames(3) 8 40
(Gary Moore) *a towards rr* **16/1**
5600 **11** 4 ½ **Candesta (USA)**[18] 8031 7-10-0 **51**........................................ MrMSHarris(5) 6 25
(Julia Feilden) *chsd ldr: rdn along over 2f out: drvn over 1f out: sn wknd* **25/1**
5400 **12** shd **Bob's Boy**[10] 8261 4-10-0 **53**...............................(vt[1]) MrHMyddelton(7) 15 26
(Oliver Greenall) *midfield: racd wd and hdwy to chse ldrs over 5f out: rdn along over 3f out: sn drvn and wknd* **66/1**
0000 **13** 4 ½ **Rock'n Gold**[21] 7960 4-10-11 **57**...............................(b[1]) MrJamesKing 1 22
(Adrian Wintle) *slowly away: a in rr* **15/2**
1330 **14** 4 ½ **Mamnoon (IRE)**[78] 6035 4-10-8 **59**...............................(b) MissLMPinchin(5) 13 15
(Roy Brotherton) *in tch: rdn along over 4f out: sn wknd* **50/1**

50F4 **15** *7* **Sakhalin Star (IRE)**[23] 7885 6-10-12 58..........................(p) MrSWalker 11
(Richard Guest) *a in rr* **16/1**
2m 15.04s (0.74) **Going Correction** -0.275s/f (Firm)
**WFA** 3 from 4yo+ 3lb **15** Ran SP% **119.1**
Speed ratings (Par 101): **86,85,84,82,82 80,80,79,76,75 71,71,67,64,58**
CSF £68.84 CT £331.48 TOTE £19.90: £5.40, £1.40, £2.10; EX 78.30 Trifecta £590.20.
**Owner** JFW Properties Ltd **Bred** Mrs T Brudenell **Trained** Middleham, N Yorks
■ Stewards' Enquiry : Mr J Brace caution: careless riding

**FOCUS**
A modest event, run at a decent gallop.
T/Plt: £28.70 to a £1 stake. Pool: £58,601.19. 1,488.65 winning units. T/Qpdt: £11.80 to a £1 stake. Pool: £5,515.65. 345.57 winning units. **Joe Rowntree**

8516 - 8523a (Foreign Racing) - See Raceform Interactive

## 8378 MAISONS-LAFFITTE (R-H)
Wednesday, November 1
**OFFICIAL GOING: Turf: very soft**

### 8524a PRIX DE CRESPIERES (CLAIMER) (2YO) (TURF) 6f
**12:10** 2-Y-O **£11,538** (£4,615; £3,461; £2,307; £1,153)

RPR
**1** **Good To Talk**[17] 2-8-7 0........................................(b) MlleAlisonMassin(4) 7 79
(Y Barberot, France) **53/10**[3]
**2** *2* **Rachael's Rocket (IRE)**[12] 8228 2-8-8 0....................(p) TonyPiccone 3 70
(C Boutin, France) **89/10**
**3** *2* **Bombetta (FR)**[17] 2-8-6 0 ow1.................................. KyllanBarbaud(8) 6 70
(N Caullery, France) **5/2**[1]
**4** *1 3/4* **So Sora (FR)**[10] 2-8-3 0.................................... MlleMickaelleMichel(10) 9 64
(M Boutin, France) **44/5**
**5** *1 1/2* **Debutante's Ball (IRE)**[14] 8154 2-8-3 0..............(p) MathieuPelletan(5) 8 54
(J S Moore) **53/10**[3]
**6** *2 1/2* **Frizzanto (FR)**[10] 2-9-5 0..........................................(p) IoritzMendizabal 5 58
(Mario Hofer, Germany) **56/10**
**7** *2* **Le Professeur (FR)**[148] 3445 2-8-2 0.............................. MlleLeaBails(9) 1 44
(C Boutin, France) **50/1**
**8** *nk* **Big Words (GER)**[11] 8253 2-8-8 0................................ RonanThomas 2 40
(J Phelippon, France) **43/10**[2]
**9** *dist* **Reine Du Lukka (FR)** 2-7-12 0................. MmeAlexiaCeccarello(10) 10
(Mme F Chenu, France) **67/1**
1m 11.98s (-1.42) **9** Ran SP% **118.1**
PARI-MUTUEL (all including 1 euro stake): WIN 6.30; PLACE 2.10, 2.60, 1.60; DF 35.20; SF 59.50.
**Owner** Ecurie Billon **Bred** O Costello & R Morehead **Trained** France

### 8525a PRIX MIESQUE (GROUP 3) (2YO FILLIES) (STRAIGHT) (TURF) 7f
**1:10** 2-Y-O **£34,188** (£13,675; £10,256; £6,837; £3,418)

RPR
**1** **Sweety Dream (FR)**[32] 7637 2-8-11 0.......................... GregoryBenoist 1 100
(P Bary, France) *trckd ldrs: effrt whn nt clr run and lost grnd over 1f out: rallied ins fnl f: styd on wl to ld towards fin* **92/10**[3]
**2** *snk* **Seaella (IRE)**[26] 2-8-11 0........................................ AntoineHamelin 7 100
(F Vermeulen, France) *led and sn swtchd to r against stands' rail: rdn along 2f out: kpt on wl fnl f: hdd towards fin* **31/10**[2]
**3** *1 1/4* **Moisson Precoce**[49] 2-8-11 0.......................... Francois-XavierBertras 6 96
(F Rohaut, France) *in tch: hdwy on outside and ev ch over 1f out to ins fnl f: kpt on same pce last 100yds* **124/10**
**4** *1 1/4* **Spaday (IRE)**[30] 2-8-11 0........................................ MaximeGuyon 4 93
(C Laffon-Parias, France) *dwlt: hld up in last pl: rdn and hdwy over 1f out: kpt on ins fnl f: nvr able to chal* **23/10**[1]
**5** *3/4* **Stella Di Camelot (IRE)**[42] 7304 2-8-11 0.............. MickaelBarzalona 5 91
(Gianluca Bietolini, Italy) *sn swtchd to r alone in centre: disp ld: edgd lft and rejnd main gp over 2f out: ev ch tl outpcd fnl f* **109/10**
**6** *shd* **Massina (FR)**[13] 8195 2-8-11 0.................................. TheoBachelot 3 91
(S Wattel, France) *trckd ldrs: rdn and outpcd whn nt clr run over 1f out: rallied ins fnl f: kpt on: no imp* **125/10**
**7** *2* **Bonita Fransisca (FR)**[74] 6228 2-8-11 0........... ChristopheSoumillon 2 85
(Antonio Marcialis, Italy) *dwlt: hld up: hdwy on outside wl over 1f out: wknd ins fnl f: eased whn btn* **23/10**[1]
1m 25.89s (-2.11) **7** Ran SP% **118.1**
PARI-MUTUEL (all including 1 euro stake): WIN 10.20; PLACE 4.00, 2.30; SF 42.90.
**Owner** Guy Pariente **Bred** Aleyrion Bloodstock Ltd **Trained** Chantilly, France

### 8526a PRIX DE SEINE-ET-OISE (GROUP 3) (3YO+) (TURF) 6f
**2:55** 3-Y-O+ **£34,188** (£13,675; £10,256; £6,837; £3,418)

RPR
**1** **The Right Man**[87] 5690 5-9-6 0.......................... Francois-XavierBertras 4 120
(D Guillemin, France) *cl up in nr-side gp: hdwy to ld as gps merged over 1f out: pushed out fnl f: comf* **3/1**[1]
**2** *1 3/4* **Gold Vibe (IRE)**[30] 7697 4-9-0 0.........................(p) ChristopheSoumillon 9 108
(P Bary, France) *hld up in centre gp: hdwy and cl up as gps merged over 1f out: chsd wnr ins fnl f: kpt on: hld nr fin* **74/10**
**3** *shd* **Son Cesio (FR)**[31] 7670 6-9-4 0.............................. MickaelBarzalona 5 112
(H-A Pantall, France) *led and overall ldr in nr side gp: rdn and hdd as gps merged over 1f out: rallied: kpt on fin* **17/2**
**4** *shd* **Spiritfix**[30] 7697 4-8-10 0........................................ MaximeGuyon 7 104
(A Fabre, France) *cl up in nr-side gp: effrt and ev ch as gps merged over 1f out: kpt on ins fnl f* **9/2**[2]
**5** *2* **Zalamea (IRE)**[31] 7671 4-9-0 0.............................. EddyHardouin 3 101+
(Carina Fey, France) *dwlt: hld up in nr-side gp: rdn over 2f out: hdwy as gps merged over 1f out: kpt on fnl f: nt pce to chal* **105/10**
**6** *nk* **Immediate**[30] 7697 5-8-10 0.................................. AurelienLemaitre 10 96
(H-F Devin, France) *cl up in centre: led that gp over 2f out to over 1f out: outpcd ins fnl f* **151/10**
**7** *3/4* **Princess Asta (FR)**[24] 4-8-10 0..............................(b) MaximPecheur 2 94
(Mario Hofer, Germany) *hld up in nr-side gp: hdwy and hung lft as gps merged over 1f out: kpt on ins fnl f: nrst fin* **34/1**
**8** *1* **Simmie (IRE)**[25] 7806 3-8-9 0.................................... TonyPiccone 12 90
(K R Burke) *cl up on far side gp: rdn over 2f out: effrt as gps merged over 1f out: wknd ins fnl f* **42/1**
**9** *1 1/4* **Downforce (IRE)**[31] 7663 5-9-0 0.......................................... WJLee 6 91
(W McCreery, Ire) *prom in nr-side gp: drvn along over 2f out: wknd over 1f out* **19/2**
**10** *hd* **Hopeless (FR)**[13] 4-9-0 0.......................................... RonanThomas 11 90
(Mme C Barande-Barbe, France) *led centre gp to over 2f out: rdn and wknd over 1f out* **106/10**
**11** *3/4* **Alwina (GER)**[29] 3-8-9 0.......................................... AntoineHamelin 8 83
(Henk Grewe, Germany) *in tch in centre gp: drvn along over 2f out: wknd over 1f out* **59/1**
**12** *2* **City Light (FR)**[21] 3-8-13 0........................................ TheoBachelot 1 80
(S Wattel, France) *hld up in tch nr-side gp: rdn and outpcd over 2f out: wknd over 1f out: eased whn btn fnl f* **69/10**[3]
1m 10.53s (-2.87) **12** Ran SP% **118.2**
PARI-MUTUEL (all including 1 euro stake): WIN 4.00; PLACE 1.80, 2.50, 2.40; DF 15.10; SF 27.30.
**Owner** Pegase Bloodstock **Bred** Mrs James Wigan **Trained** France

## 5464 MUNICH (L-H)
Wednesday, November 1
**OFFICIAL GOING: Turf: soft**

### 8527a PASTORIUS - GROSSER PREIS VON BAYERN (GROUP 1) (3YO+) (TURF) 1m 4f
**2:40** (2:40) 3-Y-O+ **£85,470** (£25,641; £12,820; £5,982; £2,564)

RPR
**1** **Guignol (GER)**[59] 6727 5-9-6 0.................................... FilipMinarik 8 117
(Jean-Pierre Carvalho, Germany) *fly-jmpd s: mde virtually all: rdn clr over 1f out: dwindling advantage ins fnl f: hld on wl* **17/5**[2]
**2** *nk* **Iquitos (GER)**[31] 7668 5-9-6 0.................................... DanielePorcu 6 117+
(H-J Groschel, Germany) *hld up in last pl: gd hdwy on wd outside wl over 1f out: chsd wnr ins fnl f: kpt on fin* **18/5**[3]
**3** *nk* **Dschingis Secret (GER)**[31] 7668 4-9-6 0........................ AdriedeVries 3 116
(Markus Klug, Germany) *hld up in tch: pushed along and outpcd over 3f out: rallied on outside wl over 1f out: kpt on fnl f: hld nr fin* **19/10**[1]
**4** *1 1/2* **Waldgeist**[25] 7805 3-9-2 0.................................. Pierre-CharlesBoudot 4 116
(A Fabre, France) *hld up: hdwy over 2f out: chsd (clr) wnr over 1f out to ins fnl f: kpt on same pce* **19/10**[1]
**5** *2* **Khan (GER)**[45] 7203 3-9-2 0..................................(p) ClementLecoeuvre 7 113
(Henk Grewe, Germany) *hld up on ins: pushed along over 3f out: effrt over 2f out: no imp fr over 1f out* **35/1**
**6** *1 1/2* **Amigo (GER)**[29] 7722 3-9-2 0............................ BauyrzhanMurzabayev 9 110
(Eva Fabianova, Germany) *racd wd of gp for over 2f: sn jnd pack: cl up: drvn and outpcd over 3f out: rallied over 2f out: no imp fr over 1f out* **42/1**
**7** *1 1/2* **Tusked Wings (IRE)**[60] 6710 3-8-13 0........................ MichaelCadeddu 1 105
(Jean-Pierre Carvalho, Germany) *in tch: effrt and chsd wnr over 2f out to over 1f out: sn wknd* **18/1**
**8** *18* **Atillio (IRE)**[60] 4-9-6 0............................................ PJMcDonald 2 77
(J D Hillis, Germany) *trckd ldrs tl rdn and wknd over 2f out* **38/1**
**9** *20* **Wild Chief (GER)**[32] 7638 6-9-6 0..............................(b[1]) KevinWoodburn 5 45
(J Hirschberger, Germany) *chsd wnr to over 2f out: sn rdn and wknd: t.o* **29/1**
2m 37.83s
**WFA** 3 from 4yo+ 5lb **9** Ran SP% **129.7**
PARI-MUTUEL (all including 10 euro stake): WIN 44 PLACE: 18, 15, 13 SF: 132.
**Owner** Stall Ullmann **Bred** Stall Ullmann **Trained** Germany

8528 - 8535a (Foreign Racing) - See Raceform Interactive

## 8371 CHELMSFORD (A.W) (L-H)
Thursday, November 2
**OFFICIAL GOING: Polytrack: standard**
Wind: light breeze Weather: cloudy, cool

### 8536 BREEDERS' CUP LIVE ON AT THE RACES NOVICE STKS 6f (P)
**5:25** (5:27) (Class 5) 2-Y-O **£4,528** (£1,347; £673; £336) **Stalls** Centre

Form RPR
3 **1** **Etisalat**[19] 8028 2-9-2 0.............................................. JimCrowley 9 79
(Owen Burrows) *chsd ldrs: hdwy into 3rd over 1f out: sn rdn: led 150yds out: kpt up to work: r.o wl* **3/1**[2]
6 **2** *1* **Jack Taylor (IRE)**[18] 8073 2-9-2 0.................................. ShaneKelly 8 76
(Richard Hughes) *chsd ldr: hdwy to ld 2f out: 1 l clr over 1f out: rdn appr fnl f: hdd 150yds out: kpt on* **25/1**
**3** *nk* **Wazin** 2-8-11 0.............................................................. RobertHavlin 2 70+
(Simon Crisford) *in rr: hdwy on outer 2f out: gd hdwy 1f out: r.o steadily fnl f* **7/1**
4123 **4** *2 1/2* **Rastacap**[24] 7891 2-9-4 80.......................................... FrannyNorton 3 69
(Mark Johnston) *broke wl: led: pushed along and hdd 2f out: rdn over 1f out: one pce* **11/10**[1]
**5** *1/2* **Taoiseach** 2-9-2 0........................................................ JamesDoyle 4 65
(Hugo Palmer) *mid-div: pushed along 2f out: reminder over 1f out: one pce under hand riding fnl f* **4/1**[3]
60 **6** *1 1/2* **Conflagration**[9] 8309 2-9-2 0...................................... JimmyQuinn 6 61
(Ed Dunlop) *hld up: pushed along over 1f out: no imp* **40/1**
6 **7** *2 3/4* **Baileys Excel**[15] 8154 2-9-2 0.................................... JoeFanning 5 52
(Chris Dwyer) *trckd ldrs: pushed along and lost pl over 2f out: no ex* **16/1**
06 **8** *1/2* **Fleeting Steps (IRE)**[9] 8309 2-9-2 0..............................(h) RyanPowell 7 50
(Sir Mark Prescott Bt) *reluctant to load: jockey mounted in stalls: a in rr* **100/1**
600 **9** *1 1/2* **Cavalry Regiment**[33] 7593 2-9-2 0................................ JasonHart 1 45
(John Quinn) *mid-div: pushed along 2f out: reminders over 1f out: fdd fnl f* **100/1**
1m 12.51s (-1.19) **Going Correction** -0.225s/f (Stan) **9** Ran SP% **119.3**
Speed ratings (Par 96): **98,96,96,92,92 90,86,85,83**
CSF £73.72 TOTE £3.90: £1.40, £4.80, £2.20; EX 68.70 Trifecta £596.10.
**Owner** Hamdan Al Maktoum **Bred** Red House Stud & Ketton Ashwell Ltd **Trained** Lambourn, Berks

**FOCUS**
Just fair novice form.

### 8537 VISIT ATTHERACES.COM/BREEDERSCUP NURSERY H'CAP 1m 2f (P)
**5:55** (5:58) (Class 5) (0-75,75) 2-Y-O **£4,528** (£1,347; £673; £336) **Stalls** Low

Form RPR
504 **1** **Baghdad (FR)**[15] 8161 2-9-6 74.................................... PJMcDonald 6 80+
(Mark Johnston) *mde all: pushed along 2f out: 1 l clr whn rdn over 1f out: r.o wl to extend advantage fnl f: readily* **7/4**[1]

0441 **2** *2* **Rustang (FR)**[7] [8371] 2-9-1 **69** 6ex....................(h) ShaneKelly 4 71
(Richard Hughes) *t.k.h: hdwy into 4th 3f out: pushed along 2f out: rdn to chse wnr 1f out: no imp ins fnl f* **9/2**[3]

4535 **3** *2* **Deadly Reel (IRE)**[35] [7552] 2-9-3 **71**.................... RichardKingscote 1 69
(Archie Watson) *trckd ldrs: pushed along in 2nd 3f out: rdn and lost 2nd 1f out: one pce fnl f* **7/1**

0323 **4** *2* **Far Dawn**[26] [7829] 2-9-1 **69**....................(v) MartinLane 8 63
(Simon Crisford) *hld up: pushed along and hdwy over 1f out: sn rdn: styd on one pce fnl f* **14/1**

0542 **5** *3/4* **Masters Apprentice (IRE)**[7] [8371] 2-8-7 **64**.............. MitchGodwin(3) 2 57
(Sylvester Kirk) *mid-div: drvn 3f out: rdn over 1f out: one pce* **7/1**

5630 **6** *2 3/4* **Ashington**[28] [7764] 2-9-3 **71**.................... JimCrowley 9 59
(Luca Cumani) *prom: 2nd 4f out: pushed along and relegated to 3rd 3f out: wknd 2f out* **10/1**

0036 **7** *1 1/4* **Mr Large (IRE)**[63] [6613] 2-9-0 **68**.................... DougieCostello 3 53
(Jamie Osborne) *in rr: drvn 2f out: rdn over 1f out: nvr a factor* **33/1**

654 **8** *1 1/4* **Falcon Eye (IRE)**[28] [7758] 2-9-7 **75**.................... JamesDoyle 7 58
(Charlie Appleby) *hld up: rdn over 2f out: no imp* **4/1**[2]

2m 5.5s (-3.10) **Going Correction** -0.225s/f (Stan) **8** Ran SP% **118.2**
Speed ratings (Par 96): **103,101,99,98,97 95,94,93**
CSF £10.25 CT £45.13 TOTE £3.00: £1.60, £1.10, £2.90; EX 12.00 Trifecta £59.30.
**Owner** Mohammed Bin Hamad Khalifa Al Attiya **Bred** S C E A Haras De Saint Pair Et Al **Trained** Middleham Moor, N Yorks

**FOCUS**
This proved straightforward for the favourite, who had an easy time of it in front.

## 8538 WATCH THE BREEDERS' CUP LIVE ON AT THE RACES H'CAP 1m (P)
6:25 (6:29) (Class 6) (0-60,62) 3-Y-O+ £3,234 (£962; £481; £240) Stalls Low

Form RPR

0532 **1** **Mach One**[7] [8376] 3-9-7 **62**....................(p) EdwardGreatrex 12 70
(Archie Watson) *trckd ldrs: pushed along and hdwy 2f out: rdn to ld over 1f out: narrow advantage ent fnl fulong: kpt on wl to assert last 150yds* **2/1**[1]

4060 **2** *1* **Never Folding (IRE)**[22] [7945] 3-8-10 **51**.................... ShaneKelly 7 57
(Seamus Durack) *reluctant to load: mid-div: drvn and hdwy over 1f out: rdn to chal ent fnl f: r.o wl to take 2nd last 100yds* **16/1**

0340 **3** *3/4* **Junoesque**[24] [7902] 3-9-3 **58**....................(p) FergusSweeney 1 62
(John Gallagher) *prom: drvn over 1f out: rdn into 2nd ent fnl f: kpt on: lost 2nd last 100yds* **16/1**

4004 **4** *1* **Samphire Coast**[9] [8328] 4-9-7 **62**....................(h) PatrickMathers 5 63
(Derek Shaw) *hld up: drvn and hdwy over 1f out: rdn and r.o ins fnl f* **5/1**[3]

3503 **5** *nk* **Miss Mirabeau**[7] [8376] 3-9-4 **59**....................(b) RyanPowell 8 61
(Sir Mark Prescott Bt) *hld up: pushed along and briefly nt clr run 1f out: r.o wl fnl f: nvr nrr* **5/1**[3]

0220 **6** *1/2* **Breaking Free**[27] [7792] 3-8-6 **47**....................(p[1]) JFEgan 6 46
(John Quinn) *mid-div: pushed along and hdwy over 1f out: rdn fnl f: no ex* **10/1**

3035 **7** *1* **Ronni Layne**[16] [8133] 3-8-10 **51**.................... RobertHavlin 9 48
(Conrad Allen) *chsd leaer: drvn and lost pl over 1f out: rdn and no ex fnl f* **16/1**

0000 **8** *2* **Cookie Ring (IRE)**[12] [8248] 6-8-7 **46** oh1....................(t) ShaneGray 11 38
(Kristin Stubbs) *hld up: drvn over 1f out: rdn fnl f: one pce* **33/1**

6-05 **9** *nk* **African Showgirl**[11] [8254] 4-9-7 **60**.................... JosephineGordon 13 52
(Ivan Furtado) *mid-div: drvn over 1f out: rdn and no ex fnl f* **33/1**

-000 **10** *3/4* **Tilly Devine**[28] [7761] 3-8-5 **46** oh1.................... KieranO'Neill 4 36
(Scott Dixon) *led: drvn 2f out: rdn and hdd over 1f out: wknd* **66/1**

0440 **11** *2 3/4* **Subotal (IRE)**[2] [8498] 4-8-0 **46** oh1.................... JackOsborn(7) 15 29
(Richard Guest) *in rr: drvn on outer 2f out: sn rdn and no imp* **40/1**

0002 **12** *nk* **Wootyhoot (FR)**[28] [7761] 3-9-1 **59**.................... GeorgeWood(3) 10 45+
(James Fanshawe) *hld up: drvn and hmpd over 1f out: sn rdn: no imp* **4/1**[2]

0520 **13** *nk* **Frangarry (IRE)**[28] [7763] 5-8-8 **52**....................(t) JoshuaBryan(5) 3 34+
(Alan Bailey) *mid-div: rdn 1f out: no imp: eased fnl f* **25/1**

3650 **14** *1/2* **Blackadder**[14] [8181] 5-8-2 **46** oh1....................(p[1]) MeganNicholls(5) 14 27
(Mark Gillard) *mid-div: hdwy on outer 2f out: wknd 1f out* **66/1**

3004 **15** *3/4* **Ripper Street (IRE)**[17] [8123] 3-8-0 **46**....................(h) JaneElliott(5) 2 25
(Christine Dunnett) *hld up: rdn over 1f out: nvr a factor* **33/1**

1m 38.98s (-0.92) **Going Correction** -0.225s/f (Stan)
**WFA** 3 from 4yo+ 2lb **15** Ran SP% **131.5**
Speed ratings (Par 101): **95,94,93,92,91 91,90,88,88,87 84,84,84,83,82**
CSF £41.73 CT £459.22 TOTE £3.10: £1.30, £4.50, £4.20; EX 53.70 Trifecta £478.70.
**Owner** Dr Bridget Drew & Partners **Bred** Mildmay Bloodstock Ltd **Trained** Upper Lambourn, W Berks

**FOCUS**
A fair handicap. The form makes sense in behind the winner.

## 8539 GET IN! BREEDERS' CUP SPECIAL FRIDAY ON ATR H'CAP 1m 6f (P)
6:55 (6:56) (Class 2) (0-105,106) 3-Y-O+
£12,450 (£3,728; £1,864; £932; £466; £234) Stalls Low

Form RPR

1100 **1** **Joshua Reynolds**[20] [8011] 3-8-9 **92**....................(b) RobertHavlin 7 100+
(John Gosden) *mid-div: pushed along and hdwy into 2nd 2f out: drvn to ld over 1f out: rdn ent fnl f: sn c clr: readily* **9/2**[3]

1260 **2** *2 1/2* **Watersmeet**[19] [8038] 6-10-1 **106**.................... JoeFanning 1 110
(Mark Johnston) *trckd ldr: tk clsr order 4f out: led over 2f out: rdn and hdd over 1f out: kpt on fnl f* **9/4**[1]

5/20 **3** *1/2* **High Secret (IRE)**[135] [3928] 6-8-13 **95**.................... MeganNicholls(5) 4 98
(Paul Nicholls) *hld up in last: effrt and drvn on outer 2f out where involved in scrimmaging w 6th home: rdn over 1f out: styd on fnl f* **9/1**

3400 **4** *3/4* **Lord George (IRE)**[48] [7115] 4-9-2 **96**.................... GeorgeWood(3) 2 98
(James Fanshawe) *trckd ldrs: drvn over 1f out: rdn and one pce fnl f* **7/2**[2]

0/60 **5** *nk* **Aussie Reigns (IRE)**[18] [8076] 7-9-1 **95**.................... HectorCrouch(3) 3 97
(Gary Moore) *hld up: drvn and n.m.r 2f out: rdn fnl f: one pce* **33/1**

-602 **6** *2 3/4* **Battersea**[48] [7124] 6-9-9 **100**.................... JackMitchell 6 98
(Roger Varian) *hld up: effrt whn involved in scrimmaging w 3rd home and n.m.r 2f out: drvn over 1f out: no imp* **7/2**[2]

6006 **7** *12* **Barye**[12] [8244] 6-9-1 **92**.................... ShaneKelly 5 73
(Richard Hughes) *led: pushed along and hdd over 2f out: sn dropped to rr* **12/1**

2m 58.05s (-5.15) **Going Correction** -0.225s/f (Stan)
**WFA** 3 from 4yo+ 6lb **7** Ran SP% **114.0**
Speed ratings (Par 109): **105,103,103,102,102 101,94**
CSF £14.99 TOTE £5.30: £2.70, £1.80; EX 17.20 Trifecta £75.80.
**Owner** Castle Down Racing & Rachel Hood **Bred** Meon Valley Stud **Trained** Newmarket, Suffolk

**FOCUS**
A decent staying contest. The runner-up has been rated to his best.

## 8540 BREEDERS' CUP STARTS FRIDAY ON AT THE RACES H'CAP 5f (P)
7:25 (7:26) (Class 4) (0-85,87) 3-Y-O+
£6,225 (£1,864; £932; £466; £233; £117) Stalls Low

Form RPR

6241 **1** **You're Cool**[37] [7486] 5-8-11 **75**.................... JoeDoyle 8 84
(John Balding) *broke wl: mde all: drvn into 1 l ld over 1f out: rdn ent fnl f: ld diminishing nr fin: jst hld on* **11/1**

1-04 **2** *shd* **Gorgeous Noora (IRE)**[16] [8129] 3-9-2 **80**.................... JimCrowley 1 88
(Luca Cumani) *trckd leaers: pushed along and hdwy over 1f out: rdn to chal ins fnl f: r.o wl and clsng on wnr nr fin: jst hld* **7/2**[2]

124 **3** *1 3/4* **Menelik (IRE)**[41] [7367] 8-9-1 **79**....................(vt) DavidProbert 3 81
(Des Donovan, Ire) *trckd ldrs: drvn over 1f out: sn rdn: kpt on one pce fnl f* **12/1**

1003 **4** *1 3/4* **Penny Dreadful**[11] [8260] 5-8-1 **72**....................(b) GabrieleMalune(7) 5 68+
(Scott Dixon) *in rr: pushed along 2f out: hdwy 1f out: rdn and r.o ins fnl f: nvr nrr* **20/1**

2500 **5** *1* **Top Boy**[20] [8012] 7-9-0 **78**....................(v) FrannyNorton 2 70
(Derek Shaw) *hld up: drvn over 1f out: rdn and kpt on fnl f* **3/1**[1]

0140 **6** *shd* **Tylery Wonder (IRE)**[12] [8238] 7-9-7 **85**....................(v) MartinLane 7 77
(Paul Midgley) *prom: drvn 1/2-way: rdn and wknd over 1f out* **16/1**

4146 **7** *1 1/4* **Dynamo Walt (IRE)**[134] [3967] 6-9-7 **85**....................(v) PatrickMathers 6 72
(Derek Shaw) *mid-div: pushed along 2f out: rdn over 1f out: no imp* **25/1**

1160 **8** *nk* **Saved My Bacon (IRE)**[20] [7994] 6-8-11 **78**.........(h) LewisEdmunds(3) 11 64
(Chris Dwyer) *in rr: racd v wd over 2f out: rdn on wd outside over 1f out: no imp* **14/1**

152 **9** *hd* **Super Julius**[61] [6695] 3-9-7 **85**....................(p) CharlesBishop 9 70
(Eve Johnson Houghton) *hld up: drvn 2f out: rdn 1f out: no imp* **8/1**

0400 **10** *1 1/2* **Gentlemen**[16] [8129] 6-9-9 **87**....................(h) JosephineGordon 10 67
(Phil McEntee) *in rr: drvn and wnt wd 2f out: nvr got involved* **25/1**

005 **11** *1* **Aleef (IRE)**[12] [8238] 4-9-5 **83**....................(h) JamesDoyle 4 59
(David O'Meara) *chsd ldr: pushed along 2f out: rdn and weakend over 1f out* **4/1**[3]

58.55s (-1.65) **Going Correction** -0.225s/f (Stan) **11** Ran SP% **119.4**
Speed ratings (Par 105): **104,103,101,98,96 96,94,94,93,91 89**
CSF £48.92 CT £484.56 TOTE £11.80: £3.30, £1.70, £3.50; EX 59.20 Trifecta £723.50.
**Owner** D Bichan & F Connor **Bred** Tirnaskea Stud **Trained** Scrooby, S Yorks

**FOCUS**
This looked quite competitive but the winner impressed in making every yard once again. A length pb from the runner-up, with the third rated to his Irish latest.

## 8541 BREEDERS' CUP TIPS ON ATTHERACES.COM H'CAP (DIV I) 6f (P)
7:55 (7:56) (Class 5) (0-75,81) 3-Y-O+ £5,175 (£1,540; £769; £384) Stalls Centre

Form RPR

211 **1** **Diagnostic**[7] [8374] 3-9-13 **81** 6ex.................... JamesDoyle 5 99+
(William Haggas) *hld up: hdwy on outer 2f out: rdn to chal over 1f out: clsd on ldr ent fnl f: led 150yds out: qckly c clr: easily* **4/9**[1]

5002 **2** *4* **Impart**[9] [8320] 3-9-6 **74**.................... JimCrowley 4 79
(David O'Meara) *disp ld tl led on own 1/2-way: rdn over 1f out: 1 l clr ent fnl f: hdd 150yds out: no ex* **6/1**[2]

262 **3** *3/4* **Logi (IRE)**[40] [7409] 3-9-4 **72**....................(b) PhillipMakin 7 75
(Richard Guest) *disp ld tl 1/2-way where settled in 2nd: rdn wl over 1f out: relegated to 3rd ent fnl f: kpt on* **11/1**

5344 **4** *nk* **Munfallet (IRE)**[32] [7653] 6-9-7 **75**.................... SeanLevey 9 77
(David Brown) *prom: pushed along 2f out: rdn over 1f out: one pce* **20/1**

5006 **5** *2 1/4* **Vroom (IRE)**[10] [8296] 4-8-12 **73**....................(e[1]) PaulHainey(7) 6 67
(Gay Kelleway) *trckd ldrs: drvn in 5th over 1f out: rdn fnl f: no ex* **66/1**

1152 **6** *3 3/4* **Deeds Not Words (IRE)**[117] [4607] 6-9-4 **72**.................... FrannyNorton 3 54
(Michael Wigham) *hld up: pushed along 2f out: drvn and mod hdwy over 1f out: one pce fnl f* **7/1**[3]

000 **7** *1 1/4* **Ruled By The Moon**[150] [3393] 3-8-9 **63**....................(p[1]) DavidProbert 1 41
(Ivan Furtado) *in rr: drvn 1/2-way: rdn over 1f out: no imp* **66/1**

00 **8** *3/4* **Malaysian Boleh**[9] [8329] 7-9-1 **69**....................(v) JosephineGordon 2 45
(Phil McEntee) *drvn in rr: brief effrt over 1f out: no imp* **50/1**

64 **9** *13* **Madame Bounty (IRE)**[26] [7811] 3-9-9 **77**.................... LiamKeniry 8 11
(Ed Walker) *trckd ldrs: pushed along 2f out: drvn and wknd qckly over 1f out* **8/1**

1m 11.42s (-2.28) **Going Correction** -0.225s/f (Stan) **9** Ran SP% **125.2**
Speed ratings (Par 103): **106,100,99,99,96 91,89,88,71**
CSF £4.29 CT £17.34 TOTE £1.40: £1.10, £1.80, £2.30; EX 4.20 Trifecta £22.60.
**Owner** Cheveley Park Stud **Bred** Cheveley Park Stud Ltd **Trained** Newmarket, Suffolk

**FOCUS**
The short-priced favourite confirmed she's well ahead of her mark. The runner-up has been rated to his latest, with the third close to form.

## 8542 BREEDERS' CUP TIPS ON ATTHERACES.COM H'CAP (DIV II) 6f (P)
8:30 (8:30) (Class 5) (0-75,77) 3-Y-O+ £5,175 (£1,540; £769; £384) Stalls Centre

Form RPR

5664 **1** **Bahamian Heights**[15] [8159] 6-8-8 **69**.................... JonathanFisher(7) 10 75
(Robert Cowell) *awkward and slowly away: latched on to pack after 1f: rdn and hdwy over 1f out: str run ins fnl f: led 50yds out* **25/1**

6303 **2** *nk* **Born To Finish (IRE)**[15] [8159] 4-9-6 **74**....................(p) DougieCostello 5 79
(Jamie Osborne) *hld up: hdwy on outer over 1f out: rdn ins fnl f: r.o wl but jst denied by fast-fining wnr* **9/2**[3]

-540 **3** *nk* **Spin Top**[257] [813] 3-8-7 **61**.................... FrannyNorton 3 65
(William Muir) *led: pushed along 2f out: 1 l clr and rdn over 1f out: hdd last 50yds: lost 2nd last few strides* **16/1**

4605 **4** *3/4* **Fredricka**[9] [8320] 6-9-6 **77**....................(p) EoinWalsh(3) 7 79
(Ivan Furtado) *trckd ldrs: 3rd 2f out: rdn into 2nd over 1f out: one pce and lost two pls fnl f* **12/1**

434 **5** *1* **Debonaire David**[5] [8433] 3-9-4 **72**....................(t[1]) ShaneKelly 2 70
(Richard Hughes) *mid-div: pushed along whn nt clr run over 1f out: sn in clr: kpt on ins fnl f* **2/1**[1]

0020 **6** *1 1/4* **Lord Cooper**[30] [7709] 3-9-8 **76**....................(tp) OscarPereira 6 70
(Jose Santos) *mid-div: pushed along 2f out: rdn over 1f out: no imp* **16/1**

5061 **7** *nk* **Love Oasis**[12] [8243] 3-9-2 **70**.................... PJMcDonald 4 63
(Mark Johnston) *trckd ldrs: rdn and ev ch over 1f out: wknd fnl f* **10/3**[2]

5300 **8** *1 1/4* **Anfaass (IRE)**[17] [8115] 3-9-7 **75**....................(p[1]) TomQueally 1 64
(George Margarson) *hld up: rdn over 1f out: no imp* **6/1**

4406 **9** 4 ½ **Nag's Wag (IRE)**[42] 7320 4-8-8 **62**.......... DavidProbert 8 37
(Conor Dore) *cl 2nd: pushed along 2f out: rdn and wknd qckly over 1f out* **28/1**

1m 11.9s (-1.80) **Going Correction** -0.225s/f (Stan) **9** Ran SP% **115.6**
Speed ratings (Par 103): **103,102,102,101,99 98,97,96,90**
CSF £134.20 CT £1899.84 TOTE £20.30: £6.50, £1.20, £4.90; EX 183.90 Trifecta £4060.70 Part Won..
**Owner** Mrs J Morley & A Rix **Bred** Pantile Stud **Trained** Six Mile Bottom, Cambs
■ Stewards' Enquiry : Jonathan Fisher two-day ban: using of whip above shoulder height (16/17 Nov)

**FOCUS**
The slower of the two divisions by 0.48sec. They didn't seem to go that quick early but the first two came from the back of the field. The runner-up has been rated to form.

## 8543 BOOK YOUR CHRISTMAS PARTY AT CHELMSFORDCITYRACECOURSE.COM H'CAP 7f (P)
**9:00** (9:02) (Class 7) (0-50,50) 3-Y-0+ **£2,911** (£866; £432; £216) **Stalls** Low

Form RPR

0000 **1** **Mr Andros**[23] 7916 4-9-5 **48**..........(bt[1]) ShaneKelly 12 58
(Brendan Powell) *hld up: hdwy on outer over 1f out: rdn and led ins fnl f: readily c clr: comf* **20/1**

0036 **2** 3 **Banta Bay**[22] 7945 3-9-4 **48**..........(p[1]) JosephineGordon 11 49
(John Best) *mid-div: drvn 3f out: hdwy 2f out: rdn and ev ch over 1f out: kpt on ins fnl f: tk 2nd nr fin* **8/1**

0205 **3** hd **Miss Uppity**[28] 7763 4-8-13 **45**.......... EoinWalsh(3) 2 46
(Ivan Furtado) *trckd ldrs: drvn to chal over 1f out: led 1f out: sn hdd: rdn and one pce: lost 2nd nr fin* **12/1**

5620 **4** 4 ½ **Dawn Goddess**[21] 7990 3-9-0 **47**.......... HectorCrouch(3) 5 35
(Gary Moore) *hld up: rdn 3f out: hdwy over 1f out: r.o ins fnl f: tk 4th on fining line* **12/1**

2444 **5** nse **Caledonian Gold**[33] 7606 4-9-4 **47**.......... JoeyHaynes 10 36
(Paul D'Arcy) *cl up in 2nd: drvn 3f out: rdn 2f out: one pce fnl f: lost 4th on fining line* **5/1[2]**

-062 **6** ¾ **Dream Revival**[28] 7763 4-9-7 **50**..........(p) PJMcDonald 9 37
(Paul Collins) *led: rdn and hdd 1f out: wknd fnl f* **5/1[2]**

300 **7** ½ **Latest Quest (IRE)**[16] 8134 3-8-8 **45**..........(b[1]) ShariqMohd(7) 1 30
(Sylvester Kirk) *trckd ldrs: 3rd gng wl 2f out: rdn and fnd nthing wl over 1f out: fdd fnl f* **7/1[3]**

0605 **8** 4 **Gog Elles (IRE)**[12] 8247 3-9-5 **49**..........(b) BenCurtis 6 23
(J S Moore) *prom: drvn over 2f out: rdn over 1f out: wknd* **12/1**

0000 **9** 2 ¼ **Parisian Chic (IRE)**[57] 6813 3-9-3 **50**.......... CharlieBennett(3) 14 18
(Lee Carter) *v.s.a fr wd draw: pushed along to join pack after 1 f: drvn in rr 2f out: no imp* **33/1**

4402 **10** ¾ **All Or Nothin (IRE)**[11] 8258 8-8-13 **45**.......... CallumShepherd(3) 7 12
(Paddy Butler) *mid-div: pushed along 2f out: sn drvn and wknd: eased fnl f* **10/1**

5022 **11** 1 **Touch The Clouds**[37] 7480 6-8-12 **46**.......... ManuelFernandes(5) 8 10
(William Stone) *hld up: drvn in rr 2f out: eased fnl f* **4/1[1]**

5405 **U** **Hidden Stash**[23] 7928 3-9-0 **49**..........(p[1]) JoshuaBryan(5) 3
(William Stone) *trckd ldrs: hdwy on outer over 1f out: u.p whn sddle slipped and jockey uns over 1f out* **11/1**

1m 25.99s (-1.21) **Going Correction** -0.225s/f (Stan)
**WFA** 3 from 4yo+ 1lb **12** Ran SP% **125.1**
Speed ratings (Par 97): **97,93,93,88,88 87,86,82,79,78 77,**
CSF £181.27 CT £2072.60 TOTE £19.70: £7.60, £3.80, £6.20; EX 236.70 Trifecta £3823.00 Part Won..
**Owner** Winterbeck Manor Stud **Bred** A Christou **Trained** Upper Lambourn, Berks
■ Sammy's Choice was withdrawn. Price at time of withdrawal 50/1. Rule 4 does not apply

**FOCUS**
A low-grade handicap. There was a nasty incident when the saddle slipped on Hidden Stash and Joshua Bryan was unseated early in the straight.
T/Plt: £53.50 to a £1 stake. Pool: £103,021.61 - 1,404.93 winning units T/Qpdt: £14.30 to a £1 stake. Pool: £11,918.25 - 616.30 winning units **Keith McHugh**

# 8153 LINGFIELD (L-H)
Thursday, November 2

**OFFICIAL GOING: Polytrack: standard**
Wind: virtually nil Weather: light cloud

## 8544 32RED CASINO/BRITISH STALLION STUDS EBF FILLIES' NOVICE STKS (PLUS 10 RACE) 7f 1y(P)
**12:15** (12:17) (Class 5) 2-Y-O **£2,911** (£866; £432; £216) **Stalls** Low

Form RPR

35 **1** **West Palm Beach (IRE)**[28] 7757 2-8-12 0.......... RobertHavlin 9 77
(John Gosden) *trckd ldng trio: effrt over 1f out: hdwy u.p 1f out: styd on strly ins fnl f to ld last strides* **8/1**

2 **2** nk **Bubble And Squeak**[15] 8148 2-8-9 0.......... MitchGodwin(3) 7 76
(Sylvester Kirk) *hld up in tch in midfield: effrt over 1f out: str run u.p ins fnl f: ev ch towards fin: kpt on* **13/2[3]**

022 **3** nk **Scandaleuse (USA)**[20] 7995 2-8-12 77.......... TedDurcan 1 75
(Sir Michael Stoute) *led: rdn over 1f out: drvn ins fnl f: hdd and lost 2 pls last strides* **11/8[1]**

4 **4** nse **Ghanimah**[20] 7995 2-8-12 0.......... JimCrowley 2 75
(William Haggas) *chsd ldr: rdn over 1f out: drvn ins fnl f: styd on u.p and ev ch towards fin: kpt on* **2/1[2]**

**5** 4 **Moon Song** 2-8-9 0.......... HectorCrouch(3) 3 64
(Clive Cox) *trckd ldng pair: effrt 2f out: no ex u.p ins fnl f: wknd fnl 100yds* **22/1**

**6** 1 ¾ **Noteworthy (IRE)** 2-8-12 0.......... ShaneKelly 6 60
(Richard Hughes) *stdd s: hld up in tch in midfield: pushed along 2f out: outpcd u.p over 1f out: no threat to ldrs but kpt on ins fnl f* **50/1**

**7** nk **Tajarrob (IRE)** 2-8-12 0.......... PJMcDonald 8 59
(Ed Dunlop) *hld up in tch in rr of main gp: pushed along 2f out: sn outpcd: no ch w ldrs but kpt on ins fnl f* **50/1**

0 **8** 7 **Edge Of The World (IRE)**[44] 7226 2-8-12 0.......... DavidProbert 5 40
(Ralph Beckett) *rn in snatches: in tch in rr of main gp: rdn 2f out: sn outpcd and wknd over 1f out* **16/1**

**9** 21 **Black Lace** 2-8-12 0.......... JackMitchell 4
(Steve Woodman) *sn dropped to rr and outpcd in detached last: t.o* **150/1**

1m 23.77s (-1.03) **Going Correction** -0.20s/f (Stan) **9** Ran SP% **114.7**
Speed ratings (Par 93): **97,96,96,96,91 89,89,81,57**
CSF £56.55 TOTE £8.70: £2.20, £1.90, £1.10; EX 37.50 Trifecta £146.20.
**Owner** Mrs Doreen Tabor **Bred** Lynch - Bages & Longfield Stud **Trained** Newmarket, Suffolk

**FOCUS**
Just a fair fillies' novice event. Five of these had run before and four of them finished in a heap, suggesting the form isn't outstanding. It's been rated with feet on the ground.

## 8545 32REDSPORT.COM / BRITISH STALLION STUDS EBF NOVICE STKS 7f 1y(P)
**12:45** (12:47) (Class 5) 2-Y-O **£2,911** (£866; £432; £216) **Stalls** Low

Form RPR

**1** **Statehood (IRE)** 2-9-2 0.......... JamesDoyle 5 82+
(Charlie Appleby) *wl in tch in midfield: effrt over 1f out: chsd wnr 1f out: styd on wl to ld last strides* **5/1[2]**

4 **2** nk **On The Warpath**[27] 7788 2-9-2 0.......... RyanPowell 11 82
(Sir Mark Prescott Bt) *hdwy to ld after 1f out: rdn over 1f out: drvn ins fnl f: kpt on tl hdd and no ex last strides* **14/1**

12 **3** nse **Il Primo Sole**[43] 7274 2-9-9 0.......... RobertHavlin 8 91+
(John Gosden) *hld up in midfield: nt clr run and swtchd rt wl over 1f out: hdwy into midfield and swtchd rt 1f out: styd on strly fnl 100yds: nt quite rch ldrs* **4/7[1]**

06 **4** 3 ½ **Metkaif**[15] 8149 2-9-2 0.......... SeanLevey 4 72
(Richard Hannon) *chsd ldrs: wnt 2nd over 3f out: rdn and unable qck over 1f out: lost 2nd 1f out: wknd ins fnl f* **7/1[3]**

**5** 2 ½ **Brigham Young** 2-9-2 0.......... LiamKeniry 9 65+
(Ed Walker) *dwlt: in tch in midfield: pushed along ent fnl 2f: outpcd over 1f out: no threat to ldrs but kpt on steadily ins fnl f* **25/1**

60 **6** ½ **Sheriff**[17] 8119 2-9-2 0.......... LouisSteward 1 67
(Michael Bell) *stdd after s: bhd: carried rt and hmpd after 1f out: clsd over 2f out: c wd and effrt over 1f out: kpt on ins fnl f: nvr trbld ldrs* **66/1**

64 **7** 1 ½ **Jeopardy John**[19] 8028 2-9-2 0.......... DavidProbert 10 60
(Michael Attwater) *in tch in midfield: rdn and outpcd 2f out: wl hld and kpt on same pce fr over 1f out* **50/1**

1 **8** 1 **N Over J**[24] 7897 2-9-6 0.......... JimCrowley 7 61
(William Knight) *t.k.h: led for 1f: chsd ldr tl over 3f out: rdn ent fnl 2f: sn struggling and outpcd over 1f out: wknd ins fnl f* **8/1**

**9** 2 ¼ **Barnay** 2-8-9 0..........(h[1]) TylerSaunders(7) 6 51
(Marcus Tregoning) *sn pushed along in last quartet: outpcd ent fnl 2f: wl btn over 1f out: wknd fnl f* **50/1**

**10** 1 ¼ **Purple Jazz (IRE)** 2-9-2 0.......... PatCosgrave 2 48
(George Baker) *sn dropped to rr: swtchd rt after 1f: rdn 2f out: sn struggling and wknd over 1f out: bhd ins fnl f* **66/1**

06 **11** 1 ¾ **Archibald Leitch**[21] 7985 2-9-2 0.......... FranBerry 3 43
(David Evans) *sn dropped towards rr: last and rdn over 3f out: swtchd rt 2f out: no imp: bhd fnl f* **150/1**

1m 23.42s (-1.38) **Going Correction** -0.20s/f (Stan) **11** Ran SP% **122.0**
Speed ratings (Par 96): **99,98,98,94,91 91,89,88,85,84 82**
CSF £68.98 TOTE £5.30: £1.50, £3.10, £1.10; EX 72.80 Trifecta £216.70.
**Owner** Godolphin **Bred** Patrick Cassidy **Trained** Newmarket, Suffolk

**FOCUS**
Not the deepest of races, but two previous winners and a couple of well-bred newcomers made it interesting. Again the principals finished close together, but a couple caught the eye and the form should work out. The winning time was 0.35sec quicker than the fillies in the opener. A step forward from the runner-up.

## 8546 32RED EBF STALLIONS FLEUR DE LYS FILLIES' STKS (LISTED RACE) (ALL-WEATHER FAST-TRACK QUALIFIER) 1m 1y(P)
**1:20** (1:26) (Class 1) 3-Y-O£22,684 (£8,600; £4,304; £2,144; £1,076; £540) **Stalls** High

4105 **1** **Muffri'Ha (IRE)**[19] 8041 5-9-3 107.......... JamesDoyle 11 100
(William Haggas) *sn pressing ldr: rdn to ld over 1f out: qcknd and asserted u.p 1f out: in command ins fnl f: r.o* **11/8[1]**

0543 **2** 1 **Zest (IRE)**[63] 6619 4-9-0 93.......... DanielMuscutt 7 94
(James Fanshawe) *chsd ldng trio: effrt over 1f out: 3rd and drvn 1f out: chsd wnr wl ins fnl f: kpt on wl but nvr getting to wnr* **20/1**

1304 **3** ½ **Promising Run (USA)**[36] 7506 4-9-0 106..........(v) PatCosgrave 8 93
(Saeed bin Suroor) *sn led: rdn and hdd over 1f out: kpt on same pce ins fnl f: lost 2nd wl ins fnl f* **11/4[2]**

6630 **4** ¾ **Mia Tesoro (IRE)**[20] 8007 4-9-0 78..........(h) PJMcDonald 2 91
(Charlie Fellowes) *taken down early: hld up in tch in midfield: effrt 2f out: swtchd rt over 1f out: hdwy to go 4th ins fnl f: kpt on wl but no threat to wnr* **50/1**

2165 **5** 1 **Pirouette**[26] 7808 4-9-3 107..........(b) CharlieBennett 9 92
(Hughie Morrison) *hld up in tch in midfield: effrt over 1f out: kpt on same pce u.p ins fnl f* **8/1**

2101 **6** ¾ **Rinaria (IRE)**[26] 7830 3-8-12 78.......... JoeyHaynes 5 87+
(K R Burke) *hld up in tch in last quintet: effrt over 1f out: hdwy ins fnl f: r.o wl fnl 100yds: nvr trbld ldrs* **50/1**

000 **7** ½ **Somethingthrilling**[34] 7576 5-9-0 90..........(t[1]) ShaneKelly 10 86
(David Elsworth) *t.k.h early: hld up in tch in rr: wd and sme hdwy bnd 2f out: styd on and swtchd rt ins fnl f: nvr trbld ldrs* **50/1**

4100 **8** ½ **Melesina (IRE)**[32] 7669 3-8-12 103.......... BarryMcHugh 3 84
(Richard Fahey) *chsd ldng pair: rdn and unable qck over 1f out: lost 3rd 1f out: wknd ins fnl f* **20/1**

0100 **9** nk **Favourite Royal (IRE)**[26] 7815 3-8-12 79..........(v[1]) CharlesBishop 1 84
(Eve Johnson Houghton) *flashing tail leaving stalls: hld up in tch in last quartet: nt clr run 2f out: effrt on inner over 1f out: no imp fnl f* **66/1**

-506 **10** ¾ **Belle Meade (IRE)**[26] 7808 3-8-12 89.......... DavidProbert 6 82
(Andrew Balding) *t.k.h: hld up in tch in rr: effrt u.p over 1f out: kpt on but nvr threatened ldrs* **25/1**

150 **11** nse **Simply Me**[37] 7484 4-9-0 80..........(p) RichardKingscote 4 82
(Tom Dascombe) *hld up in tch in midfield: rdn over 2f out: unable qck and struggling over 1f out: wknd ins fnl f* **40/1**

1641 **12** 4 ½ **Khamaary (IRE)**[26] 7823 3-8-12 100.......... JimCrowley 12 71
(Mark Johnston) *hld up in tch in last quartet and styd wd early: rdn over 2f out: sn struggling: bhd ins fnl f: fin lame* **6/1[3]**

1m 35.01s (-3.19) **Going Correction** -0.20s/f (Stan)
**WFA** 3 from 4yo+ 2lb **12** Ran SP% **117.4**
Speed ratings (Par 108): **107,106,105,104,103 103,102,102,101,100 100,96**
CSF £36.46 TOTE £2.20: £1.50, £4.50, £1.10; EX 26.30 Trifecta £80.80.
**Owner** Sheikh Juma Dalmook Al Maktoum **Bred** Lodge Park Stud **Trained** Newmarket, Suffolk

**FOCUS**
A decent Listed event and a Fast-Track Qualifier for the Fillies & Mares Championship back here on Good Friday. They bet 20-1 bar four and, with the pace far from solid, it paid to be handy with the first three always in the first four positions. The fourth, sixth and ninth suggest the form is below par for the grade. The fourth has been rated to the better view of her form.

## 8547 PLAY JACKPOT GAMES AT SUNBETS.CO.UK/VEGAS H'CAP 7f 1y(P)
1:50 (1:55) (Class 2) (0-105,99) 3-Y-O+ £11,971 (£3,583; £1,791; £896; £446) Stalls Low

Form RPR
0621 1 **Gulliver**[26] 7828 3-9-5 **95**........................(tp) JamesDoyle 3 103
(Hugo Palmer) *hld up in tch in midfield: effrt to chse ldrs and swtchd rt over 1f out: drvn to ld ins fnl f: r.o wl and a holding chalr* 9/4[1]

-036 2 *nk* **Sacred Act**[55] 6873 6-9-7 **96**........................ FranBerry 6 104
(Michael Bell) *hld up in tch in midfield: effrt to chse ldrs over 1f out: drvn and hdwy to chal ins fnl f: r.o wl and c clr w wnr: a jst hld* 12/1

3030 3 2 ¼ **Shyron**[40] 7404 6-8-9 **89**........................ JaneElliott(5) 11 91
(George Margarson) *hld up in last pair: hdwy on inner over 1f out: nt clr run and swtchd rt ins fnl f: wnt 3rd wl ins fnl f: nvr getting to ldrs* 14/1

3600 4 *nk* **Alfred Hutchinson**[187] 2141 9-9-7 **96**........................(p) KieranShoemark 7 97
(David O'Meara) *hld up in tch towards rr: effrt jst over 1f out: hdwy ins fnl f: styd on wl u.p: no threat to ldng pair* 25/1

055 5 1 **Charles Molson**[150] 3410 6-9-8 **97**........................ JimCrowley 14 95+
(Patrick Chamings) *stdd s: hld up in last pair: clsd on inner nt clr run 1f out tl swtchd rt wl ins fnl f: pushed along and styd on towards fin: nvr trbld ldrs* 9/1

0242 6 *hd* **Easy Tiger**[27] 7789 5-8-10 **85**........................ PJMcDonald 10 83+
(Malcolm Saunders) *chsd ldrs: rdn and unable qck over 1f out: kpt on u.p ins fnl f: nvr getting on terms w ldng pair* 4/1[2]

0100 7 ¾ **Highland Acclaim (IRE)**[6] 8383 6-9-1 **90**........................(h) DavidProbert 2 86
(David O'Meara) *sn bustled along to ld: drvn over 1f out: hdd ins fnl f: no ex and wknd wl ins fnl f* 66/1

2020 8 *nk* **Mutawathea**[26] 7807 6-9-10 **99**........................(p) RobertHavlin 13 94+
(Simon Crisford) *hld up in tch in midfield: nt clr run and shuffled bk to rr over 1f out: swtchd rt ins fnl f: styd on towards fin: nvr trbld ldrs* 12/1

0053 9 *hd* **Barracuda Boy (IRE)**[26] 7828 7-9-5 **94**........................ BarryMcHugh 9 89
(Marjorie Fife) *ponied to s and taken down early: chsd ldr: rdn over 1f out: unable qck 1f out: wknd ins fnl f* 28/1

200- 10 *hd* **Bobby Wheeler (IRE)**[425] 6109 4-8-12 **90**........................ HectorCrouch(3) 5 84
(Clive Cox) *t.k.h: chsd ldrs: rdn and unable qck whn swtchd rt jst over 1f out: wknd ins fnl f* 10/1

4001 11 ¾ **Miracle Of Medinah**[66] 6540 6-9-0 **94**........................ JoshuaBryan(5) 8 86
(Mark Usher) *hld up in tch towards rr: effrt over 1f out: drvn and no imp jst ins fnl f: nvr trbld ldrs* 25/1

0005 12 *hd* **Mr Bossy Boots (IRE)**[19] 8032 6-9-1 **90**........................(p) RichardKingscote 1 81+
(Amanda Perrett) *trckd ldrs: pressing ldrs whn short of room jst over 1f out: nvr enough room after and forced to ease ins fnl f* 13/2[3]

4030 13 *nse* **Chestnut Fire**[126] 4261 5-8-13 **88**........................ ShaneKelly 4 79
(Daniel Mark Loughnane) *hld up in tch in midfield: effrt over 1f out: no imp whn sltly impeded ins fnl f: wknd fnl 100yds* 50/1

1m 22.48s (-2.32) **Going Correction** -0.20s/f (Stan)
**WFA** 3 from 4yo+ 1lb 13 Ran SP% **119.8**
Speed ratings (Par 109): **105,104,102,101,100 100,99,99,98,98 97,97,97**
CSF £29.82 CT £328.45 TOTE £3.30: £1.40, £3.70, £4.40; EX 35.20 Trifecta £315.10.
**Owner** Saleh Al Homaizi & Imad Al Sagar **Bred** S A Douch **Trained** Newmarket, Suffolk

**FOCUS**
A typically competitive Lingfield handicap of its type, but the favourite did it nicely. The third has been rated close to last winter's form.

## 8548 32RED EBF STALLIONS RIVER EDEN FILLIES' STKS (LISTED RACE) 1m 5f (P)
2:25 (2:26) (Class 1) 3-Y-O+
£22,684 (£8,600; £4,304; £2,144; £1,076; £540) Stalls Low

Form RPR
1-14 1 **Daphne**[17] 8121 4-9-3 93........................ JimCrowley 2 98
(William Haggas) *trckd ldrs: swtchd rt and effrt to chal between horses over 1f out: rdn to ld jst ins fnl f: r.o wl* 7/2[2]

1132 2 1 ½ **Melodic Motion (IRE)**[49] 7089 3-8-12 102........................ JamesDoyle 4 96
(Ralph Beckett) *hld up in tch in midfield: edgd rt over 6f out: hdwy to chse ldr 5f out: rdn and ev ch over 1f out: kpt on but unable to match pce of wnr ins fnl f: wnt 2nd fnl 50yds* 9/4[1]

0121 3 ¾ **Cribbs Causeway (IRE)**[26] 7817 3-8-12 95........(p) KieranShoemark 13 95
(Roger Charlton) *dwlt: towards rr: hdwy to ld 9f out: rdn 2f out hrd pressed over 1f out: hdd jst ins fnl f: kpt on same pce and lost 2nd fnl 50yds* 5/1[3]

2522 4 1 ¼ **Gakku**[48] 7109 3-8-12 78........................(b) JackMitchell 1 93
(Roger Varian) *led tl 9f out: chsd ldr tl 5f out: styd chsng ldrs: 4th and styd on same pce u.p fr over 1f out* 33/1

1406 5 1 ¼ **Ouja**[20] 8007 3-8-12 93........................(b) RobertHavlin 11 91
(John Gosden) *stdd s: hld up in last quartet: edgd lft over 6f out: effrt and hdwy into midfield 2f out: kpt on ins fnl f: nvr threatened ldrs* 20/1

1323 6 *hd* **Pacharana**[17] 8121 4-9-3 94........................ DavidProbert 9 91
(Luca Cumani) *t.k.h: chsd ldr after 1f tl 10f out: styd chsng ldrs tl midfield and rdn 2f out: kpt on same pce ins fnl f* 9/1

4 7 1 ¾ **Val De Marne**[33] 3-8-12 0........................ RaphaelMarchelli 12 88
(A Fabre, France) *t.k.h: hld up in midfield: hdwy to chse ldrs 7f out: rdn and unable qck over 1f out: wknd ins fnl f* 7/1

0161 8 *nse* **Fire Jet (IRE)**[15] 8166 4-9-3 91........................ JimmyQuinn 7 88
(John Mackie) *hld up in tch towards rr: hdwy on outer over 4f out: rdn and unable qck 2f out: kpt on but no threat to ldrs ins fnl f* 33/1

504 9 *hd* **Santa Monica**[20] 8020 4-9-8 97........................ DeclanMcDonogh 3 93
(Charles O'Brien, Ire) *hld up in tch in midfield: effrt on inner over 1f out: no imp 1f out: wknd ins fnl f* 18/1

5040 10 ½ **Elysian Fields (GR)**[26] 7817 6-9-3 90........................ PJMcDonald 10 87
(Amanda Perrett) *hld up in last pair: impeded over 6f out: effrt wl over 1f out: nvr trbld ldrs* 66/1

524- 11 ½ **Sacrifice My Soul (IRE)**[29] 7752 5-9-3 0........................(bt[1]) PatCosgrave 6 86
(Mme Pia Brandt, France) *hld up in tch: effrt over 1f out: no imp u.p and wknd ins fnl f* 20/1

2044 12 2 **Gallifrey**[36] 7507 3-8-12 82........................(p) RichardKingscote 14 83
(Lucy Wadham) *chsd ldrs tl 5f out: steadily lost pl: towards rr and rdn over 1f out: sn wknd* 33/1

462 13 23 **Lady Makfi (IRE)**[83] 5896 5-9-3 73........................ LiamKeniry 5 49
(Johnny Farrelly) *hld up in rr: nt clr run 4f out: lost tch and eased over 1f out: t.o* 200/1

2m 40.7s (-5.30) **Going Correction** -0.20s/f (Stan)
**WFA** 3 from 4yo+ 5lb 13 Ran SP% **117.8**
Speed ratings (Par 108): **108,107,106,105,105 104,103,103,103,103 103,101,87**
CSF £10.71 TOTE £3.70: £1.50, £1.50, £1.90; EX 12.80 Trifecta £45.60.
**Owner** The Queen **Bred** The Queen **Trained** Newmarket, Suffolk

**FOCUS**
A staying Listed event for fillies and mares including three overseas challengers. It was run at a rather stop-start gallop. The bare form is open to question.

## 8549 BETWAY H'CAP (DIV I) 1m 2f (P)
2:55 (2:56) (Class 5) (0-70,69) 3-Y-O+ £2,911 (£866; £432; £216) Stalls Low

Form RPR
005 1 **What A Welcome**[28] 7768 3-8-12 **63**........................ JoeyHaynes 1 72+
(Patrick Chamings) *trckd ldrs tl rdn to ld 1f out: sn clr and in command: r.o wl: quite comf* 9/1

/4-6 2 1 ½ **Miss Blondell**[15] 8156 4-8-12 **67**........................ TylerSaunders(7) 6 71+
(Marcus Tregoning) *sn dropped towards rr: pushed along briefly over 4f out: rdn over 2f out: hdwy whn nt clr run and pushed rt 1f out: str run ins fnl f: snatched 2nd on post: nvr getting to wnr* 10/1

2250 3 *nse* **Silver Dixie (USA)**[6] 8386 7-8-13 **61**........................(p) CharlesBishop 3 65
(Peter Hedger) *dwlt: sn rcvrd and in tch in midfield on inner: effrt to chse ldrs over 1f out: chsd clr wnr 100yds out: kpt on but no imp: lost 2nd on post* 5/1[1]

1061 4 1 ¼ **Luxford**[28] 7761 3-8-10 **61**........................ RobertHavlin 2 63
(John Best) *hld up in tch in midfield: nt clr run 2f out tl swtchd rt ent fnl f: kpt on but nvr threatening wnr* 15/2

3253 5 1 ½ **Daily Trader**[24] 7902 3-8-8 **66**........................ KatherineGlenister(7) 13 65
(David Evans) *chsd ldrs: clsd to join ldr 3f out: sn rdn and ev ch tl unable to match pce of wnr jst ins fnl f: lost 2nd and wknd fnl 100yds* 17/2

3060 6 *nk* **Shifting Star (IRE)**[10] 8300 12-9-6 **68**........................(vt) JosephineGordon 4 66
(John Bridger) *t.k.h: led for 1f: chsd ldr tl 3f out: unable qck over 1f out: wknd ins fnl f* 25/1

5664 7 1 ¾ **Cadeaux Boxer**[28] 7769 4-9-2 **69**........................(h) PaddyBradley(5) 8 63
(Lee Carter) *chsd ldr tl led after 1f: rdn over 2f out: hdd 1f out: no ex and wknd ins fnl f* 9/1

6034 8 1 ½ **Unit Of Assessment (IRE)**[24] 7902 3-9-2 **67**........................(t) DavidProbert 12 58
(William Knight) *hld up in midfield: rdn over 2f out: no real imp whn pushed rt 1f out: wl hld and one pced ins fnl f* 13/2[2]

2303 9 5 **Miss Pacific**[15] 8156 3-9-3 **68**........................ KieranShoemark 10 49+
(William Jarvis) *stdd s and dropped in bhd: effrt but stl plenty to do towards inner over 1f out: nt clr run and hmpd 1f out: wl hld and eased ins fnl f* 8/1

50 10 *shd* **Solveig's Song**[146] 3519 5-8-10 **58** ow1........................(p) JackMitchell 7 39
(Steve Woodman) *in tch in midfield: swtchd rt over 2f out: unable qck u.p over 1f out: nudged rt 1f out: sn wknd* 50/1

1601 11 *hd* **Scrafton**[198] 1870 6-9-6 **68**........................ GeorgeDowning 5 49
(Tony Carroll) *stdd s: hld up towards rr: effrt over 2f out: no hdwy u.p and wknd over 1f out* 50/1

4005 12 ¾ **Rum Swizzle**[20] 8000 5-9-6 **68**........................ RichardKingscote 11 47
(Harry Dunlop) *a towards rr: effrt and wd bnd 2f out: bhd fnl f* 10/1

00-5 13 1 ¼ **Diptych (USA)**[42] 7324 3-8-2 **58**........................(p) ManuelFernandes(5) 9 36
(Sir Mark Prescott Bt) *in tch in midfield: rdn over 2f out: struggling and lost pl 2f out: bhd and wknd ins fnl f* 7/1[3]

2m 3.26s (-3.34) **Going Correction** -0.20s/f (Stan)
**WFA** 3 from 4yo+ 3lb 13 Ran SP% **121.9**
Speed ratings (Par 103): **105,103,103,102,101 101,99,98,94,94 94,93,92**
CSF £96.75 CT £507.53 TOTE £10.90: £3.70, £2.80, £2.40; EX 116.00 Trifecta £799.60.
**Owner** Mrs K Meredith **Bred** Newsells Park Stud **Trained** Baughurst, Hants

**FOCUS**
The first division of an ordinary handicap won by the far least-exposed runner in the field. The form has been rated around the third and fourth.

## 8550 BETWAY H'CAP (DIV II) 1m 2f (P)
3:30 (3:30) (Class 5) (0-70,71) 3-Y-O+ £2,911 (£866; £432; £216) Stalls Low

Form RPR
2435 1 **Circulation**[98] 5319 3-9-3 **69**........................ RichardKingscote 2 76
(Ralph Beckett) *chsd ldrs: effrt to chal 1f out: kpt on wl u.p to ld last strides: all out* 3/1[1]

0660 2 *shd* **Bleu Et Noir**[24] 7907 6-9-5 **68**........................(h) DavidProbert 9 74
(Tim Vaughan) *dwlt: midfield: hdwy on outer to join ldr 7f out: drvn to ld over 1f out: battled on wl u.p tl hdd last strides* 9/1

0523 3 *nk* **Choral Clan (IRE)**[9] 8313 6-9-6 **69**........................ JackMitchell 4 74
(Brendan Powell) *hld up in tch in midfield: effrt to chse ldrs and swtchd rt bnd 2f out: ev ch u.p jst ins fnl f: styd on: unable qck nr fin* 3/1[1]

3265 4 ½ **Sir Gnet (IRE)**[26] 7831 3-8-13 **65**........................ PJMcDonald 10 69
(Ed Dunlop) *hld up in tch in midfield: effrt 2f out: hdwy u.p towards inner and ev ch jst ins fnl f: unable qck cl home* 7/1[3]

0000 5 1 **Zoffany Bay (IRE)**[23] 7917 3-8-7 **59**........................(b) KieranO'Neill 13 61
(George Peckham) *stdd and dropped in bhd after s: hld up in last pair: clsd onto bk of field over 3f out: rdn and hdwy jst over 1f out: styd on wl ins fnl f: nt rch ldrs* 40/1

6000 6 ½ **The Gay Cavalier**[6] 8386 6-8-7 **63**........................(t) JackOsborn(7) 5 64
(John Ryan) *s.i.s and rousted along: bhd: clsd into bk of field 3f out: wd bnd 2f out: hdwy 1f out: styd on wl ins fnl f: nt rch ldrs* 10/1

6360 7 *hd* **Famous Dynasty (IRE)**[19] 8031 3-8-6 **58**........................ JosephineGordon 7 59
(Michael Blanshard) *hld up in midfield: effrt over 2f out: hdwy on inner to chse ldrs 1f out: no ex and wknd wl ins fnl f* 20/1

5500 8 ½ **Olympic Legend (IRE)**[119] 4537 3-8-5 **60**........................(t[1]) GeorgeWood(3) 6 60
(Martin Bosley) *hld up in tch in midfield: unable qck u.p over 1f out: kpt on ins fnl f* 20/1

5160 9 1 **American History (USA)**[23] 7927 3-9-2 **71**........................(p) HectorCrouch(3) 1 69
(William Muir) *hld up in last quartet: effrt over 1f out: styd on ins fnl f: nvr trbld ldrs* 11/2[2]

-016 10 1 ¼ **Rakematiz**[121] 4462 3-8-8 **63**........................ CallumShepherd(3) 3 58
(Brett Johnson) *awkward leaving stalls: hld up in last trio: pushed along and swtchd lft over 1f out: kpt on ins fnl f: nvr trbld ldrs* 20/1

6640 11 1 ½ **Orithia (USA)**[15] 8156 3-8-11 **63**........................(b) KieranShoemark 8 55
(Seamus Durack) *led: jnd 7f out: rdn and hdd over 1f out: no ex and btn jst ins fnl f: sn wknd* 20/1

0000 **12** *1 ½* **Skidby Mill (IRE)**[15] 8156 7-8-11 **65**.......................... PaddyBradley(5) 12 54
(Laura Mongan) *chsd ldr for 2f: styd chsng ldrs tl lost pl u.p over 1f out: wknd ins fnl f* **50/1**

2m 4.32s (-2.28) **Going Correction** -0.20s/f (Stan)
**WFA** 3 from 6yo+ 3lb **12** Ran SP% **120.4**
Speed ratings (Par 103): **101,100,100,100,99 99,98,98,97,96 95,94**
CSF £28.68 CT £89.91 TOTE £3.10: £1.30, £2.30, £1.40; EX 21.30 Trifecta £75.10.
**Owner** K Abdullah **Bred** Juddmonte Farms Ltd **Trained** Kimpton, Hants

**FOCUS**
As in the first leg, this went to an unexposed sort. The first four finished in a bunch and the winning time was just over a second slower than the first division. The third and fourth set the initial level.

## 8551 PLAY SLOTS AT SUNBETS.CO.UK/VEGAS APPRENTICE H'CAP 7f 1y(P)
**4:00** (4:02) (Class 6) (0-65,65) 3-Y-0+ **£2,264** (£673; £336; £168) **Stalls** Low

Form RPR
100 **1** **Garth Rockett**[19] 8031 3-9-3 **57**....................................(t[1]) BenRobinson 2 62
(Brendan Powell) *chsd ldrs: effrt over 1f out: styd on wl fnl 100yds to ld nr fin* **16/1**
13/5 **2** *½* **Exit Europe**[24] 7881 5-9-12 **65**............................................ RowanScott 8 70
(Sir Mark Prescott Bt) *t.k.h: chsd ldr: rdn and ev ch 2f: sustained duel w ldr after: battled on wl tl hdd by wnr nr fin: gained 2nd on nod* **13/8**[1]
2463 **3** *shd* **Violet's Lads (IRE)**[48] 7122 3-9-7 **61**........................... JoshuaBryan 6 65
(Brett Johnson) *led: jnd and rdn 2f out: sustained duel w chalr and battled on wl after: hdd nr fin: lost 2nd on nod* **14/1**
0050 **4** *2 ½* **Rivers Of Asia**[7] 8376 4-9-4 **64**.............................. RussellHarris(7) 5 62
(Martin Smith) *midfield: effrt ent fnl 2f: chsd clr ldng trio 1f out: kpt on but no threat to ldrs* **9/1**
6000 **5** *3 ¼* **Brother In Arms (IRE)**[64] 6581 3-8-13 **58**.................... AledBeech(5) 14 46+
(Tony Carroll) *stdd and dropped in after s t.k.h in rr: hdwy towards inner jst over 1f out: styd on ins fnl f: nvr trbld ldrs* **50/1**
3202 **6** *½* **Dream Start**[9] 8329 3-9-0 **59**.......................................(t) JackOsborn(5) 12 46+
(John Ryan) *bustled along leaving stalls: sn swtchd lft and racd off the pce in last trio: rdn over 2f out: hdwy and nt clr run jst ins fnl f: swtchd lft and styd on: nvr trbld ldrs* **8/1**
000 **7** *hd* **Pulsating (IRE)**[22] 7945 3-8-11 **51**....................................(b) JaneElliott 9 37
(Daniel Steele) *chsd ldng trio: rdn and unable qck over 1f out: 4th and btn 1f out: wknd ins fnl f* **50/1**
3-00 **8** *shd* **Touch Of Color**[35] 7539 4-8-9 **51** oh1...................... ConnorMurtagh(3) 1 38
(Richard Fahey) *hld up in midfield: effrt 2f out: drvn over 1f out: plugged on ins fnl f: nvr trbld ldrs* **25/1**
0000 **9** *1* **Secret Missile**[6] 8402 7-9-1 **57**...................................(v) FinleyMarsh(3) 3 41
(David C Griffiths) *hld up in tch in midfield: effrt 2f out: no imp u.p over 1f out: nvr trbld ldrs* **13/2**[3]
0135 **10** *nk* **Cee Jay**[46] 7191 4-9-1 **57**.................................................. WilliamCox(3) 4 41+
(Patrick Chamings) *awkward leaving stalls and dwlt: sn rcvrd and in tch in midfield: shkn up 2f out: rdn and no hdwy over 1f out: wl hld fnl f* **12/1**
1322 **11** *nk* **La Isla Bonita**[35] 7540 3-9-6 **63**.................................. CameronNoble(3) 7 45+
(Richard Spencer) *rdr late removing hood and short of room leaving stalls: sn dropped to rr: sme hdwy on outer over 2f out: wd bnd 2f out and sn edging lft u.p: nvr trbld ldrs* **6/1**[2]
3000 **12** *nk* **Noble Deed**[22] 7951 7-9-4 **57**.........................................(p) PaddyBradley 10 39
(Michael Attwater) *hld up in midfield: effrt 2f out: no hdwy and wknd ins fnl f* **33/1**
0-35 **13** *7* **Showtime Blues**[286] 332 5-8-13 **59**............................ IsobelFrancis(7) 13 22
(Jim Boyle) *sn bhd: nvr on terms and no ch whn hung lft 1f out* **33/1**

1m 24.29s (-0.51) **Going Correction** -0.20s/f (Stan)
**WFA** 3 from 4yo+ 1lb **13** Ran SP% **120.7**
Speed ratings (Par 101): **94,93,93,90,86 86,85,85,84,84 84,83,75**
CSF £41.21 CT £416.33 TOTE £17.70: £4.20, £1.20, £3.60; EX 53.60 Trifecta £718.20.
**Owner** Philip Banfield **Bred** P Banfield **Trained** Upper Lambourn, Berks

**FOCUS**
A moderate apprentice handicap and a race where you had to be handy with the first three always on the sharp end. There was precious little between the trio at the line either.
T/Jkpt: Not Won. T/Plt: £14.00 to a £1 stake. Pool: £44,687.41 - 2,324.15 winning units T/Qpdt: £11.70 to a £1 stake. Pool: £7,394.73 - 465.89 winning units **Steve Payne**

# 8314 NEWCASTLE (A.W) (L-H)
Friday, November 3

**OFFICIAL GOING: Tapeta: standard**
Wind: Almost nil Weather: Dry

## 8552 BETWAY SPRINT APPRENTICE H'CAP 6f (Tp)
**5:45** (5:45) (Class 5) (0-70,68) 3-Y-0+ **£2,911** (£866; £432; £216) **Stalls** Centre

Form RPR
021 **1** **Lady Of The Lamp (IRE)**[42] 7365 3-8-9 **63**........... SebastianWoods(7) 9 72+
(Rae Guest) *in tch in centre of gp: stdy hdwy gng wl over 1f out: shkn up to ld ins fnl f: kpt on strly* **11/2**[1]
2115 **2** *1 ¾* **Nuns Walk**[27] 7825 3-8-12 **66**............................. RobertDodsworth(7) 8 70
(Tim Easterby) *cl up in centre of gp: led 1/2-way: rdn and hdd ins fnl f: kpt on same pce* **7/1**[3]
2315 **3** *½* **Insurplus (IRE)**[45] 7249 4-8-10 **62**................................. SeanMooney(5) 3 64
(Jim Goldie) *hld up on far side of gp: rdn and hdwy over 1f out: kpt on ins fnl f: nvr able to chal* **16/1**
2022 **4** *½* **Meandmyshadow**[37] 7525 9-9-0 **64**.......................(b) CameronNoble(3) 12 65
(Alan Brown) *cl up on nr side of gp: rdn over 2f out: effrt and edgd lft over 1f out: kpt on same pce ins fnl f* **17/2**
2633 **5** *nk* **Charlie's Dreamer**[44] 7282 3-8-11 **61**........................ GabrieleMalune(3) 10 61
(Michael Appleby) *in tch on nr side of gp: rdn and effrt over 2f out: kpt on same pce fnl f* **12/1**
0004 **5** *dht* **Cosmic Chatter**[11] 8293 7-9-4 **68**............................(p) JamieGormley(3) 14 68
(Ruth Carr) *hld up on nr side of gp: rdn and hdwy over 1f out: kpt on ins fnl f: nrst fin* **9/1**
6-04 **7** *1* **Dandy Bird (IRE)**[85] 5836 3-9-0 **61**............................ CallumRodriguez 7 58
(Julie Camacho) *hld up in centre of gp: rdn over 2f out: hdwy appr fnl f: kpt on: nt pce to chal* **20/1**
4205 **8** *1 ½* **Avenue Of Stars**[14] 8211 4-8-11 **63**...........................(p) SeamusCronin(5) 4 55
(Karen McLintock) *midfield in centre of gp: rdn and hung lft over 2f out: no imp fr over 1f out* **8/1**
454 **9** *nk* **Roys Dream**[13] 8243 3-9-2 **66**............................................ GerO'Neill(3) 2 57
(Paul Collins) *prom on far side of gp: drvn along 1/2-way: wknd appr fnl f* **8/1**
0600 **10** *¾* **Tan**[3] 8484 3-9-3 **67**.................................................(t) PatrickVaughan(3) 11 56
(Tony Coyle) *hld up on nr side of gp: rdn and hdwy over 1f out: no imp fnl f* **25/1**
6410 **11** *nk* **Sexy Legs**[18] 8108 5-9-0 **66**......................................(t) BenSanderson(5) 13 54
(Rebecca Menzies) *hld up on nr side of gp: rdn over 2f out: sn n.d* **16/1**
-100 **12** *4* **Shesthedream (IRE)**[13] 8243 4-9-4 **65**.............................. BenRobinson 6 41
(David Barron) *hld up in centre: rdn over 2f out: sn no imp: btn over 1f out* **50/1**
0002 **13** *hd* **Kommander Kirkup**[15] 8194 6-8-9 **59**...................... ConnorMurtagh(3) 5 35
(Michael Herrington) *hld up on far side of gp: rdn and effrt over 2f out: edgd lft and wknd over 1f out* **6/1**[2]
0150 **14** *3* **Prazeres**[43] 7332 3-8-5 **59**.......................................... JonathanFisher(7) 1 26
(Les Eyre) *led on far side of gp to 1/2-way: cl up tl rdn and wknd over 1f out* **22/1**

1m 12.1s (-0.40) **Going Correction** +0.075s/f (Slow) **14** Ran SP% **119.3**
Speed ratings (Par 103): **105,102,102,101,100 100,99,97,97,96 95,90,90,86**
CSF £40.54 CT £603.64 TOTE £4.60: £1.50, £2.90, £6.50; EX 31.00 Trifecta £407.00.
**Owner** Sonia M Rogers & Anthony Rogers **Bred** Airlie Stud **Trained** Newmarket, Suffolk

**FOCUS**
An open handicap run at a decent pace. The field raced up the centre and the winner did it nicely. The runner-up has been rated to her Redcar win.

## 8553 32RED.COM / EBF NOVICE MEDIAN AUCTION STKS (PLUS 10 RACE) 1m 5y (Tp)
**6:15** (6:18) (Class 4) 2-Y-0 **£4,204** (£1,251; £625; £312) **Stalls** Centre

Form RPR
3 **1** **Elegiac**[16] 8155 2-9-2 0.................................................... FrannyNorton 1 83+
(Mark Johnston) *mde all: rdn over 1f out: pushed clr fnl f: readily* **11/10**[1]
2 **2** *6* **Broken Wings (IRE)**[24] 7937 2-8-11 0............................... GrahamLee 8 64
(Keith Dalgleish) *in tch: hdwy to chse wnr over 1f out: edgd lft: kpt on fnl f: no ch w ready wnr* **7/2**[2]
06 **3** *nk* **She's Royal**[24] 7937 2-8-11 0.............................................. TomEaves 5 64
(Bryan Smart) *hld up in midfield: rdn and hdwy over 1f out: kpt on ins fnl f: nt pce to chal* **66/1**
45 **4** *2* **Cracker Factory**[8] 8372 2-9-2 0............................................ BenCurtis 2 64
(William Haggas) *t.k.h: cl up on far side of gp: effrt and drvn along 2f out: outpcd in fnl f* **12/1**
4 **5** *2 ¼* **Windsor Cross (IRE)**[10] 8316 2-9-2 0............................. TonyHamilton 3 59
(Richard Fahey) *t.k.h: cl up tl rdn and outpcd over 1f out: btn fnl f* **12/1**
20 **6** *2 ¼* **Photonics (IRE)**[21] 8013 2-9-2 0...................................... PJMcDonald 6 54
(Hugo Palmer) *hld up in tch: drvn and outpcd over 2f out: n.d after* **4/1**[3]
00 **7** *nk* **Bob's Girl**[10] 8322 2-8-11 0............................................(h) JosephineGordon 10 48
(David Simcock) *dwlt: hld up: rdn and outpcd over 2f out: n.d after* **20/1**
00 **8** *hd* **Military Madame (IRE)**[13] 8236 2-8-11 0......................... JasonHart 12 47
(John Quinn) *t.k.h: hld up on nr side of gp: rdn over 2f out: sn btn* **100/1**
060 **9** *1 ½* **Blyton Lass**[14] 8208 2-8-11 48........................................ JamesSullivan 9 44
(James Given) *hld up in tch on nr side of gp: rdn and outpcd over 2f out: sn btn* **150/1**
20 **10** *10* **Sunstorm**[20] 8046 2-9-2 73............................................. PhillipMakin 4 26
(David Brown) *t.k.h: chsd wnr to over 1f out: sn wknd* **33/1**
05 **11** *27* **Praeceps (IRE)**[9] 8340 2-9-2 0........................................... RyanPowell 11
(Sir Mark Prescott Bt) *bhd: struggling over 3f out: sn btn: t.o* **66/1**
60 **12** *hd* **Daffy Grey (IRE)**[37] 7521 2-9-2 0....................................... DavidAllan 7
(Michael Easterby) *dwlt: bhd: rdn and outpcd over 3f out: btn fnl 2f: t.o* **200/1**

1m 39.08s (0.48) **Going Correction** +0.075s/f (Slow) **12** Ran SP% **118.1**
Speed ratings (Par 98): **100,94,93,91,89 87,86,86,85,75 48,48**
CSF £4.76 TOTE £2.00: £1.10, £1.40, £10.80; EX 4.90 Trifecta £145.90.
**Owner** Browne Boyce Richards & Richards **Bred** Aston House Stud **Trained** Middleham Moor, N Yorks

**FOCUS**
An interesting maiden. They went a steady pace with the winner making all for a smooth success.

## 8554 SUNBETS.CO.UK MAIDEN STKS 1m 5y (Tp)
**6:45** (6:46) (Class 5) 3-Y-0+ **£3,072** (£914; £456; £228) **Stalls** Centre

Form RPR
05 **1** **Al Galayel (IRE)**[185] 2260 3-9-5 0...................................... PJMcDonald 3 89
(Luca Cumani) *mde all: pushed along 2f out: edgd lft ins fnl f: styd on strly* **9/4**[2]
3 **2** *2 ¾* **Francis Xavier (IRE)**[29] 7768 3-9-5 0......................... JosephineGordon 2 82
(Hugo Palmer) *t.k.h: cl up: effrt and ev ch over 1f out: kpt on same pce ins fnl f* **11/10**[1]
**3** *2* **Khamry** 4-9-7 0............................................................... PhillipMakin 1 77+
(Owen Burrows) *upset in stalls: dwlt and wnt lft s: hld up in tch: smooth hdwy to chse ldrs whn rn green and drifted rt over 1f out: kpt on same pce ins fnl f: bttr for r* **5/1**[3]
0 **4** *8* **Acker Bilk (IRE)**[124] 4409 3-9-5 0...................................... GrahamLee 8 58
(Keith Dalgleish) *dwlt: hld up in tch: effrt and chsd clr ldng trio over 1f out: sn no further imp* **20/1**
**5** *1 ¼* **Li Mei (IRE)** 3-9-0 0.......................................................... BenCurtis 9 50
(William Haggas) *hld up: rn green and outpcd over 3f out: rallied wl over 1f out: sn no imp* **8/1**
0 **6** *8* **Port Soif**[35] 7574 3-9-0 0.................................................. ShaneGray 5 31
(David O'Meara) *trckd ldrs: rdn over 2f out: wknd over 1f out* **100/1**
**7** *10* **Lady Sundew (IRE)** 4-9-2 0................................................ DavidNolan 6
(Iain Jardine) *hld up: drvn and struggling over 3f out: btn fnl 2f* **50/1**
0-00 **8** *11* **Highfield Lass**[83] 5950 6-9-2 46......................................... JasonHart 7
(Tracy Waggott) *t.k.h: cl up tl rdn and wknd over 2f out* **125/1**
**9** *8* **Olimar (FR)**[473] 3-9-0 0................................................ BarryMcHugh 4
(Marjorie Fife) *dwlt: hld up: drvn along over 3f out: wknd over 2f out* **100/1**

1m 39.09s (0.49) **Going Correction** +0.075s/f (Slow)
**WFA** 3 from 4yo+ 2lb **9** Ran SP% **115.7**
Speed ratings (Par 103): **100,97,95,87,86 78,68,57,49**
CSF £5.01 TOTE £3.30: £1.20, £1.10, £1.70; EX 5.90 Trifecta £20.40.
**Owner** Al Shaqab Racing **Bred** D J Maher **Trained** Newmarket, Suffolk

**FOCUS**
An uncompetitive maiden run at a steady pace. The front three finished clear. It's been rated around the runner-up.

## 8555 32RED CASINO NOVICE AUCTION STKS (PLUS 10 RACE) 7f 14y (Tp)
**7:15** (7:16) (Class 4) 2-Y-0 **£4,204** (£1,251; £625; £312) **Stalls** Centre

Form RPR
1 **1** **Augenblick (IRE)**[25] 7875 2-8-13 0.................................... JackMitchell 1 77
(Roger Varian) *in tch: smooth hdwy to ld over 1f out: pushed clr ins fnl f: comf* **8/11**[1]
4 **2** *2* **Riverside Walk**[15] 8189 2-8-11 0...................................... GrahamLee 11 68
(Keith Dalgleish) *hld up: hdwy and prom over 1f out: chsd wnr wl ins fnl f: kpt on* **10/1**[3]

6 **3** *hd* **Ideal Candy (IRE)**$^{137}$ [3908] 2-8-5 0 ShaneGray 2 61
(Karen Tutty) *led: rdn and hdd over 1f out: rallied: one pce and lost 2nd pl wl ins fnl f* **66/1**

60 **4** *2 ¾* **Dragon Tattoo (IRE)**$^{25}$ [7875] 2-8-7 0 JosephineGordon 6 56
(Hugo Palmer) *prom: effrt and rdn wl over 1f out: outpcd ins fnl f* **20/1**

06 **5** *1* **Contrebasse**$^{21}$ [8013] 2-9-0 0 DavidAllan 10 61
(Tim Easterby) *hld up: pushed along whn checked briefly over 2f out: shkn up and styd on steadily fnl f: nvr nrr* **10/1**$^{3}$

004 **6** *¾* **Power Sail**$^{14}$ [8215] 2-8-10 65 (b) DuranFentiman 5 55
(Tim Easterby) *trckd ldr: rdn over 2f out: wknd over 1f out* **20/1**

6 **7** *1* **Wynfaul The Wizard (USA)**$^{25}$ [7883] 2-9-2 0 PhillipMakin 8 58
(Richard Guest) *s.i.s: t.k.h in rr: rdn over 2f out: effrt over 1f out: sn no imp* **66/1**

24 **8** *nk* **Glacier Fox**$^{24}$ [7929] 2-9-0 0 JamesSullivan 3 55
(Tom Tate) *t.k.h: in tch: rdn and outpcd over 2f out: wknd over 1f out* **9/4**$^{2}$

**9** *13* **Luna Lady** 2-8-5 0 FrannyNorton 7 12
(Ann Duffield) *hld up in tch: drvn and outpcd over 2f out: sn wknd* **33/1**

**10** *24* **Holte End** 2-8-5 0 RyanPowell 9
(Kevin Frost) *unruly in stalls: missed break: hld up: struggling over 3f out: btn fnl 2f: t.o* **150/1**

1m 27.3s (1.10) **Going Correction** +0.075s/f (Slow) **10** Ran SP% **123.0**
Speed ratings (Par 98): **96,93,93,90,89 88,87,86,72,44**
CSF £9.97 TOTE £1.50: £1.02, £2.50, £18.60; EX 10.70 Trifecta £340.30.
**Owner** Ajay Anne & Partner **Bred** Michael O'Mahony **Trained** Newmarket, Suffolk

**FOCUS**
An uncompetitive contest.

## 8556 SUN BETS ON THE APP H'CAP 7f 14y (Tp)

**7:45** (7:47) (Class 5) (0-75,76) 3-Y-0+ **£3,072** (£914; £456; £228) **Stalls** Centre

Form RPR

4310 **1** **Equiano Springs**$^{38}$ [7474] 3-9-3 72 JamesSullivan 8 80
(Tom Tate) *mde all in centre of gp: rdn over 1f out: hld on gamely ins fnl f* **18/1**

1315 **2** *shd* **El Principe**$^{23}$ [7958] 4-9-7 75 (t) PJMcDonald 14 83
(Les Eyre) *chsd wnr on nr side of gp: effrt and rdn over 1f out: kpt on: hld nr fin* **8/1**

0643 **3** *½* **Acrux**$^{14}$ [8209] 4-9-4 72 (h) DavidNolan 4 79+
(David O'Meara) *hld up and bhd in centre of gp: hdwy over 1f out: rdn and r.o ins fnl f: no ex nr fin* **11/2**$^{3}$

0415 **4** *2 ¼* **Deansgate (IRE)**$^{35}$ [7571] 4-9-4 72 JoeDoyle 9 73
(Julie Camacho) *t.k.h: cl up in centre: effrt and rdn over 1f out: kpt on same pce ins fnl f* **9/2**$^{2}$

4250 **5** *nk* **Alpine Dream (IRE)**$^{54}$ [6964] 4-9-5 73 (b) DavidAllan 13 73
(Tim Easterby) *hld up on nr side of gp: rdn and hdwy wl over 1f out: kpt on ins fnl f: nt pce to chal* **25/1**

516 **6** *½* **Rock Warbler (IRE)**$^{21}$ [7998] 4-9-3 76 (t) ConnorMurtagh$^{(5)}$ 11 75
(Oliver Greenall) *hld up in centre of gp: rdn and hdwy over 1f out: kpt on same pce ins fnl f* **4/1**$^{1}$

0466 **7** *2 ¼* **Madrinho (IRE)**$^{45}$ [7245] 4-9-1 72 (bt$^{1}$) TimClark$^{(3)}$ 3 65
(John Butler) *hld up bhd ldng gp: effrt on far side of gp over 2f out: no imp fr over 1f out* **12/1**

6000 **8** *1 ½* **Alfie's Angel (IRE)**$^{14}$ [8209] 3-9-3 72 (p$^{1}$) GrahamLee 7 60
(Bryan Smart) *hld up in midfield in centre of gp: rdn along over 2f out: edgd lft and wknd over 1f out* **28/1**

0214 **9** *3 ¼* **Tagur (IRE)**$^{18}$ [8108] 3-8-9 64 (v) TomEaves 10 43
(Kevin Ryan) *cl up in centre of gp: rdn over 2f out: wknd over 1f out* **14/1**

1000 **10** *8* **Prince Of Time**$^{25}$ [7881] 5-8-10 67 CallumRodriguez$^{(3)}$ 2 25
(Richard Ford) *hld up on far side of gp: struggling over 2f out: sn wknd* **66/1**

0054 **11** *nk* **Glorious Rocket**$^{105}$ [5100] 3-9-3 72 (e$^{1}$) BenCurtis 6 28
(David Barron) *hld up in centre of gp: drvn along over 2f out: sn no imp: btn over 1f out* **20/1**

0225 **12** *1* **Dandys Denouement**$^{14}$ [8217] 3-9-1 75 BenRobinson$^{(5)}$ 12 29
(Brian Ellison) *midfield in centre of gp: drvn along over 2f out: wknd wl over 1f out* **50/1**

3022 **13** *7* **Interlink (USA)**$^{45}$ [7244] 4-9-4 72 DougieCostello 1 8
(Marjorie Fife) *hld up on far side of gp: rdn and struggling 3f out: sn btn* **20/1**

04 **L** **Majdool (IRE)**$^{14}$ [8209] 4-8-13 70 (h) LewisEdmunds$^{(3)}$ 5
(Noel Wilson) *rrd s and foot wedgd over adjacent stall: tk no part* **17/2**

1m 26.23s (0.03) **Going Correction** +0.075s/f (Slow)
**WFA** 3 from 4yo+ 1lb **14** Ran SP% **115.1**
Speed ratings (Par 103): **102,101,101,98,98 97,95,93,89,80 80,79,71,**
CSF £136.82 CT £929.87 TOTE £20.60: £5.90, £2.90, £1.60; EX 200.00 Trifecta £1939.60.
**Owner** T T Racing **Bred** Paddock Space **Trained** Tadcaster, N Yorks

**FOCUS**
The pace was steady for this open handicap. The third has been rated to this year's form.

## 8557 BETWAY CASINO H'CAP 5f (Tp)

**8:15** (8:16) (Class 5) (0-70,70) 3-Y-0+ **£2,911** (£866; £432; £216) **Stalls** Centre

Form RPR

5042 **1** **Casterbridge**$^{10}$ [8321] 5-9-4 67 (p) JasonHart 3 78
(Eric Alston) *mde virtually all in centre of gp: rdn and asserted ins fnl f: kpt on wl cl home* **7/2**$^{1}$

0004 **2** *½* **Big Lachie**$^{10}$ [8311] 3-9-7 70 BenCurtis 12 79
(Daniel Mark Loughnane) *hld up: rdn 1/2-way: gd hdwy on nr side of gp over 1f out: wnt 2nd last 50yds: r.o* **7/1**$^{3}$

000 **3** *2* **First Bombardment**$^{24}$ [7939] 4-8-9 65 PatrickVaughan$^{(7)}$ 14 67
(David O'Meara) *t.k.h: disp ld on nr side of gp: rdn over 1f out: no ex and lost 2nd pl last 50yds* **14/1**

3150 **4** *½* **Hamish McGonagain**$^{14}$ [8211] 4-9-4 67 (p) DavidNolan 1 67
(David O'Meara) *in tch on far side of gp: rdn along 2f out: kpt on same pce ins fnl f* **14/1**

3334 **5** *nk* **Ambitious Icarus**$^{16}$ [8168] 8-8-10 59 (p) FrannyNorton 4 58
(Richard Guest) *hld up: pushed along 1/2-way: effrt on far side of gp over 1f out: kpt on fnl f: nvr rchd ldrs* **9/1**

2602 **6** *1* **Astrophysics**$^{27}$ [7825] 5-9-3 66 PJMcDonald 9 62
(Lynn Siddall) *slowly away: in bhd tl mde hdwy in centre over 1f out: kpt on fnl f: nvr able to chal* **5/1**$^{2}$

4323 **7** *½* **Kodicat (IRE)**$^{13}$ [8243] 3-9-7 70 (p$^{1}$) TomEaves 6 64
(Kevin Ryan) *t.k.h in midfield in centre of gp: drvn over 2f out: no imp fr over 1f out* **9/1**

2260 **8** *hd* **Pearl Acclaim (IRE)**$^{65}$ [6593] 7-9-2 65 DavidAllan 11 58
(David C Griffiths) *chsd ldrs on nr side of gp: rdn over 2f out: wknd fnl f* **22/1**

0046 **9** *nk* **Savannah Beau**$^{10}$ [8320] 5-9-3 66 (p) PhillipMakin 10 58
(Derek Shaw) *t.k.h: hld up on nr side of gp: drvn along over 1f out: sn no imp* **14/1**

4100 **10** *2 ¼* **Groundworker (IRE)**$^{25}$ [7884] 6-8-9 58 (t) JosephineGordon 5 42
(Paul Midgley) *chsd ldrs in centre of gp: rdn over 2f out: wknd fnl f* **16/1**

1300 **11** *1* **Perfect Words (IRE)**$^{27}$ [7825] 7-9-4 67 (p) JamesSullivan 8 47
(Marjorie Fife) *hld up in centre of gp: rdn along over 2f out: wknd over 1f out* **50/1**

16 **12** *¾* **Mr Strutter (IRE)**$^{41}$ [7408] 3-9-1 67 (h) CallumRodriguez$^{(3)}$ 7 45
(Ronald Thompson) *hld up in midfield in centre of gp: rdn over 2f out: wknd over 1f out* **14/1**

0600 **13** *2 ¼* **Joey's Destiny (IRE)**$^{24}$ [7932] 7-9-6 69 DougieCostello 13 38
(Kevin Frost) *bhd on nr side of gp: struggling bef 1/2-way: nvr on terms* **16/1**

3040 **14** *2* **Control Centre (IRE)**$^{14}$ [8211] 3-9-4 67 (b$^{1}$) BarryMcHugh 2 29
(Marjorie Fife) *bhd on far side of gp: struggling over 2f out: sn wknd* **25/1**

58.91s (-0.59) **Going Correction** +0.075s/f (Slow) **14** Ran SP% **120.0**
Speed ratings (Par 103): **107,106,103,102,101 100,99,99,98,94 93,92,88,85**
CSF £26.35 CT £320.28 TOTE £3.90: £1.30, £2.40, £6.20; EX 36.20 Trifecta £508.20.
**Owner** Liam & Tony Ferguson **Bred** Liam & Tony Ferguson **Trained** Longton, Lancs

**FOCUS**
Another open contest run at a sound pace. The runner-up has been rated close to his 2yo best.

## 8558 BETWAY LIVE CASINO H'CAP (DIV I) 5f (Tp)

**8:45** (8:48) (Class 6) (0-55,55) 3-Y-0+ **£2,264** (£673; £336; £168) **Stalls** Centre

Form RPR

0506 **1** **Little Miss Lola**$^{35}$ [7575] 3-9-1 52 CallumRodriguez$^{(3)}$ 8 58
(Lynn Siddall) *trckd ldrs in centre of gp: effrt and rdn over 1f out: led wl ins fnl f: kpt on wl* **11/2**$^{3}$

0520 **2** *½* **Bond Bombshell**$^{27}$ [7825] 4-9-0 55 (v) PatrickVaughan$^{(7)}$ 3 59
(David O'Meara) *walked to s: t.k.h: cl up: led over 1f out: sn hrd pressed: hdd wl ins fnl f: hld nr fin* **6/1**

5002 **3** *shd* **Windforpower (IRE)**$^{42}$ [7366] 7-9-6 54 (p) BarryMcHugh 2 58
(Tracy Waggott) *in tch: effrt on far side of gp over 1f out: ev ch ins fnl f: kpt on: no ex nr fin* **2/1**$^{1}$

4060 **4** *hd* **Racing Angel (IRE)**$^{16}$ [8168] 5-9-2 55 (b$^{1}$) BenRobinson$^{(5)}$ 9 58
(Adrian Nicholls) *t.k.h: in tch: effrt on nr side of gp over 1f out: ch ins fnl f: no ex towards fin* **11/4**$^{2}$

0006 **5** *½* **Captain Scooby**$^{10}$ [8329] 11-8-12 46 oh1 (b) FrannyNorton 6 47
(Richard Guest) *bhd and sn pushed along: hdwy on nr side of gp over 1f out: kpt on fnl f: nrst fin* **10/1**

0360 **6** *1* **Naralsaif (IRE)**$^{11}$ [8298] 3-9-2 50 PatrickMathers 4 48
(Derek Shaw) *hld up bhd ldng gp in centre: rdn over 2f out: edgd lft over 1f out: no imp fnl f* **22/1**

6000 **7** *3 ¼* **Newgate Sioux**$^{68}$ [6469] 3-8-13 47 (t) DuranFentiman 11 33
(Tony Coyle) *cl up on nr side of gp: rdn over 2f out: rallied: wknd fnl f* **50/1**

-6P0 **8** *3 ½* **Ninedarter**$^{14}$ [8217] 3-8-12 46 DavidAllan 1 19
(Antony Brittain) *hld up on far side of gp: struggling 1/2-way: sn btn* **40/1**

0-00 **9** *1* **Burnt Cream**$^{78}$ [6114] 10-8-12 46 oh1 (t) GrahamLee 5 16
(Martin Bosley) *fractious in stalls and dwlt: bhd: rdn on far side of gp 1/2-way: wknd over 1f out* **50/1**

2405 **10** *½* **Celerity (IRE)**$^{71}$ [6339] 3-8-5 46 oh1 (p$^{1}$) GabrieleMalune$^{(7)}$ 7 14
(Lisa Williamson) *led in centre to over 1f out: sn wknd* **50/1**

0500 **11** *7* **Roman Times (IRE)**$^{33}$ [7660] 4-8-9 46 oh1 (p) LewisEdmunds$^{(3)}$ 10
(Alan Berry) *cl up: drvn along on nr side of gp 1/2-way: wknd over 1f out* **14/1**

59.97s (0.47) **Going Correction** +0.075s/f (Slow) **11** Ran SP% **118.1**
Speed ratings (Par 101): **99,98,98,97,96 95,90,84,82,82 70**
CSF £37.03 CT £88.51 TOTE £7.40: £2.10, £1.80, £1.20; EX 48.20 Trifecta £86.00.
**Owner** Lynn Siddall Racing II **Bred** Aunty Ifl **Trained** Colton, N Yorks

**FOCUS**
The pace was honest for this modest handicap. The second and third have been rated near their recent best.

## 8559 BETWAY LIVE CASINO H'CAP (DIV II) 5f (Tp)

**9:15** (9:15) (Class 6) (0-55,55) 3-Y-0+ **£2,264** (£673; £336; £168) **Stalls** Centre

Form RPR

0021 **1** **Young Tiger**$^{42}$ [7366] 4-9-3 51 (h) JamesSullivan 7 67+
(Tom Tate) *trckd ldrs gng wl: smooth hdwy on nr side of gp to ld over 1f out: sn pushed clr: readily* **4/6**$^{1}$

0506 **2** *4* **Vecheka (IRE)**$^{24}$ [7926] 6-8-7 46 oh1 JamieGormley$^{(5)}$ 9 46
(Kenny Johnson) *hld up bhd ldng gp: effrt and drvn along on nr side of gp 2f out: wnt 2nd last 50yds: no ch w wnr* **20/1**

1153 **3** *nk* **Our Place In Loule**$^{25}$ [7884] 4-9-7 55 GrahamLee 10 54
(Noel Wilson) *bhd: rdn along 1/2-way: hdwy nr side of gp fnl f: kpt on: nvr able to chal* **8/1**$^{3}$

210 **4** *½* **Lady Joanna Vassa (IRE)**$^{3}$ [8494] 4-9-1 49 (v) PhillipMakin 6 46
(Richard Guest) *led in centre: rdn and hdd over 1f out: rallied: no ex and lost two pls last 50yds* **9/1**

0-06 **5** *1 ¾* **Clouded Gold**$^{12}$ [8258] 5-8-12 46 oh1 (p) TomEaves 8 37
(Michael Appleby) *disp ld in centre: rdn over 1f out: no ex ins fnl f* **33/1**

0034 **6** *½* **Imperial Legend (IRE)**$^{3}$ [8484] 8-9-4 55 (p) RachelRichardson$^{(3)}$ 5 44
(Alan Brown) *in tch: effrt on far side of gp and ev ch briefly over 1f out: wknd ins fnl f* **4/1**$^{2}$

5006 **7** *3* **Novabridge**$^{153}$ [3345] 9-9-1 54 (b) GemmaTutty$^{(5)}$ 3 32
(Karen Tutty) *in tch: effrt on far side of gp over 1f out: wknd fnl f* **20/1**

-006 **8** *2 ¾* **Kirkby's Phantom**$^{41}$ [7388] 3-8-9 46 oh1 (p$^{1}$) LewisEdmunds$^{(3)}$ 4 14
(Alan Berry) *s.i.s: bhd and sn outpcd in centre of gp: struggling 1/2-way: nvr on terms* **100/1**

0/04 **9** *4* **Encoded (IRE)**$^{42}$ [7365] 4-9-0 48 PJMcDonald 1
(Lynn Siddall) *bhd on far side of gp: struggling over 2f out: sn wknd* **16/1**

59.67s (0.17) **Going Correction** +0.075s/f (Slow) **9** Ran SP% **120.4**
Speed ratings (Par 101): **101,94,94,93,90 89,84,80,74**
CSF £22.79 CT £73.08 TOTE £1.50: £1.10, £4.40, £2.30; EX 15.80 Trifecta £98.40.
**Owner** T T Racing **Bred** Mrs J McMahon & Mickley Stud **Trained** Tadcaster, N Yorks

**FOCUS**
A modest handicap.
T/Plt: £21.40 to a £1 stake. Pool: £104,660.14 - 3,565.43 winning units. T/Qpdt: £8.20 to a £1 stake. Pool: £11,845.40 - 1,064.92 winning units. **Richard Young**

8347

# NEWMARKET (R-H)

Friday, November 3

**OFFICIAL GOING: Good to firm (good in places; watered; 8.1)**

Wind: virtually nil Weather: dry, bright spells

## 8560 EBF FRIENDS OF RACING WELFARE NOVICE STKS (PLUS 10 RACE) (C&G) 7f

**12:35** (12:39) (Class 4) 2-Y-O **£4,528** (£1,010; £1,010; £336) **Stalls** Low

Form RPR

43 **1** **Maghaweer (IRE)**[20] 8046 2-9-0 0 JimCrowley 7 81
(Richard Hannon) *led far side gp: rdn 2f out: hung lft over 1f out: led 1f out: racing against stands' rail ins fnl f: styd on: rdn out* **7/2**[2]

1 **2** *1* **Plunger**[202] 1792 2-9-6 0 PJMcDonald 5 84
(Paul Cole) *racd centre to far side: chsd ldrs: effrt 2f out: hung lft and chsd ldrs over 1f out: racing towards stands' side and kpt on u.p ins fnl f* **20/1**

2022 **2** *dht* **Porth Swtan (IRE)**[20] 8039 2-9-0 84 PaulHanagan 11 78+
(Charles Hills) *led stands' side quartet and overall ldr: rdn 2f out: hdd 1f out: kpt on u.p and swtchd rt wl ins fnl f* **5/1**

**4** *1 3/4* **Moqarrab (USA)** 2-9-0 0 KevinStott 8 74
(Saeed bin Suroor) *racd centre to far side: t.k.h: chsd ldrs: rdn: unable qck and drifting lft over 1f out: racing towards stands' side and kpt on same pce ins fnl f* **17/2**

**5** *1/2* **Tum Tum** 2-8-11 0 GeorgeWood(3) 6 72+
(Martyn Meade) *racd centre to far side: towards rr: pushed along 3f out: hdwy and drifting lft over 1f out: kpt on ins fnl f* **16/1**

5 **6** *2 1/2* **Hilborough**[16] 8162 2-9-0 0 CharlesBishop 9 65
(Mick Channon) *racd centre to far side: midfield: effrt over 1f out and sn drifting lft: racd towards stands' side and no imp fnl f* **66/1**

**7** *3/4* **Sir Hamilton (IRE)** 2-9-0 0 JFEgan 1 63
(Denis Quinn) *racd centre to far side: towards rr: pushed along 3f out: hdwy and drifting lft over 1f out and sltly impeded 1f out: racing towards stands' side and kpt on same pce ins fnl f* **200/1**

**8** *3/4* **Chief Ironside** 2-9-0 0 RichardKingscote 10 61
(William Jarvis) *racd centre to stands' side: chsd ldrs: pushed along and drifting lft over 1f out: unable qck and outpcd 1f out: wl hld and kpt on same pce ins fnl f* **10/1**

00 **9** *2 3/4* **Encryption (IRE)**[14] 8215 2-9-0 0 RobertHavlin 13 59+
(George Scott) *racd in stands' side quartet: hld up in rr: trying to cl whn squeezed for room and hmpd 2f out: swtchd rt over 1f out: pushed along and kpt on ins fnl f: no ch w ldrs* **100/1**

**10** *4* **Daltrey** 2-9-0 0 JamesDoyle 12 43
(John Gosden) *racd in stands' side quartet: rn green: midfield overall: effrt 2f out: no imp and wl hld over 1f out: eased ins fnl f* **9/2**[3]

**11** *1 1/2* **Endlessly (IRE)** 2-9-0 0 DavidProbert 14 39
(Martyn Meade) *racd in stands' side quartet: wnt lft s: rn green: chsd gp ldr but only midfield overall: pushed along and hung lft 2f out: sn btn: bhd ins fnl f* **10/3**[1]

5002 **12** *6* **Catapult**[18] 8120 2-9-1 66 ow1 (p[1]) RobertTart 3 24
(Clifford Lines) *racd centre to far side: midfield: rdn 2f out: sn struggling and wknd: bhd fnl f* **50/1**

**13** *4 1/2* **Goodwood Showman** 2-9-0 0 TomQueally 2 11
(William Knight) *racd centre to far side: s.i.s: rn green in rr thrght: lost tch 2f out* **50/1**

00 **14** *nk* **Feel The Wrath (IRE)**[9] 8350 2-8-11 0 TimClark(3) 4 10
(Denis Quinn) *racd centre to far side: t.k.h: chsd ldrs tl lost pl 2f out: wknd over 1f out and bhd ins fnl f* **250/1**

1m 25.75s (0.35) **Going Correction** +0.125s/f (Good) **14** Ran SP% **117.7**
Speed ratings (Par 98): **103,101,101,99,99 96,95,94,91,87 85,78,73,72**
WIN: Maghaweer £3.70. PLACE: Maghaweer £1.30, Plunger £5.60, Porth Swtan £1.60. EXACTA: M/P £26.30, M/PS £7.10. CSF: M/P £38.08, M/PS £10.19. TRIFECTA: M/P/PS £71.30, M/PS/P £43.00.
**Owner** Hamdan Al Maktoum **Bred** Shadwell Estate Company Limited **Trained** East Everleigh, Wilts

**FOCUS**
Stands' side course used. Stalls: far side, except 1m4f and 2m: centre. The watered ground (4mm applied on Monday) was given as good to firm, good in places (GoingStick: 8.1). The re-positioning of the bend into the home straight increased the distance of the 1m4f and 2m races by 9yds. They split into two here, the smaller group of four coming stands' side while the larger group stayed far side most of the way until edging across towards the stands' rail from the run into the Dip. The bare form may prove better than rated.

## 8561 32RED.COM H'CAP 1m 2f

**1:10** (1:13) (Class 4) (0-85,86) 3-Y-O+ **£5,175** (£1,540; £769; £384) **Stalls** Low

Form RPR

21-5 **1** **Celestial Spheres (IRE)**[215] 1518 3-9-4 **85** (p) JamesDoyle 2 93+
(Charlie Appleby) *chsd ldrs: pushed along briefly 3f out: swtchd rt and effrt on far rail over 1f out: rdn and ev ch ins fnl f: r.o to ld towards fin: hung lft cl home* **3/1**[1]

10 **2** *hd* **Garrick**[18] 8111 3-9-2 **83** RobertHavlin 4 90
(John Gosden) *chsd ldrs: effrt 3f out: clsd u.p over 1f out: led and edgd lft ins fnl f: hdd and no ex towards fin* **13/2**

1626 **3** *1/2* **Voi**[27] 7816 3-8-5 **72** (t) JimmyQuinn 5 78
(Conrad Allen) *stdd after s: hld up in midfield: effrt to chse ldrs 2f out: ev ch ins fnl f: unable qck towards fin* **25/1**

615 **4** *1/2* **Breden (IRE)**[25] 7909 7-9-8 **86** (h) RobertWinston 3 91
(Linda Jewell) *hld up in tch in last trio: clsd to trck ldrs but nt clr run over 1f out tl gap opened ins fnl f: kpt on u.p fnl 100yds* **12/1**

5-32 **5** *1* **Doctor Cross (IRE)**[38] 7476 3-8-7 **74** PaulHanagan 8 77
(Richard Fahey) *t.k.h: hld up in midfield: effrt and nt clrest of runs over 2f out: kpt on same pce u.p ins fnl f* **9/1**

1266 **6** *1* **Medalla De Oro**[21] 8005 3-8-13 **80** (h) JackMitchell 12 81+
(Peter Chapple-Hyam) *swtchd lft and racd along on stands' side: overall ldr: clr 3f out: rdn over 2f out: hdd ins fnl f: no ex and wknd fnl 100yds* **10/1**

3402 **7** *hd* **Eltezam (IRE)**[21] 7998 4-9-2 **80** (b) AdamKirby 7 81
(Amanda Perrett) *chsd ldr: rdn 3f out: clsd and ev ch whn edgd lft u.p over 1f out: no ex jst ins fnl f: outpcd fnl 100yds* **20/1**

4222 **8** *1* **Zamperini (IRE)**[17] 8142 5-8-13 **77** JimCrowley 10 76
(Mike Murphy) *stdd after s: t.k.h: hld up in tch in last trio: effrt over 1f out: kpt on ins fnl f: nvr trbld ldrs* **5/1**[3]

5051 **9** *3/4* **Tomahawk Kid**[7] 8386 4-8-12 **81** 6ex ManuelFernandes(5) 6 78
(Ian Williams) *t.k.h: hld up in midfield: effrt over 1f out: no imp: wl hld and kpt on same pce ins fnl f* **9/2**[2]

4000 **10** *2 1/4* **Count Montecristo (FR)**[39] 7452 5-9-0 **78** KevinStott 13 71
(Kevin Ryan) *stdd after s: t.k.h: hld up in rr: effrt 2f out: no imp u.p over 1f out: nvr trbld ldrs* **14/1**

1260 **11** *3* **Perfect Quest**[30] 7728 4-9-0 **78** (t) DavidProbert 9 65
(Clive Cox) *chsd ldrs: rdn and lost pl over 1f out: bhd 1f out: wknd ins fnl f* **40/1**

2m 5.51s (-0.29) **Going Correction** +0.125s/f (Good)
**WFA** 3 from 4yo+ 3lb **11** Ran SP% **117.7**
Speed ratings (Par 105): **106,105,105,105,104 103,103,102,101,100 97**
CSF £21.99 CT £413.54 TOTE £3.70: £1.80, £2.30, £7.20; EX 27.90 Trifecta £487.00.
**Owner** Godolphin **Bred** Lane Stud Farm Ltd **Trained** Newmarket, Suffolk

**FOCUS**
Not a bad handicap. Only Medalla De Oro came stands' side this time, with the rest staying far side. It's been rated around the third and fourth.

## 8562 IRISH STALLION FARMS EBF "BOSRA SHAM" FILLIES' STKS (LISTED RACE) 6f

**1:45** (1:45) (Class 1) 2-Y-O

**£17,013** (£6,450; £3,228; £1,608; £807; £405) **Stalls** Low

Form RPR

41 **1** **Alwasmiya**[23] 7953 2-9-0 0 RobertHavlin 3 100
(Simon Crisford) *trckd ldr for 1f: styd trcking ldrs and travelled strly: wnt 2nd and swtchd out lft wl over 1f out: rdn to ld jst ins fnl f: r.o strly: readily* **8/1**

3100 **2** *3* **Izzy Bizu (IRE)**[57] 6863 2-9-3 95 PJMcDonald 1 93
(Mark Johnston) *led: rdn over 1f out: drvn and hdd jst ins fnl f: outpcd by wnr but hld on for 2nd cl home* **5/1**[3]

11 **3** *nk* **All Out**[18] 8112 2-9-0 82 SeanLevey 9 89
(Richard Hannon) *in tch in midfield: effrt 2f out: unable qck u.p over 1f out: rallied ins fnl f and styd on wl fnl 100yds: no ch w wnr* **3/1**[1]

5 **4** *nk* **Aurora Eclipse (IRE)**[26] 7855 2-9-0 0 LeighRoche 4 88
(M D O'Callaghan, Ire) *hld up in tch in midfield: effrt over 1f out: drvn 1f out: hdwy ins fnl f and styd on wl fnl 100yds: no ch w wnr* **8/1**

1000 **5** *hd* **Neola**[6] 8412 2-9-0 93 JFEgan 2 87
(Mick Channon) *in tch in midfield: effrt and drifting rt over 1f out: no imp tl styd on u.p fnl 100yds: no ch w wnr* **12/1**

0503 **6** *nse* **Looks A Million**[27] 7846 2-9-0 92 PaulHanagan 10 87
(Joseph Tuite) *t.k.h: chsd ldr after 1f tl wl over 1f out: unable qck u.p over 1f out: no ch w wnr and kpt on same pce ins fnl f* **22/1**

45 **7** *hd* **Hula Girl**[52] 7021 2-9-0 0 DavidProbert 5 87
(Charles Hills) *stdd s: t.k.h: hld up in tch in midfield: effrt over 1f out: styd on ins fnl f: nvr trbld ldrs* **33/1**

1040 **8** *1 1/4* **One Minute (IRE)**[21] 8002 2-9-0 96 (p[1]) JimCrowley 7 83
(William Haggas) *taken down early: chsd ldrs: rdn 2f out: unable qck u.p over 1f out: wknd ins fnl f* **9/2**[2]

0 **9** *2* **Abamanova (IRE)**[26] 7855 2-9-0 0 WJLee 8 76
(W McCreery, Ire) *racd away fr rivals in centre: midfield tl dropped towards rr 3f out: effrt wl over 1f out: no imp and wl hld ins fnl f* **12/1**

51 **10** *1/2* **Revived**[66] 6559 2-9-0 0 JamesDoyle 6 75
(Michael Bell) *restless in stalls: stdd s: t.k.h and hld up in tch in rr: effrt 2f out: no hdwy u.p over 1f out: wknd ins fnl f* **8/1**

1m 11.78s (-0.42) **Going Correction** +0.125s/f (Good) **10** Ran SP% **115.9**
Speed ratings (Par 101): **107,103,102,102,101 101,101,99,97,96**
CSF £47.45 TOTE £10.70: £2.80, £2.00, £1.40; EX 58.30 Trifecta £272.20.
**Owner** Shaikh Duaij Al Khalifa **Bred** Bumble Bloodstock Ltd **Trained** Newmarket, Suffolk

**FOCUS**
This is rarely a strong Listed race, but the winner did it nicely, finishing clear of the rest, who finished in a heap. The runner-up helps pin the opening level.

## 8563 QUY MILL HOTEL & SPA CONDITIONS STKS 6f

**2:20** (2:20) (Class 3) 2-3-Y-O **£7,470** (£2,236; £1,118; £559) **Stalls** Low

Form RPR

2100 **1** **Consequences (IRE)**[27] 7846 2-8-5 89 DavidProbert 3 95+
(David O'Meara) *stdd s: hld up in tch in last: clsd to trck ldr wl over 1f out: swtchd lft and cruised upsides ldr over 1f out: led jst ins fnl f: sn nudged along and qcknd clr: easily* **2/1**[2]

3636 **2** *3 1/2* **Rajar**[49] 7108 3-9-5 92 (h) PaulHanagan 2 84
(Richard Fahey) *t.k.h: led for 1f: chsd ldr tl led again over 2f out: rdn 2f out: hdd jst ins fnl f: sn brushed aside: kpt on for clr 2nd* **8/11**[1]

00 **3** *4* **Star Of Siena**[10] 8323 2-7-9 0 ow2 JackOsborn(7) 5 68
(John Ryan) *t.k.h: hdwy to ld after 1f: hdd over 2f out: sn rdn: 3rd and outpcd over 1f out: wknd ins fnl f* **40/1**

0141 **4** *4* **Ocean Temptress**[24] 7932 3-9-5 72 (v) AdamKirby 1 58
(John Ryan) *dwlt: chsd ldng pair: rdn 3f out: dropped to last and btn 2f out: wknd over 1f out* **5/1**[3]

1m 12.56s (0.36) **Going Correction** +0.125s/f (Good) **4** Ran SP% **110.3**
Speed ratings: **102,97,92,86**
CSF £3.96 TOTE £3.00; EX 4.30 Trifecta £21.40.
**Owner** Nick Bradley Racing 15 **Bred** L Lynch & R Sherrard **Trained** Upper Helmsley, N Yorks

**FOCUS**
This was a race in which 2yos had a good record for many years, but 3yos had won the previous three. Normality was resumed this time, the winner having the race run to suit and proving much too good.

## 8564 EBFSTALLIONS.COM QUY MILL HOTEL & SPA FILLIES' H'CAP 1m 4f

**2:55** (2:57) (Class 3) (0-90,88) 3-Y-O+ **£9,056** (£2,695; £1,346) **Stalls** Centre

Form RPR

2362 **1** **Donnachies Girl (IRE)**[18] 8103 4-8-4 **74** oh2 (p[1]) RowanScott(3) 2 78
(Alistair Whillans) *chsd ldr: rdn over 3f out: led over 1f out: kpt on and a jst doing enough ins fnl f: rdn out* **2/1**[2]

4001 **2** *1/2* **All My Love (IRE)**[24] 7925 5-8-11 **81** CallumShepherd(3) 4 84
(Pam Sly) *hld up in 3rd tl quick move to ld over 4f out: rdn over 3f out: drvn and hdd over 1f out: rallied ins fnl f: hld towards fin* **7/2**[3]

0-24 **3** *1/2* **Star Story**[33] 7652 3-7-13 **74** GeorgeWood(3) 1 76
(Ralph Beckett) *t.k.h: led tl hdd over 4f out and sn dropped to last: rdn over 3f out: clsd u.p and cl enough 1f out: kpt on but nvr quite getting to rivals* **1/1**[1]

2m 35.33s (3.33) **Going Correction** +0.125s/f (Good)
**WFA** 3 from 4yo+ 5lb **3** Ran SP% **105.6**
Speed ratings (Par 104): **93,92,92**
CSF £7.39 TOTE £2.80; EX 6.70 Trifecta £4.90.
**Owner** Mrs Karen Spark **Bred** Darley **Trained** Newmill-On-Slitrig, Borders

**FOCUS**
Race distance increased by 9yds. A messy tactical race. The runner-up has been rated close to form.

## 8565 WINGATE SIGNS SUPPORTS #SUPERJOSH CHARITY H'CAP 2m
3:30 (3:34) (Class 3) (0-90,82) 3-Y-O+ **£7,762** (£2,310; £1,154; £577) **Stalls** Centre

Form RPR

4003 **1** **Sunblazer (IRE)**[23] 7949 7-10-0 **82**....(t) JimCrowley 1 88
(Kim Bailey) *chsd ldrs: stdd and hld up in tch: clsd and nt clrest of runs over 2f out: swtchd rt and effrt on far rail over 1f out: rdn to ld jst ins fnl f: styd on wl* **8/1**

541 **2** *3/4* **Waiting For Richie**[42] 7359 4-9-4 **72**.... AndrewMullen 9 77
(Tom Tate) *sn led: rdn over 2f out: drvn and hdd jst ins fnl f: kpt on same pce and a hld after* **9/2**[2]

4203 **3** *1* **Medburn Cutler**[19] 8072 7-9-9 **77**....(p) RobertHavlin 4 81
(Peter Hedger) *in tch in midfield: rdn 3f out: nt clrest of runs and swtchd lft over 1f out: edging bk rt and kpt on u.p ins fnl f: wnt 3rd towards fin* **9/2**[2]

0034 **4** *1/2* **Saved By The Bell (IRE)**[2] 8511 7-8-9 **70**.... HarrisonShaw(7) 7 73
(Lawrence Mullaney) *stdd s: t.k.h: hld up towards rr: hdwy to chse ldrs 6f out: rdn over 2f out: styd on same pce u.p ins fnl f* **7/1**[3]

5514 **5** *2 3/4* **Ayr Of Elegance**[29] 7766 5-9-8 **76**.... RichardKingscote 2 76
(Philip Hide) *stdd s: hld up in tch in rr: clsd 3f out: rdn to chal over 1f out: no ex u.p jst ins fnl f: wknd fnl 100yds* **8/1**

P460 **6** *6* **Lost The Moon**[20] 8047 4-9-6 **74**.... JoeyHaynes 5 67
(Mark H Tompkins) *stdd s: hld up wl in tch towards rr: rdn 4f out: unable qck u.p over 2f out: wknd over 1f out* **66/1**

1455 **7** *1* **Graceful Lady**[7] 8394 4-9-0 **75**.... DarraghKeenan(7) 6 67
(Robert Eddery) *stdd s: t.k.h: midfield tl hdwy to chse ldr 10f out tl rdn and lost pl over 2f out: sn struggling and wknd over 1f out* **4/1**[1]

343 **8** *18* **Nelson's Touch**[39] 7462 4-9-7 **75**.... TomQueally 3 45
(Denis Coakley) *chsd ldr tl 10f out: midfield and rdn 5f out: u.p and struggling 3f out: bhd 2f out: eased ins fnl f* **4/1**[1]

3m 29.26s (-1.24) **Going Correction** +0.125s/f (Good) **8 Ran SP% 112.6**
Speed ratings (Par 107): **108,107,107,106,105 102,102,93**
CSF £42.37 CT £181.42 TOTE £7.50: £2.20, £1.70, £1.80; EX 48.00 Trifecta £263.00.
**Owner** Norman Carter **Bred** Michael G Daly **Trained** Andoversford, Gloucs

**FOCUS**
Race distance increased by 9yds. A competitive staying contest. The first two raced on the far rail much of the way. It's been rated around the runner-up, with the third to his latest effort.

## 8566 NATIONAL HERITAGE CENTRE ANNIVERSARY H'CAP 1m
4:05 (4:07) (Class 3) (0-95,93) 3-Y-O+ **£7,762** (£2,310; £1,154; £577) **Stalls** Low

Form RPR

0635 **1** **Via Serendipity**[36] 7549 3-8-11 **85**....(t) SeanLevey 8 93
(Stuart Williams) *t.k.h: chsd ldrs tl wnt 2nd ent fnl 2f: effrt to chal over 1f out: drvn to ld jst ins fnl f: styd on wl: rdn out* **8/1**

1131 **2** *1 1/4* **Salt Whistle Bay (IRE)**[30] 7736 3-8-7 **81**.... JimmyQuinn 9 86
(Rae Guest) *led: rdn and hrd pressed over 1f out: hdd jst ins fnl f: no ex and styd on same pce fnl 150yds* **10/1**

460 **3** *1* **Red Tea**[34] 7619 4-9-3 **89**.... RyanTate 5 91
(Peter Hiatt) *midfield: rdn 5f out: chsd ldrs and drvn over 1f out: kpt on same pce ins fnl f* **7/1**

0300 **4** *1/2* **Sinfonietta (FR)**[34] 7619 5-9-2 **88**.... JimCrowley 1 89
(David Menuisier) *hld up in tch in last pair: clsd and nt clrest of runs over 1f out: swtchd ins fnl f: rdn and styd on fnl 100yds: no threat to ldrs* **5/1**[3]

6060 **5** *1/2* **Alejandro (IRE)**[48] 7140 8-9-1 **87**.... JFEgan 2 86
(David Loughnane) *stdd bk after s: t.k.h: hld up in tch in rr: effrt whn sltly impeded and swtchd lft over 1f out: kpt on ins fnl f* **16/1**

1143 **6** *1* **Brilliant Vanguard (IRE)**[20] 8032 4-9-7 **93**....(p) KevinStott 7 90
(Kevin Ryan) *t.k.h: hld up in tch in midfield: effrt and edgd rt wl over 1f out: no ex u.p jst ins fnl f: wknd fnl 100yds* **3/1**[1]

1200 **7** *3 1/4* **Starlight Romance (IRE)**[70] 6404 3-9-1 **89**.... PaulHanagan 6 77
(Richard Fahey) *hld up in tch towards rr: shkn up and effrt over 2f out: hung rt and no imp over 1f out: wknd ins fnl f* **9/1**

1-03 **8** *nse* **Swiss Storm**[33] 7650 3-8-12 **86**.... DavidProbert 3 74
(David Elsworth) *taken down early: t.k.h: hld up in midfield: hdwy to chse ldr over 5f out tl jst over 2f out: sn u.p and lost pl over 1f out: wknd ins fnl f* **10/3**[2]

1m 38.51s (-0.09) **Going Correction** +0.125s/f (Good)
**WFA** 3 from 4yo+ 2lb **8 Ran SP% 113.3**
Speed ratings (Par 107): **105,103,102,102,101 100,97,97**
CSF £81.68 CT £589.30 TOTE £9.30: £2.00, £2.80, £2.20; EX 87.50 Trifecta £578.70.
**Owner** Happy Valley Racing & Breeding Limited **Bred** R Shaykhutdinov **Trained** Newmarket, Suffolk

**FOCUS**
The early pace wasn't strong and the first two were prominent throughout, while the first four raced on the far rail most of the way. It's been rated around the runner-up.
T/Plt: £277.50 to a £1 stake. Pool: £71,285.80 - 187.50 winning units T/Qpdt: £30.60 to a £1 stake. Pool: £5,534.65 - 133.77 winning units **Steve Payne**

8567 - 8574a (Foreign Racing) - See Raceform Interactive

# 6733 DEL MAR (L-H)
Friday, November 3

**OFFICIAL GOING: Dirt: fast; turf: firm**

## 8575a BREEDERS' CUP JUVENILE FILLIES TURF (GRADE 1) (2YO FILLIES) (TURF) 1m (T)
9:25 2-Y-O

**£447,154** (£138,211; £73,170; £40,650; £24,390; £8,130)

RPR

**1** **Rushing Fall (USA)**[23] 2-8-10 0.... JavierCastellano 11 110+
(Chad C Brown, U.S.A) *midfield on outer: hdwy to trck ldrs 2f out: rdn under 2f out: led over 1f out: drvn ins fnl f: kpt on strly* **9/2**[2]

**2** *3/4* **Best Performance (USA)**[33] 2-8-10 0.... JoseLOrtiz 1 108+
(Christophe Clement, U.S.A) *towards rr of midfield: rdn under 2f out: styd on strly fr over 1f out: nrst fin* **16/1**

**3** *1* **September (IRE)**[21] 8004 2-8-10 0.... SeamieHeffernan 10 106+
(A P O'Brien, Ire) *missed break: s.i.s: in rr: drvn and styd on strly on outer fr 1 1/2f out: nrst fin* **9/2**[2]

**4** *3/4* **Significant Form (USA)**[33] 2-8-10 0.... IradOrtizJr 8 104
(Chad C Brown, U.S.A) *in tch on outer: prom 2f out: rdn to ld 1 1/2f out: drvn and hdd over 1f out: no ex fnl 125yds* **7/1**[3]

**5** *hd* **Fatale Bere (FR)**[24] 2-8-10 0.... KentJDesormeaux 9 104
(Leonard Powell, U.S.A) *hld up towards rr: rdn and gd hdwy on wd outside fr 2 1/2f out: chsd ldrs appr 1f out: kpt on same pce ins fnl f* **50/1**

**6** *1 1/4* **Dixie Moon (CAN)**[26] 2-8-10 0.... EuricoRosaDaSilva 12 101
(Catherine Day-Phillips, Canada) *midfield: rdn and kpt on fr under 2f out: nvr gng pce to chal* **33/1**

**7** *1/2* **Capla Temptress (IRE)**[47] 7206 2-8-10 0.... JoelRosario 7 100
(William Mott, U.S.A) *hld up towards rr: rdn and kpt on fr under 2f out: n.d* **14/1**

**8** *2 1/2* **Now You're Talking (IRE)**[34] 7617 2-8-10 0.... WayneLordan 3 94
(Joseph Patrick O'Brien, Ire) *hld up towards rr: rdn and kpt on wl fr under 2f out: n.d* **40/1**

**9** *4 1/4* **Orbolution (USA)**[33] 2-8-10 0.... JohnRVelazquez 6 84
(Todd Pletcher, U.S.A) *in tch: nt clr run appr fnl f: lost pl qckly and sn no ch* **40/1**

**10** *nk* **Moon Dash (USA)**[24] 2-8-10 0.... MikeESmith 14 83
(Michael Stidham, U.S.A) *prom tl led after 2 1/2f: rdn under 2f out: hdd 1 1/2f out: wknd qckly* **66/1**

**11** *1/2* **Juliet Capulet (IRE)**[35] 7578 2-8-10 0.... FrankieDettori 13 82
(John Gosden) *led: hdd after 2 1/2f: remained w ldr: rdn and unable qck under 2f out: wknd qckly* **20/1**

**12** *nk* **Ultima D (USA)**[58] 2-8-10 0....(b) TylerGaffalione 5 81
(Wesley A Ward, U.S.A) *trckd ldrs: rdn over 2f out: drvn under 2f out: lost pl qckly appr fnl f* **25/1**

**13** *1/2* **Madeline (IRE)**[34] 7617 2-8-10 0.... AndreaAtzeni 4 80
(Roger Varian) *in tch in midfield: rdn 2 1/2f out: drvn under 2f out: sltly hmpd over 1f out: sn outpcd and wl btn* **33/1**

**14** *3 3/4* **Happily (IRE)**[33] 7667 2-8-10 0....(t) RyanMoore 2 72
(A P O'Brien, Ire) *towards rr of midfield: nt clr run on inner fr under 2f out: lost pl qckly and sn no ch* **9/4**[1]

1m 36.09s **14 Ran SP% 115.0**
CSF: £63.14; TRICAST: £350.20.
**Owner** e Five Racing Thoroughbreds **Bred** Fred W Hertrich III & John D Fielding **Trained** USA

**FOCUS**
A solid pace: 23.04, 24.19, 24.7, with the winner home in 23.99.

## 8576a LAS VEGAS BREEDERS' CUP DIRT MILE (GRADE 1) (3YO+) (DIRT) 1m (D)
10:05 3-Y-O+

**£447,154** (£138,211; £73,170; £40,650; £24,390; £8,130)

RPR

**1** **Battle Of Midway (USA)**[39] 3-8-11 0....(b) FlavienPrat 9 122
(Jerry Hollendorfer, U.S.A) *in tch: smooth hdwy to press ldrs 2 1/2f out: rdn 2f out: led 1 1/2f out: sn drvn: chal ins fnl f: kpt on wl: asserted cl home* **18/1**

**2** *1/2* **Sharp Azteca (USA)**[41] 4-9-0 0....(b) PacoLopez 3 122
(Jorge Navarro, U.S.A) *led: rdn 2f out: hdd 1 1/2f out: drvn and rallied to chal ins fnl f: no ex cl home* **10/3**[2]

**3** *4 1/4* **Awesome Slew (USA)**[34] 4-9-0 0.... JohnRVelazquez 5 112
(Mark Casse, Canada) *midfield: rdn and effrt 2f out: wnt 3rd 1 1/2f out: sn outpcd by front pair: kpt on same pce* **18/1**

**4** *1/2* **Practical Joke (USA)**[69] 6459 3-8-11 0.... JoelRosario 10 110+
(Chad C Brown, U.S.A) *towards rr: drvn and kpt on fr 1 1/2f out: tk mod 4th ins fnl f: n.d* **6/1**

**5** *2* **Iron Fist (USA)**[40] 5-9-0 0....(b) RicardoSantanaJr 1 106
(Steven Asmussen, U.S.A) *in tch: rdn under 3f out: drvn and wknd steadily fr 1 1/2f out* **33/1**

**6** *1 1/4* **Giant Expectations (USA)**[27] 7853 4-9-0 0.... GaryStevens 2 103+
(Peter Eurton, U.S.A) *dwlt: bhd: rdn and kpt on steadily fr 2f out: nvr in contention* **33/1**

**7** *2 3/4* **Gato Del Oro (USA)**[39] 3-8-11 0.... JoseLOrtiz 4 96
(Richard Baltas, U.S.A) *chsd ldr: rdn 2f out: wknd qckly under 2f out* **66/1**

**8** *2 3/4* **Mor Spirit (USA)**[146] 3608 4-9-0 0....(b) MikeESmith 6 91
(Bob Baffert, U.S.A) *trckd ldrs: rdn and unable qck appr 2f out: sn lost pl and wl btn* **5/2**[1]

**9** *nk* **Accelerate (USA)**[75] 6252 4-9-0 0....(b) VictorEspinoza 8 90
(John W Sadler, U.S.A) *a towards rr: nvr a factor* **4/1**[3]

**10** *1/2* **Cupid (USA)**[33] 7686 4-9-0 0....(b) RafaelBejarano 7 89
(Bob Baffert, U.S.A) *midfield: rdn and lost pl 2f out: sn wl btn* **11/1**

1m 35.2s
**WFA** 3 from 4yo+ 2lb **10 Ran SP% 112.2**
CSF: £73.82; TRICAST: £1,139.96.
**Owner** Don Alberto Stable & WinStar Farm LLC **Bred** Thor-Bred Stables LLC **Trained** USA

**FOCUS**
They didn't go that fast: 22.94, 24.01, 24.18, with the winner to the line in 23.97. The third helps set the standard.

## 8577a BREEDERS' CUP JUVENILE TURF (GRADE 1) (2YO COLTS & GELDINGS) (TURF) 1m (T)
10:50 2-Y-O

**£447,154** (£138,211; £73,170; £40,650; £24,390; £8,130)

RPR

**1** **Mendelssohn (USA)**[20] 8037 2-8-10 0....(b) RyanMoore 1 115
(A P O'Brien, Ire) *trckd ldrs on ins: effrt and shkn up over 1f out: led ins fnl f: drvn out* **9/2**[2]

**2** *1* **Untamed Domain (USA)**[47] 2-8-10 0....(b) JoseLOrtiz 2 113+
(H Graham Motion, U.S.A) *hld up and bhd: hdwy on wd outside over 2f out: rdn and chsd wnr ins fnl f: kpt on fin* **16/1**

**3** *1/2* **Voting Control (USA)**[34] 7631 2-8-10 0.... JavierCastellano 8 112
(Chad C Brown, U.S.A) *in tch: effrt and drvn along over 1f out: kpt on ins fnl f: nvr able to chal* **11/1**

**4** *hd* **Catholic Boy (USA)**[65] 2-8-10 0....(b) ManuelFranco 4 111
(Jonathan Thomas, U.S.A) *hld up on ins: nt clr run briefly over 2f out: effrt over 1f out: r.o ins fnl f: nrst fin* **7/1**

**5** *1/2* **Beckford**[34] 7618 2-8-10 0.... JoelRosario 5 110+
(Gordon Elliott, Ire) *hld up and bhd: stdy hdwy whn nt clr run briefly over 2f out: effrt on ins over 1f out: kpt on fnl f: nt pce to chal* **14/1**

**6** *1/2* **Masar (IRE)**[33] 7667 2-8-10 0.... WilliamBuick 6 111+
(Charlie Appleby) *hld up: stdy hdwy whn nt clr run and checked 3f out: sn rdn along: hdwy on outside over 1f out: kpt on fnl f: nrst fin* **4/1**[1]

**7** *1/2* **My Boy Jack (USA)**[25] 2-8-10 0.... KentJDesormeaux 13 108
(J Keith Desormeaux, U.S.A) *hld up: hdwy on outside over 2f out: sn rdn along: outpcd ins fnl f* **18/1**

8 *hd* **Flameaway (CAN)**[26] 2-8-10 0 JulienRLeparoux 10 107
(Mark Casse, Canada) *pressed ldr: drvn along over 2f out: wknd ins fnl f* **40/1**
9 *nse* **Sands Of Mali (FR)**[34] 7618 2-8-10 0 FlavienPrat 3 107
(Richard Fahey) *led at ordinary gallop: rdn over 1f out: hdd ins fnl f: sn wknd* **18/1**
10 *3/4* **James Garfield (IRE)**[41] 7394 2-8-10 0 FrankieDettori 7 105
(George Scott) *hld up in rr: n.m.r over 2f out to over 1f out: sn drvn and no imp* **13/2**[3]
11 *1/2* **Rajasinghe (IRE)**[34] 7618 2-8-10 0 (b[1]) StevieDonohoe 14 104
(Richard Spencer) *s.i.s and swtchd lft s: hld up: rdn and effrt over 2f out: hung lft and wknd over 1f out* **50/1**
12 *5 3/4* **Snapper Sinclair (USA)**[58] 2-8-10 0 RicardoSantanaJr 11 91
(Steven Asmussen, U.S.A) *t.k.h early: prom: rdn and lost pl over 2f out: btn over 1f out* **20/1**
13 *6 1/4* **Encumbered (USA)**[34] 7646 2-8-10 0 MarioGutierrez 9 77
(Simon Callaghan, U.S.A) *t.k.h early: cl up tl rdn and wknd over 1f out: eased whn btn ins fnl f* **16/1**
14 *1/2* **Hemp Hemp Hurray (CAN)**[47] 2-8-10 0 (b) JohnRVelazquez 12 75
(Wesley A Ward, U.S.A) *t.k.h: hld up in tch: hdwy and prom on outside over 2f out: rdn and wknd wl over 1f out* **25/1**

1m 35.97s **14** Ran SP% **114.3**
CSF: £67.37; TRICAST: £764.69.
**Owner** Derrick Smith & Mrs John Magnier & Michael Tabor **Bred** Clarkland Farm **Trained** Cashel, Co Tipperary
**FOCUS**
This was run at a strong pace: 22.83, 24.04, 24.42, with the winner finishing in 24.49.

## 8578a LONGINES BREEDERS' CUP DISTAFF (GRADE 1) (3YO+ FILLIES & MARES) (DIRT) 1m 1f (D)
**11:35** 3-Y-O+
**£894,308** (£276,422; £146,341; £81,300; £48,780; £16,260)

RPR
1 **Forever Unbridled (USA)**[69] 6457 5-8-12 0 JohnRVelazquez 6 120
(Dallas Stewart, U.S.A) *hld up bhd ldng gp: smooth hdwy on outside over 2f out: rdn to ld over 1f out: kpt on wl fnl f* **10/3**[2]
2 *1/2* **Abel Tasman (USA)**[41] 7417 3-8-9 0 (b) MikeESmith 4 120+
(Bob Baffert, U.S.A) *bhd and sn outpcd in last pl: stdy hdwy 4f out: effrt and rdn on outside over 2f out: chsd wnr ins fnl f: clsng at fin* **13/2**
3 *3* **Paradise Woods (USA)**[34] 7644 3-8-9 0 FlavienPrat 7 114
(Richard E Mandella, U.S.A) *pressed ldr: led over 2f out to over 1f out: no ex and lost 2nd pl ins fnl f* **6/1**
4 *1* **Elate (USA)**[34] 7632 3-8-9 0 JoseLOrtiz 5 112
(William Mott, U.S.A) *prom on outside: rdn over 2f out: outpcd and edgd lft over 1f out: sn no imp* **2/1**[1]
5 *2* **Mopotism (USA)**[41] 7417 3-8-9 0 FrankieDettori 3 107
(Doug O'Neill, U.S.A) *t.k.h early: in tch: drvn and outpcd wl over 2f out: rallied ins fnl f: kpt on: nt pce to chal* **66/1**
6 *1 1/4* **Champagne Room (USA)**[39] 3-8-9 0 MarioGutierrez 1 105
(Peter Eurton, U.S.A) *led to over 2f out: rdn and wknd over 1f out* **33/1**
7 *4 3/4* **Romantic Vision (USA)**[26] 7864 5-8-12 0 BrianJosephHernandezJr 8 94
(George R Arnold II, U.S.A) *in tch on outside: lost grnd after 2f: dropped to last pl 4f out: rdn and struggling over 2f out: sn btn* **50/1**
8 *nse* **Stellar Wind (USA)**[95] 5491 5-8-12 0 VictorEspinoza 2 94
(John W Sadler, U.S.A) *trckd ldrs on ins: rdn along over 3f out: wknd fr 2f out* **4/1**[3]

1m 50.25s
**WFA** 3 from 5yo 3lb **8** Ran SP% **110.4**
CSF: £23.04; TRICAST: £115.56.
**Owner** Charles E Fipke **Bred** Charles Fipke **Trained** USA
**FOCUS**
A solid running of the Distaff.

8579 - 8582a (Foreign Racing) - See Raceform Interactive

# 1250 JEBEL ALI (L-H)
## Friday, November 3
**OFFICIAL GOING: Dirt: fast**

## 8583a COMMERCIAL BANK OF DUBAI H'CAP (DIRT) 6f (D)
**12:45** (12:45) (65-80,80) 3-Y-0+ **£10,572** (£3,524; £1,938; £1,057; £528)

RPR
1 **Shillong**[237] 1161 4-8-9 **70** (vt) PatCosgrave 1 78
(H Al Alawi, UAE) *smooth prog 2 1/2f out, led 1f out, ran on well* **11/1**
2 *2* **Denzille Lane (IRE)**[231] 1255 5-9-5 **79** PatDobbs 5 82
(Doug Watson, UAE) *always prmnt, led 1 1/2f out, hdd 100yds out but ran on* **7/1**[2]
3 *2 3/4* **Perfect Sense**[28] 7793 3-8-11 **72** (v) AdriedeVries 3 65
(Saeed bin Suroor) *mid-division, chsd leaders whn not much room 1 1/2f out, ran on fnl 1f* **9/4**[1]
4 *1 1/4* **First Down (USA)**[748] 5-9-5 **79** TadhgO'Shea 12 69
(A R Al Rayhi, UAE) *led in centre, hdd 1 1/2f out but ran on* **7/1**[2]
5 *shd* **Always Welcome (USA)**[237] 1161 4-8-13 **73** (t) RoystonFfrench 7 62
(A R Al Rayhi, UAE) *prominent til outpcd fnl 1 1/2f* **7/1**[2]
6 *2* **Kidd Malibu (USA)**[231] 1251 4-9-6 **80** (p) FernandoJara 4 63
(Maria Ritchie, UAE) *never nr to challenge* **8/1**[3]
7 *nk* **Fidaslemei (IRE)**[398] 4-9-2 **76** (t) PaoloSirigu 2 58
(M Ramadan, UAE) *never nr to challenge* **25/1**
8 *shd* **Hammurabi (IRE)**[215] 7-9-3 **77** (bt) RichardMullen 13 59
(S Seemar, UAE) *slowly into strd, settled rear, chsd leaders and ev ch 2f out, one pace fnl 1 1/2f* **9/1**
9 *5* **Corso Como (FR)**[231] 1255 6-9-4 **78** (t) AntonioFresu 11 44
(A Al Shemaili, UAE) *never better than mid-division* **25/1**
10 *1/2* **Ajwad**[231] 1255 4-8-10 **71** JBardottier 9 34
(R Bouresly, Kuwait) *prominent til wknd fnl 2 1/2f* **10/1**
11 *5 1/4* **Archers Prize (IRE)**[651] 312 8-9-5 **79** IoannisPoullis 10 26
(R Bouresly, Kuwait) *always in rear* **33/1**
12 *23* **Say No More (IRE)**[231] 1251 4-9-3 **77** SamHitchcott 8
(Doug Watson, UAE) *broke awkwardly, al in rear* **12/1**
13 *2* **Baarez (USA)**[959] 986 6-9-0 **74** (t) JRosales 6
(S H Al Mazrouei, UAE) *never nr to challenge* **40/1**

1m 13.64s (0.23) **13** Ran SP% **127.6**
CSF: 88.92; TRICAST: 224.12.
**Owner** Byerley Team **Bred** Darley **Trained** United Arab Emirates

8584 - (Foreign Racing) - See Raceform Interactive

# 8552 NEWCASTLE (A.W) (L-H)
## Saturday, November 4
**OFFICIAL GOING: Tapeta: standard**
Wind: fresh half against Weather: fine

## 8585 BETWAY LIVE CASINO MAIDEN STKS 1m 4f 98y (Tp)
**3:25** (3:27) (Class 5) 3-Y-0+ **£3,234** (£962; £481; £240) **Stalls** High

Form RPR
226 1 **Love Conquers (JPN)**[30] 7762 3-9-0 73 PhillipMakin 7 57+
(Ralph Beckett) *midfield: smooth hdwy over 3f out: led 2f out: rdn 2 l clr appr fnl f: drvn and reduced advantage fnl 75yds: all out* **1/4**[1]
4425 2 *hd* **Relevant (IRE)**[15] 8218 3-9-0 65 PJMcDonald 4 56+
(K R Burke) *prom: pushed along to ld over 3f out: rdn whn hdd 2f out: 2 l down 1f out: styd on ins fnl f* **9/2**[2]
6500 3 *4 1/2* **Archibelle**[34] 7659 3-9-0 56 JamesSullivan 2 49
(R Mike Smith) *trckd ldrs: rdn over 3f out: one pce* **25/1**
6404 4 *1* **Color Force (IRE)**[69] 6479 4-9-5 44 JosephineGordon 1 46
(Daniel Kubler) *trckd ldrs: rdn over 3f out: sn one pce* **50/1**
5 *1 1/2* **Deshan (GER)**[27] 6-9-10 0 (t) PaulHanagan 6 49
(Tim Vaughan) *v.s.a: hld up in rr: rdn over 5f out: plugged on fr over 1f out: nvr thrat* **12/1**[3]
5630 6 *1/2* **Good Man (IRE)**[14] 8241 4-9-10 44 (p) DavidNolan 5 48?
(Karen McLintock) *hld up: rdn over 3f out: sn btn* **66/1**
0055 7 *8* **Percy Verence**[10] 6560 4-9-10 46 (tp) BarryMcHugh 3 35
(Tracy Waggott) *led: rdn whn hdd over 3f out: wknd over 1f out* **66/1**

2m 44.12s (3.02) **Going Correction** +0.35s/f (Slow)
**WFA** 3 from 4yo+ 5lb **7** Ran SP% **114.7**
Speed ratings (Par 103): **103,102,99,99,98 97,92**
CSF £1.78 TOTE £1.20: £1.10, £1.80; EX 1.90 Trifecta £7.00.
**Owner** Qatar Racing Limited **Bred** Love And Bubbles Partnership **Trained** Kimpton, Hants
**FOCUS**
A modest middle-distance maiden. They went a respectable gallop on standard Tapeta which appears to be riding marginally on the slower side of that description. The long odds-on favourite had to be stoked up to hold on. Muddling form, limited by the fourth and sixth.

## 8586 SUNBETS.CO.UK NURSERY H'CAP 7f 14y (Tp)
**3:55** (3:59) (Class 4) (0-80,76) 2-Y-0 **£5,498** (£1,636; £817; £408) **Stalls** Centre

Form RPR
503 1 **Enrolment**[15] 8212 2-8-12 **67** PaulHanagan 5 71
(Richard Fahey) *hld up: pushed along over 2f out: hung lft but hdwy over 1f out: chal strly fnl 75yds: edgd lft: kpt on to ld towards fin* **20/1**
3230 2 *hd* **Move It Move It**[28] 7821 2-9-7 **76** GrahamLee 2 79
(Keith Dalgleish) *trckd ldrs: led over 2f out: sn pushed along: rdn fnl f: strly pressed fnl 75yds: carried lft and hdd towards fin* **3/1**[2]
4312 3 *2 3/4* **Fortunate Vision**[12] 8288 2-9-3 **72** (v) TomEaves 4 68
(David Brown) *in tch: rdn over 2f out: chsd ldr over 1f out: kpt on same pce* **10/1**
4304 4 *1* **Austin Powers (IRE)**[42] 7384 2-9-3 **72** AndrewMullen 9 65
(Mark Johnston) *midfield: rdn along 3f out: kpt on same pce ins fnl f* **12/1**
2100 5 *1* **Poet's Prince**[63] 6693 2-9-7 **76** JoeFanning 10 67
(Mark Johnston) *sltly awkward s: sn trckd ldrs: rdn to chal over 2f out: wknd ins fnl f* **12/1**
4011 6 *6* **Emerald Rocket (IRE)**[15] 8207 2-9-6 **75** BenCurtis 7 50
(K R Burke) *prom: rdn along 3f out: wknd over 1f out* **11/8**[1]
244 7 *1/2* **Tarnhelm**[39] 7472 2-9-4 **73** JasonHart 8 47
(Mark Johnston) *led: rdn whn hdd over 2f out: sn wknd* **28/1**
003 8 *1/2* **Urban Soul (IRE)**[81] 6042 2-9-1 **70** PJMcDonald 3 42
(James Bethell) *hld up: nvr threatened* **14/1**
043 9 *3* **Hello My Sunshine**[102] 5255 2-9-2 **71** BarryMcHugh 1 36
(Karen McLintock) *midfield: rdn over 2f out: wknd over 1f out* **33/1**
200 10 *1 1/4* **Bowler Hat**[38] 7513 2-9-6 **75** (p[1]) JosephineGordon 6 36
(Hugo Palmer) *prom tl wknd qckly over 2f out* **9/1**[3]

1m 28.38s (2.18) **Going Correction** +0.20s/f (Slow) **10** Ran SP% **119.4**
Speed ratings (Par 98): **95,94,91,90,89 82,81,81,77,76**
CSF £80.00 CT £664.23 TOTE £22.50: £5.30, £1.50, £2.40; EX 122.30 Trifecta £1063.00.
**Owner** Cheveley Park Stud **Bred** Cheveley Park Stud Ltd **Trained** Musley Bank, N Yorks
**FOCUS**
The feature contest was a fair nursery handicap. They went a respectable gallop and the second favourite got worried out of this in the final 150 yards.

## 8587 32RED.COM / EBF NOVICE MEDIAN AUCTION STKS 6f (Tp)
**4:30** (4:31) (Class 6) 2-Y-0 **£2,911** (£866; £432; £216) **Stalls** Centre

Form RPR
462 1 **Global Tango (IRE)**[19] 8112 2-9-2 79 PJMcDonald 8 80
(Charles Hills) *pressed ldr: rdn to ld over 1f out: edgd lft ins fnl f: kpt on* **2/1**[2]
0 2 *1/2* **I'm Yer Man**[22] 8010 2-9-2 0 ShaneGray 5 79
(Ann Duffield) *dwlt: hld up: pushed along and hdwy 2f out: rdn appr fnl f: kpt on wl* **50/1**
3 *shd* **Furzig** 2-9-2 0 PaulHanagan 1 78
(Richard Fahey) *dwlt: hld up: pushed along and hdwy 2f out: rdn appr fnl f: kpt on wl* **16/1**
63 4 *2 3/4* **Enzo's Lad (IRE)**[16] 8189 2-9-0 0 ow1 CliffordLee(3) 11 71
(K R Burke) *trckd ldrs: rdn over 2f out: one pce* **4/1**[3]
6222 5 *1 3/4* **Manthoor (IRE)**[38] 7511 2-9-2 78 PhillipMakin 2 65
(Owen Burrows) *led narrowly: rdn whn hdd over 1f out: wknd ins fnl f* **1/1**[1]
000 6 *3/4* **Conversant (IRE)**[19] 8119 2-9-2 65 (b[1]) JosephineGordon 3 62
(Hugo Palmer) *trckd ldrs: rdn over 2f out: wknd ins fnl f* **16/1**
7 *4 1/2* **Canufeelthelove** 2-8-11 0 GrahamLee 4 44
(Ben Haslam) *midfield: rdn over 2f out: wknd over 1f out* **66/1**
8 *1 3/4* **Lime Pickle** 2-9-2 0 SamJames 9 44+
(John Davies) *slowly away: a towards rr* **66/1**
54 9 *1* **Sienna Dream**[15] 8208 2-8-11 0 BarryMcHugh 10 36
(Alistair Whillans) *trckd ldrs: rdn over 2f out: wknd* **33/1**
6 10 *42* **Haxby Juniors**[155] 3283 2-8-11 0 DavidAllan 7
(Antony Brittain) *trckd ldrs: rdn 3f out: wknd and eased* **100/1**

1m 13.18s (0.68) **Going Correction** +0.20s/f (Slow) **10** Ran SP% **124.0**
Speed ratings (Par 94): **103,102,102,98,96 95,89,86,85,29**
CSF £109.12 TOTE £2.70: £1.10, £10.10, £5.00; EX 105.20 Trifecta £2283.70.
**Owner** Dr Johnny Hon **Bred** Ballycrighaun Stud **Trained** Lambourn, Berks

**FOCUS**
A fair juvenile novice contest. The front two in the market got racing plenty soon enough and the well-backed favourite couldn't sustain his challenge. The second and third are the keys to the level.

## 8588 32RED CASINO NURSERY H'CAP 5f (Tp)
**5:00** (5:02) (Class 6) (0-65,66) 2-Y-O **£2,587** (£770; £384; £192) **Stalls** Centre

Form RPR

0051 **1** **Cuppacoco**[16] 8191 2-8-10 **54**.......................... ShaneGray 3 65
(Ann Duffield) *mde all: racd towards far side: rdn over 1f out: strly pressed fnl 110yds: kpt on* **7/2**[1]

0406 **2** *nse* **Lord Of The Glen**[16] 8190 2-8-3 **47**..........................(v[1]) JamesSullivan 2 58
(Jim Goldie) *chsd ldr towards far side: rdn over 2f out: chal strly fnl 110yds: kpt on: btn on nod* **9/1**

5360 **3** *3 ¼* **Skyva**[43] 7363 2-8-10 **59**.......................... BenRobinson(5) 13 58
(Brian Ellison) *hld up towards stands' side: rdn and hdwy over 1f out: kpt on fnl f* **13/2**

5006 **4** *nk* **Wiff Waff**[7] 8431 2-9-2 **60**..........................(t) PJMcDonald 10 58+
(Stuart Williams) *rrd s and slowly away: hld up in rr towards stands' side: rdn and hdwy over 1f out: kpt on fnl f* **4/1**[2]

3614 **5** *1 ½* **Seen The Lyte (IRE)**[34] 7655 2-9-5 **66**.......................... CallumRodriguez(3) 12 59
(John Quinn) *racd towards stands' side: chsd ldrs: rdn over 2f out: no ex fnl f* **6/1**[3]

3014 **6** *½* **Funkadelic**[42] 7385 2-9-7 **65**.......................... TomEaves 4 56
(Ben Haslam) *chsd ldr towards far side: rdn over 2f out: no ex fnl f* **16/1**

0050 **7** *½* **Graphite Girl (IRE)**[38] 7518 2-8-4 **51**.......................... RachelRichardson(3) 6 40
(Tim Easterby) *midfield centre: rdn over 2f out: one pce and nvr threatened* **12/1**

3000 **8** *½* **Alaskan Beauty (IRE)**[34] 7655 2-8-12 **56**.......................... DavidAllan 8 43
(Tim Easterby) *midfield centre: rdn over 2f out: one pce and nvr threatened* **20/1**

006 **9** *nk* **Siena Flyer (IRE)**[61] 6755 2-8-2 **46**.......................... AndrewMullen 1 32
(Jedd O'Keeffe) *hld up towards far side: nvr threatened* **33/1**

460 **10** *¾* **Bonanza Bowls**[46] 7242 2-9-1 **62**.......................... AdamMcNamara(3) 5 46
(Bryan Smart) *dwlt: hld up: nvr threatened* **16/1**

4566 **11** *2 ¾* **Dyson's Girl**[16] 8191 2-8-11 **55**..........................(p) GrahamLee 11 29
(Bryan Smart) *midfield centre: rdn over 2f out: wknd fnl furlojg* **10/1**

0000 **12** *½* **Albarino**[16] 8191 2-8-3 **47**.......................... JoeDoyle 7 19
(Kevin Ryan) *prom centre: rdn over 2f out: wknd fnl f* **10/1**

4000 **13** *1* **Acromatic (IRE)**[17] 8145 2-8-10 **54**..........................(v[1]) JasonHart 9 22
(John Quinn) *chsd ldrs centre: rdn 2f out: wknd fnl f* **50/1**

59.59s (0.09) **Going Correction** +0.20s/f (Slow) **13 Ran SP% 127.1**
Speed ratings (Par 94): **107,106,101,101,98 98,97,96,95,94 90,89,87**
CSF £37.49 CT £213.52 TOTE £4.90: £1.90, £3.00, £3.10; EX 34.70 Trifecta £337.80.
**Owner** C A Gledhill & Partner **Bred** Llety Farms **Trained** Constable Burton, N Yorks

**FOCUS**
A modest nursery sprint handicap. The race developed far side off a decent tempo. The winner has been rated as building on her recent win here.

## 8589 SUN BETS ON THE APP H'CAP 1m 5y (Tp)
**5:30** (5:31) (Class 6) (0-65,65) 3-Y-O+ **£2,587** (£770; £384; £192) **Stalls** Centre

Form RPR

602 **1** **Rey Loopy (IRE)**[86] 5835 3-9-4 **64**.......................... TomEaves 12 71+
(Ben Haslam) *stdd s: hld up in rr: smooth and rapid hdwy 2f out: qcknd to ld appr fnl f: rdn and kpt on* **12/1**

2644 **2** *2 ¼* **Rebel State (IRE)**[45] 7271 4-8-12 **63**..........................(p) HarrisonShaw(7) 3 64
(Jedd O'Keeffe) *hld up: rdn over 2f out: hdwy over 1f out: kpt on: wnt 2nd towards fin: no ch wnr* **25/1**

0106 **3** *1* **Billy Bond**[23] 7980 5-9-1 **59**..........................(b) PaulHanagan 10 58
(Richard Fahey) *trckd ldrs: pushed along to ld 2f out: sn rdn: hdd appr fnl f: no ex fnl 110yds: lost 2nd towards fin* **12/1**

0056 **4** *3* **Magistral**[19] 8103 7-9-5 **63**..........................(p) DavidNolan 8 55
(Linda Perratt) *hld up: rdn over 2f out: kpt on fnl f: nrst fin* **25/1**

1114 **5** *nk* **Anna Medici**[74] 6288 3-9-2 **62**.......................... RyanPowell 14 53
(Sir Mark Prescott Bt) *prom: rdn 3f out: outpcd over 1f out: no ex fnl 110yds* **7/2**[1]

1002 **6** *½* **Table Manners**[43] 7364 5-9-0 **65**.......................... NicolaCurrie(7) 9 55
(Wilf Storey) *midfield: rdn over 2f out: one pce and nvr threatened* **7/1**[2]

0-01 **7** *3* **Black Hambleton**[281] 445 4-9-6 **64**.......................... GrahamLee 2 47
(Bryan Smart) *hld up: pushed along and hdwy 2f out: wknd ins fnl f* **16/1**

560 **8** *3 ¾* **Dream Team**[32] 7704 3-9-1 **64**..........................(p) CallumRodriguez(3) 1 38
(Michael Dods) *led narrowly: rdn whn hdd over 2f out: wknd over 1f out* **25/1**

5144 **9** *1 ½* **Thornaby Nash**[46] 7240 6-8-7 **56**..........................(p) GemmaTutty(5) 11 27
(Karen Tutty) *chsd ldrs: rdn to ld over 2f out: hdd 2f out: wknd over 1f out* **12/1**

3640 **10** *7* **Supreme Power (IRE)**[49] 7162 3-9-0 **60**.......................... BarryMcHugh 7 15
(Tracy Waggott) *sn midfield: rdn 3f out: wknd over 1f out* **9/1**

3030 **11** *1* **Haymarket**[15] 8219 8-9-4 **62**.......................... PJMcDonald 6 14
(R Mike Smith) *fly leapt s: hld up: rdn 3f out: sn btn* **28/1**

3500 **12** *2* **Whitkirk**[15] 8216 4-9-7 **65**.......................... JackGarritty 5 13
(Jedd O'Keeffe) *in tch: rdn 3f out: wknd over 1f out* **8/1**[3]

-600 **13** *45* **Weather Front (USA)**[15] 8209 4-9-2 **60**..........................(p) AndrewMullen 13
(Karen McLintock) *slowly away: hld up: rdn over 3f out: sn wknd: eased and t.o* **11/1**

-160 **14** *8* **Dubaitwentytwenty**[24] 7960 3-9-5 **65**..........................(t) JosephineGordon 4
(Hugo Palmer) *pressed ldr: keen early: rdn over 3f out: wknd qckly: eased and t.o* **7/2**[1]

1m 40.6s (2.00) **Going Correction** +0.20s/f (Slow)
**WFA** 3 from 4yo+ 2lb **14 Ran SP% 130.3**
Speed ratings (Par 101): **98,95,94,91,91 90,87,84,82,75 74,72,27,19**
CSF £302.14 CT £3773.12 TOTE £12.90: £3.40, £8.60, £3.30; EX 374.70 Trifecta £4467.40 Part Won..
**Owner** Daniel Shapiro & Mrs C Barclay **Bred** Worldwide Partners **Trained** Middleham Moor, N Yorks

**FOCUS**
A modest handicap. They went a respectable gallop and a strapping, improving 3yo won readily.

## 8590 SUNBETS H'CAP (DIV I) 7f 14y (Tp)
**6:00** (6:02) (Class 6) (0-60,59) 3-Y-O+ **£2,587** (£770; £384; £192) **Stalls** Centre

Form RPR

4024 **1** **Gun Case**[15] 8210 5-9-7 **59**..........................(v[1]) PhillipMakin 10 70
(Alistair Whillans) *hld up: pushed along and hdwy over 1f out: qcknd to ld ins fnl f: rdn and kpt on wl* **11/10**[1]

0550 **2** *1 ½* **Stardrifter**[23] 7979 5-8-5 **46**.......................... RachelRichardson(3) 11 53
(Linda Perratt) *s.i.s: hld up in midfield: smooth hdwy 2f out: rdn to chal ent fnl f: kpt on* **20/1**

02-6 **3** *1 ½* **Chaucer's Tale**[166] 2902 3-9-6 **59**..........................(t) DavidAllan 14 61
(Michael Easterby) *trckd ldrs: rdn over 2f out: chal strly appr fnl f: one pce ins fnl f* **9/1**[3]

-000 **4** *4* **Arizona Sunrise**[84] 5950 4-8-13 **51**.......................... JoeDoyle 13 44
(Tina Jackson) *prom: led narrowly over 2f out: sn rdn: hdd ins fnl f: wknd* **33/1**

0100 **5** *2 ¼* **Let Right Be Done**[19] 8107 5-8-10 **48**..........................(b) AndrewMullen 12 35
(Linda Perratt) *prom: rdn over 2f out: wknd fnl f* **33/1**

0005 **6** *hd* **Gaelic Wizard (IRE)**[5] 8480 9-8-10 **48**..........................(v) SamJames 3 34
(Karen Tutty) *hld up: rdn over 2f out: kpt on ins fnl f: nvr threatened* **25/1**

5000 **7** *1* **Nifty Niece (IRE)**[66] 6571 3-8-6 **45**.......................... ShaneGray 2 28
(Ann Duffield) *hld up in rr: rdn 2f out: kpt on ins fnl f* **66/1**

3056 **8** *hd* **Willbeme**[16] 8194 9-8-11 **52**..........................(bt) PhilDennis(3) 4 35
(Simon West) *dwlt: sn midfield: rdn over 2f out: wknd over 1f out* **20/1**

0034 **9** *1 ½* **Bonnie Gals**[26] 7888 3-9-4 **57**.......................... JoeFanning 1 35
(Keith Dalgleish) *dwlt: hld up: nvr threatened* **8/1**[2]

1400 **10** *2 ¼* **African Grey**[52] 7042 3-9-1 **57**.......................... CallumRodriguez(3) 9 29
(Martin Todhunter) *midfield: rdn over 2f out: wknd over 1f out* **11/1**

3314 **11** *1 ¼* **Someone Exciting**[23] 7980 4-9-1 **58**.......................... JamieGormley(5) 7 28
(David Thompson) *chsd ldrs: rdn over 2f out: wknd over 1f out* **8/1**[2]

0430 **12** *3 ¼* **Searanger (USA)**[16] 8194 4-9-3 **55**.......................... PJMcDonald 8 17
(Rebecca Menzies) *led: rdn whn hdd over 2f out: sn wknd* **10/1**

0060 **13** *10* **Nelson's Bay**[102] 5254 8-8-0 **45**.......................... NicolaCurrie(7) 5
(Wilf Storey) *midfield: rdn over 2f out: wknd* **16/1**

5000 **14** *29* **George Bailey (IRE)**[13] 8258 5-8-7 **45**..........................(p[1]) JamesSullivan 6
(Suzzanne France) *hld up: rdn over 3f out: wknd and bhd* **50/1**

1m 27.81s (1.61) **Going Correction** +0.20s/f (Slow)
**WFA** 3 from 4yo+ 1lb **14 Ran SP% 125.9**
Speed ratings (Par 101): **98,96,94,90,87 87,86,85,84,81 80,76,64,31**
CSF £33.18 CT £159.96 TOTE £1.80: £1.10, £5.70, £3.30; EX 28.80 Trifecta £323.20.
**Owner** A C Whillans **Bred** Mildmay Bloodstock Ltd **Trained** Newmill-On-Slitrig, Borders

**FOCUS**
The first division of a moderate handicap. They went a respectable gallop with the race developing towards the near side. The heavily backed favourite won well. Straightforward form, with the runner-up helping to set the standard.

## 8591 SUNBETS H'CAP (DIV II) 7f 14y (Tp)
**6:35** (6:35) (Class 6) (0-60,59) 3-Y-O+ **£2,587** (£770; £384; £192) **Stalls** Centre

Form RPR

064 **1** **Breathoffreshair**[13] 8255 3-8-11 **50**..........................(t) JoeFanning 2 56
(Richard Guest) *dwlt: hld up: hdwy over 2f out: rdn to ld appr fnl f: kpt on* **13/2**

0301 **2** *¾* **Kroy**[16] 8194 3-9-3 **59**..........................(p) AdamMcNamara(3) 1 63
(Ollie Pears) *midfield: rdn over 2f out: hdwy to chse ldr over 1f out: kpt on* **6/1**[3]

0000 **3** *nk* **Lukoutoldmakezebak**[13] 8258 4-8-2 **45**..........................(p) JamieGormley(5) 12 49
(David Thompson) *chsd ldrs: rdn over 2f out: kpt on* **66/1**

0005 **4** *1 ¼* **Little Choosey**[8] 8401 7-9-1 **56**..........................(bt) EoinWalsh(3) 13 57
(Roy Bowring) *led: rdn over 2f out: hdd appr fnl f: no ex fnl 110yds* **12/1**

0264 **5** *nse* **Broughtons Fancy**[8] 8402 4-8-10 **53**.......................... GemmaTutty(5) 7 54
(Karen Tutty) *midfield: rdn over 2f out: kpt on ins fnl f* **11/2**[2]

6560 **6** *1* **Betty Grable (IRE)**[53] 7016 3-8-11 **57**.......................... NicolaCurrie(7) 14 54
(Wilf Storey) *hld up: rdn over 2f out: kpt on ins fnl f: nvr threatened ldrs* **16/1**

0513 **7** *hd* **Intiwin (IRE)**[15] 8210 5-9-7 **59**.......................... DavidNolan 6 57
(Linda Perratt) *hld up: rdn and hdwy over 1f out: one pce ins fnl f* **9/4**[1]

4000 **8** *1 ¼* **Sugar Beach (FR)**[15] 8206 3-9-5 **58**..........................(t) ShaneGray 3 52
(Ann Duffield) *prom: rdn over 2f out: wknd ins fnl f* **33/1**

4024 **9** *½* **Jessie Allan (IRE)**[23] 7979 6-8-3 **48**.......................... SeanMooney(7) 4 41
(Jim Goldie) *midfield: rdn 3f out: outpcd over 1f out: pluged on fnl f* **12/1**

6050 **10** *3 ¼* **Nellie Deen (IRE)**[13] 8259 4-8-0 **45**..........................(p[1]) PaulaMuir(7) 9 30
(Simon West) *prom: rdn and outpcd over 3f out: wknd over 1f out* **66/1**

6550 **11** *1 ¾* **Mercers Row**[98] 5418 10-8-9 **47**.......................... JamesSullivan 8 27
(Martin Todhunter) *hld up in rr: rdn over 2f out: nvr threatened* **50/1**

6033 **12** *nk* **Peny Arcade**[14] 8248 3-8-7 **46**.......................... PaulHanagan 10 24
(Alistair Whillans) *hld up: rdn over 2f out: sn btn* **7/1**

0604 **13** *hd* **Little Kingdom (IRE)**[49] 7166 3-9-0 **53**.......................... BarryMcHugh 11 31
(Tracy Waggott) *trckd ldrs: rdn 3f out: sn wknd* **25/1**

6605 **14** *1 ¾* **Coral Princess (IRE)**[23] 7980 3-8-6 **45**.......................... AndrewMullen 5 18
(Keith Dalgleish) *hld up: rdn over 2f out: sn btn* **14/1**

1m 27.48s (1.28) **Going Correction** +0.20s/f (Slow)
**WFA** 3 from 4yo+ 1lb **14 Ran SP% 125.9**
Speed ratings (Par 101): **100,99,98,97,97 96,95,94,93,90 88,87,87,85**
CSF £46.17 CT £2482.02 TOTE £10.20: £3.60, £1.90, £12.80; EX 69.90 Trifecta £3512.80.
**Owner** Alfa Site Services Ltd/Mrs Alison Guest **Bred** D Curran **Trained** Ingmanthorpe, W Yorks

**FOCUS**
The second division of a moderate handicap. They went a respectable gallop and the winning time was marginally quicker. The third is among those that suggests the form is limited.

## 8592 BETWAY CASINO MAIDEN STKS 6f (Tp)
**7:10** (7:10) (Class 5) 3-Y-O+ **£3,234** (£962; £481; £240) **Stalls** Centre

Form RPR

4340 **1** **Envisaging (IRE)**[44] 7321 3-9-5 78..........................(t) PJMcDonald 1 79+
(James Fanshawe) *hld up: hdwy to trck ldr 2f out: rdn over 1f out: led 110yds out: kpt on* **4/11**[1]

0320 **2** *1 ¾* **Decision Maker (IRE)**[100] 5316 3-9-2 68.......................... EoinWalsh(3) 3 73
(Roy Bowring) *prom: led over 3f out: rdn over 2f out: hdd 110yds out: no ex* **6/1**[3]

0 **3** *5* **Limoncino (IRE)**[15] 8217 3-8-11 0..........................(h) CallumRodriguez(3) 4 52
(Michael Dods) *dwlt: sn trckd ldrs: rdn over 2f out: outpcd over 1f out: plugged on ins fnl f* **12/1**

25-4 **4** *2 ¼* **Andys Girl (IRE)**[16] 8194 4-8-9 59.......................... BenRobinson(5) 5 45
(Brian Ellison) *trckd ldrs: rdn over 2f out: wknd over 1f out* **11/2**[2]

6600 **5** *10* **Six Of The Best**[66] 6572 5-9-0 40..........................(p[1]) GrahamLee 2 12
(Bryan Smart) *led narrowly: hdd over 3f out: wknd over 2f out and bhd* **50/1**

1m 14.67s (2.17) **Going Correction** +0.20s/f (Slow) **5 Ran SP% 112.6**
Speed ratings (Par 103): **93,90,84,81,67**
CSF £3.32 TOTE £1.20: £1.10, £2.10; EX 2.80 Trifecta £11.00.
**Owner** Ben CM Wong **Bred** David McGuinness **Trained** Newmarket, Suffolk

**FOCUS**
An ordinary, uncompetitive little maiden. They went a modest gallop but the right two horses still came to the fore.
T/Plt: £185.60 to a £1 stake. Pool: £55,067.51 - 216.49 winning units T/Qpdt: £127.30 to a £1 stake. Pool: £9,371.56 - 54.44 winning units **Andrew Sheret**

8560 **NEWMARKET** (R-H)
Saturday, November 4

**OFFICIAL GOING: Good to soft (7.5)**
Wind: light, against Weather: rain until race 4

## 8593 PRESTIGE CLASSICS EBF FILLIES' NOVICE STKS (PLUS 10 RACE) (DIV I) 7f
**12:05** (12:05) (Class 4) 2-Y-O **£4,528** (£1,347; £673; £336) **Stalls** Low

Form RPR
0 **1** **Nawassi**84 5938 2-9-0 0 JimCrowley 4 82
(John Gosden) *sn led and mde rest: rdn over 1f out: styd on strly and drew clr ins fnl f: rdn out* **7/4**1

01 **2** 2 3/4 **Revalue**17 8148 2-9-6 0 PatSmullen 6 81
(Charles Hills) *trckd ldng pair tl clsd to chse wnr over 2f out: effrt u.p over 1f out: no ex and wandered rt jst ins fnl f: outpcd after but stl clr 2nd* **11/4**2

**3** 3 3/4 **Hateel (IRE)** 2-9-0 0 TedDurcan 1 65+
(William Haggas) *chsd ldng trio: pushed along and outpcd over 2f out: no ch w ldng pair over 1f out: wnt 3rd and kpt on same pce ins fnl f* **8/1**

**4** 3/4 **Alizeti (IRE)** 2-9-0 0 FranBerry 9 63+
(Henry Candy) *hld up in tch in rr: pushed along and hdwy into midfield over 1f out: no threat to ldrs and kpt on same pce ins fnl f* **16/1**

**5** 1/2 **Rococo** 2-9-0 0 RobertHavlin 5 62+
(John Gosden) *hld up in tch in midfield: pushed along 2f out: sme hdwy into midfield and swtchd lft 1f out: no threat to ldrs and kpt on same pce fnl 150yds* **4/1**3

0 **6** 1 1/2 **Queen Maureen (USA)**17 8147 2-9-0 0 (t) JackMitchell 8 58
(Hugo Palmer) *in tch in midfield: rdn 3f out: sn struggling and outpcd over 2f out: wl hld and plugged on same pce fnl 2f* **40/1**

5 **7** 3/4 **Fire Orchid**17 8147 2-9-0 0 SeanLevey 2 56
(Richard Hannon) *chsd wnr tl over 2f out: 3rd and btn over 1f out: wknd ins fnl f* **12/1**

**8** 3 **Love To Breeze** 2-9-0 0 ShaneKelly 7 48
(Ed Vaughan) *hld up in last pair: pushed along 1/2-way: sn struggling and wl btn over 1f out* **20/1**

**9** 7 **Ness Of Brodgar** 2-9-0 0 JoeyHaynes 3 30
(Mark H Tompkins) *midfield: rdn 1/2-way: lost pl and towards rr 2f out: sn wknd* **100/1**

1m 28.11s (2.71) **Going Correction** +0.20s/f (Good) **9** Ran SP% **115.9**
Speed ratings (Par 95): **92,88,84,83,83 81,80,77,69**
CSF £6.53 TOTE £2.50: £1.10, £1.40, £2.70; EX 8.00 Trifecta £23.00.
**Owner** Hamdan Al Maktoum **Bred** Shadwell Estate Company Limited **Trained** Newmarket, Suffolk

**FOCUS**
Stands' side course used. Stalls: far side. There was 5mm of rain overnight, and a further 3mm in the morning, resulting in the going changing from good to firm the previous day to good to soft. The market spoke strongly in favour of this winner. The level is a bit fluid.

## 8594 PRESTIGE CLASSICS EBF FILLIES' NOVICE STKS (PLUS 10 RACE) (DIV II) 7f
**12:35** (12:38) (Class 4) 2-Y-O **£4,528** (£1,347; £673; £336) **Stalls** Low

Form RPR
2324 **1** **Perfect Thought**14 8236 2-9-0 76 RichardKingscote 4 78
(William Haggas) *taken down early: mde all: rdn over 1f out: in command ins fnl f: pushed out towards fin* **15/8**1

**2** 3/4 **Worth Waiting** 2-9-0 0 TedDurcan 3 76+
(David Lanigan) *dwlt: in tch in midfield: pushed along 3f out: rdn and hdwy over 1f out: chsd wnr and swtchd rt ins fnl f: styd on wl towards fin* **33/1**

**3** 2 1/4 **Classic Charm** 2-8-11 0 JackDuern(3) 1 70
(Dean Ivory) *s.i.s: sn rcvrd to chse wnr after 1f tl 3f out: sn rdn: chsd clr wnr again briefly jst ins fnl f: 3rd and wknd fnl 100yds: swtchd rt towards fin* **66/1**

0 **4** hd **Shurooq**40 7453 2-9-0 0 JimCrowley 2 70
(Owen Burrows) *chsd wnr for 1f: styd prom: chsd wnr again 3f out: unable qck over 1f out: lost 2 pls jst ins fnl f and kpt on same pce after* **4/1**3

**5** 1 3/4 **Sary Arqa** 2-9-0 0 JackMitchell 8 65
(Roger Varian) *hld up in tch in midfield: clsd to chse ldrs 3f out: shkn up 2f out: rdn: rn green and edgd lft ent fnl f: unable qck and kpt on same pce ins fnl f* **8/1**

**6** 1/2 **Agrotera (IRE)** 2-9-0 0 LiamKeniry 7 64
(Ed Walker) *dwlt: t.k.h: hld up in tch in last pair: swtchd rt over 2f out: effrt and hdwy over 1f out: kpt on same pce and no imp ins fnl f* **16/1**

6 **7** 1 1/2 **Beautiful Artist (USA)**17 8148 2-9-0 0 NickyMackay 5 60
(John Gosden) *chsd ldng trio: rdn 3f out: unable qck over 1f out: wknd ins fnl f* **8/1**

**8** 3 1/4 **Poetic Imagination** 2-9-0 0 RobertHavlin 9 51
(John Gosden) *hld up in tch in last pair: pushed along over 2f out: no imp and btn over 1f out: wknd and edgd rt ins fnl f* **3/1**2

6 **9** 6 **Political Slot**11 8324 2-9-0 0 (h) PatrickMathers 6 36
(Derek Shaw) *hld up in tch in last trio: short of room over 4f out: swtchd rt and rdn over 2f out: outpcd and wandered 2f out: sn bhd* **100/1**

1m 27.14s (1.74) **Going Correction** +0.20s/f (Good) **9** Ran SP% **113.3**
Speed ratings (Par 95): **98,97,94,94,92 91,90,86,79**
CSF £66.83 TOTE £2.40: £1.10, £7.20, £13.70; EX 75.70 Trifecta £975.30.
**Owner** Liam Sheridan **Bred** Rabbah Bloodstock Limited **Trained** Newmarket, Suffolk

**FOCUS**
The faster of the two divisions by 0.97sec, and another all-the-way winner.

## 8595 32RED.COM NURSERY H'CAP 1m 1f
**1:10** (1:11) (Class 4) (0-85,84) 2-Y-O **£4,528** (£1,347; £673; £336) **Stalls** Low

Form RPR
0323 **1** **Shaherezada (IRE)**10 8354 2-9-1 78 AdamKirby 3 88+
(Clive Cox) *chsd ldrs: effrt to chse ldr over 2f out: drvn to chal over 1f out: led 1f out: sn edgd lft and drvn clr: styd on* **3/1**1

5000 **2** 5 **Galactic (IRE)**10 8349 2-8-0 63 (b) KieranO'Neill 6 63
(Richard Hannon) *t.k.h: led after 1f: rdn 2f out: edgd rt u.p over 1f out: hdd 1f out: no ex and sn swtchd rt: wknd fnl 100yds but stl clr 2nd* **14/1**

521 **3** 2 1/4 **Kind Act (USA)**42 7411 2-9-7 84 MartinLane 2 80
(Charlie Appleby) *led for 1f: chsd ldr: rdn over 4f out tl 3rd and unable qck over 2f out: wl hld over 1f out: plugged on* **3/1**1

656 **4** 3 1/4 **Berkshire Spirit**38 7503 2-8-5 68 RobHornby 5 57
(Andrew Balding) *squeezed for room leaving stalls: sn swtchd rt and hld up in tch: 5th and outpcd u.p over 2f out: no threat to ldrs after: wnt modest 4th ins fnl f* **9/2**2

424 **5** 1/2 **Bold Reason (GER)**18 8136 2-9-4 81 RobertHavlin 4 69
(John Gosden) *trckd ldrs: 4th and reminders over 2f out: sn struggling and wl btn over 1f out* **3/1**1

0161 **6** 2 1/2 **Enzo (IRE)**25 7915 2-9-3 80 (t) LiamKeniry 1 63
(Ed Walker) *hld up in tch in rr: effrt over 2f out: no hdwy wl btn 2f out: eased wl ins fnl f* **7/1**3

1m 54.22s (2.52) **Going Correction** +0.20s/f (Good) **6** Ran SP% **112.3**
Speed ratings (Par 98): **96,91,89,86,86 84**
CSF £42.64 TOTE £3.20: £1.70, £5.60; EX 37.20 Trifecta £92.00.
**Owner** Nurlan Bizakov **Bred** Hesmonds Stud Ltd **Trained** Lambourn, Berks

**FOCUS**
A fair nursery. The runner-up helps set the standard.

## 8596 QUY MILL HOTEL & SPA H'CAP 1m
**1:45** (1:46) (Class 4) (0-80,82) 3-Y-O+ **£5,175** (£1,540; £769; £384) **Stalls** Low

Form RPR
4324 **1** **Roll On Rory**36 7570 4-9-5 78 (b) FrannyNorton 14 88
(Jason Ward) *t.k.h: chsd ldr tl led over 6f out: drvn over 1f out: styd on u.p and forged ahd ins fnl f: rdn out* **4/1**1

0600 **2** 2 **Shamrokh (IRE)**26 7892 3-8-9 70 ow1 (t) TomQueally 13 75
(Michael Appleby) *hld up in tch in midfield: clsd to chse wnr over 3f out: drvn to press wnr over 1f out: unable qck 1f out: kpt on same pce ins fnl f* **12/1**

0321 **3** 2 **Titan Goddess**9 8376 5-8-10 69 ShaneKelly 8 69
(Mike Murphy) *hld up in tch in midfield: rdn and hdwy over 2f out: drvn to chse clr ldng pair over 1f out: kpt on but nvr threatening ldrs* **8/1**

4105 **4** 3 **Dark Intention (IRE)**22 8014 4-9-7 80 RobertWinston 12 74
(Lawrence Mullaney) *t.k.h: hld up in tch in midfield: effrt to chse ldrs 3f out: no imp and kpt on same pce fr over 1f out* **11/2**2

5403 **5** 3/4 **Plant Pot Power (IRE)**8 8392 3-9-7 82 (p1) KieranO'Neill 11 74
(Richard Hannon) *stdd s: hld up in rr: swtchd lft over 2f out: rdn and hdwy wl over 1f out: no imp fnl f* **7/1**3

5200 **6** nk **Lawmaking**19 8111 4-9-7 80 (h) LiamKeniry 7 71
(Henry Spiller) *hld up in tch in midfield: clsd to chse ldng pair 3f out: sn pushed along and unable qck: rdn 2f out: plugged on* **12/1**

3030 **7** 11 **Roman De Brut (IRE)**26 7894 5-8-13 75 CharlieBennett(3) 5 41
(Denis Quinn) *in tch in midfield: rdn 3f out: sn struggling: wknd over 1f out* **50/1**

5420 **8** 1 **Invermere**34 7658 4-8-13 72 TonyHamilton 1 35
(Richard Fahey) *in tch in midfield: rdn over 2f out: sn struggling: wknd over 1f out* **9/1**

1363 **9** 15 **Pacific Salt (IRE)**24 7957 4-8-13 75 CallumShepherd(3) 9 4
(Pam Sly) *t.k.h: chsd ldrs tl rdn and lost pl over 3f out: wknd wl over 1f out: eased ins fnl f* **8/1**

030 **10** 22 **Pecheurs De Perles (IRE)**58 6855 3-9-5 80 PatSmullen 6
(Iain Jardine) *t.k.h: led tl over 6f out: chsd wnr tl over 3f out: sn lost pl u.p: wl bhd and virtually p.u ins fnl f: t.o* **11/1**

0000 **11** 1 3/4 **Maifalki (FR)**28 7824 4-9-2 75 (h1) RobertHavlin 4
(Jason Ward) *stdd s and sn swtchd lft: t.k.h: hld up in tch in rr: pushed along 3f out: sn btn: bhd and eased over 1f out: t.o* **16/1**

0150 **12** 5 **Rubens Dream**78 6143 3-9-2 77 JimCrowley 2
(Charles Hills) *in tch in midfield: lost pl and bhd 3f out: eased over 1f out: t.o* **16/1**

1m 38.32s (-0.28) **Going Correction** +0.20s/f (Good)
**WFA** 3 from 4yo+ 2lb **12** Ran SP% **117.6**
Speed ratings (Par 105): **109,107,105,102,101 100,89,88,73,51 50,45**
CSF £52.67 CT £375.58 TOTE £4.00: £1.50, £4.00, £2.30; EX 56.80 Trifecta £571.20.
**Owner** P Adams,J Sutton,T Wickins,Jhetherington **Bred** Stuart Matheson **Trained** Middleham, N Yorks

**FOCUS**
The pace held up pretty well here. The third has been rated close to her recent form.

## 8597 BRITISH STALLION STUDS EBF MONTROSE FILLIES' STKS (LISTED RACE) 1m
**2:20** (2:25) (Class 1) 2-Y-O
**£17,013** (£6,450; £3,228; £1,608; £807; £405) **Stalls** Low

Form RPR
31 **1** **Hadith (IRE)**17 8163 2-9-0 0 AdamKirby 4 98
(Charlie Appleby) *racd towards far side: mde all: rdn over 2f out: hung lft and forged ahd 1f out: styd on: rdn out: 1st of 5 in gp* **5/2**1

**2** 1 1/4 **Baroness (IRE)**13 8264 2-9-0 90 FranBerry 9 95
(Joseph Patrick O'Brien, Ire) *racd in centre: trckd ldrs: effrt to ld gp and ev ch 2f out: hung rt over 1f out: no ex and styd on same pce ins fnl f: 1st of 6 in gp* **8/1**

10 **3** 3/4 **Herecomesthesun (IRE)**22 8002 2-9-0 0 JimCrowley 2 93
(Archie Watson) *racd towards far side: chsd ldrs: effrt over 2f out: pressed ldrs over 1f out: styd on same pce ins fnl f: 2nd of 5 in gp* **5/1**3

6211 **4** 1/2 **Awesometank**21 8045 2-9-0 93 RichardKingscote 3 92
(William Haggas) *racd towards far side: chsd ldrs: clsd to press ldrs 2f out: rdn and edgd lft over 1f out: styd on same pce ins fnl f: 3rd of 5 in gp* **9/2**2

1 **5** 3 1/4 **Orsera (IRE)**53 7022 2-9-0 0 (h) JackMitchell 12 85
(Peter Chapple-Hyam) *racd in centre: stdd s: hld up in rr: effrt 2f out: hdwy whn wnt lft u.p over 1f out: 5th and kpt on same pce fnl f: nvr trbld ldrs: 2nd of 6 in gp* **16/1**

0051 **6** 1/2 **Wild Impala (FR)**10 8347 2-9-0 85 RobertHavlin 11 84
(John Gosden) *racd in centre: in tch in midfield: keeping on same pce u.p whn hmpd over 1f out: no imp fnl f: 3rd of 6 in gp* **16/1**

3610 **7** 5 **Elysium Dream**7 8424 2-9-0 87 SeanLevey 1 72
(Richard Hannon) *racd towards far side: chsd ldrs tl over 2f out: sn outpcd u.p and wknd over 1f out: 4th of 5 in gp* **8/1**

1040 **8** 4 1/2 **Apple Anni (IRE)**7 8440 2-9-0 80 CharlesBishop 7 62
(Mick Channon) *racd towards far side: a rr: rdn over 3f out: sn struggling: bhd 2f out: 5th of 5 in gp* **100/1**

2 **9** nk **Shalailah (IRE)**22 8016 2-9-0 90 PatSmullen 6 61
(Joseph Patrick O'Brien, Ire) *racd in centre: led gp and chsd ldr overall tl over 2f out: sn u.p and lost pl over 1f out: wknd fnl f: 4th of 6 in gp* **25/1**

56 **10** 1 **Damselfly (IRE)**7 8437 2-9-0 93 JimmyQuinn 8 59
(Joseph Patrick O'Brien, Ire) *racd in centre: in tch in midfield: effrt ent fnl 2f: rdn and no hdwy over 1f out: wknd ins fnl f: 5th of 6 in gp* **20/1**

1 **11** *1* **Pioneer Spirit**[35] 7608 2-9-0 0 .......... RobertTart 10 56
(John Gosden) *v free to post: s.i.s: rn in snatches in rr: lost tch over 1f out* **8/1**

1m 38.73s (0.13) **Going Correction** +0.20s/f (Good) **11** Ran SP% **118.1**
Speed ratings (Par 101): **107,105,105,104,101 100,95,91,90,89 88**
CSF £22.87 TOTE £3.30: £1.40, £2.60, £1.90; EX 25.70 Trifecta £106.50.
**Owner** Godolphin **Bred** Godolphin **Trained** Newmarket, Suffolk

**FOCUS**
The field split into two groups but there looked to be no bias favouring one or the other. A minor pb from the runner-up.

## 8598 WEATHERBYS GENERAL STUD BOOK ONLINE JAMES SEYMOUR STKS (LISTED RACE) 1m 2f

**2:55** (2:59) (Class 1) 3-Y-O+

**£20,982** (£7,955; £3,981; £1,983; £995; £499) **Stalls** Low

Form RPR

4522 **1** **Permission**[22] 8007 4-8-13 105 .......... DanielMuscutt 2 106
(James Fanshawe) *s.i.s: hld up in tch in last pair: clsd to chsd ldrs and rdn 2f out: ev ch and short of room on far rail over 1f out: styd on gamely u.p to ld wl ins fnl f: rdn out* **7/2**[2]

1050 **2** *nk* **Air Pilot**[97] 5464 8-9-9 112 .......... RichardKingscote 1 115
(Ralph Beckett) *trckd ldrs: clsd and upsides ldr 3f out: rdn over 2f out: getting squeezed for room and swtchd lft over 1f out: ev ch wl ins fnl f: styd on* **5/1**[3]

13-2 **3** *1* **Boynton (USA)**[23] 7988 3-9-1 113 .......... AdamKirby 5 109
(Charlie Appleby) *led: rdn ent fnl 2f: drvn and hung rt over 1f out: hdd wl ins fnl f: no ex and wknd cl home* **11/2**

4613 **4** *6* **Dark Red (IRE)**[14] 8234 5-9-4 102 .......... (b) FrannyNorton 4 96
(Ed Dunlop) *hld up in tch in midfield: effrt over 2f out: no imp over 1f out: wl hld and plugged on same pce ins fnl f* **7/1**

0262 **5** *5* **Sands Chorus**[35] 7619 5-9-4 95 .......... TomQueally 3 86
(James Given) *chsd ldr tl 3f out: sn u.p and outpcd: wknd over 1f out* **16/1**

23 **6** *1* **Spark Plug (IRE)**[21] 8041 6-9-7 110 .......... PatSmullen 6 87
(Brian Meehan) *hld up wl in tch in midfield: rdn and effrt to chse ldrs 3f out: unable qck and lost pl wl over 1f out: wknd fnl f* **5/2**[1]

131 **7** *9* **Neshmeya**[28] 7816 3-8-10 88 .......... JimCrowley 7 62
(Charles Hills) *hld up in tch in last pair: effrt and drifted lft over 2f out: sn struggling: wknd over 1f out* **8/1**

2m 3.99s (-1.81) **Going Correction** +0.20s/f (Good)
**WFA** 3 from 4yo+ 3lb **7** Ran SP% **112.3**
Speed ratings (Par 111): **115,114,113,109,105 104,97**
CSF £20.41 TOTE £4.30: £2.20, £2.40; EX 25.30 Trifecta £138.90.
**Owner** Mrs J Scott, J F Dean & Lady Trenchard **Bred** Glebe Stud, J F Dean & Lady Trenchard **Trained** Newmarket, Suffolk

**FOCUS**
They went an ordinary early gallop and the first three had a good scrap inside the last. The first two have been rated to form, and the third to his AW reappearance figure.

## 8599 PRICE BAILEY BEN MARSHALL STKS (LISTED RACE) 1m

**3:30** (3:36) (Class 1) 3-Y-O+

**£20,982** (£7,955; £3,981; £1,983; £995; £499) **Stalls** Low

Form RPR

-124 **1** **Bravo Zolo (IRE)**[208] 1691 5-9-2 111 .......... AdamKirby 8 110
(Charlie Appleby) *hld up in tch in midfield: clsd to join ldrs over 2f out: rdn over 1f out: sustained chal u.p to ld ins fnl f: hld on wl: rdn out* **3/1**[2]

121 **2** *nk* **Lord Glitters (FR)**[14] 8234 4-9-2 107 .......... JimCrowley 7 109
(David O'Meara) *taken down early: stdd s and hld up in tch in rr: effrt over 1f out: rdn to chse ldrs and edgd rt over 1f out: ev ch ins fnl f: kpt on wl but hld towards fin* **4/5**[1]

1-14 **3** *1 ¼* **Via Via (IRE)**[18] 8138 5-9-2 95 .......... PatSmullen 6 106
(James Tate) *chsd ldrs tl clsd to press ldr 3f out: rdn ent fnl 2f: led wl over 1f out but hrd pressed: hdd ins fnl f: no ex and wknd towards fin* **12/1**

5312 **4** *2* **Jallota**[7] 8417 6-9-5 110 .......... FranBerry 5 105
(Charles Hills) *hld up in tch in last pair: effrt to cl over 2f out: chsng ldrs whn squeezed for room over 1f out: kpt on same pce fnl f* **8/1**[3]

0430 **5** *4 ½* **Oh This Is Us (IRE)**[14] 8234 4-9-5 106 .......... SeanLevey 3 94
(Richard Hannon) *led: rdn over 2f out: hdd wl over 1f out: no ex and wknd ins fnl f* **10/1**

05 **6** *9* **Ciaoadiosimdone (IRE)**[19] 8117 3-8-9 0 .......... JackOsborn 1 65
(John Ryan) *chsd ldr tl 3f out: sn rdn and dropped to rr: wl bhd fnl f* **100/1**

1m 39.47s (0.87) **Going Correction** +0.20s/f (Good)
**WFA** 3 from 4yo+ 2lb **6** Ran SP% **109.4**
Speed ratings (Par 111): **103,102,101,99,94 85**
CSF £5.45 TOTE £3.40: £2.00, £1.10; EX 6.80 Trifecta £26.20.
**Owner** Godolphin **Bred** Tipper House Stud **Trained** Newmarket, Suffolk
■ La Berma was withdrawn. Price at time of withdrawal 33/1. Rule 4 does not apply

**FOCUS**
The early gallop wasn't that strong and there was a bit of a sprint finish. The time was the slowest of the three races run over a mile on the card. The winner has been rated to form.

## 8600 IMP GRAPHICS H'CAP 7f

**4:00** (4:06) (Class 4) (0-85,87) 3-Y-O+ **£5,175** (£1,540; £769; £384) **Stalls** Low

Form RPR

1-11 **1** **Yellowhammer**[17] 8150 3-9-3 82 .......... JimCrowley 9 90+
(Roger Charlton) *racd in centre: keen to post: stdd s: hld up in midfield: rdn and hdwy 2f out: chsd ldrs 1f out: styd on strly ins fnl f to ld 50yds out: rdn out: 1st of 11 in gp* **2/1**[1]

541 **2** *¾* **Give It Some Teddy**[15] 8217 3-8-7 72 .......... RobHornby 3 78+
(Tim Easterby) *racd far side: hld up in rr: swtchd lft and effrt over 2f out: rdn and hdwy over 1f out: chsd ldrs 1f out: styd on wl to snatch 2nd last strides: 1st of 3 in gp* **6/1**[2]

0210 **3** *nse* **London (FR)**[18] 8138 4-9-6 87 .......... (h) CallumShepherd[(3)] 8 94
(Phil McEntee) *racd in centre: led gp and chsd ldrs overall: rdn and ev ch 2f out: kpt on wl u.p: unable qck towards fin: 2nd of 11 in gp* **14/1**

5440 **4** *hd* **Highland Colori (IRE)**[22] 8009 9-9-6 84 .......... (b) DavidProbert 7 90
(Andrew Balding) *racd far side: pressed overall ldr tl rdn to ld 2f out: kpt on wl u.p tl hdd 50yds out: no ex and lost 2 pls last strides: 2nd of 3 in gp* **7/1**[3]

1346 **5** *1 ¼* **Multicultural (IRE)**[24] 7947 3-8-6 78 .......... (v) PaulHainey[(7)] 5 80
(James Tate) *racd in centre: dwlt: sn rcvrd to chse gp ldr and prom overall: rdn and ev ch 2f out tl unable qck 1f out: outpcd ins fnl f: 3rd of 11 in gp* **8/1**

150- **6** *1 ¼* **Able Jack**[427] 6123 4-9-1 79 .......... (v) SeanLevey 6 79
(Stuart Williams) *racd in centre: in tch in midfield: effrt 2f out: kpt on u.p ins fnl f: nt rch ldrs: 4th of 11 in gp* **50/1**

5302 **7** *hd* **Right Action**[67] 6558 3-8-11 76 .......... TonyHamilton 11 74
(Richard Fahey) *racd in centre: chsd gp ldrs and prom overall: rdn ent fnl 2f: no ex over 1f out and kpt on same pce fnl f: 5th of 11 in gp* **14/1**

0005 **8** *¾* **Medburn Dream**[20] 8078 4-9-5 83 .......... FrannyNorton 20 80
(Peter Hedger) *racd nr side: led gp and chsd ldrs overall: rdn over 2f out: hung rt ent fnl 2f and unable qck over 1f out: wknd ins fnl f: 1st of 3 in gp* **16/1**

1540 **9** *¾* **Working Class**[26] 7894 3-8-8 73 .......... JackMitchell 12 67
(Peter Chapple-Hyam) *racd in centre: hld up towards rr: rdn and hdwy over 1f out: kpt on ins fnl f: nvr trbld ldrs: 6th of 11 in gp* **33/1**

0350 **10** *¾* **Welliesinthewater (IRE)**[98] 5415 7-9-6 84 .......... (v) PatrickMathers 14 77
(Derek Shaw) *racd in centre: dwlt: t.k.h: hld up in rr: effrt 2f out: hdwy u.p 1f out: styd on ins fnl f: nvr trbld ldrs: 7th of 11 in gp* **50/1**

5620 **11** *nk* **Musical Comedy**[79] 6113 6-8-9 73 .......... ShaneKelly 10 65
(Mike Murphy) *racd in centre: stdd s: t.k.h: hld up in tch towards rr: hdwy ent fnl 2f out: rdn over 1f out: no imp and wknd ins fnl f: 8th of 11 in gp* **33/1**

440 **12** *¾* **Scottish Glen**[29] 7780 11-9-2 83 .......... HectorCrouch[(3)] 17 73
(Patrick Chamings) *racd in centre: hld up towards rr: effrt 2f out: hdwy and styd on ins fnl f: nvr trbld ldrs: 9th of 11 in gp* **25/1**

3100 **13** *nk* **Lady Freyja**[10] 8351 3-8-8 80 .......... JackOsborn[(7)] 13 68
(John Ryan) *racd in centre: hld up towards rr: rdn over 2f out: no imp over 1f out: kpt on same pce: nvr trbld ldrs: 10th of 11 in centre* **33/1**

030 **14** *nse* **Firmdecisions (IRE)**[35] 7622 7-9-4 85 .......... JackDuern[(3)] 1 74
(Dean Ivory) *racd far side: overall ldrs tl 2f out: rdn and lost pl over 1f out: wknd ins fnl f: 3rd of 3 in gp* **25/1**

2103 **15** *2 ¾* **Case Key**[16] 8186 4-8-4 75 .......... (p) GabrieleMalune[(7)] 15 57
(Michael Appleby) *racd in centre: in tch in midfield: effrt over 2f out: no imp u.p over 1f out: wknd ins fnl f: 11th of 11 in gp* **33/1**

-106 **16** *2 ¼* **Dalton**[8] 8393 3-8-11 76 .......... FranBerry 19 51
(David O'Meara) *racd stands side: hld up in rr: effrt ent fnl 2f: no imp over 1f out: bhd ins fnl f: 2nd of 3 in gp* **11/1**

1600 **17** *hd* **Robin Weathers (USA)**[7] 8418 3-8-10 78 .......... GeorgiaCox[(3)] 18 52
(William Haggas) *taken down early: racd stands side: t.k.h: chsd gp ldr and midfield overall: effrt and hung rt ent fnl 2f: btn over 1f out: wknd ins fnl f: 3rd of 3 in gp* **20/1**

1m 26.49s (1.09) **Going Correction** +0.20s/f (Good)
**WFA** 3 from 4yo+ 1lb **17** Ran SP% **126.9**
Speed ratings (Par 105): **101,100,100,99,98 97,96,95,95,94 93,93,92,92,89 86,86**
CSF £11.78 CT £142.88 TOTE £2.70: £1.40, £2.00, £2.60, £1.40; EX 15.00 Trifecta £79.00.
**Owner** Lady Rothschild **Bred** Kincorth Investments Inc **Trained** Beckhampton, Wilts
■ Stewards' Enquiry : David Probert four-day ban: excessive use of whip (Nov 18, 20-22)

**FOCUS**
The field split into three bunches, three going far side, three stands' side and the rest up the middle. Only the stands' side group failed to have a representative in the finish. It's been rated around the third, with the fourth close to his penultimate C&D form.
T/Plt: £135.70 to a £1 stake. Pool: £67,857.04 - 364.82 winning units. T/Qpdt: £33.60 to a £1 stake. Pool: £5,818.93 - 127.97 winning units. **Steve Payne**

# 8575 DEL MAR (L-H)

Saturday, November 4

**OFFICIAL GOING: Dirt: fast, turf: firm**

## 8601a GOLDIKOVA STKS (GRADE 2) (3YO+ FILLIES & MARES) (TURF) 1m (T)

**5:10** 3-Y-O+

**£97,560** (£32,520; £19,512; £9,756; £3,252; £280)

RPR

**1** **Kitten's Roar (USA)**[20] 8098 5-8-9 0 .......... JohnRVelazquez 7 109
(Michael J Maker, U.S.A) **31/10**[1]

**2** *2 ¼* **Thundering Sky (USA)**[91] 4-8-9 0 .......... RajivMaragh 4 104
(George Weaver, U.S.A) **222/10**

**3** *nse* **On Leave (USA)**[49] 4-8-9 0 .......... IradOrtizJr 1 104
(Claude McGaughey III, U.S.A) **16/5**[2]

**4** *1* **Malibu Stacy (USA)**[42] 4-8-9 0 .......... ManuelFranco 3 101
(George Weaver, U.S.A) **50/1**

**5** *½* **Laseen (IRE)**[22] 6-8-9 0 .......... (b) VictorEspinoza 5 100
(James Cassidy, U.S.A) **71/1**

**6** *1 ¼* **Majestic Heat (USA)**[34] 7685 5-8-9 0 .......... FlavienPrat 9 97
(Richard E Mandella, U.S.A) **109/10**

**7** *½* **Aljazzi**[28] 7812 4-8-11 0 .......... (h) AndreaAtzeni 11 98
(Marco Botti) *off a step slow: hld up: rdn into st: swtchd out and kpt on wout ever threatening* **43/5**

**8** *¾* **Corps De Ballet (USA)**[66] 4-8-10 0 ow1 .......... (b) CoreySNakatani 13 96
(Richard Baltas, U.S.A) **41/1**

**9** *½* **Mrs McDougal (USA)**[27] 5-8-9 0 .......... JavierCastellano 12 93
(Richard E Mandella, U.S.A) **19/1**

**10** *¾* **Hillhouse High (USA)**[62] 6-8-11 0 .......... KentJDesormeaux 6 94
(Richard Baltas, U.S.A) **207/10**

**11** *hd* **Madame Stripes (ARG)**[27] 5-8-9 0 .......... JosephTalamo 10 91
(Neil Drysdale, U.S.A) **31/5**[3]

**12** *1* **Sassy Little Lila (USA)**[42] 4-8-9 0 .......... LuisSaez 14 89
(Brad H Cox, U.S.A) **128/10**

**13** *1* **Laur Net (USA)**[35] 6-8-9 0 .......... (b) KendrickCarmouche 2 87
(Robert B Hess Jr, U.S.A) **108/1**

**14** *1 ¾* **Goldy Espony (FR)**[34] 7685 6-8-9 0 .......... (b[1]) MikeESmith 8 83
(Bob Baffert, U.S.A) **44/5**

1m 35.18s **14** Ran SP% **118.9**

**Owner** Kenneth L & Sarah K Ramsey **Bred** Dapple Bloodstock **Trained** USA

## 8602a QATAR JUVENILE TURF SPRINT STKS (LISTED RACE) (2YO) (TURF) 5f (T)

**6:20** 2-Y-O

**£97,560** (£32,520; £19,512; £9,756; £3,252; £280)

RPR

**1** **Declarationofpeace (USA)**[15] 8225 2-8-8 0 .......... (t) RyanMoore 9 105
(A P O'Brien, Ire) *in rr: clsd early st: r.o and chal under hand ride fnl f: up to ld last strides: v wl timed ride* **142/10**

2 *hd* **Sound And Silence**[22] 8001 2-8-8 0............................(tp) WilliamBuick 5 104
(Charlie Appleby) *midfield in tch: rdn to chal and led fnl f: kpt on but worn down and hdd last strides* **33/10**[1]

3 *½* **Out Of The Flames**[70] 6448 2-8-5 0 ow2............................ FlavienPrat 8 99
(Richard Hannon) *dwlt and in rr: r.o st and up for 3rd towards fin: nt quite pce to chal* **19/1**

4 *1 ¼* **Corinthia Knight (IRE)**[56] 6935 2-8-8 0............................ LukeMorris 7 98
(Archie Watson) *midfield in tch: rdn into st: kpt on same pce and jst hld on for 4th* **246/10**

5 *nse* **March X Press (USA)**[48] 7206 2-8-7 0.................... JavierCastellano 10 97
(Todd Pletcher, U.S.A) **39/10**[2]

6 *½* **Elizabeth Darcy (IRE)**[70] 6448 2-8-6 0 ow3.................(b) JoseLOrtiz 11 94
(Wesley A Ward, U.S.A) **39/1**

7 *1 ¼* **Treasuring**[35] 7617 2-8-5 0................................................ OisinMurphy 6 89
(Simon Callaghan, U.S.A) **46/1**

8 *nk* **Fairyland (USA)**[80] 2-8-6 0 ow3.......................................(b) IradOrtizJr 1 88
(Wesley A Ward, U.S.A) **63/10**

9 *½* **El Dulce (USA)**[48] 2-8-6 0............................................ JohnRVelazquez 4 87
(Todd Pletcher, U.S.A) **19/2**

10 *nk* **Majestic Dunhill (USA)**[49] 2-8-6 0...........................(b) ManuelFranco 12 86
(George Weaver, U.S.A) **30/1**

11 *½* **Count Alexander (USA)**[26] 2-8-10 0 ow4.............(b) CoreySNakatani 3 88
(Vladimir Cerin, U.S.A) **49/10**[3]

12 *½* **McErin (USA)**[135] 3993 2-8-6 0.................................(b) VictorEspinoza 2 82
(Wesley A Ward, U.S.A) **73/10**

57.23s **12** Ran SP% **119.2**

**Owner** Mrs John Magnier & Michael Tabor & Derrick Smith **Bred** Dell Ridge Farm Llc Et Al **Trained** Cashel, Co Tipperary

## 8603a 14 HANDS WINERY BREEDERS' CUP JUVENILE FILLIES (GRADE 1) (2YO FILLIES) (DIRT) 1m 110y(D)

**7:00** 2-Y-0

**£894,308** (£276,422; £146,341; £81,300; £48,780; £16,260)

RPR

1 **Caledonia Road (USA)**[27] 7862 2-8-10 0....................... MikeESmith 12 114+
(Ralph E Nicks, U.S.A) *hld up on outside: pushed along and outpcd 1/2-way: gd hdwy over 2f out: rdn to ld ins fnl f: sn clr* **20/1**

2 *3 ¼* **Alluring Star (USA)**[35] 7645 2-8-10 0........................(b) JosephTalamo 9 107
(Bob Baffert, U.S.A) *w ldr: led over 3f out: drvn along 2f out: hdd ins fnl f: kpt on same pce* **9/1**

3 *nk* **Blonde Bomber (USA)**[35] 2-8-10 0............................... JoseLezcano 5 106+
(Stanley I Gold, U.S.A) *hld up: last and plenty to do whn pushed along 1/2-way: gd hdwy on outside over 2f out: kpt on to take 3rd ins fnl f: r.o fin* **33/1**

4 *1 ¾* **Separationofpowers (USA)**[27] 7862 2-8-10 0................ JoseLOrtiz 13 102
(Chad C Brown, U.S.A) *trckd ldrs: rdn over 3f out: rallied: kpt on same pce ins fnl f* **11/2**[3]

5 *½* **Piedi Bianchi (USA)**[35] 7645 2-8-10 0......................(b) MarioGutierrez 8 101
(Doug O'Neill, U.S.A) *hld up in tch: drvn and outpcd over 3f out: rallied whn nt clr run briefly over 1f out: no imp ins fnl f* **16/1**

6 *hd* **Wonder Gadot (CAN)**[28] 2-8-10 0.......................... PatrickHusbands 11 100
(Mark Casse, Canada) *hld up: pushed along over 3f out: hdwy 2f out: styng on whn hmpd and snatched up ins fnl f: n.d after* **12/1**

7 *1* **Moonshine Memories (USA)**[35] 7645 2-8-10 0.............. FlavienPrat 7 98
(Simon Callaghan, U.S.A) *led to over 3f out: pressed ldr to over 1f out: wknd fnl f* **9/4**[1]

8 *2 ¼* **Princess Warrior (USA)**[29] 7803 2-8-10 0... BrianJosephHernandezJr 3 93
(Kenneth McPeek, U.S.A) *hld up: pushed along and outpcd 1/2-way: rallied over 1f out: kpt on ins fnl f: nvr able to chal* **16/1**

9 *6 ½* **Gio Game (USA)**[29] 2-8-10 0........................................... ManuelFranco 4 79
(Mark Casse, Canada) *t.k.h early: prom: rdn over 3f out: wknd over 2f out* **12/1**

10 *nk* **Stainless (USA)**[24] 2-8-10 0........................................ JohnRVelazquez 6 78
(Todd Pletcher, U.S.A) *hld up: pushed along and outpcd 1/2-way: nvr on terms* **33/1**

11 *9 ¼* **Heavenly Love (USA)**[29] 7803 2-8-10 0.................... JulienRLeparoux 1 58
(Mark Casse, Canada) *trckd ldrs on ins: rdn along 3f out: wknd wl over 1f out* **7/2**[2]

12 *10 ¾* **Maya Malibu (USA)**[27] 7862 2-8-10 0..................(b[1]) JavierCastellano 10 34
(H Graham Motion, U.S.A) *t.k.h: hld up in midfield: drvn and outpcd wl over 2f out: sn btn* **40/1**

13 *3 ½* **Tell Your Mama (USA)**[22] 2-8-10 0........................ KentJDesormeaux 2 27
(Robert B Hess Jr, U.S.A) *hld up midfield on ins: struggling over 4f out: sn btn* **100/1**

1m 45.05s **13** Ran SP% **119.6**
CSF: £183.95; TRICAST: £6036.62.
**Owner** Zoom And Fish Stable, Charlie Spiring & Newtown An **Bred** Vegso Racing Stable **Trained** USA

**FOCUS**
They went fast and finished slowly - 22.79 (2f), 23.93 (4f), 24.66 (6f) and 26.92 (1m) - in what looked another weak running of the Juvenile Fillies.

## 8604a BREEDERS' CUP TURF SPRINT (GRADE 1) (3YO+) (TURF) 5f (T)

**7:37** 3-Y-0+

**£447,154** (£138,211; £73,170; £40,650; £24,390; £8,130)

RPR

1 **Stormy Liberal (USA)**[147] 5-9-0 0..................................... JoelRosario 4 116
(Peter Miller, U.S.A) *in tch in midfield on inner: rdn and styd on strly fr over 1f out: led cl home* **40/1**

2 *hd* **Richard's Boy (USA)**[14] 5-9-0 0......................................... FlavienPrat 7 115
(Peter Miller, U.S.A) *trckd ldrs: wnt 2nd 2 1/2f out: rdn 1 1/2f out: drvn to ld 150yds out: kpt on wl: hdd cl home* **25/1**

3 *½* **Disco Partner (USA)**[28] 5-9-0 0........................................ IradOrtizJr 1 113+
(Christophe Clement, U.S.A) *hld up towards rr: rdn over 1f out: angled out for clr run 150yds out: sn drvn and kpt on strly: nrst fin* **6/1**[2]

4 *½* **Bucchero (USA)**[28] 5-9-0 0............................(b) FernandoDeLaCruz 11 111
(Tim Glyshaw, U.S.A) *chsd ldr: dropped to 3rd 2 1/2f out: short of room appr fnl f: rdn and kpt on same pce ins fnl f* **40/1**

5 *nse* **Pure Sensation (USA)**[61] 6-9-0 0...................... KendrickCarmouche 12 111
(Christophe Clement, U.S.A) *led: rdn under 2f out: drvn 1f out: hdd 150yds out: no ex clsng stages* **14/1**[3]

6 *nse* **Marsha (IRE)**[34] 7670 4-8-11 0.......................................... LukeMorris 6 108
(Sir Mark Prescott Bt) *towards rr of midfield: rdn over 2f out: making hdwy whn pushed rt 150yds out: sn hrd drvn and styd on* **6/1**[2]

7 *½* **Holding Gold (USA)**[61] 4-9-0 0..................................... ManuelFranco 2 109
(Mark Casse, Canada) *towards rr: rdn over 1f out: styd on ins fnl f: nrst fin* **28/1**

8 *¾* **Washington DC (IRE)**[14] 8230 4-9-0 0..........................(bt) RyanMoore 5 107
(A P O'Brien, Ire) *dwlt: in rr: rdn and styd on fnl f: nrst fin* **18/1**

9 *nk* **Cotai Glory**[20] 8097 5-9-0 0................................................ OisinMurphy 8 105
(Charles Hills) *midfield: outpcd 2f out: rdn and no imp fr under 2f out* **28/1**

10 *nk* **Lady Aurelia (USA)**[71] 6402 3-8-9 0........................... JohnRVelazquez 3 99
(Wesley A Ward, U.S.A) *in tch: rdn 1 1/2f out: fdd last 150yds* **8/11**[1]

11 *½* **Hogy (USA)**[28] 8-9-0 0.................................................(b[1]) JoseLOrtiz 10 103
(Michael J Maker, U.S.A) *hld up towards rr: wd into st: rdn and no imp fr 2f out* **33/1**

12 *2* **Mongolian Saturday (USA)**[28] 7-9-0 0........................ FlorentGeroux 9 95
(Enebish Ganbat, U.S.A) *in tch in midfield: lost pl 2f out: wknd over 1f out* **66/1**

56.12s **12** Ran SP% **118.5**
CSF: £764.41; TRICAST: £6783.43.
**Owner** Rockingham Ranch **Bred** Dapple Bloodstock & Gryphon Investments LLC **Trained** USA

**FOCUS**
Fast and furious stuff around this sharp track, and they went 21.98 and 44.57 before crossing the line in 56.12. The first two have been rated as running personal bests, with the third and seventh in line with their recent form.

## 8605a BREEDERS' CUP FILLY & MARE SPRINT (GRADE 1) (3YO+ FILLIES & MARES) (DIRT) 7f (D)

**8:14** 3-Y-0+

**£447,154** (£138,211; £73,170; £40,650; £24,390; £8,130)

RPR

1 **Bar Of Gold (USA)**[27] 7864 5-8-12 0................................... IradOrtizJr 5 114
(John C Kimmel, U.S.A) *broke wl but sn lost pl and outpcd: plenty to do 1/2-way: rapid hdwy over 2f out: angled rt ent st: styd on gamely u.p to ld last stride* **66/1**

2 *nse* **Ami's Mesa (CAN)**[46] 4-8-12 0...................................... LuisContreras 14 114
(Josie Carroll, Canada) *s.i.s and hld up on outside: smooth hdwy 1/2-way: led over 1f out: sn rdn: kpt on wl fnl f: ct last stride* **16/1**

3 *1* **Carina Mia (USA)**[41] 4-8-12 0..................................... JavierCastellano 1 111
(Chad C Brown, U.S.A) *in tch: hdwy over 2f out: rdn to dispute cl 2nd pl fnl f: no ex last 75yds* **18/1**

4 *2 ½* **Skye Diamonds (USA)**[82] 4-8-12 0...................... TiagoJosuePereira 12 105
(Bill Spawr, U.S.A) *prom: effrt and drvn along over 2f out: kpt on same pce fnl f* **5/1**[2]

5 *hd* **Princess Karen (USA)**[27] 3-8-10 0.......................... JulienRLeparoux 13 102
(Jeff Bonde, U.S.A) *cl up: led briefly 2f out: rdn and outpcd ins fnl f* **66/1**

6 *2 ¾* **Paulassilverlining (USA)**[70] 6458 5-8-12 0....................... JoseLOrtiz 2 97
(Chad C Brown, U.S.A) *midfield: outpcd and drvn along over 3f out: edgd rt and rallied over 1f out: no further imp fnl f* **12/1**

7 *½* **Unique Bella (USA)**[27] 3-8-10 0........................................ MikeESmith 11 93+
(Jerry Hollendorfer, U.S.A) *led at str gallop: swtchd rt after 2f: rdn and hdd 2f out: sn wknd* **6/4**[1]

8 *2 ¼* **Finest City (USA)**[118] 5-8-12 0...................................... CoreySNakatani 4 89
(Ian Kruljac, U.S.A) *chsd ldrs: rdn over 2f out: wknd wl over 1f out* **16/1**

9 *4 ½* **Finley'sluckycharm (USA)**[28] 4-8-12 0....... BrianJosephHernandezJr 9 77
(W Bret Calhoun, U.S.A) *midfield: drvn and outpcd 1/2-way: sme late hdwy to pass btn horses ins fnl f: nvr on terms* **8/1**[3]

10 *¾* **By The Moon (USA)**[70] 6458 5-8-12 0................................ RajivMaragh 7 75
(Michelle Nevin, U.S.A) *sn bhd and outpcd: struggling 1/2-way: nvr on terms* **16/1**

11 *nse* **Highway Star (USA)**[41] 4-8-12 0.................................. AngelSArroyo 10 75
(Rodrigo Ubillo, U.S.A) *in tch: drvn and outpcd over 3f out: sn n.d: btn fnl 2f* **14/1**

12 *4 ¼* **Proper Discretion (USA)**[42] 4-8-12 0.................... KentJDesormeaux 6 63
(Philip D'Amato, U.S.A) *s.i.s: outpcd and bhd: swtchd rt after 2f: drvn on outside over 3f out: nvr on terms* **66/1**

13 *nse* **Curlin's Approval (USA)**[34] 4-8-12 0................................(b) LuisSaez 3 63
(Happy Alter, U.S.A) *s.i.s: bhd and outpcd thrght: nvr on terms* **18/1**

14 *22 ½* **Constellation (USA)**[82] 4-8-12 0........................................ FlavienPrat 8
(Bob Baffert, U.S.A) *bhd and sn outpcd: struggling fr 1/2-way: t.o* **14/1**

1m 22.63s
**WFA** 3 from 4yo+ 1lb **14** Ran SP% **121.5**
CSF: £919.19; TRICAST: £18,53953.
**Owner** Chester & Mary Broman Sr **Bred** Chester Broman & Mary R Broman **Trained** USA

**FOCUS**
This was run at a rapid pace: 21.84, 22.51, 25.21, with the late-closing winner home in 12.78.

## 8606a BREEDERS' CUP FILLY & MARE TURF (GRADE 1) (3YO+ FILLIES & MARES) (TURF) 1m 1f (T)

**9:00** 3-Y-0+

**£894,308** (£276,422; £146,341; £81,300; £48,780; £16,260)

RPR

1 **Wuheida**[34] 7669 3-8-9 0................................................(p[1]) WilliamBuick 5 115
(Charlie Appleby) *trckd ldrs: chsd ldr under 2f out: rdn to ld over 1f out: drvn clr ins fnl f: kpt on strly* **8/1**[3]

2 *1* **Rhododendron (IRE)**[34] 7669 3-8-9 0............................. RyanMoore 14 113+
(A P O'Brien, Ire) *hld up towards rr: stdy hdwy fr 2f out: rdn over 1f out: styd on strly ins fnl f: nt rch wnr* **4/1**[2]

3 *¾* **Cambodia (USA)**[62] 5-8-12 0.................................. DraydenVanDyke 6 110
(Thomas F Proctor, U.S.A) *in tch: rdn 1 1/2f out: chsd ldr 1f out: no ex and lost 2nd 50yds out: jst hld 3rd* **16/1**

4 *hd* **Dacita (CHI)**[27] 7863 6-8-12 0......................................(b) JoelRosario 7 110+
(Chad C Brown, U.S.A) *hld up in rr: rdn and jinked lft 1 1/2f out: drvn and styd on wl on outer fr 1f out: sltly hmpd 150yds out: nrst fin* **20/1**

5 *nse* **Queen's Trust**[34] 7669 4-8-12 0.................................. FrankieDettori 10 110+
(Sir Michael Stoute) *hld up towards rr: forced to check 1 1/2f out: sn rdn: styd on strly fnl f: nrst fin* **9/1**

6 *1 ¼* **War Flag (USA)**[27] 7863 4-8-12 0....................................... JoseLOrtiz 1 107
(Claude McGaughey III, U.S.A) *hld up towards rr: short of room and sltly hmpd 1f out: sn rdn and styd on: nrst fin* **22/1**

7 *½* **Lady Eli (USA)**[70] 6463 5-8-12 0........................................ IradOrtizJr 9 106
(Chad C Brown, U.S.A) *hld up in midfield: rdn and kpt on same pce fr 1 1/2f out* **9/4**[1]

8 *nse* **Senga (USA)**[34] 7669 3-8-9 0 StephanePasquier 2 107
(P Bary, France) *in tch in midfield: rdn and effrt 2f out: chsd ldrs 1f out: wknd last 150yds* **9/1**

9 *nse* **Grand Jete**[27] 7863 4-8-12 0 JavierCastellano 8 106
(Chad C Brown, U.S.A) *hld up towards rr of midfield: rdn 2f out: drvn and no imp fr 1f out* **12/1**

10 *1 ¼* **Nezwaah**[20] 8098 4-8-12 0 AndreaAtzeni 11 103
(Roger Varian) *midfield on inner: rdn and effrt under 2f out: wknd ins fnl f* **20/1**

11 *1 ½* **Zipessa (USA)**[28] 7849 5-8-12 0 JoeBravo 4 100
(Michael Stidham, U.S.A) *led: rdn under 2f out: hdd over 1f out: wknd fnl f* **33/1**

12 *1 ½* **Birdie Gold (USA)**[132] 3-8-9 0 MikeESmith 3 98
(Gary Mandella, U.S.A) *towards rr of midfield: dropped towards rr 2f out: sn btn* **50/1**

13 *1 ½* **Goodyearforroses (IRE)**[34] 7685 5-8-12 0 CoreySNakatani 13 94
(Richard Baltas, U.S.A) *midfield on outer: lost pl under 2f out: sn btn and eased* **40/1**

14 *8 ¼* **Avenge (USA)**[34] 7685 5-8-12 0 FlavienPrat 12 77
(Richard E Mandella, U.S.A) *chsd ldr: lost pl under 2f out: sn wl btn: eased over 1f out* **20/1**

1m 47.91s (0.82)
**WFA** 3 from 4yo+ 3lb **14** Ran SP% **121.4**
CSF: £36,68; TRICAST: £530.48.
**Owner** Godolphin **Bred** Darley **Trained** Newmarket, Suffolk

**FOCUS**
The closers got going too late as the winner got first run from the turn in. They went 23.86, 47.50, 1:11.42, 1:35.87 before finishing in 1:47.91. The third, fourth and sixth have been rated to form.

## 8607a TWINSPIRES BREEDERS' CUP SPRINT (GRADE 1) (3YO+) (DIRT) 6f (D)
9:37 3-Y-0+
**£670,731** (£207,317; £109,756; £60,975; £36,585; £12,195)

RPR

1 **Roy H (USA)**[28] 7853 5-9-0 0 KentJDesormeaux 8 128+
(Peter Miller, U.S.A) *prom: smooth hdwy to press ldr over 2f out: rdn to ld last 100yds: kpt on strly: eased cl home* **9/2**[2]

2 *1* **Imperial Hint (USA)**[61] 4-9-0 0 JavierCastellano 10 124
(Luis Carvajal Jr, U.S.A) *pressed ldr: led and maintained decent gallop 1/2-way: hdd last 100yds: no ex towards fin* **11/2**[3]

3 *2* **Mind Your Biscuits (USA)**[70] 6460 4-9-0 0 (b) JoelRosario 6 117+
(Chad Summers, U.S.A) *s.i.s: hld up: hdwy and plenty to do on outside over 1f out: gd hdwy to chse clr ldng pair ins fnl f: kpt on fin* **9/1**

4 *1 ¼* **American Pastime (USA)**[42] 3-8-12 0 CoreySNakatani 3 111
(Robert B Hess Jr, U.S.A) *trckd ldrs: effrt and drvn along over 1f out: kpt on same pce ins fnl f* **16/1**

5 *nk* **Ransom The Moon (CAN)**[28] 7853 5-9-0 0 (b) FlavienPrat 9 112+
(Philip D'Amato, U.S.A) *hld up in tch on wd outside: rdn along and hdwy to chse ldrs over 1f out: edgd lft and wknd ins fnl f* **22/1**

6 *3 ¼* **Drefong (USA)**[70] 6460 4-9-0 0 (b) MikeESmith 2 102
(Bob Baffert, U.S.A) *in tch on ins: nvr really travelling w any fluency: effrt and edgd rt wl over 1f out: sn no imp: btn fnl f* **11/8**[1]

7 *2 ½* **Calculator (USA)**[69] 5-9-0 0 (b) JohnRVelazquez 1 94
(Peter Miller, U.S.A) *broke wl but sn outpcd and bhd: shortlived effrt on outside over 2f out: sn btn* **33/1**

8 *2 ¼* **Whitmore (USA)**[29] 7802 4-9-0 0 (b) ManuelFranco 5 87
(Ronald Moquett, U.S.A) *in tch: blkd after 1f: drvn and outpcd 1/2-way: btn fnl 2f* **20/1**

9 *½* **B Squared (USA)**[14] 3-8-12 0 MarioGutierrez 4 83
(Doug O'Neill, U.S.A) *broke wl but blkd after 1f and sn pushed along bhd ldng gp: drvn and outpcd 1/2-way: hung rt bnd ent st: n.d* **66/1**

10 *1 ½* **Takaful (USA)**[35] 7630 3-8-12 0 JoseLOrtiz 7 78
(Kiaran McLaughlin, U.S.A) *led at str gallop to 1/2-way: cl up tl wknd and eased wl over 1f out* **9/1**

1m 8.61s **10** Ran SP% **115.1**
CSF: £27.71; TRICAST: £213.07.
**Owner** Rockingham Ranch & David A Bernsen **Bred** Ramona S Bass Llc **Trained** USA

**FOCUS**
Not much got into this. The pace was 21.84, 22.79, with the winner to the line in 23.86.

## 8608a BREEDERS' CUP MILE (GRADE 1) (3YO+) (TURF) 1m (T)
10:19 3-Y-0+
**£894,308** (£276,422; £146,341; £81,300; £48,780; £16,260)

RPR

1 **World Approval (USA)**[49] 7179 5-9-0 0 (b) JohnRVelazquez 5 121
(Mark Casse, Canada) *in tch: rdn 2f out: drvn to ld 150yds out: kpt on wl* **11/4**[1]

2 *1 ¼* **Lancaster Bomber (USA)**[14] 8232 3-8-11 0 SeamieHeffernan 4 117
(A P O'Brien, Ire) *in tch: rdn and kpt on wl fr over 1f out: no imp on wnr clsng stages* **10/1**

3 *hd* **Blackjackcat (USA)**[28] 4-9-0 0 (b) KentJDesormeaux 13 118
(Mark Glatt, U.S.A) *hld up towards rr of midfield: wd into st: rdn and hdwy fr 1 1/2f out: hung lft over 1f out: kpt on wl ins fnl f* **28/1**

4 *nk* **Suedois (FR)**[28] 7851 6-9-0 0 DanielTudhope 8 117
(David O'Meara) *midfield: rdn 2 1/2f out: nt clr run 2f out: hdwy appr fnl f: kpt on same pce ins fnl f* **9/1**

5 *nse* **Ribchester (IRE)**[14] 8232 4-9-0 0 WilliamBuick 10 117
(Richard Fahey) *hld up in midfield: rdn and kpt on fr 1 1/2f out: nrst fin* **10/3**[2]

6 *hd* **Zelzal (FR)**[34] 7671 4-9-0 0 GregoryBenoist 6 116
(J-C Rouget, France) *midfield on inner: nt clr run 1f out: rdn and kpt on ins fnl f* **15/2**

7 *nk* **Karar**[34] 7671 5-9-0 0 FrankieDettori 14 116
(F-H Graffard, France) *hld up towards rr: wd into st: rdn and styd on fr 1 1/2f out* **33/1**

8 *½* **Om (USA)**[35] 5-9-0 0 (b) DraydenVanDyke 7 114
(Dan L Hendricks, U.S.A) *midfield: drifted bk towards rr under 2f out: rdn and kpt on last 150yds* **28/1**

9 *½* **Ballagh Rocks (USA)**[28] 7851 4-9-0 0 (b) JoseLezcano 11 113+
(William Mott, U.S.A) *hld up towards rr: stdy hdwy fr 1 1/2f out: pushed along and kpt on ins fnl f* **22/1**

10 *nse* **Heart To Heart (CAN)**[28] 7851 6-9-0 0 JulienRLeparoux 2 113
(Brian A Lynch, Canada) *chsd ldr: rdn to ld 1 1/2f out: drvn over 1f out: hdd 150yds out: wknd last 100yds* **20/1**

11 *nse* **Roly Poly (USA)**[28] 7812 3-8-8 0 (p) RyanMoore 12 109+
(A P O'Brien, Ire) *hld up towards rr: rdn and kpt on fr 1 1/2f out: n.d* **7/1**[3]

12 *4 ½* **Midnight Storm (USA)**[34] 7686 6-9-0 0 TylerBaze 1 103
(Philip D'Amato, U.S.A) *led: rdn 2 1/2f out: hdd 1 1/2f out: wknd fnl f* **28/1**

13 *1 ¼* **Mr. Roary (USA)**[35] 4-9-0 0 (b) TylerConner 3 100
(George Papaprodromou, U.S.A) *towards rr of midfield: dropped towards rr 2f out: sn struggling* **80/1**

14 *1 ½* **Home Of The Brave (IRE)**[49] 7145 5-9-0 0 (t) MikeESmith 9 96
(Hugo Palmer) *trckd ldrs: wd into st and lost pl: rdn briefly 1 1/2f out: sn btn and eased* **22/1**

1m 34.55s
**WFA** 3 from 4yo+ 2lb **14** Ran SP% **121.1**
CSF: 327.53; TRICAST: £671.38.
**Owner** Live Oak Plantation **Bred** Live Oak Stud **Trained** Canada

**FOCUS**
The leaders set an honest pace, going 22.30, 45.65, 1:10.04, 1:22.36, and they finished in 1:34.55. Three of the first four raced in the second rank. The winner didn't need to match his Woodbine Mile form to take this.

## 8609a SENTIENT JET BREEDERS' CUP JUVENILE (GRADE 1) (2YO COLTS & GELDINGS) (DIRT) 1m 110y(D)
10:58 2-Y-0
**£894,308** (£276,422; £146,341; £81,300; £48,780; £16,260)

RPR

1 **Good Magic (USA)**[28] 7842 2-8-10 0 JoseLOrtiz 6 119
(Chad C Brown, U.S.A) *trckd ldrs gng wl: wnt 2nd over 2f out: rdn to ld over 1f out: drvn clr fnl f: readily* **12/1**

2 *4 ¼* **Solomini (USA)**[35] 7646 2-8-10 0 (b) FlavienPrat 2 109
(Bob Baffert, U.S.A) *pressed ldr: led over 2f out: sn rdn along: hdd over 1f out: kpt on same pce fnl f* **12/1**

3 *1* **Bolt D'Oro (USA)**[35] 7646 2-8-10 0 (b) CoreySNakatani 11 107+
(Mick Ruis, U.S.A) *racd wd thrght: hld up: hdwy over 3f out: drvn along over 2f out: kpt on steadily ins fnl f: nt pce to chal* **10/11**[1]

4 *8 ¼* **Givemeaminit (USA)**[28] 7850 2-8-10 0 JavierCastellano 4 89
(Dallas Stewart, U.S.A) *hld up in midfield: effrt and drvn along over 2f out: edgd lft and wknd over 1f out* **50/1**

5 *2 ¼* **The Tabulator (USA)**[49] 2-8-10 0 (b) JoseValdiviaJr 7 84
(Larry Rivelli, U.S.A) *trckd ldrs: drvn along over 2f out: wknd over 1f out* **25/1**

6 *hd* **Hollywood Star (USA)**[49] 2-8-10 0 JoelRosario 12 84
(Dale Romans, U.S.A) *s.i.s and swtchd lft s: hld up in last pl: rdn and hdwy wl over 2f out: kpt on fnl f: nvr rchd ldrs* **40/1**

7 *4 ¼* **Firenze Fire (USA)**[28] 7842 2-8-10 0 IradOrtizJr 3 74
(Jason Servis, U.S.A) *hld up: stdy hdwy over 3f out: rdn and wknd fr 2f out* **12/1**

8 *5 ¼* **Hazit (USA)**[28] 7842 2-8-10 0 JohnRVelazquez 9 63
(Todd Pletcher, U.S.A) *hld up in midfield: drvn and outpcd wl over 2f out: sn wknd* **40/1**

9 *4* **Free Drop Billy (USA)**[28] 7850 2-8-10 0 RobbyAlbarado 5 54
(Dale Romans, U.S.A) *hld up in midfield on ins: stdy hdwy over 3f out: rdn and wknd over 2f out* **11/2**[2]

10 *½* **U S Navy Flag (USA)**[21] 8037 2-8-10 0 (bt) RyanMoore 1 53
(A P O'Brien, Ire) *led: rdn and hdd over 2f out: wknd wl over 1f out* **6/1**[3]

11 *6 ¾* **Golden Dragon (USA)**[36] 2-8-10 0 EvinARoman 10 38
(Mikhail Yanakov, U.S.A) *hld up: drvn and struggling over 3f out: sn btn* **80/1**

12 *hd* **Bahamian (USA)**[28] 7842 2-8-10 0 MarioGutierrez 8 38
(Simon Callaghan, U.S.A) *s.i.s: hld up: stdy hdwy over 3f out: drvn and wknd over 2f out* **100/1**

1m 43.34s **12** Ran SP% **118.0**
CSF: £138.10; TRICAST: £265.20.
**Owner** e Five Racing Thoroughbreds & Stonestreet Stables **Bred** Stonestreet Thoroughbred Holdings LLC **Trained** USA

**FOCUS**
The splits were 22.83 (2f), 23.92 (4f), 25.29 (6f), 24.95 (1m), and the final time was 1.71sec quicker than the fillies' race.

## 8610a LONGINES BREEDERS' CUP TURF (GRADE 1) (3YO+) (TURF) 1m 4f (T)
11:37 3-Y-0+
**£1,788,617** (£552,845; £292,682; £162,601; £97,560; £32,520)

RPR

1 **Talismanic**[55] 6983 4-9-0 0 MickaelBarzalona 1 118
(A Fabre, France) *in tch in midfield: hdwy fr 2f out: rdn 1 1/2f out: drvn to ld 100yds out: kpt on wl* **14/1**

2 *½* **Beach Patrol (USA)**[35] 7633 4-9-0 0 (b) JoelRosario 11 117
(Chad C Brown, U.S.A) *chsd ldr: led 2f out: rdn 1 1/2f out: hdd 100yds out: sn drvn: kpt on* **6/1**[2]

3 *nk* **Highland Reel (IRE)**[14] 8233 5-9-0 0 RyanMoore 3 117
(A P O'Brien, Ire) *trckd ldrs: rdn over 2f out: drvn and kpt on fr over 1f out: nt quite able to chal* **11/10**[1]

4 *1 ½* **Sadler's Joy (USA)**[35] 7633 4-9-0 0 JulienRLeparoux 12 114
(Thomas Albertrani, U.S.A) *hld up in rr: stdy hdwy on outer fr 2 1/2f out: rdn and kpt on wl fr 1 1/2f out* **20/1**

5 *1 ½* **Seventh Heaven (IRE)**[34] 7668 4-8-11 0 SeamieHeffernan 8 109
(A P O'Brien, Ire) *hld up towards rr: rdn over 1f out: styd on wl fnl f: nrst fin* **8/1**[3]

6 *hd* **Bullards Alley (USA)**[20] 8099 5-9-0 0 (b) JavierCastellano 2 111
(Tim Glyshaw, U.S.A) *midfield: rdn and kpt on steadily fr 1 1/2f out: n.d* **33/1**

7 *1 ½* **Itsinthepost (FR)**[34] 5-9-0 0 (b) TylerBaze 6 109
(Jeff Mullins, U.S.A) *towards rr of midfield: tk clsr order appr 2f out: rdn 2f out: outpcd 1 1/2f out: wknd fnl 100yds* **66/1**

8 *1* **Cliffs Of Moher (IRE)**[14] 8233 3-8-10 0 (t) WayneLordan 5 109
(A P O'Brien, Ire) *dwlt: towards rr: rdn and no imp fr 1 1/2f out* **14/1**

9 *½* **Oscar Performance (USA)**[35] 7633 3-8-10 0 JoseLOrtiz 13 109
(Brian A Lynch, Canada) *led: rdn and hdd 2f out: wknd fnl 150yds* **25/1**

10 *nk* **Decorated Knight**[56] 6960 5-9-0 0 AndreaAtzeni 4 106
(Roger Charlton) *midfield: dropped towards rr 2f out: rdn and effrt on inner 1 1/2f out: wknd fnl 100yds* **8/1**[3]

11 *1* **Fanciful Angel (IRE)**[35] 7633 5-9-0 0 IradOrtizJr 9 105
(Chad C Brown, U.S.A) *towards rr: hdwy on outer fr 3f out: in tch 2f out: rdn and outpcd 1 1/2f out: wknd 1f out* **28/1**

12 *2 ¾* **Bigger Picture (USA)**[70] 6461 6-9-0 0 (b) JohnRVelazquez 7 100
(Michael J Maker, U.S.A) *midfield: lost pl under 2f out: sn wl btn* **50/1**

13 9 ¾ **Hunt (IRE)**34 5-9-0 0.......................................(b) FlavienPrat 10 85
(Philip D'Amato, U.S.A) *in tch: lost pl qckly 2f out: sn wl btn* **66/1**

2m 26.19s
**WFA** 3 from 4yo+ 5lb 13 Ran SP% **117.4**
CSF: £88.52; TRICAST: £170.18.
**Owner** Godolphin SNC **Bred** Darley **Trained** Chantilly, France

**FOCUS**
They went 23.69, 48.33, 1:12.86, 1:38.00, 2:02.44 before finishing in 2:26.19, and it paid to race quite handily. The third and fifth have been rated in line with their more recent form.

## 8601 DEL MAR (L-H)
Sunday, November 5
**OFFICIAL GOING: Dirt: fast**

### 8611a BREEDERS' CUP CLASSIC (GRADE 1) (3YO+) (DIRT) 1m 2f (D)
12:35 3-Y-0+
**£2,682,926** (£829,268; £439,024; £243,902; £97,560; £97,560)

RPR
1 **Gun Runner (USA)**64 6716 4-9-0 0.......................... FlorentGeroux 5 130
(Steven Asmussen, U.S.A) *mde all: hrd pressed fr over 2f out: asserted fnl f: drvn out* **11/4**2
2 2 ¼ **Collected (USA)**77 6252 4-9-0 0.......................... MartinGarcia 11 126
(Bob Baffert, U.S.A) *pressed wnr: rdn and disp ld over 2f out to over 1f out: kpt on same pce ins fnl f* **13/2**
3 1 ¼ **West Coast (USA)**43 7418 3-8-10 0.......................(b) JavierCastellano 8 123
(Bob Baffert, U.S.A) *trckd ldrs: drvn along and outpcd wl over 2f out: rallied over 1f out: kpt on same pce ins fnl f* **4/1**3
4 ½ **War Story (USA)**64 6716 5-9-0 0.......................... JoseLOrtiz 4 122
(Jorge Navarro, U.S.A) *hld up on outside: stdy hdwy 1/2-way: rdn along and outpcd over 2f out: kpt on steadily fnl f: nt pce to chal* **80/1**
5 2 ¼ **Arrogate (USA)**77 6252 4-9-0 0.......................... MikeESmith 1 118+
(Bob Baffert, U.S.A) *awkward s and nvr gng wl towards rr: laboured prog on wd outside over 2f out: plugged on fnl f: nvr on terms* **2/1**1
5 dht **Gunnevera (USA)**71 6462 3-8-10 0.......................(b) EdgardJZayas 9 118
(Antonio Sano, U.S.A) *hld up on outside: rdn and sme hdwy over 2f out: edgd lft: drvn and no imp fr over 1f out* **18/1**
7 12 ¼ **Churchill (IRE)**15 8232 3-8-10 0.......................... RyanMoore 7 93
(A P O'Brien, Ire) *t.k.h early: prom: blkd after 1f: rdn and outpcd over 3f out: wknd fr 2f out* **16/1**
8 ½ **Mubtaahij (IRE)**35 7686 5-9-0 0.......................(b) DraydenVanDyke 6 92
(Bob Baffert, U.S.A) *in tch: blkd after 1f: drvn and outpcd over 3f out: btn fnl 2f* **25/1**
9 4 ¼ **War Decree (USA)**37 7588 3-8-10 0.......................... SeamieHeffernan 2 84
(A P O'Brien, Ire) *sn bhd: struggling over 4f out: sn btn* **40/1**
10 10 ¾ **Pavel (USA)**29 7843 3-8-10 0.......................... MarioGutierrez 10 62
(Doug O'Neill, U.S.A) *hld up bhd ldng gp: drvn and outpcd over 3f out: sn n.d: btn fnl 2f* **50/1**
11 7 **Win The Space (USA)**35 7686 5-9-0 0.......................(b) JosephTalamo 3 48
(George Papaprodromou, U.S.A) *hld up: rdn along over 4f out: nvr on terms* **80/1**

2m 1.29s
**WFA** 3 from 4yo+ 3lb 11 Ran SP% **115.2**
CSF: £19.86.
**Owner** Winchell Thoroughbreds LLC & Three Chimneys Farm **Bred** Besilu Stables LLC **Trained** USA

**FOCUS**
The dirt course had been playing to outside closers, and in this the pace was really strong, yet surprisingly the first two had the race to themselves, with the winner making all and the runner-up sat second throughout. The splits were 22.5, 23.81, 24.19, 24.53, 26.26.

8612-8619a - (Foreign Racing) - See Raceform Interactive

## 8448 CAPANNELLE (R-H)
Sunday, November 5
**OFFICIAL GOING: Turf: heavy (racing abandoned after race 4)**

### 8620a PREMIO GUIDO BERARDELLI (GROUP 3) (2YO) (TURF) 1m 1f
2:10 2-Y-0 **£29,914** (£13,162; £7,179; £3,589)

RPR
1 **Wiesenbach**14 2-8-11 0.......................... FabioBranca 9 102
(Il Cavallo In Testa, Italy) *hld up in midfield: hdwy fr 3 1/2f out: chsd ldr whn rdn over 2f out: drvn and jnd ldr 1 1/2f out: kpt on wl: edgd ahd cl home* **21/10**1
2 shd **Wait Forever (IRE)** 2-8-11 0.......................... DarioVargiu 8 102
(Stefano Botti, Italy) *trckd ldrs: led gng wl over 2f out: drvn whn jnd 1 1/2f out: kpt on wl: jst hld* **63/20**2
3 2 **Old Fox (IRE)** 2-8-11 0.......................... SalvatoreSulas 5 98
(Stefano Botti, Italy) *towards rr of midfield: rdn and hdwy fr over 3f out: drvn 2f out: kpt on: no imp on front pair fnl f* **119/10**
4 9 **Frutireu (IRE)** 2-8-11 0.......................... PierreBazire 3 80
(Stefano Botti, Italy) *chsd ldr: rdn and led briefly 2 1/2f out: hdd over 2f out: wknd over 1f out* **59/10**
5 2 ½ **Undisclosed Desire (IRE)** 2-8-11 0.......................... CarloFiocchi 6 75
(Agostino Affe', Italy) *hld up towards rr: rdn and no imp fr over 3f out* **143/20**
6 2 ¼ **Domagnano (IRE)** 2-8-11 0.......................... NicolaPinna 2 70
(Stefano Botti, Italy) *midfield: rdn 3f out: wknd over 1f out: sn eased* **99/10**
7 4 **Valeria** 2-8-8 0.......................(b) SalvatoreBasile 7 59
(Fabio Marchi, Italy) *led: hdd 2 1/2f out: sn rdn and lost pl: eased fnl f* **7/2**3
8 ¾ **La Volta Buona** 2-8-11 0.......................... SamueleDiana 4 61
(F Camici, Italy) *a towards rr* **147/10**
9 ¾ **Biz Honor (IRE)** 2-8-11 0.......................... SilvanoMulas 1 59
(Stefano Botti, Italy) *a towards rr* **73/10**

1m 55.8s (1.10) 9 Ran SP% **140.7**
PARI-MUTUEL (all including 1 euro stake): WIN 3.09; PLACE 1.37, 1.82, 2.84; DF 10.67.
**Owner** Scuderia D'Altemps Srl **Bred** Gestut Ravensberg **Trained** Italy

## 2002 KREFELD (R-H)
Sunday, November 5
**OFFICIAL GOING: Turf: soft**

### 8621a GROSSER PREIS DES WEINGUTES LUCASHOF - HERZOG VON RATIBOR-RENNEN (GROUP 3) (2YO) (TURF) 1m 110y
12:30 2-Y-0 **£27,350** (£10,256; £5,128; £2,564; £1,709)

RPR
1 **Poldi's Liebling (GER)**14 2-8-11 0.......................... BauyrzhanMurzabayev 1 108
(A Wohler, Germany) *in tch: rdn 3f out: drvn and led 2 1/2f out: kpt on wl* **19/5**3
2 nk **Guiri (GER)** 2-8-11 0.......................... FilipMinarik 2 107
(Jean-Pierre Carvalho, Germany) *led: rdn 3f out: hdd 2 1/2f out: sn drvn and kpt on wl: a jst hld by wnr* **23/5**
3 9 ½ **Melodino (GER)** 2-8-11 0.......................... DanielePorcu 6 88
(K Demme, Germany) *dwlt: in rr: rdn 3 1/2f out: plugged on to take 3rd under 2f out: no ch w front pair* **112/10**
4 5 ½ **Weltstar (GER)** 2-8-11 0.......................... MaximPecheur 5 77
(Markus Klug, Germany) *trckd ldrs: rdn 2 1/2f out: wknd steadily fr 2f out* **7/5**1
5 12 **Destino (GER)** 2-8-11 0.......................... AndreasHelfenbein 3 53
(Markus Klug, Germany) *chsd ldr: rdn and outpcd over 3f out: wknd fr over 2f out* **26/5**
6 9 **Star Max (GER)** 2-8-11 0.......................... MartinSeidl 4 35
(Markus Klug, Germany) *towards rr: rdn 4f out: lost tch 3 1/2f out* **27/10**2

1m 56.72s (10.12) 6 Ran SP% **131.7**
PARI-MUTUEL (all including 10 euro stake): WIN 48; PLACE: 27, 48; SF: 382.
**Owner** Stall Audenhove **Bred** Horst-Dieter Beyer **Trained** Germany

### 8622a GROSSER PREIS VON RONDO FOOD - NIEDERRHEIN-POKAL (GROUP 3) (3YO+) (TURF) 1m 2f 55y
1:40 3-Y-0+ **£27,350** (£10,256; £5,128; £2,564; £1,709)

RPR
1 **Veneto (GER)**538 2315 4-9-1 0.......................... AlexanderPietsch 2 110+
(Andreas Suborics, Germany) *chsd ldr: taken v wd and racd alone in bk st: led after 5f: 4 l clr whn crossing to ins rail at end of bk st: rdn 2 1/2f out: drvn whn pressed 1 1/2f out: kpt on gamely: drew clr again last 100yds* **14/1**
2 3 **Devastar (GER)**14 8270 5-9-1 0.......................... MartinSeidl 5 104
(Markus Klug, Germany) *midfield: rdn and hdwy fr over 2f out: pressed ldr 1 1/2f out: no ex last 100yds* **58/10**3
3 1 **Capitano (GER)**33 7722 4-8-13 0.......................... LukasDelozier 3 100
(J Hirschberger, Germany) *led: hdd after 5f: rdn and kpt on fr 2 1/2f out: pressed ldr 1 1/2f out: wknd last 100yds* **183/10**
4 9 ¼ **Sound Check (GER)**49 7203 4-9-1 0.......................... FilipMinarik 6 84
(P Schiergen, Germany) *hld up towards rr: rdn 3f out: lost tch w front three 2f out: plugged on* **61/10**
5 3 ½ **Colomano**42 7429 3-9-2 0.......................... AndreasHelfenbein 1 82
(Markus Klug, Germany) *hld up towards rr: rdn 2 1/2f out: lost tch w front three 2f out: plugged on: eased clsng stages* **3/5**1
6 2 ½ **Navaro Girl (IRE)**14 8270 3-8-10 0.......................... DanielePorcu 4 71
(P Schiergen, Germany) *t.k.h in midfield: rdn under 3f out: lost tch w front three 2f out: eased ins fnl f* **23/10**2

PARI-MUTUEL (all including 10 euro stake): WIN 150; PLACE: 43, 29; SF: 741.
**Owner** Gestut Winterhauch **Bred** M Barth **Trained** Germany

8623 - 8632a (Foreign Racing) - See Raceform Interactive

## BENDIGO
Wednesday, November 1
**OFFICIAL GOING: Turf: good**

### 8633a JAYCO BENDIGO CUP (GROUP 3 H'CAP) (3YO+) (TURF) 1m 4f
5:00 3-Y-0+
**£107,309** (£31,578; £15,789; £7,894; £4,385; £3,508)

RPR
1 **Qewy (IRE)**92 5503 7-9-4 0.......................... KerrinMcEvoy 2 112+
(Charlie Appleby) **6/4**2
2 hd **Kiwia (AUS)**11 4-8-11 0.......................... DamianLane 5 105
(Darren Weir, Australia) **7/5**1
3 4 ¼ **Foundry (IRE)**18 8056 7-9-1 0.......................(t) MichaelDee 1 102
(Robert Hickmott, Australia) **17/2**
4 3 **Skulduggery (AUS)**18 5-8-7 0.......................(bt1) StephenBaster 7 89
(Shawn Mathrick, Australia) **100/1**
5 shd **Khartoum (AUS)**14 4-8-7 0.......................... PatrickMoloney 4 89
(Pat Carey, Australia) **40/1**
6 shd **Big Memory (FR)**13 7-8-10 0.......................(bt) AndrewMallyon 3 92
(Tony McEvoy, Australia) **7/1**3
7 1 ¼ **Meet And Greet (AUS)**14 4-8-7 0.......................(b) NoelCallow 6 87
(Chris Meagher, Australia) **20/1**

2m 27.5s 7 Ran SP% **112.9**

**Owner** Godolphin **Bred** Darley **Trained** Newmarket, Suffolk

# 8500 KEMPTON (A.W) (R-H)

Monday, November 6

**OFFICIAL GOING: Polytrack: standard**

Wind: Light, across Weather: Fine

## 8634 BREEDERS SUPPORTING RACING EBF MAIDEN STKS (PLUS 10 RACE) (SIRE/DAM-RESTRICTED RACE) 7f (P)

**1:20** (1:20) (Class 4) 2-Y-O **£6,469** (£1,925; £721; £721) **Stalls** Low

Form RPR

34 1 **George Villiers (IRE)**[20] 8140 2-9-5 0 RobertHavlin 5 77
(John Gosden) *w ldr: led 1/2-way: shkn up 2f out: hung lft fr over 1f out and hrd pressed after: hld on wl* **3/1**[2]

60 2 ½ **Medal Of Honour**[34] 7713 2-9-5 0 (t) AdamKirby 1 76
(Joseph Patrick O'Brien, Ire) *trckd ldng pair: drvn to go 2nd 2f out: hung lft over 1f out: str chal after but nt qckn ins fnl f* **5/1**[3]

2 3 ¾ **Ocala**[26] 7953 2-9-0 0 DavidProbert 3 69
(Andrew Balding) *stdd s and also s.i.s: mostly in last trio tl prog on inner 2f out: rdn and kpt on fnl f but nvr quite able to chal* **11/8**[1]

03 3 dht **Launceston Place (FR)**[30] 7819 2-9-5 0 TedDurcan 4 74
(Henry Spiller) *chsd ldrs: rdn 2f out: effrt on inner over 1f out: kpt on fnl f: nvr quite able to chal* **12/1**

5 nk **Glorious Army** 2-9-5 0 LiamKeniry 10 73
(Ed Walker) *dwlt: settled in rr: shkn up over 2f out: prog over 1f out: pushed along and kpt on to press for a pl ins fnl f* **66/1**

6 shd **Labrega** 2-9-0 0 JosephineGordon 8 70+
(Hugo Palmer) *dwlt: hld up in rr: shkn up 2f out: prog on outer over 1f out: pressed for a pl ins fnl f: pushed along and kpt on same pce last 150yds* **12/1**

00 7 1½ **Compulsive (IRE)**[20] 8140 2-9-5 0 JackMitchell 6 69
(Roger Varian) *chsd ldrs: rdn over 2f out: nt qckn wl over 1f out: fdd fnl f* **10/1**

0 8 1 **Mesquite**[11] 8373 2-9-0 0 RichardKingscote 9 61
(Ralph Beckett) *led to 1/2-way: chsd wnr tl nt qckn 2f out: wknd fnl f* **33/1**

00 9 4 **Cristal Spirit**[23] 8046 2-9-5 0 JimCrowley 2 55
(William Haggas) *a in rr: struggling in last of main gp 3f out* **16/1**

0 10 45 **Pass Mark**[21] 8119 2-9-0 0 ManuelFernandes(5) 7
(Mrs Ilka Gansera-Leveque) *bucking s and virtually ref to r: eventually consented to run after rest had covered 1f: a t.o* **66/1**

1m 26.42s (0.42) **Going Correction** -0.05s/f (Stan) 10 Ran SP% 120.1

Speed ratings (Par 98): **95,94,93,93,93 93,91,90,85,34**

PL: 2.20 Launceston Place, 0.5 Ocala; TF GV/MH/LP: 60.50, GV/MH/O 20.30; CSF £19.05 TOTE £3.30: £1.30, £2.10; EX 19.70.

**Owner** HRH Princess Haya Of Jordan **Bred** Floors Farming & The Duke Of Devonshire **Trained** Newmarket, Suffolk

**FOCUS**

This maiden was for the offspring of sires or dams who won over at least 1m1f110yds. They spread out across the track in the straight and finished in a heap, with the first six separated by little more than one and a half lengths.

## 8635 BREEDERS BACKING RACING EBF MAIDEN FILLIES' STKS 1m (P)

**1:50** (1:55) (Class 5) 3-Y-O+ **£4,528** (£1,347; £673; £336) **Stalls** Low

Form RPR

2423 1 **Cape To Cuba**[12] 8341 3-8-11 75 GeorgeWood(3) 7 81
(James Fanshawe) *trckd ldrs: clsd gng wl 2f out: pushed into the ld over 1f out: styd on and clr fnl f* **5/2**[2]

0033 2 3 **Beyond Recall**[20] 8132 3-9-0 71 (v) LukeMorris 6 74
(Luca Cumani) *reluctant to enter stalls: nt that wl away and bustled along to rch midfield: rdn and prog on inner over 2f out: chal over 1f out: chsd wnr after: hung lft and readily lft bhd fnl f* **11/2**[3]

3 3 1¼ **Sheila's Rock (IRE)**[189] 2231 3-9-0 0 ShaneKelly 11 71
(Denis Coakley) *trckd ldng trio: shkn up over 2f out: kpt on same pce fr over 1f out to take 3rd last 75yds* **6/1**

254 4 ½ **Meccabah (FR)**[30] 7824 3-9-0 80 DavidProbert 9 70
(Andrew Balding) *trckd ldr: led over 2f out: rdn and hdd over 1f out: fnd little and sn btn* **10/11**[1]

0 5 4½ **Choose**[25] 7989 3-9-0 0 RichardKingscote 3 59
(Ralph Beckett) *led to over 2f out: lost 2nd wl over 1f out: wknd fnl f* **25/1**

6500 6 1 **Love Me Again**[13] 8328 3-9-0 57 StevieDonohoe 5 57
(Charlie Fellowes) *hld up in midfield: outpcd 2f out: shkn up and no imp on ldrs after* **66/1**

04 7 6 **Saharan Star**[21] 8116 3-9-0 0 LiamKeniry 10 42
(Patrick Chamings) *t.k.h: hld up in last trio: nvr on terms* **66/1**

8 1¼ **Shadow's Girl**[26] 5-8-9 0 WilliamCox(7) 4 39
(Bernard Llewellyn) *s.s: mostly in last pair: urged along over 3f out: nvr a factor* **100/1**

00 9 17 **Maid Of Rock (IRE)**[61] 6817 3-9-0 0 RobertWinston 2
(Mike Murphy) *plld hrd early: hld up: wknd rapidly over 2f out: t.o* **100/1**

10 61 **Delicate Kiss** 3-9-0 0 JosephineGordon 1
(John Bridger) *s.s: rn green and sn t.o* **66/1**

1m 38.27s (-1.53) **Going Correction** -0.05s/f (Stan)

**WFA** 3 from 4yo+ 2lb 10 Ran SP% 120.9

Speed ratings (Par 100): **105,102,100,100,95 94,88,87,70,9**

CSF £16.88 TOTE £3.10: £1.30, £1.60, £1.80; EX 12.40 Trifecta £56.90.

**Owner** Mrs Mary Slack & Qatar Racing Ltd **Bred** Newhall Estate Farm **Trained** Newmarket, Suffolk

■ Peters Folly was withdrawn. Price at time of withdrawal 100-1. Rule 4 does not apply.

**FOCUS**

There wasn't a great deal of depth to this maiden, which was delayed by several minutes as a couple gave trouble at the stalls. The runner-up is rated to her recent C&D handicap form.

## 8636 32RED ON THE APP STORE FILLIES' H'CAP 1m (P)

**2:20** (2:21) (Class 4) (0-85,87) 3-Y-O+ **£6,469** (£1,925; £962; £481) **Stalls** Low

Form RPR

152 1 **Express Lady (IRE)**[48] 7241 3-9-0 77 (t) JosephineGordon 5 83
(Hugo Palmer) *t.k.h: hld up disputing 5th: prog over 2f out to chse ldr wl over 1f out: chal on inner after: rdn to ld last 150yds: pushed out nr fin* **6/1**

6350 2 nk **Bint Dandy (IRE)**[12] 8351 6-9-0 82 (b) NicolaCurrie(7) 7 87
(Chris Dwyer) *t.k.h: hld up disputing 5th: shkn up over 2f out: prog jst over 1f out: styd on fnl f to take 2nd last strides* **14/1**

2010 3 hd **Kitty Boo**[21] 8113 3-9-3 80 (h) JimCrowley 2 85
(Luca Cumani) *led: rdn over 1f out: hdd last 150yds: no ex and lost 2nd fnl strides* **2/1**[1]

6-10 4 nk **Influent (IRE)**[34] 7710 3-9-1 78 LukeMorris 3 82
(James Tate) *chsd ldrs: rdn and nt qckn over 2f out: kpt on again fr over 1f out: pressed for a pl u.p ins fnl f* **7/1**

1400 5 1¾ **Tai Hang Dragon (IRE)**[12] 8351 3-9-10 87 SeanLevey 8 87+
(Richard Hannon) *rrd s: t.k.h and hld up in last pair: prog 2f out: chsd ldrs over 1f out: one pce fnl f* **14/1**

6465 6 1 **Lucy The Painter (IRE)**[10] 8390 5-9-5 80 (b[1]) LiamKeniry 4 77
(Ed de Giles) *s.s: t.k.h and hld up in last pair: rdn and no rspnse over 2f out: kpt on to pass two rivals nr fin* **9/2**[3]

2-21 7 ¾ **Considered Opinion**[30] 7826 3-9-3 80 RichardKingscote 6 75
(Ralph Beckett) *chsd ldr to over 2f out: sn lost pl and btn* **4/1**[2]

4060 8 1 **Lady Lydia (IRE)**[11] 8374 6-8-13 74 (p) MartinDwyer 1 67
(Gay Kelleway) *t.k.h: trckd ldng pair: chsd ldr over 2f out to wl over 1f out: sn btn: wknd fnl f* **33/1**

1m 38.03s (-1.77) **Going Correction** -0.05s/f (Stan)

**WFA** 3 from 5yo+ 2lb 8 Ran SP% 114.6

Speed ratings (Par 102): **106,105,105,105,103 102,101,100**

CSF £83.46 CT £226.98 TOTE £5.40: £2.00, £2.80, £1.30; EX 73.80 Trifecta £240.50.

**Owner** Dr Ali Ridha **Bred** Rabbah Bloodstock Limited **Trained** Newmarket, Suffolk

**FOCUS**

A fair handicap run at a modest gallop. The winner is unexposed and may do better.

## 8637 32RED FLOODLIT STKS (LISTED RACE) 1m 3f 219y(P)

**2:50** (2:50) (Class 1) 3-Y-O+

**£25,519** (£9,675; £4,842; £2,412; £1,210; £607) **Stalls** Low

Form RPR

1263 1 **Titi Makfi**[36] 7673 3-8-8 100 FrannyNorton 5 106
(Mark Johnston) *mde virtually all: rdn over 1f out: hrd pressed ins fnl f: hld on wl* **12/1**

4263 2 hd **Red Verdon (USA)**[25] 7988 4-9-4 106 (b) PJMcDonald 4 110
(Ed Dunlop) *hld up in midfield: rdn and prog 2f out: swtchd to inner and chsd wnr fnl f: str chal last 100yds: jst hld* **8/1**

3010 3 1 **Dylan Mouth (IRE)**[44] 7393 6-9-4 110 AdamKirby 1 108
(Marco Botti) *hld up in midfield: prog over 2f out: rdn to chse wnr over 1f out: nt qckn and lost 2nd fnl f: styd on after but nvr chal* **11/2**[3]

1056 4 2½ **Soldier In Action (FR)**[27] 7931 4-9-4 107 JimCrowley 6 104
(Mark Johnston) *chsd wnr briefly after 1f: styd prom: rdn over 2f out and sn outpcd: n.d after: kpt on fnl f* **16/1**

0400 5 ¾ **Western Hymn**[9] 8421 6-9-9 107 (b) RobertHavlin 7 108
(John Gosden) *hld up in last pair: cajoled along and no rspnse over 2f out: modest late hdwy* **9/2**[2]

51/5 6 ½ **Connecticut**[38] 7581 6-9-4 106 JackMitchell 3 102
(Roger Varian) *trckd wnr 1f: styd cl up: wnt 2nd again over 2f out gng strly: sn shkn up to chal: lost 2nd and wknd tamely over 1f out* **11/2**[3]

1-0 7 1 **Crimson Rock (USA)**[24] 8007 3-8-8 84 RichardKingscote 2 97
(Ralph Beckett) *dwlt: hld up in last pair: rdn over 2f out: no significant prog* **20/1**

0343 8 1 **Best Of Days**[38] 7581 3-8-13 104 (tp) WilliamBuick 8 100
(Hugo Palmer) *chsd wnr over 10f out: rdn and nt qckn over 2f out: sn lost pl and wknd* **2/1**[1]

2m 31.91s (-2.59) **Going Correction** -0.05s/f (Stan)

**WFA** 3 from 4yo+ 5lb 8 Ran SP% 111.7

Speed ratings (Par 111): **106,105,105,103,103 102,102,101**

CSF £98.00 TOTE £11.90: £3.00, £2.30, £1.80; EX 85.10 Trifecta £529.30.

**Owner** Paul & Clare Rooney **Bred** Floors Farming **Trained** Middleham Moor, N Yorks

**FOCUS**

This is often a good Listed race although this edition - not run under floodlights - wasn't run at a true gallop. The winner is rated as though running up to form.

## 8638 32RED LONDON MIDDLE DISTANCE SERIES FINAL H'CAP 1m 2f 219y(P)

**3:20** (3:21) (Class 2) 3-Y-O+

**£43,575** (£13,048; £6,524; £3,262; £1,631; £819) **Stalls** Low

Form RPR

5311 1 **Ply**[33] 7728 3-9-10 92 WilliamBuick 3 100+
(Roger Charlton) *hld up in midfield on inner: lost pl and in last pair over 4f out: swtchd to outer 3f out: gd prog 2f out: rdn to chse clr ldr fnl f: r.o wl to ld last 100yds: readily* **10/11**[1]

2210 2 1 **Royal Reserve**[26] 7949 4-9-6 84 AdamKirby 4 89+
(David O'Meara) *dwlt: hld up in last: gd prog on inner 2f out: drvn and styd on wl to take 2nd nr fin: no real threat to wnr* **20/1**

0531 3 nk **Seniority**[26] 7949 3-9-8 90 JimCrowley 7 95
(William Haggas) *t.k.h: hld up in last tl rapid prog to ld over 6f out: kicked clr over 2f out: kpt on after but hdd and outpcd last 100yds* **5/1**[2]

2560 4 hd **X Rated (IRE)**[40] 7516 3-8-7 75 PJMcDonald 1 79
(Mark Johnston) *trckd ldrs: rdn over 2f out: pressed for 3rd fr over 1f out: styd on but nvr pce to chal* **33/1**

0341 5 hd **Western Duke (IRE)**[59] 6887 3-9-9 91 RichardKingscote 2 95
(Ralph Beckett) *pushed up to ld but set modest pce: hdd over 6f out and sn in 3rd: rdn to chse ldr over 2f out to over 1f out: one pce* **6/1**[3]

0060 6 1 **Luv U Whatever**[13] 8315 7-8-7 71 ow1 (tp) BarryMcHugh 5 73
(Marjorie Fife) *hld up towards rr: pushed along over 2f out: kpt on same pce fr over 1f out and nvr able to chal* **66/1**

2111 7 ½ **Just In Time**[27] 7927 3-9-0 82 MartinDwyer 9 83+
(Alan King) *t.k.h: hld up in tch on outer: outpcd over 2f out: n.d after but kpt on again fnl f* **8/1**

3310 8 nk **Koeman**[24] 8005 3-9-3 85 JFEgan 10 86
(Mick Channon) *trckd ldrs: rdn over 2f out: disp 3rd over 1f out: steadily lost pl after* **12/1**

222 9 2 **Desert Ruler**[33] 7728 4-8-12 76 JackGarritty 6 74
(Jedd O'Keeffe) *hld up in tch: looked to be gng wl whn nt clr run briefly over 2f out: sn no prog: fdd over 1f out* **16/1**

0530 10 5 **Azam**[59] 6887 3-9-3 85 LukeMorris 8 75
(Michael Appleby) *chsd ldr 4f and new ldr 6f out to over 2f out: sn wknd* **66/1**

2m 20.25s (-1.65) **Going Correction** -0.05s/f (Stan)

**WFA** 3 from 4yo+ 4lb 10 Ran SP% 118.7

Speed ratings (Par 109): **104,103,103,102,102 102,101,101,100,96**

CSF £27.38 CT £68.18 TOTE £1.70: £1.10, £4.40, £1.80; EX 18.70 Trifecta £70.90.

**Owner** Sheikh Hamdan bin Mohammed Al Maktoum **Bred** Carwell Equities Ltd **Trained** Beckhampton, Wilts

**FOCUS**
A very worthwhile prize for this series final, which was contested by some progressive 3yos. It wasn't truly run though, with a slow initial pace, and was something of a messy race with a relatively slow time. The first two came from the back.

## 8639 32RED.COM H'CAP 6f (P)
**3:50** (3:51) (Class 3) (0-95,101) 3-Y-O+
**£9,337** (£2,796; £1,398; £699; £349; £175) **Stalls** Low

Form RPR

6211 **1** **Gulliver**[4] 8547 3-9-13 **101** 6ex (tp) JosephineGordon 5 110
(Hugo Palmer) *trckd ldr to over 3f out and again 2f out: pushed into the ld over 1f out: rdn out and in command fnl f* **11/8**[1]

0020 **2** ¾ **Intransigent**[65] 6676 8-8-8 **89** JasonWatson(7) 6 95
(Andrew Balding) *hld up in midfield: shkn up and no prog 2f out: r.o fr jst over 1f out to take 2nd nr fin* **16/1**

416 **3** ½ **Boy In The Bar**[10] 8383 6-8-4 **83** (b) ManuelFernandes(5) 7 87+
(Ian Williams) *sn prom on outer: rdn 2f out: chsd wnr fnl f: kpt on but a hld: lost 2nd nr fin* **6/1**[2]

4000 **4** 1 ¼ **Tropics (USA)**[42] 7455 9-9-1 **89** (h) RobertWinston 4 90
(Dean Ivory) *dwlt: hld up in rr: shkn up and no prog 2f out: kpt on fnl f to take 4th last strides: n.d* **10/1**

1-00 **5** hd **Jameerah**[101] 5379 4-8-8 **82** PJMcDonald 9 82
(Bryan Smart) *wl away: led: rdn and hdd over 1f out: fdd fnl f* **33/1**

4000 **6** nk **Sir Ottoman (FR)**[30] 7828 4-8-13 **87** (p) LukeMorris 3 86
(Ivan Furtado) *chsd ldrs: drvn 2f out: tried to cl over 1f out: one pce after* **16/1**

004 **7** ½ **Parnassian (IRE)**[13] 8310 3-8-10 **84** MartinDwyer 8 81
(Amanda Perrett) *hld up in last pair: pushed along over 2f out: no prog tl shkn up and kpt on fnl f: nvr involved* **7/1**[3]

1105 **8** ¾ **Vimy Ridge**[30] 7809 5-8-9 **83** (t) DavidProbert 2 78
(Alan Bailey) *hld up in rr: shkn up and no prog 2f out: n.d after* **33/1**

205 **9** ½ **Kasbah (IRE)**[65] 6695 5-9-9 **97** JackMitchell 1 90
(Amanda Perrett) *in tch: effrt on inner 2f out: no prog over 1f out: fdd* **7/1**[3]

3330 **10** 1 **Fast Track**[142] 3827 6-8-13 **87** BenCurtis 10 77
(David Barron) *prom: chsd ldr over 3f out to 2f out: wknd over 1f out* **16/1**

1013 **11** 3 ¾ **Pettochside**[10] 8393 8-9-3 **91** WilliamCarson 11 69
(John Bridger) *stdd s fr wdst draw: t.k.h: hld up in last: no real prog* **33/1**

1m 11.19s (-1.91) **Going Correction** -0.05s/f (Stan) 11 Ran SP% **117.0**
Speed ratings (Par 107): **110,109,108,106,106 106,105,104,103,102 97**
CSF £26.27 CT £100.78 TOTE £2.00: £1.20, £3.60, £2.00; EX 25.00 Trifecta £149.00.
**Owner** Saleh Al Homaizi & Imad Al Sagar **Bred** S A Douch **Trained** Newmarket, Suffolk
■ Stewards' Enquiry : Robert Winston caution: careless riding

**FOCUS**
A decent sprint handicap, but it wasn't run at a strong gallop.

## 8640 32RED CASINO H'CAP 7f (P)
**4:20** (4:20) (Class 4) (0-80,80) 3-Y-O+ **£6,469** (£1,925; £962; £481) **Stalls** Low

Form RPR

1103 **1** **Dourado (IRE)**[26] 7947 3-9-3 **77** DavidProbert 11 84
(Patrick Chamings) *t.k.h: trckd ldr after 2f: pushed into the ld over 1f out: drvn and hrd pressed ins fnl f: jst hld on* **6/1**[2]

3341 **2** hd **Glenn Coco**[44] 7414 3-8-8 **68** LukeMorris 5 74
(Stuart Williams) *t.k.h: trckd ldr 2f: styd cl up: rdn over 2f out: chsd wnr fnl f: chal last 100yds: jst failed* **10/3**[1]

3401 **3** nk **Portledge (IRE)**[27] 7942 3-9-1 **75** TedDurcan 3 80
(James Bethell) *hld up in midfield: prog 2f out: drvn to press ldng pair fnl f: kpt on but a hld* **13/2**[3]

4015 **4** 1 ¼ **Inexes**[13] 8319 5-9-6 **79** (p) BarryMcHugh 9 82
(Marjorie Fife) *dwlt: t.k.h: hld up in midfield: prog over 1f out: kpt on same pce fnl f and nvr able to threaten* **12/1**

5400 **5** 1 **Athassel**[31] 7789 8-8-13 **79** KatherineGlenister(7) 4 79
(David Evans) *hld up in last trio: rdn and prog over 1f out: kpt on fnl f but nvr able to threaten* **14/1**

3652 **6** ½ **Black Caesar (IRE)**[18] 8184 6-8-12 **78** SebastianWoods(7) 1 77
(Philip Hide) *led at mod pce: rdn and hdd over 1f out: fdd and lost pls fnl f* **12/1**

0000 **7** nk **Presumido (IRE)**[24] 7998 7-9-3 **76** JFEgan 6 77+
(Simon Dow) *dwlt: hld up in last pair: shkn up over 2f out: kpt on fr over 1f out but no hope of rching ldrs* **8/1**

2501 **8** ¾ **Procurator (IRE)**[18] 8184 3-9-5 **79** SeanLevey 2 74
(Richard Hannon) *t.k.h: cl up on inner: rdn to try to chal over 1f out: wknd fnl f* **13/2**[3]

4500 **9** 4 **Plucky Dip**[46] 7321 6-9-2 **75** PJMcDonald 8 60
(John Ryan) *chsd ldrs: rdn and nt qckn 2f out: wknd qckly fnl f* **14/1**

4310 **10** hd **Gold Hunter (IRE)**[31] 7789 7-9-3 **79** (p) PaddyPilley(3) 7 63
(Steve Flook) *t.k.h: hld up in rr: wknd 2f out* **14/1**

-160 **11** 10 **Glorious Politics**[24] 8014 3-9-6 **80** BenCurtis 10 36
(David Barron) *hld up: hung bdly lft bnd over 4f out to 3f out: bhd and no ch after* **20/1**

1m 24.78s (-1.22) **Going Correction** -0.05s/f (Stan)
**WFA** 3 from 5yo+ 1lb 11 Ran SP% **115.3**
Speed ratings (Par 105): **104,103,103,102,100 100,99,99,94,94 82**
CSF £25.69 CT £137.33 TOTE £7.20: £2.10, £1.70, £2.90; EX 32.60 Trifecta £184.20.
**Owner** Mrs Alexandra J Chandris **Bred** Canice M Farrell Jnr **Trained** Baughurst, Hants

**FOCUS**
There wasn't a great deal of pace on and it paid to race prominently. The winner gained a small personal best.
T/Jkpt: £4,685.10 to a £1 stake. Pool: £35,138.26 - 7.50 winning units T/Plt: £18.40 to a £1 stake. Pool: £74,587.60 - 2,957.81 winning units T/Qpdt: £12.90 to a £1 stake. Pool: £7,149.38 - 407.67 winning units **Jonathan Neesom**

# 8634 KEMPTON (A.W) (R-H)
Tuesday, November 7

**OFFICIAL GOING: Polytrack: standard**
Wind: virtually nil Weather: dry, rain race from 5

## 8641 RACING UK H'CAP 1m (P)
**4:45** (4:46) (Class 6) (0-65,65) 3-Y-O+ **£2,264** (£673; £336; £168) **Stalls** Low

Form RPR

2621 **1** **Magic Mirror**[21] 8134 4-9-2 **60** (p) JimCrowley 1 67
(Mark Rimell) *hld up wl in tch in midfield: effrt to chal over 1f out: led 1f out: styd on and hld on wl ins fnl f* **7/4**[1]

0113 **2** nk **Suitsus**[82] 6102 6-9-5 **63** (t) TimmyMurphy 3 69
(Geoffrey Deacon) *hld up in tch in midfield: effrt and hdwy on inner over 1f out: str chal ins fnl f: hung lft and hld nr fin* **9/1**

4500 **3** 1 **Anastazia**[22] 8124 5-9-4 **62** JoeyHaynes 2 66
(Paul D'Arcy) *chsd ldrs: effrt over 1f out: kpt on u.p ins fnl f: wnt 3rd last stride* **8/1**

6652 **4** shd **Connemera Queen**[21] 8132 4-9-7 **65** RobertWinston 13 68
(John Butler) *chsd ldr tl over 1f out: kpt on u.p ins fnl f: lost 3rd last stride* **5/1**[2]

6005 **5** 1 ¼ **Scribner Creek (IRE)**[11] 8400 4-9-3 **64** CharlieBennett(3) 12 65
(Denis Quinn) *hld up in tch in midfield: effrt u.p over 1f out: kpt on ins fnl f: nt enough pce to threaten ldrs* **14/1**

2021 **6** nk **Pick A Little**[19] 8182 9-9-2 **60** RichardKingscote 8 60
(Michael Blake) *taken down early: led: rdn 2f out: hdd 1f out: no ex and wknd ins fnl f* **7/1**[3]

0-44 **7** shd **Tis Wonderful (IRE)**[142] 3870 3-8-9 **62** WilliamCox(7) 9 62
(Carroll Gray) *t.k.h: chsd ldng trio: effrt over 1f out: unable qck 1f out: styd on same pce ins fnl f* **40/1**

5000 **8** 2 ¾ **Galinthias**[50] 7216 5-9-1 **64** PaddyBradley(5) 11 57
(Simon Dow) *dwlt: t.k.h: hld up towards rr: effrt over 1f out: kpt on ins fnl f: nvr trbld ldrs* **25/1**

6506 **9** 1 ½ **Udogo**[9] 6139 6-9-7 **65** MartinDwyer 4 55
(Brendan Powell) *hld up in last trio: effrt 2f out: no imp over 1f out: nvr trbld ldrs* **20/1**

00 **10** 1 **Missguided (IRE)**[35] 7712 4-9-3 **61** FergusSweeney 5 49
(Alex Hales) *s.i.s: t.k.h: hld up in rr: n.d* **10/1**

6-60 **11** 26 **Seek The Fair Land**[235] 1238 11-9-1 **64** JaneElliott(5) 10
(Daniel Steele) *dwlt: sn dropped to rr and nvr on terms: lost tch over 1f out* **50/1**

1m 39.08s (-0.72) **Going Correction** -0.15s/f (Stan)
**WFA** 3 from 4yo+ 2lb 11 Ran SP% **115.4**
Speed ratings (Par 101): **97,96,95,95,94 94,93,91,89,88 62**
CSF £17.06 CT £99.03 TOTE £2.20: £1.10, £2.50, £2.40; EX 16.50 Trifecta £69.50.
**Owner** William Wood **Bred** Hesmonds Stud Ltd **Trained** Leafield, Oxon
■ Gold Dust was withdrawn. Price at time of withdrawal 20-1. Rule 4 does not apply.

**FOCUS**
Mainly exposed sorts in a modest handicap. The gallop was on the steady side and those held up were at a disadvantage. The first seven finished in a heap and the form's straightforward.

## 8642 32RED CASINO NOVICE STKS (DIV I) 1m (P)
**5:15** (5:15) (Class 5) 2-Y-O **£3,234** (£962; £481; £240) **Stalls** Low

Form RPR

**1** **Occupy (USA)** 2-9-2 0 RichardKingscote 14 81
(Ralph Beckett) *t.k.h: chsd ldrs and clr in ldng quartet: effrt over 1f out: qcknd to ld jst ins fnl f: sn in command and r.o wl: readily* **25/1**

02 **2** 2 **Blame Culture (USA)**[42] 7488 2-9-2 0 DanielMuscutt 6 76
(George Margarson) *chsd ldr and clr in ldng quartet: effrt towards inner 2f out: ev ch 1f out: chsd wnr and kpt on same pce ins fnl f* **7/1**[3]

43 **3** 2 ¼ **U S S Missouri (USA)**[20] 8149 2-9-2 0 LiamKeniry 1 71
(Ed Walker) *led and clr in ldng quartet: rdn ent fnl 2f: hdd jst ins fnl f: sn btn and wknd fnl 100yds* **3/1**[2]

5 **4** 2 **Racing Country (IRE)**[23] 8075 2-9-2 0 JimCrowley 4 66
(Saeed bin Suroor) *chsd ldrs: clr in ldng quartet: rdn ent 2f out: unable qck: wl hld 4th and kpt on same pce ins fnl f* **11/10**[1]

**5** 3 ¾ **Gaudi (IRE)** 2-9-2 0 RobertHavlin 7 60+
(John Gosden) *off the pce in midfield: effrt over 2f out: kpt on fr over 1f out: nvr trbld ldrs* **8/1**

**6** 2 **Ad Libitum** 2-9-2 0 LouisSteward 10 53+
(Hugo Palmer) *s.i.s: off the pce towards rr: sme hdwy 1/2-way: swtchd lft over 2f out: hdwy over 1f out: kpt on: nvr trbld ldrs* **20/1**

**7** 2 ¾ **Multicurrency (USA)** 2-9-2 0 MartinDwyer 2 47
(David Simcock) *chsd clr ldng quartet: effrt 2f out: no imp: wknd and lost 2 pls fnl f* **50/1**

**8** nk **Perpetrator (IRE)** 2-9-2 0 ShaneKelly 5 46
(Roger Charlton) *racd off the pce in 6th: effrt and no hdwy 2f out: nvr on terms: wknd fnl f* **25/1**

**9** 6 **Convinced (IRE)** 2-9-2 0 SeanLevey 9 32+
(Richard Hannon) *stdd s: hld up wl off the pce in last pair: effrt and sme hdwy 2f out: no imp over 1f out: wknd fnl f* **25/1**

0 **10** 1 ½ **Seinesational**[13] 8353 2-8-13 0 CallumShepherd(3) 3 29
(William Knight) *midfield but nvr on terms w ldrs: rdn over 3f out: no hdwy and bhd 2f out* **100/1**

0 **11** 4 **Vantasy**[22] 8119 2-9-2 0 JackMitchell 12 20
(Chris Wall) *midfield but nvr on terms w ldrs: rdn 1/2-way: bhd fnl 2f* **100/1**

00 **12** 2 ¼ **Clan McGregor (IRE)**[19] 8180 2-9-2 0 RobertWinston 11 14+
(Seamus Durack) *stdd after s: hld up off the pce in rr: n.d* **200/1**

**13** 12 **Seasearch** 2-8-9 0 WilliamCox(7) 13
(Andrew Balding) *s.i.s: bhd and nvr on terms: t.o* **66/1**

00 **14** 1 **Saint Anthony**[32] 7788 2-9-2 0 JoeyHaynes 8
(Mark H Tompkins) *a towards rr and nvr on terms: rdn over 3f out: t.o* **250/1**

1m 37.51s (-2.29) **Going Correction** -0.15s/f (Stan) 14 Ran SP% **118.9**
Speed ratings (Par 96): **105,103,100,98,95 93,90,89,83,82 78,76,64,63**
CSF £181.66 TOTE £26.10: £6.00, £2.00, £1.20; EX 222.50 Trifecta £1273.40.
**Owner** Highclere Thoroughbred Racing-David Weir **Bred** Forging Oaks Farm Llc **Trained** Kimpton, Hants

**FOCUS**
Those with previous experience looked no better than fair but the winner won with something in hand and he's a useful prospect for next year. The gallop was reasonable and the pace held up. The form could possibly be rated 3lb better.

## 8643 32RED CASINO NOVICE STKS (DIV II) 1m (P)
**5:45** (5:45) (Class 5) 2-Y-O **£3,234** (£962; £481; £240) **Stalls** Low

Form RPR

42 **1** **Bow Street**[13] 8352 2-9-2 0 WilliamBuick 9 85+
(Charlie Appleby) *chsd ldrs: effrt to chse clr ldr 3f out: clsd u.p over 1f out: led jst ins fnl f: styd on and sn clr* **2/7**[1]

**2** 2 ¾ **Podemos (GER)** 2-9-2 0 RichardKingscote 3 78
(Ralph Beckett) *led: clr 3f out: rdn over 1f out: hdd jst ins fnl f: sn btn: wknd towards fin but hung on to 2nd* **8/1**[2]

**3** ½ **Highbrow** 2-9-2 0 JimCrowley 1 77+
(David Simcock) *hld up in midfield: effrt 2f out: chsd ldng pair 1f out: kpt on wl and pressing for 2nd cl home: no threat to wnr* **14/1**[3]

4 3 **Sleeping Lion (USA)** 2-9-2 0 DanielMuscutt 10 70
(James Fanshawe) *dwlt and pushed along early: hdwy into midfield after 2f out: effrt 2f out: 6th and styng on 1f out: kpt on ins fnl f: no ch w wnr* 16/1

06 5 *shd* **Brexitmeansbrexit**[13] 8339 2-8-11 0 SeanLevey 4 65
(Richard Hannon) *chsd ldng trio: effrt 2f out: chsd clr ldng pair 2f out: no imp and lost 3rd 1f out: kpt on same pce fnl f* 33/1

0 6 *3/4* **Noble Expression**[28] 7929 2-9-2 0 JackMitchell 8 68
(Roger Varian) *hld up in tch in midfield: effrt over 2f out: no imp and kpt on same pce fr over 1f out* 16/1

0 7 *2 3/4* **Casa Comigo (IRE)**[45] 7391 2-9-2 0 RobertHavlin 13 62
(John Best) *hld up in midfield: effrt 2f out: no imp u.p over 1f out: wl hld and plugged on same pce fnl f* 100/1

8 *3 1/4* **World Breaker (ITY)** 2-8-13 0 MarcMonaghan(3) 7 54
(Marco Botti) *hld up towards rr of main gp: effrt over 2f out: sn outpcd and wl btn over 1f out* 33/1

06 9 *2* **Mom Said (IRE)**[21] 8140 2-9-2 0 LiamKeniry 11 50
(Ed Walker) *hld up in midfield: effrt over 2f out: sn outpcd and wknd over 1f out* 50/1

0 10 *3 1/2* **Reveleon**[13] 8339 2-9-2 0 TedDurcan 6 42
(Sir Michael Stoute) *chsd ldr tl 3f out: sn struggling and lost pl over 2f out: wl btn and eased ins fnl f* 25/1

11 *1* **Lexington Empire** 2-9-2 0 ShaneKelly 14 40
(David Lanigan) *s.i.s: rn green and outpcd in rr: nvr on terms* 50/1

06 12 *1/2* **Dagueneau (IRE)**[12] 8372 2-8-9 0 HarryBurns(7) 5 38
(Ed Dunlop) *sn dropped to rr: nvr on terms: bhd over 2f out* 100/1

13 *11* **Essendon (FR)** 2-8-9 0 JasonWatson(7) 12 13
(Andrew Balding) *dwlt: sn pushed along towards rr: bhd 1/2-way* 50/1

1m 37.3s (-2.50) **Going Correction** -0.15s/f (Stan) 13 Ran SP% **124.9**
Speed ratings (Par 96): **106,103,102,99,99 98,96,92,90,87 86,85,74**
CSF £3.19 TOTE £1.30: £1.10, £2.00, £2.90; EX 4.50 Trifecta £22.10.
**Owner** Godolphin **Bred** Godolphin **Trained** Newmarket, Suffolk

**FOCUS**
Not much in the way of strength in depth but nevertheless a useful performance from the winner, who will be suited by a bit further in due course. The third caught the eye.

## 8644 CLOSE BROTHERS BUSINESS FINANCE NURSERY H'CAP 1m (P)
6:15 (6:16) (Class 6) (0-60,62) 2-Y-O £2,587 (£770; £384; £192) Stalls Low

Form RPR

5243 1 **Secratario (FR)**[14] 8306 2-9-7 58 (p) ShaneKelly 2 63+
(Richard Hughes) *hld up in tch in midfield: nt clr run ent fnl 2f: swtchd lft and effrt jst over 1f out: r.o wl ins fnl f to ld towards fin* 5/2[1]

5000 2 *1/2* **Sotomayor**[31] 7829 2-9-10 61 (t) SeanLevey 5 63
(Richard Hannon) *dwlt: sn rcvrd and in tch in midfield: nt clr run over 2f out: rdn and hdwy to ld over 1f out: styd on wl ins fnl f tl hdd and no ex towards fin* 3/1[2]

000 3 *1 1/4* **Arigato**[29] 7877 2-9-10 61 MartinLane 4 60
(William Jarvis) *sn chsng ldrs and t.k.h: effrt on inner to chal over 1f out: unable qck and kpt on same pce ins fnl f* 18/1

561 4 *nk* **Sauchiehall Street (IRE)**[14] 8306 2-9-7 58 JimCrowley 10 56
(Sylvester Kirk) *s.i.s: hld up in rr: switching lft over 2f out: hdwy over 1f out: swtchd rt 1f out: r.o wl ins fnl f: nt rch ldrs* 5/2[1]

1555 5 *2* **That's My Girl (IRE)**[41] 7510 2-9-11 62 TimmyMurphy 3 55
(Richard Hannon) *hld up towards rr: hdwy on inner over 2f out: rdn to chse ldrs over 1f out: no ex ins fnl f* 8/1

0605 6 *nse* **Hurricane Lil (IRE)**[29] 7897 2-9-10 61 LiamKeniry 1 54
(George Baker) *hld up towards rr: clsd and nt clr run ent fnl 2f: swtchd lft over 1f out: kpt on ins fnl f: nvr trbld ldrs* 33/1

4664 7 *3 1/2* **Ladycammyofclare (IRE)**[14] 8306 2-8-8 45 JoeFanning 7 30
(Mark Johnston) *led for 1f: styd chsng ldrs: rdn and ev ch 2f out tl no ex ent fnl f: wknd ins fnl f* 10/1

2210 8 *1/2* **Dark Blue (IRE)**[8] 8467 2-9-6 62 PaddyBradley(5) 9 46
(Mick Channon) *s.i.s: hld up towards rr: effrt over 2f out: nvr trbld ldrs* 15/2[3]

5644 9 *2* **Red For Danger**[11] 8397 2-8-10 47 (h) MartinDwyer 12 26
(Eve Johnson Houghton) *plld hrd: chsd ldrs and styd wd early: hdwy to ld 5f out: rdn and hdd over 1f out: sn wknd* 25/1

0000 10 *2 3/4* **Partry Flyer (IRE)**[19] 8190 2-8-8 45 (v) NickyMackay 13 17
(Oliver Greenall) *styd wd early: midfield tl hdwy to chse ldrs 5f out: rdn 3f out: lost pl over 1f out: sn wknd* 50/1

00 11 *3* **Miss Condi**[54] 7079 2-8-8 45 JoeyHaynes 11 10
(Martin Keighley) *t.k.h: led after 1f tl 5f out: lost pl 2f out: sn wknd* 100/1

000 12 *9* **Amiirah**[111] 5030 2-8-10 47 FergusSweeney 8
(John Gallagher) *midfield on outer: lost pl and bhd over 2f out: lost tch over 1f out* 100/1

0000 R **Afterthisone**[54] 7082 2-8-1 45 (t[1]) WilliamCox(7) 6
(Robin Dickin) *ref to r* 100/1

1m 39.29s (-0.51) **Going Correction** -0.15s/f (Stan) 13 Ran SP% **131.1**
Speed ratings (Par 94): **96,95,94,93,91 91,88,87,85,83 80,71,**
CSF £11.06 CT £119.78 TOTE £3.40: £1.40, £2.00, £6.40; EX 14.30 Trifecta £177.70.
**Owner** The Queens & Partner **Bred** Remi Boucret **Trained** Upper Lambourn, Berks
■ Stewards' Enquiry : Liam Keniry caution: careless riding

**FOCUS**
A run-of-the-mill nursery in which an ordinary gallop picked up passing the intersection. A straightforward base level for the form.

## 8645 32RED.COM H'CAP 6f (P)
6:45 (6:45) (Class 4) (0-80,80) 3-Y-O+ £4,690 (£1,395; £697; £348) Stalls Low

Form RPR

3032 1 **Born To Finish (IRE)**[5] 8542 4-9-1 74 (p) DougieCostello 4 82
(Jamie Osborne) *hld up in tch in last quartet: effrt and hdwy over 1f out: str run u.p ins fnl f to ld 75yds out: sn clr* 7/2[1]

2420 2 *1 1/4* **Nezar (IRE)**[14] 8319 6-9-0 80 JackOsborn(7) 11 84
(Dean Ivory) *s.i.s and dropped in bhd: hld up in last pair: swtchd lft and effrt 2f out: hdwy over 1f out: r.o wl ins fnl f to snatch 2nd nr fin: no threat to wnr* 16/1

3455 3 *nk* **Very Honest (IRE)**[29] 7882 4-8-10 72 CallumShepherd(3) 9 75
(Brett Johnson) *chsd ldr tl 5f out: chsd ldrs: effrt to chse ldr again over 1f out tl ins fnl f: kpt on* 20/1

050 4 *1/2* **Cappananty Con**[22] 8115 3-9-5 78 RobertWinston 12 79
(Dean Ivory) *led: rdn over 1f out: hdd 75yds out: no ex and lost 2 pls nr fin* 12/1

5365 5 *hd* **Rose Berry**[10] 8418 3-9-0 80 (h) NicolaCurrie(7) 6 82+
(Chris Dwyer) *hld up in last quartet: rdn and hdwy over 1f out: nt clr run and swtchd rt 1f out: gd hdwy ins fnl f and forced to switch rt again wl ins fnl f: r.o strly towards fin* 5/1[3]

2640 6 *1 1/2* **Mr Pocket (IRE)**[14] 8310 3-9-5 78 (t[1]) RaulDaSilva 2 74
(Paul Cole) *t.k.h: hld up in tch in midfield: effrt over 1f out: keeping on same pce whn carried rt wl ins fnl f* 14/1

133 7 *nk* **Ninjago**[34] 7737 7-9-7 80 SeanLevey 7 75
(Paul Midgley) *t.k.h: hld up in tch in midfield: effrt 2f out: styd on same pce u.p ins fnl f* 5/1[3]

236 8 *2* **Hackney Road**[35] 7709 4-8-12 78 PaulHainey(7) 8 67
(John Butler) *chsd ldrs tl wnt 2nd 5f out tl over 1f out: no ex u.p: wknd ins fnl f* 9/1

-600 9 *1/2* **Dark Alliance (IRE)**[85] 5993 6-9-1 74 ShaneKelly 5 61
(Daniel Mark Loughnane) *s.i.s: hld up in last pair: effrt on inner 2f out: kpt on but nvr threatened ldrs* 25/1

1051 10 *shd* **Danecase**[20] 8158 4-9-3 76 JimCrowley 1 63
(David Dennis) *in tch in midfield: effrt 2f out: unable qck and edgd lft over 1f out: wknd ins fnl f* 4/1[2]

1235 11 *11* **Field Of Vision (IRE)**[57] 7002 4-8-13 77 PaddyBradley(5) 3 29
(Joseph Tuite) *in tch in midfield: rdn ent fnl 2f: sn struggling and lost pl: bhd ins fnl f* 16/1

1m 11.16s (-1.94) **Going Correction** -0.15s/f (Stan) 11 Ran SP% **120.3**
Speed ratings (Par 105): **106,104,103,103,103 101,100,97,97,97 82**
CSF £62.87 CT £1017.14 TOTE £4.70: £1.70, £3.00, £7.30; EX 60.40 Trifecta £1434.90.
**Owner** Crowd Racing Partnership **Bred** B Kennedy & Mrs Ann Marie Kennedy **Trained** Upper Lambourn, Berks
■ Stewards' Enquiry : Jim Crowley caution: careless riding

**FOCUS**
Mainly exposed sorts in a fair handicap and one in which the decent gallop set things up for the closers. The winner gained a small personal best.

## 8646 32RED ON THE APP STORE H'CAP 7f (P)
7:15 (7:15) (Class 5) (0-75,76) 3-Y-O+ £2,911 (£866; £432; £216) Stalls Low

Form RPR

0301 1 **Spirit Of Belle**[43] 7459 3-9-3 72 (b) RaulDaSilva 1 81
(Paul Cole) *mde all: rdn and qcknd clr over 1f out: r.o strly: eased nr fin: readily* 9/2[1]

003 2 *2* **Wicker**[154] 3438 3-9-1 70 RichardKingscote 3 74+
(Jane Chapple-Hyam) *hld up in midfield: effrt ent fnl 2f: rdn and hdwy over 1f out: chsd clr wnr ins fnl f: r.o but no threat to wnr* 14/1

1100 3 *2* **Chetan**[13] 8341 5-9-4 72 (t) DanielMuscutt 6 72
(Charlie Wallis) *taken down early: pressed wnr tl rdn and unable to match pce of wnr over 1f out: kpt on same pce and lost 2nd ins fnl f* 10/1

0010 4 *hd* **Treacherous**[34] 7723 3-8-11 66 LiamKeniry 5 64+
(Ed de Giles) *s.i.s: t.k.h in rr: hdwy into midfield 1/2-way: effrt on inner 2f out: styd on same pce ins fnl f* 6/1[2]

5050 5 *1/2* **Dutiful Son (IRE)**[35] 7709 7-9-4 72 NickyMackay 2 70
(Simon Dow) *chsd ldrs: rdn ent fnl 2f: unable qck over 1f out: kpt on same pce ins fnl f* 10/1

3152 6 *1* **Spinnaka (IRE)**[10] 8434 3-9-7 76 (v) LukeMorris 9 70
(Luca Cumani) *hld up in tch in midfield: effrt over 2f out: styd on same pce fr over 1f out* 9/2[1]

4-00 7 *shd* **Muhajjal**[12] 8375 3-9-6 75 (t[1]) MartinDwyer 8 69
(George Peckham) *hld up in last trio: rdn and hdwy over 1f out: r.o wl ins fnl f: nvr trbld ldrs* 25/1

0650 8 *nk* **Viva Verglas (IRE)**[10] 8433 6-8-12 66 ShaneKelly 7 60
(Daniel Mark Loughnane) *stdd s: hld up towards rr: rdn and hdwy over 1f out: kpt on ins fnl f: nvr trbld ldrs* 50/1

3252 9 *shd* **Haraz (IRE)**[11] 8400 4-9-0 68 (p) DougieCostello 11 62
(Jamie Osborne) *hld up in last trio: effrt on inner over 1f out: kpt on ins fnl f: nvr trbld ldrs* 6/1[2]

-416 10 *1* **Mister Freeze (IRE)**[19] 8184 3-9-1 70 (vt) JoeyHaynes 12 60
(Patrick Chamings) *chsd ldrs: rdn and unable qck 2f out: sn lost pl: wknd ins fnl f* 20/1

600 11 *1/2* **Arlecchino's Leap**[13] 8344 5-9-8 76 (p) SteveDrowne 13 66
(Mark Usher) *hld up in last trio: effrt over 2f out: no imp: nvr trbld ldrs* 50/1

3504 12 *1 1/4* **First Experience**[42] 7493 6-9-1 72 (b) CallumShepherd(3) 4 58
(Lee Carter) *hld up in tch in midfield: effrt ent fnl 2f: sn struggling and btn over 1f out: wknd fnl f* 20/1

3653 13 *nk* **Murdanova (IRE)**[10] 8434 4-9-1 72 CharlieBennett(3) 10 57
(Denis Quinn) *hld up in midfield on outer: rdn and lost pl ent fnl 2f: wknd fnl f* 7/1[3]

0000 14 *4 1/2* **Bridge Builder**[14] 8311 7-8-10 68 ow1 (p) MarcMonaghan(3) 14 40
(Peter Hedger) *dropped in bhd after s: n.d* 66/1

1m 25.19s (-0.81) **Going Correction** -0.15s/f (Stan)
**WFA** 3 from 4yo+ 1lb 14 Ran SP% **121.1**
Speed ratings (Par 103): **98,95,93,93,92 91,91,91,90,89 89,87,87,82**
CSF £65.31 CT £611.29 TOTE £5.90: £2.00, £5.60, £3.50; EX 72.40 Trifecta £629.60.
**Owner** King Power Racing Co Ltd **Bred** W Hennessey **Trained** Whatcombe, Oxon

**FOCUS**
A fair handicap but not too many progressive sorts on show. The ordinary gallop was against those held up and very few figured, and the winner collected a clear personal best on stable debut.

## 8647 100% PROFIT BOOST AT 32REDSPORT.COM H'CAP 1m 7f 218y(P)
7:45 (7:45) (Class 6) (0-65,65) 3-Y-O+ £2,264 (£673; £336; £168) Stalls Low

Form RPR

1 **Grey Waters (IRE)**[39] 7590 3-9-3 61 OisinMurphy 10 68
(Joseph Patrick O'Brien, Ire) *wl in tch in midfield: effrt to ld 2f out: edgd rt 1f out: stdy on and a doing enough ins fnl f: rdn out* 6/4[1]

6004 2 *1* **Caracas**[20] 8157 3-9-4 62 RichardKingscote 1 68
(Harry Dunlop) *hld up in midfield: hdwy over 2f out: rdn to chse wnr over 1f out: swtchd lft 1f out: kpt on u.p ins fnl f* 12/1

-204 3 *1/2* **Author's Dream**[146] 3724 4-9-6 57 (v[1]) LukeMorris 13 60
(William Knight) *hld up in midfield: hdwy over 2f out: rdn to chse ldrs over 1f out: kpt on u.p ins fnl f* 9/1[3]

2000 4 *4 1/2* **Bumble Bay**[17] 8246 7-8-10 50 (t) CallumShepherd(3) 4 48
(Robert Stephens) *hld up in last pair: hdwy over 2f out: swtchd rt and clsd wl over 1f out: 4th 1f out: no ex and outpcd ins fnl f* 33/1

4000 5 *1 1/4* **Indian Red**[32] 7790 3-8-13 57 JoeyHaynes 12 55
(Mark H Tompkins) *chsd ldrs: rdn over 2f out: unable qck and outpcd over 1f out: wl hld and kpt on same pce ins fnl f* 12/1

-000 6 *hd* **Atalanta Bay (IRE)**[20] 8157 7-9-4 55 (h) ShaneKelly 7 51
(Marcus Tregoning) *chsd ldrs: rdn and ev ch over 2f out tl unable qck 2f out: outpcd and btn over 1f out: plugged on* 12/1

40-2 7 *3 1/2* **Thankyou Very Much**[19] 8187 7-9-5 56 (bt) TedDurcan 11 48
(James Bethell) *hld up in midfield: effrt on outer over 3f out: rdn over 2f out: no imp: plugged on but nvr threatened ldrs* 10/1

0000 **8** 1 3/4 **Victor's Bet (SPA)**[20] 8157 8-9-7 **63**........................ MeganNicholls(5) 3 53
(Ralph J Smith) *hld up in last pair: clsd and nt clr run ent fnl 2f: swtchd lft and sme hdwy over 1f out: nvr trbld ldrs* **33/1**
4530 **9** 1 1/2 **Southern States**[34] 7744 4-9-6 **57**........................(p1) CharlesBishop 6 45
(Lydia Richards) *a towards rr: rdn 4f out: nvr trbld ldrs* **7/1**[2]
5310 **10** 1/2 **Woofie (IRE)**[47] 7319 5-9-10 **61**........................(p) GeorgeDowning 9 48
(Laura Mongan) *chsd ldr tl 10f out: styd chsng ldrs tl unable qck over 2f out: wknd over 1f out* **22/1**
3433 **11** 2 1/4 **Ocean Gale**[17] 8246 4-8-12 **49**........................ DavidProbert 2 34
(Richard Price) *hld up in tch in midfield tl quick move to join ldr 10f out: led 3f out: rdn and hdd over 2f out: wknd over 1f out* **7/1**[2]
0600 **12** 4 1/2 **Mayasa (IRE)**[20] 8157 4-10-0 **65**........................(t1) DanielMuscutt 5 44
(John Flint) *hld up in tch in midfield: hdwy to chse ldrs 5f out: rdn to ld over 2f out: sn hdd and outpcd: wknd over 1f out* **40/1**
6500 **13** 6 **Hatsaway (IRE)**[37] 7651 6-9-5 **61**........................ PaddyBradley(5) 8 33
(Pat Phelan) *in tch in midfield: rdn over 3f out and sn nt clr run: lost pl over 2f out: bhd over 1f out* **20/1**
56/6 **14** 7 **Marju's Quest (IRE)**[38] 6819 7-10-0 **65**........................ TimmyMurphy 14 29
(Adrian Wintle) *sn led: jnd 10f out: hdd and rdn 3f out: sn lost pl: bhd over 1f out* **66/1**

3m 28.42s (-1.68) **Going Correction** -0.15s/f (Stan)
**WFA** 3 from 4yo+ 7lb **14** Ran SP% **126.1**
Speed ratings (Par 101): **98,97,97,95,94 94,92,91,90,90 89,87,84,80**
CSF £20.77 CT £137.90 TOTE £2.20: £1.10, £2.60, £3.50; EX 25.70 Trifecta £121.70.
**Owner** Boragh Stud Syndicate **Bred** M M Sammon **Trained** Owning Hill, Co Kilkenny

**FOCUS**
A modest event run at a stop-start gallop. The first three pulled a few lengths clear of the remainder in the closing stages.

## 8648 32RED AMATEUR RIDERS' H'CAP 1m 3f 219y(P)
**8:15** (8:15) (Class 4) (0-80,79) 3-Y-O+ **£4,523** (£1,402; £701; £350) **Stalls** Low

Form RPR
0151 **1** **Snowy Winter (USA)**[18] 8204 3-10-12 **79**........................(t) MrSWalker 3 89+
(Archie Watson) *hld up in tch: clsd on inner to chse ldr over 2f out: rdn to ld over 1f out: pressed ins fnl f: kpt on: rdn out* **11/4**[2]
1142 **2** hd **Take Two**[10] 8426 8-10-9 **76**........................ MrJBrace(5) 1 84
(Alex Hales) *sn dropped to rr: rdn and hdwy on inner over 2f out: chsd clr wnr ent fnl f: styd on to press wnr 100yds: steadily clsd but a jst hld* **5/1**
2050 **3** 8 **Zambeasy**[29] 7908 6-11-0 **76**........................ MrRBirkett 6 71
(Philip Hide) *led tl rdn and hdd over 1f out: 3rd and btn 1f out: wknd ins fnl f* **16/1**
**4** 1 3/4 **French Mix (USA)**[25] 8019 3-10-4 **71**........................ MrTHamilton 2 63
(Joseph Patrick O'Brien, Ire) *chsd ldrs: effrt over 2f out: 4th and no ex over 1f out: wknd ins fnl f* **4/1**[3]
4600 **5** 11 **Biotic**[21] 8132 6-10-5 **67**........................(p) MrPMillman 7 42
(Rod Millman) *stdd and dropped in bhd after s: hld up in tch in midfield: clsd to chse ldrs 3f out: 5th and outpcd u.p 2f out: sn wknd* **10/1**
5200 **6** 3 1/2 **Methag (FR)**[132] 4222 4-10-6 **73**........................ MrSLee(5) 4 42
(Alex Hales) *chsd ldr tl rdn and lost 2nd over 3f out: lost pl over 2f out: sn bhd* **50/1**
622 **7** nk **So Celebre (GER)**[20] 8160 4-10-7 **72**........................ MissAMcCain(3) 5 41
(Ian Williams) *hld up in tch in midfield on outer: rdn and dropped to rr over 3f out: bhd over 2f out* **9/4**[1]

2m 33.3s (-1.20) **Going Correction** -0.15s/f (Stan)
**WFA** 3 from 4yo+ 5lb **7** Ran SP% **111.0**
Speed ratings (Par 105): **98,97,92,91,84 81,81**
CSF £15.80 TOTE £3.00: £2.10, £2.00; EX 13.00 Trifecta £122.00.
**Owner** Boadicea Bloodstock **Bred** Darley **Trained** Upper Lambourn, W Berks

**FOCUS**
A fair handicap but, although the gallop was on the steady side to the home turn, the field were well strung out at the finish. The winner continues to improve on the AW.
T/Jkpt: Not won. T/Plt: £140.10 to a £1 stake. Pool: £77,187.50 - 402.13 winning units T/Qpdt: £32.60 to a £1 stake. Pool: £10,781.01 - 244.26 winning units **Steve Payne**

# 8474 REDCAR (L-H)
Tuesday, November 7

**OFFICIAL GOING: Soft (7.0)**
Wind: fairly strong half behind, dropped considerably after 2nd Weather: overcast, drizzle after race 2

## 8649 BRITISH STALLIONS STUDS EBF NOVICE STKS 7f
**12:20** (12:24) (Class 5) 2-Y-O **£3,396** (£1,010; £505; £252) **Stalls** Centre

Form RPR
2422 **1** **Up Sticks And Go**[39] 7564 2-9-2 78........................ AndrewMullen 7 76
(Keith Dalgleish) *mde all: pushed along 2f out: rdn ins fnl f: edgd lft: kpt on* **11/4**[2]
25 **2** 1 **Knighted (IRE)**[27] 7953 2-9-2 0........................ KevinStott 4 73
(Kevin Ryan) *trckd ldrs: rdn over 2f out: kpt on* **15/8**[1]
23 **3** hd **Mametz Wood (IRE)**[18] 8208 2-9-2 0........................ BenCurtis 8 72
(K R Burke) *chsd ldr: rdn over 2f out: kpt on* **10/3**[3]
**4** 7 **Diplomacy (IRE)** 2-9-2 0........................ DanielTudhope 5 54
(David O'Meara) *hld up in tch: rdn over 2f out: wknd appr fnl f* **17/2**
5 **5** hd **Indian Admiral**[106] 5202 2-9-2 0........................ FrannyNorton 6 54
(Mark Johnston) *chsd ldr: rdn over 2f out: wknd over 1f out* **12/1**
**6** 4 1/2 **Camden Town (IRE)** 2-9-2 0........................ TonyHamilton 2 42
(Roger Fell) *hld up in tch: rdn over 2f out: wknd over 1f out* **16/1**
**7** 4 **Naval Officer** 2-8-13 0........................ LewisEdmunds(3) 1 32
(Nigel Tinkler) *dwlt: hld up: sn pushed along: hdwy and briefly in tch over 2f out: wknd over 1f out* **66/1**
**8** 31 **No Civil Justice** 2-8-13 0........................ CallumRodriguez(3) 3
(David Thompson) *slowly away: sn pushed along in rr: bhd fnl 4f* **150/1**

1m 26.69s (2.19) **Going Correction** +0.225s/f (Good) **8** Ran SP% **110.8**
Speed ratings (Par 96): **96,94,94,86,86 81,76,41**
CSF £7.73 TOTE £3.20: £1.30, £1.10, £1.40; EX 7.20 Trifecta £14.70.
**Owner** Paul & Clare Rooney **Bred** D R Tucker **Trained** Carluke, S Lanarks

**FOCUS**
The ground was officially soft (GoingStick: 7.0) and clerk of the course James Sanderson said: "It's a bit better in places but will probably ride dead and tacky, though they have a tailwind to help them." After riding in the opener Ben Curtis and Kevin Stott called the ground "soft" and Andrew Mullen said it was "very tacky". A fair novice, and the first three pulled well clear.

## 8650 RACING UK'S BIGGEST EVER FREE TRIAL (S) STKS 7f 219y
**12:50** (12:50) (Class 6) 3-5-Y-O **£3,234** (£962; £481; £240) **Stalls** Centre

Form RPR
0032 **1** **Catastrophe**[26] 7979 4-9-0 55........................ JasonHart 2 60+
(John Quinn) *trckd ldrs: rdn to ld wl over 1f out: edgd lft ins fnl f: kpt on* **8/13**[1]
4065 **2** 3 1/4 **Siyahamba (IRE)**[31] 7820 3-8-5 50........................ HarryRussell(7) 4 53
(Bryan Smart) *trckd ldr: rdn over 2f out: one pce and no ch w wnr fnl f: edgd lft ins fnl f* **9/1**
0300 **3** 3 1/2 **Orientelle**[16] 8255 3-8-4 46........................(b) PhilDennis(3) 5 39
(Richard Whitaker) *led: rdn over 2f out: hdd wl over 1f out: no ex* **18/1**
0420 **4** 5 **Cosmic Dust**[26] 7979 4-8-7 52 ow1........................ LewisEdmunds(3) 8 29
(Richard Whitaker) *in tch: rdn to chse ldrs over 2f out: wknd over 1f out* **9/2**[2]
5000 **5** 5 **Italian Beauty (IRE)**[38] 7598 5-8-6 55........................(v1) NoelGarbutt(3) 1 16
(John Wainwright) *hld up: sn pushed along: nvr threatened* **14/1**
606 **6** 2 1/2 **Newgate Duchess**[8] 8477 3-8-7 0........................ DuranFentiman 7 11
(Tony Coyle) *hld up: rdn over 3f out: sn btn* **50/1**
0000 **7** 3 1/2 **Bilko's Back (IRE)**[14] 8314 5-9-0 42........................(t) TonyHamilton 3 8
(Susan Corbett) *a towards rr* **100/1**
0006 **8** 4 1/2 **Fidelma Moon (IRE)**[41] 7523 5-8-9 49........................(t1) BarryMcHugh 6
(Tracy Waggott) *prom: rdn along over 3f out: sn wknd* **13/2**[3]

1m 42.3s (5.70) **Going Correction** +0.60s/f (Yiel)
**WFA** 3 from 4yo+ 2lb **8** Ran SP% **118.3**
Speed ratings (Par 101): **95,91,88,83,78 75,72,67**
CSF £7.92 TOTE £1.50: £1.10, £2.60, £2.50; EX 7.70 Trifecta £40.90.No bid for the winner.
**Owner** J N Blackburn **Bred** D R Tucker **Trained** Settrington, N Yorks

**FOCUS**
This was a weak race. Only two of the runners had achieved an RPR in the 50s in one of their last two starts (Catastrophe and Cosmic Dust), and the former had finished a long way in front of the latter at Ayr last time out. It proved easy pickings for the favourite.

## 8651 RACING UK FREE TRIAL LIMITED TIME ONLY H'CAP 7f
**1:20** (1:23) (Class 5) (0-70,69) 3-Y-O+ **£3,396** (£1,010; £505; £252) **Stalls** Centre

Form RPR
2312 **1** **Break The Silence**[6] 8513 3-8-6 **55**........................(p) KieranO'Neill 6 62
(Scott Dixon) *mde all: rdn over 2f out: strly pressed fnl 110yds: hld on gamely* **6/1**[3]
4462 **2** nse **Edgar Allan Poe (IRE)**[15] 8299 3-9-6 **69**........................ DanielTudhope 8 76
(Rebecca Bastiman) *in tch: rdn and hdwy over 1f out: chal strly fnl 110yds: kpt on* **8/1**
6622 **3** 1 1/4 **Grinty (IRE)**[18] 8216 3-9-3 **66**........................ AndrewMullen 2 70
(Michael Dods) *in tch: pushed along and hdwy 2f out: rdn and ev ch appr fnl f: one pce fnl 110yds* **9/1**
232 **4** 1 1/4 **Vive La Difference (IRE)**[8] 8479 3-9-3 **66**........................ DavidAllan 12 67
(Tim Easterby) *hld up: rdn along over 2f out: edgd lft but hdwy over 1f out: kpt on same pce fnl f* **2/1**[1]
0012 **5** 1 3/4 **Hitchcock**[6] 8514 3-9-2 **65**........................(b) KevinStott 1 61
(Kevin Ryan) *prom: rdn over 2f out: wknd fnl 110yds* **7/2**[2]
2504 **6** 1/2 **Seaview**[22] 8107 3-8-9 **65**........................ TristanPrice(7) 7 60
(David Brown) *chsd ldrs: rdn over 2f out: ev ch over 1f out: wknd ins fnl f* **33/1**
1554 **7** 2 **Stubytuesday**[18] 8216 3-9-5 **68**........................ JamesSullivan 14 58
(Michael Easterby) *hld up: sn pushed along: plugged on fr over 1f out: nvr threatened* **18/1**
5054 **8** 5 **Monte Cinq (IRE)**[31] 7825 3-9-4 **67**........................(h) FrannyNorton 10 44
(Jason Ward) *midfield: rdn along 3f out: sn outpcd and btn* **22/1**
2132 **9** 2 **Bold Spirit**[28] 7932 6-8-9 **60**........................(t) PhilDennis(3) 5 33
(Declan Carroll) *prom: rdn 3f out: sn wknd* **20/1**
4160 **10** 1 1/4 **Kiwi Bay**[29] 7894 12-9-1 **66**........................ CallumRodriguez(3) 3 35
(Michael Dods) *chsd ldrs: rdn over 2f out: sn wknd* **16/1**
5466 **11** 5 **Baron Run**[8] 8473 7-8-3 **58** oh3 ow3........................ RussellHarris(7) 13 14
(K R Burke) *dwlt: a towards rr* **50/1**
00-5 **12** nk **Servo (IRE)**[221] 1470 3-8-9 **58**........................ BarryMcHugh 4 12
(Lynn Siddall) *rrd and slowly away: a towards rr* **100/1**
0000 **13** 3 1/4 **Taskeen (IRE)**[47] 7332 4-9-0 **62**........................ TonyHamilton 9 9
(Roger Fell) *a towards rr* **40/1**
4612 **14** 2 3/4 **Point Of Woods**[8] 8480 4-8-13 **66**........................(p) RhiainIngram(5) 11 6
(Tina Jackson) *midfield: rdn over 3f out: wknd* **25/1**

1m 27.61s (3.11) **Going Correction** +0.60s/f (Yiel)
**WFA** 3 from 4yo+ 1lb **14** Ran SP% **123.4**
Speed ratings (Par 103): **106,105,104,103,101 100,98,92,90,88 83,82,79,75**
CSF £51.06 CT £452.10 TOTE £6.40: £2.20, £2.30, £2.60; EX 61.60 Trifecta £630.10.
**Owner** Winning Connections Racing **Bred** Richard Moses Bloodstock **Trained** Babworth, Notts

**FOCUS**
A modest handicap, but solid form for the grade. The winner made all for a personal best.

## 8652 RACING UK FREE FOR A MONTH H'CAP 1m 2f 1y
**1:50** (1:50) (Class 3) (0-95,90) 3-Y-O+ **£7,762** (£2,310; £1,154; £577) **Stalls** Low

Form RPR
0104 **1** **Awake My Soul (IRE)**[10] 8423 8-9-5 **88**........................ JamesSullivan 6 95
(Tom Tate) *trckd ldrs: rdn over 2f out: drvn to ld narrowly appr fnl f: kpt on: asserted towards fin* **2/1**[1]
6113 **2** 1 **Canberra Cliffs (IRE)**[11] 8385 3-9-2 **88**........................ FranBerry 5 93
(Don Cantillon) *midfield: hdwy over 2f out: rdn over 1f out: jnd ldr ins fnl f: one pce towards fin* **9/2**[2]
0000 **3** 1 1/4 **Gulf Of Poets**[24] 8048 5-9-2 **85**........................ AndrewMullen 2 88
(Michael Easterby) *trckd ldrs: pushed along and n.m.r over 1f out: rdn and kpt on ins fnl f* **14/1**
2001 **4** nse **Silvery Moon (IRE)**[15] 8289 10-9-0 **83**........................ DavidAllan 3 85
(Tim Easterby) *pressed ldr: rdn over 2f out: one pce fnl f* **9/1**
0002 **5** nse **Swift Emperor (IRE)**[24] 8048 5-9-5 **88**........................ BenCurtis 4 90
(David Barron) *midfield: rdn over 2f out: kpt on ins fnl f: nvr threatened* **9/2**[2]
6410 **6** nk **Compton Mill**[20] 8165 5-9-3 **86**........................ DanielTudhope 7 88
(Hughie Morrison) *hld up: rdn and sme hdwy over 2f out: one pce fnl f* **5/1**[3]
5140 **7** 2 3/4 **Royal Shaheen (FR)**[15] 8289 4-8-12 **81**........................(v) GrahamLee 1 77
(Alistair Whillans) *led narrowly: rdn over 2f out: hdd appr fnl f: wknd ins fnl f* **17/2**

6003 **8** *1* **Magic City (IRE)**[6] 8510 8-8-10 **82**........................ LewisEdmunds(3) 8 76
(Michael Easterby) *hld up: rdn over 2f out: nvr threatened* **20/1**
6330 **9** *27* **Qaffaal (USA)**[115] 4916 6-9-4 **90**........................ CallumRodriguez(3) 9 30
(Michael Easterby) *hld up: rdn over 3f out: wknd and bhd* **50/1**
2m 12.14s (5.04) **Going Correction** +0.70s/f (Yiel)
**WFA** 3 from 4yo+ 3lb **9** Ran SP% **120.3**
Speed ratings (Par 107): **107,106,105,105,105 104,102,101,80**
CSF £11.61 CT £102.25 TOTE £2.90: £1.20, £2.10, £4.80; EX 18.40 Trifecta £149.40.
**Owner** T T Racing **Bred** Grundy Bloodstock Srl **Trained** Tadcaster, N Yorks
**FOCUS**
Not a bad handicap, and the winner landed a bit of a gamble. The runner-up appeared to run to form.

## 8653 RACINGUK.COM/FREETRIAL CLAIMING STKS 1m 2f 1y
**2:20** (2:20) (Class 6) 3-4-Y-0 **£3,234** (£962; £481; £240) **Stalls** Low

Form RPR
1000 **1** **Metronomic (IRE)**[42] 7476 3-9-2 61........................ AndrewMullen 1 66
(Peter Niven) *bolted to post: mde all: kpt on pushed out fr over 1f out* **14/1**
6216 **2** *1 ¼* **Restive (IRE)**[14] 8315 4-9-7 67........................ CallumRodriguez(3) 4 68
(Iain Jardine) *dwlt: hld up: pushed along and hdwy to chse ldr over 2f out: rdn over 1f out: one pce* **15/8**[1]
0630 **3** *3 ¼* **Outback Blue**[7] 8497 4-8-12 69........................(t) MattCosham(3) 2 52
(David Evans) *dwlt: hld up: rdn over 2f out: plugged on in modest 3rd fr over 1f out* **9/4**[2]
5533 **4** *8* **Little Pippin**[8] 8477 4-8-2 48........................(p) RPWalsh(7) 7 31
(Tony Coyle) *trckd ldr: rdn over 3f out: wknd fnl 2f* **15/2**
1-0 **5** *4* **Coroberee (IRE)**[24] 8048 4-9-10 82........................(p[1]) BarryMcHugh 3 39
(Tony Coyle) *trckd ldr: rdn 3f out: sn lost pl and btn* **3/1**[3]
0050 **6** *6* **Clayton Hall (IRE)**[146] 3706 4-9-5 48........................(p) TonyHamilton 6 22
(John Wainwright) *midfield: rdn over 2f out: wknd* **66/1**
0006 **7** *5* **Just Heather (IRE)**[38] 7597 3-8-3 34........................ NoelGarbutt(3) 5 4
(John Wainwright) *a towards rr* **125/1**
2m 13.84s (6.74) **Going Correction** +0.825s/f (Soft)
**WFA** 3 from 4yo 3lb **7** Ran SP% **111.3**
Speed ratings (Par 101): **106,105,102,96,92 88,84**
CSF £38.58 TOTE £14.30: £5.70, £1.70; EX 41.60 Trifecta £122.00.No bid for the winner. Outback Blue was bought by Mr G.T Bewley for £6000.
**Owner** Keep The Faith Partnership **Bred** Pier House Stud **Trained** Barton-le-Street, N Yorks
**FOCUS**
Modest claiming form, rated around the first two's better recent form.

## 8654 START YOUR RACING UK FREE TRIAL NOW H'CAP (DIV I) 1m 5f 218y
**2:55** (2:56) (Class 6) (0-65,67) 3-Y-0+ **£3,234** (£962; £481; £240) **Stalls** Low

Form RPR
1364 **1** **Affair**[28] 7918 3-8-3 **52**........................ TheodoreLadd(7) 7 60
(Hughie Morrison) *prom: led 11f out: mde rest: pushed along over 2f out: rdn over 1f out: styd on* **6/1**[3]
0612 **2** *1 ¼* **Jan De Heem**[17] 8241 7-9-9 **59**........................(p) JoeDoyle 2 63
(Tina Jackson) *in tch: smooth hdwy to trck ldr 3f out: rdn over 1f out: one pce* **3/1**[2]
0030 **3** *3* **Leopard (IRE)**[31] 7820 3-8-12 **54**........................ BarryMcHugh 5 56
(Tony Coyle) *trckd ldrs: rdn over 3f out: plugged on fnl f* **20/1**
050 **4** *shd* **Apalis (FR)**[143] 3830 5-9-12 **62**........................(t) JamesSullivan 3 62
(Michael Easterby) *midfield: rdn over 3f out: styd on fnl f* **12/1**
**5** *3 ¼* **Pantomime (IRE)**[892] 2731 5-9-5 **55**........................ GrahamLee 6 51
(Rebecca Menzies) *led: hdd 11f out: prom: rdn and outpcd 3f out: wknd ins fnl f* **33/1**
0300 **6** *2 ¼* **Unonothinjonsnow**[6] 8513 3-8-3 **45**........................ AndrewMullen 9 40
(Richard Guest) *hld up in midfield: rdn over 3f out: sme hdwy over 2f out: wknd over 1f out* **10/1**
3020 **7** *1* **La Bacouetteuse (FR)**[7] 8487 12-9-2 **52**........................(b) DavidAllan 4 44
(Iain Jardine) *hld up: rdn over 5f out: nvr threatened* **14/1**
6211 **8** *1* **Four Kingdoms (IRE)**[14] 8312 3-9-1 **64**........................ PatrickO'Hanlon(7) 1 57
(K R Burke) *trckd ldrs: rdn over 3f out: wknd fnl f and eased* **5/4**[1]
100- **9** *3 ¾* **Shalamzar (FR)**[244] 7043 8-9-10 **67**........................ LaurenSteade(7) 10 53
(Micky Hammond) *hld up in midfield: rdn over 3f out: sn btn* **66/1**
5-00 **10** *2* **Dance With Kate**[26] 7990 6-8-2 **45**........................(b[1]) RPWalsh(7) 11 28
(Olly Murphy) *midfield on outside: rdn 3f out: wknd over 1f out* **66/1**
0-00 **11** *21* **Pertuis (IRE)**[14] 8314 11-9-6 **56**........................ FrannyNorton 8 12
(Micky Hammond) *a towards rr* **50/1**
3m 17.13s (12.43) **Going Correction** +0.825s/f (Soft)
**WFA** 3 from 5yo+ 6lb **11** Ran SP% **119.8**
Speed ratings (Par 101): **97,96,94,94,92 91,90,90,88,86 74**
CSF £24.03 CT £344.93 TOTE £6.70: £2.50, £1.40, £5.70; EX 25.10 Trifecta £308.50.
**Owner** H Morrison **Bred** H Morrison **Trained** East Ilsley, Berks
■ Stewards' Enquiry : Barry McHugh four-day ban: misuse of the whip (Nov 21-24)
**FOCUS**
An ordinary handicap run at a steady early pace. The winner more or less made all and is rated near this year's best form.

## 8655 START YOUR RACING UK FREE TRIAL NOW H'CAP (DIV II) 1m 5f 218y
**3:25** (3:25) (Class 6) (0-65,67) 3-Y-0+ **£3,234** (£962; £481; £240) **Stalls** Low

Form RPR
0000 **1** **Rajapur**[70] 6565 4-8-7 **45**........................(p) LewisEdmunds(3) 5 53+
(David Thompson) *in tch: racd keenly: pushed along to chal 3f out: rdn to ld wl over 1f out: styd on wl to draw clr fnl f* **33/1**
1035 **2** *4 ½* **Adrakhan (FR)**[17] 8241 6-9-0 **49**........................ KevinStott 7 50
(Wilf Storey) *led: hdd over 4f out: rdn over 3f out: outpcd 2f out: plugged on fnl f* **7/1**
3500 **3** *½* **Captain Swift (IRE)**[11] 8396 6-9-10 **59**........................(p) GrahamLee 1 59
(John Mackie) *trckd ldrs: rdn 3f out: plugged on* **4/1**[3]
4016 **4** *nk* **Ingleby Hollow**[7] 8487 5-10-4 **67**........................(t) DanielTudhope 8 67
(David O'Meara) *prom: led over 4f out: rdn 3f out: hdd wl over 1f out: wknd and lost 2 pls fnl 110yds* **3/1**[1]
5524 **5** *½* **Eyreborn (IRE)**[8] 8478 3-9-7 **62**........................ TonyHamilton 6 63
(Keith Dalgleish) *hld up in midfield: rdn 3f out: plugged on fnl f* **7/2**[2]
30-0 **6** *3 ½* **Becky The Thatcher**[28] 7922 4-9-5 **54**........................ AndrewMullen 3 48
(Micky Hammond) *hld up: rdn over 3f out: nvr threatened* **20/1**
0630 **7** *1 ¾* **Patent**[28] 7922 4-8-11 **46**........................(b) JamesSullivan 2 37
(Peter Niven) *midfield: rdn 3f out: wknd over 1f out* **8/1**
6343 **8** *21* **Dakota City**[15] 8301 6-9-12 **61**........................(p) FranBerry 9 21
(Olly Murphy) *hld up: rdn over 3f out: sn wknd* **5/1**

0000 **9** *26* **Dark Illustrator**[8] 8477 4-8-10 **45**........................ BarryMcHugh 4
(Lynn Siddall) *midfield: wknd over 4f out and bhd* **100/1**
3m 20.67s (15.97) **Going Correction** +0.825s/f (Soft)
**WFA** 3 from 4yo+ 6lb **9** Ran SP% **116.2**
Speed ratings (Par 101): **87,84,84,83,83 81,80,68,53**
CSF £246.04 CT £1144.11 TOTE £23.90: £6.80, £2.80, £1.70; EX 327.50 Trifecta £2951.10.
**Owner** B Lapham **Bred** J & W Hoyer **Trained** Bolam, Co Durham
**FOCUS**
They went steady for a long way here and it was the slower of the two divisions by 3.54sec. The first four raced in the first four positions throughout and there was a shock result.

## 8656 THANKS & SEE YOU NEXT SEASON H'CAP 5f 217y
**3:55** (3:57) (Class 6) (0-60,62) 3-Y-0+ **£3,234** (£962; £481; £240) **Stalls** Centre

Form RPR
0221 **1** **Awesome Allan (IRE)**[8] 8481 3-9-7 **62**........................(t) MattCosham(3) 4 70
(David Evans) *prom: rdn to ld 2f out: kpt on wl* **5/4**[1]
0322 **2** *1 ¾* **Nellie's Dancer**[16] 8256 3-9-4 **56**........................(p) DavidAllan 8 59
(Scott Dixon) *prom: rdn over 2f out: kpt on* **9/1**
3345 **3** *¾* **Ambitious Icarus**[4] 8557 8-9-7 **59**........................(p) FrannyNorton 2 60
(Richard Guest) *hld up: pushed along and hdwy over 2f out: rdn over 1f out: kpt on to go 3rd fnl 110yds* **10/1**
4632 **4** *1 ¾* **Cool Strutter (IRE)**[7] 8490 5-8-13 **51**........................(b) SamJames 15 47
(Karen Tutty) *midfield: rdn over 2f out: hdwy to chse ldr over 1f out: one pce ins fnl f* **15/2**[2]
5006 **5** *2* **Market Choice (IRE)**[37] 7657 4-9-6 **58**........................ BenCurtis 14 48
(Tracy Waggott) *hld up: rdn over 2f out: kpt on ins fnl f: nvr threatened* **22/1**
5403 **6** *2 ¼* **Robbian**[7] 8490 6-8-7 **48**........................ NoelGarbutt(3) 12 31
(Charles Smith) *dwlt: sn chsd ldrs: rdn over 2f out: edgd rt towards stands' rail over 1f out: wknd ins fnl f* **12/1**
0000 **7** *2* **Barkston Ash**[41] 7525 9-9-1 **53**........................(p) JasonHart 10 30
(Eric Alston) *midfield: rdn over 2f out: plugged on fnl f* **11/1**
3040 **8** *nse* **Mighty Bond**[8] 8479 5-8-9 **47**........................(p) BarryMcHugh 9 24
(Tracy Waggott) *dwlt: hld up: rdn 3f out: nvr threatened* **20/1**
0065 **9** *shd* **Captain Scooby**[4] 8558 11-8-7 **45**........................(b) KieranO'Neill 5 21
(Richard Guest) *dwlt: sn outpcd in rr: minor late hdwy: nvr threatened* **20/1**
0062 **10** *2 ½* **Racquet**[7] 8484 4-9-10 **62**........................ JamesSullivan 6 31
(Ruth Carr) *led: rdn whn hdd 2f out: wknd* **17/2**[3]
0042 **11** *1 ½* **Henrietta's Dream**[18] 8217 3-8-10 **48**........................(b) GrahamLee 11 12
(John Wainwright) *chsd ldrs: rdn over 2f out: wknd over 1f out* **33/1**
1206 **12** *2 ¾* **Mimic's Memory**[8] 8480 3-9-10 **62**........................ JackGarritty 13 18
(Ann Duffield) *midfield: rdn over 2f out: wknd over 1f out* **50/1**
0060 **13** *6* **Kirkby's Phantom**[4] 8559 3-8-7 **45**........................(p) AndrewMullen 3
(Alan Berry) *prom tl wknd 3f out* **150/1**
00-0 **14** *7* **Amherst Rock**[45] 7414 3-9-7 **59**........................(t) DannyBrock 1
(Luke McJannet) *chsd ldrs: rdn over 3f out: hung lft and wknd* **100/1**
1m 15.53s (3.73) **Going Correction** +0.60s/f (Yiel) **14** Ran SP% **122.3**
Speed ratings (Par 101): **99,96,95,93,90 87,85,84,84,81 79,75,67,58**
CSF £12.12 CT £87.37 TOTE £2.00: £1.30, £2.50, £3.20; EX 17.00 Trifecta £69.40.
**Owner** A Cooke & K McCabe **Bred** D G Iceton **Trained** Pandy, Monmouths
**FOCUS**
A moderate sprint handicap. The winner was well in at the weights.
T/Plt: £36.50 to a £1 stake. Pool: £46,266.96 - 923.28 winning units T/Qpdt: £26.30 to a £1 stake. Pool: £4,175.76 - 117.40 winning units **Andrew Sheret**

# 8491 WOLVERHAMPTON (A.W) (L-H)
## Tuesday, November 7

**OFFICIAL GOING: Tapeta: standard**
Wind: Fresh across Weather: Raining

## 8657 32RED.COM NOVICE STKS 5f 21y (Tp)
**1:10** (1:11) (Class 5) 2-Y-0 **£3,234** (£962; £481; £240) **Stalls** Low

Form RPR
6 **1** **Towelrads Boy (IRE)**[8] 8466 2-9-2 0........................ PJMcDonald 5 78+
(Paul Cole) *sn nudged along towards rr: hdwy 1/2-way: rdn to ld ins fnl f: r.o: comf* **15/2**[3]
03 **2** *1* **Axe Cap (IRE)**[15] 8294 2-8-11 0........................ OisinMurphy 8 69
(Archie Watson) *sn pushed along to chse ldrs: rdn over 1f out: edgd rt ins fnl f: styd on* **3/1**[2]
343 **3** *nk* **Militia**[25] 8010 2-9-2 77........................ PaulHanagan 4 73
(Richard Fahey) *chsd ldr: shkn up to ld over 1f out: rdn and hdd ins fnl f: styd on same pce* **4/6**[1]
626 **4** *3* **Global Academy (IRE)**[88] 5879 2-9-2 71........................ LukeMorris 10 62
(Gay Kelleway) *chsd ldrs: rdn over 1f out: sn hung lft: no ex ins fnl f* **10/1**
00 **5** *4 ½* **Alaskan Bay (IRE)**[70] 6559 2-8-11 0........................ DavidProbert 7 41
(Rae Guest) *prom: pushed along over 3f out: outpcd fr 1/2-way* **25/1**
00 **6** *3 ¼* **Rockesbury**[197] 2029 2-9-2 0........................(b[1]) DougieCostello 6 34
(Kevin Frost) *chsd ldrs: rdn 1/2-way: wknd over 1f out* **125/1**
00 **7** *nk* **Warrior's Valley**[7] 8483 2-9-2 0........................ RobertHavlin 3 33
(David C Griffiths) *led: shkn up and hdd over 1f out: wknd ins fnl f* **100/1**
3 **8** *hd* **Crikeyitswhykie**[7] 8483 2-9-2 0........................ PatrickMathers 1 33
(Derek Shaw) *s.i.s: outpcd* **25/1**
0 **9** *1 ½* **Broughton Excels**[34] 7731 2-9-2 0........................ StevieDonohoe 2 27
(Henry Spiller) *dwlt: outpcd* **33/1**
**10** *2 ½* **Born For Prosecco (IRE)** 2-8-8 0........................ EoinWalsh(3) 9 13
(Derek Shaw) *dwlt: outpcd* **200/1**
1m 1.01s (-0.89) **Going Correction** -0.025s/f (Stan) **10** Ran SP% **118.8**
Speed ratings (Par 96): **106,104,103,99,91 86,86,85,83,79**
CSF £29.91 TOTE £9.20: £1.80, £1.20, £1.10; EX 40.20 Trifecta £57.80.
**Owner** Towelrads Com Ltd **Bred** R Coffey **Trained** Whatcombe, Oxon
**FOCUS**
The surface was standard. \n\x\x Stalls: 7f 36y - outside; remainder - inside\n\x\x An ordinary juvenile contest which produced a ready winner who improved markedly on his debut run.

## 8658 32RED CASINO NURSERY H'CAP 7f 36y (Tp)
**1:40** (1:41) (Class 6) (0-65,65) 2-Y-0 **£2,425** (£721; £360; £180) **Stalls** High

Form RPR
5056 **1** **Surfa Rosa**[14] 8325 2-9-3 **64**........................ HollieDoyle(3) 11 67+
(Richard Hannon) *broke wl: sn stdd and lost pl: hld up: hdwy over 1f out: sn edgd rt: r.o to ld towards fin* **13/2**
003 **2** *nk* **Global Spirit**[14] 8308 2-9-7 **65**........................ OisinMurphy 10 67
(Ed Dunlop) *pushed along and sn wnt prom: jnd ldr 5f out: rdn to ld ins fnl f: hdd towards fin* **6/1**[3]

0640 **3** 1 ¾ **Medici Oro**[19] 8190 2-9-0 **58** ShaneGray 3 56
(David Brown) *w ldr tl led 6f out: rdn over 1f out: hdd ins fnl f: styd on same pce* **17/2**

056 **4** ½ **Mister Maestro**[11] 8382 2-9-7 **65** SeanLevey 2 61
(Richard Hannon) *hld up in tch: rdn over 1f out: styd on same pce ins fnl f* **9/4**[1]

065 **5** nk **Obrigada**[34] 7724 2-9-4 **62** StevieDonohoe 7 58
(Tom Clover) *hld up: hdwy over 1f out: nt clr run ins fnl f: nt rch ldrs* **20/1**

606 **6** ¾ **Prime Chief (IRE)**[24] 8028 2-9-2 **63** HectorCrouch(3) 4 57
(George Baker) *hld up in tch: shkn up over 2f out: rdn over 1f out: styd on same pce ins fnl f* **12/1**

066 **7** ½ **Helen Sherbet**[48] 7265 2-9-4 **65** CliffordLee(3) 1 57
(K R Burke) *led 1f: chsd ldrs: rdn over 2f out: no ex ins fnl f* **33/1**

2330 **8** 1 ¾ **Foxrush Take Time (FR)**[8] 8467 2-9-4 **62** PhillipMakin 5 50
(Richard Guest) *hld up: pushed along 1/2-way: nt trble ldrs* **5/1**[2]

350 **9** ¾ **Silvington**[35] 7707 2-9-5 **63** LukeMorris 9 49
(Tony Carroll) *chsd ldrs: rdn over 2f out: wknd fnl f* **66/1**

4604 **10** 2 ¾ **Diamond Express (IRE)**[19] 8179 2-8-10 **61** RossaRyan(7) 6 40
(Roger Teal) *hld up in tch: rdn over 2f out: wknd over 1f out* **25/1**

42 **11** 1 ¼ **Kheleyf's Girl**[51] 7196 2-9-2 **60** PJMcDonald 8 35
(David Evans) *hld up: pushed along 4f out: rdn and wknd over 1f out* **17/2**

1m 29.53s (0.73) **Going Correction** -0.025s/f (Stan) **11** Ran SP% **116.8**
Speed ratings (Par 94): **94,93,91,91,90 89,89,87,86,83 81**
CSF £43.15 CT £342.29 TOTE £8.50: £2.80, £1.90, £2.50; EX 64.10 Trifecta £583.30.
**Owner** The Delegator Partnership **Bred** Mrs Jane Patel **Trained** East Everleigh, Wilts
■ Stewards' Enquiry : Hollie Doyle caution; careless riding

**FOCUS**
Quite a competitive nursery which saw the winner come from last to first under a confident ride.

## 8659 SUNBETS.CO.UK H'CAP 7f 36y (Tp)
**2:10** (2:11) (Class 6) (0-60,60) 3-Y-O+ **£2,587** (£770; £384; £192) **Stalls High**

Form RPR

0302 **1** **Grey Destiny**[11] 8402 7-9-3 **57** CamHardie 10 65
(Antony Brittain) *hld up: hdwy over 1f out: r.o to ld wl ins fnl f: comf* **15/2**

0064 **2** ¾ **Kafoo**[11] 8401 4-9-6 **60** (vt) AlistairRawlinson 6 66
(Michael Appleby) *chsd ldrs: rdn to ld ins fnl f: sn hdd: styd on* **6/1**[3]

4543 **3** ¾ **Swot**[29] 7899 5-8-10 **57** (v[1]) RossaRyan(7) 5 61
(Roger Teal) *hld up in tch: nt clr run and swtchd lft over 1f out: sn rdn and hung lft: styd on* **10/3**[1]

6603 **4** ¾ **Soaring Spirits (IRE)**[19] 8184 7-9-4 **58** RobHornby 3 60
(Dean Ivory) *prom: chsd ldr 5f out: rdn and ev ch over 1f out: no ex wl ins fnl f* **11/1**

403 **5** 1 ¼ **Al's Memory (IRE)**[11] 8401 8-9-3 **57** PJMcDonald 8 56
(David Evans) *led over 5f out: rdn over 1f out: hdd and no ex ins fnl f* **11/2**[2]

420 **6** nk **Joys Delight**[28] 7934 3-9-5 **60** LukeMorris 1 57
(Daniel Mark Loughnane) *s.i.s: hld up: styd on u.p fr over 1f out: edgd lft ins fnl f: nt trble ldrs* **17/2**

2013 **7** ½ **Chough**[20] 8152 3-9-5 **60** RobertHavlin 11 56
(Hughie Morrison) *chsd ldrs: rdn over 1f out: no ex ins fnl f* **13/2**

0000 **8** 1 ¼ **Arcane Dancer (IRE)**[19] 8194 4-9-4 **58** (b) DavidNolan 12 52
(Lawrence Mullaney) *hld up: rdn over 1f out: nvr on terms* **25/1**

6212 **9** shd **Isntshesomething**[11] 8401 5-9-4 **58** (v) DougieCostello 9 51
(Richard Guest) *s.i.s: hld up: plld hrd: hdwy over 1f out: sn rdn: no ex ins fnl f* **10/1**

5040 **10** 9 **Nicky Baby (IRE)**[14] 8329 3-8-13 **57** (b[1]) JackDuern(3) 7 26
(Dean Ivory) *hld up: rdn on outer over 2f out: wknd over 1f out* **22/1**

-000 **11** nse **Major Assault**[175] 2709 4-9-3 **57** JohnFahy 2 27
(Matthew Salaman) *plld hrd: led: hdd over 5f out: remained handy: rdn over 1f out: wknd ins fnl f* **100/1**

1m 28.65s (-0.15) **Going Correction** -0.025s/f (Stan)
**WFA** 3 from 4yo+ 1lb **11** Ran SP% **115.0**
Speed ratings (Par 101): **99,98,97,96,95 94,94,92,92,82 82**
CSF £49.92 CT £182.19 TOTE £8.70: £2.40, £2.30, £3.10; EX 68.10 Trifecta £317.80.
**Owner** Antony Brittain **Bred** Northgate Lodge Stud Ltd **Trained** Warthill, N Yorks

**FOCUS**
A tight handicap which, like the previous race, saw the winner pass every one of his rivals in the home straight.

## 8660 BETWAY H'CAP 5f 21y (Tp)
**2:45** (2:45) (Class 3) (0-95,94) 3-Y-O **£7,246** (£2,168; £1,084; £542; £270) **Stalls Low**

Form RPR

4012 **1** **Alsvinder**[21] 8129 4-9-2 **89** DavidNolan 4 101
(David O'Meara) *mde all: shkn up over 1f out: edgd rt: rdn out* **3/1**[2]

2161 **2** 1 ½ **Landing Night (IRE)**[28] 7940 5-8-8 **81** (tp) PJMcDonald 5 87
(Rebecca Menzies) *a.p: rdn to chse wnr ins fnl f: styd on* **9/2**[3]

0040 **3** ½ **Midnight Malibu (IRE)**[17] 8238 4-8-8 **84** RachelRichardson(3) 6 88
(Tim Easterby) *chsd wnr: rdn over 1f out: styd on same pce ins fnl f* **12/1**

2000 **4** 1 ¼ **Bowson Fred**[17] 8238 5-9-0 **94** HarrisonShaw(7) 3 94+
(Michael Easterby) *wnt lft s: hld up: swtchd rt 1/2-way: hdwy over 1f out: styd on same pce ins fnl f* **5/2**[1]

0143 **5** ½ **Upavon**[65] 6720 7-8-13 **86** (t) LukeMorris 8 84
(Stuart Williams) *pushed along leaving stalls: hld up: hdwy u.p over 1f out: styd on same pce ins fnl f* **12/1**

0000 **6** 1 ½ **Coolfitch (IRE)**[10] 8416 3-8-13 **86** (v) PhillipMakin 1 79
(David O'Meara) *s.i.s: hld up: rdn over 1f out: no imp fnl f* **14/1**

0540 **7** ½ **Stanghow**[38] 7604 5-8-8 **81** CamHardie 7 72
(Antony Brittain) *half-rrd s: plld hrd and prom: rdn over 1f out: styd on same pce* **9/1**

10 **8** 1 ½ **Rosina**[69] 6593 4-8-9 **82** (p) ShaneGray 9 67
(Ann Duffield) *hld up: rdn over 1f out: nvr on terms* **40/1**

1000 **9** nk **Rich Again (IRE)**[25] 8012 8-9-1 **88** (b) OisinMurphy 2 72
(James Bethell) *s.i.s and hmpd s: hld up: nvr on terms* **9/1**

1m 0.72s (-1.18) **Going Correction** -0.025s/f (Stan) **9** Ran SP% **116.2**
Speed ratings (Par 107): **108,105,104,102,102 99,98,96,95**
CSF £17.14 CT £141.03 TOTE £4.00: £1.40, £1.70, £3.70; EX 15.20 Trifecta £170.70.
**Owner** F Gillespie **Bred** Northern Bloodstock Inc **Trained** Upper Helmsley, N Yorks

**FOCUS**
A competitive sprint handicap which produced a worthy winner who continues to show his worth on AW surfaces. It paid to be prominent.

## 8661 BETWAY CASINO H'CAP (DIV I) 1m 1f 104y (Tp)
**3:15** (3:18) (Class 6) (0-60,61) 3-Y-O+ **£2,587** (£770; £384; £192) **Stalls Low**

Form RPR

4250 **1** **Champagne Pink (FR)**[18] 8219 3-9-1 **60** (h) CliffordLee(3) 5 66
(K R Burke) *trckd ldrs: shkn up to ld 1f out: rdn out* **9/2**[2]

5361 **2** 1 ½ **Power Home (IRE)**[7] 8498 3-9-5 **61** 6ex LukeMorris 11 64
(Denis Coakley) *hld up: pushed along and hdwy over 2f out: rdn over 1f out: r.o to go 2nd nr fin* **11/4**[1]

0340 **3** ½ **Bonnie Gals**[3] 8590 3-9-1 **57** (b[1]) PhillipMakin 8 59
(Keith Dalgleish) *hld up: hdwy on outer 3f out: rdn to ld over 1f out: sn hdd: styd on same pce ins fnl f* **12/1**

053 **4** 1 ¼ **Sunshineandbubbles**[59] 6946 4-9-1 **54** DavidNolan 9 53
(Jennie Candlish) *chsd ldr tl led over 2f out: rdn and hung lft over 1f out: sn hdd: no ex ins fnl f* **18/1**

6032 **5** nk **Dor's Law**[14] 8307 4-8-12 **51** (p) RobHornby 7 49+
(Dean Ivory) *s.i.s: hld up: hdwy whn nt clr run ins fnl f: r.o: nt rch ldrs* **9/2**[2]

6415 **6** nk **Windsorlot (IRE)**[35] 7712 4-9-3 **56** GeorgeDowning 2 54
(Tony Carroll) *hld up in tch: rdn over 2f out: styd on ins fnl f* **8/1**[3]

0010 **7** nk **Unsuspected Girl (IRE)**[14] 8313 4-9-0 **60** (t) KerrieRaybould(7) 1 58
(Milton Bradley) *hld up: nt clr run over 2f out: hdwy over 1f out: nt trble ldrs* **66/1**

0200 **8** shd **Pensax Lady (IRE)**[17] 8249 4-8-6 **52** TobyEley(7) 4 49
(Daniel Mark Loughnane) *mid-div: nt clr run and lost pl whn stmbld over 7f out: styd on ins fnl f: nt trble ldrs* **16/1**

1210 **9** ¾ **Edge (IRE)**[8] 8473 6-9-7 **60** (b) DavidProbert 10 55+
(Bernard Llewellyn) *s.i.s: pushed along early in rr: nvr on terms* **16/1**

2003 **10** shd **Filament Of Gold (USA)**[17] 8249 6-8-9 **53** (p) FinleyMarsh(5) 13 48
(Roy Brotherton) *chsd ldrs: shkn up over 2f out: rdn over 1f out: sn hung lft: styd on same pce* **10/1**

4600 **11** ¾ **Petit Filous**[112] 5001 3-9-2 **58** (t[1]) PaulHanagan 6 53
(Giles Bravery) *sn led: rdn and hdd over 2f out: nt clr run over 1f out: wknd fnl f* **16/1**

000 **12** 1 ½ **Captain Cockle**[22] 8116 4-8-7 **51** BenRobinson(5) 3 42
(Roger Teal) *prom: racd keenly: rdn over 2f out: sn wknd* **50/1**

2m 1.51s (0.71) **Going Correction** -0.025s/f (Stan)
**WFA** 3 from 4yo+ 3lb **12** Ran SP% **117.3**
Speed ratings (Par 101): **95,93,93,92,91 91,91,91,90,90 89,88**
CSF £16.98 CT £139.87 TOTE £5.70: £1.90, £1.40, £3.90; EX 21.30 Trifecta £194.90.
**Owner** Nick Bradley Racing 2 & Mrs E Burke **Bred** G A E C Campos **Trained** Middleham Moor, N Yorks

**FOCUS**
A moderate early gallop saw this contest develop into a sprint from the home turn and the winner quickened up best to shed her maiden tag.

## 8662 BETWAY CASINO H'CAP (DIV II) 1m 1f 104y (Tp)
**3:45** (3:48) (Class 6) (0-60,60) 3-Y-O+ **£2,587** (£770; £288; £288) **Stalls Low**

Form RPR

6466 **1** **Rock Island Line**[18] 8218 3-9-0 **56** (b[1]) PaulHanagan 5 63
(Mark Walford) *a.p: hmpd over 4f out: led ins fnl f: sn rdn and hung lft: r.o* **11/2**[2]

2030 **2** 1 **New Abbey Angel (IRE)**[18] 8205 4-8-12 **51** PhillipMakin 7 55
(Keith Dalgleish) *hld up: plld hrd: hdwy over 1f out: r.o to go 2nd wl ins fnl f: nt rch wnr* **16/1**

5040 **3** 1 **Lord Murphy (IRE)**[73] 6443 4-9-1 **57** EoinWalsh(3) 1 59
(Daniel Mark Loughnane) *hld up in tch: racd keenly: nt clr run and lost pl over 4f out: hdwy over 1f out: sn rdn and edgd rt: r.o* **14/1**

5343 **3** dht **Indiana Dawn**[19] 8182 4-8-12 **51** (p) OisinMurphy 8 53
(Robert Stephens) *led: rdn and hdd over 1f out: styd on same pce ins fnl f* **12/1**

5550 **5** ½ **D'Waterside**[14] 8312 3-9-1 **57** LukeMorris 10 59
(David Loughnane) *chsd ldrs: rdn over 2f out: led over 1f out: hdd and no ex ins fnl f* **12/1**

0000 **6** ½ **Buthelezi (USA)**[101] 5403 9-9-6 **59** StevieDonohoe 4 59
(Brian Ellison) *hld up: hdwy and hung lft over 1f out: nt rch ldrs* **33/1**

0011 **7** nse **Born To Reason (IRE)**[17] 8247 3-9-1 **57** (b) PJMcDonald 3 60
(Kevin Frost) *hld up: hdwy and hmpd over 1f out: nt rch ldrs* **9/4**[1]

-033 **8** 2 ½ **Peak Hill**[11] 8402 4-9-0 **56** HollieDoyle(3) 2 51
(Adrian Wintle) *hld up in tch: plld hrd: edgd rt over 4f out: sn lost pl: hdwy and nt clr run over 1f out: wknd ins fnl f* **6/1**[3]

0000 **9** ½ **Threediamondrings**[14] 8313 4-9-4 **57** (vt[1]) RobHornby 6 52
(Mark Usher) *s.i.s: hdwy to chse ldr over 7f out: led over 5f out: rdn and hdd over 1f out: wknd ins fnl f* **25/1**

3300 **10** 1 **Mamnoon (IRE)**[6] 8515 4-9-1 **59** (b) FinleyMarsh(5) 12 52
(Roy Brotherton) *hld up: nvr on terms* **40/1**

0130 **11** 2 **Barista (IRE)**[51] 7198 9-9-7 **60** CharlesBishop 13 49
(Brian Forsey) *hld up: rdn over 2f out: n.d* **50/1**

-040 **12** 9 **Struck By The Moon**[56] 7032 3-9-2 **58** DavidProbert 11 31
(Charles Hills) *prom: rdn over 2f out: wknd over 1f out* **25/1**

5004 **13** 1 ½ **Sooqaan**[17] 8249 6-8-13 **52** CamHardie 9 21
(Antony Brittain) *hld up: plld hrd and hung rt thrght: hdwy over 4f out: wkng whn hmpd over 1f out* **8/1**

2m 0.91s (0.11) **Going Correction** -0.025s/f (Stan)
**WFA** 3 from 4yo+ 3lb **13** Ran SP% **114.5**
Speed ratings (Par 101): **98,97,96,96,95 95,95,93,92,91 89,81,80**WIN: 5.90 Rock Island Line; PL: 1.90 Lord Murphy, 3.20 New Abbey Angel, 1.90 Indiana Dawn, 2.40 Rock Island Line; EX: 84.00; CSF: 80.51; TC: RIL/NAA/LM 581.24, RIL/NAA/ID 504.11; TF: RIL/NAA/LM 669.70, RIL/NAA/ID 415.40; CSF £80.51 TOTE £5.90: £2.40, £3.20, £1.90, £1.90;27 Owner Trifecta £Miss Jill Gittus Bred Jill Gittus.

**FOCUS**
Not the most competitive of handicaps, but the winner won decisively in first-time blinkers and is rated to this year's best efforts.

## 8663 BETWAY MAIDEN STKS 1m 1f 104y (Tp)
**4:20** (4:22) (Class 5) 3-Y-O+ **£3,234** (£962; £481; £240) **Stalls Low**

Form RPR

**1** **Al Kout** 3-9-2 0 GeorgeWood(3) 1 79+
(Heather Main) *hld up: hdwy over 1f out: rdn to ld and edgd rt wl ins fnl f: r.o* **22/1**

2352 **2** 1 ¼ **Majboor (IRE)**[22] 8117 3-9-5 77 PhillipMakin 6 76
(Dominic Ffrench Davis) *led: rdn and hung rt wl over 1f out: hdd and unable qck wl ins fnl f* **8/11**[1]

**3** nk **Frown** 3-9-0 0 OisinMurphy 8 70
(Ralph Beckett) *hdwy to join ldr over 7f out: settled into 2nd pl over 5f out: rdn and nt clr run wl over 1f out: ev ch ins fnl f: styd on same pce towards fin* **11/2**[3]

56 **4** 2 ¼ **Nevalyashka**[20] 8151 3-8-7 0 TylerSaunders(7) 2 66
(Marcus Tregoning) *mid-div: pushed along over 2f out: hdwy over 1f out: nt rch ldrs* **14/1**

**5** hd **Monsieur Bay** 3-9-5 0 StevieDonohoe 3 70
(Ismail Mohammed) *mid-div: rdn over 1f out: styd on ins fnl f: nt trble ldrs* **14/1**

6 2 ¼ **Lunar Mist** 3-9-0 0 ........ JimmyQuinn 9 61
(Ed Dunlop) *hld up: shkn up and edgd rt over 1f out: hung lft and styd on ins fnl f: nt trble ldrs* **33/1**

7 5 **Michigan (USA)**[177] 3-9-2 75 ........ (t[1]) EoinWalsh(3) 7 55
(Mohamed Moubarak) *chsd ldrs: rdn over 2f out: wkng whn hmpd ins fnl f* **28/1**

8 1 ¼ **Sanam** 3-9-5 0 ........ PJMcDonald 5 52
(Ed Dunlop) *hld up: pushed along 4f out: nvr on terms* **5/1[2]**

0006 9 ½ **Beast**[105] 5249 3-9-2 54 ........ (t[1]) TimClark(3) 10 51
(Johnny Farrelly) *s.s: a in rr* **50/1**

60 10 2 ½ **Nagamaat (IRE)**[35] 7708 3-8-11 0 ........ HollieDoyle(3) 4 41
(Nikki Evans) *plld hrd and prom: rdn over 2f out: wknd wl over 1f out* **200/1**

2m 0.15s (-0.65) **Going Correction** -0.025s/f (Stan) **10** Ran SP% **116.5**
Speed ratings (Par 103): **101,99,99,97,97 95,91,89,89,87**
CSF £37.93 TOTE £27.30: £4.80, £1.10, £2.00; EX 52.40 Trifecta £280.60.
**Owner** John Rylands And Wetumpka Racing **Bred** Newsells Park Stud **Trained** Kingston Lisle, Oxon

**FOCUS**
The favourite came into this maiden with an official rating of 77 so the form could work out. The winner looks an intriguing prospect given his initial price tag. The runner-up set an okay standard and arrived off the back of a personal best, but it was the second time he'd been beaten at odds on.

## 8664 BET & WATCH AT SUNBETS.CO.UK APPRENTICE H'CAP 1m 142y (Tp)
4:50 (4:51) (Class 6) (0-65,67) 3-Y-0+ £2,587 (£770; £384; £192) Stalls Low

Form RPR

2504 1 **Top Offer**[17] 8247 8-9-1 55 ........ (b) GeorgeWood 5 61
(Patrick Morris) *s.s: hld up: hdwy over 2f out: led ins fnl f: hung lft: r.o: comf* **9/1**

0210 2 1 **Jack Of Diamonds (IRE)**[34] 7735 8-9-10 67 ........ BenRobinson(3) 7 71
(Roger Teal) *hld up: pushed along over 2f out: hdwy over 1f out: r.o* **9/4[1]**

0044 3 2 ¼ **Dream Free**[7] 8498 4-8-13 53 ........ (t[1]) EoinWalsh 2 52
(Mark Walford) *hld up: hdwy over 3f out: rdn over 1f out: styd on same pce fnl f* **5/1[3]**

0002 4 1 ½ **Cockney Boy**[17] 8249 4-8-5 50 oh2 ........ (v) GabrieleMalune(5) 6 46
(Michael Appleby) *w ldr tl led over 6f out: clr 4f out: rdn over 1f out: hdd & wknd ins fnl f* **7/2[2]**

0300 5 ½ **Know Your Name**[10] 8429 6-9-6 60 ........ AdamMcNamara 1 55
(Donald McCain) *led: hdd over 6f out: chsd ldr: rdn over 2f out: wknd ins fnl f* **12/1**

4-50 6 1 ¾ **Rockshine**[14] 8327 3-9-3 60 ........ HollieDoyle 8 52
(Richard Hannon) *chsd ldrs: pushed along over 3f out: lost pl over 2f out: n.d after* **10/1**

0525 7 ¾ **Misu Pete**[15] 8300 5-9-2 59 ........ (p) GeorgiaCox(3) 9 49
(Mark Usher) *sn pushed along in rr: nvr on terms* **14/1**

6400 8 6 **Claire's Secret**[14] 8328 3-8-12 60 ........ FinleyMarsh(5) 4 38
(Philip McBride) *chsd ldrs: rdn over 1f out: wknd fnl f* **14/1**

406 P **Waiting A Lot (IRE)**[68] 6633 3-9-2 64 ........ PatrickVaughan(5) 3
(David O'Meara) *hld up: pushed along over 3f out: wnt wrong and p.u over 2f out* **25/1**

1m 48.03s (-2.07) **Going Correction** -0.025s/f (Stan)
**WFA** 3 from 4yo+ 3lb **9** Ran SP% **113.6**
Speed ratings (Par 101): **108,107,105,103,103 101,101,95,**
CSF £29.10 CT £114.69 TOTE £7.80: £2.20, £1.30, £2.40; EX 30.90 Trifecta £168.60.
**Owner** Matt Watkinson **Bred** Juddmonte Farms Ltd **Trained** Prescot, Merseyside
■ Stewards' Enquiry : Adam McNamara two-day ban; careless riding (Nov 21,22)
Gabriele Malune two-day ban: careless riding (Nov 21-22)

**FOCUS**
Nothing more than an ordinary apprentice handicap, but it was run at a good pace and the winner won snugly under a cool ride.
T/Plt: £63.80 to a £1 stake. Pool: £62,799.92 - 718.10 winning units T/Qpdt: £18.80 to a £1 stake. Pool: £6,316.46 - 248.06 winning units **Colin Roberts**

# 8464 SAINT-CLOUD (L-H)
Tuesday, November 7

**OFFICIAL GOING: Turf: soft**

## 8665a PRIX ISOLA BELLA - FONDS EUROPEEN DE L'ELEVAGE (LISTED RACE) (3YO+ FILLIES & MARES) (TURF) 1m
1:50 3-Y-0+ £22,222 (£8,888; £6,666; £4,444; £2,222)

RPR

1 **Havre De Paix (FR)**[31] 7808 5-9-0 0 ........ AntoineHamelin 3 99
(David Menuisier) **136/10**

2 nk **Dallas Affair**[48] 7305 3-8-11 0 ........ AurelienLemaitre 6 97+
(F Head, France) **23/10[1]**

3 hd **Maimara (FR)**[23] 8088 5-9-0 0 ........ (b) MaximeGuyon 10 98+
(M Delzangles, France) **5/1[3]**

4 5 **La Poutanesca (IRE)**[25] 8026 3-8-11 0 ........ RonanThomas 1 85
(D Smaga, France) **16/1**

5 nk **Limited Edition (FR)**[47] 7341 3-8-11 0 ........ TonyPiccone 8 85
(E Lellouche, France) **12/1**

6 4 ½ **Speed As (FR)**[127] 4456 3-8-11 0 ........ MickaelBerto 9 74
(A De Royer-Dupre, France) **15/1**

7 1 ¼ **Bijin (FR)**[47] 7341 3-8-11 0 ........ Pierre-CharlesBoudot 7 71
(H-A Pantall, France) **5/1[3]**

8 3 ½ **Flemish Duchesse (FR)**[23] 8089 4-9-3 0 ........ FabriceVeron 2 67
(Andreas Suborics, Germany) **31/1**

9 snk **Game Theory (IRE)**[48] 7305 5-9-3 0 ........ StephanePasquier 5 67
(N Clement, France) **7/2[2]**

10 20 **Perfectly Fair**[21] 4-9-0 0 ........ FabienLefebvre 4 18
(Georgios Alimpinisis, Greece) **27/1**

1m 44.05s (-3.45)
**WFA** 3 from 4yo+ 2lb **10** Ran SP% **119.2**
PARI-MUTUEL (all including 1 euro stake): WIN 14.60; PLACE 4.00, 1.70, 2.10; DF 25.90; SF 51.40.
**Owner** Clive Washbourn **Bred** Mme Elisabeth Erbeya **Trained** Pulborough, W Sussex

## 8666a PRIX SOLITUDE (LISTED RACE) (3YO FILLIES) (TURF) 1m 2f
2:25 3-Y-0 £23,504 (£9,401; £7,051; £4,700; £2,350)

RPR

1 **Gaining**[36] 7696 3-8-13 0 ........ MaximeGuyon 8 104
(Mme C Head-Maarek, France) **19/5[2]**

2 1 ¼ **Flood Warning**[48] 7283 3-8-13 0 ........ TonyPiccone 4 102
(Clive Cox) **8/1**

3 3 ½ **Segra (USA)**[55] 3-8-13 0 ........ ThierryThulliez 3 95
(P Bary, France) **14/1**

4 nk **Panthelia (FR)**[34] 7755 3-8-13 0 ........ (b) AurelienLemaitre 2 94
(P Sogorb, France) **9/1**

5 hd **Baltic Duchess (IRE)**[38] 7635 3-8-13 0 ........ Pierre-CharlesBoudot 5 94
(A Fabre, France) **14/5[1]**

6 ¾ **Ma Cherie**[16] 8273 3-8-13 0 ........ MllePaulineDominois 1 92
(A Fabre, France) **14/1**

7 hd **Saxon Rose**[86] 5981 3-8-13 0 ........ MickaelBarzalona 7 92
(A Fabre, France) **8/1**

8 7 **Miss Germany (GER)** 3-8-13 0 ........ DanielePorcu 6 78
(P Schiergen, Germany) **13/1**

9 6 **Astronomy's Choice**[138] 3995 3-8-13 0 ........ StephanePasquier 9 66
(John Gosden) **43/10[3]**

2m 14.56s (-1.44) **9** Ran SP% **118.7**
PARI-MUTUEL (all including 1 euro stake): WIN 4.80; PLACE 1.80, 2.70, 3.70; DF 22.50; SF 38.20.
**Owner** K Abdullah **Bred** Juddmonte Farms Ltd **Trained** Chantilly, France

# 7848 FLEMINGTON (L-H)
Tuesday, November 7

**OFFICIAL GOING: Turf: good**

## 8667a EMIRATES MELBOURNE CUP (GROUP 1 H'CAP) (3YO+) (TURF) 2m
4:00 3-Y-0+
£2,251,461 (£526,315; £263,157; £146,198; £102,339; £73,099)

RPR

1 **Rekindling**[52] 7147 3-8-2 0 ........ CoreyBrown 4 121
(Joseph Patrick O'Brien, Ire) *hld up in midfield: stdy hdwy fr 4f out: chsd ldrs whn rdn under 2f out: styd on wl to ld 50yds out: rdn out* **14/1**

2 ½ **Johannes Vermeer (IRE)**[17] 8250 4-8-8 0 ........ (t) BenMelham 3 117
(A P O'Brien, Ire) *in tch: smooth hdwy appr 2f out: rdn to ld under 2f out: drvn 1f out: hdd 50yds out: kpt on* **12/1[3]**

3 2 ½ **Max Dynamite (FR)**[75] 6363 7-8-7 0 ........ ZacPurton 2 113
(W P Mullins, Ire) *in tch in midfield: rdn and hdwy fr 3f out: nt clr run whn chsng ldrs appr 2f out: kpt on wl: nt pce of front pair ins fnl f* **19/1**

4 2 ¾ **Big Duke (IRE)**[10] 8445 5-8-6 0 ........ BrentonAvdulla 5 109
(Darren Weir, Australia) *hld up in midfield: rdn and stdy hdwy fr over 2f out: drvn 1 1/2f out: kpt on* **20/1**

5 ¾ **Nakeeta**[73] 6447 6-8-5 0 ........ GlynSchofield 19 107
(Iain Jardine) *hld up towards rr: rdn and kpt on wl fr 2 1/2f out: nvr gng pce to rch ldrs* **40/1**

6 2 ¼ **Thomas Hobson**[53] 7116 7-8-3 0 ........ BenAllen 20 103
(W P Mullins, Ire) *hld up in rr: rdn 3f out: wdst into st: drvn and kpt on fr 2f out* **20/1**

7 ½ **Tiberian (FR)**[72] 6499 5-8-10 0 ........ OlivierPeslier 22 109
(Alain Couetil, France) *hld up towards rr: forward move and in tch 1/2-way: trckd ldrs 4f out: short of room whn rdn 2f out: outpcd fr 1 1/2f out* **30/1**

8 ½ **Libran (IRE)**[10] 8445 6-8-5 0 ........ (t) DwayneDunn 7 104
(Chris Waller, Australia) *hld up towards rr of midfield: hdwy fr 2 1/2f out: rdn 2f out: briefly in tch 1 1/2f out: sn outpcd* **60/1**

9 shd **Marmelo**[17] 8250 4-8-9 0 ........ HughBowman 16 108
(Hughie Morrison) *in tch: chsd ldr over 4f out: led 3f out: rdn 2 1/2f out: hdd under 2f out: sn wknd* **6/1[1]**

10 ¾ **Wicklow Brave**[17] 8250 8-8-7 0 ........ StephenBaster 8 105
(W P Mullins, Ire) *t.k.h towards rr: rdn 3f out: kpt on steadily fr 2f out: n.d* **70/1**

11 ¾ **Red Cardinal (IRE)**[79] 6250 5-8-9 0 ........ KerrinMcEvoy 23 106
(A Wohler, Germany) *hld up towards rr: rdn 2 1/2f out: kpt on steadily fr 2f out: n.d* **15/1**

12 hd **Almandin (GER)**[31] 7-8-13 0 ........ FrankieDettori 14 110
(Robert Hickmott, Australia) *midfield: rdn and effrt over 2f out: wknd 1f out* **6/1[1]**

13 ¾ **Cismontane (NZ)**[3] 5-7-12 0 ........ (b) BeauMertens 17 94
(Gai Waterhouse & Adrian Bott, Australia) *led: rdn 4f out: hdd 3f out: wknd 2f out* **40/1**

14 ¾ **Amelie's Star (AUS)**[17] 8250 6-8-0 0 ........ DeanYendall 10 95
(Darren Weir, Australia) *midfield on outer: sme hdwy appr 2f out: rdn 2f out: wknd ins fnl f* **20/1**

15 1 **Boom Time (AUS)**[17] 8250 6-8-5 0 ........ (b) CoryParish 9 99
(David A & B Hayes & Tom Dabernig, Australia) *trckd ldrs: rdn 3f out: wknd over 2f out* **30/1**

16 1 ½ **Wall Of Fire (IRE)**[24] 8056 4-8-5 0 ........ (v[1]) CraigAWilliams 15 97
(Hugo Palmer) *hld up towards rr: rdn 3f out: hdwy appr 2f out: wknd over 1f out* **10/1[2]**

17 ½ **Single Gaze (AUS)**[17] 8250 5-8-5 0 ........ KathyO'Hara 11 97
(Nick Olive, Australia) *midfield on outer: rdn 3f out: nt clr run over 2f out: sn outpcd and btn* **30/1**

18 nk **US Army Ranger (IRE)**[59] 6957 4-8-6 0 ........ JamieSpencer 21 98
(Joseph Patrick O'Brien, Ire) *hld up in rr: rdn and sme stdy hdwy fr over 2f out: nvr in contention* **70/1**

19 ½ **Humidor (NZ)**[10] 8446 5-8-11 0 ........ (bt) BlakeShinn 13 102
(Darren Weir, Australia) *t.k.h towards rr: rdn and sme hdwy 2 1/2f out: short of room under 2f out: sn btn* **10/1[2]**

20 12 **Hartnell**[24] 8058 6-9-1 0 ........ DamianLane 12 97
(James Cummings, Australia) *in tch in midfield: lost pl appr 2f out: sn btn: eased over 1f out* **25/1**

21 1 ½ **Ventura Storm (IRE)**[17] 8250 4-8-7 0 ........ GlenBoss 6 88
(David A & B Hayes & Tom Dabernig, Australia) *midfield: rdn 3f out: wknd 1 1/2f out: sn eased* **30/1**

22 1 1/4 **Bondi Beach (IRE)**[52] 5-8-7 0................................(b[1]) MichaelWalker 1 86
(Robert Hickmott, Australia) *towards rr of midfield: rdn 3 1/2f out: lost pl 2 1/2f out: sn wl btn* **70/1**

23 dist **Gallante (IRE)**[13] 8362 6-8-5 0........................................(t) MichaelDee 18
(Robert Hickmott, Australia) *chsd ldr: lost pl qckly 4f out: t.o* **90/1**

3m 21.19s (1.55)
**WFA** 3 from 4yo+ 7lb **23** Ran SP% **115.2**

**Owner** N C Williams, Mr & Mrs L J Williams Et Al **Bred** The Pocock Family **Trained** Owning Hill, Co Kilkenny

**FOCUS**
A good, competitive running of one of the world's most famous races. The winner, second and third were all trained in Ireland, with two Lloyd Williams-owned colts coming away from their rivals. All of them held an inside rail position throughout until rounding the final bend and it's noteworthy that the first four were all drawn 5 or lower. It was the first time since Vintage Crop in 1993 that the race was taken by a runner without a prep race in Australia. The riders described the pace somewhere between slow and stop-start.

## 8641 KEMPTON (A.W) (R-H)

Wednesday, November 8

**OFFICIAL GOING: Polytrack: standard**
Wind: Light, across Weather: Fine

### 8668 100% PROFIT BOOST AT 32REDSPORT.COM EBF FILLIES' NOVICE STKS (PLUS 10 RACE) (DIV I) 1m (P)
**4:40** (4:41) (Class 5) 2-Y-O **£3,234** (£962; £481; £240) **Stalls** Low

Form RPR

5 1 **Espadrille**[21] 8163 2-9-0 0.................................................. WilliamBuick 9 72+
(Charlie Appleby) *mde all: drew clr 2f out: pushed along after and in n.d* **4/7**[1]

0 2 1 1/2 **Ruffina (USA)**[26] 7995 2-9-0 0........................................ RobertHavlin 12 68
(John Gosden) *trapped out wd: chsd ldng trio: pushed along over 2f out: styd on to take 2nd last 150yds: no ch w wnr* **11/2**[2]

3 1 **Ceilidhs Dream** 2-9-0 0.................................................. OisinMurphy 3 66+
(Ralph Beckett) *free to post: slowly away: t.k.h and hld up towards rr: pushed along and prog over 1f out: styd on wl to take 3rd wl ins fnl f* **7/1**[3]

4 3/4 **Blue Reflection** 2-9-0 0................................................ DanielMuscutt 1 64+
(James Fanshawe) *hld up wl in rr: pushed along over 2f out: styd on wl fnl f: tk 4th nr fin* **20/1**

0 5 nk **Pink Phantom**[11] 8425 2-9-0 0......................................... PJMcDonald 8 63
(Paul Cole) *chsd ldrs: pushed along fr 3f out: nvr pce to threaten but kpt on* **11/1**

0 6 3/4 **Point In Time (IRE)**[25] 8029 2-9-0 0.......................... StevieDonohoe 13 61
(Mark Usher) *chsd wnr: pushed along and no imp 2f out: lost 2nd and wknd last 150yds* **66/1**

7 1/2 **Mary Elise (IRE)** 2-9-0 0.................................................. LiamKeniry 2 60+
(Ed Walker) *slowly away: wl in rr: shkn up and no prog over 2f out: kpt on ins fnl f* **66/1**

0 8 1 1/4 **Homing Star**[11] 8425 2-9-0 0............................................. RobHornby 5 57
(Jonathan Portman) *chsd ldng pair: shkn up over 2f out: wknd jst over 1f out* **100/1**

9 shd **Makin It** 2-9-0 0.................................................................. LukeMorris 4 57
(William Knight) *nvr beyond midfield: pushed along over 2f out: fdd on inner over 1f out* **66/1**

0 10 1 **Hot Off The Press (IRE)**[21] 8163 2-9-0 0........................ FranBerry 10 54
(Michael Bell) *stdd after s: hld up in last trio: pushed along and no prog over 2f out: nvr in it but kpt on late* **66/1**

11 hd **Mayaseen (FR)** 2-9-0 0...................................................... LouisSteward 7 54
(Hugo Palmer) *chsd ldrs: urged along over 2f out: wknd over 1f out* **12/1**

12 9 **Crimson Skies (IRE)** 2-9-0 0...................................... RichardKingscote 11 32
(Tom Dascombe) *slowly away: a struggling in last: bhd over 2f out* **40/1**

1m 40.2s (0.40) **Going Correction** -0.175s/f (Stan) **12** Ran SP% **121.7**
Speed ratings (Par 93): **91,89,88,87,87 86,86,84,84,83 83,74**
CSF £4.03 TOTE £1.50: £1.10, £1.70, £2.10; EX 5.10 Trifecta £22.40.
**Owner** Godolphin **Bred** J Wigan & G Strawbridge **Trained** Newmarket, Suffolk

**FOCUS**
The first division of a fair juvenile fillies' novice contest. They went an, at best, respectable gallop on standard Polytrack. The field was seriously compressed and hard to believe the bare form is worth much.

### 8669 100% PROFIT BOOST AT 32REDSPORT.COM EBF FILLIES' NOVICE STKS (PLUS 10 RACE) (DIV II) 1m (P)
**5:10** (5:12) (Class 5) 2-Y-O **£3,234** (£962; £481; £240) **Stalls** Low

Form RPR

1 **Cecchini (IRE)** 2-9-0 0............................................... RichardKingscote 1 85+
(Ralph Beckett) *mde virtually all: stretched clr fr over 2f out: styd on wl: promising debut* **9/4**[2]

22 2 1 1/4 **Bubble And Squeak**[6] 8544 2-9-0 0............................... OisinMurphy 3 82
(Sylvester Kirk) *prom: chsd wnr wl over 2f out: styd on and drew away fr the rest but nvr able to chal* **13/8**[1]

362 3 3 **Heather Lark (IRE)**[15] 8322 2-9-0 78.............................. RobertHavlin 13 75
(John Gosden) *sn in rr: shkn up over 2f out: prog to take 3rd 1f out: no ch w ldng pair but styd on* **7/1**[3]

62 4 4 **Sharp Reminder**[57] 7033 2-9-0 0....................................... LukeMorris 7 65
(James Tate) *chsd wnr 1f: styd prom: outpcd over 2f out: no ch after but kpt on* **11/1**

5 1/2 **Crystal Moonlight** 2-9-0 0.................................................. TedDurcan 5 64+
(Sir Michael Stoute) *wl in rr: pushed along over 2f out: prog towards inner wl over 1f out: no ch but kpt on* **14/1**

6 2 3/4 **Sweet Lady Rose (IRE)** 2-9-0 0.................................. DavidProbert 12 57+
(Andrew Balding) *wl in rr: pushed along and no prog over 2f out: sme hdwy over 1f out: no ch* **40/1**

7 1/2 **Astolat** 2-9-0 0.................................................................. LiamKeniry 9 56
(Ed Walker) *t.k.h early: hld up bhd ldrs: lft bhd fr 3f out: fdd* **100/1**

6 8 3 1/4 **Dawn Of Reckoning**[11] 8419 2-9-0 0................................ RyanTate 8 48
(Jonathan Portman) *detached in last and rn green: nvr a factor but passed a few late on* **20/1**

0 9 hd **Physical Power (IRE)**[11] 8425 2-9-0 0............................ SeanLevey 4 48
(Richard Hannon) *nvr beyond midfield: urged along 1/2-way: sn struggling* **66/1**

0 10 1 3/4 **Rahaaba (IRE)**[44] 7454 2-9-0 0......................................... FranBerry 6 44
(Owen Burrows) *hld up in rr and racd wd: shuffled along and no prog over 2f out* **16/1**

11 1/2 **Leigh's Law (IRE)** 2-9-0 0............................................ LouisSteward 11 43
(Hugo Palmer) *in tch in midfield to 3f out: sn wknd* **33/1**

0 12 1 **Pas De Blanc**[9] 8472 2-9-0 0...................................... StevieDonohoe 14 40
(Brian Barr) *t.k.h: chsd wnr after 1f to wl over 2f out: wknd qckly* **125/1**

1m 37.26s (-2.54) **Going Correction** -0.175s/f (Stan) 2y crse rec **12** Ran SP% **115.7**
Speed ratings (Par 93): **105,103,100,96,96 93,93,89,89,87 87,86**
CSF £5.76 TOTE £3.30: £1.20, £1.10, £1.60; EX 7.00 Trifecta £25.90.
**Owner** P D Savill **Bred** Oak Hill Stud **Trained** Kimpton, Hants

**FOCUS**
The second division of a fair juvenile fillies' novice contest which had more depth to it in terms of prior form. The heavily supported second favourite broke the juvenile course record in a taking manner from the front.

### 8670 BRITISH STALLION STUDS EBF FILLIES' NOVICE STKS (PLUS 10 RACE) 7f (P)
**5:40** (5:41) (Class 5) 2-Y-O **£3,234** (£962; £481; £240) **Stalls** Low

Form RPR

1 **Lush Life (IRE)** 2-9-0 0.................................................. DougieCostello 5 76+
(Jamie Osborne) *hld up in last trio: gd prog on inner over 2f out: pushed into ld over 1f out: kpt on wl: comf* **16/1**

0 2 1 3/4 **Briscola**[75] 6386 2-9-0 0..................................................... RobertHavlin 2 70
(John Gosden) *v.s.i.s: mostly in last pair tl pushed along and prog on inner 2f out: shkn up and styd on to take 2nd ins fnl f: no threat to wnr* **15/2**

0 3 1 1/4 **American Endeavour (USA)**[26] 7995 2-9-0 0............ DanielMuscutt 8 67
(Marco Botti) *t.k.h: w ldr: led 1/2-way: hdd over 1f out and dropped to 3rd ins fnl f but did best of those that racd promly* **11/2**

4 1/2 **Catoca (USA)** 2-9-0 0............................................................ LiamKeniry 1 66+
(Ed Walker) *s.s: hld up in last pair: nudged along and gd prog fr 2f out: tk 4th nr fin: shaped w promise* **25/1**

0 5 1 **Fondest**[21] 8148 2-8-11 0............................................... GeorgeWood[(3)] 12 63
(James Fanshawe) *trckd ldng pair: shkn up 2f out: nt qckn wl over 1f out: one pce after* **7/2**[2]

0 6 nk **Secret Eye (IRE)**[26] 7997 2-9-0 0...............................(p[1]) PJMcDonald 4 62
(Paul Cole) *trckd ldrs: shkn up and nt qckn over 2f out: one pce and no imp fr over 1f out* **40/1**

10 7 nk **Dotted Swiss (IRE)**[13] 8373 2-9-0 0.............................. RossaRyan[(7)] 7 68
(Richard Hannon) *chsd ldng pair: rdn over 2f out: stl disputing 3rd fnl f: sn wknd* **9/2**[3]

8 2 3/4 **Apache Blaze** 2-9-0 0........................................................ KieranO'Neill 14 54
(Michael Appleby) *hld up in midfield: rdn and no prog over 2f out: sn btn* **100/1**

0 9 nk **Mystique**[125] 4533 2-9-0 0................................................. DavidProbert 3 53
(Charles Hills) *a in midfield: rdn and no prog 2f out: wknd fnl f* **20/1**

0 10 1 3/4 **Supermoss**[50] 7226 2-9-0 0................................................ RyanTate 13 48
(Heather Main) *racd on outer and a towards rr: nvr a factor* **100/1**

62 11 11 **Light Relief**[21] 8147 2-9-0 0............................................. LukeMorris 6 19+
(James Tate) *led to 1/2-way: wknd rapidly over 1f out: t.o* **5/2**[1]

0 12 5 **Ocean Spray**[15] 8308 2-9-0 0............................................... SeanLevey 9
(Richard Hannon) *a in rr: wknd sn after 1/2-way: t.o* **66/1**

1m 24.97s (-1.03) **Going Correction** -0.175s/f (Stan) **12** Ran SP% **116.5**
Speed ratings (Par 93): **98,96,94,94,92 92,92,89,88,86 74,68**
CSF £122.13 TOTE £10.50: £3.00, £2.80, £2.00; EX 231.10 Trifecta £1448.50.
**Owner** Michael Buckley **Bred** Lynch Bages **Trained** Upper Lambourn, Berks

**FOCUS**
Another fair juvenile fillies' novice contest. They went a decent gallop and three of the first four home challenged towards the far rail.

### 8671 32RED.COM NURSERY H'CAP 7f (P)
**6:10** (6:10) (Class 3) (0-90,90) 2-Y-O **£6,469** (£1,925; £962; £481) **Stalls** Low

Form RPR

0064 1 **Elsaakb (USA)**[14] 8349 2-8-0 69 oh2...........................(b) NickyMackay 5 75
(John Gosden) *hld up in last: prog on inner 2f out: chal 1f out: drvn to ld last 75yds: hld on* **10/1**[2]

421 2 shd **Lady Of Aran (IRE)**[36] 7707 2-8-7 76.............................. PJMcDonald 2 82
(Charlie Fellowes) *trckd ldng pair: wnt 2nd over 2f out: clsd to ld 1f out but hrd pressed: hdd and nt qckn last 75yds: jst hld after* **9/4**[1]

4112 3 2 3/4 **Motown Mick (IRE)**[14] 8343 2-9-5 88............................... TimmyMurphy 4 87
(Richard Hannon) *hld up in 4th: dropped to last and struggling over 2f out: n.d after but kpt on to take 3rd nr fin* **9/4**[1]

1134 4 3/4 **Prestbury Park (USA)**[11] 8420 2-9-7 90........................... WilliamBuick 1 87
(Mark Johnston) *racd freely: led at str pce: hdd & wknd 1f out* **9/4**[1]

0032 5 2 1/4 **Rainbow Jazz (IRE)**[9] 8467 2-8-0 69 oh2.....................(v) KieranO'Neill 3 59
(Mark Usher) *chsd ldr: urged along 1/2-way: lost 2nd over 2f out: steadily wknd* **16/1**[3]

1m 23.79s (-2.21) **Going Correction** -0.175s/f (Stan) 2y crse rec **5** Ran SP% **107.3**
Speed ratings (Par 100): **105,104,101,100,98**
CSF £30.88 TOTE £9.60: £3.20, £1.40; EX 30.70 Trifecta £84.30.
**Owner** Ms Hissa Hamdan Al Maktoum **Bred** Wayne Lyster, Gray Lyster & Bryan Lyster **Trained** Newmarket, Suffolk

**FOCUS**
A decent little nursery handicap. They went a solid gallop and there was more evidence that the far rail is the best place to challenge. The winning time was another juvenile course record which highlights that the track is riding quick.

### 8672 32RED CASINO H'CAP 1m 3f 219y(P)
**6:40** (6:41) (Class 3) (0-95,91) 3-Y-O+
**£7,158** (£2,143; £1,071; £535; £267; £134) **Stalls** Low

Form RPR

/400 1 **Castlelyons (IRE)**[61] 6887 5-9-1 85.............................(h) OisinMurphy 4 93
(Robert Stephens) *hld up in tch: shkn up and prog on outer 2f out: rdn to ld over 1f out: styd on wl* **11/2**[3]

1 2 1 **Isaac Bell (IRE)**[36] 7708 9-8-11 81.................................(t) LukeMorris 1 87
(Alex Hales) *led for over 1f: sn in 5th: pushed along over 3f out: effrt u.p 2f out to press wnr 1f out: kpt on but readily hld fnl f* **9/1**

1034 3 3 **Berrahri (IRE)**[12] 8384 6-8-13 83...................................... RobertHavlin 8 84
(John Best) *trckd ldr after 2f: rdn to ld jst over 2f out: hdd and one pce over 1f out* **22/1**

6004 4 2 **First Flight (IRE)**[11] 8414 6-9-6 90................................. PJMcDonald 2 88
(Heather Main) *hld up in last pair: effrt on inner 2f out: sn one pce and no great prog* **10/1**

4035 5 nk **Rydan (IRE)**[7] 8511 6-9-0 87...................................(p) HectorCrouch[(3)] 5 85
(Gary Moore) *n.m.r s: hld up in last pair: effrt towards inner 2f out: sn no great prog* **4/1**[2]

4035 **6** *2 ¼* **Desert God (IND)**[30] 7908 5-9-1 **85**................................(p[1]) ShaneKelly 3 79
(Richard Hughes) *t.k.h: led briefly over 10f out: chsd ldng pair: wknd over 1f out* **10/1**

0400 **7** *1 ¾* **Elysian Fields (GR)**[6] 8548 6-9-6 **90**............................. JackMitchell 7 81
(Amanda Perrett) *led after 2f: stretched on over 3f out: hdd jst over 2f out: sn wknd* **14/1**

1025 **8** *4* **Alqamar**[48] 7337 3-9-2 **91**..............................(b) WilliamBuick 6 77
(Charlie Appleby) *trckd ldng trio: rdn and reluctant over 2f out: sn dropped to last and wl btn* **6/4[1]**

2m 29.6s (-4.90) **Going Correction** -0.175s/f (Stan)
**WFA** 3 from 5yo+ 5lb **8 Ran SP% 114.6**
Speed ratings (Par 107): **109,108,106,105,104 103,102,99**
CSF £53.34 CT £1003.24 TOTE £8.30: £2.00, £2.30, £3.90; EX 59.00 Trifecta £431.70.
**Owner** The Warriors **Bred** Highfort Stud **Trained** Penhow, Newport

**FOCUS**
A decent middle-distance handicap but the favourite was disappointing. They went a good gallop and the well-backed winner came with a sweeping winning move, central to near side on this occasion.

## 8673 RACING UK HD H'CAP 1m 3f 219y(P)
**7:10** (7:12) (Class 6) (0-55,55) 3-Y-O **£2,587** (£770; £384; £192) **Stalls** Low

Form RPR

0054 **1** **Bird For Life**[22] 8135 3-8-5 **46** oh1.................................. NicolaCurrie(7) 7 52
(Mark Usher) *hld up in 7th: rdn and prog on outer over 2f out: clsd to ld last 150yds: styd on* **11/2[2]**

4450 **2** *nk* **Iley Boy**[29] 7918 3-8-13 **47**...............................................(p[1]) JoeyHaynes 9 52
(John Gallagher) *trckd ldng quartet: prog 3f out to ld jst over 2f out: hdd last 150yds: kpt on but a hld* **9/1**

000 **3** *nse* **Mistress Viz (IRE)**[32] 7833 3-8-9 **50**.......................... TylerSaunders(7) 1 55
(Sarah Hollinshead) *hld up in last: stl last of main gp over 2f out: rdn and gd prog on outer over 1f out: styd on fnl f and nrly snatched 2nd* **12/1**

0063 **4** *2* **Spiritofedinburgh (IRE)**[14] 8346 3-9-6 **54**.......................(t) ShaneKelly 5 56
(Brendan Powell) *hld up in 8th: prog on inner over 2f out: rdn to chal over 1f out: edgd lft and nt qckn after* **2/1[1]**

0460 **5** *nk* **Hi There Silver (IRE)**[10] 2679 3-8-12 **46** oh1.................(v) KieranO'Neill 4 47
(Michael Madgwick) *led 2f: trckd ldrs: rdn and tried to chal 2f out: one pce over 1f out* **50/1**

0056 **6** *2* **Huddersfilly Town**[18] 8249 3-9-2 **50**................................ LukeMorris 2 48
(Ivan Furtado) *trckd ldrs in 6th: rdn over 2f out: nt qckn wl over 1f out: sn btn* **13/2[3]**

000 **7** *½* **Lady Of Steel**[36] 7708 3-9-7 **55**...................................... DanielMuscutt 14 52
(John Butler) *hld up in last quartet: rdn wl over 2f out: one pce and no significant prog* **22/1**

6306 **8** *½* **Scarlet Thrush (IRE)**[27] 7992 3-9-4 **52**.......................... DannyBrock 3 49
(Luke McJannet) *hld up in last trio: rdn over 2f out: no great prog u.p after* **14/1**

0000 **9** *8* **Lulu The Rocket**[33] 7790 3-8-11 **48**................................(h) TimClark(3) 13 32
(John Butler) *stdd s: plld hrd and hld up in 10th: rdn and no prog over 2f out: sn wknd* **33/1**

0500 **10** *nk* **Our Kim (IRE)**[95] 5653 3-9-1 **49**........................................ SeanLevey 6 32
(John Butler) *won battle for ld after 2f: stdd pce after 4f: rdn and hdd jst over 2f out: wknd qckly* **12/1**

5-06 **11** *13* **Skilful Lord (IRE)**[20] 2060 3-8-13 **47**...........................(bt[1]) PJMcDonald 10 9
(David Pipe) *pressed ldr after 2f: rdn over 3f out: wknd rapidly over 2f out* **16/1**

0066 **12** *60* **Follow Me (IRE)**[32] 7833 3-9-1 **49**...............................(b[1]) OisinMurphy 8
(Lee Carter) *tried to ld but unable to: pressed ldrs on outer: wkng whn hung lft bnd over 4f out: t.o and virtually p.u over 2f out* **10/1**

2m 33.26s (-1.24) **Going Correction** -0.175s/f (Stan) **12 Ran SP% 118.3**
Speed ratings (Par 98): **97,96,96,95,95 93,93,93,87,87 79,39**
CSF £53.27 CT £576.01 TOTE £7.60: £2.70, £2.90, £2.40; EX 80.60 Trifecta £856.20.
**Owner** The Mark Usher Racing Club **Bred** Mrs Robert Langton **Trained** Upper Lambourn, Berks

**FOCUS**
A moderate 3yo middle-distance handicap. They went a muddling, start-stop gallop, and it paid to be ridden more patiently.

## 8674 32RED ON THE APP STORE H'CAP 1m 7f 218y(P)
**7:40** (7:43) (Class 6) (0-65,65) 3-Y-O **£2,587** (£770; £384; £192) **Stalls** Low

Form RPR

0400 **1** **Volturnus**[41] 7537 3-8-2 **46** oh1...................................(bt) NickyMackay 4 54
(Jamie Osborne) *mde all: set modest pce and untrbld tl pressed and pushed along over 3f out: shkn up and drew clr 2f out: styd on wl* **25/1**

430 **2** *2 ¾* **Mister Chow**[15] 8312 3-9-5 **63**...................................(v) TimmyMurphy 6 68+
(Gary Moore) *t.k.h: hld up in last: nt qckn and outpcd wl over 2f out: kpt on after and tk 2nd last 150yds: no ch to chal* **5/1[3]**

503 **3** *2* **Casemates Square (IRE)**[78] 6291 3-8-8 **52**................... PJMcDonald 5 55
(Ian Williams) *difficult to load into stall: hld up disputing 4th: prog over 2f out: sn rdn and nt qckn: tk 2nd briefly 1f out but no imp wnr* **11/10[1]**

4114 **4** *4* **Navajo Star (IRE)**[18] 8246 3-8-13 **57**............................(v) KieranO'Neill 1 55
(Michael Appleby) *trckd wnr: chal over 3f out: rdn and nt qckn over 2f out: lost 2nd and wknd fnl f* **9/2[2]**

6004 **5** *4* **Percipio**[53] 7152 3-8-6 **50**.................................................. MartinDwyer 7 43
(Alan King) *t.k.h: hld up disputing 4th: effrt on outer to chal 4f out: nt qckn and btn over 2f out: wknd* **8/1**

4000 **6** *½* **Seinfeld**[40] 7561 3-9-7 **65**...............................................(p[1]) LukeMorris 2 57
(David Simcock) *trckd ldng pair to 4f out: rdn and no rspnse wl over 2f out: sn wknd* **7/1**

3m 34.28s (4.18) **Going Correction** -0.175s/f (Stan) **6 Ran SP% 109.9**
Speed ratings (Par 98): **82,80,79,77,75 75**
CSF £134.17 TOTE £16.50: £5.40, £1.90; EX 115.40 Trifecta £291.50.
**Owner** The Hon A Blyth **Bred** Lemington Grange Stud **Trained** Upper Lambourn, Berks

**FOCUS**
A modest 3yo staying handicap. They went a sedate gallop and the leader stayed in front once challenged.

## 8675 32RED H'CAP 7f (P)
**8:10** (8:12) (Class 6) (0-55,55) 3-Y-O+ **£2,587** (£770; £384; £192) **Stalls** Low

Form RPR

3000 **1** **Loveatfirstsight**[13] 8376 4-9-3 **52**..................................(p) DanielMuscutt 2 61
(Jane Chapple-Hyam) *trckd ldrs: prog fr 2f out: rdn to ld 1f out: kpt on wl fnl f* **11/4[1]**

3320 **2** *1* **Binky Blue (IRE)**[15] 8307 5-9-3 **52**..............................(h) ShaneKelly 4 58
(Daniel Mark Loughnane) *trckd ldrs: effrt and cl up over 1f out: rdn to chse wnr ins fnl f: kpt on but unable to chal* **5/1[3]**

0002 **3** *1* **Warba (IRE)**[14] 8345 3-9-3 **53**.........................................(t) SeanLevey 7 56
(Mohamed Moubarak) *trckd ldr: led over 2f out: rdn and hdd 1f out: one pce* **10/1**

3554 **4** *nk* **New Rich**[28] 7952 7-9-3 **52**...............................................(b) CharlesBishop 9 55
(Eve Johnson Houghton) *t.k.h: hld up in last trio: prog on outer over 1f out: styd on fnl f: gave himself too much to do* **4/1[2]**

0300 **5** *nse* **Dynamic Girl (IRE)**[7] 8514 4-8-10 **52**........................(t) NicolaCurrie(7) 14 55
(Brendan Powell) *dwlt: dropped in fr wdst draw and hld up in rr: prog 2f out: rdn over 1f out: kpt on fnl f but nt pce to chal* **9/1**

025 **6** *2 ½* **How's Lucy**[139] 4006 3-8-12 **53**.................................... PaddyBradley(5) 3 48
(Jane Chapple-Hyam) *trckd ldng pair: effrt 2f out: wknd fnl f* **9/1**

2230 **7** *nse* **Mowhoob**[93] 5713 7-8-12 **52**.......................................... JoshuaBryan(5) 13 48
(Brian Barr) *hld up in last: effrt on inner over 2f out: nvr on terms w ldrs and no prog fnl f* **16/1**

1250 **8** *hd* **Captain Sedgwick (IRE)**[27] 7991 3-9-2 **52**..................... LukeMorris 12 46
(John Spearing) *t.k.h: hld up in midfield: rdn and struggling over 2f out: sn btn* **16/1**

00 **9** *hd* **Gunner Moyne**[35] 7729 5-9-3 **55**..................................(b) HectorCrouch(3) 6 50
(Gary Moore) *t.k.h: trckd ldrs on outer: lost pl and rdn 2f out: n.d after* **8/1**

0030 **10** *5* **Sakhee's Jem**[15] 8329 4-9-3 **52**........................................ PJMcDonald 8 33
(Gay Kelleway) *hld up in midfield: rdn and no prog wl over 2f out: sn wknd* **20/1**

6006 **11** *½* **Iceaxe**[30] 7900 4-9-2 **54**.................................................. EoinWalsh(3) 1 34
(John Holt) *led to over 2f out: wknd qckly wl over 1f out* **25/1**

0-00 **12** *5* **Clandon**[134] 4180 4-8-13 **51**........................................ CallumShepherd(3) 5 17
(Brett Johnson) *t.k.h: hld up in tch: rdn and wknd qckly over 2f out* **33/1**

1m 25.76s (-0.24) **Going Correction** -0.175s/f (Stan)
**WFA** 3 from 4yo+ 1lb **12 Ran SP% 126.8**
Speed ratings (Par 101): **94,92,91,91,91 88,88,88,87,82 81,75**
CSF £17.17 CT £129.95 TOTE £3.10: £1.10, £2.20, £5.20; EX 19.60 Trifecta £151.00.
**Owner** Miss K Squance **Bred** Kevin Daniel Crabb **Trained** Dalham, Suffolk

**FOCUS**
A moderate handicap. They went a decent gallop and the well-backed favourite won readily. The form looks quite strong for the grade.
T/Plt: £177.40 to a £1 stake. Pool: £73,796.14 - 303.63 winning units T/Qpdt: £155.00 to a £1 stake. Pool: £8,299.61 - 39.62 winning units **Jonathan Neesom**

# 8508 NOTTINGHAM (L-H)
Wednesday, November 8

**OFFICIAL GOING: Soft (heavy in places on the back straight; 5.7)**
Wind: Virtually nil Weather: Fine & dry

## 8676 RACING UK PROFITS RETURNED TO RACING NURSERY H'CAP 1m 75y
**12:35** (12:35) (Class 5) (0-75,75) 2-Y-O **£3,234** (£962; £481; £240) **Stalls** Centre

Form RPR

3534 **1** **Regular Income (IRE)**[14] 8354 2-9-6 **74**......................(p) JimmyQuinn 11 77
(Adam West) *dwlt: sn pushed along on outer and in tch after 2f: hdwy over 2f out: rdn along to chse ldrs over 1f out: styng on whn lft in ld ins last 100yds: kpt on* **6/1[1]**

650 **2** *2 ¾* **Marble Bar**[14] 8350 2-8-11 **72**........................................ NicolaCurrie(7) 2 69
(Henry Candy) *t.k.h: trckd ldrs on inner: pushed along over 2f out: rdn over 1f out: kpt on fnl f* **6/1[1]**

030 **3** *¾* **Creel**[12] 8387 2-9-7 **75**...................................................... PhillipMakin 8 72
(David Brown) *chsd clr ldr: hdwy 3f out: rdn to ld 1 1/2f out: drvn and hdd ent fnl f: cl up whn bmpd 120yds out: sn hmpd and kpt on same pce* **20/1**

052 **4** *1 ¼* **Dance Emperor (IRE)**[35] 7740 2-9-6 **74**............................ LiamKeniry 3 67
(Ed Walker) *trckd ldrs: hdwy and cl up 2f out: sn rdn and n.m.r over 1f out: kpt on same pce* **9/1**

0102 **5** *½* **Milan Reef (IRE)**[16] 8287 2-8-7 **66** ow1...................... CameronNoble(5) 9 58
(David Loughnane) *sn led and clr: pushed along over 2f out: sn rdn and jnd: hdd 1 1/2f out: grad wknd* **6/1[1]**

600 **6** *2 ¼* **Odds On Oli**[106] 5262 2-8-1 **55** ow1............................(p[1]) JoeFanning 1 42
(Richard Fahey) *t.k.h: prom on inner: hdwy 3f out: rdn along 2f out: drvn over 1f out: sn wknd* **16/1**

363 **7** *2* **Kirbec (IRE)**[9] 8467 2-9-2 **70**.....................................(p) AndrewMullen 4 52
(Keith Dalgleish) *towards rr: effrt and sme hdwy on outer 3f out: sn rdn and n.d* **15/2[3]**

5001 **8** *2 ¼* **Burn Some Dust (IRE)**[36] 7698 2-8-8 **62**.................. JoeyHaynes 7 39
(Brian Ellison) *a in rr* **7/1[2]**

0306 **9** *2 ¾* **Gemologist (IRE)**[92] 5756 2-9-2 **70**............................ PJMcDonald 10 41
(Mark Johnston) *dwlt: a in rr* **33/1**

6400 **10** *8* **Sigrid Nansen**[26] 8006 2-8-11 **68**................................ GeorgeWood(3) 5 22
(George Scott) *a towards rr* **12/1**

0051 **R** **Blacklooks (IRE)**[9] 8467 2-9-5 **73** 6ex................................ DavidNolan 6 73
(Ivan Furtado) *in tch: hdwy on outer to chse ldrs 2f out: effrt and edgd lft over 1f out: rdn to chal and hung lft 120yds out: sn led: hung bdly lft and rn out through rail ins last 100yds* **6/1[1]**

1m 51.39s (2.39) **Going Correction** +0.375s/f (Good) **11 Ran SP% 112.7**
Speed ratings (Par 96): **103,100,99,98,97 95,93,91,88,80**
CSF £39.15 CT £681.63 TOTE £7.20: £1.80, £2.40, £6.50; EX 45.40 Trifecta £896.00.
**Owner** Ian & Amanda Maybrey John Freeze J West **Bred** Garrett O'Neill **Trained** Epsom, Surrey

**FOCUS**
Races took place on the Inner track. The rail was set out 2 yards on the home bend adding 6 yards to races 1, 2, 3 and 7. The ground was given as officially soft, heavy in places pre-racing and clerk of the course Jane Hedley said 'we had 4mm of rain the previous day and the heavy places are in the back straight'. After riding in the opener jockey Jimmy Quinn said 'the ground is testing,' Philip Makin reported 'it is heavy' and Liam Keniry said 'it is bottomless.'\n\x\x A modest-looking handicap to start the card, which saw drama in the final furlong.

## 8677 B&M INSTALLATIONS MAIDEN STKS (DIV I) 1m 75y
**1:05** (1:06) (Class 5) 2-Y-O **£3,234** (£962; £481; £240) **Stalls** Centre

Form RPR

6 **1** **My Lord And Master (IRE)**[21] 8161 2-9-5 0.............. DanielTudhope 1 89+
(William Haggas) *mde all: pushed clr over 2f out: v easily* **4/1[2]**

**2** *6* **Young Rascal (FR)** 2-9-5 0.............................................. JoeFanning 11 74+
(William Haggas) *towards rr: swtchd lft to inner and hdwy 3f out: rdn wl over 1f out: styd on fnl f: no ch w wnr* **9/1[3]**

**3** *½* **Hipster Boy** 2-9-5 0............................................................ RobertTart 13 73+
(John Gosden) *trckd ldrs on outer: hdwy 3f out: chsd wnr 2f out: sn rdn and no imp: lost 2nd towards fin* **12/1**

5 **4** *2 ¾* **Victory Chime (IRE)**[21] 8161 2-9-5 0.............................. PhillipMakin 12 67
(Ralph Beckett) *midfield: hdwy 3f out: rdn along to chse ldrs 2f out: kpt on fnl f* **4/1[2]**


The Form Book Flat, Raceform Ltd, Newbury, RG14 5SJ

| Form | Pos | Dist | Horse | RPR |
|---|---|---|---|---|
| | 5 | 1/2 | **Rhode Island (IRE)** 2-9-5 0 ... RobertHavlin 2 (John Gosden) *in tch: hdwy over 3f out: rdn along wl over 2f out: kpt on same pce* **3/1**[1] | 66 |
| 0 | 6 | 1 3/4 | **Rocky Shores (IRE)**[12] 8389 2-9-5 0 ... FrannyNorton 7 (Mick Channon) *chsd ldng pair: rdn along 3f out: grad wknd* **20/1** | 62 |
| | 7 | 3/4 | **Doctor Knox (IRE)** 2-9-5 0 ... PJMcDonald 10 (Paul Cole) *trckd ldrs: hdwy over 3f out and sn chsng wnr: rdn 2f out: sn wknd* **12/1** | 60 |
| | 8 | 1/2 | **Lopito** 2-9-5 0 ... OisinMurphy 3 (Andrew Balding) *in tch: rdn along over 3f out: sn drvn and wknd* **14/1** | 59 |
| | 9 | 1 | **Balkhash (IRE)** 2-9-2 0 ... HectorCrouch(3) 14 (Clive Cox) *midfield: hdwy to chse ldrs 3f out: rdn along over 2f out: grad wknd* **33/1** | 57 |
| | 10 | 3 3/4 | **Desert Wind (IRE)** 2-9-5 0 ... StevieDonohoe 9 (Ed Vaughan) *a towards rr* **40/1** | 49 |
| | 11 | 3/4 | **True Destiny** 2-9-5 0 ... ShaneKelly 6 (Roger Charlton) *dwlt: a in rr* **12/1** | 47+ |
| 00 | 12 | 1 1/4 | **Harry Callahan (IRE)**[12] 8382 2-9-5 0 ... BenCurtis 5 (Tom Dascombe) *a towards rr* **66/1** | 44 |
| | 13 | 4 1/2 | **Y Fyn Duw A Fydd** 2-9-0 0 ... FergusSweeney 4 (John Gallagher) *dwlt: a in rr* **100/1** | 30 |
| 00 | 14 | 1 3/4 | **Banjo's Voice**[32] 7813 2-9-0 0 ... PaddyBradley(5) 8 (Jane Chapple-Hyam) *prom: rdn along over 3f out: wknd wl over 2f out* **250/1** | 31 |

1m 51.56s (2.56) **Going Correction** +0.375s/f (Good) **14** Ran SP% **117.8**
Speed ratings (Par 96): **102,96,95,92,92 90,89,89,88,84 83,82,78,76**
CSF £37.30 TOTE £4.60: £1.60, £2.10, £3.80; EX 49.70 Trifecta £353.70.
**Owner** T Bridge **Bred** A Stroud And J Hanly **Trained** Newmarket, Suffolk

**FOCUS**
The rail was set out 2 yards on the home bend adding 6 yards to the first of the divisions of the 1m maiden. It was taken in impressive style by one of the runners who'd seen the racetrack before.

## 8678 B&M INSTALLATIONS MAIDEN STKS (DIV II) 1m 75y
**1:40** (1:41) (Class 5) 2-Y-O **£3,234** (£962; £481; £240) **Stalls** Centre

| Form | Pos | Dist | Horse | RPR |
|---|---|---|---|---|
| | 1 | | **Kinaesthesia** 2-9-0 0 ... OisinMurphy 2 (Ralph Beckett) *dwlt: sn pushed along into midfield: trckd ldrs 1/2-way: hdwy on inner over 3f out: rdn to ld wl over 2f out: drvn ins fnl f: hld on wl towards fin* **4/1**[2] | 72+ |
| | 2 | shd | **Qawamees (IRE)** 2-9-5 0 ... PhillipMakin 8 (Ed Dunlop) *hld up: hdwy on outer wl over 2f out: rdn over 1f out: chsd ldr ins fnl f: sn drvn to chal and ev ch: no ex nr fin* **33/1** | 77 |
| | 3 | 2 1/4 | **Glencadam Master** 2-9-5 0 ... RobertHavlin 9 (John Gosden) *trckd ldrs: effrt 3f out: rdn along 2f out: kpt on same pce fnl f* **3/1**[1] | 73+ |
| 0 | 4 | nk | **Oskemen**[12] 8389 2-9-2 0 ... HectorCrouch(3) 4 (Clive Cox) *.towards rr: hdwy 3f out: rdn along 2f out: styd on wl fnl f* **7/1**[3] | 71 |
| | 5 | 3/4 | **Allieyf** 2-9-5 0 ... PaulMulrennan 1 (William Haggas) *dwlt and rr: hdwy 3f out: rdn wl over 1f out: styd on wl fnl f* **17/2** | 69 |
| | 6 | hd | **Corelli (USA)** 2-9-5 0 ... RobertTart 12 (John Gosden) *dwlt and rr: pushed along and hdwy wl over 2f out: rdn wl over 1f out: styd on wl fnl f* **12/1** | 69+ |
| 6 | 7 | 1 | **Nibras Galaxy (IRE)**[22] 8136 2-9-5 0 ... StevieDonohoe 3 (Ismail Mohammed) *prom: cl up 4f out: pushed along over 3f out: rdn over 2f out: kpt on same pce* **7/1**[3] | 67 |
| | 8 | nk | **Great Beyond** 2-9-5 0 ... ShaneKelly 14 (Roger Charlton) *trckd ldrs: hdwy to ld 1/2-way: rdn along 3f out and sn hdd: drvn 2f out: kpt on same pce* **14/1** | 66 |
| | 9 | 1 | **Best Blue** 2-9-5 0 ... DanielTudhope 13 (Michael Bell) *towards rr: gd hdwy on outer over 4f out: prom 3f out: rdn along over 2f out: kpt on same pce* **9/1** | 64 |
| | 10 | 1 | **Zamandas (IRE)** 2-9-5 0 ... JoeFanning 6 (Roger Varian) *slt ld on inner: hdd 1/2-way: cl up: rdn along over 2f out: drvn over 1f out: grad wknd* **20/1** | 62 |
| | 11 | 1 3/4 | **Hombre Casado (FR)** 2-9-5 0 ... LiamKeniry 11 (Ed Walker) *cl up: rdn along 3f out: wknd 2f out* **33/1** | 58+ |
| | 12 | 3/4 | **Born To Spend (IRE)** 2-9-0 0 ... GrahamLee 5 (Ian Williams) *dwlt: rdn along and hdwy into midfield whn hmpd after 1f: rr after* **100/1** | 51 |
| | 13 | 4 1/2 | **Billie Flynn** 2-8-11 0 ... HollieDoyle(3) 7 (Harry Dunlop) *t.k.h: trckd ldrs: rdn along 4f out: wknd 3f out* **80/1** | 41 |
| 00 | 14 | 8 | **Santiago Rock (IRE)**[35] 7739 2-9-5 0 ...(p) FergusSweeney 10 (Noel Williams) *t.k.h: a towards rr* **250/1** | 29 |

1m 56.2s (7.20) **Going Correction** +0.375s/f (Good) **14** Ran SP% **118.2**
Speed ratings (Par 96): **79,78,76,76,75 75,74,74,73,72 70,69,65,57**
CSF £142.99 TOTE £5.00: £1.60, £9.00, £1.70; EX 178.30 Trifecta £1239.70.
**Owner** Miss K Rausing **Bred** Miss K Rausing **Trained** Kimpton, Hants

**FOCUS**
The rail was set out 2 yards on the home bend adding 6 yards to the second division of the 1m maiden. It was over four seconds slower than the contest that preceded it.

## 8679 LADY CECIL H'CAP 5f 8y
**2:15** (2:16) (Class 2) (0-110,100) 3-Y-O+ **£16,172** (£4,812; £2,405; £1,202) **Stalls** Centre

| Form | Pos | Dist | Horse | RPR |
|---|---|---|---|---|
| 0001 | 1 | | **Perfect Pasture**[12] 8383 7-9-6 **100** ...(v) DavidAllan 4 (Michael Easterby) *cl up: led wl over 1f out: sn rdn and kpt on strly fnl f* **5/2**[1] | 109 |
| 462 | 2 | 1 1/4 | **Clem Fandango (FR)**[30] 7887 3-9-5 **99** ... PhillipMakin 5 (Keith Dalgleish) *trckd ldrs: hdwy over 1f out: rdn to chse wnr ins fnl f: no imp towards fin* **9/2**[2] | 104 |
| 0036 | 3 | 1 | **Green Door (IRE)**[18] 8238 6-8-9 **96** ...(v) JonathanFisher(7) 8 (Robert Cowell) *t.k.h: slt ld: rdn along 2f out: sn hdd and drvn: kpt on same pce fnl f* **16/1** | 97 |
| 6604 | 4 | 1 1/2 | **Hoof It**[12] 8383 10-9-2 **96** ... PaulMulrennan 2 (Michael Easterby) *chsd ldrs: rdn along and sltly outpcd wl over 1f out: kpt on fnl f* **15/2** | 92 |
| 6351 | 5 | 3/4 | **Gracious John (IRE)**[22] 8139 4-8-11 **98** ... KatherineGlenister(7) 6 (David Evans) *cl up: rdn and ev ch over 1f out: drvn and wknd fnl f* **6/1**[3] | 91 |
| 1-00 | 5 | dht | **Spiritual Lady**[25] 8040 3-9-6 **100** ... DanielTudhope 7 (Philip McBride) *in tch: hdwy 2f out: rdn wl over 1f out: kpt on same pce* **13/2** | 93 |
| 5006 | 7 | 2 | **Atletico (IRE)**[11] 8416 5-9-2 **96** ... FrannyNorton 9 (Roger Varian) *chsd ldrs: rdn along 2f out: sn btn* **9/1** | 82 |
| 4501 | 8 | nse | **Tomily (IRE)**[11] 8416 3-8-13 **96** ... HollieDoyle(3) 3 (Richard Hannon) *rr: rdn along 1/2-way: n.d* **8/1** | 81 |
| 1031 | 9 | 2 3/4 | **Classic Pursuit**[35] 7738 6-8-9 **96** ...(b) GabrieleMalune(7) 1 (Michael Appleby) *dwlt: a towards rr* **50/1** | 72 |

1m 1.64s (0.14) **Going Correction** +0.275s/f (Good) **9** Ran SP% **115.1**
Speed ratings (Par 109): **109,107,105,103,101 101,98,98,94**
CSF £13.49 CT £147.31 TOTE £3.10: £1.50, £1.90, £5.20; EX 16.00 Trifecta £152.50.
**Owner** S Hull & S Hollings **Bred** Mrs Jean Turpin **Trained** Sheriff Hutton, N Yorks

**FOCUS**
A classy handicap in which last year's first and second were back for another go. The field headed down the middle of the track, away from either rail. It appeared to be beneficial to be up with the early pace.

## 8680 B&M INSTALLATIONS H'CAP 5f 8y
**2:50** (2:51) (Class 4) (0-85,86) 3-Y-O+ **£5,175** (£1,540; £769; £384) **Stalls** Centre

| Form | Pos | Dist | Horse | RPR |
|---|---|---|---|---|
| 2061 | 1 | | **Quick Look**[8] 8488 4-9-3 **81** 6ex ... DavidAllan 7 (Michael Easterby) *dwlt and rr: hdwy over 2f out: rdn to chse ldrs over 1f out: styd on to chal ins fnl f: led last 100 yds* **9/2**[1] | 91+ |
| 2002 | 2 | 3/4 | **Fantasy Keeper**[35] 7737 3-8-7 **72** ... AndrewMullen 2 (Michael Appleby) *chsd ldrs: hdwy 2f out: rdn over 1f out: drvn and ev ch ent fnl f: kpt on* **5/1**[2] | 79 |
| 3161 | 3 | 1/2 | **Jabbarockie**[21] 8168 4-8-7 **71** oh1 ... NeilFarley 4 (Eric Alston) *led: rdn along wl over 1f out: drvn ent fnl f: hdd last 100 yds: no ex* **6/1**[3] | 76 |
| 4045 | 4 | 1 | **Lathom**[21] 8167 4-9-0 **78** ... JoeDoyle 11 (Julie Camacho) *chsd ldrs: rdn along wl over 1f out: drvn and kpt on same pce fnl f* **8/1** | 80 |
| 5535 | 5 | 1 3/4 | **Musharrif**[17] 8260 5-9-2 **80** ... DanielTudhope 3 (Declan Carroll) *chsd ldrs: rdn and ch over 1f out: drvn and wknd fnl f* **8/1** | 75 |
| 3300 | 6 | nk | **Straightothepoint**[16] 8293 5-8-11 **75** ... GrahamLee 9 (Bryan Smart) *in tch: hdwy to chse ldrs 2f out: sn rdn and kpt on same pce* **40/1** | 69 |
| 2352 | 7 | 2 | **Bahamian Sunrise**[21] 8167 5-9-0 **81** ...(b) HectorCrouch(3) 8 (John Gallagher) *chsd ldr: rdn along wl over 1f out: drvn appr fnl f: sn wknd* **12/1** | 68 |
| 1422 | 8 | 1 1/2 | **Memories Galore (IRE)**[18] 8238 5-9-8 **86** ...(p) TonyHamilton 1 (Roger Fell) *a towards rr* **9/2**[1] | 68 |
| 4010 | 9 | 5 | **Rosabelle**[32] 7811 3-9-2 **85** ...(b) JoshuaBryan(5) 6 (Alan Bailey) *dwlt: a towards rr* **20/1** | 49 |
| 0521 | 10 | 1 | **Van Gerwen**[16] 8293 4-9-2 **80** ... JoeFanning 5 (Les Eyre) *in tch: chsd ldrs 1/2-way: rdn along 2f out: sn wknd* **12/1** | 40 |

1m 1.9s (0.40) **Going Correction** +0.275s/f (Good) **10** Ran SP% **112.1**
Speed ratings (Par 105): **107,105,105,103,100 100,96,94,86,84**
CSF £25.61 CT £136.05 TOTE £5.70: £2.30, £1.70, £2.30; EX 24.20 Trifecta £153.80.
**Owner** Golden Ratio, Hull, Hollings & Winter **Bred** Susanna Ballinger **Trained** Sheriff Hutton, N Yorks

**FOCUS**
A decent-looking sprint, but the form isn't likely to be tested again this year on turf. The time was marginally slower than the race run before it, where a gelding officially rated 100 took the prize from four with marks in the 90s.

## 8681 SUBSCRIBE TO RACING UK ON YOUTUBE H'CAP 5f 8y
**3:20** (3:20) (Class 6) (0-65,73) 3-Y-O+ **£2,587** (£770; £384; £192) **Stalls** Centre

| Form | Pos | Dist | Horse | RPR |
|---|---|---|---|---|
| 611 | 1 | | **Ebitda**[8] 8484 3-9-11 **73** 6ex ... JamieGormley(5) 8 (Scott Dixon) *sltly hmpd s: hld up: hdwy 2f out: sn chsng ldrs: rdn to chal jst over 1f out: led ent fnl f: edgd rt: kpt on* **6/5**[1] | 81 |
| 2434 | 2 | 1 1/4 | **Angel Palanas**[7] 8512 3-8-8 **58** ...(p) RussellHarris(7) 11 (K R Burke) *chsd ldrs: hdwy to chal 2f out: rdn and ev ch ent fnl f: sn drvn and kpt on* **6/1**[3] | 62 |
| 5003 | 3 | 3/4 | **Coiste Bodhar (IRE)**[8] 8484 6-8-10 **56** ...(p) PaddyPilley(3) 10 (Scott Dixon) *slt ld: rdn along wl over 1f out: hdd ent fnl f: sn drvn and kpt on same pce* **8/1** | 57 |
| 0000 | 4 | 2 | **Drop Kick Murphi (IRE)**[15] 8328 3-8-12 **55** ... GrahamLee 13 (Christine Dunnett) *towards rr: pushed along 1/2-way: hdwy wl over 1f out: sn rdn and kpt on fnl f* **50/1** | 49 |
| 4050 | 5 | 1 | **Celerity (IRE)**[5] 8558 3-8-0 **50** oh5 ...(p) GabrieleMalune(7) 1 (Lisa Williamson) *wnt lft s and bhd: rdn along and hdwy wl over: kpt on u.p fnl f* **66/1** | 40 |
| 6050 | 6 | 2 1/4 | **Borough Boy (IRE)**[21] 8168 7-9-1 **58** ...(v) PhillipMakin 2 (Derek Shaw) *wnt lft s: in tch: pushed along 1/2-way: rdn wl over 1f out: sn one pce* **14/1** | 40 |
| 1500 | 7 | 2 1/2 | **Culloden**[8] 8484 5-9-0 **64** ... TobyEley(7) 9 (Shaun Harris) *wnt lft s: cl up: disp ld 1/2-way: rdn wl over 1f out: grad wknd* **25/1** | 37 |
| 2400 | 8 | hd | **Ayresome Angel**[17] 8260 4-9-7 **64** ... JoeFanning 4 (John Mackie) *prom: rdn along 2f out: sn wknd* **4/1**[2] | 36 |
| 0502 | 9 | 3 1/2 | **Kodimoor (IRE)**[38] 7660 4-9-3 **60** ...(bt) FrannyNorton 6 (Christopher Kellett) *chsd ldrs: rdn along 2f out: sn wknd* **9/1** | 20 |

1m 3.02s (1.52) **Going Correction** +0.275s/f (Good) **9** Ran SP% **114.8**
Speed ratings (Par 101): **98,96,94,91,90 86,82,82,76**
CSF £8.65 CT £40.16 TOTE £2.10: £1.10, £1.80, £2.40; EX 9.10 Trifecta £34.60.
**Owner** Chesterfield Estates **Bred** Selwood, Hoskins & Trickledown **Trained** Babworth, Notts

**FOCUS**
A moderate-looking sprint that probably didn't take a great deal of winning.

## 8682 AJA GENTLEMAN H'CAP (FOR GENTLEMAN AMATEUR RIDERS) 1m 2f 50y
**3:55** (3:56) (Class 5) (0-75,75) 3-Y-O+ **£3,119** (£967; £483; £242) **Stalls** Low

| Form | Pos | Dist | Horse | RPR |
|---|---|---|---|---|
| -063 | 1 | | **Topamichi**[17] 8261 7-10-3 **62** ... MrJamesKendrick(5) 15 (Michael Appleby) *led 1f: cl up: led 1/2-way: wd st towards stands side: rdn along on wd outside over 2f out: drifted lft over 1f out: drvn and hung lft ins fnl f: kpt on wl towards fin* **6/1**[3] | 70 |
| 356- | 2 | 1 1/4 | **Attest**[129] 5723 4-11-1 **74** ... MrAdamElias(5) 14 (Warren Greatrex) *hld up in rr: hdwy 3f out: rdn along 2f out: chsesd ldrs over 1f out: styd on wl fnl f* **11/1** | 79 |
| 0220 | 3 | 3/4 | **Maraakib (IRE)**[12] 8386 5-10-11 **65** ... MrJamesKing 6 (David O'Meara) *hld up in rr: stdy hdwy over 4f out: cl up 3f out: chal 2f out: sn rdn: drvn and ev ch whn carried sltly lft ins fnl f: sn drvn and no ex towards fin* **9/1** | 68 |
| 4650 | 4 | 1 | **Sonnetist**[22] 8142 3-10-10 **72** ... MrLWilliams(5) 1 (David Evans) *chsd ldrs on inner: hdwy and cl up 3f out: rdn along 2f out: drvn and ev ch over 1f out: kpt on same pce fnl f* **9/1** | 74 |
| 5 | 5 | 2 | **Speciality (FR)**[50] 3-11-1 **72** ...(b[1]) MrSWalker 4 (Ralph Beckett) *hld up in tch: hdwy 4f out: sn chsng ldrs: rdn along 2f out: sn drvn and kpt on same pce* **4/1**[2] | 70 |

2103 **6** ½ **Oceanus (IRE)**[15] 8327 3-10-7 **64**........................ MrRBirkett 12 61
(Julia Feilden) *trckd ldrs: hdwy over 4f out: cl up 3f out: rdn along over 2f out: drvn over 1f out: grad wknd* **17/2**

5322 **7** 12 **England Expects**[7] 8515 3-9-13 **61**........................(h) MrJBrace(5) 13 34
(K R Burke) *trckd ldrs: hdwy and cl up 4f out: rdn along 3f out: drvn over 2f out: sn wknd* **11/4**[1]

6434 **8** 3 **Turnbury**[16] 8301 6-10-7 **61** oh7........................(p) MrJordanWilliams 11 27
(Nikki Evans) *prom: rdn along over 3f out: wknd wl over 2f out* **33/1**

5011 **9** 2 ¾ **Shining Romeo**[45] 4545 5-11-2 **70**........................ MrAlexFerguson 3 31
(Denis Quinn) *hld up towards rr: hdwy on inner to chse ldrs 3f out: rdn along over 2f out: sn btn* **16/1**

6250 **10** 2 ½ **Lazarus (IRE)**[15] 8326 3-10-13 **73**........................(t) MrBJames(3) 2 30
(Amy Murphy) *dwlt: sn in midfield: rdn along over 4f out: wknd 3f out* **28/1**

3600 **11** 5 **Paddy A (IRE)**[16] 8295 3-10-6 **70**........................ MrJamesMorley(7) 8 17
(Ian Williams) *dwlt: rapid hdwy to ld after 1f: hdd 1/2-way: rdn along over 4f out: sn wknd* **50/1**

2m 22.47s (8.17) **Going Correction** +0.375s/f (Good)
**WFA** 3 from 4yo+ 3lb **11** Ran SP% **114.0**
Speed ratings (Par 103): **82,81,80,79,78 77,68,65,63,61 57**
CSF £66.70 CT £587.64 TOTE £5.90: £2.00, £4.10, £2.40; EX 53.50 Trifecta £564.30.
**Owner** The Horse Watchers **Bred** Dullingham Park Stud & M P Bowring **Trained** Oakham, Rutland

**FOCUS**
The rail was set out 2 yards on the home bend adding 6 yards to this race. An interesting finale in which the runner-up is rated as achieving a personal best on the Flat .
T/Jkpt: Partly Won. £10,000.00 to a £1 stake. Pool: £10,000.00 - 0.5 winning unit. T/Plt: £73.10 to a £1 stake. Pool: £58,140.01 - 580.35 winning units T/Qpdt: £7.10 to a £1 stake. Pool: £6,210.88 - 638.68 winning units **Joe Rowntree**

8683 - 8690a (Foreign Racing) - See Raceform Interactive

8499
## CHANTILLY (R-H)
Wednesday, November 8

**OFFICIAL GOING: Polytrack: standard**

## 8691a PRIX DE LA CAPITAINERIE DE CHASSE (MAIDEN) (UNRACED 2YO FILLIES) (POLYTRACK) 1m 1f
1:05 2-Y-O **£11,538** (£4,615; £3,461; £2,307; £1,153)

RPR

**1** **Voladora (IRE)** 2-9-0 0........................ MickaelBarzalona 13 78
(A Fabre, France) **5/1**[3]

**2** 1 ½ **Northern Beam (IRE)** 2-9-0 0........................ Pierre-CharlesBoudot 1 75
(H-A Pantall, France) **68/10**

**3** hd **Agathe Sainte** 2-9-0 0........................ AurelienLemaitre 6 75
(F Head, France) **49/10**[2]

**4** 4 **Queen Roselyn (USA)** 2-9-0 0........................(b[1]) MickaelBerto 14 67
(A De Royer-Dupre, France) **249/10**

**5** ¾ **Duchess Of Danzig (GER)** 2-9-0 0........................ GregoryBenoist 9 65
(H-F Devin, France) **99/10**

**6** shd **Vinaccia (IRE)** 2-9-0 0........................ AnthonyCrastus 10 65
(C Lerner, France) **51/1**

**7** 1 ¾ **Melodienne (USA)** 2-9-0 0........................ ChristopheSoumillon 5 61
(C Laffon-Parias, France) **152/10**

**8** ½ **Risky Dory (FR)** 2-9-0 0........................ TheoBachelot 4 60
(S Wattel, France) **26/1**

**9** ¾ **Genereuse Lady (FR)** 2-8-6 0........................ JeremieMonteiro(8) 16 59
(Mme C Barande-Barbe, France) **33/1**

**10** ¾ **Irish Rose (IRE)** 2-9-0 0........................ EddyHardouin 15 57
(Carina Fey, France) **30/1**

**11** 4 **Taraja (GER)** 2-9-0 0........................ AntoineHamelin 3 49
(Henk Grewe, Germany) **99/10**

**12** 3 **Weetamoo (FR)** 2-9-0 0........................ ClementLecoeuvre 7 43
(J-Y Artu, France) **93/1**

**13** 2 ½ **Place Des Vosges (IRE)** 2-9-0 0........................ IoritzMendizabal 2 38
(David Menuisier) **207/10**

**14** nk **Bartaba (FR)** 2-9-0 0........................ MaximeGuyon 11 38
(A Fabre, France) **16/5**[1]

**15** 1 **Slewdra (FR)** 2-9-0 0........................ FrankPanicucci 8 36
(Remy Kennel, France) **122/1**

**16** 10 **Zaad (FR)** 2-9-0 0........................ JimmyTastayre 12 16
(Robert Collet, France) **95/1**

1m 55.32s **16** Ran SP% **117.9**
PARI-MUTUEL (all including 1 euro stake): WIN 6.00; PLACE 2.30, 2.60, 2.20; DF 20.30; SF 40.50.
**Owner** Godolphin SNC **Bred** Godolphin **Trained** Chantilly, France

## 8692a PRIX DE LA BOUCLE D'EN HAUT (MAIDEN) (3YO) (POLYTRACK) 1m 6f
1:35 3-Y-O **£10,683** (£4,273; £3,205; £2,136; £1,068)

RPR

**1** **County Fair**[21] 3-9-2 0........................ GregoryBenoist 11 80
(D Smaga, France) **11/5**[1]

**2** 1 ¼ **Cadencia**[39] 3-8-13 0........................ MickaelBarzalona 3 75
(A Fabre, France) **14/5**[2]

**3** 1 **Mutamarida (IRE)**[50] 3-8-8 0........................ SebastienMaillot 8 69
(Rod Collet, France) **37/10**[3]

**4** ½ **Rainbow Rising (FR)**[28] 7948 3-8-9 0 ow1........................ ChristopheSoumillon 4 69
(David Menuisier) **39/10**

**5** 2 ½ **Douriya (USA)** 3-8-3 0........................(b[1]) JeremieMonteiro(5) 9 64
(A De Royer-Dupre, France) **221/10**

**6** 4 **Newcomer**[59] 3-8-8 0........................(p) EddyHardouin 6 59
(E Leenders, France) **246/10**

**7** ½ **Buck's Bahkbook (FR)** 3-8-0 0........................ AlexandreChesneau(8) 5 58
(Yannick Fouin, France) **63/1**

**8** ¾ **Samba Bresilienne (FR)** 3-8-8 0........................ StephanePasquier 10 57
(Yannick Fouin, France) **175/10**

**9** 2 **Magpie (FR)** 3-8-11 0........................ AnthonyCrastus 1 57
(Gerard Martin, Austria) **112/1**

**10** 20 **Sicilia (GER)** 3-8-8 0........................ AntoineHamelin 2 26
(H Blume, Germany) **61/1**

**11** 10 **Horsili (FR)** 3-8-11 0........................ FrankPanicucci 7 15
(Mlle E Schmitt, France) **106/1**

3m 5.08s **11** Ran SP% **117.9**
PARI-MUTUEL (all including 1 euro stake): WIN 3.20; PLACE 1.30, 1.30, 1.30; DF 4.10; SF 6.60.
**Owner** K Abdullah **Bred** Juddmonte Farms Ltd **Trained** Lamorlaye, France

8693 - 8700a (Foreign Racing) - See Raceform Interactive

8536
## CHELMSFORD (A.W) (L-H)
Thursday, November 9

**OFFICIAL GOING: Polytrack: standard**
Wind: virtually nil Weather: dry

## 8701 BET TOTEPLACEPOT AT BETFRED.COM NOVICE AUCTION STKS 6f (P)
5:15 (5:16) (Class 6) 2-Y-O **£3,234** (£962; £481; £240) **Stalls** Centre

Form RPR

3 **1** **Brigand**[17] 8288 2-9-0 0........................ DanielTudhope 1 75
(William Haggas) *t.k.h: led early sn hdd and trckd ldrs: swtchd rt over 1f out: effrt to chal between horses 1f out: rdn to ld ins fnl f: styd on* **8/11**[1]

46 **2** ½ **Maypole**[15] 8350 2-8-13 0........................ SeanLevey 8 73
(Richard Hannon) *t.k.h: hld up in tch in midfield: hdwy on outer 1/2-way: rdn to chse ldr over 2f out: ev ch u.p 1f out: kpt on: unable qck towards fin* **4/1**[3]

433 **3** hd **Alba Del Sole (IRE)**[23] 8130 2-8-11 70........................ NickyMackay 9 70
(John Gosden) *sn led and crossed to inner: rdn over 1f out: edgd rt 1f out: hdd and kpt on same pce ins fnl f* **7/2**[2]

04 **4** 1 ¼ **Demons And Wizards (IRE)**[31] 7897 2-9-1 0........................ RenatoSouza 6 70
(Sylvester Kirk) *hld up in rr: clsd on inner over 1f out: chsd clr ldng trio 1f out: pushed along and styd on wl ins fnl f: gng on at fin but nvr gng rch ldrs* **50/1**

0 **5** 2 ½ **Rose Tinted Spirit**[13] 8388 2-9-1 0........................ RichardKingscote 3 63
(Ralph Beckett) *s.i.s: in tch in last trio: effrt and hdwy to chse clr ldng trio over 1f out tl 1f out: kpt on same pce and no threat to ldrs ins fnl f* **14/1**

0310 **6** 6 **Arden Pearl (IRE)**[33] 7814 2-9-3 75........................(h) LukeMorris 5 47
(Archie Watson) *t.k.h: chsd ldrs: rdn wl over 1f out: sn outpcd and btn: wknd fnl f* **6/1**

6030 **7** 2 ½ **Mother Of Dragons (IRE)**[55] 7126 2-7-13 70........................ NicolaCurrie(7) 7 28
(Phil McEntee) *rrd as stalls opened and s.i.s: in tch in last trio: short of room wl over 1f out: sn rdn and btn: wknd fnl f* **20/1**

00 **8** 2 ¾ **Sandkissed (IRE)**[16] 8324 2-8-8 0........................(h) RaulDaSilva 2 22
(Amy Murphy) *restless in stalls: chsd ldr tl rdn and lost pl over 2f out: bhd 1f out: wknd* **100/1**

1m 12.86s (-0.84) **Going Correction** -0.225s/f (Stan) **8** Ran SP% **128.8**
Speed ratings (Par 94): **96,95,95,93,90 82,78,75**
CSF £4.98 TOTE £1.50: £1.10, £1.80, £1.60; EX 5.80 Trifecta £15.80.
**Owner** Ian and Christine Beard **Bred** D R Tucker **Trained** Newmarket, Suffolk
■ Stewards' Enquiry : Raul Da Silva one-day ban: improper behaviour (Nov 13)
Renato Souza 14-day ban: rider fails to take all reasonable and permissible measures throughout the race (Nov 23-25, Nov 28-Dec 2, Dec 4-9)

**FOCUS**
An ordinary juvenile novice contest, with the winner building on his debut effort. They went a respectable gallop on standard Polytrack and the odds-on favourite won well.

## 8702 BET TOTEJACKPOT AT BETFRED.COM NURSERY H'CAP 6f (P)
5:45 (5:46) (Class 5) (0-75,75) 2-Y-O **£4,528** (£1,347; £673; £336) **Stalls** Centre

Form RPR

3621 **1** **Vegas Boy (IRE)**[35] 7756 2-9-3 **71**........................(t) DougieCostello 1 74
(Jamie Osborne) *hld up wl in tch in midfield: effrt and rdn to ld over 1f out: hld on wl u.p ins fnl f: rdn out* **9/2**[2]

30 **2** ½ **Blackheath**[48] 7351 2-9-7 **75**........................ LiamKeniry 7 76
(Ed Walker) *stdd s: hld up in tch towards rr: pushed along and hdwy on inner over 1f out: rdn to chse ldrs ent fnl f: pressing wnr ins fnl f: styd on wl but a hld* **16/1**

0630 **3** 1 **Image**[15] 8349 2-8-8 **67**........................ FinleyMarsh(5) 5 65
(Philip McBride) *chsd ldrs: rdn and sltly outpcd whn nt clr run and swtchd rt over 1f out: rallied to go 3rd ins fnl f: styd on* **12/1**

252 **4** 1 ¾ **Procedure**[16] 8308 2-9-4 **72**........................ WilliamBuick 3 65
(Sir Michael Stoute) *stdd s: t.k.h: hld up in tch towards rr: hdwy over 2f out: rdn and ev ch over 1f out tl 1f out tl no ex jst ins fnl f: wknd fnl 100yds* **15/8**[1]

3303 **5** 3 **Indian Warrior**[48] 7362 2-9-5 **73**........................ OisinMurphy 9 57
(Ed Dunlop) *sn in rr and pushed along early: effrt on inner over 1f out: kpt on to pass btn rivals ins fnl f: nvr trbld ldrs* **25/1**

2213 **6** ¾ **Swing Out Sister (IRE)**[12] 8431 2-9-7 **75**........................ LukeMorris 2 57
(Clive Cox) *led for 1f: chsd ldr tl unable qck over 1f out: wknd ins fnl f* **5/1**[3]

0445 **7** shd **Expelled**[37] 7706 2-9-1 **69**........................ DanielMuscutt 4 50
(James Fanshawe) *in tch in midfield: rdn and struggling to qckn over 2f out: lost pl over 1f out: wl hld and kpt on same pce fnl f* **8/1**

650 **8** ¾ **Carp Kid (IRE)**[22] 8149 2-9-2 **70**........................ SeanLevey 8 49
(Richard Hannon) *hld up towards rr: outpcd and hung lft over 1f out: nvr trbld ldrs* **10/1**

0105 **9** ½ **First Drive**[74] 6481 2-9-4 **72**........................(v[1]) DanielTudhope 6 49
(Michael Bell) *led after 1f: edgd rt over 1f out: sn hdd and btn: wknd fnl f* **12/1**

1m 12.75s (-0.95) **Going Correction** -0.225s/f (Stan) **9** Ran SP% **114.9**
Speed ratings (Par 96): **97,96,95,92,88 87,87,86,85**
CSF £72.15 CT £810.80 TOTE £5.60: £1.60, £3.60, £3.10; EX 74.90 Trifecta £794.20.
**Owner** The Fabulous Fifty Boys **Bred** Brian Miller **Trained** Upper Lambourn, Berks

**FOCUS**
A fair nursery handicap. They went a decent gallop and a previous C&D winner bravely defied a hefty rise in the handicap. The third helps to set the level.

## 8703 BET TOTEQUADPOT AT BETFRED.COM NOVICE STKS 1m (P)
6:15 (6:17) (Class 5) 2-Y-O **£4,528** (£1,347; £673; £336) **Stalls** Low

Form RPR

02 **1** **Gronkowski (USA)**[33] 7810 2-9-2 0........................(b[1]) SeanLevey 11 90+
(Jeremy Noseda) *chsd ldrs: wnt 2nd after 2f tl led over 2f out: rdn over 1f out: styd on strly and drew clr ins fnl f: readily* **4/1**[2]

22 **2** 4 ½ **Big Kitten (USA)**[16] 8316 2-9-2 0........................ PJMcDonald 5 79
(Mark Johnston) *trckd ldng trio: effrt to press ldrs 2f out: rdn and pressing wnr over 1f out: 2nd and unable to match pce of wnr whn hung lft ins fnl f: wl hld and eased towards fin* **11/8**[1]

05 **3** 6 **Revolutionary Man (IRE)**[28] 7987 2-9-2 0........................ OisinMurphy 4 65
(Simon Crisford) *t.k.h: chsd ldr for 2f: styd trcking ldrs: swtchd rt and effrt jst over 2f out: rdn and pressed ldrs over 1f out: sn outpcd and edgd lft: wknd ins fnl f* **10/1**

**4** nk **Light Up Dubai** 2-9-2 0........................ WilliamBuick 6 64+
(Charlie Appleby) *hld up in tch in midfield on outer: 5th and outpcd over 2f out: no threat to ldrs after: wnt 4th and bmpd ent fnl f: kpt on* **7/1**[3]

5 ¾ **Quality Seeker (USA)** 2-9-2 0........................................ LiamKeniry 10 62+
(Ed Walker) *dwlt and pushed along leaving stalls: hld up in midfield but nvr on terms w ldrs: pushed along 3f out: hdwy to pass btn horses ins fnl f: n.d* **33/1**

6 ¾ **Jamih** 2-9-2 0........................................ NickyMackay 2 60+
(John Gosden) *s.i.s: rn green in last pair: reminders over 4f out: rdn and hdwy to pass btn horses over 1f out: no imp fnl f: nvr trbld ldrs* **14/1**

7 1 ¼ **Flag Festival** 2-9-2 0........................................ MartinLane 12 57+
(Charlie Appleby) *hld up in midfield on outer: outpcd over 2f out: rdn and no hdwy over 1f out: wl btn after* **14/1**

8 1 ½ **Whitlock** 2-9-2 0........................................ RobertHavlin 7 54+
(John Gosden) *s.i.s and pushed along leaving stalls: off the pce in last pair: rdn and sme hdwy on inner over 1f out: no imp 1f out: nvr trbld ldrs* **4/1[2]**

6 9 1 ½ **Wild West Hero**[15] 8352 2-9-2 0........................................ TedDurcan 9 50
(Sir Michael Stoute) *s.i.s: pushed along leaving stalls: off the pce in last trio: pushed along on inner over 1f out: nvr trbld ldrs* **50/1**

050 10 7 **Praeceps (IRE)**[6] 8553 2-9-2 0........................................ LukeMorris 3 33
(Sir Mark Prescott Bt) *in tch in midfield: rdn over 2f out: sn struggling and btn: wl bhd and eased ins fnl f* **100/1**

00 11 2 **Tiger Lyon (USA)**[22] 8149 2-9-2 0........................................(h) RobertWinston 1 29
(John Butler) *taken down early: t.k.h: led tl over 2f out: lost pl over 1f out and edgd rt: fdd and wl bhd whn eased towards fin* **100/1**

1m 38.56s (-1.34) **Going Correction** -0.225s/f (Stan) 11 Ran SP% **123.9**
Speed ratings (Par 96): **97,92,86,86,85 84,83,81,80,73 71**
CSF £10.39 TOTE £5.60: £1.80, £1.10, £3.70; EX 11.60 Trifecta £93.00.
**Owner** Phoenix Thoroughbred Limited **Bred** Epic Thoroughbreds Llc **Trained** Newmarket, Suffolk

**FOCUS**
A fair juvenile novice contest. They went a respectable gallop and one of the main form horses won decisively. It's looked an advantage to be prominent.

## 8704 WEATHERBYS GLOBAL STALLIONS APP NOVICE STKS (PLUS 10 RACE) 1m 2f (P)
6:45 (6:46) (Class 4) 2-Y-O £7,115 (£2,117; £1,058; £529) Stalls Low

Form RPR

1 **Photographer** 2-9-2 0........................................ RobertHavlin 1 84+
(John Gosden) *t.k.h: led on suffernce for over 1f: trckd ldrs after: effrt on inner and rdn to ld jst over 1f out: r.o wl ins fnl f: rdn out* **7/4[1]**

2 1 ¼ **Silverbook** 2-9-2 0........................................ WilliamBuick 2 81+
(Charlie Appleby) *hld up in tch in last pair: swtchd rt bnd 2f out: swtchd bk lft and clsd to chse ldrs but nt clr run over 1f out: swtchd rt and chsd ldr jst ins fnl f: r.o u.p but hld by wnr* **3/1[2]**

5 3 2 ¼ **Supernova**[33] 7813 2-9-2 0........................................ JamieSpencer 4 77
(David Simcock) *hld up in tch in last pair: swtchd rt and effrt over 1f out: drvn ent fnl f: styd on same pce: snatched 3rd nr fin* **7/2[3]**

4 nk **Ulster (IRE)** 2-9-2 0........................................ DanielTudhope 3 76
(Saeed bin Suroor) *hld up in tch: effrt to press ldrs 2f out: unable qck ent fnl f: kpt on same pce ins fnl f* **7/1**

0622 5 nk **Making Miracles**[15] 8353 2-9-2 82........................................ PJMcDonald 5 76
(Mark Johnston) *led over 8f out: rdn over 2f out: hdd over 1f out: no ex u.p and lost 2nd jst ins fnl f: styd on same pce ins fnl f: lost 2 pls nr fin* **7/1**

6 4 **Smart Champion** 2-9-2 0........................................ OisinMurphy 6 68
(Simon Crisford) *chsd ldr over 8f out: rdn and ev ch over 2f out: unable qck: lost pl and short of room over 1f out: wknd ins fnl f* **16/1**

2m 8.43s (-0.17) **Going Correction** -0.225s/f (Stan) 6 Ran SP% **114.5**
Speed ratings (Par 98): **91,90,88,87,87 84**
CSF £7.48 TOTE £2.60: £2.10, £1.80; EX 8.40 Trifecta £26.70.
**Owner** Denford Stud **Bred** Denford Stud Ltd **Trained** Newmarket, Suffolk

**FOCUS**
A decent staying juvenile novice contest. They went a modest gallop but, over a stern test for these young horses, the cream still rose to the top.

## 8705 BET TOTEEXACTA AT BETFRED.COM H'CAP 1m 2f (P)
7:15 (7:17) (Class 2) (0-105,102) 3-Y£14,971 (£3,583; £1,791; £896; £446) Stalls Low

Form RPR

6136 1 **Plutonian (IRE)**[26] 8032 3-8-9 **90**........................................ PJMcDonald 1 96
(Charles Hills) *chsd ldr: rdn and ev ch 2f out: drvn to ld 1f out: hld on wl u.p fnl 100yds: gamely* **12/1**

0043 2 hd **Pactolus (IRE)**[40] 7602 6-9-3 **95**........................................(t) OisinMurphy 6 100
(Stuart Williams) *chsd ldrs: effrt over 1f out: styd on u.p and ev ch 100yds out: hld towards fin* **12/1**

1-1 3 ½ **Middle Kingdom (USA)**[204] 1886 3-8-13 **94**...............(t[1]) RobertHavlin 3 99+
(John Gosden) *dwlt: sn in tch in midfield: wnt 3rd 6f out: nt clr run on inner and swtchd rt over 1f out: gap opened and squeezed through to chse wnr jst ins fnl f: ev ch 100yds out: unable qck towards fin* **11/10[1]**

2553 4 1 **Rainbow Rebel (IRE)**[12] 8414 4-8-10 **88**........................................ JoeFanning 5 90
(Mark Johnston) *hld up in tch in rr: swtchd rt and effrt 2f out: hdwy u.p to chse ldrs ins fnl f: edgd lft and no imp fnl 100yds* **14/1**

3254 5 2 ¾ **Ickymasho**[28] 7988 5-9-5 **97**........................................ RichardKingscote 2 94
(Jonathan Portman) *led: rdn ent fnl 2f: hdd over 1f out and unable qck: wknd ins fnl f* **10/1[3]**

0201 6 ¾ **Petite Jack**[40] 7602 4-9-10 **102**........................................(p) JackMitchell 4 97
(Archie Watson) *hld up in tch towards rr: clsd and nt clr run over 1f out: rdr trying to switch rt but horse hanging lft 1f out: stl hanging and no imp fnl f* **9/4[2]**

0005 7 nk **Tha'ir (IRE)**[16] 8315 7-8-7 **85**........................................(h) LukeMorris 7 79
(Michael Appleby) *hld up in tch in midfield: effrt over 2f out: unable qck u.p over 1f out: wl hld and one pce fnl f* **33/1**

2m 4.85s (-3.75) **Going Correction** -0.225s/f (Stan)
**WFA** 3 from 4yo+ 3lb 7 Ran SP% **112.5**
Speed ratings (Par 109): **106,105,105,104,102 101,101**
CSF £133.13 TOTE £15.40: £5.20, £3.70; EX 95.10 Trifecta £373.10.
**Owner** Mrs Fitri Hay **Bred** Pier House Stud **Trained** Lambourn, Berks

**FOCUS**
A good handicap. It paid to race prominently off a controlled, even gallop.

## 8706 BET TOTETRIFECTA AT BETFRED.COM H'CAP 7f (P)
7:45 (7:47) (Class 4) (0-85,86) 3-Y-O+ £6,469 (£1,925; £962; £481) Stalls Low

Form RPR

0042 1 **Pearl Spectre (USA)**[18] 8257 6-9-0 **85**........................................ NicolaCurrie(7) 10 92
(Phil McEntee) *chsd ldr tl led over 2f out: rdn and clr over 1f out: 3 l clr 1f out: all out but a jst lasting home towards fin* **8/1**

5313 2 nk **Miracle Garden**[34] 7789 5-8-12 **76**........................................(b) StevieDonohoe 9 82
(Ian Williams) *hld up in midfield: switching rt and hdwy over 1f out: hdwy to chse ldrs ins fnl f: r.o strly fnl 100yds: wnt 2nd nr fin: nt quite rch wnr* **7/1[3]**

0454 3 ¾ **Summer Icon**[31] 7901 4-9-5 **86**........................................ CallumShepherd(3) 7 90
(Mick Channon) *dwlt: hld up in last quartet: c wd and hdwy u.p over 1f out: styd on strly ins fnl f: snatched 3rd last strides: nvr quite getting to wnr* **8/1**

0040 4 hd **Hammer Gun (USA)**[9] 8486 4-9-2 **80**........................................(v) PatrickMathers 1 84
(Derek Shaw) *pushed along leaving stalls: in tch in midfield: swtchd rt and effrt 2f out: hdwy u.p to chse clr wnr 1f out: styd on ins fnl f: nvr quite getting to wnr and lost 2 pls nr fin* **16/1**

6600 5 1 ½ **Outer Space**[15] 8344 6-9-4 **82**........................................ DougieCostello 12 82
(Jamie Osborne) *stdd and swtchd lft after s: hld up in last pair: clsd and swtchd rt over 1f out: sn rdn and hdwy to chse ldrs 1f out: kpt on: nt rch wnr* **14/1**

0003 6 hd **Call Out Loud**[20] 8216 5-9-3 **81**........................................ AlistairRawlinson 13 80
(Michael Appleby) *awkward and wnt rt leaving stalls: slowly away: sn pushed along in last pair: hdwy over 1f out: swtchd lft 1f out: kpt on ins fnl f: nt rch ldrs* **50/1**

5303 7 2 ½ **Tadaany (IRE)**[14] 8375 5-8-9 **73**........................................ JamesSullivan 2 65
(Ruth Carr) *trckd ldrs on inner: effrt to chse wnr wl over 1f out but sn unable to match pce of wnr: lost 2nd 1f out: wknd ins fnl f* **10/1**

2100 8 2 ½ **Kenstone (FR)**[26] 8032 4-9-3 **86**........................................(p) FinleyMarsh(5) 14 72
(Adrian Wintle) *hld up in tch in midfield: swtchd rt and effrt over 1f out: no imp and wl hld fnl f* **25/1**

4120 9 2 ¼ **Rouge Nuage (IRE)**[34] 7789 7-8-13 **77**........................................ JimmyQuinn 5 56
(Conrad Allen) *hld up in tch in midfield: effrt and sltly impeded over 1f out: no imp and wl hld fnl f* **25/1**

-053 10 1 **Tropical Rock**[16] 8310 3-9-4 **83**........................................ RichardKingscote 3 59
(Ralph Beckett) *wl in tch in midfield: rdn over 3f out: unable qck and btn over 1f out: wknd ins fnl f* **7/2[1]**

1144 11 3 ¼ **Lunar Deity**[24] 8126 8-9-5 **83**........................................(t) OisinMurphy 8 51
(Stuart Williams) *a towards rr: n.d* **20/1**

0030 12 3 ¼ **Tai Sing Yeh (IRE)**[29] 7947 3-8-12 **77**........................................(t) DavidProbert 6 35
(Charles Hills) *chsd ldrs: rdn over 2f out: sn struggling and lost pl over 1f out: bhd and eased wl ins fnl f* **14/1**

0300 13 3 ½ **Firmdecisions (IRE)**[5] 8600 7-9-5 **86**........................................ JackDuern(3) 11 36
(Dean Ivory) *midfield on outer: hdwy to chse ldrs 4f out: rdn and wnt 2nd 2f out: sn lost pl and wknd over 1f out: bhd and eased ins fnl f* **8/1**

0362 14 4 ½ **Midnight Macchiato (IRE)**[14] 8375 4-8-13 **77**........................................ SeanLevey 4 15
(David Brown) *led tl over 2f out: sn struggling u.p and lost pl over 1f out: bhd and eased ins fnl f* **5/1[2]**

1m 24.73s (-2.47) **Going Correction** -0.225s/f (Stan)
**WFA** 3 from 4yo+ 1lb 14 Ran SP% **127.4**
Speed ratings (Par 105): **105,104,103,103,101 101,98,95,93,92 88,84,80,75**
CSF £64.28 CT £480.84 TOTE £9.80: £3.40, £2.60, £3.70; EX 92.10 Trifecta £1234.10.
**Owner** Steve Jakes **Bred** Estate Of Edward P Evans **Trained** Newmarket, Suffolk

**FOCUS**
A decent handicap. The winner bravely saw off his opponents fom a poor draw in the quickest comparative time on the night.

## 8707 SAMARITANS, CAN I HELP YOU? MAIDEN FILLIES' STKS 7f (P)
8:15 (8:17) (Class 5) 3-Y-O+ £5,175 (£1,540; £769; £384) Stalls Low

Form RPR

-324 1 **Ifubelieveindreams (IRE)**[21] 8192 3-9-0 75........................................ SeanLevey 1 82
(Ismail Mohammed) *hld up in tch: trck ldrs 4f out: swtchd rt and clsd to chal over 1f out: rdn to ld 1f out: sn qcknd clr u.p: comf* **13/8[2]**

42 2 3 **Domitilla**[8] 8504 3-9-0 0........................................ RyanTate 2 74
(Marco Botti) *t.k.h: chsd ldr tl over 5f out: styd trcking ldrs: swtchd rt and effrt to chal between horses jst over 1f out: chsd wnr but nvr matching her pce ins fnl f: kpt on for clr 2nd* **5/6[1]**

255 3 3 ½ **Manaahil**[40] 7600 3-9-0 72........................................ DavidProbert 4 64
(Charles Hills) *t.k.h: chsd ldrs tl wnt 2nd over 5f out: led and rdn over 1f out: hdd and immediately outpcd 1f out: wknd ins fnl f* **6/1[3]**

2420 4 4 **Greenview Paradise (IRE)**[31] 7902 3-9-0 62........................................ LukeMorris 6 54
(Brian Barr) *led tl rdn and hdd over 1f out: sn outpcd and btn 1f out: wknd ins fnl f* **20/1**

046 5 6 **Spike's Princess (IRE)**[89] 5946 3-8-7 50........................................ JackOsborn(7) 8 37
(Brian Barr) *s.i.s: in tch in rr: rdn and effrt on outer over 2f out: sn outpcd and wl btn over 1f out: no ch whn swtchd rt wl ins fnl f* **100/1**

5000 6 nk **Moving Robe (IRE)**[13] 8386 4-8-8 42........................................(t[1]) NicolaCurrie(7) 7 38
(Conrad Allen) *in tch: rdn over 2f out: sn struggling and outpcd: wl hld over 1f out* **100/1**

0-60 7 2 ½ **Like Minds**[13] 8395 3-8-9 43........................................ FinleyMarsh(5) 3 30
(David Brown) *in tch in midfield: effrt in 5th over 2f out: sn struggling and wknd over 1f out* **100/1**

1m 25.61s (-1.59) **Going Correction** -0.225s/f (Stan)
**WFA** 3 from 4yo 1lb 7 Ran SP% **114.7**
Speed ratings (Par 100): **100,96,92,88,81 80,77**
CSF £3.34 TOTE £3.20: £1.70, £1.10; EX 3.50 Trifecta £6.20.
**Owner** Ismail Mohammed **Bred** Deer Forest Stud **Trained** Newmarket, Suffolk

**FOCUS**
An ordinary fillies' maiden. They went a modest gallop but the second favourite readily defeated the free-going favourite.
T/Plt: £276.00 to a £1 stake. Pool: £107,525.87 - 284.32 winning units T/Qpdt: £63.50 to a £1 stake. Pool: £11,648.14 - 135.70 winning units **Steve Payne**

8708 - 8709a (Foreign Racing) - See Raceform Interactive

# 1373 MEYDAN (L-H)
Thursday, November 9

**OFFICIAL GOING: Dirt: fast**

## 8710a EMIRATES HOLIDAYS (MAIDEN) (DIRT) 7f (D)
3:40 (3:40) 2-Y-O+ £19,823 (£6,607; £3,634; £1,982; £991)

RPR

1 **Rothenburg (USA)** 3-9-5........................................(bt) PatCosgrave 14 78
(H Al Alawi, UAE) *tracked ldr, wide, rdn 3f out, ran on wl fnl 1 1/2f, led fnl 50m* **9/2[2]**

2 1 ¼ **Street Of Dreams**[494] 3919 4-9-6........................................ SamHitchcott 3 76
(Doug Watson, UAE) *mid-division, ran on very wl fnl 1 1/2f, nrst finish* **8/1**

3 nk **Loures (IRE)**[797] 6051 4-9-6........................................(h) FernandoJara 7 75
(Maria Ritchie, UAE) *soon led, rdn 3f out, ran on but hdd fnl 50m* **20/1**

4 6 ¼ **Chess Master (IRE)**[545] 2207 4-9-0........................................(t) JoshQuinn(6) 6 58
(A bin Harmash, UAE) *mid-division, ran on fnl 2f but nvr able to challenge* **14/1**

5 3 3/4 **Russian Miner (USA)** 3-9-5 ........................................ PatDobbs 9 47
(Doug Watson, UAE) *slowly into strd, nvr able to chal but ran on fnl 2f* 11/2[3]
6 3/4 **Desert Mountain (IRE)**[104] 5365 2-8-7 ........................ AntonioFresu 11 51
(Saeed bin Suroor) *always mid-division* 4/1[1]
7 nk **Al Boraq (USA)**[357] 8000 3-8-13 ..................................(b) SeanDavis(6) 8 44
(S Seemar, UAE) *tracked ldr til wknd fnl 2 1/2f* 11/1
8 3 **A G Cohiba (USA)**[224] 3-9-1 ...............................(v) RoystonFfrench 13 32
(H Al Alawi, UAE) *tracked ldr til wknd fnl 2 1/2f* 33/1
9 1/2 **King's Shadow (USA)**[394] 7239 3-9-5 .........................(b) AdriedeVries 2 35
(S Seemar, UAE) *slowly into strd, nvr nr to challenge* 12/1
10 2 **Quartier Francais (USA)** 3-9-5 ..........................................(b) TadhgO'Shea 10 30
(A R Al Rayhi, UAE) *tracked ldr til wknd fnl 3 1/2f* 15/2
11 3/4 **Cherkes Pharoah (USA)** 3-9-5 ...........................................(vt) PaoloSirigu 1 27
(A R Al Rayhi, UAE) *slowly into strd, nvr nr to challenge* 25/1
12 1 **Rostam (IRE)** 3-9-5 .............................................................(e) TomMarquand 5 25
(Daniel J Murphy, UAE) *broke awkwardly, al in rear* 33/1
13 1/2 **Voice Of The North (USA)**[251] 1020 3-9-5 ..........(bt) GeorgeBuckell 12 23
(S Seemar, UAE) *never nr to challenge* 25/1
14 26 **Forever Song**[148] 3720 3-9-5 ......................................(p) ConnorBeasley 4
(A bin Harmash, UAE) *never better than mid-division* 12/1
1m 25.69s (0.59) 14 Ran SP% 125.2
CSF: 39.37.
**Owner** Byerley Team **Bred** Keene Ridge Racing Llc & Darley **Trained** United Arab Emirates

## 8711a EMIRATES A380 (H'CAP) (DIRT) 1m (D)
4:15 (4:15) (60-75,75) 3-Y-O+ £19,823 (£6,607; £3,634; £1,982; £991)

RPR
1 **Naaeebb (USA)**[62] 6899 3-9-2 72 ...................................... PatCosgrave 13 80
(Saeed bin Suroor) *mid-division, smooth prog 3 1/2f out, led 2f out, ran on well* 11/2[1]
2 1 1/4 **Conquerant**[236] 6-9-6 74 ...................................................(p) AdriedeVries 7 79
(Ismail Mohammed) *mid-division, ran on fnl 1 1/2f, nrst finish* 7/1
3 2 **Ballad Singer**[221] 4-8-5 60 ..........................................(v) SamHitchcott 11 60
(Doug Watson, UAE) *tracked ldr, ran on same pace fnl 2f* 12/1
4 1 1/4 **Sky Jockey**[221] 6-8-8 69 ...........................................(tp) SeanDavis(7) 10 67
(S Seemar, UAE) *rear of mid-division, ran on fnl 2f but nvr able to challenge* 6/1[2]
5 1 **Right Flank (USA)**[156] 3-9-5 75 ...................................... PatDobbs 8 70
(Doug Watson, UAE) *slowly into strd, mid-division, hmpd 4f out, nvr nr to chal but ran on fnl 2f* 13/2[3]
6 3 3/4 **Emirates Airline**[237] 1255 5-9-2 70 ..............................(b) PaoloSirigu 12 57
(E Charpy, UAE) *tracked leaders til outpcd 3f out* 33/1
7 nk **Hello (IRE)**[6] 8579 4-8-7 65 ow3 ..................................(v) JoshQuinn(6) 2 53
(A R Al Rayhi, UAE) *slowly into strd, nvr nr to challenge* 25/1
8 1/2 **Mears (USA)**[187] 3-9-4 74 .............................................. TadhgO'Shea 3 59
(A R Al Rayhi, UAE) *tracked leaders til wknd fnl 2f* 11/2[1]
9 1 1/4 **Heraldic (USA)**[237] 1250 4-9-5 73 ..............................(bt) RichardMullen 1 55
(S Seemar, UAE) *tracked leaders til wknd fnl 2 1/2f* 15/2
10 1 1/4 **Muqaatil (USA)**[6] 8580 3-9-3 73 ...............................(vt) ConnorBeasley 4 52
(A bin Harmash, UAE) *never better than mid-division* 14/1
11 1 3/4 **Moosir (USA)**[245] 1116 7-9-4 72 .......................................(v) JimCrowley 6 47
(Doug Watson, UAE) *soon led, hdd 2f out, wknd fnl 1 1/2f* 15/2
12 3 **Pinter**[221] 5-9-1 69 ................................................... AntonioFresu 14 37
(E Charpy, UAE) *never better than mid-division* 50/1
13 9 3/4 **Royal History**[237] 1255 6-9-1 69 ...............................(b) IoannisPoullis 9 15
(A Al Shamsi, UAE) *slowly into strd, al in rear* 20/1
14 1/2 **New Signal**[6] 8584 4-9-2 70 .......................................(t) XavierZiani 5 15
(S bin Ghadayer, UAE) *slowly into strd, al in rear* 20/1
1m 41.29s (3.79)
**WFA** 3 from 4yo+ 2lb 14 Ran SP% 127.0
CSF: 43.14; TRICAST: 474.35.
**Owner** Godolphin **Bred** Darley **Trained** Newmarket, Suffolk

8712-8713a - (Foreign Racing) - See Raceform Interactive

## 8714a EMIRATES SKYWARDS (H'CAP) (DIRT) 1m (D)
6:00 (6:00) (80-94,94) 3-Y-O+ £23,127 (£7,709; £4,240; £2,312; £1,156)

RPR
1 **Galvanize (USA)**[237] 1253 4-8-8 83 ................................ FernandoJara 1 94
(Doug Watson, UAE) *soon led, kicked clr 2 1/2f out, ran on well* 12/1
2 1 1/4 **Munaaser**[237] 1253 6-9-1 89 ............................................(t) JimCrowley 5 98
(A R Al Rayhi, UAE) *rear of mid-division, ran on wl fnl 1 1/2f, nrst finish* 11/2[2]
3 2 1/2 **Thegreatcollection (USA)**[250] 1040 3-9-4 94 .........(bt) SamHitchcott 11 97
(Doug Watson, UAE) *chased leaders, ev ch 2 1/2f out, ran on same pace fnl 1 1/2f* 20/1
4 1 1/2 **Nolohay (IRE)**[245] 1119 6-9-3 91 ......................................(v) PatDobbs 3 91
(Doug Watson, UAE) *never nr to chal but ran on wl fnl 2f* 8/1
5 nse **Direct Message (USA)**[209] 4-8-13 87 ..............................(t) TadhgO'Shea 8 87
(A R Al Rayhi, UAE) *chased ldr, ran on same pace fnl 2 1/2f* 14/1
6 13 **Active Spirit (IRE)**[245] 1119 6-9-0 94 ..........................(vt) JoshQuinn(6) 9 64
(Doug Watson, UAE) *tracked leaders til wknd 2 1/2f out* 8/1
7 16 **Philosopher (IRE)**[257] 939 5-8-13 87 ........................(b) RoystonFfrench 2 20
(S bin Ghadayer, UAE) *slowly into strd, never better than mid-division* 8/1
8 2 3/4 **Dowayla (IRE)**[33] 7815 3-9-1 91 ...................................... PatCosgrave 12 18
(Saeed bin Suroor) *never better than mid-division* 5/1[1]
9 2 1/4 **Secret Ambition**[237] 1251 4-8-10 85 .............................(t) RichardMullen 4 6
(S Seemar, UAE) *slowly into strd, nvr able to challenge* 6/1[3]
10 21 **Mubajal**[166] 3065 4-8-7 82 ...........................................(v) ConnorBeasley 10
(A bin Harmash, UAE) *always in rear* 25/1
11 3 **Spiritous (USA)**[400] 7073 3-8-7 84 ...................................... AntonioFresu 6
(E Charpy, UAE) *slowly into strd, al in rear* 40/1
12 12 1/2 **Bochart**[237] 1251 4-9-1 89 ............................................(t) AdriedeVries 7
(S Seemar, UAE) *tracked ldr til wknd 3 1/2f out* 7/1
P **James Lane (USA)**[187] 4-9-1 89 ...................................... XavierZiani 13
(S bin Ghadayer, UAE) *pulled up aftr 1f* 20/1
1m 38.58s (1.08)
**WFA** 3 from 4yo+ 2lb 13 Ran SP% 122.3
CSF: 74.96; TRICAST: 1379.81.
**Owner** Abdulmohsen Al Abdulkareem **Bred** Flaxman Holdings Limited **Trained** United Arab Emirates

# 8585 NEWCASTLE (A.W) (L-H)

Friday, November 10

**OFFICIAL GOING: Tapeta: standard**
Wind: light half against Weather: fine

## 8715 32RED CASINO NOVICE AUCTION STKS 7f 14y (Tp)
5:45 (5:45) (Class 6) 2-Y-O £2,264 (£673; £336; £168) Stalls Centre

Form RPR
06 1 **Blue Harmony**[20] 8235 2-8-9 0 ........................................ BenCurtis 6 65
(K R Burke) *hld up: pushed along and hdwy 3f out: rdn to chse ldr 2f out: chal fnl f: led 110yds out: kpt on* 66/1
50 2 3/4 **Sioux Frontier (IRE)**[18] 8288 2-8-13 0 ........................ TonyHamilton 9 67
(Richard Fahey) *hld up: pushed along over 2f out: rdn and kpt on wl fr over 1f out: wnt 2nd nr fin* 10/1
361 3 nk **Harbour Vision**[43] 7535 2-9-7 75 ............................ JosephineGordon 7 74
(David Brown) *led: rdn over 2f out: drvn and strly pressed fnl f: hdd 110yds out: one pce: lost 2nd nr fin* 7/1
4 10 **Maricruz (IRE)**[28] 8016 2-8-8 0 ........................................ PaulHanagan 2 34
(John C McConnell, Ire) *hld up: rdn and hdwy over 2f out: wknd over 1f out* 10/1
5 5 2 **Destinata**[38] 7707 2-8-5 0 ...............................................(t[1]) GeorgeWood(3) 4 29
(James Fanshawe) *hld up in tch: racd keenly: rdn over 2f out: wknd over 1f out* 3/1[2]
6 6 shd **Yamuna River**[105] 5372 2-8-11 0 ........................................ LukeMorris 5 31
(James Tate) *dwlt: sn trckd ldrs: rdn 3f out: wknd over 1f out* 4/1[3]
3610 7 nse **Bungee Jump (IRE)**[48] 7384 2-9-3 75 ................................ KevinStott 8 37
(Kevin Ryan) *prom: rdn over 2f out: wknd over 1f out* 2/1[1]
06 8 16 **Swiss Marlin**[48] 7383 2-8-9 0 ............................................ JasonHart 1
(John Quinn) *in tch: rdn over 2f out: wknd and bhd* 50/1
00 9 38 **Laharna (IRE)**[11] 8474 2-8-6 0 ........................................ PhilDennis(3) 3
(Noel Wilson) *prom: rdn 3f out: wknd qckly and t.o* 200/1
1m 27.17s (0.97) **Going Correction** +0.15s/f (Slow) 9 Ran SP% 113.0
Speed ratings (Par 94): **100,99,98,87,85 84,84,66,23**
CSF £609.37 TOTE £28.80: £10.50, £2.60, £1.80; EX 559.00 Trifecta £2514.40.
**Owner** Middleham Park Racing Lxviii & Mrs Burke **Bred** Hillwood Thoroughbred Breeding Ltd **Trained** Middleham Moor, N Yorks

**FOCUS**
The going was standard. Stalls - All races: centre. An ordinary novice auction race which produced a shock winner, who improved significantly but likely didn't achieve much in doing do.

## 8716 32REDSPORT.COM MAIDEN FILLIES' STKS 6f (Tp)
6:15 (6:21) (Class 5) 3-Y-O+ £3,072 (£914; £456; £228) Stalls Centre

Form RPR
36 1 **Evies Wish (IRE)**[7] 8572 3-9-0 62 ...................................... PaulHanagan 7 69
(John C McConnell, Ire) *trckd ldrs: pushed along to ld wl over 1f out: rdn and kpt on wl to draw clr* 6/4[1]
0626 2 7 **Dream Revival**[8] 8543 4-9-0 50 ........................................(p) PJMcDonald 8 47
(Paul Collins) *hld up: rdn 2f out: kpt on to go 2nd ins fnl f: no ch w wnr* 6/1
2545 3 3/4 **Charleston Belle**[56] 7122 3-9-0 62 ....................................(b[1]) KevinStott 4 44
(Giles Bravery) *in tch: rdn 2f out: edgd lft appr fnl f: kpt on same pce* 11/4[2]
/040 4 1 1/2 **Encoded (IRE)**[7] 8559 4-9-0 48 ........................................ BarryMcHugh 1 39
(Lynn Siddall) *trckd ldrs: racd keenly: rdn 2f out: wknd ins fnl f* 66/1
4004 5 3 1/4 **Undiscovered Angel (FR)**[46] 7459 3-8-7 63 .......... PatrickO'Hanlon(7) 5 29
(K R Burke) *prom: rdn 2f out: wknd fnl f* 9/2[3]
06 6 6 **Port Soif**[7] 8554 3-9-0 0 .................................................. DanielTudhope 6 10
(David O'Meara) *led: rdn whn hdd wl over 1f out: wknd fnl f* 20/1
7 1 **Dream Destroyer (IRE)** 3-9-0 0 ........................................ SamJames 2 7
(Geoffrey Harker) *dwlt: a in rr* 50/1
1m 12.28s (-0.22) **Going Correction** +0.15s/f (Slow) 7 Ran SP% 107.3
Speed ratings (Par 100): **107,97,96,94,90 82,81**
CSF £9.55 TOTE £1.90: £1.10, £3.00; EX 7.80 Trifecta £18.70.
**Owner** Ms Caroline Ahearn **Bred** Matt Duffy & Newtown Stud **Trained** Stamullen, Co Meath

**FOCUS**
Not the most competive of sprint maidens and the winner looked a class apart from her rivals. She built on her latest effort in Ireland.

## 8717 32RED.COM FILLIES' H'CAP 6f (Tp)
6:45 (6:45) (Class 4) (0-80,80) 3-Y-O+ £4,851 (£1,443; £721; £360) Stalls Centre

Form RPR
0064 1 **Tilly Trotter (IRE)**[31] 7939 3-9-6 79 ................................ DanielTudhope 5 86
(Declan Carroll) *prom: pushed along to ld wl over 1f out: sn rdn: strly pressed fnl 110yds: hld on all out* 4/1[3]
1152 2 nse **Nuns Walk**[7] 8552 3-8-7 66 ............................................ DuranFentiman 7 73
(Tim Easterby) *trckd ldrs: rdn over 1f out: chal strly fnl 110yds: kpt on* 11/4[1]
1212 3 1 **Economic Crisis (IRE)**[10] 8488 8-9-0 73 ......................... JamesSullivan 8 77
(Alan Berry) *hld up: rdn and hdwy over 1f out: kpt on fnl f* 40/1
1134 4 1 3/4 **Penny Pot Lane**[20] 8240 4-9-1 77 ..................................... LewisEdmunds(3) 1 75
(Richard Whitaker) *led: rdn whn hdd wl over 1f out: no ex fnl 110yds* 8/1
1140 5 1 1/2 **Veena (FR)**[167] 3080 4-9-5 78 ............................................ LukeMorris 4 71
(David Simcock) *hld up: rdn 2f out: one pce and nvr threatened* 9/1
1-30 6 1/2 **Cashla Bay**[146] 3822 3-9-7 80 ..........................................(t[1]) RobertHavlin 2 72
(John Gosden) *hld up in tch: rdn 2f out: edgd lft and no imp* 5/1
2500 7 2 3/4 **French**[116] 4979 4-8-4 63 ...............................................(p) CamHardie 3 46
(Antony Brittain) *trckd ldrs: rdn over 2f out: wknd over 1f out* 28/1
5061 8 18 **Fruit Salad**[17] 8320 4-9-4 77 ......................................(p) JosephineGordon 6 2
(James Bethell) *dwlt: racd alone stands' side: hld up: rdn over 3f out: sn wknd and bhd* 7/2[2]
1m 12.49s (-0.01) **Going Correction** +0.15s/f (Slow) 8 Ran SP% 112.6
Speed ratings (Par 102): **106,105,104,102,100 99,95,71**
CSF £14.91 CT £369.62 TOTE £5.30: £1.60, £1.30, £6.10; EX 16.90 Trifecta £359.50.
**Owner** F Gillespie **Bred** James Hughes **Trained** Malton, N Yorks

**FOCUS**
A competitive sprint which produced a thrilling finish and gutsy winner. This was her best run in Britain.

## 8718 SUNBETS.CO.UK H'CAP — 1m 5y (Tp)
7:15 (7:16) (Class 4) (0-85,85) 3-Y-O+ £4,851 (£1,443; £721; £360) Stalls Centre

Form — RPR

3140 **1** **Pouvoir Magique (FR)**$^{14}$ 8385 3-9-5 **85**........................ RobertHavlin 5 93+
(John Gosden) *trckd ldrs: pushed along to ld 2f out: rdn clr appr fnl f: reduced advantage nr fin but nvr in danger* **5/2$^{2}$**

0553 **2** ¾ **Alexandrakollontai (IRE)**$^{16}$ 8351 7-9-4 **82**............(b) JamesSullivan 11 88
(Alistair Whillans) *hld up: pushed along and hdwy 2f out: wnt 2nd ins fnl f: kpt on wl* **10/1**

0626 **3** ¾ **Testa Rossa (IRE)**$^{31}$ 7941 7-8-8 **79**......................(b) SeanMooney$^{(7)}$ 12 83
(Jim Goldie) *hld up: rdn and hdwy over 1f out: kpt on wl fnl f* **14/1**

040- **4** 2 ¼ **Edgar Balthazar**$^{361}$ 7958 5-9-6 **84**................................(p) PhillipMakin 4 83
(Keith Dalgleish) *midfield: rdn and hdwy to chse ldrs over 2f out: one pce ins fnl f* **33/1**

2 **5** ½ **Waarif (IRE)**$^{31}$ 7941 4-9-2 **80**.......................................(t) DanielTudhope 7 78
(David O'Meara) *s.i.s: hld up: angled lft and hdwy 3f out: drvn to chse ldr over 1f out: no ex ins fnl f* **9/4$^{1}$**

0010 **6** hd **Zabeel Star (IRE)**$^{17}$ 8315 5-8-10 **74**.............................. BarryMcHugh 2 71
(Karen McLintock) *dwlt: hld up: pushed along and sme hdwy over 1f out: kpt on ins fnl f* **22/1**

0540 **7** 1 ¾ **My Amigo**$^{35}$ 7780 4-9-3 **81**..........................................(p) PJMcDonald 14 74
(K R Burke) *prom: led 3f out: rdn and hdd 2f out: wknd ins fnl f* **9/1$^{3}$**

6526 **8** 1 ¼ **Johnny Cavagin**$^{17}$ 8319 8-8-10 **77**......................(t) LewisEdmunds$^{(3)}$ 10 68
(Ronald Thompson) *half-rrd s and s.i.s: sn in midfield racing keenly: rdn over 2f out: nvr threatened* **20/1**

6250 **9** 1 ¼ **Prying Pandora (FR)**$^{14}$ 8390 4-9-0 **78**.......................... PaulHanagan 6 66
(Richard Fahey) *trckd ldrs: rdn over 2f out: wknd ins fnl f* **12/1**

1520 **10** 5 **Espresso Freddo (IRE)**$^{19}$ 1945 3-9-0 **80**.....................(t$^{1}$) LukeMorris 3 56
(Robert Stephens) *hld up in midfield: rdn over 2f out: wknd fnl f* **40/1**

-000 **11** 8 **Planetaria (IRE)**$^{102}$ 5469 4-8-10 **74**.................................. JoeDoyle 13 32
(Julie Camacho) *trckd ldrs: rdn 3f out: wknd over 1f out* **22/1**

6- **12** 5 **Escape Clause (IRE)**$^{19}$ 8267 3-9-5 **85**................................ BenCurtis 1 31
(Grant Tuer) *slowly away: a in rr* **80/1**

0010 **13** 1 ½ **Muqarred (USA)**$^{17}$ 8315 5-8-10 **74**................................(p) JasonHart 8 17
(Roger Fell) *trckd ldrs: rdn over 3f out: sn wknd* **50/1**

3200 **14** 9 **Echo Of Lightning**$^{19}$ 8257 7-9-2 **80**..........................(p) TonyHamilton 9 2
(Roger Fell) *led: rdn whn hdd 3f out: sn wknd* **80/1**

1m 38.59s (-0.01) **Going Correction** +0.15s/f (Slow)
**WFA** 3 from 4yo+ 2lb — **14** Ran SP% **116.1**
Speed ratings (Par 105): **106,105,104,102,101 101,99,98,97,92 84,79,77,68**
CSF £23.83 CT £299.36 TOTE £3.70: £1.60, £3.10, £3.30; EX 31.50 Trifecta £270.10.
**Owner** HRH Princess Haya Of Jordan **Bred** Mme Elisabeth Vidal **Trained** Newmarket, Suffolk

**FOCUS**
A fair handicap which the winner grabbed by the scruff of the neck on his AW debut. Not the deepest of races.

## 8719 SUN BETS ON THE APP H'CAP (DIV I) — 1m 5y (Tp)
7:45 (7:47) (Class 6) (0-60,61) 3-Y-O+ £2,264 (£673; £336; £168) Stalls Centre

Form — RPR

0360 **1** **Little Jo**$^{32}$ 7895 3-8-7 **50**.............................................. BenRobinson$^{(5)}$ 5 56+
(Brian Ellison) *trckd ldrs: pushed along 3f out: drvn to ld narrowly over 1f out: kpt on* **6/1$^{3}$**

5430 **2** ¾ **Palindrome (USA)**$^{17}$ 8314 4-8-9 **45**............................ BarryMcHugh 8 49
(Marjorie Fife) *midfield: rdn and sme hdwy over 1f out: kpt on fnl f* **5/1$^{2}$**

2606 **3** shd **Lozah**$^{17}$ 8314 4-9-3 **53**................................................... TonyHamilton 10 57+
(Roger Fell) *dwlt: hld up: pushed along and hdwy 2f out: rdn appr fnl f: kpt on ins fnl f* **6/1$^{3}$**

1440 **4** ¾ **Thornaby Nash**$^{6}$ 8589 6-9-6 **56**................................(p) DanielTudhope 3 58
(Karen Tutty) *trckd ldrs: pushed along to chal over 1f out: rdn ins fnl f: no ex fnl 75yds* **5/1$^{2}$**

0610 **5** 5 **Mr Potter**$^{17}$ 8328 4-9-11 **61**............................................(e) PhillipMakin 11 51
(Richard Guest) *slowly away: hld up: hdwy 2f out: rdn over 1f out: wknd ins fnl f* **14/1**

0051 **6** 2 **Arrowzone**$^{20}$ 8249 6-9-7 **57**.......................................(b) DougieCostello 1 42
(Kevin Frost) *prom: racd keenly and led 6f out: rdn whn hdd over 2f out: wknd fnl f* **5/2$^{1}$**

400 **7** 1 ¾ **Pontecarlo Boy**$^{18}$ 8291 3-8-7 **45**....................................(b$^{1}$) CamHardie 4 26
(Richard Whitaker) *led: hdd 6f out: remained prom: rdn to ld again over 2f out: hdd over 1f out: wknd fnl f* **40/1**

5606 **8** 1 ¾ **Betty Grable (IRE)**$^{6}$ 8591 3-8-12 **57**............................ NicolaCurrie$^{(7)}$ 9 34
(Wilf Storey) *trckd ldrs: rdn 2f out: wknd over 1f out* **11/1**

0004 **9** 2 ¼ **Arizona Sunrise**$^{6}$ 8590 4-9-1 **51**.......................................... JoeDoyle 7 23
(Tina Jackson) *trckd ldrs: rdn 3f out: wknd over 1f out* **25/1**

0500 **10** nse **Nellie Deen (IRE)**$^{6}$ 8591 4-8-6 **45**..............................(h$^{1}$) PhilDennis$^{(3)}$ 6 16
(Simon West) *hld up in midfield: tk str hold: rdn over 2f out: sn wknd* **100/1**

000- **11** 11 **Rosie Hall (IRE)**$^{440}$ 5868 7-8-9 **45**............................(b) JamesSullivan 2
(John Wainwright) *hld up in midfield: rdn over 2f out: sn wknd* **200/1**

1m 41.04s (2.44) **Going Correction** +0.15s/f (Slow)
**WFA** 3 from 4yo+ 2lb — **11** Ran SP% **113.2**
Speed ratings (Par 101): **93,92,92,91,86 84,82,80,78,78 67**
CSF £34.12 CT £189.43 TOTE £6.50: £2.50, £2.20, £2.10; EX 36.20 Trifecta £201.40.
**Owner** Ian & Tom Pallas & The Mackem 2 **Bred** Sara Hattersley **Trained** Norton, N Yorks

**FOCUS**
An ordinary handicap run at a modest early gallop. The winner is unexposed on the AW and could go on from this, but this is limited form.

## 8720 SUN BETS ON THE APP H'CAP (DIV II) — 1m 5y (Tp)
8:15 (8:16) (Class 6) (0-60,60) 3-Y-O+ £2,264 (£673; £336; £168) Stalls Centre

Form — RPR

3003 **1** **Tifl**$^{11}$ 8470 4-9-1 **54**......................................................(bt) PJMcDonald 10 59
(Heather Main) *midfield: pushed along and hdwy over 2f out: rdn to chal ins fnl f: kpt on: led 30yds out* **11/1**

006 **2** nk **Street Poet (IRE)**$^{111}$ 5135 4-9-5 **58**............................ RobertWinston 1 62
(Michael Herrington) *trckd ldr: pushed along to ld 2f out: rdn and strly pressed fnl f: hdd 30yds out* **6/1$^{2}$**

6400 **3** ¾ **Supreme Power (IRE)**$^{6}$ 8589 3-9-5 **60**.....................(p$^{1}$) BarryMcHugh 6 62
(Tracy Waggott) *in tch: rdn 2f out: chal strly appr fnl f: one pce towards fin* **9/1**

0000 **4** hd **Cookie Ring (IRE)**$^{8}$ 8538 6-8-7 **46** oh1...........................(t) ShaneGray 8 48
(Kristin Stubbs) *s.i.s: hld up: hdwy 2f out: rdn to chse ldrs appr fnl f: kpt on* **7/1$^{3}$**

0600 **5** 3 **Nelson's Bay**$^{6}$ 8590 8-8-0 **46** oh1................................ NicolaCurrie$^{(7)}$ 3 40
(Wilf Storey) *s.i.s: hld up: rdn over 2f out: kpt on fnl f: nvr threatened* **33/1**

0110 **6** 1 ¼ **Born To Reason (IRE)**$^{3}$ 8662 3-9-2 **57**....................(b) DougieCostello 9 48
(Kevin Frost) *hld up: pushed along 2f out: rdn appr fnl f: nvr threatened* **2/1$^{1}$**

6054 **7** 1 ¾ **Urban Spirit (IRE)**$^{34}$ 7820 3-8-10 **51**............................ TonyHamilton 2 38
(Roger Fell) *midfield: rdn over 2f out: wknd over 1f out* **14/1**

4400 **8** 2 **Subotal (IRE)**$^{8}$ 8538 4-8-7 **46** oh1...............................(e$^{1}$) FrannyNorton 5 28
(Richard Guest) *midfield: rdn over 2f out: wknd over 1f out* **10/1**

0054 **9** 6 **Naupaka**$^{17}$ 8314 3-8-5 **46** oh1........................................ JoeyHaynes 7 14
(Brian Ellison) *in tch: rdn over 2f out: sn wknd* **6/1$^{2}$**

4204 **10** 2 ¼ **Cosmic Dust**$^{3}$ 8650 4-8-9 **51**...............................(b$^{1}$) LewisEdmunds$^{(3)}$ 4 14
(Richard Whitaker) *led: 4 l clr tl 4f out: rdn whn hdd 2f out: wknd* **25/1**

1m 40.89s (2.29) **Going Correction** +0.15s/f (Slow)
**WFA** 3 from 4yo+ 2lb — **10** Ran SP% **115.3**
Speed ratings (Par 101): **94,93,92,92,89 88,86,84,78,76**
CSF £74.71 CT £638.23 TOTE £11.00: £2.60, £3.00, £1.80; EX 104.90 Trifecta £792.40.
**Owner** Mrs Helen Adams & Mark Telfer **Bred** R F And S D Knipe **Trained** Kingston Lisle, Oxon
■ Stewards' Enquiry : Robert Winston two-day-ban; used whip above permitted level (Nov 24-25)

**FOCUS**
Only a modest handicap, but it produced a thriling finish and a determined winner. The third ran to this year's course form.

## 8721 BET & WATCH AT SUNBETS.CO.UK H'CAP — 7f 14y (Tp)
8:45 (8:47) (Class 6) (0-65,70) 3-Y-O+ £2,264 (£673; £336; £168) Stalls Centre

Form — RPR

2210 **1** **Honey Badger**$^{15}$ 8376 6-8-13 **61**...........................(p) GeorgeWood$^{(3)}$ 10 67
(Michael Herrington) *prom: rdn to ld 2f out: kpt on: hld on towards fin* **4/1$^{2}$**

0241 **2** nk **Gun Case**$^{6}$ 8590 5-9-6 **65** 6ex........................................(v) PhillipMakin 1 70
(Alistair Whillans) *hld up: pushed along and stl bit to do over 1f out: rdn and kpt on wl fnl f* **11/10$^{1}$**

3153 **3** ½ **Insurplus (IRE)**$^{7}$ 8552 4-8-10 **62**................................ SeanMooney$^{(7)}$ 8 66
(Jim Goldie) *hld up: pushed along and hdwy 2f out: sn chsd ldr: n.m.r on rail ins fnl f: swtchd lft and kpt on* **5/1$^{3}$**

2512 **4** 1 ¼ **My Girl Maisie (IRE)**$^{11}$ 8473 3-9-4 **64**.......................... FrannyNorton 3 63
(Richard Guest) *midfield on outer: pushed along and hdwy 2f out: rdn to chse ldr appr fnl f: no ex fnl 75yds* **10/1**

0330 **5** 3 ½ **Inshaa**$^{171}$ 2923 5-9-3 **62**........................................................(p) JasonHart 2 53
(Simon West) *midfield: racd keenly: pushed along over 2f out: n.m.r and lost pl over 1f out: kpt on ins fnl f* **33/1**

0330 **6** nk **Epeius (IRE)**$^{79}$ 6318 4-9-6 **65**........................................ GrahamLee 9 55
(Ben Haslam) *midfield: rdn to chse ldr over 1f out: wknd ins fnl f* **15/2**

2335 **7** 1 ¼ **Eddiebet**$^{22}$ 8193 3-9-5 **65**.............................................. DanielTudhope 5 51
(David O'Meara) *led narrowly: rdn whn hdd 2f out: wknd fnl f* **25/1**

6006 **8** 2 ¾ **Maldonado (FR)**$^{30}$ 7957 3-8-10 **63**........................... HarrisonShaw$^{(7)}$ 7 41
(Michael Easterby) *trckd ldrs: rdn over 2f out: wknd over 1f out* **14/1**

4410 **9** 17 **Night Shadow**$^{164}$ 3184 3-8-13 **62**............................... JoshDoyle$^{(3)}$ 4
(Alan Brown) *pressed ldr: rdn over 2f out: wknd* **66/1**

1m 27.3s (1.10) **Going Correction** +0.15s/f (Slow)
**WFA** 3 from 4yo+ 1lb — **9** Ran SP% **120.1**
Speed ratings (Par 101): **99,98,98,96,92 92,90,87,68**
CSF £9.05 CT £22.98 TOTE £5.30: £2.00, £1.10, £2.20; EX 12.30 Trifecta £44.60.
**Owner** Mrs Deborah Black **Bred** Mrs Deborah Black **Trained** Cold Kirby, N Yorks

**FOCUS**
Two in-form horses fought out the finish of this handicap so the form should stand up. The winner replicated his Chelmsford win.

## 8722 BETWAY CASINO H'CAP — 6f (Tp)
9:15 (9:17) (Class 5) (0-75,87) 3-Y-O+ £3,072 (£914; £456; £228) Stalls Centre

Form — RPR

0211 **1** **Lady Of The Lamp (IRE)**$^{7}$ 8552 3-8-9 **63**......................... LukeMorris 2 71+
(Rae Guest) *midfield: chsd ldrs over 2f out: rdn to ld appr fnl f: sn drvn: edgd rt: kpt on* **6/4$^{1}$**

0000 **2** ¾ **Ballymore Castle (IRE)**$^{10}$ 8489 5-9-7 **75**................(p) AndrewMullen 10 80
(Richard Fahey) *midfield: rdn and hdwy to chse ldr appr fnl f: kpt on* **20/1**

0045 **3** shd **Cosmic Chatter**$^{7}$ 8552 7-8-13 **67**...........................(p) JamesSullivan 8 72
(Ruth Carr) *led: rdn over 2f out: hdd appr fnl f: kpt on* **14/1**

0621 **4** ¾ **Major Crispies**$^{21}$ 8211 6-9-5 **73**...............................(b) DanielTudhope 7 76
(David O'Meara) *awkward s: hld up: sme hdwy and stl on bit over 1f out: pushed along appr fnl f: drvn ins fnl f: kpt on same pce* **3/1$^{2}$**

0002 **5** 1 **Samarmadi**$^{21}$ 8211 3-9-6 **74**.......................................(p) LouisSteward 6 73
(Hugo Palmer) *chsd ldrs: rdn over 2f out: one pce* **5/1$^{3}$**

2406 **6** ½ **Poppy In The Wind**$^{17}$ 8321 5-8-13 **70**........................(v) JoshDoyle$^{(3)}$ 9 68+
(Alan Brown) *dwlt: hld up: rdn over 2f out: hdwy over 1f out: one pce ins fnl f* **20/1**

3100 **7** ½ **Manatee Bay**$^{21}$ 8211 7-9-2 **70**.....................................(p) FrannyNorton 1 66
(Noel Wilson) *s.i.s: hld up: rdn 2f out: nvr threatened* **33/1**

0003 **8** hd **Start Time (IRE)**$^{9}$ 8512 4-9-4 **72**.................................... PhillipMakin 11 68
(Paul Midgley) *hld up: nvr threatened* **10/1**

5010 **9** 1 ¼ **Lucky Lodge**$^{44}$ 7525 7-8-10 **64**...................................(v) CamHardie 3 56
(Antony Brittain) *prom: rdn over 2f out: wknd fnl f* **25/1**

0050 **10** ½ **Vallarta (IRE)**$^{17}$ 8321 7-9-0 **68**........................................ JackGarritty 12 58
(Ruth Carr) *prom: rdn over 2f out: wknd fnl f* **20/1**

-506 **11** 4 ½ **Naples Bay**$^{25}$ 8106 3-8-13 **67**............................................ JasonHart 4 43
(John Quinn) *dwlt: hld up: rdn over 2f out: sn wknd* **50/1**

0450 **12** ½ **Pomme De Terre (IRE)**$^{17}$ 8321 5-9-5 **73**..................... PaulMulrennan 5 47
(Michael Dods) *dwlt: hld up: rdn over 2f out: wknd* **28/1**

1m 13.31s (0.81) **Going Correction** +0.15s/f (Slow) — **12** Ran SP% **123.9**
Speed ratings (Par 103): **100,99,98,97,96 95,95,94,93,92 86,85**
CSF £41.68 CT £345.22 TOTE £2.20: £1.40, £5.30, £4.40; EX 39.90 Trifecta £385.90.
**Owner** Sonia M Rogers & Anthony Rogers **Bred** Airlie Stud **Trained** Newmarket, Suffolk

**FOCUS**
All the right horses were involved in the finish of this sprint handicap, but the game winner might find life tougher from now on. She didn't need to improve on her previous win.

T/Plt: £684.70 to a £1 stake. Pool: £104,409.90 - 111.31 winning units T/Qpdt: £43.30 to a £1 stake. Pool: £12,878.50 - 220.00 winning units **Andrew Sheret**

8723 - 8731a (Foreign Racing) - See Raceform Interactive

8665
## SAINT-CLOUD (L-H)
### Friday, November 10

**OFFICIAL GOING: Turf: soft**

### 8732a PRIX MARGOUILLAT (CONDITIONS) (3YO) (TURF) 1m 4f
**12:00** 3-Y-O **£11,111** (£4,444; £3,333; £2,222; £1,111)

RPR

1 **Sermando (FR)**[9] 3-9-0 0 ........ AdrienMoreau 5 73
(J Phelippon, France) 2/1[2]

2 snk **Lady Valdean**[14] 8390 3-9-1 0 ........ GuillaumeTrolleyDePrevaux 3 74
(Jose Santos) *wl into stride: sn led: pushed along over 2f out: rdn to hold advantage over 1f out: drvn ins fnl f and hdd fnl 50yds* 23/5[3]

3 hd **Tres Rush (IRE)**[23] 3-9-4 0 ........(b) ThierryThulliez 1 76
(F Head, France) 6/4[1]

4 ¾ **Garopaba (IRE)** 3-8-7 0 ........ ThomasHuet 2 64
(M Delzangles, France) 6/1

5 6 **Helmsdale**[434] 6077 3-8-10 0 ........ FrankPanicucci 4 58
(S Cerulis, France) 67/10

2m 44.58s (4.18) **5 Ran SP% 118.5**
PARI-MUTUEL (all including 1 euro stake): WIN 3.00; PLACE 1.90, 3.00, SF 130.40.
**Owner** Ecurie Brillantissime **Bred** Suc. A Humeau & Mme A Humeau **Trained** France

### 8733a PRIX DENISY (LISTED RACE) (3YO+) (TURF) 1m 7f 110y
**1:35** 3-Y-O+ **£22,222** (£8,888; £6,666; £4,444; £2,222)

RPR

1 **Against Rules (FR)**[37] 7752 5-8-13 0 ........(b) TheoBachelot 3 96
(S Wattel, France) 47/10[2]

2 1 ¾ **Morgan Le Faye**[66] 6805 3-8-6 0 ........ MickaelBarzalona 10 96
(A Fabre, France) *hld up towards rr: gd hdwy to chse ldrs over 2f out: rdn to chal over 1f out: drvn ins fnl f and styd on one pce* 118/10

3 3 **Nabunga (FR)**[53] 5-9-2 0 ........ StephanePasquier 5 93
(Gianluca Bietolini, Italy) 123/10

4 nk **Nardo (FR)**[19] 7-9-2 0 ........ ChristopherGrosbois 14 93
(F Foucher, France) 89/10

5 ½ **Adler (GER)**[26] 8090 3-8-9 0 ........ MartinSeidl 9 94
(Markus Klug, Germany) 181/10

6 nk **St Mary's**[9] 8511 4-8-13 0 ........ HayleyTurner 6 89
(Andrew Balding) *settled midfield: tk clsr order 3f out: rdn over 2 out: no ex fnl f* 25/1

7 2 **Arizona Air (GER)**[66] 6805 3-8-6 0 ........ MaximeGuyon 12 89
(A Fabre, France) 77/10

8 7 **Hukamaa**[24] 8144 3-8-6 0 ........ AurelienLemaitre 8 80
(F Head, France) 13/2[3]

9 1 ¼ **Bonfire Heart (FR)**[19] 5-9-2 0 ........ TonyPiccone 13 80
(R Le Gal, France) 157/10

10 15 **Mistress Quickly (IRE)**[62] 6930 3-8-6 0 ........ FabriceVeron 1 61
(Ralph Beckett) *disp ld early: settled bhd ldr after 1f: led 3f out: sn rdn and hdd: eased ins fnl f* 241/10

11 4 **Shadow Sadness (GER)**[26] 8090 5-9-2 0 ........ IoritzMendizabal 2 57
(C Von Der Recke, Germany) 27/1

12 2 **High Jinx (IRE)**[41] 7639 9-9-2 0 ........(p) ChristopheSoumillon 4 54
(Tim Easterby) *sn front rnk: led after 1f: pushed along over 3f out: rdn and hdd over 2f out: eased heavily ins fnl f* 29/10[1]

13 8 **Chiavari (IRE)**[53] 3-8-6 0 ........ ClementLecoeuvre 11 44
(A Fabre, France) 56/1

3m 31.6s (-7.10)
**WFA** 3 from 4yo+ 6lb **13 Ran SP% 117.8**
PARI-MUTUEL (all including 1 euro stake): WIN 5.70; PLACE 1.90, 4.30, 3.20; DF 42.50; SF 78.60.
**Owner** L Haegel **Bred** J Hayoz **Trained** France

8412
## DONCASTER (L-H)
### Saturday, November 11

**OFFICIAL GOING: Soft (good to soft in places on straight course; 6.6)**
Wind: Light against Weather: Fine & dry

### 8734 BETFRED MOBILE COCK O'THE NORTH EBF MAIDEN STKS (PLUS 10 RACE) (DIV I) 6f 2y
**11:55** (11:55) (Class 4) 2-Y-O **£5,040** (£1,508; £754; £377; £188) **Stalls** Centre

Form RPR

1 **Raid (IRE)** 2-9-5 0 ........ OisinMurphy 11 85+
(David Simcock) *hld up in rr: smooth hdwy on outer to trck ldrs 2f out: rdn to chse ldr ins fnl f: led last 110 yds: sn clr* 9/2[2]

4522 2 2 ¼ **Lady Willpower**[12] 8471 2-9-0 77 ........ JasonHart 10 73
(John Quinn) *cl up: led 2f out: rdn and edgd lft over 1f out: drvn and hung lft ins fnl f: hdd last 110 yds: kpt on same pce* 9/2[2]

5 3 ¾ **Hidden Affair**[105] 5430 2-9-5 0 ........ DavidProbert 4 76
(Henry Candy) *prom: cl up 3f out: rdn along and sltly outpcd 2f out: sn rdn and kpt on wl fnl f* 5/1[3]

4 nk **Azpeitia** 2-9-0 0 ........ RichardKingscote 2 70+
(Ralph Beckett) *wnt lft s: hld up in rr: hdwy over 2f out: rdn along over 1f out: styd on fnl f* 9/1

5 ¾ **Any Little Rhyme** 2-9-0 0 ........ DanielTudhope 6 68
(Michael Bell) *trckd ldrs: hdwy 1/2-way: rdn 2f out and ev ch: wknd ent fnl f* 12/1

3 6 2 ¼ **Al Asef**[31] 7953 2-9-5 0 ........ DanielMuscutt 1 66
(Marco Botti) *wnt lft s: in tch: hdwy on inner wl over 2f out: sn pushed along: rdn over 1f out and ev ch: wknd fnl f* 11/4[1]

7 3 **Yajooll** 2-9-5 0 ........ WilliamBuick 9 57
(William Haggas) *towards rr: hdwy and in tch 3f out: green and pushed along 2f out: sn one pce* 11/2

60 8 shd **Crystal Deauville (FR)**[77] 6453 2-9-5 0 ........ MartinDwyer 5 57
(Gay Kelleway) *slt ld: rdn along over 2f out: sn hdd and grad wknd* 33/1

9 2 ½ **My Society (IRE)** 2-9-5 0 ........ BenCurtis 3 49
(David Dennis) *cl up: rdn along over 2f out: sn wknd* 66/1

10 2 ½ **Assertainty** 2-9-2 0 ........ RachelRichardson(3) 8 42
(Tim Easterby) *dwlt: t.k.h: a towards rr* 66/1

0 11 nk **Scots Snap (IRE)**[12] 8466 2-8-7 0 ........ TylerSaunders(7) 7 36
(Marcus Tregoning) *a towards rr* 100/1

1m 14.87s (1.27) **Going Correction** +0.275s/f (Good) **11 Ran SP% 119.7**
Speed ratings (Par 98): **102,99,98,97,96 93,89,89,86,82 82**
CSF £25.38 TOTE £6.30: £1.90, £1.70, £1.90; EX 31.90 Trifecta £155.90.
**Owner** Qatar Racing Limited **Bred** James Waldron **Trained** Newmarket, Suffolk

**FOCUS**
The ground was officially soft, good to soft in places on the straight course, and clerk of the course Roderick Duncan said: "It dried a bit yesterday, I'd say it's good to soft on the last three furlongs of the straight." After riding in the opener Daniel Muscutt, Richard Kingscote and William Buick all called the ground soft and Danny Tudhope said: "It's very testing." The time backed up the view that the ground was soft. This was the slower of the two divisions by 0.23sec but the winner looks useful.

### 8735 BETFRED MOBILE COCK O'THE NORTH EBF MAIDEN STKS (PLUS 10 RACE) (DIV II) 6f 2y
**12:25** (12:26) (Class 4) 2-Y-O **£5,040** (£1,508; £754; £377; £188) **Stalls** Centre

Form RPR

5 1 **Tallow (IRE)**[12] 8474 2-9-0 0 ........ JimCrowley 7 79+
(William Haggas) *hld up towards rr: hdwy over 2f out: chsd ldrs over 1f out: rdn to ld ins fnl f: kpt on* 10/3[2]

5 2 1 ½ **Ornamental**[87] 6070 2-9-5 0 ........ DavidProbert 9 79
(Henry Candy) *trckd ldrs: hdwy over 2f out: rdn to chal jst over 1f out: drvn and ev ch ins fnl f: kpt on same pce* 6/1[3]

2 3 1 ¼ **Gilded Hour (IRE)**[25] 8130 2-9-0 0 ........ OisinMurphy 6 70
(Ralph Beckett) *in tch: niggled along 4f out: hdwy to chse ldrs 2f out: rdn along on inner over 1f out: kpt on fnl f* 5/2[1]

062 4 ¾ **Scenic River**[12] 8474 2-8-11 69 ........ RachelRichardson(3) 10 68
(Tim Easterby) *prom: cl up over 2f out: led 1 1/2f out and sn rdn: drvn and hdd ins fnl f: wknd towards fin* 12/1

2 5 3 **Big Brave Bob**[19] 8294 2-9-5 0 ........ ShaneKelly 1 64
(Richard Hughes) *racd wd: led: pushed along and jnd over 2f out: rdn and hdd 1 1/2f out: sn drvn and grad wknd* 6/1[3]

6 2 ½ **Monadee** 2-9-5 0 ........ JackMitchell 2 57
(Roger Varian) *green and a towards rr* 12/1

7 4 ½ **The British Lion (IRE)** 2-9-5 0 ........ PJMcDonald 8 43
(Mark Johnston) *chsd ldrs: pushed along wl over 2f out: sn rdn and wknd* 6/1[3]

0 8 4 **Cocktail (IRE)**[31] 7953 2-9-5 0 ........ JackGarritty 4 31
(Jedd O'Keeffe) *prom: green and rdn along 3f out: sn wknd* 50/1

5 9 11 **Poppy Line**[18] 8324 2-9-0 0 ........ PatrickMathers 3
(Derek Shaw) *dwlt: a in rr* 40/1

1m 14.64s (1.04) **Going Correction** +0.275s/f (Good) **9 Ran SP% 114.3**
Speed ratings (Par 98): **104,102,100,99,95 92,86,80,66**
CSF £23.44 TOTE £4.10: £1.20, £2.50, £1.30; EX 24.40 Trifecta £77.60.
**Owner** Cheveley Park Stud **Bred** Tom Twomey **Trained** Newmarket, Suffolk

**FOCUS**
The quicker division by 0.23sec, and a 1-2 for owners Cheveley Park Stud. The front pair were improvers from their respective debuts.

### 8736 BETFRED "HOME OF GOALS GALORE" APPRENTICE H'CAP (FUTURE STARS APPRENTICE SERIES) 7f 6y
**1:00** (1:01) (Class 3) (0-90,90) 3-Y-O+
**£7,470** (£2,236; £1,118; £559; £279; £140) **Stalls** Centre

Form RPR

22-1 1 **What's The Story**[210] 1804 3-9-5 **84** ........ CallumRodriguez 15 97
(Keith Dalgleish) *trckd ldrs: smooth hdwy to ld over 2f out: rdn clr over 1f out: kpt on strly* 9/1[3]

1323 2 2 ½ **Hajjam**[14] 8418 3-9-1 **80** ........(h) ShelleyBirkett 7 87
(David O'Meara) *in tch: trckd ldrs 1/2-way: hdwy 2f out: rdn to chse wnr over 1f out: drvn and no imp fnl f* 8/1[2]

1322 3 ¾ **Pastime**[14] 8418 3-9-3 **87** ........ CameronNoble(5) 21 92+
(Gay Kelleway) *towards rr: hdwy on wd outside 3f out: rdn along and chsd ldrs whn edgd lft wl over 1f out: drvn and hung lft ent fnl f: kpt on* 10/1

1332 4 2 ¼ **Lady In Question (IRE)**[21] 8240 3-8-7 **77** ........ ConnorMurtagh(5) 5 76
(Richard Fahey) *hld up: hdwy 1/2-way: in tch and swtchd rt over 2f out: sn rdn and styd on wl appr fnl f* 9/1[3]

0600 5 nk **Twin Appeal (IRE)**[29] 8014 6-9-2 **83** ........(b) BenRobinson(3) 22 82
(David Barron) *in rr: hdwy over 2f out: rdn along and styng on whn n.m.r jst ins fnl f: sn swtchd lft and drvn: kpt on wl towards fin* 20/1

3320 6 nk **Letmestopyouthere (IRE)**[27] 8077 3-9-3 **82** ........ CallumShepherd 18 79
(David Evans) *midfield: hdwy on outer 3f out: rdn along 2f out: drvn over 1f out: kpt on fnl f* 16/1

0012 7 1 **Boots And Spurs**[11] 8486 8-9-0 **83** ........(v) JamieGormley(5) 8 79
(Scott Dixon) *prom: cl up 3f out: rdn along wl over 1f out: wknd appr fnl f* 7/1[1]

20-0 8 ½ **Weld Al Emarat**[11] 8485 5-8-9 **80** ........ HarrisonShaw(7) 4 74
(Michael Easterby) *hld up: hdwy on inner 1/2-way: in tch and rdn along 2f out: kpt on same pce* 50/1

4206 9 1 ¾ **Luis Vaz De Torres (IRE)**[29] 8014 5-8-12 **83** ..(h) SebastianWoods(7) 17 73
(Richard Fahey) *prom: cl up 1/2-way: disp ld 3f out: rdn along over 2f out: wknd over 1f out* 12/1

0406 10 ¾ **Showboating (IRE)**[21] 8240 9-9-0 **78** ........ LewisEdmunds 3 66
(John Balding) *chsd ldrs: rdn along 2f out: sn drvn and wknd* 16/1

3152 11 2 ½ **El Principe**[8] 8556 4-8-10 **77** ........(t) JaneElliott(3) 1 58
(Les Eyre) *prom: cl up 1/2-way: led 3f out: rdn and hdd over 2f out: sn wknd* 14/1

0500 12 ¾ **Fingal's Cave (IRE)**[11] 8486 5-9-6 **84** ........ AlistairRawlinson 16 63
(Philip Kirby) *in tch on outer: rdn along over 2f out: sn wknd* 16/1

5400 13 hd **Golden Amber (IRE)**[27] 8077 6-9-9 **87** ........ JackDuern 12 66
(Dean Ivory) *s.i.s: sn swtchd rt to outer: a towards rr* 20/1

0012 14 shd **Sans Souci Bay**[12] 8470 3-9-3 **82** ........(b) HollieDoyle 20 60
(Scott Dixon) *nvr bttr than midfield* 33/1

6154 15 ½ **Roaring Forties (IRE)**[11] 8486 4-9-7 **85** ........(p) PhilDennis 13 62
(Rebecca Bastiman) *chsd ldrs: rdn along wl over 2f out: sn wknd* 20/1

6146 16 ½ **Pastoral Player**[36] 7781 10-9-3 **88** ........ TheodoreLadd(7) 2 64
(Hughie Morrison) *s.i.s: a in rr* 25/1

1120 17 1 ¼ **Sir Titan**[81] 6289 3-9-4 **88** ........ TylerSaunders(5) 11 60
(Marcus Tregoning) *led: pushed along 1/2-way: rdn and hdd 3f out: sn wknd* 10/1

0000 18 1 **Khelman (IRE)**[11] 8488 7-9-2 **80** ........(p) AdamMcNamara 6 50
(Richard Fahey) *in tch: pushed along 1/2-way: sn rdn and wknd* 40/1

000- **19** *1* **Easy Victory**[379] 7667 3-9-8 **87** GeorgeWood 19 53
(Saeed bin Suroor) *midfield: pushed along on outer 3f out: sn rdn and wknd over 2f out* **12/1**

0-00 **20** *3/4* **Lost At Sea**[101] 5530 3-9-11 **90** CliffordLee 14 55
(K R Burke) *chsd ldrs: pushed along 1/2-way: rdn and wkng whn n.m.r over 2f out: sn in rr* **33/1**

1m 28.01s (1.71) **Going Correction** +0.275s/f (Good)
**WFA** 3 from 4yo+ 1lb **20** Ran SP% **127.1**
Speed ratings (Par 107): **101,98,97,94,94 94,92,92,90,89 86,85,85,85,84 84,82,81,80,79**
CSF £73.10 CT £769.56 TOTE £7.10: £2.40, £2.10, £2.70, £2.90; EX 53.30 Trifecta £223.20.
**Owner** Weldspec Glasgow Limited **Bred** Mrs Liz Nelson Mbe **Trained** Carluke, S Lanarks

**FOCUS**
A competitive handicapm with an unexposed winner and the second and third rated close to their latest C&D form.

## 8737 BETFRED "SUPPORTS JACK BERRY HOUSE" H'CAP — 7f 6y
**1:35** (1:36) (Class 2) (0-105,105) 3-Y-0+

**£12,450** (£3,728; £1,864; £932; £466; £234) **Stalls** Centre

Form RPR

2/00 **1** **Speculative Bid (IRE)**[21] 8234 6-9-10 **105** SeanLevey 13 113+
(David Elsworth) *hld up in rr: gng wl but short of room 2f out tl appr fnl f: stl plenty to do once clr: qcknd up smartly: led towards fin* **7/1**[2]

0011 **2** *nk* **Shady McCoy (USA)**[29] 8014 7-9-4 **99** RichardKingscote 1 106
(Ian Williams) *hld up in midfield: smooth hdwy over 2f out: pushed along to ld ins fnl f: sn rdn: edgd rt: kpt on but hdd towards fin* **16/1**

1003 **3** *1 1/4* **Bertiewhittle**[42] 7622 9-8-4 **92** GabrieleMalune(7) 4 96
(David Barron) *hld up: rdn over 2f out: hdwy appr fnl f: kpt on: wnt 3rd towards fin* **14/1**

0042 **4** *nk* **Right Touch**[26] 8104 7-8-8 **89** PaulHanagan 2 92
(Richard Fahey) *prom: rdn to ld over 1f out: hdd ins fnl f: sltly hmpd 110yds out: no ex and lost 3rd towards fin* **7/1**[2]

0026 **5** *1* **Bravery (IRE)**[12] 8469 4-9-2 **97** DanielTudhope 16 98
(David O'Meara) *hld up in midfield: briefly short of room 2f out: pushed along and hdwy over 1f out: kpt on ins fnl f* **8/1**[3]

460 **6** *nk* **Hells Babe**[35] 7808 4-9-0 **95** OisinMurphy 18 95
(Michael Appleby) *racd alone stands' side: chsd ldrs overall: rdn over 2f out: one pce fnl f* **25/1**

0030 **7** *nk* **Robero**[15] 8383 5-8-10 **91** BenCurtis 6 90
(Michael Easterby) *trckd ldrs: rdn 2f out: one pce fnl f* **25/1**

4356 **8** *nk* **Get Knotted (IRE)**[26] 8104 5-8-11 **95** (p) CallumRodriguez(3) 5 93
(Michael Dods) *trckd ldrs: rdn along over 3f out: plugged on* **8/1**[3]

650 **9** *shd* **Beach Bar (IRE)**[14] 8439 6-8-0 **86** oh2 KillianLeonard(5) 9 84
(Richard John O'Brien, Ire) *chsd ldrs: rdn over 2f out: outpcd over 1f out: kpt on ins fnl f* **20/1**

0340 **10** *nk* **Heaven's Guest (IRE)**[26] 8104 7-8-7 **88** PatrickMathers 15 85
(Richard Fahey) *hld up: rdn along 3f out: kpt on ins fnl f: nvr threatened* **14/1**

020 **11** *1 1/4* **Von Blucher (IRE)**[26] 8104 4-9-4 **99** (p) PJMcDonald 10 93
(Rebecca Menzies) *in tch: rdn over 2f out: no ex ins fnl f* **33/1**

0300 **12** *3/4* **Mobsta (IRE)**[15] 8383 5-8-7 **91** CallumShepherd(3) 11 83
(Mick Channon) *midfield: bit short of room and shuffled bk 2f out: kpt on same pce fnl f* **16/1**

0000 **13** *hd* **Steel Train (FR)**[29] 8009 6-8-8 **92** ShelleyBirkett(3) 3 84
(David O'Meara) *dwlt: hld up: rdn and hdwy 2f out: chsd ldrs appr fnl f: wknd fnl 75yds* **28/1**

0035 **14** *nk* **Sea Fox (IRE)**[14] 8423 3-8-9 **91** ow1 (t) ShaneKelly 17 81
(David Evans) *midfield: rdn over 2f out: wknd over 1f out* **20/1**

0600 **15** *1/2* **Gurkha Friend**[12] 8469 5-8-8 **89** BarryMcHugh 12 78
(Karen McLintock) *hld up: nvr threatened* **50/1**

113 **16** *1* **Siege Of Boston (IRE)**[17] 8344 4-8-5 **86** oh2 (t) FrannyNorton 8 73
(David C Griffiths) *midfield: rdn along 3f out: wknd over 1f out* **33/1**

2103 **17** *1/2* **London (FR)**[7] 8600 4-8-1 **89** (h) NicolaCurrie(7) 14 75
(Phil McEntee) *prom: rdn over 2f out: wknd appr fnl f* **7/1**[2]

1251 **18** *nk* **Muntadab (IRE)**[26] 8104 5-9-5 **100** TonyHamilton 7 85
(Roger Fell) *led: rdn whn hdd over 1f out: wknd* **6/1**[1]

-010 **19** *14* **Lord Of The Rock (IRE)**[42] 7609 5-8-13 **94** PaulMulrennan 19 42
(Michael Dods) *prom: rdn over 2f out: wknd and eased* **25/1**

1m 27.78s (1.48) **Going Correction** +0.275s/f (Good)
**WFA** 3 from 4yo+ 1lb **19** Ran SP% **131.5**
Speed ratings (Par 109): **102,101,100,99,98 98,98,97,97,97 95,94,94,94,93 92,92,91,75**
CSF £105.66 CT £1608.64 TOTE £7.70: £2.00, £3.60, £4.20, £1.90; EX 148.50 Trifecta £2083.40.
**Owner** K Quinn/ C Benham **Bred** Summerhill Bloodstock **Trained** Newmarket, Suffolk

**FOCUS**
A good, competitive handicap, run in a time 0.23sec quicker than the preceding Class 3 event. The winner is rated back to his best, with the form rated around the third and fourth.

## 8738 BETFRED MOBILE WENTWORTH STKS (LISTED RACE) — 6f 2y
**2:05** (2:07) (Class 1) 3-Y-0+

**£22,684** (£8,600; £4,304; £2,144; £1,076; £540) **Stalls** Centre

Form RPR

2015 **1** **Dream Of Dreams (IRE)**[50] 7356 3-9-3 107 JimCrowley 2 113
(Sir Michael Stoute) *hld up in tch: hdwy on inner over 2f out: chsd ldrs over 1f out: rdn to chal ent fnl f: sn led: drvn out* **5/1**[2]

0011 **2** *1* **Perfect Pasture**[3] 8679 7-9-6 100 (v) PhillipMakin 11 113
(Michael Easterby) *cl up: chal 2f out: rdn to ld over 1f out: drvn and edgd lft jst ins fnl f: sn hdd: kpt on* **11/1**

1040 **3** *2* **Danzeno**[21] 8230 6-9-3 108 OisinMurphy 9 104
(Michael Appleby) *dwlt and in rr: hdwy over 2f out: rdn along wl over 1f out: styd on wl fnl f* **5/1**[2]

0411 **4** *1* **Teruntum Star (FR)**[28] 8044 5-9-3 104 (p) KevinStott 4 100
(Kevin Ryan) *prom: hdwy and cl up 2f out: rdn to dispute ld over 1f out: drvn ent fnl f: kpt on same pce* **7/1**[3]

5621 **5** *nk* **Sir Dancealot (IRE)**[14] 8417 3-9-3 111 SeanLevey 14 99
(David Elsworth) *swtchd lft s and hld up in rr: hdwy over 2f out: chsd ldrs on inner over 1f out: sn rdn and kpt on same pce fnl f* **7/2**[1]

0663 **6** *1 1/4* **Gordon Lord Byron (IRE)**[29] 8003 9-9-10 112 RichardKingscote 10 102
(T Hogan, Ire) *in tch on outer: rdn along and sltly outpcd 2f out: styd on u.p fnl f* **20/1**

-004 **7** *nse* **G Force (IRE)**[28] 8050 6-9-3 98 (b) GaryCarroll 7 95
(Adrian Paul Keatley, Ire) *towards rr: hdwy 2f out: sn rdn and kpt on fnl f: eased nr line* **40/1**

5132 **8** *nse* **Flying Pursuit**[15] 8383 4-9-3 103 (p) RachelRichardson 1 95
(Tim Easterby) *led: rdn along 2f out: hdd over 1f out: sn drvn and grad wknd* **8/1**

0043 **9** *5* **Maarek**[17] 8355 10-9-3 103 KillianHennessy 13 79
(Miss Evanna McCutcheon, Ire) *a towards rr* **25/1**

1610 **10** *1/2* **Sainted**[42] 7611 4-8-12 99 WilliamBuick 3 73
(William Haggas) *a towards rr* **8/1**

2550 **11** *1* **Dark Defender**[42] 7612 4-9-3 87 (v) AndrewMullen 8 74
(Keith Dalgleish) *chsd ldrs: pushed along 1/2-way: rdn wl over 2f out: sn wknd* **100/1**

1551 **12** *nk* **Yes You (IRE)**[12] 8480 3-8-12 68 JamieGormley 6 68
(Iain Jardine) *in tch: rdn along wl over 2f out: sn wknd* **150/1**

020 **13** *1* **Perfect Angel (IRE)**[99] 5597 3-8-12 100 MartinDwyer 5 65
(Andrew Balding) *chsd ldrs: rdn along 2f out: sn wknd* **22/1**

3020 **14** *2 1/4* **Stake Acclaim (IRE)**[28] 8044 5-9-3 105 RobertWinston 12 63
(Dean Ivory) *prom on outer: rdn along 2f out: wknd over 1f out* **14/1**

1m 13.49s (-0.11) **Going Correction** +0.275s/f (Good) **14** Ran SP% **122.3**
Speed ratings (Par 111): **111,109,107,105,105 103,103,103,96,96 94,94,93,90**
CSF £56.10 TOTE £5.90: £2.30, £4.00, £2.20; EX 71.20 Trifecta £465.60.
**Owner** Saeed Suhail **Bred** Prostock Ltd **Trained** Newmarket, Suffolk
■ Stewards' Enquiry : Gary Carroll two-day ban; failing to take all reasonable and permissible measures to obtain the best possible placing (Nov 25,28)

**FOCUS**
A fair Listed sprint. The winner built on his Listed win, with the second back to his best.

## 8739 BETFRED TV EBF STALLIONS BREEDING WINNERS GILLIES FILLIES' STKS (LISTED RACE) — 1m 2f 43y
**2:40** (2:40) (Class 1) 3-Y-0+

**£23,680** (£8,956; £4,476; £2,236) **Stalls** Low

Form RPR

2113 **1** **Star Rock**[29] 8011 3-8-13 86 PJMcDonald 2 103
(Hughie Morrison) *hld up towards rr: hdwy 3f out: chsd ldrs 2f out: rdn to chse ldr over 1f out: drvn to ld ins fnl f: styd on wl* **5/1**

-202 **2** *3/4* **Vintage Folly**[52] 7283 3-8-13 102 JosephineGordon 5 101
(Hugo Palmer) *trckd ldng pair: hdwy and cl up over 3f out: led over 2f out: rdn over 1f out: drvn ent fnl f: sn hdd: kpt on* **2/1**[1]

1000 **3** *2 1/2* **Melesina (IRE)**[9] 8546 3-8-13 100 DanielTudhope 6 96
(Richard Fahey) *trckd ldrs: hdwy 3f out: rdn along 2f out: drvn over 1f out: kpt on same pce fnl f* **25/1**

1225 **4** *nk* **Empress Ali (IRE)**[24] 8165 6-9-2 91 JamesSullivan 1 94
(Tom Tate) *led 1f: trckd ldrs on inner: pushed along and sltly outpcd wl over 2f out: rdn wl over 1f out: kpt on wl u.p fnl f* **10/1**

1324 **5** *1* **Indulged**[52] 7283 4-9-2 95 WilliamBuick 7 92
(James Fanshawe) *prom: trckd ldr after 3f: pushed along and cl up over 3f out: rdn over 2f out: sn drvn and wknd* **9/2**[3]

0521 **6** *4* **Brief Visit**[44] 7550 4-9-2 87 OisinMurphy 3 84
(Andrew Balding) *cl up: led after 1f: rdn along over 3f out: hdd over 2f out: sn drvn and wknd wl over 1f out* **22/1**

-140 **7** *1/2* **Gracious Diana**[142] 3995 3-8-13 95 (t) RobertHavlin 8 84
(John Gosden) *hld up: sme hdwy 3f out: rdn along over 2f out: sn wknd* **14/1**

1113 **8** *nse* **Time Chaser**[63] 6924 3-8-13 91 JimCrowley 4 84
(Roger Charlton) *hld up in rr: sme hdwy over 3f out: rdn along wl over 2f out: n.d* **3/1**[2]

2m 14.25s (4.85) **Going Correction** +0.675s/f (Yiel)
**WFA** 3 from 4yo+ 3lb **8** Ran SP% **117.1**
Speed ratings (Par 108): **107,106,104,104,103 100,99,99**
CSF £15.86 TOTE £5.70: £1.60, £1.10, £5.30; EX 17.50 Trifecta £260.20.
**Owner** Ben & Sir Martyn Arbib **Bred** Arbib Bloodstock Partnership **Trained** East Ilsley, Berks

**FOCUS**
The first race of the day over the round course, and they stayed on the inside in the home straight. This Listed race was dominated by 3yos. The winner improved despite the drop in trip, with the second to form.

## 8740 BETFRED NOVEMBER H'CAP — 1m 3f 197y
**3:15** (3:16) (Class 2) 3-Y-0+

**£43,575** (£13,048; £6,524; £3,262; £1,631; £819) **Stalls** Low

Form RPR

0402 **1** **Saunter (FR)**[44] 7548 4-8-13 **95** JimCrowley 14 104+
(Ian Williams) *trckd ldrs: rdn over 2f out: chal appr fnl f: led ins fnl f: edgd lft: styd on wl* **6/1**[2]

3046 **2** *1 1/4* **Chelsea Lad (IRE)**[28] 8042 4-9-2 **98** JosephineGordon 9 104
(Martyn Meade) *in tch on inner: rdn 3f out: hdwy 2f out: chsd ldrs appr fnl f: styd on: edgd rt towards fin* **20/1**

1000 **3** *1 1/4* **Eddystone Rock (IRE)**[21] 8234 5-9-4 **100** RobertHavlin 15 104+
(John Best) *midfield: short of room and shuffled bk over 2f out: stl plenty to do over 1f out: styd on wl: wnt 3rd post* **33/1**

0110 **4** *shd* **Storm King**[77] 6449 8-8-10 **92** SteveDrowne 16 96
(David C Griffiths) *led: rdn whn hdd over 2f out: remained cl up: styd on fnl f* **66/1**

4464 **5** *1* **Gawdawpalin (IRE)**[12] 8468 4-8-9 **91** KieranO'Neill 19 93
(Sylvester Kirk) *prom: rdn to ld over 2f out: hdd over 1f out: no ex fnl 110yds* **25/1**

3621 **6** *1/2* **Dance The Dream**[12] 8468 4-8-12 **101** TylerSaunders(7) 23 102
(Marcus Tregoning) *prom: rdn 3f out: outpcd over 2f out: plugged on ins fnl f* **10/1**

113 **7** *shd* **Royal Line**[15] 8391 3-8-9 **96** WilliamBuick 12 98
(John Gosden) *trckd ldrs: pushed along and hdwy over 2f out: rdn to ld over 1f out: hung lft and hdd ins fnl f: wknd fnl 75yds* **5/1**[1]

5033 **8** *nk* **Wild Hacked (USA)**[50] 7354 4-9-4 **100** DanielMuscutt 10 101
(Marco Botti) *trckd ldrs: rdn over 2f out: ev ch appr fnl f: wknd fnl 75yds* **16/1**

4100 **9** *1 3/4* **Fun Mac (GER)**[28] 8038 6-9-6 **102** (t) PJMcDonald 3 100
(Hughie Morrison) *midfield on inner: rdn over 2f out: plugged on fnl f: nvr threatened* **50/1**

2362 **10** *nk* **Al Destoor**[42] 7595 7-8-8 **90** (t) FrannyNorton 11 88
(Jennie Candlish) *swtchd lft s: hld up in rr: rdn along 3f out: kpt on ins fnl f: nvr threatened* **16/1**

245 **11** *1/2* **Niblawi (IRE)**[65] 6857 5-8-2 **91** JackOsborn(7) 21 88
(Neil Mulholland) *midfield: rdn over 2f out: no imp* **16/1**

1402 **12** *nk* **Top Tug (IRE)**[12] 8468 6-9-10 **106** MartinDwyer 1 102
(Alan King) *hld up: rdn and hdwy 2f out: in tch appr fnl f: wknd fnl 110yds* **12/1**

2420 **13** *nse* **Machine Learner**[27] 8076 4-8-9 **91** (v) OisinMurphy 18 87
(Joseph Tuite) *in tch: rdn along 3f out: sn outpcd and btn* **16/1**

3140 **14** *3/4* **Cohesion**[19] 2202 4-9-5 **104** GeorgeWood(3) 4 99
(David Bridgwater) *hld up: rdn over 2f out: nvr threatened* **16/1**

0002 **15** *2 1/2* **Syphax (USA)**[28] 8042 3-8-11 **98** KevinStott 7 90
(Kevin Ryan) *midfield: rdn 3f out: wknd ins fnl f* **14/1**

4006 **16** *hd* **Master The World (IRE)**[12] 8468 6-9-10 **106**..................(p) SeanLevey 5 97
(David Elsworth) *nvr bttr than midfield* **50/1**
0130 **17** *¾* **Euchen Glen**[28] 8038 4-8-9 **91**............................... JFEgan 6 80
(Jim Goldie) *hld up: rdn over 2f out: sn no prog* **12/1**
00-0 **18** *¾* **Mirsaale**[7] 8038 7-8-12 **94**..................(p) PhillipMakin 2 82
(Keith Dalgleish) *hld up in rr: rdn over 2f out: nvr threatened* **40/1**
2-44 **19** *2½* **Minotaur (IRE)**[19] 8292 5-9-4 **100**..................(p[1]) FranBerry 20 84
(Jonjo O'Neill) *midfield on outside: brought to r alone towards stands' side 4f out: rdn over 3f out: wknd over 2f out* **33/1**
1200 **20** *½* **Azari**[28] 8042 5-8-13 **95**..................(p) RichardKingscote 17 78
(Tom Dascombe) *hld up: nvr threatened* **33/1**
/1-3 **21** *1* **Towerlands Park (IRE)**[14] 8423 4-8-10 **92**.................. DavidProbert 13 74
(Michael Bell) *in tch: rdn over 3f out: wknd over 2f out* **9/1[3]**
1126 **22** *9* **Sepal (USA)**[24] 8166 4-8-4 **91**.................. JamieGormley[(5)] 8 58
(Iain Jardine) *a towards rr* **25/1**
6200 **23** *31* **Sir Chauvelin**[42] 7619 5-9-1 **97**.................. DanielTudhope 22 15
(Jim Goldie) *in tch on outside: rdn over 3f out: wknd fnl 2f* **25/1**

2m 39.54s (4.64) **Going Correction** +0.675s/f (Yiel)
**WFA** 3 from 4yo+ 5lb **23** Ran SP% **134.5**
Speed ratings (Par 109): **111,110,109,109,108 108,108,108,106,106 106,106,106,105,103 103,103,102,101,100 100,94,73**
CSF £132.66 CT £3753.43 TOTE £7.10: £2.70, £5.10, £4.80, £10.70; EX 141.00 Trifecta £6130.40.
**Owner** Michael Watt And Billy Slater (aus) **Bred** S A R L Haras Du Cadran Et Al **Trained** Portway, Worcs

**FOCUS**
A typically open renewal of this traditional handicap. Winning trainer Ian Williams also had ante-post favourite Reshoun, but he didn't make the cut, while another leading fancy who didn't run was Duke Of Bronte. The bulk of the field raced down the centre of the track in the home straight. Saunter is rated to his best.

## 8741 BETFRED "RACING'S BIGGEST SUPPORTER" NURSERY H'CAP 6f 2y
3:50 (3:51) (Class 4) (0-85,85) 2-Y-O **£5,175** (£1,540; £769; £384) **Stalls** Centre

Form RPR
3313 **1** **Captain Jameson (IRE)**[29] 8008 2-9-3 **81**.................. JasonHart 7 86+
(John Quinn) *in tch: hdwy 2f out: rdn to chse ldrs over 1f out: led ins fnl f: sn edgd rt: drvn out* **5/1[3]**
4231 **2** *½* **Excellent Times**[12] 8475 2-8-11 **75**.................. PJMcDonald 6 78+
(Tim Easterby) *dwlt and in rr: hdwy and nt clr run over 1f out: swtchd rt and rdn jst ins fnl f: styd on wl towards fin* **9/2[2]**
4021 **3** *¾* **Gangland**[18] 8325 2-8-9 **73**..................(h) PaulHanagan 11 74
(Richard Fahey) *in tch: pushed along over 2f out: rdn and hdwy over 1f out: drvn to chal ins fnl f: sn n.m.r: no ex towards fin* **4/1[1]**
2243 **4** *1* **Kimifive (IRE)**[27] 8073 2-8-12 **76**.................. OisinMurphy 8 74
(Joseph Tuite) *hld up: hdwy wl over 1f out: sn rdn: n.m.r and swtchd lft ent fnl f: kpt on* **9/1**
2321 **5** *1* **Biddy Brady (USA)**[21] 8235 2-8-3 **70**............(h) RachelRichardson[(3)] 10 65
(Tim Easterby) *led: rdn along 2f out: drvn over 1f out: hdd ins fnl f: kpt on same pce* **9/1**
0316 **6** *2¼* **Feebs**[33] 7891 2-8-11 **75**.................. PaulMulrennan 9 63
(Michael Easterby) *chsd ldrs: hdwy wl over 1f out: sn rdn: kpt on same pce fnl f* **20/1**
203 **7** *hd* **Eva Docc (IRE)**[26] 8102 2-8-0 **64**.................. AndrewMullen 13 51
(Keith Dalgleish) *in rr: hdwy wl over 1f out: sn rdn: kpt on fnl f* **50/1**
5161 **8** *nk* **Dawn Breaking**[19] 8288 2-8-7 **74**.................. LewisEdmunds[(3)] 4 61
(Richard Whitaker) *towards rr: hdwy on inner and nt clr run over 1f out: sn swtchd lft and rdn: kpt on fnl f* **8/1**
6124 **9** *2¾* **Mable Lee (IRE)**[43] 7564 2-8-6 **70**.................. JosephineGordon 2 48
(Iain Jardine) *cl up: rdn along 2f out: drvn and edgd lft over 1f out: grad wknd* **12/1**
6110 **10** *shd* **Canford's Joy (IRE)**[29] 8008 2-9-4 **82**.................. ShaneGray 5 60
(Ann Duffield) *cl up: rdn along 2f out: grad wknd appr fnl f* **33/1**
3103 **11** *1* **Tathmeen (IRE)**[14] 8420 2-9-7 **85**.................. JimCrowley 1 60
(Richard Hannon) *cl up on inner: rdn along 2f out: sn drvn and wknd* **11/2**

1m 15.22s (1.62) **Going Correction** +0.275s/f (Good) **11** Ran SP% **118.7**
Speed ratings (Par 98): **100,99,98,97,95 92,92,92,88,88 86**
CSF £27.55 CT £102.16 TOTE £5.30: £1.90, £2.00, £2.00; EX 26.60 Trifecta £93.90.
**Owner** The Jam Partnership **Bred** Yeomanstown Stud **Trained** Settrington, N Yorks
■ Stewards' Enquiry : Jason Hart caution: careless riding

**FOCUS**
A fair nursery to conclude the 2017 turf season. The third is a decent enough guide to the form.
T/Jkpt: Not Won. T/Plt: £79.00 to a £1 stake. Pool: £134,569.56 - 1,242.0 winning units T/Qpdt: £24.20 to a £1 stake. Pool: £16,140.75 - 493.07 winning units **Joe Rowntree & Andrew Sheret**

# 8657 WOLVERHAMPTON (A.W) (L-H)
Saturday, November 11

**OFFICIAL GOING: Tapeta: standard**
Wind: Light across Weather: Cloudy

## 8742 BETWAY CASINO H'CAP (DIV I) 6f 20y (Tp)
4:20 (4:22) (Class 6) (0-65,66) 3-Y-O+ **£2,264** (£673; £336; £168) **Stalls** Low

Form RPR
360 **1** **A Sure Welcome**[72] 6638 3-9-4 **62**..................(p) LiamKeniry 2 69
(John Spearing) *a.p: racd keenly: chsd ldr 2f out: shkn up to ld over 1f out: rdn and edgd rt ins fnl f: styd on* **9/1**
440- **2** *½* **Desert Fox**[398] 7184 3-9-4 **62**.................. ShaneKelly 1 68
(Mike Murphy) *s.i.s: racd keenly and sn prom: rdn over 1f out: edgd rt and chsd wnr ins fnl f: r.o* **10/1**
0003 **3** *1¾* **Reedanjas (IRE)**[53] 7255 3-9-0 **65**..................(p) PaulHainey[(7)] 5 65
(Gay Kelleway) *hld up: hdwy over 1f out: nt rch ldrs* **10/1**
0501 **4** *¾* **Zenovia (IRE)**[11] 8496 3-9-2 **60**..................(tp) LukeMorris 4 58
(Archie Watson) *sn pushed along and prom: shkn up over 2f out: styd on u.p* **11/4[1]**
5050 **5** *2* **The Hooded Claw (IRE)**[33] 7910 6-9-0 **58**..................(b) GrahamLee 10 50
(Patrick Morris) *s.i.s: hld up: hdwy over 1f out: styd on same pce ins fnl f* **20/1**
6603 **6** *shd* **Swanton Blue (IRE)**[24] 8158 4-9-5 **66**.................. CallumShepherd[(3)] 8 58
(Ed de Giles) *led: rdn and hdd over 1f out: no ex ins fnl f* **7/2[2]**
0030 **7** *¾* **Nuzha**[19] 8298 3-8-11 **58**.................. EoinWalsh[(3)] 3 47
(Tony Newcombe) *s.i.s: hld up: nt clr run over 1f out: sn hung lft: nvr nr to chal* **33/1**
5000 **8** *1¼* **Kachess**[21] 8243 3-8-12 **63**.................. NicolaCurrie[(7)] 12 49
(David Loughnane) *sn led: hdd 5f out: chsd ldrs: rdn over 1f out: wknd fnl f* **18/1**
-005 **9** *¾* **Portrush Storm**[112] 5146 12-8-4 **51** oh6.................. PhilDennis[(3)] 7 34
(Ray Peacock) *s.i.s: hld up: nt clr run over 1f out: n.d* **100/1**
0224 **10** *1¼* **Meandmyshadow**[8] 8552 9-9-2 **63**..................(b) JoshDoyle[(3)] 13 43+
(Alan Brown) *sn pushed along and prom: racd wd tl crossed over to chse ldr over 4f out: rdn over 2f out: wknd over 1f out* **6/1[3]**
0400 **11** *2½* **Sophisticated Heir (IRE)**[14] 8427 7-9-3 **61**.................. DougieCostello 6 33
(Kevin Frost) *broke wl: sn lost pl: hld up: shkn up over 1f out: nvr nr to chal* **7/1**
0-00 **12** *4½* **Singula**[21] 8242 3-8-11 **55**.................. WilliamCarson 9 14
(Alan King) *dwlt: hld up: plld hrd: rdn over 2f out: wknd over 1f out* **50/1**
0521 **13** *1¾* **Toolatetodelegate**[14] 8428 3-8-10 **59**..................(tp) JoshuaBryan[(5)] 11 12
(Brian Barr) *hld up: hung rt over 2f out: wknd over 1f out* **16/1**

1m 13.19s (-1.31) **Going Correction** -0.175s/f (Stan) **13** Ran SP% **125.7**
Speed ratings (Par 101): **101,100,98,97,94 94,93,91,90,88 85,79,77**
CSF £98.42 CT £652.99 TOTE £10.70: £2.40, £3.00, £3.80; EX 153.60 Trifecta £2294.10.
**Owner** Kinnersley Partnership 3 **Bred** Richard Evans Bloodstock **Trained** Kinnersley, Worcs

**FOCUS**
Dry, relatively still conditions at the start of this eight-race early evening fixture. The first four home in this first division of a moderate sprint handicap came from the first five stalls, but none were involved in the early pace battle.

## 8743 BETWAY CASINO H'CAP (DIV II) 6f 20y (Tp)
4:50 (4:51) (Class 6) (0-65,65) 3-Y-O+ **£2,264** (£673; £336; £168) **Stalls** Low

Form RPR
4300 **1** **Searanger (USA)**[7] 8590 4-8-11 **55**.................. DougieCostello 1 63
(Rebecca Menzies) *s.i.s: sn prom: swtchd lft over 1f out: rdn to ld wl ins fnl f: jst hld on* **22/1**
600 **2** *hd* **Rockley Point**[18] 8327 4-9-7 **65**..................(b[1]) JoeyHaynes 9 72
(Paul D'Arcy) *hld up: nt clr run over 1f out: rdn and r.o wl ins fnl f: nt quite get there* **15/2[3]**
0213 **3** *¾* **Nutini (IRE)**[14] 8427 4-9-5 **63**.................. LiamKeniry 2 68
(Malcolm Saunders) *chsd ldrs: rdn to ld wl ins fnl f: sn hdd and unable qck* **11/8[1]**
0322 **4** *1½* **Kyllukey**[25] 8128 4-9-4 **62**..................(v) LukeMorris 5 63
(Milton Bradley) *chsd ldr tl led 1/2-way: rdn over 1f out: hdd and no ex wl ins fnl f* **10/1**
3345 **5** *2* **Pushkin Museum (IRE)**[42] 7607 6-9-7 **65**..................(h) GrahamLee 8 60
(Patrick Morris) *hld up: plld hrd: nt clr run over 1f out: sn rdn: styd on: nt trble ldrs* **12/1**
0300 **6** *½* **Top Of The Bank**[37] 7767 4-9-4 **62**..................(p) TonyHamilton 3 55
(Kristin Stubbs) *chsd ldrs: rdn over 1f out: no ex ins fnl f* **14/1**
4413 **7** *1¼* **Wotadoll**[24] 8168 3-9-5 **63**.................. RobertWinston 4 52
(Dean Ivory) *s.i.s: hld up: plld hrd: shkn up over 1f out: styd on same pce* **9/2[2]**
5004 **8** *2¾* **Monarch Maid**[11] 8496 6-8-11 **55**.................. WilliamCarson 13 36
(Peter Hiatt) *plld hrd: led to 1/2-way: rdn and hung rt over 1f out: wknd ins fnl f* **33/1**
4532 **9** *¾* **Fairway To Heaven (IRE)**[11] 8495 8-9-3 **61**............(v[1]) MartinHarley 11 40+
(Lee Carter) *hld up: shkn up over 2f out: rdn: hung lft and eased wl ins fnl f* **8/1**
4400 **10** *16* **Jacksonfire**[11] 8495 5-8-4 **51** oh6..................(p) PhilDennis[(3)] 7
(Michael Mullineaux) *s.i.s: hld up: hdwy whn nt clr run 1f out: eased ins fnl f* **80/1**

1m 13.59s (-0.91) **Going Correction** -0.175s/f (Stan) **10** Ran SP% **115.1**
Speed ratings (Par 101): **99,98,97,95,93 92,90,87,86,64**
CSF £174.01 CT £391.49 TOTE £27.00: £6.00, £2.60, £1.30; EX 225.90 Trifecta £945.60.
**Owner** ICM Racing and Partner **Bred** Phoenix Rising Farms **Trained** Mordon, Durham

**FOCUS**
The slower division by 0.4 seconds, but as with division one the first two home had declined the early pace.

## 8744 BETWAY LIVE CASINO MAIDEN STKS 1m 5f 219y (Tp)
5:20 (5:20) (Class 5) 3-Y-O+ **£2,911** (£866; £432; £216) **Stalls** Low

Form RPR
2246 **1** **Silver Link (IRE)**[12] 8478 3-9-0 75..................(p[1]) BenCurtis 2 79
(Marcus Tregoning) *hld up: hdwy over 2f out: shkn up to ld over 1f out: pushed clr fnl f* **6/4[1]**
4-3 **2** *6* **Ocean Of Love**[16] 8377 3-9-0 0.................. WilliamCarson 4 71
(Saeed bin Suroor) *plld hrd early in 2nd pl: shkn up to ld over 2f out: rdn: edgd lft and hdd over 1f out: no ex ins fnl f* **13/8[2]**
6022 **3** *1¾* **Stylish Dancer**[24] 8157 3-9-0 70.................. LukeMorris 6 68
(Luca Cumani) *led at stdy pce: shkn up over 4f out: rdn and hdd over 2f out: no ex fnl f* **7/2[3]**
5032 **4** *10* **My Illusionist**[31] 7948 3-9-5 71.................. StevieDonohoe 1 63
(Harry Dunlop) *chsd ldrs: rdn over 2f out: wknd over 1f out* **14/1**
**5** *17* **Samson's Reach**[21] 4-9-6 0.................. JoshuaBryan[(5)] 7 33
(Richard Price) *dwlt: hld up: pushed along over 5f out: sn lost tch* **66/1**

3m 0.12s (-7.88) **Going Correction** -0.175s/f (Stan)
**WFA** 3 from 4yo 6lb **5** Ran SP% **108.5**
Speed ratings (Par 103): **115,111,110,104,95**
CSF £4.11 TOTE £2.10: £1.10, £1.30; EX 4.00 Trifecta £6.30.
**Owner** Sir Thomas Pilkington & Mrs Sonia Rogers **Bred** Mrs S M Rogers & Sir Thomas Pilkington **Trained** Whitsbury, Hants

**FOCUS**
Not too bad a stayers' maiden for the time of year, but the pace was uneven.

## 8745 BETWAY SPRINT H'CAP 5f 21y (Tp)
5:50 (5:50) (Class 5) (0-75,76) 3-Y-O+ **£2,911** (£866; £432; £216) **Stalls** Low

Form RPR
2562 **1** **Blazed (IRE)**[21] 8242 3-8-12 **69**.................. PaddyPilley[(3)] 2 76
(Roger Charlton) *s.i.s: hld up: hdwy: nt clr run and swtchd lft over 1f out: rdn and r.o to ld post* **5/2[2]**
0005 **2** *nse* **Fast Act (IRE)**[26] 8106 5-9-2 **70**..................(p[1]) JoeDoyle 1 77
(Kevin Ryan) *led: rdn and edgd lft over 1f out: edgd rt ins fnl f: hdd post* **7/1**
5000 **3** *nk* **Invincible Ridge (IRE)**[24] 8167 9-9-2 **70**.................. NeilFarley 4 76
(Eric Alston) *chsd ldrs: nt clr run over 1f out and ins fnl f: r.o* **13/8[1]**
-040 **4** *2¾* **Bondi Beach Boy**[18] 8320 8-9-2 **70**.................. LukeMorris 10 66
(Antony Brittain) *sn prom: plld hrd: rdn and hung lft fr over 1f out: styd on same pce ins fnl f* **11/1**
-300 **5** *2¼* **Mysterious Look**[24] 8167 4-9-2 **70**..................(p[1]) RobHornby 6 58
(Sarah Hollinshead) *hld up: rdn over 1f out: styd on ins fnl f: nvr on terms* **40/1**
-000 **6** *1* **Mysterious Glance**[21] 8243 4-8-8 **62**.................. KieranO'Neill 8 46
(Sarah Hollinshead) *sn chsng ldr: rdn over 1f out: wknd ins fnl f* **50/1**



The Form Book Flat, Raceform Ltd, Newbury, RG14 5SJ

0301 **7** 1 3/4 **Seamster**10 8512 10-9-2 **75**.....................................(t) CameronNoble(5) 5 53
(David Loughnane) *hld up: hdwy 1/2-way: rdn over 1f out: wknd ins fnl f* **5/1**3

0215 **8** 6 **Point North (IRE)**123 4724 10-9-0 **68**........................(b) RobertWinston 3 24
(John Balding) *s.i.s: in rr whn hung rt over 3f out: wknd 1/2-way* **20/1**

1m 0.95s (-0.95) **Going Correction** -0.175s/f (Stan) 8 Ran SP% **113.3**
Speed ratings (Par 103): **100,99,99,95,91 89,87,77**
CSF £19.59 CT £35.05 TOTE £3.50: £1.40, £2.50, £1.10; EX 20.50 Trifecta £50.40.
**Owner** H R H Sultan Ahmad Shah **Bred** Knocktoran Stud **Trained** Beckhampton, Wilts

**FOCUS**
Low-drawn horses locked out the frame in this modest sprint, which was decided on the nod.

## 8746 32RED CASINO NURSERY H'CAP 5f 21y (Tp)
**6:20** (6:20) (Class 5) (0-75,76) 2-Y-O **£2,911** (£866; £432; £216) **Stalls** Low

Form RPR

6303 **1** **Joegogo (IRE)**40 7690 2-9-0 **67**.............................................. FranBerry 7 73
(David Evans) *mde all: rdn over 1f out: styd on wl* **4/1**3

5040 **2** 1 3/4 **Nampara**35 7814 2-8-9 **62**.................................................. JoeyHaynes 4 62
(Paul D'Arcy) *prom: chsd wnr over 3f out: rdn and ev ch over 1f out: styng on same pce whn edgd lft ins fnl f* **6/1**

2012 **3** 2 **Ghepardo**46 7482 2-9-2 **76**............................................. RossaRyan(7) 3 69
(Richard Hannon) *hld up: nt clr run 4f out: hdwy 2f out: sn rdn: styd on same pce ins fnl f* **5/2**1

4460 **4** 1/2 **Villa Tora**62 6977 2-9-1 **68**............................................ JoeFanning 2 59
(Mark Johnston) *chsd wnr tl over 3f out: rdn over 1f out: no ex ins fnl f* **8/1**

2056 **5** 1/2 **Tonkolili (IRE)**26 8110 2-8-13 **66**..............................(h) FrannyNorton 1 55
(William Muir) *hld up: nt clr run wl over 2f out: rdn over 1f out: no imp fnl f* **17/2**

6121 **6** 1 1/4 **Global Exceed**26 8110 2-9-7 **74**....................................(b) LukeMorris 5 58
(Ed Dunlop) *sn drvn along in rr: nvr trbld ldrs* **11/4**2

3160 **7** 6 **Haveoneyerself (IRE)**25 8131 2-9-3 **70**........................ TonyHamilton 6 33
(John Butler) *pushed along early in rr: hdwy over 3f out: rdn and wknd over 1f out* **28/1**

1m 0.95s (-0.95) **Going Correction** -0.175s/f (Stan) 7 Ran SP% **114.6**
Speed ratings (Par 96): **100,97,94,93,92 90,80**
CSF £27.93 TOTE £6.50: £2.70, £3.10; EX 26.30 Trifecta £90.70.
**Owner** Wayne Clifford **Bred** Barry Noonan And Denis Noonan **Trained** Pandy, Monmouths

**FOCUS**
A sprint nursery won in an identical time to that of the preceding C&D 0-75 for older horses and decided by a smart piece of pace scrambling. The winner is rated as running close to his best.

## 8747 32RED.COM FILLIES' CONDITIONS STKS 7f 36y (Tp)
**6:50** (6:51) (Class 2) 3-Y-0+
**£11,827** (£3,541; £1,770; £885; £442; £222) **Stalls** High

Form RPR

2210 **1** **Bumptious**35 7808 4-9-1 84.........................................(p) StevieDonohoe 1 90
(Ismail Mohammed) *chsd ldrs: shkn up over 1f out: rdn to ld wl ins fnl f: r.o* **5/1**3

6125 **2** nk **Pepita (IRE)**56 7155 3-9-0 82............................................... FranBerry 5 88
(Richard Hannon) *a.p: rdn and hung lft ins fnl f: r.o wl* **16/1**

0211 **3** 3/4 **Peach Melba**13 8463 3-9-2 98.......................................... FrannyNorton 4 88
(Mark Johnston) *led: rdn over 1f out: hdd wl ins fnl f* **8/11**1

6362 **4** hd **Rajar**8 8563 3-9-0 91.......................................................(h) DanielTudhope 8 86
(Richard Fahey) *racd keenly in 2nd pl: rdn and ev ch fr over 1f out: hung lft and no ex wl ins fnl f* **9/2**2

4011 **5** 3/4 **Toy Theatre**14 8418 3-9-0 79............................................. OisinMurphy 7 84
(Michael Appleby) *hld up: hdwy over 1f out: sn rdn: r.o: nt pce to chal* **8/1**

4100 **6** 9 **Sexy Legs**8 8552 5-9-1 62.........................................(tp1) DougieCostello 6 60
(Rebecca Menzies) *s.i.s: hld up: shkn up over 2f out: wknd over 1f out* **100/1**

1m 26.76s (-2.04) **Going Correction** -0.175s/f (Stan)
**WFA** 3 from 4yo+ 1lb 6 Ran SP% **110.7**
Speed ratings (Par 96): **104,103,102,102,101 91**
CSF £67.90 TOTE £4.90: £1.90, £4.40; EX 70.30 Trifecta £159.00.
**Owner** Abdulla Al Mansoori **Bred** Swettenham Stud **Trained** Newmarket, Suffolk

**FOCUS**
A fair conditions event, with the first two home appearing to profit from declining the worst excesses of the pace.

## 8748 32RED.COM NOVICE AUCTION STKS 1m 142y (Tp)
**7:20** (7:23) (Class 6) 2-Y-0 **£2,264** (£673; £336; £168) **Stalls** Low

Form RPR

42 **1** **Guvenor's Choice (IRE)**100 5557 2-9-2 0....................(t) MartinHarley 3 77+
(K R Burke) *mde all: shkn up over 1f out: reminder and flashed tail ins fnl f: r.o: comf* **10/11**1

14 **2** 1 1/2 **Ocean Voyage (IRE)**21 8245 2-9-4 0............................ TonyHamilton 1 74
(Richard Fahey) *chsd ldrs: rdn over 2f out: chsd wnr ins fnl f: styd on* **6/1**3

432 **3** nk **Sassie (IRE)**15 8399 2-8-11 72......................................... OisinMurphy 8 66
(Sylvester Kirk) *chsd wnr: rdn over 2f out: edgd lft and styd on same pce ins fnl f* **2/1**2

**4** 3 **Capriolette (IRE)** 2-8-11 0.............................................. LiamKeniry 4 60+
(Ed Walker) *s.i.s: hld up: hdwy and hung lft fr over 1f out: nt trble ldrs* **16/1**

**5** 2 1/2 **Destinys Rock** 2-8-11 0.................................................. ShaneKelly 6 54+
(Daniel Mark Loughnane) *hld up: shkn up and hung lft over 1f out: nt trble ldrs* **50/1**

10 **6** 1 **N Over J**9 8545 2-9-6 0............................................ CallumShepherd(3) 7 64
(William Knight) *plld hrd and prom: hung rt wl over 6f out: rdn over 2f out: hung lft and wknd fnl f* **14/1**

00 **7** 1 1/4 **Wowsham (IRE)**18 8316 2-9-2 0.................................... AndrewMullen 2 55
(Keith Dalgleish) *hld up: rdn over 2f out: hung lft over 1f out: sn wknd* **80/1**

00 **8** nk **Balgowlah (IRE)**10 8501 2-9-2 0................................. StevieDonohoe 5 54
(David Lanigan) *hld up: rdn over 2f out: nvr on terms* **50/1**

60 **9** 1 1/4 **Trick Shot Jenny**10 8502 2-8-11 0............................... DougieCostello 9 46
(Jamie Osborne) *hld up: shkn up over 2f out: nvr nr to chal* **50/1**

1m 50.09s (-0.01) **Going Correction** -0.175s/f (Stan) 9 Ran SP% **119.7**
Speed ratings (Par 94): **93,91,91,88,86 85,84,84,83**
CSF £7.67 TOTE £1.80: £1.10, £1.70, £1.10; EX 8.50 Trifecta £13.50.
**Owner** I McInnes, Dr M Glaze & E Burke **Bred** Noel Finegan **Trained** Middleham Moor, N Yorks

**FOCUS**
Very few got into this juvenile novice event and it all proved pretty straightforward for the well-supported favourite. The first two home are rated to have taken a small step forward in form.

## 8749 SUNBETS.CO.UK H'CAP 1m 142y (Tp)
**7:50** (7:52) (Class 5) (0-75,75) 3-Y-0+ **£2,911** (£866; £432; £216) **Stalls** Low

Form RPR

0001 **1** **Fire Diamond**15 8401 4-8-12 **66**.............................(p) RichardKingscote 2 74
(Tom Dascombe) *hld up: hdwy over 1f out: rdn to ld wl ins fnl f: edgd lft: r.o* **6/1**3

4031 **2** 1 1/2 **Luang Prabang (IRE)**15 8400 4-9-0 **71**........................ HollieDoyle(3) 5 76
(Chris Wall) *hld up in tch: nt clr run wl over 1f out: sn shkn up and hung lft: styd on same pce wl ins fnl f* **5/2**1

5166 **3** 3/4 **Rock Warbler (IRE)**8 8556 4-9-7 **75**................................(t) KevinStott 6 78+
(Oliver Greenall) *hld up: hdwy and nt clr run over 1f out: r.o to go 3rd nr fin: nt rch ldrs* **10/1**

0065 **4** 1/2 **Rock N Rolla (IRE)**14 8433 3-9-3 **74**........................(v) AndrewMullen 13 77
(Keith Dalgleish) *plld hrd and prom: rdn and hung lft over 1f out: styd on same pce ins fnl f* **12/1**

3031 **5** nk **Doria Road (USA)**23 8192 3-8-8 **65**.................................. ShaneGray 8 67
(Kevin Ryan) *chsd ldr: rdn to ld over 1f out: hdd and no ex wl ins fnl f* **20/1**

6023 **6** nk **Epitaph (IRE)**11 8497 3-8-12 **69**......................................(v1) LukeMorris 7 70
(Michael Appleby) *chsd ldrs: rdn over 2f out: sn hung lft: no ex wl ins fnl f* **15/2**

6433 **7** 1 1/2 **Acrux**8 8556 4-9-5 **73**.................................................(h) DanielTudhope 12 70
(David O'Meara) *hld up: shkn up over 1f out: nvr on terms* **7/2**2

6200 **8** 1 1/2 **Chosen Character (IRE)**43 7566 9-9-0 **75**......(vt) ElishaWhittington(7) 3 68
(Tom Dascombe) *hld up in tch: rdn over 1f out: wknd ins fnl f* **50/1**

25 **9** 3/4 **Black Dave (IRE)**106 5359 7-8-10 **67**........................... MattCosham(3) 1 59
(David Evans) *led: rdn and hdd over 1f out: wknd ins fnl f* **25/1**

03 **10** 1 1/2 **Spiritual Star (IRE)**46 7493 8-9-4 **72**............................. OisinMurphy 10 60
(Lee Carter) *hld up: effrt: nt clr run and edgd rt over 1f out: wknd ins fnl f* **20/1**

-022 **11** nk **Energia Flavio (BRZ)**72 6637 7-9-7 **75**................................ FranBerry 9 63
(Patrick Morris) *hld up: hdwy over 1f out: wknd ins fnl f* **16/1**

6310 **12** 1 1/4 **Bell Heather (IRE)**57 7111 4-8-7 **66**........................ ConnorMurtagh(5) 11 51
(Patrick Morris) *hld up: hmpd over 1f out: n.d* **18/1**

5330 **13** 18 **Dana's Present**19 8299 8-8-11 **68**..................................... EoinWalsh(3) 4 11
(Tony Newcombe) *s.s: a in rr: bhd fr 1/2-way* **66/1**

1m 47.97s (-2.13) **Going Correction** -0.175s/f (Stan)
**WFA** 3 from 4yo+ 3lb 13 Ran SP% **121.6**
Speed ratings (Par 103): **102,100,100,99,99 97,97,96,95,94 94,92,76**
CSF £20.43 CT £153.93 TOTE £6.90: £2.30, £1.60, £3.80; EX 26.70 Trifecta £238.50.
**Owner** John Brown **Bred** John Brown **Trained** Malpas, Cheshire

**FOCUS**
A winning time 2.12 seconds faster than that of the novice auction race which preceded it, courtesy of a strong early pace which burned most of those associated with it.
T/Plt: £241.60 to a £1 stake. Pool: £94,754.01 - 286.20 winning units T/Qpdt: £51.00 to a £1 stake. Pool: £15,903.36 - 230.61 winning units **Colin Roberts**

# 8667 FLEMINGTON (L-H)
Saturday, November 11
**OFFICIAL GOING: Turf: good**

## 8750a MELBOURNE'S OWN 3AW TROPHY (H'CAP) (4YO+) (TURF) 1m
**2:30** 4-Y-0+
**£39,473** (£12,631; £6,315; £3,508; £2,105; £1,403)

RPR

**1** **Fastnet Tempest (IRE)**13 4-9-4 **0**..............................(b) KerrinMcEvoy 6 101
(William Haggas) **17/10**1

**2** shd **Raw Impulse**13 5-9-3 **0**................................................... DamianLane 1 100
(Darren Weir, Australia) **13/2**

**3** 3/4 **Jacquinot Bay (AUS)**28 8059 10-9-2 **0**..........................(v) BlakeShinn 5 97
(David A & B Hayes & Tom Dabernig, Australia) **19/5**2

**4** 1 **Coldstone (FR)**28 8057 5-9-0 **0**..................................... DwayneDunn 4 93
(Michael Kent, Australia) **6/1**

**5** hd **Master Reset (AUS)**175 6-9-1 **0**.................................(p) BenMelham 7 93
(Matt Laurie, Australia) **18/1**

**6** 1/2 **Man Of His Word (AUS)**14 5-9-3 **0**.........................(p) BrentonAvdulla 3 94
(Bruce W Hill, Australia) **4/1**3

**7** 3 **Aurum Spirit (AUS)**31 9-8-7 **0**.....................................(bt) CoreyBrown 2 77
(Robbie Griffiths, Australia) **25/1**

1m 36.8s 7 Ran SP% **114.6**

**Owner** Oti Racing, L Webb Et Al **Bred** Rockhart Trading Ltd **Trained** Newmarket, Suffolk

## 8751a QUEEN ELIZABETH STKS (GROUP 3 H'CAP) (3YO+) (TURF) 1m 5f
**3:50** 3-Y-0+
**£106,140** (£31,578; £15,789; £7,894; £4,385; £3,508)

RPR

**1** **Vengeur Masque (IRE)**7 5-8-8 **0**................................ PatrickMoloney 9 106
(Michael Moroney, Australia) **11/2**3

**2** 3/4 **Grey Lion (IRE)**17 8362 5-8-7 **0**..............................(b) JordanChilds 5 104
(Matt Cumani, Australia) **25/1**

**3** 1/2 **Wheal Leisure (AUS)**17 8362 4-8-7 **0**............................. DeanYendall 2 103
(Archie Alexander, Australia) **17/2**

**4** 3 1/2 **Violate (AUS)**17 8362 4-8-7 **0**......................................(p) JamesWinks 6 98
(Brent Stanley, Australia) **25/1**

**5** shd **Gallic Chieftain (FR)**17 8362 4-8-7 **0**.........................(b1) MichaelDee 7 98
(Darren Weir, Australia) **4/1**2

**6** 2 1/4 **Qewy (IRE)**10 8633 7-9-4 **0**........................................ KerrinMcEvoy 10 105
(Charlie Appleby) **11/5**1

**7** 1 1/2 **Kiwia (AUS)**10 8633 4-8-9 **0**........................................... DamianLane 4 94
(Darren Weir, Australia) **4/1**2

**8** shd **Bettyrae Ruby (AUS)**217 4-8-7 **0**.................................(t) CoreyBrown 1 92
(Tim Hughes, Australia) **100/1**

**9** 8 **Cool Chap (AUS)**14 8445 5-8-7 **0**................................(p) DwayneDunn 8 80
(David A & B Hayes & Tom Dabernig, Australia) **15/1**

10 *12* **Tunes (AUS)**[243] 9-8-7 0....................(p) NoelCallow 3 62
(Grant Young, Australia) 100/1
2m 42.99s 10 Ran SP% 113.1

**Owner** R & C Legh Racing Pty Ltd, G G Syndicate Ltd Et Al **Bred** Dayton Investments Ltd **Trained** Australia

8752a - (Foreign Racing) - See Raceform Interactive

## 8753a EMIRATES STKS (GROUP 1) (3YO+) (TURF) 1m 2f
5:55 3-Y-O+
£704,678 (£210,526; £105,263; £52,631; £29,239; £23,391)

RPR
1 **Tosen Stardom (JPN)**[7] 6-9-4 0....................(bt) DamianLane 4 113
(Darren Weir, Australia) 11/2[2]
2 *1 ½* **Happy Clapper (AUS)**[14] 8446 7-9-4 0....................(b) BlakeShinn 5 110
(Patrick Webster, Australia) 7/1[3]
3 *hd* **It's Somewhat (USA)**[14] 6-9-4 0.................... BrentonAvdulla 10 110
(James Cummings, Australia) 17/1
4 *shd* **The Taj Mahal (IRE)**[28] 8058 3-9-1 0....................(b[1]) BenMelham 2 110
(A P O'Brien, Ire) 15/1
5 *shd* **Folkswood**[14] 8446 4-9-4 0....................(p) KerrinMcEvoy 12 109
(Charlie Appleby) 13/5[1]
6 *hd* **Cliff's Edge (AUS)**[14] 3-8-0 0.................... DeanYendall 9 106
(Darren Weir, Australia) 11/2[2]
7 *hd* **Harlem**[7] 5-9-4 0....................(b) ReganBayliss 7 108
(David A & B Hayes & Tom Dabernig, Australia) 30/1
8 *hd* **Odeon (NZ)**[4] 4-9-3 0.................... ChrisSymons 3 107
(Mathew Ellerton & Simon Zahra, Australia) 13/1
9 *hd* **Sense Of Occasion (AUS)**[7] 7-9-4 0.................... CoreyBrown 6 108
(Kris Lees, Australia) 50/1
10 *½* **So Si Bon (AUS)**[7] 4-9-3 0....................(b) NoelCallow 1 106
(Robbie Laing, Australia) 60/1
11 *shd* **Gailo Chop (FR)**[14] 8446 6-9-4 0.................... JohnAllen 8 106
(Darren Weir, Australia) 7/1[3]
12 *¾* **Samovare (AUS)**[21] 4-8-13 0....................(b[1]) DwayneDunn 11 100
(David A & B Hayes & Tom Dabernig, Australia) 50/1
2m 1.22s
**WFA** 3 from 4yo+ 3lb 12 Ran SP% 111.3

**Owner** Australian Bloodstock No 2 Syndicate, Doonaree Rac **Bred** Northern Racing **Trained** Australia

8754a (Foreign Racing) - See Raceform Interactive 7755

# TOULOUSE
Saturday, November 11
**OFFICIAL GOING: Turf: soft**

## 8755a PRIX FILLE DE L'AIR (GROUP 3) (3YO+ FILLIES & MARES) (TURF) 1m 2f 110y
2:50 3-Y-O+ £34,188 (£13,675; £10,256; £6,837; £3,418)

RPR
1 **Haggle**[56] 7177 4-8-13 0.................... Pierre-CharlesBoudot 3 109
(H-F Devin, France) *led first 150yds: hdd and settled in 4th: dropped to 5th 1/2-way: shkn up turning in: hdwy to chal 1f out: led 100yds out: pushed out* 48/10[3]
2 *1* **Son Macia (GER)**[20] 8273 4-8-13 0....................(b) MickaelBarzalona 7 107
(Andreas Suborics, Germany) *settled in 2nd: pushed along turning in: sn rdn: led over 1f out: immediately pressed: hdd 100yds out: no ex* 4/1[2]
3 *¾* **Via Firenze (IRE)**[52] 7305 4-8-13 0.................... MaximeGuyon 2 106+
(Mme Pia Brandt, France) *trckd ldr in 3rd: effrt fr 2f out: nt clrest of runs: kpt on wl* 53/10
4 *1 ½* **Rosental**[38] 7753 5-8-13 0.................... JamieSpencer 6 103+
(Luca Cumani) *settled towards rr: shkn up and hdwy fr 2f out: nt pce to rch ldrs: styd on for 4th* 13/2
5 *nse* **Louversey**[51] 7341 3-8-9 0.................... AnthonyCrastus 8 104
(P Sogorb, France) *led after 150yds: rdn and hdd over 1f out: wknd fnl f* 23/1
6 *1 ½* **Hebah (IRE)**[38] 7755 3-8-11 0 ow2.................... ChristopheSoumillon 4 103
(J-C Rouget, France) *slt stumble s: racd rr of midfield: rdn over 1 1/2f out: nt qckn: n.d* 23/10[1]
7 *nk* **Layali (FR)**[38] 7755 3-8-9 0.................... GregoryBenoist 1 100
(F Rohaut, France) *mid-div on inner: effrt fr over 2f out: nvr able to get on terms* 12/1
8 *snk* **Style Icon (FR)**[40] 7696 3-8-9 0.................... AurelienLemaitre 9 100
(H-F Devin, France) *awkward s and s.i.s: a towards rr* 13/1
9 *15* **Astral Merit (FR)**[14] 8444 7-8-13 0.........(b) Roberto-CarlosMontenegro 5 70
(F Monnier, France) *midfield: 4th 1/2-way: pushed along and wknd 2f out: eased* 33/1
2m 11.38s
**WFA** 3 from 4yo+ 3lb 9 Ran SP% 118.7
PARI-MUTUEL (all including 1 euro stake): WIN 5.80; PLACE 1.90, 1.70, 2.00; DF 11.20; SF 27.60.
**Owner** Mrs R G Hillen **Bred** Fittocks Stud **Trained** France

8756 - 8769a (Foreign Racing) - See Raceform Interactive

# 8254 SOUTHWELL (L-H)
Monday, November 13
**OFFICIAL GOING: Fibresand: standard**
Wind: Light behind Weather: Cloudy

## 8770 BETWAY MEDIAN AUCTION MAIDEN STKS 1m 3f 23y(F)
12:40 (12:40) (Class 5) 3-5-Y-O £3,234 (£962; £481; £240) Stalls Low

Form RPR
664 1 **Second Page**[33] 7948 3-8-12 70....................(b[1]) RossaRyan(7) 9 75
(Richard Hannon) *dwlt and towards rr: hdwy and in tch after 3f: trckd ldng pair 5f out: hdwy to chal 2f out: rdn to ld 1 1/2f out: drvn and edgd lft ins fnl f: kpt on wl* 15/8[1]
0236 2 *3* **Epitaph (IRE)**[2] 8749 3-9-5 69....................(v) LukeMorris 10 70
(Michael Appleby) *cl up: rdn along over 3f out: rdn to chal over 2f out: drvn and led briefly wl over 1f out: sn hdd: hld whn sltly hmpd ins fnl f: one pce* 2/1[2]
5220 3 *12* **Line Of Beauty**[54] 7279 3-9-0 68.................... RobertHavlin 6 46
(Simon Crisford) *cl up: led after 3f: jnd and rdn over 2f out: drvn and hdd wl over 1f out: kpt on same pce* 5/2[3]
0 4 *3 ¾* **Hewouldwouldnthe**[48] 7492 3-9-0 0.................... RobHornby 4 40
(Jonathan Portman) *chsd ldrs: rdn along 4f out: plugged on one pce* 50/1
24 5 *½* **Swiss Vinnare**[44] 7600 3-8-12 0.................... NicolaCurrie(7) 1 44
(Phil McEntee) *dwlt and bhd: hdwy 1/2-way: in tch over 4f out: sn rdn along and n.d* 7/1
5340 6 *hd* **Dragonite (IRE)**[48] 7478 3-9-5 43.................... PaulMulrennan 2 44
(Daniel Mark Loughnane) *towards rr: hdwy 1/2-way: rdn along over 4f out: n.d* 33/1
7 *26* **Bury The Evidence**[7] 4-9-4 0....................(h) PatrickMathers 3
(Derek Shaw) *a towards rr: outpcd and bhd fnl 3f* 100/1
000 8 *1 ¼* **Somepink (IRE)**[39] 7761 4-9-1 39....................(b[1]) EoinWalsh(3) 8
(Daniel Mark Loughnane) *a towards rr: outpcd and bhd fnl 3f* 150/1
000 9 *1 ½* **Jungle George**[25] 8183 3-9-5 40....................(p) BenCurtis 5
(Scott Dixon) *chsd ldrs: lost pl and rdn along after 3f: bhd fr 1/2-way* 100/1
0 10 *26* **Born For Champagne (IRE)**[22] 8256 3-9-0 0...........(h) TonyHamilton 7
(Derek Shaw) *t.k.h: slt ld 3f: prom: rdn along 5f out: sn lost pl and bhd: t.o fnl 3f* 150/1
2m 23.77s (-4.23) **Going Correction** -0.20s/f (Stan)
**WFA** 3 from 4yo 4lb 10 Ran SP% 117.4
Speed ratings (Par 103): **107,104,96,93,93 92,73,73,71,53**
CSF £6.03 TOTE £2.50: £1.10, £1.30, £1.10; EX 5.40 Trifecta £10.90.
**Owner** Middleham Park Racing LXIV **Bred** Whitwell Bloodstock **Trained** East Everleigh, Wilts
**FOCUS**
An uncompetitive maiden run at a steady pace. The front two pulled a long way clear and the race has been rated around them.

## 8771 BETWAY STAYERS H'CAP 2m 102y(F)
1:10 (1:10) (Class 5) (0-75,76) 3-Y-O+ £2,911 (£866; £432; £216) Stalls Low

Form RPR
5434 1 **Gabrial's Star**[17] 8394 8-9-7 70....................(b) TonyHamilton 3 83
(Richard Fahey) *trckd ldrs: smooth hdwy 3f out: cl up over 2f out: rdn to ld over 1f out: sn clr: kpt on strly* 4/1[3]
4000 2 *11* **Bertie Moon**[12] 8511 7-9-8 71.................... LukeMorris 7 71
(Michael Appleby) *led: pushed along 3f out: jnd and rdn over 2f out: hdd and drvn over 1f out: kpt on same pce* 15/2
0000 3 *3 ¾* **Rite To Reign**[17] 8398 6-9-6 76....................(v) RossaRyan(7) 2 71
(Philip McBride) *hld up in tch: hdwy on inner 7f out: trckd ldrs over 5f out: chsd ldng pair over 3f out: rdn along on inner over 2f out: drvn wl over 1f out: kpt on one pce* 5/1
4206 4 *6* **Ruler Of The Nile**[94] 5896 5-8-13 69....................(p) WilliamCox(7) 5 57
(Robert Stephens) *hld up in tch: hdwy to trck ldrs 5f out: pushed along over 3f out: rdn wl over 2f out: sn one pce* 17/2
3423 5 *9* **Hurricane Hollow**[13] 8487 7-9-6 69.................... BenCurtis 4 46
(David Barron) *hld up in rr: hdwy on outer and prom 1/2-way: chsd ldr 6f out: cl up 4f out: rdn along 3f out: drvn over 2f out and sn wknd* 10/3[2]
5000 6 *99* **Sleep Easy**[17] 8394 5-9-10 73....................(tp) RobertWinston 6
(Neil Mulholland) *trckd ldrs: cl up after 6f: pushed along over 6f out: rdn and wknd 5f out: sn bhd: t.o fnl 3f* 11/4[1]
000- P **Giant Redwood (IRE)**[208] 7507 5-8-13 62....................(t) FranBerry 1
(Ben Haslam) *cl up: rdn along and lost pl 1/2-way: sn bhd and t.o whn p.u 4f out: dismntd* 66/1
3m 39.26s (-6.24) **Going Correction** -0.20s/f (Stan) 7 Ran SP% 110.2
Speed ratings (Par 103): **107,101,99,96,92 42,**
CSF £30.73 TOTE £4.00: £1.60, £2.20; EX 23.50 Trifecta £110.70.
**Owner** Dr Marwan Koukash **Bred** Miss K Rausing **Trained** Musley Bank, N Yorks
**FOCUS**
Plenty to prove for most of the field. It was run at a steady pace and the winner scored impressively. He has been rated back to last winter's form.

## 8772 BETWAY DASH H'CAP 6f 16y(F)
1:40 (1:41) (Class 6) (0-65,67) 4-Y-O+ £2,264 (£673; £336; £168) Stalls Low

Form RPR
0406 1 **First Excel**[16] 8427 5-9-3 61....................(b) JimmyQuinn 6 68
(Roy Bowring) *mde all: rdn wl over 1f out: drvn and hung lft ins fnl f: hld on wl towards fin* 13/2[3]
1320 2 *nk* **Bold Spirit**[6] 8651 6-9-2 60....................(t) BarryMcHugh 2 67
(Declan Carroll) *trckd ldrs on inner: hdwy and n.m.r bnd 3f out: rdn ent fnl f: sn chsng wnr: swtchd rt and drvn last 100yds: kpt on* 5/1[1]
5046 3 *2* **Sarabi**[13] 8484 4-8-6 55....................(p) JamieGormley(5) 4 55
(Scott Dixon) *midfield: hdwy and n.m.r bnd 3f out: rdn to chse ldrs over 1f out: drvn and kpt on same pce fnl f* 16/1
5526 4 *nk* **Tasaaboq**[13] 8496 6-8-1 52....................(tp) NicolaCurrie(7) 7 51
(Phil McEntee) *dwlt and bhd: hdwy and wd st to stands' rail: rdn along 2f out: hdwy over 1f out: styd on strly fnl f* 14/1
2003 5 *1* **Ticks The Boxes (IRE)**[14] 8480 5-9-9 67....................(p) PaulMulrennan 13 63
(John Wainwright) *prom: cl up on outer 1/2-way: rdn 2f out: sn edgd lft: drvn and edgd lft ent fnl f: kpt on same pce* 9/1
1050 6 *2* **Fortinbrass (IRE)**[77] 6531 7-9-2 60.................... RobertWinston 3 50
(John Balding) *chsd ldrs: rdn along over 2f out: sn drvn and kpt on same pce* 20/1
2010 7 *1 ¾* **Corporal Maddox**[40] 7723 10-9-4 62....................(p) LukeMorris 10 47
(Ronald Harris) *towards rr: rdn along and wd st: kpt on u.p fnl 2f* 11/1
2520 8 *½* **Unnoticed**[265] 850 5-9-7 65.................... FrannyNorton 12 48
(Ollie Pears) *chsd ldrs towards outer: rdn along over 2f out: sn btn* 8/1
0005 9 *shd* **Big Amigo (IRE)**[16] 8427 4-9-1 62.................... EoinWalsh(3) 11 51+
(Daniel Mark Loughnane) *trckd ldrs whn n.m.r and lost pl after 1f: t.k.h after and a towards rr* 11/2[2]
0001 10 *¾* **Bingo George (IRE)**[22] 8259 4-8-9 53....................(t) RobHornby 9 34
(Mark Rimell) *chsd wnr: rdn wl over 2f out: drvn wl over 1f out: grad wknd* 13/2[3]
36 11 *4 ½* **Wimboldsley**[77] 6531 6-8-0 51 oh5.................... GabrieleMalune(7) 1 18
(Scott Dixon) *chsd ldrs on inner: rdn along over 2f out: sn wknd* 40/1
5552 12 *1 ½* **Fantasy Justifier (IRE)**[13] 8496 6-8-13 57....................(p) BenCurtis 8 20
(Ronald Harris) *a towards rr* 8/1
00-5 13 *6* **Interchoice Star**[22] 8258 12-8-7 51 oh6....................(p) JamesSullivan 5
(Ray Peacock) *in tch: rdn along wl over 2f out: sn wknd* 66/1
1m 15.64s (-0.86) **Going Correction** -0.20s/f (Stan) 13 Ran SP% 120.5
Speed ratings (Par 101): **97,96,93,93,92 89,87,86,86,85 79,77,69**
CSF £38.73 CT £509.90 TOTE £8.80: £2.20, £2.00, £5.00; EX 52.90 Trifecta £684.50.

**Owner** S R Bowring **Bred** S R Bowring **Trained** Edwinstowe, Notts
**FOCUS**
The pace was sound for this modest handicap.

## 8773 SUNBETS H'CAP — 1m 13y(F)
2:15 (2:17) (Class 5) (0-70,72) 3-Y-O+ £3,234 (£962; £481; £240) Stalls Low

Form RPR
3412 1 **Medici Moon**[13] 8498 3-8-10 **60**....................(p) LukeMorris 11 70
(Scott Dixon) *mde all: rdn along over 2f out: drvn over 1f out: kpt on wl u.p fnl f* **6/1**[3]
0606 2 1 1/4 **Red Touch (USA)**[17] 8400 5-9-6 **68**....................(p) AlistairRawlinson 8 75
(Michael Appleby) *dwlt and towards rr: hdwy 3f out: rdn along towards inner 2f out: styd on wl fnl f* **7/2**[2]
0044 3 3/4 **Samphire Coast**[11] 8538 4-9-0 **62**....................(h) PatrickMathers 12 67
(Derek Shaw) *prom: cl up 3f out: rdn to chal 2f out: ev ch: drvn and kpt on same pce fnl f* **7/1**
0650 4 5 **Zaeem**[88] 6111 8-9-5 **72**....................(t) JaneElliott(5) 14 66
(Ivan Furtado) *trckd ldrs on outer: cl up 3f out: rdn over 2f out: drvn wl over 1f out: kpt on same pce* **14/1**
0006 5 1 **Shearian**[22] 8254 7-8-11 **66**.................... GerO'Neill(7) 2 58
(Declan Carroll) *prom on inner: pushed along 3f out: rdn wl over 1f out: hld whn n.m.r and swtchd rt ent fnl f: one pce* **33/1**
1 6 nse **Straight Away**[14] 8479 3-9-6 **70**.................... RobHornby 6 61
(Andrew Balding) *dwlt: sn trcking ldrs: smooth hdwy over 2f out: cl up and rdn over 1f out: hung lft ent fnl f: sn wknd* **13/8**[1]
6640 7 1 3/4 **Cadeaux Boxer**[11] 8549 4-9-6 **68**.................... FranBerry 7 55
(Lee Carter) *chsd ldrs: rdn along over 3f out: wknd wl over 2f out* **16/1**
0200 8 nse **Hernando Torres**[24] 8209 9-9-5 **67**....................(tp) JamesSullivan 13 54
(Michael Easterby) *nvr bttr than midfield* **50/1**
6442 9 2 1/4 **Rebel State (IRE)**[9] 8589 4-8-9 **64**....................(p) HarrisonShaw(7) 3 46
(Jedd O'Keeffe) *midfield: effrt 3f out: sn rdn and no hdwy* **22/1**
5560 10 5 **Livella Fella (IRE)**[24] 8206 4-9-7 **69**.................... PhillipMakin 4 40
(Keith Dalgleish) *chsd ldrs: pushed along 1/2-way: sn rdn and lost pl: bhd fr over 2f out* **40/1**
-100 11 3/4 **American Patrol (IRE)**[181] 2711 3-8-10 **60**.................... BenCurtis 10 29
(Neil Mulholland) *a in rr* **25/1**
4401 12 2 1/2 **Sunnua (IRE)**[12] 8513 4-8-12 **60**.................... TonyHamilton 1 23
(Richard Fahey) *chsd ldrs on inner: rdn along over 3f out: sn wknd* **25/1**
2400 13 8 **Dream Magic (IRE)**[27] 8132 3-8-10 **63**.................... EoinWalsh(3) 5 8
(Daniel Mark Loughnane) *a in rr: bhd fnl 3f* **40/1**
1m 42.27s (-1.43) **Going Correction** -0.20s/f (Stan)
**WFA** 3 from 4yo+ 2lb **13 Ran SP% 121.5**
Speed ratings (Par 103): **99,97,97,92,91 90,89,89,86,81 81,78,70**
CSF £25.83 CT £155.45 TOTE £5.30: £1.70, £1.30, £2.30; EX 30.40 Trifecta £169.20.
**Owner** D Sharp and Partners **Bred** G E Amey **Trained** Babworth, Notts
**FOCUS**
A strongly run handicap with the first three finishing clear. The race has been rated through the third.

## 8774 BETWAY MAIDEN STKS — 4f 214y(F)
2:45 (2:46) (Class 5) 3-Y-O+ £2,911 (£866; £432; £216) Stalls Centre

Form RPR
0644 1 **Know The Truth**[22] 8256 3-8-7 59.................... WilliamCarver(7) 6 55
(Andrew Balding) *prom: chal over 1f out: sn rdn: styd on wl fnl f to ld nr line* **4/1**[3]
0440 2 nk **Excellent World (IRE)**[13] 8490 4-9-0 40....................(t) BarryMcHugh 5 54
(Tony Coyle) *cl up: chal 1/2-way: led wl over 1f out: rdn appr fnl f and sn edgd lft: drvn ins fnl f: hdd and no ex nr line* **12/1**
3222 3 2 3/4 **Nellie's Dancer**[6] 8656 3-9-0 56....................(p) LukeMorris 8 44
(Scott Dixon) *trckd ldrs: hdwy and cl up 2f out: rdn wl over 1f out: ev ch: drvn and kpt on same pce fnl f* **5/4**[1]
0- 4 1 **Lyin Eyes**[10] 8568 3-9-0 0.................... ShaneFoley 4 41
(K J Condon, Ire) *slt ld: rdn along over 2f out: hdd wl over 1f out: sn drvn and grad wknd* **9/4**[2]
0500 5 2 1/4 **Red Shanghai (IRE)**[14] 8481 3-8-11 39....................(v[1]) NoelGarbutt(3) 7 32
(Charles Smith) *in tch: rdn along 1/2-way: n.d* **100/1**
0600 6 3/4 **Dollywaggon Pike**[21] 8298 3-9-0 45.................... FrannyNorton 2 30
(J R Jenkins) *cl up: rdn along 1/2-way: sn wknd* **20/1**
0650 7 7 **Nitro**[28] 8117 3-9-5 29.................... BenCurtis 1 10
(Roy Brotherton) *dwlt: a in rr* **150/1**
59.61s (-0.09) **Going Correction** 0.0s/f (Stan) **7 Ran SP% 109.3**
Speed ratings (Par 103): **100,99,95,93,89 88,77**
CSF £42.03 TOTE £4.00: £1.60, £5.00; EX 37.00 Trifecta £70.40.
**Owner** A M Balding **Bred** George Strawbridge **Trained** Kingsclere, Hants
**FOCUS**
A weak maiden. The winner stayed on well to give William Carver victory on his first ride under rules. The runner-up is the key to the form.

## 8775 BETWAY APPRENTICE CLASSIFIED CLAIMING STKS — 4f 214y(F)
3:20 (3:26) (Class 6) 3-Y-O+ £2,264 (£673; £336; £168) Stalls Centre

Form RPR
3130 1 **Roaring Rory**[72] 6670 4-8-8 64....................(p) JamieGormley(5) 8 69
(Ollie Pears) *cl up: led wl over 1f out: rdn clr ent fnl f: kpt on strly* **20/1**
/6-0 2 2 1/4 **Strategic Heights (IRE)**[69] 6798 8-8-10 69..........(p) JackDinsmore(7) 6 65
(Jamie Osborne) *towards rr: hdwy 2f out: rdn along over 1f out: chsd wnr and edgd rt ins fnl f: kpt on same pce* **12/1**[3]
3002 3 1 **The Big Lad**[21] 8296 5-8-6 69....................(e) NicolaCurrie(5) 4 55
(Richard Hughes) *towards rr: hdwy wl over 1f out: sn rdn to chse ldrs: no imp fnl f* **4/6**[1]
6000 4 1 1/2 **Tan**[10] 8552 3-9-0 63....................(vt[1]) PatrickVaughan(5) 1 58
(Tony Coyle) *cl up: led over 2f out: hdd wl over 1f out: sn rdn and edgd lft: wknd fnl f* **14/1**
0065 5 1 1/4 **Vroom (IRE)**[11] 8541 4-8-8 70....................(p) PaulHainey(7) 2 49
(Gay Kelleway) *prom: rdn along 2f out: wknd over 1f out* **3/1**[2]
3130 6 1/2 **Absolutely Awesome**[48] 7486 3-9-3 67.................... TimClark 3 50
(John Butler) *prom: rdn along over 2f out: sn wknd* **12/1**[3]
060- 7 4 1/2 **Monsieur Jamie**[391] 7444 9-8-4 55.................... WilliamCox(5) 5 25
(Clare Ellam) *a in rr* **66/1**
59.52s (-0.18) **Going Correction** 0.0s/f (Stan) **7 Ran SP% 113.3**
Speed ratings (Par 101): **101,97,95,93,91 90,83**
CSF £219.33 TOTE £12.90: £5.40, £3.60; EX 98.90 Trifecta £264.40.
**Owner** Ownaracehorse Ltd & Ollie Pears **Bred** R S Hoskins & Hermes Services **Trained** Norton, N Yorks
■ Red Flute was withdrawn. Price at time of withdrawal 25-1. Rule 4 does not apply.
**FOCUS**
The pace was sound for this uncompetitive claimer.

## 8776 BETWAY H'CAP — 4f 214y(F)
3:50 (3:51) (Class 6) (0-60,59) 3-Y-O+ £2,587 (£770; £384; £192) Stalls Centre

Form RPR
4400 1 **Broadhaven Honey (IRE)**[13] 8495 3-9-5 **57**....................(v) BenCurtis 14 72
(Ronald Harris) *prom on stands' side: hdwy wl over 1f out: rdn and hung bdly lft ent fnl f: led last 110yds: sn clr* **20/1**
0060 2 3 1/2 **Novabridge**[10] 8559 9-8-13 **51**....................(b) PaulMulrennan 1 53
(Karen Tutty) *racd nr far rail: prom: hdwy to ld 2f out: rdn and edgd rt to centre over 1f out: hdd and sltly hmpd ins fnl f: kpt on: no ch w wnr* **16/1**
6000 3 1 1/4 **Chillililli**[16] 8428 3-8-2 **45**....................(b[1]) JaneElliott(5) 8 43
(Michael Appleby) *racd towards stands' side: chsd ldrs: hdwy wl over 1f out: rdn to chse ldr ent fnl f: kpt on same pce* **100/1**
1000 4 nk **Snoozy Sioux (IRE)**[48] 7494 3-9-5 **57**....................(b[1]) RobertWinston 12 53
(Martin Smith) *racd towards stands' side: hld up towards rr: hdwy wl over 1f out: sn rdn and styd on wl fnl f* **12/1**
4016 5 hd **Mr Enthusiastic**[16] 8428 3-8-11 **49**.................... BarryMcHugh 10 45
(Noel Wilson) *racd towards stands' side: chsd ldrs: rdn along wl over 1f out: kpt on u.p fnl f* **33/1**
0033 6 nk **Coiste Bodhar (IRE)**[5] 8681 6-8-6 **51**....................(p) GabrieleMalune(7) 2 46
(Scott Dixon) *racd far side: prom: cl up 1/2-way: rdn along wl over 1f out: drvn appr fnl f and grad wknd* **4/1**[2]
5000 7 hd **Only Ten Per Cent (IRE)**[88] 6114 9-9-0 **52**....................(v) FrannyNorton 9 46
(J R Jenkins) *racd centre: midfield: hdwy wl over 1f out: sn rdn and kpt on fnl f: n.d* **12/1**
0346 8 nk **Imperial Legend (IRE)**[10] 8559 8-8-12 **53**...(b[1]) RachelRichardson(3) 13 46
(Alan Brown) *towards rr nr stands' side: rdn along 2f out: sme late hdwy* **20/1**
0506 9 nk **Borough Boy (IRE)**[5] 8681 7-9-6 **58**....................(v) PatrickMathers 3 50
(Derek Shaw) *trckd ldrs far side: hdwy 2f out: rdn over 1f out: sn drvn and wknd fnl f* **9/4**[1]
0104 10 1 1/2 **Llewellyn**[167] 3186 9-9-0 **59**.................... GerO'Neill(7) 7 45+
(Declan Carroll) *racd centre: chsd ldrs: rdn along 2f out: sn drvn and wknd* **10/1**[3]
1533 11 2 **Our Place In Loule**[10] 8559 4-9-3 **55**.................... TonyHamilton 6 34
(Noel Wilson) *racd towards far side: cl up: rdn 2f out and ev ch: wknd appr fnl f* **10/1**[3]
0450 12 hd **Le Laitier (FR)**[13] 8490 6-8-2 **45**....................(b) JamieGormley(5) 11 23
(Scott Dixon) *dwlt: a towards rr stands' side* **25/1**
-065 13 1 1/2 **Clouded Gold**[10] 8559 5-8-7 **45**....................(p) LukeMorris 5 18
(Michael Appleby) *racd towards far side: slt ld: rdn along and hdd 2f out: sn wknd* **16/1**
-000 14 5 **Miss Mayson**[13] 8484 3-8-12 **50**.................... JamesSullivan 4 5
(Karen Tutty) *racd centre: a towards rr* **16/1**
58.92s (-0.78) **Going Correction** 0.0s/f (Stan) **14 Ran SP% 119.3**
Speed ratings (Par 101): **106,100,98,97,97 97,96,96,95,93 90,89,87,79**
CSF £292.07 CT £27600.16 TOTE £22.20: £5.70, £4.60, £18.80; EX 440.20.
**Owner** M Doocey, S Doocey & P J Doocey **Bred** James F Hanly **Trained** Earlswood, Monmouths
**FOCUS**
An open handicap run at a strong pace. The winner bounced back to last autumn's form.
T/Jkpt: Not won. T/Plt: £583.60 to a £1 stake. Pool: £76,157.67 - 95.25 winning units T/Qpdt: £333.90 to a £1 stake. Pool: £8,077.45 - 17.90 winning units **Joe Rowntree**

# 8691 CHANTILLY (R-H)
Monday, November 13
**OFFICIAL GOING: Polytrack: standard, turf: heavy**

## 8777a PRIX YACOWLEF (LISTED RACE) (2YO) (TURF) — 5f 110y
1:35 2-Y-O £25,641 (£10,256; £7,692; £5,128; £2,564)

RPR
1 **Absolute City (FR)**[37] 7846 2-8-9 0.................... NicolasPerret 4 96
(J-P Gauvin, France) **5/2**[1]
2 1 1/4 **Fastidious (FR)**[14] 2-8-13 0.................... Pierre-CharlesBoudot 5 96
(Louis Baudron, France) **155/10**
3 1 1/2 **The Broghie Man**[19] 8356 2-8-13 0....................(b) ChristopheSoumillon 3 91
(Adrian Paul Keatley, Ire) **37/10**[2]
4 1 **Arecibo (FR)**[14] 2-8-13 0.................... MaximeGuyon 8 88
(C Laffon-Parias, France) **53/10**[3]
5 1 **Drummore (IRE)**[21] 8302 2-8-13 0.................... MickaelBarzalona 7 84
(A Fabre, France) **58/10**
6 hd **Blue Tango (GER)**[14] 2-8-13 0.................... FabriceVeron 6 84
(M Munch, Germany) **51/1**
7 1 1/2 **Moses (FR)**[33] 2-8-13 0.................... EddyHardouin 9 79
(Mario Hofer, Germany) **15/2**
8 3/4 **Rioticism (FR)**[18] 8378 2-8-13 0.................... AntoineHamelin 1 76
(Matthieu Palussiere, France) **66/10**
9 7 **Zinia Dei Grif (ITY)**[135] 2-8-13 0.................... TonyPiccone 2 53
(Antonio Marcialis, Italy) **47/1**
10 6 **Silver Stripes (IRE)**[23] 8252 2-8-9 0....................(p) IoritzMendizabal 10 29
(P Vovcenko, Germany) **30/1**
1m 6.6s (2.10) **10 Ran SP% 118.6**
PARI-MUTUEL (all including 1 euro stake): WIN 3.50; PLACE 1.60, 3.70, 1.80; DF 21.50; SF 28.30.
**Owner** Jean-Claude Seroul **Bred** J-C Seroul **Trained** France

# 8715 NEWCASTLE (A.W) (L-H)
Wednesday, November 15
**OFFICIAL GOING: Tapeta: standard**
Wind: Virtually nil Weather: Cloudy

## 8778 BETWAY CASINO H'CAP — 2m 56y (Tp)
3:40 (3:43) (Class 4) (0-85,85) 3-Y-O+ £7,561 (£2,263; £1,131; £566; £282) Stalls Low

Form RPR
140 1 **Mobbhij**[37] 7880 3-9-7 **85**.................... JimmyQuinn 3 91+
(Saeed bin Suroor) *trckd ldrs on inner: swtchd rt and hdwy over 2f out: pushed along wl over 1f out: rdn to chse ldr appr fnl f: styd on wl to ld towards fin* **7/2**[2]

1466 **2** 3/4 **Montanna**26 8214 3-8-11 **75**....(b1) JackGarritty 11 80
(Jedd O'Keeffe) *trckd clr ldr: tk clsr order over 6f out: led 3f out: rdn clr 2f out: jnd and drvn ins fnl f: hdd and no ex towards fin* 11/1
412 **3** 1 **Waiting For Richie**12 8565 4-9-2 **73**.... AndrewMullen 1 77
(Tom Tate) *trckd ldrs: hdwy over 3f out: rdn wl over 1f out: drvn and kpt on same pce fnl f* 11/41
3063 **4** hd **Stormin Tom (IRE)**14 8511 5-8-12 **72**.... RachelRichardson(3) 13 76
(Tim Easterby) *trckd ldrs: effrt over 3f out and sn pushed along: rdn 2f out: drvn and kpt on same pce fnl f* 33/1
2322 **5** nk **Innoko (FR)**14 8505 7-8-9 **66**....(p) LukeMorris 5 69
(Robert Stephens) *hld up in midfield: hdwy 6f out: chsd ldrs wl over 2f out: sn rdn along: drvn over 1f out: kpt on same pce* 12/1
1540 **6** 3/4 **Wordiness**28 8157 9-8-8 **68**.... MattCosham(3) 9 70
(David Evans) *hld up towards rr: hdwy on inner 3f out: rdn along to chse ldrs wl over 1f out: sn drvn and kpt on fnl f* 33/1
0344 **7** 1/2 **Saved By The Bell (IRE)**12 8565 7-8-13 **70**.... PaulMulrennan 14 72
(Lawrence Mullaney) *trckd ldrs: pushed along 3f out: rdn over 2f out: sn drvn and no imp* 14/1
350 **8** 1 1/4 **Airton**27 8188 4-9-7 **78**.... JosephineGordon 10 78
(James Bethell) *hld up: a towards rr* 7/1
4/02 **9** 1/2 **Zaidiyn (FR)**19 8384 7-9-9 **80**.... StevieDonohoe 8 80
(Brian Ellison) *hld up and bhd: hdwy on outer over 3f out: in tch and rdn along 2f out: sn btn* 6/1
0500 **10** nse **Belle De Lawers**27 8192 6-9-2 **73**.... DanielTudhope 4 73
(James Bethell) *in tch: effrt over 3f out: sn rdn along and grad wknd* 50/1
0514 **11** 1 **Lady Clitico (IRE)**165 3338 6-8-10 **67**.... GrahamLee 12 65
(Rebecca Menzies) *hld up: a in rr* 125/1
0000 **12** 2 1/2 **Samtu (IRE)**27 8188 6-9-8 **79**.... BarryMcHugh 7 74
(Marjorie Fife) *hld up: a towards rr* 125/1
0011 **13** 7 **Tonto's Spirit**15 8487 5-8-12 **76**....(h) SeamusCronin(7) 6 63
(Kenneth Slack) *led and sn clr: pushed along 4f out: rdn and hdd 3f out: sn wknd* 11/23

3m 32.67s (-2.53) **Going Correction** -0.025s/f (Stan)
**WFA** 3 from 4yo+ 7lb 13 Ran SP% 123.2
Speed ratings (Par 105): **105,104,104,104,103 103,103,102,102,102 101,100,97**
CSF £42.50 CT £124.30 TOTE £4.80: £1.50, £3.30, £2.20; EX 60.00 Trifecta £254.00.
**Owner** Godolphin **Bred** Darley **Trained** Newmarket, Suffolk

**FOCUS**
A fairly decent staying handicap. They went a respectable gallop on a standard Tapeta surface, but the form is pretty sound rated around the third.

## 8779 32RED.COM NOVICE STKS 7f 14y (Tp)
4:15 (4:16) (Class 5) 2-Y-O £2,911 (£866; £432; £216) Stalls Centre

Form RPR
**1** **Kings Shield (USA)** 2-9-2 0.... RobertHavlin 4 87+
(John Gosden) *trckd ldrs: swtchd rt: green and niggled along 3f out: hdwy 2f out: rdn to chal appr fnl f: sn rdn and hung lft: led ins fnl f: kpt on wl* 8/111
2 **2** 1 1/4 **Ostilio**29 8140 2-9-2 0....(h1) PaulMulrennan 6 82+
(Simon Crisford) *sn trcking ldrs: hdwy over 2f out: rdn to chal over 1f out: led briefly ent fnl f: sn hdd and kpt on same pce towards fin* 13/82
2 **3** 5 **Illusional**65 7001 2-9-2 0.... JoeFanning 7 67
(Mark Johnston) *cl up: led after 2f: rdn along wl over 1f out: drvn and hdd ent fnl f: wknd* 4/13
0550 **4** 4 1/2 **Snaffled (IRE)**21 8340 2-9-2 0.... TomEaves 5 54
(David Brown) *hld up in rr: hdwy wl over 2f out: rdn to chse ldrs wl over 1f out: sn no imp* 125/1
0 **5** 2 1/4 **Altra Vita**33 7995 2-8-11 0.... LukeMorris 9 43
(Sir Mark Prescott Bt) *chsd ldrs: rdn along over 2f out: sn wknd* 66/1
55 **6** 3/4 **Mafdet**26 8215 2-8-11 0.... GrahamLee 10 41
(Bryan Smart) *chsd ldrs: rdn along wl over 2f out: sn wknd* 33/1
0 **7** 3 **Amadeus (IRE)**27 8189 2-9-2 0.... TonyHamilton 2 38
(Richard Fahey) *in tch: effrt and sme hdwy 1/2-way: rdn along 3f out: sn wknd* 40/1
0 **8** 1 **Whatwouldyouknow (IRE)**16 8474 2-9-2 0.... PhillipMakin 8 35
(Richard Guest) *trckd ldrs: pushed along 21/2f out: sn wknd* 33/1
0 **9** 4 **Ayton (IRE)**25 8236 2-8-11 0.... AndrewMullen 3 20
(Ollie Pears) *a in rr* 100/1
0 **10** 12 **Swissie**16 8474 2-9-2 0.... StevieDonohoe 1
(Ivan Furtado) *led 2f: cl up: rdn along 3f out: sn wknd* 150/1

1m 25.68s (-0.52) **Going Correction** -0.10s/f (Stan) 10 Ran SP% 128.3
Speed ratings (Par 96): **98,96,90,85,83 82,78,77,73,59**
CSF £2.49 TOTE £2.00: £1.10, £1.02, £1.70; EX 3.50 Trifecta £5.80.
**Owner** Qatar Racing Limited **Bred** Rosemont Farm Llc **Trained** Newmarket, Suffolk

**FOCUS**
A fair juvenile novice contest. They went a decent gallop and a heavily supported newcomer won well. The race has been rated around the second and fourth.

## 8780 32RED CASINO NURSERY H'CAP 5f (Tp)
4:45 (4:49) (Class 6) (0-55,55) 2-Y-O £2,385 (£704; £352) Stalls Centre

Form RPR
4062 **1** **Lord Of The Glen**11 8588 2-9-6 **54**....(v) DanielTudhope 9 61
(Jim Goldie) *cl up: led 3f out: rdn ent fnl f: kpt on wl* 11/81
0460 **2** 1/2 **Rock On Baileys**22 8325 2-9-2 **50**....(p) JosephineGordon 3 55
(Chris Dwyer) *chsd ldrs: hdwy 2f out: rdn over 1f out: drvn and ev ch ins fnl f: kpt on* 6/12
0462 **3** 1 1/2 **Lady Lintera (IRE)**19 8397 2-9-2 **50**....(h) LukeMorris 5 50
(Ann Duffield) *t.k.h: hld up towards rr: hdwy 2f out: sn rdn : styd on u.p fnl f* 13/23
0355 **4** hd **Cherry Oak (IRE)**89 6154 2-9-7 **55**.... PaulMulrennan 1 54
(Ben Haslam) *hld up towards rr: hdwy 2f out: rdn over 1f out: kpt on fnl f* 14/1
606 **5** 1/2 **Harvest Day**160 3495 2-9-3 **51**....(t) PhillipMakin 4 48
(Michael Easterby) *dwlt and rr: hdwy 2f out: sn rdn and styd on wl fnl f: nrst fin* 15/2
0500 **6** nk **Poppy Jag (IRE)**14 8500 2-9-2 **50**....(p1) DougieCostello 8 46
(Kevin Frost) *cl up: rdn over 2f out: drvn wl over 1f out: grad wknd* 33/1
0600 **7** 3 **Furni Factors**49 7518 2-9-5 **53**.... FrannyNorton 10 38
(Ronald Thompson) *in tch: hdwy to chse ldrs 1/2-way: sn rdn and wknd wl over 1f out* 10/1
5500 **8** 1/2 **Monkey Magic**57 7242 2-9-4 **52**....(t1) TomEaves 11 36
(Nigel Tinkler) *trckd ldrs: hdwy and cl up 1/2-way: rdn along 2f out: sn wknd* 16/1
044 **9** 3 1/4 **Sitsi**76 6624 2-9-5 **53**.... GrahamLee 12 25
(Bryan Smart) *a in rr* 28/1
0043 **10** hd **Laydee Victoria (IRE)**116 5161 2-9-5 **53**....(p1) AndrewMullen 7 27
(Ollie Pears) *chsd ldrs: rdn over 2f out: sn wknd* 12/1
3003 **11** nk **Casey Banter**71 6790 2-8-9 **50**.... MillyNaseb(7) 13 20
(Julia Feilden) *a towards rr* 12/1
0000 **12** 3/4 **Dark Hedges**15 8483 2-8-7 **46** oh1.... ConnorMurtagh(5) 6 13
(Olly Williams) *cl up: rdn along over 2f out: sn wknd* 100/1

59.49s (-0.01) **Going Correction** -0.10s/f (Stan) 12 Ran SP% 125.9
Speed ratings (Par 94): **96,95,92,92,91 91,86,85,80,80 79,78**
CSF £10.27 CT £46.48 TOTE £2.30: £1.10, £2.60, £2.30; EX 14.90 Trifecta £70.60.
**Owner** Johnnie Delta Racing **Bred** Goldie Racing Limited **Trained** Uplawmoor, E Renfrews

**FOCUS**
A moderate sprint nursery. The market got this race spot-on off a decent gallop and the form looks straightforward.

## 8781 SUNBETS.CO.UK MAIDEN STKS 1m 5y (Tp)
5:15 (5:17) (Class 5) 3-Y-O+ £3,234 (£962; £481; £240) Stalls Centre

Form RPR
32 **1** **Francis Xavier (IRE)**12 8554 3-9-5 0.... JosephineGordon 3 72+
(Hugo Palmer) *cl up: led wl over 1f out: rdn clr ins fnl f* 1/121
5 **2** 3 **Flying Raconteur**16 8479 3-9-5 0....(t1) TomEaves 6 65
(Nigel Tinkler) *trckd ldrs: hdwy over 2f out: rdn wl over 1f out: chsd wnr ins fnl f: kpt on same pce* 5/12
04 **3** 2 3/4 **Acker Bilk (IRE)**12 8554 3-9-5 0.... GrahamLee 1 58
(Keith Dalgleish) *led: rdn along over 2f out: hdd wl over 1f out: sn drvn and kpt on same pce* 6/13
**4** 7 **Majestic Man (IRE)**20 4-9-7 0.... FrannyNorton 7 41
(Ronald Thompson) *hld up in rr: sme late hdwy: nvr a factor* 50/1
0 **5** 2 3/4 **My Distant Murphy**89 6129 3-9-5 0....(t1) CamHardie 8 35
(Jacqueline Coward) *t.k.h early: in tch: rdn along 3f out: sn outpcd* 66/1
00 **6** hd **Wind Turbine (IRE)**16 8479 3-9-5 0.... DuranFentiman 5 34
(Tim Easterby) *chsd ldrs: rdn along 3f out: sn wknd* 25/1
00- **7** 17 **Thornton Frank**344 8237 3-9-5 0.... BarryMcHugh 4
(Brian Rothwell) *in tch: rdn along 3f out: sn outpcd and bhd* 80/1
0 **8** 10 **Lady Sundew (IRE)**12 8554 4-9-2 0.... PaulMulrennan 2
(Iain Jardine) *t.k.h: trckd ldng pair: pushed along 3f out: rdn over 2f out: sn wknd* 25/1

1m 38.78s (0.18) **Going Correction** -0.10s/f (Stan)
**WFA** 3 from 4yo 2lb 8 Ran SP% 135.7
Speed ratings (Par 103): **95,92,89,82,79 79,62,52**
CSF £2.02 TOTE £1.10: £1.02, £1.20, £1.30; EX 2.30 Trifecta £5.00.
**Owner** The Missionary Hymn Partnership **Bred** Rockhart Trading Ltd **Trained** Newmarket, Suffolk

**FOCUS**
An ordinary maiden. They went a respectable gallop, but the long odds-on favourite easily defeated the right two horses in second and third. The race has been rated through the latter.

## 8782 32RED ON THE APP STORE NOVICE AUCTION STKS 1m 5y (Tp)
5:45 (5:47) (Class 6) 2-Y-O £2,385 (£704; £352) Stalls Centre

Form RPR
0 **1** **Trevithick**14 8509 2-9-2 0.... GrahamLee 5 81
(Bryan Smart) *trckd ldrs: pushed along 3f out: hdwy 2f out: sn cl up: rdn to ld appr fnl f: kpt on strly* 22/1
43 **2** 3 1/2 **Rare Groove (IRE)**29 8140 2-8-13 0.... CliffordLee(3) 4 73
(Jedd O'Keeffe) *trckd ldr: cl up over 2f out: rdn to take slt ld wl over 1f out: drvn and hdd appr fnl f: kpt on same pce* 5/23
3 **3** 1 1/4 **The Lincoln Lawyer**14 8509 2-9-2 0.... FrannyNorton 1 70
(Mark Johnston) *led: jnd and pushed along over 2f out: rdn and hdd wl over 1f out: drvn and wknd ent fnl f* 6/41
22 **4** 2 3/4 **Broken Wings (IRE)**12 8553 2-8-11 0.... PaulMulrennan 6 59
(Keith Dalgleish) *trckd ldrs: hdwy over 2f out: rdn along wl over 1f out: sn drvn: edgd lft and no imp* 7/42
40 **5** 7 **Golden Guide**19 8380 2-8-11 0.... BenCurtis 3 43
(K R Burke) *trckd ldng pair: cl up 1/2-way: rdn along wl over 2f out: sn wknd* 28/1
60 **6** 11 **Wynfaul The Wizard (USA)**12 8555 2-9-2 0.... PhillipMakin 7 22
(Richard Guest) *dwlt: a rr* 80/1

1m 37.7s (-0.90) **Going Correction** -0.10s/f (Stan) 6 Ran SP% 114.0
Speed ratings (Par 94): **100,96,95,92,85 74**
CSF £76.97 TOTE £21.30: £7.60, £1.90; EX 68.40 Trifecta £199.00.
**Owner** Mrs P A Clark **Bred** Mrs P A Clark **Trained** Hambleton, N Yorks

**FOCUS**
A fair juvenile novice contest and they went a respectable gallop. There was no fluke about the shock outcome and the race has been rated at face value.

## 8783 32REDSPORT.COM NURSERY H'CAP 7f 14y (Tp)
6:15 (6:17) (Class 6) (0-55,56) 2-Y-O £2,385 (£704; £352) Stalls Centre

Form RPR
600 **1** **Lord Caprio (IRE)**68 6897 2-9-7 **55**....(t1) PaulMulrennan 14 65+
(Ben Haslam) *stdd s: hld up and bhd: gd hdwy on stands rail 2f out: chsd ldrs over 1f out: rdn to ld jst ins fnl f: kpt on strly* 33/1
3355 **2** 3 **Rock On Bertie (IRE)**49 7518 2-9-5 **53**....(p) TomEaves 12 52
(Nigel Tinkler) *led: rdn along over 2f out: drvn over 1f out: hdd jst ins fnl f: kpt on u.p* 10/1
000 **3** 3/4 **Lady Jayne (IRE)**19 8381 2-8-12 **46**.... JosephineGordon 11 43
(Ian Williams) *towards rr: hdwy to chse ldrs over 2f out: rdn wl over 1f out: edgd lft to far rail and drvn ent fnl f: styd on* 7/13
500 **4** 1/2 **Blue Havana (IRE)**133 4502 2-9-8 **56**.... JasonHart 9 52
(John Quinn) *hld up towards rr: hdwy over 2f out: rdn wl over 1f out: styd on fnl f* 18/1
0000 **5** 1/2 **Partry Flyer (IRE)**8 8644 2-8-12 **46** oh1....(b1) KevinStott 2 40
(Oliver Greenall) *midfield: hdwy to chse ldrs over 2f out: rdn wl over 1f out: drvn and ch ent fnl f: kpt on same pce* 25/1
0532 **6** 2 1/2 **Istanbul Pasha (IRE)**16 8475 2-9-6 **54**....(v) DanielTudhope 8 41
(David Evans) *cl up: chal over 2f out: rdn and ev ch over 1f out: drvn ent fnl f: kpt on same pce* 3/11
0050 **7** 2 **Navarra Princess (IRE)**76 6609 2-9-3 **51**.... StevieDonohoe 5 33
(Don Cantillon) *prom: cl up over 2f out: rdn wl over 1f out: wknd fnl f* 8/1
4450 **8** nk **Call Dawn**47 7563 2-9-8 **56**.... PhillipMakin 10 37
(Michael Easterby) *trckd ldrs: hdwy over 2f out: rdn to chal over 1f out: ev ch: drvn ent fnl f: sn wknd* 16/1
300 **9** 3/4 **Fabella Bere (FR)**26 8213 2-9-5 **56**.... CliffordLee(3) 1 35
(K R Burke) *in tch: rdn along 2f out: sn btn* 22/1
5006 **10** 1 **Lady Sandy (IRE)**49 7518 2-9-5 **53**.... BenCurtis 4 29
(David Barron) *in tch: rdn along wl over 2f out: sn wknd* 15/2
3003 **11** 1/2 **Mr Carbonator**16 8475 2-9-7 **55**.... JimmyQuinn 3 30
(Philip Kirby) *prom: rdn along wl over 2f out: sn drvn and grad wknd* 6/12

4436 **12** *shd* **Avenging Red (IRE)**[28] 8145 2-9-6 **54**.........................(p) FrannyNorton 7 29+
(Adam West) *t.k.h: cl up: ev ch 2f out: sn rdn and wknd over 1f out* **10/1**

650 **13** *6* **Out Last**[78] 6545 2-9-2 **50**.............................................(p[1]) AndrewMullen 13 9
(Keith Dalgleish) *a towards rr* **33/1**

0004 **14** *12* **Salty Sugar**[14] 8500 2-9-8 **56**.............................................(t[1]) LukeMorris 6 7
(Paul Cole) *dwlt: sn trcking ldrs: rdn along 3f out: sn lost pl and bhd* **9/1**

1m 26.44s (0.24) **Going Correction** -0.10s/f (Stan) 14 Ran SP% **128.1**
Speed ratings (Par 94): **94,90,89,89,88 85,83,83,82,81 80,80,73,59**
CSF £344.35 CT £1700.26 TOTE £20.90: £5.90, £3.40, £2.70; EX 221.40 Trifecta £2758.80.
**Owner** Blue Lion Racing IX **Bred** Kildaragh Stud **Trained** Middleham Moor, N Yorks

**FOCUS**
A moderate nursery. They went a respectable gallop and the shock winner proved something of a revelation on his fourth start.

## 8784 BET & WATCH AT SUNBETS.CO.UK H'CAP 7f 14y (Tp)
6:45 (6:47) (Class 7) (0-50,50) 3-Y-O+ £2,264 (£673; £336; £168) Stalls Centre

Form RPR

6245 **1** **Pitch High (IRE)**[56] 7271 3-8-12 **50**............................ MillyNaseb(7) 6 55
(Julia Feilden) *led 2f: cl up: led again over 2f out: rdn wl over 1f out: drvn and kpt on wl fnl f* **12/1**

5502 **2** *½* **Stardrifter**[11] 8590 5-9-0 **47**.................................. RachelRichardson(3) 13 53
(Linda Perratt) *hld up in rr: hdwy over 2f out: n.m.r and swtchd rt ent fnl f sn rdn and styd on wl towards fin* **5/2[1]**

6262 **3** *nk* **Dream Revival**[5] 8716 4-9-5 **49**..................................(p) StevieDonohoe 5 53
(Paul Collins) *in tch towards far side: hdwy 2f out: rdn to chse wnr ent fnl f: sn drvn and ev ch: no ex nr fin* **8/1**

4004 **4** *1* **Jennies Gem**[79] 6529 4-9-2 **46**....................................... AndrewMullen 3 47
(Ollie Pears) *prom: rdn along over 2f out: sn sltly outpcd: kpt on wl u.p fnl f* **12/1**

3100 **5** *3 ½* **Zebelini (IRE)**[50] 7481 5-9-0 **47**.................................. EoinWalsh(3) 12 39
(Roy Bowring) *prom nr stands' rail: led after 2f: hdd over 2f out and sn rdn: wknd appr fnl f* **15/2[3]**

340 **6** *¾* **Ypres**[49] 7525 8-9-6 **50**..............................................(p[1]) KevinStott 8 40
(Jason Ward) *dwlt and in rr: hdwy over 2f out: rdn wl over 1f out: styd on fnl f* **10/1**

/5-0 **7** *1 ¾* **Dazeekha**[204] 2063 4-9-6 **50**............................................ TomEaves 4 35
(Michael Herrington) *t.k.h: hld up in tch: hdwy over 2f out: sn chsng ldrs: rdn over 1f out: kpt on same pce fnl f* **28/1**

004 **8** *1 ¼* **Linda Doris (IRE)**[21] 8342 3-9-3 **48**.......................... DanielMuscutt 9 29
(Gay Kelleway) *in tch: rdn along 3f out: sn wknd* **25/1**

0604 **9** *½* **Diamond Avalanche (IRE)**[27] 8193 4-9-2 **46**.................. JackGarritty 2 27
(Kristin Stubbs) *trckd ldrs: hdwy over 2f out: rdn wl over 1f out: wknd appr fnl f* **5/1[2]**

0040 **10** *1* **Arizona Sunrise**[5] 8719 4-9-5 **49**............................... ConnorMurtagh 11 27
(Tina Jackson) *nvr bttr than midfield* **16/1**

0 **11** *nk* **Reason To Believe (FR)**[22] 8307 3-9-4 **49**...................(p) JimmyQuinn 1 25
(David Bridgwater) *trckd ldrs towards far side: rdn along over 2f out: sn wknd* **11/1**

6066 **12** *1 ½* **Prisom (IRE)**[24] 8259 4-9-6 **50**................................ JosephineGordon 14 23
(Gay Kelleway) *hld up: a towards rr* **9/1**

0400 **13** *2 ½* **Mighty Bond**[8] 8656 5-9-3 **47**........................................(p) BarryMcHugh 7 13
(Tracy Waggott) *trckd ldrs: effrt 2f out: sn rdn: wknd over 1f out* **33/1**

00-5 **14** *13* **Echoism (IRE)**[29] 8137 3-9-5 **50**.......................................... LukeMorris 10
(Peter Hiatt) *chsd ldrs: rdn along 3f out: sn wknd* **16/1**

1m 26.43s (0.23) **Going Correction** -0.10s/f (Stan)
**WFA** 3 from 4yo+ 1lb 14 Ran SP% **132.9**
Speed ratings (Par 97): **94,93,93,91,87 87,85,83,83,81 81,79,77,62**
CSF £45.66 CT £285.87 TOTE £14.80: £4.50, £1.80, £3.20; EX 64.70 Trifecta £436.90.
**Owner** Stowstowquickquickstow Partnership **Bred** T Purcell & K Purcell **Trained** Exning, Suffolk

**FOCUS**
A moderate handicap and the form looks straightforward. The winning time was virtually identical to that clocked by the juveniles in the 7f nursery half an hour earlier off a respectable gallop.
T/Plt: £53.00 to a £1 stake. Pool: £61,618.08 - 1,161.23 winning units T/Qpdt: £20.70 to a £1 stake. Pool: £8,388.72 - 403.78 winning units **Joe Rowntree**

8785 - 8792a (Foreign Racing) - See Raceform Interactive

# 8701 CHELMSFORD (A.W) (L-H)
Thursday, November 16

**OFFICIAL GOING: Polytrack: standard**
Wind: light, half against Weather: showers

## 8793 TOTESCOOP6 MAGIC MILLION THIS SATURDAY NURSERY H'CAP 6f (P)
5:25 (5:27) (Class 6) (0-60,60) 2-Y-O £3,234 (£962; £481; £240) Stalls Centre

Form RPR

0005 **1** **Mosskeeter**[29] 8145 2-9-5 **58**........................................... RobertHavlin 3 68
(John Best) *hld up in tch in midfield: clsd to trck ldrs and travelling strly over 2f out: effrt to chse ldr over 1f out: led ins fnl f: edgd lft but r.o strly: readily* **9/2[2]**

0501 **2** *3* **Hic Bibi**[15] 8500 2-9-7 **60**........................................... JosephineGordon 4 61
(David Brown) *dwlt: rousted along and sn rcvrd to ld: hdd after 1f: chsd ldr tl rdn to ld again over 1f out: hdd ins fnl f: sn outpcd but kpt on for 2nd* **9/4[1]**

0503 **3** *1 ¾* **Watching Spirits**[19] 8432 2-9-7 **60**.................................... RyanTate 10 56+
(Michael Appleby) *s.i.s and bmpd leaving stalls: hdwy into midfield 4f out: swtchd rt and effrt wl over 1f out: kpt on u.p ins fnl f to snatch 3rd last strides: nvr threatened ldrs* **5/1[3]**

030 **4** *nk* **Moremoneymoreparty (IRE)**[17] 8475 2-9-3 **56**.............. PhillipMakin 6 51
(Richard Guest) *chsd ldrs: effrt ent fnl 2f: 3rd and unable qck u.p ent fnl f: no imp and lost 3rd last strides* **12/1**

6500 **5** *nse* **Roseau City**[23] 8325 2-9-5 **58**.......................................(b[1]) SeanLevey 7 53
(David Elsworth) *midfield: rdn over 2f out: drvn and hdwy over 1f out: chsd ldrs but no imp ins fnl f* **10/1**

050 **6** *1 ¾* **Grasmere (IRE)**[61] 7141 2-9-4 **60**........................ CallumShepherd(3) 13 49
(Alan Bailey) *towards rr and on outer: rdn 3f out: styd on ins fnl f: nvr trbld ldrs* **33/1**

000 **7** *1 ½* **Jazzy Girl (IRE)**[24] 8294 2-8-13 **52**................................... BenCurtis 9 37
(Brendan Powell) *s.i.s: sn pushed along in rr: hdwy 1f out: kpt on ins fnl f: nvr trbld ldrs* **14/1**

000 **8** *½* **Royal Wave**[91] 6100 2-8-6 **45**........................................... JimmyQuinn 5 28
(William Knight) *chsd ldrs: 5th and rdn over 2f out: unable qck over 1f out: wknd ins fnl f* **16/1**

560 **9** *1 ½* **Shadow Seeker (IRE)**[17] 8467 2-9-4 **57**.....................(b[1]) ShaneKelly 2 36
(Paul D'Arcy) *s.i.s and rousted along early: hld up in rr: effrt over 2f out: nvr trbld ldrs* **9/1**

000 **10** *2 ¾* **Lastoneforthecraic (IRE)**[136] 4440 2-8-6 **52**.... KatherineGlenister(7) 12 23
(David Evans) *hld up in rr: effrt over 2f out: nvr trbld ldrs* **66/1**

3660 **11** *5* **Royal Crown (IRE)**[61] 7159 2-9-7 **60**............................ DanielTudhope 1 16
(David O'Meara) *a in rr: n.d* **12/1**

0650 **12** *1 ¾* **Mirek (IRE)**[37] 7914 2-8-11 **50**........................................ DanielMuscutt 8
(Patrick Chamings) *taken down early: t.k.h: led after 1f: rdn and hdd over 1f out: sn struggling: fdd fnl f* **10/1**

1m 13.94s (0.24) **Going Correction** -0.125s/f (Stan) 12 Ran SP% **126.2**
Speed ratings (Par 94): **93,89,86,86,86 83,81,81,79,75 68,66**
CSF £16.03 CT £56.79 TOTE £5.40: £1.80, £1.50, £2.60; EX 19.50 Trifecta £75.90.
**Owner** Lingfield Park Owners Group 2016 **Bred** D R Tucker **Trained** Oad Street, Kent

**FOCUS**
A modest nursery with the winner taking a step forward. They went a decent gallop on standard Polytrack.

## 8794 TOTESCOOP6 £1 MILLION THIS SATURDAY NOVICE MEDIAN AUCTION STKS 7f (P)
5:55 (5:57) (Class 6) 2-Y-O £3,234 (£962; £481; £240) Stalls Low

Form RPR

2 **1** **Music Society (IRE)**[119] 5047 2-9-2 0.............................. BenCurtis 10 85+
(Sylvester Kirk) *t.k.h: mde all: rdn and clr over 1f out: r.o wl: eased towards fin: easily* **5/1[2]**

05 **2** *4 ½* **Blue Candy**[22] 8339 2-9-2 0........................................... DanielTudhope 6 72
(Archie Watson) *chsd wnr thrght: rdn over 2f out: drvn and no imp over 1f out: kpt on same pce ins fnl f* **5/1[2]**

**3** *1* **Strange Society (IRE)** 2-9-2 0............................... JosephineGordon 1 69+
(Hugo Palmer) *s.i.s: sn rcvrd and wl in tch in midfield: effrt in 4th and drifted rt wl over 1f out: wnt 3rd ins fnl f: kpt on but no threat to wnr* **5/2[1]**

**4** *3 ¼* **Jahaafel (FR)** 2-9-2 0......................................................... JimCrowley 5 61+
(William Haggas) *s.i.s: rn green: hld up off the pce in last quintet: effrt in 7th but plenty to do over 2f out: kpt on steadily to go 4th wl ins fnl f: nvr trbld ldrs* **5/2[1]**

606 **5** *1 ½* **Sheriff**[14] 8545 2-9-2 0........................................................ SeanLevey 2 56
(Michael Bell) *chsd ldng pair: effrt over 1f out: unable qck u.p: lost 3rd and wknd ins fnl f* **8/1[3]**

0 **6** *½* **Financial Crime (IRE)**[20] 8388 2-8-13 0............(v[1]) CallumShepherd(3) 8 55
(Mick Channon) *midfield but nvr on terms w ldrs: 6th and rdn over 2f out: plugged on same pce and nvr threatened ldrs* **40/1**

**7** *1 ½* **Father Ailbe (IRE)** 2-8-13 0.............................................. TimClark(3) 13 51
(John Butler) *t.k.h: rn green: hld up off the pce in last pair: effrt and sme hdwy whn hung lft over 1f out: wl hld whn nt clr run whn swtchd rt 1f out: nvr trbld ldrs* **66/1**

0020 **8** *3* **Catapult**[13] 8560 2-9-2 65.............................................(t[1]) ShaneKelly 3 43
(Clifford Lines) *hld up off the pce in last pair: rdn and sme hdwy into midfield 1f out: nvr getting on terms* **25/1**

**9** *1* **Shyjack** 2-9-2 0......................................................... DanielMuscutt 11 40
(George Margarson) *s.i.s: rn v green in rr: swtchd lft over 1f out: nvr trbld ldrs* **18/1**

00 **10** *4* **Wilfred Owen**[29] 8162 2-9-2 0.....................................(p[1]) RobertHavlin 7 29
(John Gosden) *chsd ldrs: rdn and outpcd over 2f out: wl hld over 1f out: wknd fnl f* **25/1**

**11** *2 ½* **Inch Pincher** 2-8-11 0........................................................ DavidProbert 9 18
(Rae Guest) *squeezed for room leaving stall: rn green: in tch in midfield on outer: rdn 3f out and sn struggling: steadily lost pl and bhd ins fnl f* **33/1**

0 **12** *2 ¼* **Essendon (FR)**[9] 8643 2-8-9 0...................................... JasonWatson(7) 4 17
(Andrew Balding) *hld up off the pce in last quintet: pushed along over 2f out: 8th and drifted rt bnd 2f out: sn rdn and no imp after: wknd fnl f* **66/1**

1m 25.63s (-1.57) **Going Correction** -0.125s/f (Stan) 12 Ran SP% **122.9**
Speed ratings (Par 94): **103,97,96,93,91 90,89,85,84,79 77,74**
CSF £29.72 TOTE £6.10: £1.90, £1.90, £1.50; EX 34.80 Trifecta £118.80.
**Owner** Des Kavanagh & Derrick Murphy **Bred** Pier House Stud **Trained** Upper Lambourn, Berks

**FOCUS**
A fair juvenile novice contest. The winner controlled the race from the front and took a clear step forward.

## 8795 TOTESCOOP6 PLAY FOR £2 THIS SATURDAY NURSERY H'CAP 5f (P)
6:25 (6:27) (Class 6) (0-65,67) 2-Y-O £3,234 (£962; £481; £240) Stalls Low

Form RPR

0042 **1** **Magic Pulse (IRE)**[29] 8145 2-9-1 **58**............................ DougieCostello 1 61
(David C Griffiths) *trckd ldrs and travelled strly: swtchd out rt and chsd ldr 2f out: rdn to ld 1f out: hung rt and hrd pressed wl ins fnl f: a jst holding on* **13/8[1]**

0044 **2** *shd* **Avon Green**[23] 8309 2-9-6 **63**........................................... LiamKeniry 3 66
(Joseph Tuite) *t.k.h: hld up in tch in last trio: hdwy over 2f out: chsd ldrs and swtchd rt 1f out: styd on and str chal ins fnl f: a jst hld* **7/1**

040 **3** *1 ¾* **Blessed To Empress (IRE)**[51] 7491 2-9-7 **64**............... DavidProbert 8 60
(Amy Murphy) *swtchd lft after s: racd in last trio: rdn and hdwy over 1f out: kpt on wl ins fnl f to go 3rd towards fin* **9/2[3]**

0504 **4** *¾* **Swift Fox**[33] 8027 2-8-7 **50**............................................(b) KieranO'Neill 4 44
(Gary Moore) *sn bustled along to ld: rdn over 1f out: hdd 1f out: wknd ins fnl f* **14/1**

046 **5** *nk* **Cool Baby**[24] 8294 2-8-10 **56**........................................... EoinWalsh(3) 5 49
(Robert Cowell) *dwlt: sn rcvrd and hld up in tch in midfield: effrt u.p over 1f out: styd on same pce ins fnl f* **14/1**

2000 **6** *2* **Red Snapper**[42] 7756 2-8-7 **50**......................................(p[1]) NickyMackay 6 35
(William Stone) *chsd ldr tl unable qck u.p over 1f out: wknd ins fnl f* **40/1**

000 **7** *¾* **Kylie Style**[36] 7953 2-9-0 **57** ow2........................................ RobertTart 9 40
(Steph Hollinshead) *wd and racd in last trio: rdn over 2f out: kpt on but nvr enough pce to get on terms* **50/1**

1051 **8** *3* **Just For The Craic (IRE)**[45] 7695 2-9-10 **67**.................... JimCrowley 2 39
(Neil Mulholland) *chsd ldng trio tl unable qck u.p over 1f out: wknd ins fnl f* **3/1[2]**

566 **9** *nk* **Chizz De Biz (IRE)**[19] 8432 2-9-4 **61**.............................(p[1]) RobHornby 7 32
(Daniel Kubler) *midfield: rdn and dropped to last trio 3f out: bhd over 1f out* **22/1**

1m 0.53s (0.33) **Going Correction** -0.125s/f (Stan) 9 Ran SP% **115.9**
Speed ratings (Par 94): **92,91,89,87,87 84,82,78,77**
CSF £13.71 CT £43.87 TOTE £2.60: £1.10, £2.50, £1.10; EX 15.30 Trifecta £49.00.
**Owner** Craig Buckingham **Bred** J & S Bishop & J Cronin **Trained** Bawtry, S Yorks

**FOCUS**
A modest nursery with the winner building on latest promise. They went a decent gallop and the favourite narrowly prevailed.

## 8796 TOTESCOOP6 THREE WAYS TO WIN FILLIES' NOVICE STKS (PLUS 10 RACE) 1m (P)

6:55 (6:58) (Class 4) 2-Y-O £7,115 (£2,117; £1,058; £529) Stalls Low

Form RPR

6 **1** **Flora Sandes (USA)**[21] 8373 2-9-0 0............................(h) WilliamBuick 3 83
(Charlie Appleby) *t.k.h: mde all: rdn over 1f out: hld on wl towards fin* 11/2[3]

222 **2** ½ **Bubble And Squeak**[8] 8669 2-9-0 0.......................... BenCurtis 10 81
(Sylvester Kirk) *chsd ldng trio: effrt over 1f out: chsd wnr ins fnl f: kpt on u.p and chalng wl ins fnl f: kpt on but a hld* 8/1

3342 **3** 3 ½ **Fleeting Freedom**[42] 7764 2-9-0 78....................... JosephineGordon 14 73
(Alan Bailey) *chsd wnr: rdn over 1f out: lost 2nd and no ex u.p ins fnl f: wknd wl ins fnl f* 33/1

**4** 1 **Perfection** 2-9-0 0............................................. RobertHavlin 4 71
(John Gosden) *trckd ldrs: nt clrest of runs briefly over 1f out: sn rdn and unable qck: wknd wl ins fnl f* 11/10[1]

0 **5** nk **Desert Diamond**[21] 8373 2-9-0 0.............................. TedDurcan 9 70
(Sir Michael Stoute) *midfield: 9th and rdn over 1f out: hdwy jst over 1f out: styd on steadily ins fnl f: nvr trbld ldrs* 16/1

3 **6** 1 ½ **Jamaican Jill**[21] 8373 2-9-0 0.............................. PhillipMakin 12 66
(William Muir) *t.k.h: hld up in tch in midfield: effrt in 6th over 2f out: kpt on same pce and no imp fr over 1f out* 20/1

60 **7** 2 ¼ **Beautiful Artist (USA)**[12] 8594 2-9-0 0....................... RobertTart 1 61
(John Gosden) *chsd ldng quartet: effrt in 5th over 2f out: unable qck and drifted rt ent fnl f: wknd ins fnl f* 25/1

43 **8** 1 **Final Treat (IRE)**[34] 8006 2-9-0 0.......................... DanielTudhope 8 58
(William Haggas) *midfield: effrt in 7th over 2f out: no imp and btn over 1f out* 4/1[2]

0 **9** ¾ **Qaswarah (IRE)**[20] 8380 2-9-0 0.............................. JimCrowley 2 57
(Ed Dunlop) *midfield: 8th and effrt over 2f out: no imp and swtchd lft 1f out: kpt on same pce* 50/1

**10** 3 ½ **Cape Liberty (IRE)** 2-9-0 0................................ JackMitchell 11 48
(Simon Crisford) *dwlt and squeezed for room leaving stalls: rn green and a towards rr: rdn and outpcd over 2f out: no ch after* 33/1

**11** 1 ¾ **Phantasmic** 2-9-0 0........................................... DavidProbert 5 44
(Sir Michael Stoute) *rn green: midfield and pushed along: rdn and outpcd over 2f out: no ch after* 12/1

**12** nk **Diablery** 2-9-0 0.............................................. NickyMackay 13 43
(John Gosden) *s.i.s: a bhd* 33/1

03 **13** 4 **North Bay Sunrise (IRE)**[51] 7489 2-9-0 0...................... SeanLevey 15 34
(Ed Vaughan) *t.k.h: hld up in last trio: outpcd over 2f out: no ch after* 80/1

0 **14** 3 ½ **Snatty Dancer**[19] 8419 2-9-0 0................................ LiamKeniry 7 25
(Hughie Morrison) *midfield but sn pushed along: struggling and losing pl 3f out: bhd fnl f* 66/1

1m 38.75s (-1.15) **Going Correction** -0.125s/f (Stan) 14 Ran SP% 129.8
Speed ratings (Par 95): **100,99,96,95,94 93,90,89,89,85 83,83,79,76**
CSF £49.47 TOTE £6.90: £2.10, £2.30, £7.00; EX 48.50 Trifecta £544.20.
**Owner** Godolphin **Bred** Whisper Hill Farm Llc **Trained** Newmarket, Suffolk

**FOCUS**
A decent juvenile fillies' novice contest. On a night where it has paid to be up there, the winner made all in tough fashion. The placed horses set the level.

## 8797 TOTESCOOP6 THE MILLIONAIRE MAKER H'CAP 1m (P)

7:25 (7:28) (Class 5) (0-75,77) 3-Y-O+ £5,175 (£1,540; £769; £384) Stalls Low

Form RPR

0102 **1** **Pinnata (IRE)**[52] 7457 3-9-4 73...............................(t) SeanLevey 4 81+
(Stuart Williams) *dwlt: rousted along and sn rcvrd: hld up in tch in midfield: switching rt and hdwy over 1f out: styd on u.p to ld 100yds out: a doing enough towards fin: rdn out* 9/2[2]

3000 **2** nk **Carnival King (IRE)**[19] 8434 5-9-4 71..................... JosephineGordon 2 79
(Amy Murphy) *in tch towards rr: effrt over 2f out: hdwy u.p over 1f out: styd on to chse wnr wl ins fnl f: kpt on but nvr quite getting to wnr* 25/1

0210 **3** 1 ¼ **Dashing Poet**[15] 8503 3-8-11 66.......................... DanielMuscutt 12 70
(Heather Main) *t.k.h: chsd ldr tl rdn to ld over 1f out: hdd and no ex 100yds out: sn lost 2nd and wknd towards fin* 25/1

6002 **4** ¾ **Shamrokh (IRE)**[12] 8596 3-9-4 73.......................... DougieCostello 8 75+
(Michael Appleby) *t.k.h: hld up in tch: clsd and swtchd lft over 1f out: chsd ldrs and drvn ins fnl f: wknd wl ins fnl f* 9/2[2]

3132 **5** 2 ¼ **Miracle Garden**[7] 8706 5-9-9 76..........................(v) StevieDonohoe 1 74
(Ian Williams) *trckd ldrs: effrt over 1f out: chsd ldr briefly 1f out: sn no ex and wknd fnl 100yds* 9/4[1]

4000 **6** 3 ½ **Muthraab Aldaar (IRE)**[24] 8299 4-8-9 62.................... JackMitchell 7 52
(Jim Boyle) *s.i.s: detached in last and rdn along: swtchd rt and v wd wl over 1f out: hung lft over 1f out: kpt on to pass btn rivals: nvr trbld ldrs* 100/1

0552 **7** shd **Zafaranah (USA)**[29] 8156 3-8-12 67........................... RobHornby 9 56
(Pam Sly) *in tch in midfield on outer: unable qck u.p over 1f out: wknd ins fnl f* 20/1

1655 **8** ¾ **Highland Pass**[20] 8392 3-9-5 74.............................. DavidProbert 5 61
(Andrew Balding) *s.i.s and rdn along early: racd in last pair: effrt on inner over 1f out: nvr getting on terms and wl btn 1f out* 10/1

0016 **9** nk **Harlequin Striker (IRE)**[24] 8297 5-9-10 77..........(p) CharlesBishop 3 64
(Dean Ivory) *led tl rdn and hdd over 1f out: wknd ins fnl f* 12/1

3213 **10** 3 ½ **Titan Goddess**[12] 8596 5-9-2 69............................. ShaneKelly 11 48
(Mike Murphy) *s.i.s: t.k.h: hdwy to chse ldrs 5f out: rdn over 1f out: sn btn and wknd fnl f* 14/1

6311 **11** 3 **Dreaming Time**[19] 8433 3-9-8 77............................... JoeFanning 6 48
(James Tate) *hld up in tch in midfield: effrt u.p over 1f out: unable qck and wknd ins fnl f* 9/1

010 **12** 3 ¼ **William Sayle**[36] 7959 3-9-8 77..........................(p[1]) WilliamBuick 10 41
(John Gosden) *chsd ldrs: rdn and lost pl over 2f out: bhd over 1f out: eased wl ins fnl f* 6/1[3]

1m 38.94s (-0.96) **Going Correction** -0.125s/f (Stan)
**WFA** 3 from 4yo+ 2lb 12 Ran SP% 128.3
Speed ratings (Par 103): **99,98,97,96,94 90,90,90,89,86 83,80**
CSF £124.31 CT £2638.64 TOTE £6.30: £2.00, £7.00, £3.30; EX 127.20 Trifecta £6140.10.
**Owner** David N Reynolds & C D Watkins **Bred** Ammerland Verwaltung Gmbh & Co Kg **Trained** Newmarket, Suffolk

**FOCUS**
A fair handicap. They went a respectable gallop and there is no obvious reason to doubt the form.

## 8798 TOTESCOOP6 RESULTS AT TOTEPOOLLIVEINFO.COM H'CAP 7f (P)

7:55 (7:56) (Class 5) (0-75,77) 3-Y-O+ £5,175 (£1,540; £769; £384) Stalls Low

Form RPR

6054 **1** **Fredricka**[14] 8542 6-9-7 75.................................(v) RenatoSouza 1 84
(Ivan Furtado) *t.k.h: trckd ldrs: swtchd out rt and effrt wl over 1f out: rdn and ev ch 1f out: led ins fnl f: edgd lft and hld on wl towards fin* 10/1

4020 **2** hd **Kreb's Cycle (IRE)**[27] 8209 3-9-6 75...................(p) JosephineGordon 4 82
(Ian Williams) *hld up in tch in midfield: swtchd lft and hdwy over 1f out: str chal jst ins fnl f: kpt on wl but hld towards fin* 9/4[1]

3120 **3** 1 ¼ **Lucymai**[22] 8341 4-9-0 71.................................. JackDuern[(3)] 14 76
(Dean Ivory) *w ldr tl rdn to ld over 1f out: hdd and no ex ins fnl f: outpcd fnl 75yds* 10/1

0006 **4** 1 **Maggie Pink**[21] 8374 8-8-9 63.................................. RyanTate 9 65
(Michael Appleby) *taken down early: chsd ldrs: rdn ent fnl f: wnt 4th 100yds out and and kpt on towards fin: nvr quite enough pce to rch ldrs* 16/1

6244 **5** 3 **African Blessing**[30] 8132 4-9-0 68............................ BenCurtis 12 62
(Charlie Wallis) *sn led tl hdd 2f out: sn drvn and unable qck: wknd ins fnl f* 6/1[3]

5061 **6** 1 ¼ **Champagne Bob**[17] 8473 5-8-6 67.................(p) JonathanFisher[(7)] 6 58
(Richard Price) *hld up in tch towards rr: shkn up over 1f out: sn rdn and no imp: kpt on same pce fnl f: nvr trbld ldrs* 16/1

6050 **7** 2 ¾ **Thaqaffa (IRE)**[19] 8433 4-9-4 72..........................(p) DanielMuscutt 7 55
(Amy Murphy) *dwlt and jostled leaving stalls: hld up in midfield: effrt u.p but unable qck over 1f out: wknd ins fnl f* 10/1

-230 **8** ¾ **Wild Acclaim (IRE)**[160] 3524 3-9-1 70.................... AlistairRawlinson 2 50
(Michael Appleby) *hld up in tch: effrt ent fnl 2f: unable qck and btn 1f out: wknd ins fnl f* 12/1

1514 **9** 3 ¼ **Wahaab (IRE)**[28] 8184 6-9-6 74................................(t) TimmyMurphy 8 47
(Sophie Leech) *hld up in tch in rr: wd bnd 2f out: nvr trbld ldrs* 25/1

6124 **10** nse **Daring Guest (IRE)**[19] 8434 3-8-12 72.................... JaneElliott[(5)] 5 44
(George Margarson) *t.k.h: chsd ldrs early: steadily shuffled bk towards rr: effrt over 1f out: no hdwy and wknd fnl f* 7/2[2]

0005 **11** ½ **El Torito (IRE)**[24] 8296 3-8-5 63..................(p) CharlieBennett[(3)] 10 33
(Jim Boyle) *dwlt and rousted along leaving stalls: pushed rt over 5f out: hdwy to join ldrs on outer over 4f out: rdn and lost pl ent fnl 2f: wknd over 1f out* 25/1

**12** 16 **Syndex (IRE)**[272] 792 4-8-7 61 oh1.............................. KieranO'Neill 3
(Johnny Farrelly) *a bhd: lost tch 2f out: eased ins fnl f* 33/1

1m 25.45s (-1.75) **Going Correction** -0.125s/f (Stan)
**WFA** 3 from 4yo+ 1lb 12 Ran SP% 124.6
Speed ratings (Par 103): **105,104,103,102,98 97,94,93,89,89 89,70**
CSF £33.79 CT £250.92 TOTE £9.30: £3.00, £1.40, £4.00; EX 31.40 Trifecta £471.10.
**Owner** J Melo **Bred** J C Parsons & J J Gilmartin **Trained** Wiseton, Nottinghamshire

**FOCUS**
A fair handicap. They went a respectable gallop and the favourite couldn't quite get up.

## 8799 BOOK TICKETS AT CHELMSFORDCITYRACECOURSE.COM H'CAP (DIV I) 1m 2f (P)

8:25 (8:28) (Class 6) (0-55,57) 3-Y-O+ £3,234 (£962; £481; £240) Stalls Low

Form RPR

0566 **1** **Huddersfilly Town**[8] 8673 3-8-13 50......................(p[1]) PhillipMakin 1 59
(Ivan Furtado) *chsd ldrs: effrt and rdn to ld over 1f out: clr and styd on wl ins fnl f* 6/1

0602 **2** 3 **Never Folding (IRE)**[14] 8538 3-9-2 53........................ ShaneKelly 5 56
(Seamus Durack) *taken down early and led to post: in tch in midfield: effrt in 4th over 2f out: swtchd rt and then bk lft over 1f out: chsd clr wnr 1f out: no imp but kpt on for clr 2nd* 3/1[2]

0550 **3** 2 ¾ **Awesome Rock (IRE)**[155] 3726 8-8-12 46 oh1............... RobertHavlin 2 43
(Roger Ingram) *hld up in tch: hdwy over 1f out: styd on to go 3rd 100yds: nvr threatened ldng pair* 33/1

546 **4** 1 **Sheer Intensity (IRE)**[103] 5653 4-8-8 49........... KatherineGlenister[(7)] 11 44+
(David Evans) *tried to get under front of stalls bef they opened and veered rt: s.i.s: sn swtchd lft and bhd: rdn and hdwy over 1f out: styd on wl ins fnl f to go 4th wl ins fnl f: nvr trbld ldrs* 28/1

0000 **5** 1 **Optima Petamus**[8] 8219 5-9-4 52...........................(v[1]) DougieCostello 6 45
(Patrick Holmes) *s.i.s: hld up in tch: 5th and effrt over 2f out: swtchd rt wl over 1f out: no imp* 8/1

0020 **6** 2 **Tarseekh**[23] 8307 4-9-7 55.................................(v) CharlesBishop 4 44
(Chris Gordon) *led: rdn ent fnl 2f: hdd over 1f out: no ex: wknd ins fnl f* 14/1

3533 **7** 3 ¼ **Master Of Heaven**[35] 7990 4-9-0 48........................(p) DavidProbert 14 31
(Jim Boyle) *pushed rt leaving stalls: hdwy to join ldr after 2f: rdn and ev ch 2f out tl no ex 1f out: wknd ins fnl f* 5/1[3]

4304 **8** 1 ¾ **McDelta**[22] 8346 7-9-4 52................................ JosephineGordon 3 32
(Geoffrey Deacon) *midfield: lost pl and rdn 7f out: bhd 6f out: rdn and sme hdwy over 1f out: nvr getting on terms: wknd fnl f* 11/4[1]

/0-0 **9** 1 ½ **Ambuscade**[36] 7952 4-8-12 46 oh1.......................... StevieDonohoe 12 23
(Neil Mulholland) *pushed rt s: in tch: rdn and struggling 3f out: sn outpcd and wl bhd fnl 2f* 40/1

6204 **10** 1 ¼ **Dawn Goddess**[14] 8543 3-8-6 46............................ NoelGarbutt[(3)] 9 21
(Gary Moore) *s.i.s and short of room leaving stalls: swtchd lft and t.k.h towards rr: hdwy on outer 6f out: rdn and struggling over 2f out: wknd 2f out* 22/1

0-P0 **11** 27 **Power Up**[241] 1284 6-9-6 57.................................. CharlieBennett[(3)] 10
(Luke McJannet) *chsd ldrs: rdn 3f out: sn struggling and lost pl: bhd and eased over 1f out: t.o* 33/1

4000 **12** 29 **Subotal (IRE)**[6] 8720 4-8-12 46 oh1..........................(e) JoeFanning 8
(Richard Guest) *awkward leaving stalls and s.i.s: hld up in tch: dropped to rr 3f out: sn eased: t.o* 20/1

2m 7.92s (-0.68) **Going Correction** -0.125s/f (Stan)
**WFA** 3 from 4yo+ 3lb 12 Ran SP% 121.3
Speed ratings (Par 101): **97,94,92,91,90 89,86,85,84,83 61,38**
CSF £22.91 CT £566.53 TOTE £8.10: £2.60, £2.10, £6.60; EX 33.70 Trifecta £438.80.
**Owner** BGC Racing XI & Partner **Bred** Bearstone Stud Ltd **Trained** Wiseton, Nottinghamshire

**FOCUS**
The first division of a moderate handicap. They went a respectable gallop, but a couple of the more likely types still came to the fore and a personal best from the winner.

## 8800 BOOK TICKETS AT CHELMSFORDCITYRACECOURSE.COM H'CAP (DIV II) 1m 2f (P)
8:55 (9:00) (Class 6) (0-55,56) 3-Y-0+ **£3,234** (£962; £481; £240) Stalls Low

Form RPR
5033 1 **King Kevin**[31] 8123 3-8-12 **48**.....(b) RobertHavlin 13 57
(Ed Dunlop) *s.i.s: off the pce in last pair: clsd but stl plenty to do over 2f out: swtchd rt 2f out: hanging lft but hdwy over 1f out rdn to ld and stl hanging ins fnl f: sn clr* 7/2[2]
05-0 2 2¼ **Hediddodinthe (IRE)**[27] 8205 3-9-3 **53**..... PhillipMakin 5 58
(Richard Guest) *hld up off the pce: clsd but stl plenty to do over 2f out: chsd clr ldrs over 1f out: hdwy to trck ldr and swtchd rt 1f out: chsd wnr ins fnl f: no threat but kpt on for clr 2nd* 11/4[1]
000 3 6 **Win Lose Draw (IRE)**[90] 6131 5-9-7 **54**.....(p) AlistairRawlinson 1 47+
(Michael Appleby) *chsd ldrs: wnt 2nd 4f out: clsd to trck ldr 2f out: rdn and ev ch over 1f out tl ins fnl f: wknd fnl 100yds* 7/1
0000 4 nse **Outlaw Torn (IRE)**[26] 8249 8-9-2 **49**.....(e) DougieCostello 9 42+
(Richard Guest) *taken down early: led: rdn ent fnl 2f: hdd ins fnl f: no ex and wknd fnl 100yds* 16/1
2000 5 4½ **Pensax Lady (IRE)**[9] 8661 4-9-5 **52**..... SteveDrowne 3 36
(Daniel Mark Loughnane) *rdn along in midfield: drvn over 2f out: no imp and wl hld fr over 1f out* 12/1
4205 6 nk **Haldaw**[16] 8498 3-8-11 **50**..... CallumShepherd(3) 6 34
(Mick Channon) *stall opened early and wnt 100yds bef returning to s and reloaded: in tch in midfield: effrt to chse clr ldng pair 2f out:* 6/1[3]
3254 7 4 **Just Fab (IRE)**[29] 8152 4-9-2 **52**.....(b) CharlieBennett(3) 10 28
(Lee Carter) *hld up in last quartet: effrt over 2f out: no imp: nvr trbld ldrs* 14/1
0005 8 9 **Whip Up A Frenzy (IRE)**[26] 8248 5-8-9 **45**.....(p) ShelleyBirkett(3) 4 4
(David O'Meara) *hld up in midfield: rdn and wknd over 2f out: wl bhd over 1f out* 8/1
0060 9 2¼ **Rubheira**[42] 7760 5-8-12 **45**..... StevieDonohoe 2
(Neil Mulholland) *hld up in last trio: rdn and lost tch over 2f out* 66/1
5000 10 5 **Lesanti**[26] 8248 3-8-10 **46**.....(p[1]) JoeFanning 12
(Ed de Giles) *chse ldr tl 4f out: rdn and outpcd over 2f out: wknd over 1f out* 20/1
5000 11 ½ **La Goulue**[143] 4164 3-8-9 **45**.....(p) JoeyHaynes 11
(John Gallagher) *chsd ldrs: rdn over 3f out: lost pl and bhd over 1f out* 50/1
-050 12 34 **African Showgirl**[14] 8538 4-9-9 **56**..... JosephineGordon 7
(Ivan Furtado) *wd in midfield: lost pl 3f out: bhd and eased over 1f out: t.o* 10/1

2m 7.29s (-1.31) **Going Correction** -0.125s/f (Stan)
**WFA** 3 from 4yo+ 3lb 12 Ran SP% **124.3**
Speed ratings (Par 101): **100,98,93,93,89 89,86,79,77,73 72,45**
CSF £14.10 CT £67.26 TOTE £4.50: £1.70, £1.70, £2.90; EX 18.40 Trifecta £113.00.
**Owner** E A L Dunlop **Bred** Denford Stud Ltd **Trained** Newmarket, Suffolk

**FOCUS**
The second division of a moderate handicap. The winning time was nearly a second quicker.
T/Jkpt: Not Won. T/Plt: £251.00 to a £1 stake. Pool: £107,739.78 - 313.31 winning units T/Qpdt: £75.30 to a £1 stake. Pool: £13,279.35 - 130.39 winning units **Steve Payne**

# 8770 SOUTHWELL (L-H)
Thursday, November 16

**OFFICIAL GOING: Fibresand: standard**
Wind: Moderate half behind Weather: Cloudy

## 8801 SUNBETS.CO.UK H'CAP 1m 13y(F)
12:40 (12:40) (Class 6) (0-65,66) 3-Y-0+ **£2,264** (£673; £336; £168) Stalls Low

Form RPR
0102 1 **Monsieur Jimmy**[25] 8254 5-9-0 **65**..... GerO'Neill(7) 4 73
(Declan Carroll) *towards rr: swtchd rt and hdwy on outer 3f out: chsd ldrs 2f out: rdn wl over 1f out: styd on strly fnl f to ld nr line* 6/1[3]
5321 2 nse **Mach One**[14] 8538 3-9-6 **66**.....(p) AndrewMullen 13 73
(Archie Watson) *dwlt: sn cl up: chal over 2f out: rdn to ld over 1f out: drvn and edgd rt ins fnl f: hdd nr line* 9/4[1]
6460 3 2¼ **Luath**[27] 8210 4-8-13 **57**..... NickyMackay 8 59
(Suzzanne France) *towards rr and swtchd rt to outer after 2f: hdwy on outer and wd st: sn chsng ldrs: rdn along and cl up wl over 1f out: ev ch whn drvn ent fnl f: n.m.r and swtchd lft last 75yds: kpt on* 11/1
3121 4 nk **Break The Silence**[9] 8651 3-9-2 **62** 6ex.....(p) KieranO'Neill 6 63
(Scott Dixon) *led: rdn along 2f out: drvn and hdd over 1f out: kpt on u.p fnl f* 13/2
0010 5 2¾ **Noble Ballad**[23] 8328 3-9-1 **61**.....(b) GrahamLee 3 55
(Ralph Beckett) *trckd ldrs: hdwy 3f out: cl up 2f out: sn rdn and ev ch: wknd ent fnl f* 14/1
5003 6 1¾ **Anastazia**[9] 8641 5-9-4 **62**..... JoeyHaynes 2 53
(Paul D'Arcy) *in tch: hdwy 3f out: chsd ldrs over 2f out: rdn wl over 1f out: sn no imp* 22/1
4400 7 7 **Appleberry (IRE)**[25] 8260 5-9-8 **66**.....(p) AlistairRawlinson 11 40
(Michael Appleby) *cl up: disp ld 3f out: rdn over 2f out: drvn wl over 1f out: grad wknd* 33/1
0300 8 3 **True Colors**[27] 8218 3-9-2 **62**..... TonyHamilton 10 28
(Richard Fahey) *dwlt and a towards rr* 16/1
566 9 2¼ **Wardy (IRE)**[15] 8504 3-9-5 **65**..... FranBerry 5 26
(Peter Chapple-Hyam) *a towards rr* 16/1
4405 10 4½ **Luna Magic**[31] 8125 3-9-0 **63**.....(h) SimonPearce(3) 12 13
(Lydia Pearce) *dwlt: sn chsng ldrs: rdn along 3f out: sn wknd* 33/1
4504 11 3¼ **Scent Of Power**[17] 8477 5-8-2 **51** oh6..... JaneElliott(5) 1
(Barry Leavy) *a towards rr* 100/1
3000 12 shd **Secret Glance**[68] 6947 5-8-10 **54**..... TomEaves 14
(Adrian Wintle) *dwlt: a towards rr* 22/1
2312 13 nk **Quiet Moment (IRE)**[25] 8255 3-8-7 **53**..... JoeFanning 7
(Keith Dalgleish) *trckd ldrs: pushed along 3f out: rdn over 2f out: sn wknd* 9/2[2]
0000 14 1¼ **Tilly Devine**[14] 8538 3-8-5 **51** oh6.....(v[1]) FrannyNorton 9
(Scott Dixon) *chsd ldrs: rdn along 1/2-way: sn wknd* 100/1

1m 42.4s (-1.30) **Going Correction** -0.175s/f (Stan)
**WFA** 3 from 4yo+ 2lb 14 Ran SP% **119.9**
Speed ratings (Par 101): **99,98,96,96,93 91,84,81,79,75 71,71,71,70**
CSF £18.54 CT £153.13 TOTE £7.40: £2.10, £1.30, £3.00; EX 26.00 Trifecta £216.30.
**Owner** Ray Flegg & John Bousfield **Bred** J Repard & M Stokes **Trained** Malton, N Yorks

■ Stewards' Enquiry : Andrew Mullen caution: careless riding

**FOCUS**
The going was standard. Stalls: race 3 centre, remainder inside. An ordinary handicap which produced a tight finish and a fifth course success for the winner, who has been rated back to his best.

## 8802 32RED CASINO NOVICE AUCTION STKS 7f 14y(F)
1:15 (1:17) (Class 5) 2-Y-0 **£2,911** (£866; £432; £216) Stalls Low

Form RPR
1 **German Bight (IRE)** 2-8-9 **0**..... TomEaves 4 75+
(Keith Dalgleish) *dwlt: sn prom and led over 5f out: pushed clr over 2f out: rdn ins fnl f: kpt on* 7/1
2 ¾ **The Jungle VIP** 2-8-10 **0**..... FrannyNorton 5 74+
(Mark Johnston) *green and sn pushed along towards rr: hdwy on inner 3f out: rdn along 2f out: hdwy to chse wnr wl over 1f out: kpt on wl fnl f* 9/2
0 3 6 **Amity Island**[27] 8208 2-8-8 **0**..... CamHardie 8 56
(Ollie Pears) *towards rr: pushed along 3f out: swtchd rt to outer 2f out and sn rdn: kpt on fnl f* 25/1
6 4 hd **Goldfox Girl**[22] 8347 2-8-3 **0**..... AndrewMullen 6 50
(Michael Appleby) *trckd ldrs: hdwy towards outer 3f out and wd st: chsd wnr wl over 2f out and sn rdn: drvn wl over 1f out: kpt on same pce* 3/1[2]
36 5 7 **Ipcress File**[15] 8502 2-8-8 **0**..... KieranO'Neill 3 36
(Scott Dixon) *prom: rdn along wl over 2f out: sn drvn and wknd* 4/1[3]
6 ½ **Mischievous Rock** 2-7-12 **0**..... JaneElliott(5) 7 30
(Michael Appleby) *trckd ldrs: hdwy on outer and wd st: sn prom: rdn along 2f out: sn edgd lft and wknd* 14/1
063 7 8 **She's Royal**[13] 8553 2-8-3 **70**..... JoeFanning 1 8
(Bryan Smart) *led: hdd over 5f out: rdn along on inner 3f out: wknd 2f out* 11/4[1]
00 8 21 **Molliana**[15] 8501 2-8-3 **0**..... NickyMackay 2
(Neil Mulholland) *a in rr: outpcd and bhd fnl 3f* 100/1

1m 29.57s (-0.73) **Going Correction** -0.175s/f (Stan) 8 Ran SP% **113.9**
Speed ratings (Par 96): **97,96,89,89,81 80,71,47**
CSF £38.06 TOTE £9.80: £2.00, £1.40, £5.00; EX 40.20 Trifecta £653.40.
**Owner** Michael Beaumont **Bred** Alan O'Flynn **Trained** Carluke, S Lanarks

**FOCUS**
A moderate maiden which was dominated by the winner, who was perfectly streetwise on debut and always had matters in hand.

## 8803 BETWAY SPRINT H'CAP 4f 214y(F)
1:45 (1:46) (Class 4) (0-85,85) 3-Y-0+ **£4,690** (£1,395; £697; £348) Stalls Centre

Form RPR
0403 1 **Midnight Malibu (IRE)**[9] 8660 4-9-6 **84**..... DavidAllan 9 93
(Tim Easterby) *cl up centre: rdn to ld jst over 1f out: drvn ins fnl f: kpt on wl* 10/1
2346 2 ½ **Arzaak (IRE)**[30] 8129 3-9-7 **85**.....(b) JosephineGordon 11 92
(Chris Dwyer) *racd towards stands side: chsd ldrs: hdwy wl over 1f out: rdn ent fnl f: sn ev ch: drvn and no ex towards fin* 7/1[3]
0063 3 ½ **Crosse Fire**[16] 8488 5-8-8 **72**.....(p) KieranO'Neill 4 77
(Scott Dixon) *cl up centre: rdn along and ev ch over 1f out: drvn and kpt on fnl f* 11/1
200 4 1¼ **Razin' Hell**[72] 6794 6-9-5 **83**.....(v) BenCurtis 8 84
(John Balding) *sn led in centre: rdn along 2f out: hdd over 1f out: grad wknd* 9/1
5355 5 nk **Musharrif**[8] 8680 5-8-9 **80**.....(b[1]) GerO'Neill(7) 2 80
(Declan Carroll) *racd towards far side: chsd ldrs: rdn along 2f out: drvn and wknd fnl f* 3/1[1]
U110 6 ¾ **Gnaad (IRE)**[67] 6970 3-8-13 **77**..... FranBerry 7 74
(Alan Bailey) *dwlt and rr whn swtchd markedly lft to r nr far rail: hdwy over 2f out: rdn wl over 1f out: kpt on* 10/1
0302 7 nk **Treaty Of Rome (USA)**[25] 8260 5-8-11 **75**.....(v) TonyHamilton 6 71
(Derek Shaw) *towards rr: rdn along 1/2-way: styd on fr over 1f out: n.d* 11/2[2]
0206 8 hd **Mujassam**[16] 8486 5-8-11 **82**.....(b) PatrickVaughan(7) 3 77
(David O'Meara) *towards rr: rdn along 2f out: sme late hdwy* 16/1
6004 9 nk **Zapper Cass (FR)**[31] 8105 4-8-13 **77**.....(t) BarryMcHugh 5 71
(Tony Coyle) *dwlt: a in rr* 20/1
1151 10 2 **Piazon**[25] 8260 6-9-1 **82**.....(be) TimClark(3) 14 69
(John Butler) *sn swtchd lft and chsd ldrs centre: rdn along 2f out: sn wknd* 9/1
000 11 1 **Bosham**[75] 6669 7-9-7 **85**.....(bt) PaulMulrennan 10 68
(Michael Easterby) *racd towards stands side: prom: rdn along 2f out: sn wknd* 33/1
1000 12 3½ **Alpha Tauri (USA)**[25] 8257 11-9-1 **79**..... JoeyHaynes 13 50
(Charles Smith) *a towards rr* 80/1
045 13 nse **Dungannon**[158] 3617 10-9-0 **85**.....(b) WilliamCox(7) 12 55
(Andrew Balding) *a in rr* 14/1

57.82s (-1.88) **Going Correction** -0.25s/f (Stan) 13 Ran SP% **120.9**
Speed ratings (Par 105): **105,104,103,101,100 99,99,98,98,95 93,88,87**
CSF £78.14 CT £824.45 TOTE £11.40: £4.10, £1.90, £3.90; EX 73.00 Trifecta £966.00.
**Owner** D A West & Partner **Bred** Kabansk Ltd & Rathbarry Stud **Trained** Great Habton, N Yorks

**FOCUS**
A decent sprint handicap and a willing winner who seems to be well suited by AW surfaces.

## 8804 32RED.COM NURSERY H'CAP 6f 16y(F)
2:15 (2:15) (Class 5) (0-75,70) 2-Y-0 **£2,835** (£848; £424; £212; £105) Stalls Low

Form RPR
0660 1 **Helen Sherbet**[9] 8658 2-9-2 **65**..... BenCurtis 3 68
(K R Burke) *trckd ldrs on inner: rdn along and sltly outpcd 2f out: styd on wl u.p fnl f: led nr line* 10/1
5616 2 hd **Give Em A Clump (IRE)**[17] 8475 2-9-2 **65**.....(v) FranBerry 7 67
(David Evans) *cl up: led after 2f: rdn along 2f out: hrd pressed and drvn over 1f out: kpt on gamely u.p ins fnl f: hdd nr line* 5/1[2]
6000 3 nk **Our Kid (IRE)**[46] 7655 2-8-9 **58**.....(b) BarryMcHugh 5 59
(Richard Fahey) *trckd ldng pair: hdwy and cl up on outer 2f out: rdn to chal ent fnl f: ev ch: drvn and no ex nr fin* 5/1[2]
040 4 nk **Optimickstickhill**[91] 6085 2-8-8 **57**..... KieranO'Neill 4 57
(Scott Dixon) *slt ld: hdd after 2f: cl up: rdn along 2f out: drvn over 1f out: ev ch ins fnl f: no ex towards fin* 16/1
0430 5 4 **Show Princess**[29] 8164 2-8-13 **62**..... DougieCostello 1 49
(Michael Appleby) *in tch: rdn along wl over 2f out: sn drvn and one pce* 9/1
2030 6 2½ **Eva Docc (IRE)**[5] 8741 2-9-1 **64**..... AndrewMullen 2 43
(Keith Dalgleish) *dwlt and rr: rdn along and sme hdwy wl over 2f out: n.d* 7/1

0500 7 7 **Corton Lass**[17] 8475 2-8-9 58 (p) JoeFanning 6 15
(Keith Dalgleish) *trckd ldrs on outer: rdn along over 3f out: sn lost pl and wd st: sn bhd* 3/1[1]

2440 U **Tarnhelm**[12] 8586 2-9-7 70 FrannyNorton 8
(Mark Johnston) *stmbld and uns rdr s* 11/2[3]

1m 15.96s (-0.54) **Going Correction** -0.175s/f (Stan) 8 Ran SP% **111.2**
Speed ratings (Par 96): **96,95,95,94,89 86,76,**
CSF £55.80 CT £274.96 TOTE £9.80: £2.50, £1.90, £2.00; EX 68.60 Trifecta £432.50.
**Owner** S Lock, J Craft & E Burke **Bred** Steve Lock **Trained** Middleham Moor, N Yorks

**FOCUS**
Only a fair nursery, but one which produced the exciting sight of four runnners in a line entering the last 100yds. The winner knuckled down well.

## 8805 SUNBETS.CO.UK DOWNLOAD THE APP MAIDEN STKS 7f 14y(F)
**2:45** (2:45) (Class 5) 3-Y-0+ **£2,911** (£866; £432; £216) **Stalls** Low

Form RPR

1 **Abraj Dubai (USA)** 3-9-0 0 GrahamLee 2 84+
(David O'Meara) *trckd ldrs: smooth hdwy to trck ldr 3f out: led on bit 2f out: sn clr: easily* 7/2[3]

6335 2 8 **Charlie's Dreamer**[13] 8552 3-8-9 60 JaneElliott[(5)] 4 59
(Michael Appleby) *led after 1f: jnd and rdn over 2f out: sn hdd and drvn: kpt on: no ch w wnr* 4/1

0460 3 10 **Ejabah (IRE)**[25] 8255 3-9-0 44 (v[1]) JoeyHaynes 3 32
(Charles Smith) *led 1f: chsd ldrs on inner: rdn along wl over 2f out: kpt on one pce* 50/1

2520 4 ½ **Haraz (IRE)**[9] 8646 4-9-6 68 (v) DougieCostello 8 36
(Jamie Osborne) *prom: cl up on outer 1/2-way: rdn along wl over 2f out: sn edgd lft and drvn: plodded on one pce* 11/4[2]

5 ¾ **Take The High Road**[36] 7967 3-9-5 0 (p[1]) TomEaves 1 33
(Keith Dalgleish) *trckd ldrs: effrt 3f out: rdn along over 2f out: sn one pce* 13/8[1]

5660 6 nk **Fivos**[20] 8395 3-9-5 44 (v) AlistairRawlinson 9 33
(David Bridgwater) *towards rr: rdn along and sme hdwy on inner wl over 2f out: n.d* 50/1

0 7 8 **Lady Carduros (IRE)**[15] 8504 3-9-0 0 StevieDonohoe 7 6
(Neil Mulholland) *dwlt: a in rr* 66/1

0000 8 ¾ **Zarkavon**[62] 7109 3-9-0 23 (p[1]) AndrewMullen 5 4
(John Wainwright) *racd wd: a in rr* 100/1

6 9 11 **Ritas Legacy**[37] 7930 3-9-5 0 PaulMulrennan 6
(Roy Brotherton) *cl up: rdn along 3f out: wknd qckly and sn bhd* 66/1

1m 28.14s (-2.16) **Going Correction** -0.175s/f (Stan)
**WFA** 3 from 4yo 1lb 9 Ran SP% **114.9**
Speed ratings (Par 103): **105,95,84,83,83 82,73,72,60**
CSF £17.49 TOTE £4.60: £1.40, £1.30, £13.10; EX 21.50 Trifecta £460.90.
**Owner** Hambleton Racing Ltd XXV **Bred** Darley **Trained** Upper Helmsley, N Yorks

**FOCUS**
A moderate maiden which rather fell apart, but the easy winner was in a different league to her rivals.

## 8806 BETWAY H'CAP 1m 4f 14y(F)
**3:20** (3:20) (Class 5) (0-75,74) 3-Y-0+ **£2,911** (£866; £432; £216) **Stalls** Low

Form RPR

0050 1 **Throckley**[40] 7824 6-9-7 74 GrahamLee 11 87
(Conor Dore) *trckd ldrs: hdwy over 3f out: cl up over 2f out: led wl over 1f out: sn rdn and kpt on strly* 25/1

0631 2 2 ¼ **Topamichi**[8] 8682 7-9-1 68 6ex CharlesBishop 1 77
(Michael Appleby) *trckd ldrs: hdwy over 3f out: led over 2f out: sn jnd and rdn: hdd wl over 1f out: drvn and kpt on same pce fnl f* 11/4[1]

3010 3 ½ **Good Time Ahead (IRE)**[17] 8478 3-8-0 65 KeelanBaker[(7)] 3 74
(Philip Kirby) *hld up towards rr: stdy hdwy 1/2-way chsd ldrs 3f out: rdn over 2f out: styd on wl fnl f* 14/1

2535 4 6 **Daily Trader**[14] 8549 3-8-5 66 MattCosham[(3)] 6 65
(David Evans) *rr and reminders after 3f: hdwy over 5f out: in tch and rdn along over 2f out: sn no imp* 5/1[3]

62-1 5 3 **Mister Showman**[25] 8261 4-8-12 65 (p) TomEaves 2 59
(Keith Dalgleish) *prom: hdwy to ld over 4f out: rdn along 3f out: sn hdd and grad wknd* 4/1[2]

420 6 4 ½ **Assiduous**[21] 8377 3-9-1 73 FranBerry 10 61
(Mark Johnston) *chsd ldrs: rdn along 5f out: drvn over 3f out: sn outpcd* 10/1

5010 7 1 ¼ **Deep Challenger (IRE)**[27] 8214 5-9-6 73 (t[1]) DougieCostello 13 58
(Jamie Osborne) *hld up towards rr: hdwy over 3f out: kpt on fnl 2f: n.d* 13/2

0060 8 1 **Up Ten Down Two (IRE)**[37] 7924 8-9-0 67 CamHardie 7 50
(Michael Easterby) *a towards rr* 40/1

5245 9 8 **Eyreborn (IRE)**[9] 8655 3-8-4 62 JoeFanning 9 34
(Keith Dalgleish) *a towards rr* 16/1

6600 10 14 **The Lock Master (IRE)**[31] 8122 10-9-2 69 (p) AlistairRawlinson 12 17
(Michael Appleby) *a towards rr* 25/1

0102 11 5 **Miningrocks (FR)**[17] 8477 5-9-3 70 (v) PaulMulrennan 4 10
(Conor Dore) *led and sn clr: pushed along 5f out: hdd and rdn over 4f out: wknd 3f out* 40/1

-203 12 24 **Young Tom**[161] 3501 4-8-2 60 oh1 JaneElliott[(5)] 8
(Sue Smith) *chsd ldrs: rdn along 4f out: sn wknd* 16/1

4040 13 32 **Tristram**[38] 7895 3-8-9 67 AndrewMullen 5
(John Mackie) *prom: rdn along wl over 4f out: sn wknd* 16/1

2m 36.46s (-4.54) **Going Correction** -0.175s/f (Stan)
**WFA** 3 from 4yo+ 5lb 13 Ran SP% **122.6**
Speed ratings (Par 103): **108,106,106,102,100 97,96,95,90,81 77,61,40**
CSF £93.06 CT £1051.72 TOTE £25.30: £7.20, £1.40, £4.00; EX 231.90 Trifecta £3835.40.
**Owner** Mrs Louise Marsh **Bred** The Maroon Stud **Trained** Hubbert's Bridge, Lincs

**FOCUS**
Quite a competitive handicap for the grade and a decisive winner.

## 8807 SUNBETS.CO.UK TOP PRICE ON ALL FAVOURITES ALL-WEATHER "HANDS AND HEELS" APPRENTICE H'CAP 7f 14y(F)
**3:50** (3:52) (Class 6) (0-60,60) 3-Y-0+ **£2,264** (£673; £336; £168) **Stalls** Low

Form RPR

3410 1 **Queens Royale**[20] 8402 3-9-2 58 (v[1]) TheodoreLadd[(5)] 13 65
(Michael Appleby) *qckly away: mde all: pushed along 2f out: kpt on wl fnl f* 12/1

2-63 2 1 ¼ **Chaucer's Tale**[12] 8590 3-9-3 59 RyanTimby[(5)] 2 63
(Michael Easterby) *prom on inner: chsd wnr wl over 1f out: kpt on fnl f* 14/1

6044 3 1 ¼ **Gatillo**[17] 8473 4-9-4 54 StephenCummins 4 55
(Julia Feilden) *hld up and bhd: hdwy on inner 3f out: chsd ldrs 1 1/2f out: sn rdn and kpt on fnl f* 6/1[2]

4445 4 ¾ **Caledonian Gold**[14] 8543 4-8-3 46 oh1 (b) OliverDaykin[(7)] 1 45
(Paul D'Arcy) *chsd ldrs on inner: : hdwy over 3f out: swtchd lft and rdn wl over 1f out: kpt on fnl f* 16/1

2206 5 1 ¾ **Breaking Free**[14] 8538 3-8-9 46 (p) SeanMooney 3 40
(John Quinn) *midfield on inner: pushed along o ver 3f out: switc hed rt and rdn to chse ldrs 2f out: no imp fnl f* 15/2[3]

5200 6 hd **Frangarry (IRE)**[14] 8538 5-8-9 50 (t) PaulHainey[(5)] 6 44
(Alan Bailey) *towards rr: hdwy and wd st: rdn along 2f out: kpt on fnl f* 20/1

3012 7 2 ¼ **Kroy**[12] 8591 3-9-9 60 (p) SeamusCronin 10 52
(Ollie Pears) *trckd ldrs whn bmpd after 1 1/2f: t.k.h after: in tch whn n.m.r 1/2-way: wd st: hdwy on outer to chse ldrs 2f out: sn rdn and btn* 2/1[1]

4603 8 4 ½ **Quadriga (IRE)**[25] 8259 7-8-10 46 oh1 (b) BenSanderson 14 22
(Chris Grant) *trckd ldrs: hdwy and cl up 4f out: rdn along over 2f out: wknd wl over 1f out* 12/1

0/0- 9 4 **Hugie Boy (IRE)**[483] 4544 5-9-10 60 (t[1]) JackOsborn 7 25
(Scott Dixon) *chsd ldrs: rdn along 3f out: sn wknd* 40/1

650- 10 2 ¼ **Melcano**[421] 6681 3-8-7 49 TobyEley[(5)] 9 7
(Shaun Harris) *a towards rr* 66/1

3403 11 ¾ **Bonnie Gals**[9] 8661 3-9-4 55 (b) SebastianWoods 12 11
(Keith Dalgleish) *in tch on outer: rdn along 1/2-way: sn wknd* 8/1

2223 12 5 **Nellie's Dancer**[3] 8774 3-9-0 56 (p) PatrickO'Hanlon[(5)] 11
(Scott Dixon) *a in rr* 9/1

1m 29.76s (-0.54) **Going Correction** -0.175s/f (Stan)
**WFA** 3 from 4yo+ 1lb 12 Ran SP% **117.1**
Speed ratings (Par 101): **96,94,93,92,90 90,87,82,77,75 74,68**
CSF £164.01 CT £1129.35 TOTE £10.30: £3.30, £4.00, £2.00; EX 138.70 Trifecta £1001.90.
**Owner** Wayne Brackstone, Steve Whitear **Bred** W Brackstone & S J Whitear **Trained** Oakham, Rutland

■ Stewards' Enquiry : Sean Mooney three-day ban: careless riding (Nov 30-Dec 2)
Seamus Cronin seven-day ban: used whip down shoulder (Nov 30-Dec 1,5,8,13,15,20)
Theodore Ladd four-day ban: careless riding (Nov 30, Dec 1,2,4)

**FOCUS**
A modest handicap in which it paid to be up with the pace.
T/Plt: £1,341.40 to a £1 stake. Pool: £63,398.62 - 34.50 winning units T/Qpdt: £291.40 to a £1 stake. Pool: £7,976.34 - 20.25 winning units **Joe Rowntree**

8808 - (Foreign Racing) - See Raceform Interactive

# [8793]CHELMSFORD (A.W) (L-H)
Friday, November 17

**OFFICIAL GOING: Polytrack: standard**
Wind: virtually nil Weather: dry, chilly

## 8809 TOTESCOOP6 MAGIC MILLION THIS SATURDAY NOVICE STKS 6f (P)
**5:45** (5:48) (Class 5) 2-Y-0 **£4,528** (£1,347; £673; £336) **Stalls** Centre

Form RPR

3 1 **Red Cymbal**[18] 8466 2-9-2 0 DanielTudhope 4 80
(William Haggas) *mde all: rdn over 1f out: forged ahd u.p ins fnl f: styd on wl to assert towards fin* 4/5[1]

2 2 ¾ **Fakhoor (IRE)**[51] 7513 2-9-2 0 DavidProbert 3 78
(Owen Burrows) *pressed wnr thrght: rdn wl over 1f out: sn drvn: jst outpcd by wnr fnl 100yds* 11/4[2]

3 5 **Midnight Guest (IRE)** 2-8-11 0 DanielMuscutt 2 58+
(George Margarson) *trckd ldrs: effrt 2f out: outpcd by ldng pair over 1f out: kpt on same pce ins fnl f* 25/1

4 1 ¼ **Filbert Street** 2-9-2 0 LukeMorris 6 59+
(Robert Cowell) *in tch in midfield: effrt in 5th ent fnl 2f: outpcd over 1f out: kpt on same pce ins fnl f* 12/1

52 5 1 ¾ **Haylah (IRE)**[46] 7688 2-8-11 0 SeanLevey 8 49
(Richard Hannon) *chsd ldrs: effrt ent fnl 2f: outpcd and btn over 1f out: wknd ins fnl f* 9/2[3]

30 6 3 **Crikeyitswhykie**[10] 8657 2-9-2 0 PatrickMathers 1 45
(Derek Shaw) *in tch in midfield: pushed along over 3f out: rdn 3f out: outpcd and struggling over 1f out: wknd fnl f* 100/1

7 ½ **Kachumba** 2-8-11 0 JimmyQuinn 7 38
(Rae Guest) *s.i.s: hld up in rr: lost tch in last trio over 2f out: swtchd lft over 1f out: nudged along and kpt on ins fnl f: nvr trbld ldrs* 33/1

00 8 ¾ **Broughton Excels**[10] 8657 2-9-2 0 StevieDonohoe 5 41
(Henry Spiller) *hld up in last trio: lost tch over 2f out* 150/1

60 9 4 ½ **Baileys Excel**[15] 8536 2-9-2 0 (h[1]) JoeFanning 9 28
(Chris Dwyer) *taken down early: off the pce in last trio: lost tch over 2f out* 25/1

1m 12.32s (-1.38) **Going Correction** -0.20s/f (Stan) 9 Ran SP% **120.4**
Speed ratings (Par 96): **101,100,93,91,89 85,84,83,77**
CSF £3.27 TOTE £1.70: £1.10, £1.10, £6.30; EX 3.70 Trifecta £29.80.
**Owner** Cheveley Park Stud **Bred** Cheveley Park Stud Ltd **Trained** Newmarket, Suffolk

**FOCUS**
A fair juvenile novice contest. The heavily backed favourite made all at a decent tempo.

## 8810 TOTESCOOP6 £1 MILLION THIS SATURDAY MAIDEN STKS 1m 2f (P)
**6:15** (6:17) (Class 5) 3-Y-0+ **£5,040** (£1,508; £754; £377) **Stalls** Low

Form RPR

3-22 1 **Corked (IRE)**[29] 8192 4-9-3 75 JamesDoyle 1 76
(Hugo Palmer) *t.k.h: mde all: rdn over 1f out: asserted u.p and in command 1f out: styd on wl: comf* 1/5[1]

3032 2 3 **Sugardrop**[74] 6750 3-9-0 74 RobertHavlin 2 70
(Amanda Perrett) *t.k.h: trckd ldrs: wnt 2nd and swtchd out rt 2f out: unable qck and hung lft 1f out: clr 2nd and kpt on same pce ins fnl f* 6/1[2]

404 3 14 **Wannabe Like You**[16] 8504 3-9-5 69 LukeMorris 3 57
(Archie Watson) *chsd wnr: shkn up over 3f out: rdn and lost 2nd 2f out: sn btn and wknd over 1f out: eased wl ins fnl f* 10/1[3]

0 4 8 **I Should Coco**[30] 8151 4-8-12 0 (p[1]) RhiainIngram[(5)] 4 25
(Karen George) *wnt rt s: t.k.h: hld up in tch in rr: rdn over 3f out: lost tch 2f out* 66/1

2m 7.17s (-1.43) **Going Correction** -0.20s/f (Stan)
**WFA** 3 from 4yo 3lb 4 Ran SP% **108.2**
Speed ratings (Par 103): **97,94,83,77**
CSF £1.88 TOTE £1.10; EX 1.90 Trifecta £2.20.
**Owner** The Corked Partnership **Bred** Lisieux Stud **Trained** Newmarket, Suffolk

**FOCUS**
An ordinary, uncompetitive maiden. The long odds-on favourite made all in straightforward fashion. The second has been rated to her penultimate C&D form.

## 8811 TOTESCOOP6 PLAY FOR £2 THIS SATURDAY CLAIMING STKS 1m (P)
6:45 (6:46) (Class 6) 3-Y-O+ £3,234 (£962; £481; £240) Stalls Low

Form RPR
6356 **1** **Big Baz (IRE)**[44] 7727 7-9-12 91 DougieCostello 2 96+
(William Muir) *chsd ldrs tl wnt 2nd 4f out: pushed along to ld 2f out: rdn and qcknd clr over 1f out: v easily* **2/5**[1]

1600 **2** 3 ¾ **Georgian Bay (IRE)**[31] 8138 7-9-5 88 (v) PatrickO'Hanlon(7) 4 87
(K R Burke) *dwlt: hld up in tch: swtchd rt 2f out: rdn to go 2nd but wnr clr over 1f out: kpt on but no ch w wnr* **3/1**[2]

0004 **3** 5 **Michele Strogoff**[23] 6949 4-9-12 83 (b) BenCurtis 5 75
(Tony Coyle) *led: rdn and hdd 2f out: outpcd and btn over 1f out: wknd ins fnl f* **10/1**[3]

0300 **4** 9 **Just Surprise Me (IRE)**[81] 6527 4-9-0 70 (t[1]) SeanLevey 1 41
(Mohamed Moubarak) *t.k.h: chsd ldr tl 6f out: styd prom: effrt 2f out: rdn and outpcd jst over 1f out: fdd fnl f: burst blood vessel* **20/1**

U160 **5** 14 **Secret Lightning (FR)**[218] 1755 5-8-2 51 (p) KeelanBaker(7) 3 3
(Michael Appleby) *restless in stalls: hld up in tch: rdn and struggling 3f out: bhd over 1f out* **100/1**

1m 38.3s (-1.60) **Going Correction** -0.20s/f (Stan) 5 Ran SP% **111.3**
Speed ratings (Par 101): **100,96,91,82,68**
CSF £1.94 TOTE £1.40: £1.10, £1.40; EX 2.00 Trifecta £3.50.Big Baz was claimed by Mr Dan Gilbert for £12000
**Owner** The Big Baz Partnership **Bred** Haras De La Perelle **Trained** Lambourn, Berks

**FOCUS**
A decent claimer. They went a respectable gallop and the likeable favourite outclassed the opposition. The race has been given a token rating around the winner's recent level.

## 8812 TOTESCOOP6 THREE WAYS TO WIN H'CAP 7f (P)
7:15 (7:17) (Class 3) (0-95,95) 3-Y-O+ £9,703 (£2,887; £1,443; £721) Stalls Low

Form RPR
4163 **1** **Boy In The Bar**[11] 8639 6-8-9 83 (v) JosephineGordon 3 92
(Ian Williams) *t.k.h: chsd ldrs: swtchd rt and effrt over 1f out: rdn and sn chalng: led ins fnl f: r.o wl: rdn out* **4/1**[2]

21-1 **2** 1 **Cliffs Of Capri**[23] 8344 3-9-3 92 DougieCostello 1 98+
(Jamie Osborne) *hld up in tch in midfield: nt clr run and swtchd rt over 1f out: hdwy u.p ins fnl f: wnt 2nd wl ins fnl f: r.o but nvr getting to wnr* **9/4**[1]

0605 **3** 1 **Alejandro (IRE)**[14] 8566 8-8-13 87 LukeMorris 10 91
(David Loughnane) *t.k.h: chsd ldr after 1f: rdn to ld over 1f out: hdd ins fnl f: no ex and outpcd wl ins fnl f* **33/1**

-111 **4** ½ **Gilgamesh**[197] 2348 3-9-3 92 RobertHavlin 4 94+
(George Scott) *hld up in tch in last quintet: nt clr run jst over 2f out: clsd and nt clr run again over 1f out: rdn and hdwy ins fnl f: styd on wl towards fin: nvr getting to ldrs* **6/1**

0421 **5** ½ **Pearl Spectre (USA)**[8] 8706 6-8-10 91 6ex NicolaCurrie(7) 7 92
(Phil McEntee) *led early: sn hdd and chsd ldrs: rdn ent fnl 2f: kpt on same pce ins fnl f* **7/1**

1610 **6** ¾ **Golden Goal (IRE)**[42] 7781 3-8-11 89 (h[1]) CallumShepherd(3) 11 87
(Saeed bin Suroor) *chsd ldrs: effrt u.p to press ldrs over 1f out: no ex ins fnl f: wknd towards fin* **9/2**[3]

0000 **7** 1 ¾ **Kickboxer (IRE)**[21] 8383 6-8-13 94 GabrieleMalune(7) 5 89
(Michael Appleby) *hld up in tch in last quartet: rdn and hdwy over 1f out: kpt on ins fnl f: nvr trbld ldrs* **33/1**

0303 **8** 1 ½ **Shyron**[15] 8547 6-8-8 87 JaneElliott(5) 12 78
(George Margarson) *hld up in last pair: nt clr run and swtchd lft over 1f out: nvr trbld ldrs* **14/1**

3500 **9** nse **Welliesinthewater (IRE)**[13] 8600 7-8-12 86 (v) PatrickMathers 6 76
(Derek Shaw) *hld up in tch in midfield: unable qck u.p over 1f out: wknd ins fnl f* **33/1**

6500 **10** 3 ¼ **Holiday Magic (IRE)**[26] 8257 6-9-7 95 CamHardie 9 77
(Michael Easterby) *dwlt: hld up in tch in last quintet: swtchd rt and effrt over 1f out: nvr trbld ldrs* **50/1**

6004 **11** 1 ½ **Alfred Hutchinson**[15] 8547 9-9-6 94 (p) DanielTudhope 14 72
(David O'Meara) *hld up in tch in last quartet: effrt and wd bnd 2f out: no imp: nvr trbld ldrs* **14/1**

0404 **12** 1 ¼ **Hammer Gun (USA)**[8] 8706 4-8-7 81 oh1 (v) JoeFanning 8 55
(Derek Shaw) *t.k.h: hld up in tch in midfield: unable qck over 1f out: wknd ins fnl f* **12/1**

1000 **13** ¾ **Highland Acclaim (IRE)**[15] 8547 6-8-13 87 (h) DavidProbert 13 59
(David O'Meara) *sn led: rdn and hdd over 1f out: wknd ins fnl f* **50/1**

1m 24.24s (-2.96) **Going Correction** -0.20s/f (Stan)
**WFA** 3 from 4yo+ 1lb 13 Ran SP% **129.5**
Speed ratings (Par 107): **108,106,105,105,104 103,101,100,99,96 94,93,92**
CSF £14.18 CT £287.84 TOTE £5.10: £1.90, £1.20, £7.80; EX 21.60 Trifecta £779.00.
**Owner** Sovereign Racing **Bred** Brinkley Stud S R L **Trained** Portway, Worcs

**FOCUS**
A good handicap. They went a decent gallop and it is sound form. The third has been rated to last winter's AW form.

## 8813 TOTESCOOP6 THE MILLIONAIRE MAKER H'CAP (DIV I) 1m 2f (P)
7:45 (7:47) (Class 5) (0-70,69) 3-Y-O+ £5,175 (£1,540; £769; £384) Stalls Low

Form RPR
2424 **1** **Rayaa**[31] 8143 4-9-7 69 (t) DanielTudhope 11 76
(Michael Appleby) *chsd ldrs: wnt 2nd over 3f out: rdn to ld ent fnl f: styd on wl: rdn out* **7/2**[1]

2102 **2** 1 **Jack Of Diamonds (IRE)**[10] 8664 8-9-5 67 DavidProbert 7 72
(Roger Teal) *hld up in tch: trckd ldrs over 2f out: effrt over 1f out: rdn and kpt on same pce ins fnl f: wnt 2nd last stride* **5/1**[3]

5600 **3** shd **Livella Fella (IRE)**[4] 8773 4-9-4 69 CallumRodriguez(3) 1 74
(Keith Dalgleish) *chsd ldr: rdn over 2f out: kpt on u.p: lost 2nd last stride* **20/1**

2545 **4** 1 ¼ **Hard Toffee (IRE)**[21] 8386 6-9-5 67 RobertTart 8 69
(Louise Allan) *led: rdn over 2f out: hdd ent fnl f: styd on same pce u.p after* **8/1**

3004 **5** hd **Bollihope**[28] 8206 5-9-2 64 PhillipMakin 10 66
(Richard Guest) *hld up in tch in midfield: effrt and hdwy over 2f out: clsd to chse ldrs 1f out: kpt on same pce u.p ins fnl f* **10/1**

0200 **6** 8 **Berlusca (IRE)**[17] 8497 8-9-3 65 JosephineGordon 5 51
(David Loughnane) *taken down early: hld up in midfield: hdwy over 2f out: no imp over 1f out: wknd ins fnl f* **14/1**

0000 **7** 5 **Accurate**[48] 7601 4-8-12 60 (p) StevieDonohoe 3 36
(Ian Williams) *chsd ldng trio: rdn 3f out: unable qck and btn over 1f out: wknd fnl f* **9/2**[2]

3363 **8** 1 **Millie's Kiss**[21] 8400 3-8-10 68 RossaRyan(7) 9 43
(Philip McBride) *hld up in tch in midfield: effrt over 2f out: no imp and btn u.p over 1f out: wknd fnl f* **10/1**

0614 **9** 15 **Luxford**[15] 8549 3-8-10 61 RobertHavlin 6 6
(John Best) *wnt lft s: in tch in midfield: lost pl and wd bnd 2f out: sn wl btn and eased* **8/1**

4520 **10** 9 **Right About Now (IRE)**[64] 7083 3-8-10 68 NicolaCurrie(7) 4
(Chris Dwyer) *bmpd s: hld up in last trio: rdn over 3f out: lost tch over 1f out: eased fnl f* **20/1**

505 **P** **The Salmon Man**[16] 6610 5-9-2 64 ShaneKelly 2
(Brendan Powell) *a towards rr: rdn 4f out: lost tch and eased 2f out: p.u 1f out* **20/1**

2m 5.13s (-3.47) **Going Correction** -0.20s/f (Stan)
**WFA** 3 from 4yo+ 3lb 11 Ran SP% **118.4**
Speed ratings (Par 103): **105,104,104,103,102 96,92,91,79,72**
CSF £20.06 CT £296.39 TOTE £3.70: £1.30, £2.10, £6.70; EX 21.50 Trifecta £318.80.
**Owner** Abdullateef Al Zeer **Bred** World Racing Network **Trained** Oakham, Rutland

**FOCUS**
The first division of a modest handicap. They went a respectable gallop and the favourite did well to win from an awkward draw. The runner-up helps set the standard.

## 8814 TOTESCOOP6 THE MILLIONAIRE MAKER H'CAP (DIV II) 1m 2f (P)
8:15 (8:19) (Class 5) (0-70,72) 3-Y-O+ £5,175 (£1,540; £769; £384) Stalls Low

Form RPR
1325 **1** **Dangerous Ends**[65] 7063 3-9-1 70 (p) CallumShepherd(3) 6 78
(Brett Johnson) *hld up in tch in midfield: effrt over 2f out: led u.p 100yds: sn edgd lft but r.o wl: rdn out* **8/1**

5233 **2** ½ **Choral Clan (IRE)**[15] 8550 6-9-6 69 JackMitchell 3 75
(Brendan Powell) *t.k.h: chsd ldrs: effrt on inner over 1f out: ev ch 1f out: kpt on wl u.p: hld towards fin* **5/1**[2]

5050 **3** 1 ¼ **Mullarkey**[35] 8000 3-9-2 68 JoeyHaynes 7 73
(John Best) *chsd ldrs: effrt over 2f out: hdwy and drvn to ld 1f out: hdd 100yds out: sn squeezed for room and no ex towards fin* **10/1**

2203 **4** nk **Maraakib (IRE)**[9] 8682 5-9-2 65 DanielTudhope 10 68
(David O'Meara) *hld up in tch in midfield: effrt to chse ldrs 2f out: kpt on u.p ins fnl f* **6/1**[3]

5035 **5** 2 ¼ **Miss Mirabeau**[15] 8538 3-8-8 60 (b) LukeMorris 8 58
(Sir Mark Prescott Bt) *dwlt and short of room leaving stalls: t.k.h: hld up in tch: effrt 2f out: kpt on same pce u.p ins fnl f* **5/1**[2]

1-50 **6** 1 ¾ **Intermodal**[32] 8111 3-9-6 72 DougieCostello 9 67
(Jamie Osborne) *t.k.h: w ldr tl led 7f out: rdn over 1f out: hdd 1f out: wknd ins fnl f* **8/1**

0004 **7** nse **Never A Word (USA)**[17] 8497 3-9-1 67 (bt) KevinStott 5 62
(Oliver Greenall) *rousted along leaving stalls: effrt and swtchd rt bnd 2f out: no imp u.p over 1f out: nvr trbld ldrs* **16/1**

6260 **8** 2 **Bartholomew J (IRE)**[31] 8142 3-9-0 66 SimonPearce 11 57
(Lydia Pearce) *hld up in rr: effrt on inner over 1f out: no imp 1f out: nvr trbld ldrs* **33/1**

3034 **9** 1 **William Booth (IRE)**[25] 8300 3-9-1 67 DavidProbert 1 56
(Ivan Furtado) *t.k.h: hld up in tch in midfield: swtchd rt over 2f out: no imp u.p over 1f out: wknd ins fnl f* **3/1**[1]

0060 **10** ¾ **Auntie Barber (IRE)**[30] 8156 4-9-4 67 (vt[1]) SeanLevey 4 54
(Stuart Williams) *t.k.h: led tl 7f out: chsd ldr tl rdn and lost pl over 1f out: wknd fnl f* **16/1**

6000 **11** 10 **Miss Danby (IRE)**[39] 7895 3-8-10 62 JoeFanning 2 30
(Mark Johnston) *in tch in midfield: rdn and lost pl over 2f out: bhd and wknd fnl f* **25/1**

2m 6.89s (-1.71) **Going Correction** -0.20s/f (Stan)
**WFA** 3 from 4yo+ 3lb 11 Ran SP% **122.5**
Speed ratings (Par 103): **98,97,96,96,94 93,93,91,90,90 82**
CSF £49.87 CT £416.88 TOTE £9.50: £2.70, £2.30, £4.10; EX 40.60 Trifecta £591.60.
**Owner** Colin Westley **Bred** R S Cockerill (farms) Ltd **Trained** Epsom, Surrey
■ Stewards' Enquiry : Callum Shepherd three-day ban: careless riding (Dec 1,2,4)

**FOCUS**
The second division of a modest handicap. They went a muddling gallop and the winning time was nearly two seconds slower. The runner-up has been rated to his recent form.

## 8815 LASER SENSORY H'CAP 1m 5f 66y(P)
8:45 (8:49) (Class 7) (0-50,51) 3-Y-O+ £2,911 (£866; £432; £216) Stalls Low

Form RPR
5002 **1** **Kaisan**[20] 8430 4-9-7 50 (t) DavidProbert 14 56
(Bernard Llewellyn) *rousted along early: in tch in midfield: clsd to chse ldrs and wnt clr in ldng quintet over 3f out: effrt to chse ldrs and edgd lft over 1f out: led ins fnl f: styd on* **10/1**

0504 **2** 1 ¼ **Dibloam (USA)**[36] 7991 4-8-13 45 (h) MattCosham(3) 2 49
(David Evans) *s.i.s: hld up in rr: nt clr run 4f out: swtchd rt over 3f out: hdwy but stl plenty to do 2f out: r.o v strly ins fnl f: snatched 2nd last stride* **8/1**

4001 **3** shd **Volturnus**[9] 8674 3-9-3 51 6ex (bt) DougieCostello 5 57
(Jamie Osborne) *chsd ldr: wnt clr in ldng quintet over 3f out: led over 2f out: rdn over 1f out: hdd 100yds out: no ex and lost 2nd last stride* **4/1**[1]

0000 **4** 2 ½ **Koubba (IRE)**[86] 6305 4-9-2 45 (t) StevieDonohoe 12 45
(Neil Mulholland) *hld up in rr: hdwy but stl plenty to do over 2f out: styd on wl fnl f: nvr gng to rch ldrs* **50/1**

0004 **5** 3 **Babette (IRE)**[16] 8507 3-9-1 49 (v) JosephineGordon 11 47
(Alan Bailey) *chsd ldrs: wnt clr in ldng quintet over 3f out: rdn and getting outpcd whn swtchd lft over 1f out: wknd ins fnl f* **7/1**

4502 **6** 2 **Iley Boy**[9] 8673 3-8-13 47 (p) JoeyHaynes 6 42
(John Gallagher) *chsd ldrs: wnt clr in ldng quintet over 3f out: 3rd and outpcd over 1f out: wknd ins fnl f* **5/1**[3]

5360 **7** 4 ½ **Oyster Card**[193] 2460 4-9-2 45 (p) AlistairRawlinson 1 32
(Michael Appleby) *led: rdn and hdd over 2f out: wknd fnl f* **16/1**

2-06 **8** 3 ¾ **Moon Arrow (IRE)**[36] 7991 4-9-5 48 (v) LukeMorris 3 30
(Michael Blake) *hld up towards rr: hdwy into midfield and rdn 3f out: nvr getting on terms and wl btn fnl 2f* **7/1**

0366 **9** 2 ¾ **Briac (FR)**[44] 7730 6-9-0 48 PaddyBradley(5) 10 26
(Mark Pattinson) *t.k.h: hld up in tch in last quartet: effrt into midfield 3f out: no imp and nvr getting on terms w ldrs: plugged on same pce fr over 1f out* **9/2**[2]

3466 **10** 1 ½ **Rezwaan**[169] 3251 10-9-2 45 ShaneKelly 4 21
(Murty McGrath) *in tch in midfield: 6th and outpcd over 3f out: wl btn 2f out: wknd* **33/1**

3006 **11** 1 **The Last Melon**[21] 8396 5-9-2 50 RachealKneller(5) 9 24
(James Bennett) *midfield: rdn and outpcd over 3f out: no ch fnl 2f* **16/1**

0035 **12** 14 **Galuppi**[36] 6109 6-9-3 46 (v) DanielTudhope 7
(J R Jenkins) *hld up in rr: nvr on terms: lost tch 2f out: eased ins fnl f* **16/1**

0540 **13** *6* **Tayaar (IRE)**[43] 6293 4-9-7 **50** CamHardie 8
(John Ryan) *midfield: rdn over 3f out: sn struggling: bhd 2f out: eased ins fnl f: t.o* **33/1**

0063 **14** *64* **Netley Abbey**[99] 5846 3-8-13 **47** (p) JoeFanning 13
(Karen George) *chsd ldrs tl 5f out: sn lost pl: t.o and eased fnl 2f* **16/1**

2m 50.9s (-2.70) **Going Correction** -0.20s/f (Stan)
**WFA** 3 from 4yo+ 5lb **14** Ran SP% **131.4**
Speed ratings (Par 97): **100,99,99,97,95 94,91,89,87,86 86,77,73,34**
CSF £95.03 CT £389.24 TOTE £8.20: £3.20, £3.40, £1.60; EX 119.40 Trifecta £738.40.
**Owner** B J Llewellyn **Bred** Lady Bamford **Trained** Fochriw, Caerphilly

**FOCUS**
A moderate staying handicap. They went a respectable gallop and a few of the more likely candidates came to the fore. A minor pb from the second.

## 8816 GERRY MCCARTHY 40TH ANNIVERSARY H'CAP 5f (P)
**9:15** (9:17) (Class 6) (0-65,67) 3-Y-O+ **£3,234** (£962; £360; £360) **Stalls Low**

Form RPR

5501 **1** **Entertaining Ben**[43] 7767 4-9-6 **64** (p) KevinStott 6 73
(Amy Murphy) *mde all: rdn over 1f out: styd on wl: nvr seriously chal* **8/1**

5403 **2** *2 1/4* **Spin Top**[15] 8542 3-9-3 **61** DougieCostello 7 62
(William Muir) *hld up in tch in midfield on inner: effrt and hdwy over 1f out: chsd wnr ins fnl f: no imp* **6/1**[3]

2600 **3** *1 1/4* **Pearl Acclaim (IRE)**[14] 8557 7-9-5 **63** (p) SteveDrowne 1 59
(David C Griffiths) *t.k.h: chsd ldrs: wnt 2nd over 2f out: drifted rt wl over 1f out: no imp: lost 2nd ins fnl f: wknd towards fin* **8/1**

0530 **3** *dht* **Firesnake (IRE)**[17] 8490 4-8-2 **53** (v) GabrieleMalune(7) 9 49
(Lisa Williamson) *dwlt: hld up in last trio: effrt on inner over 1f out: kpt on ins fnl f: nvr threatening wnr* **16/1**

0015 **5** *1/2* **Red Stripes (USA)**[30] 8159 5-9-3 **61** (b) DavidProbert 4 56
(Lisa Williamson) *dwlt and short of room leaving stalls: rdn and effrt over 1f out: hdwy and swtchd lft ins fnl f: styd on: nvr trbld ldrs* **4/1**[2]

000 **6** *1 1/2* **Malaysian Boleh**[15] 8541 7-9-0 **65** (p) NicolaCurrie(7) 11 54+
(Phil McEntee) *s.i.s: outpcd in rr: styd on ins fnl f: nvr trbld ldrs* **33/1**

4303 **7** *1/2* **Frank The Barber (IRE)**[17] 8494 5-8-10 **54** (tp) LukeMorris 2 41
(Steph Hollinshead) *in tch in midfield: effrt over 1f out: sn drvn and unable qck: no imp ins fnl f* **12/1**

0445 **8** *1/2* **Roundabout Magic (IRE)**[43] 7767 3-9-5 **63** NickyMackay 8 49
(Simon Dow) *t.k.h: chsd ldrs: rdn and unable qck over 1f out: wknd ins fnl f* **12/1**

3400 **9** *4* **Mossgo (IRE)**[146] 4093 7-9-9 **67** (t) RobertHavlin 3 38
(John Best) *hld up in midfield: effrt over 1f out: unable qck: wknd ins fnl f* **12/1**

0003 **10** *1 1/2* **First Bombardment**[14] 8557 4-9-5 **63** DanielTudhope 5 29
(David O'Meara) *t.k.h: chsd ldr tl over 2f out: squeezed for room and lost pl 2f out: sn btn: wknd fnl f* **2/1**[1]

59.32s (-0.88) **Going Correction** -0.20s/f (Stan) **10** Ran SP% **121.7**
Speed ratings (Par 101): **99,95,93,93,92 90,89,88,82,79**
TC: EB/ST/PA 209.21, EB/ST/FS 383.77; TF: EB/ST/PA 400.90, EB/ST/FS 454.20; CSF £57.96 TOTE £7.60: £2.90, £2.80, £1.30, £1.60; EX 46.40.
**Owner** Amy Murphy Racing Club **Bred** C J Mills **Trained** Newmarket, Suffolk

**FOCUS**
A modest sprint handicap. The winner made all in convincing fashion. The winner has been rated back towards his best.
T/Plt: £13.10 to a £1 stake. Pool: £99,028.07 - 5,487.85 winning units. T/Qpdt: £12.00 to a £1 stake. Pool: £10,334.47 - 636.36 winning units. **Steve Payne**

# 8544 LINGFIELD (L-H)
Friday, November 17

**OFFICIAL GOING: Polytrack: standard**
Wind: Bright, clear sky Weather: Nil

## 8817 £10 FREE AT 32RED.COM NURSERY H'CAP 7f 1y(P)
**11:50** (11:52) (Class 5) (0-75,77) 2-Y-O **£2,911** (£866; £432; £216) **Stalls Low**

Form RPR

060 **1** **Insurgence**[72] 6827 2-9-4 **71** DanielMuscutt 1 77+
(James Fanshawe) *settled bhd ldr: rdn over 1f out: kpt on wl and led 110yds out: in control and pushed out nr fin* **13/2**[2]

0250 **2** *1* **Zalshah**[21] 8387 2-9-6 **73** (p) TomMarquand 9 76
(Richard Hannon) *in rr-div and t.k.h early: rdn over 1f out between horses: kpt on wl at fin to take 2nd fnl strides* **14/1**

006 **3** *nk* **Grace's Secret**[35] 7995 2-9-1 **68** LiamKeniry 4 70
(Ed Walker) *racd between horses bhd ldrs: rdn wl over 1f out on outer: kpt on ins fnl f to take 3rd* **10/1**

5031 **4** *1 1/2* **Enrolment**[13] 8586 2-9-5 **72** TonyHamilton 11 70
(Richard Fahey) *quick away: sn pressed ldr on outer: rdn along wl over 1f out: ev ch in 2nd ent fnl f: no ex sn after and kpt on one pce* **10/1**

6131 **5** *1/2* **Montague (IRE)**[17] 8493 2-9-10 **77** DougieCostello 3 74
(Jamie Osborne) *pushed along leaving stalls and sn led on rail: rdn wl over 1f out: kpt on tl hdd & wknd qckly fnl 110yds* **7/1**[3]

4100 **6** *2* **Straight Ash (IRE)**[23] 8349 2-9-1 **71** HollieDoyle(3) 8 63
(Richard Hannon) *in rr: shkn up over 2f out on rail: stuck to inner and rdn wl over 1f out: kpt on one pce ins fnl f* **13/2**[2]

0032 **7** *nk* **Global Spirit**[10] 8658 2-8-12 **65** RobertHavlin 5 56
(Ed Dunlop) *racd in mid-div: rdn over 1f out: kpt on one pce after* **11/2**[1]

000 **8** *1* **Bessie Warfield**[44] 7733 2-8-13 **66** LukeMorris 12 54
(Luca Cumani) *c across fr wd draw and w ldrs on outer: rdn wl over 2f out and losing pl: plugged on in st* **22/1**

**9** *shd* **Dream Malfunction (IRE)**[111] 5442 2-9-7 **74** JosephineGordon 7 62
(Joseph Tuite) *in rr: rdn over 2f out: plugged on at one pce fr over 1f out* **40/1**

042 **10** *3/4* **Cwynar**[22] 8373 2-9-7 **74** DavidProbert 2 60
(Charles Hills) *bhd ldr on inner: rdn wl over 1f out: sn no ex and wknd* **7/1**[3]

642 **11** *1* **High Seas (IRE)**[23] 8347 2-9-7 **74** JamesDoyle 13 57
(Hugo Palmer) *racd in rr-div on outer: rdn along over 2f out: c wd st: no prog after* **15/2**

3202 **12** *1/2* **Not After Midnight (IRE)**[30] 8153 2-9-9 **76** RobHornby 10 58
(Daniel Kubler) *bhd ldrs and racd wd: shkn up over 2f out and c v wd into st: sn rdn: no ex and wknd sn after* **20/1**

000 **13** *2* **Pescedora (IRE)**[20] 8425 2-8-13 **66** ShaneKelly 6 42
(Roger Charlton) *in rr: rdn along to hold tch over 2f out: no ex st* **40/1**

1m 24.4s (-0.40) **Going Correction** +0.05s/f (Slow) **13** Ran SP% **117.7**
Speed ratings (Par 96): **104,102,102,100,100 97,97,96,96,95 94,93,91**
CSF £88.22 CT £927.44 TOTE £8.60: £3.10, £4.50, £4.10; EX 98.40 Trifecta £1716.70.
**Owner** Dr Catherine Wills & Frederik Tylicki **Bred** St Clare Hall Stud **Trained** Newmarket, Suffolk

**FOCUS**
An ordinary nursery, but wide open. Seven of the 13 runners were making their nursery debuts after the prerequisite three runs, including the winner and third. Only three of these had won before. The second has been rated near his best.

## 8818 BETWAY H'CAP 6f 1y(P)
**12:20** (12:21) (Class 5) (0-75,77) 3-Y-O+ **£2,911** (£866; £432; £216) **Stalls Low**

Form RPR

44 **1** **Sword Exceed (GER)**[132] 4616 3-9-9 **77** LukeMorris 5 88+
(Ivan Furtado) *racd in mid-div on outer: gng wl on outer over 2f out: smooth prog fr over 1f: cruised into contention and upsides ent fnl f: pushed into ld 100yds out: sn clr: easily* **7/2**[2]

6564 **2** *1 1/2* **Pretty Bubbles**[22] 8374 8-9-2 **70** (v) JosephineGordon 8 75
(J R Jenkins) *in rr and t.k.h between horses: rdn wl over 1f out: kpt on wl ins fnl f to take 2nd fnl strides: no ch w easy wnr* **14/1**

1534 **3** *nk* **Geoff Potts (IRE)**[38] 7923 4-9-4 **72** TonyHamilton 4 76
(Richard Fahey) *bhd ldr early: pressed ldr by 1/2-way and t.k.h: upsides and hanging rt whn rdn ent fnl f: wnr sn wnt by: kpt on tl lost 2nd fnl strides* **9/4**[1]

0002 **4** *1/2* **Ballymore Castle (IRE)**[7] 8722 5-9-5 **73** (p) AndrewMullen 7 75+
(Richard Fahey) *racd in rr-div on inner: rdn along over 1f out: plenty to do whn swtchd off rail ent fnl f: gd prog fnl 110yds to take 4th nr fin* **8/1**

0453 **5** *1/2* **Cosmic Chatter**[7] 8722 7-8-12 **66** (p) JackGarritty 9 67
(Ruth Carr) *in rr: shkn up w plenty to do over 2f out: c wd into st: rdn over 1f out: kpt on wl ins fnl f: nrst fin* **14/1**

1526 **6** *nk* **Deeds Not Words (IRE)**[15] 8541 6-9-4 **72** (p) RobertHavlin 1 74+
(Michael Wigham) *bhd ldr on inner: gng wl and boxed in fr over 1f out: swtchd out ent fnl f: hmpd again sn after and eased* **9/1**

0610 **7** *nk* **Love Oasis**[15] 8542 3-9-1 **69** JoeFanning 11 68
(Mark Johnston) *sn led and set str pce: slowed tempo by 1/2-way: rdn over 2f out: plugged on tl hdd 110yds out and wknd qckly* **20/1**

1266 **8** *3/4* **Contentment**[62] 7161 3-9-7 **75** (t[1]) JamesDoyle 10 71
(William Haggas) *in rr: rdn along over 2f out and c wd st: no ex and pushed out over 1f out* **7/1**[3]

3520 **9** *nk* **Miss Icon**[44] 7723 3-8-8 **62** DavidProbert 3 58
(Patrick Chamings) *racd in mid-div on rail: rdn over 1f out and sn one pce* **14/1**

4231 **10** *hd* **Ballesteros**[25] 8296 8-8-5 **64** RhiainIngram(5) 2 59
(Roger Ingram) *settled bhd ldrs on outer: ev ch over 1f out: sn shkn up: fnd nil and n.m.r: no ex ins fnl f* **25/1**

0200 **11** *8* **Kingsley Klarion (IRE)**[43] 7759 4-9-3 **74** TimClark(3) 6 43
(John Butler) *bdly missed break and a detached in rr: tried to cl at 1/2-way: sn no ex: lost ch at s* **50/1**

1m 11.81s (-0.09) **Going Correction** +0.05s/f (Slow) **11** Ran SP% **117.2**
Speed ratings (Par 103): **102,100,99,98,98 97,97,96,96,95 85**
CSF £50.24 CT £133.89 TOTE £4.50: £1.70, £2.90, £1.30; EX 50.40 Trifecta £177.10.
**Owner** 21st Century Racing, C Hodgson & Bgc **Bred** Gestut Wittekindshof **Trained** Wiseton, Nottinghamshire

**FOCUS**
An ordinary sprint handicap. The third has been rated close to form.

## 8819 32RED CASINO/EBF NOVICE STKS 5f 6y(P)
**12:50** (12:50) (Class 5) 2-Y-O **£2,911** (£866; £432; £216) **Stalls High**

Form RPR

35 **1** **Drakefell (IRE)**[21] 8388 2-9-2 0 SeanLevey 1 79
(Richard Hannon) *mde all: marginal ldr on rail: increased pce wl over 1f out and 3 l ld ent fnl f: rdn ins fnl f w runner-up clsng: on top and pushed out nr fin* **10/11**[1]

4224 **2** *1 1/4* **Choice Encounter**[165] 3406 2-8-13 76 CallumShepherd(3) 5 74
(Michael Bell) *racd in last trio: stl in tch: rdn over 1f out: kpt on wl and chsd clr ldr ent fnl f: keeping on wl at fin* **7/2**[2]

**3** *2* **Mosseyb (IRE)** 2-9-2 0 JamesDoyle 8 69+
(William Haggas) *missed break and wnt rt s: detached in rr and green: nudged and niggled to take clsr order fr wl over 3f out: rdn in last over 2f out and began to cl on outer: encouraging hdwy fnl f under hands and heels to take 3rd* **9/2**[3]

**4** *1/2* **Dubai Silk** 2-8-11 0 LukeMorris 2 60
(Robert Cowell) *pressed ldr between horses: rdn over 2f out: lost 2nd ent fnl f and ct for 3rd fnl strides* **9/1**

00 **5** *2 1/2* **Hornby**[142] 4213 2-9-2 0 RobertHavlin 4 56
(Michael Attwater) *bhd ldr on inner: rdn over 1f out: nt qckn and plugged on one pce ins fnl f* **66/1**

4 **6** *1 3/4* **No More Commisery (IRE)**[53] 7450 2-8-11 0 ShaneKelly 3 45
(Mick Quinn) *pressed ldr on outer: wnt wd ent st and sn rdn: noe ex and pushed out ins fnl f* **6/1**

**7** *3 3/4* **Perambulation** 2-8-11 0 KieranO'Neill 6 31
(Stuart Kittow) *in rr: pushed along wl over 2f out: no ex fr over 1f out* **33/1**

00 **8** *nk* **May Spirit**[60] 7211 2-8-11 0 RobHornby 7 30
(Michael Blanshard) *bhd ldr on outer: rdn along fr 1/2-way: no ex fr over 1f out* **100/1**

59.71s (0.91) **Going Correction** +0.05s/f (Slow) **8** Ran SP% **122.5**
Speed ratings (Par 96): **94,92,88,88,84 81,75,74**
CSF £4.89 TOTE £2.30: £1.10, £1.40, £1.60; EX 5.10 Trifecta £14.80.
**Owner** Des Anderson **Bred** D J Anderson **Trained** East Everleigh, Wilts

**FOCUS**
A moderate and uncompetitive novice event. Few got into it and the runner-up's mark of 76 sets the standard. The runner-up has been rated close to his pre-race mark, but the level is a bit fluid.

## 8820 32RED.COM/ BRITISH STALLION STUDS EBF FILLIES' H'CAP 1m 2f (P)
**1:25** (1:25) (Class 3) (0-90,88) 3-Y-O **£9,766** (£2,923; £1,461; £731; £364) **Stalls Low**

Form RPR

-351 **1** *hd* **Crimson Rosette (IRE)**[32] 8117 3-8-11 **78** (h) StevieDonohoe 7 84
(Charlie Fellowes) *hld up in rr on outer: tk clsr order on outer over 3f out: picked up wl and ev ch ent fnl f: bmpd by ldr fnl 50yds and unbalanced rdr: nt rcvrd: fin 2nd: awrdd r* **5/1**[2]

1505 **2** **Stellar Surprise**[50] 7545 3-9-0 **81** (t) SeanLevey 2 88
(Stuart Williams) *hld up in mid-div: prog and ev ch ent fnl f: rdn between horses and led jst ins fnl f: edgd rt fnl 50yds and bmpd runner-up: fin first: disqualified and plcd 2nd - caused interference* **20/1**

1006 **3** *1/2* **Glenys The Menace (FR)**[21] 8385 3-9-2 **83** RobertHavlin 5 88
(John Best) *hld up in rr-div on rail: shuffled bk and in last but in tch over 1f out: slipped in and prog ent fnl f on heels of ldrs: shot through gap 1f out: ev ch tl no ex nr fin* **10/1**[3]

6263 **4** ¾ **Voi**[14] 8561 3-8-0 **74** oh2 (t) NicolaCurrie(7) 6 78+
(Conrad Allen) *racd in last: rdn and c wd wl over 1f out: chsd eventual wnr ent fnl f: keeping on fnl 100yds wnt clipped heels 50yds out and eased fnl strides* **16/1**

5515 **5** 3 ¼ **Hidden Steps**[23] 8351 3-9-5 **86** (h) DavidProbert 4 83
(Andrew Balding) *t.k.h: pressed ldr and briefly led tl settled bhd ldng pair after 7f out: rdn wl over 1f out between horses: sltly unbalanced sn after and lost pl: kpt on one pce after* **10/1**[3]

1601 **6** 3 ¾ **Villette (IRE)**[31] 8143 3-8-13 **80** RobHornby 3 69
(Dean Ivory) *bhd ldr on rail: rdn wl over 1f out on inner: fnd nil ent fnl f and plugged on after* **16/1**

1132 **7** 1 ¼ **Canberra Cliffs (IRE)**[10] 8652 3-9-7 **88** FranBerry 8 75
(Don Cantillon) *racd in cl up 3rd on outer tl pressed ldr 7f out: hrd rdn over 1f out: sn swamped either side and wknd fnl f* **12/1**

1 **8** 2 ¾ **Part Exchange**[52] 7492 3-9-6 **87** JamesDoyle 1 68
(Hugo Palmer) *marginal ldr on rail: rdn along over 3f out: fnd nil over 1f out: hdd ent fnl f and wknd v qckly* **4/9**[1]

2m 4.49s (-2.11) **Going Correction** +0.05s/f (Slow) 8 Ran SP% **128.3**
Speed ratings (Par 103): **109,110,109,108,106 103,102,100**
CSF £104.81 CT £999.62 TOTE £5.70: £1.10, £8.00, £3.10; EX 233.10 Trifecta £684.20.
**Owner** A E Oppenheimer **Bred** Hascombe & Valiant Studs **Trained** Newmarket, Suffolk

**FOCUS**
A decent 3yo fillies' handicap which was a one-horse race according to the market, but backers of the short-price favourite got their fingers burnt. The pace didn't look that strong and all eight fillies' were still closely bunched after turning in. There was some argy-bargy between the first two well inside the last furlong and it was serious enough for the Stewards to reverse their placings. It's been rated around the third and fourth.

## 8821 PLAY JACKPOT GAMES AT SUNBETS.CO.UK/VEGAS H'CAP 1m 1y(P)
**2:00** (2:01) (Class 4) (0-85,84) 3-Y-0+ **£4,690** (£1,395; £697; £348) **Stalls** High

Form RPR

051 **1** **Al Galayel (IRE)**[14] 8554 3-9-2 **82** LukeMorris 12 92+
(Luca Cumani) *kpt st fr wd draw tl c over to pack after 1f: w ldrs on outer: pressed ldr at 1/2-way: led over 2f out and sn kicked for home: kpt on wl fr over 1f out: plld out more whn chal ins fnl f: progive* **4/1**[2]

-231 **2** 1 **Top Mission**[169] 3234 3-9-4 **84** WilliamCarson 9 92
(Saeed bin Suroor) *between horses bhd ldrs: rdn wl over 1f out and chsd wnr: kpt on one pce ins fnl f for 2nd: nt get to wnr* **11/4**[1]

11-0 **3** 1 **Tiercel**[38] 7941 4-9-6 **84** SilvestreDeSousa 4 91+
(Roger Varian) *hld up on rail bhd ldr: shkn up over 1f out and racd awkward angling for gap ent fnl f: sn rdn between horses: stuck on and briefly tk 2nd ins fnl f: lost 2nd wl ins fnl f and kpt on one pce* **4/1**[2]

0210 **4** nk **Intense Style (IRE)**[27] 8240 5-8-9 **80** FayeMcManoman(7) 10 86
(Les Eyre) *settled in mid-div: rdn over 2f out: kpt on ins fnl f and jst hld 4th* **50/1**

4000 **5** nk **Ice Royal (IRE)**[42] 7789 4-9-5 **83** DougieCostello 3 88
(Jamie Osborne) *in mid-divsion on inner: swtchd off rail and rdn wl over 2f out to chse ldrs: kpt on ins fnl f* **9/1**

040 **6** ½ **Parnassian (IRE)**[11] 8639 3-9-4 **84** RobertHavlin 7 87
(Amanda Perrett) *racd in rr-div on inner and plld hrd early: rdn over 2f out and clung to rail ent st: n.m.r ent fnl f and jockey briefly stopped riding: swiched out and kpt on ins fnl f* **10/1**

50-0 **7** 1 ¼ **Wimpole Hall**[25] 8297 4-9-4 **82** DavidProbert 8 83
(William Jarvis) *in rr-div between horses: rdn over 2f out: kpt on one pce fr over 1f out* **8/1**[3]

4400 **8** 1 **Scottish Glen**[13] 8600 11-8-13 **80** HectorCrouch(3) 1 79
(Patrick Chamings) *in rr on inner: rdn over 2f out: kpt on one pce in st* **14/1**

0000 **9** ½ **In The Red (IRE)**[68] 6964 4-9-4 **82** TomMarquand 5 80
(Martin Smith) *led on rail: pressed fr 1/2-way: rdn to hold pl and* **66/1**

0530 **10** nse **Areen Heart (FR)**[21] 8392 3-9-3 **83** (h) PhillipMakin 6 80
(David O'Meara) *mid-div on outer: rdn over 2f out: plugged on* **9/1**

3000 **11** 1 ¼ **Van Huysen (IRE)**[176] 2999 5-9-6 **84** SeanLevey 2 79
(Dominic Ffrench Davis) *a in rr: rdn over 2f out: one pce st* **28/1**

15-0 **12** 4 ½ **Toriano**[170] 3214 4-9-2 **80** JoeFanning 11 64
(Nick Littmoden) *racd in rr-div on outer: rdn and wnt v wd st: no ex sn after* **25/1**

1m 36.9s (-1.30) **Going Correction** +0.05s/f (Slow)
**WFA** 3 from 4yo+ 2lb 12 Ran SP% **124.3**
Speed ratings (Par 105): **108,107,106,105,105 104,103,102,102,102 100,96**
CSF £15.83 CT £49.68 TOTE £5.00: £1.60, £1.80, £1.10; EX 18.90 Trifecta £27.10.
**Owner** Al Shaqab Racing **Bred** D J Maher **Trained** Newmarket, Suffolk

**FOCUS**
A fair handicap and it paid to be handy with the first three always close to the pace. It's been rated around the fourth.

## 8822 BETWAY MAIDEN STKS 1m 4f (P)
**2:35** (2:35) (Class 5) 3-Y-0+ **£2,911** (£866; £432; £216) **Stalls** Low

Form RPR

4353 **1** **Persistence (IRE)**[21] 8390 3-9-0 75 RichardKingscote 9 74+
(Ralph Beckett) *racd in 3rd bhd ldng pair: shkn up and prog to ld 3f out: sn rdn and kpt on wl fr over 1f to fend off plcd horses* **11/4**[2]

4234 **2** 1 **Nurse Nightingale**[17] 8485 3-9-0 71 (h) JamesDoyle 6 72
(Michael Bell) *reluctantly led tl hdd and settled bhd ldr after 2f: rdn in 3rd over 2f out: kpt chalng fr over 1f out: no ex nr fin* **5/2**[1]

0-44 **3** shd **Soghan (IRE)**[30] 8151 3-9-5 75 (t) ShaneKelly 3 77
(Richard Hughes) *racd in mid-div: rdn wl over 2f out to chse ldng trio: plenty to do over 1f out: kpt on strly ins fnl f to snatch 3rd post: gng on at fin* **7/2**[3]

62 **4** ½ **Warm Oasis**[30] 8151 3-9-5 0 DanielMuscutt 11 76+
(James Fanshawe) *in mid-div: impr fr over 3f out and travelling sweetly bhd ldng pair over 2f out: shkn up and racd awkwardly fr over 1f out: nvr able to chal and lost 3rd in fnl strides* **11/4**[2]

**5** 10 **Emerald Cross (IRE)** 4-9-10 0 SteveDrowne 8 59
(Adam West) *s.s: sn in rr-div: rdn wl over 3f out: lft bhd sn after* **33/1**

0 **6** 12 **Rosie Lea (FR)**[30] 8151 4-9-5 0 LiamKeniry 4 35
(Stuart Kittow) *in rr-div on inner and plld hrd early: rdn wl over 3f out: no ex sn after* **66/1**

0 **7** 1 **Amajari (FR)**[32] 8116 3-9-5 0 FranBerry 2 39
(Gary Moore) *in rr: rdn over 3f out: plugged on after* **66/1**

0 **8** ½ **Mr Boycie Quest**[30] 8151 3-9-2 0 HectorCrouch(3) 10 38
(Gary Moore) *bhd ldr tl led after 2f: rdn wl over 3f out: hdd over 2f out: no ex and wknd sn after* **50/1**

0 **9** ¾ **Delicate Kiss**[11] 8635 3-9-0 0 (b[1]) WilliamCarson 7 32
(John Bridger) *in rr-div on outer: tk clsr over 4f out to keep tabs on ldrs: sn struggling and plugged on* **100/1**

**10** ¾ **Celsiana**[24] 3-8-7 0 (b[1]) TylerSaunders(7) 5 31
(Marcus Tregoning) *mid-div on inner tl sed to struggled after 2f: sn dropped to rr and rdn to hold tch: one pce fr over 3f out* **25/1**

2m 32.42s (-0.58) **Going Correction** +0.05s/f (Slow)
**WFA** 3 from 4yo 5lb 10 Ran SP% **116.9**
Speed ratings (Par 103): **103,102,102,101,95 87,86,86,85,85**
CSF £9.76 TOTE £3.50: £1.40, £1.50, £1.30; EX 10.50 Trifecta £27.00.
**Owner** Duke Of Roxburghe & James Wigan **Bred** Floors Farming & London Thoroughbred Services Ltd **Trained** Kimpton, Hants

**FOCUS**
An uncompetitive older-horse maiden in which they bet 25-1 bar four and those at the head of the market dominated the finish. Adjusted official ratings had it pretty much spot-on. The second has been rated close to form, and the third and fourth similar to their Kempton latest.

## 8823 BETWAY APPRENTICE H'CAP (DIV I) 6f 1y(P)
**3:10** (3:11) (Class 6) (0-60,60) 3-Y-0+ **£2,264** (£673; £336; £168) **Stalls** Low

Form RPR

1663 **1** **Wild Flower (IRE)**[17] 8495 5-9-1 **56** RossaRyan(5) 9 61
(Jimmy Fox) *w ldr on outer: rdn and narrowly led over 1f out: briefly hdd 1f out: picked up wl ins fnl f to regain ld w runner-up pressing all the way to line: jst hld on* **7/1**[3]

3410 **2** shd **Arcanista (IRE)**[18] 8473 4-9-1 **58** (p) PaulHainey(7) 8 63
(Chris Dwyer) *cl up on outer: rdn and pressed wnr wl over 1f out: briefly led 1f out: sn hdd but remained pressing wnr all the way to line: jst hld* **8/1**

535 **3** hd **Napping**[146] 4092 4-9-5 **55** (h[1]) PaddyPilley 6 59
(Anabel K Murphy) *mid-div between horses: shkn up wl over 2f out and prog: angled wd into st: kpt on wl fr 1f out on outer to take 3rd nr fin: nvr nrr* **20/1**

2534 **4** nk **Mercers**[25] 8298 3-9-9 **59** CallumShepherd 5 62
(Paddy Butler) *racd in mid-div on outer: rdn wl over 1f out: kpt on wl tl one pce wl ins fnl f* **14/1**

5014 **5** hd **Zenovia (IRE)**[6] 8742 3-9-10 **60** (tp) HollieDoyle 2 64+
(Archie Watson) *racd in mid-div between horses: rdn 1f out and ev ch: nt clrest run after: pushed out wl ins fnl f: can do bttr* **1/1**[1]

0000 **6** 1 ¾ **Rapid Rise (IRE)**[21] 8395 3-8-9 **48** (v) GeorgiaCox(3) 11 45
(Milton Bradley) *sluggish s and wnt st to rail: in rr and outpcd: rdn along in last w plenty to do 3f out: kpt on steadily tl styd on strly past btn horses ins fnl f: nvr nrr* **25/1**

0001 **7** ½ **Deer Song**[45] 7705 4-8-11 **50** JaneElliott(3) 3 47
(John Bridger) *led early: sn settled bhd ldr on rail: rdn wl over 2f out: kpt on one pce after* **16/1**

4221 **8** nse **Flowing Clarets**[25] 8298 4-9-5 **55** HectorCrouch 4 50
(John Bridger) *bhd ldrs between horses: shkn up 3f out to hold pl: rdn wl over 1f out: plugging on fr 1f out: n.m.r ins fnl f: rdr stood up in iron and lost two pls nr fin* **5/1**[2]

0465 **9** 2 ¼ **Multi Quest**[17] 8496 5-8-5 **46** oh1 (b) NicolaCurrie(5) 1 34
(John E Long) *racd in mid-div on inner: rdn 3f out to hold pl: kpt on tl one pce fr 1f out* **16/1**

0000 **10** nk **Encapsulated**[37] 7945 7-8-8 **49** RhiainIngram(5) 10 36
(Roger Ingram) *wnt to post early: in rr of pack: rdn on outer wl over 2f to hold pl: dropped to rr ent st: pushed out after* **25/1**

0060 **11** 11 **Dramatic Voice**[78] 6635 4-8-10 **46** oh1 CharlieBennett 7
(Ken Cunningham-Brown) *sn led: rdn to hold pl wl over 3f out: hdd over 2f out: wknd through pack fr over 1f out* **100/1**

1m 12.83s (0.93) **Going Correction** +0.05s/f (Slow) 11 Ran SP% **122.2**
Speed ratings (Par 101): **95,94,94,94,93 91,90,90,87,87 72**
CSF £61.73 CT £1089.34 TOTE £9.60: £2.20, £2.60, £4.50; EX 74.90 Trifecta £2022.40.
**Owner** Mrs Sarah-Jane Fox **Bred** Peter Harms **Trained** Collingbourne Ducis, Wilts

**FOCUS**
The first division of a moderate apprentice sprint handicap featuring a short-price favourite, but a typical race for the track as not only did the principals finish in a heap, there was also trouble. Limited form.

## 8824 BETWAY APPRENTICE H'CAP (DIV II) 6f 1y(P)
**3:45** (3:48) (Class 6) (0-60,59) 3-Y-0+ **£2,264** (£673; £336; £168) **Stalls** Low

Form RPR

2250 **1** **Mistry**[17] 8496 4-8-5 **45** (p) NicolaCurrie(5) 3 51
(Mark Usher) *mde all: slt ld thrght: hld together tl rdn over 1f out: kpt on wl ins fnl f: a doing enough* **18/1**

5005 **2** ½ **Termsnconditions (IRE)**[29] 8194 3-9-4 **58** (v) WilliamCox(5) 10 62
(Tim Vaughan) *pressed wnr on outer: rdn wl over 1f out: kpt on wl thrght fnl f: wnr a doing enough* **5/1**[3]

0023 **3** ½ **Dontforgettocall**[20] 8428 3-9-6 **55** (v) PaddyPilley 11 58
(Joseph Tuite) *between horses in mid-div: angled out ent st and rdn: sltly hmpd sn after: kpt on wl fr 1f out on outer to take 3rd fnl strides* **10/1**

0602 **4** hd **Spitfire Limited**[20] 8428 3-9-1 **50** (h) HectorCrouch 6 52
(George Baker) *in rr-div on inner: shkn up and prog 2f out: sltly hmpd ent st: swtchd off inner and rdn over 1f out: kpt on wl ins fnl f and jst failed for 3rd* **7/1**

6500 **5** nk **Blackadder**[15] 8538 5-8-3 **45** KeelanBaker(7) 8 46
(Mark Gillard) *hld up in rr: shkn up wl over 1f out and prog: swtchd to inner over 1f out: rdn 1f out: kpt on wl ins fnl f between horses* **50/1**

3245 **6** nk **Exquisite Ruby**[37] 7951 3-9-10 **59** CallumShepherd 1 59
(Charles Hills) *racd bhd ldrs on rail: rdn over 1f out: kpt on wl tl one pce nring fin* **4/1**[2]

0600 **7** ¾ **Compton Prince**[91] 6157 8-9-3 **59** (b) KerrieRaybould(7) 2 57
(Milton Bradley) *sltly rrd s: sn in mid-div on rail: shkn up wl over 1f out and clung to inner: ev ch in 3rd 1f out: wknd sn after* **16/1**

6305 **8** 1 ½ **Flying Sakhee**[39] 7910 4-8-12 **48** ow2 (p) PaddyBradley(3) 12 43
(John Bridger) *in rr on outer and t.k.h at times: rdn out wd wl over 1f out: plugged on in st* **33/1**

5040 **9** 2 **Quite A Story**[17] 8495 5-9-6 **55** (p[1]) CharlieBennett 5 42
(Archie Watson) *racd in mid-div on outer: rdn along over 2f out: pl ch over 1f out: no ex ins fnl f* **2/1**[1]

1060 **10** nk **Krazy Paving**[51] 7517 5-9-1 **55** (b) RossaRyan(5) 9 41
(Anabel K Murphy) *mid-div on outer: rdn to hold pl wl over 2f out: sltly bmpd ent st: plugged on* **10/1**

0000 **11** 4 ½ **Autumn Tonic (IRE)**[26] 8258 5-9-0 **49** (be[1]) CliffordLee 4 20+
(Charlie Wallis) *racd in mid-div between horses and squeezed up on first bnd: sn bhd ldrs on outer: rdn along jst over 2f out and struggling to hold pl: wknd over 1f out* **20/1**

00-0 **12** *2 ¼* **Aegean Boy**[31] 8128 4-8-13 48 ........................ HollieDoyle 7 12
(John Bridger) *a in rr and t.k.h at times: lost tch and wl bhd over 2f out: pushed along and one pce fr over 1f out* **33/1**

1m 12.52s (0.62) **Going Correction** +0.05s/f (Slow) **12** Ran SP% **124.4**
Speed ratings (Par 101): **97,96,95,95,95 94,93,91,88,88 82,79**
CSF £107.68 CT £999.02 TOTE £21.20: £5.20, £1.60, £3.00; EX 149.00 Trifecta £2370.00.
**Owner** Ushers Court **Bred** Mrs Jane Patel **Trained** Upper Lambourn, Berks

**FOCUS**
The pace held up here with the first two holding those positions throughout. The winning time was 0.31sec quicker than the first division. The first three have been rated near their best.
T/Plt: £73.60 to a £1 stake. Pool: £53,412.85 529.54 winning units. T/Qpdt: £8.20 to a £1 stake. Pool: £6,820.61 - 614.69 winning units. **Cathal Gahan**

8825-8835a - (Foreign Racing) - See Raceform Interactive

## 8579 JEBEL ALI (L-H)
Friday, November 17

**OFFICIAL GOING: Dirt: fast**

### 8836a ORIENT IRRIGATION SERVICES (H'CAP) (DIRT) 1m 1f
**12:35** (12:35) (71-84,84) 3-Y-0+ **£11,233** (£3,744; £2,059; £1,123; £561)

RPR

**1** **Galles (USA)**[112] 3-9-1 82 ........................ RoystonFfrench 1 97
(S bin Ghadayer, UAE) *soon led, rdn 2 1/2f out, skipped clr 1f out, easily* **7/1**[3]

**2** *4 ½* **Aslan (USA)**[14] 8579 6-8-7 72 ........................(b) XavierZiani 8 77
(S bin Ghadayer, UAE) *tracked ldr, rdn to chal 3f out, outpcd fnl 1 1/2f but ran on well* **9/2**[2]

**3** *3 ½* **Long Water (USA)**[14] 8580 6-9-2 80 ........................(b) PatCosgrave 10 78
(H Al Alawi, UAE) *tracked ldg pair, ev ch 3f out, ran on same pace fnl 2f* **10/1**

**4** *2 ¾* **Fast Enough (IRE)**[14] 8581 4-9-6 84 ........................(v) PatDobbs 4 76
(Doug Watson, UAE) *slowly into strd, nvr nr to chal but ran on fnl 2f* **20/1**

**5** *2 ½* **Cross Step (USA)**[13] 3-9-2 83 ........................(p) TadhgO'Shea 3 70
(A R Al Rayhi, UAE) *never better than mid-division* **11/1**

**6** *¾* **Gavroche (USA)**[13] 6-9-1 79 ........................(h) FernandoJara 6 65
(Maria Ritchie, UAE) *never nr to challenge* **9/2**[2]

**7** *1 ½* **Strong Chemistry**[245] 1254 5-9-6 84 ........................ RichardMullen 9 66
(K Al Neyadi, UAE) *never better than mid-division* **25/1**

**8** *8 ½* **Al Barez (USA)**[258] 1040 3-8-13 80 ........................(tp) DaneO'Neill 5 45
(A bin Harmash, UAE) *slowly into strd, al in rear* **20/1**

**9** *3 ¼* **Say No More (IRE)**[14] 8583 4-8-13 77 ........................(h) SamHitchcott 2 35
(Doug Watson, UAE) *mid-division, hrd rdn 3 1/2f out, sn beaten* **20/1**

**10** *12* **Finishing Touch**[113] 5324 3-9-0 81 ........................(t) OisinMurphy 7
(Saeed bin Suroor) *slowly into strd, al in rear* **7/4**[1]

1m 51.37s
**WFA** 3 from 4yo+ 3lb **10** Ran SP% **120.8**
CSF: 37.62; TRICAST: 330.18.
**Owner** Mohammad Farooq **Bred** Darley **Trained** United Arab Emirates

8837 - (Foreign Racing) - See Raceform Interactive

## 8732 SAINT-CLOUD (L-H)
Friday, November 17

**OFFICIAL GOING: Turf: very soft**

### 8838a PRIX BELLE DE NUIT - FONDS EUROPEEN DE L'ELEVAGE (LISTED RACE) (3YO+ FILLIES & MARES) (TURF) 1m 4f 110y
**12:40** 3-Y-0+ **£22,222** (£8,888; £6,666; £4,444; £2,222)

RPR

**1** **Bebe D'Amour (FR)**[26] 8273 3-8-13 0 ........................ StephanePasquier 11 102
(J-Y Artu, France) **6/4**[1]

**2** *snk* **Zouk (FR)**[10] 3-8-13 0 ........................ MaximeGuyon 7 101
(P Adda, France) **19/5**[2]

**3** *1 ½* **Agathonia (USA)**[19] 8462 3-8-13 0 ........................ MickaelBarzalona 2 99
(H-A Pantall, France) **124/10**

**4** *1 ¾* **Gambia Bird (IRE)**[46] 7696 3-8-13 0 ........................ EddyHardouin 1 96
(Lennart Hammer-Hansen, Germany) **31/1**

**5** *¾* **Mahati (FR)**[44] 7753 4-9-4 0 ........................ Pierre-CharlesBoudot 9 93
(A Fabre, France) **28/1**

**6** *2 ½* **Not After Hours (FR)**[85] 6364 3-8-13 0 ........................ Francois-XavierBertras 10 91
(F Rohaut, France) **116/10**

**7** *3* **Roche Rose (IRE)**[23] 4-9-4 0 ........................ ClementLecoeuvre 4 84
(E Lellouche, France) **81/1**

**8** *6* **Mam'Selle (IRE)**[69] 6920 3-8-13 0 ........................ AurelienLemaitre 12 77
(William Haggas) **99/10**

**9** *2* **Lawless Secret**[20] 8414 3-8-13 0 ........................ FranckBlondel 5 73
(Simon Crisford) **118/10**

**10** *nk* **Vienna Woods (FR)**[46] 7696 3-8-13 0 ........................ TheoBachelot 6 73
(Y Barberot, France) **32/1**

**11** *8* **Precious Ramotswe**[21] 8390 3-8-13 0 ........................ IoritzMendizabal 3 60
(John Gosden) **36/5**[3]

**12** *snk* **Pacharana**[15] 8548 4-9-4 0 ........................ AntoineHamelin 8 58
(Luca Cumani) **39/1**

2m 55.1s
**WFA** 3 from 4yo 5lb **12** Ran SP% **118.7**
PARI-MUTUEL (all including 1 euro stake): WIN 2.50; PLACE 1.20, 1.60, 2.30; DF 5.60; SF 6.50.
**Owner** J Y Artu **Bred** J-Y Artu, D Artu & Mlle M Artu **Trained** France

## 8817 LINGFIELD (L-H)
Saturday, November 18

**OFFICIAL GOING: Polytrack: standard**
Wind: medium, across Weather: overcast, rain from race 3

### 8839 32RED.COM / EBF NOVICE STKS (DIV I) 1m 1y(P)
**11:55** (11:57) (Class 5) 2-Y-0 **£2,911** (£866; £432; £216) **Stalls High**

Form RPR

4 **1** **Rusper (IRE)**[56] 7411 2-9-2 0 ........................ DougieCostello 8 74
(Jamie Osborne) *hld up in tch in midfield: effrt and hdwy on outer over 1f out: drvn to chse ldng pair 1f out: styd on strly to ld last stride* **7/1**

5 **2** *shd* **Gaudi (IRE)**[11] 8642 2-9-2 0 ........................ RobertHavlin 7 74
(John Gosden) *led: pushed along ent fnl 2f: drvn and hrd pressed ins fnl f: kpt on u.p: hdd last stride* **5/4**[1]

6 **3** *½* **Alpine Peak (USA)**[18] 8492 2-9-2 0 ........................ SilvestreDeSousa 1 73
(Roger Varian) *chsd ldrs: wnt 2nd and swtchd out rt over 1f out: sn drvn and chalng ins fnl f: unable qck towards fin* **6/1**[3]

00 **4** *2 ¼* **Aiya (IRE)**[169] 3305 2-9-2 0 ........................(h[1]) RobHornby 4 67
(Andrew Balding) *stdd after s: t.k.h: hld up in tch in midfield: effrt and hdwy over 1f out: chsd clr ldng trio ins fnl f: styd on but nvr getting on terms* **16/1**

05 **5** *2 ¼* **Dubai Frame**[17] 8508 2-9-2 0 ........................ JimmyQuinn 5 62
(Ed Dunlop) *t.k.h: hdwy to chse ldr after 2f tl unable qck over 1f out: wknd ins fnl f* **33/1**

**6** *½* **Lady Noorah** 2-8-12 0 ow1 ........................ JackGarritty 6 57+
(Richard Fahey) *s.i.s: hld up in last trio: pushed along and hdwy whn swtchd lft 1f out: kpt on ins fnl f: nvr trbld ldrs* **25/1**

**7** *shd* **Ventura Magic** 2-9-2 0 ........................ TomMarquand 9 60+
(Richard Hannon) *t.k.h: hld up in tch in midfield: rdn over 2f out: unable qck and kpt on same pce fr over 1f out* **25/1**

**8** *nk* **Temur Khan** 2-9-2 0 ........................ JamesDoyle 3 60+
(Hugo Palmer) *s.i.s: rn green and pushed along in rr: rdn over 1f out: swtchd rt ins fnl f: nvr trbld ldrs* **5/1**[2]

6 **9** *shd* **Island Court (IRE)**[169] 3305 2-9-2 0 ........................ LiamKeniry 10 59
(J S Moore) *dwlt and pushed along leaving stalls: sn rcvrd to chse ldr for 2f: settled bk into 4th: rdn and unable qck over 1f out: wknd ins fnl f* **33/1**

0 **10** *1 ¼* **Iconic Boy**[50] 7580 2-9-2 0 ........................(h[1]) SeanLevey 11 56
(David Elsworth) *taken down early: stdd after s: hld up in last trio: effrt wl over 1f out: no imp: nvr trbld ldrs* **11/1**

00 **11** *1 ¾* **Reveleon**[11] 8643 2-9-2 0 ........................ TedDurcan 2 52
(Sir Michael Stoute) *taken down early: in tch in midfield: rdn over 2f out: struggling and lost pl over 1f out: bhd ins fnl f* **25/1**

1m 38.73s (0.53) **Going Correction** -0.05s/f (Stan) **11** Ran SP% **119.5**
Speed ratings (Par 96): **95,94,94,92,89 89,89,89,88,87 85**
CSF £15.48 TOTE £7.70: £2.10, £1.10, £2.10; EX 20.30 Trifecta £37.20.
**Owner** B Spiers, I Barratt, S Short & A Signy **Bred** Barronstown Stud **Trained** Upper Lambourn, Berks

**FOCUS**
The first division of a modest novice event. Only one of the eight to have run before had made the frame and he proved good enough.

### 8840 32RED.COM / EBF NOVICE STKS (DIV II) 1m 1y(P)
**12:25** (12:28) (Class 5) 2-Y-0 **£2,911** (£866; £432; £216) **Stalls High**

Form RPR

3 **1** **Masaarr (USA)**[24] 8350 2-9-2 0 ........................ JackMitchell 5 84+
(Roger Varian) *trckd ldrs: shkn up and qcknd to ld jst over 1f out: r.o strly: easily* **1/3**[1]

0 **2** *4 ½* **Poetic Imagination**[14] 8594 2-8-11 0 ........................ WilliamBuick 4 64
(John Gosden) *led and set stdy gallop: rdn and qcknd ent fnl 2f: hdd over 1f out: nt match pce of wnr and kpt on same pce fnl f* **6/1**[2]

**3** *1* **Winged Spur (IRE)** 2-8-11 0 ........................ SilvestreDeSousa 9 62
(Mark Johnston) *chsd ldr: rdn ent fnl 2f: drvn and unable qck over 1f out: edgd lft 1f out and kpt on same pce fnl f* **10/1**

50 **4** *1 ¼* **Fire Orchid**[14] 8593 2-8-11 0 ........................ SeanLevey 10 59
(Richard Hannon) *chsd ldng trio: effrt ent fnl 2f: nt match pce of wnr over 1f out: styd on same pce u.p ins fnl f* **25/1**

0 **5** *1 ¼* **Goodwood Showman**[15] 8560 2-9-2 0 ........................ MartinHarley 1 61
(William Knight) *broke wl: sn stdd and wl in tch in midfield: effrt in 5th ent fnl 2f: outpcd over 1f out and wl hld whn swtchd rt ins fnl f* **66/1**

**6** *½* **Cross My Mind (IRE)** 2-8-11 0 ........................ GrahamLee 2 55+
(Ralph Beckett) *dwlt: hld up in tch: pushed along jst over 2f out: no ch w wnr but kpt on steadily ins fnl f* **8/1**[3]

0 **7** *hd* **Barnay**[16] 8545 2-8-9 0 ........................ TylerSaunders(7) 8 59
(Marcus Tregoning) *dwlt: hld up in tch towards rr: swtchd rt and pushed along over 2f out: hdwy and swtchd lft 1f out: no ch w wnr but kpt on steadily ins fnl f* **25/1**

00 **8** *1 ¾* **Highcastle (IRE)**[24] 8353 2-8-9 0 ........................ HarryBurns(7) 6 55
(Ed Dunlop) *broke okay but sn dropped into midfield: in tch: pushed along over 2f out: drifted rt and outpcd bnd 2f out: wl hld after* **66/1**

**9** *6* **Daddy Tyrrell (USA)** 2-9-2 0 ........................ LiamKeniry 11 41
(J S Moore) *dwlt: hld up in tch in rr: rn green and outpcd jst over 2f out: wknd over 1f out* **33/1**

0 **10** *½* **True Destiny**[10] 8677 2-9-2 0 ........................ TomMarquand 3 40
(Roger Charlton) *s.i.s: rn green in detached last: n.d* **16/1**

0 **11** *nk* **Seasearch**[11] 8642 2-8-9 0 ........................ WilliamCox(7) 7 39
(Andrew Balding) *dwlt: in tch: pushed along and outpcd over 2f out: wknd over 1f out* **66/1**

1m 40.09s (1.89) **Going Correction** -0.05s/f (Stan) **11** Ran SP% **130.5**
Speed ratings (Par 96): **88,83,82,81,80 79,79,77,71,71 70**
CSF £3.42 TOTE £1.20: £1.10, £1.60, £2.50; EX 4.20 Trifecta £16.20.
**Owner** Sheikh Ahmed Al Maktoum **Bred** Godolphin **Trained** Newmarket, Suffolk

**FOCUS**
Again only one of the eight to have run before in this division had made the frame and he emphatically proved too good for the others. The winning time was 1.36sec slower than the first leg.

### 8841 SUNBETS.CO.UK DOWNLOAD THE APP CLAIMING STKS 1m 1y(P)
**1:00** (1:00) (Class 6) 3-Y-0 **£2,264** (£673; £336; £168) **Stalls High**

Form RPR

4-1 **1** **Enigmatic (IRE)**[58] 7322 3-9-5 73 ........................ DougieCostello 4 72
(Jamie Osborne) *t.k.h: led and set stdy gallop: rdn wl over 1f out: drvn 1f out: hdd ins fnl f: rallied u.p to ld again last stride* **2/1**[2]

3403 **2** *shd* **Junoesque**[16] 8538 3-8-8 58 ........................(p) JoeyHaynes 1 61
(John Gallagher) *trckd ldrs: effrt on inner wl over 1f out: drvn and ev ch 1f out: led ins fnl f: r.o: hdd last strides* **9/2**[3]

1060 **3** *nk* **Mutineer**[24] 8341 3-9-8 72 ........................ RobHornby 6 75
(Daniel Kubler) *stdd s: hld up in tch in rr: pushed up to press ldrs and wd bnd 2f out: sltly outpcd over 1f out: rallied and ev ch wl ins fnl f: r.o* **11/8**[1]

1251 **4** *1 ¾* **Topmeup**[19] 8470 3-8-12 60 ........................(v) LukeMorris 5 60
(Gay Kelleway) *chsd wnr tl outpcd u.p over 1f out: kpt on same pce ins fnl f* **9/2**[3]

1m 40.85s (2.65) **Going Correction** -0.05s/f (Stan) **4** Ran SP% **111.8**
Speed ratings (Par 98): **84,83,83,81**
CSF £10.72 TOTE £2.20; EX 7.60 Trifecta £18.30.
**Owner** Melbourne 10 Racing **Bred** Stonepark Farms **Trained** Upper Lambourn, Berks

**FOCUS**
A moderate 3yo claimer, reduced to just the four runners, and a messy race with no pace on early. The front three finished in a heap.

## 8842 BETWAY MEDIAN AUCTION MAIDEN STKS — 6f 1y(P)
**1:35** (1:36) (Class 6) 3-5-Y-O — **£2,264** (£673; £336; £168) **Stalls** Low

Form — RPR

**1** **Temeraire (FR)**[148] 3-9-0 76 ........ JamesDoyle 4 — 77+
(Hugo Palmer) *mde all: rdn and qcknd clr over 1f out: r.o strly: readily* **11/10**[1]

2402 **2** *4 ½* **Trotter**[25] 8311 3-9-5 70 ........ (b) LukeMorris 11 — 65
(Stuart Kittow) *chsd ldrs: effrt ent fnl 2f: outpcd by wnr over 1f out: kpt on u.p to go 2nd last strides: no threat to wnr* **5/1**[3]

306 **3** *nk* **Canadian Royal**[71] 6904 3-9-5 60 ........ (t[1]) SeanLevey 7 — 64
(Stuart Williams) *chsd ldrs: effrt to go 2nd 2f out: outpcd over 1f out: kpt on same pce fnl f: lost 2nd last strides* **14/1**

40 **4** *2 ¾* **Divine Messenger**[24] 8342 3-9-5 0 ........ RobertHavlin 8 — 55
(Emma Owen) *midfield: outpcd over 2f out: hdwy 1f out to go 4th ins fnl f: keeping on towards fin: no threat to ldrs* **100/1**

0-24 **5** *2 ¾* **Amenta (IRE)**[94] 6066 3-9-0 65 ........ (t[1]) JoeyHaynes 1 — 41
(John Berry) *taken down early: t.k.h: hld up in tch in midfield: effrt over 2f out: sn struggling and outpcd: wl hld and one pce fr over 1f out* **20/1**

**6** *hd* **Jakeboy** 3-9-5 0 ........ RenatoSouza 10 — 45
(Sylvester Kirk) *chsd wnr tl 2f out: lost pl u.p over 1f out: wknd fnl f* **33/1**

00 **7** *¾* **Dilinger**[40] 7907 3-9-5 0 ........ LiamKeniry 6 — 43
(Stuart Kittow) *stdd s: t.k.h: hld up in tch in last quintet: pushed along and outpcd over 2f out: n.d after* **25/1**

03 **8** *nk* **Irish Sky (IRE)**[225] 1605 3-8-7 0 ........ JackOsborn(7) 2 — 37
(Henry Spiller) *hld up in last pair: effrt and stl plenty to do wl over 1f out: no hdwy: n.d* **20/1**

0 **9** *1* **Sanches**[309] 221 3-9-2 0 ........ MattCosham(3) 9 — 39+
(Dr Jeremy Naylor) *hld up in tch in last quintet: rdn over 2f out: v wd bnd 2f out: no ch after* **100/1**

22-5 **10** *10* **Port Isaac (IRE)**[175] 3085 4-9-5 75 ........ (h[1]) BenCurtis 5 — 7
(Marcus Tregoning) *rousted along leaving stalls: in tch in last quintet: rdn 3f out: drvn and no hdwy over 2f out: wl btn over 1f out: wknd: fin lame* **5/2**[2]

**11** *1 ¾* **We Win** 3-8-7 0 ........ GinaMangan(7) 3
(J R Jenkins) *s.i.s: pushed along in rr: lost tch 2f out* **100/1**

0 **12** *6* **Cymru Lady**[73] 6808 3-9-0 0 ........ RyanTate 12
(Nikki Evans) *in tch in midfield on outer: rdn and struggling whn wd bnd 2f out: bhd after* **100/1**

1m 11.21s (-0.69) **Going Correction** -0.05s/f (Stan) — **12** Ran SP% **119.8**
Speed ratings (Par 101): **102,96,95,91,88 88,87,86,85,71 69,61**
CSF £6.66 TOTE £2.10: £1.10, £1.50, £2.90; EX 8.00 Trifecta £45.70.
**Owner** Blessingndisguise Partnership **Bred** S C Famille Rothschild **Trained** Newmarket, Suffolk

**FOCUS**
A moderate and uncompetitive older-horse sprint maiden, but an interesting winner.

## 8843 SUNBETS.CO.UK H'CAP — 1m 1y(P)
**2:10** (2:13) (Class 2) (0-105,104) 3-Y£01,971 (£3,583; £1,791; £896; £446) **Stalls** High

Form — RPR

200 **1** **Arcanada (IRE)**[42] 7807 4-9-9 **103** ........ (p[1]) RichardKingscote 8 — 112
(Tom Dascombe) *chsd ldr: pushed into ld over 1f out: clr and rdn 100yds out: a doing enough and pushed out towards fin* **7/1**

0362 **2** *1* **Sacred Act**[16] 8547 6-9-5 **99** ........ JamesDoyle 4 — 106
(Michael Bell) *hld up in tch in midfield: effrt over 1f out: hdwy u.p 1f out: chsd clr wnr ins fnl f: styd on wl but nvr quite getting to wnr* **9/2**[3]

5505 **3** *¾* **Gabrial (IRE)**[28] 8234 8-9-10 **104** ........ JackGarritty 2 — 109
(Richard Fahey) *t.k.h: hld up in tch in midfield: rdn and hdwy to chse ldrs over 1f out: kpt on u.p ins fnl f* **20/1**

1-3 **4** *hd* **Utmost (USA)**[218] 1780 3-9-4 **100** ........ RobertHavlin 7 — 104
(John Gosden) *chsd ldrs: rdn and unable qck over 1f out: rallied ins fnl f: styd on fnl 100yds: nvr getting to wnr* **4/1**[2]

052 **5** *1 ½* **Belgian Bill**[45] 7727 9-9-2 **96** ........ LiamKeniry 1 — 97
(George Baker) *t.k.h: chsd ldrs: effrt u.p over 1f out: unable qck and wknd wl ins fnl f* **12/1**

555 **6** *nk* **Charles Molson**[16] 8547 6-9-3 **97** ........ JimCrowley 9 — 97
(Patrick Chamings) *hld up in tch in last to: nt clrest of runs but hdwy on inner over 1f out: pushed along and styd on ins fnl f: nvr trbld ldrs* **8/1**

0112 **7** *½* **Shady McCoy (USA)**[7] 8737 7-9-8 **102** ........ WilliamBuick 11 — 101+
(Ian Williams) *stdd s: hld up in tch in rr: stuck bhd a wall of horses over 2f out: hdwy over 1f out: swtchd rt ins fnl f: styd on wl: nvr trbld ldrs* **10/1**

1104 **8** *3* **Forceful Appeal (USA)**[169] 3298 9-8-11 **96** ........ PaddyBradley(5) 5 — 88
(Simon Dow) *stdd s: hld up in tch towards rr: switching rt and pushed along over 1f out: rdn and no imp ins fnl f: nvr trbld ldrs* **50/1**

1305 **9** *1* **Third Time Lucky (IRE)**[218] 1775 5-9-0 **101** ....(h) SebastianWoods(7) 12 — 91
(Richard Fahey) *stdd s: hld up in tch in last trio: nt clrest of runs over 1f out: no imp: nvr trbld ldrs* **33/1**

0203 **10** *shd* **Eagle Creek (IRE)**[45] 7727 3-9-0 **96** ........ SilvestreDeSousa 3 — 85
(Simon Crisford) *led tl rdn and hdd over 1f out: btn 1f out: sn wknd: heavily eased wl ins fnl f* **2/1**[1]

1600 **11** *7* **Swift Approval (IRE)**[77] 6685 5-8-12 **92** ........ (t) LukeMorris 10 — 66
(Stuart Williams) *chsd ldrs: rdn over 2f out: sn struggling and lost pl: bhd ins fnl f* **40/1**

1m 35.06s (-3.14) **Going Correction** -0.05s/f (Stan)
**WFA** 3 from 4yo+ 2lb — **11** Ran SP% **124.0**
Speed ratings (Par 109): **113,112,111,111,109 109,108,105,104,104 97**
CSF £39.56 CT £633.76 TOTE £7.80: £2.40, £1.50, £4.70; EX 48.80 Trifecta £578.20.
**Owner** The Arcanada Partnership **Bred** C J Foy **Trained** Malpas, Cheshire

**FOCUS**
A warm handicap and they went a good pace. Solid form. The winner has been rated back to his best, and the third to his latest.

## 8844 BETWAY CHURCHILL STKS (LISTED RACE) (ALL-WEATHER FAST TRACK QUALIFIER) — 1m 2f (P)
**2:45** (2:47) (Class 1) 3-Y-O+
**£22,684** (£8,600; £4,304; £1,610; £1,610; £540) **Stalls** Low

Form — RPR

0060 **1** **Master The World (IRE)**[7] 8740 6-9-2 105 ........ (p) SeanLevey 7 — 108
(David Elsworth) *hld up in tch in midfield: hdwy to chse ldrs over 1f out: led ins fnl f: sn in command and r.o wl: rdn out* **10/1**

4001 **2** *1 ¾* **Victory Bond**[37] 7988 4-9-2 107 ........ JamesDoyle 2 — 105
(William Haggas) *squeezed for room and dropped to last trio sn after s: in tch: hdwy and swtchd lft over 1f out: r.o u.p ins fnl f to go 2nd fnl 50yds: nvr getting to wnr* **13/8**[1]

6304 **3** *¾* **Mia Tesoro (IRE)**[16] 8546 4-8-11 87 ........ (h) StevieDonohoe 1 — 98
(Charlie Fellowes) *hld up in tch in midfield: effrt to chse ldrs u.p over 1f out: kpt on same pce ins fnl f: lost 2nd last 50yds* **50/1**

2016 **4** *shd* **Petite Jack**[9] 8705 4-9-2 102 ........ (p) LukeMorris 4 — 103
(Archie Watson) *chsd ldng trio: swtchd lft and wnt 2nd 2f out: rdn to ld over 1f out: hdd ins fnl f: outpcd fnl 100yds* **7/1**[3]

**4** *dht* **In The Lope (IRE)**[34] 3-8-13 89 ........ AurelienLemaitre 3 — 104
(Mme Pia Brandt, France) *squeezed for room sn after s and dropped to last pair: effrt and switching rt bnd 2f out: styd on u.p ins fnl f: nvr getting to ldrs* **16/1**

-360 **6** *2 ¼* **Battalion (IRE)**[218] 1775 7-9-2 107 ........ DougieCostello 6 — 98
(Jamie Osborne) *s.i.s: in tch in rr: hdwy on inner over 1f out: no imp ins fnl f* **16/1**

3-23 **7** *3* **Boynton (USA)**[14] 8598 3-8-13 109 ........ WilliamBuick 9 — 93
(Charlie Appleby) *t.k.h: hdwy to chse ldrs on outer after 1f: led over 6f out: rdn and hdd over 1f out: sn btn and wknd ins fnl f* **9/4**[2]

0410 **8** *7* **Ayrad (IRE)**[21] 8421 6-9-2 109 ........ (b) RichardKingscote 8 — 78
(Roger Charlton) *chsd ldr tl 2f out: sn lost pl: bhd ins fnl f* **10/1**

2625 **9** *2 ¼* **Sands Chorus**[14] 8598 5-9-2 95 ........ SilvestreDeSousa 5 — 74
(James Given) *stmbld leaving stalls: led tl over 6f out: jst beginning to struggle whn hmpd 2f out: sn lost pl: bhd ins fnl f* **33/1**

2m 1.14s (-5.46) **Going Correction** -0.05s/f (Stan)
**WFA** 3 from 4yo+ 3lb — **9** Ran SP% **116.2**
Speed ratings (Par 111): **119,117,117,116,116 115,112,107,105**
CSF £26.84 TOTE £11.70: £3.00, £1.20, £10.10; EX 36.20 Trifecta £769.60.
**Owner** K Quinn/ C Benham **Bred** A Hanahoe **Trained** Newmarket, Suffolk
■ Stewards' Enquiry : Luke Morris two-day ban: careless riding (Dec 2,4)

**FOCUS**
A decent Listed event and a Fast Track Qualifier for the Middle Distance Championship on Good Friday. The race had gone to a 3yo six times in the last nine runnings, but this was one for the older brigade. The third and fourth dictate the level.

## 8845 BETWAY GOLDEN ROSE STKS (LISTED RACE) (ALL-WEATHER FAST TRACK QUALIFIER) — 6f 1y(P)
**3:15** (3:20) (Class 1) 3-Y-O+
**£20,982** (£7,955; £3,981; £1,983; £995; £499) **Stalls** Low

Form — RPR

0110 **1** **Gifted Master (IRE)**[36] 8003 4-9-6 109 ........ (b) JamesDoyle 12 — 114
(Hugo Palmer) *chsd ldr and sn clr of field: rdn over 1f out: styd on u.p to ld 100yds out: sn clr and kpt on* **9/2**[2]

5120 **2** *1 ½* **Mythmaker**[84] 6428 5-9-3 105 ........ GrahamLee 3 — 106
(Bryan Smart) *chsd clr ldng pair: effrt over 1f out: clsd u.p ins fnl f: styd on to go 2nd towards fin: nvr getting to wnr* **8/1**

005 **3** *nk* **Out Do**[38] 7950 8-9-3 104 ........ (v) DanielTudhope 1 — 105
(David O'Meara) *hld up in midfield: effrt over 1f out: hdwy and swtchd rt ins fnl f: styd on to go 3rd cl home: nvr getting to wnr* **12/1**

3464 **4** *hd* **Intisaab**[21] 8417 6-9-3 105 ........ (p) MartinHarley 7 — 105+
(David O'Meara) *hld up in last trio: effrt over 1f out: hdwy u.p ins fnl f: r.o strly fnl 100yds: wnt 4th last strides: nvr threatened wnr* **9/1**

4140 **5** *nk* **Caspian Prince (IRE)**[56] 7396 8-9-10 113 ........ (t) BenCurtis 10 — 111
(Tony Coyle) *sn pushed into ld and wnt clr w wnr: rdn ent fnl 2f: drifted rt u.p over 1f out: hdd 100yds out: no ex and lost 3 pls towards fin* **33/1**

3120 **6** *nse* **Spring Loaded (IRE)**[21] 8416 5-9-3 105 ........ JoeyHaynes 8 — 103+
(Paul D'Arcy) *hld up in rr: effrt and hdwy over 1f out: styd on wl ins fnl f: nvr trbld ldrs* **5/1**[3]

622 **7** *3* **Clem Fandango (FR)**[10] 8679 3-8-12 100 ........ PhillipMakin 4 — 89
(Keith Dalgleish) *prom in chsng gp: hung rt and lost pl bnd 2f out: wl hld after and kpt on same pce* **10/1**

2056 **8** *½* **Royal Birth**[77] 6685 6-9-3 102 ........ (t) JimCrowley 2 — 92
(Stuart Williams) *t.k.h: hld up in midfield: effrt u.p over 1f out: no imp fnl f: nvr trbld ldrs* **7/1**

05-5 **9** *½* **Making Trouble (GER)**[20] 5-9-3 104 ........ LukeMorris 6 — 91
(D Moser, Germany) *s.i.s: hld up in last trio: effrt on inner over 1f out: no imp 1f out and wl hld ins fnl f* **25/1**

1332 **10** *1 ½* **Mazzini**[49] 7603 4-9-3 100 ........ (p) GeorgeWood 5 — 86
(James Fanshawe) *hld up off the pce in midfield: wd and lost pl bnd 2f out: bhd and no hdwy whn rdn over 1f out* **3/1**[1]

1m 9.68s (-2.22) **Going Correction** -0.05s/f (Stan) — **10** Ran SP% **117.0**
Speed ratings (Par 111): **112,110,109,109,108 108,104,104,103,101**
CSF £40.58 TOTE £5.90: £2.00, £2.50, £3.30; EX 42.80 Trifecta £413.60.
**Owner** Dr Ali Ridha **Bred** Tally-Ho Stud **Trained** Newmarket, Suffolk

**FOCUS**
A fascinating Listed contest and a Fast Track Qualifier for the Sprint Championship back here next Easter. Remarkably for a race like this few got into it, as two (the pair drawn widest) went scorching off in front, including the winner. The others were always playing catch-up. The winner has been rated back to his best.

## 8846 BETWAY H'CAP — 1m 4f (P)
**3:45** (3:47) (Class 6) (0-60,60) 3-Y-O+ — **£2,264** (£673; £336; £168) **Stalls** Low

Form — RPR

0111 **1** **Raashdy (IRE)**[21] 8430 4-9-7 **59** ........ (p) WilliamCarson 4 — 65
(Peter Hiatt) *chsd ldr for 1f: styd trcking ldrs and travelled strly: effrt over 1f out: ev ch ins fnl f: led 50yds out: rdn out* **11/4**[1]

0451 **2** *nk* **Betsalottie**[26] 8301 4-9-0 **55** ........ HectorCrouch(3) 5 — 61
(John Bridger) *hld up in tch in midfield: clsd over 2f out: effrt on inner over 1f out: ev ch and drvn 1f out: led ins fnl f: hdd 50yds out: kpt on* **8/1**

0006 **3** *1 ¼* **The Gay Cavalier**[16] 8550 6-9-1 **60** ........ (t) RossaRyan(7) 10 — 64
(John Ryan) *dwlt and rousted along leaving stalls: hld up towards rr: hdwy into midfield 1/2-way: rdn and hdwy over 1f out: styd on u.p ins fnl f: wnt 3rd last strides* **4/1**[2]

5000 **4** *nk* **Olympic Legend (IRE)**[16] 8550 3-9-0 **57** ........ (t) GrahamLee 16 — 61
(Martin Bosley) *chsd ldr after 1f: rdn to ld over 1f out: hdd ins fnl f: no ex and one pced fnl 100yds* **16/1**

043 **5** *1* **Bergholt (IRE)**[45] 7729 4-9-5 **57** ........ (p) KieranO'Neill 8 — 58
(Tim Vaughan) *led: rdn ent fnl 2f: hdd over 1f out: kpt on tl no ex and one pced ins fnl f* **15/2**

0000 **6** *1 ¾* **Karam Albaari (IRE)**[94] 6069 9-9-6 **58** ........ (v) SeanLevey 3 — 57+
(J R Jenkins) *hld up in midfield: clsd 2f out: effrt ent fnl f: kpt on same pce ins fnl f* **20/1**

5046 **7** *hd* **Garcon De Soleil**[32] 8135 4-8-8 **46** oh1 ........ RobHornby 15 — 44
(Michael Blanshard) *hld up in tch in midfield: shuffled bk towards rr 4f out: swtchd rt and hdwy over 1f out: styd on wl ins fnl f: nvr trbld ldrs* **25/1**

0003 **8** *2* **Hong Kong Joe**[17] 8507 7-8-8 **46**..........................(e) JoeyHaynes 9 41
(Lydia Richards) *hld up in midfield: effrt and hung rt bnd 2f out: kpt on same pce fr over 1f out* **20/1**

35 **9** *¾* **London Grammar (IRE)**[42] 7833 3-8-6 **52**.................. HollieDoyle(3) 7 47
(Ralph J Smith) *t.k.h: hld up in last trio: effrt and nt clr run whn swtchd rt over 1f out: styd on ins fnl f: nvr trbld ldrs* **16/1**

6300 **10** *shd* **Marmion**[22] 8386 5-9-8 **60**..........................(h) PatrickMathers 2 54
(Les Eyre) *t.k.h: hld up in tch in midfield: effrt whn squeezed for room and hmpd 2f out: no imp over 1f out: wknd ins fnl f* **7/1**[3]

0440 **11** *nk* **Just Fred (IRE)**[44] 7761 4-8-8 **46** oh1..........................(t) JimmyQuinn 12 39
(Neil Mulholland) *hld up towards rr: nt clr run and swtchd rt over 2f out: effrt u.p over 1f out: no imp 1f out: nvr trbld ldrs* **25/1**

-100 **12** *1 ¾* **Stand Guard**[27] 8261 13-9-8 **60**.................. LiamKeniry 6 50
(John Butler) *hld up in last trio: effrt over 1f out: no imp: nvr trbld ldrs* **33/1**

5220 **13** *¾* **Tommys Geal**[30] 8183 5-8-11 **56**.................. NicolaCurrie(7) 14 45
(Michael Madgwick) *hld up in midfield: effrt u.p and wd bnd 2f out: wl hld and no imp after* **20/1**

5050 **14** *¾* **Elusive Cowboy (USA)**[26] 7712 4-8-10 **55**..............(p) WilliamCox(7) 1 43
(Chris Gordon) *hld up in midfield: rdn over 3f out: wknd u.p over 1f out* **25/1**

40 **15** *5* **Tuolumne Meadows**[74] 6796 4-9-4 **59**..............(p[1]) EoinWalsh(3) 11 39
(Tony Newcombe) *v.s.a: hdwy to chse ldrs after 2f: rdn 3f out: lost pl 2f out: sn wknd* **16/1**

46P0 **16** *7* **L'Ami De Rouge**[24] 8346 4-8-9 **47**.................. RyanTate 13 16
(Ralph J Smith) *hld up in last trio: pushed along over 1f out: sn wknd: burst blood vessel* **50/1**

2m 31.64s (-1.36) **Going Correction** -0.05s/f (Stan)
**WFA** 3 from 4yo+ 5lb **16 Ran SP% 130.4**
Speed ratings (Par 101): **102,101,100,100,100 98,98,97,96,96 96,95,95,94,91 86**
CSF £23.54 CT £95.32 TOTE £2.90: £1.30, £2.40, £1.70, £4.00; EX 25.90 Trifecta £113.90.
**Owner** P W Hiatt **Bred** Shadwell Estate Company Limited **Trained** Hook Norton, Oxon

**FOCUS**
A moderate handicap, but won by a bang-in-form gelding.
T/Plt: £26.20 to a £1 stake. Pool: £63,675.04 - 1,769.99 winning units T/Qpdt: £29.30 to a £1 stake. Pool: £5,314.20 - 133.88 winning units **Steve Payne**

## [8742] WOLVERHAMPTON (A.W) (L-H)

Saturday, November 18

**OFFICIAL GOING: Tapeta: standard**
Wind: Light across Weather: Overcast

### 8847 32REDSPORT.COM NURSERY H'CAP 7f 36y (Tp)

5:45 (5:46) (Class 6) (0-60,60) 2-Y-O £2,587 (£770; £384; £192) **Stalls High**

Form RPR

0345 **1** **Zapateado**[17] 8500 2-9-2 **55**.................. ShaneKelly 2 60+
(Richard Hughes) *hld up: nt clr run over 2f out: swtchd rt and hdwy wl over 1f out: swtchd lft 1f out: r.o to ld wl ins fnl f: comf* **14/1**

4500 **2** *1 ¾* **Call Dawn**[3] 8783 2-9-3 **56**..........................(h[1]) CamHardie 8 57
(Michael Easterby) *hld up: rdn over 2f out: hdwy over 1f out: r.o to go 2nd nr fin* **40/1**

3300 **3** *½* **Foxrush Take Time (FR)**[11] 8658 2-9-4 **60**.................. CliffordLee(3) 10 60
(Richard Guest) *a.p: chsd ldr 4f out: rdn to ld over 2f out: hdd and unable qck wl ins fnl f* **13/2**[3]

6006 **4** *½* **Odds On Oli**[10] 8676 2-9-0 **53**.................. TonyHamilton 4 52
(Richard Fahey) *plld hrd and prom: rdn over 1f out: styd on same pce ins fnl f* **10/1**

4603 **5** *2 ¼* **Arty But Poor**[30] 8191 2-9-5 **58**..........................(p[1]) KevinStott 3 51
(Oliver Greenall) *sn led: hdd over 5f out: remained handy: rdn to chse ldr over 1f out: no ex ins fnl f* **4/1**[2]

0425 **6** *1* **Puramente**[32] 8141 2-9-6 **59**.................. JoeFanning 9 50
(Jo Hughes) *hld up: rdn over 1f out: styd on ins fnl f: nvr on terms* **11/4**[1]

0006 **7** *¾* **Jazz Affair (IRE)**[17] 8500 2-9-1 **54**.................. DougieCostello 7 43
(Jamie Osborne) *hld up in tch: n.m.r over 6f out: rdn over 2f out: hung lft over 1f out: wknd ins fnl f* **18/1**

5005 **8** *1 ¼* **Long Embrace**[44] 7756 2-9-5 **58**.................. RobertHavlin 5 44
(Simon Crisford) *in tch whn hmpd and lost pl over 6f out: in rr and rdn over 2f out: n.d* **8/1**

604 **9** *1* **Dragon Tattoo (IRE)**[15] 8555 2-9-6 **59**.................. JosephineGordon 1 42
(Hugo Palmer) *pushed along to chse ldrs: rdn over 1f out: wknd ins fnl f* **9/1**

0000 **10** *3* **Bodie And Doyle**[32] 8131 2-8-13 **59**..........................(b[1]) JasonWatson(7) 6 35
(Andrew Balding) *chsd ldrs: led over 5f out: rdn and hdd over 2f out: wknd fnl f* **9/1**

000 **11** *10* **Arlecchino's Arc (IRE)**[22] 8387 2-9-2 **55**..........................(p) SteveDrowne 12 6
(Mark Usher) *s.i.s: sn pushed along in rr: bhd fnl 4f* **33/1**

1m 29.72s (0.92) **Going Correction** -0.15s/f (Stan) **11 Ran SP% 117.5**
Speed ratings (Par 94): **88,86,85,84,82 81,80,78,77,74 62**
CSF £457.34 CT £4001.45 TOTE £11.10: £3.20, £7.50, £2.30; EX 439.60 Trifecta £2780.80.
**Owner** Don Churston & Ray Greatorex **Bred** Honeypuddle Stud **Trained** Upper Lambourn, Berks

**FOCUS**
The first of five juvenile races on this eight-race card. Not many got into this low-grade nursery despite the fact that they appeared to go an even gallop.

### 8848 £10 FREE AT 32RED.COM NURSERY H'CAP 1m 142y (Tp)

6:15 (6:17) (Class 5) (0-75,75) 2-Y-O £3,234 (£962; £481; £240) **Stalls Low**

Form RPR

3552 **1** **La La Land (IRE)**[18] 8491 2-9-7 **75**..........................(p) TimmyMurphy 9 82+
(Jamie Osborne) *hld up: hdwy over 3f out: rdn over 2f out: led over 1f out: hung lft ins fnl f: r.o* **6/1**[3]

0000 **2** *1 ½* **Gembari**[23] 8371 2-7-13 **58**..........................(v[1]) JaneElliott(5) 4 61
(Ivan Furtado) *w ldr: led over 3f out: rdn over 2f out: hdd wl over 1f out: styd on same pce ins fnl f* **40/1**

643 **3** *1 ¼* **Handsome Bob (IRE)**[18] 8493 2-8-13 **70**..........(p) CallumRodriguez(3) 8 70
(Keith Dalgleish) *hld up: pushed along over 5f out: hdwy over 1f out: r.o to go 3rd wl ins fnl f: nt rch ldrs* **8/1**

0030 **4** *nk* **Urban Soul (IRE)**[14] 8586 2-8-13 **67**..........................(p[1]) KevinStott 10 67
(James Bethell) *prom: lost pl over 6f out: hdwy 3f out: rdn over 1f out: styd on* **40/1**

3234 **5** *nse* **Far Dawn**[16] 8537 2-8-13 **67**..........................(v) RobertHavlin 11 67
(Simon Crisford) *wnt lft s: sn pushed along towards rr: pulling hrd and nt clr run over 5f out: shkn up over 2f out: rdn and r.o ins fnl f: nt rch ldrs* **5/1**[2]

025 **6** *1 ¾* **Compliance (IRE)**[60] 7237 2-9-4 **72**.................. JoeFanning 6 68
(James Tate) *chsd ldrs: led wl over 1f out: sn rdn and hdd: no ex ins fnl f* **4/1**[1]

02 **7** *¾* **Jo's Girl (IRE)**[39] 7914 2-9-1 **69**.................. DougieCostello 5 63
(Jamie Osborne) *s.s: hld up: pushed along over 2f out: rdn ins fnl f: styd on: nvr nrr* **8/1**

6114 **8** *hd* **Kikini Bamalaam (IRE)**[70] 6940 2-9-0 **68**.................. JasonHart 3 62
(Keith Dalgleish) *hld up in tch: rdn over 2f out: styd on same pce fr over 1f out* **18/1**

650 **9** *½* **Global Wonder (IRE)**[25] 8309 2-8-12 **66**.................. FranBerry 1 59
(Ed Dunlop) *s.i.s: hld up: rdn over 1f out: nvr on terms* **25/1**

0514 **10** *4* **El Borracho (IRE)**[70] 6934 2-8-10 **69**.................. PaddyBradley(5) 2 54
(Simon Dow) *led: racd keenly: hdd over 3f out: sn rdn: wknd over 1f out* **5/1**[2]

313 **11** *4 ½* **Voicemail**[80] 6575 2-9-7 **75**.................. TonyHamilton 12 50
(James Tate) *chsd ldrs: rdn over 2f out: wknd over 1f out* **10/1**

3344 **12** *shd* **Calling Rio (IRE)**[18] 8491 2-9-5 **73**.................. JosephineGordon 7 48
(David Loughnane) *w ldrs tl pushed along 7f out: remained handy: rdn over 2f out: sn wknd* **25/1**

1m 49.21s (-0.89) **Going Correction** -0.15s/f (Stan) **12 Ran SP% 116.8**
Speed ratings (Par 96): **97,95,94,94,94 92,92,91,91,87 83,83**
CSF £232.61 CT £1942.31 TOTE £5.80: £2.10, £10.90, £2.60; EX 279.80 Trifecta £7526.70 Part won..
**Owner** Michael Buckley & Charles E Noell **Bred** Yeomanstown Stud **Trained** Upper Lambourn, Berks

**FOCUS**
Quite a competitive 0-75 nursery, but the winner looks value for more than the winning margin and is the one to concentrate on.

### 8849 32RED.COM EBF NOVICE STKS 1m 1f 104y (Tp)

6:45 (6:48) (Class 5) 2-Y-O £4,528 (£1,347; £673; £336) **Stalls Low**

Form RPR

6 **1** **Corelli (USA)**[10] 8678 2-9-2 0.................. RobertHavlin 2 79+
(John Gosden) *hld up: hdwy over 2f out: shkn up over 1f out: r.o to ld wl ins fnl f* **4/1**[2]

42 **2** *nk* **Craving (IRE)**[28] 8245 2-9-2 0.................. SilvestreDeSousa 12 78
(Simon Crisford) *sn led: rdn over 2f out: edgd rt over 1f out: hdd wl ins fnl f* **2/1**[1]

4 **3** *3* **Talas (IRE)**[24] 8352 2-9-2 0.................. JackMitchell 4 72
(Roger Varian) *trckd ldrs: racd keenly: chsd ldr over 1f out: sn rdn and hung lft: no ex ins fnl f* **9/2**[3]

**4** *3* **Silver Character (IRE)** 2-9-2 0.................. RichardKingscote 13 67
(Tom Dascombe) *sn pushed along and prom: rn green: reminder over 5f out: rdn over 2f out: styd on same pce fr over 1f out* **66/1**

0 **5** *½* **King Tut (USA)**[24] 8339 2-9-2 0.................. ShaneKelly 3 66
(Roger Charlton) *hld up: pushed along and hdwy over 1f out: no ex ins fnl f* **14/1**

0 **6** *1* **Highland Sky (IRE)**[74] 6777 2-9-2 0.................. LukeMorris 6 64+
(David Simcock) *s.i.s: hld up: shkn up over 2f out: styd on fr over 1f out: nvr nrr* **7/1**

04 **7** *½* **Time To Perfection (IRE)**[22] 8399 2-8-11 0.................. RenatoSouza 11 58
(Sylvester Kirk) *hld up: effrt over 2f out: wknd over 1f out* **40/1**

52 **8** *¾* **I'm A Star (IRE)**[81] 6553 2-9-2 0.................. MartinHarley 8 61
(Stuart Williams) *chsd ldr: rdn over 2f out: wknd fnl f* **7/1**

**9** *½* **Bill Cody (IRE)** 2-9-2 0.................. DougieCostello 5 60
(Jamie Osborne) *hld up: shkn up over 1f out: nvr on terms* **33/1**

**10** *6* **Houlton** 2-9-2 0..........................(t[1]) DanielMuscutt 7 49
(Marco Botti) *s.i.s: hld up: rdn over 2f out: sn wknd* **40/1**

**11** *3 ¼* **River Of Gold (IRE)** 2-9-2 0.................. NickyMackay 10 43
(John Gosden) *s.i.s: hld up: hung rt and wknd over 2f out* **20/1**

63 **12** *1* **Perfect Blue (IRE)**[22] 8399 2-9-2 0.................. JoeFanning 9 41
(Mark Johnston) *chsd ldrs: rdn over 2f out: wknd over 1f out* **25/1**

**13** *19* **Come On Sal** 2-8-11 0.................. FranBerry 1
(Daniel Mark Loughnane) *sn pushed along in rr: bhd fnl 5f* **200/1**

1m 59.96s (-0.84) **Going Correction** -0.15s/f (Stan) **13 Ran SP% 121.6**
Speed ratings (Par 96): **97,96,94,91,90 90,89,88,88,83 80,79,62**
CSF £11.93 TOTE £5.10: £2.20, £1.40, £2.00; EX 15.50 Trifecta £83.90.
**Owner** George Strawbridge **Bred** George Strawbridge Jr **Trained** Newmarket, Suffolk

**FOCUS**
Not a particularly deep maiden, but the front two came clear in the closing stages and the winner looks a really nice prospect over further next year.

### 8850 32RED CASINO EBF FILLIES' NOVICE STKS (PLUS 10 RACE) (DIV I) 6f 20y (Tp)

7:15 (7:19) (Class 5) 2-Y-O £4,528 (£1,347; £673; £336) **Stalls Low**

Form RPR

2222 **1** **Gold Filigree (IRE)**[31] 8154 2-8-9 **75**.................. FinleyMarsh(5) 7 76
(Richard Hughes) *led early: racd keenly in 2nd: chal over 1f out: styd on u.p to ld wl ins fnl f* **9/2**[3]

02 **2** *nk* **Puds**[25] 8324 2-9-0 0.................. SteveDrowne 2 75
(Charles Hills) *sn led: rdn over 1f out: hdd wl ins fnl f* **18/1**

**3** *5* **It's A Wish** 2-9-0 0.................. SilvestreDeSousa 9 60
(Clive Cox) *prom: racd keenly: settled and lost pl over 4f out: pushed along: hdwy and hung rt over 1f out: r.o to go 3rd nr fin* **7/1**

62 **4** *nk* **Musical Theatre**[37] 7986 2-9-0 0..........................(h) StevieDonohoe 8 60
(David Simcock) *hld up in tch: racd keenly: shkn up and hmpd over 1f out: hung rt and no ex ins fnl f* **12/1**

**5** *1 ½* **Autumn Snow** 2-9-0 0.................. JosephineGordon 6 55+
(Saeed bin Suroor) *hld up: pushed along over 3f out: sme hdwy and hung lft over 1f out: nt trble ldrs* **9/4**[2]

0 **6** *nk* **Spanish Mane (IRE)**[19] 8474 2-9-0 0.................. TonyHamilton 4 54+
(Richard Fahey) *sn pushed along in rr: rdn over 1f out: n.d* **50/1**

2 **7** *hd* **Cirrus Minor (FR)**[60] 7238 2-9-0 0.................. MartinHarley 3 53
(K R Burke) *prom: shkn up over 2f out: rdn and hung lft over 1f out: wknd ins fnl f* **2/1**[1]

6 **8** *1* **Lethal Angel**[24] 8348 2-9-0 0.................. FranBerry 12 50
(Stuart Williams) *hld up: pushed along 1/2-way: nvr on terms* **28/1**

0 **9** *6* **Queen Of Dreams (IRE)**[24] 8347 2-9-0 0.................. LukeMorris 5 32
(William Knight) *s.i.s: hld up: pushed along 1/2-way: wknd over 2f out* **50/1**

60 **10** *1 ¾* **Cat Ballou**[80] 6567 2-9-0 0.................. DanielTudhope 1 27
(David O'Meara) *chsd ldrs: shkn up over 2f out: wknd over 1f out* **150/1**

**11** *7* **Crazie Maisie** 2-8-7 0.................. JackOsborn(7) 11 6
(Brian Barr) *s.i.s: sn pushed along in rr: bhd 1/2-way* **200/1**

1m 13.84s (-0.66) **Going Correction** -0.15s/f (Stan) **11 Ran SP% 116.3**
Speed ratings (Par 93): **98,97,90,90,88 88,87,86,78,76 66**
CSF £76.29 TOTE £5.50: £1.50, £3.70, £2.10; EX 67.40 Trifecta £481.30.

**Owner** Galloway,Lawrence,Merritt & Mrs Blake **Bred** Grangecon Holdings Ltd **Trained** Upper Lambourn, Berks
■ Stewards' Enquiry : Finley Marsh one-day ban: failed to ride to draw (Dec 2)

**FOCUS**
Some promising types on paper in here, but very little got into it and the front two had it between them from over a furlong out.

## 8851 32RED CASINO EBF FILLIES' NOVICE STKS (PLUS 10 RACE) (DIV II) 6f 20y (Tp)
7:45 (7:50) (Class 5) 2-Y-O **£4,528** (£1,347; £673; £336) **Stalls** Low

Form RPR
5 **1** **Two Weeks**[92] 6138 2-8-11 0 HectorCrouch(3) 5 78
(Clive Cox) *sn led: rdn and edgd lft over 1f out: styd on u.p* **8/1**
4 **2** 3/4 **Rizzle Dizzle**[26] 8288 2-8-11 0 CliffordLee(3) 9 76
(K R Burke) *chsd ldrs: rdn to chse wnr over 1f out: styd on* **5/1**
10 **3** 1 1/2 **Crotchet**[28] 8236 2-9-7 0 TonyHamilton 6 78
(Richard Fahey) *hld up in tch: nt clr run and swtchd rt over 1f out: styd on* **20/1**
3 **4** 2 1/4 **Wazin**[16] 8536 2-9-0 0 RobertHavlin 4 64
(Simon Crisford) *sn chsng wnr: rdn and ev ch over 1f out: no ex ins fnl f* **3/1**[2]
**5** 1 1/2 **Sooda (USA)** 2-9-0 0 SilvestreDeSousa 3 60+
(Roger Varian) *s.i.s: hld up: shkn up and edgd lft over 1f out: r.o ins fnl f: nt rch ldrs* **11/4**[1]
00 **6** nk **Lady Sophiebella**[19] 8474 2-9-0 0 TomEaves 1 59
(Bryan Smart) *prom: rdn over 2f out: wknd ins fnl f* **200/1**
3 **7** hd **Moretti (IRE)**[19] 8471 2-9-0 0 (h[1]) DanielTudhope 2 58
(David O'Meara) *s.i.s: hld up: styd on ins fnl f: nvr nrr* **10/1**
**8** 1 1/2 **L'Age D'Or** 2-9-0 0 LukeMorris 10 54
(Robert Cowell) *s.i.s: hld up: shkn up over 2f out: nvr on terms* **33/1**
2 **9** nk **Popsicle (IRE)**[140] 4367 2-9-0 0 TomMarquand 8 53
(Richard Hannon) *prom: racd keenly: lost pl 4f out: shkn up over 2f out: wknd over 1f out* **7/2**[3]
06 **10** nk **Glamorous Dream (IRE)**[45] 7725 2-9-0 0 BenCurtis 11 52
(Ronald Harris) *led early: chsd ldrs: rdn over 2f out: wknd fnl f* **66/1**
**11** 1 1/2 **Bella Ferrari** 2-9-0 0 MartinHarley 7 47
(George Scott) *s.i.s: hld up: plld hrd: shkn up over 1f out: wknd fnl f* **33/1**
1m 13.29s (-1.21) **Going Correction** -0.15s/f (Stan) 11 Ran SP% **123.4**
Speed ratings (Par 93): **102,101,99,96,94 93,93,91,90,90 88**
CSF £48.47 TOTE £8.90: £2.50, £2.30, £4.10; EX 54.20 Trifecta £608.50.
**Owner** Apple Tree Stud **Bred** Limestone And Tara Studs **Trained** Lambourn, Berks

**FOCUS**
Some reasonably promising fillies on show here and this looks a race that could throw up a few winners.

## 8852 BETWAY LIVE CASINO MAIDEN STKS 1m 1f 104y (Tp)
8:15 (8:15) (Class 5) 3-Y-O+ **£3,234** (£962; £481; £240) **Stalls** Low

Form RPR
6602 **1** **Bleu Et Noir**[16] 8550 6-9-8 69 (h) KieranO'Neill 7 78+
(Tim Vaughan) *hld up in tch: racd keenly: shkn up over 2f out: led over 1f out: sn clr: easily* **15/8**[2]
0620 **2** 6 **Luminous**[44] 7762 3-9-0 70 SilvestreDeSousa 2 57
(Simon Crisford) *led: hung rt 7f out: rdn over 2f out: hung rt and hdd over 1f out: wknd ins fnl f* **10/11**[1]
**3** 2 1/2 **Remember Nerja (IRE)**[71] 6910 3-8-9 43 JaneElliott(5) 1 52?
(Barry Leavy) *s.i.s: hld up: styd on to go 3rd wl ins fnl f: nt trble ldrs* **100/1**
-356 **4** 1 3/4 **Deliberator**[38] 7948 3-9-5 71 (h) MartinHarley 5 53
(William Knight) *chsd ldr: rdn and ev ch fr over 2f out tl wl over 1f out: hmpd sn after: wknd fnl f* **7/2**[3]
0 **5** 10 **Shadow's Girl**[12] 8635 5-8-10 0 WilliamCox(7) 3 27
(Bernard Llewellyn) *chsd ldrs: rdn over 3f out: sn wknd* **66/1**
000 **6** 11 **Shanghai Shane (IRE)**[17] 8504 3-8-12 0 JackOsborn(7) 6 9
(Brian Barr) *prom: pushed along and lost pl over 7f out: bhd fnl 4f* **200/1**
1m 59.57s (-1.23) **Going Correction** -0.15s/f (Stan)
**WFA** 3 from 5yo+ 3lb 6 Ran SP% **112.4**
Speed ratings (Par 103): **99,93,91,89,81 71**
CSF £3.97 TOTE £2.30: £1.40, £1.20; EX 4.60 Trifecta £70.20.
**Owner** Alan Peterson **Bred** Upton Viva Stud **Trained** Aberthin, Vale of Glamorgan

**FOCUS**
A weak maiden in which they finished well strung out. The winner has been rated to the better view of his latest effort.

## 8853 BETWAY CASINO H'CAP 5f 21y (Tp)
8:45 (8:45) (Class 5) (0-70,71) 3-Y-O+ **£3,234** (£962; £481; £240) **Stalls** Low

Form RPR
2456 **1** **Berryessa (IRE)**[53] 7486 3-9-6 69 LukeMorris 7 77
(Rae Guest) *hld up in tch: rdn and nt clr run over 1f out: led ins fnl f: r.o* **10/1**
3224 **2** 1/2 **Kyllukey**[7] 8743 4-8-10 62 (v) CallumShepherd(3) 9 68
(Milton Bradley) *sn prom: rdn and nt clr run over 1f out: ev ch ins fnl f: styd on* **17/2**
040 **3** 3/4 **Powerful Dream (IRE)**[79] 6612 4-9-6 69 (p) BenCurtis 3 73+
(Ronald Harris) *hld up: hdwy and nt clr run fr over 1f out tl wl ins fnl f: r.o: nt rch ldrs* **14/1**
1112 **4** 1 1/4 **Lydiate Lady**[17] 8512 5-9-6 69 JasonHart 10 68
(Eric Alston) *chsd ldrs: rdn over 1f out: sn ev ch: styd on same pce ins fnl f* **10/1**
3455 **5** nk **Pushkin Museum (IRE)**[7] 8743 6-9-0 63 (h) ShaneKelly 5 61
(Patrick Morris) *broke wl: sn stdd to trck ldrs: rdn and ev ch ins fnl f: styd on same pce* **7/1**[3]
0560 **6** shd **Krystallite**[53] 7486 4-8-13 62 JosephineGordon 4 59
(Scott Dixon) *s.i.s: hld up: nt clr run over 1f out: r.o ins fnl f: nt rch ldrs* **16/1**
0052 **7** hd **Fast Act (IRE)**[7] 8745 5-9-8 71 (p) KevinStott 8 68
(Kevin Ryan) *sn chsng ldr: rdn to ld over 1f out: hdd and no ex ins fnl f* **7/2**[2]
1335 **8** shd **Annie Salts**[36] 7994 4-8-13 69 (h) NicolaCurrie(7) 1 67+
(Chris Dwyer) *hld up: hdwy and nt clr run over 1f out: nt clr run and swtchd rt ins fnl f: nvr able to chal* **3/1**[1]
3400 **9** 3/4 **Temple Road (IRE)**[210] 1981 9-8-13 62 (bt) LiamKeniry 11 56
(Milton Bradley) *s.i.s: hld up: nt clr run ins fnl f: n.d* **66/1**
1000 **10** nk **Red Invader (IRE)**[25] 8311 7-9-0 66 TimClark(3) 6 59
(John Butler) *s.i.s: hld up: r.o ins fnl f: nvr on terms* **20/1**
032 **11** 2 1/2 **Cruise Tothelimit (IRE)**[40] 7911 9-8-13 62 (b) FranBerry 2 46
(Patrick Morris) *sn led: rdn and hdd over 1f out: wknd ins fnl f* **8/1**
1m 1.03s (-0.87) **Going Correction** -0.15s/f (Stan) 11 Ran SP% **118.3**
Speed ratings (Par 103): **100,99,98,96,95 95,95,94,93,93 89**
CSF £92.85 CT £1219.48 TOTE £12.70: £3.50, £2.80, £4.10; EX 103.60 Trifecta £2197.00.
**Owner** RGRL Syndicate 2 **Bred** Samuel William Ormsby **Trained** Newmarket, Suffolk

**FOCUS**
A wide-open low-grade sprint. The pace collapsed and it set things up for the finishers. The third horse looked a bit unlucky. The runner-up helps set the standard.

## 8854 SUNBETS.CO.UK H'CAP 1m 142y (Tp)
9:15 (9:17) (Class 6) (0-60,63) 3-Y-O+ **£2,587** (£770; £384; £192) **Stalls** Low

Form RPR
2501 **1** **Champagne Pink (FR)**[11] 8661 3-9-3 63 (h) CliffordLee(3) 4 70+
(K R Burke) *prom: rdn to ld over 1f out: edgd lft: r.o* **4/1**[3]
4303 **2** 1 1/4 **Ingleby Angel (IRE)**[17] 8514 8-9-4 58 DanielTudhope 13 62
(David O'Meara) *hld up: hdwy over 1f out: edgd lft and r.o u.p to go 2nd post: nt rch wnr* **7/2**[2]
2100 **3** shd **Edge (IRE)**[11] 8661 6-9-6 60 (b) StevieDonohoe 7 64
(Bernard Llewellyn) *hld up: hdwy over 2f out: rdn over 1f out: styd on u.p* **25/1**
0516 **4** 1 1/2 **Arrowzone**[8] 8719 6-9-2 56 (b) DougieCostello 12 57
(Kevin Frost) *s.i.s and swtchd lft sn after s: hld up: rdn and r.o ins fnl f: nt rch ldrs* **12/1**
2060 **5** nk **Mimic's Memory**[11] 8656 3-9-3 60 JackGarritty 1 60
(Ann Duffield) *hld up: nt clr run over 2f out: hdwy over 1f out: swtchd rt ins fnl f: nt trble ldrs* **33/1**
3005 **6** 4 **Know Your Name**[11] 8664 6-9-3 57 TomEaves 3 49
(Donald McCain) *led 1f: chsd ldr: led 2f out: rdn and hdd over 1f out: wknd ins fnl f* **25/1**
5041 **7** nk **Top Offer**[11] 8664 8-9-5 59 (b) FranBerry 5 50
(Patrick Morris) *hld up: rdn over 1f out: nvr on terms* **10/1**
0005 **8** 3 **Different Journey**[17] 8515 4-9-4 58 (b) PhillipMakin 6 43
(Michael Easterby) *led after 1f: rdn and hdd 2f out: wknd fnl f* **5/2**[1]
0040 **9** 1/2 **Sky Marshal (IRE)**[26] 8299 3-9-3 60 LiamKeniry 2 44
(Ed Walker) *prom: rdn over 2f out: wknd over 1f out* **14/1**
4335 **10** 10 **Log Off (IRE)**[131] 4697 3-8-11 59 RhiainIngram(5) 9 22
(Karen George) *s.i.s: hld up: hdwy 3f out: wknd over 2f out* **66/1**
5401 **11** 2 **Hot Mustard**[28] 8248 7-9-3 57 (h) JosephineGordon 8 16
(William Muir) *chsd ldrs: rdn over 3f out: wknd over 1f out* **9/1**
1063 **12** 3 1/2 **Billy Bond**[14] 8589 5-9-5 59 (b) TonyHamilton 10 10
(Richard Fahey) *prom: rdn over 2f out: sn wknd* **12/1**
1m 48.58s (-1.52) **Going Correction** -0.15s/f (Stan)
**WFA** 3 from 4yo+ 3lb 12 Ran SP% **124.1**
Speed ratings (Par 101): **100,98,98,97,97 93,93,90,90,81 79,76**
CSF £18.75 CT £328.03 TOTE £4.50: £1.30, £2.00, £7.70; EX 21.00 Trifecta £458.60.
**Owner** Nick Bradley Racing 2 & Mrs E Burke **Bred** G A E C Campos **Trained** Middleham Moor, N Yorks

**FOCUS**
Another wide-open low-grade event run at a sound gallop.
T/Plt: £463.70 to a £1 stake. Pool: £116,402.29 - 183.22 winning units T/Qpdt: £17.20 to a £1 stake. Pool: £16,216.42 - 695.68 winning units **Colin Roberts**

8855-8856a (Foreign Racing) - See Raceform Interactive

# SANDOWN (AUS) (L-H)
Saturday, November 18

**OFFICIAL GOING: Turf: good to soft changing to good from race 6 (4.25am)**

## 8857a MYPUNTER.COM ECLIPSE STKS (GROUP 3 H'CAP) (2YO+) (TURF) 1m 1f
6:20 2-Y-O+
**£53,070** (£15,789; £7,894; £3,947; £2,192; £1,754)

RPR
**1** **Payroll (AUS)**[7] 5-8-8 0 (tp) DamienOliver 6 99
(Richard Laming, Australia) **11/2**[3]
**2** shd **Kidmenever (IRE)**[35] 8056 4-9-4 0 (p) KerrinMcEvoy 7 109
(Charlie Appleby) **13/2**
**3** 3 3/4 **Jacquinot Bay (AUS)**[7] 8750 10-8-9 0 (v) CoryParish 8 92
(David A & B Hayes & Tom Dabernig, Australia) **12/1**
**4** nk **Raw Impulse**[7] 8750 5-8-11 0 DamianLane 1 93
(Darren Weir, Australia) **9/2**[1]
**5** 1/2 **Von Tunzelman (NZ)**[9] 5-8-7 0 MichaelDee 2 88
(Roger James, New Zealand) **11/1**
**6** nk **Pure Pride (NZ)**[11] 5-8-9 0 (vt) StephenBaster 10 90
(Murray Johnson, Australia) **15/1**
**7** 3 **Khartoum (AUS)**[17] 8633 4-8-7 0 PatrickMoloney 3 82
(Pat Carey, Australia) **100/1**
**8** 1 1/4 **Nozomi (AUS)**[11] 6-8-11 0 MarkZahra 13 83
(Anthony Freedman, Australia) **5/1**[2]
**9** hd **Balf's Choice (AUS)**[11] 5-9-1 0 (p) JamieKah 12 86
(Ryan Balfour, Australia) **8/1**
**10** hd **Dodging Bullets (AUS)**[22] 6-8-10 0 (p) ReganBayliss 9 81
(Symon Wilde, Australia) **10/1**
**11** 2 3/4 **Lord Durante (AUS)**[22] 9-8-7 0 StanTsaikos 4 72
(Simone Ferchie, Australia) **50/1**
**12** 1 1/4 **Foundation (IRE)**[35] 4-9-1 0 (b) NoelCallow 11 78
(David A & B Hayes & Tom Dabernig, Australia) **25/1**
**13** 15 **Raghu (NZ)**[244] 1278 5-8-7 0 (p) BenEThompson 5 38
(Jason Warren, Australia) **40/1**
1m 51.45s 13 Ran SP% **115.3**
**Owner** Mrs J Laming, J R Brockmuller Et Al **Bred** Macquarie Stud **Trained** Australia

8858 - 8868a (Foreign Racing) - See Raceform Interactive

# [8847] WOLVERHAMPTON (A.W) (L-H)

Monday, November 20

**OFFICIAL GOING: Tapeta: standard**

Wind: Breezy, against in straight Weather: Cloudy and damp, occasional showers, cool

## 8869 32REDSPORT.COM MAIDEN FILLIES' STKS — 1m 142y (Tp)

1:00 (1:01) (Class 5) 3-Y-O+ — £3,234 (£962; £481; £240) Stalls Low

Form — RPR

056 **1** **Ciaoadiosimdone (IRE)**[16] [8599] 3-9-0 85 SilvestreDeSousa 3 — 71
(John Ryan) *trckd ldrs: hdwy into 2nd 1/2-way: led over 2f out: rdn and chal by runner-up 1f out: r.o wl to assert last 100yds* **2/1**[2]

544 **2** ¾ **Meccabah (FR)**[14] [8635] 3-9-0 75 (b[1]) PhillipMakin 2 — 69
(Andrew Balding) *trckd ldrs: hdwy into 2nd over 1f out: chal wnr 1f out: sn rdn: hld last 100yds* **11/10**[1]

**3** 1¾ **Ladies First** 3-9-0 0 CamHardie 1 — 65
(Michael Easterby) *hld up: hdwy on inner over 1f out: sn rdn and kpt on to take 3rd ins fnl f* **28/1**

**4** 1½ **Mundersfield** 3-9-0 0 MartinHarley 7 — 61
(David Simcock) *hld up: pushed along and hdwy over 1f out: r.o: tk 4th ins fnl f* **6/1**[3]

6 **5** 1¾ **Deauville Diva (IRE)**[35] [8116] 3-8-7 0 TylerSaunders(7) 4 — 57
(Marcus Tregoning) *mid-div: pushed along over 2f out: rdn and hdwy into 3rd over 1f out: wknd and lost pl ins fnl f* **12/1**

5400 **6** 2¼ **Cloud Nine (FR)**[40] [7948] 4-9-3 47 TomMarquand 11 — 52
(Tony Carroll) *mid-div: pushed along over 2f out: drvn 2f out: rdn over 1f out: one pce* **100/1**

00- **7** ¾ **Freediver**[361] [8081] 3-8-7 0 NicolaCurrie(7) 12 — 50
(John Berry) *hld up: hdwy on outer 2f out: sn rdn and one pce* **33/1**

3433 **8** 2 **Indiana Dawn**[13] [8662] 4-8-10 51 (v[1]) WilliamCox(7) 5 — 46
(Robert Stephens) *led: hdd after 3f: remained prom trcking ldrs: drvn 2f out: rdn over 1f out: wknd* **16/1**

0 **9** 2¼ **Bury The Evidence**[7] [8770] 4-9-3 0 (h) PatrickMathers 6 — 41
(Derek Shaw) *hld up: drvn 2f out: rdn over 1f out: no imp* **100/1**

5 **10** 11 **Little Miss Tango**[138] [4490] 3-8-7 0 Pierre-LouisJamin(7) 8 — 15
(Roger Teal) *in rr: rdn 2f out: no imp* **100/1**

0 **11** 10 **Paco Filly**[40] [7948] 3-9-0 0 CharlesBishop 9
(Nikki Evans) *prom: drvn and wknd 3f out* **100/1**

0450 **12** 1¼ **Thechampagnesonice**[40] [7945] 4-9-3 49 (p[1]) LiamKeniry 10
(Malcolm Saunders) *t.k.h: led after 3f: pushed along and hdd over 2f out: wknd qckly* **66/1**

1m 48.22s (-1.88) **Going Correction** -0.15s/f (Stan)
**WFA** 3 from 4yo 3lb — 12 Ran SP% 120.7
Speed ratings (Par 100): **102,101,99,98,96 94,94,92,90,80 71,70**
CSF £4.52 TOTE £2.20: £1.10, £1.10, £8.70; EX 5.80 Trifecta £56.20.
**Owner** Pull It Right Back Partnership **Bred** D Farrington And Canning Downs **Trained** Newmarket, Suffolk

**FOCUS**
Just a modest maiden, this only concerned the first two from the home turn. The pace had slowed down the back straight. The sixth is key to the level. The first two have been rated below their best.

## 8870 32RED.COM NURSERY H'CAP — 1m 1f 104y (Tp)

1:30 (1:31) (Class 6) (0-65,66) 2-Y-O — £2,587 (£770; £384; £192) Stalls Low

Form — RPR

2050 **1** **Mouchee (IRE)**[25] [8371] 2-8-11 58 MattCosham(3) 2 — 61
(David Evans) *mid-div: hdwy on inner 2f out: pushed into 3rd over 1f out: swtchd to chal and rdn ent fnl f: r.o wl to ld nr fin* **4/1**[2]

0332 **2** nk **Progressive Jazz (IRE)**[27] [8306] 2-8-8 52 (v) JoeyHaynes 4 — 54
(K R Burke) *led: rdn over 1f out: 1 l clr ent fnl f: r.o but hdd nr fin* **5/1**[3]

000 **3** 1 **Ahfad**[107] [5655] 2-8-6 50 LukeMorris 1 — 51
(Stuart Williams) *trckd ldrs: rdn in 3rd 2f out: drvn to chal 1f out: sn rdn: one pce* **12/1**

4000 **4** nk **Sigrid Nansen**[12] [8676] 2-9-8 66 SilvestreDeSousa 11 — 66
(George Scott) *mid-div: drvn and hdwy 2f out: rdn 1f out: kpt on* **12/1**

0360 **5** 1 **Mr Large (IRE)**[18] [8537] 2-9-7 65 DougieCostello 6 — 64
(Jamie Osborne) *hld up on inner: pushed along and effrt 2f out: drvn over 1f out: swtchd to outer and rdn ent fnl f: briefly n.m.r: kpt on* **7/1**

614 **6** ½ **Sauchiehall Street (IRE)**[13] [8644] 2-9-1 59 BenCurtis 3 — 56+
(Sylvester Kirk) *in rr: rdn and hdwy on outer 2f out: kpt on fnl f* **3/1**[1]

0005 **7** nk **Global Angel**[25] [8371] 2-8-13 64 (b) HarryBurns(7) 12 — 61
(Ed Dunlop) *prom: cl 2nd whn drvn 2f out: wknd and lost pl ent fnl f* **12/1**

0046 **8** 7 **Power Sail**[17] [8555] 2-9-6 64 DuranFentiman 10 — 47
(Tim Easterby) *mid-div: pushed along 2f out: rdn over 1f out: no imp* **16/1**

000R **9** 2 **Afterthisone**[13] [8644] 2-8-2 45 ow1 CamHardie 9 — 25
(Robin Dickin) *mid-div: rdn 2f out: drvn and no imp fr over 1f out* **150/1**

5504 **10** 1¼ **Onefootinfront**[33] [8164] 2-9-3 61 SteveDrowne 7 — 38
(Daniel Mark Loughnane) *hld up: rdn and effrt on outer 2f out: wknd fnl f* **10/1**

0500 **11** 20 **Misty Breese (IRE)**[25] [8371] 2-8-1 45 (h) AndrewMullen 8
(Paul D'Arcy) *prom: drvn and lost pl 3f out: wknd* **40/1**

0000 **12** 1¾ **Amiirah**[13] [8644] 2-8-1 45 (b[1]) JimmyQuinn 13
(John Gallagher) *prom: drvn and rdn over 3f out: fdd qckly* **125/1**

0000 **13** 99 **Caviar Royale**[38] [8013] 2-9-6 64 (p) CharlesBishop 5
(Nikki Evans) *in rr: drvn and lost tch 4f out: virtually p.u 2f out: allowed to come home in own time* **125/1**

2m 0.78s (-0.02) **Going Correction** -0.15s/f (Stan) — 13 Ran SP% 116.9
Speed ratings (Par 94): **94,93,92,92,91 91,90,84,82,81 64,62,**
CSF £23.77 CT £221.71 TOTE £4.60: £2.00, £1.50, £4.00; EX 23.20 Trifecta £159.50.
**Owner** E R Griffiths **Bred** T Mooney & Ms O Flores **Trained** Pandy, Monmouths

**FOCUS**
A weak, late-season nursery. The first seven finished in a heap. The winner has been rated within 2lb of his best.

## 8871 32RED CASINO NURSERY H'CAP — 7f 36y (Tp)

2:00 (2:01) (Class 4) (0-85,84) 2-Y-O — £4,528 (£1,347; £673; £336) Stalls High

Form — RPR

0012 **1** **Our Man In Havana**[23] [8431] 2-8-7 77 WilliamCox(7) 6 — 78
(Richard Price) *cl up in 2nd: pushed along to dispute ld 2f out: rdn into ld over 1f out: hld on wl fnl f* **5/1**[3]

2162 **2** nk **Central City (IRE)**[45] [7787] 2-9-4 81 JosephineGordon 2 — 81
(Hugo Palmer) *led: jnd by wnr 2f out: hdd and rdn over 1f out: kpt on wl fnl f: jst hld* **7/4**[1]

2140 **3** shd **Escape The City**[23] [8424] 2-9-0 80 CharlieBennett(3) 3 — 80
(Hughie Morrison) *trckd ldrs: pushed along 2f out: rdn and ev ch ent fnl f: r.o* **9/4**[2]

0303 **4** 1¾ **Havana Mariposa**[27] [8325] 2-8-5 68 JoeyHaynes 7 — 64
(K R Burke) *hld up in last: drvn into 4th over 1f out: rdn ent fnl f: no imp* **11/2**

0230 **5** 1¾ **New Empire**[23] [8420] 2-9-0 77 LukeMorris 5 — 68
(Peter Chapple-Hyam) *hld up in 4th: rdn and relegated to last over 1f out: no ex fnl f* **10/1**

1m 28.21s (-0.59) **Going Correction** -0.15s/f (Stan) — 5 Ran SP% 108.3
Speed ratings (Par 98): **97,96,96,94,92**
CSF £13.74 TOTE £6.60: £2.10, £1.10; EX 12.60 Trifecta £22.80.
**Owner** D J Oseman **Bred** Alvediston Stud & Partners **Trained** Ullingswick, H'fords

**FOCUS**
Just a fair nursery. Straightforward form.

## 8872 SUNBETS.CO.UK H'CAP — 7f 36y (Tp)

2:30 (2:31) (Class 4) (0-85,85) 3-Y-O+ — £5,175 (£1,540; £769; £384) Stalls High

Form — RPR

6020 **1** **Makaarim**[24] [8392] 3-9-5 84 RichardKingscote 2 — 92+
(Hughie Morrison) *trckd ldrs gng wl: pushed along and hdwy over 1f out: chal fnl f: rdn briefly: led last 50yds: pushed out to assert* **7/2**[1]

6005 **2** nk **Twin Appeal (IRE)**[9] [8736] 6-9-3 81 (b) BenCurtis 8 — 89
(David Barron) *trckd ldrs: pushed along and hdwy 2f out: rdn to ld ent fnl f: r.o wl: hdd last 50yds* **6/1**[3]

2426 **3** 1¼ **Easy Tiger**[18] [8547] 5-9-7 85 (p) LiamKeniry 9 — 90
(Malcolm Saunders) *prom: pushed along to ld over 1f out: rdn and hdd ent fnl f: kpt on* **7/1**

130 **4** ½ **Siege Of Boston (IRE)**[9] [8737] 4-9-6 84 (t) TomMarquand 3 — 87
(David C Griffiths) *trckd ldrs: pushed along 2f out: rdn over 1f out: one pce fnl f* **16/1**

-114 **5** nk **Boost**[254] [1149] 3-9-2 81 (p[1]) LukeMorris 6 — 82+
(Sir Mark Prescott Bt) *trckd ldrs: drvn over 1f out: sn rdn: no ex fnl f* **7/1**

0154 **6** ¾ **Inexes**[14] [8640] 5-9-1 79 (p) PhillipMakin 1 — 79
(Marjorie Fife) *hld up: pushed along and hdwy over 1f out: rdn ins fnl f: no ex* **8/1**

0314 **7** 1 **Florencio**[27] [8319] 4-9-6 84 (p) TonyHamilton 12 — 82
(Roger Fell) *hld up: pushed along 2f out: rdn and mod hdwy over 1f out: no ex fnl f* **14/1**

2606 **8** 2¼ **Custard The Dragon**[29] [8257] 4-9-4 82 (p) JoeFanning 5 — 74
(John Mackie) *hld up: rdn and hdwy on outer 2f out: no ex fnl f* **14/1**

4000 **9** 1¼ **Gentlemen**[18] [8540] 6-9-6 84 (h) JosephineGordon 4 — 72
(Phil McEntee) *hld up: drvn 2f out: rdn and racd wd over 1f out: no imp* **25/1**

620- **10** 1 **Whirl Me Round**[394] [7536] 3-9-6 85 (h[1]) AndrewMullen 10 — 70
(George Peckham) *towards rr: pushed along 2f out: reminders and wknd wl over 1f out* **50/1**

002- **11** 1¼ **Exchequer (IRE)**[370] [7968] 6-9-7 85 DanielTudhope 7 — 67
(David O'Meara) *led: drvn 2f out: hdd over 1f out: sn rdn and wknd* **9/2**[2]

1m 27.13s (-1.67) **Going Correction** -0.15s/f (Stan)
**WFA** 3 from 4yo+ 1lb — 11 Ran SP% 115.8
Speed ratings (Par 105): **103,102,101,100,100 99,98,95,94,93 91**
CSF £23.87 CT £142.03 TOTE £4.60: £1.70, £2.20, £2.00; EX 32.10 Trifecta £202.10.
**Owner** Thurloe Thoroughbreds Xliv **Bred** Essafinaat Ltd **Trained** East Ilsley, Berks

**FOCUS**
A fair handicap. It's been rated around the third and fourth.

## 8873 BETWAY DASH H'CAP — 5f 21y (Tp)

3:00 (3:02) (Class 6) (0-60,63) 3-Y-O+ — £2,587 (£770; £384; £192) Stalls Low

Form — RPR

251 **1** **Swendab (IRE)**[20] [8494] 9-8-12 58 (b) RossaRyan(7) 9 — 66
(John O'Shea) *prom: led after 1f: mde rest: pushed along 2f out: drvn over 1f out: rdn and jst over 1 l clr ent fnl f: hld on wl* **8/1**

051- **2** 1¼ **Gorgeous (FR)**[335] [8472] 4-9-2 55 TomMarquand 8 — 61+
(Tony Carroll) *slowly away: last 2f out: drvn and gd hdwy over 1f out: rdn ent fnl f: str run to take 2nd nr fin* **66/1**

0 **3** ½ **Eternalist**[91] [6267] 4-9-0 60 SeanMooney(7) 7 — 62
(Jim Goldie) *led tl hdd after 1f: sn trcking ldrs: 3rd 2f out: rdn fnl f: kpt on* **10/1**

4001 **4** nk **Broadhaven Honey (IRE)**[7] [8776] 3-9-10 63 6ex (v) BenCurtis 10 — 64
(Ronald Harris) *chsd ldrs: pushed along in 4th 2f out: rdn 1f out: kpt on* **6/1**[3]

636 **5** hd **Billyoakes (IRE)**[40] [7951] 5-9-6 59 (p) LukeMorris 6 — 59
(Charlie Wallis) *hld up: drvn and hdwy over 1f out: sn rdn: r.o ins fnl f* **11/1**

5202 **6** ¾ **Bond Bombshell**[17] [8558] 4-8-9 55 (p) PatrickVaughan(7) 3 — 52
(David O'Meara) *mid-div: pushed along 2f out: rdn over 1f out: one pce fnl f* **12/1**

0000 **7** hd **Waneen (IRE)**[180] [2962] 4-9-5 58 LiamKeniry 11 — 54
(John Butler) *prom: cl 2nd after 1f: rdn and wknd over 1f out* **2/1**[1]

0505 **8** nk **The Hooded Claw (IRE)**[9] [8742] 6-9-2 55 TomEaves 2 — 56
(Patrick Morris) *slowly away: hdwy on inner 2f out: drvn over 1f out: briefly n.m.r ins fnl f: kpt on* **9/2**[2]

0-60 **9** 1 **Storm Lightning**[20] [8496] 8-9-0 56 EoinWalsh(3) 4 — 48
(Mark Brisbourne) *hld up: pushed along on outer 2f out: reminder ent fnl f: no imp* **16/1**

1150 **10** ½ **Teepee Time**[20] [8494] 4-9-2 58 (b) PhilDennis(3) 1 — 48
(Michael Mullineaux) *mid-div: chsd along 2f out: rdn and wknd over 1f out* **22/1**

4060 **11** 6 **Nag's Wag (IRE)**[18] [8542] 4-9-7 60 PaulMulrennan 5 — 28
(Conor Dore) *mid-div: pushed along on outer 2f out: sn drvn and wknd* **22/1**

1m 0.95s (-0.95) **Going Correction** -0.15s/f (Stan) — 11 Ran SP% 118.1
Speed ratings (Par 101): **101,99,98,97,97 96,95,95,93,93 83**
CSF £457.82 CT £5232.29 TOTE £7.20: £1.90, £7.80, £2.80; EX 225.60 Trifecta £1501.80.
**Owner** E&G Racing: Swendab **Bred** P Brady **Trained** Elton, Gloucs

**FOCUS**
A low-grade sprint handicap. The third has been rated near her best.

## 8874 BETWAY SPRINT H'CAP (DIV I) — 6f 20y (Tp)

3:30 (3:30) (Class 5) (0-70,70) 3-Y-O+ — £3,234 (£962; £481; £240) Stalls Low

Form — RPR

0003 **1** **Invincible Ridge (IRE)**[9] [8745] 9-9-7 70 JasonHart 3 — 78
(Eric Alston) *mid-div: pushed along and hdwy 2 out: wnt 3rd over 1f out: drvn into ld jst ins fnl f: rdn and hld on wl* **6/1**[2]



The Form Book Flat, Raceform Ltd, Newbury, RG14 5SJ

2020 **2** *hd* **Arnarson**[21] 8479 3-9-5 **68**................(b[1]) LukeMorris 2 75
(Ed Dunlop) *slowly away: hld up: pushed along and hdwy 2f out: drvn into 2nd ins fnl f: rdn and r.o wl: hld by wnr cl home* **8/1**
1504 **3** *1 ¾* **Hamish McGonagain**[17] 8557 4-9-2 **65**................ DanielTudhope 7 66
(David O'Meara) *hld up: pushed along 2f out: hdwy ent fnl f: sn rdn: r.o wl* **7/1**[3]
2202 **4** *nk* **Indian Affair**[23] 8427 7-8-11 **67**................(bt) KerrieRaybould[(7)] 1 67
(Milton Bradley) *hld up: hdwy on inner over 1f out: reminders ins fnl f: r.o* **20/1**
6-02 **5** *1* **Strategic Heights (IRE)**[7] 8775 8-9-6 **69**................(p) DougieCostello 8 66
(Jamie Osborne) *chsd ldrs: pushed along in 4th 2f out: drvn over 1f out: rdn and one pce fnl f* **20/1**
6131 **6** *½* **Inlawed**[27] 8311 3-9-5 **68**................ RichardKingscote 4 64
(Ed Walker) *trckd ldrs: pushed along in 3rd 2f out: reminder and wknd over 1f out* **2/1**[1]
5320 **7** *hd* **Essential**[31] 8216 3-9-2 **65**................(v[1]) SilvestreDeSousa 9 60
(George Scott) *chsd ldr: drvn over 2f out: rdn and no ex ent fnl f* **7/1**[3]
1400 **8** *1 ¼* **Newstead Abbey**[23] 8434 7-9-4 **67**................(v[1]) TomEaves 6 58
(Michael Herrington) *hld up: pushed along over 2f out: swtchd to outer over 1f out: sn rdn and no imp* **10/1**
0400 **9** *1 ½* **Control Centre (IRE)**[17] 8557 3-9-2 **65**................ PhillipMakin 11 51
(Marjorie Fife) *hld up: pushed along 2f out: no imp* **66/1**
5060 **10** *1 ½* **Fareeq**[42] 7881 3-9-4 **67**................(vt[1]) BenCurtis 10 48
(Charlie Wallis) *towards rr: rdn on outer over 2f out: no imp* **25/1**
4002 **11** *1 ½* **Danish Duke (IRE)**[21] 8481 6-8-10 **66**................(b) SeamusCronin[(7)] 5 43
(Ruth Carr) *led: 3 l clr 2f out: much reduced ld over 1f out: hdd jst ins fnl f: wknd qckly* **12/1**
160 **12** *1 ¾* **Mr Strutter (IRE)**[17] 8557 3-9-1 **64**................(h) JimmyQuinn 13 35
(Ronald Thompson) *mid-div: pushed along and lost pl over 2f out* **50/1**

1m 13.06s (-1.44) **Going Correction** -0.15s/f (Stan) **12** Ran SP% **117.3**
Speed ratings (Par 103): **103,102,100,100,98 98,97,96,94,92 90,87**
CSF £49.24 CT £350.81 TOTE £6.50: £1.80, £2.70, £2.20; EX 53.30 Trifecta £462.60.
**Owner** Paul Buist & John Thompson **Bred** Con Harrington **Trained** Longton, Lancs

**FOCUS**
The leaders came back in this modest handicap, which was only 0.86sec outside the standard. The winner has been rated close to last winter's form, and the runner-up to his maiden best.

## 8875 BETWAY SPRINT H'CAP (DIV II) 6f 20y (Tp)
**4:00** (4:00) (Class 5) (0-70,70) 3-Y-O+ **£3,234** (£962; £481; £240) **Stalls** Low

Form RPR
2310 **1** **Rapid Ranger**[23] 8427 3-9-2 **65**................(h) DanielTudhope 8 73+
(David O'Meara) *hld up: hdwy and stl plenty to do over 1f out: pushed along to chal ins fnl f: str run to ld last 50yds: cosily* **5/1**[3]
4000 **2** *¾* **Lady Cristal (IRE)**[27] 8321 3-8-12 **64**................(p) CliffordLee[(3)] 4 70
(K R Burke) *trckd ldrs: pushed along and hdwy into 3rd over 1f out: sn rdn and ev ch ins fnl f: r.o wl: tk 2nd nr fin* **14/1**
0006 **3** *nk* **Don't Blame Me**[27] 8311 4-9-5 **68**................ MartinHarley 3 73
(Clive Cox) *led tl hdd after 1f: settled in 2nd: pushed along to ld again over 1f out: sn rdn: hdd last 50yds: lost 2nd nr fin* **11/2**
2211 **4** *½* **Awesome Allan (IRE)**[13] 8656 3-8-11 **67**................(t) KatherineGlenister[(7)] 1 71
(David Evans) *trckd ldrs: pushed along in 3rd 2f out: 3rd and ev ch 1f out: rdn and kpt on fnl f* **9/2**[2]
3601 **5** *nk* **Our Greta (IRE)**[27] 8328 3-9-3 **66**................ LukeMorris 7 69
(Michael Appleby) *mid-div: pushed along and effrt over 1f out: sn rdn: kpt on steadily fnl f* **8/1**
002 **6** *2 ¼* **Rockley Point**[9] 8743 4-9-4 **67**................(b) JoeyHaynes 6 63
(Paul D'Arcy) *mid-div: drvn in 5th wl over 1f out: rdn and n.m.r ent fnl f: kpt on* **3/1**[1]
6000 **7** *shd* **Joey's Destiny (IRE)**[17] 8557 7-9-5 **68**................ DougieCostello 5 64
(Kevin Frost) *hld up: drvn over 1f out: reminders and sme hdwy fnl f* **22/1**
3006 **8** *2 ¾* **Top Of The Bank**[9] 8743 4-8-10 **59**................(p) TonyHamilton 2 46
(Kristin Stubbs) *cl 2nd tl led after 1f: pushed along and hdd over 1f out: fdd* **10/1**
0606 **9** *nse* **Peachey Carnehan**[20] 8489 3-9-1 **67**................(v) PhilDennis[(3)] 12 54
(Michael Mullineaux) *hld up: drvn on outer wl over 1f out: sn rdn: no imp* **20/1**
0500 **10** *1 ¾* **Vallarta (IRE)**[10] 8722 7-9-2 **65**................ JackGarritty 11 47
(Ruth Carr) *mid-div: pushed along over 1f out: sn rdn: no imp* **20/1**
134P **11** *1 ¾* **Assertive Agent**[210] 2043 7-9-2 **65**................ TomMarquand 9 42
(Tony Carroll) *hld up: pushed along 2f out: hdwy over 1f out: no ex fnl f* **66/1**
**12** *1 ¾* **Buddha Boy**[79] 6704 3-9-1 **64**................ BenCurtis 13 36
(Miss Tracy M Reilly, Ire) *prom: drvn 2f out: sn rdn and wknd* **25/1**
2530 **13** *nk* **One Big Surprise**[46] 7771 5-9-7 **70**................(tp) ShaneKelly 10 41
(Richard Hughes) *mid-div: pushed along on outer 2f out: drvn and wknd over 1f out* **22/1**

1m 13.36s (-1.14) **Going Correction** -0.15s/f (Stan) **13** Ran SP% **125.7**
Speed ratings (Par 103): **101,100,99,98,98 95,95,91,91,89 87,84,84**
CSF £68.33 CT £412.45 TOTE £6.10: £2.20, £5.00, £2.00; EX 88.40 Trifecta £695.10.
**Owner** Kristen McEwen & Caroline Head **Bred** Clive Dennett **Trained** Upper Helmsley, N Yorks

**FOCUS**
This was run at a decent clip and in a time 1.16sec outside standard, although it was the slower division by 0.36sec. The runner-up has been rated near her best.

## 8876 BETWAY APPRENTICE H'CAP 2m 120y (Tp)
**4:30** (4:30) (Class 5) (0-70,76) 3-Y-O+ **£3,234** (£962; £481; £240) **Stalls** Low

Form RPR
205 **1** **Omotesando**[20] 8497 7-9-10 **66**................(p) CharlieBennett 13 74
(Oliver Greenall) *mid-div: hdwy 3f out: wnt 3rd 2f out: pushed along to chal over 1f out: sn rdn: led ent fnl f: styd on wl* **12/1**
6513 **2** *1* **Hallstatt (IRE)**[32] 8187 11-9-4 **64**................(t) TobyEley[(4)] 3 71
(John Mackie) *trckd ldrs: 3rd 3f out: pushed along into 2nd 2f out: rdn and ev ch over 1f out: styd on to establish clr 2nd ins fnl f* **20/1**
3216 **3** *4* **Alternate Route**[45] 7790 3-9-5 **68**................(p) HectorCrouch 10 70
(Sir Mark Prescott Bt) *cl up in 2nd tl led over 3f out: pushed along over 2f out where 2 l ld: reduced advantage whn rdn over 1f out: hdd ent fnl f: no ex* **15/8**[2]
4341 **4** *1 ¾* **Gabrial's Star**[7] 8771 8-10-4 **76** 6ex................(b) SebastianWoods[(2)] 2 76
(Richard Fahey) *trckd ldrs: pushed along 3f out: drvn in 4th over 2f out: rdn over 1f out: no imp* **7/4**[1]
5503 **5** *5* **Itlaaq**[24] 8386 11-9-9 **69**................(t) RyanTimby[(4)] 7 63
(Michael Easterby) *hld up: pushed along and effrt over 2f out: reminder 1f out: kpt on* **20/1**
3516 **6** *1* **Sheriff Of Nawton (IRE)**[72] 6944 6-9-12 **70**................ BenSanderson[(2)] 4 63
(Roger Fell) *hld up: effrt on inner 2f out: sn rdn: no ex* **22/1**
5406 **7** *1 ¼* **Wordiness**[5] 8778 9-9-12 **68**................ CallumShepherd 5 59
(David Evans) *mid-div: drvn 2f out: rdn wl over 1f out: no ex* **7/1**[3]
**8** *1* **Kalamkan (USA)**[318] 107 4-8-13 **55**................(v[1]) PatrickVaughan 12 45
(T G McCourt, Ire) *mid-div: drvn 3f: rdn 2f out: one pce* **50/1**
00/ **9** *hd* **Dalasiri (IRE)**[743] 7152 8-9-11 **67**................(t) TimClark 9 57
(Johnny Farrelly) *hld up: last 3f out: drvn and styd on past btn horses fr over 1f out: nvr a factor* **40/1**
3430 **10** *4* **Dakota City**[13] 8655 6-9-9 **65**................(b) RossaRyan 11 50
(Olly Murphy) *dwlt leaving stalls and lost many l: in rr: rdn to join rest after 2f: racd in rr: drvn 3f out: no imp* **25/1**
2000 **11** *1 ½* **Dream Serenade**[24] 8396 4-8-11 **53**................(h) AlistairRawlinson 1 36
(Michael Appleby) *led: hdd and drvn over 3f out: sn rdn and wknd* **28/1**
4630 **12** *5* **Bamako Du Chatelet (FR)**[36] 8072 6-9-5 **67**................(v) LukeCatton[(6)] 6 44
(Ian Williams) *mid-div: pushed along and lost pl over 3f out: wkng whn reminder over 1f out* **12/1**

3m 37.45s (-6.25) **Going Correction** -0.15s/f (Stan)
**WFA** 3 from 4yo+ 7lb **12** Ran SP% **124.6**
Speed ratings (Par 103): **108,107,105,104,102 102,101,100,100,98 98,95**
CSF £230.39 CT £661.11 TOTE £16.30: £3.30, £2.60, £1.30; EX 192.10 Trifecta £2166.80.
**Owner** Phil Evans **Bred** Darley **Trained** Oldcastle Heath, Cheshire

**FOCUS**
This moderate staying handicap was run at a fairly steady gallop. The runner-up is the key to the level - he's been rated to his best since 2015, with the winner close to his old best.
T/Jkpt: Not Won. T/Plt: £85.00 to a £1 stake. Pool: £79,549.47 - 682.96 winning units T/Qpdt: £30.00 to a £1 stake. Pool: £8,226.38 - 202.51 winning units **Keith McHugh**

# 8839 LINGFIELD (L-H)
Tuesday, November 21

**OFFICIAL GOING: Polytrack: standard**
Wind: Fresh, half behind in home straight Weather: Overcast

## 8877 32RED.COM/EBF NOVICE STKS 1m 1y(P)
**12:40** (12:42) (Class 5) 2-Y-O **£2,911** (£866; £432; £216) **Stalls** High

Form RPR
**1** **Rajaam (IRE)** 2-9-2 0................ SeanLevey 2 77+
(Richard Hannon) *s.i.s: sn in midfield: prog on inner to trck ldng pair over 2f out: shkn up to ld over 1f out but hrd pressed: hung rt fnl f: styd on wl* **7/1**
25 **2** *¾* **Key Player**[33] 8180 2-9-2 0................ CharlesBishop 10 75
(Eve Johnson Houghton) *trckd ldr: chal over 1f out: w wnr to 100yds out: nt qckn after* **16/1**
**3** *3* **Sweet Charity** 2-8-11 0................ FranBerry 1 63
(Denis Coakley) *hld up towards rr: prog on inner over 2f out: chsd ldng pair fnl f: no imp but shaped wl* **22/1**
**4** *nk* **Elhafei (USA)** 2-9-2 0................ JimCrowley 12 67+
(John Gosden) *t.k.h: hld up in last pair: prog on wd outside over 1f out: shkn up and styd on encouragingly fnl f* **6/1**[3]
5 **5** *2* **Rhode Island (IRE)**[13] 8677 2-9-2 0................ RobertHavlin 8 62
(John Gosden) *trckd ldng pair: nt qckn and lost pl over 2f out: one pce and n.d after* **3/1**[2]
1 **6** *nk* **Kassar (IRE)**[48] 7726 2-9-9 0................ KieranShoemark 7 69
(Roger Charlton) *blindfold and blanket on for entry: racd on outer: trckd ldrs: nudged by rival over 5f out: shkn up and nt qckn over 2f out: one pce and n.d after* **5/4**[1]
0 **7** *1* **Dawn Dash**[35] 8136 2-8-11 0................ RichardKingscote 9 54
(Ralph Beckett) *led: rdn and hdd over 1f out: wknd w tail swishing* **33/1**
**8** *¾* **Visor** 2-9-2 0................(h[1]) DanielMuscutt 3 57
(James Fanshawe) *hld up in rr: shkn up over 2f out: no real prog* **66/1**
**9** *1* **Outlane** 2-8-11 0................ LukeMorris 6 50
(Luca Cumani) *nvr beyond midfield: pushed along over 3f out: no real prog* **66/1**
**10** *7* **Villa Maria** 2-8-11 0................ BenCurtis 11 33
(K R Burke) *slowly away: a in last pair: t.o* **33/1**
04 **11** *1 ¾* **Spring Ability (IRE)**[20] 8502 2-8-13 0................ CallumShepherd[(3)] 5 34
(Laura Mongan) *free to post: plld hrd: chsd ldrs to 2f out: wknd rapidly: t.o* **66/1**

1m 38.36s (0.16) **Going Correction** -0.075s/f (Stan) **11** Ran SP% **116.8**
Speed ratings (Par 96): **96,95,92,91,89 89,88,87,86,79 78**
CSF £98.78 TOTE £7.50: £2.10, £3.80, £6.10; EX 95.50 Trifecta £4226.90.
**Owner** Hamdan Al Maktoum **Bred** Peter J Doyle Bloodstock Ltd **Trained** East Everleigh, Wilts

**FOCUS**
A fair novice in which the early gallop wasn't that strong. The opening level is a bit fluid.

## 8878 BETWAY H'CAP 1m 7f 169y(P)
**1:10** (1:12) (Class 6) (0-60,61) 3-Y-O+ **£2,264** (£673; £336; £168) **Stalls** Low

Form RPR
6/00 **1** **Lake Shore Drive (IRE)**[63] 7233 5-9-6 **56**................ StevieDonohoe 11 68+
(Johnny Farrelly) *hld up in midfield: prog on outer over 3f out: led wl over 2f out and shifted lft sn after: drvn clr and in n.d over 1f out* **6/1**[3]
0/0- **2** *4 ½* **Ding Ding**[15] 3401 6-9-0 **50**................ CharlesBishop 8 54
(Sheena West) *hld up in midfield: prog over 3f out: tried to chal over 2f out but qckly outpcd by wnr: one pce after* **5/1**[1]
3003 **3** *1* **Wintour Leap**[48] 7730 6-8-12 **55**................(p) WilliamCox[(7)] 1 58
(Robert Stephens) *trckd ldrs: lost pl over 3f out: effrt on outer over 2f out: drvn to take 3rd jst over 1f out: kpt on* **6/1**[3]
0004 **4** *3* **Bumble Bay**[14] 8647 7-8-9 **48**................(tp[1]) CallumShepherd[(3)] 4 47
(Robert Stephens) *hld up in rr: prog whn sltly impeded over 2f out: chal for 3rd 1f out: one pce after* **8/1**
5000 **5** *1 ¾* **Hatsaway (IRE)**[14] 8647 6-9-3 **58**................ PaddyBradley[(5)] 6 55
(Pat Phelan) *led 3f: styd handy: sltly impeded over 2f out and sn outpcd: n.d after* **16/1**
4-10 **6** *1 ¼* **Shan Dun na nGall (IRE)**[272] 859 6-9-3 **60**................(t) NicolaCurrie[(7)] 12 56
(Amy Murphy) *hld up in rr: effrt on outer over 3f out: outpcd 2f out: no ch after* **8/1**
0000 **7** *1* **Victor's Bet (SPA)**[14] 8647 8-9-11 **61**................ RyanTate 10 56
(Ralph J Smith) *stdd s: hld up in detached last: stl last whn sltly impeded over 2f out: pushed along on inner and modest late prog: nvr involved* **16/1**
-050 **8** *hd* **Meetings Man (IRE)**[56] 7490 10-9-5 **55**................(p) TomMarquand 2 49
(Ali Stronge) *t.k.h: prom: chsd ldr 7f out to 3f out: wkng whn sltly impeded over 2f out* **10/1**
023- **9** *1 ¼* **Canford Thompson**[340] 8410 4-9-3 **60**................ RossaRyan[(7)] 5 53
(Daniel Steele) *stdd s: t.k.h: hld up in rr: prog on outer 4f out to chse ldng pair over 2f out: lost 3rd and wknd qckly jst over 1f out* **16/1**

3044 **10** *10* **Marshall Aid (IRE)**[155] 3916 4-9-10 **60** LiamKeniry 3 41
(Mark Usher) *hld up in tch: wknd over 2f out: bhd fnl f* **11/2**[2]

4044 **11** *13* **Color Force (IRE)**[17] 8585 4-9-0 **50** (t) JosephineGordon 7 45+
(Daniel Kubler) *t.k.h: w ldrs: led after 7f to wl over 2f out: wkng whn bdly hmpd sn after: rdr all but off and miraculous rcvry: t.o after* **20/1**

2640 **12** *3* **Chestnut Storm (IRE)**[29] 8301 4-9-7 **57** LukeMorris 9 29+
(Brian Barr) *led after 3f to after 7f: drvn 5f out: wkng whn hmpd over 2f out: eased and t.o* **33/1**

3m 24.69s (-1.01) **Going Correction** -0.075s/f (Stan) **12** Ran SP% **117.3**
Speed ratings (Par 101): **99,96,96,94,93 93,92,92,92,87 80,79**
CSF £35.64 CT £189.92 TOTE £10.00: £3.50, £2.40, £2.00; EX 51.90 Trifecta £341.10.
**Owner** P Tosh **Bred** Barronstown Stud And Cobra **Trained** Enmore, Somerset
■ Stewards' Enquiry : Stevie Donohoe seven-day ban: careless riding (Dec 5-9, 11-12)

**FOCUS**
A moderate staying contest. It's been rated around the third and the second's previous Flat form.

## 8879 BETWAY SPRINT H'CAP 6f 1y(P)
**1:40** (1:41) (Class 4) (0-85,87) 3-Y-O+ **£4,690** (£1,395; £697; £348) **Stalls Low**

Form RPR

-042 **1** **Gorgeous Noora (IRE)**[19] 8540 3-9-5 **83** LukeMorris 6 91
(Luca Cumani) *trckd ldrs: rdn over 1f out: clsd fnl f to ld last 75yds: drvn out* **11/4**[1]

3655 **2** *½* **Rose Berry**[14] 8645 3-8-9 **80** (h) NicolaCurrie(7) 2 86
(Chris Dwyer) *hld up in last trio: shkn up and nt qckn over 2f out: picked up fnl f: fin wl to take 2nd last strides but jst too late* **9/2**[2]

0200 **3** *1* **Diamond Lady**[34] 8167 6-9-1 **82** HollieDoyle(3) 5 85
(William Stone) *trckd ldr: drvn to ld jst over 1f out: hdd last 75yds: one pce and lost 2nd fnl strides* **25/1**

6055 **4** *shd* **Kodiline (IRE)**[35] 8129 3-9-8 **86** (v) AdamKirby 7 89
(Clive Cox) *dwlt: sn in 6th: rdn and outpcd wl over 1f out: styd on again u.p fnl f: clsng at fin* **6/1**

0346 **5** *½* **Shamsaya (IRE)**[72] 6970 3-9-5 **83** SilvestreDeSousa 4 84
(Simon Crisford) *trckd ldrs: cl up and drvn over 1f out: nt qckn and kpt on same pce fnl f* **7/1**

520 **6** *½* **Super Julius**[19] 8540 3-9-7 **85** (p) CharlesBishop 10 84
(Eve Johnson Houghton) *hld up in rr: rdn 2f out and sn outpcd: kpt on u.p on outer fnl f: nvr able to chal* **20/1**

0000 **7** *½* **Highland Acclaim (IRE)**[4] 8812 6-9-9 **87** (h) SeanLevey 1 85
(David O'Meara) *led: rdn and hdd jst over 1f out: no ex and lost several pls last 100yds* **16/1**

1131 **8** *1 ¾* **Short Work**[21] 8489 4-9-5 **83** (b) DanielTudhope 8 75
(David O'Meara) *trckd ldrs: rdn 2f out: lost pl and wknd over 1f out* **11/2**

3640 **9** *¾* **Medici Banchiere**[24] 8418 3-9-5 **83** BenCurtis 3 73
(K R Burke) *nvr gng wl: sn shoved along in last trio: nvr a factor* **5/1**[3]

4300 **10** *2 ¾* **Just An Idea (IRE)**[28] 8310 3-9-1 **79** StevieDonohoe 9 60
(Harry Dunlop) *sn in last: nvr a factor* **100/1**

1m 10.49s (-1.41) **Going Correction** -0.075s/f (Stan) **10** Ran SP% **119.2**
Speed ratings (Par 105): **106,105,104,103,103 102,101,99,98,94**
CSF £15.13 CT £259.36 TOTE £3.60: £1.60, £1.80, £5.30; EX 21.20 Trifecta £333.40.
**Owner** Saleh Al Homaizi & Imad Al Sagar **Bred** Kabansk Ltd & Rathbarry Stud **Trained** Newmarket, Suffolk

**FOCUS**
There was a typically bunched finish to this sprint handicap. The second has been rated pretty much to her best.

## 8880 BETWAY H'CAP 1m 2f (P)
**2:10** (2:11) (Class 3) (0-95,94) 3-Y-O-**£7,246** (£2,168; £1,084; £542; £270) **Stalls Low**

Form RPR

4513 **1** **Fayez (IRE)**[28] 8315 3-9-0 **90** DanielTudhope 7 99+
(David O'Meara) *hld up in midfield: gng strly 2f out: prog on outer over 1f out and qckly clsd to chal: hung lft but drvn to edge ahd last 75yds* **10/1**

0000 **2** *nk* **Brex Drago (ITY)**[52] 7602 5-9-3 **90** (b[1]) TomMarquand 1 98
(Marco Botti) *cl up on inner: rdn 2f out: led jst ins fnl f but pressed: drvn and hdd last 75yds* **33/1**

0303 **3** *1 ¾* **Emenem**[51] 7649 3-9-0 **90** SilvestreDeSousa 10 95
(Simon Dow) *prog on outer to trck ldr after 2f: chal over 2f out: stl upsides 1f out: one pce fnl f* **8/1**[3]

1-13 **4** *¾* **Middle Kingdom (USA)**[12] 8705 3-9-4 **94** (t) RobertHavlin 2 97
(John Gosden) *pushed up to ld: pressed and rdn 2f out: hdd and no rspnse jst ins fnl f* **11/10**[1]

3242 **5** *nse* **Cape Peninsular**[63] 7234 4-9-0 **87** (b[1]) LukeMorris 5 90
(James Tate) *dwlt and urged along early to chse ldrs: rdn over 2f out: hanging lft and hld whn nt clr run ins fnl f: drvn and kpt on* **12/1**

5501 **6** *2* **Ay Ay (IRE)**[41] 7959 3-8-7 **86** HollieDoyle(3) 4 85
(David Elsworth) *t.k.h: trapped out wd and hld up: effrt 2f out: nvr able to threaten* **9/1**

1200 **7** *1* **Sir Titan**[10] 8736 3-8-8 **84** BenCurtis 3 81
(Marcus Tregoning) *t.k.h: prom: trapped out wd bnd 2f out: no prog over 1f out* **20/1**

6660 **8** *¾* **Coillte Cailin (IRE)**[31] 8244 7-9-0 **87** KieranShoemark 8 82
(David O'Meara) *slowly away: hld up in rr: drvn and modest prog on inner wl over 1f out: nvr a threat* **40/1**

4603 **9** *1* **Red Tea**[18] 8566 4-9-2 **89** FranBerry 6 82
(Peter Hiatt) *chsd ldr 2f: styd prom: drvn over 2f out: lost pl and fdd over 1f out* **33/1**

0504 **10** *¾* **Gothic Empire (IRE)**[27] 8344 5-8-8 **81** RyanTate 12 73
(Richard Rowe) *stdd s: hld up in last pair: pushed along and no real prog 2f out: nvr remotely involved* **66/1**

0000 **11** *hd* **Vettori Rules**[54] 7558 4-9-1 **88** JosephineGordon 11 80
(Gay Kelleway) *t.k.h: hld up towards rr: rdn and no prog over 2f out: wl btn after* **66/1**

1-51 **12** *½* **Celestial Spheres (IRE)**[18] 8561 3-8-11 **87** (p) WilliamBuick 13 78
(Charlie Appleby) *bustled along fr wdst draw: trapped out wd and a in rr: nvr able to make prog* **11/2**[2]

200 **13** *2* **Believe It (IRE)**[73] 6933 5-8-9 **89** (p) StephenCummins(7) 9 76
(Richard Hughes) *stdd s: hld up in last pair: pushed along over 2f out: no prog and nvr involved* **50/1**

2m 4.24s (-2.36) **Going Correction** -0.075s/f (Stan) **13** Ran SP% **118.9**
**WFA** 3 from 4yo+ 3lb
Speed ratings (Par 107): **106,105,104,103,103 102,101,100,99,99 99,98,97**
CSF £302.94 CT £2751.10 TOTE £10.40: £2.30, £6.90, £2.10; EX 314.40 Trifecta £5886.30.
**Owner** Northern Lads & Nawton Racing **Bred** Miss Siobhan Ryan **Trained** Upper Helmsley, N Yorks

**FOCUS**
Quite a good handicap, and an impressive winner. It's been rated around the third.

## 8881 PLAY JACKPOT GAMES AT SUNBETS.CO.UK/VEGAS CLAIMING STKS 7f 1y(P)
**2:40** (2:40) (Class 6) 3-Y-O+ **£2,264** (£673; £336; £168) **Stalls Low**

Form RPR

-001 **1** **Unforgiving Minute**[73] 6949 6-9-7 87 AdamKirby 9 84
(John Butler) *trckd ldrs: rousted to chal 2f out: led over 1f out and drvn: decisive move and hld on as others clsd at fin* **9/4**[1]

4202 **2** *½* **Nezar (IRE)**[14] 8645 6-8-13 80 JackOsborn(7) 4 81
(Dean Ivory) *hld up in last trio: prog on inner over 1f out: chsd wnr ins fnl f: r.o and clsng at fin: too much to do* **11/2**[3]

0505 **3** *½* **Dutiful Son (IRE)**[14] 8646 7-8-12 70 SilvestreDeSousa 5 72
(Simon Dow) *trckd ldrs: rdn wl over 1f out: prog to dispute 2nd fnl f: kpt on but nvr able to chal* **14/1**

2560 **4** *nse* **Al Khan (IRE)**[21] 8486 8-8-11 75 (tp) KevinStott 3 71
(Kevin Ryan) *t.k.h: hld up in midfield: hrd rdn fr 2f out: hanging lft bhd rival over 1f out: styd on fnl f: nrst fin* **7/1**

6005 **5** *shd* **Outer Space**[12] 8706 6-9-3 78 DougieCostello 2 77
(Jamie Osborne) *hld up in midfield: gng strly 2f out: effrt over 1f out: styd on to press for a pl fnl f: too much to do* **3/1**[2]

3206 **6** *1 ½* **Letmestopyouthere (IRE)**[10] 8736 3-9-1 80 MattCosham(3) 7 74
(David Evans) *racd on outer: hld up in last trio: rdn 2f out: kpt on fr over 1f out: nvr enough pce to chal* **11/2**[3]

1303 **7** *1 ½* **Morache Music**[29] 8296 9-8-11 72 (p) LiamKeniry 10 63
(Patrick Chamings) *t.k.h: hld up in rr: no prog 2f out: one pce and no threat after* **20/1**

3-00 **8** *hd* **Fullon Clarets**[29] 8296 5-8-2 62 (p) NicolaCurrie(7) 6 60
(Laura Mongan) *led to over 1f out: wknd fnl f* **66/1**

1440 **9** *½* **Lunar Deity**[12] 8706 8-8-12 80 (t) MillyNaseb(7) 8 69
(Stuart Williams) *s.s: mostly in last: nvr a factor* **20/1**

3004 **10** *nk* **Yeeoow (IRE)**[69] 7056 8-8-13 70 (v) BenCurtis 12 62
(K R Burke) *pressed ldr to 2f out: wknd over 1f out: dismntd after fin* **25/1**

0010 **11** *4 ½* **Bingo George (IRE)**[8] 8772 4-8-11 53 (t) TomMarquand 1 48
(Mark Rimell) *chsd ldng pair to over 2f out: wknd qckly* **100/1**

1m 24.45s (-0.35) **Going Correction** -0.075s/f (Stan)
**WFA** 3 from 4yo+ 1lb **11** Ran SP% **121.6**
Speed ratings (Par 101): **99,98,97,97,97 95,94,94,93,93 87**
CSF £14.78 TOTE £2.90: £1.30, £1.90, £3.10; EX 16.30 Trifecta £116.90.There was no bid for the winner.
**Owner** Power Geneva Ltd **Bred** Equine Breeding Limited **Trained** Newmarket, Suffolk

**FOCUS**
A decent, competitive claimer, and jockeyship proved the difference. The weaker members and compressed nature of the field govern the level.

## 8882 32RED CASINO NURSERY H'CAP 5f 6y(P)
**3:10** (3:10) (Class 5) (0-75,77) 2-Y-O **£2,911** (£866; £432; £216) **Stalls High**

Form RPR

3031 **1** **Joegogo (IRE)**[10] 8746 2-9-6 **73** FranBerry 2 78
(David Evans) *mde all: drvn over 1f out: kpt on wl fnl f* **5/4**[1]

100 **2** *1* **Dotted Swiss (IRE)**[13] 8670 2-9-7 **74** SeanLevey 5 75
(Richard Hannon) *hld up in 4th: gng strly 2f out: shkn up over 1f out: nt qckn but kpt on fnl f to snatch 2nd last stride* **3/1**[2]

6441 **3** *shd* **Inuk (IRE)**[38] 8027 2-7-12 **58** (p) NicolaCurrie(7) 1 59
(Richard Hughes) *s.i.s and urged along to chse ldng pair: gng bttr after 2f: drvn to chse wnr 1f out: kpt on but a hld: lost 2nd post* **9/2**[3]

2623 **4** *3 ½* **Deviate (IRE)**[57] 7450 2-9-7 **77** PaddyPilley(3) 6 65
(Tom Dascombe) *pressed wnr to over 1f out: lost 2nd and wknd fnl f* **13/2**

1000 **5** *1 ¾* **Brockey Rise (IRE)**[63] 7228 2-8-11 **67** MattCosham(3) 3 49+
(David Evans) *sn last: outpcd: no imp* **10/1**

58.7s (-0.10) **Going Correction** -0.075s/f (Stan) **5** Ran SP% **110.1**
Speed ratings (Par 96): **97,95,95,89,86**
CSF £5.21 TOTE £2.40: £1.60, £1.30; EX 5.40 Trifecta £11.40.
**Owner** Wayne Clifford **Bred** Barry Noonan And Denis Noonan **Trained** Pandy, Monmouths

**FOCUS**
A fair nursery. The second has been rated to her best.

## 8883 BETWAY APPRENTICE H'CAP 1m 4f (P)
**3:40** (3:40) (Class 6) (0-65,67) 3-Y-O **£2,264** (£673; £336; £168) **Stalls Low**

Form RPR

0051 **1** **What A Welcome**[19] 8549 3-10-0 **67** CharlieBennett 5 78+
(Patrick Chamings) *trckd ldng pair: wnt 2nd 2f out: rdn to ld over 1f out: drvn 3 l clr fnl f: hld on nr fin* **13/8**[1]

0-16 **2** *¾* **Kohinoor Diamond (IRE)**[40] 7990 3-9-9 **62** (p[1]) HectorCrouch 6 70+
(Sir Mark Prescott Bt) *hld up in last trio: racd awkwardly whn asked for effrt over 2f out: consented to run on fnl f but hanging and stl racd awkwardly: tk 2nd last 100yds: clsd on wnr nr fin* **7/2**[2]

1005 **3** *2 ¾* **I'm Running Late**[34] 8160 3-9-13 **66** JackDuern 1 69
(Dean Ivory) *led: rdn and hdd over 1f out: qckly outpcd by clung on to 3rd* **6/1**[3]

3326 **4** *nk* **Ode To Glory**[45] 7831 3-9-5 **65** SebastianWoods(7) 4 68
(Rae Guest) *trckd ldrs: rdn over 2f out: nt qckn over 1f out and safely btn after: one pce* **8/1**

4004 **5** *nk* **Widnes**[28] 8327 3-9-8 **61** (b) TimClark 3 63
(Alan Bailey) *hld up: stmbld sn after s: rdn over 2f out: outpcd after: kpt on u.p but no ch* **12/1**

6002 **6** *½* **Desert Song**[27] 8346 3-9-0 **56** PaddyBradley(3) 9 58
(Pat Phelan) *trckd ldrs: rdn and nt qckn 2f out: one pce after and safely btn* **14/1**

160 **7** *5* **Enola (IRE)**[132] 4761 3-9-9 **62** KieranShoemark 2 56
(Amy Murphy) *hld up in last trio: brief effrt on inner 2f out: sn no prog and wknd* **33/1**

4252 **8** *2 ¼* **Relevant (IRE)**[17] 8585 3-9-12 **65** (p[1]) PaddyPilley 10 55
(K R Burke) *trckd ldr to 2f out: wknd qckly* **20/1**

0040 **9** *5* **Ripper Street (IRE)**[19] 8538 3-8-4 **46** oh1 (h) JaneElliott(3) 8 28
(Christine Dunnett) *hld up in last trio: shkn up and wknd over 3f out: bhd fnl 2f* **80/1**

0541 **10** *9* **Bird For Life**[13] 8673 3-8-4 **48** NicolaCurrie(5) 7 16
(Mark Usher) *t.k.h: hld up in midfield on outer: lost pl fr 5f out: bhd 2f out: t.o* **12/1**

2m 30.63s (-2.37) **Going Correction** -0.075s/f (Stan) **10** Ran SP% **116.7**
Speed ratings (Par 98): **104,103,101,101,101 100,97,96,92,86**
CSF £6.94 CT £26.91 TOTE £2.50: £1.20, £1.50, £2.30; EX 7.30 Trifecta £35.00.
**Owner** Mrs K Meredith **Bred** Newsells Park Stud **Trained** Baughurst, Hants

**FOCUS**
A modest affair, but the first two finished nicely clear.

T/Jkpt: Not Won. T/Plt: £2,401.70 to a £1 stake. Pool: £75,507.68 - 22.95 winning units. T/Qpdt: £56.10 to a £1 stake. Pool: £11,289.82 - 148.90 winning units. **Jonathan Neesom**

## 8777 CHANTILLY (R-H)

Tuesday, November 21

**OFFICIAL GOING: Polytrack: standard; turf: very soft**

### 8884a PRIX HEROD (LISTED RACE) (2YO) (TURF) 7f

1:20 2-Y-O **£25,641** (£10,256; £7,692; £5,128; £2,564)

RPR

1 **Wind Chimes**[22] 2-8-9 0 Pierre-CharlesBoudot 11 100
(A Fabre, France) **19/10**[1]

2 3 ½ **Louis D'Or (IRE)**[33] 8195 2-8-13 0 MaximeGuyon 2 95
(T Castanheira, France) **29/10**[2]

3 3 ½ **Omaha Beach (IRE)**[14] 2-8-9 0 (p) MickaelBarzalona 10 82
(Mme Pia Brandt, France) **77/10**

4 hd **Beau Massagot (FR)** 2-8-13 0 FranckBlondel 7 85
(C Escuder, France) **26/1**

5 ¾ **Palya (FR)**[14] 2-8-9 0 (b) ClementLecoeuvre 5 79
(B Legros, France) **48/1**

6 snk **Salt Lake City (FR)**[12] 2-8-13 0 SebastienMaillot 1 83
(Robert Collet, France) **221/10**

7 2 ½ **Forza Capitano (FR)**[22] 2-8-13 0 AurelienLemaitre 4 76
(H-A Pantall, France) **106/10**

8 7 **Arrogant (IRE)**[30] 8271 2-8-13 0 TheoBachelot 6 58
(Jose Santos) *dwlt: in rr early: nvr a factor* **144/10**

9 2 ½ **Dusky Dance (IRE)**[79] 6726 2-8-13 0 EddyHardouin 8 52
(P Schiergen, Germany) **33/1**

10 nse **Fou Rire (IRE)**[22] 2-8-9 0 StephanePasquier 3 48
(F Chappet, France) **13/2**[3]

11 1 ½ **Shrewd Approach (IRE)**[51] 7647 2-8-9 0 GregoryBenoist 9 44
(Simon Crisford) *sn trcking ldrs: rdn over 2f out: limited rspnse and eased fnl f* **195/10**

1m 29.78s (3.68) **11** Ran SP% **118.0**

PARI-MUTUEL (all including 1 euro stake): WIN 2.90; PLACE 1.30, 1.40, 2.00; DF 4.50; SF 10.10.

**Owner** Derrick Smith & Mrs John Magnier & Michael Tabor **Bred** Ecurie Des Monceaux **Trained** Chantilly, France

### 8885a PRIX DE L'OAK TREE (CONDITIONS) (3YO) (POLYTRACK) 1m 1f

1:50 3-Y-O **£11,111** (£4,444; £3,333; £2,222; £1,111)

RPR

1 **Passion Nonantaise (FR)**[37] 3-8-10 0 Pierre-CharlesBoudot 5 82
(J-P Gauvin, France) **31/10**[1]

2 ¾ **Nonza (FR)**[213] 3-8-10 0 MlleZoePfeil(5) 12 85
(H-F Devin, France) **67/10**

3 hd **Mightily**[15] 3-9-2 0 (p) MickaelBarzalona 4 86
(A Fabre, France) *settled bhd ldrs: tk clsr order 3f out: rdn to chal over 1f out: briefly led: sn hdd and lost 2nd on post* **18/5**[2]

4 ¾ **Silver Express (FR)**[197] 3-8-10 0 (p) GregoryBenoist 3 78
(Mme Pia Brandt, France) **26/1**

5 ½ **Snirvana (IRE)**[46] 3-8-7 0 JeromeMoutard(6) 8 80
(F Head, France) **49/10**[3]

6 snk **Assanilka (FR)**[27] 8351 3-8-3 0 (p) HayleyTurner(4) 2 74
(Harry Dunlop) *led: hdd after 3f: remained cl up: rdn to chal 2f out: rdn over 1f out: wknd ins fnl f* **83/10**

7 nk **Opinion Maker (IRE)**[20] 3-8-6 0 AlexandreChesneau(8) 1 80
(G Botti, France) **99/10**

8 1 ½ **Blues Music (FR)**[85] 3-8-10 0 IoritzMendizabal 13 73
(Simone Brogi, France) **179/10**

9 4 ½ **Alexandrite**[20] 3-8-10 0 StephanePasquier 11 64
(Mme C Head-Maarek, France) **18/1**

10 5 ½ **Cyelia (FR)**[20] 3-8-8 0 ow1 TristanBaron(3) 9 53
(Arry Benillouche, France) **103/1**

11 snk **Savile Row (FR)**[152] 3994 3-9-0 0 (p) EddyHardouin 6 56
(Frau Erika Mader, Germany) **27/1**

12 dist **Fond Du Coeur (IRE)**[83] 3-8-7 0 MaximeGuyon 10
(Mme Pia Brandt, France) **31/1**

1m 50.53s **12** Ran SP% **117.9**

PARI-MUTUEL (all including 1 euro stake): WIN 4.10; PLACE 1.50, 2.30, 1.70; DF 11.50; SF 24.50.

**Owner** Jean-Paul Gauvin **Bred** J-P Gauvin & Earl Haras De Nonant Le Pin **Trained** France

## 8668 KEMPTON (A.W) (R-H)

Wednesday, November 22

**OFFICIAL GOING: Polytrack: standard to slow**

Wind: Fresh, behind Weather: Clear

### 8886 32RED ON THE APP STORE H'CAP 1m 1f 219y(P)

4:10 (4:10) (Class 5) (0-75,77) 3-Y-O+ **£3,234** (£962; £481; £240) **Stalls** Low

Form RPR

0332 1 **Peace And Plenty**[22] 8497 3-9-2 **73** SilvestreDeSousa 11 83
(William Muir) *trckd ldng trio: hung lft and wd bnd 2f out: lost grnd and sn drvn: clsd fr over 1f out: tk 2nd 150yds out: styd on to ld last strides* **11/4**[2]

2332 2 ½ **Hairdryer**[230] 1583 4-9-7 **75** OisinMurphy 2 84
(Andrew Balding) *trckd ldng trio: prog on inner and gd run through fr 2f out: rdn to ld over 1f out: fnd little in front and hdd last strides* **5/2**[1]

4046 3 2 ¼ **Jive Talking (IRE)**[46] 7817 3-9-4 **75** (h) AdamKirby 12 80
(Michael Bell) *prog fr wdst draw to ld after 2f: rdn and hdd over 1f out: one pce* **8/1**[3]

4300 4 4 **Sufi**[146] 4267 3-9-1 **75** HectorCrouch(3) 1 72
(Ken Cunningham-Brown) *disp ld 2f: chsd ldr to 2f out: wknd over 1f out* **8/1**[3]

3600 5 2 ¼ **Buckland Beau**[22] 8497 6-9-2 **70** StevieDonohoe 5 62
(Charlie Fellowes) *hld up in last pair: prog on outer over 2f out: rchd 5th over 1f out but no ch: no hdwy after* **8/1**[3]

4500 6 3 ¼ **The Yellow Bus**[30] 8295 4-9-2 **70** KieranO'Neill 7 56
(Daniel Steele) *disp ld 2f: chsd ldr after: rdn over 3f out: wknd 2f out* **25/1**

4140 7 ½ **Tee It Up Tommo (IRE)**[40] 7999 8-9-0 **75** (t) WilliamCox(7) 4 60
(Daniel Steele) *mostly in last pair: rdn 3f out: no real prog* **50/1**

0215 8 2 **Rubis**[29] 8327 4-8-8 **62** PatrickMathers 9 43
(Richard Fahey) *hld up towards rr and racd wd: dropped to last u.p over 2f out: no ch after* **16/1**

5040 9 nk **First Experience**[15] 8646 6-8-12 **69** CharlieBennett(3) 3 49
(Lee Carter) *hld up towards rr: rdn and no prog 3f out* **50/1**

6005 10 4 ½ **Biotic**[15] 8648 6-8-11 **65** (b[1]) RyanTate 8 36
(Rod Millman) *hld up towards rr: pushed along and no prog over 2f out: eased over 1f out* **14/1**

0450 R **Plead**[96] 6160 3-9-6 **77** JackMitchell 10
(Archie Watson) *ref to r: tk no part* **10/1**

2m 5.9s (-2.10) **Going Correction** 0.0s/f (Stan)

**WFA** 3 from 4yo+ 3lb **11** Ran SP% **118.0**

Speed ratings (Par 103): **108,107,105,102,100 98,97,96,95,92**

CSF £9.94 CT £47.65 TOTE £3.90: £1.60, £1.10, £2.30; EX 9.30 Trifecta £37.50.

**Owner** Muir Racing Partnership - Doncaster **Bred** Newsells Park Stud **Trained** Lambourn, Berks

**FOCUS**

A fair handicap.

### 8887 CLOSE BROTHERS BUSINESS FINANCE NURSERY H'CAP 7f (P)

4:40 (4:40) (Class 6) (0-65,65) 2-Y-O **£2,587** (£770; £384; £192) **Stalls** Low

Form RPR

6122 1 **Roman Spinner**[49] 7734 2-9-7 **65** (t) LukeMorris 14 70
(Rae Guest) *hld up in last pair fr wdst draw: prog and taken to outer wl over 1f out: r.o fnl f to ld last 75yds: won gng away* **9/2**[3]

045 2 1 **Crystal Casque**[36] 8130 2-9-4 **62** OisinMurphy 4 64
(Rod Millman) *t.k.h: trckd ldrs: wnt 2nd 2f out: drvn to ld 1f out: hdd and outpcd last 75yds* **14/1**

0655 3 1 ¾ **Obrigada**[15] 8658 2-9-3 **61** JosephineGordon 10 58
(Tom Clover) *dwlt: t.k.h: hld up towards rr: n.m.r 1/2-way: prog over 2f out to chse ldrs over 1f out: kpt on same pce fnl f and unable to chal* **10/1**

644 4 nse **Dashing Dusty (IRE)**[55] 7535 2-9-3 **61** DougieCostello 11 58
(Jamie Osborne) *pressed ldr to 2f out: stl chalng 1f out: one pce fnl f* **25/1**

0000 5 ½ **Jazzy Girl (IRE)**[6] 8793 2-8-8 **52** EdwardGreatrex 5 48
(Brendan Powell) *led: rdn 2f out: hdd and fdd 1f out* **33/1**

2431 6 nk **Secratario (FR)**[15] 8644 2-9-7 **65** (p) ShaneKelly 9 60+
(Richard Hughes) *trckd ldrs disputing 5th: rdn and fnd nil 2f out: kpt on again fnl f but nvr able to chal* **3/1**[2]

0002 7 ¾ **Sotomayor**[15] 8644 2-9-6 **64** SeanLevey 6 57
(Richard Hannon) *s.s: mostly in last: urged along over 2f out: prog u.p over 1f out: chsd ldrs fnl f: one pce after* **11/4**[1]

600 8 4 ½ **Golden Deal (IRE)**[49] 7725 2-9-4 **62** (h) TimmyMurphy 1 43
(Richard Phillips) *trckd ldrs disputing 5th: shkn up over 2f out: wknd over 1f out* **40/1**

0000 9 5 **Blackwood**[21] 8500 2-8-5 **49** RobHornby 13 16
(Michael Blanshard) *in tch to over 2f out: sn wknd qckly* **100/1**

6162 10 2 **Give Em A Clump (IRE)**[6] 8804 2-9-7 **65** (v) AdamKirby 2 27
(David Evans) *t.k.h: trckd ldrs tl wknd qckly 2f out* **9/2**[3]

000 11 1 ¾ **Miss Condi**[15] 8644 2-8-1 **45** (h[1]) KieranO'Neill 12 2
(Martin Keighley) *a in rr: rdn 1/2-way: wknd over 2f out* **100/1**

1m 27.76s (1.76) **Going Correction** 0.0s/f (Stan) **11** Ran SP% **115.0**

Speed ratings (Par 94): **89,87,85,85,85 84,84,78,73,70 68**

CSF £60.25 CT £609.69 TOTE £5.00: £1.90, £4.30, £2.70; EX 62.50 Trifecta £300.10.

**Owner** Reprobates Too **Bred** Ashbrittle Stud **Trained** Newmarket, Suffolk

**FOCUS**

The early pace wasn't that strong and the winner found the best turn of foot, building on her recent form.

### 8888 32RED CASINO/EBFSTALLIONS.COM NOVICE STKS (DIV I) 7f (P)

5:10 (5:13) (Class 5) 2-Y-O **£3,234** (£962; £481; £240) **Stalls** Low

Form RPR

02 1 **Flavius Titus**[26] 8381 2-9-2 0 JackMitchell 2 80
(Roger Varian) *wl in tch disputing 6th: prog over 2f out to chse ldr wl over 1f out: wandered whn shkn up but narrow ld fnl f: asserted last 75yds despite rdr dropping whip* **13/2**[3]

3 2 1 **Salute The Soldier (GER)**[26] 8388 2-9-2 0 AdamKirby 12 77
(Clive Cox) *sn led: rdn 2f out: narrowly hdd fnl f: kpt on wl but hld last 75yds* **11/8**[1]

3 3 ½ **I Can (IRE)** 2-9-2 0 FranBerry 9 69+
(Henry Candy) *hld up in 10th: prog 2f out: pushed along and styd on to take 3rd last 150yds: no threat to ldng pair but shaped wl* **33/1**

4 1 ½ **Mushtaq (IRE)** 2-9-2 0 SeanLevey 6 64
(Richard Hannon) *chsd ldr to wl over 1f out: one pce after and steadily lft bhd* **4/1**[2]

0 5 1 ¼ **Doctor Knox (IRE)**[14] 8677 2-9-2 0 (t[1]) JimCrowley 10 60+
(Paul Cole) *in tch disputing 6th: nt qckn over 2f out: one pce fr over 1f out* **20/1**

0 6 nk **Daltrey**[19] 8560 2-9-2 0 JamesDoyle 8 60
(John Gosden) *trckd ldrs disputing 4th: shkn up over 2f out: fdd over 1f out* **7/1**

5 7 2 **Brigham Young**[20] 8545 2-9-2 0 LiamKeniry 13 54
(Ed Walker) *dropped in fr wd draw and disp 8th: pushed along over 2f out: no real prog whn reminders fnl f* **20/1**

8 1 **Three Weeks (USA)** 2-9-2 0 DanielTudhope 7 52
(William Haggas) *slowly away: rn green in last trio and long way off the pce: sme late hdwy: bttr for experience* **8/1**

0 9 ½ **Purple Jazz (IRE)**[20] 8545 2-9-2 0 KieranO'Neill 4 50
(George Baker) *trckd ldrs disputing 4th: wknd wl over 1f out* **150/1**

3 10 3 ¼ **Classic Charm**[18] 8594 2-8-8 0 JackDuern(3) 11 36
(Dean Ivory) *t.k.h: trckd ldng pair to 2f out: sn wknd* **25/1**

11 1 ½ **Sheila Rose (IRE)** 2-8-11 0 OisinMurphy 5 32
(Denis Coakley) *in tch disputing 8th: pushed along sn after 1/2-way: wknd on inner over 2f out* **50/1**

12 1 ½ **My Heart** 2-8-11 0 StevieDonohoe 14 28
(Ismail Mohammed) *dwlt fr wdst draw: a wl in rr* **50/1**

13 10 **More Harry** 2-9-2 0 DougieCostello 3 6
(Neil Mulholland) *difficult to load into stall: dwlt: t.k.h and hld up in rr: wknd over 2f out: t.o* **200/1**

14 2 ½ **Cativo Ragazzo** 2-9-2 0 RobertHavlin 1
(John E Long) *dwlt: v green and a last: t.o* **250/1**

1m 25.9s (-0.10) **Going Correction** 0.0s/f (Stan) **14** Ran SP% **120.8**

Speed ratings (Par 96): **100,98,94,93,91 91,89,87,87,83 81,80,68,65**

CSF £14.85 TOTE £7.60: £2.00, £1.20, £8.00; EX 20.20 Trifecta £523.60.

**Owner** Sheikh Mohammed Obaid Al Maktoum **Bred** Cheveley Park Stud Ltd **Trained** Newmarket, Suffolk

**FOCUS**
Not a bad novice, and there were one or two noteworthy performances. A step forward from the winner, with the runner-up rated as replicating his debut form.

## 8889 32RED CASINO/EBFSTALLIONS.COM NOVICE STKS (DIV II) 7f (P)
5:40 (5:46) (Class 5) 2-Y-O £3,234 (£962; £481; £120; £120) Stalls Low

Form RPR
2 1 **Qaysar (FR)**[28] 8350 2-9-2 0 SeanLevey 8 85+
(Richard Hannon) *trckd ldrs: shkn up over 2f out: stl only 6th over 1f out: clsd qckly after to ld 150yds out: on top at fin* 1/2[1]
55 2 1 **Crack On Crack On**[28] 8350 2-9-2 0 AdamKirby 9 80
(Clive Cox) *t.k.h: trckd ldrs: shkn up over 2f out: prog to ld briefly 1f out: outpcd last 100yds* 9/2[2]
3 1 3/4 **Employer (IRE)** 2-9-2 0 JosephineGordon 3 75+
(Hugo Palmer) *trckd ldrs on inner: prog 2f out: chal 1f out: styd on same pce fnl f* 7/1[3]
6 4 3/4 **Mrs Benson (IRE)**[44] 7875 2-8-11 0 RobHornby 4 68
(Michael Blanshard) *led 1f: trckd ldr: rdn over 2f out: stl on terms jst over 1f out: fdd* 66/1
4 dht **La Maquina** 2-9-2 0 LiamKeniry 10 73+
(George Baker) *slowly away: t.k.h and sn in midfield: pushed along over 2f out: no imp on ldrs over 1f out: styd on encouragingly ins fnl f* 20/1
6 1/2 **Tribal Warrior** 2-9-2 0 LukeMorris 14 72
(James Tate) *pressed ldrs: rdn 2f out: stl cl up over 1f out: fdd fnl f* 33/1
0 7 1 1/4 **Rux Ruxx (IRE)**[23] 8474 2-8-11 0 OisinMurphy 12 64
(Andrew Balding) *racd keenly: led after 1f: rdn 2f out: hdd & wknd 1f out* 20/1
06 8 4 **Corazon Espinado (IRE)**[144] 4349 2-8-11 0 PaddyBradley(5) 2 58
(Simon Dow) *a in abt 8th: nudged along and lft bhd by ldrs fr 2f out: no ch whn shkn up ins fnl f* 100/1
9 3/4 **Duke Of Alba (IRE)** 2-9-2 0 DougieCostello 1 56+
(Jamie Osborne) *slowly away: a in rr: nvr a real factor* 50/1
10 shd **Ragstone Ridge (FR)** 2-9-2 0 ShaneKelly 6 55
(Richard Hughes) *dwlt: a in rr: nvr a factor* 66/1
11 1 1/4 **Jal Mahal** 2-8-11 0 RobertHavlin 13 47
(John Gosden) *v difficult to load into stall: slowly away: a wl in rr* 12/1
12 7 **Bayards Cove** 2-8-8 0 HollieDoyle(3) 7 28
(Brian Barr) *t.k.h: hld up in rr: wknd over 2f out: sn bhd* 100/1
13 5 **One More Dawn** 2-8-11 0 DannyBrock 11 15
(Mark Pattinson) *difficult to load into stall: slowly away: a in rr: t.o* 100/1
1m 26.95s (0.95) **Going Correction** 0.0s/f (Stan) 13 Ran SP% **125.4**
Speed ratings (Par 96): **94,92,90,90,90 89,88,83,82,82 81,73,67**
CSF £2.96 TOTE £1.40: £1.10, £1.80, £2.00; EX 3.60 Trifecta £11.50.
**Owner** Al Shaqab Racing **Bred** S N C Scuderia Waldeck **Trained** East Everleigh, Wilts

**FOCUS**
The early gallop wasn't strong and it turned into a bit of a dash. The time was the slower of the two divisions by 1.05sec. The runner-up has been rated to his mark.

## 8890 100% PROFIT BOOST AT 32REDSPORT.COM NOVICE MEDIAN AUCTION STKS 1m (P)
6:10 (6:14) (Class 6) 2-Y-O £2,587 (£770; £384; £192) Stalls Low

Form RPR
23 1 **Tanseeq**[75] 6885 2-9-2 0 JimCrowley 3 83
(William Haggas) *trckd ldng pair: rdn over 2f out: clsd over 1f out: edgd lft but led ins fnl f: styd on wl* 11/4[2]
62 2 1 1/2 **Savaanah (IRE)**[56] 7504 2-8-11 0 SilvestreDeSousa 9 74
(Roger Varian) *chsd ldr to wl over 1f out: kpt on wl to take 2nd again wl ins fnl f* 10/1
12 3 1 1/2 **Blue Mist**[26] 8387 2-9-9 0 KieranShoemark 13 83
(Roger Charlton) *led but pestered by loose horse: rdn 2f out: hdd and edgd lft ins fnl f: fin weakly* 11/8[1]
4 1 1/4 **Paddy The Chef (IRE)** 2-9-2 0 StevieDonohoe 8 73+
(Ian Williams) *dwlt: wl in rr: long way off the pce over 2f out: gd prog over 1f out: tk 4th fnl f and styd on wl* 100/1
5 4 1/2 **Pilgrim Soul** 2-8-11 0 OisinMurphy 12 57
(Andrew Balding) *hld up in last trio: wl bhd over 2f out: styd on w sme purpose fr over 1f out: fin wl* 66/1
03 6 shd **Icart Point**[21] 8501 2-9-2 0 AdamKirby 14 62
(Clive Cox) *t.k.h early: chsd ldrs: lft bhd fr over 2f out* 16/1
64 7 nk **Canimar**[28] 8348 2-8-11 0 JoeFanning 7 56
(Ed Dunlop) *chsd ldrs in 5th: outpcd fr over 2f out: no ch after* 20/1
2 8 1 **Bodes Well (IRE)**[44] 7897 2-9-2 0 EdwardGreatrex 5 59
(Warren Greatrex) *t.k.h early: in tch: shkn up 3f out: steadily fdd* 20/1
54 9 5 **Victory Chime (IRE)**[14] 8677 2-9-2 0 RichardKingscote 6 47
(Ralph Beckett) *dwlt: in tch in midfield: pushed along over 3f out: wknd 2f out* 6/1[3]
20 10 1 3/4 **Is It Off (IRE)**[26] 8388 2-9-2 0 FranBerry 2 42
(Gary Moore) *restrained after s into last pair: nvr any real prog and nvr involved* 16/1
64 11 3 **Pepper Street (IRE)**[39] 8030 2-8-11 0 (h) JosephineGordon 4 30
(Hugo Palmer) *nvr bttr than midfield: pushed along sn after 1/2-way: wknd 2f out* 50/1
12 4 **Enchanting Enya (IRE)** 2-9-0 0 ow3 DougieCostello 10 24
(Steph Hollinshead) *s.v.s: a bhd* 100/1
13 28 **Billy Star** 2-9-2 0 KieranO'Neill 1
(Jimmy Fox) *dwlt: a wl in rr: t.o* 100/1
01 U **Indiscretion (IRE)**[39] 8029 2-9-4 0 DanielMuscutt 11
(Jonathan Portman) *stmbld and uns rdr s* 33/1
1m 39.41s (-0.39) **Going Correction** 0.0s/f (Stan) 14 Ran SP% **122.8**
Speed ratings (Par 94): **101,99,98,96,92 92,91,90,85,84 81,77,49,**
CSF £29.30 TOTE £3.80: £1.80, £2.80, £1.10; EX 31.20 Trifecta £92.70.
**Owner** Hamdan Al Maktoum **Bred** Shortgrove Manor Stud **Trained** Newmarket, Suffolk

**FOCUS**
A fair novice. The opening level is a bit fluid.

## 8891 BRITISH STALLION STUDS EBF HYDE STKS (LISTED RACE) (ALL-WEATHER FAST TRACK QUALIFIER) 1m (P)
6:40 (6:42) (Class 1) 3-Y-O+
£22,684 (£8,600; £4,304; £2,144; £1,076; £540) Stalls Low

Form RPR
1265 1 **Second Thought (IRE)**[46] 7806 3-9-0 105 JamesDoyle 5 109
(William Haggas) *racd in 7th on inner: prog 2f out: drvn to chal jst over 1f out: disp ld ins fnl f: r.o to gain upper hand nr fin* 5/1[2]
-126 2 1/2 **Keystroke**[222] 1773 5-9-2 103 AdamKirby 8 109
(Jeremy Noseda) *hld up in abt 8th: prog 2f out: drvn and clsd between rivals fnl f: jnd ldng pair 100yds out: jst outpcd nr fin* 10/1
-003 3 nk **Mr Owen (USA)**[25] 8417 5-9-2 105 OisinMurphy 1 108
(David Simcock) *trckd ldrs: drvn to chal over 1f out: disp ld ins fnl f: jst outpcd nr fin* 16/1
5101 4 1/2 **Khafoo Shememi (IRE)**[63] 7275 3-9-3 107 SeanLevey 9 109
(Richard Hannon) *trckd ldr: narrow ld 2f out but hrd pressed: hdd ins fnl f: kpt on* 8/1
1011 5 1 **Archetype (FR)**[58] 7471 3-9-0 103 SilvestreDeSousa 11 104
(Simon Crisford) *trckd ldrs: rdn and clsd on outer over 1f out: one pce last 150yds* 8/1
2301 6 1/2 **Stormy Antarctic**[38] 8089 4-9-5 111 JamieSpencer 10 109+
(Ed Walker) *hld up in rr: trying to cl on ldrs and stl gng strly whn nowhere to go jst over 1f out: nt rcvr but styd on nr fin* 6/1[3]
-143 7 1 1/2 **Via Via (IRE)**[18] 8599 5-9-2 104 LukeMorris 6 100
(James Tate) *chsd ldrs: rdn 2f out: nt qckn over 1f out: one pce after* 20/1
1214 8 hd **Accidental Agent**[32] 8234 3-9-0 110 CharlesBishop 2 99
(Eve Johnson Houghton) *hld up in last pair: shkn up and no prog over 2f out: stl only 10th over 1f out: styd on wl last 150yds* 11/4[1]
5424 9 1 1/2 **So Beloved**[25] 8438 7-9-2 112 DanielTudhope 4 96
(David O'Meara) *trckd ldr: chal jst over 2f out: upsides tl jst over 1f out: wknd qckly* 12/1
5406 10 1 3/4 **Glastonbury Song (IRE)**[74] 6961 3-9-0 104 JimCrowley 12 91
(G M Lyons, Ire) *dropped in fr wdst draw and hld up in last: shkn up and no prog over 2f out* 12/1
0410 11 1 3/4 **London Protocol (FR)**[23] 8469 4-9-2 102 TonyPiccone 3 88
(K R Burke) *kpt away fr inner: led to 2f out: sn wknd* 33/1
0405 12 2 1/2 **Battle Of Marathon (USA)**[25] 8417 5-9-2 92 DanielMuscutt 7 83
(John Ryan) *hld up in last trio: rdn over 2f out: hanging and no prog* 100/1
1m 37.71s (-2.09) **Going Correction** 0.0s/f (Stan)
**WFA** 3 from 4yo+ 2lb 12 Ran SP% **118.9**
Speed ratings (Par 111): **110,109,109,108,107 107,105,105,104,102 100,98**
CSF £53.63 TOTE £6.00: £2.00, £3.70, £5.20; EX 67.20 Trifecta £2078.30.
**Owner** Liam Sheridan **Bred** Tally-Ho Stud **Trained** Newmarket, Suffolk

**FOCUS**
A good, competitive Listed race, and there were four in line with half a furlong to run.

## 8892 32RED H'CAP 1m 7f 218y(P)
7:10 (7:10) (Class 2) (0-105,106) 3-Y-O+
£11,827 (£3,541; £1,770; £885; £442; £222) Stalls Low

Form RPR
0564 1 **Soldier In Action (FR)**[16] 8637 4-10-1 **106** JimCrowley 3 113
(Mark Johnston) *mde all: untrbld in front despite mod pce: kicked on 3f out: hrd pressed over 1f out: kpt edging lft after but hld on wl* 6/1
4004 2 1/2 **Lord George (IRE)**[20] 8539 4-9-4 **95** (t[1]) DanielMuscutt 7 101
(James Fanshawe) *trckd wnr: rdn over 2f out: chal over 1f out: sltly impeded fnl f and nvr able to get past* 7/2[2]
2102 3 2 1/4 **Royal Reserve**[16] 8638 4-8-9 **86** oh1 SilvestreDeSousa 9 89+
(David O'Meara) *hld up in last in modly run event: rdn over 2f out: prog to take 3rd fnl f: no ch of threatening ldng pair* 3/1[1]
5216 4 3/4 **St Mary's**[12] 8733 4-8-6 **90** WilliamCox(7) 4 92
(Andrew Balding) *t.k.h: trckd ldng pair: shkn up and nt qckn over 2f out: kpt on fr over 1f out but nt pce to chal* 13/2
/10- 5 1 **Boite (IRE)**[214] 4581 7-9-2 **93** EdwardGreatrex 6 94
(Warren Greatrex) *hld up in 5th: rdn over 2f out whn pce lifted: nvr able to chal* 25/1
02-6 6 1 1/4 **Continuum**[26] 8384 8-8-9 **86** (p) TomMarquand 8 86
(Peter Hedger) *slowly away: hld up in 7th: lft w little ch once pce lifted over 2f out: nvr able to threaten* 25/1
0532 7 1 1/2 **Suegioo (FR)**[30] 8292 8-8-12 **89** (p) TonyHamilton 2 87
(Richard Fahey) *hld up in 8th: urged along over 3f out: outpcd over 2f out: tried to make prog over 1f out: wknd fnl f* 10/1
3140 8 16 **Every Chance (IRE)**[29] 8315 4-8-13 **90** (t[1]) DougieCostello 5 69
(Jamie Osborne) *hld up in 6th: effrt on inner over 2f out but ldrs already gone: wknd over 1f out: heavily eased and t.o* 14/1
-250 9 1 3/4 **Rock Steady (IRE)**[23] 8468 4-9-7 **98** KieranShoemark 1 75
(Roger Charlton) *taken down early: hld up in 4th: rdn and nt qckn over 2f out: wknd over 1f out: virtually p.u ins fnl f* 11/2[3]
3m 34.05s (3.95) **Going Correction** 0.0s/f (Stan) 9 Ran SP% **113.7**
Speed ratings (Par 109): **90,89,88,88,87 87,86,78,77**
CSF £26.83 CT £74.08 TOTE £6.10: £2.10, £1.50, £1.60; EX 24.00 Trifecta £125.70.
**Owner** A D Spence **Bred** Randolf Peters **Trained** Middleham Moor, N Yorks

**FOCUS**
A steadily run staying handicap, and the winner dominated throughout.

## 8893 32RED.COM H'CAP 1m 3f 219y(P)
7:40 (7:44) (Class 4) (0-85,85) 3-Y-O+ £4,690 (£1,395; £697; £348) Stalls Low

Form RPR
0211 1 **Entangling (IRE)**[36] 8143 3-8-13 **79** SilvestreDeSousa 5 93+
(Chris Wall) *hld up in last trio: pushed along 3f out: rapid prog on outer over 2f out: led over 1f out and shot clr in a matter of strides: eased nr fin* 6/1[3]
0000 2 3 1/4 **Cliff Face (IRE)**[32] 8244 4-9-10 **85** (b[1]) LukeMorris 6 91
(Sir Mark Prescott Bt) *s.i.s: t.k.h: hld up: effrt over 2f out: prog over 1f out but wnr sn shot past: kpt on to win battle for 2nd fnl f but no ch* 9/1
0031 3 hd **Sunblazer (IRE)**[19] 8565 7-9-10 **85** (t) JimCrowley 12 90
(Kim Bailey) *hld up in last trio: rdn and no prog over 2f out: styd on fr over 1f out to chal for 2nd ins fnl f: kpt on* 6/1[3]
1634 4 1 1/2 **Yamarhaba Malayeen (IRE)**[21] 8506 3-9-0 **80** DanielTudhope 7 83
(Michael Bell) *t.k.h: prom tl restrained bhd ldrs after 4f: rdn over 2f out: no ch w wnr but stl disputing 2nd 1f out: one pce after* 4/1[1]
1511 5 1 1/4 **Snowy Winter (USA)**[15] 8648 3-9-3 **83** (t) AndrewMullen 4 84
(Archie Watson) *hld up in tch: nt clr run over 2f out: swtchd ins over 1f out and effrt to dispute 2nd sn after: fdd ins fnl f* 5/1[2]
12 6 shd **Isaac Bell (IRE)**[14] 8672 9-9-8 **83** (t) FranBerry 13 84
(Alex Hales) *prog to go prom after 4f: rdn to chse ldr 2f out but hanging: wnr shot past sn after: wknd fnl f* 6/1[3]
2040 7 hd **Northwest Frontier (IRE)**[32] 8239 3-8-12 **78** (b[1]) TonyHamilton 11 79
(Richard Fahey) *led after 2f: tried to kick on over 2f out but limited rspnse: hdd over 1f out: wknd fnl f* 16/1
530P 8 9 **Kath's Legacy**[26] 8390 4-8-3 **71** oh1 NicolaCurrie(7) 8 57
(Richard Hughes) *mostly in last and nvr really gng: nvr a factor* 12/1
1500 9 5 **Langlauf (USA)**[35] 8166 4-9-3 **85** (p) JackOsborn(7) 9 63
(Rod Millman) *chsd ldrs: rdn over 2f out: wknd rapidly wl over 1f out* 20/1

6424 **10** 2 1/4 **Vogueatti (USA)**[81] 6687 4-9-4 79 ........ AdamKirby 10 54
(Marco Botti) *prog to trck ldr after 3f: lost 2nd and wknd rapidly 2f out* **12/1**

0460 **11** 1/2 **Song Of Love (IRE)**[89] 6399 5-9-0 78 ........ CharlieBennett(3) 1 52
(Shaun Harris) *led 2f: styd prom tl wknd rapidly wl over 1f out* **66/1**

2m 33.06s (-1.44) **Going Correction** 0.0s/f (Stan)
**WFA** 3 from 4yo+ 5lb 11 Ran SP% **117.0**
Speed ratings (Par 105): **104,101,101,100,99 99,99,93,90,88 88**
CSF £58.80 CT £340.48 TOTE £6.50: £2.40, £2.80, £2.30; EX 57.60 Trifecta £465.70.
**Owner** Ben CM Wong **Bred** Sweetmans Bloodstock **Trained** Newmarket, Suffolk
■ Stewards' Enquiry : Nicola Currie caution: entered wrong stall

**FOCUS**
A few of the ones up front raced keenly in the early stages, and it was the hold-up horses who came through at the finish, the winner bolting up.
T/Jkpt: Not won. T/Plt: £22.70 to a £1 stake. Pool: £84,765.86 - 2,715.52 winning units T/Qpdt: £6.60 to a £1 stake. Pool: £11,368.52 - 1,265.49 winning units **Jonathan Neesom**

8894 - 8901a (Foreign Racing) - See Raceform Interactive

## [8809] CHELMSFORD (A.W) (L-H)
Thursday, November 23

**OFFICIAL GOING: Polytrack: standard**
Wind: medium, half behind Weather: dry

### 8902 BET TOTEPLACEPOT AT BETFRED.COM NURSERY H'CAP 5f (P)
5:55 (6:01) (Class 6) (0-65,67) 2-Y-O £3,234 (£962; £481; £240) Stalls Low

Form RPR

4602 **1** **Rock On Baileys**[8] 8780 2-8-6 50 ........ (b[1]) SilvestreDeSousa 6 61
(Chris Dwyer) *chsd ldr tl led over 3f out: rdn and kicked clr over 1f out: in n.d and r.o wl ins fnl f: comf* **9/4[1]**

0300 **2** 3 3/4 **Mother Of Dragons (IRE)**[14] 8701 2-9-2 67 ........ NicolaCurrie(7) 9 64
(Phil McEntee) *sn pushed along in midfield: hdwy to chse clr wnr 1f out: kpt on to hold 2nd but no imp on wnr fnl f* **33/1**

4000 **3** 1/2 **Bomad**[30] 8325 2-9-7 65 ........ (v[1]) PatrickMathers 7 60
(Derek Shaw) *s.i.s: bustled along in rr: rdn over 2f out: clsd and nt clr run 1f out: swtchd rt and styd on wl towards fin: no ch w wnr* **16/1**

6065 **4** 1/2 **Harvest Day**[8] 8780 2-8-7 51 ........ (t) JosephineGordon 10 44+
(Michael Easterby) *s.i.s and wnt rt s: pushed along in last pair: rdn over 2f out: hdwy on outer 1f out: styd on ins fnl f: no ch w wnr* **11/1**

0465 **5** 1/2 **Cool Baby**[7] 8795 2-8-12 56 ........ (p[1]) LukeMorris 2 48
(Robert Cowell) *t.k.h: chsd ldrs: swtchd rt after 1f out: effrt over 1f out: sn outpcd by wnr and btn 1f out: kpt on same pce ins fnl f* **7/1[3]**

0442 **6** 1/2 **Avon Green**[7] 8795 2-9-5 63 ........ LiamKeniry 5 53
(Joseph Tuite) *t.k.h: nt clr run over 1f out: sn rdn and unable qck: no ch w wnr and one pced ins fnl f* **4/1[2]**

0565 **7** 5 **Tonkolili (IRE)**[12] 8746 2-9-5 63 ........ (h) KieranShoemark 8 35
(William Muir) *led for over 1f: chsd wnr: rdn and unable qck over 1f out: sn lost 2nd and btn: wknd ins fnl f* **12/1**

59.83s (-0.37) **Going Correction** -0.075s/f (Stan) 7 Ran SP% **88.1**
Speed ratings (Par 94): **99,93,92,91,90 89,81**
CSF £41.44 CT £360.81 TOTE £2.50: £1.50, £6.80; EX 30.00 Trifecta £176.10.
**Owner** G R Bailey Ltd (Baileys Horse Feeds) **Bred** Petches Farm Ltd **Trained** Newmarket, Suffolk
■ Blessed To Empress and Llamrei were withdrawn. Price at time of withdrawal 5/2 and 14/1. Rule 4 applies to all bets - deduction 25p in the pound. Rule 4 applies to board prices prior to withdrawal - deduction 30p in the pound.

**FOCUS**
This proved straightforward for the well-in winner.

### 8903 WEATHERBYS GENERAL STUD BOOK ONLINE EBF NOVICE STKS (PLUS 10 RACE) (SIRE/DAM-RESTRICTED RACE) 1m (P)
6:30 (6:34) (Class 3) 2-Y-O £7,762 (£2,310; £1,154; £577) Stalls Low

Form RPR

06 **1** **Noble Expression**[16] 8643 2-9-2 0 ........ JackMitchell 2 79+
(Roger Varian) *trckd ldrs: nt clr run over 1f out: swtchd rt and chal ent fnl f: pushed into ld ins fnl f: sn rdn and asserted towards fin* **7/2[1]**

0 **2** 1 1/4 **Best Blue**[15] 8678 2-9-2 0 ........ SilvestreDeSousa 8 74
(Michael Bell) *led: hung rt off bnd wl over 1f out: sn rdn: hdd ins fnl f: styd on same pce after: eased cl home* **4/1[2]**

60 **3** 1 3/4 **Nibras Galaxy (IRE)**[15] 8678 2-9-2 0 ........ SeanLevey 11 70
(Ismail Mohammed) *chsd ldr: effrt over 1f out: sn nudged rt and unable qck: kpt on same pce ins fnl f* **10/1**

**4** shd **Hasanoanda** 2-9-2 0 ........ NickyMackay 3 70+
(John Gosden) *rn green: s.i.s: hld up in tch in midfield: swtchd rt over 1f out: pushed along and styd on wl ins fnl f* **16/1**

02 **5** 4 **Briscola**[15] 8670 2-8-11 0 ........ RobertHavlin 1 55
(John Gosden) *hld up in tch in midfield: effrt over 1f out: edgd lft and no imp 1f out: wknd ins fnl f* **7/2[1]**

**6** 3 3/4 **Msaikah (IRE)** 2-8-11 0 ........ LukeMorris 10 46
(Luca Cumani) *swtchd lft after s: hld up in tch in midfield: effrt and outpcd over 1f out: wknd ins fnl f* **12/1**

0510 **7** 1 **Blacklooks (IRE)**[15] 8676 2-9-2 79 ........ JosephineGordon 9 49
(Ivan Furtado) *t.k.h early: chsd ldrs tl unable qck and hung lft over 1f out: sn lost pl and wknd fnl f* **6/1[3]**

**8** 3 1/4 **Beloved Knight** 2-9-2 0 ........ TomMarquand 4 41
(Laura Mongan) *dwlt: hld up in tch in last trio: rdn over 2f out: sn struggling: wknd over 1f out* **66/1**

0 **9** 8 **Balkhash (IRE)**[15] 8677 2-8-13 0 ........ HectorCrouch(3) 5 22
(Clive Cox) *stdd s: t.k.h: hld up in tch in last trio: effrt and no imp over 2f out: wknd over 1f out* **10/1**

00 **10** 6 **Kiss Me Daily (FR)**[26] 8419 2-8-11 0 ........ RichardKingscote 6 +
(Ralph Beckett) *t.k.h: hld up in tch in midfield: effrt over 2f out: no imp and eased over 1f out: fin lame* **20/1**

1m 40.76s (0.86) **Going Correction** -0.075s/f (Stan) 10 Ran SP% **116.7**
Speed ratings (Par 100): **92,90,89,88,84 81,80,76,68,62**
CSF £17.49 TOTE £4.30: £1.60, £1.80, £3.60; EX 22.20 Trifecta £168.20.
**Owner** Sheikh Mohammed Obaid Al Maktoum **Bred** Horizon Bloodstock Limited **Trained** Newmarket, Suffolk

**FOCUS**
This was fairly steadily run in the early stages and the first three home raced in the first three positions virtually throughout.

### 8904 BET TOTEQUADPOT AT BETFRED.COM CONDITIONS STKS (PLUS 10 RACE) 1m 2f (P)
7:00 (7:01) (Class 3) 2-Y-O £9,703 (£2,887; £1,443; £721) Stalls Low

Form RPR

3 **1** **Lucky Deal**[24] 8476 2-9-2 0 ........ SilvestreDeSousa 3 83
(Mark Johnston) *mde all: rdn ent fnl 3f: drvn and kpt finding ex over 1f out: styd on strly and clr ins fnl f: eased nr fin* **5/1[3]**

1 **2** 2 **Wissahickon (USA)**[33] 8245 2-9-6 0 ........ RobertHavlin 1 83
(John Gosden) *chsd wnr: effrt 3f out: drvn and unable qck over 1f out: kpt on same pce ins fnl f* **1/1[1]**

2222 **3** 3/4 **Bubble And Squeak**[7] 8796 2-8-8 84 ........ MitchGodwin(3) 2 73
(Sylvester Kirk) *stdd after s: hld up in 3rd: effrt 3f out: swtchd lft and drvn over 1f out: unable qck and styd on same pce ins fnl f* **9/4[2]**

0 **4** 6 **Future Score (IRE)**[50] 7726 2-9-2 0 ........ JimmyQuinn 4 66
(Saeed bin Suroor) *wnt rt s: in tch in rr: rdn and outpcd over 2f out: wl hld over 1f out* **9/1**

2m 9.0s (0.40) **Going Correction** -0.075s/f (Stan) 4 Ran SP% **107.4**
Speed ratings (Par 100): **95,93,92,88**
CSF £10.52 TOTE £4.90; EX 11.70 Trifecta £18.10.
**Owner** Kai Fai Leung **Bred** Fittocks Stud **Trained** Middleham Moor, N Yorks

**FOCUS**
The winner had his own way in front but still impressed in seeing his race out strongly.

### 8905 BET TOTEEXACTA AT BETFRED.COM H'CAP 7f (P)
7:30 (7:31) (Class 2) (0-105,102) 3-Y-O+ £12,938 (£3,850; £1,924; £962) Stalls Low

Form RPR

0000 **1** **Steel Train (FR)**[12] 8737 6-9-3 95 ........ MartinHarley 1 104
(David O'Meara) *hld up in midfield and travelled strly: nt clr run ent fnl 2f: swtchd lft over 1f out: clsd to trck ldrs and swtchd rt ins fnl f: sn pushed along and qcknd to ld: r.o wl* **8/1**

6000 **2** 1 **Swift Approval (IRE)**[5] 8843 5-9-0 92 ........ (v[1]) SeanLevey 5 98
(Stuart Williams) *t.k.h: w ldr tl led 1/2-way: rdn over 1f out: drvn 1f out: hdd and one pce ins fnl f* **8/1**

3300 **3** hd **Qaffaal (USA)**[16] 8652 6-8-12 90 ........ SilvestreDeSousa 7 95
(Michael Easterby) *hld up in last pair: swtchd rt and hdwy on outer bnd 2f out: hdwy u.p 1f out: styd on wl ins fnl f* **7/1[3]**

1120 **4** nse **Shady McCoy (USA)**[5] 8843 7-9-10 102 ........ RichardKingscote 6 107
(Ian Williams) *hld up in tch in rr: wd and effrt bnd 2f out: hdwy 1f out: styd on wl u.p ins fnl f* **7/2[1]**

5050 **5** 2 **Loyalty**[184] 2922 10-8-8 89 ........ (v) CallumShepherd(3) 9 89
(Derek Shaw) *hld up wl in tch in midfield: effrt over 1f: drvn to chse ldr 1f out: sn edgd lft u.p* **50/1**

0032 **6** 2 **Show Stealer**[30] 8310 4-8-7 85 ........ (p) LukeMorris 8 80
(Rae Guest) *hld up in tch in midfield: effrt over 2f out: unable qck u.p over 1f out: kpt on same pce ins fnl f* **7/1[3]**

4215 **7** 1/2 **Pearl Spectre (USA)**[6] 8812 6-8-2 87 ........ NicolaCurrie(7) 10 80
(Phil McEntee) *led tl 1/2-way: rdn and unable qck over 1f out: lost 2nd 1f out: no ex and outpcd whn impeded and wknd ins fnl f* **6/1[2]**

3624 **8** 1 **Rajar**[12] 8747 3-8-9 88 ........ (h) PatrickMathers 4 77
(Richard Fahey) *taken down early: t.k.h: chsd ldrs: effrt to press ldr over 1f out: getting outpcd whn squeezed for room and bmpd ins fnl f: wknd after* **20/1**

3030 **9** 9 **Shyron**[6] 8812 6-8-4 87 ........ JaneElliott(5) 12 53
(George Margarson) *chsd ldrs on outer: hung lft and outpcd over 2f out: lost pl and bhd over 1f out: wknd ins fnl f* **16/1**

3223 **10** 1 **Pastime**[12] 8736 3-8-8 87 ........ JosephineGordon 11 49
(Gay Kelleway) *chsd ldrs tl rdn and struggling over 2f out: bhd and swtchd lft over 1f out: wknd ins fnl f* **7/2[1]**

0000 **U** **Gentlemen**[3] 8872 6-8-3 84 ........ (b) HollieDoyle(3) 3
(Phil McEntee) *ducked rt: ref to r and uns rdr leaving stalls* **12/1**

1m 25.08s (-2.12) **Going Correction** -0.075s/f (Stan)
**WFA** 3 from 4yo+ 1lb 11 Ran SP% **126.2**
Speed ratings (Par 109): **109,107,107,107,105 103,102,101,91,89**
CSF £75.98 CT £494.99 TOTE £9.40: £3.90, £3.80, £2.00; EX 111.80 Trifecta £1182.00.
**Owner** Rasio Cymru I & Dutch Rose Partnerhsip **Bred** Erich Schmid **Trained** Upper Helmsley, N Yorks

**FOCUS**
A good, competitive handicap. It's been rated around the runner-up. The winner has been rated back to his best, and the third and fourth close to their best.

### 8906 BET TOTETRIFECTA AT BETFRED.COM CLAIMING STKS 6f (P)
8:00 (8:00) (Class 6) 3-Y-O+ £3,234 (£962; £481; £240) Stalls Centre

Form RPR

0000 **1** **Captain Lars (SAF)**[32] 8260 8-9-0 75 ........ (v) PatrickMathers 6 83
(Derek Shaw) *mde all: rein broke after 1f and dashed clr: shkn up over 1f out: kpt on wl ins fnl f: unchal* **10/1**

2110 **2** 4 **Captain Bob (IRE)**[79] 6797 6-8-11 72 ........ (p) EmmaTaff(7) 2 75
(Jamie Osborne) *hmpd leaving stall: hld up in midfield: effrt on inner over 1f out: rdn to chse clr wnr 1f out: kpt on but nvr a threat* **8/1**

3620 **3** 2 3/4 **Tatlisu (IRE)**[23] 8486 7-9-4 85 ........ SebastianWoods(7) 3 74
(Richard Fahey) *stdd and hmpd leaving stalls: hld up in last pair: effrt over 1f out: flashing tail u.p: swtchd rt ins fnl f: wnt 3rd wl ins fnl f: nvr nr wnr* **15/8[1]**

2350 **4** 2 **Field Of Vision (IRE)**[16] 8645 4-9-2 74 ........ LiamKeniry 1 59
(Joseph Tuite) *w wnr for 1f: chsd clr wnr after: no imp u.p over 1f out: wknd ins fnl f* **8/1**

031- **5** 3 1/2 **Golden Steps (FR)**[308] 6-9-12 100 ........ (h) DougieCostello 5 58
(Jamie Osborne) *off the pce in 3rd: no imp over 1f out: wknd fnl f* **9/4[2]**

2026 **6** 18 **Dream Start**[21] 8551 3-8-7 60 ........ (t) SilvestreDeSousa 7
(John Ryan) *dwlt: nvr gng wl in last pair: bhd and eased over 1f out* **6/1[3]**

1m 12.1s (-1.60) **Going Correction** -0.075s/f (Stan) 6 Ran SP% **111.2**
Speed ratings (Par 101): **107,101,98,95,90 66**
CSF £79.52 TOTE £5.70: £7.90, £3.70; EX 53.70 Trifecta £284.50.Captain Bob was claimed by Mr P. Kirby for £8,000. Field of Vision was claimed by Mr J. L. Flint for £7,000. Golden Steps was claimed by Mr J. S. Goldie for £12,000.
**Owner** Chris Hamilton **Bred** Klawervlei Stud **Trained** Sproxton, Leics

**FOCUS**
A bit of a strange race, the winner scooting clear after the reins broke early on, and perhaps the other riders assumed he would come back to them. As it was, he was never in danger.

## 8907 BET TOTEWIN AT BETFRED.COM H'CAP 7f (P)
**8:30** (8:30) (Class 5) (0-75,81) 3-Y-O+ **£5,175** (£1,540; £769; £384) **Stalls Low**

Form RPR
1203 **1** **Lucymai**[7] 8798 4-9-0 **71**........................................ JackDuern(3) 10 86
(Dean Ivory) *rousted along leaving stalls: led after 1f and mde rest: wnt clr over 2f out: rdn over 1f out: styd on wl and unchal after: comf* **8/1**
0443 **2** *4 ½* **Samphire Coast**[10] 8773 4-8-8 **62**..............................(v[1]) PatrickMathers 2 65
(Derek Shaw) *wnt rt s: hld up in tch in midfield: hdwy u.p over 1f out: chsd clr wnr and kpt on u.p ins fnl f: nvr threatened* **9/1**
5000 **3** *3* **Plucky Dip**[17] 8640 6-9-5 **73**.............................. SilvestreDeSousa 1 68
(John Ryan) *in tch in midfield: effrt over 2f out: hdwy u.p over 1f out: chsd clr wnr 1f out: no imp and lost 2nd ins fnl f* **10/1**
5000 **4** *nk* **Round The Island**[26] 8427 4-8-10 **64**.............................. RobertHavlin 6 58
(Richard Whitaker) *led for 1f: styd chsng ldrs: wnt 2nd but wnr gng clr over 1f out: unable qck over 1f out: no imp and kpt on same pce ins fnl f* **33/1**
0541 **5** *4* **Fredricka**[7] 8798 6-9-8 **81** 6ex..............................(v) JaneElliott(5) 12 65
(Ivan Furtado) *t.k.h: hld up in tch in midfield: rdn and outpcd over 2f out: wl hld and plugged on same pce fr over 1f out* **20/1**
3621 **6** *nk* **Medicean El Diablo**[37] 8132 4-9-5 **73**.............................. TomMarquand 3 56
(Jimmy Fox) *short of room and hmpd leaving stalls: hld up in tch in rr: clsd on inner and nt clr run briefly 2f out: rdn and hdwy over 1f out: battling for placing but no imp on wnr 1f out: wknd fnl 100yds* **7/2**[1]
4330 **7** *¾* **Acrux**[12] 8749 4-9-5 **73**..............................(h) MartinHarley 7 54
(David O'Meara) *hld up in tch in rr: nt clr run and swtchd rt over 2f out: sme hdwy over 1f out: nvr trbld ldrs* **8/1**
0224 **8** *¾* **Clef**[26] 8418 3-8-13 **75**.............................. SebastianWoods(7) 8 53
(Richard Fahey) *hld up in tch in midfield: effrt and unable qck over 1f out: sn btn and wknd fnl f* **7/1**[3]
-000 **9** *2 ½* **Muhajjal**[16] 8646 3-9-3 **72**..............................(t) KieranO'Neill 4 44
(George Peckham) *short of room and hmpd leaving stalls: sme hdwy over 1f out: nvr trbld ldr* **20/1**
1200 **10** *¾* **Rouge Nuage (IRE)**[14] 8706 7-9-1 **76**.............................. NicolaCurrie(7) 13 47
(Conrad Allen) *in tch in midfield but stuck on outer: rdn ent fnl 2f: sn outpcd: wknd u.p over 1f out* **40/1**
6001 **11** *14* **Ebbisham (IRE)**[26] 8434 4-9-3 **71**.............................. JimmyQuinn 11 5
(John Mackie) *t.k.h: hld up in tch in midfield: lost pl over 2f out: bhd over 1f out* **12/1**
3/52 **12** *1* **Exit Europe**[21] 8551 5-8-12 **66**.............................. LukeMorris 9
(Sir Mark Prescott Bt) *chsd ldrs: unable qck u.p and lost pl over 2f out: bhd and eased 1f out* **5/1**[2]
0064 **13** *21* **Maggie Pink**[7] 8798 8-8-9 **63**..............................(p[1]) RyanTate 16
(Michael Appleby) *chsd wnr after 1f tl lost pl u.p over 2f out: bhd over 1f out: t.o* **20/1**
6602 **14** *8* **Out Of The Ashes**[155] 3971 4-9-0 **68**..............................(t) SeanLevey 14
(Mohamed Moubarak) *chsd ldrs on outer tl rdn and lost pl qckly over 2f out: bhd over 1f out: t.o* **16/1**

1m 25.08s (-2.12) **Going Correction** -0.075s/f (Stan)
**WFA** 3 from 4yo+ 1lb **14 Ran SP% 125.9**
Speed ratings (Par 103): **109,103,100,100,95 95,94,93,90,89 73,72,48,39**
CSF £76.09 CT £769.58 TOTE £10.30: £3.50, £4.10, £3.00; EX 120.40 Trifecta £1812.50.
**Owner** Roger S Beadle **Bred** Richard Kent **Trained** Radlett, Herts

**FOCUS**
Another race dominated from the front. A clear pb from the winner, with the runner-up rated a bit below form.

## 8908 BOOK TICKETS AT CHELMSFORDCITYRACECOURSE.COM H'CAP 1m (P)
**9:00** (9:02) (Class 6) (0-60,61) 3-Y-O+ **£3,234** (£962; £481; £240) **Stalls Low**

Form RPR
1145 **1** **Anna Medici**[19] 8589 3-9-6 **61**..............................(p[1]) LukeMorris 8 69
(Sir Mark Prescott Bt) *trckd ldrs: effrt to ld over 1f out: drvn clr ins fnl f: styd on* **11/4**[2]
0325 **2** *1* **Dor's Law**[16] 8661 4-8-12 **51**..............................(p) RobHornby 9 58
(Dean Ivory) *dwlt: in tch in rr: effrt on outer over 1f out: hdwy and edgd lft u.p ins fnl f: wnt 2nd wl ins fnl f: styd on wl but nvr getting to wnr* **9/1**
5500 **3** *1 ½* **Gracious George (IRE)**[30] 8313 7-9-4 **57**.............................. KieranO'Neill 1 60
(Jimmy Fox) *in tch in midfield: swtchd lft and effrt over 1f out: chsd clr wnr 1f out: no imp and lost 2nd wl ins fnl f* **6/1**[3]
0000 **4** *hd* **Sugar Beach (FR)**[19] 8591 3-9-0 **55**..............................(h[1]) JimmyQuinn 5 56
(Ann Duffield) *hld up in tch in midfield: effrt over 1f out: chsd ldrs and drvn 1f out: kpt on same pce ins fnl f* **20/1**
0362 **5** *hd* **Banta Bay**[21] 8543 3-8-7 **48**..............................(p) JoeyHaynes 10 49
(John Best) *s.i.s and rousted along: hdwy into midfield 1/2-way: rdn over 1f out: styd on sane pce u.p ins fnl f* **12/1**
5264 **6** *3* **Tasaaboq**[10] 8772 6-8-13 **52**..............................(t) JosephineGordon 16 49+
(Phil McEntee) *t.k.h: hld up in tch in midfield on outer: effrt over 1f out: no imp whn nudged lft ins fnl f: wknd wl ins fnl f* **16/1**
0220 **7** *hd* **Touch The Clouds**[21] 8543 6-8-2 **46**.............................. JaneElliott(5) 4 40
(William Stone) *chsd ldrs on inner: effrt u.p over 1f out: no ex u.p 1f out: wknd ins fnl f* **16/1**
4300 **8** *½* **Characterized**[44] 7916 3-9-5 **60**.............................. TimmyMurphy 14 52
(Geoffrey Deacon) *hld up wl in tch in midfield: effrt over 2f out: no imp over 1f out and hld whn nudged lft ins fnl f: kpt on same pce* **25/1**
1305 **9** *6* **With Approval (IRE)**[35] 8182 5-9-1 **57**..............................(p) CallumShepherd(3) 7 36
(Laura Mongan) *chsd ldr tl led 2f out: sn rdn and hdd: no ex u.p ent fnl f: btn whn nudged lft ins fnl f* **20/1**
3051 **10** *nse* **Belgravian (FR)**[29] 8345 3-9-2 **57**..............................(tp) EdwardGreatrex 2 45+
(Archie Watson) *stdd s: t.k.h: hld up in tch in rr: switching rt over 2f out: nt clr run over 1f out tl effrt ent fnl f: midfield whn nt clr run again ins fnl f: eased* **5/2**[1]
0504 **11** *hd* **Rivers Of Asia**[21] 8551 4-9-7 **60**.............................. TomMarquand 13 38
(Martin Smith) *a towards rr: rdn over 2f out: no imp: wknd over 1f out* **14/1**
3003 **12** *3 ¼* **Orientelle**[16] 8650 3-8-5 **46** oh1..............................(b) PatrickMathers 6 15
(Richard Whitaker) *led tl 2f out: sn hung rt and rdn: lost pl and sn btn: wknd fnl f* **50/1**
-030 **13** *7* **Mr Mac**[173] 3327 3-9-2 **57**..............................(h) CharlesBishop 12 10
(Peter Hedger) *chsd ldrs: rdn ent fnl 2f: sn struggling and lost pl over 1f out: wknd* **10/1**
0024 **14** *4 ½* **Tawfeer**[24] 8470 3-8-0 **48**..............................(p) NicolaCurrie(7) 3
(Phil McEntee) *restless in stalls: dwlt: a towards rr: rdn and struggling over 2f out: bhd over 1f out* **14/1**
15 **15** *5* **Lady Morel (IRE)**[66] 7212 3-9-1 **56**.............................. LiamKeniry 11
(Joseph Tuite) *dwlt: a towards rr: bhd over 1f out* **33/1**
0000 **16** *8* **Poet's Quest**[77] 6847 3-8-5 **46** oh1.............................. RyanTate 15
(Michael Appleby) *a rr: u.p and struggling 3f: lost tch over 1f out: t.o* **33/1**

1m 40.21s (0.31) **Going Correction** -0.075s/f (Stan)
**WFA** 3 from 4yo+ 2lb **16 Ran SP% 142.6**
Speed ratings (Par 101): **95,94,92,92,92 89,88,88,82,82 82,78,71,67,62 54**
CSF £31.26 CT £164.50 TOTE £5.40: £1.60, £3.10, £1.80, £4.60; EX 49.60 Trifecta £513.80.
**Owner** Neil Greig **Bred** W N Greig **Trained** Newmarket, Suffolk

**FOCUS**
A moderate affair.
T/Plt: £8,198.70 to a £1 stake. Pool: £106,134.57 - 9.45 winning units T/Qpdt: £3,002.20 to a £1 stake. Pool: £9,737.09 - 2.40 winning units **Steve Payne**

# 8778 NEWCASTLE (A.W) (L-H)
Thursday, November 23

**OFFICIAL GOING: Tapeta: standard**
Wind: Breezy, half against Weather: Overcast

## 8909 BETWAY H'CAP 1m 4f 98y (Tp)
**1:50** (1:50) (Class 6) (0-65,65) 3-Y-O+ **£2,911** (£866; £432; £216) **Stalls High**

Form RPR
50/1 **1** **British Art**[51] 7719 5-9-3 **58**..............................(v) KevinStott 5 68+
(R K Watson, Ire) *trckd ldrs gng wl: led on bit over 2f out: rdn clr fr over 1f out* **2/1**[1]
1160 **2** *2 ½* **Exclusive Waters (IRE)**[34] 8205 7-9-9 **64**.............................. AndrewMullen 9 70
(Tina Jackson) *hld up in midfield on outside: effrt and pushed along over 2f out: hdwy to chse (clr) wnr appr fnl f: kpt on: nt pce to chal* **11/1**[3]
0000 **3** *¾* **Galilee Chapel (IRE)**[45] 7885 8-9-2 **60**..............................(b) RowanScott(3) 8 65
(Alistair Whillans) *t.k.h: hld up in tch: effrt and rdn 2f out: kpt on ins fnl f* **50/1**
1200 **4** *1 ¼* **London Glory**[32] 8261 4-9-0 **60**..............................(b) JamieGormley(5) 13 63
(David Thompson) *hld up: stdy hdwy over 2f out: sn pushed along: kpt on fnl f: nrst fin* **12/1**
6640 **5** *1 ¼* **Senatus (FR)**[170] 3432 5-9-10 **65**..............................(h) DanielMuscutt 3 66
(Karen McLintock) *led to over 2f out: chsd wnr to appr fnl f: sn rdn and outpcd* **11/1**[3]
1420 **6** *1 ¼* **Life Knowledge (IRE)**[58] 7479 5-8-13 **57**.............................. CliffordLee(3) 11 56
(Patrick Holmes) *dwlt and swtchd lft s: hld up: rdn and hdwy 2f out: no imp fnl f* **12/1**
0000 **7** *2 ½* **Almutamarred (USA)**[33] 8246 5-9-2 **57**.............................. TomEaves 2 52
(James Unett) *dwlt: hld up: effrt over 2f out: kpt on fnl f: no imp* **16/1**
0331 **8** *¾* **Traveltalk (IRE)**[24] 8477 3-9-3 **63**.............................. StevieDonohoe 1 58
(Brian Ellison) *trckd ldrs: rdn over 2f out: wknd fnl f* **12/1**
200 **9** *shd* **Tectonic (IRE)**[24] 8109 8-9-5 **60**..............................(v) JoeFanning 6 53
(Keith Dalgleish) *hld up midfield: nt clr run over 2f out to over 1f out: sn rdn and outpcd* **33/1**
0603 **10** *2* **Hayward Field (IRE)**[41] 8000 4-9-6 **64**.............................. PhilDennis(3) 4 54
(Noel Wilson) *hld up in tch on ins: rdn over 2f out: wknd over 1f out* **12/1**
0050 **11** *½* **Calvinist**[22] 8505 4-9-10 **65**..............................(tp) JackGarritty 7 54
(Ruth Carr) *in tch: rdn over 2f out: wknd over 1f out* **33/1**
0000 **12** *½* **Etaad (USA)**[34] 8206 6-9-2 **64**.............................. SebastianWoods(7) 12 53
(Lucinda Egerton) *hld up towards rr: rdn over 3f out: btn fnl 2f* **66/1**
2110 **13** *2 ¼* **Four Kingdoms (IRE)**[16] 8654 3-8-11 **64**.............................. PatrickO'Hanlon(7) 10 50
(K R Burke) *in tch: rdn and outpcd over 2f out: hung lft and btn over 1f out* **7/2**[2]
0604 **14** *6* **Melabi (IRE)**[81] 6723 4-9-6 **61**.............................. GrahamLee 14 36
(Richard Ford) *hld up towards rr: rdn over 3f out: nvr on terms* **25/1**

2m 40.47s (-0.63) **Going Correction** +0.15s/f (Slow)
**WFA** 3 from 4yo+ 5lb **14 Ran SP% 122.1**
Speed ratings (Par 101): **108,106,105,105,104 103,101,101,101,99 99,99,97,93**
CSF £24.80 CT £875.98 TOTE £3.30: £1.60, £2.90, £12.40; EX 31.80 Trifecta £1131.70.
**Owner** Cousins Plus One Syndicate **Bred** Rabbah Bloodstock Limited **Trained** Killylea, Co Armagh

**FOCUS**
A modest handicap run at an ordinary pace. Despite the size of the field, they bet 11-1 bar two but the market was right as the well-backed favourite hosed up.

## 8910 BETWAY LIVE CASINO H'CAP 1m 4f 98y (Tp)
**2:20** (2:23) (Class 2) (0-105,96) 3-Y-O+ **£16,172** (£4,812; £2,405; £1,202) **Stalls High**

Form RPR
2000 **1** **Sir Chauvelin**[12] 8740 5-9-10 **95**.............................. DanielTudhope 5 102
(Jim Goldie) *hld up: swtchd rt and hdwy to ld over 1f out: rdn out ins fnl f* **4/1**[3]
5534 **2** *1* **Rainbow Rebel (IRE)**[14] 8705 4-9-2 **87**.............................. JoeFanning 4 92
(Mark Johnston) *led: rdn and hdd over 1f out: rallied fnl f: tk 2nd cl home: nt pce of wnr* **11/2**
1-02 **3** *hd* **Burcan (FR)**[30] 8315 5-9-6 **91**.............................. DanielMuscutt 1 96
(Marco Botti) *trckd ldrs: effrt and ev ch over 1f out: sn chsng wnr: kpt on fnl f: lost 2nd cl home* **3/1**[2]
2- **4** *2 ½* **Diodorus (IRE)**[134] 4772 3-9-4 **94**..............................(b) KevinStott 7 96
(Karen McLintock) *dwlt: sn trcking ldr: ev ch and rdn over 2f out: no ex fr over 1f out* **16/1**
0001 **5** *½* **Master Singer (USA)**[33] 8244 3-9-6 **96**..............................(b) RobertTart 2 97
(John Gosden) *trckd ldrs: stdy hdwy over 2f out: rdn and outpcd over 1f out: sn n.d* **5/4**[1]
30-6 **6** *5* **Pearl Castle (IRE)**[266] 985 7-9-4 **92**.............................. CliffordLee(3) 6 84
(K R Burke) *hld up in tch: rdn and outpcd over 2f out: sn btn* **50/1**
6000 **7** *½* **Gurkha Friend**[12] 8737 5-9-2 **87**.............................. TomEaves 3 78
(Karen McLintock) *plld hrd: hld up: rdn and struggling over 2f out: sn btn* **50/1**

2m 43.04s (1.94) **Going Correction** +0.15s/f (Slow)
**WFA** 3 from 4yo+ 5lb **7 Ran SP% 114.6**
Speed ratings (Par 109): **99,98,98,96,96 92,92**
CSF £26.09 TOTE £5.70: £2.80, £2.50; EX 20.10 Trifecta £54.60.
**Owner** J Fyffe, Mrs M Craig, G Thomson **Bred** W M Johnstone **Trained** Uplawmoor, E Renfrews


The Form Book Flat, Raceform Ltd, Newbury, RG14 5SJ

**FOCUS**
A valuable handicap, but a disappointing turnout with the highest-rated horse (the 3yo Master Singer) 9lb below the race ceiling. The pace was modest and the winning time was 2.57sec slower than the preceding 0-65. The second has been rated close to his best, with the winner to form.

## 8911 32RED CASINO MAIDEN FILLIES' STKS 1m 2f 42y (Tp)
2:55 (2:56) (Class 4) 3-Y-0+ £4,851 (£1,443; £721; £360) Stalls High

Form RPR
3352 1 **Tranquil Star (IRE)**[31] 8291 3-9-0 77 DanielTudhope 4 82+
(Jeremy Noseda) *mde all at stdy gallop: niggled briefly and qcknd clr 2f out: unchal* 2/5[1]
0-42 2 7 **Ebqaa (IRE)**[54] 7597 3-9-0 74 TomEaves 2 65
(James Unett) *prom: hdwy on outside to chse wnr over 2f out: rdn and outpcd fr over 1f out* 7/2[2]
442 3 6 **Lewinsky (IRE)**[35] 8193 3-9-0 63 CamHardie 3 53
(Antony Brittain) *dwlt: t.k.h and sn chsng wnr: drvn along over 2f out: wknd over 1f out* 33/1
6 4 2 **Lunar Mist**[16] 8663 3-9-0 0 JoeFanning 1 49
(Ed Dunlop) *t.k.h: trckd ldrs: drvn and outpcd over 2f out: sn wknd* 8/1[3]
2m 12.88s (2.48) **Going Correction** +0.15s/f (Slow) 4 Ran SP% **107.7**
Speed ratings (Par 102): **96,90,85,84**
CSF £2.08 TOTE £1.40; EX 2.10 Trifecta £6.70.
**Owner** P Makin **Bred** Paulyn Limited **Trained** Newmarket, Suffolk

**FOCUS**
A weak and uncompetitive older-fillies' maiden which the red-hot favourite took easily.

## 8912 BETWAY H'CAP 1m 2f 42y (Tp)
3:30 (3:32) (Class 4) (0-85,85) 3-Y-0+ £4,851 (£1,443; £721; £360) Stalls High

Form RPR
1 1 **Paddyplex**[198] 2496 4-9-4 82 PhillipMakin 2 90
(Keith Dalgleish) *chsd ldng pair: stdy hdwy over 2f out: rdn to ld over 1f out: edgd lft ins fnl f: hld on wl cl home* 12/1
3340 2 hd **Andok (IRE)**[27] 8385 3-8-11 78 TonyHamilton 8 85
(Richard Fahey) *hld up midfield: drvn and effrt over 2f out: rallied to chse wnr 1f out: kpt on: hld cl home* 11/1
25 3 1 ¼ **Waarif (IRE)**[13] 8718 4-9-2 80 (t) DanielTudhope 7 85
(David O'Meara) *missed break: hld up: effrt and angled rt 2f out: kpt on wl fnl f: hld towards fin* 3/1[1]
0106 4 hd **Zabeel Star (IRE)**[13] 8718 5-8-10 74 TomEaves 4 78
(Karen McLintock) *dwlt: hld up: rdn and hdwy over 1f out: kpt on ins fnl f: nvr able to chal* 16/1
6263 5 ½ **Testa Rossa (IRE)**[13] 8718 7-8-7 78 (b) SeanMooney(7) 9 81
(Jim Goldie) *hld up on outside: rdn and outpcd over 2f out: rallied over 1f out: kpt on: no further imp wl ins fnl f* 11/2[2]
1-60 6 3 **Daisy Bere (FR)**[47] 7815 4-8-10 81 (p) RussellHarris(7) 10 78
(K R Burke) *t.k.h: prom: smooth hdwy over 2f out: rdn and led briefly over 1f out: edgd lft and wknd ins fnl f* 20/1
5604 7 2 **X Rated (IRE)**[17] 8638 3-8-8 75 JoeFanning 1 68
(Mark Johnston) *chsd clr ldr: hdwy over 2f out: cl up and rdn over 1f out: sn wknd* 13/2
5535 8 hd **Corton Lad**[35] 8188 7-9-4 85 (bt) RowanScott(3) 11 78
(Keith Dalgleish) *t.k.h: led and sn clr: hdd over 1f out: sn wknd* 12/1
5505 9 ¾ **Archipeligo**[34] 8205 6-8-2 71 oh3 JamieGormley(5) 12 62
(Iain Jardine) *hld up in tch: rdn over 2f out: wknd over 1f out* 14/1
0646 10 1 ¼ **Purple Rock (IRE)**[31] 8289 5-8-12 76 (t) CamHardie 5 68
(Michael Easterby) *hld up: pushed along over 2f out: sn no imp: btn over 1f out* 6/1[3]
4220 11 1 **Henpecked**[23] 8485 7-8-7 71 oh1 (p) AndrewMullen 3 58
(Alistair Whillans) *hld up: drvn and outpcd over 2f out: sn btn* 33/1
5532 12 5 **Alexandrakollontai (IRE)**[13] 8718 7-9-2 83 (b) CharlieBennett(3) 6 60
(Alistair Whillans) *hld up: rdn and struggling over 3f out: btn fnl 2f* 11/1
2m 9.06s (-1.34) **Going Correction** +0.15s/f (Slow)
**WFA** 3 from 4yo+ 3lb 12 Ran SP% **120.3**
Speed ratings (Par 105): **111,110,109,109,109 106,105,105,104,103 102,98**
CSF £139.47 CT £505.28 TOTE £10.60: £3.80, £3.00, £1.30; EX 106.40 Trifecta £427.70.
**Owner** G & J Park **Bred** Jill Park **Trained** Carluke, S Lanarks

**FOCUS**
A fair handicap run at a decent pace. The second has been rated close to his best, with a small pb from the third, and the fourth close to form.

## 8913 BETWAY SPRINT H'CAP 5f (Tp)
4:05 (4:07) (Class 3) (0-95,95) 3-Y-0 £8,191 (£2,451; £1,225; £613; £305) Stalls Centre

Form RPR
0060 1 **Atletico (IRE)**[15] 8679 5-9-2 90 DanielTudhope 13 103+
(Roger Varian) *hld up on nr side of gp: shkn up and gd hdwy over 1f out: edgd lft and led ins fnl f: pushed out: comf* 11/4[1]
0004 2 1 ¼ **Bowson Fred**[16] 8660 5-9-4 92 PaulMulrennan 3 100
(Michael Easterby) *cl up in centre of gp: led over 1f out to ins fnl f: kpt on: nt pce of wnr* 5/1[2]
0051 3 1 ¼ **Hilary J**[30] 8321 4-8-7 81 oh1 ShaneGray 14 85
(Ann Duffield) *prom on nr side of gp: effrt and hdwy over 1f out: edgd lft and one pce ins fnl f* 13/2[3]
4220 4 1 **Memories Galore (IRE)**[15] 8680 5-9-1 89 (p) TonyHamilton 9 89
(Roger Fell) *hld up in centre of gp: rdn and hdwy over 1f out: kpt on ins fnl f: nrst fin* 13/2[3]
1612 5 ¾ **Landing Night (IRE)**[16] 8660 5-8-4 81 (tp) RowanScott(3) 10 78
(Rebecca Menzies) *hld up in centre of gp: nt clr run over 2f out to over 1f out: rdn and kpt on fnl f: nvr able to chal* 7/1
0000 6 nk **Rich Again (IRE)**[16] 8660 8-8-11 85 (b) KevinStott 5 81
(James Bethell) *s.i.s: hld up: effrt on far side of gp over 1f out: kpt on fnl f: no imp* 20/1
0363 7 ½ **Green Door (IRE)**[15] 8679 6-9-0 95 (v) JonathanFisher(7) 2 89
(Robert Cowell) *in tch: effrt and rdn in centre of gp over 1f out: outpcd ins fnl f* 11/1
100 8 1 ¼ **Rosina**[16] 8660 4-8-7 81 oh1 (p) JoeFanning 7 71
(Ann Duffield) *hld up in centre of gp: effrt and pushed along over 1f out: no imp fnl f* 40/1
000 9 1 ¾ **Old Fashioned (CHI)**[219] 1863 5-9-1 89 (vt[1]) DavidProbert 4 73
(Luke McJannet) *led on far side of gp: rdn and hdd over 1f out: wknd ins fnl f* 100/1
3300 10 nse **Fast Track**[17] 8639 6-8-4 85 GabrieleMalune(7) 6 68
(David Barron) *prom in centre: drvn over 2f out: wknd appr fnl f* 14/1
005 11 ½ **Jameerah**[17] 8639 4-8-2 81 oh1 JamieGormley(5) 11 63
(Bryan Smart) *prom in centre of gp: drvn and outpcd over 2f out: btn over 1f out* 16/1
42- 12 1 ¼ **Ziggy Lee**[419] 6926 11-8-7 81 CamHardie 12 58
(Lawrence Mullaney) *hld up towards nr side of gp: drvn and outpcd 1/2-way: sn wknd* 66/1
0144 13 nk **Equimou**[33] 8238 3-9-7 95 PhillipMakin 1 71
(Robert Eddery) *prom on far side of gp: effrt and pushed along over 2f out: wknd over 1f out* 11/1
59.45s (-0.05) **Going Correction** +0.175s/f (Slow) 13 Ran SP% **121.4**
Speed ratings (Par 107): **107,105,103,101,100 99,98,96,94,94 93,91,90**
CSF £15.59 CT £87.17 TOTE £3.90: £1.90, £2.00, £2.70; EX 21.30 Trifecta £119.10.
**Owner** A D Spence **Bred** Tally-Ho Stud **Trained** Newmarket, Suffolk

**FOCUS**
A decent sprint handicap and predictably no hanging about. There was no draw bias, with the principals drawn on either flank. It's been rated on the positive side, with the third matching her latest back-to-form win.

## 8914 32RED.COM FILLIES' NOVICE AUCTION STKS 7f 14y (Tp)
4:35 (4:36) (Class 6) 2-Y-0 £2,911 (£866; £432; £216) Stalls Centre

Form RPR
26 1 **Great Shot Sam (USA)**[56] 7556 2-9-0 0 DavidProbert 2 70
(Andrew Balding) *cl up on far side of gp: chal over 2f out: led over 1f out: rdn out fnl f* 3/1[2]
63 2 1 ½ **Ideal Candy (IRE)**[20] 8555 2-9-0 0 ShaneGray 1 66
(Karen Tutty) *hld up: rdn and hdwy wl over 1f out: chsd wnr ins fnl f: r.o* 12/1
5 3 nk **Strawberryandcream**[34] 8208 2-9-0 0 KevinStott 9 65
(James Bethell) *prom: effrt and rdn 2f out: kpt on same pce ins fnl f* 5/1[3]
42 4 ½ **Riverside Walk**[20] 8555 2-9-0 0 DanielTudhope 7 64
(Keith Dalgleish) *t.k.h early: cl up: led over 3f out to over 1f out: no ex ins fnl f* 7/4[1]
5 1 ¼ **Wherearainbowsend (IRE)** 2-9-0 0 (h[1]) GrahamLee 5 60
(Bryan Smart) *s.i.s: hld up: rn green and outpcd over 2f out: rallied over 1f out: kpt on ins fnl f* 33/1
061 6 ½ **Blue Harmony**[13] 8715 2-9-4 67 CliffordLee(3) 3 66
(K R Burke) *prom: rdn over 2f out: edgd lft and wknd over 1f out* 5/1[3]
0 7 18 **Leahcar**[30] 8316 2-9-0 0 TomEaves 8 10
(James Ewart) *cl up: rdn and outpcd over 2f out: sn wknd* 100/1
00 8 10 **Miss Van Winkle**[164] 3662 2-9-0 0 JoeFanning 6
(Mark Johnston) *t.k.h: led to over 3f out: sn lost pl and struggling* 10/1
1m 28.89s (2.69) **Going Correction** +0.175s/f (Slow) 8 Ran SP% **115.4**
Speed ratings (Par 91): **91,89,88,88,86 86,65,54**
CSF £38.53 TOTE £3.40: £1.20, £2.50, £1.80; EX 37.80 Trifecta £216.20.
**Owner** L L Register **Bred** Lannister Holdings Llc, D Brown Et Al **Trained** Kingsclere, Hants

**FOCUS**
A modest fillies' novice event.

## 8915 32RED.COM EBF NOVICE STKS (PLUS 10 RACE) (DIV I) 6f (Tp)
5:10 (5:16) (Class 4) 2-Y-0 £3,946 (£1,174; £586; £293) Stalls Centre

Form RPR
5 1 **Gowanbuster**[30] 8316 2-9-2 0 (t) PaulMulrennan 6 70+
(Susan Corbett) *t.k.h: hld up: hdwy in centre of gp to ld over 1f out: pushed out fnl f* 10/1
00 2 1 ¾ **Cocktail (IRE)**[12] 8735 2-9-2 0 JackGarritty 10 65
(Jedd O'Keeffe) *hld up nr side of gp: hdwy to chse wnr over 1f out: kpt on ins fnl f: nt pce to chal* 66/1
0 3 1 ¼ **Nice Shot (IRE)**[57] 7513 2-9-2 0 DanielTudhope 1 61
(David Simcock) *plld hrd: cl up on far side of gp: ev ch over 2f out to over 1f out: rallied ins fnl f: kpt on fin* 13/8[1]
0 4 nse **Naval Officer**[16] 8649 2-9-2 0 ShaneGray 3 62+
(Nigel Tinkler) *dwlt and blkd s: hld up: pushed along and edgd lft over 2f out: styd on steadily fnl f: nvr nr ldrs* 100/1
4 5 ½ **Takeonefortheteam**[24] 8466 2-9-2 0 DavidProbert 5 59
(Daniel Mark Loughnane) *t.k.h: prom: effrt on far side of gp over 1f out: outpcd fnl f* 9/2[3]
23 6 ½ **Illusional**[8] 8779 2-9-2 0 JoeFanning 2 58
(Mark Johnston) *t.k.h: led in centre of gp: rdn and hdd over 1f out: outpcd ins fnl f* 15/8[2]
200 7 5 **Sunstorm**[20] 8553 2-9-2 71 TomEaves 9 43
(David Brown) *prom on nr side of gp: rdn over 2f out: wknd over 1f out* 22/1
00 8 3 **Symphonic**[24] 8474 2-8-11 0 GrahamLee 8 29
(Ann Duffield) *prom in centre of gp: lost pl over 2f out: sn wknd* 100/1
9 2 ¼ **Alabanza** 2-8-13 0 RowanScott(3) 4 27
(Keith Dalgleish) *dwlt and blkd s: bhd and green: effrt over 3f out: wknd over 2f out* 28/1
6 10 3 ¾ **Camden Town (IRE)**[16] 8649 2-9-2 0 TonyHamilton 7 16
(Roger Fell) *in tch in centre of gp tl rdn and wknd over 2f out* 25/1
11 34 **Aonedamproofing** 2-9-2 0 AndrewMullen 11
(Lisa Williamson) *walked to s: unruly in stalls: s.v.s: t.o thrght* 100/1
1m 14.12s (1.62) **Going Correction** +0.175s/f (Slow) 11 Ran SP% **116.3**
Speed ratings (Par 98): **96,93,92,91,91 90,83,79,76,71 26**
CSF £505.78 TOTE £10.10: £2.30, £15.90, £1.10; EX 360.80 Trifecta £11133.30 Part won..
**Owner** Hassle-Free Racing **Bred** L Waugh **Trained** Otterburn, Northumberland

**FOCUS**
The first division of an ordinary novice event, but the winner did it nicely.

## 8916 32RED.COM EBF NOVICE STKS (PLUS 10 RACE) (DIV II) 6f (Tp)
5:40 (5:42) (Class 4) 2-Y-0 £3,946 (£1,174; £586; £293) Stalls Centre

Form RPR
64 1 **Royal Prospect (IRE)**[24] 8474 2-9-2 0 PaulMulrennan 10 77
(Julie Camacho) *s.i.s: hld up: hdwy nr side of gp over 2f out: led and blkd over 1f out: drvn out fnl f* 4/1[3]
0 2 ¾ **The British Lion (IRE)**[12] 8735 2-9-2 0 JoeFanning 9 76
(Mark Johnston) *hld up: hdwy nr side of gp to chse ldr over 2f out: cl 3rd and keeping on whn hmpd and snatched up over 1f out: rallied ins fnl f: fin 3rd: promoted to 2nd* 7/1
2622 3 1 ¼ **Midsummer Knight**[26] 8432 2-8-13 78 CliffordLee(3) 6 73
(K R Burke) *t.k.h: led in centre of gp: rdn: drifted rt and hdd over 1f out: rallied ins fnl f: fin 2nd: demoted to 3rd* 13/8[1]
0330 4 1 **Laubali**[30] 8325 2-9-2 69 DanielTudhope 2 68
(David O'Meara) *hld up bhd ldng gp: rdn along over 2f out: hdwy over 1f out: kpt on: nt pce to chal* 9/1
3 5 4 ½ **Furzig**[19] 8587 2-9-2 0 TonyHamilton 3 55
(Richard Fahey) *t.k.h: cl up towards far side of gp: rdn and outpcd over 2f out: btn over 1f out* 5/2[2]

00 6 4 ½ **Balmec (IRE)**[56] 7551 2-9-2 0 ShaneGray 4 41
(Ann Duffield) *in tch in centre of gp: rdn and lost pl over 2f out: sn struggling* **100/1**

05 7 7 **Ideal Spirit**[127] 5015 2-8-11 0 SamJames 8 15
(Karen Tutty) *trckd ldrs in centre of gp: struggling over 2f out: sn wknd* **40/1**

0 8 5 **Assertainty**[12] 8734 2-9-2 0 DuranFentiman 1 5
(Tim Easterby) *hld up in tch on far side of gp: struggling over 2f out: sn btn* **40/1**

9 11 **Matilda Grace (IRE)** 2-8-4 0 GabrieleMalune(7) 5
(Lisa Williamson) *dwlt: a bhd and struggling in centre of trck* **100/1**

1m 13.1s (0.60) **Going Correction** +0.175s/f (Slow) 9 Ran SP% **116.0**
Speed ratings (Par 98): **103,100,101,99,93 87,77,71,56**
CSF £31.43 TOTE £4.70: £1.30, £1.20; EX 32.10 Trifecta £122.30.
**Owner** Geoff & Sandra Turnbull **Bred** Highpark Bloodstock Ltd **Trained** Norton, N Yorks

**FOCUS**
A rough race with the main action unfolding close to the nearside rail.
T/Jkpt: Partly Won. £10,000.00 to a £1 stake. Pool: £10,000.00 - 0.5 winning unit. T/Plt: £103.40 to a £1 stake. Pool: £64,918.00 - 458.30 winning units T/Qpdt: £12.80 to a £1 stake. Pool: £7,428.46 - 427.16 winning units **Richard Young**

8917 - 8923a (Foreign Racing) - See Raceform Interactive

8909

# NEWCASTLE (A.W) (L-H)

Friday, November 24

**OFFICIAL GOING: Tapeta: standard**
Wind: Almost nil Weather: Cold, dry

## 8924 BETWAY APPRENTICE H'CAP 6f (Tp)
**5:45** (5:45) (Class 6) (0-55,55) 3-Y-0+ **£2,587** (£770; £384; £192) **Stalls** Centre

Form RPR

641 1 **Breathoffreshair**[20] 8591 3-9-5 **53** JackOsborn 10 62
(Richard Guest) *hld up on nr side of gp: pushed along and hdwy to ld 2f out: sn clr: kpt on wl fnl f: comf* **2/1**[1]

0240 2 2 **Jessie Allan (IRE)**[20] 8591 6-8-12 **46** SeanMooney 2 49
(Jim Goldie) *s.i.s: hld up on far side of gp: effrt and hdwy over 1f out: chsd (clr) wnr ins fnl f: kpt on: nt pce to chal* **16/1**

2623 3 nk **Dream Revival**[9] 8784 4-9-2 **50** (p) SebastianWoods 7 52
(Paul Collins) *s.i.s: hld up: pushed along and hdwy nr side of gp over 1f out: disp 2nd pl ins fnl f: kpt on same pce nr fin* **7/1**[2]

2645 4 2 ½ **Broughtons Fancy**[20] 8591 4-9-5 **53** HarrisonShaw 4 48
(Karen Tutty) *prom on far side of gp: effrt and chsd (clr) wnr over 1f out to ins fnl f: edgd rt and kpt on same pce* **8/1**[3]

-033 5 2 **Guiding Star**[14] 8730 3-8-7 **46** oh1 (p) RussellHarris(5) 6 35
(Patrick J McKenna, Ire) *hld up in centre of gp: rdn and hdwy over 1f out: no further imp ins fnl f* **16/1**

2000 6 shd **Kyllach Me (IRE)**[36] 8194 5-9-0 **55** (v) HarryRussell(7) 1 43
(Bryan Smart) *hld up in tch on outside of gp: rdn over 2f out: sn edgd lft: no imp over 1f out* **33/1**

5062 7 hd **Vecheka (IRE)**[21] 8559 6-8-12 **46** (p) AledBeech 12 34
(Kenny Johnson) *cl up on nr side of gp: ev ch briefly 2f out: rdn and outpcd fnl f* **28/1**

0560 8 ¾ **Willbeme**[20] 8590 9-8-10 **49** (bt) FayeMcManoman(5) 5 34
(Simon West) *in tch in centre of gp: drvn over 2f out: outpcd fr over 1f out* **20/1**

0604 9 2 ¼ **Racing Angel (IRE)**[21] 8558 5-9-7 **55** (b) BenSanderson 9 34
(Adrian Nicholls) *midfield in centre of gp: drvn and outpcd 2f out: btn fnl f* **9/1**

0050 10 hd **Wilde Extravagance (IRE)**[25] 8481 4-9-2 **50** (h) HarryBurns 8 28
(Julie Camacho) *t.k.h: led in centre of gp to 2f out: sn rdn: wknd fnl f* **10/1**

6040 11 3 ½ **Little Kingdom (IRE)**[20] 8591 3-9-2 **50** JonathanFisher 3 18
(Tracy Waggott) *prom on far side of gp: drvn and outpcd over 2f out: sn btn* **33/1**

0024 12 6 **Jorvik Prince**[24] 8490 3-9-2 **55** (b) PatrickO'Hanlon(5) 11 5
(Karen Tutty) *t.k.h: prom in centre of gp: rdn along over 2f out: wknd wl over 1f out* **14/1**

5005 13 5 **Media World (IRE)**[55] 7605 4-9-0 **48** SeamusCronin 13
(Julie Camacho) *bhd on nr side of gp: struggling 1/2-way: nvr on terms* **8/1**[3]

1m 12.33s (-0.17) **Going Correction** +0.075s/f (Slow) 13 Ran SP% **119.7**
Speed ratings (Par 101): **104,101,100,97,94 94,94,93,90,90 85,77,70**
CSF £36.22 CT £199.57 TOTE £2.10: £1.10, £6.30, £1.80; EX 38.70 Trifecta £367.20.
**Owner** Alfa Site Services Ltd/Mrs Alison Guest **Bred** D Curran **Trained** Ingmanthorpe, W Yorks

**FOCUS**
A cold evening with temperatures around 3C. A modest sprint handicap for apprentice riders and the winner did it well.

## 8925 32RED.COM NURSERY H'CAP 1m 5y (Tp)
**6:15** (6:16) (Class 5) (0-75,76) 2-Y-0 **£3,557** (£1,058; £529; £264) **Stalls** Centre

Form RPR

6001 1 **Lord Caprio (IRE)**[9] 8783 2-8-11 **61** 6ex (t) TomEaves 1 65
(Ben Haslam) *hld up in last pl: swtchd lft and hdwy over 2f out: led over 1f out: edgd lft ins fnl f: drvn out* **7/2**[2]

534 2 ¾ **Canadian George (FR)**[46] 7883 2-9-3 **67** PaulMulrennan 4 69
(Keith Dalgleish) *in tch: hdwy to chal over 1f out: edgd lft ins fnl f: kpt on: hld nr fin* **6/1**

0303 3 2 ¾ **Creel**[16] 8676 2-9-12 **76** PhillipMakin 3 72
(David Brown) *carried lft s: sn cl up: ev ch over 2f out: rdn and kpt on same pce fr over 1f out* **9/2**[3]

6433 4 1 ¾ **Handsome Bob (IRE)**[6] 8848 2-9-6 **70** (v[1]) DanielTudhope 5 62
(Keith Dalgleish) *t.k.h: disp ld to 2f out: sn rdn and outpcd* **15/8**[1]

3044 5 ¾ **Austin Powers (IRE)**[20] 8586 2-9-7 **71** AndrewMullen 6 61
(Mark Johnston) *mde most tl rdn and hdd over 1f out: sn wknd* **9/2**[3]

0630 6 3 ¼ **She's Royal**[8] 8802 2-9-6 **70** GrahamLee 2 52
(Bryan Smart) *dwlt: t.k.h: sn prom: rdn over 2f out: edgd lft and wknd over 1f out* **25/1**

1m 39.59s (0.99) **Going Correction** +0.075s/f (Slow) 6 Ran SP% **111.5**
Speed ratings (Par 96): **98,97,94,92,92 88**
CSF £23.61 TOTE £5.00: £2.10, £4.20; EX 24.60 Trifecta £118.00.
**Owner** Blue Lion Racing IX **Bred** Kildaragh Stud **Trained** Middleham Moor, N Yorks
■ Stewards' Enquiry : Paul Mulrennan 18-day ban (six days deferred for two months): excessive use of the whip - totting up procedure (Dec 15-29)

**FOCUS**
A straightforward nursery; not much depth.

## 8926 32RED.COM NOVICE AUCTION STKS 7f 14y (Tp)
**6:45** (6:45) (Class 6) 2-Y-O **£2,587** (£770; £384; £192) **Stalls** Centre

Form RPR

45 1 **Windsor Cross (IRE)**[21] 8553 2-9-2 0 (b[1]) TonyHamilton 3 77
(Richard Fahey) *mde all: drvn along over 1f out: kpt on wl fnl f* **4/1**[3]

2 1 ½ **Fascinator** 2-8-11 0 GrahamLee 1 68+
(Ann Duffield) *t.k.h: stdd in last pl: shkn up and green over 1f out: no imp tl picked up under hands and heels last 100yds: wnt 2nd nr fin: improve* **20/1**

3 ½ **Darkolva (IRE)**[16] 8684 2-9-2 0 JimmyQuinn 4 72
(Joseph Patrick O'Brien, Ire) *t.k.h: pressed wnr: drvn along fr 2f out: kpt on same pce fnl f: lost 2nd towards fin* **10/11**[1]

02 4 ½ **I'm Yer Man**[20] 8587 2-9-2 0 ShaneGray 2 71
(Ann Duffield) *t.k.h early: cl up: drvn and effrt over 1f out: one pce ins fnl f* **9/4**[2]

1m 27.17s (0.97) **Going Correction** +0.075s/f (Slow) 4 Ran SP% **107.9**
Speed ratings (Par 94): **97,95,94,94**
CSF £41.46 TOTE £5.00; EX 26.10 Trifecta £97.10.
**Owner** Alan Harte **Bred** Mrs Louise Quinn **Trained** Musley Bank, N Yorks

**FOCUS**
An interesting novices' auction race and the pace was genuine enough, with the winner making all.

## 8927 BETWAY H'CAP 5f (Tp)
**7:15** (7:16) (Class 5) (0-75,76) 3-Y-0+ **£3,881** (£1,155; £577; £288) **Stalls** Centre

Form RPR

0421 1 **Casterbridge**[21] 8557 5-9-3 **71** (p) TomEaves 6 81
(Eric Alston) *mde all in centre of gp: rdn and drifted rt over 1f out: kpt on wl fnl f* **4/1**[1]

2000 2 1 ½ **Dundunah (USA)**[45] 7940 3-9-4 **72** (t) DanielTudhope 11 77
(David O'Meara) *hld up: hdwy on nr side of gp and chsd wnr over 1f out: kpt on ins fnl f: nt pce to chal* **25/1**

2530 3 nk **Oriental Lilly**[54] 7657 3-8-1 **62** SeanMooney(7) 4 66
(Jim Goldie) *hld up: hdwy far side of gp over 1f out: wnt 3rd ins fnl f: kpt on: nt pce to chal* **40/1**

0310 4 1 **Apricot Sky**[23] 8512 7-9-7 **75** (p) PaulMulrennan 12 75
(Michael Dods) *chsd wnr to over 1f out: drvn and kpt on same pce fnl f* **25/1**

0404 5 ½ **Bondi Beach Boy**[13] 8745 8-9-1 **69** CamHardie 14 67
(Antony Brittain) *prom on nr side of gp: pushed along over 2f out: kpt on same pce ins fnl f* **25/1**

4066 6 ½ **Poppy In The Wind**[14] 8722 5-9-0 **68** (v) JimmyQuinn 2 64
(Alan Brown) *hld up on far side of gp: rdn along 1/2-way: hdwy over 1f out: kpt on fnl f: no imp* **9/1**

1301 7 shd **Roaring Rory**[11] 8775 4-8-5 **64** (p) JamieGormley(5) 9 60
(Ollie Pears) *in tch towards nr side of gp: drvn and outpcd 1/2-way: rallied fnl f: kpt on* **14/1**

0454 8 2 ¼ **Lathom**[16] 8680 4-9-8 **76** GrahamLee 8 64
(Julie Camacho) *in tch in centre of gp: rdn along 1/2-way: wknd over 1f out* **4/1**[1]

5060 9 ¾ **Naples Bay**[14] 8722 3-8-8 **62** JasonHart 13 47
(John Quinn) *bhd on nr side of gp: rdn and carried hd high fr 1/2-way: sme late hdwy: nvr on terms* **66/1**

0042 10 ¾ **Big Lachie**[21] 8557 3-9-4 **72** JackGarritty 7 54
(Daniel Mark Loughnane) *prom in centre of gp tl rdn and wknd over 1f out* **7/1**[3]

6026 11 3 **Astrophysics**[21] 8557 5-8-10 **64** JoeFanning 1 36
(Lynn Siddall) *in tch on far side of gp: drvn over 2f out: wknd wl over 1f out* **10/1**

0211 12 2 ¾ **Young Tiger**[21] 8559 4-8-9 **63** (h) AndrewMullen 5 25
(Tom Tate) *dwlt: t.k.h and sn in tch in centre of gp: rdn over 2f out: wknd wl over 1f out* **11/2**[2]

103- 13 1 ¼ **Coto (IRE)**[7] 8825 5-9-3 **74** CharlieBennett(3) 3 31
(M J Tynan, Ire) *hld up on far side of gp: struggling over 2f out: sn btn* **10/1**

58.81s (-0.69) **Going Correction** +0.075s/f (Slow) 13 Ran SP% **118.2**
Speed ratings (Par 103): **108,105,105,103,102 101,101,98,96,95 90,86,84**
CSF £114.32 CT £3615.60 TOTE £4.70: £1.40, £6.10, £11.80; EX 127.60 Trifecta £2712.10.
**Owner** Liam & Tony Ferguson **Bred** Liam & Tony Ferguson **Trained** Longton, Lancs

**FOCUS**
A competitive sprint handicap with the in-form winner making virtually all the running. He has been rated close to his old best.

## 8928 SUNBETS H'CAP (DIV I) 1m 5y (Tp)
**7:45** (7:45) (Class 5) (0-75,77) 3-Y-0+ **£3,881** (£1,155; £577; £288) **Stalls** Centre

Form RPR

31 1 **Malaspina (ITY)**[64] 7342 5-9-9 **77** (p[1]) PhillipMakin 7 88
(Ivan Furtado) *mde all: set stdy pce: rdn and qcknd over 1f out: edgd rt: kpt on wl fnl f: unchal* **9/2**

0000 2 1 ¾ **Planetaria (IRE)**[14] 8718 4-9-2 **70** JasonHart 9 77
(Julie Camacho) *hld up: hdwy nr side of gp to chse wnr over 1f out: kpt on: nt pce to chal* **28/1**

2412 3 1 ¾ **Gun Case**[14] 8721 5-8-10 **67** (v) RowanScott(3) 4 70
(Alistair Whillans) *dwlt: hld up bhd ldng gp: rdn and outpcd over 2f out: rallied over 1f out: kpt on fnl f: nvr able to chal* **10/3**[2]

020 4 ½ **Always Thankful**[29] 8374 3-9-5 **75** (p) StevieDonohoe 6 76
(Ismail Mohammed) *hld up in tch: effrt and rdn 2f out: kpt on same pce fnl f* **16/1**

3136 5 ¾ **Off Art**[23] 8510 7-9-2 **70** (p) DuranFentiman 3 70
(Tim Easterby) *dwlt: hld up: drvn and outpcd over 2f out: rallied whn blkd ins fnl f: sn n.d* **11/1**

562 6 ½ **Thello**[35] 8209 5-8-12 **69** PhilDennis(3) 1 68
(Jim Goldie) *t.k.h: hld up: hdwy on outside to dispute 2nd pl over 1f out: outpcd ins fnl f* **4/1**[3]

2130 7 3 ¼ **Clock Chimes**[30] 8341 3-9-4 **74** AndrewMullen 8 65
(David Brown) *chsd ldrs: wnt 2nd over 2f out to over 1f out: wknd fnl f* **3/1**[1]

3001 8 ¾ **Teomaria**[23] 8514 3-8-11 **67** GrahamLee 10 56
(K R Burke) *hld up on nr side of gp: drvn and outpcd over 2f out: sn btn* **12/1**

4600 **9** ½ **Town Charter (USA)**[48] 7824 3-9-3 **73**........................(t) DougieCostello 2 61
(Tony Coyle) *chsd wnr to over 2f out: rdn and wknd wl over 1f out* **33/1**
1m 38.83s (0.23) **Going Correction** +0.075s/f (Slow)
**WFA** 3 from 4yo+ 2lb 9 Ran SP% **114.6**
Speed ratings (Par 103): **101,99,97,97,96 95,92,91,91**
CSF £114.94 CT £474.25 TOTE £5.70: £1.70, £4.10, £1.70; EX 103.60 Trifecta £478.50.
**Owner** BGC Racing, C Hodgson & Giggle Factor **Bred** Scuderia Fert Di Ferrario Paolo Et Al **Trained** Wiseton, Nottinghamshire

**FOCUS**
The early pace was not strong in division one of this modest mile handicap and again, the winner made all.

## 8929 SUNBETS H'CAP (DIV II) 1m 5y (Tp)
**8:15** (8:15) (Class 5) (0-75,75) 3-Y-0+ **£3,881** (£1,155; £577; £288) **Stalls** Centre

Form RPR
0402 **1** **Breanski**[31] 8318 3-9-5 **75**..........................................(v) DanielTudhope 10 84
(David O'Meara) *hld up: hdwy to chse clr ldng pair over 2f out: rdn to ld appr fnl f: kpt on strly* **6/4**[1]
021 **2** 2 ¼ **Rey Loopy (IRE)**[20] 8589 3-9-0 **70**........................................ TomEaves 1 73
(Ben Haslam) *hld up: hdwy and rdn over 2f out: styd on fnl f to take 2nd nr fin: no ch w wnr* **9/2**[3]
0241 **3** nse **Newmarket Warrior (IRE)**[35] 8209 6-9-0 **73**.........(p) JamieGormley(5) 8 77
(Iain Jardine) *t.k.h: led 2f: pressed ldr: clr of rest 1/2-way: rdn and chsd wnr over 1f out: no ex and lost 2nd nr fin* **5/2**[2]
4000 **4** 1 ¾ **Sumner Beach**[31] 8319 3-9-5 **75**................................(t¹) StevieDonohoe 3 74
(Brian Ellison) *hld up in tch: effrt and chsd clr ldng pair 1/2-way to over 2f out: rallied over 1f out: kpt on ins fnl f: nt pce to chal* **20/1**
2500 **5** ¾ **Fire Palace**[23] 7881 3-8-10 **66**.............................................. JoeFanning 9 63
(Robert Eddery) *t.k.h: prom in chsng gp: drvn along over 2f out: sn outpcd: rallied fnl f: no imp* **25/1**
04L **6** nk **Majdool (IRE)**[21] 8556 4-8-13 **70**........................................ PhilDennis(3) 4 67
(Noel Wilson) *dwlt: t.k.h: led after 2f and maintained decent gallop: rdn and hdd appr fnl f: sn btn* **8/1**
2505 **7** 2 ¾ **Alpine Dream (IRE)**[21] 8556 4-9-4 **72**...............................(b) JasonHart 2 63
(Tim Easterby) *hld up: effrt and hung lft over 2f out: wknd over 1f out* **12/1**
11- **8** 37 **Nice Vintage (IRE)**[11] 7478 5-8-13 **70**.......................... RowanScott(3) 6
(Katie Scott) *chsd ldng pair to 1/2-way: sn lost pl and struggling: t.o* **100/1**
1m 40.12s (1.52) **Going Correction** +0.075s/f (Slow)
**WFA** 3 from 4yo+ 2lb 8 Ran SP% **115.2**
Speed ratings (Par 103): **95,92,92,90,90 89,87,50**
CSF £8.61 CT £15.64 TOTE £2.00: £1.10, £1.50, £1.20; EX 9.70 Trifecta £19.80.
**Owner** Mrs P Good **Bred** Mrs P Good **Trained** Upper Helmsley, N Yorks

**FOCUS**
The early pace for division two of the 1m handicap was not strong and two went off in front, setting up the race for the favourite, who came from off the pace. Fair form.

## 8930 SUNBETS.CO.UK H'CAP 7f 14y (Tp)
**8:45** (8:46) (Class 6) (0-65,65) 3-Y-0+ **£2,264** (£673; £336; £168) **Stalls** Centre

Form RPR
1533 **1** **Insurplus (IRE)**[14] 8721 4-9-5 **63**..................................... DanielTudhope 8 72
(Jim Goldie) *hld up in centre of gp: weaved through over 2f out: led over 1f out: drvn out* **3/1**[1]
6005 **2** 1 **Tellovoi (IRE)**[24] 8490 9-9-0 **65**....................................(v) JackOsborn(7) 1 71
(Richard Guest) *missed break: t.k.h and led after 1f on far side of gp: rdn and hdd over 1f out: rallied: kpt on same pce last 100yds* **33/1**
2101 **3** 2 ¾ **Honey Badger**[14] 8721 6-9-6 **64**........................................(p) TomEaves 13 63
(Michael Herrington) *prom on nr side of gp: rdn to chal over 1f out: no ex ins fnl f* **5/1**[2]
2050 **4** 2 **Avenue Of Stars**[21] 8552 4-9-2 **60**.............................(p) AndrewMullen 14 53
(Karen McLintock) *hld up on nr side of gp: hdwy over 2f out: sn rdn: kpt on ins fnl f: nt pce to chal* **12/1**
0600 **5** 1 ½ **Ad Vitam (IRE)**[90] 6435 9-9-3 **61**................................(bt) PatrickMathers 9 50
(Suzzanne France) *hld up in midfield in centre of gp: rdn over 2f out: one pce fr over 1f out* **33/1**
3305 **6** 1 ¾ **Inshaa**[14] 8721 5-9-2 **60**...........................................................(p) JasonHart 10 44
(Simon West) *hld up towards nr side of gp: rdn along over 2f out: kpt on ins fnl f: nvr able to chal* **16/1**
6524 **7** hd **Connemera Queen**[17] 8641 4-9-7 **65**.............................. DougieCostello 2 49
(John Butler) *in tch on far side of gp: rdn over 2f out: wknd over 1f out* **9/1**[3]
0205 **8** ½ **Spun Gold**[23] 8503 3-9-5 **64**..........................................(v¹) StevieDonohoe 6 46
(Charlie Fellowes) *s.i.s: hld up on far side of gp: drvn along over 2f out: wknd over 1f out* **3/1**[1]
6105 **9** ¾ **Mr Potter**[14] 8719 4-9-2 **60**..................................................(e) PhillipMakin 7 40
(Richard Guest) *hld up: rdn on far side of gp over 2f out: sn no imp: btn over 1f out* **20/1**
-010 **10** 1 ½ **Black Hambleton**[20] 8589 4-9-6 **64**........................................ GrahamLee 5 40
(Bryan Smart) *in tch in centre of gp: lost pl over 2f out: sn btn* **9/1**[3]
4100 **11** ¾ **Night Shadow**[14] 8721 3-9-1 **60**.............................................. JimmyQuinn 4 33
(Alan Brown) *hld up in centre of gp: drvn and outpcd over 2f out: sn btn* **66/1**
0000 **12** 1 ¾ **Kachess**[13] 8742 3-8-8 **60**................................................ NicolaCurrie(7) 12 29
(David Loughnane) *led 1f on nr side of gp: cl up tl wknd over 2f out* **33/1**
1600 **13** 1 ¾ **Kiwi Bay**[17] 8651 12-9-6 **64**............................................ PaulMulrennan 11 29
(Michael Dods) *prom in centre of gp: lost pl qckly 3f out: sn btn* **25/1**
1m 26.44s (0.24) **Going Correction** +0.075s/f (Slow)
**WFA** 3 from 4yo+ 1lb 13 Ran SP% **119.2**
Speed ratings (Par 101): **101,99,96,94,92 90,90,89,89,87 86,84,82**
CSF £124.55 CT £509.15 TOTE £4.10: £1.20, £10.20, £1.50; EX 115.50 Trifecta £2386.90.
**Owner** Mr & Mrs G Grant & Partner **Bred** Patrick J Monahan **Trained** Uplawmoor, E Renfrews

**FOCUS**
An even pace for this low-key handicap and the winner came from off the pace to score readily - he has been rated to his best.

## 8931 BETWAY MAIDEN STKS 6f (Tp)
**9:15** (9:16) (Class 5) 3-Y-0+ **£3,881** (£1,155; £577; £288) **Stalls** Centre

Form RPR
**1** **Bobby Joe Leg** 3-9-5 0............................................................ TomEaves 2 74+
(Ruth Carr) *stdd in last pl: shkn up and hdwy over 1f out: led ins fnl f: comf* **33/1**
034- **2** ¾ **Kingofmerrows (IRE)**[340] 8454 3-9-5 77.......................... DougieCostello 4 71
(Jamie Osborne) *cl up: led over 2f out: rdn and edgd lft over 1f out: hdd ins fnl f: kpt on: hld nr fin* **9/2**
03 **3** hd **Limoncino (IRE)**[20] 8592 3-9-0 0...................................(h) PaulMulrennan 1 65
(Michael Dods) *racd on outside of main gp: overall ldr to over 2f out: rallied: kpt on same pce ins fnl f* **20/1**
3202 **4** 1 ¼ **Decision Maker (IRE)**[20] 8592 3-9-2 70............................ EoinWalsh(3) 6 66
(Roy Bowring) *t.k.h: trckd ldrs: rdn whn edgd lft and outpcd over 1f out: rallied: kpt on ins fnl f* **9/4**[1]
4-30 **5** ½ **Pudding Chare (IRE)**[25] 8479 3-9-5 66............................ JackGarritty 7 65
(Richard Fahey) *in tch: rdn along over 2f out: edgd lft and no imp over 1f out* **5/2**[2]
-306 **6** ½ **Bequia (IRE)**[143] 4463 3-9-0 69.......................................... DanielTudhope 8 58
(David O'Meara) *hld up: effrt over 2f out: rdn and no imp over 1f out* **3/1**[3]
46 **7** 2 ¼ **Captain Bond**[35] 8217 3-8-12 0........................................ ZakWheatley(7) 5 56
(David O'Meara) *hld up: rdn and hung lft over 2f out: sn no imp: btn over 1f out* **22/1**
0 **8** 5 **Dream Destroyer (IRE)**[14] 8716 3-9-0 0............................. SamJames 3 35
(Geoffrey Harker) *s.i.s: hld up in tch: struggling 3f out: sn btn* **125/1**
1m 13.21s (0.71) **Going Correction** +0.075s/f (Slow) 8 Ran SP% **115.4**
Speed ratings (Par 103): **98,97,96,95,94 93,90,84**
CSF £170.60 TOTE £31.10: £7.90, £1.80, £1.50; EX 150.60 Trifecta £2042.70.
**Owner** Mrs Angela Clark **Bred** Angela Clark **Trained** Huby, N Yorks

**FOCUS**
A modest maiden run at a fair pace. The front-running 3rd is possibly the key to the form, but the race has been rated a bit cautiously.
T/Plt: £284.80 to a £1 stake. Pool: £97,561.75 - 250.05 winning units. T/Qpdt: £57.80 to a £1 stake. Pool: £9,785.76 - 125.18 winning units. **Richard Young**

8932 - 8942a (Foreign Racing) - See Raceform Interactive

# 8877 LINGFIELD (L-H)
Saturday, November 25

**OFFICIAL GOING: Polytrack: standard**
Wind: very light across Weather: Sunny

## 8943 £10 FREE AT 32RED.COM (S) STKS 1m 1y(P)
**11:45** (11:46) (Class 6) 2-Y-O **£2,264** (£673; £336; £168) **Stalls** High

Form RPR
6500 **1** **Carp Kid (IRE)**[16] 8702 2-8-11 68........................................ SeanLevey 2 67
(Richard Hannon) *mde all: rdn over 1f out: drvn ins fnl f: hld on towards fin* **13/8**[1]
3605 **2** nk **Mr Large (IRE)**[5] 8870 2-8-11 65.................................... DougieCostello 1 66
(Jamie Osborne) *trckd ldrs: rdn to chse ldr over 1f out: kpt on: nvr quite getting there* **9/4**[2]
6056 **3** 7 **Hurricane Lil (IRE)**[18] 8644 2-8-6 58.............................. KieranO'Neill 3 44
(George Baker) *prom: rdn over 2f out: wknd over 1f out* **10/1**
055 **4** 3 ¼ **Rose Of Shiraz**[35] 8253 2-8-6 0.................................................. LukeMorris 5 36
(J S Moore) *trckd ldrs: rdn over 2f out: sn outpcd and btn* **40/1**
06 **5** ¾ **Financial Crime (IRE)**[9] 8794 2-8-8 0...................(v) CallumShepherd(3) 7 40
(Mick Channon) *sn chsd ldrs towards outer: rdn over 3f out: sn outpcd: btn wl over 1f out* **14/1**
0045 **6** 1 **Counterfeit**[29] 8397 2-7-13 61...........................................(p) NicolaCurrie(7) 6 32
(Richard Hughes) *hld up towards outer: rdn 2f out: nvr threatened* **12/1**
**7** 4 **Bond Do Tigrao**[52] 7745 2-8-11 0..............................(t) SilvestreDeSousa 4 28
(Sylvester Kirk) *dwlt: hld up towards inner: rdn along over 3f out: no imp whn sltly checked over 2f out* **5/1**[3]
**8** ½ **Cornish Point (IRE)** 2-8-11 0........................................... DavidProbert 8 26
(J S Moore) *dwlt: a towards rr* **40/1**
1m 36.61s (-1.59) **Going Correction** -0.075s/f (Stan) 8 Ran SP% **113.9**
Speed ratings (Par 94): **104,103,96,93,92 91,87,87**
CSF £5.33 TOTE £2.20: £1.10, £1.30, £3.40; EX 5.80 Trifecta £26.20.The winner was sold for 7,200
**Owner** Sullivan Ltd, Blunt, Palmer-Brown, Ensor **Bred** Acorn Stud **Trained** East Everleigh, Wilts

**FOCUS**
A moderate 2yo seller and they finished well spread out behind the front two. Few got into it.

## 8944 PLAY SLOTS AT SUNBETS.CO.UK/VEGAS CONDITIONS STKS 7f 1y(P)
**12:15** (12:15) (Class 3) 3-Y-0+ **£7,246** (£2,168; £1,084; £542; £270) **Stalls** Low

Form RPR
000 **1** **Early Morning (IRE)**[52] 7727 6-8-11 92..................... HectorCrouch(3) 3 103
(Harry Dunlop) *mde all: rdn clr appr fnl f: easily* **12/1**
1005 **2** 5 **Chevallier**[176] 3298 5-9-0 91..................................................(p¹) LukeMorris 2 90
(Archie Watson) *trckd ldrs: rdn over 1f out: one pce* **10/1**
06 **3** nk **Hakam (USA)**[49] 7828 5-9-0 95.............................(p) SilvestreDeSousa 4 89
(Michael Appleby) *in tch: rdn over 2f out: kpt on ins fnl f* **7/2**[2]
2101 **4** ½ **Bumptious**[14] 8747 4-9-2 86..................................................(p) SeanLevey 6 89
(Ismail Mohammed) *prom: rdn over 2f out: sn one pce: no ex towards fin* **12/1**
1-10 **5** hd **Brittanic (IRE)**[59] 7506 3-9-4 97........................................... MartinHarley 5 91
(David Simcock) *dwlt: hld up in rr: pushed along 2f out: kpt on ins fnl f* **7/1**[3]
066- **6** ½ **C Note (IRE)**[338] 8489 4-9-0 97........................................(t¹) DanielMuscutt 1 85
(Heather Main) *hld up in tch: pushed along over 1f out: bit short of room appr fnl f: keeping on whn short of room again towards fin and eased* **20/1**
2111 **7** ½ **Gulliver**[19] 8639 3-8-13 105.......................................(tp) JosephineGordon 7 83
(Hugo Palmer) *chsd ldrs on outside: pushed along over 3f out: rdn over 2f out: sn no prog: wknd ins fnl f* **11/10**[1]
1m 23.14s (-1.66) **Going Correction** -0.075s/f (Stan)
**WFA** 3 from 4yo+ 1lb 7 Ran SP% **111.6**
Speed ratings (Par 107): **106,100,99,99,99 98,98**
CSF £113.89 TOTE £14.00: £5.90, £5.40; EX 123.70 Trifecta £1466.70.
**Owner** Early Risers **Bred** Lakin Bloodstock/Wardley Bloodstock **Trained** Lambourn, Berks

**FOCUS**
A decent conditions event, but the enterprisingly ridden winner bolted up and has been rated back to something like his best.

## 8945 32RED CASINO/EBF STALLIONS NOVICE STKS 5f 6y(P)
**12:50** (12:50) (Class 5) 2-Y-O **£2,911** (£866; £432; £216) **Stalls** High

Form RPR
4 **1** **Hit The Beat**[39] 8130 2-8-11 0............................................... MartinHarley 1 73
(Clive Cox) *mde all: rdn over 1f out: kpt on wl* **15/8**[2]
351 **2** 2 **Drakefell (IRE)**[8] 8819 2-9-2 78.................................... RossaRyan(7) 4 78
(Richard Hannon) *prom: rdn 2f out: kpt on but a hld* **11/10**[1]
**3** 4 ½ **Galloway Hills** 2-9-2 0............................................. SilvestreDeSousa 8 55+
(David Elsworth) *dwlt: green and outpcd in rr tl r.o wl fnl f: wnt 3rd post* **7/1**[3]

0 **4** *nk* **Eesha Says (IRE)**[29] 8397 2-8-11 0 ......... DavidProbert 2 49
(Tony Carroll) *dwlt: sn chsd ldrs on inner: rdn over 2f out: outpcd by ldng pair over 1f out: one pce and lost 3rd post* **100/1**

600 **5** *1 ½* **Crystal Deauville (FR)**[14] 8734 2-9-2 0 ......... (p[1]) MartinDwyer 7 48
(Gay Kelleway) *chsd ldrs on outside: rdn over 2f out: sn outpcd: hung lft over 1f out: no ex ins fnl f* **12/1**

0 **6** *1 ¼* **Gunnar Julius (USA)**[72] 7079 2-9-2 0 ......... LiamKeniry 3 44
(Ed Walker) *dwlt: sn in tch: rdn over 2f out: outpcd whn carried lft appr fnl f: no ex ins fnl f* **14/1**

6650 **7** *1 ¾* **Mocead Cappall**[38] 8145 2-8-8 52 ......... EoinWalsh(3) 9 33
(John Holt) *hld up: rdn over 2f out: nvr threatened* **100/1**

600 **8** *½* **Swiss Psalm**[59] 7512 2-8-11 39 ......... KieranO'Neill 5 31
(Mark Gillard) *midfield: rdn over 2f out: sltly short of room appr fnl f: sn wknd* **100/1**

54 **9** *nk* **Zouch**[35] 8252 2-9-2 0 ......... LukeMorris 6 35
(J S Moore) *midfield: rdn over 2f out: wknd over 1f out* **12/1**

58.25s (-0.55) **Going Correction** -0.075s/f (Stan) **9** Ran SP% **119.9**
Speed ratings (Par 96): **101,97,90,90,87 85,82,82,81**
CSF £4.49 TOTE £2.80: £1.10, £1.10, £2.00; EX 4.90 Trifecta £17.80.
**Owner** Clive Cox Racing Ltd **Bred** Mrs Tina Cox **Trained** Lambourn, Berks

**FOCUS**
A modest sprint novice event. The third winner to make all on the card and again few got into it, with the front two holding those places throughout.

## 8946 BETWAY H'CAP 1m 2f (P)
**1:25** (1:25) (Class 6) (0-65,65) 3-Y-O+ **£2,264** (£673; £336; £168) **Stalls** Low

Form RPR

6000 **1** **Music Major**[24] 8503 4-9-6 **64** ......... LukeMorris 13 70
(Michael Attwater) *swtchd lft s: hld up: rdn and hdwy over 1f out: r.o wl: led 50yds out* **20/1**

4450 **2** *nk* **Pink Ribbon (IRE)**[60] 7495 5-9-3 **61** ......... (p) SilvestreDeSousa 6 66
(Sylvester Kirk) *trckd ldrs: rdn over 2f out: edgd ahd 75yds out: sn hdd: kpt on* **4/1**[2]

0314 **3** *nk* **Beepeecee**[30] 8376 3-9-3 **64** ......... (b) ShaneKelly 9 70
(Richard Hughes) *dwlt: hld up in rr: angled rt and hdwy whn short of room of room 1f out: swtchd rt: r.o strly fnl 110yds: gaining at fin* **10/1**

5303 **4** *½* **Bayston Hill**[28] 8429 3-9-3 **64** ......... DanielMuscutt 14 69
(Mark Usher) *across fr wd stall to sn ld: rdn over 2f out: hdd 75yds out: no ex* **7/1**[3]

2503 **5** *1 ¼* **Silver Dixie (USA)**[23] 8549 7-9-3 **61** ......... (p) CharlesBishop 2 63
(Peter Hedger) *midfield: rdn over 2f out: hdwy over 1f out: one pce ins fnl f* **7/2**[1]

0503 **6** *nse* **Falcon's Fire (IRE)**[46] 7936 4-9-3 **61** ......... (b) PhillipMakin 8 62
(Keith Dalgleish) *midfield towards outer: rdn over 2f out: bmpd by 3rd ins fnl f: kpt on* **12/1**

6400 **7** *¾* **Attain**[100] 6109 8-9-3 **61** ......... EdwardGreatrex 12 61
(Archie Watson) *hld up: rdn 2f out: kpt on ins fnl f: nrst fin* **12/1**

2006 **8** *1* **Chelwood Gate (IRE)**[28] 8429 7-9-4 **62** ......... (v) PaulMulrennan 4 60
(Conor Dore) *trckd ldrs: rdn over 2f out: wknd fnl 110yds* **10/1**

436 **9** *nse* **Yogiyogiyogi (IRE)**[51] 7768 3-9-4 **65** ......... MartinHarley 7 64
(Denis Coakley) *prom: rdn over 2f out: wknd fnl 110yds* **14/1**

3665 **10** *nk* **Sheila's Fancy (IRE)**[108] 5780 3-9-2 **63** ......... LiamKeniry 3 61
(J S Moore) *hld up: rdn over 2f out: nvr threatened* **25/1**

4004 **11** *¾* **Berkeley Vale**[24] 8513 6-9-2 **60** ......... DavidProbert 1 56
(Roger Teal) *midfield on inner: rdn over 2f out: wknd fnl 110yds* **14/1**

0000 **12** *6* **Idol Deputy (FR)**[29] 8400 11-9-1 **64** ......... (p) RachealKneller(5) 10 49
(James Bennett) *trckd ldrs: rdn over 2f out: wknd over 1f out* **66/1**

1132 **13** *2* **Suitsus**[18] 8641 6-9-7 **65** ......... (t) TimmyMurphy 5 46
(Geoffrey Deacon) *in tch on outside: rdn over 2f out: wknd over 1f out* **7/1**[3]

2m 5.44s (-1.16) **Going Correction** -0.075s/f (Stan)
**WFA** 3 from 4yo+ 3lb **13** Ran SP% **124.2**
Speed ratings (Par 101): **101,100,100,100,99 99,98,97,97,97 96,92,90**
CSF £100.75 CT £885.76 TOTE £14.80: £4.40, £2.40, £4.30; EX 152.70 Trifecta £349.90.
**Owner** The Attwater Partnership **Bred** Kevin Daniel Crabb **Trained** Epsom, Surrey
■ Stewards' Enquiry : Shane Kelly caution: careless riding

**FOCUS**
A moderate handicap run at a steady pace.

## 8947 32RED.COM/EBF FILLIES' H'CAP 1m 1y(P)
**2:00** (2:01) (Class 4) (0-85,83) 3-Y-O+ **£6,145** (£1,828; £913; £456) **Stalls** High

Form RPR

1000 **1** **Favourite Royal (IRE)**[23] 8546 3-9-1 **79** ......... (v) CharlesBishop 4 84
(Eve Johnson Houghton) *midfield on inner: gng wl whn bit short of room 2f out: rdn and hdwy appr fnl f: sn chsd ldr: kpt on to ld 50yds out* **14/1**

3241 **2** *¾* **Ifubelieveindreams (IRE)**[16] 8707 3-9-1 **79** ......... SeanLevey 3 82
(Ismail Mohammed) *hld up: rdn and r.o strly fnl f: wnt 2nd post* **7/1**[3]

4231 **3** *nse* **Cape To Cuba**[19] 8635 3-8-10 **77** ......... GeorgeWood(3) 5 80
(James Fanshawe) *dwlt: hld up: rdn and gd hdwy on inner over 1f out: kpt on* **3/1**[1]

0143 **4** *nse* **Lady Perignon**[34] 8257 4-9-1 **77** ......... DavidProbert 2 81
(Andrew Balding) *led: rdn 2f out: edgd rt ins fnl f: hdd 50yds out: no ex* **6/1**[2]

3465 **5** *shd* **Multicultural (IRE)**[21] 8600 3-8-13 **77** ......... (v) LukeMorris 7 80+
(James Tate) *hld up: rdn and hdwy on outside appr fnl f: r.o: nrst fin* **8/1**

0633 **6** *½* **Hawatif (IRE)**[53] 7710 4-9-0 **76** ......... PaulMulrennan 1 79
(Anthony Carson) *trckd ldrs: rdn over 2f out: chal 1f out: no ex fnl 50yds* **25/1**

3502 **7** *1 ¼* **Bint Dandy (IRE)**[19] 8636 6-9-0 **83** ......... (b) NicolaCurrie(7) 6 83
(Chris Dwyer) *midfield towards outer: rdn 2f out: one pce and nvr threatened* **8/1**

0312 **8** *2 ¼* **Luang Prabang (IRE)**[14] 8749 4-8-7 **72** ......... HollieDoyle(3) 10 67
(Chris Wall) *prom: rdn over 2f out: wknd fnl f* **8/1**

61 **9** *2 ¼* **Labhay (IRE)**[141] 4565 3-8-12 **79** ......... GeorgiaCox(3) 9 67
(William Haggas) *chsd ldrs on outer: rdn 2f out: wknd over 1f out* **10/1**

5461 **10** *2 ½* **Dealer's Choice (IRE)**[51] 7771 3-8-10 **74** ......... SilvestreDeSousa 8 57
(Roger Varian) *chsd ldrs: hrd rdn over 2f out: wknd over 1f out* **15/2**

1m 36.78s (-1.42) **Going Correction** -0.075s/f (Stan)
**WFA** 3 from 4yo+ 2lb **10** Ran SP% **116.5**
Speed ratings (Par 102): **104,103,103,103,103 102,101,99,96,94**
CSF £108.39 CT £377.55 TOTE £16.90: £4.30, £2.20, £1.80; EX 169.20 Trifecta £968.50.
**Owner** J Cross,M Duckham,L Godfrey,P Wollaston **Bred** Emma Capon Bloodstock **Trained** Blewbury, Oxon

**FOCUS**
A fair handicap with eight of the ten fillies either winning or being placed in their most recent start, but a messy race with both the leaders pulling hard in front. It became a sprint from the home bend and the first six finished in a heap, so it has to be rated to an ordinary level.

## 8948 PLAY STARBURST SLOT AT SUNBETS.CO.UK/VEGAS H'CAP (DIV I) 7f 1y(P)
**2:35** (2:35) (Class 6) (0-55,55) 3-Y-O+ **£2,264** (£673; £336; £168) **Stalls** Low

Form RPR

0001 **1** **Loveatfirstsight**[17] 8675 4-9-7 **55** ......... (p) DanielMuscutt 4 62
(Jane Chapple-Hyam) *in tch: drvn and hdwy to chse ldr jst ins fnl f: edgd rt and led 50yds out: kpt on* **3/1**[1]

0040 **2** *nk* **Jack Blane**[29] 8401 3-9-4 **53** ......... (p) PhillipMakin 3 58
(Keith Dalgleish) *midfield: pushed along and hdwy over 1f out: rdn to chse ldrs ins fnl f: sltly impeded 50yds out: kpt on* **3/1**[1]

4043 **3** *½* **Black Truffle (FR)**[39] 8134 7-8-6 **47** ......... (v) NicolaCurrie(7) 8 52
(Mark Usher) *chsd ldrs: rdn over 2f out: kpt on* **12/1**

0350 **4** *nse* **Ronni Layne**[23] 8538 3-9-0 **49** ......... (b[1]) PaulMulrennan 12 53
(Louise Allan) *chsd ldrs: rdn over 2f out: kpt on* **10/1**

0300 **5** *hd* **Locommotion**[45] 7952 5-9-2 **50** ......... WilliamCarson 13 54
(Matthew Salaman) *dwlt but sn led: rdn 2f out: edgd rt ins fnl f: hdd 50yds out: no ex* **25/1**

0053 **6** *¾* **Lucky Di**[39] 8133 7-8-13 **47** ......... CharlesBishop 2 49
(Peter Hedger) *hld up: rdn over 2f out: kpt on ins fnl f: nrst fin* **8/1**[3]

0006 **7** *shd* **Rapid Rise (IRE)**[8] 8823 3-8-10 **48** ......... (v) GeorgiaCox(3) 10 49
(Milton Bradley) *s.i.s: hld up in rr: rdn along over 3f out: kpt on ins fnl f: nrst fin* **25/1**

000- **8** *¾* **Last Word**[394] 7647 3-9-6 **55** ......... LiamKeniry 7 55
(Joseph Tuite) *trckd ldrs: rdn 2f out: sltly short of room ins fnl f: wknd fnl 75yds* **33/1**

1260 **9** *¾* **Tigerfish (IRE)**[68] 7212 3-9-0 **52** ......... (p) HollieDoyle(3) 11 49
(William Stone) *hld up: sme late hdwy: nvr threatened* **12/1**

3520 **10** *hd* **Luduamf (IRE)**[58] 7540 3-8-7 **49** ......... RossaRyan(7) 14 45
(Richard Hannon) *midfield towards outer: rdn 2f out: nvr threatened* **14/1**

0001 **11** *nk* **Mr Andros**[23] 8543 4-9-7 **55** ......... (bt) ShaneKelly 6 51
(Brendan Powell) *in tch: rdn over 2f out: wknd fnl f* **7/2**[2]

2200 **12** *2* **Harlequin Rose (IRE)**[60] 7487 3-9-3 **52** ......... (v) DavidProbert 9 42
(Patrick Chamings) *midfield: rdn over 2f out: wknd fnl f* **33/1**

00-0 **13** *2 ¼* **Alligator**[49] 7833 3-9-3 **52** ......... SteveDrowne 5 36
(Tony Carroll) *hld up in midfield: rdn over 2f out: wknd over 1f out* **50/1**

1m 24.29s (-0.51) **Going Correction** -0.075s/f (Stan)
**WFA** 3 from 4yo+ 1lb **13** Ran SP% **130.0**
Speed ratings (Par 101): **99,98,98,98,97 96,96,95,95,94 94,92,89**
CSF £12.40 CT £103.35 TOTE £3.80: £1.60, £2.20, £4.20; EX 13.90 Trifecta £139.60.
**Owner** Miss K Squance **Bred** Kevin Daniel Crabb **Trained** Dalham, Suffolk
■ Stewards' Enquiry : Daniel Muscutt two-day ban: careless riding (Dec 9, 11)

**FOCUS**
Low-grade fare and a typical Lingfield finish, with plenty still in with a chance late on. There was a bit of trouble between the front pair to boot, but the Stewards allowed the result to stand. It has been rated to an ordinary level around the 2nd-4th.

## 8949 PLAY STARBURST SLOT AT SUNBETS.CO.UK/VEGAS H'CAP (DIV II) 7f 1y(P)
**3:10** (3:11) (Class 6) (0-55,55) 3-Y-O+ **£2,264** (£673; £336; £168) **Stalls** Low

Form RPR

405U **1** **Hidden Stash**[23] 8543 3-8-11 **49** ......... (p) HollieDoyle(3) 7 56
(William Stone) *mde all: rdn over 2f out: strly pressed wl over 1f out: hld on wl* **11/1**

0023 **2** *nk* **Warba (IRE)**[17] 8675 3-9-3 **52** ......... (t) SeanLevey 9 58
(Mohamed Moubarak) *prom: rdn to chal strly wl over 1f out: kpt on* **7/1**

4064 **3** *hd* **Hisar (IRE)**[25] 8495 3-9-4 **53** ......... AlistairRawlinson 12 58
(Michael Appleby) *trckd ldrs: rdn over 1f out: kpt on fnl f* **5/2**[1]

5544 **4** *¾* **New Rich**[17] 8675 7-9-3 **51** ......... (b) EdwardGreatrex 3 55
(Eve Johnson Houghton) *midfield: rdn and hdwy appr fnl f: kpt on ins fnl f* **11/4**[2]

6430 **5** *½* **Monsieur Royale**[56] 7606 7-9-2 **50** ......... WilliamCarson 4 53
(Clive Drew) *trckd ldrs: rdn 2f out: no ex fnl 75yds* **20/1**

3005 **6** *2 ½* **Dynamic Girl (IRE)**[17] 8675 4-8-10 **51** ......... (t) NicolaCurrie(7) 1 47
(Brendan Powell) *slowly away: hld up: rdn over 2f out: sme late hdwy: nvr threatened* **7/2**[3]

-000 **7** *nse* **Mette**[59] 7514 4-8-12 **46** ......... (t[1]) DanielMuscutt 8 42
(Mark Usher) *in tch: keen early: rdn and outpcd over 2f out: no threat after* **66/1**

3200 **8** *4 ½* **Wedgewood Estates**[37] 8185 6-9-0 **48** ......... SteveDrowne 11 32
(Tony Carroll) *midfield: rdn over 2f out: wknd ins fnl f* **33/1**

0400 **9** *1 ¾* **Nicky Baby (IRE)**[18] 8659 3-9-6 **55** ......... (h[1]) ShaneKelly 5 33
(Dean Ivory) *dwlt: hld up: rdn over 3f out: sn btn* **12/1**

-000 **10** *hd* **Clandon**[17] 8675 4-8-9 **46** oh1 ......... (v[1]) CallumShepherd(3) 6 25
(Brett Johnson) *hld up: rdn over 2f out: sn btn* **50/1**

1m 24.39s (-0.41) **Going Correction** -0.075s/f (Stan)
**WFA** 3 from 4yo+ 1lb **10** Ran SP% **117.1**
Speed ratings (Par 101): **99,98,98,97,97 94,94,88,86,86**
CSF £83.06 CT £256.37 TOTE £11.40: £3.60, £2.40, £1.10; EX 90.20 Trifecta £458.00.
**Owner** Miss Caroline Scott **Bred** Kingsclere Stud **Trained** West Wickham, Cambs

**FOCUS**
This division was hit by four non-runners. Another race where those at the front were greatly favoured, with the order of the first three never changing. The winning time was 1/10 of a second slower than the first leg.

## 8950 BETWAY SPRINT H'CAP 5f 6y(P)
**3:40** (3:40) (Class 4) (0-85,81) 3-Y-O+ **£4,690** (£1,395; £697; £348) **Stalls** High

Form RPR

2033 **1** **Come On Dave (IRE)**[43] 7994 8-9-3 **77** ......... (v) LiamKeniry 4 84
(John Butler) *prom: rdn 2f out: led ins fnl f: kpt on* **9/2**[2]

5621 **2** *½* **Blazed (IRE)**[14] 8745 3-8-11 **71** ......... SilvestreDeSousa 6 76+
(Roger Charlton) *s.i.s: sn in tch: chsd ldr 2f out: rdn over 1f out: no immediate rspnse: kpt on wl fnl 110yds* **11/10**[1]

3350 **3** *½* **Annie Salts**[7] 8853 4-8-0 **67** ......... (h) NicolaCurrie(7) 2 70
(Chris Dwyer) *hld up in tch: rdn and hdwy on inner appr fnl f: kpt on* **7/1**[3]

0034 **4** *½* **Penny Dreadful**[23] 8540 5-8-10 **70** ......... (b) KieranO'Neill 5 72
(Scott Dixon) *led: hung repeatedly rt: rdn over 1f out: hdd ins fnl f: no ex* **10/1**

5264 **5** *hd* **Zipedeedodah (IRE)**[68] 7217 5-9-3 **77** ......... (t) ShaneKelly 1 78
(Joseph Tuite) *hld up: pushed along and hdwy 1f out: rdn and one pce fnl 110yds* **14/1**

6406 **6** *1 ¼* **Mr Pocket (IRE)**[18] 8645 3-9-1 **75**....................(bt) SeanLevey 7 71
(Paul Cole) *sn chsd ldrs on outer: rdn 2f out: wknd fnl f* **9/2**[2]
58.15s (-0.65) **Going Correction** -0.075s/f (Stan) 6 Ran SP% **112.2**
Speed ratings (Par 105): **102,101,100,99,99 97**
CSF £9.93 TOTE £5.50: £2.50, £1.10; EX 10.10 Trifecta £54.30.
**Owner** Royale Racing Syndicate **Bred** Mrs Eithne Hamilton **Trained** Newmarket, Suffolk

**FOCUS**
A fair little sprint handicap to end with plenty of pace on. The winner has been rated to last winter's form.
T/Plt: £512.00 to a £1 stake. Pool: £57,023.40 - 81.30 winning units T/Qpdt: £12.80 to a £1 stake. Pool: £7,578.73 - 435.02 winning units **Andrew Sheret**

# [8869] WOLVERHAMPTON (A.W) (L-H)

Saturday, November 25

**OFFICIAL GOING: Tapeta: standard**
Wind: Fresh half behind Weather: Fine

## 8951 32RED.COM EBF STALLIONS NOVICE STKS (DIV I) 1m 142y (Tp)
**5:45** (5:47) (Class 5) 2-Y-O **£3,881** (£1,155; £577; £288) **Stalls** Low

Form RPR
0 **1** **Thunderbolt Rocks**[29] 8387 2-9-2 0.................... JosephineGordon 2 76
(Hugo Palmer) *s.i.s: pushed along early in rr: swtchd rt and hdwy over 1f out: edgd lft and r.o to ld towards fin* **10/1**
34 **2** *¾* **Dance Me (USA)**[30] 8373 2-8-8 0.................... MitchGodwin(3) 10 69
(Sylvester Kirk) *hld up in tch: rdn over 1f out: led wl ins fnl f: hdd towards fin* **9/1**
60 **3** *1 ¼* **Island Court (IRE)**[7] 8839 2-9-2 0.................... TomMarquand 5 71
(J S Moore) *chsd ldrs: rdn over 2f out: ev ch ins fnl f: sn carried lft: styd on same pce* **50/1**
33 **4** *½* **The Lincoln Lawyer**[10] 8782 2-9-2 0.................... JoeFanning 7 70
(Mark Johnston) *led 1f: chsd ldr: rdn over 2f out: led ins fnl f: sn hdd: styd on same pce: fin 5th: plcd 4th* **3/1**[2]
421 **5** *1 ¼* **Guvenor's Choice (IRE)**[14] 8748 2-9-3 82....................(t) CliffordLee(3) 6 72
(K R Burke) *pushed along to ld after 1f: rdn over 1f out: hdd and no ex ins fnl f: fin 6th: plcd 5th* **9/4**[1]
**6** *2 ¾* **Shakour (IRE)** 2-9-2 0....................(t[1]) RobertHavlin 9 62
(John Gosden) *s.i.s: hld up: styd on ins fnl f: nvr on terms: fin 7th: plcd 6th* **6/1**[3]
0 **7** *nk* **Crimson Skies (IRE)**[17] 8668 2-8-11 0.................... RichardKingscote 3 56
(Tom Dascombe) *chsd ldrs: rdn over 2f out: wknd over 1f out: fin 8th: plcd 7th* **66/1**
60 **8** *½* **Wild West Hero**[16] 8703 2-9-2 0.................... TedDurcan 1 60
(Sir Michael Stoute) *hld up in tch: rdn over 2f out: wknd over 1f out: fin 9th: plcd 8th* **33/1**
**9** *3 ¼* **Black Medusa (IRE)** 2-9-2 0.................... RaulDaSilva 8 53
(Paul Cole) *prom: lost pl after 1f: n.d after: fin 10th: plcd 9th* **33/1**
00 **10** *nk* **Connoisseur**[51] 7757 2-8-11 0.................... LukeMorris 4 48
(Sir Mark Prescott Bt) *prom: lost pl after 1f: nvr on terms after: fin 11th: plcd 10th* **100/1**
00 **11** *3* **Parisian (IRE)**[31] 8340 2-9-2 0.................... FranBerry 13 46
(Ralph Beckett) *s.i.s: hdwy over 3f out: wknd over 1f out: fin 12th: plcd 11th* **8/1**
5 **D** *¾* **Mr Reckless (IRE)**[60] 7488 2-9-2 0.................... DougieCostello 11 74
(Jamie Osborne) *hld up: hdwy and hung lft over 1f out: nt clr run ins fnl f: r.o: fin 4th: disqualified* **17/2**
1m 50.16s (0.06) **Going Correction** -0.05s/f (Stan) 12 Ran SP% **121.1**
Speed ratings (Par 96): **97,96,95,94,93 90,90,89,86,86 84,94**
CSF £96.07 TOTE £8.00: £2.70, £3.00, £10.80; EX 90.80 Trifecta £3746.40.
**Owner** Nick Bradley 45 & Partner **Bred** Hall Of Fame Stud Ltd **Trained** Newmarket, Suffolk
■ Stewards' Enquiry : Dougie Costello three-day ban: failed to weigh-in (Dec 9, 11, 12)

**FOCUS**
This looks modest form.

## 8952 32RED.COM EBF STALLIONS NOVICE STKS (DIV II) 1m 142y (Tp)
**6:15** (6:15) (Class 5) 2-Y-O **£3,881** (£1,155; £577; £288) **Stalls** Low

Form RPR
3 **1** **Hipster Boy**[17] 8677 2-9-2 0.................... RobertHavlin 2 77+
(John Gosden) *sn led: hdd over 6f out: chsd ldrs: rdn and r.o to ld wl ins fnl f* **6/4**[1]
05 **2** *hd* **Profound (IRE)**[29] 8387 2-9-2 0.................... JackMitchell 6 77
(Roger Varian) *chsd ldrs: rdn to ld and hung lft over 1f out: hdd wl ins fnl f* **7/2**[2]
**3** *2 ¾* **Voyager Blue** 2-9-2 0.................... JasonHart 9 71+
(Jamie Osborne) *hmpd sn after s: hld up: hdwy over 1f out: r.o* **40/1**
**4** *shd* **Angelina D'Or (GER)** 2-8-11 0.................... PJMcDonald 8 66+
(Mark Johnston) *s.i.s: hld up: hdwy and hung lft over 1f out: r.o* **18/1**
00 **5** *3* **Silver Crescent**[58] 7543 2-9-2 0.................... RichardKingscote 12 64
(Ralph Beckett) *s.i.s: hld up: r.o ins fnl f: nvr nrr* **17/2**[3]
52 **6** *1 ¼* **Dukeofwallingford**[46] 7915 2-9-2 0.................... CharlesBishop 11 62
(Eve Johnson Houghton) *w ldrs: led over 6f out: rdn and hdd over 1f out: wknd ins fnl f* **10/1**
**7** *¾* **The Bearfighter (IRE)** 2-9-2 0.................... StevieDonohoe 1 60
(Charlie Fellowes) *mid-div: hdwy over 2f out: rdn over 1f out: wknd ins fnl f* **33/1**
05 **8** *1 ½* **Real Estate (IRE)**[84] 6683 2-9-2 0.................... LukeMorris 13 57
(James Tate) *w ldrs: rdn and ev ch over 1f out: wknd ins fnl f* **25/1**
6 **9** *5* **Ad Libitum**[18] 8642 2-9-2 0.................... JosephineGordon 10 46
(Hugo Palmer) *mid-div: pushed along over 3f out: sme hdwy over 2f out: wknd over 1f out* **10/1**
0 **10** *4* **Lexington Empire**[18] 8643 2-9-2 0.................... TedDurcan 4 38
(David Lanigan) *w ldrs: lost pl 7f out: rdn and wknd over 2f out* **50/1**
45 **11** *2* **Elusif (IRE)**[29] 8382 2-9-2 0.................... TomMarquand 7 34
(Marco Botti) *prom: rdn over 2f out: wknd over 1f out* **12/1**
00 **12** *3 ¼* **Spring Praise (IRE)**[29] 8382 2-8-13 0....................(t) MarcMonaghan(3) 3 27
(Marco Botti) *s.i.s: hld up: nvr on terms* **100/1**
**13** *11* **Garsington** 2-9-2 0.................... PhillipMakin 5
(Ed Dunlop) *hld up: rdn and wknd over 2f out* **100/1**
1m 50.22s (0.12) **Going Correction** -0.05s/f (Stan) 13 Ran SP% **117.1**
Speed ratings (Par 96): **97,96,94,94,91 90,89,88,84,80 78,75,66**
CSF £5.75 TOTE £2.20: £1.20, £1.50, £7.00; EX 7.60 Trifecta £201.00.
**Owner** HH Sheikha Al Jalila Racing **Bred** Godolphin **Trained** Newmarket, Suffolk

**FOCUS**
Run in a similar time to the earlier division, the first two in the market had it between them in the straight.

## 8953 32RED CASINO FILLIES' H'CAP 5f 21y (Tp)
**6:45** (6:45) (Class 5) (0-70,71) 3-Y-O+ **£3,234** (£962; £481; £240) **Stalls** Low

Form RPR
1124 **1** **Lydiate Lady**[7] 8853 5-9-5 **68**.................... JasonHart 7 74
(Eric Alston) *mde all: rdn and edgd rt fr over 1f out: jst hld on* **8/1**
5210 **2** *nk* **Toolatetodelegate**[14] 8742 3-8-5 **57**....................(tp) HollieDoyle(3) 3 62
(Brian Barr) *hld up: hdwy 2f out: hung rt over 1f out: sn rdn: r.o* **16/1**
1465 **3** *hd* **Look Surprised**[35] 8243 4-8-13 **65**.................... MitchGodwin(3) 6 69
(Roger Teal) *hld up: hdwy over 1f out: nt clr run ins fnl f: r.o* **17/2**
1454 **4** *hd* **Cool Breeze (IRE)**[25] 8494 3-8-6 **55**.................... JosephineGordon 8 58
(David Simcock) *hld up: hdwy over 1f out: rdn and edgd lft ins fnl f: r.o* **7/1**[3]
4561 **5** *nk* **Berryessa (IRE)**[7] 8853 3-9-8 **71**.................... LukeMorris 2 73
(Rae Guest) *prom: rdn over 1f out: r.o* **6/4**[1]
403 **6** *½* **Powerful Dream (IRE)**[7] 8853 4-9-6 **69**....................(p) DavidProbert 1 69
(Ronald Harris) *chsd ldrs: rdn and edgd rt over 1f out: nt clr run ins fnl f: styd on* **9/2**[2]
0006 **7** *4* **Mysterious Glance**[14] 8745 4-8-1 **57**.................... WilliamCox(7) 10 43
(Sarah Hollinshead) *s.i.s: hld up: hdwy over 1f out: wknd wl ins fnl f* **50/1**
0-0 **8** *4* **Rocking Rudolph (USA)**[303] 416 4-9-7 **70**.......(h[1]) RichardKingscote 4 42
(Robert Cowell) *chsd wnr: hung rt 1/2-way: sn lost 2nd: wknd fnl f* **14/1**
3200 **9** *½* **Little Miss Daisy**[46] 7912 3-9-5 **68**.................... PhillipMakin 11 38
(William Muir) *s.i.s: hld up: nvr on terms* **16/1**
1060 **10** *1 ¾* **Beau Mistral (IRE)**[35] 8243 8-9-1 **64**.................... TomMarquand 9 28
(Tony Carroll) *chsd ldrs: rdn 1/2-way: wknd over 1f out* **66/1**
3005 **11** *6* **Mysterious Look**[14] 8745 4-9-4 **67**....................(p) RobHornby 5 9
(Sarah Hollinshead) *prom: rdn 1/2-way: wknd over 1f out* **28/1**
1m 1.77s (-0.13) **Going Correction** -0.05s/f (Stan) 11 Ran SP% **117.7**
Speed ratings (Par 100): **99,98,98,97,97 96,90,83,83,80 70**
CSF £125.95 CT £1120.43 TOTE £7.20: £2.30, £3.60, £2.30; EX 115.40 Trifecta £875.00.
**Owner** The Scotch Piper Racing **Bred** Catridge Farm Stud **Trained** Longton, Lancs

**FOCUS**
The winner made all, reversing latest form with the 5th/6th for a length pb.

## 8954 32REDSPORT.COM NURSERY H'CAP 6f 20y (Tp)
**7:15** (7:16) (Class 5) (0-75,79) 2-Y-O **£3,234** (£962; £481; £240) **Stalls** Low

Form RPR
0311 **1** **Joegogo (IRE)**[4] 8882 2-9-13 **79** 6ex.................... FranBerry 8 83
(David Evans) *mde all: rdn over 1f out: styd on u.p* **7/2**[3]
3106 **2** *1* **Arden Pearl (IRE)**[16] 8701 2-9-7 **73**....................(p[1]) EdwardGreatrex 1 74
(Archie Watson) *a.p: racd keenly: chsd wnr over 1f out: r.o u.p* **12/1**
6211 **3** *¾* **Vegas Boy (IRE)**[16] 8702 2-9-11 **77**....................(t) DougieCostello 3 76
(Jamie Osborne) *trckd ldrs: rdn over 1f out: edgd lft: r.o* **5/2**[2]
440U **4** *2* **Tarnhelm**[9] 8804 2-9-4 **70**.................... PJMcDonald 6 63
(Mark Johnston) *s.i.s: pushed along in rr: hdwy u.p over 1f out: nt rch ldrs* **28/1**
032 **5** *1 ¾* **Axe Cap (IRE)**[18] 8657 2-9-3 **69**.................... LukeMorris 7 57
(Archie Watson) *plld hrd in 2nd: rdn and hung rt over 1f out: no ex fnl f* **2/1**[1]
006 **6** *8* **La Cabana**[26] 8472 2-8-9 **61**.................... BarryMcHugh 2 25
(Richard Fahey) *s.i.s: pushed along over 3f out: wknd over 2f out* **14/1**
3231 **7** *9* **Lina's Star (IRE)**[64] 7363 2-9-1 **67**.................... PhillipMakin 4 4
(David O'Meara) *s.i.s: pushed along and hdwy over 2f out: wknd wl over 1f out* **8/1**
1m 14.57s (0.07) **Going Correction** -0.05s/f (Stan) 7 Ran SP% **113.0**
Speed ratings (Par 96): **97,95,94,92,89 79,67**
CSF £41.78 CT £120.93 TOTE £4.50: £2.50, £5.30; EX 51.90 Trifecta £147.70.
**Owner** Wayne Clifford **Bred** Barry Noonan And Denis Noonan **Trained** Pandy, Monmouths

**FOCUS**
This proved straightforward for the winner, who enjoyed the run of the race.

## 8955 BETWAY LIVE CASINO H'CAP 1m 5f 219y (Tp)
**7:45** (7:46) (Class 6) (0-65,65) 3-Y-O+ **£2,587** (£770; £384; £192) **Stalls** Low

Form RPR
5003 **1** **Captain Swift (IRE)**[18] 8655 6-9-6 **58**....................(p) JoeFanning 12 68
(John Mackie) *sn chsng ldr: lost pl 7f out but remained handy: led over 2f out: rdn over 1f out: styd on* **12/1**
/001 **2** *2* **Lake Shore Drive (IRE)**[4] 8878 5-9-10 **62** 6ex.......... StevieDonohoe 10 69
(Johnny Farrelly) *prom: racd keenly: jnd ldrs over 7f out: led over 3f out: rdn and hdd over 2f out: styng on same pce whn edgd rt wl ins fnl f* **7/4**[1]
1111 **3** *1* **Raashdy (IRE)**[7] 8846 4-9-11 **63**....................(p) LukeMorris 7 69
(Peter Hiatt) *hld up: hdwy over 7f out: rdn over 2f out: styd on same pce fnl f* **7/2**[3]
-333 **4** *nk* **Singular Quest**[29] 8396 5-9-7 **59**.................... RichardKingscote 3 64
(Daniel Mark Loughnane) *chsd ldrs: rdn over 1f out: styd on same pce fnl f* **11/4**[2]
0200 **5** *3 ¼* **Howardian Hills (IRE)**[24] 8507 4-9-7 **59**....................(h) KieranShoemark 5 60
(Victor Dartnall) *hld up: hdwy u.p over 2f out: hung lft over 1f out: no ex fnl f* **20/1**
460 **6** *2* **Anton Chigurh**[107] 5824 8-9-13 **65**....................(h[1]) CharlesBishop 2 63
(Nikki Evans) *hld up in tch: rdn over 1f out: wknd fnl f* **100/1**
2053 **7** *2* **Gabrial The Terror (IRE)**[86] 6632 7-9-13 **65**.................... LiamKeniry 9 60
(Patrick Morris) *s.s: hld up: shkn up over 1f out: nvr on terms* **40/1**
0455 **8** *½* **Poppyinthepark**[81] 6788 4-8-13 **54**....................(h[1]) PhilDennis(3) 1 49
(Michael Mullineaux) *s.i.s: hld up: shkn up over 2f out: n.d* **66/1**
0/0- **9** *¾* **Boethius**[33] 7280 4-9-10 **62**.................... KieranO'Neill 8 55
(Tim Vaughan) *s.i.s: hld up: rdn over 2f out: n.d* **66/1**
64-2 **10** *9* **Shoofly (IRE)**[43] 8022 4-9-11 **63**.................... AlistairRawlinson 4 44
(David Harry Kelly, Ire) *sn led: hdd over 3f out: wknd over 1f out* **16/1**
-110 **11** *1 ¼* **Miss Dusky Diva (IRE)**[285] 721 5-9-5 **61**.................... DavidProbert 13 40
(David W Drinkwater) *hld up: rdn over 2f out: n.d* **50/1**
0546 **12** *30* **Modernism**[46] 7925 8-9-13 **65**....................(p) FranBerry 11 2
(Ian Williams) *broke wl: sn stdd to trck ldrs: rdn and wknd over 2f out: eased* **9/1**
3m 4.01s (-3.99) **Going Correction** -0.05s/f (Stan) 12 Ran SP% **122.0**
Speed ratings (Par 101): **109,107,107,107,105 104,102,102,102,97 96,79**
CSF £33.54 CT £96.26 TOTE £16.40: £2.90, £1.30, £1.60; EX 59.20 Trifecta £198.60.
**Owner** Mrs Sue Adams & S P Adams **Bred** Mrs Michele Craig White **Trained** Church Broughton , Derbys

**FOCUS**
The front four were clear; not a bad race for the grade.

## 8956 BETWAY CLAIMING STKS — 1m 1f 104y (Tp)
8:15 (8:15) (Class 5) 3-Y-O+ — £3,234 (£962; £481; £240) Stalls Low

Form — RPR

1005 1 **General Hazard (IRE)**[137] 4712 4-9-7 84 ........ LukeMorris 4 79+
(Archie Watson) *pushed along to go prom after 1f: jnd ldr over 4f out: led over 3f out: rdn over 1f out: styd on* **13/8**[1]

0050 2 1 ¼ **Tha'ir (IRE)**[16] 8705 7-9-3 80 ........(h) GabrieleMalune(7) 7 79
(Michael Appleby) *hld up: hdwy 1/2-way: chsd wnr over 2f out: rdn over 1f out: styd on* **5/1**[3]

1400 3 shd **Every Chance (IRE)**[3] 8892 4-9-10 90 ........(t) DougieCostello 6 79+
(Jamie Osborne) *s.i.s: hld up: hdwy over 1f out: sn rdn and edgd lft: r.o wl towards fin: nt rch ldrs* **9/2**[2]

0043 4 1 ¾ **Michele Strogoff**[8] 8811 4-9-1 82 ........(p) JoshDoyle(3) 3 69
(Tony Coyle) *plld hrd and prom: nt clr run over 2f out: rdn over 1f out: edgd rt wl ins fnl f: styd on* **6/1**

3030 5 2 ¼ **Tadaany (IRE)**[16] 8706 5-8-7 72 ........ JaneElliott(5) 5 59
(Ruth Carr) *chsd ldr to 1/2-way: remained handy: rdn over 1f out: no ex fnl f* **8/1**

0000 6 3 ½ **La Goulue**[9] 8800 3-7-13 38 ........(v¹) HollieDoyle(3) 8 44
(John Gallagher) *hld up: shkn up over 2f out: nvr on terms* **150/1**

116- 7 12 **Ocean Eleven**[20] 7816 4-9-2 79 ........ TomMarquand 1 30
(Martin Keighley) *unruly in stalls: s.i.s and pushed along early in rr: rdn and wknd over 2f out* **12/1**

0060 8 ½ **Niqnaaqpaadiwaaq**[44] 7980 5-9-0 46 ........(p¹) JasonHart 2 27
(Eric Alston) *led: plld hrd: clr 8f out tl over 5f out: hdd over 3f out: wknd over 1f out* **50/1**

50 9 1 ¼ **Black Dave (IRE)**[14] 8749 7-8-5 65 ........ KatherineGlenister(7) 9 23
(David Evans) *hld up: racd keenly: rdn over 2f out: sn hung rt and wknd* **25/1**

1m 59.78s (-1.02) **Going Correction** -0.05s/f (Stan)
**WFA** 3 from 4yo+ 3lb — 9 Ran SP% **112.5**
Speed ratings (Par 103): **102,100,100,99,97 94,83,83,81**
CSF £9.45 TOTE £2.40: £1.10, £2.60, £1.80; EX 10.60 Trifecta £38.20.
**Owner** Boadicea Bloodstock **Bred** London Thoroughbred Services Ltd **Trained** Upper Lambourn, W Berks

**FOCUS**
A decent claimer but Luke Morris always had things in hand on the winner.

## 8957 BETWAY CASINO H'CAP — 1m 1f 104y (Tp)
8:45 (8:46) (Class 6) (0-60,60) 3-Y-O+ — £2,587 (£770; £384; £192) Stalls Low

Form — RPR

5164 1 **Arrowzone**[7] 8854 6-9-3 56 ........(b) DougieCostello 6 62
(Kevin Frost) *hld up in tch: nt clr run wl over 1f out: rdn to ld ins fnl f: r.o* **11/4**[1]

0355 2 1 ¼ **Miss Mirabeau**[8] 8814 3-9-3 59 ........(b) LukeMorris 2 63
(Sir Mark Prescott Bt) *chsd ldrs: wnt 2nd over 2f out: rdn and ev ch ins fnl f: styd on same pce* **7/2**[2]

206 3 nk **Joys Delight**[18] 8659 3-9-2 58 ........ RichardKingscote 4 61
(Daniel Mark Loughnane) *hld up: nt clr run over 2f out: hdwy over 1f out: r.o* **10/1**

0330 4 1 ½ **Peak Hill**[18] 8662 4-9-3 56 ........ TimmyMurphy 1 56
(Adrian Wintle) *led 1f: led again over 6f out: rdn over 1f out: hdd and no ex ins fnl f* **33/1**

3032 5 1 ¼ **Ingleby Angel (IRE)**[7] 8854 8-9-2 58 ........ JoshDoyle(3) 13 56
(David O'Meara) *hld up: plld hrd: hdwy and hung lft fr over 1f out: nt rch ldrs* **9/2**[3]

4156 6 3 **Windsorlot (IRE)**[18] 8661 4-9-3 56 ........ TomMarquand 3 48
(Tony Carroll) *prom: pushed along over 3f out: rdn and edgd lft over 1f out: wknd ins fnl f* **14/1**

403 7 ½ **Lord Murphy (IRE)**[18] 8662 4-9-1 57 ........ EoinWalsh(3) 9 49
(Daniel Mark Loughnane) *hld up: hdwy u.p and hung lft over 1f out: nt clr run and wknd ins fnl f* **12/1**

0100 8 1 ½ **Unsuspected Girl (IRE)**[18] 8661 4-9-2 58 ........(t) CallumShepherd(3) 7 46
(Milton Bradley) *hld up: nt clr run over 2f out: hdwy over 1f out: hung lft and wknd ins fnl f* **33/1**

4640 9 hd **Critical Thinking (IRE)**[99] 6160 3-9-2 58 ........ JosephineGordon 8 46
(David Loughnane) *hld up: plld hrd: rdn over 1f out: nt trble ldrs* **7/1**

000- 10 3 **Premier Currency (IRE)**[255] 8458 4-9-0 56 ........(t) HollieDoyle(3) 10 38
(Mike Murphy) *led after 1f: hdd over 6f out: chsd ldr tl over 2f out: nt clr run and wknd fnl f* **66/1**

000 11 nk **Missguided (IRE)**[18] 8641 4-9-6 59 ........(b) DavidProbert 5 41
(Alex Hales) *s.i.s: a in rr* **22/1**

3000 12 1 ¾ **Mamnoon (IRE)**[18] 8662 4-9-2 55 ........(b) FranBerry 12 33
(Roy Brotherton) *sn prom: rdn over 2f out: hmpd and wknd over 1f out* **40/1**

4204 13 20 **Greenview Paradise (IRE)**[16] 8707 3-8-11 60 ........ GabrieleMalune(7) 11
(Brian Barr) *hld up in tch: lost pl 4f out: wknd over 2f out* **66/1**

1m 59.85s (-0.95) **Going Correction** -0.05s/f (Stan)
**WFA** 3 from 4yo+ 3lb — 13 Ran SP% **118.7**
Speed ratings (Par 101): **102,100,100,99,98 95,95,93,93,90 90,89,71**
CSF £11.26 CT £83.54 TOTE £3.20: £1.70, £1.70, £2.90; EX 15.00 Trifecta £155.60.
**Owner** C & D Racing **Bred** J K Beckitt & Son **Trained** Market Drayton, Shropshire

**FOCUS**
Moderate handicap form; the 2nd/3rd help set the level.

## 8958 SUNBETS.CO.UK H'CAP — 7f 36y (Tp)
9:15 (9:16) (Class 5) (0-70,70) 3-Y-O+ — £3,234 (£962; £481; £240) Stalls High

Form — RPR

5001 1 **Tuscany (IRE)**[52] 7723 3-9-3 68 ........ RaulDaSilva 5 76+
(Paul Cole) *a.p: chsd ldr 1/2-way: rdn and r.o to ld wl ins fnl f* **9/4**[1]

6100 2 nk **Baltic Prince (IRE)**[26] 8473 7-9-5 69 ........ TomMarquand 8 77
(Tony Carroll) *led: shkn up over 2f out: rdn and hdd wl ins fnl f* **18/1**

6504 3 4 **Zaeem**[12] 8773 8-9-1 70 ........(t) JaneElliott(5) 3 67
(Ivan Furtado) *chsd ldrs: rdn over 1f out: styd on same pce fnl f* **13/2**[3]

3201 4 1 ½ **Inglorious**[40] 8108 3-9-4 69 ........(v) AndrewMullen 2 61
(Keith Dalgleish) *hld up: hdwy over 1f out: sn rdn: no imp fnl f* **12/1**

0405 5 2 **Lanjano**[36] 8216 3-9-3 68 ........ KevinStott 4 55
(Kevin Ryan) *prom: rdn over 1f out: wknd fnl f* **4/1**[2]

4660 6 1 **Madrinho (IRE)**[22] 8556 4-9-2 69 ........(bt) TimClark(3) 6 54
(John Butler) *s.i.s: hld up: rdn over 1f out: nt trble ldrs* **7/1**

1003 7 nk **Chetan**[18] 8646 5-9-6 70 ........(t) LukeMorris 11 54
(Charlie Wallis) *chsd ldr to 1/2-way: sn rdn: wknd fnl f* **14/1**

0554 8 2 ½ **Perfect Symphony (IRE)**[36] 8211 3-9-5 70 ........(p) DavidProbert 1 46
(Sophie Leech) *hld up: hmpd sn after s: nvr on terms* **12/1**

6-46 9 4 **Frozen Lake (USA)**[210] 2133 5-9-2 66 ........ FranBerry 7 33
(John O'Shea) *hld up: pushed along and sme hdwy on outer over 2f out: sn rdn and wknd* **12/1**

0000 10 ½ **Berlios (IRE)**[32] 8321 4-9-4 68 ........ PhillipMakin 10 33
(Rebecca Bastiman) *hld up: nvr on terms* **28/1**

0600 11 1 ¾ **Weloof (FR)**[81] 6792 3-9-4 69 ........ LiamKeniry 12 29
(John Butler) *s.i.s: hld up: rdn over 1f out: sn wknd and eased* **20/1**

1m 28.47s (-0.33) **Going Correction** -0.05s/f (Stan)
**WFA** 3 from 4yo+ 1lb — 11 Ran SP% **119.8**
Speed ratings (Par 103): **99,98,94,92,90 88,88,85,81,80 78**
CSF £48.86 CT £245.57 TOTE £3.10: £1.10, £5.20, £2.90; EX 52.80 Trifecta £252.10.
**Owner** P F I Cole Ltd **Bred** Kildaragh Stud & M Downey **Trained** Whatcombe, Oxon

**FOCUS**
Few got into this.
T/Plt: £298.90 to a £1 stake. Pool: £117,354.62 - 286.59 winning units T/Qpdt: £44.10 to a £1 stake. Pool: £14,396.70 - 241.30 winning units **Colin Roberts**

# 8252 LE CROISE-LAROCHE
Saturday, November 25

**OFFICIAL GOING: Turf: heavy**

## 8959a PRIX D'HEM (CLAIMER) (3YO) (TURF) — 1m 1f
7:15 3-Y-O — £7,264 (£2,905; £2,179; £1,452; £726)

RPR

1 **Guanacaste (IRE)**[18] 3-9-2 0 ........ ChristopheSoumillon 7
(H-A Pantall, France) **5/2**[1]

2 2 ½ **Dominique (FR)** 3-9-2 0 ........ JakubPavlicek 3
(Pavel Tuma, Czech Republic) **39/1**

3 nk **Bar Mina (IRE)**[171] 3-7-12 0 ........ MlleCoraliePacaut(10) 12
(H-A Pantall, France) **43/10**[2]

4 ½ **Esperitum (FR)**[57] 3-8-7 0 ........ MlleAlisonMassin(4) 14
(D & P Prod'Homme, France) **15/1**

5 1 ½ **A Head Ahead (GER)**[15] 3-8-10 0 ........(p) MlleAudeDuporte(5) 6
(Gianluca Bietolini, Italy) **14/1**

6 2 ½ **Autarcie**[113] 3-8-8 0 ........ TheoBachelot 13
(S Wattel, France) **9/2**[3]

7 1 ½ **Sampaquita (FR)**[68] 7215 3-8-5 0 ........ JeromeMoutard(3) 11
(J-M Lefebvre, France) **61/1**

8 3 ½ **Silver Casina (IRE)**[18] 3-8-4 0 ........ AlexandreChesneau(7) 5
(G Botti, France) **8/1**

9 20 **Silver Saint (FR)**[69] 3-8-11 0 ........(b) StephaneBreux 1
(F Foresi, France) **43/1**

10 hd **Caroline Piano (FR)**[70] 3-8-7 0 ........ HayleyTurner(4) 2
(Henk Grewe, Germany) **38/1**

11 8 **Baileys Apprentice**[192] 3-7-12 0 ........ MlleMickaelleMichel(10) 4
(P Adda, France) **47/1**

12 nk **La Michodiere (IRE)**[45] 3-8-11 0 ........ DavidBreux 8
(Henk Grewe, Germany) **10/1**

13 1 **Doctor Chalnetta (FR)**[18] 3-8-8 0 ........ EddyHardouin 10
(P Adda, France) **19/1**

14 dist **Guiding Passion (FR)**[47] 7896 3-8-9 0 ow1 ........(p) TonyPiccone 9
(K R Burke) *a towards rr: wl btn into st: eased and tailed rt off* **30/1**

2m 4.2s — 14 Ran SP% **118.0**
PARI-MUTUEL (all including 1 euro stake): WIN 3.50; PLACE 1.80, 9.20, 2.00; DF 54.20; SF 85.00.
**Owner** Haras Du Grand Courgeon **Bred** Haras Du Mezeray **Trained** France

## 8960a PRIX DE LA PISCINE DE ROUBAIX (CLAIMER) (3YO) (TURF) — 5f 110y
7:45 3-Y-O — £6,410 (£2,564; £1,923; £1,282; £641)

RPR

1 **Castle Dream (FR)**[121] 3-9-2 0 ........ EddyHardouin 2 76
(K Borgel, France) **8/1**

2 1 ½ **Elusiva (FR)**[33] 8304 3-8-8 0 ........ SoufianeSaadi 3 63
(H-A Pantall, France) **19/1**

3 1 ¼ **Happy Dream (ITY)**[33] 8305 3-8-6 0 ........ MlleCoraliePacaut(10) 11 67
(J Parize, France) **2/1**[1]

4 2 **Makhzen (FR)**[25] 3-8-10 0 ........ MlleMickaelleMichel(10) 10 64
(M Boutin, France) **53/10**

5 1 ½ **Secret Lady**[24] 3-9-3 0 ........ ChristopheSoumillon 4 56
(Mme M Bollack-Badel, France) **7/2**[2]

6 ¾ **Undiscovered Angel (FR)**[15] 8716 3-8-9 0 ow1 ........ TonyPiccone 1 46
(K R Burke) *hld up: rdn into st: sn outpcd and btn* **14/1**

7 hd **Lord Cooper**[23] 8542 3-9-2 0 ........(p) TheoBachelot 9 47
(Jose Santos) *a towards rr: rdn home bnd: no imp and wl btn st: fin 8th plcd 7th* **43/10**[3]

8 2 ½ **Mystery Sky (FR)**[24] 3-8-8 0 ........(p) JimmyTastayre 8 31
(Mme F Chenu, France) **132/1**

9 10 **Chaplin (FR)**[43] 3-8-13 0 ........(b) JeromeMoutard(3) 5 6
(G Radovic, France) **57/1**

D 1 ½ **If I Say So**[37] 3-8-13 0 ........ GuillaumeNugou(7) 6 52
(M Boutin, France) **47/1**

PARI-MUTUEL (all including 1 euro stake): WIN 9.00; PLACE 2.10, 3.20, 1.50; DF 41.30; SF 82.50.
**Owner** Jacques Piasco **Bred** Bel Becq & Haras D'Etreham **Trained** France

8961 - 8962a (Foreign Racing) - See Raceform Interactive

# 8620 CAPANNELLE (R-H)
Sunday, November 26

**OFFICIAL GOING: Turf: heavy**

## 8963a PREMIO ROMA GBI RACING (GROUP 2) (3YO+) (TURF) — 1m 2f
2:45 3-Y-O+ — £100,000 (£44,000; £24,000; £12,000)

RPR

1 **Anda Muchacho (IRE)**[42] 8095 3-9-0 0 ........ DarioVargiu 8 110
(Nicolo Simondi, Italy) *travelled wl in midfield: clsd fr 3f out: str run u.p fnl f: led last 100yds: drvn out* **6/5**[1]



The Form Book Flat, Raceform Ltd, Newbury, RG14 5SJ

2 ½ **Mac Mahon (ITY)**[70] 7205 3-9-0 0.................... NicolaPinna 10 109
(Stefano Botti, Italy) *w.w in fnl pair: hdwy 3f out: styd on fnl f: nt quite pce of wnr and a jst hld* **15/4[3]**

3 1 **Presley (ITY)**[553] 2517 4-9-3 0.................... LucaManiezzi 3 106
(Stefano Botti, Italy) *settled in 4th: drvn to ld 2 1/2f out: styd on u.p fnl f: hdd last 110yds: no ex* **36/5**

4 1 ½ **Time To Choose**[28] 8448 4-9-3 0.................... Pierre-CharlesBoudot 1 103
(Stefano Botti, Italy) *chsd ldng pair: pressed ldr under 4f out: rdn and nt qckn 2f out: kpt on at one pce fnl f: jst hld 4th* **71/20[2]**

5 nse **Red Label (IRE)**[42] 8095 3-9-0 0.................... FabioBranca 7 104
(Marco Botti) *settled in fnl trio: tk clsr order 3f out: drvn and styd on 2f out: edgd lft whn rdn 1 1/2f out and nt pce of ldrs: styd on fnl f: jst missed 4th* **123/20**

6 5 ½ **Wireless (FR)**[57] 7640 6-9-3 0.................... TheoBachelot 4 92
(V Luka Jr, Czech Republic) *racd in midfield: rdn and nt qckn 2f out: sn outpcd by ldrs: wl hld fnl f* **17/4**

7 10 **Aspettatemi (ITY)**[15] 3-9-0 0.................... SalvatoreBasile 6 73
(D Grilli, Italy) *sn led: hdd after 3f: chsd ldr: rdn and edgd lft 2f out: sn wknd* **47/1**

8 3 **Voice Of Love (IRE)**[42] 8095 4-9-3 0.................... PierreBazire 9 66
(Stefano Botti, Italy) *pressed ldr on outer: led after 3f: pressed and rdn over 3f out: hdd 2 1/2f out: wknd fnl 1 1/2f* **71/20[2]**

9 2 **Shamshad (FR)**[14] 4-9-3 0.................... SamueleDiana 5 62
(V di Napoli, Italy) *settled in rr: moved up a couple of pls bef 1/2-way: outpcd and drvn 3 1/2f out: bhd fnl 2f* **193/10**

2m 3.6s (0.30)
**WFA** 3 from 4yo+ 3lb **9** Ran SP% **162.7**
PARI-MUTUEL (all including 1 euro stake): WIN 2.18 PLACE 1.28, 1.56, 2.02 DF 9.42.
**Owner** Scuderia Incolinx & Diego Romeo **Bred** Thomas Hassett **Trained** Italy

8964 - 8974a (Foreign Racing) - See Raceform Interactive

## 8465 TOKYO (L-H)

### Sunday, November 26

**OFFICIAL GOING: Turf: firm**

## 8975a JAPAN CUP (GRADE 1) (3YO+) (TURF) 1m 4f

6:40 3-Y-O+ £2,101,411 (£837,674; £522,643; £311,418; £207,612)

RPR

1 **Cheval Grand (JPN)**[48] 5-9-0 0.................... HughBowman 1 123
(Yasuo Tomomichi, Japan) **123/10**

2 1 ¼ **Rey De Oro (JPN)**[63] 3-8-9 0.................... Christophe-PatriceLemaire 2 122+
(Kazuo Fujisawa, Japan) **14/5[2]**

3 nk **Kitasan Black (JPN)**[28] 8465 5-9-0 0.................... YutakaTake 4 121
(Hisashi Shimizu, Japan) **11/10[1]**

4 4 **Makahiki (JPN)**[28] 8465 4-9-0 0.................... HiroyukiUchida 11 115
(Yasuo Tomomichi, Japan) **14/1**

5 nk **Idaho (IRE)**[42] 8099 4-9-0 0.................... RyanMoore 14 114
(A P O'Brien, Ire) *dwlt: towards rr early: impr to take clsr order over 2f out: drvn over 1f out: styd on fnl f* **100/1**

6 nk **Rainbow Line (JPN)**[28] 8465 4-9-0 0.................... YasunariIwata 9 114
(Hidekazu Asami, Japan) **57/1**

7 1 **Soul Stirring (JPN)**[28] 8465 3-8-5 0.................... CristianDemuro 8 109
(Kazuo Fujisawa, Japan) **83/10**

8 ½ **Yamakatsu Ace (JPN)**[28] 8465 5-9-0 0.................... KenichiIkezoe 16 111
(Kaneo Ikezoe, Japan) **116/1**

9 nk **Guignol (GER)**[25] 8527 5-9-0 0.................... FilipMinarik 3 111
(Jean-Pierre Carvalho, Germany) **71/1**

10 1 ¼ **Satono Crown (JPN)**[28] 8465 5-9-0 0.................... MircoDemuro 12 109
(Noriyuki Hori, Japan) **47/10[3]**

11 nk **Sciacchetra (JPN)**[28] 8465 4-9-0 0.................... YuichiFukunaga 13 108
(Katsuhiko Sumii, Japan) **47/1**

12 hd **Sounds Of Earth (JPN)**[48] 6-9-0 0.................... HironobuTanabe 5 108
(Kenichi Fujioka, Japan) **101/1**

12 dht **Boom Time (AUS)**[19] 8667 6-9-0 0....................(b) CoryParish 10 108
(David A Hayes, Australia) **321/1**

14 nk **Last Impact (JPN)**[48] 7-9-0 0.................... KeitaTosaki 17 107
(Katsuhiko Sumii, Japan) **274/1**

15 1 ¼ **Iquitos (GER)**[25] 8527 5-9-0 0.................... DanielePorcu 6 105
(H-J Groschel, Germany) **122/1**

16 1 ¼ **One And Only (JPN)**[28] 8465 6-9-0 0.................... NorihiroYokoyama 15 103
(Shinsuke Hashiguchi, Japan) **284/1**

17 2 **Decipher (JPN)**[28] 8465 8-9-0 0.................... YuichiShibayama 7 100
(Futoshi Kojima, Japan) **415/1**

2m 23.7s (-1.80)
**WFA** 3 from 4yo+ 5lb **17** Ran SP% **126.5**
PARI-MUTUEL (all including 100 jpy stake): WIN 1330; SHOW 190, 140, 120; DF 1770; SF 5250.
**Owner** Kazuhiro Sasaki **Bred** Northern Racing **Trained** Japan

**FOCUS**
Some decent international performers took their chance in this well-established contest, but it was the home team that filled the first four positions. A pb from the winner, with the runner-up in line with the best view of his Classic form and the third just off his best; they were clear.

## 8195 DEAUVILLE (R-H)

### Monday, November 27

**OFFICIAL GOING: Polytrack: standard**

## 8976a PRIX DE BURSARD (CONDITIONS) (3YO) (POLYTRACK) 1m 4f 110y

11:25 3-Y-O

£14,059 (£5,683; £4,188; £2,692; £1,645; £1,047)

RPR

1 **Nagano Gold** 3-8-13 0.................... DavidLiska 2 90
(V Luka Jr, Czech Republic) **33/1**

2 1 ¼ **Azuro (FR)**[26] 3-8-13 0.................... ChristopheSoumillon 3 88
(C Lotoux, France) **1/1[1]**

3 1 ½ **Pascasha D'Or (FR)**[54] 3-8-13 0.................... TheoBachelot 1 86
(S Wattel, France) **27/10[2]**

4 3 **Vienna Woods (FR)**[10] 8838 3-8-9 0.................... MaximeGuyon 7 77
(Y Barberot, France) **104/10**

5 ¾ **Greshnitsia (FR)**[54] 3-8-9 0.................... StephanePasquier 6 76
(V Luka Jr, Czech Republic) **49/1**

6 shd **Lady Valdean**[17] 8732 3-8-9 0.................... MickaelBarzalona 4 76
(Jose Santos) *wl into stride: led: hdd after 1f: remained cl up: pushed along over 2f out to briefly ld: sn hdd and rdn: drvn over 1f out: styd on one pce fnl f* **13/2**

7 3 ½ **Paul's Saga (FR)**[20] 3-8-11 0 ow2.................... Pierre-CharlesBoudot 5 72
(J-P Gauvin, France) **56/10[3]**

PARI-MUTUEL (all including 1 euro stake): WIN 33.50; PLACE 7.50, 1.60; SF 80.10.
**Owner** Syndikat V3J **Bred** J Knight & E Cantillon **Trained** Czech Republic

8977 - (Foreign Racing) - See Raceform Interactive

## 8801 SOUTHWELL (L-H)

### Tuesday, November 28

**OFFICIAL GOING: Fibresand: standard**
Wind: Fresh behind Weather: Fine & dry

## 8978 BETWAY H'CAP 1m 4f 14y(F)

12:10 (12:10) (Class 5) (0-75,75) 3-Y-O+ £2,911 (£866; £432; £216) Stalls Low

Form RPR

0103 1 **Good Time Ahead (IRE)**[12] 8806 3-8-4 **65**.................... JamieGormley(5) 8 74
(Philip Kirby) *trckd ldrs: hdwy 4f out: swtchd lft towards inner over 2f out: rdn to chal over 1f out: led ent fnl f: kpt on wl* **5/2[1]**

1422 2 2 **Ominotago**[151] 4319 5-9-3 **68**.................... LukeMorris 6 73
(Michael Appleby) *trckd ldr: cl up 4f out: led 3f out and sn rdn: jnd and drvn over 1f out: hdd ent fnl f: kpt on same pce* **5/1[2]**

5 3 2 ¼ **Speciality (FR)**[20] 8682 3-9-0 **70**....................(b) RichardKingscote 5 72
(Ralph Beckett) *prom: effrt and cl up over 2f out: rdn wl over 1f out: drvn and kpt on same pce fnl f* **5/1[2]**

5566 4 1 **Cousin Khee**[55] 7744 10-8-7 **65**.................... TheodoreLadd(7) 3 65
(Hughie Morrison) *hld up in rr: hdwy over 3f out: rdn along 2f out: kpt on fnl f* **10/1**

-603 5 ¾ **Swift Cedar (IRE)**[42] 8143 7-9-10 **75**.................... FranBerry 10 73
(David Evans) *towards rr: hdwy on outer over 5f out: chsd ldrs and wd st: rdn along over 2f out: drvn and ch over 1f out: kpt on one pce* **7/1**

0003 6 4 ½ **Rite To Reign**[15] 8771 6-9-1 **73**....................(v) RossaRyan(7) 2 64
(Philip McBride) *towards rr: hdwy to trck ldrs 7f out: pushed along 4f out: rdn 3f out: sn drvn and grad wknd* **13/2[3]**

0504 7 8 **Apalis (FR)**[21] 8654 5-8-10 **61** oh1....................(t) CamHardie 4 39
(Michael Easterby) *trckd ldrs: pushed along 4f out: rdn over 3f out: sn wknd* **20/1**

0313 8 6 **Rita's Man (IRE)**[30] 8464 3-9-3 **73**.................... PhillipMakin 1 43
(Keith Dalgleish) *led: pushed along over 4f out: rdn over 3f out: sn hdd & wknd* **14/1**

6010 9 3 **Scrafton**[26] 8549 6-8-10 **68**.................... AledBeech(7) 7 32
(Tony Carroll) *trckd ldrs: pushed along over 5f out: rdn along 4f out: sn lost pl and bhd* **28/1**

2m 38.36s (-2.64) **Going Correction** -0.025s/f (Stan)
**WFA** 3 from 5yo+ 5lb **9** Ran SP% **111.7**
Speed ratings (Par 103): **107,105,104,103,103 100,94,90,88**
CSF £14.00 CT £55.35 TOTE £3.00: £1.20, £2.00, £2.20; EX 14.70 Trifecta £65.60.
**Owner** Greenbank, Fairhurst & Fletcher **Bred** Mrs M Dowdall Blake **Trained** East Appleton, N Yorks
■ Stewards' Enquiry : Rossa Ryan two-day ban: careless riding (Dec 12-13)

**FOCUS**
A modest handicap. The winner perhaps has a bit more to offer on this surface.

## 8979 BETWAY CASINO MAIDEN STKS 1m 4f 14y(F)

12:40 (12:42) (Class 5) 3-Y-O+ £2,911 (£866; £432; £216) Stalls Low

Form RPR

1 **Summer Name (IRE)**[605] 5-9-10 0....................(t[1]) TimmyMurphy 7 78
(Rebecca Curtis) *towards rr: hdwy 1/2-way: chsd ldrs over 3f out: wd st and sn chsng ldng pair: rdn: green and wandered over 1f out: sn led: kpt on strly* **33/1**

2362 2 4 ½ **Epitaph (IRE)**[15] 8770 3-9-5 70....................(v) LukeMorris 5 72
(Michael Appleby) *trckd ldrs: hdwy over 4f out: sn cl up: chal 3f out and sn rdn: drvn and ev ch over 1f out: kpt on same pce fnl f* **9/2[2]**

5224 3 6 **Gakku**[26] 8548 3-9-0 93....................(b) JackMitchell 11 57
(Roger Varian) *led: jnd 4f out: pushed along 3f out: sn rdn: drvn wl over 1f out: sn hdd and one pce* **4/6[1]**

4 12 **Qasr**[13] 3-9-5 0....................(h) PhillipMakin 3 43
(Keith Dalgleish) *chsd ldrs: rdn along and outpcd over 4f out: plugged on u.p fnl 2f* **8/1[3]**

0 5 10 **Leodis (IRE)**[144] 4569 5-9-10 0.................... AndrewMullen 4 26
(Tom Tate) *in tch: rdn along and outpcd over 5f out: sn bhd* **50/1**

6-00 6 6 **Chelsea Corsage (IRE)**[28] 8497 3-9-0 70.................... EdwardGreatrex 10 13
(Paul D'Arcy) *chsd ldr: rdn along over 4f out: drvn over 3f out: sn wknd* **25/1**

0000 7 26 **Zarkavon**[12] 8805 3-9-0 23....................(p) TomEaves 9
(John Wainwright) *prom: rdn along over 5f out: sn lost pl and bhd* **200/1**

8 20 **Run For Eva**[33] 4-9-5 0....................(h) SamJames 1
(Olly Williams) *s.i.s: a bhd* **150/1**

05 9 1 ¼ **My Distant Murphy**[13] 8781 3-9-5 0....................(t) CamHardie 12
(Jacqueline Coward) *a in rr* **200/1**

4 10 60 **Seirios (IRE)**[130] 5128 3-9-5 0....................(e[1]) PaulMulrennan 6
(Jane Chapple-Hyam) *chsd ldrs: rdn along over 5f out: sn lost pl and bhd* **66/1**

2m 39.99s (-1.01) **Going Correction** -0.025s/f (Stan)
**WFA** 3 from 4yo+ 5lb **10** Ran SP% **101.2**
Speed ratings (Par 103): **102,99,95,87,80 76,59,45,44,4**
CSF £106.92 TOTE £33.50: £6.10, £1.30, £1.02; EX 155.50 Trifecta £286.60.
**Owner** Ramsden, Morecombe & JCM Retail **Bred** Lakin Bloodstock/Wardley Bloodstock **Trained** Newport, Pembrokeshire
■ Frown was withdrawn. Price at time of withdrawal 3-1. Rule 4 applies to all bets - deduction 25p in the pound

**FOCUS**
Not much depth to this, with \bFrown\p refusing to enter the stalls and the favourite nowhere near her best, but this still looked a fair performance from the winner. The form is rated around the runner-up with the favourite disappointing.

## 8980 BETWAY SPRINT H'CAP 6f 16y(F)

1:10 (1:12) (Class 6) (0-60,60) 3-Y-O+ £2,587 (£770; £384; £192) Stalls Low

Form RPR

0020 1 **Kommander Kirkup**[25] 8552 6-9-6 **59**....................(p) TomEaves 13 67
(Michael Herrington) *trckd ldrs on outer: hdwy 3f out and sn cl up: rdn to chal wl over 1f out: led appr fnl f: kpt on strly* **22/1**

5060 **2** *1 ¼* **Borough Boy (IRE)**[15] 8776 7-9-2 **55**............................(v) PhillipMakin 2 59
(Derek Shaw) *trckd ldr: hdwy and cl up 3f out: rdn to chal over 2f out: led briefly wl over 1f out: sn hdd: drvn and kpt on same pce fnl f* **12/1**

1040 **3** *½* **Llewellyn**[15] 8776 9-9-1 **57**..........................................(v) PhilDennis(3) 1 60
(Declan Carroll) *led on inner: pushed along 3f out and sn jnd: rdn over 2f out: hdd wl over 1f out: sn drvn and kpt on same pce* **20/1**

0336 **4** *hd* **Coiste Bodhar (IRE)**[15] 8776 6-8-10 **49**.............................. LukeMorris 3 51
(Scott Dixon) *chsd ldrs: rdn along over 2f out: drvn over 1f out: kpt on fnl f* **16/1**

0506 **5** *¾* **Fortinbrass (IRE)**[15] 8772 7-9-0 **58**........................ BenRobinson(5) 8 58
(John Balding) *chsd ldrs: rdn along over 2f out: drvn over 1f out: kpt on u.p fnl f* **8/1**

2646 **6** *1 ¾* **Tasaaboq**[5] 8908 6-8-12 **51**..................................(tp) JosephineGordon 4 46+
(Phil McEntee) *dwlt and towards rr: hdwy over 2f out: sn rdn: styd on fnl f* **11/2[3]**

0145 **7** *1 ¼* **Zenovia (IRE)**[11] 8823 3-9-7 **60**..........................(tp) EdwardGreatrex 11 51
(Archie Watson) *dwlt and towards rr: hdwy over 2f out: sn rdn: styd on fnl f* **5/1[2]**

0000 **8** *1* **Sir Harry Collins (IRE)**[168] 3703 3-8-9 **48**........................ CamHardie 7 36
(Michael Appleby) *in tch: rdn along 3f out: sn no imp* **50/1**

0100 **9** *nk* **Bingo George (IRE)**[7] 8881 4-8-13 **52**......................(t) TomMarquand 12 39
(Mark Rimell) *chsd ldrs: rdn along over 2f out: sn drvn and wknd* **14/1**

0000 **10** *¾* **Kensington Palace (IRE)**[38] 8247 4-8-8 **47**............(p) BarryMcHugh 10 32
(Marjorie Fife) *a in rr* **14/1**

406 **11** *3* **Ypres**[13] 8784 8-8-9 **48**..............................................(e[1]) AndrewMullen 6 24
(Jason Ward) *swtchd lft sn after s: a towards rr* **16/1**

0-50 **12** *¾* **Oh So Dandy (IRE)**[35] 8329 3-9-1 **54**.....................(v) PatrickMathers 5 28
(Derek Shaw) *chsd ldrs: rdn along 3f out: sn wknd* **25/1**

1001 **13** *1* **Kaaber (USA)**[37] 8258 6-9-2 **58**................................(bt) MitchGodwin(3) 9 29
(Michael Blake) *a in rr* **5/2[1]**

3000 **14** *11* **Mad Rose (IRE)**[29] 8480 3-9-5 **58**...........................(b[1]) DanielMuscutt 14
(Denis Quinn) *dwlt: a in rr* **100/1**

1m 16.66s (0.16) **Going Correction** -0.025s/f (Stan) **14** Ran SP% **120.4**
Speed ratings (Par 101): **97,95,94,94,93 91,89,88,87,86 82,81,80,65**
CSF £255.01 CT £5447.67 TOTE £19.30: £5.20, £3.50, £6.70; EX 173.50 Trifecta £4534.60.
**Owner** Stuart Herrington & Pete Forster **Bred** W M Lidsey **Trained** Cold Kirby, N Yorks

**FOCUS**
A moderate sprint handicap in which the principals were always prominent.

## 8981 32RED CASINO NOVICE STKS (DIV I) 7f 14y(F)
**1:40** (1:41) (Class 5) 2-Y-O **£2,911** (£866; £432; £216) **Stalls** Low

Form RPR

51 **1** **Tallow (IRE)**[17] 8735 2-9-4 0........................................ RichardKingscote 5 81+
(William Haggas) *trckd ldrs: hdwy on inner 2f out: rdn over 1f out: drvn to chal ent fnl f: sn edgd rt: kpt on to ld last 100yds* **4/6[1]**

**2** *1* **Magnetic Boundary (USA)** 2-9-2 0..................................(t[1]) FranBerry 1 75
(George Scott) *dwlt: sn swtchd rt to outer and hdwy to join ldrs after 1f: cl up tl rdn to ld wl* **5/1[3]**

00 **3** *9* **Dorian Gray (IRE)**[63] 7489 2-8-13 0.......................... CharlieBennett(3) 8 51
(Hughie Morrison) *trckd ldrs: pushed along over 3f out: rdn over 2f out: plugged on one pce u.p fr wl over 1f out* **40/1**

0 **4** *¾* **Samovar**[31] 8432 2-9-2 0.............................................. KieranO'Neill 9 49
(Scott Dixon) *cl up: rdn to take slt ld over 2f out: drvn and hdd wl over 1f out: sn wknd* **50/1**

44 **5** *½* **Consultant**[32] 8382 2-9-2 0.......................................... DavidProbert 2 48
(Andrew Balding) *hld up: a towards rr* **9/2[2]**

0 **6** *hd* **Shyjack**[12] 8794 2-8-11 0.............................................. JaneElliott(5) 4 47
(George Margarson) *a towards rr* **22/1**

4200 **7** *6* **Miss Mo Brown Bear (IRE)**[74] 7123 2-8-8 67..........(b[1]) HollieDoyle(3) 3 26
(Richard Hannon) *led: rdn along 3f out: hdd over 2f out and sn wknd* **7/1**

1m 29.57s (-0.73) **Going Correction** -0.025s/f (Stan) **7** Ran SP% **116.1**
Speed ratings (Par 96): **103,101,91,90,90 89,83**
CSF £4.61 TOTE £1.40: £1.10, £2.40; EX 5.40 Trifecta £116.80.
**Owner** Cheveley Park Stud **Bred** Tom Twomey **Trained** Newmarket, Suffolk
■ Serabrina was withdrawn. Pirce at time of withdrawal 18-1. Rule 4 does not apply.

**FOCUS**
The first two, well clear, look useful. The winner more than confirmed her latest form.

## 8982 32RED CASINO NOVICE STKS (DIV II) 7f 14y(F)
**2:10** (2:14) (Class 5) 2-Y-O **£2,911** (£866; £432; £216) **Stalls** Low

Form RPR

42 **1** **On The Warpath**[26] 8545 2-9-2 0...................................... LukeMorris 4 82+
(Sir Mark Prescott Bt) *slt ld: cruised clr 2f out: heavily eased towards fin* **4/7[1]**

0 **2** *2 ¾* **Dawn Dancer**[27] 8509 2-9-2 0...................................... DavidProbert 6 64
(Andrew Balding) *dwlt and towards rr: hdwy over 2f out: rdn wl over 1f out: styd on fnl f: no ch w wnr* **7/1**

0 **3** *1 ½* **Desert Wind (IRE)**[20] 8677 2-9-2 0............................ StevieDonohoe 7 60
(Ed Vaughan) *towards rr: hdwy 1/2-way: wd st: rdn to chse ldrs over 2f out: kpt on same pce u.p fnl f* **25/1**

0 **4** *shd* **G Eye Joe**[123] 5350 2-9-2 0...................................... PaulMulrennan 8 60
(James Given) *cl up on outer: rdn along wl over 2f out: drvn wl over 1f out: kpt on same pce* **13/2[3]**

4502 **5** *3* **Zabaletaswansong (GER)**[35] 8325 2-8-9 71.............. RossaRyan(7) 2 52
(Richard Hannon) *prom on inner: rdn along 3f out: wknd fnl 2f* **11/2[2]**

56 **6** *1 ¼* **Jackpot Royale**[49] 7929 2-9-2 0...................................... PhillipMakin 1 48
(Michael Appleby) *trckd ldrs: cl up 3f out and sn rdn along: drvn wl over 1f out: grad wknd* **16/1**

**7** *2* **Iron Sky** 2-9-2 0.............................................................. AndrewMullen 9 43
(Keith Dalgleish) *dwlt: hdwy on outer and wd st: rdn over 2f out: n.d* **14/1**

060 **8** *9* **Thundercloud**[144] 4567 2-8-11 61.............................. KieranO'Neill 5 14
(Scott Dixon) *cl up: rdn along 1/2-way: sn wknd* **50/1**

0 **9** *13* **More Harry**[6] 8888 2-9-2 0........................................ DougieCostello 3
(Neil Mulholland) *a in rr: outpcd and bhd fnl 3f* **100/1**

1m 30.03s (-0.27) **Going Correction** -0.025s/f (Stan) **9** Ran SP% **124.2**
Speed ratings (Par 96): **100,96,95,95,91 90,87,77,62**
CSF £6.12 TOTE £1.50: £1.10, £1.90, £6.30; EX 6.40 Trifecta £96.90.
**Owner** Charles C Walker - Osborne House II **Bred** Sahara Group & Eurowest Bloodstock **Trained** Newmarket, Suffolk

**FOCUS**
The winner had loads in hand. He was value for plenty more than the bare form but there's a question over what depth there was behind.

## 8983 32RED.COM CLAIMING STKS 7f 14y(F)
**2:40** (2:40) (Class 5) 2-Y-O **£2,911** (£866; £432; £216) **Stalls** Low

Form RPR

4315 **1** **Powerful Society (IRE)**[48] 7956 2-8-8 72.................... BarryMcHugh 4 68
(Richard Fahey) *dwlt: sn cl up on outer: rdn to ld wl over 1f out: styd on wl* **11/8[1]**

20 **2** *2 ½* **Kheleyf's Girl**[21] 8658 2-8-3 59..................................(v[1]) MattCosham(3) 1 58
(David Evans) *prom on inner: hdwy 2f out: rdn to chse wnr ent fnl f: kpt on same pce* **13/2**

03 **3** *5* **Amity Island**[12] 8802 2-9-3 0.......................................... AndrewMullen 5 56
(Ollie Pears) *cl up: rdn along and sltly outpcd 2f out: kpt on fnl f* **4/1[3]**

000 **4** *½* **Tea Rattle**[85] 6755 2-8-0 51.......................................... KieranO'Neill 3 37
(Scott Dixon) *led: rdn along over 2f out: hdd wl over 1f out: sn drvn and grad wknd* **20/1**

1140 **5** *3 ¼* **Kikini Bamalaam (IRE)**[10] 8848 2-8-9 67........................ JasonHart 2 37
(Keith Dalgleish) *cl up: rdn along over 2f out: sn drvn and wknd wl over 1f out* **9/4[2]**

1m 30.5s (0.20) **Going Correction** -0.025s/f (Stan) **5** Ran SP% **111.0**
Speed ratings (Par 96): **97,94,88,87,84**
CSF £10.78 TOTE £2.10: £1.20, £2.30; EX 8.30 Trifecta £29.60.Powerful Society was claimed by Mr T. Vaughan for £6000
**Owner** Crown Select **Bred** Gigginstown House Stud **Trained** Musley Bank, N Yorks

**FOCUS**
A weak claimer but the form makes sense as rated.

## 8984 SUNBETS.CO.UK MAIDEN STKS 1m 13y(F)
**3:10** (3:10) (Class 5) 3-Y-O+ **£2,911** (£866; £324; £324) **Stalls** Low

Form RPR

0006 **1** **Moving Robe (IRE)**[19] 8707 4-8-9 42....................(tp) DarraghKeenan(7) 3 54
(Conrad Allen) *t.k.h: trckd ldrs on inner: hdwy wl over 2f out: rdn to ld ent fnl f: kpt on wl* **20/1**

3026 **2** *2 ¼* **Bo Selecta (IRE)**[37] 8256 3-9-5 60..............................(p) StevieDonohoe 1 53
(Richard Spencer) *slt ld: hmpd by loose horse over 4f out: rdn along 3f out: drvn and hdd narrowly 2f out: rallied to ld again 1 1/2f out: hdd ent fnl f: kpt on same pce* **4/1[3]**

0024 **3** *1* **Cockney Boy**[21] 8664 4-9-7 47..................................(v) AlistairRawlinson 8 52
(Michael Appleby) *cl up: chal 3f out: rdn to ld narrowly 2f out: sn drvn and hdd 1 1/2f out: kpt on same pce* **7/4[2]**

0- **3** *dht* **Ignacio Zuloaga (IRE)**[353] 8305 3-9-5 0................... RichardKingscote 5 51
(Jo Hughes) *prom: rdn along and outpcd over 2f out: drvn and kpt on wl fnl f* **13/8[1]**

6502 **5** *3* **Cool Echo**[83] 6828 3-8-7 56.......................................... GinaMangan(7) 4 39
(J R Jenkins) *in tch: hdwy 3f out: rdn 2f out: plugged on same pce* **12/1**

0000 **6** *3 ¼* **Slipalongtrevaskis**[34] 8345 4-9-7 36............................... TimmyMurphy 7 38
(J R Jenkins) *t.k.h early: towards rr: rdn along and sme hdwy 2f out: sn edgd lft and n.d* **25/1**

5005 **7** *23* **Red Shanghai (IRE)**[15] 8774 3-8-11 41.......................(v) NoelGarbutt(3) 10
(Charles Smith) *prom on outer: pushed along 1/2-way: sn rdn and wknd* **50/1**

00 **8** *25* **Lady Carduros (IRE)**[12] 8805 3-9-2 0 ow2................ DougieCostello 6
(Neil Mulholland) *dwlt: a bhd* **40/1**

6606 **U** **Fivos**[12] 8805 3-9-5 44..................................................(b[1]) TomMarquand 2
(David Bridgwater) *uns rdr s* **25/1**

1m 44.92s (1.22) **Going Correction** -0.025s/f (Stan)
**WFA** 3 from 4yo 2lb **9** Ran SP% **119.0**
Speed ratings (Par 103): **92,89,88,88,85 82,59,34,**
WIN: 13.20 Moving Robe; PL: .50 Cockney Boy, 1.30 Bo Selecta, 3.40 Moving Robe, .50 Ignacio Zuloaga; EX: 92.00; CSF: 96.37; TC: ; TF: 167.40, 209.10;.
**Owner** sportsdays.co.uk **Bred** Cooneen Stud **Trained** Newmarket, Suffolk

**FOCUS**
A weak maiden, and a couple of the placed runners looked to do too much up front, but still the winner seemed to improve a bit for the switch to Fibresand. It seemed no fluke.

## 8985 SUNBETS.CO.UK DOWNLOAD THE APP AMATEUR RIDERS' H'CAP 1m 13y(F)
**3:40** (3:42) (Class 6) (0-60,60) 3-Y-O+ **£2,183** (£677; £338; £169) **Stalls** Low

Form RPR

0510 **1** **Belgravian (FR)**[5] 8908 3-10-11 **57**..................................(tp) MrSWalker 1 65
(Archie Watson) *prom: led after 3f: rdn along 2f out: drvn and edgd rt ent fnl f: kpt on wl* **7/2[2]**

0016 **2** *1 ¼* **Ingleby Spring (IRE)**[27] 8515 5-10-4 **53**.................. MrBillyGarritty(5) 2 59
(Richard Fahey) *a.p: cl up 3f out: rdn wl over 1f out: ev ch: drvn and kpt on same pce ins fnl f* **12/1**

0010 **3** *2 ¼* **Mr Andros**[3] 8948 4-10-4 **55**......................................(bt) MissMStratton(7) 5 56
(Brendan Powell) *cl up on outer: chal over 2f out: rdn wl over 1f out: ev ch whn swtchd lft and drvn fnl f: kpt on same pce* **16/1**

003 **4** *2* **Win Lose Draw (IRE)**[12] 8800 5-10-9 **53**...........(p) MissSBrotherton 7 49
(Michael Appleby) *trckd ldrs on inner: hdwy over 2f out: rdn along wl over 1f out: no imp fnl f* **5/1[3]**

6000 **5** *1 ¼* **Candesta (USA)**[27] 8515 7-10-6 **55**..............................(t) MrMSHarris(5) 3 48+
(Julia Feilden) *in tch on inner: pushed along and lost pl over 3f out: rdn and hdwy 2f out: styd on wl fnl f: nrst fin* **16/1**

2006 **6** *nk* **Frangarry (IRE)**[12] 8807 5-9-13 **48**............................(t) MissJCooley(5) 8 40
(Alan Bailey) *racd wd: in tch: hdwy 2f out: rdn to chse ldrs over 1f out: drvn and no imp fnl f* **20/1**

515 **7** *2* **Masquerade Bling (IRE)**[60] 7573 3-11-0 **60**..............(p) MrJamesKing 4 46
(Neil Mulholland) *in tch: hdwy over 2f out: sn rdn: drvn over 1f out: kpt on one pce* **7/1**

0002 **8** *shd* **Pindaric**[39] 8219 3-10-0 **51**..................................(p) MissEmilyBullock(5) 13 37
(Alan Lockwood) *chsd ldrs: rdn along 2f out: sn drvn and no imp appr fnl f* **10/1**

0443 **9** *2 ¼* **Gatillo**[12] 8807 4-10-10 **54**.............................................. MrRBirkett 12 36
(Julia Feilden) *in tch: hdwy on inner to chse ldrs 2f out: sn rdn: drvn and wknd appr fnl f: sn eased* **10/3[1]**

0506 **10** *4 ½* **Clayton Hall (IRE)**[21] 8653 4-10-4 **48**............................ MissCWalton 11 19
(John Wainwright) *racd wd: a towards rr* **66/1**

1000 **11** *1* **American Patrol (IRE)**[15] 8773 3-10-12 **58**...... MissBrodieHampson 10 25
(Neil Mulholland) *a in rr* **22/1**

-000 **12** *8* **Royal Rettie**[237] 1557 5-10-5 **54**..................................(h) MissMBryant(5) 9
(Paddy Butler) *chsd ldrs: rdn along over 3f out: sn wknd* **50/1**

0304 **13** *8* **Port Lairge**[40] 8182 7-9-8 45.......................................(v) MrDannyKerr(7) 6
(Michael Chapman) *rel to r and lost 20 l s: a t.o* **33/1**
1m 44.65s (0.95) **Going Correction** -0.025s/f (Stan)
**WFA** 3 from 4yo+ 2lb **13** Ran SP% **118.5**
Speed ratings (Par 101): **94,92,90,88,87 86,84,84,82,78 77,69,61**
CSF £42.05 CT £462.57 TOTE £4.60: £2.10, £3.40, £4.40; EX 40.20 Trifecta £759.00.
**Owner** Greenfield Racing **Bred** Al Asayl Bloodstock **Trained** Upper Lambourn, W Berks
**FOCUS**
A moderate handicap. The winner enjoyed a softish lead and the second took a small step forward.
T/Plt: £40.20 to a £1 stake. Pool: £62,006.10 - 1,124.72 winning units T/Qpdt: £29.10 to a £1 stake. Pool: £4,885.50 - 124.06 winning units **Joe Rowntree**

## 8976 DEAUVILLE (R-H)

Tuesday, November 28

**OFFICIAL GOING: Polytrack: standard**

### 8986a PRIX PETITE ETOILE (LISTED RACE) (3YO FILLIES) (POLYTRACK) 1m 1f 110y(P)

**12:47** 3-Y-O **£23,504** (£9,401; £7,051; £4,700; £2,350)

RPR

**1** **Indian Blessing**[52] 7815 3-9-2 0.................................. GregoryBenoist 8 105
(Ed Walker) *a.p: chsd ldrs 2 1/2f out: rdn to follow ldr into fnl f: sustained run to ld last 100yds: drvn out: readily* **148/10**
**2** *2* **Vintage Folly**[17] 8739 3-9-2 0........................... Pierre-CharlesBoudot 14 101
(Hugo Palmer) *w.w towards rr on outer: hdwy on wd outside fnl bnd: styd on wl u.p fr over 1f out: nrest at fin* **4/1**[2]
**3** *hd* **Garance (FR)**[44] 8088 3-9-2 0.............................. ChristopheSoumillon 6 101
(J-C Rouget, France) **16/5**[1]
**4** *3/4* **Louversey**[17] 8755 3-9-2 0............................................ AnthonyCrastus 9 99
(P Sogorb, France) **11/1**
**5** *shd* **Illaunmore (USA)**[29] 3-9-2 0.................................... MickaelBarzalona 16 99
(Mme Pia Brandt, France) **34/1**
**6** *1 1/4* **Ashtaneh (USA)**[19] 3-9-2 0............................................ MickaelBerto 11 96
(A De Royer-Dupre, France) **35/1**
**7** *1* **Chabelita**[152] 3-9-2 0...................................... Francois-XavierBertras 15 94
(F Rohaut, France) **18/1**
**8** *3/4* **Ouja**[26] 8548 3-9-2 0.........................................................(b) TonyPiccone 1 93
(John Gosden) *led: drvn along whn jnd wl over 2f out: hdd appr 1 1/2f out: kpt on at same pce* **24/1**
**9** *3/4* **Niedziela (IRE)**[28] 8499 3-9-2 0.................................... AntoineHamelin 3 91
(C Lerner, France) **50/1**
**10** *1 1/4* **Turf Laurel (IRE)**[12] 8808 3-9-2 0.................................. AurelienLemaitre 7 89
(S Kobayashi, France) **19/1**
**11** *3/4* **Waltz Key (FR)**[80] 6963 3-9-2 0.......................... Jean-BernardEyquem 4 87
(J-C Rouget, France) **15/1**
**12** *nk* **Diablesse**[28] 8499 3-9-2 0............................................... MaximeGuyon 10 86
(F Head, France) **36/5**[3]
**13** *shd* **Speed As (FR)**[21] 8665 3-9-2 0................................ StephanePasquier 2 86
(A De Royer-Dupre, France) **17/1**
**14** *1 3/4* **Gracious Diana**[17] 8739 3-9-2 0.................................. IoritzMendizabal 13 83
(John Gosden) *settled towards rr of midfield: prog on outer to chse ldrs fnl bnd: sn rdn and btn: wknd fnl f* **47/1**
**15** *2 1/2* **Front Contender (IRE)**[59] 3-9-2 0................................... JulienAuge 12 78
(C Ferland, France) **89/10**
**16** *10* **White Rosa (IRE)**[58] 7673 3-9-2 0...............................(h) TheoBachelot 5 57
(Hugo Palmer) *a in rr: wl bhd fnl 1 1/2f: nvr a factor* **52/1**
1m 55.27s **16** Ran SP% **118.4**
PARI-MUTUEL (all including 1 euro stake): WIN 15.80; PLACE 4.30, 2.00, 1.90; DF 55.90; SF 131.20.
**Owner** P K Siu **Bred** Jocelyn Targett **Trained** Upper Lambourn, Berks
**FOCUS**
A 1-2 for British trainers in a bunchy finish behind the winner.

## 8886 KEMPTON (A.W) (R-H)

Wednesday, November 29

**OFFICIAL GOING: Polytrack: standard**
Wind: Fresh, against in home straight Weather: Overcast, cold

### 8987 CLOSE BROTHERS BUSINESS FINANCE MAIDEN STKS 1m 1f 219y(P)

**4:10** (4:12) (Class 5) 2-Y-O **£3,234** (£962; £481; £240) **Stalls** Low

Form RPR

4 **1** **Ispolini**[28] 8509 2-9-5 0...................................................(t) WilliamBuick 12 79+
(Charlie Appleby) *sn trckd ldr: jinked sltly bnd over 6f out: chal and upsides fr 3f out tl led 1f out: asserted last 150yds* **10/11**[1]
3 **2** *2* **Glencadam Master**[21] 8678 2-9-5 0................................ RobertHavlin 9 75+
(John Gosden) *sn led: jnd 3f out: clr of rest over 2f out and kpt on tl hdd 1f out: no ex* **9/4**[2]
3 **3** *1* **Grecian Spirit**[29] 8492 2-9-5 0......................................... LukeMorris 8 73
(James Tate) *chsd ldrs: rdn 4f out: prog over 2f out: chsd clr ldng pair over 1f out: styd on fnl f: nrst fin* **12/1**
0 **4** *1/2* **Fenisa's Hook**[33] 8389 2-9-5 0.................................... EdwardGreatrex 1 72
(Warren Greatrex) *chsd ldrs: prog on inner to dispute 3rd bhd clr ldng pair over 1f out: styd on fnl f: nrst fin* **20/1**
**5** *4* **Harbour Breeze (IRE)** 2-9-5 0...................................... DavidProbert 3 65+
(Lucy Wadham) *dwlt: t.k.h: hld up in midfield and rn green: prog 2f out: rchd 5th fnl f: n.d but shaped w sme promise* **66/1**
6 **6** *1 3/4* **Volevo Lui**[69] 7333 2-9-2 0...................................... MarcMonaghan(3) 11 61
(Marco Botti) *in tch on outer: outpcd fr 3f out: n.d after but kpt on* **80/1**
**7** *nk* **Overtrumped** 2-9-0 0.................................................. DanielMuscutt 13 56
(Mike Murphy) *sn in last trio: pushed along and prog wl over 1f out: kpt on steadily fnl f: nt disgracd* **100/1**
50 **8** *1/2* **Harbour Nights**[42] 8155 2-9-5 0...........................(b[1]) JosephineGordon 7 60
(Hugo Palmer) *nvr beyond midfield: outpcd and struggling over 2f out: one pce after* **50/1**
6 **9** *4* **Jamih**[20] 8703 2-9-5 0...................................................... NickyMackay 6 53
(John Gosden) *trapped out wd in midfield: lost grnd bnd 2f out: no ch after* **16/1**
**10** *1 1/4* **Cleverley (IRE)** 2-9-0 0.................................................. FranBerry 4 45
(Henry Candy) *dwlt: hld up in last pair: pushed along and sme prog 2f out: no hdwy whn swtchd lft fnl f* **33/1**
2 **11** *1 1/4* **Equidae**[162] 3930 2-9-5 0......................................................... AdamKirby 5 48
(James Tate) *prom: rdn to chse clr ldng pair over 2f out to over 1f out: wknd qckly* **10/1**[3]
**12** *11* **Singer In The Sand (IRE)** 2-9-0 0...............................(h[1]) ShaneKelly 10 23
(Pat Phelan) *dwlt: a bhd in last trio: t.o* **150/1**
06 **13** *5* **Boss For A Day**[28] 8501 2-9-5 0...................................... SeanLevey 2 18
(J S Moore) *chsd ldng pair to over 2f out: wknd rapidly: t.o* **100/1**
2m 5.25s (-2.75) **Going Correction** -0.075s/f (Stan) **13** Ran SP% **120.9**
Speed ratings (Par 96): **108,106,105,105,102 100,100,99,96,95 94,85,81**
CSF £2.82 TOTE £1.80: £1.10, £1.30, £2.60; EX 3.90 Trifecta £15.50.
**Owner** Godolphin **Bred** Newsells Park Stud **Trained** Newmarket, Suffolk
**FOCUS**
The first two had this between them from a long way out, but they got racing soon enough and those in behind finished closer than they merited.

### 8988 32RED.COM/BRITISH STALLION STUDS EBF NOVICE STKS (DIV I) 6f (P)

**4:40** (4:43) (Class 5) 2-Y-O **£3,234** (£962; £481; £240) **Stalls** Low

Form RPR

3 **1** **Desert Doctor (IRE)**[83] 6853 2-9-2 0................................ LiamKeniry 9 73
(Ed Walker) *t.k.h early: trckd ldr: led wl over 1f out: rdn fnl f: pressed 75yds out: kpt on wl* **4/1**[2]
**2** *nk* **Lashabeeh (IRE)** 2-9-2 0............................................... FranBerry 5 72+
(Roger Varian) *in tch in 6th: shkn up jst over 2f out: prog over 1f out: tk 2nd last 150yds and pressed wnr 75yds out: nt qckn nr fin* **4/1**[2]
**3** *1 1/2* **Sir Commander (IRE)** 2-9-2 0...................................... MartinHarley 7 68+
(William Haggas) *hld up in 7th: prog over 2f out: shkn up to take 3rd ins fnl f: styd on but unable to threaten* **11/4**[1]
00 **4** *2* **Pas De Blanc**[21] 8669 2-8-11 0...................................... HollieDoyle 8 57
(Brian Barr) *led to wl over 1f out: stl disputing 2nd jst ins fnl f: fdd* **100/1**
**5** *1/2* **Dollar Value (USA)** 2-9-2 0........................................... LukeMorris 2 60
(Robert Cowell) *trckd ldng pair: shkn up and lost pl 2f out: n.d after: kpt on again last 100yds* **9/2**[3]
**6** *hd* **Sea Ess Seas (IRE)** 2-9-2 0....................................(t[1]) DougieCostello 1 60
(Jamie Osborne) *hld up in 8th: pushed along over 2f out: styd on fr over 1f out: nrst fin* **16/1**
**7** *3/4* **Sweet And Dandy (IRE)** 2-8-11 0.................................. KieranO'Neill 3 52
(Jimmy Fox) *trckd ldrs in 5th: prog on inner to chse wnr over 1f out to fnl f: wknd* **5/1**
**8** *2* **Cloud Eight (IRE)** 2-9-2 0.......................................(t[1]) DanielMuscutt 10 51
(Marco Botti) *dwlt: t.k.h and trckd ldng trio: shkn up over 2f out: wknd over 1f out* **16/1**
**9** *2* **Little Aub** 2-9-2 0.............................................................. SteveDrowne 4 45
(Mark Usher) *dwlt: a in last pair: no prog fnl 2f* **66/1**
0 **10** *8* **Black Lace**[27] 8544 2-8-11 0....................................(p[1]) EdwardGreatrex 6 16
(Steve Woodman) *dwlt: sn scrubbed along: nvr gng wl: wknd 2f out: t.o* **250/1**
1m 13.33s (0.23) **Going Correction** -0.075s/f (Stan) **10** Ran SP% **116.2**
Speed ratings (Par 96): **95,94,92,89,89 89,88,85,82,72**
CSF £20.40 TOTE £4.70: £1.50, £1.60, £1.50; EX 19.80 Trifecta £61.90.
**Owner** Mrs Fitri Hay **Bred** Skeaghmore Hill **Trained** Upper Lambourn, Berks
**FOCUS**
An ordinary novice.

### 8989 32RED.COM/BRITISH STALLION STUDS EBF NOVICE STKS (DIV II) 6f (P)

**5:10** (5:12) (Class 5) 2-Y-O **£3,234** (£962; £481; £240) **Stalls** Low

Form RPR

0 **1** **Count Otto (IRE)**[100] 6272 2-9-2 0...............................(h[1]) JoeyHaynes 9 82
(Amanda Perrett) *dwlt: sn pressed ldr: carried lft 2f out: led over 1f out: styd on wl and drew clr fnl f* **16/1**
0423 **2** *2 3/4* **City Gent**[57] 7706 2-9-2 76................................... RichardKingscote 8 74
(Ralph Beckett) *led: rdn and hung lft 2f out: hdd and nt qckn over 1f out: wl hld after* **1/1**[1]
6 **3** *1 1/2* **Monadee**[18] 8735 2-9-2 0............................................... JackMitchell 5 70
(Roger Varian) *trckd ldng pair: hung lft 2f out: nt qckn over 1f out: kpt on same pce after and jst won battle for 3rd* **2/1**[2]
**4** *shd* **Global Pass** 2-9-2 0.............................................................(h[1]) LiamKeniry 4 69
(Ed Walker) *unruly bef ent stalls: chsd ldng trio: shkn up over 2f out: effrt to press for 3rd over 1f out: kpt on* **7/1**[3]
00 **5** *3 3/4* **Ede's A Winner**[64] 7488 2-8-4 0................................ SophieRalston(7) 6 53+
(Pat Phelan) *chsd ldrs in 5th: wd bnd 3f out and lost grnd: no ch after: tk modest 5th again fnl f: kpt on* **200/1**
**6** *2 1/2* **Ellen Gates** 2-8-11 0........................................................ ShaneKelly 2 45
(Richard Hughes) *hld up in 8th: effrt on inner 2f out: no prog over 1f out: fdd fnl f* **16/1**
**7** *1* **Jampower** 2-9-2 0.................................................................. FranBerry 3 48
(Stuart Williams) *jst in tch in 6th: shkn up and no prog over 2f out: wknd over 1f out* **25/1**
05 **8** *3* **Powerful Rose**[140] 4757 2-8-11 0...................................... DavidProbert 7 33
(Michael Blanshard) *dwlt: t.k.h and racd awkwardly: mostly in last: nvr a factor* **100/1**
**9** *1 1/2* **Darkest Light** 2-9-2 0..................................................(t[1]) DougieCostello 1 34
(Jamie Osborne) *nvr bttr than last trio: wknd over 1f out* **12/1**
1m 12.85s (-0.25) **Going Correction** -0.075s/f (Stan) **9** Ran SP% **120.6**
Speed ratings (Par 96): **98,94,92,92,87 83,82,78,76**
CSF £34.14 TOTE £24.30: £4.90, £1.02, £1.10; EX 54.80 Trifecta £140.20.
**Owner** Count Otto Partnership **Bred** Noel Finegan **Trained** Pulborough, W Sussex
**FOCUS**
The faster of the two divisions by 0.48sec.

### 8990 32RED ON THE APP STORE H'CAP 6f (P)

**5:40** (5:40) (Class 5) (0-75,75) 3-Y-O+ **£3,234** (£962; £481; £240) **Stalls** Low

Form RPR

201 **1** **Higher Court (USA)**[51] 7882 9-9-4 72................................ AdamKirby 11 79
(Emma Owen) *fast away fr wd draw: mde all: rdn over 1f out: hld on wl* **9/1**
6641 **2** *1/2* **Bahamian Heights**[27] 8542 6-8-10 71..................... JonathanFisher(7) 12 77
(Robert Cowell) *dwlt: hld up in midfield on outer: shkn up wl over 1f out: gd prog after: r.o to take 2nd nr fin: too late to chal* **20/1**
4553 **3** *1/2* **Very Honest (IRE)**[22] 8645 4-9-1 72...................... CallumShepherd(3) 4 76
(Brett Johnson) *mostly chsd wnr: rdn 2f out: tried to chal over 1f out: hld fnl f and lost 2nd nr fin* **7/1**
5266 **4** *1 1/2* **Deeds Not Words (IRE)**[12] 8818 6-9-4 72.................(p) DavidProbert 2 71
(Michael Wigham) *hld up in midfield: gng wl enough over 2f out: rdn and nt qckn wl over 1f out: one pce after* **13/2**

0202 **5** *hd* **Arnarson**[9] 8874 3-9-0 **68**..........(b) LukeMorris 8 67
(Ed Dunlop) *pushed along early to chse ldrs: effrt jst over 2f out: nt qckn over 1f out: one pce after* **11/2**[2]

5642 **6** *nk* **Pretty Bubbles**[12] 8818 8-9-3 **71**..........(v) JosephineGordon 6 69
(J R Jenkins) *hld up in last trio: sme prog on inner fr 2f out: no imp on ldrs and one pce fnl f* **8/1**

5343 **7** *1* **Geoff Potts (IRE)**[12] 8818 4-9-4 **72**.......... JackGarritty 3 66
(Richard Fahey) *t.k.h: trckd ldrs: tried to cl 2f out: nt qckn over 1f out: fdd ins fnl f* **11/4**[1]

260 **8** *nk* **Kinglami**[60] 7610 8-9-7 **75**..........(p) FranBerry 10 68
(John O'Shea) *hld up in last trio: trying to make prog whn nt clr run over 1f out: nvr in it* **33/1**

16 **9** *½* **Straight Away**[16] 8773 3-9-2 **70**.......... LiamKeniry 5 62
(Andrew Balding) *trckd ldng pair: disp 2nd over 2f out gng strly: shkn up wl over 1f out and wknd tamely* **6/1**[3]

6000 **10** *1* **Arlecchino's Leap**[22] 8646 5-9-6 **74**..........(p) SteveDrowne 1 63
(Mark Usher) *dwlt: hld up in last: shkn up and no prog over 2f out* **25/1**

4160 **11** *¾* **Mister Freeze (IRE)**[22] 8646 3-9-0 **68**..........(t) JoeyHaynes 9 54
(Patrick Chamings) *chsd ldrs on outer: rdn over 2f out: sn lost pl and wknd* **40/1**

1m 12.61s (-0.49) **Going Correction** -0.075s/f (Stan) **11** Ran SP% **117.3**
Speed ratings (Par 103): **100,99,98,96,96 96,94,94,93,92 91**
CSF £176.42 CT £1361.09 TOTE £11.30: £3.20, £5.70, £2.70; EX 177.70 Trifecta £1999.10.
**Owner** Miss Emma L Owen **Bred** Darley **Trained** Nether Winchendon, Bucks

**FOCUS**
This sprint was dominated from the front. The winner was up a length on his British form, the third helping with the standard.

## 8991 32RED CASINO H'CAP 6f (P)
**6:10** (6:12) (Class 2) (0-105,105) 3-Y-O+
**£11,827** (£3,541; £1,770; £885; £442; £222) **Stalls** Low

Form RPR

4-52 **1** **Double Up**[201] 2573 6-9-2 **100**..........(t) JimCrowley 5 111
(Roger Varian) *t.k.h: mde all: shkn up to drew 2 l clr over 1f out: rdn out fnl f* **8/1**

4644 **2** *¾* **Intisaab**[11] 8845 6-9-7 **105**..........(p) MartinHarley 1 114
(David O'Meara) *hld up in midfield: prog over 2f out: rdn to chse wnr fnl f: clsd nr fin but nvr quite able to chal* **4/1**[1]

3-00 **3** *2½* **Reckless Endeavour (IRE)**[61] 7587 4-9-0 **98**.......... DougieCostello 4 99
(Jamie Osborne) *hld up towards rr: prog and weaved through fr 2f out: styd on fnl f to take 3rd last 100yds: nvr able to threaten* **8/1**

0530 **4** *nk* **Straight Right (FR)**[53] 7807 3-9-5 **103**..........(h[1]) LiamKeniry 8 103+
(Andrew Balding) *dwlt: hld up in last: prog on inner fr 2f out: styd on u.p fnl f to press for 3rd last 100yds* **7/1**

053 **5** *1¼* **Out Do**[11] 8845 8-9-6 **104**..........(v) AdamKirby 3 100
(David O'Meara) *prom: chsd wnr 2f out: sn outpcd: lost 2nd 1f out: fdd last 100yds* **8/1**

3320 **6** *nk* **Mazzini**[11] 8845 4-8-13 **100**..........(p) GeorgeWood(3) 12 95+
(James Fanshawe) *blindfold off sme time bef stalls opened: dwlt: racd wd towards rr: shkn up 2f out: kpt on same pce fr over 1f out* **6/1**[2]

0030 **7** *hd* **Stellarta**[45] 8077 6-8-6 **90**.......... RobHornby 11 84
(Michael Blanshard) *chsd ldrs: nt qckn 2f out and sn lost pl: kpt on again fnl f but no ch* **25/1**

0050 **8** *1¼* **Outback Traveller (IRE)**[33] 8383 6-8-11 **95**..........(v) LukeMorris 6 85
(Robert Cowell) *trckd ldrs: rdn and nt qckn over 2f out: fdd fr over 1f out* **12/1**

3102 **9** *1* **Cartographer**[123] 5422 3-8-8 **92**.......... JosephineGordon 7 79
(Martyn Meade) *pressed ldrs on outer: lost pl jst over 2f out: steadily wknd* **13/2**[3]

5010 **10** *¾* **Tomily (IRE)**[21] 8679 3-8-11 **95**.......... TomMarquand 10 80
(Richard Hannon) *a in last trio: no prog 2f out and nvr a factor* **20/1**

050 **11** *3* **Kasbah (IRE)**[23] 8639 5-8-11 **95**.......... JackMitchell 9 70
(Amanda Perrett) *t.k.h: chsd wnr to 2f out: sn wknd* **33/1**

03- **12** *nk* **Leo Minor (USA)**[418] 7130 3-8-11 **95**.......... PJMcDonald 2 69
(Robert Cowell) *a in rr: no prog over 2f out: sn wl btn* **20/1**

1m 11.55s (-1.55) **Going Correction** -0.075s/f (Stan) **12** Ran SP% **117.5**
Speed ratings (Par 109): **107,106,102,102,100 100,99,98,96,95 91,91**
CSF £37.52 CT £269.29 TOTE £6.90: £2.80, £1.80, £2.00; EX 39.30 Trifecta £278.20.
**Owner** A D Spence & M B Spence **Bred** Mount Coote New England Barton & Myriad **Trained** Newmarket, Suffolk

**FOCUS**
A good, competitive handicap, but the first two pulled nicely clear. The winner is rated back to his best.

## 8992 32RED WILD FLOWER STKS (LISTED RACE) 1m 3f 219y(P)
**6:40** (6:43) (Class 1) 3-Y-O+
**£22,684** (£8,600; £4,304; £2,144; £1,076; £540) **Stalls** Low

Form RPR

2632 **1** **Red Verdon (USA)**[23] 8637 4-9-6 107..........(b) PJMcDonald 2 108
(Ed Dunlop) *hld up in rr: gd prog on inner over 2f out to ld wl over 1f out: drvn fnl f: hld on wl* **5/2**[1]

0601 **2** *½* **Master The World (IRE)**[11] 8844 6-9-9 105..........(p) SeanLevey 5 110
(David Elsworth) *chsd ldrs: rdn to cl fr over 2f out: tk 2nd fnl f: pressed wnr last 100yds but a hld* **7/1**

-141 **3** *¾* **Daphne**[27] 8548 4-9-4 98.......... JimCrowley 7 104
(William Haggas) *trckd clr ldr: clsd to ld 2f out: sn hdd and nt qckn: lost 2nd fnl f: kpt on but readily hld after* **7/2**[3]

12-4 **4** *nk* **Mountain Bell**[32] 8421 4-9-1 107.......... MartinHarley 6 100
(Ralph Beckett) *hld up in midfield: nt qckn whn rdn over 2f out: styd on fr over 1f out: nvr quite able to rch ldrs* **3/1**[2]

0-01 **5** *2½* **Not So Sleepy**[180] 3300 5-9-6 100..........(t) AdamKirby 1 101
(Hughie Morrison) *trckd ldrs: outpcd and rdn over 2f out: nvr on terms after but kpt on fnl f* **20/1**

-300 **6** *¾* **Astronomy's Choice**[22] 8666 3-8-10 95..........(b[1]) NickyMackay 8 96
(John Gosden) *sn led: clr after 4f: c bk to rivals qckly and hdd 2f out: sn btn and steadily wknd* **40/1**

1251 **7** *½* **Great Court (IRE)**[33] 8398 3-8-10 89.......... JackMitchell 3 95
(Roger Varian) *hld up in last: prog on inner over 2f out: rchd 5th over 1f out: no hdwy after* **12/1**

4005 **8** *4½* **Western Hymn**[23] 8637 6-9-11 107..........(b) RobertHavlin 4 97
(John Gosden) *hld up in rr: shkn up and no prog over 2f out: wl btn after* **11/1**

3245 **9** *3* **Indulged**[18] 8739 4-9-1 95.......... GeorgeWood 10 82
(James Fanshawe) *racd wd: hld up: rdn and no prog 3f out: wl btn after* **20/1**

**10** *20* **Tenerife Song**[416] 4-9-1 92.......... DougieCostello 9 50
(Jamie Osborne) *chsd ldng pair to over 3f out: wknd rapidly: t.o* **100/1**

2m 29.67s (-4.83) **Going Correction** -0.075s/f (Stan)
**WFA** 3 from 4yo+ 5lb **10** Ran SP% **117.3**
Speed ratings (Par 111): **113,112,112,111,110 109,109,106,104,91**
CSF £19.98 TOTE £3.20: £1.20, £2.40, £1.60; EX 19.00 Trifecta £76.50.
**Owner** The Hon R J Arculli **Bred** Liberty Road Stables **Trained** Newmarket, Suffolk

**FOCUS**
There was a good gallop on thanks to Astronomy's Choice, and this looks solid Listed form. The form is rated around the runner-up with the winner not quite needing to match his recent level.

## 8993 NICOLA SHEPHERD-BANKS H'CAP 1m 3f 219y(P)
**7:10** (7:15) (Class 6) (0-65,65) 3-Y-O+ **£2,587** (£770; £384; £192) **Stalls** Low

Form RPR

0342 **1** **Sky Eagle (IRE)**[36] 8312 3-9-5 **65**.......... LiamKeniry 12 71
(Ed Walker) *racd in 5th bhd clr ldrs: clsd over 2f out: drvn to ld wl over 1f out: hrd pressed after but asserted last 150yds* **5/2**[1]

6620 **2** *1¼* **Malt Teaser (FR)**[42] 8160 3-9-2 **62**.......... RobertHavlin 1 66
(John Best) *hld up in rr: prog on inner over 2f out: hanging lft over 1f out: styd on fnl f to take 2nd last strides* **6/1**

3415 **3** *hd* **Katabatika**[43] 8135 3-9-0 **60**.......... PJMcDonald 10 64
(Hughie Morrison) *hld up in 6th: clsd over 2f out: threaten over 1f out but nt qckn: styd on to press ldrs ins fnl f but effrt rather petered out nr fin* **9/2**[3]

-440 **4** *hd* **Tis Wonderful (IRE)**[22] 8641 3-8-7 **60**.......... WilliamCox(7) 6 63
(Carroll Gray) *chsd clr ldng pair: tk 2nd over 2f out: chal and upsides wl over 1f out: pressed wnr after tl no ex last 150yds* **66/1**

3064 **5** *3¼* **Art Of Swing (IRE)**[85] 6781 5-9-10 **65**.......... ShaneKelly 2 62
(Gary Moore) *chsd clr ldng trio: rdn to cl over 2f out: no imp over 1f out: fdd* **10/3**[2]

0606 **6** *2¾* **Tyrsal (IRE)**[36] 8326 6-9-7 **62**.......... HollieDoyle 5 55
(Clifford Lines) *hld up: dropped to last pair 4f out: wl btn in 10th 2f out: passed a few after* **20/1**

6066 **7** *hd* **Runaiocht (IRE)**[28] 8503 7-9-4 **59**.......... JimmyQuinn 4 51
(Paul Burgoyne) *hld up in rr: effrt wl over 2f out and gng bttr than sme: shkn up and fnd nil sn after* **40/1**

0040 **8** *2½* **Never A Word (USA)**[12] 8814 3-9-5 **65**..........(bt) NickyMackay 3 54
(Oliver Greenall) *led and sn clr: c bk to rivals over 2f out: tried to kick on again but hdd & wknd wl over 1f out* **16/1**

26-0 **9** *1* **Gracesome (IRE)**[57] 7711 6-9-4 **59**.......... TomMarquand 14 46
(Michael Blanshard) *hld up in rr: rdn 4f out: sn struggling* **66/1**

3612 **10** *4* **Power Home (IRE)**[22] 8661 3-9-1 **61**.......... FranBerry 13 42
(Denis Coakley) *hld up in last pair: brief effrt over 2f out: sn wknd* **10/1**

1304 **11** *14* **Cat Royale (IRE)**[32] 8429 4-9-9 **64**..........(p) DannyBrock 9 22
(John Butler) *chsd clr ldr and wl ahd of rest after 4f: rdn over 3f out: lost 2nd and wknd rapidly over 2f out: t.o* **20/1**

2m 32.86s (-1.64) **Going Correction** -0.075s/f (Stan)
**WFA** 3 from 4yo+ 5lb **11** Ran SP% **114.0**
Speed ratings (Par 101): **102,101,101,100,98 96,96,95,94,91 82**
CSF £16.19 CT £62.25 TOTE £3.40: £1.30, £2.10, £1.40; EX 19.30 Trifecta £90.40.
**Owner** M Betamar **Bred** Richard Ahern **Trained** Upper Lambourn, Berks

**FOCUS**
This was well run and set up for those held up.

## 8994 ALL WEATHER "HANDS AND HEELS" APPRENTICE SERIES H'CAP (PART OF THE RACING EXCELLENCE INITIATIVE) 1m (P)
**7:40** (7:42) (Class 7) (0-50,50) 3-Y-O+ **£1,940** (£577; £288; £144) **Stalls** Low

Form RPR

0004 **1** **Cookie Ring (IRE)**[19] 8720 6-8-12 **46**..........(t) FayeMcManoman(5) 10 52
(Kristin Stubbs) *t.k.h early: trckd ldrs: prog over 2f out: chsd ldr over 1f out: nudged into the ld 100yds out: hld on* **7/2**[1]

3050 **2** *nk* **Flying Sakhee**[12] 8824 4-9-4 **47**.......... StephenCummins 2 52
(John Bridger) *hld up wl in rr: stl only 12th 2f out: urged along and rapid prog on outer over 1f out: r.o to take 2nd nr fin: jst too late* **12/1**

3006 **3** *½* **Sonnet Rose (IRE)**[36] 8307 3-9-4 **49**..........(bt[1]) SebastianWoods 6 52
(Conrad Allen) *pressed ldrs on inner: led over 2f out: kpt on but hdd last 100yds: lost 2nd nr fin* **8/1**

4203 **4** *½* **Lutine Charlie (IRE)**[41] 8185 10-9-3 **46**..........(p) DarraghKeenan 7 49
(Emma Owen) *led to over 2f out: chsd ldr to over 1f out: kpt on same pce after* **9/1**

0040 **5** *¾* **Linda Doris (IRE)**[14] 8784 3-8-10 **46**..........(t) PaulHainey(5) 4 46
(Gay Kelleway) *hld up in midfield: effrt over 2f out: kpt on fr over 1f out: nrst fin but nvr able to chal* **25/1**

2300 **6** *¾* **Mowhoob**[21] 8675 7-9-7 **50**..........(p) JonathanFisher 5 50
(Brian Barr) *pressed ldng pair: nt qckn 2f out: kpt on same pce fr over 1f out* **10/1**

5330 **7** *2* **Master Of Heaven**[13] 8799 4-9-4 **47**..........(p) HarryBurns 14 42
(Jim Boyle) *t.k.h: racd wd and sn pressed ldrs: lost grnd bnd 3f out: nt on terms fnl 2f: one pce* **7/1**[3]

0600 **8** *nk* **Palace Moon**[183] 3172 12-8-13 **47**..........(t) WilliamCarver(5) 1 41
(Michael Attwater) *hld up in rr: pushed along and no imp on ldrs fnl 2f* **14/1**

5000 **9** *¾* **Golden Cannon**[41] 8185 6-9-4 **50**.......... SophieRalston(3) 13 43
(Sheena West) *reluctant to enter stalls: t.k.h: hld up and racd wd: last and no ch whn c to nr side in st: styd on fnl f* **66/1**

655 **10** *hd* **Sir Jamie**[83] 6846 4-9-6 **49**.......... AledBeech 12 41
(Tony Carroll) *a in rr: no real prog fnl 2f* **14/1**

0450 **11** *3* **Suni Dancer**[72] 7213 6-9-5 **48**.......... BenSanderson 8 33
(Tony Carroll) *slowly away: rchd midfield by 1/2-way: no hdwy and btn 2f out* **25/1**

2540 **12** *nk* **Just Fab (IRE)**[13] 8800 4-9-2 **50**..........(b) JasonWatson(5) 9 34
(Lee Carter) *s.s: a wl in rr: pushed along and no great prog 2f out* **12/1**

5-00 **13** *2¾* **Mellow**[43] 8134 3-9-0 **48**.......... TheodoreLadd(3) 3 25
(Hughie Morrison) *reluctant to go to post or enter the stalls: trckd ldrs: lost pl over 3f out: wknd tamely over 2f out* **5/1**[2]

1m 39.7s (-0.10) **Going Correction** -0.075s/f (Stan)
**WFA** 3 from 4yo+ 2lb **13** Ran SP% **119.5**
Speed ratings (Par 97): **97,96,96,95,94 94,92,91,91,90 87,87,84**
CSF £46.06 CT £330.83 TOTE £4.80: £1.90, £4.20, £3.10; EX 56.40 Trifecta £466.70.
**Owner** Mrs Ailsa Stirling **Bred** Gerard Brady **Trained** Norton, N Yorks

**FOCUS**
A low-grade handicap.
T/Plt: £21.40 to a £1 stake. Pool: £88,423.06 - 3,014.61 winning units T/Qpdt: £16.30 to a £1 stake. Pool: £11,602.42 - 524.16 winning units **Jonathan Neesom**

# [8951]WOLVERHAMPTON (A.W) (L-H)

Wednesday, November 29

**OFFICIAL GOING: Tapeta: standard**

Wind: Fresh across Weather: Cloudy with sunny spells

## 8995 SUNBETS.CO.UK MAIDEN STKS 7f 36y (Tp)

**12:15** (12:16) (Class 5) 3-Y-O+ **£3,234** (£962; £481; £240) **Stalls** High

Form RPR

64 **1** **Delilah Park**[140] 4764 3-9-0 0 ............ MartinHarley 9 75
(Clive Cox) *a.p: led over 1f out: rdn out* **6/1**

4 **2** 2 ½ **Gustavo Fring (IRE)**[217] 2090 3-9-5 0 ............ StevieDonohoe 1 73
(Richard Spencer) *led: rdn: edgd rt and hdd over 1f out: styd on same pce ins fnl f* **11/4**[2]

2 **3** nk **Secret Return (IRE)**[53] 7826 4-9-1 0 ............ LukeMorris 2 68
(Karen George) *chsd ldr: rdn and edgd rt over 1f out: styd on same pce fnl f* **4/1**[3]

35 **4** 5 **Hi Ho Silver**[28] 8504 3-9-5 0 ............ ShaneKelly 5 59
(Chris Wall) *s.i.s: hld up: hdwy over 2f out: shkn up over 1f out: no ex fnl f* **14/1**

433 **5** 5 **Colourful Career (USA)**[44] 8116 3-9-5 73 ............ JimCrowley 8 45
(Ed Dunlop) *plld hrd and prom: rdn over 1f out: wknd fnl f* **13/8**[1]

03- **6** 1 ¾ **De Little Engine (IRE)**[384] 7883 3-9-5 0 ............ DougieCostello 10 40
(Jamie Osborne) *hld up: sme hdwy over 2f out: wknd wl over 1f out* **28/1**

05 **7** 6 **Shadow's Girl**[11] 8852 5-8-8 0 ............ WilliamCox(7) 7 20
(Bernard Llewellyn) *s.i.s: hld up: rdn 1/2-way: sn wknd* **250/1**

00 **8** 5 **Born For Champagne (IRE)**[16] 8770 3-9-0 0 .........(h) PatrickMathers 3 6
(Derek Shaw) *plld hrd and prom: pushed along 1/2-way: wknd 2f out* **250/1**

**9** 6 **Georgiezar** 4-9-1 0 ............ HollieDoyle 6
(Brian Forsey) *a in rr: rdn and wknd 1/2-way* **250/1**

6500 **10** 1 ½ **Nitro**[16] 8774 3-9-2 29 ............ MitchGodwin(3) 4
(Roy Brotherton) *s.i.s: a in rr: wknd 1/2-way* **250/1**

1m 28.41s (-0.39) **Going Correction** -0.025s/f (Stan)
**WFA** 3 from 4yo+ 1lb 10 Ran SP% **110.8**
Speed ratings (Par 103): **101,98,97,92,86 84,77,71,64,63**
CSF £21.44 TOTE £6.80: £1.70, £1.30, £1.60; EX 26.60 Trifecta £100.60.
**Owner** Mr & Mrs De & J Cash And P Turner **Bred** Derra Park Stud **Trained** Lambourn, Berks

**FOCUS**
They were racing on standard Tapeta. The track had been cultivated to a depth of four inches and had been reinstated with a gallop master finish. A modest older-horse maiden to start with three of these having been gelded since last seen. Not many got into it and the form is ordinary, but the winner did it nicely. The form is rated around the runner-up.

## 8996 32RED ON THE APP STORE NURSERY H'CAP 7f 36y (Tp)

**12:45** (12:46) (Class 6) (0-65,65) 2-Y-O **£2,587** (£770; £384; £192) **Stalls** High

Form RPR

0245 **1** **Diamond Pursuit**[42] 8153 2-9-7 65 ............ DougieCostello 8 70
(Jo Hughes) *hld up in tch: shkn up over 1f out: rdn: hung lft and r.o to ld wl ins fnl f* **9/1**

504 **2** ½ **Fire Orchid**[11] 8840 2-9-5 63 ............ TomMarquand 7 67
(Richard Hannon) *hld up: hdwy over 4f out: jnd ldr 1/2-way: shkn up to ld over 1f out: rdn and hdd wl ins fnl f* **9/1**

4450 **3** 2 ¼ **Expelled**[20] 8702 2-9-7 65 ............ DanielMuscutt 5 63
(James Fanshawe) *chsd ldr to 1/2-way: remained handy: shkn up over 1f out: rdn and edgd lft ins fnl f: styd on same pce* **6/4**[1]

0000 **4** hd **Philamundo (IRE)**[36] 8308 2-9-7 65 ............ StevieDonohoe 9 63+
(Richard Spencer) *hld up: hdwy u.p and hung lft fr over 1f out: r.o* **14/1**

0350 **5** ¾ **Salire (IRE)**[39] 8236 2-9-3 61 ............ JackGarritty 3 57
(Ann Duffield) *prom: rdn over 1f out: no ex ins fnl f* **22/1**

0030 **6** ½ **Westfield Wonder**[106] 6043 2-9-0 58 ............ JimmyQuinn 2 53
(Ronald Thompson) *sn pushed along to ld: rdn: edgd rt and hdd over 1f out: wknd wl ins fnl f* **100/1**

3451 **7** ¾ **Zapateado**[11] 8847 2-9-5 63 ............ ShaneKelly 11 56
(Richard Hughes) *hld up: shkn up and hdwy over 1f out: nt trble ldrs* **11/2**[3]

600 **8** 2 **Shadow Seeker (IRE)**[13] 8793 2-8-11 55 ............ LukeMorris 10 43
(Paul D'Arcy) *hld up: pushed along and hdwy 2f out: styd on same pce fnl f* **40/1**

6002 **9** 7 **Where's Jeff**[59] 7655 2-9-3 61 ............ CamHardie 4 32
(Michael Easterby) *hld up: pushed along 1/2-way: rdn and wknd over 1f out* **5/1**[2]

5420 **10** nk **Still Got It**[29] 8491 2-9-4 62 ............ RobHornby 12 32
(Daniel Mark Loughnane) *chsd ldrs: pushed along over 2f out: rdn and wknd over 1f out* **28/1**

000 **11** 7 **See The Tar (IRE)**[42] 8155 2-8-12 56 ............ MartinDwyer 6 9
(Jo Hughes) *hld up: plld hrd: rdn and wknd over 2f out* **16/1**

1m 30.13s (1.33) **Going Correction** -0.025s/f (Stan) 11 Ran SP% **115.8**
Speed ratings (Par 94): **91,90,87,87,86 86,85,83,75,74 66**
CSF £82.92 CT £188.87 TOTE £10.60: £2.40, £2.50, £1.70; EX 94.80 Trifecta £323.10.
**Owner** David Klein & Jo Hughes **Bred** Broughton Bloodstock **Trained** Lambourn. Berks

**FOCUS**
A moderate nursery, with only two of these having hit the target before, and a gamble went astray.

## 8997 32RED CASINO FILLIES' NOVICE STKS (PLUS 10 RACE) (DIV I) 1m 142y (Tp)

**1:15** (1:16) (Class 5) 2-Y-O **£3,234** (£962; £481; £240) **Stalls** Low

Form RPR

351 **1** **West Palm Beach (IRE)**[27] 8544 2-9-7 78 ............ JimCrowley 10 81
(John Gosden) *chsd ldrs: shkn up over 1f out: hmpd ins fnl f: rdn and r.o to ld nr fin* **11/4**[2]

**2** hd **Heeyaam** 2-9-0 0 ............ DanielMuscutt 1 74+
(Marco Botti) *s.i.s: hld up: hdwy over 2f out: swtchd rt over 1f out: edgd rt ins fnl f: sn led: hdd nr fin* **18/1**

66 **3** 1 ½ **Yamuna River**[19] 8715 2-9-0 0 ............ JoeFanning 6 70
(James Tate) *chsd ldr tl wnt upsides over 6f out: rdn to ld over 1f out: edgd lft and hdd wl ins fnl f* **33/1**

**4** 2 **Calypso Blue (IRE)** 2-9-0 0 ............ PhillipMakin 5 66
(Charlie Appleby) *led: shkn up and hdd over 1f out: styd on same pce ins fnl f* **9/4**[1]

**5** nk **Morning Beauty** 2-9-0 0 ............ JosephineGordon 2 66+
(Hugo Palmer) *s.i.s: rn green early in rr: hdwy over 1f out: r.o: nt rch ldrs* **9/1**[3]

5 **6** 2 ¼ **Destinys Rock**[18] 8748 2-9-0 0 ............ PJMcDonald 3 61
(Daniel Mark Loughnane) *prom: racd keenly: rdn over 1f out: wknd wl ins fnl f* **66/1**

0 **7** 2 ¼ **Mille Tank**[32] 8419 2-9-0 0 ............ MartinDwyer 4 56
(William Muir) *s.i.s: hld up: swtchd rt over 2f out: shkn up over 1f out: nt trble ldrs* **66/1**

**8** ¾ **Marie Toulouse (IRE)** 2-8-13 0 ow2 ............ CliffordLee(3) 12 57
(K R Burke) *hld up in tch: rdn over 2f out: wknd over 1f out* **28/1**

05 **9** 5 **Altra Vita**[14] 8779 2-9-0 0 ............ LukeMorris 9 44
(Sir Mark Prescott Bt) *prom: rdn over 2f out: wknd wl over 1f out* **150/1**

60 **10** 2 ½ **Political Slot**[25] 8594 2-9-0 0 ............(h) PatrickMathers 11 39
(Derek Shaw) *s.i.s: pushed along early in rr: rdn and wknd over 2f out* **200/1**

**11** shd **Love Is Enough (JPN)** 2-9-0 0 ............ KieranShoemark 7 39+
(John Gosden) *s.s: clsd to latch on to the bk markers over 5f out: pushed along and wknd over 2f out* **12/1**

1m 51.89s (1.79) **Going Correction** -0.025s/f (Stan) 11 Ran SP% **90.9**
Speed ratings (Par 93): **91,90,89,87,87 85,83,82,78,76 76**
CSF £27.81 TOTE £3.00: £1.10, £3.50, £4.20; EX 39.80 Trifecta £162.20.
**Owner** Mrs Doreen Tabor **Bred** Lynch - Bages & Longfield Stud **Trained** Newmarket, Suffolk

■ Monteja was withdrawn. Price at time of withdrawal 4-1. Rule 4 applies to all bets - deduction 20p in the pound

**FOCUS**
An interesting fillies' novice event with several top stables represented. The race was weakened slightly when the third-favourite Monteja was withdrawn after getting upset in the stalls, but the race should still produce winners.

## 8998 32RED CASINO FILLIES' NOVICE STKS (PLUS 10 RACE) (DIV II) 1m 142y (Tp)

**1:45** (1:45) (Class 5) 2-Y-O **£3,234** (£962; £481; £240) **Stalls** Low

Form RPR

44 **1** **Ghanimah**[27] 8544 2-9-0 0 ............ JimCrowley 9 75
(William Haggas) *chsd ldr: rdn to ld over 1f out: r.o* **10/11**[1]

0 **2** 1 ¼ **Spring Waterfall (IRE)**[34] 8373 2-9-0 0 ............ KieranShoemark 3 72
(Saeed bin Suroor) *led: rdn and hdd over 1f out: styd on same pce ins fnl f* **8/1**[3]

00 **3** 1 **Physical Power (IRE)**[21] 8669 2-9-0 0 ............ HollieDoyle 6 70
(Richard Hannon) *chsd ldrs: pushed along over 2f out: rdn and hung rt ins fnl f: styd on* **80/1**

**4** 1 ¼ **Dorella (GER)** 2-9-0 0 ............ CharlesBishop 7 68
(Eve Johnson Houghton) *mid-div: hdwy over 2f out: rdn and hung lft over 1f out: nt clr run ins fnl f: nt rch ldrs* **16/1**

06 **5** ¾ **Point In Time (IRE)**[21] 8668 2-9-0 0 ............ StevieDonohoe 10 66
(Mark Usher) *chsd ldrs: rdn over 2f out: no ex ins fnl f* **100/1**

**6** 1 ¼ **Chloris** 2-9-0 0 ............ TedDurcan 1 63+
(John Gosden) *s.i.s: hld up: hdwy over 1f out: hung lft ins fnl f: nt trble ldrs* **8/1**[3]

40 **7** ¾ **River Cafe (IRE)**[51] 7898 2-8-11 0 ............ MitchGodwin(3) 13 62
(Sylvester Kirk) *s.i.s: hld up: effrt and nt clr run 1f out: nvr on terms* **50/1**

**8** shd **Realpolitik (IRE)** 2-9-0 0 ............ JackMitchell 12 62
(Roger Varian) *mid-div: pushed along over 2f out: sn lost pl* **22/1**

**9** 1 **Blame Me Forever (USA)** 2-9-0 0 ............ RyanTate 11 60+
(Marco Botti) *s.s: nvr on terms* **40/1**

502 **10** 1 ½ **Come With Me**[36] 8323 2-9-0 78 ............(t) JoeFanning 8 56
(John Gosden) *mid-div: shkn up and lost pl over 2f out: n.d after* **7/2**[2]

**11** 1 ¼ **Cue's Folly** 2-9-0 0 ............ PJMcDonald 5 54+
(Ed Dunlop) *s.s: a in rr* **40/1**

1m 52.29s (2.19) **Going Correction** -0.025s/f (Stan) 11 Ran SP% **116.1**
Speed ratings (Par 93): **89,87,87,85,85 84,83,83,82,81 80**
CSF £8.47 TOTE £1.90: £1.10, £1.80, £6.30; EX 10.10 Trifecta £419.80.
**Owner** Hamdan Al Maktoum **Bred** Shadwell Estate Company Limited **Trained** Newmarket, Suffolk

**FOCUS**
Very few ever got into this division and the order didn't change that much. The winning time was 0.4sec slower than the first leg.

## 8999 BETWAY H'CAP 1m 1f 104y (Tp)

**2:20** (2:21) (Class 2) (0-105,100) 3-Y-O+
**£15,562** (£4,660; £2,330; £1,165; £582; £292) **Stalls** Low

Form RPR

0432 **1** **Pactolus (IRE)**[20] 8705 6-9-5 96 ............(t) AaronJones(3) 5 104
(Stuart Williams) *hld up in tch: led over 1f out: rdn and edgd lft wl ins fnl f: jst hld on* **7/1**[2]

04P0 **2** nk **Mount Tahan (IRE)**[60] 7622 5-9-3 91 ............ KevinStott 7 98
(Kevin Ryan) *s.i.s: hld up: rdn and r.o wl ins fnl f: jst failed* **9/1**[3]

4050 **3** ½ **Battle Of Marathon (USA)**[7] 8891 5-9-4 92 ............ PaulMulrennan 8 98
(John Ryan) *hld up: hdwy and nt clr run over 1f out: r.o* **40/1**

0360 **4** 1 ½ **Kyllachy Gala**[46] 8032 4-9-10 98 ............ TomMarquand 1 101
(Marco Botti) *prom: rdn and nt clr run over 1f out: styd on same pce wl ins fnl f* **16/1**

02 **5** shd **Primero (FR)**[159] 4-9-12 100 ............ PhillipMakin 10 103
(David O'Meara) *hld up: hdwy over 1f out: sn rdn: styd on same pce wl ins fnl f* **9/1**[3]

0000 **6** hd **Mythical Madness**[97] 6355 6-9-10 98 ............(v) KieranShoemark 2 101
(David O'Meara) *prom: sn stdd and lost pl: hld up: hdwy and nt clr run over 1f out: edgd lft and no ex wl ins fnl f* **10/1**

5342 **7** ¾ **Rainbow Rebel (IRE)**[6] 8910 4-8-13 87 ............ PJMcDonald 9 88
(Mark Johnston) *chsd ldrs: led over 1f out: sn rdn and hdd: styd on same pce* **7/1**[2]

5313 **8** nk **Seniority**[23] 8638 3-8-13 90 ............ JimCrowley 4 90
(William Haggas) *plld hrd and prom: nt clr run wl over 1f out: ev ch 1f out: no ex ins fnl f* **15/8**[1]

3050 **9** ½ **Third Time Lucky (IRE)**[11] 8843 5-9-12 100 ............(h) TonyHamilton 3 99
(Richard Fahey) *hld up: plld hrd: nt clr run over 1f out: nt trble ldrs* **25/1**

0303 **10** hd **Bronze Angel (IRE)**[30] 8469 8-9-0 95 ............(v) TylerSaunders(7) 12 94
(Marcus Tregoning) *s.i.s: hld up: hdwy over 1f out: no ex wl ins fnl f* **18/1**

1040 **11** 2 ¼ **Forceful Appeal (USA)**[11] 8843 9-9-2 95 ............ PaddyBradley(5) 11 89
(Simon Dow) *hld up: shkn up over 2f out: nvr on terms* **80/1**

3241 **12** ½ **Roll On Rory**[25] 8596 4-8-11 85 ............(b) TomEaves 6 78
(Jason Ward) *led 1f: chsd ldr tl led again over 2f out: rdn and hdd over 1f out: wknd wl ins fnl f* **10/1**

6250 **13** hd **Sands Chorus**[11] 8844 5-9-7 95 ............ BarryMcHugh 13 88
(James Given) *led after 1f: rdn and hdd over 2f out: wknd ins fnl f* **40/1**

1m 58.71s (-2.09) **Going Correction** -0.025s/f (Stan)
**WFA** 3 from 4yo+ 3lb 13 Ran SP% **119.1**
Speed ratings (Par 109): **108,107,107,105,105 105,105,104,104,104 102,101,101**
CSF £66.73 CT £2354.53 TOTE £7.80: £2.80, £4.20, £12.20; EX 84.10 Trifecta £2515.10.
**Owner** T W Morley & Mrs J Morley **Bred** Tom McDonald **Trained** Newmarket, Suffolk

**FOCUS**
A warm handicap and almost the entire field were in a line across the track coming to the last furlong. The main action unfolded down the centre of the track and the placed horses may have been a bit unlucky. The winner was better to score off a career-high mark.

## 9000 BETWAY CASINO H'CAP 1m 4f 51y (Tp)
2:50 (2:52) (Class 4) (0-80,80) 3-Y-O+ £5,175 (£1,540; £769; £384) Stalls Low

Form RPR
6001 1 **Island Brave (IRE)**[29] 8497 3-9-1 **76** PJMcDonald 5 83+
(Heather Main) *hld up: shkn up over 4f out: pushed along and hdwy over 2f out: rdn and r.o to ld wl ins fnl f* **3/1**[1]
-243 2 1 **Star Story**[26] 8564 3-8-13 **74** PhillipMakin 4 80
(Ralph Beckett) *plld hrd and prom: stdd and lost pl over 9f out: hdwy u.p over 1f out: r.o to go 2nd nr fin* **13/2**
1 3 ¾ **Spinning Melody (USA)**[48] 7989 3-9-5 **80** KieranShoemark 11 84
(Simon Crisford) *chsd ldr: rdn over 2f out: hung rt ins fnl f: styd on same pce* **11/2**[3]
0000 4 nk **Maifalki (FR)**[25] 8596 4-9-9 **79** TomEaves 12 83
(Jason Ward) *led: pushed clr 2f out: rdn over 1f out: hdd and no ex wl ins fnl f* **20/1**
1422 5 ¾ **Take Two**[22] 8648 8-9-8 **78** JoeFanning 7 81
(Alex Hales) *s.i.s: hld up: hdwy over 1f out: styd on same pce wl ins fnl f* **8/1**
5300 6 hd **Azam**[23] 8638 3-9-5 **80** AlistairRawlinson 10 82
(Michael Appleby) *s.i.s: hld up: rdn over 2f out: r.o ins fnl f: nvr nrr* **33/1**
0400 7 nk **Tangramm**[37] 8295 5-9-8 **78** (p) CharlesBishop 9 80
(Dean Ivory) *hld up: hdwy: hung lft and nt clr run over 1f out: nt trble ldrs* **16/1**
6016 8 ¾ **Villette (IRE)**[12] 8820 3-9-5 **80** RobHornby 1 81
(Dean Ivory) *hld up in tch: shkn up over 2f out: styd on same pce fnl f* **20/1**
2051 9 2 **Omotesando**[9] 8876 7-8-7 **66** (p) CharlieBennett(3) 3 64
(Oliver Greenall) *chsd ldrs: rdn over 3f out: styd on same pce fr over 1f out* **9/2**[2]
014 10 2½ **Thistimenextyear**[106] 6033 3-9-5 **80** StevieDonohoe 2 74
(Richard Spencer) *trckd ldrs: racd keenly: rdn over 2f out: wknd fnl f* **14/1**
353- 11 16 **Lungarno Palace (USA)**[486] 4912 6-9-2 **75** (b) HectorCrouch(3) 6 43
(John Gallagher) *hld up: pushed along over 3f out: wknd over 2f out* **50/1**
0501 12 24 **Throckley**[13] 8806 6-9-10 **80** PaulMulrennan 8 10
(Conor Dore) *hld up: hdwy over 9f out: rdn and wknd over 2f out* **12/1**
2m 36.13s (-4.67) **Going Correction** -0.025s/f (Stan)
**WFA** 3 from 4yo+ 5lb **12 Ran SP% 117.7**
Speed ratings (Par 105): **114,113,112,112,112 112,111,111,109,108 97,81**
CSF £21.08 CT £103.51 TOTE £3.70: £1.60, £1.60, £2.80; EX 27.80 Trifecta £124.40.
**Owner** Donald M Kerr **Bred** Tally-Ho Stud **Trained** Kingston Lisle, Oxon

**FOCUS**
A fair middle-distance handicap and they went a solid pace. The finish was pretty compressed and it's hard to be positive overall.

## 9001 BETWAY DASH H'CAP 5f 21y (Tp)
3:25 (3:25) (Class 6) (0-65,65) 3-Y-O+ £2,587 (£770; £384; £192) Stalls Low

Form RPR
5043 1 **Hamish McGonagain**[9] 8874 4-9-7 **65** (p) KieranShoemark 3 72
(David O'Meara) *broke wl: sn stdd and lost pl: hdwy over 1f out: hung rt and r.o to ld towards fin* **5/2**[1]
03 2 ½ **Eternalist**[9] 8873 4-8-9 **60** SeanMooney(7) 9 65
(Jim Goldie) *broke wl: stdd and lost pl sn after s: hdwy over 1f out: r.o to go 2nd nr fin* **10/1**
0155 3 ½ **Red Stripes (USA)**[12] 8816 5-8-9 **60** (b) GabrieleMalune(7) 2 63
(Lisa Williamson) *plld hrd: trckd ldrs: wnt 2nd over 1f out: rdn to ld wl ins fnl f: hdd towards fin* **8/1**
5606 4 1 **Krystallite**[11] 8853 4-9-2 **60** TomEaves 7 60
(Scott Dixon) *sn pushed along to ld: rdn and hung rt fr over 1f out: hdd and unable qck wl ins fnl f* **16/1**
2242 5 ½ **Kyllukey**[11] 8853 4-9-1 **62** (v) HectorCrouch(3) 1 60
(Milton Bradley) *trckd ldrs: shkn up over 1f out: no ex wl ins fnl f* **9/2**[3]
1600 6 ½ **Mr Strutter (IRE)**[9] 8874 3-8-13 **64** (h) WilliamCox(7) 4 60
(Ronald Thompson) *prom: pushed along 1/2-way: styd on same pce fr over 1f out* **40/1**
4032 7 nk **Spin Top**[12] 8816 3-9-3 **61** MartinDwyer 6 56
(William Muir) *hld up: rdn: edgd rt and r.o towards fin: nvr nrr* **4/1**[2]
0030 8 2 **First Bombardment**[12] 8816 4-8-10 **61** (t) PatrickVaughan(7) 11 49
(David O'Meara) *s.s: hld up: n.d* **18/1**
1306 9 ½ **Absolutely Awesome**[16] 8775 3-9-7 **65** StevieDonohoe 10 51
(John Butler) *hld up: nvr on terms* **20/1**
6055 10 2¼ **Shackled N Drawn (USA)**[64] 7486 5-9-7 **65** (p) CharlesBishop 8 43
(Peter Hedger) *chsd ldr 4f out tl rdn over 1f out: wknd ins fnl f* **9/1**
2150 11 1¼ **Point North (IRE)**[18] 8745 10-9-2 **65** (b) BenRobinson(5) 5 39
(John Balding) *s.i.s: n.d* **40/1**
1m 1.15s (-0.75) **Going Correction** -0.025s/f (Stan) **11 Ran SP% 117.7**
Speed ratings (Par 101): **105,104,103,101,101 100,99,96,95,92 90**
CSF £28.44 CT £178.27 TOTE £3.10: £1.10, £2.90, £3.00; EX 28.80 Trifecta £209.00.
**Owner** The Lawton Bamforth Partnership **Bred** Llety Farms **Trained** Upper Helmsley, N Yorks
■ Stewards' Enquiry : Kieran Shoemark caution: careless riding

**FOCUS**
A modest sprint handicap in which they went a blistering pace, but the leaders may have gone off a bit too quick.

## 9002 32REDSPORT.COM NURSERY H'CAP 6f 20y (Tp)
3:55 (3:57) (Class 6) (0-60,59) 2-Y-O £2,587 (£770; £384; £192) Stalls Low

Form RPR
3603 1 **Skyva**[25] 8588 2-9-2 **59** BenRobinson(5) 2 63
(Brian Ellison) *chsd ldrs: rdn to ld wl ins fnl f: jst hld on* **7/2**[1]
005 2 hd **Alaskan Bay (IRE)**[22] 8657 2-9-2 **54** PaulMulrennan 11 57
(Rae Guest) *led: hdd over 3f out: remained w ldr: shkn up to ld again over 1f out: rdn: hung lft and hdd wl ins fnl f: r.o* **20/1**
0003 3 shd **Our Kid (IRE)**[13] 8804 2-9-7 **59** (b) TonyHamilton 10 62
(Richard Fahey) *s.i.s: hld up: hdwy over 1f out: rdn and hung lft ins fnl f: r.o* **13/2**
4623 4 1¼ **Lady Lintera (IRE)**[14] 8780 2-8-12 **50** (h) ShaneGray 1 49
(Ann Duffield) *chsd ldrs: rdn over 1f out: r.o* **7/1**
0000 5 1 **Kylie Style**[13] 8795 2-8-8 **53** (p[1]) PatrickVaughan(7) 4 49
(Steph Hollinshead) *w ldr: led over 3f out: rdn and hdd over 1f out: no ex wl ins fnl f* **33/1**
5006 6 ¾ **Poppy Jag (IRE)**[14] 8780 2-8-11 **49** (p) RyanPowell 9 43
(Kevin Frost) *mid-div: rdn over 2f out: styd on ins fnl f* **40/1**
0060 7 2¼ **Jazz Affair (IRE)**[11] 8847 2-9-0 **52** (v[1]) JoeFanning 12 39
(Jamie Osborne) *prom: racd keenly: rdn over 1f out: no ex fnl f* **9/1**
6035 8 nk **Arty But Poor**[11] 8847 2-9-6 **58** (p) KevinStott 13 44
(Oliver Greenall) *hld up: rdn over 2f out: styd on ins fnl f: nt trble ldrs* **7/1**
600 9 3½ **Haven's View**[151] 4367 2-9-5 **57** StevieDonohoe 5 33
(Richard Hughes) *s.i.s: hld up: n.d* **6/1**[3]
5326 10 ½ **Istanbul Pasha (IRE)**[14] 8783 2-9-2 **54** (v) KieranShoemark 3 28
(David Evans) *mid-div: rdn over 2f out: sme hdwy over 1f out: wknd fnl f* **9/2**[2]
4500 11 3¾ **Ben My Chree**[50] 7920 2-9-6 **58** (b[1]) TomEaves 8 21
(Bryan Smart) *hld up: rdn over 2f out: sn wknd* **22/1**
1m 14.82s (0.32) **Going Correction** -0.025s/f (Stan) **11 Ran SP% 117.5**
Speed ratings (Par 94): **96,95,95,93,92 91,88,88,83,82 77**
CSF £79.16 CT £448.51 TOTE £4.20: £1.60, £4.30, £2.20; EX 59.20 Trifecta £374.60.
**Owner** Facts & Figures **Bred** Facts & Figures **Trained** Norton, N Yorks
■ Watch Tan was withdrawn. Price at time of withdrawal 18-1. Rule 4 does not apply.

**FOCUS**
A moderate nursery with only one previous winner in the field. Again they went a serious gallop, but this time the pace held up.
T/Jkpt: Not won. T/Plt: £262.00 to a £1 stake. Pool: £59,329.39 - 165.28 winning units T/Qpdt: £78.80 to a £1 stake. Pool: £7,546.54 - 70.82 winning units **Colin Roberts**

# 8986 DEAUVILLE (R-H)
Wednesday, November 29

**OFFICIAL GOING: Polytrack: fast**

## 9003a PRIX LYPHARD (LISTED RACE) (3YO+) (POLYTRACK) 1m 1f 110y(P)
2:05 3-Y-O+ £22,222 (£8,888; £6,666; £4,444; £2,222)

RPR
1 **Astral Merit (FR)**[18] 8755 7-8-10 0 (b) StephanePasquier 4 98
(F Monnier, France) **128/10**
2 snk **Syrita (FR)**[70] 7305 4-9-0 0 (p) OlivierPeslier 16 102
(M Nigge, France) **11/1**
3 ½ **Replenish (FR)**[46] 8032 4-9-0 0 AurelienLemaitre 11 101
(S Cerulis, France) **86/1**
4 hd **Caravagio (FR)**[43] 4-9-0 0 (p) MathieuAndrouin 10 100
(Alain Couetil, France) **12/1**
5 2½ **Time Shanakill (IRE)**[43] 4-9-0 0 PierreBazire 14 95
(G Botti, France) **13/1**
6 snk **Subway Dancer (IRE)**[17] 8769 5-9-0 0 ChristopheSoumillon 8 95
(Z Koplik, Czech Republic) **3/1**[1]
7 ¾ **Abareeq**[180] 3300 4-9-0 0 IoritzMendizabal 7 93
(Mark Johnston) *midfield: rdn over 1f out: outpcd fnl f* **32/1**
8 hd **Utmost (USA)**[11] 8843 3-8-11 0 TonyPiccone 15 94
(John Gosden) *in tch on outer: rdn and effrt into st: outpcd but keeping on whn sltly hmpd ent fnl f: no threat after* **68/10**[3]
9 snk **Skiperia (FR)**[60] 6-8-10 0 (p) LukasDelozier 9 89
(Y Barberot, France) **49/1**
10 ¾ **Sinfonietta (FR)**[26] 8566 5-9-0 0 FranckBlondel 5 91
(David Menuisier) *hld up in midfield: swtchd ins and rdn to chal over 1f out: no ex fnl f: wknd* **67/1**
11 nse **Jasmiralda (FR)**[29] 4-8-10 0 (b) TheoBachelot 6 87
(S Wattel, France) **13/2**[2]
12 snk **Promise Of Peace (JPN)**[38] 8270 3-8-11 0 (b[1]) ThierryThulliez 2 92
(A Wohler, Germany) **27/1**
13 3½ **Royal Julius (IRE)**[31] 8448 4-9-3 0 ClementLecoeuvre 13 86
(J Reynier, France) **68/10**[3]
14 5 **Silver Look (ARG)**[212] 4-8-10 0 FabriceVeron 1 69
(S Kobayashi, France) **31/1**
15 ¾ **Licinius (GER)**[55] 4-9-0 0 EddyHardouin 3 72
(Yasmin Almenrader, Germany) **22/1**
16 snk **Prost (GER)**[50] 7941 3-8-11 0 GregoryBenoist 12 72
(Ed Vaughan) *prom: rdn and effrt early st: no ex over 1f out: wknd and eased: dropped to last* **19/1**
1m 54.75s
**WFA** 3 from 4yo+ 3lb **16 Ran SP% 118.1**
PARI-MUTUEL (all including 1 euro stake): WIN 13.80; PLACE 4.80, 4.30, 23.10; DF 75.90; SF 217.00.
**Owner** Bruno Foucher **Bred** Bruno Foucher **Trained** France

9004-9011a (Foreign Racing) - See Raceform Interactive

# 8924 NEWCASTLE (A.W) (L-H)
Thursday, November 30

**OFFICIAL GOING: Tapeta: standard**
Wind: fresh half against Weather: Unsettled with sleet showers

## 9012 SUNBETS.CO.UK APPRENTICE H'CAP (DIV I) 7f 14y (Tp)
5:45 (5:45) (Class 6) (0-60,62) 3-Y-O+ £2,264 (£673; £336; £168) Stalls Centre

Form RPR
-632 1 **Chaucer's Tale**[14] 8807 3-9-6 **60** (t) HarrisonShaw(3) 9 66
(Michael Easterby) *w ldr: led over 3f out: rdn over 2f out: kpt on* **9/4**[1]
2402 2 ¾ **Jessie Allan (IRE)**[6] 8924 6-8-10 **46** RowanScott 7 51
(Jim Goldie) *in tch: hdwy to trck ldr gng wl 2f out: rdn over 1f out: kpt on* **9/2**[3]
4000 3 1¾ **Miss Bates**[47] 8031 3-9-5 **56** CliffordLee 10 55
(Ann Duffield) *hld up: pushed along and hdwy 2f out: chsd ldr appr fnl f: sn rdn: one pce fnl 110yds* **6/1**
-040 4 3 **Dandy Bird (IRE)**[27] 8552 3-9-8 **59** PhilDennis 4 50
(Julie Camacho) *hld up: rdn over 2f out: kpt on fnl f: nvr threatened ldrs* **9/1**
0642 5 2¼ **Kafoo**[23] 8659 4-9-12 **62** (vt) AlistairRawlinson 3 48
(Michael Appleby) *chsd ldrs: rdn over 2f out: no imp* **4/1**[2]
0400 6 nk **Arizona Sunrise**[15] 8784 4-8-5 **46** oh1 SophieRalston(5) 11 31
(Tina Jackson) *hld up: rdn over 2f out: sme late hdwy: nvr threatened* **25/1**
210 7 1 **Justice Pleasing**[112] 5835 4-9-8 **61** (p) BenSanderson(3) 8 44
(Roger Fell) *trckd ldrs: rdn over 2f out: wknd fnl f* **11/1**
2305 8 2½ **Tom's Anna (IRE)**[108] 6003 7-8-10 **46** oh1 JackDuern 2 22
(Sean Regan) *led narrowly: hdd over 3f out: wknd over 2f out* **33/1**
0440 9 3¼ **She's Zoff (IRE)**[96] 6437 3-8-4 **46** oh1 WilliamCarver(5) 6 12
(John Quinn) *prom: rdn over 2f out: wknd over 1f out* **20/1**


The Form Book Flat, Raceform Ltd, Newbury, RG14 5SJ

4600 **10** ½ **Fast Kar (IRE)**[103] 6216 3-8-9 **46** oh1 EdwardGreatrex 1 11
(Barry John Murphy, Ire) *chsd ldrs: rdn 3f out: sn wknd* **33/1**
1m 28.79s (2.59) **Going Correction** +0.35s/f (Slow)
**WFA** 3 from 4yo+ 1lb **10** Ran SP% **116.1**
Speed ratings (Par 101): **99,98,96,92,90 89,88,85,82,81**
CSF £11.62 CT £51.67 TOTE £3.00: £1.30, £1.90, £2.30; EX 13.10 Trifecta £65.50.
**Owner** A N C Bengough & Stittenham Racing **Bred** T M Jennings **Trained** Sheriff Hutton, N Yorks
**FOCUS**
A moderate contest. The winner looks to have taken a fractional step forward.

## 9013 SUNBETS.CO.UK APPRENTICE H'CAP (DIV II) 7f 14y (Tp)
**6:15** (6:16) (Class 6) (0-60,62) 3-Y-0+ **£2,264** (£673; £336; £168) **Stalls** Centre

Form RPR
5050 **1** **Lotara**[30] 8496 5-8-10 **46** oh1 PhilDennis 8 52
(Jim Goldie) *hld up: pushed along and hdwy over 2f out: led over 1f out: edgd rt: kpt on* **12/1**
000- **2** 1¼ **Western Way (IRE)**[442] 6490 8-9-9 **62** (p) NicolaCurrie(3) 5 65
(Don Cantillon) *hld up: rdn and outpcd in rr over 2f out: hdwy over 1f out: kpt on* **12/1**
0003 **3** 1¼ **Lukoutoldmakezebak**[26] 8591 4-8-7 **46** oh1 (p) JamieGormley(3) 3 45
(David Thompson) *chsd ldrs: rdn and outpcd 3f out: rallied over 1f out: kpt on fnl f* **8/1**[2]
0643 **4** 1 **Hisar (IRE)**[5] 8949 3-9-2 **53** (p) AlistairRawlinson 4 49
(Michael Appleby) *in tch: rdn over 2f out: chsd ldr appr fnl f: one pce* **5/6**[1]
0-60 **5** 1½ **Shudbeme**[89] 6673 4-8-7 **46** oh1 (p) HarrisonShaw(3) 7 39
(Neville Bycroft) *midfield: rdn over 3f out: one pce and nvr threatened* **50/1**
0620 **6** nk **Vecheka (IRE)**[6] 8924 6-8-7 **46** (p) AledBeech(3) 10 38
(Kenny Johnson) *dwlt: hld up: rdn over 3f out: plugged on fr over 1f out: nvr threatened* **20/1**
1050 **7** 7 **Mr Potter**[6] 8930 4-9-7 **60** (v) JackOsborn(3) 1 33
(Richard Guest) *dwlt but sn pressed ldr racing keenly: led 5f out: clr over 3f out tl 2f out: rdn whn hdd over 1f out: wknd* **8/1**[2]
0000 **8** 3¼ **Taskeen (IRE)**[23] 8651 4-9-5 **58** (p[1]) BenSanderson(3) 6 22
(Roger Fell) *in tch: rdn over 2f out: wknd over 1f out* **11/1**[3]
0004 **9** nk **Tan**[17] 8775 3-9-6 **60** (t) PatrickVaughan(3) 9 22
(Tony Coyle) *hld up: nvr threatened* **14/1**
0330 **10** 4 **Peny Arcade**[26] 8591 3-8-9 **46** oh1 (v[1]) RowanScott 2
(Alistair Whillans) *led: hdd 5f out: rdn over 2f out: wknd* **14/1**
1m 29.22s (3.02) **Going Correction** +0.35s/f (Slow)
**WFA** 3 from 4yo+ 1lb **10** Ran SP% **120.6**
Speed ratings (Par 101): **96,94,93,92,90 89,81,78,77,73**
CSF £151.37 CT £1263.87 TOTE £13.60: £3.00, £3.20, £1.50; EX 140.70 Trifecta £549.30.
**Owner** Mrs Lucille Bone **Bred** Triple H Stud Ltd **Trained** Uplawmoor, E Renfrews
**FOCUS**
The slower of the two divisions by 0.43sec. Low-grade form with a fractional step up from the winner.

## 9014 32RED.COM NURSERY H'CAP 1m 5y (Tp)
**6:45** (6:46) (Class 6) (0-60,61) 2-Y-0 **£2,264** (£673; £336; £168) **Stalls** Centre

Form RPR
600 **1** **Trick Shot Jenny**[19] 8748 2-9-1 **54** DougieCostello 6 56
(Jamie Osborne) *in tch: rdn to chse ldr over 1f out: ev ch ins fnl f: kpt on: led post* **33/1**
0030 **2** shd **Mr Carbonator**[15] 8783 2-9-0 **53** JimmyQuinn 7 55
(Philip Kirby) *hld up: rdn and hdwy 2f out: led narrowly 1f out: sn drvn: kpt on: hdd post* **8/1**
3552 **3** shd **Rock On Bertie (IRE)**[15] 8783 2-9-1 **54** (p) TomEaves 5 56
(Nigel Tinkler) *led: rdn 2f out: hdd 1f out: kpt on* **9/2**[2]
5004 **4** 2½ **Blue Havana (IRE)**[15] 8783 2-9-2 **55** JasonHart 3 51
(John Quinn) *hld up in tch: pushed along over 2f out: rdn and one pce in 4th fr appr fnl f* **11/2**[3]
3003 **5** 10 **Foxrush Take Time (FR)**[12] 8847 2-9-7 **60** PhillipMakin 1 33
(Richard Guest) *midfield: rdn over 2f out: wknd over 1f out* **11/2**[3]
6553 **6** 3¼ **Obrigada**[8] 8887 2-9-8 **61** JosephineGordon 8 27
(Tom Clover) *chsd ldrs: rdn over 2f out: wknd over 1f out* **10/3**[1]
0003 **7** 1¾ **Ahfad**[10] 8870 2-8-11 **50** PJMcDonald 2 12
(Stuart Williams) *s.i.s: rdn along to sn chse ldr: rdn 3f out: wknd fnl 2f* **10/3**[1]
5040 **8** ½ **Onefootinfront**[10] 8870 2-9-8 **61** AndrewMullen 4 22
(Daniel Mark Loughnane) *dwlt: sn chsd ldrs: rdn over 3f out: sn wknd* **16/1**
1m 42.98s (4.38) **Going Correction** +0.35s/f (Slow) **8** Ran SP% **115.0**
Speed ratings (Par 94): **92,91,91,89,79 76,74,73**
CSF £272.92 CT £1431.12 TOTE £16.50: £5.60, £3.20, £1.20; EX 182.50 Trifecta £730.70.
**Owner** Melbourne 10 Racing **Bred** Glebe Farm Stud **Trained** Upper Lambourn, Berks
■ Stewards' Enquiry : Jimmy Quinn four-day ban: using his whip down the shoulder in the forehand and above the permitted level from inside the final furlong (Dec 14-16/18)
**FOCUS**
A modest nursery and the first four finished a mile clear of the rest. Straightforward, limited form at face value.

## 9015 32RED CASINO EBF NOVICE MEDIAN AUCTION STKS 7f 14y (Tp)
**7:15** (7:16) (Class 6) 2-Y-0 **£2,911** (£866; £432; £216) **Stalls** Centre

Form RPR
3 **1** **Strange Society (IRE)**[14] 8794 2-9-2 0 JosephineGordon 4 76+
(Hugo Palmer) *chsd ldrs: pushed along to chal over 1f out: rdn to ld 110yds out: kpt on pushed out: shade cosily* **5/6**[1]
25 **2** nk **Ambient (IRE)**[101] 6260 2-9-2 0 JackMitchell 3 75
(Roger Varian) *hld up in tch: hdwy 2f out: pushed along to ld appr fnl f: sn rdn: hdd 110yds out: one pce* **5/2**[2]
2020 **3** 4½ **Not After Midnight (IRE)**[13] 8817 2-8-11 74 GeorgeDowning 6 58
(Daniel Kubler) *prom: rdn to ld 2f out: hdd appr fnl f: wknd ins fnl f* **4/1**[3]
32 **4** 1 **Sunhill Lad (IRE)**[63] 7556 2-9-2 0 ShaneGray 5 60
(Ann Duffield) *led: rdn whn hdd 2f out: wknd ins fnl f* **12/1**
**5** 8 **Hocus Focus (IRE)** 2-9-2 0 PhillipMakin 1 39
(Richard Guest) *dwlt: sn in tch: rdn over 2f out: sn wknd* **33/1**
1m 29.18s (2.98) **Going Correction** +0.35s/f (Slow) **5** Ran SP% **113.8**
Speed ratings (Par 94): **97,96,91,90,81**
CSF £3.37 TOTE £1.60: £1.10, £1.50; EX 3.50 Trifecta £7.80.
**Owner** M M Stables **Bred** Gortskagh House Stud & Tally Ho Stud **Trained** Newmarket, Suffolk
**FOCUS**
An ordinary novice in which the first two showed improvement.

## 9016 BETWAY CASINO H'CAP 6f (Tp)
**7:45** (7:46) (Class 3) (0-90,90) 3-Y-0 **£7,246** (£2,168; £1,084; £542; £270) **Stalls** Centre

Form RPR
141 **1** **Glenamoy Lad**[68] 7405 3-9-2 **85** (t) PhillipMakin 13 102+
(Michael Wigham) *dwlt: hld up: smooth hdwy 2f out: qcknd to ld 75yds out: c clr pushed out: comf* **6/1**[2]
0004 **2** 2¾ **Tropics (USA)**[24] 8639 9-9-1 **87** (h) JackDuern(3) 8 93
(Dean Ivory) *trckd ldrs: sn rdn: hdd 75yds out: kpt on but no ch w wnr* **9/2**[1]
2603 **3** 1 **Eccleston**[38] 8293 6-9-0 **83** (v) GrahamLee 1 86
(Julie Camacho) *hld up: pushed along 2f out: r.o wl fnl f: wnt 3rd post* **28/1**
0033 **4** shd **Bertiewhittle**[19] 8737 9-8-11 **87** GabrieleMalune(7) 3 89
(David Barron) *dwlt: hld up: rdn over 3f out: kpt on fnl f: nrst fin* **10/1**
2402 **5** ½ **Kenny The Captain (IRE)**[37] 8319 6-8-10 **82** RachelRichardson(3) 10 83
(Tim Easterby) *prom: rdn over 2f out: one pce fnl f: lost 2 pls nr fin* **9/2**[1]
3140 **6** hd **Florencio**[10] 8872 4-9-1 **84** (p) DougieCostello 5 84
(Roger Fell) *dwlt: hld up: rdn and sme hdwy over 1f out: kpt on fnl f* **14/1**
0641 **7** 1½ **Tilly Trotter (IRE)**[20] 8717 3-8-13 **82** TomEaves 6 77
(Declan Carroll) *trckd ldrs: rdn 2f out: no ex fnl f* **16/1**
000- **8** ½ **Ustinov**[412] 7315 5-9-5 **88** (h) KieranShoemark 2 82
(David O'Meara) *hld up in midfield: pushed along over 2f out: no imp* **33/1**
0424 **9** ¾ **Right Touch**[19] 8737 7-9-6 **89** TonyHamilton 4 80
(Richard Fahey) *nvr bttr than midfield* **7/1**[3]
6004 **10** 3½ **Kadrizzi (FR)**[128] 5241 4-9-7 **90** RobHornby 9 70
(Dean Ivory) *hld up: nvr threatened* **10/1**
0142 **11** 1 **Mont Kiara (FR)**[68] 7405 4-9-5 **88** ShaneGray 7 65
(Kevin Ryan) *midfield: rdn over 2f out: sn wknd* **7/1**[3]
000 **12** 3 **Bosham**[14] 8803 7-8-6 **82** (bt) HarrisonShaw(7) 14 49
(Michael Easterby) *prom: rdn over 2f out: sn wknd* **40/1**
0210 **13** 1¾ **Handsome Dude**[61] 7612 5-9-3 **86** (b) JosephineGordon 11 48
(David Barron) *led: rdn whn hdd over 2f out: wknd* **7/1**[3]
1m 12.08s (-0.42) **Going Correction** +0.35s/f (Slow) **13** Ran SP% **127.7**
Speed ratings (Par 107): **116,112,111,110,110 109,107,107,106,101 100,96,93**
CSF £35.10 CT £760.58 TOTE £7.20: £2.30, £2.70, £5.80; EX 51.40 Trifecta £973.60.
**Owner** V Healy **Bred** Mrs T A Foreman **Trained** Newmarket, Suffolk
**FOCUS**
This was run at a good gallop and the winner impressed. The second is rated close to his recent effort.

## 9017 SUN BETS ON THE APP STORE CLASSIFIED CLAIMING STKS 1m 5y (Tp)
**8:15** (8:15) (Class 5) 3-Y-0+ **£2,911** (£866; £432; £216) **Stalls** Centre

Form RPR
2332 **1** **Choral Clan (IRE)**[13] 8814 6-9-0 69 JackMitchell 1 67
(Brendan Powell) *dwlt: hld up: hdwy 2f out: pushed along to chse ldr over 1f out: led ins fnl f: kpt on* **3/1**[2]
2034 **2** 1½ **Maraakib (IRE)**[13] 8814 5-9-4 64 KieranShoemark 2 67
(David O'Meara) *trckd ldrs: rdn to ld 2f out: hdd ins fnl f one pce* **4/1**[3]
0325 **3** nse **Ingleby Angel (IRE)**[5] 8957 8-8-7 58 PatrickVaughan(7) 5 63
(David O'Meara) *hld up in tch: racd keenly: rdn 2f out: kpt on fnl f* **2/1**[1]
0345 **4** nk **Hellavashock**[49] 7979 4-8-2 46 (b) AndrewMullen 4 50
(Alistair Whillans) *led: rdn whn hdd 2f out: kpt on* **28/1**
-506 **5** 8 **Intermodal**[13] 8814 3-9-2 69 DougieCostello 8 46
(Jamie Osborne) *trckd ldrs: rdn over 2f out: sn wknd* **9/2**
5600 **6** 3 **George Reme (IRE)**[106] 6067 3-8-12 66 (p) JasonHart 7 35
(John Quinn) *prom: rdn over 2f out: wknd* **15/2**
0-60 **7** 1¼ **Austerity (IRE)**[44] 8143 4-9-10 60 PJMcDonald 6 43
(Sally Haynes) *hld up in tch: rdn over 2f out: sn wknd* **50/1**
1m 41.53s (2.93) **Going Correction** +0.35s/f (Slow)
**WFA** 3 from 4yo+ 2lb **7** Ran SP% **113.7**
Speed ratings (Par 103): **99,97,97,97,89 86,84**
CSF £15.23 TOTE £4.00: £1.80, £2.20; EX 14.20 Trifecta £37.20.There was no bid for the winner.
**Owner** Bob Harris & Patricia Mitchell **Bred** L Queally **Trained** Upper Lambourn, Berks
**FOCUS**
This was steadily run and a few threw their chances away by failing to settle. The form is rated around the third and fourth.

## 9018 BET & WATCH AT SUNBETS.CO.UK MAIDEN STKS 1m 5y (Tp)
**8:45** (8:45) (Class 5) 3-4-Y-0 **£2,911** (£866; £432; £216) **Stalls** Centre

Form RPR
2223 **1** **Ambrosia**[68] 7388 3-9-0 73 (h[1]) KieranShoemark 8 49
(Roger Charlton) *dwlt: hld up in tch: racd keenly: pushed along and qcknd to ld 110yds out: rdn out* **9/4**[2]
35 **2** ½ **Valley Of Light**[49] 7989 3-9-0 0 (v[1]) TomMarquand 3 47
(Saeed bin Suroor) *led narrowly: rdn 2f out: hdd 110yds out: one pce* **3/1**[3]
0-50 **3** hd **Servo (IRE)**[23] 8651 3-9-5 53 JackGarritty 5 52
(Lynn Siddall) *rrd s: sn trckd ldrs racing keenly: rdn over 1f out: ev ch ins fnl f: one pce* **40/1**
0540 **4** 1½ **Urban Spirit (IRE)**[20] 8720 3-9-5 50 TonyHamilton 1 48
(Roger Fell) *dwlt: hld up: rdn and sme hdwy over 1f out: one pce fnl f* **33/1**
**5** 1½ **Middle Creek** 3-9-0 0 RobertHavlin 6 40
(John Gosden) *dwlt: sn in tch: hdwy and prom 3f out: rdn 2f out: edgd lft and no ex ins fnl f* **6/4**[1]
4003 **6** 2½ **Supreme Power (IRE)**[20] 8720 3-9-5 60 (p) BarryMcHugh 4 39
(Tracy Waggott) *prom: rdn 2f out: wknd ins fnl f* **8/1**
00 **7** 2½ **Dream Destroyer (IRE)**[6] 8931 3-9-0 0 SamJames 2 28
(Geoffrey Harker) *prom: rdn over 2f out: wknd over 1f out* **125/1**
1m 43.54s (4.94) **Going Correction** +0.35s/f (Slow) **7** Ran SP% **113.1**
Speed ratings (Par 103): **89,88,88,86,85 82,80**
CSF £9.19 TOTE £2.50: £1.10, £1.80; EX 11.50 Trifecta £231.90.
**Owner** Saleh Al Homaizi & Imad Al Sagar **Bred** Saleh Al Homaizi & Imad Al Sagar **Trained** Beckhampton, Wilts
**FOCUS**
Not a particularly convincing piece of maiden form and it's rated negatively.

## 9019 BETWAY LIVE CASINO H'CAP 6f (Tp)
**9:15** (9:16) (Class 6) (0-60,62) 3-Y-0 **£2,264** (£673; £336; £168) **Stalls** Centre

Form RPR
6411 **1** **Breathoffreshair**[6] 8924 3-9-0 **53** (t) JoeFanning 11 62+
(Richard Guest) *trckd ldrs: pushed along to ld 2f out: rdn out fnl 110yds: shade cosily* **4/7**[1]

3606 2 3/4 **Naralsaif (IRE)**[27] 8558 3-8-7 **46** oh1..........................(v) PatrickMathers 13 53
(Derek Shaw) *midfield: rdn and hdwy over 1f out: chsd ldr ins fnl f: kpt on but a hld* **25/1**

0000 3 1 1/2 **Fintry Flyer**[75] 7164 3-8-4 **46** oh1..........................(p) PhilDennis(3) 6 48
(Jim Goldie) *hld up: gng wl and n.m.r over 1f out: pushed along and hdwy appr fnl f: swtchd lft: kpt on* **50/1**

0410 4 1 **Fikhaar**[50] 7951 3-9-5 **58**.......................... TomEaves 8 57
(Kevin Ryan) *trckd ldr: rdn 2f out: no ex ins fnl f* **14/1**

0120 5 1/2 **Kroy**[14] 8807 3-9-7 **60**..........................(p) AndrewMullen 7 58
(Ollie Pears) *in tch: rdn 2f out: edgd lft and kpt on same pce ins fnl f* **9/2**[2]

5061 6 2 **Little Miss Lola**[27] 8558 3-8-10 **54**.......................... JamieGormley(5) 14 46
(Lynn Siddall) *prom: rdn over 2f out: wknd ins fnl f* **11/1**[3]

0266 7 3/4 **Dream Start**[7] 8906 3-9-7 **60**..........................(t) TomMarquand 9 50
(John Ryan) *dwlt: hld up: rdn along over 3f out: sme hdwy over 1f out: nvr threatened* **25/1**

0550 8 1 1/2 **Santafiora**[33] 8427 3-9-9 **62**.......................... GrahamLee 1 47
(Julie Camacho) *hld up: nvr threatened* **25/1**

0400 9 1/2 **Little Kingdom (IRE)**[6] 8924 3-8-11 **50**.......................... JasonHart 4 34
(Tracy Waggott) *hld up in midfield: rdn 2f out: nvr threatened* **66/1**

0060 10 3 **Maldonado (FR)**[20] 8721 3-8-13 **59**.......................... HarrisonShaw(7) 5 34
(Michael Easterby) *hld up: racd keenly: nvr threatened* **16/1**

1000 11 1/2 **Night Shadow**[6] 8930 3-9-7 **60**.......................... JimmyQuinn 3 33
(Alan Brown) *midfield: rdn over 2f out: wknd over 1f out* **50/1**

0165 12 2 **Mr Enthusiastic**[17] 8776 3-8-9 **48**.......................... BarryMcHugh 10 15
(Noel Wilson) *led: rdn whn hdd 2f out: wknd* **50/1**

4505 13 1 **Night Law**[20] 8729 3-9-4 **57**.......................... PJMcDonald 2 21
(Barry John Murphy, Ire) *dwlt: sn midfield: rdn over 2f out: wknd over 1f out* **12/1**

1m 12.91s (0.41) **Going Correction** +0.35s/f (Slow) **13** Ran SP% **129.3**
Speed ratings (Par 98): **111,110,108,106,106 103,102,100,99,95 95,92,91**
CSF £29.00 CT £521.55 TOTE £1.40: £1.10, £6.00, £11.60; EX 24.90 Trifecta £1160.30.
**Owner** Alfa Site Services Ltd/Mrs Alison Guest **Bred** D Curran **Trained** Ingmanthorpe, W Yorks

**FOCUS**
A moderate sprint handicap but quite a deep race for the grade.
T/Jkpt: Not Won. T/Plt: £144.80 to a £1 stake. Pool: £129,223.28 - 651.28 winning units T/Qpdt: £18.70 to a £1 stake. Pool: £15,096.66 - 596.70 winning units **Andrew Sheret**

# 8902 CHELMSFORD (A.W) (L-H)
## Friday, December 1

**OFFICIAL GOING: Polytrack: standard**
Wind: VIRTUALLY NIL Weather: DRY, COLD

## 9020 BET TOTEPLACEPOT AT BETFRED.COM APPRENTICE H'CAP 7f (P)
**5:45** (5:47) (Class 4) (0-85,87) 3-Y-0+ **£6,469** (£1,925; £962; £481) **Stalls** Low

Form RPR

0036 1 **Call Out Loud**[22] 8706 5-9-3 **81**..........................(vt) AlistairRawlinson 5 89
(Michael Appleby) *trckd ldr: effrt and chal over 1f out: drvn ins fnl f: led on post* **5/1**[1]

1402 2 nse **Human Nature (IRE)**[37] 8344 4-9-0 **83**..........................(t) MillyNaseb(5) 10 90
(Stuart Williams) *led: jnd over 1f out: rdn 1f out: kpt on u.p: hdd on post* **8/1**[3]

4543 3 1 1/4 **Summer Icon**[22] 8706 4-9-4 **85**.......................... PaddyBradley(3) 12 89+
(Mick Channon) *hld up in rr: effrt over 1f out: hdwy u.p 1f out: styd on strly to go 3rd towards fin: nt rch ldrs* **5/1**[1]

6000 4 1 **Robin Weathers (USA)**[27] 8600 3-8-9 **76**.......................... GeorgiaCox(3) 6 77+
(William Haggas) *taken down early: rrd as stalls opened and s.i.s: t.k.h towards rr: hdwy 3f out: swtchd rt over 1f out: styd on u.p ins fnl f: nt rch ldrs* **5/1**[1]

3000 5 nse **Firmdecisions (IRE)**[22] 8706 7-9-5 **83**.......................... JackDuern 4 84
(Dean Ivory) *chsd ldrs: effrt to chse ldng pair 2f out: styd on same pce ins fnl f: lost 2 pls towards fin* **5/1**[1]

5000 6 nk **Welliesinthewater (IRE)**[14] 8812 7-9-6 **84**..........................(v) EoinWalsh 2 84
(Derek Shaw) *midfield: rdn 3f out: kpt on u.p ins fnl f: nvr enough pce to rch ldrs* **7/1**[2]

5136 7 4 1/2 **Phalaborwa**[83] 6936 3-9-1 **84**.......................... CameronNoble(5) 15 72+
(Ed Vaughan) *wnt rt s: stuck out wd and towards rr: effrt bnd 2f out: plugged on but nvr trbld ldrs* **12/1**

0064 8 1/2 **Juan Horsepower**[44] 8158 3-8-13 **77**..........................(p) HollieDoyle 9 63
(Richard Hannon) *chsd ldng pair tl lost pl u.p ent fnl 2f: wknd fnl f* **12/1**

0003 9 3/4 **Plucky Dip**[8] 8907 6-8-4 **73**.......................... NicolaCurrie(5) 13 57
(John Ryan) *off the pce in last pair: u.p over 2f out: nvr trbld ldrs* **20/1**

510 10 hd **Dark Magic**[35] 8393 3-8-10 **79**.......................... WilliamCox(5) 7 63
(Dean Ivory) *led to post: midfield: rdn wl over 2f out: no imp and wl hld over 1f out* **12/1**

3100 11 3 1/2 **Gold Hunter (IRE)**[25] 8640 7-8-9 **78**..........................(p) FinleyMarsh(5) 3 52
(Adrian Wintle) *trckd ldrs: effrt over 1f out: fnd nil and sn btn: fdd fnl f* **20/1**

0600 12 17 **Lady Lydia (IRE)**[25] 8636 6-8-0 **71**.......................... AledBeech(7) 8
(Hugo Froud) *sn pushed along and off the pce towards rr: lost tch 2f out* **66/1**

1m 25.6s (-1.60) **Going Correction** -0.125s/f (Stan) **12** Ran SP% **124.4**
Speed ratings (Par 105): **104,103,102,101,101 100,95,95,94,94 90,70**
CSF £46.62 CT £220.25 TOTE £6.80: £3.50, £2.90, £2.00; EX 57.90 Trifecta £442.10.
**Owner** Kings Head Duffield Racing Partnership **Bred** Rabbah Bloodstock Limited **Trained** Oakham, Rutland

**FOCUS**
The pace held up. The winner has been rated to his Southwell form, and the runner-up a length up on his 2017 form.

## 9021 BET TOTEJACKPOT AT BETFRED.COM NURSERY H'CAP 7f (P)
**6:15** (6:16) (Class 5) (0-75,77) 2-Y-0 **£4,528** (£1,347; £673; £336) **Stalls** Low

Form RPR

2502 1 **Zalshah**[14] 8817 2-9-9 **77**..........................(p) TomMarquand 4 80
(Richard Hannon) *trckd ldrs: effrt over 1f out: rdn to chal jst ins fnl f: led 75yds out: styd on wl: rdn out* **5/1**[3]

0524 2 1 **Dance Emperor (IRE)**[23] 8676 2-9-5 **73**.......................... PJMcDonald 8 73
(Ed Walker) *chsd ldr tl rdn to ld over 1f out: hdd 75yds out: kpt on same pce after* **7/1**

0051 3 1 1/4 **Mossketeer**[15] 8793 2-9-1 **69**.......................... RobertHavlin 3 66
(John Best) *hld up wl in tch in midfield: nt clr run ent fnl 2f: swtchd rt over 1f out: effrt to chse ldrs 1f out: styd on same pce ins fnl f* **11/1**

3613 4 1 3/4 **Harbour Vision**[21] 8715 2-9-8 **76**.......................... AdamKirby 2 68
(David Brown) *chsd ldrs: effrt over 1f out: unable qck 1f out: wknd wl ins fnl f* **10/3**[2]

5300 5 2 1/2 **Strategic (IRE)**[32] 8467 2-8-13 **67**.......................... SeanLevey 7 52
(Richard Hannon) *midfield: rdn over 2f out: swtchd rt and drvn over 1f out: no imp and nvr pced after* **16/1**

0641 6 1 1/2 **Elsaakb (USA)**[23] 8671 2-9-7 **75**..........................(b) JimCrowley 6 56
(John Gosden) *t.k.h: hld up in tch in last trio: effrt over 1f out: no imp: wl hld and plugged on same pce ins fnl f* **7/4**[1]

052 7 1 **Blue Candy**[15] 8794 2-9-7 **75**.......................... EdwardGreatrex 9 54
(Archie Watson) *led tl rdn and hdd over 1f out: no ex and btn 1f out: wknd ins fnl f* **12/1**

0330 8 shd **Lamb Chop**[34] 8419 2-9-4 **72**..........................(p) WilliamCarson 1 50
(Rod Millman) *niggled along thrght: in tch in last pair: no imp and hung lft over 1f out: wl hld whn swtchd rt ins fnl f* **33/1**

6406 9 1 1/4 **Polar Light**[44] 8164 2-9-0 **68**..........................(b1) DavidProbert 5 43
(David Elsworth) *s.i.s: a rr: reminder over 3f out: n.d* **25/1**

1m 26.2s (-1.00) **Going Correction** -0.125s/f (Stan) **9** Ran SP% **117.3**
Speed ratings (Par 96): **100,98,97,95,92 90,89,89,88**
CSF £40.47 CT £373.73 TOTE £7.30: £2.50, £2.40, £2.70; EX 52.10 Trifecta £482.50.
**Owner** Burnham P & D ltd **Bred** Clarendon Farm **Trained** East Everleigh, Wilts

**FOCUS**
A fair nursery. The form is possibly worth a shade more.

## 9022 BET TOTEQUADPOT AT BETFRED.COM FILLIES' NOVICE STKS (PLUS 10 RACE) (DIV I) 6f (P)
**6:45** (6:46) (Class 5) 2-Y-O **£4,528** (£1,347; £673; £336) **Stalls** Centre

Form RPR

5222 1 **Lady Willpower**[20] 8734 2-8-7 77.......................... WilliamCox(7) 10 75
(John Quinn) *midfield tl hdwy to ld over 4f out: mde rest: rdn over 1f out: kpt on wl ins fnl f: rdn out* **7/1**[3]

5 2 1/2 **Moon Song**[29] 8544 2-8-11 0.......................... HectorCrouch(3) 3 74
(Clive Cox) *mostly 2nd: effrt to chal over 1f out: kpt on wl u.p ins fnl f but a jst hld* **4/1**[2]

0160 3 1/2 **The Mums**[37] 8343 2-9-7 79..........................(v1) RobertHavlin 5 79
(John Gosden) *trckd ldrs: shkn up over 1f out: drvn 1f out: kpt on ins fnl f* **12/1**

5 4 1/2 **Any Little Rhyme**[20] 8734 2-9-0 0.......................... LukeMorris 8 71
(Michael Bell) *in tch in midfield: effrt over 2f out: drvn 1f out: kpt on ins fnl f* **8/1**

5 1 **Queen Of Desire (IRE)** 2-9-0 0.......................... JackMitchell 6 68
(Roger Varian) *t.k.h: led tl over 4f out: trckd ldrs: effrt over 1f out: no ex ins fnl f: lost 2 pls and wknd towards fin* **11/1**

422 6 nse **Daybreak**[88] 6747 2-9-0 83.......................... PJMcDonald 1 67+
(Hughie Morrison) *s.i.s: rousted along in rr early: swtchd rt and hdwy 4f out: swtchd rt over 1f out: hung lft and kpt on ins fnl f: nvr threatened ldrs* **1/1**[1]

20 7 2 1/4 **Popsicle (IRE)**[13] 8851 2-9-0 0.......................... TomMarquand 7 61
(Richard Hannon) *hld up in tch: sltly hmpd 4f out: rdn over 2f out: drvn and no imp over 1f out: kpt on same pce ins fnl f* **20/1**

0 8 shd **French Sparkle**[32] 8472 2-8-7 0.......................... JonathanFisher(7) 9 60
(Robert Cowell) *stdd s: hld up in rr: pushed along and sme hdwy over 1f out: styd on steadily ins fnl f: nvr threatened ldrs* **50/1**

9 8 **Seek The Moon (USA)** 2-9-0 0.......................... PhillipMakin 11 36
(David O'Meara) *s.i.s and rn green early: hdwy on outer over 3f out: sltly impeded and lost pl over 2f out: wknd over 1f out* **28/1**

00 10 9 **Ocean Spray**[23] 8670 2-9-0 0.......................... SeanLevey 4 9
(Richard Hannon) *broke wl and chsd ldrs early: sn pushed and lost pl: rdn 4f out and dropped towards rr over 2f out: wknd over 1f out* **66/1**

1m 14.24s (0.54) **Going Correction** -0.125s/f (Stan) **10** Ran SP% **121.3**
Speed ratings (Par 93): **91,90,89,89,87 87,84,84,73,61**
CSF £35.60 TOTE £12.30: £2.50, £1.70, £3.60; EX 57.20 Trifecta £401.40.
**Owner** P Wilkins & Mickley Stud **Bred** Mickley Stud And Sarah Taylor **Trained** Settrington, N Yorks

**FOCUS**
A positive ride and the jockey's 7lb allowance were key to the winner's success here. The third and fourth help with the level.

## 9023 BET TOTEQUADPOT AT BETFRED.COM FILLIES' NOVICE STKS (PLUS 10 RACE) (DIV II) 6f (P)
**7:15** (7:15) (Class 5) 2-Y-O **£4,528** (£1,347; £673; £336) **Stalls** Centre

Form RPR

6 1 **Restless Rose**[84] 6867 2-9-0 0.......................... PJMcDonald 6 77+
(Stuart Williams) *sn w ldr: led over 2f out: rdn over 1f out: drvn 1f out: edgd lft but forged ahd ins fnl f: styd on strly and gng away at fin* **4/1**[2]

0123 2 2 1/4 **Ghepardo**[20] 8746 2-9-4 75.......................... TomMarquand 8 74
(Richard Hannon) *led and crossed to inner: hdd over 2f out: sn rdn: drvn ent fnl f: no ex and outpcd fnl 100yds* **5/1**[3]

4333 3 1 **Alba Del Sole (IRE)**[22] 8701 2-9-0 70.......................... NickyMackay 4 67
(John Gosden) *trckd ldrs: effrt wl over 1f out: sn rdn: drvn and styd on same pce fnl f* **4/5**[1]

6 4 1/2 **Mischievous Rock**[15] 8802 2-9-0 0.......................... LukeMorris 2 66
(Michael Appleby) *hld up wl in tch in midfield: clsd to trck ldrs and nt clrest of runs over 1f out: sn swtchd rt and rdn ent fnl f: kpt on same pce ins fnl f* **25/1**

0 5 2 **Oneroa (IRE)**[165] 3902 2-9-0 0.......................... PhillipMakin 5 60
(Ivan Furtado) *chsd ldrs: rdn and outpcd over 1f out: wl hld and kpt on same pce ins fnl f* **14/1**

3 6 2 **Midnight Guest (IRE)**[14] 8809 2-8-9 0.......................... JaneElliott(5) 7 54
(George Margarson) *hld up in tch in midfield on outer: shkn up over 1f out: no imp and wknd ins fnl f* **7/1**

00 7 2 1/2 **Queen Of Dreams (IRE)**[13] 8850 2-9-0 0.......................... MartinHarley 9 46
(William Knight) *in tch in midfield: struggling u.p over 1f out: sn wknd* **66/1**

00 8 10 **Poorauldjosephine**[45] 8130 2-8-7 0.......................... GinaMangan(7) 3 16
(J R Jenkins) *sn dropped towards rr: lost tch 2f out* **100/1**

00 9 7 **Aldbury Lass (IRE)**[38] 8323 2-8-7 0.......................... DarraghKeenan(7) 10
(Robert Eddery) *stdd s: hld up in last pair: lost tch 2f out* **66/1**

1m 13.2s (-0.50) **Going Correction** -0.125s/f (Stan) **9** Ran SP% **119.2**
Speed ratings (Par 93): **98,95,93,93,90 87,84,71,61**
CSF £24.73 TOTE £4.70: £1.70, £1.50, £1.10; EX 30.40 Trifecta £64.80.
**Owner** Happy Valley Racing & Breeding Limited **Bred** M E Broughton **Trained** Newmarket, Suffolk


The Form Book Flat, Raceform Ltd, Newbury, RG14 5SJ

**FOCUS**
The faster of the two divisions by 1.04sec, and the first two were in the front rank throughout. The form is rated around the second and third.

## 9024 BET TOTEEXACTA AT BETFRED.COM NURSERY H'CAP 6f (P)
**7:45** (7:45) (Class 6) (0-65,67) 2-Y-O **£3,234** (£962; £481; £240) **Stalls** Centre

Form RPR

0042 **1** **Swissal (IRE)**[30] 8500 2-9-4 **62**.......................... DougieCostello 4 66
(David Dennis) *chsd ldrs tl effrt to chal over 1f out: rdn to ld 1f out: styd on wl* **7/2**[1]

3002 **2** *1 1/4* **Mother Of Dragons (IRE)**[8] 8902 2-9-2 **67**................. NicolaCurrie(7) 3 67
(Phil McEntee) *in tch in midfield: nt clr run on inner over 2f out: hdwy to chse ldrs and switching rt over 1f out: styd on u.p to go 2nd towards fin* **8/1**[3]

000 **3** *1 1/4* **Tiger Lyon (USA)**[22] 8703 2-9-5 **63**..............................(h) AdamKirby 10 60
(John Butler) *taken down early: led: rdn over 1f out: hdd 1f out: no ex: wknd and lost 2nd towards fin* **7/2**[1]

4250 **4** *1 1/2* **Bombshell Bay**[53] 7890 2-9-5 **63**...............................(p) TomMarquand 2 55
(Richard Hannon) *hld up in tch in last quartet: effrt and hdwy u.p towards inner over 1f out: kpt on same pce ins fnl f* **4/1**[2]

0003 **5** *3/4* **Bomad**[8] 8902 2-9-7 **65**................................................(v) PatrickMathers 8 55
(Derek Shaw) *s.i.s: in rr: hdwy on outer 3f out: chsd ldrs but unable qck u.p over 1f out: btn whn impeded ins fnl f* **9/1**

5005 **6** *3/4* **Roseau City**[15] 8793 2-8-13 **57**........................................(b) HollieDoyle 6 45
(David Elsworth) *t.k.h: hld up in tch: swtchd rt and effrt over 1f out: swtchd lft and no imp ins fnl f* **14/1**

400 **7** *1 1/2* **Shamrock Emma (IRE)**[39] 8294 2-8-11 **55**............. JosephineGordon 7 38
(John Best) *hld up in last trio: effrt on outer jst over 2f out: no imp: nvr trbld ldrs* **16/1**

606 **8** *2* **Conflagration**[29] 8536 2-9-8 **66**........................................ JimCrowley 5 43
(Ed Dunlop) *a towards rr: nvr trbld ldrs* **4/1**[2]

600 **9** *6* **Cat Ballou**[13] 8850 2-8-1 **45**............................................ JimmyQuinn 11 4
(David O'Meara) *chsd ldr tl wl over 1f out: sn wknd: bhd ins fnl f* **33/1**

1m 13.59s (-0.11) **Going Correction** -0.125s/f (Stan) **9** Ran SP% **121.0**
Speed ratings (Par 94): **95,93,91,89,88 87,85,83,75**
CSF £33.96 CT £108.24 TOTE £3.30: £1.50, £4.70, £2.20; EX 27.30 Trifecta £147.40.
**Owner** Tyre Hill Farm Ltd **Bred** Deal Gharrafa Syndicate **Trained** Hanley Swan, Worcestershire
■ Stewards' Enquiry : Nicola Currie caution: careless riding

**FOCUS**
A modest nursery with the winner rated to his best form to date.

## 9025 BET TOTETRIFECTA AT BETFRED.COM H'CAP 1m (P)
**8:15** (8:16) (Class 4) (0-85,87) 3-Y-O+ **£6,469** (£1,925; £962; £481) **Stalls** Low

Form RPR

0005 **1** **Ice Royal (IRE)**[14] 8821 4-9-4 **82**.................................. DougieCostello 2 92
(Jamie Osborne) *hld up in tch in midfield: swtchd rt and hdwy wl over 1f out: sn rdn and chsd ldr: styd on wl to ld ins fnl f: sn in command* **7/1**[2]

-221 **2** *1 1/2* **Corked (IRE)**[14] 8810 4-8-11 **75**................................ JosephineGordon 3 82
(Hugo Palmer) *led: rdn and kicked clr over 1f out: hdd ins fnl f: no ex* **7/1**[2]

6240 **3** *1 3/4* **Lagenda**[49] 8014 4-9-0 **78**..............................................(p) PJMcDonald 6 81
(Kristin Stubbs) *hld up in tch in midfield: effrt and swtchd lft over 1f out: kpt on ins fnl f to go 3rd wl ins fnl f: no threat to ldrs* **33/1**

0430 **4** *1 1/4* **Maratha (IRE)**[30] 8510 3-9-0 **79**.......................................(t) SeanLevey 12 79
(Stuart Williams) *hld up in tch in midfield: nt clrest of runs 2f out: effrt and hdwy u.p over 1f out: chsd ldrs 1f out: no imp fnl f* **20/1**

253 **5** *nk* **Waarif (IRE)**[8] 8912 4-9-2 **80**......................................(p[1]) MartinHarley 8 79+
(David O'Meara) *s.i.s: bhd and pushed along: hdwy u.p 1f out: styd on wl ins fnl f: nvr trbld ldrs* **8/1**[3]

3221 **6** *2 1/2* **Glendun (USA)**[37] 8341 3-8-12 **77**..................................(p) RyanTate 5 70
(James Eustace) *chsd ldr for 1f: styd chsng ldrs tl effrt whn short of room and hmpd over 1f out: wknd ins fnl f* **8/1**[3]

6101 **7** *hd* **Blaze Of Hearts (IRE)**[46] 8126 4-8-11 **78**.................... JackDuern(3) 9 71
(Dean Ivory) *jnd ldr after 1f tl unable qck and hung lft over 1f out: wandered bk rt 1f out: wknd ins fnl f* **25/1**

0300 **8** *nk* **Chestnut Fire**[29] 8547 5-9-7 **85**...................................... ShaneKelly 1 77
(Daniel Mark Loughnane) *hld up in tch in last quintet: swtchd rt and effrt over 1f out: swtchd lft 1f out: kpt on same pce and no imp ins fnl f* **20/1**

1- **9** *nk* **Samharry**[498] 4545 3-9-4 **83**.......................................... JimCrowley 7 74+
(John Gosden) *bmpd leaving stalls: swtchd rt and effrt wd bnd wl over 1f out: swtchd rt over 1f out: n.d* **11/10**[1]

4530 **10** *nk* **Family Fortunes**[37] 8344 3-9-6 **85**............................ TomMarquand 11 76
(Sylvester Kirk) *in midfield on outer: rdn over 2f out: no imp and btn over 1f out: wknd ins fnl f* **16/1**

4040 **11** *9* **Hammer Gun (USA)**[14] 8812 4-9-0 **78**.....................(v) PatrickMathers 10 48
(Derek Shaw) *awkward leaving stalls: t.k.h: hld up in tch in last quintet: effrt wl over 1f out: no hdwy: wknd fnl f* **20/1**

-040 **12** *1/2* **Fighting Temeraire (IRE)**[62] 7622 4-9-9 **87**..................... AdamKirby 14 56
(Dean Ivory) *chsd ldrs tl lost pl qckly wl over 1f out: wknd* **20/1**

1m 38.19s (-1.71) **Going Correction** -0.125s/f (Stan)
**WFA** 3 from 4yo+ 1lb **12** Ran SP% **126.6**
Speed ratings (Par 105): **103,101,99,98,98 95,95,95,94,94 85,85**
CSF £52.52 CT £1561.58 TOTE £8.60: £2.10, £1.90, £7.30; EX 61.80 Trifecta £617.10.
**Owner** A Taylor & J A Osborne **Bred** Corrin Stud **Trained** Upper Lambourn, Berks

**FOCUS**
With the favourite disappointing, this was fought out by the next two in the betting. The winner has been rated back to his spring form, and the runner-up to a length pb.

## 9026 BET TOTEWIN AT BETFRED.COM H'CAP 1m 5f 66y(P)
**8:45** (8:46) (Class 6) (0-65,66) 3-Y-O **£3,234** (£962; £481; £240) **Stalls** Low

Form RPR

302 **1** **Mister Chow**[23] 8674 3-9-7 **65**........................................(v) AdamKirby 10 73
(Gary Moore) *hld up in tch in midfield: hdwy 3f out: rdn and clsd to chal 1f out: led 100yds out: styd on* **5/2**[2]

0004 **2** *3/4* **Olympic Legend (IRE)**[13] 8846 3-8-13 **57**....................(t) RobertHavlin 2 64
(Martin Bosley) *t.k.h: hld up in tch in midfield: clsd to trck ldrs and nt clr run 2f out: rdn to chal 1f out: kpt on same pce fnl 100yds* **12/1**

0331 **3** *nse* **Beatisa**[58] 7729 3-9-5 **66**..................................... HectorCrouch(3) 9 73
(Christine Dunnett) *sn led: hdd 8f out: styd chsng ldrs tl swtchd rt and rdn to ld 2f out: edgd lft u.p over 1f out: hdd 100yds out: kpt on same pce* **25/1**

0013 **4** *11* **Volturnus**[14] 8815 3-8-7 **51**..........................................(bt) NickyMackay 11 42
(Jamie Osborne) *hld up in midfield: hdwy to ld 8f out: rdn and hdd 2f out: outpcd over 1f out: wknd fnl f* **5/1**[3]

0114 **5** *2 1/2* **Send Up (IRE)**[55] 7832 3-9-8 **66**.....................................(b[1]) LukeMorris 5 53
(Sir Mark Prescott Bt) *t.k.h: chsd ldr tl 9f out: styd prom tl unable qck u.p over 2f out: wknd fnl f* **9/4**[1]

1600 **6** *1 1/4* **Enola (IRE)**[10] 8883 3-9-4 **62**.................................... KieranShoemark 8 48
(Amy Murphy) *hld up in tch in midfield: rdn 3f out: no imp and wl hld over 1f out* **50/1**

3320 **7** *1 1/2* **Too Many Shots**[38] 8312 3-8-11 **55**................................ JoeyHaynes 13 38
(John Best) *hld up in tch in last quartet: effrt u.p over 2f out: nvr on terms* **20/1**

0045 **8** *1 1/2* **Percipio**[23] 8674 3-8-4 **48**............................................. MartinDwyer 6 29
(Alan King) *hld up in tch in last quartet: rdn 4f out: sme hdwy into midfield over 2f out: no imp after* **25/1**

0003 **9** *1 1/4* **Mistress Viz (IRE)**[23] 8673 3-8-0 **51**........................ NicolaCurrie(7) 3 30
(Sarah Hollinshead) *hld up in midfield: rdn over 3f out: sn struggling and wl btn 2f out* **16/1**

0540 **10** *13* **Naupaka**[21] 8720 3-8-2 **46** oh1............................................. KieranO'Neill 4 7
(Brian Ellison) *stdd s: t.k.h: hld up in rr: lost tch 2f out: eased fnl f* **33/1**

0053 **11** *11* **I'm Running Late**[10] 8883 3-9-5 **66**.............................(p[1]) JackDuern(3) 12 11
(Dean Ivory) *mostly chsd ldr tl lost pl u.p over 2f out: eased over 1f out: t.o* **10/1**

3006 **12** *3* **Unonothinjonsnow**[24] 8654 3-7-11 **48** oh1 ow2.....(p[1]) JackOsborn(7) 14
(Richard Guest) *taken down early: t.k.h: hld up in tch in midfield: u.p and dropped to rr over 2f out: bhd and eased fnl f: t.o* **33/1**

3264 **13** *2 1/4* **Ode To Glory**[10] 8883 3-9-7 **65**..................................... DavidProbert 7
(Rae Guest) *awkward leaving stalls and s.i.s: a rr: lost tch 2f out: eased: t.o* **10/1**

0-40 **14** *nk* **Autumn Glow**[162] 4003 3-8-12 **59**................................... RosieJessop(3) 1
(Miss Joey Ellis) *wl in tch in midfield: rdn 7f out: lost pl over 3f out: lost tch 2f out: eased: t.o* **80/1**

2m 52.59s (-1.01) **Going Correction** -0.125s/f (Stan) **14** Ran SP% **129.3**
Speed ratings (Par 98): **98,97,97,90,89 88,87,86,85,77 71,69,67,67**
CSF £33.30 CT £661.15 TOTE £3.80: £2.00, £3.10, £6.10; EX 34.50 Trifecta £710.10.
**Owner** G L Moore **Bred** The Pocock Family **Trained** Lower Beeding, W Sussex

**FOCUS**
This set up for those ridden off the pace and the third did well to hang in there, finishing clear of the rest.

## 9027 BOOK TICKETS ONLINE AT CHELMSFORDCITYRACECOURSE.COM H'CAP 1m 2f (P)
**9:15** (9:17) (Class 5) (0-70,75) 3-Y-O+ **£5,175** (£1,540; £769; £384) **Stalls** Low

Form RPR

3552 **1** **Miss Mirabeau**[6] 8957 3-8-8 **59**.......................................(v) LukeMorris 3 70
(Sir Mark Prescott Bt) *travelled strly: wl in tch in midfield: clsd to trck ldng pair over 2f out: swtchd lft and rdn hands and heels to chal 1f out: led ins fnl f: styd on* **4/1**[2]

3251 **2** *1 1/4* **Dangerous Ends**[14] 8814 3-9-0 **72**..............................(p) RossaRyan(7) 1 80
(Brett Johnson) *t.k.h: led for 2f: chsd ldr tl rdn to ld over 1f out: hdd and kpt on same pce ins fnl f* **5/2**[1]

0500 **3** *3 1/2* **Thaqaffa (IRE)**[15] 8798 4-9-6 **69**............................... KieranShoemark 2 69
(Amy Murphy) *stdd s: hld up in midfield: effrt to chse ldng trio over 2f out: drifted rt over 1f out and bk lft ins fnl f: kpt on* **11/1**

5454 **4** *3* **Hard Toffee (IRE)**[14] 8813 6-9-2 **65**............................... RobertTart 10 59
(Louise Allan) *hdwy to ld after 2f: rdn over 2f out: hdd over 1f out: sn outpcd and drifted rt: wknd ins fnl f* **10/1**

0005 **5** *1* **Zoffany Bay (IRE)**[29] 8550 3-8-7 **58**..........................(b) KieranO'Neill 13 51
(George Peckham) *hld up towards rr: rdn and hdwy u.p over 1f out: kpt on ins fnl f: nvr trbld ldrs* **33/1**

2050 **6** *1* **Spun Gold**[7] 8930 3-8-13 **64**.......................................... JimCrowley 7 55
(Charlie Fellowes) *pushed along early: sn t.k.h and hld up in tch in midfield: no hdwy u.p over 1f out: wknd ins fnl f* **9/2**[3]

0063 **7** *1* **The Gay Cavalier**[13] 8846 6-8-4 **60**.............................(t) JackOsborn(7) 9 48
(John Ryan) *s.i.s and rousted along early: clsd onto bk of field 7f out: hdwy into midfield u.p over 1f out: plugged on but nvr on terms w ldrs* **16/1**

061 **8** *6* **Miss M (IRE)**[50] 7990 3-8-6 **57**...................................... MartinDwyer 8 34
(William Muir) *hld up in last quartet: effrt on outer over 1f out: no imp and sn btn: wknd fnl f* **8/1**

6003 **9** *4 1/2* **Livella Fella (IRE)**[14] 8813 4-9-6 **69**............................. PhillipMakin 4 36
(Keith Dalgleish) *chsd ldrs tl lost pl u.p over 2f out: wknd over 1f out* **10/1**

564 **10** *3 1/4* **Nevalyashka**[24] 8663 3-8-9 **67**................................ TylerSaunders(7) 6 29
(Marcus Tregoning) *rousted along leaving stalls: in tch in last quartet: rdn and struggling over 2f out: wl btn over 1f out* **20/1**

0236 **11** *32* **Shimmering Light**[31] 8497 3-9-5 **70**...............................(v) AdamKirby 14
(Michael Bell) *chsd ldrs: rdn and swtchd to outer 5f out: dropped to rr and lost tch over 2f out: eased fnl f: t.o* **20/1**

2m 6.33s (-2.27) **Going Correction** -0.125s/f (Stan)
**WFA** 3 from 4yo+ 2lb **11** Ran SP% **122.7**
Speed ratings (Par 103): **104,103,100,97,97 96,95,90,87,84 58**
CSF £14.71 CT £106.17 TOTE £5.20: £1.70, £1.40, £4.60; EX 15.00 Trifecta £109.20.
**Owner** Exors Of The Late J L C Pearce **Bred** J L C Pearce **Trained** Newmarket, Suffolk
■ Stewards' Enquiry : Jack Osborn two-day ban; used whip without giving mount time to respond (Dec 15-16)

**FOCUS**
A modest handicap. A clear pb from the winner, with the runner-up rated a length up on his latest C&D win.
T/Plt: £181.50 to a £1 stake. Pool of £112,340.44 - 451.65 winning tickets. T/Qpdt: £23.40 to a £1 stake. Pool of £11,939.27 - 377.42 winning tickets. **Steve Payne**

# 8978 SOUTHWELL (L-H)
Friday, December 1

**OFFICIAL GOING: Fibresand: standard**
Wind: Fresh behind Weather: Fine & dry

## 9028 BETWAY H'CAP 1m 4f 14y(F)
**12:10** (12:10) (Class 5) (0-75,75) 4-Y-O+ **£3,234** (£962; £481; £240) **Stalls** Low

Form RPR

2162 **1** **Restive (IRE)**[24] 8653 4-8-13 **67**..................................... LukeMorris 7 79
(Iain Jardine) *trckd ldrs: hdwy on inner over 3f out and sn cl up: led wl over 2f out: rdn clr over 1f out: edgd rt ins fnl f: kpt on strly* **7/2**[2]

0606 **2** *7* **Luv U Whatever**[25] 8638 7-9-2 **70**................................(tp) BarryMcHugh 6 71
(Marjorie Fife) *trckd ldng pair: cl up 4f out: chal on outer over 3f out: rdn and ev ch over 2f out: drvn wl over 1f out: kpt on same pce* **11/10**[1]

3422 **3** *1 1/4* **Sugarloaf Mountain (IRE)**[227] 1870 4-9-0 **73**........... BenRobinson(5) 1 72
(Brian Ellison) *slt ld: pushed along 4f out: jnd over 3f out and sn rdn: hdd wl over 2f out: drvn wl over 1f out: kpt on same pce* **7/1**[3]

1-05 **4** ½ **Coroberee (IRE)**[24] 8653 4-9-7 **75**.............................(p) DougieCostello 8 73
(Tony Coyle) *hld up: hdwy over 4f out: in tch 3f out: rdn along to chse ldrs 2f out: swtchd lft and drvn over 1f out: kpt on towards fin* **22/1**

-325 **5** 9 **Katie Gale**[260] 1223 7-9-5 **73**.............................(v[1]) AndrewMullen 4 57
(Michael Appleby) *cl up: rdn along 4f out: drvn 3f out: sn one pce* **14/1**

6000 **6** 8 **The Lock Master (IRE)**[15] 8806 10-8-12 **66**......(be[1]) AlistairRawlinson 3 37
(Michael Appleby) *rr and niggled along after 3f: pushed along on outer and sme hdwy over 4f out: drvn along over 3f out: nvr a factor* **22/1**

0503 **7** 15 **Zambeasy**[24] 8648 6-8-13 **74**.............................(p[1]) SebastianWoods(7) 2 21
(Philip Hide) *awkward s: sn trcking ldrs on inner: pushed along 1/2-way: rdn along and lost pl over 4f out:. sn bhd* **7/1**[3]

2m 37.6s (-3.40) **Going Correction** -0.10s/f (Stan) 7 Ran SP% **110.2**
Speed ratings (Par 103): **107,102,101,101,95 89,79**
CSF £7.13 CT £21.06 TOTE £3.40: £1.60, £2.00; EX 9.70 Trifecta £33.60.
**Owner** I J Jardine **Bred** Epona Bloodstock Ltd **Trained** Carruthertown, D'fries & G'way

**FOCUS**
An ordinary middle-distance handicap, but an impressive winner. He's been rated cautiously given the lack of depth in behind.

## 9029 SUNBETS H'CAP — 7f 14y(F)
**12:40** (12:40) (Class 5) (0-75,83) 4-Y-0+ **£3,234** (£962; £481; £240) **Stalls** Low

Form RPR

311 **1** **Malaspina (ITY)**[7] 8928 5-10-1 **83** 6ex.............................(p) PhillipMakin 5 94
(Ivan Furtado) *trckd ldrs: hdwy over 2f out: led 1 1/2f out: sn rdn and edgd lft: drvn ins fnl f: hld on wl towards fin* **5/2**[1]

0000 **2** hd **Mr Christopher (IRE)**[34] 8433 5-9-4 **72**.............(p) RichardKingscote 7 82
(Tom Dascombe) *prom: cl up on inner 3f out: rdn to ld 2f out: hdd 1 1/2f out and sn drvn: ev ch ins fnl f: no ex nr fin* **12/1**

0054 **3** 2½ **Majestic Moon (IRE)**[40] 8254 7-9-4 **75**.................... ShelleyBirkett(3) 3 78
(Julia Feilden) *hld up in midfield: hdwy 3f out: rdn to chse ldrs wl over 1f out: drvn and edgd lft appr fnl f: kpt on same pce* **12/1**

3202 **4** nk **Bold Spirit**[18] 8772 6-8-5 **62**.............................(t) PhilDennis(3) 4 65
(Declan Carroll) *trckd ldrs on inner: hdwy over 2f out: nt clr run wl over 1f out: rdn and kpt on fnl f* **7/1**[3]

0160 **5** 3¼ **Harlequin Striker (IRE)**[15] 8797 5-9-8 **76**.............(p) CharlesBishop 11 69
(Dean Ivory) *prom: rdn along to chse ldrs 2f out: n.m.r and swtchd rt jst over 1f out: sn drvn and wknd* **14/1**

000 **6** 3 **Captain Revelation**[35] 8386 5-9-7 **75**.............................(t[1]) JasonHart 1 60
(Michael Mullineaux) *towards rr and rdn along on inner 1/2-way: hdwy 2f out: kpt on fnl f: nrst fin* **20/1**

2000 **7** hd **Hernando Torres**[18] 8773 9-8-5 **66**.....................(t) HarrisonShaw(7) 13 51
(Michael Easterby) *bhd tl styd on fnl 2f: nrst fin* **33/1**

1020 **8** ¾ **Miningrocks (FR)**[15] 8806 5-9-1 **69**............................ TomEaves 8 52
(Conor Dore) *sn led: rdn along 3f out: hdd 2f out: sn drvn and wknd over 1f out* **80/1**

1102 **9** ½ **Captain Bob (IRE)**[8] 8906 6-8-11 **72**..................(p) JonathanFisher(7) 12 53
(Philip Kirby) *dwlt: sn chsng ldrs: cl up 1/2-way: rdn and ev ch over 2f out: drvn and wknd over 1f out* **20/1**

6526 **10** 4 **Black Caesar (IRE)**[25] 8640 6-9-0 **75**.................... SebastianWoods(7) 2 46
(Philip Hide) *a towards rr* **20/1**

100 **11** nk **Muqarred (USA)**[21] 8718 5-9-5 **73**.............................(p) TonyHamilton 10 43
(Roger Fell) *dwlt: a in rr* **13/2**[2]

5220 **12** 1¾ **Stosur (IRE)**[55] 7830 6-8-13 **74**.............................(b) RossaRyan(7) 6 39
(Gay Kelleway) *midfield: rdn along over 3f out: wknd over 2f out* **25/1**

2621 **13** 1 **Bounty Pursuit**[53] 7881 5-9-0 **71**............................ MitchGodwin(3) 14 33
(Michael Blake) *dwlt: a in rr* **7/1**[3]

6200 **14** 2¾ **Musical Comedy**[27] 8600 6-9-2 **70**............................ FranBerry 9 25
(Mike Murphy) *chsd ldrs: wd st: rdn along wl over 2f out: sn drvn and wknd* **25/1**

1m 28.12s (-2.18) **Going Correction** -0.10s/f (Stan) 14 Ran SP% **115.1**
Speed ratings (Par 103): **108,107,104,104,100 97,97,96,95,91 90,88,87,84**
CSF £28.44 CT £304.26 TOTE £3.50: £1.70, £3.60, £3.40; EX 36.80 Trifecta £171.50.
**Owner** BGC Racing, C Hodgson & Giggle Factor **Bred** Scuderia Fert Di Ferrario Paolo Et Al **Trained** Wiseton, Nottinghamshire

**FOCUS**
An ordinary handicap in which those held up or outpaced early had no chance. This went to the one progressive runner in the field. The runner-up has been rated back to her best, and the third to his 1m latest here.

## 9030 SUNBETS MAIDEN AUCTION STKS — 1m 13y(F)
**1:10** (1:10) (Class 5) 3-Y-0 **£3,234** (£962; £481; £240) **Stalls** Low

Form RPR

0562 **1** **Isstoora (IRE)**[36] 8374 3-9-0 67............................ LukeMorris 1 66
(Archie Watson) *trckd ldng pair: hdwy 3f out: sn cl up: led jst over 2f out: rdn over 1f out: drvn and edgd lft ins fnl f: kpt on wl towards fin* **8/13**[1]

52 **2** ¾ **Flying Raconteur**[16] 8781 3-9-5 0.............................(t) TomEaves 2 69
(Nigel Tinkler) *trckd ldrs: hdwy 3f out: chsd wnr and swtchd lft wl over 1f out: sn chal: rdn over 1f out: drvn and ev ch ins fnl f: no ex towards fin* **9/4**[2]

0652 **3** 12 **Siyahamba (IRE)**[24] 8650 3-8-12 50............................ HarryRussell(7) 4 41
(Bryan Smart) *hld up in rr: pushed along over 3f out: rdn and hdwy wl over 2f: kpt on fnl f* **10/1**[3]

0300 **4** 6 **New Tale**[35] 8395 3-9-5 46.............................(b[1]) SamJames 3 28
(Olly Williams) *led: rdn along 3f out: sn drvn and hdd jst over 2f out: sn wknd* **40/1**

0000 **5** 3¼ **Stragar**[37] 8345 3-9-5 44.............................(b[1]) PhillipMakin 5 20
(Michael Appleby) *cl up: rdn along 3f out: sn wknd* **20/1**

0060 **6** 7 **Just Heather (IRE)**[24] 8653 3-9-0 31............................ HollieDoyle 6
(John Wainwright) *sn rdn along and outpcd in rr: bhd fnl 3f* **150/1**

1m 43.26s (-0.44) **Going Correction** -0.10s/f (Stan) 6 Ran SP% **109.6**
Speed ratings (Par 102): **98,97,85,79,76 69**
CSF £2.04 TOTE £1.50: £1.10, £1.40; EX 2.30 Trifecta £4.90.
**Owner** Greenfield Racing **Bred** Essafinaat Ltd **Trained** Upper Lambourn, W Berks

**FOCUS**
An uncompetitive 3yo maiden auction contest and it turned out just as the market predicted. The winner has been rated close to form.

## 9031 SUNBETS.CO.UK (S) STKS — 7f 14y(F)
**1:40** (1:40) (Class 6) 3-Y-0+ **£2,264** (£673; £336; £168) **Stalls** Low

Form RPR

5043 **1** **Zaeem**[6] 8958 8-9-2 70............................ TonyHamilton 4 68
(Ivan Furtado) *trckd ldng pair: hdwy over 3f out: led wl over 2f out: rdn and edgd lft 1f out: sn drvn and kpt on* **7/4**[2]

0-20 **2** 1½ **Pearl Nation (USA)**[291] 720 8-9-2 92.............................(h) LukeMorris 1 64
(Michael Appleby) *trckd ldrs: hdwy 3f out: chsd wnr 2f out: sn rdn: drvn over 1f out: edgd rt ins fnl f: kpt on same pce* **5/6**[1]

000 **3** 1¼ **Ace Master**[30] 8513 9-8-13 64.............................(b) EoinWalsh(3) 6 61
(Roy Bowring) *sn led: rdn along over 3f out: hdd wl over 2f out: cl up tl drvn over 1f out and kpt on same pce* **8/1**[3]

5000 **4** 22 **Nellie Deen (IRE)**[21] 8719 4-8-11 40.............................(e[1]) JasonHart 3
(Simon West) *prom: rdn along 1/2-way: sn wknd* **250/1**

6-0 **5** 17 **Escape Clause (IRE)**[21] 8718 3-9-2 80............................ PhillipMakin 5
(Grant Tuer) *a rr: bhd fnl 3f* **16/1**

1m 29.35s (-0.95) **Going Correction** -0.10s/f (Stan) 5 Ran SP% **108.3**
Speed ratings (Par 101): **101,99,97,72,53**
CSF £3.41 TOTE £2.60: £1.50, £1.10; EX 3.80 Trifecta £7.10.
**Owner** 21st Century Racing & Nigel Sennett **Bred** Umm Qarn Management Co Ltd **Trained** Wiseton, Nottinghamshire

**FOCUS**
An uncompetitive seller with the five runners officially rated between 40 and 92. The runner-up was weak in the market and the form has been rated with feet on the ground.

## 9032 SUNBETS.CO.UK H'CAP — 1m 13y(F)
**2:10** (2:11) (Class 6) (0-65,65) 4-Y-0+ **£2,587** (£770; £384; £192) **Stalls** Low

Form RPR

0065 **1** **Shearian**[18] 8773 7-8-13 **64**............................ GerO'Neill(7) 7 73
(Declan Carroll) *trckd ldrs: hdwy over 3f out: cl up over 2f out: rdn to ld 1 1/2f: out: drvn out* **11/2**

4603 **2** ¾ **Luath**[15] 8801 4-8-13 **57**............................ NickyMackay 3 64
(Suzzanne France) *bhd on inner and sn niggled along: swtchd to outer and rdn along 3f out: gd hdwy 2f out: styd on u.p fnl f* **11/4**[1]

5433 **3** ¾ **Swot**[24] 8659 5-8-6 **57**.............................(v) RossaRyan(7) 8 62
(Roger Teal) *dwlt: sn trcking ldrs: cl up 1/2-way: chal 3f out: rdn 2f out: drvn and ev ch over 1f out: kpt on same pce* **9/2**[3]

0263 **4** shd **Ubla (IRE)**[38] 8328 4-8-11 **62**............................ PaulHainey(7) 4 67
(Gay Kelleway) *trckd ldr: hdwy and cl up over 3f out: rdn to take slt ld over 2f out: hdd 1 1/2f out: sn drvn and kpt on same pce* **8/1**

0000 **5** hd **Ravenhoe (IRE)**[36] 8376 4-8-4 **55**............................ AndrewBreslin(7) 9 60
(Mark Johnston) *trckd ldrs: pushed along and lost pl 1/2-way: hdwy over 2f out: rdn to chse ldrs over 1f out: kpt on u.p fnl f* **10/1**

0052 **6** 8 **Tellovoi (IRE)**[7] 8930 9-9-0 **65**.............................(v) JackOsborn(7) 1 50
(Richard Guest) *led: rdn along 3f out: hdd over 2f out: sn wknd* **3/1**[2]

3056 **7** 1 **Inshaa**[7] 8930 5-9-2 **60**.............................(p) JasonHart 2 43
(Simon West) *chsd ldrs: rdn along 3f out: wknd 2f out* **25/1**

0005 **8** 5 **Italian Beauty (IRE)**[24] 8650 5-8-7 **51** oh1.....................(p) HollieDoyle 6 22
(John Wainwright) *sn outpcd and a bhd* **66/1**

1m 43.0s (-0.70) **Going Correction** -0.10s/f (Stan) 8 Ran SP% **110.8**
Speed ratings (Par 101): **99,98,97,97,97 89,88,83**
CSF £19.66 CT £69.51 TOTE £6.20: £2.40, £1.30, £1.80; EX 22.30 Trifecta £121.20.
**Owner** Mrs Sarah Bryan **Bred** Minehart Developments Ltd **Trained** Malton, N Yorks
■ Stewards' Enquiry : Andrew Breslin seven-day ban: used whip above the permitted level (Dec 15-16, 18-22)
Nicky Mackay two-day ban: used whip above the permitted level (Dec 15-16)

**FOCUS**
A modest handicap with not much covering the front five at the line. Straightforward form.

## 9033 BETWAY SPRINT H'CAP — 6f 16y(F)
**2:45** (2:46) (Class 6) (0-65,67) 4-Y-0+ **£2,587** (£770; £384; £192) **Stalls** Low

Form RPR

4061 **1** **First Excel**[18] 8772 5-9-7 **64**.............................(b) JimmyQuinn 4 73
(Roy Bowring) *mde all: rdn wl over 1f out: drvn and edgd lft ins fnl f: kpt on wl* **11/4**[1]

-000 **2** 1¾ **Declamation (IRE)**[130] 5205 7-8-7 **50**............................ KieranO'Neill 1 54
(John Butler) *chsd wnr: cl up over 2f out: rdn wl over 1f out and ev ch: swtchd rt and drvn jst ins fnl f: kpt on same pce* **7/1**

2240 **3** ½ **Meandmyshadow**[20] 8742 9-9-5 **62**.............................(b) CamHardie 2 65
(Alan Brown) *in tch on inner: rdn along and outpcd over 3f out: hdwy 2f out: sn drvn and styd on u.p fnl f* **18/1**

2445 **4** 3½ **African Blessing**[15] 8798 4-9-3 **67**............................ RossaRyan(7) 3 59
(Charlie Wallis) *chsd ldrs: rdn along over 2f out: drvn over 1f out: kpt on one pce* **7/2**[2]

6003 **5** nk **Pearl Acclaim (IRE)**[14] 8816 7-9-5 **62**............................ SteveDrowne 7 53
(David C Griffiths) *chsd ldng pair: rdn along over 2f out: drvn wl over 1f out: grad wknd appr fnl f* **16/1**

0655 **6** 1½ **Vroom (IRE)**[18] 8775 4-9-2 **66**.............................(e) PaulHainey(7) 9 53
(Gay Kelleway) *in tch: rdn along and wd st: drvn 2f out: kpt on u.p appr fnl f* **10/1**

6500 **7** shd **Viva Verglas (IRE)**[24] 8646 6-9-7 **64**............................ LukeMorris 8 50
(Daniel Mark Loughnane) *dwlt sn rdn along and towards rr tl styd on fnl 2f* **4/1**[3]

1106 **8** nk **Dodgy Bob**[52] 7932 4-9-7 **67**.............................(v) PhilDennis(3) 11 52
(Michael Mullineaux) *racd wd: in tch: wd st: sn rdn and n.d* **16/1**

4000 **9** ¾ **Appleberry (IRE)**[15] 8801 5-9-7 **64**.............................(p) AndrewMullen 10 47
(Michael Appleby) *in tch towards outer: rdn along and wd st: n.d* **16/1**

5600 **10** 16 **Willbeme**[7] 8924 9-8-7 **50** oh1.............................(e[1]) JoeyHaynes 5
(Simon West) *dwlt: a in rr* **40/1**

1m 15.85s (-0.65) **Going Correction** -0.10s/f (Stan) 10 Ran SP% **115.8**
Speed ratings (Par 101): **100,97,97,92,91 89,89,89,88,67**
CSF £22.37 CT £249.45 TOTE £3.10: £1.30, £2.50, £4.70; EX 29.00 Trifecta £515.70.
**Owner** S R Bowring **Bred** S R Bowring **Trained** Edwinstowe, Notts

**FOCUS**
A modest sprint handicap and the front pair dominated the contest from the start. Those held up had no chance. The form looks straightforward.

## 9034 SUNBETS H'CAP — 1m 13y(F)
**3:20** (3:20) (Class 6) (0-60,67) 3-Y-0 **£2,264** (£673; £336; £168) **Stalls** Low

Form RPR

0000 **1** **Tilly Devine**[15] 8801 3-8-7 **46** oh1.............................(b[1]) KieranO'Neill 1 55
(Scott Dixon) *mde all: rdn clr over 2f out: drvn and edgd lft ins fnl f: kpt on wl towards fin* **100/1**

1451 **2** 2 **Anna Medici**[8] 8908 3-10-0 **67** 6ex.............................(p) LukeMorris 12 71
(Sir Mark Prescott Bt) *towards rr: hdwy on outer over 3f out: rdn over 2f out: drvn to chse wnr and edgd lft ins fnl f: no imp towards fin* **10/3**[2]

0605 **3** 1½ **Mimic's Memory**[13] 8854 3-9-6 **59**............................ ShaneGray 11 60
(Ann Duffield) *in tch: hdwy over 2f out: sn rdn and kpt on fnl f* **8/1**

2065 **4** nk **Breaking Free**[15] 8807 3-8-7 **46** oh1.............................(p) CamHardie 4 46
(John Quinn) *trckd ldrs towards inner: hdwy 3f out: rdn along 2f out: sn drvn and kpt on same pce* **20/1**

0000 **5** 2 **Sir Harry Collins (IRE)**[3] 8980 3-8-2 **48**.............. GabrieleMalune(7) 13 43
(Michael Appleby) *dwlt: sn chsng ldrs towards outer: hdwy over 2f out: rdn wl over 1f out: sn drvn and wknd* **25/1**

2514 **6** 1 ¾ **Topmeup**[13] 8841 3-9-0 **60**..............................(v) RossaRyan(7) 5 51
(Gay Kelleway) *in tch: hdwy 3f out: rdn along 2f out: sn drvn and btn* **16/1**
40-0 **7** 7 **Red Douglas**[137] 4968 3-8-9 **48**.............................. TomEaves 2 22
(Scott Dixon) *chsd wnr: rdn over 2f out: wknd over 1f out out* **40/1**
5046 **8** 3 ¾ **Seaview**[24] 8651 3-9-6 **62**.............................. AaronJones(3) 3 27
(David Brown) *chsd ldrs: rdn along over 2f out: sn wknd* **7/2**[3]
5000 **9** 10 **Our Kim (IRE)**[23] 8673 3-8-5 **47**.............................. TimClark(3) 9
(John Butler) *chsd ldrs: rdn along over 2f out: sn wknd* **40/1**
3000 **10** 9 **True Colors**[15] 8801 3-9-5 **58**..............................(p[1]) TonyHamilton 10
(Richard Fahey) *a towards rr* **14/1**
50-0 **11** 20 **Melcano**[15] 8807 3-8-4 **46**..............................(v[1]) CharlieBennett(3) 7
(Shaun Harris) *chsd ldrs on inner: rdn along wl over 3f out: sn lost pl and bhd* **100/1**
5101 **P** **Belgravian (FR)**[3] 8985 3-9-10 **63** 6ex..............................(tp) AndrewMullen 6
(Archie Watson) *.dwlt: swtchd lft towards outer whn lost action and p.u after 11/2f* **13/8**[1]

1m 43.19s (-0.51) **Going Correction** -0.10s/f (Stan) **12** Ran SP% **122.5**
Speed ratings (Par 98): **98,96,94,94,92 90,83,79,69,60 40,**
CSF £415.54 CT £3135.44 TOTE £89.30: £16.40, £1.60, £2.60; EX 755.80 Trifecta £5983.80 Part won..
**Owner** Winning Connections Racing **Bred** Mrs Yvette Dixon **Trained** Babworth, Notts

**FOCUS**
A modest 3yo handicap and a complete boil-over, but a race marred by the favourite \bBelgravian\p sadly going wrong and being pulled up after a furlong. The form helps set the level.
T/Plt: £9.00 to a £1 stake. Pool of £51,253.25 - 4,141.34 winning tickets. T/Qpdt: £3.30 to a £1 stake. Pool of £4,885.78 - 1,091.61 winning tickets. **Joe Rowntree**

9035 - 9048a (Foreign Racing) - See Raceform Interactive

## 8995 WOLVERHAMPTON (A.W) (L-H)

Saturday, December 2

**OFFICIAL GOING: Tapeta: standard**
Wind: Fresh across Weather: Showers

### 9049 32RED CASINO NOVICE STKS 5f 21y (Tp)
**5:45** (5:45) (Class 5) 2-Y-O **£3,234** (£962; £481; £240) **Stalls** Low

Form RPR
36 **1** **Al Asef**[21] 8734 2-9-2 0.............................. DanielMuscutt 5 83+
(Marco Botti) *a.p: chsd ldr 1/2-way: shkn up to ld 1f out: r.o wl: comf* **5/4**[1]
6222 **2** 3 ¼ **Midsummer Knight**[9] 8916 2-8-13 77..............................(p[1]) CliffordLee(3) 6 71
(K R Burke) *sn led: rdn and hdd 1f out: styd on same pce ins fnl f* **15/8**[2]
**3** 5 **Madame Ritz (IRE)** 2-8-11 0..............................(h[1]) RobertHavlin 2 48
(Richard Phillips) *prom: rdn over 1f out: styd on same pce* **80/1**
**4** 2 ¾ **Ingleby Molly (IRE)** 2-8-11 0.............................. ShaneGray 4 38
(David O'Meara) *hld up: plld hrd: shkn up 1/2-way: sn outpcd* **33/1**
0 **5** 1 **Straffan (IRE)**[147] 4598 2-8-11 0.............................. DavidProbert 7 35
(David O'Meara) *prom: pushed along 1/2-way: wknd over 1f out* **18/1**
06 **6** ½ **Spanish Mane (IRE)**[14] 8850 2-8-12 0 ow1.............................. JackGarritty 3 34
(Richard Fahey) *lost pl sn after s: nvr on terms after* **40/1**
3 **7** ½ **It's A Wish**[14] 8850 2-8-8 0.............................. HectorCrouch(3) 11 31
(Clive Cox) *plld hrd: w ldr tl wl over 3f out: lost 2nd 1/2-way: rdn and wknd over 1f out* **5/1**[3]
**8** 3 ¼ **Argon** 2-9-2 0.............................. RyanPowell 9 25
(Sir Mark Prescott Bt) *s.s: outpcd* **33/1**
60 **9** nk **Haxby Juniors**[28] 8587 2-8-11 0..............................(h[1]) CamHardie 8 18
(Antony Brittain) *hld up: racd keenly: n.d* **200/1**
0 **10** 1 ½ **Born For Prosecco (IRE)**[25] 8657 2-8-11 0.............................. PatrickMathers 10 13
(Derek Shaw) *prom to 1/2-way* **200/1**
**11** 2 **Our Tony** 2-8-11 0.............................. JoeFanning 1 6
(Keith Dalgleish) *s.s: outpcd: bhd whn hung lft over 1f out* **20/1**

1m 0.52s (-1.38) **Going Correction** -0.175s/f (Stan) **11** Ran SP% **116.5**
Speed ratings (Par 96): **104,98,90,86,84 84,83,78,77,75 71**
CSF £3.47 TOTE £2.10: £1.10, £1.10, £10.20; EX 4.20 Trifecta £102.10.
**Owner** Raed El Youssef **Bred** Aislabie Bloodstock Ltd **Trained** Newmarket, Suffolk

**FOCUS**
They finished pretty well strung out in this novice. The winner is possibly value for being a bit better than rated.

### 9050 32RED.COM EBF NOVICE STKS (PLUS 10 RACE) (DIV I) 7f 36y (Tp)
**6:15** (6:17) (Class 4) 2-Y-O **£4,528** (£1,347; £673; £336) **Stalls** High

Form RPR
4 **1** **Moqarrab (USA)**[29] 8560 2-9-2 0.............................. WilliamCarson 4 80+
(Saeed bin Suroor) *trckd ldr tl led over 1f out: sn edgd lft: rdn clr ins fnl f* **13/8**[1]
32 **2** 4 ½ **Epic Fantasy**[36] 8382 2-9-2 0.............................. PJMcDonald 10 69
(Charles Hills) *sn led: rdn: hung lft and hdd over 1f out: no ex ins fnl f* **11/4**[2]
**3** 2 **Native Appeal (IRE)** 2-9-2 0..............................(t[1]) AdamKirby 2 64+
(Charlie Appleby) *hld up: pushed along and hdwy over 2f out: rdn and hung lft over 1f out: styd on to go 3rd wl ins fnl f* **7/2**[3]
0 **4** ¾ **Black Medusa (IRE)**[7] 8951 2-9-2 0.............................. RaulDaSilva 7 62
(Paul Cole) *chsd ldrs: pushed along 1/2-way: styd on same pce fr over 1f out* **66/1**
**5** nk **Glorious Player (IRE)** 2-9-2 0.............................. RichardKingscote 8 61+
(Tom Dascombe) *s.i.s: hld up: r.o ins fnl f: nvr nrr* **25/1**
252 **6** 1 **Key Player**[11] 8877 2-9-2 78.............................. CharlesBishop 5 59
(Eve Johnson Houghton) *chsd ldrs: rdn over 2f out: wknd ins fnl f* **11/2**
00 **7** 2 ½ **Edge Of The World (IRE)**[30] 8544 2-8-11 0.............................. DavidProbert 3 48
(Ralph Beckett) *pushed along at various stages towards rr: nvr on terms* **66/1**
5 **8** shd **Valentino Dancer**[58] 7765 2-9-2 0.............................. ShaneGray 11 52
(David O'Meara) *s.i.s: a in rr* **50/1**
30 **9** 3 **Taghee**[36] 8381 2-9-2 0.............................. RyanTate 1 45
(Marco Botti) *chsd ldrs: pushed along 1/2-way: wknd over 1f out* **25/1**
0 **10** 49 **Aonedamproofing**[9] 8915 2-8-9 0..............................(h[1]) GabrieleMalune(7) 6
(Lisa Williamson) *s.i.s: a in rr: bhd fr 1/2-way* **250/1**

1m 27.63s (-1.17) **Going Correction** -0.175s/f (Stan) **10** Ran SP% **115.4**
Speed ratings (Par 98): **99,93,91,90,90 89,86,86,82,26**
CSF £5.93 TOTE £2.60: £1.30, £1.20, £1.50; EX 7.50 Trifecta £18.30.
**Owner** Godolphin **Bred** WinStar Farm LLC **Trained** Newmarket, Suffolk

**FOCUS**
A nice performance from the winner, who put his stamp on the race in the straight. The opening level is fluid.

### 9051 32RED.COM EBF NOVICE STKS (PLUS 10 RACE) (DIV II) 7f 36y (Tp)
**6:45** (6:48) (Class 4) 2-Y-O **£4,528** (£1,347; £673; £336) **Stalls** High

Form RPR
3220 **1** **Jellmood**[134] 5109 2-8-13 90..............................(h[1]) MarcMonaghan(3) 2 82
(Marco Botti) *a.p: hung lft fr over 1f out: rdn to ld ins fnl f: styd on* **3/1**[2]
**2** nk **Swiss Knight** 2-9-2 0.............................. AdamKirby 1 81+
(Charlie Appleby) *sn led: hdd 6f out: remained handy: rdn to ld again over 1f out: hdd ins fnl f: kpt on* **15/8**[1]
**3** 4 **Chingachgook** 2-9-2 0.............................. JackGarritty 7 71+
(Richard Fahey) *hld up in tch: shkn up over 1f out: styd on same pce ins fnl f* **18/1**
0 **4** 2 ¾ **Rogue Hero (IRE)**[71] 7352 2-9-2 0..............................(t[1]) PJMcDonald 4 65
(Paul Cole) *hld up: hdwy and hung lft fr over 1f out: styd on same pce fnl f* **18/1**
**5** nk **Sun Hat (IRE)** 2-8-11 0.............................. RobertHavlin 8 59
(Simon Crisford) *led 6f out: rdn and hdd over 1f out: nt clr run sn after: wknd ins fnl f* **25/1**
**6** hd **Mewtow** 2-9-2 0..............................(h[1]) FranBerry 6 64
(George Scott) *prom: hmpd 6f out: chsd ldr over 5f out: rdn and ev ch wl over 1f out: nt clr run sn after: wknd ins fnl f* **40/1**
00 **7** 2 ¾ **Demurrer (USA)**[49] 8030 2-9-2 0.............................. DannyBrock 10 57
(Michael Bell) *s.i.s: hld up: rdn over 2f out: nvr on terms* **80/1**
0 **8** ½ **Imperial Red (IRE)**[36] 8389 2-8-13 0.............................. GeorgiaCox(3) 3 56
(William Haggas) *s.i.s: a in rr* **9/2**[3]
**9** ¾ **Marshal Dan (IRE)** 2-8-13 0.............................. HectorCrouch(3) 9 54
(Heather Main) *s.i.s: a in rr* **33/1**
**10** 1 ¾ **Refrain (IRE)** 2-9-2 0.............................. TedDurcan 5 49
(Sir Michael Stoute) *rn green towards rr: pushed along over 2f out: wknd over 1f out* **9/2**[3]

1m 27.75s (-1.05) **Going Correction** -0.175s/f (Stan) **10** Ran SP% **117.1**
Speed ratings (Par 98): **99,98,94,90,90 90,87,86,85,83**
CSF £8.83 TOTE £4.10: £1.50, £1.20, £3.80; EX 11.30 Trifecta £144.50.
**Owner** Sheikh Mohammed Bin Khalifa Al Maktoum **Bred** Essafinaat Ltd **Trained** Newmarket, Suffolk

**FOCUS**
Marginally the slower of the two divisions, by 0.12sec, but the first two put distance between themselves and the third. The winner has been rated below his best.

### 9052 SUNBETS.CO.UK H'CAP 7f 36y (Tp)
**7:15** (7:16) (Class 6) (0-55,55) 3-Y-O+ **£2,749** (£818; £408; £204) **Stalls** High

Form RPR
0000 **1** **Herm (IRE)**[54] 7911 3-9-4 **52**.............................. FranBerry 1 58
(David Evans) *a.p: rdn to ld 1f out: styd on* **11/1**
2110 **2** ¾ **Prince Jai**[52] 7952 4-9-7 **55**..............................(v) AdamKirby 8 59
(Ian Williams) *sn pushed along to ld: rdn over 2f out: hdd 1f out: styd on u.p* **4/1**[3]
6454 **3** 1 ½ **Broughtons Fancy**[8] 8924 4-8-13 **52**.............................. GemmaTutty(5) 11 52
(Karen Tutty) *chsd ldr 6f out tl over 4f out: remained handy: rdn over 1f out: no ex wl ins fnl f* **16/1**
0000 **4** nk **Mossy's Lodge**[59] 7723 4-9-7 **55**.............................. DavidProbert 5 55
(Anthony Carson) *hmpd s: sn pushed along: hdwy over 4f out: chsd ldr over 4f out tl rdn over 1f out: styd on same pce ins fnl f* **33/1**
0402 **5** nse **Jack Blane**[7] 8948 3-9-7 **55**..............................(p) PhillipMakin 2 55
(Keith Dalgleish) *hld up: nt clr run 1/2-way: hdwy over 1f out: rdn and hung lft ins fnl f: nt rch ldrs* **3/1**[2]
21 **6** nk **Secret Memories (IRE)**[22] 8730 3-9-7 **55**..............................(t[1]) PJMcDonald 6 54
(Miss Katy Brown, Ire) *s.i.s: hld up: r.o ins fnl f: nvr nrr* **7/1**
-064 **7** ¾ **Rosenborg Rider (IRE)**[22] 8730 4-9-5 **53**..............................(p) RichardKingscote 7 50
(Adrian McGuinness, Ire) *wnt lft s: sn prom: rdn over 1f out: styd on same pce* **9/4**[1]
0000 **8** ¾ **Sunnyside Bob (IRE)**[42] 8247 4-8-9 **50**.............................. FayeMcManoman(7) 4 45
(Neville Bycroft) *hld up: hdwy over 1f out: no ex ins fnl f* **28/1**
3202 **9** 6 **Binky Blue (IRE)**[24] 8675 5-9-5 **53**..............................(h) ShaneKelly 10 34
(Daniel Mark Loughnane) *hld up: pushed along over 2f out: wknd over 1f out* **12/1**

1m 29.87s (1.07) **Going Correction** -0.175s/f (Stan) **9** Ran SP% **116.6**
Speed ratings (Par 101): **86,85,83,83,83 82,81,80,74**
CSF £55.22 CT £719.57 TOTE £11.60: £2.80, £1.80, £2.90; EX 80.00 Trifecta £484.30.
**Owner** Trevor Gallienne **Bred** Mountarmstrong Stud **Trained** Pandy, Monmouths
■ Stewards' Enquiry : Fran Berry trainer rep said, regarding improved form shown, gelding appreciated 54-day break which freshened him up, and that hey may have benefited from being schooled over hurdles

**FOCUS**
This was steadily run, several failed to settle and it turned into a dash up the straight. It's been rated around the recent form of the placed horses.

### 9053 BETWAY CASINO H'CAP 1m 1f 104y (Tp)
**7:45** (7:46) (Class 3) (0-95,95) 3-Y-O **£7,246** (£2,168; £1,084; £542; £270) **Stalls** Low

Form RPR
0503 **1** **Battle Of Marathon (USA)**[3] 8999 5-8-11 **92**.............................. JackOsborn(7) 1 101
(John Ryan) *hld up: hdwy 1/2-way: rdn and r.o to ld wl ins fnl f* **7/1**[3]
3033 **2** 1 ¼ **Emenem**[11] 8880 3-9-0 **90**.............................. KieranShoemark 4 96
(Simon Dow) *hld up in tch: rdn over 2f out: r.o to go 2nd nr fin* **5/1**[2]
1-30 **3** ¾ **Towerlands Park (IRE)**[21] 8740 4-9-3 **91**..............................(p[1]) RichardKingscote 6 95
(Michael Bell) *a.p: chsd ldr over 5f out: shkn up to ld over 1f out: rdn and hdd wl ins fnl f* **11/4**[1]
0044 **4** ¾ **First Flight (IRE)**[24] 8672 6-8-13 **87**.............................. PJMcDonald 2 90
(Heather Main) *hld up: pushed along over 3f out: rdn and r.o ins fnl f: nt rch ldrs* **8/1**
5200 **5** ½ **Espresso Freddo (IRE)**[22] 8718 3-8-5 **81** oh3..............................(h[1]) KieranO'Neill 7 83
(Robert Stephens) *hld up: racd keenly: hdwy over 1f out: styd on* **80/1**
0002 **6** ¾ **Brex Drago (ITY)**[11] 8880 5-9-5 **93**..............................(b) TomMarquand 10 93
(Marco Botti) *sn led: hdd 8f out: chsd ldr tl over 5f out: remained handy: rdn and nt clr run over 1f out: styd on same pce* **11/1**
6053 **7** nk **Alejandro (IRE)**[15] 8812 8-8-13 **87**.............................. DougieCostello 13 87
(David Loughnane) *led 8f out: rdn over 2f out: hdd over 1f out: no ex ins fnl f* **50/1**
4655 **8** hd **Multicultural (IRE)**[7] 8947 3-8-5 **81** oh4..............................(v) JoeFanning 5 80
(James Tate) *hld up: rdn over 1f out: nt trble ldrs* **8/1**
6510 **9** ½ **Pensax Boy**[78] 7129 5-8-13 **87**.............................. SteveDrowne 9 85
(Daniel Mark Loughnane) *hld up: shkn up and nt clr run ent fnl f: nt trble ldrs* **22/1**

0025 **10** *1* **Swift Emperor (IRE)**[25] 8652 5-9-0 **88** ........ FranBerry 11 84
(David Barron) *s.i.s: hld up: rdn over 1f out: nvr on terms* **16/1**

-363 **11** *1 ½* **Perfect Cracker**[259] 1258 9-9-1 **89** ........ AdamKirby 3 82
(Clive Cox) *prom: shkn up over 1f out: wknd and eased ins fnl f* **22/1**

5131 **12** *6* **Fayez (IRE)**[11] 8880 3-9-5 **95** ........ DavidProbert 12 75
(David O'Meara) *hld up: rdn over 2f out: wknd over 1f out* **7/1**[3]

1m 57.64s (-3.16) **Going Correction** -0.175s/f (Stan)
**WFA** 3 from 4yo+ 2lb **12** Ran SP% **116.7**
Speed ratings (Par 107): **107,105,105,104,104 103,103,103,102,101 100,95**
CSF £39.84 CT £120.49 TOTE £7.70: £2.00, £2.30, £1.80; EX 58.90 Trifecta £228.90.
**Owner** G Smith-Bernal **Bred** Galleria Bloodstock & Rhinestone B/Stock **Trained** Newmarket, Suffolk

**FOCUS**
A good, competitive handicap run at a decent clip. The runner-up has been rated to form.

## 9054 BETWAY LIVE CASINO H'CAP — 1m 4f 51y (Tp)
**8:15** (8:15) (Class 5) (0-70,70) 3-Y-O+ **£3,234** (£962; £481; £240) Stalls Low

Form RPR

5550 **1** **Tan Arabiq**[47] 8124 4-9-3 **66** ........ TomMarquand 1 74
(Michael Appleby) *chsd ldrs: wnt 2nd over 2f out: rdn to ld ins fnl f: jst hld on* **9/1**

0006 **2** *nk* **Belabour**[39] 8313 4-9-2 **65** ........ PJMcDonald 5 72+
(Mark Brisbourne) *hld up: hdwy and nt clr run over 1f out: sn rdn: edgd lft and r.o wl towards fin: nt quite rch wnr* **3/1**[1]

**3** *¾* **Ice Canyon**[117] 5727 3-9-0 **70** ........ EoinWalsh(3) 12 76
(Mark Brisbourne) *s.i.s: hld up: hdwy and nt clr run over 1f out: swtchd lft: r.o* **50/1**

0424 **4** *hd* **Deeley's Double (FR)**[36] 8386 4-9-3 **66** ........ RichardKingscote 10 71
(Daniel Mark Loughnane) *led after 1f: rdn over 1f out: hdd ins fnl f: styd on same pce* **9/2**[2]

2266 **5** *nk* **Best Example (USA)**[45] 8160 5-8-13 **65** ........ ShelleyBirkett(3) 9 70
(Julia Feilden) *chsd ldrs: effrt and nt clr run over 1f out: styd on* **8/1**

1420 **6** *1* **My Brother Mike (IRE)**[32] 8497 3-9-3 **70** ........ DougieCostello 11 73
(Kevin Frost) *hld up: hdwy 2f out: rdn: nt clr run and swtchd rt over 1f out: styd on same pce wl ins fnl f* **12/1**

0164 **7** *1 ¾* **Ingleby Hollow**[25] 8655 5-8-10 **66** ........(t) PatrickVaughan(7) 7 67
(David O'Meara) *s.i.s: hld up: hdwy over 1f out: no ex ins fnl f* **33/1**

0006 **8** *6* **Dolphin Village (IRE)**[32] 8485 7-9-1 **67** ........ CharlieBennett(3) 3 58
(Shaun Harris) *hld up in tch: rdn over 1f out: wknd ins fnl f* **7/1**[3]

-050 **9** *2* **Mister Fizz**[9] 8426 9-9-3 **66** ........ HollieDoyle 8 54
(Miss Imogen Pickard) *pushed along and prom: hmpd and lost pl after 1f: n.d after* **40/1**

1124 **10** *1 ¾* **Favorite Girl (GER)**[154] 4344 9-9-6 **69** ........ AdamKirby 4 54
(Michael Appleby) *led 1f: chsd ldr tl rdn over 2f out: wkng whn hmpd over 1f out* **8/1**

4461 **11** *3 ½* **Hussar Ballad (USA)**[36] 8396 8-9-4 **67** ........ CamHardie 2 46
(Antony Brittain) *hld up in tch: plld hrd: rdn over 2f out: wknd over 1f out* **7/1**[3]

0050 **12** *34* **Rum Swizzle**[30] 8549 5-9-0 **66** ........(p[1]) HectorCrouch(3) 6
(Harry Dunlop) *w ldrs: stdd and hld up in tch after 1f: rdn over 3f out: wknd over 2f out* **25/1**

2m 36.46s (-4.34) **Going Correction** -0.175s/f (Stan)
**WFA** 3 from 4yo+ 4lb **12** Ran SP% **119.3**
Speed ratings (Par 103): **107,106,106,106,105 105,104,100,98,97 95,72**
CSF £35.40 CT £1313.45 TOTE £10.50: £2.90, £2.80, £11.00; EX 53.40 Trifecta £2710.50.
**Owner** Sarnian Racing **Bred** Michael Appleby **Trained** Oakham, Rutland

**FOCUS**
The pace steadied in the middle of the race and the winner and fourth got first run on the closers. There was a bit of a bunched finish. The winner has been rated to his best, and the fourth helps set the standard.

## 9055 BETWAY FREE BET CLUB H'CAP — 1m 4f 51y (Tp)
**8:45** (8:46) (Class 2) (0-105,104) 3-Y-O+
**£11,827** (£3,541; £1,770; £885; £442; £111) Stalls Low

Form RPR

4001 **1** **Castlelyons (IRE)**[24] 8672 5-8-11 **89** ........(h) RichardKingscote 2 95+
(Robert Stephens) *hld up: shkn up over 1f out: rdn and r.o to ld nr fin* **2/1**[1]

5251 **2** *nk* **Al Hamdany (IRE)**[31] 8506 3-8-11 **93** ........ KieranShoemark 9 98
(Marco Botti) *hld up: hdwy over 8f out: rdn to ld wl ins fnl f: hdd nr fin* **7/1**

0034 **3** *¾* **Crowned Eagle**[50] 8005 3-8-13 **95** ........ TomMarquand 8 99
(Marco Botti) *chsd ldr: rdn to ld and hung lft over 1f out: hdd and unable qck wl ins fnl f* **9/2**

1400 **4** *1 ¼* **Cohesion**[21] 8740 4-9-12 **104** ........(p[1]) AdamKirby 6 106
(David Bridgwater) *chsd ldrs: rdn over 1f out: styd on same pce ins fnl f* **4/1**[3]

1320 **5** *1* **Canberra Cliffs (IRE)**[15] 8820 3-8-8 **90** ........ DavidProbert 7 90
(Don Cantillon) *prom: rdn over 1f out: no ex wl ins fnl f* **40/1**

4050 **6** *1 ½* **Afonso De Sousa (USA)**[65] 7548 7-8-9 **87** ........ RyanTate 1 85
(Michael Appleby) *hld up: styng on whn nt clr run ins fnl f: nvr trbld ldrs* **40/1**

151 **6** *dht* **Mixboy (FR)**[32] 8485 7-8-11 **89** ........ JoeFanning 5 87
(Keith Dalgleish) *led: hdd over 1f out: no ex ins fnl f* **3/1**[2]

-300 **8** *4* **Nonios (IRE)**[48] 8078 5-8-7 **85** oh1 ........(h) KieranO'Neill 4 77
(David Simcock) *s.i.s: hld up: sme hdwy over 1f out: wknd ins fnl f* **25/1**

2m 36.8s (-4.00) **Going Correction** -0.175s/f (Stan)
**WFA** 3 from 4yo+ 4lb **8** Ran SP% **117.7**
Speed ratings (Par 109): **106,105,105,104,103 102,102,100**
CSF £17.26 CT £56.53 TOTE £2.90: £1.20, £2.10, £1.50; EX 16.80 Trifecta £104.50.
**Owner** The Warriors **Bred** Highfort Stud **Trained** Penhow, Newport

**FOCUS**
A good race and a thrilling finish, the well-backed winner getting up in the final strides. It's been rated around the third to his latest effort.

## 9056 BETWAY H'CAP — 1m 1f 104y (Tp)
**9:15** (9:17) (Class 6) (0-55,55) 3-Y-O+ **£2,587** (£770; £384; £192) Stalls Low

Form RPR

0331 **1** **King Kevin**[16] 8800 3-9-2 **55** ........(b) RobertHavlin 4 62+
(Ed Dunlop) *s.i.s: hld up: hdwy over 1f out: rdn to ld ins fnl f: r.o* **5/4**[1]

1566 **2** *nk* **Windsorlot (IRE)**[7] 8957 4-9-4 **55** ........ GeorgeDowning 8 61
(Tony Carroll) *hld up in tch: rdn over 1f out: edgd lft ins fnl f: r.o* **16/1**

0320 **3** *1 ½* **Weardiditallgorong**[29] 6035 5-9-4 **55** ........(b) DavidProbert 6 59
(Des Donovan, Ire) *chsd ldrs: rdn over 1f out: ev ch ins fnl f: styd on same pce* **20/1**

534 **4** *1 ½* **Sunshineandbubbles**[25] 8661 4-9-2 **53** ........ JoeFanning 2 54
(Jennie Candlish) *led: rdn over 1f out: hdd and no ex ins fnl f* **6/1**[2]

464/ **5** *nse* **Romantic (IRE)**[133] 5170 8-9-4 **55** ........ AdamKirby 11 56
(Noel C Kelly, Ire) *hld up: rdn over 1f out: r.o ins fnl f: nt rch ldrs* **16/1**

5505 **6** *nse* **D'Waterside**[25] 8662 3-9-2 **55** ........ DougieCostello 7 56
(David Loughnane) *w ldr: rdn and ev ch over 1f out: no ex ins fnl f* **8/1**[3]

6640 **7** *½* **Rowlestonerendezvu**[39] 8327 4-9-3 **54** ........ TomMarquand 12 54
(Tony Carroll) *hld up: rdn and r.o ins fnl f: nvr nrr* **25/1**

4030 **8** *1 ½* **Bonnie Gals**[16] 8807 3-9-2 **55** ........(b) PhillipMakin 3 52
(Keith Dalgleish) *hld up: rdn over 1f out: nvr trbld ldrs* **8/1**[3]

060 **9** *nk* **Peter Stuyvesant (IRE)**[47] 8116 3-9-2 **55** ........ FranBerry 10 51
(Denis Coakley) *chsd ldrs: rdn over 1f out: edgd lft and wknd ins fnl f* **16/1**

6050 **10** *6* **Camaradorie (IRE)**[144] 4727 3-9-2 **55** ........ SimonPearce 1 40
(Lydia Pearce) *hld up: hdwy over 1f out: wknd ins fnl f* **66/1**

0054 **11** *8* **Little Choosey**[28] 8591 7-9-4 **55** ........(b) JimmyQuinn 13 25
(Roy Bowring) *prom: rdn over 2f out: wknd over 1f out* **12/1**

4000 **12** *3 ¾* **Claire's Secret**[25] 8664 3-8-9 **55** ........ RossaRyan(7) 9 17
(Philip McBride) *hld up: rdn and wknd over 2f out* **50/1**

2m 0.15s (-0.65) **Going Correction** -0.175s/f (Stan)
**WFA** 3 from 4yo+ 2lb **12** Ran SP% **118.4**
Speed ratings (Par 101): **95,94,93,92,92 91,91,90,89,84 77,74**
CSF £23.45 CT £288.05 TOTE £2.30: £1.40, £2.80, £4.10; EX 21.80 Trifecta £308.70.
**Owner** E A L Dunlop **Bred** Denford Stud Ltd **Trained** Newmarket, Suffolk

**FOCUS**
A moderate heat.
T/Plt: £41.00 to a £1 stake. Pool: £123,714.54 - 2,202.05 winning tickets. T/Qpdt: £34.90 to a £1 stake. Pool: £11,580.11 - 245.22 winning tickets. **Colin Roberts**

9057 - 9069a (Foreign Racing) - See Raceform Interactive

# 9028 SOUTHWELL (L-H)
Monday, December 4

**OFFICIAL GOING: Fibresand: standard**
Wind: Light behind Weather: Fine & dry

## 9070 BETWAY H'CAP — 1m 4f 14y(F)
**11:50** (11:50) (Class 5) (0-70,73) 4-Y-O+ **£2,911** (£866; £432; £216) Stalls Low

Form RPR

1621 **1** **Restive (IRE)**[3] 9028 4-9-10 **73** 6ex ........ LukeMorris 3 83
(Iain Jardine) *trckd ldng pair: hdwy over 3f out: sn cl up: led 1 1/2f out: sn rdn: edgd rt ent fnl f: kpt on strly* **8/11**[1]

6062 **2** *4* **Luv U Whatever**[3] 9028 7-9-7 **70** ........(tp) JoeyHaynes 5 74
(Marjorie Fife) *trckd ldrs: hdwy on outer and cl up 7f out: led over 5f out: pushed along 3f out: rdn over 2f out: hdd 1 1/2f out: sn drvn and kpt on same pce* **7/2**[2]

1015 **3** *1* **Percys Princess**[55] 7925 6-9-3 **71** ........ JaneElliott(5) 1 73
(Michael Appleby) *led 2f: cl up on inner: rdn along and ev ch wl over 2f out: drvn over 1f out: kpt on same pce* **33/1**

0001 **4** *13* **Rajapur**[27] 8655 4-8-7 **56** oh5 ........(p) JoeFanning 7 37
(David Thompson) *trckd ldrs: pushed along and outpcd 4f out: plugged on u.p fnl 2f* **20/1**

6021 **5** *7* **Bleu Et Noir**[16] 8852 6-9-9 **72** ........(h) KieranO'Neill 4 42
(Tim Vaughan) *trckd ldng pair: pushed along over 4f out: rdn over 3f out: sn wknd* **9/2**[3]

0600 **6** *3 ¼* **Masterful Act (USA)**[199] 2787 10-9-1 **64** ........ AndrewMullen 2 29
(John Balding) *cl up: slt ld after 2f: pushed along and hdd over 5 out: rdn wl over 3f out: sn wknd* **20/1**

1660 **7** *25* **Kay Sera**[145] 4733 9-8-9 **61** ........ EoinWalsh(3) 6
(Tony Newcombe) *a towards rr: rdn along 1/2-way: sn outpcd and bhd* **66/1**

2m 36.28s (-4.72) **Going Correction** -0.10s/f (Stan) **7** Ran SP% **112.3**
Speed ratings (Par 103): **111,108,107,99,94 92,75**
CSF £3.25 TOTE £1.30: £1.10, £1.70; EX 3.00 Trifecta £28.20.
**Owner** I J Jardine **Bred** Epona Bloodstock Ltd **Trained** Carrutherstown, D'fries & G'way

**FOCUS**
An ordinary middle-distance handicap. They went a respectable gallop on standard Fibresand and the favourite won readily. He has been rated back to his 3yo form.

## 9071 BETWAY SPRINT MAIDEN STKS — 6f 16y(F)
**12:20** (12:22) (Class 5) 3-Y-O+ **£2,911** (£866; £432; £216) Stalls Low

Form RPR

0303 **1** **Ghaseedah**[59] 7793 3-9-0 67 ........(b) TimmyMurphy 5 76
(Simon Crisford) *cl up: led 2f out: sn qcknd clr: v readily* **3/1**[2]

3 **2** *5* **Ladies First**[14] 8869 3-9-0 0 ........ CamHardie 3 60+
(Michael Easterby) *towards rr and sn pushed along on inner: hdwy 3f out: rdn wl over 1f out: styd on fnl f: no ch w wnr* **3/1**[2]

0260 **3** *5* **Gettin' Lucky**[60] 7763 4-9-5 46 ........(p) AndrewMullen 2 49
(John Balding) *broke wl and led at gd pce: jnd and rdn over 2f out: sn hdd: drvn wl over 1f out: kpt on one pce* **16/1**

4603 **4** *1* **Ejabah (IRE)**[18] 8805 3-9-0 44 ........(v) JoeyHaynes 8 41
(Charles Smith) *towards rr: rdn along and n.m.r bnd 1/2-way: styd on u.p fnl 2f: nrst fin* **33/1**

3352 **5** *1 ¼* **Charlie's Dreamer**[18] 8805 3-8-9 60 ........ JaneElliott(5) 1 37
(Michael Appleby) *chsd ldrs: rdn along wl over 2f out: sn one pce* **9/4**[1]

00-0 **6** *2* **Take This Waltz**[43] 8255 3-8-11 39 ........ PhilDennis(3) 4 30
(Bill Turner) *chsd ldrs: rdn along over 3f out: no hdwy* **100/1**

4- **7** *¾* **Thunderbell**[370] 8139 3-9-0 0 ........(be[1]) KieranO'Neill 6 28
(Scott Dixon) *chsd ldrs: rdn along 1/2-way: no hdwy* **14/1**

**8** *2* **Romantic Story** 3-9-0 0 ........ LukeMorris 9 22
(Robert Cowell) *dwlt and towards rr: hdwy and in tch after 2f: chsd ldrs 3f out: wknd over 2f out* **5/1**[3]

0400 **9** *6* **Danica Ashton**[48] 8134 3-8-11 42 ........(vt[1]) RosieJessop(3) 11
(Miss Joey Ellis) *dwlt: a in rr* **100/1**

043 **10** *3 ½* **Hell Of A Lady**[185] 3279 3-9-0 44 ........ WilliamCarson 7
(Michael Attwater) *midfield: rdn along bef 1/2-way: sn wknd* **40/1**

1m 15.01s (-1.49) **Going Correction** -0.10s/f (Stan) **10** Ran SP% **117.3**
Speed ratings (Par 103): **105,98,91,90,88 86,85,82,74,69**
CSF £12.43 TOTE £4.00: £1.70, £1.80, £3.70; EX 16.80 Trifecta £120.20.
**Owner** Abdulla Al Mansoori **Bred** Whatton Manor Stud **Trained** Newmarket, Suffolk
■ Caledonian Gold was withdrawn. Price at time of withdrawal 8-1. Rule 4\n\x\x applies to bets placed prior to withdrawal but not to SP bets. Deduction 10p in the pound. New market formed

**FOCUS**
An ordinary maiden, but a good time. They went a decent gallop and one of the joint-second favourites stormed to victory.

## 9072 SUNBETS.CO.UK MAIDEN H'CAP (DIV I) — 1m 13y(F)
**12:50** (12:51) (Class 6) (0-55,56) 3-Y-0+ — £2,264 (£673; £336; £168) Stalls Low

Form — RPR

0654 **1** **Breaking Free**[3] 9034 3-8-13 **45**.....(p) JasonHart 3 — 55
(John Quinn) *trckd ldrs on inner: effrt whn nt clr run and hmpd on inner 3f out: sn cl up: led 2f out: rdn over 1f out: drvn and edgd rt ins fnl f: hld on wl towards fin* **6/1**

0040 **2** ¾ **Mr Coco Bean (USA)**[76] 7240 3-9-10 **56**..... BenCurtis 8 — 64
(David Barron) *dwlt: hld up towards rr: hdwy 3f out: chsd wnr wl over 1f out: rdn to chal appr fnl f: sn drvn and ev ch: no ex last 75yds* **13/8**[1]

0605 **3** 9 **Quick Monet (IRE)**[40] 8345 4-8-11 **45**..... CharlieBennett(3) 7 — 31
(Shaun Harris) *trckd ldrs: hdwy over 3f out: rdn and hung lft wl over 2f out: drvn wl over 1f out: kpt on same pce* **40/1**

0243 **4** 3 **Cockney Boy**[6] 8984 4-9-2 **47**.....(vt) LukeMorris 6 — 26
(Michael Appleby) *in tch: pushed along and hdwy over 3f out: wd st and sn chsng ldrs: rdn wl over 1f out: sn drvn and one pce* **9/2**[3]

0044 **5** 4 **Jennies Gem**[19] 8784 4-9-1 **46**..... AndrewMullen 12 — 16
(Ollie Pears) *towards rr: pushed along and hdwy on outer over 3f out: wd st and sn rdn: plugged on one pce fnl 2f* **10/1**

0-00 **6** ¾ **Red Douglas**[3] 9034 3-9-2 **48**.....(p[1]) KieranO'Neill 11 — 16
(Scott Dixon) *dwlt: hdwy to chse ldrs after 3f: prom over 3f out: rdn along wl over 2f out: sn drvn and wknd* **25/1**

3406 **7** nk **Dragonite (IRE)**[21] 8770 3-9-0 **46** ow1..... DougieCostello 1 — 13
(Daniel Mark Loughnane) *a towards rr* **25/1**

0-30 **8** ½ **Poppy May (IRE)**[315] 377 3-9-4 **50**..... TomEaves 4 — 16
(James Given) *slt ld 2f: cl up: rdn along whn bmpd wl over 2f out: sn drvn and wknd* **33/1**

0000 **9** nk **Nifty Niece (IRE)**[30] 8590 3-8-13 **45**..... ShaneGray 9 — 10
(Ann Duffield) *prom: rdn along over 3f out: sn wknd* **50/1**

65-4 **10** nk **Jock Talk (IRE)**[38] 8406 3-9-6 **52**.....(t) JoeFanning 10 — 16
(Gordon Elliott, Ire) *dwlt: sn rdn along: a in rr* **7/2**[2]

000/ **11** 1 ¼ **Madame Mime Artist**[1342] 1235 6-9-5 **50**..... RaulDaSilva 5 — 11
(Natalie Lloyd-Beavis) *cl up: slt ld after 2f: rdn along 3f out: sn hdd & wknd* **100/1**

1m 43.62s (-0.08) **Going Correction** -0.10s/f (Stan)
**WFA** 3 from 4yo+ 1lb — 11 Ran SP% **117.9**
Speed ratings (Par 101): **96,95,86,83,79 78,78,77,77,77 75**
CSF £15.45 CT £376.10 TOTE £6.60: £1.70, £1.10, £7.20; EX 21.80 Trifecta £414.60.
**Owner** Adams, Allen, Blades, Bruton & Ellis **Bred** A S Denniff **Trained** Settrington, N Yorks

**FOCUS**
The first division of a moderate maiden handicap. They went a respectable gallop and the hot favourite couldn't quite pick up the new leader in the second part of the straight. A step up from the winner.

## 9073 SUNBETS.CO.UK MAIDEN H'CAP (DIV II) — 1m 13y(F)
**1:20** (1:20) (Class 6) (0-55,54) 3-Y-0+ — £2,264 (£673; £336; £168) Stalls Low

Form — RPR

0063 **1** **Sonnet Rose (IRE)**[5] 8994 3-8-8 **49**.....(bt) SebastianWoods(7) 10 — 60+
(Conrad Allen) *cl up: led over 3f out: clr 2f out: rdn ins fnl f: edgd lft and kpt on wl* **9/2**[3]

0006 **2** 4 ½ **Trois Bon Amis (IRE)**[46] 8193 3-8-12 **46**.....(t) KieranO'Neill 3 — 46
(Mark Campion) *prom: cl up over 3f out: rdn over 2f out: sn chsng wnr: drvn and kpt on same pce fnl f* **50/1**

6500 **3** 4 ½ **Pentito Rap (USA)**[170] 3819 3-8-11 **45**..... DanielMuscutt 9 — 34
(Rod Millman) *trckd ldrs: hdwy over 3f out: rdn along over 2f out: drvn wl over 1f out: kpt on same pce* **9/2**[3]

4453 **4** 2 ¼ **Queen Moon (IRE)**[43] 8255 3-9-2 **50**..... DavidProbert 6 — 34
(Andrew Balding) *n.m.r after s and sn towards rr: rdn along wl over 3f out: hdwy over 2f out: kpt on fr over 1f out: n.d* **11/4**[2]

5000 **5** 1 **Holyroman Princess**[152] 4494 3-8-11 **45**.....(v) GeorgeDowning 11 — 27
(Daniel Kubler) *towards rr: rdn along and wd st: styd on u.p fnl 2f* **33/1**

**6** ¾ **Emigrated (IRE)**[134] 4549 4-8-12 **45**.....(v) PatrickMathers 7 — 25
(Derek Shaw) *n.m.r and hmpd sn after s: towards rr and sn swtchd rt to outer: hdwy and wd st: rdn to chse ldrs 2f out: drvn and no imp over 1f out* **25/1**

0000 **7** 4 ½ **Kensington Palace (IRE)**[6] 8980 4-9-0 **47**.....(p) JoeyHaynes 5 — 16
(Marjorie Fife) *sn outpcd and a bhd* **16/1**

0000 **8** shd **Poet's Quest**[11] 8908 3-8-11 **45**.....(v[1]) LukeMorris 4 — 14
(Michael Appleby) *cl up: slt ld 1/2-way: rdn along and hdd over 3f out: sn drvn and wknd over 2f out* **50/1**

000 **9** hd **Three's A Crowd (IRE)**[74] 7323 3-9-4 **52**..... LiamKeniry 1 — 20
(Ed de Giles) *slt ld: hdd 1/2-way: cl up: rdn along 3f out and sn wknd* **22/1**

4050 **10** nk **Machiavelian Storm (IRE)**[109] 6102 5-8-5 **45**.....(t[1]) WilliamCox(7) 2 — 13
(Richard Mitchell) *sn outpcd and a bhd* **100/1**

-000 **11** 3 ¾ **Touch Of Color**[32] 8551 4-9-0 **47**..... JackGarritty 12 — 6
(Richard Fahey) *chsd ldrs: rdn along 3f out: sn wknd* **16/1**

4430 **12** 7 **Gatillo**[6] 8985 4-9-4 **54**.....(p[1]) ShelleyBirkett(3) 8
(Julia Feilden) *dwlt: sn chsng ldrs on outer: hdwy 3f out: rdn over 2f out: sn wknd* **9/4**[1]

1m 43.39s (-0.31) **Going Correction** -0.10s/f (Stan)
**WFA** 3 from 4yo+ 1lb — 12 Ran SP% **121.6**
Speed ratings (Par 101): **97,92,88,85,84 84,79,79,79,78 75,68**
CSF £227.84 CT £1109.11 TOTE £5.00: £1.70, £12.70, £1.80; EX 173.20 Trifecta £1703.80.
**Owner** John C Davies **Bred** J C Davies **Trained** Newmarket, Suffolk

**FOCUS**
The second division of a moderate maiden handicap. The winning time was marginally quicker and a personal best from the winner.

## 9074 BETWAY SPRINT H'CAP — 6f 16y(F)
**1:50** (1:52) (Class 4) (0-85,87) 3-Y-0+ — £4,690 (£1,395; £697; £348) Stalls Low

Form — RPR

2060 **1** **Mujassam**[18] 8803 5-8-12 **80**.....(b) PatrickVaughan(7) 1 — 90
(David O'Meara) *midfield: hdwy 2f out: chsd ldrs over 1f out: rdn ent fnl f: qcknd to ld last 75yds* **25/1**

1035 **2** 1 **Tricky Dicky**[34] 8489 4-9-5 **80**..... SamJames 11 — 87
(Olly Williams) *prom: chal wl over 1f out: rdn to ld ent fnl f: sn drvn: hdd and no ex last 75yds* **5/1**[2]

3020 **3** ¾ **Treaty Of Rome (USA)**[18] 8803 5-8-13 **74**.....(v) PatrickMathers 5 — 78
(Derek Shaw) *hld up towards rr: hdwy on inner 2f out: rdn over 1f out: drvn and styd on wl fnl f* **15/2**[3]

-306 **4** 1 ¼ **Cashla Bay**[24] 8717 3-9-3 **78**.....(bt[1]) RobertHavlin 4 — 78
(John Gosden) *t.k.h: trckd ldrs: hdwy 2f out: rdn over 1f out: sn drvn and kpt on same pce fnl f* **12/1**

1106 **5** nk **Gnaad (IRE)**[18] 8803 3-9-1 **76**..... LiamKeniry 6 — 75
(Alan Bailey) *dwlt and towards rr: hdwy towards inner over 2f out: rdn to chse ldrs over 1f out: drvn and kpt on same pce fnl f* **16/1**

0361 **6** 1 **Call Out Loud**[3] 9020 5-9-6 **81**.....(vt) AlistairRawlinson 13 — 77
(Michael Appleby) *chsd ldrs: rdn along over 2f out: drvn over 1f out: kpt on same pce* **4/1**[1]

0040 **7** ¾ **Zapper Cass (FR)**[18] 8803 4-8-13 **74**.....(t) BenCurtis 7 — 68
(Tony Coyle) *towards rr: hdwy over 2f out: sn rdn and kpt on fnl f* **25/1**

2060 **8** ½ **Gin In The Inn (IRE)**[38] 8393 4-9-12 **87**..... JackGarritty 8 — 79
(Richard Fahey) *dwlt: a towards rr* **12/1**

2004 **9** ½ **Razin' Hell**[18] 8803 6-9-7 **82**.....(v) AndrewMullen 3 — 73
(John Balding) *slt ld: rdn along wl over 2f out: drvn over 1f out: hdd ent fnl f: sn wknd* **10/1**

0633 **10** 1 ¾ **Crosse Fire**[18] 8803 5-8-12 **73**.....(p) KieranO'Neill 10 — 58
(Scott Dixon) *cl up: rdn along over 2f out: drvn wl over 1f out: grad wknd* **10/1**

0344 **11** shd **Penny Dreadful**[9] 8950 5-8-3 **69**.....(p) JamieGormley(5) 14 — 54
(Scott Dixon) *dwlt: sn cl up on outer: rdn along over 2f out: sn drvn and wknd* **33/1**

3550 **12** nk **Aguerooo (IRE)**[133] 5211 4-9-6 **81**.....(p) HollieDoyle 9 — 65
(Ollie Pears) *a towards rr* **16/1**

6502 **13** 1 ¼ **Adam's Ale**[34] 8489 8-9-3 **78**.....(p) CamHardie 12 — 58
(Marjorie Fife) *a towards rr* **40/1**

1145 **14** 11 **Boost**[14] 8872 3-9-6 **81**.....(v[1]) LukeMorris 2 — 26
(Sir Mark Prescott Bt) *chsd ldrs on inner: pushed along over 3f out: rdn wl over 2f out: sn wknd* **15/2**[3]

1m 15.38s (-1.12) **Going Correction** -0.10s/f (Stan) — 14 Ran SP% **118.6**
Speed ratings (Par 105): **103,101,100,99,98 97,96,95,94,92 92,92,90,75**
CSF £140.07 CT £1080.89 TOTE £32.90: £7.60, £2.10, £2.30; EX 236.20 Trifecta £1666.80.
**Owner** Thoroughbred British Racing **Bred** Bumble Bs, D F Powell & S Nicholls **Trained** Upper Helmsley, N Yorks

**FOCUS**
The feature contest was a decent sprint handicap. They went a respectable gallop and there is no obvious reason to doubt the form despite the lengthy price of the winner. He has been rated similar to the last time he ran over 6f.

## 9075 BETWAY DASH H'CAP — 4f 214y(F)
**2:20** (2:26) (Class 6) (0-55,55) 3-Y-0+ — £2,264 (£673; £336; £168) Stalls Centre

Form — RPR

0036 **1** **Archie Stevens**[34] 8494 7-9-0 **51**..... PaddyPilley(3) 10 — 62
(Clare Ellam) *racd towards stands' side: cl up: led 3f out: rdn over 1f out: hung lft ins fnl f: drvn out* **22/1**

0005 **2** 1 **Something Lucky (IRE)**[55] 7912 5-9-0 **48**.....(p) LukeMorris 1 — 55
(Michael Appleby) *racd towards far side: prom: hdwy 2f out: rdn over 1f out: chal ent fnl f: ev ch and drvn: flashed tail and no ex towards fin* **2/1**[1]

0423 **3** 1 ½ **Silver Penny**[42] 8298 3-8-12 **46**.....(p) DavidProbert 6 — 48
(Jim Boyle) *chsd ldrs centre: hdwy 2f out: swtchd rt and rdn over 1f out: kpt on fnl f* **8/1**[3]

2026 **4** nk **Bond Bombshell**[14] 8873 4-9-0 **55**.....(b[1]) PatrickVaughan(7) 2 — 56
(David O'Meara) *dwlt: in tch nr far rail: rdn along to chse ldrs over 1f out: n.m.r and swtchd rt ins fnl f: kpt on towards fin* **11/1**

6040 **5** ½ **Racing Angel (IRE)**[10] 8924 5-9-6 **54**..... AndrewMullen 4 — 53+
(Adrian Nicholls) *dwlt and in rr towards far side: swtchd rt and hdwy wl over 1f out: rdn and kpt on fnl f* **10/1**

0050 **6** 1 ½ **Roy's Legacy**[55] 7926 8-8-11 **48**..... CharlieBennett(3) 7 — 42
(Shaun Harris) *cl up centre: rdn along 2f out: drvn over 1f out: grad wknd* **25/1**

0000 **7** ¾ **Lackaday**[34] 8490 5-9-2 **50**.....(p) JoeFanning 3 — 41
(Noel Wilson) *racd towards far side: slt ld: hdd over 3f out: rdn wl over 1f out: grad wknd* **7/1**[2]

0463 **8** nk **Sarabi**[21] 8772 4-9-1 **54**.....(bt) JamieGormley(5) 13 — 44
(Scott Dixon) *dwlt: a towards stands' side* **7/1**[2]

4265 **9** ½ **Excellent Aim**[250] 1435 10-9-2 **55**..... JaneElliott(5) 11 — 43
(George Margarson) *chsd ldrs towards centre: rdn along over 2f out: sn no imp* **33/1**

0602 **10** 1 ½ **Novabridge**[21] 8776 9-8-12 **51**.....(b) GemmaTutty(5) 5 — 34
(Karen Tutty) *racd towards far side: chsd ldrs: rdn wl over 1f out: wknd appr fnl f* **11/1**

1000 **11** 1 ½ **Tea El Tee (IRE)**[63] 7692 3-9-5 **53**.....(v) MartinDwyer 8 — 30
(Gay Kelleway) *dwlt: sn outpcd and a bhd* **16/1**

-000 **12** 3 **Roger Thorpe**[98] 6528 8-9-1 **49**..... BenCurtis 12 — 16
(John Balding) *a towards rr stands' side* **25/1**

60-0 **13** 9 **Monsieur Jamie**[21] 8775 9-8-11 **52**..... WilliamCox(7) 14
(Clare Ellam) *dwlt: a towards rr stands' side* **66/1**

59.4s (-0.30) **Going Correction** -0.025s/f (Stan) — 13 Ran SP% **117.6**
Speed ratings (Par 101): **101,99,97,96,95 93,92,91,90,88 86,81,66**
CSF £62.34 CT £418.09 TOTE £22.50: £5.30, £1.20, £2.90; EX 97.70 Trifecta £1165.90.
**Owner** Miss Clare Louise Ellam **Bred** Howard Barton Stud **Trained** Market Drayton, Shropshire

**FOCUS**
A moderate sprint handicap. The main action unfolded towards the far rail. The winner has fallen a long way in the weights.

## 9076 SUNBETS.CO.UK H'CAP — 7f 14y(F)
**2:50** (2:53) (Class 6) (0-60,62) 4-Y-0+ — £2,264 (£673; £336; £168) Stalls Low

Form — RPR

2024 **1** **Bold Spirit**[3] 9029 6-9-6 **62**.....(t) PhilDennis(3) 5 — 72
(Declan Carroll) *trckd ldrs: smooth hdwy to ld 2f out: rdn appr fnl f: kpt on strly* **7/4**[1]

/- **2** 3 ¾ **Why Me**[54] 7966 7-8-8 **47**..... BenCurtis 3 — 47
(Gavin Cromwell, Ire) *midfield: hdwy 3f out: chsd ldrs wl over 1f out: sn rdn: styd on fnl f* **2/1**[2]

1300 **3** ½ **Barista (IRE)**[27] 8662 9-9-6 **59**..... HollieDoyle 10 — 58
(Brian Forsey) *dwlt and towards rr: hdwy on inner over 2f out: rdn to chse ldrs over 1f out: drvn and kpt on fnl f* **25/1**

0050 **4** 1 ¼ **Big Amigo (IRE)**[21] 8772 4-9-4 **60**..... EoinWalsh(3) 9 — 55
(Daniel Mark Loughnane) *chsd ldrs: rdn along over 3f out: drvn wl over 1f out: kpt on fnl f* **14/1**

1000 **5** 1 ¾ **Bingo George (IRE)**[6] 8980 4-8-13 **52**.....(t[1]) RobHornby 11 — 42
(Mark Rimell) *chsd ldrs on outer: wd st: rdn along 2f out: drvn over 1f out: kpt on one pce* **28/1**

4352 **6** nk **Limerick Lord (IRE)**[77] 7212 5-8-4 **46**.....(p) ShelleyBirkett(3) 13 — 36
(Julia Feilden) *cl up: led 3f out: rdn along over 2f out: sn hdd: drvn over 1f out: sn wknd and edgd rt ins fnl f* **12/1**

4500 **7** *hd* **Sir Lancelott**[44] 8248 5-9-0 **53** ........................(b[1]) JoeFanning 14 42
(Adrian Nicholls) *cl up on outer: chal wl over 2f out: sn rdn and ev ch: drvn and wknd over 1f out* **25/1**

/0-0 **8** *3 ¼* **Hugie Boy (IRE)**[18] 8807 5-9-4 **57**........................(tp) KieranO'Neill 6 37
(Scott Dixon) *slt ld: rdn along and hdd over 3f out: sn drvn and wknd* **66/1**

0640 **9** *nk* **Maggie Pink**[11] 8907 8-9-7 **60**........................ AlistairRawlinson 8 39
(Michael Appleby) *chsd ldrs: rdn along over 3f out: wd st: sn drvn and wknd* **9/1[3]**

040- **10** *2 ¼* **Madakheel (USA)**[636] 867 6-8-7 **46** oh1........................ JimmyQuinn 12 19
(Simon West) *a towards rr* **100/1**

0000 **11** *6* **Mette**[9] 8949 4-8-0 **46** oh1........................(t) NicolaCurrie[(7)] 2
(Mark Usher) *in tch on inner: rdn along over 3f out: sn wknd* **66/1**

4500 **12** *3 ½* **Le Laitier (FR)**[21] 8776 6-8-7 **46** oh1........................(p[1]) LukeMorris 4
(Scott Dixon) *a towards rr* **50/1**

0060 **13** *½* **Royal Holiday (IRE)**[53] 7979 10-8-13 **52**........................(p) JoeyHaynes 1
(Marjorie Fife) *v.s.a: a bhd* **25/1**

4250 **14** *9* **Trust Me Boy**[98] 6529 9-8-12 **51**........................(p[1]) RobertHavlin 7
(John E Long) *a towards rr* **25/1**

1m 29.21s (-1.09) **Going Correction** -0.10s/f (Stan) **14 Ran SP% 118.8**
Speed ratings (Par 101): **102,97,97,95,93 93,93,89,89,86 79,75,75,64**
CSF £4.57 CT £63.03 TOTE £2.50: £1.30, £1.60, £4.10; EX 6.50 Trifecta £66.00.
**Owner** Mrs Sarah Bryan **Bred** The Queen **Trained** Malton, N Yorks

**FOCUS**
A modest handicap. The favourite outclassed this opposition off a respectable tempo and has been rated to his highest mark since 2014.

## 9077 BETWAY CASINO H'CAP 1m 3f 23y(F)
**3:20** (3:22) (Class 6) (0-60,60) 4-Y-O+ **£2,264** (£673; £336; £168) **Stalls** Low

Form RPR

4554 **1** **Star Ascending (IRE)**[37] 8430 5-8-9 **48**........................(b[1]) JoeFanning 7 57
(Jennie Candlish) *dwlt: hdwy into midfield after 3f: trckd ldrs 4f out: chsd ldr over 2f out: rdn to ld over 1f out: edgd lft ins fnl f: drvn out* **10/3[2]**

0420 **2** *2 ¼* **Lean On Pete (IRE)**[69] 7479 8-9-6 **59**........................ AndrewMullen 8 64
(Ollie Pears) *led: pushed along over 3f out: rdn over 2f out: hdd and drvn over 1f out: swtchd rt ins fnl f: kpt on* **8/1[3]**

0000 **3** *6* **Dream Serenade**[14] 8876 4-8-12 **51**........................(p[1]) LukeMorris 13 47
(Michael Appleby) *cl up on outer: chal over 3f out: rdn and ev ch over 2f out: drvn over 1f out: kpt on one pce* **20/1**

4400 **4** *1 ¼* **Just Fred (IRE)**[16] 8846 4-8-7 **46** oh1........................(t) JimmyQuinn 3 40
(Neil Mulholland) *hld up in tch: hdwy over 3f out: chsd ldrs over 2f out: sn rdn: drvn over 1f out: no imp* **16/1**

0000 **5** *6* **Etaad (USA)**[11] 8909 6-9-7 **60**........................(b) JasonHart 10 44
(Lucinda Egerton) *sn pushed along in rr: rdn along and hdwy 3f out: drvn and plugged on u.p fnl 2f* **25/1**

6000 **6** *4* **St Patrick's Day (IRE)**[45] 7792 5-9-4 **57**........................(v) DougieCostello 5 35
(J R Jenkins) *towards rr tl styd on fnl 3f: n.d* **8/1[3]**

4006 **7** *1* **Saga Sprint (IRE)**[40] 8346 4-8-11 **50**........................(p) ShaneGray 9 26
(J R Jenkins) *chsd ldrs: rdn along 3f out: sn drvn and wknd fnl 2f* **22/1**

5500 **8** *1 ¼* **Highwayman**[45] 8218 4-9-1 **54**........................(p[1]) RobertHavlin 1 28
(David Thompson) *in tch: rdn along 4f out: sn outpcd* **33/1**

3040 **9** *4 ½* **Port Lairge**[6] 8985 7-8-4 **46** oh1........................ PhilDennis[(3)] 14 13
(Michael Chapman) *a towards rr* **50/1**

0305 **10** *¾* **Flying Power**[37] 8430 9-8-7 **46** oh1........................(p) PatrickMathers 2 12
(John Norton) *chsd ldrs on inner: rdn along over 3f out: sn drvn and wknd* **12/1**

5220 **11** *16* **Never Say (IRE)**[140] 4980 4-8-2 **46**........................(p) JaneElliott[(5)] 12
(Sam England) *racd in midfield: rdn along over 3f out: sn wknd* **25/1**

0600 **12** *¾* **Arquus (IRE)**[40] 8345 4-8-7 **46** oh1........................ RobHornby 11
(Ed de Giles) *cl up: rdn along on inner over 3f out: sn drvn and wknd* **33/1**

00 **13** *58* **Tuolumne Meadows**[16] 8846 4-9-1 **52**........................ EoinWalsh[(3)] 6
(Tony Newcombe) *a towards rr: bhd fnl 3f* **25/1**

**U** **Siempre Amigos (IRE)**[16] 8337 4-9-3 **56**........................ BenCurtis 4
(Gavin Cromwell, Ire) *hld up: hdwy on outer over 5f out: in tch and rdn along on outer whn uns rdr 3f out* **2/1[1]**

2m 25.64s (-2.36) **Going Correction** -0.10s/f (Stan) **14 Ran SP% 120.7**
Speed ratings (Par 101): **104,102,98,97,92 89,89,88,84,84 72,72,30,**
CSF £26.50 CT £473.86 TOTE £4.50: £2.10, £2.40, £4.40; EX 35.30 Trifecta £353.70.
**Owner** Paul Wright-Bevans **Bred** Philip Gilligan & Anne Gilligan **Trained** Basford Green, Staffs
■ Stewards' Enquiry : Dougie Costello two-day ban: caused interference (Dec 18-19)

**FOCUS**
A modest middle-distance handicap. They went a respectable gallop and the second-favourite was well on top by the finish. The runner-up is a fair guide to the form.
T/Jkpt: Not Won. T/Plt: £107.50 to a £1 stake. Pool: £56,477.03 - 383.18 winning units T/Qpdt: £31.10 to a £1 stake. Pool: £8,706.30 - 206.51 winning units **Joe Rowntree**

# 9049 WOLVERHAMPTON (A.W) (L-H)
Tuesday, December 5

**OFFICIAL GOING: Tapeta: standard**
Wind: Light, behind Weather: Overcast

## 9078 BETWAY APPRENTICE H'CAP 1m 1f 104y (Tp)
**12:40** (12:41) (Class 5) (0-75,74) 4-Y-O+ **£3,234** (£962; £481; £240) **Stalls** Low

Form RPR

4502 **1** **Pink Ribbon (IRE)**[10] 8946 5-8-10 **63**........................ FinleyMarsh 8 68
(Sylvester Kirk) *t.k.h: led tl 8f out: chsd ldr tl over 5f out: styd handy tl effrt to chse ldr again over 1f out: styd on u.p ins fnl f to ld towards fin* **13/2**

2006 **2** *½* **Berlusca (IRE)**[18] 8813 8-8-9 **62**........................ NicolaCurrie 7 66
(David Loughnane) *stdd s: t.k.h: hdwy to ld 8f out: rdn over 1f out: kpt on u.p tl hdd and no ex towards fin* **10/1**

1022 **3** *shd* **Jack Of Diamonds (IRE)**[18] 8813 8-9-1 **68**........................ TylerSaunders 3 72
(Roger Teal) *s.i.s: hld up in last trio: effrt on outer 3f out: edging lft over 1f out: hdwy to chse ldrs 1f out: kpt on wl ins fnl f: nvr quite getting to ldrs* **9/4[1]**

5050 **4** *1* **Archipeligo**[12] 8912 6-9-1 **68**........................(p) JamieGormley 2 70
(Iain Jardine) *hld up in tch in midfield: swtchd rt and effrt over 1f out: kpt on ins fnl f: chsng ldrs and keeping on same pce whn nt clrest of runs towards fin* **5/1[3]**

4020 **5** *shd* **Perceived**[55] 7960 5-8-11 **64**........................ WilliamCox 5 66
(Antony Brittain) *hld up in tch in midfield: effrt whn nt clr run and swtchd rt over 1f out: hdwy ins fnl f: styd on wl u.p fnl 100yds: nt rch ldrs* **25/1**

0630 **6** *nk* **The Gay Cavalier**[4] 9027 6-8-7 **60**........................(t) JackOsborn 6 61
(John Ryan) *s.i.s: hld up in tch in last pair: effrt whn nt clr run over 1f out: swtchd lft jst ins fnl f: kpt on fnl 100yds: nt rch ldrs* **8/1**

0500 **7** *¾* **Boycie**[62] 7735 4-9-7 **74**........................ RossaRyan 4 73
(Richard Hannon) *chsd ldr tl over 8f out: styd chsng ldrs: wnt 2nd again over 5f out tl 4f out: rdn over 2f out: struggling to qckn whn squeezed for room over 1f out: kpt on same pce ins fnl f* **4/1[2]**

4646 **8** *2 ¼* **Tigerwolf (IRE)**[41] 8341 4-8-9 **67**........................ TobyEley[(5)] 1 62
(Daniel Mark Loughnane) *stdd after s: t.k.h: hld up in tch in rr: swtchd rt and hdwy on outer as sddle shifted forward 5f out: chsd ldr 4f out tl lost 2nd and drifted rt over 1f out: wknd ins fnl f* **13/2**

2m 2.93s (2.13) **Going Correction** -0.075s/f (Stan) **8 Ran SP% 118.2**
Speed ratings (Par 103): **87,86,86,85,85 85,84,82**
CSF £70.45 CT £192.60 TOTE £3.40: £1.02, £4.30, £2.20; EX 74.80 Trifecta £262.50.
**Owner** T R Lock **Bred** Ann & Joe Hallinan **Trained** Upper Lambourn, Berks

**FOCUS**
This ordinary handicap was steadily run and suited those ridden prominently.

## 9079 BETWAY DASH H'CAP 5f 21y (Tp)
**1:10** (1:10) (Class 4) (0-85,85) 3-Y-O+ **£4,851** (£1,082; £1,082; £360) **Stalls** Low

Form RPR

4500 **1** **Union Rose**[48] 8167 5-9-3 **81**........................(p[1]) DavidProbert 4 88
(Ronald Harris) *chsd ldrs: effrt over 1f out: nt clr run 1f out: gap opened and hdwy to chse ldr wl ins fnl f: r.o strly u.p to ld towards fin* **9/1**

3000 **2** *nk* **Fast Track**[12] 8913 6-9-4 **82**........................ BenCurtis 1 88
(David Barron) *stmbld leaving stalls: hld up in tch in last trio: effrt on inner over 1f out: hdwy u.p and ev ch wl ins fnl f: styd on* **10/3[2]**

6410 **2** *dht* **Tilly Trotter (IRE)**[5] 9016 3-9-4 **82**........................ TomEaves 10 88
(Declan Carroll) *taken down early: w ldr tl led over 1f out: sn rdn: drvn ins fnl f: kpt on tl hdd and no ex towards fin* **13/2[3]**

1460 **4** *1* **Dynamo Walt (IRE)**[33] 8540 6-9-7 **85**........................(v) PatrickMathers 3 87
(Derek Shaw) *chsd ldng trio: effrt over 1f out: rdn to chse ldr 1f out: sn drvn and unable qck: kpt on same pce and lost 2 pls wl ins fnl f* **16/1**

6125 **5** *1* **Landing Night (IRE)**[12] 8913 5-9-3 **81**........................(tp) PJMcDonald 2 80
(Rebecca Menzies) *hld up in tch in midfield: effrt over 1f out: hanging lft 1f out: kpt on towards fin: unable to threaten ldrs* **2/1[1]**

5005 **6** *1 ¼* **Top Boy**[33] 8540 7-8-10 **77**........................(v) CallumShepherd[(3)] 7 71
(Derek Shaw) *bmpd s: hld up in last pair: effrt over 1f out: swtchd lft ent fnl f: kpt on ins fnl f: nvr trbld ldrs* **9/1**

0000 **7** *½* **Old Fashioned (CHI)**[12] 8913 5-9-7 **85**........................(bt) EdwardGreatrex 5 77
(Luke McJannet) *taken down early: mde most tl rdn and hdd over 1f out: wknd ins fnl f* **66/1**

1435 **8** *2* **Upavon**[28] 8660 7-9-3 **84**........................(t) AaronJones[(3)] 9 69
(Stuart Williams) *hld up in tch in midfield: effrt over 1f out: no imp: nvr threatened ldrs: burst blood vessel* **9/1**

0006 **9** *4* **Rich Again (IRE)**[12] 8913 8-9-5 **83**........................(b) JoeFanning 8 54
(James Bethell) *stdd and short of room leaving stalls: sn swtchd lft and hld up in rr: n.d* **10/1**

1m 1.01s (-0.89) **Going Correction** -0.075s/f (Stan) **9 Ran SP% 116.2**
Speed ratings (Par 105): **104,103,103,101,100 98,97,94,87**
WIN: Union Rose 12.70; PL: Fast Track 1.30, Union Rose 3.00, Tilly Trotter 2.20; EX: UR/TT 38.00, UR/FT 24.50; CSF: UR/TT 33.27, UR/FT 19.70; TC: UR/TT/FT 119.04, UR/FT/TT 106.56; TF: UR/TT/FT 161.80, UR/FT/TT 166.60.
**Owner** Adrian Evans **Bred** Home Farm **Trained** Earlswood, Monmouths

**FOCUS**
A competitive sprint handicap with the fourth helping set the standard.

## 9080 32RED CASINO FILLIES' NOVICE STKS (PLUS 10 RACE) (DIV I) 7f 36y (Tp)
**1:40** (1:40) (Class 5) 2-Y-O **£3,234** (£962; £481; £240) **Stalls** High

Form RPR

03 **1** **American Endeavour (USA)**[27] 8670 2-9-0 0........................ DanielMuscutt 5 71
(Marco Botti) *chsd clr ldr: clsd to ld and drifted rt whn shkn up 1f out: rdn ins fnl f: styd on and a doing enough* **7/2[2]**

6 **2** *nk* **Lady Noorah**[17] 8839 2-9-0 0........................ JackGarritty 6 70
(Richard Fahey) *chsd ldng pair: clsd over 1f out and chsd wnr whn edgd lft and sltly impeded 1f out: kpt on ins fnl f: a hld* **40/1**

6211 **3** *2* **Bath And Tennis (IRE)**[40] 8373 2-10-0 **82**........................(b) LukeMorris 2 79
(Sir Mark Prescott Bt) *racd v freely: led and sn dashed clr: rdn and hdd 1f out: no ex and wknd ins fnl f* **7/4[1]**

**4** *1 ½* **Sun Maiden** 2-9-0 0........................ DavidProbert 8 61
(Sir Michael Stoute) *s.i.s: rn green early and wl off the pce in rr: hdwy and swtchd rt over 2f out: styd on strly ins fnl f: nvr trbld ldrs* **7/2[2]**

**5** *½* **Nautica (IRE)** 2-9-0 0........................ RobHornby 4 60
(Jonathan Portman) *prom in chsng gp but nvr on terms w ldrs: rdn and rn green over 2f out: kpt on ins fnl f: nvr trbld ldrs* **66/1**

**6** *2* **Smart Dart** 2-9-0 0........................ RichardKingscote 10 55
(Ralph Beckett) *midfield but nvr on terms w ldrs: rdn over 2f out: kpt on but nvr trbld ldrs* **17/2**

546 **7** *6* **Diva Star**[77] 7226 2-8-7 **70**........................(t[1]) TylerSaunders[(7)] 11 41
(Marcus Tregoning) *s.i.s: off the pce towards rr: hung lft u.p over 1f out: nvr trbld ldrs* **16/1**

**8** *5* **Wallflower (IRE)** 2-9-0 0........................ MartinDwyer 1 28
(Rae Guest) *sn off the pce in rr: n.d* **50/1**

0 **9** *1 ½* **Matilda Grace (IRE)**[12] 8916 2-9-0 0........................ RyanPowell 7 25
(Lisa Williamson) *s.i.s: midfield but nvr on terms w ldrs: rdn 3f out: sn struggling and wl btn over 1f out* **100/1**

**10** *14* **Just Right** 2-8-9 0........................ WilliamCox[(5)] 3
(John Flint) *v.s.a: a wl bhd* **100/1**

5 **P** **Fyxenna**[36] 8472 2-9-0 0........................(p[1]) MartinHarley 9
(Clive Cox) *chsd ldrs: lost action sn after s and p.u over 6f out: dismntd* **15/2[3]**

1m 29.22s (0.42) **Going Correction** -0.075s/f (Stan) **11 Ran SP% 116.9**
Speed ratings (Par 93): **94,93,91,89,89 86,79,74,72,56**
CSF £137.97 TOTE £5.50: £1.50, £3.80, £1.10; EX 89.30 Trifecta £378.50.
**Owner** A J Suited & Gute Freunde Partnership **Bred** Baumann Stables **Trained** Newmarket, Suffolk
■ Stewards' Enquiry : Daniel Muscutt caution: allowed mount to hang right-handed into the whip without timely correction

**FOCUS**
This was run at a good gallop thanks to the free-running favourite.

## 9081 32RED CASINO FILLIES' NOVICE STKS (PLUS 10 RACE) (DIV II) 7f 36y (Tp)
**2:10** (2:15) (Class 5) 2-Y-O **£3,234** (£962; £481; £240) **Stalls** High

Form RPR

3 **1** **Point Hope (IRE)**[171] 3815 2-9-0 0........................ TomMarquand 2 70
(Richard Hannon) *chsd ldrs: rdn and clsd to chal 2f out: led 1f out: hld on wl ins fnl f: rdn out* **9/4[1]**

0 **2** *nk* **Allante (IRE)**[71] 7453 2-9-0 0........................ KieranShoemark 10 70
(Sir Michael Stoute) *hld up in tch: effrt and hdwy over 1f out: chsd wnr jst ins fnl f: ev ch ins fnl f: kpt on wl but hld towards fin* **12/1**

000 **3** 1 3/4 **Lady Of Authority**139 [5026] 2-9-0 49 ShaneKelly 4 65
(Murty McGrath) *hld up in tch in midfield: nt clr run and swtchd rt wl over 1f out: rdn and hdwy 1f out: kpt on wl to go 3rd towards fin* **200/1**

02 **4** 1/2 **Poetic Imagination**17 [8840] 2-9-0 0 RobertHavlin 11 64
(John Gosden) *chsd ldr tl led ent fnl 2f: rdn over 1f out: hdd 1f out: no ex and outpcd fnl 100yds* **3/1**2

**5** 1/2 **La Mernancia (IRE)** 2-9-0 0 DougieCostello 5 63
(Jamie Osborne) *s.i.s: rn green and hld up in last trio: hdwy over 1f out: rdn ins fnl f: kpt on: nt rch ldrs* **33/1**

**6** *nk* **Fresh Terms** 2-9-0 0 RichardKingscote 1 62
(Ralph Beckett) *chsd ldrs: effrt on inner but unable qck over 1f out: kpt on same pce ins fnl f* **6/1**3

0 **7** 3/4 **Astroblaze**41 [8347] 2-9-0 0 JoeyHaynes 8 60
(Mark H Tompkins) *hld up in midfield: effrt on outer over 2f out: kpt on ins fnl f: nvr trbld ldrs* **200/1**

4 **8** 1 3/4 **Catoca (USA)**27 [8670] 2-9-0 0 LiamKeniry 7 56
(Ed Walker) *s.i.s: hld up in last trio: rdn and effrt on outer wl over 2f out: kpt on but nvr threatened ldrs* **9/4**1

6 **9** 1/2 **Thistimelastyear**48 [8147] 2-9-0 0 TomEaves 6 55
(Philip Hide) *hld up in tch towards rr: effrt and rdn over 1f out: no imp* **80/1**

0 **10** 1 **Inch Pincher**19 [8794] 2-9-0 0 DavidProbert 9 52
(Rae Guest) *stdd after s: hld up in rr: n.d* **100/1**

00 **11** 24 **Supermoss**27 [8670] 2-9-0 0 PJMcDonald 3
(Heather Main) *led tl rdn and hdd ent fnl 2f: sn dropped out: wl bhd and virtually p.u ins fnl f* **40/1**

1m 29.33s (0.53) **Going Correction** -0.075s/f (Stan) 11 Ran SP% **117.1**
Speed ratings (Par 93): **94,93,91,91,90 90,89,87,86,85 58**
CSF £30.79 TOTE £2.90: £1.40, £4.00, £13.50; EX 34.00 Trifecta £2235.20.
**Owner** Denford Stud **Bred** Knocktartan House Stud **Trained** East Everleigh, Wilts
**FOCUS**
The slower of the two divisions by 0.11sec.

## 9082 BETWAY STAYERS H'CAP 2m 120y (Tp)
**2:40** (2:41) (Class 4) (0-85,87) 3-Y-O+ **£4,851** (£1,443; £721; £360) **Stalls** Low

Form RPR
-001 **1** **Captain Navarre**34 [8505] 5-9-10 **81** (v) ShaneKelly 1 89+
(Charlie Fellowes) *hld up off the pce in midfield: wnt 3rd 10f out: clsd to press ldng pair 2f out: pushed into ld ins fnl f: asserted fnl 75yds: comf* **13/8**1

4606 **2** 1 1/2 **Lost The Moon**32 [8565] 4-9-0 **71** JoeyHaynes 10 76
(Mark H Tompkins) *hld up off the pce in last trio: rdn and hdwy over 2f out: chsd ldrs 1f out: kpt on wl to go 2nd last strides* **50/1**

0065 **3** *nk* **Start Seven**45 [8244] 5-10-2 **87** DougieCostello 5 92
(Jamie Osborne) *led for 1f: chsd clr ldr after: rdn and clsd to ld 2f out: hdd ins fnl f: kpt on same pce: lost 2nd last strides* **12/1**

2064 **4** 2 3/4 **Ruler Of The Nile**22 [8771] 5-8-6 **66** CallumShepherd(3) 3 68
(Robert Stephens) *racd off the pce in 4th: effrt u.p over 2f out: kpt on same pce ins fnl f* **33/1**

1460 **5** 3/4 **Frederic**52 [8038] 6-10-2 **87** JoeFanning 7 88
(Keith Dalgleish) *squeezed for room sn after s: swtchd lft and hld up off the pce in last trio: hdwy on outer 3f out: kpt on same pce ins fnl f* **13/2**

120 **6** 1/2 **Takbeer (IRE)**88 [6880] 5-9-3 **74** (p) CharlesBishop 6 74
(Nikki Evans) *swtchd rt and hdwy to ld after 1f: rdn and hdd 2f out: no ex and wknd ins fnl f* **28/1**

4351 **7** 14 **Steaming (IRE)**40 [8377] 3-9-1 **78** (p) RichardKingscote 9 63
(Ralph Beckett) *hld up off the pce in last trio: rdn 3f out: no hdwy and wl btn 2f out* **7/2**2

2461 **8** 1 **Silver Link (IRE)**24 [8744] 3-9-3 **80** (p) BenCurtis 4 64
(Marcus Tregoning) *off the pce in midfield: rdn and dropped to last trio 3f out: lost tch over 1f out* **4/1**3

3414 **9** *nk* **Gabrial's Star**15 [8876] 8-9-7 **78** (b) JackGarritty 8 60
(Richard Fahey) *racd off the pce in 3rd tl 10f out: lost pl over 3f out: bhd fnl 2f* **18/1**

3m 37.8s (-5.90) **Going Correction** -0.075s/f (Stan)
**WFA** 3 from 4yo+ 6lb 9 Ran SP% **115.0**
Speed ratings (Par 105): **110,109,109,107,107 107,100,100,100**
CSF £106.72 CT £756.25 TOTE £2.70: £1.10, £8.60, £3.40; EX 124.20 Trifecta £2020.80.
**Owner** The Johnson'S **Bred** Shortgrove Manor Stud **Trained** Newmarket, Suffolk
**FOCUS**
A well-run staying handicap rated around the third..

## 9083 FOLLOW SUNBETS ON TWITTER CLAIMING STKS 7f 36y (Tp)
**3:10** (3:10) (Class 6) 3-Y-O+ **£2,587** (£770; £384; £192) **Stalls** High

Form RPR
6203 **1** **Tatlisu (IRE)**12 [8906] 7-8-11 82 SebastianWoods(7) 8 83
(Richard Fahey) *hld up in midfield: clsd and swtchd lft 1f out: chsd wnr ins fnl f: r.o u.p to ld last strides* **7/1**

0011 **2** *nk* **Unforgiving Minute**14 [8881] 6-10-0 85 AdamKirby 5 92
(John Butler) *chsd ldrs: effrt over 2f out: rdn to ld 1f out: drvn ins fnl f: kpt on: hdd last strides* **9/4**2

1325 **3** 2 1/4 **Miracle Garden**19 [8797] 5-9-0 77 (v) RichardKingscote 9 73
(Ian Williams) *chsd ldr: rdn and ev ch over 1f out tl no ex jst ins fnl f: wknd fnl 100yds* **13/8**1

4005 **4** 1 **Athassel**29 [8640] 8-9-3 78 KatherineGlenister(7) 1 80
(David Evans) *hld up in midfield: effrt on inner 2f out: kpt on same pce u.p ins fnl f* **11/1**

0200 **5** *nse* **Light From Mars**192 [3084] 12-8-10 65 (p) DavidProbert 2 66
(Ronald Harris) *led: rdn over 1f out: hdd 1f out: no ex and wknd fnl 100yds* **50/1**

0055 **6** 1 1/4 **Outer Space**14 [8881] 6-9-6 77 DougieCostello 3 73
(Jamie Osborne) *stmbld leaving stalls: hld up in last trio: hdwy 2f out: rdn over 1f out: kpt on u.p ins fnl f: swtchd rt towards fin: nvr trbld ldrs* **5/1**3

5140 **7** 2 **Wahaab (IRE)**19 [8798] 6-8-11 70 (t) JackOsborn(7) 6 66
(Sophie Leech) *bhd: effrt over 2f out: kpt on ins fnl f: nvr trbld ldrs* **40/1**

0100 **8** 4 1/2 **Corporal Maddox**22 [8772] 10-8-10 60 (p) BenCurtis 7 47
(Ronald Harris) *midfield: effrt u.p and wd bnd 2f out: sn btn and wknd fnl f* **40/1**

00 **9** 11 **Latest Quest (IRE)**33 [8543] 3-8-5 43 MartinDwyer 10 15
(Sylvester Kirk) *t.k.h: chsd ldrs tl lost pl u.p over 2f out: bhd and eased ins fnl f* **100/1**

000- **10** 13 **Seraphima**444 [6586] 7-8-0 41 (h1) RyanPowell 4
(Lisa Williamson) *a last trio: struggling u.p over 2f out: sn lost tch: t.o* **250/1**

1m 27.76s (-1.04) **Going Correction** -0.075s/f (Stan) 10 Ran SP% **114.6**
Speed ratings (Par 101): **102,101,99,97,97 96,94,89,76,61**
CSF £22.61 TOTE £7.60: £1.50, £1.40, £1.70; EX 28.20 Trifecta £71.30.
**Owner** Middleham Park Racing LIV **Bred** J C And Rocal Bloodstock **Trained** Musley Bank, N Yorks
**FOCUS**
Not a bad claimer and it was run at a decent clip.

## 9084 SUNBETS.CO.UK H'CAP 1m 142y (Tp)
**3:40** (3:40) (Class 6) (0-55,55) 3-Y-O+ **£2,587** (£770; £384; £192) **Stalls** Low

Form RPR
6006 **1** **Big Bad Lol (IRE)**34 [8514] 3-9-3 **54** RichardKingscote 3 61+
(Ed Walker) *hld up in tch in last quartet: switching rt and effrt ent fnl 2f: rdn and hdwy to ld ins fnl f: rn green in front but kpt on: rdn out* **7/4**1

-000 **2** 1/2 **Shamlan (IRE)**194 [3001] 5-9-6 **55** (p) DougieCostello 11 59
(Kevin Frost) *stdd after s: hld up in last quartet: hdwy on inner over 2f out: swtchd rt over 1f out: nt clr run 1f out: hdwy to chse wnr wl ins fnl f: kpt on wl* **33/1**

0003 **3** 2 1/2 **Ixelles Diamond (IRE)**42 [8307] 6-8-13 **51** (h) CharlieBennett(3) 6 50
(Lee Carter) *hld up wl in tch in midfield: effrt to chse ldrs over 2f out: rdn and ev ch over 1f out: led 1f out: sn hdd and outpcd wl ins fnl f* **22/1**

0004 **4** 3/4 **Sugar Beach (FR)**12 [8908] 3-9-3 **54** (h) JimmyQuinn 8 51
(Ann Duffield) *hld up in tch in midfield: hdwy and chsng ldrs 2f out: nt clr run ent fnl f: swtchd rt and kpt on same pce fnl 100yds* **12/1**

2451 **5** 1 **Pitch High (IRE)**20 [8784] 3-8-9 **53** MillyNaseb(7) 1 48
(Julia Feilden) *t.k.h: led: rdn wl over 1f out: hdd 1f out: no ex and wknd ins fnl f* **8/1**

500 **6** 2 **Living Leader**42 [8307] 8-9-2 **51** EdwardGreatrex 4 42
(Grace Harris) *chsd ldrs: effrt on inner over 1f out: unable qck 1f out: wknd ins fnl f* **50/1**

6063 **7** 1 1/4 **Lozah**25 [8719] 4-9-5 **54** JasonHart 5 42
(Roger Fell) *s.i.s: hld up in last quartet: nt clr run over 2f out: hdwy u.p over 1f out: kpt on: nvr trbld ldrs* **10/1**

0664 **8** *nse* **Caribbean Spring (IRE)**42 [8307] 4-8-13 **53** JaneElliott(5) 9 41
(George Margarson) *hld up in tch in midfield: effrt over 1f out: swtchd rt 1f out: nvr threatened ldrs* **13/2**3

000- **9** *nk* **Shackles**399 [7741] 3-9-4 **55** TomEaves 7 43
(Nicky Richards) *squeezed for room leaving stalls: hld up in rr: effrt over 1f out: swtchd lft 1f out: nvr trbld ldrs* **40/1**

0606 **10** 2 3/4 **Life Of Luxury**34 [8507] 4-9-3 **52** WilliamCarson 2 34
(Mark Brisbourne) *chsd ldr: rdn over 2f out: lost 2nd over 1f out and losing pl whn squeezed for room 1f out: wknd ins fnl f* **5/1**2

3304 **11** 29 **Peak Hill**10 [8957] 4-9-6 **55** (p1) TimmyMurphy 10
(Adrian Wintle) *hld up wl in tch in midfield: lost pl u.p over 2f out: wl bhd and eased ins fnl f: t.o* **10/1**

5200 **12** 11 **Fleeting Glimpse**64 [7692] 4-9-6 **55** DavidProbert 13
(Dai Burchell) *plld hrd and ref to settle: midfield and wd: hdwy to chse ldrs 7f out: lost pl over 3f out: t.o and virtually p.u ins fnl f* **80/1**

1m 49.32s (-0.78) **Going Correction** -0.075s/f (Stan)
**WFA** 3 from 4yo+ 2lb 12 Ran SP% **116.3**
Speed ratings (Par 101): **100,99,97,96,95 94,92,92,92,90 64,54**
CSF £79.88 CT £986.11 TOTE £2.40: £1.30, £9.00, £4.40; EX 68.30 Trifecta £1842.10.
**Owner** Laurence Bellman **Bred** Jaykayenn Syndicate **Trained** Upper Lambourn, Berks
**FOCUS**
A moderate affair with improved form from the winner.

## 9085 BET & WATCH AT SUNBETS.CO.UK MEDIAN AUCTION MAIDEN STKS 1m 142y (Tp)
**4:10** (4:10) (Class 6) 3-5-Y-O **£2,587** (£770; £384; £192) **Stalls** Low

Form RPR
6040 **1** **Diamond Avalanche (IRE)**20 [8784] 4-9-7 46 JackGarritty 8 62
(Kristin Stubbs) *mde all: shkn up over 1f out: drifting rt but in command ins fnl f: styd on* **12/1**

063 **2** 1 1/2 **Joys Delight**10 [8957] 3-9-0 58 RichardKingscote 6 54
(Daniel Mark Loughnane) *chsd wnr: effrt wl over 1f out: unable qck and swtchd lft jst ins fnl f: kpt on same pce* **15/8**2

0004 **3** 6 **Compton Brave**41 [8345] 3-9-5 45 AdamKirby 2 46
(J R Jenkins) *hld up in midfield: effrt to go 3rd but ldng pair clr wl over 1f out: no imp but kpt on to hold 3rd ins fnl f* **10/1**3

0006 **4** 1/2 **La Goulue**10 [8956] 3-9-0 43 (v) HollieDoyle 3 40
(John Gallagher) *chsd ldng pair: effrt over 2f out: outpcd by ldng pair over 1f out: battling for wl hld 3rd and kpt on same pce ins fnl f* **20/1**

**5** 1/2 **Peters Folly** 4-9-2 0 (h1) WilliamCarson 1 39
(Peter Hiatt) *s.i.s: rn green in rr: nt clr run over 2f out: switching rt and sme hdwy wl over 1f out: no ch w ldng pair and kpt on same pce ins fnl f* **33/1**

00 **6** *nk* **Sanches**17 [8842] 3-9-2 0 MattCosham(3) 4 43
(Dr Jeremy Naylor) *hld up in midfield: effrt on outer over 2f out: no threat to ldrs and plugged on same pce ins fnl f* **40/1**

4 **7** 3/4 **My Brunette (IRE)**50 [8117] 3-9-0 0 TimmyMurphy 7 36
(Geoffrey Deacon) *s.i.s: dropped into last pair: hdwy on outer to chse ldrs 4f out: 5th and struggling over 2f out: wl btn and swtchd lft over 1f out* **1/1**1

6-00 **8** 19 **Polkadot Princess (IRE)**110 [6099] 3-9-0 49 CharlesBishop 5
(Nikki Evans) *chsd ldng trio tl lost pl u.p over 2f out: bhd and lost tch over 1f out* **22/1**

1m 49.46s (-0.64) **Going Correction** -0.075s/f (Stan)
**WFA** 3 from 4yo 2lb 8 Ran SP% **116.1**
Speed ratings (Par 101): **99,97,92,91,91 91,90,73**
CSF £34.33 TOTE £14.80: £3.70, £1.10, £3.00; EX 42.20 Trifecta £224.20.
**Owner** Mrs C M Clarke, Foulrice Park Racing Ltd **Bred** Mrs Vera Deegan **Trained** Norton, N Yorks
**FOCUS**
Moderate maiden form.
T/Jkpt: Not Won. T/Plt: £110.10 to a £1 stake. Pool: £74,377.14 - 492.87 winning units T/Qpdt: £13.00 to a £1 stake. Pool: £9,372.97 - 532.50 winning units **Steve Payne**

# 9003 DEAUVILLE (R-H)
Tuesday, December 5
**OFFICIAL GOING: Polytrack: standard**

## 9086a PRIX DE MAROLLES (CLAIMER) (2YO) (POLYTRACK) 7f 110y(P)
**10:55** 2-Y-O **£8,547** (£3,418; £2,564; £1,709; £854)

RPR
**1** **Favoritisme (FR)**67 2-8-11 0 (b) EnzoCorallo 3 73
(C Ferland, France) **22/5**2

**2** 2 **Dragon's Teeth (IRE)**44 2-9-1 0 (b) MlleCharleneMannier(4) 13 76
(R Le Gal, France) **15/2**3

3 nk **Arrogant (IRE)**[14] 8884 2-9-4 0 ThomasHuet 10 75
(Jose Santos) *sn prom: trckd ldrs: pushed along over 2f out: rdn over 1f out: drvn and styd on same pce fnl f* **7/5**[1]
4 1 ¾ **Swansea Beach (FR)**[26] 2-9-1 0 ClementGuitraud 14 67
(Y Barberot, France) **28/1**
5 1 ½ **Valhala (FR)**[36] 8482 2-8-11 0 (p) GuillaumeTrolleyDePrevaux 9 60
(T Castanheira, France) **12/1**
6 ¾ **Vida Loca (FR)**[44] 2-8-4 0 MlleMickaelleMichel(4) 1 55
(M Boutin, France) **15/2**[3]
7 1 **Digha (FR)**[22] 2-8-11 0 ThierryThulliez 15 56
(P Demercastel, France) **22/1**
8 hd **Norwegian Lord (FR)**[56] 8101 2-8-11 0 (p) ThomasMessina 8 55
(M Boutin, France) **22/1**
9 1 ¼ **Ma Lougie (FR)** 2-8-9 0 ow1 RichardJuteau 5 50
(J-L Dehez, France) **145/1**
10 3 **French Reflection (IRE)**[40] 2-8-8 0 JimmyTastayre 4 42
(G Botti, France) **84/1**
11 snk **Golden Frost (FR)** 2-8-8 0 (b[1]) QuentinPerrette 11 42
(H De Nicolay, France) **110/1**
12 2 ½ **Qatar Magic (FR)** 2-8-8 0 (p) MatthiasLauron 2 36
(Yannick Fouin, France) **51/1**
13 4 **Peterhof (FR)**[55] 2-9-1 0 FredericChampagne 12 34
(M Lehmann, France) **13/1**
14 snk **Julietta (FR)** 2-8-8 0 AntonioPolli 16 26
(Mario Hofer, Germany) **47/1**
15 2 ½ **Paulina Dream (FR)** 2-8-11 0 ErwannLebreton 7 24
(Edouard Thueux, France) **102/1**

1m 29.26s **15 Ran SP% 118.4**
PARI-MUTUEL (all including 1 euro stake): WIN 5.40; PLACE 1.50, 1.80, 1.30; DF 16.60; SF 28.40.
**Owner** Haras D'Etreham **Bred** Haras D'Etreham & C Ferland **Trained** France

## 9087a PRIX DE MONDEVILLE (MAIDEN) (2YO) (POLYTRACK) 6f 110y(P)
1:05 2-Y-O £11,538 (£4,615; £3,461; £2,307; £1,153)

RPR
1 **Jack Taylor (IRE)**[33] 8536 2-9-2 0 FabriceVeron 9 76
(Richard Hughes) *wl into stride: trckd ldrs: swtchd and rdn to ld over 1f out: drvn whn chal ins fnl f: hld on gamely* **5/1**[3]
2 nse **Rozanne (IRE)**[62] 7731 2-8-13 0 EddyHardouin 4 73
(P Monfort, France) **28/1**
3 ¾ **Senza Fine (FR)**[36] 2-8-13 0 GregoryBenoist 5 71
(Mme Pia Brandt, France) **11/5**[1]
4 1 **Taxman (USA)**[22] 2-9-2 0 AurelienLemaitre 12 71
(H-F Devin, France) **23/5**[2]
5 ¾ **Corantin (FR)**[40] 8378 2-9-2 0 StephanePasquier 6 69
(J-Y Artu, France) **13/2**
6 nse **Baystone (FR)**[71] 7470 2-8-7 0 TristanBaron(6) 16 66
(H-A Pantall, France) **96/1**
7 hd **Mariobasset (FR)**[52] 2-9-2 0 ChristopherGrosbois 3 68
(J Boisnard, France) **32/1**
8 ½ **Venussio (FR)**[26] 2-9-2 0 (b[1]) MathieuAndrouin 13 67
(J-L Delaplace, France) **93/1**
9 ½ **Red Vancouver (FR)**[208] 2-8-13 0 AnthonyCrastus 2 62
(C Lerner, France) **14/1**
10 3 **Jinx (FR)**[22] 2-9-2 0 (p) JeromeCabre 8 57
(J Boisnard, France) **90/1**
11 5 **Briateke (FR)**[51] 8094 2-8-13 0 FabioBranca 1 40
(Antonio Marcialis, Italy) **42/1**
12 ¾ **Cunningly (FR)**[43] 2-8-13 0 (b) IoritzMendizabal 14 38
(F Chappet, France) **9/1**
13 ¾ **Tishka (FR)** 2-8-8 0 JulienAuge 10 31
(C Ferland, France) **15/1**
14 1 ¾ **En Dansant (FR)**[25] 2-8-7 0 GabrielLeDevehat(6) 11 31
(H-A Pantall, France) **132/1**
15 1 ¼ **Onesarnieshort (FR)**[36] 8475 2-9-2 0 AntoineHamelin 7 30
(Mme G Rarick, France) **37/1**
16 1 ½ **Houlanbator (FR)**[34] 2-8-8 0 DelphineSantiago(5) 15 23
(Mlle G Meijer, France) **114/1**

1m 17.17s **16 Ran SP% 118.3**
PARI-MUTUEL (all including 1 euro stake): WIN 6.00; PLACE 2.30, 5.30, 1.50; DF 79.50; SF 157.90.
**Owner** Anthony Hogarth **Bred** Qatar Bloodstock & Ecurie Des Charmes **Trained** Upper Lambourn, Berks

# 8943 LINGFIELD (L-H)
Wednesday, December 6

**OFFICIAL GOING: Polytrack: standard**
Wind: Fresh, mostly behind in home straight Weather: Overcast

## 9088 PLAY SLOTS AT SUNBETS.CO.UK/VEGAS EBF MAIDEN STKS 1m 1y(P)
11:40 (11:40) (Class 5) 3-Y-O+ £2,911 (£866; £432; £216) Stalls High

Form RPR
1 **Mordin (IRE)** 3-9-5 0 FrankieDettori 8 83+
(Simon Crisford) *wl in tch: prog over 2f out: rn green whn asked to cl on ldrs over 1f out: picked up smartly fnl f to ld last 100yds: scooted clr* **1/2**[1]
3236 2 2 ¼ **Narjes**[49] 8150 3-9-0 75 (h) JimCrowley 1 67
(Laura Mongan) *t.k.h: trckd ldrs: wnt 2nd over 2f out: rdn to chal over 1f out: upsides whn wnr shot by 100yds out: kpt on* **11/4**[2]
3564 3 ¾ **Deliberator**[18] 8852 3-9-5 68 MartinHarley 9 70
(William Knight) *sn trckd ldr: led wl over 2f out: hrd pressed fnl f: hdd and outpcd last 100yds* **7/1**[3]
6 4 3 ¼ **Ginger Lady (IRE)**[183] 3438 3-9-0 0 JoeyHaynes 2 57
(Mark H Tompkins) *hld up early: chsd ldrs 5f out: rdn 2f out: one pce and no imp* **50/1**
4043 5 ½ **Wannabe Like You**[19] 8810 3-9-5 67 (p[1]) EdwardGreatrex 3 61
(Archie Watson) *prom: rdn 2f out: wknd fnl f on inner* **12/1**
5P 6 ½ **I'm Right On Time**[189] 3209 3-9-2 0 JackDuern(3) 11 60
(Dean Ivory) *hld up in 9th: pushed along over 2f out: shkn up and no great prog over 1f out: kpt on* **50/1**
7 5 **Napoleon (IRE)** 4-9-6 0 FranBerry 6 48
(Laura Mongan) *dwlt: mostly in last pair: outpcd fr 3f out: no great prog after* **50/1**
5-00 8 4 ½ **Annabella**[300] 644 4-9-1 43 RyanTate 5 32
(Tim McCarthy) *hld up towards rr: outpcd 3f out: pushed along and no hdwy after* **100/1**
0 9 ½ **Sanam**[29] 8663 3-9-5 0 AdamKirby 7 36
(Ed Dunlop) *s.i.s: a wl in rr: bhd over 2f out* **10/1**
0000 10 10 **Moorea**[42] 8342 3-9-2 44 MitchGodwin(3) 10 12
(John Bridger) *led to wl over 2f out: wknd rapidly* **100/1**
50 11 34 **Watar Day**[216] 2330 3-8-9 0 AliceMills(5) 4
(Linda Jewell) *chsd ldrs 3f: sn wknd: t.o* **100/1**

1m 36.87s (-1.33) **Going Correction** -0.05s/f (Stan)
**WFA** 3 from 4yo 1lb **11 Ran SP% 131.5**
Speed ratings (Par 103): **104,101,101,97,97 96,91,87,86,76 42**
CSF £2.61 TOTE £1.40: £1.10, £1.10, £3.10; EX 2.50 Trifecta £9.60.
**Owner** Abdullah Saeed Al Naboodah **Bred** Bernard Cooke **Trained** Newmarket, Suffolk

**FOCUS**
A nice performance from the winner, albeit in just an ordinary maiden. The runner-up sets the standard.

## 9089 32RED.COM FILLIES' H'CAP 7f 1y(P)
12:10 (12:10) (Class 3) (0-90,87) 3-Y-O+ £7,246 (£2,168; £1,084; £542; £270) Stalls Low

Form RPR
422 1 **Domitilla**[27] 8707 3-8-8 74 (h[1]) TomMarquand 5 83
(Marco Botti) *trckd ldr: rdn to chal 2f out: hanging but led 1f out: styd on wl* **8/1**
1 2 2 ¼ **Temeraire (FR)**[18] 8842 3-8-10 76 JosephineGordon 6 79
(Hugo Palmer) *t.k.h: led: pressed 2f out: hdd and nt qckn 1f out: hld on for 2nd* **5/2**[1]
4046 3 ¾ **Yeah Baby Yeah (IRE)**[92] 6787 4-9-2 82 MartinDwyer 8 83
(Gay Kelleway) *stdd s: hld up in last: nudged along 2f out: nt clr run 1f out: styd on to win battle for 3rd ins fnl f: nvr nr to chal* **33/1**
5433 4 hd **Summer Icon**[5] 9020 4-9-0 85 PaddyBradley(5) 9 85
(Mick Channon) *hld up in last trio: rdn 2f out: effrt on outer over 1f out: pressed for 3rd ins fnl f but no ch to threaten* **3/1**[2]
0001 5 1 ¼ **Favourite Royal (IRE)**[11] 8947 3-9-2 82 (v) CharlesBishop 2 79
(Eve Johnson Houghton) *hld up in last trio: rdn 2f out: effrt to dispute 3rd fnl f but no ch: one pce last 100yds* **9/2**[3]
2040 6 1 **Clear Water (IRE)**[60] 7811 4-9-7 87 DavidProbert 3 81
(Michael Wigham) *trckd ldrs: rdn to chse ldng pair jst over 2f out: sn outpcd: lost 3rd ins fnl f: fdd* **11/2**
604 7 1 **Turanga Leela**[36] 8488 3-8-13 79 (v) JimCrowley 4 71
(Ian Williams) *chsd ldng pair to jst over 2f out: sn btn* **12/1**
1405 8 shd **Veena (FR)**[26] 8717 4-8-11 77 LukeMorris 1 68
(David Simcock) *racd in 5th: rdn over 2f out: no prog and sn btn* **25/1**

1m 23.5s (-1.30) **Going Correction** -0.05s/f (Stan) **8 Ran SP% 112.7**
Speed ratings (Par 104): **105,102,101,101,99 98,97,97**
CSF £27.55 CT £624.22 TOTE £7.40: £3.00, £1.02, £6.20; EX 23.40 Trifecta £400.80.
**Owner** Scuderia Blueberry S R L & Partner 2 **Bred** Razza Del Sole Societa Agricola Srl **Trained** Newmarket, Suffolk

**FOCUS**
Few got into this, the front two having the race between them from the turn in.

## 9090 32REDPOKER.COM NURSERY H'CAP 7f 1y(P)
12:40 (12:42) (Class 6) (0-65,71) 2-Y-O £2,264 (£673; £336; £168) Stalls Low

Form RPR
5042 1 **Fire Orchid**[7] 8996 2-8-12 63 RossaRyan(7) 4 67
(Richard Hannon) *nt that wl away but sn chsd ldrs: clsd 2f out: led over 1f out: drvn and kpt on wl whn pressed last 100yds* **4/1**[1]
060 2 ½ **Corazon Espinado (IRE)**[14] 8889 2-8-13 62 PaddyBradley(5) 3 65
(Simon Dow) *trckd ldrs: shkn up wl over 1f out: clsd fnl f: tk 2nd last 100yds and sn chalng: nt qckn nr fin* **12/1**
1444 3 1 **Felisa**[37] 8467 2-9-6 64 (v) FranBerry 6 64
(David Evans) *led 1f: sn in 3rd: wd bnd 2f out and lost grnd: styd on again fnl f to take 3rd last stride* **8/1**
0300 4 shd **Little Miss Lilly**[50] 8131 2-9-8 66 AdamKirby 8 66
(Clive Cox) *wl in tch: prog over 2f out: rdn over 1f out: tk 2nd briefly ins fnl f and tried to chal: one pce last 100yds* **5/1**[3]
0003 5 1 ¼ **Lady Jayne (IRE)**[21] 8783 2-8-2 46 JosephineGordon 2 42
(Ian Williams) *chsd ldr after 1f: rdn over 2f out: lost 2nd and one pce wl over 1f out* **4/1**[1]
2451 6 ½ **Diamond Pursuit**[7] 8996 2-9-13 71 6ex MartinDwyer 5 66
(Jo Hughes) *t.k.h: hld up in last trio: shuffled along 2f out and sme prog into midfield: no ch whn drvn last 100yds* **9/2**[2]
0563 7 ¾ **Hurricane Lil (IRE)**[11] 8943 2-8-10 57 (b[1]) HectorCrouch(3) 9 50
(George Baker) *hld up in midfield: rdn over 2f out: plugged on fr over 1f out but n.d* **33/1**
555 8 1 ¼ **That's My Girl (IRE)**[29] 8644 2-9-3 61 (b[1]) KieranO'Neill 1 51
(Richard Hannon) *led after 1f to over 1f out: wknd on inner sn after* **11/1**
0043 9 1 ¼ **Isoletta**[131] 5366 2-9-8 66 LiamKeniry 11 52
(Ed Walker) *trapped out wd early then hld up in last trio: shkn up and no prog 2f out: nvr in it* **12/1**
6444 10 ½ **Dashing Dusty (IRE)**[14] 8887 2-9-2 60 TimmyMurphy 10 45
(Jamie Osborne) *trapped out wd: nvr bttr than midfield: shkn up in rr 2f out: no prog* **12/1**
0500 11 13 **Raven's Girl**[135] 5216 2-8-1 45 RyanPowell 7
(Michael Madgwick) *s.v.s: ct up after 2f: rdn and wknd over 3f out: t.o* **100/1**

1m 24.75s (-0.05) **Going Correction** -0.05s/f (Stan) **11 Ran SP% 121.3**
Speed ratings (Par 94): **98,97,96,96,94 94,93,91,90,89 75**
CSF £55.03 CT £376.43 TOTE £4.50: £1.50, £6.80, £3.30; EX 59.40 Trifecta £545.80.
**Owner** Rockcliffe Stud **Bred** P And Mrs A G Venner **Trained** East Everleigh, Wilts

**FOCUS**
A modest nursery.

## 9091 BETWAY CONDITIONS STKS 1m 2f (P)
1:10 (1:10) (Class 2) 3-Y-O+ £11,827 (£3,541; £1,770; £885) Stalls Low

Form RPR
622/ 1 **Toast Of New York (USA)**[1130] 7614 6-9-4 0 (h[1]) FrankieDettori 5 106
(Jamie Osborne) *led 3f: trckd ldr tl led again over 2f out: shkn up whn pressed over 1f out: pushed out fnl f* **2/1**[2]
0164 2 1 **Petite Jack**[18] 8844 4-9-4 102 (b[1]) LukeMorris 2 104
(Archie Watson) *trckd ldng pair: shkn up to chse wnr 2f out: chal over 1f out: hanging and readily outbattled after* **7/4**[1]
3-20 3 ¾ **Intern (IRE)**[166] 4029 3-9-2 103 FranBerry 4 104
(David Simcock) *stdd s: hld up in last: rdn over 2f out: tk 3rd over 1f out: styd on and clsd on ldng pair wout posing a threat* **5/2**[3]

006 **4** 4½ **Mr Scaramanga**[94] 6746 3-9-5 102 ........................ AdamKirby 1 98
(Simon Dow) *t.k.h: led after 3f to over 2f out: wknd on inner over 1f out* **9/1**

2m 4.01s (-2.59) **Going Correction** -0.05s/f (Stan)
**WFA** 3 from 4yo+ 2lb **4** Ran SP% **108.3**
Speed ratings (Par 109): **108,107,106,103**
CSF £5.85 TOTE £2.00; EX 5.20 Trifecta £5.80.
**Owner** Al Shaqab Racing **Bred** Ashleigh Stud, F Ramos And J Ramos **Trained** Upper Lambourn, Berks

**FOCUS**
While Toast Of New York didn't need to be anywhere near his best to take this, he could easily have been beaten and no-one would have been shocked following such a long absence, so a winning return can only be a positive as connections mull bigger targets ahead.

## 9092 BETWAY H'CAP 1m 4f (P)
**1:45** (1:46) (Class 6) (0-60,60) 3-Y-0+ **£2,264** (£673; £336; £168) **Stalls** Low

Form RPR
0400 **1** **Sky Marshal (IRE)**[18] 8854 3-8-12 55 ........................ LiamKeniry 11 61
(Ed Walker) *hld up in midfield: rdn 2f out: prog on outer over 1f out: styd on wl fnl f to ld last strides* **16/1**

0000 **2** hd **Rock'n Gold**[35] 8515 4-9-0 53 ........................ TimmyMurphy 7 58
(Adrian Wintle) *reluctant to go to post or in the stall: dwlt: hld up in last trio: prog on outer to trck ldrs 5f out: rdn 2f out: clsd on outer to ld ins fnl f: kpt on but hdd last strides* **20/1**

4000 **3** hd **Attain**[11] 8946 8-9-6 59 ........................ EdwardGreatrex 8 63
(Archie Watson) *trckd ldrs: prog to chal on inner jst over 1f out: upsides ins fnl f: jst outpcd* **5/1**[2]

0006 **4** 1 **Karam Albaari (IRE)**[18] 8846 9-9-3 56 ........................(v) MartinHarley 2 62
(J R Jenkins) *hld up in midfield: prog on inner over 1f out gng wl: trying to cl whn nt clr run ins fnl f: r.o nr fin but unable to rcvr* **7/1**

4512 **5** nk **Betsalottie**[18] 8846 4-9-1 57 ........................ MitchGodwin(3) 4 59
(John Bridger) *hld up towards rr: rdn over 2f out: prog jst over 1f out: styd on wl fnl f: gaining at fin* **5/1**[2]

0045 **6** hd **Widnes**[15] 8883 3-9-3 60 ........................(vt[1]) JosephineGordon 6 63
(Alan Bailey) *rrd s: hld up in last trio: stl wl in rr 2f out: drvn on outer over 1f out: r.o fnl f: fin wl but too late* **9/2**[1]

250 **7** hd **Saint Helena (IRE)**[48] 8183 9-9-0 53 ........................(b) MartinDwyer 15 55
(Mark Gillard) *t.k.h: pressed ldr: narrow ld over 2f out: hdd ins fnl f: one pce and lost several pls nr fin* **50/1**

2200 **8** nk **Tommys Geal**[18] 8846 5-8-8 54 ........................ NicolaCurrie(7) 12 55
(Michael Madgwick) *hld up in midfield: forced to come wdst of all whn trying to make grnd 2f out: styd on fnl f: nt pce to threaten* **25/1**

0006 **9** nk **Atalanta Bay (IRE)**[29] 8647 7-8-7 53 ........................(p[1]) TylerSaunders(7) 13 54
(Marcus Tregoning) *rousted along to ld: narrowly hdd over 2f out: stl upsides 1f out: fdd last 100yds* **8/1**

1113 **10** ¾ **Hermosa Vaquera (IRE)**[48] 8183 7-9-4 60 ........................(p) HectorCrouch(3) 16 59
(Gary Moore) *pressed ldng pair: stl cl up over 1f out: fdd ins fnl f* **14/1**

23-0 **11** 2 **Canford Thompson**[15] 8878 4-9-5 58 ........................ AdamKirby 14 54
(Daniel Steele) *hld up wl in rr: drvn on wd outside and prog over 3f out to press ldrs 2f out: wknd jst over 1f out* **14/1**

0000 **12** nk **Lady Of Steel**[28] 8673 3-8-10 53 ........................ DanielMuscutt 9 50
(John Butler) *chsd ldrs: rdn over 2f out: wknd wl over 1f out* **33/1**

4534 **13** hd **Loving Your Work**[123] 5653 6-9-3 56 ........................ KieranShoemark 10 51
(Ken Cunningham-Brown) *hld up in rr: shkn up on inner over 2f out: nvr able to make much prog* **25/1**

0-66 **13** dht **General Brook (IRE)**[220] 2178 7-8-9 48 ........................ LukeMorris 3 43
(John O'Shea) *prom tl steadily wknd fr 2f out* **33/1**

1000 **15** 1¾ **Stand Guard**[18] 8846 13-9-1 57 ........................ TimClark(3) 5 50
(John Butler) *hld up in last: nvr mde any prog* **25/1**

5035 **P** **Silver Dixie (USA)**[11] 8946 7-9-7 60 ........................(v) CharlesBishop 1
(Peter Hedger) *chsd ldrs: rdn and wknd rapidly over 4f out: t.o whn p.u 3f out* **11/2**[3]

2m 31.81s (-1.19) **Going Correction** -0.05s/f (Stan)
**WFA** 3 from 4yo+ 4lb **16** Ran SP% **133.9**
Speed ratings (Par 101): **101,100,100,100,99 99,99,99,99,98 97,97,97,97,95**
CSF £321.99 CT £1866.30 TOTE £20.70: £4.20, £5.00, £1.90, £2.20; EX 558.70 Trifecta £6364.70.
**Owner** Dubai Thoroughbred Racing **Bred** Roundhill Stud **Trained** Upper Lambourn, Berks

**FOCUS**
An ordinary handicap, but a competitive one, and it produced a typical Lingfield finish.

## 9093 PLAY JACKPOT GAMES AT SUNBETS.CO.UK/VEGAS H'CAP (DIV I) 7f 1y(P)
**2:15** (2:16) (Class 5) (0-70,72) 3-Y-0+ **£2,911** (£866; £432; £216) **Stalls** Low

Form RPR
4000 **1** **Varsovian**[112] 6068 7-9-4 70 ........................ JackDuern(3) 3 78
(Dean Ivory) *racd keenly: mde all: kicked 2 l clr over 1f out: drifted rt fnl f but kpt on wl* **6/1**

0066 **2** 1¼ **Spirit Of Sarwan (IRE)**[118] 5821 3-9-2 72 ........................ MillyNaseb(7) 2 77
(Julia Feilden) *dwlt: hld up towards rr: prog on inner wl over 1f out: chsd wnr fnl f: kpt on but nvr quite able to chal* **9/2**[3]

3350 **3** ½ **Eddiebet**[26] 8721 3-8-13 62 ........................ MartinHarley 1 65
(David O'Meara) *trckd ldrs: wnt 3rd over 2f out: rdn to dispute 2nd 1f out: one pce fnl f* **8/1**

1001 **4** 2¼ **Garth Rockett**[34] 8551 3-8-11 60 ........................(tp) MartinDwyer 7 57
(Brendan Powell) *t.k.h: trckd wnr: rdn 2f out: lost 2nd and fdd fnl f* **7/2**[2]

0400 **5** nk **First Experience**[14] 8886 6-9-0 66 ........................ CharlieBennett(3) 6 62
(Lee Carter) *trckd ldng pair on outer to over 2f out: pushed along and lost pl over 1f out: reminder ins fnl f: kpt on* **16/1**

1000 **6** ¾ **War Of Succession**[54] 7998 3-9-2 68 ........................ EoinWalsh(3) 5 62
(Tony Newcombe) *stdd s: hld up in last: encouraged along 3f out: stl no prog over 1f out: styd on ins fnl f: gaining at fin* **25/1**

3000 **7** hd **Anonymous John (IRE)**[147] 4746 5-9-8 71 ........................ KieranShoemark 4 65
(Dominic Ffrench Davis) *hld up in midfield: stl gng wl enough over 2f out: rchd 5th and shkn up 1f out: no prog after: nvr posed a threat* **8/1**

0026 **8** nk **Rockley Point**[16] 8875 4-9-3 66 ........................(b) FranBerry 8 59
(Paul D'Arcy) *hld up in midfield on outer: shkn up and in tch over 2f out: fdd over 1f out* **3/1**[1]

5006 **9** ½ **The Yellow Bus**[14] 8886 4-9-4 67 ........................ KieranO'Neill 10 59
(Daniel Steele) *hld up in last fr wd draw: shkn up and no prog over 2f out: nvr a factor* **14/1**

/62- **10** 1¼ **Sahalin**[75] 565 4-9-2 65 ........................ DanielMuscutt 9 53
(John Flint) *pushed along in midfield: nvr able to make any prog fr 2f out* **33/1**

1m 24.6s (-0.20) **Going Correction** -0.05s/f (Stan) **10** Ran SP% **121.2**
Speed ratings (Par 103): **99,97,97,94,94 93,93,92,92,90**
CSF £34.63 CT £190.58 TOTE £7.20: £2.90, £2.80, £3.10; EX 38.70 Trifecta £384.90.
**Owner** Radlett Racing **Bred** Darley **Trained** Radlett, Herts

**FOCUS**
The early pace wasn't strong and the winner dominated throughout.

## 9094 PLAY JACKPOT GAMES AT SUNBETS.CO.UK/VEGAS H'CAP (DIV II) 7f 1y(P)
**2:50** (2:50) (Class 5) (0-70,71) 3-Y-0+ **£2,911** (£866; £432; £216) **Stalls** Low

Form RPR
5053 **1** **Dutiful Son (IRE)**[15] 8881 7-9-8 71 ........................ JimCrowley 5 79
(Simon Dow) *trckd ldng trio: clsd on outer to ld jst over 1f out: drvn fnl f: jst clung on* **7/2**[3]

00 **2** nse **Mansfield**[44] 8295 4-9-2 65 ........................(h[1]) DavidProbert 3 73
(Michael Wigham) *trckd ldrs in 5th: effrt on outer over 1f out: prog to chse wnr 150yds out: rdn and clsd after: needed one more stride* **13/8**[1]

1614 **3** 1½ **The Special One (IRE)**[57] 7916 4-8-10 59 ........................(t) TomMarquand 6 63
(Ali Stronge) *hld up and last to 1/2-way: shkn up wl over 1f out: gd prog on outer fnl f: tk 3rd nr fin: too late to chal* **16/1**

2103 **4** 1 **Dashing Poet**[20] 8797 3-9-3 66 ........................ LukeMorris 1 67
(Heather Main) *trckd ldng pair: drvn to try to chal over 1f out: one pce fnl f* **3/1**[2]

4620 **5** 1 **Passing Star**[40] 8400 6-9-4 67 ........................(tp) GeorgeDowning 9 66
(Daniel Kubler) *hld up in last pair: sme prog towards inner over 1f out: shkn up and kpt on same fnl f: nvr involved* **12/1**

0000 **6** hd **Muhajjal**[13] 8907 3-9-0 70 ........................(t) RossaRyan(7) 10 68
(George Peckham) *hld up in 7th: shkn up and no prog wl over 1f out: n.d after* **16/1**

-500 **7** hd **German Whip**[62] 7769 4-9-0 66 ........................ HectorCrouch(3) 7 64
(Gary Moore) *hld up in 6th: shkn up and no prog 2f out: rdn and one pce fnl f: nvr a threat* **20/1**

0000 **8** nk **Bridge Builder**[29] 8646 7-9-2 65 ........................(p) CharlesBishop 8 62
(Peter Hedger) *pressed ldr: rdn to chal over 1f out: lost pl and btn jst ins fnl f* **50/1**

-000 **9** 3 **Fullon Clarets**[15] 8881 5-8-6 62 ........................(p) NicolaCurrie(7) 2 51
(Laura Mongan) *led: styd on inner ini st: hdd & wknd jst over 1f out* **25/1**

30 **10** 15 **Spiritual Star (IRE)**[25] 8749 8-9-5 71 ........................ CharlieBennett(3) 4 19
(Lee Carter) *hld up: dropped to last and jinked 3f out: sn bhd* **20/1**

1m 23.63s (-1.17) **Going Correction** -0.05s/f (Stan) **10** Ran SP% **120.1**
Speed ratings (Par 103): **104,103,102,101,99 99,99,99,95,78**
CSF £9.42 CT £81.45 TOTE £4.50: £1.70, £1.20, £3.60; EX 15.40 Trifecta £123.80.
**Owner** J C G Chua & Partner **Bred** Lodge Park Stud **Trained** Ashtead, Surrey
■ Stewards' Enquiry : George Downing caution: careless riding

**FOCUS**
The faster of the two divisions by 0.97sec with the winner earning his best figure since March.

## 9095 BETWAY STAYERS AMATEUR RIDERS' H'CAP 1m 7f 169y(P)
**3:20** (3:20) (Class 6) (0-60,60) 3-Y-0+ **£2,183** (£677; £338; £169) **Stalls** Low

Form RPR
6122 **1** **Strictly Art (IRE)**[40] 8396 4-10-6 57 ........................ MissJCooley(5) 4 65
(Alan Bailey) *trckd ldng pair: led over 6f out: sent for home over 2f out: clr fnl f: styd on wl* **13/2**

0021 **2** 3¼ **Kaisan**[19] 8815 4-10-6 52 ........................(t) MissSBrotherton 1 56
(Bernard Llewellyn) *t.k.h: trckd ldr to 7f out: lost pl over 4f out: renewed effrt on inner over 2f out: pushed along and kpt on to take 2nd nr fin* **3/1**[2]

6005 **3** nk **Great Return**[165] 4088 4-10-11 60 ........................ MrAdamElias(3) 6 64
(Warren Greatrex) *hld up in midfield: prog over 4f out: chsd ldng pair 3f out: effrt on outer over 1f out: kpt on to press for 2nd nr fin* **10/1**

005 **4** hd **Bohemian Rhapsody (IRE)**[20] 5274 8-10-2 55 ........................(p) MrCJTodd(7) 10 59
(Brian Barr) *trckd ldrs: wnt 2nd over 3f out: rdn and no imp wnr over 1f out: lost 2 pls nr fin* **40/1**

5042 **5** 2¼ **Dibloam (USA)**[19] 8815 4-10-1 47 ow1 ........................(h) MrSWalker 2 48
(David Evans) *hld up in last trio: sme prog over 3f out: nvr on terms w ldrs: rchd 5th over 1f out: styd on* **9/4**[1]

-106 **6** 6 **Shan Dun na nGall (IRE)**[15] 8878 6-10-12 58 ........................(v) MrJamesKing 12 52
(Amy Murphy) *hld up towards rr: prog on outer over 3f out: wknd 2f out* **12/1**

4231 **7** shd **General Allenby**[57] 7922 3-9-12 55 ........................(be) MrWillPettis(5) 14 50
(Henry Tett) *racd wd tl past 1/2-way: trckd ldrs: wnt 2nd over 6f out to over 3f out: sn wknd* **5/1**[3]

0000 **8** 2¾ **Victor's Bet (SPA)**[15] 8878 8-10-8 59 ........................ MissEllaSmith(5) 5 49
(Ralph J Smith) *hld up and detached in last to over 2f out: stl last whn swtchd sharply rt 1f out: passed a few rivals fnl f: nvr in it* **25/1**

0500 **9** ½ **Elusive Cowboy (USA)**[18] 8846 4-10-5 51 ........................(p) MrAlexFerguson 13 41
(Chris Gordon) *hld up towards rr on outer: outpcd fr 3f out: no ch after* **25/1**

0440 **10** ½ **Marshall Aid (IRE)**[15] 8878 4-10-7 58 ........................(t) MissEMacKenzie(5) 9 47
(Mark Usher) *hld up in rr: ift bhd over 3f out: no ch after* **33/1**

0300 **11** 2¾ **My Lord**[16] 6754 9-10-4 55 ........................ MissMBryant(5) 3 41
(Paddy Butler) *hld up in last pair: nvr a factor* **66/1**

3641 **12** 2¼ **Affair**[29] 8654 3-9-10 55 ........................ MissGDucker(7) 7 40
(Hughie Morrison) *t.k.h: led to over 6f out: wknd 4f out* **25/1**

3m 24.38s (-1.32) **Going Correction** -0.05s/f (Stan)
**WFA** 3 from 4yo+ 6lb **12** Ran SP% **121.0**
Speed ratings (Par 101): **101,99,99,99,98 95,94,93,93,93 91,90**
CSF £25.14 CT £200.43 TOTE £5.40: £1.30, £1.30, £4.00; EX 25.30 Trifecta £367.80.
**Owner** AB Racing Limited **Bred** Lismacue Mare Syndicate **Trained** Newmarket, Suffolk
■ Stewards' Enquiry : Miss Ella Smith 10-day ban: failing take all reasonable and permissible measures to obtain best possible position (21 Dec, 3,5,10,11,26,29 Jan, 10,15,20 Feb)

**FOCUS**
The early leader didn't settle and dropped right out, but otherwise the pace held up pretty well.
T/Jkpt: Not won. T/Plt: £109.80 to a £1 stake. Pool: £55,298.41. 367.58 winning units. T/Qpdt: £79.90 to a £1 stake. Pool: £5,652.08. 52.29 winning units. **Jonathan Neesom**

# 9012 NEWCASTLE (A.W) (L-H)
Wednesday, December 6

**OFFICIAL GOING: Tapeta: standard**
Wind: Fairly strong, half against Weather: Dry

## 9096 BETWAY CASINO H'CAP 1m 4f 98y (Tp)
**3:25** (3:25) (Class 4) (0-85,86) 3-Y-0+ **£4,851** (£1,443; £721; £360) **Stalls** High

Form RPR
0440 **1** **Gallifrey**[34] 8548 3-9-0 82 ........................(b[1]) RichardKingscote 5 88
(Lucy Wadham) *t.k.h: trckd ldrs: drvn and outpcd over 2f out: rallied over 1f out: kpt on to ld towards fin* **2/1**[1]

1064 **2** ½ **Zabeel Star (IRE)**[13] 8912 5-8-10 **74** TomEaves 1 79
(Karen McLintock) *missed break: hld up: smooth hdwy on outside over 2f out: rdn to ld appr fnl f: edgd lft ins fnl f: hdd and no ex towards fin* **11/1**

6040 **3** ¾ **X Rated (IRE)**[13] 8912 3-8-6 **74** AndrewMullen 8 78
(Mark Johnston) *led: rdn and hdd appr fnl f: rallied: one pce last 75yds* **13/2**[3]

-430 **4** ¾ **Always Resolute**[53] 8047 6-8-13 **77** BenCurtis 9 79
(Brian Ellison) *chsd ldrs: drvn along over 2f out: rallied over 1f out: kpt on ins fnl f* **17/2**

5000 **5** 1 **Belle De Lawers**[21] 8778 6-8-7 **71** oh1 (p[1]) HollieDoyle 2 72
(James Bethell) *pressed ldr to over 1f out: drvn and no ex ins fnl f* **25/1**

24-0 **6** hd **Mustaaqeem (USA)**[137] 5164 5-9-8 **86** JackGarritty 6 86
(Richard Fahey) *hld up midfield on ins: pushed along over 2f out: kpt on fnl f: nvr able to chal* **8/1**

-061 **7** hd **Wishing Well**[182] 3464 5-8-10 **74** PJMcDonald 7 74
(Micky Hammond) *hld up midfield: hdwy over 2f out: rdn and outpcd fnl f* **33/1**

2200 **8** ¾ **Henpecked**[13] 8912 7-8-7 **71** oh3 (p) JoeDoyle 3 70
(Alistair Whillans) *hld up: rdn and outpcd over 2f out: plugged on same pce fnl f* **40/1**

1023 **9** 55 **Royal Reserve**[14] 8892 4-9-7 **85** ShaneGray 4
(David O'Meara) *hld up: rdn and outpcd over 2f out: lost tch and eased fr over 1f out* **5/2**[2]

2m 40.21s (-0.89) **Going Correction** +0.075s/f (Slow)
**WFA** 3 from 4yo+ 4lb **9 Ran SP% 114.4**
Speed ratings (Par 105): **105,104,104,103,103 102,102,102,65**
CSF £24.44 CT £121.64 TOTE £3.40: £1.10, £3.80, £1.40; EX 35.00 Trifecta £131.20.
**Owner** Chasemore Farm **Bred** Mr & Mrs A E Pakenham **Trained** Newmarket, Suffolk

**FOCUS**
This competitive handicap proved a lively betting heat and it saw a bunched finish.

## 9097 32RED CASINO NURSERY H'CAP — 1m 5y (Tp)
**4:00** (4:02) (Class 5) (0-75,77) 2-Y-O — **£3,234** (£962; £481; £240) **Stalls** Centre

Form — RPR

4245 **1** **Bold Reason (GER)**[32] 8595 2-9-9 **77** (b[1]) RobertHavlin 12 83+
(John Gosden) *hld up in tch nr side of gp: smooth hdwy to ld over 1f out: shkn up and edgd rt ins fnl f: styd on strly* **4/1**[2]

4500 **2** 2¼ **Bajan Gold (IRE)**[42] 8354 2-8-8 **65** (t) AaronJones(3) 14 66
(Stuart Williams) *dwlt: hld up: hdwy nr side of gp and prom over 1f out: kpt on fnl f to take 2nd last stride* **12/1**

624 **3** nse **Sharp Reminder**[28] 8669 2-9-2 **70** PhillipMakin 11 72
(James Tate) *hld up: hdwy on nr side of gp to press wnr over 1f out: kpt on same pce last 100yds: lost 2nd last stride* **16/1**

2345 **4** 3¼ **Far Dawn**[18] 8848 2-8-13 **67** (b[1]) JackMitchell 8 60
(Simon Crisford) *hld up midfield: smooth hdwy and prom in centre of gp whn nt clr run briefly and stmbld over 1f out: sn rdn: no imp fnl f* **8/1**[3]

632 **5** ¾ **Ideal Candy (IRE)**[13] 8914 2-9-0 **68** ShaneGray 10 60
(Karen Tutty) *hld up: rdn over 2f out: hdwy in centre of gp over 1f out: kpt on fnl f: nvr able to chal* **40/1**

020 **6** 1 **Jo's Girl (IRE)**[18] 8848 2-9-1 **69** (t[1]) AndrewMullen 13 58
(Micky Hammond) *hld up in rr: rdn over 2f out: hdwy on nr side of gp over 1f out: kpt on fnl f: no imp* **40/1**

**7** 3 **Papa Stour (USA)**[64] 7713 2-9-7 **75** RobHornby 1 57
(Andrew Balding) *prom on far side of gp: rdn and outpcd over 1f out: btn fnl f* **11/4**[1]

502 **8** ¾ **Sioux Frontier (IRE)**[26] 8715 2-9-1 **69** JackGarritty 5 50
(Richard Fahey) *taken early to post: t.k.h: hld up midfield in centre of gp: outpcd over 2f out: rallied ins fnl f: no imp* **10/1**

5001 **9** hd **Carp Kid (IRE)**[11] 8943 2-9-0 **68** DougieCostello 9 48
(Jamie Osborne) *cl up on nr side of gp: ev ch over 2f out to over 1f out: sn outpcd: btn ins fnl f* **9/1**

0063 **10** 1¾ **Grace's Secret**[19] 8817 2-9-3 **71** GrahamLee 7 47
(Ed Walker) *trckd ldrs in centre of gp: rdn over 2f out: wknd over 1f out* **8/1**[3]

5110 **11** nse **Sunbreak (IRE)**[53] 8045 2-9-5 **73** RichardKingscote 6 49
(Mark Johnston) *led in centre of gp: rdn and hdd over 1f out: sn btn* **14/1**

206 **12** 6 **Photonics (IRE)**[33] 8553 2-9-5 **73** PJMcDonald 3 35
(Hugo Palmer) *midfield on far side of gp: drvn and outpcd over 2f out: wknd wl over 1f out* **20/1**

606 **13** 8 **Wynfaul The Wizard (USA)**[21] 8782 2-8-5 **59** PatrickMathers 2 3
(Richard Guest) *dwlt: t.k.h: hld up on far side of gp: struggling over 2f out: sn btn* **100/1**

600 **14** 18 **Squirrelheed**[138] 5127 2-8-0 **54** oh8 HollieDoyle 4
(Richard Guest) *rrd s: bhd on far side of gp: struggling 3f out: lost tch fnl 2f* **100/1**

1m 38.98s (0.38) **Going Correction** +0.075s/f (Slow) **14 Ran SP% 119.8**
Speed ratings (Par 96): **101,98,98,95,94 93,90,89,89,88 87,81,73,55**
CSF £49.47 CT £520.80 TOTE £4.90: £1.90, £2.90, £4.40; EX 59.10 Trifecta £716.50.
**Owner** B E Nielsen **Bred** Bjorn E Nielsen **Trained** Newmarket, Suffolk
■ Stewards' Enquiry : Robert Havlin two-day ban: careless riding (Dec 20-21)

**FOCUS**
An open-looking nursery. A strong headwind was evident inside the final 2f and the principals were drawn high.

## 9098 32RED.COM NURSERY H'CAP — 6f (Tp)
**4:30** (4:35) (Class 4) (0-85,81) 2-Y-O — **£4,204** (£1,251; £625; £312) **Stalls** Centre

Form — RPR

1361 **1** **Armed Response**[75] 7362 2-9-7 **81** JackGarritty 5 84
(Jedd O'Keeffe) *w ldrs: led over 2f out to over 1f out: rallied and regained ld ins fnl f: hld on gamely* **7/2**[2]

0621 **2** hd **Lord Of The Glen**[21] 8780 2-8-1 **61** (v) HollieDoyle 6 63
(Jim Goldie) *in tch: hdwy to ld over 1f out: edgd lft and hdd ins fnl f: rallied: hld nr fin* **11/2**

024 **3** ½ **I'm Yer Man**[12] 8926 2-9-2 **76** ShaneGray 1 77
(Ann Duffield) *hld up: rdn and hdwy over 1f out: kpt on ins fnl f: nt rch first two* **16/1**

2302 **4** ½ **Move It Move It**[32] 8586 2-9-6 **80** PhillipMakin 2 79
(Keith Dalgleish) *hld up: hdwy over 2f out: rdn over 1f out: kpt on same pce fnl f* **11/8**[1]

3316 **5** ½ **Big Les (IRE)**[39] 8413 2-9-5 **79** PJMcDonald 4 77
(Karen McLintock) *hld up in tch: rdn over 2f out: hdwy over 1f out: kpt on same pce fnl f* **5/1**[3]

5430 **6** 3¾ **Gorse (IRE)**[37] 8475 2-8-2 **62** (p) JimmyQuinn 3 48
(Ann Duffield) *uns rdr and loose bef s: in tch: hdwy and cl up over 2f out: wknd over 1f out* **25/1**

0430 **7** 1¾ **Hello My Sunshine**[32] 8586 2-8-7 **67** AndrewMullen 8 48
(Karen McLintock) *w ldr to over 2f out: rdn and wknd wl over 1f out* **33/1**

5100 **8** 9 **Blacklooks (IRE)**[13] 8903 2-9-5 **79** (p[1]) TomEaves 7 33
(Ivan Furtado) *led to over 2f out: sn rdn and wknd* **14/1**

1m 13.04s (0.54) **Going Correction** +0.075s/f (Slow) **8 Ran SP% 115.7**
Speed ratings (Par 98): **99,98,98,97,96 91,89,77**
CSF £23.39 CT £273.44 TOTE £3.50: £1.20, £1.40, £3.60; EX 20.20 Trifecta £145.60.
**Owner** Caron & Paul Chapman **Bred** Alvediston Stud **Trained** Middleham Moor, N Yorks

**FOCUS**
A tight-looking nursery that saw another bunched finish.

## 9099 32RED.COM MAIDEN FILLIES' STKS (PLUS 10 RACE) — 1m 5y (Tp)
**5:00** (5:04) (Class 5) 2-Y-O — **£2,911** (£866; £432; £216) **Stalls** Centre

Form — RPR

**1** **Caring Touch (USA)** 2-9-0 0 JimmyQuinn 8 80+
(Saeed bin Suroor) *in tch: effrt and pushed along 2f out: led ins fnl f: styd on strly* **10/3**[3]

4 **2** 2½ **Angelina D'Or (GER)**[11] 8952 2-9-0 0 PJMcDonald 6 74
(Mark Johnston) *led: rdn 2f out: hdd ins fnl f: kpt on: nt pce of wnr* **3/1**[2]

02 **3** 3½ **Ruffina (USA)**[28] 8668 2-9-0 0 RobertHavlin 7 66
(John Gosden) *trckd ldr: effrt and rdn 2f out: outpcd fnl f* **11/10**[1]

00 **4** 2¾ **Leahcar**[13] 8914 2-9-0 0 TomEaves 11 60
(James Ewart) *hld up: pushed along over 2f out: hdwy over 1f out: kpt on fnl f: nvr able to chal* **100/1**

0 **5** ½ **Astolat**[28] 8669 2-9-0 0 RichardKingscote 2 58
(Ed Walker) *trckd ldrs: drvn along over 2f out: wknd over 1f out* **20/1**

**6** 2 **Catch The Tide (FR)** 2-9-0 0 (h[1]) DougieCostello 12 54
(Henry Spiller) *t.k.h: hld up: rdn over 2f out: hdwy over 1f out: sn no imp* **40/1**

**7** 1¼ **Now Say Yes (IRE)** 2-9-0 0 PaulMulrennan 5 51
(David Lanigan) *t.k.h in midfield: pushed along and outpcd over 2f out: btn over 1f out* **25/1**

0 **8** 3 **Born To Spend (IRE)**[28] 8678 2-9-0 0 PhillipMakin 4 44
(Ian Williams) *dwlt: sn prom: drvn and outpcd over 2f out: wknd over 1f out* **66/1**

**9** 3½ **Lady Grigio (IRE)** 2-9-0 0 GrahamLee 1 36
(Iain Jardine) *hld up towards rr: drvn and struggling over 2f out: sn btn* **50/1**

**10** 3½ **Streets Of Joy** 2-9-0 0 BenCurtis 9 28
(Henry Spiller) *hld up: rdn over 2f out: sn btn* **33/1**

**11** 9 **Arahat (USA)** 2-9-0 0 NickyMackay 10
(John Gosden) *awkward s: rn green in rr: struggling fr 1/2-way* **12/1**

1m 42.46s (3.86) **Going Correction** +0.075s/f (Slow) **11 Ran SP% 121.8**
Speed ratings (Par 93): **83,80,77,74,73 71,70,67,64,60 51**
CSF £13.62 TOTE £4.00: £1.10, £1.60, £1.10; EX 16.80 Trifecta £31.80.
**Owner** Godolphin **Bred** Godolphin **Trained** Newmarket, Suffolk

**FOCUS**
A fair 2yo fillies maiden, rated around the third. They went steadily until halfway.

## 9100 BET & WATCH AT SUNBETS.CO.UK H'CAP — 1m 5y (Tp)
**5:30** (5:34) (Class 5) (0-75,75) 3-Y-O+ — **£2,911** (£866; £432; £216) **Stalls** Centre

Form — RPR

5626 **1** **Thello**[12] 8928 5-8-11 **68** PhilDennis(3) 14 81
(Jim Goldie) *t.k.h: hld up: smooth hdwy on nr side of gp to ld over 1f out: shkn up and qcknd clr run-in: readily* **9/2**[2]

4-11 **2** 3 **Enigmatic (IRE)**[18] 8841 3-9-4 **73** DougieCostello 12 79
(Jamie Osborne) *prom on nr side of gp: effrt and chsd wnr over 1f out: kpt on ins fnl f: nt pce of wnr* **10/1**

1365 **3** 2 **Off Art**[12] 8928 7-8-12 **69** (p) RachelRichardson(3) 5 70
(Tim Easterby) *prom on far side of gp: drvn along over 2f out: kpt on ins fnl f: nt rch first two* **10/1**

2413 **4** nse **Newmarket Warrior (IRE)**[12] 8929 6-9-5 **73** (p) GrahamLee 10 74
(Iain Jardine) *hld up: pushed along over 2f out: kpt on fnl f: nrst fin* **4/1**[1]

0100 **5** ½ **William Sayle**[20] 8797 3-9-6 **75** (p) RobertHavlin 7 75
(John Gosden) *t.k.h: prom: led on nr side of gp over 2f out: hdd over 1f out: outpcd fnl f* **20/1**

0002 **6** 1 **Planetaria (IRE)**[12] 8928 4-9-4 **72** JasonHart 3 70
(Julie Camacho) *prom in centre of gp: rdn over 2f out: no ex fnl f* **8/1**[3]

1663 **7** ½ **Rock Warbler (IRE)**[25] 8749 4-9-7 **75** (t) PaulMulrennan 4 72
(Oliver Greenall) *hld up in centre of gp: rdn and hdwy 2f out: no imp fnl f* **4/1**[1]

0004 **8** nk **Sumner Beach**[12] 8929 3-9-4 **73** (tp) BenCurtis 9 69
(Brian Ellison) *midfield in centre of gp: drvn and effrt over 2f out: no imp over 1f out* **14/1**

0-00 **9** 1¾ **Le Roi Du Temps (USA)**[205] 2684 4-9-3 **71** AndrewMullen 8 63
(Tom Tate) *hld up in centre of gp: drvn along over 2f out: sn btn* **25/1**

5454 **10** 4½ **Rockwood**[128] 5469 6-9-7 **75** (v) PJMcDonald 2 57
(Karen McLintock) *missed break: hld up on far side of gp: struggling over 2f out: sn btn* **9/1**

1/0- **11** 17 **Scrutiny**[231] 1221 6-9-0 **68** JoeDoyle 1 11
(Kevin Ryan) *led on far side of gp to over 2f out: rdn and wknd qckly wl over 1f out* **33/1**

11-0 **12** 9 **Nice Vintage (IRE)**[12] 8929 5-8-6 **63** RowanScott(3) 11
(Katie Scott) *bhd in centre of gp: struggling over 2f out: sn btn* **100/1**

1m 38.72s (0.12) **Going Correction** +0.075s/f (Slow)
**WFA** 3 from 4yo+ 1lb **12 Ran SP% 116.7**
Speed ratings (Par 103): **102,99,97,96,96 95,94,94,92,88 71,62**
CSF £46.20 CT £434.62 TOTE £5.10: £1.10, £2.50, £3.70; EX 50.90 Trifecta £523.90.
**Owner** James Gaffney **Bred** Mickley Stud & Mr W T Whittle **Trained** Uplawmoor, E Renfrews

**FOCUS**
Another competitive handicap on the card. The main action came stands' side.

## 9101 SUNBETS.CO.UK H'CAP — 7f 14y (Tp)
**6:00** (6:03) (Class 5) (0-75,77) 3-Y-O+ — **£2,911** (£866; £432; £216) **Stalls** Centre

Form — RPR

3101 **1** **Equiano Springs**[33] 8556 3-9-7 **75** AndrewMullen 4 84
(Tom Tate) *mde all in centre: rdn over 1f out: hld on wl fnl f* **9/1**

4154 **2** ½ **Deansgate (IRE)**[33] 8556 4-9-4 **72** PaulMulrennan 7 80
(Julie Camacho) *dwlt: hld up in centre of gp: hdwy and edgd lft over 1f out: chsd wnr ins fnl f: kpt on: hld towards fin* **8/1**[3]

5400 **3** 2¼ **My Amigo**[26] 8718 4-9-9 **77** (p) PJMcDonald 14 79
(K R Burke) *chsd wnr on nr side: rdn over 2f out: no ex and lost 2nd ins fnl f* **9/2**[1]

50-6 **4** ¾ **Able Jack**[32] 8600 4-9-5 **76** (v) AaronJones(3) 12 76
(Stuart Williams) *hld up: hdwy nr side of gp and prom 2f out: rdn and one pce fnl f* **10/1**

2000 **5** ½ **Tommy G**[43] 8319 4-9-1 **76**... SeanMooney(7) 6 75
(Jim Goldie) *hld up in centre of gp: rdn over 2f out: hdwy over 1f out: no imp fnl f* **14/1**

3300 **6** 2½ **Acrux**[13] 8907 4-9-3 **71**...(h) RichardKingscote 13 63
(David O'Meara) *hld up: hdwy nr side of gp and prom over 2f out: rdn over 1f out: wknd fnl f* **9/2**[1]

31-0 **7** ¾ **King Of Nepal**[221] 2151 3-9-6 **74**... JackGarritty 2 64
(Henry Candy) *t.k.h: cl up on far side of gp: rdn over 2f out: btn ins fnl f* **5/1**[2]

1 **8** ½ **Bobby Joe Leg**[12] 8931 3-9-7 **75**... TomEaves 10 63
(Ruth Carr) *hld up: stdy hdwy on nr side of gp wl over 1f out: sn rdn and edgd lft: no imp fnl f* **16/1**

4123 **9** 1 **Gun Case**[12] 8928 5-8-10 **67**... RowanScott(3) 1 53
(Alistair Whillans) *hld up on far side of gp: drvn and outpcd over 2f out: n.d after* **9/1**

6015 **10** ½ **Our Greta (IRE)**[16] 8875 3-8-12 **66**... BenCurtis 9 50
(Michael Appleby) *prom in centre of gp: rdn over 2f out: edgd lft and wknd over 1f out* **20/1**

0564 **11** 4½ **Magistral**[32] 8589 7-8-2 **61**...(p) JamieGormley(5) 11 33
(Linda Perratt) *midfield in centre of trck: drvn and outpcd over 2f out: sn wknd* **20/1**

6000 **12** 17 **Zoravan (USA)**[155] 4475 4-9-9 **77**...(v) PhillipMakin 8 3
(Keith Dalgleish) *hld up on far side of gp: struggling 3f out: sn wknd: eased whn no ch fnl f* **18/1**

1130 **13** 8 **Spinwheel**[270] 1149 3-9-6 **74**... SamJames 5
(John Davies) *cl up in centre of gp tl rdn and wknd over 2f out: eased whn no ch fnl f* **100/1**

04L6 **14** 11 **Majdool (IRE)**[12] 8929 4-8-10 **67**... PhilDennis(3) 3
(Noel Wilson) *rrd and lost many l s: nvr on terms: eased whn no ch fnl 2f* **28/1**

1m 25.03s (-1.17) **Going Correction** +0.075s/f (Slow) **14** Ran SP% **125.0**
Speed ratings (Par 103): **109,108,105,105,104 101,100,100,99,98 93,73,64,52**
CSF £79.19 CT £386.53 TOTE £10.00: £3.30, £3.50, £1.50; EX 93.30 Trifecta £926.50.
**Owner** T T Racing **Bred** Paddock Space **Trained** Tadcaster, N Yorks

**FOCUS**
This looked wide-open, but few landed a blow. Straightforward form.

## 9102 BETWAY H'CAP 6f (Tp)
**6:30** (6:32) (Class 6) (0-55,57) 3-Y-O+ **£2,264** (£673; £336; £168) **Stalls** Centre

Form RPR

6060 **1** **Star Cracker (IRE)**[37] 8480 5-9-9 **57**...(p) PJMcDonald 11 65
(Jim Goldie) *prom: hdwy on nr side of gp to ld over 1f out: drvn out fnl f* **12/1**

4543 **2** ½ **Broughtons Fancy**[4] 9052 4-8-11 **52**...(p[1]) HarrisonShaw(7) 12 59
(Karen Tutty) *prom: effrt on nr side of gp and chsd wnr over 1f out: kpt on ins fnl f* **7/2**[2]

0602 **3** 1¾ **Borough Boy (IRE)**[8] 8980 7-9-7 **55**...(v) PatrickMathers 9 56
(Derek Shaw) *t.k.h: hld up in tch in centre of gp: hdwy over 1f out: kpt on same pce ins fnl f* **5/1**[3]

0005 **4** 3½ **Sir Harry Collins (IRE)**[5] 9034 3-9-0 **48**...(v[1]) PhillipMakin 4 39
(Michael Appleby) *t.k.h: led at decent gallop in centre of gp: rdn and hdd over 1f out: outpcd fnl f* **10/1**

0650 **5** nk **Captain Scooby**[29] 8656 11-8-12 **46** oh1...(b) JasonHart 10 36
(Richard Guest) *dwlt: bhd: drvn along 1/2-way: hdwy on nr side of gp fnl f: kpt on: nvr able to chal* **20/1**

5-00 **6** 1¼ **Dazeekha**[21] 8784 4-8-13 **47**... TomEaves 2 33
(Michael Herrington) *hld up towards rr: shortlived effrt in centre of gp over 1f out: sn no imp* **25/1**

0501 **7** nk **Lotara**[6] 9013 5-8-9 **46** oh1... PhilDennis(3) 1 31
(Jim Goldie) *taken early to post: hld up on far side of gp: drvn and outpcd over 2f out: n.d after* **7/4**[1]

0065 **8** 2¾ **Market Choice (IRE)**[29] 8656 4-9-7 **55**... BenCurtis 7 32
(Tracy Waggott) *t.k.h: chsd ldr in centre of gp to 1/2-way: rdn and wknd over 1f out* **7/1**

500- **9** 13 **Go Charlie**[481] 5378 6-8-12 **46**...(h) JoeDoyle 8
(Lisa Williamson) *taken early to post: hld up on far side of gp: struggling over 2f out: sn btn* **66/1**

1m 12.3s (-0.20) **Going Correction** +0.075s/f (Slow) **9** Ran SP% **114.6**
Speed ratings (Par 101): **104,103,101,96,95 94,93,90,72**
CSF £52.47 CT £241.80 TOTE £7.40: £2.50, £1.10, £2.00; EX 51.20 Trifecta £201.10.
**Owner** The Vital Sparks **Bred** James Mc Claren **Trained** Uplawmoor, E Renfrews

**FOCUS**
They went a solid pace in this moderate sprint handicap.

## 9103 BETWAY MEDIAN AUCTION MAIDEN STKS 5f (Tp)
**7:00** (7:00) (Class 6) 3-5-Y-O **£2,264** (£673; £336; £168) **Stalls** Centre

Form RPR

6233 **1** **Dream Revival**[12] 8924 4-9-0 50...(p) PJMcDonald 2 59
(Paul Collins) *s.i.s: in tch: hdwy nr side of gp to ld over 1f out: edgd lft ins fnl f: rdn out* **8/11**[1]

-500 **2** 3 **Oh So Dandy (IRE)**[8] 8980 3-9-5 54...(v) PatrickMathers 1 53
(Derek Shaw) *t.k.h: prom: hdwy on outside of gp and chsd wnr over 1f out: kpt on same pce ins fnl f* **8/1**

030 **3** 3 **Irish Sky (IRE)**[18] 8842 3-9-0 52...(p[1]) BenCurtis 5 37
(Henry Spiller) *t.k.h: cl up: led 1/2-way to over 1f out: rdn and wknd ins fnl f* **3/1**[2]

0600 **4** 1¼ **Kirkby's Phantom**[29] 8656 3-9-0 20...(p) AndrewMullen 3 33
(Alan Berry) *led to 1/2-way: rdn and wknd over 1f out* **100/1**

4402 **5** 3½ **Excellent World (IRE)**[23] 8774 4-9-0 46...(t) DougieCostello 4 20
(Tony Coyle) *t.k.h: cl up tl rdn and wknd over 1f out* **6/1**[3]

1m 1.62s (2.12) **Going Correction** +0.075s/f (Slow) **5** Ran SP% **109.3**
Speed ratings (Par 101): **86,81,76,74,68**
CSF £7.24 TOTE £1.40: £1.10, £2.70; EX 6.60 Trifecta £13.10.
**Owner** Ms R Taylor **Bred** Knockroon Stud **Trained** Saltburn, Cleveland

**FOCUS**
A desperately weak sprint maiden.

T/Plt: £122.40 to a £1 stake. Pool: £77,783.62. 463.56 winning units. T/Qpdt: £15.40 to a £1 stake. Pool: £13,359.29. 640.33 winning units. **Richard Young**

9104 - 9111a (Foreign Racing) - See Raceform Interactive

# 9086 DEAUVILLE (R-H)
Wednesday, December 6

**OFFICIAL GOING: Polytrack: standard**

## 9112a PRIX DES PERRETS (CLAIMER) (4YO+) (LADY RIDERS) (POLYTRACK) 1m 1f 110y(P)
**10:50** 4-Y-0+ **£7,692** (£3,076; £2,307; £1,538; £769)

RPR

**1** **Zariyano (FR)**[50] 5-9-0 0... MlleMickaelleMichel(5) 13 77
(Carina Fey, France) **27/10**[1]

**2** 1¼ **Sky Bolt (FR)**[116] 4-8-4 0...(b) MlleLucieOger(7) 2 66
(H-A Pantall, France) **12/1**

**3** snk **Barye**[34] 8539 6-8-6 0...(p) MlleLeaBails(5) 4 66
(Richard Hughes) *sn led on inner: wnt 2l clr wl over 2 1/2f out: c towards stands' side st: jnd appr 1 1/2f out: hdd ins fnl f: kpt on under hands and heels* **17/5**[2]

**4** snk **Dakarus Fritz (GER)**[196] 4-8-11 0... MllePaulineDominois 11 66
(M Figge, Germany) **56/10**

**5** 1¾ **Tour**[5] 4-8-6 0...(p) MlleRomaneViolet(5) 6 62
(M Nigge, France) **36/1**

**6** 2½ **Basileus (IRE)**[28] 4-9-4 0... DelphineSantiago 3 64
(A Giorgi, Italy) **6/1**

**7** 1 **Federico**[23] 4-9-3 0...(b) MlleMarionLanave(5) 12 66
(Mlle C Nicot, France) **18/5**[3]

**8** 2 **Barocca (GER)**[267] 1196 5-8-3 0... MlleCoraliePacaut(5) 1 48
(S Smrczek, Germany) **22/1**

**9** hd **Lions Hill (GER)** 4-8-13 0... MlleLauraPoggionovo(5) 8 58
(J-Y Artu, France) **81/1**

**10** 12 **House Captain**[29] 6-9-4 0... MlleMarylineEon 7 33
(Georgios Alimpinisis, Greece) **68/1**

1m 55.78s **10** Ran SP% **118.3**
PARI-MUTUEL (all including 1 euro stake): WIN 3.70; PLACE 1.90, 3.10, 2.10; DF 22.40; SF 38.80.
**Owner** Torsten Raber **Bred** Appapays Racing Club **Trained** France

9113 - 9121a (Foreign Racing) - See Raceform Interactive

# 9020 CHELMSFORD (A.W) (L-H)
Thursday, December 7

**OFFICIAL GOING: Polytrack: standard**
Wind: light to medium, across Weather: dry

## 9122 BET TOTEPLACEPOT AT BETFRED.COM NURSERY H'CAP 5f (P)
**5:25** (5:26) (Class 5) (0-75,70) 2-Y-O **£3,234** (£962; £481; £240) **Stalls** Low

Form RPR

264 **1** **Global Academy (IRE)**[30] 8657 2-9-6 **69**...(p[1]) MartinHarley 6 79
(Gay Kelleway) *mde all: 5 l clr 2f out: rdn and styd on wl fr over 1f out: unchal* **6/1**

3000 **2** 4 **Angel Of The South (IRE)**[77] 7334 2-9-7 **70**... RobertWinston 2 66+
(Dean Ivory) *s.i.s: swtchd rt and effrt over 1f out: chsd clr wnr 150yds: kpt on but nvr a threat* **3/1**[2]

0022 **3** 3¼ **Mother Of Dragons (IRE)**[6] 9024 2-8-11 **67**... NicolaCurrie(7) 4 51
(Phil McEntee) *sn pushed along and outpcd: nt clrest of runs wl over 1f out: effrt over 1f out: no imp* **5/1**[3]

0052 **4** 1 **Alaskan Bay (IRE)**[8] 9002 2-8-5 **54**... HollieDoyle 1 35
(Rae Guest) *chsd wnr: pushed along wl over 2f out: sn outpcd by wnr: wl btn 1f out: lost 2 pls ins fnl f* **15/8**[1]

0421 **5** ½ **Magic Pulse (IRE)**[21] 8795 2-9-0 **63**... DougieCostello 5 42
(David C Griffiths) *s.i.s and wnt rt s: off the pce in last pair: effrt over 1f out: no imp* **5/1**[3]

6000 **6** 1¾ **Cardaw Lily (IRE)**[43] 8349 2-9-0 **68**...(p[1]) FinleyMarsh(5) 7 41
(Richard Hughes) *t.k.h early: chsd ldng pair: outpcd over 2f out: no threat to wnr after: wknd ins fnl f* **25/1**

59.63s (-0.57) **Going Correction** -0.10s/f (Stan) **6** Ran SP% **111.2**
Speed ratings (Par 96): **100,93,88,86,86 83**
CSF £23.71 TOTE £6.70: £2.90, £2.00; EX 26.00 Trifecta £115.00.
**Owner** Dr Johnny Hon **Bred** Noel Brosnan **Trained** Exning, Suffolk

**FOCUS**
A modest sprint nursery. The winner broke well and never saw another rival in a thoroughly dominant display.

## 9123 BET TOTEJACKPOT AT BETFRED.COM EBF NOVICE STKS (PLUS 10 RACE) 6f (P)
**5:55** (5:57) (Class 4) 2-Y-O **£7,115** (£2,117; £1,058; £529) **Stalls** Centre

Form RPR

4 **1** **Mushtaq (IRE)**[15] 8888 2-9-2 0... TomMarquand 6 81
(Richard Hannon) *sn dropped to last pair: pushed along and hdwy on outer bnd 2f out: carried rt wl over 1f out: rdn and hdwy to chal ins fnl f: drvn to ld wl ins fnl f: styd on* **4/1**[2]

2242 **2** ¾ **Choice Encounter**[20] 8819 2-8-13 75... CallumShepherd(3) 5 79
(Michael Bell) *bmpd s and dwlt: sn swtchd lft: hdwy into midfield 4f out: rdn to ld over 1f out: sn drifted rt: kpt on: hdd and nt quite match pce of wnr towards fin* **6/1**[3]

60 **3** 2¼ **Lethal Angel**[19] 8850 2-8-11 0... FranBerry 7 67
(Stuart Williams) *styd wd: hld up towards rr: effrt over 1f out: kpt on ins fnl f: wnt 3rd on post: nvr getting on terms w ldng pair* **33/1**

31 **4** nse **Red Cymbal**[20] 8809 2-9-6 0... GeorgiaCox(3) 4 79
(William Haggas) *in tch: effrt and swtchd wl over 1f out: chsd ldrs and kpt on same pce ins fnl f: lost 3rd on post* **4/6**[1]

**5** 2½ **Grandfather Tom** 2-8-13 0... EoinWalsh(3) 8 65
(Robert Cowell) *in tch in midfield: clsd to chse ldng pair over 1f out: rdn and unable qck over 1f out: wknd ins fnl f* **50/1**

4 **6** 6 **Filbert Street**[20] 8809 2-9-2 0... LukeMorris 1 47
(Robert Cowell) *prom tl led 4f out: rdn and hdd over 1f out: wknd ins fnl f* **8/1**

1062 **7** 1¼ **Arden Pearl (IRE)**[12] 8954 2-9-0 74...(p) EdwardGreatrex 3 41
(Archie Watson) *taken down early: led tl 4f out: losing pl and impeded jst over 1f out: wknd ins fnl f* **6/1**[3]

0 **8** *3 1/4* **Sir Hector (IRE)**[209] 2577 2-9-2 0 ........................ DanielMuscutt 2 33
(Charlie Wallis) *chsd ldrs tl rdn and lost pl qckly over 2f out: bhd whn hung lft over 1f out: wknd ins fnl f* **150/1**

1m 12.93s (-0.77) **Going Correction** -0.10s/f (Stan) 8 Ran SP% **125.2**
Speed ratings (Par 98): **101,100,97,96,93 85,83,79**
CSF £30.69 TOTE £4.80: £1.90, £1.70, £5.80; EX 34.00 Trifecta £542.30.
**Owner** Al Shaqab Racing **Bred** M Phelan **Trained** East Everleigh, Wilts

**FOCUS**
A fair juvenile novice contest. They went a contested gallop and the first three home came through from off the pace.

## 9124 BET TOTEQUADPOT AT BETFRED.COM H'CAP 6f (P)
**6:30** (6:30) (Class 4) (0-80,81) 3-Y-O+ **£7,762** (£2,310; £1,154; £577) **Stalls** Centre

Form RPR

0504 **1** **Cappananty Con**[30] 8645 3-9-4 **77** ........................ RobertWinston 7 85
(Dean Ivory) *t.k.h: broke wl: sn restrained to chse ldrs: effrt over 1f out: rdn to press ldr ent fnl f: led ins fnl f: styd on wl* **6/1**[2]

0321 **2** *3/4* **Born To Finish (IRE)**[30] 8645 4-9-4 **77** ........................(p) DougieCostello 5 82+
(Jamie Osborne) *in tch towards rr: rdn and gd hdwy towards inner over 1f out: chsd ldrs and swtchd rt ins fnl f: styd on strly to go 2nd last strides* **7/2**[1]

0020 **3** *nk* **Red Tycoon (IRE)**[69] 7571 5-8-11 **70** ........................ HollieDoyle 1 74
(Ken Cunningham-Brown) *t.k.h: trckd ldrs: effrt on inner over 1f out: styd on same pce wl ins fnl f* **9/1**

050 **4** *nk* **Aleef (IRE)**[35] 8540 4-9-6 **79** ........................(t[1]) MartinHarley 3 82
(David O'Meara) *led: rdn over 1f out: hdd ins fnl f: no ex and lost 2 pls towards fin* **6/1**[2]

2022 **5** *2 1/4* **Nezar (IRE)**[16] 8881 6-9-4 **80** ........................ JackDuern[(3)] 8 75
(Dean Ivory) *hld up in tch towards rr: gd hdwy on outer 3f out: chsd ldrs and rdn 2f out: unable qck 1f out: wknd ins fnl f* **6/1**[2]

0001 **6** *1/2* **Captain Lars (SAF)**[14] 8906 8-9-5 **78** ........................(v) PatrickMathers 9 72
(Derek Shaw) *chsd ldrs: rdn over 1f out: unable qck and wknd wl ins fnl f* **7/1**[3]

0510 **7** *1 3/4* **Danecase**[30] 8645 4-8-10 **76** ........................ RossaRyan[(7)] 10 64
(David Dennis) *hld up in tch in midfield: effrt u.p over 1f out: styd on same pce and no imp ins fnl f* **25/1**

5030 **8** *hd* **Curious Fox**[64] 7737 4-9-7 **80** ........................ DavidProbert 2 68
(Anthony Carson) *hld up in tch in midfield: edgd lft and no imp ins fnl f* **14/1**

1546 **9** *shd* **Inexes**[17] 8872 5-9-4 **77** ........................(p) PhillipMakin 13 64
(Marjorie Fife) *hld up in tch towards rr: nt clrest of runs over 1f out: modest late hdwy: nvr trbld ldrs* **8/1**

050 **10** *hd* **Jameerah**[14] 8913 4-9-5 **78** ........................ GrahamLee 14 65
(Bryan Smart) *hld up in midfield: effrt over 1f out: no imp: nvr trbld ldrs* **25/1**

0540 **11** *2 3/4* **Monte Cinq (IRE)**[30] 8651 3-9-7 **80** ........................ TomEaves 6 58
(Jason Ward) *stdd after s: hld up in rr: swtchd rt over 1f out: no prog: n.d* **16/1**

600 **12** *nk* **Kinglami**[8] 8990 8-9-2 **75** ........................(p) FranBerry 11 52
(John O'Shea) *dwlt: hld up in rr: n.d* **40/1**

20-0 **13** *10* **Whirl Me Round**[17] 8872 3-9-8 **81** ........................ LukeMorris 4 26
(George Peckham) *taken down early: chsd ldr tl lost pl wl over 1f out: bhd and eased ins fnl f* **20/1**

4000 **14** *11* **Gold Flash**[199] 2893 5-9-2 **75** ........................ JimmyQuinn 12
(Richenda Ford) *chsd ldrs tl lost pl over 2f out: bhd over 1f out* **66/1**

1m 12.1s (-1.60) **Going Correction** -0.10s/f (Stan) 14 Ran SP% **127.6**
Speed ratings (Par 105): **106,105,104,104,101 100,98,97,97,97 93,93,80,65**
CSF £27.46 CT £204.86 TOTE £8.90: £2.80, £1.80, £2.40; EX 40.00 Trifecta £388.20.
**Owner** Jim Biggane, John Waterfall & Dean Ivory **Bred** Miss H Botterill & Mr D R Botterill **Trained** Radlett, Herts

**FOCUS**
A fair handicap. They went a decent gallop and it is sound form.

## 9125 BET TOTEEXACTA AT BETFRED.COM H'CAP 1m (P)
**7:00** (7:01) (Class 3) (0-95,95) 3-Y-O+ **£9,703** (£2,887; £1,443; £721) **Stalls** Low

Form RPR

2-1 **1** **Bowerman**[246] 1551 3-8-12 **87** ........................ JackMitchell 2 99+
(Roger Varian) *hld up wl in tch in midfield: clsd to trck ldrs ent fnl 2f: shkn up to chal jst over 1f out: pushed into ld ins fnl f: sn in command and r.o wl: readily* **5/6**[1]

2000 **2** *2 3/4* **Believe It (IRE)**[16] 8880 5-8-6 **87** ........................ StephenCummins[(7)] 6 93+
(Richard Hughes) *squeezed for room leaving stalls: t.k.h: hld up in tch in rr: hdwy and nt clr run on inner over 1f out swtchd rt 1f out: r.o wl ins fnl f to go 2nd last strides* **66/1**

3003 **3** *hd* **Sibilance**[62] 7781 3-8-13 **88** ........................ RichardKingscote 5 94
(Ralph Beckett) *chsd ldr: rdn and ev ch over 1f out tl unable to match pce of wnr ins fnl f: kpt on same pce fnl 100yds: lost 2nd last strides* **10/3**[2]

66-6 **4** *3/4* **C Note (IRE)**[12] 8944 4-9-7 **95** ........................(t) TomMarquand 10 99
(Heather Main) *hld up in tch in midfield: effrt over 1f out: hdwy u.p 1f out: kpt on wl ins fnl f: no threat to wnr* **40/1**

1030 **5** *nk* **London (FR)**[26] 8737 4-9-1 **89** ........................(h) JosephineGordon 4 92
(Phil McEntee) *led: rdn and hrd pressed over 1f out: hdd and immediately outpcd by wnr ins fnl f: kpt on same pce and lost 3 pls ins fnl f* **14/1**

0505 **6** *2 3/4* **Loyalty**[14] 8905 10-8-11 **85** ........................(v) PatrickMathers 11 82+
(Derek Shaw) *hld up in tch towards rr: effrt on outer bnd 2f out: hdwy u.p 1f out: edgd lft but kpt on ins fnl f: no threat to wnr* **25/1**

5000 **7** *1/2* **Holiday Magic (IRE)**[20] 8812 6-8-11 **92** ........................ HarrisonShaw[(7)] 9 88
(Michael Easterby) *hld up in tch in midfield: shuffled bk to rr over 2f out: pushed along and sme hdwy whn nt clr run over 1f out: keeping on same pce whn nt clr run again ins fnl f: nvr threatened ldrs* **50/1**

0000 **8** *3 1/4* **Kickboxer (IRE)**[20] 8812 6-9-2 **90** ........................ DanielMuscutt 3 78
(Michael Appleby) *hld up in tch in midfield: effrt ent fnl 2f: drvn and unable qck over 1f out: wknd ins fnl f* **33/1**

0050 **9** *1 3/4* **Mr Bossy Boots (IRE)**[35] 8547 6-9-2 **90** ........................(p) JoeyHaynes 12 74
(Amanda Perrett) *t.k.h: chsd ldrs on outer tl lost pl over 2f out: bhd ins fnl f* **25/1**

0525 **10** *nk* **Belgian Bill**[19] 8843 9-9-7 **95** ........................ LiamKeniry 1 78
(George Baker) *dwlt: sn rcvrd to trck ldrs: effrt over 1f out: unable qck and btn 1f out: wknd ins fnl f* **7/1**[3]

0052 **11** *6* **Chevallier**[12] 8944 5-9-2 **90** ........................(p) LukeMorris 7 60
(Archie Watson) *wl in tch in midfield tl shuffled bk towards rr over 2f out: swtchd rt and effrt ent fnl 2f: sn btn and bhd fnl f* **10/1**

5200 **12** *2* **Kentuckyconnection (USA)**[64] 7727 4-9-1 **89** ........................ GrahamLee 8 54
(Bryan Smart) *chsd ldrs tl lost pl qckly over 2f out: bhd fnl f* **25/1**

1m 38.47s (-1.43) **Going Correction** -0.10s/f (Stan)
**WFA** 3 from 4yo+ 1lb 12 Ran SP% **126.3**
Speed ratings (Par 107): **103,100,100,99,99 96,95,92,90,90 84,82**
CSF £113.08 CT £168.06 TOTE £1.90: £1.10, £12.50, £1.30; EX 97.40 Trifecta £398.80.
**Owner** Paul Smith **Bred** Cheveley Park Stud Ltd **Trained** Newmarket, Suffolk

**FOCUS**
The feature contest was a good handicap. The favourite showed a touch of class in justifying strong market support.

## 9126 BET TOTETRIFECTA AT BETFRED.COM H'CAP 1m (P)
**7:30** (7:30) (Class 5) (0-70,72) 3-Y-O+ **£5,175** (£1,540; £769; £384) **Stalls** Low

Form RPR

3412 **1** **Glenn Coco**[31] 8640 3-9-3 **70** ........................ AaronJones[(3)] 6 82+
(Stuart Williams) *mde all: rdn and fnd ex over 1f out: clr and pushed along hands and heels ins fnl f: comf* **7/2**[2]

4432 **2** *2 3/4* **Samphire Coast**[14] 8907 4-9-0 **63** ........................(v) PatrickMathers 5 69
(Derek Shaw) *restless in stalls: t.k.h: wl in tch in midfield: effrt to press wnr and kicked clr jst over 2f out: unable to match pce of wnr 1f out: kpt on same pce ins fnl f* **6/1**

0032 **3** *2* **Wicker**[30] 8646 3-9-8 **72** ........................ MartinHarley 1 73
(Jane Chapple-Hyam) *hld up wl in tch in midfield: nt clr run and shuffled bk towards rr over 2f out: swtchd rt and hdwy over 1f out: kpt on ins fnl f to go 3rd towards fin: no threat to ldrs* **5/1**[3]

4351 **4** *3/4* **Broughtons Knight**[54] 8031 3-8-13 **63** ........................ JackMitchell 3 63
(Jim Boyle) *hld up in tch in last trio: rdn and hdwy 2f out: chsd clr ldng pair ent fnl f: kpt on same pce: lost 3rd towards fin* **10/3**[1]

0341 **5** *nk* **Pass The Cristal (IRE)**[62] 7791 3-9-3 **67** ........................ DougieCostello 4 66
(William Muir) *hld up in tch in last pair: effrt on outer over 1f out: kpt on ins fnl f: nvr trbld ldrs* **8/1**

0011 **6** *5* **Fire Diamond**[26] 8749 4-9-8 **71** ........................(p) RichardKingscote 7 58
(Tom Dascombe) *t.k.h: hld up in tch last trio: effrt ent fnl 2f: no imp and btn over 1f out: wknd fnl f* **7/1**

6020 **7** *1 1/4* **Out Of The Ashes**[14] 8907 4-9-2 **68** ........................(t) EoinWalsh[(3)] 8 53
(Mohamed Moubarak) *t.k.h: chsd wnr tl over 2f out: sn lost pl u.p: bhd ins fnl f* **33/1**

6000 **8** *1/2* **Ready (IRE)**[37] 8497 7-9-5 **68** ........................(p) DannyBrock 2 51
(Mark Pattinson) *chsd ldng pair: unable qck u.p over 1f out: wknd fnl f* **6/1**

1m 39.59s (-0.31) **Going Correction** -0.10s/f (Stan)
**WFA** 3 from 4yo+ 1lb 8 Ran SP% **117.1**
Speed ratings (Par 103): **97,94,92,91,91 86,84,84**
CSF £25.44 CT £105.99 TOTE £3.60: £1.70, £2.00, £1.20; EX 25.80 Trifecta £144.10.
**Owner** Miss Emily Stevens Partnership **Bred** Old Mill Stud And S C Williams **Trained** Newmarket, Suffolk

■ Stewards' Enquiry : Danny Brock two-day ban: using his whip above shoulder height (Dec 21-22)

**FOCUS**
An ordinary handicap. The second-favourite won well off his own respectable tempo.

## 9127 BET TOTEWIN AT BETFRED.COM H'CAP (DIV I) 1m 2f (P)
**8:00** (8:02) (Class 6) (0-60,62) 3-Y-O+ **£3,234** (£962; £481; £240) **Stalls** Low

Form RPR

5050 **1** **Ceyhan**[93] 6799 5-9-8 **61** ........................ DougieCostello 2 68
(Jamie Osborne) *hld up in tch in midfield: clsd on inner over 2f out: rdn to chal over 1f out: kpt on u.p to ld towards fin* **6/1**

6321 **2** *1/2* **Chaucer's Tale**[7] 9012 3-8-12 **60** ........................(t) HarrisonShaw[(7)] 10 67
(Michael Easterby) *t.k.h: led: drifted rt off bnd wl over 1f out: rdn over 1f out: kpt on u.p tl hdd and no ex wl ins fnl f* **3/1**[2]

1033 **3** *2 3/4* **Venetian Proposal (IRE)**[108] 6257 3-9-1 **56** ........................(p) KieranO'Neill 9 58
(Zoe Davison) *t.k.h: pressed ldr for 2f: chsd ldr pair after: rdn over 1f out: unable qck and edgd lft 1f out: outpcd ins fnl f* **20/1**

5661 **4** *2* **Huddersfilly Town**[21] 8799 3-9-1 **56** ........................(p) PhillipMakin 7 56+
(Ivan Furtado) *dwlt and pushed along early: hld up in tch in last trio: effrt wd over 1f out: kpt on ins fnl f: nvr threatened ldrs* **4/1**[3]

0000 **5** *3 1/4* **Diana Lady (CHI)**[36] 8513 5-9-9 **62** ........................(t[1]) EdwardGreatrex 1 53
(Luke McJannet) *stdd s: t.k.h: hld up in tch in rr: effrt 2f out: sme hdwy u.p over 1f out: no imp ins fnl f: nvr trbld ldrs* **50/1**

0005 **6** *2 3/4* **Optima Petamus**[21] 8799 5-8-11 **50** ........................(p) JoeyHaynes 6 36
(Patrick Holmes) *hld up in tch in midfield: effrt u.p over 2f out: no imp and btn over 1f out: wknd ins fnl f* **20/1**

3614 **7** *4 1/2* **Arcadian Sea (IRE)**[63] 7761 3-9-3 **58** ........................ JosephineGordon 4 36
(William Jarvis) *t.k.h: chsd ldrs: rdn and unable qck over 2f out: lost pl over 1f out: wknd ins fnl f* **15/8**[1]

6060 **8** *shd* **Fairy Mist (IRE)**[119] 5817 10-8-6 **48** oh1 ow2........................(v) MitchGodwin[(3)] 3 25
(John Bridger) *t.k.h: hld up in tch in last trio: effrt over 2f out: no imp and swtchd lft over 1f out: wknd ins fnl f* **66/1**

5006 **9** *2 1/2* **Love Me Again**[31] 8635 3-9-2 **57** ........................ DanielMuscutt 5 30
(Charlie Fellowes) *dwlt and short of room leaving stall: hld up in tch in midfield: effrt jst over 2f out: no imp and btn over 1f out: wknd ins fnl f* **18/1**

0400 **10** *4 1/2* **Lord Of The Storm**[49] 8183 9-8-9 **48** ........................ LukeMorris 8 12
(Michael Attwater) *midfield tl hdwy to chse ldr after 2f tl over 2f out: lost pl u.p over 1f out: bhd ins fnl f* **16/1**

00-6 **11** *1 3/4* **Life Happens**[307] 552 3-8-11 **52** ........................(p[1]) RobHornby 11 13
(Jonathan Portman) *wnt rt s: hdwy into midfield: lost pl over 2f out: bhd 1f out* **40/1**

2m 7.95s (-0.65) **Going Correction** -0.10s/f (Stan)
**WFA** 3 from 5yo+ 2lb 11 Ran SP% **120.6**
Speed ratings (Par 101): **98,97,95,93,91 89,85,85,83,79 78**
CSF £23.82 CT £349.08 TOTE £6.70: £2.30, £1.60, £7.00; EX 28.90 Trifecta £427.80.
**Owner** Melbourne 10 Racing **Bred** Ashbrittle Stud **Trained** Upper Lambourn, Berks

**FOCUS**
The first division of a modest handicap. They went a muddling gallop, but the the winner made the most of his decreasing mark in game enough fashion.

## 9128 BET TOTEWIN AT BETFRED.COM H'CAP (DIV II) 1m 2f (P)
**8:30** (8:33) (Class 6) (0-60,62) 3-Y-O+ **£3,234** (£962; £481; £240) **Stalls** Low

Form RPR

0055 **1** **Zoffany Bay (IRE)**[6] 9027 3-9-4 **58** ........................(p[1]) KieranO'Neill 1 68
(George Peckham) *chsd ldrs: effrt to chse ldr and kicked clr ent fnl 2f: rdn and chalng 1f out: led ins fnl f: pricked ears in front but c clr* **5/2**[2]

0400 **2** *1 1/2* **Fintech (IRE)**[40] 8429 3-9-5 **62** ........................(t) HectorCrouch[(3)] 5 69
(Philip Hide) *led: rdn and kicked clr w wnr ent fnl 2f: hdd and kpt on same pce fnl 100yds* **7/1**

060 **3** 3 ¾ **Captain Peaky**[135] 5258 4-8-13 **51** ow1 DougieCostello 2 50
(Patrick Holmes) *t.k.h: in tch in midfield: effrt over 2f out: chsd clr ldng pair over 1f out: no imp* **25/1**

3000 **4** ½ **Characterized**[14] 8908 3-9-3 **57** TimmyMurphy 6 56
(Geoffrey Deacon) *chsd ldrs: rdn and unable qck over 2f out: no threat to ldrs and kpt on same pce fr over 1f out* **14/1**

0020 **5** *hd* **Wootyhoot (FR)**[35] 8538 3-9-5 **59** DanielMuscutt 8 58
(James Fanshawe) *hld up towards rr: effrt and switching rt bnd 2f out: no ch w ldng pair: edging lft and kpt on same pce ins fnl f* **5/1**[3]

3350 **6** *nk* **Log Off (IRE)**[19] 8854 3-9-2 **56** LukeMorris 10 54
(Karen George) *hld up in tch in midfield: rdn and unable qck over 2f out: drvn and no imp over 1f out: wl hld and kpt on same pce fnl f* **33/1**

4000 **7** ¾ **Nicky Baby (IRE)**[12] 8949 3-8-3 **50** (p) JackOsborn(7) 3 47
(Dean Ivory) *t.k.h: hld up in last trio: no hdwy u.p over 1f out: wl hld and kpt on same pce ins fnl f* **33/1**

31-1 **8** ¾ **Victoriously**[225] 2095 5-9-9 **61** (p) MartinLane 4 55
(Andi Brown) *bmpd s: hld up in tch in rr: clsd but stuck bhd horses over 2f out: nvr clr run after and no imp* **5/1**[3]

5-02 **9** 4 ½ **Hediddodinthe (IRE)**[21] 8800 3-9-1 **55** PhillipMakin 7 42
(Richard Guest) *hld up in tch in midfield on outer: rdn and unable qck over 2f out: wknd and bhd over 1f out* **15/8**[1]

0600 **10** *56* **Rubheira**[21] 8800 5-8-7 **45** RobHornby 9
(Neil Mulholland) *t.k.h: sn chsng ldr tl lost pl u.p over 2f out: bhd and eased ins fnl f: t.o* **100/1**

2m 8.1s (-0.50) **Going Correction** -0.10s/f (Stan)
**WFA** 3 from 4yo+ 2lb **10** Ran SP% **126.6**
Speed ratings (Par 101): **98,96,93,93,93 93,92,91,88,43**
CSF £22.04 CT £380.17 TOTE £3.90: £1.30, £2.10, £4.90; EX 23.20 Trifecta £327.70.
**Owner** Fawzi Abdulla Nass **Bred** Camas Park Stud **Trained** Newmarket, Suffolk
■ Stewards' Enquiry : Kieran O'Neill two-day ban: using his whip above the permitted level (Dec 21-22)

**FOCUS**
The second division of a modest handicap. They went another muddling tempo and the winning time was virtually identical.

## 9129 GO HOMES LAND H'CAP 6f (P)
**9:00** (9:02) (Class 7) (0-50,50) 3-Y-0+ **£2,911** (£866; £432; £216) **Stalls** Centre

Form RPR

300- **1** **Mercury**[34] 8568 5-9-3 **46** (bt) MartinHarley 10 55
(Adrian Brendan Joyce, Ire) *chsd ldrs: effrt over 1f out: rdn to ld 1f out: styd on: rdn out* **5/1**[3]

000 **2** *1* **Pulsating (IRE)**[35] 8551 3-9-5 **48** (p) EdwardGreatrex 4 54
(Archie Watson) *in tch in midfield: effrt to chse ldrs over 2f out: clsd u.p to press ldng pair 1f out: chsd wnr ins fnl f: kpt on* **9/4**[1]

4233 **3** 1 ¼ **Silver Penny**[3] 9075 3-8-12 **46** (p) PaddyBradley(5) 6 48
(Jim Boyle) *chsd ldrs: sltly outpcd over 2f out: rallied u.p 1f out: kpt on ins fnl f* **6/1**

65 **4** *nk* **Olaudah**[72] 7497 3-9-4 **47** FranBerry 2 48+
(Henry Candy) *stdd bk to rr sn after s: t.k.h: hdwy over 1f out: styd on wl ins fnl f: nt rch ldrs* **11/4**[2]

6024 **5** *hd* **Spitfire Limited**[20] 8824 3-9-4 **50** (h) HectorCrouch(3) 8 51
(George Baker) *taken down early: hld up in tch in midfield: effrt and swtchd rt over 1f out: kpt on ins fnl f: nt rch ldrs* **8/1**

-000 **6** 1 ¾ **La Fortuna**[41] 8395 4-9-7 **50** DanielMuscutt 13 46
(Charlie Wallis) *led tl over 3f out: rdn to ld over 1f out: hdd 1f out: no ex and wknd fnl 100yds* **33/1**

0420 **7** 4 ½ **Quintus Cerialis (IRE)**[127] 5535 5-9-6 **49** (tp) LukeMorris 5 31
(Karen George) *s.i.s: hld up in rr: effrt and switching rt bnd 2f out: no imp and wl hld fnl f* **20/1**

0020 **8** *1* **Louis Vee (IRE)**[46] 8259 9-8-10 **46** (b) RossaRyan(7) 1 25
(John O'Shea) *rousted along leaving stalls: sn w ldr tl led over 3f out: rdn and hdd over 1f out: wknd ins fnl f* **16/1**

-504 **9** ¾ **Noneedtotellme (IRE)**[47] 8242 4-8-11 **45** (v) WilliamCox(5) 3 22
(James Unett) *hld up in midfield: effrt and wnt lft u.p over 1f out: hung rt 1f out: no imp* **16/1**

0036 **10** 1 ½ **Whaleweigh Station**[51] 8134 6-9-5 **48** (v) DougieCostello 11 20
(J R Jenkins) *s.i.s: a towards rr: no imp over 1f out: wknd fnl f* **25/1**

0040 **11** ¾ **Joshlee (IRE)**[55] 7993 3-8-11 **47** NicolaCurrie(7) 12 17
(Emma Owen) *hld up in midfield on outer: no hdwy u.p over 1f out: wknd ins fnl f* **40/1**

4060 **12** *16* **Emilysbutterscotch**[40] 8428 3-9-5 **48** DavidProbert 9
(Rae Guest) *midfield tl lost pl jst over 2f out: bhd and eased ins fnl f* **25/1**

0-00 **13** *14* **Aegean Boy**[20] 8824 4-8-13 **45** (t) MitchGodwin(3) 7
(John Bridger) *hld up in rr: eased over 1f out: t.o* **66/1**

1m 12.5s (-1.20) **Going Correction** -0.10s/f (Stan) **13** Ran SP% **130.6**
Speed ratings (Par 97): **104,102,101,100,100 98,92,90,89,87 86,65,46**
CSF £17.14 CT £77.98 TOTE £11.60: £3.30, £1.40, £1.90; EX 44.80 Trifecta £337.90.
**Owner** Mrs Christina Joyce **Bred** Park Farm Racing **Trained** Athlone, Co Roscommon

**FOCUS**
A moderate sprint handicap. The winner showed the right attitude from the front.
T/Plt: £153.60 to a £1 stake. Pool: £111,269.49 - 528.80 winning units T/Qpdt: £11.80 to a £1 stake. Pool: £15,969.96 - 998.31 winning units **Steve Payne**

9130 - 9135a (Foreign Racing) - See Raceform Interactive

# 9122 CHELMSFORD (A.W) (L-H)
Friday, December 8

**OFFICIAL GOING: Polytrack: standard**
Wind: MEDIUM, HALF AGAINST Weather: DRY, COLD

## 9136 BET TOTEPLACEPOT AT BETFRED.COM APPRENTICE H'CAP 5f (P)
**5:45** (5:45) (Class 5) (0-75,75) 3-Y-0+ **£5,175** (£1,540; £769; £384) **Stalls** Low

Form RPR

6412 **1** **Bahamian Heights**[9] 8990 6-8-10 **71** JonathanFisher(7) 4 80+
(Robert Cowell) *taken down early and walked rdrless to s: s.i.s: bhd: hdwy 2f out: swtchd rt over 1f out: rdn to ld ins fnl f: in command and pushed out towards fin* **9/4**[1]

511 **2** *1* **Swendab (IRE)**[18] 8873 9-8-9 **63** (b) MitchGodwin 1 68
(John O'Shea) *led: rdn wl over 1f out: kpt on wl u.p tl hdd and one pced ins fnl f* **8/1**

1553 **3** 1 ½ **Red Stripes (USA)**[9] 9001 5-8-2 **61** oh1 (b) GabrieleMalune(5) 7 61
(Lisa Williamson) *w ldr: rdn wl over 1f out: sustained duel w ldr tl no ex ins fnl f: wknd wl ins fnl f* **10/1**

3440 **4** 2 ¼ **Penny Dreadful**[4] 9074 5-9-1 **69** (p) PaddyPilley 8 61
(Scott Dixon) *chsd ldng trio: effrt wl over 1f out: drvn and no ex ent fnl f: wknd ins fnl f* **12/1**

2645 **5** ¾ **Zipedeedodah (IRE)**[13] 8950 5-9-2 **75** (t) NicolaCurrie(5) 2 64
(Joseph Tuite) *chsd ldrs: rdn over 1f out: no ex u.p 1f out: wknd ins fnl f* **5/1**[3]

2340 **6** *1* **Yorkee Mo Sabee (IRE)**[76] 7405 4-8-11 **70** (t) MillyNaseb(5) 3 55
(Stuart Williams) *restless jst bef stalls opened and awkward whn stalls opened and rdr lost nr side iron: hdwy into midfield and rdr kicked other foot out of iron over 3f out: rdn over 1f out: wknd ins fnl f* **9/2**[2]

5615 **7** ¾ **Berryessa (IRE)**[13] 8953 3-8-10 **71** SebastianWoods(7) 6 54
(Rae Guest) *midfield: effrt over 1f out: no imp: nvr trbld ldrs* **7/1**

1300 **8** *5* **Mighty Zip (USA)**[155] 4531 5-8-2 **61** oh2 (p) WilliamCox(5) 5 26
(Lisa Williamson) *midfield: hung rt 3f out: sn struggling: bhd over 1f out* **33/1**

0002 **9** *6* **Dundunah (USA)**[14] 8927 3-9-5 **73** (t) KieranShoemark 10 16
(David O'Meara) *sn outpcd in rr: n.d* **10/1**

59.29s (-0.91) **Going Correction** -0.10s/f (Stan) **9** Ran SP% **118.0**
Speed ratings (Par 103): **103,101,99,95,94 92,91,83,73**
CSF £21.75 CT £154.41 TOTE £3.30: £1.60, £2.40, £2.90; EX 20.40 Trifecta £122.50.
**Owner** Mrs J Morley & A Rix **Bred** Pantile Stud **Trained** Six Mile Bottom, Cambs

**FOCUS**
A fair sprint handicap for apprentice riders. They went a decent gallop on standard Polytrack and the favourite picked up strongly from off the pace in the straight.

## 9137 BET TOTEJACKPOT AT BETFRED.COM NOVICE STKS 7f (P)
**6:15** (6:15) (Class 5) 2-Y-O **£4,528** (£1,347; £673; £336) **Stalls** Low

Form RPR

03 **1** **Nice Shot (IRE)**[15] 8915 2-9-2 0 (h[1]) MartinHarley 6 81
(David Simcock) *t.k.h: mde all: rdn over 1f out: in command and styd on wl ins fnl f* **10/3**[2]

6 **2** 2 ¾ **Court House (IRE)**[72] 7511 2-9-2 0 RobertHavlin 1 74+
(John Gosden) *s.i.s: racd in last pair: swtchd rt and hdwy wl over 1f out: chsd ldng pair over 1f out: kpt on to go 2nd wl ins fnl f: nvr threatened wnr* **2/5**[1]

**3** 1 ¼ **Artieshow (USA)** 2-9-2 0 DanielMuscutt 7 71
(Marco Botti) *chsd wnr for 2f: styd chsng ldrs tl wnt 2nd again over 2f out: rdn over 1f out: rn green: awkward hd carriage and wandered ins fnl f: no imp and lost 2nd wl ins fnl f* **10/1**

0 **4** 4 ½ **Father Ailbe (IRE)**[22] 8794 2-8-13 0 TimClark(3) 9 58
(John Butler) *in tch in midfield: rdn and outpcd whn hung lft over 1f out: wl hld 4th and kpt on same pce ins fnl f* **50/1**

56 **5** *2* **Hilborough**[35] 8560 2-9-2 0 CharlesBishop 3 53
(Mick Channon) *hld up in last trio: rdn over 1f out: no imp and wl hld fnl f* **12/1**

**6** *nse* **Suprematism (USA)** 2-9-2 0 RyanTate 2 53
(Marco Botti) *pushed along in midfield: rdn over 1f out: sn outpcd and wknd fnl f* **16/1**

0 **7** *6* **Garsington**[13] 8952 2-9-2 0 LukeMorris 5 37
(Ed Dunlop) *trckd ldrs tl outpcd and pushed along over 1f out: sn btn and wknd ins fnl f* **100/1**

00 **8** *7* **Imperial Red (IRE)**[6] 9051 2-8-13 0 GeorgiaCox(3) 4 18
(William Haggas) *s.i.s: a pushed along towards rr: n.d* **8/1**[3]

6 **9** *14* **Astrobreeze**[59] 7915 2-8-11 0 JoeyHaynes 8
(Mark H Tompkins) *t.k.h: chsd ldrs on outer: hdwy to chse wnr after 2f tl lost pl qckly over 2f out: bhd over 1f out: wknd fnl f* **66/1**

1m 25.95s (-1.25) **Going Correction** -0.10s/f (Stan) **9** Ran SP% **132.7**
Speed ratings (Par 96): **103,99,98,93,91 90,84,76,60**
CSF £5.83 TOTE £5.40: £1.30, £1.02, £3.00; EX 9.90 Trifecta £43.20.
**Owner** Orbis Bloodstock (uk) Limited **Bred** Cooneen Stud **Trained** Newmarket, Suffolk

**FOCUS**
An ordinary juvenile novice contest. The second-favourite made all after breaking sharply from the gates.

## 9138 BET TOTEQUADPOT AT BETFRED.COM (S) STKS 1m (P)
**6:45** (6:45) (Class 5) 3-Y-0+ **£5,175** (£1,540; £769; £384) **Stalls** Low

Form RPR

2130 **1** **Titan Goddess**[22] 8797 5-8-12 **69** ShaneKelly 3 68
(Mike Murphy) *dwlt and niggled along early: sn in tch in midfield: effrt to chal ent fnl f: rdn to ld ins fnl f: styd on wl* **5/2**[1]

4032 **2** 1 ¼ **Junoesque**[20] 8841 3-8-8 **58** (p) JoeyHaynes 1 62
(John Gallagher) *trckd ldrs: effrt u.p to chal over 1f out: no ex and kpt on same pce fnl 100yds* **7/1**

5065 **3** *nse* **Intermodal**[8] 9017 3-8-13 **69** DougieCostello 2 67
(Jamie Osborne) *t.k.h: chsd ldr: rdn and ev ch over 1f out: no ex and outpcd fnl 100yds: burst blood vessel* **7/2**[3]

0305 **4** 1 ½ **Tadaany (IRE)**[13] 8956 5-8-9 **70** JaneElliott(5) 4 63
(Ruth Carr) *taken down early: led: rdn over 1f out: hdd ins fnl f: no ex and wknd towards fin* **11/4**[2]

0603 **5** *7* **Mutineer**[20] 8841 3-9-5 **72** GeorgeDowning 7 52
(Daniel Kubler) *in tch in rr but nvr travelling wl: rdn over 2f out: no imp: wknd ins fnl f* **5/1**

00 **P** **Black Dave (IRE)**[13] 8956 7-9-6 **63** AdamKirby 6
(David Evans) *in tch in last pair: lost tch and hung rt 3f out: sn eased and p.u 1f out* **16/1**

1m 38.92s (-0.98) **Going Correction** -0.10s/f (Stan)
**WFA** 3 from 5yo+ 1lb **6** Ran SP% **112.5**
Speed ratings (Par 103): **100,98,98,97,90**
CSF £20.04 TOTE £4.10: £2.50, £3.30; EX 17.60 Trifecta £63.40.There was no bid for the winner. Intermodal was claimed by Mr J. Tuite for £6,000.
**Owner** Phoebe's Friends **Bred** Mrs A D Bourne **Trained** Westoning, Beds

**FOCUS**
A modest seller. They went a respectable gallop and the favourite came through centrally for a straightforward victory.

## 9139 BET TOTEEXACTA AT BETFRED.COM MAIDEN STKS 6f (P)
**7:15** (7:15) (Class 5) 3-Y-0+ **£5,175** (£1,540; £769; £384) **Stalls** Centre

Form RPR

36 **1** **Karijini (GER)**[192] 3188 3-9-0 0 EdwardGreatrex 3 76+
(Archie Watson) *mde all: gng best over 2f out: pushed along and clr over 1f out: in command whn rdr dropped whip wl ins fnl f: eased towards fin: dismntd after fin: burst blood vessel* **11/10**[1]

34-2 **2** *2* **Kingofmerrows (IRE)**[14] 8931 3-9-5 **73** DougieCostello 5 73
(Jamie Osborne) *chsd wnr: effrt over 2f out: drvn and unable qck over 1f out: kpt on same pce ins fnl f* **9/4**[2]

3063 **3** *6* **Canadian Royal**[20] 8842 3-9-5 **60** (t) AdamKirby 7 54
(Stuart Williams) *t.k.h: tracd ldrs: unable qck u.p over 2f out: outpcd wl over 1f out: wnt modest 3rd ins fnl f* **8/1**

4 4 1/2 **Dirayah (IRE)** 3-9-0 0..........(b[1]) LukeMorris 2 34
(George Peckham) *s.i.s: rn green and rousted along early: in tch in rr of main gp: rdn over 2f out: sn outpcd and wl hld over 1f out* 7/2[3]

0006 5 1 1/4 **Tilsworth Lukey**[80] 7254 4-8-12 38.......... GinaMangan(7) 1 35
(J R Jenkins) *chsd ldrs: rdn over 2f out: sn outpcd and btn over 1f out: wknd and lost 2 pls ins fnl f* 150/1

6 24 **Fireguard** 4-9-5 0.......... ShaneKelly 6
(Emma Owen) *s.i.s: sn outpcd and t.o after 2f: hung rt over 1f out* 33/1

000 7 shd **Eye Burner**[48] 8242 3-9-5 0.......... TimmyMurphy 4
(J R Jenkins) *t.k.h: hld up in tch: rdn over 2f out: sn outpcd and btn: wl bhd fnl f* 150/1

1m 11.79s (-1.91) **Going Correction** -0.10s/f (Stan) 7 Ran SP% 116.0
Speed ratings (Par 103): **108,105,97,91,89 57,57**
CSF £3.99 TOTE £1.70: £1.30, £1.90; EX 3.60 Trifecta £9.50.
**Owner** Greenfield Racing **Bred** Graf U Grafin V Stauffenberg **Trained** Upper Lambourn, W Berks

**FOCUS**
A fair maiden. The favourite never looked likely to get caught from the front.

## 9140 BET TOTETRIFECTA AT BETFRED.COM H'CAP 1m 2f (P)
7:45 (7:46) (Class 4) (0-80,88) 3-Y-0+ £8,086 (£2,406; £1,202; £601) Stalls Low

Form RPR

4000 1 **Tangramm**[9] 9000 5-9-5 78..........(p) CharlesBishop 9 84
(Dean Ivory) *stdd and dropped in bhd after s: hld up in tch in last trio: effrt wd and hdwy over 1f out: edgd lft u.p but styd on to ld wl ins fnl f* 16/1

4020 2 3/4 **Eltezam (IRE)**[35] 8561 4-9-7 80..........(h) JoeyHaynes 3 84
(Amanda Perrett) *led for 2f: styd trcking ldrs tl effrt to chse ldr wl over 1f out: sn drvn and chalng: kpt on same pce wl ins fnl f* 10/1

0-00 3 nk **Wimpole Hall**[21] 8821 4-9-6 79.......... DavidProbert 7 82
(William Jarvis) *t.k.h: chsd ldr tl led after 2f: rdn and hrd pressed over 1f out: hdd and kpt on same pce wl ins fnl f* 12/1

6110 4 1 **Ourmullion**[46] 8295 3-9-4 79..........(p) JosephineGordon 8 81
(John Best) *chsd ldrs: rdn 4f out: kpt on wl u.p and stl pressing ldrs 1f out: no ex and one pced ins fnl f* 8/1[3]

0051 5 1/2 **Ice Royal (IRE)**[7] 9025 4-10-1 88 6ex.......... DougieCostello 4 88
(Jamie Osborne) *hld up in tch in midfield: nt clr and travelling wl over 2f out: swtchd rt and effrt over 1f out: hdwy u.p 1f out: kpt on ins fnl f* 7/2[1]

0502 6 nk **Tha'ir (IRE)**[13] 8956 7-9-7 80..........(h) LukeMorris 6 80
(Michael Appleby) *hld up in tch in midfield: clsd to trck ldrs and nt clr run jst over 2f out: effrt u.p to chse ldrs over 1f out: kpt on same pce ins fnl f* 10/1

2535 7 1/2 **Waarif (IRE)**[7] 9025 4-9-7 80..........(p) MartinHarley 5 79
(David O'Meara) *s.i.s: hld up in rr: pushed along and hdwy over 1f out: kpt on ins fnl f: nvr trbld ldrs* 6/1[2]

3321 8 7 **Peace And Plenty**[16] 8886 3-9-2 77.......... MartinDwyer 11 63
(William Muir) *midfield tl hdwy to chse ldr over 7f out tl wl over 1f out: unable qck u.p: wknd ins fnl f* 6/1[2]

1 9 1 **Al Kout**[31] 8663 3-9-5 80.......... TomMarquand 2 64
(Heather Main) *t.k.h: hld up in tch in last trio: rdn 4f out: dropped to last and struggling u.p 3f out: n.d after* 8/1[3]

4021 10 7 **Breanski**[14] 8929 3-9-5 80..........(v) AdamKirby 12 50
(David O'Meara) *hld up in tch in midfield: rdn over 3f out: no imp and struggling whn carried rt over 1f out: sn wknd and bhd 1f out* 12/1

4240 11 1 1/4 **Vogueatti (USA)**[16] 8893 4-9-4 77.......... DanielMuscutt 1 43
(Marco Botti) *hld up in tch in midfield: rdn ent fnl 3f: sn struggling and btn over 1f out: bhd fnl f* 8/1[3]

2m 6.87s (-1.73) **Going Correction** -0.10s/f (Stan)
**WFA** 3 from 4yo+ 2lb 11 Ran SP% 123.6
Speed ratings (Par 105): **102,101,101,100,99 99,99,93,92,87 86**
CSF £174.86 CT £2014.07 TOTE £21.70: £4.90, £4.20, £3.60; EX 271.60 Trifecta £4650.60 Part won..
**Owner** John Marsden **Bred** W G H Barrons **Trained** Radlett, Herts

**FOCUS**
The feature contest was a decent handicap. They went a respectable gallop and the winner was another horse on the night to pick up particularly well centrally from off the pace.

## 9141 BET TOTEWIN AT BETFRED.COM H'CAP 1m (P)
8:15 (8:18) (Class 6) (0-55,60) 3-Y-0+ £3,234 (£962; £481; £240) Stalls Low

Form RPR

6030 1 **Ertidaad (IRE)**[236] 1818 5-8-12 46 oh1..........(v[1]) CharlesBishop 12 51
(Suzi Best) *hld up in tch in midfield: effrt over 1f out: drvn and styd on wl ins fnl f to ld nr fin* 14/1

0436 2 nk **Dukes Meadow**[48] 8248 6-8-10 49.......... RhiainIngram(5) 14 53
(Roger Ingram) *chsd ldrs: rdn to ld over 1f out: kpt on wl u.p ins fnl f: hdd nr fin* 14/1

256 3 hd **How's Lucy**[30] 8675 3-9-3 52.......... MartinHarley 16 56
(Jane Chapple-Hyam) *chsd ldr tl 4f out: styd prom: rdn and chal over 1f out: kpt on wl u.p: no ex nr fin* 14/1

3252 4 1 1/2 **Dor's Law**[15] 8908 4-9-4 52..........(p) RobHornby 11 52
(Dean Ivory) *dwlt: hld up in tch towards rr: hdwy into midfield 3f out: effrt over 1f out: swtchd rt and rdn ins fnl f: styd on: nt rch ldrs* 4/1[1]

6 5 3/4 **Emigrated (IRE)**[4] 9073 4-8-12 46 oh1..........(v) PatrickMathers 9 44
(Derek Shaw) *in tch in midfield: effrt over 1f out: kpt on u.p ins fnl f* 20/1

6 nse **Boketto (IRE)**[308] 560 3-8-10 48..........(t[1]) EoinWalsh(3) 3 46
(Derek Shaw) *hld up in tch in last quartet: swtchd lft and gd hdwy over 1f out: kpt on u.p ins fnl f* 7/1[3]

000 7 1/2 **Gunner Moyne**[30] 8675 5-9-6 54..........(v) AdamKirby 8 51
(Emma Owen) *broke wl: sn rdn and dropped to last quartet: effrt on outer over 2f out: kpt on u.p ins fnl f: nvr trbld ldrs* 8/1

0056 8 1/2 **Dynamic Girl (IRE)**[13] 8949 4-8-9 50..........(t) NicolaCurrie(7) 7 46
(Brendan Powell) *s.i.s: nt clr run 2f out: hdwy and swtchd rt ent fnl f: styd on: nvr trbld ldrs* 14/1

0103 9 1 **Mr Andros**[10] 8985 4-9-7 55..........(bt) ShaneKelly 13 48
(Brendan Powell) *dwlt: t.k.h: sn in tch in midfield on outer: hdwy to chse ldr 4f out: rdn and ev ch whn drifted rt wl over 1 out: unable qck and wknd ins fnl f* 8/1

2034 10 1/2 **Lutine Charlie (IRE)**[9] 8994 10-8-12 46..........(p) MartinDwyer 2 38
(Emma Owen) *in tch in midfield: effrt over 1f out: styd on same pce and no imp ins fnl f* 14/1

3006 11 shd **Mowhoob**[9] 8994 7-9-2 50.......... LukeMorris 10 42
(Brian Barr) *in tch in midfield: rdn over 2f out: no rspnse and sn struggling: kpt on same pce fr over 1f out* 12/1

1060 12 1 **Henry Grace (IRE)**[226] 2095 6-9-6 54..........(b) KieranO'Neill 4 44
(Jimmy Fox) *t.k.h early: hld up in tch in last quartet: effrt over 1f out: swtchd lft over 1f out: nvr trbld ldrs* 14/1

035 13 4 **Al's Memory (IRE)**[31] 8659 8-9-8 56.......... FranBerry 5 36
(David Evans) *chsd ldrs: short of room and hmpd over 3f out: rdn and losing pl 3f out: wknd over 1f out* 6/1[2]

0600 14 7 **Rosie Crowe (IRE)**[69] 7605 5-8-9 46 oh1..........(v) CharlieBennett(3) 6 9
(Shaun Harris) *led tl over 1f out: wknd fnl f: fin lame* 20/1

1m 40.21s (0.31) **Going Correction** -0.10s/f (Stan)
**WFA** 3 from 4yo+ 1lb 14 Ran SP% 126.2
Speed ratings (Par 101): **94,93,93,92,91 91,90,90,89,88 88,87,83,76**
CSF £206.20 CT £1701.96 TOTE £15.80: £5.10, £4.10, £7.10; EX 220.40 Trifecta £2596.20 Part won..
**Owner** A Cullen & Ms F A O'Sullivan **Bred** Cloneymore Farms Ltd & James C Murtagh **Trained** Lewes, East Sussex

**FOCUS**
A moderate handicap. They went a respectable gallop and another winner on the night challenged late on the outside.

## 9142 BOOK ONLINE AT CHELMSFORDCITYRACECOURSE.COM H'CAP 7f (P)
8:45 (8:48) (Class 6) (0-65,67) 3-Y-0+ £3,234 (£962; £481; £240) Stalls Low

Form RPR

2060 1 **Captain Pugwash (IRE)**[45] 8327 3-9-4 62.......... LiamKeniry 8 68
(Henry Spiller) *in tch towards rr: swtchd lft and gd hdwy over 1f out: rdn to chal 1f out: led 100yds: edgd rt and styd on to assert towards fin* 9/2[1]

0526 2 1 **Viola Park**[42] 8401 3-8-13 57..........(p[1]) LukeMorris 6 60
(Ronald Harris) *in tch in midfield: rdn over 2f out: swtchd rt and hdwy 2f out: drvn and ev ch over 1f out: kpt on same pce fnl 100yds* 6/1[3]

0260 3 hd **Rockley Point**[7] 9093 4-9-8 66..........(b) AdamKirby 15 69
(Paul D'Arcy) *rousted along leaving stalls: w ldr tl led 2f out: sn rdn: hdd 100yds out: styd on same pce after: lost 2nd last strides* 7/1

0500 4 1 3/4 **Mr Potter**[8] 9013 4-9-0 58..........(v) DougieCostello 5 56
(Richard Guest) *restless in stalls: stdd s: hld up off the pce in rr: clsd and nt clrest of runs over 1f out: hdwy to chse ldrs and rdn ins fnl f: kpt on same pce towards fin* 14/1

0011 5 1 **Loveatfirstsight**[13] 8948 4-9-0 58..........(p) DanielMuscutt 9 55
(Jane Chapple-Hyam) *in tch in midfield: pushed along over 2f out: nt clr run over 1f out: hdwy 1f out: chsng ldrs and keeping on same pce whn sltly impeded wl ins fnl f* 5/1[2]

0526 6 2 3/4 **Tellovoi (IRE)**[7] 9032 9-9-2 67..........(v) JackOsborn(7) 11 55
(Richard Guest) *squeezed for room leaving stalls: hld up off the pce towards rr: hdwy and v wd bnd 2f out: kpt on ins fnl f: nvr trbld ldrs* 12/1

4101 7 4 1/2 **Queens Royale**[22] 8807 3-9-4 62..........(v) RobertWinston 10 38
(Michael Appleby) *in tch in midfield: effrt u.p over 2f out: unable qck: wl hld and kpt on same pce ins fnl f* 8/1

2100 8 shd **Robbie Roo Roo**[48] 8243 4-9-5 63..........(vt) RobertTart 14 38
(Mrs Ilka Gansera-Leveque) *sn off the pce in rr: sme hdwy ent fnl f: swtchd lft and kpt onins fnl f: nvr trbld ldrs* 12/1

6000 9 3/4 **Weloof (FR)**[13] 8958 3-9-4 65.......... TimClark(3) 7 38
(John Butler) *wl off the pce in rr: pushed along and sme hdwy jst over 1f out: nvr trbld ldrs* 33/1

0600 10 2 3/4 **Fareeq**[18] 8874 3-9-5 63..........(vt) DavidProbert 3 29
(Charlie Wallis) *chsd ldrs: rdn and unable qck over 1f out: edgd rt and wknd ins fnl f* 16/1

6034 11 6 **Soaring Spirits (IRE)**[31] 8659 7-8-13 57..........(p) RobHornby 13 7
(Dean Ivory) *in tch in midfield: rdn over 2f out: unable qck and wknd over 1f out* 16/1

0660 12 1 1/2 **Marbooh (IRE)**[41] 8429 4-9-1 62.......... RosieJessop(3) 4 8
(Miss Joey Ellis) *chsd ldrs: rdn over 3f out: lost pl and bhd over 1f out: wknd fnl f* 16/1

2044 13 7 **Forever Yours (IRE)**[134] 5341 4-9-0 61.......... JackDuern(3) 12
(Dean Ivory) *led tl 2f out: sn rdn and lost pl over 1f out: bhd ins fnl f* 8/1

1m 25.69s (-1.51) **Going Correction** -0.10s/f (Stan) 13 Ran SP% 126.5
Speed ratings (Par 101): **104,102,102,100,99 96,91,91,90,87 80,78,70**
CSF £32.98 CT £202.76 TOTE £5.70: £2.30, £2.80, £3.90; EX 37.10 Trifecta £262.80.
**Owner** Miss A Jones **Bred** Ardrums House Stud **Trained** Newmarket, Suffolk

**FOCUS**
A modest handicap. The favourite came through late off a respectable tempo to get on top.
T/Plt: £374.60 to a £1 stake. Pool: £108,121.85 - 210.66 winning units T/Qpdt: £301.40 to a £1 stake. Pool: £10,457.65 - 25.67 winning units **Steve Payne**

9143 - 9151a (Foreign Racing) - See Raceform Interactive

# 9078 WOLVERHAMPTON (A.W) (L-H)
Saturday, December 9

**OFFICIAL GOING: Tapeta: standard**
Wind: LIGHT, BEHIND Weather: DRY, COLD

## 9152 BETWAY SPRINT H'CAP 6f 20y (Tp)
5:45 (5:46) (Class 5) (0-75,74) 3-Y-0+ £3,881 (£1,155; £577; £288) Stalls Low

Form RPR

3101 1 **Rapid Ranger**[19] 8875 3-9-3 70..........(h) MartinHarley 7 79+
(David O'Meara) *hld up in tch and travelled strly: wnt 3rd 2f out: swtchd rt and effrt jst ins fnl f: rdn and hdwy to ld 50yds out: kpt on* 4/1[2]

601 2 3/4 **A Sure Welcome**[28] 8742 3-9-0 67..........(p) LiamKeniry 13 73
(John Spearing) *t.k.h: w ldr: rdn over 1f out: styd on to ld ins fnl f: hdd and one pce fnl 50yds* 12/1

4022 3 3/4 **Trotter**[21] 8842 3-9-3 70..........(b) LukeMorris 4 74
(Stuart Kittow) *in tch in midfield: effrt over 1f out: hdwy and kpt on wl u.p ins fnl f: nt rch ldrs* 8/1

6212 4 1/2 **Blazed (IRE)**[14] 8950 3-9-5 72.......... KieranShoemark 2 74
(Roger Charlton) *s.i.s: sn rcvrd and in tch in midfield: nt clr run ent fnl 2f: effrt on inner over 1f out: hdwy ins fnl f: styd on wl fnl 100yds* 10/3[1]

6214 5 nk **Major Crispies**[29] 8722 6-9-6 73..........(b) AdamKirby 8 74
(David O'Meara) *restless in stalls and rdr struggling to remove hood: s.i.s: bhd: swtchd rt over 1f out: hdwy ins fnl f: styd on wl fnl 100yds: nt rch ldrs* 10/1

4045 6 3/4 **Bondi Beach Boy**[15] 8927 8-9-0 67.......... CamHardie 12 66
(Antony Brittain) *stdd s: hld up in last trio: nt clrest of runs and swtchd rt over 1f out: hdwy 1f out: kpt on ins fnl f: nvr trbld ldrs* 50/1

6324 7 1/2 **Duke Cosimo**[46] 8320 7-9-3 70..........(p) TomEaves 3 67
(Michael Herrington) *in tch in midfield: effrt over 1f out: kpt on same pce ins fnl f* 8/1

0400 8 1 **Zapper Cass (FR)**[5] 9074 4-9-7 74..........(t[1]) BenCurtis 9 68
(Tony Coyle) *chsd ldrs: unable qck u.p 2f out: wknd ins fnl f* 10/1

2114 9 shd **Awesome Allan (IRE)**[19] 8875 3-9-0 67..........(t) FranBerry 5 61
(David Evans) *sn led: rdn over 1f out: hdd ins fnl f: fdd wl ins fnl f* 10/1

0031 **10** *3 ¼* **Invincible Ridge (IRE)**[19] 8874 9-9-6 **73**.................... JasonHart 1 56
(Eric Alston) *trckd ldrs: rdn 2f out: unable qck and outpcd over 1f out: wknd ins fnl f* **9/2**[3]

0060 **11** *7* **Mysterious Glance**[14] 8953 4-8-2 **60** oh6.................... WilliamCox(5) 10 21
(Sarah Hollinshead) *in tch in midfield: unable qck u.p 2f out: lost pl and wknd ins fnl f* **100/1**

00-0 **12** *3 ½* **Seraphima**[4] 9083 7-8-0 **60** oh15....................(h) KeelanBaker(7) 11 10
(Lisa Williamson) *hld up in last trio: rdn wl over 1f out: sn btn and wknd fnl f* **100/1**

1m 14.21s (-0.29) **Going Correction** 0.0s/f (Stan) **12** Ran SP% **122.4**
Speed ratings (Par 103): **101,100,99,98,97 96,96,94,94,90 81,76**
CSF £53.36 CT £381.94 TOTE £4.90: £1.90, £3.60, £2.50; EX 62.50 Trifecta £439.20.
**Owner** Kristen McEwen & Caroline Head **Bred** Clive Dennett **Trained** Upper Helmsley, N Yorks

**FOCUS**
A fair sprint handicap, but few got involved.

## 9153 BET & WATCH AT SUNBETS.CO.UK H'CAP 1m 142y (Tp)
**6:15** (6:15) (Class 6) (0-65,65) 3-Y-0+ **£2,749** (£818; £408; £204) **Stalls** Low

Form RPR

0623 **1** **Dellaguista (IRE)**[38] 8513 3-9-5 **65**.................... AndrewMullen 8 76+
(Tim Easterby) *trckd ldng trio: pushed along and qcknd to ld 1f out: sn rdn and readily asserted: r.o wl: readily* **7/2**[2]

3555 **2** *3* **King Oswald (USA)**[130] 5510 4-9-3 **61**....................(p) GeorgeDowning 13 66
(James Unett) *dropped in bhd after s: hld up in tch in rr: clsd and nt clr run whn swtchd rt ent fnl f: hdwy to chse clr wnr ins fnl f: kpt on and edgd lft u.p: no threat to wnr* **20/1**

6553 **3** *nk* **Mac O'Polo (IRE)**[140] 5139 3-9-4 **64**.................... RichardKingscote 7 68
(Tom Dascombe) *chsd ldr: clsd and upsides over 3f out: rdn wl over 1f out: unable to match pce of wnr jst ins fnl f: kpt on same pce fnl 100yds* **4/1**[3]

425U **4** *1* **Beatbybeatbybeat**[43] 8400 4-9-4 **62**....................(v) CamHardie 5 64
(Antony Brittain) *t.k.h: hld up wl in tch in midfield: effrt over 1f out: kpt on u.p ins fnl f: no threat to wnr* **16/1**

1003 **5** *½* **Edge (IRE)**[21] 8854 6-9-2 **60**....................(b) DavidProbert 4 61
(Bernard Llewellyn) *hld up in tch towards rr: hdwy on inner 3f out: swtchd rt and chsd ldrs over 1f out: kpt on same pce u.p ins fnl f* **15/2**

0342 **6** *¾* **Maraakib (IRE)**[9] 9017 5-9-6 **64**.................... KieranShoemark 9 63
(David O'Meara) *hld up in tch in rr: effrt and hdwy over 1f out: kpt on ins fnl f: no threat to wnr* **11/2**

5403 **7** *¾* **Mio Ragazzo**[38] 8503 3-9-2 **62**.................... RyanTate 1 60
(Marco Botti) *restrained sn after s: t.k.h and trckd ldng pair: effrt over 1f out: sn rdn and fnd little: wknd wl ins fnl f* **5/2**[1]

0250 **8** *1 ¾* **Harry Beau**[40] 8473 3-9-3 **63**.................... FranBerry 3 57
(David Evans) *led and set stdy gallop: rdn and qcknd 2f out: hdd 1f out: sn outpcd and wknd ins fnl f* **12/1**

0000 **9** *2 ¾* **Idol Deputy (FR)**[14] 8946 11-8-11 **60**....................(p) RachealKneller(5) 6 48
(James Bennett) *sn stdd bk into midfield: nt clr run and shuffled bk towards rr over 2f out: effrt over 1f out: no imp* **25/1**

3060 **10** *¾* **World Of Good**[53] 8132 4-9-4 **62**....................(b) JosephineGordon 11 49
(Anabel K Murphy) *hld up in tch in last quartet: effrt on outer 2f out: no imp: wknd fnl f* **50/1**

200 **11** *1* **Makhfar (IRE)**[42] 8429 6-9-4 **62**....................(p) SteveDrowne 10 47
(Mark Usher) *in tch in midfield: rdn over 2f out: lost pl over 1f out: wknd fnl f* **33/1**

1m 52.98s (2.88) **Going Correction** 0.0s/f (Stan)
**WFA** 3 from 4yo+ 2lb **11** Ran SP% **125.0**
Speed ratings (Par 101): **87,84,84,83,82 82,81,79,77,76 75**
CSF £79.25 CT £310.02 TOTE £4.40: £1.90, £4.40, £2.40; EX 85.00 Trifecta £1514.20.
**Owner** David & Yvonne Blunt **Bred** M Gittins **Trained** Great Habton, N Yorks

**FOCUS**
A modest handicap run at a muddling pace.

## 9154 32RED.COM EBF NOVICE STKS (DIV I) 1m 142y (Tp)
**6:45** (6:46) (Class 5) 2-Y-0 **£3,881** (£1,155; £577; £288) **Stalls** Low

Form RPR

54 **1** **Mr Reckless (IRE)**[14] 8951 2-9-2 0.................... TimmyMurphy 7 76+
(Jamie Osborne) *broke wl: sn restrained to trck ldrs and t.k.h: effrt on inner and qcknd to ld 1f out: sn rdn and asserted: r.o wl: readily* **4/1**[2]

**2** *1 ½* **Galactic Spirit** 2-9-2 0.................... DanielMuscutt 1 73+
(Marco Botti) *hld up in tch in midfield: effrt over 2f out: wnt 3rd and swtchd rt jst ins fnl f: sn drvn: chsd wnr ins fnl f: kpt on* **7/1**

**3** *2 ¼* **Holy Heart (IRE)** 2-9-2 0.................... RobertHavlin 3 68+
(John Gosden) *s.i.s: hld up in tch: effrt on outer bnd 2f out: styd on to go 3rd wl ins fnl f: no threat to wnr* **13/2**[3]

04 **4** *1 ½* **Rogue Hero (IRE)**[7] 9051 2-9-2 0....................(t) LukeMorris 8 65
(Paul Cole) *sn led: rdn and hdd over 1f out: sn outpcd by wnr: lost 2nd ins fnl f: wknd towards fin* **12/1**

63 **5** *1 ¼* **Alpine Peak (USA)**[21] 8839 2-9-2 0.................... FranBerry 10 62
(Roger Varian) *chsd ldr 8f out tl unable qck over 1f out: edgd lft and btn jst ins fnl f: wknd fnl 100yds* **4/1**[2]

**6** *1 ¼* **Elapidae** 2-9-2 0.................... ShaneKelly 9 60+
(David Lanigan) *dwlt: sn rcvrd and in tch in midfield: effrt but unable qck whn rn green over 1f out: wknd ins fnl f* **40/1**

**7** *4 ½* **Winds Of Fire (USA)** 2-9-2 0.................... AdamKirby 2 50+
(Charlie Appleby) *rn green: sn dropped to last trio and pushed along at times: outpcd over 2f out: wl hld whn swtchd rt 1f out* **9/4**[1]

00 **8** *hd* **Seasearch**[21] 8840 2-8-11 0.................... WilliamCox(5) 4 50
(Andrew Balding) *in tch in last trio: pushed along and outpcd over 2f out: wknd over 1f out* **100/1**

55 **9** *½* **Indian Admiral**[32] 8649 2-9-2 0.................... RichardKingscote 5 49
(Mark Johnston) *chsd ldrs: rdn over 3f out: lost pl over 2f out: bhd ins fnl f* **9/1**

1m 52.42s (2.32) **Going Correction** 0.0s/f (Stan) **9** Ran SP% **117.7**
Speed ratings (Par 96): **89,87,85,84,83 82,78,77,77**
CSF £32.82 TOTE £5.20: £1.80, £2.10, £1.90; EX 37.70 Trifecta £288.50.
**Owner** The Q Party **Bred** Mrs T E K Squarey **Trained** Upper Lambourn, Berks

**FOCUS**
Another muddling-looking pace, but a race that should produce winners.

## 9155 32RED.COM EBF NOVICE STKS (DIV II) 1m 142y (Tp)
**7:15** (7:15) (Class 5) 2-Y-0 **£3,881** (£1,155; £577; £288) **Stalls** Low

Form RPR

**1** **Cross Counter** 2-9-2 0.................... AdamKirby 8 83+
(Charlie Appleby) *s.i.s: rn green early: in tch towards rr: hdwy into midfield over 3f out: effrt in 4th and swtchd rt over 1f out: str run to ld and edgd lft ins fnl f: sn clr* **7/2**[2]

**2** *2 ¼* **Kaser (IRE)** 2-9-2 0.................... TomMarquand 4 78
(Saeed bin Suroor) *chsd ldrs: wnt 3rd over 2f out: effrt and pressing ldng pair over 1f out: ev ch briefly ins fnl f: 2nd but unable to match pce of wnr fnl 100yds* **1/1**[1]

**3** *2 ½* **Barbara Villiers** 2-8-11 0.................... RichardKingscote 9 68
(Mark Johnston) *chsd ldr tl rdn to ld over 1f out: hdd ins fnl f: sn outpcd* **20/1**

**4** *½* **Antonian** 2-9-2 0.................... RobertHavlin 2 72
(John Gosden) *led: rdn and hdd over 1f out: ev ch tl outpcd fnl 100yds* **7/2**[2]

0 **5** *9* **Bill Cody (IRE)**[21] 8849 2-9-2 0.................... TimmyMurphy 5 53
(Jamie Osborne) *hld up in tch in midfield: hdwy to chse ldrs 4f out tl rdn and unable qck over 2f out: wknd over 1f out* **20/1**

**6** *1 ¼* **Roundabout Kitten (USA)** 2-9-2 0.................... ShaneKelly 7 50
(David Lanigan) *dwlt: rn green in last trio and rn in snatches: reminder 4f out: rdn and outpcd over 2f out: wknd over 1f out* **40/1**

**7** *1 ¾* **Kolo Tamam** 2-9-2 0.................... KieranShoemark 1 47
(Roger Charlton) *got loose in paddock: s.i.s: rn v green in rr: rdn over 2f out: no imp and hung lft over 1f out: wknd fnl f* **8/1**[3]

00 **8** *9* **Essendon (FR)**[23] 8794 2-8-9 0.................... JasonWatson(7) 3 28
(Andrew Balding) *chsd ldrs tl 4f out: rdn and lost pl over 2f out: wknd over 1f out* **100/1**

**9** *14* **Approaching Menace** 2-8-11 0.................... DavidProbert 6
(Amy Murphy) *hld up in tch towards rr: rdn over 2f out: sn struggling: lost tch over 1f out* **50/1**

1m 50.51s (0.41) **Going Correction** 0.0s/f (Stan) **9** Ran SP% **120.5**
Speed ratings (Par 96): **98,96,93,93,85 84,82,74,62**
CSF £7.46 TOTE £4.20: £1.50, £1.20, £3.80; EX 7.80 Trifecta £75.70.
**Owner** Godolphin **Bred** Godolphin **Trained** Newmarket, Suffolk

**FOCUS**
No worthwhile form to go on pre-race, so we'll have to see how it works out.

## 9156 32RED.COM CONDITIONS STKS (PLUS 10 RACE) (ALL-WEATHER FAST TRACK QUALIFIER) 6f 20y (Tp)
**7:45** (7:46) (Class 2) 2-Y-0 **£9,451** (£2,829; £1,414; £708; £352) **Stalls** Low

Form RPR

2165 **1** **Never Back Down (IRE)**[42] 8412 2-9-2 94.................... JosephineGordon 2 100
(Hugo Palmer) *pushed along leaving stalls: squeezed for room: hmpd and dropped to rr after 1f: bhd and hmpd again 4f out: effrt and plenty to do wl over 1f out: str run ins fnl f to ld towards fin* **10/1**[3]

21 **2** *1* **Music Society (IRE)**[23] 8794 2-9-2 0.................... BenCurtis 4 97
(Sylvester Kirk) *s.i.s and pushed along early: clsd onto bk of field and swtchd rt after 1f: t.k.h after and hdwy into midfield: effrt in 5th 2f out: swtchd rt and hdwy to chal ins fnl f: wnt 2nd last strides* **14/1**

4124 **3** *hd* **Corinthia Knight (IRE)**[35] 8602 2-9-2 105.................... LukeMorris 6 96
(Archie Watson) *pushed along leaving stalls: trckd ldrs after 1f: rdn ent fnl 2f: led ins fnl f: rdn on u.p: hdd and lost 2 pls towards fin* **7/4**[2]

2122 **4** *2 ¼* **Sound And Silence**[35] 8602 2-9-9 107....................(tp) AdamKirby 1 97
(Charlie Appleby) *trckd ldrs: squeezed for room and hmpd after 1f: sn trcking ldrs: effrt over 1f out: pressed ldrs but unable qck jst ins fnl f: sn wknd* **10/11**[1]

3111 **5** *2 ¼* **Joegogo (IRE)**[14] 8954 2-9-2 83.................... FranBerry 7 83
(David Evans) *jnd ldr after 1f: rdn to ld over 1f out: hdd ins fnl f: sn btn and wknd* **25/1**

1002 **6** *2 ¾* **Izzy Bizu (IRE)**[36] 8562 2-9-0 93.................... RichardKingscote 8 73
(Mark Johnston) *led: rdn and hdd over 1f out: wknd ins fnl f* **18/1**

4300 **7** *6* **Yogi's Girl (IRE)**[46] 8317 2-8-11 85.................... AndrewMullen 3 52
(David Evans) *chsd ldr: carried lft and hmpd after 1f: dropped towards rr: rdn and wknd over 1f out* **66/1**

1m 13.72s (-0.78) **Going Correction** 0.0s/f (Stan) **7** Ran SP% **115.1**
Speed ratings (Par 102): **105,103,103,100,97 93,85**
CSF £131.49 TOTE £9.00: £2.20, £4.20; EX 95.90 Trifecta £334.20.
**Owner** M M Stables **Bred** Cooneen Stud **Trained** Newmarket, Suffolk

■ Stewards' Enquiry : Richard Kingscote eight-day ban: careless riding (27th Dec - 1st Jan); two-day: careless riding (23rd,26th Dec)

**FOCUS**
A decent conditions race, but it set up for the closers.

## 9157 BETWAY CASINO H'CAP 1m 5f 219y (Tp)
**8:15** (8:16) (Class 2) (0-105,106) 3-Y-0+ **£12,450** (£3,728; £1,864; £932; £466) **Stalls** Low

Form RPR

0012 **1** **Velvet Revolution**[95] 6793 4-8-9 **86** oh1.................... JosephineGordon 6 93
(Marco Botti) *stdd s: hld up off the pce in last pair: pushed along and hdwy over 2f out: wnt 3rd and swtchd rt over 1f out: chsd ldr jst ins fnl f: styd on wl u.p to ld last stride* **9/2**[2]

4004 **2** *shd* **Cohesion**[7] 9055 4-9-11 **102**.................... AdamKirby 3 108
(David Bridgwater) *chsd clr ldr: pushed along and clsd 3f out: rdn to ld wl over 1f out: sn drvn: kpt on u.p: hdd last stride* **11/4**[1]

0000 **3** *7* **Cosmelli (ITY)**[114] 6123 4-9-2 **93**....................(b) TomEaves 4 89
(Gay Kelleway) *stdd after s: racd off the pce in 3rd: clsd 3f out: rdn 2f out: unable qck and sltly impeded over 1f out: wknd ins fnl f* **20/1**

1110 **4** *nse* **Brandon Castle**[48] 8274 5-9-8 **99**....................(t) AndrewMullen 7 95
(Archie Watson) *taken down early: led and sn clr: rdn over 2f out: hdd wl over 1f out: unable qck and swtchd rt over 1f out: wknd ins fnl f* **5/1**[3]

-160 **5** *10* **Haines**[239] 1770 6-8-12 **94**.................... WilliamCox(5) 1 76
(Andrew Balding) *stdd after s: hld up off the pce in last pair: effrt over 2f out: no imp: wknd over 1f out* **12/1**

3m 1.84s (-6.16) **Going Correction** 0.0s/f (Stan) **5** Ran SP% **74.0**
Speed ratings (Par 109): **117,116,112,112,107**
CSF £7.47 TOTE £3.30: £1.40, £1.70; EX 7.60 Trifecta £22.70.
**Owner** Heart Of The South Racing 104 & Partner **Bred** Newsells Park Stud **Trained** Newmarket, Suffolk

■ Watersmeet was withdrawn. Price at time of withdrawal 13-8F. Rule 4 applies to all bets - deduction 35p in the pound.

**FOCUS**
A race weakened by the late withdrawal of the previous year's winner Watersmeet, who would have been favourite, but still decent form from the first two.

## 9158 BETWAY LIVE CASINO H'CAP 2m 120y (Tp)
**8:45** (8:46) (Class 6) (0-65,66) 3-Y-0+ **£2,749** (£818; £408; £204) **Stalls** Low

Form RPR

2043 **1** **Author's Dream**[32] 8647 4-9-6 **57**....................(v) MartinHarley 3 72+
(William Knight) *s.i.s: swtchd rt and hdwy to chse ldr after 3f tl 10f out: styd chsng ldrs tl effrt to go 2nd and wnt clr w ldr over 2f out: rdn to ld over 1f out: styd on strly and drew wl clr* **4/1**[2]

6650 **2** *11* **Sheila's Fancy (IRE)**[14] 8946 3-9-2 **59**.................... LiamKeniry 2 63
(J S Moore) *s.i.s: hld up in last pair: clsd and nt clr run over 2f out: swtchd lft and effrt over 1f out: styd on ins fnl f to go 2nd nr fin: no ch w wnr* **28/1**

4060 **3** *nse* **Wordiness**[19] 8876 9-10-1 **66**.................... FranBerry 1 68
(David Evans) *t.k.h: hld up towards rr: nt clr run and swtchd rt over 2f out: hdwy u.p over 1f out: styd on ins fnl f: wnt 3rd nr fin: no ch w wnr* **16/1**

5132 **4** *nk* **Hallstatt (IRE)**[19] 8876 11-10-0 **65**....................(t) LukeMorris 7 67
(John Mackie) *hld up in midfield: effrt to chse clr ldng pair over 2f out: kpt on u.p: no ch w wnr* **7/1**

666 **5** *½* **Spin Point (IRE)**[38] 7936 5-9-10 **61**....................(v[1]) AdamKirby 5 62
(Ian Williams) *led for 1f: styd prom: chsd ldr again 10f out: led over 3f out: rdn and wnt clr w wnr over 2f out: hdd over 1f out: sn outpcd: lost 3 pls towards fin* **5/1**

00/0 **6** *1 ¾* **Dalasiri (IRE)**[19] 8876 8-9-10 **64**....................(t) TimClark(3) 8 63
(Johnny Farrelly) *stdd s: hld up in rr: sme hdwy over 2f out: swtchd rt and rdn wl over 1f out: no imp after: nvr trbld ldrs* **25/1**

0042 **7** *4 ½* **Caracas**[32] 8647 3-9-6 **63**.................... RichardKingscote 13 58
(Harry Dunlop) *hld up in midfield: effrt over 2f out: no imp and wl hld over 1f out: wknd fnl f* **9/2[3]**

1100 **8** *4* **Miss Dusky Diva (IRE)**[14] 8955 5-9-7 **58**.................... WilliamCarson 6 47
(David W Drinkwater) *taken down early: hld up in midfield: hdwy 3f out: rdn to go prom in chsng gp over 2f out: no imp over 1f out: wknd ins fnl f* **25/1**

0460 **9** *8* **Garcon De Soleil**[21] 8846 4-8-9 **46** oh1.................... RobHornby 12 25
(Michael Blanshard) *chsd ldrs early: in tch in midfield after 3f: no hdwy over 2f out: wknd over 1f out* **20/1**

0000 **10** *14* **Desktop**[51] 8187 5-8-11 **48**.................... CamHardie 9 10
(Antony Brittain) *t.k.h: hld up in tch in midfield on outer: hdwy to chse ldrs 10f out: lost pl qckly and bhd 3f out: t.o* **33/1**

0134 **11** *nse* **Volturnus**[8] 9026 3-8-8 **51**....................(vt[1]) NickyMackay 11 15
(Jamie Osborne) *s.i.s: hdwy on outer to ld after 2f: rdn and hdd over 3f out: lost pl over 2f out: bhd and eased over 1f out: t.o* **7/2[1]**

0033 **12** *58* **Wintour Leap**[18] 8878 6-9-0 **54**....................(p) CallumShepherd(3) 4
(Robert Stephens) *hld up in tch in midfield: rdn 4f out: bhd and lost tch 2f out: eased: t.o* **10/1**

-R44 **13** *48* **Katalan (GER)**[288] 893 4-8-9 **46** oh1....................(h) DannyBrock 10
(John Butler) *hdwy to chse ldr after 1f tl 14f out: styd chsng ldrs tl lost pl qckly 5f out: bhd 4f: sn lost tch: t.o* **50/1**

3m 40.22s (-3.48) **Going Correction** 0.0s/f (Stan)
**WFA** 3 from 4yo+ 6lb **13** Ran SP% **125.3**
Speed ratings (Par 101): **108,102,102,102,102 101,99,97,93,87 87,59,37**
CSF £124.98 CT £1670.65 TOTE £5.00: £2.00, £7.80, £3.40; EX 149.90 Trifecta £936.40.
**Owner** Heseltine & Conroy **Bred** Spring Bloodstock Ltd **Trained** Patching, W Sussex
■ Stewards' Enquiry : Danny Brock four-day ban: using whip above shoulder height (23rd, 26th-28th Dec)

**FOCUS**
A moderate staying handicap.

## 9159 BETWAY MAIDEN STKS 1m 4f 51y (Tp)
**9:15** (9:16) (Class 5) 3-Y-0+ **£3,557** (£1,058; £529; £264) **Stalls** Low

Form RPR

-443 **1** **Soghan (IRE)**[22] 8822 3-9-5 75....................(t) ShaneKelly 2 83
(Richard Hughes) *t.k.h early: chsd ldrs: effrt in 3rd 3f out: chsd clr ldr u.p over 2f out: styd on to ld ins fnl f: drew clr towards fin* **15/8[2]**

4-32 **2** *2 ¾* **Ocean Of Love**[28] 8744 3-9-0 73.................... WilliamCarson 5 73
(Saeed bin Suroor) *led for 2f: chsd ldr tl led again 6f out: rdn and kicked on 3f out: drvn and hdd ins fnl f: one pced* **11/8[1]**

04 **3** *6* **Hewouldwouldnthe**[26] 8770 3-8-7 0.................... Pierre-LouisJamin(7) 7 63
(Jonathan Portman) *hld up towards rr: effrt over 2f out: kpt on ins fnl f to go 3rd fnl 50yds: no ch w ldng pair* **66/1**

-422 **4** *1 ¼* **Ebqaa (IRE)**[16] 8911 3-9-0 72.................... TomEaves 6 61
(James Unett) *in tch in midfield: effrt to chse ldr over 3f out tl 3rd and outpcd over 2f out: wknd ins fnl f* **8/1**

5620 **5** *2* **Sula Island**[57] 8000 3-9-0 70.................... TomMarquand 10 58
(Alan King) *chsd ldr for 2f: styd chsng ldrs: rdn and unable qck 3f out: wl hld and plugged on same pce fnl 2f* **14/1**

6504 **6** *2 ¼* **Sonnetist**[31] 8682 3-9-5 71.................... FranBerry 3 59
(David Evans) *stdd s: t.k.h: hld up in rr: swtchd rt and effrt wd over 2f out: nvr threatened ldrs* **5/1[3]**

0 **7** *¾* **Gealach Ghorm (IRE)**[39] 8497 3-9-0 71.................... WilliamCox(5) 1 58
(Sarah Hollinshead) *hld up in midfield: effrt 3f out: sn outpcd and wl hld over 1f out* **25/1**

06 **8** *11* **Rosie Lea (FR)**[22] 8822 4-9-4 0.................... LiamKeniry 11 34
(Stuart Kittow) *hld up in last trio: rdn 3f out: sn bhd* **100/1**

60 **9** *½* **Kwikstep**[75] 7462 3-9-0 0.................... MartinLane 4 35
(Andi Brown) *s.i.s: hld up in last trio: hdwy on outer 5f out: struggling u.p over 3f out: wknd over 2f out: bhd fnl f* **100/1**

**10** *37* **Sutoor (IRE)**[25] 3-9-5 0.................... DanielMuscutt 9
(Mark Brisbourne) *s.i.s: hdwy to ld after 2f: hdd 6f out: chsd ldr tl over 3f out: sn dropped out and bhd: t.o* **66/1**

2m 40.31s (-0.49) **Going Correction** 0.0s/f (Stan)
**WFA** 3 from 4yo 4lb **10** Ran SP% **120.1**
Speed ratings (Par 103): **101,99,95,94,93 91,91,83,83,58**
CSF £4.94 TOTE £2.90: £1.20, £1.20, £7.80; EX 5.70 Trifecta £244.90.
**Owner** The Queens **Bred** Ballyreddin Stud **Trained** Upper Lambourn, Berks

**FOCUS**
Not much depth to this maiden.
T/Plt: £287.50 to a £1 stake. Pool: £122,583.13 - 311.20 winning units T/Qpdt: £37.10 to a £1 stake. Pool: £14,867.22 - 296.32 winning units **Steve Payne**

9160 - 9166a (Foreign Racing) - See Raceform Interactive

# 9060 SHA TIN (R-H)
Sunday, December 10

**OFFICIAL GOING: Turf: good**

## 9167a LONGINES HONG KONG VASE (GROUP 1) (3YO+) (COURSE A) (TURF) 1m 4f
**6:00** 3-Y-0+ **£1,072,100** (£413,793; £216,300; £112,852; £65,830)

RPR

**1** **Highland Reel (IRE)**[36] 8610 5-9-0 0.................... RyanMoore 8 119
(A P O'Brien, Ire) *chsd ldr: rdn to ld 2 1/2f out: drvn 1 1/2f out: strly pressed ins fnl f: rallied and fnd ex last 150yds: drvn out* **43/20[1]**

**2** *1 ¾* **Talismanic**[36] 8610 4-9-0 0.................... MaximeGuyon 1 116+
(A Fabre, France) *in tch in 3rd: trckd ldrs gng wl 2 1/2f out: rdn over 1f out: pressed ldr strly ins fnl f: no ex last 150yds* **43/10[3]**

**3** *¾* **Tosen Basil (JPN)**[62] 5-9-0 0.................... JoaoMoreira 7 115
(Hideaki Fujiwara, Japan) *hld up in midfield: stdy hdwy fr 3f out: chsd ldrs whn rdn 2f out: ev ch 1f out: no ex last 100yds* **84/10**

**4** *nk* **Chemical Charge (IRE)**[56] 8099 5-9-0 0.................... OisinMurphy 4 115
(Ralph Beckett) *hld up towards rr of midfield: rdn and hdwy fr 2f out: nt clr run 1 1/2f out: drvn and kpt on fr over 1f out* **87/1**

**5** *¾* **Gold Mount**[21] 8864 4-9-0 0....................(t) ZacPurton 12 113
(A S Cruz, Hong Kong) *hld up towards rr: nt clr run 2f out: rdn under 2f out: kpt on fr over 1f out* **81/10**

**6** *nk* **Max Dynamite (FR)**[33] 8667 7-9-0 0.................... GlynSchofield 2 113
(W P Mullins, Ire) *hld up in midfield: pushed along over 3f out: rdn and effrt 2f out: chsd ldrs 1 1/2f out: wknd steadily fnl f* **42/1**

**7** *3* **Smart Call (SAF)**[91] 6972 6-8-10 0.................... JimCrowley 11 104
(Sir Michael Stoute) *hld up towards rr: rdn over 3f out: kpt on steadily fr over 2f out to ins fnl f: no ex last 150yds* **155/1**

**8** *2* **Eagle Way (AUS)**[35] 8629 5-9-0 0....................(b) TommyBerry 5 105
(John Moore, Hong Kong) *in tch in midfield: tk clsr order 3f out: rdn 2 1/2f out: wknd 1 1/2f out* **13/1**

**9** *¾* **Kiseki (JPN)**[49] 8272 3-8-9 0.................... MircoDemuro 3 104
(Katsuhiko Sumii, Japan) *hld up in rr: forward move into midfield 5f out: rdn 2 1/2f out: wknd appr fnl f* **13/5[2]**

**10** *2* **Danehill Kodiac (IRE)**[43] 8421 4-9-0 0.................... SeanLevey 10 100
(Richard Hannon) *in tch in midfield: rdn over 3f out: lost pl 2 1/2f out: sn btn* **121/1**

**11** *1 ¼* **Tiberian (FR)**[33] 8667 5-9-0 0.................... OlivierPeslier 9 98
(Alain Couetil, France) *a towards rr* **12/1**

**12** *8 ½* **Helene Charisma (FR)**[21] 8864 4-9-0 0....................(bt[1]) SamClipperton 6 85
(John Moore, Hong Kong) *led: hdd 2 1/2f out: sn rdn: wknd 2f out: eased 1 1/2f out* **39/1**

2m 26.23s (-1.97)
**WFA** 3 from 4yo+ 4lb **12** Ran SP% **122.3**
PARI-MUTUEL (all including 10 hkd stake): WIN 31.50; PLACE 13.00, 15.50, 28.50; DF 70.50.
**Owner** Derrick Smith & Mrs John Magnier & Michael Tabor **Bred** Hveger Syndicate **Trained** Cashel, Co Tipperary

**FOCUS**
A decent field lined up for a big prize, and it saw a perfect send off for one of Aidan O'Brien's most popular horses of recent years.

## 9168a LONGINES HONG KONG SPRINT (GROUP 1) (3YO+) (COURSE A) (TURF) 6f
**6:40** 3-Y-0+ **£1,101,880** (£425,287; £222,309; £115,987; £67,659)

RPR

**1** **Mr Stunning (AUS)**[21] 8865 5-9-0 0.................... NashRawiller 4 122+
(J Size, Hong Kong) *trckd ldrs: led gng wl 1 1/2f out: sn rdn: drvn and hld on wl last 100yds* **19/20[1]**

**2** *nk* **D B Pin (NZ)**[21] 8865 5-9-0 0.................... OlivierDoleuze 12 121+
(J Size, Hong Kong) *midfield: wd into st: gd hdwy over 2f out: chsd ldr whn rdn 1 1/2f out: drvn and kpt on wl last 150yds: a jst hld* **20/1**

**3** *1 ½* **Blizzard (AUS)**[70] 7674 6-9-0 0.................... GeraldMosse 3 116
(P F Yiu, Hong Kong) *midfield: rdn and hdwy fr under 2f out: kpt on wl: no imp on front pair fnl f* **44/1**

**4** *¾* **Lucky Bubbles (AUS)**[21] 8865 6-9-0 0.................... HughBowman 1 114
(K W Lui, Hong Kong) *in tch in midfield: rdn and kpt on fr 1 1/2f out: nvr gng pce to chal* **5/2[2]**

**5** *½* **Amazing Kids (NZ)**[21] 8865 6-9-0 0.................... BrettPrebble 6 112
(J Size, Hong Kong) *towards rr of midfield: wd into st: rdn 2f out: kpt on fr over 1f out* **17/1**

**6** *nk* **Let's Go Donki (JPN)**[43] 5-8-10 0.................... Yasunarilwata 7 107+
(Tomoyuki Umeda, Japan) *dwlt: in rr: rdn 2f out: styd on fnl f: nrst fin* **46/1**

**7** *½* **Thewizardofoz (AUS)**[21] 8865 6-9-0 0....................(b) JoaoMoreira 8 110
(J Size, Hong Kong) *midfield: rdn and kpt on steadily fr under 2f out* **36/5[3]**

**8** *1 ¼* **The Right Man**[39] 8526 5-9-0 0.................... Francois-XavierBertras 13 106
(D Guillemin, France) *hld up towards rr: rdn under 2f out: kpt on ins fnl f: n.d* **183/1**

**9** *¾* **Peniaphobia (IRE)**[21] 8865 6-9-0 0....................(tp) MatthewChadwick 9 103
(A S Cruz, Hong Kong) *chsd ldr: led 4f out: rdn under 2f out: hdd 1 1/2f out: wknd fnl f* **22/1**

**10** *2 ½* **Not Listenin'tome (AUS)**[21] 8865 7-9-0 0....................(t) TommyBerry 10 95
(John Moore, Hong Kong) *in tch: rdn 2f out: wknd over 1f out* **33/1**

**11** *2 ¾* **Stormy Liberal (USA)**[36] 8604 5-9-0 0....................(t) SilvestreDeSousa 11 86
(Peter Miller, U.S.A) *a towards rr* **83/1**

**12** *2 ¼* **Once In A Moon (JPN)**[70] 7674 4-8-10 0.................... ZacPurton 2 75
(Makoto Saito, Japan) *led: hdd 4f out: rdn under 2f out: lost pl 1 1/2f out: sn wl btn* **20/1**

**13** *10* **Signs Of Blessing (IRE)**[70] 7670 6-9-0 0.................... StephanePasquier 5 47
(F Rohaut, France) *in tch in midfield: rdn and outpcd 2f out: wknd 1 1/2f out: sn eased* **84/1**

1m 8.4s **13** Ran SP% **121.7**
PARI-MUTUEL (all including 10 hkd stake): WIN 19.50; PLACE 11.50, 37.50, 73.00; DF 140.50.
**Owner** Maurice Koo Win Chong **Bred** Makybe Racing & Breeding **Trained** Hong Kong

**FOCUS**
Plenty of early speed on for this sprint, and it proved to be a good race for trainer John Size, who had the first two home.

## 9170a LONGINES HONG KONG MILE (GROUP 1) (3YO+) (COURSE A) (TURF) 1m
**7:50** 3-Y-0+ **£1,369,905** (£528,735; £276,384; £144,200; £84,117)

RPR

**1** **Beauty Generation (NZ)**[21] 8866 5-9-0 0....................(bt) KCLeung 9 119
(John Moore, Hong Kong) *mde all: wnt 2 l clr 2f out: rdn 1 1/2f out: drvn over 1f out: kpt on wl* **74/10**

**2** *1* **Western Express (AUS)**[21] 8866 5-9-0 0.................... SamClipperton 7 117
(J Size, Hong Kong) *in tch: rdn 2f out: kpt on wl fnl f: nt rch wnr* **35/1**

**3** *nk* **Helene Paragon (FR)**[21] 8866 5-9-0 0....................(h) TommyBerry 2 116
(John Moore, Hong Kong) *hld up towards rr: wd into st: rdn and styd on wl fr 2f out: nrst fin* **59/10[3]**

**4** *1 ¼* **Seasons Bloom (AUS)**[21] 8866 5-9-0 0....................(t) JoaoMoreira 5 113+
(C S Shum, Hong Kong) *hld up towards rr: rdn over 2f out: drvn 1 1/2f out: styd on on fnl f: nrst fin* **8/5[1]**

**5** *¾* **Lancaster Bomber (USA)**[36] 8608 3-8-13 0.................... RyanMoore 11 112
(A P O'Brien, Ire) *midfield: rdn over 2f out: kpt on fr over 1f out: nvr gng pce to chal* **14/1**

6 ¾ **Horse Of Fortune (SAF)**[21] 8866 7-9-0 0 .................. UmbertoRispoli 13 110
(A T Millard, Hong Kong) *chsd ldr: rdn over 2f out: wknd steadily fr over 1f out* **49/1**

7 shd **Beauty Only (IRE)**[21] 8866 6-9-0 0 ..................................(t) ZacPurton 12 110
(A S Cruz, Hong Kong) *hld up towards rr: hdwy on outer into midfield 2 1/2f out: rdn and kpt on same pce fr 2f out* **7/2**[2]

8 ½ **Sichuan Dar (AUS)**[21] 8866 6-9-0 0 ...........................(t) NashRawiller 6 109
(A T Millard, Hong Kong) *towards rr of midfield: rdn 2f out: nt clr run under 2f out: kpt on steadily ins fnl f: n.d* **29/1**

9 ¾ **Joyful Trinity (IRE)**[21] 8866 5-9-0 0 ................ GeraldMosse 10 107
(John Moore, Hong Kong) *towards rr of midfield: rdn over 2f out: sme hdwy 1 1/2f out: no imp ins fnl f* **29/1**

10 ¾ **Lightning Spear**[50] 8232 6-9-0 0 ........................ OisinMurphy 1 105
(David Simcock) *in tch in midfield: rdn 2f out: wknd steadily fr 1 1/2f out* **139/1**

11 1 **Satono Aladdin (JPN)**[21] 8858 6-9-0 0 ....................(bt) HughBowman 4 103
(Yasutoshi Ikee, Japan) *t.k.h in rr: quick hdwy to take much clsr order 3f out: rdn and outpcd 2f out: wknd over 1f out* **13/1**

12 2½ **Contentment (AUS)**[70] 7682 7-9-0 0 ..........................(e) BrettPrebble 8 97
(J Size, Hong Kong) *in tch: rdn and lost pl 2f out: wknd over 1f out: eased last 100yds* **23/1**

13 1 **Karar**[36] 8608 5-9-0 0 ............................................ Pierre-CharlesBoudot 3 95
(F-H Graffard, France) *trckd ldrs: racd keenly: rdn over 2f out: wknd 1 1/2f out* **128/1**

14 1 **Roly Poly (USA)**[36] 8608 3-8-9 0 ........................(p) SeamieHeffernan 14 89
(A P O'Brien, Ire) *towards rr of midfield: rdn and lost pl appr 2f out: sn struggling* **24/1**

1m 33.72s (-0.98)
**WFA** 3 from 5yo+ 1lb **14** Ran SP% **122.0**
PARI-MUTUEL (all including 10 hkd stake): WIN 84.00; PLACE 24.00, 83.00, 21.00; DF 1235.00.
**Owner** Patrick Kwok Ho Chuen **Bred** Nearco Stud Limited **Trained** Hong Kong

**FOCUS**
This was the first of two races where the jockey on the winner deserves lots of praise for stacking his rivals up behind before gaining an advantage at the right time.

## 9171a LONGINES HONG KONG CUP (GROUP 1) (3YO+) (COURSE A) (TURF) 1m 2f
8:30 3-Y-O+ £1,489,028 (£574,712; £300,417; £156,739; £91,431)

RPR

1 **Time Warp**[21] 8864 4-9-0 0 ....................................................(t) ZacPurton 5 119
(A S Cruz, Hong Kong) *mde all: rdn clr under 2f out: kpt on strly* **61/20**[2]

2 2¼ **Werther (NZ)**[21] 8864 6-9-0 0 ................................ TommyBerry 3 115+
(John Moore, Hong Kong) *midfield: rdn 2f out: drvn and styd on fr under 2f out: no imp on wnr ins fnl f* **6/5**[1]

3 1½ **Neorealism (JPN)**[42] 8465 6-9-0 0 .......................... JoaoMoreira 1 112
(Noriyuki Hori, Japan) *t.k.h: trckd ldrs: rdn under 2f out: kpt on tl no ex last 75yds* **63/10**[3]

4 ½ **Staphanos (JPN)**[42] 8465 6-9-0 0 ............................(h) HughBowman 8 111
(Hideaki Fujiwara, Japan) *towards rr of midfield: rdn under 2f out: drvn and kpt on fr 1 1/2f out* **15/1**

5 ½ **Smart Layer (JPN)**[28] 8767 7-8-10 0 ..............................(t) YutakaTake 9 106
(Ryuji Okubo, Japan) *chsd ldr: rdn 2f out: wknd steadily fr 1 1/2f out* **27/1**

6 nk **Poet's Word (IRE)**[50] 8233 4-9-0 0 ............................ AndreaAtzeni 12 109
(Sir Michael Stoute) *hld up towards rr: rdn 2 1/2f out: wd into st: kpt on steadily fr under 2f out* **36/5**

7 2 **Secret Weapon**[21] 8864 7-9-0 0 .................................(t) NashRawiller 11 105
(C H Yip, Hong Kong) *hld up towards rr: rdn and kpt on steadily fr 2f out: n.d* **37/1**

8 shd **Robin Of Navan (FR)**[57] 8041 4-9-0 0 ........................ SamClipperton 4 105
(Harry Dunlop) *racd keenly in midfield: stdy hdwy fr over 3f out: chsd ldrs whn rdn under 2f out: wknd fnl f* **104/1**

9 ½ **Garlingari (FR)**[71] 7638 6-9-0 0 ...........................(p) StephanePasquier 6 104
(Mme C Barande-Barbe, France) *in tch: rdn over 2f out: lost pl under 2f out: sn no imp* **94/1**

10 nk **War Decree (USA)**[35] 8611 3-8-11 0 ........................ SeamieHeffernan 7 103
(A P O'Brien, Ire) *towards rr of midfield: rdn and no imp fr 2f out* **77/1**

11 1¼ **Deauville (IRE)**[85] 7179 4-9-0 0 ...............................(b) RyanMoore 2 101
(A P O'Brien, Ire) *in tch: dropped to midfield 2 1/2f out: rdn 2f out: wknd fnl f* **10/1**

12 1 **Blond Me (IRE)**[56] 8098 5-8-10 0 ............................. OisinMurphy 10 95
(Andrew Balding) *squeezed out at s: a towards rr* **51/1**

2m 1.63s (0.23)
**WFA** 3 from 4yo+ 2lb **12** Ran SP% **122.8**
PARI-MUTUEL (all including 10 hkd stake): WIN 40.50; PLACE 14.50, 12.50, 20.00; DF 44.50.
**Owner** Martin Siu Kim Sun **Bred** Miss K Rausing **Trained** Hong Kong

**FOCUS**
This looked a competitive contest but it was completely stolen from the front under a fine tactical ride.

9169 - 9174a (Foreign Racing) - See Raceform Interactive

# 9070 SOUTHWELL (L-H)
Monday, December 11

**OFFICIAL GOING: Fibresand: standard**
Wind: Fresh behind Weather: Cloudy

## 9175 32RED CASINO NURSERY H'CAP 1m 13y(F)
12:30 (12:31) (Class 6) (0-60,59) 2-Y-O £2,264 (£673; £336; £168) Stalls Low

Form RPR

0302 1 **Mr Carbonator**[11] 9014 2-8-12 **55** ............................ JamieGormley(5) 11 62+
(Philip Kirby) *hld up in rr: hdwy over 3f out: n.m.r and hmpd on home turn: chsd ldrs and rdn wl over 1f out: chsd ldr and drvn ins fnl f: kpt on wl to ld last 50yds* **4/1**[2]

6403 2 ½ **Medici Oro**[34] 8658 2-9-6 **58** ................................ PhillipMakin 6 64
(David Brown) *cl up: led 3f out: rdn wl over 1f out: drvn ins fnl f: hdd and no ex last 50yds* **4/1**[2]

0044 3 5 **Blue Havana (IRE)**[11] 9014 2-9-2 **54** ........................(v¹) JasonHart 13 48
(John Quinn) *dwlt and in rr: sn swtchd lft towards inner: hdwy to trck ldrs over 4f out: rdn along to chse ldr over 2f out: drvn over 1f out: kpt on same pce* **7/1**[3]

3000 4 3 **Fabella Bere (FR)**[26] 8783 2-9-1 **53** ............................ BenCurtis 12 40
(K R Burke) *towards rr: pushed along and hdwy on outer 1/2-way: rdn 3f out: drvn and edgd lft wl over 1f out: kpt on* **12/1**

0600 5 2¾ **Thundercloud**[13] 8982 2-9-5 **57** ............................ PaulMulrennan 2 37
(Scott Dixon) *cl up: rdn to ld briefly 3 1/2f out: hdd 3f out: sn rdn: grad wknd fnl 2f* **66/1**

003 6 2¼ **Dorian Gray (IRE)**[13] 8981 2-9-3 **58** ........................ CharlieBennett(3) 10 33
(Hughie Morrison) *midfield: hdwy on outer 3f out: rdn along over 2f out: sn no imp* **7/1**[3]

5523 7 6 **Rock On Bertie (IRE)**[11] 9014 2-9-4 **56** ........................(p) TomEaves 5 16
(Nigel Tinkler) *towards rr: sme hdwy 3f out: rdn along over 2f out: n.d* **7/2**[1]

3505 8 2½ **Salire (IRE)**[12] 8996 2-9-7 **59** ..................................... GrahamLee 4 13
(Ann Duffield) *chsd ldrs: rdn along over 3f out: wknd over 2f out* **20/1**

00R0 9 1¾ **Afterthisone**[21] 8870 2-8-7 **45** ........................................ CamHardie 7
(Robin Dickin) *chsd ldrs: rdn along wl over 3f out: sn wknd* **66/1**

0004 10 6 **Tea Rattle**[13] 8983 2-8-10 **48** ...................................... KieranO'Neill 1
(Scott Dixon) *led: rdn along and hdd 3 1/2f out: wknd over 2f out* **50/1**

6040 11 6 **Dragon Tattoo (IRE)**[23] 8847 2-9-5 **57** ...............(p¹) JosephineGordon 9
(Hugo Palmer) *prom: rdn along over 3f out: sn wknd* **20/1**

000 12 6 **Mops Tango**[163] 4340 2-8-11 **49** ...................................... LukeMorris 14
(Michael Appleby) *dwlt: sn chsng ldrs on outer: rdn along wl over 3f out: sn wknd* **25/1**

0066 13 15 **La Cabana**[16] 8954 2-9-5 **57** ........................................ JackGarritty 8
(Richard Fahey) *a in rr* **33/1**

1m 46.26s (2.56) **Going Correction** +0.025s/f (Slow) **13** Ran SP% **116.2**
Speed ratings (Par 94): **88,87,82,79,76 74,68,66,64,58 52,46,31**
CSF £18.18 CT £110.43 TOTE £4.70: £1.70, £1.70, £2.80; EX 25.60 Trifecta £147.40.
**Owner** Alan Fairhurst and Peter Sharp **Bred** Mel Roberts & Ms Nicola Meese **Trained** East Appleton, N Yorks

■ Stewards' Enquiry : Jack Garritty two-day ban: using his whip arm above shoulder height (Dec 26-27)

**FOCUS**
A modest nursery. They went an, at best, respectable gallop on standard Fibresand but it is sound enough form. It's been rated slightly negatively.

## 9176 BETWAY CLASSIFIED CLAIMING STKS 6f 16y(F)
1:00 (1:00) (Class 6) 3-Y-O+ £2,264 (£673; £336; £168) Stalls Low

Form RPR

4000 1 **Newstead Abbey**[21] 8874 7-9-3 65 ..................................(b) TomEaves 1 73
(Michael Herrington) *mde all: rdn wl over 1f out: drvn out* **8/1**

314 2 1¾ **Bernie's Boy**[79] 7389 4-9-3 67 ..................................(p) LukeMorris 11 67
(Iain Jardine) *cl up: rdn to chal 2f out: drvn over 1f out: ch ent fnl f: kpt on same pce* **7/2**[1]

0-00 3 3 **Hugie Boy (IRE)**[7] 9076 5-8-12 57 ..................................(bt¹) KieranO'Neill 2 53
(Scott Dixon) *prom on inner: rdn along over 2f out: drvn and edgd rt over 1f out: kpt on same pce* **40/1**

003 4 ½ **Ace Master**[10] 9031 9-8-12 62 ...........................................(b) EoinWalsh(3) 9 54
(Roy Bowring) *t.k.h: trckd ldrs: pushed along and hdwy over 2f out: rdn wl over 1f out: kpt on same pce* **11/2**[3]

1020 5 2 **Captain Bob (IRE)**[10] 9029 6-8-10 70 ..................... JonathanFisher(7) 7 50
(Philip Kirby) *dwlt and in rr: hdwy 3f out: rdn along 2f out: drvn over 1f out: kpt on fnl f* **13/2**

6060 6 1¼ **Peachey Carnehan**[21] 8875 3-9-2 64 ..........................(be¹) PhilDennis(3) 3 48
(Michael Mullineaux) *in rr tl kpt on u.p fnl 2f: n.d* **14/1**

0540 7 ½ **Glorious Rocket**[38] 8556 3-9-1 69 ...................................(h) BenCurtis 4 42
(David Barron) *a towards rr* **9/2**[2]

4630 8 5 **Sarabi**[7] 9075 4-8-11 54 .................................................(tp) PaddyPilley(3) 5 25
(Scott Dixon) *t.k.h: chsd ldrs: rdn along over 2f out: drvn wl over 1f out: sn wknd* **25/1**

-025 9 ½ **Strategic Heights (IRE)**[21] 8874 8-8-8 67 ...........(p) JackDinsmore(7) 10 25
(Jamie Osborne) *chsd ldrs on outer: wd st: rdn over 2f out: sn wknd* **9/2**[2]

0200 10 12 **Miningrocks (FR)**[10] 9029 5-9-0 65 ............................(v) PaulMulrennan 6
(Conor Dore) *dwlt and in rr: rdn along and wd st: nvr a factor* **25/1**

1m 16.17s (-0.33) **Going Correction** +0.025s/f (Slow) **10** Ran SP% **115.2**
Speed ratings (Par 101): **103,100,96,96,93 91,91,84,83,67**
CSF £35.02 TOTE £8.90: £2.30, £1.60, £8.20; EX 54.20 Trifecta £2047.80.There was no bid for the winner.
**Owner** Tony Culhane Racing Club **Bred** Grasshopper 2000 Ltd **Trained** Cold Kirby, N Yorks

**FOCUS**
An ordinary claimer. The winner made all at a decent tempo and there was little change in the early, prominent order throughout. The winner has been rated in line with his better recent form.

## 9177 32RED.COM BRITISH STALLION STUDS EBF NOVICE STKS 7f 14y(F)
1:30 (1:33) (Class 5) 2-Y-O £2,911 (£866; £432; £216) Stalls Low

Form RPR

421 1 **On The Warpath**[13] 8982 2-9-9 85 ...................................... LukeMorris 6 92+
(Sir Mark Prescott Bt) *trckd ldrs: pushed along and sltly outpcd over 2f out: rdn and hdwy wl over 1f out: drvn to chal ent fnl f: sn led and styd on strly* **4/6**[1]

341 2 3½ **Line House**[52] 8208 2-9-1 75 ............................................ BenCurtis 13 72
(K R Burke) *cl up: led wl over 2f out: rdn over 1f out: drvn and hdd ins fnl f: kpt on same pce* **5/1**[3]

2 3 1¾ **Magnetic Boundary (USA)**[13] 8981 2-9-2 0 ......................(t) FranBerry 3 68
(George Scott) *trckd ldrs: hdwy 3f out: rdn along wl over 1f out: sn drvn and kpt on same pce* **11/4**[2]

4 1¼ **One More Chance (IRE)** 2-8-11 0 ...................................... JasonHart 2 60+
(David Brown) *dwlt and bhd: hdwy on inner 3f out: swtchd rt to centre and rdn wl over 1f out: styd on wl fnl f* **50/1**

5 nse **Love Rat** 2-9-2 0 ............................................................... TomEaves 4 65+
(Scott Dixon) *dwlt and in rr: sn swtchd rt to outer and hdwy to chse ldrs 4f out: rdn along over 2f out: drvn wl over 1f out: kpt on same pce* **100/1**

04 6 2¼ **Samovar**[13] 8981 2-9-2 0 ........................................... KieranO'Neill 12 59
(Scott Dixon) *cl up: slt ld over 4f out: rdn along 3f out: sn hdd: drvn over 2f out: grad wknd* **100/1**

0540 7 6 **Jaffar**[147] 4963 2-9-2 65 ................................................... GrahamLee 7 42
(Scott Dixon) *chsd ldrs: rdn along 3f out: wknd over 2f out* **100/1**

8 ½ **Team Showme** 2-8-11 0 ........................................... AndrewMullen 5 36
(Michael Dods) *dwlt and in rr: rdn along and hdwy 3f out: no imp fnl 2f* **66/1**

3366 9 3½ **Raven's Raft (IRE)**[111] 6285 2-8-11 63 .............(h¹) JosephineGordon 11 27
(Michael Appleby) *slt ld: hdd over 4f out: cl up: rdn along 3f out: drvn over 2f out and sn wknd* **25/1**

10 1¾ **Traumatised** 2-8-6 0 ................................................ KevinLundie(5) 9 22
(Michael Appleby) *in rr: wd st and bhd* **100/1**

04 11 ½ **Serabrina (IRE)**[41] 8483 2-8-11 0 ...................................(t¹) ShaneGray 8 21
(David Menuisier) *dwlt: a towards rr* **40/1**

00 12 4 **Amadeus (IRE)**[26] 8779 2-9-2 0 ...................................... JackGarritty 10 15
(Richard Fahey) *chsd ldrs: rdn along on outer 1/2-way: wd st and sn wknd* **50/1**

04 **13** 4 **G Eye Joe**[13] 8982 2-9-2 0 PaulMulrennan 1 4
(James Given) *dwlt: a towards rr* **16/1**
1m 29.31s (-0.99) **Going Correction** +0.025s/f (Slow) **13** Ran SP% **124.9**
Speed ratings (Par 96): **106,102,100,98,98 95,89,88,84,82 81,77,72**
CSF £4.83 TOTE £1.50: £1.10, £1.80, £1.10; EX 5.90 Trifecta £9.60.
**Owner** Charles C Walker - Osborne House II **Bred** Sahara Group & Eurowest Bloodstock **Trained** Newmarket, Suffolk

**FOCUS**
A fair juvenile novice contest. The odds-on favourite came nicely clear of the right two horses in second and third. The fourth and sixth are key to the level. The second and third would support the race being rated 4lb higher.

## 9178 BETWAY CASINO H'CAP 1m 6f 21y(F)
**2:00** (2:00) (Class 5) (0-75,75) 3-Y-O+ **£2,911** (£866; £432; £216) **Stalls** Low

Form RPR
1031 **1** **Good Time Ahead (IRE)**[13] 8978 3-8-12 69 JamieGormley(5) 7 82
(Philip Kirby) *trckd ldrs: smooth hdwy over 3f out: sn cl up: led 2f out and sn rdn: styd on strly fnl f* **6/4**[1]
5664 **2** 3 ¾ **Cousin Khee**[13] 8978 10-8-9 63 TheodoreLadd(7) 1 69
(Hughie Morrison) *hld up towards rr: hdwy on inner over 4f out: cl up 3f out: cl up 2f out: sn rdn to chse wnr and ev ch: drvn appr fnl f and kpt on same pce* **6/1**[3]
0000 **3** 11 **Samtu (IRE)**[26] 8778 6-10-0 75 JoeyHaynes 9 66
(Marjorie Fife) *prom: cl up over 4f out: rdn to take slt ld 3f out: hdd 2f out: sn drvn and kpt on one pce* **6/1**[3]
0002 **4** 4 ½ **Bertie Moon**[28] 8771 7-9-9 70 AndrewMullen 3 54
(Michael Appleby) *led: rdn along over 3f out: sn hdd: drvn 2f out and grad wknd* **5/1**[2]
0005 **5** 8 **Etaad (USA)**[7] 9077 6-8-13 60 (b) JasonHart 11 33
(Lucinda Egerton) *hld up towards rr: hdwy over 4f out: rdn along over 3f out: nvr nr ldrs* **50/1**
-054 **6** 1 ¼ **Coroberee (IRE)**[10] 9028 4-9-11 72 (p) GrahamLee 8 43
(Tony Coyle) *cl up: rdn along over 3f out: sn drvn and wknd* **9/1**
0006 **7** 5 **Sleep Easy**[28] 8771 5-9-12 73 RobertWinston 10 37
(Neil Mulholland) *hld up in tch: hdwy on outer to chse ldrs 1/2-way: rdn along wl over 3f out: sn wknd* **9/1**
1320 **8** 99 **Newt**[41] 8487 3-9-1 67 FranBerry 5
(Chris Wall) *in tch on inner: pushed along 1/2-way: rdn and lost pl 5f out: sn bhd* **20/1**
0303 **9** 20 **Golden Set**[52] 8204 3-9-1 67 EdwardGreatrex 2
(Eve Johnson Houghton) *chsd ldng pair: rdn along over 5f out: wknd 4f out* **20/1**
3m 7.8s (-0.50) **Going Correction** +0.025s/f (Slow)
**WFA** 3 from 4yo+ 5lb **9** Ran SP% **116.7**
Speed ratings (Par 103): **102,99,93,91,86 85,82,26,14**
CSF £10.66 CT £43.07 TOTE £2.40: £1.30, £2.20, £2.20; EX 10.10 Trifecta £50.90.
**Owner** Greenbank, Fairhurst & Fletcher **Bred** Mrs M Dowdall Blake **Trained** East Appleton, N Yorks
■ Alternate Route was withdrawn. Price at time of withdrawal 7/2. Rule 4 applies to board prices before withdrawal. Deduction - 20p in the pound. New market formed.

**FOCUS**
A fair staying handicap. They went a respectable gallop and the strong favourite found the anticipated progression to win readily back over 1m6f. A clear pb from the winner.

## 9179 SUNBETS.CO.UK H'CAP 7f 14y(F)
**2:30** (2:32) (Class 4) (0-80,81) 3-Y-O+ **£4,690** (£1,395; £697; £348) **Stalls** Low

Form RPR
0400 **1** **Hammer Gun (USA)**[10] 9025 4-9-2 76 (v) PatrickMathers 6 87
(Derek Shaw) *trckd ldrs: hdwy over 2f out: swtchd lft and rdn over 1f out: led ins fnl f: drvn out* **5/1**[2]
6060 **2** 1 **Custard The Dragon**[21] 8872 4-9-6 80 (p) AndrewMullen 2 88
(John Mackie) *sn pushed along in rr: hdwy 1/2-way: rdn to chse ldrs wl over 1f out: drvn to ins fnl f: kpt on wl* **15/2**
0012 **3** ¾ **Monteverdi (FR)**[61] 7947 4-9-7 81 TimmyMurphy 8 87
(Jamie Osborne) *led: hdd briefly 3f out: led again over 2f out: rdn wl over 1f out: drvn and hdd ins fnl f: kpt on* **5/1**[2]
2310 **4** 1 **Cainhoe Star**[46] 8375 4-9-4 78 LukeMorris 11 82
(Anthony Carson) *dwlt and towards rr: hdwy on outer wl over 2f out: rdn to chse ldrs whn edgd lft over 1f out: sn drvn and kpt on same pce* **7/1**[3]
3555 **5** 1 ½ **Musharrif**[25] 8803 5-9-4 78 TomEaves 4 78
(Declan Carroll) *cl up on inner: slt ld 3f out: rdn along and hdd over 2f out: cl up and drvn wl over 1f out: wknd fnl f* **16/1**
0115 **6** 1 ¾ **Toy Theatre**[30] 8747 3-9-5 79 AlistairRawlinson 5 74
(Michael Appleby) *chsd ldrs: rdn along wl over 2f out: drvn wl over 1f out: kpt on one pce* **12/1**
0000 **7** nk **Alpha Tauri (USA)**[25] 8803 11-8-12 77 BenRobinson(5) 9 72
(Charles Smith) *cl up: rdn along over 2f out: sn drvn and grad wknd* **50/1**
0434 **8** 4 **Michele Strogoff**[16] 8956 4-9-4 78 (p) BenCurtis 1 62
(Tony Coyle) *chsd ldrs on inner: rdn along 3f out: sn drvn and wknd* **25/1**
3620 **9** ½ **Midnight Macchiato (IRE)**[32] 8706 4-9-3 77 PhillipMakin 10 60
(David Brown) *cl up on outer: rdn along over 2f out: sn wknd* **20/1**
1 **10** 1 ¼ **Abraj Dubai (USA)**[25] 8805 3-9-6 80 GrahamLee 7 60
(David O'Meara) *dwlt: sn trcking ldrs: rdn along over 3f out: sn btn* **2/1**[1]
0000 **11** ½ **Bouclier (IRE)**[51] 8240 7-9-5 79 CamHardie 3 57
(Michael Easterby) *sn outpcd and a bhd* **66/1**
1m 29.24s (-1.06) **Going Correction** +0.025s/f (Slow) **11** Ran SP% **116.6**
Speed ratings (Par 105): **107,105,105,103,102 100,99,95,94,93 92**
CSF £40.30 CT £202.79 TOTE £6.00: £2.00, £2.50, £1.80; EX 43.00 Trifecta £412.70.
**Owner** A Flint **Bred** Her Majesty The Queen **Trained** Sproxton, Leics

**FOCUS**
The feature contest was a fairly decent handicap. A couple of horses previously well suited to Fibresand came to the fore off a solid tempo. The winner has been rated to his best.

## 9180 SUN BETS ON THE APP STORE H'CAP 1m 13y(F)
**3:00** (3:02) (Class 5) (0-70,72) 3-Y-O+ **£2,911** (£866; £432; £216) **Stalls** Low

Form RPR
3212 **1** **Mach One**[25] 8801 3-9-6 70 (p) EdwardGreatrex 2 80+
(Archie Watson) *dwlt and in rr: sn swtchd lft to inner: hdwy on inner 3f out: swtchd rt and rdn to chse ldrs wl over 1f out: drvn ent fnl f: styd on wl to ld last 80yds* **5/2**[1]
1000 **2** 1 ½ **Muqarred (USA)**[10] 9029 5-9-9 72 (p) BenCurtis 4 79
(Roger Fell) *in tch: hdwy wl over 2f out: sn cl up: rdn to ld jst over 1f out: drvn ins fnl f: hdd and no ex last 80yds* **14/1**
443- **3** ¾ **Best Tamayuz**[363] 8351 6-8-7 56 oh1 (p) KieranO'Neill 5 61
(Scott Dixon) *slt ld: rdn along over 2f out: drvn over 1f out: hdd appr fnl f: kpt on wl u.p* **28/1**
0006 **4** 2 ½ **Captain Revelation**[10] 9029 5-9-6 72 (bt[1]) PhilDennis(3) 7 72
(Michael Mullineaux) *trckd ldrs: cl up and wd st: sn rdn to chal: ev ch tl drvn and wknd over 1f out* **20/1**
1600 **5** 1 ¾ **Dubaitwentytwenty**[37] 8589 3-9-1 65 (t[1]) JosephineGordon 1 61
(Hugo Palmer) *trckd ldrs on inner: hdwy over 2f out and sn cl up: rdn wl over 1f out: drvn appr fnl f: kpt on same pce* **28/1**
0651 **6** 3 ¼ **Shearian**[10] 9032 7-8-11 67 GerO'Neill(7) 11 55
(Declan Carroll) *trckd ldrs: hdwy over 3f out: rdn and cl up over 2f out: drvn wl over 1f out: grad wknd* **11/1**
3000 **7** ¾ **Dubai Waves**[45] 8400 3-8-13 66 EoinWalsh(3) 9 52
(Tony Newcombe) *in rr: hdwy and n.m.r on bnd 3f out: rdn over 2f out: n.d* **80/1**
0631 **8** ½ **Sonnet Rose (IRE)**[7] 9073 3-7-13 56 6ex (bt) NicolaCurrie(7) 3 41
(Conrad Allen) *in tch: pushed along over 3f out: sn rdn and wknd over 2f out* **13/2**
0024 **9** shd **Shamrokh (IRE)**[25] 8797 3-9-8 72 GrahamLee 14 57
(Michael Appleby) *chsd ldrs: cl up on outer over 3 1/2f out: sn rdn and wd st: sn wknd* **7/2**[2]
4121 **10** 2 ¾ **Medici Moon**[28] 8773 3-9-1 65 (p) LukeMorris 6 44
(Scott Dixon) *cl up: rdn along over 3f out: drvn and wknd over 2f out* **9/2**[3]
60-6 **11** 6 **Gone With The Wind (GER)**[216] 2501 6-9-1 64 JasonHart 10 29
(Rebecca Bastiman) *dwlt: a in rr* **66/1**
3220 **12** nk **Showdance Kid**[52] 8216 3-9-3 67 RyanPowell 12 31
(Kevin Frost) *chsd ldrs: rdn along wl over 3f out: sn wknd* **33/1**
1m 43.59s (-0.11) **Going Correction** +0.025s/f (Slow)
**WFA** 3 from 5yo+ 1lb **12** Ran SP% **114.6**
Speed ratings (Par 103): **101,99,98,96,94 91,90,90,89,87 81,80**
CSF £35.21 CT £789.30 TOTE £3.30: £1.40, £3.50, £6.70; EX 39.70 Trifecta £718.80.
**Owner** Dr Bridget Drew & Partners **Bred** Mildmay Bloodstock Ltd **Trained** Upper Lambourn, W Berks

**FOCUS**
An ordinary handicap. They went a respectable gallop and the favourite came through to win despite a modest beginning. It's been rated around the runner-up, with the third to his recent form.

## 9181 BETWAY H'CAP 4f 214y(F)
**3:30** (3:31) (Class 6) (0-60,60) 3-Y-O+ **£2,264** (£673; £336; £168) **Stalls** Centre

Form RPR
0035 **1** **Pearl Acclaim (IRE)**[10] 9033 7-9-6 59 (p) SteveDrowne 1 73
(David C Griffiths) *racd towards far side: cl up: led over 3f out: rdn and edgd rt wl over 1f out: drvn out* **11/2**[3]
0361 **2** 2 ½ **Archie Stevens**[7] 9075 7-9-1 57 6ex PaddyPilley(3) 7 62
(Clare Ellam) *slt ld in centre: hdd over 3f out: rdn along and swtchd lft wl over 1f out: sn drvn and chsd wnr ent fnl f: kpt on same pce* **4/1**[1]
0000 **3** 1 ¾ **Very First Blade**[50] 8258 8-8-4 46 oh1 (be) PhilDennis(3) 4 45
(Michael Mullineaux) *racd towards far side: chsd ldrs: rdn along wl over 1f out: styd on wl fnl f* **33/1**
4025 **4** 1 ½ **Excellent World (IRE)**[5] 9103 4-8-7 46 (t) DuranFentiman 9 40
(Tony Coyle) *in tch centre: hdwy 2f out: sn rdn: kpt on fnl f* **12/1**
3364 **5** ½ **Coiste Bodhar (IRE)**[13] 8980 6-8-10 49 (p) LukeMorris 10 41
(Scott Dixon) *racd towards stands' side: in tch: rdn along 2f out: kpt on fnl f* **5/1**[2]
6064 **6** hd **Krystallite**[12] 9001 4-9-6 59 (p) BenCurtis 5 50
(Scott Dixon) *chsd ldrs centre: hdwy 1/2-way: sn rdn and edgd rt: drvn wl over 1f out: sn wknd* **5/1**[2]
0200 **7** 1 ¾ **Men United (FR)**[44] 8428 4-8-11 50 (v[1]) JimmyQuinn 3 35
(Roy Bowring) *racd towards far side: cl up: rdn along 2f out: drvn and wknd over 1f out* **11/2**[3]
2310 **8** hd **Ballesteros**[24] 8818 8-9-2 60 RhiainIngram(5) 6 44
(Roger Ingram) *racd towards far side: chsd ldrs: rdn along 2f out: sn wknd* **14/1**
2660 **9** 1 ¾ **Red Flute**[217] 2472 5-8-0 46 oh1 KeelanBaker(7) 12 24
(Michael Appleby) *racd nr stands' rail: in tch: rdn along over 2f out: sn wknd* **8/1**
0003 **10** 5 **Chillililli**[28] 8776 3-8-2 46 oh1 (b) JaneElliott(5) 11 6
(Michael Appleby) *racd towards stands' rail: in tch: rdn along over 2f out: sn wknd* **40/1**
59.93s (0.23) **Going Correction** +0.075s/f (Slow) **10** Ran SP% **115.0**
Speed ratings (Par 101): **101,97,94,91,91 90,87,87,84,76**
CSF £27.35 CT £676.81 TOTE £7.00: £2.30, £2.00, £5.40; EX 35.70 Trifecta £936.80.
**Owner** Ontoawinner 2 & Partner **Bred** Awbeg Stud **Trained** Bawtry, S Yorks

**FOCUS**
A modest sprint handicap. They went a respectable tempo right across the course and two of the more fancied horses filled the first two placings. The winner has been rated to the best of his 2017 form.
T/Jkpt: £11,615.50 to a £1 stake. Pool: £16,359.94 - 1.0 winning unit. T/Plt: £57.10 to a £1 stake. Pool: £94,986.29 - 1,213.53 winning units. T/Qpdt: £7.40 to a £1 stake. Pool: £13,405.66 - 1,337.53 winning units. **Joe Rowntree**

# 9088 LINGFIELD (L-H)
Tuesday, December 12

**OFFICIAL GOING: Polytrack: standard**
Wind: Light, across Weather: Fine, 1 degree

## 9182 32REDSPORT.COM (S) STKS 6f 1y(P)
**11:30** (11:31) (Class 6) 2-Y-O **£2,458** (£731; £365; £182) **Stalls** Low

Form RPR
413 **1** **Inuk (IRE)**[21] 8882 2-8-6 59 (p) NicolaCurrie(7) 6 56
(Richard Hughes) *mde all: shkn up whn pressed 2f out: def advantage over 1f out: rdn out* **9/5**[2]
0223 **2** 1 **Mother Of Dragons (IRE)**[5] 9122 2-8-9 70 (p[1]) JosephineGordon 3 49
(Phil McEntee) *chsd wnr: rdn to chal 2f out: nt qckn over 1f out: kpt on but nvr threatened to overtake after* **4/6**[1]
0600 **3** 1 ½ **Jazz Affair (IRE)**[13] 9002 2-8-7 50 EmmaTaff(7) 1 49
(Jamie Osborne) *t.k.h: hld up in 4th: lft bhd fr 1/2-way but stl gng wl enough: pushed along over 1f out: styd on to take 3rd ins fnl f: clsng at fin but no ch* **8/1**[3]
6000 **4** 3 ¾ **Swiss Psalm**[17] 8945 2-8-9 39 RobHornby 5 32
(Mark Gillard) *trckd ldrs: rdn over 2f out: wknd fnl f* **66/1**
00 **5** 31 **Aonedampproofing**[10] 9050 2-9-0 0 (h) DannyBrock 2
(Lisa Williamson) *slowly away: racd awkwardly and hanging thrght: lost tch 1/2-way: t.o* **80/1**
1m 11.38s (-0.52) **Going Correction** -0.10s/f (Stan) **5** Ran SP% **109.5**
Speed ratings (Par 94): **99,97,95,90,49**
CSF £3.28 TOTE £2.60: £1.20, £1.10; EX 3.10 Trifecta £4.10.There was no bid for the winner.
**Owner** Richard Hughes Racing Club **Bred** Tally-Ho Stud **Trained** Upper Lambourn, Berks

**FOCUS**
A moderate contest that only ever concerned the front two in the market. Straightforward form rated around the winner, third and fourth.

## 9183 BETWAY SPRINT H'CAP (DIV I) — 6f 1y(P)
**12:00** (12:02) (Class 6) (0-65,66) 3-Y-0+ **£3,234** (£962; £481; £240) **Stalls** Low

Form | | | | RPR
---|---|---|---|---
2024 | 1 | | **Indian Affair**[22] 8874 7-9-1 **66**.......................(bt) KerrieRaybould(7) 3 (Milton Bradley) *trckd ldr after 1f: pushed along to chal over 1f out: kpt on wl to edge ahd last 50yds* **5/1**[3] | 73
6030 | 2 | hd | **Gold Club**[90] 7058 6-9-5 **63**.......................AdamKirby 7 (Lee Carter) *led after 1f: drvn over 1f out: kpt on u.p but hdd last 50yds* **4/1**[2] | 69
0000 | 3 | 1 | **Strictly Carter**[49] 8329 4-8-13 **57**.......................(t[1]) FranBerry 5 (Alan Bailey) *hld up in midfield on inner: prog over 1f out: tk 3rd ins fnl f: kpt on but unable to chal* **6/1** | 60
6631 | 4 | 1 ¼ | **Wild Flower (IRE)**[25] 8823 5-9-0 **58**.......................KieranO'Neill 2 (Jimmy Fox) *led 1f: chsd ldng pair after: rdn 2f out: one pce and lost 3rd ins fnl f* **3/1**[1] | 57
4102 | 5 | nk | **Arcanista (IRE)**[25] 8823 4-8-8 **59**.......................(p) PaulHainey(7) 9 (Chris Dwyer) *t.k.h: chsd ldrs on outer: nt qckn wl over 1f out: one pce fnl f* **8/1** | 57
3100 | 6 | nk | **Everkyllachy (IRE)**[41] 8512 3-9-7 **65**.......................(b) TomMarquand 4 (J S Moore) *sn in last trio: rdn and no prog wl over 1f out: styd on last 150yds on inner but no ch* **20/1** | 62
2425 | 7 | 1 | **Kyllukey**[13] 9001 4-9-3 **61**.......................(v) LukeMorris 1 (Milton Bradley) *t.k.h: trckd ldrs: rdn and nt qckn wl over 1f out: wl hld whn nt clr run last 100yds: eased* **4/1**[2] | 55
1640 | 8 | ½ | **Justice Rock**[42] 8495 4-8-0 **51**.......................(t) NicolaCurrie(7) 10 (Phil McEntee) *t.k.h and sn buried away in midfield: rdn and no prog wl over 1f out* **20/1** | 43
5560 | 9 | 2 ¾ | **Delahay**[71] 7694 3-8-7 **51** oh5.......................HollieDoyle 8 (Michael Blanshard) *sn in last: struggling fr 1/2-way: no real prog* **50/1** | 35
0000 | 10 | 3 ¼ | **Taurean Gold**[200] 3035 3-8-0 **51** oh6.......................KeelanBaker(7) 6 (John Bridger) *free to post: plld hrd: hld up in last trio: no prog 2f out* **100/1** | 24

1m 11.52s (-0.38) **Going Correction** -0.10s/f (Stan) **10** Ran **SP% 119.5**
Speed ratings (Par 101): **98,97,96,94,94 93,92,91,88,83**
CSF £25.14 CT £125.23 TOTE £6.50: £1.80, £1.70, £2.40; EX 29.70 Trifecta £256.30.
**Owner** J M Bradley **Bred** Mette Campbell-Andenaes **Trained** Sedbury, Gloucs

**FOCUS**
They went steady early and the front two were up there throughout. The winner has been rated near the best of recent years.

## 9184 BETWAY SPRINT H'CAP (DIV II) — 6f 1y(P)
**12:30** (12:30) (Class 6) (0-65,65) 3-Y-0+ **£3,234** (£962; £481; £240) **Stalls** Low

Form | | | | RPR
---|---|---|---|---
6000 | 1 | | **Compton Prince**[25] 8824 8-9-0 **58**.......................(b) TomMarquand 2 (Milton Bradley) *mde virtually all: rdn 2f out: drew 2 l clr over 1f out: hld on nr fin* **10/1** | 65
1600 | 2 | ½ | **Mister Freeze (IRE)**[13] 8990 3-9-7 **65**.......................(t) JoeyHaynes 1 (Patrick Chamings) *trckd ldng pair on inner: rdn to take 2nd 1f out: kpt on and clsd on wnr nr fin* **5/1**[2] | 70
365 | 3 | 1 | **Billyoakes (IRE)**[22] 8873 5-9-0 **58**.......................(p) LukeMorris 8 (Charlie Wallis) *trckd ldrs: drvn and nt qckn wl over 1f out: kpt on again fnl f to take 3rd last 50yds* **13/2**[3] | 60
0410 | 4 | ¾ | **Chip Or Pellet**[42] 8494 4-8-12 **56**.......................DannyBrock 4 (Mark Pattinson) *w wnr: stl upsides 2f out: nt qckn wl over 1f out: lost 2nd and fdd fnl f* **20/1** | 56
006 | 5 | ½ | **Malaysian Boleh**[25] 8816 7-8-11 **62**.......................(v) NicolaCurrie(7) 9 (Phil McEntee) *trckd ldrs on outer: lost grnd bnd 2f out: no rspnse whn drvn over 1f out: kpt on fnl f* **14/1** | 60
2056 | 6 | 1 | **Met By Moonlight**[189] 3423 3-9-3 **61**.......................SteveDrowne 6 (Ron Hodges) *hld up towards rr: pushed along fnl 2f: nvr threatened ldrs* **10/1** | 56
0010 | 7 | ¾ | **Deer Song**[25] 8823 4-8-7 **51** oh1.......................JosephineGordon 5 (John Bridger) *hld up towards rr: rdn and no prog over 1f out* **14/1** | 44
0305 | 8 | ½ | **Merdon Castle (IRE)**[54] 8186 5-9-7 **65**.......................MartinHarley 3 (Jane Chapple-Hyam) *missed break: detached in last most of way: rdn over 2f out: no significant prog* **11/10**[1] | 56
5005 | 9 | 2 ½ | **Blackadder**[25] 8824 5-8-0 **51** oh6.......................KeelanBaker(7) 7 (Mark Gillard) *racd wd in rr: no prog 2f out: fdd* **25/1** | 34

1m 11.63s (-0.27) **Going Correction** -0.10s/f (Stan) **9** Ran **SP% 117.7**
Speed ratings (Par 101): **97,96,95,94,93 92,91,90,87**
CSF £60.49 CT £358.10 TOTE £12.70: £2.40, £2.00, £1.90; EX 75.50 Trifecta £420.30.
**Owner** E A Hayward **Bred** Whitsbury Manor Stud **Trained** Sedbury, Gloucs

**FOCUS**
As in the first division it paid to be handy. The time was 0.11sec slower. The third helps set the level.

## 9185 32RED ON THE APP STORE FILLIES' H'CAP — 6f 1y(P)
**1:00** (1:00) (Class 4) (0-85,84) 3-Y-0+ **£4,916** (£1,463; £731; £365) **Stalls** Low

Form | | | | RPR
---|---|---|---|---
0326 | 1 | | **Show Stealer**[19] 8905 4-9-7 **84**.......................(p) MartinHarley 3 (Rae Guest) *wl in tch: trckd ldng pair 2f out: drvn and r.o fr over 1f out to ld last 100yds: sn clr* **6/4**[1] | 92
3465 | 2 | 1 ½ | **Shamsaya (IRE)**[21] 8879 3-9-5 **82**.......................RobertHavlin 6 (Simon Crisford) *trckd ldng pair to 1/2-way: sn dropped to 5th: pushed along over 1f out: r.o whn rdn last 150yds: fin wl to take 2nd fnl stride* **6/1**[3] | 86
5533 | 3 | hd | **Very Honest (IRE)**[13] 8990 4-8-9 **72**.......................(v) LukeMorris 2 (Brett Johnson) *drvn to ld at str pce: rdn 2f out: hdd and outpcd 100yds out: lost 2nd last stride* **9/2**[2] | 75
2003 | 4 | 1 | **Diamond Lady**[21] 8879 6-9-5 **82**.......................HollieDoyle 1 (William Stone) *tried to ld but unable to: chsd ldr: rdn 2f out: lost 2nd and one pce fnl f* **9/2**[2] | 82
6426 | 5 | 2 ½ | **Pretty Bubbles**[13] 8990 8-8-7 **70**.......................(v) JosephineGordon 5 (J R Jenkins) *hld up in last pair: tried to make prog on inner over 1f out: pushed along and no hdwy fnl f* **12/1** | 62
6125 | 6 | 1 ¼ | **Dusky Maid (IRE)**[103] 6619 3-9-1 **78**.......................FrannyNorton 7 (James Given) *sn in last pair: nvr a factor and no prog fnl 2f* **10/1** | 66
0100 | 7 | 18 | **Rosabelle**[34] 8680 3-9-6 **83**.......................(b) AdamKirby 4 (Alan Bailey) *urged along but nt pce to be prom early: prog on outer to chse ldng pair 1/2-way to 2f out: wknd rapidly: t.o* **14/1** | 13

1m 10.23s (-1.67) **Going Correction** -0.10s/f (Stan) **7** Ran **SP% 114.1**
Speed ratings (Par 102): **107,105,104,103,100 98,74**
CSF £10.98 TOTE £2.40: £1.90, £2.50; EX 11.70 Trifecta £42.40.
**Owner** Colin Joseph **Bred** Max Weston **Trained** Newmarket, Suffolk

**FOCUS**
There was a bit of competition for the early lead and that played into the hands of the winner. The second and third have been rated close to their recent AW form.

## 9186 BETWAY CASINO H'CAP — 1m 2f (P)
**1:35** (1:35) (Class 3) (0-95,96) 3-Y-0- **£7,561** (£2,263; £1,131; £566; £282) **Stalls** Low

Form | | | | RPR
---|---|---|---|---
0332 | 1 | | **Emenem**[10] 9053 3-9-2 **90**.......................AdamKirby 6 (Simon Dow) *trckd ldrs: clsd on inner 2f out: led jst ins fnl f: drvn and hrd pressed last 100yds: hld on wl* **2/1**[1] | 98
3604 | 2 | shd | **Kyllachy Gala**[13] 8999 4-9-10 **96**.......................KieranShoemark 5 (Marco Botti) *t.k.h early: trckd ldrs: prog to chal over 1f out: pressed wnr last 100yds: jst hld* **9/2**[3] | 103
3030 | 3 | 1 ½ | **Bronze Angel (IRE)**[13] 8999 8-8-13 **92**.......................(b) TylerSaunders(7) 1 (Marcus Tregoning) *trckd ldng pair: led wl over 1f out: hdd and no ex jst ins fnl f* **8/1** | 96
4100 | 4 | 1 ¼ | **Intrepidly (USA)**[60] 8005 3-9-3 **91**.......................SeanLevey 9 (Jeremy Noseda) *hld up in midfield: rdn on outer over 2f out: no prog tl styd on fnl f to take 4th nr fin* **7/2**[2] | 94
0003 | 5 | shd | **Cosmeapolitan**[10] 5781 4-9-2 **88**.......................MartinDwyer 8 (Alan King) *slowly away and urged along early: mostly in last: detached and rdn over 3f out: fnlly styd on fr over 1f out: nrst fin* **15/2** | 89
6451 | 6 | nk | **Noble Peace**[58] 8078 4-9-4 **90**.......................MartinHarley 3 (Lydia Pearce) *stdd s: hld up in last pair: sme prog towards inner 2f out: nt on terms w ldrs over 1f out: shkn up and tk 4th briefly ins fnl f: nvr really involved* **20/1** | 91
0000 | 7 | 2 | **Van Huysen (IRE)**[25] 8821 5-8-8 **83**.......................CallumShepherd(3) 7 (Dominic Ffrench Davis) *trckd ldr: led wl over 2f out to wl over 1f out: wknd fnl f* **25/1** | 80
1104 | 8 | 3 ¼ | **Storm King**[31] 8740 8-9-6 **92**.......................SteveDrowne 2 (David C Griffiths) *led at mod pce: edgd rt over 3f out: hdd wl over 2f out and sn lost pl: eased whn no ch over 1f out* **8/1** | 82
/2-5 | 9 | 5 | **Fanoulpifer**[106] 6514 6-9-7 **93**.......................(h[1]) LukeMorris 4 (Michael Attwater) *hld up in last trio: rdn whn wd bnd 2f out: hd high and fnd nil after* **50/1** | 73

2m 4.67s (-1.93) **Going Correction** -0.10s/f (Stan)
**WFA** 3 from 4yo+ 2lb **9** Ran **SP% 118.3**
Speed ratings (Par 107): **103,102,101,100,100 100,98,96,92**
CSF £11.27 CT £60.20 TOTE £2.80: £1.20, £1.50, £2.80; EX 12.40 Trifecta £85.90.
**Owner** Robert Moss And Damien Brennan **Bred** D R Tucker **Trained** Ashtead, Surrey

**FOCUS**
A good handicap, but there wasn't much pace on early. Muddling form. It's been rated around the principals, with the runner-up to his recent form.

## 9187 BETWAY DASH H'CAP — 5f 6y(P)
**2:10** (2:10) (Class 2) (0-105,103) 3-Y-0+ **£12,602** (£3,772; £1,886; £944; £470) **Stalls** High

Form | | | | RPR
---|---|---|---|---
3515 | 1 | | **Gracious John (IRE)**[34] 8679 4-9-5 **101**.......................FranBerry 5 (David Evans) *pushed up to press ldr: rdn to take narrow ld 1f out: drvn and asserted last 150yds* **3/1**[2] | 110
0560 | 2 | 1 | **Royal Birth**[24] 8845 6-9-1 **100**.......................(t) AaronJones(3) 9 (Stuart Williams) *racd in last pair fr wdst draw: rdn on wd outside over 1f out: styd on wl fnl f to take 2nd last strides* **5/1** | 105
0121 | 3 | nk | **Alsvinder**[35] 8660 4-8-12 **94**.......................MartinHarley 3 (David O'Meara) *mde most: drvn and hdd 1f out: styd on same pce after: lost 2nd last strides* **11/4**[1] | 98
4063 | 4 | hd | **Shamshon (IRE)**[56] 8129 6-8-3 **85**.......................(t) JosephineGordon 1 (Stuart Williams) *trckd ldng pair: chal on inner over 1f out: disp 2nd fnl f but nt pce of wnr and lost pl nr fin* **4/1**[3] | 88
4031 | 5 | ¾ | **Midnight Malibu (IRE)**[26] 8803 4-8-6 **88**.......................LukeMorris 4 (Tim Easterby) *t.k.h: hld up disputing 5th: rdn and nt qckn over 1f out: styd on ins fnl f but nvr able to chal* **10/1** | 89
500 | 6 | hd | **Kasbah (IRE)**[13] 8991 5-8-10 **92**.......................JackMitchell 7 (Amanda Perrett) *racd in last pair fr wd draw: rdn 2f out: styd on fnl f but nvr able to rch ldrs* **10/1** | 92
203 | 7 | 2 | **Sir Maximilian (IRE)**[306] 651 8-9-7 **103**.......................AdamKirby 6 (Ian Williams) *hld up disputing 5th: no imp on ldrs on inner jst over 1f out: fdd ins fnl f* **14/1** | 96
2660 | 8 | nk | **Zac Brown (IRE)**[119] 6025 6-9-0 **96**.......................(t) DanielMuscutt 2 (Charlie Wallis) *t.k.h: trckd ldng pair: stl cl up jst over 1f out: fdd fnl f* **25/1** | 88

56.75s (-2.05) **Going Correction** -0.10s/f (Stan) **8** Ran **SP% 117.0**
Speed ratings (Par 109): **112,110,109,109,108 108,104,104**
CSF £18.98 CT £45.93 TOTE £4.10: £1.70, £2.10, £1.10; EX 23.80 Trifecta £79.40.
**Owner** Terry Reffell **Bred** Skeaghmore Hill **Trained** Pandy, Monmouths

**FOCUS**
The gallop wasn't overly strong, the winner and third racing on the pace throughout. The winner has been rated close to form.

## 9188 32RED.COM / EBF NOVICE STKS (PLUS 10 RACE) — 5f 6y(P)
**2:45** (2:46) (Class 4) 2-Y-0 **£4,916** (£1,463; £731; £365) **Stalls** High

Form | | | | RPR
---|---|---|---|---
22 | 1 | | **Little Boy Blue**[69] 7731 2-9-2 0.......................LukeMorris 4 (Bill Turner) *hld up bhd ldrs: prog and squeezed between rivals 1f out: drvn to ld 100yds out: hld on* **5/4**[1] | 70+
1232 | 2 | hd | **Ghepardo**[11] 9023 2-9-0 76.......................TomMarquand 5 (Richard Hannon) *w ldrs early but sn in 5th: rdn over 2f out: clsd fnl f: drvn to take 2nd nr fin and clsd on wnr last strides* **2/1**[2] | 67
4426 | 3 | ¾ | **Avon Green**[19] 8902 2-8-11 67.......................JosephineGordon 3 (Joseph Tuite) *chsd ldr: rdn to ld jst over 1f out: hdd and one pce last 100yds: lost 2nd nr fin* **13/2**[3] | 61
0530 | 4 | ¾ | **Llamrei**[41] 8500 2-8-11 54.......................MartinDwyer 8 (Jo Hughes) *mounted on crse and taken down early: pressed ldng pair but trapped out wd: rdn 2f out: no ex fnl f* **25/1** | 59
46 | 5 | 3 ½ | **No More Commisery (IRE)**[25] 8819 2-8-11 0.......................FranBerry 2 (Mick Quinn) *led: gng wl 2f out: hdd jst over 1f out: wknd qckly* **14/1** | 46
005 | 6 | 2 ½ | **Hornby**[25] 8819 2-9-2 58.......................RobertHavlin 6 (Michael Attwater) *hld up fr wd draw: shkn up and no prog fr last pair over 1f out* **33/1** | 42
0 | 7 | 1 | **Shimmy Shoes (IRE)**[48] 8356 2-8-11 0.......................RobHornby 1 (Jamie Osborne) *outpcd in last: nvr a factor* **17/2** | 33

58.39s (-0.41) **Going Correction** -0.10s/f (Stan) **7** Ran **SP% 115.1**
Speed ratings (Par 98): **99,98,97,96,90 86,85**
CSF £3.99 TOTE £2.00: £1.50, £1.40; EX 4.10 Trifecta £7.80.
**Owner** Mrs Tracy Turner **Bred** Mrs P A Turner **Trained** Sigwells, Somerset

**FOCUS**
A modest novice race, with the form seemingly limited by the fourth. The runner-up has been rated a few pounds off her recent form.

## 9189 BETWAY H'CAP — 5f 6y(P)
3:15 (3:16) (Class 5) (0-70,70) 3-Y-O+ — £3,234 (£962; £481; £240) Stalls High

Form — RPR

4000 1 **Temple Road (IRE)**[24] [8853] 9-8-11 60 (bt) TomMarquand 8 — 73
(Milton Bradley) *hld up fr wd draw and sn dropped in: gd prog on inner over 1f out: pushed into the ld ins fnl f and sn clr: rdn out nr fin* **16/1**

4450 2 1 1/2 **Roundabout Magic (IRE)**[25] [8816] 3-8-11 60 NickyMackay 4 — 67
(Simon Dow) *chsd ldng pair: rdn to cl jst over 1f out but wnr sn shot past: tk 2nd ins fnl f and styd on but no ch to chal* **9/2**[2]

0550 3 1 3/4 **Shackled N Drawn (USA)**[13] [9001] 5-8-13 62 (b[1]) CharlesBishop 2 — 63
(Peter Hedger) *blasted off in front: 3 l clr 2f out: c bk to rivals over 1f out: hdd ins fnl f: all out but clung on for 3rd* **7/1**[3]

5011 4 nk **Entertaining Ben**[25] [8816] 4-9-7 70 (p) KieranShoemark 1 — 70
(Amy Murphy) *chsd clr ldr: rdn to cl over 1f out whn wnr shot past: no ex fnl f* **3/1**[1]

40 5 nk **Sandfrankskipsgo**[85] [7217] 8-9-5 68 ShaneKelly 10 — 67
(Peter Crate) *hld up on outer fr wd draw: shkn up and no prog wl over 1f out: kpt on ins fnl f: no ch* **20/1**

036 6 nk **Powerful Dream (IRE)**[17] [8953] 4-9-5 68 (v[1]) LukeMorris 5 — 65
(Ronald Harris) *chsd ldrs: urged along by 1/2-way: rchd 4th 2f out but nvr a threat: one pce after* **7/1**[3]

0000 7 1 1/2 **Red Invader (IRE)**[24] [8853] 7-9-1 64 LiamKeniry 6 — 56
(John Butler) *s.i.s: hld up in last: rdn over 1f out: modest late prog* **10/1**

0063 8 1 3/4 **Don't Blame Me**[22] [8875] 4-9-6 69 AdamKirby 9 — 55
(Clive Cox) *nvr beyond midfield: no prog wl over 1f out: fdd* **3/1**[1]

-150 9 3 **Dreams Of Glory**[292] [886] 9-9-4 67 SteveDrowne 3 — 42
(Ron Hodges) *a wl in rr: shkn up and no prog 2f out* **25/1**

4000 10 1 **Mossgo (IRE)**[25] [8816] 7-9-2 65 (t) JosephineGordon 7 — 36
(John Best) *sltly awkward s: sn chsd ldrs: wknd qckly 2f out* **25/1**

57.85s (-0.95) **Going Correction** -0.10s/f (Stan) — **10** Ran SP% **120.6**
Speed ratings (Par 103): **103,100,97,97,96 96,93,91,86,84**
CSF £87.47 CT £574.23 TOTE £17.10: £4.50, £1.90, £2.50; EX 118.40 Trifecta £752.30.
**Owner** J M Bradley **Bred** Paul Monaghan **Trained** Sedbury, Gloucs

**FOCUS**
A modest sprint handicap. The winner has been rated back to last winter's form.
T/Jkpt: Part won. £10,000.00 to a £1 stake - 0.50 winning units. T/Plt: £18.00 to a £1 stake. Pool: £86,895.04 - 3,508.81 winning units T/Qpdt: £10.00 to a £1 stake. Pool: £14,670.95 - 1,076.47 winning units **Jonathan Neesom**

# 9152 WOLVERHAMPTON (A.W) (L-H)
Tuesday, December 12

**9190 Meeting Abandoned -** Public and other equine areas unsafe

# 8987 KEMPTON (A.W) (R-H)
Wednesday, December 13

**OFFICIAL GOING: Polytrack: standard**
Wind: Strong in front, easing after race 3 Weather: Heavy rain early, dark cloud by race 3

## 9198 BETHANY & THEODORE FITCHIE NOVICE STKS — 6f (P)
3:40 (3:45) (Class 5) 2-Y-O — £3,234 (£962; £481; £240) Stalls Low

Form — RPR

63 1 **Monadee**[14] [8989] 2-9-2 0 JackMitchell 4 — 77
(Roger Varian) *broke wl and sn led: mde all: shkn up 2f out: sn rdn and wnt clr ins fnl f: pushed out fnl 100yds: comf* **5/2**[2]

2 1 1/2 **Breathless Times** 2-9-2 0 KieranShoemark 12 — 73+
(Roger Charlton) *dropped in leaving stalls: hld up in rr and sltly bhd: shkn up and prog between horses over 2f out: in tch over 1f out: no catching wnr ent fnl f: but kpt on wl and shaped w plenty of promise* **9/2**[3]

0 3 2 1/4 **Kachumba**[26] [8809] 2-8-11 0 MartinLane 9 — 61
(Rae Guest) *settled in rr: shkn up over 2f out: effrt wl over 1f out and c wdst: gd prog ins fnl f to take 3rd nr fin: nvr nrr* **33/1**

4 1/2 **Dubai Acclaim (IRE)** 2-9-2 0 JackGarritty 3 — 64
(Richard Fahey) *replated in stables and last to post: hld up in mid-div between horses: rdn over 1f out and tk 2nd ent fnl f: grad wknd ins fnl f and lost 3rd nr fin* **10/1**

00 5 2 3/4 **Sir Hector (IRE)**[6] [9123] 2-9-2 0 DanielMuscutt 1 — 56
(Charlie Wallis) *fly-leaped s: sn settled bhd ldr: effrt over 2f out: no ex ent fnl f: pushed out wl ins fnl f* **100/1**

6 1 1/4 **Nikita (IRE)** 2-8-11 0 (h[1]) JosephineGordon 6 — 47
(Hughie Morrison) *hld up in mid-div on inner: scrubbed along to take clsr order over 2f out: swtchd to inner and gd prog sn after: no ex ent fnl f and wknd* **25/1**

4 7 5 **Azpeitia**[32] [8734] 2-8-11 0 RichardKingscote 8 — 32
(Ralph Beckett) *pressed ldr on outer: racd keenly and plld hrd: effrt wl over 1f out: fnd nil and wknd ent fnl f: eased sn after* **4/6**[1]

8 8 **Silverturnstogold** 2-9-2 0 RobHornby 7 — 13
(Neil Mulholland) *missed break and struggling: bhd at 1/2-way: kpt on one pce fr over 1f out* **50/1**

04 9 5 **Eesha Says (IRE)**[18] [8945] 2-8-11 0 WilliamCarson 11
(Tony Carroll) *cl up on outer w no cover: rdn over 2f out: no ex fr over 1f out and wknd* **100/1**

1m 13.02s (-0.08) **Going Correction** -0.05s/f (Stan) — **9** Ran SP% **126.6**
Speed ratings (Par 96): **98,96,93,92,88 87,80,69,63**
CSF £15.40 TOTE £3.40: £1.20, £1.60, £6.20; EX 20.20 Trifecta £215.50.
**Owner** Sheikh Ahmed Al Maktoum **Bred** Litex Commerce **Trained** Newmarket, Suffolk

**FOCUS**
There was a decent pace on in this modest novice event.

## 9199 BETTER ODDS WITH MATCHBOOK NURSERY H'CAP — 7f (P)
4:10 (4:10) (Class 5) (0-75,76) 2-Y-O — £3,234 (£962; £481; £240) Stalls Low

Form — RPR

460 1 **Cristal Pallas Cat (IRE)**[78] [7482] 2-8-4 62 (h[1]) RhiainIngram[(5)] 5 — 67
(Roger Ingram) *sn led and mde all: kicked for home 2f out: kpt on wl ent fnl f: hrd pressed by runner-up fr 100yds out: fought on gamely and jst prevailed* **40/1**

633 2 nk **Mr Gent (IRE)**[55] [8179] 2-9-6 73 (b[1]) PJMcDonald 2 — 77
(Ed Dunlop) *mid-div on inner and niggled along sn after s: shkn up over 2f out: rdn 2f out and swtchd to inner: tk 2nd ent fnl f: kpt on wl and upsides wnr 100yds out: wnt hd to hd sn after: nt get past game wnr post* **6/1**[2]

640 3 3 1/4 **Jeopardy John**[41] [8545] 2-9-2 69 WilliamCarson 6 — 64
(Michael Attwater) *w ldr on outer: rdn 2f out to chse wnr in centre of crse: kpt on tl lost 2nd ent fnl f: plugged on after* **12/1**

600 4 1 1/2 **Beautiful Artist (USA)**[27] [8796] 2-9-2 69 RobertHavlin 10 — 60
(John Gosden) *awkward leaving stalls and settled in rr: edgd to outer wl over 2f out where shkn up: rdn over 1f out in rr: grad drifted rt to rail but kpt on wl ins fnl f* **11/1**

5242 5 hd **Dance Emperor (IRE)**[12] [9021] 2-9-9 76 LukeMorris 4 — 67
(Ed Walker) *cl up and racd on outer w no cover: plld hrd most of way: travelled wl over 2f out: rdn 2f out: kpt on fr over 1f out: wknd nr fin: can do bttr* **1/1**[1]

4550 6 nse **Hollywood Dream**[56] [8153] 2-9-0 67 RobHornby 9 — 58
(Neil Mulholland) *mid-div on outer: rdn wl over 1f out w plenty to do: picked up wl ins fnl f: nvr nrr* **66/1**

2504 7 shd **Bombshell Bay**[12] [9024] 2-8-10 63 TomMarquand 1 — 53
(Richard Hannon) *settled bhd ldr on rail: rdn 2f out: no ex and wknd sn after* **10/1**

200 8 2 1/4 **Is It Off (IRE)**[21] [8890] 2-9-7 74 AdamKirby 7 — 58
(Gary Moore) *sluggish s and pushed along to racd in rr on inner: shuffled along and swtchd to inner over 1f out: one pce fnl f* **7/1**[3]

1055 9 1/2 **Boomerang Betty (IRE)**[100] [6749] 2-9-2 69 DougieCostello 8 — 52
(Jamie Osborne) *sluggish s and in rr: rdn wl over 1f out between horses: plugged on one pce ins fnl f* **20/1**

0243 10 3 3/4 **Coal Stock (IRE)**[120] [6029] 2-9-5 72 JamieSpencer 3 — 45
(Christian Williams) *hld up in rr-div: rdn 2f out: no ex sn after* **14/1**

005 11 1 **Ede's A Winner**[14] [8989] 2-7-11 57 SophieRalston[(7)] 11 — 27
(Pat Phelan) *kpt st fr wd draw tl c across after 1f to r in mid-div: rdn over 2f out: no ex fr 2f out* **40/1**

1m 27.28s (1.28) **Going Correction** -0.05s/f (Stan) — **11** Ran SP% **119.7**
Speed ratings (Par 96): **90,89,85,84,84 83,83,81,80,76 75**
CSF £264.90 CT £3097.90 TOTE £41.60: £9.10, £2.60, £3.60; EX 405.50 Trifecta £1914.40.
**Owner** Titan Partnership **Bred** Joseph Broderick **Trained** Epsom, Surrey

**FOCUS**
This ordinary nursery saw another winner make all.

## 9200 MATCHBOOK VIP NOVICE STKS (DIV I) — 1m (P)
4:40 (4:42) (Class 5) 2-Y-O — £3,234 (£962; £481; £240) Stalls Low

Form — RPR

41 1 **Rusper (IRE)**[25] [8839] 2-9-9 0 DougieCostello 4 — 83
(Jamie Osborne) *broke wl and sn hld up bhd ldrs: rdn 2f out and led over 1f out: edgd lft u.p and plld out plenty whn strly chal nr fin* **7/2**[2]

2 shd **Sod's Law** 2-9-2 0 PJMcDonald 12 — 75
(Hughie Morrison) *racd in mid-div: rdn wl over 1f out and swtchd to inner: gd prog ent fnl f: ev ch fnl 110yds: no ex nr fin* **50/1**

0 3 1 **Stylehunter**[49] [8350] 2-9-2 0 (b[1]) RobertHavlin 10 — 73
(John Gosden) *wl away: sn hld up bhd ldrs: rdn over 1f out: kpt on strly ins fnl f and clsng on ldr whn checked in run nr fin and eased* **9/1**

5 4 shd **Tum Tum**[40] [8560] 2-9-2 0 JosephineGordon 6 — 72
(Martyn Meade) *racd in mid-div: rdn wdst of all wl over 1f out: ev ch ins fnl f: no ex nr fin* **6/4**[1]

5 2 1/4 **Holy Shambles (IRE)** 2-8-13 0 MarcMonaghan[(3)] 8 — 67+
(Marco Botti) *racd in rr-div between horses: shkn up and swtchd to outer over 2f out: picked up wl whn rdn over 1f out: c bk to centre sn after and pushed out fnl f: keeping on at fin: nvr involved* **25/1**

4 6 nk **Dorella (GER)**[14] [8998] 2-8-11 0 CharlesBishop 13 — 61
(Eve Johnson Houghton) *pressed ldr on outer: rdn 2f out: sn no ex and wknd* **20/1**

7 1 1/2 **Sovereign Duke (GER)** 2-9-2 0 FranBerry 3 — 63+
(Henry Candy) *in rr and rn v green early: rdn over 2f out: swtchd to inner and c home wl ins fnl f* **7/1**[3]

6 8 3 1/2 **Tribal Warrior**[21] [8889] 2-9-2 0 LukeMorris 9 — 55
(James Tate) *t.k.h and plld way into ld: rdn 2f out and hdd over 1f out: sn wknd* **10/1**

9 3/4 **Storm Again** 2-8-13 0 HectorCrouch[(3)] 5 — 53
(Philip Hide) *in rr-div on outer: rn green and pushed along at times: rdn over 2f out and sn struggling: plugged on past btn horse fr over 1f out* **66/1**

0 10 hd **Ragstone Ridge (FR)**[21] [8889] 2-9-2 0 ShaneKelly 11 — 53
(Richard Hughes) *chsd ldrs: rdn 2f out: sn no ex and plugged on* **66/1**

0 11 1 3/4 **Singer In The Sand (IRE)**[14] [8987] 2-8-4 0 SophieRalston[(7)] 2 — 44
(Pat Phelan) *mid-div on inner: shuffled along on inner wl over 1f out: one pce fnl f* **200/1**

12 6 **French Cricket (FR)** 2-9-2 0 LiamKeniry 7 — 35
(George Baker) *racd in mid-div on inner: rdn over 2f out: no picked up* **40/1**

13 3 1/4 **Kevlar** 2-9-2 0 RobHornby 14 — 27
(Jonathan Portman) *bdly missed break and a in rr: nvr involved* **100/1**

14 3/4 **Mayer** 2-9-2 0 AdamKirby 1 — 26
(Luca Cumani) *early pce: sn dropped to rr: bhd wl over 3f out: nvr involved after* **10/1**

1m 40.07s (0.27) **Going Correction** -0.05s/f (Stan) — **14** Ran SP% **120.4**
Speed ratings (Par 96): **96,95,94,94,92 92,90,87,86,86 84,78,75,74**
CSF £182.79 TOTE £4.50: £1.70, £6.90, £3.20; EX 84.30 Trifecta £1971.90.
**Owner** Melbourne 10 Racing **Bred** Barronstown Stud **Trained** Upper Lambourn, Berks

**FOCUS**
They were well strung out heading into the home bend in this first division of the 1m novice event.

## 9201 MATCHBOOK VIP NOVICE STKS (DIV II) — 1m (P)
5:10 (5:12) (Class 5) 2-Y-O — £3,234 (£962; £481; £240) Stalls Low

Form — RPR

3 1 **Highbrow**[36] [8643] 2-9-2 0 JamieSpencer 11 — 81+
(David Simcock) *racd in mid-div on outer: shkn up and smooth prog wl over 2f out: rdn in centre of trck 2f out: kpt on strly fr over 1f out and led ent fnl f: drew clr sn after: pushed out nr fin: comf* **8/11**[1]

2 4 1/2 **Returning Glory** 2-9-2 0 JimmyQuinn 14 — 71
(Saeed bin Suroor) *broke wl fr wd draw: t.k.h and plld way to dispute ld: clr ldr 5f out: nursed along and hld together wl over 1f out: sn rdn: hdd ent fnl f: plugged on after and kpt on to hold runner-up spot* **7/2**[2]

0 **3** *hd* **Shakour (IRE)**[18] 8951 2-9-2 0 (t) RobertHavlin 3 70
(John Gosden) *pushed along leaving stalls and sn led: pressed sn after: hdd over 5f out but remained bhd ldr: rdn wl over 1f out: kpt on wl ins fnl f pressing for runner-up spot tl no ex nr fin* **6/1**[3]

**4** *nk* **Caradoc (IRE)** 2-9-2 0 LiamKeniry 9 72+
(Ed Walker) *racd in rr-div on outer: travelling wl and impr into mid-div wl over 2f out: swtchd to inner and pushed along: effrt over 1f out: kpt on wl ins fnl f: nvr nrr* **20/1**

**5** *2 1/2* **Morning Has Broken (IRE)** 2-8-11 0 SeanLevey 8 59+
(David Elsworth) *bhd ldrs and t.k.h: rdn over 2f out: plugged on fr over 1f out* **33/1**

0 **6** *3* **Hackbridge**[42] 8501 2-9-2 0 ShaneKelly 6 57
(Pat Phelan) *bhd ldrs on inner: lost pl wl over 4f out: rdn 3f out: plugged on after* **100/1**

04 **7** *1* **Black Medusa (IRE)**[11] 9050 2-9-2 0 RaulDaSilva 13 55
(Paul Cole) *cl up bhd ldrs on outer: rdn over 2f out: no ex nt long after* **25/1**

**8** *1/2* **Teaser** 2-9-2 0 (h[1]) DanielMuscutt 1 53
(James Fanshawe) *s.s and in rr: rdn over 2f out: no ex* **20/1**

0 **9** *5* **Beloved Knight**[20] 8903 2-9-2 0 TomMarquand 12 42
(Laura Mongan) *r in mid-div on outer: rdn over 2f out: hld over 1f out* **66/1**

**10** *shd* **Oi The Clubb Oi'S** 2-9-2 0 RichardKingscote 10 42
(Ian Williams) *in rr-div: no ex fr wl over 1f out* **28/1**

**11** *3* **Betjeman** 2-9-2 0 PJMcDonald 7 35
(Hughie Morrison) *in rr-div: struggling fr over 2f out* **33/1**

**12** *3* **Dame Nellie** 2-8-11 0 (h[1]) StevieDonohoe 4 23
(Rae Guest) *rrd leaving stalls: rn green: outpcd and a in rr* **50/1**

1m 38.98s (-0.82) **Going Correction** -0.05s/f (Stan) **12** Ran SP% **121.6**
Speed ratings (Par 96): **102,97,97,97,94 91,90,90,85,84 81,78**
CSF £2.93 TOTE £1.60: £1.10, £1.40, £1.60; EX 4.60 Trifecta £12.40.
**Owner** Sheikh Juma Dalmook Al Maktoum **Bred** Mrs C R Philipson & Lofts Hall Stud **Trained** Newmarket, Suffolk

**FOCUS**
This second division of the 1m novice event was run in a time 1.09secs quicker. The opening level is a bit fluid.

## 9202 SMARTER BETS WITH MATCHBOOK MAIDEN STKS 1m (P)
**5:40** (5:47) (Class 5) 3-Y-O+ £3,234 (£962; £481; £240) **Stalls Low**

Form RPR

26- **1** **Humbert (IRE)**[458] 6388 3-9-5 0 JosephineGordon 13 89+
(Hugo Palmer) *t.k.h bhd ldr: shkn up to chse ldr over 2f out: rdn 2f out and sn in tch: led ent fnl f: wnt clr* **7/4**[1]

**2** *4 1/2* **Maximinus Thrax (FR)** 3-9-5 0 JamieSpencer 5 78+
(David Simcock) *racd in mid-div between horses: rdn over 2f out w plenty to do: kpt on strly fr pack: tk 2nd wl ins fnl f: nvr nrr* **3/1**[2]

-260 **3** *1 3/4* **Pure Shores**[209] 2754 3-9-0 75 PJMcDonald 14 69
(Ian Williams) *sn led and set gd pce: wnt 3 l clr over 3f out: rdn over 1f out: hdd ent fnl f: lost 2nd wl ins fnl f: no ex* **4/1**[3]

**4** *9* **Compton Abbey** 3-8-11 0 CallumShepherd(3) 2 47
(Brett Johnson) *racd bhd ldrs: rdn over 3f out: plugged on* **50/1**

0-3 **5** *shd* **Ignacio Zuloaga (IRE)**[15] 8984 3-9-5 0 RichardKingscote 9 52
(Jo Hughes) *chsd ldrs: rdn wl over 3f out to hold pl: no ex and plugged on one pce fr over 2f out* **10/1**

5 **6** *2 1/4* **Peters Folly**[8] 9085 4-9-1 0 (h) WilliamCarson 6 42
(Peter Hiatt) *in rr-div: effrt 3f out: sn hld* **66/1**

00 **7** *1/2* **Sanam**[7] 9088 3-9-5 0 AdamKirby 11 46
(Ed Dunlop) *racd in rr: pushed along sn wl 3f out: no ex* **33/1**

606U **8** *1/2* **Fivos**[15] 8984 3-8-12 44 (p) PoppyBridgwater(7) 7 44
(David Bridgwater) *racd in mid-div on outer: effrt wl over 2f out: lft bhd sn after* **100/1**

64 **9** *2 1/4* **Ginger Lady (IRE)**[7] 9088 3-9-0 0 JoeyHaynes 3 34
(Mark H Tompkins) *racd in rr-div: shkn up over 2f out: no ex sn after* **25/1**

**10** *6* **Hail Cloud (IRE)** 3-9-2 0 MarcMonaghan(3) 1 25
(Marco Botti) *t.k.h early: in mid-div on inner: shaekn up over 3f out: struggling and one pce fr over 2f out* **7/1**

04 **11** *2* **I Should Coco**[26] 8810 4-8-10 0 RhiainIngram(5) 4 15
(Karen George) *a in rr* **200/1**

**12** *shd* **Catherinethegrace (IRE)** 3-9-0 0 KieranO'Neill 12 15
(Jimmy Fox) *completely missed break: detached in rr: grad mde up grnd fr wl over 3f out: nvr involved* **66/1**

**13** *1/2* **Mr Brownstone**[13] 3-9-5 0 (t) MartinDwyer 10 18
(Brendan Powell) *racd in rr-div on outer: t.k.h: no ex fr over 2f out* **50/1**

1m 38.47s (-1.33) **Going Correction** -0.05s/f (Stan)
**WFA** 3 from 4yo 1lb **13** Ran SP% **118.1**
Speed ratings (Par 103): **104,99,97,88,88 86,85,85,83,77 75,75,74**
CSF £6.52 TOTE £2.70: £1.40, £1.50, £1.50; EX 9.80 Trifecta £23.20.
**Owner** Woodhurst Construction Ltd **Bred** Tally-Ho Stud **Trained** Newmarket, Suffolk

**FOCUS**
No strength in depth here and the principals dominated.

## 9203 CLOSE BROTHERS BUSINESS FINANCE H'CAP 7f (P)
**6:10** (6:14) (Class 6) (0-65,67) 3-Y-O £2,587 (£770; £384; £192) **Stalls Low**

Form RPR

0300 **1** **Mr Mac**[20] 8908 3-8-11 55 (t[1]) TomMarquand 7 64
(Peter Hedger) *hld up in rr: shkn up and swtchd wdst of all over 2f out: rdn 2f out: qcknd up wl and sustained run fr over 1f out to ld jst ins fnl f: kpt on wl* **20/1**

5262 **2** *1 3/4* **Viola Park**[5] 9142 3-8-13 57 (p) LukeMorris 1 61
(Ronald Harris) *bhd ldr on rail: rdn over 2f out and swtchd to inner: prog fr over 1f out: led briefly 1f out: sn hdd: kpt on after* **7/2**[1]

002 **3** *3/4* **Happy Escape**[168] 4211 3-9-5 63 (t) AdamKirby 11 65
(Neil Mulholland) *early pce fr wd draw and disp ld: led over 4f out: rdn 2f out: pressed all rnd over 1f out: stuck on tl hdd 1f out: plugged on gamely after* **14/1**

5150 **4** *hd* **Masquerade Bling (IRE)**[15] 8985 3-9-1 59 RobHornby 9 60
(Neil Mulholland) *in rr-div on outer: rdn 2f out and chal between horses over 1f out: kpt on ins fnl f* **12/1**

0005 **5** *1* **Brother In Arms (IRE)**[41] 8551 3-8-12 56 JosephineGordon 2 55
(Tony Carroll) *settled in mid-div on inner: rdn 2f out: kpt on and ev ch ent fnl f: no ex and one pce* **12/1**

0421 **6** *hd* **Vixen (IRE)**[65] 7899 3-9-1 59 (h) EdwardGreatrex 10 57
(Eve Johnson Houghton) *bucking to post: cl up w ldrs on outer w no cover: rdn wl over 3f out to hold pl: plugged on fr over 1f out* **13/2**[2]

2660 **7** *nk* **Dragon Dream (IRE)**[64] 7934 3-8-12 61 RhiainIngram(5) 3 58
(Roger Ingram) *in rr: tk clsr order wl over 2f out: nt clr run tl 2f out: rdn and one pce fr over 1f out* **11/1**

0000 **8** *1 3/4* **Kachess**[19] 8930 3-8-6 57 NicolaCurrie(7) 4 50
(David Loughnane) *between horses in rr-div: rdn over 2f out: kpt on one pce* **33/1**

4633 **9** *1 3/4* **Violet's Lads (IRE)**[41] 8551 3-9-1 62 CallumShepherd(3) 8 50
(Brett Johnson) *t.k.h bhd ldrs: gng okay on heels of ldrs ent fnl f: nt asked whn nt clr run ins fnl f and eased* **8/1**[3]

2300 **10** *3/4* **Wild Acclaim (IRE)**[27] 8798 3-9-9 67 CharlesBishop 5 53
(Michael Appleby) *mid-div on outer: rdn wl over 1f out: one pce fnl f* **12/1**

40-2 **11** *2* **Desert Fox**[32] 8742 3-9-7 65 ShaneKelly 6 46
(Mike Murphy) *t.k.h and disp ld: hdd over 4f out: remained prom: rdn wl over 2f out: wknd qckly through pack ins fnl f* **7/2**[1]

1m 25.52s (-0.48) **Going Correction** -0.05s/f (Stan) **11** Ran SP% **114.7**
Speed ratings (Par 98): **100,98,97,96,95 95,95,93,91,90 88**
CSF £86.85 CT £1053.76 TOTE £26.70: £5.80, £1.80, £3.30; EX 122.90 Trifecta £2146.10.
**Owner** P C F Racing Ltd **Bred** J J Whelan **Trained** Hook, Hampshire

**FOCUS**
A moderate 3yo handicap, run at a fair pace. The consistent runner-up and those close up support this level.

## 9204 DOWNLOAD THE MATCHBOOK APP H'CAP 1m 7f 218y(P)
**6:40** (6:43) (Class 4) (0-85,86) 3-Y-O+ £4,690 (£1,395; £697; £348) **Stalls Low**

Form RPR

0313 **1** **Sunblazer (IRE)**[21] 8893 7-10-0 85 (t) RichardKingscote 8 92
(Kim Bailey) *settled in mid-div on outer: shkn up and gd prog over 2f out: rdn 2f out and led ent fnl f: kpt on wl* **3/1**[1]

0355 **2** *1* **Rydan (IRE)**[35] 8672 6-9-13 84 (p) AdamKirby 10 89
(Gary Moore) *hld up in rr between horses: shkn up and smooth prog fr over 2f out: rdn on inner over 1f out: swtchd off rail sn after: keeping on ins fnl f: tk 2nd nr fin but wnr a doing enough* **7/1**

0000 **3** *3/4* **Vettori Rules**[22] 8880 4-9-13 84 JosephineGordon 11 88
(Gay Kelleway) *pressed ldr tl led after 6f: rdn 2f out: kpt on tl hdd ent fnl f: lost 2nd nr fin* **33/1**

2-66 **4** *nk* **Continuum**[21] 8892 8-9-12 83 (p) TomMarquand 1 87
(Peter Hedger) *in rr: rdn wl over 2f out: kpt on wl fr pack over 1f out: nt gng pce of plcd horses* **10/1**

126 **5** *6* **Isaac Bell (IRE)**[21] 8893 9-9-11 82 (t) LukeMorris 9 78
(Alex Hales) *cl up racing on outer: shkn up ent st where nt clr run and hmpd: lost momentum and hung rt after: nt rcvrd and pushed out fr over 1f out* **5/1**[2]

0356 **6** *1/2* **Desert God (IND)**[35] 8672 5-9-4 82 (p) StephenCummins(7) 3 78
(Richard Hughes) *led tl 6f: remained bhd ldr: rdn over 2f out: sn hld* **6/1**[3]

3006 **7** *nk* **Azam**[14] 9000 3-9-2 79 AlistairRawlinson 5 76
(Michael Appleby) *in rr-div on inner: gng wl on inner over 2f out: sn rdn: fnd little and plugged on* **7/1**

0604 **8** *10* **Poyle Thomas**[42] 8505 8-9-9 80 FranBerry 4 63
(Michael Madgwick) *bhd ldr on inner: shkn up wl over 2f out: wknd qckly over 1f out* **7/1**

1000 **9** *4 1/2* **Royal Marskell**[103] 4355 8-9-8 86 NicolaCurrie(7) 2 64
(Gay Kelleway) *in rr: t.k.h at times: c wdst into st: sn hld* **33/1**

03-1 **R** **Song Light**[15] 8072 7-9-11 82 RobHornby 6
(Seamus Mullins) *ref to r* **20/1**

3m 29.96s (-0.14) **Going Correction** -0.05s/f (Stan)
**WFA** 3 from 4yo+ 6lb **10** Ran SP% **113.2**
Speed ratings (Par 105): **98,97,97,96,93 93,93,88,86,**
CSF £22.80 CT £561.04 TOTE £3.80: £1.60, £2.10, £7.10; EX 25.80 Trifecta £245.10.
**Owner** Norman Carter **Bred** Michael G Daly **Trained** Andoversford, Gloucs

**FOCUS**
Not a bad staying handicap. It was run at an uneven pace.

## 9205 MATCHBOOK BETTING PODCAST H'CAP 1m 2f 219y(P)
**7:10** (7:13) (Class 4) (0-85,86) 3-Y-O+ £4,690 (£1,395; £697; £348) **Stalls Low**

Form RPR

0051 **1** **General Hazard (IRE)**[18] 8956 4-9-6 84 EdwardGreatrex 8 91
(Archie Watson) *pressed ldr on outer: rdn over 2f out: kpt on wl and led 1f out: hrd pressed nr fin: jst hld on* **8/1**

-211 **2** *nse* **Enfolding (IRE)**[261] 1404 3-9-2 83 AdamKirby 2 91+
(James Fanshawe) *racd in mid-div on inner: rdn 2f out: gd prog to chse ldng pair on inner: kpt on strly fnl 110yds: jst failed* **10/3**[1]

0343 **3** *1* **Berrahri (IRE)**[35] 8672 6-9-3 81 JosephineGordon 10 86
(John Best) *sn led: rdn over 2f out: kpt on wl tl hdd 1f out: lost 2nd sn after: one pce fnl 55yds* **11/1**

0002 **4** *1 3/4* **Cliff Face (IRE)**[21] 8893 4-9-7 85 (b) LukeMorris 11 87
(Sir Mark Prescott Bt) *sluggish s: hld up in rr-div on inner: rdn 2f out: outpcd tl kpt on strly ent fnl f: nvr nrr* **8/1**

5040 **5** *3/4* **Gothic Empire (IRE)**[22] 8880 5-9-3 81 RyanTate 14 82
(Richard Rowe) *hld up in last pair: swtchd wd ent st: sn rdn w plenty to do: qcknd up wl over 1f out: no ch w plcd horses fnl f and pushed out: nvr nrr* **40/1**

5016 **6** *nk* **Ay Ay (IRE)**[22] 8880 3-9-5 86 HollieDoyle 6 87
(David Elsworth) *bhd ldrs on outer: rdn along wl over 1f out: no ex and kpt on one pce* **5/1**[2]

1400 **7** *3/4* **Graceful James (IRE)**[63] 7949 4-9-2 80 KieranO'Neill 12 79
(Jimmy Fox) *in rr: rdn over 2f out: kpt on over 1f out tl no ex fnl f* **20/1**

0063 **8** *1 1/2* **Glenys The Menace (FR)**[26] 8820 3-9-3 84 SteveDrowne 13 81
(John Best) *racd in mid-div on outer: lost pl wl over 2f out: hld together tl over 1f out whn briefly shuffled along: eased ins fnl f: nvr involved* **14/1**

0444 **9** *1 3/4* **First Flight (IRE)**[11] 9053 6-9-8 86 PJMcDonald 1 79
(Heather Main) *racd in mid-div: rdn over 2f out: plugged on* **6/1**[3]

0-05 **10** *2* **Argus (IRE)**[70] 7231 5-9-5 83 DougieCostello 9 73
(Alexandra Dunn) *bhd ldrs on outer: rdn over 2f out: sn one pce and wknd* **40/1**

3201 **11** *7* **Bristol Missile (USA)**[179] 3839 3-8-13 80 TomMarquand 5 59
(Richard Hannon) *bhd ldrs on inner: struggling to hold pl over 2f out: shkn up and no ex fr over 1f out: wknd fnl f* **8/1**

0330 **12** *hd* **Storm Rock**[46] 8423 5-8-13 77 RichardKingscote 4 55
(Harry Dunlop) *in rr: lost pl and no ex fr over 3f out* **20/1**

2m 19.57s (-2.33) **Going Correction** -0.05s/f (Stan)
**WFA** 3 from 4yo+ 3lb **12** Ran SP% **116.8**
Speed ratings (Par 105): **106,105,105,103,103 103,102,101,100,98 93,93**
CSF £32.74 CT £295.85 TOTE £9.10: £2.70, £1.90, £2.80; EX 39.10 Trifecta £352.90.
**Owner** Boadicea Bloodstock **Bred** London Thoroughbred Services Ltd **Trained** Upper Lambourn, W Berks

**FOCUS**
It paid to be handy in this fair handicap.
T/Plt: £90.60 to a £1 stake. Pool: £67,037.27 - 539.93 winning units. T/Qpdt: £8.70 to a £1 stake. Pool: £11,451.39 - 963.64 winning units. **Cathal Gahan**

# [9182]LINGFIELD (L-H)

Wednesday, December 13

**OFFICIAL GOING: Polytrack: standard**

Wind: Fresh, half behind in straight Weather: Overcast

## 9206 PLAY FOR FREE AT SUNBETS.CO.UK/VEGAS H'CAP 1m 1y(P)

12:00 (Class 4) (0-85,84) 3-Y-0+ £4,690 (£1,395; £697; £348) Stalls Low

Form RPR

0156 1 **Goring (GER)**[50] 8310 5-9-6 83 ....................(v) CharlesBishop 6 92
(Eve Johnson Houghton) *trckd ldrs: clsd on outer over 1f out: shkn up to ld jst ins fnl f: sn clr: rdn out* 11/2[3]

4263 2 2 **Easy Tiger**[23] 8872 5-9-7 84 .................... LiamKeniry 7 88
(Malcolm Saunders) *trckd ldr 2f: styd cl up: rdn over 2f out: trying to cl whn wnr wnt past jst over 1f out: styd on to take 2nd nr fin* 3/1[2]

4304 3 hd **Maratha (IRE)**[12] 9025 3-9-0 78 ....................(t) SeanLevey 3 82
(Stuart Williams) *trckd ldng pair: poised to chal 2f out: shkn up between rivals over 1f out: nt qckn as wnr wnt past: no imp after and lost 2nd last strides* 5/2[1]

4000 4 1 **Scottish Glen**[26] 8821 11-8-10 76 .................... HectorCrouch(3) 5 77
(Patrick Chamings) *racd in 7th: rdn wl over 2f out: no great prog tl styd on fnl f: tk 4th last stride and nrst fin* 9/1

0-00 5 nk **Genetics (FR)**[46] 8423 3-9-2 80 ....................(h[1]) RobHornby 1 81
(Andrew Balding) *hld up off the pce in last quartet: pushed along and no real prog over 2f out: rdn fnl f and styd on: nrst fin but nvr in it* 15/2

000U 6 shd **Gentlemen**[20] 8905 6-9-4 81 ....................(h) DannyBrock 4 81
(Phil McEntee) *s.i.s and pushed up into midfield: rdn over 2f out: no imp tl kpt on fnl f: nvr able to chal* 33/1

5-00 7 ¾ **Toriano**[26] 8821 4-8-12 75 .................... TomMarquand 12 74
(Nick Littmoden) *trckd ldr after 2f: chal and upsides over 1f out tl jst ins fnl f: outpcd and then fdd nr fin* 25/1

420 8 nse **Cricklewood Green (USA)**[68] 7780 6-8-12 78 .......... MitchGodwin(3) 10 76
(Sylvester Kirk) *s.i.s: off the pce in last pair: rdn on inner over 2f out: no prog tl styd on fnl f: nrst fin* 25/1

1010 9 hd **Blaze Of Hearts (IRE)**[12] 9025 4-8-12 78 .................... JackDuern(3) 2 76
(Dean Ivory) *led at gd pce: rdn 2f out: hdd and fdd jst ins fnl f* 7/1

1400 10 1 ¾ **Tee It Up Tommo (IRE)**[21] 8886 8-8-11 74 .................... HollieDoyle 8 68
(Daniel Steele) *hld up in last quartet and off the pce: tried to cl over 2f out: sn rdn and no prog* 33/1

4400 11 2 ¼ **Lunar Deity**[22] 8881 8-8-12 78 .................... AaronJones(3) 9 67
(Stuart Williams) *slowly away: a in last pair: rdn and no prog over 2f out* 20/1

1m 35.45s (-2.75) **Going Correction** -0.025s/f (Stan)

**WFA** 3 from 4yo+ 1lb 11 Ran SP% 121.6

Speed ratings (Par 105): **112,110,109,108,108 108,107,107,107,105 103**

CSF £21.68 CT £52.23 TOTE £6.70: £2.40, £1.40, £1.20; EX 25.20 Trifecta £113.50.

**Owner** G C Stevens **Bred** Westminster Race Horses Gmbh **Trained** Blewbury, Oxon

**FOCUS**

A decent handicap. They went a good gallop and it is sound form. A small pb from the winner, with the runner-up rated close to form and the fourth close to his latest effort.

## 9207 PLAY JACKPOT GAMES AT SUNBETS.CO.UK/VEGAS (S) STKS 7f 1y(P)

12:30 (12:31) (Class 6) 3-Y-0+ £2,264 (£673; £336; £168) Stalls Low

Form RPR

0531 1 **Dutiful Son (IRE)**[7] 9094 7-9-10 71 .................... AdamKirby 3 75
(Simon Dow) *trckd ldng pair: wnt 2nd over 1f out: shkn up to ld 150yds out: urged along and sn drew away* 4/7[1]

5204 2 1 ¾ **Haraz (IRE)**[27] 8805 4-9-0 66 ....................(p) DougieCostello 6 60
(Jamie Osborne) *hld up in last pair: prog over 1f out: styd on to take 2nd nr fin: no ch w wnr* 7/2[2]

0000 3 ½ **Bridge Builder**[7] 9094 7-9-6 65 ....................(p) CharlesBishop 2 65
(Peter Hedger) *led: rdn over 1f out: hdd 150yds out: no ex and lost 2nd nr fin* 12/1[3]

1000 4 ½ **Corporal Maddox**[8] 9083 10-9-6 60 ....................(p) LukeMorris 7 64
(Ronald Harris) *trckd ldng pair: rdn whn wd bnd 2f out: kpt on one pce after* 20/1

0/1- 5 1 **Footstepsintherain (IRE)**[609] 1416 7-8-9 72 .................... JaneElliott(5) 5 55
(Daniel Steele) *chsd ldr to over 1f out: sn fdd* 12/1[3]

0536 6 nk **Lucky Di**[18] 8948 7-8-9 45 .................... TomMarquand 1 49
(Peter Hedger) *hld up in last pair: rdn on inner wl over 1f out: no prog* 16/1

1m 24.09s (-0.71) **Going Correction** -0.025s/f (Stan) 6 Ran SP% 111.9

Speed ratings (Par 101): **103,101,100,99,98 98**

CSF £2.80 TOTE £1.30: £1.02, £2.30; EX 3.30 Trifecta £12.50.

**Owner** J C G Chua & Partner **Bred** Lodge Park Stud **Trained** Ashtead, Surrey

**FOCUS**

An ordinary seller. It turned into a tactical race but the odds-on favourite won cosily. Straightforward form.

## 9208 BETWAY CASINO H'CAP 1m 4f (P)

1:00 (1:02) (Class 5) (0-75,77) 3-Y-0+ £2,911 (£866; £432; £216) Stalls Low

Form RPR

4225 1 **Take Two**[14] 9000 8-9-12 77 .................... MartinHarley 8 83
(Alex Hales) *hld up in last pair tl rapid prog 8f out to join ldr 6f out: led 3f out: drvn over 1f out: hld on wl fnl f* 9/2[2]

330 2 ¾ **Miss Liguria**[105] 6578 3-8-13 68 .................... LiamKeniry 6 72
(Ed Walker) *hld up in midfield: rdn and in tch over 2f out: styd on fr over 1f out to take 2nd last stride* 16/1

0/32 3 shd **Volpone Jelois (FR)**[20] 3086 4-9-3 73 ....................(p) MeganNicholls(5) 10 77
(Paul Nicholls) *racd wd: trckd ldrs: rdn over 2f out: prog over 1f out to chse wnr last 100yds: a hld and lost 2nd last stride* 7/1[3]

6004 4 nk **Top Beak (IRE)**[69] 7770 4-9-6 71 ....................(t[1]) RobertHavlin 7 74+
(Michael Attwater) *stdd s: hld up in last: stl only 13th 2f out but gng wl: rapid prog on outer over 1f out: r.o to take 4th last strides: too late* 10/1

3000 5 nk **Ardamir (FR)**[24] 7096 5-9-10 75 .................... FranBerry 3 78+
(Laura Mongan) *hld up wl in rr: prog on inner fr 2f out: rdn and styd on fnl f: nrst fin but nvr rchd ldrs* 50/1

-104 6 nk **Erinyes (IRE)**[104] 6628 3-9-6 75 ....................(p) EdwardGreatrex 4 78
(Archie Watson) *wl in tch: prog on inner and rdn 2f out: tried to chal jst over 1f out: one pce last 150yds* 7/1[3]

3004 7 hd **Sufi**[21] 8886 3-9-0 72 .................... HectorCrouch(3) 2 74
(Ken Cunningham-Brown) *led 2f: trckd ldr to 6f out: rdn over 2f out: rallied to chse wnr over 1f out to 100yds out: wknd nr fin* 12/1

-162 8 1 **Kohinoor Diamond (IRE)**[22] 8883 3-8-10 65 ....................(b[1]) LukeMorris 5 66
(Sir Mark Prescott Bt) *trckd ldrs: rdn over 2f out: cl enough over 1f out: fnd nil and racd w hd at v awkward angle after: fdd* 5/2[1]

0324 9 ¾ **My Illusionist**[32] 8744 3-9-1 70 .................... StevieDonohoe 9 69
(Harry Dunlop) *towards rr: rdn wl over 2f out and nt on terms w ldrs: plugged on fr over 1f out: n.d* 25/1

0622 10 1 **Luv U Whatever**[9] 9070 7-9-4 69 ....................(tp) JoeyHaynes 11 67
(Marjorie Fife) *hld up wl in rr: rdn over 3f out: no prog and wl hld fr 2f out* 12/1

5-04 11 2 ¾ **Tower Power**[63] 7960 6-9-8 73 .................... HollieDoyle 15 66
(Phil McEntee) *quick move fr wd draw to ld after 2f: hdd 3f out: lost 2nd and wknd qckly over 1f out* 25/1

0 12 1 **Michigan (USA)**[36] 8663 3-9-3 72 ....................(t) SeanLevey 12 64
(Mohamed Moubarak) *prom: lost pl 5f out: rdn over 3f out: sn wknd* 50/1

53-0 13 1 **Lungarno Palace (USA)**[14] 9000 6-9-6 71 ....................(b) PJMcDonald 13 61
(John Gallagher) *racd wd: in tch: rdn over 3f out: wknd over 2f out* 33/1

5052 14 55 **Pack It In (IRE)**[21] 6176 4-9-4 69 .................... DougieCostello 14
(Alexandra Dunn) *racd wd: in tch to 5f out: wknd rapidly 4f out: sn t.o and eased* 50/1

0336 15 15 **Musikel (IRE)**[166] 4295 3-9-3 72 ....................(p) AdamKirby 1
(Chris Gordon) *prom early but sn lost pl and urged along: last and wkng 5f out: sn t.o* 12/1

2m 30.63s (-2.37) **Going Correction** -0.025s/f (Stan)

**WFA** 3 from 4yo+ 4lb 15 Ran SP% 126.3

Speed ratings (Par 103): **106,105,105,105,105 104,104,104,103,102 101,100,99,63,53**

CSF £73.22 CT £510.55 TOTE £5.40: £1.70, £5.60, £3.00; EX 98.00 Trifecta £712.90.

**Owner** Edging Ahead **Bred** Steven & Petra Wallace **Trained** Edgcote, Northamptonshire

**FOCUS**

A fair middle-distance handicap. They went a muddling gallop and the winner's rider was alert to the situation from over 3f out. The winner has been rated to his recent form.

## 9209 BETWAY MAIDEN STKS 1m 2f (P)

1:30 (1:32) (Class 5) 3-Y-0+ £2,911 (£866; £432; £216) Stalls Low

Form RPR

42 1 **Dash Of Spice**[73] 7652 3-9-5 0 .................... SeanLevey 1 76+
(David Elsworth) *led 1f: trckd ldr: led again wl over 2f out: shkn up and drew clr wl over 1f out: in n.d after* 11/10[1]

34/ 2 3 ¾ **Past Master**[805] 6864 4-9-7 0 .................... FranBerry 8 69+
(Henry Candy) *hld up in midfield: shkn up over 2f out: styd on steadily fr over 1f out to take 2nd last strides: shaped wl* 6/1

245 3 nk **Swiss Vinnare**[30] 8770 3-8-12 69 ....................(h[1]) NicolaCurrie(7) 7 68
(Phil McEntee) *t.k.h: led after 1f to wl over 2f out: chsd wnr after but no ch over 1f out: lost 2nd last strides* 20/1

00 4 1 ¼ **Delicate Kiss**[26] 8822 3-9-0 0 ....................(b) WilliamCarson 3 61
(John Bridger) *prom: chsd ldng pair 1/2-way: rdn to press for 2nd over 1f out: no ex ins fnl f: short of room nr fin* 200/1

5 5 2 **Monsieur Bay**[36] 8663 3-9-5 0 .................... StevieDonohoe 4 62
(Ismail Mohammed) *chsd ldrs: rdn and no imp over 2f out* 7/2[2]

4 6 shd **Mundersfield**[23] 8869 3-9-0 0 .................... JamieSpencer 5 56+
(David Simcock) *hld up towards rr: nudged along and no imp ldrs fnl 2f: could do bttr* 8/1

7 1 ½ **Duhr (IRE)**[242] 3-9-5 0 .................... RyanTate 2 58
(Ralph J Smith) *t.k.h: hld up in last pair: stl there 2f out: nudged along and no real prog: likely improver* 66/1

442 8 7 **Meccabah (FR)**[23] 8869 3-9-0 75 ....................(b) PJMcDonald 6 39
(Andrew Balding) *prom tl wknd wl over 2f out* 9/2[3]

42/ 9 15 **Diamond Reflection (IRE)**[91] 3361 5-9-7 0 ....................(t) DougieCostello 9 13
(Alexandra Dunn) *a in rr: wknd 3f out: t.o* 100/1

2m 6.03s (-0.57) **Going Correction** -0.025s/f (Stan)

**WFA** 3 from 4yo+ 2lb 9 Ran SP% 121.2

Speed ratings (Par 103): **101,98,97,96,95 95,93,88,76**

CSF £9.08 TOTE £1.80: £1.10, £1.70, £6.00; EX 9.90 Trifecta £90.10.

**Owner** J C Smith **Bred** Littleton Stud **Trained** Newmarket, Suffolk

**FOCUS**

A fair maiden. They went a modest gallop but the favourite still managed to show off his superiority. It's been rated around the third.

## 9210 PLAY STARBURST SLOT AT SUNBETS.CO.UK/VEGAS H'CAP 7f 1y(P)

2:00 (2:01) (Class 3) (0-95,93) 3-Y-0+ £7,246 (£2,168; £1,084; £542; £270) Stalls Low

Form RPR

0300 1 **Shyron**[20] 8905 6-8-5 82 .................... JaneElliott(5) 2 90
(George Margarson) *hld up in last quartet: prog wl over 1f out: dream run through on inner fnl f: pushed into the ld 75yds out: hung rt after but in command* 5/1[2]

4240 2 ½ **Right Touch**[13] 9016 7-9-1 87 .................... JackGarritty 8 94
(Richard Fahey) *trckd ldrs: gng strly 2f out: shkn up to cl 1f out but wnr wnt past sn after: rdn and styd on to take 2nd nr fin* 16/1

2150 3 ½ **Pearl Spectre (USA)**[20] 8905 6-8-8 87 .................... NicolaCurrie(7) 9 93
(Phil McEntee) *led at str pce: tried to kick on again 2f out: hdd last 75yds: lost 2nd nr fin* 11/1

5142 4 hd **Make Music**[221] 2390 4-8-11 90 .................... JasonWatson(7) 5 95
(Andrew Balding) *chsd ldng pair: rdn to chse ldr over 1f out: kpt on but lost 2nd ins fnl f* 25/1

0201 5 ¾ **Makaarim**[23] 8872 3-9-2 88 .................... FranBerry 3 91+
(Hughie Morrison) *dwlt: hld up in last quartet: stl there over 1f out: shkn up and r.o fnl f: too late to chal* 3/1[1]

0530 6 hd **Alejandro (IRE)**[11] 9053 8-9-0 86 .................... LukeMorris 1 89
(David Loughnane) *chsd ldng trio: rdn over 2f out: one pce over 1f out and lost pls ins fnl f* 8/1[3]

0040 7 hd **Alfred Hutchinson**[26] 8812 9-9-6 92 ....................(p) MartinHarley 12 94
(David O'Meara) *chsd ldrs: rdn 2f out: no imp over 1f out: fdd* 14/1

0040 8 ¾ **Kadrizzi (FR)**[13] 9016 4-8-12 87 ....................(p) JackDuern(3) 4 87
(Dean Ivory) *hld up in midfield: pushed along 2f out: kpt on one pce fnl f and nvr posed a threat* 12/1

0500 9 ¾ **Mr Bossy Boots (IRE)**[6] 9125 6-9-4 90 ....................(p) JoeyHaynes 11 88
(Amanda Perrett) *nvr beyond midfield: rdn and no prog over 2f out: one pce after* 20/1

0050 10 ½ **Eljaddaaf (IRE)**[191] 3410 6-9-2 88 ....................(h) RobertWinston 13 85
(Dean Ivory) *racd wd: hld up in rr: prog on outer 3f out: rdn over 2f out: fdd over 1f out* 33/1

220- 11 ¾ **Mickey (IRE)**[458] 6371 4-9-2 88 ....................(t) RichardKingscote 6 83
(Tom Dascombe) *dwlt: a in rr: rdn and no prog over 2f out* 5/1[2]

00-0 12 shd **Bobby Wheeler (IRE)**[41] 8547 4-9-1 87 .................... AdamKirby 14 81
(Clive Cox) *chsd ldr to over 1f out: lost pl rapidly* 11/1

0400 **13** *2* **Forceful Appeal (USA)**[14] 8999 9-9-2 **93**.................. PaddyBradley(5) 7 82
(Simon Dow) *hld up in last trio: shkn up and no prog over 2f out* **20/1**

1m 22.48s (-2.32) **Going Correction** -0.025s/f (Stan) **13** Ran SP% **122.7**
Speed ratings (Par 107): **112,111,110,110,109 109,109,108,107,107 106,106,103**
CSF £79.95 CT £886.30 TOTE £7.10: £2.30, £4.70, £3.70; EX 122.80 Trifecta £1399.90.

**Owner** F Butler **Bred** F Butler **Trained** Newmarket, Suffolk

■ Stewards' Enquiry : Jason Watson caution: careless riding

**FOCUS**
The feature contest was a good handicap. They went a decent gallop and one of the joint second-favourites won well. The third has been rated to form.

## 9211 BETWAY H'CAP (DIV I) 1m 2f (P)
**2:30** (2:30) (Class 6) (0-65,67) 3-Y-O+ **£2,264** (£673; £336; £168) **Stalls** Low

Form RPR
3034 **1** **Bayston Hill**[18] 8946 3-8-11 **64**...................................... NicolaCurrie(7) 4 72
(Mark Usher) *trckd ldrs: wnt 2nd 2f out: led over 1f out: sn rdn clr: comf* **5/2**[1]

0001 **2** *2 ½* **Music Major**[18] 8946 4-9-9 **67**.......................................... RobertHavlin 3 71
(Michael Attwater) *hld up in 8th: effrt on inner whn nt clr run and snatched up wl over 1f out: rdn and r.o fnl f to take 2nd last strides* **5/1**[3]

0340 **3** *½* **Unit Of Assessment (IRE)**[41] 8549 3-9-6 **66**.............(vt) MartinHarley 9 68
(William Knight) *trckd ldrs: swift move to ld 6f out: rdn over 2f out: hdd over 1f out: no ch w wnr after and lost 2nd last strides* **7/1**

5125 **4** *nk* **Betsalottie**[7] 9092 4-8-10 **57**...................................... MitchGodwin(3) 11 58
(John Bridger) *racd wd: in tch: rdn over 2f out: kpt on u.p to press for a pl fnl f: one pce nr fin* **8/1**

0160 **5** *½* **Rakematiz**[41] 8550 3-8-13 **62**.............................. CallumShepherd(3) 12 63
(Brett Johnson) *chsd ldr to 6f out and new ldr over 4f out to 2f out: one pce u.p* **14/1**

3625 **6** *nse* **Banta Bay**[20] 8908 3-8-5 **51** oh4.......................................(p) JoeyHaynes 5 52
(John Best) *towards rr: pushed along over 3f out: rdn and effrt 2f out: one pce fr over 1f out* **16/1**

6306 **7** *½* **The Gay Cavalier**[8] 9078 6-8-8 **59**.............................(t) JackOsborn(7) 10 58
(John Ryan) *dwlt: hld up in last pair: rdn wl over 1f out: kpt on fnl f but nvr able to threaten* **8/1**

000U **8** *1 ¼* **Exspectation (IRE)**[49] 8346 3-8-8 **54**................................ HollieDoyle 1 51
(Michael Blanshard) *led to 6f out: chsd ldr to over 4f out: styd cl up tl wknd 2f out* **33/1**

0 **9** *1 ¼* **Solveig's Song**[41] 8549 5-8-11 **55**............................(p) EdwardGreatrex 7 49
(Steve Woodman) *hld up in last pair: rdn and no prog on outer 2f out* **33/1**

0050 **10** *½* **The Dancing Lord**[179] 3823 8-8-7 **51** oh1......................(t) JimmyQuinn 8 44
(Adam West) *hld up wl in rr: stl there whn two reminders wl over 1f out: no prog and nudged along after* **50/1**

4661 **11** *1* **Estibdaad (IRE)**[83] 7325 7-9-0 **58**...................................(t) DannyBrock 6 49
(Paddy Butler) *dwlt: a in rr: shkn up 3f out: nt clr run briefly 2f out on inner: no prog after* **12/1**

6400 **12** *½* **Cadeaux Boxer**[30] 8773 4-9-7 **65**........................................ AdamKirby 2 55
(Lee Carter) *plld hrd: trckd ldrs: wknd over 2f out* **4/1**[2]

2m 4.56s (-2.04) **Going Correction** -0.025s/f (Stan)
**WFA** 3 from 4yo+ 2lb **12** Ran SP% **128.0**
Speed ratings (Par 101): **107,105,104,104,103 103,103,102,101,101 100,99**
CSF £16.09 CT £84.38 TOTE £3.70: £1.30, £2.30, £2.60; EX 16.30 Trifecta £105.30.

**Owner** High Five Racing and Partners **Bred** Selwood Bloodstock & Mrs S Read **Trained** Upper Lambourn, Berks

**FOCUS**
The first division of a modest handicap. They went a muddling gallop but the well-backed favourite ran out a ready winner. A minor pb from the winner, while the second, third and fourth suggest this is a sensible starting point.

## 9212 BETWAY H'CAP (DIV II) 1m 2f (P)
**3:00** (3:00) (Class 6) (0-65,67) 3-Y-O+ **£2,264** (£673; £336; £168) **Stalls** Low

Form RPR
000 **1** **Miss Minuty**[95] 6948 5-9-2 **67**...................................... JasonWatson(7) 10 74
(Jeremy Scott) *blindfold off sltly late and dwlt: sn in midfield: prog 3f out: rdn wl over 1f out: chsd ldr fnl f: r.o to edge ahd last 75yds* **16/1**

4060 **2** *nk* **Squire**[65] 7878 6-9-7 **65**...................................................(t) StevieDonohoe 5 71
(Michael Attwater) *led at mod pce: kicked on over 2f out: drvn fnl f: worn down last 75yds* **9/2**[3]

0003 **3** *¾* **Attain**[7] 9092 8-9-1 **59**...................................................... EdwardGreatrex 2 64
(Archie Watson) *trckd ldng pair: rdn over 2f out: disp 2nd 1f out: one pce last 100yds* **11/4**[1]

0162 **4** *1 ¼* **Ingleby Spring (IRE)**[15] 8985 5-8-11 **55**....................... PatrickMathers 7 58
(Richard Fahey) *trckd ldrs on outer: rdn over 2f out: nt qckn and btn over 1f out: kpt on again ins fnl f* **6/1**

6140 **5** *1* **Luxford**[26] 8813 3-9-0 **60**.................................................. MartinDwyer 8 62
(John Best) *trckd ldr: rdn over 2f out: lost 2nd and wknd fnl f* **11/1**

4360 **6** *1 ¾* **Yogiyogiyogi (IRE)**[18] 8946 3-9-3 **63**...........................(v[1]) RobertWinston 12 61
(Denis Coakley) *t.k.h: hld up in rr: tried to make prog over 2f out but only limited hdwy over 1f out: n.d* **14/1**

0660 **7** *½* **Runaiocht (IRE)**[14] 8993 7-8-12 **56**..................................... JimmyQuinn 4 52
(Paul Burgoyne) *wl in tch: 5th whn shkn up and no rspnse over 2f out: one pce after* **7/1**

5021 **8** *¾* **Pink Ribbon (IRE)**[8] 9078 5-9-2 **63**............................(p) MitchGodwin(3) 6 58
(Sylvester Kirk) *t.k.h: hld up in tch: rdn and no prog over 2f out: wknd over 1f out* **7/2**[2]

0000 **9** *8* **Genuine Approval (IRE)**[149] 4982 4-8-13 **57**................. LiamKeniry 11 37
(John Butler) *hld up in rr: pushed along over 3f out: no prog and sn btn* **33/1**

030- **10** *½* **Aspasius (GER)**[457] 6406 5-8-7 **51** oh1........................... KieranO'Neill 9 30
(Gary Moore) *hld up towards rr: rdn and wknd 3f out* **50/1**

0000 **11** *5* **Moorea**[7] 9088 3-8-5 **51** oh6.............................................. HollieDoyle 3 21
(John Bridger) *stdd s: plld hrd in last: lost tch over 3f out: bhd after* **100/1**

2m 9.19s (2.59) **Going Correction** -0.025s/f (Stan)
**WFA** 3 from 4yo+ 2lb **11** Ran SP% **120.6**
Speed ratings (Par 101): **88,87,87,86,85 83,83,82,76,76 72**
CSF £88.48 CT £266.74 TOTE £11.60: £3.10, £2.10, £1.40; EX 104.80 Trifecta £815.80.

**Owner** Miss Jennifer Dorey **Bred** J L C Pearce **Trained** Brompton Regis, Somerset

**FOCUS**
The second division of a modest handicap. The winning time was over four seconds slower than the other division. Straightforward form, with the third and fourth helping to pin the level.

## 9213 SUNBETS.CO.UK ALL-WEATHER "HANDS AND HEELS" APPRENTICE SERIES H'CAP (EXCELLENCE INITIATIVE) 1m 1y(P)
**3:30** (3:33) (Class 6) (0-60,58) 3-Y-O+ **£2,264** (£673; £336; £168) **Stalls** Low

Form RPR
5650 **1** **Stringybark Creek**[51] 8300 3-9-1 **48**.......................(p[1]) DarraghKeenan 4 54
(Daniel Steele) *t.k.h: trckd ldng trio: clsd fr over 1f out: styd on to ld last 50yds: jst hld on* **8/1**

5146 **2** *nk* **Topmeup**[12] 9034 3-9-8 **58**.............................................(v) PaulHainey(3) 8 63
(Gay Kelleway) *trckd ldrs: pushed along over 1f out: clsd fnl f: tk 2nd last stride but jst too late* **6/1**[3]

330 **3** *shd* **Bloodsweatandtears**[55] 8181 9-9-12 **58**........................... JackOsborn 2 63
(William Knight) *trckd ldng trio: wnt 2nd over 2f out: led 1f out: kpt on but hdd 50yds out: lost 2nd last stride* **8/1**

0206 **4** *1 ¼* **Tarseekh**[27] 8799 4-9-4 **53**.....................................(b[1]) TheodoreLadd(3) 9 55
(Chris Gordon) *t.k.h: led: urged along and hdd 1f out: one pce and lost pls last 100yds* **7/1**

0-13 **5** *nk* **Rock Icon**[105] 6588 4-9-7 **58**...............................(h) GeorgiaDobie(5) 3 59
(J S Moore) *t.k.h: trckd ldr to over 2f out: styd cl up but one pce after* **4/1**[2]

0005 **6** *½* **Ravenhoe (IRE)**[12] 9032 4-9-3 **54**.......................... SharnaArmstrong(5) 7 54+
(Mark Johnston) *hld up off the pce towards rr: plenty to do 2f out: pushed along and styd on fr over 1f out: nrst fin but too late* **11/4**[1]

2500 **7** *1* **Aye Aye Skipper (IRE)**[107] 6503 7-9-5 **54**...............(b) KeelanBaker(3) 5 52
(Ken Cunningham-Brown) *awkward s and slowly away: rchd midfield after 2f: tried to make prog on inner 2f out: no real hdwy fnl f* **16/1**

0000 **8** *2* **Golden Cannon**[14] 8994 6-8-13 **45**............................. BenSanderson 10 38
(Sheena West) *wl in rr: tried to cl fr 2f out: nvr really a factor* **50/1**

0502 **9** *2 ¼* **Flying Sakhee**[14] 8994 4-9-2 **48**............................. StephenCummins 12 36
(John Bridger) *hld up towards rr: urged along and no prog over 2f out* **10/1**

0-00 **10** *¾* **No Refund (IRE)**[44] 8473 6-8-11 **46**........................ RussellHarris(3) 6 32
(Martin Smith) *slowly away: mostly in last pair: wl off the pce over 2f out* **33/1**

350 **11** *23* **London Grammar (IRE)**[25] 8846 3-9-1 **51**..............(h) JasonWatson(3) 1 +
(Ralph J Smith) *whipped rnd leaving stalls: nvr able to catch up: t.o* **12/1**

1m 41.14s (2.94) **Going Correction** -0.025s/f (Stan)
**WFA** 3 from 4yo+ 1lb **11** Ran SP% **123.2**
Speed ratings (Par 101): **84,83,83,82,82 81,80,78,76,75 52**
CSF £58.25 CT £415.70 TOTE £10.10: £2.70, £2.00, £3.30; EX 67.20 Trifecta £568.00.

**Owner** Alex Percy **Bred** Whatton Manor Stud **Trained** Henfield, W Sussex

**FOCUS**
A moderate apprentice riders' handicap. They went a sedate gallop and they finished in a bit of a heap. Straightforward form rated around the third and fourth.

T/Jkpt: £10,000.00 to a £1 stake. Pool: £14,084.51 - 1 winning unit. T/Plt: £33.50 to a £1 stake. Pool: £165,241.86 - 3600.50 winning units T/Qpdt: £52.50 to a £1 stake. Pool: £8,715.70 - 122.72 winning units. **Jonathan Neesom**

# 9152 WOLVERHAMPTON (A.W) (L-H)
Wednesday, December 13

**OFFICIAL GOING: Tapeta: standard**
Wind: Fresh across Weather: Showers clearing to leave a fine day

## 9214 BETWAY SPRINT H'CAP 5f 21y (Tp)
**1:45** (1:46) (Class 6) (0-59,58) 3-Y-O+ **£2,587** (£770; £384; £192) **Stalls** Low

Form RPR
0506 **1** **Roy's Legacy**[9] 9075 8-8-8 **48**................................... CharlieBennett(3) 6 56
(Shaun Harris) *w ldr tl led 3f out: rdn over 1f out: styd on gamely u.p* **25/1**

0052 **2** *hd* **Something Lucky (IRE)**[9] 9075 5-8-11 **48**............(v[1]) AndrewMullen 11 55
(Michael Appleby) *s.i.s: hld up: racd keenly: hdwy 2f out: shkn up and ev ch ins fnl f: styd on* **3/1**[2]

2102 **3** *3* **Toolatetodelegate**[18] 8953 3-9-0 **58**.....................(tp) WilliamCarver(7) 8 54
(Brian Barr) *hmpd s: hld up: r.o to go 3rd wl ins fnl f: nt trble ldrs* **10/1**

51-2 **4** *1* **Gorgeous (FR)**[23] 8873 4-9-5 **56**...................................... FrannyNorton 5 49
(Tony Carroll) *chsd ldrs: pushed along 1/2-way: styd on same pce ins fnl f* **3/1**[2]

65 **5** *1 ¾* **Your Gifted (IRE)**[43] 8494 10-9-1 **52**...............................(v) RaulDaSilva 9 39
(Lisa Williamson) *prom: rdn over 1f out: no ex fnl f* **22/1**

4104 **6** *1* **Fikhaar**[13] 9019 3-9-6 **57**.................................................... TomEaves 3 41
(Kevin Ryan) *chsd ldrs: hmpd 1/2-way: rdn over 1f out: wknd ins fnl f* **11/4**[1]

5002 **7** *1 ¼* **Oh So Dandy (IRE)**[7] 9103 3-9-0 **51**...............................(v) PhillipMakin 7 29
(Derek Shaw) *s.i.s and wnt rt s: hld up: plld hrd: bhd 1/2-way* **7/1**[3]

4400 **8** *8* **Mags Well (IRE)**[63] 7951 3-9-6 **57**................................... TimmyMurphy 2 7
(Geoffrey Deacon) *led 2f: wknd over 1f out* **50/1**

1m 2.46s (0.56) **Going Correction** +0.20s/f (Slow) **8** Ran SP% **108.4**
Speed ratings (Par 101): **103,102,97,96,93 91,89,77**
CSF £89.21 CT £736.90 TOTE £18.70: £4.40, £2.00, £2.10; EX 72.00 Trifecta £396.40.

**Owner** Notts Racing, S Mohammed & S Rowley **Bred** A Christou **Trained** Carburton, Notts

**FOCUS**
The going was standard. Rails - outside for races 6 and 7; inside for remainder. An ordinary sprint handicap which saw the winner bounce back to form following a spell in the doldrums. The first two have been rated near their recent best.

## 9215 BETWAY H'CAP (DIV I) 6f 20y (Tp)
**2:15** (2:16) (Class 6) (0-62,64) 3-Y-O+ **£2,587** (£770; £384; £192) **Stalls** Low

Form RPR
4025 **1** **Jack Blane**[11] 9052 3-9-0 **55**............................................(p) PhillipMakin 6 61
(Keith Dalgleish) *hld up: hdwy over 1f out: rdn to ld ins fnl f: r.o* **9/4**[2]

064P **2** *½* **Snow Excuse**[43] 8490 3-8-7 **48**........................................(t) ShaneGray 7 52
(Bryan Smart) *hld up: hdwy over 1f out: rdn: edgd lft lft and r.o to go 2nd post: nt rch wnr* **14/1**

5000 **3** *shd* **French**[33] 8717 4-9-5 **60**..................................................(p) CamHardie 4 64
(Antony Brittain) *trckd ldrs: wnt 2nd over 4f out: rdn to ld over 1f out: hdd ins fnl f: r.o* **5/1**[3]

0054 **4** *½* **Sir Harry Collins (IRE)**[7] 9102 3-8-7 **48** oh2............(v) AndrewMullen 8 50
(Michael Appleby) *hld up in tch: shkn up: nt clr run and hung lft over 1f out: r.o* **10/1**

1450 **5** *nk* **Zenovia (IRE)**[15] 8980 3-9-5 **60**....................................(tp) BenCurtis 3 64
(Archie Watson) *pushed along and prom: hmpd and lost pl sn after s: rdn over 1f out: r.o ins fnl f: nt rch ldrs* **7/4**[1]

0-00 **6** ½ **Dalness Express**[313] 544 4-8-2 **48** oh3 (t[1]) WilliamCox(5) 2 48
(John O'Shea) *chsd ldr tl over 4f out: remained handy: rdn over 1f out: styd on same pce wl ins fnl f* **150/1**

1060 **7** 1½ **Dodgy Bob**[12] 9033 4-9-6 **64** (v) PhilDennis(3) 10 59
(Michael Mullineaux) *prom: rdn over 1f out: styd on same pce fnl f* **11/1**

0600 **8** 2¼ **Blistering Dancer (IRE)**[55] 8185 7-8-7 **48** oh3 (b) FrannyNorton 5 36
(Tony Carroll) *led: rdn over 2f out: hdd over 1f out: wknd ins fnl f* **25/1**

1m 15.72s (1.22) **Going Correction** +0.20s/f (Slow) **8 Ran SP% 112.4**
Speed ratings (Par 101): **99,98,98,97,97 96,94,91**
CSF £32.01 CT £141.62 TOTE £3.10: £1.10, £3.40, £1.70; EX 31.40 Trifecta £170.80.
**Owner** Ronnie Docherty **Bred** P J H Whitten **Trained** Carluke, S Lanarks

**FOCUS**
Not the strongest of handicaps, but the winner did it well and can remain competitive if the handicapper is not too harsh. Ordinary form.

## 9216 BETWAY H'CAP (DIV II) 6f 20y (Tp)
**2:45** (2:48) (Class 6) (0-62,63) 3-Y-0+ **£2,587** (£770; £384; £192) **Stalls Low**

Form RPR

6556 **1** **Vroom (IRE)**[12] 9033 4-9-2 **63** (p) HarrisonShaw(7) 6 72
(Gay Kelleway) *trckd ldrs: racd keenly: shkn up to ld wl ins fnl f: r.o* **5/1**[3]

5000 **2** 1½ **Viva Verglas (IRE)**[12] 9033 6-9-7 **61** BenCurtis 10 65
(Daniel Mark Loughnane) *sn led: rdn and hdd ins fnl f: styd on same pce* **4/1**[2]

0003 **3** shd **Tally's Song**[43] 8496 4-8-4 **47** oh2 (p) GeorgiaCox(3) 8 51
(Grace Harris) *prom: chsd ldr over 4f out: rdn to ld ins fnl f: sn hdd: styd on same pce* **16/1**

0300 **4** ½ **Scotch Myst**[50] 8329 3-8-9 **56** SebastianWoods(7) 7 58
(Richard Fahey) *hld up in tch: lost pl wl over 3f out: hung lft and r.o ins fnl f* **11/4**[1]

0006 **5** ¾ **Kyllach Me (IRE)**[19] 8924 5-8-6 **53** (v) HarryRussell(7) 4 53
(Bryan Smart) *hld up: rdn over 2f out: r.o ins fnl f: nvr nrr* **8/1**

460 **6** 1¾ **Captain Bond**[19] 8931 3-9-6 **60** ShaneGray 1 54
(David O'Meara) *hld up: shkn up over 2f out: no imp fnl f* **8/1**

4066 **7** 2 **Ambitious Boy**[43] 8495 8-8-7 **47** oh2 (p) FrannyNorton 3 35
(John O'Shea) *s.i.s: nt clr run 1f out: nvr on terms* **6/1**

0600 **8** 1 **Beau Mistral (IRE)**[18] 8953 8-9-6 **60** GeorgeDowning 2 44
(Tony Carroll) *plld hrd and prom: rdn over 1f out: wknd ins fnl f* **20/1**

000- **9** 1 **Fred's Filly**[384] 8079 4-8-2 **47** oh2 (v) WilliamCox(5) 5 28
(Nick Mitchell) *s.i.s: hdwy over 3f out: shkn up over 1f out: wkng whn hmpd ins fnl f* **100/1**

1m 15.65s (1.15) **Going Correction** +0.20s/f (Slow) **9 Ran SP% 111.5**
Speed ratings (Par 101): **100,98,97,97,96 93,91,89,88**
CSF £24.01 CT £286.73 TOTE £6.50: £2.00, £1.70, £3.60; EX 32.30 Trifecta £320.40.
**Owner** Buy, Clarke, Sparham & Presland **Bred** Paul & T J Monaghan **Trained** Exning, Suffolk

**FOCUS**
A run-of-the-mill sprint handicap which saw the top weight show a little too much class for his rivals. The third, who has been rated to her best, limits the level.

## 9217 FOLLOW SUN BETS ON TWITTER H'CAP (DIV I) 1m 142y (Tp)
**3:15** (3:16) (Class 6) (0-53,53) 3-Y-0+ **£2,587** (£770; £384; £192) **Stalls Low**

Form RPR

0040 **1** **Sooqaan**[36] 8662 6-9-5 **51** CamHardie 5 58
(Antony Brittain) *hld up: racd keenly: hdwy over 3f out: rdn to ld over 1f out: styd on* **6/1**[3]

-422 **2** nk **Stamp Duty (IRE)**[53] 8247 9-9-0 **46** TomEaves 10 52
(Suzzanne France) *s.i.s: hld up: hdwy over 2f out: rdn over 1f out: sn hung lft: kpt on* **11/1**

524 **3** ½ **Satchville Flyer**[63] 7945 6-9-4 **53** MattCosham(3) 8 58
(David Evans) *hld up: hdwy on outer over 2f out: rdn and hung lft fr over 1f out: nt trble ldrs* **13/2**

5056 **4** nk **D'Waterside**[11] 9056 3-9-5 **53** (b[1]) BenCurtis 12 58
(David Loughnane) *w ldr tl led over 3f out: rdn: edgd rt and hdd over 1f out: styd on same pce wl ins fnl f* **4/1**[1]

3454 **5** 6 **Hellavashock**[13] 9017 4-8-11 **46** (v[1]) RowanScott(3) 6 38
(Alistair Whillans) *prom: rdn over 2f out: nt clr run over 1f out: wknd ins fnl f* **4/1**[1]

2500 **6** hd **Captain Sedgwick (IRE)**[35] 8675 3-9-0 **51** GeorgiaCox(3) 1 43
(John Spearing) *hld up: pushed along over 3f out: sme hdwy u.p over 1f out: styng on same pce whn hmpd ins fnl f* **16/1**

5053 **7** 1¼ **Joyful Dream (IRE)**[43] 8498 3-9-5 **53** PaulMulrennan 2 48
(John Butler) *trckd ldrs: racd keenly: shkn up whn hmpd over 1f out: sn hung lft and wknd* **11/2**[2]

050 **8** 2½ **Shadow's Girl**[14] 8995 5-8-9 **46** oh1 WilliamCox(5) 7 30
(Bernard Llewellyn) *hld up: rdn over 2f out: nvr on terms* **150/1**

4006 **9** 3½ **Cloud Nine (FR)**[23] 8869 4-9-1 **47** FrannyNorton 13 23
(Tony Carroll) *hld up in tch: stdd and lost pl over 6f out: n.d after* **18/1**

054 **10** 2½ **Spring Beauty**[75] 7574 3-8-9 **46** oh1 PhilDennis(3) 3 17
(John Weymes) *trckd ldrs: racd keenly: rdn and wknd over 2f out* **28/1**

6053 **11** 4 **Quick Monet (IRE)**[9] 9072 4-8-11 **46** oh1 CharlieBennett(3) 9 9
(Shaun Harris) *sn led: hdd over 3f out: sn rdn: wknd over 1f out* **22/1**

600 **12** 6 **Nagamaat (IRE)**[27] 8663 3-9-4 **52** (t[1]) GeorgeDowning 11 2
(Nikki Evans) *sn pushed along towards rr: bhd fnl 3f* **200/1**

1m 51.64s (1.54) **Going Correction** +0.20s/f (Slow)
**WFA** 3 from 4yo+ 2lb **12 Ran SP% 111.4**
Speed ratings (Par 101): **101,100,100,100,94 94,93,91,88,85 82,76**
CSF £64.09 CT £436.78 TOTE £9.30: £2.70, £2.50, £1.90; EX 85.10 Trifecta £389.80.
**Owner** Antony Brittain **Bred** J A And Mrs Duffy **Trained** Warthill, N Yorks
■ Stewards' Enquiry : Ben Curtis two-day ban: careless riding (Dec 27-28)

**FOCUS**
Ordinary fare. One or two of these were quite keen early on which suggests they did not go much of a gallop. It's been rated around the balance of the first four.

## 9218 FOLLOW SUN BETS ON TWITTER H'CAP (DIV II) 1m 142y (Tp)
**3:50** (3:52) (Class 6) (0-53,53) 3-Y-0+ **£2,587** (£770; £384; £192) **Stalls Low**

Form RPR

1605 **1** **Secret Lightning (FR)**[26] 8811 5-9-0 **51** (b) KevinLundie(5) 11 57
(Michael Appleby) *a.p: chsd ldr 2f out: rdn to ld over 1f out: r.o* **40/1**

464 **2** 2 **Sheer Intensity (IRE)**[27] 8799 4-9-0 **49** MattCosham(3) 6 51+
(David Evans) *hld up: hdwy u.p over 1f out: r.o to go 2nd nr fin: nt rch wnr* **9/1**

006 **3** ½ **Living Leader**[8] 9084 8-9-0 **51** BenRobinson(5) 12 52
(Grace Harris) *prom: chsd ldr over 5f out: led over 2f out: rdn and hdd over 1f out: styd on same pce ins fnl f* **16/1**

0-00 **4** 2 **Alligator**[18] 8948 3-8-12 **46** oh1 (b) GeorgeDowning 7 43
(Tony Carroll) *trckd ldrs: rdn over 1f out: styd on same pce fnl f* **33/1**

0041 **5** hd **Cookie Ring (IRE)**[14] 8994 6-8-9 **48** (t) FayeMcManoman(7) 10 44+
(Kristin Stubbs) *s.i.s: hld up: r.o ins fnl f: nt trble ldrs* **13/2**

5344 **6** 1 **Sunshineandbubbles**[11] 9056 4-9-5 **51** (p) PaulMulrennan 4 45
(Jennie Candlish) *led early: sn lost pl: shkn up over 1f out: styd on: nt trble ldrs* **11/4**[1]

0005 **7** ½ **Pensax Lady (IRE)**[27] 8800 4-9-4 **50** BenCurtis 5 43
(Daniel Mark Loughnane) *hld up: hdwy over 4f out: rdn over 2f out: styd on same pce fr over 1f out* **11/2**[3]

550 **8** 2 **Sir Jamie**[14] 8994 4-9-1 **47** (p[1]) FrannyNorton 1 36
(Tony Carroll) *hld up: rdn over 1f out: nvr on terms* **9/2**[2]

0000 **9** 5 **Chookie Valentine**[71] 7704 4-9-0 **46** oh1 (p) JasonHart 9 24
(Keith Dalgleish) *racd keenly: sn led: hdd over 6f out: remained handy: nt clr run fr over 2f out tl swtchd rt over 1f out: wknd fnl f* **11/1**

0400 **10** 1½ **Peak Storm**[25] 8299 8-9-7 **53** (tp) TimmyMurphy 3 28
(John O'Shea) *hld up: nvr nr to chal* **20/1**

0500 **11** 8 **Machiavelian Storm (IRE)**[9] 9073 5-8-9 **46** oh1 (tp) WilliamCox(5) 8 4
(Richard Mitchell) *hld up: hdwy over 5f out: wknd over 2f out* **150/1**

000 **12** 2¾ **Sunset Bounty**[42] 8504 3-8-5 **46** oh1 MillyNaseb(7) 13
(Julia Feilden) *pushed along to chse ldrs: led over 6f out: rdn and hdd over 2f out: wknd over 1f out* **50/1**

1m 52.49s (2.39) **Going Correction** +0.20s/f (Slow)
**WFA** 3 from 4yo+ 2lb **12 Ran SP% 110.5**
Speed ratings (Par 101): **97,95,94,93,92 91,91,89,85,83 76,74**
CSF £336.06 CT £5730.93 TOTE £17.90: £5.80, £2.40, £4.00; EX 226.30 Trifecta £2230.80.
**Owner** Mick Appleby Racing **Bred** Jeffrey Colin Smith **Trained** Oakham, Rutland

**FOCUS**
Not a strong gallop again and, unsurprisingly, most of those who raced prominently fared best. It's been rated around the first two.

## 9219 BET & WATCH AT SUNBETS.CO.UK H'CAP 7f 36y (Tp)
**4:25** (4:29) (Class 5) (0-66,66) 3-Y-0+ **£3,557** (£1,058; £529; £264) **Stalls High**

Form RPR

3021 **1** **Grey Destiny**[36] 8659 7-9-2 **61** CamHardie 3 71
(Antony Brittain) *s.i.s: hld up: hdwy and edgd lft over 1f out: r.o to ld wl ins fnl f* **6/1**[2]

02 **2** ½ **Mansfield**[7] 9094 4-9-6 **65** (h) FrannyNorton 9 73
(Michael Wigham) *plld hrd and prom: wnt 2nd over 5f out tl led over 2f out: rdn over 1f out: hdd wl ins fnl f* **4/5**[1]

2634 **3** 1¾ **Ubla (IRE)**[12] 9032 4-8-12 **62** (p) WilliamCox(5) 7 66
(Gay Kelleway) *trckd ldrs: racd keenly: nt clr run and swtchd rt over 2f out: chsd ldr over 1f out tl rdn ins fnl f: styd on same pce* **18/1**

-305 **4** 4 **Pudding Chare (IRE)**[19] 8931 3-9-0 **66** SebastianWoods(7) 6 60
(Richard Fahey) *hld up: hdwy over 1f out: edgd lft ins fnl f: nt rch ldrs* **18/1**

0060 **5** 1 **Chelwood Gate (IRE)**[18] 8946 7-9-0 **59** (v) PaulMulrennan 2 56
(Conor Dore) *hld up: hdwy and hmpd over 1f out: swtchd rt: r.o ins fnl f: nt rch ldrs* **16/1**

**6** ½ **Butoolat**[33] 8730 3-8-11 **56** JasonHart 8 47
(Keith Dalgleish) *led over 6f out: hdd over 5f out: remained handy: rdn over 1f out: wknd fnl f* **15/2**[3]

6005 **7** 1¼ **Ad Vitam (IRE)**[19] 8930 9-8-13 **58** (bt) TomEaves 5 45
(Suzzanne France) *hld up: hdwy 1/2-way: carried rt over 2f out: rdn over 1f out: edgd lft and wknd fnl f* **22/1**

460 **8** 1¾ **Frozen Lake (USA)**[18] 8958 5-8-13 **63** (h[1]) BenRobinson(5) 12 46
(John O'Shea) *s.s: hld up: shkn up over 2f out: nvr on terms* **20/1**

0000 **9** 1 **Appleberry (IRE)**[12] 9033 5-9-1 **60** AndrewMullen 4 41
(Michael Appleby) *led early: chsd ldrs: rdn over 2f out: nt clr run wl over 1f out: wkng whn hmpd ins fnl f* **40/1**

**10** 3¾ **One Liner**[40] 8569 3-9-0 **59** (p) TimmyMurphy 1 31
(John O'Shea) *sn outpcd* **100/1**

6 **11** 1¾ **Evanescent (IRE)**[72] 7691 8-9-1 **60** GeorgeDowning 11 27
(Tony Carroll) *racd keenly: led over 5f out: hdd over 2f out: wknd over 1f out* **100/1**

1m 29.36s (0.56) **Going Correction** +0.20s/f (Slow) **11 Ran SP% 111.5**
Speed ratings (Par 103): **104,103,101,96,95 95,93,91,90,86 84**
CSF £10.05 CT £78.34 TOTE £6.90: £1.90, £1.02, £4.30; EX 15.90 Trifecta £99.70.
**Owner** Antony Brittain **Bred** Northgate Lodge Stud Ltd **Trained** Warthill, N Yorks

**FOCUS**
A fair handicap which saw two in-form rivals fight out the finish. The form has a solid look to it. A clear pb from the winner, with the runner-up rated to his latest effort.

## 9220 SUNBETS.CO.UK H'CAP 7f 36y (Tp)
**4:55** (4:58) (Class 4) (0-79,79) 3-Y-0+ **£5,498** (£1,636; £817; £408) **Stalls High**

Form RPR

2000 **1** **Rouge Nuage (IRE)**[20] 8907 7-9-2 **74** TomEaves 10 82
(Conrad Allen) *hld up: hdwy over 2f out: rdn to chse ldr and edgd lft over 1f out: r.o to ld wl ins fnl f* **18/1**

4450 **2** hd **Inaam (IRE)**[137] 5415 4-9-0 **79** SebastianWoods(7) 5 86
(Richard Fahey) *trckd ldrs: racd keenly: wnt 2nd over 2f out: led over 1f out: rdn and hdd wl ins fnl f* **8/1**

2403 **3** 2¾ **Lagenda**[12] 9025 4-9-5 **77** (p) ShaneGray 7 77
(Kristin Stubbs) *hld up: hdwy over 1f out: r.o: nt rch ldrs* **7/2**[1]

6630 **4** ½ **Rock Warbler (IRE)**[7] 9100 4-9-3 **75** (t) PaulMulrennan 3 74
(Oliver Greenall) *hld up: hdwy and nt clr run over 1f out: swtchd lft: styd on* **15/2**

0024 **5** 1½ **Ballymore Castle (IRE)**[26] 8818 5-9-3 **75** (p) AndrewMullen 1 70
(Richard Fahey) *chsd ldrs: hmpd after 1f: rdn over 2f out: no ex ins fnl f* **15/2**

0054 **6** 1¼ **Athassel**[8] 9083 8-9-3 **78** MattCosham(3) 4 69
(David Evans) *s.i.s: hld up: rdn over 2f out: r.o ins fnl f: nvr nrr* **11/2**[3]

0002 **7** ¾ **Mr Christopher (IRE)**[12] 9029 5-9-0 **75** (p) PaddyPilley(3) 11 64
(Tom Dascombe) *led 1f: chsd ldr tl led again 3f out: rdn and hdd over 1f out: wknd ins fnl f* **4/1**[2]

1002 **8** 8 **Baltic Prince (IRE)**[18] 8958 7-9-0 **72** GeorgeDowning 2 40
(Tony Carroll) *led 6f out tl 3f out: sn rdn: wknd over 1f out* **9/1**

0002 **9** 5 **Alkashaaf (USA)**[56] 8158 3-8-9 **74** (t) TobyEley(7) 6 28
(Daniel Mark Loughnane) *s.s: a in rr* **40/1**

1030 **10** 1 **Case Key**[39] 8600 4-9-3 **75** (p) BenCurtis 12 26
(Michael Appleby) *prom: pushed along and lost pl 1/2-way: wknd over 2f out* **22/1**

1m 28.18s (-0.62) **Going Correction** +0.20s/f (Slow) **10 Ran SP% 114.3**
Speed ratings (Par 105): **111,110,107,107,105 103,103,93,88,87**
CSF £151.61 CT £627.41 TOTE £21.80: £5.40, £2.40, £1.80; EX 123.40 Trifecta £838.00.
**Owner** sportsdays.co.uk **Bred** Dermot Farrington **Trained** Newmarket, Suffolk
■ Stewards' Enquiry : Paddy Pilley two-day ban: careless riding (Dec 27-28)
Paul Mulrennan caution: careless riding

**FOCUS**
Quite a competitive handicap which produced a good finish and a determined winner. The winner has been rated to his September form and the runner-up close to form.

## 9221 BETWAY CASINO H'CAP 1m 4f 51y (Tp)
5:25 (5:26) (Class 6) (0-52,52) 3-Y-O+ £2,587 (£770; £384; £192) Stalls Low

Form RPR
5026 1 **Iley Boy**[26] 8815 3-8-12 **47**....................(p) BenCurtis 7 54
(John Gallagher) *hld up: hdwy over 3f out: rdn to ld wl ins fnl f: edgd lft: styd on* **13/2**[3]
0302 2 1 **New Abbey Angel (IRE)**[36] 8662 4-9-7 **52**.................... PhillipMakin 12 56
(Keith Dalgleish) *dwlt: hld up: hdwy and hung lft over 1f out: styd on* **8/1**
0003 3 nk **Dream Serenade**[9] 9077 4-9-6 **51**....................(p) AndrewMullen 10 55
(Michael Appleby) *led after 1f: rdn over 1f out: hung rt and hdd wl ins fnl f: styng on same pce whn hung lft towards fin* **25/1**
0212 4 2 ½ **Kaisan**[7] 9095 4-9-7 **52**....................(t) TimmyMurphy 9 52
(Bernard Llewellyn) *prom: pushed along 4f out: rdn and hung lft over 1f out: styd on same pce fnl f* **2/1**[1]
6400 5 1 **Rowlestonerendezvu**[11] 9056 4-9-7 **52**.................... GeorgeDowning 4 50
(Tony Carroll) *chsd ldrs: wnt 2nd 3f out: sn rdn and ev ch: no ex wl ins fnl f* **9/1**
0056 6 ¾ **Bridal March**[83] 7325 3-8-11 **46**....................(p) FrannyNorton 3 44
(John Mackie) *chsd ldrs: nt clr run and lost pl over 2f out: styd on ins fnl f* **33/1**
3 7 2 ¼ **Remember Nerja (IRE)**[25] 8852 3-8-9 **47**.................... EoinWalsh[(3)] 1 42
(Barry Leavy) *hld up: pushed along over 2f out: nvr on terns* **20/1**
0425 8 6 **Dibloam (USA)**[7] 9095 4-8-12 **46**....................(h) MattCosham[(3)] 8 30
(David Evans) *hld up: racd keenly: hdwy over 9f out: chsd ldr 8f out tl rdn 3f out: wkng whn hmpd over 1f out* **7/2**[2]
6523 9 hd **Siyahamba (IRE)**[12] 9030 3-8-8 **50**.................... HarryRussell[(7)] 11 35
(Bryan Smart) *hld up: pushed along over 5f out: n.d* **25/1**
5420 10 ½ **Anton Dolin (IRE)**[55] 2272 9-9-3 **51**....................(be) PhilDennis[(3)] 2 34
(Michael Mullineaux) *prom: lost pl 9f out: rdn over 3f out: wknd over 2f out* **66/1**
2056 11 3 **Haldaw**[27] 8800 3-8-9 **49**.................... WilliamCox[(5)] 6 28
(Mick Channon) *led 1f: chsd ldr tl 8f out: remained handy: rdn over 2f out: wkng whn nt clr run over 1f out* **22/1**
0630 12 2 ¾ **Netley Abbey**[26] 8815 3-8-8 **46**....................(p) GeorgiaCox[(3)] 5 21
(Karen George) *prom: lost pl over 4f out: wknd over 3f out* **16/1**
2m 42.37s (1.57) **Going Correction** +0.20s/f (Slow)
**WFA** 3 from 4yo+ 4lb 12 Ran SP% **117.1**
Speed ratings (Par 101): **102,101,101,99,98 98,96,92,92,92 90,88**
CSF £51.21 CT £1223.92 TOTE £7.20: £2.20, £3.40, £4.40; EX 63.30 Trifecta £269.40.
**Owner** J Gallagher **Bred** C R Marks (Banbury) **Trained** Chastleton, Oxon

**FOCUS**
A fairly moderate middle-distance handicap, but the winner has time on his side and may be improving. Straightforward form.
T/Plt: £250.60 to a £1 stake. Pool: £82,841.98 - 241.24 winning units. T/Qpdt: £53.50 to a £1 stake. Pool: £9,036.90 - 124.93 winning units. **Colin Roberts**

9222 - 9229a (Foreign Racing) - See Raceform Interactive

# 9136 CHELMSFORD (A.W) (L-H)
Thursday, December 14

**OFFICIAL GOING: Polytrack: standard**
Wind: light, half behind Weather: dry

## 9230 BET TOTEPLACEPOT AT BETFRED.COM NURSERY H'CAP 7f (P)
5:45 (5:45) (Class 6) (0-60,62) 2-Y-O £3,234 (£962; £481; £240) Stalls Low

Form RPR
0056 1 **Roseau City**[13] 9024 2-9-2 **55**....................(b) SeanLevey 6 62
(David Elsworth) *rousted along leaving stalls: sn trcking ldrs: swtchd rt and effrt over 1f out: hdwy u.p to chal ins fnl f: led 50yds: styd on strly and gng away at fin* **10/1**
3004 2 1 ¾ **Bezos (IRE)**[111] 6366 2-9-2 **62**....................(p[1]) RossaRyan[(7)] 1 64
(Richard Hannon) *trckd ldrs: effrt and rdn to ld over 1f out: drvn ins fnl f: hdd and nt match pce of wnr fnl 50yds* **11/4**[1]
6600 3 1 **Bad Dog**[121] 6022 2-9-3 **56**....................(v[1]) TomEaves 10 56
(Michael Easterby) *midfield: hdwy to trck ldrs after 2f: ev ch 2f out: edging lft u.p over 1f out: no ex and btn 100yds out: wknd towards fin* **28/1**
000 4 2 ¼ **Wilfred Owen**[28] 8794 2-8-11 **50**....................(b[1]) RobertHavlin 3 44
(John Gosden) *t.k.h: hld up in tch in midfield: swtchd rt and nt clr run over 1f out: sn rdn on ins fnl f: nvr threatened ldrs* **5/1**[3]
0306 5 ½ **Westfield Wonder**[15] 8996 2-9-1 **54**.................... FrannyNorton 2 46
(Ronald Thompson) *dwlt and bustled along leaving stalls: in tch in midfield: swtchd rt and effrt over 1f out: kpt on same pce ins fnl f* **8/1**
6000 6 ¾ **Haven's View**[15] 9002 2-9-2 **55**.................... ShaneKelly 9 45
(Richard Hughes) *s.i.s and squeezed for room leaving stalls: sn swtchd lft and in tch in last trio: effrt over 1f out: rdn and hdwy 1f out: pushed along and kpt on fnl 100yds: nvr trbld ldrs* **12/1**
0506 7 nk **Grasmere (IRE)**[28] 8793 2-9-4 **57**.................... RobertWinston 11 46
(Alan Bailey) *w ldr: rdn and ev ch over 2f out tl lost pl ent fnl f: wknd ins fnl f* **14/1**
006 8 3 **Pammi**[99] 6816 2-8-9 **48**.................... LukeMorris 7 29
(Anthony Carson) *dwlt and bustled along early: in tch in last trio: rdn 2f out: no imp: n.d* **18/1**
4440 9 hd **Dashing Dusty (IRE)**[8] 9090 2-9-7 **60**....................(p[1]) DougieCostello 5 41
(Jamie Osborne) *led tl rdn and hdd over 1f out: sn outpcd and btn 1f out: wknd ins fnl f* **9/2**[2]
000 10 ½ **Broughton Excels**[27] 8809 2-8-13 **52**.................... StevieDonohoe 4 31
(Henry Spiller) *hld up in tch in midfield: effrt over 1f out: awkward hd carriage and no imp: wknd ins fnl f* **6/1**
0554 11 8 **Rose Of Shiraz**[19] 8943 2-9-0 **53**....................(p[1]) LiamKeniry 8 11
(J S Moore) *in tch in last pair: swtchd rt and effrt wl over 1f out: no imp: wknd fnl f* **33/1**
1m 26.67s (-0.53) **Going Correction** -0.15s/f (Stan) 11 Ran SP% **122.0**
Speed ratings (Par 94): **97,95,93,91,90 89,89,86,85,85 76**
CSF £39.09 CT £792.90 TOTE £12.30: £2.90, £1.50, £7.00; EX 46.10 Trifecta £1177.00.
**Owner** Hot To Trot Syndicate - Roseau City **Bred** Stowell Hill Ltd **Trained** Newmarket, Suffolk

**FOCUS**
A low-grade nursery. A filly in second-time blinkers came home in front of three rivals wearing headgear for the first time. The winner has been rated to her best, and the runner-up close to his best.

## 9231 BET TOTEJACKPOT AT BETFRED.COM NOVICE AUCTION STKS 7f (P)
6:15 (6:17) (Class 6) 2-Y-O £3,234 (£962; £481; £240) Stalls Low

Form RPR
0243 1 **I'm Yer Man**[8] 9098 2-8-10 76.................... ShaneGray 1 74
(Ann Duffield) *trckd ldrs: effrt to chal over 1f out: rdn to ld 1f out: styd on to assert ins fnl f* **5/4**[1]
044 2 1 **Demons And Wizards (IRE)**[35] 8701 2-9-0 0.................... MartinDwyer 2 75
(Sylvester Kirk) *trckd ldrs: effrt to press ldng pair 1f out: drvn and kpt on same pce ins fnl f: wnt 2nd towards fin* **11/4**[2]
3 ¾ **Precious Silk (IRE)** 2-8-7 0.................... OscarPereira 8 66
(Jose Santos) *w ldr tl led 2f out: sn rdn: hdd 1f out: unable qck and one pced ins fnl f: lost 2nd towards fin* **14/1**
4 ¾ **Racehorse** 2-8-5 0.................... KieranO'Neill 9 62
(Hughie Morrison) *s.i.s: t.k.h and rn green in last trio: effrt over 1f out: hdwy to chse clr ldng trio 1f out: kpt on ins fnl f: nvr threatened ldrs* **12/1**
0 5 ½ **Haverland (IRE)**[59] 8112 2-9-0 0.................... StevieDonohoe 4 70
(Charlie Fellowes) *stdd s: t.k.h: hld up in last pair: effrt and c wd bnd 2f out: hdwy over 1f out: kpt on ins fnl f: nvr threatened ldrs* **7/2**[3]
0 6 3 **Little Aub**[15] 8988 2-8-3 0.................... NicolaCurrie[(7)] 3 58
(Mark Usher) *bmpd leaving stalls: midfield: rdn and outpcd over 2f out: wknd ins fnl f* **33/1**
7 6 **Lenin (IRE)** 2-8-12 0.................... LiamKeniry 6 45
(J S Moore) *s.i.s: rn green and on and off the bridle in rr: outpcd over 2f out: bhd whn swtchd lft ins fnl f* **25/1**
00 8 1 ¾ **Pretty Pearl**[50] 8347 2-7-12 0.................... DarraghKeenan[(7)] 5 32
(Robert Eddery) *in tch in midfield: 5th and unable qck u.p over 2f out: lost pl and wl hld over 1f out: wknd fnl f* **40/1**
060 9 1 ¾ **Boss For A Day**[15] 8987 2-8-12 0....................(p[1]) JosephineGordon 7 37
(J S Moore) *led tl 2f out: sn lost pl: bhd ins fnl f* **20/1**
1m 26.62s (-0.58) **Going Correction** -0.15s/f (Stan) 9 Ran SP% **121.7**
Speed ratings (Par 94): **97,95,95,94,93 90,83,81,79**
CSF £4.92 TOTE £2.00: £1.10, £1.40, £4.70; EX 5.90 Trifecta £40.10.
**Owner** The Birrafun Partnership **Bred** W H R John And Partners **Trained** Constable Burton, N Yorks

**FOCUS**
They went steady early and it was an advantage to be handy. The level is a bit fluid. The runner-up has been rated as taking a small step forward.

## 9232 BET TOTEQUADPOT AT BETFRED.COM H'CAP 7f (P)
6:45 (6:47) (Class 7) (0-50,52) 3-Y-O+ £2,587 (£770; £384; £192) Stalls Low

Form RPR
05U1 1 **Hidden Stash**[19] 8949 3-9-8 **51**....................(p) HollieDoyle 14 62
(William Stone) *broke wl to ld fr wd draw and crossed to inner: mde all: rdn and kicked clr wl over 1f out: in command after: styd on wl* **7/1**[3]
0433 2 2 ½ **Black Truffle (FR)**[19] 8948 7-8-11 **47**....................(v) NicolaCurrie[(7)] 8 51
(Mark Usher) *t.k.h: trckd ldrs: effrt to chse clr wnr wl over 1f out: clr 2nd but no imp after: kpt on* **4/1**[1]
6466 3 2 **Tasaaboq**[16] 8980 6-9-6 **49**....................(t) JosephineGordon 10 48
(Phil McEntee) *hld up wl in tch in midfield and travelled strly: effrt to chse clr ldng pair over 1f out: kpt on same pce and no imp after* **4/1**[1]
5200 4 2 ¾ **Luduamf (IRE)**[19] 8948 3-8-9 **45**.................... RossaRyan[(7)] 1 36
(Richard Hannon) *hld up off the pce in last quintet: clsd over 2f out: rdn and effrt over 1f out: swed rt 1f out: kpt on same pce ins fnl f: nvr threatened ldrs* **9/2**[2]
000- 5 hd **Gift From God**[50] 7754 4-9-0 **50**....................(t) AledBeech[(7)] 9 41
(Hugo Froud) *hld up off the pce in last pair: shkn up over 1f out: rdn and hdwy 1f out: styd on wl ins fnl f: nvr trbld ldrs* **25/1**
0-45 6 nse **Harvest Ranger**[53] 8255 3-9-2 **45**.................... KieranShoemark 6 36
(Michael Appleby) *chsd wnr tl over 5f out: styd trcking ldrs tl outpcd u.p over 1f out: wknd ins fnl f* **10/1**
6505 7 1 ¾ **Captain Scooby**[8] 9102 11-9-2 **45**....................(b) FrannyNorton 4 31
(Richard Guest) *stdd s: hld up in rr: clsd onto bk of main gp: effrt and sme hdwy over 1f out: sn no imp and wl hld fnl f* **11/1**
0340 8 nk **Lutine Charlie (IRE)**[6] 9141 10-9-2 **45**....................(p) MartinDwyer 12 30
(Emma Owen) *trckd ldrs: effrt and rdn over 1f out: fnd little and sn btn: wknd ins fnl f* **14/1**
0000 9 3 ½ **Encapsulated**[27] 8823 7-8-13 **47**.................... RhiainIngram[(5)] 5 23
(Roger Ingram) *taken down early and led rdrless to post: off the pce in last quintet: effrt and swtchd rt over 1f out: nvr trbld ldrs* **9/1**
0000 10 10 **Royal Rettie**[16] 8985 5-9-7 **50**....................(h) DannyBrock 13
(Paddy Butler) *taken down early: pushed along in midfield on outer: lost pl over 2f out: bhd over 1f out* **33/1**
11 3 ½ **Sharp Operator**[145] 5172 4-9-9 **52**.................... LukeMorris 11
(Charlie Wallis) *s.i.s: sn rcvrd and hdwy to chse wnr over 5f out tl wl over 1f out: sn dropped out: bhd and eased ins fnl f* **12/1**
0/0- 12 55 **Sweet Piccolo**[534] 3734 7-8-13 **45**.................... CallumShepherd[(3)] 2
(Paddy Butler) *a off the pce in rr: lost tch and eased over 1f out: t.o* **66/1**
1m 26.82s (-0.38) **Going Correction** -0.15s/f (Stan) 12 Ran SP% **120.7**
Speed ratings (Par 97): **96,93,90,87,87 87,85,85,81,69 65,2**
CSF £35.31 CT £133.00 TOTE £7.40: £2.20, £1.70, £1.90; EX 38.80 Trifecta £112.40.
**Owner** Miss Caroline Scott **Bred** Kingsclere Stud **Trained** West Wickham, Cambs

**FOCUS**
Despite the big field, few got into this. The winner has been rated back to his early 2017 form.

## 9233 BET TOTEEXACTA AT BETFRED.COM H'CAP 1m (P)
7:15 (7:17) (Class 2) (0-105,102) 3-Y-O+ £12,938 (£3,850; £1,924; £962) Stalls Low

Form RPR
0200 1 **Mutawathea**[42] 8547 6-9-5 **97**....................(p) RobertHavlin 3 106
(Simon Crisford) *chsd ldr tl rdn to chal over 1f out: led 1f out: styd on wl* **10/3**[2]
0305 2 1 ¾ **London (FR)**[7] 9125 4-8-4 **89**....................(h) NicolaCurrie[(7)] 9 94
(Phil McEntee) *led: rdn and jnd over 1f out: styd on same pce ins fnl f* **11/1**
2-00 3 nk **Abe Lincoln (USA)**[152] 4916 4-9-5 **97**....................(tp) KieranShoemark 6 101
(Jeremy Noseda) *chsd ldrs: effrt over 1f out: hung rt and kpt on same pce ins fnl f* **10/3**[2]
4321 4 ¾ **Pactolus (IRE)**[15] 8999 6-9-4 **99**....................(t) AaronJones[(3)] 2 102
(Stuart Williams) *chsd ldrs: effrt over 1f out: kpt on same pce u.p ins fnl f* **5/2**[1]
0006 5 1 **Mythical Madness**[15] 8999 6-9-5 **97**....................(v) TomEaves 8 97
(David O'Meara) *stdd s: hld up in tch in last pair: pushed along over 2f out: kpt on same pce u.p ins fnl f: nvr threatened ldrs* **14/1**

0-12 **6** ½ **Calling Out (FR)**[301] 767 6-9-10 **102**.......................... LiamKeniry 1 101
(David Simcock) *hld up in tch in midfield: effrt over 1f out: rdn 1f out: kpt on ins fnl f: nvr threatened ldrs* **14/1**

0001 **7** 8 **Steel Train (FR)**[21] 8905 6-9-7 **99**.......................... MartinHarley 5 80
(David O'Meara) *hld up in tch towards rr: sltly impeded after 1f out: effrt over 2f out: keeping on same pce and no imp whn edgd lft ins fnl f: eased fnl 100yds* **6/1**[3]

4003 **8** 1 **Certificate**[75] 7603 6-9-10 **102**.......................... JosephineGordon 7 80
(Conor Dore) *chsd ldrs: unable qck u.p over 1f out: wknd fnl f* **25/1**

3000 **9** 17 **Bancnuanaheireann (IRE)**[131] 5643 10-9-0 **92**....... AlistairRawlinson 4 31
(Michael Appleby) *dwlt and pushed along leaving stalls: swtchd rt and hdwy into midfield after 1f: rdn over 3f out: dropped to last 2f out: sn wl btn: eased fnl f* **33/1**

1m 37.36s (-2.54) **Going Correction** -0.15s/f (Stan) **9** Ran SP% **117.5**
Speed ratings (Par 109): **106,104,103,103,102 101,93,92,75**
CSF £40.42 CT £133.36 TOTE £4.40: £1.70, £3.10, £1.60; EX 44.10 Trifecta £202.30.
**Owner** Sultan Ali **Bred** Genesis Green Stud & P Scott **Trained** Newmarket, Suffolk

**FOCUS**
A good handicap in which it paid to race close to the pace. The winner has been rated back to his best, and the runner-up to form.

## 9234 BET TOTETRIFECTA AT BETFRED.COM H'CAP 5f (P)
7:45 (7:45) (Class 4) (0-80,87) 3-Y-0+ **£6,469** (£1,925; £962; £481) **Stalls** Low

Form RPR

000 **1** **Rosina**[21] 8913 4-9-5 **78**.......................... (p) FrannyNorton 4 86
(Ann Duffield) *restless in stalls: hld up in rr: clsd to chse ldrs and swtchd rt 1f out: str run to ld 100yds out: sn in command and r.o wl* **12/1**

4066 **2** 1½ **Mr Pocket (IRE)**[19] 8950 3-8-11 **70**.......................... (b) RaulDaSilva 2 73
(Paul Cole) *short of room and snatched up sn after s: midfield: effrt to chse ldrs on inner over 1f out: ev ch ins fnl f: chsd wnr and kpt on same pce fnl 100yds* **7/2**[2]

2411 **3** 1¾ **You're Cool**[42] 8540 5-9-6 **79**.......................... JoeDoyle 7 75
(John Balding) *sn led: rdn over 1f out: hdd 100yds out: no ex and wknd towards fin* **5/2**[1]

4404 **4** hd **Penny Dreadful**[6] 9136 5-8-10 **69**.......................... (p) KieranO'Neill 5 65
(Scott Dixon) *hung rt: led early: sn hdd and chsd ldr: effrt over 1f out: no ex ins fnl f: wknd towards fin* **11/1**

2256 **5** 3 **Monumental Man**[77] 7538 8-9-7 **80**.......................... (p) WilliamCarson 1 65
(Michael Attwater) *chsd ldrs: unable qck over 1f out: wknd ins fnl f* **6/1**[3]

5001 **6** 2¾ **Union Rose**[9] 9079 5-10-0 **87** 6ex.......................... (p) LukeMorris 3 62
(Ronald Harris) *midfield: rdn over 2f out: unable qck and outpcd over 1f out: wknd ins fnl f* **7/2**[2]

0640 **7** 6 **Juan Horsepower**[13] 9020 3-9-2 **75**.......................... (p) TomMarquand 6 28
(Richard Hannon) *wnt rt s: sn bustled in last trio: struggling in last 2f out: wknd over 1f out* **8/1**

58.6s (-1.60) **Going Correction** -0.15s/f (Stan) **7** Ran SP% **114.4**
Speed ratings (Par 105): **106,103,100,100,95 91,81**
CSF £53.56 TOTE £7.90: £5.70, £2.70; EX 61.40 Trifecta £445.50.
**Owner** Ms J Bianco **Bred** Charley Knoll Partnership **Trained** Constable Burton, N Yorks

**FOCUS**
This was run at a good gallop and the hold-up horses came to the fore. The winner has been rated to the level of her Ayr win in August.

## 9235 BET TOTEWIN AT BETFRED.COM MEDIAN AUCTION MAIDEN STKS 1m 5f 66y(P)
8:15 (8:16) (Class 6) 3-5-Y-0 **£3,234** (£962; £481; £240) **Stalls** Low

Form RPR

**1** **Bardd (IRE)**[23] 5-9-9 0.......................... LukeMorris 7 74
(Nicky Henderson) *hld up in tch in midfield and travelled strly: hdwy to trck ldr 5f out: rdn to ld over 1f out: sn asserted and hung lft: styd on* **2/1**[2]

5322 **2** 1¾ **Prerogative (IRE)**[15] 7905 3-9-5 73.......................... (p) TomMarquand 3 73
(Tony Carroll) *trckd ldrs: effrt in 3rd over 2f out: chsd wnr over 1f out: kpt on same pce u.p ins fnl f* **5/1**[3]

30 **3** 3 **Tiar Na Nog (IRE)**[64] 7948 5-9-4 0.......................... RobertWinston 2 62
(Denis Coakley) *t.k.h: hld up in tch in last pair: shkn up over 1f out: wnt 3rd 1f out: nudged along and kpt on same pce ins fnl f: eased towards fin* **8/1**

**4** 3½ **Shaella (IRE)**[30] 3-9-0 0.......................... MartinHarley 1 59
(Jane Chapple-Hyam) *t.k.h: hld up in tch in last pair: effrt in 4th 2f out: no imp over 1f out: 4th and wknd ins fnl f* **15/8**[1]

5640 **5** 8 **Nevalyashka**[13] 9027 3-9-0 65.......................... (b[1]) MartinDwyer 6 47
(Marcus Tregoning) *t.k.h: hld up in midfield on outer: hdwy to join ldr 9f out tl led 5f out: rdn and hdd over 1f out: sn btn and edgd rt: wknd fnl f* **8/1**

**6** 17 **Whitmel**[49] 4-9-9 0.......................... AlistairRawlinson 5 25
(Michael Appleby) *t.k.h: chsd ldr tl 9f out: styd in tch in midfield: rdn over 3f out: wknd over 1f out: bhd fnl f* **33/1**

**7** 15 **Miss Tenacity** 4-9-4 0.......................... DannyBrock 4
(Jane Chapple-Hyam) *rn green thrght: led tl 5f out: sn rdn: dropped out qckly 2f out: eased over 1f out: t.o* **25/1**

2m 56.44s (2.84) **Going Correction** -0.15s/f (Stan) **7** Ran SP% **113.8**
**WFA** 3 from 4yo+ 4lb
Speed ratings (Par 101): **85,83,82,79,75 64,55**
CSF £12.39 TOTE £2.70: £1.40, £2.30; EX 10.50 Trifecta £41.40.
**Owner** Elite Racing Club **Bred** Tullamaine Castle Stud **Trained** Upper Lambourn, Berks

**FOCUS**
A weak maiden.

## 9236 BOOK TICKETS AT CHELMSFORDCITYRACECOURSE.COM H'CAP 1m 2f (P)
8:45 (8:45) (Class 5) (0-75,77) 3-Y-0+ **£5,175** (£1,540; £769; £384) **Stalls** Low

Form RPR

0503 **1** **Mullarkey**[27] 8814 3-9-0 **68**.......................... JosephineGordon 4 76
(John Best) *wnt rt s: dropped to rr after 1f: hld up in tch: effrt 2f out: clsd to chse ldrs u.p 1f out: styd on to ld wl ins fnl f: r.o wl* **4/1**[2]

1021 **2** 1 **Pinnata (IRE)**[28] 8797 3-9-9 **77**.......................... (t) SeanLevey 9 83
(Stuart Williams) *stdd and swtchd lft after s: t.k.h: hld up in tch in last trio: effrt to chse ldrs and swtchd rt 2f out: kpt on u.p and ev ch ins fnl f: kpt on same pce fnl 75yds* **5/2**[1]

2216 **3** hd **Glendun (USA)**[13] 9025 3-9-9 **77**.......................... (p) RyanTate 1 82
(James Eustace) *led for 2f: chsd ldr: rdn over 1f out: kpt on u.p to ld ins fnl f: hdd and one pced wl ins fnl f* **4/1**[2]

-112 **4** 2 **Enigmatic (IRE)**[8] 9100 3-9-5 **73**.......................... DougieCostello 2 74
(Jamie Osborne) *t.k.h: chsd ldrs: effrt and swtchd rt bnd 2f out: drvn over 1f out: no ex and hld whn swtchd lft ins fnl f: wknd towards fin* **4/1**[2]

4002 **5** 2 **Fintech (IRE)**[7] 9128 3-8-1 **62**.......................... (t) NicolaCurrie[(7)] 8 59
(Philip Hide) *wnt rt s: hdwy to ld after 2f: rdn and kicked on over 1f out: drvn and hdd ins fnl f: wknd towards fin* **8/1**[3]

0210 **6** shd **Pink Ribbon (IRE)**[1] 9212 5-8-8 **63**.......................... (p) MitchGodwin[(3)] 3 59
(Sylvester Kirk) *t.k.h: wl in tch in midfield: effrt over 2f out: unable qck over 1f out: wknd ins fnl f* **10/1**

-335 **7** 57 **Sea Dweller**[79] 7477 4-9-1 **67**.......................... LukeMorris 7
(Anthony Carson) *wnt rt s: hdwy to chse ldrs 7f out: lost pl u.p over 2f out: lost tch over 1f out: eased: t.o* **22/1**

0000 **8** 1½ **Pivotman**[122] 6014 9-8-13 **72**.......................... (bt) HarrisonShaw[(7)] 10
(Michael Easterby) *midfield tl stdd bk to last trio after 2f: tongue strap c loose: dropped to rr and rdn over 2f out: lost tch over 1f out: eased: t.o* **33/1**

2m 5.93s (-2.67) **Going Correction** -0.15s/f (Stan)
**WFA** 3 from 4yo+ 2lb **8** Ran SP% **116.1**
Speed ratings (Par 103): **104,103,103,101,99 99,54,52**
CSF £14.70 CT £42.11 TOTE £7.30: £2.00, £1.70, £2.10; EX 19.10 Trifecta £69.60.
**Owner** Thomson, Tobin & Sheridan **Bred** Best Breeding **Trained** Oad Street, Kent

**FOCUS**
A fair handicap, the pace picked up a fair way out and the first two came from behind.
T/Jkpt: Not Won. T/Plt: £89.40 to a £1 stake. Pool: £131,901.52 - 1,076.58 winning units T/Qpdt: £28.70 to a £1 stake. Pool: £15,029.13 - 386.50 winning units **Steve Payne**

# 9230 CHELMSFORD (A.W) (L-H)
Friday, December 15

**OFFICIAL GOING: Polytrack: standard**
Wind: LIGHT, HALF AGAINST Weather: DRY, COLD, RAIN from RACE 3

## 9237 BET TOTEPLACEPOT AT BETFRED.COM ALL-WEATHER "HANDS AND HEELS" APPRENTICE H'CAP 1m 2f (P)
5:45 (5:45) (Class 7) (0-50,51) 3-Y-0+ **£2,587** (£770; £384; £192) **Stalls** Low

Form RPR

2250 **1** **Ted's Brother (IRE)**[48] 8430 9-9-1 **47**.......................... (v[1]) PoppyBridgwater[(3)] 11 61
(Laura Morgan) *stdd s: t.k.h: hld up in rr: hdwy into midfield 7f out: clsd to chse ldrs over 2f out: pushed into ld over 1f out: sn edgd but sn clr: r.o strly: easily* **14/1**

2040 **2** 9 **Dawn Goddess**[29] 8799 3-8-11 **45**.......................... JasonWatson[(3)] 3 43
(Gary Moore) *stdd and short of room leaving stalls: hld up in rr: clsd into midfield over 2f out: effrt and hdwy over 1f out: nt clr 1f out: styd on to go 2nd towards fin: no ch w wnr* **14/1**

4012 **3** ½ **The King's Steed**[55] 8248 4-9-7 **50**.......................... HarrisonShaw 14 46
(Shaun Lycett) *hld up wl in tch in midfield: effrt to chse ldrs over 2f out: outpcd by wnr over 1f out: chsd clr wnr ins fnl f: no imp and lost 2nd towards fin* **7/1**[3]

0030 **4** 1½ **Hong Kong Joe**[27] 8846 7-9-2 **45**.......................... (e) HarryBurns 16 38
(Lydia Richards) *styd wd early: in tch in midfield: effrt ent fnl 2f: no ch w wnr and kpt on same pce fr over 1f out* **10/1**

0301 **5** ½ **Ertidaad (IRE)**[7] 9141 5-9-8 **51** 6ex.......................... (v) SebastianWoods 9 43
(Suzi Best) *wl in tch in midfield: pushed along 4f out: rdn and unable qck over 2f out: no ch w wnr and keeping on same pce whn nt clr run ins fnl f* **5/2**[1]

0004 **6** 1¼ **Outlaw Torn (IRE)**[29] 8800 8-9-5 **48**.......................... (e) BenSanderson 12 38
(Richard Guest) *t.k.h: pressed ldrs tl wnt 2nd 5f out: led over 3f out: rdn and hdd over 1f out: sn outpcd by wnr: wknd ins fnl f* **8/1**

0405 **7** 1 **Linda Doris (IRE)**[16] 8994 3-8-11 **45**.......................... (t) PaulHainey[(3)] 8 34
(Gay Kelleway) *hld up towards rr: effrt over 2f out: no imp and plugged on same pce fr over 1f out* **16/1**

0465 **8** ¾ **Spike's Princess (IRE)**[36] 8707 3-9-2 **50**.......................... WilliamCarver[(3)] 4 37
(Brian Barr) *trckd ldrs: rdn over 2f out: outpcd and btn over 1f out: wknd ins fnl f* **20/1**

0440 **9** ½ **Understory (USA)**[64] 7990 10-8-13 **45**.......................... SophieRalston[(3)] 6 31
(Tim McCarthy) *led tl over 3f out: lost pl over 1f out: wknd ins fnl f* **14/1**

0-00 **10** ½ **Charlie Chaplin (GER)**[20] 6621 3-9-4 **49**.......................... (p) DarraghKeenan 5 35
(Robert Eddery) *hld up towards rr: effrt and sme hdwy over 2f out: no imp over 1f out: nvr trbld ldrs* **7/1**[3]

65 **11** 7 **Emigrated (IRE)**[7] 9141 4-8-11 **45**.......................... (v) CharlotteMcFarland[(5)] 1 16
(Derek Shaw) *dropped towards rr after 1f: n.d: lost tch over 1f out* **6/1**[2]

0-00 **12** 8 **Melcano**[14] 9034 3-8-11 **45**.......................... TheodoreLadd[(3)] 2 2
(Shaun Harris) *midfield: dropped to rr and struggling u.p 4f out: wl bhd over 1f out* **66/1**

0-06 **13** 35 **Sixth Of June**[51] 8345 3-9-3 **48**.......................... JonathanFisher 10
(Rod Millman) *t.k.h: w ldr tl 5f out: sn pushed along: dropped out rapidly over 3f out: t.o and eased over 1f out* **20/1**

2m 7.52s (-1.08) **Going Correction** -0.20s/f (Stan)
**WFA** 3 from 4yo+ 2lb **13** Ran SP% **125.0**
Speed ratings (Par 97): **96,88,88,87,86 85,85,84,84,83 78,71,43**
CSF £200.71 CT £1510.75 TOTE £18.70: £6.30, £4.50, £2.50; EX 346.20 Trifecta £1312.70.
**Owner** Laura Morgan Racing Club **Bred** T Counihan **Trained** Grantham, Lincolnshire

**FOCUS**
Fairly still but very cold conditions for this evening fixture. A basement-grade hands and heels handicap to start with, in which the emphatic winner sat a long way off the initial contested lead.

## 9238 BET TOTEJACKPOT AT BETFRED.COM NURSERY H'CAP 1m 2f (P)
6:15 (6:16) (Class 6) (0-65,67) 2-Y-0 **£3,234** (£962; £481; £240) **Stalls** Low

Form RPR

0002 **1** **Gembari**[27] 8848 2-8-12 **61**.......................... (v) JaneElliott[(5)] 3 62
(Ivan Furtado) *chsd ldr after 2f: effrt to chal over 1f out: led and hung lft 1f out: styd on and forged ahd towards fin* **5/1**

0304 **2** ¾ **Urban Soul (IRE)**[27] 8848 2-9-6 **67**.......................... (p) CliffordLee[(3)] 7 67
(James Bethell) *chsd ldng pair after 2f: effrt on inner to chal over 1f out: ev ch but awkward hd carriage ins fnl f: no ex and jst outpcd wl ins fnl f* **4/1**[2]

3322 **3** 3 **Progressive Jazz (IRE)**[25] 8870 2-8-11 **55**.......................... (v) JoeyHaynes 2 50
(K R Burke) *led: rdn and hrd pressed over 1f out: hdd 1f out: no ex and short of room sn after: wknd fnl 100yds* **9/4**[1]

6500 **4** 4 **Global Wonder (IRE)**[27] 8848 2-9-7 **65**.......................... MartinHarley 4 51
(Ed Dunlop) *stdd s: t.k.h: hld up in last pair: effrt 2f out: chsd clr ldng trio 1f out: kpt on same pce and nvr threatening ldrs* **9/2**[3]

6600 **5** 1¾ **Prince Consort (IRE)**[51] 8349 2-9-3 **61**.......................... (p[1]) TomMarquand 5 44
(Brian Meehan) *chsd ldr for 2f: sn dropped to 4th: rdn and outpcd over 2f out: btn over 1f out: wknd ins fnl f* **8/1**

6001 **6** ¾ **Trick Shot Jenny**[15] 9014 2-8-13 **57**.......................... DougieCostello 6 39
(Jamie Osborne) *swtchd lft after s: hld up in midfield: effrt to chse clr ldng trio over 2f out: no imp and wl hld over 1f out* **8/1**

000 **7** *18* **Miss Van Winkle**$^{22}$ 8914 2-8-11 **55**................................ FrannyNorton 1 2
(Mark Johnston) *taken down early: t.k.h: hld up in last pair: racd awkwardly bnd 8f out: shkn up over 2f out: sn btn and lost tch over 1f out* **16/1**

2m 8.91s (0.31) **Going Correction** -0.20s/f (Stan) **7** Ran SP% **113.7**
Speed ratings (Par 94): **90,89,87,83,82 81,67**
CSF £24.87 TOTE £6.20: £2.80, £2.50; EX 28.00 Trifecta £87.80.
**Owner** Ron Hull **Bred** A C Cook **Trained** Wiseton, Nottinghamshire

**FOCUS**
An unexceptional late-season nursery, and a winning time 1.39 seconds slower than that of the previous race. Ordinary form.

## 9239 BET TOTEQUADPOT AT BETFRED.COM EBF FILLIES' NOVICE STKS (PLUS 10 RACE) 7f (P)
**6:45** (6:46) (Class 4) 2-Y-O **£6,469** (£1,925; £962; £481) **Stalls** Low

Form RPR
**1** **Crown Walk** 2-9-0 0.......................................................(h$^{1}$) MartinLane 6 79+
(Charlie Appleby) *chsd ldrs: wnt 2nd 5f out: effrt and chal over 2f out: edgd lft and led over 1f out: sn asserted u.p: r.o strly and drew clr ins fnl f: readily* **7/2**$^{2}$

025 **2** *4½* **Briscola**$^{22}$ 8903 2-9-0 75.................................................. RobertHavlin 5 65
(John Gosden) *hld up in tch in midfield: effrt ent fnl 2f: chsd clr ldng pair over 1f out: no ch w wnr but kpt to go 2nd last strides* **6/1**$^{3}$

2 **3** *hd* **Dance Me (USA)**$^{20}$ 8951 2-8-11 72.............................. MitchGodwin$^{(3)}$ 8 64
(Sylvester Kirk) *led after 1f: pressed over 2f out: sn rdn: hdd and unable qck over 1f out: no ch w wnr and kpt in same pce ins fnl f:* **11/10**$^{1}$

**4** *1½* **Miss Milla B** 2-9-0 0.................................................... StevieDonohoe 2 60
(Ed Vaughan) *hld up in tch in last pair: effrt over 1f out: wnt 4th 1f out: no threat to wnr and kpt on same pce ins fnl f* **25/1**

**5** *6* **Flora Tristan** 2-9-0 0.................................................... DanielMuscutt 3 44
(Marco Botti) *s.i.s and pushed along early: clsd onto bk of field and t.k.h after 2f: swtchd rt over 1f out: no imp* **12/1**

00 **6** *6* **Astrofire**$^{71}$ 7758 2-9-0 0.................................................. JoeyHaynes 1 28
(Mark H Tompkins) *t.k.h: hld up in tch: outpcd over 2f out: btn and eased over 1f out: sddle slipped* **100/1**

20 **7** *2¼* **Cirrus Minor (FR)**$^{27}$ 8850 2-9-0 0.................................... MartinHarley 7 22
(K R Burke) *led for 1f: chsd ldng pair 5f out tl outpcd and lost 3rd over 1f out: sn wknd* **6/1**$^{3}$

1m 25.36s (-1.84) **Going Correction** -0.20s/f (Stan) **7** Ran SP% **110.9**
Speed ratings (Par 95): **102,96,96,94,88 81,78**
CSF £22.94 TOTE £4.00: £1.50, £2.60; EX 15.70 Trifecta £39.70.
**Owner** Godolphin **Bred** Godolphin **Trained** Newmarket, Suffolk

**FOCUS**
A modest fillies' juvenile novice event, run in steady rain. The second and third would back the winner being rated 4lb higher but it's questionable whether they were at their best here.

## 9240 BET TOTEEXACTA AT BETFRED.COM NOVICE AUCTION STKS 1m (P)
**7:15** (7:15) (Class 5) 2-Y-O **£4,528** (£1,347; £673; £336) **Stalls** Low

Form RPR
0 **1** **Sir Hamilton (IRE)**$^{42}$ 8560 2-8-11 0.................................... LukeMorris 2 81
(Denis Quinn) *t.k.h: led for 1f: chsd ldr after: rdn and chalng over 2f out: led 1f out: sn in command and styd on strly: rdn out* **12/1**

4 **2** *3* **Paddy The Chef (IRE)**$^{23}$ 8890 2-8-11 0............................ StevieDonohoe 3 74
(Ian Williams) *trckd ldrs: effrt ent fnl 2f: unable qck over 1f out: chsd clr wnr 100yds out: kpt on same pce* **1/1**$^{1}$

42 **3** *1¼* **Angelina D'Or (GER)**$^{9}$ 9099 2-8-6 0.............................. FrannyNorton 5 66
(Mark Johnston) *hld up in tch: reminders over 2f out: unable qck u.p over 1f out: no threat to wnr and kpt on same pce ins fnl f: wnt 3rd fnl 75yds* **7/2**$^{3}$

1403 **4** *2¼* **Escape The City**$^{25}$ 8871 2-8-11 80............................ CharlieBennett$^{(3)}$ 1 69
(Hughie Morrison) *led after 1f: travelling bttr than wnr over 2f out: pushed along over 1f out: hdd and rdn 1f out: wknd ins fnl f* **5/2**$^{2}$

**5** *9* **Knight Errant (IRE)** 2-8-11 0.......................................... TomMarquand 4 44
(William Jarvis) *dwlt and stmbld sn after s: rn green in rr: rdn and no imp over 2f out: wknd over 1f out* **25/1**

1m 38.33s (-1.57) **Going Correction** -0.20s/f (Stan) **5** Ran SP% **112.3**
Speed ratings (Par 96): **99,96,94,92,83**
CSF £25.53 TOTE £10.90: £4.80, £2.20; EX 37.70 Trifecta £119.10.
**Owner** B Syversen **Bred** B Minde **Trained** Newmarket, Suffolk

**FOCUS**
A reasonable little novice event. The runner-up has been rated as improving slightly.

## 9241 BET TOTETRIFECTA AT BETFRED.COM H'CAP 6f (P)
**7:45** (7:48) (Class 4) (0-85,87) 3-Y-O+ **£6,469** (£1,925; £962; £481) **Stalls** Low

Form RPR
4022 **1** **Human Nature (IRE)**$^{14}$ 9020 4-9-0 **85**........................(t) MillyNaseb$^{(7)}$ 4 95
(Stuart Williams) *chsd ldrs: wnt 2nd wl over 1f out and sn rdn to chal: led ins fnl f: styd on wl* **9/2**$^{2}$

0-10 **2** *1¼* **Nautical Haven**$^{209}$ 2831 3-9-4 **82**...................................... TomEaves 7 88
(Kevin Ryan) *led: rdn over 1f out: hdd and kpt on same pce ins fnl f* **8/1**

3212 **3** *1* **Born To Finish (IRE)**$^{8}$ 9124 4-8-13 **77**..................(p) DougieCostello 10 80+
(Jamie Osborne) *swtchd lft after s: hld up in last quartet: clsd and swtchd lft over 1f out: hdwy 1f out: chsd ldng pair ins fnl f: styd on u.p: nvr getting to ldrs* **5/1**$^{3}$

1503 **4** *1½* **Pearl Spectre (USA)**$^{2}$ 9210 6-9-2 **87**......................... NicolaCurrie$^{(7)}$ 3 85+
(Phil McEntee) *bustled along in midfield: c wd and rdn bnd 2f out: kpt on u.p ins fnl f: nvr enough pce to threaten ldrs* **11/4**$^{1}$

4121 **5** *1* **Bahamian Heights**$^{7}$ 9136 6-8-1 **72**........................ JonathanFisher$^{(7)}$ 9 67
(Robert Cowell) *taken down early: s.i.s: hld up in last pair: effrt over 1f out: hdwy between horses ins fnl f: styd on: nvr trbld ldrs* **6/1**

304 **6** *¾* **Siege Of Boston (IRE)**$^{25}$ 8872 4-9-5 **83**......................(t) PJMcDonald 5 76
(David C Griffiths) *chsd ldng trio: effrt ent fnl 2f: unable qck u.p over 1f out: wknd ins fnl f* **8/1**

0000 **7** *1¼* **Highland Acclaim (IRE)**$^{24}$ 8879 6-9-6 **84**....................(h) SeanLevey 2 73
(David O'Meara) *t.k.h: in tch in midfield: effrt over 1f out: unable qck u.p 1f out: no imp ins fnl f* **20/1**

5260 **8** *nk* **Johnny Cavagin**$^{35}$ 8718 8-8-13 **77**..........................(t) RobertWinston 6 65
(Ronald Thompson) *hld up in last pair: effrt wl over 1f out: no imp: nvr trbld ldrs* **25/1**

0006 **9** *2* **Sir Ottoman (FR)**$^{39}$ 8639 4-9-6 **84**............................(p) LukeMorris 8 65
(Ivan Furtado) *sn pushed along to chse ldr: rdn over 2f out: lost 2nd and unable to wl over 1f out: wknd ins fnl f* **16/1**

2664 **10** *3½* **Deeds Not Words (IRE)**$^{16}$ 8990 6-8-7 **71**..................(p) FrannyNorton 1 41
(Michael Wigham) *hld up in tch in last quartet: effrt on inner over 1f out: no imp ins fnl f* **16/1**

1m 11.12s (-2.58) **Going Correction** -0.20s/f (Stan) **10** Ran SP% **118.4**
Speed ratings (Par 105): **109,107,106,104,102 101,100,99,96,92**
CSF £41.11 CT £192.67 TOTE £5.60: £2.00, £4.10, £1.50; EX 68.30 Trifecta £435.10.
**Owner** Enticknap, Reynolds & Watkins **Bred** Tally-Ho Stud **Trained** Newmarket, Suffolk

**FOCUS**
A competitive sprint handicap on paper, and a good contest with no obvious excuses in practice. Another step forward from the winner, with the runner-up rated to his figure from the void race here in February.

## 9242 BET TOTEWIN AT BETFRED.COM H'CAP 2m (P)
**8:15** (8:17) (Class 5) (0-70,72) 3-Y-O+ **£5,175** (£1,540; £769; £384) **Stalls** Low

Form RPR
0-64 **1** **Caged Lightning (IRE)**$^{42}$ 8214 7-10-0 **70**..................(p) PJMcDonald 3 76
(Steve Gollings) *hld up in tch in midfield: rdn 3f out: hdwy to press ldrs over 1f out: styd on to ld ins fnl f: hld on wl towards fin* **4/1**$^{1}$

0503 **2** *hd* **Fitzwilly**$^{49}$ 8394 7-9-6 **67**........................................ PaddyBradley$^{(5)}$ 8 72
(Mick Channon) *hld up in last pair: hdwy 3f out: rdn and hdwy over 1f out: str chal ins fnl f: kpt on but hld towards fin* **12/1**

3/5- **3** *2* **Argante (FR)**$^{135}$ 4941 8-10-2 **72**.......................................(b) FranBerry 2 75
(Henry Spiller) *hld up in rr: nt clr run over 2f out: hdwy on outer 2f out: styd on u.p to go 3rd wl ins fnl f: nvr getting to ldng pair* **25/1**

0644 **4** *2¾* **Ruler Of The Nile**$^{10}$ 9082 5-9-7 **66**........................ CallumShepherd$^{(3)}$ 6 65
(Robert Stephens) *in tch in midfield: clsd to trck ldrs 5f out: chal 3f out: sn rdn to ld: drvn and hdd ins fnl f: wknd wl ins fnl f* **8/1**

-602 **5** *shd* **Tynecastle Park**$^{26}$ 6530 4-8-5 **54**........................(p$^{1}$) DarraghKeenan$^{(7)}$ 11 53
(Robert Eddery) *dwlt: rcvrd to chse ldrs after 2f: chsd ldr 5f out tl led 3f out: hdd and unable qck u.p over 1f out: wknd ins fnl f* **5/1**$^{2}$

5323 **6** *nk* **Angel In The Snow**$^{48}$ 8430 4-8-9 **51** oh2................. JosephineGordon 7 50
(Brian Ellison) *hld up towards rr: rdn over 3f out: hdwy over 1f out: swtchd rt ins fnl f: kpt on but nvr getting on terms w ldrs* **5/1**$^{2}$

R060 **7** *hd* **Retrieve (AUS)**$^{72}$ 7744 10-10-1 **71**...........................(tp) CharlesBishop 1 70
(Johnny Farrelly) *chsd ldrs: rdn 3f out: unable qck over 2f out: wknd ins fnl f* **6/1**$^{3}$

0223 **8** *16* **Stylish Dancer**$^{34}$ 8744 3-9-8 **70**.......................................... LukeMorris 4 51
(Luca Cumani) *s.i.s: sn bustled along: hdwy into midfield after 3f: clsd to chse ldrs 4f out: rdn over 3f out: wknd over 1f out* **4/1**$^{1}$

4550 **9** *27* **Bracken Brae**$^{44}$ 8505 5-9-13 **69**........................................ JoeyHaynes 10 16
(Mark H Tompkins) *hld up in tch: hdwy to chse ldrs over 4f out: effrt over 3f out: sn struggling and lost pl over 2f out: bhd over 1f out: t.o* **20/1**

4640 **10** *12* **Conkering Hero (IRE)**$^{85}$ 7319 3-9-7 **69**............................ LiamKeniry 9 4
(Joseph Tuite) *mostly chsd ldr tl led 5f out: hdd 3f out: sn rdn and dropped out: bhd over 1f out: t.o* **14/1**

3255 **11** *43* **Katie Gale**$^{14}$ 9028 7-10-0 **70**.............................................. ShaneKelly 5
(Michael Appleby) *led: reminders 6f out: hdd and drvn 5f out: sn dropped out: t.o and eased wl over 1f out* **25/1**

3m 29.82s (-0.18) **Going Correction** -0.20s/f (Stan)
**WFA** 3 from 4yo+ 6lb **11** Ran SP% **125.5**
Speed ratings (Par 103): **92,91,90,89,89 89,89,81,67,61 40**
CSF £56.27 CT £1085.56 TOTE £5.10: £2.00, £3.10, £5.20; EX 58.00 Trifecta £630.40.
**Owner** Four Men & A Little Lady **Bred** Miss A Prendergast **Trained** Scamblesby, Lincs

**FOCUS**
A moderate but competitive marathon event, in which held-up horses locked out the frame. The winner has been rated to form, and the runner-up to this year's form.

## 9243 CHELMSFORD CITY SUPPORTING THE HORSE COMES FIRST H'CAP 1m (P)
**8:45** (8:46) (Class 6) (0-65,67) 3-Y-O+ **£3,234** (£962; £481; £240) **Stalls** Low

Form RPR
4322 **1** **Samphire Coast**$^{8}$ 9126 4-9-5 **63**..............................(v) PatrickMathers 3 71
(Derek Shaw) *hld up in tch: nt clr run over 2f out: swtchd rt and hdwy over 1f out: hdwy between horses 1f out and str run to ld ins fnl f: r.o wl* **7/4**$^{1}$

6330 **2** *1¾* **Ross Raith Rover**$^{132}$ 5664 4-9-1 **66**........................ DarraghKeenan$^{(7)}$ 7 70
(Robert Eddery) *trckd ldrs: swtchd lft and effrt over 1f out: hdwy to chal 1f out: chsd wnr and kpt on same pce ins fnl f* **8/1**$^{3}$

5004 **3** *½* **Mr Potter**$^{7}$ 9142 4-9-0 **58**.......................................(v) RobertWinston 11 61
(Richard Guest) *plld hrd early: hld up in rr: clsd over 2f out: rdn and hdwy over 1f out: ev ch ins fnl f: no ex and one pce towards fin* **14/1**

3415 **4** *4* **Pass The Cristal (IRE)**$^{8}$ 9126 3-9-8 **67**.......................... DougieCostello 8 61
(William Muir) *stdd and swtchd lft after s: hld up in last pair: effrt and hdwy on inner over 1f out: kpt on same pce and no imp ins fnl f: snatched 4th last strides* **10/1**

6053 **5** *½* **Mimic's Memory**$^{14}$ 9034 3-8-10 **58**.............................. CliffordLee$^{(3)}$ 12 51
(Ann Duffield) *t.k.h: chsd ldrs tl led 4f out: rdn over 1f out: hdd jst ins fnl f: wknd* **10/1**

3200 **6** *1½* **Essential**$^{25}$ 8874 3-9-3 **62**..................................................(v) FranBerry 2 51
(George Scott) *hld up wl in tch in midfield: effrt to chse ldng pair over 2f out: unable qck over 1f out and btn whn hung lft and hmpd ins fnl f: stl hanging and wknd wl ins fnl f* **10/1**

1102 **7** *1¼* **Prince Jai**$^{13}$ 9052 4-8-13 **57**.......................................(v) StevieDonohoe 1 43
(Ian Williams) *led for 1f: mostly chsd ldr after: rdn and ev ch over 1f out tl no ex jst ins fnl f: wknd wl ins fnl f* **4/1**$^{2}$

130 **8** *5* **Almanack**$^{132}$ 5651 7-9-2 **63**........................................ NathanAlison$^{(3)}$ 6 38
(Mark Pattinson) *t.k.h: hld up in tch in midfield: effrt u.p on outer over 2f out: no imp and btn over 1f out: wknd ins fnl f* **25/1**

0-43 **9** *¾* **Zulu**$^{213}$ 2707 3-9-5 **64**..................................................... WilliamCarson 5 37
(Rod Millman) *a towards rr: effrt over 1f out: no imp: wknd fnl f* **20/1**

0560 **10** *4½* **Sea Tea Dea**$^{81}$ 7464 3-9-6 **65**............................................. LukeMorris 4 28
(Anthony Carson) *t.k.h: chsd ldrs: rdn and unable qck over 2f out: lost pl and wknd over 1f out* **16/1**

5005 **11** *1¼* **Fire Palace**$^{21}$ 8929 3-9-4 **63**.............................................. MartinHarley 9 23
(Robert Eddery) *taken down early: s.i.s: styd wd and steadily rcvrd to ld after 1f: hdd 4f out: rdn over 2f out: lost pl over 1f out: sn bhd and wknd fnl f* **25/1**

1m 38.68s (-1.22) **Going Correction** -0.20s/f (Stan)
**WFA** 3 from 4yo+ 1lb **11** Ran SP% **119.8**
Speed ratings (Par 101): **98,96,95,91,91 89,88,83,82,78 77**
CSF £16.17 CT £152.53 TOTE £2.60: £1.30, £2.50, £4.70; EX 17.50 Trifecta £159.40.
**Owner** Paddy Barrett **Bred** P E Barrett **Trained** Sproxton, Leics

**FOCUS**
A contested lead in this concluding mile handicap, and a winning time 0.35 seconds slower than that of Sir Hamilton in the 2yo novice event earlier.
T/Plt: £1,192.10 to a £1 stake. Pool: £103,554.34 - 63.41 winning units T/Qpdt: £85.00 to a £1 stake. Pool: £13,189.89 - 114.74 winning units **Steve Payne**

## 9143 DUNDALK (A.W) (L-H)
Friday, December 15

**OFFICIAL GOING: Polytrack: standard**

### 9244a CROWNE PLAZA RACE & STAY H'CAP 5f (P)
5:30 (5:30) 3-Y-O+ £5,791 (£1,795; £855; £385; £150)

RPR

1 **Chicago School (IRE)**21 8939 4-8-9 **56**............(vt) ConorMcGovern(5) 7 64
(Anthony McCann, Ire) *hld up in tch: 6th 1/2-way: rdn 2f out and sn swtchd rt: r.o wl u.p nr side ins fnl f to ld fnl strides* **8/1**

2 *hd* **Bluesbreaker (IRE)**9 9106 5-8-1 **53**..................(bt) AndrewSlattery(10) 13 60
(Damian Joseph English, Ire) *chsd ldrs: 3rd 1/2-way: gd hdwy on outer to ld ins fnl f where edgd sltly lft: rdn clr briefly tl reduced advantage nr fin and hdd fnl strides* **25/1**

3 *nk* **Flawlessly (FR)**21 8932 3-8-11 **60**............................... GavinRyan(7) 14 66
(Ms Sheila Lavery, Ire) *dwlt and in rr: hdwy 2f out to chse ldrs ins fnl f: wnt 3rd wl ins fnl f and r.o cl home: hld* **6/1**3

4 *1 3/4* **Brave Display (IRE)**9 9108 3-9-5 **66**................(v) DerekMcCormack(5) 1 66+
(P J Prendergast, Ire) *in tch: rdn fr 1/2-way and u.p whn tk clsr order and hmpd ins fnl f: swtchd rt and r.o into nvr threatening 4th* **11/2**2

5 *1/2* **Fast Act (IRE)**27 8853 5-9-7 **70**........................................(p) BenCoen(7) 12 68
(Kevin Ryan) *broke wl to ld: rdn under 2f out and hdd u.p ins fnl f: sn no ex and one pce clsng stages* **14/1**

6 *nk* **Billyfairplay (IRE)**21 8939 3-8-4 **53** ow1.............(p1) GearoidBrouder(7) 3 50
(W J Martin, Ire) *cl up: pushed along in 2nd early: rdn 2f out and no ex whn sltly hmpd ins fnl f: wknd* **10/1**

7 *1/2* **Danz Gift (IRE)**28 8825 6-9-2 **63**..........................(t) KillianHennessy(5) 6 58
(Ms Sheila Lavery, Ire) *hld up towards rr: rdn under 2f out and sme late hdwy ins fnl f: nvr nrr* **4/1**1

8 *1 1/4* **Mo Henry**9 9107 5-9-9 **68**...................................................(v) SeanCorby(5) 4 59
(Adrian Paul Keatley, Ire) *mid-div: rdn 2f out and no imp ins fnl f: kpt on one pce* **8/1**

9 *nk* **My Good Brother (IRE)**9 9107 8-9-3 **64**............ DylanRobinson(5) 11 53
(T G McCourt, Ire) *mid-div: rdn over 2f out and no imp on ldrs over 1f out: one pce after* **10/1**

10 *1 1/4* **Coto (IRE)**21 8927 5-9-7 **70**........................................... RonanShort(7) 5 55
(M J Tynan, Ire) *towards rr: tk clsr order over 1f out: kpt on one pce ins fnl f* **25/1**

11 *nk* **Arc Royal**112 6397 3-10-3 **73**................................ EmmetMcNamara 10 57
(Richard John O'Brien, Ire) *hld up: pushed along in 10th bef 1/2-way and no imp u.p in rr over 1f out: kpt on clsng stages* **14/1**

12 *hd* **Hot Stuff**42 8569 4-7-13 **48**.......................................(bt1) DamienMelia(7) 2 31
(James McAuley, Ire) *chsd ldrs: 4th 3f out: rdn over 2f out and wknd far side under 1f out where n.m.r on inner* **33/1**

13 *nk* **Dream Dreamer**21 8932 4-8-13 **55**......................................(e1) PBBeggy 9 37
(Jack W Davison, Ire) *chsd ldrs: 5th 3f out: tk clsr order bhd ldrs 2f out where swtchd lft: sn rdn and no ex 1f out: wknd qckly ins fnl f* **25/1**

14 *1* **Jenniechild (IRE)**21 8932 4-8-8 **57**........................... NathanCrosse(7) 8 35
(Peter Fahey, Ire) *hld up mid-div: racd keenly: 8th 3f out: rdn under 2f out and sn wknd: eased clsng stages* **6/1**3

59.56s (0.16) **Going Correction** 0.0s/f (Stan) **14 Ran SP% 132.2**
Speed ratings: **99,98,98,95,94 94,93,91,90,88 88,88,87,85**
CSF £211.92 CT £1355.93 TOTE £9.70: £2.70, £7.50, £2.50; DF 205.50 Trifecta £1774.10.
**Owner** Miss Rita Shah **Bred** Miss Eileen Farrelly **Trained** Castleblaney, Co. Monaghan
■ Stewards' Enquiry : Andrew Slattery caution: careless riding

**FOCUS**
The winner was delivering for the second time since joining this stable earlier in the year and has proved a very decent recruit for small money. The winner has been rated in line with his recent course win and the runner-up to this year's best.

9245-9246a (Foreign Racing) - See Raceform Interactive

### 9247a CROWNE PLAZA LEADING JOCKEY & TRAINER AWARDS 2017 H'CAP 6f (P)
7:00 (7:00) 3-Y-O+ £13,141 (£4,059; £1,923; £854; £320)

RPR

1 **Togoville (IRE)**28 8825 7-8-9 **86**.....................(b) ConorMcGovern(5) 6 96
(Anthony McCann, Ire) *mde all: over 1 l clr at 1/2-way: rdn and pressed 2f out: kpt on wl u.p ins fnl f: all out* **7/1**3

2 *1/2* **Geological (IRE)**7 9149 5-8-8 **80**....................................... RoryCleary 8 88
(Damian Joseph English, Ire) *cl up early tl sn settled bhd ldrs: disp 2nd fr 1/2-way: rdn into 2nd wl ins fnl f and kpt on wl clsng stages: hld* **20/1**

3 *1/2* **Alfredo Arcano (IRE)**14 9036 3-8-10 **82**......................(h) WayneLordan 4 89
(David Marnane, Ire) *chsd ldrs: 4th 1/2-way: hdwy far side 2f out: sn rdn in 2nd and no imp on wnr wl ins fnl f where dropped to 3rd* **7/2**2

4 *nk* **Rivellino**21 8938 7-8-0 **77**........................................... KillianLeonard(5) 10 83
(Adrian McGuinness, Ire) *hld up: 8th 1/2-way: rdn 2f out and sme hdwy to chse ldrs u.p ent fnl f: kpt on same pce far side in 4th clsng stages* **9/1**

5 *3/4* **Russian Soul (IRE)**119 6141 9-9-5 **91**........................... ConorHoban 1 94
(M Halford, Ire) *s.i.s and towards rr: 9th 1/2-way: tk clsr order 2f out and sme hdwy to chse ldrs 1f out: rdn bhd ldrs far side ins fnl f and no imp on wnr in 5th clsng stages: kpt on same pce* **25/1**

6 *1/2* **Naadirr (IRE)**49 8383 6-9-7 **93**.......................................(v) PatSmullen 7 95
(Kevin Ryan) *mid-div: disp 6th at 1/2-way: rdn 2f out and no imp on ldrs u.p in 8th ins fnl f: kpt on nr side clsng stages* **11/4**1

7 *1/2* **Have A Nice Day**42 8573 7-8-5 **82**.........................(v1) DannySheehy(5) 3 82
(John James Feane, Ire) *hld up: disp 6th at 1/2-way: rdn 2f out and sme hdwy far side over 1f out: no ex wl ins fnl f* **8/1**

8 *1* **Captain Dion**14 9036 4-9-4 **90**.............................................(vt) PBBeggy 5 87
(F Birrane, Ire) *sn trckd ldr: jnd for 2nd at 1/2-way: rdn 2f out and sn no ex: wknd 1f out* **14/1**

9 *1/2* **Confrontational (IRE)**42 8573 3-8-8 **80** ow1.............(p) ShaneFoley 11 75
(John Joseph Murphy, Ire) *chsd ldrs: pushed along in 5th after 1/2-way and no imp on wnr 2f out: wknd* **7/1**3

10 *2 3/4* **G Force (IRE)**34 8738 6-9-10 **96**....................................(b) ColinKeane 9 83
(Adrian Paul Keatley, Ire) *dwlt and settled towards rr: 10th 1/2-way: rdn and no imp 2f out: one pce after* **10/1**

11 *2* **Golden Pearl**28 8825 4-8-4 **76** oh8.............................(t) NGMcCullagh 2 56
(M Halford, Ire) *v s.i.s and detached in rr: no imp at 1/2-way: kpt on one pce fnl 2f: nvr a factor* **25/1**

1m 11.73s (-0.67) **Going Correction** 0.0s/f (Stan) **11 Ran SP% 123.2**
Speed ratings: **103,102,101,101,100 99,98,97,96,93 90**
CSF £144.71 CT £577.62 TOTE £9.60: £3.00, £1.80, £1.50; DF 94.90 Trifecta £775.20.
**Owner** Patrick Joseph McCann **Bred** Steven Nolan **Trained** Castleblaney, Co. Monaghan

**FOCUS**
An eighth course success for the likeable Togoville. It's been rated around the balance of the first four.

9248 - 9256a (Foreign Racing) - See Raceform Interactive

## 9043 JEBEL ALI (L-H)
Friday, December 15

**OFFICIAL GOING: Dirt: fast**

### 9257a SHADWELL (MAIDEN) (DIRT) 1m (D)
1:00 (1:00) 2-Y-O+ £8,590 (£2,863; £1,574; £859; £429)

RPR

1 **Au Coeur (IRE)**212 3-8-13 70........................................ RichardMullen 1 67
(S Seemar, UAE) *tracked ldr, led 3f out, ran on wl , easlily* **10/3**2

2 *6 1/2* **Cherkes Pharoah (USA)**7 9151 3-8-13 ..................(vt) TadhgO'Shea 4 52
(A R Al Rayhi, UAE) *slowly away, rear of mid-division, ran on fnl 2 1/2f but no ch wth winner* **10/1**

3 *1* **Dubawi's Thunder**301 800 6-9-0 62........................................ JFEgan 3 50
(R Bouresly, Kuwait) *mid-division, chsd leaders 3f out, one pace fnl 2f* **33/1**

4 *1/2* **Dangerous Thought (USA)**27 8856 4-9-0 62................(v) PatDobbs 10 49
(Doug Watson, UAE) *soon led, hdd 3f out but ran on same pace* **12/1**

5 *5 1/4* **Al Boraq (USA)**21 8940 3-8-13 60..........................(v) SamHitchcott 5 37
(S Seemar, UAE) *never better than mid-division* **33/1**

6 *3 1/4* **Muqaatil (USA)**7 9151 3-8-13 66..........................(bt) SilvestreDeSousa 6 29
(A bin Harmash, UAE) *never better than mid-division* **20/1**

7 *2 3/4* **Eagle's Stare (IRE)**398 7940 3-8-13 ..............................(t) AntonioFresu 8 23
(S Seemar, UAE) *never nr to challenge* **7/1**3

8 *hd* **Nalout (USA)**27 8856 3-8-2 57........................................(v) SeanDavis(6) 9 17
(S Seemar, UAE) *always in rear* **40/1**

9 *1 3/4* **Al Whaad (USA)**21 8940 3-8-8 ..................................(t) ConnorBeasley 2 13
(A bin Harmash, UAE) *always in rear* **25/1**

10 *16 1/2* **Nomadic (IRE)**28 8835 4-8-7 55...............................(p) AdamMcLean(7) 11
(Miss B Deutrom, UAE) *never nr to challenge* **66/1**

11 *24* **Perfect Sense**42 8583 3-8-13 72.....................................(p) PatCosgrave 7
(Saeed bin Suroor) *slowly into strd, al in rear* **4/5**1

1m 38.08s
**WFA** 3 from 4yo+ 1lb **11 Ran SP% 126.3**
CSF: 35.88.
**Owner** Touch Gold Racing **Bred** Darley **Trained** United Arab Emirates

## 9096 NEWCASTLE (A.W) (L-H)
Saturday, December 16

**OFFICIAL GOING: Tapeta: standard**
Wind: Almost nil Weather: Overcast, cold

### 9258 BETWAY STAYERS H'CAP 2m 56y (Tp)
12:40 (12:41) (Class 6) (0-65,67) 3-Y-O+ £3,234 (£962; £481; £240) Stalls Low

Form RPR

5040 1 **Apalis (FR)**18 8978 5-8-13 **58**................................(t) HarrisonShaw(7) 12 64
(Michael Easterby) *hld up: hdwy on outside over 2f out: led over 1f out: sn hrd pressed: hld on wl fnl f* **25/1**

1221 2 *1/2* **Strictly Art (IRE)**10 9095 4-9-3 **62**..................................... HarryBurns(7) 3 67
(Alan Bailey) *hld up in tch: hdwy over 2f out: effrt and ev ch over 1f out: kpt on fnl f: hld nr fin* **6/1**

2536 3 *shd* **Uptown Funk (IRE)**61 8114 3-9-9 **67**........................(p) AndrewMullen 13 74
(Keith Dalgleish) *hld up: hdwy on outside over 2f out: rdn over 1f out: kpt on ins fnl f* **15/2**

6405 4 *3* **Senatus (FR)**23 8909 5-9-12 **64**......................................(h) DanielMuscutt 8 65
(Karen McLintock) *dwlt: t.k.h: hld up: stdy hdwy on ins over 2f out: rdn wl over 1f out: kpt on same pce ins fnl f* **4/1**2

6350 5 *3/4* **Traditional Dancer (IRE)**58 8187 5-8-11 **49**............. FrannyNorton 11 49
(Iain Jardine) *sn chsng ldrs: wnt 2nd 6f out: led over 2f out to over 1f out: rdn and outpcd fnl f* **5/1**3

0/11 6 *1 1/4* **British Art**23 8909 5-9-13 **65**................................................(v) GrahamLee 4 64
(R K Watson, Ire) *prom: stdy hdwy over 2f out: rdn wl over 1f out: wknd ins fnl f* **11/4**1

6-65 7 *3 3/4* **Shulammite Man (IRE)**209 1197 4-8-9 **47**.............. JosephineGordon 9 41
(Sally Haynes) *hld up midfield: hdwy on outside over 2f out: sn rdn: outpcd fr over 1f out* **40/1**

0055 8 *2* **Etaad (USA)**5 9178 6-8-12 **57**........................................(b) PaulaMuir(7) 14 49
(Lucinda Egerton) *hld up: rdn and outpcd over 2f out: n.d after* **80/1**

5140 9 *1* **Lady Clitico (IRE)**31 8778 6-9-13 **65**...........................(p) DougieCostello 10 56
(Rebecca Menzies) *t.k.h: hld up towards rr: drvn along over 2f out: sn no imp: btn over 1f out* **14/1**

5456 10 *2 3/4* **Braes Of Lochalsh**31 7983 6-9-13 **65**.............................(p) PJMcDonald 5 52
(Jim Goldie) *hld up: rdn and outpcd over 2f out: sn btn* **14/1**

0200 11 *1 1/2* **La Bacouetteuse (FR)**39 8654 12-8-5 **48**.............(b) JamieGormley(5) 7 34
(Iain Jardine) *awkward s: hld up: rdn over 4f out: no imp fr 3f out* **50/1**

2200 12 *1/2* **Crakehall Lad (IRE)**109 6565 6-8-5 **46** oh1.................(b) PhilDennis(3) 2 31
(Andrew Crook) *chsd ldr to 6f out: rdn and outpcd over 2f out: wknd over 1f out* **50/1**

340 13 *nk* **Teak (IRE)**19 4120 10-9-8 **60**........................................(v) StevieDonohoe 1 45
(Ian Williams) *led to over 2f out: sn rdn and wknd* **33/1**

1066 14 *10* **Shan Dun na nGall (IRE)**10 9095 6-8-11 **56**.....(vt) GabrieleMalune(7) 6 29
(Amy Murphy) *hld up midfield: drvn and struggling over 2f out: sn wknd* **18/1**

3m 33.37s (-1.83) **Going Correction** +0.10s/f (Slow)
**WFA** 3 from 4yo+ 6lb **14 Ran SP% 122.4**
Speed ratings (Par 101): **108,107,107,106,105 105,103,102,101,100 99,99,99,94**
CSF £166.94 CT £1268.86 TOTE £19.70: £5.00, £2.80, £2.20; EX 219.60 Trifecta £2499.50.
**Owner** J Blackburn Racing **Bred** Mise De Moratalla **Trained** Sheriff Hutton, N Yorks

**FOCUS**
This looked a decent enough race for the grade. Straightforward form rated around the first four.

## 9259 BETWAY CONDITIONS STKS (ALL-WEATHER FAST TRACK QUALIFIER) 2m 56y (Tp)
**1:15** (1:15) (Class 2) 3-Y-O+ **£16,172** (£4,812; £2,405; £1,202) **Stalls** Low

Form RPR
2-44 **1** **Mountain Bell**[17] 8992 4-8-12 105............................ JosephineGordon 3 98+
(Ralph Beckett) *t.k.h: hld up in last pl: pushed along over 4f out: hdwy 2f out: led ins fnl f: pushed out: comf* **2/1**[1]

-430 **2** *2* **Cape Cova (IRE)**[176] 4033 4-9-3 102......................... DougieCostello 1 101
(Michael Appleby) *t.k.h early: trckd ldrs: effrt and rdn over 2f out: styd on fnl f to take 2nd nr fin: no ch w wnr* **33/1**

2602 **3** *shd* **Watersmeet**[44] 8539 6-9-3 106......................................... PJMcDonald 7 101
(Mark Johnston) *led: rdn and hrd pressed over 1f out: hdd ins fnl f: kpt on same pce: lost 2nd cl home* **5/2**[2]

0042 **4** *1* **Lord George (IRE)**[24] 8892 4-9-3 96......................... DanielMuscutt 5 100
(James Fanshawe) *prom: effrt and ev ch over 1f out: kpt on same pce ins fnl f* **4/1**[3]

0015 **5** *3* **Master Singer (USA)**[23] 8910 3-8-11 96....................(b) RobertHavlin 4 96
(John Gosden) *t.k.h: hld up: effrt on outside over 2f out: outpcd fr over 1f out* **8/1**

0003 **6** *1 ¾* **Cosmelli (ITY)**[7] 9157 4-9-3 90........................................(v) TomEaves 2 94?
(Gay Kelleway) *hld up in tch: drvn and outpcd over 2f out: n.d after* **50/1**

0042 **7** *1 ½* **Cohesion**[7] 9157 4-9-3 103.............................................. GrahamLee 6 92
(David Bridgwater) *pressed ldr to over 2f out: drvn and sn outpcd: btn fnl f* **5/1**

3m 31.36s (-3.84) **Going Correction** +0.10s/f (Slow)
**WFA** 3 from 4yo+ 6lb 7 Ran SP% **114.6**
Speed ratings (Par 109): **113,112,111,111,109 109,108**
CSF £60.55 TOTE £2.30: £1.50, £8.60; EX 41.70 Trifecta £181.00.
**Owner** Qatar Racing Limited **Bred** Theakston Stud **Trained** Kimpton, Hants

**FOCUS**
A decent conditions race. Muddling form. The fourth has been rated to his handicap latest for now.

## 9260 BETWAY MAIDEN STKS 1m 4f 98y (Tp)
**1:50** (1:50) (Class 5) 3-4-Y-O **£4,528** (£1,347; £673; £336) **Stalls** High

Form RPR
624 **1** **Warm Oasis**[29] 8822 3-9-5 75......................................... DanielMuscutt 6 79+
(James Fanshawe) *t.k.h: hld up: effrt and swtchd rt over 1f out: hung lft and led ins fnl f: continued to hang lft: kpt on wl cl home* **7/4**[2]

5 **2** *nk* **Emerald Cross (IRE)**[29] 8822 4-9-6 0......................... CliffordLee(3) 3 73
(Adam West) *trckd ldrs: effrt and ev ch over 1f out: wnt 2nd wl ins fnl f: kpt on* **18/1**

2432 **3** *1 ¼* **Star Story**[17] 9000 3-9-0 76....................................... JosephineGordon 5 69
(Ralph Beckett) *t.k.h: prom: hdwy on outside to ld 2f out: edgd lft and hdd ins fnl f: 3rd and one pce whn n.m.r and eased nr fin* **5/4**[1]

4223 **4** *1* **Sugarloaf Mountain (IRE)**[15] 9028 4-9-4 71..........(t) BenRobinson(5) 1 69
(Brian Ellison) *led at ordinary gallop: qcknd 3f out: hdd 2f out: rdn and one pce fnl f* **12/1**

**5** *1 ¾* **Cuckoo's Calling**[24] 3-9-0 0....................................... PJMcDonald 4 62
(James Bethell) *hld up in tch: effrt and hung lft over 2f out: rdn and no imp over 1f out* **5/1**[3]

650 **6** *4 ½* **The Foozler**[86] 7331 4-9-9 0........................................ AndrewMullen 2 59?
(Peter Niven) *trckd ldr to over 2f out: rdn and wknd over 1f out* **250/1**

2m 47.98s (6.88) **Going Correction** +0.10s/f (Slow)
**WFA** 3 from 4yo 4lb 6 Ran SP% **110.8**
Speed ratings (Par 103): **81,80,79,79,78 75**
CSF £28.92 TOTE £2.80: £1.60, £7.40; EX 31.70 Trifecta £63.80.
**Owner** The Cool Silk Partnership **Bred** Ashbrittle Stud **Trained** Newmarket, Suffolk

**FOCUS**
A muddling maiden run in a slow time. Muddling form, with the fourth rated close to form for now.

## 9261 BETWAY H'CAP (DIV I) 1m 4f 98y (Tp)
**2:25** (2:26) (Class 6) (0-60,62) 3-Y-O+ **£3,234** (£962; £481; £240) **Stalls** High

Form RPR
0311 **1** **Esspeegee**[67] 7918 4-8-10 54......................................(p) PaulHainey(7) 4 61
(Alan Bailey) *prom: effrt and rdn over 1f out: led wl ins fnl f: kpt on wl* **13/2**

5640 **2** *hd* **Magistral**[10] 9101 7-9-7 58........................................(p) PJMcDonald 12 65
(Linda Perratt) *hld up in midfield on outside: hdwy to ld over 1f out: sn hrd pressed: hdd wl ins fnl f: kpt on* **14/1**

4206 **3** *2 ¼* **Life Knowledge (IRE)**[23] 8909 5-9-1 55..................... CliffordLee(3) 8 58
(Patrick Holmes) *hld up: hdwy 2f out: kpt on ins fnl f: nt rch first two* **15/2**

50/6 **4** *hd* **Mitcd (IRE)**[44] 8187 6-8-6 48.................................... JamieGormley(5) 1 51
(George Bewley) *prom: rdn over 2f out: rallied over 1f out: kpt on same pce ins fnl f* **20/1**

0550 **5** *hd* **Percy Verence**[42] 8585 4-8-6 46 oh1...............(tp) RachelRichardson(3) 7 48
(Tracy Waggott) *prom: led gng wl over 2f out: rdn and hdd over 1f out: kpt on same pce fnl f* **66/1**

1634 **6** *1 ¾* **Bigbadboy (IRE)**[45] 8515 4-8-9 53.......................(h[1]) HarrisonShaw(7) 9 53
(Clive Mulhall) *hld up in midfield: effrt and rdn over 2f out: no imp fnl f* **8/1**

045 **7** *nk* **Bollihope**[29] 8813 5-9-11 62........................................ DougieCostello 10 61
(Richard Guest) *dwlt: hld up: stdy hdwy 2f out: sn rdn: no further imp fnl f* **9/2**[2]

00-2 **8** *1* **Western Way (IRE)**[16] 9013 8-9-4 62.......................(p) NicolaCurrie(7) 6 59
(Don Cantillon) *plld hrd early: cl up: led briefly over 2f out: wknd over 1f out* **3/1**[1]

4- **9** *½* **Noble Aussie (IRE)**[105] 6709 6-8-9 46 oh1................... TomEaves 3 43
(Miss Nicole McKenna, Ire) *t.k.h: hld up: rdn along over 2f out: sn n.d* **33/1**

0566 **10** *shd* **Leonard Thomas**[111] 6470 7-9-2 56.......................... RowanScott(3) 5 53
(Rebecca Menzies) *dwlt: hld up: effrt and rdn wl over 1f out: sn no imp: btn fnl f* **20/1**

5036 **11** *4* **Falcon's Fire (IRE)**[21] 8946 4-9-9 60..........................(b) GrahamLee 11 50
(Keith Dalgleish) *hld up: stdy hdwy over 2f out: rdn and wknd over 1f out* **5/1**[3]

006 **12** *13* **Wind Turbine (IRE)**[31] 8781 3-8-5 46 oh1.................... DuranFentiman 2 16
(Tim Easterby) *led to over 2f out: rdn and wknd wl over 1f out* **33/1**

2m 41.35s (0.25) **Going Correction** +0.10s/f (Slow)
**WFA** 3 from 4yo+ 4lb 12 Ran SP% **119.6**
Speed ratings (Par 101): **103,102,101,101,101 99,99,99,98,98 96,87**
CSF £87.42 CT £705.42 TOTE £5.70: £2.10, £4.60, £2.70; EX 73.40 Trifecta £569.70.
**Owner** The Skills People Group Ltd **Bred** Trinity Park Stud **Trained** Newmarket, Suffolk

**FOCUS**
A moderate handicap. The winner has been rated as building on his turf form.

## 9262 BETWAY H'CAP (DIV II) 1m 4f 98y (Tp)
**3:00** (3:00) (Class 6) (0-60,62) 3-Y-O+ **£3,234** (£962; £481; £240) **Stalls** High

Form RPR
2045 **1** **Theglasgowwarrior**[47] 8478 3-9-4 59............................ PJMcDonald 3 66
(Jim Goldie) *hld up: hdwy on outside over 2f out: led and rdn over 1f out: edgd lft ins fnl f: kpt on wl* **5/1**[3]

3311 **2** *½* **King Kevin**[14] 9056 3-9-4 59...........................................(b) RobertHavlin 1 65
(Ed Dunlop) *wnt lft s: hld up: stdy hdwy 2f out: squeezed through against far rail and chsd wnr ins fnl f: kpt on: hld cl home* **4/1**[2]

50/1 **3** *hd* **Manomine**[15] 9042 8-9-6 57........................................ ShaneGray 6 62
(R K Watson, Ire) *led to 1/2-way: cl up: ev ch over 2f out to over 1f out: edgd lft: rallied: kpt on ins fnl f* **16/1**

043 **4** *nse* **Acker Bilk (IRE)**[31] 8781 3-9-3 58................................ GrahamLee 11 64
(Keith Dalgleish) *hld up in midfield on outside: hdwy to dispute ld briefly over 1f out: sn rdn: kpt on ins fnl f* **6/1**

36 **5** *3* **Lucky Ellen (IRE)**[46] 8498 3-8-8 49............................. FrannyNorton 5 50
(Jennie Candlish) *t.k.h: cl up: rdn along 2f out: kpt on same pce fnl f* **9/4**[1]

0- **6** *nk* **Blue Skimmer (IRE)**[118] 6244 5-9-10 61......................... TomEaves 7 61
(Miss Nicole McKenna, Ire) *plld hrd in tch: effrt and rdn 2f out: outpcd fnl f* **16/1**

5003 **7** *1 ½* **Archibelle**[42] 8585 3-9-1 56................................................ JackGarritty 2 54
(R Mike Smith) *hld up in tch: effrt and hung lft over 2f out: wknd appr fnl f* **33/1**

6000 **8** *1 ¼* **Fillydelphia (IRE)**[23] 8241 6-8-2 46 oh1........................(h) PaulaMuir(7) 4 41
(Patrick Holmes) *hld up: rdn over 2f out: sn no imp: btn fnl f* **80/1**

5460 **9** *nk* **Modernism**[21] 8955 8-9-11 62.......................................(v) StevieDonohoe 10 57
(Ian Williams) *trckd ldrs: led over 2f out to over 1f out: sn wknd* **16/1**

-360 **10** *¾* **Aneedh**[56] 8241 7-8-11 48...............................................(p[1]) CamHardie 9 41
(Clive Mulhall) *t.k.h: hld up: rdn and outpcd over 2f out: btn over 1f out* **50/1**

0003 **11** *6* **Galilee Chapel (IRE)**[23] 8909 8-9-6 60.......................(b) RowanScott(3) 8 44
(Alistair Whillans) *t.k.h: hld up: hdwy to ld 1/2-way: hdd over 2f out: sn wknd* **8/1**

2m 42.88s (1.78) **Going Correction** +0.10s/f (Slow)
**WFA** 3 from 5yo+ 4lb 11 Ran SP% **116.6**
Speed ratings (Par 101): **98,97,97,97,95 95,94,93,93,92 88**
CSF £24.89 CT £299.34 TOTE £5.50: £1.60, £2.40, £3.20; EX 25.50 Trifecta £414.20.
**Owner** Mrs Lucille Bone **Bred** Mrs Lucille Bone **Trained** Uplawmoor, E Renfrews
■ Stewards' Enquiry : P J McDonald two-day ban: careless riding (Dec 30-31)

**FOCUS**
The second leg of a moderate handicap, but this one looked the better of the two. The third helps pin the opening level.

## 9263 32RED.COM NOVICE STKS 1m 5y (Tp)
**3:35** (3:35) (Class 5) 2-Y-O **£4,528** (£1,347; £673; £336) **Stalls** Centre

Form RPR
**1** **Without Parole** 2-9-2 0................................................ RobertHavlin 2 92+
(John Gosden) *prom: shkn up to ld over 1f out: qcknd clr fnl f: promising* **8/13**[1]

01 **2** *6* **Trevithick**[31] 8782 2-9-6 0........................................... GrahamLee 7 79
(Bryan Smart) *chsd ldrs: ev ch over 2f out: chsd wnr over 1f out: kpt on: nt pce to chal* **11/4**[2]

451 **3** *¾* **Windsor Cross (IRE)**[22] 8926 2-9-6 81.......................(b) JackGarritty 5 77
(Richard Fahey) *cl up: led over 2f out to over 1f out: outpcd fnl f* **10/1**

3 **4** *7* **Winged Spur (IRE)**[28] 8840 2-8-11 0............................ PJMcDonald 6 52
(Mark Johnston) *prom: lost pl 3f out: sn outpcd: rallied over 1f out: sn no imp* **9/1**[3]

60 **5** *3* **Camden Town (IRE)**[23] 8915 2-8-9 0........................ BenSanderson(7) 3 50
(Roger Fell) *sn pushed along in rr: effrt and rdn wl over 2f out: sn no imp: btn over 1f out* **100/1**

324 **6** *10* **Sunhill Lad (IRE)**[16] 9015 2-9-2 68................................. TomEaves 1 27
(Ann Duffield) *stdd s: hld up: struggling over 3f out: btn fnl 2f* **25/1**

**7** *3 ¾* **Blue Petal (IRE)**[36] 8724 2-8-11 0................................(b[1]) ShaneGray 4 13
(R K Watson, Ire) *led to over 2f out: sn wknd* **40/1**

1m 38.74s (0.14) **Going Correction** +0.10s/f (Slow) 7 Ran SP% **115.0**
Speed ratings (Par 96): **103,97,96,89,86 76,72**
CSF £2.55 TOTE £1.60: £1.20, £1.50; EX 2.90 Trifecta £8.80.
**Owner** John Gunther & Tanya Gunther **Bred** John Gunther **Trained** Newmarket, Suffolk

**FOCUS**
The second and third had already shown a fair level of ability, and the winner, who was the sole newcomer, looked smart, albeit he was getting weight.

## 9264 SUNBETS.CO.UK H'CAP 7f 14y (Tp)
**4:05** (4:06) (Class 2) (0-105,98) 3-Y-O+ **£15,752** (£4,715; £2,357; £1,180; £587) **Stalls** Centre

Form RPR
556 **1** **Charles Molson**[28] 8843 6-9-5 96................................ DanielMuscutt 6 103
(Patrick Chamings) *prom: hdwy to ld over 1f out: drvn out fnl f* **5/1**[2]

3400 **2** *½* **Heaven's Guest (IRE)**[35] 8737 7-8-8 85..................... PatrickMathers 10 91
(Richard Fahey) *prom: effrt and rdn over 1f out: chsd wnr ins fnl f: kpt on: hld nr fin* **8/1**

2230 **3** *shd* **Pastime**[23] 8905 3-8-10 87........................................... JosephineGordon 1 92+
(Gay Kelleway) *t.k.h: cl up: ev ch and rdn over 1f out: kpt on ins fnl f* **9/1**

3003 **4** *½* **Qaffaal (USA)**[23] 8905 6-8-6 90................................ HarrisonShaw(7) 8 94+
(Michael Easterby) *hld up: nt clr run over 2f out to over 1f out: kpt on fnl f: nvr able to chal* **10/1**

-003 **5** *shd* **Reckless Endeavour (IRE)**[17] 8991 4-9-7 98............ DougieCostello 5 102
(Jamie Osborne) *hld up: effrt and rdn over 1f out: kpt on ins fnl f: nt pce to chal* **9/1**

063 **6** *hd* **Hakam (USA)**[21] 8944 5-9-2 93......................................(p) AndrewMullen 3 96
(Michael Appleby) *hld up: rdn and hdwy over 1f out: kpt on same pce ins fnl f* **12/1**

-105 **7** *hd* **Brittanic (IRE)**[21] 8944 3-9-4 95...................................... TomEaves 7 98+
(David Simcock) *s.i.s: hld up: hdwy and swtchd lft over 1f out: rdn and no imp fnl f* **3/1**[1]

0334 **8** *1 ¾* **Bertiewhittle**[16] 9016 9-8-3 87................................. GabrieleMalune(7) 2 85
(David Barron) *hld up on outside: drvn along over 2f out: no imp fr over 1f out* **16/1**

0002 **9** *nse* **Swift Approval (IRE)**[23] 8905 5-8-12 92..................(vt) AaronJones(3) 11 90
(Stuart Williams) *t.k.h: led on nr side of gp: rdn and hdd over 1f out: wknd ins fnl f* **11/2**[3]

5320 **10** *1 ¼* **Alexandrakollontai (IRE)**[23] 8912 7-8-5 82.................(b) CamHardie 4 76
(Alistair Whillans) *prom on outside: rdn over 2f out: wknd over 1f out* **33/1**

0105 11 *nk* **Rene Mathis (GER)**60 8138 7-9-4 **95** JackGarritty 9 89
(Richard Fahey) *t.k.h: cl up: outpcd over 2f out: btn over 1f out* **9/1**
1m 27.09s (0.89) **Going Correction** +0.10s/f (Slow) **11** Ran SP% **123.8**
Speed ratings (Par 109): **98,97,97,96,96 96,96,94,94,92 92**
CSF £47.43 CT £369.22 TOTE £6.10: £2.10, £3.00, £2.10; EX 54.40 Trifecta £501.10.
**Owner** Trolley Action **Bred** Mrs Sheila Oakes **Trained** Baughurst, Hants

**FOCUS**
The pace was slow early so not form to rely on. The winner has been rated to his best and the runner-up close to this year's level.

## 9265 BETWAY DASH H'CAP 5f (Tp)
**4:35** (4:35) (Class 6) (0-55,54) 3-Y-O+ **£3,234** (£962; £481; £240) **Stalls** Centre

Form RPR
0023 1 **Windforpower (IRE)**43 8558 7-9-1 **53** (v) BenRobinson(5) 8 60
(Tracy Waggott) *prom: hdwy far side of gp over 1f out: led ins fnl f: drvn out* **5/1**3
0616 2 ½ **Little Miss Lola**16 9019 3-9-1 **53** JamieGormley(5) 2 58
(Lynn Siddall) *led at decent gallop: rdn 2f out: hdd ins fnl f: kpt on same pce towards fin* **14/1**
0003 3 ½ **Fintry Flyer**16 9019 3-8-9 **45** (p) PhilDennis(3) 6 48
(Jim Goldie) *hld up in midfield: hdwy nr side of gp over 1f out: kpt on fnl f: nrst fin* **12/1**
6020 4 1 ¼ **Novabridge**12 9075 9-8-12 **50** (b) GemmaTutty(5) 7 49
(Karen Tutty) *hld up: hdwy nr side of gp over 1f out: kpt on fnl f: nt pce to chal* **28/1**
0522 5 1 ¾ **Something Lucky (IRE)**3 9214 5-9-3 **50** (v) AndrewMullen 11 43
(Michael Appleby) *cl up: drvn along over 2f out: no ex ins fnl f* **6/4**1
4000 6 *nk* **Little Kingdom (IRE)**16 9019 3-8-10 **46** RachelRichardson(3) 3 38
(Tracy Waggott) *hld up on far side of gp: rdn and outpcd 1/2-way: sme late hdwy: nvr on terms* **40/1**
5061 7 1 **Roy's Legacy**3 9214 8-9-2 **52** 6ex CharlieBennett(3) 10 40
(Shaun Harris) *cl up: rdn over 2f out: wknd ins fnl f* **8/1**
5050 8 *nk* **Captain Scooby**2 9232 11-8-7 **47** ow2 (b) BenSanderson(7) 1 34
(Richard Guest) *dwlt: bhd on far side of gp: rdn 1/2-way: sme late hdwy: nvr on terms* **28/1**
6206 9 ½ **Vecheka (IRE)**16 9013 6-8-12 **45** (p) TomEaves 5 30
(Kenny Johnson) *hld up: effrt 1/2-way: drvn and no imp over 1f out: btn fnl f* **33/1**
2331 10 *hd* **Dream Revival**10 9103 4-9-0 **54** (p) SebastianWoods(7) 9 38
(Paul Collins) *dwlt: bhd: rdn and drifted lft over 1f out: nvr on terms* **9/2**2
4300 11 11 **Storm Trooper (IRE)**155 4847 6-9-7 **54** (t1) PatrickMathers 4
(Adam West) *in tch: drvn and struggling 1/2-way: sn btn* **20/1**
59.47s (-0.03) **Going Correction** +0.10s/f (Slow) **11** Ran SP% **117.4**
Speed ratings (Par 101): **104,103,102,100,97 97,95,95,94,93 76**
CSF £65.85 CT £813.99 TOTE £5.50: £1.60, £3.50, £3.50; EX 69.00 Trifecta £812.20.
**Owner** David Tate **Bred** Tally-Ho Stud **Trained** Spennymoor, Co Durham

**FOCUS**
A moderate sprint handicap. The second and third have been rated to their recent C&D form.
T/Plt: £383.90 to a £1 stake. Pool: £59,124.30 - 112.40 winning units T/Qpdt: £35.20 to a £1 stkae. Pool: £5,139.73 - 107.81 winning units **Richard Young**

# 9214 WOLVERHAMPTON (A.W) (L-H)
Saturday, December 16

**OFFICIAL GOING: Tapeta: standard**
Wind: Light across Weather: Overcast

## 9266 32RED.COM NOVICE AUCTION STKS 5f 21y (Tp)
**5:45** (5:47) (Class 5) 2-Y-O **£3,881** (£1,155; £577; £288) **Stalls** Low

Form RPR
54 1 **Ty Rock Brandy (IRE)**8 9146 2-8-11 0 RichardKingscote 3 62
(Lee Smyth, Ire) *pushed along to chse ldrs: rdn and r.o to ld wl ins fnl f* **7/2**2
2 1 **Los Camachos (IRE)** 2-9-2 0 FranBerry 6 63+
(David Evans) *s.i.s: sn pushed along in rr: rdn and r.o to go 2nd wl ins fnl f* **8/1**
050 3 1 ¾ **Ideal Spirit**23 8916 2-8-11 52 SamJames 1 52
(Karen Tutty) *chsd ldrs: pushed along 1/2-way: rdn over 1f out: styd on same pce ins fnl f* **40/1**
4 ½ **A Few Good Men** 2-9-2 0 (p1) SteveDrowne 2 55
(Jose Santos) *sn w ldr: led over 3f out: rdn over 1f out: hdd and no ex wl ins fnl f* **15/2**3
05 5 1 ¾ **Straffan (IRE)**14 9049 2-8-11 0 BenCurtis 8 44
(David O'Meara) *sn pushed along to ld: hdd over 3f out: rdn and ev ch fr over 1f out tl no ex ins fnl f* **14/1**
6005 6 1 ½ **Crystal Deauville (FR)**21 8945 2-9-2 0 MartinDwyer 7 44
(Gay Kelleway) *trckd ldrs: racd keenly: rdn over 1f out: wknd ins fnl f* **7/2**2
0 7 2 ¼ **Argon**14 9049 2-9-2 0 LukeMorris 4 36
(Sir Mark Prescott Bt) *sn drvn along in rr: edgd lft over 1f out: eased whn btn ins fnl f* **11/1**
8 5 **Street Sensation (IRE)** 2-9-2 0 ShaneKelly 5 18
(Richard Fahey) *s.s: outpcd* **11/4**1
1m 1.57s (-0.33) **Going Correction** +0.025s/f (Slow) **8** Ran SP% **111.4**
Speed ratings (Par 96): **103,101,98,97,95 92,89,81**
CSF £29.64 TOTE £4.40: £1.50, £2.50, £6.30; EX 38.90 Trifecta £582.10.
**Owner** T Heatrick **Bred** D Laverty **Trained** Magheralin, Co Down

**FOCUS**
A modest novice in which the first two came from off the pace. Weak form.

## 9267 BETWAY H'CAP (DIV I) 6f 20y (Tp)
**6:15** (6:18) (Class 6) (0-55,55) 3-Y-O+ **£2,749** (£818; £408; £204) **Stalls** Low

Form RPR
6434 1 **Hisar (IRE)**16 9013 3-9-5 **53** (p) LukeMorris 1 60
(Michael Appleby) *a.p: shkn up over 2f out: rdn to chse ldr over 1f out: styd on u.p to ld nr fin* **2/1**1
3030 2 *nk* **Frank The Barber (IRE)**29 8816 5-9-2 **50** (t) LiamKeniry 12 56
(Steph Hollinshead) *w ldr tl led over 2f out: rdn and flashed tail fr over 1f out: edgd rt and hdd nr fin* **12/1**
5040 3 1 ¾ **Noneedtotellme (IRE)**9 9129 4-8-12 **46** oh1 GeorgeDowning 6 47
(James Unett) *chsd ldrs: rdn over 2f out: styd on same pce ins fnl f* **25/1**
4022 4 ¾ **Jessie Allan (IRE)**16 9012 6-8-5 **46** SeanMooney(7) 7 45
(Jim Goldie) *hld up: pushed along over 2f out: rdn: hung lft and r.o ins fnl f: nt rch ldrs* **10/3**2
5050 5 ½ **The Hooded Claw (IRE)**26 8873 6-9-6 **54** FranBerry 13 51
(Patrick Morris) *broke wl: sn stdd and lost pl: hld up: plld hrd: nt clr run over 1f out: r.o ins fnl f* **8/1**3
-050 6 1 **Whispering Soul (IRE)**295 899 4-9-0 **48** ow2 RobertTart 4 42
(Brian Baugh) *hld up: hdwy over 1f out: sn rdn: styd on same pce ins fnl f* **33/1**
0060 7 1 ¼ **Tink**60 8133 3-8-12 **46** oh1 KieranO'Neill 3 36
(Mark Brisbourne) *prom: rdn over 2f out: edgd rt and no ex fnl f* **100/1**
5303 8 1 **Firesnake (IRE)**29 8816 4-9-4 **52** (v) BenCurtis 9 39
(Lisa Williamson) *hld up: plld hrd: rdn over 1f out: no imp* **8/1**3
0000 9 *nk* **Night Shadow**16 9019 3-9-7 **55** (b1) ShaneKelly 5 41
(Alan Brown) *s.i.s: hld up: nvr nrr* **14/1**
4000 10 2 ¼ **Jacksonfire**35 8743 5-8-12 **46** oh1 (p) EdwardGreatrex 2 26
(Michael Mullineaux) *hld up: sme hdwy over 1f out: wknd wl ins fnl f* **40/1**
2053 11 6 **Miss Uppity**44 8543 4-8-9 **46** oh1 EoinWalsh(3) 10 8
(Ivan Furtado) *chsd ldrs: rdn over 2f out: wknd over 1f out* **12/1**
0040 12 *shd* **Monarch Maid**35 8743 6-8-13 **52** (p1) WilliamCox(5) 8 13
(Peter Hiatt) *led: rdn and hdd over 2f out: wknd over 1f out* **16/1**
1m 14.74s (0.24) **Going Correction** +0.025s/f (Slow) **12** Ran SP% **116.8**
Speed ratings (Par 101): **99,98,96,95,94 93,91,90,89,86 78,78**
CSF £26.74 CT £475.75 TOTE £2.90: £1.30, £3.40, £5.80; EX 28.10 Trifecta £449.50.
**Owner** The Horse Watchers **Bred** N Hartery **Trained** Oakham, Rutland

**FOCUS**
It didn't pay to be too far off the pace here, the first three racing in the first five throughout. The second and third pin the straightforward level.

## 9268 BETWAY H'CAP (DIV II) 6f 20y (Tp)
**6:45** (6:46) (Class 6) (0-55,54) 3-Y-O+ **£2,749** (£818; £408; £204) **Stalls** Low

Form RPR
0002 1 **Pulsating (IRE)**9 9129 3-9-3 **50** (p) EdwardGreatrex 9 62+
(Archie Watson) *hld up: shkn up and hdwy over 1f out: rdn: hung lft and r.o to ld wl ins fnl f: comf* **5/4**1
0240 2 1 ¼ **Jorvik Prince**22 8924 3-9-6 **53** SamJames 4 58
(Karen Tutty) *sn led: rdn and edgd lft over 1f out: hdd and unable qck wl ins fnl f* **8/1**3
0004 3 1 ½ **Mossy's Lodge**14 9052 4-9-7 **54** LukeMorris 13 55
(Anthony Carson) *prom: chsd ldr and edgd lft 4f out: rdn 2f out: styd on same pce ins fnl f* **11/1**
0060 4 *nk* **Rapid Rise (IRE)**21 8948 3-8-13 **46** (v) TomMarquand 2 46
(Milton Bradley) *pushed along towards rr early: swtchd rt and hdwy over 1f out: sn rdn: styd on same pce ins fnl f* **6/1**2
00-0 5 2 **Go Charlie**10 9102 6-8-12 **45** (h) RaulDaSilva 8 39+
(Lisa Williamson) *s.s: shkn up and nt clr run over 1f out: r.o ins fnl f: nvr nrr* **100/1**
0000 6 *nse* **Three's A Crowd (IRE)**12 9073 3-9-0 **47** (b1) LiamKeniry 7 41
(Ed de Giles) *s.i.s: hld up: rdn over 1f out: nt trble ldrs* **28/1**
0232 7 *nk* **Warba (IRE)**21 8949 3-9-1 **53** (t1) WilliamCox(5) 1 46
(Mohamed Moubarak) *chsd ldrs: rdn over 2f out: no ex fnl f* **8/1**3
4434 7 *dht* **Princess Way (IRE)**50 8395 3-9-5 **52** (v) FranBerry 6 45
(David Evans) *led early: chsd ldr tl n.m.r and lost pl 4f out: rdn over 2f out: styng on same pce whn hung lft ins fnl f* **11/1**
-600 9 2 ¾ **Storm Lightning**26 8873 8-9-3 **53** EoinWalsh(3) 10 38
(Mark Brisbourne) *prom: lost pl 5f out: rdn over 2f out: n.d after* **25/1**
0430 10 ¾ **Hell Of A Lady**12 9071 3-8-12 **45** SteveDrowne 3 32
(Michael Attwater) *chsd ldrs: rdn over 2f out: wknd fnl f* **66/1**
000 11 ½ **Latest Quest (IRE)**11 9083 3-8-12 **45** (b) MartinDwyer 11 26
(Sylvester Kirk) *hdwy over 4f out: rdn over 1f out: wknd fnl f* **20/1**
1m 14.88s (0.38) **Going Correction** +0.025s/f (Slow) **11** Ran SP% **112.2**
Speed ratings (Par 101): **98,96,94,93,91 91,90,90,87,86 85**
CSF £10.07 CT £75.07 TOTE £2.00: £1.40, £2.40, £2.80; EX 12.10 Trifecta £96.20.
**Owner** Dream Racing Club **Bred** Mrs Margaret Sinanan **Trained** Upper Lambourn, W Berks

**FOCUS**
A nice performance from the well-treated winner, but it was the slower of the two divisions by 0.14sec. The second and third help set the level.

## 9269 BETWAY SPRINT H'CAP 6f 20y (Tp)
**7:15** (7:16) (Class 3) (0-95,95) 3-Y-O- **£9,451** (£2,829; £1,414; £708; £352) **Stalls** Low

Form RPR
0042 1 **Tropics (USA)**16 9016 9-8-11 **88** (h) JackDuern(3) 4 98
(Dean Ivory) *trckd ldrs: racd keenly: rdn to ld 1f out: edgd lft: r.o* **11/4**1
6240 2 1 ½ **Rajar**23 8905 3-8-11 **85** (h) FrannyNorton 8 90
(Richard Fahey) *hld up in tch: shkn up over 1f out: rdn to chse wnr ins fnl f: styd on* **17/2**
3000 3 *shd* **Suzi's Connoisseur**77 7622 6-9-7 **95** (t1) FranBerry 1 100
(Stuart Williams) *hld up: rdn over 1f out: r.o to go 3rd nr fin: nt rch ldrs* **15/2**
0002 4 *nk* **Fast Track**11 9079 6-8-9 **83** BenCurtis 6 87
(David Barron) *hld up: hdwy over 1f out: sn rdn: styd on* **7/2**2
0530 5 1 ¾ **Barracuda Boy (IRE)**44 8547 7-9-3 **91** JoeyHaynes 3 89
(Marjorie Fife) *s.i.s: shkn up over 2f out: r.o ins fnl f: nt trble ldrs* **11/1**
6040 6 *hd* **Turanga Leela**10 9089 3-8-4 **81** oh3 (v) GeorgiaCox(3) 7 79
(Ian Williams) *led 5f out: rdn over 2f out: hdd 1f out: styd on same pce* **66/1**
1425 7 *shd* **Seeking Magic**70 7828 9-9-3 **91** (t) RyanTate 9 88
(Clive Cox) *led 1f: chsd ldr: rdn over 2f out: no ex fnl f* **10/1**
1300 8 *hd* **Reflektor (IRE)**98 6927 4-9-5 **93** RichardKingscote 5 90
(Tom Dascombe) *prom: pushed along over 2f out: styd on same pce fnl f* **12/1**
0143 9 3 ¾ **Coronation Day**66 7950 4-9-0 **88** LukeMorris 2 73
(James Tate) *chsd ldrs: rdn over 1f out: wknd wl ins fnl f* **13/2**3
1m 13.69s (-0.81) **Going Correction** +0.025s/f (Slow) **9** Ran SP% **111.1**
Speed ratings (Par 107): **106,104,103,103,101 100,100,100,95**
CSF £25.17 CT £150.80 TOTE £3.50: £1.70, £2.40, £2.30; EX 29.30 Trifecta £200.00.
**Owner** Dean Ivory **Bred** D Konecny, S Branch & A Branch **Trained** Radlett, Herts
■ Stewards' Enquiry : Georgia Cox one-day ban: failed to take all reasonable and permissible measures to obtain the best possible placing (Dec 30)

**FOCUS**
A good sprint and solid form for the grade.

## 9270 BETWAY LIVE CASINO H'CAP 1m 4f 51y (Tp)
**7:45** (7:45) (Class 6) (0-65,67) 3-Y-O+ **£2,749** (£818; £408; £204) **Stalls** Low

Form RPR
5354 1 **Daily Trader**30 8806 3-9-3 **65** FranBerry 1 72
(David Evans) *hld up: hdwy over 3f out: rdn to ld wl ins fnl f: styd on* **4/1**2



The Form Book Flat, Raceform Ltd, Newbury, RG14 5SJ

1113 **2** 1 **Raashdy (IRE)**[21] 8955 4-9-5 **63**........................................ LukeMorris 5 67
(Peter Hiatt) *hld up in tch: chsd ldr over 5f out: rdn to ld over 1f out: hdd wl ins fnl f* **2/1**[1]

0060 **3** nk **Dolphin Village (IRE)**[14] 9054 7-9-6 **64**........................................ BenCurtis 3 68+
(Shaun Harris) *prom: lost pl over 7f out: rdn over 1f out: r.o ins fnl f* **11/2**[3]

5532 **4** 1 **Excellent Puck (IRE)**[129] 5810 7-9-5 **66**................ CallumShepherd(3) 6 68
(Shaun Lycett) *led 1f: chsd ldrs: nt clr run over 2f out: rdn over 1f out: edgd lft ins fnl f: styd on* **7/1**

0530 **5** shd **Gabrial The Terror (IRE)**[21] 8955 7-9-4 **62**........................ LiamKeniry 2 64
(Patrick Morris) *dwlt: hld up: rdn and hung lft over 1f out: r.o ins fnl f: nt trble ldrs* **22/1**

0400 **6** hd **Never A Word (USA)**[17] 8993 3-9-2 **64**..................(tp) TomMarquand 10 67
(Oliver Greenall) *led after 1f: hdd 8f out: remained handy: rdn over 1f out: styd on same pce wl ins fnl f* **9/1**

4335 **7** 3/4 **Pour L'Amour (IRE)**[138] 5483 4-9-6 **64**........................ ShaneKelly 11 65
(Daniel Mark Loughnane) *hld up: hdwy over 4f out: rdn over 1f out: styd on same pce ins fnl f* **14/1**

1336 **8** 1 3/4 **Inflexiball**[78] 7567 5-9-4 **62**........................................ FrannyNorton 8 60
(John Mackie) *trckd ldrs: racd keenly: shkn up over 2f out: no ex ins fnl f* **16/1**

060 **9** 1 **Udogo**[39] 8641 6-9-4 **62**........................................(p) MartinDwyer 4 58
(Brendan Powell) *hld up: rdn over 2f out: nvr on terms* **16/1**

0064 **10** 1 **La Goulue**[11] 9085 3-8-3 **51** oh6........................(v) HollieDoyle 12 47
(John Gallagher) *hdwy to chse ldr 10f out: led 8f out: rdn and hdd over 1f out: wkng whn n.m.r ins fnl f* **66/1**

2m 45.36s (4.56) **Going Correction** +0.025s/f (Slow)
**WFA** 3 from 4yo+ 4lb **10** Ran SP% **115.5**
Speed ratings (Par 101): **85,84,84,83,83 83,82,81,80,80**
CSF £12.23 CT £43.38 TOTE £4.90: £1.80, £1.30, £2.20; EX 15.90 Trifecta £79.10.
**Owner** Mrs Penny Keble-White & B J Mould **Bred** Cheveley Park Stud Ltd **Trained** Pandy, Monmouths

**FOCUS**
A bit of a tactical affair. The winner has been rated near the best of his recent form.

## 9271 BETWAY CASINO H'CAP — 1m 1f 104y (Tp)
**8:15** (8:16) (Class 4) (0-85,87) 3-Y-0+ **£5,175** (£1,540; £769; £384) **Stalls** Low

Form RPR

0250 **1** **Swift Emperor (IRE)**[14] 9053 5-9-8 **86**........................ BenCurtis 9 94
(David Barron) *a.p: rdn over 1f out: r.o to ld wl ins fnl f* **11/1**

3402 **2** 1 1/4 **Andok (IRE)**[23] 8912 3-9-0 **80**........................ JackGarritty 7 85
(Richard Fahey) *led 1f: chsd ldr tl rdn to ld over 1f out: edgd rt and hdd wl ins fnl f* **13/2**[3]

-104 **3** 1 1/4 **Influent (IRE)**[40] 8636 3-8-11 **77**........................ PJMcDonald 5 79
(James Tate) *hld up in tch: rdn over 1f out: styd on same pce wl ins fnl f* **7/1**

3420 **4** hd **Rainbow Rebel (IRE)**[17] 8999 4-9-8 **86**........................ FrannyNorton 2 88+
(Mark Johnston) *s.i.s: hld up: hdwy over 1f out: edgd rt wl ins fnl f: r.o: nt rch ldrs* **7/1**

3000 **5** 1 3/4 **Nonios (IRE)**[14] 9055 5-9-3 **81**........................(h) LiamKeniry 4 80
(David Simcock) *s.i.s: hld up: hdwy over 1f out: sn rdn: styd on same pce wl ins fnl f* **20/1**

6600 **6** nk **Coillte Cailin (IRE)**[25] 8880 7-9-6 **84**........................ MartinHarley 3 82
(David O'Meara) *hld up: hdwy over 2f out: rdn over 1f out: styd on same pce fnl f* **14/1**

0040 **7** 1 **Dutch Uncle**[54] 8297 5-9-5 **83**........................ LukeMorris 1 79
(Archie Watson) *hld up: hdwy u.p over 1f out: no ex fnl f* **10/3**[1]

5100 **8** 1 **Pensax Boy**[14] 9053 5-9-7 **85**........................ SteveDrowne 12 79
(Daniel Mark Loughnane) *hld up: rdn over 2f out: nvr nrr* **20/1**

-556 **9** nk **Sindarban (IRE)**[38] 3716 6-9-6 **87**..........(t) RowanScott(3) 10 80
(Keith Dalgleish) *dwlt: hld up: rdn over 2f out: nvr on terms* **40/1**

0004 **10** 1/2 **Maifalki (FR)**[17] 9000 4-9-1 **79**........................ DougieCostello 8 71
(Jason Ward) *w ldr tl led 8f out: rdn and hdd over 1f out: wknd ins fnl f* **11/2**[2]

3630 **11** hd **Perfect Cracker**[14] 9053 9-9-4 **87**........................ WilliamCox(5) 11 79
(Clive Cox) *hld up: rdn over 1f out: n.d* **33/1**

2005 **12** 4 **Espresso Freddo (IRE)**[14] 9053 3-8-12 **78**..........(h) KieranO'Neill 6 62
(Robert Stephens) *prom: racd keenly: rdn over 2f out: wknd fnl f* **18/1**

0506 **13** 7 **Afonso De Sousa (USA)**[14] 9055 7-9-7 **85**.......... AlistairRawlinson 13 55
(Michael Appleby) *chsd ldrs: rdn over 3f out: wknd over 2f out* **40/1**

1m 58.64s (-2.16) **Going Correction** +0.025s/f (Slow)
**WFA** 3 from 4yo+ 2lb **13** Ran SP% **114.4**
Speed ratings (Par 105): **110,108,107,107,106 105,104,104,103,103 103,99,93**
CSF £72.32 CT £536.38 TOTE £12.80: £3.80, £2.40, £2.30; EX 103.60 Trifecta £819.50.
**Owner** DC Racing Partnership **Bred** John Davison **Trained** Maunby, N Yorks

**FOCUS**
Not a bad handicap.

## 9272 SUNBETS.CO.UK H'CAP — 7f 36y (Tp)
**8:45** (8:48) (Class 4) (0-85,86) 3-Y-0+ **£5,175** (£1,540; £769; £384) **Stalls** High

Form RPR

0052 **1** **Twin Appeal (IRE)**[26] 8872 6-9-5 **83**........................(b) BenCurtis 3 91
(David Barron) *hld up in tch: rdn and edgd lft fr over 1f out: r.o to ld towards fin* **5/2**[1]

-204 **2** 3/4 **Shepherd's Purse**[102] 6801 5-9-0 **78**........................ PJMcDonald 6 84
(David Loughnane) *chsd ldrs: rdn to ld ins fnl f: hdd towards fin* **12/1**

02-0 **3** 1/2 **Exchequer (IRE)**[26] 8872 6-9-7 **85**........................ MartinHarley 9 92+
(David O'Meara) *hld up: hdwy and nt clr run over 1f out: nt clr run again ins fnl f: r.o to go 3rd nr fin: nvr able to chal* **28/1**

5306 **4** 1/2 **Alejandro (IRE)**[3] 9210 8-9-8 **86**........................ TomMarquand 12 89
(David Loughnane) *prom: chsd ldr over 5f out: rdn to ld over 1f out: hdd ins fnl f: styd on same pce towards fin* **11/1**

5056 **5** nk **Loyalty**[9] 9125 10-9-5 **83**........................(v) PatrickMathers 2 85+
(Derek Shaw) *hld up: hdwy 1/2-way: effrt and nt clr run over 1f out: styd on* **20/1**

6033 **6** hd **Eccleston**[16] 9016 6-9-5 **83**........................(v) RichardKingscote 8 85
(Julie Camacho) *s.i.s: hld up: hdwy and nt clr run over 1f out: styd on* **15/2**[3]

3310 **7** nk **The Feathered Nest (IRE)**[71] 7782 3-9-8 **86**........................ JackGarritty 10 87
(Richard Fahey) *hld up: shkn up over 1f out: r.o towards fin: nvr nrr* **16/1**

0202 **8** hd **Kreb's Cycle (IRE)**[30] 8798 3-8-12 **76**........................(p) StevieDonohoe 7 77
(Ian Williams) *prom: shkn up over 2f out: styd on same pce fnl f* **8/1**

0005 **9** shd **Firmdecisions (IRE)**[15] 9020 7-9-1 **82**........................(b) JackDuern(3) 5 82
(Dean Ivory) *hld up: plld hrd: rdn and hung lft 1f out: nvr trbld ldrs* **12/1**

0220 **10** shd **Energia Flavio (BRZ)**[35] 8749 7-8-11 **75**........................(h[1]) ShaneKelly 1 75
(Patrick Morris) *chsd ldrs: rdn over 1f out: no ex wl ins fnl f* **33/1**

441 **11** 1 1/4 **Sword Exceed (GER)**[29] 8818 3-9-5 **83**........................ LukeMorris 11 80
(Ivan Furtado) *dwlt: hld up: rdn over 1f out: n.d* **5/1**[2]

3616 **12** 3 **Call Out Loud**[12] 9074 5-9-6 **84**........................(v) AlistairRawlinson 4 73
(Michael Appleby) *led: rdn and hdd over 1f out: wknd ins fnl f* **10/1**

1m 27.81s (-0.99) **Going Correction** +0.025s/f (Slow) **12** Ran SP% **118.0**
Speed ratings (Par 105): **106,105,104,104,103 103,103,102,102,102 101,97**
CSF £33.30 CT £699.93 TOTE £3.40: £1.40, £3.60, £6.50; EX 39.00 Trifecta £546.70.
**Owner** Twinacre Nurseries Ltd Partnership **Bred** Glashare House Stud **Trained** Maunby, N Yorks
■ Stewards' Enquiry : Patrick Mathers two-day ban: careless riding (Dec 30-31)

**FOCUS**
They didn't go that quick early, it turned into a dash and they finished in a bit of a heap.

## 9273 BET & WATCH AT SUNBETS.CO.UK MAIDEN STKS — 7f 36y (Tp)
**9:15** (9:18) (Class 5) 3-Y-0+ **£3,881** (£1,155; £577; £288) **Stalls** High

Form RPR

0 **1** **Star Quality**[196] 3353 3-9-0 0........................ BenCurtis 1 73
(David Loughnane) *chsd ldr to 1/2-way: remained handy: rdn to ld over 1f out: styd on* **40/1**

3 **2** nk **Peace Terms (IRE)**[45] 8504 3-9-0 0........................ PJMcDonald 5 72
(Ralph Beckett) *s.i.s: hld up: swtchd rt and hdwy over 1f out: rdn to chse wnr fnl f: styd on* **6/4**[1]

4-22 **3** 3 3/4 **Kingofmerrows (IRE)**[8] 9139 3-9-5 71........................ DougieCostello 3 67
(Jamie Osborne) *prom: edgd rt 5f out: rdn over 1f out: styng on same pce whn hung rt ins fnl f* **3/1**[3]

4 **3** 3/4 **Perfect Lady** 3-9-0 0........................ MartinHarley 4 52
(Clive Cox) *chsd ldrs: wnt 2nd 1/2-way: led over 2f out: hdd over 1f out: wknd ins fnl f* **13/2**

0332 **5** nse **Beyond Recall**[40] 8635 3-9-0 71........................(b[1]) LukeMorris 6 52
(Archie Watson) *hld up: bmpd 5f out: hdwy 1/2-way: rdn over 2f out: wknd fnl f* **11/4**[2]

6 **6** 9 **Jakeboy**[28] 8842 3-9-5 0........................ RenatoSouza 2 32
(Sylvester Kirk) *led: rdn and hdd over 2f out: wknd over 1f out* **28/1**

1m 28.59s (-0.21) **Going Correction** +0.025s/f (Slow) **6** Ran SP% **110.9**
Speed ratings (Par 103): **102,101,97,93,93 82**
CSF £98.65 TOTE £20.00: £7.60, £1.50; EX 47.70 Trifecta £381.40.
**Owner** Miss Sarah Hoyland **Bred** Juddmonte Farms Ltd **Trained** Market Drayton, Shropshire

**FOCUS**
The first two came clear in this maiden and there was a surprising result.
T/Plt: £96.40 to a £1 stake. Pool: £105,592.12 - 799.11 winning units T/Qpdt: £10.00 to a £1 stake. Pool: £12,618.20 - 925.42 winning units **Colin Roberts**

# [9112] DEAUVILLE (R-H)
## Saturday, December 16
**OFFICIAL GOING: Polytrack: standard**

## 9274a PRIX LUTHIER (LISTED RACE) (3YO+) (POLYTRACK) — 7f 110y(P)
**12:50** 3-Y-0+ **£22,222** (£8,888; £6,666; £4,444; £2,222)

RPR

**1** **Mr Owen (USA)**[24] 8891 5-8-13 0........................ ChristopheSoumillon 6 107+
(David Simcock) **17/10**[1]

**2** 1 3/4 **City Light (FR)**[45] 8526 3-8-13 0........................ MaximeGuyon 4 102
(S Wattel, France) **11/1**

**3** 3/4 **Early Morning (IRE)**[21] 8944 6-8-13 0........................ IoritzMendizabal 11 100
(Harry Dunlop) **32/1**

**4** shd **Lucky Team (FR)**[11] 5-8-13 0........................(p) HugoJourniac 10 100+
(J Boisnard, France) **11/1**

**5** nk **Nice To See You (FR)**[22] 8942 4-9-2 0........................(b) GregoryBenoist 3 102+
(Robert Collet, France) **10/1**

**6** hd **Speculative Bid (IRE)**[35] 8737 6-8-13 0........................ SeanLevey 5 99
(David Elsworth) **81/10**[3]

**7** 1 1/4 **King Malpic (FR)**[56] 8251 4-8-13 0........................ OlivierPeslier 8 96
(T Lemer, France) **84/10**

**8** shd **Snaad**[56] 8251 5-8-13 0........................ StephanePasquier 9 95
(F-H Graffard, France) **25/1**

**9** shd **Zalamea (IRE)**[45] 8526 4-8-13 0........................ EddyHardouin 7 95
(Carina Fey, France) **10/1**

**10** 1 **Ross (IRE)**[84] 5-8-13 0........................ AntoineHamelin 12 93
(P Schiergen, Germany) **15/2**[2]

**11** shd **Art Collection (FR)**[30] 4-8-13 0........................ MlleAlisonMassin 1 92
(Andrew Hollinshead, France) **86/1**

**12** 3/4 **Miracle Des Aigles (FR)**[22] 8942 4-8-13 0........................ RonanThomas 2 90
(Mme C Barande-Barbe, France) **15/1**

1m 26.09s **12** Ran SP% **119.6**
PARI-MUTUEL (all including 1 euro stake): WIN 2.70; PLACE 1.50, 3.10, 7.40; DF 15.40; SF 18.40.
**Owner** Qatar Racing Limited **Bred** Derry Meeting Farm **Trained** Newmarket, Suffolk

9275 - (Foreign Racing) - See Raceform Interactive

# [9237] CHELMSFORD (A.W) (L-H)
## Sunday, December 17
**OFFICIAL GOING: Polytrack: standard**
Wind: Almost nil Weather: Misty, overcast, raining after race 1

## 9276 BET TOTEPLACEPOT AT BETFRED.COM MAIDEN FILLIES' STKS — 1m (P)
**12:45** (12:47) (Class 5) 3-Y-0+ **£3,234** (£962; £481; £240) **Stalls** Low

Form RPR

0323 **1** **Wicker**[10] 9126 3-9-0 72........................ StevieDonohoe 5 63
(Jane Chapple-Hyam) *trckd ldr: rdn wl over 1f out: chal fnl f: drvn and kpt on to ld last strides* **2/1**[1]

2203 **2** hd **Line Of Beauty**[34] 8770 3-9-0 66........................ RobertHavlin 2 62
(Simon Crisford) *led: rdn over 1f out: kpt on u.p fnl f but worn down last strides* **2/1**[1]

2362 **3** 1/2 **Narjes**[11] 9088 3-9-0 73........................(h) FranBerry 3 61
(Laura Mongan) *hld up in last: plld out wd and effrt 2f out: rdn to chse ldng pair fnl f: grad clsd nr fin* **5/2**[2]

3504 **4** 2 **Ronni Layne**[22] 8948 3-9-0 49........................(b) LukeMorris 4 56?
(Louise Allan) *in tch: rdn over 2f out: nt qckn over 1f out: one pce and wl hld after* **20/1**

64 **5** 3 ¾ **Lunar Mist**[24] 8911 3-9-0 0........................ FrannyNorton 1 47
(Ed Dunlop) *chsd ldng pair to over 1f out: wknd* 9/1[3]
1m 39.69s (-0.21) **Going Correction** -0.075s/f (Stan) 5 Ran SP% **110.0**
Speed ratings (Par 100): **98,97,97,95,91**
CSF £6.30 TOTE £2.40: £1.30, £1.10; EX 6.40 Trifecta £10.50.
**Owner** Mrs T Brudenell & Mrs J Chapple-Hyam **Bred** Lady Berta Partnership **Trained** Dalham, Suffolk
**FOCUS**
An ordinary little maiden.

## 9277 TOTEJACKPOT AT BETFRED.COM FILLIES' NOVICE STKS (PLUS 10 RACE) 1m (P)
**1:15** (1:17) (Class 5) 2-Y-O £3,234 (£962; £481; £240) **Stalls** Low

Form RPR
**1** **Ejtyah** 2-9-0 0........................ JamieSpencer 3 77+
(David Simcock) *hld up in last: prog to chse ldr over 1f out: rdn to chal fnl f: led last 75yds: shade cleverly* 7/2[3]
4 **2** ½ **Calypso Blue (IRE)**[18] 8997 2-9-0 0........................(p[1]) MartinHarley 6 76
(Charlie Appleby) *trckd ldr: rdn to ld wl over 1f out: styd on u.p fnl f but hdd and hld last 75yds* 15/8[2]
3 **3** 4 **Barbara Villiers**[8] 9155 2-9-0 0........................ FrannyNorton 1 66
(Mark Johnston) *sn led at mod pce: rdn and hdd wl over 1f out: no rspnse and sn btn* 13/8[1]
5020 **4** hd **Come With Me**[18] 8998 2-9-0 76........................(t) RobertHavlin 5 66
(John Gosden) *chsd ldng pair: pushed along wl over 2f out: outpcd wl over 1f out: n.d after* 8/1
**5** 8 **Braganza** 2-9-0 0........................ LukeMorris 4 47
(Ed Dunlop) *t.k.h: racd wd: in tch: rn green and hung rt bnd 2f out: sn wknd* 20/1
1m 40.78s (0.88) **Going Correction** -0.075s/f (Stan) 5 Ran SP% **111.0**
Speed ratings (Par 93): **92,91,87,87,79**
CSF £10.59 TOTE £5.10: £2.60, £1.10; EX 12.70 Trifecta £21.00.
**Owner** Abdullah Saeed Al Naboodah **Bred** Good Breeding **Trained** Newmarket, Suffolk
**FOCUS**
The first pair came clear in what wasn't a bad little novice event for fillies.

## 9278 BET TOTEEXACTA AT BETFRED.COM H'CAP 1m 2f (P)
**1:50** (1:51) (Class 6) (0-55,56) 3-Y-O+ £2,587 (£770; £384; £192) **Stalls** Low

Form RPR
6614 **1** **Huddersfilly Town**[10] 9127 3-9-10 56........................(p) LukeMorris 2 62
(Ivan Furtado) *nt that wl away: mostly in last trio tl rdn and prog on outer bnd 2f out: drvn to chse ldr fnl f: edgd ahd last 75yds* 5/4[1]
0000 **2** nk **Our Kim (IRE)**[16] 9034 3-8-10 45........................ TimClark(3) 3 50
(John Butler) *trckd ldrs: wnt 2nd over 2f out: rdn to ld over 1f out: kpt on but hdd last 75yds* 20/1
3300 **3** 2 **Master Of Heaven**[18] 8994 4-8-12 45........................(p) CharlieBennett(3) 6 46
(Jim Boyle) *led: rdn and hdd over 1f out: nt qckn and wl hld in 3rd fnl f* 3/1[2]
00 **4** 2 ¼ **Reason To Believe (FR)**[32] 8784 3-8-6 45........................ PoppyBridgwater(7) 9 42
(David Bridgwater) *t.k.h: hld up in last trio: gng wl enough 3f out: rdn and fnd nil 2f out: wl hld after* 16/1
0560 **5** ½ **Haldaw**[4] 9221 3-8-12 49........................ PaddyBradley(5) 1 45
(Mick Channon) *trckd ldrs on inner: rdn and nt qckn 2f out: steadily outpcd* 9/2[3]
0060 **6** 3 ¼ **Saga Sprint (IRE)**[13] 9077 4-9-4 48........................(v) TimmyMurphy 7 37
(J R Jenkins) *early reminders: mostly chsd ldr to over 2f out: wknd quite qckly* 8/1
/00- **7** 13 **Summerling (IRE)**[522] 4267 6-9-1 45........................ StevieDonohoe 8 10
(Rae Guest) *a last: wknd 2f out: t.o* 20/1
2m 7.81s (-0.79) **Going Correction** -0.075s/f (Stan)
**WFA** 3 from 4yo+ 2lb 7 Ran SP% **114.1**
Speed ratings (Par 101): **100,99,98,96,95 93,82**
CSF £29.43 CT £63.91 TOTE £2.20: £1.50, £7.90; EX 30.60 Trifecta £129.50.
**Owner** BGC Racing XI & Partner **Bred** Bearstone Stud Ltd **Trained** Wiseton, Nottinghamshire
**FOCUS**
There was a fair pace on in this moderate handicap.

## 9279 BET TOTEQUADPOT AT BETFRED.COM H'CAP 7f (P)
**2:25** (2:25) (Class 5) (0-70,71) 3-Y-O+ £3,234 (£962; £481; £240) **Stalls** Low

Form RPR
3514 **1** **Broughtons Knight**[10] 9126 3-9-1 63........................(p) JackMitchell 4 71
(Jim Boyle) *mde all: pushed clr over 2f out: 4 l ahd and rdn over 1f out: unchal* 9/4[1]
5-33 **2** 2 ½ **Ebtkaar (IRE)**[174] 4152 3-9-9 71........................ RobertHavlin 1 71
(Michael Appleby) *mostly chsd wnr: rdn and outpcd over 2f out: nt qckn and no imp fr over 1f out* 6/1
5266 **3** 1 **Tellovoi (IRE)**[9] 9142 9-8-10 65........................(v) JackOsborn(7) 5 62
(Richard Guest) *s.i.s: t.k.h early: in tch: rdn over 2f out: chsd ldng pair over 1f out: one pce after* 9/2[3]
501 **4** 3 ½ **Amazing Grazing (IRE)**[96] 7035 3-9-0 69........................(e[1]) BenSanderson(7) 2 57
(Richard Guest) *t.k.h: trckd ldrs: outpcd over 2f out: hanging and no prog over 1f out* 10/1
4256 **5** 1 ½ **Tulip Dress**[80] 7539 4-8-13 61........................ LukeMorris 6 45
(Anthony Carson) *hld up in last pair: rdn and lft bhd wl over 2f out: nvr on terms* 25/1
4663 **6** ½ **Tasaaboq**[3] 9232 6-8-0 55 oh6........................(tp[1]) NicolaCurrie(7) 7 37
(Phil McEntee) *sn pushed along in last pair and nvr gng the pce: no prog fnl 2f* 10/1
6606 **7** 6 **Madrinho (IRE)**[22] 8958 4-9-5 67........................ LiamKeniry 3 33
(John Butler) *short of room briefly after s: chsd ldrs: lost plr qckly over 2f out: sn wknd* 5/2[2]
1m 25.2s (-2.00) **Going Correction** -0.075s/f (Stan) 7 Ran SP% **113.8**
Speed ratings (Par 103): **108,105,104,100,98 97,90**
CSF £16.09 TOTE £3.30: £1.60, £3.20; EX 18.00 Trifecta £62.70.
**Owner** M B Spence **Bred** Broughton Bloodstock **Trained** Epsom, Surrey
**FOCUS**
This was highly tactical and it's form to treat with caution.

## 9280 BET TOTETRIFECTA AT BETFRED.COM H'CAP 6f (P)
**2:55** (2:55) (Class 5) (0-75,77) 3-Y-O+ £3,234 (£962; £481; £240) **Stalls** Centre

Form RPR
2450 **1** **Excellent George**[113] 6430 5-9-4 75........................(t) AaronJones(3) 7 84
(Stuart Williams) *trckd ldr: pushed into the ld over 1f out: rdn out fnl f: readily* 5/1[3]
1215 **2** 1 ¼ **Bahamian Heights**[2] 9241 6-9-0 75........................ JonathanFisher(7) 6 80
(Robert Cowell) *s.s: stdy prog fr rr 1/2-way: rdn 2f out: chsd wnr fnl f: styd on but nvr able to chal* 9/4[1]
2025 **3** 1 **Arnarson**[18] 8990 3-9-2 70........................(b) LukeMorris 8 72
(Ed Dunlop) *chsd ldrs on outer: drvn and nt qckn over 1f out: one pce after* 5/1[3]
5350 **4** ½ **Courier**[80] 7553 5-9-0 73........................ KevinLundie(5) 3 73+
(Michael Appleby) *chsd ldrs: pushed along over 2f out: no prog over 1f out: styd on last 150yds: nvr nrr* 6/1
5415 **5** 1 ½ **Fredricka**[24] 8907 6-9-9 77........................(v) RenatoSouza 4 72
(Ivan Furtado) *t.k.h early: trckd ldrs: rdn 2f out: fdd fnl f* 3/1[2]
5533 **6** ¾ **Red Stripes (USA)**[9] 9136 5-8-0 61 oh1........................(b) GabrieleMalune(7) 5 54
(Lisa Williamson) *racd keenly: led to over 1f out: steadily wknd* 9/1
0000 **7** 4 ½ **Gold Flash**[10] 9124 5-9-2 70........................ KieranO'Neill 2 49
(Richenda Ford) *a in last pair: struggling over 2f out: sn no ch* 33/1
0-00 **8** 20 **Seraphima**[8] 9152 7-8-7 61 oh16........................(h) RyanPowell 9
(Lisa Williamson) *s.i.s: racd wd: in tch to 1/2-way: wknd rapidly: t.o* 100/1
1m 11.58s (-2.12) **Going Correction** -0.075s/f (Stan) 8 Ran SP% **117.3**
Speed ratings (Par 103): **111,109,108,107,105 104,98,71**
CSF £17.18 CT £59.78 TOTE £6.70: £2.20, £1.30, £1.80; EX 25.20 Trifecta £129.40.
**Owner** D A Shekells,J W Parry,Stuartc Williams **Bred** Old Mill Stud & S Williams & J Parry **Trained** Newmarket, Suffolk
**FOCUS**
A modest sprint handicap, but sound form for the class.

## 9281 BET TOTEWIN AT BETFRED.COM H'CAP 1m (P)
**3:25** (3:25) (Class 4) (0-78,77) 3-Y-O+ £5,175 (£1,540; £769; £384) **Stalls** Low

Form RPR
441 **1** **The Eagle's Nest (IRE)**[58] 8206 3-9-2 73........................ MartinHarley 2 79+
(Rae Guest) *t.k.h: trckd ldng pair: plld out wd and rdn to cl over 1f out: led last 150yds: styd on wl* 11/4[2]
4033 **2** ¾ **Lagenda**[4] 9220 4-9-7 77........................(p) ShaneGray 6 82
(Kristin Stubbs) *pressed ldr: rdn to chal over 1f out: upsides tl outpcd by wnr ins fnl f* 7/2[3]
4121 **3** nse **Glenn Coco**[10] 9126 3-9-3 77........................ AaronJones(3) 4 81
(Stuart Williams) *led but pressed: rdn 2f out: jnd over 1f out: hdd and nt qckn last 150yds* 10/11[1]
4335 **4** 3 ¼ **Colourful Career (USA)**[18] 8995 3-9-2 73........................(p[1]) RobertHavlin 1 69
(Ed Dunlop) *trckd ldng pair: shkn up wl over 1f out: no rspnse and sn btn* 16/1
5130 **5** 2 ½ **Anif (IRE)**[37] 4631 3-9-6 77........................(t) HollieDoyle 5 67
(Jean-Rene Auvray) *a last: pushed along 3f out: no prog and wl btn over 1f out* 25/1
1m 39.64s (-0.26) **Going Correction** -0.075s/f (Stan)
**WFA** 3 from 4yo+ 1lb 5 Ran SP% **111.0**
Speed ratings (Par 105): **98,97,97,93,91**
CSF £12.62 TOTE £3.10: £1.50, £1.70; EX 12.00 Trifecta £21.10.
**Owner** The Eagle Has Landed **Bred** Kevin & Meta Cullen **Trained** Newmarket, Suffolk
**FOCUS**
Another tactical affair.

## 9282 MERRY CHRISTMAS FROM CHELMSFORD CITY RACECOURSE H'CAP 1m (P)
**4:00** (4:00) (Class 7) (0-50,57) 3-Y-O+ £1,940 (£577; £288; £144) **Stalls** Low

Form RPR
0415 **1** **Cookie Ring (IRE)**[4] 9218 6-8-12 48........................(t) FayeMcManoman(7) 2 54
(Kristin Stubbs) *hld up in rr: prog and nt clr run over 1f out: chsd ldr ins fnl f: pushed along and styd on wl to ld last strides* 10/3[2]
2200 **2** hd **Touch The Clouds**[24] 8908 6-9-2 45........................ HollieDoyle 9 50
(William Stone) *mde most: rdn over 1f out: kpt on but hdd last strides* 7/1
2563 **3** 2 **How's Lucy**[9] 9141 3-9-3 52........................ PaddyBradley(5) 4 51
(Jane Chapple-Hyam) *hld up in midfield: effrt and swtchd to inner jst over 1f out: rdn and kpt on to take 3rd nr fin: nt quite pce to chal* 4/1[3]
6051 **4** hd **Secret Lightning (FR)**[4] 9218 5-9-9 57 6ex........................(b) KevinLundie(5) 6 57
(Michael Appleby) *t.k.h: trckd ldrs on outer: rdn wl over 1f out: cl up but nt qckn jst ins fnl f: one pce after* 8/1
0033 **5** hd **Ixelles Diamond (IRE)**[12] 9084 6-9-5 51........................ CharlieBennett(3) 7 50
(Lee Carter) *chsd ldr after 1f: rdn 2f out: lost 2nd and no ex ins fnl f* 10/1
4362 **6** 3 **Dukes Meadow**[9] 9141 6-9-2 50........................ RhiainIngram(5) 1 42
(Roger Ingram) *dwlt: hld up in last: nvr on terms: modest late prog* 5/2[1]
0560 **7** 3 ½ **Dynamic Girl (IRE)**[9] 9141 4-8-11 47........................(t) NicolaCurrie(7) 8 31
(Brendan Powell) *s.s: t.k.h and rapid prog to press ldng pair after 2f: wknd qckly over 1f out: hung lft after* 11/1
06U0 **8** 3 **Fivos**[4] 9202 3-8-8 45........................(p) PoppyBridgwater(7) 10 20
(David Bridgwater) *dwlt: t.k.h: hld up in rr and racd wd: no prog 2f out: wl btn after* 25/1
-000 **9** 3 ½ **Annabella**[11] 9088 4-9-2 45........................ RyanTate 3 13+
(Tim McCarthy) *in tch in midfield: sddle slipped 1/2-way: in rr and rdr wout irons over 2f out* 50/1
0/0- **10** 5 **Sammy's Choice**[690] 341 5-9-3 46........................ TimmyMurphy 5 2
(J R Jenkins) *plld hrd: chsd ldr 1f: prom tl wknd rapidly 2f out* 50/1
1m 40.18s (0.28) **Going Correction** -0.075s/f (Stan)
**WFA** 3 from 4yo+ 1lb 10 Ran SP% **120.5**
Speed ratings (Par 97): **95,94,92,92,92 89,85,82,79,74**
CSF £27.69 CT £99.50 TOTE £5.20: £1.70, £3.10, £1.90; EX 32.80 Trifecta £173.20.
**Owner** Mrs Ailsa Stirling **Bred** Gerard Brady **Trained** Norton, N Yorks
**FOCUS**
A weak handicap.
T/Plt: £22.70 to a £1 stake. Pool: £72,941.64 - 2,340.15 winning units T/Qpdt: £7.90 to a £1 stake. Pool: £7,009.57 - 654.19 winning units **Jonathan Neesom**

9283-9294a (Foreign Racing) - See Raceform Interactive

# 9266 WOLVERHAMPTON (A.W) (L-H)
Monday, December 18
**OFFICIAL GOING: Tapeta: standard**
Wind: Light across Weather: Overcast

## 9295 BETWAY AMATEUR RIDERS' H'CAP 1m 1f 104y (Tp)
**2:00** (2:00) (Class 5) (0-75,77) 3-Y-O+ £3,119 (£967; £483; £242) **Stalls** Low

Form RPR
0504 **1** **Archipeligo**[13] 9078 6-10-4 67........................(p) MrBLynn(3) 3 74
(Iain Jardine) *hld up: hdwy over 1f out: rdn and r.o to ld nr fin* 14/1
4651 **2** nk **Quoteline Direct**[47] 8515 4-10-2 62........................(h) MissBeckySmith 8 68
(Micky Hammond) *chsd ldrs: rdn to ld and edgd rt wl ins fnl f: hdd nr fin* 10/1


The Form Book Flat, Raceform Ltd, Newbury, RG14 5SJ

6220 **3** 1 **Luv U Whatever**[5] 9208 7-10-5 70..........................(tp) MrBillyGarritty(5) 7 74
(Marjorie Fife) *s.i.s: hld up: edgd lft over 4f out: hdwy over 2f out: rdn over 1f out: hung lft ins fnl f: styd on* **8/1**

0403 **4** ½ **X Rated (IRE)**[12] 9096 3-10-7 74.......................... MissEmmaBedford(5) 5 77
(Mark Johnston) *led: hdd 8f out: led again 6f out: rdn over 1f out: hdd wl ins fnl f: styd on same pce* **6/1**

6460 **5** hd **Purple Rock (IRE)**[25] 8912 5-11-0 74......................(t) MissSBrotherton 1 76
(Michael Easterby) *hld up: hmpd over 4f out: hdwy wl over 2f out: shkn up over 1f out: nt clr run ins fnl f: styd on* **7/2**[1]

5621 **6** 3½ **Isstoora (IRE)**[17] 9030 3-10-5 67.................................... MrSWalker 12 62
(Archie Watson) *hld up in tch: chsd ldr over 2f out: rdn over 1f out: no ex ins fnl f* **9/2**[2]

0162 **7** shd **Barnaby Brook (CAN)**[51] 8429 7-10-6 66....................(b) MissADeniel 2 61
(Tom Dascombe) *hld up: pushed along over 5f out: styd on fr over 1f out: nvr nrr* **7/1**

3143 **8** 4 **Beepeecee**[23] 8946 3-9-11 66.........................................(b) MrCJTodd(7) 6 52
(Richard Hughes) *chsd ldrs: wnt 2nd over 3f out tl over 2f out: sn rdn: wknd fnl f* **11/2**[3]

-400 **9** 3½ **Jersey Jewel (FR)**[75] 5968 5-10-2 67...............(t[1]) MissCAGreenway(5) 9 46
(Peter Bowen) *chsd ldrs: rdn over 3f out: wknd over 2f out* **100/1**

5500 **10** 4 **Venutius**[111] 6564 10-10-0 67................................ MrKaiLenihan(7) 11 38
(Charles Hills) *hld up: nvr on terms* **150/1**

6130 **11** 4½ **Mr Red Clubs (IRE)**[82] 7505 8-11-3 77...............................(p) MrFTett 10 38
(Henry Tett) *hld up: hdwy 4f out: rdn and wknd over 2f out* **40/1**

10-6 **12** 2¼ **Sadhbh (IRE)**[325] 439 3-9-12 65.................................... MrCPrice(5) 4 22
(John Flint) *prom: n.m.r and lost pl after 1f: n.d after* **150/1**

0062 **13** 7 **Berlusca (IRE)**[13] 9078 8-9-13 62................................ MissJCooley(3) 13 4
(David Loughnane) *plld hrd and prom: led 8f out: hdd 6f out: chsd ldr tl over 3f out: wknd over 2f out* **25/1**

2m 0.9s (0.10) **Going Correction** +0.075s/f (Slow)
**WFA** 3 from 4yo+ 2lb **13** Ran SP% **118.0**
Speed ratings (Par 103): **102,101,100,100,100 97,97,93,90,86 82,80,74**
CSF £142.72 CT £1206.01 TOTE £14.60: £3.90, £3.40, £3.20; EX 232.20 Trifecta £2824.30.
**Owner** Top Of The Hill Racing Club **Bred** Dachel Stud **Trained** Carrutherstown, D'fries & G'way

**FOCUS**
Mainly exposed sorts in this amateur riders' event which was run at a decent gallop. The winner is back to his autumn form.

## 9296 BETWAY (S) STKS 6f 20y (Tp)
**2:35** (2:36) (Class 6) 3-5-Y-O **£2,749** (£818; £408) **Stalls Low**

Form RPR

0245 **1** **Ballymore Castle (IRE)**[5] 9220 5-8-12 75.................(p) AndrewMullen 1 65+
(Richard Fahey) *chsd ldr over 3f: shkn up over 1f out: rdn and r.o to ld wl ins fnl f* **5/6**[1]

142 **2** ¾ **Bernie's Boy**[7] 9176 4-9-2 67............................................(p) LukeMorris 5 67
(Iain Jardine) *sn led: shkn up over 2f out: rdn over 1f out: hdd and unable qck wl ins fnl f* **9/4**[2]

2042 **3** hd **Haraz (IRE)**[5] 9207 4-8-12 66......................................(p) DougieCostello 3 62
(Jamie Osborne) *hld up: hdwy to chse ldr over 2f out: rdn and ev ch ins fnl f: styd on same pce* **4/1**[3]

1m 15.87s (1.37) **Going Correction** +0.075s/f (Slow) **3** Ran SP% **105.3**
Speed ratings (Par 101): **93,92,91**
CSF £2.84 TOTE £1.70; EX 2.60 Trifecta £2.00.The winner was bought in for 9,000gns. Bernie's Boy was bought by Mr P. S. McEntee for £6,000. Haraz was the subject of a friendly claim.
**Owner** Middleham Park Racing XXVI **Bred** Mogeely Stud **Trained** Musley Bank, N Yorks

**FOCUS**
Just three runners for this 6f conditions seller and it developed into a sprint up the straight after a steady early gallop. A token figure for the race.

## 9297 BETWAY H'CAP 6f 20y (Tp)
**3:10** (3:11) (Class 5) (0-70,72) 3-Y-O+ **£3,557** (£1,058; £529; £264) **Stalls Low**

Form RPR

0666 **1** **Poppy In The Wind**[24] 8927 5-9-3 66..............................(v) HollieDoyle 6 75
(Alan Brown) *hld up: hdwy over 1f out: r.o to ld nr fin* **8/1**

0431 **2** hd **Hamish McGonagain**[19] 9001 4-9-5 68................(p) KieranShoemark 10 76
(David O'Meara) *broke wl: sn stdd and lost pl: hdwy over 1f out: rdn to ld wl ins fnl f: hdd nr fin* **7/1**

6012 **3** 2¼ **A Sure Welcome**[9] 9152 3-9-6 69..................................(p) LiamKeniry 7 70
(John Spearing) *chsd ldrs: led over 2f out: rdn and hdd wl ins fnl f: no ex* **7/4**[1]

2040 **4** nk **Picks Pinta**[107] 6688 6-8-5 59...................................... JamieGormley(5) 8 59
(John David Riches) *prom: jnd ldr over 2f out: stl ev ch ins fnl f: styd on same pce* **33/1**

3504 **5** nk **Field Of Vision (IRE)**[25] 8906 4-9-7 70......................(t[1]) DanielMuscutt 5 69
(John Flint) *hld up in tch: rdn over 1f out: styd on same pce ins fnl f* **16/1**

4140 **6** ¾ **Air Of York (IRE)**[51] 8434 5-9-5 68..............................(p) LukeMorris 3 64
(John Flint) *plld hrd: w ldr 2f: remained handy: rdn over 1f out: edgd lft ins fnl f: styd on same pce* **16/1**

6-01 **7** 1½ **Run With Pride (IRE)**[68] 7951 7-9-2 65...................... PatrickMathers 1 57
(Derek Shaw) *prom: rdn over 1f out: no ex fnl f* **11/2**[3]

0030 **8** ½ **Plucky Dip**[17] 9020 6-9-0 70.......................................... JackOsborn(7) 2 60
(John Ryan) *hld up: racd keenly: rdn over 1f out: nvr on terms* **7/2**[2]

5540 **9** 3¼ **Perfect Symphony (IRE)**[23] 8958 3-9-5 68.................(p) ShaneKelly 9 48
(Sophie Leech) *s.i.s: hld up: n.d* **25/1**

2000 **10** 6 **Kingsley Klarion (IRE)**[31] 8818 4-9-7 70.................... RobertWinston 11 30
(John Butler) *led over 3f: wknd over 1f out* **28/1**

1m 14.7s (0.20) **Going Correction** +0.075s/f (Slow) **10** Ran SP% **119.6**
Speed ratings (Par 103): **101,100,97,97,96 95,93,93,88,80**
CSF £63.18 CT £144.08 TOTE £9.80: £2.50, £1.90, £1.40; EX 70.00 Trifecta £191.10.
**Owner** Mrs M Doherty & Mrs W A D Dyason **Bred** P Balding **Trained** Yedingham, N Yorks

**FOCUS**
Quite a competitive sprint for the grade with several having form on the course. The pace wasn't strong.

## 9298 32RED CASINO NURSERY H'CAP 5f 21y (Tp)
**3:40** (3:40) (Class 5) (0-75,75) 2-Y-O **£3,557** (£1,058; £529; £264) **Stalls Low**

Form RPR

0003 **1** **Tiger Lyon (USA)**[17] 9024 2-8-9 63..............................(h) AndrewMullen 2 65
(John Butler) *edgd rt s: sn led: rdn and hung rt over 1f out: sn hdd: rallied to ld nr fin* **5/2**[2]

0035 **2** hd **Bomad**[17] 9024 2-8-9 63.............................................(v) PatrickMathers 1 64
(Derek Shaw) *prom: outpcd 4f out: hdwy 2f out: shkn up to ld over 1f out: rdn and hung rt ins fnl f: carried hd high and nt run on: hdd nr fin* **5/1**

3366 **3** ½ **Magic Mark**[111] 6547 2-9-0 71.......................................... CliffordLee(3) 5 70
(K R Burke) *chsd ldrs: hmpd over 1f out: sn rdn: r.o* **2/1**[1]

0U50 **4** 1¼ **Peas On Earth**[100] 6950 2-7-11 54 oh6.............................. NoelGarbutt(3) 3 49
(Derek Shaw) *hld up: hdwy on outer over 2f out: hmpd over 1f out: styd on same pce ins fnl f* **50/1**

6234 **5** 2½ **Deviate (IRE)**[27] 8882 2-9-7 75.................................. RichardKingscote 7 62
(Tom Dascombe) *w ldr: ev ch whn hmpd over 1f out: wknd wl ins fnl f* **4/1**[3]

0005 **6** 3¼ **Brockey Rise (IRE)**[27] 8882 2-8-11 65............................ PJMcDonald 4 39
(David Evans) *sn outpcd* **8/1**

1m 2.76s (0.86) **Going Correction** +0.075s/f (Slow) **6** Ran SP% **111.6**
Speed ratings (Par 96): **96,95,94,92,88 83**
CSF £15.00 CT £27.62 TOTE £3.80: £2.00, £2.40; EX 14.90 Trifecta £43.90.
**Owner** M McKay & T Cassidy **Bred** Kelly G Ramsey **Trained** Newmarket, Suffolk

**FOCUS**
Not much strength to this nursery but the pace was sound.

## 9299 32RED.COM EBF NOVICE MEDIAN AUCTION STKS 1m 1f 104y (Tp)
**4:10** (4:12) (Class 5) 2-Y-O **£3,881** (£1,155; £577; £288) **Stalls Low**

Form RPR

50 **1** **Jackfinbar (FR)**[79] 7637 2-8-13 0................................ HectorCrouch(3) 1 77
(Harry Dunlop) *hld up: hdwy over 2f out: rdn and edgd lft over 1f out: nt clr run wl ins fnl f: r.o to ld nr fin* **16/1**

3 **2** nk **Voyager Blue**[23] 8952 2-9-2 0................................... RichardKingscote 2 76
(Jamie Osborne) *trckd ldrs: racd keenly: shkn up over 3f out: rdn and edgd lft ins fnl f: ev ch towards fin: r.o* **13/8**[1]

422 **3** shd **Craving (IRE)**[30] 8849 2-9-2 81.................................... TimmyMurphy 13 76
(Simon Crisford) *led: rdn over 1f out: hdd nr fin* **4/1**[3]

0 **4** nk **Realpolitik (IRE)**[19] 8998 2-8-11 0................................ JackMitchell 12 70
(Roger Varian) *hld up: hdwy and hung lft fr over 1f out: sn rdn: r.o wl towards fin* **33/1**

**5** nk **That's So Cool (IRE)** 2-9-2 0........................................ PJMcDonald 8 75
(David Simcock) *hld up in tch: rdn over 2f out: r.o* **28/1**

4 **6** ¾ **Hasanoanda**[25] 8903 2-9-2 0.......................................... RobertHavlin 7 74
(John Gosden) *chsd ldr: rdn and ev ch over 1f out: styng on same pce whn hmpd wl ins fnl f* **15/8**[2]

663 **7** ¾ **Yamuna River**[19] 8997 2-8-11 74.......................................... LukeMorris 5 67
(James Tate) *chsd ldrs: pushed along over 3f out: rdn and edgd lft over 1f out: styd on* **22/1**

**8** 10 **Stirling Value** 2-9-2 0........................................................ JoeyHaynes 11 53
(David Simcock) *s.i.s: rn green in rr: nvr nrr* **50/1**

00 **9** 4 **Purple Jazz (IRE)**[26] 8888 2-9-2 0...................................... LiamKeniry 10 45
(George Baker) *hld up: nvr on terms* **200/1**

0 **10** 1¼ **Overtrumped**[19] 8987 2-8-11 0.................................... DanielMuscutt 3 38
(Mike Murphy) *hld up in tch: rdn and wknd over 2f out* **33/1**

**11** 6 **Mochalov** 2-9-2 0................................................................ DannyBrock 4 32
(Jane Chapple-Hyam) *unruly in stalls: s.i.s: hld up: rdn and wknd over 2f out* **125/1**

**12** 11 **The Wire Flyer** 2-9-2 0.................................................. KieranShoemark 6 11
(Amy Murphy) *s.i.s: rn green and a in rr* **100/1**

1m 59.54s (-1.26) **Going Correction** +0.075s/f (Slow) **12** Ran SP% **116.7**
Speed ratings (Par 96): **108,107,107,107,107 106,105,96,93,92 86,77**
CSF £40.45 TOTE £18.50: £5.00, £1.10, £1.10; EX 53.90 Trifecta £271.60.
**Owner** Haven't A Pot **Bred** Larissa Kneip & Sandrine Grevet **Trained** Lambourn, Berks

**FOCUS**
Quite an interesting median auction event. The pace was sound and, although just over a length covered the first five home, there were some promising sorts and it should throw up a few winners. The form makes some sense.

## 9300 32REDSPORT.COM CLAIMING STKS 1m 142y (Tp)
**4:40** (4:41) (Class 5) 2-Y-O **£3,396** (£1,010; £505; £252) **Stalls Low**

Form RPR

0010 **1** **Carp Kid (IRE)**[12] 9097 2-8-13 67................................... DougieCostello 7 69
(Jamie Osborne) *s.i.s: hdwy over 6f out: led over 1f out: hrd rdn and hung lft ins fnl f: styd on* **5/2**[1]

4510 **2** 1½ **Zapateado**[19] 8996 2-7-13 63.......................................... NicolaCurrie(7) 5 60
(Richard Hughes) *trckd ldrs: hmpd and lost pl 2f out: hdwy over 1f out: r.o* **11/4**[2]

0616 **3** hd **Blue Harmony**[25] 8914 2-8-12 69............................................ BenCurtis 6 64
(K R Burke) *hld up: pushed along over 3f out: hdwy over 1f out: r.o* **8/1**

565 **4** 1½ **Hilborough**[10] 9137 2-8-10 69.................................... CallumShepherd(3) 8 62
(Mick Channon) *sn pushed along in rr: hdwy 2f out: rdn and edgd lft over 1f out: styd on* **7/1**[3]

300 **5** 1¼ **Taghee**[16] 9050 2-9-4 74................................................ MarcMonaghan(3) 3 68
(Marco Botti) *hld up: nt clr run over 2f out: hdwy over 1f out: sn rdn and edgd lft: nt trble ldrs* **12/1**

02 **6** 2½ **Kheleyf's Girl**[20] 8983 2-8-2 60....................................(v) KieranO'Neill 1 43
(David Evans) *led: rdn: hdd and hung rt over 1f out: wknd ins fnl f* **10/1**

0016 **7** 10 **Trick Shot Jenny**[3] 9238 2-8-5 57....................................... LukeMorris 9 25
(Jamie Osborne) *chsd ldrs: rdn over 2f out: wknd over 1f out: eased* **7/1**[3]

0 **8** 22 **Bond Do Tigrao**[23] 8943 2-8-0 50....................................(t[1]) JaneElliott(5) 2
(Sylvester Kirk) *plld hrd: w ldr: ev ch over 2f out: sn rdn and wknd* **22/1**

1m 50.69s (0.59) **Going Correction** +0.075s/f (Slow) **8** Ran SP% **112.5**
Speed ratings (Par 96): **100,98,98,97,96 93,84,65**
CSF £9.20 TOTE £3.20: £1.30, £1.40, £2.10; EX 9.70 Trifecta £49.90.Hilborough was claimed by Mr J. L. Eyre for £8,000.
**Owner** Melbourne 10 Racing **Bred** Acorn Stud **Trained** Upper Lambourn, Berks

**FOCUS**
Mainly exposed sorts in this juvenile claimer which was run at a muddling gallop, but a minor pb from the winner.

## 9301 SUNBETS.CO.UK MAIDEN STKS 1m 142y (Tp)
**5:10** (5:11) (Class 5) 3-Y-O+ **£3,234** (£962; £481; £240) **Stalls Low**

Form RPR

2603 **1** **Pure Shores**[5] 9202 3-9-0 75........................................... PJMcDonald 6 73
(Ian Williams) *hld up in tch: chsd ldr over 2f out: rdn to ld ins fnl f: edgd lft: r.o* **9/4**[2]

4222 **2** 1¾ **Wonderfillo (IRE)**[166] 4490 3-9-5 74.................................. MartinHarley 4 74
(David O'Meara) *chsd ldr tl led over 3f out: rdn and edgd lft over 1f out: hdd ins fnl f: styd on same pce* **10/11**[1]

**3** 3¼ **Crumblecreek (IRE)** 3-8-11 0...................................... HectorCrouch(3) 3 62
(Clive Cox) *chsd ldrs: rdn over 2f out: styd on same pce fr over 1f out* **10/1**

5 **4** ¾ **Middle Creek**[18] 9018 3-9-0 0......................................... RobertHavlin 2 60
(John Gosden) *hld up: shkn up over 2f out: sn outpcd: styd on ins fnl f* **7/2**[3]

0 **5** *11* **Sutoor (IRE)**[9] 9159 3-9-5 0 ShaneKelly 1 40
(Mark Brisbourne) *led: drvn along over 5f out: hdd over 3f out: wknd wl over 1f out* **100/1**

**6** *1* **Motley Crew**[10] 4-9-7 0 CamHardie 5 37
(Michael Easterby) *s.s: hld up: wknd over 2f out* **28/1**

1m 50.0s (-0.10) **Going Correction** +0.075s/f (Slow)
**WFA** 3 from 4yo 2lb **6** Ran SP% **118.9**
Speed ratings (Par 103): **103,101,98,97,88 87**
CSF £5.04 TOTE £3.30: £1.50, £1.10; EX 5.40 Trifecta £21.40.
**Owner** Fergus Anstock **Bred** The Kathryn Stud **Trained** Portway, Worcs

**FOCUS**
The form horses came to the fore in this modest maiden.
T/Jkpt: Not Won. T/Plt: £118.60 to a £1 stake. Pool: £72,162.64 - 444.00 winning units T/Qpdt: £8.70 to a £1 stake. Pool: £10,768.83 - 908.36 winning units **Colin Roberts**

# 9175 SOUTHWELL (L-H)
## Tuesday, December 19

**OFFICIAL GOING: Fibresand: standard**
Wind: Virtually nil Weather: Cloudy

## 9302 32RED CASINO NURSERY H'CAP 6f 16y(F)
12:30 (12:32) (Class 6) (0-60,60) 2-Y-O **£2,264** (£673; £336; £168) **Stalls** Low

Form RPR

046 **1** **Shades Of Mist**[147] 5262 2-9-7 **60** PJMcDonald 13 66
(Tony Coyle) *trckd ldrs: hdwy on outer 1/2-way: rdn to ld wl over 1f out: drvn ins fnl f: kpt on wl* **16/1**

000 **2** *½* **Good Impression**[50] 8466 2-9-5 **58** (b) TomMarquand 5 62
(Ali Stronge) *towards rr: hdwy 1/2-way: chsd ldrs 2f out: rdn over 1f out: drvn and ev ch ins fnl f: kpt on* **7/1**[3]

6234 **3** *1* **Lady Lintera (IRE)**[20] 9002 2-8-11 **50** (p[1]) ShaneGray 8 51
(Ann Duffield) *in tch: hdwy over 2f out: rdn to chse ldrs over 1f out: drvn and kpt on fnl f* **7/1**[3]

0060 **4** *shd* **Lady Sandy (IRE)**[34] 8783 2-8-13 **52** BenCurtis 14 53
(David Barron) *in tch: wd st: hdwy over 2f out: rdn along to chse ldrs wl over 1f out: drvn and kpt on fnl f* **10/1**

0430 **5** *nk* **Laydee Victoria (IRE)**[34] 8780 2-8-12 **51** AndrewMullen 3 51
(Ollie Pears) *in tch on inner: hdwy wl over 2f out: rdn to chse ldng pair over 1f out: drvn and kpt on same pce fnl f* **18/1**

0500 **6** *nk* **Navarra Princess (IRE)**[34] 8783 2-8-3 **49** NicolaCurrie(7) 7 48+
(Don Cantillon) *towards rr: swtchd rt towards outer after 1f: hdwy and wd st: rdn to chse ldrs over 1f out: drvn and edgd lft ent fnl f: sn no imp* **5/1**[1]

0654 **7** *2 ¼* **Harvest Day**[26] 8902 2-8-11 **50** (t[1]) CamHardie 9 42
(Michael Easterby) *towards rr: pushed along and hdwy over 2f out: rdn wl over 1f out: kpt on same pce* **8/1**

4200 **8** *3 ½* **Still Got It**[20] 8996 2-9-6 **59** FranBerry 6 39
(Daniel Mark Loughnane) *a towards rr* **16/1**

0404 **9** *¾* **Optimickstickhill**[33] 8804 2-9-4 **57** TomEaves 4 35
(Scott Dixon) *slt ld: rdn along over 2f out: hdd wl over 1f out: sn drvn and wknd appr fnl f* **13/2**[2]

0000 **10** *1* **Elixsoft (IRE)**[152] 5056 2-8-9 **55** BenSanderson(7) 10 30
(Roger Fell) *dwlt: a towards rr* **20/1**

004 **11** *4* **Pas De Blanc**[20] 8988 2-9-5 **58** HollieDoyle 12 20
(Brian Barr) *cl up: rdn along 3f out: drvn over 2f out: sn wknd* **12/1**

0040 **12** *1 ¼* **Tea Rattle**[8] 9175 2-8-9 **48** KieranO'Neill 11 6
(Scott Dixon) *cl up: disp ld over 3f out: sn rdn along and wknd* **50/1**

000 **13** *1 ½* **Shadow Seeker (IRE)**[20] 8996 2-8-13 **52** (b) LukeMorris 1 5
(Paul D'Arcy) *chsd ldrs: rdn along wl over 2f out: sn drvn and wknd* **25/1**

0005 **14** *7* **Kylie Style**[20] 9002 2-8-8 **54** ow3 PatrickVaughan(7) 2
(Steph Hollinshead) *a towards rr* **14/1**

1m 17.13s (0.63) **Going Correction** -0.05s/f (Stan) **14** Ran SP% **117.2**
Speed ratings (Par 94): **93,92,91,90,90 90,87,82,81,80 74,73,71,61**
CSF £118.33 CT £892.91 TOTE £13.40: £2.90, £2.70, £2.40; EX 149.90 Trifecta £3137.20.
**Owner** Craig Buckingham **Bred** Talqaa Partnership **Trained** Norton, N Yorks
■ Stewards' Enquiry : Kieran O'Neill caution: careless riding

**FOCUS**
A moderate nursery. The 3rd-5th set base level; one-two improvers off three runs.

## 9303 SUNBETS.CO.UK DOWNLOAD THE APP H'CAP 1m 13y(F)
1:00 (1:02) (Class 5) (0-70,76) 3-Y-O+ **£2,911** (£866; £432; £216) **Stalls** Low

Form RPR

0201 **1** **Mama Africa (IRE)**[58] 8256 3-9-1 **70** JaneElliott(5) 4 81
(David Barron) *t.k.h early: cl up: led over 3f out: pushed clr wl over 1f out: rdn ins fnl f: kpt on wl* **11/1**

0002 **2** *2 ¼* **Muqarred (USA)**[8] 9180 5-9-9 **72** (p) BenCurtis 1 78
(Roger Fell) *trckd ldrs: hdwy over 2f out: sn chsng wnr: rdn over 1f out: drvn and rdn on same pce fnl f* **13/2**[3]

2121 **3** *nk* **Mach One**[8] 9180 3-9-12 **76** 6ex (p) EdwardGreatrex 6 80
(Archie Watson) *in tch: pushed along after 2f: rdn along wl over 2f out: drvn wl over 1f out: kpt on same pce fnl f* **11/8**[1]

0064 **4** *4* **Captain Revelation**[8] 9180 5-9-6 **72** (bt) PhilDennis(3) 2 68
(Michael Mullineaux) *n.m.r sn after s then swtchd rt: trckd ldrs: rdn over 3f out: one pce 2f out: no ex ins fnl f* **20/1**

0040 **5** *1 ¾* **Sumner Beach**[13] 9100 3-9-6 **70** (t) StevieDonohoe 8 61
(Brian Ellison) *a towards rr* **12/1**

6460 **6** *2 ¼* **Tigerwolf (IRE)**[14] 9078 4-9-2 **65** PJMcDonald 7 52
(Daniel Mark Loughnane) *a towards rr* **16/1**

6062 **7** *4* **Red Touch (USA)**[36] 8773 5-9-7 **70** (v) AlistairRawlinson 5 48
(Michael Appleby) *dwlt: hdwy on inner 1/2-way: rdn along to chse ldrs wl over 2f out: drvn wl over 1f out: sn wknd* **7/2**[2]

1210 **8** *4 ½* **Medici Moon**[8] 9180 3-9-1 **65** (p) LukeMorris 3 31
(Scott Dixon) *slt ld: rdn along and hdd over 3f out: sn drvn and wknd* **14/1**

1m 42.28s (-1.42) **Going Correction** -0.05s/f (Stan)
**WFA** 3 from 4yo+ 1lb **8** Ran SP% **111.0**
Speed ratings (Par 103): **105,102,102,98,96 94,90,85**
CSF £75.18 CT £156.14 TOTE £7.90: £2.30, £1.80, £1.10; EX 38.60 Trifecta £192.40.
**Owner** M Rozenbroek & Harrowgate Bloodstock Ltd **Bred** G J King **Trained** Maunby, N Yorks

**FOCUS**
A good effort from the winner to see off two in-form rivals, and this has been rated around the 2nd/3rd.

## 9304 BETWAY MEDIAN AUCTION MAIDEN STKS 6f 16y(F)
1:30 (2:02) (Class 6) 3-5-Y-O **£2,264** (£673; £336; £168) **Stalls** Low

Form RPR

42 **1** **Jack The Truth (IRE)**[298] 904 3-9-5 0 FranBerry 6 73
(George Scott) *mde all: rdn clr 2f out: kpt on strly* **13/8**[1]

32 **2** *3* **Ladies First**[15] 9071 3-9-0 0 CamHardie 9 58
(Michael Easterby) *chsd ldrs: hdwy over 2f out: sn rdn along to chse wnr: no imp fnl f* **11/4**[3]

0633 **3** *½* **Canadian Royal**[11] 9139 3-9-5 58 (t[1]) PJMcDonald 5 61
(Stuart Williams) *trckd ldrs: hdwy 1/2-way: rdn along to chse wnr 2f out: drvn and no imp fnl f* **5/2**[2]

033 **4** *4* **Limoncino (IRE)**[25] 8931 3-9-0 65 (h) AndrewMullen 2 44
(Michael Dods) *awkward s and green in rr: hdwy and in tch 1/2-way: rdn along over 2f out: sn one pce* **6/1**

0065 **5** *3 ¾* **Tilsworth Lukey**[11] 9139 4-9-5 42 TomMarquand 10 37
(J R Jenkins) *cl up: rdn along 3f out: drvn over 2f out: sn wknd* **50/1**

0 **6** *5* **Georgiezar**[20] 8995 4-9-0 0 HollieDoyle 8 16
(Brian Forsey) *prom: rdn along 3f out: drvn and wknd fnl 2f* **200/1**

6 **7** *5* **Fireguard**[11] 9139 4-9-5 0 StevieDonohoe 1 5
(Emma Owen) *a outpcd in rr* **100/1**

00-0 **8** *2 ¼* **Thornton Frank**[34] 8781 3-9-0 0 JamieGormley(5) 3
(Brian Rothwell) *a outpcd in rr* **100/1**

1m 16.44s (-0.06) **Going Correction** -0.05s/f (Stan) **8** Ran SP% **112.1**
Speed ratings (Par 101): **98,94,93,88,83 76,69,66**
CSF £6.13 TOTE £2.50: £1.10, £1.10, £1.30; EX 7.70 Trifecta £16.50.
**Owner** Jack Stephenson **Bred** Michael G Daly **Trained** Newmarket, Suffolk
■ Khaleefa Bay was withdrawn. Price at time of withdrawal 33-1. Rule 4 does not apply.

**FOCUS**
There was a delay after Khaleefa Bay, who had a blindfold on, burst through the stalls, smashed through the rail and went straight into the ditch at the side of the track, not for the first time highlighting the danger of using blindfolds for stalls entry. The filly was fatally injured. The race itself proved pretty straightforward for the favourite. Weak form.

## 9305 BETWAY H'CAP 6f 16y(F)
2:00 (2:22) (Class 4) (0-85,85) 3-Y-O+ **£4,690** (£1,395; £697; £348) **Stalls** Low

Form RPR

0016 **1** **Captain Lars (SAF)**[12] 9124 8-8-5 **76** (v) GabrieleMalune(7) 5 87
(Derek Shaw) *trckd ldrs: hdwy on inner over 2f out: rdn over 1f out: led ins fnl f: drvn out* **9/1**

0352 **2** *1 ¼* **Tricky Dicky**[15] 9074 4-9-4 **82** SamJames 1 89
(Olly Williams) *cl up: rdn along 2f out: led jst over 1f out: drvn and hdd ins fnl f: kpt on same pce* **11/4**[1]

2100 **3** *1* **Handsome Dude**[19] 9016 5-9-7 **85** (b) BenCurtis 4 89
(David Barron) *led: rdn wl over 1f out: hdd appr fnl f: kpt on same pce* **9/1**

4001 **4** *1 ¼* **Hammer Gun (USA)**[8] 9179 4-9-4 **82** 6ex (v) PatrickMathers 9 82
(Derek Shaw) *in tch: hdwy over 2f out: rdn wl over 1f out: sn drvn and kpt on fnl f* **7/2**[2]

2066 **5** *½* **Letmestopyouthere (IRE)**[28] 8881 3-9-0 **78** FranBerry 7 76
(David Evans) *towards rr: hdwy and wd st: rdn along 2f out: kpt on fnl f* **7/1**

0601 **6** *hd* **Mujassam**[15] 9074 5-9-0 **85** (b) PatrickVaughan(7) 2 83
(David O'Meara) *in tch: hdwy over 2f out: n.m.r and swtchd lft wl over 1f out: sn drvn and no imp* **4/1**[3]

-202 **7** *3 ½* **Pearl Nation (USA)**[18] 9031 8-9-7 **85** LukeMorris 8 71
(Michael Appleby) *chsd ldrs: rdn along over 2f out: wknd wl over 1f out* **14/1**

6330 **8** *7* **Crosse Fire**[15] 9074 5-8-8 **72** KieranO'Neill 3 36
(Scott Dixon) *cl up: rdn along wl over 2f out: wknd wl over 1f out* **20/1**

10 **9** *nse* **Bobby Joe Leg**[13] 9101 3-8-10 **74** TomEaves 6 38
(Ruth Carr) *hld up: a towards rr* **20/1**

1m 15.18s (-1.32) **Going Correction** -0.05s/f (Stan) **9** Ran SP% **117.6**
Speed ratings (Par 105): **106,104,103,101,100 100,95,86,86**
CSF £34.67 CT £231.36 TOTE £11.00: £2.70, £1.40, £3.10; EX 44.60 Trifecta £533.80.
**Owner** Chris Hamilton **Bred** Klawervlei Stud **Trained** Sproxton, Leics

**FOCUS**
A fairly competitive sprint handicap and the winner has been rated to his best.

## 9306 BETWAY CLAIMING STKS 1m 3f 23y(F)
2:30 (2:40) (Class 6) 3-Y-O+ **£2,264** (£673; £336; £168) **Stalls** Low

Form RPR

5010 **1** **Throckley**[20] 9000 6-9-5 80 GrahamLee 1 87
(Conor Dore) *trckd ldng pair: cl up on inner 3f out: led 1 1/2f out: rdn and kpt on wl fnl f* **15/8**[2]

4003 **2** *2* **Every Chance (IRE)**[24] 8956 4-9-10 86 (t) TimmyMurphy 4 89
(Jamie Osborne) *cl up: led briefly 2f out: sn rdn and hdd: drvn and hung lft ent fnl f: kpt on same pce* **5/4**[1]

2323 **3** *7* **Brigadoon**[220] 2622 10-9-3 78 RobertWinston 2 71
(Michael Appleby) *led: rdn along 3f out: drvn and hdd 2f out: sn one pce* **7/2**[3]

1303 **4** *40* **Vivat Rex (IRE)**[323] 478 6-9-4 80 (t) TomEaves 5 8
(Conor Dore) *in tch: pushed along 4f out: rdn over 3f out: wd st: sn outpcd and bhd* **20/1**

2m 28.07s (0.07) **Going Correction** -0.05s/f (Stan) **4** Ran SP% **106.2**
Speed ratings (Par 101): **97,95,90,61**
CSF £4.46 TOTE £3.50; EX 7.50 Trifecta £7.70.The winner was claimed by Mrs S. V. O. Leech for £8,000.
**Owner** Mrs Louise Marsh **Bred** The Maroon Stud **Trained** Hubbert's Bridge, Lincs

**FOCUS**
Despite the small field this was a decent claimer, and a nice performance from the winner.

## 9307 SUNBETS.CO.UK H'CAP 7f 14y(F)
3:00 (3:04) (Class 6) (0-65,66) 3-Y-O+ **£2,264** (£673; £336; £168) **Stalls** Low

Form RPR

1010 **1** **Queens Royale**[11] 9142 3-9-6 **62** (v) RobertWinston 7 71
(Michael Appleby) *mde all: rdn wl over 1f out: drvn and kpt on wl fnl f* **11/1**

43-3 **2** *2* **Best Tamayuz**[8] 9180 6-8-13 **55** (p) KieranO'Neill 8 59
(Scott Dixon) *clsd up: rdn along over 2f out: drvn over 1f out: kpt on u.p fnl f* **11/4**[1]

0504 **3** *2 ½* **Big Amigo (IRE)**[15] 9076 4-9-3 **59** (e) PJMcDonald 4 56
(Daniel Mark Loughnane) *chsd ldrs: hdwy over 2f out: rdn wl over 1f out: drvn and kpt on same pce fnl f* **8/1**[3]

5200 **4** ¾ **Unnoticed**[36] 8772 5-9-6 **62**..........(t) AndrewMullen 2 57
(Ollie Pears) *trckd ldrs on inner: hdwy over 2f out: rdn to chse ldng pair over 1f out: kpt on one pce fnl f* **12/1**

6343 **5** 1 ½ **Ubla (IRE)**[6] 9219 4-9-6 **62**..........(p) LukeMorris 10 53
(Gay Kelleway) *midfield on outer: wd st: rdn and hdwy 2f out: drvn and no imp fnl f* **9/2**[2]

5065 **6** 1 ¾ **Fortinbrass (IRE)**[21] 8980 7-9-1 **57**.......... ShaneGray 3 43
(John Balding) *prom: rdn along wl over 2f out: drvn wl over 1f out: grad wknd* **16/1**

0105 **7** nk **Noble Ballad**[33] 8801 3-9-5 **61**..........(b) GrahamLee 9 46
(Ralph Beckett) *chsd ldrs on outer: wd st: rdn along over 2f out: grad wknd* **9/2**[2]

0460 **8** 2 **Seaview**[18] 9034 3-9-0 **59**.......... AaronJones(3) 5 39
(David Brown) *a towards rr* **11/1**

0000 **9** ¾ **Hernando Torres**[18] 9029 9-9-0 **63**..........(tp) RyanTimby(7) 1 41
(Michael Easterby) *dwlt: a in rr* **33/1**

0035 **10** 3 ¼ **Ticks The Boxes (IRE)**[36] 8772 5-9-10 **66**..........(p) TomEaves 6 35
(John Wainwright) *a towards rr* **14/1**

1m 29.52s (-0.78) **Going Correction** -0.05s/f (Stan) **10 Ran SP% 114.0**
Speed ratings (Par 101): **102,99,96,96,94 92,91,89,88,85**
CSF £40.44 CT £259.90 TOTE £11.30: £3.00, £1.30, £2.50; EX 49.90 Trifecta £488.60.
**Owner** Wayne Brackstone, Steve Whitear **Bred** W Brackstone & S J Whitear **Trained** Oakham, Rutland

**FOCUS**
A modest affair in which the pace held up.

## 9308 BETWAY SPRINT H'CAP 4f 214y(F)
**3:30** (3:30) (Class 5) (0-75,75) 3-Y-0+ **£2,911** (£866; £432; £216) **Stalls** Centre

Form RPR

0351 **1** **Pearl Acclaim (IRE)**[8] 9181 7-8-11 **65** 6ex..........(p) TomMarquand 5 74
(David C Griffiths) *prom: cl up 1/2-way: rdn to chal and ev ch over 1f out: n.m.r and drvn ins fnl f: kpt on wl to ld nr fin* **5/1**[2]

5336 **2** shd **Red Stripes (USA)**[2] 9280 5-8-0 **61** oh1..........(b) GabrieleMalune(7) 9 69
(Lisa Williamson) *cl up: slt ld over 2f out: rdn and edgd lft over 1f out: drvn and hung lft ins fnl f: hdd and no ex nr line* **10/1**

1065 **3** 1 ¾ **Gnaad (IRE)**[15] 9074 3-9-7 **75**.......... LiamKeniry 1 77
(Alan Bailey) *racd towards far side: trckd ldrs: hdwy and cl up 1/2-way: rdn along wl over 1f out: ev ch tl drvn ins fnl f and kpt on same pce* **9/4**[1]

3104 **4** 1 ¼ **Apricot Sky**[25] 8927 7-9-6 **74**..........(p) AndrewMullen 8 71
(Michael Dods) *led centre: hdd over 2f out: cl up and pushed along: rdn over 1f out: n.m.r and swtchd rt ins fnl f: kpt on same pce* **16/1**

5400 **5** 2 ½ **Monte Cinq (IRE)**[12] 9124 3-9-7 **75**.......... TomEaves 7 63
(Jason Ward) *racd towards stands' side: in tch: hdwy 2f out: rdn over 1f out: no imp fnl f* **16/1**

3052 **6** 1 ¼ **Kody Ridge (IRE)**[118] 6313 3-9-4 **72**.......... BenCurtis 4 56
(Roger Fell) *racd towards far side: chsd ldrs: rdn along 2f out: sn drvn and grad wknd* **5/1**[2]

0014 **7** shd **Broadhaven Honey (IRE)**[29] 8873 3-8-11 **65**..........(v) LukeMorris 10 48
(Ronald Harris) *racd towards stands' side: chsd ldrs: cl up 1/2-way: rdn along wl over 1f out: wknd fnl f* **17/2**[3]

4342 **7** dht **Angel Palanas**[41] 8681 3-8-7 **61** oh2..........(p) JoeyHaynes 2 44
(K R Burke) *racd towards far side: in tch: rdn along 2f out: no hdwy* **10/1**

3010 **9** ½ **Roaring Rory**[25] 8927 4-8-5 **64**..........(p) JamieGormley(5) 6 46
(Ollie Pears) *dwlt: sn outpcd and a in rr* **10/1**

0006 **10** 1 ¾ **Fly True**[180] 4011 4-8-10 **64**..........(p1) NickyMackay 3 39
(Suzzanne France) *dwlt: a bhd nr stands' side* **33/1**

59.29s (-0.41) **Going Correction** 0.0s/f (Stan) **10 Ran SP% 116.6**
Speed ratings (Par 103): **103,102,100,98,94 92,91,91,91,88**
CSF £54.12 CT £146.51 TOTE £5.00: £1.50, £2.80, £1.60; EX 49.30 Trifecta £245.90.
**Owner** Ontoawinner 2 & Partner **Bred** Awbeg Stud **Trained** Bawtry, S Yorks

**FOCUS**
A competitive heat and a tight finish. The winner replicated last week's win here.
T/Jkpt: Not Won. T/Plt: £76.40 to a £1 stake. Pool: £75,739.28 - 723.27 winning units T/Qpdt: £19.50 to a £1 stake. Pool: £8,716.47 - 329.91 winning units **Joe Rowntree**

# 8884 CHANTILLY (R-H)
### Tuesday, December 19
**OFFICIAL GOING: Polytrack: standard**

## 9309a PRIX DE LA ROUTE DU BERCEAU (CLAIMER) (4YO+) (POLYTRACK) 7f 110y(P)
**10:25** 4-Y-0+ **£7,692** (£3,076; £2,307; £1,538; £769)

RPR

**1** **See You Soon (FR)**[102] 6-8-11 0.......... NicolasLarenaudie 2 67
(P Sobry, France) **7/2**[2]

**2** nse **Well Fleeced**[14] 5-9-5 0.......... WilliamsSaraiva 12 75
(Carina Fey, France) **43/10**[3]

**3** hd **Honiara**[55] 8344 4-9-4 0..........(p) ThomasMessina 1 73
(J-M Capitte, France) **10/1**

**4** 1 ½ **Heir To A Throne (FR)**[67] 8014 4-9-4 0.......... FrankPanicucci 14 70
(Leo Braem, Belgium) **23/1**

**5** 5 **Spirit Of Nayef (FR)**[386] 4-9-1 0.......... ThierryThulliez 7 54
(F Vermeulen, France) **31/10**[1]

**6** ¾ **Ducale Di Maremma (ITY)**[78] 4-9-4 0.......... JimmyTastayre 3 55
(Frank Sheridan, Italy) **46/1**

**7** ¾ **Shaslika (FR)**[55] 7-8-11 0.......... PaulineProd'homme(5) 5 51
(D & P Prod'Homme, France) **17/1**

**8** nse **Arineo (GER)**[13] 4-8-11 0..........(p) MatthiasLauron 13 46
(Yasmin Almenrader, Germany) **13/2**

**9** nk **Bat Aloufat (FR)**[63] 4-8-11 0.......... GabrielLeDevehat 11 46
(M Pimbonnet, France) **24/1**

**10** 1 ¼ **Rip Van Suzy (IRE)**[446] 6912 4-8-11 0.......... GuillaumeTrolleyDePrevaux 8 42
(Jo Hughes) *visibility poor due to fog: trckd ldrs into st: rdn over 1f out: wknd fnl f* **55/1**

**11** 4 ½ **Dazari (FR)**[143] 4-8-11 0..........(p) RichardJuteau 9 31
(S Gouyette, France) **29/1**

**12** snk **Lions Hill (GER)**[13] 9112 4-9-0 0.......... MlleMelineeKuntz(4) 4 38
(J-Y Artu, France) **65/1**

**13** 2 ½ **Dumbarton Rock**[1582] 5617 7-8-11 0.......... ThomasHuet 15 25
(Georgios Alimpinisis, Greece) **41/1**

**14** 3 ½ **Sopran Anny (ITY)**[245] 4-8-8 0.......... AdrienMoreau 10 13
(Frank Sheridan, Italy) **107/1**

**15** 2 **Polarstern (GER)** 5-8-11 0.......... ErwannLebreton 16 11
(U Schwinn, Germany) **58/1**

**16** 3 ½ **Luminous Mind (USA)**[22] 9-8-11 0.......... StephaneLaurent 6 2
(F-X Belvisi, France) **53/1**

**17** 20 **S Grillo**[288] 1070 9-8-11 0.......... AntonioPolli 17
(G Bernaud, Belgium) **68/1**

1m 29.8s **17 Ran SP% 118.7**
PARI-MUTUEL (all including 1 euro stake): WIN 4.50; PLACE 1.80, 1.90, 2.90; DF 11.80; SF 23.70.
**Owner** Antoine Boucher **Bred** Mme A Tamagni **Trained** France

# 9198 KEMPTON (A.W) (R-H)
### Wednesday, December 20
**OFFICIAL GOING: Polytrack: standard**
Wind: Nil Weather: Cloudy

## 9310 CINDY FULLER NOVICE MEDIAN AUCTION STKS 6f (P)
**4:10** (4:13) (Class 6) 2-Y-O **£2,587** (£770; £384; £192) **Stalls** Low

Form RPR

**1** **Worship (IRE)** 2-8-11 0.......... OisinMurphy 2 73+
(David Simcock) *settled bhd ldrs on rail: shkn up wl over 1f out to chse clr ldr: gradual prog ins fnl f u.str hands and heels riding: upsides 110yds out: rdn nr fin to ld: progive* **11/4**[2]

31 **2** ½ **Desert Doctor (IRE)**[21] 8988 2-9-9 0.......... LiamKeniry 5 83
(Ed Walker) *sn led: clr ldr at 1/2-way and set gd pce: shkn up and 3 l ld ent fnl f where flashed tail: hrd pressed 110yds out: kpt on wl tl hdd nr fin* **8/1**[3]

01 **3** 2 ¾ **Count Otto (IRE)**[21] 8989 2-9-9 0..........(h) JoeyHaynes 3 75
(Amanda Perrett) *settled bhd ldr: rdn along 2f out: nt gng pce of ldng pair: kpt on fr over 1f out to take 3rd* **6/5**[1]

34 **4** 1 ¼ **Lady Al Thumama**[56] 8347 2-8-11 0..........(t1) StevieDonohoe 7 59
(Charlie Fellowes) *between horses chsng ldrs and ref to settle: shkn up over 2f out: rdn over 1f out: plugged on one pce ins fnl f* **9/1**

6 **5** ½ **Sea Ess Seas (IRE)**[21] 8988 2-9-2 0..........(t) DougieCostello 1 63+
(Jamie Osborne) *on rail in mid-div: rdn 2f out and chsd ldr over 1f out: kpt on one pce tl wknd ins fnl f* **20/1**

52 **6** 2 ¾ **Moon Song**[19] 9022 2-8-8 0.......... HectorCrouch(3) 11 49
(Clive Cox) *chsd ldrs and racd wdst: rdn along over 2f out: sn one pce* **12/1**

64 **7** 3 ¾ **Mischievous Rock**[19] 9023 2-8-6 0.......... JaneElliott(5) 4 38
(Michael Appleby) *chsd ldr on outer: rdn jst over 2f out: nt qckn and plugged on fr over 1f out* **40/1**

0 **8** 1 **Bayards Cove**[28] 8889 2-8-11 0.......... HollieDoyle 8 35
(Brian Barr) *in rr-div on inner: rdn along wl over 2f out and bhd: plugged on* **200/1**

**9** 1 **Woggle (IRE)** 2-8-11 0.......... JosephineGordon 12 32
(Geoffrey Deacon) *in rr: pushed along at 1/2-way: rdn over 2f out: sn help* **100/1**

**10** 2 **Pak Choi** 2-9-2 0.......... RobHornby 9 31
(Andrew Balding) *restless and wnt down in stalls: s.s and a in rr* **25/1**

0 **11** 2 ¾ **One More Dawn**[28] 8889 2-8-11 0..........(h1) DannyBrock 10 18
(Mark Pattinson) *missed break and a in rr* **250/1**

1m 12.14s (-0.96) **Going Correction** -0.125s/f (Stan) **11 Ran SP% 113.9**
Speed ratings (Par 94): **101,100,96,95,94 90,85,84,83,80 76**
CSF £22.71 TOTE £3.50: £1.50, £2.10, £1.10; EX 21.00 Trifecta £38.70.
**Owner** Qatar Racing Ltd & Kin Hung Kei **Bred** Roundhill Stud & J S Investments **Trained** Newmarket, Suffolk
■ Ambroise was withdrawn not under orders. Price at time of withdrawal 12-1. Rule 4 applies to board prices prior to withdrawal. Deduction - 5p in the pound. New market formed.

**FOCUS**
A fair novice, and the first two finished nicely clear.

## 9311 32RED/BRITISH STALLION STUDS EBF NOVICE STKS 7f (P)
**4:40** (4:43) (Class 5) 2-Y-O **£3,234** (£962; £481; £240) **Stalls** Low

Form RPR

**1** **Mr Ritz** 2-9-2 0.......... MartinHarley 14 84+
(Jeremy Noseda) *broke wl fr wd draw and sn bhd ldr on outer: shkn up wl over 1f out and wnt clr of pack w ldr: rdn and nosed ahd ent fnl f: rn green tl on top fnl 100yds and pushed out* **6/1**

4 **2** 1 **La Maquina**[28] 8889 2-9-2 0.......... LiamKeniry 11 81
(George Baker) *sn led and racd keenly: shkn up wl over 1f out and wnt clr of pack w wnr in cl pursuit: rdn and marginally hdd ent fnl f: kpt on pressing wnr tl no ex fnl 100yds* **9/2**[3]

**3** 10 **My Boy Sepoy** 2-9-2 0.......... DanielMuscutt 4 58+
(Stuart Williams) *hld up in rr: gng wl and plenty to do whn shkn up over 2f out: sn hmpd and slowed for a couple of strides: pushed along and gd hdwy through pack to take modest 3rd wl ins fnl f: nvr involved* **50/1**

62 **4** shd **Royal Residence**[62] 8189 2-9-2 0..........(v1) LukeMorris 7 54+
(James Tate) *hmpd s: hld up in mid-div: rdn 2f out on outer and prog to go modest 3rd over 1f out: kpt on fnl f tl lost 3rd nr fin* **9/4**[1]

**5** shd **Stealth** 2-9-2 0.......... RobertHavlin 8 53+
(John Gosden) *hmpd s: in rr: shkn up wl over 2f out on inner and prog: pushed out fr over 1f out and kpt on wl ins fnl f* **4/1**[2]

0 **6** 1 ¼ **Silverturnstogold**[7] 9198 2-9-2 0.......... RobHornby 12 50
(Neil Mulholland) *bhd ldrs on rail: shkn up and n.m.r 2f out: plugged on under hands and heels fr over 1f out* **150/1**

0 **7** 2 **Sheila Rose (IRE)**[28] 8888 2-8-11 0.......... ShaneKelly 13 40
(Denis Coakley) *chsd ldrs on outer: rdn over 2f out: sn lft bhd by ldng pce: plugged on tl wknd fr over 1f out* **150/1**

**8** 1 ¼ **Arnoul Of Metz** 2-9-2 0.......... FranBerry 3 41
(Henry Spiller) *settled in rr-div: rdn over 2f out: plugged on one pce fr over 1f out* **20/1**

**9** 1 ¾ **Craftiness** 2-8-11 0..........(h1) KieranShoemark 9 32
(Roger Charlton) *wnt bdly rt s and hmpd rivals: effrt over 2f out: nt qckn and kpt on one pce* **16/1**

0 **10** hd **Jampower**[21] 8989 2-8-13 0.......... AaronJones(3) 2 36
(Stuart Williams) *bhd ldr on rail and t.k.h: lft bhd by ldng pair 2f out: no ex: pushed out and wknd fr over 1f out* **66/1**

0 **11** 1 ¼ **Crazie Maisie**[32] 8850 2-8-11 0.......... HollieDoyle 6 28
(Brian Barr) *racd in mid-div on inner: rdn 2f out: nt qckn and one pce fnl f* **250/1**

12 *1* **Dubai Landmark (IRE)** 2-9-2 0 JosephineGordon 10 30
(Hugo Palmer) *in rr-div on outer: hrd rdn on outer fr over 2f out: no ex fr over 1f out* 13/2

13 *9* **Paco Style** 2-9-2 0 KierenFox 5
(Michael Attwater) *awkward s: detached and rn green: no ch fr over 4f out* 66/1

1m 26.62s (0.62) **Going Correction** -0.125s/f (Stan) 13 Ran SP% 113.9
Speed ratings (Par 96): **91,89,78,78,78 76,74,73,71,70 69,68,57**
CSF £30.90 TOTE £7.10: £2.70, £1.60, £5.60; EX 31.90 Trifecta £837.60.
**Owner** The Honorable Earle I Mack **Bred** E I Mack **Trained** Newmarket, Suffolk

**FOCUS**
This was steadily run early on and it was an advantage to race handily. Nevertheless, the first two pulled miles clear of the rest and look useful sorts.

## 9312 32RED ON THE APP STORE NOVICE STKS (DIV I) 1m (P)
**5:10** (5:15) (Class 5) 2-Y-O £3,234 (£962; £481; £240) **Stalls** Low

Form RPR

32 **1** **Glencadam Master**[21] [8987] 2-9-2 0 RobertHavlin 1 83
(John Gosden) *wl away and sn led: rdn 2f out: kpt on wl fr over 1f out: plld out plenty whn pressed ent fnl f: wl on top cl home* 13/8[2]

54 **2** *1 ¾* **Tum Tum**[7] [9200] 2-9-2 0 FrannyNorton 2 79
(Martyn Meade) *bhd ldr on rail: shkn up and chsd wnr 2f out: rdn over 1f out and ev ch ent fnl f: briefly threatened tl no ex 100yds out* 6/1[3]

00 **3** *2 ½* **Battle Lines**[60] [8245] 2-9-2 0 FranBerry 7 73+
(James Tate) *hld up in rr: sltly squeezed up between horses in rr over 2f out: pushed along and prog fr pack 2f out: wnt to inner: no threat to ldng pair: kpt on w promise fr over 1f out to line* 25/1

1 **4** *1 ¼* **Statehood (IRE)**[48] [8545] 2-9-9 0 AdamKirby 3 78
(Charlie Appleby) *sn bhd ldr on outer: rdn 2f out and ev ch over 1f out: one pce ent fnl f and lost 3rd fnl 110yds* 11/8[1]

**5** *2 ¼* **Valyrian** 2-9-2 0 LukeMorris 10 65+
(Luca Cumani) *racd in mid-div: rdn 2f out: plugged on fr over 1f out* 20/1

0 **6** *3 ¾* **Braemar**[125] [6108] 2-9-2 0 OisinMurphy 11 57
(Sir Michael Stoute) *in rr-div and racd wd: rdn on bnd appr st: plenty to do and pushed along in rr 2f out: pleasing hdwy fr over 1f out: nvr nrr* 12/1

3 **7** *hd* **Passing Clouds**[56] [8340] 2-9-2 0 KierenFox 8 56
(Michael Attwater) *wl away tl restrained into rr after 3f: effrt over 2f out on outer: no ex sn after* 40/1

**8** *1* **Thama** 2-8-11 0 (h[1]) EdwardGreatrex 6 49
(Mrs Ilka Gansera-Leveque) *racd in mid-div on rail: rdn over 2f out on inner: one pce after* 100/1

**9** *1 ¾* **Pastoral Dreams** 2-9-2 0 HollieDoyle 4 50
(Simon Dow) *a in rr: effrt fr over 2f out: one pce* 100/1

00 **10** *¾* **Dawn Dash**[29] [8877] 2-8-11 0 JosephineGordon 12 43
(Ralph Beckett) *chsd ldrs and racd on outer: rdn along wl over 2f out: sn struggling* 50/1

0 **11** *2 ¼* **Billy Star**[28] [8890] 2-9-2 0 KieranO'Neill 9 43
(Jimmy Fox) *racd in mid-div between horses: t.k.h early: rdn along over 2f out: fnd little* 200/1

0 **12** *2* **Houlton**[32] [8849] 2-9-2 0 (t) KieranShoemark 5 38
(Marco Botti) *missed break and rdn to hold tch: in rr: shkn up and fnd nil over 2f out: pushed out* 80/1

1m 37.89s (-1.91) **Going Correction** -0.125s/f (Stan) 12 Ran SP% 118.9
Speed ratings (Par 96): **104,102,99,98,96 92,92,91,89,88 86,84**
CSF £11.35 TOTE £2.40: £1.10, £1.60, £6.70; EX 12.00 Trifecta £123.70.
**Owner** Angus Dundee Distillers plc **Bred** Lord Margadale & Mr & Mrs A Scott **Trained** Newmarket, Suffolk

**FOCUS**
Few got into this.

## 9313 32RED ON THE APP STORE NOVICE STKS (DIV II) 1m (P)
**5:40** (5:43) (Class 5) 2-Y-O £3,234 (£962; £481; £240) **Stalls** Low

Form RPR

3 **1** **Native Appeal (IRE)**[18] [9050] 2-9-2 0 (t) AdamKirby 9 79+
(Charlie Appleby) *w ldr on outer: rdn 2f out in centre: knuckled down ins fnl f and led 100yds out: pushed out nr fin: snug* 9/4[1]

2260 **2** *¾* **Albishr (IRE)**[67] [8035] 2-9-9 101 TomMarquand 13 84
(Simon Dow) *sn led: rdn 2f out: kpt on wl tl hdd last 100yds: no ex* 11/2[3]

43 **3** *1 ½* **Talas (IRE)**[32] [8849] 2-9-2 0 JackMitchell 6 74
(Roger Varian) *chsd ldrs on rail: rdn 2f out on inner: ev ch over 1f out: one pce ins fnl f and jst hld 3rd* 3/1[2]

**4** *½* **Qayed (CAN)** 2-9-2 0 JamieSpencer 7 72+
(David Simcock) *in mid-div on outer: shkn up over 2f out w plenty to do: rn green tl kpt on past horses under hands and heels fr over 1f out: sn shuffled along: shaped w plenty of promise and picked up wl ins fnl f: nvr involved* 12/1

0 **5** *1 ½* **Gattaia (USA)**[112] [6575] 2-8-11 0 OisinMurphy 4 64
(Ralph Beckett) *bhd ldrs on outer: effrt 2f out: kpt on one pce fr over 1f out* 14/1

0 **6** *1 ¼* **Apache Blaze**[42] [8670] 2-8-11 0 AndrewMullen 3 61
(Michael Appleby) *chsd ldr on rail: effrt on inner 2f out: kpt on one pce* 66/1

**7** *hd* **Scottish Jig (USA)** 2-8-11 0 RobertHavlin 1 61
(John Gosden) *in rr-div on rail: squeezed along w plenty to do over 2f out: effrt 2f out: shuffled along after* 11/2[3]

**8** *nse* **Legal History (IRE)** 2-9-2 0 LiamKeniry 10 66+
(Ed Walker) *in rr: shuffled along in rr fr 2f out w plenty to do: pushed out fr over 1f out: can do bttr* 25/1

00 **9** *1 ¾* **Vice Marshal (IRE)**[187] [3783] 2-9-2 0 StevieDonohoe 8 61
(Charlie Fellowes) *mid-div on outer: rdn 2f out: sn kpt on one pce* 125/1

**10** *2 ½* **Allegiant (USA)** 2-9-2 0 KieranShoemark 12 56
(Roger Charlton) *slowly away and checked early which unbalanced rdr briefly: shuffled along fr 2f out and swtchd to outer: gng on after the line* 20/1

05 **11** *5* **Bill Cody (IRE)**[11] [9155] 2-9-2 0 DougieCostello 2 44
(Jamie Osborne) *racd in mid-div on rail: effrt over 2f out: sn struggling: pushed out* 33/1

0 **12** *2 ¾* **Forricherforpoorer (IRE)**[54] [8387] 2-9-2 0 MartinHarley 11 38
(William Knight) *a in rr: effrt over 3f out: pushed out fr over 1f out* 100/1

1m 39.84s (0.04) **Going Correction** -0.125s/f (Stan) 12 Ran SP% 115.7
Speed ratings (Par 96): **94,93,91,91,89 88,88,88,86,84 79,76**
CSF £13.69 TOTE £3.20: £1.40, £1.80, £1.50; EX 14.30 Trifecta £36.50.
**Owner** Godolphin **Bred** Godolphin **Trained** Newmarket, Suffolk

**FOCUS**
This was run in a much slower time (1.95sec) than the first division. Once again it paid to race handily.

## 9314 ROA/RACING POST OWNERS' JACKPOT H'CAP 1m (P)
**6:10** (6:13) (Class 4) (0-85,87) 3-Y-O+ £4,690 (£1,395; £697; £348) **Stalls** Low

Form RPR

621 **1** **Dance Teacher (IRE)**[121] [6268] 3-8-13 78 LiamKeniry 6 86
(David Elsworth) *bhd ldrs on outer: shkn up and smooth prog 2f out in centre: rdn over 1f out: led jst ins fnl f: kpt on wl to fend off chalrs* 14/1

3000 **2** *1* **Chestnut Fire**[19] [9025] 5-9-4 82 JosephineGordon 2 88
(Daniel Mark Loughnane) *racd in mid-div on rail: rdn over 1f out: kpt on wl between horses and tk 2nd 100yds out: styd on* 10/1

0515 **3** *nk* **Ice Royal (IRE)**[12] [9140] 4-9-9 87 DougieCostello 13 92
(Jamie Osborne) *racd in mid-div between horses: effrt 2f out and kpt on wl: ev ch ent fnl f where shifted sltly rt: one pce nr fin* 15/2

0051 **4** *nk* **Lacan (IRE)**[49] [8503] 6-8-10 74 LukeMorris 7 78
(Brett Johnson) *in rr-div on inner: travelling wl whn swtchd out 2f out: sn rdn: kpt on ins fnl f: styd on wl fnl 100yds* 9/2[1]

0202 **5** *hd* **Eltezam (IRE)**[12] [9140] 4-9-2 80 JoeyHaynes 10 84
(Amanda Perrett) *w ldr on outer: rdn 2f out and led ent fnl f: sn hdd: kpt on tl wknd nr fin and lost three pls* 5/1[2]

1526 **6** *1* **Bluff Crag**[68] [7999] 4-8-10 74 StevieDonohoe 1 76
(Philip McBride) *bhd ldrs on rail: gng okay and kpt to centre 2f out: shuffled along and n.m.r on heels fr over 1f out tl fin: eased nrr fin* 33/1

0446 **7** *½* **Assanilka (FR)**[29] [8885] 3-8-9 74 (p) KieranO'Neill 3 73
(Harry Dunlop) *led for 2f: remained handy: rdn over 2f out and swtchd to inner: ev ch sn after: kpt on tl 1f out where grad wknd* 11/1

0126 **8** *nk* **Jumping Jack (IRE)**[37] [4698] 3-8-12 77 KieranShoemark 4 76
(Chris Gordon) *s.s: pushed along early to sit in rr-div: rdn on inner 3f out: keeping on tl short of room ins fnl f: pushed out nr fin: nvr nrr* 20/1

4300 **9** *hd* **Golden Wedding (IRE)**[58] [8297] 5-9-2 80 (p) CharlesBishop 8 79
(Eve Johnson Houghton) *led after 2f: rdn 2f out and hdd ent fnl f: wknd sn after* 7/1[3]

0400 **10** *1 ¾* **Fighting Temeraire (IRE)**[19] [9025] 4-9-5 83 AdamKirby 5 78
(Dean Ivory) *missed break: hld up in rr: rdn on outer over 2f out and sn one pce: pushed out fnl f* 14/1

3016 **11** *3 ¾* **Intimate Art (IRE)**[144] [5400] 3-8-13 85 JasonWatson[(7)] 14 71
(Andrew Balding) *in rr-div and racd wd: rdn out wd fr over 3f out: one pce fr over 1f out* 11/1

1400 **12** *3 ¼* **Native Soldier (IRE)**[40] [7781] 3-8-11 76 (b[1]) DanielMuscutt 9 54
(John Flint) *between horses in mid-div: effrt wl over 2f out: sn struggling* 28/1

6216 **13** *hd* **Medicean El Diablo**[27] [8907] 4-8-9 73 TomMarquand 12 52
(Jimmy Fox) *in rr and plld hrd early: rdn over 2f out: no ex and one pce fr over 1f out: pushed out* 15/2

1m 37.13s (-2.67) **Going Correction** -0.125s/f (Stan)
**WFA** 3 from 4yo+ 1lb 13 Ran SP% 121.1
Speed ratings (Par 105): **108,107,106,106,106 105,104,104,104,102 98,95,95**
CSF £145.98 CT £1185.86 TOTE £9.10: £3.60, £4.00, £2.70; EX 192.00 Trifecta £1548.10.
**Owner** Simon Lockyer & Tim Clark **Bred** Oakhill Stud **Trained** Newmarket, Suffolk

**FOCUS**
A competitive handicap and they finished in a heap.

## 9315 32RED CASINO FILLIES' H'CAP 6f (P)
**6:40** (6:42) (Class 5) (0-70,70) 3-Y-O+ £3,234 (£962; £481; £240) **Stalls** Low

Form RPR

4544 **1** **Cool Breeze (IRE)**[25] [8953] 3-8-0 56 oh1 MillyNaseb[(7)] 5 67+
(David Simcock) *hld up in mid-div on outer: shkn up wdst over 2f out: led ent fnl f: sn in complete control: nudged out: readily* 11/2[2]

4265 **2** *2 ¼* **Pretty Bubbles**[8] [9185] 8-9-7 70 (v) JosephineGordon 8 73
(J R Jenkins) *racd in rr on inner: rdn 2f out: kpt on wl and tk 2nd nr fin: no ch w wnr* 11/2[2]

1023 **3** *½* **Toolatetodelegate**[7] [9214] 3-8-9 58 (tp) HollieDoyle 4 59
(Brian Barr) *cl up bhd ldrs: rdn between horses 2f out: kpt on wl and tk 2nd jst ins fnl f: no ex nr fin and lost 2nd* 8/1

0002 **4** *1 ½* **Lady Cristal (IRE)**[30] [8875] 3-9-0 66 (p) CliffordLee[(3)] 3 63
(K R Burke) *sn led and ref to settle: hdd wl over 2f out but remained upsides: rdn 2f out and plugged on one pce after* 5/2[1]

0366 **5** *nk* **Powerful Dream (IRE)**[8] [9189] 4-9-5 68 (p[1]) LukeMorris 6 64
(Ronald Harris) *hld up in rr on outer: rdn out wd fr wl over 1f out: lugging rt ins fnl f and pushed out* 16/1

**6** *hd* **Natalie Express (FR)**[87] 3-9-4 67 (h[1]) FranBerry 1 62
(Henry Spiller) *hld up in last: rdn 2f out: one pce* 14/1

4653 **7** *1 ¾* **Look Surprised**[25] [8953] 4-8-13 65 MitchGodwin[(3)] 7 54
(Roger Teal) *w ldrs on outer: led over 2f out: effrt wl over 1f out: sn hdd: wknd qckly fnl f* 6/1[3]

0033 **8** *5* **Reedanjas (IRE)**[39] [8742] 3-8-9 65 (p) HarrisonShaw[(7)] 2 38
(Gay Kelleway) *cl up on outer: rdn over 2f out: sn hld* 11/2[2]

1m 12.49s (-0.61) **Going Correction** -0.125s/f (Stan) 8 Ran SP% 112.7
Speed ratings (Par 100): **99,96,95,93,92 92,90,83**
CSF £34.52 CT £240.20 TOTE £5.30: £1.70, £1.90, £2.30; EX 36.20 Trifecta £167.10.
**Owner** Khalifa Dasmal **Bred** K A Dasmal **Trained** Newmarket, Suffolk

**FOCUS**
With competition for the lead, this set up for a finisher.

## 9316 100% PROFIT BOOST AT 32REDSPORT.COM FILLIES' H'CAP 7f (P)
**7:10** (7:13) (Class 5) (0-75,75) 3-Y-O+ £3,234 (£962; £360; £360) **Stalls** Low

Form RPR

4050 **1** **Veena (FR)**[14] [9089] 4-9-7 75 (p[1]) OisinMurphy 10 82
(David Simcock) *w ldr: shkn up over 1f out on outer: pushed along and upsides ent fnl f: rdn to ld nr fin* 10/1

45 **2** *hd* **Groundfrost (IRE)**[49] [8519] 3-9-7 75 StevieDonohoe 3 81
(John James Feane, Ire) *t.k.h early in mid-div on rail: settled bttr by 1/2-way: rdn between horses 2f out: kpt on wl ent fnl f: hrd rdn on rail fnl 150yds in three way fin: jst hld* 7/2[2]

3504 **3** *hd* **Courier**[3] [9280] 5-9-5 73 LukeMorris 2 79
(Michael Appleby) *sn led: rdn 2f out: kpt on wl fr over 1f out tl 100yds out: stuck on between horses: no ex at line and dead-heated for 3rd* 4/1[3]

6211 **3** *dht* **Magic Mirror**[43] [8641] 4-8-9 63 (p) TomMarquand 7 69+
(Mark Rimell) *hld up in last: shkn up over 2f out: rdn and swtchd wdst 2f out: kpt on strly ins fnl f to dead-heat for 3rd on line* 3/1[1]

00 **5** *2* **Little Miss Kodi (IRE)**[128] [6015] 4-9-4 72 SteveDrowne 1 73
(Daniel Mark Loughnane) *in rr-div on rail: shkn up 2f out: kpt on one pce ins fnl f* 20/1

0115 6 1 3/4 **Loveatfirstsight**[12] 9142 4-8-7 61 oh3......................(p) EdwardGreatrex 6 57
(Jane Chapple-Hyam) *in rr-div on outer: rdn wdst over 2f out: sn one pce* 10/1

4005 7 4 **First Experience**[14] 9093 6-8-7 64.............................. CharlieBennett(3) 8 49
(Lee Carter) *chsd ldr on outer: shkn up 2f out: no ex and wknd sn after* 25/1

6000 8 1 1/4 **Lady Lydia (IRE)**[19] 9020 6-8-6 67.................................... AledBeech(7) 5 49
(Hugo Froud) *bhd ldrs between horses: shkn up 2f out: nt qckn and pushed out fr 1f out* 50/1

1m 27.21s (1.21) **Going Correction** -0.125s/f (Stan) 8 Ran SP% **96.0**
Speed ratings (Par 100): **88,87,87,87,85 83,78,77**
WIN: 8.10 Veena; PL: .60 Magic Mirror, 1.70 Groundfrost, .70 Courier, 1.90 Veena; EX: 35.00; CSF: 30.02; TC: 35.54, 43.9; TF: 69.80, 74.40;.
**Owner** Chola Dynasty **Bred** Ecurie Haras De Beauvoir **Trained** Newmarket, Suffolk

**FOCUS**
A steadily run affair that turned into a 2f sprint, and there was little to separate the first four at the line.

## 9317 32RED.COM H'CAP 1m 7f 218y(P)
**7:40** (7:41) (Class 6) (0-60,60) 3-Y-0+ **£2,587** (£770; £384; £192) **Stalls** Low

Form RPR

5256 1 **Aumerle**[59] 8261 5-9-8 58...................................................... LukeMorris 8 66
(Shaun Lycett) *chsd ldrs: rdn 3f out: kpt on wl on outer fr over 1f out wdst of all and led 110yds out: drew clr* 7/1

0053 2 3 **Great Return**[14] 9095 4-9-10 60.................................... EdwardGreatrex 2 64
(Warren Greatrex) *racd in mid-div: rdn 3f out: led 2f out: hdd fnl 110yds: plugged on* 4/1[2]

5550 3 hd **Spiritoftomintoul**[54] 8394 8-9-10 60............................(b) GeorgeDowning 3 64
(Tony Carroll) *in rr: rdn 3f out on inner: kpt on wl fr over 1f out to take 3rd nr fin* 14/1

3031 4 shd **Black Prince (FR)**[52] 7790 3-9-0 56..............................(t) DougieCostello 7 62
(Anthony Honeyball) *chsd ldrs on outer: rdn 3f out: plugged on fr over 1f out: one pce fnl f: fin 5th: plcd 4th* 5/2[1]

0-00 5 1/2 **Unblinking**[70] 7960 4-9-7 57............................................ LiamKeniry 11 60+
(Nigel Twiston-Davies) *in rr: prog fr over 3f out: kpt on strly fnl f and fin wl nr line: fin 6th: plcd 5th* 20/1

6006 6 1 1/4 **Enola (IRE)**[19] 9026 3-9-2 58................................(p[1]) JosephineGordon 1 62
(Amy Murphy) *mid-div: rdn wl over 2f out: plugged on: fin 7th: plcd 6th* 33/1

0/6- 7 hd **Sea's Aria (IRE)**[69] 2355 6-9-1 51..................................(t) RobertHavlin 12 53
(Mark Hoad) *chsd ldrs: rdn over 3f out: nt qckn and plugged one pce: fin 8th: plcd 7th* 16/1

2005 8 3/4 **Howardian Hills (IRE)**[25] 8955 4-9-7 57.................(h) KieranShoemark 4 58
(Victor Dartnall) *mid-div: rdn 3f out: styd on one pce: fin 9th: plcd 8th* 14/1

/0-2 9 1/2 **Ding Ding**[16] 8878 6-9-0 50............................................ StevieDonohoe 6 50
(Sheena West) *hld up towards rr: rdn over 3f out: plugged on: fin 10th: plcd 9th* 5/1[3]

1144 10 3/4 **Navajo Star (IRE)**[42] 8674 3-9-0 56.............................(v) AndrewMullen 5 57
(Michael Appleby) *sn led: hdd 2f out: wknd qckly: fin 11th: plcd 10th* 12/1

310- 11 18 **Maid Of Tuscany (IRE)**[29] 7367 6-9-5 55.......................(b) AdamKirby 9 33
(Neil Mulholland) *hld up in rr: struggling fr over 3f out: t.o: fin 12th: plcd 11th* 33/1

3050 12 7 **Grey Diamond**[121] 6257 3-9-1 57.................................... DannyBrock 10 28
(Denis Quinn) *sluggish s: in rr-div: no ex fr over 3f out: t.o: fin 13th: plcd 12th* 100/1

0330 13 22 **Wintour Leap**[11] 9158 6-9-2 52.......................................(p) OisinMurphy 13
(Robert Stephens) *racd in mid-div: pushed along to hold tch fr 6f out: bhd fr over 2f out: no ex and eased: t.o: fin 14th: plcd 13th* 20/1

2000 D nk **Tommys Geal**[14] 9092 5-8-10 53..................................... NicolaCurrie(7) 14 56
(Michael Madgwick) *racd in last: rdn w plenty to 3f out: styd on strly fnl f to take nvr nrr 4th nr fin: fin 4th: disqualified: jockey failed to weigh-in* 25/1

3m 27.44s (-2.66) **Going Correction** -0.125s/f (Stan)
**WFA** 3 from 4yo+ 6lb 14 Ran SP% **124.9**
Speed ratings (Par 101): **101,99,99,99,98 98,98,97,97,97 88,84,73,99**
CSF £33.73 CT £398.75 TOTE £8.20: £2.60, £2.00, £4.40; EX 43.70 Trifecta £353.40.
**Owner** D Teevan **Bred** St Clare Hall Stud **Trained** Leafield, Oxon
■ Stewards' Enquiry : Nicola Currie three-day ban: failed to weigh in (Jan 3-5)

**FOCUS**
A moderate staying contest.
T/Plt: £58.40 to a £1 stake. Pool: £92,395.78 - 1,154.05 winning units. T/Qpdt: £21.50 to a £1 stake. Pool: £12,897.55 - 443.80 winning units. **Cathal Gahan**

# 9206 LINGFIELD (L-H)
Wednesday, December 20

**OFFICIAL GOING: Polytrack: standard**
Wind: light, across Weather: overcast, gloomy

## 9318 32RED.COM EBF NOVICE STKS (DIV I) 1m 1y(P)
**11:40** (11:40) (Class 5) 2-Y-O **£2,911** (£866; £432; £216) **Stalls** High

Form RPR

0 1 **Three Weeks (USA)**[28] 8888 2-9-2 0................................ MartinHarley 2 78+
(William Haggas) *dwlt: sn rcvrd and hld up in tch in midfield: clsd to trck ldrs over 3f out: chsd clr ldr 2f out: rdn over 1f out: swtchd rt ins fnl f: str run to ld 50yds out: sn in command* 8/11[1]

50 2 3/4 **Brigham Young**[28] 8888 2-9-2 0.......................................... LiamKeniry 8 76
(Ed Walker) *led and set stdy gallop: pushed along and qcknd clr wl over 1f out: rdn ent fnl f: hdd and no ex fnl 50yds* 7/2[2]

60 3 7 **Thistimelastyear**[15] 9081 2-8-8 0................................ HectorCrouch(3) 6 54
(Philip Hide) *chsd ldr: rdn over 3f out: lost 2nd 2f out and sn outpcd: wknd fnl f* 33/1

0 4 1 1/4 **Diablery**[34] 8796 2-8-11 0.............................................. NickyMackay 3 51
(John Gosden) *trckd ldrs: swtchd rt over 2f out: sn rdn and outpcd in 4th 2f out: wknd fnl f* 10/1

5 hd **Culpability (USA)** 2-9-2 0................................................ RobertHavlin 10 56
(John Gosden) *wl in tch in midfield: rdn and outpcd over 2f out: no ch w ldrs and kpt on same pce fr over 1f out* 9/2[3]

00 6 2 1/4 **Balkhash (IRE)**[27] 8903 2-9-2 0........................................ AdamKirby 7 50
(Clive Cox) *hld up in tch in midfield: rdn and outpcd over 2f out: no ch but kpt on ins fnl f* 14/1

00 7 2 3/4 **Beloved Knight**[7] 9201 2-9-2 0...................................... TomMarquand 5 44
(Laura Mongan) *dropped to rr over 4f out: rdn and outpcd over 2f out: no ch after* 50/1

8 hd **Argent Bleu** 2-9-2 0........................................................... SteveDrowne 9 43
(Roger Ingram) *stdd s: hld up in last pair: pushed along and outpcd over 2f out: no ch after* 40/1

00 9 1 3/4 **Born To Spend (IRE)**[14] 9099 2-8-12 0 ow1................ StevieDonohoe 4 35
(Ian Williams) *stdd s: t.k.h: hld up in tch towards rr: outpcd over 2f out: wknd over 1f out* 66/1

000 10 12 **Amenhotepthethird**[71] 7915 2-8-13 13.......................... NoelGarbutt(3) 1
(Mark Gillard) *led ldrs: rdn over 3f out: 5th and outpcd over 2f out: wknd over 1f out: bhd ins fnl f* 100/1

1m 41.38s (3.18) **Going Correction** +0.175s/f (Slow) 10 Ran SP% **123.9**
Speed ratings (Par 96): **91,90,83,82,81 79,76,76,74,62**
CSF £3.81 TOTE £1.50: £1.10, £1.20, £12.70; EX 4.10 Trifecta £86.70.
**Owner** Apple Tree Stud **Bred** Apple Tree Stud **Trained** Newmarket, Suffolk

**FOCUS**
The first division of a modest novice event in which half the field needed this for a handicap mark and few ever got into it. The first two finished well clear.

## 9319 32RED.COM EBF NOVICE STKS (DIV II) 1m 1y(P)
**12:10** (12:12) (Class 5) 2-Y-O **£2,911** (£866; £432; £216) **Stalls** High

Form RPR

6 1 **Mewtow**[18] 9051 2-9-2 0..................................................(h) OisinMurphy 3 76
(George Scott) *racd keenly: mde all: pushed along and kicked clr over 1f out: in command and styd on ins fnl f* 7/1

04 2 1 1/2 **Oskemen**[42] 8678 2-9-2 0.................................................. AdamKirby 4 72
(Clive Cox) *trckd ldng pair: effrt to chse wnr 2f out: sn drvn and unable to match pce of wnr over 1f out: kpt on but a hld ins fnl f* 13/8[1]

3 3 1 1/2 **Sweet Charity**[29] 8877 2-8-11 0......................................... FranBerry 5 63
(Denis Coakley) *chsd ldng trio: effrt ent fnl 2f: wnt 3rd and hung lft ent fnl f: kpt on same pce and no imp fnl f* 7/2[2]

00 4 2 1/4 **Barnay**[32] 8840 2-9-2 0...................................................... MartinDwyer 7 63
(Marcus Tregoning) *t.k.h: hld up in tch in last trio: swtchd rt and effrt jst over 1f out: hdwy ins fnl f: styd on fnl 100yds: nvr trbld ldrs* 33/1

0 5 1 1/4 **Cleverley (IRE)**[21] 8987 2-8-12 0 ow1............................ KieranShoemark 1 56
(Henry Candy) *in tch in midfield: effrt ent fnl 2f: unable qck and btn over 1f out: kpt on same pce after* 25/1

30 6 hd **Classic Charm**[28] 8888 2-8-8 0........................................ JackDuern(3) 6 55
(Dean Ivory) *hld up in tch in midfield: swtchd rt and effrt over 1f out: no imp and kpt on same pce ins fnl f* 16/1

7 nse **Sophie Gray (IRE)** 2-8-11 0............................................... RobertHavlin 2 54+
(John Gosden) *v.s.a and rn green in detached last early: clsd to bk of field 5f out: pushed along over 1f out: styd on and nt clrest of runs ins fnl f: nvr trbld ldrs* 9/2[3]

0 8 hd **Ventura Magic**[32] 8839 2-9-2 0........................................ TomMarquand 8 59
(Richard Hannon) *chsd wnr tl 2f out: unable qck and btn over 1f out: wknd ins fnl f* 9/1

0 9 17 **Jetpac**[84] 7512 2-9-2 0..................................................... GeorgeDowning 9 18
(Laura Mongan) *hld up in tch in last trio: lost tch u.p over 1f out* 150/1

1m 40.15s (1.95) **Going Correction** +0.175s/f (Slow) 9 Ran SP% **114.3**
Speed ratings (Par 96): **97,95,94,91,90 90,90,90,73**
CSF £18.42 TOTE £7.10: £2.00, £1.10, £1.20; EX 20.90 Trifecta £67.30.
**Owner** Alrabban Racing **Bred** Patrick B Doyle (construction) Ltd **Trained** Newmarket, Suffolk

**FOCUS**
Unlike in the first division a couple of these had already shown reasonable ability, but this was another race where you had to be handy. It's been rated around the balance of the 2nd/3rd. The winning time was 1.23sec quicker than the first leg.

## 9320 32RED CASINO EBF FILLIES' NOVICE STKS (PLUS 10 RACE) 7f 1y(P)
**12:40** (12:41) (Class 5) 2-Y-O **£2,911** (£866; £432; £216) **Stalls** Low

Form RPR

1 **Dancing Brave Bear (USA)** 2-8-12 0......................... StevieDonohoe 3 77+
(Ed Vaughan) *hld up in tch in midfield: swtchd rt and hdwy over 1f out: str run to ld 150yds out: sn in command and r.o wl* 20/1

2 1 **Cosmic Love** 2-8-9 0............................................................ GeorgiaCox(3) 5 74
(William Haggas) *t.k.h: hld up in tch in last quartet: clsd 2f out: nt clr run over 1f out tl hdwy 1f out: chsd clr wnr 100yds out: styd on wl but nvr getting to wnr* 12/1

4 3 1 1/2 **Perfection**[34] 8796 2-8-12 0.............................................. RobertHavlin 4 70
(John Gosden) *t.k.h: chsd ldrs: effrt ent fnl 2f: edgd rt u.p 1f out: 3rd and styd on same pce ins fnl f* 5/4[1]

4 1 1/2 **Renny's Lady (IRE)** 2-8-12 0............................................. FranBerry 6 66
(David Evans) *hld up in last pair: pushed along and effrt wd over 2f out: hdwy ent fnl f: kpt on wl ins fnl f: no threat to ldrs* 50/1

5 hd **Suhayl Moon (IRE)** 2-8-12 0............................................. MartinHarley 7 68+
(Charlie Appleby) *t.k.h early: chsd ldr tl over 5f out: effrt in cl 3rd whn nt clr run and snatched up over 1f out: kpt on same pce ins fnl f* 11/8[2]

364 6 1/2 **Katie Lee (IRE)**[51] 8472 2-8-5 0...................................... NicolaCurrie(7) 2 64
(Henry Candy) *in tch in last quartet: rdn and hdwy towards inner over 1f out: swtchd rt ins fnl f: kpt on: nvr trbld ldrs* 16/1

4226 7 3/4 **Daybreak**[19] 9022 2-8-12 82............................................... OisinMurphy 12 62
(Hughie Morrison) *dwlt and flashing tail leaving stalls: hdwy to chse ldr over 5f out: rdn to ld jst over 1f out: hdd 150yds: sn wknd* 8/1[3]

0 8 3 **Marilyn M (IRE)**[203] 3215 2-8-12 0............................ KieranShoemark 8 54
(George Scott) *led: rdn and hdd ent fnl f: wknd ins fnl f* 33/1

00 9 2 3/4 **Astroblaze**[15] 9081 2-8-12 0.............................................. JoeyHaynes 11 47
(Mark H Tompkins) *t.k.h: chsd ldrs: rdn over 2f out: lost pl over 1f out: wknd ins fnl f* 100/1

10 1/2 **Tough Lass (IRE)** 2-8-12 0................................................. LukeMorris 9 45
(George Peckham) *t.k.h: hld up in tch in midfield: rdn and lost pl ent fnl 2f: bhd whn hung lft over 1f out* 66/1

11 9 **Tornequeta May** 2-8-12 0.................................................(p[1]) JimmyQuinn 10 21
(Adam West) *s.i.s: a in rr: rdn and lost tch over 1f out* 50/1

1m 26.29s (1.49) **Going Correction** +0.175s/f (Slow) 11 Ran SP% **125.3**
Speed ratings (Par 93): **98,96,95,93,93 92,91,88,85,84 74**
CSF £239.29 TOTE £30.00: £5.70, £2.20, £1.20; EX 246.00 Trifecta £793.80.
**Owner** Ballymore Sterling Syndicate **Bred** CASA Farms I LLC **Trained** Newmarket, Suffolk
■ Stewards' Enquiry : Oisin Murphy caution: careless riding

**FOCUS**
An interesting fillies' novice event with newcomers filling four of the first five places. Fair form for the time of year.

## 9321 BETWAY CLASSIFIED (S) STKS 1m 2f (P)
**1:10** (1:10) (Class 6) 3-Y-0+ **£2,264** (£673; £336; £168) **Stalls** Low

Form RPR

00P 1 **Black Dave (IRE)**[12] 9138 7-9-3 63.................................(v) FranBerry 4 56
(David Evans) *t.k.h: mde all: rdn ent fnl 2f: drifted rt and drvn over 1f out: styd on wl ins fnl f* 3/1[2]

2500 **2** 1 ½ **Lazarus (IRE)**[16] 8682 3-9-1 69........(t) KieranShoemark 2 54
(Amy Murphy) *hld up in tch in last: rdn and outpcd in 4th over 1f out: rallied 1f out: styd on strly ins fnl f: snatched 2nd on post* **9/2**[3]

000 **3** nse **Top Diktat**[49] 8515 9-9-0 54........(v[1]) HectorCrouch(3) 5 53
(Gary Moore) *dwlt and swtchd lft after s: hld up in tch in last pair: effrt to chse ldng pair over 2f out: wnt 2nd and pressing wnr 1f out: no ex fnl 100yds: lost 2nd on post* **14/1**

1046 **4** ½ **Drumochter**[54] 8390 3-9-1 70........ DougieCostello 3 53
(Jamie Osborne) *chsd wnr: effrt and ev ch 2f out: unable qck u.p and lost 2nd 1f out: kpt on same pce ins fnl f* **4/6**[1]

0000 **5** 21 **Moorea**[7] 9212 3-8-12 42........ MitchGodwin(3) 1 13
(John Bridger) *chsd ldng pair tl rdn and dropped to rr over 2f out: wknd over 1f out* **50/1**

2m 10.49s (3.89) **Going Correction** +0.175s/f (Slow)
**WFA** 3 from 7yo+ 2lb **5** Ran SP% **111.8**
Speed ratings (Par 101): **91,89,89,89,72**
CSF £16.44 TOTE £3.90: £2.40, £1.90; EX 14.60 Trifecta £48.40.There was no bid for the winner
**Owner** Mrs E Evans **Bred** Richard Frayne **Trained** Pandy, Monmouths

**FOCUS**
A weak classified seller with the winning rider judging things to perfection from the front. Not form to trust at all.

## 9322 32RED.COM NURSERY H'CAP — 7f 1y(P)
**1:45** (1:45) (Class 4) (0-85,87) 2-Y-O **£3,946** (£1,174; £586; £293) **Stalls** Low

Form RPR

1123 **1** **Motown Mick (IRE)**[42] 8671 2-9-10 87........ TimmyMurphy 6 89
(Richard Hannon) *w ldr tl rdn to ld jst over 2f out: hrd pressed ins fnl f: kpt on u.p: won on the nod* **13/8**[1]

0561 **2** shd **Roseau City**[6] 9230 2-8-0 63 6ex........(b) HollieDoyle 3 65
(David Elsworth) *t.k.h: chsd ldrs: effrt 2f out: chsd wnr 1f out: sn chalng and kpt on u.p: lost on the nod* **11/2**

1603 **3** nse **The Mums**[19] 9022 2-9-3 80........(v) RobertHavlin 7 82
(John Gosden) *stdd and dropped in bhd after s: hld up in tch in rr: effrt over 1f out: rdn and hdwy to chse ldrs ins fnl f: kpt on wl fnl 100yds* **10/1**

4516 **4** 3 ½ **Diamond Pursuit**[14] 9090 2-8-1 71........ NicolaCurrie(7) 2 63
(Jo Hughes) *chsd ldrs: rdn ent fnl 2f: unable qck and swtchd rt 1f out: wknd ins fnl f* **9/2**[3]

0121 **5** ¾ **Our Man In Havana**[30] 8871 2-8-10 78........ WilliamCox(5) 1 68
(Richard Price) *t.k.h: led: rdn and hdd jst over 2f out: wknd ins fnl f* **9/4**[2]

1m 26.36s (1.56) **Going Correction** +0.175s/f (Slow) **5** Ran SP% **111.5**
Speed ratings (Par 98): **98,97,97,93,92**
CSF £10.97 TOTE £2.30: £1.50, £2.00; EX 11.30 Trifecta £40.10.
**Owner** N Woodcock & M Daniels **Bred** Top Row Partnership **Trained** East Everleigh, Wilts

**FOCUS**
A fair nursery, with all five remaining runners coming into the race in some sort of form, and a thrilling finish with little covering the first three at the line. The front pair came close together nearing the post.

## 9323 BETWAY SPRINT H'CAP — 6f 1y(P)
**2:20** (2:20) (Class 6) (0-60,60) 3-Y-O+ **£2,264** (£673; £336; £168) **Stalls** Low

Form RPR

3653 **1** **Billyoakes (IRE)**[8] 9184 5-9-5 58........(p) LukeMorris 8 65
(Charlie Wallis) *led after 1f: mde rest: rdn and kicked clr over 1f out: kpt on u.p and a holding on ins fnl f* **7/1**

0003 **2** ¾ **Strictly Carter**[8] 9183 4-8-11 57........(t) HarryBurns(7) 1 62
(Alan Bailey) *chsd ldrs: swtchd rt and effrt over 1f out: chsd wnr ins fnl f: kpt on* **4/1**[2]

0600 **3** ½ **Krazy Paving**[33] 8824 5-9-0 53........(v[1]) JosephineGordon 3 56
(Anabel K Murphy) *led for 1f: chsd ldrs: effrt and chsd wnr over 1f out: kpt on same pce and lost 2nd ins fnl f* **16/1**

0430 **4** ½ **Bobby Vee**[173] 4303 3-9-3 59........ JackDuern(3) 6 61+
(Dean Ivory) *hld up in tch in last trio: effrt 2f out: hdwy u.p on inner 1f out: kpt on ins fnl f* **33/1**

5353 **5** nk **Napping**[33] 8823 4-9-3 56........(h) MartinHarley 4 57
(Anabel K Murphy) *trckd ldrs: effrt over 1f out: kpt on same pce ins fnl f* **6/1**[3]

1025 **6** hd **Arcanista (IRE)**[8] 9183 4-8-13 59........(p) PaulHainey(7) 7 59+
(Chris Dwyer) *hld up in last pair: effrt over 1f out: sltly impeded 1f out: hdwy ins fnl f: styd on wl fnl 100yds: nvr trbld ldrs* **8/1**

0050 **7** nk **El Torito (IRE)**[34] 8798 3-9-6 59........(p) AdamKirby 2 58+
(Jim Boyle) *sn dropped to rr and rousted along early: in rr: drvn over 1f out: sn swtchd rt: hdwy ins fnl f: styd on wl fnl 100yds: nvr trbld ldrs* **9/4**[1]

4505 **8** ¾ **Zenovia (IRE)**[7] 9215 3-9-7 60........(bt[1]) EdwardGreatrex 9 57
(Archie Watson) *mounted on crse: t.k.h: hld up in tch in midfield: nt clr run over 1f out: swtchd rt 1f out: kpt on same pce ins fnl f* **7/1**

0000 **9** ¾ **Fullon Clarets**[14] 9094 5-9-7 60........(p) FranBerry 10 54
(Laura Mongan) *chsd ldrs tl wnt 2nd over 4f out: hung lft and lost 2nd over 1f out: wknd ins fnl f* **22/1**

5344 **10** ½ **Mercers**[33] 8823 3-8-13 59........ NicolaCurrie(7) 11 52
(Paddy Butler) *in tch in midfield on outer: rdn 2f out: unable qck and lost pl bnd wl over 1f out: kpt on same pce after* **20/1**

1m 13.29s (1.39) **Going Correction** +0.175s/f (Slow) **10** Ran SP% **119.1**
Speed ratings (Par 101): **97,96,95,94,94 94,93,92,91,90**
CSF £35.07 CT £450.20 TOTE £7.70: £2.20, £1.50, £4.40; EX 35.40 Trifecta £264.20.
**Owner** Roalco Limited **Bred** Mrs M Cusack **Trained** Ardleigh, Essex

**FOCUS**
A moderate sprint handicap with recent winning form thin on the ground. The gallop was ordinary and yet another race where the pace held up, while the first four raced closest to the inside rail.

## 9324 BETWAY STAYERS H'CAP — 1m 7f 169y(P)
**2:55** (2:56) (Class 5) (0-75,77) 3-Y-O+ **£2,911** (£866; £432; £216) **Stalls** Low

Form RPR

0111 **1** **Noble Behest**[88] 7412 3-9-6 73........(p) AdamKirby 3 79
(Robert Stephens) *chsd ldrs: nt clrest of runs over 2f out: effrt and swtchd rt over 1f out: sn drvn and ev ch 1f out: led ins fnl f: kpt on wl u.p* **2/1**[1]

6062 **2** nk **Lost The Moon**[15] 9082 4-9-10 71........ ShaneKelly 4 76
(Mark H Tompkins) *chsd ldrs tl wnt 2nd over 3f out: rdn and ev ch over 1f out: kpt on u.p ins fnl f* **4/1**[3]

/323 **3** 1 ¼ **Volpone Jelois (FR)**[7] 9208 4-9-7 73........(p) MeganNicholls(5) 7 77
(Paul Nicholls) *pressed ldr tl led 5f out: rdn over 1f out: hdd ins fnl f: no ex and wknd towards fin* **7/2**[2]

5145 **4** 1 ½ **Ayr Of Elegance**[47] 8565 5-10-0 75........ FranBerry 5 77
(Philip Hide) *hld up in tch: effrt and rdn to chse ldrs 2f out: unable qck over 1f out: kpt on same pce ins fnl f* **6/1**

6502 **5** ½ **Sheila's Fancy (IRE)**[11] 9158 3-8-6 59........ LukeMorris 1 60
(J S Moore) *hld up in tch: rdn ent fnl 3f: kpt on same pce u.p fnl f* **6/1**

343/ **6** 9 **Jalingo (IRE)**[886] 7203 6-10-2 77........ TimmyMurphy 6 67
(Ali Stronge) *stdd and dropped in bhd after s: hld up in rr: pushed along and wnt 6th over 2f out: no imp: wknd ins fnl f* **20/1**

2300 **7** 7 **Night Generation (GER)**[23] 8072 5-9-0 61........(tp) MartinHarley 2 43
(Chris Gordon) *led tl 5f out: lost pl u.p over 2f out: bhd over 1f out* **16/1**

3m 25.01s (-0.69) **Going Correction** +0.175s/f (Slow)
**WFA** 3 from 4yo+ 6lb **7** Ran SP% **114.8**
Speed ratings (Par 103): **108,107,107,106,106 101,98**
CSF £10.35 TOTE £2.80: £1.70, £2.10; EX 10.80 Trifecta £22.20.
**Owner** A C Elliott **Bred** Mr & Mrs A E Pakenham **Trained** Penhow, Newport

**FOCUS**
They only went steady in this staying handicap and there were three in a line entering the last furlong. The winner remains progressive, with the 2nd/3rd to their latest form.

## 9325 BETWAY APPRENTICE H'CAP — 1m 4f (P)
**3:25** (3:25) (Class 5) (0-70,72) 3-Y-O+ **£2,911** (£866; £432; £216) **Stalls** Low

Form RPR

6300 **1** **Bamako Du Chatelet (FR)**[30] 8876 6-9-0 65........(v) LukeCatton(7) 10 74
(Ian Williams) *s.i.s: sn swtchd lft and rousted along: hdwy into midfield after 2f: effrt 2f out: nt clr run and swtchd rt over 1f out: str run to ld wl ins fnl f: sn clr* **20/1**

2163 **2** 2 ¼ **Alternate Route**[30] 8876 3-8-12 67........(b[1]) GavinAshton(7) 8 73
(Sir Mark Prescott Bt) *midfield: hdwy on outer to chse ldrs 8f out: wnt 2nd over 5f out: rdn over 1f out: led 100yds out: sn hdd and outpcd by wnr* **11/2**

5030 **3** 1 **Zambeasy**[19] 9028 6-9-9 72........(p) SebastianWoods(5) 6 76
(Philip Hide) *led: rdn over 1f out: hdd 100yds out: no ex and outpcd after* **10/1**

4206 **4** 1 **My Brother Mike (IRE)**[18] 9054 3-9-7 69........ PaddyBradley 9 72
(Kevin Frost) *hld up in last pair: hdwy 2f out: styd on wl ins fnl f: nt rch ldrs* **9/2**[3]

30P0 **5** ½ **Kath's Legacy**[28] 8893 4-9-4 67........ StephenCummins(5) 4 68
(Richard Hughes) *hld up in last pair: nt clr run and swtchd rt jst over 2f out: hdwy 1f out: styd on strly ins fnl f: nt rch ldrs* **8/1**

2342 **6** ½ **Nurse Nightingale**[33] 8822 3-9-6 71........(h) CameronNoble(3) 2 73
(Michael Bell) *t.k.h: chsd ldr for 2f: styd handy: effrt on inner to chse ldrs over 1f out: no ex ins fnl f: wknd wl ins fnl f* **11/4**[1]

4324 **7** ¾ **Moneyoryourlife**[208] 3041 3-9-3 68........ RossaRyan(3) 5 68
(Richard Hannon) *t.k.h: chsd ldr after 2f tl over 5f out: styd chsng ldrs: rdn and pressing ldrs over 1f out: no ex 1f out: wknd ins fnl f* **4/1**[2]

**8** ¾ **Quebec**[61] 6-9-9 70........ RhiainIngram(3) 11 68
(Roger Ingram) *chsd ldrs: rdn over 2f out: unable qck and edgd lft ent fnl f: kpt on same pce after* **25/1**

203 **9** 2 ½ **Heron (USA)**[90] 7331 3-9-6 71........ WilliamCox(3) 7 66
(Brett Johnson) *hld up in tch in last quartet: pushed along over 2f out: no imp* **20/1**

3000 **10** nse **My Lord**[14] 9095 9-8-5 56 oh4........(p[1]) PoppyBridgwater(7) 3 50
(Paddy Butler) *hld up in tch in midfield: rdn and unable qck over 2f out: wknd ins fnl f* **50/1**

5/4- **11** nk **Deebaj (IRE)**[189] 6765 5-9-0 65........ JasonWatson(7) 1 59
(Gary Moore) *hld up in tch in last quartet: rdn over 2f out: no imp* **16/1**

2m 33.5s (0.50) **Going Correction** +0.175s/f (Slow)
**WFA** 3 from 4yo+ 4lb **11** Ran SP% **121.6**
Speed ratings (Par 103): **105,103,102,102,101 101,101,100,98,98 98**
CSF £125.94 CT £1197.13 TOTE £17.00: £4.70, £1.60, £3.70; EX 71.20 Trifecta £2371.20.
**Owner** Macable Partnership **Bred** S N C Ecurie Jouenne Gerard **Trained** Portway, Worcs

**FOCUS**
An ordinary apprentice handicap but the winner looked as good as ever.
T/Plt: £30.20 to a £1 stake. Pool: £54,819.76 - 1,322.03 winning units. T/Qpdt: £17.80 to a £1 stake. Pool: £5,870.52 - 243.32 winning units. **Steve Payne**

9326 - 9333a (Foreign Racing) - See Raceform Interactive

# 9276 CHELMSFORD (A.W) (L-H)
### Thursday, December 21

**OFFICIAL GOING: Polytrack: standard**
Wind: light, half behind Weather: dry

## 9334 BET TOTEPLACEPOT AT BETFRED.COM AMATEUR RIDERS' H'CAP — 7f (P)
**5:45** (5:46) (Class 6) (0-60,61) 3-Y-O+ **£3,119** (£967; £483; £242) **Stalls** Low

Form RPR

060- **1** **Complicit (IRE)**[15] 9105 6-11-1 61........(p) MrAlexFerguson 7 67
(J F Levins, Ire) *awkward leaving stalls: hld up in midfield: effrt in 4th 2f out: clsd to chse ldrs and swtchd rt over 1f out: styd on ins fnl f to ld towards fin* **2/1**[1]

5250 **2** ½ **Misu Pete**[44] 8664 5-10-7 58........(p) MissEMacKenzie(5) 4 63
(Mark Usher) *led early: sn stdd bk into midfield: hdwy to chse clr ldng pair over 2f out: clsd on inner over 1f out: rdn to ld ins fnl f: hdd and no ex towards fin* **8/1**

1030 **3** 1 ½ **Mr Andros**[13] 9141 4-10-2 55........(bt) MissMStratton(7) 2 56
(Brendan Powell) *sn led: clr w rival 1/2-way: rdn over 1f out: hdd ins fnl f: no ex and styd on same pce fnl 100yds* **5/1**[3]

0060 **4** shd **Mowhoob**[13] 9141 7-9-7 46........(p) MrCAJones(7) 8 47
(Brian Barr) *nt rr s: styd wd early: chsd ldrs tl hdwy to join ldr 5f out: wnt clr w ldr 1/2-way: rdn over 1f out: no ex and styd on same pce fnl 100yds* **33/1**

3040 **5** 8 **Moi Aussie**[87] 7465 4-10-12 58........(p) MissSBrotherton 3 37
(Michael Appleby) *pressed ldrs early: midfield and outpcd over 2f out: no hdwy u.p over 1f out: wl hld fnl f* **8/1**

0364 **6** 1 ½ **Hint Of Grey (IRE)**[37] 8122 4-10-7 53........(v[1]) MrSWalker 1 28
(Don Cantillon) *sn dropped to rr and bustled along: no imp u.p over 1f out: n.d* **9/4**[2]

4020 **7** 3 ½ **All Or Nothin (IRE)**[49] 8543 8-9-12 49 oh1 ow3........ MissMBryant(5) 9 15
(Paddy Butler) *impeded leaving stalls: hld up in rr: stl plenty to do whn nt clr run and swtchd lft over 1f out: nvr on terms* **33/1**

4515 **8** 1 **Pitch High (IRE)**[16] 9084 3-10-4 53........ MissJCooley(3) 5 16
(Julia Feilden) *racd wd: chsd ldrs: rdn and outpcd jst over 2f out: btn over 1f out: wknd fnl f* **6/1**

0034 **9** 3 ¼ **Twiggy**[52] 8479 3-10-11 60........(h) MrBLynn(3) 6 14
(Iain Jardine) *dwlt: hld up towards rr: effrt over 2f out: no hdwy and wl btn over 1f out* **7/1**

1m 26.28s (-0.92) **Going Correction** -0.25s/f (Stan) **9** Ran SP% **135.7**
Speed ratings (Par 101): **95,94,92,92,83 81,77,76,72**
CSF £23.47 CT £80.91 TOTE £3.00: £1.30, £2.60, £1.80; EX 23.00 Trifecta £132.40.
**Owner** J F Levins **Bred** Barouche Stud Ireland Ltd **Trained** The Curragh, Co Kildare

■ Stewards' Enquiry : Mr Alex Ferguson two-day ban: using whip above the permitted level (Jan 5,10)

**FOCUS**
A modest amateur riders' handicap. They went a contested gallop on standard Polytrack and the favourite came through to win narrowly, just matching his recent form.

## 9335 TOTEJACKPOT AT BETFRED.COM NOVICE MEDIAN AUCTION STKS 7f (P)

**6:15** (6:17) (Class 5) 2-Y-O **£4,528** (£1,347; £673; £336) **Stalls** Low

Form RPR

1 **Move Swiftly** 2-8-11 0........ TomMarquand 5 79+
(William Haggas) *stdd sn after s: t.k.h: hld up in midfield: effrt over 1f out: chsd clr ldr jst ins fnl f: r.o strly to ld last strides* **7/2**[2]

3 2 *hd* **Artieshow (USA)**[13] 9137 2-9-2 0........ DanielMuscutt 1 84
(Marco Botti) *led: rdn and kicked clr over 1f out despite awkward hd carriage: wnt lft u.p jst ins fnl f: pushed out fnl 75yds: hdd last strides* **7/2**[2]

03 3 *8* **The British Lion (IRE)**[28] 8916 2-9-2 0........ PJMcDonald 9 62
(Mark Johnston) *sn chsng ldr: rdn and unable qck whn hung lft over 1f out: lost btn 2nd jst ins fnl f: sn wknd* **9/4**[1]

5 4 *½* **Dollar Value (USA)**[22] 8988 2-9-2 0........ LukeMorris 10 61
(Robert Cowell) *trckd ldrs: rdn over 2f out: outpcd u.p and edgd lft over 1f out: no ch w ldng pair and kpt on same pce ins fnl f* **8/1**

05 5 *¾* **Haverland (IRE)**[7] 9231 2-9-2 0........ StevieDonohoe 3 59
(Charlie Fellowes) *hld up in midfield: effrt and nt clrest of runs over 1f out: kpt on ins fnl f: nvr trbld ldrs* **6/1**[3]

6 6 *1 ¼* **Ellen Gates**[22] 8989 2-8-11 0........ ShaneKelly 7 51+
(Richard Hughes) *stdd sn after s: t.k.h: trckd ldrs: rdn and unable qck over 1f out: wknd ins fnl f* **20/1**

000 7 *4 ½* **Demurrer (USA)**[19] 9051 2-9-2 0........ KieranShoemark 4 43
(Michael Bell) *hld up in tch in midfield: rdn and struggling over 2f out: hung lft and lost pl u.p over 1f out: sn wknd* **33/1**

0 8 *4 ½* **Carolyn's Voice**[57] 8347 2-8-8 0........ AaronJones(3) 6 26
(Stuart Williams) *midfield: 7th and rdn over 2f out: no imp and wl hld over 1f out: n.d* **33/1**

9 *1 ½* **Irish Times** 2-9-2 0........ FranBerry 8 27
(Henry Spiller) *dwlt: hld up off the pce in last trio: wd and no hdwy bnd 2f out: n.d* **33/1**

10 *1 ¼* **Falling Wood (IRE)** 2-8-13 0........ MarcMonaghan(3) 11 24
(Marco Botti) *s.i.s: rn green and a wl off the pce in last trio: n.d* **20/1**

06 11 *1 ¾* **Shyjack**[23] 8981 2-8-11 0........ JaneElliott(5) 2 19
(George Margarson) *s.i.s: a off the pce in last trio: n.d* **50/1**

1m 25.01s (-2.19) **Going Correction** -0.25s/f (Stan) 11 Ran SP% **120.9**
Speed ratings (Par 96): **102,101,92,92,91 89,84,79,77,76 74**
CSF £15.30 TOTE £4.40: £1.40, £1.50, £1.20; EX 17.20 Trifecta £26.80.
**Owner** Sheikh Rashid Dalmook Al Maktoum **Bred** Mrs K E Collie **Trained** Newmarket, Suffolk

**FOCUS**
A fair juvenile novice contest. The level is fluid and this could be rated higher.

## 9336 WEATHERBYS GENERAL STUD BOOK ONLINE BRITISH EBF MAIDEN STKS (PLUS 10 RACE) (SIRE/DAM-RESTRICTED) 1m (P)

**6:45** (6:47) (Class 3) 2-Y-O **£7,762** (£2,310; £1,154; £577) **Stalls** Low

Form RPR

02 1 **Best Blue**[28] 8903 2-9-0 0........ CameronNoble(5) 8 78
(Michael Bell) *mde all: wnt clr w rival over 2f out: rdn over 1f out: edging rt ins fnl f: kpt on and a jst holding on cl home* **7/2**[2]

3423 2 *hd* **Fleeting Freedom**[35] 8796 2-9-0 78........ RobertWinston 5 73
(Alan Bailey) *chsd wnr: wnt clr w wnr and drvn over 2f out: carried rt ins fnl f: kpt on and clsd towards fin: nvr quite getting to wnr* **6/1**

0 3 *hd* **Winds Of Fire (USA)**[12] 9154 2-9-5 0........ AdamKirby 2 78
(Charlie Appleby) *chsd ldng pair tl 5f out: rdn 3f out: 4th and unable qck over 2f out: no imp tl styd on fnl 100yds: clsng qckly on ldng pair cl home: nt quite rch ldng pair* **3/1**[1]

4 *¾* **Natch** 2-9-5 0........ NickyMackay 1 76+
(John Gosden) *midfield: hdwy to chse ldrs 5f out: rdn and unable qck over 2f out: no imp tl clsd to press ldrs towards fin: nvr quite getting to ldrs* **5/1**

603 5 *6* **Island Court (IRE)**[26] 8951 2-9-5 74........ TomMarquand 3 61
(J S Moore) *hld up in midfield: effrt over 2f out: no imp over 1f out: wl hld and kpt on same pce ins fnl f* **12/1**

0 6 *¾* **Ttmab**[57] 8352 2-9-5 0........ JoeyHaynes 6 60
(Mark H Tompkins) *hld up in tch in rr of main gp: effrt and swtchd rt over 1f out: 6th and no imp fnl f* **100/1**

2 7 *7* **The Jungle VIP**[35] 8802 2-9-5 0........ PJMcDonald 4 43
(Mark Johnston) *chsd ldrs early: sn dropped bk into midfield: effrt over 2f out: no prog and sn outpcd: wknd over 1f out* **4/1**[3]

00 8 *6* **Mythological (IRE)**[57] 8353 2-9-5 0........ LukeMorris 9 28
(Peter Chapple-Hyam) *dwlt: swtchd lft after 1f: a in rr of main gp: wknd over 1f out* **40/1**

9 *1 ¼* **Mood For Mischief** 2-9-5 0........ LiamKeniry 7 25
(Ed Walker) *v.s.a: sn detached in last: nvr on terms* **12/1**

1m 38.55s (-1.35) **Going Correction** -0.25s/f (Stan) 9 Ran SP% **117.0**
Speed ratings (Par 100): **96,95,95,94,88 88,81,75,73**
CSF £25.25 TOTE £3.90: £1.40, £1.70, £1.50; EX 22.70 Trifecta £88.30.
**Owner** W J & T C O Gredley & Lord Derby **Bred** Stanley House Stud **Trained** Newmarket, Suffolk

**FOCUS**
A fair juvenile maiden for horses whose sire/dam won over 1m4f plus. This could be rated up to 5lb higher.

## 9337 BET TOTEQUADPOT AT BETFRED.COM FILLIES' H'CAP 1m (P)

**7:15** (7:17) (Class 5) (0-75,76) 3-Y-O+ **£5,175** (£1,540; £769; £384) **Stalls** Low

Form RPR

6231 1 **Dellaguista (IRE)**[12] 9153 3-9-3 72........ PJMcDonald 2 79+
(Tim Easterby) *hld up in tch in midfield: nt clr run over 2f out: swtchd rt and upsides ldr on bridle over 1f out: shkn up to ld ins fnl f: rdn 75yds: kpt on and holding chalr after* **2/1**[2]

1301 2 *nk* **Titan Goddess**[13] 9138 5-9-1 69........ ShaneKelly 3 76
(Mike Murphy) *t.k.h: stdd and dropped in bhd after s: nt clr run over 2f out: effrt on inner to press ldrs over 1f out: ev ch ins fnl f: kpt on u.p but hld cl home* **6/1**[3]

2212 3 *1* **Corked (IRE)**[20] 9025 4-9-8 76........ LiamKeniry 1 81
(Ed Walker) *led: rdn over 1f out: hdd ins fnl f: no ex and outpcd towards fin* **13/8**[1]

2200 4 *5* **Stosur (IRE)**[20] 9029 6-9-4 72........(v) AdamKirby 5 65
(Gay Kelleway) *pressed ldr tl unable qck over 1f out: wknd ins fnl f* **10/1**

6-2 5 *1* **Palavicini Run (IRE)**[13] 9150 4-8-10 69 ow2........ DonaghO'Connor(5) 4 60
(J F Levins, Ire) *t.k.h: hld up wl in tch: unable qck over 1f out: sn btn and wknd ins fnl f* **14/1**

1206 6 *1 ¼* **Indigo Princess**[149] 5261 4-8-5 64........ KevinLundie(5) 6 52
(Michael Appleby) *t.k.h: hld up in tch: clsd to chse ldrs 3f out: rdn and unable qck over 1f out: wknd ins fnl f* **40/1**

6336 7 *8* **Hawatif (IRE)**[26] 8947 4-9-7 75........ LukeMorris 7 45
(Anthony Carson) *chsd ldrs on outer: lost pl u.p over 2f out: bhd 1f out: wknd* **8/1**

1m 37.9s (-2.00) **Going Correction** -0.25s/f (Stan)
**WFA** 3 from 4yo+ 1lb 7 Ran SP% **115.0**
Speed ratings (Par 100): **100,99,98,93,92 91,83**
CSF £14.69 TOTE £2.60: £1.30, £3.00; EX 17.20 Trifecta £30.30.
**Owner** David & Yvonne Blunt **Bred** M Gittins **Trained** Great Habton, N Yorks

**FOCUS**
A fair fillies' handicap. They went a respectable gallop and the right three horses came to the fore.

## 9338 BET TOTEEXACTA AT BETFRED.COM H'CAP 1m 2f (P)

**7:45** (7:47) (Class 5) (0-70,72) 3-Y-O+ **£5,175** (£1,540; £769; £384) **Stalls** Low

Form RPR

0223 1 **Jack Of Diamonds (IRE)**[16] 9078 8-8-13 68........ RossaRyan(7) 2 74
(Roger Teal) *dwlt: hld up in tch in last pair: effrt and swtchd rt over 1f out: drvn and chal ins fnl f: led 50yd out: styd on* **11/4**[1]

3321 2 *nk* **Choral Clan (IRE)**[21] 9017 6-9-7 69........ JackMitchell 4 75
(Brendan Powell) *trckd ldrs: swtchd rt and effrt over 1f out: sn rdn to chal: led ins fnl f: hdd 50yds out: kpt on same pce after* **3/1**[2]

2520 3 *1 ¼* **Relevant (IRE)**[30] 8883 3-8-8 61........(t[1]) AaronJones(3) 6 64
(Stuart Williams) *led: rdn over 1f out: hdd ins fnl f: no ex and outpcd fnl 50yds* **12/1**

4512 4 *¾* **Anna Medici**[20] 9034 3-9-4 68........(p) LukeMorris 1 70
(Mike Murphy) *chsd ldrs: unable qck u.p over 1f out: kpt on u.p wl ins fnl f: nt enough pce to threaten ldrs* **5/1**[3]

5003 5 *nk* **Thaqaffa (IRE)**[20] 9027 4-9-5 67........ KieranShoemark 3 68
(Amy Murphy) *stdd after s: hld up wl in tch: effrt 2f out: rdn over 1f out: kpt on ins fnl f: nt enough pce to chal* **3/1**[2]

3541 6 *nk* **Il Sicario (IRE)**[53] 3813 3-9-1 72........ SebastianWoods(7) 7 72
(Bill Turner) *sn w ldr: rdn over 1f out: no ex 100yds out: wknd towards fin* **25/1**

0540 7 *31* **Bridge Of Sighs**[58] 8313 5-9-2 67........(p) CharlieBennett(3) 5 5
(Lee Carter) *chsd ldrs on outer tl dropped to rr u.p over 2f out: wknd over 1f out: bhd and eased ins fnl f* **9/1**

2m 6.03s (-2.57) **Going Correction** -0.25s/f (Stan)
**WFA** 3 from 4yo+ 2lb 7 Ran SP% **114.9**
Speed ratings (Par 103): **100,99,98,98,97 97,72**
CSF £11.43 TOTE £3.30: £1.60, £2.20; EX 12.80 Trifecta £130.60.
**Owner** Inside Track Racing Club **Bred** Gigginstown House Stud **Trained** Great Shefford, Berks

**FOCUS**
An ordinary handicap. They went an, at best, respectable gallop but the consistent favourite gained another deserved victory.

## 9339 BET TOTETRIFECTA AT BETFRED.COM H'CAP 6f (P)

**8:15** (8:16) (Class 4) (0-80,82) 3-Y-O+ **£8,086** (£2,406; £1,202; £601) **Stalls** Centre

Form RPR

504 1 **Aleef (IRE)**[14] 9124 4-9-6 79........(t) AdamKirby 5 88
(David O'Meara) *mde all: rdn and drifted rt wl over 1f out: hld on wl u.p wl ins fnl f: rdn out* **9/2**[3]

3401 2 *½* **Envisaging (IRE)**[47] 8592 3-9-5 78........(t) PJMcDonald 7 85
(James Fanshawe) *stdd s: hld up in last pair: effrt and swtchd rt over 1f out: swtchd lft and wnt 2nd ins fnl f: kpt on u.p but hld towards fin* **5/1**

4350 3 *¾* **Upavon**[16] 9079 7-9-7 80........(t) FranBerry 6 85
(Stuart Williams) *hld up in tch in midfield: effrt over 1f out: hdwy u.p to chse ldrs 100yds out: kpt on but nvr getting to ldrs: eased cl home* **12/1**

0034 4 *2 ¼* **Diamond Lady**[9] 9185 6-9-9 82........ HollieDoyle 2 79
(William Stone) *t.k.h: chsd ldr tl over 4f out: styd chsng ldrs: effrt u.p over 1f out: no ex and outpcd ins fnl f* **7/1**

0225 5 *1 ¾* **Nezar (IRE)**[14] 9124 6-9-3 79........ JackDuern(3) 1 71
(Dean Ivory) *chsd ldr over 4f out: rdn over 1f out: no ex and lost 2nd ins fnl f: wknd fnl 100yds* **11/4**[1]

5500 6 *1* **Aguerooo (IRE)**[17] 9074 4-9-5 78........(p) ShaneKelly 4 67
(Ollie Pears) *dwlt and bustled along early: in tch in last pair: effrt u.p on inner over 1f out: no imp ins fnl f* **14/1**

0203 7 *hd* **Red Tycoon (IRE)**[14] 9124 5-8-8 70........ HectorCrouch(3) 3 58
(Ken Cunningham-Brown) *hld up in tch in midfield: effrt u.p over 1f out: unable qck: wl hld and kpt on same pce ins fnl f* **7/1**

5041 8 *1 ¾* **Cappananty Con**[14] 9124 3-9-7 80........ RobertWinston 8 62
(Dean Ivory) *chsd ldrs on outer: rdn and lost pl ent fnl 2f: bhd 1f out: wknd ins fnl f* **7/2**[2]

1m 10.35s (-3.35) **Going Correction** -0.25s/f (Stan) 8 Ran SP% **123.1**
Speed ratings (Par 105): **112,111,110,107,105 103,103,101**
CSF £29.53 CT £261.85 TOTE £5.50: £1.60, £2.30, £3.30; EX 35.00 Trifecta £550.20.
**Owner** Nick Bradley Racing 8 **Bred** Sarah Fortune **Trained** Upper Helmsley, N Yorks

**FOCUS**
The feature contest was a decent sprint handicap. The third favourite made all in under standard time.

## 9340 ALEXANDRA AND SOFIA BABY TEXO H'CAP 6f (P)

**8:45** (8:47) (Class 7) (0-50,56) 3-Y-O+ **£2,911** (£866; £432; £216) **Stalls** Centre

Form RPR

4332 1 **Black Truffle (FR)**[7] 9232 7-8-11 47........(p) NicolaCurrie(7) 5 54
(Mark Usher) *chsd ldrs: effrt to chse ldr over 1f out: kpt on wl u.p ins fnl f to ld last strides* **5/1**[3]

654 2 *nk* **Olaudah**[14] 9129 3-9-4 47........ AdamKirby 3 53
(Henry Candy) *led: rdn over 1f out: drvn ins fnl f: hdd last strides* **15/8**[2]

6062 3 *1 ¼* **Naralsaif (IRE)**[21] 9019 3-9-6 49........(v) PatrickMathers 7 51
(Derek Shaw) *hld up in midfield: effrt on outer 2f out: hdwy u.p over 1f out: chsd ldng pair ins fnl f: kpt on* **8/1**

0021 4 *1 ¼* **Pulsating (IRE)**[5] 9268 3-9-13 56 6ex........(p) EdwardGreatrex 1 54+
(Archie Watson) *restless in stalls: v awkward leaving stalls and slowly away: bhd: hdwy after 2f: clsd and nt clr run 1f out: kpt on ins fnl f: nvr trbld ldrs* **5/4**[1]

0006 5 *½* **La Fortuna**[14] 9129 4-9-5 48........ DanielMuscutt 6 44
(Charlie Wallis) *wl in tch in midfield: pushed up to chse ldrs and rdn over 2f out: unable qck and edgd lft 1f out: kpt on same pce ins fnl f* **14/1**

3000 6 *½* **Head Space (IRE)**[59] 8296 9-9-5 48........(vt) HollieDoyle 10 43
(Brian Barr) *hld up in tch in midfield on outer: effrt over 1f out: kpt on same pce ins fnl f* **33/1**

0500 7 1 3/4 **Captain Scooby**[5] 9265 11-9-2 **45**.................................(b) LukeMorris 14 34
(Richard Guest) *sn bustled along towards rr: sme hdwy and nt clr run 1f out: kpt on same pce ins fnl f* **16/1**
0000 8 1 **Tea El Tee (IRE)**[17] 9075 3-9-1 **49**.................................(p) WilliamCox(5) 13 35
(Gay Kelleway) *chsd ldr tl over 1f out: no ex u.p and wknd ins fnl f* **40/1**
0000 9 1/2 **Only Ten Per Cent (IRE)**[38] 8776 9-9-7 **50**...........(v) AlistairRawlinson 4 34
(J R Jenkins) *s.i.s: sn rcvrd and in tch in midfield: unable qck u.p over 1f out: wknd ins fnl f* **28/1**
0303 10 4 **Irish Sky (IRE)**[15] 9103 3-9-6 **49**.................................(t[1]) FranBerry 12 21
(Henry Spiller) *in tch towards rr: effrt wd over 1f out: no imp: wl hld and eased wl ins fnl f* **20/1**
2000 11 6 **Bubbly Bailey**[69] 7993 7-8-9 **45**.................................(v) GinaMangan(7) 2
(J R Jenkins) *restless in stalls: a bhd: lost tch over 1f out* **66/1**
0000 12 4 **Silver Springs (IRE)**[77] 7763 4-8-13 **47**.................................RhiainIngram(5) 11
(Roger Ingram) *chsd ldrs tl shuffled bk and hmpd over 2f out: bhd and lost tch over 1f out* **50/1**

1m 12.3s (-1.40) **Going Correction** -0.25s/f (Stan) **12** Ran SP% **136.6**
Speed ratings (Par 97): **99,98,96,95,94 93,91,90,89,84 76,70**
CSF £16.53 CT £84.94 TOTE £7.90: £2.00, £1.10, £2.80; EX 30.20 Trifecta £202.80.
**Owner** The Mark Usher Racing Club **Bred** Peter Harris **Trained** Upper Lambourn, Berks

**FOCUS**
This looked a strong enough race for the grade. The right horse filled the first four placings.
T/Plt: £35.80 to a £1 stake. Pool: £99,272.76 - 2,019.09 winning units T/Qpdt: £22.80 to a £1 stake. Pool: £7,069.54 - 228.56 winning units **Steve Payne**

# 9302 SOUTHWELL (L-H)
## Thursday, December 21

**OFFICIAL GOING: Fibresand: standard**
Wind: Virtually nil Weather: Heavy cloud

## 9341 BETWAY CASINO H'CAP 1m 4f 14y(F)
**11:45** (11:45) (Class 4) (0-85,87) 3-Y-0+ **£4,690** (£1,395; £697; £348) **Stalls** Low

Form RPR
5115 1 **Snowy Winter (USA)**[29] 8893 3-9-5 **82**.................................(t) AndrewMullen 3 94+
(Archie Watson) *trckd ldrs: hdwy over 3f out: led over 2f out: rdn clr over 1f out: kpt on strly* **9/1**
0311 2 4 **Good Time Ahead (IRE)**[10] 9178 3-8-7 **75** 6ex......... JamieGormley(5) 8 80
(Philip Kirby) *prom early: stdd and in tch after 3f: pushed along over 4f out: rdn along to chse ldrs over 2f out: drvn wl over 1f out: kpt on u.p fnl f* **5/2**[1]
3622 3 1 3/4 **Epitaph (IRE)**[23] 8979 3-8-7 **70**.................................(v) JimmyQuinn 6 72
(Michael Appleby) *cl up: rdn along 3f out: drvn wl over 1f out: kpt on same pce* **11/1**
13 4 3 1/4 **Spinning Melody (USA)**[22] 9000 3-9-3 **80**...........(p[1]) KieranShoemark 9 77
(Simon Crisford) *sn led: pushed along over 3f out: rdn and hdd over 2f out: sn drvn and wknd over 1f out* **9/2**[2]
0653 5 2 1/4 **Start Seven**[16] 9082 5-10-0 **87**................................. DougieCostello 2 79
(Jamie Osborne) *hld up towards rr: hdwy to chse ldrs over 3f out: rdn along on outer over 2f out: sn drvn and no imp* **12/1**
5121 6 2 1/4 **Moabit (GER)**[73] 7903 5-9-4 **82**.................................(t) MeganNicholls(5) 5 71
(Paul Nicholls) *in rr: hdwy on inner and in tch over 3f out: rdn along over 2f out: sn btn* **11/2**[3]
6211 7 16 **Restive (IRE)**[17] 9070 4-9-6 **79**................................. LukeMorris 1 42
(Iain Jardine) *prom on inner: pushed along over 4f out: rdn 3f out: sn drvn and wknd wl over 1f out* **9/2**[2]
400- 8 19 **Alton Bay (IRE)**[63] 6223 9-9-0 **73**................................. MartinHarley 7 6
(Peter Fahey, Ire) *chsd ldrs on outer: rdn along over 3f out: sn wknd* **14/1**
0000 R **Royal Marskell**[8] 9204 8-9-6 **86**................................. HarrisonShaw(7) 4
(Gay Kelleway) *ref to r* **40/1**

2m 35.94s (-5.06) **Going Correction** -0.025s/f (Stan)
**WFA** 3 from 4yo+ 4lb **9** Ran SP% **115.5**
Speed ratings (Par 105): **115,112,111,109,107 106,95,82,**
CSF £31.81 CT £255.23 TOTE £10.00: £2.60, £1.20, £2.40; EX 36.70 Trifecta £276.10.
**Owner** Boadicea Bloodstock **Bred** Darley **Trained** Upper Lambourn, W Berks

**FOCUS**
Not a bad middle-distance handicap to start and an impressive winner.

## 9342 SUNBETS.CO.UK H'CAP (DIV I) 1m 13y(F)
**12:15** (12:17) (Class 6) (0-55,54) 3-Y-0+ **£2,264** (£673; £336; £168) **Stalls** Low

Form RPR
0005 1 **Candesta (USA)**[23] 8985 7-9-6 **53**.................................(t) DanielMuscutt 9 66
(Julia Feilden) *in tch: hdwy on inner over 3f out: chsd ldrs over 2f out: led 2f out and sn rdn: kpt on strly* **5/1**[3]
243 2 5 **Satchville Flyer**[8] 9217 6-9-6 **53**................................. FranBerry 11 53
(David Evans) *trckd ldrs on outer: hdwy over 3f out: rdn over 2f out: edgd lft wl over 1f out: chsd wnr and carried hd high over 1f out: sn edgd lft and kpt on same pce* **7/2**[1]
0006 3 2 **St Patrick's Day (IRE)**[17] 9077 5-9-7 **54**.................................(v) TimmyMurphy 8 49
(J R Jenkins) *v.s.a and lost six l at s: pushed along and bhd: hdwy and wd st: rdn over 2f out: styd on u.p appr fnl f: nrst fin* **4/1**[2]
0640 4 1 1/4 **Monzino (USA)**[174] 4047 9-8-9 **45**................................. PhilDennis(3) 7 37
(Michael Chapman) *towards rr: hdwy and wd st: rdn over 2f out: kpt on u.p appr fnl f* **100/1**
0001 5 3/4 **Tilly Devine**[20] 9034 3-9-3 **51**.................................(b) LukeMorris 3 40
(Scott Dixon) *cl up: rdn along 3f out: drvn wl over 1f out: grad wknd* **7/1**
0061 6 2 1/2 **Moving Robe (IRE)**[23] 8984 4-8-10 **50**.................................(tp) DarraghKeenan(7) 4 34
(Conrad Allen) *chsd ldrs: rdn along and outpcd over 2f out: kpt on u.p fnl f* **5/1**[3]
1005 7 hd **Zebelini (IRE)**[36] 8784 5-8-13 **46**.................................(t) JimmyQuinn 2 30
(Roy Bowring) *led: rdn along 3f out: hdd 2f out: sn drvn: edgd lft and wknd* **25/1**
5000 8 2 1/2 **Sir Lancelott**[17] 9076 5-9-4 **51**.................................(v[1]) AndrewMullen 10 29
(Adrian Nicholls) *cl up: pushed along on outer 3f out: rdn over 2f out: swtchd rt wl over 1f out: sn drvn and wknd* **10/1**
0530 9 2 **Quick Monet (IRE)**[8] 9217 4-8-9 **45**................................. CharlieBennett(3) 1 18
(Shaun Harris) *chsd ldrs on inner: rdn along 3f out: sn wknd* **33/1**
5334 10 2 1/2 **Little Pippin**[33] 8653 4-9-1 **48**.................................(p) PJMcDonald 5 15
(Tony Coyle) *a in rr* **12/1**
000 11 3 1/4 **Dream Destroyer (IRE)**[21] 9018 3-8-11 **45**................................. SamJames 6
(Geoffrey Harker) *a in rr* **66/1**

1m 43.74s (0.04) **Going Correction** -0.025s/f (Stan)
**WFA** 3 from 4yo+ 1lb **11** Ran SP% **114.1**
Speed ratings (Par 101): **98,93,91,89,89 86,86,83,81,79 76**
CSF £21.61 CT £75.20 TOTE £4.60: £2.10, £1.70, £1.30; EX 20.90 Trifecta £75.10.
**Owner** Mrs Jo Lambert **Bred** Juddmonte Farms Inc **Trained** Exning, Suffolk

**FOCUS**
The first division of a moderate handicap, but the winner was well treated on his early 2017 form and has been rated back near that level.

## 9343 SUNBETS.CO.UK H'CAP (DIV II) 1m 13y(F)
**12:45** (12:45) (Class 6) (0-55,53) 3-Y-0+ **£2,264** (£673; £336; £168) **Stalls** Low

Form RPR
3446 1 **Sunshineandbubbles**[8] 9218 4-8-12 **51**.................................(p) RossaRyan(7) 6 57
(Jennie Candlish) *trckd ldrs on inner: hdwy over 2f out: sn cl up: rdn over 1f out: drvn ins fnl f: led last 100yds* **12/1**[3]
3526 2 1/2 **Limerick Lord (IRE)**[17] 9076 5-8-11 **46**.................(p) ShelleyBirkett(3) 11 51
(Julia Feilden) *cl up: slt ld over 3f out: rdn along over 2f out: hdd wl over 1f out: drvn and led again jst ins fnl f: hdd and no ex last 100yds* **12/1**[3]
0000 3 1 **Gunner Moyne**[13] 9141 5-9-6 **52**.................................(v) PJMcDonald 8 54
(Emma Owen) *n.m.r and pushed along sn after s: sn swtchd rt to outer and hdwy to trck ldrs after 1 1/2f: cl up 1/2-way: rdn to take slt ld wl over 1f out: drvn and hdd jst ins fnl f: kpt on same pce* **12/1**[3]
/-2 4 1 **Why Me**[17] 9076 7-9-1 **47**.................................(t) MartinHarley 10 47
(Gavin Cromwell, Ire) *prom: cl up over 3f out: effrt to chal 2f out: ev ch: rdn over 1f out: drvn and n.m.r ins fnl f: wknd towards fin* **5/6**[1]
3460 5 2 1/4 **General Tufto**[206] 3137 12-9-3 **49**.................................(b) JoeyHaynes 5 44
(Charles Smith) *dwlt and towards rr: hdwy and wd st: rdn 2f out: sn chsng ldrs: kpt on same pce* **16/1**
6541 6 6 **Breaking Free**[17] 9072 3-9-4 **51**.................................(p) TomEaves 4 30
(John Quinn) *dwlt and towards rr: hdwy wl over 2f out: sn rdn and no imp* **9/2**[2]
0540 7 4 1/2 **Little Choosey**[19] 9056 7-9-2 **53**.................................(vt[1]) KevinLundie(5) 3 22
(Roy Bowring) *a towards rr* **25/1**
0000 8 6 **Roger Thorpe**[17] 9075 8-8-10 **45**................................. JackDuern(3) 7
(John Balding) *led: rdn along and hdd over 3f out: wknd over 2f out* **25/1**
0500 9 2 **African Showgirl**[35] 8800 4-9-2 **53**................................. JaneElliott(5) 1 3
(Ivan Furtado) *a towards rr* **14/1**
000- 10 2 3/4 **Can Can Dream**[456] 6678 3-8-12 **45**................................. SamJames 2
(Olly Williams) *a towards rr* **100/1**
40-0 11 2 **Madakheel (USA)**[17] 9076 6-8-13 **45**.................................(p[1]) JimmyQuinn 9
(Simon West) *chsd ldrs: rdn along 3f out: sn wknd* **100/1**

1m 44.25s (0.55) **Going Correction** -0.025s/f (Stan)
**WFA** 3 from 4yo+ 1lb **11** Ran SP% **118.0**
Speed ratings (Par 101): **96,95,94,93,91 85,80,74,72,70 68**
CSF £142.95 CT £1794.57 TOTE £12.50: £2.40, £2.90, £2.30; EX 144.60 Trifecta £494.20.
**Owner** Amazing Racing **Bred** Mickley Stud **Trained** Basford Green, Staffs

**FOCUS**
There were four in a line passing the furlong pole in this division and the form is limited. The winning time was around half a second slower than the first leg.

## 9344 BETWAY DASH MAIDEN STKS 4f 214y(F)
**1:15** (1:15) (Class 5) 3-Y-0+ **£2,911** (£866; £432; £216) **Stalls** Centre

Form RPR
42 1 **Gustavo Fring (IRE)**[22] 8995 3-9-5 0................................. FranBerry 1 65+
(Richard Spencer) *bmpd and wnt lft s: racd far side: chsd ldrs: led over 3f out: rdn along and hdd wl over 1f out: drvn to chal ent fnl f: styd on to ld last 75yds* **4/9**[1]
2024 2 1/2 **Decision Maker (IRE)**[27] 8931 3-9-5 70.................................(t[1]) JimmyQuinn 7 63
(Roy Bowring) *racd towards stands' side: chsd ldrs: gd hdwy at 1/2-way: led wl over 1f out: drvn and edgd lft ins fnl f: jst ahd whn rdr dropped whip 75yds out: sn hdd and no ex* **5/2**[2]
2603 3 2 1/2 **Gettin' Lucky**[17] 9071 4-9-5 46................................. AndrewMullen 10 54
(John Balding) *racd towards stands' side: led: hdd over 3f out: cl up: rdn wl over 1f out: drvn and edgd lft ent fnl f: kpt on same pce* **7/1**[3]
0254 4 3 1/2 **Excellent World (IRE)**[10] 9181 4-9-0 46.................................(p) DuranFentiman 4 36
(Tony Coyle) *prom: rdn along 2f out: sn drvn and grad wknd* **10/1**
0030 5 1 1/4 **Chillililli**[10] 9181 3-8-9 43.................................(b) JaneElliott(5) 3 32
(Michael Appleby) *prom centre: rdn along 2f out: sn wknd* **20/1**
0400 6 3 **Joshlee (IRE)**[14] 9129 3-9-0 44................................. PJMcDonald 6 21
(Emma Owen) *sn outpcd and bhd* **25/1**
0600 7 6 **Dramatic Voice**[34] 8823 4-9-0 29................................. HollieDoyle 2
(Ken Cunningham-Brown) *wnt lft s: racd towards far side: cl up: rdn along 1/2-way: sn wknd* **100/1**
0000 8 4 1/2 **Eye Burner**[13] 9139 3-9-5 30................................. TimmyMurphy 8
(J R Jenkins) *sn outpcd and bhd* **66/1**

59.09s (-0.61) **Going Correction** -0.025s/f (Stan) **8** Ran SP% **130.5**
Speed ratings (Par 103): **103,102,98,92,90 85,76,69**
CSF £2.33 TOTE £1.30: £1.02, £1.10, £1.60; EX 2.20 Trifecta £5.80.
**Owner** Rebel Racing (2) **Bred** Tally-Ho Stud **Trained** Newmarket, Suffolk

**FOCUS**
Older-horse maidens don't come much weaker than this and the market got it right.

## 9345 32RED.COM NURSERY H'CAP 6f 16y(F)
**1:45** (1:45) (Class 5) (0-75,76) 2-Y-O **£2,911** (£866; £432; £216) **Stalls** Low

Form RPR
4500 1 **Hard Graft**[57] 8349 2-9-2 **69**................................. PJMcDonald 3 75
(David Brown) *trckd ldrs: swtchd rt and hdwy 2f out: rdn to chse ldr and edgd lft ent fnl f: sn drvn to chal: kpt on to ld last 75yds* **3/1**[2]
1315 2 3/4 **Montague (IRE)**[34] 8817 2-9-9 **76**................................. DougieCostello 1 80
(Jamie Osborne) *led: rdn along 2f out: drvn and edgd rt over 1f out: drvn and hung rt ins fnl f: hdd and no ex last 75yds* **11/4**[1]
006 3 3 1/2 **Lady Sophiebella**[33] 8851 2-8-9 **62** ow1................................. TomEaves 10 55
(Bryan Smart) *cl up: rdn along 2f out: swtchd lft jst over 1f out: kpt on same pce fnl f* **25/1**
0033 4 2 1/4 **Our Kid (IRE)**[22] 9002 2-8-12 **64** ow1.................................(b) JackGarritty 2 52
(Richard Fahey) *pushed along early and trckd ldrs on inner: effrt over 2f out: rdn wl over 1f out: sn drvn and one pce* **5/1**[3]
6601 5 nk **Helen Sherbet**[35] 8804 2-8-11 **67**................................. CliffordLee(3) 8 53
(K R Burke) *towards rr: hdwy over 2f out: sn rdn and kpt on fnl f* **7/1**
2310 6 3 3/4 **Lina's Star (IRE)**[26] 8954 2-8-13 **66**................................. MartinHarley 7 40
(David O'Meara) *dwlt: sn swtchd rt to outer: hdwy and cl up over 3f out: rdn over 2f out: drvn wl over 1f out: sn wknd* **22/1**
5400 7 1/2 **Jaffar**[10] 9177 2-8-12 **65**.................................(be) LukeMorris 9 38
(Scott Dixon) *a towards rr* **25/1**
0620 8 1 1/4 **Arden Pearl (IRE)**[14] 9123 2-9-7 **74**.................................(p) EdwardGreatrex 5 43
(Archie Watson) *a towards rr* **11/1**
1620 9 1 3/4 **Give Em A Clump (IRE)**[29] 8887 2-8-13 **66**.................................(v) FranBerry 4 30
(David Evans) *chsd ldrs: rdn along 3f out: wknd 2f out* **15/2**

1m 16.39s (-0.11) **Going Correction** -0.025s/f (Stan) **9** Ran SP% **113.0**
Speed ratings (Par 96): **99,98,93,90,89 84,84,82,80**
CSF £11.04 CT £164.00 TOTE £4.40: £1.40, £1.20, £6.30; EX 14.50 Trifecta £242.10.
**Owner** J C Fretwell **Bred** Biddestone Stud **Trained** Averham Park, Notts

**FOCUS**
An ordinary nursery and a gamble landed. The winner has been rated back to his early season form, with a minor pb from the runner-up.

## 9346 BETWAY STAYERS H'CAP — 1m 3f 23y(F)
2:15 (2:15) (Class 6) (0-65,65) 3-Y-0+ — £2,264 (£673; £336; £168) Stalls Low

Form — RPR

4202 **1** **Lean On Pete (IRE)**[17] 9077 8-9-4 **60**.......................... AndrewMullen 8 66
(Ollie Pears) *led 1f: cl up: led 2f out and sn rdn: drvn ins fnl f: edgd rt and kpt on* **7/2**[2]

2-15 **2** *1* **Mister Showman**[35] 8806 4-9-9 **65**..............................(p) LukeMorris 11 69
(Keith Dalgleish) *trckd ldrs: pushed along 3f out: rdn over 2f out: drvn over 1f out: kpt on u.p fnl f* **2/1**[1]

0600 **3** *nk* **Up Ten Down Two (IRE)**[35] 8806 8-9-2 **65**.................. RyanTimby(7) 9 69
(Michael Easterby) *prom: rdn along over 2f out: drvn over 1f out: kpt on same pce* **25/1**

2000 **4** *nse* **Havelock (IRE)**[33] 5624 3-9-6 **65**................................ DougieCostello 10 70
(Peter Fahey, Ire) *hld up towards rr: hdwy 3f out: rdn to chse ldrs wl over 1f out: kpt on fnl f* **14/1**

3426 **5** *2 ¼* **Maraakib (IRE)**[12] 9153 5-9-6 **62**................................ KieranShoemark 4 62
(David O'Meara) *trckd ldrs on inner: hdwy 3f out: chal 2f out: sn rdn and ev ch: drvn appr fnl f and kpt on one pce* **15/2**

0- **6** *nk* **Cresendo (IRE)**[55] 8410 4-9-2 **58**..............................(t) MartinHarley 12 58
(Gavin Cromwell, Ire) *led after 1f: rdn along 3f out: hdd 2f out: sn drvn: wknd appr fnl f* **11/2**[3]

0006 **7** *4* **The Lock Master (IRE)**[20] 9028 10-9-6 **62**...........(v) AlistairRawlinson 7 57
(Michael Appleby) *chsd ldrs on outer: rdn along 3f out: wknd fnl 2f* **20/1**

0006 **8** *11* **Buthelezi (USA)**[44] 8662 9-9-1 **57**................................ StevieDonohoe 5 33
(Brian Ellison) *a towards rr* **14/1**

6600 **9** *7* **Kay Sera**[17] 9070 9-9-0 **59**........................................ EoinWalsh(3) 6 24
(Tony Newcombe) *a towards rr* **50/1**

606 **10** *15* **Anton Chigurh**[26] 8955 8-9-7 **63**..............................(h) CharlesBishop 1 4
(Nikki Evans) *midfield: rdn along over 4f out: sn outpcd* **33/1**

/0-0 **11** *20* **Scrutiny**[15] 9100 6-9-6 **65**........................................ ShelleyBirkett(3) 3
(Kevin Ryan) *in tch on inner: rdn along over 4f out: sn outpcd and bhd* **50/1**

-051 **12** *hd* **Bushel (USA)**[247] 1864 7-9-2 **58**.................................. TomEaves 2
(Tony Newcombe) *a in rr: outpcd and bhd fr over 4f out* **25/1**

2m 26.42s (-1.58) **Going Correction** -0.025s/f (Stan)
**WFA** 3 from 4yo+ 3lb — 12 Ran SP% **115.4**
Speed ratings (Par 101): **104,103,103,103,101 101,98,90,85,74 59,59**
CSF £9.62 CT £143.89 TOTE £4.50: £1.70, £1.10, £5.90; EX 13.50 Trifecta £243.60.
**Owner** Keith West & Ollie Pears Racing Club **Bred** Mrs T Mahon **Trained** Norton, N Yorks

**FOCUS**
A modest handicap. The winner basically replicated April's C&D form, with this making sense around the 2nd-4th.

## 9347 BETWAY SPRINT H'CAP — 6f 16y(F)
2:50 (2:50) (Class 6) (0-65,69) 3-Y-0+ — £2,264 (£673; £336; £168) Stalls Low

Form — RPR

0201 **1** **Kommander Kirkup**[23] 8980 6-9-7 **63**.........................(p) AndrewMullen 4 71
(Michael Herrington) *dwlt: sn trcking ldrs: hdwy 1/2-way: led 2f out: sn rdn: drvn and edgd lft ins fnl f: kpt on* **4/1**[2]

2565 **2** *nk* **The Amber Fort (USA)**[54] 8434 3-9-11 **67**.................. MartinHarley 2 74
(David O'Meara) *trckd ldrs on inner: hdwy over 2f out: rdn wl over 1f out: chal ins fnl f: sn drvn and kpt on* **5/2**[1]

2403 **3** *2* **Meandmyshadow**[20] 9033 9-9-5 **61**............................(b) CamHardie 8 62
(Alan Brown) *led 2f: cl up: rdn along over 2f out: drvn wl over 1f out: kpt on same pce fnl f* **15/2**

2140 **4** *1 ¾* **Tagur (IRE)**[48] 8556 3-9-7 **63**..................................(p) TomEaves 1 58
(Kevin Ryan) *trckd ldrs: hdwy on inner to ld 4f out: pushed along 3f out: hdd 2f out: sn rdn and kpt on one pce* **9/1**

0002 **5** *1 ¼* **Viva Verglas (IRE)**[8] 9216 6-9-5 **61**............................ LukeMorris 3 52
(Daniel Mark Loughnane) *prom: rdn along wl over 2f out: sn drvn and one pce* **9/2**[3]

-003 **6** *nk* **Hugie Boy (IRE)**[10] 9176 5-8-3 **50**......................(bt) JamieGormley(5) 10 40
(Scott Dixon) *in tch on outer wd st: sn rdn and n.d* **11/1**

5561 **7** *2 ¾* **Vroom (IRE)**[8] 9216 4-9-6 **69** 6ex........................(p) HarrisonShaw(7) 5 50
(Gay Kelleway) *prom: rdn along wl over 2f out: sn drvn and wknd* **5/1**

0000 **8** *nse* **Jacksonfire**[5] 9267 5-8-4 **49** oh4............................(be) PhilDennis(3) 6 30
(Michael Mullineaux) *dwlt: a towards rr* **50/1**

6200 **9** *1* **Bop It**[81] 7660 8-8-13 **58**..................................(t) RachelRichardson(3) 9 36
(Michael Easterby) *prom: rdn along over 3f out: sn wknd* **20/1**

1m 16.22s (-0.28) **Going Correction** -0.025s/f (Stan) — 9 Ran SP% **120.2**
Speed ratings (Par 101): **100,99,96,94,92 92,88,88,87**
CSF £15.12 CT £74.28 TOTE £5.80: £2.00, £1.30, £2.30; EX 24.10 Trifecta £125.80.
**Owner** Stuart Herrington & Pete Forster **Bred** W M Lidsey **Trained** Cold Kirby, N Yorks

**FOCUS**
A modest sprint handicap weakened further by the absence of Ghaseedah, who would probably have started a warm favourite. Limited form.

## 9348 BETWAY H'CAP — 4f 214y(F)
3:25 (3:27) (Class 6) (0-58,71) 3-Y-0+ — £2,264 (£673; £336; £168) Stalls Centre

Form — RPR

3645 **1** **Coiste Bodhar (IRE)**[10] 9181 6-8-9 **49**..................(p) JamieGormley(5) 2 57
(Scott Dixon) *cl up towards far side: rdn along 2f out: styd on u.p ent fnl f: led last 50yds* **7/1**

3511 **2** *¾* **Pearl Acclaim (IRE)**[2] 9308 7-10-8 **71** 12ex...............(p) SteveDrowne 3 76
(David C Griffiths) *sn cl up: chal 1/2-way: rdn to ld 1 1/2f out: drvn ent fnl f: hdd and no ex last 50yds* **2/1**[1]

3612 **3** *¾* **Archie Stevens**[10] 9181 7-9-4 **56**................................ PaddyPilley(3) 7 58
(Clare Ellam) *racd centre: slt ld: rdn along and hdd 1 1/2f out: drvn ent fnl f: kpt on same pce* **4/1**[2]

-006 **4** *nse* **Dazeekha**[15] 9102 4-8-10 **45**........................................ TomEaves 6 47
(Michael Herrington) *chsd ldrs centre: hdwy wl over 1f out: swtchd lft and rdn appr fnl f: kpt on u.p* **20/1**

2000 **5** *3 ¾* **Men United (FR)**[10] 9181 4-9-1 **50**............................(t) JimmyQuinn 1 39
(Roy Bowring) *wnt lft s: in tch: hdwy on far side over 2f out: rdn wl over 1f out: kpt on fnl f* **10/1**

0264 **6** *¾* **Bond Bombshell**[17] 9075 4-8-12 **54**....................(v) PatrickVaughan(7) 11 40
(David O'Meara) *racd towards stands' side: prom: cl up 1/2-way: rdn along wl over 1f out: grad wknd* **12/1**

0610 **7** *1 ¼* **Roy's Legacy**[5] 9265 8-9-0 **52** 6ex.......................... CharlieBennett(3) 5 33
(Shaun Harris) *racd centre: in tch: rdn along 2f out: no hdwy* **12/1**

0544 **8** *hd* **Sir Harry Collins (IRE)**[8] 9215 3-8-11 **46**..................(v) AndrewMullen 4 27
(Michael Appleby) *chsd ldrs towards far side: rdn along 2f out: sn wknd* **6/1**[3]

0003 **9** *2 ¾* **Very First Blade**[10] 9181 8-8-7 **45**..........................(be) PhilDennis(3) 8 16
(Michael Mullineaux) *racd towards stands' side: outpcd and bhd fr 1/2-way* **20/1**

06-6 **10** *10* **Secret Striker**[145] 5431 5-8-10 **45**................................ HollieDoyle 9
(Ken Cunningham-Brown) *dwlt: racd stands' side: outpcd and bhd fr 1/2-way* **25/1**

59.36s (-0.34) **Going Correction** -0.025s/f (Stan) — 10 Ran SP% **118.0**
Speed ratings (Par 101): **101,99,98,98,92 91,89,89,84,68**
CSF £21.02 CT £66.80 TOTE £8.30: £2.20, £1.30, £1.80; EX 33.00 Trifecta £144.70.
**Owner** Yvonne Lowe & W A Robinson **Bred** C Amerian **Trained** Babworth, Notts

**FOCUS**
A top-heavy and moderate sprint handicap. Five of these met over C&D ten days earlier including the first three here. That trio disputed the lead throughout. A fine effort for the grade from the runner-up in defeat.
T/Jkpt: Not Won. T/Plt: £116.20 to a £1 stake. Pool: £61,218.84 - 384.57 winning units T/Qpdt: £46.90 to a £1 stkae. Pool: £7,073.60 - 111.51 winning units **Joe Rowntree**

9349 - 9359a (Foreign Racing) - See Raceform Interactive

# 9130 MEYDAN (L-H)
Thursday, December 21

**OFFICIAL GOING: Dirt: fast**

## 9360a ENTISAR SPONSORED BY AL TAYER MOTORS (LISTED RACE) (DIRT) — 1m 2f (D)
4:50 (4:50) 3-Y-0+

£33,039 (£11,013; £5,506; £2,753; £1,651; £1,101)

RPR

**1** **Etijaah (USA)**[28] 8921 7-9-0 105..............................(h) DaneO'Neill 3 106+
(Doug Watson, UAE) *tracked ldr, rdn 2f out, sprinted clr 1 1/2f out, won easily* **16/1**

**2** *6* **Barreesh (IRE)**[356] 5-9-0 95..................................(t) ColmO'Donoghue 1 92
(Jaber Ramadhan, Bahrain) *mid-division, kpt on wl fnl 2f but no ch wth winner* **66/1**

**3** *1 ¾* **Faulkner**[28] 8921 7-9-0 110........................................ SamHitchcott 12 89
(Doug Watson, UAE) *tracked leaders, rdn 3 1/2f out, kpt on fnl 2f* **4/1**[3]

**4** *1 ½* **Los Barbados (IRE)**[301] 890 5-9-0 97........................(v) AdriedeVries 9 86
(Fawzi Abdulla Nass, Bahrain) *mid-division, ran on same pace fnl 2f* **28/1**

**5** *¾* **Storm Belt (USA)**[42] 8712 8-9-0 100.............................. FernandoJara 4 84
(Doug Watson, UAE) *mid-division, kpt on same pace fnl 3f* **12/1**

**6** *1 ½* **Fly At Dawn (USA)**[271] 1375 3-8-11 108........................(t) WilliamBuick 10 81
(Charlie Appleby) *tracked ldr, ev ch 3f out, ran on same pace fnl 2f* **11/8**[1]

**7** *2* **Farrier (USA)**[271] 1373 9-9-0 108............................(p) RichardMullen 13 77
(S Seemar, UAE) *soon led, hdd 2f out, wknd fnl 1 1/2f* **20/1**

**8** *nk* **Second Summer (USA)**[271] 1373 5-9-3 113..................(vt) PatDobbs 11 79
(Doug Watson, UAE) *slowly away, nvr better than mid-division* **3/1**[2]

**9** *25* **Top Clearance (USA)**[279] 1253 5-9-0 100..............(t) SilvestreDeSousa 8 26
(G Selvaratnam, UAE) *never better than mid-division* **22/1**

**10** *5 ½* **Tannaaf (IRE)**[18] 9058 5-9-0 99........................................ LSalles 2 15
(R Bouresly, Kuwait) *never able to challenge* **66/1**

**11** *nse* **Linguistic (IRE)**[61] 8234 4-9-0 102.............................. RoystonFfrench 5 15
(S bin Ghadayer, UAE) *tracked ldr til wknd fnl 3f* **20/1**

**12** *4 ¼* **Khusoosy (USA)**[308] 776 5-9-0 100..............................(t) TadhgO'Shea 6 7
(A R Al Rayhi, UAE) *never better than mid-division* **25/1**

**13** *11 ½* **Good Contact (USA)**[665] 722 5-9-0 99.............................. PatCosgrave 7
(S Seemar, UAE) *never better than mid-division* **25/1**

2m 5.6s (0.90)
**WFA** 3 from 4yo+ 2lb — 13 Ran SP% **128.7**
CSF: 822.43.
**Owner** Hamdan Al Maktoum **Bred** Shadwell Farm LLC **Trained** United Arab Emirates

## 9361a GARHOUD SPRINT SPONSORED BY LINCOLN NAVIGATOR (LISTED RACE) (DIRT) — 6f (D)
5:25 (5:25) 3-Y-0+

£33,039 (£11,013; £5,506; £2,753; £1,651; £1,101)

RPR

**1** **Muarrab**[271] 1377 8-9-0 108.............................................. DaneO'Neill 9 116
(A R Al Rayhi, UAE) *tracked ldr, led 2 1/2f out, ran on well* **11/1**[3]

**2** *6* **Comicas (USA)**[180] 4071 4-9-0 111..............................(b) WilliamBuick 6 97+
(Charlie Appleby) *tracked ldr, ev ch 3f out, ran on same pace fnl 2f* **15/8**[1]

**3** *shd* **My Catch (IRE)**[271] 1377 6-9-0 110.................................. PatDobbs 2 96
(Doug Watson, UAE) *chased ldr, ran on same pace fnl 2 1/2f* **5/2**[2]

**4** *¾* **Yalta (IRE)**[20] 9048 3-9-0 101.................................... RoystonFfrench 5 94
(S bin Ghadayer, UAE) *soon led, hdd 2 1/2f out but ran on well* **14/1**

**5** *2* **Krypton Factor**[279] 1252 9-9-0 99..............................(v) AdriedeVries 4 88
(Fawzi Abdulla Nass, Bahrain) *never better than mid-division* **33/1**

**6** *3 ¼* **Fitzgerald (USA)**[271] 1373 5-9-0 108....................(t) SilvestreDeSousa 12 77
(A bin Harmash, UAE) *never better than mid-division* **14/1**

**7** *4 ¼* **Nawwaar (USA)**[714] 90 8-9-0 102.................................... AntonioFresu 3 64
(A R Al Rayhi, UAE) *never nr to challenge* **33/1**

**8** *nk* **Portamento (IRE)**[48] 8581 5-9-0 101..............................(t) TadhgO'Shea 1 63
(A R Al Rayhi, UAE) *never better than mid-division* **25/1**

**9** *8 ¾* **Desert Force**[313] 695 5-9-0 108.................................... SamHitchcott 10 35
(Doug Watson, UAE) *never nr to challenge* **20/1**

**10** *29* **Satwa Story**[48] 8581 7-9-0 98........................................(t) PatCosgrave 8
(S Seemar, UAE) *never nr to challenge* **50/1**

**11** *39* **Ennobled Friend (USA)**[14] 9133 7-9-0 96..............(bt) ConnorBeasley 11
(A bin Harmash, UAE) *very slwly away, nvr in contention* **25/1**

1m 11.61s (0.01) — 11 Ran SP% **105.3**
CSF: 21.74.
**Owner** Hamdan Al Maktoum **Bred** Stratford Place Stud **Trained** UAE
■ Raven's Corner was withdrawn. Price at time of withdrawal 7/2. Rule 4 applies to all bets - deduction 20p in the pound.

9362 - (Foreign Racing) - See Raceform Interactive

9341

# SOUTHWELL (L-H)

Friday, December 22

**OFFICIAL GOING: Fibresand: standard**

Wind: Virtually nil Weather: Fine & dry

## 9363 SUNBETS.CO.UK H'CAP 7f 14y(F)

11:50 (11:50) (Class 5) (0-75,76) 3-Y-O+ £2,911 (£866; £432; £216) Stalls Low

Form RPR

0101 1 **Queens Royale**[3] 9307 3-9-2 **68** 6ex.....(v) RobertWinston 3 75
(Michael Appleby) *t.k.h early: n.m.r and swtchd lft to inner after 1f: trckd ldrs: effrt on far rail over 2f out: cl up and rdn wl over 1f out: drvn ins fnl f: kpt on gamely to ld nr line* 3/1[2]

0241 2 nse **Bold Spirit**[18] 9076 6-9-0 **69**.....(t) PhilDennis(3) 4 76
(Declan Carroll) *t.k.h early: prom: cl up 3f out: chal 2f out: rdn to ld jst over 1f out: drvn ins fnl f: edgd lft and hdd nr line* 7/2[3]

0000 3 6 **Count Montecristo (FR)**[49] 8561 5-9-10 **76**.....(p) TomEaves 2 67
(Kevin Ryan) *cl up: led wl over 2f out: rdn wl over 1f out: hdd appr fnl f: kpt on same pce* 8/1

1300 4 3 1/4 **Clock Chimes**[28] 8928 3-9-6 **72**.....(v[1]) PJMcDonald 7 55
(David Brown) *chsd ldrs on outer: cl up 1/2-way: rdn along and wd st: drvn wl over 1f out: sn btn* 7/4[1]

6210 5 7 **Bounty Pursuit**[21] 9029 5-9-2 **71**..... MitchGodwin(3) 6 36
(Michael Blake) *a towards rr* 20/1

0611 6 16 **First Excel**[21] 9033 5-9-3 **69**.....(b) JimmyQuinn 1
(Roy Bowring) *dwlt: sn slt ld on inner: pushed along over 3f out: hdd wl over 2f out: sn rdn and wknd: eased over 1f out* 15/2

1m 29.25s (-1.05) **Going Correction** -0.075s/f (Stan) **6** Ran SP% **111.2**

Speed ratings (Par 103): **103,102,96,92,84 66**

CSF £13.56 TOTE £3.00: £2.60, £1.70; EX 9.50 Trifecta £62.10.

**Owner** Wayne Brackstone, Steve Whitear **Bred** W Brackstone & S J Whitear **Trained** Oakham, Rutland

■ Stewards' Enquiry : Robert Winston two-day ban: using whip above the permitted level (Jan 5-6)

**FOCUS**

A routine Fibresand handicap, though half the field were last-time-out winners and it provided a tight finish. The winner stuck to the inside rail, while the others came up to middle in the straight.

## 9364 SUNBETS.CO.UK DOWNLOAD THE APP H'CAP 1m 13y(F)

12:25 (12:27) (Class 6) (0-65,67) 3-Y-O+ £2,587 (£770; £384; £192) Stalls Low

Form RPR

0506 1 **Spun Gold**[21] 9027 3-9-3 **61**.....(bt[1]) StevieDonohoe 14 68
(Charlie Fellowes) *dwlt and wnt rt s: wd and racd keenly: sn cl up: led after 1f: rdn along and clr whn edgd rt 1/2f out: hung rt to stands rail ins fnl f: kpt on* 7/1[3]

6005 2 2 **Dubaitwentytwenty**[11] 9180 3-9-7 **65**.....(tp) JosephineGordon 11 67
(Hugo Palmer) *prom: chsd wnr over 4f out: rdn along and rdr dropped whip 2f out: kpt on* 10/1

6516 3 3 3/4 **Shearian**[11] 9180 7-9-3 **67**..... GerO'Neill(7) 13 61
(Declan Carroll) *in tch: hdwy 3f out: rdn over 2f out: kpt on u.p appr fnl f* 12/1

3-32 4 1 3/4 **Best Tamayuz**[3] 9307 6-8-12 **55**.....(p) KieranO'Neill 8 45
(Scott Dixon) *led 1f: chsd ldng pair: rdn along 3f out: drvn over 2f out: kpt on one pce* 5/2[1]

062 5 1/2 **Street Poet (IRE)**[42] 8720 4-9-2 **59**..... RobertWinston 10 48
(Michael Herrington) *midfield: hdwy 1/2-way: chsd ldrs 3f out: rdn over 2f out: sn drvn and no imp* 7/2[2]

3525 6 2 3/4 **Charlie's Dreamer**[18] 9071 3-9-1 **59**..... LukeMorris 9 40
(Michael Appleby) *prom: rdn along wl over 2f out: grad wknd* 25/1

3534 7 1/2 **Dose**[237] 2153 4-8-12 **62**..... SebastianWoods(7) 4 43
(Richard Fahey) *towards rr: hdwy 3f out: rdn along 2f out: kpt on fnl f: nrst fin* 20/1

5042 8 2 **Stoneboat Bill**[24] 7567 5-9-3 **63**..... PhilDennis(3) 1 39
(Declan Carroll) *dwlt: a towards rr* 8/1

0034 9 3/4 **Ace Master**[11] 9176 9-9-0 **62**.....(b) KevinLundie(5) 3 36
(Roy Bowring) *in tch on inner: rdn along over 3f out: n.d* 14/1

0060 10 11 **The Yellow Bus**[16] 9093 4-9-9 **66**..... RyanPowell 6 14
(Daniel Steele) *dwlt: a towards rr* 40/1

6050 11 24 **Coral Princess (IRE)**[48] 8591 3-8-7 **51** oh6.....(b[1]) AndrewMullen 7
(Keith Dalgleish) *a towards rr* 50/1

0435 12 2 **Wannabe Like You**[16] 9088 3-9-8 **66**.....(p) EdwardGreatrex 12
(Archie Watson) *chsd ldrs: rdn along 3f out: sn drvn and wknd* 14/1

1m 41.46s (-2.24) **Going Correction** -0.075s/f (Stan)

**WFA** 3 from 4yo+ 1lb **12** Ran SP% **117.5**

Speed ratings (Par 101): **108,106,102,100,100 97,96,94,94,83 59,57**

CSF £71.33 CT £591.38 TOTE £8.40: £2.40, £3.00, £3.50; EX 97.40 Trifecta £1687.40.

**Owner** Joe Soiza & Mason Soiza **Bred** Fittocks Stud & Arrow Farm & Stud **Trained** Newmarket, Suffolk

**FOCUS**

A modest handicap and not many got into it. The first three were drawn 14, 11 and 13 which shows that a high draw need not be an issue over the mile here.

## 9365 SUNBETS.CO.UK TOP PRICE ON ALL FAVOURITES H'CAP 7f 14y(F)

1:00 (1:01) (Class 6) (0-55,55) 3-Y-O £2,264 (£673; £336; £168) Stalls Low

Form RPR

4340 1 **Princess Way (IRE)**[6] 9268 3-9-4 **52**.....(v) FranBerry 6 60
(David Evans) *mde all: rdn along 2f out: drvn ins fnl f: kpt on wl towards fin* 10/1

5044 2 1 3/4 **Ronni Layne**[5] 9276 3-9-1 **49**.....(b) LukeMorris 5 52
(Louise Allan) *trckd ldrs: hdwy over 2f out: swtchd lft and rdn over 1f out: drvn and kpt on fnl f* 9/2[2]

3004 3 3/4 **New Tale**[21] 9030 3-8-12 **46**.....(b) SamJames 4 47
(Olly Williams) *chsd wnr: rdn along 2f out: edgd rt over 1f out: drvn and kpt on same pce fnl f* 16/1

0262 4 5 **Bo Selecta (IRE)**[24] 8984 3-9-7 **55**.....(p) StevieDonohoe 11 43
(Richard Spencer) *trckd ldrs on outer: hdwy over 2f out: rdn wl over 1f out: sn drvn and one pce* 4/1[1]

0015 5 nk **Tilly Devine**[1] 9342 3-9-3 **51**.....(b) KieranO'Neill 2 38
(Scott Dixon) *dwlt and sn rdn along on inner towards rr: hdwy on inner over 3f out: rdn to chse ldrs 2f out: sn drvn and no imp* 5/1[3]

-006 6 1/2 **Red Douglas**[18] 9072 3-8-12 **46** oh1.....(p) TomEaves 9 32
(Scott Dixon) *dwlt and towards rr: hdwy 4f out: rdn over 1f out: kpt on u.p fnl f* 25/1

6501 7 1/2 **Stringybark Creek**[9] 9213 3-8-7 **48**.....(p) DarraghKeenan(7) 10 32
(Daniel Steele) *dwlt and bhd tl styd on fnl 2f* 11/2

-456 8 2 3/4 **Harvest Ranger**[8] 9232 3-8-12 **46** oh1..... KieranShoemark 1 23
(Michael Appleby) *a in rr* 10/1

6034 9 12 **Ejabah (IRE)**[18] 9071 3-8-12 **46** oh1.....(v) JoeyHaynes 8
(Charles Smith) *n.m.r and swtchd rt over 5f out: sn rdn along and bhd after* 16/1

0043 10 3 **Compton Brave**[17] 9085 3-8-12 **46** oh1..... JosephineGordon 7
(J R Jenkins) *trckd ldrs whn n.m.r and hmpd over 5f out: sn lost pl and bhd* 8/1

0600 11 4 **Tink**[6] 9267 3-8-9 **46** oh1..... CharlieBennett(3) 3
(Mark Brisbourne) *chsd ldrs: rdn along over 3f out: sn wknd* 50/1

1m 29.58s (-0.72) **Going Correction** -0.075s/f (Stan) **11** Ran SP% **117.1**

Speed ratings (Par 98): **101,99,98,92,92 91,90,87,74,70 66**

CSF £54.38 CT £725.49 TOTE £11.60: £3.70, £1.50, £4.80; EX 59.60 Trifecta £1063.90.

**Owner** Mrs I M Folkes **Bred** Tally-Ho Stud **Trained** Pandy, Monmouths

■ Stewards' Enquiry : Stevie Donohoe caution: careless riding

**FOCUS**

A poor handicap with this lot having a combined record of 4-136. This was another race dominated by those ridden prominently.

## 9366 BETWAY DASH H'CAP 4f 214y(F)

1:35 (1:35) (Class 4) (0-85,87) 3-Y-O+ £4,690 (£1,046; £1,046; £348) Stalls Centre

Form RPR

4102 1 **Tilly Trotter (IRE)**[17] 9079 3-9-7 **83**..... TomEaves 7 90
(Declan Carroll) *cl up: rdn over 1f out: drvn to chal ins fnl f: kpt on wl to ld nr line* 7/1

0000 2 hd **Kickboxer (IRE)**[15] 9125 6-9-4 **87**..... GabrieleMalune(7) 2 93
(Michael Appleby) *racd towards far side: dwlt and outpcd in rr: rdn along and hdwy wl over 1f out: swtchd rt ins fnl f: fin v strly* 9/2[3]

0040 2 dht **Razin' Hell**[18] 9074 6-9-4 **80**.....(v) AndrewMullen 3 86
(John Balding) *racd towards centre: led: rdn and edgd lft over 1f out: drvn ins fnl f: sn hung lft to far rail: hdd and no ex nr line* 7/2[2]

3300 4 1 1/4 **Crosse Fire**[3] 9305 5-8-10 **72**.....(v) KieranO'Neill 4 74
(Scott Dixon) *prom towards far side: rdn along wl over 1f out: drvn fnl f and kpt on same pce* 13/2

4211 5 2 **Casterbridge**[28] 8927 5-9-1 **77**.....(p) RobertWinston 5 71
(Eric Alston) *racd centre: chsd ldrs: rdn wl over 1f out: wknd appr fnl f* 11/4[1]

1510 6 3/4 **Piazon**[36] 8803 6-9-2 **81**.....(be) TimClark(3) 1 73
(John Butler) *dwlt and towards rr far side: hdwy to chse ldrs 3f out: rdn along 2f out: sn drvn and wknd* 6/1

0000 7 4 **Bosham**[22] 9016 7-8-8 **77**.....(bt) HarrisonShaw(7) 8 54
(Michael Easterby) *racd centre: in tch: rdn along 1/2-way: sn outpcd* 25/1

58.66s (-1.04) **Going Correction** -0.075s/f (Stan) **7** Ran SP% **111.0**

Speed ratings (Par 105): **105,104,104,102,99 98,91**

PL: 1.40 Kickboxer, 0.80 Razin' Hell; EX: TT & KB: £16.50, TT & RH: £12.80 ; CSF: TT & KB: £17.94, TT & RH: £14.86; TC: TT & KB & RH: £61.93, TT& RH & KB £58.82; TF: 2-1-4 £33.00 2-4-1 £27.00; TOTE £6.80: £3.30.

**Owner** F Gillespie **Bred** James Hughes **Trained** Malton, N Yorks

**FOCUS**

A fair sprint handicap and with a few confirmed trailblazers in opposition there was never going to be any hanging about.

## 9367 BETWAY CLASSIFIED CLAIMING STKS 1m 6f 21y(F)

2:10 (2:10) (Class 6) 3-Y-O+ £2,264 (£673; £336; £168) Stalls Low

Form RPR

4140 1 **Gabrial's Star**[17] 9082 8-9-6 75.....(b) JackGarritty 2 74+
(Richard Fahey) *cl up: led 3f out: pushed clr wl over 1f out: v readily* 4/6[1]

0003 2 4 **Samtu (IRE)**[11] 9178 6-9-12 75..... JoeyHaynes 1 72
(Marjorie Fife) *sn led: pushed along 4f out: rdn and hdd 3f out: drvn wl over 1f out: kpt on same pce* 7/1

524 3 hd **Iniesta (IRE)**[16] 4750 6-9-5 68.....(b[1]) TomMarquand 3 65
(Fergal O'Brien) *trckd ldng pair: effrt over 3f out: rdn along over 2f out: drvn over 1f out: kpt on same pce* 6/1[3]

0024 4 1 **Bertie Moon**[11] 9178 7-9-9 70..... LukeMorris 4 67
(Michael Appleby) *trckd ldng pair: effrt over 3f out: rdn along wl over 2f out: drvn over 1f out: one pce fnl f* 4/1[2]

3m 7.38s (-0.92) **Going Correction** -0.075s/f (Stan) **4** Ran SP% **106.8**

Speed ratings (Par 101): **99,96,96,96**

CSF £5.49 TOTE £1.50; EX 4.20 Trifecta £12.20.

**Owner** Dr Marwan Koukash **Bred** Miss K Rausing **Trained** Musley Bank, N Yorks

**FOCUS**

A moderate classified claimer and straightforward for the warm favourite.

## 9368 BETWAY LIVE CASINO H'CAP 1m 3f 23y(F)

2:45 (2:46) (Class 6) (0-55,55) 4-Y-O+ £2,264 (£673; £336; £168) Stalls Low

Form RPR

033- 1 **Ochos Rios**[26] 5204 4-9-6 **54**..... FranBerry 1 61
(Neil Mulholland) *s.i.s and lost 6 l s: awkward and pushed along in rr: hdwy on outer into midfield over 7f out: chsd ldrs over 4f out: rdn along and cl up 3f out: styd on to ld appr fnl f: sn drvn kpt on wl* 12/1

5541 2 nk **Star Ascending (IRE)**[18] 9077 5-8-12 **53**.....(b) RossaRyan(7) 9 60
(Jennie Candlish) *t.k.h: trckd ldrs on outer: hdwy over 4f out: pushed along and wd st: rdn over 2f out: chal over 1f out: drvn and ev ch ins fnl f: no ex towards fin* 10/11[1]

0033 3 2 3/4 **Dream Serenade**[9] 9221 4-9-1 **49**.....(p) LukeMorris 7 51
(Michael Appleby) *led: pushed along 4f out: rdn along 3f out: hdd wl over 2f out: cl up and drvn wl over 1f out: kpt on same pce fnl f* 5/1[2]

0000 4 1/2 **Mamnoon (IRE)**[27] 8957 4-9-3 **51**.....(b) KieranShoemark 12 52
(Roy Brotherton) *prom: trckd ldr after 3f: cl up 4f out: rdn to ld wl over 2f out: drvn wl over 1f out: hdd appr fnl f: kpt on same pce* 20/1

4004 5 4 **Just Fred (IRE)**[18] 9077 4-8-12 **46** oh1.....(t) JimmyQuinn 8 41
(Neil Mulholland) *chsd ldrs: rdn along over 3f out: drvn over 2f out: grad wknd* 12/1

5 6 1/2 **Pantomime (IRE)**[23] 8654 5-9-1 **52**..... PhilDennis(3) 5 46
(Rebecca Menzies) *prom: rdn along over 3f out: wknd over 2f out* 12/1

6030 7 3 3/4 **Quadriga (IRE)**[36] 8807 7-8-12 **46** oh1..... KieranO'Neill 10 34
(Chris Grant) *chsd ldrs: rdn along wl over 3f out: sn wknd* 25/1

4200 8 1 3/4 **Tred Softly (IRE)**[52] 8487 4-9-7 **55**.....(b) DougieCostello 6 40
(John Quinn) *towards rr: sme hdwy 3f out: sn rdn along and nvr a factor* 10/1[3]

5060 9 1 **Clayton Hall (IRE)**[24] 8985 4-8-7 **46** oh1.....(p) WilliamCox(5) 11 30
(John Wainwright) *a towards rr* 66/1

0400 10 15 **Port Lairge**[18] 9077 7-8-12 **46** oh1..... JoeyHaynes 13 6
(Michael Chapman) *v.s.a: a bhd* 50/1



The Form Book Flat, Raceform Ltd, Newbury, RG14 5SJ

2200 **11** *2 ¼* **Never Say (IRE)**[18] 9077 4-8-7 **46** oh1..............................(p) JaneElliott(5) 2 2
(Sam England) *in tch on inner: rdn along over 5f out: sn outpcd and bhd fnl 3f* **40/1**

0445 **12** *8* **Jennies Gem**[18] 9072 4-8-12 **46** oh1.............................. AndrewMullen 4
(Ollie Pears) *hld up: swtchd rt to outer over 6f out: rdn along over 4f out: sn lost pl and bhd fnl 3f* **16/1**

0-00 **13** *12* **Kazoey**[202] 3340 4-8-12 **46** oh1.............................. DuranFentiman 3
(Chris Fairhurst) *a in rr* **66/1**

2m 26.21s (-1.79) **Going Correction** -0.075s/f (Stan) **13** Ran SP% **123.1**
Speed ratings (Par 101): **103,102,100,100,97 97,94,93,92,81 79,74,65**
CSF £22.96 CT £70.57 TOTE £15.60: £3.70, £1.10, £1.70; EX 45.80 Trifecta £174.80.
**Owner** Wayne Clifford **Bred** Mrs S Clifford **Trained** Limpley Stoke, Wilts
■ Stewards' Enquiry : Rossa Ryan four-day ban: using whip above the permitted level (Jan 5,6,8,9)

**FOCUS**
Rock-bottom stuff containing a bunch of infrequent winners and seven of the 13 runners were out of the weights, but a quite remarkable performance from the winner.

## 9369 BETWAY CASINO H'CAP 1m 3f 23y(F)
**3:20** (3:20) (Class 5) (0-75,77) 3-Y-0+ **£2,911** (£866; £432; £216) **Stalls** Low

Form RPR

5046 **1** **Sonnetist**[13] 9159 3-9-1 **70**.............................. FranBerry 6 75
(David Evans) *trckd ldng pair: hdwy and cl up on outer over 3f out: led wl over 2f out and sn rdn: drvn ent fnl f: hld on wl towards fin* **5/1**[3]

6035 **2** *½* **Swift Cedar (IRE)**[24] 8978 7-9-6 **72**.............................. StevieDonohoe 3 76
(David Evans) *hld up in rr: pushed along wl over 3f out: wd st and rdn over 2f out: str run nr stands rail appr fnl f: tk 2nd nr fin* **11/4**[2]

6312 **3** *1* **Topamichi**[36] 8806 7-9-3 **69**.............................. LukeMorris 1 72
(Michael Appleby) *t.k.h: trckd ldrs: hdwy over 3f out: rdn 2f out: chal over 1f out: drvn and ev ch ent fnl f: wknd towards fin* **10/11**[1]

600 **4** *2 ¼* **Song Of Love (IRE)**[30] 8893 5-9-4 **73**..............................(p) PaddyPilley(3) 2 72
(Shaun Harris) *hld up in rr: hdwy on inner to trck ldrs over 4f out: rdn along wl over 2f out: sn drvn and no imp* **20/1**

3502 **5** *1 ¾* **Vigee Le Brun (IRE)**[167] 4633 3-9-2 **71**.............................. SamJames 4 67
(Olly Williams) *led: rdn along over 3f out: hdd wl over 2f out: sn drvn and grad wknd* **12/1**

436/ **6** *½* **Brotherly Company (IRE)**[6] 5-9-8 **77**.............................. PhilDennis(3) 5 72
(Joanne Foster) *trckd ldr: cl up 4f out: rdn along 3f out: drvn over 2f out: grad wknd* **66/1**

2m 26.54s (-1.46) **Going Correction** -0.075s/f (Stan)
**WFA** 3 from 5yo+ 3lb **6** Ran SP% **109.7**
Speed ratings (Par 103): **102,101,100,99,98 97**
CSF £18.15 TOTE £5.10: £2.40, £1.10; EX 18.30 Trifecta £44.30.
**Owner** Wayne Clifford **Bred** Mrs S Clifford **Trained** Pandy, Monmouths
■ Stewards' Enquiry : Sam James two-day ban: using whip above the permitted level (Jan 5-6)

**FOCUS**
An ordinary handicap and a 1-2 for trainer David Evans.
T/Plt: £223.80 to a £1 stake. Pool: £50,329.70 - 164.13 winning units T/Qpdt: £21.40 to a £1 stake. Pool: £4,890.02 - 168.86 winning units **Joe Rowntree**

# 9295 WOLVERHAMPTON (A.W) (L-H)
Friday, December 22

**OFFICIAL GOING: Tapeta: standard**
Wind: Overcast Weather: Light behind

## 9370 32RED.COM NURSERY H'CAP 7f 36y (Tp)
**5:45** (5:46) (Class 5) (0-75,77) 2-Y-0 **£2,911** (£866; £432; £216) **Stalls** High

Form RPR

1000 **1** **Blacklooks (IRE)**[16] 9098 2-9-6 **77**.............................. JaneElliott(5) 2 83+
(Ivan Furtado) *hld up: hdwy whn hmpd over 1f out: swtchd rt: r.o to ld wl ins fnl f: comf* **14/1**

0421 **2** *1 ¼* **Swissal (IRE)**[21] 9024 2-9-2 **68**.............................. DougieCostello 10 70
(David Dennis) *hld up: hung lft fr over 1f out: swtchd rt and r.o ins fnl f: wnt 2nd nr fin* **9/1**

3304 **3** *½* **Laubali**[29] 8916 2-9-3 **69**.............................. MartinHarley 4 70
(David O'Meara) *prom: rdn over 1f out: styd on* **11/2**[3]

0042 **4** *nk* **Bezos (IRE)**[8] 9230 2-8-10 **62**..............................(p) TomMarquand 7 62+
(Richard Hannon) *sn chsng ldr: led over 2f out: rdn and edgd lft over 1f out: hdd wl ins fnl f* **8/1**

024 **5** *1* **Poetic Imagination**[17] 9081 2-9-6 **72**..............................(v[1]) RobertHavlin 5 70
(John Gosden) *chsd ldrs: nt clr run over 2f out: sn ev ch: rdn over 1f out: no ex wl ins fnl f* **4/1**[2]

3200 **6** *1 ¼* **Phoenix Lightning (IRE)**[82] 7647 2-9-5 **71**..............................(p) GrahamLee 1 66
(Rebecca Menzies) *hld up: racd keenly: hdwy over 1f out: sn rdn and hung lft: no ex ins fnl f* **8/1**

6332 **7** *1* **Mr Gent (IRE)**[9] 9199 2-9-7 **73**..............................(b) PJMcDonald 3 65
(Ed Dunlop) *pushed along sn after leaving stalls: hdwy over 5f out: rdn over 1f out: no ex ins fnl f* **2/1**[1]

0440 **8** *4 ½* **By Royal Approval (IRE)**[58] 8349 2-9-6 **72**.............. JosephineGordon 9 53
(Michael Appleby) *sn pushed along to go prom: rdn 1/2-way: wknd over 1f out* **8/1**

003 **9** *33* **Equilibrium**[94] 7250 2-8-12 **64**.............................. TomEaves 6 +
(Ivan Furtado) *led over 4f: n.m.r and wknd sn after: eased* **40/1**

1m 29.56s (0.76) **Going Correction** 0.0s/f (Stan) **9** Ran SP% **121.2**
Speed ratings (Par 96): **95,93,93,92,91 90,88,83,46**
CSF £138.82 CT £795.73 TOTE £17.70: £4.30, £2.40, £2.00; EX 160.90 Trifecta £1396.70.
**Owner** John L Marriott **Bred** Premier Bloodstock **Trained** Wiseton, Nottinghamshire

**FOCUS**
The going was standard\n\x\x For races 1 and 2, the stalls were on the outside. For all other races, the stalls were on the inside\n\x\x A run-of-the-mill nursery which was run at a decent clip and suited the hold-up horses.

## 9371 32RED CASINO FILLIES' NOVICE AUCTION STKS (PLUS 10 RACE) 7f 36y (Tp)
**6:15** (6:18) (Class 5) 2-Y-0 **£2,911** (£866; £432; £216) **Stalls** High

Form RPR

**1** **Unveiling** 2-8-10 0.............................. RobHornby 4 71
(Jonathan Portman) *hld up: pushed along 4f out: hdwy over 2f out: led over 1f out: rdn out* **12/1**

30 **2** *½* **Golden Image**[107] 6824 2-8-8 0.............................. EdwardGreatrex 5 68
(Jonathan Portman) *prom: pushed along over 2f out: sn outpcd: hrd rdn fr over 1f out: edgd lft and r.o ins fnl f: wnt 2nd nr fin* **5/2**[1]

6325 **3** *nk* **Ideal Candy (IRE)**[16] 9097 2-8-9 67.............................. SamJames 1 68
(Karen Tutty) *led: rdn and hdd over 1f out: styd on same pce ins fnl f* **10/3**[2]

**4** *1 ¾* **Dillie Dallie (IRE)** 2-9-0 0.............................. FranBerry 9 69
(Henry Spiller) *s.i.s: hdwy over 1f out: sn rdn and edgd lft: styd on same pce ins fnl f* **16/1**

4 **5** *2* **Racehorse**[8] 9231 2-8-5 0.............................. CharlieBennett(3) 3 58
(Hughie Morrison) *chsd ldrs: wnt 2nd 3f out: rdn over 1f out: edgd lft and no ex ins fnl f* **4/1**[3]

5 **6** *3 ½* **Wherearainbowsend (IRE)**[29] 8914 2-8-8 0..............................(h) TomEaves 7 50
(Bryan Smart) *chsd ldr 4f: wknd fnl f* **10/1**

**7** *1 ½* **Culture Shock** 2-9-0 0.............................. TomMarquand 8 52
(Richard Hannon) *s.i.s: a in rr: rdn: hung lft and wknd over 1f out* **11/2**

1m 29.92s (1.12) **Going Correction** 0.0s/f (Stan) **7** Ran SP% **109.7**
Speed ratings (Par 93): **93,92,92,90,87 83,82**
CSF £38.82 TOTE £16.60: £6.80, £1.90; EX 54.40 Trifecta £173.80.
**Owner** J G B Portman **Bred** D R Botterill **Trained** Upper Lambourn, Berks

**FOCUS**
An ordinary novice auction race which produced a 1-2 for the Jonathan Portman stable. The winner should go on to better things.

## 9372 32REDSPORT.COM NOVICE STKS 6f 20y (Tp)
**6:45** (6:47) (Class 5) 2-Y-0 **£2,911** (£866; £432; £216) **Stalls** Low

Form RPR

0 **1** **Mount Wellington (IRE)**[116] 6532 2-9-2 85..............................(v[1]) FranBerry 1 79
(Henry Spiller) *prom: chsd ldr 4f out: rdn over 1f out: styd on u.p to ld nr fin* **8/1**[3]

322 **2** *½* **Epic Fantasy**[20] 9050 2-9-2 78.............................. PJMcDonald 3 77
(Charles Hills) *led 5f out: rdn and edgd lft ins fnl f: hdd nr fin* **4/6**[1]

05 **3** *3 ¼* **Rose Tinted Spirit**[43] 8701 2-9-2 0.............................. JosephineGordon 6 67
(Ralph Beckett) *prom: pushed along and outpcd over 2f out: styd on ins fnl f* **11/1**

05 **4** *hd* **Oneroa (IRE)**[21] 9023 2-8-11 0.............................. TomEaves 2 61
(Ivan Furtado) *hld up: hdwy and hung lft over 1f out: styd on: nt rch ldrs* **28/1**

65 **5** *nk* **Becker**[52] 8493 2-9-2 0.............................. GrahamLee 8 65
(James Given) *prom: racd keenly: rdn over 1f out: edgd lft and no ex ins fnl f* **20/1**

5 **6** *9* **Hocus Focus (IRE)**[22] 9015 2-9-2 0.............................. DougieCostello 7 37
(Richard Guest) *s.i.s: hld up: nvr on terms* **80/1**

31 **7** *nse* **Brigand**[43] 8701 2-9-3 0.............................. GeorgiaCox(3) 11 40
(William Haggas) *broke wl enough: sn lost pl: n.d after* **3/1**[2]

**8** *2 ¼* **Harbour Pilot** 2-9-2 0.............................. HollieDoyle 4 29
(David Loughnane) *s.i.s: a in rr: hung lft fr over 2f out* **50/1**

0 **9** *6* **Keynote (IRE)**[179] 4151 2-9-2 0.............................. TomMarquand 5 10
(David C Griffiths) *led 1f: chsd ldrs: rdn over 3f out: wknd over 2f out* **25/1**

006 **10** *2 ¾* **Balmec (IRE)**[29] 8916 2-9-2 50.............................. JimmyQuinn 9 1
(Ann Duffield) *hld up: pushed along over 3f out: wknd over 2f out* **100/1**

1m 14.73s (0.23) **Going Correction** 0.0s/f (Stan) **10** Ran SP% **120.7**
Speed ratings (Par 96): **98,97,93,92,92 80,80,77,69,65**
CSF £13.87 TOTE £6.90: £2.00, £1.10, £3.00; EX 16.80 Trifecta £71.10.
**Owner** Dethrone Racing **Bred** Alan O'Flynn **Trained** Newmarket, Suffolk

**FOCUS**
A fair novice event. The first two dominated and should remain competitive.

## 9373 BETWAY SPRINT H'CAP 5f 21y (Tp)
**7:15** (7:15) (Class 2) (0-105,107) 3-Y£01,971 (£3,583; £1,791; £896; £446) **Stalls** Low

Form RPR

5151 **1** **Gracious John (IRE)**[10] 9187 4-9-9 **107** 6ex.............................. FranBerry 5 114
(David Evans) *half-rrd s: rcvrd to ld 4f out: rdn over 1f out: all out* **3/1**[1]

0100 **2** *shd* **Tomily (IRE)**[23] 8991 3-8-10 **94**.............................. HollieDoyle 2 100
(Richard Hannon) *chsd ldrs: pushed along 3f out: rdn and ev ch wl ins fnl f: r.o* **5/1**

0042 **3** *½* **Bowson Fred**[29] 8913 5-8-10 **94**.............................. CamHardie 4 98
(Michael Easterby) *chsd ldrs: rdn over 1f out: r.o* **7/2**[2]

0101 **4** *¾* **Doctor Sardonicus**[129] 6025 6-9-7 **105**.............................. MartinHarley 3 106
(David Simcock) *led 1f: chsd ldrs: rdn over 1f out: r.o* **4/1**[3]

1150 **5** *1* **Compas Scoobie**[97] 7144 4-8-6 **93**..............................(t[1]) AaronJones(3) 6 91
(Stuart Williams) *hld up: hdwy u.p: hung lft and nt clr run ins fnl f: r.o: nt rch ldrs* **14/1**

6652 **6** *shd* **Sign Of The Kodiac (IRE)**[76] 7828 4-8-7 **94**.................. EoinWalsh(3) 8 91
(Tony Newcombe) *prom: chsd wnr over 3f out: rdn and ev ch over 1f out: styd on same pce ins fnl f* **20/1**

0600 **7** *1 ¼* **Doc Sportello (IRE)**[83] 7611 5-8-11 **95**..................(p) GeorgeDowning 1 88
(Tony Carroll) *hld up: rdn over 1f out: hung lft ins fnl f: nt trble ldrs* **50/1**

0634 **8** *nk* **Shamshon (IRE)**[10] 9187 6-8-2 **86** oh1..............................(t) JosephineGordon 7 78
(Stuart Williams) *hld up: pushed along 1/2-way: rdn over 1f out: nvr on terms* **7/1**

1m 0.84s (-1.06) **Going Correction** 0.0s/f (Stan) **8** Ran SP% **109.8**
Speed ratings (Par 109): **108,107,107,105,104 104,102,101**
CSF £16.73 CT £48.72 TOTE £3.90: £1.30, £1.90, £1.50; EX 20.70 Trifecta £78.00.
**Owner** Terry Reffell **Bred** Skeaghmore Hill **Trained** Pandy, Monmouths

**FOCUS**
An above-average sprint handicap which produced a determined winner. The form looks solid.

## 9374 BETWAY DASH H'CAP 5f 21y (Tp)
**7:45** (7:46) (Class 6) (0-55,55) 3-Y-0+ **£2,264** (£673; £336; £168) **Stalls** Low

Form RPR

2402 **1** **Jorvik Prince**[6] 9268 3-9-5 **53**.............................. SamJames 10 68
(Karen Tutty) *mde all: rdn clr over 1f out: comf* **10/3**[2]

655 **2** *4 ½* **Your Gifted (IRE)**[9] 9214 10-9-4 **52**..............................(v) RaulDaSilva 9 51
(Lisa Williamson) *hld up: hdwy 2f out: rdn and r.o to go 2nd nr fin: no ch w wnr* **25/1**

6000 **3** *nk* **Storm Lightning**[6] 9268 8-9-2 **53**.............................. EoinWalsh(3) 11 51
(Mark Brisbourne) *s.i.s: outpcd: rdn and r.o wl ins fnl f to go 3rd nr fin* **33/1**

0302 **4** *½* **Frank The Barber (IRE)**[6] 9267 5-9-2 **50**..............................(t) LiamKeniry 8 46
(Steph Hollinshead) *chsd ldrs: chsd wnr over 2f out: rdn and hung lft over 1f out: styd on same pce* **3/1**[1]

5000 **5** *hd* **Captain Scooby**[1] 9340 11-8-12 **46** oh1..............................(b) FrannyNorton 2 41
(Richard Guest) *s.i.s: outpcd: r.o ins fnl f: nvr nrr* **11/2**

5060 **6** *hd* **Roubles (USA)**[52] 8494 3-9-2 **50**.............................. GrahamLee 3 44
(Julie Camacho) *trckd ldrs: plld hrd: shkn up over 1f out: rdn and styng on same pce whn hung rt wl ins fnl f* **5/1**[3]

0204 **7** *nk* **Novabridge**[6] 9265 9-9-2 **50**..............................(b) JimmyQuinn 4 43
(Karen Tutty) *s.i.s: sn prom: rdn over 1f out: styd on same pce* **8/1**

1500 **8** *1* **Teepee Time**[32] 8873 4-9-4 **55**.......................................(b) PhilDennis(3) 5 45
(Michael Mullineaux) *chsd wnr over 2f: rdn over 1f out: wknd fnl f* **20/1**

6444 **9** *1 ¾* **Barnsdale**[156] 5027 4-8-5 **46** oh1................ MeganEllingworth(7) 6 30
(John Holt) *hld up: pushed along 1/2-way: nvr on terms* **50/1**

0506 **10** *2 ½* **Whispering Soul (IRE)**[6] 9267 4-8-12 **46**....................(p) PJMcDonald 7 21
(Brian Baugh) *hld up in tch: rdn 1/2-way: wknd fnl f* **14/1**

02 **11** *2 ½* **Imbucato**[71] 6341 3-9-5 **53**............................................ GeorgeDowning 1 19
(Tony Carroll) *s.i.s: outpcd* **14/1**

1m 1.55s (-0.35) **Going Correction** 0.0s/f (Stan) **11** Ran SP% **118.1**
Speed ratings (Par 101): **102,94,94,93,93 92,92,90,88,84 80**
CSF £90.20 CT £1701.80 TOTE £4.60: £1.50, £3.60, £8.10; EX 82.50 Trifecta £1781.00.
**Owner** Thoroughbred Homes Ltd **Bred** Hellwood Stud Farm & Mrs Jill Willows **Trained** Osmotherley, N Yorks

**FOCUS**
A low-grade handicap which featured a sparkling display from the well-backed winner.

## 9375 BETWAY CASINO H'CAP — 1m 4f 51y (Tp)
**8:15** (8:15) (Class 6) (0-60,60) 3-Y-O+ **£2,264** (£673; £336; £168) **Stalls** Low

Form RPR

4000 **1** **Dream Magic (IRE)**[39] 8773 3-9-2 **59**........................ AndrewMullen 11 72
(Daniel Mark Loughnane) *led: hdd over 9f out: chsd ldr tl led again over 3f out: rdn clr fr over 2f out: eased nr fin* **9/1**

4404 **2** *8* **Tis Wonderful (IRE)**[23] 8993 3-8-12 **60**........................ WilliamCox(5) 7 60
(Carroll Gray) *prom: racd keenly: chsd wnr over 3f out: rdn: hung lft and flashed tail over 1f out: no ex* **7/1**[3]

2501 **3** *4* **Ted's Brother (IRE)**[7] 9237 9-8-1 **47**..................(v) PoppyBridgwater(7) 8 40
(Laura Morgan) *s.i.s: hld up: hdwy and nt clr run over 3f out: nt clr run again over 2f out: rdn: nt clr run and swtchd rt over 1f out: styd on to go 3rd nr fin* **3/1**[2]

0360 **4** *hd* **Falcon's Fire (IRE)**[6] 9261 4-9-4 **60**...........................(b) RowanScott(3) 1 52
(Keith Dalgleish) *chsd ldrs: rdn and hung lft over 1f out: no ex* **7/1**[3]

2020 **5** *1 ½* **Mr Frankie**[59] 8327 6-9-6 **59**................................................ LiamKeniry 3 49
(Adrian Wintle) *prom: lost pl over 6f out: nt clr run 3f out: hdwy 2f out: sn rdn and hung lft: wknd fnl f* **10/1**

2203 **6** *½* **Cool Music (IRE)**[127] 6088 7-9-1 **54**..................................(p) CamHardie 10 43
(Antony Brittain) *hld up: rdn over 2f out: nvr nrr* **20/1**

0005 **7** *nk* **Diana Lady (CHI)**[15] 9127 5-9-3 **59**................................(t) EoinWalsh(3) 5 48
(Luke McJannet) *hld up: rdn over 2f out: nvr on terms* **66/1**

0566 **8** *7* **Bridal March**[9] 9221 3-8-3 **46**.........................................(p) JimmyQuinn 2 25
(John Mackie) *hld up: hdwy over 6f out: pushed along over 3f out: rdn and wknd over 1f out* **22/1**

4400 **9** *7* **Marshall Aid (IRE)**[16] 9095 4-9-2 **55**..........................(vt) KieranO'Neill 12 21
(Mark Usher) *hld up: rdn over 3f out: wknd over 2f out* **10/1**

365 **10** *35* **Lucky Ellen (IRE)**[6] 9262 3-8-6 **49**.................................. FrannyNorton 4
(Jennie Candlish) *hld up in tch: plld hrd: shkn up and n.m.r 3f out: wknd over 2f out* **5/2**[1]

6500 **11** *8* **Poet's Charm (IRE)**[26] 7712 3-8-8 **51**.................................(h) TomEaves 6
(Martin Hill) *chsd ldrs: led over 9f out: hdd & wknd over 3f out: eased* **33/1**

2m 38.68s (-2.12) **Going Correction** 0.0s/f (Stan)
**WFA** 3 from 4yo+ 4lb **11** Ran SP% **120.3**
Speed ratings (Par 101): **107,101,99,98,97 97,97,92,88,64 59**
CSF £69.34 CT £238.32 TOTE £12.00: £3.50, £1.70, £1.90; EX 90.10 Trifecta £384.80.
**Owner** Mrs C Loughnane **Bred** Paul V Jackson & Janet P Jackson **Trained** Rock, Worcs

**FOCUS**
What looked to be a tight handicap was turned into a procession by the aggressively-ridden winner. The form may be best treated with caution.

## 9376 BETWAY H'CAP — 1m 1f 104y (Tp)
**8:45** (8:46) (Class 6) (0-65,67) 3-Y-O **£2,264** (£673; £336; £168) **Stalls** Low

Form RPR

5011 **1** **Champagne Pink (FR)**[34] 8854 3-9-6 **67**.........................(h) CliffordLee(3) 3 76
(K R Burke) *hld up in tch: rdn over 1f out: edgd lft and r.o to ld wl ins fnl f* **5/2**[1]

5533 **2** *1 ¼* **Mac O'Polo (IRE)**[13] 9153 3-9-3 **64**.................................. PaddyPilley(3) 9 71
(Tom Dascombe) *chsd ldrs: rdn to ld ins fnl f: sn edgd lft and hdd: styd on same pce* **10/1**

0340 **3** *4* **William Booth (IRE)**[35] 8814 3-9-8 **66**............................... TomEaves 10 65
(Ivan Furtado) *sn prom: led over 6f out: rdn and edgd rt over 1f out: hdd and no ex ins fnl f* **12/1**

0151 **4** *¾* **Broughtons Story**[67] 8123 3-8-11 **62**................................ JackOsborn(7) 8 60
(Philip McBride) *led after 1f: hdd over 6f out: chsd ldrs: rdn over 1f out: ev ch ins fnl f: wknd towards fin* **8/1**

0551 **5** *nk* **Zoffany Bay (IRE)**[15] 9128 3-9-6 **64**.........................(p) KieranO'Neill 7 61
(George Peckham) *racd keenly: led 1f: chsd ldrs: rdn over 1f out: styng on same pce whn hung rt ins fnl f* **8/1**

6400 **6** *1 ¼* **Critical Thinking (IRE)**[27] 8957 3-8-11 **55**.................. TomMarquand 1 50
(David Loughnane) *prom: hmpd and lost pl after 1f: rdn over 2f out: styd on ins fnl f* **5/1**[3]

2654 **7** *2 ¾* **Sir Gnet (IRE)**[50] 8550 3-9-6 **64**....................................(h) PJMcDonald 11 54
(Ed Dunlop) *hld up: shkn up over 2f out: nvr on terms* **5/1**[3]

0006 **8** *1 ¾* **War Of Succession**[16] 9093 3-9-4 **65**.............................. EoinWalsh(3) 6 51
(Tony Newcombe) *s.i.s: hmpd over 7f out: rdn over 2f out: n.d* **4/1**[2]

600 **9** *2 ¼* **Fortuities (IRE)**[14] 9144 3-9-2 **60**.......................................... LiamKeniry 5 42
(John James Feane, Ire) *hld up in tch: rdn over 3f out: hung lft and wknd over 1f out* **20/1**

00-0 **10** *1 ¾* **Freediver**[32] 8869 3-8-9 **60**.............................................. NicolaCurrie(7) 12 39
(John Berry) *hld up: rdn over 2f out: wkng whn hmpd over 1f out* **40/1**

4423 **11** *½* **Lewinsky (IRE)**[29] 8911 3-9-5 **63**...................................... CamHardie 4 41
(Antony Brittain) *s.i.s: hld up: hmpd over 6f out: a in rr* **40/1**

3000 **12** *¾* **Wild Acclaim (IRE)**[9] 9203 3-9-9 **67**............................ AndrewMullen 2 44
(Michael Appleby) *prom: hmpd and lost pl after 1f: hmpd again 7f out: rdn over 2f out: wknd over 1f out* **50/1**

2m 0.63s (-0.17) **Going Correction** 0.0s/f (Stan) **12** Ran SP% **132.5**
Speed ratings (Par 98): **100,98,95,94,94 93,90,89,87,85 85,84**
CSF £32.84 CT £280.66 TOTE £3.30: £1.50, £2.50, £3.90; EX 27.00 Trifecta £285.80.
**Owner** Nick Bradley Racing 2 & Mrs E Burke **Bred** G A E C Campos **Trained** Middleham Moor, N Yorks

**FOCUS**
Not the most competitive of handicaps, but it produced a progressive winner who may have even more to offer.

T/Jkpt: Not won. T/Plt: £232.10 to a £1 stake. Pool: £112,615.42 - 354.14 winning units T/Qpdt: £14.30 to a £1 stake. Pool: £10,166.40 - 524.00 winning units **Colin Roberts**

9377-9384a (Foreign Racing) - See Raceform Interactive

# [9318]LINGFIELD (L-H)
## Saturday, December 23

**OFFICIAL GOING: Polytrack: standard**
Wind: Medium, across Weather: Overcast

## 9385 32RED.COM NOVICE AUCTION STKS — 1m 1y(P)
**12:00** (12:01) (Class 5) 2-Y-O **£2,911** (£866; £432; £216) **Stalls** High

Form RPR

**1** **Lawn Ranger** 2-9-2 0.................................................. KierenFox 7 74+
(Michael Attwater) *s.i.s: sn rcvrd and in tch: hdwy into midfield 1/2-way: effrt and rn green bnd 2f out: chsd ldng pair ent fnl f: styd on strly to ld towards fin* **20/1**

0442 **2** *½* **Demons And Wizards (IRE)**[9] 9231 2-9-2 74............... MartinDwyer 2 73
(Sylvester Kirk) *t.k.h: pressed ldr tl pushed into ld 2f out: drvn and forged ahd ins fnl f: hdd and one pce towards fin* **8/13**[1]

34 **3** *1 ¾* **Winged Spur (IRE)**[7] 9263 2-8-11 0................................ FrannyNorton 6 64
(Mark Johnston) *led: rdn and hdd 2f out: no ex u.p jst ins fnl f: wknd towards fin* **11/4**[2]

50 **4** *2 ½* **Ainne**[75] 7875 2-8-11 0..................................................... LukeMorris 3 58
(Sylvester Kirk) *hld up in tch in last pair: rdn and outpcd over 2f out: rallied 1f out: kpt on ins fnl f to go 4th towards fin: no threat to ldrs* **20/1**

0 **5** *½* **Now Say Yes (IRE)**[17] 9099 2-8-11 0.......................... StevieDonohoe 5 57
(David Lanigan) *hld up in tch in rr: swtchd rt and hdwy 6f out: chsd ldrs 5f out: pushed along to chal over 2f out: unable qck u.p and lost pl over 1f out: wknd ins fnl f* **7/1**[3]

0 **6** *1 ½* **Lenin (IRE)**[9] 9231 2-9-2 0................................................ LiamKeniry 1 58
(J S Moore) *dwlt: sn rcvrd to chse ldrs: unable qck u.p over 1f out: wknd ins fnl f* **20/1**

**7** *nse* **Maytheorsebewithu (IRE)** 2-8-8 0......................... CharlieBennett(3) 4 53
(Pat Phelan) *in tch in midfield: rdn and outpcd over 2f out: wl hld and kpt on same pce fr over 1f out* **33/1**

00 **8** *¾* **Ragstone Sand (IRE)**[75] 7897 2-9-2 0............................ ShaneKelly 9 56
(Gary Moore) *in tch towards rr: pushed along over 2f out: wd bnd and lost pl 2f out: no threat to ldrs but kpt on ins fnl f* **25/1**

0 **9** *6* **Cornish Point (IRE)**[28] 8943 2-9-2 0.............................. TomMarquand 8 42
(J S Moore) *in tch: rdn and dropped to rr over 4f out: bhd over 1f out* **66/1**

1m 41.13s (2.93) **Going Correction** +0.175s/f (Slow) **9** Ran SP% **123.7**
Speed ratings (Par 96): **92,91,89,87,86 85,85,84,78**
CSF £33.76 TOTE £17.70: £5.90, £1.10, £1.10; EX 59.40 Trifecta £250.10.
**Owner** Canisbay Bloodstock **Bred** Jacqueline Doyle **Trained** Epsom, Surrey

**FOCUS**
An ordinary maiden, but a nice debut from the winner, who is very much a work in progress.

## 9386 32RED.COM / EBF STALLIONS BREEDING WINNERS FILLIES' CONDITIONS STKS — 1m 1y(P)
**12:35** (12:35) (Class 3) 3-Y-O+ **£9,766** (£2,923; £1,461; £731) **Stalls** High

Form RPR

5432 **1** **Zest (IRE)**[51] 8546 4-9-0 93.......................................... DanielMuscutt 3 89
(James Fanshawe) *trckd ldr: rdn and ev ch wl over 1f out: sustained chal u.p to ld wl ins fnl f: hld on wl towards fin* **4/7**[1]

1320 **2** *nk* **Singyoursong (IRE)**[140] 5658 4-9-0 97..........................(h) LukeMorris 1 89
(David Simcock) *s.i.s: hld up wl in tch in rr: effrt to press ldng pair over 2f out: sltly outpcd over 1f out: rallied to chal wl ins fnl f: kpt on u.p: hld towards fin* **11/4**[2]

4334 **3** *nk* **Summer Icon**[17] 9089 4-9-0 84....................................... ShaneKelly 2 88
(Mick Channon) *t.k.h: trckd ldr: dropped to last and over 2f out: rallied and swtchd rt jst ins fnl f: kpt on wl fnl 100yds* **7/1**[3]

1014 **4** *¾* **Bumptious**[28] 8944 4-9-7 86.......................................(p) StevieDonohoe 4 93
(Ismail Mohammed) *led: rdn and qcknd wl over 1f out: hdd wl ins fnl f: no ex and lost 2 pls towards fin* **16/1**

1m 39.49s (1.29) **Going Correction** +0.175s/f (Slow) **4** Ran SP% **108.7**
Speed ratings (Par 104): **100,99,99,98**
CSF £2.42 TOTE £1.50; EX 2.60 Trifecta £3.70.
**Owner** Elite Racing Club **Bred** Elite Racing Club **Trained** Newmarket, Suffolk

**FOCUS**
A tactical affair. The early gallop wasn't strong and it turned into a bit of a dash, with little separating the four fillies at the line.

## 9387 32RED CASINO (S) STKS — 5f 6y(P)
**1:10** (1:10) (Class 6) 2-Y-O **£2,264** (£673; £336; £168) **Stalls** Low

Form RPR

0056 **1** **Crystal Deauville (FR)**[7] 9266 2-9-0 62............................(t[1]) MartinDwyer 5 61
(Gay Kelleway) *sn led and mde rest: rdn over 2f out: asserted u.p ins fnl f: in command wl ins fnl f: eased towards fin* **3/1**[3]

0006 **2** *1 ¾* **Red Snapper**[37] 8795 2-8-9 48.........................................(p) HollieDoyle 3 50
(William Stone) *broke in front but wnt rt and sn hdd: sn dropped to rr and outpcd in last: pushed along and clsd 2f out: swtchd rt jst ins fnl f: styd on u.p to go 2nd last strides: no threat to wnr* **10/1**

5650 **3** *nk* **Tonkolili (IRE)**[30] 8902 2-8-9 60..................................(b[1]) FrannyNorton 4 49
(William Muir) *taken down early: squeezed for room leaving stalls: sn rcvrd to chse ldrs: effrt to chal over 2f out: edgd lft u.p 1f out: no ex and outpcd fnl 100yds: lost 2nd last strides* **5/2**[2]

3000 **4** *1 ¼* **Yogi's Girl (IRE)**[14] 9156 2-9-3 82.................................... FranBerry 2 52
(David Evans) *nt that wl away: sn rcvrd to chse ldr tl 2f out: cl 3rd whn squeezed for room and swtchd lft over 1f out: unable qck u.p and wknd wl ins fnl f* **5/4**[1]

0000 **5** *5* **Butterfly Spirit**[119] 6417 2-8-9 48.................................... LukeMorris 1 26
(Michael Attwater) *awkward leaving stalls: in tch in last pair: rdn 2f out: unable qck and wknd ins fnl f* **25/1**

59.54s (0.74) **Going Correction** +0.175s/f (Slow) **5** Ran SP% **111.0**
Speed ratings (Par 94): **101,98,97,95,87**
CSF £28.54 TOTE £3.80: £1.70, £5.00; EX 28.50 Trifecta £72.40.Tonkolili was bought by Mr Matt Watkinson for £7,500.
**Owner** Iboxit Ltd & Partner 2 **Bred** Lotfi Kohli **Trained** Exning, Suffolk



The Form Book Flat, Raceform Ltd, Newbury, RG14 5SJ

**FOCUS**
With the favourite underperforming, this took little winning.

## 9388 BETWAY QUEBEC STKS (LISTED RACE) 1m 2f (P)
**1:45** (1:45) (Class 1) 3-Y-0+
**£20,982** (£7,955; £3,981; £1,983; £995; £499) **Stalls** Low

Form RPR
1642 **1** **Petite Jack**[17] 9091 4-9-3 102....(b) LukeMorris 2 105
(Archie Watson) *trckd ldrs: nt clr run ent fnl 2f: rdn and wnt between horses to chal ent fnl f: led ins fnl f: r.o wl* **7/2**[2]
3043 **2** *nk* **Mia Tesoro (IRE)**[35] 8844 4-8-12 92....(h) StevieDonohoe 4 99
(Charlie Fellowes) *broke wl to ld: sn restrained and t.k.h in midfield: nt clr run ent fnl 2f: hdwy 1f out: chal wl ins fnl f: r.o* **16/1**
-340 **3** *hd* **Utmost (USA)**[24] 9003 3-9-1 100.... RobertHavlin 6 104
(John Gosden) *sn trcking ldr: led 2f out: sn rdn: hdd ins fnl f: kpt on u.p* **4/1**[3]
-203 **4** *½* **Intern (IRE)**[17] 9091 3-9-1 102.... FranBerry 9 103
(David Simcock) *t.k.h: hld up in tch in last pair: effrt and clsd on outer over 2f out: kpt on u.p ins fnl f* **8/1**
5061 **5** *½* **Dolphin Vista (IRE)**[84] 7619 4-9-3 102.... GeorgeWood 1 102
(Martyn Meade) *hld up in tch in midfield: effrt jst over 2f out: kpt on ins fnl f* **8/1**
3606 **6** *½* **Battalion (IRE)**[35] 8844 7-9-3 105.... DougieCostello 8 101
(Jamie Osborne) *s.i.s: hld up in tch in rr: stuck bhd a wall of horses over 1f out: swtchd lft and shkn up 1f out: pushed along and kpt on ins fnl f: nvr trbld ldrs* **16/1**
6012 **7** *¾* **Master The World (IRE)**[24] 8992 6-9-6 107....(p) JosephineGordon 7 103
(David Elsworth) *trckd ldrs on outer: effrt to press ldrs ent fnl 2f: unable qck u.p and outpcd 1f out: wknd wl ins fnl f* **9/4**[1]
-015 **8** *¾* **Not So Sleepy**[24] 8992 5-9-3 100....(t) AdamKirby 5 98
(Hughie Morrison) *sn led: hdd and rdn 2f out: no ex u.p and wknd ins fnl f* **9/1**

2m 5.39s (-1.21) **Going Correction** +0.175s/f (Slow)
**WFA** 3 from 4yo+ 2lb **8** Ran SP% **117.0**
Speed ratings (Par 111): **111,110,110,110,109 109,108,108**
CSF £57.42 TOTE £4.60: £1.60, £4.50, £1.90; EX 59.70 Trifecta £404.60.
**Owner** W Burn **Bred** Mrs Liz Nelson Mbe **Trained** Upper Lambourn, W Berks
**FOCUS**
A competitive Listed contest.

## 9389 BETWAY DASH H'CAP 5f 6y(P)
**2:20** (2:23) (Class 5) (0-70,70) 3-Y-0+ **£2,911** (£866; £432; £216) **Stalls** Low

Form RPR
4502 **1** **Roundabout Magic (IRE)**[11] 9189 3-8-12 61.... NickyMackay 7 69
(Simon Dow) *stdd after s and t.k.h: hld up in tch tch towards rr: nt clr run and swtchd rt 2f out: rdn and hdwy ent fnl f: chsd ldr jst ins fnl f: str run to ld fnl 50yds* **5/1**[3]
5503 **2** *¾* **Shackled N Drawn (USA)**[11] 9189 5-8-12 61....(bt) CharlesBishop 8 66
(Peter Hedger) *taken down early: raced freely: led after 1f: rdn over 1f out: kpt on wl u.p under tl hdd and no ex fnl 50yds* **10/1**
0001 **3** *½* **Temple Road (IRE)**[11] 9189 9-9-3 66....(bt) TomMarquand 2 70
(Milton Bradley) *hld up in tch towards rr: nt clr run 2f out: swtchd rt ent fnl f: r.o strly fnl 100yds: nvr quite getting to ldrs* **9/2**[2]
1140 **4** *hd* **Awesome Allan (IRE)**[14] 9152 3-9-3 66.... FranBerry 3 69
(David Evans) *hld up in tch towards rr: effrt on inner ent fnl f: r.o wl fnl 100yds: nvr quite getting to ldrs* **5/1**[3]
0000 **5** *hd* **Mossgo (IRE)**[11] 9189 7-8-13 62....(t) LukeMorris 4 64
(John Best) *led for 1f: chsd ldng pair after: edgd lft over 2f out: rdn over 1f out: kpt on same pce ins fnl f* **25/1**
0114 **6** *½* **Entertaining Ben**[11] 9189 4-8-13 69....(p) NicolaCurrie(7) 10 69
(Amy Murphy) *bustled along leaving stalls: chsd ldr after 1f tl jst ins fnl f: kpt on same pce after* **14/1**
1001 **7** *½* **Ask The Guru**[66] 8146 7-8-7 56....(b) KierenFox 9 54
(Michael Attwater) *chsd ldrs on outer: unable qck u.p over 1f out: kpt on same pce ins fnl f* **25/1**
0662 **8** *1* **Mr Pocket (IRE)**[9] 9234 3-9-7 70....(b) RaulDaSilva 6 65
(Paul Cole) *s.i.s: hld up in tch in rr: effrt over 1f out: swtchd rt jst ins fnl f: styd on fnl 100yds: nvr trbld ldrs* **3/1**[1]
05 **9** *¾* **Sandfrankskipsgo**[11] 9189 8-9-2 65.... ShaneKelly 1 57
(Peter Crate) *t.k.h: hld up in tch in midfield: short of room and hmpd over 2f out: swtchd rt and effrt over 1f out: wknd ins fnl f* **13/2**
5000 **10** *1 ¼* **Culloden**[45] 8681 5-8-10 62.... CharlieBennett(3) 5 50
(Shaun Harris) *wl in tch in midfield: rdn and losing pl whn squeezed for room ent fnl f: wknd* **33/1**

58.77s (-0.03) **Going Correction** +0.175s/f (Slow) **10** Ran SP% **116.2**
Speed ratings (Par 103): **107,105,105,104,104 103,102,101,99,97**
CSF £52.39 CT £247.69 TOTE £5.90: £1.90, £3.30, £1.50; EX 56.80 Trifecta £270.80.
**Owner** Six Mile Hill Racing **Bred** T F Lacy **Trained** Ashtead, Surrey
**FOCUS**
A modest sprint. The first three finished 2-3-1 in a similar race here 11 days earlier.

## 9390 BETWAY H'CAP 1m 4f (P)
**2:55** (2:55) (Class 2) (0-105,101) 3-Y-£01,971 (£3,583; £1,791; £896; £446) **Stalls** Low

Form RPR
1115 **1** **Hajaam (IRE)**[52] 8506 3-8-9 88....(t[1]) StevieDonohoe 1 96
(Charlie Fellowes) *hld for 2f: chsd ldr tl over 7f out: styd trcking ldrs: effrt and swtchd rt over 1f out: styd on u.p to ld 100yds out: kpt on* **13/2**[3]
025 **2** *¾* **Primero (FR)**[24] 8999 4-9-9 98.... AdamKirby 6 105
(David O'Meara) *hld up in last pair: nt clr run over 2f out: swtchd rt and effrt wl over 1f out hdwy u.p 1f out: chsd wnr wl ins fnl f: kpt on* **6/4**[1]
4000 **3** *1* **Abareeq**[24] 9003 4-9-8 97.... FrannyNorton 8 102
(Mark Johnston) *hld up in tch in midfield: effrt over 2f out: swtchd rt and hdwy to chse ldrs wl ins fnl f: kpt on* **5/1**[2]
4000 **4** *2 ¾* **Elysian Fields (GR)**[45] 8672 6-8-12 87....(p[1]) JackMitchell 4 88
(Amanda Perrett) *hld up in tch in midfield: effrt towards inner over 1f out: swtchd rt 1f out: no imp ins fnl f* **14/1**
00-5 **5** *½* **Ming Dynasty (FR)**[104] 6984 5-9-8 97.... JosephineGordon 5 97
(Marco Botti) *t.k.h: hld up in midfield: swtchd rt and hdwy over 7f out: led over 6f out: rdn over 1f out: hdd 100yds out: sn btn and wknd* **5/1**[2]
1104 **6** *hd* **Brandon Castle**[14] 9157 5-9-8 97....(t) EdwardGreatrex 7 97
(Archie Watson) *taken down early: chsd ldrs: hdwy to ld 10f out tl over 6f out: chsd ldr after: rdn and ev ch 2f out tl no ex ent fnl f: wknd ins fnl f* **14/1**
0206 **7** *3 ¼* **Majeed**[141] 5592 7-9-5 101.... GeorgeBass(7) 3 96
(David Simcock) *s.i.s: hld up in rr: effrt wd and bmpd wl over 1f out: nvr trbld ldrs* **12/1**
1040 **8** *5* **Storm King**[11] 9186 8-9-3 92.... TomMarquand 2 79
(David C Griffiths) *chsd ldr for over 1f: styd chsng ldrs tl rdn and lost pl over 2f out: towards rr whn hung rt and bmpd wl over 1f out: sn wknd* **20/1**

2m 32.64s (-0.36) **Going Correction** +0.175s/f (Slow)
**WFA** 3 from 4yo+ 4lb **8** Ran SP% **112.5**
Speed ratings (Par 109): **108,107,106,105,104 104,102,99**
CSF £16.11 CT £52.13 TOTE £5.90: £2.20, £1.10, £1.50; EX 18.80 Trifecta £77.40.
**Owner** Khalifa Bin Hamad Al Attiyah **Bred** Marston Stud **Trained** Newmarket, Suffolk
**FOCUS**
The front two got racing a fair way out and had a gap on the rest turning in, but they didn't last home.

## 9391 BETWAY CASINO H'CAP 1m 4f (P)
**3:30** (3:30) (Class 6) (0-65,67) 3-Y-0 **£2,264** (£673; £336; £168) **Stalls** Low

Form RPR
006 **1** **Sanches**[18] 9085 3-8-7 50.... HollieDoyle 1 58+
(Dr Jeremy Naylor) *hld up in tch in midfield: clsd to chse ldrs over 2f out: effrt over 1f out: hdwy to ld 75yds out: r.o wl* **66/1**
0456 **2** *½* **Widnes**[17] 9092 3-9-3 60....(vt) JosephineGordon 3 66
(Alan Bailey) *led tl over 8f out: chsd ldr tl over 3f out: styd prom: swtchd rt and hdwy u.p to chse wnr wl ins fnl f: kpt on but nvr getting to wnr* **3/1**[1]
4605 **3** *1* **Hi There Silver (IRE)**[45] 8673 3-7-9 45....(v) NicolaCurrie(7) 9 48
(Michael Madgwick) *chsd ldrs tl wnt 2nd over 3f out: rdn to ld 2f out: drvn over 1f out: hdd 75yds out: no ex* **25/1**
6202 **4** *shd* **Malt Teaser (FR)**[24] 8993 3-9-6 63.... SteveDrowne 6 66
(John Best) *hld up in tch towards rr: effrt u.p over 1f out: kpt on ins fnl f: nvr quite getting on terms w ldrs* **5/1**[3]
2600 **5** *¾* **Bartholomew J (IRE)**[36] 8814 3-9-7 64.... SimonPearce 11 66
(Lydia Pearce) *hld up in tch in midfield: hdwy to chse ldrs 4f out: rdn and ev ch 2f out tl no ex ins fnl f: wknd wl ins fnl f* **14/1**
0261 **6** *¾* **Iley Boy**[10] 9221 3-8-6 49....(p) JoeyHaynes 4 50
(John Gallagher) *hld up in tch: nt clrest of runs over 2f out: pushed along and hdwy 1f out: nt clr run and swtchd lft ins fnl f: kpt on: nvr trbld ldrs* **4/1**[2]
4153 **7** *2 ½* **Katabatika**[24] 8993 3-9-4 61.... AdamKirby 10 58
(Hughie Morrison) *hld up in tch in midfield on outer: rdn over 2f out: unable qck over 1f out: kpt on same pce fnl f* **4/1**[2]
4066 **8** *nk* **Presence Process**[131] 6006 3-8-13 56.... ShaneKelly 8 52
(Pat Phelan) *hld up in tch in rr of main gp: effrt over 1f out: nvr trbld ldrs* **16/1**
0000 **9** *1 ¼* **Nicky Baby (IRE)**[16] 9128 3-7-12 48....(p) JackOsborn(7) 7 42
(Dean Ivory) *t.k.h: chsd ldr tl led over 8f out: hdd 2f out: wknd ins fnl f* **33/1**
0205 **10** *hd* **Wootyhoot (FR)**[16] 9128 3-9-0 57.... DanielMuscutt 5 51
(James Fanshawe) *dwlt: sn rcvrd to chse ldrs: shuffled bk and nt clr run over 2f out: wknd fnl f* **13/2**
0000 **11** *32* **Investigation**[80] 7744 3-9-7 67....(h) CharlieBennett(3) 2 10
(Shaun Harris) *v.s.a and lost over 100yds: clsd onto bk of field and t.k.h 8f out: rdn over 3f out: lost tch 2f out: t.o* **66/1**

2m 34.68s (1.68) **Going Correction** +0.175s/f (Slow) **11** Ran SP% **117.3**
Speed ratings (Par 98): **101,100,100,99,99 98,97,97,96,96 74**
CSF £254.45 CT £5187.39 TOTE £24.00: £10.70, £1.50, £5.70; EX 110.80 Trifecta £2276.80.
**Owner** Mrs Rebekah Swift **Bred** Mrs P Good **Trained** Shrewton, Wilts
**FOCUS**
An ordinary handicap which went to the least exposed runner in the line-up.
T/Plt: £100.90 to a £1 stake. Pool: £61,067.91 - 441.72 winning units T/Qpdt: £39.30 to a £1 stake. Pool: £3,833.68 - 72.16 winning units **Steve Payne**

9392 - 9403a (Foreign Racing) - See Raceform Interactive

# 9370 WOLVERHAMPTON (A.W) (L-H)
Tuesday, December 26

**OFFICIAL GOING: Tapeta: standard**
Wind: Light behind Weather: Fine

## 9404 32RED CASINO EBF NOVICE STKS 5f 21y (Tp)
**12:05** (12:05) (Class 5) 2-Y-0 **£4,204** (£1,251; £625; £312) **Stalls** Low

Form RPR
**1** **Reiffa (IRE)** 2-8-8 0.... GeorgiaCox(3) 7 73+
(William Haggas) *s.i.s: pushed along towards rr and edgd lft over 3f out: hdwy over 1f out: shkn up and r.o to ld wl ins fnl f* **15/2**
2222 **2** *1* **Midsummer Knight**[24] 9049 2-8-13 77....(t[1]) CliffordLee(3) 8 74
(K R Burke) *led: pushed clr over 1f out: rdn and hdd wl ins fnl f* **15/8**[1]
221 **3** *nse* **Little Boy Blue**[14] 9188 2-9-9 80.... LukeMorris 6 81
(Bill Turner) *chsd ldr: rdn over 1f out: ev ch wl ins fnl f: styd on* **11/2**[2]
0 **4** *2 ¾* **Cloud Eight (IRE)**[27] 8988 2-9-2 0....(t) DanielMuscutt 3 64
(Marco Botti) *hld up: hdwy 2f out: shkn up over 1f out: styd on* **10/1**
4263 **5** *4 ½* **Avon Green**[14] 9188 2-8-11 67.... JosephineGordon 2 43
(Joseph Tuite) *prom: rdn over 1f out: wknd ins fnl f* **16/1**
2 **6** *1* **Los Camachos (IRE)**[10] 9266 2-9-2 0.... FranBerry 4 44
(David Evans) *hmpd s: prom: rdn 1/2-way: wknd over 1f out* **7/1**
5 **7** *2 ¾* **Royal Pursuit (USA)**[109] 6897 2-9-2 0.... TomEaves 9 34
(Kevin Ryan) *hld up in tch: rdn and wknd 1/2-way* **6/1**[3]
06 **8** *4 ½* **Gunnar Julius (USA)**[31] 8945 2-9-2 0.... KieranShoemark 10 18
(Ed Walker) *s.i.s: outpcd* **33/1**
06 **9** *nk* **Rusty Blade (IRE)**[207] 3277 2-8-10 0 ow1.... TobyEley(7) 5 18
(Daniel Mark Loughnane) *edgd lft s: prom: racd keenly: rdn and wknd over 1f out* **66/1**
00 **10** *¾* **Tommy Boy**[88] 7580 2-9-2 0.... StevieDonohoe 1 14
(Ian Williams) *sn pushed along in rr: hmpd over 3f out: wknd 1/2-way* **11/1**

1m 1.09s (-0.81) **Going Correction** -0.025s/f (Stan) **10** Ran SP% **116.5**
Speed ratings (Par 96): **105,103,103,98,91 90,85,78,78,76**
CSF £21.86 TOTE £9.80: £3.30, £1.20, £1.60; EX 25.40 Trifecta £100.30.
**Owner** Abdulla Al Khalifa **Bred** Wardstown Stud Ltd **Trained** Newmarket, Suffolk
■ Stewards' Enquiry : Toby Eley three-day ban: careless riding (Jan 9-11)
Georgia Cox four-day ban: careless riding (Jan 9-12)
**FOCUS**
A well-run novice with the placed horses setting the level.

## 9405 32RED.COM NURSERY H'CAP 1m 142y (Tp)
**12:40** (12:40) (Class 3) (0-95,90) 2-Y-£8,821 (£2,640; £1,320; £660; £329) **Stalls** Low

Form RPR
4216 **1** **Guvenor's Choice (IRE)**[31] 8951 2-8-12 81....(t) LukeMorris 5 84
(K R Burke) *trckd ldrs: shkn up to ld and edgd lft 1f out: drvn out* **5/2**[2]

2201 **2** *nk* **Jellmood**[24] 9051 2-9-4 **90**........................(h) MarcMonaghan(3) 6 92
(Marco Botti) *hld up: hdwy: nt clr run and swtchd lft over 1f out: sn rdn: r.o* **9/4**[1]

6163 **3** *shd* **Blue Harmony**[8] 9300 2-8-0 **69**........................(v[1]) HollieDoyle 4 71
(K R Burke) *edgd lft sn after s: chsd ldr: shkn up and ev ch fr over 1f out: sn edgd rt: r.o* **9/1**

4513 **4** *3* **Windsor Cross (IRE)**[10] 9263 2-8-12 **81**........................(b) TomEaves 2 77
(Richard Fahey) *trckd ldrs: rdn over 1f out: styd on same pce ins fnl f* **4/1**[3]

610 **5** *¾* **Pastamakesufaster**[68] 8196 2-8-7 **79**........................ MattCosham(3) 1 73
(David Evans) *free to post: led at stdy pce: rdn 2f out: hdd 1f out: no ex* **14/1**

6035 **6** *2¾* **Island Court (IRE)**[5] 9336 2-8-6 **75**........................ JosephineGordon 3 63
(J S Moore) *hmpd sn after s: hld up: rdn over 2f out: outpcd fr over 1f out* **11/2**

1m 51.66s (1.56) **Going Correction** -0.025s/f (Stan) **6** Ran SP% **111.4**
Speed ratings (Par 100): **92,91,91,88,88 85**
CSF £8.41 TOTE £2.80: £1.80, £1.70; EX 8.70 Trifecta £41.60.
**Owner** I McInnes, Dr M Glaze & E Burke **Bred** Noel Finegan **Trained** Middleham Moor, N Yorks

**FOCUS**
A steadily run nursery, with the winner looking the type to rate higher when winning here last time

## 9406 BETWAY LIVE CASINO H'CAP — 1m 1f 104y (Tp)

**1:10** (1:10) (Class 6) (0-60,60) 3-Y-0+ **£2,911** (£866; £432; £216) **Stalls** Low

Form RPR

3112 **1** **King Kevin**[10] 9262 3-9-5 **60**........................(b) RobertHavlin 4 68+
(Ed Dunlop) *hld up: hdwy over 1f out: led and hung lft ins fnl f: rdn out* **5/2**[1]

1-10 **2** *2½* **Victoriously**[19] 9128 5-9-7 **60**........................(p) LukeMorris 9 63
(Andi Brown) *hld up: rdn over 2f out: hdwy u.p over 1f out: r.o to go 2nd nr fin* **6/1**[3]

5662 **3** *nk* **Windsorlot (IRE)**[24] 9056 4-9-4 **57**........................ GeorgeDowning 7 60
(Tony Carroll) *chsd ldrs: rdn over 2f out: styd on* **12/1**

1462 **4** *hd* **Topmeup**[13] 9213 3-9-4 **59**........................(v) JosephineGordon 13 61
(Gay Kelleway) *hld up: rdn over 1f out: hung lft and r.o ins fnl f: nt rch ldrs* **25/1**

3253 **5** *nk* **Ingleby Angel (IRE)**[26] 9017 8-9-5 **58**........................ FranBerry 2 60
(David O'Meara) *s.i.s: hld up: hdwy over 1f out: sn rdn: styd on* **5/1**[2]

0632 **6** *¾* **Joys Delight**[21] 9085 3-8-10 **58**........................ TobyEley(7) 10 58
(Daniel Mark Loughnane) *chsd ldr: rdn to ld over 1f out: hdd and no ex ins fnl f* **20/1**

0205 **7** *nk* **Mr Frankie**[4] 9375 6-9-1 **59**........................ WilliamCox(5) 1 60
(Adrian Wintle) *chsd ldrs: rdn whn hmpd over 1f out: no ex ins fnl f* **12/1**

0410 **8** *1* **Top Offer**[38] 8854 8-9-6 **59**........................(b) KieranShoemark 11 57
(Patrick Morris) *hld up in tch: rdn over 1f out: no ex fnl f* **25/1**

533- **9** *3¼* **Hold Hands**[391] 8155 6-8-11 **55**........................(t[1]) JennyPowell(5) 5 47
(Brendan Powell) *a in rr* **33/1**

060 **10** *hd* **The Gay Cavalier**[13] 9211 6-9-6 **59**........................(t) JackMitchell 8 50
(John Ryan) *sn pushed along and a in rr* **14/1**

4030 **11** *2* **Lord Murphy (IRE)**[31] 8957 4-9-3 **56**........................ TomEaves 3 43
(Daniel Mark Loughnane) *plld hrd and prom: rdn over 2f out: wknd fnl f* **11/1**

1106 **12** *¾* **Born To Reason (IRE)**[46] 8720 3-9-2 **57**........................(b) DougieCostello 12 43
(Kevin Frost) *stdd s: hld up: rdn over 1f out: n.d* **12/1**

4030 **13** *shd* **Mio Ragazzo**[17] 9153 3-9-2 **60**........................(h[1]) MarcMonaghan(3) 6 46
(Marco Botti) *led: rdn: edgd rt and hdd over 1f out: wknd ins fnl f* **8/1**

1m 59.55s (-1.25) **Going Correction** -0.025s/f (Stan)
**WFA** 3 from 4yo+ 2lb **13** Ran SP% **124.1**
Speed ratings (Par 101): **104,101,101,101,101 100,100,99,96,96 94,93,93**
CSF £16.67 CT £160.42 TOTE £2.80: £1.30, £2.70, £5.00; EX 18.50 Trifecta £105.80.
**Owner** E A L Dunlop **Bred** Denford Stud Ltd **Trained** Newmarket, Suffolk
■ Stewards' Enquiry : George Downing four-day ban: used whip above permitted level (Jan 9-12)

**FOCUS**
This was run at a good gallop with the winner continuing his upturn in form.

## 9407 BETWAY H'CAP — 1m 1f 104y (Tp)

**1:45** (1:45) (Class 2) (0-105,104) 3-Y-0+
**£12,450** (£3,728; £1,864; £932; £466; £234) **Stalls** Low

Form RPR

4P02 **1** **Mount Tahan (IRE)**[27] 8999 5-8-13 **93**........................ ShaneGray 7 100
(Kevin Ryan) *hld up: hdwy over 1f out: rdn and r.o to ld wl ins fnl f* **11/2**

1223 **2** *½* **Born To Be Alive (IRE)**[90] 7506 3-9-5 **104**........................ CliffordLee(3) 2 110
(K R Burke) *pushed along leaving stalls: hld up: hdwy over 1f out: rdn to chse ldr fnl f: r.o* **6/1**

6042 **3** *½* **Kyllachy Gala**[14] 9186 4-9-4 **98**........................ KieranShoemark 5 103
(Marco Botti) *led at stdy pce: qcknd 3f out: rdn over 1f out: hdd wl ins fnl f* **5/1**[3]

3321 **4** *1* **Emenem**[14] 9186 3-8-11 **93**........................ LukeMorris 4 96
(Simon Dow) *chsd ldr tl rdn over 1f out: styd on* **7/2**[2]

0065 **5** *1¼* **Mythical Madness**[12] 9233 6-9-2 **96**........................(v) FranBerry 8 96
(David O'Meara) *chsd ldrs: rdn over 2f out: styd on same pce fnl f* **8/1**

5031 **6** *¾* **Battle Of Marathon (USA)**[24] 9053 5-8-8 **95**........................ JackOsborn(7) 3 94
(John Ryan) *hld up: pushed along on outer over 2f out: no imp fnl f* **3/1**[1]

0303 **7** *1¼* **Bronze Angel (IRE)**[14] 9186 8-8-12 **92**........................(b) MartinDwyer 1 88
(Marcus Tregoning) *prom: rdn over 2f out: no ex fnl f* **16/1**

3441 **8** *5* **Grand Inquisitor**[31] 8048 5-8-12 **92**........................(p) JosephineGordon 6 77
(Ian Williams) *s.i.s: hld up: rdn and wknd over 1f out* **12/1**

2m 1.24s (0.44) **Going Correction** -0.025s/f (Stan)
**WFA** 3 from 4yo+ 2lb **8** Ran SP% **118.2**
Speed ratings (Par 109): **97,96,96,95,94 93,92,87**
CSF £39.60 CT £177.78 TOTE £6.10: £2.10, £1.80, £2.20; EX 41.60 Trifecta £222.20.
**Owner** T A Rahman **Bred** S F Bloodstock **Trained** Hambleton, N Yorks

**FOCUS**
A good handicap. The early gallop was modest, but it picked up leaving the back straight. The third and fourth set the standard.

## 9408 BETWAY CASINO H'CAP — 1m 4f 51y (Tp)

**2:15** (2:15) (Class 5) (0-75,73) 3-Y-0+ **£4,204** (£1,251; £625; £312) **Stalls** Low

Form RPR

-322 **1** **Ocean Of Love**[17] 9159 3-9-0 **73**........................(h[1]) HectorCrouch(3) 4 89
(Saeed bin Suroor) *trckd ldrs: pushed along on outer to ld over 2f out: rdn clr fr over 1f out* **11/4**[2]

5501 **2** *8* **Tan Arabiq**[24] 9054 4-9-3 **69**........................ TomMarquand 7 71
(Michael Appleby) *hld up: plld hrd: hdwy over 2f out: rdn to chse wnr over 1f out: styd on same pce fnl f* **5/1**[3]

5324 **3** *1½* **Excellent Puck (IRE)**[10] 9270 7-8-13 **65**........................ JosephineGordon 5 65
(Shaun Lycett) *led: hdd over 10f out: chsd ldr tl over 3f out: nt clr run and lost pl over 2f out: styng on same pce whn rdn and hung lft over 1f out* **9/1**

3313 **4** *shd* **Beatisa**[25] 9026 3-8-6 **69**........................ JacobMitchell(7) 8 69
(Christine Dunnett) *s.i.s: hdwy to ld 10f out: rdn and hdd over 2f out: wknd fnl f* **18/1**

0603 **5** *hd* **Dolphin Village (IRE)**[10] 9270 7-8-9 **64**........................(h) CharlieBennett(3) 2 63
(Shaun Harris) *hld up: rdn over 2f out: hdwy over 1f out: nt trble ldrs* **16/1**

0036 **6** *3½* **Rite To Reign**[28] 8978 6-9-4 **70**........................(v) GrahamLee 9 64
(Philip McBride) *s.i.s: hld up: pushed along on outer over 2f out: nvr on terms* **14/1**

302 **7** *nk* **Miss Liguria**[13] 9208 3-8-12 **68**........................ HollieDoyle 6 62
(Ed Walker) *chsd ldrs: rdn over 2f out: wknd over 1f out* **6/1**

062 **8** *6* **Belabour**[24] 9054 4-9-1 **67**........................ LukeMorris 3 50
(Mark Brisbourne) *chsd ldrs: pushed along over 3f out: hmpd over 2f out: wknd over 1f out* **9/4**[1]

-000 **9** *1¼* **Freud (FR)**[265] 1562 7-9-2 **68**........................(t) GeorgeDowning 1 49
(Ian Williams) *hld up: pushed along over 2f out: sn wknd* **50/1**

2m 39.03s (-1.77) **Going Correction** -0.025s/f (Stan)
**WFA** 3 from 4yo+ 4lb **9** Ran SP% **118.2**
Speed ratings (Par 103): **104,98,97,97,97 95,94,90,90**
CSF £17.53 CT £110.29 TOTE £3.60: £1.80, £1.30, £2.00; EX 22.30 Trifecta £132.10.
**Owner** Godolphin **Bred** Darley **Trained** Newmarket, Suffolk

**FOCUS**
This looked competitive beforehand, but the winner found a deal of improvement for the fitting of a first-time hood. The placed horses have been rated close to their recent C&D efforts.

## 9409 BETWAY CONDITIONS STKS — 6f 20y (Tp)

**2:50** (2:53) (Class 2) 3-Y-0+
**£12,450** (£3,728; £1,864; £932; £466; £234) **Stalls** Low

Form RPR

6442 **1** **Intisaab**[27] 8991 6-9-3 107........................(p) KieranShoemark 4 112
(David O'Meara) *hld up: plld hrd: hdwy over 1f out: rdn to ld wl ins fnl f: r.o: edgd lft towards fin* **7/2**[2]

1110 **2** *1* **Gulliver**[31] 8944 3-9-3 105........................(tp) JosephineGordon 3 109
(Hugo Palmer) *chsd ldrs: rdn to ld wl ins fnl f: sn hdd: styd on* **7/2**[2]

1202 **3** *hd* **Mythmaker**[38] 8845 5-9-3 105........................ GrahamLee 7 108
(Bryan Smart) *chsd ldr 5f out: rdn over 2f out: edgd rt ins fnl f: styd on* **14/1**

-521 **4** *nse* **Double Up**[27] 8991 6-9-3 105........................(t) JackMitchell 6 108+
(Roger Varian) *chsd ldr 1f: remained handy and racd keenly: rdn over 1f out: styd on* **10/3**[1]

3420 **5** *nse* **Polybius**[122] 6428 6-9-3 106........................ StevieDonohoe 1 108
(David Simcock) *hld up: hdwy over 1f out: r.o: nt mot much room towards fin* **9/1**

3522 **6** *½* **Salateen**[121] 6476 5-9-6 107........................ FranBerry 2 109
(David O'Meara) *led: rdn over 1f out: hdd and unable qck wl ins fnl f* **4/1**[3]

1040 **7** *¾* **Kimberella**[108] 6926 7-9-6 109........................ TomEaves 8 107
(Richard Fahey) *hld up: shkn up over 1f out: nt trble ldrs* **12/1**

0002 **8** *2½* **Line Of Reason (IRE)**[91] 7475 7-9-3 100........................ LukeMorris 5 96
(Paul Midgley) *hld up: rdn over 1f out: no ex fnl f* **25/1**

1m 12.84s (-1.66) **Going Correction** -0.025s/f (Stan) **8** Ran SP% **115.7**
Speed ratings (Par 109): **110,108,108,108,108 107,106,103**
CSF £16.44 TOTE £5.00: £1.40, £1.70, £3.30; EX 24.30 Trifecta £167.50.
**Owner** Stuart Graham **Bred** Shadwell Estate Company Limited **Trained** Upper Helmsley, N Yorks

**FOCUS**
All eight of the runners in this conditions race were rated in three figures, and there wasn't much to choose between several of them beforehand. The early pace wasn't strong and there was a bit of a bunched finish. The winner has been rated close to his best.

## 9410 SUNBETS.CO.UK H'CAP (DIV I) — 7f 36y (Tp)

**3:25** (3:27) (Class 5) (0-75,75) 3-Y-0+ **£4,204** (£1,251; £625; £312) **Stalls** High

Form RPR

1-00 **1** **King Of Nepal**[20] 9101 3-9-2 **70**........................ FranBerry 5 79
(Henry Candy) *hld up: racd keenly: shkn up and hdwy over 2f out: rdn: edgd lft and r.o to ld wl ins fnl f* **11/4**[1]

0116 **2** *1¼* **Fire Diamond**[19] 9126 4-9-0 **71**........................(p) PaddyPilley(3) 2 77
(Tom Dascombe) *hld up: hdwy over 1f out: rdn and swtchd rt ins fnl f: r.o to go 2nd nr fin: nt rch wnr* **13/2**[3]

0010 **3** *nk* **Ebbisham (IRE)**[33] 8907 4-9-2 **70**........................ TomMarquand 3 75
(John Mackie) *chsd ldrs: rdn over 2f out: styd on u.p* **7/1**

0020 **4** *2* **Baltic Prince (IRE)**[13] 9220 7-9-4 **72**........................ GeorgeDowning 4 71
(Tony Carroll) *led: rdn over 1f out: hdd wl ins fnl f: no ex towards fin* **25/1**

6000 **5** *½* **Dark Alliance (IRE)**[49] 8645 6-9-2 **70**........................ TomEaves 7 68
(Daniel Mark Loughnane) *hld up: hdwy over 1f out: r.o: nt rch ldrs* **10/1**

0020 **6** *hd* **Mr Christopher (IRE)**[13] 9220 5-9-7 **75**........................(p) AlistairRawlinson 6 73
(Tom Dascombe) *chsd ldr: rdn and edgd rt over 2f out: no ex wl ins fnl f* **11/1**

4003 **7** *½* **My Amigo**[20] 9101 4-9-0 **75**........................(p) PatrickO'Hanlon(7) 11 71
(K R Burke) *s.i.s: hdwy over 5f out: pushed along on outer over 2f out: sn outpcd: styd on towards fin* **17/2**

5311 **8** *1½* **Dutiful Son (IRE)**[13] 9207 7-9-6 **74**........................ LukeMorris 10 66
(Simon Dow) *hld up in tch: rdn over 2f out: no ex fnl f* **17/2**

4-40 **9** *1* **Clement (IRE)**[299] 984 7-9-1 **72**........................ GeorgiaCox(3) 1 61
(John O'Shea) *s.i.s: in rr: sme hdwy over 1f out: no ex ins fnl f* **50/1**

1011 **10** *2* **Rapid Ranger**[17] 9152 3-9-7 **75**........................(h) KieranShoemark 12 59
(David O'Meara) *s.i.s: in rr: rdn and hung lft over 2f out: n.d* **11/2**[2]

6000 **11** *4½* **Paddy A (IRE)**[48] 8682 3-8-12 **66**........................ StevieDonohoe 8 38
(Ian Williams) *sn pushed along and a in rr* **16/1**

5400 **12** *3* **Perfect Symphony (IRE)**[8] 9297 3-9-0 **68**........................(v[1]) DougieCostello 9 32
(Sophie Leech) *chsd ldrs: shkn up over 2f out: wknd over 1f out* **50/1**

1m 27.35s (-1.45) **Going Correction** -0.025s/f (Stan) **12** Ran SP% **120.0**
Speed ratings (Par 103): **107,105,105,102,102 102,101,99,98,96 91,87**
CSF £20.24 CT £115.11 TOTE £3.90: £1.60, £2.40, £3.10; EX 25.30 Trifecta £162.70.
**Owner** First Of Many **Bred** Sir Eric Parker **Trained** Kingston Warren, Oxon

**FOCUS**
A fair handicap, and the quicker of the two divisions. The third sets the standard.

## 9411 SUNBETS.CO.UK H'CAP (DIV II) — 7f 36y (Tp)

**4:00** (4:01) (Class 5) (0-75,75) 3-Y-0+ **£4,204** (£1,251; £625; £312) **Stalls** High

Form RPR

3020 **1** **Right Action**[52] 8600 3-9-0 **75**........................ SebastianWoods(7) 1 82
(Richard Fahey) *chsd ldrs: nt clr run over 1f out: rdn to ld 1f out: styd on* **9/2**[2]

0000 **2** *hd* **Steal The Scene (IRE)**[59] 8434 5-8-10 **67**..................(p[1]) CliffordLee(3) 8 73
(Kevin Frost) *s.i.s: hld up: rdn and r.o wl ins fnl f: nt quite get there* **10/1**

0556 **3** *¾* **Outer Space**[21] 9083 6-9-7 **75**.................................. DougieCostello 2 79
(Jamie Osborne) *hld up: hdwy over 1f out: sn rdn: styd on* **9/2[2]**

2145 **4** *¾* **Major Crispies**[17] 9152 6-8-11 **72**...................(b) PatrickVaughan(7) 11 74
(David O'Meara) *s.i.s: hld up: hdwy over 1f out: styd on* **18/1**

**5** *1* **Smugglers Creek (IRE)**[81] 7795 3-9-1 **69**.......................... LukeMorris 10 68
(Iain Jardine) *sn chsng ldr: hung rt 1/2-way: rdn and ev ch over 1f out: styd on same pce ins fnl f* **9/4[1]**

2000 **6** *1* **Chosen Character (IRE)**[45] 8749 9-8-11 **72**....(vt) ElishaWhittington(7) 3 69
(Tom Dascombe) *prom: shkn up over 2f out: edgd lft and styd on same pce fnl f* **33/1**

5-04 **7** *½* **Smokethatthunders (IRE)**[330] 478 7-9-3 **71**.......... GeorgeDowning 5 66
(James Unett) *hld up: rdn over 1f out: nt trble ldrs* **25/1**

6304 **8** *shd* **Rock Warbler (IRE)**[13] 9220 4-9-6 **74**..................................(t) TomEaves 7 69
(Oliver Greenall) *prom: rdn and ev ch over 1f out: no ex ins fnl f* **11/2[3]**

0000 **9** *hd* **Anonymous John (IRE)**[20] 9093 5-9-2 **70**.............. JosephineGordon 9 64
(Dominic Ffrench Davis) *hld up: rdn over 1f out: n.d* **16/1**

1 **10** *1½* **Our Oystercatcher**[78] 7907 3-8-13 **70**......................(h) HectorCrouch(3) 6 60
(Philip Hide) *led: rdn over 2f out: hdd 1f out: wknd wl ins fnl f* **8/1**

1m 28.33s (-0.47) **Going Correction** -0.025s/f (Stan) **10** Ran SP% **120.7**
Speed ratings (Par 103): **101,100,99,99,97 96,96,96,95,94**
CSF £50.83 CT £223.40 TOTE £5.50: £1.80, £3.00, £1.90; EX 64.10 Trifecta £287.60.
**Owner** Middleham Park Racing LVII & Partner **Bred** Aunty Ifl **Trained** Musley Bank, N Yorks

**FOCUS**
The slower of the two divisions by 0.98sec. The winner has been rated to his turf form.
T/Plt: £43.00 to a £1 stake. Pool: £55,338.51 - 938.39 winning units T/Qpdt: £20.10 to a £1 stake. Pool: £4,777.22 - 175.19 winning units **Colin Roberts**

9412 - 9413a (Foreign Racing) - See Raceform Interactive

## 9404 WOLVERHAMPTON (A.W) (L-H)
### Wednesday, December 27

**OFFICIAL GOING: Tapeta: standard**
Wind: Light across Weather: Cloudy

## 9414 BETWAY DASH H'CAP 5f 21y (Tp)
**1:45** (1:46) (Class 6) (0-65,65) 3-Y-O+ **£2,587** (£770; £384; £192) **Stalls** Low

Form RPR

112 **1** **Swendab (IRE)**[19] 9136 9-8-13 **64**...................................(b) RossaRyan(7) 9 71
(John O'Shea) *pushed along to chse ldr: rdn to ld over 1f out: hung lft ins fnl f: jst hld on* **9/2[2]**

010 **2** *nk* **Run With Pride (IRE)**[9] 9297 7-9-7 **65**.................. PatrickMathers 3 71
(Derek Shaw) *mid-div: sn pushed along: hdwy over 1f out: rdn to chse wnr wl ins fnl f: r.o: flashed tail nr fin* **7/2[1]**

1006 **3** *½* **Everkyllachy (IRE)**[15] 9183 3-9-6 **64**..............................(b) HollieDoyle 2 68
(J S Moore) *pushed along in rr: hdwy over 1f out: r.o: nt rch ldrs* **13/2[3]**

1500 **4** *1¼* **Point North (IRE)**[28] 9001 10-9-2 **60**.........................(b) RobertWinston 4 60
(John Balding) *hmpd s: hld up: hdwy over 1f out: r.o* **25/1**

032 **5** *hd* **Eternalist**[28] 9001 4-8-10 **61**........................................... SeanMooney(7) 7 60
(Jim Goldie) *sn prom: pushed along 1/2-way: rdn over 1f out: styd on* **7/2[1]**

3200 **6** *nk* **Jumping Around (IRE)**[70] 8158 3-9-2 **60**...............(p) StevieDonohoe 10 58
(Ian Williams) *hld up: rdn over 1f out: r.o ins fnl f: nt rch ldrs* **14/1**

6552 **7** *1¾* **Your Gifted (IRE)**[5] 9374 10-8-7 51 oh1...........................(v) RaulDaSilva 1 43
(Lisa Williamson) *chsd ldrs: rdn over 1f out: no ex wl ins fnl f* **14/1**

6110 **8** *1* **Dream Ally (IRE)**[180] 4310 7-9-3 **64**.................................. PhilDennis(3) 8 52
(John Weymes) *hld up: pushed along 1/2-way: nvr trbld ldrs* **14/1**

0320 **9** *shd* **Cruise Tothelimit (IRE)**[39] 8853 9-8-9 **60**.......(bt) SebastianWoods(7) 5 48
(Patrick Morris) *chsd ldrs: rdn 1/2-way: wknd fnl f* **14/1**

0646 **10** *1½* **Krystallite**[16] 9181 4-8-13 **57**......................................(p) JosephineGordon 6 39
(Scott Dixon) *led: rdn and hdd over 1f out: wknd ins fnl f* **8/1**

1m 1.71s (-0.19) **Going Correction** 0.0s/f (Stan) **10** Ran SP% **117.6**
Speed ratings (Par 101): **101,100,99,97,97 96,94,92,92,89**
CSF £20.84 CT £105.06 TOTE £5.60: £2.50, £1.30, £2.40; EX 23.60 Trifecta £198.70.
**Owner** E&G Racing: Swendab **Bred** P Brady **Trained** Elton, Gloucs

**FOCUS**
The track was cultivated to a depth of about four inches and then reinstated with a gallop master finish. Travel issues due to the bad weather resulted in several non-runners throughout the afternoon. A modest sprint handicap to start in which the early pace was always likely to be quick.

## 9415 32REDSPORT.COM FILLIES' NOVICE STKS (PLUS 10 RACE) (DIV I) 6f 20y (Tp)
**2:15** (2:16) (Class 5) 2-Y-O **£3,557** (£1,058; £529; £264) **Stalls** Low

Form RPR

**1** **Hello Brigette (IRE)**[49] 8683 2-9-0 0............................ DougieCostello 9 79
(M D O'Callaghan, Ire) *racd keenly: prom: led over 4f out: rdn clr and hung lft fr over 1f out: eased towards fin* **7/2[2]**

**2** *4* **Sugar Coating** 2-9-0 0.................................................. JackGarritty 6 67+
(Richard Fahey) *s.i.s: hld up: hdwy over 1f out: r.o to go 2nd wl ins fnl f: no ch w wnr* **13/8[1]**

2322 **3** *1¾* **Ghepardo**[15] 9188 2-9-4 76.................................. TomMarquand 4 66
(Richard Hannon) *trckd ldrs: shkn up over 2f out: rdn over 1f out: styd on same pce* **13/8[1]**

4 **4** *5* **Ingleby Molly (IRE)**[25] 9049 2-9-0 0.................. KieranShoemark 11 47
(David O'Meara) *hld up: hdwy over 4f out: chsd wnr over 3f out tl rdn over 1f out: wknd fnl f* **22/1[3]**

00 **5** *2¾* **Displaying Amber**[110] 6897 2-9-0 0............................... LukeMorris 5 39
(Ben Haslam) *sn led: hdd over 4f out: remained handy tl rdn and wknd over 1f out* **66/1**

**6** *1¾* **Miss Mollie** 2-9-0 0...................................................... TomEaves 2 33
(James Given) *s.i.s: sn pushed along in rr: wknd 2f out* **22/1[3]**

00 **7** *8* **Amazing Amaya**[84] 7731 2-9-0 0.............................. PatrickMathers 8 9
(Derek Shaw) *prom: lost pl 4f out: sn hung rt: wknd over 2f out* **100/1**

1m 15.14s (0.64) **Going Correction** 0.0s/f (Stan) **7** Ran SP% **109.6**
Speed ratings (Par 93): **95,89,87,80,77 74,64**
CSF £8.76 TOTE £3.60: £1.70, £1.50; EX 12.10 Trifecta £20.20.
**Owner** Anthony F O'Callaghan **Bred** Jack Lynch **Trained** The Curragh, Co. Kildare

**FOCUS**
This first division of the fillies' novice event was hit by non-runners. They finished well spread out and few got into it.

## 9416 32REDSPORT.COM FILLIES' NOVICE STKS (PLUS 10 RACE) (DIV II) 6f 20y (Tp)
**2:45** (2:52) (Class 5) 2-Y-O **£3,557** (£1,058; £529; £264) **Stalls** Low

Form RPR

0002 **1** **Angel Of The South (IRE)**[20] 9122 2-9-0 70.............. RobertWinston 2 75
(Dean Ivory) *mde all: shkn up over 1f out: rdn out: edgd lft towards fin* **9/2[2]**

4 **2** *2¾* **I Was Only Joking (IRE)**[67] 8235 2-9-0 0........................ JackGarritty 1 67
(Richard Fahey) *chsd ldrs: rdn to chse wnr over 1f out: styd on same pce ins fnl f* **6/1[3]**

230 **3** *8* **Vodka Pigeon**[160] 5056 2-8-11 71................................. AaronJones(3) 6 43
(Adam West) *prom: sn lost pl: pushed along 4f out: r.o to go 3rd nr fin* **20/1**

42 **4** *½* **Rizzle Dizzle**[39] 8851 2-9-0 0....................................... PJMcDonald 7 41
(K R Burke) *racd keenly: w wnr tl rdn over 2f out: wknd fnl f* **4/7[1]**

**5** *1¼* **Nalaini (IRE)** 2-8-11 0..................................................... PhilDennis(3) 8 38
(Declan Carroll) *chsd ldrs: pushed along 1/2-way: wknd 2f out* **22/1**

0 **6** *2* **Canufeelthelove**[53] 8587 2-9-0 0....................................... TomEaves 10 32
(Ben Haslam) *s.i.s: a in rr* **100/1**

00 **7** *1* **French Sparkle**[26] 9022 2-8-7 0.............................. JonathanFisher(7) 5 29
(Robert Cowell) *hld up in tch: pushed along and wknd over 2f out* **50/1**

234 **8** *5* **Global Rose (IRE)**[112] 6806 2-9-0 72..........................(h[1]) MartinDwyer 4 14
(Gay Kelleway) *s.i.s: plld hrd and sn prom: rdn and hung lft over 2f out: sn wknd* **7/1**

1m 14.76s (0.26) **Going Correction** 0.0s/f (Stan) **8** Ran SP% **120.7**
Speed ratings (Par 93): **98,94,83,83,81 78,77,70**
CSF £31.38 TOTE £5.20: £1.30, £1.50, £3.10; EX 29.10 Trifecta £321.00.
**Owner** Heather & Michael Yarrow **Bred** Castle Estates **Trained** Radlett, Herts

**FOCUS**
This division was also hit by non-runners. The winning time was 0.38sec quicker than the first leg and the race has been rated around the winner.

## 9417 32RED CASINO NOVICE STKS 1m 142y (Tp)
**3:25** (3:31) (Class 5) 2-Y-O **£3,234** (£962; £481; £240) **Stalls** Low

Form RPR

4 **1** **Antonian**[18] 9155 2-9-2 0............................................ RobertHavlin 10 71+
(John Gosden) *trckd ldrs: wnt 2nd over 5f out: led over 4f out: rdn clr fr over 1f out* **6/5[1]**

**2** *2½* **Danzay (IRE)** 2-9-2 0.................................................. FrannyNorton 4 65
(Mark Johnston) *chsd ldr 3f: remained handy: pushed along over 4f out: chsd wnr over 3f out tl over 2f out: wnt 2nd again over 1f out: rdn and hung rt ins fnl f: styd on same pce* **11/4[2]**

04 **3** *1* **Father Ailbe (IRE)**[19] 9137 2-8-13 0.............................. TimClark(3) 2 63
(John Butler) *trckd ldrs: rdn over 1f out: nt clr run ins fnl f: styd on* **33/1**

6 **4** *1¾* **Roundabout Kitten (USA)**[18] 9155 2-9-2 0........... StevieDonohoe 7 59
(David Lanigan) *prom: chsd wnr over 2f out tl rdn over 1f out: hmpd ins fnl f: no ex* **40/1**

5 **5** *nk* **La Mernancia (IRE)**[22] 9081 2-8-11 0......................... DougieCostello 1 54
(Jamie Osborne) *hld up: rdn over 2f out: styd on ins fnl f: nt trble ldrs* **12/1**

0 **6** *1* **Oi The Clubb Oi'S**[14] 9201 2-9-2 0.................................. TomEaves 12 57
(Ian Williams) *s.i.s: hld up: hung lft and r.o ins fnl f: nvr nrr* **100/1**

0 **7** *3¾* **Night Spark (GER)**[117] 6653 2-9-2 0....................... JosephineGordon 5 49
(Ralph Beckett) *racd keenly: led: hdd over 4f out: pushed along over 2f out: wknd over 1f out* **11/2[3]**

**8** *shd* **Atticus Boy (IRE)** 2-9-2 0............................................ KieranShoemark 9 49
(David Lanigan) *hld up: nvr on terms* **12/1**

6 **9** *½* **Elapidae**[18] 9154 2-9-2 0..................................................... FranBerry 13 47
(David Lanigan) *s.i.s: hld up: rdn over 1f out: sn hung lft: n.d* **25/1**

0 **10** *1¾* **Mayer**[14] 9200 2-9-2 0..................................................... LukeMorris 8 44
(Luca Cumani) *hld up: rdn over 3f out: wknd over 2f out* **40/1**

1m 52.48s (2.38) **Going Correction** 0.0s/f (Stan) **10** Ran SP% **115.5**
Speed ratings (Par 96): **89,86,85,84,84 83,79,79,79,77**
CSF £4.20 TOTE £2.20: £1.10, £1.40, £6.20; EX 7.00 Trifecta £62.60.
**Owner** Denford Stud **Bred** Denford Stud Ltd **Trained** Newmarket, Suffolk

**FOCUS**
An already uncompetitive contest was weakened further by the absence of Kaser, who would have been sent off a red-hot favourite. This race was won by Jack Hobbs when it was run as a proper maiden three years ago.

## 9418 32RED.COM EBF FILLIES' H'CAP 1m 142y (Tp)
**3:55** (3:56) (Class 2) (0-105,90) 3-Y-O+
**£16,807** (£5,032; £2,516; £1,258; £629; £315) **Stalls** Low

Form RPR

5051 **1** **Stellar Surprise**[40] 8820 3-9-0 **83**..............................(t) PJMcDonald 2 90+
(Stuart Williams) *a.p: rdn to chse ldr and edgd lft over 1f out: led ins fnl f: drvn out* **5/2[1]**

01 **2** *shd* **Star Quality**[11] 9273 3-7-12 **74**................................ NicolaCurrie(7) 5 80
(David Loughnane) *led at stdy pce: shkn up and qcknd over 1f out: hdd ins fnl f: r.o* **11/2**

6320 **3** *1½* **Carolinae**[154] 5308 5-9-7 **88**.......................................(h) StevieDonohoe 1 91
(Charlie Fellowes) *trckd ldrs: rdn and swtchd rt over 1f out: r.o* **9/2[3]**

6040 **4** *1¼* **Soul Silver (IRE)**[81] 7815 3-9-4 **90**......................... CallumShepherd(3) 6 90
(David Simcock) *hld up: rdn over 1f out: styd on: nt rch ldrs* **8/1**

-606 **5** *1* **Daisy Bere (FR)**[34] 8912 4-8-13 **80**...............................(p) JoeyHaynes 7 78
(K R Burke) *hld up: rdn over 1f out: nvr on terms* **4/1[2]**

6031 **6** *1* **Pure Shores**[9] 9301 3-8-8 **77** 6ex............................... LukeMorris 4 73
(Ian Williams) *chsd wnr: rdn and ev ch over 1f out: no ex ins fnl f* **4/1[2]**

1m 51.76s (1.66) **Going Correction** 0.0s/f (Stan)
**WFA** 3 from 4yo+ 2lb **6** Ran SP% **113.2**
Speed ratings (Par 96): **92,91,90,89,88 87**
CSF £16.79 TOTE £3.50: £1.60, £2.20; EX 14.30 Trifecta £55.90.
**Owner** J W Parry & Robert Levitt **Bred** Southcourt Stud **Trained** Newmarket, Suffolk

**FOCUS**
A valuable fillies' handicap in which last year's first and second re-opposed, but they could only manage fifth and third this time. The pace was steady and it developed into something of a sprint.

## 9419 BETWAY CASINO H'CAP — 1m 1f 104y (Tp)
4:25 (4:28) (Class 4) (0-85,82) 3-Y-O+ £4,851 (£1,443; £721; £360) Stalls Low

Form RPR

3043 1 **Maratha (IRE)**[14] 9206 3-9-1 78.....................(t) PJMcDonald 5 85
(Stuart Williams) *chsd ldrs: nt clr run and swtchd rt wl over 1f out: sn led: drvn out* 9/4[1]

2 2 **Perfect Soldier (IRE)**[66] 8267 3-9-1 78..................... DougieCostello 6 81
(M D O'Callaghan, Ire) *pushed along to join ldr after 1f: pushed along over 3f out: rdn and hmpd over 1f out: styd on same pce ins fnl f* 7/2[3]

0626 3 hd **First Up (IRE)**[20] 5484 3-9-5 82.....................(t) TomEaves 8 84
(Oliver Greenall) *chsd ldrs: rdn over 2f out: styd on u.p* 16/1

5350 4 nk **Waarif (IRE)**[19] 9140 4-9-3 78.....................(t[1]) FranBerry 3 80
(David O'Meara) *hld up in tch: rdn over 1f out: kpt on* 11/4[2]

4332 5 2 ¼ **Toga Tiger (IRE)**[83] 7759 10-9-5 80..................... RobertWinston 2 77
(Daniel Mark Loughnane) *hld up: rdn over 1f out: nt trble ldrs* 8/1

0405 6 2 **Sumner Beach**[8] 9303 3-8-7 70.....................(t) JosephineGordon 4 63
(Brian Ellison) *hld up: pushed along over 4f out: n.d* 12/1

1605 7 6 **Harlequin Striker (IRE)**[26] 9029 5-9-0 75.....................(p) CharlesBishop 1 55
(Dean Ivory) *led: rdn and hdd over 1f out: wknd and eased ins fnl f* 12/1

1m 59.59s (-1.21) **Going Correction** 0.0s/f (Stan)
**WFA** 3 from 4yo+ 2lb 7 Ran SP% 112.0
Speed ratings (Par 105): **105,103,103,102,100 99,93**
CSF £9.95 CT £95.02 TOTE £2.70: £1.50, £2.30; EX 11.40 Trifecta £72.60.
**Owner** Happy Valley Racing & Breeding Limited **Bred** Castlemartin Sky & Skymarc Farm **Trained** Newmarket, Suffolk

**FOCUS**
A fair handicap and a nice winner.

## 9420 BETWAY SPRINT H'CAP — 6f 20y (Tp)
4:55 (4:56) (Class 6) (0-55,61) 3-Y-O+ £2,587 (£770; £384; £192) Stalls Low

Form RPR

4021 1 **Jorvik Prince**[5] 9374 3-9-8 61 6ex..................... GemmaTutty(5) 2 68
(Karen Tutty) *mde all: rdn over 1f out: styd on u.p* 13/8[1]

6636 2 1 ½ **Tasaaboq**[10] 9279 6-9-0 48.....................(t) JosephineGordon 3 51
(Phil McEntee) *s.i.s: hld up: hdwy over 1f out: sn rdn and edgd lft: chsd wnr ins fnl f: styd on* 9/2[2]

0224 3 shd **Jessie Allan (IRE)**[11] 9267 6-8-12 46..................... PJMcDonald 7 48
(Jim Goldie) *hld up: pushed along over 2f out: hdwy over 1f out: sn rdn and hung lft: r.o* 9/2[2]

0403 4 3 **Noneedtotellme (IRE)**[11] 9267 4-8-12 46 oh1..................... AndrewMullen 1 39
(James Unett) *s.i.s: sn prom: rdn over 1f out: styng on same pce whn nt clr run ins fnl f* 16/1

060 5 ½ **Goadby**[57] 8496 6-8-12 46 oh1.....................(v) RobHornby 5 38
(John Holt) *chsd ldrs: rdn over 1f out: styd on same pce fnl f* 66/1

6400 6 shd **Justice Rock**[15] 9183 4-8-9 50.....................(t) NicolaCurrie(7) 13 41
(Phil McEntee) *sn pushed along to go prom: chsd ldr 4f out: rdn over 1f out: no ex ins fnl f* 25/1

64P2 7 hd **Snow Excuse**[14] 9215 3-9-0 48.....................(t) TomEaves 6 39
(Bryan Smart) *chsd ldr 2f: remained handy: rdn and hung lft over 2f out: no ex fnl f* 11/2[3]

0003 8 6 **Storm Lightning**[5] 9374 8-8-13 50..................... EoinWalsh(3) 12 23
(Mark Brisbourne) *trckd ldrs: racd keenly: shkn up and wknd over 1f out* 22/1

2206 9 ½ **Deben**[119] 6571 4-9-1 49..................... LukeMorris 9 20
(John Weymes) *hld up: shkn up over 2f out: n.d* 16/1

205 10 nk **Spoken Words**[155] 5260 8-8-12 46 oh1.....................(p) PatrickMathers 11 16
(John David Riches) *broke wl enough but awkward sn after s and lost pl: nvr on terms after* 80/1

3000 11 8 **Storm Trooper (IRE)**[11] 9265 6-9-1 52..................... AaronJones(3) 8
(Adam West) *free to post: prom: lost pl 1/2-way: sn rdn: wknd 2f out* 40/1

1m 14.25s (-0.25) **Going Correction** 0.0s/f (Stan) 11 Ran SP% 115.0
Speed ratings (Par 101): **101,99,98,94,94 94,93,85,85,84 74**
CSF £8.10 CT £27.10 TOTE £2.50: £1.20, £1.60, £1.50; EX 9.80 Trifecta £33.50.
**Owner** Thoroughbred Homes Ltd **Bred** Hellwood Stud Farm & Mrs Jill Willows **Trained** Osmotherley, N Yorks

**FOCUS**
A poor sprint handicap, full of infrequent winners, but won by an in-form gelding. The placed horses pin the level.

## 9421 BETWAY LIVE CASINO H'CAP — 1m 5f 219y (Tp)
5:25 (5:25) (Class 6) (0-65,65) 3-Y-O+ £2,587 (£770; £384; £192) Stalls Low

Form RPR

1212 1 **Willyegolassiego**[27] 3026 4-9-12 63..................... DougieCostello 9 74
(Neil Mulholland) *hld up: hdwy 2f out: rdn to ld ins fnl f: edgd rt: styd on* 18/1

3001 2 1 ½ **Bamako Du Chatelet (FR)**[7] 9325 6-10-0 65.....................(v) StevieDonohoe 3 74
(Ian Williams) *s.i.s: hld up: hdwy over 6f out: chsd ldr over 2f out: rdn to ld 1f out: sn hung lft and hdd: styd on same pce* 6/4[1]

1132 3 3 ¾ **Raashdy (IRE)**[11] 9270 4-9-12 63.....................(p) LukeMorris 5 66
(Peter Hiatt) *prom: led over 2f out: rdn and hdd 1f out: no ex ins fnl f* 4/1[2]

0031 4 15 **Captain Swift (IRE)**[32] 8955 6-9-11 62.....................(p) AndrewMullen 11 43
(John Mackie) *chsd ldrs: rdn over 3f out: wknd over 1f out* 7/1

6004 5 1 ¾ **Slaying The Dragon (IRE)**[13] 2591 4-8-8 48 ow1.....................(b[1]) TimClark(3) 7 26
(Martin Hill) *s.i.s: hld up: rdn over 3f out: n.d* 66/1

3334 6 6 **Singular Quest**[32] 8955 5-9-7 58..................... RobertWinston 13 27
(Daniel Mark Loughnane) *chsd ldrs: lft 2nd over 6f out tl rdn over 2f out: wknd over 1f out* 6/1[3]

3236 7 2 ¾ **Angel In The Snow**[12] 9242 4-8-11 48.....................(p[1]) JosephineGordon 4 13
(Brian Ellison) *led: hdd over 11f out: chsd ldr: lft in ld over 6f out: rdn and hdd over 2f out: wknd over 1f out* 4/1[2]

14-2 8 9 **Major Ben**[343] 290 4-9-11 65..................... MitchGodwin(3) 8 16
(Michael Blake) *chsd ldrs: hit rails 10f out: lft 3rd over 6f out: rdn over 2f out: sn wknd* 20/1

0-00 9 2 ½ **Zarliman (IRE)**[23] 8135 7-8-9 51.....................(p) RhiainIngram(5) 1
(Roger Ingram) *sn pushed along and a in rr: wknd over 3f out* 125/1

0000 10 41 **Almutamarred (USA)**[34] 8909 5-9-3 54.....................(b[1]) RobHornby 10 +
(James Unett) *sn pushed along to chse ldrs: led over 11f out: rdn clr 9f out: eased over 7f out: hdd over 6f out: lost tch fr over 4f out: rdr rode a fin a circ to early* 16/1

1000 U **Miss Dusky Diva (IRE)**[18] 9158 5-9-4 55..................... WilliamCarson 6 +
(David W Drinkwater) *hld up: gng wl whn clipped heels and uns rdr wl over 3f out* 40/1

3m 4.02s (-3.98) **Going Correction** 0.0s/f (Stan) 11 Ran SP% 127.4
Speed ratings (Par 101): **111,110,108,99,98 95,93,88,86,63**
CSF £48.70 CT £146.74 TOTE £12.40: £3.10, £1.20, £1.90; EX 53.50 Trifecta £282.10.
**Owner** John Hobbs **Bred** Southcourt Stud **Trained** Limpley Stoke, Wilts
■ Stewards' Enquiry : Rob Hornby 12-day ban: appeared to ride a finish a circuit too soon (Jan 10-20, 22)

**FOCUS**
A modest staying handicap, but no shortage of drama with one jockey riding a finish a circuit early and another being unseated half a mile from home. The first three finished well clear.
T/Plt: £137.40 to a £1 stake. Pool: £92,781.21 - 492.77 winning units T/Qpdt: £16.20 to a £1 stake. Pool: £10,497.34 - 477.64 winning units **Colin Roberts**

9422 - 9429a (Foreign Racing) - See Raceform Interactive

9385
# LINGFIELD (L-H)
Thursday, December 28

**OFFICIAL GOING: Polytrack: standard**
Wind: Light to moderate, across Weather: Sunny, crisp

## 9430 BETWAY APPRENTICE (S) STKS — 1m 4f (P)
11:40 (11:40) (Class 6) 3-Y-O+ £2,264 (£673; £336; £168) Stalls Low

Form RPR

0244 1 **Bertie Moon**[6] 9367 7-8-9 67.....................(v) KeelanBaker(8) 6 60
(Michael Appleby) *t.k.h: mde all: kicked on 4f out: pressed and rdn 2f out: styd on wl and in command fnl f* 4/1[3]

0501 2 2 ¾ **Ceyhan**[21] 9127 5-9-7 65..................... KieranShoemark 4 59
(Jamie Osborne) *trckd ldrs: wnt 2nd wl over 3f out: clsd to press wnr 2f out: rdn and fnd little over 1f out: wl hld fnl f* 5/4[1]

5503 3 4 **Awesome Rock (IRE)**[42] 8799 8-8-11 42..................... RhiainIngram(6) 1 49
(Roger Ingram) *hld up in last pair: lot to do whn prog 3f out: chsd ldng pair 2f out: one pce and no imp over 1f out* 40/1

0640 4 ½ **La Goulue**[12] 9270 3-8-3 40.....................(v) PoppyBridgwater(5) 8 44
(John Gallagher) *hld up: rdn and prog to chse ldng pair 3f out to 2f out: kpt on one pce* 66/1

2640 5 6 **Ode To Glory**[27] 9026 3-8-5 63..................... JackOsborn(3) 3 35
(Rae Guest) *hld up in last pair: rdn and no prog over 4f out: plugged on one pce fr over 2f out* 9/4[2]

0000 6 29 **My Lord**[8] 9325 9-9-3 52.....................(p) CallumShepherd 2
(Paddy Butler) *chsd ldrs tl wknd qckly 3f out: t.o* 33/1

00 7 87 **Michigan (USA)**[15] 9208 3-8-13 67.....................(t[1]) EdwardGreatrex 7
(Mohamed Moubarak) *chsd wnr to wl over 3f out: wknd rapidly and sn t.o* 8/1

0500 P **The Dancing Lord**[15] 9211 8-9-0 46.....................(tp) NicolaCurrie(3) 5
(Adam West) *wl bhd whn fatally injured over 2f out* 20/1

2m 31.74s (-1.26) **Going Correction** -0.075s/f (Stan)
**WFA** 3 from 5yo+ 4lb 8 Ran SP% 118.0
Speed ratings (Par 101): **101,99,96,96,92 72,14,**
CSF £9.55 TOTE £4.30: £1.50, £1.10, £3.70; EX 11.90 Trifecta £75.40.The winner was bought in for 5,000gns. Ceyhan was bought by Mr F. J. Brennan for £5,000.
**Owner** SC Oliver Racing Limited **Bred** M E Wates **Trained** Oakham, Rutland
■ Stewards' Enquiry : Keelan Baker four-day ban: used whip above the permitted level (Jan 11-14)

**FOCUS**
A moderate seller with a horse who wanted to win beating one who didn't.

## 9431 PLAY JACKPOT GAMES AT SUNBETS.CO.UK/VEGAS H'CAP (DIV I) — 7f 1y(P)
12:10 (12:14) (Class 6) (0-65,67) 3-Y-O+ £2,264 (£673; £336; £168) Stalls Low

Form RPR

0006 1 **Muhajjal**[22] 9094 3-9-0 65.....................(t) RossaRyan(7) 5 71
(George Peckham) *hld up towards rr: gng strly whn waiting for room 2f out: prog over 1f out: rdn to chse ldr ins fnl f: styd on wl to ld last strides* 3/1[1]

1504 2 nk **Masquerade Bling (IRE)**[15] 9203 3-9-1 59..................... RobHornby 7 64
(Neil Mulholland) *trckd ldng pair: clsd to ld jst over 1f out: rdn fnl f: styd on but hdd last strides* 7/1

6143 3 1 ¼ **The Special One (IRE)**[22] 9094 4-9-1 59.....................(t) TomMarquand 6 61
(Ali Stronge) *hld up in last: gd prog jst over 1f out: chsd ldng pair ins fnl f: no imp last 75yds* 4/1[2]

6330 4 1 ¼ **Violet's Lads (IRE)**[15] 9203 3-9-1 62..................... CallumShepherd(3) 4 60
(Brett Johnson) *s.i.s: hld up towards rr: gng strly whn waiting for room 2f out: prog over 1f out: tried to cl on ldrs ins fnl f: nt qckn last 100yds* 10/1

0304 5 ¾ **Smart Mover (IRE)**[125] 6393 4-8-0 51 oh2.....................(p) NicolaCurrie(7) 9 47
(Nikki Evans) *racd on outer: in tch: rdn over 2f out: no prog over 1f out: kpt on ins fnl f* 80/1

5600 6 1 ½ **Sea Tea Dea**[13] 9243 3-9-4 62..................... LukeMorris 10 54
(Anthony Carson) *chsd ldrs: rdn over 2f out: fdd jst over 1f out* 25/1

106- 7 nk **Bobby Benton (IRE)**[374] 8455 6-9-9 67.....................(v[1]) TimmyMurphy 2 58
(Suzi Best) *mde most: rdn 2f out: hdd jst over 1f out: wknd fnl f* 5/1[3]

/50- 8 1 ¾ **Sea Of Hope (IRE)**[82] 7840 4-9-2 60..................... FranBerry 8 47+
(Henry Candy) *w ldr: rdn 2f out: stl upsides jst over 1f out but hanging bdly: lost pl qckly fnl f and continued to hang* 6/1

5000 9 nk **German Whip**[22] 9094 4-9-3 64..................... HectorCrouch(3) 1 50
(Gary Moore) *chsd ldrs on inner: rdn over 2f out: wknd jst over 1f out* 6/1

1m 24.69s (-0.11) **Going Correction** -0.075s/f (Stan) 9 Ran SP% 116.9
Speed ratings (Par 101): **97,96,95,93,92 91,90,88,88**
CSF £24.99 CT £85.42 TOTE £4.30: £1.70, £2.40, £1.40; EX 26.00 Trifecta £150.20.
**Owner** Fawzi Abdulla Nass **Bred** Aislabie Bloodstock Ltd **Trained** Newmarket, Suffolk

**FOCUS**
The first division of a modest handicap, but an exciting finish. The placed horses set the level.

## 9432 PLAY JACKPOT GAMES AT SUNBETS.CO.UK/VEGAS H'CAP (DIV II) — 7f 1y(P)
12:45 (12:46) (Class 6) (0-65,66) 3-Y-O+ £2,264 (£673; £336; £168) Stalls Low

Form RPR

3435 1 **Ubla (IRE)**[9] 9307 4-8-12 61.....................(p) WilliamCox(5) 5 67
(Gay Kelleway) *trckd ldrs: rdn and clsd on outer to ld jst over 1f out: drvn and styd on fnl f* 10/1

0601 2 ½ **Captain Pugwash (IRE)**[20] 9142 3-9-7 65..................... LiamKeniry 4 72
(Henry Spiller) *hld up in midfield: prog whn nt clr run and bmpd over 1f out: r.o to take 2nd last 100yds: no imp on wnr nr fin* 7/4[1]

0423 3 ¾ **Haraz (IRE)**[10] 9296 4-9-5 63.....................(v) DougieCostello 1 67
(Jamie Osborne) *trckd ldng pair: poised in bhd them whn nt clr run and bmpd over 1f out: r.o to press for 2nd ins fnl f: nt qckn last 75yds* 8/1



The Form Book Flat, Raceform Ltd, Newbury, RG14 5SJ

0500 **4** 3/4 **El Torito (IRE)**[8] 9323 3-8-12 **59**............................(b[1]) CharlieBennett(3) 8 60
(Jim Boyle) *t.k.h: hld up in rr: wdst of all bnd 2f out and lost grnd: styd on fnl f: nrst fin* **16/1**
6425 **5** hd **Kafoo**[28] 9012 4-9-4 **62**.................................(vt) LukeMorris 3 62
(Michael Appleby) *mostly trckd ldr: rdn to ld wl over 1f out: racd awkwardly and hdd jst over 1f out: lost pls last 100yds* **8/1**
0052 **6** 1/2 **Termsnconditions (IRE)**[41] 8824 3-9-1 **59**..................(v) KieranO'Neill 2 58
(Tim Vaughan) *t.k.h early: hld up in midfield: trying to make grnd on inner whn nt clr run over 1f out: swtchd out and kpt on but nt pce to threaten* **7/1**[3]
0065 **7** 3 1/4 **Malaysian Boleh**[16] 9184 7-9-2 **60**.........................(v) JosephineGordon 9 50
(Phil McEntee) *led to wl over 1f out: wknd* **25/1**
0520 **8** 4 **Waqt (IRE)**[72] 8132 3-9-1 **66**.............................. TylerSaunders(7) 6 45
(Marcus Tregoning) *t.k.h: hld up in rr: rdn and struggling over 2f out: sn no ch* **11/2**[2]
3503 **9** 22 **Eddiebet**[22] 9093 3-9-4 **62**.............................. KieranShoemark 7
(David O'Meara) *n.m.r after s: hld up in last pair: rdn and struggling 3f out: wknd and t.o* **10/1**

1m 24.03s (-0.77) **Going Correction** -0.075s/f (Stan) 9 Ran SP% **114.4**
Speed ratings (Par 101): **101,100,99,98,98 97,94,89,64**
CSF £27.62 CT £152.31 TOTE £13.70: £3.90, £1.10, £2.50; EX 39.90 Trifecta £265.30.
**Owner** Peter Petrovic **Bred** Tenuta Genzianella **Trained** Exning, Suffolk

**FOCUS**
A rather messy race with the second and third getting into all sorts of trouble. The winning time was 0.66sec quicker than the first division and the winner has been rated to his better recent form.

## 9433 32RED.COM EBF NOVICE STKS 7f 1y(P)
**1:15** (1:19) (Class 5) 2-Y-O **£2,911** (£866; £432; £216) **Stalls** Low

Form RPR
05 **1** **Maverick Officer**[125] 6367 2-9-2 0.............................. StevieDonohoe 1 77
(David Simcock) *hld up in 6th: gng strly over 2f out: encouraged along over 1f out: picked up wl fnl f and r.o to ld last 75yds* **14/1**
226 **2** 3/4 **Ode To Autumn**[125] 6388 2-9-2 82.............................. RobertHavlin 10 75
(John Gosden) *racd wd early: w ldr: led wl over 1f out but sn drvn and making heavy weather of it: kpt on but hdd and outpcd last 75yds* **11/8**[1]
021 **3** nk **Zalshah**[27] 9021 2-9-9 84.................................(p) TomMarquand 8 81
(Richard Hannon) *trckd ldng pair: wnt 2nd over 1f out: drvn to chal fnl f: nt qckn last 100yds* **9/4**[2]
3 **4** 1/2 **Chingachgook**[26] 9051 2-9-2 0.............................. JackGarritty 3 73
(Richard Fahey) *trckd ldrs on inner: clsd 2f out: rdn to chal fnl f: nt qckn last 100yds* **13/2**[3]
**5** 5 **Breaking Records (IRE)** 2-9-2 0.......................... JosephineGordon 9 59
(Hugo Palmer) *mde most to wl over 1f out: sn wknd* **12/1**
0 **6** hd **Marshal Dan (IRE)**[26] 9051 2-8-13 0.......................... HectorCrouch(3) 6 59
(Heather Main) *chsd ldrs: rdn over 2f out: wknd over 1f out* **66/1**
**7** 3 **Liberty Lynx** 2-8-8 0........................................ GeorgiaCox(3) 4 46
(William Haggas) *s.s: wl off the pce in last: nudged along and kpt on steadily fnl 2f* **12/1**
0 **8** 1 1/4 **Dubai Landmark (IRE)**[8] 9311 2-9-2 0.......................... JackMitchell 11 47
(Hugo Palmer) *dwlt: off the pce in rr: rchd 7th 1/2-way but nt on terms: rn green bnd 2f out: wknd fnl f* **33/1**
**9** 3 **Licinius** 2-9-2 0........................................ LukeMorris 2 39
(Charles Hills) *dwlt: a off the pce in rr: rdn and no prog 1/2-way* **33/1**
00 **10** 8 **Garsington**[20] 9137 2-9-2 0.............................. ShaneKelly 7 17
(Ed Dunlop) *off the pce towards rr: shkn up 1/2-way: wknd over 2f out: t.o* **80/1**

1m 23.07s (-1.73) **Going Correction** -0.075s/f (Stan) 10 Ran SP% **116.9**
Speed ratings (Par 96): **106,105,104,104,98 98,94,93,90,80**
CSF £33.52 TOTE £15.30: £3.40, £1.10, £1.60; EX 49.20 Trifecta £126.80.
**Owner** Mrs Fitri Hay **Bred** Haras De La Perelle **Trained** Newmarket, Suffolk

**FOCUS**
Quite an interesting novice event with several top stables represented, but the first four finished in a heap suggesting the form isn't anything special.

## 9434 BETWAY STAYERS H'CAP 1m 7f 169y(P)
**1:45** (1:49) (Class 4) (0-85,85) 3-Y-O+ **£4,690** (£1,395; £697; £348) **Stalls** Low

Form RPR
0230 **1** **Royal Reserve**[22] 9096 4-10-0 **85**.............................. KieranShoemark 5 89+
(David O'Meara) *stdd s: hld up and last tl 3f out: prog 2f out: cajoled along and gd run to ld 100yds out: idled in front and jst clung on* **10/1**
3552 **2** shd **Rydan (IRE)**[15] 9204 6-10-0 **85**...............................(p) AdamKirby 7 89
(Gary Moore) *wl plcd: drvn to chse ldr over 1f out tl ins fnl f: rallied last 75yds: jst failed* **11/2**[3]
0011 **3** shd **Island Brave (IRE)**[29] 9000 3-9-3 **80**.............................. LukeMorris 4 84
(Heather Main) *trckd ldr: led 3f out but pressed: drvn 2f out: hdd last 100yds: kpt on u.p but jst hld* **7/2**[2]
0011 **4** 1 3/4 **Captain Navarre**[23] 9082 5-10-0 **85**.......................(v) StevieDonohoe 8 87
(Charlie Fellowes) *trckd ldrs: chal fr 3f out to wl over 1f out: nt qckn and one pce fnl f* **11/10**[1]
-664 **5** 1/2 **Continuum**[15] 9204 8-9-12 **83**...............................(v) TomMarquand 6 84
(Peter Hedger) *hld up in tch: drvn wl over 2f out: nvr able to chal but kpt on fr over 1f out* **8/1**
6040 **6** 7 **Poyle Thomas**[15] 9204 8-9-5 **76**...............................(h[1]) FranBerry 3 69
(Michael Madgwick) *hld up: shkn up 3f out and no prog: steadily fdd* **25/1**
146- **7** 35 **Aristocles (IRE)**[28] 7320 4-8-13 **70**..........................(v[1]) CharlesBishop 1 21
(Nikki Evans) *led and clr: c bk to rivals 1/2-way: hdd & wknd 3f out: eased 2f out: t.o* **66/1**

3m 27.32s (1.62) **Going Correction** -0.075s/f (Stan)
**WFA** 3 from 4yo+ 6lb 7 Ran SP% **110.8**
Speed ratings (Par 105): **92,91,91,91,90 87,69**
CSF £59.00 CT £222.40 TOTE £7.70: £3.60, £2.10; EX 30.10 Trifecta £148.50.
**Owner** Royal Guinness Reserve Partnership **Bred** New England, Myriad & Watership Down **Trained** Upper Helmsley, N Yorks

**FOCUS**
Quite a decent staying handicap, but with the bulk of the field inclined to ignore the clear leader this developed into a bit of a sprint. It produced a cracking finish between the first three, though.

## 9435 PLAY SLOTS AT SUNBETS.CO.UK/VEGAS MAIDEN STKS 1m 1y(P)
**2:20** (2:22) (Class 5) 3-Y-O+ **£2,911** (£866; £432; £216) **Stalls** High

Form RPR
2453 **1** **Swiss Vinnare**[15] 9209 3-8-12 71..............................(h) NicolaCurrie(7) 5 74
(Phil McEntee) *urged along early to get gng: chsd ldr after 1f: led jst over 2f out: rdn and edgd rt fnl f but styd on wl* **4/1**[3]
-362 **2** 3 1/4 **Paradise Lake (IRE)**[73] 8116 3-9-5 76.............................. LiamKeniry 4 66
(Ed Walker) *t.k.h: trckd ldrs: wnt 2nd 2f out: rdn and fnd little over 1f out: readily hld after* **10/11**[1]
5643 **3** 3/4 **Deliberator**[22] 9088 3-9-5 73.............................. AdamKirby 1 65
(William Knight) *trckd ldrs: hmpd on inner over 5f out: effrt over 2f out: rdn to take 3rd over 1f out: pressed runner-up after but nvr finding enough to threaten* **5/2**[2]
**4** 1 1/2 **Elite Treaty** 3-9-5 0.............................. FranBerry 3 61
(Gay Kelleway) *mostly in 6th: shkn up 2f out: styd on steadily to take 4th ins fnl f: nt disgracd* **10/1**
0000 **5** 4 1/2 **Annabella**[11] 9282 4-9-1 43.............................. RobertHavlin 9 46
(Tim McCarthy) *chsd ldr 1f: edgd lft over 5f out: wknd 2f out* **100/1**
0 **6** 5 **Duhr (IRE)**[15] 9209 3-9-5 68.............................. TimmyMurphy 7 38
(Ralph J Smith) *sn wl bhd in last: modest late hdwy: nvr in it* **16/1**
56 **7** nk **Peters Folly**[15] 9202 4-9-1 0..................................(h) LukeMorris 6 33
(Peter Hiatt) *a in last trio and sn wl off the pce: nvr a factor* **40/1**
406/ **8** 4 1/2 **Nelson's Hill**[945] 2637 7-9-3 49.............................. AaronJones(3) 8 28
(William de Best-Turner) *led and stretched field: hdd & wknd rapidly jst over 2f out* **66/1**
**9** 1/2 **Uptown Girl** 3-9-0 0.............................. SimonPearce 2 20
(Lydia Pearce) *slowly away: a wl bhd in last trio* **33/1**

1m 37.33s (-0.87) **Going Correction** -0.075s/f (Stan)
**WFA** 3 from 4yo+ 1lb 9 Ran SP% **123.8**
Speed ratings (Par 103): **101,97,97,95,91 86,85,81,80**
CSF £8.63 TOTE £4.80: £1.10, £1.10, £1.30; EX 10.90 Trifecta £17.50.
**Owner** Steve Jakes **Bred** A C M Spalding **Trained** Newmarket, Suffolk

**FOCUS**
A moderate maiden with the big two in the market putting in laboured efforts.

## 9436 32RED CASINO NURSERY H'CAP 7f 1y(P)
**2:55** (2:56) (Class 6) (0-65,67) 2-Y-O **£2,264** (£673; £336; £168) **Stalls** Low

Form RPR
0424 **1** **Bezos (IRE)**[6] 9370 2-9-2 **67**..............................(p) RossaRyan(7) 9 77
(Richard Hannon) *trckd ldr: shkn up to ld jst over 1f out: sn rdn clr: comf* **5/1**[2]
0602 **2** 2 **Corazon Espinado (IRE)**[22] 9090 2-9-2 **65**.............. PaddyBradley(5) 2 70
(Simon Dow) *trckd ldrs on inner: effrt jst over 1f out and plld off rail: rdn to chse wnr ins fnl f: styd on but no imp* **13/8**[1]
0430 **3** 2 1/4 **Isoletta**[22] 9090 2-9-6 **64**.............................. LiamKeniry 3 63
(Ed Walker) *hld up in midfield: urged along over 2f out: prog on outer over 1f out: styd on to take 3rd ins fnl f* **8/1**[3]
0003 **4** 1 **Lady Of Authority**[23] 9081 2-9-8 **66**.............................. ShaneKelly 7 62
(Murty McGrath) *chsd ldrs: pushed along fr 3f out: lost pl wl over 1f out: styd on again ins fnl f* **20/1**
0000 **5** 1/2 **Royal Wave**[42] 8793 2-8-1 **45**.............................. KieranO'Neill 4 40
(William Knight) *t.k.h: hld up in rr: 9th jst over 2f out: prog wl over 1f out: kpt on but nvr enough pce to threaten* **25/1**
065 **6** 1/2 **Free Talkin**[80] 7875 2-8-11 **55**.............................. KierenFox 1 49
(Michael Attwater) *dwlt: sn in midfield: prog on inner 2f out: cl up jst over 1f out: fdd* **20/1**
0550 **7** nk **Boomerang Betty (IRE)**[15] 9199 2-9-8 **66**................ DougieCostello 11 59
(Jamie Osborne) *hld up in last pair: shkn up over 2f out: kpt on steadily fr over 1f out: nvr really involved* **16/1**
000 **8** nk **Amadeus (IRE)**[17] 9177 2-8-7 **51**...............................(b[1]) PatrickMathers 6 43
(Richard Fahey) *in rr and nt gng wl: last wl over 1f out: kpt on fnl 100yds* **8/1**[3]
0050 **9** nk **Kylie Style**[9] 9302 2-8-0 **51**...............................(p) NicolaCurrie(7) 10 42
(Steph Hollinshead) *t.k.h: led: clr after 2f: hdd & wknd jst over 1f out* **40/1**
6060 **10** 1/2 **Conflagration**[27] 9024 2-9-6 **64**.............................. AdamKirby 12 54
(Ed Dunlop) *disp 2nd pl to 2f out: sn drvn: wknd fnl f* **10/1**
0006 **11** 1/2 **Dark Freedom (IRE)**[102] 7196 2-9-1 **59**.............................. LukeMorris 5 47
(Charles Hills) *dwlt: urged along early: a towards rr: nvr a factor* **9/1**
5506 **12** 26 **Hollywood Dream**[15] 9199 2-9-7 **65**.............................. FranBerry 8
(Neil Mulholland) *chsd ldrs on outer: wkng whn rn v wd bnd 2f out: t.o* **12/1**

1m 24.35s (-0.45) **Going Correction** -0.075s/f (Stan) 12 Ran SP% **125.5**
Speed ratings (Par 94): **99,96,94,93,92 91,91,91,90,90 89,59**
CSF £13.63 CT £70.04 TOTE £5.00: £1.60, £1.60, £2.60; EX 16.60 Trifecta £67.10.
**Owner** Middleham Park Racing LIII & K Sohi **Bred** Kevin Blake **Trained** East Everleigh, Wilts

**FOCUS**
A modest nursery containing just one previous winner.

## 9437 BETWAY H'CAP 6f 1y(P)
**3:30** (3:32) (Class 5) (0-75,76) 3-Y-O+ **£2,911** (£866; £432; £216) **Stalls** Low

Form RPR
0 **1** **Art Nouvelle (IRE)**[34] 8938 3-9-8 **76**.............................. AdamKirby 3 84
(Joseph Patrick O'Brien, Ire) *trckd ldrs: prog to go 2nd 2f out: rdn to ld narrowly 1f out: drvn and grad asserted last 100yds* **9/2**[3]
6400 **2** 1 **Juan Horsepower**[14] 9234 3-8-11 **72**..........................(p) RossaRyan(7) 4 77
(Richard Hannon) *urged along to ld but hdd after 1f: rdn to ld again over 2f out: hdd 1f out: kpt on but hld last 100yds* **7/1**
4312 **3** 3/4 **Hamish McGonagain**[10] 9297 4-9-0 **68**..................(p) KieranShoemark 2 71+
(David O'Meara) *hld up in midfield: rdn and no prog 2f out: styd on wl fnl f to take 3rd last stride* **5/2**[1]
0001 **4** nse **Varsovian**[22] 9093 7-9-3 **74**.............................. JackDuern(3) 8 76
(Dean Ivory) *trckd ldrs on outer: rdn 2f out: prog to chse ldng pair ins fnl f: no imp and lost 3rd last stride* **5/1**
5333 **5** 3/4 **Very Honest (IRE)**[16] 9185 4-9-4 **72**.............................. LukeMorris 5 72+
(Brett Johnson) *chsd ldrs: hmpd 2f out and lost pl: tried to rally over 1f out: kpt on same pce fnl f* **7/2**[2]
5100 **6** 1/2 **Danecase**[21] 9124 4-9-7 **75**...............................(p[1]) DougieCostello 1 73
(David Dennis) *dwlt: in rr: prog on inner wl over 1f out: chsd ldrs fnl f: fdd nr fin* **15/2**
0-00 **7** 4 **Whirl Me Round**[21] 9124 3-9-7 **75**..............................(b[1]) KieranO'Neill 9 61
(George Peckham) *restless stalls: sn in last: struggling fr 1/2-way: nvr a factor* **25/1**
6455 **8** 6 **Zipedeedodah (IRE)**[20] 9136 5-9-5 **73**..............................(t) ShaneKelly 7 39
(Joseph Tuite) *chsd ldng pair on outer to 2f out: sn wknd* **25/1**
0/ **9** 1/2 **Helis (FR)**[536] 4-9-7 **75**.............................. LiamKeniry 6 40
(Michael Scudamore) *led after 1f to over 2f out: wknd qckly* **40/1**

1m 10.92s (-0.98) **Going Correction** -0.075s/f (Stan) 9 Ran SP% **120.0**
Speed ratings (Par 103): **103,101,100,100,99 98,93,85,84**
CSF £36.56 CT £97.24 TOTE £4.80: £1.60, £2.30, £1.40; EX 43.10 Trifecta £140.00.
**Owner** Geansai Nua Syndicate **Bred** Cloughmealy Stud **Trained** Owning Hill, Co Kilkenny

**FOCUS**
An ordinary sprint handicap, won by an intriguing Irish challenger.
T/Jkpt: Not won. T/Plt: £19.70 to a £1 stake. Pool: £78,762.96 - 2,906.39 winning units T/Qpdt: £7.00 to a £1 stake. Pool: £11,102.17 - 1169.46 winning units **Jonathan Neesom**

9438 - (Foreign Racing) - See Raceform Interactive

# 9363 SOUTHWELL (L-H)

Friday, December 29

**OFFICIAL GOING: Fibresand: standard**

Wind: Virtually nil freshening to light half behind after race 3 Weather: Heavy cloud

## 9439 32RED CASINO NURSERY H'CAP — 1m 13y(F)

12:15 (12:17) (Class 6) (0-65,65) 2-Y-O — £2,264 (£673; £336; £168) Stalls Low

Form / RPR

4036 1 **Couldn't Could She**[64] 8371 2-8-13 60 ow2 CliffordLee(3) 2 66
(Adam West) *trckd ldrs: hdwy 3f out: led 2f out: sn rdn clr: styd on wl* 12/1

4443 2 3 **Felisa**[23] 9090 2-9-6 64 (v) FranBerry 6 63
(David Evans) *towards rr on inner: hdwy 3f out: swtchd markedly rt to outer and chsd ldrs 2f out: rdn to chse wnr over 1f out: drvn ins fnl f: no imp towards fin* 15/2

3021 3 2 **Mr Carbonator**[18] 9175 2-8-13 62 JamieGormley(5) 7 58+
(Philip Kirby) *towards rr: hdwy 3f out: swtchd lft and rdn to chse ldrs 2f out: drvn and no imp fnl f* 9/4[1]

4032 4 7 **Medici Oro**[18] 9175 2-9-5 63 TomEaves 3 40
(David Brown) *cl up: led 1/2-way: pushed along and hdd over 3f out: sn rdn: drvn wl over 1f out: grad wknd* 7/2[2]

3223 5 3/4 **Progressive Jazz (IRE)**[14] 9238 2-8-6 55 (v) RhiainIngram(5) 12 30
(K R Burke) *trckd ldrs on outer: hdwy and cl up 1/2-way: led over 3f out: rdn along and hdd 2f out: sn drvn and grad wknd* 7/1[3]

3246 6 1/2 **Sunhill Lad (IRE)**[13] 9263 2-9-7 65 ShaneGray 8 39
(Ann Duffield) *dwlt and towards rr: hdwy on inner 2f out: sn rdn and kpt on wl fnl f* 25/1

4040 7 nk **Optimickstickhill**[10] 9302 2-8-13 57 LukeMorris 1 30
(Scott Dixon) *slt ld: pushed along and hdd over 4f out: rdn along 3f out: drvn over 2f out: sn wknd* 40/1

5050 8 1 1/4 **Salire (IRE)**[18] 9175 2-8-13 57 JackGarritty 4 27
(Ann Duffield) *midfield: sme hdwy over 3f out: rdn along wl over 2f out: sn wknd* 80/1

0443 9 nk **Blue Havana (IRE)**[18] 9175 2-8-9 53 (v) JasonHart 10 23
(John Quinn) *prom: rdn along over 3f out: sn wknd* 7/1[3]

3660 10 1 1/4 **Raven's Raft (IRE)**[18] 9177 2-9-3 61 (p[1]) AndrewMullen 11 28
(Michael Appleby) *in tch on outer: pushed along 1/2-way: sn rdn and lost pl: bhd fnl 2f* 20/1

4000 11 1/2 **Jaffar**[8] 9345 2-9-2 60 (b) DougieCostello 9 26
(Scott Dixon) *chsd ldrs: rdn along over 3f out: sn drvn and wknd* 33/1

6005 12 25 **Thundercloud**[18] 9175 2-8-10 54 (p[1]) KieranO'Neill 5
(Scott Dixon) *chsd ldrs towards inner: rdn along wl over 3f out: sn outpcd and bhd* 40/1

1m 43.3s (-0.40) **Going Correction** -0.175s/f (Stan) 12 Ran SP% 115.1
Speed ratings (Par 94): **95,92,90,83,82 81,81,80,79,78 78,53**
CSF £89.12 CT £282.61 TOTE £12.50: £2.70, £2.50, £1.40; EX 104.20 Trifecta £424.20.
**Owner** Ross Deacon & Partners **Bred** D R Botterill & E Boumans **Trained** Epsom, Surrey

**FOCUS**
A modest nursery with the winner recording a personal best and the second setting the level.

## 9440 32RED.COM NOVICE AUCTION STKS — 4f 214y(F)

12:45 (12:47) (Class 5) 2-Y-O — £2,911 (£866; £432; £216) Stalls Centre

Form / RPR

4 1 **A Few Good Men**[13] 9266 2-8-7 0 RossaRyan(7) 8 65
(Jose Santos) *racd towards stands' side: chsd ldrs: hdwy 2f out: rdn over 1f out: styd on wl to ld nr fin* 7/1[3]

215 2 shd **Magic Pulse (IRE)**[22] 9122 2-8-13 63 DougieCostello 5 64
(David C Griffiths) *racd centre: cl up: pushed along and carried bdly lft to far rail ent fnl f: sn rdn to ld and edgd rt: drvn: hung rt and hdd nr fin* 7/1[3]

0561 3 2 **Crystal Deauville (FR)**[6] 9387 2-8-5 62 (bt[1]) HarrisonShaw(7) 6 56
(Gay Kelleway) *slt ld centre: pushed along 2f out: rdn and hung bdly lft to far rail ent fnl f: sn hdd: drvn and kpt on same pce* 4/1[2]

0503 4 2 3/4 **Ideal Spirit**[13] 9266 2-8-5 54 ShaneGray 4 39
(Karen Tutty) *chsd ldrs centre: rdn along 2f out: kpt on same pce* 16/1

45 5 1 **Takeonefortheteam**[36] 8915 2-9-1 0 AndrewMullen 2 45
(Daniel Mark Loughnane) *cl up centre: rdn along 2f out: wkng whn n.m.r and swtchd rt ins fnl f* 3/1[1]

0 6 4 **Street Sensation (IRE)**[13] 9266 2-8-13 0 JackGarritty 7 29
(Richard Fahey) *dwlt: green and a outpcd in rr* 12/1

4210 7 nk **Magic Applause (IRE)**[183] 4252 2-9-3 70 (h[1]) FranBerry 1 32
(George Scott) *racd towards far side: prom: rdn along 2f out: sn wknd* 3/1[1]

00 8 1/2 **Argon**[13] 9266 2-9-0 0 (p[1]) LukeMorris 3 27
(Sir Mark Prescott Bt) *sn rdn along and outpcd centre: swtchd lft towards far side after 1f: a bhd* 33/1

59.65s (-0.05) **Going Correction** -0.175s/f (Stan) 8 Ran SP% 111.5
Speed ratings (Par 96): **93,92,89,85,83 77,76,75**
CSF £51.89 TOTE £7.70: £2.10, £1.80, £2.00; EX 46.50 Trifecta £170.80.
**Owner** The Villains **Bred** W H R John And Partners **Trained** Upper Lambourn, Berks

■ Stewards' Enquiry : Harrison Shaw three-day ban: careless riding (Jan 12-14)

**FOCUS**
A modest novice auction event with the runner-up rated in line with earlier form.

## 9441 SUNBETS.CO.UK MAIDEN STKS — 7f 14y(F)

1:15 (1:17) (Class 5) 3-Y-O+ — £2,911 (£866; £432; £216) Stalls Low

Form / RPR

1 **The Great Wall (USA)**[133] 6168 3-9-5 72 AndrewMullen 1 88+
(Michael Appleby) *mde all: qcknd clr wl over 2f out: unchal* 2/5[1]

2 19 **Riverside Bridge (IRE)**[36] 5-9-5 0 StevieDonohoe 4 31+
(Brian Ellison) *s.i.s and bhd: rdn along 1/2-way: hdwy 2f out: styd on to take remote 2nd ins fnl f* 12/1[3]

3 3 **Di's Pride** 4-9-0 0 RobHornby 5 18
(David Bridgwater) *chsd ldrs: hdwy 3f out and sn rdn along: drvn to chse wnr wl over 1f out: kpt on one pce and lost remote 2nd ins fnl f* 33/1

055/ 4 2 1/4 **My Girl Jo (FR)**[891] 4512 5-9-0 46 RobertWinston 3 12
(John Balding) *prom: chsd ldng pair 1/2-way: rdn along 3f out: chsd wnr 2f out: sn drvn and kpt on one pce* 40/1

60 5 1/2 **Fireguard**[10] 9304 4-9-5 0 FranBerry 6 16
(Emma Owen) *a in rr* 66/1

3325 6 15 **Beyond Recall**[13] 9273 3-9-0 69 (b) LukeMorris 7
(Archie Watson) *wnt rt s and rdn along on wd outside: sn cl up: drvn along 3f out: lost pl wl over 1f out and sn eased* 11/4[2]

1m 28.76s (-1.54) **Going Correction** -0.175s/f (Stan) 6 Ran SP% 112.7
Speed ratings (Par 103): **101,79,75,73,72 55**
CSF £6.76 TOTE £1.20: £1.10, £4.50; EX 6.70 Trifecta £44.30.
**Owner** The Horse Watchers **Bred** WinStar Farm LLC **Trained** Oakham, Rutland

**FOCUS**
With the second-favourite struggling this form is worth little, but the winner did it easily.

## 9442 BETWAY STAYER'S H'CAP — 2m 102y(F)

1:50 (1:50) (Class 5) (0-75,75) 3-Y-O+ — £2,911 (£866; £432; £216) Stalls Low

Form / RPR

0044 1 **Serenity Now (IRE)**[22] 8261 9-9-3 64 (p) StevieDonohoe 8 71+
(Brian Ellison) *trckd ldrs: hdwy 4f out: led wl over 2f out: drvn and edgd lft ent fnl f: kpt on wl towards fin* 7/1

6444 2 1 3/4 **Ruler Of The Nile**[14] 9242 5-9-0 64 CallumShepherd(3) 1 68
(Robert Stephens) *trckd ldrs: hdwy 4f out: chsd ldng pair over 2f out: rdn to chse wnr 1 1/2f out: sn drvn and kpt on same pce* 5/1[3]

3306 3 3 1/4 **Deep Resolve (IRE)**[115] 6789 6-9-4 65 BenCurtis 5 65
(Sally Haynes) *hld up in tch: hdwy over 5f out: chsd ldrs 3f out: sn rdn: drvn and kpt on one pce fnl 2f* 6/1

0603 4 7 **Wordiness**[20] 9158 9-9-4 65 FranBerry 2 57
(David Evans) *hld up in tch: hdwy over 4f out: rdn along to chse ldrs 3f out: drvn 2f out: sn one pce* 11/1

4116 5 4 1/2 **Vercingetorix (IRE)**[29] 5438 6-9-7 75 (p) RossaRyan(7) 4 61
(Iain Jardine) *cl up: led over 4f out: rdn along 3f out: sn hdd and drvn: grad wknd fnl 2f* 4/1[2]

2550 6 2 **Katie Gale**[14] 9242 7-9-5 66 AndrewMullen 7 50
(Michael Appleby) *trckd ldng pair: pushed along over 4f out: rdn along over 3f out: sn drvn and btn* 10/1

004 7 3 3/4 **Song Of Love (IRE)**[7] 9369 5-9-12 73 (p) DougieCostello 3 52
(Shaun Harris) *hld up in rr: hdwy over 4f out: rdn along and in tch 3f out: sn drvn and wknd* 20/1

1620 8 47 **Kohinoor Diamond (IRE)**[16] 9208 3-8-11 64 (b) LukeMorris 6
(Sir Mark Prescott Bt) *sn led: pushed along and hdd over 4f out: rdn along over 3f out: sn lost pl and bhd whn eased fnl 2f* 11/4[1]

3m 41.98s (-3.52) **Going Correction** -0.175s/f (Stan)
**WFA** 3 from 5yo+ 6lb 8 Ran SP% 112.3
Speed ratings (Par 103): **101,100,98,95,92 91,89,66**
CSF £40.18 CT £220.88 TOTE £6.00: £1.70, £1.70, £2.00; EX 25.80 Trifecta £173.80.
**Owner** Brian Ellison Racing Club **Bred** Citadel Stud **Trained** Norton, N Yorks

**FOCUS**
A modest staying handicap.

## 9443 BETWAY DASH H'CAP — 4f 214y(F)

2:25 (2:26) (Class 4) (0-80,82) 3-Y-O+ — £4,690 (£1,395; £697; £348) Stalls Centre

Form / RPR

1133 1 **Foolaad**[223] 2840 6-9-12 82 (t) RobertWinston 6 93
(Roy Bowring) *racd towards stands' side: cl up: led 1 1/2f out: rdn and kpt on strly fnl f* 10/1

6460 2 1 3/4 **Brother Tiger**[125] 6411 8-9-7 77 FranBerry 1 81
(David C Griffiths) *racd towards far side: cl up: rdn along 2f out: drvn and kpt on same pce fnl f* 8/1

3362 3 nk **Red Stripes (USA)**[10] 9308 5-8-7 63 oh3 (b) AndrewMullen 7 66
(Lisa Williamson) *chsd ldrs towards stands' side: rdn and hdwy over 1f out: kpt on fnl f* 6/1[3]

3004 4 nk **Crosse Fire**[7] 9366 5-9-2 72 (v) KieranO'Neill 2 74
(Scott Dixon) *cl up: led over 3f out: rdn 2f out: hdd 1 1/2f out: sn drvn and edgd lft: kpt on same pce* 4/1[2]

0161 5 1 **Captain Lars (SAF)**[10] 9305 8-9-5 82 6ex (v) NicolaCurrie(7) 4 80
(Derek Shaw) *trckd ldrs: pushed along over 2f out: rdn wl over 1f out: no imp* 15/8[1]

5106 6 2 1/4 **Piazon**[7] 9366 6-9-4 81 (be) RossaRyan(7) 8 71
(John Butler) *racd towards stands' side: prom: rdn along 2f out: sn edgd lft and wknd* 9/1

6200 7 1 1/4 **Midnight Macchiato (IRE)**[18] 9179 4-9-5 75 TomEaves 5 61
(David Brown) *sn outpcd and a in rr* 25/1

4044 8 1 **Penny Dreadful**[15] 9234 5-8-11 67 (b) LukeMorris 3 49
(Scott Dixon) *narrow ld: hdd over 3f: cl up: rdn along over 2f out: sn drvn and wknd* 10/1

57.6s (-2.10) **Going Correction** -0.175s/f (Stan) 8 Ran SP% 112.2
Speed ratings (Par 105): **109,106,105,105,103 100,98,96**
CSF £82.80 CT £526.34 TOTE £7.10: £1.90, £2.90, £1.90; EX 101.70 Trifecta £615.50.
**Owner** K Nicholls **Bred** Darley **Trained** Edwinstowe, Notts

**FOCUS**
A fair sprint handicap, with the winner back to his best.

## 9444 BETWAY SPRINT CLASSIFIED STKS — 6f 16y(F)

3:00 (3:03) (Class 6) 3-Y-O+ — £2,264 (£673; £336; £168) Stalls Low

Form / RPR

0002 1 **Declamation (IRE)**[28] 9033 7-9-0 50 RobertWinston 3 69
(John Butler) *cl up: led over 4f out: rdn clr over 1f out: readily* 5/2[1]

5-42 2 6 **Clergyman**[261] 1720 5-8-11 53 PhilDennis(3) 1 49
(Rebecca Bastiman) *chsd ldrs on inner: pushed along over 2f out: rdn wl over 1f out: kpt on fnl f* 9/1

3004 3 nk **Scotch Myst**[16] 9216 3-9-0 55 JackGarritty 7 48
(Richard Fahey) *led 1 1/2f: cl up: rdn along over 2f out: drvn over 1f out: kpt on same pce* 3/1[2]

0405 4 nk **Racing Angel (IRE)**[25] 9075 5-9-0 52 AndrewMullen 8 47
(Adrian Nicholls) *in tch: hdwy towards outer over 2f out: rdn to chse ldrs over 1f out: drvn and kpt on same pce fnl f* 12/1

432 5 4 1/2 **Satchville Flyer**[8] 9342 6-9-0 54 FranBerry 6 34
(David Evans) *awkward s and t.k.h early: in tch: pushed along and wd st: sn rdn and n.d* 7/2[3]

6033 6 2 3/4 **Gettin' Lucky**[8] 9344 4-9-0 46 (p) TomEaves 9 25
(John Balding) *cl up: rdn along 3f out: drvn over 2f out: wknd wl over 1f out* 12/1

0036 7 3/4 **Hugie Boy (IRE)**[8] 9347 5-8-9 50 (bt) JamieGormley(5) 4 23
(Scott Dixon) *a towards rr* 12/1

650 8 8 **Dusty Bin**[186] 4162 3-8-9 55 (h[1]) KevinLundie(5) 2
(Roy Bowring) *s.i.s: a bhd* 20/1

1m 15.29s (-1.21) **Going Correction** -0.175s/f (Stan) 8 Ran SP% 113.6
Speed ratings (Par 101): **101,93,92,92,86 82,81,70**
CSF £25.42 TOTE £3.60: £1.50, £2.60, £1.10; EX 27.20 Trifecta £113.60.
**Owner** J Butler **Bred** Darley **Trained** Newmarket, Suffolk

**FOCUS**
A moderate classified sprint, but the winner took it well.

## 9445 BETWAY H'CAP 1m 3f 23y(F)
**3:30** (3:31) (Class 6) (0-60,65) 3-Y-O+ **£2,264** (£673; £336; £168) **Stalls** Low

Form RPR
1624 **1** **Ingleby Spring (IRE)**[16] 9212 5-8-10 **54**............. SebastianWoods(7) 12 63
(Richard Fahey) *trckd ldrs: hdwy over 4f out: chal over 2f out: led wl over 1f out: sn rdn: drvn and edgd rt ins fnl f: kpt on wl towards fin* **13/2**[3]

5412 **2** *2 ½* **Star Ascending (IRE)**[7] 9368 5-8-9 **53**.....................(b) RossaRyan(7) 10 58
(Jennie Candlish) *t.k.h early: in tch: hdwy on outer to trck ldrs after 3f: hdwy 4f out: led 3f out: sn jnd and rdn: hdd wl over 1f out: sn drvn and kpt on same pce u.p fnl f* **11/8**[1]

-003 **3** *4 ½* **Master Of Song**[58] 8258 10-8-9 **46** oh1.........................(p) KieranO'Neill 3 44
(Roy Bowring) *midfield: effrt and n.m.r home turn: hdwy on inner over 2f out: rdn to chse ldng pair over 1f out: kpt on same pce fnl f* **22/1**

4551 **4** *5* **Go On Gal (IRE)**[123] 6524 4-8-13 **57**...........................(p) MillyNaseb(7) 4 47
(Julia Feilden) *prom: effrt to chse ldng pair 3f out: sn rdn along: drvn 2f out: grad wknd* **15/2**

0001 **5** *1 ¼* **Dream Magic (IRE)**[7] 9375 3-9-11 **65** 6ex.................... AndrewMullen 7 54
(Daniel Mark Loughnane) *cl up: led briefly 3f out: sn hdd and rdn: drvn and wknd fnl 2f* **5/2**[2]

0060 **6** *1* **The Lock Master (IRE)**[8] 9346 10-9-11 **62**....................(v) LukeMorris 1 48
(Michael Appleby) *chsd ldrs: rdn along 5f out: plugged on u.p fnl 3f* **20/1**

0-00 **7** *1* **Ambuscade**[43] 8799 4-8-9 **46** oh1.................................. RobHornby 11 31
(Neil Mulholland) *chsd ldrs: rdn along wl over 3f out: sn wknd* **40/1**

6404 **8** *nse* **Monzino (USA)**[8] 9342 9-8-6 **46** oh1................................ PhilDennis(3) 9 31
(Michael Chapman) *towards rr: wd st and rdn over 2f out: n.d* **50/1**

**9** *12* **Mangata (FR)**[30] 3-9-1 **60**............................................ JamieGormley(5) 8 26
(Philip Kirby) *midfield: rdn along 5f out: sn lost pl and bhd* **25/1**

0020 **10** *5* **Pindaric**[31] 8985 3-8-11 **51**.................................................(p) CamHardie 2 9
(Alan Lockwood) *led: rdn along 4f out: hdd over 3f out: sn wknd* **33/1**

6006 **11** *16* **Masterful Act (USA)**[25] 9070 10-9-8 **59**............................. TomEaves 5
(John Balding) *a towards rr: rdn along 5f out: sn outpcd and bhd* **14/1**

2000 **12** *27* **Crakehall Lad (IRE)**[13] 9258 6-8-9 **46** oh1........................(v) JasonHart 6
(Andrew Crook) *a towards rr: rdn along 1/2-way: lost tch and bhd over 3f out* **66/1**

2m 24.6s (-3.40) **Going Correction** -0.175s/f (Stan)
**WFA** 3 from 4yo+ 3lb 12 Ran SP% **124.2**
Speed ratings (Par 101): **105,103,99,96,95 94,93,93,85,81 69,50**
CSF £15.61 CT £202.38 TOTE £7.10: £2.40, £1.10, £5.20; EX 19.80 Trifecta £197.60.
**Owner** Percy Green Racing 3 **Bred** Stephanie Von Schilcher & Gavan Kinch **Trained** Musley Bank, N Yorks

**FOCUS**
A moderate handicap with the winner finding a bit on her recent best.
T/Jkpt: Not won. T/Plt: £81.20 to a £1 stake. Pool: £126,961.23 - 1,140.28 winning units T/Qpdt: £17.30 to a £1 stake. Pool: £14,608.26 - 622.39 winning units **Joe Rowntree**

# 932 DOHA
Friday, December 29
**OFFICIAL GOING: Turf: good**

## 9446a AL RAYYAN STKS (CONDITIONS RACE) (2YO) (TURF) 7f (T)
**3:15** 2-Y-O **£46,341** (£17,886; £8,943; £4,878; £3,252)

RPR
**1** **Tip Two Win**[92] 7546 2-9-2 0.............................................. DavidProbert 4 96
(Roger Teal) *dwlt: scrubbed along early: sn racing keenly in midfield: 5th and drvn to cl 2f out: led ent fnl f: rdn clr*

**2** *4 ½* **Anima Rock (FR)**[150] 5694 2-9-2 0.................................... HarryBentley 3 84
(Jassim Mohammed Ghazali, Qatar)

**3** *1* **Poets Dream (IRE)**[67] 8290 2-9-2 0............................... GeraldAvranche 8 81
(Mohammed Hussain Afroz, Qatar)

**4** *3 ½* **Es'hail (USA)** 2-9-2 0............................................... StephaneLadjadj 10 72
(R Al Jehani, Qatar)

**5** *½* **Shawwal**[176] 4520 2-9-2 0................................................. CarloFiocchi 9 71
(S Ibido, Qatar)

**6** *nk* **Black Orange**[233] 2522 2-9-2 0........................................ FalehBughanaim 5 70
(Debbie Mountain, Qatar)

**7** *¾* **Al Modajal (FR)**[75] 2-9-2 0...............................(b) PierantonioConvertino 2 68
(Jassim Mohammed Ghazali, Qatar)

**8** *¾* **Kynoch (USA)** 2-9-2 0................................................ TheoBachelot 11 66
(J Smart, Qatar)

**9** *2 ¾* **Berkeley Square (IRE)**[110] 6975 2-9-2 0........................ TomLukasek 13 58
(H Al Ramzani, Qatar)

**10** *2 ¼* **Albassel** 2-9-2 0............................................... Jean-BaptisteHamel 6 52
(M Al Attiya, Qatar)

**11** *3* **Tamboureen (IRE)**[175] 4588 2-9-2 0.....................(bt) J-PGuillambert 12 44
(Mohammed Jassim Ghazali, Qatar)

**12** *2 ¼* **Rockin Fella (IRE)**[179] 4427 2-9-2 0............................ EduardoPedroza 7 38
(H Al Ramzani, Qatar)

**13** *11* **Dawn Trader** 2-9-2 0................................................. DarrenWilliams 1 8
(A Al Kathiri, Qatar)

1m 25.41s 13 Ran
**Owner** Mrs Anne Cowley **Bred** Mrs Anne Cowley **Trained** Great Shefford, Berks

9447-9451a (Foreign Racing) - See Raceform Interactive

# 9430 LINGFIELD (L-H)
Saturday, December 30
**OFFICIAL GOING: Polytrack: standard**
Wind: Strong across into the stands'

## 9452 32RED.COM NURSERY H'CAP 6f 1y(P)
**11:30** (11:30) (Class 4) (0-85,83) 2-Y-O **£3,946** (£1,174; £586; £293) **Stalls** Low

Form RPR
232 **1** **City Gent**[31] 8989 2-9-0 **76**...........................................(b[1]) OisinMurphy 1 85
(Ralph Beckett) *trckd ldrs: swtchd rt and chsd ldr over 1f out: led ins fnl f: rdn clr* **2/1**[1]

1115 **2** *3 ¾* **Joegogo (IRE)**[21] 9156 2-9-7 **83**........................................... FranBerry 3 80
(David Evans) *led: racd keenly: rdn over 1f out: edgd rt: hdd and no ex ins fnl f* **11/4**[2]

3152 **3** *1 ¾* **Montague (IRE)**[9] 9345 2-9-4 **80**................................ DougieCostello 5 71
(Jamie Osborne) *hld up in tch: racd keenly: jnd ldr over 3f out tl rdn wl over 1f out: styd on same pce fnl f* **9/2**

0513 **4** *½* **Mossketeer**[29] 9021 2-8-8 **70**...................................... JosephineGordon 2 60
(John Best) *prom: sn lost pl: pushed along over 4f out: sn outpcd: r.o ins fnl f* **7/2**[3]

5025 **5** *1 ¼* **Zabaletaswansong (GER)**[32] 8982 2-8-9 **71**..........(p[1]) TomMarquand 4 57
(Richard Hannon) *chsd ldr tl wnt upsides over 3f out: ev ch 2f out: sn rdn: nt clr run over 1f out: wknd ins fnl f* **10/1**

1m 11.26s (-0.64) **Going Correction** -0.025s/f (Stan) 5 Ran SP% **109.5**
Speed ratings (Par 98): **103,98,95,95,93**
CSF £7.65 TOTE £2.40: £1.70, £1.50; EX 7.20 Trifecta £12.20.
**Owner** J C Smith **Bred** Littleton Stud **Trained** Kimpton, Hants

**FOCUS**
An ordinary-looking nursery for the grade.

## 9453 BETWAY SPRINT H'CAP 6f 1y(P)
**12:00** (Class 3) (0-95,97) 3-Y-O+ **£7,246** (£2,168; £1,084; £542; £270) **Stalls** Low

Form RPR
1-10 **1** **Dubai One (IRE)**[260] 1774 3-9-5 **92**.................................. OisinMurphy 1 102+
(Saeed bin Suroor) *hld up: hdwy over 1f out: shkn up to ld ins fnl f: r.o* **7/2**[2]

5006 **2** *½* **Kasbah (IRE)**[18] 9187 5-9-3 **90**........................................... JackMitchell 8 98
(Amanda Perrett) *hld up: hdwy over 1f out: rdn and ev ch ins fnl f: styd on* **7/1**

0035 **3** *½* **Reckless Endeavour (IRE)**[14] 9264 4-9-10 **97**.......... DougieCostello 2 103
(Jamie Osborne) *hld up: shkn up and hdwy 1f out: nt clr run sn after: rdn and r.o wl towards fin: nt rch ldrs* **3/1**[1]

0421 **4** *1* **Tropics (USA)**[14] 9269 9-9-2 **92**.....................................(h) JackDuern(3) 6 95
(Dean Ivory) *led over 3f: remained w ldr: rdn and ev ch ins fnl f: no ex towards fin* **4/1**[3]

5034 **5** *½* **Pearl Spectre (USA)**[15] 9241 6-8-7 **87**......................... NicolaCurrie(7) 5 88
(Phil McEntee) *pushed along to chse ldrs: rdn over 1f out: no ex wl ins fnl f* **5/1**

03-0 **6** *½* **Leo Minor (USA)**[31] 8991 3-9-3 **90**..................................... FranBerry 10 90
(Robert Cowell) *trckd ldrs: shkn up: hung lft and flashed tail over 1f out: no ex ins fnl f* **40/1**

6600 **7** *½* **Zac Brown (IRE)**[18] 9187 6-9-7 **94**...............................(t) DanielMuscutt 7 92
(Charlie Wallis) *racd keenly: w ldr tl led over 2f out: rdn: hdd and no ex ins fnl f* **50/1**

6000 **8** *4* **Doc Sportello (IRE)**[8] 9373 5-9-3 **90**........................(p) RobertWinston 3 75
(Tony Carroll) *hmpd sn after s: hld up: shkn up over 1f out: nvr on terms* **18/1**

0300 **9** *¾* **Stellarta**[31] 8991 6-9-1 **88**.............................................. TomMarquand 4 71
(Michael Blanshard) *sn pushed along in rr: rdn over 2f out: n.d* **12/1**

0406 **10** *33* **Turanga Leela**[14] 9269 3-8-4 **80** oh2............................(v) GeorgiaCox(3) 9
(Ian Williams) *dwlt: outpcd* **66/1**

1m 10.32s (-1.58) **Going Correction** -0.025s/f (Stan) 10 Ran SP% **115.2**
Speed ratings (Par 107): **109,108,107,106,105 105,104,99,98,54**
CSF £27.68 CT £83.42 TOTE £3.30: £1.20, £2.30, £1.30; EX 23.50 Trifecta £94.00.
**Owner** Godolphin **Bred** Darley **Trained** Newmarket, Suffolk

**FOCUS**
A decent, well-run sprint handicap. The winner continued her progress, well on top of a couple of nicely treated rivals.

## 9454 PLAY JACKPOT GAMES AT SUNBETS.CO.UK/VEGAS H'CAP 7f 1y(P)
**12:35** (12:36) (Class 6) (0-55,55) 3-Y-O+ **£2,264** (£673; £336; £168) **Stalls** Low

Form RPR
3005 **1** **Locommotion**[35] 8948 5-9-2 **50**........................................... LukeMorris 7 57
(Matthew Salaman) *a.p: chsd ldr over 5f out: shkn up over 1f out: styd on to ld post* **9/1**

0340 **2** *nse* **Soaring Spirits (IRE)**[22] 9142 7-9-7 **55**...................(p) RobertWinston 9 62
(Dean Ivory) *sn led: rdn over 1f out: hdd post* **12/1**

4006 **3** *1 ½* **Critical Thinking (IRE)**[8] 9376 3-9-6 **54**.................. StevieDonohoe 12 57+
(David Loughnane) *hld up: pushed along and hdwy over 1f out: r.o to go 3rd wl ins fnl f: nt rch ldrs* **5/1**[2]

2600 **4** *1 ¼* **Tigerfish (IRE)**[35] 8948 3-9-2 **50**....................................(p) HollieDoyle 2 50
(William Stone) *hld up in tch: rdn over 1f out: styd on same pce ins fnl f* **7/1**

0564 **5** *shd* **D'Waterside**[17] 9217 3-9-5 **53**...................................(b) JosephineGordon 3 52
(David Loughnane) *trckd ldrs: rdn over 1f out: styd on same pce ins fnl f* **7/2**[1]

0604 **6** *½* **Rapid Rise (IRE)**[14] 9268 3-8-12 **46**...........................(v) TomMarquand 1 44
(Milton Bradley) *hld up: hdwy over 1f out: sn rdn: styd on same pce ins fnl f* **12/1**

0000 **7** *1 ¼* **Mad Rose (IRE)**[32] 8980 3-9-6 **54**..................................(t[1]) DanielMuscutt 8 49
(Denis Quinn) *hmpd sn after s: hld up: hdwy over 1f out: no imp ins fnl f* **50/1**

2020 **8** *3 ½* **Binky Blue (IRE)**[28] 9052 5-9-5 **53**.....................................(h) ShaneKelly 4 38
(Daniel Mark Loughnane) *hld up: rdn over 1f out: n.d* **16/1**

5000 **9** *½* **Aye Aye Skipper (IRE)**[17] 9213 7-8-13 **50**.......(b) AdamMcNamara(3) 14 34
(Ken Cunningham-Brown) *s.s: in rr: sme hdwy over 1f out: n.d* **33/1**

500 **10** *nk* **Sir Jamie**[17] 9218 4-8-12 **46** oh1................................(p) GeorgeDowning 5 29
(Tony Carroll) *hld up: rdn over 1f out: a in rr* **22/1**

0055 **11** *2 ½* **Brother In Arms (IRE)**[17] 9203 3-9-7 **55**............................ AdamKirby 13 31
(Tony Carroll) *hld up: shkn up over 2f out: nvr on terms* **11/1**

0600 **12** *nse* **Fairy Mist (IRE)**[23] 9127 10-8-12 **46** oh1..................(b) WilliamCarson 10 22
(John Bridger) *hmpd s: hld up: pushed along over 2f out: n.d* **66/1**

0006 **13** *½* **Three's A Crowd (IRE)**[14] 9268 3-8-7 **46** oh1............(b) JaneElliott(5) 11 21
(Ed de Giles) *sn pushed along in rr and nvr gng* **33/1**

0600 **14** *hd* **Peter Stuyvesant (IRE)**[28] 9056 3-9-4 **52**....................(v[1]) OisinMurphy 6 26
(Denis Coakley) *racd keenly: prom: rdn over 2f out: wknd over 1f out* **13/2**[3]

1m 24.77s (-0.03) **Going Correction** -0.025s/f (Stan) 14 Ran SP% **118.0**
Speed ratings (Par 101): **99,98,97,95,95 95,93,89,89,88 85,85,85,85**
CSF £105.17 CT £605.33 TOTE £9.00: £3.50, £4.10, £2.20; EX 139.10 Trifecta £1418.60.
**Owner** Susannah Green & Debbie Hughes **Bred** Gracelands Stud **Trained** Tonyrefail, Rhondda Cynon Taff

**FOCUS**
The first five finishers were positioned in the first six after about a couple of furlongs. The winner has been rated to form.

## 9455 BETWAY MAIDEN STKS 1m 2f (P)
1:10 (1:11) (Class 5) 3-Y-O+ £2,911 (£866; £432; £216) Stalls Low

Form RPR
3354 1 **Colourful Career (USA)**[13] 9281 3-9-5 70 AdamKirby 3 71
(Ed Dunlop) *mde all: shkn up and qcknd over 2f out: rdn clr over 1f out: hung rt u.p ins fnl f: styd on* 11/4[1]
5203 2 ¾ **Relevant (IRE)**[9] 9338 3-8-11 60 (t) AaronJones(3) 1 64
(Stuart Williams) *chsd ldrs: shkn up over 2f out: rdn and r.o to go 2nd wl ins fnl f: nt rch wnr* 9/2[3]
2032 3 1 ¼ **Line Of Beauty**[13] 9276 3-9-0 66 RobertHavlin 6 62
(Simon Crisford) *sn chsng wnr: lost 2nd over 5f out: chsd wnr again over 3f out: rdn over 1f out: styd on same pce ins fnl f* 10/3[2]
4 2 ½ **Barrsbrook**[23] 3-9-5 0 ShaneKelly 2 62
(Gary Moore) *hld up in tch: pushed along and outpcd over 2f out: rallied over 1f out: styd on* 33/1
5P6 5 2 **I'm Right On Time**[24] 9088 3-9-2 0 JackDuern(3) 5 58
(Dean Ivory) *hld up in tch: lost grnd 1/2-way: r.o ins fnl f* 15/2
6 nk **Burrumbeet (IRE)** 3-9-5 0 (b[1]) LiamKeniry 12 57
(Ed Walker) *s.i.s: hld up: pushed along over 2f out: r.o ins fnl f: nvr nrr* 6/1
0 7 ½ **Hail Cloud (IRE)**[17] 9202 3-9-2 0 MarcMonaghan(3) 11 56
(Marco Botti) *prom: rdn over 3f out: wknd over 1f out* 20/1
8 8 **Faheem**[30] 6-9-7 0 CharlesBishop 9 39
(Lydia Richards) *s.i.s: hld up: rdn over 2f out: n.d* 20/1
4 9 ½ **Shaella (IRE)**[16] 9235 3-8-11 0 CharlieBennett(3) 10 34
(Jane Chapple-Hyam) *hld up: hdwy 7f out: chsd wnr over 5f out tl rdn over 3f out: wknd over 2f out* 14/1
0 10 5 **Catherinethegrace (IRE)**[17] 9202 3-9-0 0 KieranO'Neill 8 24
(Jimmy Fox) *s.s: a bhd* 80/1
0 11 1 ½ **Napoleon (IRE)**[24] 9088 4-9-7 0 FranBerry 4 25
(Laura Mongan) *hld up: rdn and wknd over 3f out* 25/1

2m 6.39s (-0.21) **Going Correction** -0.025s/f (Stan)
**WFA** 3 from 4yo+ 2lb 11 Ran SP% **118.2**
Speed ratings (Par 103): **99,98,97,95,93 93,93,86,86,82 81**
CSF £14.26 TOTE £3.60: £1.50, £1.60, £1.40; EX 15.80 Trifecta £40.80.
**Owner** Melbourne 10 Racing **Bred** Three Chimneys Farm Llc **Trained** Newmarket, Suffolk

**FOCUS**
A weak, muddling maiden with the first five finishers in the first six positions after a couple of furlongs or so, with the 1-2-3 sat 1-3-2. That was until an also-ran joined in the party down the back straight, before fading. The winner didn't need to improve.

## 9456 PLAY STARBURST SLOT AT SUNBETS.CO.UK/VEGAS H'CAP (DIV I) 1m 1y(P)
1:45 (1:45) (Class 6) (0-60,60) 3-Y-O+ £2,264 (£673; £336; £168) Stalls High

Form RPR
621 1 **Kafeel (USA)**[67] 8307 6-9-5 58 (b) AdamKirby 6 67+
(Gary Moore) *chsd ldrs: shkn up to ld over 1f out: hrd rdn ins fnl f: styd on* 11/8[1]
1605 2 ¾ **Rakematiz**[17] 9211 3-9-3 60 CallumShepherd(3) 11 67
(Brett Johnson) *racd keenly and sn prom: carried rt turning for home: sn rdn: r.o* 8/1
2040 3 nk **Spare Parts (IRE)**[135] 6101 3-8-2 49 NicolaCurrie(7) 5 55
(Phil McEntee) *led: rdn and hdd over 1f out: styd on* 20/1
3001 4 4 **Mr Mac**[17] 9203 3-9-6 60 (t) TomMarquand 1 57
(Peter Hedger) *hld up: rdn over 1f out: styd on fnl f: nt rch ldrs* 7/2[2]
3050 5 ½ **With Approval (IRE)**[37] 8908 5-9-3 56 (p) FranBerry 2 53
(Laura Mongan) *hld up: hdwy over 1f out: sn rdn: edgd rt and styd on same pce ins fnl f* 16/1
5003 6 ¾ **Gracious George (IRE)**[37] 8908 7-9-3 56 KieranO'Neill 3 51
(Jimmy Fox) *hld up: rdn over 1f out: styd on ins fnl f: nvr nrr* 11/2[3]
0000 7 nk **Kachess**[17] 9203 3-9-0 54 JosephineGordon 8 47
(David Loughnane) *awkward leaving stalls: racd keenly in 2nd pl: ev ch 2f out: sn rdn and edgd rt: wknd ins fnl f* 40/1
6000 8 1 ¼ **Rising Sunshine (IRE)**[74] 8134 4-8-7 46 oh1 (t[1]) LukeMorris 10 37
(Milton Bradley) *hld up in tch: rdn over 1f out: edgd lft and wknd ins fnl f* 40/1
6600 9 1 ¾ **Runaiocht (IRE)**[17] 9212 7-9-1 54 LiamKeniry 7 41
(Paul Burgoyne) *hld up: rdn over 1f out: n.d* 12/1
6000 10 2 ¼ **Palace Moon**[31] 8994 12-8-7 46 oh1 (t) KierenFox 4 28
(Michael Attwater) *hld up: rdn over 1f out: a in rr* 25/1

1m 38.25s (0.05) **Going Correction** -0.025s/f (Stan)
**WFA** 3 from 4yo+ 1lb 10 Ran SP% **117.9**
Speed ratings (Par 101): **98,97,96,92,92 91,91,90,88,86**
CSF £12.94 CT £158.26 TOTE £2.10: £1.10, £2.70, £5.30; EX 15.60 Trifecta £180.80.
**Owner** K Johnson & K Jessup **Bred** Shadwell Farm LLC **Trained** Lower Beeding, W Sussex

**FOCUS**
Few got into this moderate handicap.

## 9457 PLAY STARBURST SLOT AT SUNBETS.CO.UK/VEGAS H'CAP (DIV II) 1m 1y(P)
2:20 (2:21) (Class 6) (0-60,60) 3-Y-O+ £2,264 (£673; £336; £168) Stalls High

Form RPR
4050 1 **Luna Magic**[44] 8801 3-9-6 60 (h) SimonPearce 6 65
(Lydia Pearce) *s.i.s: hld up: hdwy u.p over 2f out: r.o to ld wl ins fnl f* 16/1
0063 2 1 ¼ **Living Leader**[17] 9218 8-8-11 50 LukeMorris 9 53
(Grace Harris) *a.p: chsd ldr 3f out: rdn to ld over 1f out: hdd wl ins fnl f* 11/2[3]
0605 3 hd **Chelwood Gate (IRE)**[17] 9219 7-9-4 57 (v) JosephineGordon 8 60
(Conor Dore) *mid-div: hdwy over 2f out: swtchd rt over 1f out: rdn and ev ch wl ins fnl f: styd on same pce* 7/2[1]
2256 4 nse **Baby Gal**[124] 6511 3-9-0 57 CharlieBennett(3) 4 58
(Jim Boyle) *hld up: hdwy and swtchd lft over 1f out: kpt on* 11/2[3]
00U0 5 ½ **Expectation (IRE)**[17] 9211 3-9-0 54 RobHornby 7 54
(Michael Blanshard) *hld up: hdwy over 1f out: nt rch ldrs* 10/1
303 6 1 **Bloodsweatandtears**[17] 9213 9-9-6 59 KierenFox 2 58
(William Knight) *mid-div: hdwy 2f out: sn rdn: no ex ins fnl f* 5/1[2]
0060 7 2 ¾ **Spirit Of Gondree (IRE)**[74] 8133 9-8-2 46 oh1 (v[1]) WilliamCox(5) 3 39
(Milton Bradley) *chsd ldr 1f: remained handy: rdn over 1f out: wknd ins fnl f* 16/1
-245 8 1 ¾ **Amenta (IRE)**[42] 8842 3-9-5 59 (t) JoeyHaynes 5 47
(John Berry) *hld up: rdn over 2f out: nvr on terms* 12/1
60 9 2 ½ **Evanescent (IRE)**[17] 9219 8-9-2 55 RobertWinston 1 38
(Tony Carroll) *led: clr 1/2-way tl rdn over 2f out: hdd over 1f out: wknd ins fnl f* 10/1
000 10 7 **Leonardo (GER)**[88] 7705 5-8-1 47 NicolaCurrie(7) 10 14
(Shaun Lycett) *chsd ldr 7f out tl 3f out: wknd over 1f out* 14/1

1m 37.7s (-0.50) **Going Correction** -0.025s/f (Stan)
**WFA** 3 from 5yo+ 1lb 10 Ran SP% **114.0**
Speed ratings (Par 101): **101,99,99,99,99 98,95,93,91,84**
CSF £99.33 CT £383.06 TOTE £17.10: £4.50, £1.70, £1.50; EX 104.70 Trifecta £466.60.
**Owner** Lady Green **Bred** Lady Jennifer Green **Trained** Newmarket, Suffolk

**FOCUS**
The second leg of a moderate handicap. Sound if limited form.

## 9458 BETWAY CASINO H'CAP 1m 4f (P)
2:55 (2:55) (Class 4) (0-85,87) 3-Y-O+ £4,787 (£1,424; £711; £355) Stalls Low

Form RPR
3330 1 **Lexington Law (IRE)**[44] 6273 4-9-4 79 (p) TomMarquand 7 90
(Alan King) *hld up: hdwy and edgd lft over 1f out: rdn and r.o to ld towards fin* 14/1
122 2 ½ **Zubayr (IRE)**[21] 5924 5-9-6 86 MeganNicholls(5) 12 96
(Paul Nicholls) *s.i.s: sn hld up in tch: shkn up over 2f out: rdn to ld ins fnl f: hdd towards fin* 13/2
2425 3 2 ¾ **Cape Peninsular**[39] 8880 4-9-12 87 OisinMurphy 3 93
(James Tate) *chsd ldr 2f: remained handy: rdn and ev ch ins fnl f: edgd lft and styd on same pce* 7/2[1]
0032 4 2 ¾ **Every Chance (IRE)**[11] 9306 4-9-8 83 (t) DougieCostello 10 84
(Jamie Osborne) *chsd ldrs: rdn and ev ch over 1f out: no ex ins fnl f* 16/1
0004 5 ¾ **Elysian Fields (GR)**[7] 9390 6-9-10 85 (p) JackMitchell 11 85
(Amanda Perrett) *prom: chsd ldr 10f out tl led over 2f out: rdn over 1f out: hdd ins fnl f: wknd towards fin* 12/1
0044 6 ¾ **Top Beak (IRE)**[17] 9208 4-8-10 71 (t) RobertHavlin 5 70
(Michael Attwater) *hld up: hdwy: nt clr run and swtchd lft over 1f out: no imp ins fnl f* 11/2[3]
0603 7 2 **Barye**[24] 9112 6-9-10 85 (p) ShaneKelly 8 81
(Richard Hughes) *hld up: hdwy 2f out: sn rdn: hung lft and wknd ins fnl f* 5/1[2]
/6-6 8 ½ **East Indies**[46] 6515 4-9-7 82 AdamKirby 4 77
(Gary Moore) *s.i.s: hld up: pushed along over 2f out: nvr on terms* 11/1
-050 9 ½ **Argus (IRE)**[17] 9205 5-9-5 80 LiamKeniry 6 74
(Alexandra Dunn) *hld up: rdn over 1f out: n.d* 80/1
0100 10 shd **Blaze Of Hearts (IRE)**[17] 9206 4-8-12 76 JackDuern(3) 9 70
(Dean Ivory) *hld up: hdwy 4f out: rdn over 1f out: wknd fnl f* 20/1
5000 11 ½ **Langlauf (USA)**[38] 8893 4-9-7 82 (p) RobertWinston 1 75
(Rod Millman) *hld up: shkn up over 2f out: n.d* 33/1
1104 12 2 ¾ **Ourmullion**[22] 9140 3-9-0 79 (p) JosephineGordon 2 69
(John Best) *led over 9f: wknd fnl f* 6/1

2m 29.25s (-3.75) **Going Correction** -0.025s/f (Stan)
**WFA** 3 from 4yo+ 4lb 12 Ran SP% **119.4**
Speed ratings (Par 105): **111,110,108,107,106 106,104,104,104,103 103,101**
CSF £101.53 CT £397.31 TOTE £15.80: £3.90, £2.10, £1.60; EX 135.70 Trifecta £485.40.
**Owner** Middleham Park Racing XXXIX **Bred** Mary Kinsella & Brian O'Connor **Trained** Barbury Castle, Wilts

**FOCUS**
A fair handicap, although lacking in unexposed types.

## 9459 BETWAY H'CAP 1m 2f (P)
3:30 (3:31) (Class 6) (0-65,65) 3-Y-O+ £2,264 (£673; £336; £168) Stalls Low

Form RPR
1420 1 **Ban Shoof**[81] 7917 4-9-7 65 (b) RobertWinston 14 71
(Gary Moore) *hdwy to go prom over 7f out: shkn up over 1f out: rdn and r.o to ld nr fin* 6/1
3403 2 nk **Unit Of Assessment (IRE)**[17] 9211 3-9-5 65 (vt) AdamKirby 9 70
(William Knight) *led after 1f: sn hdd: chsd ldr tl over 6f out: remained handy: rdn over 1f out: r.o to ld wl ins fnl f: hdd nr fin* 7/2[1]
2306 3 hd **Zephyros (GER)**[115] 6807 6-8-11 62 PoppyBridgwater(7) 3 66
(David Bridgwater) *hld up: hdwy over 1f out: r.o wl* 16/1
2106 4 shd **Pink Ribbon (IRE)**[16] 9236 5-9-6 64 LukeMorris 7 68
(Sylvester Kirk) *chsd ldrs: wnt 2nd over 6f out: rdn over 1f out: ev ch ins fnl f: styd on* 10/1
6610 5 ½ **Estibdaad (IRE)**[17] 9211 7-8-11 58 (t) CallumShepherd(3) 10 61
(Paddy Butler) *chsd ldrs: led over 8f out: rdn over 1f out: hdd u.p wl ins fnl f* 25/1
0033 6 ½ **Attain**[17] 9212 8-8-9 60 NicolaCurrie(7) 5 62
(Archie Watson) *prom: lost pl over 6f out: hdwy 2f out: sn rdn: r.o* 4/1[2]
1430 7 ¾ **Beepeecee**[12] 9295 3-9-5 65 (b) ShaneKelly 4 66+
(Richard Hughes) *hld up: hdwy over 3f out: running on whn nt clr run wl ins fnl f: nvr able to chal* 5/1[3]
5515 8 1 ¾ **Zoffany Bay (IRE)**[8] 9376 3-9-3 63 (p) KieranO'Neill 11 60
(George Peckham) *hld up: r.o u.p ins fnl f: nvr nrr* 10/1
600 9 ¾ **Udogo**[14] 9270 6-9-4 62 MartinDwyer 6 58
(Brendan Powell) *hld up: rdn over 2f out: r.o ins fnl f: nvr on terms* 25/1
135 10 hd **Hallingham**[39] 6280 7-9-1 59 HollieDoyle 8 54
(Ken Cunningham-Brown) *s.i.s: hld up: styd on towards fin* 14/1
42/0 11 4 **Diamond Reflection (IRE)**[17] 9209 5-9-7 65 (t) LiamKeniry 1 52
(Alexandra Dunn) *s.i.s: hld up: n.d* 66/1
-430 12 73 **Zulu**[15] 9243 3-9-2 62 OisinMurphy 2
(Rod Millman) *racd keenly: led 1f: chsd ldrs: hung lft fnl 6f: eased fnl 3f* 14/1

2m 8.46s (1.86) **Going Correction** -0.025s/f (Stan)
**WFA** 3 from 4yo+ 2lb 12 Ran SP% **119.8**
Speed ratings (Par 101): **91,90,90,90,90 89,89,87,87,86 83,25**
CSF £27.08 CT £327.43 TOTE £6.70: £2.40, £1.70, £4.50; EX 34.60 Trifecta £456.00.
**Owner** Tommy Ware & Bob Pettett **Bred** Lady Legard **Trained** Lower Beeding, W Sussex
■ Stewards' Enquiry : Callum Shepherd six-day ban: misuse of whip (Jan 13-18)
Robert Winston two-day ban: used whip above permitted level (Jan 15th-16th)

**FOCUS**
A bunched finish to this moderate handicap. The front-running 5th has been rated to his recent best.
T/Plt: £26.60 to a £1 stake. Pool: £79,122.48 - 2,170.50 winning units T/Qpdt: £12.50 to a £1 stake. Pool: £8,801.19 - 520.97 winning units **Colin Roberts**

9460 - 9463a (Foreign Racing) - See Raceform Interactive

# [9452]LINGFIELD (L-H)

Sunday, December 31

**OFFICIAL GOING: Polytrack: standard**

Wind: Strong, across, half behind from race 3 Weather: Overcast, rain from after race 3

## 9464 PLAY JACKPOT GAMES AT SUNBETS.CO.UK/VEGAS H'CAP 1m 1y(P)

**11:40** (11:41) (Class 5) (0-75,76) 3-Y-O **£3,881** (£1,155; £577; £288) **Stalls** High

Form RPR

3215 **1** **Shadow Warrior**[176] 4632 3-9-5 **73**.................................. AdamKirby 4 80
(Paul D'Arcy) *taken down early: hld up in tch in midfield: clsd to chse ldrs over 2f out: swtchd rt and effrt over 1f out: r.o wl u.p ins fnl f to ld 50yds out: sn in command* **8/1**

5100 **2** 1 **Dark Magic**[30] 9020 3-9-4 **75**.......................................... JackDuern(3) 11 80
(Dean Ivory) *hdwy to join ldr after 1f: shkn up wl over 1f out: sn rdn to ld over 1f out: hdd and kpt on same pce ins fnl f* **20/1**

1003 **3** ½ **Nick Vedder**[184] 4304 3-9-5 **73**.................................. DavidProbert 6 77
(Michael Wigham) *hld up in tch in midfield: effrt ent fnl 2f: hdwy u.p 1f out: nt clr run and swtchd rt ins fnl f: r.o wl to snatch 3rd last strides* **4/1**[2]

0050 **4** hd **Espresso Freddo (IRE)**[15] 9271 3-9-8 **76**........................(p) LukeMorris 1 79
(Robert Stephens) *broke wl: sn restrained to trck ldrs: effrt to chal on inner over 1f out: drvn to ld ins fnl f: hdd and no ex 50yds out: lost 2 pls nr fin* **10/1**

1213 **5** ¾ **Mach One**[12] 9303 3-9-8 **76**.........................................(b) EdwardGreatrex 7 78
(Archie Watson) *led: rdn ent fnl 2f: hdd over 1f out and no ex u.p: kpt on same pce ins fnl f* **7/2**[1]

0662 **6** ¾ **Spirit Of Sarwan (IRE)**[25] 9093 3-8-12 **73**.......................... MillyNaseb(7) 5 73
(Julia Feilden) *s.i.s: hld up in tch in rr: effrt and hdwy on inner over 1f out: kpt on ins fnl f: nvr threatened ldrs* **9/1**

452 **7** 1 ½ **Groundfrost (IRE)**[11] 9316 3-9-7 **75**............................ StevieDonohoe 2 71
(John James Feane, Ire) *chsd ldrs: rdn over 2f out: unable qck u.p over 1f out: wknd ins fnl f* **7/1**[3]

1124 **8** ¾ **Enigmatic (IRE)**[17] 9236 3-9-6 **74**............................... DougieCostello 10 69
(Jamie Osborne) *s.i.s: sn rcvrd and in midfield on outer: clsd to chse ldrs 5f out: lost pl bnd 2f out: kpt on same pce and no threat to ldrs after* **7/1**[3]

322 **9** shd **Ladies First**[12] 9304 3-8-10 **64**........................................ CamHardie 8 59
(Michael Easterby) *in tch in midfield: lost pl over 2f out: swtchd lft and no imp over 1f out: kpt on same pce* **25/1**

1 **10** 9 **La Sioux (IRE)**[123] 6568 3-8-11 **65**........................................ FranBerry 9 39
(Richard Fahey) *s.i.s: nvr travelling wl in rr: lost tch over 1f out* **15/2**

1m 37.26s (-0.94) **Going Correction** -0.05s/f (Stan) **10** Ran SP% **117.8**

Speed ratings (Par 102): **102,101,100,100,99 98,97,96,96,87**

CSF £154.96 CT £759.33 TOTE £7.40: £3.40, £5.90, £2.10; EX 205.20 Trifecta £1502.20.

**Owner** Mrs Jan Harris & Mrs M Doyle **Bred** Mrs L H Field **Trained** Newmarket, Suffolk

**FOCUS**

A fair handicap.

## 9465 32RED CASINO NOVICE MEDIAN AUCTION STKS 7f 1y(P)

**12:10** (12:11) (Class 6) 2-Y-O **£3,234** (£962; £481; £240) **Stalls** Low

Form RPR

35 **1** **Furzig**[38] 8916 2-9-2 0.............................................. TonyHamilton 3 74+
(Richard Fahey) *hld up wl in tch in midfield: pushed along and clsd to chse ldrs ent fnl 2f: swtchd rt and chsd ldr wl over 1f out: r.o to ld ins fnl f: sn rdn clr* **7/2**[2]

0 **2** 1 ¼ **Kath's Lustre**[132] 6272 2-8-11 0........................................ ShaneKelly 2 65
(Richard Hughes) *hld up in tch towards rr: clsd and nt clrest of runs jst over 2f out: swtchd rt over 1f out: hdwy 1f out: r.o wl to chse wnr wl ins fnl f: nvr getting to wnr* **16/1**

6403 **3** 1 ¼ **Jeopardy John**[18] 9199 2-9-2 69........................................ KierenFox 10 67
(Michael Attwater) *led: rdn ent fnl 2f: hdd and no ex ins fnl f: kpt on same pce and lost 2nd wl ins fnl f* **6/1**[3]

**4** nse **General Jack (IRE)** 2-9-2 0.............................................. CharlesBishop 4 67+
(Eve Johnson Houghton) *t.k.h: hld up in tch towards rr: hdwy over 1f out: rdn and kpt on wl ins fnl f* **2/1**[1]

3 **5** ½ **Precious Silk (IRE)**[17] 9231 2-8-11 0................................... OscarPereira 6 61
(Jose Santos) *t.k.h: trckd ldrs: pressed ldng pair and rdn over 1f out: unable qck and kpt on same pce ins fnl f* **10/1**

03 **6** 3 **Kachumba**[18] 9198 2-8-11 0................................................ LukeMorris 5 52
(Rae Guest) *hld up in tch in rr: nt clr run and swtchd lft over 1f out: sn hung lft and kpt on ins fnl f: nvr trbld ldrs* **7/1**

65 **7** 1 ¾ **Sea Ess Seas (IRE)**[11] 9310 2-9-2 0...........................(t) DougieCostello 8 53
(Jamie Osborne) *stdd s: t.k.h: hld up in tch in midfield: effrt over 1f out: kpt on same pce: nvr threatened ldrs* **16/1**

4 **8** 1 ¼ **Renny's Lady (IRE)**[11] 9320 2-8-11 0.................................... FranBerry 9 44
(David Evans) *chsd ldrs on outer: 3rd and rdn 2f out: sn carried rt and lost pl bnd wl over 1f out: wknd ins fnl f* **8/1**

0 **9** 1 ¼ **French Cricket (FR)**[18] 9200 2-9-2 0.................................. LiamKeniry 7 46
(George Baker) *chsd ldr tl drifted rt and lost pl bnd wl over 1f out: wknd ins fnl f* **66/1**

00 **10** 19 **Matilda Grace (IRE)**[26] 9080 2-8-11 0.............................. RyanPowell 11
(Lisa Williamson) *s.i.s: rcvrd and in tch in midfield on outer after 2f: rdn over 3f out: lost pl and bhd 2f out: sn wknd* **100/1**

1m 24.91s (0.11) **Going Correction** -0.05s/f (Stan) **10** Ran SP% **116.8**

Speed ratings (Par 94): **97,95,94,94,93 90,88,86,85,63**

CSF £58.18 TOTE £4.10: £1.40, £4.20, £2.30; EX 56.30 Trifecta £368.30.

**Owner** Mr & Mrs P Ashton **Bred** Mr & Mrs P Ashton **Trained** Musley Bank, N Yorks

■ Irish Times was withdrawn. Price at time of withdrawal 66-1. Rule 4 does not apply.

**FOCUS**

A weak-looking novice.

## 9466 32RED.COM NURSERY H'CAP 7f 1y(P)

**12:40** (12:43) (Class 4) (0-80,77) 2-Y-O **£6,301** (£1,886; £943; £472; £235) **Stalls** Low

Form RPR

0361 **1** **Ojala (IRE)**[107] 7121 2-9-7 **77**........................................... AdamKirby 3 79
(Simon Dow) *t.k.h: chsd ldr: effrt over 1f out: rdn to ld 1f out: kpt on to maintain narrow advantage ins fnl f: rdn out* **7/4**[1]

4601 **2** ½ **Cristal Pallas Cat (IRE)**[18] 9199 2-8-9 **70**..............(h) RhiainIngram(5) 4 71
(Roger Ingram) *led: pushed along ent fnl 2f: rdn hdd 1f out: kpt on but a hld ins fnl f* **10/1**

1221 **3** ½ **Roman Spinner**[39] 8887 2-9-2 **72**....................................(t) LukeMorris 5 72
(Rae Guest) *stdd and dropped in bhd after s: hld up in tch in last pair: effrt 2f out: kpt on u.p ins fnl f* **4/1**[3]

0101 **4** nk **Carp Kid (IRE)**[13] 9300 2-9-1 **71**.................................. DougieCostello 1 70
(Jamie Osborne) *trckd ldrs on inner: nt clr run over 2f out tl effrt to press ldrs over 1f out: rdn and kpt on same pce ins fnl f* **15/8**[2]

2000 **5** 1 ¾ **Is It Off (IRE)**[18] 9199 2-9-1 **71**........................................ FranBerry 2 65
(Gary Moore) *stdd after s: hld up in tch in rr: rdn over 2f out: kpt on fr over 1f out: nvr enough pce to get on terms* **11/1**

1m 25.87s (1.07) **Going Correction** -0.05s/f (Stan) **5** Ran SP% **108.6**

Speed ratings (Par 98): **91,90,89,89,87**

CSF £17.38 TOTE £2.20: £1.10, £3.40; EX 15.70 Trifecta £44.60.

**Owner** Robert Moss **Bred** Ballyphilip Stud **Trained** Ashtead, Surrey

**FOCUS**

The time was 0.96sec slower than the preceding modest-looking novice race and the 1-2 raced 2-1, so the bare form does not look solid.

## 9467 BETWAY H'CAP 1m 4f (P)

**1:15** (1:15) (Class 3) (0-95,94) 3-Y-O+ **£10,081** (£3,017; £1,508; £755; £376) **Stalls** Low

Form RPR

-510 **1** **Celestial Spheres (IRE)**[40] 8880 3-8-10 **87**...............(p) TomMarquand 1 94+
(Charlie Appleby) *t.k.h: chsd ldrs for 3f: wl in tch in midfield after tl pushed along and clsd to chse ldrs over 2f out: rdn to ld over 1f out: edgd lft jst ins fnl f: r.o wl* **5/2**[2]

2512 **2** 1 ¼ **Al Hamdany (IRE)**[29] 9055 3-9-3 **94**.................................... AdamKirby 6 99
(Marco Botti) *stdd s: hld up in tch in last pair: clsd and nt clrest of runs 2f out: swtchd rt and effrt over 1f out: hdwy u.p to chse wnr 100yds out: no imp and eased nr fin* **6/4**[1]

4204 **3** 1 ½ **Rainbow Rebel (IRE)**[15] 9271 4-8-12 **85**........................... LukeMorris 3 88
(Mark Johnston) *in tch in midfield: hdwy to chse ldr over 6f out tl led 2f out: sn rdn and hdd over 1f out: struggling to qckn and sltly impeded jst ins fnl f: lost 2nd and outpcd fnl 100yds* **9/2**[3]

3205 **4** nk **Canberra Cliffs (IRE)**[29] 9055 3-8-10 **87**............................. FranBerry 2 89
(Don Cantillon) *stdd s: hld up in rr: nt clr run 2f out: swtchd rt and effrt over 1f out: kpt on same pce ins fnl f* **16/1**

3433 **5** nk **Berrahri (IRE)**[18] 9205 6-8-2 **82**................................ NicolaCurrie(7) 4 84
(John Best) *led tl 9f out: chsd ldr tl over 6f out: styd trcking ldrs: nt clr run 2f out: effrt to chal on inner over 1f out tl unable qck: outpcd fnl 100yds* **11/2**

2-50 **6** 13 **Fanoulpifer**[19] 9186 6-9-0 **87**................................................(h) KierenFox 5 68
(Michael Attwater) *chsd ldr tl led 9f out: rdn and hdd 2f out: high hd carriage and sn lost pl: bhd ins fnl f* **50/1**

2m 30.69s (-2.31) **Going Correction** -0.05s/f (Stan)

**WFA** 3 from 4yo+ 4lb **6** Ran SP% **110.0**

Speed ratings (Par 107): **105,104,103,102,102 94**

CSF £6.36 TOTE £3.40: £1.70, £1.60; EX 6.60 Trifecta £21.70.

**Owner** Godolphin **Bred** Lane Stud Farm Ltd **Trained** Newmarket, Suffolk

**FOCUS**

Just six runners but still useful-looking form.

## 9468 PLAY FOR FREE AT SUNBETS.CO.UK/VEGAS H'CAP 1m 1y(P)

**1:45** (1:47) (Class 2) (0-105,105) 3-Y-O+ **£13,862** (£4,149; £2,074; £1,038; £517) **Stalls** High

Form RPR

1561 **1** **Goring (GER)**[18] 9206 5-8-7 **88**.................................(v) EdwardGreatrex 3 100
(Eve Johnson Houghton) *trckd ldrs and travelled wl: swtchd rt and clsd over 1f out: pushed into ld 1f out: sn rdn and readily wnt clr: r.o* **11/2**[2]

0400 **2** 2 **Alfred Hutchinson**[18] 9210 9-8-10 **91** ow1.......................(p) FranBerry 9 98
(David O'Meara) *dwlt: sn rcvrd and in tch in midfield: effrt to chse ldrs over 1f out: hdwy u.p to chse clr wnr ins fnl f: no imp* **20/1**

0500 **3** 1 **Third Time Lucky (IRE)**[32] 8999 5-9-3 **98**...................... TonyHamilton 2 103
(Richard Fahey) *s.i.s: hld up in tch in rr: hdwy over 1f out: swtchd rt ins fnl f: styd on wl: no threat to wnr* **8/1**

112 **4** 1 ½ **Mystique Moon**[248] 2117 3-8-11 **93**.................................. TomMarquand 5 93
(Charlie Appleby) *broke wl and w ldrs early: sn stdd and hld up in tch in midfield: effrt jst over 2f out: unable qck over 1f out: kpt on same pce u.p fnl f* **7/4**[1]

1-12 **5** nk **Cliffs Of Capri**[44] 8812 3-8-12 **94**.................................. DougieCostello 10 94
(Jamie Osborne) *in tch in midfield on outer: effrt wl over 1f out: kpt on same pce ins fnl f* **7/1**

2001 **6** 1 **Mutawathea**[17] 9233 6-9-6 **101**.........................................(p) RobertHavlin 7 99
(Simon Crisford) *chsd ldr after 1f tl rdn to ld over 1f out: hdd 1f out and unable to match pce of wnr: wknd fnl 100yds* **13/2**[3]

0026 **7** ½ **Brex Drago (ITY)**[29] 9053 5-8-12 **93**.............................(b) DanielMuscutt 4 90
(Marco Botti) *broke wl: sn stdd to trck ldrs and t.k.h: nt clrest of runs over 2f out: effrt between horses 1f out: no imp* **9/1**

064 **8** ½ **Mr Scaramanga**[25] 9091 3-9-3 **99**........................................ AdamKirby 12 94
(Simon Dow) *hld up in tch in last quartet: nt clrest of runs ent fnl 2f: sme hdwy over 1f out: nvr enough room: pushed along and no imp ins fnl f* **25/1**

3052 **9** 2 ½ **London (FR)**[17] 9233 4-8-8 **89**........................................(h) LukeMorris 6 79
(Phil McEntee) *chsd ldrs: lost pl u.p over 1f out: wknd ins fnl f* **20/1**

6000 **10** ¾ **My Target (IRE)**[193] 3963 6-9-10 **105**................................ DavidProbert 8 93
(Michael Wigham) *hld up in tch in midfield: shuffled bk and no hdwy u.p over 1f out: wl hld ins fnl f* **16/1**

0002 **11** nse **Believe It (IRE)**[24] 9125 5-8-0 **88**................................(b) NicolaCurrie(7) 1 76
(Richard Hughes) *led: rdn ent fnl 2f: hdd over 1f out: sn btn and wknd fnl f* **33/1**

260 **12** 3 ½ **Cherbourg (FR)**[97] 7456 5-8-5 **86** oh4.................................... HollieDoyle 11 66
(Dr Jon Scargill) *dwlt: hld up in rr: n.d* **50/1**

1m 34.69s (-3.51) **Going Correction** -0.05s/f (Stan)

**WFA** 3 from 4yo+ 1lb **12** Ran SP% **122.8**

Speed ratings (Par 109): **115,113,112,110,110 109,108,108,105,104 104,101**

CSF £118.02 CT £909.37 TOTE £7.20: £2.30, £5.60, £2.40; EX 159.90 Trifecta £1532.70.

**Owner** G C Stevens **Bred** Westminster Race Horses Gmbh **Trained** Blewbury, Oxon

**FOCUS**

A decent handicap run at a good pace, and the time was 0.35sec outside the track record.

## 9469 BETWAY SPRINT H'CAP (DIV I) 6f 1y(P)

**2:15** (2:16) (Class 6) (0-65,67) 3-Y-O+ **£3,234** (£962; £481; £240) **Stalls** Low

Form RPR

3403 **1** **Pride Of Angels**[82] 7912 4-9-4 **62**........................................ AdamKirby 7 69
(Gary Moore) *hld up in tch in midfield: clsd to chse ldrs and swtchd lft 1f out: rdn and r.o wl to ld 50yds out: sn in command* **5/1**[2]

0250 **2** ¾ **Strategic Heights (IRE)**[20] 9176 8-9-6 **64**...............(v[1]) DougieCostello 2 68
(Jamie Osborne) *led: rdn and edgd rt over 1f out: drvn ins fnl f: hdd and no ex 50yds out* **13/2**

063/ **3** 1 ½ **Stoic Boy**[802] 7385 5-8-10 **57**........................................ GeorgiaCox(3) 1 56
(Henry Candy) *hld up in tch in midfield: nt clr run on inner over 2f out: effrt to chse ldrs 1f out: no ex ins fnl f: wknd towards fin* **7/1**

0000 **4** ¾ **Weloof (FR)**[23] 9142 3-9-3 **61** LiamKeniry 9 57+
(John Butler) *stdd s: hld up in tch in rr of main gp: effrt over 1f out: hdwy and nt clr run ins fnl f: rdn and styd on wl fnl 100yds: no threat to ldrs* **16/1**

0003 **5** 1¼ **Bridge Builder**[18] 9207 7-9-2 **60** (p) CharlesBishop 6 52
(Peter Hedger) *chsd ldrs but wd: effrt over 1f out: unable qck and wknd ins fnl f* **9/2**[1]

6000 **6** ½ **Fareeq**[23] 9142 3-9-2 **60** (vt) LukeMorris 3 51
(Charlie Wallis) *chsd ldr: rdn ent fnl 2f: drvn and unable qck 1f out: lost 2nd and wknd ins fnl f* **12/1**

6002 **7** 1½ **Mister Freeze (IRE)**[19] 9184 3-9-9 **67** (t) JoeyHaynes 5 53
(Patrick Chamings) *sn bustled along in midfield: rdn and no imp over 1f out: wknd ins fnl f* **5/1**[2]

6003 **8** ½ **Krazy Paving**[11] 9323 5-8-2 **53** (v) DarraghKeenan(7) 4 37
(Anabel K Murphy) *chsd ldrs tl 2f out: lost pl over 1f out: wknd ins fnl f* **8/1**

0000 **9** 2¼ **Taurean Gold**[19] 9183 3-8-7 **51** oh6 HollieDoyle 8 28
(John Bridger) *w ldrs and wd for 1f: steadily lost pl: towards rr of main gp over 1f out: wknd ins fnl f* **80/1**

1422 **10** 7 **Bernie's Boy**[13] 9296 4-9-0 **65** (v[1]) NicolaCurrie(7) 10 20
(Phil McEntee) *hood stuck on visor and rdr struggling to remove it: v.s.a: nvr rcvrd and a detached in last* **11/2**[3]

1m 11.71s (-0.19) **Going Correction** -0.05s/f (Stan) **10** Ran SP% **118.7**
Speed ratings (Par 101): **99,98,96,95,93 92,90,90,87,77**
CSF £38.27 CT £236.93 TOTE £4.90: £2.60, £1.80, £3.00; EX 41.60 Trifecta £332.10.
**Owner** Michael Baldry **Bred** Ed's Stud Ltd **Trained** Lower Beeding, W Sussex

**FOCUS**
A modest handicap.

## 9470 BETWAY SPRINT H'CAP (DIV II) 6f 1y(P)
2:50 (2:50) (Class 6) (0-65,65) 3-Y-0+ **£3,234** (£962; £481; £240) **Stalls** Low

Form RPR

0302 **1** **Gold Club**[19] 9183 6-9-4 **65** CharlieBennett(3) 6 71
(Lee Carter) *chsd ldr: clsd to join ldr and wnt clr 2f out: rdn to ld over 1f out: rdn out* **15/2**

4233 **2** *nk* **Haraz (IRE)**[3] 9432 4-9-3 **61** (b[1]) DougieCostello 2 66
(Jamie Osborne) *t.k.h: hld up in last pair: effrt on outer over 1f out: chsd clr ldng pair ins fnl f: edgd lft but str run fnl 100yds: wnt 2nd towards fin: nvr quite getting to wnr* **6/4**[1]

0440 **3** ¾ **Forever Yours (IRE)**[23] 9142 4-8-11 **58** JackDuern(3) 1 61+
(Dean Ivory) *t.k.h: hld up in last pair: nt clr run on inner 2f out: pushed along over 1f out: rdn and hdwy ins fnl f: r.o strly fnl 100yds: nt rch ldrs* **11/4**[2]

6314 **4** *nk* **Wild Flower (IRE)**[19] 9183 5-8-6 **57** RossaRyan(7) 5 59
(Jimmy Fox) *led: wnt clr w wnr 2f out: rdn and hdd over 1f out: kpt on u.p tl one pce fnl 100yds: lost two pls nr fin* **5/1**[3]

6531 **5** ½ **Billyoakes (IRE)**[11] 9323 5-9-3 **61** (p) LukeMorris 9 61
(Charlie Wallis) *chsd ldrs: outpcd and rdn 2f out: kpt on u.p ins fnl f* **10/1**

0000 **6** *hd* **Noble Deed**[59] 8551 7-8-8 **52** KierenFox 4 51
(Michael Attwater) *in tch in midfield: effrt over 1f out: keeping on and clsng whn nt clr run and hmpd ins fnl f: styd on fnl 75yds* **14/1**

1500 **7** 13 **Dreams Of Glory**[19] 9189 9-9-7 **65** SteveDrowne 3 23
(Ron Hodges) *in tch in midfield: rdn over 2f out: lost pl and in rr 1f out: bhd and eased ins fnl f* **33/1**

1m 11.65s (-0.25) **Going Correction** -0.05s/f (Stan) 7 Ran SP% **113.8**
Speed ratings (Par 101): **99,98,97,97,96 96,78**
CSF £19.07 CT £38.95 TOTE £5.20: £2.40, £1.90; EX 18.80 Trifecta £71.70.
**Owner** Tattenham Corner Racing IV **Bred** The C H F Partnership **Trained** Epsom, Surrey

**FOCUS**
The second division of a moderate sprint.

## 9471 BETWAY DASH H'CAP 5f 6y(P)
3:20 (3:21) (Class 6) (0-60,62) 3-Y-0+ **£3,234** (£962; £481; £240) **Stalls** Low

Form RPR

0566 **1** **Met By Moonlight**[19] 9184 3-9-6 **59** SteveDrowne 9 70
(Ron Hodges) *dwlt: pushed along on outer: hdwy into midfield over 2f out: rdn and clsd over 1f out: led ins fnl f: r.o strly and drew clr fnl 100yds* **6/1**[3]

5032 **2** 2¾ **Shackled N Drawn (USA)**[8] 9389 5-9-9 **62** (bt) CharlesBishop 6 63
(Peter Hedger) *taken down early: nt that wl away: t.k.h and hdwy to join ldr after 1f: led 2f out: sn rdn: hdd ins fnl f: nt match pce of wnr* **11/8**[1]

0020 **3** ½ **Grand Myla (IRE)**[87] 7767 3-9-7 **60** (p) AdamKirby 2 59
(Gary Moore) *led: hung rt and hdd bnd 2f out: drvn and stl ev ch over 1f out tl outpcd by wnr ins fnl f* **5/2**[2]

3440 **4** 1 **Mercers**[11] 9323 3-9-1 **57** (p[1]) CallumShepherd(3) 4 53
(Paddy Butler) *chsd ldrs: rdn ent fnl 2f: drvn and kpt on same pce fr over 1f out* **16/1**

5200 **5** ¾ **Regal Miss**[61] 8494 5-8-13 **52** DavidProbert 3 45
(Patrick Chamings) *chsd ldrs: rdn and unable qck over 1f out: kpt on same pce* **20/1**

5466 **6** ¾ **Pharoh Jake**[165] 5027 9-8-12 **51** WilliamCarson 7 41
(John Bridger) *sn bustled along in midfield: no imp u.p over 1f out* **33/1**

0010 **7** 2¼ **Ask The Guru**[8] 9389 7-9-3 **56** (b) KierenFox 10 38
(Michael Attwater) *dwlt: a in rr of main gp: n.d* **8/1**

0-05 **8** ¾ **Go Charlie**[15] 9268 6-8-7 **46** oh1 (h) RaulDaSilva 5 26
(Lisa Williamson) *taken down early: restless in stalls: v.s.a: n.d* **20/1**

58.31s (-0.49) **Going Correction** -0.05s/f (Stan) 8 Ran SP% **114.4**
Speed ratings (Par 101): **101,96,95,94,93 91,88,87**
CSF £14.37 CT £26.12 TOTE £6.60: £1.70, £1.20, £1.20; EX 22.80 Trifecta £51.30.
**Owner** P E Axon **Bred** John Frampton & Paul Frampton **Trained** Charlton Mackrell, Somerset

**FOCUS**
A moderate sprint handicap.
T/Jkpt: Not Won. T/Plt: £624.80 to a £1 stake. Pool: £86,405.18 - 100.95 winning units T/Qpdt: £54.60 to a £1 stake. Pool: £11,521.60 - 155.97 winning units **Steve Payne**

# Index to meetings Flat 2017



† Abandoned
* All-Weather
(M) Mixed meeting

# INDEX TO FLAT RACING

Horses are shown in alphabetical order; the trainer's name follows the name of the horse. The figures to the right are current master ratings for all-weather and turf; the all-weather rating is preceded by the letter 'a'.Underneath the horse's name is its age, colour and sex in abbreviated format e.g. 6 b g indicates the horse is six-years-old, bay in colour, and a gelding.The descriptive details are followed by the race numbers of the races in which it has taken part in chronological order; a superscript figure indicates its finishing position in that race (brackets indicate it was the winner of the race). Bold figure represents performance with highest RPR. A diamond represents a race in which the horse's performance is deemed especially noteworthy.

**Aardwolf (USA)** *Mark Johnston* a83 92
3 b g Cape Cross(IRE) Desert Gazelle (USA) (Smart Strike (CAN))
2106$^{2}$ **(2384)** 3071$^{10}$ 3303$^{11}$ 4075$^{6}$ 4475$^{5}$ 5434$^{8}$ 6026$^{9}$ 7234$^{6}$ 7927$^{3}$ 8289$^{5}$

**Abaad (IRE)** *Mohamed Moubarak* a74 71
3 ch g Bated Breath Condition (Deploy)
237$^{6}$ 437$^{4}$ 3682$^{3}$ **7989**$^{4}$

**Abamanova (IRE)** *W McCreery* 86
2 b f Camacho Abama Lady (CAN) (Mr Greeley (USA))
7855a$^{10}$ **8562**$^{9}$

**Abandon Ship (IRE)** *Paul Cole* 78
2 b c Mastercraftsman(IRE) No Explaining (IRE) (Azamour (IRE))
4068$^{15}$ **6142**$^{2}$ 6859$^{P}$ (Dead)

**Abareeq** *Mark Johnston* a104 90
4 ch g Haatef(USA) Hafawa (IRE) (Intikhab (USA))
(1079) 1148$^{7}$ **(1341)**◆ **1446**$^{5}$ 1779$^{10}$ 2086$^{9}$ 2396$^{4}$ 2999$^{8}$ 3300$^{14}$ 9003a$^{7}$ 9390$^{3}$

**Abatement** *Roger Charlton* a90 81
3 b g Bated Breath Iwunder (IRE) (King's Best (USA))
(464) 1945$^{13}$ 3211$^{3}$ **4215**$^{2}$◆ 4831$^{4}$ 6387$^{4}$

**Abbey Marie (AUS)** *Michael Kent* 106
4 b m Redoute's Choice(AUS) Catshaan (AUS) (Catrail (USA))
8058a$^{8}$ **8250a**$^{6}$

**Abdon** *Sir Michael Stoute* a106 113
4 b g Cacique(IRE) Kinnaird (IRE) (Dr Devious (IRE))
1882$^{4}$◆ 3069$^{6}$ 5500$^{14}$ 6698$^{13}$ 7602$^{2}$ **8423**$^{2}$

**Abel Handy (IRE)** *Declan Carroll* 104
2 b c Arcano(IRE) Belle Isle (Pastoral Pursuits)
(3622) 4862$^{2}$ (5665) 6448$^{2}$ **(8001)**

**Abe Lincoln (USA)** *Jeremy Noseda* a101 94
4 b h Discreet Cat(USA) Truly Blushed (USA) (Yes It's True (USA))
3963$^{15}$ 4916$^{13}$ **9233**$^{3}$

**Abel Tasman** *Ed Walker* a74 67
3 b g Mount Nelson Helena Molony (IRE) (Sadler's Wells (USA))
552$^{3}$◆ 5220$^{10}$ 5931$^{7}$ 6443$^{3}$ 7712$^{2}$ **8313**$^{2}$

**Abel Tasman (USA)** *Bob Baffert* a120
3 b f Quality Road(USA) Vargas Girl (USA) (Deputy Minister (CAN))
**8578a**$^{2}$

**Aberdonian** *Jeremy Gask* a52 48
3 b g Royal Applause Delaware Dancer (IRE) (Danehill Dancer (IRE))
126$^{8}$ **2911**$^{5}$ 3661$^{6}$

**Abertillery** *Michael Blanshard* a57 47
5 b g Shamardal(USA) Nantyglo (Mark Of Esteem (IRE))
274$^{10}$ **1082**$^{10}$ 1698$^{8}$

**Abiento (IRE)** *Ed Walker* a64 79
3 b g Requinto(IRE) Nose One's Way (IRE) (Revoque (IRE))
1841$^{7}$ 2506$^{4}$◆ 2927$^{4}$ 5253$^{4}$ 5814$^{2}$ **(6442)** 7508$^{3}$ 8115$^{6}$

**Abingdon (USA)** *Sir Michael Stoute* a101 111
4 b m Street Cry(IRE) Justlookdontouch (IRE) (Galileo (IRE))
**(4119)** 4613$^{2}$ 5691a$^{3}$ 6356$^{6}$ 7588a$^{3}$

**A Bit Of A Touch (IRE)**
*Richard Fahey* 63
2 b g Arcano(IRE) La Vita E Bella (IRE) (Definite Article)
6057$^{6}$ **6938**$^{5}$ 7613$^{5}$

**A Bit Of Ginger** *Ann Duffield* a59 57
3 b f Camacho Hel's Angel (IRE) (Pyrus (USA))
**1596**$^{2}$ 2077$^{4}$ 2349$^{8}$ 3191$^{5}$ 3832$^{9}$ 4262$^{13}$ 4743$^{10}$ 5016$^{7}$

**Abjar** *Sir Michael Stoute* a89
3 b c Nathaniel(IRE) Kinnaird (IRE) (Dr Devious (IRE))
2260$^{6}$ 3342$^{2}$ (5894) **6952**$^{2}$

**Ablaze** *Laura Mongan* a53 62
3 ch f Arcano(IRE) Angry Bark (USA) (Woodman (USA))
89$^{10}$ 305$^{9}$ **(4346)** 5405$^{2}$ 6259$^{5}$ 7003$^{3}$ 7537$^{12}$ 8507$^{9}$

**Able Jack** *Stuart Williams* a85 79
4 b g Iffraaj Solva (Singspiel (IRE))
**8600**$^{6}$ 9101$^{4}$

**About Glory** *Richard Hannon* a63 61
3 b g Nayef(USA) Lemon Rock (Green Desert (USA))
1906$^{10}$ 2783$^{15}$ 3250$^{10}$ (3657) 5023$^{7}$ 8183$^{5}$ **8312**$^{3}$ **8396**$^{4}$

**Above Normal** *Saeed bin Suroor* a83 80
3 b g Street Cry(IRE) Saoirse Abu (USA) (Mr Greeley (USA))
**(1701)** 2149$^{4}$ 2784$^{7}$

**Above The Rest (IRE)** *David Barron* a84 110
6 b g Excellent Art Aspasias Tizzy (USA) (Tiznow (USA))
2156$^{4}$ 2606$^{15}$ 3064$^{4}$ 3842$^{4}$ **(4905)** 5393$^{24}$ 6401$^{8}$

**A Boy Named Sue** *Peter Niven* a54 51
4 b g Monsieur Bond(IRE) Elusive Sue (USA) (Elusive Quality (USA))
400$^{4}$ 579$^{8}$ **655**$^{2}$ 1125$^{3}$ 1298$^{7}$ 2378$^{9}$

**Abraj Dubai (USA)** *David O'Meara* a84
3 b f Street Cry(IRE) Pulitzer (USA) (Bernardini (USA))
**(8805)**◆ 9179$^{10}$

**Absalon (USA)** *F Head* a103 98
6 ch g Giant's Causeway(USA) Wakigoer (USA) (Miswaki (USA))
**6540a**$^{2}$

**Absolute Angel** *Peter Niven* a56 43
6 b m Primo Valentino(IRE) Send Me An Angel (IRE) (Lycius (USA))
993$^{5}$ **1308**$^{6}$ 1830$^{9}$ 3340$^{6}$ 5267$^{10}$

**Absolute Blast (IRE)** *Archie Watson* a106 103
5 b m Kodiac Perfect Fun (Marju (IRE))
(99)◆ (285) 499$^{2}$ **919**$^{3}$ (1500)◆ 1775$^{2}$ 3319$^{2}$ 4518a$^{3}$ 4934a$^{6}$ 6717a$^{3}$ 7588a$^{2}$ 8450a$^{3}$

**Absolute Champion (USA)**
*George Peckham* a48 57
5 b g Henrythenavigator(USA) Alegendinmyownmind (Cape Cross (IRE))
**8310**$^{10}$

**Absolute City (FR)** *J-P Gauvin* 96
2 bb f Elusive City(USA) Absolutely True (Westerner)
7846a$^{2}$ **(8777a)**

**Absolutely Awesome** *John Butler* a68 60
3 ch g Choisir(AUS) Milton Of Campsie (Medicean)
357$^{3}$ **(3186)**◆ **4005**$^{3}$◆ 7486$^{10}$ 8775$^{6}$ 9001$^{9}$

**Absolutely So (IRE)**
*Andrew Balding* a91 113
7 b g Acclamation Week End (Selkirk (USA))
1491$^{12}$ 2114$^{4}$ **2610**$^{2}$ (3587) 8003$^{9}$

**Abstraction (IRE)** *J S Moore* a95 95
7 b h Majestic Missile(IRE) Bronze Queen (IRE) (Invincible Spirit (IRE))
**3873a**$^{3}$ 7396$^{17}$ 7604$^{9}$

**Abu Dhabi Doo** *K R Burke* 40
2 ch f Red Jazz(USA) No Nightmare (USA) (Lion Heart (USA))
**1873**$^{7}$ 2890$^{9}$ 4504$^{6}$ 5161$^{6}$

**Abushamah (IRE)** *Ruth Carr* a79 89
6 b g Nayef(USA) Adaala (USA) (Sahm (USA))
1472$^{6}$ **1677**$^{6}$◆ 2030$^{12}$ 2586$^{5}$ 2838$^{8}$ 3204$^{5}$ 3589$^{3}$ 3743$^{3}$ 4057$^{3}$ 4661$^{2}$ 5469$^{5}$ 5993$^{3}$ 6434$^{7}$ 7225$^{2}$ 7524$^{9}$

**Acadian Angel (IRE)** *John Quinn* a69 80
3 b f Dark Angel(IRE) Bon Ton Roulet (Hawk Wing (USA))
1199$^{2}$ (1705) 2885$^{3}$◆ 3828$^{5}$ 4437$^{2}$ **(4797)** 6358$^{12}$ 7016$^{6}$

**Acapella Style (FR)**
*Matthieu Palussiere* 57
2 bl f Style Vendome(FR) Sunrise Song (IRE) (Invincible Spirit (IRE))
**1335a**$^{10}$ 1594a$^{10}$ 2321a$^{8}$

**Acapulco (USA)** *A P O'Brien* a84 107
4 ch m Scat Daddy(USA) Global Finance (USA) (End Sweep (USA))
**(2657a)**

**Accalia (IRE)** *J C Hayden* a55 83
4 b m Holy Roman Emperor(IRE) Valentine Hill (IRE) (Mujadil (USA))
2656a$^{5}$ **4416a**$^{12}$

**Accelerate (USA)** *John W Sadler* a117
4 ch h Lookin At Lucky(USA) Issues (USA) (Awesome Again (CAN))
**(5194a)** **6252a**$^{3}$ 8576a$^{9}$

**Accento** *Hugo Palmer* a49 70
3 b g Elusive Quality(USA) Azameera (IRE) (Azamour (IRE))
**2260**$^{9}$

**Accession (IRE)** *Charlie Fellowes* a91 104
8 b g Acclamation Pivotal's Princess (IRE) (Pivotal)
1902$^{5}$ 3003$^{8}$ 4264$^{7}$ **(5942)** 6856$^{6}$ 7622$^{13}$

**Accessor (IRE)** *Richard Hannon* a65 80
2 b c Exceed And Excel(AUS) Amarette (GER) (Monsun (GER))
7726$^{8}$ **(8140)**

**Accidental Agent**
*Eve Johnson Houghton* a99 113
3 b c Delegator Roodle (Xaar)
2122$^{5}$ 2565$^{7}$ (6936)◆ 7356$^{2}$ **(7807)** **8234**$^{4}$◆ 8891$^{8}$

**Acclaim The Nation (IRE)**
*Eric Alston* a80 82
4 b g Acclamation Dani Ridge (IRE) (Indian Ridge (IRE))
**(2123)** 2835$^{6}$

**Accomplice** *Michael Blanshard* a63 70
3 b f Sakhee's Secret Witness (Efisio)
681$^{4}$◆ 1083$^{7}$ 2957$^{7}$ 4150$^{7}$ 4754$^{3}$ 5266$^{2}$◆ **(5783)** 6274$^{7}$ 6792$^{11}$ 7463$^{6}$

**Accurate** *Ian Williams* a95 49
4 b g Zoffany(IRE) More Respect (IRE) (Spectrum (IRE))
3589$^{13}$ **4001**$^{9}$ 4578$^{8}$ 5396$^{12}$ 6637$^{10}$ 6948$^{7}$ 7601$^{8}$ 8813$^{7}$

**Ace Master** *Roy Bowring* a61 54
9 ch g Ballet Master(USA) Ace Maite (Komaite (USA))
4277$^{8}$ 5263$^{5}$ 5760$^{5}$ 6669$^{8}$ **8260**$^{8}$ 8513$^{10}$ **9031**$^{3}$ 9176$^{4}$ 9364$^{9}$

**Ace Of Aces (FR)** *J-P Gallorini* 66
2 ch c No Risk At All(FR) Libranous (FR) (Ballingarry (IRE))
**5989a**$^{7}$

**Ace Of Diamonds (IRE)** *D K Weld* 79
4 b g Oasis Dream Perfect Touch (USA) (Miswaki (USA))
**5582a**$^{4}$ 6978a$^{10}$

**Ace Of Spades (USA)** *George Scott* a63 61
2 br c Street Cry(IRE) Force One (Dansili)
7513$^{12}$ **7876**$^{5}$ 8102$^{2}$

**Ace Ventura** *Roger Varian* 77
2 b c Mayson Ventura Highway (Machiavellian (USA))
7117$^{5}$ **(7739)**

**Achianna (USA)** *Rod Millman* 52
2 ch f Gemologist(USA) Adoradancer (USA) (Danzig Connection (USA))
5321$^{4}$ 6394$^{7}$ **6868**$^{5}$

**Acid Test** *Jedd O'Keeffe* 36
3 b g Bated Breath Cresta Gold (Halling (USA))
1829$^{10}$ **2429**$^{9}$

**Acker Bilk (IRE)** *Keith Dalgleish* a76
3 ch g Rip Van Winkle(IRE) Portentous (Selkirk (USA))
4409$^{9}$ 8554$^{4}$ 8781$^{3}$ **9262**$^{4}$

**Aclaim (IRE)** *Martyn Meade* a79 119
4 b h Acclamation Aris (IRE) (Danroad (AUS))
2825$^{6}$ 4071$^{8}$ 5502$^{6}$ **5690a**$^{2}$◆ (7145) (7671a)

**Aclimatise** *Mark Johnston* a55 81
3 b g Acclamation Favourita (Diktat)
4309$^{10}$ 4693$^{2}$ **(5003)**

**Acolyte (IRE)** *Saeed bin Suroor* a101 102
5 b g Acclamation Obsara (Observatory (USA))
**(250a)** 694a$^{7}$

**Acquirer (IRE)** *Richard Hughes* 55
2 b g Zoffany(IRE) See Emily Play (IRE) (Galileo (IRE))
**8387**$^{9}$

**Acromatic (IRE)** *John Quinn* a22 57
2 br g Poet's Voice Natalisa (IRE) (Green Desert (USA))
2771$^{10}$ **3399**$^{4}$ 4205$^{7}$ 7041$^{11}$ 8145$^{10}$ 8588$^{13}$

**Across Dubai** *William Haggas* a84 104
3 b g Cape Cross(IRE) Saadiah (IRE) (Dubai Destination (USA))
(2284) (4618) **5639**$^{5}$ 6698$^{6}$

**Across The Stars (IRE)**
*Sir Michael Stoute* a77 113
4 b g Sea The Stars(IRE) Victoria Cross (IRE) (Mark Of Esteem (IRE))
2822$^{5}$ 4070$^{8}$ 6440$^{8}$ **7139**$^{2}$ 7393$^{7}$ 8421$^{7}$

**Acrux** *David O'Meara* a84 79
4 b g Dansili Ikat (IRE) (Pivotal)
1969$^{14}$ 3723$^{8}$ 4629$^{11}$ **6182**$^{2}$ 6570$^{9}$ 7034$^{6}$ 7571$^{4}$ 8209$^{3}$ **8556**$^{3}$ 8749$^{7}$ 8907$^{7}$ 9101$^{6}$

**Active Approach** *J S Bolger* a68 85
2 ch f New Approach(IRE) Saoirse Abu (USA) (Mr Greeley (USA))
**6974a**$^{8}$

**Active Spirit (IRE)** *Doug Watson* a101 87
6 ch g Pivotal Local Spirit (USA) (Lion Cavern (USA))
**316a**$^{4}$ 8714a$^{6}$

**Act Of Valour** *M D O'Callaghan* a95 98
3 b g Harbour Watch(IRE) B Berry Brandy (USA) (Event Of The Year (USA))
**3109a**$^{7}$

**Actress (IRE)** *A P O'Brien* 106
2 b f Declaration Of War(USA) Nasty Storm (USA) (Gulch (USA))
2862a$^{2}$ 4028$^{6}$ (4926a) **5973a**$^{3}$ 6354$^{9}$

**Act Swiftly (IRE)** *J S Moore* a28 49
3 b g Requinto(IRE) Silk Point (IRE) (Barathea (IRE))
2707$^{6}$ **3248**$^{6}$ 3720$^{11}$ 4978$^{11}$

**Actualisation** *John Quinn* 74
3 b g Exceed And Excel(AUS) Eluding (Street Cry (IRE))
1878$^{P}$

**Adamant (GER)** *Sir Michael Stoute* 87
3 gr g Dalakhani(IRE) Attima (Zafonic (USA))
**(2174)**

**Ada Misobel (IRE)** *Roy Bowring* a55 43
4 b m Alfred Nobel(IRE) Startarette (USA) (Dixieland Band (USA))
**332**$^{6}$ 1544$^{8}$ 2626$^{8}$ 3137$^{15}$

**Adam's Ale** *Marjorie Fife* a58 81
8 b g Ishiguru(USA) Aqua (Mister Baileys)
**(3492)** 3741$^{8}$ 5947$^{8}$ 6570$^{6}$ 7086$^{5}$ 7557$^{11}$ 8489$^{2}$ 9074$^{13}$

**Adams Park** *Roger Varian* 79
2 b g Mastercraftsman(IRE) Ile Deserte (Green Desert (USA))
5709$^{3}$◆ **6374**$^{3}$ 7273$^{4}$ 7956$^{4}$

**Addeybb (IRE)** *William Haggas* 104
3 ch g Pivotal Bush Cat (USA) (Kingmambo (USA))
2778$^{4}$◆ (3714) (4831)◆ 5568$^{3}$ **(7582)**

**Addicted To You (IRE)**
*Mark Johnston* a80 91
3 ch g Medicean Adalawa (IRE) (Barathea (IRE))
(1001) 2264$^{3}$ 3528$^{4}$ 4476$^{2}$ (4742)◆ 5468$^{P}$ **5944**$^{2}$

**A Definite Diamond** *Grace Harris* 15
4 ch m Assertive By Definition (IRE) (Definite Article)
1729$^{13}$ **2709**$^{11}$ 3084$^{11}$ 4148$^{10}$ 4968$^{12}$ 6102$^{12}$

**Adherence** *Tony Coyle* 64
4 b g Sir Percy Straight Laced (Refuse To Bend (IRE))
2183$^{10}$ 3155$^{8}$ **(3436)** 5951$^{6}$ 6788$^{6}$ 7922$^{4}$ (7982)

**Adiator** *Neville Bycroft* a36 63
9 b m Needwood Blade Retaliator (Rudimentary (USA))
**1456**$^{9}$ 2082$^{9}$

**Adirato (JPN)** *Naosuke Sugai* a102
3 b c Rulership(JPN) Narita Blue Star (JPN) (Manhattan Cafe (JPN))
**1375a**$^{12}$

**Adjacent** *Charlie Appleby* 65
3 b g Teofilo(IRE) Local Spirit (USA) (Lion Cavern (USA))
**5220**$^{6}$

**Adjective** *James Fanshawe* 83
4 b m Dansili Binche (USA) (Woodman (USA))
(2971)◆ **5155**$^{9}$

**Adjutant** *David O'Meara* 58
2 b c Champs Elysees Jubilee (Selkirk (USA))
**6854**$^{7}$

**Adler (GER)** *Markus Klug* 103
3 ch c Adlerflug(GER) Azalee (GER) (Lando (GER))
**8090a**$^{2}$ 8733a$^{5}$

**Ad Libitum** *Hugo Palmer* a53
2 b g Elusive Quality(USA) Sarmad (USA) (Dynaformer (USA))
**8642**$^{6}$ 8952$^{9}$

**Admirable Art (IRE)** *Tony Carroll* a70 79
7 b g Excellent Art Demi Voix (Halling (USA))
166$^{9}$ (954) 1419$^{4}$ 2974$^{5}$ **(3422)** 5049$^{4}$◆ 5788$^{12}$

**Admiral Rooke (IRE)** *Michael Dods* a36 66
2 b g Rock Of Gibraltar(IRE) Qenaa (Royal Applause)
2786$^{11}$ **3430**$^{4}$ 4204$^{7}$ **5373**$^{3}$ 6087$^{7}$ 7041$^{9}$ 7698$^{4}$

**Admiral Spice (IRE)**
*Tom Dascombe* a65 59
2 gr g Lethal Force(IRE) Rustam (Dansili)
2299$^{7}$ 3164$^{7}$ 4526$^{7}$ 5685$^{8}$ 7030$^{4}$ **7239**$^{3}$◆ **7938**$^{2}$

**Admiral's Sunset** *Hughie Morrison* a79 86
4 b m Mount Nelson Early Evening (Daylami (IRE))
**(2723)**◆ 3534$^{7}$ 4206$^{4}$ 5108$^{8}$ 7728$^{7}$

**Admiralty Arch** *C Boutin* a87 89
3 b c Archipenko(USA) Aldeburgh Music (IRE) (In The Wings)
272a$^{4}$ **(427a)** 4289a$^{12}$

**Admired** *Sir Michael Stoute* a71 68
2 gr f Oasis Dream Souviens Toi (Dalakhani (IRE))
6385$^{7}$ 6861$^{4}$ **8148**$^{3}$

**Admire Deus (JPN)**
*Tomoyuki Umeda* 117
6 ch h Admire Don(JPN) Royal Card (JPN) (Sunday Silence (USA))
**2203a**$^{4}$

**Admire Fuji (IRE)** *D De Waele* a85 76
7 b h Oasis Dream Sun Bittern (USA) (Seeking The Gold (USA))
**5490a**$^{5}$

**Admissible** *Richard Hughes*
2 b g Excelebration(IRE) Admirable Spirit (Invincible Spirit (IRE))
3467$^{12}$

**Adnap (IRE)** *Gavin Cromwell* 64
2 b c Casamento(IRE) Crystal Morning (IRE) (Cape Cross (IRE))
**4020a**$^{6}$

**Adona (FR)** *J Parize* a38 57
4 b m Creachadoir(IRE) Aduna (FR) (Iron Mask (USA))
713a$^{11}$ **930a**$^{10}$

**Adrakhan (FR)** *Wilf Storey* a44 54
6 b g Martaline Annee De La Femme (IRE) (Common Grounds)
610$^{5}$ 1197$^{9}$ 1834$^{6}$ 2549$^{5}$ 3155$^{3}$ (4102) 4853$^{6}$ 5186$^{4}$ **(6595)** 7360$^{12}$ 7922$^{3}$ 8241$^{5}$ 8655$^{2}$

**Adulate** *Hugo Palmer* a64 69
2 b c Acclamation Paradise Sea (USA) (Stormy Atlantic (USA))
5036$^{9}$ 5476$^{5}$ **6260**$^{3}$ 6860$^{12}$ 7491$^{6}$ 8110$^{9}$

**Adventureman** *Ruth Carr* a61 66
5 b g Kyllachy Constitute (USA) (Gone West (USA))
969$^{10}$ 1473$^{6}$ 1735$^{4}$ 2140$^{9}$ **2378**$^{2}$ 3048$^{2}$ 3628$^{11}$ **4298**$^{4}$ 4556$^{8}$ 5254$^{9}$ 5880$^{2}$ 6143$^{8}$ 6523$^{4}$ 7235$^{7}$ 7761$^{6}$

**Adventure Zone (IRE)** *Lee Carter* a27 12
4 b g Elnadim(USA) Eliza Doolittle (Royal Applause)
**811**$^{5}$ 1186$^{9}$

**Ad Vitam (IRE)** *Suzzanne France* a67 58
9 ch g Ad Valorem(USA) Love Sonnet (Singspiel (IRE))
**1106**$^{2}$ 1833$^{11}$ 4625$^{6}$ 5836$^{8}$ 6435$^{7}$ 8930$^{5}$ 9219$^{7}$

**Aegean Bounty (IRE)** *John Bridger*
3 b f Bahamian Bounty Royal Consort (IRE) (Green Desert (USA))
8504$^{14}$

**Aegean Boy** *John Bridger* a20 11
4 b g Paco Boy(IRE) Anosti (Act One)
**8128**$^{8}$ 8824$^{12}$ 9129$^{13}$

**Aegean Legend** *John Bridger* 69
2 b g Mayson Aegean Mystery (Dr Fong (USA))
5408$^{3}$ **6921**$^{5}$

**Aegean Secret** *John Bridger* 31
3 b g Equiano(FR) Aegean Mystery (Dr Fong (USA))
**3407**$^{6}$ 3823$^{13}$

**Aelius** *Michael Easterby* 72
3 ch g Sepoy(AUS) Syvilla (Nayef (USA))
1513$^{7}$ 2625$^{9}$ 3047$^{3}$◆ 3862$^{6}$ **(4633)**◆ 5163$^{5}$ 6210$^{8}$

**Aeolus** *Ed Walker* a107 112
6 b g Araafa(IRE) Bright Moll (Mind Games)
1903$^{6}$ 2611$^{2}$ 4354$^{4}$ **5640**$^{2}$ 6401$^{14}$ 7611$^{13}$ 8383$^{5}$

**Aethos (IRE)** *Stefano Botti* 99
3 ch c Dragon Pulse(IRE) Quela (GER) (Acatenango (GER))
2868a$^{11}$ **7205a**$^{4}$ 8275a$^{4}$

**Afaak** *Charles Hills* 102
3 b c Oasis Dream Ghanaati (USA) (Giant's Causeway (USA))
1862$^{4}$◆ (2632) (3317)◆ 3997$^{7}$ 4904$^{4}$ 6873$^{4}$◆ **7582**$^{2}$

**Afandem (FR)** *J-C Rouget* a95 110
3 b c Zoffany(IRE) Miryale (FR) (Anabaa (USA))
(3680a) **4941a**$^{2}$ 5953a$^{3}$ **7176a**$^{3}$

**Afandem (IRE)** *Hugo Palmer* a56 107
3 b g Vale Of York(IRE) Al Mahmeyah (Teofilo (IRE))
2561a$^{8}$ 4306$^{12}$ **4813**$^{8}$ 5354$^{9}$ 6325$^{16}$ 6923$^{10}$

**A Few Dollars More (IRE)**
*Andrew Slattery* a60 55
5 b g Moss Vale(IRE) Lady Naomi (USA) (Distant View (USA))
2656a[3] 7425a[11]

**A Few Good Men** *Jose Santos* a65
2 b g Compton Place Slap And Tickle (IRE) (Exceed And Excel (AUS))
9266[4] (9440)

**Affair** *Hughie Morrison* a49 60
3 b f Sakhee's Secret Supatov (USA) (Johannesburg (USA))
627[6] 766[5] 1331[8] 2371[9] (3247) 4087[7] 4804[4] (6180) 6611[3] 7336[6] 7918[4] (8654) 9095[12]

**Affectionate Lady (IRE)**
*Paul Collins* a62 23
6 b m Dandy Man(IRE) Agouti (Pennekamp (USA))
2919[8]

**Affina (IRE)** *Simon Crisford* 83
2 b f Kodiac Epistoliere (IRE) (Alzao (USA))
4786[4] (5371) (5990) 6425[4]

**Affluence (IRE)** *Martin Smith* a53 64
2 b c Thewayyouare(USA) Castalian Spring (IRE) (Oasis Dream)
5749[5] 6472[4] 6916[8] 7829[10] 8467[16]

**Affordability** *Daniel Mark Loughnane* a62 60
3 b g Bushranger(IRE) Munaa's Dream (Oasis Dream)
179[5]

**Afjaan (IRE)** *William Haggas* a106 111
5 b g Henrythenavigator(USA) Elusive Galaxy (IRE) (Elusive City (USA))
(2142) 7603[P] (Dead)

**Afkar (IRE)** *Ivan Furtado* a75 51
9 b g Invincible Spirit(IRE) Indienne (IRE) (Indian Ridge (IRE))
274[2] 400[3] 614[6]

**Afonso De Sousa (USA)**
*Michael Appleby* a95 90
7 br g Henrythenavigator(USA) Mien (USA) (Nureyev (USA))
467[3] (683) 5966[4] 6482[8] 6952[5] 7548[7] 9055[6] 9271[13]

**African** *Charlie Fellowes* a73 77
3 b c Dubawi(IRE) Pink Symphony (Montjeu (IRE))
(3922)◆ 4640[4] 6160[5]

**African Beat (IRE)** *Richard Hughes* a77 79
3 b f Cape Cross(IRE) Rythmic (Dubai Destination (USA))
392[3] 647[3] 4450[2]◆ 4966[3] 6013[4]

**African Blessing** *Charlie Wallis* a72 62
4 ch g Mount Nelson Bella Beguine (Komaite (USA))
1296[7] 1971[4] (2119) 2888[5] 3899[7] 5119[4] 5288[5] (5958) 6485[5] 7058[6] 7791[2] 7878[4] 8132[4] 8798[5] 9033[4]

**African Friend (IRE)** *Henry Candy* 83
4 b g Equiano(FR) Fontanally Springs (IRE) (Namid)
(4368) 6267[3] 6874[9] 7272[2] 8167[13]

**African Girl** *Lydia Pearce* a50 51
3 b f Equiano(FR) Tychy (Suave Dancer (USA))
393[4] 1371[8] 2507[8] 3703[4] 5040[3]◆ 6114[5]◆

**African Grey** *Martin Todhunter* a62 38
3 gr g Kheleyf(USA) Elbow Beach (Choisir (AUS))
(1034) 1123[4] 1968[13] 7042[12] 8590[10]

**African Quest** *Gary Moore* a10 41
3 b f Air Quest Pursuit Of Purpose (Dansili)
2580[6] 3309[7] 4152[6] 5791[4] 6751[3] 7003[4] 7991[12]

**African Ride** *C Laffon-Parias* a100 112
3 b c Candy Ride(ARG) Paiota Falls (USA) (Kris S (USA))
1689a[3] 2666a[7] 4390a[2] 6729a[6]

**African Showgirl** *Ivan Furtado* a66 40
4 ch m Showcasing Georgie The Fourth (IRE) (Cadeaux Genereux)
7916[12] 8254[5] 8538[9] 8800[12] 9343[9]

**African Sky** *A Fabre* 93
2 b c Shamardal(USA) Angelita (IRE) (Alzao (USA))
(6017a) 8196a[3]

**African Trader (USA)**
*Daniel Mark Loughnane* a47 60
4 bb g Lonhro(AUS) Nasaieb (IRE) (Fairy King (USA))
3702[6] 4625[4] 4968[10]

**Afterburner** *Hugo Palmer* a21 65
3 b g Kyllachy Singed (Zamindar (USA))
4562[8] 5577[7] 6150[5] 6767[7] 7936[14]

**Afterthisone** *Robin Dickin* a25 14
2 ch g Pastoral Pursuits Mandolin Wind (Haafhd)
1495[10] 1792[5] 2029[10] 6063[12] 6815[11] 7082[10] 8644[RR] 8870[9] 9175[9]

**After Tonight (FR)** *Gillian Boanas* a71
7 b g Lando(GER) Affair (FR) (Montjeu (IRE))
195[2] 780[3]

**Against Rules (FR)** *S Wattel* a71 96
5 b m Aussie Rules(USA) Around Me (IRE) (Johannesburg (USA))
(4457a) (8733a)

**Against The Odds** *Paul Cole* a89 90
4 b g Champs Elysees Generous Diana (Generous (IRE))
1798[8] 2752[3]

**Agar's Plough** *Ed Dunlop* 77
2 ch g Dutch Art Cloud's End (Dubawi (IRE))
6388[7] 6921[2] 8046[5] 8509[5]

**Agathe Sainte** *F Head* a75
2 b f Holy Roman Emperor(IRE) Agathe Rare (IRE) (Sadler's Wells (USA))
8691a[3]

**Agathonia (USA)** *H-A Pantall* a82 99
3 b f Street Cry(IRE) Regency Romance (Diktat)
(1900) 2447a[9] 5982a[5] 7673a[2] 8462a[2] 8838a[3]

**A G Cohiba (USA)** *H Al Alawi* a32
3 b f Custom For Carlos(USA) Electric Cove (USA) (Spinning World (USA))
8710a[8]

**Agent Error (IRE)** *David Simcock* 62
2 b f Iffraaj Oasis Sunset (IRE) (Oasis Dream)
6876[7] 7334[8] 7563[7]

**Agent Murphy** *Brian Meehan* 100
6 b h Cape Cross(IRE) Raskutani (Dansili)
6191[6] 6440[6] 6857[4] 7402[14]

**Agent Of Fortune** *Christine Dunnett* a52 54
2 ch f Kheleyf(USA) Royal Bloom (IRE) (Royal Applause)
5334[5] 6199[5] 6844[6] 7756[3]◆ 8120[9]

**Age Of Elegance (IRE)** *Roger Fell* a83 84
5 b m Makfi Elegant Pride (Beat Hollow)
2629[5] 2953[9] 3341[7] (3910) 4893[3]

**Age Of Wisdom (IRE)** *Gary Moore* a78 83
4 ch g Pivotal Learned Friend (GER) (Seeking The Gold (USA))
3534[8] 4499[3] 5432[11] 6323[7] 6889[3] 8072[9]

**Agnes Champ (FR)** *M Boutin* a59 57
11 b g Agnes Kamikaze(JPN) Antilles (IRE) (Danehill (USA))
4955a[4] 5176a[5]

**Agnethe (IRE)** *Paul D'Arcy* a45 66
3 b f Requinto(IRE) Abbasharjah (GER) (Tiger Hill (IRE))
1619[6] 2316[5]◆ 2970[3] 3703[2] 5339[5] 5812[2] 6298[4] 7539[7] 8342[5]

**Agreement (IRE)** *Nikki Evans* a43 62
7 b g Galileo(IRE) Cozzene's Angel (USA) (Cozzene (USA))
2059[6]

**Agrotera (IRE)** *Ed Walker* 64
2 ch f Mastercraftsman(IRE) Lombatina (FR) (King's Best (USA))
8594[6]

**Aguerooo (IRE)** *Ollie Pears* a96 78
4 b g Monsieur Bond(IRE) Vision Of Peace (IRE) (Invincible Spirit (IRE))
81a[6] 275[9] 326[5] 1103[6] 1454[5]◆ 2683[5] 2883[3] 3707[5] 4600[5] 5211[7] 9074[12] 9339[6]

**A Head Ahead (GER)**
*Gianluca Bietolini* a68 73
3 b c Makfi Allegro Vivace (FR) (Muhtathir)
5909a[4] 6084a[5] 6650a[10] 8959a[5]

**Ahead Of Time** *David Simcock* a70
3 b g Dream Ahead(USA) Malladore (IRE) (Lawman (FR))
758[6] 997[3]

**Ahfad** *Stuart Williams* a51 44
2 br g Dick Turpin(IRE) Big Moza (Pastoral Pursuits)
4583[10] 5301[8] 5655[8] 8870[3] 9014[7]

**Ahlan Bil Zain (FR)** *David Simcock* a84 84
3 bb c Elusive City(USA) Fall View (Pivotal)
2084[7] 2818[4] 3592[7] 4491[3] 5849[4] 6322[3] 7998[4]

**Ahlan Emarati (IRE)** *S Seemar* a59 107
5 b g Holy Roman Emperor(IRE) Indaba (IRE) (Indian Ridge (IRE))
84a[15]

**Ahorita (FR)** *J-M Lefebvre* a47 52
2 b f Pour Moi(IRE) Miss Penelope (FR) (Kendor (FR))
7637a[16]

**Ahundrednotout** *John James Feane* a63 46
3 ch g Mount Nelson Forest Express (AUS) (Kaaptive Edition (NZ))
4473[3] (8242)◆

**Aiguille Rouge (FR)** *Gary Moore* 76
3 ch f Falco(USA) Avanguardia (GER) (Choisir (AUS))
8142[5]

**Aimez La Vie (IRE)** *Richard Fahey* 90
3 br f Arcano(IRE) La Vita E Bella (IRE) (Definite Article)
2078[2] (3044) 3869[9] (5376) 7016[5] (7656) 8351[9]

**Aiming For Rio (FR)** *A Fabre* 106
3 ch f Rio De La Plata(USA) Tevara (Compton Place)
(3613a) 6497a[6]

**Aim Of Artemis (IRE)**
*Sir Michael Stoute* 85
2 ch f Leroidesanimaux(BRZ) Justlookdontouch (IRE) (Galileo (IRE))
6138[3] (7021)◆

**Aim To Please (FR)** *K R Burke* a87 109
4 b m Excellent Art Midnight Flash (IRE) (Anabaa Blue)
1531a[8] 2432[3] 3961[5] 5381[6] 6490a[12]

**Ainne** *Sylvester Kirk* a58 48
2 ch f Cityscape Ayun (USA) (Swain (IRE))
6504[5] 7875[10] 9385[4]

**Airlie Beach (IRE)** *W P Mullins* 98
7 b m Shantou(USA) Screaming Witness (IRE) (Shernazar)
(7261a)

**Airmax (GER)** *Ralph Beckett* 67
2 br c Maxios Artica (GER) (Pentire)
6869[6] 8389[6]

**Air Ministry (IRE)** *Michael Bell* 64
3 b g High Chaparral(IRE) Hadarama (IRE) (Sinndar (IRE))
1497[12] 2314[5] 2584[8] 3276[5] 4045[5]

**Air Of York (IRE)** *John Flint* a74 68
5 b g Vale Of York(IRE) State Secret (Green Desert (USA))
641[8] 929[11] 1890[3] 2256[5] 2297[4] 2961[2]◆ (3265) 3532[6] 3573[10] 5587[8] 6099[4] 6502[9] 7465[4] (7693) 7899[4] 8434[7] 9297[6]

**Airpearl (FR)** *X Richard*
3 b g Air Chief Marshal(IRE) Cat's Pearl (FR) (Enrique)
6256a[14]

**Air Pilot** *Ralph Beckett* 115
8 b g Zamindar(USA) Countess Sybil (IRE) (Dr Devious (IRE))
(1654a) 3299[8] 4417a[5] 5464a[8] 8598[2]

**Airplane (IRE)** *Tim Easterby* 59
2 b g Pour Moi(IRE) Abyssinie (IRE) (Danehill Dancer (IRE))
5631[14] 6204[5] 6658[5] 7519[15]

**Air Raid** *Jedd O'Keeffe* 81
2 b c Raven's Pass(USA) Siren Sound (Singspiel (IRE))
(6939) 8046[4]

**Airshow** *Rod Millman* a69 74
2 ch g Showcasing Belle Des Airs (IRE) (Dr Fong (USA))
1604[3]◆ 1767[9] 3769[2] 4466[2] 4972[6] 6030[3] 8131[3]◆ (8420)

**Airton** *James Bethell* a83 84
4 b g Champs Elysees Fly In Style (Hernando (FR))
1719[12] 1976[2] 2629[7] (4357) 5403[10] 6232[3] 7387[5] 8188[8] 8778[8]

**Airway** *James Fanshawe* a83 78
3 b g Poet's Voice Air Kiss (Red Ransom (USA))
4274[3] (6851) 7949[9]

**Aislin Moon (IRE)** *Les Eyre* 46
2 b f Sleeping Indian Shamrock Lady (IRE) (Orpen (USA))
4996[8]◆ 5494[7] 8288[8]◆

**Aiya (IRE)** *Andrew Balding* a76 36
2 ch c Declaration Of War(USA) Flamingo Sea (USA) (Woodman (USA))
2779[12] 3305[8] 8839[4]

**Aiyana Rose (FR)**
*Matthieu Palussiere* 69
2 b f Shamalgan(FR) Bint Makbul (Makbul)
5816a[3]

**Ajasam** *M Weiss* 88
6 b g King's Best(USA) Funseeker (UAE) (Halling (USA))
714a[7]

**A J Cook (IRE)** *Ron Barr* a48 46
7 b g Mujadil(USA) Undertone (IRE) (Noverre (USA))
1006[14] 1674[3] 1978[9] 2628[10] 5418[7] 5542[4] 5695[10] 6271[3] 6688[9]

**Ajjlan (FR)** *J-C Rouget* 84
3 b c Zoffany(IRE) La Jalousie (FR) (Muhtathir)
5777a[DSQ]

**Ajmal (IRE)** *A Fabre* 103
3 b g Shamardal(USA) Adja (IRE) (Rock Of Gibraltar (IRE))
1689a[5] 3103a[5]

**Ajman King (IRE)** *Roger Varian* 99
3 ch c Lope De Vega(IRE) Third Dimension (FR) (Suave Dancer (USA))
7125[2]◆ (7652) (8385)◆

**Ajman Princess (IRE)** *Roger Varian* a64 113
4 b m Teofilo(IRE) Reem Three (Mark Of Esteem (IRE))
(1468) (2389) 3586[3] 4613[3] 5381[2] (6248a) 6981a[7]

**Ajraam (USA)** *M Al Mheiri* a85 85
7 b g Daaher(CAN) Abby Road (IRE) (Danehill (USA))
250a[14]

**Ajwad** *R Bouresly* a74 86
4 b h Rock Of Gibraltar(IRE) Afrodita (IRE) (Montjeu (IRE))
8583a[10]

**Ajwan** *Richard Fahey* 67
2 rg f Helmet(AUS) Rock Ace (IRE) (Verglas (IRE))
2836[2]◆ 3483[2]

**Akamanto (IRE)** *R Mike Smith* a61 76
3 b c Cape Cross(IRE) Allofus (IRE) (Celtic Swing)
1624[5] 1963[7] 2721[5] 3291[8] 5066[5] (5532) 5921[4] 7162[11] 8218[4]

**Akavit (IRE)** *Ed de Giles* a41 79
5 b g Vale Of York(IRE) Along Came Molly (Dr Fong (USA))
1469[9] 1935[2] (2363) 3004[4] 3464[2] (3685) (4120) 5524[13]

**Akbulat** *A Savujev* 60
4 b g Invincible Spirit(IRE) Summer's Lease (Pivotal)
4955a[9]

**Akdaar** *Roger Varian* 73
3 b g Dubawi(IRE) Min Banat Alreeh (IRE) (Oasis Dream)
2135[5]◆ 3948[4]

**Akeed Champion** *S Seemar* a71 100
5 b h Dubawi(IRE) Shy Lady (FR) (Kaldoun (FR))
250a[7] 892a[9]

**Akhlaaq** *Owen Burrows* 90
3 b g New Approach(IRE) Misheer (Oasis Dream)
1901[4] 3836[4]

**Akihiro (JPN)** *A Fabre* 113
3 b c Deep Impact(JPN) Baahama (IRE) (Anabaa (USA))
1826a[2] 2483a[3] 8087a[2]

**Akinspirit (IRE)** *Nikki Evans* a52 32
13 b g Invincible Spirit(IRE) Akebia (USA) (Trempolino (USA))
839[10] 1082[13]

**Akkadian Empire** *Iain Jardine* a67 74
3 b g Arabian Gleam Floral Beauty (Shamardal (USA))
1300[3] 3291[12] 3975[6] 4432[4] 5131[2] 5950[7] 7162[7]

**Akula (IRE)** *Barry Leavy*
10 ch g Soviet Star(USA) Danielli (IRE) (Danehill (USA))
8430[9]

**Akuna Mattatta (IRE)** *Ralph J Smith* a39
3 b g Approve(IRE) Akuna Magic (IRE) (Whipper (USA))
397[7] 679[5] 863[9] 7322[9] 7907[U] 8428[RR]

**Akvavera** *Ralph Beckett* 78
2 ch f Leroidesanimaux(BRZ) Akdarena (Hernando (FR))
4528[2]◆ 5371[2] (6666)

**Alaadel** *William Haggas* a73 88
4 ch g Dubawi(IRE) Infallible (Pivotal)
(2819) 3572[5] 4752[8] 5564[2]◆ 6874[2] 7780[4]◆ (8393)

**Alabanza** *Keith Dalgleish* a27
2 b c Big Bad Bob(IRE) Tahfeez (IRE) (Alhaarth (IRE))
8915[9]

**Alabaster** *Sir Mark Prescott Bt* a92 87
3 gr g Archipenko(USA) Alvarita (Selkirk (USA))
466[5] 758[4] (855) (2264)◆ 3335[2] (4004)◆

**Alabaster (USA)** *Saeed bin Suroor* a103
5 br g Medaglia d'Oro(USA) Lady Pegasus (USA) (Fusaichi Pegasus (USA))
432a[3] (650a) 891a[3] 1043a[3]

**Alacovia (FR)** *P Bary* a86 83
3 b f Motivator Pomonia (FR) (Anabaa (USA))
(4232a)

**Alacritas** *David Simcock* a54 22
2 gr f Leroidesanimaux(BRZ) Albaraka (Selkirk (USA))
3697[10] 7033[9] 8147[7]

**Aladdine** *F Head* 107
3 b f Naaqoos Katerini (FR) (Cacique (IRE))
(2561a) 3370a[6] 4390a[3]

**Aladdin Sane (IRE)** *Brian Meehan* 60
3 b g Teofilo(IRE) Aqua Aura (USA) (Distorted Humor (USA))
2231[9] 2751[6] 3394[6] 4968[9]

**Alambra (IRE)** *Stefano Botti* 97
3 ch f Shamardal(USA) Secret Fashion (King's Best (USA))
3121a[3] 8096a[2] 8450a[5]

**Alandil (FR)** *T de Vlaminck* a59
5 ch g Muhaymin(USA) Alanna (FR) (Bering)
1070a[10]

**A L'Anglaise** *Rae Guest* a83 50
4 b m Invincible Spirit(IRE) Alabelle (Galileo (IRE))
599[4] 9921[2]

**Alareef (SAF)** *M F De Kock* a93
6 b g Stronghold Modraj (Machiavellian (USA))
316a[10]

**Al Asef** *Marco Botti* a83 79
2 br c Kyllachy Hot Reply (Notnowcato)
7953[3] 8734[6] (9049)

**Alaska (IRE)** *Sylvester Kirk* a68 73
2 b c Kodiac Sunny Hollow (Beat Hollow)
2816[4] 3169[3] 3655[2] (3936) 4367[3] 4827[4] 5322[2] 6036[11] 6951[4] 7734[13]

**Alaskan Bay (IRE)** *Rae Guest* a57 48
2 b f Kodiac Party Appeal (USA) (Mr Greeley (USA))
4972[7] 6559[10] 8657[5] 9002[2] 9122[4]

**Alaskan Beauty (IRE)** *Tim Easterby* a43 60
2 b f Kodiac My American Beauty (Wolfhound (USA))
4555[10] 5162[3] 5702[8] 7159[10] 7655[7] 8588[8]

**Alaskan Star (IRE)** *Amanda Perrett* a19 63
2 b g Kodiac Lightwood Lady (IRE) (Anabaa (USA))
3029[6] 3328[7] 5865[7] 6609[7] 7081[14] 7510[12]

**Alba Del Sole (IRE)** *John Gosden* a70 68
2 b f Dandy Man(IRE) Winterwell (USA) (First Defence (USA))
3215[4] 7732[3] 8130[3]◆ 8701[3] 9023[3]

**Alba Power (IRE)** *Hugo Palmer* 98
2 b c Fast Company(IRE) Shehila (IRE) (Zamindar (USA))
3868[6] (4318) 4812[5] 5395[3] 6353[4] 7090[3] 7754a[2] 8196a[4]

**Al Barez (USA)** *A bin Harmash* a45
3 gr g Big Brown(USA) Juncture (USA) (El Prado (IRE))
1040a[8] 8836a[8]

**Al Barg (IRE)** *Richard Hannon* 82
2 b g Acclamation Miss Hawai (FR) (Peintre Celebre (USA))
5136[2]◆ (5476) 6388[8]

**Albarino** *Kevin Ryan* a44 42
2 b g Equiano(FR) Cocabana (Captain Rio)
1803[7] 2882[7] 6264[10] 7363[8] 8191[8] 8588[12]

**Albassel** *M Al Attiya* 52
2 b c Pastoral Pursuits Oh So Saucy (Imperial Ballet (IRE))
9446a[10]

**Alberobello (FR)**
*M Delcher Sanchez* a88 49
4 b g Fuisse(FR) Ashkiyra (FR) (Marju (IRE))
1920a[2] 6302a[2]

**Albert (JPN)** *Noriyuki Hori* 119
6 ch h Admire Don(JPN) Folklore (JPN) (Dance In The Dark (JPN))
2203a[5]

**Albert Boy (IRE)** *Scott Dixon* a61 73
4 ch g Falco(USA) Trumbaka (IRE) (In The Wings)
390[7] 1545[4] (2295) 2815[5] (3148) 3439[2] 3740[5] 4345[9] 5080[3] 5706[7] 6109[3]◆ 6524[9]

**Alberto** *Lisa Williamson* a4
7 b g Bertolini(USA) Al Awaalah (Mukaddamah (USA))
309[P]

**Albert's Back** *Michael Easterby* a37 73
3 b g Champs Elysees Neath (Rainbow Quest (USA))
1497[6] 1818[6] 2467[3] 3335[7] 7627[8]

**Albert Street (IRE)** *Michael Dods* 69
2 b c Acclamation Chroussa (IRE) (Holy Roman Emperor (IRE))
4598[4] 5068[2] 6312[5] 7269[7]

**Albishr (IRE)** *Simon Dow* a84 101
2 b c Clodovil(IRE) Casual Remark (IRE) (Trans Island)
(4083) 5106[2] 6396[2] 7546[6] 8035[7] 9313[2]

**Albizu Campos** *Lawrence Mullaney* a48 45
3 b g Mastercraftsman(IRE) Lolita Lebron (IRE) (Royal Applause)
848[11] 1034[3] 1835[15] 2228[7] 2349[9] 3525[4] 4744[8] 5374[10]

**Albizzia** *Ralph Beckett* 68
3 b f Archipenko(USA) Altitude (Green Desert (USA))
1609[4]◆

**Al Boraq (USA)** *S Seemar* a44
3 br g Archarcharch(USA) There I Go (USA) (Hennessy (USA))
8710a[7] 9257a[5]

**Alcatraz (IRE)** *George Baker* a75 84
5 b g Camacho Spring Opera (IRE) (Sadler's Wells (USA))
173[2] 507[2] 809[4] 1289[6] 1932a[2] 2752[2] 5397[14] 6543a[5] 7070a[9]

**Aldbury Lass (IRE)** *Robert Eddery* 36
2 b f Dark Angel(IRE) Heeby Jeeby (Lawman (FR))
2750[12] 8323[9] 9023[9]

**Aldeburgh** *Nigel Twiston-Davies* a85 86
8 b g Oasis Dream Orford Ness (Selkirk (USA))
1504[2] 1788[4]

**Al Destoor** *Jennie Candlish* a85 96
7 ch g Teofilo(IRE) In A Silent Way (IRE) (Desert Prince (IRE))
2787[4] (3582) 4429[2] 5634[3] 6881[6] 7595[2] 8740[10]

**Aldreth** *Michael Easterby* a88 76
6 b g Champs Elysees Rowan Flower (IRE) (Ashkalani (IRE))
(62) 759[2] 1002[3] (1223) 1405[7]

**Aldrin (FR)** *David Pipe* 74
4 b g New Approach(IRE) Trip To The Moon (Fasliyev (USA))
3062[5]

**Aleef (IRE)** *David O'Meara* a99 75
4 b h Kodiac Okba (USA) (Diesis)
6758[9] 7144[14] 7604[8] 8238[5] 8540[11] 9124[4] (9339)◆

**Alejandro (IRE)** *David Loughnane* a92 96
8 b g Dark Angel(IRE) Carallia (IRE) (Common Grounds)
598[8] (736) 1288[3] 1422[7] 2030[7] (2226) 3014[6] 3837[7] 4017[6] 7140[8] 8566[5] 8812[3] 9053[7] 9210[6] 9272[4]

**Alemaratalyoum (IRE)** *Ed Dunlop* a76 83
3 ch c Lope De Vega(IRE) Heart Of Ice (IRE) (Montjeu (IRE))
(1306) 1550[6] 3162[9] 3621[2] (4542) 4983[4]◆ 5333[3] 5961[4] (7083) 7909[8]

**Al Erayg (IRE)** *F-H Graffard* 95
4 b h Oasis Dream Vallee Des Reves (USA) (Kingmambo (USA))
4454a[2] 5269a[4]

**Alessa (GER)** *Henk Grewe* a56 40
3 bb f Scalo All About Love (GER) (Winged Love (IRE))
6225a[11]

**Alets (FR)** *C Baillet* 60
2 ch f Maiguri(IRE) Atabaska (FR) (Ashkalani (IRE))
1335a[8] 2073a[4]

**Alexander M (IRE)** *Mark Johnston* a65 102
3 gr c Mastercraftsman(IRE) Naomh Geileis (USA) (Grand Slam (USA))
503[4] 737[4] 1591[2] 2395[2] 2588[3] 3041[3] 3531[2] (3859) 5404[5] (5686) 6059[3] (6416) 6563[4] (7107) (7595)

**Alexandrakollontai (IRE)**
*Alistair Whillans* a89 86
7 b m Amadeus Wolf Story (Observatory (USA))
1677[15] 2155[12] 2789[2] 3451[8] 3828[4] 4475[8] 4883[7] (5185) 5881[7] 6208[6] 7161[7] 7658[5] 7941[5] 8351[3] 8718[2] 8912[12] 9264[10]

**Alexandrite** *Mme C Head-Maarek* a65 59
3 b f Oasis Dream Argumentative (Observatory (USA))
8885a[9]

**Alexios Komnenos (IRE)** *J A Stack* 111
3 b c Choisir(AUS) Alexiade (IRE) (Montjeu (IRE))
4383a[3] (6119a) 6959a[6]

**Alexis Des Fosses (FR)**
*J Phelippon* a60 69
3 bb g Alex The Winner(USA) L'Hommee (FR) (Voix Du Nord (FR))
748a[7]

**Alfa Manifesto (FR)**
*Matthieu Palussiere* a68 79
3 b g Whipper(USA) Fairy Dress (USA) (Fasliyev (USA))
427a[5] 748a[3]

**Alfa McGuire (IRE)** *Bryan Smart* 86
2 b c Lord Shanakill(USA) Watsdaplan (IRE) (Verglas (IRE))
3895[5] (4597) 5314[3] (6465)◆ 7090[7] 8415[10]

**Alfa Queen (IRE)** *Iain Jardine* a76 34
3 b f Intikhab(USA) Insaaf (Averti (IRE))
3649[4] 4729[2] 6161[4] 7032[3] 8204[2]◆

**Alfarqad (USA)** *Owen Burrows* 78
2 bb c War Front(USA) Love And Pride (USA) (A.P. Indy (USA))
7391[3] 8119[4]

**Alfarris (FR)** *William Haggas* a92 93
3 b g Shamardal(USA) Rose Et Noire (IRE) (Dansili)
(2260)◆ 2998[2] 4886[4] (6187) 7516[4]

**Alf Guineas (IRE)** *John Gosden* a90 73
4 b m Sea The Stars(IRE) Sayyedati Storm (USA) (Storm Cat (USA))
(1583)◆ 2389[8] 3219[8]

**Alfieri (FR)** *T Castanheira* a85 81
4 b g Naaqoos Jolie Et Belle (FR) (Oratorio (IRE))
391a[3] 6454a[6] 7636a[15]

**Alfie's Angel (IRE)** *Bryan Smart* a66 79
3 b g Dark Angel(IRE) Penolva (IRE) (Galileo (IRE))
(4122) 4610[6] 5132[6] (5994) 6348[6] 7245[10] 7942[7] 8209[8] 8556[8]

**Alfolk (IRE)** *David Simcock* a55
3 b g Invincible Spirit(IRE) Elmaam (Nayef (USA))
127[6] 310[5] 642[7] 1034[6] 1193[6] 1363[8]

**Alfonsine (IRE)** *Stefano Botti* 95
3 b f Approve(IRE) Statenice (Montjeu (IRE))
2244a[7]

**Alfonso Manana (IRE)**
*James Given* a71 68
3 ch g Dutch Art Chance For Romance (Entrepreneur)
244[2] 656[2] 878[3] 920[3] 1782[5] 2180[6] 2630[3] 3296[7] (4161) 5759[6] 6620[13]

**Alfred Hutchinson** *David O'Meara* a103 89
9 ch g Monsieur Bond(IRE) Chez Cherie (Wolfhound (USA))
(118) 680[3] 1023[6] 1773[9] 2141[8] 8547[4] 8812[11] 9210[7] 9468[2]

**Alfredo Arcano (IRE)**
*David Marnane* a91 87
3 b g Arcano(IRE) Cheherazad (IRE) (Elusive City (USA))
6971a[22] 9247a[3]

**Alfred Richardson** *John Davies* a70 77
3 ch g Dapper Vera Richardson (IRE) (Dutch Art)
1347[4] (2035) 3461[3] (3934) 6518[5] 7328[5]

**Al Fujairah** *Richard Hannon* 72
2 b c Showcasing First Term (Acclamation)
3037[5] 3590[6]

**Algaith (USA)** *Owen Burrows* a104 109
5 b g Dubawi(IRE) Atayeb (USA) (Rahy (USA))
2290[4] 3218[4]

**Al Galayel (IRE)** *Luca Cumani* a92 62
3 b g Zoffany(IRE) Glympse (IRE) (Spectrum (IRE))
1730[8] 2260[5] (8554)◆ (8821)◆

**Algam (IRE)** *Richard Hannon* a85 88
2 b c Kodiac Evangeline (Sadler's Wells (USA))
5063[2] 5504[6] (5960) 6683[2] 7741[2] 8379[4]

**Algebra** *John Joseph Murphy* a45 59
3 b g Dark Angel(IRE) Paracel (USA) (Gone West (USA))
1389a[15]

**Algometer** *David Simcock* 115
4 gr h Archipenko(USA) Albanova (Alzao (USA))
3012[2] 4814[3] 5436[7]

**Alhadab (FR)** *A Fabre* 100
2 b c Camelot Grace Lady (FR) (Muhtathir)
5776a[2]

**Al Hajar (IRE)** *Charlie Appleby* 97
2 b c Dark Angel(IRE) Warshah (IRE) (Shamardal (USA))
5420[2]◆ 6388[4] (7520) (8413)

**Alhajjaj** *Andrew Balding* a72
4 gr g Cacique(IRE) Strawberry Morn (CAN) (Travelling Victor (CAN))
37[4] 479[5] (747)

**Al Hamdany (IRE)** *Marco Botti* a99 93
3 b g Kodiac Easy Times (Nayef (USA))
1861[6] 2569[5] 2824[10] 5634[7] 6887[5] 7516[2] 8385[5] (8506) 9055[2] 9467[2]

**Al Hareth (IRE)** *George Peckham* a53
2 b c Take Charge Indy(USA) Pure Symmetry (USA) (Storm Cat (USA))
7511[10] 7788[9]

**Alhawdaj (USA)** *Mark Johnston* a56
2 ch f Speightstown(USA) Baragah (USA) (Awesome Again (CAN))
7238[9]

**Al Hawraa** *Kevin Ryan* a43 67
4 b m Iffraaj Kashoof (Green Desert (USA))
1201[5] 2430[10] 6047[8] (6690) 8103[3]

**Ali Bin Nayef** *Michael Wigham* a59 45
5 b g Nayef(USA) Maimoona (IRE) (Pivotal)
35[8] 279[3] 462[2] 738[6] 924[8] 1081[6] 1256[4]

**Alicante (GER)** *Markus Klug* 99
3 b f Lando(GER) Annouche (GER) (Unfuwain (USA))
1846a[2] 4393a[4] 5693a[8] 7203a[7] 8462a[7]

**Alice Springs (IRE)** *A P O'Brien* 118
4 ch m Galileo(IRE) Aleagueoftheirown (IRE) (Danehill Dancer (IRE))
1653a[2]

**Alidara (IRE)** *Emma Owen* a37 26
5 ch m Manduro(GER) Artisia (IRE) (Peintre Celebre (USA))
2468[P]

**Aliento** *Ollie Pears* 50
2 ch f Bated Breath Scarlet Royal (Red Ransom (USA))
3398[9] 4502[8] 6264[8]

**Alifax** *Jamie Osborne* a73 72
2 gr c Mayson Scrupulous (Dansili)
3390[10] 3689[5] 3965[2] (4291) 4858[6] 5572[3] 6050a[8] 7121[3] 7647[11]

**Alignement** *C Laffon-Parias* 109
4 b h Pivotal Soldata (USA) (Maria's Mon (USA))
6052a[5] 6915a[P]

**Alinstante** *Sir Mark Prescott Bt* a96 88
4 b m Archipenko(USA) Algarade (Green Desert (USA))
269[3]

**Ali Spirit (IRE)** *F Vermeulen* a78 81
4 b h Invincible Spirit(IRE) Citron Presse (USA) (Lemon Drop Kid (USA))
(6302a)

**Ali The Hunter (IRE)**
*Johnny Farrelly*
4 ch m Papal Bull Polish Spring (IRE) (Polish Precedent (USA))
7492[10]

**Alizeti (IRE)** *Henry Candy* 63
2 b f Dutch Art Ushindi (IRE) (Montjeu (IRE))
8593[4]

**Aljady (FR)** *Richard Fahey* 77
2 b c Bated Breath No Truth (IRE) (Galileo (IRE))
(8474)

**Al Jawza** *Richard Hannon* a63 63
3 b f Nathaniel(IRE) Mosqueras Romance (Rock Of Gibraltar (IRE))
1401[6] 2019[6] 2585[6] 3024[8] 5024[7]

**Al Jazi (IRE)** *F Rohaut* 111
4 b m Canford Cliffs(IRE) Rainbow Crossing (Cape Cross (IRE))
4071[9] (5597)

**Aljazzi** *Marco Botti* a105 114
4 b m Shamardal(USA) Nouriya (Danehill Dancer (IRE))
(1795) 2432[5] 3961[2] (6697) 7812[9] 8601a[7]

**Al Jellaby** *Clive Cox* 84
2 b c Exceed And Excel(AUS) Dolphina (USA) (Kingmambo (USA))
4218[3] 5105[3] (6859)

**Aljezeera** *Luca Cumani* 104
3 b f Frankel Dynaforce (USA) (Dynaformer (USA))
2827[3] 6357[3] 7089[2]◆ (8121)

**Al Johrah** *H-F Devin* 108
3 b f Bated Breath Bea Remembered (Doyen (IRE))
7697a[5]

**Aljuljalah (USA)** *Roger Varian* a98 102
4 b m Exchange Rate(USA) Ruler's Charm (USA) (Cape Town (USA))
3395[4] 4617[2] (6619) 7603[5]

**Alkashaaf (USA)**
*Daniel Mark Loughnane* a82 28
3 b g More Than Ready(USA) Abby Road (IRE) (Danehill (USA))
31[3] 329[3] 458[4] (578) 87[7] 1124[9] 3303[12] 4736[7] 6637[7] 7569[10] 8158[2] 9220[9]

**Alketios (GR)** *Chris Gordon* a59 56
6 b g Kavafi(IRE) Mazea (IRE) (Montjeu (IRE))
2915[5] 3688[4] 4180[4] 6752[7]

**Al Khafji** *Jeremy Gask* a74 70
4 ch g New Approach(IRE) Wadaat (Diktat)
769[7] 1085[6] 1498[6] 1684[5] 2622[9] 3820[7]

**Alkhalifa (IRE)** *Brian Meehan* 81
2 gr c Kodiac Bridal Path (Groom Dancer (USA))
4534[3] (5151) 6207[3] 6699[7] 8008[4]

**Al Khan (IRE)** *Kevin Ryan* a95 92
8 b g Elnadim(USA) Popolo (IRE) (Fasliyev (USA))
5[8] 199[3] 459[6] 730[5] 1769[13] 4293[8] 4961[5]◆ 5434[9] 6464[2] 6949[5] 7886[6] 8486[12] 8881[4]

**Alkhawaneej Boy (IRE)** *Kevin Ryan* 84
2 b c Elzaam(AUS) Kaplinsky (IRE) (Fath (USA))
6938[4]◆ (7460)

**Alkhor** *J Phelippon* a61 64
4 b g Exceed And Excel(AUS) Ruse (Diktat)
(1696) 1910[3] 2113[3] 2692[3] 4955a[2]

**Al Kout** *Heather Main* a79
3 gr g Oasis Dream Honorlina (FR) (Linamix (FR))
(8663) 9140[9]

**All About The Pace** *Mark Usher* a57 41
3 ch f Sixties Icon Phoebe Woodstock (IRE) (Grand Lodge (USA))
2060[3] 3261[4] 4012[4] 4978[8]

**Allante (IRE)** *Sir Michael Stoute* a70
2 b f Pivotal Have Faith (IRE) (Machiavellian (USA))
7453[12] 9081[2]

**All Dolled Up (IRE)**
*Sarah-Jayne Davies* a46 55
5 b m Aussie Rules(USA) All On Sugar (GER) (Red Ransom (USA))
146[10]

**All Dynamite (FR)** *Leo Braem* a57 53
8 b g Kentucky Dynamite(USA) All Risk (BEL) (Pyramus (USA))
6018a[7]

**Allee Bleue (IRE)** *Philip Hobbs* a77 79
7 ch g Mount Nelson Murrieta (Docksider (USA))
6889[2]

**Allegheny Bay (IRE)** *J S Moore* a63 54
3 b g Power Allegheny Creek (IRE) (Teofilo (IRE))
140[2] 393[2] 642[5] 902[4] 1024[2] 1463[2] 2536a[5] 3166[3]

**Allegiant (USA)** *Roger Charlton* a56
2 b g City Zip(USA) Preferential (Dansili)
9313[10]

**Allegio (IRE)** *Denis Gerard Hogan* a67 83
4 b g Galileo(IRE) Song Of My Heart (IRE) (Footstepsinthesand)
5519a[2]

**Allegramente** *Sir Michael Stoute* 14
2 b f Dansili Allegretto (IRE) (Galileo (IRE))
5660[10]

**Allegro Lady (GER)** *Dr A Bolte* 66
3 rg f Santiago(GER) Adelma (GER) (Sternkoenig (IRE))
5693a[14]

**Allen's Folly** *Peter Hiatt* a42 50
4 b m Captain Gerrard(IRE) Rabarama (Xaar)
1[6] 153[13] 923[9] 1112[9] 1192[5] 1452[9] 1887[9] 5535[8] 5784[10]

**Allergic (AUS)** *James Cummings* 105
5 b g Street Cry(IRE) Cajou (AUS) (Encosta De Lago (AUS))
6714a[10]

**Allez Henri (IRE)**
*D & P Prod'Homme* a99 97
6 b g Footstepsinthesand Macotte (FR) (Nicolotte)
1775[3] 4069[14]

**All For Nothing (IRE)**
*John C McConnell* 68
4 b g Bushranger(IRE) Allofus (IRE) (Celtic Swing)
(6126) 6523[2]

**All For The Best (IRE)**
*Robert Stephens* a77 79
5 b g Rip Van Winkle(IRE) Alleluia (Caerleon (USA))
1405[2] 3663[2] 6096[7]

**Allfredandnobell (IRE)**
*Micky Hammond* a26 57
4 b g Alfred Nobel(IRE) Its In The Air (IRE) (Whipper (USA))
7360[11] 7922[5] 8241[4]

**Alliance Secrete (FR)** *T Castanheira* a85 95
3 bb c Sageburg(IRE) Gentle Tap (Beat Hollow)
5521a[11] 5909a[2] 6650a[5] 8025a[9]

**Allied** *Sir Michael Stoute* 57
2 ch c Dawn Approach(IRE) Mambo Halo (USA) (Southern Halo (USA))
8389[14]

**Allieyf** *William Haggas* 69
2 b c New Approach(IRE) Sajjhaa (King's Best (USA))
8678[5]◆

**Alligator** *Tony Carroll* a60 37
3 ch g Sepoy(AUS) See You Later (Emarati (USA))
7833[11] 8948[13] 9218[4]

**All My Love (IRE)** *Pam Sly* a80 85
5 b m Lord Shanakill(USA) Afilla (Dansili)
2061[2] 2965[2] 3684[4] 4216[8] 7024[9] (7925) 8564[2]

**Allnite (IRE)** *Tom Dascombe* 44
2 b g Arcano(IRE) Paint The Town (IRE) (Sadler's Wells (USA))
6410[5] 7266[8]

**Allofmelovesallofu**
*Ken Cunningham-Brown* a41 62
3 ch g Sakhee's Secret La Palma (Sinndar (IRE))
2957[10] 3691[7] 4562[6] 5783[10] 6502[11]

**Allons Y (FR)** *F Rossi* 90
3 b f Soldier Of Fortune(IRE) Absolutely True (Westerner)
3103a[6]

**All Or Nothin (IRE)** *Paddy Butler* a54 84
8 b g Majestic Missile(IRE) Lady Peculiar (CAN) (Sunshine Forever (USA))
167[2] (309) 620[8] 1075[6] 1593[2] 1979[5] 2469[4] 5146[7] 5410[4] 5657[4] 7910[8] 8258[2] 8543[10] 9334[7]

**All Out** *Richard Hannon* 89
2 b f Acclamation Time Over (Mark Of Esteem (IRE))
(7731) (8112) 8562[3]

**All This Time (GER)** *D Guillemin* 91
2 b f Dabirsim(FR) Amazing Bounty (FR) (Tertullian (USA))
4166a[2]

**All To The Red (FR)**
*R Le Dren Doleuze* a71 54
4 ch g Naaqoos Naralina (FR) (Linamix (FR))
1078a[9]

**Allumage** *Sylvester Kirk* a81 85
5 b m Montjeu(IRE) Alaia (IRE) (Sinndar (IRE))
1079[6] 3033[7] 4829[4]

**Alluringly (USA)** *A P O'Brien* 109
3 b f Fastnet Rock(AUS) All For Glory (USA) (Giant's Causeway (USA))
2523[2] 3301[3] 3995[6] 4928a[6] (6080a) 6356[5] 6972a[8] 7171a[5] 7812[8]

**Alluring Star (USA)** *Bob Baffert* a107
2 b f Exchange Rate(USA) Spring Jump (USA) (Jump Start (USA))
8603a[2]

**Allux Boy (IRE)** *Nigel Tinkler* 72
3 b g Iffraaj Ms Victoria (IRE) (Fasliyev (USA))
2145[8] 3296[8] 4058[7] 5122[4] 5826[8]

**All You (IRE)** *David O'Meara* a73 77
5 b g Siyouni(FR) Diamond Light (USA) (Fantastic Light (USA))
42[7] 382[6] 928[9] 1334[2]◆ 1409[3] 1700[11] 2108[8] 2224[5] 3205[2] 3560[8] 3935[3] 4572[5]

**Almagest** *Robert Stephens*
9 br g Galileo(IRE) Arabesque (Zafonic (USA))
4120[10]

**Almanack** *Mark Pattinson* a67 69
7 b g Haatef(USA) Openness (Grand Lodge (USA))
90[10] 1186[4] 1449[2]◆ 1603[5] (2178) 4587[3] 5651[8] 9243[8]

**Almandin (GER)** *Robert Hickmott* 121
7 b g Monsun(GER) Anatola (GER) (Tiger Hill (IRE))
8667a[12]

**Almane (IRE)** *Richard Fahey* a53 78
2 ch g Sir Prancealot(IRE) Red Rosanna (Bertolini (USA))
1495[4]◆ (1872) 3254[6]

**Al Mansor (IRE)** *Richard Hannon* a70 65
3 gr c Dark Angel(IRE) Atullia (GER) (Tertullian (USA))
1550[3] 1888[7] 2794[8] 3937[4]

**Almanzor (FR)** *J-C Rouget* 129
4 b h Wootton Bassett Darkova (USA) (Maria's Mon (USA))
6052a[5]

**Almargo (IRE)** *A bin Harmash* a92 90
6 b g Invincible Spirit(IRE) Alexander Youth (IRE) (Exceed And Excel (AUS))
250a[3]

**Al Mashrab** *J-C Rouget* 64
2 b c Style Vendome(FR) Candicans (Dansili)
6170a[6]

**Al Mayda (USA)** *Hugo Palmer* a72 91
3 ch f Distorted Humor(USA) Ms. Margaret H (USA) (Point Given (USA))
(5220) 6152[5] 7283[8] 8007[12]

**Almerita Moon (IRE)** *Marco Botti* a40
3 b f Henrythenavigator(USA) Moonboat (Starcraft (NZ))
1333[10]

**Almizhar (IRE)** *R Bouresly* a23 46
3 b c Dark Angel(IRE) La Reine Mambo (USA) (High Yield (USA))
649a[9]

**Al Modajal (FR)**
*Jassim Mohammed Ghazali* 76
2 b g Dawn Approach(IRE) Bush Cat (USA) (Kingmambo (USA))
9446a[7]

**Almoner** *Tracey Collins* a80
5 b m Oasis Dream Alumni (Selkirk (USA))
(168)

**Almoonqith (USA)**
*David A & B Hayes & Tom Dabern* a88 112
7 bb h Dynaformer(USA) Bohemian Lady (USA) (Carson City (USA))
1400a[7] (Dead)

**Almoqatel (IRE)** *Tony Newcombe* a31 32
5 b g Clodovil(IRE) Majestic Night (IRE) (Mujadil (USA))
4713[8] 6748[9] 7212[9]

**Almoreb (IRE)** *Richard Hannon* a98 100
3 b c Raven's Pass(USA) Macadamia (IRE) (Classic Cliche (IRE))
(2778) 3504[4] 4634[6] (5300) 5849[2] (6617) 7129[3] 7743[2]

**Almost Gemini (IRE)** *Kenneth Slack* a71 77
8 gr g Dylan Thomas(IRE) Streetcar (IRE) (In The Wings)
4742[6] 5700[3] 6233[2] 7330[3]

**Al Muffrih (IRE)** *William Haggas* 85
2 b c Sea The Stars(IRE) Scarlet And Gold (IRE) (Peintre Celebre (USA))
8352[3]

**Almunther (IRE)** *Micky Hammond* 66
4 b g Invincible Spirit(IRE) Adaala (USA) (Sahm (USA))
2547[4] 3095[13] 4019[5] 5131[9] 7478[3] 8218[2]

**Al Murqab (IRE)** *J Phelippon* a80 62
7 b g Danehill Dancer(IRE) Champaka (IRE) (Caerleon (USA))
(8303a)

**Al Mustashar (IRE)**
*Saeed bin Suroor* a55 65
2 b g Shamardal(USA) Dresden Doll (USA) (Elusive Quality (USA))
6264[6] 8149[11]

**Almutamarred (USA)** *James Unett* a72 56
5 ch g Street Cry(IRE) Sortita (GER) (Monsun (GER))
3252[6] 5284[3] 5872[8] 7413[9] 7832[10] 8246[10] 8909[7] 9421[10]

**Alnaas** *John Gosden* a81 79
3 b f Dansili Hedaaya (IRE) (Indian Ridge (IRE))
1948[2] (2463) 3031[4]

**Al Nafoorah** *Ed Dunlop* a71 89
3 b f Bated Breath Cat O' Nine Tails (Motivator)
2274[2] 2587[2] 2931[2] 3656[2] (3911) 4372[4] (5265)◆ 5506[11] (6700) 7276[6] 8351[2]

**Alnashama** *Charles Hills* a95 92
5 b g Dubawi(IRE) Ghanaati (USA) (Giant's Causeway (USA))
2384[3] 3212[3] 3837[5] 4578[5]

**Alnasl (IRE)** *Archie Watson* a78 84
3 b f Tamayuz Arwaah (IRE) (Dalakhani (IRE))
2110[3] (2296) 3088[7] 3425[8] 4184[11] 4697[3] 5249[2] 5565[4] (5895) (6594) 6948[4] (7095)◆ 7830[4]

**Al Neksh** *William Haggas* 99
4 b g Zoffany(IRE) Mount Crystal (IRE) (Montjeu (IRE))
2735[2]◆ 4316[6] 6399[4] 7091[3] 7395[10]

**Alniyat** *Ed Dunlop* a44 45
3 ch f Sepoy(AUS) Agata Laguna (IRE) (Elnadim (USA))
2572[7]

**Aloft (IRE)** *Robert Hickmott* 103
5 b g Galileo(IRE) Dietrich (USA) (Storm Cat (USA))
8056a[9]

**Alouja (IRE)** *Hugo Palmer* a71 76
3 ch f Raven's Pass(USA) Artisti (Cape Cross (IRE))
2585[3] 3039[3] 3595[2] 4903[9] 6015[5] 7364[4]

**Alounak (FR)** *Jean-Pierre Carvalho* 95
2 b c Camelot Awe Struck (Rail Link)
6229a[4] (6985a)

**Al Ozzdi** *Simon Crisford* a70 72
2 b g Acclamation Zibeling (IRE) (Cape Cross (IRE))
4860[10] (5786) 6279[4] 6934[5]

**Alphabet** *A P O'Brien* 109
3 b f Lawman(FR) Applauded (IRE) (Royal Applause)
3078[7] 3632a[3] 3873a[3] 4927a[6] 6640a[9] 6973a[2] 7424a[2] 7670a[10] 7856a[5] 8230[11]

**Alphabetical Order** *David O'Meara* a62 79
9 b g Alflora(IRE) Lady Turk (FR) (Baby Turk)
3795[10] 4301[3] 4684[11] 5313[6] 6061[2]◆ 6467[4]

**Alpha Centauri (IRE)**
*Mrs John Harrington* 106
2 gr f Mastercraftsman(IRE) Alpha Lupi (IRE) (Rahy (USA))
(2862a) 4028[2]◆ 6974a[5]

**Alpha Delphini** *Bryan Smart* 113
6 b g Captain Gerrard(IRE) Easy To Imagine (USA) (Cozzene (USA))
2397[8]◆ 3079[3] 3926[6]◆ 4635[9] 5647[2] 6402[8] 6668[7] (7475) (8105)◆

**Alpha Tauri (USA)** *Charles Smith* a83 76
11 b g Aldebaran(USA) Seven Moons (JPN) (Sunday Silence (USA))
67[5] (419) 527[2] 850[3] (2466) 4293[9] 4766[8] 8257[10] 8803[12] 9179[7]

**Alpine Dream (IRE)** *Tim Easterby* a73 81
4 b m Dream Ahead(USA) Infamous Angel (Exceed And Excel (AUS))
1971[6] 2548[3] 3095[4] (3577) 4121[5] 4375[2] 5399[4] 5881[2] 6629[5] 6964[13] 8556[5] 8929[7]

**Alpine Peak (USA)** *Roger Varian* a73
2 gr c Mizzen Mast(USA) Affectionately (Galileo (IRE))
8492[6] 8839[3] 9154[5]

**Al Qahwa (IRE)** *David O'Meara* a75 103
4 b g Fast Company(IRE) Cappuccino (IRE) (Mujadil (USA))
(2736) 3593[8] 4353[9] 5435[2] 5640[23] 6206[10] 6971a[2] 8044[10] 8383[10]

**Alqalsar (IRE)** *Brian Meehan* 74
3 ch c Bahamian Bounty With Colour (Rainbow Quest (USA))
1961[5] 2782[2] 3755[2]

**Alqamar** *Charlie Appleby* a77 94
3 b g Dubawi(IRE) Moonsail (Monsun (GER))
(2807) 4032[9] 6872[2] 7337[5] 8672[8]

**Alraased (USA)** *A R Al Rayhi* a72 82
8 br g Exchange Rate(USA) Alabaq (USA) (Riverman (USA))
203a[2]

**Alrahaal (IRE)** *Marcus Tregoning* 80
2 ch c Raven's Pass(USA) Loose Julie (IRE) (Cape Cross (IRE))
3305[2] 5504[4]

**Al Reeh (IRE)** *Marco Botti* a81 83
3 br c Invincible Spirit(IRE) Dffra (IRE) (Refuse To Bend (IRE))
3211[4] 5245[7]

**Alright Dave** *Ronald Harris*
2 ch g Frozen Power(IRE) Crazy Hazy (IRE) (Sakhee's Secret)
8493[7]

**Al Sail (FR)** *Richard Hannon* a73
3 b g Kendargent(FR) Golden Lily (FR) (Dolphin Street (FR))
307[2] 807[2]

**Alshan Fajer** *J R Jenkins* a82 55
7 ch g Lemon Drop Kid(USA) Illuminise (IRE) (Grand Lodge (USA))
1182[5] 1292[5] 1697[9] 2022[7] 2471[4] 3208[11] 4980[6]

**Alshibaa (IRE)** *William Haggas* a71 77
3 br g New Approach(IRE) Amjaad (Dansili)
2854[6] (4186)

**Al's Memory (IRE)** *David Evans* a62 58
8 b g Red Clubs(IRE) Consensus (IRE) (Common Grounds)
6503[4] 6866[8] 8401[3] 8659[5] 9141[13]

**Alsvinder** *David O'Meara* a101 73
4 b h Footstepsinthesand Notting Hill (BRZ) (Jules (USA))
2341[7] 4566[2] 5602[9] 6267[4] 6891[8] (7538) 8129[2] (8660) 9187[3]

**Altaayil (IRE)** *Gary Moore* a88 94
6 br g Sea The Stars(IRE) Alleluia (Caerleon (USA))
7096[2]◆ 7785[2]◆

**Altaira** *Tony Carroll* a52 54
6 b g Dubawi(IRE) Peach Pearl (Invincible Spirit (IRE))
274[6] 544[5] 854[13] 1298[2] 5050[6] 5713[10] (6305) 7215[12] 8182[7]

**Altavilla (IRE)** *F Chappet* 62
2 b f Big Bad Bob(IRE) Anamarka (Mark Of Esteem (IRE))
5907a[10] 6409a[5]

**Altea (FR)** *P Sogorb* 97
2 b f Siyouni(FR) Ensis (SPA) (Zieten (USA))
8170a[2]

**Altered Method (IRE)** *Hugo Palmer* a55 38
2 ch g Dawn Approach(IRE) Swift Action (IRE) (Invincible Spirit (IRE))
7383[8] 8316[9]

**Alternate Route** *Sir Mark Prescott Bt* a73 65
3 b g New Approach(IRE) Almamia (Hernando (FR))
4562[10] 5243[8] 5746[7] 6293[10] 6820[3] 7233[2] (7490) 7790[6] 8876[3] 9325[2]

**Alternative Fact** *Ed Dunlop* 94
2 b c Dalakhani(IRE) O Fourlunda (Halling (USA))
6140[2]◆ (7120) 8196a[2]

**Altharoos (IRE)** *Micky Hammond* a64 85
7 br g Sakhee(USA) Thamara (USA) (Street Cry (IRE))
3204[3] 3559[6]

**Altiko Tommy (IRE)** *George Baker* a70 40
3 b g Kodiac Altishaan (Darshaan)
(1242)◆ 1888[6] 3173[3] 4748[10] 6076[13] 7916[13] 8503[4]

**Alton Bay (IRE)** *Peter Fahey* a84 83
9 b g Pushkin(IRE) Miss Chapman (IRE) (Imperial Ballet (IRE))
9341[8]

**Altra Vita** *Sir Mark Prescott Bt* a44
2 b f Animal Kingdom(USA) Alma Mater (Sadler's Wells (USA))
7995[12] 8779[5] 8997[9]

**Altyn Alqa** *Clive Cox* a43
3 b f High Chaparral(IRE) Albanka (USA) (Giant's Causeway (USA))
1420[8]

**Altyn Orda (IRE)** *Roger Varian* 106
2 ch f Kyllachy Albanka (USA) (Giant's Causeway (USA))
5938[2] 7620[2] (8002)

**Al Udeid (IRE)** *R Le Gal* a35 37
7 gr g Verglas(IRE) Gold Strike (IRE) (Rainbow Quest (USA))
6018a[10]

**Alwahsh (IRE)** *William Haggas* 89
3 b c Dubawi(IRE) Gile Na Greine (IRE) (Galileo (IRE))
2066[2] 2681[4] (3755) 5392[9] 5841[4] 6671[5] 8048[3]

**Alwasmiya** *Simon Crisford* a67 100
2 b f Kyllachy Miss Bunter (Bahamian Bounty)
7238[4] (7953) (8562)

**Always Amazing** *Robert Cowell* a83 84
3 ch g Kyllachy Amazed (Clantime)
(3259) 4098[3]◆ 6430[9]

**Alwaysandforever (IRE)**
*Luca Cumani* 87
3 b f Teofilo(IRE) Deep Winter (Pivotal)
(6750)

**Always Dreaming (USA)**
*Todd Pletcher* a124
3 bb c Bodemeister(USA) Above Perfection (USA) (In Excess I (IRE))
(2420a) 2851a[8]

**Always Resolute** *Brian Ellison* a79 81
6 b g Refuse To Bend(IRE) Mad Annie (USA) (Anabaa (USA))
6317[4] 6880[3] 8047[11] 9096[4]

**Always Thankful** *Ismail Mohammed* a76 79
3 b f Showcasing Thankful (Diesis)
1705[2] 2474[4] 3246[8] (3443) (5829)◆ 6697[11] 7130[2] 8374[8] 8928[4]

**Always Welcome (USA)**
*A R Al Rayhi* a77 36
4 ch g Elusive Quality(USA) No Matter What (USA) (Nureyev (USA))
316a[6] 8583a[5]

**Al Whaad (USA)** *A bin Harmash* a44
3 b f Pioneerof The Nile(USA) Red Cognac (USA) (Hennessy (USA))
9257a[9]

**Alwina (GER)** *Henk Grewe* 98
3 b f Areion(GER) Alte Dame (GER) (Dashing Blade)
1846a[8] 3882a[6] 4517a[5] 6495a[6] 8526a[11]

**Al Wukair (IRE)** *A Fabre* 120
3 b c Dream Ahead(USA) Macheera (IRE) (Machiavellian (USA))
(1689a) 2399[3] 4942a[2] (5980a) 8232[7]

**Al Yarmouk** *John Gosden* a78
3 b c Holy Roman Emperor(IRE) Disco Volante (Sadler's Wells (USA))
354[2]

**Alyce (IRE)** *N Branchu* a22 18
4 ch m Soave(GER) Newcastle (FR) (High Yield (USA))
4955a[14] 6125a[16]

**Alyssa** *Ralph Beckett* a74 105
4 b m Sir Percy Almiranta (Galileo (IRE))
3090[10] 4639[3] (7089) 8231[7]

**Al Zaman (IRE)** *Simon Crisford* a86 85
3 bb c Cacique(IRE) Flowers Of Spring (IRE) (Celtic Swing)
(1984) 2526[5] 3081[5] 5686[7] 6423[2] 7627[6] 8188[4]

**Amaani (FR)** *G E Mikhalides* a80 82
3 b f Le Havre(IRE) Moony Face (FR) (Bering)
2644a[13] 7471a[7]

**Amabilis** *Ralph Beckett* a96 105
3 b f Champs Elysees Pure Joy (Zamindar (USA))
(3233) 5506[7]◆ (6919) 7576[9]

**Amadeus (IRE)** *Richard Fahey* a46
2 gr c Fastnet Rock(AUS) Alegra (Galileo (IRE))
8189[9] 8779[7] 9177[12] 9436[8]

**Amadeus Rox (FR)** *Alan King* a59 59
3 b g Falco(USA) Vittoria Vetra (Danehill Dancer (IRE))
2027[3] 2705[4] 3220[3] 4623[5]

**Amadeus Wolfe Tone (IRE)**
*Leo Braem* a69 71
8 b g Amadeus Wolf Slieve (Selkirk (USA))
4233a[11]

**A Magic Man (IRE)** *Henk Grewe* 73
3 gr g Lawman(FR) Ayun Tara (FR) (Martaline)
2697a[6] 3310a[5]

**Amajari (FR)** *Gary Moore* a39 13
3 b c Lonhro(AUS) Angalia (IRE) (High Chaparral (IRE))
8116[9] 8822[7]

**Amandine** *David Elsworth* a76 71
2 b f Shamardal(USA) Kissable (IRE) (Danehill Dancer (IRE))
4815[9] 5531[3] 6064[2]

**Amanto (GER)** *Ali Stronge* a80 74
7 b g Medicean Amore (GER) (Lando (GER))
(965) 1466[2] (1697) 3004[6] 4095[2]

**Amaretto** *Jim Boyle* 56
2 b c Kyllachy Dan Loose Daughter (Sakhee (USA))
4583[7] 5709[6] 6827[8]

**Amarone Red (IRE)** *Tom Dascombe* 51
2 ch f Harbour Watch(IRE) Lisa's Strong (IRE) (Kalanisi (IRE))
4806[12] 5963[5] 6410[6] 7082[8]

**Amazigh World (FR)** *P Monfort*
3 bb c Sandwaki(USA) Singapore Treat (FR) (Sagacity (FR))
6455a[15]

**Amazing (FR)** *F Vermeulen* a90 103
3 ch g Kentucky Dynamite(USA) Little Jaw (Footstepsinthesand)
1826a[5] 2250a[7]

**Amazing Alice** *Archie Watson* a82 51
2 b f Sayif(IRE) Dot Hill (Refuse To Bend (IRE))
2037[8] 2750[9] 3174[2] 3576[5] (3999) (4977)◆ 5240[2] (5844) 6684[3] 7536[2] 7814[21]

**Amazing Amaya** *Derek Shaw* a9 35
2 b f New Approach(IRE) Faslen (USA) (Fasliyev (USA))
6876[11] 7731[8] 9415[7]

**Amazing Grazing (IRE)**
*Richard Guest* a71 64
3 b g Intense Focus(USA) North Light Rose (USA) (North Light (IRE))
3435[3] 4611[5] 5757[7] (7035) 9279[4]

**Amazing Kids (NZ)** *J Size* 123
5 b g Falkirk(NZ) Cadence (NZ) (Rhythm (USA))
1376a[6] 9168a[5]

**Amazing Michele (FR)**
*Richard Fahey* 78
2 gr f Mastercraftsman(IRE) Holy Freud (USA) (Freud (USA))
5631[4] 6183[3] (6875) 7552[8] 8379[7]

**Amazing Red (IRE)** *Ed Dunlop* a93 94
4 b g Teofilo(IRE) Artisia (IRE) (Peintre Celebre (USA))
2165[3]◆ 2774[6] 3594[9] (5663) 6399[9] 7150[2] 7614[4]

**Amazing Rock (SWI)**
*Mark Johnston* a58 59
2 ch g Rock Of Gibraltar(IRE) Adalawa (IRE) (Barathea (IRE))
5735[5] 6590[6] 7237[11] 7829[6] 8141[4]

**Amazing Steps (IRE)**
*Charlie Fellowes* 66
3 b c Footstepsinthesand Fiordiligi (Mozart (IRE))
3921[7] 4611[4]

**Amazour (IRE)** *Ismail Mohammed* a106 108
5 b g Azamour(IRE) Choose Me (IRE) (Choisir (AUS))
572[7] 1150[4] 1769[11] 2611[3] 4072[11] 4353[7] (7118) 7807[15]

**Ambassadorial (USA)** *M Halford* a105
3 b g Elusive Quality(USA) Tactfully (IRE) (Discreet Cat (USA))
1742a[3]

**Amber Flush** *Clare Ellam* a13 77
8 b m Sir Harry Lewis(USA) Sari Rose (FR) (Vertical Speed (FR))
74[8] 666[8]

**Amberine** *Malcolm Saunders* 35
3 b f Equiano(FR) Crimson Fern (IRE) (Titus Livius (FR))
1761[6] 6174[9]

**Amber Mischief** *Adam West* a23
3 ch f Mayson Grand Lucre (Grand Slam (USA))
1024[8] 7459[11]

**Amber Morning** *Roger Charlton* a37 58
3 b f Nathaniel(IRE) Amber Queen (IRE) (Cadeaux Genereux)
2783[10] 3209[10] 4497[13]

**Amber Mystique** *Kristin Stubbs* a79 74
4 ch m Sakhee(USA) Dame De Noche (Lion Cavern (USA))
97[6] 1032[2]◆ 1245[2] 3147[3] 3828[9] 4344[3] 4722[7]

**Ambiance (IRE)** *Katharina Stenefeldt* a45 98
6 b g Camacho Thawrah (IRE) (Green Desert (USA))
4940a[13]

**Ambient (IRE)** *Roger Varian* a77 68
2 b g Born To Sea(IRE) Undulant Way (Hurricane Run (IRE))
5655[2] 6260[5] 9015[2]

**Ambitious Boy** *John O'Shea* a49 45
8 bl g Striking Ambition Cherished Love (IRE) (Tomba)
270[6] 899[6] 1247[10] 5892[4] 6615[9] 7694[6] 8495[6] 9216[7]

**Ambitious Icarus** *Richard Guest* a69 76
8 b g Striking Ambition Nesting Box (Grand Lodge (USA))
(1031) 1203[4] 1475[4] 1721[5] 1965[8] 2424[5] 2843[3] 3563[10] 3758[6] 3914[2] 4561[11] 5340[2] (5418) 5750[3] 6040[3] 6148[4] 7366[3] 7575[3] 7694[3] 8168[4] 8557[5] 8656[3]

**Ambitious Rosie** *Tony Carroll* a41 49
6 b m Striking Ambition Cerulean Rose (Bluegrass Prince (IRE))
414[10] 733[12] 880[14]

**Ambivalence (IRE)** *H-A Pantall* a77 105
3 gr f Invincible Spirit(IRE) Alpine Snow (IRE) (Verglas (IRE))
3612a[2]

**Ambrosia** *Roger Charlton* a75 76
3 b f Frankel Pearling (USA) (Storm Cat (USA))
5712[2] 6287[2] 6941[2] 7388[3] (9018)

**Ambuscade** *Neil Mulholland* a37
4 b m Dick Turpin(IRE) Tarqua (IRE) (King Charlemagne (USA))
7952[9] 8799[9] 9445[7]

**Amelia Dream** *Mick Channon* a63 77
3 ch f Kyllachy Lady Scarlett (Woodman (USA))
1907[8] 2395[4] 3088[4] 3542[3] 4012[5] (4623) 5153[2] 5682[4] 5932[3] 6415[3] 7163[7] 7599[7] 8000[9]

**Amelie's Star (AUS)** *Darren Weir* 106
5 b m Testa Rossa(AUS) Zazita (AUS) (Zabeel (NZ))
8250a[11] 8667a[14]

**Amenhotepthethird** *Mark Gillard*
2 b c Motivator Autumn Wealth (IRE) (Cadeaux Genereux)
4909[12] 6859[10] 7503[11] 7915[8] 9318[10]

**Amenta (IRE)** *John Berry* a55 59
3 b f Roderic O'Connor(IRE) Pale Light (USA) (Lemon Drop Kid (USA))
3571[2] 6066[4] 8842[5] 9457[8]

**American Craftsman (IRE)**
*Jedd O'Keeffe* a34 64
3 gr g Mastercraftsman(IRE) Quiet Mouse (USA) (Quiet American (USA))
1914[3] 2349[6] 2702[5] (3207) 3489[5] 6002[5] 6892[6]

**American Day (GER)** *A Kleinkorres*
6 ch g Toylsome Alia (GER) (Tertullian (USA))
1196a[10]

**American Endeavour (USA)**
*Marco Botti* a71
2 ch f Distorted Humor(USA) Crazy Party (USA) (A.P. Indy (USA))
7995[7] 8670[3]◆ (9080)

**American History (USA)**
*William Muir* a73 76
3 bb g High Chaparral(IRE) Spinning Time (USA) (Giant's Causeway (USA))
437[2] 5061[2] 5707[5] (6281) 7063[6] 7927[7] 8550[9]

**American Hope (USA)**
*Saeed bin Suroor* a103 109
6 b g Lemon Drop Kid(USA) Cedrat (FR) (Enrique)
87a[14] 538a[3] 775a[5]

**American Hustle (IRE)** *Brian Ellison* a59 56
5 b m Jeremy(USA) Love In May (IRE) (City On A Hill (USA))
3577[6] 3912[13] 5002[9] 7240[3]◆ 8193[3]

**American Oxygen** *C Von Der Recke* 87
2 b f Bahamian Bounty Amalfi (IRE) (Acclamation)
6494a[3]

**American Pastime (USA)**
*Robert B Hess Jr* a111
3 bb c Tapizar(USA) Ryan's Inheritance (USA) (Valid Expectations (USA))
8607a[4]

**American Patriot (USA)**
*Todd Pletcher* 112
4 bb h War Front(USA) Life Well Lived (USA) (Tiznow (USA))
3924[11] 7851a[10]

**American Patrol (IRE)**
*Neil Mulholland* a63 58
3 ch g Rio De La Plata(USA) Gutter Press (IRE) (Raise A Grand (IRE))
(376) 502[7] 2711[13] 8773[11] 8985[11]

**American Ruby (USA)** *Roger Fell* 34
2 b f Data Link(USA) Fifth Avenue Doll (USA) (Marquetry (USA))
4963[6] 5600[7] 5999[5] 7030[11]

**Amherst Rock** *Luke McJannet* a39 61
3 ch g Exceed And Excel(AUS) Frigid (Indian Ridge (IRE))
7414[9] 8656[14]

**Amiga Intima (FR)** *C Plisson* a66 64
7 b m Dylan Thomas(IRE) Maitresse (FR) (Singspiel (IRE))
798a[8]

**Amigo (GER)** *Eva Fabianova* 110
3 ch c Lord Of England(GER) All Night Long (GER) (Ransom O'War (USA))
(4931a) 6255a[3] 7722a[3] 8527a[6]

**Amiirah** *John Gallagher* a22 41
2 b f Helmet(AUS) Aalya (IRE) (Peintre Celebre (USA))
2037[10] 3210[10] 5030[10] 8644[12] 8870[12]

**Amiral** *J-F Doucet* a69 60
4 gr g Siyouni(FR) Attachante (IRE) (Teofilo (IRE))
3274a[4]

**Amiral Chop (FR)** *A Chopard* a37 73
2 ch c Deportivo Lonsome Drive (FR) (Domedriver (IRE))
3445a[4] 8482a[9]

**Ami's Mesa (CAN)** *Josie Carroll* a114 92
4 bb m Sky Mesa(USA) Victorious Ami (CAN) (Victory Gallop (CAN))
8605a[2]

**Amitie Waltz (FR)** *Richard Hughes* a77
5 b g Sinndar(IRE) Lia Waltz (FR) (Linamix (FR))
1069[5] 1866[2]◆

**Amity Island** *Ollie Pears* a56
2 ch c Harbour Watch(IRE) Mylington Light (Mount Nelson)
8208[9] 8802[3] 8983[3]

**Amlad (IRE)** *Ed Dunlop* a92 90
3 ch g Lope De Vega(IRE) Pietra Dura (Cadeaux Genereux)
1499[3] (1874) (3596) 4701[2] 5525[8] 6232[4] 7031[2] 7548[8]

**A Momentofmadness** *Charles Hills* a94 100
4 b g Elnadim(USA) Royal Blush (Royal Applause)
(1793) 2391[2] 3321[4] 3967[3] 4816[3] 5505[2] 6325[4] 7144[6] 7804[5]

**Among Angels**
*Daniel Mark Loughnane* a85 61
5 b g Acclamation Love Action (IRE) (Motivator)
25[5] 159[2] 312[7] 660[5] (850) 1074[10] 1185[7] 1867[3] 2608[12] 3214[7] 3723[7]

**Amood (IRE)** *Archie Watson* a86 81
6 ch g Elnadim(USA) Amanah (USA) (Mr Prospector (USA))
1472[8] 1778[7] 2133[10] 2684[9] 2922[3] 3492[3] 3847[5] 4304[2] 4999[7]◆ 5415[4] 5827[2] 6807[3] 7099[3] 7742[7]

**Amore Hass (IRE)** *Stefano Botti* 108
3 b g Azamour(IRE) Hassaya (IRE) (King's Best (USA))
2245a[3] 2868a[4] 4941a[6] **(7442a)** 8448a[7]

**Amoretti (FR)** *M Creveau*
13 b h Lac Ladoga Lakarifair (IRE) (Always Fair (USA))
6543a[6]

**Amor Invicto (IRE)** *Daniel Kubler* a65 67
4 b g Holy Roman Emperor(IRE) Love In The Mist (USA) (Silver Hawk (USA))
***239[5]*** *420[8]*

**Amourice (IRE)** *Jane Chapple-Hyam* 81
2 b f Authorized(IRE) Amancaya (GER) (Dai Jin)
3590[4] 4361[9] 5660[2] **6200[2]**

**Amplification (USA)** *Ed Dunlop* 77
2 b g Lonhro(AUS) Our Drama Queen (IRE) (Danehill Dancer (IRE))
8119[3]◆ **(8382)**

**Amun (GER)** *C Von Der Recke* 104
3 b c Soldier Hollow Albula (GER) (Dashing Blade)
**4422a[9]**

**Amy Blair** *Keith Dalgleish* a28 79
4 b g Captain Gerrard(IRE) Shalad'Or (Golden Heights)
*1823[10]* 2430[5] 2773[2] 3048[7] (3242) 3450[4] (4432) 4893[11] **(5097)** 5650[7] 6349[13]

**Anaakeed** *Owen Burrows* 57
2 ch f Dubawi(IRE) Daymooma (Pivotal)
**8322[5]◆**

**Anaerobio (ARG)** *M F De Kock* a78 110
9 b h Catcher In The Rye(IRE) Potra Anala (ARG) (Potrillon (ARG))
**87a[7]** 320a[4] 653a[6]

**Anahita (FR)** *S bin Ghadayer* 92
6 b m Turtle Bowl(IRE) Nazlia (FR) (Polish Precedent (USA))
**431a[9]**

**Anakin Skywalker (GER)** *W Mongil* a35 71
8 b g Soldier Hollow Aughamore Beauty (IRE) (Dara Monarch)
***8303a[10]***

**Anapa (FR)** *W Delalande*
2 b g Elusive City(USA) Anasy (USA) (Gone West (USA))
6409a[10]

**Anastazia** *Paul D'Arcy* a74 72
5 br m Kyllachy Meddle (Diktat)
*1618[2]* **(2318)** 2974[4] 3730[4] **4542[3]** 5337[4] 6656[5] *7771[9]* 8124[7] *8641[3] 8801[6]*

**Ancient Astronaut** *John Quinn* a64 81
4 b g Kodiac Tatora (Selkirk (USA))
**(1972) 2800[2]** 3847[10] **4629[3]** 5280[3] 7405[6] *7940[13]*

**Ancient Foe** *Andrew Balding* a81 42
3 b g Shamardal(USA) Pearl Dance (USA) (Nureyev (USA))
4332[6] ***5243[3]*** *5794[4]*

**Ancient Longing** *Roger Charlton* 70
3 b f Nathaniel(IRE) Longing To Dance (Danehill Dancer (IRE))
5428[5] **6194[4]** 6775[4] 7279[7]

**Ancient Spirit (GER)**
*Jean-Pierre Carvalho*
2 bb c Invincible Spirit(IRE) Assisi (GER) (Galileo (IRE))
8091a[5]

**Andalouse Eria (FR)** *C Escuder* a69 66
3 bb f Rio De La Plata(USA) Berroscoberro (FR) (Octagonal (NZ))
**8025a[8]**

**Andalusite** *John Gallagher* a66 70
4 br m Equiano(FR) Kammaan (Diktat)
*1220[5] 1599[7]* 1785[3] (2056) 2511[4] *2996[2]* 3522[7] (4711) 5558[3] 5789[3] 6555[9] **(7216)** *7484[10] 8156[7]*

**Anda Muchacho (IRE)**
*Nicolo Simondi* 110
3 b c Helmet(AUS) Montefino (IRE) (Shamardal (USA))
(2245a) 2868a[3] **(8095a) (8963a)**

**Andanotherone (IRE)** *Denis Quinn* a58 66
4 b m Kodiac Itsanothergirl (Reprimand)
***624[5]*** *883[5] 964[3]*

**Andastra (GER)** *Ralph Beckett* a90 85
4 b m Kamsin(GER) Arpista (GER) (Chief Singer)
***744[4]*** *1258[8]*

**Andok (IRE)** *Richard Fahey* a85 85
3 b g Elzaam(AUS) My Causeway Dream (IRE) (Giant's Causeway (USA))
**2402[5]** 2824[13] 4507[5] 6942[3] **7555[3]** 8111[4] 8385[10] ***8912[2] 9271[2]***

**Andrassy Avenue (USA)**
*Charlie Appleby* a79
3 b g Street Cry(IRE) Suez (Green Desert (USA))
***1725[5]*** (Dead)

**Andys Girl (IRE)** *Brian Ellison* a63 61
4 gr m Clodovil(IRE) Fishy (Irish River (FR))
***8194[4]*** *8592[4]*

**Aneedh** *Clive Mulhall* a57 49
7 b g Lucky Story(USA) Seed Al Maha (USA) (Seeking The Gold (USA))
**3436[3]** 4558[6] 8241[7] *9262[10]*

**Aneen (IRE)** *Kevin Prendergast* a98 97
3 bb f Lawman(FR) Asheerah (Shamardal (USA))
3110a[7] ***7588a[6]*** *8407a[2]*

**Anfaass (IRE)** *George Margarson* a64 80
3 ro c Vale Of York(IRE) Webcast (IRE) (Verglas (IRE))
4100[7] 4887[14] 5159[5] **5606[3]** 6297[7] 8115[11] *8542[8]*

**An Fear Cluin (IRE)** *R Mike Smith* a62 83
6 b g Galileo(IRE) Potion (Pivotal)
***3[6] 666[6]*** **3830[10]**

**Angel Baby (FR)** *Alex Fracas* a75 75
3 b f Canford Cliffs(IRE) Shabanou (FR) (Shamardal (USA))
***4289a[2]*** **6650a[3]**

**Angel Carlotta (IRE)** *Nigel Tinkler* 23
2 b f Camelot Stravina (GER) (Platini (GER))
**7521[9]** 8046[10]

**Angel Down** *Henry Candy* a78 90
3 b g Kyllachy Falling Angel (Kylian (USA))
*2334[6] 3211[7]* (4313) 5115[3] **(5966)** 7129[7]

**Angel Force (IRE)** *David C Griffiths* 87
2 ch f Lethal Force(IRE) Indian Angel (Indian Ridge (IRE))
2134[7] 2988[4] 3333[5] 4739[6] 4922[4] (5440) 5615[2] **6448[5]** 7138[5] 8001[12]

**Angel Gabriel (IRE)** *Richard Fahey* a74 103
8 b g Hurricane Run(IRE) Causeway Song (USA) (Giant's Causeway (USA))
**1802[4]** 2525[8] 3073[6] 3594[11] 4338[5] 4998[2]◆ 5438[2] 5912[5] 6680[3] 7599[3] 8047[8]

**Angelical (IRE)**
*Daniel Mark Loughnane* a59 64
4 b m Dark Angel(IRE) Ladylishandra (IRE) (Mujadil (USA))
**(2153) 2710[3]** 3148[4] **3628[4] 4088[3]** 5290[4] 6109[4] 6811[2] 7567[9]

**Angelical Eve (IRE)** *George Baker* a53 35
3 gr f Dark Angel(IRE) First Lady (IRE) (Indian Ridge (IRE))
***2112[6]*** 5050[11] 6748[14] *8134[5] 8345[11]*

**Angelic Lord (IRE)** *Tom Dascombe* a99 105
5 b g Dark Angel(IRE) Divine Design (IRE) (Barathea (IRE))
***730[9]*** *999[6]*

**Angelina D'Or (GER)**
*Mark Johnston* a74
2 ch f Casamento(IRE) Ange Doree (FR) (Sinyar (IRE))
*8952[4]* ***9099[2]*** *9240[3]*

**Angel In Disguise (IRE)**
*Philip McBride* a49 43
3 b f Vale Of York(IRE) Meynell (Sakhee (USA))
2585[13]

**Angel In The Snow** *Brian Ellison* a55 52
4 ch g Haafhd Chilly Filly (IRE) (Montjeu (IRE))
3756[6] **5284[2]** 5740[5] ***7360[3]*** *8314[2]* ***8430[3]*** *9242[6] 9421[7]*

**Angel Island (IRE)** *J A Stack* 86
3 b f So You Think(NZ) Dombeya (IRE) (Danehill (USA))
**3109a[8]**

**Angel Islington (IRE)**
*Andrew Balding* a74 73
2 gr f Dark Angel(IRE) Doregan (IRE) (Bahhare (USA))
2905[5] 3421[4] ***4749[2]*** 5685[3]

**Angelita (GER)** *P Schiergen* 99
2 b f Areion(GER) Angel Dragon (GER) (Royal Dragon (USA))
**8269a[3]**

**Angelito** *Tony Newcombe* a51 65
8 ch g Primo Valentino(IRE) Supreme Angel (Beveled (USA))
*602[10]* 2724[11] 4735[3] **7191[3]**

**Angel Meadow** *Micky Hammond* 86
3 b f Mayson Memo (Groom Dancer (USA))
2806[12] **3462[5]** 3709[8] 5806[6]

**Angel Of Darkness** *Charles Hills* a80 88
3 b f Dark Angel(IRE) Chelsea Morning (USA) (Giant's Causeway (USA))
*168[2] (1693) 2094[2]* (3307) 4051[2] 4536[4] 5117[8] **5965[2]** 6358[3] 7155[6]

**Angel Of Light (IRE)** *Jo Hughes* a44 4
5 b m Dark Angel(IRE) Riymaisa (IRE) (Traditionally (USA))
***69[7]***

**Angel Of Rome (IRE)**
*Richard Hughes* a69 30
3 gr f Mastercraftsman(IRE) Bright Sapphire (IRE) (Galileo (IRE))
***1333[3]*** *2019[11] 3178[6]* 4442[8] 5565[6]

**Angel Of The South (IRE)**
*Dean Ivory* a75 75
2 gr f Dark Angel(IRE) Oeuvre D'Art (IRE) (Marju (IRE))
**1681[2]** 2563[7] **2905[2] 3668[3]◆** 4253[11] 6353[15] 7334[9] *9122[2]* ***(9416)***

**Angelou** *David O'Meara* a46 36
3 b f Poet's Voice Quiz Show (Primo Dominie)
***612[6]*** 5006[5]

**Angel Palanas** *K R Burke* a64 64
3 b g Mayson Scottish Exile (IRE) (Ashkalani (IRE))
2927[10] 3313[3] 3709[7] 4428[4] 5636[3] **5962[2]** *6904[4]* 7218[3] 8512[4] 8681[2] *9308[7]*

**Angel's Acclaim (IRE)** *Kevin Ryan* a70 64
3 gr f Dark Angel(IRE) Miss Otis (Danetime (IRE))
*1782[4]* 2180[4] 4688[4] ***(5835)***

**Angel's Glory** *Roger Varian* 76
2 b f Invincible Spirit(IRE) Dutch Diamond (Dutch Art)
**7563[3]** 8006[4]

**Angel's Quest (FR)** *Richard Hughes* a73 79
3 b f Dark Angel(IRE) Lilac Charm (IRE) (Marju (IRE))
3007[5] *3472[3]*◆ **4096[2]** 4975[5] 5506[8] (5969)

**Angel's Whisper (IRE)**
*Jeremy Noseda* a61 70
2 gr f Dark Angel(IRE) Tasheyaat (Sakhee (USA))
**6438[2]** 7269[8] *7986[4]*

**Angie B (IRE)** *John Wainwright* a29 45
2 b f Acclamation Musical Peace (IRE) (Oratorio (IRE))
4502[10] 5179[7] 5613[4] **5945[3]** *7029[8]* 7518[8]

**Anginola (IRE)** *Julia Brooke* a40 36
8 b m Kodiac Lady Montekin (Montekin)
**7220[10]**

**Angrywhitepyjamas (IRE)**
*William Muir* a89 85
4 b g Manduro(GER) Ornellaia (IRE) (Mujadil (USA))
***(3966)*** 4882[5] *6952[6]* 7959[7] 8295[12]

**Anieres Boy** *Oliver Greenall* a61 60
5 b g Kheleyf(USA) Place Morny (IRE) (Cadeaux Genereux)
***21[9]***

**Anif (IRE)** *Jean-Rene Auvray* a76 75
3 b g Cape Cross(IRE) Cadenza (FR) (Dansili)
1962[5] **(3500)** 4084[3] 4631[8] *9281[5]*

**Anima Rock (FR)**
*Jassim Mohammed Ghazali* 94
2 b c Shamalgan(FR) Carnet De Bal (Kingsalsa (USA))
**9446a[2]**

**Annabella** *Tim McCarthy* a46
4 b m Approve(IRE) Ashlinn (IRE) (Ashkalani (IRE))
*139[7] 644[8] 9088[8] 9282[9]* ***9435[5]***

**Anna Briggs** *Michael Blanshard* a23 29
2 b f Havana Gold(IRE) Netta (IRE) (Barathea (IRE))
*3210[9]* **5216[13]**

**Annagassan** *Donal Kinsella* a48 43
4 ch m Art Connoisseur(IRE) Amatara (IRE) (Indian Haven)
***6798a[8]***

**Anna Jammeela** *A Wohler* 52
2 b f Big Bad Bob(IRE) All Annalena (IRE) (Dubai Destination (USA))
**6494a[10]**

**Anna Medici** *Mike Murphy* a71 65
3 b f Sir Percy Florentia (Medicean)
*1064[7] 1179[6]*◆ *1401[9] 4982[3] (5239)*◆ (5511) *(6016) 6288[4] 8589[5] (8908)* ***9034[2]*** *9338[4]*

**Anna Nerium** *Richard Hannon* 100
2 ch f Dubawi(IRE) Anna Oleanda (IRE) (Old Vic)
3746[6] 4815[3] (5420) **(6863)** 8002[9]

**Anna's Legacy** *Jim Goldie* 17
4 b m Shirocco(GER) Gargoyle Girl (Be My Chief (USA))
**4657[6]** 6044[8] **6350[5]** 6788[9]

**Anne's Valentino** *Rebecca Menzies* 9
7 b m Primo Valentino(IRE) Annie's Gift (IRE) (Presenting)
**7922[10]**

**Annie Fior (IRE)**
*Thomas P O'Connor* a75 82
3 ch f Finsceal Fior(IRE) Annamanamoux (USA) (Leroidesanimaux (BRZ))
*1026[9] 1582[6] 3262[9]* 4621[4] **5589[3]** *8225a[12]*

**Annie Salts** *Chris Dwyer* a73 76
4 b m Zebedee Dazzling View (USA) (Distant View (USA))
*327[2] (604) 961[5]* 1328[4] *1547[8] (1981)* 3331[6] 4081[4] **(5514)** 7256[3] *7486[3] 7994[5]* 8853[8] *8950[3]*

**Annoushka**
*Mrs Ilka Gansera-Leveque* a43 57
4 b m Proclamation(IRE) Anapola (GER) (Polish Precedent (USA))
2908[10] 4323[10] 5080[2]◆ 5508[7] **7015[4]** 8122[10]

**Annus Mirabilis (IRE)** *Stuart Webb* 101
6 b g Montjeu(IRE) Love Me True (USA) (Kingmambo (USA))
1400a[13] 1994a[4] **8056a[5]**

**Ann Without An E** *Mick Channon* 84
2 b f Rip Van Winkle(IRE) Visanilla (FR) (Danehill (USA))
5573[3] **6190[5]** 6659[6] 7045[4] 8074[6]

**Anonymous John (IRE)**
*Dominic Ffrench Davis* a81 66
5 gr g Baltic King Helibel (IRE) (Pivotal)
*506[7] 808[4] 1467[4]* ***(1890)*** 2582[6] *3214[3]* 3696[8] 4251[8] *4746[9] 9093[7] 9411[9]*

**Another Angel (IRE)** *Antony Brittain* 67
3 b g Dark Angel(IRE) Kermana (IRE) (Selkirk (USA))
6062[9]

**Another Batt (IRE)** *George Scott* 99
2 ch g Windsor Knot(IRE) Mrs Batt (IRE) (Medecis)
(3460) 3929[8] (4681) 5109[3] **5395[2]** 6190[3] **(6745a)**

**Another Boy** *Ralph Beckett* a69 79
4 ch g Paco Boy(IRE) Kurtanella (Pastoral Pursuits)
2795[4] 3396[10] 4810[4] **(5333)** 6378[3] 7229[7] **7780[3]**

**Another Day Of Sun (IRE)**
*Mick Channon* a74 71
2 ch g Camacho Sunblush (UAE) (Timber Country (USA))
3002[8] (3398) 4220[6] 4716[3] 5366[6] ***5844[3] 6636[5] 7363[3]*** *7787[4] 8208[6]*

**Another Desperado (IRE)**
*Rebecca Bastiman* 42
4 b g Approve(IRE) Kind Regards (IRE) (Unfuwain (USA))
**2453[4]**

**Another Eclipse (IRE)**
*David Simcock* a78 94
3 b g Lope De Vega(IRE) Black Dahlia (Dansili)
2857[2]◆ 3583[3] (4460) 5634[2] 6482[3] **7091[2]**

**Anotherfortheroad**
*Matthieu Palussiere* 71
2 ch c Dutch Art Sacred Aspect (IRE) (Haatef (USA))
**7012a[7]** 8253a[3]

**Another Go (IRE)** *Sally Haynes* a16 66
4 gr g Strategic Prince Golden Rose (GER) (Winged Love (IRE))
**1517[11]** 3486[5] 6784[5]

**Another Situation (USA)**
*Richard Guest* a21
2 ch f Trappe Shot(USA) Return The Jewel (USA) (Broken Vow (USA))
***7450[8]***

**Another Story (IRE)**
*Ms Sheila Lavery* a90 97
4 b m Rip Van Winkle(IRE) Chronicle (Observatory (USA))
2241a[5] **6491a[8]** 6642a[8]

**Another Touch** *Richard Fahey* 109
4 b g Arcano(IRE) Alsalwa (IRE) (Nayef (USA))
1492[17] 1960[2] 2767[4] (3218) 3963[11] 4918[8] **(5456)**

**Another Wise Kid (IRE)**
*Paul Midgley* a81 97
9 b g Whipper(USA) Romancing (Dr Devious (IRE))
**1515[9]** 2031[7] 3463[5] 4477[3] 5379[13]

**Ansaab** *Marjorie Fife* a98 87
9 b g Cape Cross(IRE) Dawn Raid (IRE) (Docksider (USA))
*359[9] 524[5]* ***(648)***◆

**An Saighdiur (IRE)** *Andrew Slattery* a68 88
10 b g Acclamation Brief Sentiment (IRE) (Brief Truce (USA))
1385a[16] ***6801a[5]***

**Anse De Bel'Amande (FR)**
*F Lemercier* 60
3 b f No Risk At All(FR) Tracy Eria (FR) (Loup Solitaire (USA))
3134a[8] **4232a[11]**

**Anse Marcel (FR)** *J-P Gauvin* a67 58
4 bl m Naaqoos Curves In Control (USA) (Arch (USA))
***837a[2]***

**Antagonist** *Roger Charlton* a68 69
2 b c Dansili Melodramatic (IRE) (Sadler's Wells (USA))
5710[6]◆ **6921[4]** *7511[7]*

**Antiquarium (IRE)** *Charlie Appleby* a112 101
5 b g New Approach(IRE) Antillia (Red Ransom (USA))
***(268)***◆ (Dead)

**Anton Chigurh** *Nikki Evans* a79 70
8 b g Oasis Dream Barathiki (Barathea (IRE))
***6[2]*** *419[4] 1074[11] 1329[5] 1695[2]* 3168[4] 4802[6] 5824[7] *8955[6] 9346[10]*

**Anton Dolin (IRE)**
*Michael Mullineaux* a56 58
9 ch g Danehill Dancer(IRE) Ski For Gold (Shirley Heights)
*241[7] 423[5] 721[4]* ***839[2]*** *2272[10] 9221[10]*

**Antonian** *John Gosden* a72
2 b c Intello(GER) Highest (Dynaformer (USA))
***9155[4]*** *(9417)*

**Antonio Giuseppe (NZ)**
*Chris Waller* 107
4 br g Shocking(AUS) Crystalthecowgirl (NZ) (High Chaparral (IRE))
**6714a[4]**

**Any Joy (IRE)** *Ben Haslam* a34 57
4 b m Zoffany(IRE) For Joy (Singspiel (IRE))
***883[6] 1408[9]***

**Any Little Rhyme** *Michael Bell* a71 68
2 b f Shamardal(USA) Free Verse (Danehill Dancer (IRE))
8734[5] ***9022[4]***

**Anythingtoday (IRE)** *Hugo Palmer* a82 105
3 b g Zoffany(IRE) Corking (IRE) (Montjeu (IRE))
2132[8] 3778[4] 4443[2] (5421)◆ (5781)◆ **5940[3]** 6474[2] 6920[10] 7395[3] 8042[9]

**Anythingwithapulse (IRE)**
*Daniel Mark Loughnane*
2 br f Dragon Pulse(IRE) Mahatta (IRE) (Halling (USA))
*3467[11]*

**Aonedamproofing** *Lisa Williamson*
2 b g Westlake Pinball (IRE) (Namid)
*8915[11] 9050[10] 9182[5]*

**Aothea (GER)** *Carmen Bocskai*
3 b f Areion(GER) Aotearoa (FR) (Doyen (IRE))
*4288a[P]*

**Apache Blaze** *Michael Appleby* a61
2 b f Champs Elysees Polar Circle (USA) (Royal Academy (USA))
*8670[8]* ***9313[6]***

**Apalis (FR)** *Michael Easterby* a67 62
5 gr m Mastercraftsman(IRE) Parcimonie (Nombre Premier)
***3252[7]*** 3432[5] 3830[9] 8654[4] *8978[7]* ***(9258)***◆

**Apero Time (FR)** *D Windrif* a31 47
3 ch f Air Chief Marshal(IRE) Holiday Snap (American Post)
**4783a[11]**

**Apex King (IRE)** *Ed Dunlop* 97
3 b g Kodiac Rainbowskia (FR) (Rainbow Quest (USA))
**1861[5]** 2614[5] 7400[5]

**Apex Predator (IRE)**
*Seamus Durack* a65 67
2 b c Acclamation Key Girl (IRE) (Key Of Luck (USA))
**6133[7]** *6885[6]*

**Aphaea** *Michael Easterby* 54
2 b f Farhh Wood Chorus (Singspiel (IRE))
**6938[6]** 8013[10] 8236[7]

**Apilobar (FR)** *F Vermeulen* a105 108
4 b h Slickly(FR) Popee (FR) (Take Risks (FR))
1871a[3] 2559a[2] **3369a[3]**

**Apoleon (GER)**
*Frau Anna Schleusner-Fruhriep* 99
7 br g Ogatonango(GER) Abisou (GER) (Goofalik (USA))
**2667a[10]** 4487a[5] 7722a[9] 8463a[4]

**Apollo (GER)** *J Hirschberger*
2 bb c Maxios Adela (GER) (Tannenkonig (IRE))
6986a[12]

**Apollo Kentucky (USA)**
*Kenji Yamauchi* a118
5 bb h Langfuhr(CAN) Dixiana Delight (USA) (Gone West (USA))
***1380a[9]***

**Appalachian Spring (IRE)**
*H-A Pantall* a65 83
3 b c Redoute's Choice(AUS) Alpensinfonie (IRE) (Montjeu (IRE))
**6225a[2]**

**Apparition (IRE)**
*Joseph Patrick O'Brien* a75 94
3 br g Dream Ahead(USA) Bluebell Park (USA) (Gulch (USA))
**6978a[4]**

**Appeared** *Roger Varian* a90 108
5 b g Dubawi(IRE) Appearance (Galileo (IRE))
**(2603)◆ 4033[2] 5353[5]** 6399[8]

**Appease** *Julia Feilden* a49 52
8 b g Oasis Dream Penchee (Grand Lodge (USA))
*1456[3]* 5509[6] **(6296) 7216[4]**

**Appelina (DEN)** *Wido Neuroth*
4 ch m Appel Au Maitre(FR) Wings Of A Dove (Hernando (FR))
*2942a[6]*

**Appenzeller (USA)** *Richard Hughes* 58
2 gr g Mizzen Mast(USA) Uforia (USA) (Zilzal (USA))
6093[6] 7351[10] 8112[5]

**Apphia (IRE)** *Hugo Palmer* 107
3 b f High Chaparral(IRE) Mixed Blessing (Lujain (USA))
2131[2]◆ (3007) 3995[5] 5155[4] 5658[6] 6675[4] (7577)

**Apple Anni (IRE)** *Mick Channon* 83
2 b f Fast Company(IRE) Common Cause (Polish Patriot (USA))
6824[3] (7266) 7423a[9] 8082a[4] 8440a[7] 8597[8]

**Appleberry (IRE)** *Michael Appleby* a76 74
5 b m Approve(IRE) Passage To India (IRE) (Indian Ridge (IRE))
1542[3] 2683[4] 2821[7] 3541[4] 7738[4] 8167[11] 8260[11] 8801[7] 9033[9] 9219[9]

**Applicator (USA)** *Mikhail Yanakov* 104
4 b g Henrythenavigator(USA) River Flower (USA) (Strodes Creek (USA))
7851a[12]

**Appointed** *Tim Easterby* 97
3 b f Delegator Celestial Harmony (Polish Precedent (USA))
3094[2] 4376[6] (5439) 5915[5] 6404[12] 6671[3] 6924[6] 7816[11]

**Appreciating** *Kevin Ryan* a59
3 b f New Approach(IRE) Star Value (IRE) (Danehill Dancer (IRE))
612[5] 1151[5]

**Approaching Menace** *Amy Murphy* a11
2 b f Cityscape Candle (Dansili)
9155[9]

**Appy Days (IRE)** *Ian Williams* a66
7 b m King's Theatre(IRE) A-To-Z (IRE) (Ahonoora)
576[3] 894[2]

**Apres Midi (IRE)** *K R Burke* 82
4 b m Galileo(IRE) Rose Bonheur (Danehill Dancer (IRE))
1938[3] 3158[3] 4118[6] 4908[8] (5475) 6349[7]

**Apricot Sky** *Michael Dods* a75 78
7 ch g Pastoral Pursuits Miss Apricot (Indian Ridge (IRE))
4379[14] 5426[4] 5602[10] 6670[11] 7657[7] 7923[3] (8237) 8512[7] 8927[4] 9308[4]

**April Angel (FR)** *P Demercastel* a53 63
3 b f Spirit One(FR) Lady Verde (FR) (Meshaheer (USA))
3353a[9] 4455a[10] 6084a[8]

**Aprilios (FR)** *J-M Lefebvre* a87 83
5 gr g Desert Style(IRE) Allegria (FR) (Verglas (IRE))
5979a[4] 6648a[13] 7636a[13]

**Aprovado (IRE)** *Michael Dods* a86 88
5 b g Approve(IRE) Aldburgh (Bluebird (USA))
443[8] 660[3] 995[2] (1346) 1777[12] 2951[2] 3386[3] 4337[10] 4787[2] 5471[5] 5947[9] 6943[9] 7940[6]

**Aqabah (USA)** *Charlie Appleby* 103
2 gr c Exchange Rate(USA) Fast Tip (USA) (Najran (USA))
(2607) 3098a[4] 3925[5] 4906[9] 7112[3] 7754a[4]

**Aqshion Stations** *Richard Price* a42 41
3 b g Aqlaam Shersha (IRE) (Priolo (USA))
139[11] 4633[10] 6034[5] 6502[12]

**Aqua Ardens (GER)** *George Baker* a92 79
9 b g Nayef(USA) Arduinna (GER) (Winged Love (IRE))
528[2] 1074[7] 1238[7]

**Aquadabra (IRE)** *Mick Channon* a70 72
2 b f Born To Sea(IRE) Amazing Win (IRE) (Marju (IRE))
1627[3] 2037[3] 2265[3] 3690[3] 4204[4] 4488[2] (4991) 5270[4] 5614[6] 6651[5] 7159[7] 7814[8] 8110[2] 8154[4]

**Aqua Libre** *Jennie Candlish* a62 85
4 b m Aqlaam Be Free (Selkirk (USA))
304[7] 551[9] 1238[3] 1718[7] 3441[4] 4542[6] 5039[5] 5895[5] 6369[6] 7015[10] 7478[8] 7934[11]

**Aquamarina** *Robyn Brisland* a76 55
3 b f Kheleyf(USA) Reeling N' Rocking (IRE) (Mr Greeley (USA))
(1199) 7576[12] 8150[8] 8374[11]

**A Quiet Man (IRE)** *F Chappet* 95
2 gr c Literato(FR) Priceless Baby (IRE) (Peintre Celebre (USA))
(6247a) 6912a[3]

**Araaja (IRE)** *A De Watrigant* 102
3 ch f Iffraaj Roshanak (IRE) (Spinning World (USA))
(4988a) 6227a[5] 7305a[4]

**Arabda** *Patrick Wahl* 95
6 br m Elnadim(USA) Ghizlaan (USA) (Seeking The Gold (USA))
205a[12] 431a[10]

**Arabela Dawn (IRE)** *John Quinn* a43 47
3 b f Delegator Arabela (IRE) (Medicean)
3150[6] 4743[11] 7980[11]

**Arabella Rose** *Ivan Furtado* a53
3 b f Monsieur Bond(IRE) Moorhouse Girl (Makbul)
331[4] 600[5] 1004[8]

**Arabellas Fortune** *James Ewart*
2 b f Haafhd Finellas Fortune (Elmaamul (USA))
5278[10] 6057[12]

**Arabian Gift (IRE)** *Charlie Appleby* 81
2 br f Dubawi(IRE) Gift Range (IRE) (Spectrum (IRE))
3858[2]

**Arabian Hope (USA)**
*Saeed bin Suroor* a99 110
3 b f Distorted Humor(USA) Achieving (USA) (Bernardini (USA))
(1503) (2117) (3843) 4857[3]◆ 5460a[10] (6718a) 7812[13]

**Arabian Jazz (IRE)** *Michael Bell* 69
2 b f Red Jazz(USA) Queen Of Rap (IRE) (Alhaarth (IRE))
2258[U] 2502[2] 2910[3] 4167[2] 4858[9] 6087[4] (6890)

**Arabian Oasis** *Philip Kirby* a62 79
5 b g Oasis Dream Love Divine (Diesis)
1561[4] 4358[9] 5021[8]

**Arabian Sea (USA)** *Roger Charlton* a50 56
2 b f Point Of Entry(USA) Galanty Show (Danehill (USA))
6917[7] 7997[9]

**Arabica** *Simone Brogi* 86
2 b f Style Vendome(FR) Besito (IRE) (Kodiac)
6251a[2]

**Arabic Culture (USA)**
*Saeed bin Suroor* 70
3 b g Lonhro(AUS) Kydd Gloves (USA) (Dubai Millennium)
3755[4]◆

**Arab Moon** *William Knight* a97 84
3 b g Elnadim(USA) Albeed (Tiger Hill (IRE))
(1726)◆ (2371) 2395[5] (3457)◆ 4314[3] (5798)◆ 6887[2] 8005[11]

**Arab Spring (IRE)**
*Sir Michael Stoute* a116 114
7 b h Monsun(GER) Spring Symphony (IRE) (Darshaan)
574[2] 934a[10]

**Arachina (IRE)** *Harry Dunlop* a56 55
2 ch f Arakan(USA) Tibouchina (IRE) (Daylami (IRE))
4253[16] 5216[14] 7211[5] 7756[8] 7996[3] 8500[10]

**Aragon Knight** *Daniel Steele* a75 59
4 b g Kheleyf(USA) Midnight Allure (Aragon)
330[7] 575[3] 1062[7] 1339[8] 6888[9]

**Arahat (USA)** *John Gosden*
2 b f Temple City(USA) Perfect Rah (USA) (Perfect Soul (IRE))
9099[11]

**Aramist (IRE)** *Sally Haynes* a57 84
7 gr g Aussie Rules(USA) Mistic Sun (Dashing Blade)
2928[6] 5438[4] 5873[3] 6317[7] 6968[7]

**A Raving Beauty (GER)**
*Andreas Suborics* 104
4 rg m Mastercraftsman(IRE) Anabasis (GER) (High Chaparral (IRE))
3019a[5] 4518a[5] 6647a[4] 7672a[2] 8450a[2]

**Arawak (USA)** *Wesley A Ward* a90 90
2 b c Uncle Mo(USA) Spicy Teddy (USA) (Spanish Steps (USA))
3925[12]

**Arazza (GER)** *J Hirschberger* 99
3 b f Areion(GER) Aloe (GER) (Lomitas)
1846a[5] 3882a[3] 5196a[8] 6254a[9] 6987a[3] 7672a[4] 8462a[8]

**Arbalet (IRE)** *Hugo Palmer* 99
2 gr c Dark Angel(IRE) Miss Beatrix (IRE) (Danehill Dancer (IRE))
3846[2] 4539[2] (5179) 6696[3]◆ 8036[6]

**Arborist (IRE)** *A R Al Rayhi* a61 74
3 gr g Dark Angel(IRE) Ride For Roses (IRE) (Barathea (IRE))
649a[8]

**Arcadian Cat (USA)** *Ralph Beckett* 73
2 b f Kitten's Joy(USA) Calissa (IRE) (Danehill Dancer (IRE))
8425[3]

**Arcadian Sea (IRE)** *William Jarvis* a62 58
3 b g Born To Sea(IRE) Drombeg Dawn (IRE) (Orpen (USA))
2521[4] 2997[8] 4156[6] 4978[3] 5406[3] 6048[3]◆ 6524[6] (7324) 7761[4] 9127[7]

**Arcanada (IRE)** *Tom Dascombe* a112 112
4 ch g Arcano(IRE) Bond Deal (IRE) (Pivotal)
87a[13] 538a[4] 4916[2] 6746a[8] 7807[17] (8843)

**Arcane Dancer (IRE)**
*Lawrence Mullaney* a60 66
4 b m Arcano(IRE) La Reine Mambo (USA) (High Yield (USA))
69[4] 2224[2] 3203[4] 3577[5] 4601[3] 4900[3] (5214) 5802[8] 6047[7] 6471[8] 7476[11] 8194[8] 8659[8]

**Arcanista (IRE)** *Chris Dwyer* a63 62
4 ch m Arcano(IRE) Cattiva Generosa (Cadeaux Genereux)
293[8] 481[13] 684[4] 811[2] 1249[9] 1603[10] 2024[4] 2312[8] 5854[7] 6318[2]◆ 6814[3] 7282[4] (7911) 8473[10] 8823[2] 9183[5] 9323[6]

**Arcavallo (IRE)** *Michael Dods* 84
2 ch c Arcano(IRE) Pashmina (IRE) (Barathea (IRE))
2896[9] 3895[2] 4502[2] (5494) (6055) 7814[2]

**Archangel Raphael (IRE)**
*Amanda Perrett* a78 87
5 b g Montjeu(IRE) La Sylvia (IRE) (Oasis Dream)
467[5] 809[6] 1504[3] 1788[9] 2369[7] 3616[5] 4755[6] 6781[6] 7490[3] 8426[9]

**Archer's Arrow (USA)**
*Saeed bin Suroor* a84 79
3 b c Lonhro(AUS) Midnight Music (IRE) (Dubawi (IRE))
(1552) 1895[2] 3211[12] 5416[8] 6882[2] 7789[6]

**Archers Prize (IRE)** *R Bouresly* a29 26
8 b h Dark Angel(IRE) Silver Arrow (USA) (Shadeed (USA))
8583a[11]

**Archetype (FR)** *Simon Crisford* a104 104
3 b c Le Havre(IRE) Angel Rose (IRE) (Definite Article)
1962[4] (2997) 3787[2] (4640) 5568[7] (6655) (7471a) 8891[5]

**Arch Gold (USA)** *Mark Johnston* a67 62
2 b c Arch(USA) Trepidation (USA) (Seeking The Gold (USA))
4245[3] 8492[4]

**Archibald Leitch** *David Evans* a43 54
2 b g Archipenko(USA) Aubrietia (Dutch Art)
7280[8] 7985[6] 8545[11]

**Archibelle** *R Mike Smith* a59 69
3 b f Archipenko(USA) Cloud Hill (Danehill (USA))
175[8] 658[6] 1122[3] 2137[2] 2496[3] 4476[4] 5096[6] 5401[5] 6436[8] 7659[8] 8585[3] 9262[7]

**Archie (IRE)** *Tom Clover* a83 83
5 b g Fast Company(IRE) Winnifred (Green Desert (USA))
2232[9] 2730[3] 4321[5] 4832[8] 6134[7]◆ 6855[5]◆ 7582[13] 7998[8] 8341[2]

**Archie McKellar** *Ralph Beckett* a83 102
2 b c Archipenko(USA) Desert Berry (Green Desert (USA))
5710[3]◆ 6869[3] (8149) 8422[4]

**Archie Perkins (IRE)** *Nigel Tinkler* a64 63
2 b g Arcano(IRE) Sidney Girl (Azamour (IRE))
2221[10] 2698[8] 3398[4] 4273[4] 5373[8] 5878[5] 6625[6] 7029[2] (7239)

**Archie's Advice** *Keith Dalgleish* a69 83
6 b g Archipenko(USA) Flylowflylong (IRE) (Danetime (IRE))
2497[4] 2772[6] 3240[6] 3451[6] 3976[5] 4658[9] 5650[3] 6316[7] 6349[8] 7700[5]

**Archie Stevens** *Clare Ellam* a76 60
7 b g Pastoral Pursuits Miss Wells (IRE) (Sadler's Wells (USA))
71[5] 194[5] 330[3] 387[2] 665[2] 886[3] 955[6] 1147[5] 1722[12] 1896[4] 3186[9] 3942[2] 4174[4] 4458[10] 6896[7] 7575[10] 8146[3] 8494[6] (9075) 9181[2] 9348[3]

**Archimedes (IRE)** *David C Griffiths* a73 70
4 b g Invincible Spirit(IRE) Waveband (Exceed And Excel (AUS))
22[13] (416) 523[6] 851[5] 2967[9] 3201[3] 3667[8] 3758[7] 4531[5] 4795[3] (4993) 5055[5] 5587[9] 6478[8] 6612[5] 7767[9] 8168[15]

**Archimento** *Philip Hide* a70 72
4 ch g Archipenko(USA) Caribana (Hernando (FR))
1324[6] 2233[8] 5299[4] 6258[4] 6781[7] 7601[2] 8160[8]

**Archipeligo** *Iain Jardine* a77 75
6 b g Archipenko(USA) Red Slew (Red Ransom (USA))
968[7] 1201[7] 1519[9] 1891[7] 2308[8] 3242[2]◆ (3343) 4260[9] 4358[6] 4608[2] 4899[5] 5097[2] (5417) 5921[5] 6431[7] 6948[5] 7234[5] 7569[5] 7831[8] 8205[5] 8912[9] 9078[4] (9295)

**Archipentura** *J R Jenkins* a44 59
5 b m Archipenko(USA) Bookiesindex Girl (IRE) (Rakti)
311[10] 761[7]

**Archi Pink** *M Weiss*
5 gr g Archipenko(USA) In The Pink (IRE) (Indian Ridge (IRE))
835a[6]

**Archippos** *Philip Kirby* 86
4 b g Archipenko(USA) Sparkling Clear (Efisio)
(1517) 2574[4] 3315[5] 7615[3] 8047[5]

**Archi's Affaire** *Michael Dods* a63 93
3 ch g Archipenko(USA) Affaire D'Amour (Hernando (FR))
1782[7] (3243)◆ (3484)◆ 4430[2] (4899) 6383[4] 6930[10]

**Architecture (IRE)** *Hugo Palmer* 115
4 b m Zoffany(IRE) Brigayev (ITY) (Fasliyev (USA))
7393[4] 8007[3] 8421[11]

**Arch Villain (IRE)** *Amanda Perrett* a103 108
8 b g Arch(USA) Barzah (IRE) (Darshaan)
6447[4] 7547[8]

**Arc Royal** *Richard John O'Brien* a57 77
3 ch g Arcano(IRE) Royal Blush (Royal Applause)
1702[5] 2106[3] 2554[8] 3082[4] 3588[3] 4290[8] 5400[9] 6397[6] 9244a[11]

**Arctic Angel (IRE)** *James Fanshawe* a71
4 b g Dark Angel(IRE) Charlene Lacy (IRE) (Pips Pride)
2962[2] 3758[14] 4724[4]

**Arctic Flower (IRE)** *John Bridger* a48 66
4 gr m Roderic O'Connor(IRE) Just In Love (FR) (Highest Honor (FR))
3688[8] 3823[3] 4350[4] (5145) (5410) (5651) (6263) 6439[6] 7157[10] 8113[9]

**Arctic Sea** *Paul Cole* a82 79
3 bb c Oasis Dream Rainbow Dancing (Rainbow Quest (USA))
198[5] 863[3] (1550) (2361) 3457[7] 4736[2] 6579[4]

**Arctic Treasure (IRE)**
*Richard Fahey* a57 61
2 b g Iffraaj Street Star (USA) (Street Cry (IRE))
5537[5] 6432[7] 7242[7] 7938[5]

**Ardad (IRE)** *John Gosden* 107
3 b c Kodiac Good Clodora (IRE) (Red Clubs (IRE))
2768[4] 3835[5] 5595[11]

**Ardamir (FR)** *Laura Mongan* a87 58
5 b g Deportivo Kiss And Cry (FR) (Nikos)
163[6]◆ 353[3] 1153[2] 1628[3] 2125[3] 4222[11] 5798[9] 7096[7] 9208[5]

**Ardeatina** *A Giorgi* a78 52
2 ch f Harbour Watch(IRE) May West (Act One)
4166a[5]

**Ardenode (IRE)** *E J O'Neill* 100
2 b g Hellvelyn Coconut Kisses (Bahamian Bounty)
(3611a) 4391a[3]

**Arden Pearl (IRE)** *Archie Watson* a74 76
2 b f Swiss Spirit Music Pearl (IRE) (Oratorio (IRE))
3821[11] 4757[3] (5717) 7814[18] 8701[6] 8954[2] 9123[7] 9345[8]

**Ardhoomey (IRE)** *G M Lyons* a99 115
5 b g Dark Angel(IRE) Moy Joy (IRE) (Orpen (USA))
2657a[2] 3926[11] 4927a[3] 6640a[3] 6973a[6] 7424a[3] 7856a[6] 8225a[5]

**Arecibo (FR)** *C Laffon-Parias* a93 95
2 b c Invincible Spirit(IRE) Oceanique (USA) (Forest Wildcat (USA))
(4782a) 6728a[5] 7306a[4] 8777a[4]

**Areen Faisal (IRE)** *David O'Meara* 82
2 ch g Bahamian Bounty Yellow Trumpet (Petong)
1858[3]◆ 3556[5] 3929[15] (4716) 6330[3] 7090[19]

**Areen Heart (FR)** *David O'Meara* a82 91
3 b g Exceed And Excel(AUS) Reine Zao (FR) (Alzao (USA))
1878[2] 2554[3]◆ 3232[6] 4578[2] 5165[2] 6404[8] 7656[5] 7892[8] 8392[7] 8821[10]

**Arendelle** *Ed Walker* 66
2 b f Camelot Ape Attack (Nayef (USA))
7733[12] 8419[5]

**Areyoutheway (IRE)**
*Michael Appleby* a63 65
3 ch g Thewayyouare(USA) Grenouillere (USA) (Alysheba (USA))
100[7] 305[8]

**Argaki (IRE)** *Keith Dalgleish* a74 85
7 ch g Strategic Prince Amathusia (Selkirk (USA))
363[9] 841[9] 4210[11] 4661[6] 5206[4] 5917[8] 6346[2] 6893[6]

**Argante (FR)** *Henry Spiller* a75 72
8 bb g Singspiel(IRE) Abyaan (IRE) (Ela-Mana-Mou)
9242[3]

**Argent Bleu** *Roger Ingram* a43
2 b c Steele Tango(USA) Silver Marizah (IRE) (Manduro (GER))
9318[8]

**Argenterie** *Marcus Tregoning* 89
3 ch f Archipenko(USA) Sterling Sound (USA) (Street Cry (IRE))
2523[6] 6422[12]

**Argentic (FR)** *F Head* a95 104
3 gr g Kendargent(FR) Soft Lips (Rahy (USA))
2484a[5] 5522a[4] 6963a[2]

**Argon** *Sir Mark Prescott Bt* a36
2 b c Kyllachy Cool Question (Polar Falcon (USA))
9049[8] 9266[7] 9440[8]

**Arguin (FR)** *C Ferland* a80 78
2 b g Manduro(GER) Olonella (Selkirk (USA))
7470a[3]

**Argus (IRE)** *Alexandra Dunn* a74 86
5 b g Rip Van Winkle(IRE) Steel Princess (IRE) (Danehill (USA))
5488a[18] 7231[5] 9205[10] 9458[9]

**Argyle (IRE)** *Gary Moore* a20 72
4 gr g Lawman(FR) All Hallows (IRE) (Dalakhani (IRE))
8301[11]

**Aria Laforlongeuse (FR)** *S Wattel* a59 71
2 b f Masterstroke(USA) Wonderful Life (GER) (Tiger Hill (IRE))
8169a[10]

**Ariena (IRE)** *Clive Cox* a75 83
3 b f Arcano(IRE) Xena (IRE) (Mull Of Kintyre (USA))
3822[4] 4634[5] 6426[3] 7398[7] 7830[5] 8374[3]

**Arigato** *William Jarvis* a60 58
2 b c Poet's Voice Xtrasensory (Royal Applause)
6826[10] 7280[7] 7877[8]◆ 8644[3]

**Arineo (GER)** *Yasmin Almenrader* a66 46
4 b h Areion(GER) Arabella (GER) (Trempolino (USA))
9309a[8]

**Ariost (GER)** *C Von Der Recke* a37
3 b g Nicaron(GER) Antique Rose (GER) (Desert King (IRE))
7534a[6]

**Aristocles (IRE)** *Nikki Evans* a21 40
4 b g High Chaparral(IRE) Amathusia (Selkirk (USA))
9434[7]

**Aristocracy** *Fergal O'Brien* a43 53
6 b g Royal Applause Pure Speculation (Salse (USA))
2712[6]◆ 3436[6] 5361[4]

**Aristocratic** *Sir Michael Stoute* a85 86
4 b m Exceed And Excel(AUS) Peeress (Pivotal)
2177[2] 2605[6] 4121[3]

**Aristodemus (IRE)** *Tim Easterby* 59
2 b g Camacho Sceal Nua (IRE) (Iffraaj)
2154[3] 2590[7] 4502[5] 5279[7] 6043[6]

**Aristo Du Plessis (FR)**
*James Ewart* 64
7 b g Voix Du Nord(FR) J'Aime (FR) (Royal Charter (FR))
8291[5]

**Arithmetic (IRE)** *Ruth Carr* 73
4 b g Invincible Spirit(IRE) Multiplication (Marju (IRE))
1706[13] 2108[5] 2498[3]◆ 2953[8] 3432[2] 3744[9] 4185[2] 4575[7] 5261[7] 5807[8] 6269[6] 6673[10]

**Arize (IRE)** *Jim Boyle* a71 48
4 b m Approve(IRE) Raise (USA) (Seattle Slew (USA))
151[2] 394[4] 1599[9] 1899[7] 2335[6] 2962[9] 4726[11]

**Arizona Air (GER)** *A Fabre* 89
3 b f Hurricane Run(IRE) Arizona Sun (IRE) (Spinning World (USA))
8733a[7]

**Arizona Mist (IRE)** *Simon Crisford* a50 70
2 bg f Exceed And Excel(AUS) Phoenix City (USA) (El Prado (IRE))
3687[6] 4628[4] 5162[2]◆ 6950[10] (Dead)

**Arizona Run (FR)** *C Scandella* a58 84
9 b h Hurricane Run(IRE) Arizona Sun (IRE) (Spinning World (USA))
364a[4]

**Arizona Snow** *Ronald Harris* a53 52
5 b g Phoenix Reach(IRE) Calgary (Pivotal)
20[10] 455[11] 640[13] 1112[6] 2724[7] 3569[14] 7191[11] 7694[5]

**Arizona Sunrise** *Tina Jackson* a44 45
4 b g Sakhee's Secret Phoenix Rising (Dr Fong (USA))
4690[12] 5540[10] 5950[11] 8590[4] 8719[9] 8784[10] 9012[6]

**Arklow (USA)** *Brad H Cox* a96 107
3 b c Arch(USA) Unbridled Empire (USA) (Empire Maker (USA))
4652a[11]

**Arlecchino's Arc (IRE)** *Mark Usher* a43 46
2 ch g Arcano(IRE) Sir Cecil's Girl (IRE) (Thunder Gulch (USA))
7391[16] 8030[9] 8387[14] 8847[11]

**Arlecchino's Leap** *Mark Usher* a88 58
5 br g Kheleyf(USA) Donna Giovanna (Mozart (IRE))
2054[7] 6014[6] 7321[13] 8344[11] 8646[11] 8990[10]

**Arlecchino's Rock** *Patrick Martin* a57 57
4 ch g Rock Of Gibraltar(IRE) Xtra Special (Xaar)
6800a[2]

**Armagnac (IRE)** *Michael Bell* a71 69
3 br g Arcano(IRE) Folle Blanche (USA) (Elusive Quality (USA))
1410[3] 2266[5] 2931[4] 4446[7] 5077[4] 5545[10] 6091[4] (6664) 6893[3]

**Armande (IRE)** *A Fabre* 113
4 b m Sea The Stars(IRE) Alpine Snow (IRE) (Verglas (IRE))
2201a[2] (2946a) 4423a[3]

**Armandihan (IRE)** *Kevin Ryan* a72 88
3 b g Zoffany(IRE) Flying Flag (IRE) (Entrepreneur)
970[6] 1829[2] (2547) 5400[7] 6617[7] 7824[2] 8385[4]

**Armed Response** *Jedd O'Keeffe* a84 79
2 b c Sepoy(AUS) Respondez (Oasis Dream)
2299[4] 2771[3] (3973)◆ 4472[3] 5127[6] (7362) (9098)◆

**Armelle (FR)** *Scott Dixon* a48 61
6 b m Milk It Mick Park Ave Princess (IRE) (Titus Livius (FR))
21[10]

**Armenian Girl (FR)** *A Lyon* a62 65
3 ch f Soldier Of Fortune(IRE) Everblue (IRE) (Green Tune (USA))
4455a[9]

**Armondo (TUR)** *T Turkmen* 95
2 b c Mehmet Bora(TUR) Judiana (IRE) (Dolphin Street (FR))
6745a[2]

**Armoricaine** *C Ferland* 93
2 gr f Kendargent(FR) Last Born (FR) (Monsun (GER))
(5815a)

**Armum (IRE)** *Ed Dunlop* a69 79
2 b f Society Rock(IRE) Good Clodora (IRE) (Red Clubs (IRE))
3135[4] (3576) 4028[20] 6778[8] 7123[4]

**Arnarson** *Ed Dunlop* a84 66
3 b c Exceed And Excel(AUS) Islandia (USA) (Johar (USA))
464[3] 1358[4] 1692[3] 2087[6] 3259[3] 4784[2] 6268[10] 7574[2] 8479[9] 8874[2] 8990[5] 9280[3]

**Arnold** *Ann Duffield* 67
3 b g Equiano(FR) Azurinta (IRE) (Azamour (IRE))
2181[2]◆ 2455[4] (2853) 3403[11] 3974[8]

**Arnoul Of Metz** *Henry Spiller* a54
2 b g Kyllachy Appointee (IRE) (Exceed And Excel (AUS))
9311[8]

**Arod (IRE)** *David Simcock* a61 115
6 b h Teofilo(IRE) My Personal Space (USA) (Rahy (USA))
7179a[5]

**Arpani (FR)** *T Castanheira* a79 74
3 b f Tin Horse(IRE) Mariposa (IRE) (Oasis Dream)
2484a[7] 4289a[10]

**Arquus (IRE)** *Ed de Giles* a41 48
4 b g Lilbourne Lad(IRE) Charaig (Rainbow Quest (USA))
2231[12] 3435[9] 6752[6] 7212[7] 8345[10] 9077[12]

**Arriviste (FR)** *J-M Lefebvre* a60
2 bl c Fuisse(FR) Irrationnelle (IRE) (Astronomer Royal (USA))
5952a[9]

**Arrogant (IRE)** *Jose Santos* a75 80
2 b g Haatef(USA) Keep Baccinhit (IRE) (Raise A Grand (IRE))
4044[4] 5063[4] 6403[8] 7012a[5] (7470a) 8271a[2] 8884a[8] 9086a[3]

**Arrogate (USA)** *Bob Baffert* a136
4 rg h Unbridled's Song(USA) Bubbler (USA) (Distorted Humor (USA))
(469a) (1380a) 5194a[4] 6252a[2] 8611a[5]

**Arrowtown** *Michael Easterby* a75 83
5 b m Rail Link Protectress (Hector Protector (USA))
2815[2] 4380[6] (7558) 8047[2]

**Arrowzone** *Kevin Frost* a81 59
6 b g Iffraaj Donna Giovanna (Mozart (IRE))
117[8] 885[7] 1178[7] 1422[10] 1706[14] 2163[8] 3820[5] 4575[9] 5053[6] 6060[8] 7729[9] 7991[5] (8249) 8719[6] 8854[4] (8957)

**Arrucian** *Ms N M Hugo* a17 32
4 b m Medicean Arruhan (IRE) (Mujtahid (USA))
6277[8] 7600[8]

**Arsenio Lupin** *Denis Quinn* a73 80
3 b c Delegator Tenebrae (IRE) (In The Wings)
115[3]◆ 466[4] 1089[3] 2625[2]◆ 3412[13] 5115[5]

**Artarmon (IRE)** *Michael Bell* 69
2 b c So You Think(NZ) Aljumar (IRE) (Marju (IRE))
7955[8] 8508[3]◆

**Art Collection (FR)**
*Andrew Hollinshead* a92 80
4 b g Shakespearean(IRE) Renascent Rahy (Rahy (USA))
(1475) (1777) 2031[6] 2381[4] 3492[6] 5705[6] 6662[6] 8251a[8] 9274a[11]

**Art Echo** *John Mackie* a79 84
4 b g Art Connoisseur(IRE) Madhaaq (IRE) (Medicean)
(2120) 2505[3] (2795) 3471[4] (4339) 4622[7] 5610[5] 6964[11] 7594[4] 8108[2]

**Artful Artist (IRE)** *A J Martin* a37 89
8 b g Excellent Art Silly Goose (IRE) (Sadler's Wells (USA))
6956a[4] 7860a[8]

**Artful Charlie (FR)** *E J O'Neill*
2 b c Myboycharlie(IRE) Famous Portrait (FR) (Kendor (FR))
4782a[5]

**Artful Rogue (IRE)** *Amanda Perrett* a85 87
6 b g Excellent Art Szabo (IRE) (Anabaa (USA))
38[3] 3785[2]◆ 4216[6] 5330[7] 5798[3] 6819[5] 7728[4]

**Arthenia (IRE)** *Charles Hills* 70
2 b f Camelot Miss Intimate (USA) (War Chant (USA))
6132[7] 6917[6] 7810[3]

**Arthenus** *James Fanshawe* a91 107
5 b g Dutch Art Lady Hen (Efisio)
2127[6] 4070[12] 5148[2] 5925[6] 6915a[3] 7805[7] 8468[5]

**Art History (IRE)** *Philip Kirby* a57 53
9 gr g Dalakhani(IRE) What A Picture (FR) (Peintre Celebre (USA))
1028[8] 1303[5] 4345[5] 4791[6]

**Arthur Mc Bride (IRE)**
*Nigel Twiston-Davies* 91
8 bb g Royal Anthem(USA) Lucky Diverse (IRE) (Lucky Guest)
2562[7] 3076[4] 3527[3] 4073[9] 5524[3] 6680[2] (6779) 7402[11] 8038[12]

**Arthur's Queen (FR)** *Carroll Gray* a43 61
6 b m Soldier Of Fortune(IRE) Tintagel (Oasis Dream)
4469[7] 5054[5]

**Arthurthedelegator** *Oliver Greenall* a67 69
3 b g Delegator Markova's Dance (Mark Of Esteem (IRE))
1550[9] 2228[3] 2886[2] 3774[5]

**Artic Nel** *Ian Williams* a39 55
3 ch f Haafhd Artic Bliss (Fraam)
3615[9] 4274[6] 4729[6] 6180[5] 7232[5] 7537[7]

**Artieshow (USA)** *Marco Botti* a84
2 b c Artie Schiller(USA) Garden Music (USA) (Pivotal)
9137[3] 9335[2]

**Artifix (IRE)** *F Head* 38
3 b f Lawman(FR) Houleuse (USA) (Dynaformer (USA))
3275a[7]

**Artigiano (USA)** *Charlie Appleby* a102 106
7 ch g Distorted Humor(USA) Angel Craft (USA) (A.P. Indy (USA))
(322a)

**Artistica (GER)** *D Moser* 103
3 bb f Areion(GER) Artica (GER) (Pentire)
(2623)◆ (3105a) 4864[6]

**Art Nouvelle (IRE)**
*Joseph Patrick O'Brien* a84 90
3 b f Art Connoisseur(IRE) Van De Cappelle (IRE) (Pivotal)
4385a[11] (9437)

**Art Obsession (IRE)** *Paul Midgley* a80 87
6 b g Excellent Art Ghana (IRE) (Lahib (USA))
514[3]◆ 971[2] (2404) 3195[5] (4343) 5457[11] 6205[8] 6971a[15] 8319[10]

**Art Of Swing (IRE)** *Gary Moore* a76 72
5 b g Excellent Art Shahmina (IRE) (Danehill (USA))
2388[4] 2781[3] 3616[10] 5320[6] 6781[4]◆ 8993[5]

**Artscape** *Dean Ivory* a75 81
5 b g Iffraaj Artisti (Cape Cross (IRE))
(807) 1302[5] 2230[8] 2932[4]◆ (3532)◆ 4277[6] 5369[5] 5814[3] 6442[6] 6780[6]◆ 7272[9] 8311[5]

**Art Scholar (IRE)** *Michael Appleby* a53 67
10 b g Pyrus(USA) Marigold (FR) (Marju (IRE))
2504[6] 3907[4] 5267[4] 5809[5] 6109[6]

**Art's Desire (IRE)** *Ed Walker* a68 66
3 ch f Dutch Art Zenella (Kyllachy)
1401[3]◆ 2121[4] 2782[4] 3422[8]◆ 4214[3] 4797[3] 5485[7] 6638[6] 7157[5] (7539) 8376[6]

**Artsteelwork** *John Butler* a23 31
3 b f Fast Company(IRE) Etymology (Rail Link)
1600[11] 2090[12] 3141[8] 3545[9] 5239[10]

**Art Wave (IRE)** *M Al Mheiri* a100 97
6 ch h Art Connoisseur(IRE) Musical Review (UAE) (Jade Robbery (USA))
205a[5]

**Arty But Poor** *Oliver Greenall* a55 53
2 b g Dutch Art Libys Dream (IRE) (Invincible Spirit (IRE))
3467[4] 4160[6] 4526[11] 8191[3]◆ 8847[5] 9002[8]

**Arty Campbell (IRE)**
*Bernard Llewellyn* a85 87
7 b g Dylan Thomas(IRE) Kincob (USA) (Kingmambo (USA))
6096[3] 6508[3] 6779[5] (7110) 7599[9]

**Arvios** *F-X Belvisi* a86 86
5 ch g Medicean Akrivi (IRE) (Tobougg (IRE))
6648a[2] 7636a[3]

**Arwa (IRE)** *Charles Hills* 90
3 b f Holy Roman Emperor(IRE) Another Storm (USA) (Gone West (USA))
1958[8] 3167[10]

**Arya Stark** *Tony Carroll* a49
3 b f Piccolo Night Affair (Bold Edge)
76[8] 376[5] 546[3] 897[7]

**Aryeh (IRE)** *Hugo Palmer* a61
3 ch f Exceed And Excel(AUS) Height Of Summer (IRE) (Alhaarth (IRE))
168[8] 424[4]

**Arzaak (IRE)** *Chris Dwyer* a92 91
3 br g Casamento(IRE) Dixieland Kiss (USA) (Dixie Union (USA))
307[3] 578[3] 765[4] 972[2] 1332[5] (1543) 1774[6] 2271[2] (2992) 3672[4] 4992[2] 5811[2] 6758[3] 7286[4] 8129[6] 8803[2]

**Asaas (USA)** *Roger Varian* a86 83
3 ch g Distorted Humor(USA) Affectionately (Galileo (IRE))
3682[2] (4444)◆ 6468[4] 7452[3]

**Asanta Sana (IRE)** *John Gosden* a55 59
3 b f Galileo(IRE) Milanova (AUS) (Danehill (USA))
1342[4] 1701[4]

**Asara (GER)** *H-F Devin* 59
3 b f Soldier Hollow Avanti Polonia (GER) (Polish Precedent (USA))
6566a[5]

**Ascend (USA)** *H Graham Motion* 111
5 rg g Candy Ride(ARG) Ghost Dancing (USA) (Silver Ghost (USA))
5977a[5] 7633a[5]

**Ascendant** *Johnny Farrelly* a64 73
11 ch g Medicean Ascendancy (Sadler's Wells (USA))
721[3] (859) 1870[7] 2332[2] 4217[6]

**Ascot Day (IRE)** *David Simcock* a96 81
3 b g Kheleyf(USA) My Lucky Liz (IRE) (Exceed And Excel (AUS))
(72)◆ (291)◆ 3159[6] 4098[4] 5029[6] (5416)

**Ascot Week (USA)** *John Quinn* a68 80
3 br g Lonhro(AUS) Millenia (Unfuwain (USA))
2260[7] 3062[4] 3862[3] 6236[10]

**Ascription (IRE)** *Keith Dalgleish* a79 75
8 b g Dansili Lady Elgar (IRE) (Sadler's Wells (USA))
1295[7]

**Ashadihan** *Kevin Ryan* a108 105
4 b m Kyllachy Miss Delila (USA) (Malibu Moon (USA))
(617) 1771[3] 2616[5]

**Ashazuri** *Jonathan Portman* a69 70
3 b f Dick Turpin(IRE) Shesha Bear (Tobougg (IRE))
1550[10] 2394[9] 3163[3] 3656[3] (3870) 5067[3]◆ 5545[5] 6139[3] 6866[7] 8156[4]

**Asheena** *Paul D'Arcy* a37 42
2 gr f Lethal Force(IRE) Meddle (Diktat)
1873[6] 2258[5] 8347[10]

**Ashford Island** *Adam West* a38 56
4 b g Munnings(USA) Falling Angel (Kylian (USA))
3001[6] 3137[14] 3823[11] 4458[14]

**Ashiana (GER)** *P Schiergen* 108
3 ch f Mastercraftsman(IRE) Ashantee (GER) (Areion (GER))
( ) 5693a[5] (6710a) 7669a[6] 8450a[8]

**Ashington** *Luca Cumani* a67 67
2 b g Canford Cliffs(IRE) Kadoma (Danehill Dancer (IRE))
5743[5] 6616[6] 7001[3] 7764[7]◆ 8537[6]

**Ashkoul (FR)** *Michael Appleby* 95
4 b g Tamayuz Asharna (IRE) (Darshaan)
1704[8] 2136[3] 2804[7] 3154[9]

**Ashpan Sam** *David W Drinkwater* a59 96
8 b g Firebreak Sweet Patoopie (Indian Ridge (IRE))
2780[8] 3324[7] 3861[9] (4521)◆ 4803[3] 5402[5] 5720[7]

**Ashtaneh (USA)** *A De Royer-Dupre* a96 30
3 b f More Than Ready(USA) Ashiyla (FR) (Rock Of Gibraltar (IRE))
8986a[6]

**Ashwaq** *Richard Hannon* a70 75
3 ch f Sepoy(AUS) Blaugrana (IRE) (Exceed And Excel (AUS))
(1287) 1940[6] 3038[6] 4298[11] 5358[4] 5748[8]

**Ashwass (USA)** *Roger Varian* a70 91
3 bb g Lonhro(AUS) Alzerra (UAE) (Pivotal)
5794[6] (7080)

**Asian Wing (IRE)**
*John James Feane* a65 44
8 ch g Hawk Wing(USA) Blue Beacon (Fantastic Light (USA))
900[3] 8246[13]

**Asidious Alexander (IRE)**
*Simon Crisford* 101
3 ch f Windsor Knot(IRE) Birthday Present (Cadeaux Genereux)
2644a[12] 4208[7]

**Askari** *Tom Clover* a69 71
4 b g Sea The Stars(IRE) Loulwa (IRE) (Montjeu (IRE))
333[3] 856[7] 2042[4] 2615[7] (3439) 4345[8]

**Asking (IRE)** *A P O'Brien* a93 100
3 b f Zoffany(IRE) Roselita (IRE) (Sadler's Wells (USA))
2441a[2] 2665a[9] 3110a[8] 3964[6] (4385a) 4512a[3] 5308a[7] 5597[8]

**Ask The Guru** *Michael Attwater* a59 58
7 b g Ishiguru(USA) Tharwa (IRE) (Last Tycoon)
215[7] 327[8] 1022[5] 1340[8] 3942[4] 4731[2] (5027) (5871) 6478[9] 7494[8] (8146) 9389[7] 9471[7]

**Aslan (USA)** *S bin Ghadayer* a91
6 br g A.P. Indy(USA) Satin Kiss (USA) (Seeking The Gold (USA))
8836a[2]

**Asmahan** *Simon Crisford*
3 b f Casamento(IRE) Finnmark (Halling (USA))
2307[U]

**Aspasius (GER)** *Gary Moore* a30 49
5 b g Desert Prince(IRE) Aspasia Lunata (GER) (Tiger Hill (IRE))
9212[10]

**Aspettatemi (ITY)** *D Grilli* 100
3 ch c Red Rocks(IRE) Fly Queen (Dashing Blade)
2245a[4] 8448a[3] 8963a[7]

**Assad Lawal (FR)** *S Jeddari* a21 38
2 ch g Bernebeau(FR) Tardoune (FR) (Spadoun (FR))
7592a[9]

**Assanilka (FR)** *Harry Dunlop* a80 78
3 b f Diamond Green(FR) Regal Step (Royal Applause)
1796[7] 2978a[8] 7276[9] 7710[4] 8351[4]◆ 8885a[6] 9314[7]

**Assertainty** *Tim Easterby* a5 42
2 b g Assertive Layla's Oasis (Oasis Dream)
8734[10] 8916[8]

**Assertive Agent** *Tony Carroll* a71 66
7 b m Assertive Agent Kensington (Mujahid (USA))
308[2] (735) 1326[3] 1599[4] 2043[P] 8875[11]

**Assertor** *Tony Carroll* 51
3 b f Assertive Blue Goddess (IRE) (Blues Traveller (IRE))
4964[4] 5969[6] 6368[3] 6828[3] 7199[8] 8181[7]

**Assiduous** *Mark Johnston* a61 78
3 b g Sir Percy Suzi Spends (IRE) (Royal Applause)
3717[4] 4146[2] 8377[7] 8806[6]

**Assonance (FR)** *H-F Devin* 58
2 gr f Saonois(FR) Agosta (FR) (Ange Gabriel (FR))
3679a[8]

**Asterina** *A De Royer-Dupre* a74 93
4 ch m Dalakhani(IRE) Altamira (Peintre Celebre (USA))
6226a[7]

**Astolat** *Ed Walker* a58
2 b f Camelot Sablonne (USA) (Silver Hawk (USA))
8669[7] 9099[5]

**Astone Man (FR)** *Tony Carroll* 62
3 gr c Rajsaman(FR) Astonia (FR) (Astarabad (USA))
3407[4] 5247[3] 6368[4]

**Astraea** *Michael Easterby* 70
2 b f Cityscape Rapid Revalation (USA) (Bianconi (USA))
3179[3] 3846[3] 5380[8] 6940[12] 8008[8]

**Astral Merit (FR)** *F Monnier* a98 95
7 b m Apsis Luminescence (FR) (Signe Divin (USA))
3883a[5] 4679a[2] 8444a[8] 8755a[9] (9003a)

**Astroblaze** *Mark H Tompkins* a60
2 ch f Havana Gold(IRE) Astrodonna (Carnival Dancer)
8347[12] 9081[7] 9320[9]

**Astrobreeze** *Mark H Tompkins* 32
2 b f Lawman(FR) Astromagick (Rainbow Quest (USA))
7915[6] 9137[9]

**Astrofire** *Mark H Tompkins* a28 37
2 b f Kheleyf(USA) Astromancer (USA) (Silver Hawk (USA))
7022[8] 7758[8] 9239[6]

**Astrojewel** *Mark H Tompkins* 23
2 b f Havana Gold(IRE) Astrolibra (Sakhee (USA))
5534[10]

**Astrologist (IRE)** *Clive Cox* 75
2 b c Sea The Stars(IRE) Jumooh (Monsun (GER))
7813[8] 8162[2]

**Astronomy's Choice** *John Gosden* a96 95
3 b f Redoute's Choice(AUS) Astronomy Domine (Galileo (IRE))
2436[3] 3995[11] 8666a[9] 8992[6]

**Astrophysics** *Lynn Siddall* a79 73
5 ch g Paco Boy(IRE) Jodrell Bank (IRE) (Observatory (USA))
3052[12] 3667[5] 4428[7] 4850[8] 5211[2] 5459[2] 6089[2] 6670[6] 7268[8] 7825[2] 8557[6] 8927[11]

**Astrosecret** *Mark H Tompkins* a66 66
4 b m Halling(USA) Optimistic (Reprimand)
2460[7] 2728[6] 3292[5] 4756[8] 5080[10] 6109[9]

**Astroshadow** *Mark H Tompkins* a11 49
3 gr f Aussie Rules(USA) Astrodiva (Where Or When (IRE))
2515[8] 3145[8] 3720[12] 5209[2] 6530[12] 7490[10]

**Astrostorm** *Mark H Tompkins* a48 46
3 b g Medicean Astrolibra (Sakhee (USA))
437[8] 855[6] 1414[4] 3220[4]◆ 4978[7]

**Astute Boy (IRE)** *Ed Vaughan* a79 80
3 b g Arcano(IRE) Spa (Sadler's Wells (USA))
4348[2] 5652[2] (6293) 6880[2] 7568[5]

**Asulaman (GER)** *S Cerulis* a77 69
10 b g Sulamani(IRE) Andrelhina (Tirol (IRE))
6300a[5]

**A Sure Welcome** *John Spearing* a73 61
3 b g Pastoral Pursuits Croeso Bach (Bertolini (USA))
(1564) (2016) 3173[7] 4350[3] 6016[6] 6638[11] (8742) 9152[2] 9297[3]

**Atalanta Bay (IRE)**
*Marcus Tregoning* a59 49
7 b m Strategic Prince Wood Sprite (Mister Baileys)
7232[12] 7483[8] 8157[7] 8647[6] 9092[9]

**Atalanta Queen** *Michael Appleby* 64
2 b f Canford Cliffs(IRE) Champagne Aerial (IRE) (Night Shift (USA))
2832[5] 3023[6] 3712[7] 4527[9] 5161[2] (5293) 5933[4] 7082[9] 7458[8]

**Atalante** *Jeremy Noseda* a79 69
4 b m Cape Cross(IRE) Sabria (USA) (Miswaki (USA))
(983) (1326)

**Ataman (IRE)** *Chris Wall* a78 82
5 b g Sholokhov(IRE) Diora (IRE) (Dashing Blade)
1706[9] 2333[2] 3009[8] 3718[5] 4804[12] 5760[3]

**Ateem (FR)** *Richard Hannon* 78
2 b c Dark Angel(IRE) Jeu De Plume (IRE) (Montjeu (IRE))
5709[4] 6132[3] 6674[4] 7392[7]

**Athas An Bhean** *Adrian Paul Keatley* 82
4 b m Royal Applause Dusty Moon (Dr Fong (USA))
1385a[2]

**Athassel** *David Evans* a88 85
8 ch g Dalakhani(IRE) Hope Island (IRE) (Titus Livius (FR))
(51) 282[2] (332)◆ 482[3] 684[2] 841[4] (1063) (1080) (1219) 1290[3] 1365[6] 1586[6] 1890[4] (2064) 2582[3] 3095[11] (3214) 3620[7] 3808[8] 4521[5] 4844[3] 5059[2] 5396[9] 5519a[9] 5821[5] 6289[4] 6672[8] 7789[11] 8640[5] 9083[4] 9220[6]

**Athena (IRE)** *A P O'Brien* 83
2 b f Camelot Cherry Hinton (Green Desert (USA))
7421a[7]

**Athenian Garden (USA)**
*Paddy Butler* a54 47
10 b m Royal Academy(USA) Webee (USA) (Kingmambo (USA))
440[11] 733[13] 1082[6] 1699[6]

**Athletic** *David Evans* a78 56
8 b g Doyen(IRE) Gentle Irony (Mazilier (USA))
214[3]◆ 426[2] 501[7] 685[7] 929[8] 969[6] (1325) 1427[P] (Dead)

**Atholblair Boy (IRE)** *Nigel Tinkler* a79 73
4 ch g Frozen Power(IRE) Ellxell (IRE) (Exceed And Excel (AUS))
1472[4] 1735[12] 2120[6] 2731[7] 3758[2] 4310[4] 4695[2] 5318[11] 6181[2] (7572) 8211[3]

**Atillio (IRE)** *J D Hillis* 92
4 b h Lawman(FR) Councilofconstance (IRE) (Footstepsinthesand)
8527a[8]

**Atkinson Grimshaw (FR)**
*Andrew Balding* a90 92
3 ch g Rio De La Plata(USA) Cosabawn (IRE) (Barathea (IRE))
(959) (3068) 4856[3] 5940[2] 6579[3]

**Atlanta Belle (IRE)** *Chris Wall* a65 52
3 ch f Zebedee Tara Too (IRE) (Danetime (IRE))
140[4] 1192[3] 1693[5] 2235[11] 4723[7] 5812[3] (6324) 7517[2] 8128[6]

**Atlantic Jet (IRE)**
*Eugene M O'Sullivan* a38 48
4 b g Approve(IRE) Ishimagic (Ishiguru (USA))
6802a[7]

**Atlantik Cup (GER)** *A Kleinkorres* a82 64
4 rg g Electric Beat Adora (GER) (Danehill (USA))
1920a[10] 5269a[7] 6226a[6]

**Atlas (IRE)** *Denis Gerard Hogan* a90 86
4 b g Acclamation Sheer Bliss (IRE) (Sadler's Wells (USA))
5518a[4] 8222a[5]

**Atletico (IRE)** *Roger Varian* a107 98
5 b g Kodiac Queenofthefairies (Pivotal)
3463[3]◆ 4830[5] (5219)◆ 5505[5] 6275[13] 8012[8]◆ 8416[6] 8679[7] (8913)◆
**Atnaga (FR)** *C Boutin* a67 3
3 gr f Maiguri(IRE) Dykam (FR) (Dylan Thomas (IRE))
838a[8]
**Atomic Jack** *George Baker* 37
2 b g Nathaniel(IRE) Indigo River (IRE) (Kodiac)
6374[8]
**Atrafan (IRE)** *Alan Brown* a60 56
3 b g Atraf Up Front (IRE) (Up And At 'Em)
3525[6] 4302[4] 4694[5] 5182[9] 6437[9]
**Atreju (GER)** *Waldemar Hickst* 41
5 b h Wiesenpfad(FR) Adorata (GER) (Tannenkonig (IRE))
7342a[9]
**Attain** *Archie Watson* a75 72
8 b g Dansili Achieve (Rainbow Quest (USA))
44[13] 351[4]◆ (440) 555[4] 965[5] 1028[2] 1364[3] 1430[4] 1937[3] 2336[3] (2512) 2722[2] 3028[3] 3753[4] 4041[4] 4492[6] 5183[4] 5599[8] 6109[7] 8946[7] 9092[3] 9212[3] 9459[6]
**Attendu (FR)** *C Laffon-Parias* 113
4 b h Acclamation Gwenseb (FR) (Green Tune (USA))
1531a[3] 2248a[7] 3354a[2] 4234a[3] 4942a[3] (6498a) 7671a[9]
**Attention (AUS)**
*Peter & Paul Snowden* 105
3 ch c Stratum(AUS) Flamboyance (AUS) (Snowland (AUS))
8057a[9]
**Attention Baileys (FR)** *P Monfort* a52 40
7 b g Dubai Destination(USA) Baileys Outshine (Inchinor)
691a[8] 822a[7]
**Attention Seaker** *Tim Easterby* 77
7 b m Bollin Eric Pay Attention (Revoque (IRE))
3311[4] (5740) (6090) 6968[9] 8487[2]
**Atteq** *Richard Fahey* a76 84
3 b c Invincible Spirit(IRE) Wallis (King's Best (USA))
31[4] 329[4] 657[3] 1244[3] (2107) 2374[2] 3303[8] 4075[3] 4334[6]
**Attest** *Warren Greatrex* a65 79
4 b g Cacique(IRE) Change Course (Sadler's Wells (USA))
8682[2]
**Attica** *Markus Klug* 95
3 b f Tai Chi(GER) Anna Desta (GER) (Desert Style (IRE))
7672a[6]
**Atticus Boy (IRE)** *David Lanigan* a49
2 b c Cape Cross(IRE) Satwa Pearl (Rock Of Gibraltar (IRE))
9417[8]
**Attilia (IRE)** *A Giorgi* a61 62
2 b f Fast Company(IRE) Cut The Cackle (IRE) (Danetime (IRE))
4389a[2]
**Atty Persse (IRE)** *Roger Charlton* 104
3 b g Frankel Dorcas Lane (Norse Dancer (IRE))
(2126) 3042[2] (3998) 4811[9] 6327[6]
**At Your Service** *W P Browne* a62 72
3 b c Frankel Crystal Gaze (IRE) (Rainbow Quest (USA))
7656[10]
**Auckland (IRE)** *A P O'Brien* 88
3 b c Galileo(IRE) Airwave (Air Express (IRE))
6491a[15]
**Au Coeur (IRE)** *S Seemar* a67 68
3 b g Invincible Spirit(IRE) Botanique (IRE) (Pivotal)
(9257a)
**Audacious Girl (FR)** *E Lellouche* 81
2 b f Dabirsim(FR) Firuza (Oasis Dream)
5978a[5]
**Auenperle (GER)** *Christina Bucher* 97
2 ch f Areion(GER) Aotearoa (FR) (Doyen (IRE))
6726a[2] 8170a[7]
**Aufsteiger (FR)** *P Schiergen* a71 95
3 b g Meshaheer(USA) Moon Romance (FR) (Nayef (USA))
3613a[7] 4939a[9]
**Augenblick (IRE)** *Roger Varian* a77
2 b f Epaulette(AUS) Freezing Love (USA) (Danzig (USA))
(7875) (8555)
**Auguri Pyla (FR)** *C Baillet*
2 ch f Maiguri(IRE) Desert City (FR) (Simon Du Desert (FR))
1282a[9]
**Augustini (FR)** *H De Nicolay* a69 62
3 bl g Slickly(FR) Augusta Lucilla (USA) (Mr Greeley (USA))
5523a[6] 6225a[7]
**Aumerle** *Shaun Lycett* a71 66
5 b g Authorized(IRE) Succinct (Hector Protector (USA))
1027[6] 1697[4] 2111[5] 3623[5] 4545[2] 5508[5] 8261[6] (9317)
**Aumit Hill** *John Quinn* a20 23
4 b g Authorized(IRE) Eurolinka (IRE) (Tirol (IRE))
3389[6]
**Auntie Barber (IRE)** *Stuart Williams* a80 74
4 b m Elusive City(USA) Lady Stardust (Spinning World (USA))
885[5] (1245) 1368[2] 2254[5] 4010[4] 4096[4] 4621[10] 5113[8] 5745[8] 6578[6] 8156[8] 8814[10]
**Auntie Pam (IRE)** *Tom Dascombe* a67 65
2 b f Sir Prancealot(IRE) Sans Reserve (IRE) (Foxhound (USA))
1627[2] 2015[4] 2556[2] 3306[3] 5479[6] 5685[4] 5751[4] 6379[4] 7410[8]
**Auric Goldfinger (IRE)**
*Richard Hannon* a65 67
3 b g Kyllachy Ghenwah (FR) (Selkirk (USA))
377[2] (463) 763[4] 895[3] 1242[10] 1625[6] 1790[2] 4144[6] 6681[9] 7062[12] 7216[12]
**Aurora Butterfly (IRE)** *W McCreery* 103
3 gr f Born To Sea(IRE) Diamonaka (FR) (Akarad (FR))
4208[3]◆ 4928a[5] 6080a[9] 6490a[9]
**Aurora Eclipse (IRE)**
*M D O'Callaghan* 88
2 b f Kodiac Tiltili (IRE) (Spectrum (IRE))
7855a[5] 8562[4]
**Aurora Gray** *Hughie Morrison* a84 90
4 gr m Rip Van Winkle(IRE) Summer's Eve (Singspiel (IRE))
(141) (280)◆ 3663[3] 4120[3] 5110[2] 5524[2] 6779[2] 8038[20]
**Aurum Spirit (AUS)** *Robbie Griffiths* 77
8 b g Bel Esprit(AUS) Lakemba Gold (AUS) (Made Of Gold (USA))
8750a[7]
**Aury Touch (ITY)** *Stefano Botti* 103
5 ch m Pounced(USA) A Touch Wild (USA) (Touch Gold (USA))
8096a[6]
**Auspicion** *Tom Tate* a83 77
5 b g Dansili Superstar Leo (IRE) (College Chapel)
2685[6] (3252) 4260[8] (4358) 5417[7] 5704[3] 6349[9] (7034) 7569[4] 7941[12]
**Aussi Celebre (IRE)** *C Martinon* a55 95
8 gr g Aussie Rules(USA) Femme Celebre (IRE) (Peintre Celebre (USA))
7639a[6]
**Aussie Andre** *Roger Ingram* a92 60
6 b g High Chaparral(IRE) Hana Dee (Cadeaux Genereux)
467[8] 683[P]
**Aussie Lyrics (FR)** *Mrs C Gilbert* a67 74
7 gr g Aussie Rules(USA) Operam (Kris)
(2671a) 5987a[2]
**Aussie Reigns (IRE)** *Gary Moore* a97 85
7 b g Aussie Rules(USA) Rohain (IRE) (Singspiel (IRE))
6214a[6] 8076[8] 8539[5]
**Aussie Valentine (IRE)** *P D Deegan* a91 95
6 b g Aussie Rules(USA) Love Valentine (IRE) (Fruits Of Love (USA))
1388a[2] 5582a[11] 7066a[9]
**Aussie Wind** *Hugo Palmer* a88 59
2 b c Aussie Rules(USA) Ride The Wind (Cozzene (USA))
4291[6] (5412) (5743) 6229a[P] (Dead)
**Austerity (IRE)** *Sally Haynes* a43 58
4 br g Elnadim(USA) Royal Reprieve (FR) (Celtic Swing)
2467[6] 8143[12] 9017[7]
**Austin Powers (IRE)** *Mark Johnston* a65 72
2 ch g Power My Lass (Elmaamul (USA))
3165[7] 4472[2] 5092[3] 5644[4] 6481[3] 6977a[14] 7384[4] 8586[4] 8925[5]
**Austrian School (IRE)**
*Mark Johnston* a74 77
2 b c Teofilo(IRE) Swiss Roll (IRE) (Entrepreneur)
(6204)◆ 6616[5] 7556[3] (7890)
**Autarcie** *S Wattel* a76 80
3 b f Henrythenavigator(USA) Alloway (Rahy (USA))
8959a[6]
**Authentic Art** *Ralph Beckett* a59 53
2 ch g Dutch Art Tahirah (Green Desert (USA))
5531[6] 6761[5] 7352[11]
**Authorative (IRE)** *Anthony McCann* a46 51
7 b g Refuse To Bend(IRE) Reasonably Devout (CAN) (St Jovite (USA))
2162[6]
**Authorized Too** *Noel Williams* a83 82
6 b g Authorized(IRE) Audaz (Oasis Dream)
3840[7] (4750) (5251)
**Author's Dream** *William Knight* a72 59
4 gr g Authorized(IRE) Spring Dream (IRE) (Kalanisi (IRE))
1369[2] 2332[9] 3724[4] 8647[3] (9158)
**Autocratic** *Sir Michael Stoute* a82 115
4 b h Dubawi(IRE) Canda (USA) (Storm Cat (USA))
1882[6] (3012) 5925[7] 6441[6]
**Automated** *Gordon Elliott* a69 84
6 b g Authorized(IRE) Red Blooded Woman (USA) (Red Ransom (USA))
5488a[12]
**Autumn Belle** *Ollie Pears* 44
2 b f Canford Cliffs(IRE) Ballyea (IRE) (Acclamation)
1908[5] 3200[6]
**Autumn Glow** *Miss Joey Ellis* a54 31
3 b f Sir Percy Steady Rain (Zafonic (USA))
3175[4] 4003[9] 9026[14]
**Autumn Leaves** *Clive Cox* 77
2 b f Helmet(AUS) Jadwiga (Pivotal)
3689[2] 4806[2] (6100)
**Autumn Lodge** *R Le Gal* a45 64
2 b g Stimulation(IRE) Timeless Elegance (IRE) (Invincible Spirit (IRE))
1495[5] 1767[3] 2015[2] 3156[3] 3929[16] 4044[2] 4758[5] 4991[9] 5627a[2] 6017a[4] 6247a[4] 6409a[3] 8101a[5]
**Autumn Snow** *Saeed bin Suroor* a55
2 b f Invincible Spirit(IRE) Epic Similie (Lomitas)
8850[5]
**Autumn Tonic (IRE)** *Charlie Wallis* a45 36
5 b g Approve(IRE) Trempjane (Lujain (USA))
67[7] 311[2] 494[7] 852[5] (1112) 1759[11] 2367[5] 3001[9] 3728[10] 4179[8] 8258[11] 8824[11]
**Auxiliary** *Patrick Holmes* a71 75
4 b g Fast Company(IRE) Lady Xara (IRE) (Xaar)
2430[8] 3205[7] (3432) 4430[7] 5313[5] 5872[6] 7267[5] 7567[5] 7925[8]
**Avago Josh** *Ivan Furtado* a5
3 ch g Aqlaam Heart Stopping (USA) (Chester House (USA))
1497[P] 1866[6] 3054[P]
**Avalanche** *T J O'Mara* a56 80
8 gr g Three Valleys(USA) Silent Waters (Polish Precedent (USA))
5519a[4]
**Avantgardist (GER)** *Pat Phelan* a60 62
3 ch g Campanologist(USA) Avocette (GER) (Kings Lake (USA))
959[3] 3503[6] 5034[7] 6443[5] 7152[5]
**Av A Word** *Daniel Kubler* a75 73
3 b g Aussie Rules(USA) Real Me (Mark Of Esteem (IRE))
89[6] 305[4]◆ 637[5] 1107[2] 1331[2] 1623[5] (2679) 3250[7] 3674[3] (4177) 4494[6] (5867) (6557) 7004[4] 7568[3]
**Avenge (USA)** *Richard E Mandella* 112
5 bb m War Front(USA) Lerici (USA) (Woodman (USA))
8606a[14]
**Avenging Red (IRE)** *Adam West* a52 57
2 b c Red Jazz(USA) Lorena (IRE) (Bishop Of Cashel)
4044[3] 4972[8] 5586[4] 7756[4] 8027[3] 8145[6] 8783[12]
**Aventinus (IRE)** *Hugo Palmer* a93 89
3 b g Zoffany(IRE) Luminous Gold (Fantastic Light (USA))
(1895) 2554[9] (3620) 5642[5] 6026[2] 7118[5] 8222a[10]
**Aventus (IRE)** *Jane Chapple-Hyam* a51 53
3 b c Zebedee Irish Design (IRE) (Alhaarth (IRE))
305[3]
**Avenue Dargent (FR)** *J-M Osorio* 95
4 ch m Kendargent(FR) Corfu (IRE) (Daylami (IRE))
6665a[4]
**Avenue Des Champs**
*Jane Chapple-Hyam* a70 70
5 b g Champs Elysees Penang Cry (Barathea (IRE))
(4762) 5454[9] 6259[3] 6889[10] 7483[2] 8157[5] (Dead)
**Avenue Du Monde (FR)**
*Laura Grizzetti* a29 50
5 ch m Champs Elysees Marla (GER) (Pentire)
515a[2]
**Avenue Of Stars** *Karen McLintock* a70 68
4 b g Makfi Clifton Dancer (Fraam)
1472[7] 2776[7] 4310[12] 6237[4] 6786[2] 7017[8] 8211[5] 8552[8] 8930[4]
**Ave Sothia (FR)** *T Castanheira* a60 67
3 b f Soave(GER) Bithia (IRE) (Vettori (IRE))
3275a[2]
**Aviator (GER)** *James Eustace* a65 91
9 br g Motivator Amore (GER) (Lando (GER))
6889[8]
**Avilius** *A Fabre* a88 113
3 b g Pivotal Alessandria (Sunday Silence (USA))
4941a[3] 6053a[3] 6980a[2] 7638a[6]
**Avocadeau (IRE)** *Stuart Kittow* a50 61
6 b g Lawman(FR) Christmas Cracker (FR) (Alhaarth (IRE))
(1937) 2295[4] 3251[3] 4040[3] (5053) 6175[4] 7729[6]
**Avocet (USA)** *Julia Feilden* a49 40
4 b m Artie Schiller(USA) Striking Example (USA) (Empire Maker (USA))
3440[4] 4187[9] 4967[10] 6622[3] 7324[6] 7991[10]
**Avoidable** *David Simcock* a69
4 b g Iffraaj Ever Rigg (Dubai Destination (USA))
29[5]
**Avon Breeze** *Richard Whitaker* a71 98
8 b m Avonbridge African Breeze (Atraf)
(4435) 4719[4]◆ 4889[2] (5129) 5457[6] 5684[5] (5705)
**Avon Green** *Joseph Tuite* a66 57
2 ch f Avonbridge Greenery (IRE) (Green Desert (USA))
6005[6] 6338[7] 7351[9] 8191[4] 8309[4] 8795[2] 8902[6] 9188[3] 9404[5]
**Awake My Soul (IRE)** *Tom Tate* a58 101
8 ch g Teofilo(IRE) Field Of Hope (IRE) (Selkirk (USA))
2735[4]◆ 3597[10] 5421[7] 6449[8] (6881) 8165[14] 8423[4] (8652)
**Awardee (USA)** *Mikio Matsunaga* a115 103
7 b h Jungle Pocket(JPN) Heavenly Romance (JPN) (Sunday Silence (USA))
1380a[5]
**Aware (IRE)** *Charles Hills* a52 68
3 b g Lawman(FR) Viz (IRE) (Darshaan)
1939[4] 2997[7] 3520[5] 4492[7]
**Awesome** *Clive Cox* 79
2 ch f Bahamian Bounty Ballymore Celebre (IRE) (Peintre Celebre (USA))
2563[9] 3022[2] 3807[4] (6806) (8010)
**Awesome Allan (IRE)** *David Evans* a71 70
3 b g Acclamation Spring Approach (Tiger Hill (IRE))
1731[11] 2557[7] 3411[2] 3584[7] 4333[10] 4835[7] 5253[5] 6276[5] 6949[7] 7156[6] 7398[13] 7723[13] 8168[2] 8298[2] (8481) (8656) 8875[4] 9152[9] 9389[4]
**Awesome Rock (IRE)**
*Roger Ingram* a49 44
8 ch g Rock Of Gibraltar(IRE) Dangerous Diva (IRE) (Royal Academy (USA))
279[2] 621[5] 880[12] 1081[8] 1322[10] 2219[5] 3026[5] 3726[7] 8799[3] 9430[3]
**Awesome Slew (USA)** *Mark Casse* a115
4 b h Awesome Again(CAN) Slewfoundmoney (USA) (Seeking The Gold (USA))
8576a[3]
**Awesometank** *William Haggas* a57 92
2 br f Intense Focus(USA) Janey Muddles (IRE) (Lawman (FR))
4972[4]◆ 5834[6] 6584[2] (7621) (8045) 8597[4]
**Awfaa (IRE)** *Sir Michael Stoute* a55 80
3 b f Shamardal(USA) Elraabeya (CAN) (Seeking The Gold (USA))
5118[2] 5712[4] 6614[5]
**Awsaaf** *Simon Crisford* a76 73
2 b c Swiss Spirit Atheera (IRE) (Shamardal (USA))
(3187)◆ 3576[4] 6231[4] 7318[9]
**Axe Cap (IRE)** *Archie Watson* a69 60
2 b f Zebedee Clouded Leopard (USA) (Danehill (USA))
3023[7] 8294[3]◆ 8657[2] 8954[5]
**Ay Ay (IRE)** *David Elsworth* a92 92
3 b g Pour Moi(IRE) Chatline (IRE) (One Cool Cat (USA))
177[2]◆ 626[4] 1621[6] 5421[5] 5940[5] 7400[8] (7959) 8880[6] 9205[6]
**Aye Aye Skipper (IRE)**
*Ken Cunningham-Brown* a52 60
7 b g Captain Marvelous(IRE) Queenfisher (Scottish Reel I (IRE))
52[4]◆ 214[8] 293[6] 2294[6] 3522[3] (3809) 4203[2] 5823[5]◆ 6102[8] 6503[7] 9213[7] 9454[9]
**Ayguemorte (FR)** *P-L Guerin* a64 58
4 b g Vertigineux(FR) Aiguille Du Midi (FR) (Fly To The Stars)
6125a[11]
**Ayla's Emperor** *John Flint* a42 54
8 b m Holy Roman Emperor(IRE) Ayla (IRE) (Daylami (IRE))
4966[7] 5361[6] 6309[11]
**Ayrad (IRE)** *Roger Charlton* a78 112
6 ch g Dalakhani(IRE) Sweet Firebird (IRE) (Sadler's Wells (USA))
4069[5] 4584[5] 5925[9] 6514[4] (7743) 8421[9] 8844[8]
**Ayresome Angel** *John Mackie* a42 72
4 ch m Captain Gerrard(IRE) Almunia (IRE) (Mujadil (USA))
5134[3] 5580[2] 5877[4] 7522[8] 8260[12] 8681[8]
**Ayr Of Elegance** *Philip Hide* a77 78
5 b m Motivator Gaelic Swan (IRE) (Nashwan (USA))
92[5] (289) (1092) 1505[4] 2388[2] 3004[5] 3840[5] (5025) 7766[4] 8565[5] 9324[4]
**Ayton (IRE)** *Ollie Pears* a20 44
2 b f Declaration Of War(USA) Mubashera (USA) (Medaglia d'Oro (USA))
8236[9] 8779[9]
**Ay Up Mrs** *Rebecca Bastiman*
4 b m Monsieur Bond(IRE) Smiddy Hill (Factual (USA))
1680[16]
**Ayutthaya (IRE)** *Kevin Ryan* 85
2 ch c Lope De Vega(IRE) Pivotal Role (Pivotal)
6380[2] 6967[2] (7593)
**Azaly (IRE)** *Owen Burrows* a86 82
3 ch g Sepoy(AUS) Azzoom (IRE) (Cadeaux Genereux)
1692[4] 3293[4] (4579) 5664[2] (7998)◆
**Azam** *Michael Appleby* a82 76
3 b g Dansili Giants Play (USA) (Giant's Causeway (USA))
1886[6] 2784[9] 4701[5] 5803[3] 6887[13] 8638[10] 9000[6] 9204[7]
**Azamesse (IRE)** *J R Jenkins* a60 60
5 b m Azamour(IRE) Jeunesse Doree (IRE) (Rock Of Gibraltar (IRE))
98[4] 315[8] 646[9] 762[5] 2972[8]
**Azamix (FR)** *R Le Gal* 74
3 gr c Azamour(IRE) Casta Diva (FR) (Linamix (FR))
6225a[5]
**Azari** *Tom Dascombe* a87 101
5 b g Azamour(IRE) Atasari (IRE) (Whipper (USA))
(3470) 3841[3] 4380[2] 4863[6] (5924) 6857[2] 7395[12] 8042[8] 8740[20]
**Azezati (IRE)** *David Simcock* a59 67
2 ch f Dream Ahead(USA) Sweet Nicole (Okawango (USA))
5507[2] 6319[3]
**Azpeitia** *Ralph Beckett* a32 70
2 ch f Showcasing Leaves You Baby (IRE) (Pivotal)
8734[4]◆ 9198[7]
**Azuro (FR)** *C Lotoux* a88 84
3 b g Myboycharlie(IRE) Anthropologie (IRE) (Okawango (USA))
8976a[2]
**Azzeccagarbugli (IRE)**
*Stefano Botti* 101
4 b h Kodiac Consultant Stylist (IRE) (Desert Style (IRE))
3120a[4]
**Azzir (IRE)** *K R Burke* a75 82
5 gr g Echo Of Light Lady Georgina (Linamix (FR))
3315[3] 3744[3] 5579[2] 5830[4] 7328[9] 7524[14]
**Azzuri** *Dan Skelton* a47 68
5 b g Azamour(IRE) Folly Lodge (Grand Lodge (USA))
3616[9]
**Baarez (USA)** *S H Al Mazrouei*
6 ch g Hard Spun(USA) Sortita (GER) (Monsun (GER))
8583a[13]
**Baasha** *Ed Dunlop* 66
2 b g Havana Gold(IRE) Tawaasul (Haafhd)
7128[13] 7543[6] 7915[3]
**Baashiq (IRE)** *Roger Varian* 88
3 b g New Approach(IRE) Fatanah (IRE) (Green Desert (USA))
4618[3] 5323[5] 6073[7]
**Babalugats (IRE)** *Tim Easterby* 43
3 br f Elzaam(AUS) Ellanova (Kyllachy)
2137[7] 2705[11]
**Babamunchkin** *Michael Bell* a45 65
3 b f Henrythenavigator(USA) Babycakes (IRE) (Marju (IRE))
2475[8] 3053[4] 5001[8]
**Babar (FR)** *A Fabre* 59
2 b c Motivator Bargouzine (USA) (Stravinsky (USA))
7592a[8]
**Babel's Book (FR)** *F-H Graffard* 78
4 b g Iffraaj Ponentina (FR) (Lando (GER))
6648a[6]
**Babette (IRE)** *Alan Bailey* a52 48
3 b f Cape Cross(IRE) Crinoline (USA) (Street Cry (IRE))
2172[7] 2620[8] 3085[8] 6112[9] 7833[8] 8507[4] 8815[5]
**Babouska** *Michael Easterby* a58 47
3 b f Monsieur Bond(IRE) Prices Lane (Gentleman's Deal (IRE))
(149) 434[4]
**Babyfact** *Malcolm Saunders* a30 84
6 b m Piccolo Pennyspider (IRE) (Redback)
1768[7] 2360[3] (2725) 3278[5] 3696[9] 4532[3] 4993[3] (5271)◆ 6652[6]

**Baby Gal** *Jim Boyle* a63 63
3 b f Royal Applause Our Gal (Kyllachy)
625[4] 1242[7] 2252[3] 3246[8] 3941[5] 5028[2] 5295[2]◆ 6106[5] 6511[6] 9457[4]
**Baby Helmet** *Karen Tutty* a59 52
3 ch g Helmet(AUS) Lady Gorgeous (Compton Place)
48[6] 378[3]◆ 895[9] 3461[9] 3913[11] 4743[7] 5182[11] 6903[11]
**Babylon Lane** *Michael Dods* 44
2 gr f Lethal Force(IRE) Crinkle (IRE) (Distant Relative)
5210[8]
**Babylove (FR)** *H-A Pantall* a65
3 b f Zafeen(FR) Bainorama (FR) (Anabaa (USA))
1459a[8] 4288a[7]
**Baby Love (GER)** *R Dzubasz* 49
4 ch m It's Gino(GER) Beltana (GER) (Areion (GER))
7673a[11]
**Baby Say Yes** *John Norton* a6
3 b f Sayif(IRE) Baby Princess (BRZ) (Crimson Tide (IRE))
3258[4] 3984[8]
**Bacacarat (IRE)** *Andrew Balding* 72
2 b c Raven's Pass(USA) Mathuna (IRE) (Tagula (IRE))
7580[12] 8387[4]
**Baccarat (IRE)** *Charlie Appleby* a72 114
8 ch g Dutch Art Zut Alors (IRE) (Pivotal)
(433a) 1044a[2] 1376a[11] 2737[11]
**Bacchus** *Brian Meehan* 109
3 b g Kheleyf(USA) Rumbled (Halling (USA))
(1945) 2565[3] 3959[9] 4813[5] 5423[3] (6198) 7782[4]
**Backinanger** *Kevin Ryan* a57 58
3 b g Royal Applause Giusina Mia (USA) (Diesis)
787[6] 1005[3] 1127[3] 1835[11] 2897[7] 2949[3] 4303[11]
**Back On Board (IRE)** *Stefano Botti* 103
3 b c Nathaniel(IRE) Holy Moon (IRE) (Hernando (FR))
2868a[2] 4941a[8]
**Back To Love (CAN)** *Mark Gillard* a42 35
4 b m Street Cry(IRE) Song And Danz (USA) (Unbridled's Song (USA))
2087[9] 2679[14] 2916[11] 5823[10] 7480[10] 7711[12]
**Bad Dog** *Michael Easterby* a56 56
2 ch g Pastoral Pursuits Movie Star (IRE) (Barathea (IRE))
3149[9] 3429[6] 3789[6] 5878[9] 6022[8] 9230[3]◆
**Badenscoth** *Dean Ivory* a84 86
3 b g Foxwedge(AUS) Twice Upon A Time (Primo Dominie)
916[5] 1141[4] 1488[7] (2018) 3162[2]◆ 3627[7] 4255[7] 4748[2] (5242) 5578[3] 6576[6] 7131[2] 7759[10]
**Bad Girl Caoimhe (IRE)**
*Marjorie Fife* a59 26
4 br m Big Bad Bob(IRE) Sumostars (IRE) (Refuse To Bend (IRE))
152[9] 444[7] 684[10] 5215[10] 6131[12]
**Baghdad (FR)** *Mark Johnston* a80 71
2 b c Frankel Funny Girl (IRE) (Darshaan)
5036[5] 5504[11] 8161[4] (8537)
**Bahaarah (IRE)** *Richard Hannon* a94 101
4 b m Iffraaj Love Intrigue (IRE) (Marju (IRE))
617[5] 1795[6]
**Bahamadam** *Eve Johnson Houghton* a82 91
3 b f Bahamian Bounty Pelagia (IRE) (Lycius (USA))
(3167) 4208[8] 5294[4] 6377[5]
**Bahama Moon (IRE)** *David Barron* a66 93
5 b g Lope De Vega(IRE) Bahama Bay (GER) (Dansili)
1208[6] 1704[4] 3498[10] 4658[10] 5163[4] 5496[3] 5996[7] 6416[6] (7142) 7595[6]
**Bahamian (USA)** *Simon Callaghan* a87
2 ch c Freedom Child(USA) Final Humor (USA) (Distorted Humor (USA))
8609a[12]
**Bahamian Bird** *Richard Fahey* a77 81
4 b m Bahamian Bounty Ride The Wind (Cozzene (USA))
(1717) 2120[4] (2548) 3095[8] 3577[7] 5078[2] 5754[3] 6570[8] 8318[3]
**Bahamian C** *Richard Fahey* a52 67
6 b g Bahamian Bounty Amandian (IRE) (Indian Ridge (IRE))
1498[19] 2108[3] 3036[7] 3935[7] 4627[10] 5097[6] 8205[7]
**Bahamian Dollar** *David Evans* a83 86
4 b g Bahamian Bounty Penny Ha'penny (Bishop Of Cashel)
275[12] 783[2]◆ 1185[10] 2608[14] 3161[2] 3696[2] (3919) 4343[8] (5051) 5720[3] 6429[5] 6506[5] 7737[6] 8115[3] 8319[12]
**Bahamian Heights** *Robert Cowell* a80 72
6 b g Bahamian Bounty Tahirah (Green Desert (USA))
2038[9] 3170[5] 3518[5] 4629[6] 5514[6] 8159[4] (8542) 8990[2]◆ (9136) 9241[5] 9280[2]
**Bahamian Paradise**
*Hughie Morrison* a62 59
3 ch f Bahamian Bounty Amanjena (Beat Hollow)
1762[2] 2474[9]◆ 3184[5] 7320[2] 8328[12]
**Bahamian Sunrise** *John Gallagher* a80 86
5 ch g Bahamian Bounty Tagula Sunrise (IRE) (Tagula (IRE))
2058[2] 2253[6] 3021[7] (5304) 6282[2] 6695[3]◆ 7508[5] 8167[2] 8680[7]
**Bahamian Sunshine** *Lee Smyth* a42 71
4 ch g Bahamian Bounty Tagula Sunrise (IRE) (Tagula (IRE))
2950[8] 3704[6] 4682[5]
**Bahango (IRE)** *Patrick Morris* a78 62
5 b g Bahamian Bounty Last Tango (IRE) (Lion Cavern (USA))
(45) 443[4] 955[2] (1558) 1836[7] 7939[10]
**Bahar (USA)** *Richard Hannon* a72 61
3 b g First Defence(USA) La Rignana (USA) (Galileo (IRE))
1485[3] 2087[4]
**Bahkit (IRE)** *Sally Haynes* a70 70
3 b g Intikhab(USA) Pink Moon (IRE) (Namid)
(6518) (7236)

**Bahuta Acha** *David Loughnane* 73
2 b g Captain Gerrard(IRE) Rosein (Komaite (USA))
1873[11] 2148[7] 2590[2] 2816[7] 6756[7] 7041[5] (7385) 7690[5] 8483[2]
**Baileys Apprentice** *P Adda* a45 60
3 gr f Mastercraftsman(IRE) Jalissa (Mister Baileys)
385[5] 881[8] 8959a[11]
**Baileys Excel** *Chris Dwyer* a64
2 b c Exceed And Excel(AUS) Baileys Jubilee (Bahamian Bounty)
8154[6] 8536[7] 8809[9]
**Baileys Excelerate (FR)**
*Mark Johnston* a82 84
2 gr c Excelebration(IRE) Cruel Sea (USA) (Mizzen Mast (USA))
5600[3]◆ (6057)◆ 7451[2] 7956[2]
**Baileys Pursuit** *Gay Kelleway* a67 43
5 ch m Pastoral Pursuits Royal Mistress (Fasliyev (USA))
67[11] 217[7] 601[9]
**Baileys Rockstar** *James Given* a42
2 b f Rock Of Gibraltar(IRE) Biased (Haafhd)
5998[8] 7535[8] 8208[10]
**Baileys Showgirl (FR)**
*Mark Johnston* a69 99
3 b f Sepoy(AUS) Tanguista (FR) (War Chant (USA))
1621[7] 3013[6] 3964[17]
**Baillolet (FR)** *Mme Pia Brandt* 90
2 b c Le Havre(IRE) Coutances (Shamardal (USA))
5989a[2] (7175a) 7754a[6]
**Baiyouna (FR)** *A De Royer-Dupre* 95
3 b f Sea The Stars(IRE) Balankiya (IRE) (Darshaan)
4424a[5] 6981a[9] 7635a[7]
**Bajan Beacon** *Iain Jardine* a24 15
4 gr g Hellvelyn Bajan Rose (Dashing Blade)
2429[11] 2791[8] 3151[9]
**Bajan Gold (IRE)** *Stuart Williams* a66 66
2 ch c Lope De Vega(IRE) Charmgoer (USA) (Nureyev (USA))
5036[4] 6367[4] 7281[5]◆ 7764[8] 8354[9] 9097[2]◆
**Bajazzo (GER)** *H-A Pantall* a78 78
3 b c Amico Fritz(GER) Brangane (IRE) (Anita's Prince)
6455a[12]
**Bakchich Game (FR)** *G Botti* 99
2 b c Shakespearean(IRE) Baffle Creek (Refuse To Bend (IRE))
8276a[6]
**Baker Street** *Tom Dascombe* a53 62
3 ch g Bahamian Bounty Aliante (Sir Percy)
1428[7] 1968[3] 2349[14] 2527[6] 3041[8] 4453[9]
**Bakht Khan (IRE)** *Kevin Ryan* a69 51
2 ch g Sepoy(AUS) Naddwah (Pivotal)
5825[6] 6950[3]◆ 7876[9]
**Balancing Time** *Amanda Perrett* a77 78
4 b g Pivotal Time On (Sadler's Wells (USA))
(1430) 3308[4] 3616[11] 4809[13]
**Balashakh (USA)** *David Simcock* a75 78
3 b g Blame(USA) She Has Aptitude (USA) (Aptitude (USA))
855[3]◆ 1239[2] 4913[2] 6389[5] 7935[6]
**Bal De Rio (FR)** *Brian Ellison* a73 76
4 b g Vertigineux(FR) Baldoranic (FR) (Panoramic)
5212[5] 5701[3]
**Balducci** *Roger Fell* a70 77
10 b g Dansili Miss Meltemi (IRE) (Miswaki Tern (USA))
1187[7] 1549[5]
**Balestra** *Charles Hills* a84 82
3 b c Bated Breath Nimble Thimble (USA) (Mizzen Mast (USA))
2090[6] 2782[8] (4490) 6404[13] 7759[5]
**Balf's Choice (AUS)** *Ryan Balfour* 102
4 bb g Written Tycoon(AUS) Not Jude's Choice (AUS) (Celtic Swing)
8857a[9]
**Balgair** *Tom Clover* a74 71
3 ch g Foxwedge(AUS) Glencal (Compton Place)
2088[7] 2894[5] 4311[7] 5218[7] 7062[2]◆ 7881[3]◆ 8503[2]
**Balgowlah (IRE)** *David Lanigan* a54
2 b g Thewayyouare(USA) Rohain (IRE) (Singspiel (IRE))
8340[10] 8501[8] 8748[8]
**Balkhash (IRE)** *Clive Cox* a50 57
2 b g Champs Elysees Balatoma (IRE) (Mr Greeley (USA))
8677[9] 8903[9] 9318[6]
**Balkinstown (IRE)** *Robert Stephens* 51
7 b g Westerner Graffogue (IRE) (Red Sunset)
6343[3]
**Ballad Singer** *Doug Watson* a67 53
4 ch g Kyllachy Clear Voice (USA) (Cryptoclearance (USA))
8711a[3]
**Ballagh Rocks (USA)** *William Mott* 115
4 b h Stormy Atlantic(USA) Bells Are Ringing (USA) (Sadler's Wells (USA))
7851a[3] 8608a[9]
**Ballard Down (IRE)** *William Knight* a98 105
4 b g Canford Cliffs(IRE) Mackenzie's Friend (Selkirk (USA))
1422[2] (2310) 3212[5] 4001[2] (5157)
**Ballesteros** *Roger Ingram* a79 80
8 ch g Tomba Flamenco Dancer (Mark Of Esteem (IRE))
234[9] 358[6] 682[3] 971[12] 1370[6] 1696[11] 2524[7] 3231[5] 3581[5] 4333[6] 5098[9] 5402[12] 6062[3]◆ 6411[2] 7137[4] 7625[2] 8106[3] (8296) 8818[10] 9181[8]
**Ballet Concerto** *Sir Michael Stoute* a91 120
4 b g Dansili Ballet Ballon (USA) (Rahy (USA))
(1492) 2396[5] 3320[6] 3963[4] (4918)◆ (6105) (6928) (Dead)
**Ballet De La Reine (USA)**
*J-C Rouget* 74
2 b f War Front(USA) All For Glory (USA) (Giant's Causeway (USA))
5988a[5]

**Balletomane** *Richard Hannon* a68 68
2 b c Exceed And Excel(AUS) Alexander Ballet (Mind Games)
6424[4] 7810[7] 8028[2] 8309[3]
**Ballet Shoes (IRE)** *A P O'Brien* 102
2 b f Galileo(IRE) Emerald Ring (IRE) (Johannesburg (USA))
6487a[2] 6974a[7] 7421a[3] 7859a[3]
**Ball Girl (IRE)** *G M Lyons* 92
2 b f Tagula(IRE) Love Thirty (Mister Baileys)
6488a[3] 7421a[9] 8082a[16]
**Balliol** *Ronald Harris* a72 62
5 b g Exceed And Excel(AUS) Cinerama (IRE) (Machiavellian (USA))
551[10]
**Ball Lightning (FR)** *E Libaud* a70 74
7 b g Sir Percy Tunguska (Silver Patriarch (IRE))
8303a[2]
**Ballot Box** *Mrs John Harrington* 76
2 br f Big Bad Bob(IRE) Represent (IRE) (Exceed And Excel (AUS))
6977a[21]
**Ballyfarsoon (IRE)** *Ian Williams* a63 60
6 ch g Medicean Amzara (IRE) (Montjeu (IRE))
1985[8] 5483[11] 6820[8] 7483[5] 7992[2] (8246)
**Ballylare** *Lee Carter* a84 83
4 b g Mullionmileanhour(IRE) Retainage (USA) (Polish Numbers (USA))
66[5]
**Ballymore Castle (IRE)**
*Richard Fahey* a75 84
5 br g Invincible Spirit(IRE) Ballymore Lady (USA) (War Chant (USA))
1512[4] 2081[5] 2833[6] 3294[3] 3792[11] 4270[8] 8115[14] 8489[8] 8722[2] 8818[4] 9220[5] (9296)
**Ballymount** *E J O'Neill* 98
2 ch g Cityscape Symphony Star (IRE) (Amadeus Wolf)
(5816a)
**Ballynanty (IRE)** *Andrew Balding* a99 66
5 gr g Yeats(IRE) Reina Blanca (Darshaan)
1341[5] 1779[13] 2519[5] 3073[11]
**Ballyquin (IRE)** *Andrew Balding* 73
2 b c Acclamation Something Mon (USA) (Maria's Mon (USA))
8388[4]
**Ballysampson** *Simon Dow* a39 25
3 b c Equiano(FR) The Fugative (Nicholas (USA))
2674[5]
**Balmec (IRE)** *Ann Duffield* a41 42
2 bl g Society Rock(IRE) Crossreadh (USA) (Sahm (USA))
7383[7] 7551[7] 8916[6] 9372[10]
**Balmont Belle (IRE)** *Barry Leavy* a51 45
7 b m Balmont(USA) Social Set (IRE) (Key Of Luck (USA))
1403[8] 1985[6] 3628[9] 4840[6] 6153[RR] 7028[9]
**Balmoral Castle** *Jonathan Portman* a53 98
8 b g Royal Applause Mimiteh (USA) (Maria's Mon (USA))
1964[7] 2291[10] 4832[3] 5643[11] 6422[10] 7358[8]
**Balsa Baie (FR)** *D Meslin* a67
6 gr m Crillon(FR) Biquette (Octagonal (NZ))
8303a[3]
**Baltic Duchess (IRE)** *A Fabre* 104
3 b f Lope De Vega(IRE) Born Wild (GER) (Sadler's Wells (USA))
1459a[2] 4988a[6] 6732a[2] 7635a[5] 8666a[5]
**Baltic Eagle (GER)** *Rune Haugen* a68 69
3 ch g Adlerflug(GER) Baltic Gift (Cadeaux Genereux)
881[2] 1877[3] 2137[5]
**Baltic Knight (IRE)** *Husain Aldailami* a90 103
7 b g Baltic King Night Of Joy (IRE) (King's Best (USA))
914a[8]
**Baltic Prince (IRE)** *Tony Carroll* a77 69
7 b g Baltic King Brunswick (Warning)
277[8] 516[5] 1105[6] 1189[3] 3589[10] 4529[9] 5699[10] 6345[6] (7212) 8184[9] 8473[9] 8958[2] 9220[8] 9410[4]
**Balty Boys (IRE)** *Brian Ellison* a58 69
8 b g Cape Cross(IRE) Chatham Islands (USA) (Elusive Quality (USA))
8315[12]
**Bamako Du Chatelet (FR)**
*Ian Williams* a77 74
6 gr g Voix Du Nord(FR) Royale Du Chatelet (FR) (Sleeping Car (FR))
30[2] (220) 440[4] 861[2] 965[4] 1364[7] 1891[4] 2111[2] 2336[7] 3685[4] 5024[4] 6259[6] 7096[3] 8072[10] 8876[12] (9325) 9421[2]
**Bamber Bridge (IRE)** *Michael Dods* 94
3 gr c Dark Angel(IRE) Nashira (Prince Sabo)
4719[8] 5669[5] 6434[4] 7702[4] 8289[10]
**Bambino Lola** *Adam West* 89
2 b f Helmet(AUS) Lifetime Romance (IRE) (Mozart (IRE))
(4090)◆ 5154[3] (6394)◆ 6863[8]
**Bamo Mc** *Mike Murphy* 51
3 gr g Hellvelyn Soft Touch (IRE) (Petorius (IRE))
4764[7] 5577[12] 6103[11]
**Banaadeer (AUS)** *M F De Kock* 105
5 br g More Than Ready(USA) Provence (AUS) (Redoute's Choice (AUS))
87a[6] 433a[14]
**Bancnuanaheireann (IRE)**
*Michael Appleby* a99 88
10 b g Chevalier(IRE) Alamanta (IRE) (Ali-Royal (IRE))
744[3] 2396[7] 2999[11] 5643[13] 9233[9]
**Banditry (IRE)** *Ian Williams* a99 101
5 b g Iffraaj Badalona (Cape Cross (IRE))
(963) 2086[2] 2431[6] 3154[4] 4002[2]◆ (4316) 4882[2]
**Banff (IRE)** *Olly Murphy* a56 56
4 b g Papal Bull Hugs 'n Kisses (IRE) (Noverre (USA))
(5413) 5716[4]
**Banish (USA)** *Hugo Palmer* a97 92
4 b g Smart Strike(CAN) Beyond Our Reach (IRE) (Danehill Dancer (IRE))
2136[5] 2558[5] 4585[6] 5798[4] 6887[7] 7234[4] (7515) 7880[5] 8188[12]

**Banjo's Voice** *Jane Chapple-Hyam* 31
2 ch g Poet's Voice La Jwaab (Alhaarth (IRE))
6388[12] 7813[9] 8677[14]
**Bank Bonus** *Brian Ellison* a72 79
8 b g Motivator Small Fortune (Anabaa (USA))
991[8] 4357[8]
**Banksea** *Luca Cumani* 109
4 b g Lawman(FR) Stars In Your Eyes (Galileo (IRE))
(1960) 3963[26] 6873[8] 7395[5]
**Bannock (IRE)** *A bin Harmash* a86 86
8 b g Bertolini(USA) Laoub (USA) (Red Ransom (USA))
316a[3]
**Ban Shoof** *Gary Moore* a77 74
4 b g Shirocco(GER) Pasithea (IRE) (Celtic Swing)
122[5] 380[6] 2913[10] 3616[8] 4809[7] 5142[3] (5866) 6588[4] 7495[2] 7917[9] (9459)
**Bansuri** *Jo Hughes* a26
2 ch f Piccolo Trina's Pet (Efisio)
4452[8]
**Banta Bay** *John Best* a56 54
3 b g Kheleyf(USA) Atnab (USA) (Riverman (USA))
2507[6] 3442[8] 4006[8] 6324[10] 6791[8] 7763[3] 7945[6] 8543[2] 8908[5] 9211[6]
**Banzari** *H-F Devin* 110
5 b m Motivator Bantu (Cape Cross (IRE))
1271a[7]
**Bapak Asmara (IRE)** *Kevin Ryan* a69 87
5 ro g Zebedee Sheba Five (USA) (Five Star Day (USA))
1777[8] 2899[10] 4477[8] 5211[13] 5994[8] 6574[8]
**Bapak Bangsawan** *Ann Stokell* a77 53
7 b g Pastoral Pursuits Nsx (Roi Danzig (USA))
153[5]
**Barag (IRE)** *J-C Rouget* 65
2 gr c Myboycharlie(IRE) Aliyeska (IRE) (Fasliyev (USA))
5989a[6]
**Baraweez (IRE)** *Brian Ellison* a100 107
7 b g Cape Cross(IRE) Aquarelle Bleue (Sadler's Wells (USA))
999[7] 1148[5] 1769[8] 3842[10] 4377[11] 5517a[6] 5688a[2] 6355[4] 6685[4] 6961a[8] 8009[6]
**Barbados Bob (USA)** *Ecurie Fievez* a58 58
7 b g Speightstown(USA) Lemon Lady (USA) (Lemon Drop Kid (USA))
(1070a)
**Barbara Villiers** *Mark Johnston* a68
2 b f Champs Elysees Frances Stuart (IRE) (King's Best (USA))
9155[3] 9277[3]
**Barbarianatthegate** *Brian Meehan* a73 74
2 ch c Lethal Force(IRE) Poetic Dancer (Byron)
3156[9] 3965[5] 4560[2]◆ 5179[2] 5572[14] 6008[4] (6410)
**Barbary Prince** *Shaun Harris* a11 41
5 ch g Dapper La Vie Est Belle (Makbul)
479[9] 747[9] 4346[5] 5267[12] 5850[11] 6088[6] 6589[7] 7215[10]
**Bardd (IRE)** *Nicky Henderson* a74
5 b g Dylan Thomas(IRE) Zarawa (IRE) (Kahyasi (IRE))
(9235)
**Barefoot Baby (IRE)** *Richard Fahey* a60 64
2 ch f Choisir(AUS) Gwen Lady Byron (IRE) (Dandy Man (IRE))
5437[6] 6311[5] 6938[2] 7552[7] 7829[4] 8013[13]
**Barford (IRE)** *Pam Sly* 89
2 b c Big Bad Bob(IRE) Rupa (IRE) (Acclamation)
3908[4] 4583[2] (5808) 6699[5]◆ 7384[5] (8013)
**Bargain Buy** *William Haggas* a91 84
4 ch m Tamayuz Peace Summit (Cape Cross (IRE))
8101[10] 994[3]
**Barig Al Thumama** *Marco Botti* a74 74
2 ch c Kyllachy Self Centred (Medicean)
5120[2]◆ 6146[3] 7788[2] 8343[3]
**Barista (GER)** *J Hirschberger* 88
2 ch f Rock Of Gibraltar(IRE) Basilea Gold (GER) (Monsun (GER))
8269a[7]
**Barista (IRE)** *Brian Forsey* a67 67
9 b g Titus Livius(FR) Cappuccino (IRE) (Mujadil (USA))
2708[3] 3422[6] 5793[9] (6101) 6503[3] 7198[11] 8662[11] 9076[3]
**Baritone (IRE)** *Sir Michael Stoute* 61
2 b c Camelot Star Ruby (IRE) (Rock Of Gibraltar (IRE))
7392[5]◆
**Barizan (IRE)** *Brendan Powell* 74
11 b g Kalanisi(IRE) Behra (IRE) (Grand Lodge (USA))
2357[9] 2928[3] 3494[2] 4791[4]
**Barkston Ash** *Eric Alston* 78
9 b g Kyllachy Ae Kae Ae (USA) (King Of Kings (IRE))
5806[7] 6546[13] 7018[8] 7525[12] 8656[7]
**Bar Mina (IRE)** *H-A Pantall* 77
3 b f Falco(USA) Maisha (GER) (Platini (GER))
8959a[3]
**Barnaby Brook (CAN)**
*Tom Dascombe* a71 54
7 b g North Light(IRE) Mascara (USA) (Milwaukee Brew (USA))
6523[7] (6948) 7495[6] 8429[2] 9295[7]
**Barnacle** *Emma Owen* a47 47
8 b g Compton Place Bombalarina (IRE) (Barathea (IRE))
278[2] 395[5] 741[5] 859[11] 1081[11] 1207[8] 1985[7]
**Barnay** *Marcus Tregoning* a63
2 b g Nayef(USA) Barnezet (GR) (Invincible Spirit (IRE))
8545[9] 8840[7] 9319[4]
**Barney Bullet (IRE)** *Noel Wilson* 53
2 b g Havana Gold(IRE) Lalinde (Tiger Hill (IRE))
6055[7] 6432[8] 7242[6]
**Barney George** *Iain Jardine* 61
2 ch c Cityscape Romantic Retreat (Rainbow Quest (USA))
3973[7] 4956[8] 5918[5] 7698[8] 8287[11]

**Barney Roy** *Richard Hannon* 124
3 b c Excelebration(IRE) Alina (IRE) (Galileo (IRE)) (1959)◆ 2399[2] (3927) 4638[2]◆ 6328[3] 8233[9]
**Barnsdale** *John Holt* a47 48
4 b g Stimulation(IRE) Seren Teg (Timeless Times (USA))
386[11] 601[10] 874[3] 1006[12] 1247[11] 1759[7] 2370[6] 2995[6] 3466[4] 3545[4] 5027[4] 9374[9]
**Barocca (GER)** *S Smrczek* a48
5 b m It's Gino(GER) Bromelia (GER) (Platini (GER))
1196a[2] 9112a[8]
**Bar Of Gold (USA)** *John C Kimmel* a114 106
5 bb m Medaglia d'Oro(USA) Khancord Kid (USA) (Lemon Drop Kid (USA))
(8605a)
**Baron Bolt** *Paul Cole* a90 96
4 br g Kheleyf(USA) Scarlet Royal (Red Ransom (USA))
2390[8] 2833[3] 3565[5] 4321[3] 6068[6]◆ (6506) 7622[5] 8077[2]◆ 8393[2]
**Baroncello (GER)** *Andreas Suborics* a86 94
4 b h Medecis Balsamia (GER) (Speedmaster (GER))
1661a[8]
**Baroness (IRE)**
*Joseph Patrick O'Brien* a71 95
2 b f Declaration Of War(USA) Charroux (IRE) (Darshaan)
8597[2]
**Baron Run** *K R Burke* a45 56
7 ch g Bertolini(USA) Bhima (Polar Falcon (USA))
312[10] 514[8] 1296[9] 3239[9] 4897[4] 5285[5] 5750[4] 6688[6] 8473[6] 8651[11]
**Barracuda Boy (IRE)** *Marjorie Fife* a103 84
7 b g Bahamian Bounty Madame Boulangere (Royal Applause)
6186[8] 6484[7] 7455[5] 7828[3] 8547[9] 9269[5]
**Barraquero (IRE)** *Brian Meehan* 110
2 b c Zebedee Chica Whopa (IRE) (Oasis Dream)
3747[3] (4466)◆ (5570)
**Barreesh (IRE)** *Jaber Ramadhan* a92 89
5 ch g Giant's Causeway(USA) Astrologie (FR) (Polish Precedent (USA))
9360a[2]
**Barren Brook** *Laura Mongan* a71 77
10 b g Beat Hollow Carinthia (IRE) (Tirol (IRE))
351[9]
**Barrington (IRE)** *Charles Hills* a86 99
3 b c Casamento(IRE) Mia Divina (Exceed And Excel (AUS))
2823[6]◆ 3959[18] 4992[3] 5513[4] 6922[12] 7455[9]
**Barron's Lad** *Mark Michael McNiff* 77
4 ch g Compton Place Dance Away (Pivotal)
1385a[10]
**Barrsbrook** *Gary Moore* a62
3 b g Doyen(IRE) Sayrianna (Sayaarr (USA))
9455[4]
**Barsanti (IRE)** *Roger Varian* a100 118
5 b g Champs Elysees Silver Star (Zafonic (USA))
3072[3] 4070[2] 4917[2]
**Bartaba (FR)** *A Fabre* a38
2 b f Deep Impact(JPN) Baahama (IRE) (Anabaa (USA))
8691a[14]
**Bartholomeu Dias** *Charles Hills* 91
2 b c Mount Nelson Lady Francesca (Montjeu (IRE))
3002[3] 4068[4]◆ 5808[3]
**Bartholomew J (IRE)** *Lydia Pearce* a66 71
3 ch g Fast Company(IRE) Mana (IRE) (Motivator)
377[3] 644[6] 897[8] 987[6] (1623) 2027[5]◆ (2315) 3041[2]◆ 3752[6] 4320[2] 6144[6] 8142[8] 8814[8] 9391[5]
**Barton Mills** *William Haggas* a83 69
2 b c Iffraaj Balladonia (Primo Dominie)
6884[2]◆ (7512) 8043[9]
**Barwah (USA)** *Peter Niven* a76 62
6 b m Discreet Cat(USA) Enfiraaj (USA) (Kingmambo (USA))
(444) 729[2] 1032[7] 1104[2] 2685[10] (3344) 3845[16]
**Barwell (IRE)** *Michael Dods* a61 95
3 b g Rock Of Gibraltar(IRE) Agata (FR) (Poliglote)
1366[3] 1782[6] 2186[3] (3499) (3745) 6187[2] (6944)
**Barwick** *George Baker* a64 90
9 b g Beat Hollow Tenpence (Bob Back (USA))
2085[3] 3323[7] 4457a[4] 5397[13] (5987a) 7430a[3] (7534a) 8303a[5]
**Barwod** *J Smart* 108
4 b h Lope De Vega(IRE) Atlanda (FR) (Hernando (FR))
914a[6]
**Barye** *Richard Hughes* a107 82
6 b g Archipenko(USA) Oblige (Robellino (USA))
197[5] 1068[5] 1341[6] 1798[7] 7397[9] 8244[6] 8539[7] 9112a[3] 9458[7]
**Basateen (IRE)** *Doug Watson* 108
5 ch g Teofilo(IRE) Tasha's Dream (USA) (Woodman (USA))
208a[4] 699a[7] 890a[4] 1374a[8]
**Basheer** *Marco Botti* a69
3 b g Dubawi(IRE) Reem (AUS) (Galileo (IRE))
127[10] 545[4] 878[5]
**Bashiba (IRE)** *Nigel Tinkler* 94
6 ch g Iffraaj Nightswimmer (IRE) (Noverre (USA))
1876[5] 2123[2] 2899[6] 3295[3] 3741[3] 4379[3] 4867[3] 6185[11] 8012[10]
**Basic Trilogy (NZ)** *John Moore* 110
5 cg g Mastercraftsman(IRE) Gold Class (NZ) (Gold Brose (AUS))
3129a[6]
**Basil Berry** *Chris Dwyer* a100 101
6 b g Tobougg(IRE) Dolly Coughdrop (IRE) (Titus Livius (FR))
1794[6] 2518[6] 4321[4] 5037[6] 5914[10]
**Basileus (IRE)** *A Giorgi* a74 106
4 ch h Dream Ahead(USA) Miss Mariduff (USA) (Hussonet (USA))
2004a[3] 2663a[4] 9112a[6]
**Basingstoke (IRE)**
*Daniel Mark Loughnane* a55 44
8 b g Elusive City(USA) Ryninch (IRE) (Dr Devious (IRE))
26[6] 222[8]

**Bassino (USA)** *James Bennett* a57 37
4 b g Street Cry(IRE) Show Me The Roses (USA) (Storm Cat (USA))
124[5] 383[2] 605[6] 740[7] 1406[11] 2095[10] 2916[9] 3823[10]
**Bassmah** *Ismail Mohammed* 83
3 b f Harbour Watch(IRE) Secret Night (Dansili)
3171[2] 3869[2] 4351[2] (5946)
**Bastia** *Martyn Meade* a68
3 br f Paco Boy(IRE) Miliana (IRE) (Polar Falcon (USA))
(520) 1005[5] 1194[2]
**Bataka** *Harry Dunlop* a49 60
3 ch f Mount Nelson Dominica (Alhaarth (IRE))
150[3]
**Bat Aloufat (FR)** *M Pimbonnet* a73 67
4 b m Way Of Light(USA) Schicky Micky (FR) (Testa Rossa (AUS))
6302a[3] 9309a[9]
**Bateel (IRE)** *F-H Graffard* 117
5 b m Dubawi(IRE) Attractive Crown (USA) (Chief's Crown (USA))
2202a[2] (3586) (5691a) (6981a) 8231[2]
**Bath And Tennis (IRE)**
*Sir Mark Prescott Bt* a79 78
2 bb f Footstepsinthesand Goldamour (IRE) (Fasliyev (USA))
3135[3] 3516[2] 3960[17] 4598[5] 6338[6] 7706[2] (8131) (8373) 9080[3]
**Bathsheba Bay (IRE)**
*Richard Hannon* 87
2 b c Footstepsinthesand Valamareha (IRE) (Val Royal (FR))
4583[5] 5301[2]◆ 5641[2] (6654)
**Battaash (IRE)** *Charles Hills* 128
3 b g Dark Angel(IRE) Anna Law (IRE) (Lawman (FR))
(3835) (4635) (5595) 6402[4] (7670a)
**Battalion (IRE)** *Jamie Osborne* a110 113
7 b g Authorized(IRE) Zigarra (Halling (USA))
574[3] 919[6] 1775[9] 8844[6] 9388[6]
**Batten The Hatches** *David Barron* a76 95
3 b g Harbour Watch(IRE) Our Little Secret (IRE) (Rossini (USA))
(731) 2271[5] 3038[4] (4104)◆ 5383[2] 6450[18]
**Battered** *William Haggas* a85 104
3 b g Foxwedge(AUS) Swan Wings (Bahamian Bounty)
1702[5] 2334[4] (2739)◆ 3836[3] 5434[5] (5642) 6404[2] 7149[2]
**Battersea** *Roger Varian* a98 104
6 b g Galileo(IRE) Gino's Spirits (Perugino (USA))
2288[6] 6447[8] 7124[2] 8539[6]
**Battle Commence (IRE)**
*David O'Meara* 65
2 b g Declaration Of War(USA) Invincible Ash (IRE) (Invincible Spirit (IRE))
6146[5]
**Battle In Seattle (FR)**
*A De Royer-Dupre* a97 100
3 ch c Naaqoos Boa Vinda (FR) (High Yield (USA))
3613a[4]
**Battle Lines** *James Tate* a73 63
2 ch c Sepoy(AUS) Goslar (In The Wings)
7391[10] 8245[7] 9312[3]◆
**Battle Of Jericho (USA)**
*A P O'Brien* a99 99
2 b c War Front(USA) Together (IRE) (Galileo (IRE))
7797a[2] 8001[7]
**Battle Of Marathon (USA)**
*John Ryan* a101 97
5 b g War Front(USA) Sayedah (IRE) (Darshaan)
1494[22] 5456[5] 6024[13] 7149[4] 7619[15] 8417[5] 8891[12] 8999[3] (9053) 9407[6]
**Battle Of Midway (USA)**
*Jerry Hollendorfer* a122
3 b c Smart Strike(CAN) Rigoletta (USA) (Concerto (USA))
2420a[3] 5463a[6] (8576a)
**Battle Of Wits (IRE)**
*Frau R Weissmeier* a46 50
3 b g Fast Company(IRE) Mirandassister (IRE) (Titus Livius (FR))
838a[16]
**Battleoftheboyne (IRE)**
*Eamonn O'Connell* a58 70
8 b g Majestic Missile(IRE) Khaytada (IRE) (Doyoun)
2656a[13]
**Batts Rock (IRE)** *Michael Bell* a88 91
4 b g Fastnet Rock(AUS) Be My Queen (IRE) (Sadler's Wells (USA))
2603[2]◆ 3073[7] 3594[5] 4908[2] 6952[4] 7515[4]
**Bayards Cove** *Brian Barr* a35
2 b f Harbour Watch(IRE) Acicula (IRE) (Night Shift (USA))
8889[12] 9310[8]
**Baydar** *Ian Williams* a75 111
4 b g Rock Of Gibraltar(IRE) Splashdown (Falbrav (IRE))
3012[7] 4033[13] 4614[11] 5500[11] 6449[18] 7395[19]
**Bayelsa Boy (IRE)** *Tim Easterby*
2 b g Elzaam(AUS) Extraordinary (IRE) (Swain (IRE))
6432[15]
**Bayezid (IRE)** *S Tasbek* 77
2 b c Most Improved(IRE) Hurrem Sultan (IRE) (Dylan Thomas (IRE))
6745a[4]
**Bay Of Biscaine (FR)** *Mario Hofer* a76 93
3 gr g Mastercraftsman(IRE) Britney (FR) (Kheleyf (USA))
5777a[9] 8305a[4]
**Bay Of Poets (IRE)** *Charlie Appleby* a83 110
3 b g Lope De Vega(IRE) Bristol Bay (IRE) (Montjeu (IRE))
2084[3]◆ 2569[2] 3368a[7] 3994[12] 5522a[2] (6172a) 7176a[4]
**Bay Station** *Jason Ward* a21 74
3 b f Camacho Hazelhurst (IRE) (Night Shift (USA))
657[5] 3184[7] 4107[4]◆ 4717[4] 5134[5] 6469[4] 7014[6] 7525[17]

**Baystone (FR)** *H-A Pantall* a67 22
2 b f Kendargent(FR) Little Stone (FR) (One Cool Cat (USA))
7470a[10] 9087a[6]
**Bayston Hill** *Mark Usher* a72 71
3 br g Big Bad Bob(IRE) Jessica Ennis (USA) (English Channel (USA))
1686[6] 2088[11] (3024) 3752[5] 4492[3] 5718[6] 6557[5] 7495[3] 7917[7] 8429[3] 8946[4]◆ (9211)
**Bay Watch (IRE)** *Andrew Balding* a62 58
3 b g Harbour Watch(IRE) Karuga (Kyllachy)
27[4] 763[9] 3870[7] 4542[5]
**Baz (FR)** *F-H Graffard* a78 98
7 b g Mount Nelson Zelah (IRE) (Alzao (USA))
8444a[9]
**Bazooka (IRE)** *David Flood* a68 82
6 b g Camacho Janadam (IRE) (Mukaddamah (USA))
47[9] 6763[7] (7202) 7651[3] 8295[2]
**Bazwind (IRE)** *David Evans* a67 70
3 b g Lilbourne Lad(IRE) Gay Heroine (Caerleon (USA))
100[2] 292[3] 766[3] (846) 1411[5] 1888[5] 3627[8]
**Bazzat (IRE)** *John Ryan* a67 55
4 ch g Roderic O'Connor(IRE) Compradore (Mujtahid (USA))
166[6]
**Bbob Alula** *Bill Turner* 63
2 ch g Showcasing Island Rhapsody (Bahamian Bounty)
6178[3] 6826[8]
**Beach Bar (IRE)**
*Richard John O'Brien* a90 87
6 b g Azamour(IRE) Toasted Special (USA) (Johannesburg (USA))
204a[9] 319a[6] 540a[9] 891a[10] 2968[6] 4017[5] 4563[12] 8737[9]
**Beach Break** *Ralph Beckett* a73 83
3 b g Cacique(IRE) Wemyss Bay (Sadler's Wells (USA))
2721[2] (3286) 4796[6] 6415[6]
**Beachcomber Bay (IRE)**
*Charlie Appleby* 52
2 b c Invincible Spirit(IRE) Beach Bunny (IRE) (High Chaparral (IRE))
7460[7]
**Beach Dancer (IRE)** *William Knight* a59 51
3 b g Footstepsinthesand All Night Dancer (IRE) (Danehill Dancer (IRE))
819[6] 1024[7] 1688[3] 2235[8] 2362[7] 2957[6] 3719[7] 4714[6]
**Beach Party** *Hughie Morrison* a53 43
3 b f Dutch Art Musical Sands (Green Desert (USA))
3456[6] 4565[8] 5247[6] 6524[P]
**Beach Patrol (USA)** *Chad C Brown* 117
4 bb h Lemon Drop Kid(USA) Bashful Bertie (USA) (Quiet American (USA))
(5977a) (7633a) 8610a[2]
**Beach Samba (IRE)**
*Ibrahim Al Malki* a71 98
5 ch h Lope De Vega(IRE) Braziliz (USA) (Kingmambo (USA))
932a[6]
**Beachwalk** *Sir Michael Stoute* a72 59
2 b g Showcasing Esplanade (Danehill (USA))
6653[11] 7765[6] 8493[4]
**Beach Wedding (IRE)** *J P Murtagh* 75
2 b f Footstepsinthesand Lovers Peace (IRE) (Oratorio (IRE))
6487a[5] 8082a[10]
**Beachy Head (IRE)** *A R Al Rayhi* a103 72
6 b h Shamardal(USA) Chaquiras (USA) (Seeking The Gold (USA))
250a[11] 694a[6] 775a[P]
**Beaconsfield** *Hughie Morrison* a57 69
3 b g Foxwedge(AUS) Italian Connection (Cadeaux Genereux)
4748[8] 5221[8] 7095[7] 7483[9] 7879[12]
**Beadlam (IRE)** *Roger Fell* a67 67
4 ch m Frozen Power(IRE) Pivotal Role (Pivotal)
1879[5] 2430[9] 3432[8] 3934[7] (4727) 5185[9] (5897) 6003[3] 6638[5] 7476[8]
**Beama (FR)** *H-A Pantall* a86 78
4 b m Elusive City(USA) High Will (FR) (High Chaparral (IRE))
7636a[5]
**Bean Feasa** *J S Bolger* 104
3 b f Dubawi(IRE) Speirbhean (IRE) (Danehill (USA))
1634a[5] (2441a) 3110a[5] 3964[12] 4928a[8] 6958a[10]
**Bearag** *David O'Meara* a62 52
3 b f Dutch Art Cats Eyes (Echo Of Light)
2228[9] 2993[7] 3543[6] 5836[7] 7945[12] 8247[10]
**Beardwood** *Mark Johnston* a96 91
5 ch g Dutch Art Valentina Guest (IRE) (Be My Guest (USA))
2431[8] 2735[12] 3154[5] 3597[3] 4002[4] 4118[4] 4585[2] 4863[5] 6449[13] 6887[11]
**Bear Faced** *A bin Harmash* a94 89
4 b g Intikhab(USA) Hulcote Rose (IRE) (Rock Of Gibraltar (IRE))
204a[14]
**Bear Valley (IRE)** *Mark Johnston* a83 93
3 b g Manduro(GER) Shane (GER) (Kornado)
2132[6] 3778[2] 3998[3] 4376[12] 4886[8] 5598[8] 5915[3] 6232[7] 6671[8] 6920[14] 8005[7] 8244[8]
**Beast** *Johnny Farrelly* a54 70
3 b g Makfi Wunders Dream (IRE) (Averti (IRE))
2474[12] 3173[8] 4006[7] 5249[6] 8663[9]
**Beat Baby (IRE)** *Niels Petersen* a88 98
10 ch g Johannesburg(USA) Najiya (Nashwan (USA))
2943a[11]
**Beatbox Rhythm (IRE)** *K R Burke* a100 99
2 ch c Beat Hollow Birthday Present (Cadeaux Genereux)
5058[2] (5801) 6326[7] 7049[3] (8008)◆ (8317)
**Beatbybeatbybeat** *Antony Brittain* a75 69
4 ch m Poet's Voice Beat As One (Medicean)
1717[8] 2587[5] 3189[4] 3911[5] 4168[5] 5185[10] 5835[9] 7474[4] 7958[2] 8192[5] 8400[U] 9153[4]

**Beatisa** *Christine Dunnett* a73 61
3 b f Intikhab(USA) Bea Menace (USA) (Mizzen Mast (USA))
466[6] 814[5] 5249[8] 6101[3] 7278[3] (7729) 9026[3]◆ 9408[4]
**Beat Route** *Michael Attwater*
10 ch g Beat Hollow Steppin Out (First Trump)
6398[7]
**Beat The Bank** *Andrew Balding* a86 123
3 b g Paco Boy(IRE) Tiana (Diktat)
(1859)◆ 3959[10] (4817) (5593) (7579) 8232[10]
**Beat The Blues** *Miss Joey Ellis* a35 33
5 b m Aqlaam Beat As One (Medicean)
2281[10]
**Beau Amadeus (IRE)**
*Susan Corbett* a49 68
8 b g Amadeus Wolf Degree Of Honor (FR) (Highest Honor (FR))
362[6] 583[9]
**Beauchamp Opal** *Charlie Fellowes* a60 56
3 b f Pastoral Pursuits Orange Sunset (IRE) (Roanoke (USA))
89[3] 502[3] 895[4]◆ 1445[5] 2790[10] 3674[11]
**Beauchamp Rose** *Charlie Fellowes* a18
3 b f Pastoral Pursuits Ashford Castle (USA) (Bates Motel (USA))
4449[6] 5022[11]
**Beauden Barrett** *John Quinn* a72 74
4 b g Dick Turpin(IRE) Riccoche (IRE) (Oasis Dream)
3696[12] 4495[10] 4728[3] 5650[5] 5921[2] 6431[9] 6784[6] 8205[8]
**Beau Et Sublime (FR)** *A J Martin* 74
7 b g Saddler Maker(IRE) Jolie Jouvencelle (FR) (Sandhurst Prince)
5582a[18]
**Beau Ideal** *A Fabre* 97
2 b c Exceed And Excel(AUS) Lay Time (Galileo (IRE))
7011a[2] (7846a)
**Beau Massagot (FR)** *C Escuder* 85
2 ch c Panis(USA) In Memory (FR) (Chimes Band (USA))
8884a[4]
**Beau Mistral (IRE)** *Tony Carroll* a69 72
8 ch m Windsor Knot(IRE) Carpet Lover (IRE) (Fayruz)
(161) (308) 735[7] 879[2] 1066[6] 1219[2] (1791) 1979[8] 7689[6] 8243[12] 8953[10] 9216[8]
**Beaumont's Party (IRE)**
*Laura Morgan* a47 32
10 b g High Chaparral(IRE) Miss Champagne (FR) (Bering)
4181[7] 4791[8]
**Beau Recall (IRE)** *Simon Callaghan* 106
3 b f Sir Prancealot(IRE) Greta D'Argent (IRE) (Great Commotion (USA))
4650a[6] 8071a[5]
**Beauregard** *N Clement* a67 79
3 ch g Choisir(AUS) Beaute Divine (Peintre Celebre (USA))
2697a[9]
**Beau Satchel** *Adrian McGuinness* a71 84
7 b g Indesatchel(IRE) Sweet Patoopie (Indian Ridge (IRE))
5519a[6]
**Beaute Absolue (FR)** *F Vermeulen* a11 40
2 gr f Rajsaman(FR) Malinday (FR) (Lord Of Men)
6452a[9]
**Beau Temps (FR)** *S Smrczek* a73 81
4 b h Rip Van Winkle(IRE) Blue Ciel (Oasis Dream)
3274a[7]
**Beautiful Artist (USA)** *John Gosden* a65 60
2 b f Lonhro(AUS) She's A Beauty (USA) (Storm Cat (USA))
8148[6] 8594[7] 8796[7] 9199[4]◆
**Beautiful Destiny (IRE)**
*Matthieu Palussiere* 85
2 ch f Haatef(USA) Milana (FR) (Mark Of Esteem (IRE))
5090a[5]
**Beautiful Memory (IRE)**
*Saeed bin Suroor* a74 74
2 b f Invincible Spirit(IRE) Express Way (ARG) (Ahmad (ARG))
7022[3] 7757[3]
**Beautiful Morning**
*Mrs John Harrington* 106
4 b m Galileo(IRE) Date With Destiny (IRE) (George Washington (IRE))
2637a[4] 6490a[5] 6972a[2] (7283)
**Beautiful Romance**
*Saeed bin Suroor* 114
5 b m New Approach(IRE) Mazuna (IRE) (Cape Cross (IRE))
(890a) 1374a[2]
**Beautiful Stranger (IRE)**
*Keith Dalgleish* a76 78
6 b g Iffraaj Monarchy (IRE) (Common Grounds)
49[3] 382[10]
**Beautiful Vintage (IRE)**
*Stefano Botti* 101
2 gr c Zebedee High Vintage (IRE) (High Chaparral (IRE))
8276a[3]
**Beau Times (IRE)** *Tim Easterby* 9
2 b f Sepoy(AUS) Timeless Dream (Oasis Dream)
1908[9] 4296[10]
**Beauty Filly** *William Haggas* 79
2 b f Invincible Spirit(IRE) Miss Delila (USA) (Malibu Moon (USA))
(7334)◆
**Beauty Generation (NZ)**
*John Moore* 119
4 b g Road To Rock(AUS) Stylish Bel (AUS) (Bel Esprit (AUS))
(9170a)
**Beauty Of Love** *Mme Pia Brandt* a90 83
3 b f Elusive City(USA) Breath Of Love (USA) (Mutakddim (USA))
1825a[6]

**Beauty Only (IRE)** *A S Cruz* 125
6 b g Holy Roman Emperor(IRE) Goldendale (IRE) (Ali-Royal (IRE))
2492a[2] 9170a[7]

**Bebe Cherie (FR)** *Markus Klug* 92
5 b m Youmzain(IRE) Shamaniya (IRE) (Doyoun)
2667a[14]

**Bebe D'Amour (FR)** *J-Y Artu* a72 107
3 ro f Montmartre(FR) Prudence Royale (FR) (Loup Solitaire (USA))
3366a[2] 7635a[4] 8273a[4] (8838a)

**Be Be King (IRE)**
*Eve Johnson Houghton* a67
3 b g Bated Breath Champion Place (Compton Place)
2090[7] 6526[8]

**Be Bold** *Rebecca Bastiman* a52 58
5 ch g Assertive Marysienka (Primo Dominie)
971[11] 1431[11] 1971[11] 3666[10] 4509[13] 4997[7]◆ (5283) 5542[5] 6238[7] 6660[4] 6786[5] 7389[6] 7979[7] 8259[8]

**Becca Campbell (IRE)**
*Eve Johnson Houghton* a46 76
4 b m Roderic O'Connor(IRE) Scottendale (Zilzal (USA))
1789[5] 2055[7] (2615) 2913[7] 3683[6] 4442[2] 4994[3] 5556[3] (6095) 7278[5]

**Beck And Call** *Henry Candy* 82
3 b f Holy Roman Emperor(IRE) Gosbeck (Dubawi (IRE))
2121[3] 3157[2] (3822) 5325[6] 6276[3] 7155[2]

**Becker** *James Given* a70 43
2 b c Delegator Mosa Mine (Exceed And Excel (AUS))
8212[6] 8493[5] 9372[5]

**Beckford** *Gordon Elliott* 113
2 b c Bated Breath Whirly Dancer (Danehill Dancer (IRE))
(4386a) 5973a[2] 6975a[2] 7618[5] 8577a[5]

**Beckton** *Robyn Brisland* a75 73
2 b f Finjaan Stormy Weather (Nashwan (USA))
6875[2] 7997[2]

**Becky Sharp** *Jim Boyle* 59
2 b f Foxwedge(AUS) Perfect Practice (Medicean)
5655[6] 6653[16] 7153[5]

**Becky The Thatcher**
*Micky Hammond* 65
4 b m Mastercraftsman(IRE) Fairmont (IRE) (Kingmambo (USA))
7922[11] 8655[6]

**Becquamis (FR)** *T Lemer* a71 95
3 bb g Vertigineux(FR) Becquamour (FR) (Septieme Ciel (USA))
2561a[6] 3614a[8]

**Becquarius (FR)** *Eric Saint-Martin* a63 62
7 b g Medecis Berangele (FR) (Medaaly)
515a[4]

**Becquasiki (FR)** *T Lemer*
2 b f Reply(IRE) Becquarine (FR) (Deportivo)
1594a[13]

**Becuna (USA)** *Michael Bell* a55 67
3 b f Elusive Quality(USA) Badalona (Cape Cross (IRE))
1143[4] 3542[6] 4700[4] 5331[9] 6006[4]

**Bedazzling Lady (IRE)**
*Robert Eddery* a48 48
4 rg m Zebedee Malta (USA) (Gone West (USA))
311[6] 438[9]

**Bed Of Diamonds** *Adam West* a44 46
3 ch f Bated Breath Bedara (Barathea (IRE))
2371[8] 2711[6] 5142[8] 5787[10] 7212[11] 7990[9] 8247[6]

**Bedouin (IRE)** *Luca Cumani* a66 89
3 b g High Chaparral(IRE) Jewel In The Sand (IRE) (Bluebird (USA))
1737[2]◆ 2807[4] 3596[6] (4632) 5323[4] (5868) 6701[6] 7358[2] 8048[5]

**Bedouin's Story** *Saeed bin Suroor* 63
2 b c Farhh Time Crystal (IRE) (Sadler's Wells (USA))
8350[7]

**Bee Case** *Simon Dow* a83 72
3 br f Showcasing Binabee (Galileo (IRE))
350[3] 458[10] 4351[6]

**Bee Ina Bonnet** *Tim Easterby* 71
2 ch f Helmet(AUS) Rosabee (IRE) (No Excuse Needed)
6086[5] 6559[9] 6876[3] (7265) 7621[11] 8413[8]

**Bee Jersey (USA)** *Doug Watson* a100
3 ch c Jersey Town(USA) Bees (USA) (Rahy (USA))
201a[2] 697a[2]◆ 1375a[15]

**Bee Machine (IRE)** *Declan Carroll* a24 45
2 b g Footstepsinthesand Lady Royale (Monsieur Bond (IRE))
1496[9] 3622[7] 4598[11] 7239[10] 7519[5] 8287[6]

**Beepeecee** *Richard Hughes* a70 68
3 b g Henrythenavigator(USA) Roedean (IRE) (Oratorio (IRE))
(377) 1428[5] 2903[10] (3695) 3937[3]◆ 4350[11] 5031[8] 5411[7] 6502[7] 6866[9] 7540[3]◆ (7792) 8376[4] 8946[3] 9295[8] 9459[7]

**Be Famous (GER)** *Frau S Steinberg* 105
5 b g Kamsin(GER) Bandeira (GER) (Law Society (USA))
2667a[11]

**Begging Bowl** *Michael Easterby* a70
2 br f Pastoral Pursuits Bow Bridge (Bertolini (USA))
4359[3]◆

**Being There (FR)** *Charlie Appleby* 89
2 b c Dubawi(IRE) Beauty Parlour (Deep Impact (JPN))
3746[2]◆ (4859) 5395[6]

**Be Kool (IRE)** *Brian Ellison* a71 95
4 b g Approve(IRE) Accounting (Sillery (USA))
1677[14] 2430[2] 3049[5] (3792) 4377[4] (4957) 5582a[6] 5688a[3] 7594[12]

**Belabour** *Mark Brisbourne* a79 77
4 b g Bernardini(USA) Criticism (Machiavellian (USA))
165[3] (457) 3794[6] 5403[9] 6196[7] 7515[9] 7880[12] 8313[6] 9054[2] 9408[8]

**Beleave** *Luke Dace* a75 78
4 gr m Avonbridge Grezie (Mark Of Esteem (IRE))
736[5] 1085[10]

**Belfast (FR)** *F-H Graffard* 79
3 ch f Manduro(GER) Beringold (Bering)
3353a[7]

**Belgian Bill** *George Baker* a106 103
9 b h Exceed And Excel(AUS) Gay Romance (Singspiel (IRE))
205a[3] 542a[3] 698a[4] 3963[21] 6186[9] 6717a[5] 7727[2] 8843[5] 9125[10]

**Belgrano (FR)** *C Lerner* a74 66
2 b c Tin Horse(IRE) Oakcabin (IRE) (Refuse To Bend (IRE))
1335a[9] 4678a[2] 8169a[8]

**Belgravia (IRE)** *A P O'Brien* 99
3 b c Galileo(IRE) Love Me True (USA) (Kingmambo (USA))
4032[4] 4420a[6]

**Belgravian (FR)** *Archie Watson* a65 60
3 b g Pivotal Elle Galante (GER) (Galileo (IRE))
1830[5] 2359[5] 2842[U] 3426[5] 4150[10] 5935[6] 6847[3] 7323[12] 7945[5] (8345) 8908[10] (8985) 9034[P]

**Believe It (IRE)** *Richard Hughes* a95 80
5 b h Rip Van Winkle(IRE) Have Faith (IRE) (Machiavellian (USA))
36[4] 516[12] (1085) (1598) 2163[4] (3454) (3718) 5821[2] 6475[10] 6933[16] 8880[13] 9125[2]◆ 9468[11]

**Belisa (IRE)** *Ivan Furtado* a65 70
3 ch f Lope De Vega(IRE) Fleche Brisee (USA) (Dynaformer (USA))
1730[10] (4263) 4900[2] (5536)

**Bella Alissa** *Robert Cowell* 80
3 b f Dutch Art Crazy Too (IRE) (Invincible Spirit (IRE))
2344[4] (3806) 4990[6] (7217)◆ 8186[2]

**Bellabel (FR)** *Stephane Chevalier* a58 29
3 b f Slickly(FR) Arosana (GER) (Tertullian (USA))
5910a[9]

**Bella Duchess (IRE)**
*David C Griffiths* a36 41
3 b f Big Bad Bob(IRE) Spinning Gold (Spinning World (USA))
73[7]

**Bella Ferrari** *George Scott* a47
2 b f Bated Breath Massarossa (Mr Prospector (USA))
8851[11]

**Bella Figura (IRE)**
*Mrs John Harrington* 75
2 b f Mastercraftsman(IRE) Ebony Street (USA) (Street Cry (IRE))
4020a[3]

**Bellamay** *John Weymes* a16 44
3 b f Foxwedge(AUS) Steeple (Selkirk (USA))
510[8]

**Bella Noche (FR)** *P Monfort* a59 59
4 bl m Country Reel(USA) Nabella (Rock Of Gibraltar (IRE))
7069a[9]

**Bella's Boy (IRE)** *John Ryan* a37 52
4 b g Lovelace Cosa Deasa (IRE) (Barathea (IRE))
761[13] 982[9] 1139[9] 1406[P] 2024[RR]

**Bella's Venture** *John Gallagher* a55 64
4 gr m Hellvelyn Fayre Bella (Zafeen (FR))
1899[5] 2763[3] 3773[4] 5829[6] 6283[2] 6807[10] 7213[3] 7899[8] 8185[13]

**Bellcanto (GER)** *J Hirschberger* a61 65
5 b g Areion(GER) Bergwelt (GER) (Solarstern (FR))
4955a[6] 7307a[2]

**Belle Boyd** *W McCreery* a94 81
3 b f Oasis Dream Portrayal (USA) (Saint Ballado (CAN))
8407a[3]

**Belle De Lawers** *James Bethell* a82 52
6 b m Black Sam Bellamy(IRE) Scotland The Brave (Zilzal (USA))
1781[7] 2787[5] 5469[10] 8192[7] 8778[10] 9096[5]

**Belledesert** *Steph Hollinshead* 90
4 b m Pastoral Pursuits Ocean Blaze (Polar Prince (IRE))
1936[4] 2623[11] 3307[3] 4201[3] 4536[3] 5117[7]

**Belle Diva (IRE)** *Ralph Beckett* a75 56
3 b f Dark Angel(IRE) Red Intrigue (IRE) (Selkirk (USA))
2094[10]

**Belleire (FR)** *M Nigge* a75 76
3 ch f Soldier Of Fortune(IRE) Eire (Medicean)
2978a[6] 4232a[4]

**Belle Meade (IRE)** *Andrew Balding* a82 92
3 ch f Roderic O'Connor(IRE) Hazardous (Night Shift (USA))
5916[5]◆ 6619[7] 7808[6] 8546[10]

**Belle Peinture (FR)** *Alan Lockwood* a17 41
6 ch m Peintre Celebre(USA) Grosgrain (USA) (Diesis)
5002[12] 5498[8] 7015[13]

**Bellevarde (IRE)** *Richard Price* a71 73
3 b f Kodiac Pearl Mountain (IRE) (Pearl Of Love (IRE))
288[4] 2271[7] 2927[5] 3584[2] 4188[5] 4843[6] 5325[2] 5606[2] (6098) 7192[2] 7689[7]

**Belle Vendome (FR)** *M Pimbonnet* a56
2 b f Kendargent(FR) Bye Bye Fuji (USA) (Elusive Quality (USA))
6456a[6]

**Bell Heather (IRE)** *Patrick Morris* a75 75
4 b m Iffraaj Burren Rose (USA) (Storm Cat (USA))
152[5]◆ 360[7] 729[3] (4726)◆ 5399[6] 6638[3] (6946) 7111[8] 8749[12]

**Bell Of The Ball (IRE)** *Liam Lennon* 58
7 b m Bachelor Duke(USA) Grangehill Dancer (IRE) (Danehill Dancer (IRE))
4962[6]

**Bell Weir** *Kenneth Slack* 72
9 gr g Tobougg(IRE) Belly Dancer (IRE) (Danehill Dancer (IRE))
1716[14]

**Belobog (FR)** *M Boutin* 59
2 b g Whipper(USA) Divinatrice (FR) (Numerous (USA))
5627a[6] 8253a[7]

**Beloved Knight** *Laura Mongan* a44
2 ch c Sir Percy Silent Decision (USA) (Mr Greeley (USA))
8903[8] 9201[9] 9318[7]

**Beltor** *Robert Stephens* a86 80
6 b g Authorized(IRE) Carahill (AUS) (Danehill (USA))
1798[6]

**Be Mindful (IRE)** *Charles Hills* a54 56
2 b f Invincible Spirit(IRE) Strawberry Roan (IRE) (Sadler's Wells (USA))
3815[6] 4496[10] 7898[8]

**Be My Sea (IRE)** *Tony Carroll* a84 84
6 b g Sea The Stars(IRE) Bitooh (Diktat)
381[6] 2021[6]

**Be My Sheriff (GER)** *M Rulec* a99 105
3 b c Lawman(FR) Bezzaaf (Machiavellian (USA))
1658a[6] 3368a[9]

**Benadalid** *Chris Fairhurst* a80 72
2 b g Assertive Gambatte (One Cool Cat (USA))
1495[3] 2896[4] (3339) 4258[3] 6432[6] 7050[6]

**Benaras (USA)** *Tim Easterby* 49
2 b f Gio Ponti(USA) Brocatelle (Green Desert (USA))
2836[6]

**Benbatl** *Saeed bin Suroor* 115
3 b c Dubawi(IRE) Nahrain (Selkirk (USA))
(1513) 1904[3] 2766[2] 3322[5] (3994) 5394[5]◆ 6928[6]

**Benbecula** *Richard Mitchell* a71 69
8 b g Motivator Isle Of Flame (Shirley Heights)
3694[3] 4519[4] 5432[5]

**Bengala (FR)** *John M Oxx* 95
3 ch f Pivotal Bright Sky (IRE) (Wolfhound (USA))
3874a[5] 4928a[9] 7066a[7]

**Bengali Boys (IRE)** *Richard Fahey* 100
2 gr c Clodovil(IRE) Caherassdotcom (Compton Place)
(1873) 2382[2] 3149[2] (5150)◆ 6448[4]

**Bengal Lancer** *Ian Williams* 92
3 gr g Hellvelyn Bens Georgie (IRE) (Opening Verse (USA))
4268[4] 5333[2] (6076) (6397) 7053[2] 7784[5]

**Benger's Pursuit** *Jo Hughes* a31
2 ch f Pastoral Pursuits Bengers Lass (USA) (Orientate (USA))
7454[12] 8228a[14]

**Benissimo (IRE)** *Tony Forbes* a62 40
7 b g Beneficial Fennor Rose (IRE) (Kotashaan (FR))
1984[4] 2164[7] 4274[10] 4630[8] 6038[7] 8430[7]

**Benjamin Thomas (IRE)**
*John Quinn* a43 78
3 b g Mayson Strudel (IRE) (Spectrum (IRE))
1680[2] 2682[3] 3054[2] 3493[3] (3568) 4616[9] 5560[2] 5994[5] 6663[12] 8211[12]

**Benkei (IRE)** *H Rogers* 103
7 b g Galileo(IRE) Bywayofthestars (Danehill (USA))
5488a[8] 6976a[9] 7860a[10]

**Ben My Chree** *Bryan Smart* a21 61
2 gr f Lethal Force(IRE) Steal The Curtain (Royal Applause)
4555[4] 4995[5] 5494[8] 7920[10] 9002[11]

**Bennelong** *Lee Carter* a65 51
11 b g Bahamian Bounty Bundle Up (USA) (Miner's Mark (USA))
1699[7]

**Benoordenhout (IRE)** *T Le Brocq* a63 54
6 br g Footstepsinthesand Tara Too (IRE) (Danetime (IRE))
1931a[4] 2670a[8] 3958a[4] 5986a[2]

**Be On The Bell** *C Biancheri* a50 25
7 b m Byron Bella Beguine (Komaite (USA))
930a[7]

**Be Perfect (USA)** *Ruth Carr* a86 88
8 b g Street Cry(IRE) Binya (GER) (Royal Solo (IRE))
991[10] 1307[4] (1719) (2109) 2386[8] 3091[9] 3841[11] (4429) 5071[4] 5737[6] 6383[9] 6944[11] 7234[11]

**Bequia (IRE)** *David O'Meara* a58 72
3 ch f Helmet(AUS) Bunditten (IRE) (Soviet Star (USA))
2280[3] 3784[9]◆ 4463[6] 8931[6]

**Beraymi (IRE)** *J Reynier* 97
4 b m Manduro(GER) Tempete (Dubai Millennium)
3637a[7]

**Berdibek (FR)** *M Delzangles* 106
3 gr g Dark Angel(IRE) Beraviyna (IRE) (Zamindar (USA))
4941a[7] 5692a[4]

**Berengaria (IRE)** *Mark Johnston* a83 86
3 b f Teofilo(IRE) Belle Josephine (Dubawi (IRE))
2817[3] 3535[5] 4701[4] 5207[5] 5868[3]

**Berghain (IRE)** *J Hirschberger* 100
4 ch h Medicean Basilea Gold (GER) (Monsun (GER))
3011[5]

**Bergholt (IRE)** *Tim Vaughan* a62 57
4 b g Sir Percy Sularina (IRE) (Alhaarth (IRE))
2022[9] 3773[8] 6673[4] 7729[3] 8846[5]

**Beringer** *Alan King* a74 78
2 b g Sea The Stars(IRE) Edaraat (USA) (Rahy (USA))
4218[13] (4909) 5743[3] 6375[6]

**Berisha (AUS)** *Robert Smerdon* 102
5 b g Al Samer(AUS) Beheshta (IRE) (Brief Truce (USA))
8100a[2]

**Berjou (FR)** *Mme Pia Brandt* a70 65
3 b g Holy Roman Emperor(IRE) Bernieres (IRE) (Montjeu (IRE))
3446a[3]

**Berkeley Square (IRE)**
*H Al Ramzani* 101
2 ch c Galileo(IRE) Homecoming Queen (IRE) (Holy Roman Emperor (IRE))
5345a[5] 6240a[3] 6975a[7] 9446a[9]

**Berkeley Vale** *Roger Teal* a70 76
6 b g Three Valleys(USA) Intriguing Glimpse (Piccolo)
1983[6] (2722) 3753[14] 4802[5] 5427[4] 7495[9] 8313[14] 8513[4] 8946[11]

**Berkshire (IRE)** *Paul Cole* a100 111
6 b h Mount Nelson Kinnaird (IRE) (Dr Devious (IRE))
2552[4] 3069[5] 3597[5] 5634[8]

**Berkshire Boy (IRE)**
*Andrew Balding* a83 91
3 b g Elzaam(AUS) Circuit City (IRE) (Exit To Nowhere (USA))
1501[2] 1841[4] 2565[4] 3504[7] (7229) 7784[7]

**Berkshire Royal** *Andrew Balding* 66
2 b g Sir Percy Forest Express (AUS) (Kaaptive Edition (NZ))
4218[8] 5934[6] 6777[5] 7904[5]

**Berkshire Spirit** *Andrew Balding* 67
2 gr c Mastercraftsman(IRE) Rebecca Rolfe (Pivotal)
5840[6] 6553[5] 7503[6] 8595[4]

**Berlin Calling (IRE)** *Gerald Geisler* a53 50
3 ch f Dandy Man(IRE) Dolce Attesa (Dr Fong (USA))
3275a[6]

**Berling (IRE)** *Jessica Long* a84 102
10 gr g Montjeu(IRE) Danaskaya (IRE) (Danehill (USA))
5676a[8] 6501a[8]

**Berlios (IRE)** *Rebecca Bastiman* a79 55
4 b g Excellent Art Endless Peace (IRE) (Russian Revival (USA))
416[5] 843[2]◆ 971[7] 7557[12] 7923[11] 8321[7] 8958[10]

**Berlusca (IRE)** *David Loughnane* a87 70
8 b g Holy Roman Emperor(IRE) Shemanikha (FR) (Sendawar (IRE))
306[3] 599[8] 885[6] 1065[3] 3744[8] 4082[6] 5849[7] 6416[2] 7832[9] 8497[7] 8813[6] 9078[2] 9295[13]

**Bermondsey Belle (IRE)**
*Lucy Wadham* a63 67
3 b f Sir Percy Bermondsey Girl (Bertolini (USA))
3408[5] 4347[2] 5024[6] 7537[9] 8157[6] 8507[11]

**Bermonville (FR)** *W Walton* 75
2 b f Air Chief Marshal(IRE) Belliflore (FR) (Verglas (IRE))
8443a[9]

**Bernardo O'Reilly** *Richard Spencer* 84
3 b g Intikhab(USA) Baldovina (Tale Of The Cat (USA))
(4759) 5433[3] 6426[5] 7404[8] 8115[5]

**Bernie's Boy** *Phil McEntee* a67 72
4 b g Lilbourne Lad(IRE) Stoney Cove (IRE) (Needwood Blade)
1677[10] 2339[5] 2888[10] 3401[7] 4013[3] 4509[5] 4743[3] (5280) 7389[4] 9176[2] 9296[2] 9469[10]

**Bernina Range (FR)** *J-M Lefebvre* a57 62
5 b g Elusive City(USA) Belle Chasse (Kyllachy)
713a[3] 930a[6]

**Be Royale** *Michael Appleby* a76 76
7 b m Byron Sofia Royale (Royal Applause)
308[5] 1489[3] 1599[6] 1890[9] 2548[5] 2974[2] 3287[4] 3718[9] 4184[9]

**Berrahri (IRE)** *John Best* a86 90
6 b g Bahri(USA) Band Of Colour (IRE) (Spectrum (IRE))
277[7] 714a[5] 835a[4] (915a) 1178[6] 1422[6] 1687[9] (2369) 2685[3] 3441[2] 4522[2] (4802) (5403) 5912[10] 7143[8] 8384[4] 8672[3] 9205[3] 9467[5]

**Berryessa (IRE)** *Rae Guest* a77 76
3 b f Dandy Man(IRE) Carrauntoohil (IRE) (Marju (IRE))
288[2]◆ (679) 3285[2] 3904[4] 4574[5] 7486[6] (8853) 8953[5] 9136[7]

**Bertha Burnett (IRE)** *Brian Rothwell* 55
6 gr m Verglas(IRE) Starsazi (Observatory (USA))
3529[8] 4105[10] 4344[5] 5807[6]

**Bertie Blu Boy** *Lisa Williamson* a88 50
9 b g Central Park(IRE) Shaymee's Girl (Wizard King)
575[9] 682[2]◆ 1140[7] 1467[8] 1696[10]

**Bertie Moon** *Michael Appleby* a67 86
7 b g Bertolini(USA) Fleeting Moon (Fleetwood (IRE))
1153[8] 2068[6] 2752[4] 3315[8] 5873[7] 8511[7] 8771[2]◆ 9178[4] 9367[4] (9430)

**Bertie Wallace (IRE)** *Keith Dalgleish* 52
2 b g Fast Company(IRE) Six Diamonds (Exceed And Excel (AUS))
2771[8] 6042[5] 7013[5] 7519[18]

**Bertiewhittle** *David Barron* a89 98
9 ch g Bahamian Bounty Minette (Bishop Of Cashel)
1208[7] 1799[6] 2606[20] 3294[5] 3792[5] 5396[2] 5669[7] (6186) 6419[12] 6918[8] 7622[3] 8737[3] 9016[4] 9264[8]

**Bertog** *John Mackie* 73
2 ch c Sepoy(AUS) Lucky Token (IRE) (Key Of Luck (USA))
5631[11] 6854[5] 7819[6]◆ 8349[3]

**Beruska (FR)** *Carina Fey* a68 81
4 ch m Literato(FR) Al Ribh (USA) (A.P. Indy (USA))
6541a[6]

**Be Seeing You** *Trevor Wall* a26 31
6 ch g Medicean Oshiponga (Barathea (IRE))
5053[7]

**Beshaayir** *William Haggas* 82
2 b f Iffraaj Bahia Breeze (Mister Baileys)
6138[2] (7352)

**Bessemer Lady** *Ralph Beckett* a61
3 b f Cacique(IRE) Blast Furnace (IRE) (Sadler's Wells (USA))
236[9] 437[9] (881) 1331[4]

**Bessie Warfield** *Luca Cumani* a54 62
2 b f Oasis Dream Wallis (King's Best (USA))
4902[12] 6183[7] 7733[10] 8817[8]

**Best Bard (CAN)** *Norman McKnight* 87
7 b g Shakespeare(USA) Chamul (CAN) (Mutakddim (USA))
7179a[10]

**Best Blue** *Michael Bell* a78 64
2 b c Oasis Dream Filia Regina (Galileo (IRE))
8678[9] 8903[2] (9336)

**Best Company (IRE)** *Dean Ivory* 43
2 b g Fast Company(IRE) Story (Observatory (USA))
6108[14] 6761[7]

**Best Example (USA)** *Julia Feilden* a78 73
5 ch g King's Best(USA) Born Something (IRE) (Caerleon (USA))
349[7] 2477[7] 2971[4] 3753[10] 4573[4] 5508[3]◆ 6109[2] 6632[2] 7483[6] 8160[6] 9054[5]

**Best Fouad (FR)** *F Rohaut* a111 112
6 bb g King's Best(USA) Raheefa (USA) (Riverman (USA))
1659a[6] 3104a[3] (5046a)

**Best Of Days** *Hugo Palmer* a100 110
3 b c Azamour(IRE) Baisse (High Chaparral (IRE))
4029[12] 5148[3] 6441[4] 7581[3] 8637[8]

**Best Of My Love (IRE)**
*Mick Channon* 74
3 b f Canford Cliffs(IRE) Announcing Peace (Danehill (USA))
3039[8] 3404[4] (3626) 4208[10] 5139[8]

**Best Of Times** *Saeed bin Suroor* 107
5 b g Dubawi(IRE) Nabati (USA) (Rahy (USA))
654a[P] (Dead)

**Best Performance (USA)**
*Christophe Clement* a74 108
2 ch f Broken Vow(USA) Give My Regards (USA) (Smart Strike (CAN))
8575a[2]

**Best Solution (IRE)**
*Saeed bin Suroor* a84 114
3 b c Kodiac Al Andalyya (USA) (Kingmambo (USA))
430a[4] 697a[8] (2614) 3322[8] 4029[10] 5464a[2] 6727a[5] (8421)

**Best Tamayuz** *Scott Dixon* a62 54
6 ch g Tamayuz Pink Ivory (Sakhee (USA))
9180[3] 9307[2] 9364[4]

**Best Trip (IRE)** *Marjorie Fife* a57 91
10 b g Whipper(USA) Tereed Elhawa (Cadeaux Genereux)
1910[11] 2081[10] 2550[8] 3095[17]

**Best Vision (FR)** *J-M Capitte*
3 gr c Vision D'Etat(FR) Isarwelle (GER) (Sternkoenig (IRE))
584a[8]

**Betjeman** *Hughie Morrison* a35
2 b c Poet's Voice Respectfilly (Mark Of Esteem (IRE))
9201[11]

**Betsalottie** *John Bridger* a61 61
4 gr g Aqlaam Si Belle (IRE) (Dalakhani (IRE))
812[3] 966[4] 1284[7] 1556[6] 2679[2] 3519[7] 4088[2] 4461[3] 5023[5] 5653[5] 6101[11] 7905[4] 8152[5] (8301) 8846[2] 9092[5] 9211[4]

**Betsey Trotter (IRE)** *D K Weld* 79
2 b f Camacho Inourthoughts (IRE) (Desert Style (IRE))
6488a[8]

**Betty F** *Jeremy Noseda* 94
2 ch f Frankel Instance (Invincible Spirit (IRE))
(6424)◆ 7617[8]◆

**Betty Grable (IRE)** *Wilf Storey* a54 59
3 b f Delegator Danella (IRE) (Platini (GER))
5538[6] 5946[5] 6184[6] 7016[8] 8591[6] 8719[8]

**Betty Loch** *M Halford* a71 78
3 b f Pivotal Etive (USA) (Elusive Quality (USA))
4385a[7]

**Bettyrae Ruby (AUS)** *Tim Hughes* 92
3 b f O'Lonhro(AUS) Fee Mail (Danehill (USA))
8751a[8]

**Beverley Bullet** *Lawrence Mullaney* a62 71
4 b g Makfi Don't Tell Mary (IRE) (Starcraft (NZ))
2179[7] 2918[4] (3529) 4262[2] 4690[3] 5126[3] (5455) 6060[5] (7223) 7567[4] 7894[6]

**Beyond Beyond** *Hughie Morrison* a51 42
3 b g Shirocco(GER) Riverine (Risk Me (FR))
3674[9]

**Beyond Conceit (IRE)**
*Nicky Henderson*
8 b g Galileo(IRE) Baraka (IRE) (Danehill (USA))
3928[16]

**Beyond Equal** *Stuart Kittow* 69
2 b g Kheleyf(USA) Samasana (IRE) (Redback)
6394[8] 7079[2] 7897[6]

**Beyond Recall** *Archie Watson* a74 68
3 b f Cacique(IRE) Forgotten Dreams (IRE) (Olden Times)
2144[2] 3727[5] 5331[10] 6139[7] 7770[3] 8132[3] 8635[2] 9273[5] 9441[6]

**Beyond The Sea (USA)** *A Fabre* 102
3 bb f Sea The Stars(IRE) Devil By Design (USA) (Medaglia d'Oro (USA))
4665a[4] 5449a[4]

**Beywin (FR)** *H-A Pantall* 49
2 bb f Rip Van Winkle(IRE) Beyond The Dream (USA) (Fusaichi Pegasus (USA))
6171a[9]

**Bezos (IRE)** *Richard Hannon* a77 62
2 b g Famous Name Midnight Oasis (Oasis Dream)
4696[7] 5047[3] 5430[8] 5756[7] 6366[4] 9230[2] 9370[4] (9436)

**B Fifty Two (IRE)** *Marjorie Fife* a44 102
8 br g Dark Angel(IRE) Petite Maxine (Sharpo)
1799[11] 2381[15] 3052[5] 3324[11] 3847[9] 4379[5] 5379[3] 5696[6] 6267[15] 6943[3] 7111[4] 7572[13] 7628[2] 8106[4]

**Bharuch (IRE)** *P Aragoni* 100
5 gr h Footstepsinthesand Bysshe (Linamix (FR))
3104a[6]

**Bhindi** *Eve Johnson Houghton* 68
2 b f Casamento(IRE) Palkin (Singspiel (IRE))
4806[15] 5216[2] 5717[2] 6417[7] 7228[5]

**Bhodi (IRE)** *Sir Michael Stoute* 49
2 b c Dark Angel(IRE) Modesty's Way (USA) (Giant's Causeway (USA))
4534[6]

**Bhutan (IRE)** *Joseph Patrick O'Brien* 86
4 gr g Galileo(IRE) Ecology (USA) (Unbridled's Song (USA))
7860a[24]

**Bianca Minola (FR)** *David Menuisier* a63 77
3 ch f Shakespearean(IRE) Transylvania (FR) (Motivator)
2711[10] 4761[10] 5249[3] (6032) 8204[4] 8487[7]

**Biba** *Keith Dalgleish* 43
3 ch f Harbour Watch(IRE) Acicula (IRE) (Night Shift (USA))
6044[5] 6350[4] 6548[5] 7885[12]

**Bib And Tucker** *David Brown* 51
2 br g Dandy Man(IRE) Dhuyoof (IRE) (Sinndar (IRE))
3754[8] 4291[9] 5047[8]

**Bibbidibobbidiboo (IRE)**
*Ann Duffield* a59 61
2 b f Red Jazz(USA) Provence (Averti (IRE))
3943[7] 4834[4] 5600[4] 6561[4] 7384[7] 8190[3]

**Bibby (USA)** *Victoria H Oliver* 66
5 bb m Stormy Atlantic(USA) Love Cove (USA) (Not For Love (USA))
1813a[10]

**Bibione (FR)** *J Parize* a69 67
4 gr m Never On Sunday(FR) Hermanville (IRE) (Hurricane Run (IRE))
606a[4]

**Bibliotheca (JPN)** *W P Browne* a50 71
4 b m Harbinger Taygete (USA) (Miswaki (USA))
1207[9] 7659[10]

**Bicolour (USA)** *Mark Johnston* a56 59
3 b f Tiznow(USA) Burmilla (USA) (Storm Cat (USA))
2681[10] 3472[5] 3945[6] 4493[4] 4734[7]

**Bidding War** *James Tate* 71
2 ch f Champs Elysees Locharia (Wolfhound (USA))
7334[5]◆

**Biddy Brady (USA)** *Tim Easterby* 69
2 ch f Street Boss(USA) October Tempest (USA) (Theatrical (IRE))
5494[5] 6055[2] 6755[3] 7242[2] (8235) 8741[5]

**Bien Chase (IRE)** *Adrian McAllister* a73 66
6 ch g Bienamado(USA) General Chase (Scottish Reel I (IRE))
6797a[3]

**Big Amigo (IRE)**
*Daniel Mark Loughnane* a77 57
4 b g Bahamian Bounty Goldamour (IRE) (Fasliyev (USA))
(21) (158) 480[5] 971[8] 1147[3] (1296) 1542[4] 1819[3] 2064[8] 2469[6] 4310[10] 5587[10] 5930[7] 7525[15] 8427[5] 8772[9]◆ 9076[4] 9307[3]

**Bigbadboy (IRE)** *Clive Mulhall* a56 60
4 b g Big Bad Bob(IRE) Elegantly (IRE) (Rock Of Gibraltar (IRE))
4262[14] (5831) (6092) 6346[6] 8218[3] 8515[4] 9261[6]

**Big Bad Lol (IRE)** *Ed Walker* a62 52
3 b g Big Bad Bob(IRE) Indienne (IRE) (Indian Ridge (IRE))
4444[6] 5577[10] 6368[7] 8514[6] (9084)

**Big Baz (IRE)** *William Muir* a96 105
7 b g Pivotal Gracefully (IRE) (Orpen (USA))
1493[10] 1960[9] 3218[5] 3963[24] 6355[6] 6873[3] 7149[5] 7727[6] (8811)◆

**Big Bear (FR)** *N Caullery* a64 62
5 b g Thewayyouare(USA) Alivera (FR) (Danehill (USA))
822a[2]

**Big Brave Bob** *Richard Hughes* 67
2 br c Big Bad Bob(IRE) Namaadhej (USA) (Swain (IRE))
8294[2]◆ 8735[5]

**Big Challenge (IRE)**
*Saeed bin Suroor* a91 87
3 ch c Sea The Stars(IRE) Something Mon (USA) (Maria's Mon (USA))
1725[2]

**Big Chill (IRE)** *Patrick Chamings* a69 80
5 b g Acclamation Royal Consort (IRE) (Green Desert (USA))
2618[5] 3396[7] 4446[6] 5111[7] 6345[12]

**Big City Boy (IRE)** *Phil McEntee*
9 b g Tamarisk(IRE) Cuddles (IRE) (Taufan (USA))
5339[10]

**Big Country (IRE)** *Michael Appleby* a98 105
4 b g High Chaparral(IRE) Mount Eliza (IRE) (Danehill (USA))
(687) (1502)◆ 2431[4] (3790) 4614[8] 4918[2]◆ 7619[16] 8042[5]

**Bigdabog** *Eric Alston* 23
2 b g Sayif(IRE) Alice's Girl (Galileo (IRE))
4014[7] 4834[10]

**Big Duke (IRE)** *Darren Weir* a73 110
5 b g Raven's Pass(USA) Hazarayna (Polish Precedent (USA))
1994a[3] 8667a[4]

**Big Easy (GER)** *Ian Williams* 85
10 b g Ransom O'War(USA) Basilea Gold (GER) (Monsun (GER))
7785[6]

**Bigger Picture (USA)**
*Michael J Maker* 116
6 ch g Badge Of Silver(USA) Glory Dancer (CAN) (Honour And Glory (USA))
6461a[3] 8610a[12]

**Big Kitten (USA)** *Mark Johnston* a79 77
2 ch c Kitten's Joy(USA) Queen Martha (USA) (Rahy (USA))
7473[2]◆ 8316[2] 8703[2]

**Big Lachie** *Daniel Mark Loughnane* a80 74
3 b g Camacho Ryan's Quest (IRE) (Mukaddamah (USA))
1820[5] 2215[8] 3411[5] 5272[4] 6113[6] 7127[7] 7409[7] 7882[9] 8311[4] 8557[2]◆ 8927[10]

**Big Les (IRE)** *Karen McLintock* a77 77
2 b c Big Bad Bob(IRE) Love Match (Danehill Dancer (IRE))
3254[4] 4259[3] 4862[3] (7891) 8413[6] 9098[5]

**Big Mec (FR)** *Mlle B Renk* a45 20
6 b g Champs Elysees Fonage (Zafonic (USA))
8303a[9]

**Big Memory (FR)** *Tony McEvoy* 102
7 b g Duke Of Marmalade(IRE) Nicara (GER) (Nebos (GER))
1400a[12] 8633a[6]

**Big Orange** *Michael Bell* a82 119
6 b g Duke Of Marmalade(IRE) Miss Brown To You (IRE) (Fasliyev (USA))
1374a[4] (3011) (3996) 5503[2] 8229[11]

**Big Score (USA)** *Tim Yakteen* 108
3 bk c Mr. Big(USA) Not Unusual (USA) (Unusual Heat (USA))
4652a[8]

**Big Sigh (IRE)** *Ismail Mohammed* a68 74
3 ch c Raven's Pass(USA) Sospira (Cape Cross (IRE))
201a[8] 7085[2] (7561) 8326[5]

**Big Storm Coming** *David Brown* a81 83
7 b g Indesatchel(IRE) Amber Valley (Foxhound (USA))
(3833) 4837[2] 6434[9]

**Big Time (IRE)** *Kevin Ryan* a106 103
6 br g Kheleyf(USA) Beguine (USA) (Green Dancer (USA))
326[2] 2433[11] 4925a[13] 5393[20] 7626[7] 8383[7]

**Big Time Dancer (IRE)** *Brian Ellison* 72
4 b g Zoffany(IRE) Final Opinion (IRE) (King's Theatre (IRE))
4210[6]◆ 5000[5] 5699[6] 6434[8] (7028) 7824[12] 8214[5]

**Big Time Maybe (IRE)**
*Tom Dascombe* a90 77
2 b g Dandy Man(IRE) Divine Design (IRE) (Barathea (IRE))
1934[2] 2522[9] 3490[4] 5398[3] 6021[3] 7194[3] (7706) (8431)◆

**Big Tour (IRE)** *Saeed bin Suroor* a93 101
3 b c Dubawi(IRE) Alsindi (IRE) (Acclamation)
4086[2] (4700)◆ 5323[2]◆ 6014[4] (6686) (7340)◆ 8104[10]

**Big Whiskey (IRE)** *Clare Ellam* a99 87
7 ch g Ad Valorem(USA) El Opera (IRE) (Sadler's Wells (USA))
304[8]

**Big Words (GER)** *J Phelippon* 68
2 b f Whipper(USA) Big Monologue (IRE) (Testa Rossa (AUS))
2073a[3] 8253a[2] 8524a[8]

**Bijin (FR)** *H-A Pantall* a81 93
3 b f Holy Roman Emperor(IRE) Hayaku (USA) (Arch (USA))
7341a[3] 8665a[7]

**Bilash** *Sarah Hollinshead* a47 34
10 gr g Choisir(AUS) Goldeva (Makbul)
270[8] 901[8] 1965[12] 6148[9]

**Bilko's Back (IRE)** *Susan Corbett* a37 38
5 b g Big Bad Bob(IRE) Chica Roca (USA) (Woodman (USA))
990[7] 1312[8] 1469[11] 8314[14] 8650[7]

**Bill Cody (IRE)** *Jamie Osborne* a60
2 b g Declaration Of War(USA) Call This Cat (IRE) (One Cool Cat (USA))
8849[9] 9155[5] 9313[11]

**Billesdon Bess** *Richard Hannon* 102
3 br f Dick Turpin(IRE) Coplow (Manduro (GER))
2177[5] 2761[2] (3693) 4915[2] (5529) (6074) 7506[5]

**Billesdon Brook** *Richard Hannon* a87 101
2 ch f Champs Elysees Coplow (Manduro (GER))
2173[3]◆ 3070[2] 3868[2] (4496) 5329[3] (5572) (6418) 7088[5]

**Billiebrookedit (IRE)**
*Steph Hollinshead* 65
2 ch c Dragon Pulse(IRE) Klang (IRE) (Night Shift (USA))
1495[6] 2706[3]◆ 5099[7] 5839[4] 6547[9] 7954[6]

**Billie Flynn** *Harry Dunlop* 41
2 b f Lawman(FR) Lyric Art (USA) (Red Ransom (USA))
8678[13]

**Bills Delight** *Bill Turner* 38
3 b f Compton Place Sing Alana Sing (Singspiel (IRE))
5252[11] 6339[12]

**Billy Bond** *Richard Fahey* a71 66
5 b g Monsieur Bond(IRE) Princess Cocoa (IRE) (Desert Sun)
1610[6] 2276[8] 2773[3] 3242[5] 4019[2] 4960[2] 5497[10] 6003[7] (7225) 7703[11] 7980[6] 8589[3] 8854[12]

**Billy Booth (IRE)** *Gay Kelleway* 56
2 br g Big Bad Bob(IRE) Lady Natilda (First Trump)
3390[15] 4074[5] 4598[10]

**Billycock Hill** *Tom Dascombe* a57 67
2 b c Kyllachy Red Kyte (Hawk Wing (USA))
7352[7] 7788[8]

**Billy Dylan (IRE)** *Richard Hannon* a85 83
2 b g Excelebration(IRE) It's True (IRE) (Kheleyf (USA))
2779[6] (3516) 3993[11] (4335) 5424[3] 6682[2] 7821[15]

**Billyfairplay (IRE)** *W J Martin* a58 51
3 b g Dark Angel(IRE) Nurture (IRE) (Bachelor Duke (USA))
9244a[6]

**Billyoakes (IRE)** *Charlie Wallis* a75 59
5 b g Kodiac Reality Check (IRE) (Sri Pekan (USA))
116[3] 355[4] 501[5] 844[6] 2680[3] 3140[7] 5297[3] 5748[7] 5962[6] 7320[3] 7951[6] 8873[5] 9184[3] (9323) 9470[5]

**Billy Ray** *Mick Channon* a61 34
2 b c Sixties Icon Fiumicino (Danehill Dancer (IRE))
7503[10] 8030[6]

**Billy Roberts (IRE)** *Richard Guest* a54 85
4 b g Multiplex Mi Amor (IRE) (Alzao (USA))
1032[8] (1700) 2226[8] 2884[11] 4631[7] 5337[3] 6591[8]◆

**Billy's Boots** *J R Jenkins* a62 43
3 ch g Winker Watson Solmorin (Fraam)
496[5] 813[7] 960[8]◆ 1363[2]◆ 1474[4] 1821[3] 2252[6] 3703[10] 4008[3] 5028[4] 5419[8] 6339[6] 7705[2]

**Billys Connoisseur (IRE)**
*Tim Easterby* a59
4 b g Art Connoisseur(IRE) Tarziyma (IRE) (Kalanisi (IRE))
402[5] 580[12] 1293[6]

**Billy Star** *Jimmy Fox* a43
2 b g Sixties Icon Appreciative (Cockney Rebel (IRE))
8890[13] 9312[11]

**Bin Battuta** *Saeed bin Suroor* 107
3 ch c Dubawi(IRE) Land Of Dreams (Cadeaux Genereux)
(1518) 1886[3] 2437[4] 3998[8] (4886) 6445[2]

**Bin Daahir** *Charles Hills* 57
2 b c Exceed And Excel(AUS) Beach Frolic (Nayef (USA))
3025[7] 3769[4]

**Bing Bang Bank (IRE)**
*David Barron* 59
3 br g Big Bad Bob(IRE) Causeway Charm (USA) (Giant's Causeway (USA))
1675[5]◆ 2159[5]

**Bingo George (IRE)** *Mark Rimell* a59 48
4 b g Holy Roman Emperor(IRE) Kalleidoscope (Pivotal)
139[6] 2763[9] 2917[5] 3185[3]◆ 4723[8] 5050[13] 5542[6] 6046[5] 6437[10] 7190[10] 8117[8] (8259) 8772[10] 8881[11] 8980[9] 9076[5]

**Binky Blue (IRE)**
*Daniel Mark Loughnane* a64 57
5 b m Approve(IRE) Sabander Bay (USA) (Lear Fan (USA))
145[6] 426[9] 602[7] 784[8] 1842[5] 2023[2] 2278[9] 3172[5]◆ 3473[7] 3906[3] 4459[5] 5897[9] 6502[5] 7606[3] 7945[3] 8133[2] 8307[9] 8675[2] 9052[9] 9454[8]

**Bint Arcano (FR)** *Julie Camacho* a87 93
4 ch m Arcano(IRE) Rosa Mundi (Alhaarth (IRE))
(151) 581[6] (994) 1261[4] 2081[7] 2805[4] (3287) 4617[3] (5317) 6358[4]

**Bint Dandy (IRE)** *Chris Dwyer* a102 87
6 b m Dandy Man(IRE) Ceol Loch Aoidh (IRE) (Medecis)
142[3] 285[2] 810[13] 1368[3] 1771[6] 2093[6] (2973) 4001[7] 4763[6] 5369[4] 5789[2] 6145[6] 6261[3] 7484[5] 8351[7] 8636[2] 8947[7]

**Bint Huwaar (USA)**
*George Peckham* a47 53
2 b f More Than Ready(USA) Miss Mary Apples (USA) (Clever Trick (USA))
6438[5] 7757[7]

**Binti Al Nar (GER)** *P Schiergen* 92
2 ch f Areion(GER) Best Moving (GER) (Reset (AUS))
6494a[2] 8094a[2]

**Biotic** *Rod Millman* a76 81
6 b g Aqlaam Bramaputra (IRE) (Choisir (AUS))
2233[3] 3670[2] 4443[4] 6075[4] 6475[6]◆ 7452[12] 8132[8] 8648[5] 8886[10]

**Birch Grove (IRE)** *David Simcock* 68
2 b f Galileo(IRE) Danehurst (Danehill (USA))
8419[4]

**Birchwood (IRE)** *Richard Fahey* 110
4 b h Dark Angel(IRE) Layla Jamil (IRE) (Exceed And Excel (AUS))
1491[8] 2610[6] 4072[19] 5594[3]◆ 6918[7] 7807[13]

**Birdcage** *Patrick Morris* a6 64
4 b m Showcasing Trinny (Rainbow Quest (USA))
2631[8]

**Birdette (IRE)** *Mark Johnston* 65
2 b f Epaulette(AUS) Madam Ninette (Mark Of Esteem (IRE))
4205[4] 5127[12] 8380[6]

**Bird For Life** *Mark Usher* a52 30
3 b f Delegator Birdolini (Bertolini (USA))
3279[4] 3669[6] 4164[6] 6814[8] 7323[9] 7761[5] 8135[4] (8673) 8883[10]

**Birdie Gold (USA)** *Gary Mandella* a90 102
3 ch f Birdstone(USA) Gold Revenue (USA) (Touch Gold (USA))
8606a[12]

**Birdie Must Fly** *Jimmy Fox* a33 24
5 ch m Major Cadeaux Musical Day (Singspiel (IRE))
51[9] 274[11]

**Birikyno** *Matthew Salaman* a40 42
6 b g Piccolo Alvarinho Lady (Royal Applause)
7198[7] 8124[9]

**Biri's Angel (IRE)** *Simone Langiano* 82
3 b f Sir Prancealot(IRE) Phi Phi (IRE) (Fasliyev (USA))
2244a[11]

**Birmano (USA)** *A Fabre* a90 96
3 ch c Elusive Quality(USA) Que Piensa Cat (ARG) (Easing Along (USA))
1337a[5]

**Birthday Girl (IRE)** *Amanda Perrett* 36
2 b f Excelebration(IRE) Street Style (IRE) (Rock Of Gibraltar (IRE))
7898[9]

**Birthright** *Richard Hannon* 68
2 b c Mawatheeq(USA) Pooka's Daughter (IRE) (Eagle Eyed (USA))
7273[6]

**Bishop Of Bling (IRE)** *Chris Wall* a63 71
4 b g Big Bad Bob(IRE) Convent Girl (IRE) (Bishop Of Cashel)
2468[3] 4260[12] 5362[4] 5824[6]

**Bishops Cannings (IRE)**
*David Elsworth* a72
3 b f Cape Blanco(IRE) Carini (Vettori (IRE))
642[3] 862[2]◆ 1001[3] (1424)

**Bismarck The Flyer (IRE)**
*Ollie Pears* a60 65
3 b g Requinto(IRE) Livia's Wake (IRE) (Galileo (IRE))
264[3] 511[5] 903[5] 2077[3] 2182[5] 3289[5] 4161[8]

**Bite My Tongue (IRE)** *Tony Carroll*
4 b g Vale Of York(IRE) Near Relation (Distant Relative)
1410[7] 1984[10]

**Bithynia (IRE)** *Christopher Kellett* a55 68
3 b f Kodiac Alexander Confranc (IRE) (Magical Wonder (USA))
75[3] 212[3] 288[4] 3063[10] 3624[2] 4107[6] 4531[8] 5580[7] 6526[3] 7014[5]

**Bit Of A Quirke** *Mark Walford* 70
4 ch g Monsieur Bond(IRE) Silk (IRE) (Machiavellian (USA))
1707[2] (2108) 2953[5] (3935) 4439[4] 5540[8] 5807[4] 6470[5]

**Bittersweet (IRE)** *Jason Ward* 37
3 ch f Power Jessie Jane (IRE) (Dylan Thomas (IRE))
7896[5]

**Bizet (IRE)** *John Ryan* a59 65
3 b g Helmet(AUS) Morinda (Selkirk (USA))
15844 19681 43276 36746 43116 47533 52097 54067 57872 60235 62815 64732 65876 68213 72536 81227

**Biz Honor (IRE)** *Stefano Botti* 59
2 b c Dawn Approach(IRE) Biz Bar (Tobougg (IRE))
8620a9

**Biz Power (IRE)** *Stefano Botti* 78
3 b g Power Biz Bar (Tobougg (IRE))
2245a7

**Blackadder** *Mark Gillard* a46 42
5 b g Myboycharlie(IRE) Famcred (Inchinor)
505015 54318 65073 67486 72135 818110 853814 88245 91849

**Black Agnes (IRE)** *Lee Smyth* a68 63
4 b m Holy Roman Emperor(IRE) Nice To Know (FR) (Machiavellian (USA))
24987 32413

**Black Bess** *Jim Boyle* a80 97
4 br m Dick Turpin(IRE) Spring Clean (FR) (Danehill (USA))
13017 (2618) 29122 33077 52943 (5842) 63773 69196 79012

**Black Bolt (IRE)** *Richard Hannon* a82 53
3 br c Cape Cross(IRE) Safiya Song (IRE) (Intikhab (USA))
61958 64268

**Black Bubba (IRE)** *David Evans* a46 70
3 b g Arcano(IRE) Assumption (IRE) (Beckett (IRE))
27583 29892 31662 33915 38107 41615

**Black Caesar (IRE)** *Philip Hide* a77 85
6 b g Bushranger(IRE) Evictress (IRE) (Sharp Victor (USA))
(116) 2879 5703 26763 29172 (3518) 39383 43732 (6753) 70023 70946 77805 81842 86406 902910

**Black Dave (IRE)** *David Evans* a76 67
7 b g Excellent Art Miss Latina (IRE) (Mozart (IRE))
(49) 2674 5078 6483 7694 9985 14228 18936 23464 (2968) 33255 42516 50492 53595 87499 89569 9138P (9321)

**Black Dream (IRE)** *Mlle B Renk* a70 74
3 b c Born To Sea(IRE) Undulant Way (Hurricane Run (IRE))
838a4

**Black Friday** *Karen McLintock* 78
2 b c Equiano(FR) The Clan Macdonald (Intikhab (USA))
50924 58793 73262 800811

**Black Granite (IRE)**
*Jassim Mohammed Ghazali* a98 106
5 b g Dark Angel(IRE) Glisten (Oasis Dream)
932a2

**Black Grass** *Michael Easterby* a79 85
4 b g Monsieur Bond(IRE) Alustar (Emarati (USA))
(1915) 305210 31834 37416 42492 43796 48679

**Black Hambleton** *Bryan Smart* a65 67
4 b g Dick Turpin(IRE) Duena (Grand Lodge (USA))
679 (445) 85897 893010

**Blackheath** *Ed Walker* a76 75
2 b g Excelebration(IRE) Da's Wish (IRE) (Sadler's Wells (USA))
49097 63943 73518 87022◆

**Black Hole Sun** *Ian Williams* a56
5 ch m Black Sam Bellamy(IRE) Black Annie (IRE) (Anshan)
(420) 5493

**Black Iceman** *Lydia Pearce* a37 4
9 gr g Iceman Slite (Mind Games)
58509

**Black Isle Boy (IRE)** *David O'Meara* a59 89
3 b g Elzaam(AUS) Shadow Mountain (Selkirk (USA))
(2033) (2775) (3195)◆ 36646 51002 53837 645017

**Blackjackcat (USA)** *Mark Glatt* a106 118
4 bb g Tale Of The Cat(USA) Bootleg Annie (USA) (Go For Gin (USA))
8608a3

**Black Label** *Adrian McGuinness* a72 70
6 b g Medicean Black Belt Shopper (IRE) (Desert Prince (IRE))
227a6

**Black Lace** *Steve Woodman* a16
2 b f Showcasing Ivory Lace (Atraf)
85449 898810

**Blacklooks (IRE)** *Ivan Furtado* a83 73
2 b g Society Rock(IRE) Mosaique Beauty (IRE) (Sadler's Wells (USA))
59606 665313 68977 74605 (8467) 86760 89037 90988 (9370)

**Black Lotus** *Chris Wall* a64 60
2 b f Declaration Of War(USA) Ravensburg (Raven's Pass (USA))
74546 81196◆

**Black Max (FR)** *H-A Pantall* 103
4 b g Fuisse(FR) Okapina (FR) (Okawango (USA))
3880a4 4653a3 5690a11 6729aRR

**Black Medusa (IRE)** *Paul Cole* a62
2 b c Canford Cliffs(IRE) Dancer's Leap (Pivotal)
89519 90504 92017

**Black Night (IRE)** *J Moon* a81 94
5 b h Excellent Art Starfish (IRE) (Galileo (IRE))
81744 (2670a) 5692a7 8444a6

**Black Orange** *Debbie Mountain* a50 70
2 br c Pastoral Pursuits Mrs Snaffles (IRE) (Indian Danehill (IRE))
14963 16942 (2154) 25222 9446a6

**Black Prince (FR)**
*Anthony Honeyball* a62 57
3 b g Falco(USA) Thamara (USA) (Street Cry (IRE))
17263◆ 271111 38643 520911 68203 (7790) 93174

**Black Redstart** *Alan Bailey* a55 59
3 b f Big Bad Bob(IRE) Red Roxanne (Rock Of Gibraltar (IRE))
1574

**Black Ruby (IRE)**
*Mrs John Harrington* 95
3 b f Dansili Green Room (USA) (Theatrical (IRE))
6080a6

**Black Sails** *G M Lyons* 91
2 br f Lope De Vega(IRE) Missouri Belle (Invincible Spirit (IRE))
402811 6242a6 6487a6

**Black Salt** *David Barron* a52 73
3 b g Equiano(FR) Marine Girl (Shamardal (USA))
25952◆ (3150) 426510 53166

**Blacksou (FR)** *F Vermeulen* a64 55
7 b g Blackdoun(FR) Cadline (FR) (Cardoun (FR))
6300a8

**Blackthorn Stick (IRE)**
*Paul Burgoyne* a65 58
8 b g Elusive City(USA) Hi Lyla (IRE) (Lahib (USA))
4688 7244 8605 11395 14277 16037 31726

**Black Trilby (IRE)** *Clive Cox* 89
3 ch c Helmet(AUS) Reine De Romance (IRE) (Vettori (IRE))
28942◆ 33033 38362 44903 60736 790910

**Black Truffle (FR)** *Mark Usher* a55 36
7 b g Kyllachy Some Diva (Dr Fong (USA))
227812 29616◆ 32658 41632 47274 52394 57928 68134 81343 89483 92322 (9340)

**Blackwood** *Michael Blanshard* a40 43
2 b g Firebreak Witness (Efisio)
57098 70799 802912 85009 88879

**Blaine** *Brian Barr* a82 104
7 ch g Avonbridge Lauren Louise (Tagula (IRE))
(2780)◆ 332414 441110 591110 692213 745512

**Blair House (IRE)** *Charlie Appleby* 106
4 ch g Pivotal Patroness (Dubawi (IRE))
39632◆ 559411 635516

**Blairmayne (IRE)**
*Miss Natalia Lupini* a63 83
4 b g Zebedee Amended (Beat Hollow)
2656a4 6971a3

**Blake Dean** *Chris Gordon* a35 65
9 b g Halling(USA) Antediluvian (Air Express (IRE))
64510

**Blakeney Point** *Roger Charlton* a99 108
4 b g Sir Percy Cartoon (Danehill Dancer (IRE))
(1798) 252512 30734 46144 56382 64274 (7354) (7931)

**Blame Culture (USA)**
*George Margarson* a76 56
2 b c Blame(USA) Pearl In The Sand (IRE) (Footstepsinthesand)
58878 74882◆ 86422

**Blame Me Forever (USA)**
*Marco Botti* a60
2 b f Blame(USA) Empress Josephine (USA) (Empire Maker (USA))
89989

**Blanchefleur (IRE)** *Richard Hannon* a35 80
2 b f Camelot Portrait Of A Lady (IRE) (Peintre Celebre (USA))
59342◆ 63853 68612 800211 83409

**Blanco (USA)** *George Baker* a50
4 b g Cape Blanco(IRE) Nimue (USA) (Speightstown (USA))
27414

**Blankiedoodie** *John C McConnell* a40 54
4 b g Halling(USA) Our Day Will Come (Red Ransom (USA))
46592◆ 52495

**Blastofmagic** *David Dennis* a46 46
3 gr g Hellvelyn Elegant Pursuit (Pastoral Pursuits)
11932 13727

**Blazed (IRE)** *Roger Charlton* a76 70
3 gr g Dark Angel(IRE) Sudden Blaze (IRE) (Soviet Star (USA))
31888 36912 61845 72556 82422 (8745) 89502 91524

**Blaze Of Glory (FR)** *Jamie Osborne* a87
3 ch g Excelebration(IRE) Roche Ambeau (FR) (Chichicastenango (FR))
343◆ (236)◆ 5533 7883 321110

**Blaze Of Hearts (IRE)** *Dean Ivory* a76 82
4 b g Canford Cliffs(IRE) Shesthebiscuit (Diktat)
29655 36706 52186 (6294) 713112 (8126) 90257 92069 945810

**Blaze To Win (TUR)**
*Aydin Kucukaksoy* 103
6 b h Win River Win(USA) Lovely Blaze (TUR) (Sri Pekan (USA))
6744a5

**Blazing Beryl (IRE)** *Brian Meehan* a45 55
2 b f Most Improved(IRE) Lady Gray (IRE) (High Chaparral (IRE))
38155 54304 600511 681510 70826 78277

**Blazing Speed** *A S Cruz* 120
8 b g Dylan Thomas(IRE) Leukippids (IRE) (Sadler's Wells (USA))
3129a2

**Blazing Tunder (IRE)** *Henry Candy* 76
2 gr c Casamento(IRE) La Chita Bonita (IRE) (Verglas (IRE))
(8162)

**Blending** *John Gosden* a83 85
3 b f Medicean Panzanella (Dansili)
17964 22875 74065

**Blessed Silence (FR)**
*J-M Beguigne* a89 99
4 ch m Siyouni(FR) Blanc Sur Blanc (IRE) (Hold That Tiger (USA))
3354a6 (5979a) 8089a2

**Blessed To Empress (IRE)**
*Amy Murphy* a66 61
2 b f Holy Roman Emperor(IRE) Blessing Box (Bahamian Bounty)
(2258) 280113 32304 60368 67494 74917 87953

**Bless Him (IRE)** *David Simcock* a82 102
3 b c Sea The Stars(IRE) Happy Land (IRE) (Refuse To Bend (IRE))
12412 (1485) 23853 30715 (3997) 64765

**Bletchley** *Ralph Beckett* 104
3 b f Makfi An Ghalanta (IRE) (Holy Roman Emperor (IRE))
(3395) 42082 55977 78082

**Bleu Et Noir** *Tim Vaughan* a78 61
6 b g Enrique Gastina (FR) (Pistolet Bleu (IRE))
579410 61506 70806 79077 85502 (8852)◆ 90705

**Blind Faith (IRE)** *Luca Cumani* a83 83
4 ch m Zoffany(IRE) Guajira (FR) (Mtoto)
29735 38572 46215 57453 62087

**Bling King** *Geoffrey Harker* a61 66
8 b g Haafhd Bling Bling (IRE) (Indian Ridge (IRE))
13292 17356 21084 26882 37602 39772 55392 59505

**Blink (FR)** *N Caullery* a66 57
4 b m Pour Moi(IRE) Blue Blue Sky (IRE) (Anabaa (USA))
3274a9

**Blistering Dancer (IRE)**
*Tony Carroll* a48 42
7 b g Moss Vale(IRE) Datura (Darshaan)
7424 9827 13043 22985 356911 46957 514511 70176 71909 818510 92158

**Blithe Spirit** *Eric Alston* a50 100
6 b m Byron Damalis (IRE) (Mukaddamah (USA))
193612 25248 28569 332118 43337 54022 667712 713710

**Blitz** *Clive Cox* a84 85
3 b f Exceed And Excel(AUS) Photo Flash (IRE) (Bahamian Bounty)
9262 17314 21306 (3411) 50295 61774 66796

**Blizzard (AUS)** *P F Yiu* 119
5 ch g Starcraft(NZ) Stormy Choice (AUS) (Redoute's Choice (AUS))
9168a3

**Blonde Bomber (USA)**
*Stanley I Gold* a106
2 rg f Fort Larned(USA) Girl Can Rock (USA) (El Prado (IRE))
8603a3

**Blond Magicien (FR)** *F Lenglart*
4 ch h Ballingarry(IRE) Aurore Fleurie (FR) (Cadoudal (FR))
8303a11

**Blond Me (IRE)** *Andrew Balding* 113
5 ch m Tamayuz Holda (IRE) (Docksider (USA))
(2765) 55712 6981a11 (8098a) 9171a12

**Bloodsweatandtears** *William Knight* a65 71
9 b g Barathea(IRE) Celestial Princess (Observatory (USA))
2149 8113 13383 81819 92133 94576

**Bloomfield (IRE)** *W McCreery* 101
3 b f Teofilo(IRE) Ramona (Desert King (IRE))
5766a2

**Bloomin Lovely (IRE)** *John Quinn* a70 71
3 b f Helmet(AUS) Dorothy Dene (Red Ransom (USA))
4013 5102 7313 12435 33848

**Blooriedotcom (IRE)**
*Peter Chapple-Hyam* 73
2 b g Holy Roman Emperor(IRE) Peaceful Kingdom (USA) (King Of Kings (IRE))
64247 73333◆ 79154 83548

**Blue Bahia (IRE)** *Mark Johnston* a72 76
3 b f Big Bad Bob(IRE) Brazilian Bride (IRE) (Pivotal)
762 6004 (845) 11248 16255

**Blue Bayou** *Brian Meehan* 96
4 ch m Bahamian Bounty Oshiponga (Barathea (IRE))
14914◆ 261610

**Blue Bounty** *J H Culloty* a51 47
6 ch g Bahamian Bounty Laheen (IRE) (Bluebird (USA))
2656a19

**Blue Candy** *Archie Watson* a72
2 b c Bahamian Bounty Sally Can Wait (Sakhee (USA))
776511 83395 87942 90217

**Blue De Vega (GER)** *Robert Cowell* a101 112
4 b h Lope De Vega(IRE) Burning Heights (GER) (Montjeu (IRE))
1653a3 3099a6 79502

**Blue Diamond (FR)** *J Hirschberger* a49 78
5 b g King's Best(USA) Ripley (GER) (Platini (GER))
(7721a)

**Blue Harmony** *K R Burke* a71 37
2 b f Bahamian Bounty Fascination Street (IRE) (Mujadil (USA))
687610 82356 (8715) 89146 93003 94053

**Blue Havana (IRE)** *John Quinn* a52 51
2 b f Havana Gold(IRE) Labyrinthine (IRE) (Pivotal)
33905 38958 450211 87834 90144 91753 94399

**Blue Hills (FR)** *Y Barberot* a80 85
3 b f Myboycharlie(IRE) Acentela (IRE) (Shirocco (GER))
799a8

**Blue Hussar (IRE)** *Micky Hammond* 92
6 b g Montjeu(IRE) Metaphor (USA) (Woodman (USA))
27703 (6968) 80479

**Blue Jacket (USA)** *Dianne Sayer* a56 69
6 ro m Mizzen Mast(USA) Complex (USA) (Unbridled's Song (USA))
6847 (1721) 21407 28435 46876 64358

**Blue Laureate** *Clive Cox* 87
2 b g Poet's Voice Powder Blue (Daylami (IRE))
53013◆ 61324 65053 (7117) 75444

**Blue Link (FR)** *T Castanheira* 80
2 b c Air Chief Marshal(IRE) La Barrique (IRE) (Indian Ridge (IRE))
8196a6

**Blue Mist** *Roger Charlton* a83 84
2 ch g Makfi Namaskar (Dansili)
(8030)◆ 83872 88903

**Blue Moon Rising (IRE)**
*Christos Kouvaras* a72 71
4 ch m Dream Ahead(USA) Wedding Gown (Dubai Destination (USA))
6302a4

**Blue On Blue (USA)** *John Gosden* a85 79
3 ch g More Than Ready(USA) Alina (USA) (Came Home (USA))
15513 (2071) 45003 73214 (7789)

**Blue Petal (IRE)** *R K Watson* a13 64
2 ch f Haatef(USA) Sapphire Spray (IRE) (Viking Ruler (AUS))
92637

**Blue Point (IRE)** *Charlie Appleby* 119
3 b c Shamardal(USA) Scarlett Rose (Royal Applause)
(2289) 40303 69264 (7806)◆

**Blue Rambler** *Ian Williams* 106
7 b g Monsun(GER) La Nuit Rose (FR) (Rainbow Quest (USA))
202a5 540a7 359413

**Blue Reflection** *James Fanshawe* a64
2 br f Dansili Alvee (IRE) (Key Of Luck (USA))
86684◆

**Blue Revelation** *Paul Webber* a75 47
4 b g Exceed And Excel(AUS) Epiphany (Zafonic (USA))
5488 32494

**Blue Rocks** *Lisa Williamson* a61 59
3 b g Indesatchel(IRE) Mabinia (IRE) (Cape Cross (IRE))
(2065) 35434 41597 42906 48946 58265 59563 63397 66799

**Bluesacha Rosetgri (FR)** *R Le Gal* 65
3 ch f Recharge(IRE) Blue Saga (FR) (Sagacity (FR))
3366a8

**Bluesbreaker (IRE)**
*Damian Joseph English* a60 55
5 b g Fastnet Rock(AUS) Jalisco (IRE) (Machiavellian (USA))
1385a14 9244a2

**Blue Sea Of Ibrox (IRE)**
*Mrs A Corson* 40
9 gr m Subtle Power(IRE) Jerpoint Rose (IRE) (Roselier (FR))
3958a8 5986aP

**Blue Skimmer (IRE)**
*Miss Nicole McKenna* a61 63
5 b g Arcano(IRE) Cattiva Generosa (Cadeaux Genereux)
92626

**Blues Music (FR)** *Simone Brogi* a83 73
3 b f Motivator Blanc Sur Blanc (IRE) (Hold That Tiger (USA))
8885a8

**Blue Soave (FR)** *F Chappet* a88 102
9 ch g Soave(GER) Rhapsody In Blue (FR) (Bering)
6729a7 8127a3

**Blue Suede (IRE)** *Richard Fahey* a76 49
3 b f Requinto(IRE) Shoooz (IRE) (Soviet Star (USA))
17317 19757 29926

**Blue Surf** *Amanda Perrett* a104 97
8 ch g Excellent Art Wavy Up (IRE) (Brustolon)
3525 9212

**Blue Tango (GER)** *M Munch* a82 84
2 gr c Zebedee Beatify (IRE) (Big Bad Bob (IRE))
4596a4 5461a7 7011a9 8777a6

**Blue Top** *Dai Burchell* a64 60
8 b g Millkom Pompey Blue (Abou Zouz (USA))
1623 6034

**Blue Uluru (IRE)** *G M Lyons* a64 90
2 b f Choisir(AUS) Lady Of Beauty (USA) (Coronado's Quest (USA))
7855a8 8225a8

**Blue Valentino** *Lisa Williamson* a32 26
8 b g Primo Valentino(IRE) Blue Water (Shaamit (IRE))
17546 32646

**Blue Whisper** *James Eustace* a61
2 ch g Bated Breath Vivid Blue (Haafhd)
68857

**Bluff (USA)** *D Selvaratnam* a101
5 ch g Tapit(USA) Ermine Slippers (USA) (El Prado (IRE))
204a13

**Bluff Crag** *Philip McBride* a79 77
4 b g Canford Cliffs(IRE) Camp Riverside (USA) (Forest Camp (USA))
10858 13232 16844 23362 278510 531311 (6288) 67955 74932 79996 93146

**Blushing Red (FR)** *Ed Dunlop* a74 80
3 ch g Le Havre(IRE) Boliche (Key Of Luck (USA))
9592 (1122) 27844 32914 37885 50057 (6094) 670110 74528 814311

**Blushing Rose** *Sir Michael Stoute* a94 95
3 ch f Dalakhani(IRE) Russelliana (Medicean)
38385 45644 49753 (5745) (6687) 78162

**Bluvida (FR)** *Pascal Vannereux* a62 20
6 ch m Gentlewave(IRE) Dolce Nera (Dansili)
7430a8

**Blyton Lass** *James Given* a44 14
2 ch f Havana Gold(IRE) Cesseras (IRE) (Cape Cross (IRE))
70137 75516 82087 85539

**Boater (IRE)** *Mark Johnston* a83 83
3 b f Helmet(AUS) Cercle D'Amour (USA) (Storm Cat (USA))
3125 (1000)

**Bobbie Green (IRE)** *Tim Easterby*
2 br f Big Bad Bob(IRE) Sticky Green (Lion Cavern (USA))
82139

**Bobbio (IRE)** *Marco Botti* a27
3 ch c Choisir(AUS) Balladiene (IRE) (Noverre (USA))
11416 14889

**Bobby Benton (IRE)** *Suzi Best* a58 53
6 b g Invincible Spirit(IRE) Remarkable Story (Mark Of Esteem (IRE))
94317

**Bobby Biscuit (USA)** *Simon Dow* a70
2 b c Scat Daddy(USA) Poupee Flash (USA) (Elusive Quality (USA))
68854

**Bobby Joe Leg** *Ruth Carr* a74
3 ch g Pastoral Pursuits China Cherub (Inchinor)
(8931) 91018 93059

**Bobby's Charm (USA)** *Robert Cowell* a68 66
2 b g Shanghai Bobby(USA) Magic Charm (USA) (Horse Greeley (USA))
4534[4] 5480[5] 7513[11]

**Bobbys Helmet (IRE)** *David C Griffiths*
3 b g Helmet(AUS) Ready When You Are (IRE) (Royal Applause)
1676[8]

**Bobby Vee** *Dean Ivory* a61 62
3 ch f Camacho Miss Lesley (Needwood Blade)
1332[8] 1554[8] 2474[10] 3331[4]◆ 3624[3] 4303[16] 9323[4]◆

**Bobby Wheeler (IRE)** *Clive Cox* a84 96
4 b g Pivotal Regal Rose (Danehill (USA))
8547[10] 9210[12]

**Bob Hopeful** *Mike Murphy* a65
4 b g Big Bad Bob(IRE) Trick (IRE) (Shirley Heights)
165[5] 747[4] 1299[8] 1728[4] 2024[5]

**Bob Maxwell (IRE)** *David Barron* a77 68
3 b g Big Bad Bob(IRE) Catching Stars (IRE) (Halling (USA))
1513[5] 2791[2] 3500[4] 4610[8]

**Boboli Gardens** *Iain Jardine* a27 33
7 b g Medicean Park Crystal (IRE) (Danehill (USA))
425[9] 579[13]

**Bo Bridget (IRE)** *Adrian Murray* a37 63
4 gr m Mastercraftsman(IRE) Greta D'Argent (IRE) (Great Commotion (USA))
7984[8]

**Bob's Boy** *Oliver Greenall* a43 61
4 b g Showcasing Tech Zinne (Zinaad)
3028[6] 5021[15] 6153[5] 7478[4] 7990[8] 8261[12] 8515[12]

**Bob's Girl** *David Simcock* a48 55
2 b f Big Bad Bob(IRE) Linda (FR) (Tamayuz)
7403[7] 8322[7] 8553[7]

**Boccaccina (FR)** *Mme A Engels* 25
6 b m Librettist(USA) Brailovskaya (ITY) (Darshaan)
6543a[3]

**Bochart** *S Seemar* a92 78
4 ch g Dubawi(IRE) Camlet (Green Desert (USA))
8714a[12]

**Bodacious Name (IRE)** *John Quinn* a53 72
3 b g Famous Name Nice Wee Girl (IRE) (Clodovil (IRE))
3180[4]◆ 4962[5] (5581)◆ 5740[2] 7048[2] 7983[4] 8478[7]

**Bodes Well (IRE)** *Warren Greatrex* a59 73
2 b g Rock Of Gibraltar(IRE) Gypsie Queen (IRE) (Xaar)
7897[2] 8890[8]

**Bodie And Doyle** *Andrew Balding* a46 63
2 ch g Raven's Pass(USA) Queenofthenorth (IRE) (Halling (USA))
6133[8] 6869[7] 7460[8] 8131[9] 8847[10]

**Bodybuilder** *Richard Hannon* a54 67
2 b c Power Looks All Right (IRE) (Danehill Dancer (IRE))
2756[7] 3083[5] 3622[3] 4527[12] 5408[2] 6749[7] 7023[5] 7410[4] 7690[4] 8145[8]

**Body Sculpt (FR)** *S Kobayashi* 98
3 gr f Kendargent(FR) Vital Body (FR) (Gold Away (IRE))
1270a[5] 1825a[5] 2665a[7] 6227a[9] 7341a[8]

**Boethius** *Tim Vaughan* a64
4 b g Manduro(GER) Perfect Note (Shamardal (USA))
8955[9]

**Bogardus (IRE)** *Patrick Holmes* a61 64
6 b g Dalakhani(IRE) Sugar Mint (IRE) (High Chaparral (IRE))
1101[5]

**Bogart** *Kevin Ryan* a59 93
8 ch g Bahamian Bounty Lauren Louise (Tagula (IRE))
1515[11] 1876[4] 2404[7] 2837[3] 5379[10] 5671[2] 6267[2] 6593[6] 7055[14] 8012[9]

**Bogsnog (IRE)** *Ruth Carr* a63 62
7 b g Moss Vale(IRE) Lovers Kiss (Night Shift (USA))
1006[9] 1247[7] (1371) 1721[4] 2179[4] 2589[4] 3758[8] 4162[2] (4723) 5482[7] (5892) 6635[4] 7525[8] 7933[4]

**Bohemian Flame (IRE)** *Andrew Balding* 94
3 b g Zoffany(IRE) Red Japonica (Daylami (IRE))
5916[9] 6426[7]

**Bohemian Rhapsody (IRE)** *Brian Barr* a66 49
8 b g Galileo(IRE) Quiet Mouse (USA) (Quiet American (USA))
1684[7] 2153[7] 3428[10] 5274[5] 9095[4]

**Bohemien (IRE)** *Alain Couetil* a87 101
4 b h Acclamation Blagueuse (IRE) (Statue Of Liberty (USA))
5628a[6]

**Bois D'Ebene (IRE)** *John O'Shea* a67 63
3 b f Big Bad Bob(IRE) Mpumalanga (Observatory (USA))
2778[7] 3246[10] 4214[9] 4468[6] 5783[4] 6345[9] 7199[7] 8031[13]

**Bois de Boulogne (USA)** *John Gosden* a65
3 b c Street Cry(IRE) Rosa Parks (Sadler's Wells (USA))
(504)

**Boite (IRE)** *Warren Greatrex* a94 100
7 b g Authorized(IRE) Albiatra (USA) (Dixieland Band (USA))
8892[5]

**Bokan (FR)** *Wido Neuroth* a100 100
5 b g Soldier Of Fortune(IRE) Paree (IRE) (Desert Prince (IRE))
4825a[5] 6501a[6] 7428a[2]

**Boker Mazal (FR)** *F Foresi* a37 18
6 b g Daramsar(FR) Killdora (FR) (Kendor (FR))
364a[14]

**Boketto (IRE)** *Derek Shaw* a48
3 b f Canford Cliffs(IRE) Olimpic Girl (IRE) (Darshaan)
9141[6]◆

**Boko Fittleworth (IRE)** *Jonjo O'Neill* 54
2 b g Most Improved(IRE) Sycamores (FR) (Gold Away (IRE))
7079[12] 7391[13] 8162[6]

**Bold** *Stuart Williams* a78 54
5 b g Oasis Dream Minority (Generous (IRE))
358[5]

**Bolder Bob (IRE)** *David Barron* 87
3 b g Big Bad Bob(IRE) Semiquaver (IRE) (Mark Of Esteem (IRE))
3182[3] 4036[3]◆ 4623[4] (5753) (7267)◆ 8011[11]

**Bold Grove** *Edward Bevan* a49 45
5 b g Proclamation(IRE) Trysting Grove (IRE) (Cape Cross (IRE))
1075[7] 1456[10] 4149[11] 4625[RR]

**Bold Max** *Zoe Davison* a48 46
6 b g Assertive Jane's Payoff (IRE) (Danetime (IRE))
52[8] 644[3] 860[6] 966[3] 1451[3] 2916[7] 3522[10]

**Bold Prediction (IRE)** *Ed Walker* a94 84
7 b g Kodiac Alexander Eliott (IRE) (Night Shift (USA))
235[3] 465[4] 1177[3] 1546[4] 1766[6] 2310[3] 2828[10] 4001[5] 4563[8]

**Bold Reason (GER)** *John Gosden* a83 75
2 b c Invincible Spirit(IRE) Bufera (IRE) (King's Best (USA))
5301[4] 7613[2] 8136[4] 8595[5] (9097)

**Bold Spirit** *Declan Carroll* a76 65
6 b g Invincible Spirit(IRE) Far Shores (USA) (Distant View (USA))
1720[7] 2990[4] 3402[5] 4509[10] 4743[8] 5016[6] 5283[5] 5802[9] 6058[3] 6464[8] 6572[2] (7018) 7389[3] 7932[2] 8651[9] 8772[2]◆ 9029[4] (9076)◆ 9363[2]

**Bollihope** *Richard Guest* a77 73
5 ch g Medicean Hazy Dancer (Oasis Dream)
42[3] 2685[5] 2920[5] 3910[4] 4446[5] 5091[2] 5221[3] 5363[7] 7567[8] 8206[4] 8813[5] 9261[7]

**Bollin Joan** *Tim Easterby* 59
2 b f Mount Nelson Bollin Greta (Mtoto)
6659[5] 6938[8]

**Bollin Ted** *Tim Easterby* a59 63
3 b g Haafhd Bollin Greta (Mtoto)
1914[9] 3207[4] 4171[2] 4839[5] (5001) (5215) 5800[3] 6048[6] (6470) 7325[5] 7479[4] 8218[8]

**Boltcity (FR)** *M Boutin* a58 58
10 b g Elusive City(USA) Combloux (USA) (Southern Halo (USA))
930a[3]

**Bolt D'Oro (USA)** *Mick Ruis* a121
2 b c Medaglia d'Oro(USA) Globe Trot (USA) (A.P. Indy (USA))
8609a[3]

**Bomad** *Derek Shaw* a67 70
2 b g Kheleyf(USA) Fenella Fudge (Rock Hard Ten (USA))
4792[2] 5240[4] 6147[8] 7050[9] 8325[10] 8902[3] 9024[5] 9298[2]

**Bombastic (IRE)** *Ed de Giles* 81
2 ch c Raven's Pass(USA) Star Of The West (Galileo (IRE))
4805[2] 5504[3] 6394[2] 7353[4]

**Bombay (IRE)** *David O'Meara* 71
3 b g High Chaparral(IRE) Cleide Da Silva (USA) (Monarchos (USA))
6522[2] 6782[2] 7896[3]

**Bombay Dream** *William Haggas* a63 65
3 ch f Sepoy(AUS) Indiana Blues (Indian Ridge (IRE))
3536[7] 4157[7]

**Bombay Rascal** *Robert Walford* a6
4 ch m Indian Haven Kohiba (IRE) (Rock Of Gibraltar (IRE))
7492[12] 8151[12]

**Bombero (IRE)** *Ed de Giles* 68
3 b g Dragon Pulse(IRE) Mathool (IRE) (Alhaarth (IRE))
2930[9] 3435[7] 3755[8] 4914[7] (5761) 6144[9]

**Bombetta (FR)** *N Caullery* a65 75
2 b f George Vancouver(USA) Salvia (FR) (Septieme Ciel (USA))
5629a[4] 6017a[3] 6452a[6] 8524a[3]

**Bombshell Bay** *Richard Hannon* a63 62
2 b c Foxwedge(AUS) Cumana Bay (Dansili)
4567[11] 5105[6] 5557[4] 6022[2] 6762[5] 7890[9] 9024[4] 9199[7]

**Bombyx** *James Fanshawe* 82
2 ch c Sir Percy Bombazine (IRE) (Generous (IRE))
7543[3] (8136)◆

**Bonanza Bowls** *Bryan Smart* a46 59
2 b g Zebedee Twilight Belle (IRE) (Fasliyev (USA))
6055[4] 6545[6] 7242[8] 8588[10]

**Bond Angel** *David Evans* a36 35
2 gr f Monsieur Bond(IRE) Angel Grigio (Dark Angel (IRE))
2691[6] 3023[5] 3467[8]

**Bond Bombshell** *David O'Meara* a59 69
4 ch m Monsieur Bond(IRE) Fashion Icon (USA) (Van Nistelrooy (USA))
1828[9] 2305[5] 2700[9] 3667[12] 4015[5] 4664[7] 5055[3] 5260[4] 5736[10] 6089[5] 6670[10] 7366[5] 7575[2] 7825[17] 8558[2] 8873[6] 9075[4] 9348[6]

**Bond Do Tigrao** *Sylvester Kirk* a28 40
2 b c Monsieur Bond(IRE) Bahama Bay (Bahamian Bounty)
8943[7] 9300[8]

**Bondi Beach (IRE)** *Robert Hickmott* 114
5 b g Galileo(IRE) One Moment In Time (IRE) (Danehill (USA))
8667a[22]

**Bondi Beach Boy** *Antony Brittain* a78 85
8 b g Misu Bond(IRE) Nice One (Almaty (IRE))
7137[11] 7940[4]◆ 8320[7] 8745[4] 8927[5] 9152[6]

**Bond Street Beau** *Philip McBride* 51
2 ch g Dandy Man(IRE) Loveleaves (Polar Falcon (USA))
8350[10]

**Bonfire Heart (FR)** *R Le Gal* a96 92
5 b g Falco(USA) Arlecchina (GER) (Mtoto)
8733a[9]

**Boniface (IRE)** *Robert Eddery* 61
2 b c Born To Sea(IRE) Sassy (FR) (Sinndar (IRE))
4859[8] 5964[4] 7543[16]

**Bonita Chica (FR)** *F Monnier* a60 57
5 ch m Paco Boy(IRE) Forewarned (IRE) (Grand Lodge (USA))
4233a[5]

**Bonita Fransisca (FR)** *Antonio Marcialis* 98
2 b f Pedro The Great(USA) Siendra (IRE) (Refuse To Bend (IRE))
4131a[3] 6228a[3] 8525a[7]

**Bonjour Baileys (FR)** *J-V Toux* 46
2 bb f Kyllachy I Stand Corrected (Exceed And Excel (AUS))
2321a[3]

**Bonjour Steve** *Richard Price* a67 70
6 b g Bahamian Bounty Anthea (Tobougg (IRE))
(20) 2709[7] 2932[3] 3424[3] 4278[5] 4842[5] 5051[4] 5564[3] 6099[5] 6810[5] 7099[9]

**Bonneval (NZ)** *Murray Baker & Andrew Forsman* 110
3 b f Makfi Imposingly (AUS) (Zabeel (NZ))
8058a[6] 8250a[14]

**Bonnie Arlene (IRE)** *Mark Johnston* a79 78
3 b f Excelebration(IRE) Pioneer Bride (USA) (Gone West (USA))
1297[2] 1445[3] 1726[2] (3053) 3721[3] 4012[3] 4439[3] 5096[4] (5549) 6002[3] (6628)◆ 6937[6] 7338[6] 7735[10] 8143[5]

**Bonnie Gals** *Keith Dalgleish* a61 61
3 b f Delegator Esteraad (IRE) (Cadeaux Genereux)
96[7] 310[2] 1033[2] 2338[5] 3387[9] 3708[3] 3977[8] 4473[9] 6784[3] 7888[4]◆ 8590[9] 8661[3] 8807[11] 9056[8]

**Bonsai (FR)** *Robert Collet* a63 49
5 b g Fastnet Rock(AUS) Banderille (IRE) (Red Ransom (USA))
822a[6]

**Bon Scotte (IRE)** *Richard Hannon* 86
2 b c Kodiac Bonne (Namid)
(6374) 7355[5]

**Bonusdargent (FR)** *Mme Pia Brandt* a95 99
5 b h Kendargent(FR) Quadded Bere (FR) (Epistolaire (IRE))
1691a[10] 4130a[9]

**Booborowie (IRE)** *Ali Stronge* a45 72
4 bb g Big Bad Bob(IRE) Rejuvenation (IRE) (Singspiel (IRE))
8142[7]

**Boogey Wonderland** *Scott Dixon* 45
3 b f Paco Boy(IRE) Western Eyes (IRE) (Rock Of Gibraltar (IRE))
4445[6] 6268[7]

**Boogie Babe** *Richard Fahey* a48 57
3 b f Aqlaam Bahamian Babe (Bahamian Bounty)
442[6] 731[6] 1064[6] 5472[2]◆ 6148[2]◆ 7036[9] 7889[8] 8481[5]

**Bookmaker** *John Bridger* a62 47
7 b g Byron Cankara (IRE) (Daggers Drawn (USA))
238[11] (398) 570[2] 734[7] 966[2] 1427[3] 1898[4] 2367[3] 3686[3] 4350[7] 5145[10]

**Book Of Days (FR)** *N Caullery* a64 69
6 bb m Definite Article Jetarsu (IRE) (King's Theatre (IRE))
8303a[6]

**Book Of Dreams (IRE)** *Mark Johnston* 82
2 b g Dream Ahead(USA) Moonbi Ridge (IRE) (Definite Article)
(5755)◆ 6465[2] 7221[2] 7593[4] 8045[6]

**Book Of Dust** *Giles Bravery* a49 51
3 ch f Pastoral Pursuits Northern Bows (Bertolini (USA))
1609[10] 2092[6] 4173[4] 5336[13]

**Boomerang Betty (IRE)** *Jamie Osborne* a59 69
2 b f Havana Gold(IRE) Arbeel (Royal Applause)
(4151) 4806[7] 5144[5] 6749[5] 9199[9] 9436[7]

**Boomerang Bob (IRE)** *Jamie Osborne* a104 93
8 b h Aussie Rules(USA) Cozzene's Pride (USA) (Cozzene (USA))
234[4] (639)◆ 953a[F] (Dead)

**Boomshackerlacker (IRE)** *George Baker* a96 104
7 gr g Dark Angel(IRE) Allegrina (IRE) (Barathea (IRE))
1960[17] 3963[16] 4905[11] 5594[8] 6173a[2] 7416a[8] 8127a[P]

**Boom The Groom (IRE)** *Tony Carroll* a110 106
6 b g Kodiac Ecco Mi (IRE) (Priolo (USA))
572[3]◆ 842[6] 917[4] 1772[8] 3321[6] 4072[21] 5505[13] 6025[9] 6512[U] 6927[11]

**Boom Time (AUS)** *David A Hayes* 111
5 b h Flying Spur(AUS) Bit Of A Ride (AUS) (Snippets (AUS))
1400a[5] 1994a[11] 8056a[4] (8250a) 8667a[15] 8975a[12]

**Booshbash (IRE)** *Ed Dunlop* a62 57
3 gr f Dark Angel(IRE) Surrey Storm (Montjeu (IRE))
284[4] 439[4]

**Boost** *Sir Mark Prescott Bt* a84
3 b f Pivotal Hooray (Invincible Spirit (IRE))
(244) (788) 1149[4] 8872[5] 9074[14]

**Boots And Spurs** *Scott Dixon* a86 88
8 b g Oasis Dream Arctic Char (Polar Falcon (USA))
5[2] 25[6] 156[4] 528[4] 850[8] 1074[4] 1109[3] 1433[6] 1512[5] 2133[13] 2466[5] 2838[2] 3144[4] (3498) 4017[7] 4207[8] 4377[3] 5382[4] 5643[3] 6209[5] 6965[12] 7582[12] 8009[10] (8240) 8486[2] 8736[7]

**Bop It** *Michael Easterby* a47 61
8 b g Misu Bond(IRE) Forever Bond (Danetime (IRE))
1833[13] 1972[7] 2305[8] 3186[6] 6271[2] 6572[8] 7660[11] 9347[9]

**Boragh Steps (IRE)** *Joseph Patrick O'Brien* a83 84
2 br f Footstepsinthesand Boragh Jamal (IRE) (Namid)
6136[14]

**Border Bandit (USA)** *Tracy Waggott* a61 89
9 b g Selkirk(USA) Coretta (IRE) (Caerleon (USA))
1544[6]

**Borders Dream** *Donald Whillans* 2
2 b c Dream Ahead(USA) Songseeker (IRE) (Oasis Dream)
6311[9]

**Boreagh Lass (IRE)** *Henry Candy* 76
2 b f Fast Company(IRE) Jalasaat (USA) (Lemon Drop Kid (USA))
3390[7] (5963) 7357[5]

**Born For Champagne (IRE)** *Derek Shaw* a14
3 b f Born To Sea(IRE) Roman Locket (IRE) (Holy Roman Emperor (IRE))
8256[7] 8770[10] 8995[8]

**Born For Prosecco (IRE)** *Derek Shaw* a13
2 ch f Red Jazz(USA) Kelso Magic (USA) (Distant View (USA))
8657[10] 9049[10]

**Born Legend (IRE)** *Charles Hills* a68 64
3 b g Born To Sea(IRE) Hallowed Park (IRE) (Barathea (IRE))
265[8] 437[3]◆ 1239[4] 4462[4]

**Born On The Clyde (IRE)** *John Patrick Shanahan* a48 4
3 b g The Carbon Unit(USA) There's A Light (IRE) (Fantastic Light (USA))
5427[9] 5649[10]

**Born To Be Alive (IRE)** *K R Burke* a110 105
3 b g Born To Sea(IRE) Yaria (IRE) (Danehill (USA))
2681[2]◆ (3383) 5643[2] 6172a[2] 7506[3] 9407[2]

**Born To Boogie** *Chris Grant* a43 54
3 b f Bahri(USA) Turtle Dove (Tobougg (IRE))
1123[8] 2470[9] 4473[7]

**Born To Boom (IRE)** *K R Burke* a55 78
3 b g Born To Sea(IRE) La Belle Maison (IRE) (Titus Livius (FR))
1730[3]◆ 2185[3]◆ 3485[5] 4036[7] (6315) 7162[6] 8318[6]

**Born To Finish (IRE)** *Jamie Osborne* a82 73
4 b g Dark Angel(IRE) Music Pearl (IRE) (Oratorio (IRE))
(80) (171) 547[3] (682) 1696[6] 2147[5] 2608[9] 3696[4] 4256[7] 4851[5] 6076[9] 6503[6] 7409[3] 7882[7] 8159[3] 8542[2] (8645) 9124[2] 9241[3]

**Born To Please** *Mark Usher* a41 58
3 b f Stimulation(IRE) Heart Felt (Beat Hollow)
3024[4] 3752[8] 4493[7] 5266[3] (5545) 5790[8] 7199[2] 8152[6] 8299[3]

**Born To Reason (IRE)** *Kevin Frost* a60 48
3 b g Born To Sea(IRE) Laureldean Lady (IRE) (Statue Of Liberty (USA))
265[4] 840[4] 959[4] 1195[6] 1968[9] 3819[7] 4262[3] 5897[7] 7323[10] (7833) (8247) 8662[7] 8720[6] 9406[12]

**Borntosin (IRE)** *Marco Botti* a46 63
3 b g Born To Sea(IRE) Mrs Beeton (IRE) (Dansili)
2260[8] 2521[7] 4540[2]

**Born To Spend (IRE)** *Ian Williams* a44 51
2 ch f Born To Sea(IRE) Banco Suivi (IRE) (Nashwan (USA))
8678[12] 9099[8] 9318[9]

**Borough Boy (IRE)** *Derek Shaw* a71 71
7 b g Jeremy(USA) Ostrusa (AUT) (Rustan (HUN))
4[12] 312[11] 480[6] 815[7] 1076[4] 1184[2] 1490[4] 1547[4] (1869) 2263[4] 2932[2] 3170[4] 3466[8] 4005[6] 7738[8] 7933[5] 8168[9] 8681[6] 8776[9] 8980[2] 9102[3]

**Borsakov (IRE)** *V Luka Jr* a87 87
5 b g Dylan Thomas(IRE) Million Wishes (Darshaan)
(2696a) 8251a[6]

**Borthwen (IRE)** *Charles Hills* 18
3 b f Lawman(FR) Apticanti (USA) (Aptitude (USA))
1857[14]

**Boscaccio (GER)** *Christian Sprengel* 105
4 b h Mount Nelson Bianca De Medici (Medicean)
4130a[8] 5464a[9]

**Boscastle (USA)** *Hughie Morrison* 62
2 ch f Sea The Stars(IRE) Imprecation (USA) (First Defence (USA))
7399[7] 7733[9] 8425[14]

**Bo Selecta (IRE)** *Richard Spencer* a64 64
3 b c Dream Ahead(USA) Chicane (Motivator)
119[6] 415[3]◆ 848[9] 5512[3] 6131[13] 6529[2] 8256[6] 8984[2] 9365[4]

**Bosham** *Michael Easterby* a98 81
7 b g Shamardal(USA) Awwal Malika (USA) (Kingmambo (USA))
63[4] 326[6] 957[11] 1222[6] 2104[2] (2551) 3337[8] 3967[9] 4600[8] 6062[7] 6669[10] 8803[11] 9016[12] 9366[7]

**Bosphorus Prince (IRE)** *Matthew Salaman* a77 73
5 b h Hurricane Run(IRE) Bosphorus Queen (IRE) (Sri Pekan (USA))
1069[3] 1551[4] 1892[2] (2336)

**Boss For A Day** *J S Moore* a55
2 ch g Mastercraftsman(IRE) Santa Agata (FR) (Anabaa (USA))
8195a[8] 8501[6] 8987[13] 9231[9]

**Bossiney Bay (IRE)** *Hughie Morrison* 50
2 b f Camelot Ursula Minor (IRE) (Footstepsinthesand)
7733[13]

**Bossipop** *Tim Easterby* a52 95
4 ch g Assertive Opopmil (IRE) (Pips Pride)
1831[11] 2524[5] 3861[8] 4505[2] 4787[3] (5457) 5705[2] 6205[16] 6412[2] 6922[5] 7144[22] 7626[8] 8012[19]

**Boss Koko** *Tim Easterby* 43
2 ch f Cityscape Speedy Utmost Meg (Medicean)
3312[11] 3662[10] 4167[6]

**Bossy Guest (IRE)** *Mick Channon* 109
5 b g Medicean Ros The Boss (IRE) (Danehill (USA))
1960[5] 2606[7] 3963[14] 4905[14] 5157[11]

**Bostonian** *Shaun Lycett* a78 79
7 b g Dubawi(IRE) Bolshaya (Cadeaux Genereux)
1289[7] 1602[4] 2059[5] 3308[5] 3698[2]

**Bottleofsmoke (IRE)**
*Gavin Cromwell* a65 70
4 b g Big Bad Bob(IRE) Testimonial (Singspiel (IRE))
(1402) 1985[2] 5689a[3]

**Bouclier (IRE)** *Michael Easterby* a89 82
7 ch h Zamindar(USA) Bastet (IRE) (Giant's Causeway (USA))
94[9] 989[3] (1302) (2026) 5949[3] 6414[11] 7612[14] 8014[14] 8240[9] 9179[11]

**Boudica Bay (IRE)** *Eric Alston*
2 b f Rip Van Winkle(IRE) White Shift (IRE) (Night Shift (USA))
7013[8]

**Bounce** *Henry Candy* a89 100
4 b m Bahamian Bounty Black Belt Shopper (IRE) (Desert Prince (IRE))
2623[3] 3080[2] 4920[9] 6039[4] 6864[8]

**Bound (IRE)** *A P O'Brien* 100
3 ch f Galileo(IRE) Remember When (IRE) (Danehill Dancer (IRE))
8086a[4]

**Bound For Nowhere (USA)**
*Wesley A Ward* 109
3 b c The Factor(USA) Fancy Deed (USA) (Alydeed (CAN))
4030[4]◆ 5690a[10]

**Boundsy (IRE)** *Richard Fahey* a88 93
3 ch g Dandy Man(IRE) Chiba (UAE) (Timber Country (USA))
2271[4] 2806[7] 3152[2] 4433[2] (4892) 5416[2] (6679) (7610) 8416[3]

**Bounty Pursuit** *Michael Blake* a76 73
5 b g Pastoral Pursuits Poyle Dee Dee (Oasis Dream)
(724) (852) 1109[9] 1285[2] 1334[5] 3773[2] 5111[6] 6502[2] (7881) 9029[13] 9363[5]

**Bourbonisto** *Ben Haslam* a62 62
3 ch g Stimulation(IRE) Psychic's Dream (Oasis Dream)
3391[4] 4302[3] 5703[7] 6435[14]

**Bourne** *Donald McCain* a37 57
11 gr g Linamix(FR) L'Affaire Monique (Machiavellian (USA))
6317[6] 7047[5]

**Bowban** *Brian Ellison* a72
3 b c Makfi Serafina's Flight (Fantastic Light (USA))
175[2] 777[2] 4307[8]

**Bow Belles** *Tim Easterby* 74
2 ch f Kyllachy Rockme Cockney (Cockney Rebel (IRE))
1909[5] (5162) 5665[3] 6466[8] 7385[3] 7954[2]

**Bowditch (IRE)** *John Gosden* a81 74
2 b c Nathaniel(IRE) Kate The Great (Xaar)
6374[5] 7333[4] 7648[5] (8155)

**Bowerman** *Roger Varian* a99
3 b c Dutch Art Jamboretta (IRE) (Danehill (USA))
(1551) (9125)◆

**Bowgey Man** *Michael Easterby* 1
2 b g Pastoral Pursuits Black Annis Bower (Proclamation (IRE))
5162[11]

**Bowler Hat** *Hugo Palmer* a63 74
2 b g Helmet(AUS) Fatima's Gift (Dalakhani (IRE))
6147[2] 6885[8] 7513[7] 8586[10]

**Bowsers Bold** *Roger Ingram* a52 56
6 gr g Firebreak Cristal Clear (IRE) (Clodovil (IRE))
7325[11]

**Bowson Fred** *Michael Easterby* a105 104
5 b g Monsieur Bond(IRE) Bow Bridge (Bertolini (USA))
200[5] 388[3] 842[2] 1152[5] 1362[2] 1946[2] 3321[16] 3829[16] 8238[10] 8660[4] 8913[2] 9373[3]

**Bow Street** *Charlie Appleby* a85 92
2 ch c New Approach(IRE) Favourable Terms (Selkirk (USA))
7726[3] 8352[2] (8643)

**Boxer Dunford (IRE)** *D P Coakley* a63 42
4 b g Lilbourne Lad(IRE) Maid Of Ailsa (USA) (Pivotal)
6798a[2]

**Boxeur (IRE)** *F Rossi* 99
4 b h Slickly(FR) Joha (FR) (Johann Quatz (FR))
4454a[9]

**Boychick (IRE)** *Ed Walker* a75 75
4 b g Holy Roman Emperor(IRE) Al Saqiya (USA) (Woodman (USA))
(124) (421) (517) 806[2] 1498[5] 2956[2] 3547[2] 4573[2] (5477)

**Boycie** *Richard Hannon* a75 85
4 b g Paco Boy(IRE) Eve (Rainbow Quest (USA))
517[6] (1498) 1788[3] 2146[4] (3009) 3744[2] 4254[7] 5060[8] 6273[5] 6848[10] 7735[8] 9078[7]

**Boy In The Bar** *Ian Williams* a92 97
6 ch g Dutch Art Lipsia (IRE) (Dubai Destination (USA))
2391[9] 2780[3] (3034)◆ 3593[3] 4830[6] 6686[4] (8319) 8383[6] 8639[3] (8812)

**Boynton (USA)** *Charlie Appleby* a109 109
3 ch g More Than Ready(USA) Baffled (USA) (Distorted Humor (USA))
7988[2] 8598[3] 8844[7]

**Boy Royal (FR)** *Alain Couetil* 97
3 b c Myboycharlie(IRE) Viola Royale (IRE) (Royal Academy (USA))
7634a[9]

**Brabbham (USA)** *A bin Harmash* a99 85
7 b h Bernardini(USA) Easter Bunnette (USA) (Carson City (USA))
203a[5] 537a[8]

**Bracken Brae** *Mark H Tompkins* a80 61
5 b m Champs Elysees Azure Mist (Bahamian Bounty)
62[2] (616) 1175[6] 1223[2] (1561) 2059[4] 4762[5] 6618[5] 8505[8] 9242[9]

**Bradfield Magic (IRE)** *Charles Hills* a63 62
3 b f Holy Roman Emperor(IRE) Magic Eye (IRE) (Nayef (USA))
3473[9] 4714[3] 5357[7] 6102[2] 6340[4] (6847) 7279[4] 7917[11]

**Braemar** *Sir Michael Stoute* a57 61
2 b c Oasis Dream Spectacle (Dalakhani (IRE))
6108[8]◆ 9312[6]

**Braes Of Lochalsh** *Jim Goldie* a52 76
6 b g Tiger Hill(IRE) Gargoyle Girl (Be My Chief (USA))
2125[5] 2609[5] 3389[2] 4038[2] 4301[2] 4684[5] 5208[2] 5468[5] 6661[4] 7701[5] 7983[6] 9258[10]

**Braganza** *Ed Dunlop* a47
2 b f Nathaniel(IRE) Amber Queen (IRE) (Cadeaux Genereux)
9277[5]

**Brahma** *Hughie Morrison* a36 60
4 b g Mount Nelson Swan Queen (In The Wings)
1072[5] 1556[13]

**Brametot (IRE)** *J-C Rouget* 121
3 b c Rajsaman(FR) Morning Light (GER) (Law Society (USA))
(1824a) (2666a) (3368a)◆ 6053a[5] 7668a[5] 8233[6]

**Brando** *Kevin Ryan* 120
5 ch g Pivotal Argent Du Bois (USA) (Silver Hawk (USA))
(1903) 2737[12] 4907[3] (5690a) 6926[9] 7671a[7] 8230[6]

**Brandon Castle** *Archie Watson* a97 100
5 b g Dylan Thomas(IRE) Chelsey Jayne (IRE) (Galileo (IRE))
1716[8] 3486[6] 3744[10] 4336[8] (5483) (6398) 6895[2] (7386)◆ (7599) (7701) 8274a[9] 9157[4] 9390[6]

**Brandy Station (IRE)**
*Lisa Williamson* a76 77
2 b c Fast Company(IRE) Kardyls Hope (IRE) (Fath (USA))
1673[10] (2299) 3333[4] 6330[11] 6624[2] 7318[3] 7954[3] 8154[5]

**Branscombe** *Mark Johnston* a78 77
2 b g Invincible Spirit(IRE) Lacily (USA) (Elusive Quality (USA))
2459[6] 3254[5] (3782) 4160[2] 4866[7] 5322[6]

**Brassbound (USA)** *Michael Appleby* a92 39
9 b g Redoute's Choice(AUS) In A Bound (AUS) (Ashkalani (IRE))
1108[4] 1590[4]

**Brass Ring** *Ismail Mohammed* a81 90
7 b g Rail Link Moraine (Rainbow Quest (USA))
202a[6]

**Brasted (IRE)** *Lee Carter* a63 50
5 ch g Footstepsinthesand Ellen (IRE) (Machiavellian (USA))
2365[5] 2996[10] 7062[8] 7791[9]

**Brave Anna (USA)** *A P O'Brien* 112
3 b f War Front(USA) Liscanna (IRE) (Sadler's Wells (USA))
1883[10]

**Brave Display (IRE)**
*P J Prendergast* a71 76
3 b g Requinto(IRE) Ashtown Girl (IRE) (Exceed And Excel (AUS))
9244a[4]

**Brave Impact** *Mme Pia Brandt* a81 94
6 b g Montjeu(IRE) Bellona (IRE) (Bering)
1871a[6]

**Bravery (IRE)** *David O'Meara* a76 108
4 b g Galileo(IRE) Lady Icarus (Rainbow Quest (USA))
(1494) 1882[7] 2767[8] 3963[17] 4918[16] 5500[9] 6355[7] 6449[7] 7619[13] 8009[2]◆ 8469[6] 8737[5]

**Brave Tart** *Martin Smith* a36 19
3 b f Pastoral Pursuits Poyle Kiera (Diktat)
3748[11] 4565[10] 4764[12]

**Bravo Zolo (IRE)** *Charlie Appleby* a105 110
5 b g Rip Van Winkle(IRE) Set Fire (IRE) (Bertolini (USA))
(698a) 892a[2] 1691a[4] (8599)

**Braztime** *Richard Hannon* a79 78
3 b f Canford Cliffs(IRE) Briery (IRE) (Salse (USA))
2094[6] (2587) 3031[8] 4501[4] 4794[6] 5331[7] 6818[7] 7493[7] 7710[8]

**Breakable** *Tim Easterby* a86 100
6 ch m Firebreak Magic Myth (IRE) (Revoque (IRE))
2115[10] 4890[7] 5422[4] (5683) 5914[5] 6358[2] 6676[3] 6918[9] 7113[7]

**Breakdancer (FR)**
*Fredrik Reuterskiold* a56 87
4 b g Tale Of Ekati(USA) Fancy Clancy (USA) (Rahy (USA))
694a[8] 2943a[2] 6500a[6]

**Breakheart (IRE)** *Andrew Balding* a54 57
10 b g Sakhee(USA) Exorcet (FR) (Selkirk (USA))
46[6] 636[9] 854[2] 966[10] 1298[13] 4804[10] (5299) 6035[6] 6475[11]

**Breaking Bread** *John Gosden* 67
3 b c Nathaniel(IRE) American Spirit (IRE) (Rock Of Gibraltar (IRE))
1682[6]

**Breaking Free** *John Quinn* a56 50
3 ch g Kyllachy Hill Welcome (Most Welcome)
2077[6] 2455[10] 4900[8] 5239[2]◆ 6528[2] 7792[8] 8538[6] 8807[5] 9034[4] (9072) 9343[6]

**Breaking Lucky (CAN)**
*Reade Baker* a115
5 ch h Lookin At Lucky(USA) Shooting Party (USA) (Sky Classic (CAN))
469a[8]

**Breaking Records (IRE)**
*Hugo Palmer* a59
2 b c Kodiac Querulous (USA) (Raven's Pass (USA))
9433[5]

**Break The Silence** *Scott Dixon* a63 62
3 b g Rip Van Winkle(IRE) In A Silent Way (IRE) (Desert Prince (IRE))
2296[3] 3442[2] 3701[3] 4298[9] 4765[6] 5802[5] 6529[3] 6846[3] 7216[2] 7791[3] (8181) 8513[2] (8651) 8801[4]

**Breakwater Bay (IRE)** *Tim Easterby* 73
3 b g Lilbourne Lad(IRE) Aqualina (IRE) (King's Theatre (IRE))
1678[5] 2347[5] 2705[2] 2991[2] 3909[8] (4436) 4898[4] 5706[8] 6573[6]

**Brean Flyer** *Bill Turner* a50
3 b f Phenomena Lois Lane (Striking Ambition)
76[6] 288[7]

**Breanski** *David O'Meara* a84 79
3 b g Delegator Jubilee (Selkirk (USA))
3745[2] 3975[2] (5009) 5378[2] 5993[7] 6518[4] 7824[7] 8318[2] (8929) 9140[10]

**Breathable** *Tim Easterby* 64
2 b g Bated Breath Cassique Lady (IRE) (Langfuhr (CAN))
5876[7] 6204[3] 6658[3]

**Breath Caught** *Ralph Beckett* 86
2 b c Bated Breath Double Crossed (Caerleon (USA))
4465[8] 6654[2] (8381)

**Breathe Easy (IRE)** *Gavin Cromwell* a63 92
7 ch g Redback Inishmac (IRE) (Danehill Dancer (IRE))
6491a[7] 6978a[6]

**Breathless** *Clive Mulhall* a53 15
5 b g Royal Applause Ada River (Dansili)
7[11] 147[7] 400[11] 610[6] 839[11]

**Breathless Times** *Roger Charlton* a75
2 b c Bated Breath Bea Menace (USA) (Mizzen Mast (USA))
9198[2]◆

**Breathoffreshair** *Richard Guest* a62 14
3 b g Bated Breath Stormy Weather (Nashwan (USA))
2790[13] 7791[6] 8255[4] (8591) (8924) (9019)

**Breden (IRE)** *Linda Jewell* a88 92
7 b g Shamardal(USA) Perfect Touch (USA) (Miswaki (USA))
2232[2] 3160[4] 6007[6] 6887[6] (7358) 7909[5] 8561[4]

**Breeze (IRE)** *J A Stack* a75 74
3 b f Sea The Stars(IRE) Kitty Matcham (IRE) (Rock Of Gibraltar (IRE))
(6899)

**Breeze Up** *Ed de Giles* a28 24
3 b g Shirocco(GER) Lucky Breeze (IRE) (Key Of Luck (USA))
4808[13] 5428[10] 6277[9] 7085[8] 7537[14] 8157[13]

**Breezolini** *Adrian Brendan Joyce* a54 67
9 b m Bertolini(USA) African Breeze (Atraf)
(6688)

**Brendan (IRE)** *Jim Goldie* 48
4 b g Elnadim(USA) My (King's Best (USA))
3383[7] 4682[11] 5260[3] 5605[6] 5995[7] 6631[5] 6896[8]

**Brendan Brackan (IRE)** *G M Lyons* a108 114
8 b g Big Bad Bob(IRE) Abeyr (Unfuwain (USA))
(1388a) 2240a[3] 5087a[4]

**Bretherton**
*Mohammed Jassim Ghazali* a81 98
6 ch g Exceed And Excel(AUS) Cliche (IRE) (Diktat)
914a[11]

**Breton Belle (IRE)** *David Simcock* a51 52
3 ch f Nathaniel(IRE) Cream Tease (Pursuit Of Love)
2307[7] 2834[7] 3542[7] 5846[7] 6820[10]

**Breton Blues** *Fred Watson* a47 41
7 b g Street Cry(IRE) Many Colours (Green Desert (USA))
2183[14] 4055[10] 5544[14]

**Breton Rock (IRE)** *David Simcock* 116
7 b g Bahamian Bounty Anna's Rock (IRE) (Rock Of Gibraltar (IRE))
2825[3] 3587[5] 4362[3] (5502) 6193[4] 7145[5] 8232[12]

**Brex Drago (ITY)** *Marco Botti* a100 97
5 b g Mujahid(USA) Shibuni's Thea (IRE) (Barathea (IRE))
322a[3] 654a[6] 775a[3] 1043a[12] 1860[10] 2828[14] 7602[8] 8880[2] 9053[6] 9468[7]

**Brexit** *Pat Phelan* a37 57
3 b f Bahamian Bounty Famcred (Inchinor)
2018[8] 3246[12]

**Brexitmeansbrexit** *Richard Hannon* a65
2 b f Helmet(AUS) Lady Scarlett (Woodman (USA))
7995[10] 8339[6] 8643[5]◆

**Briac (FR)** *Mark Pattinson* a57 53
6 b g Kapgarde(FR) Jarwin Do (FR) (Grand Tresor (FR))
646[8] (1081) (1303) 1556[10] 2332[4] 3724[12] 4217[10] 5716[3] 6309[6] 7730[6] 8815[9]

**Brian Ryan** *Robyn Brisland* a50
2 b c Finjaan Touching (IRE) (Kheleyf (USA))
1694[5]

**Brian The Snail (IRE)**
*Richard Fahey* 102
3 gr g Zebedee Sweet Irish (Shamardal (USA))
(1702) 2768[5] 3078[6] 4813[19] 5640[21] 7626[11]

**Briardale (IRE)** *James Bethell* a95 104
5 b g Arcano(IRE) Marine City (JPN) (Carnegie (IRE))
156[5] 1517[6] (1781) 2855[2] (3154) 4261[12] 4918[19] 7619[34]

**Briateke (FR)** *Antonio Marcialis* a78 70
2 bl f Dabirsim(FR) Queen Of Poland (Halling (USA))
6171a[5] 8094a[7] 9087a[11]

**Brick By Brick (IRE)**
*Mrs John Harrington* 100
2 b g Big Bad Bob(IRE) Pivka (Pivotal)
(7290a) 7855a[3]

**Bridal March** *John Mackie* a63 44
3 ch f Casamento(IRE) Exultate Jubilate (USA) (With Approval (CAN))
2309[4] 2886[8] 3627[10] 4163[8] 4727[12] 5761[5] 7325[6] 9221[6] 9375[8]

**Bridey's Lettuce (IRE)** *Ivan Furtado* a72 73
5 b g Iffraaj Its On The Air (IRE) (King's Theatre (IRE))
70[6] 525[2] 993[3] 1072[3] 2022[4] 2460[2] 2781[7]◆ 3685[5] 5208[3] (5493)

**Bridge Builder** *Peter Hedger* a77 56
7 b g Avonbridge Amazing Dream (IRE) (Thatching)
94[4] (355) 570[5] 808[6] 1339[5] 5711[9] 6780[7] 7099[11] 8311[11] 8646[14] 9094[8] 9207[3] 9469[5]◆

**Bridge Of Sighs** *Lee Carter* a79 75
5 ch g Avonbridge Ashantiana (Ashkalani (IRE))
92[3] 1430[3] 2333[6] 2913[3] 3817[4] 5843[3] 6848[11] 7098[5]◆ 8000[4] 8313[8] 9338[7]

**Bridge That Gap** *Roger Ingram* a47 46
9 b g Avonbridge Figura (Rudimentary (USA))
121[10] 636[11] 865[11]

**Brief Visit** *Andrew Balding* a79 90
4 b m Fastnet Rock(AUS) Brevity (USA) (Street Cry (IRE))
1504[4] 4915[9] 5533[5] 6369[2] (7550) 8739[6]

**Brigadoon** *Michael Appleby* a83 83
10 b g Compton Place Briggsmaid (Elegant Air)
3[2] 477[2] 958[3] (1207) 1291[2] 1865[3] 2270[2] 2622[3] 9306[3]

**Brigand** *William Haggas* a75 67
2 b g Dick Turpin(IRE) Juncea (Elnadim (USA))
8288[3]◆ (8701) 9372[7]

**Brigham Young** *Ed Walker* a76
2 br c Street Cry(IRE) Bible Belt (IRE) (Big Bad Bob (IRE))
8545[5]◆ 8888[7] 9318[2]

**Brigliadoro (IRE)** *Philip McBride* a103 99
6 ch g Excellent Art Milady's Pride (Machiavellian (USA))
1860[5] 2828[2] 4321[2] 4854[11] 5914[4] (6483) (7727) 8234[18]

**Brilliant Vanguard (IRE)**
*Kevin Ryan* a98 96
4 b g Fast Company(IRE) Alyska (IRE) (Owington)
1512[10] 1969[4] 2772[5] 4215[8] 4832[2] 5425[4] (6209) (6520)◆ (6933)◆ 7727[4] 8032[3] 8566[6]

**Brimham Rocks** *Ralph Beckett* a69 101
3 b g Fastnet Rock(AUS) Colima (IRE) (Authorized (IRE))
(2273) 2807[6] (3489) 3752[4] (4898) 5525[10] 6383[2] (8011)

**Bringit (IRE)** *Jamie Osborne* 64
3 b g Holy Roman Emperor(IRE) Challow Hills (USA) (Woodman (USA))
2580[7] 3921[6] 4490[4]◆

**Bring On A Spinner** *Stuart Williams* a84 61
4 b g Kheleyf(USA) Posy Fossil (USA) (Malibu Moon (USA))
4[5] (312) 664[6] 984[6] 1185[8] 1296[6] 4752[5]

**Briscola** *John Gosden* a70
2 b f Redoute's Choice(AUS) La Concorde (FR) (Sadler's Wells (USA))
6386[9] 8670[2]◆ 8903[5] 9239[2]

**Brise De Mer (FR)** *George Baker* a74 74
3 b g Miesque's Son(USA) Lisselan Firefly (IRE) (Monashee Mountain (USA))
2484a[13] 3781[4] 4943a[7]

**Brisk Tempo (FR)** *Richard Fahey* a75
2 b g Dabirsim(FR) Allegro Vivace (FR) (Muhtathir)
7707[7] 8208[2]

**Bristol Missile (USA)**
*Richard Hannon* a59 82
3 bb c Kitten's Joy(USA) Dearest Girl (IRE) (Galileo (IRE))
1682[3] 2143[3] 2527[2] 3318[8] (3839) 9205[11]

**British Art** *R K Watson* a68 47
5 b g Iffraaj Bush Cat (USA) (Kingmambo (USA))
(7360) (8909) 9258[6]

**British Embassy (IRE)** *Bill Turner* a75 73
5 b g Clodovil(IRE) Embassy Belle (IRE) (Marju (IRE))
1969[6] 2677[6] 3030[10] 3282[2] 4294[6] 4912[5] 5276[4] 6310[7]

**Brittanic (IRE)** *David Simcock* a101 65
3 ch c Excelebration(IRE) Fountain Of Peace (USA) (Kris S (USA))
(177)◆ 7506[7] 8944[5]◆ 9264[7]◆

**Briyouni (FR)** *Kevin Ryan* a76 91
4 b g Siyouni(FR) Brianza (USA) (Thunder Gulch (USA))
1860[12] 2406[10] 2838[13] 4207[5] 5926[4] 6266[2] 6965[11] 7570[7]

**Broad Appeal** *Jonathan Portman* a67 64
3 ch g Medicean Shy Appeal (IRE) (Barathea (IRE))
(503)◆ 1686[7] 2931[8] 3922[5] 5565[5] 6006[3] 6767[6] 8000[6] 8312[12]

**Broadchurch (FR)** *D Allard* 44
2 br f Reply(IRE) Gwenhwyfar (IRE) (Cacique (IRE))
2321a[5] 8228a[12]

**Broadhaven Honey (IRE)**
*Ronald Harris* a72 58
3 b f Harbour Watch(IRE) Honeymead (IRE) (Pivotal)
2631[7] 3672[6] 4200[4] 4574[8] 6612[7] 7689[4] 7767[4] 8168[11] 8495[10] (8776)◆ 8873[4] 9308[7]

**Broadway Dreams** *Marjorie Fife* 79
3 b g Oasis Dream Rosa Eglanteria (Nayef (USA))
4055[6] 4474[2] 4720[4] 6431[2]

**Brockey Rise (IRE)** *David Evans* a49 69
2 ch g Zebedee Age Of Diplomacy (Araafa (IRE))
3037[10] 3538[6] 4335[4] 5143[2]◆ 5562[5] (6043) 6547[7] 6977a[24] 7228[9] 8882[5] 9298[6]

**Brockholes** *Bryan Smart* a74 75
4 ch m Equiano(FR) Rivalry (Medicean)
416[4]

**Broctune Papa Gio** *Gillian Boanas* a66 58
10 b g Tobougg(IRE) Fairlie (Halling (USA))
361[2] 2919[3] 4263[10] 4743[5] 5544[4] 6435[6] (6903) 7573[7]

**Brogan** *Tom Dascombe* a66 83
3 b f Pivotal Roger Sez (IRE) (Red Clubs (IRE))
1878[6] 3167[9] 3715[2] 4617[7] 7130[4] 7656[4] 8150[11]

**Broken Force (USA)** *K R Burke* a65 64
2 ch g Broken Vow(USA) New Girlfriend (IRE) (Diesis)
6403[12] 7237[7]

**Broken Wings (IRE)** *Keith Dalgleish* a73
2 b f Canford Cliffs(IRE) Moss Top (IRE) (Moss Vale (IRE))
7937[2]◆ 8553[2] 8782[4]

**Brokopondo (IRE)** *J F Levins* a85 87
5 b g Bushranger(IRE) Saramacca (IRE) (Kahyasi (IRE))
1388a[6]

**Bromance** *Peter Niven* a60 65
4 b g Showcasing Romantic Destiny (Dubai Destination (USA))
360[9] (3205) 3935[2] 4170[7] 5212[7] 6471[9]

**Bronze Angel (IRE)**
*Marcus Tregoning* a96 98
8 b g Dark Angel(IRE) Rihana (IRE) (Priolo (USA))
7149[8] 7549[3] 8032[7] 8469[3] 8999[10] 9186[3] 9407[7]

**Bronze Beau** *Kristin Stubbs* a52 77
10 ch g Compton Place Bella Cantata (Singspiel (IRE))
2777[2] (3238) 3707[8] 4182[5] (4428) 4607[4] 4896[2] 5211[12] 5818[2] 6267[12] 6574[9] 7055[12] 7522[12] 7825[3]

**Brooke's Point** *Neil Mulholland* a48 52
4 b g Cape Cross(IRE) Forest Pearl (USA) (Woodman (USA))
281[5] 646[5] 1402[5] 2964[7] 3575[13]

**Brorocco** *Andrew Balding* a88 98
4 b g Shirocco(GER) Lady Brora (Dashing Blade)
1757[5] (2086) 2552[2] 3300[5] 4614[13] 5037[3] 5609[2] 6449[4] (7395) 7619[5]

**Brother Bear (IRE)**
*Mrs John Harrington* 106
2 b c Kodiac Hurricane Emma (USA) (Mr Greeley (USA))
(3098a) 3925[4] 4926a[3] 6975a[6] 7855a[7]

**Brother In Arms (IRE)** *Tony Carroll* a66 61
3 b g Kodiac Cool Cousin (IRE) (Distant Relative)
265[6] 435[5] 1088[8] (1418) 1580[4] 2474[6] 3870[8] 5291[7] 6581[9] 8551[5] 9203[5] 9454[11]

**Brotherly Company (IRE)**
*Joanne Foster* a72 83
5 b g Fast Company(IRE) Good Lady (IRE) (Barathea (IRE))
9369[6]

**Brother McGonagall** *Tim Easterby* a59 79
3 b r Equiano(FR) Anatase (Danehill (USA))
404[5] 2223[4] 2630[7] 2853[3]◆ (3431) (3708)◆ 4557[3]◆ (4838) 5378[5] 6001[3] 6315[5] 7162[8] 7524[13]

**Brother Ralph (IRE)** *Brian Meehan* 64
2 b g Redoute's Choice(AUS) Fusion (IRE) (Cape Cross (IRE))
7392[4] 8387[11]

**Brother Tiger** *David C Griffiths* a84 79
8 b g Singspiel(IRE) Three Secrets (IRE) (Danehill (USA))
1222[11] 1586[7] 1833[14] (2368) 3176[5] 3967[5] 4566[6] 4979[4] 5241[6] 6411[11] 9443[2]

**Brough Lane Lass (IRE)**
*John Weymes* a33 47
2 b f Big Bad Bob(IRE) Place De Moscou (IRE) (Rock Of Gibraltar (IRE))
3339[6] 3943[8] 4259[8]

**Broughton Excels** *Henry Spiller* a41 42
2 b c Kyllachy Excello (Exceed And Excel (AUS))
7731[7] 8657[9] 8809[8] 9230[10]

**Broughtons Admiral** *Henry Spiller* a65 65
3 b g Born To Sea(IRE) Chanter (Lomitas)
3327[9] 3819[2] 5336[3] 6048[4] 7003[2] 7253[2] 7790[3]

**Broughtons Fancy** *Karen Tutty* a59 49
4 b m Pastoral Pursuits Lifetime Romance (IRE) (Mozart (IRE))
166[11] 383[9] 640[4] (1247) 1298[4] 2278[2] 2675[3] 2961[9] 3522[11] 4561[8] 6131[7] 6528[10] 6902[2] 7573[6] 8402[4] 8591[5] 8924[4] 9052[3] 9102[2]

**Broughtons Knight** *Jim Boyle* a71 67
3 b g Foxwedge(AUS) Disco Ball (Fantastic Light (USA))
2793[5] 3412[8] 4365[6] 5131[6] 5618[5] 6293[4] 6766[3] 7760[5]◆ (8031) 9126[4] (9279)

**Broughtons Sport** *Andi Brown* 63
3 b g Showcasing Ginger Cookie (Bold Edge)
7459[10] 8117[6]

**Broughtons Story** *Philip McBride* a64 62
3 b g Royal Applause News Desk (Cape Cross (IRE))
100[4]◆ 637[2]◆ 5888[7] 6518[8] (7271) 7917[5] (8123) 9376[4]

**Brownie (FR)** *Bent Olsen* a75 106
5 b h Sunday Break(JPN) Tropical Mark (Mark Of Esteem (IRE))
(2942a) 6501a[3]

**Brown Velvet** *Mrs C Gilbert* a43 47
5 b m Kodiac Silkenveil (IRE) (Indian Ridge (IRE))
1931a[5] 2672a[3] 4143a[3] (4656a) 5201a[2] (5986a)

**Brundtland (IRE)** *Charlie Appleby* 82
2 bb c Dubawi(IRE) Future Generation (IRE) (Hurricane Run (IRE))
(8353)

**Bruny Island (IRE)** *Charlie Fellowes* a67 64
3 ch g Bahamian Bounty Prianca (GER) (Diktat)
323[4] 2794[2] 3296[3] 4447[3] 4727[2]◆ 4983[7]

**Brutal (IRE)** *G M Lyons* 100
3 b g Pivotal Loreto (IRE) (Holy Roman Emperor (IRE))
1636a[7]

**Bryght Boy** *Ed Walker* a67 66
4 b g Paco Boy(IRE) Bright Moll (Mind Games)
3396[4] 4298[7] 5145[2] 7198[6]

**B Squared (USA)** *Doug O'Neill* a109 104
3 b c Square Eddie(CAN) Silar Rules (USA) (Ten Most Wanted (USA))
8607a[9]

**Bubble And Squeak** *Sylvester Kirk* a82
2 b f Mastercraftsman(IRE) Comeback Queen (Nayef (USA))
8148[2] 8544[2] 8669[2] 8796[2] 8904[3]

**Bubble Bath** *M Pimbonnet* a71 67
3 br f Big Bad Bob(IRE) Plume (Pastoral Pursuits)
(4455a) 5268a[3]

**Bubbles Arcade** *Rod Millman* 58
5 b m Arkadian Hero(USA) Alwariah (Xaar)
5428[11] 5712[8] 6150[8]

**Bubbly Bailey** *J R Jenkins* a48 39
7 b g Byron Night Gypsy (Mind Games)
143[9] 1221[2] 2370[9] 7705[8] 7993[9] 9340[11]

**Bubbly Bellini (IRE)**
*Adrian McGuinness* a69 82
10 b g Mull Of Kintyre(USA) Gwapa (IRE) (Imperial Frontier (USA))
1385a[5]

**Buccaneers Cove (IRE)**
*Richard Fahey* a65 65
3 b g Footstepsinthesand Primissima (GER) (Second Set (IRE))
2035[8] 5378[7] 5807[7]

**Buccaneers Vault (IRE)**
*Paul Midgley* a80 84
5 gr g Aussie Rules(USA) Heaven's Vault (IRE) (Hernando (FR))
403[5] 783[6] 1091[5] 1833[6] 2428[3] 3095[5] 3401[4] 5070[4] 5318[2] 5696[8] 6197[4] (7086) 8115[2]

**Bucchero (USA)** *Tim Glyshaw* a96 117
5 ch h Kantharos(USA) Meetmeontime (USA) (General Meeting (USA))
8604a[4]

**Buckland Beau** *Charlie Fellowes* a85 78
6 b g Rock Of Gibraltar(IRE) Heavenly Whisper (IRE) (Halling (USA))
1706[3] 3750[5] 4523[7] 5510[3] 6111[6] 7759[8] 8497[12] 8886[5]

**Buckle Street** *Martin Keighley* a67 57
4 br g Cacique(IRE) Rose Row (Act One)
4222[6]

**Bucklow Brook** *David Brown* a42
2 ch f Sepoy(AUS) Rivalry (Medicean)
8189[8] 8373[13]

**Buck's Bahkbook (FR)**
*Yannick Fouin* a58
3 gr f Martaline Buck's Brook (FR) (Turgeon (USA))
8692a[7]

**Bucks Frizz (IRE)** *David Evans* a4 41
2 b f Havana Gold(IRE) Frizzante (Efisio)
3815[12] 4440[9] 5356[7] 6790[10] 7695[7]

**Buckstay (IRE)** *Peter Chapple-Hyam* a110 114
7 b g Lawman(FR) Stella Del Mattino (USA) (Golden Gear (USA))
4072[25] 4905[17] 5393[25]

**Buckstopper Kit (USA)**
*Richard Fahey* 78
2 b c Kitten's Joy(USA) Prime Silver (USA) (Silver Hawk (USA))
6380[5] 6967[3] (7473) 8045[5]

**Budarri** *Stuart Coltherd* 52
4 b g Supreme Sound Amtaar (Nayef (USA))
5003[7]

**Buddha Boy** *Miss Tracy M Reilly* a66 66
3 b g Bated Breath Midnight Fantasy (Oasis Dream)
8875[12]

**Budgie** *Mark H Tompkins* a42 29
2 b c Excelebration(IRE) Lady Bellatrix (Singspiel (IRE))
2459[5] 3165[9] 3791[14]

**Buffer Zone** *Roger Charlton* a83 73
2 br c Bated Breath Buffering (Beat Hollow)
6071[4]◆ 7351[5] (7877)

**Bulas Belle** *Grant Tuer* 83
7 b m Rob Roy(USA) Bula Rose (IRE) (Alphabatim (USA))
5438[5] 5737[3] 6090[6] 6569[3] 7330[6]

**Buldan** *Sir Michael Stoute* a48 58
3 b c New Approach(IRE) Meeznah (USA) (Dynaformer (USA))
1857[7] 2751[5] 3720[10]

**Bullards Alley (USA)** *Tim Glyshaw* 116
5 bb g Flower Alley(USA) Flower Forest (USA) (Kris S (USA))
3553a[6] (8099a) 8610a[6]

**Bullingdon** *Richard Hannon* 82
2 b c Dansili Rimth (Oasis Dream)
5151[3]◆ (5710)

**Bullington Bandit (IRE)**
*Jane Chapple-Hyam* 95
2 br c Canford Cliffs(IRE) Spiritual Flame (Invincible Spirit (IRE))
(3746) 4906[7] 5570[7] (Dead)

**Bullington Bear (FR)**
*Jane Chapple-Hyam* a75 64
4 b g Youmzain(IRE) Maternelle (FR) (Machiavellian (USA))
2689[7]

**Bullseye Bullet** *Mark Usher* a54 50
2 ch g Kheleyf(USA) Satin Doll (Diktat)
3390[16] 4725[7] 4977[6] 6063[9] 6634[10] 7196[3]

**Bumbasina (IRE)** *W McCreery* 94
3 b f Canford Cliffs(IRE) New Plays (IRE) (Oratorio (IRE))
4512a[5] 6334a[2] 7171a[7]

**Bumble Bay** *Robert Stephens* a55 53
7 b g Trade Fair Amica (Averti (IRE))
5894[6] 6129[2] 6623[7] 7490[12] 8246[8] 8647[4] 8878[4]

**Bumble Beeze (IRE)**
*Tom Dascombe* a43 44
2 ch g Zebedee Choose Me Please (IRE) (Choisir (AUS))
3467[9] 3918[7] 4291[10]

**Bumptious** *Ismail Mohammed* a93 84
4 b m Acclamation Cast In Gold (USA) (Elusive Quality (USA))
1830[6] 2369[4] 2975[2] 3454[10] (5247) (5789) 6619[2] 7094[2] (7484) 7808[10] (8747)◆ 8944[4] 9386[4]

**Bunbury** *Richard Hughes* a96 89
5 b g Dansili Ithaca (USA) (Distant View (USA))
306[2] 1023[7] 1258[2] 1766[9] 2291[4] 4563[5]

**Bunce (IRE)** *Linda Perratt* a59 69
9 b g Good Reward(USA) Bold Desire (Cadeaux Genereux)
2776[8] 3238[3] 3385 [3] 3653[4] 4246[4] 4682[4] 4847[5]

**Bunch Of Thyme (IRE)** *Bill Turner* 39
2 b g Elzaam(AUS) Goodie Goodie (Shirocco (GER))
1604[10] 5655[10] 6505[6]

**Bungee Jump (IRE)** *Kevin Ryan* a72 77
2 b f Canford Cliffs(IRE) Starchy (Cadeaux Genereux)
5412[4] 5998[3] 6666[6] (7045) 7384[9] 8715[7]

**Buonarroti (IRE)** *Declan Carroll* a76 93
6 b g Galileo(IRE) Beauty Is Truth (IRE) (Pivotal)
1517[18] 2770[12] 3240[4]◆ 3582[7] 4206[11] 4796[8] 5313[4] 6188[7] 7561[2] (7983)

**Burauq** *Milton Bradley* a56 56
5 b g Kyllachy Riccoche (IRE) (Oasis Dream)
88[4] 216[4] 438[8] 2214[12] 2509[4] 2724[5] 3280[5] 3811[9] 4467[4] (4735) 5271[9] 5892[2] 6174[3] 6615[3] 7195[10]

**Burcan (FR)** *Marco Botti* a98
5 ch g Astronomer Royal(USA) Sentimental Union (USA) (Dixie Union (USA))
7602[7] 8315[2] 8910[3]

**Burford Brown** *Hugo Palmer* 57
2 br c Swiss Spirit Sareb (FR) (Indian Ridge (IRE))
7580[8]

**Burguillos** *Alan King* 101
4 ch g Lope De Vega(IRE) Hazy Dancer (Oasis Dream)
(2504)◆ 2804[2] 3790[2] 4882[11] 8414[5]

**Burgundy Boy (IRE)**
*Ms Sheila Lavery* 98
2 gr c Red Jazz(USA) Zibaline (FR) (Linamix (FR))
5345a[4] 8440a[4]

**Buridan (FR)** *Richard Hannon* 82
2 b c Choisir(AUS) Lady McKell (IRE) (Raven's Pass (USA))
(3668) 5398[5]

**Burlington (IRE)** *John Gosden* a66 51
2 b g Zoffany(IRE) Peig (IRE) (Refuse To Bend (IRE))
7512[7] 7946[7] 8350[9]

**Burmese Blazer (IRE)** *G M Lyons* 71
2 bb g Arakan(USA) Sr Pius (IRE) (Antonius Pius (USA))
8082a[11]

**Burnieboozle (IRE)** *John Quinn* 65
2 b g Frozen Power(IRE) Tea Chest (IRE) (In The Wings)
4597[4] 5127[8] 5735[3] 6625[3]◆ 6940[13]

**Burning Heat (IRE)**
*Mohamed Moubarak* a72 73
4 b g Rock Of Gibraltar(IRE) Burning Damask (USA) (Thunder Gulch (USA))
91[3] 616[6] 4762[3] 7924[9]

**Burning Thread (IRE)**
*David Elsworth* a80 84
10 b g Captain Rio Desert Rose (Green Desert (USA))
194[2] 573[3] 1087[5] 1465[5] 3278[9] 4219[6] 5263[7]

**Burnside (FR)**
*Daniel Mark Loughnane* a79 68
4 gr g Kendargent(FR) Tishkara (FR) (Xaar)
28[5] 423[2] (555)◆ (837a)

**Burn Some Dust (IRE)** *Brian Ellison* a42 59
2 b g Shirocco(GER) Chilly Filly (IRE) (Montjeu (IRE))
3523[5] 4259[7] 5162[10] (7698) 8676[8]

**Burns Supper (IRE)** *James Ewart* 54
2 ch g Poet's Voice Charming (IRE) (Invincible Spirit (IRE))
3149[7]

**Burnt Cream** *Martin Bosley* a36 40
10 b m Exceed And Excel(AUS) Basbousate Nadia (Wolfhound (USA))
622[9] 6114[13] 8558[9]

**Burn The Boats (IRE)**
*John James Feane* a84 76
8 br g Big Bad Bob(IRE) Forever Phoenix (Shareef Dancer (USA))
6801a[8]

**Burnt Sugar (IRE)** *Roger Fell* a105 107
5 b g Lope De Vega(IRE) Lady Livius (IRE) (Titus Livius (FR))
1876[12] 2031[5] 2381[7] (3294) 3842[16] 4505[6] 5393[12] 5669[2] 6419[2] (6961a) 7807[16]

**Burren View Lady (IRE)**
*Denis Gerard Hogan* a75 67
7 br m Dansili Westerly Gale (USA) (Gone West (USA))
(1618) (3198) 7771[8]

**Burrishoole Abbey (IRE)** *K R Burke* a67 86
3 b g Acclamation Xeralda (IRE) (Xaar)
1841[6] (2499) 3038[8] (3836)

**Burrumbeet (IRE)** *Ed Walker* a57
3 b g Fastnet Rock(AUS) Bright Bank (IRE) (Sadler's Wells (USA))
9455[6]

**Burtonwood** *Julie Camacho* a70 72
5 b g Acclamation Green Poppy (Green Desert (USA))
242[4] (514) 732[5] 971[9] 1346[2] 1887[5] 2305[6] 2923[2] 3170[3] 3812[2] 5318[6] 5620[8] 6670[4] 7628[7]

**Bury The Evidence** *Derek Shaw* a41
4 b m Phoenix Reach(IRE) Madam Bijou (Atraf)
8770[7] 8869[9]

**Bush Beauty (IRE)** *Eric Alston* a63 70
6 b m Bushranger(IRE) Scottendale (Zilzal (USA))
1842[4] 2278[10] 3147[4] 3577[3] 4165[5] 4209[3] 4837[5] 5399[3] 5829[3] 6550[4] 7241[7]

**Bushel (USA)** *Tony Newcombe* a62 75
7 b g Street Cry(IRE) Melhor Ainda (USA) (Pulpit (USA))
806[11] 1207[5] (1864) 9346[12]

**Bush House (IRE)** *Hugo Palmer* a93 84
3 b g Canford Cliffs(IRE) Magena (USA) (Kingmambo (USA))
265[2] (840) 1518[4] 2824[8] (4751)◆ 6445[17] 6887[3] 7516[3]

**Bush Warrior (IRE)**
*Anabel K Murphy* a74 55
6 b g Bushranger(IRE) Lady Corduff (IRE) (Titus Livius (FR))
355[8] 1087[3] 1290[10] 1896[2] 2161[4] 3021[5]

**Bushwise (IRE)** *Milton Bradley* a58 61
4 b m Bushranger(IRE) Validate (Alhaarth (IRE))
217[9] 2675[8] 3569[9] 3758[10] 5429[4] 5651[6] 5784[6] 6174[7] 8137[6]

**Busker (USA)** *A bin Harmash* a81 99
9 ch h Street Cry(IRE) Adonesque (IRE) (Sadler's Wells (USA))
322a[6] 428a[5] 699a[9] 888a[11]

**Buskin River (IRE)** *James Eustace* a60 68
3 b g Kodiac Miss Smilla (Red Ransom (USA))
2259[7] 6153[7] (7005) 7916[10]

**Bustam (IRE)** *John Quinn* a67 86
2 b g Worthadd(IRE) Malayan Mist (IRE) (Dansili)
2948[2]◆ 3339[3] 4068[6] 4860[3] 5465[4] 7623[5]

**Busted Ice (IRE)** *A Wohler* 63
2 b c Falco(USA) Sansiwa (IRE) (Dansili)
5776a[12]

**Busy Street** *Sally Haynes* a81 84
5 b g Champs Elysees Allegro Viva (USA) (Distant View (USA))
1182[2] 1292[2] 1719[3] 2426[4] 2741[13] 4796[4] 5830[3]◆ 6757[2]

**Buthela (FR)** *A Fabre* a77 113
3 b c Acclamation Tribune (FR) (Grand Slam (USA))
5777a[2] 7640a[2]

**Buthelezi (USA)** *Brian Ellison* a72 58
9 b g Dynaformer(USA) Ntombi (USA) (Quiet American (USA))
779[8] 1002[8] 1307[9] 1608[9] 2386[7] 5021[11] 5403[12] 8662[6] 9346[8]

**Butoolat** *Keith Dalgleish* a59 61
3 b f Oasis Dream Handassa (Dubawi (IRE))
9219[6]

**Butte Montmartre (FR)** *R Le Gal* a74 79
6 gr m Montmartre(FR) Dark Beauty (Singspiel (IRE))
(515a)

**Butterflies (IRE)** *A P O'Brien* 99
3 b f Galileo(IRE) Mariah's Storm (USA) (Rahy (USA))
2637a[6] 3874a[2]

**Butterfly Lily** *Ralph Beckett* 66
3 gr f Lawman(FR) Bruxcalina (FR) (Linamix (FR))
1947[6]◆

**Butterfly Spirit** *Michael Attwater* a47 52
2 gr f Lethal Force(IRE) Zubova (Dubawi (IRE))
2015[5] 3029[8] 3516[8] 5479[9] 6417[10] 9387[5]

**Butterscotch (IRE)** *A P O'Brien* 99
2 b f Galileo(IRE) Lesson In Humility (IRE) (Mujadil (USA))
4418a[2] 7578[5] 8002[4]

**Butterworth Brow** *Bryan Smart* 45
3 b f Acclamation Rivalry (Medicean)
3896[4]

**Button Up (IRE)** *Sir Michael Stoute* a60 55
3 b f So You Think(NZ) Star Ruby (IRE) (Rock Of Gibraltar (IRE))
3007[7]◆ 4497[8]

**Buttonwood** *Antonio Marcialis* a58 61
3 b g Sakhee's Secret Broughtons Motto (Mtoto)
2536a[6] 3310a[6]

**Butzje (GER)** *Markus Klug* 52
2 b f It's Gino(GER) Beltana (GER) (Areion (GER))
8269a[6]

**Buxted Dream (USA)** *Luca Cumani* a83 86
3 gr g Dream Ahead(USA) America Nova (FR) (Verglas (IRE))
2066[4]◆ 2581[2] 3234[2] 3825[2] 5158[2] (5937) (6282) 7709[4] 8115[7]

**Buyer Beware (IRE)** *Patrick Holmes* a68 73
5 br g Big Bad Bob(IRE) Adoring (IRE) (One Cool Cat (USA))
1719[9] 3046[6] 3830[5] 4852[4] 5700[9]

**Buying Trouble (USA)** *David Evans* a89 106
4 b m Hat Trick(JPN) Lotus Sutra (USA) (Kingmambo (USA))
617[6] 917[7] 1491[6] 1936[8] 2623[5] (3080) 3632a[10] 4864[4] 6234[9] 6864[10]

**Buzet (FR)** *F Foresi*
3 ch c Execute(FR) Safayeli (TUR) (Down The Flag (USA))
847a[3]

**Buzz (FR)** *Hughie Morrison* a78 88
3 gr g Motivator Tiysha (IRE) (Araafa (IRE))
2690[11] 5033[2]◆

**Buzz Boy (ITY)** *Adrian Paul Keatley* a33 61
4 ch g Buzzword Echad (IRE) (Kris Kin (USA))
3193[2] 3389[4] 5208[6]

**Buzz Lightyere** *Philip Hide* a56 67
4 b g Royal Applause Lady Gloria (Diktat)
(2255) 2916[3] 3688[5] 4461[2]◆ 5023[4] 5790[7] (5823) 6284[2] (6725) 7098[9] 7916[5]

**Bybrook** *David Simcock* a75 78
4 b m Dubawi(IRE) Diary (IRE) (Green Desert (USA))
5414[5] 5957[3] 7201[2] (8426)

**Bye Bye Baby (IRE)** *A P O'Brien* 100
2 b f Galileo(IRE) Remember When (IRE) (Danehill Dancer (IRE))
6487a[4] (7620) (7859a) 8265a[3]

**Byres Road** *Mark Johnston* a88 84
4 ch g Pivotal Croeso Cariad (Most Welcome)
240[2] 266[4] 349[5] 782[2] 876[5] 1032[4] 1224[6] 1457[4] 1788[6] 4685[6]

**Byron Blue (IRE)** *Brian Barr* a47 43
8 br g Dylan Thomas(IRE) High Society (IRE) (Key Of Luck (USA))
395[7] 988[5] 5244[6]

**Byronegetonefree** *Stuart Coltherd* a55 55
6 b g Byron Lefty's Dollbaby (USA) (Brocco (USA))
3340[7] 4018[4] 5008[6] 5257[5] 5413[2] 6898[12]

**Byron Flyer** *Ian Williams* a92 102
6 b g Byron Nursling (IRE) (Kahyasi (IRE))
(571) 746[2]◆ 1309[4] 3067[7]◆ 3594[2] 4921[2] 5912[2] 7115[2] 8038[7]

**Byron's Choice** *Michael Dods* a54 77
2 b g Poet's Voice Byrony (IRE) (Byron)
3398[6] (4205) 5412[6] 6379[3] 7243[2]

**By Royal Approval (IRE)**
*Michael Appleby* a71 75
2 b g Approve(IRE) Spring Bouquet (IRE) (King's Best (USA))
5278[6] 6432[10] 7126[4] 7877[4] 8349[11] 9370[8]

**By The Law** *Tim Easterby* 67
4 b g New Approach(IRE) Walk On Bye (IRE) (Danehill Dancer (IRE))
2119[8] 3181[12] 4060[6]

**By The Moon (USA)** *Michelle Nevin* a112
5 bb m Indian Charlie(USA) By The Light (USA) (Malibu Moon (USA))
8605a[10]

**Cabal** *Geoffrey Harker* a68 65
10 br m Kyllachy Secret Flame (Machiavellian (USA))
527[7] 729[6] 968[4] 1334[8]◆ 1879[2] 2346[2] 2900[3] 3181[3] 3912[5] 4059[3] 5007[8] 5880[10]

**Cabanon Bay** *Malcolm Saunders* 59
2 b g Dandy Man(IRE) Eventfull Meet (IRE) (Dalakhani (IRE))
2756[11] 3083[6] 4466[7]

**Cabarita (GER)** *H-J Groschel* 93
2 ch f Areion(GER) Caesarina (Hernando (FR))
(6494a) 8269a[5]

**Cable Car** *John Flint* a49
6 gr g Pastoral Pursuits Nina Fontenail (FR) (Kaldounevees (FR))
5563[7] 6633[9]

**Cabotin (FR)** *A Fabre* a79 79
2 gr c Kendargent(FR) Zoubrovka (USA) (Proud Citizen (USA))
5952a[10] 6453a[2] 7012a[2]

**Caccini (FR)** *Adam Wyrzyk* 105
4 b h American Post Courances (FR) (Simon Du Desert (FR))
2667a[8]

**Cadeau Magnifique** *Richard Fahey* a82 73
5 b g Dutch Art Cadeau Speciale (Cadeaux Genereux)
359[8] 992[2]◆

**Cadeaux Boxer** *Lee Carter* a73 77
4 ch g Major Cadeaux Ashantiana (Ashkalani (IRE))
4277[9] 4810[2] 5111[5] 6134[6] 6795[6] 7769[4] 8549[7] 8773[7] 9211[12]

**Cadeaux Pearl** *Scott Dixon* a51 39
9 b g Acclamation Anneliina (Cadeaux Genereux)
311[4] 386[2] 481[5] 852[4] 1076[7] 1209[2] 1593[9] 1978[15]

**Cadela Rica** *Gay Kelleway* a22 30
3 b f Compton Place Millennium Heiress (Singspiel (IRE))
2296[4] 4759[8]

**Cadencia** *A Fabre* a75 71
3 ch f Shamardal(USA) Baila Me (GER) (Samum (GER))
8692a[2]

**Cadillac Mountain (AUS)**
*Darren Weir* 92
6 b g Reset(AUS) Picholine (AUS) (Dehere (USA))
1400a[8]

**Cadmium** *Micky Hammond* a52 71
6 b m Major Cadeaux Miss Mirasol (Sheikh Albadou)
3405[7]◆ 3706[5] 4439[8] 5498[6] 5802[4] 6346[11]

**Cadore (IRE)** *Lucy Normile* 26
9 b g Hurricane Run(IRE) Mansiya (Vettori (IRE))
2456[5] 3389[7]

**Caesar's Comet (IRE)** *Paul Midgley* a66 65
3 b g Acclamation Star Now (Librettist (USA))
5020[3] 5708[4] 8115[8]

**Caeser The Gaeser (IRE)**
*Nigel Tinkler* a73 70
5 b g Captain Rio Alchimie (IRE) (Sri Pekan (USA))
2923[5] 4789[7] 5620[9] 5836[5] 6435[11] 7332[9] 7571[14]

**Cafe Royal (GER)** *A Schutz* a83 107
6 ch g Nicaron(GER) Cariera (GER) (Macanal (USA))
1271a[3] 1659a[8] 2485a[5] 3856a[6] 6173a[4]

**Caged Lightning (IRE)**
*Steve Gollings* a76 73
7 b g Haatef(USA) Rainbow Melody (IRE) (Rainbows For Life (CAN))
7319[6] 8214[4] (9242)

**Cagliari** *Simon Crisford* a52 21
3 gr f Bahamian Bounty Crocus Rose (Royal Applause)
6161[5] 6473[5]

**Cahar Fad (IRE)** *Steph Hollinshead* a62 45
5 b g Bushranger(IRE) Tarbiyah (Singspiel (IRE))
334[3] 689[7] 820[6] 1145[2] 1322[2] 1402[8] 2626[11] 3264[5] 6622[13]

**Cainhoe Star** *Anthony Carson* a84 70
4 ch g Pivotal Celeste (Green Desert (USA))
2732[3] 3688[2] (4323) (4561) 5363[6] 6620[2]◆ 7321[3] (7947) 8375[8] 9179[4]

**Cairdiuil (IRE)** *I Madden* a53 77
11 b g Bachelor Duke(USA) Lilabelle (IRE) (Lil's Boy (USA))
5582a[2]

**Caius College Girl (IRE)**
*Adrian Wintle* a62 52
5 b m Royal Applause Galeaza (Galileo (IRE))
282[11] 605[5] 1298[6] 2672a[4] 6341[7] 7693[9] 8133[12]

**Caiya** *Eve Johnson Houghton* 72
2 b f Casamento(IRE) Louverissa (IRE) (Verglas (IRE))
(7898)

**Cajmere** *Tom Dascombe* a80 70
3 b g Kyllachy Percolator (Kheleyf (USA))
41[2] (379) 657[4] 3719[2]

**Calaconta (FR)** *F Foucher* 61
2 b f Muhtathir Triki Miki (FR) (Della Francesca (USA))
7470a[4]

**Calajani (FR)** *Andrew Hollinshead* a8 57
4 b g Azamour(IRE) Clarinda (AUS) (Sir Dapper (AUS))
6365a[5] 7069a[2]

**Calare (IRE)** *Charlie Appleby* a90 98
3 ch f Dubawi(IRE) Calando (USA) (Storm Cat (USA))
317a[5] 652a[7] 889a[5]

**Calayana (FR)** *A De Royer-Dupre* 102
3 b f Sinndar(IRE) Clariyn (FR) (Acclamation)
5981a[2]

**Calculator (USA)** *Peter Miller* a114 102
5 rg h In Summation(USA) Back To Basics (USA) (Alphabet Soup (USA))
8607a[7]

**Calderon (IRE)** *Tony McEvoy* a96 115
4 b h Lope De Vega(IRE) Bibury (Royal Applause)
(1882) 3012[3] 4371[5] 8058a[11]

**Calder Prince (IRE)** *Tom Dascombe* a85 103
4 gr g Dark Angel(IRE) Flame Of Ireland (IRE) (Fasliyev (USA))
321a[8] 775a[6] 2142[4] 2568[8] 3294[11] 3743[2] (4578)◆ 5382[3] 5683[5] 5926[2] 6414[4] 6879[3] 7108[4] 7609[6]

**Caledonia Duchess** *Jo Hughes* a69 63
4 b m Dutch Art Granuaile O'Malley (IRE) (Mark Of Esteem (IRE))
5794[5] 7061[2] 7710[5] 8300[3]

**Caledonia Laird** *Jo Hughes* a66 64
6 b g Firebreak Granuaile O'Malley (IRE) (Mark Of Esteem (IRE))
1474 (1842) 2511[3] 3265[2] 3912[10] 5039[3] 6014[7] 6638[9] 7323[11] 8402[5]

**Caledonian Gold** *Paul D'Arcy* a55 54
4 b m Acclamation Moonlight Rhapsody (IRE) (Danehill Dancer (IRE))
1180[5] 1285[5] 1407[4] 1587[3] 1894[8] 3001[4] 3522[4] 4561[5] 5239[3] 5857[2] 6112[4] 7481[4] 7606[4] 8543[5] 8807[4]

**Caledonia Road (USA)**
*Ralph E Nicks* a114
2 b f Quality Road(USA) Come A Callin (USA) (Dixie Union (USA))
(8603a)

**Calibration (IRE)** *Martyn Meade* 90
3 b c Excelebration(IRE) Dance Troupe (Rainbow Quest (USA))
(5075)◆

**California Chrome (USA)**
*Art Sherman* a135 116
6 ch h Lucky Pulpit(USA) Love The Chase (USA) (Not For Love (USA))
469a[9]

**California Cliffs (IRE)** *Rae Guest* a54 57
3 b f Canford Cliffs(IRE) Quiet Waters (USA) (Quiet American (USA))
1151[6] 1609[8] 2316[6] 3657[2] 5532[6] 6257[5] 6560[4] 7325[2] 7991[13]

**California Lad** *F Birrane* a66 59
4 b g Aussie Rules(USA) Medaille D'Or (With Approval (CAN))
5518a[18]

**California Tee** *Matthieu Palussiere* 89
3 ch f Kheleyf(USA) Quintrell (Royal Applause)
3614a[5] 5450a[6] 6979a[9]

**Caliste** *H-A Pantall* a72 42
2 b c Intense Focus(USA) Russian Hill (Indian Ridge (IRE))
6247a[5]

**Callaghan (GER)** *Tom Gretton* a58 42
4 b g Cacique(IRE) Cent Cheveux Blanc (GER) (Pentire)
2308[5] 3501[7] 4627[11] 6069[12] 6305[5] 6953[7] 8430[10]

**Callaloo** *Tony Coyle* 17
3 ch f Rip Van Winkle(IRE) In The Soup (USA) (Alphabet Soup (USA))
5458[11] 5670[9]

**Call Dawn** *Michael Easterby* a57 58
2 b f Helmet(AUS) Authoritative (Diktat)
3460[4] 6086[4] 6755[5] 7563[9] 8783[8] 8847[2]

**Called To The Bar (IRE)**
*Mme Pia Brandt* 111
3 b g Henrythenavigator(USA) Perfect Hedge (Unfuwain (USA))
1460a[2] (2947a) 4652a[2]

**Calling Out (FR)** *David Simcock* a103 112
6 bb g Martaline Exit The Straight (IRE) (Exit To Nowhere (USA))
(148) 767[2] 9233[6]

**Calling Rio (IRE)** *David Loughnane* a73 75
2 b f Canford Cliffs(IRE) Rio's Pearl (Captain Rio)
6010[8] 6666[5] 7045[3] 7521[3] 7733[3] 8163[4] 8491[4] 8848[12]

**Calliope** *Kenneth Slack* a53 70
4 b m Poet's Voice Costa Brava (IRE) (Sadler's Wells (USA))
1679[9] 3343[7] 5951[3] 6270[5]

**Call Me Grumpy (IRE)**
*Roger Varian* a59 84
3 b g Holy Roman Emperor(IRE) Miss Rochester (IRE) (Montjeu (IRE))
(3784)◆ 4058[2] 4837[4] 6111[2] 7131[3]

**Call Out Loud** *Michael Appleby* a90 78
5 b g Aqlaam Winner's Call (Indian Ridge (IRE))
67[4] (159) 312[6] 528[3] (745) (1189) (1365) 1546[2] 2528[7] 6414[12] 7108[9] 8216[3] 8706[6] (9020) 9074[6] 9272[12]

**Call To Mind** *William Haggas* 109
3 b c Galileo(IRE) Memory (IRE) (Danehill Dancer (IRE))
(1961) 2829[3] 4029[6] 5095[3] (6421) 7634a[2]

**Calm Charm (IRE)** *Chris Wall* a58 50
3 ch f Teofilo(IRE) Mango Lady (Dalakhani (IRE))
6817[8] 7485[8] 8116[5]

**Calva D'Auge (FR)** *B De Montzey* 90
2 b c Air Chief Marshal(IRE) Hill Ou Elle (FR) (Tiger Hill (IRE))
6912a[4] 7592a[7]

**Calvados Spirit** *William Muir* a90 90
4 b g Invincible Spirit(IRE) Putois Peace (Pivotal)
(1562)◆ 2828[8] 3298[11] 3808[4] 4443[3] 4976[3] 7129[8] 7950[7]

**Calvin (FR)** *Y Durepaire* 101
4 b g Whipper(USA) Celestina Agostino (USA) (Street Cry (IRE))
7416a[5]

**Calvinist** *Ruth Carr* a95 70
4 b g Holy Roman Emperor(IRE) Sharp Relief (IRE) (Galileo (IRE))
746[5] 985[5] 1309[7] 4002[9] 4828[9] 5397[12] 6398[5] 8505[10] 8909[11]

**Calvin's Gal (IRE)** *Luke McJannet* a41 17
2 ch f Casamento(IRE) Spirit of Hope (IRE) (Danehill Dancer (IRE))
4972[11] 6636[10] 6950[6]

**Calypso Blue (IRE)** *Charlie Appleby* a76
2 b f Dubawi(IRE) Dark Orchid (USA) (Dansili)
8997[4] 9277[2]

**Calypso Choir** *Sylvester Kirk* a85 85
4 ch m Bahamian Bounty Heavenly Song (IRE) (Oratorio (IRE))
94[10]

**Calypso Delegator (IRE)**
*Micky Hammond* 56
4 b g Lilbourne Lad(IRE) Amber Nectar (IRE) (Barathea (IRE))
2591[3] 5802[10] (6560)

**Calypso Jo** *Kevin Ryan* a68 39
3 b g Bahamian Bounty Cha Cha Cha (Efisio)
878[2]◆ 1837[4] 4341[11]

**Camacho Chief (IRE)** *Michael Dods* 85
2 b g Camacho Passage To India (IRE) (Indian Ridge (IRE))
3460[5] 3705[2] (4895) (5603) 6693[3] 6977a[5] 7891[2]

**Camacho Dancer (IRE)**
*Keith Henry Clarke* a50 56
2 b f Camacho Dazzling Day (Hernando (FR))
2862a[5]

**Camakasi (IRE)** *Ali Stronge* a77 81
6 b g Camacho Innocence (Unfuwain (USA))
(169) 286[5] 507[7] 2020[3] 2971[3] 4257[8] 4699[4] 5477[3] (6175)

**Camanche Grey (IRE)** *Ben Haslam* a47 60
6 gr g Camacho Sense Of Greeting (IRE) (Key Of Luck (USA))
3944[9] (4478) 5069[3] 5418[3] 6351[2]

**Camaradorie (IRE)** *Lydia Pearce* a59 48
3 ch f Camacho Lady Duxyana (Most Welcome)
96[3]◆ 763[6] 2734[9] 3701[5] 4727[7] 9056[10]

**Camargue** *Mark Johnston* a81 84
3 b f Invincible Spirit(IRE) Chaquiras (USA) (Seeking The Gold (USA))
1294[3] 1724[5]

**Cambiko (FR)** *M Le Forestier* 48
2 ch c Balko(FR) Candid (Lion Cavern (USA))
3679a[9]

**Cambodia (IRE)** *Chris Wall* a76 76
4 ch g Fast Company(IRE) Remarkable Story (Mark Of Esteem (IRE))
122[8] 1224[P] 2685[16]

**Cambodia (USA)** *Thomas F Proctor* 110
5 b m War Front(USA) Sassifaction (USA) (Smart Strike (CAN))
8606a[3]

**Camden Town (IRE)** *Roger Fell* a50 42
2 ch g New Approach(IRE) Antique (IRE) (Dubai Millennium)
8649[6] 8915[10] 9263[5]

**Camdora (IRE)** *Jamie Osborne* a67 57
5 b m Arcano(IRE) Crimphill (IRE) (Sadler's Wells (USA))
303[3] 521[4]

**Camelback (USA)** *G M Lyons* 101
2 b g Exchange Rate(USA) Pick And Choose (USA) (Street Cry (IRE))
6240a[4] 6955a[5]

**Camellia Japonica (IRE)**
*Joseph G Murphy* 82
4 b m Zoffany(IRE) Red Japonica (Daylami (IRE))
1387a[12]

**Cameo Star (IRE)** *Richard Fahey* a75 71
2 ch g Camacho Passionforfashion (IRE) (Fasliyev (USA))
3895[7] (4995) 5370[9] 6065[4] 7734[11]

**Camerone (IRE)** *Ralph Beckett* 93
3 b f Galileo(IRE) Louvain (IRE) (Sinndar (IRE))
2613[4] (3933) 4829[6] (6307)◆ 7092[4]

**Camino** *Andi Brown* a49 50
4 b m Equiano(FR) Juncea (Elnadim (USA))
455[10] 640[14] 1452[2] 1759[9] 2370[3] (3942) 5027[2] 5871[7] 6114[2]

**Camiyra (IRE)** *J P Murtagh* a71 70
3 b f Henrythenavigator(USA) Myrica (Dansili)
6345[3]

**Camomile Lawn (IRE)**
*Ralph Beckett* a70 49
2 b f Camelot Endure (IRE) (Green Desert (USA))
4212[2] 4909[8] 6883[8] 7552[10]

**Camp Creek (CAN)** *Kevin Attard* 100
4 rg g Dunkirk(USA) Go Go Neigh (CAN) (Storm Boot (USA))
7178a[8]

**Campion** *Richard Hannon* a51 76
2 b f Exceed And Excel(AUS) Princess Janie (USA) (Elusive Quality (USA))
1627[8] 2173[4] (3022) 3297[3] 4361[7]◆ 5329[10] 6338[5] 6778[5]

**Canadian Diamond (IRE)**
*Richard Rowe* a73 67
10 ch g Halling(USA) Six Nations (USA) (Danzig (USA))
(19) (508) 1505[6] (Dead)

**Canadian George (FR)**
*Keith Dalgleish* a69 66
2 b c George Vancouver(USA) Connaissance (IRE) (Choisir (AUS))
6890[5] 7520[3] 7883[4] 8925[2]

**Canadian Royal** *Stuart Williams* a64 65
3 b g Royal Applause Emily Carr (IRE) (Teofilo (IRE))
3438[8] 5040[2]◆ 5291[6] 6295[3] 6581[8] 6904[6] 8842[3] 9139[3] 9304[3]

**Canary Row (IRE)** *P J Prendergast* 101
7 b g Holy Roman Emperor(IRE) Fresh Mint (IRE) (Sadler's Wells (USA))
1388a[7] 5688a[4] (6334a) 7066a[4]

**Canberra Cliffs (IRE)** *Don Cantillon* a90 93
3 b f Canford Cliffs(IRE) Gloved Hand (Royal Applause)
1088[6]◆ 1348[5] (1968) 2269[3] (2702)◆ 3094[3] 4722[2] 4975[6] (5838) (6176) 8385[3] 8652[2] 8820[7] 9055[5] 9467[4]

**Can Can Dream** *Olly Williams*
3 b f Stimulation(IRE) Can Can Dancer (Fantastic Light (USA))
9343[10]

**Can Can Sixty Two** *Mick Channon* 53
2 b f Sixties Icon Natalie Jay (Ballacashtal (CAN))
8425[9]

**Candelaria** *Jonjo O'Neill* 77
4 b g Kyllachy Gleam Of Light (IRE) (Danehill (USA))
3903[8] 4467[11] 5252[8] 5657[7] 6612[6] 7190[12]

**Candelisa (IRE)** *Tony Coyle* a78 99
4 br g Dream Ahead(USA) Vasilia (Dansili)
1492[3]◆ 2828[13] 3498[4] 4077[7] 6349[5] 7044[5] (7523) 7981[8]

**Candesta (USA)** *Julia Feilden* a68 59
7 b g First Defence(USA) Wandesta (Nashwan (USA))
351[7] 516[6] 1735[8] 2318[5] 4446[8] 5002[5] 6143[6] 7062[7] 8031[12] 8515[11] 8985[5] (9342)

**Candidate (IRE)** *Hughie Morrison* 72
2 b c Camelot Miss Mariduff (USA) (Hussonet (USA))
7355[7] 7906[4] 8353[11]

**Candyman Can (IRE)** *Henry Spiller* a62 57
7 b g Holy Roman Emperor(IRE) Palwina (FR) (Unfuwain (USA))
3308[10]

**Candy Store (IRE)** *Stefano Botti* 99
3 ch f Lope De Vega(IRE) March Madness (Noverre (USA))
2244a[5] 3121a[5] (7441a) 8450a[4]

**Canessar (FR)** *H-F Devin* 105
4 rg g Kendargent(FR) Candara (FR) (Barathea (IRE))
4879a[8]

**Canford Bay (IRE)** *Antony Brittain* a66 55
3 b c Canford Cliffs(IRE) Maundays Bay (IRE) (Invincible Spirit (IRE))
5006[2] 5619[5] 6062[6] 6469[7] 7036[3] 7366[9] (7575) 8194[3]◆ 8321[4]

**Canford Belle** *Grant Tuer* a59 58
4 b m Canford Cliffs(IRE) Ballyea (IRE) (Acclamation)
400[2] 579[4] 605[8] 1260[4] 1456[7] 1823[2] 6528[13]

**Canford's Joy (IRE)** *Ann Duffield* 80
2 b g Canford Cliffs(IRE) Joyful (IRE) (Green Desert (USA))
5494[6] (6312) (7383) 8008[17] 8741[10]

**Canford Thompson** *Daniel Steele* a65 35
4 b g Canford Cliffs(IRE) Sadie Thompson (IRE) (King's Best (USA))
8878[9] 9092[11]

**Canford Tor (IRE)** *Henry Candy* 60
3 b g Canford Cliffs(IRE) Igreja (ARG) (Southern Halo (USA))
2172[6] 2782[9] 3691[10] 4255[10] 5049[5]

**Canimar** *Ed Dunlop* a56 73
2 b f Havana Gold(IRE) Acquifer (Oasis Dream)
8006[6] 8348[4] 8890[7]

**Canizay (IRE)** *Roger Fell* 33
3 ch g Tagula(IRE) Baltic Dip (IRE) (Benny The Dip (USA))
3342[12] 4508[6] 5374[7]

**Canndera (FR)** *A De Royer-Dupre* 99
3 b f Dalakhani(IRE) Candara (FR) (Barathea (IRE))
5982a[2]

**Cannonball (IRE)** *G M Lyons* 107
3 b c Lope De Vega(IRE) Two Sets To Love (IRE) (Cadeaux Genereux)
6957a[4] 7837a[2]

**Canny Kool** *Brian Ellison* a31 90
5 b g Kheleyf(USA) Kool Acclaim (Royal Applause)
2573[3] 3539[8] 4353[12] 4890[RR]

**Canny Style** *Kevin Ryan* a70 77
4 b m Canford Cliffs(IRE) Stylish One (IRE) (Invincible Spirit (IRE))
1679[3] 2061[3] 2815[3] 4244[2] 4571[5] (5284) (5599) 6895[3] 7560[2]

**Canouville (FR)** *P Sogorb* a73 82
2 b f Air Chief Marshal(IRE) Our Dream Queen (Oasis Dream)
1594a[3] (2321a)

**Canterbury Quad (FR)**
*Henry Spiller* a66 80
3 b f Motivator Coiffure (King's Best (USA))
1459a[6] 2929[3] 4003[3] 4365[8] 6340[7]

**Can't Explain** *Michael Bell* 74
2 cg f Lethal Force(IRE) Miss Universe (IRE) (Warning)
5365[2]

**Canufeelthelove** *Ben Haslam* a44
2 b f Sayif(IRE) Lady-Love (Pursuit Of Love)
8587[7] 9416[6]

**Canyon City** *Neil King* a21 87
4 b g Authorized(IRE) Colorado Dawn (Fantastic Light (USA))
6344[9]

**Capchop (FR)** *P Sogorb* a78 95
3 b g Captain Chop(FR) Gooseley Lane (Pyramus (USA))
1660a[4] 2561a[9]

**Cape Banjo (USA)** *Ralph Beckett* a86 85
4 ch g Cape Blanco(IRE) Magic Of Love (Magic Ring (IRE))
1598[2] 2233[4] 2960[5] 3785[4] 4413[9] 4893[7] 5747[7]

**Cape Bunting (IRE)** *Mark Johnston* a89 85
2 b f Cape Cross(IRE) Bergamask (USA) (Kingmambo (USA))
(4094)◆ (4848)◆ 5329[7] (6684)

**Cape Byron** *Roger Varian* 103
3 ch c Shamardal(USA) Reem Three (Mark Of Esteem (IRE))
(6870) 7845a[3]

**Cape Caster (IRE)** *Evan Williams* a67 87
6 br g Cape Cross(IRE) Playboy Mansion (IRE) (Grand Lodge (USA))
8038[9]

**Cape Coast** *Mark Johnston* a80 97
3 b c Cape Cross(IRE) Famusa (Medicean)
3342[6] 3720[4]◆ (4117) (4691) 4886[2]◆ 6675[2]

**Cape Cova (IRE)** *Michael Appleby* a101 108
4 b g Cape Cross(IRE) Sina Cova (IRE) (Barathea (IRE))
2797[4] 3594[3] 4033[17] 9259[2]◆

**Cape Cruiser (USA)** *Ralph Beckett* a62 54
3 ch g Cape Blanco(IRE) Skip A Dare (USA) (Skip Away (USA))
2711[8]◆ 3326[8]

**Cape Discovery** *Richard Hughes* a88 79
5 ch g Shamardal(USA) Kotsi (IRE) (Nayef (USA))
38[6] 173[8] 2041[4] 2752[11] 4712[4]

**Cape Hideaway** *Mark Walford* a55 66
5 b g Mount Nelson Amiata (Pennekamp (USA))
3340[5]

**Cape Icon** *Clive Cox* a93 78
6 b g Mount Nelson Cape Merino (Clantime)
4631[3] 6289[10]

**Cape Liberty (IRE)** *Simon Crisford* a48
2 b f Cape Cross(IRE) Sharqawiyah (Dubawi (IRE))
8796[10]

**Cape Love (USA)** *Mark Johnston* 64
4 ch g Cape Blanco(IRE) Matroshka (IRE) (Red Ransom (USA))
2079[8] 2773[8]

**Cape Of Eagles (USA)** *Fawzi Abdulla Nass* a71 59
3 b c Cape Blanco(IRE) Aj's Gal (USA) (Monashee Mountain (USA))
201a[9]

**Cape Of Glory (IRE)** *Keith Dalgleish* a89 91
4 br g Cape Cross(IRE) Stairway To Glory (IRE) (Kalanisi (IRE))
779[4] 4076[6] 4429[7]

**Cape Peninsular** *James Tate* a93 65
4 b m Cape Cross(IRE) Najam (Singspiel (IRE))
1583[3] (2164) 3235[3] 4357[2]◆ 5414[4] 7234[2] 8880[5] 9458[3]

**Cape Spirit (IRE)** *Andrew Balding* a59 59
5 b m Cape Cross(IRE) Fearless Spirit (USA) (Spinning World (USA))
121[2] 290[4] 741[2] 1191[9] 1369[6] 1458[5] 1754[5] 2272[5] 3026[12]

**Capesthorne (IRE)** *Sir Michael Stoute* 42
2 b f Oasis Dream Eleanora Duse (IRE) (Azamour (IRE))
5885[8]

**Cape To Cuba** *James Fanshawe* a81 82
3 b f Harbour Watch(IRE) Czarna Roza (Polish Precedent (USA))
2019[8] 3293[2] 4275[2] 6941[4] 7514[2] 8341[3] (8635) 8947[3]

**Capezzano (USA)** *Charlie Appleby* a92 77
3 b g Bernardini(USA) Cableknit (USA) (Unbridled's Song (USA))
697a[3] 1040a[3] 3997[18]

**Capital Flight (IRE)** *Paul Cole* 79
2 ch g Zoffany(IRE) Mackenzie's Friend (Selkirk (USA))
5641[3] 6403[7] 7392[8]

**Capital Gearing** *Leo Braem* a58 69
4 b g Makfi Dicara (GER) (Royal Applause)
26[5] 663[4] 1070a[5] 6125a[2] 6543a[8]

**Capitano (GER)** *J Hirschberger* 106
4 b h Paolini(GER) Carabiola (FR) (Grape Tree Road)
6987a[7] 7722a[6] 8622a[3]

**Capla Dancer (IRE)** *K R Burke* 73
2 ch f Red Jazz(USA) Greatest Dancer (IRE) (Iffraaj)
(1909) 2890[6] 4689[5]

**Capla Temptress (IRE)** *William Mott* a68 101
2 b f Lope De Vega(IRE) Mrs Beeton (IRE) (Dansili)
(3965) (5154) 5941[3]◆ (7206a) 8575a[7]

**Cap'N (IRE)** *Brendan Powell*
6 b g Gamut(IRE) Dawn Princess (IRE) (Old Vic)
8229[13]

**Capolavoro (FR)** *Robert Cowell* a79 73
6 b g Sulamani(IRE) Farnesina (FR) (Anabaa (USA))
513[5] 1450[2] 2064[5] (2346)

**Capomento (IRE)** *Tom Dascombe* 97
2 b f Casamento(IRE) Satin Cape (IRE) (Cape Cross (IRE))
(4689) 5329[2]◆ 6228a[4] 7578[7]

**Caponova (IRE)** *Tom Dascombe* a66 87
4 b g Bushranger(IRE) Satin Cape (IRE) (Cape Cross (IRE))
(2146)◆ 2558[6] 3744[7] 5330[6] 5924[5] 7024[10]

**Cappadocia (IRE)** *John James Feane* a66 70
7 b g Mujadil(USA) Green Vision (IRE) (Green Desert (USA))
5519a[7] 6797a[10]

**Cappananty Con** *Dean Ivory* a85 79
3 gr g Zebedee Fairmont (IRE) (Kingmambo (USA))
(264) 765[2] 877 1332[2] 2927[6] 3673[2] 4268[5] 4752[4] (5481) 6442[7] 7709[5] 8115[12] 8645[4] (9124) 9339[8]

**Cappielow Park** *Ali Stronge* a49 41
8 b g Exceed And Excel(AUS) Barakat (Bustino)
281[7] 508[4] 733[8]

**Capri (IRE)** *A P O'Brien* 121
3 gr c Galileo(IRE) Dialafara (FR) (Anabaa (USA))
1636a[4] 2442a[3] 3322[6] (4387a) (7147) 7668a[17]

**Capricious Cantor (IRE)** *Ed Dunlop* a95 99
4 b m Cape Cross(IRE) Alleluia (Caerleon (USA))
2999[5] 3883a[2] 5155[5] 5658[8] 6665a[6] 8121[2]◆

**Capriolette (IRE)** *Ed Walker* a60
2 b f Most Improved(IRE) Greta D'Argent (IRE) (Great Commotion (USA))
8748[4]

**Cap Rocat (FR)** *F-H Graffard* a74 98
4 ch g Siyouni(FR) Spain (FR) (Bering)
2696a[11]

**Captain America (SWE)** *Annike Bye Hansen* a78 100
7 b g Academy Award(IRE) Muja Maiy (IRE) (Mujadil (USA))
2943a[7] 6500a[2]

**Captain Bob (IRE)** *Philip Kirby* a75 76
6 b g Dark Angel(IRE) Birthday Present (Cadeaux Genereux)
501[3] 929[3] 1431[2] 2058[3] 2469[2] (2800) (4373) 6797a[7] 8906[2] 9029[9] 9176[5]

**Captain Bond** *David O'Meara* a61 35
3 b g Captain Gerrard(IRE) Forever's Girl (Monsieur Bond (IRE))
878[4]◆ 8217[6] 8931[7] 9216[6]

**Captain Cat (IRE)** *Tony Carroll* a101 82
8 bb g Dylan Thomas(IRE) Mother Of Pearl (IRE) (Sadler's Wells (USA))
118[5] 465[5] 680[6] 1079[4] 6873[11] 7619[19]

**Captain Cirdan (IRE)** *Marco Gasparini* 93
2 b c Big Bad Bob(IRE) Malikayah (IRE) (Fasliyev (USA))
4131a[5]

**Captain Cockle** *Roger Teal* a45 49
4 b g Indian Haven Demand (Red Ransom (USA))
5794[11] 7514[9] 8116[8] 8661[12]

**Captain Colby (USA)** *Ed Walker* a85 107
5 b g Bernstein(USA) Escape To Victory (Salse (USA))
1491[2] 2433[13] 2780[10] 4072[22] 5513[7] 7144[7] 8138[6] 8383[11]

**Captain Courageous (IRE)** *Ed Walker* a80 93
4 b g Canford Cliffs(IRE) Annacloy Pearl (IRE) (Mull Of Kintyre (USA))
164[2] (641)◆ 1462[5] 2477[5] (3036) 3282[4] (4085) 5032[3] 6422[4] 7582[15]

**Captain Dion** *F Birrane* a93 95
4 gr g Equiano(FR) Bandanna (Bandmaster (USA))
219[3] (403)◆ 598[3] 1103[2] 1454[6] 1794[4] 5705[7] 6662[11] (7553) 7594[5] 9247a[8]

**Captain Felix** *James Eustace* a78 76
5 b g Captain Gerrard(IRE) Sweet Applause (IRE) (Acclamation)
4699[3]◆ 5477[6]

**Captain George (IRE)** *Michael Blake* a69 67
6 b g Bushranger(IRE) High Society Girl (IRE) (Key Of Luck (USA))
1937[5] 4840[4] 5274[3] 6309[7]

**Captain Hawk** *Ian Williams* a67 69
3 b g Acclamation Vintage Gardenia (Selkirk (USA))
2927[7] 3715[5] 4610[7] 5326[4] 6016[8] 6638[7] 7323[4] (8210) 8401[7]

**Captain James (FR)** *Mrs C Gilbert* a18 49
7 bb g Linngari(IRE) Chopassing (FR) (Indian Rocket)
(2672a) (3958a) (4143a)

**Captain Jameson (IRE)** *John Quinn* 86
2 b g Camacho Cross Section (USA) (Cape Cross (IRE))
5576[3] 6312[3] (7013) 8008[3] (8741)

**Captain Joe** *Brian Barr* a6 70
6 ch g Captain Gerrard(IRE) Bond Shakira (Daggers Drawn (USA))
1603[14]

**Captain K (IRE)** *Gordon Elliott* a51 46
5 b g Captain Rio Zenana (IRE) (Lucky Guest)
51[7]◆ 123[5] 222[5] 334[2] 614[4] 644[5] 1563[3]

**Captain Kendall (IRE)** *Harry Chisman* a49 19
8 b g Clodovil(IRE) Queen's Lace (IRE) (King's Best (USA))
167[4] 544[7] 860[13] 8473[12]

**Captain Kissinger** *Jo Hughes* a53 56
2 b g Captain Gerrard(IRE) Nigella (Band On The Run)
1496[8] 2277[5] 2292[4] 5627a[5] 6613[9]

**Captain Lars (SAF)** *Derek Shaw* a88 82
7 b g Captain Al(SAF) Polar Charge (Polar Falcon (USA))
71[6] 851[4] 1185[5] (1487) 1586[5] 5241[11] 5612[4] 5929[2] 6185[5] 6794[6] 7137[8] 7405[9] 7738[9] 8260[9] (8906) 9124[6] (9305) 9443[5]

**Captain Marmalade (IRE)** *Jimmy Fox* a51 60
5 gr g Duke Of Marmalade(IRE) Elisium (Proclamation (IRE))
2763[8] 3661[5] 4180[3] 4713[6] 5713[5] 6503[5] (6751) 7216[10]

**Captain Morley** *David Simcock* a81 104
6 b g Hernando(FR) Oval Office (Pursuit Of Love)
8468[9]

**Captain Navarre** *Charlie Fellowes* a89 78
5 b g Excellent Art Quantum (IRE) (Alhaarth (IRE))
7024[8] 8047[7] (8505) (9082) 9434[4]

**Captain Peacock** *William Knight* a90 83
4 b g Champs Elysees Blast Furnace (IRE) (Sadler's Wells (USA))
(1684) (2020) 2752[8] 3458[6] 4370[9] 5303[5] 6273[8] 7096[6] 7880[4]

**Captain Peaky** *Patrick Holmes* a64 60
4 b g Captain Gerrard(IRE) Multi-Sofft (Northern State (USA))
2140[13] 2996[4] 3196[3] 4687[10] 4851[6] 5258[8] 9128[3]

**Captain Pugwash (IRE)** *Henry Spiller* a72 68
3 b g Sir Prancealot(IRE) Liscoa (IRE) (Foxhound (USA))
5031[2]◆ 5783[2] 6387[8] 7061[6] 8327[11] (9142) 9432[2]

**Captain Revelation** *Michael Mullineaux* a90 76
5 ch g Captain Rio Agony Aunt (Formidable I (USA))
5[5] 156[6] 1074[3] 1562[7] 2685[7] 3540[4] 4529[3] 6014[8] 6564[8] 8386[18] 9029[6]◆ 9180[4] 9303[4]

**Captain Ryan** *Geoffrey Deacon* a64 67
6 b g Captain Gerrard(IRE) Ryan's Quest (IRE) (Mukaddamah (USA))
2214[5] 2509[2] 3008[3] 3811[2] 4731[3] 5429[8] 6004[2] 6478[7] 7694[2] 8298[8]

**Captain Scooby** *Richard Guest* a61 49
11 b g Captain Rio Scooby Dooby Do (Atraf)
21[7] 2034[10] 2589[8] 3256[7] 3468[9] 3915[10] 4478[5] 4789[9] 5252[5] 5377[6] 5567[3] 6041[9] 6148[7] 7191[6] 7693[3] 7926[10] 8128[7] 8298[12] 8329[6] 8558[5] 8656[9] 9102[5] 9232[7] 9265[8] 9340[7] 9374[5]

**Captain Sedgwick (IRE)** *John Spearing* a50 56
3 b f Approve(IRE) Alinda (IRE) (Revoque (IRE))
600[8] 764[4] 1192[DSQ] 1428[8] 2309[3] 3823[U] 4150[5] (4968) 5714[2] 7005[5] 7991[8] 8675[8] 9217[6]

**Captain Sue (IRE)** *Ian Williams* a68 67
3 ch f Tamayuz Correct (Oasis Dream)
1601[7] 4892[10] 7911[10]

**Captain Swift (IRE)** *John Mackie* a69 59
6 br g Captain Rio Grannys Reluctance (IRE) (Anita's Prince)
218[2] 423[3] 616[4] 2162[3] 7413[5] 7983[7] 8396[7] 8655[3] (8955) 9421[4]

**Captain Vancouver (FR)** *M D O'Callaghan* a79 79
2 b g George Vancouver(USA) Asiana (FR) (Westerner)
8082a[7]

**Captive (FR)** *Richard Hannon* a56 20
3 b g Kyllachy Ukraine (IRE) (Cape Cross (IRE))
2782[10] 3691[13]

**Capton** *Henry Candy* a64 96
4 b g Cape Cross(IRE) Flavian (Catrail (USA))
1683[2] 3750[12] 5363[2] (6195) (7132) 8165[2]

**Captor** *David Simcock* a58 63
3 b g Frankel Hasten (IRE) (Montjeu (IRE))
3342[7] 4808[10] 5364[9]

**Cap Verite (IRE)** *N Clement* a67 100
3 b f Cape Cross(IRE) Ghar Shoop (IRE) (Dubai Destination (USA))
4654a[6] (6914a) 7634a[8]

**Caracas** *Harry Dunlop* a68
3 b g Cacique(IRE) Bourbonella (Rainbow Quest (USA))
328[6] 6623[8] 7711[8] 8157[4] 8647[2] 9158[7]

**Caradoc (IRE)** *Ed Walker* a72
2 b c Camelot Applause (IRE) (Danehill Dancer (IRE))
9201[4]◆

**Caramuru (IRE)** *Richard Hannon* a71 27
3 b g Casamento(IRE) Zaynaba (IRE) (Traditionally (USA))
2152[11]

**Caravaggio (USA)** *A P O'Brien* a94 124
3 gr c Scat Daddy(USA) Mekko Hokte (USA) (Holy Bull (USA))
(2863a) (4030) 4907[4] 5690a[6] (6973a) 8230[3]

**Caravagio (FR)** *Alain Couetil* a100 87
4 ch h American Post Semire (FR) (Mizoram (USA))
9003a[4]

**Caravela (IRE)** *Mick Channon* 78
3 b f Henrythenavigator(USA) Stella Point (IRE) (Pivotal)
3309[3]◆ 6236[2] (6941) 7598[7]

**Carbon Dating (IRE)** *John Patrick Shanahan* a42 110
5 b g The Carbon Unit(USA) Advertising Space (IRE) (Galileo (IRE))
82a[2] 202a[2] 540a[4] 699a[5] 890a[8] (1802) 2571[7] 3057a[5] 6440[7]

**Carbutt's Ridge (IRE)** *N Caullery* a59 59
4 br g Alfred Nobel(IRE) Tallassee (Indian Ridge (IRE))
6125a[6]

**Carcharias (IRE)** *Ed de Giles* a56 68
4 b g Kodiac Princess Atoosa (USA) (Gone West (USA))
1729[11] 3906[5] 4459[2] 4846[2] 5049[7] 6102[10] 6503[2] 6725[4] 7770[9]

**Cardaw Lily (IRE)** *Richard Hughes* a52 71
2 b f Lawman(FR) Chervil (Dansili)
2563[4] 2905[6] 7126[11] 7876[7] 8349[19] 9122[6]

**Card High (IRE)** *Wilf Storey* a79 81
7 b g Red Clubs(IRE) Think (FR) (Marchand De Sable (USA))
509[7] 1307[6] 1719[4] 3046[7] 3527[2]

**Cardsharp** *Mark Johnston* 110
2 b c Lonhro(AUS) Pure Illusion (IRE) (Danehill (USA))
(2292) 2607[4] (3297) (3556)◆ 3993[3] (4812) 5570[3] 6446[3] 7618[3] 8037[5]

**Carducci** *Richard Hannon* a67 80
3 b f Poet's Voice Gee Kel (IRE) (Danehill Dancer (IRE))
2274[8] 2754[2] (3217) 4050[6] 5113[4] 5549[2] 6274[8] 7710[10]

**Careyanne** *Brian Baugh* a42 46
3 ch f Mount Nelson Mayaar (USA) (Grand Slam (USA))
1889[9] 3393[8] 4332[7] 5898[9]

**Caribbean Spring (IRE)** *George Margarson* a63 59
4 b g Dark Angel(IRE) Bogini (IRE) (Holy Roman Emperor (IRE))
1894[4] (2312) 2976[7] 3263[4] 4627[13] 4971[12] 6112[7] 6847[6] 8031[6] 8307[4] 9084[8]

**Caridade (USA)** *Kevin Ryan* 81
3 b f Medaglia d'Oro(USA) Raffle Ticket (USA) (A.P. Indy (USA))
2898[4]◆ 4378[4] (5538)◆ 6358[5] 7130[6] 7822[9]

**Carigrad (IRE)** *Hugo Palmer* a71 88
3 b g Excelebration(IRE) Blissful Beat (Beat Hollow)
1488[3] (1829) 2612[3] 4048[4] 4580[2] 4618[2]

**Carina Mia (USA)** *Chad C Brown* a113
4 bb m Malibu Moon(USA) Miss Simpatia (ARG) (Southern Halo (USA))
8605a[3]

**Caring Touch (USA)** *Saeed bin Suroor* a80
2 b f Elusive Quality(USA) Blue Petrel (USA) (Distorted Humor (USA))
(9099)◆

**Carlini (IRE)** *Brian Meehan* 61
2 b c Zoffany(IRE) Taking Liberties (IRE) (Royal Academy (USA))
5105[9] 6057[8] 6921[7]

**Carlovian** *Mark Walford* a53 57
4 b g Acclamation Mimisel (Selkirk (USA))
1978[12] 2989[3] 3979[3] (4743) (5285) 5848[3] 6131[5] 6783[2] 7389[5] 7703[4] 7980[7]

**Carlton Choice (IRE)** *Louis Baudron* a84 84
3 b g Bushranger(IRE) Choice House (USA) (Chester House (USA))
1774[10] 5521a[5]

**Carlton Frankie** *Michael Easterby* 90
3 b f Equiano(FR) Valiant Runner (Haafhd)
(1828) (2271) 3844[15] 5574[8] 6450[14] 8012[13]

**Carnageo (FR)** *Richard Fahey* a55 92
4 b g Pivotal Sudarynya (IRE) (Sadler's Wells (USA))
1517[8] 2226[7] 2838[4]◆ 3451[3] (4207) 5668[14] 6349[4] (6965) 7555[5] 8048[9]

**Carnival King (IRE)** *Amy Murphy* a79 84
5 b g Arcano(IRE) Validate (Alhaarth (IRE))
2081[8] 2833[9] 5064[5] 5719[3] 6273[7] 7759[9] 8434[9] 8797[2]◆

**Carntop** *Ralph Beckett* 106
4 b g Dansili Milford Sound (Barathea (IRE))
2604[9] 3323[3] 4614[10] 5638[8]

**Carol (IRE)** *Ed Dunlop* a74 78
3 b f Acclamation Miss Topsy Turvy (IRE) (Mr Greeley (USA))
2269[4]◆ 2929[2] 3507[4] (4145) 4845[4] 6818[4] 7364[6]

**Carolinae** *Charlie Fellowes* a91 89
5 ch m Makfi You Too (Monsun (GER))
(499) (964) 1771[7] 2805[6] 4051[3] 4536[2] 5308a[11] 9418[3]

**Caroline Piano (FR)** *Henk Grewe* a60 67
3 bb f Campanologist(USA) Mei (FR) (Shamardal (USA))
8959a[10]

**Carolyn's Voice** *Stuart Williams* a26 29
2 br f Poet's Voice Two Days In Paris (FR) (Authorized (IRE))
8347[11] 9335[8]

**Carouse (IRE)** *Andrew Balding* 83
2 b g Excelebration(IRE) Terre Du Vent (FR) (Kutub (IRE))
2607[6] 3576[2] 4799[3] 5596[5] 6674[7]

**Carpathian (FR)** *Jean-Pierre Carvalho* 99
4 b h Elusive City(USA) Comnena (Tiger Hill (IRE))
2667a[9]

**Carpe Diem Lady (IRE)** *Ralph Beckett* a68 81
4 b m Acclamation Greenisland (IRE) (Fasliyev (USA))
2087[3] (3773)◆ 4536[5] 4910[7] 6555[10]

**Carpet Time (IRE)** *David Barron* 18
2 b g Intense Focus(USA) Beal Ban (IRE) (Daggers Drawn (USA))
6056[7]

**Carp Kid (IRE)** *Jamie Osborne* a70 68
2 b c Lope De Vega(IRE) Homegrown (IRE) (Mujadil (USA))
7391[6] 7739[5] 8149[7] 8702[8] (8943) 9097[9] (9300) 9466[4]◆

**Carragold** *Antony Brittain* a74 74
11 b g Diktat Shadow Roll (IRE) (Mark Of Esteem (IRE))
1864[8]

**Carrera** *Mrs A Malzard* a30 48
7 b g Sixties Icon Aileen's Gift (IRE) (Rainbow Quest (USA))
1933a[4] 2672a[7] 3958a[3]

**Carricklane** *Richard Hughes* a65
2 b f Zoffany(IRE) New River (IRE) (Montjeu (IRE))
4007[2]

**Carrigeen Prince (IRE)** *Garvan Donnelly* a72 72
5 ch g Strategic Prince Hi Lyla (IRE) (Lahib (USA))
3197[6]

**Carrington (FR)** *Charlie Appleby* a86 91
4 b g New Approach(IRE) Winning Family (IRE) (Fasliyev (USA))
1608[5]

**Carrouges (IRE)** *Simone Brogi* 68
2 b f So You Think(NZ) Castle Cross (IRE) (Cape Cross (IRE))
5815a[4]

**Carry On Deryck** *Saeed bin Suroor* a93 113
5 b g Halling(USA) Mullein (Oasis Dream)
6105[3] 6746a[5] 7619[8]

**Cartavio (IRE)** *Andrew Balding* a64 72
3 b g Cacique(IRE) Star Cluster (Observatory (USA))
40[5] 437[5] 737[8] (3088) 3484[8] 4082[5]

**Carthage (IRE)** *Brian Ellison* a69 71
6 b g Mastercraftsman(IRE) Pitrizzia (Lando (GER))
2741[10] 3947[4] 4357[5] 5008[8] 6901[6] 7359[7]

**Cartographer** *Martyn Meade* a79 97
3 b f Henrythenavigator(USA) Right Answer (Lujain (USA))
(2970) 3822[3] (4317) 4813[13] 5422[2] 8991[9]

**Cartwright** *Sir Mark Prescott Bt* a101 91
4 b g High Chaparral(IRE) One So Marvellous (Nashwan (USA))
(2461)◆ 2797[5] 3928[13] (6793)

**Carvelas (IRE)** *P J F Murphy* a64 61
8 b g Cape Cross(IRE) Caraiyma (IRE) (Shahrastani (USA))
(924) 1191[5]

**Casablanca (IRE)** *Andrew Balding* a77 77
4 b m Cape Blanco(IRE) Wonderful Town (USA) (Bernstein (USA))
576[4] 780[2] (894) 1175[3]

**Casaclare (IRE)** *Jonjo O'Neill* 66
3 b g Casamento(IRE) Sarah Ann (IRE) (Orpen (USA))
3431[6] 6509[2] 7085[10]

**Casa Comigo (IRE)** *John Best* a62 49
2 b c Cape Cross(IRE) Belanoiva (IRE) (Motivator)
7391[12] 8643[7]

**Casado (IRE)** *John Best* a64 53
3 b g Casamento(IRE) Sense Of Greeting (IRE) (Key Of Luck (USA))
1736[11] 2315[6] 4006[3] 4748[5] 5793[8] 6257[10]

**Cascadian** *A Fabre* 98
2 ch c New Approach(IRE) Falls Of Lora (IRE) (Street Cry (IRE))
5978a[2]

**Case Key** *Michael Appleby* a45 78
4 gr g Showcasing Fluttering Rose (Compton Place)
3816[5] 4201[4] 4489[2] 5035[2] (6197) 7086[11] 8186[3] 8600[15] 9220[10]

**Casemates Square (IRE)** *Ian Williams* a58 46
3 b g Casamento(IRE) Marhaba (Nayef (USA))
5757[5] 5894[7] 6291[3] 8674[3]

**Casement (IRE)** *Roger Charlton* 84
3 b g Casamento(IRE) Kirk Wynd (Selkirk (USA))
2476[7]◆ 5611[3] (6368) 7132[7] 8078[2]

**Casey Banter** *Julia Feilden* a46 45
2 bb f Holy Roman Emperor(IRE) Sinister Ruckus (USA) (Trippi (USA))
4620[3] 5507[7] 6140[10] 6790[3] 8780[11]

**Cashla Bay** *John Gosden* a78 81
3 b f Fastnet Rock(AUS) Rose Blossom (Pastoral Pursuits)
3167[3] 3822[8] 8717[6] 9074[4]

**Cashman (FR)** *A Wohler* a72 102
4 ch h Soldier Of Fortune(IRE) Crystals Sky (FR) (Hernando (FR))
4130a[2] 4931a[2] 6173a[5] 6987a[5] 8463a[10]

**Casima** *Clive Cox* a60 56
2 b f Dark Angel(IRE) Caskelena (IRE) (Galileo (IRE))
5660[8] 6575[6] 7997[10]

**Casimiro (IRE)** *Roger Charlton* a88 87
3 ch g Casamento(IRE) Glyndebourne (USA) (Rahy (USA))
(2090) 3578[4] 5744[6] 7736[4]

**Casina Di Notte (IRE)** *Marco Botti* a82 80
3 ch g Casamento(IRE) Nightswimmer (IRE) (Noverre (USA))
2145[6] 3443[2] 4050[10] 4983[9] (5510) 7759[7]

**Casou (FR)** *L Gadbin* a40 27
3 b c Casamento(IRE) Ourika (IRE) (Danehill Dancer (IRE))
4943a[11]

**Caspian Gold (IRE)**
*Richard Hughes* a38 46
3 ch g Born To Sea(IRE) Eminence Gift (Cadeaux Genereux)
1790[9] 2371[10] 3250[13] 4180[11]

**Caspian Prince (IRE)** *Tony Coyle* a115 116
8 ch g Dylan Thomas(IRE) Crystal Gaze (IRE) (Rainbow Quest (USA))
84a[3] 543a[5] 773a[3] 932a[3] 1044a[7] 2573[5] 3092[9] (3321) 3829[4] (4927a) 6973a[4] 7396[10] 8845[5]

**Cassilero (GER)** *K Demme* a65 28
6 b h Creachadoir(IRE) Cassilera (GER) (Anzillero (GER))
8463a[8]

**Cassini (IRE)** *John Gosden* 77
2 b c Galileo(IRE) Chrysanthemum (IRE) (Danehill Dancer (IRE))
5840[3] 7128[3]

**Castanea** *Ronald Harris* a46 25
5 ch g Pivotal Invitee (Medicean)
425[6] 621[4] 880[5] 1082[11] 4470[8]

**Castellated** *Richard Hannon* a72 78
3 b f Teofilo(IRE) Portal (Hernando (FR))
2118[9] 3291[6] 3721[6] (4442)

**Casterbridge** *Eric Alston* a81 80
5 b g Pastoral Pursuits Damalis (IRE) (Mukaddamah (USA))
1805[U] 2184[4] 2621[5] (3170) 3239[5] 3707[4] 4249[8] 5580[5] 5827[5] 7137[7] 7737[4] 8321[2] (8557) (8927) 9366[5]

**Casterton (IRE)** *A Fabre* 104
3 b c Fastnet Rock(AUS) Chenchikova (IRE) (Sadler's Wells (USA))
6913a[3] 7634a[6]

**Castilo Del Diablo (IRE)**
*David Simcock* a86 74
8 br g Teofilo(IRE) Hundred Year Flood (USA) (Giant's Causeway (USA))
197[8] 746[8] 1027[5] 1240[4] 1457[6] 4519[6] 5663[8]

**Castleacre** *James Tate* a80 90
3 ch f Exceed And Excel(AUS) Cloud Castle (In The Wings)
1901[6] 3159[4] 6619[6]

**Castle Dream (FR)** *K Borgel* 76
3 b g Wootton Bassett Haut La Main (IRE) (Beat Hollow)
4783a[5] (8960a)

**Castle Guest (IRE)** *M Halford* a75 96
8 b g Rock Of Gibraltar(IRE) Castelletto (Komaite (USA))
4822a[11]

**Castle Harbour** *John Gosden* a96 105
4 b g Kyllachy Gypsy Carnival (Trade Fair)
1493[9] 1902[3] 3003[5] 3963[27]

**Castle Hill Cassie (IRE)**
*Ben Haslam* a82 77
3 ch f Casamento(IRE) Angel Bright (IRE) (Dark Angel (IRE))
1401[2] 2078[3] (3054) 5697[2] 6149[4] (7241) 8150[4]

**Castlelyons (IRE)** *Robert Stephens* a95 76
5 br g Papal Bull Summercove (IRE) (Cape Cross (IRE))
4216[4] 5397[8] 6887[10] (8672) (9055)

**Castlerea Tess** *Sarah Hollinshead* a61 66
4 ch m Pastoral Pursuits Zartwyda (IRE) (Mozart (IRE))
51[2] (494) 1062[3] 1246[4] 1842[8] (1979) 2306[7] (3290) 3666[7] (4149) 4844[7] 8427[13]

**Castle Talbot (IRE)** *Tom Clover* a60 70
5 b g Rock Of Gibraltar(IRE) Louve Sacree (USA) (Seeking The Gold (USA))
2731[3] 4320[4] 5261[2] 5854[2] 7028[6] 8327[6]

**Catalinas Diamond (IRE)**
*Pat Murphy* a50 62
9 b m One Cool Cat(USA) Diamondiferous (USA) (Danzig (USA))
2043[6] 2509[5] 2724[4] 3280[6] 3811[5] 4148[6] 4735[5]

**Catalyze** *Paddy Butler* a41 62
9 b g Tumblebrutus(USA) Clarita Dear (CHI) (Hussonet (USA))
211[7] 438[10] 544[8] 644[9] 1219[8] 1304[5] 1723[10]

**Catapult** *Clifford Lines* a53 69
2 b g Equiano(FR) Alectrona (FR) (Invincible Spirit (IRE))
3169[4] 3516[5] 4696[5] 5440[8] 7491[9] 8120[2]◆ 8560[12] 8794[8]

**Catastrophe** *John Quinn* a65 65
4 b g Intikhab(USA) Mrs Snaffles (IRE) (Indian Danehill (IRE))
68[4] 361[7] 3048[8] 4432[2] 5074[2] 5649[2] 6092[10] 6549[12] 7271[3] 7979[2] (8650)

**Cat Ballou** *David O'Meara* a27 41
2 ch f Equiano(FR) Flamenco Dancer (Mark Of Esteem (IRE))
6086[6] 6567[10] 8850[10] 9024[9]

**Cat Burglar (USA)** *Bob Baffert* a105
7 ch h Unbridled's Song(USA) Be My Prospect (USA) (Forest Wildcat (USA))
5194a[3]

**Catch A Wave (IRE)**
*Debbie Mountain* 84
3 b g Approve(IRE) Casablanca Jewel (IRE) (Kalanisi (IRE))
933a[10]

**Catcher On The Go (IRE)**
*Evan Williams* 82
7 b g Catcher In The Rye(IRE) Suspicious Minds (Anabaa (USA))
(5563) 6033[5]

**Catch The Pigeon** *Ed de Giles* a52 52
2 ch f Paco Boy(IRE) Jasmick (IRE) (Definite Article)
4749[6] 5216[6] 5356[6] 6063[5] 6585[13] 7057[12] 8027[8]

**Catch The Tide (FR)** *Henry Spiller* a54
2 ch f Kendargent(FR) Coiffure (King's Best (USA))
9099[6]

**Catchy Lass (IRE)**
*Anthony Mulholland* a79 57
8 b m Catcher In The Rye(IRE) Liseraw Lass (IRE) (Grand Lodge (USA))
3341[9]

**Catheadans Fury** *Martin Bosley*
3 ch f Firebreak Dualagi (Royal Applause)
8504[12]

**Catherinethegrace (IRE)**
*Jimmy Fox* a24
3 gr f Duke Of Marmalade(IRE) Little Miss Gracie (Efisio)
9202[12] 9455[10]

**Cathie's Dream (USA)** *Noel Wilson* 23
2 b f More Than Ready(USA) Mantilla (USA) (Gone West (USA))
2988[8] 3846[8] 8483[7]

**Catholic Boy (USA)**
*Jonathan Thomas* a112 111
2 b c More Than Ready(USA) Song Of Bernadette (USA) (Bernardini (USA))
8577a[4]

**Cativo Ragazzo** *John E Long*
2 b c Multiplex Sea Isle (Selkirk (USA))
8888[14]

**Catoca (USA)** *Ed Walker* a66
2 b f Lemon Drop Kid(USA) Catrageous (USA) (Tale Of The Cat (USA))
8670[4] 9081[8]

**Cat Royale (IRE)** *John Butler* a72 72
4 b g Lilbourne Lad(IRE) Call This Cat (IRE) (One Cool Cat (USA))
47[2] 954[7] 1449[3] 1729[8] 2615[12] 3208[14] (4982) 5895[3] 7495[10] 8429[4] 8993[11]

**Cat Silver** *Charlie Wallis* a66 74
4 b g Dansili Catopuma (USA) (Elusive Quality (USA))
2291[5] 2960[12] 3718[7] (4695) 6113[5] 6442[5] 7408[9] 8158[11]

**Catskill** *Wilf Storey* a12
3 b f Dutch Art Catfish (IRE) (One Cool Cat (USA))
357[7] 2924[9] 3404[10] 4105[13]

**Catwilldo (IRE)** *Garvan Donnelly* a65 58
7 b m One Cool Cat(USA) Hypocrisy (Bertolini (USA))
5995[4] 6798a[6]

**Cavalieri (IRE)** *Philip Kirby* a72 66
7 b g Oratorio(IRE) Always Attractive (IRE) (King's Best (USA))
28[3] 399[3] 519[7] 759[6] 1344[3] (1834) 2549[4] 3464[7] 3566[3] 5008[10] 5896[3] 6569[5] 7248[9] 8187[8]

**Cavalry Regiment** *John Quinn* a45 42
2 gr g Lethal Force(IRE) Saddlers Bend (IRE) (Refuse To Bend (IRE))
5755[6] 6853[7] 7593[9] 8536[9]

**Cavalseulles (FR)** *L Gadbin* a77 64
3 bl f Le Havre(IRE) Courseulles (FR) (Monsun (GER))
4232a[9]

**Cavaprun (FR)** *D Guillemin* a95 80
3 b g Siyouni(FR) Atabaska (FR) (Ashkalani (IRE))
(8305a)

**Cavatina** *William Haggas* a76 70
2 b f Lethal Force(IRE) Piano (Azamour (IRE))
6064[4] 6875[3] (7995)

**Cavendish Place** *David Brown* 44
2 b g Doncaster Rover(USA) Beauty Pageant (IRE) (Bahamian Bounty)
4996[9] 5537[9]

**Caviar Royale** *Nikki Evans* 63
2 b g Royal Applause Precious Secret (IRE) (Fusaichi Pegasus (USA))
6070[10] 6654[10] 6867[8] 8013[12] 8870[13]

**Caymus** *Tracy Waggott* a29 50
4 b m Compton Place Midnight Sky (Desert Prince (IRE))
1828[11] 2994[10] 3563[9]

**Cead Mile Failte (FR)**
*Matthieu Palussiere* 83
2 b f Dabirsim(FR) Wave City (IRE) (Elusive City (USA))
(3515a) 4596a[3] 5448a[7]

**Cecchini (IRE)** *Ralph Beckett* a85
2 br f Rip Van Winkle(IRE) Urban Daydream (IRE) (Oasis Dream)
(8669)◆

**Cecilator** *Noel Williams* 61
3 b f Delegator Cecily Parsley (Fantastic Light (USA))
1944[14] 2468[4] 2760[4] 3425[9] 3864[8] 4914[6] 5986a[3]

**Ce De Nullis (IRE)** *Paul Midgley* 70
2 ch f Dandy Man(IRE) Plym (Notnowcato)
3557[3] 3826[4] 4555[5] 5440[4] 6036[2] 7734[14] 8288[11]

**Cee Jay** *Patrick Chamings* a63 60
4 ch g Kyllachy Intermission (IRE) (Royal Applause)
217[3] 604[5] 2214[4] 2724[10] (4458) 6004[3] 7191[5] 8551[10]

**Ceilidhs Dream** *Ralph Beckett* a66
2 b f Oasis Dream Ceilidh House (Selkirk (USA))
8668[3]

**Ce La Vie** *Keith Dalgleish* 82
3 ch f Dutch Art Chase The Lady (USA) (Atticus (USA))
1387a[7] 2434[13] 2817[4] 7702[5] 8385[8]

**Celebration** *G M Lyons* 103
4 b g Equiano(FR) Bold Bidder (Indesatchel (IRE))
4416a[6] 4925a[3] 6971a[14]

**Celebration Day (IRE)**
*Simon Crisford* a90 93
4 b g Raven's Pass(USA) Bunting (Shaadi (USA))
(1323) 2068[2] (3235) 4002[7] (4976) 6007[8]

**Celebrity (GER)** *D Moser* 94
3 b f Shamardal(USA) Cherry Danon (IRE) (Rock Of Gibraltar (IRE))
3882a[7] (6605a)

**Celerity (IRE)** *Lisa Williamson* a52 49
3 ch f Casamento(IRE) Shinko Dancer (IRE) (Shinko Forest (IRE))
76[7] 264[9] 496[3] 787[4] 960[2] 1127[2] 1221[6] 1363[6] 1418[4] 1580[5] 1688[9] 2065[8] 2362[6] 3544[6] 4148[9] 5052[7] 5252[2] 5703[4] 6004[10] 6339[5] 8558[10] 8681[5]

**Celestation** *Mark Johnston* a78 80
3 b f Excelebration(IRE) Coventina (IRE) (Daylami (IRE))
2302[2]◆ 2513[3] 2929[8] 4056[2] 4431[2] 4798[3] 5163[3] 5439[7] 5650[12] 7142[8] 7762[4] (8205)

**Celeste Mogador (FR)**
*T Castanheira*
4 b m Alexandros Gentle Tap (Beat Hollow)
1181a[7]

**Celestial Bay** *Sylvester Kirk* a80 75
8 b m Septieme Ciel(USA) Snowy Mantle (Siberian Express (USA))
38[7] 213[4] 497[9]

**Celestial Dancer (FR)**
*Nigel Twiston-Davies* a52 24
5 bb m Dr Fong(USA) Rabeera (Beat Hollow)
98[9] 508[6] 741[6] 1402[6]

**Celestial Spheres (IRE)**
*Charlie Appleby* a94 93
3 b g Redoute's Choice(AUS) Copernica (IRE) (Galileo (IRE))
1518[5] (8561) 8880[12] (9467)

**Celestin's** *William Haggas* 71
2 b f Cacique(IRE) Veenwouden (Desert Prince (IRE))
7265[2]◆ 7906[2] 8323[4]

**Celsiana** *Marcus Tregoning* a31
3 ch f Sepoy(AUS) Generous Lady (Generous (IRE))
8822[10]

**Celtic Artisan (IRE)**
*Rebecca Menzies* a74 72
6 ch g Dylan Thomas(IRE) Perfectly Clear (USA) (Woodman (USA))
147[5] 361[8] (605) (636) 757[4] (1334) 1449[5] 2301[3] 3898[5] 4893[9] 5510[6] 6266[4] 6946[7] 7792[3]

**Celtic Ava (IRE)** *Pat Phelan* a66 56
5 b m Peintre Celebre(USA) Denices Desert (Green Desert (USA))
120[4]

**Celtic Power** *Jim Goldie* a47 70
5 b g Rail Link Biloxi (Caerleon (USA))
2427[5] 3043[10] 3978[7] 4244[4] 5008[4] 5413[6] 5923[5] 7248[8] 7982[8]

**Celtik Secret** *Hughie Morrison* 63
3 ro f Sakhee's Secret Cill Rialaig (Environment Friend)
2908[6] 3615[10] 4224[7] 5867[5] 6812[5]

**Cenotaph (USA)** *A P O'Brien* a93 93
5 b g War Front(USA) Sanserif (IRE) (Fasliyev (USA))
4416a[15] 5530[12] 8222a[3]

**Cent Flying** *William Muir* 53
2 b g Sepoy(AUS) Sea Of Leaves (USA) (Stormy Atlantic (USA))
2750[10] 3622[6] 3917[9] 6609[4] 7081[11]

**Central City (IRE)** *Hugo Palmer* a81 78
2 b g Kodiac She Basic (IRE) (Desert Prince (IRE))
2134[4] 2522[3]◆ 3754[4] 3999[4] 5572[9] 6128[2] (6951)◆ 7335[6] 7787[2] 8871[2]

**Central Square (IRE)** *Roger Varian* 111
5 b g Azamour(IRE) Lucky Clio (IRE) (Key Of Luck (USA))
2396[3] 4069[11] 4918[9] 5436[4] 6243a[3] 7619[32]

**Centre Haafhd** *Kenneth Slack* a46 53
6 b g Haafhd Deira Dubai (Green Desert (USA))
579[11] 1106[7] 5467[11]

**Century Dream (IRE)**
*Simon Crisford* 111
3 b c Cape Cross(IRE) Salacia (IRE) (Echo Of Light)
2132[3] 2824[4] (4299) (4961) 5392[6] (7609) (8423)

**Ceol Na Nog (IRE)** *J S Bolger* 95
4 b m Teofilo(IRE) Ard Fheis (IRE) (Lil's Boy (USA))
4822a[2] 6334a[6]

**Ceramist** *John Gosden* 72
2 b f Mastercraftsman(IRE) Dalasyla (IRE) (Marju (IRE))
6037[3]◆

**Cerastes (TUR)**
*Ibrahim Bekirogullari* a104
3 b c Always A Classic(CAN) Alcina (TUR) (Beau Genius (CAN))
6717a[2]

**Cersei** *F Rohaut* a92 98
4 b m Invincible Spirit(IRE) Elle Galante (GER) (Galileo (IRE))
1159a[5] 4234a[5]

**Certaldo (FR)** *C Ferland* 63
3 b g Wootton Bassett Cazorla (IRE) (Entrepreneur)
6084a[4]

**Certificate** *Conor Dore* a103 94
6 ch g Pivotal Graduation (Lomitas)
2610[4] 4072[24] 6419[14] 7603[3] 9233[8]

**Cerulean Silk** *Tony Carroll* a51 44
7 b m Striking Ambition Cerulean Rose (Bluegrass Prince (IRE))
311[11]

**C'Est No Mour (GER)** *Peter Hedger* a48 89
4 b h Champs Elysees C'Est L'Amour (GER) (Whipper (USA))
1420[9] 2039[11] 2689[6] (3683) (4413) 5663[3] (6513) (7096)◆ 7651[6]

**Ceyhan** *Jamie Osborne* a79 66
5 ch g Rock Of Gibraltar(IRE) Alla Prima (IRE) (In The Wings)
353[2]◆ 457[3] 687[2] 1818[5] 4202[5] 4840[8] 6076[5] 6799a[7] (9127) 9430[2]

**Chabelita** *F Rohaut* a94 90
3 b f Lawman(FR) Chabelle (Shirocco (GER))
8986a[7]

**Chagatai (IRE)** *Clive Cox* 88
2 b g Kodiac Golden Shine (Royal Applause)
(1767)◆ 3010[5]

**Chai Chai (IRE)** *Andrew Balding* a54 76
2 b g Zoffany(IRE) Flamenco Red (Warning)
3066[5] 4083[3]◆ 4560[9] 5572[7] 6375[5] 6860[3] (7106)◆ 7914[8]

**Chain Of Daisies** *Henry Candy* a104 111
5 b m Rail Link Puya (Kris)
3012[6] 4308[2] 6441[3] (8007)

**Chalco (FR)** *A Bonin* a59 63
2 gr g Elusive City(USA) Lady Time (FR) (Orpen (USA))
6170a[7]

**Chalky (IRE)** *Martyn Meade* 75
3 gr f Canford Cliffs(IRE) Beautiful Hill (IRE) (Danehill (USA))
5038[2] 5712[3] 6614[2]

**Challow (IRE)** *Sylvester Kirk* a63 72
3 b g Acclamation Starlight Smile (USA) (Green Dancer (USA))
1554[5] 1888[9] 2220[3] 2588[10] 3162[6] 4255[3] 5053[3] 5753[5] 6556[3] 7414[5] 7537[5] 8114[9]

**Chamasay** *David Evans* a68 45
3 b g Sayif(IRE) Miss Chamanda (IRE) (Choisir (AUS))
1107[6] (1297)◆ 1421[9] (1545) 1817[3] 3423[11]

**Champagne Bob** *Richard Price* a61 71
5 gr g Big Bad Bob(IRE) Exclusive Approval (USA) (With Approval (CAN))
3084[12] 3573[3] 4373[3] (4467) (5112) 5264[4] 5827[7] 6197[9] 6807[2] 7046[5] 7465[9] 7934[6] (8473) 8798[6]

**Champagne Champ** *Rod Millman* a95 96
5 b g Champs Elysees Maramba (Rainbow Quest (USA))
1942[2] 2788[3] 3534[3] 4356[14] 5110[3] 6151[5] 7200[2] 7903[2]

**Champagne Freddie** *John O'Shea* a61 34
4 b g Sleeping Indian Shes Minnie (Bertolini (USA))
127[4] 221[7] 684[12] 6035[12] 6503[8] 6813[8]

**Champagne Pink (FR)** *K R Burke* a76 61
3 b f Teofilo(IRE) Carruba (IRE) (Marju (IRE))
484[4]◆ 5829[5] 6947[4]◆ 7235[2] 7936[5] 8219[8] (8661) (8854) (9376)

**Champagne Queen** *Rae Guest* a47 55
3 ch f Showcasing Night Haven (Night Shift (USA))
126[6] 456[3] 1193[5] 1605[2] 1835[F] 2507[17]

**Champagne Reign (IRE)**
*J S Moore* a57 40
3 b f Casamento(IRE) Reign Of Fire (IRE) (Perugino (USA))
2726[8] 3657[15]

**Champagne Room (USA)**
*Peter Eurton* a112
3 b f Broken Vow(USA) Lucky To Be Me (USA) (Bernstein (USA))
8578a[6]

**Champagne Rules** *Sharon Watt* a63 54
6 gr g Aussie Rules(USA) Garabelle (IRE) (Galileo (IRE))
2272[12] (5261) 6035[3] 6788[10] 7235[5] 7760[4] (8314) (8507)

**Champarisi** *Grant Tuer* a69 68
2 b f Champs Elysees Parisi (Rahy (USA))
5998[6] 6264[3] 7033[3]◆ (7361) 7937[5]

**Champion Harbour (IRE)**
*Richard Fahey* a65 62
3 b g Harbour Watch(IRE) Drastic Measure (Pivotal)
1970[8] 2349[3] (2790) 3561[5] 4265[3] 4304[4] 4837[3] 5467[13] 6315[4] 7166[2] 7942[11]

**Championship (IRE)** *A bin Harmash* a90 118
6 ch g Exceed And Excel(AUS) Aljafliyah (Halling (USA))
86a[2] (320a) (774a)

**Champs De Reves**
*Marcus Tregoning* 71
2 b c Champs Elysees Joyeaux (Mark Of Esteem (IRE))
4218[11] 4465[3] 4885[5]

**Champs Inblue** *Pat Phelan* 50
2 ch g Champs Elysees Ellablue (Bahamian Bounty)
3776[6] 5030[11]

**Chancellor (FR)** *C Ferland* a46 79
3 ch f Stormy River(FR) Exgray (IRE) (Exceed And Excel (AUS))
5523a[8]

**Chancery (USA)** *David O'Meara* a62 89
9 bb g Street Cry(IRE) Follow That Dream (Darshaan)
1517[3] 1911[10] 2741[5] 3091[2] 3315[4] 3841[6] 4206[3] 4796[2] 5287[4] 6000[4] 6944[7] 7234[9] 7824[5] 8188[11]

**Chance To Dance (IRE)**
*Stephen Autridge & Jamie Richa* a102 103
7 b g Teofilo(IRE) Crystal Ballet (USA) (Royal Academy (USA))
1994a[5]

**Chance To Dream (IRE)** *John Best* a62 78
3 b g Dream Ahead(USA) Kerry Gal (IRE) (Galileo (IRE))
1299[6] 1551[5] 2231[5] (3162) 3504[8] 5033[4]

**Chanche The Life (IRE)** *K Borgel* a68 87
4 b m Frozen Power(IRE) Pivot D'Amour (Pivotal)
384a[8]

**Chandon Elysees** *Gary Moore* a67 62
4 b m Champs Elysees Upstream (Prince Sabo)
39[4] 738[8]

**Chandrayaan** *John E Long* a50 24
10 ch g Bertolini(USA) Muffled (USA) (Mizaaya)
167[12] 274[5] 544[4] 644[7] 740[3] 854[9] 1084[10] 2733[8] 3442[5]

**Chandresh** *Robert Cowell* a49 59
4 b m Holy Roman Emperor(IRE) Cloud's End (Dubawi (IRE))
143[4] 270[5] 722[4] 2069[4] 2994[8] 3545[6]

**Change Maker** *Andrew Balding* 56
2 ch c Havana Gold(IRE) Belle Allemande (CAN) (Royal Academy (USA))
8508[7]

**Changing (IRE)** *Daniel Kubler* a12 48
2 b f Intense Focus(USA) Penny Rose (Danehill Dancer (IRE))
4252[11] 6093[5] 6517[7] 8306[10]

**Channel Maker (CAN)** *William Mott* a102 108
3 ch g English Channel(USA) In Return (USA) (Horse Chestnut (SAF))
7633a[6]

**Channel Packet** *Michael Appleby* a69 65
3 b c Champs Elysees Etarre (IRE) (Giant's Causeway (USA))
731[5] 1244[4] 1584[5] 2186[8] 2794[9] 5182[4]

**Chanson De La Mer (IRE)** *David Menuisier* 40
2 b f Le Havre(IRE) Easy To Sing (Johannesburg (USA))
6824[11]

**Chant (IRE)** *Ann Duffield* a80 74
7 b g Oratorio(IRE) Akarita (IRE) (Akarad (FR))
3983[2] (5832)

**Chante Blu (FR)** *A Giorgi* a67 59
2 b c Elusive City(USA) Chanson Celeste (Oratorio (IRE))
1919a[10] 5627a[4] 8101a[7] 8482a[7]

**Chantecler** *Neil Mulholland* a72 75
6 b g Authorized(IRE) Snow Goose (Polar Falcon (USA))
220[4]

**Chantresse (IRE)** *K R Burke* 68
2 b f Holy Roman Emperor(IRE) Woodland Chant (USA) (War Chant (USA))
6876[4] 7818[8] 8236[5]

**Chapa (FR)** *N Bellanger* 79
3 b c Wootton Bassett La Buena (IRE) (Big Shuffle (USA))
1658a[10]

**Chaparrachik (IRE)** *Amanda Perrett* a70 75
3 b g High Chaparral(IRE) Chocolat Chaud (IRE) (Excellent Art)
1736[7] 2394[3] 3520[2] 3788[4] 5298[6] 6023[3] 6423[6]

**Chaparral Prince (IRE)** *Charles Hills* 58
2 b g High Chaparral(IRE) Snow Gretel (IRE) (Green Desert (USA))
4859[9] 8389[13]

**Chapeau Bleu (IRE)** *Mrs C Gilbert* a69 53
5 b m Haatef(USA) La Petite Bleue (GER) (Fantastic Light (USA))
2670a[5] 5201a[8] (5984a)

**Chaplin (FR)** *G Radovic* a9 91
3 b g Myboycharlie(IRE) Lady Oriande (Makbul)
8960a[9]

**Chaplin Bay (IRE)** *Ruth Carr* a81 81
5 b g Fastnet Rock(AUS) Green Castle (IRE) (Indian Ridge (IRE))
(1778) 2133[9] 2500[5] 3045[3] 3388[2] 3792[8] 4103[7] 4685[5] 5213[7] 5922[3] 6663[11] 6964[7] 7474[9]

**Characterized** *Geoffrey Deacon* a61 69
3 b f Oasis Dream Hypnology (USA) (Gone West (USA))
2908[5] 3309[2] 4145[3] 5357[6] 6076[4] 6681[3] 7457[13] 7916[9] 8908[8] 9128[4]

**Character Onesie (IRE)** *Richard Fahey* a76 81
5 b g Dark Angel(IRE) Flame Keeper (IRE) (Pivotal)
1677[4] 1969[9] 2500[4] 3144[5] 3560[2] 4609[2]◆ 5077[3] 5496[6] 6158[2] 6516[6] 7052[3] 7770[10]

**Character Witness (IRE)** *Roger Varian* a77 75
2 b g Casamento(IRE) She's A Character (Invincible Spirit (IRE))
4805[6] 5365[4] 5834[3] 8039[5] 8379[6]

**Charava (IRE)** *Patrick Holmes* a54 68
5 br g Captain Marvelous(IRE) Sweet Compliance (Safawan)
2224[11] 3198[7] 4688[11]

**Charismatic Man (IRE)** *Ralph Beckett* a93 81
4 b g Dalakhani(IRE) On Fair Stage (IRE) (Sadler's Wells (USA))
422[4] (1248) 3213[2] 3841[5]

**Charles Fox** *James Fanshawe* a60 63
2 b g Power Jouet (Reprimand)
5576[7] 6146[6]

**Charles Molson** *Patrick Chamings* a103 95
6 b g Monsieur Bond(IRE) Arculinge (Paris House)
1769[3] 2390[10] 2606[5] 3410[5] 8547[5] 8843[6] (9264)

**Charleston Belle** *Giles Bravery* a44 67
3 b f Danehill Dancer(IRE) Blanche Dubawi (IRE) (Dubawi (IRE))
4445[2] 5335[5] 5937[4] 7122[5] 8716[3]

**Charlie Alpha (IRE)** *Roger Ingram* 31
3 b g Dandy Man(IRE) Maroussies Rock (Rock Of Gibraltar (IRE))
1600[12] 2171[6] 6791[11]

**Charlie Chaplin (GER)** *Robert Eddery* a37 36
3 b g Lope De Vega(IRE) Campina (Oasis Dream)
5511[7] 6621[9] 9237[10]

**Charlie Lad** *Daniel Mark Loughnane* a64 64
5 b g Myboycharlie(IRE) Night Owl (Night Shift (USA))
153[4] 327[5] 523[7]

**Charlie Rascal (FR)** *Peter Chapple-Hyam* a62 61
3 b g Myboycharlie(IRE) Rascafria (USA) (Johannesburg (USA))
378[5] 3087[6] 3326[6]

**Charlie's Dreamer** *Michael Appleby* a61 65
3 ch f Equiano(FR) Enford Princess (Pivotal)
4568[6] 5969[2] 6268[6] 7014[3] 7282[3] 8552[5] 8805[2] 9071[5] 9364[6]

**Charlie The Lad (FR)** *Matthieu Palussiere* a74
3 b g Myboycharlie(IRE) Paree (IRE) (Desert Prince (IRE))
427a[2]

**Charlie Victor** *Malcolm Saunders* a51 41
3 b g Myboycharlie(IRE) Audrey Brown (Mind Games)
1453[4] 2362[12] 5567[8] 6174[11]

**Charlot The Kid (FR)** *C Delcher-Sanchez* 87
3 gr c Evasive Hickory Spinny (USA) (Cozzene (USA))
6963a[5]

**Charly Nova (FR)** *F Rossi* 97
3 b f Myboycharlie(IRE) Terra Nova (FR) (American Post)
1337a[3] 3612a[4]

**Charm Appeal (FR)** *H-F Devin* 104
3 b f Canford Cliffs(IRE) Tara's Force (IRE) (Acclamation)
2644a[15] 6054a[8]

**Charming Guest (IRE)** *Mick Channon* 52
2 b f Kodiac Na Zdorovie (Cockney Rebel (IRE))
2563[8]

**Charming Ka (FR)** *H Fortineau* a9 57
2 ch f No Risk At All(FR) Social Butterfly (FR) (Gold Away (IRE))
4677a[8] 8228a[8]

**Charming Kitten (USA)** *Michael J Maker* a106 106
7 bb h Kitten's Joy(USA) Iteration (USA) (Wild Again (USA))
2641a[4]

**Charming Loza** *Charlie Fellowes* a68 54
3 b f Lawman(FR) Ellbeedee (IRE) (Dalakhani (IRE))
1885[12] 2311[6] 2760[7] 4012[7]

**Charming Power (IRE)** *Ann Duffield* 17
2 b g Power Always Attractive (IRE) (King's Best (USA))
5180[8] 5492[9] 7890[10]

**Charnock Richard** *David Brown* a63 81
2 b c Mayson Velvet Band (Verglas (IRE))
3169[9] 3523[2] 4606[3] 5398[2] 5603[4] 6353[7] 7013[3] 7731[4] 7919[5]

**Chartbreaker (FR)** *Chris Gordon* a70 84
6 b g Shirocco(GER) Caucasienne (FR) (Galileo (IRE))
759[9] 1466[5] (3004) 3618[9]

**Chartbuster (IRE)** *Julie Camacho* a75 72
3 b g Mastercraftsman(IRE) Gift Dancer (Imperial Dancer)
4055[4]◆ 4569[5] 5632[5] 8205[3]

**Chatburn (IRE)** *David O'Meara* a74 82
2 b c Dream Ahead(USA) Mistress Of Rome (Holy Roman Emperor (IRE))
2403[7] 2896[2]◆ (3149)◆ 3556[4] (4760) 5440[3] 6353[14] 7318[5] 7821[22]

**Chatez (IRE)** *Alan King* 101
6 b g Dandy Man(IRE) Glory Days (GER) (Tiger Hill (IRE))
8469[2]

**Chatoyer (FR)** *J S Moore* a65 72
3 ch c Siyouni(FR) Polyegos (IRE) (Hawk Wing (USA))
1600[4] 1762[4] 4341[7] 4793[3] 6157[3]◆ (6502) 7058[9] 7308a[8] 8025a[4] 8305a[10]

**Chatting (IRE)** *Hugo Palmer* a66
3 b f Intikhab(USA) Kesh Kumay (IRE) (Danehill (USA))
(2957)◆

**Chaucer's Tale** *Michael Easterby* a67 49
3 b g Poet's Voice Grand Slam Maria (FR) (Anabaa (USA))
2902[6] 8590[3] 8807[2] (9012) 9127[2]

**Chauvelin** *Nigel Tinkler* a48 60
6 b g Sir Percy Enforce (USA) (Kalanisi (IRE))
2546[6] 3155[9] 4102[6] 4558[3] 4839[2] 6088[7] 6471[5] 7360[4] 8122[5]

**Cheapo** *Brett Johnson*
4 ch g Aqlaam Shy Appeal (IRE) (Barathea (IRE))
916[8]

**Che Bella (IRE)** *Keith Dalgleish* 85
2 gr f Holy Roman Emperor(IRE) Satwa Ruby (FR) (Verglas (IRE))
1908[4] 2452[5] 2801[9] 5990[3] (6940) 7552[4] 7921[2] 8379[2]

**Chebsey Beau** *John Quinn* a71 81
7 b g Multiplex Chebsey Belle (IRE) (Karinga Bay)
2622[10] 3315[6] (5923) (6895) 7330[11] 8109[3]

**Check 'Em Tuesday (IRE)** *Daniel Mark Loughnane* a47 43
4 b m Kodiac Wait Watcher (IRE) (Fath (USA))
90[5] 655[4] 3912[14] 4747[12]

**Checkpoint Charlie (IRE)** *E J O'Neill* a78 78
2 gr c Foxwedge(AUS) Guiletta (IRE) (Dalakhani (IRE))
7175a[3]

**Cheeky Kiki (IRE)** *Giles Bravery* a54
2 b f Makfi Manoeuvre (IRE) (Galileo (IRE))
7361[4] 7937[10]

**Cheeky Rascal (IRE)** *Richard Hannon* 74
2 b c Most Improved(IRE) Bessie Lou (IRE) (Montjeu (IRE))
3390[9] 4520[3]◆ 5030[5] 5572[2] 6699[3] 8354[10]

**Cheeni** *Jim Goldie* 52
5 ch m Orientor Class Wan (Safawan)
2453[2] 2777[3] 2950[2] 3710[2] 4478[3] 4847[4] (5203) 5472[5] 5919[3] 6384[4] 6785[5] 7164[6]

**Cheerfilly (IRE)** *Tom Dascombe* a61 85
3 br f Excelebration(IRE) Classic Remark (IRE) (Dr Fong (USA))
2572[3] 3044[2] 3911[3] (4624) (5078)◆ 5324[4] 7830[8]

**Cheers Buddy (IRE)** *Lee Smyth* a49 57
9 b g Acclamation Victorian Dancer (IRE) (Groom Dancer (USA))
5992[5]

**Cheers Monsieur** *Tim Easterby* a18
2 ch g Monsieur Bond(IRE) Cheers For Thea (IRE) (Distant Music (USA))
2786[12]

**Cheeseandpickle** *Keith Dalgleish* a67
2 ch f Helmet(AUS) Branston Gem (So Factual (USA))
(1776) 7946[10]

**Chef Oui Chef (FR)** *M Boutin* a62 53
7 b g Medecis Romantic Pearl (FR) (Kahyasi (IRE))
4233a[7]

**Chef United** *Roger Fell* a49 30
2 b f Swiss Spirit Eurolinka (IRE) (Tirol (IRE))
6264[11] 7033[10] 7238[12] 7698[10] 8190[13]

**Chelabella** *Derek Shaw* a65 61
4 b m Medicean Agrippina (Timeless Times (USA))
1447[5] 1758[6] 1983[7] (2319)

**Chelsea Corsage (IRE)** *Paul D'Arcy* a76 66
3 b f Teofilo(IRE) Galley (Zamindar (USA))
7321[14] 8497[11] 8979[6]

**Chelsea Lad (IRE)** *Martyn Meade* 104
4 b g Clodovil(IRE) Yali (IRE) (Orpen (USA))
1960[P] 2767[2] 4410[3] 6355[9] 7619[4] 8042[6] 8740[2]

**Chelsea's Boy (IRE)** *Donald McCain* a78 80
4 gr g Rip Van Winkle(IRE) St Roch (IRE) (Danehill (USA))
2021[3]◆ 2928[7] 3459[5] 4346[6] 5700[8] 6551[7] 7048[8]

**Chelwood Gate (IRE)** *Conor Dore* a74 69
7 gr g Aussie Rules(USA) Jusoor (USA) (El Prado (IRE))
267[6] 1238[8] 1728[9] (2365) 2968[2] 3344[7] 3966[7] 4538[2] 5183[6] 5895[2] 6153[9] 6946[12] 8429[6] 8946[8] 9219[5] 9457[3]

**Chemical Charge (IRE)** *Ralph Beckett* a112 116
5 ch h Sea The Stars(IRE) Jakonda (USA) (Kingmambo (USA))
(1516) 1957[2] 2822[6] 4070[3] (4849) (6931) 8099a[6] 9167a[4]

**Cherbourg (FR)** *Dr Jon Scargill* a81 81
5 b g Dunkerque(FR) Seduisante (FR) (Anabaa (USA))
465[2] 736[6] 7456[8] 9468[12]

**Cheri Cheri Lady (TUR)** *Ibrahim Bekirogullari* 101
5 b m Luxor(TUR) Uni Baby (IRE) (Flying Spur (AUS))
6718a[2]

**Cheries Amours (FR)** *T Castanheira* a79 88
3 b f Air Chief Marshal(IRE) Cherie Bibie (FR) (Statue Of Liberty (USA))
2484a[3]

**Cherina Dynamite (SPA)** *V Luka Jr* a64 69
2 b f Kodiac Carefree Smile (IRE) (Invincible Spirit (IRE))
6494a[8]

**Cherished (IRE)** *Geoffrey Deacon* 63
3 b f Kodiac Marasem (Cadeaux Genereux)
4445[5] 5969[3] 6808[2] 7227[6] 7907[6]

**Cherkes Pharoah (USA)** *A R Al Rayhi* a52
3 b c Candy Ride(ARG) Coral Sea (USA) (Rubiano (USA))
8710a[11] 9257a[2]

**Cherry Kool** *Stuart Williams* a52 66
4 b m Kheleyf(USA) Pretty Kool (Inchinor)
1429[8] 2680[4] 3331[9] 3812[7] 4053[8] (4543)

**Cherry Leyf** *Stuart Williams* a57 51
3 b f Kheleyf(USA) Pretty Kool (Inchinor)
288[10] 624[7] 1363[5] 3818[4] 4714[8] 5041[5] 6324[9] 6724[9] 7705[7] 8134[11]

**Cherry Lips (ITY)** *A Giorgi* a37
2 b f Blu Air Force(IRE) Cryadora (IRE) (Street Cry (IRE))
6456a[10]

**Cherry Oak (IRE)** *Ben Haslam* a54 54
2 b f Society Rock(IRE) Blue Holly (IRE) (Blues Traveller (IRE))
4628[7] 5015[3] 5575[5] 6154[5] 8780[4]◆

**Cherubic** *Charles Hills* a48 52
2 b f Dark Angel(IRE) Doula (USA) (Gone West (USA))
1884[7] 2832[7] 6005[9] 6845[4] 7239[12]

**Chesham Rose (IRE)** *Dave Roberts* a47 50
4 gr m Mastercraftsman(IRE) Rose's Destination (IRE) (Dubai Destination (USA))
70[9]

**Chessman (IRE)** *John Gosden* a83 98
3 b c Acclamation Dulcian (IRE) (Shamardal (USA))
1945[2]◆ 3082[2]◆ 3959[7]

**Chess Master (IRE)** *A bin Harmash* a76 75
4 br g Shamardal(USA) Cassandra Go (IRE) (Indian Ridge (IRE))
8710a[4]

**Chess Move (IRE)** *George Baker* a66 76
2 b g Kodiac Azia (IRE) (Desert Story (IRE))
4007[6] (4799) 6745a[8]

**Chester Deelyte (IRE)** *Lisa Williamson* a54 47
9 b m Desert Style(IRE) Bakewell Tart (IRE) (Tagula (IRE))
167[13]

**Chester'slittlegem (IRE)** *Mrs A Corson* a26 17
8 b m Atraf Ceylon Round (FR) (Royal Applause)
1933a[8]

**Chester Street** *Roger Charlton* a92 83
4 b g Invincible Spirit(IRE) Expressive (Falbrav (IRE))
235[7] 918[7] 8032[4]◆

**Chestnut Fire** *Daniel Mark Loughnane* a99 70
5 ch g Showcasing Music In Exile (USA) (Diesis)
2093[4] 2606[19] 3255[3] 4261[9] 8547[13] 9025[8] 9314[2]

**Chestnut Storm (IRE)** *Brian Barr* a66 42
4 ch m Rip Van Winkle(IRE) Always Attractive (IRE) (King's Best (USA))
19[2] 241[6] 741[4] 8301[9] 8878[12]

**Chetan** *Charlie Wallis* a78 69
5 b g Alfred Nobel(IRE) Island Music (IRE) (Mujahid (USA))
1140[6] 1467[6] 1728[6] 2058[4] 2514[4] 3084[4] 3702[7] 4256[8] 4695[5] 5339[7] 5793[3] 6112[6] (6813) (7061) (7323) 7759[11] 8341[12] 8646[3] 8958[7]

**Cheval Blanche (USA)** *Michael Bell* a78 85
3 gr f Stay Thirsty(USA) Primrose Hill (USA) (Giant's Causeway (USA))
(1343)◆ 1470[2] (2177) 3964[10] 4903[6] 6358[10]

**Cheval Grand (JPN)** *Yasuo Tomomichi* 123
5 ch h Heart's Cry(JPN) Halwa Sweet (JPN) (Machiavellian (USA))
2203a[2] (8975a)

**Chevalgris** *Dai Burchell* a61 82
7 gr g Verglas(IRE) Danzelline (Danzero (AUS))
5896[7] 6343[6]

**Chevalier Du Lac (IRE)** *Conor Dore* a66 76
3 b g Sir Prancealot(IRE) Crimson Sunrise (IRE) (Holy Roman Emperor (IRE))
4447[11] 5004[6] 5374[13]

**Chevallier** *Archie Watson* a96 93
5 b g Invincible Spirit(IRE) Magical Romance (IRE) (Barathea (IRE))
43[3] 349[2] (465) (918) 1023[9] 1177[8] 3298[5] 8944[2] 9125[11]

**Chiarush (IRE)** *G Botti* a72 82
3 gr f Dark Angel(IRE) Laetoli (ITY) (Footstepsinthesand)
2484a[4]

**Chiavari (IRE)** *A Fabre* 83
3 b f Born To Sea(IRE) Chiarezza (AUS) (Fantastic Light (USA))
8733a[13]

**Chica De La Noche** *Simon Dow* a67 77
3 b f Teofilo(IRE) Welsh Cake (Fantastic Light (USA))
392[5] 3869[7] 4251[7] 4711[3] (6106) 6511[U]

**Chicago School (IRE)** *Anthony McCann* a64 66
4 ch g Approve(IRE) Ms Sasha Malia (IRE) (Verglas (IRE))
8194[10] (9244a)

**Chicago Star** *Mick Channon* a68 73
3 b f Exceed And Excel(AUS) Librettista (AUS) (Elusive Quality (USA))
1705[7] 2503[6] 2885[4] 3246[5] (4150) 4846[8] 6106[7] 7058[5] 7457[5] 7771[10]

**Chica La Habana (IRE)** *Robert Cowell* 81
2 ch f Havana Gold(IRE) Esloob (USA) (Diesis)
(3557)◆ 3960[21] 7617[11]

**Chicissime (FR)** *J-P Gauvin* a75 65
3 b f Sunday Break(JPN) Belle Dame (GER) (Pilsudski (IRE))
5523a[5]

**Chickenfortea (IRE)** *Eric Alston* a49 72
3 gr g Clodovil(IRE) Kardyls Hope (IRE) (Fath (USA))
1835[14] 2993[3] 4576[7] (4745) 5291[3] 5826[9] 6679[8] (7389) 8488[6]

**Chickpea** *Michael Bell* 43
2 b f Rip Van Winkle(IRE) Tahlia Ree (IRE) (Acclamation)
5534[9] 6100[6] 6510[7]

**Chiclet (IRE)** *Tracey Collins* a103 100
6 b m Dandy Man(IRE) Springfort (IRE) (Captain Rio)
200[9]

**Chief Craftsman** *Luca Cumani* 80
3 b g Mastercraftsman(IRE) Eurolink Raindance (IRE) (Alzao (USA))
1967[6] 2584[2] 3860[2] 4569[3] 5364[8]

**Chief Ironside** *William Jarvis* 61
2 b c Lawman(FR) Moment Of Time (Rainbow Quest (USA))
8560[8]

**Chief Justice** *Richard Fahey* a77 78
2 b g Acclamation Freedom Pass (USA) (Gulch (USA))
5801[2] 6326[RR] 6897[2] 8046[2]◆

**Chiefofchiefs** *Charlie Fellowes* a90 94
4 b g Royal Applause Danvers (Cape Cross (IRE))
2476[P] (2689) 3730[2] (4215) (4916) 5668[3] 6007[4] 6933[14] 7582[4]

**Chief's App (FR)** *Y Barberot* a58 53
4 ch m Air Chief Marshal(IRE) Appearance (GER) (Monsun (GER))
1181a[4]

**Chika Dream (FR)** *N Leenders* a72 98
7 ch g Danehill Dancer(IRE) Smala Tica (FR) (Loup Solitaire (USA))
7416a[7]

**Chikoko Trail** *Mick Channon* 58
2 ch c Sixties Icon Search Party (Rainbow Quest (USA))
8140[8] 8509[7]

**Childesplay** *Heather Main* a80 84
6 ch m Byron Parting Gift (Cadeaux Genereux)
506[3] 810[6] 1066[4] 1599[3] 3518[6] 4051[4]◆ 4746[3] (5326) 5754[2]

**Chilean** *Martyn Meade* a83 105
2 b c Iffraaj Childa (IRE) (Duke Of Marmalade (IRE))
5887[4] (6616) (6925)◆ 8415[6]

**Chillala (IRE)** *Harry Dunlop* 71
2 b f Requinto(IRE) Positive Step (IRE) (Footstepsinthesand)
4533[5] 6070[7] 7357[6] 8472[3]

**Chilli Jam** *Ed de Giles* a61 58
4 b g Mastercraftsman(IRE) Wosaita (Generous (IRE))
6035[4] 6306[3] (6622) 7360[5] 7711[3] 7991[3]

**Chillililli** *Michael Appleby* a48 10
3 ch f Monsieur Bond(IRE) Stunning Icon (Dr Fong (USA))
73[9] 385[9] 1545[8] 2065[7] 2306[6] 2734[11] 8242[8] 8428[10] 8776[3] 9181[10] 9344[5]

**Chilli Spice (IRE)** *J P Murtagh* a81 92
4 ch m Manduro(GER) Contrary (IRE) (Mark Of Esteem (IRE))
1387a[9] 2637a[9]

**Chill Wind (FR)** *D & P Prod'Homme* a71 83
6 ch g Halling(USA) Lakuta (IRE) (Pivotal)
7070a[6]

**Chilworth Icon** *Debbie Mountain* a91 96
7 b g Sixties Icon Tamara Moon (IRE) (Acclamation)
914a[9]

**China Excels** *Mandy Rowland* a68 74
10 b g Exceed And Excel(AUS) China Beauty (Slip Anchor)
1558[5] 1965[4]

**Chinese Spirit (IRE)** *R Mike Smith* a32 74
3 gr g Clodovil(IRE) In The Ribbons (In The Wings)
4036[5] 4474[4] 4899[4] 5466[11] (5993) 6692[4] 7656[7] (7984) 8209[13]

**Chingachgook** *Richard Fahey* a73
2 b c Al Kazeem Natty Bumppo (IRE) (Kheleyf (USA))
9051[3] 9433[4]

**Ching Ching Lor (IRE)**
*Declan Carroll* a65 57
3 b g Elzaam(AUS) Art Critic (USA) (Fusaichi Pegasus (USA))
1680[9] 2077[7] (2455) (3191) 4721[6] 5666[9] 6470[11] 6893[9]

**Chinoiseries** *David Simcock* 84
4 b m Archipenko(USA) Robe Chinoise (Robellino (USA))
2389[7] 3586[9]

**Chionodoxa** *Tim Easterby* 46
3 ch f Haafhd Bollin Nellie (Rock Hopper)
1680[14] 1914[8] 3207[5] 5017[7] 5209[9] 6892[7] 7219[5]

**Chipolata (FR)** *J Reynier* 90
2 ch f Muhtathir Chicago May (FR) (Numerous (USA))
6731a[4] 7637a[4]

**Chip Or Pellet** *Mark Pattinson* a58 50
4 b g Hellvelyn Concentration (IRE) (Mind Games)
1965[6] 2633[11] 2923[6] 3202[6] 3915[8] 4174[13] 5004[4] (5419) 8494[9] 9184[4]

**Chippenham (IRE)** *John Gosden*
3 ch c Casamento(IRE) Ohiyesa (IRE) (Noverre (USA))
882[8] 1190[3] 1420[2] 1874[4]

**Chipping (IRE)** *Michael Dods* a69 75
3 b g Dark Angel(IRE) Bean Uasal (IRE) (Oasis Dream)
1702[8] 2820[9] 4080[2] 4694[8] 5182[6] 5922[9]

**Chiquit Indian (FR)** *E Caroux* a55 80
3 b f Indian Danehill(IRE) Chiquitita (IRE) (Oratorio (IRE))
6649a[4]

**Chiswick Bey (IRE)** *Richard Fahey* a73 75
9 b g Elusive City(USA) Victoria Lodge (IRE) (Grand Lodge (USA))
361[3] (655) 968[9] 1706[2] 2140[5] 3049[3] 3487[5] (4554) 5091[3] 5805[3] 6058[2] 6464[3] 6964[10] 7476[9] 8124[5]

**Chiverny (FR)** *F Chappet* 107
5 b g Whipper(USA) Courances (FR) (Simon Du Desert (FR))
(3104a)

**Chivers (IRE)** *Daniel Steele* a59 83
6 b g Duke Of Marmalade(IRE) Thara (USA) (Hennessy (USA))
1870[4] 2111[8]

**Chizz De Biz (IRE)** *Daniel Kubler* a54 60
2 b f Zebedee Chizzler (IRE) (Baltic King)
6417[5]◆ 7724[6] 8432[6] 8795[9]

**Chloellie** *J R Jenkins* 35
2 b f Delegator Caramelita (Deportivo)
5534[8] 6480[13] 8471[6]

**Chloris** *John Gosden* a63
2 b f Dansili Primevere (IRE) (Singspiel (IRE))
8998[6]

**Chocante (NZ)** *Stephen Marsh* 107
4 b g Shocking(AUS) Strictly Maternal (NZ) (O'Reilly (NZ))
6714a[3]

**Chocolate Account (USA)**
*Ed Dunlop* a41 29
3 rg f Exchange Rate(USA) Western Vision (USA) (Gone West (USA))
4300[10] 4729[5] 5118[7] 6847[5]

**Chocolate Box (IRE)** *Luca Cumani* a85 77
3 b c Zoffany(IRE) Chocolate Mauk (USA) (Cozzene (USA))
2588[8] 3291[7] 3752[2] 4809[5] 6210[2] (6849) 7359[5] 8398[3]

**Chocolat Noir (IRE)**
*Martin Todhunter* 77
4 b m Yeats(IRE) Valrhona (IRE) (Spectrum (IRE))
8485[7]

**Choice Encounter** *Michael Bell* a81 76
2 ch g Choisir(AUS) Gimme Some Lovin (IRE) (Desert Style (IRE))
1966[4] 2279[2] 2691[2] 3406[4] 8819[2] 9123[2]

**Chookie Dunedin** *Keith Dalgleish* 92
2 b c Epaulette(AUS) Lady Of Windsor (IRE) (Woods Of Windsor (USA))
(2948) 3925[10] 6521[7] 7090[20]

**Chookie Valentine** *Keith Dalgleish* a24 33
4 b g Approve(IRE) Lady Of Windsor (IRE) (Woods Of Windsor (USA))
6131[15] 6690[9] 7219[11] 7704[10] 9218[9]

**Choose** *Ralph Beckett* a59
3 b f Dansili Insinuate (USA) (Mr Prospector (USA))
7989[7] 8635[5]

**Choosey (IRE)** *Henry Candy* 70
2 ch g Choisir(AUS) Petit Chou (IRE) (Captain Rio)
4805[7] 5494[3] 6178[4]

**Chopemoi (FR)** *Mlle A Pelletant* 32
2 b f Deportivo Wa Zine (FR) (Iron Mask (USA))
8482a[15]

**Chopin (GER)** *Abdulla Kuwaiti* 110
7 b g Santiago(GER) Caucasienne (FR) (Galileo (IRE))
(934a)

**Choral Clan (IRE)** *Brendan Powell* a78 67
6 b g Oratorio(IRE) Campbellite (Desert Prince (IRE))
90[2] (286) 1602[6] 2477[8] 4751[7] 5718[7] 6620[7] 7493[5] 7878[2] 8313[3] 8550[3] 8814[2] (9017) 9338[2]

**Choral Music** *Jonathan Portman* 51
2 b f Equiano(FR) Gospel Music (Beat Hollow)
3815[8] 5107[11] 8294[10]

**Chosen Character (IRE)**
*Tom Dascombe* a69 82
9 b g Choisir(AUS) Out Of Thanks (IRE) (Sadler's Wells (USA))
3540[2] 4085[4] 5062[2] 5683[6] 6725[2] 7108[8] 7566[8] 8749[8] 9411[6]

**Chosen World** *Julie Camacho* 65
3 b g Intikhab(USA) Panoptic (Dubawi (IRE))
5315[6] 5946[3] 6268[5]

**Chough** *Hughie Morrison* a65 61
3 b f Dutch Art Port Charlotte (Oasis Dream)
89[5] 209[6] 637[3] 881[4] 4713[2] 5266[6] 5713[2]◆ 6751[2] 7323[7] (7952) 8152[3] 8659[7]

**Choumicha** *Hugo Palmer* a66 87
3 b f Paco Boy(IRE) Galicuix (Galileo (IRE))
1883[11]

**Chrisellaine (IRE)** *Charles Hills* a74 69
2 b f Iffraaj Janicellaine (IRE) (Beat Hollow)
5990[4]◆ (7033)◆

**Christian C (USA)** *Wayne Catalano* 99
4 ch g Kitalpha(USA) Elle Belle (USA) (El Prado (IRE))
7851a[11]

**Christmas Night** *Ollie Pears* a59 62
2 ch g Compton Place Night Haven (Night Shift (USA))
3200[7] 3791[4]◆ 4620[2] 6011[2] 6634[9] 7264[6] 8190[8]

**Christopher Wood (IRE)**
*Ralph Beckett* 78
2 b c Fast Company(IRE) Surf The Web (IRE) (Ela-Mana-Mou)
(4218) 4885[4] 7197[2]

**Chunkyfunkymonkey** *John Ryan* a49 71
3 ch g Kheleyf(USA) Give Me High Five (Dubawi (IRE))
1514[6] 1804[7] 2066[10] 3327[5] 3531[4] 3939[6] 4177[2] (4320) 4697[4] (5337) 5722[8] 5853[3] 6587[7]

**Chupalla** *David Evans* a74 83
3 b f Helmet(AUS) Dubai Sunrise (USA) (Seeking The Gold (USA))
125[4] 291[5] 678[5] 1801[12] (4556) 5965[3] 6321[8] 7155[7]

**Churchill (IRE)** *A P O'Brien* a93 125
3 b c Galileo(IRE) Meow (IRE) (Storm Cat (USA))
(2399) (3100a) 3927[4] 6328[2] 6960a[7] 8232[3] 8611a[7]

**Ciaoadiosimdone (IRE)** *John Ryan* a71 93
3 ch f Arcano(IRE) Croque Madame (IRE) (Galileo (IRE))
7576[7] 8117[5] 8599[6] (8869)

**Ciaras Cookie (IRE)**
*Mandy Rowland* a16 1
5 b m Approve(IRE) Preach (IRE) (Danehill Dancer (IRE))
153[14] 4726[10] 6041[11]

**Cidjle Dangles (FR)** *C Plisson* 29
2 b f Meshaheer(USA) Augira (FR) (Sternkoenig (IRE))
6409a[4]

**Ciel Rouge** *Charlie Wallis* a51 56
3 b f Champs Elysees Artistic Blue (USA) (Diesis)
1428[9] 1726[8] 2056[8]

**Ciel Russe (FR)** *Edouard Thueux* a64 55
4 b g Kingsalsa(USA) L'Aiglone (FR) (Lost World (IRE))
1078a[8]

**Cima Da Conegliano (FR)**
*M Arienti* 85
3 b c Cima De Triomphe(IRE) Fiona Rae (IRE) (Invincible Spirit (IRE))
584a[5]

**Cimeara (IRE)** *J S Bolger* 74
2 b f Vocalised(USA) Gold Mirage (IRE) (Galileo (IRE))
8440a[9]

**Cincuenta Pasos (IRE)**
*Joseph Tuite* a65 93
6 ch g Footstepsinthesand Sweet Nicole (Okawango (USA))
2113[7] 3424[7]◆ 3572[7]

**Cinque Port** *Richard Hughes* a81 60
3 ch g Compton Place Jump Ship (Night Shift (USA))
(1179) 1895[5] 2567[14] 5051[7]

**Circle Of Friends (CAN)**
*Robert Tiller* a82 31
3 bb g Midnight Lute(USA) She Ain't Much (USA) (Phone Trick (USA))
8097a[8]

**Circling Vultures** *Antony Brittain* a59 53
3 ch g Monsieur Bond(IRE) Knavesmire (IRE) (One Cool Cat (USA))
1347[5] 2584[6] 2921[5] 5319[10]

**Circuit** *Wilf Storey* a41 28
3 br f Foxwedge(AUS) Lady Circe (USA) (Spinning World (USA))
393[7] 615[5] 2507[16] 4263[11] 5618[9]

**Circuit Judge** *William Knight* a68 66
3 b c Lawman(FR) Gimasha (Cadeaux Genereux)
5220[5] 6103[6] 6817[5]

**Circuit Land (USA)** *C S Shum* a88 117
6 bb g Mizzen Mast(USA) Storm Dove (USA) (Storm Bird (CAN))
2492a[4]

**Circuitous** *Keith Dalgleish* a42 65
9 b g Fasliyev(USA) Seren Devious (Dr Devious (IRE))
4039[10] 4833[6] 4958[3] 5203[6] 6550[5] 7889[9] 8107[5]

**Circulate** *Tom Clover* a69 2
3 b f Dutch Art Royal Whisper (Royal Applause)
96[2] 393[5] 520[3] 5007[12] 6016[10] 6847[9]

**Circulation** *Ralph Beckett* a76 71
3 b f Oasis Dream Double Crossed (Caerleon (USA))
2760[2]◆ 3465[4] 4611[3] 5319[5] (8550)

**Circumcanes (IRE)** *M Nigge* 13
3 ch f Dragon Pulse(IRE) Et Dona Ferentes (Green Desert (USA))
3353a[13]

**Circus Couture (IRE)** *Stefano Botti* 110
5 ch h Intikhab(USA) Bois Joli (IRE) (Orpen (USA))
2004a[2] (3120a) 3

**Circus Ring (IRE)**
*Joseph Patrick O'Brien* a84 78
3 b g Fastnet Rock(AUS) Arabian Mirage (Oasis Dream)
1386a[7]

**Cirencester** *Henry Candy* 76
3 b f Sea The Stars(IRE) Columella (Kyllachy)
2287[7]

**Cirin Toinne (IRE)** *J S Bolger* a84 97
4 ch m Galileo(IRE) Sister Angelina (USA) (Saint Ballado (CAN))
1387a[11] 2637a[8] 8086a[12]

**Cirrus Minor (FR)** *K R Burke* a74
2 b f George Vancouver(USA) Porza (FR) (Septieme Ciel (USA))
7238[2]◆ 8850[7] 9239[7]

**Cismontane (NZ)**
*Gai Waterhouse & Adrian Bott* 105
4 b g High Chaparral(IRE) Viviane (NZ) (Volksraad)
8667a[13]

**City Dreamer (IRE)** *Alan King* 69
3 ch g Casamento(IRE) Cadescia (IRE) (Cadeaux Genereux)
2118[7] 2588[5]

**City Gent** *Ralph Beckett* a85 76
2 b g Holy Roman Emperor(IRE) City Girl (IRE) (Elusive City (USA))
5151[7] 6304[4] 6826[2] 7706[3] 8989[2] (9452)

**City Ground (USA)** *Michael Appleby* a69 74
10 bb g Orientate(USA) Magnet (USA) (Seeking The Gold (USA))
(1932a) 4439[9] 5968[8] 6475[2]

**City Guest (IRE)** *George Margarson* 74
2 b g Epaulette(AUS) Union City Blues (IRE) (Encosta De Lago (AUS))
2279[6] 3164[8] 3516[3] 3929[19] 4827[5] (5474) 6481[6]

**City Light (FR)** *S Wattel* a102 105
3 b c Siyouni(FR) Light Saber (FR) (Kendor (FR))
2561a[2] 3613a[2] 8526a[12] 9274a[2]

**City Limits** *Luca Cumani* a48 75
3 ch c Nathaniel(IRE) Wait It Out (USA) (Swain (IRE))
3779[7] 4314[5]

**City Money (IRE)**
*M Delcher Sanchez* a94 105
5 b h Elusive City(USA) Peachmelba (USA) (Theatrical (IRE))
2643a[9] 5628a[5]

**City Of Angkor Wat (IRE)**
*Conor Dore* a75 53
7 b g Elusive City(USA) Kathleen Rafferty (IRE) (Marju (IRE))
216[6] 293[5] 482[11] 1887[8] 2063[8] 2312[9]

**City Of Joy** *Sir Michael Stoute* a97 95
3 b g Elusive City(USA) Ammo (IRE) (Sadler's Wells (USA))
(2385) (3232)◆ 3997[10] 4904[10] 6404[5] 7400[4]

**Claim The Roses (USA)**
*Ed Vaughan* a95 52
6 b g Speightstown(USA) Reboot (USA) (Rubiano (USA))
4261[5] 4570[7] 6289[7]

**Claire's Secret** *Philip McBride* a66 60
3 ch f Sakhee's Secret Akathea (Barathea (IRE))
1685[12] 2274[6] 2794[4] 4050[9] 8328[11] 8664[8] 9056[12]

**Clairette (IRE)** *Roger Charlton* a75 83
2 b f Al Kazeem Petit Calva (FR) (Desert King (IRE))
5938[4]◆ (6862) 7995[3]

**Clandon** *Brett Johnson* a40 57
4 b g Sakhee's Secret Whassup (FR) (Midyan (USA))
3824[7] 4180[12] 8675[12] 8949[10]

**Clan McGregor (IRE)**
*Seamus Durack* a14 55
2 b c Dragon Pulse(IRE) Riymaisa (IRE) (Traditionally (USA))
7503[8] 8180[7] 8642[12]

**Clanvellyn** *K R Burke* a24
3 b f Hellvelyn Clancassie (Clantime)
244[7]

**Clarabel** *John Weymes* a23 58
4 b m Major Cadeaux Neardown Beauty (IRE) (Bahhare (USA))
4247[4] 5997[6]

**Claramara (IRE)** *Mark Johnston* 64
2 b f Epaulette(AUS) Yaqootah (USA) (Gone West (USA))
5356[5] 5702[10] 6042[2] 6626[7] 7222[2] 7938[P]

**Claregate Street (IRE)** *M Halford* a73 74
3 b f Helmet(AUS) Eaton Street (Discreet Cat (USA))
1389a[17]

**Classica (FR)** *J-P Gauvin* 19
3 gr f Deportivo Effet De Loupe (Dalakhani (IRE))
3275a[13]

**Classical Times**
*Peter Chapple-Hyam* 97
3 b f Lawman(FR) Sunday Times (Holy Roman Emperor (IRE))
(2344) 2802[4] 3964[5] 6234[3] 7113[9] 8040[7]

**Classic Charm** *Dean Ivory* a55 70
2 b f Rip Van Winkle(IRE) Classic Lass (Dr Fong (USA))
8594[3] 8888[10] 9319[6]

**Classic Collection**
*Saeed bin Suroor* a89 102
5 b g Cape Cross(IRE) Local Spirit (USA) (Lion Cavern (USA))
654a[13] 888a[6]

**Classic Empire (USA)** *Mark Casse* a123
3 b c Pioneerof The Nile(USA) Sambuca Classica (USA) (Cat Thief (USA))
2420a[4] 2851a[2]

**Classic Flyer** *Christine Dunnett* a72 50
5 b g Stimulation(IRE) Tranquil Flight (Oasis Dream)
2263[6] 2621[7] 2967[6] 3468[6] 3728[11] 5657[8] 5748[5] 6531[7] 6850[7]

**Classic Mission** *Jonathan Portman* a41 72
6 ch g Bahamian Bounty Triple Cee (IRE) (Cape Cross (IRE))
3208[13] 3753[13] 4257[9]

**Classic Pursuit** *Michael Appleby* a69 81
6 b g Pastoral Pursuits Snake's Head (Golden Snake (USA))
1290[6] 1419[6] 1971[7] (2263) 2621[2] 4005[7] 4182[3] 5211[11] 5459[6] 5962[3] (6040) 6670[7] 7522[3] (7738) 8679[9]

**Classic Seniority** *Marjorie Fife* a80 100
5 b g Kyllachy Dramatic Solo (Nayef (USA))
2381[5] 2840[6] 3792[3] (4570) (5094) 5396[5] 5640[10] 6206[11] 6662[2] 7626[9] 8009[14]

**Classic Villager** *Dean Ivory* a83 82
5 b g Authorized(IRE) Sablonne (USA) (Silver Hawk (USA))
3966[2] 4976[6] 6848[13]

**Claude Greenwood** *Tony Carroll* a46 45
7 b g Lucky Story(USA) Greenmeadow (Sure Blade (USA))
167[6] 334[8]

**Claudine (IRE)** *Henry Candy* a68 65
2 b f Zoffany(IRE) Hamalka (IRE) (Alhaarth (IRE))
6394[6] (6824) 7707[6]

**Clayton Hall (IRE)** *John Wainwright* a55 60
4 b g Lilbourne Lad(IRE) Hawk Dance (IRE) (Hawk Wing (USA))
1498[10] 1707[9] 2108[9] 2591[5] 3706[9] 8653[6] 8985[10] 9368[9]

**Clean Cut** *Ivan Furtado* a43 49
3 b f Kheleyf(USA) Regal Asset (USA) (Regal Classic (CAN))
307[7] 612[7] 819[8] 1544[7] 2228[4] 2732[4] 4171[6]

**Clearance** *Mark H Tompkins* 51
3 b g Authorized(IRE) Four Miracles (Vettori (IRE))
3682[8] 4274[7] 4569[12] 5581[7] 7253[7] 7918[7]

**Clear As A Bell (IRE)** *Tim Easterby* a64 69
3 ch f Choisir(AUS) Brilliant Crystal (Compton Place)
1835[12] 2853[9] (3832) 4184[2] 4262[8] (4602) (5182) 6015[4] 6265[8] 7017[7]

**Clear For Take Off** *F Head* a92 91
3 gr f Soldier Hollow Chantra (GER) (Lando (GER))
4988a[7]

**Clearly** *John Gosden* a74 85
3 b f Invincible Spirit(IRE) Concordia (Pivotal)
5220[12] (6817) 7276[3] 7815[5] 8351[10]

**Clear Spring (IRE)** *John Spearing* a86 106
9 b g Chineur(FR) Holly Springs (Efisio)
2433[8] 2780[4] 3034[7] 3324[15] 4505[4] 5612[2] 5929[5]◆ 6794[3] 7084[2] (7742) 8077[6] 8393[5]

**Clear Water (IRE)** *Michael Wigham* a97 90
4 b m Hard Spun(USA) Storm Lily (USA) (Storm Cat (USA))
4051[8] 4889[6] 5435[15] 5828[2]◆ 6358[11] 6864[4] 7811[10] 9089[6]

**Clef** *Richard Fahey* a53 82
3 b f Dutch Art Humouresque (Pivotal)
3094[8] 7044[7] 7702[2] 8113[2] 8418[4] 8907[8]

**Clemency** *Donald McCain* 68
6 b m Halling(USA) China Tea (USA) (High Chaparral (IRE))
6413[2] 7109[5] 7477[3]

**Clement (IRE)** *John O'Shea* a76 68
7 b g Clodovil(IRE) Winnifred (Green Desert (USA))
685[4] 984[10] 9410[9]

**Clemento (IRE)** *Roger Charlton* a74 74
3 b g Canford Cliffs(IRE) Street Style (IRE) (Rock Of Gibraltar (IRE))
2476[5] 3533[4] 7125[4] 7561[3] 8160[3]

**Clem Fandango (FR)**
*Keith Dalgleish* a89 104
3 b f Elzaam(AUS) Question (USA) (Coronado's Quest (USA))
2561a[4] 3614a[4] 7697a[6] 7887[2] 8679[2] 8845[7]

**Clemmie (IRE)** *A P O'Brien* 114
2 b f Galileo(IRE) Meow (IRE) (Storm Cat (USA))
4028[7]◆ (4418a) (4855)◆ (7617)◆

**Clenymistra (IRE)** *David O'Meara* a59 71
3 ch f Poet's Voice Expedience (USA) (With Approval (CAN))
(2903) 3977[3] 4690[5] 5001[2] 5618[3] (6048) 6436[2] 7568[7] 7924[5]

**Cleonte (IRE)** *Andrew Balding* 101
4 ch g Sir Percy Key Figure (Beat Hollow)
2398[5] 3928[12] 5638[10] 6929[4] 7614[6]

**Clergyman** *Rebecca Bastiman* a50 57
5 b g Pastoral Pursuits Doctor's Note (Pursuit Of Love)
1209[4] 1720[2] 9444[2]

**Cleverconversation (IRE)**
*Jane Chapple-Hyam* a63 74
4 ro m Thewayyouare(USA) Monet's Lady (IRE) (Daylami (IRE))
1225[4] 1484[5] 2023[7]

**Clever Cookie** *Peter Niven* a110 115
9 b g Primo Valentino(IRE) Mystic Memory (Ela-Mana-Mou)
2803[6] 3090[9] 4356[9] 4917[3] 6447[6] 7116[4] 8229[6]

**Clever Divya** *J R Jenkins* a57 40
4 b m Archipenko(USA) Clever Omneya (USA) (Toccet (USA))
481[12] 735[4] 4323[8]

**Clever Lady (IRE)** *David Evans* a35 46
3 b f Big Bad Bob(IRE) Muneera (USA) (Green Dancer (USA))
1762[6] 2090[8] 2463[6] 3569[6] 3774[6] 4625[3] 4968[11]

**Cleverley (IRE)** *Henry Candy* a56
2 gr f Mastercraftsman(IRE) Turning Point (Dalakhani (IRE))
8987[10] 9319[5]

**Cliff (IRE)** *Nigel Tinkler* a77 73
7 b g Bachelor Duke(USA) Silesian (IRE) (Singspiel (IRE))
50[2] (145) 501[6] 2684[11] 3095[9] 3666[8] (3979) 4605[2] 5379[4] (5696) 6237[6] 6546[2] 6964[6] 7332[3] 7628[5]

**Cliff Bay (IRE)** *Keith Dalgleish* a64 70
3 b g Elzaam(AUS) Lost Highway (IRE) (Danehill Dancer (IRE))
1817[2] 2347[2] 3243[5] **(3975)** 4838[5] 5097[5] 5466[5] 5880[5] 6381[4] 6783[3] **(7704)** 7984[3]

**Cliff Face (IRE)** *Sir Mark Prescott Bt* a98 97
4 b m Canford Cliffs(IRE) Kotdiji (Mtoto)
3968[6] 4364[5] **4829**[2] 5658[13] 6675[8] 7337[7] 8244[9] 8893[2] 9205[4]

**Cliffhanger** *Paul Cole* a69 67
4 b m Canford Cliffs(IRE) Copy-Cat (Lion Cavern (USA))
**6321**[9]

**Cliff's Edge (AUS)** *Darren Weir* 110
2 b c Canford Cliffs(IRE) Simulation (AUS) (Snaadee (USA))
**8753a**[6]

**Cliffs Of Capri** *Jamie Osborne* a98
3 b g Canford Cliffs(IRE) Shannon Spree (Royal Applause)
(8344)◆ **8812**[2]◆ 9468[5]◆

**Cliffs Of Moher (IRE)** *A P O'Brien* 119
3 b c Galileo(IRE) Wave (IRE) (Dansili)
(2569) **3322**[2] 4638[4]◆ 6328[4] 6960a[6] 8233[7] 8610a[8]

**Cline** *Kevin Ryan* a56 62
4 ch m Pivotal Graduation (Lomitas)
1243[6] 2430[12] 4263[8] **(4900)** 5074[10] 6047[11]

**Clip Art** *Jamie Osborne* a13 42
3 b f Acclamation Semaphore (Zamindar (USA))
**3085**[11] 3259[7] 4211[14]

**Cloak And Degas (IRE)**
*Tim McCarthy* a49 48
5 b g Sakhee's Secret Coup De Torchon (FR) (Namid)
**7605**[12]

**Clock Chimes** *David Brown* a78
3 b g Foxwedge(AUS) Passing Hour (USA) (Red Ransom (USA))
1111[2] (1205) **7942**[3] 8341[8] 8928[7] 9363[4]

**Clonard Street** *A J Martin* 80
5 b g Archipenko(USA) Moi Aussi (USA) (Mt. Livermore (USA))
**5582a**[10]

**Clon Coulis (IRE)** *David Barron* 101
3 b f Vale Of York(IRE) Cloneden (IRE) (Definite Article)
(3896) 5117[2]◆ **(6382)**

**Clondaw Banker (IRE)**
*Nicky Henderson* a57
8 b g Court Cave(IRE) Freya Alex (Makbul)
**780**[5]

**Clondaw Warrior (IRE)** *W P Mullins* a49 107
10 br g Overbury(IRE) Thespian (IRE) (Tiraaz (USA))
**3553a**[10]

**Clongowes (IRE)** *J S Bolger* 104
3 b c New Approach(IRE) Punctilious (Danehill (USA))
**6956a**[3]

**Clon Rocket (IRE)** *John Holt* a60 67
4 b g Lilbourne Lad(IRE) Ryalahna (IRE) (High Chaparral (IRE))
**1371**[5] 1887[10] 1965[10] 2589[10]

**Cloth Of Stars (IRE)** *A Fabre* 126
4 b h Sea The Stars(IRE) Strawberry Fledge (USA) (Kingmambo (USA))
(1271a) (1659a) (2249a) 6983a[2] **7668a**[2]◆

**Cloud Computing (USA)**
*Chad C Brown* a118
3 bb c Maclean's Music(USA) Quick Temper (USA) (A.P. Indy (USA))
**(2851a)**

**Cloud Dragon (IRE)** *Hugo Palmer* a73 70
3 br g Dark Angel(IRE) Karliysha (IRE) (Kalanisi (IRE))
237[3] **(681)** 2145[7] 3392[10]

**Clouded Gold** *Michael Appleby* a37 26
5 ch g Resplendent Glory(IRE) Segretezza (IRE) (Perugino (USA))
7017[11] 8258[6] **8559**[5] 8776[13]

**Cloud Eight (IRE)** *Marco Botti* a64
2 b c Dream Ahead(USA) Night Cam (IRE) (Night Shift (USA))
8988[8] **9404**[4]

**Cloud Monkey (IRE)**
*Martin Todhunter* a59 73
7 bb g Marju(IRE) Sweet Clover (Rainbow Quest (USA))
**1716**[13] 5284[11]

**Cloud Nine (FR)** *Tony Carroll* a52 54
4 b m Sakhee(USA) Heaven (Reel Buddy (USA))
764[5] **2319**[5] 2763[5] 3442[9] 3809[5] 4968[4] 6847[7] 7948[7] 8869[6] 9217[9]

**Clovelly Bay (IRE)**
*Marcus Tregoning* a80 80
6 b g Bushranger(IRE) Crystalline Stream (FR) (Polish Precedent (USA))
163[8] **381**[2] 619[6] **1602**[2] 4413[6] 6135[9] 6819[4]

**Clowance One** *Roger Charlton* a94 88
5 b g Oasis Dream Clowance (Montjeu (IRE))
3458[3]◆ 4216[3] (4499) 5303[4] **(5799) 6793**[4]

**Clubbable** *Richard Fahey* 80
2 b f Mayson Invitee (Medicean)
4116[3] 5092[2] 5702[3] 6693[2] 7087[2]◆ **7621**[2] 8039[6] (8471)

**Club House (IRE)** *Kevin Frost* a41 37
7 b g Marju(IRE) Idesia (IRE) (Green Desert (USA))
**52**[10]

**Clubland (IRE)** *Roy Bowring* a74 66
8 b g Red Clubs(IRE) Racjilanemm (Kyllachy)
**22**[7] 3397[10] 5542[14]

**Club Tropicana** *Richard Spencer* a80 89
2 ch f Helmet(AUS) Twenty Seven (IRE) (Efisio)
6480[6] 6886[3] **7578**[9] 7995[11]

**C Note (IRE)** *Heather Main* a99 103
4 b g Iffraaj Alexander Queen (IRE) (King's Best (USA))
8944[6] **9125**[4]

**Coach Bombay (IRE)**
*Adrian Brendan Joyce* a64 48
9 b g Ad Valorem(USA) Molly-O (IRE) (Dolphin Street (FR))
**1260**[10]

**Coachella (IRE)** *Ed de Giles* a35 45
3 gr g Kyllachy Indian Belle (IRE) (Indian Ridge (IRE))
2790[11] **3695**[4] 4211[10] 4970[7] 5791[6] 6041[6] 6342[7] 7324[11]

**Coal Stock (IRE)** *Christian Williams* a45 70
2 ch g Red Jazz(USA) Scar Tissue (Medicean)
3668[7] 4465[10] **4963**[2] 5246[4] 6029[3] 9199[10]

**Coastal Cyclone** *Harry Dunlop* a46 76
3 b g Canford Cliffs(IRE) Seasonal Cross (Cape Cross (IRE))
2757[4] 3211[11] **4251**[3] 4910[4] 5253[6] 6768[3] 7127[4] 7272[7] 8115[10]

**Coastal Drive** *Richard Hannon* a25 73
2 gr c Harbour Watch(IRE) Added Attraction (FR) (Kendor (FR))
**3742**[3] 4297[5] 4909[2] 5742[6]

**Coasted (USA)** *Leah Gyarmati* 101
3 b f Tizway(USA) Malibu Pier (USA) (Malibu Moon (USA))
**4650a**[7]

**Coast Guard** *Tom Dascombe* a65 52
2 b f Harbour Watch(IRE) Epernay (Tiger Hill (IRE))
6410[3] 6875[7] **7707**[3] 8153[11]

**Coat Of Arms (IRE)** *A P O'Brien* 106
2 b c Galileo(IRE) La Traviata (USA) (Johannesburg (USA))
**6240a**[2] 6975a[4] 7580[3] 8415[11]

**Cobalty Isle (IRE)** *Henry Candy* a71 78
3 b g Kodiac Shamarlane (Shamardal (USA))
3085[2]◆ **3669**[2] 4309[4]

**Cobbler Quinn (IRE)**
*Keith Dalgleish* 33
2 b g Tagula(IRE) Skyscape (Zafonic (USA))
**3283**[7]

**Cockney Boy** *Michael Appleby* a54 46
4 ch g Cockney Rebel(IRE) Menha (Dubawi (IRE))
1556[12] **1937**[2] 2295[7] 3143[7] 5284[9] 5895[8] 6524[7] 8249[2] 8664[4] 8984[3] 9072[4]

**Cockney Cracker (FR)**
*Cathrine Witso Slettemark* 93
6 b g Cockney Rebel(IRE) Lady An Co (FR) (Lavirco (GER))
**4825a**[4]

**Cocktail (IRE)** *Jedd O'Keeffe* a65 43
2 ch c Dream Ahead(USA) Pina Colada (Sabrehill (USA))
7953[9] 8735[8] **8915**[2]

**Cocohulababy (IRE)** *Noel Meade* a75 71
2 ch f Casamento(IRE) Rockahoolababy (IRE) (Kalanisi (IRE))
**8082a**[14]

**Coconut Creme** *William Haggas* 96
3 b f Cape Cross(IRE) Soft Centre (Zafonic (USA))
(2227)◆ 3006[2] 3995[7] **6074**[4] 8007[4]

**Codeshare** *Sally Haynes* a88 88
5 b g Dansili Clepsydra (Sadler's Wells (USA))
195[3] (780) **(991) 1307**[3] 1781[4] **2386**[2] 3527[8] 5438[3] 5882[4] 6427[9]

**Codicil** *Sir Mark Prescott Bt* a83 79
2 b f Lawman(FR) Macleya (GER) (Winged Love (IRE))
(4212) (5492) (6008)◆ **(6900)**

**Coeur D'Amour (IRE)**
*Madeleine Tylicki* 95
2 b f Zoffany(IRE) Adoring (IRE) (One Cool Cat (USA))
**7859a**[2]

**Coeur De Beaute (FR)**
*M Delcher Sanchez* 99
2 b f Dabirsim(FR) Twilight Tear (Rock Of Gibraltar (IRE))
**6051a**[2] 7306a[2]

**Coeur De Lion** *Alan King* a66 88
4 b g Pour Moi(IRE) Hora (Hernando (FR))
(2928) **7402**[2] **8047**[3]

**Cohesion** *David Bridgwater* a109 99
4 b g Champs Elysees Winter Bloom (USA) (Aptitude (USA))
3524◆ 7673 **(1068)** 1770[4] 2202a[7] 8740[14] 9055[4] 9157[2] 9259[7]

**Coillte Cailin (IRE)** *David O'Meara* a99 83
7 b m Oratorio(IRE) Forest Walk (IRE) (Shinko Forest (IRE))
(117) 396[5] **720**[3] 963[4] 1258[7] 3981[5] 4718[6] 5704[6] 6687[6] 8244[11] 8880[8] 9271[6]

**Coiste Bodhar (IRE)** *Scott Dixon* a72 60
6 b g Camacho Nortolixa (FR) (Linamix (FR))
1296[10] 1431[10] 1869[7] **2932**[7] 3667[10] 7020[5] 7825[14] 8258[10] 8484[3] 8681[3] 8776[6] 8980[4] 9181[5] (9348)

**Cold Fire (IRE)** *Jeremy Gask* a62
4 ch g Frozen Power(IRE) Eleanor Eloise (USA) (Minardi (USA))
**807**[4] 1024[9]

**Cold Fusion (IRE)** *David Flood* a72 55
4 b m Frozen Power(IRE) Tuscania (USA) (Woodman (USA))
**49**[7] 233[5] 383[5] 482[6] 605[9] 988[2] 1082[7] 1369[4] 1486[5] 1629[4] 1937[6] 2272[9] 2364[2] 2712[2] 3251[5]

**Cold Shoulder** *Andrew Balding* 73
3 b g Passing Glance Averami (Averti (IRE))
**3427**[4]◆ 4611[9]

**Cold Snap (IRE)** *William Jarvis* a71 86
4 b g Medicean Shivering (Royal Applause)
2040[10] **4099**[2] 6141[4]

**Cold Stare (IRE)** *E J O'Neill* 98
2 b g Intense Focus(USA) Ziria (IRE) (Danehill Dancer (IRE))
5501[9] **7754a**[8]

**Coldstone (FR)** *Michael Kent* a88 93
5 ch g Gold Away(IRE) Vraona (Fantastic Light (USA))
8057a[4] **8750a**[4]

**Colibri (IRE)** *Hugo Palmer* 96
3 b g Redoute's Choice(AUS) High Days (IRE) (Hennessy (USA))
**2126**[4] 3997[16] 4856[11] 5943[4] 7566[3]

**Collateral (IRE)** *James Tate* a74 75
2 b g Reckless Abandon May Day Queen (IRE) (Danetime (IRE))
3305[4] 4101[6] **4577**[2] 5600[5] 6438[6] 6932[2] 7764[10]

**Collateral Beauty** *Richard Fahey* 66
2 b f Pastoral Pursuits Nicola's Dream (Alhaarth (IRE))
**4116**[4] 4919[5] 5534[3] 6200[8] 7222[6]

**Collected (USA)** *Bob Baffert* a126 96
4 ch h City Zip(USA) Helena Bay (Johannesburg (USA))
**(6252a) 8611a**[2]

**College King** *Christine Dunnett* a16 4
2 b g Baltic King Flaming Telepath (Storming Home)
**7788**[11] 8161[10]

**Collegiate (IRE)** *Sir Michael Stoute* a40
2 b f Declaration Of War(USA) Cochabamba (IRE) (Hurricane Run (IRE))
**8373**[11]

**Colleville (FR)** *N Caullery* a71 45
2 b f Literato(FR) Isalou (FR) (Unfuwain (USA))
**6251a**[9]

**Collingham Park (IRE)**
*Jedd O'Keeffe* 77
2 b g Dragon Pulse(IRE) Curraline (IRE) (Bachelor Duke (USA))
2029[5] 2452[3] (3495) **4014**[2] 4716[6] 7596[3] 8008[12]

**Collision Course (IRE)** *A Oliver* a70 92
4 gr g Fast Company(IRE) Anam Chara (IRE) (Soviet Star (USA))
**5582a**[12]

**Collodi (GER)** *Neil Mulholland* a77 77
8 b g Konigstiger(GER) Codera (GER) (Zilzal (USA))
**(3564)**

**Colomano** *Markus Klug* 113
3 b c Cacique(IRE) Codera (GER) (Zilzal (USA))
2002a[4] (3636a) 4422a[13] 5983a[4] **6727a**[3] 7429a[3] 8622a[5]

**Colonel Frank** *Ed Walker* a78 86
3 b g Dutch Art Loquacity (Diktat)
5642[6]◆ 7094[5]◆ 7553[4] **(8392)**

**Colonel Maximus (IRE)**
*Gordon Elliott* a41 66
4 gr g Zebedee Lella Beya (Diktat)
**5518a**[9]

**Colonial Classic (FR)**
*James Fanshawe* a90 97
4 br m Dansili Flame Of Hestia (IRE) (Giant's Causeway (USA))
**2389**[4] 4119[8] 7581[4] 8121[5]

**Colorado Dream** *George Baker* 66
2 b g Oasis Dream Colorado Dawn (Fantastic Light (USA))
2148[8] 4218[5] 4880[9] 6553[8] **8164**[2]

**Color Force (IRE)** *Daniel Kubler* a49 46
4 gr m Dark Angel(IRE) Amistad (GER) (Winged Love (IRE))
139[8] 733[5] **988**[6] **5809**[4] 6306[10] 6479[4] **8585**[4] 8878[11]

**Colourbearer (IRE)** *Charlie Wallis* a75 59
10 ch g Pivotal Centifolia (FR) (Kendor (FR))
242[5] **(302)** 480[10] 682[6] 843[6] 1140[5] 1339[3]

**Colour Contrast (IRE)** *Iain Jardine* 62
4 b g Rock Of Gibraltar(IRE) Colour Coordinated (IRE) (Spectrum (IRE))
**2955**[5] **3530**[2] 3977[6] 4034[3] 4660[4] 5096[5] 5649[7] 6346[3] 6690[4] 7219[9] 7478[13]

**Colourfield (IRE)** *Ed Vaughan* 70
2 b f Makfi Rainbow Desert (USA) (Dynaformer (USA))
8006[9] **8347**[3]

**Colourful Career (USA)** *Ed Dunlop* a73 72
3 bb g More Than Ready(USA) Rainbow Luck (USA) (Honour And Glory (USA))
2167[4] **7600**[3] 8116[3] 8995[5] 9281[4] (9455)

**Columbia Kid (IRE)** *Lee Smyth* 72
2 b f Big Bad Bob(IRE) Tinaheely (IRE) (Intikhab (USA))
**2948**[3]

**Columbian Cartel** *J S Moore* a46
4 b g Indesatchel(IRE) Find The Answer (Vital Equine (IRE))
**2957**[9] **3470**[6] 3813[8]

**Combe Hay (FR)** *Henry Spiller* 65
4 b m Elusive City(USA) Coiffure (King's Best (USA))
**39**[7]

**Come Back King (IRE)**
*Michael Appleby* a81 69
4 ch g Pivotal Queen Consort (USA) (Kingmambo (USA))
**154**[2] 603[3]

**Comedia Eria (FR)** *P Monfort* a79 79
5 b m Lope De Vega(IRE) Vola Vola (IRE) (Danehill Dancer (IRE))
**81a**[3] 2696a[7]

**Comedy House** *Michael Madgwick* a68 58
9 b g Auction House(USA) Kyle Akin (Vettori (IRE))
**35**[9]

**Comedy School (USA)**
*Mark Johnston* a70 80
3 b f Distorted Humor(USA) Cheeky Charm (USA) (A.P. Indy (USA))
2115[11] 3033[8] 3838[8] **4377**[5] 4631[4]

**Come On Come On (IRE)**
*Clive Cox* 78
3 br c Lord Shanakill(USA) Maridiyna (IRE) (Sinndar (IRE))
2567P

**Come On Dave (IRE)** *John Butler* a84 81
8 b g Red Clubs(IRE) Desert Sprite (IRE) (Tagula (IRE))
573[8] 816[4] 1327[4] 1836[3] 3176[6] (3659) (4352) 4464[2] 6411[7] 7137[3] 7994[3] **(8950)**

**Come On Percy** *Richard Fahey* a54 68
3 b c Sir Percy Collette's Choice (Royal Applause)
**73**[2] 385[8]

**Come On Sal**
*Daniel Mark Loughnane*
2 b f Sayif(IRE) Immortelle (Arazi (USA))
884[13]

**Come On Tier (FR)** *David Simcock* 81
2 b c Kendargent(FR) Milwaukee (FR) (Desert King (IRE))
7906[3]◆ **(8509)**

**Come With Me** *John Gosden* a66 71
2 b f Dansili Fantasia (Sadler's Wells (USA))
6292[5] 7733[16] **8323**[2] 8998[10] 9277[4]

**Comhghairdeas (IRE)**
*Andrew Slattery* 84
3 b g Acclamation Maid To Order (IRE) (Zafonic (USA))
**6971a**[9]

**Comicas (USA)** *Charlie Appleby* a113 105
4 ch g Distorted Humor(USA) Abby's Angel (USA) (Touch Gold (USA))
(694a) 1041a[4] **1377a**[2] 2737[3] 4071[13] 9361a[2]

**Cominols (SWI)** *A Schaerer* a69
6 b g Vespone(IRE) Chapadinha (SWI) (Beldale Flutter (USA))
835a[5]

**Comin' Through (AUS)**
*Chris Waller* 108
3 b c Fastnet Rock(AUS) Mica's Pride (AUS) (Bite The Bullet (USA))
**8059a**[15]

**Commanche** *Chris Dwyer* a72 64
8 ch g Sleeping Indian Happy Memories (IRE) (Thatching)
302[4] 583[2] **(843)** 1219[6] 1631[6] 4766[4] 5119[5] 5511[5] 6113[3] 6635[6] 7320[10] 7933[8] 8329[5] 8490[6]

**Commander** *Roger Varian* 88
3 b c Frankel Model Queen (USA) (Kingmambo (USA))
1961[2] **(3293)**

**Commander Grigio (IRE)** *J A Stack* 98
2 b c Holy Roman Emperor(IRE) Many Hearts (USA) (Distorted Humor (USA))
**4386a**[7] 4926a[4]

**Commander Han (FR)** *Kevin Ryan* 72
2 ch c Siyouni(FR) Acentela (IRE) (Shirocco (GER))
6403[9] **7819**[4]

**Commissar** *Mandy Rowland* a56 9
8 b g Soviet Star(USA) Sari (Faustus (USA))
**70**[4] 421[5] 661[5] 1081[7] 1864[5]◆ 2166[11] 2729[12]

**Commodity (IRE)** *Sir Michael Stoute* a89 82
4 ch g Dutch Art Royale Danehill (IRE) (Danehill (USA))
(1687) (2317) (2960) 3589[4] **6014**[3] 6933[6]

**Communique (IRE)** *Mark Johnston* a83
2 ch c Casamento(IRE) Midnight Line (USA) (Kris S (USA))
8030[2]◆ **8372**[2]

**Compainville (FR)**
*X Thomas-Demeaulte* 78
2 b f Rajsaman(FR) Luna Celtica (IRE) (Celtic Swing)
**7637a**[15]

**Company Asset (IRE)** *Kevin Ryan* a78 103
4 ch m Fast Company(IRE) Changari (USA) (Gulch (USA))
2138[3] 2805[3] (4248) (4431) 5439[6] 6349[3] **(6924)** 7753a[2] 8273a[11]

**Company Trader (IRE)**
*Sharon Watt* 45
3 b g Fast Company(IRE) Akariyda (IRE) (Salse (USA))
1701[6] 2300[5] **2841**[7] 3489[11] 5581[9]

**Comparative** *C Von Der Recke* a62 61
5 b g Oasis Dream Indication (Sadler's Wells (USA))
1070a[2]

**Compas Scoobie** *Stuart Williams* a95 101
4 br g Kheleyf(USA) Fantastic Santanyi (Fantastic Light (USA))
(2161) 2320[5] 3330[2]◆ 4272[2] 4816[9] (5426) **(6177)** 6512[5]◆ 7144[20] 9373[5]

**Compass Point** *Laura Mongan* 44
2 b c Helmet(AUS) Takarna (IRE) (Mark Of Esteem (IRE))
**6260**[9] 7128[14]

**Compass Rose (IRE)** *Scott Dixon* a50 36
3 b f Henrythenavigator(USA) Raydaniya (IRE) (In The Wings)
4568[8] 5003[9] **7035**[4] 7480[12] 8255[12]

**Compatriot (IRE)**
*John Joseph Murphy* a61 53
3 b g Pour Moi(IRE) Wooded Glade (Oasis Dream)
1389a[19]

**Competent** *Tim Fitzgerald* a71
5 b g Compton Place Pantita (Polish Precedent (USA))
1864[9] 2308[10]

**Competition** *Brian Rothwell* a54 63
5 b g Multiplex Compolina (Compton Place)
1984[6] **2632**[5] 2791[7] **3537**[4] 3898[6] 4575[6] 5284[5]

**Compliance (IRE)** *James Tate* a71 58
2 b c Exceed And Excel(AUS) Saadiah (IRE) (Dubai Destination (USA))
6108[10] **6883**[2] 7237[5] 8848[6]

**Complicit (IRE)** *J F Levins* a75 66
6 b g Captain Rio Molomo (Barathea (IRE))
**(9334)**

**Complimenti (USA)** *Doug Watson* a92
3 ch f Congrats(USA) Goldilocks' Cat (USA) (Seeking The Gold (USA))
317a[2] **652a**[4] **889a**[3]

**Comporta** *Ismail Mohammed* 63
2 b c Iffraaj Hot Wired (Rock Of Gibraltar (IRE))
**7281**[7] 7819[11]

**Comprise** *Michael Bell* a86 77
3 b g Pivotal Constitute (USA) (Gone West (USA))
(1432) 2072[2] 2806[11] 3673[3] **(4500)** 4892[9] 5416[4] 7287[5]

**Compton Abbey** *Brett Johnson* a50
3 b f Compton Place Bolsena (USA) (Red Ransom (USA))
**9202**[4]

**Compton Brave** *J R Jenkins* a46 39
3 b g Compton Place Willmar (IRE) (Zafonic (USA))
2734[13] 3703[7] **7514**[7] **8345**[4] **9085**[3] 9365[10]

**Compton Grace** *Mick Channon* 46
2 ch f Compton Place Janet Girl (Polar Falcon (USA))
5216[8] 5717[7] 5779[5] 6815[12]

**Compton Lane** *Rod Millman* a62 74
3 b g Compton Place Dubai Affair (Dubawi (IRE))
1332[6] 2271[6] 2758[6] 3692[9]

**Compton Mill** *Hughie Morrison* a77 89
5 b g Compton Place Classic Millennium (Midyan (USA))
2504[3] 2893[3] 4522[6] (5287) 6929[6] 7651[4] (7735) 8165[8] 8652[6]

**Compton Park** *Les Eyre* a70 73
10 ch h Compton Place Corps De Ballet (IRE) (Fasliyev (USA))
1310[3] 1631[7] 1971[3] 2104[8] 3666[9] 3949[5] 4506[11] 5836[10] 8194[12]

**Compton Poppy** *Tony Carroll* a58 82
3 b f Compton Place Miss Poppy (Averti (IRE))
2407[6] 3517[3] 3865[8] 4842[2] 5360[4]

**Compton Prince** *Milton Bradley* a67 59
8 ch g Compton Place Malelane (IRE) (Prince Sabo)
(172) 355[7] 468[5] 768[3] 1080[4] 1339[6] 1723[2] 2214[3] (2509) 2962[10] (3280) 3811[12] 4467[6] 4735[7] 6157[8] 8824[7] (9184)

**Compton River** *Bryan Smart* a77 69
5 b g Compton Place Inagh River (Fasliyev (USA))
886[6] 1031[6] 1558[6] 2551[4] 4428[5] 4896[3] 5804[7] 6351[3] 7020[2] 7522[18] 7884[7] 8237[3] 8484[5]

**Compulsive (IRE)** *Roger Varian* a70 61
2 ch c Lope De Vega(IRE) Fand (USA) (Kingmambo (USA))
6884[7] 8140[7] 8634[7]

**Computable** *Tim Easterby* 84
3 ch g Compton Place Kummel Excess (IRE) (Exceed And Excel (AUS))
1975[2] 2806[8] 4835[6] 6185[12]

**Comrade Conrad (IRE)**
*Roger Charlton* 85
3 br c Canford Cliffs(IRE) View (IRE) (Galileo (IRE))
(1682) 2690[5] 3392[5] 6135[2] 6865[6] 7565[7]

**Comrade In Arms (USA)**
*Sir Michael Stoute* a73 65
2 b g War Front(USA) Maryinsky (IRE) (Sadler's Wells (USA))
5960[5] 8149[9] 8493[2]

**Comselle** *Stuart Kittow* 59
2 b f Compton Place M'selle (IRE) (Elnadim (USA))
2563[11] 5327[4]◆ 6178[6] 6651[7] 7228[8] 8110[10]

**Concur (IRE)** *Rod Millman* a47 56
4 ch g Approve(IRE) Tradmagic (IRE) (Traditionally (USA))
2043[8] 2178[5] (3185) (3704) 4426[4] 5146[8] 7694[9] 7911[9]

**Condamine (IRE)** *Jeremy Gask* a77
4 b g Duke Of Marmalade(IRE) Miracolia (IRE) (Montjeu (IRE))
91[2]

**Confessional** *Tim Easterby* a75 97
10 b g Dubawi(IRE) Golden Nun (Bishop Of Cashel)
2524[3] 3092[13] 3625[3] 3829[10] 4306[8] 4686[7] (5402) 5505[9] 6314[3] 6412[3] 6677[7] 6927[3] 7610[4] 8238[3] 8416[4]

**Conflagration** *Ed Dunlop* a61 49
2 b c Exceed And Excel(AUS) Please Sing (Royal Applause)
8112[6] 8309[7] 8536[6] 9024[8] 9436[10]

**Confrontation (USA)**
*Saeed bin Suroor* a109
7 br g War Pass(USA) Successfully Sweet (USA) (Successful Appeal (USA))
695a[8]

**Confrontational (IRE)**
*John Joseph Murphy* a94 84
3 b g Footstepsinthesand Chevanah (IRE) (Chevalier (IRE))
8225a[9] 9247a[9]

**Conistone** *James Bethell* a56 66
3 ch f Poet's Voice Protectress (Hector Protector (USA))
1678[7] 2702[4] 3207[3] 4603[4] 6048[13] (6587)

**Conjuror's Bluff** *Fred Watson* a29 27
9 b g Tiger Hill(IRE) Portmeirion (Polish Precedent (USA))
1473[11] 2342[6] 4105[11]

**Conkering Hero (IRE)** *Joseph Tuite* a76 44
3 ch g Arakan(USA) Brioney (IRE) (Barathea (IRE))
284[7] 1445[4] (3326)◆ 4307[4] 5932[6] 6618[4] 7319[9] 9242[10]

**Connacht Girl (IRE)**
*Adrian Paul Keatley* 79
3 b f Dark Angel(IRE) Fairy Flight (USA) (Fusaichi Pegasus (USA))
1634a[11] 3194[4]

**Connaught Ranger (IRE)**
*Denis Coakley* a76 69
2 ch g Finsceal Fior(IRE) Mona Brown (IRE) (Dylan Thomas (IRE))
5710[5] 6885[5] (7489) 8030[3]

**Connect** *Clive Cox* 100
2 b c Roderic O'Connor(IRE) Robema (Cadeaux Genereux)
3783[4]◆ (5547) 6696[6] (8290)

**Connecticut** *Roger Varian* a102 95
6 b g New Approach(IRE) Craigmill (Slip Anchor)
7581[5] 8637[6]

**Connemera Queen** *John Butler* a69 70
4 ch m Major Cadeaux Cashleen (USA) (Lemon Drop Kid (USA))
4059[2] 5185[6] 7249[6] 7723[5] 8132[2] 8641[4] 8930[7]

**Connery (IRE)** *Sylvester Kirk* a60 83
2 gr g Clodovil(IRE) Ringarooma (Erhaab (USA))
3328[2] 3925[15] (4488) 4582[5] 5150[18] 6935[8] 7814[12]

**Connivence (FR)** *A Fabre* 94
2 ch f Motivator Terrienne (FR) (Henny Hughes (USA))
(7415a) 8170a[4]

**Connoisseur** *Sir Mark Prescott Bt* a48 49
2 gr f Mastercraftsman(IRE) Critical Acclaim (Peintre Celebre (USA))
7334[11] 7757[9] 8951[10]

**Conquerant** *Ismail Mohammed* a79 79
6 ch g Dubawi(IRE) The World (Dubai Destination (USA))
8711a[2]

**Conqueress (IRE)** *Tom Dascombe* a59 69
3 ch f Dandy Man(IRE) Sesmen (Inchinor)
2754[9] 3246[11] 4525[5] 5139[4]◆ 6439[2] 7241[9] 8427[8]

**Conquest Mo Money (USA)**
*Miguel L Hernandez* a115
3 b c Uncle Mo(USA) Stirring (USA) (Seeking The Gold (USA))
2851a[7]

**Conquest Panthera (USA)**
*Mark Casse* a77 111
5 ch g Kitten's Joy(USA) Lastofthsummerwine (USA) (Sky Mesa (USA))
7179a[7]

**Conquest Tsunami (CAN)**
*Mark Casse* a102 77
5 b g Stormy Atlantic(USA) Classic Neel (USA) (El Corredor (USA))
8097a[5]

**Conron (IRE)** *M Halford* 51
3 b g Mastercraftsman(IRE) Numbers Game (Rainbow Quest (USA))
1389a[18]

**Conselice** *K R Burke* 91
4 gr m Showcasing Dictatrix (Diktat)
3334[8] 5927[4] 6804a[8]

**Consequences (IRE)**
*David O'Meara* 95
2 b c Dandy Man(IRE) Originate (Oasis Dream)
2740[2]◆ (3283) 3993[9] 7846a[10] (8563)◆

**Conset Bay** *P Bary* 70
2 br f Poet's Voice Abandagold (IRE) (Orpen (USA))
1919a[13]

**Considered Opinion** *Ralph Beckett* a75 82
3 b f Redoute's Choice(AUS) Forest Crown (Royal Applause)
7485[2] (7826) 8636[7]

**Consolida** *Luca Cumani* a79 69
2 b f Sir Percy Red Larkspur (IRE) (Red Clubs (IRE))
7403[5] (7937)◆

**Consortium (IRE)**
*Miss Imogen Pickard* a73 65
5 b g Teofilo(IRE) Wish List (IRE) (Mujadil (USA))
786[4] 1330[7]

**Constantino (IRE)** *Richard Fahey* a98 83
4 b g Danehill Dancer(IRE) Messias Da Silva (USA) (Tale Of The Cat (USA))
43[2] 918[2] (4261)◆ 4916[14] 6685[5]◆ 7609[12]

**Constellation (USA)** *Bob Baffert* a115
4 ch m Bellamy Road(USA) For Royalty (USA) (Not For Love (USA))
8605a[14]

**Construct** *Ralph Beckett* 51
2 b c Maxios Airfield (Dansili)
7120[7]

**Consultant** *Andrew Balding* a48 66
2 b g Kodiac Mary Goodnight (King's Best (USA))
7740[4] 8382[4] 8981[5]

**Consulting** *Stuart Williams* a77 78
4 ch g Kyllachy Doctor's Note (Pursuit Of Love)
93[6] 2835[9] 3330[8] 3816[7] 4099[10] 5156[3]◆ 5936[6]

**Contango (IRE)** *Andrew Balding* 98
3 ch g Casamento(IRE) Call Later (USA) (Gone West (USA))
(3393) (4295) (5160) 5915[2]

**Conte Fleurette (FR)**
*Mlle V Mercader* a57 46
4 b m Slickly(FR) Pretty As Can Be (Giant's Causeway (USA))
7069a[7]

**Contentment (AUS)** *J Size* 119
6 ch g Hussonet(USA) Jemison (AUS) (Commands (AUS))
(2492a) 9170a[12]

**Contentment** *William Haggas* a78 80
3 b f Cacique(IRE) Cartimandua (Medicean)
(3075) 3900[2] 4564[6] 7161[6] 8818[8]

**Con Te Partiro (USA)**
*Wesley A Ward* a69 110
3 bb f Scat Daddy(USA) Temple Street (USA) (Street Cry (IRE))
(3964) 8071a[9]

**Continuum** *Peter Hedger* a87 67
8 bb g Dansili Clepsydra (Sadler's Wells (USA))
8384[6] 8892[6] 9204[4] 9434[5]

**Contortioniste** *C Laffon-Parias* 91
2 ch c Pivotal Distortion (Distorted Humor (USA))
(4596a) 5461a[6] 6730a[5]

**Contrapposto (IRE)**
*David Menuisier* 101
3 b c Cacique(IRE) Interim Payment (USA) (Red Ransom (USA))
1904[4] 2766[10]

**Contrast (IRE)** *Richard Hannon* 96
3 ch g Dutch Art Israar (Machiavellian (USA))
2126[6] 2824[7]

**Contrebasse** *Tim Easterby* a61 59
2 b g Champs Elysees Viola Da Braccio (IRE) (Vettori (IRE))
7043[7] 8013[6] 8555[5]◆

**Contribute** *Martyn Meade* a60 66
2 ch g Bahamian Bounty Myth And Magic (IRE) (Namid)
1858[8] 2279[5] 4094[4] 4922[6] 6036[3] 7938[3]◆ 8349[12]

**Control Centre (IRE)** *Marjorie Fife* a68 78
3 b g Dragon Pulse(IRE) Margaux Magique (IRE) (Xaar)
(3239) 3496[6] 4250[3] 4663[11] 5697[4] 8211[11] 8557[14] 8874[9]

**Controversial Lady (IRE)**
*J S Moore* a63 73
2 b f Holy Roman Emperor(IRE) Eleanor Roosevelt (IRE) (Dalakhani (IRE))
1681[8] 1776[5] 2052[4] 2750[4] 4252[2] 4858[4]◆ 5585a[5] (5907a) (6050a) 6452a[4] 6977a[7] 7592a[5] 8169a[7]

**Converge (USA)**
*Naipaul Chatterpaul* 101
4 b g Sidney's Candy(USA) Atlantic Ocean (USA) (Stormy Atlantic (USA))
7633a[11]

**Conversant (IRE)** *Hugo Palmer* a62 60
2 gr g Zebedee Tea Cup (Danehill Dancer (IRE))
6938[9] 7765[7] 8119[8] 8587[6]

**Convey** *Sir Michael Stoute* a110 117
5 b g Dansili Insinuate (USA) (Mr Prospector (USA))
(919) (1775) 2492a[6]

**Convinced (IRE)** *Richard Hannon* a32
2 b c Invincible Spirit(IRE) Personified (GER) (Doyen (IRE))
8642[9]

**Cookie Ring (IRE)** *Kristin Stubbs* a54 42
6 b g Moss Vale(IRE) Talah (Danehill (USA))
2120[10] 2633[15] 3001[11] 3344[9] 3935[13] 5239[7] 6621[11] 8248[7] 8538[8] 8720[4] (8994) 9218[5] (9282)

**Cookie's Star** *Philip McBride* a56 36
3 b f Kyllachy Bling Bling (IRE) (Indian Ridge (IRE))
1089[5] 1342[6] 2062[4] 3166[4] 3701[7]

**Cool (FR)** *F Rossi* 86
3 b c Footstepsinthesand Coremis (FR) (Bering)
847a[4]

**Cool Baby** *Robert Cowell* a49 53
2 b f Intense Focus(USA) Dead Cool (Kyllachy)
5015[9] 6567[4]◆ 8294[6] 8795[5] 8902[5]

**Cool Bahamian (IRE)**
*Eve Johnson Houghton* a70 90
6 b g Bahamian Bounty Keritana (FR) (One Cool Cat (USA))
2040[4] 2618[4] 3161[5] 3919[3] 4719[5] 5156[2] 6429[6] 6874[4]

**Cool Breeze (IRE)** *David Simcock* a67 61
3 b f Dream Ahead(USA) Dead Cool (Kyllachy)
2463[5] 3536[8] 4053[2] (5041) 5418[4] 5812[5] 8494[4]◆ 8953[4] (9315)

**Cool Chap (AUS)**
*David A & B Hayes & Tom Dabern* 104
4 b g High Chaparral(IRE) Cherishing (USA) (Johannesburg (USA))
8100a[6] 8751a[9]

**Cool Cowboy (USA)** *Doug Watson* a115
6 ch h Kodiak Kowboy(USA) Grand Breeze (USA) (Grand Slam (USA))
85a[5] (539a) 1041a[2] 1377a[5]

**Cool Echo** *J R Jenkins* a54 56
3 b f Mount Nelson Ellcon (IRE) (Royal Applause)
1[4] 418[5] 764[6] 5122[5] 5855[8] 6828[2] 8984[5]

**Coolfitch (IRE)** *David O'Meara* a85 96
3 b f Roderic O'Connor(IRE) Farbenspiel (IRE) (Desert Prince (IRE))
1731[6] 2160[6] (2806) 3295[5] 3741[2] (4079) 4412[5] 4867[2] 5354[12] 6450[11] 7610[10] 7887[7] 8416[15] 8660[6]

**Cool Macavity (IRE)**
*Nicky Henderson* a73 91
9 b g One Cool Cat(USA) Cause Celebre (IRE) (Peintre Celebre (USA))
6135[6]

**Cool Music (IRE)** *Antony Brittain* a62 55
7 b m One Cool Cat(USA) Musicology (USA) (Singspiel (IRE))
1629[8] 2272[6] 3192[3] 3760[3] 4169[6] (4558) 5017[2] 5493[2] 5832[8] 6088[3] 9375[6]

**Coolongolook** *Luca Cumani* a76 74
2 b c Invincible Spirit(IRE) Cascata (IRE) (Montjeu (IRE))
7813[3]◆ 8339[2]

**Cool Run Girl (IRE)** *Iain Jardine* a30 55
3 br f Lord Shanakill(USA) Fantastic Anna (IRE) (Fantastic Light (USA))
179[6] 4479[3] 4958[8] 5203[9] 5542[10] 6381[5] 7220[9]

**Cool Sky** *Ian Williams* a86 88
8 b g Millkom Intersky High (USA) (Royal Anthem (USA))
3076[6] 3840[6] (5524)

**Cool Spirit** *James Given* 84
2 b g Swiss Spirit Marmot Bay (IRE) (Kodiac)
3556[3]◆ 5825[3] (6567)

**Cool Strutter (IRE)** *Karen Tutty* a59 68
5 b g Kodiac Cassava (IRE) (Vettori (IRE))
44[6] 445[5] 579[6] 969[5] 2179[3] 2633[3] 3256[6] 3488[2] 3979[2] 4263[4] 4744[4] 5544[10] 6131[4] 6903[6] 8481[3] 8490[2] 8656[4]

**Cool Team (IRE)** *Hugo Palmer* a89 80
3 b g Tamayuz Coolminx (IRE) (One Cool Cat (USA))
2231[2] 2997[2] 3781[3] (4764) 5849[5] 6882[3] (7570) (7999)◆

**Cooperate (IRE)** *E J O'Neill* a68 27
2 b f Excelebration(IRE) Phillippa (IRE) (Galileo (IRE))
7470a[9]

**Cooperess** *Dai Burchell* a51 61
4 b m Sixties Icon Vilnius (Imperial Dancer)
7241[11] 1246[9] 2298[6] 2733[7] 4710[4] 5357[3] 5791[11] 7199[6]

**Cooptado (ARG)** *P Schiergen* a90 92
6 b g Equal Stripes(ARG) Coordinada (ARG) (Ride The Rails (USA))
1042a[8]

**Copa Beech** *Olly Williams* 13
3 ch g Paco Boy(IRE) My Girl Jode (Haafhd)
73[10]

**Coping Stone** *David Brown* a66 51
3 b f Bahamian Bounty Brick Tops (Danehill Dancer (IRE))
1088[4] 1418[6] 2065[5]

**Copper Baked (FR)** *K R Burke* a63 71
3 bb f Never On Sunday(FR) Shakila (Cadeaux Genereux)
(1589) 2035[3] 2703[4] 3554a[4] 4455a[2]

**Copperfield (TUR)** *S Tasbek* 94
3 ch c Three Valleys(USA) Shall We Dance (TUR) (Unaccounted For (USA))
6746a[7]

**Copper Knight (IRE)** *Tim Easterby* 104
3 b g Sir Prancealot(IRE) Mystic Dream (Oasis Dream)
2160[2] (2570) (3092) 3835[3] 4920[10] 5354[4] 6450[6] 6927[7]

**Coprah** *Cathrine Erichsen* a87 102
9 b g Bertolini(USA) Oatcake (Selkirk (USA))
6501a[9]

**Copying** *C Lerner* 89
3 b f Choisir(AUS) Epistole (IRE) (Alzao (USA))
2003a[7]

**Coquine** *David O'Meara* a69 63
4 b m Monsieur Bond(IRE) Stolen Glance (Mujahid (USA))
161[3] 929[6] 1243[2] 1720[5]

**Coral Caye** *Steph Hollinshead* 49
3 b f Pastoral Pursuits Vermilion Creek (Makbul)
2895[5] 5958[7] 6507[9] 7694[4] 8185[4]

**Coral Princess (IRE)**
*Keith Dalgleish* a50 47
3 b f Elzaam(AUS) Ohwhatalady (IRE) (Invincible Spirit (IRE))
777[5] 970[8] 1102[4] 3196[5] 3484[7] 3832[8]◆ 4263[7]◆ 4688[7] 4900[5] 5254[3] 5604[6] 5922[6] 7889[7] 7980[5] 8591[14] 9364[11]

**Coral Sea** *Charles Hills* a70 84
3 gr f Excelebration(IRE) Tropical Paradise (IRE) (Verglas (IRE))
119[7] (3536) 4317[6] 5316[5] (5558) 6555[8] 7156[4]

**Coral Slipper (FR)**
*Matthieu Palussiere* 64
2 b f Sea's Legacy(IRE) Anaboo (IRE) (Cape Cross (IRE))
1929a[9] 8228a[4]

**Corantin (FR)** *J-Y Artu* a69 77
2 bb c Tin Horse(IRE) Coraloune (FR) (Valanour (IRE))
9087a[5]

**Corazon Espinado (IRE)**
*Simon Dow* a70 52
2 b c Iffraaj Three Decades (IRE) (Invincible Spirit (IRE))
3747[7] 4349[6] 8889[8] 9090[2] 9436[2]

**Corbellina (FR)** *F Cheyer* 68
6 gr m Montmartre(FR) Corbelle (FR) (Air Du Nord (USA))
4457a[6]

**Cordite (IRE)** *Jim Boyle* a64 84
6 ch g Footstepsinthesand Marion Haste (IRE) (Ali-Royal (IRE))
1683[3] 2233[6] 3009[5] 3616[3] 4413[5] 5477[4] (6556) 7096[8] 7651[5] 8326[9]◆

**Coreczka (IRE)**
*Miss Clare Louise Cannon* a78 72
6 b m Intense Focus(USA) Szewinska (Green Desert (USA))
5469[7] (6797a)

**Corelli (USA)** *John Gosden* a79 69
2 b c Point Of Entry(USA) Vignette (USA) (Diesis)
8678[6]◆ (8849)◆

**Corgi** *Hughie Morrison* 73
2 b c So You Think(NZ) Ermyn Express (Selkirk (USA))
7739[4] 8161[2]

**Corinthia Knight (IRE)**
*Archie Watson* a104 98
2 ch c Society Rock(IRE) Victoria Lodge (IRE) (Grand Lodge (USA))
(1694)◆ (2015) 2286[2] 3929[9] 5150[4] (5891) 6935[2]◆ 8602a[4] 9156[3]

**Corked (IRE)** *Ed Walker* a82 72
4 b m Mastercraftsman(IRE) Dama'A (IRE) (Green Desert (USA))
7541[2] 8192[2] (8810) 9025[2] 9337[3]

**Cornborough** *Mark Walford* 81
6 ch g Sir Percy Emirates First (IRE) (In The Wings)
1706[11] 2624[7] (3153) 4893[4] (5135) 5704[4] 6467[3]

**Cornelious (IRE)** *Clifford Lines* a68 72
5 b g Cape Cross(IRE) Fantastic Spring (USA) (Fantastic Light (USA))
154[5] 517[10] 7958[7]

**Cornelius (FR)** *Jonathan Geake* a32 37
5 b g Country Reel(USA) Dinaha (FR) (Octagonal (NZ))
279[10] 462[8] 988[13] 5722[9]

**Cornerstone Lad** *Micky Hammond* 70
3 b g Delegator Chapel Corner (IRE) (Alhaarth (IRE))
2185[7] 3499[2]◆ 4436[3] 5454[8] 7019[5] (7895) 8478[3]

**Cornish Point (IRE)** *J S Moore* a42
2 b g Thewayyouare(USA) Griffin Point (IRE) (Tagula (IRE))
8943[8] 9385[9]

**Cornwallville (IRE)** *Roger Fell* a104 99
5 ch h Makfi Morinqua (IRE) (Cadeaux Genereux)
205a[8] 698a[14] 775a[8]

**Coroberee (IRE)** *Tony Coyle* a73 70
4 b g Dansili Cabaret (IRE) (Galileo (IRE))
8048[14] 8653[5] 9028[4] 9178[6]

**Coronation Cottage**
*Malcolm Saunders* a65 76
3 b f Pastoral Pursuits Avrilo (Piccolo)
1837[5] 3692[3] 4200[3] (4990) 5588[6] 6097[6] (6612) 7195[8] 8159[7]

**Coronation Day** *James Tate* a94 94
4 b m Bahamian Bounty Queensgate (Compton Place)
2054[2] 2548[4] 5245[10] (5869) 6554[4] 7950[3] 9269[9]

**Coronet** *John Gosden* 115
3 gr f Dubawi(IRE) Approach (Darshaan)
2665a[3] 3301[5] (3995) 4928a[4] 6356[2] 7147[5] 8231[3]

**Corporal Maddox** *Ronald Harris* a64 67
10 b g Royal Applause Noble View (USA) (Distant View (USA))
267[7] 551[5] 1365[7] 2256[3] 2968[3] 3454[13] 3773[7] 4251[14] 5145[5] 5817[2] 6345[8] (6503) 7723[10] 8772[7] 9083[8] 9207[4]

**Corps De Ballet (USA)** *Richard Baltas* 96
4 b m Speightstown(USA) Private Banking (FR) (Anabaa (USA))
8601a[8]

**Corpus Chorister (FR)** *David Menuisier* a85 90
4 b m Soldier Of Fortune(IRE) Bridge Of Peace (Anabaa (USA))
1466[4] 2622[2] 4338[2] (4998)◆ 6323[6] 7402[18]

**Corredordel Viento (USA)** *Simon Dow* a45 53
3 bb g Lonhro(AUS) Asheville (USA) (Clever Trick (USA))
2087[5] 2783[14] 3839[9] 7729[8] 8312[14]

**Correggio** *Micky Hammond* 74
7 ch g Bertolini(USA) Arian Da (Superlative)
2108[7] 3400[8] 4169[6] 5005[2] 5455[2] 6269[4] 7925[9]

**Corridor Kid (IRE)** *Derek Shaw* a68 74
4 b g Kodiac All In Clover (IRE) (Bahri (USA))
1819[6] 2263[3] 2932[5] 4005[8] 5962[5] 6148[6] 7320[8]

**Corrosive (USA)** *Hugo Palmer* a84 78
2 b c Uncle Mo(USA) Lovely Syn (USA) (Freud (USA))
6403[5] (7511)

**Corsen** *A Fabre* a65 86
2 b c Cape Cross(IRE) Dream Play (IRE) (In The Wings)
7844a[2]

**Corso Como (FR)** *A Al Shemaili* a74 74
6 b g Lawman(FR) Via Milano (FR) (Singspiel (IRE))
8583a[9]

**Corton Lad** *Keith Dalgleish* a88 95
7 b g Refuse To Bend(IRE) Kelucia (IRE) (Grand Lodge (USA))
(2375) (2426) 2774[5] 3841[10] 4356[19] 5164[8] 5996[5] 6383[5] 7701[3] 8188[5] 8912[8]

**Corton Lass** *Keith Dalgleish* a15 61
2 gr f Showcasing Elbow Beach (Choisir (AUS))
3980[4] 4427[3] 4895[7] 6379[5] 6693[7] 8475[7] 8804[7]

**Cosa Nostra (IRE)** *Richard Fahey* 77
2 ch c Society Rock(IRE) Gilded Truffle (IRE) (Peintre Celebre (USA))
3754[5] 4681[2] 5465[2] 6204[2] 6674[3] 7090[17] 8013[3]

**Cosmeapolitan** *Alan King* a100 92
4 b g Mawatheeq(USA) Cosmea (Compton Place)
2431[7] 2735[17] 4614[15] 5781[3] 9186[5]

**Cosmelli (ITY)** *Gay Kelleway* a102 96
4 b g Mr Vegas(IRE) Victorian Girl (GER) (Lomitas)
3073[10] 3594[8] 4356[8]◆ 5351[7] 5912[8] 6123a[7] 9157[3] 9259[6]

**Cosmica Sidera (IRE)** *D Smaga* 95
4 b m Galileo(IRE) Bywayofthestars (Danehill (USA))
6914a[5]

**Cosmic Chatter** *Ruth Carr* a76 83
7 b g Paris House Paradise Eve (Bahamian Bounty)
1454[7] 1831[8] 2184[9] 2840[9] 3288[7] 3585[8] 3974[2]◆ 5264[2] (5806) 6141[6] 6877[9] 7244[7] 7923[7] 8293[4] 8552[5] 8722[3] 8818[5]

**Cosmic City** *J-P Gauvin* a57 70
5 gr g Elusive City(USA) Cosmic Fire (FR) (Dalakhani (IRE))
7721a[3]

**Cosmic Dust** *Richard Whitaker* a47 54
4 b m Equiano(FR) Cosmic Song (Cosmonaut)
3760[8] 5181[8] 6003[4] 7270[2] 7979[11] 8650[4] 8720[10]

**Cosmic Love** *William Haggas* a74
2 ch f Sea The Stars(IRE) Soodad (King's Best (USA))
9320[2]◆

**Cosmic Ray** *Les Eyre* a63 82
5 b g Phoenix Reach(IRE) Beat Seven (Beat Hollow)
419[10] 811[6] 1086[6] 1403[7] 1610[2] (1735) 2140[4] (2378) (3048) 3451[4] (4019) 4294[5]

**Cosmic Sky** *Tim Easterby* a35 55
3 b f Harbour Watch(IRE) Foolish Lady (IRE) (Exceed And Excel (AUS))
1835[6] 2349[5] 2792[6] 3543[7] 4603[6] (5374) 6630[5] 7165[5]

**Cosmic Tigress** *John Quinn* a62 65
6 b m Tiger Hill(IRE) Cosmic Case (Casteddu)
990[8] (1256) 1436[8] 2340[3] 3046[2] 3830[6] 4684[6] 5257[4] 5599[6]

**Cosmo Charlie (USA)**
*Doug Watson* a110
3 br c Stay Thirsty(USA) Lake Como (USA) (Salt Lake (USA))
430a[2] 697a[6] (1040a) 1375a[13]

**Cosmopolitan Girl (IRE)**
*Robert Cowell* a74 91
4 b m Dream Ahead(USA) Absolute Music (USA) (Consolidator (USA))
(2253)◆ 4078[5] 5355[5] 7887[5]

**Cosmopolitan Queen**
*David Elsworth* a72 77
2 ch f Dubawi(IRE) Barshiba (IRE) (Barathea (IRE))
3590[7] 4213[2] 4855[8] 5572[5] 6037[2] 6575[4] 7621[13]

**Costa Filey** *Ed Vaughan* a71 72
6 b g Pastoral Pursuits Cosmic Destiny (IRE) (Soviet Star (USA))
327[6]

**Costa Percy** *Jennie Candlish* a69 66
3 b g Sir Percy Costa Brava (IRE) (Sadler's Wells (USA))
265[7] 580[5] 1736[12] 2686[6] (6892) 7895[3] 8396[5]

**Cosy Club (IRE)** *Adrian Paul Keatley* a47 59
3 br g So You Think(NZ) Bali Breeze (IRE) (Common Grounds)
3196[7] (5205)

**Cotai Glory** *Charles Hills* 117
5 ch h Exceed And Excel(AUS) Continua (USA) (Elusive Quality (USA))
2397[9]◆ 3079[11] 3926[7] 4920[3] 5684[4] 6402[3] 6973a[5] 7396[2] 8097a[2] 8604a[9]

**Cote D'Azur** *Les Eyre* a88 101
4 ch g Champs Elysees Florentia (Medicean)
1258[9] 1704[5] (2406)◆ 2767[6] 3963[18] 4578[6] 5130[7] 7619[3] 8009[11]

**Cotinga** *Ralph Beckett* a59 79
3 ch f Paco Boy(IRE) Hobby (Robellino (USA))
2761[4] 3392[2] 4336[6] 5533[3] 6369[4] 7201[3] 7902[8]

**Coto (IRE)** *M J Tynan* a71 76
5 b m Fast Company(IRE) Let Me Shine (USA) (Dixie Union (USA))
8927[13] 9244a[10]

**Cottesloe (IRE)** *Neil Mulholland* a65 81
8 b g Teofilo(IRE) Vignelaure (IRE) (Royal Academy (USA))
220[6] 4346[8]

**Cotton Club (IRE)** *Rod Millman* a89 82
6 b g Amadeus Wolf Slow Jazz (USA) (Chief's Crown (USA))
62[7] (422) 759[4] 2176[5] 3004[7] (3694) 4222[3] 4913[3] 5820[3] 6513[6]

**Cougar Kid (IRE)** *John O'Shea* a48 43
6 b g Yeats(IRE) Western Skylark (IRE) (Westerner)
4967[7]

**Cougar Mountain (IRE)** *A P O'Brien* 118
6 b h Fastnet Rock(AUS) Descant (USA) (Nureyev (USA))
914a[2] 1378a[8] 2129[6] 2440a[3] 3924[7] 4935a[5] 5974a[2] 6926[5] 7424a[4] 7856a[8] 8003[5]

**Couldn't Could She** *Adam West* a66 61
2 b f Sixties Icon Emperatriz (Holy Roman Emperor (IRE))
3576[7] 4520[5] 5786[8] 6825[5]◆ 7057[4] 7196[7] 8141[3] 8371[6] (9439)

**Count Alexander (USA)**
*Vladimir Cerin* 104
2 ch c Scat Daddy(USA) Intelyhente (USA) (Smart Strike (CAN))
8602a[11]

**Count Calabash (IRE)**
*Eve Johnson Houghton* 92
3 b g Big Bad Bob(IRE) Tinaheely (IRE) (Intikhab (USA))
1886[5] 2824[6] 4408[3] 5598[5] 6515[3]

**Counterfeit** *Richard Hughes* a46 59
2 b f Iffraaj Money Note (Librettist (USA))
4533[14] 5327[8] 6721[4] 8397[5] 8943[6]

**Counter Spirit (IRE)**
*Ismail Mohammed* a71 57
3 b f Invincible Spirit(IRE) Counterclaim (Pivotal)
5335[4] 6066[3]

**Count Montecristo (FR)** *Kevin Ryan* a88 89
5 b g Siyouni(FR) Blackberry Pie (USA) (Gulch (USA))
(599) 885[2]◆ 1911[3] 2310[4] 4685[8] 5484[7] 7452[10] 8561[10] 9363[3]

**Count Octave** *Andrew Balding* a92 112
3 b c Frankel Honorine (IRE) (Mark Of Esteem (IRE))
(1414) 2555[5] 4032[2] 6421[2]◆ 7147[6]

**Count Otto (IRE)** *Amanda Perrett* a82 51
2 b g Sir Prancealot(IRE) Dessert Flower (IRE) (Intikhab (USA))
6272[9] (8989) 9310[3]

**Country Blue (FR)** *Mrs A Malzard* 60
8 bl g Country Reel(USA) Exica (FR) (Exit To Nowhere (USA))
1931a[3] 2669a[2] 4142a[4] 4655a[2] 5200a[2] 5984a[7] 6544a[2]

**Country'N'Western (FR)**
*David Elsworth* a63
5 b g Samum(GER) Cracking Melody (Shamardal (USA))
7708[7]

**Count Simon (IRE)** *Andrew Balding* 83
3 b g Rip Van Winkle(IRE) Wedding Cake (IRE) (Groom Dancer (USA))
3182[4]◆ 4117[2] 5128[2] 5753[4] 6196[3] 6871[3] (7560) 8011[7]

**County Fair** *D Smaga* a80 79
3 b c Nayef(USA) Village Fete (Singspiel (IRE))
(8692a)

**County Show** *Joseph G Murphy* 65
4 b g Showcasing Cheeky Girl (College Chapel)
5518a[15]

**Coup De Vent** *John O'Shea* a46 59
6 b m Tobougg(IRE) Pigment (Zamindar (USA))
1425[7] 1894[7] 2358[6] 4087[8] 5653[9] 5782[4]

**Coup Fatale (FR)**
*Ecurie Avant-Garde* a33 64
5 ch g Air Chief Marshal(IRE) Territorial (Selkirk (USA))
6300a[11]

**Courier** *Michael Appleby* a79 86
5 b m Equiano(FR) Pivotal Drive (IRE) (Pivotal)
1778[13] 2548[2] 2884[9] (3541) 4375[8] 4719[6] 5317[4] 5828[5] 6382[3] 6787[5] 7553[7] 9280[4]◆ 9316[3]

**Courteous Crown** *Richard Hannon* a52 60
2 ch f Helmet(AUS) Speak Softly To Me (USA) (Ogygian (USA))
5586[7] 6100[7] 6824[7] 7510[6] 7829[8]

**Court House (IRE)** *John Gosden* a82
2 b c Dawn Approach(IRE) Crossanza (IRE) (Cape Cross (IRE))
7511[6]◆ 9137[2]

**Court Of Justice (FR)**
*David Simcock* 79
2 b c Dabirsim(FR) Great News (FR) (Bering)
6916[2]

**Courtside (FR)** *David Simcock* 72
2 ch g Siyouni(FR) Memoire (FR) (Sadler's Wells (USA))
7810[5]◆ 8353[6]

**Cousin Khee** *Hughie Morrison* a72 67
10 b g Sakhee(USA) Cugina (Distant Relative)
4380[7] 5110[5] 6038[5] 6968[6] 7744[6] 8978[4]◆ 9178[2]

**Cove Beach** *Paul Cole* a56 59
2 ch f Harbour Watch(IRE) Dubai Affair (Dubawi (IRE))
2502[13] 3807[5] 4252[9] 4991[8] 7081[3] 7695[8] 8145[3] 8500[7]

**Coverham (IRE)** *James Eustace* a64 71
3 b g Bated Breath Mark Too (IRE) (Mark Of Esteem (IRE))
1580[3]◆ 2016[2]◆ 2507[2] 3296[2] 4050[3] 7062[6] 7465[5] 8124[3]

**Coviglia (IRE)** *David O'Meara* a6 43
3 ro c Invincible Spirit(IRE) Bright Snow (USA) (Gulch (USA))
6184[10] 6667[4] 7574[7]

**Cowboy Soldier (IRE)**
*Robert Cowell* 76
2 b c Kodiac Urgele (FR) (Zafonic (USA))
7732[2]◆

**Cox Bazar (FR)** *C Ferland* 108
3 b g Nombre Premier Dame De Montlebeau (FR) (Dyhim Diamond (IRE))
(5450a) 6979a[6]

**Coya** *Charles Hills* a63 19
3 b f Paco Boy(IRE) Toffee Vodka (IRE) (Danehill Dancer (IRE))
1503[8] 1692[6] 1905[8] 6439[8]

**Cozy Girl (FR)** *F Vermeulen* a84 96
5 b m Footstepsinthesand Kalambaka (FR) (Dansili)
6665a[3]

**Cracker Factory** *William Haggas* a64 64
2 b g Poet's Voice Pure Song (Singspiel (IRE))
6108[4] 8372[5] 8553[4]

**Cracker'star (FR)** *C Plisson* a45 56
4 ch g Muhtathir Star Davis (FR) (Starborough)
4233a[6] 5176a[P]

**Cracking Art** *Il Cavallo In Testa* 58
2 b c Dutch Art Tamathea (IRE) (Barathea (IRE))
4131a[7]

**Crack On Crack On** *Clive Cox* a80 77
2 ch c Havana Gold(IRE) Almunia (IRE) (Mujadil (USA))
6005[5] 8350[5] 8889[2]

**Cracksman** *John Gosden* 131
3 b c Frankel Rhadegunda (Pivotal)
(2084) 3322[3] 4387a[2] (6327)◆ (6980a) (8233)

**Craftiness** *Roger Charlton* a32
2 b f Al Kazeem Artful (IRE) (Green Desert (USA))
9311[9]

**Craftsmanship (FR)** *Robert Eddery* a88 86
6 ch g Mastercraftsman(IRE) Jennie Jerome (IRE) (Pivotal)
599[7] 1178[5] 1788[5] 3168[3] 3966[9] 4443[5] 4699[6] 5065[4] 5337[5]

**Crafty Madam (IRE)** *Clive Cox* a85 83
3 gr f Mastercraftsman(IRE) Dani Ridge (IRE) (Indian Ridge (IRE))
2383[2] (3085) 3621[7] (7130) 7780[9] 8150[3]

**Craggaknock** *Mark Walford* a74 88
6 b g Authorized(IRE) Goodie Twosues (Fraam)
991[5] 6944[8]

**Crakehall Lad (IRE)** *Andrew Crook* a46 50
6 ch g Manduro(GER) My Uptown Girl (Dubai Destination (USA))
414[4]◆ 1188[6] 1436[7] 2549[2] 3756[2] 4102[9] 6565[8] 9258[12] 9445[12]

**Cranwell** *George Baker* a42 58
5 b m Nayef(USA) First Bloom (USA) (Fusaichi Pegasus (USA))
1081[12] 2679[13] 4087[11]

**Cranworth Phoenix** *Brian Barr* 50
2 b f Lilbourne Lad(IRE) Kahalah (IRE) (Darshaan)
2217[4] 2756[10] 3619[6] 5293[2] 5933[10] 7081[13] 8306[11]

**Craving (IRE)** *Simon Crisford* a78
2 b c Equiano(FR) Pretty Bonnie (Kyllachy)
7488[4] 8245[2] 8849[2] 9299[3]

**Cray (IRE)** *James Bethell* a79 78
3 b g Rip Van Winkle(IRE) Amaya (USA) (Kingmambo (USA))
970[3]◆ 1308[4] 1701[3] (2686) 3335[6] 4004[2] 4612[6] 5682[6] 6090[5]

**Crazie Maisie** *Brian Barr* a28
2 ch f Intikhab(USA) Maisie's Moon (USA) (Curlin (USA))
8850[11] 9311[11]

**Crazy Horse** *John Gosden* 115
4 b g Sleeping Indian Mainstay (Elmaamul (USA))
1493[8]

**Crazy Tornado (IRE)**
*Keith Dalgleish* a67 75
4 b g Big Bad Bob(IRE) All Day (CHI) (Jaded Dancer (USA))
1717[6] 2140[6] 2339[2] 2773[5] 2952[7] 3488[4] 3833[7] 4661[5] (5206) 5469[2] 5993[4] 6591[5] 7042[7] 7699[6] 7981[3]

**Crazy World** *Declan Carroll* 51
2 b g Sleeping Indian Mis Chicaf (IRE) (Prince Sabo)
4599[11] 5179[8] 5755[7] (7518)

**Creek Walk (USA)** *Saeed bin Suroor* a74 71
3 b g Street Cry(IRE) Badminton (Zieten (USA))
3682[4] 6791[5]

**Creel** *David Brown* a72 72
2 b c Aussie Rules(USA) Spate Rise (Speightstown (USA))
6854[9] 7613[3] 8387[7] 8676[3] 8925[3]

**Creggs Pipes (IRE)** *Andrew Slattery* a73 110
5 ch m Rip Van Winkle(IRE) Sophie Germain (IRE) (Indian Ridge (IRE))
2637a[3] (3101a) 4419a[11]

**Crepusculedesdieux (FR)** *P Sobry* a90 75
6 b g Honours List(IRE) Pousselea (IRE) (Dockside (USA))
2696a[2] 5490a[8] 7636a[12]

**Crescendo Forte (FR)** *F Foresi* a35 48
8 b g Green Tune(USA) Nee Brune (FR) (Akarad (FR))
364a[15]

**Crescent (IRE)** *Ahmed Kobeissi* 94
5 ch h Galileo(IRE) Coralita (IRE) (Night Shift (USA))
914a[14]

**Cresendo (IRE)** *Gavin Cromwell* a65 44
4 b g Vocalised(USA) Rachida (IRE) (Hurricane Run (IRE))
9346[6]

**Cribbs Causeway (IRE)**
*Roger Charlton* a95 100
3 b f Rip Van Winkle(IRE) Bristol Fashion (Dansili)
1730[5] 2585[8] 3024[5] (3721) (4012) (4319) 4612[8] (6104) 7401[2] (7817) 8548[3]

**Cricklewood Green (USA)**
*Sylvester Kirk* a84 83
6 ch g Bob And John(USA) B Berry Brandy (USA) (Event Of The Year (USA))
235[8] 3014[9] 3298[10] 3750[6] 4254[9] (4887) 5788[4] 6134[2] 7780[14] 9206[8]

**Crikeyitswhykie** *Derek Shaw* a45 49
2 b g Piccolo Kitty Kitty Cancan (Warrshan (USA))
8483[3]◆ 8657[8] 8809[6]

**Crimean Tatar (TUR)** *Hugo Palmer* a110 110
4 b h Sea The Stars(IRE) Unity (IRE) (Sadler's Wells (USA))
1957[4] 2803[8] 6191[4] 6744a[4]

**Crimson Rock (USA)** *Ralph Beckett* a97 56
3 b f Fastnet Rock(AUS) Maryinsky (IRE) (Sadler's Wells (USA))
8007[10] 8637[7]

**Crimson Rosette (IRE)**
*Charlie Fellowes* a84 80
3 b f Teofilo(IRE) Crimson Ribbon (USA) (Lemon Drop Kid (USA))
1885[3] 3094[5] (8117) (8820)

**Crimson Skies (IRE)**
*Tom Dascombe* a56
2 ch f Declaration Of War(USA) Emily Blake (IRE) (Lend A Hand)
8668[12] 8951[7]

**Crindle Carr (IRE)** *David Barron* a60 48
3 ch g Compton Place Arley Hall (Excellent Art)
40[8] 198[2] 580[4] 925[3] 2591[2]

**Cristal Fizz (IRE)** *William Haggas* 100
3 ch f Power Effervesce (IRE) (Galileo (IRE))
2644a[8] 3882a[5] 6358[8]

**Cristal Pallas Cat (IRE)**
*Roger Ingram* a71 58
2 b g Kodiac Flower Of Kent (USA) (Diesis)
6319[4] 6827[6] 7482[9] (9199) 9466[2]

**Cristal Spirit** *William Haggas* a55 48
2 b g Nathaniel(IRE) Celestial Girl (Dubai Destination (USA))
7580[14] 8046[7] 8634[9]

**Cristot (FR)** *J-C Rouget* a85 92
2 b c Siyouni(FR) Count The Cost (USA) (Cozzene (USA))
2664a[4] 3445a[10] 7470a[2]

**Critical Thinking (IRE)**
*David Loughnane* a60 65
3 b g Art Connoisseur(IRE) Cookie Cutter (IRE) (Fasliyev (USA))
115[6] 435[2] 552[4] (766) 1195[3] 2036[3] 3041[5] 3489[10] 4144[3] 4295[4] 5404[6] 5895[4] 6160[7] 8957[9] 9376[6] 9454[3]

**Cromer (IRE)** *Martyn Meade* a43
2 b c Footstepsinthesand Boga (IRE) (Invincible Spirit (IRE))
3135[7]

**Cropley (IRE)** *Dai Burchell* a17 32
8 gr g Galileo(IRE) Niyla (IRE) (Darshaan)
7233[9]

**Cropus (FR)** *R Le Gal* a64 72
3 ch g Le Havre(IRE) Sabi Sabi (FR) (Orpen (USA))
(4943a) 6084a[6]

**Croquembouche (IRE)** *Ed de Giles* a45 93
8 b g Acclamation Wedding Cake (IRE) (Groom Dancer (USA))
2234[2] 2574[7] 3409[4] 3671[4] (6232) 7096[5] 7397[12]

**Cross Counter** *Charlie Appleby* a83
2 b c Teofilo(IRE) Waitress (USA) (Kingmambo (USA))
(9155)

**Crossed Baton** *John Gosden* 84
2 b c Dansili Sacred Shield (Beat Hollow)
6142[6] (7128)◆

**Crosse Fire** *Scott Dixon* a83 73
5 b g Monsieur Bond(IRE) Watersilk (IRE) (Fasliyev (USA))
4[6] 71[4] 159[6] 312[3] 416[9] 480[4]◆ 851[2] 1071[3] (1185) 1296[5] (1542) 1820[6] (3202) 3667[4] 3946[8] 4278[4] 5211[10] (5459) 5804[8] 6062[8] 6574[4] 7055[13] 7557[13] 7939[11] 8260[6] 8488[3] 8803[3] 9074[10] 9305[8] 9366[4] 9443[4]

**Crossing The Line** *Andrew Balding* 91
2 br f Cape Cross(IRE) Terentia (Diktat)
(5608) 6863[6] 7617[10]

**Crossley** *Neville Bycroft* a22 31
8 ch g Monsieur Bond(IRE) Dispol Diamond (Sharpo)
2919[12] 3263[7]

**Cross My Mind (IRE)** *Ralph Beckett* a55
2 b f Cape Cross(IRE) Zaaqya (Nayef (USA))
8840[6]

**Cross Step (USA)** *A R Al Rayhi* a70 83
3 b g Kitten's Joy(USA) Maid Service (USA) (Arch (USA))
2476[2] (2963) 4535[5] 5598[10] 8836a[5]

**Crotchet** *Richard Fahey* a78 78
2 gr f Lethal Force(IRE) Humouresque (Pivotal)
(5575)◆ 8236[10] 8851[3]

**Crowned Eagle** *Marco Botti* a99 100
3 b g Oasis Dream Gull Wing (IRE) (In The Wings)
(2690)◆ 3322[15] 4811[7] 7400[3] 8005[4] 9055[3]

**Crowning Glory (FR)** *Ralph Beckett* a95 102
4 b m Speightstown(USA) Forest Crown (Royal Applause)
1795[8] 2392[4] 3319[5] (5130) 7815[12] 8407a[6]

**Crown Of Cortez** *Richard Fahey* a70 53
2 ch g Pivotal Bahia Emerald (IRE) (Bahamian Bounty)
2771[6] 3648[6] 6590[7] (7030) (8190)◆

**Crownthorpe** *Richard Fahey* a69 86
2 b g Monsieur Bond(IRE) Normandy Maid (American Post)
1694[3]◆ 2221[8] 3187[3] 5279[2] 6087[2] (6699) 7050[2] 7821[11]

**Crown Vallary (FR)** *K R Burke* 88
2 b f Manduro(GER) Troiecat (FR) (One Cool Cat (USA))
5372[2] (6171a) 6803a[2] 7637a[8]

**Crown Walk** *Charlie Appleby* a79
2 ch f Dubawi(IRE) Dunnes River (USA) (Danzig (USA))
(9239)◆

**Crucial Moment** *Bill Turner* a61 62
3 b g Pivotal Moonglow (Nayef (USA))
1597$^{5}$ (1817) 2726$^{6}$ 3024$^{6}$ 6180$^{6}$

**Cruel Clever Cat** *John Gallagher* a21 50
2 b f Bated Breath Satin Braid (Diktat)
1496$^{5}$ 2037$^{7}$ 4175$^{5}$ 4973$^{6}$ 5546$^{4}$ 6790$^{9}$

**Cruise Tothelimit (IRE)** *Patrick Morris* a69 65
9 b g Le Vie Dei Colori Kiva (Indian Ridge (IRE))
45$^{8}$ 602$^{6}$ 901$^{2}$◆ 1062$^{8}$ (1413) 1722$^{10}$ 3186$^{2}$ 3466$^{2}$ 5098$^{8}$ 7020$^{3}$ 7911$^{2}$ 8853$^{11}$ 9414$^{9}$

**Crumblecreek (IRE)** *Clive Cox* a62
3 b f Sir Prancealot(IRE) Larkfield Empress (IRE) (Holy Roman Emperor (IRE))
9301$^{3}$

**Crushed (IRE)** *William Haggas* a68 80
3 b g Beat Hollow Sel (Salse (USA))
3859$^{2}$ 4691$^{4}$ 5753$^{3}$ (6766) 7358$^{10}$ 7925$^{3}$

**Cruzador (IRE)** *S Gouyette* a8 28
9 b g Holy Roman Emperor(IRE) Mona Stella (USA) (Nureyev (USA))
4233a$^{12}$

**Cry Baby (IRE)** *Y Barberot* a85 84
3 b f Power Monteleone (IRE) (Montjeu (IRE))
2484a$^{8}$ 6455a$^{7}$

**Cry Fury** *Matt Sheppard* 9
9 b g Beat Hollow Cantanta (Top Ville)
6811$^{7}$

**Cryptonite (IRE)** *Michael Appleby* a62 60
3 gr g Dark Angel(IRE) Bowness (Efisio)
1730$^{12}$ (2309) 2470$^{6}$ 3184$^{3}$ 3624$^{11}$ 4726$^{6}$ 4983$^{8}$ 5283$^{4}$ 5542$^{8}$ (6174) 6437$^{6}$ 7525$^{11}$

**Crystal Casque** *Rod Millman* a64 17
2 ch f Helmet(AUS) Crystal Moments (Haafhd)
3390$^{12}$ 7707$^{4}$ 8130$^{5}$ 8887$^{2}$

**Crystal Deauville (FR)** *Gay Kelleway* a72 57
2 b g Equiano(FR) Crystal Plum (IRE) (Rock Of Gibraltar (IRE))
5952a$^{5}$ 6453a$^{6}$ 8734$^{8}$ 8945$^{5}$ 9266$^{6}$ (9387) 9440$^{3}$

**Crystal Dolois (FR)** *A Bonin* 31
2 ch c Tin Horse(IRE) Crystal Fire (FR) (Green Tune (USA))
7844a$^{6}$

**Crystal Gazing (FR)** *C Escuder* a78 58
5 b m Diamond Green(FR) Meditative (FR) (Daylami (IRE))
515a$^{10}$

**Crystal Hope** *Sir Michael Stoute* 67
2 ch f Nathaniel(IRE) Crystal Etoile (Dansili)
8163$^{6}$

**Crystal Moonlight** *Sir Michael Stoute* a64
2 ch f New Approach(IRE) Crystal Capella (Cape Cross (IRE))
8669$^{5}$◆

**Crystal Ocean** *Sir Michael Stoute* 120
3 b c Sea The Stars(IRE) Crystal Star (Mark Of Esteem (IRE))
(1967)◆ 2766$^{3}$ 4029$^{3}$ (5639) 7147$^{2}$

**Crystal River** *William Haggas* a68 106
3 b f Dubawi(IRE) Inner Secret (USA) (Singspiel (IRE))
(6782) (8088a)

**Crystal Secret** *John Bridger* a50 49
3 b f Sayif(IRE) Laser Crystal (IRE) (King's Theatre (IRE))
2087$^{7}$ 2393$^{7}$ 3007$^{9}$ 3674$^{4}$◆ 4087$^{5}$ 4348$^{9}$ 4914$^{3}$ 5067$^{6}$ 5718$^{5}$ 6006$^{8}$ 6320$^{6}$ 6473$^{6}$ 7490$^{9}$ 7712$^{11}$

**Crystal Stanza (IRE)** *Charlie Fellowes* a61
3 b g Poet's Voice Clear Impression (IRE) (Danehill (USA))
150$^{2}$

**Crystal Sunstone** *Eve Johnson Houghton* a59 66
3 b g Henrythenavigator(USA) Crystal Power (USA) (Pleasant Colony (USA))
5794$^{9}$ 6633$^{8}$ 7125$^{5}$ 7917$^{8}$ 8181$^{2}$

**Cry Wolf** *James Evans* a73
4 ch g Street Cry(IRE) Love Charm (Singspiel (IRE))
7515$^{10}$

**Cthulhu (USA)** *William Muir* a36 61
3 b f Henrythenavigator(USA) So Stylish (USA) (Johannesburg (USA))
3248$^{5}$ 4449$^{4}$ 7948$^{9}$

**Cuban Heel** *Clive Cox* 77
2 gr g Havana Gold(IRE) Tipping Over (IRE) (Aussie Rules (USA))
3747$^{8}$ 4885$^{2}$ 5960$^{3}$ 7391$^{4}$ 7929$^{2}$

**Cuban Queen (USA)** *Julia Feilden* a44 37
4 ro m Elusive Quality(USA) One Smokin' Lady (USA) (Smoke Glacken (USA))
167$^{3}$ 398$^{7}$ 544$^{10}$ 854$^{6}$ 1587$^{4}$ 1887$^{6}$ 2319$^{7}$

**Cubswin (IRE)** *Roger Charlton* a71 76
3 b f Zamindar(USA) Moonlight Rhapsody (IRE) (Danehill Dancer (IRE))
1944$^{4}$ 2564$^{4}$ 3596$^{3}$ 4450$^{5}$ (4989)

**Cuckoo's Calling** *James Bethell* a62
3 b f So You Think(NZ) Sinndarina (FR) (Sinndar (IRE))
9260$^{5}$

**Cuddington (IRE)** *Tom Dascombe* 70
2 gr c Dark Angel(IRE) Pindrop (Exceed And Excel (AUS))
5874$^{4}$◆

**Cue's Folly** *Ed Dunlop* a54
2 b f Nathaniel(IRE) Island Odyssey (Dansili)
8998$^{11}$

**Cuillin Hills** *Keith Dalgleish* 60
2 ch g Pastoral Pursuits Justbetweenfriends (USA) (Diesis)
3339$^{8}$ 4681$^{4}$ 5465$^{3}$ 6625$^{7}$ 7698$^{7}$

**Cullingworth (IRE)** *Richard Fahey* a32 95
3 b g Kodiac Think (FR) (Marchand De Sable (USA))
(1801) 2126$^{12}$ 3077$^{10}$ 4376$^{5}$ 4856$^{6}$◆ 5392$^{7}$◆ (6001)

**Culloden** *Shaun Harris* a63 69
5 b g Kyllachy Mamounia (IRE) (Green Desert (USA))
20$^{11}$ 852$^{10}$ (1220) 1359$^{5}$ 1722$^{2}$ 1869$^{4}$ 2076$^{9}$ 2628$^{3}$ 3563$^{2}$ 3914$^{3}$ 4478$^{8}$ (4847) (5377) (5605) 6040$^{5}$ 8168$^{7}$ 8484$^{10}$ 8681$^{7}$ 9389$^{10}$

**Culmination** *Donald McCain* 99
5 b g Beat Hollow Apogee (Shirley Heights)
1733$^{5}$ 2571$^{9}$

**Culpability (USA)** *John Gosden* a56
2 b c Blame(USA) Princess Consort (USA) (Dixieland Band (USA))
9318$^{5}$

**Cultivator (FR)** *F Rossi* 101
3 b g Motivator Tounsia (FR) (Desert Style (IRE))
3680a$^{4}$

**Culturati** *Charlie Appleby* 107
4 b g Dubawi(IRE) Whazzis (Desert Prince (IRE))
(3593)◆

**Cultured Knight** *Richard Hughes* a83 80
4 ch g Compton Place Cultured Pride (IRE) (King's Best (USA))
1302$^{2}$◆ 1768$^{5}$ 2161$^{2}$ 2516$^{2}$ 3176$^{P}$ (Dead)

**Culture Shock** *Richard Hannon* a52
2 b f Zoffany(IRE) No Song (Zamindar (USA))
9371$^{7}$

**Cum Spiro Spero (IRE)** *Tony Coyle* 56
2 ch f Casamento(IRE) Bon Ton Roulet (Hawk Wing (USA))
5372$^{8}$ 5492$^{5}$ 6057$^{9}$

**Cunco (IRE)** *John Gosden* 105
3 b c Frankel Chrysanthemum (IRE) (Danehill Dancer (IRE))
(2128) 2555$^{6}$

**Cunningly (FR)** *F Chappet* a55
2 bl f Amadeus Wolf Seguida (USA) (Vindication (USA))
9087a$^{12}$

**Cupid (USA)** *Bob Baffert* a119
4 rg h Tapit(USA) Pretty N Smart (USA) (Beau Genius (CAN))
8576a$^{10}$

**Cupid's Arrow (IRE)** *Ruth Carr* a61 65
3 b g Majestic Missile(IRE) Kiss And Don'Tell (USA) (Rahy (USA))
1913$^{10}$◆ 2304$^{11}$ 2630$^{4}$ 2993$^{4}$ 3403$^{4}$◆ 4265$^{4}$ 4744$^{2}$ (5282) 5741$^{3}$ 6265$^{10}$ 7017$^{3}$ 7932$^{5}$

**Cuppacoco** *Ann Duffield* a65 43
2 b f Stimulation(IRE) Glen Molly (IRE) (Danetime (IRE))
5735$^{8}$ 6939$^{11}$ 7269$^{5}$ (8191) (8588)

**Curbyourenthusiasm (IRE)** *David Simcock* a113 114
6 gr g Mastercraftsman(IRE) Mohican Princess (Shirley Heights)
202a$^{7}$ 540a$^{8}$ 3090$^{6}$

**Curiosity (IRE)** *Hugo Palmer* a80 86
2 b g High Chaparral(IRE) Precautionary (Green Desert (USA))
3746$^{3}$◆ (4259) (4880) 5501$^{6}$ 6900$^{7}$

**Curious Fox** *Anthony Carson* a80 88
4 b m Bertolini(USA) Doric Lady (Kyllachy)
2124$^{6}$ (3177) 3532$^{2}$ (5156) 5758$^{5}$ 6429$^{7}$ 7155$^{3}$ 7737$^{14}$ 9124$^{8}$

**Curlew River** *Mark Johnston* a81 97
3 b f Casamento(IRE) Dubai Opera (USA) (Dubai Millennium)
(1756) 2520$^{7}$ (5533) (5820)◆ 6357$^{8}$ 6675$^{5}$ 6924$^{5}$ 7395$^{13}$ 7817$^{5}$

**Curlin Road (USA)** *Doug O'Neill* a104
4 b g Curlin(USA) Spread (USA) (Coronado's Quest (USA))
6252a$^{4}$

**Curlin's Approval (USA)** *Happy Alter* a112
4 bb m Curlin(USA) Withmom'sapproval (USA) (With Approval (CAN))
8605a$^{13}$

**Curtsy (IRE)** *Hughie Morrison* a60 62
3 ch f Galileo(IRE) Acts Of Grace (USA) (Bahri (USA))
2027$^{4}$ 2371$^{7}$ 3180$^{3}$◆ 4978$^{10}$ 5361$^{5}$ 6180$^{4}$

**Curzon (IRE)** *David O'Meara* 67
2 b c Roderic O'Connor(IRE) Anna Karenina (USA) (Atticus (USA))
3399$^{9}$ 3972$^{4}$ 4996$^{3}$ 5603$^{3}$

**Curzon Line** *Michael Easterby* a82 77
8 b g Dubawi(IRE) Polska (USA) (Danzig (USA))
363$^{3}$ 581$^{2}$ 760$^{7}$ 1717$^{5}$ 2161$^{7}$ 3181$^{5}$ 3899$^{5}$ 4833$^{2}$ 5601$^{5}$

**Custard The Dragon** *John Mackie* a92 84
4 b g Kyllachy Autumn Pearl (Orpen (USA))
(25) 441$^{3}$ (663) 850$^{4}$ 1365$^{2}$ (1546) (1867)◆ 2922$^{2}$ 7780$^{6}$ 8014$^{12}$ 8257$^{6}$ 8872$^{8}$ 9179$^{2}$

**Custom Cut (IRE)** *David O'Meara* a97 117
8 b g Notnowcato Polished Gem (IRE) (Danehill (USA))
1493$^{6}$ 1974$^{2}$ (2440a) 3320$^{7}$ 3843$^{8}$ 5456$^{2}$ 6119a$^{3}$ 6959a$^{7}$ 7579$^{5}$ 8138$^{10}$

**Cwynar** *Charles Hills* a70 55
2 b f Kodiac Modern Art (New Approach (IRE))
4533$^{12}$ 7724$^{4}$ 8373$^{2}$ 8817$^{10}$

**Cyelia (FR)** *Arry Benillouche* a72 75
3 b f Intense Focus(USA) Aaliyah (GER) (Anabaa (USA))
8885a$^{10}$

**Cyflymder (IRE)** *David C Griffiths* a49 57
11 b g Mujadil(USA) Nashwan Star (IRE) (Nashwan (USA))
614$^{14}$ 2023$^{4}$ 2342$^{7}$ 3048$^{6}$ 3832$^{3}$ (4350) 4688$^{5}$ 4851$^{4}$ 5145$^{3}$ 5410$^{3}$ 6263$^{3}$ 6591$^{7}$

**Cymric (USA)** *Charlie Appleby* 112
4 b g Kitten's Joy(USA) Fastbridled (USA) (Unbridled's Song (USA))
(538a) 774a$^{3}$ 1493$^{7}$

**Cymro (IRE)** *Tom Dascombe* 108
5 gr g Dark Angel(IRE) Dictatrice (FR) (Anabaa (USA))
1704$^{6}$ 2804$^{5}$

**Cymru Lady** *Nikki Evans* 4
3 ch f Equiano(FR) Racina (Bluebird (USA))
6808$^{7}$ 8842$^{12}$ (Dead)

**Cypria Charis (IRE)** *Sir Michael Stoute* 24
2 b f Henrythenavigator(USA) Amathusia (Selkirk (USA))
6583$^{9}$

**Cyrus Dallin** *William Muir* a64 81
3 b g Roderic O'Connor(IRE) Munaawashat (IRE) (Marju (IRE))
(466) 927$^{4}$ 3040$^{9}$ (3621) 4313$^{4}$ 5242$^{9}$ 6203$^{4}$

**Cytringan** *Lydia Pearce* a42 48
4 b m Equiano(FR) Scisciabubu (IRE) (Danehill (USA))
52$^{7}$ 217$^{6}$ 1220$^{6}$

**Czabo** *Mick Channon* 104
4 b m Sixties Icon Fiumicino (Danehill Dancer (IRE))
1159a$^{6}$ (1387a) 3319$^{10}$

**Daawy (IRE)** *William Haggas* 93
3 ch g Teofilo(IRE) Juno Marlowe (IRE) (Danehill (USA))
1906$^{6}$ (2159) 3316$^{2}$ 4856$^{8}$ 6482$^{6}$

**Dabadiyan (IRE)** *C Von Der Recke* a43 44
7 b g Zamindar(USA) Dabista (IRE) (Highest Honor (FR))
7534a$^{3}$

**Daban (IRE)** *John Gosden* a78 111
3 b f Acclamation Malaspina (IRE) (Whipper (USA))
(1883) 2434$^{3}$ 3959$^{6}$ 6401$^{P}$

**Dabulena (IRE)** *D K Weld* 97
3 gr f Siyouni(FR) Dabista (IRE) (Highest Honor (FR))
7171a$^{10}$

**Dabyah (IRE)** *John Gosden* 111
3 b f Sepoy(AUS) Samdaniya (Machiavellian (USA))
(1958) 4031$^{4}$ 8003$^{10}$

**Dacita (CHI)** *Chad C Brown* 114
5 ch m Scat Daddy(USA) Daja (CHI) (Seeker's Reward (CAN))
(5954a) 8606a$^{4}$

**Daddies Girl (IRE)** *Rod Millman* 92
2 b f Elzaam(AUS) La Cuvee (Mark Of Esteem (IRE))
1681$^{3}$ 2037$^{4}$ (2173) 2801$^{5}$ 4361$^{10}$ 4841$^{3}$ 5875$^{8}$ 6395$^{4}$ (7123) (7734)◆ 8043$^{6}$ 8424$^{4}$

**Daddys Lil Darling (USA)** *Kenneth McPeek* a109 109
3 b f Scat Daddy(USA) Miss Hot Salsa (USA) (Houston (USA))
4650a$^{4}$ 8071a$^{2}$

**Daddys Poppit (USA)** *William Haggas* a62 55
2 ch f Scat Daddy(USA) Valiant Girl (Lemon Drop Kid (USA))
6138$^{9}$ 7033$^{6}$ 8466$^{8}$

**Daddy Tyrrell (USA)** *J S Moore* a41
2 b c Scat Daddy(USA) My Hopeful Heart (USA) (Strong Hope (USA))
8840$^{9}$

**Daffrah** *James Tate* a55 56
2 b f Dawn Approach(IRE) Island Babe (USA) (Kingmambo (USA))
3312$^{8}$ 3858$^{7}$ 4709$^{6}$ 6022$^{7}$ 6815$^{8}$ 8141$^{2}$ 8371$^{4}$

**Daffy Grey (IRE)** *Michael Easterby* 43
2 ro g Zebedee Pahokee (IRE) (Almutawakel)
6939$^{6}$ 7521$^{8}$ 8553$^{12}$

**Daffy Jane** *Nigel Tinkler* 68
2 b f Excelebration(IRE) Final Dynasty (Komaite (USA))
3980$^{7}$ 4555$^{7}$ 4862$^{4}$ 5210$^{6}$ 6756$^{3}$ (7159)

**Daghash** *Stuart Kittow* a75 78
8 b g Tiger Hill(IRE) Zibet (Kris)
2622$^{6}$ 3685$^{7}$ 4630$^{7}$ 5590$^{8}$

**Dagian (IRE)** *Amanda Perrett* a66 60
2 ch g Dawn Approach(IRE) Hen Night (IRE) (Danehill Dancer (IRE))
7580$^{7}$ 7946$^{5}$

**Dagobert Duke** *P Sobry* a88 82
7 ch g Duke Of Marmalade(IRE) Victoria Page (FR) (Anabaa (USA))
6123a$^{4}$

**Dagonet (IRE)** *Roger Charlton* a83 68
3 b g Sir Prancealot(IRE) Dubai Diamond (Octagonal (NZ))
3038$^{12}$ 3672$^{7}$

**Dagueneau (IRE)** *Ed Dunlop* a51 57
2 b g Champs Elysees Bright Enough (Fantastic Light (USA))
7117$^{10}$ 8372$^{6}$ 8643$^{12}$

**Dahik (IRE)** *Roger Varian* a72 81
2 ch c Society Rock(IRE) Bishop's Lake (Lake Coniston (IRE))
2134$^{2}$ 2556$^{4}$ (3277)◆ 3929$^{20}$ 7318$^{6}$

**Daily Trader** *David Evans* a72 71
3 ch g Medicean Danehill Destiny (Danehill Dancer (IRE))
(385) (967) 1736$^{6}$ 2711$^{7}$ 3422$^{4}$ 4633$^{4}$ 5824$^{3}$ 6139$^{2}$ 7711$^{5}$ 7902$^{3}$ 8549$^{5}$ 8806$^{4}$ (9270)

**Daimochi (IRE)** *Clive Cox* a67 73
3 b c Excelebration(IRE) Quiritis (Galileo (IRE))
1692$^{7}$ 2361$^{3}$ 3005$^{8}$ 4492$^{4}$

**Dainty Dandy (IRE)** *Paul Cole* 95
3 b f Dandy Man(IRE) Pinewoods Lily (IRE) (Indian Ridge (IRE))
3307$^{5}$ 3672$^{8}$ 4081$^{3}$ 4536$^{9}$

**Daira Bridge (IRE)** *David O'Meara* 70
3 b g Dream Ahead(USA) Lady Livius (IRE) (Titus Livius (FR))
2345$^{3}$◆

**Dairam (USA)** *M Al Mheiri* a82 61
7 b h Jazil(USA) Tarteel (USA) (Bahri (USA))
250a$^{12}$

**Daira Prince (IRE)** *Roger Varian* 88
3 b g Dubawi(IRE) Chiang Mai (IRE) (Sadler's Wells (USA))
2475$^{2}$ (3727) 4544$^{4}$◆ (5077) 7582$^{10}$

**Daisy Bere (FR)** *K R Burke* a84 73
4 b m Peer Gynt(JPN) Jackette (USA) (Mr Greeley (USA))
99$^{6}$ 7815$^{10}$ 8912$^{6}$◆ 9418$^{5}$

**Daisy Boy (IRE)** *Stuart Williams* a81 82
6 b g Cape Cross(IRE) Muluk (IRE) (Rainbow Quest (USA))
38$^{5}$ 507$^{6}$ 2562$^{9}$ 3683$^{4}$ 3817$^{2}$ 4095$^{4}$ 4762$^{4}$

**Dakarus Fritz (GER)** *M Figge* a77 70
4 b h Konigstiger(GER) Dakara (Dansili)
81a$^{8}$ 9112a$^{4}$

**Dakota City** *Olly Murphy* a79 66
6 b g Three Valleys(USA) West Dakota (USA) (Gone West (USA))
122$^{4}$ 507$^{5}$ 861$^{4}$ 2042$^{6}$ 2461$^{3}$ 3470$^{4}$ 8301$^{3}$ 8655$^{8}$ 8876$^{10}$

**Dakota Gold** *Michael Dods* 106
3 b g Equiano(FR) Joyeaux (Mark Of Esteem (IRE)) (1975) 2899$^{2}$ (5383) 6198$^{2}$ 6970$^{2}$ 7286$^{3}$

**Dalakania (IRE)** *C Laffon-Parias* a75 69
3 rg f Dalakhani(IRE) Arme Ancienne (Sillery (USA))
3353a$^{12}$

**Dalalah** *Richard Guest* a48 50
4 b m Exceed And Excel(AUS) Bashasha (USA) (Kingmambo (USA))
1720$^{8}$ 1978$^{5}$ 2306$^{4}$ 2633$^{12}$ 3185$^{11}$ 7705$^{5}$ 7993$^{4}$ 8133$^{8}$ 8495$^{11}$

**Dalasiri (IRE)** *Johnny Farrelly* a63 84
8 gr g Dylan Thomas(IRE) Dalataya (IRE) (Sadler's Wells (USA))
8876$^{9}$ 9158$^{6}$

**Dalavand (IRE)** *Laura Mongan* a53 61
4 ch g Tamayuz Kirunavaara (IRE) (Galileo (IRE))
123$^{7}$ 233$^{4}$ 646$^{4}$ 988$^{12}$ 1697$^{8}$ 2914$^{11}$ 3251$^{9}$

**Dalavida (FR)** *David Simcock* a61 34
3 gr f Kendargent(FR) Dalawysa (FR) (Dalakhani (IRE))
658$^{3}$ 1143$^{3}$ 1259$^{5}$ 5607$^{7}$

**Dalawyna (FR)** *Kevin Ryan* 60
2 gr f Kendargent(FR) Dalawysa (FR) (Dalakhani (IRE))
4528$^{6}$ 7383$^{4}$

**Daleelak (IRE)** *Mark Johnston* a63 72
4 b g Arcano(IRE) Alshamatry (USA) (Seeking The Gold (USA))
2381$^{2}$ 5791$^{2}$ 7979$^{14}$ 8249$^{11}$

**Dalgig** *Jennie Candlish* a37 20
7 b g New Approach(IRE) Bright Halo (IRE) (Bigstone (IRE))
4470$^{6}$ 4980$^{7}$

**Dal Harraild** *William Haggas* 115
4 ch g Champs Elysees Dalvina (Grand Lodge (USA))
1957$^{6}$ (3090) 4070$^{6}$ 6400$^{6}$

**Dali (USA)** *A P O'Brien* a80 92
2 b c Scat Daddy(USA) Alegendinmyownmind (Cape Cross (IRE))
2861a$^{7}$ 7855a$^{4}$

**Dalila (GER)** *P Schiergen* 93
3 b f Rock Of Gibraltar(IRE) Douala (Dubawi (IRE))
6254a$^{6}$ 7204a$^{5}$ 8463a$^{9}$

**Dalileo (IRE)** *Mark Johnston* a80 67
2 b c Galileo(IRE) Snow Queen (IRE) (Danehill Dancer (IRE))
7160$^{4}$ 7758$^{2}$

**Dallas Affair** *F Head* a74 104
3 b f Soldier Hollow Daytona (GER) (Lando (GER))
(1459a) (4027a) 4665a$^{3}$ 7305a$^{6}$ 8665a$^{2}$

**Dalness Express** *John O'Shea* a48 29
4 b g Firebreak Under My Spell (Wizard King)
167$^{7}$ 544$^{12}$ 9215$^{6}$

**Dalshand (FR)** *David O'Meara* 98
4 ch g New Approach(IRE) Daltaiyma (IRE) (Doyoun)
8047$^{16}$ 8485$^{8}$

**Dalton** *David O'Meara* 84
3 b c Mayson Pious (Bishop Of Cashel)
(2495)◆ 3038$^{11}$ 8393$^{6}$ 8600$^{16}$

**Dalton Highway (IRE)** *D K Weld* 84
4 b g Zoffany(IRE) Poinsettia (IRE) (Galileo (IRE))
6956a$^{12}$

**Daltrey** *John Gosden* a75 43
2 b c Iffraaj Roger Sez (IRE) (Red Clubs (IRE))
8560$^{10}$ 8888$^{6}$

**Damasia (FR)** *F Vermeulen* 61
4 b m American Post Mona Des Sables (IRE) (Marchand De Sable (USA))
1181a$^{6}$

**Dame Du Roi (IRE)** *F Head* 109
3 b f Dark Angel(IRE) Uruguay (IRE) (Authorized (IRE))
5460a$^{8}$ 6729a$^{3}$ 7671a$^{4}$◆

**Dame Nellie** *Rae Guest* a44
2 b f Aussie Rules(USA) Eminencia (Sadler's Wells (USA))
9201$^{12}$

**Dameron (FR)** *C Ferland* a74 84
2 b c Dabirsim(FR) Maka (FR) (Slickly (FR))
6249a$^{8}$

**Damo** *Simon Dow* a60
3 ch g New Approach(IRE) Umlilo (Mtoto)
237$^{7}$ 378$^{4}$ 545$^{9}$ 5898$^{8}$

**Damocles (GER)** *John Gosden* a85 73
3 b c Siyouni(FR) Duty And Destiny (IRE) (Montjeu (IRE))
1857$^{4}$ 2231$^{4}$ (8504)

**Damselfly (IRE)** *Joseph Patrick O'Brien* a72 89
2 b f Power Flavia Tatiana (IRE) (Holy Roman Emperor (IRE))
7290a$^{5}$ 7797a$^{6}$ 8597$^{10}$

**Danarosa (IRE)** *Simone Brogi* 94
3 b c Clodovil(IRE) Duna (GER) (Lomitas)
1417a$^{7}$

**Dana's Present** *Tony Newcombe* a76 32
8 ch g Osorio(GER) Euro Empire (USA) (Bartok I (IRE))
49$^{5}$◆ 267$^{5}$ 1065$^{5}$ 1982$^{3}$ 2365$^{3}$ 8299$^{10}$ 8749$^{13}$

**Dance Alone** *Damian Joseph English* a78 76
4 gr g Bahamian Bounty Palais Glide (Proclamation (IRE))
5519a$^{12}$

**Dance Colony** *F Vermeulen* a74 70
2 b f Lawman(FR) Vologda (IRE) (Red Ransom (USA))
5988a$^{8}$

**Dance Dan Dan (IRE)**
Mark Johnston a61
3 b c Danehill Dancer(IRE) Justly Royal (USA) (Royal Academy (USA))
198[4] 328[5] 437[7]

**Dance Diva** Richard Fahey 97
2 b f Mayson Dance East (Shamardal (USA))
(3179)◆ (3712) (4361)◆ 5391[2] 5941[8] 8043[7]

**Dance Emperor (IRE)** Ed Walker a73 73
2 b c Holy Roman Emperor(IRE) Dance Avenue (IRE) (Sadler's Wells (USA))
6071[9] 6827[5] 7740[2] 8676[4] 9021[2] 9199[5]

**Dance King** Tim Easterby a74 94
7 ch g Danehill Dancer(IRE) One So Wonderful (Nashwan (USA))
1911[9] 2593[2] 3091[4] 3790[3]◆ 4076[4] (4206) 5924[8] 6399[6] 6965[4] (7555) 8048[4]

**Dance Me (USA)** Sylvester Kirk a69 69
2 b f Bernardini(USA) Stormy Saturday (USA) (Stormy Atlantic (USA))
4253[3]◆ 8373[4] 8951[2] 9239[3]

**Dance Of Fire** N W Alexander a56 59
5 b g Norse Dancer(IRE) Strictly Dancing (IRE) (Danehill Dancer (IRE))
8315[13]

**Dance On The Day (IRE)**
Tom Dascombe 57
2 b f Epaulette(AUS) Skeleton (IRE) (Tobougg (IRE))
8348[7]

**Dancer Cross** Stefano Botti 90
2 b f Cape Cross(IRE) Dancer Destination (Dubai Destination (USA))
8094a[3]

**Dance Rebel** Dr Jon Scargill a67
4 b g Cockney Rebel(IRE) Slave To The Rythm (IRE) (Hamas (IRE))
807[3] 1339[7] 1755[6]

**Dance Rock** Neil Mulholland a60 67
4 b g Oasis Dream Zee Zee Top (Zafonic (USA))
2721[7] 6775[6] 7080[3] 7712[7]

**Dance Teacher (IRE)**
David Elsworth a86 80
3 ch f Lope De Vega(IRE) Fairnilee (Selkirk (USA))
2793[3] 3461[7] 4255[6] 5111[2] (6268) (9314)

**Danceteria (FR)** David Menuisier 77
2 b c Redoute's Choice(AUS) Bal De La Rose (IRE) (Cadeaux Genereux)
6374[6] 6916[3] 7955[4]

**Dance The Dream**
Marcus Tregoning 106
4 b m Sir Percy Shadow Dancing (Unfuwain (USA))
2389[3] 7354[6] 7931[2] (8468) 8740[6]

**Dance To Paris** Lucy Wadham a68 70
2 b f Champs Elysees Riabouchinska (Fantastic Light (USA))
3662[2] 5030[8] 7403[4] 7786[2]

**Dance With Kate** Olly Murphy a27 28
6 b m Hamairi(IRE) Vercheny (Petoski)
2581[9] 7990[11] 8654[10]

**Dancin Alpha** Alan Swinbank a56 49
6 ch g Bahamian Bounty Phoebe Woodstock (IRE) (Grand Lodge (USA))
44[3] 314[5] 1101[4]

**Dancing Brave Bear (USA)**
Ed Vaughan a77
2 b f Street Cry(IRE) Baghdaria (USA) (Royal Academy (USA))
(9320)◆

**Dancing Break (FR)** A Schutz a42
3 ch f Sunday Break(JPN) Dancing Amber (GER) (Ashkalani (IRE))
4288a[8]

**Dancing Breeze (IRE)** John Gosden 100
3 ch f New Approach(IRE) Posterity (IRE) (Indian Ridge (IRE))
(1885) 2802[6] 3504[5] 3964[7] 4637[3] 5927[3] 6697[6]

**Dancing Diamond (GER)**
P Schaerer
5 b m Arcano(IRE) Dancing Flower (IRE) (Compton Place)
714a[6]

**Dancing Dragon (IRE)**
George Baker 58
3 b f Dragon Pulse(IRE) Abbeyleix Lady (IRE) (Montjeu (IRE))
2585[7] 3748[10] 4754[5] 5722[7] 6754[4]

**Dancing Hawk (GER)**
Andreas Suborics a64
4 b h Soldier Hollow Dyveke (GER) (Lando (GER))
6454a[8]

**Dancing Master (FR)** E J O'Neill a56 42
2 b g George Vancouver(USA) Lindfield Dancer (Byron)
4678a[8] 6017a[5]

**Dancing Rainbow (GR)**
Amanda Perrett a49 47
4 b m Tiantai(USA) Rainbow Way (High Chaparral (IRE))
278[13]

**Dancing Star** Andrew Balding 113
4 b m Aqlaam Strictly Dancing (IRE) (Danehill Dancer (IRE))
2397[11] 2907[2] 4071[14]

**Dandies (IRE)** A Giorgi a71 37
2 ch c Dandy Man(IRE) Porta Portese (Zamindar (USA))
2073a[8]

**Dandiesque (IRE)** Richard Hannon a53 69
2 b f Dandy Man(IRE) Marigold (FR) (Marju (IRE))
5534[6] 5844[6] 6147[3] 6860[2] 7121[4] 8153[9]

**Dandilion (IRE)** Alex Hales a63 68
4 b m Dandy Man(IRE) Free Angel (USA) (Mystery Storm (USA))
271[2]◆ 722[3] (901) 1126[7] 1722[9] 1980[5] 2370[2] 3186[3] (3545) 4053[3] (4559) 6612[2] 7195[9]

**Dandy Bird (IRE)** Julie Camacho a67 45
3 b f Dandy Man(IRE) Labba (Tiger Hill (IRE))
5375[8] 5836[4] 8552[7] 9012[4]

**Dandy Dude (IRE)**
Keith Henry Clarke a68 68
4 b g Dandy Man(IRE) Queen Of Fibres (IRE) (Scenic)
3452[4]

**Dandy Flame (IRE)** Richard Hughes a81 85
3 ch g Dandy Man(IRE) Nouveau Riche (IRE) (Entrepreneur)
(78) (435) (496) 1838[7] 2215[5] 2757[3] 3424[5] 4500[10] (4910) (5473) 6072[5] 7742[8]

**Dandy Highwayman (IRE)**
Ollie Pears 90
3 ch g Dandy Man(IRE) Paradise Blue (IRE) (Bluebird (USA))
(1913) 2775[3] 3462[2] (3709) 4080[6]

**Dandyleekie (IRE)** David O'Meara a73 69
5 b g Dandy Man(IRE) Cockaleekie (USA) (Alphabet Soup (USA))
2821[3]◆ 3452[3] 3585[11] 4250[6] 4616[7] 4958[7] 5318[7] 5807[2] 6564[9] 7327[8] 7523[3] 7894[15] 8254[7]

**Dandyman Port (IRE)** Des Donovan 89
3 b f Dandy Man(IRE) Fillthegobletagain (IRE) (Byron)
1520a[4] 2573[9] 5355[9] 8418[11]

**Dandy Rock (IRE)** T Hogan a55 52
4 b g Dandy Man(IRE) Balgren (IRE) (Ballad Rock)
6799a[5]

**Dandy's Beano (IRE)** Kevin Ryan 76
2 ch f Dandy Man(IRE) Hear My Cry (USA) (Giant's Causeway (USA))
4996[6] 5575[2]◆ 6055[8] (7242)

**Dandys Denouement** Brian Ellison a29 74
3 b g Pastoral Pursuits Engaging (Oasis Dream)
3568[8] 3948[2] 5019[2] 8217[5] 8556[12]

**Danecase** David Dennis a79 78
4 ch g Showcasing Yding (IRE) (Danehill (USA))
2147[6] 2762[2] (3008) 3696[7] 4251[5] (8158) 8645[10] 9124[7] 9437[6]

**Danehill Desert (IRE)**
Richard Fahey a63 70
2 b g Clodovil(IRE) Misplace (IRE) (Green Desert (USA))
2403[4]◆ 2890[5] (3705) 5150[16] 6951[7] 7264[3] 7891[4]

**Danehill Kodiac (IRE)**
Richard Hannon a109 112
4 b h Kodiac Meadow (Green Desert (USA))
(6201) 6931[4] 7354[2] (7805) 8421[3] 9167a[10]

**Dan Emmett (USA)**
Michael Scudamore a55 67
7 ch g Flower Alley(USA) Singing Dixie (USA) (Dixieland Band (USA))
2032[7] 2928[4] 7893[9]

**Dangerous Ends** Brett Johnson a80 54
3 b g Monsieur Bond(IRE) Stolen Glance (Mujahid (USA))
(89) (502) 864[3] 3163[6] (4747)◆ 6067[3] 6288[2]◆ 7063[5] (8814) 9027[2]

**Dangerous Lady** Tim Easterby 69
2 b f Bahamian Bounty Purple Silk (Holy Roman Emperor (IRE))
5665[5] 5998[2]◆ 6559[8] 7326[6]

**Dangerous Thought (USA)**
Doug Watson a62
4 ch g Super Saver(USA) Trepidation (USA) (Seeking The Gold (USA))
9257a[4]

**Danglydontask** David Arbuthnot a64 66
6 b g Lucky Story(USA) Strat's Quest (Nicholas (USA))
(1935) 3685[3] 4471[8] 6343[9] 8157[8] 8505[11]

**Dani Blue (FR)** Mme P Butel a71 71
4 gr m Slickly(FR) Angelic Girl (USA) (Swain (IRE))
3274a[5]

**Danica Ashton** Miss Joey Ellis a32 38
3 b f Fast Company(IRE) Spirit Of Success (Invincible Spirit (IRE))
6295[7] 6828[4] 7322[10] 8134[14] 9071[9]

**Danielsflyer (IRE)** David Barron a69 103
3 b g Dandy Man(IRE) Warm Welcome (Motivator)
(2400) 3844[12] 4813[18] 5423[8] 6198[5]

**Danish Dancer (IRE)** Ed Walker a31 27
2 ch g Sir Prancealot(IRE) Daneville (IRE) (Danetime (IRE))
7120[12] 7765[10]

**Danish Duke (IRE)** Ruth Carr a75 76
6 ch g Duke Of Marmalade(IRE) Bridge Note (USA) (Stravinsky (USA))
2923[3] 3386[6] 3897[8] 4343[7] 4958[6] (5620)◆ 5827[3] 6527[4] 7245[4] 7628[9] 8107[8] 8481[2] 8874[11]

**Dankara (FR)** E Leray 38
3 ch f Medecis Lasdramad (FR) (Mount Nelson)
4943a[8]

**Dann (FR)** D Guillemin 91
2 ch c Muhaymin(USA) Dykam (FR) (Dylan Thomas (IRE))
1335a[4] (1929a) (2881a) 5679a[7]

**Danny Mc D** Iain Jardine 53
4 b g Kheleyf(USA) Thorntoun Piccolo (Groom Dancer (USA))
3448[5] 5003[6] 5458[6] 5917[11] 5997[12] 6591[10] 6901[14]

**Danot (IRE)** Jedd O'Keeffe a61 64
5 ch g Zebedee Hapipi (Bertolini (USA))
1473[9] 1823[5] 3203[6] 3912[7] 4743[4] 5285[2] 5848[2] 6131[2] 6435[5] 7390[5] 7889[2] 8402[9]

**Dan's Dream** Mick Channon 56
2 br f Cityscape Royal Ffanci (Royal Applause)
5047[4]

**Dan's Hopeforglory** Peter Niven a50 31
5 b m Bahri(USA) Silvan Stream (Observatory (USA))
993[4] 1308[9] 1829[9] 2688[8] 3343[8] 3978[9]

**Dan Troop** Richard Fahey a70 101
3 b g Lawman(FR) Full Mandate (IRE) (Acclamation)
(2338) (3434) 4556[2] (5400) (7140)

**Danzan (IRE)** Andrew Balding a71 104
2 b c Lawman(FR) Charanga (Cadeaux Genereux)
3965[6] 4725[3] (5127) 6326[5] 7090[2] 7618[8]

**Danzay (IRE)** Mark Johnston a74
2 b c Raven's Pass(USA) La Chapelle (IRE) (Holy Roman Emperor (IRE))
9417[2]◆

**Danzella** Chris Fairhurst a46 45
5 b m Desideratum Danzatrice (Tamure (IRE))
3400[5] 3740[9]

**Danzeno** Michael Appleby 114
6 b g Denounce Danzanora (Groom Dancer (USA))
3089[6] 4072[5] (4881)◆ 5640[7] 7806[4] 8230[10] 8738[3]

**Danz Gift (IRE)** Ms Sheila Lavery a75 68
6 ch g Haatef(USA) Gracious Gift (Cadeaux Genereux)
9244a[7]

**Danzig Spring (FR)** J-C Rouget 60
2 b f Motivator Smyrnes (FR) (Anabaa (USA))
5816a[4]

**Daphne** William Haggas a104 97
4 b m Duke Of Marmalade(IRE) Daring Aim (Daylami (IRE))
(7397) 8121[4] (8548) 8992[3]

**Dapper Man (IRE)** Roger Fell a53 63
3 b g Dandy Man(IRE) Gist (IRE) (Namid)
1470[6] 2107[2] 2374[7] 2885[6] 3403[8] (3914) 4107[3] 4174[2] 4717[6] 5377[4] 5919[10] 6148[8] 6469[6] 6660[2]

**Daqeeq (AUS)** M F De Kock 80
3 br c Medaglia d'Oro(USA) Eight Eighty Eight (USA) (Maria's Mon (USA))
649a[3]

**Dara Tango (FR)** A J Martin a58 62
10 b g Lando(GER) Dara Dancer (Batshoof)
(5689a)

**Darbuzan (FR)** M Delzangles 108
3 gr c Zamindar(USA) Darbaza (FR) (Verglas (IRE))
(5982a) (6913a) 7634a[3]

**Darcey Lou** John Best a44 44
3 b f Mullionmileanhour(IRE) Balletlou (IRE) (Peintre Celebre (USA))
1552[7] 2315[5] 3674[10]

**Darebin (GER)** Gary Moore a81 72
5 ch g It's Gino(GER) Delightful Sofie (GER) (Grand Lodge (USA))
289[3] (576) 856[2]

**Daring Guest (IRE)**
George Margarson a76 70
3 b g Fast Company(IRE) Balm (Oasis Dream)
(1024) 2474[5]◆ 3173[6] 4186[5] (4766) 5341[6] (7058) 7881[2] 8434[4] 8798[10]

**Daring Knight** Clare Ellam a24 56
4 b g Dick Turpin(IRE) Fairy Slipper (Singspiel (IRE))
2993[12] 3726[11]

**Daring Lion (GER)** A Kleinkorres a86 67
4 b h Areion(GER) Daring Action (Arazi (USA))
5628a[8]

**Daring Match (GER)** J Hirschberger a88 110
6 ch h Call Me Big(GER) Daring Action (Arazi (USA))
3370a[9] 4517a[2] 6495a[2]

**Daring Storm (GER)** F Cheyer a41 63
7 b g Big Shuffle(USA) Daring Action (Arazi (USA))
(713a) 6541a[12]

**Dark Acclaim (IRE)** Marco Botti 95
2 gr c Dark Angel(IRE) Sistine (Dubai Destination (USA))
4083[4] (5314) 6925[4] 8290[3]

**Dark Alliance (IRE)**
Daniel Mark Loughnane a85 47
6 b g Dark Angel(IRE) Alinda (IRE) (Revoque (IRE))
2608[6] 5396[11] 5993[9] 8645[9] 9410[5]◆

**Dark Amber** Damian Joseph English a59 57
7 b m Sakhee(USA) Donna Vita (Vettori (IRE))
238[2] 497[7] 1014a[6]

**Dark American (FR)** J-C Rouget a84 95
3 gr g Dark Angel(IRE) Tres Americanqueen (FR) (American Post)
(3355a)

**Darkanna (IRE)** Richard Fahey 102
2 gr f Dark Angel(IRE) Jadanna (IRE) (Mujadil (USA))
2134[9] 2904[6] (3490) 3960[7] 4855[7] 5461a[2] 6353[5] 7617[5] (7821)

**Dark Blue (IRE)** Mick Channon a61 60
2 b f Dark Angel(IRE) Lapis Blue (IRE) (Invincible Spirit (IRE))
4253[12] 4709[7] 5144[4] 5752[7] 6613[2] 7082[2] (7996) 8467[7] 8644[8]

**Dark Confidant (IRE)**
Donald McCain a64 67
4 b g Royal Applause Sleek Gold (Dansili)
501[11] 929[12] 2082[5] 2633[5] 3265[5] 3652[8] 4163[4] 4451[3] (4833) 5285[7] 5917[7] (6049) 6318[8]

**Dark Crystal** Linda Perratt a58 77
6 b m Multiplex Glitz (IRE) (Hawk Wing (USA))
2339[3] 2955[7] 3241[4] (3450) (3652) 3976[3] 4248[3] 4663[5] 5469[8] 5650[2] 5922[8]

**Dark Defender** Keith Dalgleish a71 94
4 b g Pastoral Pursuits Oh So Saucy (Imperial Ballet (IRE))
1385a[9] 1880[7] 2528[12] 3653[2] 4080[3] 4343[4] (4683) 5094[2] 5647[5] 6923[5] 7612[8] 8738[11]

**Dark Destroyer (IRE)** Joseph Tuite a82 74
3 b g Helmet(AUS) Oeuvre D'Art (IRE) (Marju (IRE))
119[2] (545) (1411) 1945[8] 3621[11] 6203[8] 7398[11] 7947[7]

**Dark Devil (IRE)** Richard Fahey a87 90
4 gr g Dark Angel(IRE) Ride For Roses (IRE) (Barathea (IRE))
3212[6] 3651[7] 4207[11] 5926[6] 6414[3]◆ (7111)◆ 7594[2] 7981[9] 8297[2]◆

**Dark Emerald (IRE)** Brendan Powell a80 112
7 gr g Dark Angel(IRE) Xema (Danehill (USA))
320a[5] 538a[8] 892a[8] 1493[11] 3867[7] 4410[10]

**Darkest Light** Jamie Osborne a34
2 b c Lethal Force(IRE) Deora De (Night Shift (USA))
8989[9]

**Dark Eyes (AUS)**
Gai Waterhouse & Adrian Bott 96
4 b g Snitzel(AUS) Cinnamon Dove (USA) (Gulch (USA))
1400a[11]

**Dark Forest** Marjorie Fife a72 74
4 b g Iffraaj Through The Forest (USA) (Forestry (USA))
44[11] (481) 663[3] 929[7] 1187[3] (1593) 1820[3] 2120[2] 3095[19] 4210[7] 5070[2] 6348[8] 7249[9]

**Dark Freedom (IRE)** Charles Hills a47 57
2 b g Canford Cliffs(IRE) Arctic Freedom (USA) (War Chant (USA))
3846[7] 5365[9] 5755[8] 7196[6] 9436[11]

**Dark Hedges** Olly Williams a13 45
2 b f Zebedee Bella Chica (IRE) (Bigstone (IRE))
1873[10] 2502[15] 2988[3] 3662[9] 4599[9] 5015[7] 6285[11] 7264[7] 8483[9] 8780[12]

**Dark Illustrator** Lynn Siddall a45 37
4 b m Dutch Art Xtrasensory (Royal Applause)
3550[11] 6346[12] 6690[8] 7220[12] 7523[9] 8477[7] 8655[9]

**Dark Intention (IRE)**
Lawrence Mullaney a80 85
4 b m High Chaparral(IRE) Ajiaal (Cape Cross (IRE))
2805[5] 3065[4] 3845[3] 4899[6] 5455[4] (6964) 7594[9] 8014[5] 8596[4]

**Dark Liberty (IRE)** Simon Crisford a59 96
2 gr f Dark Angel(IRE) Extricate (IRE) (Exceed And Excel (AUS))
4560[3]◆ 5114[6] 6037[4] (7243) 7621[3] 8045[2] (8461a)

**Dark Magic** Dean Ivory a80 75
3 b g Invincible Spirit(IRE) Dark Promise (Shamardal (USA))
3669[5]◆ (5158) 8393[14] 9020[10] 9464[2]

**Darkolva (IRE)**
Joseph Patrick O'Brien a79 86
2 gr c Dark Angel(IRE) Penolva (IRE) (Galileo (IRE))
8926[3]

**Dark Pearl (IRE)** Ed Walker 89
3 b g Born To Sea(IRE) Luanas Pearl (IRE) (Bahri (USA))
2783[3] 3426[2] (4146) 5397[3]◆ 6445[7]◆

**Dark Phantom (IRE)**
Eve Johnson Houghton a58 43
6 b g Dark Angel(IRE) Stoneware (Bigstone (IRE))
2056[5] 2956[3] 3251[8] 4971[8]

**Dark Power (IRE)** Clive Cox 94
3 gr g Dark Angel(IRE) Sixfields Flyer (IRE) (Desert Style (IRE))
4407[5] (5264) (5959) 6197[8] 7782[7]

**Dark Profit (IRE)** Keith Dalgleish a72 92
5 gr g Dark Angel(IRE) Goldthroat (IRE) (Zafonic (USA))
1109[2]◆ 1296[4] 3833[3] (4039) 4663[9] (4837) 6672[6] (6894) 7886[11]

**Dark Red (IRE)** Ed Dunlop a100 108
5 gr g Dark Angel(IRE) Essexford (IRE) (Spinning World (USA))
2828[4] 2999[4] 4918[13] 5421[3] 5500[2] 6449[3] 7091[4] 7602[6]◆ (8042) 8234[3] 8598[4]

**Dark Road (IRE)** P Monfort a68 54
4 b g Alfred Nobel(IRE) Denices Desert (Green Desert (USA))
391a[5]

**Darkroom Angel** Philip Hide a61 78
3 gr f Dark Angel(IRE) Framed (Elnadim (USA))
(1790) (2395) 3033[6] 4798[4] 5506[10] 5822[6] 7276[7] 7762[10]

**Dark Rose Angel (IRE)**
Simon Crisford 105
2 b f Dark Angel(IRE) Roseraie (IRE) (Lawman (FR))
5660[5] (6183) 7088[2] 8002[12]

**Dark Shot** Andrew Balding a77 97
4 b g Acclamation Dark Missile (Night Shift (USA))
2038[4] 2391[3] 3321[2]◆ 3867[5] 4411[5] 4974[4] 5505[14]

**Dark Side Dream** Chris Dwyer a85 79
5 b g Equiano(FR) Dream Day (Oasis Dream)
45[3] 403[2] 783[3] 995[5] (1980) 2462[2] (3140) 3969[3] 5245[3] 6290[2] 6686[3] 7321[5] (7709) 8310[5]

**Dark Side Jazz (IRE)** John Ryan 64
2 ch g Red Jazz(USA) Marianne's Dancer (IRE) (Bold Fact (USA))
8119[7] 8350[11]

**Darksideoftarnside (IRE)**
Sally Haynes a79 86
3 b g Intense Focus(USA) Beautiful Dancer (IRE) (Danehill Dancer (IRE))
7935[2] (8291)

**Dark Spec** Pam Sly 78
2 b c Dark Angel(IRE) Speciosa (IRE) (Danehill Dancer (IRE))
5036[8] 5960[2] 6653[6] 7580[4]

**Dark Titan (IRE)** Ed Walker a74
3 b g Sepoy(AUS) Kournikova (SAF) (Sportsworld (USA))
127[9] 354[3] (882) 1195[2] 7452[11]

**Darling Baie (FR)** Mrs A Malzard 30
4 b m Crillon(FR) Bring It Back (FR) (Wathik (USA))
5986a[6]

**Darma (IRE)** Martyn Meade a79 86
5 b m Acclamation Dark Dancer (FR) (Danehill (USA))
547[8]

**Dartmoor Girl (IRE)** Mark Gillard a45
3 b f So You Think(NZ) Preveza (FR) (Dalakhani (IRE))
2175[6] 4224[9] 5796[4] 7059[5] 7232[11]

**Dartmouth** Sir Michael Stoute a111 121
5 b h Dubawi(IRE) Galatee (FR) (Galileo (IRE))
(2803) 4070[4] 6400[2] 6976a[8] 8229[10]

**Darvie** David Barron a62 62
3 b g Stimulation(IRE) Timeless Elegance (IRE) (Invincible Spirit (IRE))
1183[3] 1349[3] 2182[6] 2897[12] 4303[5] 5182[2] 5992[7] 6182[4] 6902[3]

**Darwasl** Brian Meehan 66
3 b f Sepoy(AUS) Hakeeka (Cape Cross (IRE))
2564[7] 3759[7]

**Daschas** Stuart Williams a81 67
3 b g Oasis Dream Canada Water (Dansili)
1582[7] 4501[8] 7404[9] 7780[16]

**Dashanti** *Jonathan Portman* a34
3 gr f Medicean Daheeya (Daylami (IRE))
*862[6] 1342[7]* ***2062[5]***

**Dasheen** *Adrian McAllister* a54 85
4 b g Bahamian Bounty Caribbean Dancer (USA) (Theatrical (IRE))
**8438a[10]**

**Dashing Dusty (IRE)**
*Jamie Osborne* a58 59
2 b g Elzaam(AUS) Zuppa Inglese (IRE) (Orpen (USA))
**5749[6]** 6262[4] *7535[4] 8887[4] 9090[10] 9230[9]*

**Dashing Poet** *Heather Main* a71 53
3 b f Poet's Voice Millisecond (Royal Applause)
*75[6] 3248 456[2]*◆ *813[8] (1221) (1328)* 1688[5] 2271[3] 2720[6] *3466[3]* 3692[8] 7127[9] *7771[2]* ***(8156)*** *8503[7] 8797[3] 9094[4]*

**Dashing Star** *David Elsworth* a93 102
7 b g Teofilo(IRE) Dashiba (Dashing Blade)
*7675* ***1341[8]***

**Dash Of Spice** *David Elsworth* a76 81
3 br c Teofilo(IRE) Dashiba (Dashing Blade)
6390[4] **7652[2]** *(9209)*◆

**Data Protection** *William Muir* a63 59
2 b g Foxwedge(AUS) Midnight Sky (Desert Prince (IRE))
*2277[4]* 2706[4] 3277[5] 4758[6] 5933[6] (6366) ***6815[2]*** *7829[9]*

**Dathanna (IRE)** *Charlie Appleby* 87
2 b f Dubawi(IRE) Colour (AUS) (More Than Ready (USA))
2905[7] 3712[4] (5660) (6200) **7552[2]**

**David Fallow** *Paul Midgley*
2 b g Assertive Dimashq (Mtoto)
4014[10] 5179[10]

**David's Beauty (IRE)** *Brian Baugh* a62 64
4 b m Kodiac Thaisy (USA) (Tabasco Cat (USA))
***95[3]*** *743[5]* *901[4]* *1126[6]* *1372[5]* 3201[4] 3524[5] 4148[5] 5052[3] 5459[7] 5778[3] 6179[2] (6810) 7191[4] *7407[6]*

**Davina** *Jeremy Scott* a25
2 b f Delegator Devon Diva (Systematic)
***8029[11]***

**Davinci Dawn** *Ann Duffield* a47 25
3 b f Poet's Voice Bonnie Brae (Mujahid (USA))
***1471[6]*** *1818[11]* 2950[9]

**Davy's Dilemma** *Michael Dods* a52 88
3 b g Sixties Icon Wansdyke Lass (Josr Algarhoud (IRE))
2376[4] (3909) **(4476)**

**Dawaaleeb (USA)** *Charles Hills* a79 83
3 b c Invincible Spirit(IRE) Plaza (USA) (Chester House (USA))
1857[5]◆ 2681[7] **5611[2]** 6150[3] *(7768)*

**Dawerann (IRE)** *Gordon Elliott* 57
8 b g Medicean Dawera (IRE) (Spinning World (USA))
**5689a[11]**

**Dawn Breaking** *Richard Whitaker* 73
2 b g Firebreak Jubilee Dawn (Mark Of Esteem (IRE))
6939[5] **(7551)** 8046[6] **(8288)** 8741[8]

**Dawn Dancer** *Andrew Balding* a64 54
2 b c Dawn Approach(IRE) Ballet Ballon (USA) (Rahy (USA))
8509[9] ***8982[2]***

**Dawn Dash** *Ralph Beckett* a54 42
2 ch f Dawn Approach(IRE) Dashiba (Dashing Blade)
8136[10] ***8877[7]*** *9312[10]*

**Dawn Delivers** *J S Bolger* 89
2 ch f Dawn Approach(IRE) Siyasa (USA) (Rahy (USA))
**5344a[3]** 6242a[7]

**Dawn Goddess** *Gary Moore* a43 50
3 b f Dick Turpin(IRE) Aurora Sky (IRE) (Hawk Wing (USA))
*2371[0]* 3825[4] 4735[8] 5410[7] 5790[5] 6281[6] **7005[2]** *7990[13] 8543[4] 8799[10] 9237[2]*

**Dawn Horizons** *William Haggas* 94
4 ch m New Approach(IRE) Hidden Hope (Daylami (IRE))
**(4829)** 5569[8]

**Dawn Of Hope (IRE)** *Roger Varian* a96 110
4 ch m Mastercraftsman(IRE) Sweet Firebird (IRE) (Sadler's Wells (USA))
1493[3] 2129[7] 3961[7] 4718[2] 6490a[3] 7305a[5] **7812[5]**

**Dawn Of Reckoning**
*Jonathan Portman* a48 60
2 b f Dawn Approach(IRE) Reckoning (IRE) (Danehill Dancer (IRE))
**8419[6]** *8669[8]*

**Dawn Trader** *A Al Kathiri* 8
2 b c Nathaniel(IRE) Amelia May (Dansili)
**9446a[13]**

**Dawoodi** *Linda Perratt* a52 77
3 ch g Exceed And Excel(AUS) Anna Amalia (IRE) (In The Wings)
3195[6] 3386[7] 4039[12] 4683[13] 4896[4] 5204[4] 5471[7] 5995[6] 6694[3] 6896[5] (7164) *7575[7]* **7660[3]** 7884[4]

**Dawwass (USA)** *S Seemar* a79
3 ch g Speightstown(USA) Quaintly (USA) (Giant's Causeway (USA))
*201a[4]* ***1040a[6]***

**Daybreak** *Hughie Morrison* a67 83
2 b f Dawn Approach(IRE) Walk On Bye (IRE) (Danehill Dancer (IRE))
5107[4] **5885[2]** 6747[2] *9022[6] 9320[7]*

**Daybreak Boy (IRE)**
*Henry De Bromhead* a82 96
4 bb g Kingsalsa(USA) Aloisi (Kalanisi (IRE))
6956a[7] **7837a[4]**

**Daydream (IRE)** *Tony Newcombe* a46
4 b m Dream Ahead(USA) Intricate Dance (USA) (Aptitude (USA))
***95[6]*** *2731[0]* *3001[13]*

**Dayking** *Saeed bin Suroor* a85
3 b c Dubawi(IRE) Birjand (Green Desert (USA))
***2167[2]***◆

**Daynawar (FR)** *Andrew Hollinshead* 82
3 ch g Zamindar(USA) Dayita (FR) (Dansili)
**(6256a)**

**Day Of Rest (FR)** *George Baker* a70 79
2 ro g Sunday Break(JPN) Nakiya (FR) (Kendor (FR))
3445a[3] 4090[4] 5520a[4] **6170a[2]** 7175a[5] 8101a[3]

**Dazacam** *Michael Herrington* a87 80
3 b f Camacho Dazakhee (Sakhee (USA))
*125[3] (243) 678[3]* ***778[2]*** *926[3] 1124[4]* 1732[6] 2122[6]

**Dazari (FR)** *S Gouyette* a45 36
4 b g Paco Boy(IRE) Darbaza (FR) (Verglas (IRE))
***9309a[11]***

**Dazeekha** *Michael Herrington* a47 15
4 b m Captain Gerrard(IRE) Dazakhee (Sakhee (USA))
*2063[7] 8784[7] 9102[6]* ***9348[4]***◆

**Dazzle Gold (USA)** *Robert Cowell* a72 63
2 b c Lemon Drop Kid(USA) Tustarta (USA) (Trempolino (USA))
4567[5] ***7512[3]*** *8340[7]*

**D'bai (IRE)** *Charlie Appleby* 115
3 b g Dubawi(IRE) Savannah Belle (Green Desert (USA))
2944a[2] 3368a[10] 4817[3] **(5392)**◆ 6963a[3] 7275[6] 7845a[5]

**D B Pin (NZ)** *J Size* a106 121
4 b g Darci Brahma(NZ) Pins 'N' Needles (NZ) (Pins (AUS))
**9168a[2]**

**Deadly Accurate** *Hughie Morrison* 75
2 br g Lethal Force(IRE) Riccoche (IRE) (Oasis Dream)
5709[9] **6132[5]** **(6510)** **7353[3]** 8074[7]

**Deadly Reel (IRE)** *Archie Watson* a69 71
2 b f Pour Moi(IRE) Lady Ederle (USA) (English Channel (USA))
3312[6] **3908[3]** 4465[4] 4786[5] **6395[3]** 7552[5] *8537[3]*

**Dealer's Choice (IRE)** *Roger Varian* a78 80
3 gr f Exchange Rate(USA) Micaela's Moon (USA) (Malibu Moon (USA))
2619[2] 3279[2] **(4092)** 4788[5] 5758[4] *7056[6] (7771) 8947[10]*

**Deansgate (IRE)** *Julie Camacho* a80 78
4 b g Dandy Man(IRE) Romarca (IRE) (Raise A Grand (IRE))
*1778[4]* 2348[7] *2791[4]* 4168[8] 4529[4] (6181) *7571[5] 8556[4]* ***9101[2]***

**Dear Django (FR)**
*D & P Prod'Homme* 70
3 b g Rajsaman(FR) Dear Maria (FR) (Kendor (FR))
**6650a[12]**

**Deauville (IRE)** *A P O'Brien* 121
4 b h Galileo(IRE) Walklikeanegyptian (IRE) (Danehill (USA))
1378a[7] 2127[2] (2553) 3108a[3] **3924[3]** 5087a[2] 5977a[3] 7179a[11] 9171a[11]

**Deauville Diva (IRE)**
*Marcus Tregoning* a57 49
3 b f Lawman(FR) Sheila Toss (IRE) (Galileo (IRE))
8116[6] ***8869[5]***

**Deauville Society (IRE)**
*Sir Mark Prescott Bt* a39 55
2 b f Society Rock(IRE) Dorothy Dene (Red Ransom (USA))
3179[10] *3687[11]* 3902[5] **5717[5]** 6585[10] *7996[7]*

**Debawtry (IRE)** *David O'Meara* 69
2 b f Camacho Muluk (IRE) (Rainbow Quest (USA))
**6086[2]** (6624)◆

**Deben** *John Weymes* a44 57
4 b g Lilbourne Lad(IRE) Mocca (IRE) (Sri Pekan (USA))
2989[6] 3290[4] 3832[10] **5016[2]** 5283[2] 5738[2] 6131[8] 6571[6] *9420[9]*

**Debonaire David** *Richard Hughes* a76 73
3 b c Sir Prancealot(IRE) Peyto Princess (Bold Arrangement)
*(4011)*◆ *(4447)*◆ 5271[8] 5606[4] ***7882[3]***◆ ***8433[4]***◆ *8542[5]*

**De Bruyne Horse** *Richard Hannon* 100
2 b c Showcasing Right Rave (IRE) (Soviet Star (USA))
2435[5] (2852)◆ **3297[DSQ]** 3925[8] 4386a[4] 5195a[6] (5679a) 6353[18] 6696[7] 7112[8] 7821[8] 8276a[7]

**Debt Collector (NZ)** *Cliff Brown* 110
4 b g Thorn Park(AUS) Prompt Payment (IRE) (In The Wings)
**1378a[9]**

**Debt Of Honour (FR)** *C Boutin* a54 53
4 b g Makfi Ammo (IRE) (Sadler's Wells (USA))
*1920a[15]* 6365a[9] **7069a[4]**

**Debutante's Ball (IRE)** *J S Moore* a60 90
2 ch f Society Rock(IRE) Query (USA) (Distant View (USA))
(2706) 3960[19] **4391a[5]** 5150[14] **5461a[4]** 5978a[6] 6228a[10] *8154[7]* 8524a[5]

**Decadent Times (IRE)** *Marjorie Fife* a64 54
3 b g Art Connoisseur(IRE) Be Special (IRE) (Sri Pekan (USA))
**1913[8]** 2993[11] 3403[7] 4107[12]

**Deccan Queen** *D Smaga* 80
3 b f Rail Link Trellis Bay (Sadler's Wells (USA))
**6566a[2]**

**Decidement (FR)** *E Lellouche* 62
3 b f Montmartre(FR) Arisk (FR) (My Risk (FR))
**6566a[11]**

**Deciding Vote** *Chris Wall* 64
3 b f Pivotal Clincher Club (Polish Patriot (USA))
2727[5] 3595[10] 4341[6] 5291[2] **(5855)** 7122[7]

**Decima (IRE)** *Michael Easterby* 69
3 b f Dream Ahead(USA) Snowtime (IRE) (Galileo (IRE))
1705[9] 2078[4] 2547[8] 5498[3]◆ 6269[5] **(7478)** 7960[10] 8219[3]

**Decipher (JPN)** *Futoshi Kojima* 114
8 b h Deep Impact(JPN) Mizna (USA) (Dubai Millennium)
**8975a[17]**

**Decision Maker (IRE)** *Roy Bowring* a73 70
3 b g Iffraaj Consensus (IRE) (Common Grounds)
3755[9] 4275[3] 4793[2] 5316[8] ***8592[2]*** *8931[4] 9344[2]*

**Declamation (IRE)** *John Butler* a76 49
7 ch g Shamardal(USA) Dignify (IRE) (Rainbow Quest (USA))
*724[9]* 4039[9] 5205[8] *9033[2]* ***(9444)***

**Declarationoflove (IRE)**
*Tom Clover* a73 80
2 b c Declaration Of War(USA) Mary's Daughter (Royal Applause)
1681[4] 2052[3] **(2473)** 3929[13] **5150[2]** 6448[12] *6935[7] 7536[7]*

**Declarationofpeace (USA)**
*A P O'Brien* a98 105
2 bb c War Front(USA) Serena's Cat (USA) (Storm Cat (USA))
3929[22] **5973a[7]** **7618[7]** *8225a[3]* **(8602a)**

**Decorated Knight** *Roger Charlton* a116 121
5 ch h Galileo(IRE) Pearling (USA) (Storm Cat (USA))
*(574)* (1046a) 1378a[6] (3108a) 3962[2] 4638[6] 6328[5] **(6960a)** 8610a[10]

**De Coronado (USA)** *A P O'Brien* a97 85
4 b h Street Cry(IRE) Vertigineux (USA) (Kris S (USA))
6956a[19] ***7588a[7]***

**Decruz (IRE)** *R Bouresly*
3 gr f Dark Angel(IRE) Yazmin (IRE) (Green Desert (USA))
*317a[14]*

**Deduce (FR)** *James Eustace* a69 68
4 b m Iffraaj Count The Cost (USA) (Cozzene (USA))
***7762[9]***

**Deebaj (IRE)** *Gary Moore* a59 74
5 br g Authorized(IRE) Athreyaa (Singspiel (IRE))
***9325[11]***

**Deecider** *Tom Dascombe* 55
2 b c Captain Gerrard(IRE) Plead (FR) (Bering)
**6853[4]** 7141[8] 7562[6]

**Deeds Not Words (IRE)**
*Michael Wigham* a78 77
6 b g Royal Applause Wars (IRE) (Green Desert (USA))
2319[4] 2589[2] *(2962)* ***(3469)***◆ (3660) 4256[5] 4607[2] *8541[6]*◆ *8818[6]*◆ *8990[4]* *9241[10]*

**Dee Ex Bee** *Mark Johnston* 99
2 b c Farhh Dubai Sunrise (USA) (Seeking The Gold (USA))
(5641) 6326[6] 6925[3] **(7648)** **8035[2]**

**Deeley's Double (FR)**
*Daniel Mark Loughnane* a71 66
4 ch g Makfi Habilea (FR) (Grand Lodge (USA))
*2443 4268 1085[4]* 1498[2]◆ 8386[4] ***9054[4]***

**Dee Majesty (JPN)**
*Yoshitaka Ninomiya* 122
4 b h Deep Impact(JPN) Hermes Tiara (JPN) (Brian's Time (USA))
**2203a[6]**

**Deep Challenger (IRE)**
*Jamie Osborne* a78 77
5 b g Galileo(IRE) Healing Music (FR) (Bering)
*1205[4]*◆ *1299[4]* *(1839)* **2163[2]** 2913[2]◆ 3308[3]◆ 3817[5] *4730[9]* ***(7832)*** 8214[10] *8806[7]*

**Deep Dream** *Andrew Balding* a63
4 b m Dream Ahead(USA) Jessica's Dream (IRE) (Desert Style (IRE))
***612[4]*** *807[8]*

**Deep Inside (FR)** *Mme Pia Brandt* a53 93
3 b f Redoute's Choice(AUS) Well Spoken (IRE) (Sadler's Wells (USA))
**1690a[8]**

**Deep Resolve (IRE)** *Sally Haynes* a71 61
6 b g Intense Focus(USA) I'll Be Waiting (Vettori (IRE))
***(1072)*** 1519[3] *2471[3]* 5701[8] 6789[6] *9442[3]*

**Deer Song** *John Bridger* a58 61
4 b g Piccolo Turkish Delight (Prince Sabo)
*554[3]* 1022[8] *1080[7]* *1557[10]* 2298[3] **3008[2]** 3942[6] 4532[8] 4695[9] 6009[5] 6373[9] 6478[12] *6813[9] (7705) 8823[7] 9184[7]*

**Defining Moment** *Rae Guest* a45 73
3 b f Camacho Elfine (IRE) (Invincible Spirit (IRE))
*1[5]* 2734[5] 3818[2] (5339) 5871[4] **(6298)**◆

**Definitely Maybe (IRE)**
*Keith Dalgleish* a13
3 b g Elusive Quality(USA) Ebony Street (USA) (Street Cry (IRE))
***1782[10]***

**Defoe (IRE)** *Roger Varian* 116
3 gr c Dalakhani(IRE) Dulkashe (IRE) (Pivotal)
(2824) (4376)◆ (5095)◆ **(6191)**◆ 7147[10]

**Deftera Fantutte (IRE)**
*Natalie Lloyd-Beavis* a30
6 b m Amadeus Wolf Carranza (IRE) (Lead On Time (USA))
***274[12]*** *739[11]* *3001[8]*

**Deftera Lad (IRE)**
*Natalie Lloyd-Beavis* a60 50
5 b g Fast Company(IRE) Speedbird (USA) (Sky Classic (CAN))
***123[2]***

**Degas (GER)** *Markus Klug* 109
4 ch h Exceed And Excel(AUS) Diatribe (Tertullian (USA))
1661a[2] **3019a[2]** 4939a[6] 6647a[6]

**Deimos (FR)** *K Borgel* a58 82
3 b c Stormy River(FR) Danse Du Soir (FR) (Nombre Premier)
847a[2] **2697a[5]** *5521a[12]*

**Deinonychus** *Michael Appleby* a50 73
6 b g Authorized(IRE) Sharp Dresser (USA) (Diesis)
*1561[5]* 1716[15] 3153[8] 4279[2] **5287[2]** **(5579)** 6038[6]

**Deja (FR)** *Jeremy Noseda* a76 84
2 b c Youmzain(IRE) Atarfe (IRE) (Anabaa (USA))
**4859[5]** *(6159)*

**Delagate This Lord**
*Michael Attwater* a57 84
3 b g Delegator Lady Filly (Atraf)
*2017[7] 2309[7]* 2507[3] 3085[3] (4256) (6308)◆ **(7192)**◆ 7809[8]◆

**Delagoa Bay (IRE)** *Sylvester Kirk* a63 60
9 b m Encosta De Lago(AUS) Amory (GER) (Goofalik (USA))
*35[3] 241[3]* ***721[2]*** *859[6]*

**Delahay** *Michael Blanshard* a35 45
3 b f Delegator Harryana To (Compton Place)
1761[5] **2393[5]** 7122[6] 7694[8] *9183[9]*

**Delamar (USA)** *Roger L Attfield* 86
2 b f Into Mischief(USA) Delmarva (USA) (Unbridled's Song (USA))
**7206a[8]**

**Delannoy** *Neil Mulholland* a59 71
3 ch g Le Havre(IRE) Raving Monsun (Monsun (GER))
*1551[6]* 2137[8] **2394[4]** 4633[8] 5275[4] 5780[9] **(6473)** ***7336[7]***◆

**Delano Roosevelt (IRE)**
*A P O'Brien* 105
2 b c Galileo(IRE) Again (IRE) (Danehill Dancer (IRE))
6955a[3] **7426a[2]**

**Delectation** *A Wohler* 110
3 b f Delegator Chushka (Pivotal)
(1846a) 2644a[16] 3882a[4] 4857[5] **(6987a)**

**Delegation (FR)** *J Albrecht* a69 74
7 b m Mount Nelson Delta Diva (USA) (Victory Gallop (CAN))
**3637a[DSQ]**

**Delegation** *Tim Easterby* 48
3 b g Delegator Rosabee (IRE) (No Excuse Needed)
**2857[8]** 4693[6] 5019[8] 7980[13]

**De Lesseps (USA)** *John Murray* a63 20
9 ch g Selkirk(USA) Suez (Green Desert (USA))
***26[10]***

**Deleyla** *Roger Varian* a71 71
3 b f Acclamation Alwarga (USA) (Street Sense (USA))
3075[3] **3748[6]** ***6577[2]*** *7364[5]*

**Deleyll** *John Butler* a57 59
3 ch g Sepoy(AUS) Strings (Unfuwain (USA))
*2091[0] 7631[2]* 2315[7] *(3327)* **3674[2]**

**Delfie Lane** *Richard Hughes* a69 77
3 b g Harbour Watch(IRE) Anneliina (Cadeaux Genereux)
*522[2] 895[2] (987)*◆ *1343[3]* 1685[2] 2474[2] 3774[2] 4251[2] **(4715)**

**Deliberator** *William Knight* a71
3 b g Delegator Purest (Shamardal (USA))
***2330[3]*** *7322[5]*◆ *7948[6] 8852[4] 9088[3] 9435[3]*

**Delicate Kiss** *John Bridger* a61
3 b f Delegator Desert Kiss (Cape Cross (IRE))
*8635[10] 8822[9]* ***9209[4]***

**Delilah Park** *Clive Cox* a75 65
3 b f Delegator Sarah Park (IRE) (Redback)
*3472[6]* 4764[4] ***(8995)***

**Delirium (IRE)** *Ed de Giles* a49 59
3 b f Tamayuz Coeur De La Mer (IRE) (Caerleon (USA))
3142[12] 4184[6] **4845[2]**◆ 5713[7] 6340[6] *6818[9]* **(7279)** *7879[7]*

**De Little Engine (IRE)**
*Jamie Osborne* a66
3 ch g Power Reveuse De Jour (IRE) (Sadler's Wells (USA))
***8995[6]***

**Dellaguista (IRE)** *Tim Easterby* a87 73
3 gr f Sea The Stars(IRE) Lady Springbank (IRE) (Choisir (AUS))
3031[3] 3862[8] 4437[4] 6047[5] 7046[7] 7598[6] 7984[2] 8513[3] *(9153)* ***(9337)***

**Della Valle (GER)** *Mike Murphy* a59 83
4 b m Lando(GER) Denial (Sadler's Wells (USA))
1683[16] 2785[5] **4344[2]** 5113[7] 5477[7] 7278[6]

**Del Parco** *Clive Cox* a73 77
3 b g Delegator Sparkle Park (Kyllachy)
*1727[2]* 2172[2] 2895[3] 4198[4] **5253[2]** 6099[8]

**Delph Crescent (IRE)**
*Richard Fahey* 68
2 gr g Dark Angel(IRE) Zut Alors (IRE) (Pivotal)
**4577[3]**◆ 5680[6] **6939[4]**

**Delphyne** *Shaun Harris* a63 41
5 ch m Mount Nelson Darmiana (USA) (Lemon Drop Kid (USA))
*6621[0]* ***1069[4]*** ***1308[3]*** 1679[8]

**Delsheer (FR)** *Hugo Palmer* 76
2 b c Iffraaj Rose Et Noire (IRE) (Dansili)
6653[8] 7273[3] **(7906)**

**Demand Respect** *Henry Spiller* a37 37
4 ch g Paco Boy(IRE) Brilliance (Cadeaux Genereux)
*4621[0]* ***1545[5]*** *1868[10]*

**Dembaba (IRE)** *Gordon Elliott* a46 27
5 b g Moss Vale(IRE) Wildsplash (USA) (Deputy Minister (CAN))
***1560[7]***

**Demi's Quest** *Tony Carroll* a30
3 b f Roderic O'Connor(IRE) Demi Voix (Halling (USA))
***377[11]*** *987[9]*

**Demographic (USA)** *Emma Lavelle* a46
8 b g Aptitude(USA) Private Line (USA) (Private Account (USA))
***353[7]***

**Demons And Wizards (IRE)**
*Sylvester Kirk* a75 63
2 b g Elnadim(USA) Crystal Theatre (IRE) (King's Theatre (IRE))
*7488[8] 7897[4] 8701[4]* ***9231[2]*** *9385[2]*

**Demons Rock (IRE)**
*Tom Dascombe* 100
2 b c Requinto(IRE) Afnoon (USA) (Street Cry (IRE))
1767[10] 2577[3] 3169[2] 3917[5] 4335[2] (5047) (5685) (6128)◆ **(6330)** 7049[4]

**Demurrer (USA)** *Michael Bell* a57
2 br c First Defence(USA) Seeking Ema (USA) (Seeking The Gold (USA))
*7489[7]* ***8030[8]*** ***9051[7]*** *9335[7]*

**Denaar (IRE)** *Antonio Marcialis* a93 90
2 b c Acclamation Clever Millie (USA) (Cape Canaveral (USA))
(2459)◆ (2826)◆ 3925[11] 4812[9] 5526[8] 6051a[4] (6452a) 8195a[2]

**Denham** *Michael Appleby* a35
2 b f Denounce Fareham (Komaite (USA))
7986[7]

**Denitza (FR)** *C Ferland* a81 88
3 b f Wootton Bassett Comnena (Tiger Hill (IRE))
4027a[6]

**Denmead** *John Butler* a83 79
4 b g Champs Elysees Glorious Dreams (USA) (Honour And Glory (USA))
1207[2] 1548[4] (2275) 2388[3] (3459) 5524[5] 6323[2] 7402[13]

**Denver Spirit (IRE)** *Luca Cumani* a48 42
3 b f Invincible Spirit(IRE) Leavingonajetplane (IRE) (Danehill (USA))
2753[7] 3329[9]

**Denzille Lane (IRE)** *Doug Watson* a89 68
5 ch g Iffraaj Alexander Youth (IRE) (Exceed And Excel (AUS))
8583a[2]

**Dependable (GER)** *Charles Hills* a51
2 ch f Reliable Man Dessau (GER) (Soldier Hollow)
6575[9]

**Derek Duval (USA)** *Stuart Williams* a76 82
3 b g Lope De Vega(IRE) Lady Raj (USA) (El Prado (IRE))
(1064) 1332[3]◆ 3784[8]◆ (4100) 4868[2] 5661[5] 6145[7] 7131[8] 7569[9] 8341[5]◆

**Der Graue (IRE)** *B Mohamed* a73 86
6 gr g Kandahar Run Denial (Sadler's Wells (USA))
7670a[13]

**Dervish** *John Berry* a38
3 b g Cacique(IRE) Doggerbank (IRE) (Oasis Dream)
464[9]

**Desaguadero (FR)**
*Matthieu Palussiere* a71 66
3 gr g Tin Horse(IRE) Finest Cape (Anabaa (USA))
427a[3]

**Des Annees Folles (FR)** *P Adda* a64 73
4 ch m Bernebeau(FR) Celere (FR) (Kabool)
(7307a)

**Desert Ace (IRE)** *Paul Midgley* a66 86
6 ch g Kheleyf(USA) Champion Place (Compton Place)
1915[4] 2341[4] 3183[8] 3337[7] 3707[7] (4249) 4379[9] 4850[6] 5204[2] 5920[2] 6314[2] 7137[2] 8237[2]

**Desert Blanc** *C Baillet* a87 92
9 b h Desert Style(IRE) Lumiere Rouge (FR) (Indian Ridge (IRE))
81a[4]

**Desert Chief** *Michael Appleby* a49 53
5 b g Kheleyf(USA) African Breeze (Atraf)
68[8] 311[9] 614[RR]

**Desert Cross** *Jonjo O'Neill* a68 71
4 b g Arcano(IRE) Secret Happiness (Cape Cross (IRE))
1556[2]◆ (2042) 2781[12] 3817[3] 4630[3] (5274) 7336[10]◆ 7925[2] 8326[3]

**Desert Diamond** *Sir Michael Stoute* a70
2 b f Dubawi(IRE) Arizona Jewel (Dansili)
8373[8] 8796[5]◆

**Desert Doctor (IRE)** *Ed Walker* a83 60
2 ch g Society Rock(IRE) Dorn Hill (Lujain (USA))
6853[3] (8988) 9310[2]

**Desert Dream** *Sir Michael Stoute* 79
3 b c Oasis Dream Rosika (Sakhee (USA))
1609[5] (2231)◆ 3336[5] 5404[8] 6389[6]

**Desert Dune (FR)** *Y Fertillet* a56 61
5 b g Whipper(USA) Arosana (GER) (Tertullian (USA))
364a[3]

**Desert Encounter (IRE)**
*David Simcock* 116
5 b g Halling(USA) La Chicana (IRE) (Invincible Spirit (IRE))
(2604) 3072[2] 4638[3] 5394[6] (7393) 8233[5]

**Desert Explorer (IRE)**
*Eve Johnson Houghton* a69 71
3 b g Henrythenavigator(USA) Bee Eater (IRE) (Green Desert (USA))
1552[3] 1939[3] 2266[4] 3248[P]

**Desert Force** *Doug Watson* a114 100
5 b g Equiano(FR) Mail The Desert (IRE) (Desert Prince (IRE))
206a[4] 695a[5] 9361a[9]

**Desert Fox** *Mike Murphy* a68 51
3 b g Foxwedge(AUS) Snow Moccasin (IRE) (Oasis Dream)
8742[2]◆ 9203[11]

**Desert Frost (IRE)**
*Saeed bin Suroor* 85
3 b c Dark Angel(IRE) Layla Jamil (IRE) (Exceed And Excel (AUS))
(2383) 2830[6]

**Desert God (IND)** *Richard Hughes* a79 98
5 ch h Burden Of Proof(IRE) Running Flame (IND) (Steinbeck (USA))
82a[7] 428a[7] 4370[4]◆ 5351[4] 6151[9] 7200[3] 7908[5] 8672[6] 9204[6]

**Desert Grey (IRE)** *Roger Charlton* a73 36
3 bz g Mastercraftsman(IRE) Endure (IRE) (Green Desert (USA))
5797[12] 6792[7] 8159[2] 8311[10]

**Desert Haze** *Ralph Beckett* a100 98
4 br m New Approach(IRE) Ensemble (FR) (Iron Mask (USA))
1795[10] 2392[3] 4679a[6] 7576[11]

**Desert Heights (IRE)** *N Caullery* a62 53
3 b g So You Think(NZ) Desert Fantasy (Oasis Dream)
3446a[6]

**Desert Law (IRE)** *Paul Midgley* a82 103
9 b g Oasis Dream Speed Cop (Cadeaux Genereux)
(1800) 3321[7] 3829[14] 4416a[8] 4867[11] 5602[5] (6185) (6325) 6668[6] 7051[6]

**Desert Mountain (IRE)**
*Saeed bin Suroor* a51 62
2 b g Epaulette(AUS) Al Andalyya (USA) (Kingmambo (USA))
5365[7] 8710a[6]

**Desert Path** *Amanda Perrett* a70
2 ch g Champs Elysees Desert Image (Beat Hollow)
7726[7] 8339[4]◆

**Desert Rain (IRE)** *Saeed bin Suroor* a82 78
3 b f Invincible Spirit(IRE) Ballantrae (IRE) (Diktat)
1600[2] 2121[2] 2572[5] (4979)

**Desert River (IRE)**
*Mark H Tompkins* a66 68
4 b g Showcasing Kathy's Rocket (USA) (Gold Legend (USA))
2320[3]◆

**Desert Ruler** *Jedd O'Keeffe* a80 82
4 b g Kheleyf(USA) Desert Royalty (IRE) (Alhaarth (IRE))
1700[2]◆ 2133[3] 2685[2] 5072[2] 7524[2] 7728[2] 8638[9]

**Desert Skyline (IRE)** *David Elsworth* a55 115
3 ch g Tamayuz Diamond Tango (FR) (Acatenango (GER))
2829[2]◆ 3318[3] 4032[6] 4811[2] 5503[3] 6250a[2] (7116) 8229[9]

**Desert Song** *Pat Phelan* a61 54
3 b g Makfi Lyra's Daemon (Singspiel (IRE))
2689[11] 3408[6] 4224[8] 5545[9] 8346[2]◆ 8883[6]

**Desert Sport (USA)** *Robert Cowell* a73 79
3 b g Hat Trick(JPN) Desert Sky (IRE) (Green Desert (USA))
1970[4] (2508) 4104[6] 7538[11]

**Desert Strike** *Conor Dore* a84 59
11 b g Bertolini(USA) Mary Jane (Tina's Pet)
152[8] 468[9] 961[7]

**Desert Trip (FR)** *David Menuisier* 58
2 b g Fuisse(FR) Sea Life (FR) (Anabaa (USA))
8112[8] 8388[9]

**Desert Water (IRE)** *Richard Hannon* 75
3 b f Sepoy(AUS) Desert Sunrise (Green Desert (USA))
3094[10]

**Desert Way (IRE)** *Rebecca Menzies* 87
4 ch m Giant's Causeway(USA) Desert Sage (Selkirk (USA))
2302[4] 3947[3] 4170[6] (5060) 5996[9]

**Desert Wind (IRE)** *Ed Vaughan* a79 49
2 b c Worthadd(IRE) Matula (IRE) (Halling (USA))
8677[10] 8982[3]

**Deshan (GER)** *Tim Vaughan* a49
6 b g Soldier Hollow Desimona (GER) (Monsun (GER))
8585[5]

**Desi Daru (IRE)** *Conrad Allen* a26 46
5 b g Indian Haven Daiquiri (IRE) (Houmayoun (FR))
4274[8] 5141[8] 6150[11] 7605[10]

**Desidero (SPA)** *Pat Phelan* a3 45
3 b f Sixties Icon Atasari (IRE) (Whipper (USA))
6257[11]

**Designamento (IRE)** *Ed de Giles* a34 46
3 b g Casamento(IRE) Designed (Zamindar (USA))
6153[10] 7216[8] 8152[11] 8514[10]

**Designs On Rome (IRE)**
*John Moore* 121
7 b g Holy Roman Emperor(IRE) Summer Trysting (USA) (Alleged (USA))
3129a[6]

**Desirable** *Brian Barr* a49 46
4 b m Stimulation(IRE) Hot Pursuits (Pastoral Pursuits)
387[6]

**Desktop** *Antony Brittain* a60 54
5 b g Desideratum First Harmony (First Trump)
3756[8] 5244[2]◆ 5740[3] 6530[8] 6898[7] 7360[10] 8187[12] 9158[10]

**Despacito** *Brendan Powell* 62
2 b f Equiano(FR) Dongola (IRE) (Xaar)
6761[3] 7197[3]

**Desperados Destiny** *Michael Dods* a67 70
3 b g Delegator Muara (Wolfhound (USA))
2499[7] 3584[8] 4958[10] 5837[4] 7218[2]

**Destinata** *James Fanshawe* a62
2 b f Canford Cliffs(IRE) Hurricane Lady (IRE) (Hurricane Run (IRE))
7707[5] 8715[5]

**Destination Aim** *Fred Watson* a50 67
10 b g Dubai Destination(USA) Tessa Reef (IRE) (Mark Of Esteem (IRE))
2179[2]◆ 3344[8] 4663[4]◆ (5258) 5835[11]

**Destino (GER)** *Markus Klug* 53
2 b c Soldier Hollow Divya (GER) (Platini (GER))
8621a[5]

**Destinys Rock**
*Daniel Mark Loughnane* a61
2 b f Zoffany(IRE) Special Destiny (Tobougg (IRE))
8748[5] 8997[6]

**Destroyer** *Tom Tate* a85 83
4 b g Royal Applause Good Girl (IRE) (College Chapel)
3095[2] 3845[4] (4438) 5130[4] 6266[9] 6964[8]

**Detachment** *Les Eyre* a79 73
4 b g Motivator Argumentative (Observatory (USA))
1358[2]◆ 1781[5] 2226[6] 2701[9] 7052[4]◆ 7894[11]

**Detailed (IRE)**
*Joseph Patrick O'Brien* a65 103
3 b f Motivator Seraya (FR) (Danehill (USA))
4899[2] 7089[4] (7837a) 8086a[4]

**De Treville** *A Wohler* 100
5 b h Oasis Dream Dar Re Mi (Singspiel (IRE))
1661a[5]

**Devamani (FR)** *A De Royer-Dupre* a88 97
3 ch c Dubawi(IRE) Daryakana (FR) (Selkirk (USA))
7176a[6]

**Devastar (GER)** *Markus Klug* 105
5 b h Areion(GER) Deva (GER) (Platini (GER))
3116a[4] 4487a[4] 4931a[3] 6451a[2] 7722a[5] 8270a[2] 8622a[2]

**Devastating Power (IRE)**
*Brendan W Duke* 69
2 ch g Excelebration(IRE) Acago (USA) (Royal Academy (USA))
4386a[8]

**De Vegas Kid (IRE)** *Tony Carroll* a59 69
3 ch c Lope De Vega(IRE) Fravolina (USA) (Lemon Drop Kid (USA))
313[5] 846[7] 1123[3] 1421[5] 2017[4] 2315[4] 3627[11] 4542[7] 4970[3] 5791[2] 6587[5] 6752[2]

**Deviate (IRE)** *Tom Dascombe* a71 79
2 b f Acclamation Divert (IRE) (Averti (IRE))
4806[11] (5480) 6559[2] 6678[6] 7193[2] 7450[3] 8882[4] 9298[5]

**Devil Or Angel** *Bill Turner* a35 60
2 ch f Assertive Level Pegging (IRE) (Common Grounds)
2756[9] 3029[5] 4740[7] 8145[7]

**Devil's Bridge (IRE)**
*Richard Hannon* a86 89
3 b c Casamento(IRE) Cantaloupe (Priolo (USA))
1518[9] 1912[2] 2612[5] 3578[3] 4215[7] 4736[4] 5541[7] 6158[3] 8375[9]

**Devil's Cowboy (IRE)** *Charles Hills* 64
2 b c Helmet(AUS) Naseem Sea (IRE) (Bahri (USA))
1858[7] 3591[7] 4049[6] 5572[11] 6481[7]

**Devil's Eye (IRE)**
*Mlle L-L Rohn-Pelvin* a62 48
5 b g Danehill Dancer(IRE) Danse Grecque (USA) (Hold That Tiger (USA))
364a[9]

**Devil's Guard (IRE)** *Keith Dalgleish* a44 57
3 br g Dark Angel(IRE) Visual Element (USA) (Distant View (USA))
3484[6] 3831[4] 4473[2] 5649[9] 6594[7] 8247[9]

**Devious Spirit (IRE)** *Iain Jardine* a54 62
5 br g Intikhab(USA) Unintentional (Dr Devious (IRE))
174[10] 383[P] 400[5] 579[10] 2179[9]

**Devon Finestra** *T Poche*
3 b f Harbour Watch(IRE) Ulla (Singspiel (IRE))
3134a[15]

**Dew Line (IRE)** *Michael Mulvany* a63 95
5 bb m Vale Of York(IRE) Begin The Beguine (IRE) (Peintre Celebre (USA))
1387a[10] 1808a[7] 1999a[7] 7066a[3] 7261a[6] 8086a[3]

**Dewpoint (IRE)** *Patrick Tallis* 64
3 br f Kyllachy Late Night Movie (IRE) (Holy Roman Emperor (IRE))
2656a[15]

**Deyaarna (USA)** *Saeed bin Suroor* a84 77
2 b c Kitten's Joy(USA) Tanaami (USA) (Elusive Quality (USA))
6388[5] 7120[2] (7758) (8399)

**Dhahmaan (IRE)** *David O'Meara* a102 102
4 b h Kodiac Heroine Chic (IRE) (Big Bad Bob (IRE))
326[4]

**Dhalam (USA)** *John Gosden* a86 77
3 bb c Lonhro(AUS) War Tigress (USA) (War Chant (USA))
1552[2]◆ 1962[3] (3188) 8375[4]

**Dharoos (IRE)** *Nigel Hawke* a85 48
4 ch g New Approach(IRE) Cailiocht (USA) (Elusive Quality (USA))
6849[5]

**Dhevanafushi** *H-A Pantall* a101 102
4 gr h Kendargent(FR) Tejaara (USA) (Kingmambo (USA))
1159a[4] 1531a[5] (4454a) 7636a[14]

**Diable D'Or (IRE)**
*Eve Johnson Houghton* a75 84
3 gr g Clodovil(IRE) Caherassdotcom (Compton Place)
1731[12] 2215[7] 3621[4] 4251[4]◆ 4810[5] 4983[5] 5797[6] 6310[6] 6888[3] 8186[6]

**Diablery** *John Gosden* a51
2 b f Dalakhani(IRE) Magical Romance (IRE) (Barathea (IRE))
8796[12] 9318[4]

**Diablesse** *F Head* a86 101
3 b f High Chaparral(IRE) Vraiment Rouge (FR) (Red Ransom (USA))
6732a[5] 8986a[12]

**Dia Del Sol** *Markus Klug* 84
3 b c Soldier Hollow Diatribe (Tertullian (USA))
2002a[9] 2869a[8]

**Diagnostic** *William Haggas* a99 80
3 gr f Dutch Art Holistic (Pivotal)
7227[2]◆ (7793) (8374) (8541)◆

**Di Alta (IRE)** *Ed Walker* a61 85
3 b f High Chaparral(IRE) Dibiya (IRE) (Caerleon (USA))
2929[5] 3341[6] 4571[2] (5217) 5715[5] 6968[5]

**Diamant De Vati (FR)** *S Wattel* a80 53
6 b g Kingsalsa(USA) Reine De Vati (FR) (Take Risks (FR))
6300a[4] 6648a[15]

**Diamante (IRE)** *Daniel Kubler* a48 49
3 b f Big Bad Bob(IRE) Miracle Steps (CAN) (Theatrical (IRE))
814[8] 1410[5] 2705[9] 3657[8]

**Diamond Avalanche (IRE)**
*Kristin Stubbs* a62 47
4 b g Alfred Nobel(IRE) Queens Flight (King's Best (USA))
2429[8] 3387[11] 3832[7] 5019[6] 5283[8] 8193[4] 8784[9] (9085)

**Diamond Bear (USA)**
*Sir Mark Prescott Bt* a76 72
3 bb f First Dude(USA) Lady Mariah (USA) (Giant's Causeway (USA))
2677[5] 3727[10] 7095[4] 7452[4] 7762[11] 8313[4]

**Diamond Charlie (IRE)** *Simon Dow* a84 62
9 br g Diamond Green(FR) Rosy Lydgate (Last Tycoon)
171[4]

**Diamond Daisy (GER)**
*Ferdinand J Leve* 83
4 bb m Shirocco(GER) Daytona (GER) (Lando (GER))
7204a[4] 8088a[8]

**Diamond Dougal (IRE)**
*Mick Channon* 77
2 b g Zebedee Blue Saphire (Acclamation)
1934[3] 5654[3] 5755[5] 6375[7] (6749) 7041[2] 7228[4] (7564) 7734[4] 8420[5]

**Diamond Eagle (IRE)** *Shaun Harris* a36
5 b g Moss Vale(IRE) Purify (Sinndar (IRE))
580[8]

**Diamond Express (IRE)** *Roger Teal* a54 66
2 b f Fast Company(IRE) South Ring (IRE) (Titus Livius (FR))
3807[6] 4799[2]◆ 5561[4] 5586[6] 7491[10] 8179[4] 8658[10]

**Diamond Fields (IRE)** *J A Stack* a92 105
4 b m Fastnet Rock(AUS) Question Times (Shamardal (USA))
(1653a) 2241a[6] 6119a[6] 6958a[9]

**Diamond Indulgence** *Derek Shaw* a50 25
4 b m Cockney Rebel(IRE) Shaws Diamond (USA) (Ecton Park (USA))
362[4] 455[4] 761[11] 5535[6] 6045[8]

**Diamond Joel** *David Dennis*
5 b g Youmzain(IRE) Miss Lacroix (Picea)
6889[12]

**Diamond Kut** *Andrew Balding* a73 67
4 gr g Rock Of Gibraltar(IRE) Diamond Line (FR) (Linamix (FR))
(29)

**Diamond Lady** *William Stone* a86 89
6 b m Multiplex Ellen Mooney (Efisio)
(1899) 2147[4] 3074[5] (3330) 4099[7] 5035[5] 5426[2] 6141[8] 6430[2] 7538[8] 8167[8] 8879[3] 9185[4] 9339[4]

**Diamond Penny (IRE)**
*Mrs A Corson* 6
9 b g Diamond Green(FR) Penny Fan (Nomination)
2670a[9]

**Diamond Princess** *Michael Appleby* 33
3 b f Bahri(USA) Rainbow's Destiny (Dubai Destination (USA))
848[13]

**Diamond Pursuit** *Jo Hughes* a70 69
2 b f Pastoral Pursuits Broughtons Jewel (IRE) (Bahri (USA))
1627[5] (2052) 3025[4] 3297[4] 4361[11] 4991[4] 5629a[8] 6552[7] 7690[2] 7914[4] 8153[5] (8996) 9090[6] 9322[4]

**Diamond Reflection (IRE)**
*Alexandra Dunn* a52 75
5 b g Oasis Dream Briolette (IRE) (Sadler's Wells (USA))
9209[9] 9459[11]

**Diamond Runner (IRE)**
*Lawrence Mullaney* a57 63
5 b g Amadeus Wolf Hawk Eyed Lady (IRE) (Hawk Wing (USA))
2687[9] 3343[2] (3761) 3935[5] 4558[5] 5454[3] (5950) 6188[3] 7052[13] 7479[13] 8205[12]

**Diamonds A Dancing**
*Donald McCain* a74 78
7 ch g Delta Dancer Zing (Zilzal (USA))
3198[6] 4034[5] (4627) 5002[3] (5701) 6153[2] 6858[7]

**Diamondsaretrumps (IRE)**
*Phil McEntee* a52 26
4 b m Dick Turpin(IRE) Serial Sinner (IRE) (High Chaparral (IRE))
3728[13] 4180[9] 4561[10]

**Diamond Set** *Tom Dascombe* 74
2 b c Dutch Art Asaawir (Royal Applause)
5099[2] 5825[5]

**Diamonds Pour Moi** *Ralph Beckett* a77 103
4 b m Pour Moi(IRE) Diamond Light (USA) (Fantastic Light (USA))
2571[8] 5569[6]

**Diamond Vendome (FR)** *C Ferland* 92
2 b c Style Vendome(FR) Ordargent (FR) (Kendargent (FR))
(5626a) 6730a[4]

**Diamond Vine (IRE)** *Ronald Harris* a44 57
9 b g Diamond Green(FR) Glasnas Giant (Giant's Causeway (USA))
88[7] 217[5] 438[7] 602[8] 1359[7] 2724[2] 3569[4] 3774[8] 4467[7] 4735[6] 5146[9] 5271[11]

**Diana Lady (CHI)** *Luke McJannet* a68 48
4 gr m Dunkirk(USA) Lady Kitty Karson (USA) (Carson City (USA))
1502[14] 1757[9] 2093[7] 7601[10] 8513[7] 9127[5] 9375[7]

**Diana Storm (GER)**
*Waldemar Hickst* 103
3 b f Soldier Hollow Divya (GER) (Platini (GER))
4393a[2] 5693a[6] 6710a[2] 7673a[7] 8462a[4]

**Diaphora (GER)** *Markus Klug* 78
3 b f Pivotal Diacada (GER) (Cadeaux Genereux)
3882a[10]

**Dibayani (IRE)**
*David A & B Hayes & Tom Dabern* 114
7 b g Shamardal(USA) Dibiya (IRE) (Caerleon (USA))
8057a[3]

**Dibazari (FR)** *G Botti* a76 56
3 b g Zanzibari(USA) Diba (GER) (Big Shuffle (USA))
584a[3] 8305a[2]

**Dibloam (USA)** *David Evans* a49
4 ch g Hard Spun(USA) Nuqoosh (Machiavellian (USA))
331[6] 580[6] 849[5] 1249[12] 1563[7] 1985[5] 7761[11] 7991[4] 8815[2]◆ 9095[5] 9221[8]

**Dice Roll (FR)** *F Chappet* 93
2 ch c Showcasing Schlague (FR) (Pulpit (USA))
5978a[4] (7637a)

**Dichato (USA)** *John Gosden* a69 80
2 b g Scat Daddy(USA) Dolce Lemone (CAN) (Lemon Drop Kid (USA))
3037[8] 3591[3]◆ 4266[2] 5063[3]

**Dicktation** *Richard Whitaker* 25
2 b g Dick Turpin(IRE) Curly Come Home (Notnowcato)
6938[12] 7978[5]

**Dicton** *Gianluca Bietolini* a85 117
4 b h Lawman(FR) Saying (USA) (Giant's Causeway (USA))
1531a[2] 3118a[4] 6498a[3] 7640a[8]

**Diditi** *Il Cavallo In Testa* 87
3 b c Elusive City(USA) Hideaway Heroine (IRE) (Hernando (FR))
2868a[7]

**Di Fede (IRE)** *Ralph Beckett* a91 82
2 b f Shamardal(USA) Dibiya (IRE) (Caerleon (USA))
2173[5] (2958) 4068[14] 5366[2] 6934[3] 7552[3] (8343)

**Diferent Dimension (USA)** *Peter Wolsley* a95 97
5 b g Into Mischief(USA) Pardon My Sarong (USA) (Souvenir Copy (USA))
204a[7] 698a[3] 775a[7]

**Different Journey** *Michael Easterby* a49 74
4 b g Poet's Voice Vintage Gardenia (Selkirk (USA))
2632[4] 2887[7] 6266[12] 6855[9] 7235[9] 8515[5] 8854[8]

**Different League (FR)** *Matthieu Palussiere* 109
2 b f Dabirsim(FR) Danseuse Corse (IRE) (Danehill Dancer (IRE))
(4028)◆ 6249a[3] 7617[2]

**Different Views (USA)** *Gay Kelleway* a68 68
3 bb g Proud Citizen(USA) Elite (Invincible Spirit (IRE))
584a[7] 748a[4] 847a[7]

**Digeanta (IRE)** *W P Mullins* 93
10 b g Helissio(FR) Scolboa Gold (IRE) (Accordion)
5488a[4] 8038[27]

**Digha (FR)** *P Demercastel* a58 61
2 bb f Denon(USA) Higha (FR) (Vettori (IRE))
6171a[7] 9086a[7]

**Digicode (FR)** *Matthieu Palussiere* 64
2 ch c Soul City(IRE) Solitudine (Inchinor)
3445a[7]

**Digital Revolution** *Antony Brittain* a56 38
3 ch f Monsieur Bond(IRE) Lujiana (Lujain (USA))
2699[6] 3258[3] 4447[7] 5419[4] 5736[6] 6469[5] 7407[4]

**Dilinger** *Stuart Kittow* a43 45
3 b g Equiano(FR) Dilys (Efisio)
7080[7] 7907[8] 8842[7]

**Dillie Dallie (IRE)** *Henry Spiller* a69
2 b f Zoffany(IRE) Dalliefour (IRE) (Cape Cross (IRE))
9371[4]

**Dilmun (USA)** *Joseph Patrick O'Brien* a85 90
3 b f War Front(USA) Pachattack (USA) (Pulpit (USA))
6490a[10] 7588a[10] 8407a[12]

**Dimaie (FR)** *Y Barberot* a48
2 ch f My Risk(FR) De Broceliande (FR) (Woodman (USA))
4677a[6]

**Dimension** *Conor Murphy* a75 101
9 bb g Medicean Palatial (Green Desert (USA))
7851a[14]

**Diminutive (IRE)** *Grace Harris* a46 53
5 ch m Fast Company(IRE) Take It Easee (IRE) (Noverre (USA))
2589[13] 3391[9] 3569[5] 4467[10] 5252[6] 5567[7] 6028[4] 6507[7] 7190[11]

**Dimitre** *Henry Candy* a76 72
3 gr g Showcasing Devoted (IRE) (Dalakhani (IRE))
3719[3]

**Dina (GER)** *Markus Klug* 91
2 b f Nathaniel(IRE) Diatribe (Tertullian (USA))
6985a[3] 8269a[4]

**Ding Ding** *Sheena West* a54 57
6 ch m Winker Watson Five Bells (IRE) (Rock Of Gibraltar (IRE))
8878[2] 9317[9]

**Dinkum Diamond (IRE)** *Andrew Slattery* 106
9 b g Aussie Rules(USA) Moving Diamonds (Lomitas)
1385a[7] 5582a[8] 6491a[12]

**Dinneratmidnight** *Richard Guest* a74 88
6 b g Kyllachy The Terrier (Foxhound (USA))
1836[4] 2161[5] 2837[10] 3401[8] 4433[11]

**Dinsdale** *Michael Scudamore* a66
4 b g Cape Cross(IRE) Emmy Award (IRE) (Sadler's Wells (USA))
7708[8]

**Diocles Of Rome (IRE)** *Ralph Beckett* 59
2 b c Holy Roman Emperor(IRE) Serisia (FR) (Exit To Nowhere (USA))
7392[6]

**Diocletian (IRE)** *Andrew Balding* 72
2 b c Camelot Saturday Girl (Peintre Celebre (USA))
7128[9] 7813[6] 8353[5]

**Diodorus (IRE)** *Karen McLintock* a96 79
3 b c Galileo(IRE) Divine Proportions (USA) (Kingmambo (USA))
8910[4]

**Diore Lia (IRE)** *Jane Chapple-Hyam* 52
3 b f Yeats(IRE) Cyclonic Storm (Catrail (USA))
2087[8] 2576[5]

**Dios Corrida (JPN)** *Yoshitada Takahashi* a102
3 bb c Kane Hekili(JPN) Erimo Today (JPN) (Wild Rush (USA))
1041a[7] 1377a[11]

**Diplomacy (IRE)** *David O'Meara* 54
2 b g Champs Elysees Winter Bloom (USA) (Aptitude (USA))
8649[4]◆

**Diplomat (GER)** *Mario Hofer* 108
6 b h Teofilo(IRE) Desidera (IRE) (Shaadi (USA))
914a[4] 1661a[3] 3019a[4] 4939a[4] 6746a[10] 8095a[7]

**Diptych (USA)** *Sir Mark Prescott Bt* a61 5
3 bb f Hat Trick(JPN) Fork Lightning (USA) (Storm Cat (USA))
7324[5] 8549[13]

**Dirayah (IRE)** *George Peckham* a34
3 b f Dark Angel(IRE) Folga (Atraf)
9139[4]

**Dirchill (IRE)** *David Barron* 79
3 b g Power Bawaakeer (USA) (Kingmambo (USA))
2383[3] 2819[3] 3407[2] 4341[2] 5264[3] (5645) 6348[3] 7268[6]

**Direct Message (USA)** *A R Al Rayhi* a92
4 b h Bernardini(USA) Tweeter (USA) (Unbridled's Song (USA))
8714a[5]

**Directorship** *Patrick Chamings* a75 91
11 br g Diktat Away To Me (Exit To Nowhere (USA))
2291[2] 3144[2] 3750[10] 4861[5] 6134[14] 6700[6] 7131[5]

**Direct Times (IRE)** *Peter Chapple-Hyam* 87
6 b g Acclamation Elegant Times (IRE) (Dansili)
4581[7]

**Dire Straits (IRE)** *Stuart Kittow* a44 57
6 b g Teofilo(IRE) Kalagold (IRE) (Magical Strike (USA))
3213[9] 5251[7]

**Dirty Randy (IRE)** *Keith Dalgleish* a63 62
3 b g Notnowcato Regal Fairy (IRE) (Desert King (IRE))
1822[2] 3180[6] 7885[6]

**Disapproval (IRE)** *Daniel Kubler* a47 54
2 b f Approve(IRE) Disko (IRE) (Kodiac)
2910[7] 3821[10] 6816[5] 7756[9] 7996[9]

**Disclosure** *Declan Carroll* a60 65
6 b g Indesatchel(IRE) Gemini Gold (IRE) (King's Best (USA))
80[2] 222[9] 579[3] 768[5]◆ 1203[10] 1310[5] 1721[7] 2179[8] 3001[12] 3290[6]

**Disco Partner (USA)** *Christophe Clement* a89 118
5 rg h Disco Rico(USA) Lulu's Number (USA) (Numerous (USA))
8604a[3]

**Discovered (IRE)** *Roger Charlton* a52 68
3 ch g Bated Breath Sandglass (Zafonic (USA))
1961[7] 5611[6] 6182[6] 7457[8]

**Discreet Hero (IRE)** *Simon Crisford* a79 90
4 ch g Siyouni(FR) Alfaguara (USA) (Red Ransom (USA))
4732[3]◆ (5811)◆ 6512[4]◆

**Discursus** *H-A Pantall* a58 102
3 b f Dubawi(IRE) Discourse (USA) (Street Cry (IRE))
(7204a) 8448a[6]

**Displaying Amber** *Ben Haslam* a48
2 ch f Showcasing Amber Lane (Compton Place)
6010[7] 6897[12] 9415[5]

**Di's Pride** *David Bridgwater* a45
4 b m Paco Boy(IRE) Bramalea (Whitmore's Conn (USA))
9441[3]

**Distain** *Frau S Steinberg* 97
5 b m Champs Elysees Market Forces (Lomitas)
6710a[9] (8096a) 8450a[10]

**Distant (USA)** *Roger Charlton* a83
3 br f First Defence(USA) Ventoux (Galileo (IRE))
3209[5] (4003) 4751[4] 5798[7] 7710[12]

**Distant High** *Richard Price* a40 68
6 b m High Chaparral(IRE) Distant Dreamer (USA) (Rahy (USA))
2358[4] 3425[7] 3771[7] 4470[3] 4840[7]

**Distant Past** *Kevin Ryan* a96 95
6 b g Pastoral Pursuits Faraway Lass (Distant Relative)
63[5] 388[5] 664[2]◆ 2156[13] 2578[3] 4306[11] 6348[2] 6927[9]

**Disturb** *Andrew Crook* a23
5 ch g Halling(USA) Ataraxy (Zamindar (USA))
7935[8]

**Diva Star** *Marcus Tregoning* a41 68
2 ch f Siyouni(FR) Kissin Sign (Turtle Bowl (IRE))
3747[5] 6386[4] 7226[6] 9080[7]

**Divine Call** *Milton Bradley* a66 70
10 b g Pivotal Pious (Bishop Of Cashel)
242[7] 303[6] 843[10] 2043[11] 2709[5] 3084[9] 3774[9] 4256[10] 5271[10] 5848[8] 6582[4]

**Divine Intuition (IRE)** *Kevin Ryan* 69
2 b g Showcasing Sea Fret (Nayef (USA))
3690[6] 5058[3] 7221[4] 8120[10]

**Divine Messenger** *Emma Owen* a55 28
3 b c Firebreak Resentful Angel (Danehill Dancer (IRE))
7930[4] 8342[8] 8842[4]◆

**Divine Prince (GR)** *Amanda Perrett* a54
4 ch g Apotheosis(USA) Pringipessa's Way (Machiavellian (USA))
35[11] 279[7] 462[9]

**Divisidero (USA)** *William Bradley* 115
5 b h Kitten's Joy(USA) Madame Du Lac (USA) (Lemon Drop Kid (USA))
5977a[7] 7851a[4]

**Diwan Senora (FR)** *Y Barberot* a86 87
4 b h Youmzain(IRE) Kiss Senora (FR) (Chichicastenango (FR))
4454a[6] 5979a[17]

**Dixieland Diva (USA)** *Andrew Balding* 72
2 b f Cape Blanco(IRE) Winnie Dixie (USA) (Dixie Union (USA))
5114[2]

**Dixie Moon (CAN)** *Catherine Day-Phillips* a86 101
2 ch f Curlin(USA) Dixie Chicken (USA) (Rahy (USA))
7206a[2] 8575a[6]

**Dixie's Double** *Daniel Kubler* a62 69
3 b f Multiplex Dress Design (IRE) (Brief Truce (USA))
313[6] 1088[5] 1242[8] 1418[8] 1715[13]

**Dixon** *Mark H Tompkins* a59 59
3 b c Lawman(FR) Pure Song (Singspiel (IRE))
2314[6] 3438[10] 4569[10] 7325[4] 7833[2] 8123[5] 8312[7] 8507[8]

**Dizoard** *Iain Jardine* a36 53
7 b m Desideratum Riviere (Meadowbrook)
1834[10] 3706[8] 5413[9]

**Dizzey Heights (IRE)** *Stuart Kittow* a66 74
5 b m Halling(USA) Extreme Pleasure (IRE) (High Chaparral (IRE))
144[9] 526[4] 2710[5] 3428[3]

**Dizzy G (IRE)** *K R Burke* 54
2 b f Red Jazz(USA) Altogether (IRE) (King's Best (USA))
5528[11] 6304[6]

**Djiguite (FR)** *D Smaga* a89 111
5 b h Makfi Envoutement (FR) (Vettori (IRE))
1159a[2] 1531a[6] 2248a[4] 3354a[5] 6173a[6]

**Djumay (GER)** *Andreas Suborics* 95
3 b f Shamardal(USA) Djumama (IRE) (Aussie Rules (USA))
1846a[9] 4518a[6] 7305a[7]

**D K Travel (IRE)** *John James Feane* a53 51
3 b g Jeremy(USA) Guth Na Gaoithe (IRE) (Invincible Spirit (IRE))
7165[3]

**Dltripleseven (IRE)** *Richard Hughes* a67 63
4 gr g Dark Angel(IRE) Namu (Mujahid (USA))
141[3]

**Dobby First (FR)** *Mlle V Dissaux* a48 50
4 b h Dobby Road(FR) My First Love (FR) (Northern Crystal)
713a[12] 930a[13]

**Dock Of The Bay** *Mick Channon* 65
3 b g Sixties Icon Kaylianni (Kalanisi (IRE))
6194[10]

**Doc Sportello (IRE)** *Tony Carroll* a107 92
5 b g Majestic Missile(IRE) Queen Of Silk (IRE) (Brief Truce (USA))
33[2]◆ (200) 842[10] 1772[12] 4306[10] 5911[6]◆ 6922[7] 7611[15] 9373[7] 9453[8]

**Doctor Bartolo (IRE)** *Charles Hills* a87 87
3 gr g Sir Prancealot(IRE) Operissimo (Singspiel (IRE))
(175) 1764[6] 2755[3] 3583[8] (4254) 6189[2] 7031[3]

**Doctor Bong** *Grace Harris* a60 59
5 b g Sleeping Indian Vax Rapide (Sharpo)
3397[8] 3773[6] 4846[6] 4970[5] 5791[10] (6342) 6807[5] 7198[9] 8031[2]◆ 8307[13]

**Doctor Chalnetta (FR)** *P Adda* a46 76
3 bb f Doctor Dino(FR) Maharina (FR) (Medaaly)
8959a[13]

**Doctor Cross (IRE)** *Richard Fahey* a70 79
3 b g Cape Cross(IRE) Doctrine (Barathea (IRE))
3206[3] 7476[2]◆ 8561[5]

**Doctor Dynamite (IRE)** *Tim Easterby* 56
3 b g Alfred Nobel(IRE) Alhaadh (USA) (Diesis)
4171[8]

**Doctor Jazz (IRE)** *Richard Hannon* a61
2 b c Most Improved(IRE) Daliyana (IRE) (Cadeaux Genereux)
8029[7]

**Doctor Kehoe** *Mme A-M Verschueren* a52 51
5 b g Cockney Rebel(IRE) Ogre (USA) (Tale Of The Cat (USA))
121[9] 7534a[4]

**Doctor Knox (IRE)** *Paul Cole* a60 60
2 b c Dawn Approach(IRE) Queen Of Carthage (USA) (Cape Cross (IRE))
8677[7] 8888[5]

**Doctor Parkes** *Natalie Lloyd-Beavis* a78 79
11 b g Diktat Lucky Parkes (Full Extent (USA))
211[5] 387[5] 518[4] 844[7] 1147[6] 1328[8] 1791[2] 1965[7] 2995[2] 3469[5] 4149[3] 4695[10] 5146[6] 7487[6]

**Doctor Sardonicus** *David Simcock* a110 82
6 ch g Medicean Never A Doubt (Night Shift (USA))
63[2] 818[7] (1222) 4881[12] (6025) 9373[4]

**Dodging Bullets (AUS)** *Symon Wilde* 103
5 b g Dash For Cash(AUS) Young Love (AUS) (Danzero (AUS))
8857a[10]

**Dodgy Bob** *Michael Mullineaux* a79 71
4 b g Royal Applause Rustam (Dansili)
159[4] 514[6] 745[4] 2216[4] 2776[4] 3203[9] 4182[2] 4664[4] 4844[5] 5396[13] 5827[6] 6097[2] (6318) (6785) 7628[10] 7932[6] 9033[8] 9215[7]

**Doeadeer (IRE)** *Keith Dalgleish* a63 32
4 b m Dandy Man(IRE) Bloomsday Babe (USA) (Cherokee Run (USA))
26[12] 161[2] 724[7] 843[7] 1076[11] 1720[11]

**Doha Dream (FR)** *A Fabre* 116
4 b h Shamardal(USA) Crystal Reef (King's Best (USA))
3369a[5] 4423a[U]◆ 5692a[2] 6499a[2] 7668a[12]

**Dollar And A Dream (IRE)** *Michael Mullineaux* 23
8 b g Fruits Of Love(USA) Gorgeous Georgina (IRE) (Tirol (IRE))
7629[6]

**Dollar Reward** *Stuart Williams* a74 74
4 b g Shamardal(USA) Cape Dollar (IRE) (Cape Cross (IRE))
118[3]

**Dollar Value (USA)** *Robert Cowell* a61
2 gr c Exchange Rate(USA) Makoma (USA) (Malibu Moon (USA))
8988[5] 9335[4]

**Dolly Dagger** *Mark Usher* 50
2 ch f Pastoral Pursuits Dance Away (Pivotal)
2173[9] 2801[12] 3619[4]

**Dolly Dimples** *William Jarvis* a59 34
3 gr f Sir Percy Brave Mave (Daylami (IRE))
139[9]

**Dollywaggon Pike** *J R Jenkins* a30 43
3 b f Hellvelyn Once Removed (Distant Relative)
5969[7] 6569[5] 6526[10] 8298[7] 8774[6]

**Dolokhov** *J Phelippon* a70 65
3 b g Harbour Watch(IRE) Forest Prize (Charnwood Forest (IRE))
7308a[7] 8305a[3]

**Dolphin Village (IRE)** *Shaun Harris* a80 83
7 b g Cape Cross(IRE) Reform Act (USA) (Lemon Drop Kid (USA))
38[2] 1248[4] 1504[5] 1976[3] 3091[8] 4357[7] 6202[7] 6848[8] 7728[9] 8326[8] 8485[6] 9054[8] 9270[3]◆ 9408[5]

**Dolphin Vista (IRE)** *Martyn Meade* a102 107
4 b g Zoffany(IRE) Flordiligi (Mozart (IRE))
1494[5] 2396[9] 5940[6] (7619) 9388[5]

**Dolydaydream** *Pat Phelan* a43 30
2 b f Equiano(FR) Ellie In The Pink (IRE) (Johannesburg (USA))
5216[11] 7875[8] 8502[10]

**Domacasi (FR)** *S Renaud*
3 bl f Hurricane Cat(USA) Maguilor Floo (FR) (Goldneyev (USA))
3134a[11]

**Domagnano (IRE)** *Stefano Botti* 70
2 b c Planteur(IRE) Daloisi (FR) (Marchand De Sable (USA))
8620a[6]

**Domberg (GER)** *C Zschache* 76
2 b c Champs Elysees Diaccia (GER) (High Chaparral (IRE))
6726a[5]

**Domfront (IRE)** *N Clement* a94 90
3 b c Royal Applause Debuetantin (Big Shuffle (USA))
799a[3]

**Dominannie (IRE)** *Sally Haynes* a53 68
4 b m Paco Boy(IRE) English Rose (USA) (Kafwain (USA))
360[8] 4661[4]◆ 4960[4]◆ 5578[4] 6047[3] 6564[6]

**Dominating (GER)** *Mark Johnston* a89 97
3 ch g Jukebox Jury(IRE) Dominante (GER) (Monsun (GER))
2394[6] 2807[8] (3220)◆ (3788) 4612[2] (4852) 5799[2] 6445[10] 7163[2] 7359[3] (7785) 8011[9] (8292)

**Dominique (FR)** *Pavel Tuma*
3 b g Motivator Dentelle I (FR) (Apeldoorn (FR))
8959a[2]

**Dominium (USA)** *Jeremy Gask* a71 74
10 b g E Dubai(USA) Sudenlylastsummer (USA) (Rinka Das (USA))
50[4] 242[6] 501[9] 734[5] 1080[9] 1419[8]

**Domitilla** *Marco Botti* a83 71
3 b f Cape Cross(IRE) Dan Loose Daughter (Sakhee (USA))
1948[4] 8504[2] 8707[2] (9089)

**Dona Bruja (ARG)** *Ignacio Correas IV* a90 109
4 b m Storm Embrujado(ARG) This Is Crazy (AUS) (Nureyev (USA))
5954a[2]

**Doneraile (IRE)** *Robert Eddery* a21 53
3 b g Requinto(IRE) Yaky Romani (IRE) (Victory Note (USA))
157[6]

**Donjuan Triumphant (IRE)** *Andrew Balding* a89 118
4 b h Dream Ahead(USA) Mathuna (IRE) (Tagula (IRE))
1773[11] 2150[3] 5640[9] (6856) (7611) 8230[8]

**Don Mimi (ITY)** *Gianluca Bietolini* a59 72
5 b h Pounced(USA) Petite Sophie (FR) (Linamix (FR))
6300a[9]

**Donnachies Girl (IRE)** *Alistair Whillans* a75 78
4 b m Manduro(GER) Russian Society (Darshaan)
2408[7] 2887[8] 3383[4] (3978) (4244) 4962[2]◆ (5414) 5872[2] 6383[3] 7701[6] 8103[2] (8564)

**Donna Finchella (IRE)** *Brian Meehan* 52
3 b f Casamento(IRE) Air Maze (Dansili)
2231[14] 2475[7] 2759[8]

**Donncha (IRE)** *Robert Eddery* a80 106
6 br g Captain Marvelous(IRE) Seasonal Style (IRE) (Generous (IRE))
1494[3] 1960[7] 2767[16] 4410[8] 4905[13]

**Donnelly's Rainbow (IRE)** *Rebecca Bastiman* 72
4 b g Lilbourne Lad(IRE) Donnelly's Hollow (IRE) (Docksider (USA))
2377[7] 4506[4] 6182[7] 7390[2]◆ 7934[3] 8108[3]

**Donnerschlag** *Jean-Pierre Carvalho* 107
7 ch g Bahamian Bounty Dame Hester (IRE) (Diktat)
3105a[4] 6495a[11]

**Donny Belle** *David Brown* 70
2 b f Doncaster Rover(USA) Speedy Senorita (IRE) (Fayruz)
2836[3] 3215[2] 3826[5] 5057[6] 6756[8]

**Don Padeja** *Fergal O'Brien*
7 br g Dansili La Leuze (IRE) (Caerleon (USA))
4469[12]

**Don Pepe (IRE)** *Richard Hannon* 60
2 b c Havana Gold(IRE) Woodmaven (USA) (Woodman (USA))
3846[6]

**Don't Blame Me** *Clive Cox* a80 61
4 b g Captain Gerrard(IRE) Dragon Flyer (IRE) (Tagula (IRE))
1467[2] 2692[9] 7408[10] 7882[12] 8311[6] 8875[3] 9189[8]

**Don't Cry About It (IRE)** *Ali Stronge* a58
2 ch g Casamento(IRE) Back At De Front (IRE) (Cape Cross (IRE))
7513[10] 7877[6] 8149[12]

**Dontforgettocall** *Joseph Tuite* a59 66
3 ch g Foxwedge(AUS) Shaken And Stirred (Cadeaux Genereux)
1474[6] 1605[7] 7122[9] 8146[2] 8428[3] 8824[3]

**Don't Give Up** *Saeed bin Suroor* a98 100
3 b c Dubawi(IRE) Avongrove (Tiger Hill (IRE))
(3456) 5425[2]◆ (6007) 6881[7] 7727[5]

**Dontgiveuponbob** *Richard Fahey* 73
2 b g Pastoral Pursuits Parsonagehotelyork (IRE) (Danehill (USA))
2134[5] 2769[4] 3429[3] 4374[2] 5255[5] 6425[7] 6940[3] 7384[8] 7890[3]

**Don't Lie Kitten (USA)** *A bin Harmash* a55
3 b f Kitten's Joy(USA) Southern Alibi (USA) (Elusive Quality (USA))
317a[13] 889a[8]

**Don't Tell Nik (IRE)** *Roger Fell* a18 44
4 b m Lawman(FR) Karliysha (IRE) (Kalanisi (IRE))
176[12]

**Don't Touch** *Richard Fahey* a88 115
5 b g Dutch Art Expressive (Falbrav (IRE))
3765a[2] 4354[8] 6401[9] 6966[6] 7822[6]

**Donttouchthechips (IRE)**
Nikki Evans a37 64
4 b g Lilbourne Lad(IRE) Trim (IRE) (Ela-Mana-Mou)
2709[12] 4470[9]

**Donuts Reyor (FR)** V Luka Jr a85 82
4 gr g Cat Junior(USA) Elegante Lady (FR) (Verglas (IRE))
7636a[4]

**Don Valentino (IRE)** David O'Meara 86
3 b g Dandy Man(IRE) My Funny Valentine (IRE) (Mukaddamah (USA))
2338[4] 3150[3] 3448[2] (3984) (4437)◆

**Donworth (USA)** Doug O'Neill a98
5 bb h Tiznow(USA) Temple Street (USA) (Street Cry (IRE))
5194a[2] 6252a[7]

**Dooder (USA)** Chad C Brown 88
2 bb f Flatter(USA) Wild Grace (USA) (Forest Wildcat (USA))
7206a[9]

**Doodle Dandy (IRE)**
David Bridgwater a61 55
4 b m Starspangledbanner(AUS) Grid Lock (IRE) (Van Nistelrooy (USA))
1552[6] 1818[10] 2231[8] 2961[5] 3397[11] 6439[4] 7279[9]

**Dora Bruder (FR)** D Cottin 72
3 b f Le Havre(IRE) Fashion School (Shamardal (USA))
(5910a) 6650a[7]

**Dora's Field (IRE)** Stuart Kittow a55 76
4 b m Rip Van Winkle(IRE) Rydal Mount (IRE) (Cape Cross (IRE))
2710[2]◆ 3168[6] 5290[9] 8143[7]

**Dorcas** James Given a47 68
2 b f Havana Gold(IRE) Mortitia (Dansili)
2258[4] 5334[4] (5998) 6433[7] 7593[6]

**Dorcia** Lennart Reuterskiold Jr 106
3 b f Henrythenavigator(USA) Spinola (FR) (Spinning World (USA))
(7428a)

**Doreen** Sir Michael Stoute a58 55
3 b f Dansili Hi Calypso (IRE) (In The Wings)
2307[3] 3145[9] 4012[8]

**Dorella (GER)**
Eve Johnson Houghton a68
2 b f Reliable Man Diacada (GER) (Cadeaux Genereux)
8998[4]◆ 9200[6]

**Do Re Mi Fa Sol (FR)** P Decouz 105
4 b m Wootton Bassett Maitresse (FR) (Singspiel (IRE))
2201a[9]

**Dorian Gray (IRE)** Hughie Morrison a51
2 b g So You Think(NZ) Flawless Beauty (Excellent Art)
6885[10] 7489[8] 8981[3] 9175[6]

**Doria Road (USA)** Kevin Ryan a69 64
3 b f Quality Road(USA) Celestic (USA) (Sky Classic (CAN))
1705[3] 4214[6] 5009[3] 5666[10] 7061[3] (8192) 8749[5]

**Dormello (IRE)** D Selvaratnam a102 106
9 b h Dansili Field Of Hope (IRE) (Selkirk (USA))
86a[8] 542a[6] 699a[10]

**Dor's Law** Dean Ivory a59 56
4 b m Lawman(FR) Law Of Chance (Pennekamp (USA))
147[8] 420[7] 636[12] 5336[4] 6296[5] 6622[6] 7324[10]
8125[3] 8307[2] 8661[5] 8908[2] 9141[4]

**Dose** Richard Fahey a67 64
4 b m Teofilo(IRE) Prescription (Pivotal)
46[3] (390) 883[2] 1007[3] 1186[5] 1879[3] 2153[4] 9364[7]

**Dostoyevsky (IRE)** N Caullery a59 59
4 b g Galileo(IRE) My Branch (Distant Relative)
(6365a)

**Doswell (USA)** John Gosden 87
2 br g Giant's Causeway(USA) Ballet Pacifica (USA) (Minardi (USA))
4859[2]

**Dot Green (IRE)** Mark H Tompkins a72 85
4 b m Lawman(FR) Katajan (Halling (USA))
2317[5] 4631[6] 4999[8]◆ 6111[11]

**Dotted Swiss (IRE)** Richard Hannon a75
2 b f Swiss Spirit Luxuria (IRE) (Kheleyf (USA))
(3174) 8373[7] 8670[7] 8882[2]

**Double Dutch** John Butler a32 33
3 ch g Dutch Art Duchess Dora (IRE) (Tagula (IRE))
1287[12] 1818[12] 5145[9]

**Double Lady (FR)** A Fabre 93
3 gr f Stormy River(FR) Montagne Magique (IRE) (King's Best (USA))
1690a[7]

**Double Pouvoir (FR)**
A De Watrigant
2 b f Rajsaman(FR) Cloudracer (IRE) (Rail Link)
1282a[6]

**Double Reflection** K R Burke 73
2 b f Showcasing Green And Bleue (Green Tune (USA))
3237[4]◆ (5356) 5990[7] 6504[3] 7552[6]

**Double Spin** Robert Cowell a69 55
3 b f Hard Spun(USA) Dear Lavinia (USA) (Grand Slam (USA))
1286[6] 2112[5] 2924[2] 3313[4] 4731[9] 6004[5] 6324[8]

**Doublet (IRE)** Mark Johnston a78 87
2 b c Epaulette(AUS) Biaraafa (IRE) (Araafa (IRE))
4520[6] (5063) (5557)

**Double Up** Roger Varian a111 96
6 b g Exceed And Excel(AUS) My Love Thomas (IRE) (Cadeaux Genereux)
1946[5] 2573[2] (8991) 9409[4]

**Double Variance (FR)** S Wattel a76 88
2 b f Orpen(USA) Life Of Risks (FR) (Take Risks (FR))
4596a[5] 5090a[4]

**Douceur Angevine (FR)** J-F Doucet 29
3 b f Duke Of Marmalade(IRE) Nelly Dean (Pivotal)
4943a[10]

**Douceur D'Antan (FR)** P Adda a68 69
3 ch f Never On Sunday(FR) Inassouvie (FR) (Lord Of Men)
2536a[7] 3446a[2] 4455a[7]

**Dougan** David Evans a105 99
5 b g Dutch Art Vive Les Rouges (Acclamation)
200[3] 1501[10] 1769[12] 3410[6] 3861[2] 4411[9] 4881[6]
5435[5] 6275[8] 7118[3] 7950[8] 8383[16]

**Douglas Macarthur (IRE)**
A P O'Brien 113
3 b c Galileo(IRE) Alluring Park (IRE) (Green Desert (USA))
1636a[2] (2442a) 3322[7] 4387a[5] 6327[4] 7147[9]

**Dourado (IRE)** Patrick Chamings a84 82
3 b c Dark Angel(IRE) Skehana (IRE) (Mukaddamah (USA))
2506[5]◆ (5560) (6558) 7398[10] 7947[3] (8640)

**Douriya (USA)** A De Royer-Dupre a71
3 b f Giant's Causeway(USA) Darma (FR) (Danehill Dancer (IRE))
8692a[5]

**Dove Mountain (IRE)** Olly Murphy a65 65
6 b g Danehill Dancer(IRE) Virginia Waters (USA) (Kingmambo (USA))
46[4] 239[2] 420[6] 1249[10] 3192[7] 3726[3] (4461) 5080[7]

**Dovils Date** Tim Vaughan a75 72
8 gr g Clodovil(IRE) Lucky Date (IRE) (Halling (USA))
688[9] 1153[9] 1257[10] 1364[6] (2966) (3775) (8157)

**Dovil's Duel (IRE)** Gavin Cromwell a65 54
6 b g Clodovil(IRE) Duelling (Diesis)
49[6] 690[4] 3197[2] 6800a[9]

**Dowayla (IRE)** Saeed bin Suroor a96 95
3 b f Sepoy(AUS) Baheeja (Dubawi (IRE))
3262[6] 3981[2] (4736) 6145[2] 6687[3] 7815[3] 8714a[8]

**Dowitcher (USA)** Mark Johnston 14
2 b f Lonhro(AUS) Danelagh (AUS) (Danehill (USA))
5801[6]

**Downforce (IRE)** W McCreery a62 111
5 b g Fast Company(IRE) Spinning Ruby (Pivotal)
(1520a) 3099a[4] 6966[2]◆ 7424a[5] 7663a[2] 8526a[9]

**Down Time (USA)** Paul Midgley a17 45
7 b g Harlan's Holiday(USA) Frappay (USA) (Deputy Minister (CAN))
8109[6] 8386[15] 8515[9]

**Downton Kitten (USA)**
David Lanigan 74
3 b f Kitten's Joy(USA) Manda Bay (USA) (Empire Maker (USA))
(2144)

**Downtown Mombasa (IRE)**
Eve Johnson Houghton a66 67
2 b f Lord Shanakill(USA) Mattinata (Tiger Hill (IRE))
4151[3]◆ 4749[4]

**Downtown Rebel (USA)**
Andrew Slattery 53
3 bb g Arch(USA) Downtown Drifter (USA) (Devil His Due (USA))
4045[6]

**Dowse's Beach (USA)** Brad H Cox 109
6 rg g Disco Rico(USA) Mary Lou's Magic (USA) (Concorde's Tune (USA))
8097a[6]

**Do You Know (IRE)** Marco Botti a67 57
3 b f So You Think(NZ) Queen Of Lyons (USA) (Dubai Destination (USA))
48[3] 392[4] 2587[12] 3473[3] 3971[8] 4748[7] 5076[3]
5852[4]

**Dracarys** Jose Santos a36 50
2 b c Sepoy(AUS) Fen Guest (Woodborough (USA))
6826[7] 7351[13] 7946[11]

**Drago (IRE)** David O'Meara a70 56
5 b g Cape Cross(IRE) Eden (USA) (Holy Bull (USA))
1329[4] 2163[7] 3065[7] 4059[5]

**Dragon Bay (USA)** Stuart C Simon a92 103
4 ch g Parading(USA) Cologne (USA) (Horse Chestnut (SAF))
7179a[12]

**Dragon Dream (IRE)** Roger Ingram a66 67
3 b f Dragon Pulse(IRE) Night Scent (IRE) (Scenic)
89[9] 763[7] 1000[8] 1421[6] (4211) 5031[3] 5545[2] 6321[6]
6558[6] 7934[9] 9203[7]

**Dragon Falls (IRE)** R Bouresly a54 100
8 b g Distorted Humor(USA) Tizdubai (USA) (Cee's Tizzy (USA))
316a[13] 773a[10]

**Dragon Fei (IRE)**
Dermot Anthony McLoughlin a68 95
7 b m Jeremy(USA) Wallonia (IRE) (Barathea (IRE))
4383a[8] 5766a[9] 6080a[14]

**Dragonfly Dream** John Best a28
2 b f Sepoy(AUS) Tartaria (Oasis Dream)
7757[10]

**Dragonite (IRE)**
Daniel Mark Loughnane a46 48
3 ch g Dragon Pulse(IRE) Glamorous (GER) (Red Ransom (USA))
149[9] 3939[5] 5790[3] 7253[4] 7478[9] 8770[6] 9072[7]

**Dragon Khan (IRE)** John O'Shea 67
8 b g Dr Fong(USA) Desert Magic (IRE) (Green Desert (USA))
1610[7] 2294[9]

**Dragon King (IRE)** Iain Jardine a85 94
5 ch g Dylan Thomas(IRE) Alexander Queen (IRE) (King's Best (USA))
1910[14] 3199[9] (3581) 4343[9] 4683[8]

**Dragon Lips (GER)**
Andreas Suborics 108
3 bb g Footstepsinthesand Devilish Lips (GER) (Konigstiger (GER))
(2002a) 2869a[4] 4130a[4] (4939a)

**Dragon Mall (USA)** David Simcock a106 102
4 b g Blame(USA) Petition The Lady (USA) (Petionville (USA))
320a[6] 698a[5] 888a[7] 3218[3] 4069[9] 4918[18]

**Dragon Mountain** Hugo Palmer a71
2 b c Sir Percy Rouge Dancer (Elusive City (USA))
6883[3] 7726[DSQ] 8029[5]

**Dragons Tail (IRE)** Tom Dascombe 90
2 b c Dragon Pulse(IRE) Mastoora (IRE) (Acclamation)
2148[3] (2556) 3929[7] 4827[2] 5681[4] 5939[2] 6977a[3]
7353[6]

**Dragon's Teeth (IRE)** R Le Gal a79 76
2 b g Dragon Pulse(IRE) Lamassu (IRE) (Entrepreneur)
1495[9] 1792[2] 3490[5] 3936[5] 4196a[2] 5626a[4] 6409a[2]
9086a[2]

**Dragons Thunder (IRE)**
Brian Ellison 1
3 ch g Dragon Pulse(IRE) Boschendal (IRE) (Zamindar (USA))
3555[8]

**Dragons Voice** Philip Hide a71 84
3 b g Poet's Voice China (Royal Academy (USA))
354[6] 1083[3] (2931) 3627[3] (5221) 6134[13] 6700[8]
(7909)

**Dragon Tattoo (IRE)** Hugo Palmer a56 36
2 b f Zoffany(IRE) Geisha Lily (FR) (Gone West (USA))
7266[6] 7875[9] 8555[4] 8847[9] 9175[11]

**Drakefell (IRE)** Richard Hannon a79 70
2 b c Canford Cliffs(IRE) Cake (IRE) (Acclamation)
8154[3] 8388[5] (8819) 8945[2]

**Dramatically (USA)** A P O'Brien a62 96
2 b f War Front(USA) Wonder Of Wonders (USA) (Kingmambo (USA))
8265a[5]

**Dramatic Queen (USA)**
William Haggas 75
2 ch f Kitten's Joy(USA) Midnight Music (IRE) (Dubawi (IRE))
7608[3] (8322)

**Dramatic Voice**
Ken Cunningham-Brown a19 34
4 ch m Poet's Voice Darwinia (GER) (Acatenango (GER))
1075[13] 1305[9] 5778[6] 6635[11] 8823[11] 9344[7]

**Dravid** Rod Millman a36 48
3 b g Famous Name Sweet Power (Pivotal)
2018[7] 2507[11] 2758[7] 4188[4]

**Draw Swords** John Gosden a79
3 br c Dansili Sacred Shield (Beat Hollow)
65[2] 265[5]

**Dr Doro (IRE)** Ian Williams a61 48
4 b m Holy Roman Emperor(IRE) Stellarina (IRE) (Night Shift (USA))
816[10] 1261[10] 1365[9] 4616[8]

**Dream Ally (IRE)** John Weymes a67 67
7 b g Oasis Dream Alexander Alliance (IRE) (Danetime (IRE))
723[3] 901[5] (981) 1246[6] (3256) (3544) 4310[8]
9414[8]

**Dream Awhile (USA)** J-C Rouget a78 94
3 b f War Front(USA) Baroness Richter (IRE) (Montjeu (IRE))
3103a[3] 4988a[3]

**Dream Ballad (IRE)** Hugo Palmer a52 65
3 b c Dream Ahead(USA) Royal Alchemist (Kingsinger (IRE))
4309[11] 4579[4]

**Dreamboat Annie** Mark Usher a43 68
2 b f Piccolo Bold Rose (Bold Edge)
3156[5] 3821[7] (4044) 4991[2] 6012[5] 6651[4] 7194[4]

**Dream Bounty** Michael Appleby 2
5 b m Bahamian Bounty Dream In Waiting (Oasis Dream)
6237[9] 7255[9]

**Dream Castle** Saeed bin Suroor 114
3 b c Frankel Sand Vixen (Dubawi (IRE))
(1514) 1959[2] 2399[5]◆ 3959[5] 5502[7] 6746a[2]

**Dreamdancer (IRE)** Joseph Tuite a22
2 b f Rip Van Winkle(IRE) Silver Samba (Dalakhani (IRE))
7946[12]

**Dream Dancing (USA)** Mark Casse a92 106
3 rg f Tapit(USA) To Dream About (USA) (Monarchos (USA))
8071a[7]

**Dream D'Ange (FR)** C Ferland a43 68
2 b f Sageburg(IRE) Fantastic Filly (FR) (Myrakalu (FR))
4677a[7]

**Dream Destroyer (IRE)**
Geoffrey Harker a35
3 gr f Vale Of York(IRE) Lady Georgina (Linamix (FR))
8716[7] 8931[8] 9018[7] 9342[11]

**Dream Dreamer** Jack W Davison a58 62
4 b m Dream Ahead(USA) Moonlit Garden (IRE) (Exceed And Excel (AUS))
9244a[13]

**Dream Dubai** M F De Kock a88 103
4 b h Kyllachy Welsh Anthem (Singspiel (IRE))
318a[13] 696a[8]

**Dream Dy (FR)** C Ferland a88 104
4 ch g Dream Ahead(USA) Diyakalanie (FR) (Ashkalani (IRE))
1159a[3]

**Dream Factory (IRE)** Marco Botti a79 73
4 ch g Manduro(GER) Istishaara (USA) (Kingmambo (USA))
(92) 381[3] (Dead)

**Dream Farr (IRE)** Ed Walker a81 72
4 b g Dream Ahead(USA) French Lady (NZ) (Entrepreneur)
(242) 518[3] (808) 1467[5] 2821[5] 3454[8] 4495[3]
5326[3] 5936[3] 6507[2] 7056[8]

**Dream Free** Mark Walford a68 67
4 b g Oasis Dream Freedonia (Selkirk (USA))
3205[3] 3559[7] 4345[3] 5824[8] 6270[3] 6788[7] 7236[8]
8219[4] 8498[4] 8664[3]

**Dreaming Of Paris** William Haggas a76
3 b f Oasis Dream Parisi (Rahy (USA))
168[3] (283)

**Dreaming Time** James Tate a81 73
3 b f Oasis Dream Maskunah (IRE) (Sadler's Wells (USA))
500[5] (814) 1142[5] 6160[6] 6664[3] (7770) (8433)
8797[11]

**Dream Love** Simon Dow a78 32
4 b m Rail Link Love Always (Piccolo)
213[3] 1555[4] 2041[7]

**Dream Machine (IRE)** Michael Bell a53 82
3 ch g Dream Ahead(USA) Last Cry (FR) (Peintre Celebre (USA))
(3041) 3787[3] 4798[2] 5838[2] 6518[3] (7097)◆ 7824[3]

**Dream Magic (IRE)**
Daniel Mark Loughnane a72 56
3 b g Lord Shanakill(USA) Pursuit of Passion (Pastoral Pursuits)
265[3] 552[2] 2395[8] 3175[2] 5485[4] 6947[10] 8132[11]
8773[13] (9375) 9445[5]

**Dream Malfunction (IRE)**
Joseph Tuite a62 75
2 ch f Mastercraftsman(IRE) Limetree Lady (Selkirk (USA))
8817[9]

**Dream Mount (IRE)** Marco Botti a75 45
2 b c Dream Ahead(USA) Mistify (IRE) (Elusive Quality (USA))
5631[10] 6883[7] (7488) 8491[5]

**Dream Of Camelot (IRE)**
Gary Moore 73
2 b f Camelot Definite Opinion (IRE) (Kheleyf (USA))
7898[3] 8425[4]

**Dream Of Delphi (IRE)**
William Haggas a59 62
2 b f Camacho Kitty Softpaws (IRE) (Royal Applause)
3390[13] 3776[7] 4116[11] (6585) 6845[2] 7519[12] 8141[9]

**Dreamofdiscovery (IRE)**
Julie Camacho a60 60
3 b g Henrythenavigator(USA) Dreamwriter (USA) (Tale Of The Cat (USA))
40[7] 1470[3] 2902[3] (5286) 6091[5] 7042[5]

**Dream Of Dreams (IRE)**
Sir Michael Stoute 113
3 ch c Dream Ahead(USA) Vasilia (Dansili)
2425[2]◆ 6428[10] (7154) 7356[5] (8738)

**Dream Of Joy (IRE)** Roger Varian a66 78
3 b f Dream Ahead(USA) Love And Laughter (IRE) (Theatrical (IRE))
5335[2]

**Dream Of Summer (IRE)**
Jeremy Noseda a85 79
4 b g Canford Cliffs(IRE) Danehill's Dream (IRE) (Danehill (USA))
2026[3] 2617[5] 4001[10] 6882[7] 7759[13]

**Dream On Dreamer (IRE)**
Antony Brittain 65
3 b f Dream Ahead(USA) Marula (IRE) (Sadler's Wells (USA))
5009[6]

**Dream Prospect** Roger Charlton 61
2 b g Invincible Spirit(IRE) Turama (Pivotal)
3782[6]◆ 4466[4] 5474[3] 6609[6]

**Dream Reversion** Tom Dascombe a61 64
3 b c Oasis Dream Last Second (IRE) (Alzao (USA))
324[7] 463[2]

**Dream Revival** Paul Collins a59 43
4 br m Captain Gerrard(IRE) Passkey (Medicean)
6903[10] 7270[6] 7763[2] 8543[6] 8716[2] 8784[3] 8924[3]
(9103) 9265[10]

**Dream Serenade** Michael Appleby a55 58
4 b m Dream Eater(IRE) Lady Santana (IRE) (Doyoun)
98[3]◆ 218[4] (721) 900[5] 1486[7] 1703[4] 2549[3] 2972[2]
3436[7] 7483[10] 8396[9] 8876[11] 9077[3] 9221[3] 9368[3]

**Dreams Of Glory** Ron Hodges a73 73
9 ch g Resplendent Glory(IRE) Pip's Dream (Glint Of Gold)
(95) 575[5] 886[7] 9189[9] 9470[7]

**Dream Start** John Ryan a60 65
3 b f Exceed And Excel(AUS) Calipatria (Shamardal (USA))
1857[13] 2434[14] 4269[4] 5158[5] 5793[4] 6850[3]◆
7282[2] 7480[7] 8329[2] 8551[6] 8906[6] 9019[7]

**Dream Team** Michael Dods a55 56
3 b g Captain Gerrard(IRE) Mimi Mouse (Diktat)
417[5] 1029[4] 3484[5] 4785[5] 6058[6] 7704[9] 8589[8]

**Dreamtide** Amanda Perrett 64
3 b f Champs Elysees Moraine (Rainbow Quest (USA))
2576[6] 3145[6] 4202[3]

**Dream Today (IRE)** Mark Johnston 107
2 b c Dream Ahead(USA) Macheera (IRE) (Machiavellian (USA))
(6403) 7146[5] 8036[2]◆ 8422[6]

**Dream Walker (FR)** Brian Ellison a99 99
8 gr g Gold Away(IRE) Minnie's Mystery (FR) (Highest Honor (FR))
1148[8] 1494[19] 2406[15] 3587[8] 4293[4] 5157[9]
5517a[3] (5688a) 6491a[11] 7066a[5] 7609[10]

**Dream Warrior** Charlie Appleby 85
2 b c Dubawi(IRE) I'm A Dreamer (IRE) (Noverre (USA))
6921[3] 7281[3] (7844a)

**Drefong (USA)** Bob Baffert a126
4 b h Gio Ponti(USA) Eltimaas (USA) (Ghostzapper (USA))
8607a[6]

**Dr Goodhead (FR)** Charles Hills a49 56
3 b f Zoffany(IRE) Whoosh (FR) (Muhtathir)
1948[8] 2753[3] 3329[6] 4214[11] 4971[11]

**Drill** Luca Cumani 54
2 b c Dansili Pongee (Barathea (IRE))
4860[8]

**Driver's Girl (USA)** Marco Botti a72
3 bb f Candy Ride(ARG) Sharbat (USA) (Dynaformer (USA))
283[2] (615)

**Dr Julius No** Richard Hughes a92 94
3 b g Dick Turpin(IRE) Royal Assent (Royal Applause)
31[2]◆ 1026[7] 1801[3] 2126[9] 3303[4] 3838[3] 4861[2]
5609[4] 6422[3]◆ 6870[6] 7650[4]

**Drochaid** Andrew Balding a89 97
3 ch c Mastercraftsman(IRE) Avon Lady (Avonbridge)
1582[2] (2520) (3318) 3998[4]

**Drombeg Dream (IRE)** *Augustine Leahy* 88
2 b f Arcano(IRE) Drombeg Dawn (IRE) (Orpen (USA))
4418a7

**Drop Kick Murphi (IRE)** *Christine Dunnett* a29 49
3 b g Sir Prancealot(IRE) Rindiseyda (IRE) (Arakan (USA))
4357 7656 687410 72558 79337 832814 86814

**Drover** *Keith Dalgleish* 53
2 ch g Foxwedge(AUS) Brooksby (Diktat)
39736 45776 52026

**Dr Red Eye** *Scott Dixon* a56 69
9 ch g Dr Fong(USA) Camp Fire (IRE) (Lahib (USA))
268 (222) 7845 14088 18689 22943

**Dr Richard Kimble (IRE)** *Mark Johnston* a73 69
2 b g Lawman(FR) Aoife Alainn (IRE) (Dr Fong (USA))
59187 63807 70433 (8491)

**Dr Shepherd (FR)** *C Scandella* 38
2 ch c Evasive Dame Du Floc (IRE) (Peintre Celebre (USA))
6170a8

**Druids Cross (IRE)** *Joseph Patrick O'Brien* a83 90
3 b c Cape Cross(IRE) Shell Garland (USA) (Sadler's Wells (USA))
25558

**Druid's Diamond** *Mark Walford* a19 57
4 b g Piccolo Faithful Beauty (IRE) (Last Tycoon)
16767 26885 29558 334310 41694 48394 52152 60352 61536 79827

**Druids Ridge** *M Al Mheiri* a84 85
5 b h Paco Boy(IRE) Miss Queen (USA) (Miswaki (USA))
316a9

**Drumfad Bay (IRE)** *Mrs John Harrington* 99
3 b f Acclamation Manieree (IRE) (Medicean)
1634a8 396419 6642a2 711310

**Drummore (IRE)** *A Fabre* a80 84
2 b c Dubawi(IRE) Rahiyah (USA) (Rahy (USA))
7844a4 (8302a) 8777a5

**Drumochter** *Jamie Osborne* a53 78
3 br f Bated Breath Dixey (Diktat)
5037 33833 43785 53673 (5782) 63898 71074 83906 93214

**Dschingis Secret (GER)** *Markus Klug* 120
4 b h Soldier Hollow Divya (GER) (Platini (GER))
(2450a) 3116a5 (4392a) (5983a) (6983a) 7668a6◆ 8527a3

**Dubai Acclaim (IRE)** *Richard Fahey* a64
2 b c Acclamation Bahati (IRE) (Intikhab (USA))
91984

**Dubai Art** *Richard Fahey* a77 47
3 b c Dutch Art Enact (Kyllachy)
(34) 32119 37099 47284

**Dubai Celebrity** *Chris Grant*
5 b g Sakhee(USA) Aljana (IRE) (Exceed And Excel (AUS))
5413P (Dead)

**Dubai Classic (IRE)** *K R Burke* 61
2 b f Fast Company(IRE) Dubai Pearl (IRE) (Refuse To Bend (IRE))
28365 331213

**Dubai Dynamo** *Ruth Carr* a82 92
12 b g Kyllachy Miss Mercy (IRE) (Law Society (USA))
151213 18324 222610

**Dubai Elegance** *Saeed bin Suroor* a83 75
3 ch f Sepoy(AUS) Some Sunny Day (Where Or When (IRE))
54844 63214 75696

**Dubai Empire (FR)** *John Quinn* 80
2 ch c Motivator Cable Beach (USA) (Langfuhr (CAN))
53805 64034 (7160) 80356

**Dubai Frame** *Ed Dunlop* a62 62
2 b c Sixties Icon Strictly Lambada (Red Ransom (USA))
835013 85085 88395

**Dubai Horizon (IRE)** *Saeed bin Suroor* a90 100
3 b g Poet's Voice Chibola (ARG) (Roy (USA))
(1624) 24372

**Dubai Knights (IRE)** *P Monfort* a67 73
3 b g Sir Prancealot(IRE) Dubai Princess (IRE) (Dubai Destination (USA))
8305a8

**Dubai Landmark (IRE)** *Hugo Palmer* a47
2 b c Helmet(AUS) Cairncross (IRE) (Cape Cross (IRE))
931112 94338

**Dubai One (IRE)** *Saeed bin Suroor* a102 70
3 ch f Exceed And Excel(AUS) Dresden Doll (USA) (Elusive Quality (USA))
(1454) 17748 (9453)

**Dubai Sand (IRE)** *J S Bolger* 103
3 ch c Teofilo(IRE) Bring Back Matron (IRE) (Rock Of Gibraltar (IRE))
1636a5 2442a5 4387a7 (Dead)

**Dubai Silk** *Robert Cowell* a60
2 ch f Helmet(AUS) Silken Express (IRE) (Speightstown (USA))
88194

**Dubai's Secret** *David Brown* a82 85
4 ch g Paco Boy(IRE) Lilli Marlane (Sri Pekan (USA))
21556 296011 375011 42933 53006 62974 65164 782413 83757

**Dubai Thunder** *Saeed bin Suroor* 106
3 b c Dubawi(IRE) Gonbarda (GER) (Lando (GER))
(2783)◆ 332211

**Dubaitwentytwenty** *Hugo Palmer* a67 63
3 br f Poet's Voice Cairncross (IRE) (Cape Cross (IRE))
(40) 72796 79607 858914 91805 93642◆

**Dubai Waves** *Tony Newcombe* a73 42
3 b f Poet's Voice Pencarrow (Green Desert (USA))
7582 11435 15813 22846 341210 84009 91807

**Dubara** *Luca Cumani* a78 95
3 b f Dubawi(IRE) Kibara (Sadler's Wells (USA))
19073◆ 36932 47634 (6377) 74063 780813

**Dubawi Fifty** *Karen McLintock* a96 93
4 b g Dubawi(IRE) Plethora (Sadler's Wells (USA))
(5468) (6151)◆ 80384◆

**Dubawi Flame** *H Al Ramzani* 94
4 b g Dubawi(IRE) Flame Of Gibraltar (IRE) (Rock Of Gibraltar (IRE))
934a15

**Dubawi Prince** *Roger Varian* 85
3 b c Dubawi(IRE) Flawly (Old Vic)
(1497) 19436

**Dubawi's Thunder** *R Bouresly* a61
6 b g Dubawi(IRE) Eclaircie (IRE) (Thunder Gulch (USA))
9257a3

**Dubhe** *Charlie Appleby* 90
2 b c Dubawi(IRE) Great Heavens (Galileo (IRE))
51054◆ (5840)◆ 69255 83795

**Dubka** *Sir Michael Stoute* 108
4 b m Dubawi(IRE) Rosika (Sakhee (USA))
23896 35862 46137 55692 644711 70896 81216

**Ducale Di Maremma (ITY)** *Frank Sheridan* a73 71
4 b h Showcasing Sadhya (FR) (Prince Sabo)
9309a6

**Duc De Seville (IRE)** *Michael Chapman* a27 53
5 b g Duke Of Marmalade(IRE) Splendid (IRE) (Mujtahid (USA))
14369 203210

**Duchess Of Danzig (GER)** *H-F Devin* a65
2 ch f Sea The Stars(IRE) Djumama (IRE) (Aussie Rules (USA))
8691a5

**Duchess Of Fife** *William Knight* a47 69
3 ch f Dutch Art La Adelita (IRE) (Anabaa (USA))
239413 31895 41862 512611 54785 (5961) 68224 74634 830012

**Duchess Of France (IRE)** *Adrian Paul Keatley* 95
4 b m Dylan Thomas(IRE) Miss Champagne (FR) (Bering)
33842 4385a3 6334a3 6642a9 6961a18 7856a10

**Duchy** *Michael Bell* a51 75
4 b m Kyllachy Albavilla (Spectrum (IRE))
51135 55496 61442

**Ducissa** *Daniel Kubler* a63 38
3 b m Exceed And Excel(AUS) Baize (Efisio)
9299 11809

**Duck A L'Orange (IRE)** *Michael Bell* a79 78
4 ch g Duke Of Marmalade(IRE) Incheni (IRE) (Nashwan (USA))
924 6195 13642

**Duckanddive (IRE)** *Mrs Denise Foster* a47 44
4 b m Kodiac Lady Ingabelle (IRE) (Catrail (USA))
6798a9

**Duck Egg Blue (IRE)** *Patrick Holmes* a53 76
3 b f Haatef(USA) Sapphire Spray (IRE) (Viking Ruler (AUS))
32878 42482 49015 53193 62082 63163 66923 773514

**Ducky Mallon (IRE)** *Donal Kinsella* a80 85
6 gr g Jeremy(USA) Indus Ridge (IRE) (Indian Ridge (IRE))
1233a5 1385a6 4327a4 6971a18 7425a7

**Duffy** *Richard Fahey* 42
2 b c Redoute's Choice(AUS) Kunegunda (Pivotal)
685411 75216

**Duggary** *Kevin Frost* a43 61
2 b g Champs Elysees Waitingonacloud (In The Wings)
44527 53809 58766 70308 74518 78905

**Duhr (IRE)** *Ralph J Smith* a58 67
3 b g Mawatheeq(USA) Dijlah (Linamix (FR))
92097 94356

**Duke Cosimo** *Michael Herrington* a83 78
7 ch g Pivotal Nannina (Medicean)
21847 384716 43435 46839 51843 545713 59474 68745 72446 75723 79402 83204 91527

**Duke Of Alba (IRE)** *Jamie Osborne* a56
2 b c Lope De Vega(IRE) Royal Alchemist (Kingsinger (IRE))
88899

**Duke Of Bronte** *Rod Millman* a51 97
3 b g Mount Nelson Reaf (In The Wings)
129910 169210 (1962) 28245 37794 (4535) 53284 (6920) 80053 83912

**Duke Of Brunswick (AUS)** *Mick Price* 83
5 b g Magnus(AUS) Tristabeel (AUS) (Zabeel (NZ))
8057a12

**Duke Of Clarence (IRE)** *Ian Williams* a59 91
8 gr g Verglas(IRE) Special Lady (FR) (Kaldoun (FR))
252513

**Duke Of Diamonds** *Julia Feilden* a56 79
5 gr g Duke Of Marmalade(IRE) Diamond Line (FR) (Linamix (FR))
16084 27529

**Duke Of Dorset** *Harry Fry* a60
2 b c Sepoy(AUS) Zuleika Dobson (Cadeaux Genereux)
77079 85017

**Duke Of Dundee (FR)** *A De Mieulle* 106
5 b g Duke Of Marmalade(IRE) Santa Louisia (Highest Honor (FR))
934a6

**Duke Of Firenze** *David C Griffiths* a97 113
8 ch g Pivotal Nannina (Medicean)
19466 25734 (2764) 33213 382915 407216 51165 564016 6973a10 71449 7670a4

**Duke Of Freedom** *Ann Duffield* a44 60
2 b g Equiano(FR) Duchess Of Seville (Duke Of Marmalade (IRE))
41673 45976 52785 73628 792011 819110 83976

**Duke Of North (IRE)** *Jim Boyle* a62 73
5 b g Danehill Dancer(IRE) Althea Rose (IRE) (Green Desert (USA))
13244 16874 22562◆ (2582) 29176 53336 628811 70984 71574 76536 791611 83008

**Duke Of Sonning** *Shaun Harris* a55 59
5 ch g Duke Of Marmalade(IRE) Moonshadow (Diesis)
18705 35665 45453 701512 74127

**Dukeofwallingford** *Eve Johnson Houghton* a62 67
2 b g Equiano(FR) Hazelberry (Bertolini (USA))
70935 79152 89526

**Duke Of Yorkshire** *Tim Easterby* a75 73
7 b g Duke Of Marmalade(IRE) Dame Edith (FR) (Top Ville (IRE))
151915 33252 37533 42445 48015 541710 61266 82199

**Duke's Girl** *Michael Bell* a55 71
3 b f Poet's Voice Juniper Girl (IRE) (Revoque (IRE))
14485 27615 34052◆ 37112 54065 61074 70193 78952

**Dukes Meadow** *Roger Ingram* a62 35
6 b g Pastoral Pursuits Figura (Rudimentary (USA))
1233 3836 7392 9669 13387 17295 23123 313713 47655 57909 66224 73233 82486 91412 92826

**Duke Street (IRE)** *Dr Richard Newland* a91 87
5 b g Duke Of Marmalade(IRE) Act Of The Pace (IRE) (King's Theatre (IRE))
(759)◆ 80388

**Dukhan** *Hugo Palmer* a85 84
2 br c Teofilo(IRE) Vedela (FR) (Selkirk (USA))
43632 48594◆ (8372)

**Dukinta (IRE)** *Hugo Palmer* a71 79
3 b f Dubawi(IRE) Misskinta (IRE) (Desert Sun)
361511 43006 50227 (5780) 66186 733612

**Dulciboy** *Stefano Botti* 91
3 b c Paco Boy(IRE) Dulcify (IRE) (Dubawi (IRE))
2245a5 8095a6

**Dulcina** *R P McNamara* a51 44
3 b f Compton Place Alushta (Royal Applause)
14182

**Dumbarton Rock** *Georgios Alimpinisis* a25 41
7 b g Kyllachy Ellablue (Bahamian Bounty)
9309a13

**Duncan Of Scotland (IRE)** *Lee Smyth* a65 67
4 ch g Roderic O'Connor(IRE) Cantando (IRE) (Hamas (IRE))
(2454) 29497 49582 59943

**Dundonnell (USA)** *C Fownes* a105 106
7 b g First Defence(USA) Family (USA) (Danzig (USA))
694a2 1041a3 1377a9

**Dundunah (USA)** *David O'Meara* a77 80
3 ch f Sidney's Candy(USA) Sealedwithapproval (USA) (With Approval (CAN))
20803 26309 29253 32022◆ 40605 (4576) 53382 58377 66697 79407 89272 91369

**Dungannon** *Andrew Balding* a93 80
10 b g Monsieur Bond(IRE) May Light (Midyan (USA))
712 (387) 6644 8516 (1110) 18638 23684 36175 880313

**Dunleer (IRE)** *Donal Kinsella* a40
3 b f Invincible Spirit(IRE) Alioonagh (USA) (Giant's Causeway (USA))
2656a20

**Dunquin (IRE)** *John Mackie* a76 75
5 b g Cape Cross(IRE) Last Resort (Lahib (USA))
4710 (841) (1330) 18918 343211 45735

**Duplication (IRE)** *Joseph Patrick O'Brien* a94 89
3 b c Requinto(IRE) Primeshade Promise (Opening Verse (USA))
8225a7

**Du Pyla (FR)** *Z Koplik* 74
4 b h Vertigineux(FR) Do I Worry (FR) (Charge D'Affaires)
7307a12

**Duquesa Penguin** *D & P Prod'Homme* a45 47
5 ch g Winker Watson Quaker Parrot (Compton Place)
4955a15

**Duretto** *Andrew Balding* a83 114
5 ch g Manduro(GER) Landinium (ITY) (Lando (GER))
25713 (7139) 82295

**Dusky Dance (IRE)** *P Schiergen* 73
2 gr c Lope De Vega(IRE) Dawn Dew (GER) (Montjeu (IRE))
6726a8 8884a9

**Dusky Dawn** *Alan Swinbank* a82 47
5 b m Kheleyf(USA) Piddies Pride (IRE) (Indian Lodge (IRE))
435 6113 8505 9944 (1104) 12956 15923

**Dusky Maid (IRE)** *James Given* a84 66
3 b f Dark Angel(IRE) Dream Scape (Oasis Dream)
8454 11022 13337 14714 (2993) (3473) 42142 47976 (5845) 60152 66195 91856

**Dusty** *Mick Channon* 65
2 ch f Paco Boy(IRE) Hairspray (Bahamian Bounty)
38218 44403◆ 756310

**Dusty Berry** *Eve Johnson Houghton* a32 62
3 ch f Sixties Icon Hazelberry (Bertolini (USA))
6277

**Dusty Bin** *Roy Bowring* a45 48
3 b g Sepoy(AUS) Short Affair (Singspiel (IRE))
4016 8758 32966 36245 41627 94448

**Dusty Blue** *Michael Easterby* a72 74
5 ch m Medicean Jazz Jam (Pivotal)
2211 (1071) 15473 (2025) 40158 443310 53759

**Dutch Academy** *K R Burke* a46 61
2 b c Dutch Art Katimont (IRE) (Montjeu (IRE))
73835◆ 80735 82088

**Dutch Art Dealer** *Ivan Furtado* a91 79
6 b g Dutch Art Lawyers Choice (Namid)
(32)◆ 27513 9894 151217 38576 43399 58054

**Dutch Artist (IRE)** *Alan Brown* 84
5 ch g Dutch Art Baltic Princess (FR) (Peintre Celebre (USA))
17173 26847 34332 365211 416812 51833 55785 675711 71429 78943 821610

**Dutch Barney** *Barry Leavy* a17 11
7 b g Dutch Art Celeb Style (IRE) (Tagula (IRE))
214014 340010

**Dutch Breeze** *S Cannavo* 90
6 ch g Dutch Art Oasis Breeze (Oasis Dream)
2867a5

**Dutch Connection** *Charles Hills* 119
5 ch h Dutch Art Endless Love (IRE) (Dubai Destination (USA))
39246 4935a6 (6476) 7179a6 8003P

**Dutch Desire** *William Haggas* 52
2 b f Dutch Art Danehill Destiny (Danehill Dancer (IRE))
53277

**Dutch Dream** *Linda Perratt* a33 57
4 ch m Dutch Art Starry Sky (Oasis Dream)
24548 27776 29507 (3710) 44782 (4896) 54727 63847 67869

**Dutch Golden Age (IRE)** *Gary Moore* a94 43
5 b g Kodiac Magic Melody (Petong)
(93) 2877 (547) 15016 17948 32582

**Dutch Melody** *Chris Wall* 20
3 b f Dutch Art Mystic Melody (IRE) (Montjeu (IRE))
293010 430011

**Dutch Mist** *Kevin Ryan* a72 88
4 ch m Dutch Art Solstice (Dubawi (IRE))
1425 45911

**Dutch Quality** *Marco Botti* a71 69
3 b g Dutch Art Miss Quality (USA) (Elusive Quality (USA))
20667 30419

**Dutch Stranger** *Harry Dunlop* 61
2 b f Dutch Art Passing Stranger (IRE) (Dixie Union (USA))
24734◆

**Dutch Uncle** *Archie Watson* a79 77
5 b g Dutch Art Evasive Quality (FR) (Highest Honor (FR))
362 2666 (719) 9632 12585 20866 392416 485413 53026 632210 71567 79094 829711 92717

**Dutiful Son (IRE)** *Simon Dow* a85 47
7 b g Invincible Spirit(IRE) Grecian Dancer (Dansili)
3493 46011 5068 13013 (1423) 208310 296010 34716 47529 52415◆ 606810 67945 770911 86465 88813 (9094) (9207)◆ 94108

**Duxbury** *Richard Fahey* a24
3 b c Dutch Art Triskel (Hawk Wing (USA))
47910

**D'Waterside** *David Loughnane* a61 57
3 b g Sir Percy Santorini Sunset (Haafhd)
26207 34937 52474 59355 70615 79485 831211 86625 90566 92174 94545

**Dwight D** *Stuart Coltherd* a59 90
4 b g Duke Of Marmalade(IRE) Almatinka (IRE) (Indian Ridge (IRE))
688110 756611 79846 828911

**Dylaban (IRE)** *Alain Couetil* a85 65
5 b g Dylan Thomas(IRE) La Bastoche (IRE) (Kaldoun (FR))
(6454a) 7636a7

**Dylan Dancing (IRE)** *C Le Veel* a81 97
4 b h Dylan Thomas(IRE) Raindancing (IRE) (Tirol (IRE))
(5490a) 5979a15

**Dylan Mouth (IRE)** *Marco Botti* a108 115
6 b h Dylan Thomas(IRE) Cottonmouth (IRE) (Noverre (USA))
542a2 699a3 1042a5 19577 25193 30907 (4614) 739310 86373

**Dylan's Centenary** *Phil McEntee* a27 21
6 b g Kyllachy Sheka (Ishiguru (USA))
611215 721310 7323RR 793414

**Dylan's Storm (IRE)** *Peter Niven* a37 43
5 b g Zebedee Storm Lady (IRE) (Alhaarth (IRE))
318110 391212 39348 51819 554412

**Dyllan (IRE)** *Ruth Carr* a71 77
4 b g Zebedee Luvmedo (IRE) (One Cool Cat (USA))
39037 44898 52802 57397 62375

**Dynamic** *William Haggas* 88
3 b f Teofilo(IRE) White Cay (Dalakhani (IRE))
(6390)◆ 72765 (8351)

**Dynamic Girl (IRE)** *Brendan Powell* a67 56
4 b m Holy Roman Emperor(IRE) Boca Dancer (IRE) (Indian Ridge (IRE))
18994 22297 386910 49757 55588 715811 74653 78997 85148 86755 89496 91418 92827

**Dyna Might** *Ollie Pears* a59 61
3 b f Foxwedge(AUS) Dyna Bowl (USA) (Dynaformer (USA))
206010 (2705) 32072 (3405) 43364 49784 561710 788510 831412

**Dynamo (IRE)** *Richard Hughes* a55 61
6 b g Galileo(IRE) Trading Places (Dansili)
2186 82012 9657

**Dynamo Walt (IRE)** *Derek Shaw* a89 71
6 b g Acclamation Cambara (Dancing Brave (USA))
3584 6182 8167 10255 12225 22624 (2516) 32314 39676 85407 90794

**Dynatail (USA)** *Michael Dini* 96
3 bb f Hightail(USA) Southern Dynamo (USA) (Dynaformer (USA))
4650a10

**Dyson's Girl** *Bryan Smart* a48 65
2 ch f Equiano(FR) Choisette (Choisir (AUS))
187210 31794 40144 47392 53734 56144 71595 77566 81916 858811

**Eadaoins Pet (IRE)** *John James Feane* a65 67
4 b m Tagula(IRE) Ice Rock (IRE) (Rock Of Gibraltar (IRE))
29935

**Eadbhard (IRE)** *M C Grassick* a43 55
2 b g Elzaam(AUS) Only Exception (IRE) (Jeremy (USA))
7423a[11]

**Eagle Creek (IRE)** *Simon Crisford* a103 98
3 b g Raven's Pass(USA) Blue Angel (IRE) (Oratorio (IRE))
(1692)◆ 2402[9] 6235[2] 6873[7] 7727[3] 8843[10]

**Eagle Eyes (GER)** *Jean-Pierre Carvalho* a74 90
4 ch m Adlerflug(GER) Evening Breeze (GER) (Surumu (GER))
7203a[6]

**Eagle's Stare (IRE)** *S Seemar* a23 5
3 b c Bernardini(USA) Sander Camillo (USA) (Dixie Union (USA))
9257a[7]

**Eagle Way (AUS)** *John Moore* 115
4 ch g More Than Ready(USA) Wedgetail Eagle (AUS) (Lure (USA))
3129a[3] 9167a[8]

**Early Dawn** *Marco Botti* 68
2 ch f Dawn Approach(IRE) Born Something (IRE) (Caerleon (USA))
3697[4] 4533[4]

**Early Morning (IRE)** *Harry Dunlop* a103 102
6 gr g New Approach(IRE) Summer's Eve (Singspiel (IRE))
2141[2] 3963[28] 5914[8] 6918[17] 7727[10] (8944) 9274a[3]

**Earnshaw (USA)** *S bin Ghadayer* a73 111
6 gr h Medaglia d'Oro(USA) Emily Bronte (Machiavellian (USA))
86a[3] 429a[3] 776a[2] 1046a[5] 1379a[5]

**Earth (FR)** *H De Nicolay* a33
3 b f Myboycharlie(IRE) Rolled Gold (USA) (Giant's Causeway (USA))
3134a[14]

**Eartha Kitt** *Tom Dascombe* 102
3 bb f Pivotal Ceiling Kitty (Red Clubs (IRE))
2616[8] (3793)◆ 4864[3]◆ 6234[2]◆ 7356[10] 7811[3] (8040)

**Earthly (USA)** *Bernard Llewellyn* a81 71
3 b c Spring At Last(USA) Geographic (USA) (Empire Maker (USA))
(552) 1404[5] 2174[6] (3178) 6176[5] 7231[7] 7599[6] 8506[6]

**Earthwindorfire** *Geoffrey Deacon* a64 65
6 br g High Chaparral(IRE) Elemental (Rudimentary (USA))
218[10]

**East Coast Lady (IRE)** *William Stone* a77 76
5 b m Kodiac Alexander Anapolis (IRE) (Spectrum (IRE))
50[6] 505[6] 883[3] 1066[2] 1489[2] 2464[7] 2800[3] (3139) 4317[5] 5295[7] 5750[5] 7002[6] (7465) (8300)

**Easter Lily (IRE)** *A P O'Brien* 85
2 ch f Galileo(IRE) Chanting (USA) (Danehill (USA))
5344a[5]

**Eastern (IRE)** *Andrew Balding* 68
3 b f Shamardal(USA) Thought Is Free (Cadeaux Genereux)
6614[4] 7125[6]

**Eastern Dragon (IRE)** *Iain Jardine* a84 81
7 b g Elnadim(USA) Shulammite Woman (IRE) (Desert Sun)
(359) 611[5] 782[5] 1032[6] 1832[8] 5207[7] 5667[8]

**Eastern Impact (IRE)** *Richard Fahey* a105 110
6 b g Bahamian Bounty Kate The Great (Xaar)
207a[11] 433a[8] 651a[14] 1152[3]◆ 2433[2] 4072[7] 5640[11] 6206[13] 7144[17] 8044[4]

**Eastern Lady (IND)** *Richard Price* a46 58
4 ch m Dancing Forever(USA) Oriental Lady (IRE) (King's Best (USA))
4279[4] 5049[6] 5607[6] 6095[6]

**Eastern Racer (IRE)** *Brian Ellison* 89
5 b g Bushranger(IRE) Queen Cobra (IRE) (Indian Rocket)
1512[16] 1910[6]

**Eastern Sunrise** *Richard Hannon* 58
2 b f Dawn Approach(IRE) Desert Sunrise (Green Desert (USA))
5114[7] 5660[9] 6806[8] (Dead)

**East India** *George Baker* a53 74
5 ch g Galileo(IRE) Field Of Hope (IRE) (Selkirk (USA))
2512[3] 3308[6] 4802[3] (6018a)

**East Indies** *Gary Moore* a77 69
4 b g Authorized(IRE) Elan (Dansili)
6515[6] 9458[8]

**East Of The Nile** *E J O'Neill* 57
2 b f Helmet(AUS) Temple Of Thebes (IRE) (Bahri (USA))
8252a[6]

**East Street Revue** *Tim Easterby* 99
4 ch g Pastoral Pursuits Revue Princess (IRE) (Mull Of Kintyre (USA))
1876[2]◆ 2433[4] 3092[12] 3829[8] 4867[6] 6677[4] (8012) 8416[13]

**East Wind** *Tony Coyle*
2 b f Dick Turpin(IRE) Angel Rays (Unfuwain (USA))
7890[8]

**Easy Break (FR)** *F Chappet* 74
2 b f Sunday Break(JPN) Entre Deux Mers (FR) (Saint Estephe (FR))
6251a[6]

**Easy Code** *William Haggas* a78 75
4 b g Bahamian Bounty Skirrid (Halling (USA))
3008[7] 3718[3] 4311[4] 5145[4] (5482) 5870[3] 7058[3] (7493) 7769[5]

**Easyrider (FR)** *J-M Lefebvre* a58 62
2 b g Dream Ahead(USA) Hashbrown (GER) (Big Shuffle (USA))
5952a[11] 7012a[9]

**Easy Tiger** *Malcolm Saunders* a91 89
5 b g Refuse To Bend(IRE) Extremely Rare (IRE) (Mark Of Esteem (IRE))
4410[2]◆ (4622)◆ 5842[4] 6419[8] 7025[2] 7404[4] 7789[2] 8547[6] 8872[3] 9206[2]

**Easy Victory** *Saeed bin Suroor* 87
3 b f Dubawi(IRE) Independence (Selkirk (USA))
8736[19]

**Easy Wind** *Sir Mark Prescott Bt* a63 65
3 br f Shirocco(GER) Attainable (Kalanisi (IRE))
3317[11] 3472[10] 3824[5] 4962[3]◆ 5361[2]◆ 5846[2]

**Eaton Square** *John Gosden* 94
3 b g Invincible Spirit(IRE) Loch Jipp (USA) (Belong To Me (USA))
3303[10]

**Ebbesbourne (IRE)** *Sir Michael Stoute* a70 92
3 b f Teofilo(IRE) Ebble (Oasis Dream)
2117[5] (3094) 3749[2] 5658[7] 7817[9]

**Ebbisham (IRE)** *John Mackie* a75 61
4 b g Holy Roman Emperor(IRE) Balting Lass (IRE) (Orpen (USA))
641[9] (1729) 2909[6] 3718[11] 4501[7] (8434) 8907[11] 9410[3]

**Eben Dubai (IRE)** *John Flint* a41 59
5 b g New Approach(IRE) Eldalil (Singspiel (IRE))
1939[6] 2219[6] 2722[3]◆ 3428[8] 3575[5] 4040[2] 4494[2] 4734[5] 6305[3] 7336[3] 7567[3] 7918[6]

**Ebitda** *Scott Dixon* a46 81
3 b f Compton Place Tipsy Girl (Haafhd)
415[5] 600[7] 904[6] (2897) 3703[6] 3914[4] 4107[7] (5703) (6114)◆ 6574[6] (7014) (8484) (8681)

**Ebony N Ivory** *Archie Watson* a74 76
4 b g Equiano(FR) Ile Deserte (Green Desert (USA))
242[3] 518[8] 843[4] 955[7] 1219[5] 1296[8]

**Ebony Princess (IRE)** *Kieran P Cotter* a47 48
7 b m Camacho Maripova (IRE) (Marju (IRE))
2955[9]

**Ebqaa (IRE)** *James Unett* a65 73
3 b f Cape Cross(IRE) Estedaama (IRE) (Marju (IRE))
7109[4] 7597[2] 8911[2] 9159[4]

**Ebtkaar (IRE)** *Michael Appleby* a71 58
3 b g Cape Cross(IRE) Clare Glen (IRE) (Sakhee (USA))
3393[3] 4152[3] 9279[2]

**Eburaci (IRE)** *Charlie Fellowes* a58 61
3 b c Vale Of York(IRE) Dubai Pearl (IRE) (Refuse To Bend (IRE))
1513[8] 1866[4] 2793[11]

**Eccleston** *Julie Camacho* a86 92
6 b g Acclamation Miss Meggy (Pivotal)
1515[8] 2840[4] 3463[4] 3585[7] 4343[2] 5093[6] 7612[10] 8293[3]◆ 9016[3] 9272[6]

**Echauffour (FR)** *J-C Rouget* a87 85
4 b h Le Havre(IRE) Langrune (IRE) (Fasliyev (USA))
6123a[2]

**Echo (IRE)** *Jedd O'Keeffe* a54 57
2 b g Zoffany(IRE) Aweebounce (IRE) (Dubawi (IRE))
5180[7] 5492[7] 6465[5] 7239[7] (7519)

**Echo Cove (IRE)** *Jane Chapple-Hyam* 73
2 ch c Roderic O'Connor(IRE) Russian Rave (Danehill Dancer (IRE))
6654[7] 7520[7] 7810[4]

**Echoism (IRE)** *Peter Hiatt* a14 30
3 ch f Casamento(IRE) Epic Similie (Lomitas)
8137[5] 8784[14]

**Echo Of Lightning** *Roger Fell* a66 86
7 b g Echo Of Light Classic Lass (Dr Fong (USA))
3581[9] 4339[8] (4851) 5601[3] (5805) 6414[8] 7111[7] 7327[3]◆ 8014[2] 8240[14] 8257[11] 8718[14]

**Eclipse De Sivola (FR)** *K Borgel* a50 56
3 ch f Noroit(GER) Magic Fairy (FR) (Ski Chief (USA))
3275a[4]

**Economic Crisis (IRE)** *Alan Berry* a77 79
8 ch m Excellent Art Try The Air (IRE) (Foxhound (USA))
3183[2]◆ 3707[10] 4249[5] 4850[3] 5256[6] 5602[6] 5920[4] 6351[5] 6593[7] 6891[5] (7657) 7884[2] (8106) 8488[2] 8717[3]

**Ecrin Des Bieffes (FR)** *J A Remolina Diez* a93 93
3 b c Shakespearean(IRE) Nova Luz (Divine Light (JPN))
(272a) 6455a[13]

**Eddiebet** *David O'Meara* a71 66
3 ch g Monsieur Bond(IRE) Champagne Katie (Medicean)
956[6]◆ 1179[5] 1589[2] 1866[3] 2901[3] 8193[5] 8721[7] 9093[3] 9432[9]

**Eddiemaurice (IRE)** *John Flint* a71 78
6 ch g Captain Rio Annals (Lujain (USA))
1763[2]

**Eddiethebung (IRE)** *Nigel Tinkler*
2 ch g Casamento(IRE) Ma Paloma (FR) (Highest Honor (FR))
7623[9] 8013[16]

**Eddy Mercs** *Michael Appleby* a9
5 bl g Striking Ambition Bella Tutrice (IRE) (Woodborough (USA))
222[10]

**Eddystone Rock (IRE)** *John Best* a103 106
5 ch g Rock Of Gibraltar(IRE) Bayberry (UAE) (Bering)
396[3] 716a[4] 835a[7] 1494[6] 2086[8] 3323[2] 4033[10] 4918[6] 5500[8] 5940[4] (6449) 7395[7] 7619[11] 8234[13] 8740[3]

**Eden Rose** *Mick Channon* 42
2 b f Dansili Gallic Star (IRE) (Galileo (IRE))
8163[13]

**Ede's A Winner** *Pat Phelan* a53 17
2 ch f Archipenko(USA) Run For Ede's (Peintre Celebre (USA))
5717[9] 7488[9] 8989[5] 9199[11]

**Ede's E Rider** *Pat Phelan* a54
3 b g Equiano(FR) Run For Ede's (Peintre Celebre (USA))
502[9] 3412[11] 7945[13]

**Ede's The Mover** *Pat Phelan* a55 48
4 b m Bahamian Bounty Run For Ede's (Peintre Celebre (USA))
2257[8] 3172[3] 4010[5] 5062[6] 7006[9]

**Edgar (GER)** *David Bridgwater* a77
7 b g Big Shuffle(USA) Estella (GER) (Acatenango (GER))
3[7]

**Edgar Allan Poe (IRE)** *Rebecca Bastiman* a55 76
3 b g Zoffany(IRE) Swingsky (IRE) (Indian Ridge (IRE))
3403[10] 3913[6] (4473) (4721) 6893[4] 7699[4] 7958[6] 8299[2] 8651[2]

**Edgar Balthazar** *Keith Dalgleish* a88 92
5 b g Pastoral Pursuits Assistacat (IRE) (Lend A Hand)
8718[4]

**Edge (IRE)** *Bernard Llewellyn* a64 61
6 b g Acclamation Chanter (Lomitas)
2762[5] 3422[12] 4203[7] 4968[6] 5427[5] 5713[3] 6306[2]◆ (6754) 7210[2] (7900) 8473[7] 8661[9] 8854[3] 9153[5]

**Edged In Blue** *K R Burke* a57 65
3 b f Acclamation Dutch Diamond (Dutch Art)
397[2] 875[6] (2072) 3822[6] 4542[4]

**Edged Out** *Christopher Mason* 80
7 b m Piccolo Edge Of Light (Xaar)
2360[7] 3281[3] (3865)

**Edge Of Heaven** *Jonathan Portman* a89 71
5 b m Pastoral Pursuits Halfwaytoparadise (Observatory (USA))
99[5]

**Edge Of Sanity (IRE)** *Iain Jardine* a79 99
8 b g Invincible Spirit(IRE) Saor Sinn (IRE) (Galileo (IRE))
4921[3] 6329[11]

**Edge Of The World (IRE)** *Ralph Beckett* a48 52
2 b f Fastnet Rock(AUS) Lady Links (Bahamian Bounty)
7226[7] 8544[8] 9050[7]

**Edification** *R P McNamara* a72 61
4 b g Dream Ahead(USA) Elegant Pride (Beat Hollow)
6802a[2]

**Edith Weston** *Robert Cowell* a48 50
4 b m Showcasing Twitch Hill (Piccolo)
271[10] 723[9] 2069[9]

**Edward Lewis** *David O'Meara* 106
4 b g Kyllachy Tahirah (Green Desert (USA))
(1876) 2031[2] (2578) 2839[4] 3321[5]◆ 4072[6] 4881[9] 5640[18] 6325[2] 7475[5] 8044[14]

**Edwin** *Mario Hofer* 81
3 ch c Excelebration(IRE) Edallora (IRE) (Refuse To Bend (IRE))
2002a[10]

**Eeh Bah Gum (IRE)** *David O'Meara* 43
2 b g Dandy Man(IRE) Moonline Dancer (FR) (Royal Academy (USA))
6264[13] 7326[11] 7818[9]

**Eeny Mac (IRE)** *John Wainwright* a2 52
10 ch g Redback Sally Green (IRE) (Common Grounds)
2378[8] 3530[7] 4554[7]

**Eesha Beauty (IRE)** *Marco Botti* a67 66
2 b f Born To Sea(IRE) Eastern Glow (Cape Cross (IRE))
3902[8] 5717[3] (6636)

**Eesha Says (IRE)** *Tony Carroll* a49
2 b f Fast Company(IRE) Admire The View (IRE) (Dubawi (IRE))
8397[9] 8945[4] 9198[9]

**Eez Eh (IRE)** *Keith Dalgleish* 78
4 b g Jeremy(USA) Step With Style (USA) (Gulch (USA))
1683[9] 2497[5] 2953[6] 3432[9] 3898[3] 4608[5] 5540[7]

**Efaadah (IRE)** *F Head* 102
2 b f Dansili Albaraah (IRE) (Oasis Dream)
6731a[2] 8004[8]

**Effywind (FR)** *K Borgel* 61
4 gr m Diamond Green(FR) Halix (FR) (Tropular)
3274a[8]

**Efily (FR)** *Z Koplik* 36
4 b m Slickly(FR) Efisia (FR) (Efisio)
7307a[10]

**Eggesford** *Martyn Meade* a59
3 b g Foxwedge(AUS) Elegant Pride (Beat Hollow)
855[4]

**Egg Tart (AUS)** *Chris Waller* 104
3 b f Sebring(AUS) Mrs Windsor (AUS) (King's Best (USA))
8059a[7]

**Ehtedaam (USA)** *A R Al Rayhi* a30 66
8 br g Arch(USA) Bow River Gold (Rainbow Quest (USA))
203a[14]

**Ehtiraas** *Owen Burrows* a88 87
4 b g Oasis Dream Kareemah (IRE) (Peintre Celebre (USA))
5125[2] 6809[5]

**Einstein** *Mrs Ilka Gansera-Leveque* a65 54
4 b h Aqlaam Park Crystal (IRE) (Danehill (USA))
68[6] 390[4] 481[7] 689[5] 924[9] 1758[3] 3628[8] (4165)

**Eirene** *Dean Ivory* 99
2 b f Declaration Of War(USA) Za Za Zoom (IRE) (Le Vie Dei Colori)
3697[3] (4296) 5576[2] (6136) 6863[2] 7617[6]◆

**Eium Mac** *Neville Bycroft* a55 52
8 b g Presidium Efipetite (Efisio)
1868[7] 2466[7] 4263[6] 6947[2] 8248[9]

**Ejaaby** *Roger Varian* a72 86
3 ch g Helmet(AUS) Vivid Blue (Haafhd)
(1889) 2506[2] 3146[3] 3592[14]

**Ejabah (IRE)** *Charles Smith* a54 45
3 b f Iffraaj Relinquished (Royal Applause)
1205[6] 1432[4] 2182[7] 2853[7] 6526[4] 7109[6] 8255[7] 8805[3] 9071[4]◆ 9365[9]

**Ejayteekay** *Hughie Morrison* a79 77
4 b m Big Bad Bob(IRE) Lovely Dream (IRE) (Elnadim (USA))
(1447) 1897[7] 2605[8] 3507[8] 4372[P] 4746[6] 5290[3] (6034) (6821) 7151[2] 7721a[8]

**Ejtyah** *David Simcock* a77
2 b f Frankel Darysina (USA) (Smart Strike (CAN))
(9277)◆

**Ekhtiyaar** *Roger Varian* 106
3 b c Bated Breath Bayja (IRE) (Giant's Causeway (USA))
2122[2] (2831)◆ 3844[5] (4813) 7782[5]

**Eland Ally** *Anabel K Murphy* a65 50
9 b g Striking Ambition Dream Rose (IRE) (Anabaa (USA))
143[2] 270[10] 2370[8]

**Elapidae** *David Lanigan* a60
2 b c Helmet(AUS) Al Cobra (IRE) (Sadler's Wells (USA))
9154[6]◆ 9417[9]

**Elarqam** *Mark Johnston* 111
2 b c Frankel Attraction (Efisio)
(6967)◆ (7546)

**Elas Ruby** *John Gosden* a78 101
3 b f Raven's Pass(USA) Elas Diamond (Danehill Dancer (IRE))
2174[2] 3006[4] (3749) 4424a[3] 5981a[4] 7577[7]

**El Astronaute (IRE)** *John Quinn* a100 100
4 ch g Approve(IRE) Drumcliffe Dancer (IRE) (Footstepsinthesand)
(1863) (2524) 3321[8] 3829[7] 4881[16] (5505) 6025[2] 6677[2] 7604[5]

**Elate (USA)** *William Mott* a120
3 bb f Medaglia d'Oro(USA) Cheery (USA) (Distorted Humor (USA))
8578a[4]

**Elation (IRE)** *Roger Varian* 77
2 b f Invincible Spirit(IRE) Hallowed Park (IRE) (Barathea (IRE))
5107[5]◆ (5702) 7623[3]

**Elbereth** *Andrew Balding* a102 109
6 b m Mount Nelson Masandra (IRE) (Desert Prince (IRE))
(1355a) 1775[4] 2432[2] 3299[4] 4069[12] 5436[6] 6744a[2] 7577[9]

**El Bertie (IRE)** *Tim Easterby* a54 44
2 b g Elzaam(AUS) Emily Jane (IRE) (Acclamation)
2816[10] 5412[8] 5834[9] 7363[5] 7920[6] 8287[13]

**El Borracho (IRE)** *Simon Dow* a65 69
2 br g Society Rock(IRE) Flame Of Hibernia (IRE) (One Cool Cat (USA))
3746[7] 4213[7] 4709[5] (6395) 6934[4] 8848[10]

**El Campeon** *Simon Dow* a82 59
5 bb g Multiplex Villabella (FR) (Hernando (FR))
280[2]◆ 519[5] 1153[5] 1464[2]

**El Cap (USA)** *Sir Michael Stoute* a78 105
3 b g Speightstown(USA) Divine Presence (USA) (A.P. Indy (USA))
1889[3] 3262[5] (4508) 5496[2] (5926)

**El Cat Bere (FR)** *M Rolland* a70 78
3 b g Hurricane Cat(USA) Valibi Bere (FR) (Russian Blue (IRE))
6496a[4]

**El Chapo** *Richard Fahey* a60 79
2 b g Lethal Force(IRE) Never Lose (Diktat)
4297[4] 4848[3] 5412[5] 6425[5] 6940[2] (7384) (7921)

**El Divo (FR)** *N Caullery* 65
2 b c Dabirsim(FR) Ellary (FR) (Equerry (USA))
8482a[13]

**Eldritch (IRE)** *John Gosden* a94 85
3 b g Dark Angel(IRE) Henties Bay (IRE) (Cape Cross (IRE))
(2118) 3005[5] 7949[4] 8188[2]◆ 8398[2]

**El Dulce (USA)** *Todd Pletcher* a83 103
2 b c Twirling Candy(USA) Figureta (ARG) (The Leopard (USA))
8602a[9]

**Election Day** *Mark Johnston* a82 83
3 b g Invincible Spirit(IRE) Missisipi Star (IRE) (Mujahid (USA))
1875[2]◆ 2376[3] 3232[4] 4215[3] 6468[2] 7327[5] 7728[8] 8375[6]

**Elector** *Sir Michael Stoute* 78
2 b c Dansili Enticement (Montjeu (IRE))
(6921)

**Electric Landlady (IRE)** *Denis Coakley* a77 80
2 b f Red Jazz(USA) Margie (IRE) (Marju (IRE))
(3210)◆ 4028[18] (4806) 6200[4]

**Elegance (IRE)** *Martin Smith* a46 36
2 ch f Famous Name Royal Crescent (IRE) (Spectrum (IRE))
6584[8] 7707[13]

**Elegante Bere (FR)** *D Guillemin* 97
3 b f Peer Gynt(JPN) Particuliere (Spectrum (IRE))
4027a[9]

**Elegant Joan** *Kevin Frost* a20 22
2 ch f Assertive Fangfoss Girls (Monsieur Bond (IRE))
3815[11] 4466[8]

**Elegantly Bound (IRE)** *James Given* a77 35
3 b g Choisir(AUS) Boundless Joy (AUS) (Montjeu (IRE))
385[2]◆ 662[2] 849[2]

**Elegant Pose (IRE)** *G M Lyons* 104
3 b f Elusive Pimpernel(USA) Abeyr (Unfuwain (USA))
6080a[3] (8083a)

**Elegiac** *Mark Johnston* a83
2 b c Farhh Lamentation (Singspiel (IRE))
8155[3]◆ (8553)◆

**Elementary** *Michael Bell* a71 71
3 b g Exceed And Excel(AUS) Humdrum (Dr Fong (USA))
(210) 350[2]

**Elemento** *Phil McEntee* a14 28
3 ch g Assertive Black Baccara (Superior Premium)
956[7] 1183[5] 6295[8]

**Elements Legacy** *Tracy Waggott* a51 60
3 b g Kheleyf(USA) New Romantic (Singspiel (IRE))
73[11] 178[6] 970[9] 2346[7]

**Elements Quest (IRE)** *K R Burke* 49
2 b f Elzaam(AUS) Sweet Chilli (IRE) (Intikhab (USA))
4204[10] 4606[4] 5068[4] 7518[14]

**Elevaz (IRE)** *C Le Veel* a54 60
4 gr m Rock Of Gibraltar(IRE) Entreves (Montjeu (IRE))
6125a[14]

**Elfend** *Rod Collet* 77
2 b f Invincible Spirit(IRE) Alsindi (IRE) (Acclamation)
4595a[3]

**El Footstep (GER)** *Mario Hofer*
2 b c Footstepsinthesand Elle Danzig (GER) (Roi Danzig (USA))
6986a[14]

**Elhaame (IRE)** *Saeed bin Suroor* a26 112
7 b g Acclamation Gold Hush (USA) (Seeking The Gold (USA))
(208a)

**Elhafei (USA)** *John Gosden* a67
2 br c Speightstown(USA) Albamara (Galileo (IRE))
8877[4]◆

**El Hayem (IRE)** *Sir Michael Stoute* a54 101
4 b g Invincible Spirit(IRE) Winning Sequence (FR) (Zafonic (USA))
1960[6] 2568[2]◆ 2828[11] (4636) 6355[5] 7619[29]

**El Hombre** *Keith Dalgleish* a75 98
3 ch c Camacho Nigella (Band On The Run)
972[4] 1625[3] 2499[2] (2776) (3038) 3664[3] 4079[2] (4787) (6662)

**El Huerfano (USA)** *Peter Miller* a108 101
5 b g Tannersmyman(USA) Adriftinthebay (USA) (Capsized (USA))
5194a[5]

**Elidor** *Mick Channon* 114
7 br g Cape Cross(IRE) Honorine (IRE) (Mark Of Esteem (IRE))
(1733) 3011[6] 4420a[3] 6447[16] 7115[5]

**Elishpour (IRE)** *Alan Fleming* a90 58
7 b g Oasis Dream Elbasana (IRE) (Indian Ridge (IRE))
5488a[16]

**Elite Excalibur (AUS)** *S Burridge* 109
4 b g Fastnet Rock(AUS) Romantic River (USA) (Irish River (FR))
87a[5] 429a[4] 538a[2] 776a[6] 888a[14]

**Elite Icon** *Iain Jardine* a50 59
3 b g Sixties Icon Sailing Days (Kris)
40[6] 777[6] 1414[3] 3484[4]◆ 3901[4] 5850[5] 6352[4] 6892[4]◆ (7048)

**Elite Shadow** *Gay Kelleway* 70
2 gr g Finjaan Silver Elite (Forzando)
8118[2] 8294[8]

**Elite Treaty** *Gay Kelleway* a61
3 b g Mawatheeq(USA) Silver Elite (Forzando)
9435[4]

**Elixsoft (IRE)** *Roger Fell* a30 50
2 b f Elzaam(AUS) Grandegrandegrande (IRE) (High Chaparral (IRE))
2502[10] 2896[13] 3430[7] 5056[9] 9302[10]

**Elizabeth Bennet (IRE)**
*Charles Hills* a88 95
2 b f Acclamation Littlepromisedland (IRE) (Titus Livius (FR))
3070[3] (3687) 4361[5]◆ 5329[9] (6065) 7578[6] 8002[8]

**Elizabeth Browning (IRE)**
*A P O'Brien* a58 105
3 b f Galileo(IRE) Inca Princess (IRE) (Holy Roman Emperor (IRE))
2241a[4] 2441a[6] (4934a)

**Elizabeth Darcy (IRE)**
*Wesley A Ward* 101
2 b f Camacho Regency Girl (IRE) (Pivotal)
3929[6] 4391a[2] 6448[7] 8602a[6]

**Eljaddaaf (IRE)** *Dean Ivory* a95 83
6 b g Shamardal(USA) Almansoora (USA) (Bahri (USA))
(94) 639[3] 957[8] 1794[10] 2780[5] 3410[9] 9210[10]

**Ellaal** *Ruth Carr* a61 81
8 b g Oasis Dream Capistrano Day (USA) (Diesis)
1433[7] 1700[13] 1969[12] 2339[7] 3048[4] 3332[4] 3899[8] 4601[5] 4960[7] (5544) 6092[8] 6591[2] 6893[8] 7792[5] 8216[16]

**Ellen Gates** *Richard Hughes* a51
2 b f Mayson Mrs Greeley (Mr Greeley (USA))
8989[6] 9335[6]

**Eller Brook** *Michael Dods* 61
2 ch f Sepoy(AUS) Haigh Hall (Kyllachy)
4555[6] 5370[7] 6085[5] 7159[3] 7655[3]

**Elleval (IRE)** *David Marnane* a103 104
7 b g Kodiac Penny Rouge (IRE) (Pennekamp (USA))
208a[5] 428a[9] 654a[2] 888a[8] 1046a[10] 1355a[3] 2440a[6] 3963[10] 4822a[8]

**Elliptique (IRE)** *S Seemar* a113 114
6 br h New Approach(IRE) Uryale (FR) (Kendor (FR))
776a[10] 1046a[9]

**El Loco (GER)** *Markus Klug* 104
4 b h Lope De Vega(IRE) Elora (GER) (Alkalde (GER))
3019a[6] 4130a[5] 4487a[3] 6451a[5]

**Ellthea (IRE)** *K R Burke* 110
2 b f Kodiac Tropical Lady (IRE) (Sri Pekan (USA))
2904[4] (3482)◆ 5329[6] 6228a[9] (7087) (7421a) 8004[5]

**El Mansour (FR)** *D Retif* a53 14
4 b h Lawman(FR) Equity (FR) (Anabaa (USA))
1078a[10]

**Elm Grove (IRE)** *W McCreery* 93
5 b m Arcano(IRE) Ladytown (IRE) (Bertolini (USA))
2954[5] 5582a[13]

**Elmley Queen** *Roy Brotherton* a27 45
3 b f Piccolo All Business (Entrepreneur)
126[10] 960[10]

**Elnadim Star (IRE)** *Kevin Ryan* 78
2 ch f Elnadim(USA) Fancy Feathers (IRE) (Redback)
4555[8] (6085)◆ (7269)◆

**El Nefous (IRE)** *George Peckham* a55
3 rg f Choisir(AUS) Light And Airy (Linamix (FR))
3259[4]

**El Nino Sea (IRE)** *Richard Fahey* 61
3 b g Sea The Stars(IRE) Mayano Sophia (IRE) (Rock Of Gibraltar (IRE))
1914[4] 2429[4] 2857[7]

**El Principe** *Les Eyre* a83 80
4 b g Strategic Prince Shamrock Lady (IRE) (Orpen (USA))
1080[2] 1339[2] 1833[3] 2034[6] 2923[4] 4426[2] (5213) 5497[3] (5699) 7958[5] 8556[2] 8736[11]

**Elpy Bere (FR)** *J-P Dubois* 29
3 b f Hurricane Cat(USA) Help From Heaven (IRE) (Titus Livius (FR))
3353a[11]

**Elsaakb (USA)** *John Gosden* a75 65
2 ch g Exchange Rate(USA) Bella Jolie (USA) (Broken Vow (USA))
5106[8] 6260[8] 7788[6] 8349[4] (8671) 9021[6]

**Elsie's Indian (FR)** *E Kurdu* a77 63
7 ch g Linngari(IRE) Elsie (GER) (Barathea (IRE))
4955a[11]

**Eltanin (IRE)** *John Quinn* a70 68
3 ch g Dragon Pulse(IRE) Maigh Nuad (IRE) (Alhaarth (IRE))
1782[3] 3184[6] 3709[3] 4265[5] 5919[6] 6786[3] 7365[3]

**El Tel** *Shaun Harris* a58 16
5 ch g Sixties Icon Chelsea (USA) (Miswaki (USA))
724[8] 969[11] 1249[6] 1406[10]

**Eltezam (IRE)** *Amanda Perrett* a85 89
4 b g Kodiac Tymora (USA) (Giant's Causeway (USA))
1150[10] 1794[5] 2390[9] 2833[5] 3585[12] 4570[5] 6322[9] 6809[3] 7285[4] 7549[8] 7998[2] 8561[7] 9140[2] 9314[5]

**El Torito (IRE)** *Jim Boyle* a72 63
3 ch g Tagula(IRE) April Green (FR) (Green Tune (USA))
1000[4]◆ 1176[4] 1724[6] (2293) 3412[12] 4251[13] 4983[10] 5560[4] 7002[8] 7094[11] 7653[9] 8184[10] 8296[5] 8798[11] 9323[7] 9432[4]◆

**Elucidation (IRE)** *Sir Michael Stoute* a81 89
3 b g Oasis Dream Mimalia (USA) (Silver Hawk (USA))
1886[7] 2520[5] 6655[4]

**Elusif (IRE)** *Marco Botti* a34 68
2 b c Elusive Quality(USA) Appealing (IRE) (Bertolini (USA))
6916[4] 8382[5] 8952[11]

**Elusiva (FR)** *H-A Pantall* a70 71
3 b f Elusive City(USA) Ypomoni (Green Tune (USA))
8304a[8] 8960a[2]

**Elusive Beauty (IRE)** *K J Condon* a87 95
3 b f Elusive Pimpernel(USA) Lost Icon (IRE) (Intikhab (USA))
1386a[6] 3632a[5] (4208) 4512a[7] 6491a[19] 6642a[7] 6961a[15]

**Elusive Bird** *Giles Bravery* a39 53
2 ch f Choisir(AUS) Ermena (Dalakhani (IRE))
3215[10] 4539[5] 6480[11] 7362[10] 7756[7] 7996[8] 8306[8]

**Elusive Blue (GER)** *J Phelippon* a74 75
3 b c Harbour Watch(IRE) Elusive Feeling (USA) (Elusive Quality (USA))
1417a[3]

**Elusive Cowboy (USA)**
*Chris Gordon* a76 67
4 ch g Elusive Quality(USA) Sarmad (USA) (Dynaformer (USA))
74[6] 507[12] 3308[8] 4257[5] 5320[8] 6588[5] 7712[13] 8846[14] 9095[9]

**Elusive Duchess (IRE)**
*Adrian Paul Keatley* 82
3 gr f Elusive Pimpernel(USA) Minema (FR) (Linamix (FR))
6956a[20]

**Elusive Heights (IRE)** *G M Lyons* a104 101
4 b g Elusive Pimpernel(USA) Berg Bahn (IRE) (Big Bad Bob (IRE))
4822a[9] 7588a[8]

**Elusive Olivia (USA)** *Joseph Tuite* a70 57
3 b f Elusive Quality(USA) Kenza (USA) (Menifee (USA))
(510) 1470[4] 2274[4] 2587[7] 4184[8]

**Elusive Time (IRE)** *Takashi Kodama* a95 99
9 b g Elusive City(USA) Brosna Time (IRE) (Danetime (IRE))
(6491a) 6961a[7]

**Elusivity (IRE)** *Conor Dore* a86 78
9 b g Elusive City(USA) Tough Chic (IRE) (Indian Ridge (IRE))
45[12] 330[8] (480) 665[3] 923[4] 1109[10] 2161[9] 2469[8] 2932[6] 3466[7] 4009[3] 4724[2] 5081[6] 5892[8] 6529[11] 7407[10]

**El Vip (IRE)** *Luca Cumani* a107 99
4 b g Pivotal Elle Danzig (GER) (Roi Danzig (USA))
1766[3]◆ 2141[10] (3255) 3963[20] 6355[17]

**Elwazir** *Owen Burrows* 84
2 ch c Frankel Dash To The Front (Diktat)
7580[2] 8350[4]

**Elyaasaat (USA)** *William Haggas* 68
3 b c Frankel Lahudood (Singspiel (IRE))
1857[6]

**Elysee Star** *Ben Haslam* a26 64
2 b f Champs Elysees Alushta (Royal Applause)
3943[2] 4502[3] 6433[3] 7222[4] 7938[11]

**Elysian Fields (GR)** *Amanda Perrett* a91 98
6 ch m Champs Elysees Second Of May (Lion Cavern (USA))
2389[2] 3968[5] 6104[7] 7401[4] 7817[8] 8548[10] 8672[7] 9390[4] 9458[5]

**Elysian Flyer (IRE)** *Paul Midgley* a81 88
5 b g Majestic Missile(IRE) Starisa (IRE) (College Chapel)
660[4]◆ 1103[10] (2837)◆ 3625[4] 4416a[13] 5426[7] 5647[3] 6267[7] 6878[5] 7475[4] 7557[10]

**Elysian Prince** *Neil King* a86 66
6 b g Champs Elysees Trinkila (USA) (Cat Thief (USA))
(36) 467[7] 1289[3] 7515[11]

**Elysium Dream** *Richard Hannon* 88
2 b f Champs Elysees Dream Of Wunders (Cape Cross (IRE))
2577[4] (2905) 4068[5] 4858[11] 5659[4] 6200[3] 7090[6] (7814) 8424[7] 8597[7]

**Emadee (IRE)** *Andrew Slattery* 83
2 b f Zebedee Kenema (IRE) (Petardia)
6241a[5]

**Emaraaty** *John Gosden* 96
2 b c Dubawi(IRE) Zee Zee Top (Zafonic (USA))
6653[4]◆ (7392)◆ 8037[8]

**Embankment** *Michael Attwater* a63 50
8 b g Zamindar(USA) Esplanade (Danehill (USA))
812[4] 1107[3] (1620) 2615[10] 3208[12] 4747[7] 5299[9]

**Ember's Glow** *Jason Ward* 70
3 ch g Sepoy(AUS) Fading Light (King's Best (USA))
4508[5] 5073[5] 5538[2] 6203[6] 6667[3] 7388[4]

**Embleton** *Charlie Wallis* a57
3 b f Cacique(IRE) Morzine (Miswaki (USA))
2734[14] 3191[9] 4493[9] 5028[8]

**Embour (IRE)** *Richard Hannon* 82
2 b c Acclamation Carpet Lady (IRE) (Night Shift (USA))
1941[3]

**Emell** *Tim Vaughan* a92 94
7 ch g Medicean Londonnetdotcom (IRE) (Night Shift (USA))
1148[9] 1494[15] 2907[8] 6873[9] 8032[13]

**Emenem** *Simon Dow* a98 96
3 b c Sir Percy Kahalah (IRE) (Darshaan)
(439)◆ 1764[5] (2088) 3318[2] 4376[3] 5568[9] 6474[3] 7516[8] 7649[3] 8880[3] 9053[2] (9186) 9407[4]

**Emerald Bay** *Ronald Thompson* a59 60
4 b m Kyllachy Bahia Emerald (IRE) (Bahamian Bounty)
523[10] 981[7]

**Emerald Cross (IRE)** *Adam West* a73
4 b g Cape Cross(IRE) Yaqootah (USA) (Gone West (USA))
8822[5] 9260[2]

**Emerald Master (GER)** *Mario Hofer* 80
2 ch c Mastercraftsman(IRE) Emerald Art (IRE) (Excellent Art)
6986a[7]

**Emerald Rocket (IRE)** *K R Burke* a75 64
2 b g Society Rock(IRE) Lady From Limerick (IRE) (Rainbows For Life (CAN))
2896[12] 3398[3] 6432[4] 7243[4] 7519[14] (7938) (8207) 8586[6]

**Emerald Secret (IRE)** *Paul Midgley* a61 65
3 b f Arcano(IRE) Limit (IRE) (Barathea (IRE))
1474[3] 1828[8] 2182[8] 4559[7] 5004[5] 5283[10] 5605[7]

**Emiglia (GER)** *Frau S Weis*
8 ch m Lateral Estelle (Emarati (USA))
1196a[7]

**Emigrated (IRE)** *Derek Shaw* a44 63
4 b g Fastnet Rock(AUS) Ecoutila (USA) (Rahy (USA))
9073[6] 9141[5] 9237[11]

**Emilene** *Mark Brisbourne* a53 18
3 b f Clodovil(IRE) Spark Up (Lahib (USA))
3188[10] 3472[7] 4164[10] 7692[10] 8395[8]

**Emilia James** *Mark Johnston* a85 78
2 ch f Poet's Voice Dozy (IRE) (Exceed And Excel (AUS))
1872[2] (2105)◆ 2522[4] (3230) 3960[23] 6494a[7] 7318[2] 7787[6]

**Emily Goldfinch** *Phil McEntee* a55 65
4 ch m Prime Defender Lakelands Lady (IRE) (Woodborough (USA))
80[6] 273[8] 521[6] 3137[2] (3823) 4561[4] 5119[2] 6656[7] 7282[7]

**Emilysbutterscotch** *Rae Guest* a45 52
3 ch f Kyllachy Solfilia (Teofilo (IRE))
3970[7] 6009[4] 6791[10] 8146[6] 8428[7] 9129[12]

**Eminent (IRE)** *Martyn Meade* 117
3 b c Frankel You'll Be Mine (USA) (Kingmambo (USA))
(1904) 2399[6] 3322[4] 4638[5] (6053a) 6960a[3]

**Emirates Airline** *E Charpy* a66 81
5 b g Dubawi(IRE) Moonlife (IRE) (Invincible Spirit (IRE))
203a[11] 316a[7] 8711a[6]

**Emirates Flight** *Saeed bin Suroor* a70
3 ch f New Approach(IRE) Flying Cloud (IRE) (Storming Home)
2576[8]

**Emirates Flyer** *Saeed bin Suroor* a104 100
6 b g Acclamation Galapagar (USA) (Miswaki (USA))
82a[6]

**Emjayem** *John Holt* a71 83
7 ch g Needwood Blade Distant Stars (IRE) (Distant Music (USA))
955[5] 1147[4] 2253[4] 2621[8] 3812[5] 4531[9] 4993[5] 5542[7]

**Emmaus (IRE)** *Roger Varian* 105
3 b c Invincible Spirit(IRE) Prima Luce (IRE) (Galileo (IRE))
(8138)◆

**Emotionless (IRE)** *Charlie Appleby* a110 117
4 b g Shamardal(USA) Unbridled Elaine (USA) (Unbridled's Song (USA))
85a[6] 650a[2]◆ 1042a[3]

**Emperor Bob (IRE)**
*Patrick J McKenna* a73 71
5 b g Big Bad Bob(IRE) Simonda (Singspiel (IRE))
6800a[7]

**Emperor Napoleon** *Andrew Balding* a64 93
4 b g Champs Elysees Amarullah (FR) (Daylami (IRE))
3067[4]

**Emphatic (IRE)** *Robert Cowell* 70
2 bb c Epaulette(AUS) Wild Ocean (Pivotal)
4599[10] 7383[3] 8235[2]

**Empire Of The Star (FR)** *A Wohler* 109
3 b g Siyouni(FR) Etoile Nocturne (FR) (Medicean)
2869a[3] 5522a[3] 6729a[2]

**Employer (IRE)** *Hugo Palmer* a75
2 b c Camelot Close Regards (IRE) (Danehill (USA))
8889[3]

**Empress Ali (IRE)** *Tom Tate* 96
6 b m Holy Roman Emperor(IRE) Almansa (IRE) (Dr Devious (IRE))
2855[5] 4292[3] 5439[4] (6152) 6924[2] 7555[2] 8165[5] 8739[4]

**Empress Rose** *Richard Hughes* 33
2 ch f Makfi Ittasal (Any Given Saturday (USA))
6862[10]

**Enable** *John Gosden* a83 129
3 b f Nathaniel(IRE) Concentric (Sadler's Wells (USA))
1943[3]◆ (2523)◆ (3301) (4928a) (5394) (6356) (7668a)

**Encapsulated** *Roger Ingram* a67 43
7 b g Zamindar(USA) Star Cluster (Observatory (USA))
293[7] (521) 768[8] 1304[2] 1723[12] 2367[6] 4162[10] 6850[9] 7481[7] 7945[10] 8823[10] 9232[9]

**Enchanted Moment** *Olly Murphy* a62 54
5 b m Lawman(FR) Gentle Thoughts (Darshaan)
4627[12] 5290[5] 5895[10]

**Enchanting Enya (IRE)**
*Steph Hollinshead* a24
2 ch f Champs Elysees Miss Honorine (IRE) (Highest Honor (FR))
8890[12]

**Encipher (USA)** *A R Al Rayhi* a98 98
8 b h Elusive Quality(USA) Secret Charm (IRE) (Green Desert (USA))
87a[10] 205a[6] 653a[8] 772a[3]

**Encoded (IRE)** *Lynn Siddall* a44 39
4 ch m Sakhee's Secret Confidentiality (IRE) (Desert Style (IRE))
5946[10] 7365[4] 8559[9] 8716[4]

**Encore D'Or** *Robert Cowell* a110 106
5 b g Oasis Dream Entente Cordiale (IRE) (Ela-Mana-Mou)
388[8] 842[5] (1025) 1772[3] 3079[8] (3967) 4920[7] 5450a[3] 6025[7] (7051) 7396[9]

**Encrypted** *Hugo Palmer* a90 83
2 b c Showcasing Disclose (Dansili)
3591[9] (4213)◆ 4919[3] 5526[9] 6448[11] (7318) 8317[9]

**Encryption (IRE)** *George Scott* a62 59
2 b g High Chaparral(IRE) Challow Hills (USA) (Woodman (USA))
7237[9] 8215[7] 8560[9]

**Encumbered (USA)**
*Simon Callaghan* a67 99
2 b c Violence(USA) Dying To Dance (USA) (Street Cry (IRE))
8577a[13]

**En Dansant (FR)** *H-A Pantall* a46 50
2 b f Zoffany(IRE) Madeenh (FR) (Pivotal)
9087a[14]

**Endeavour (IRE)** *Marjorie Fife* a64 67
3 b g Acclamation Miss Hawai (FR) (Peintre Celebre (USA))
623[3]◆ 819[5] 1310[6] (1605) (1786) 3184[4] 3949[9] 4303[15] 6156[8]

**Endless Acres (IRE)**
*Charlie Fellowes* a101 105
4 b g Champs Elysees Eternity Ring (Alzao (USA))
(1505)◆ 1798[3] 2788[2] 3928[2] 8038[P]

**Endless Charm** *Charlie Appleby* a75
3 ch f Dubawi(IRE) Whazzis (Desert Prince (IRE))
2334[10]

**Endless Gold** *Charlie Appleby* a52 87
3 b g Dubawi(IRE) Love Charm (Singspiel (IRE))
1730[2] 2567[7] 3784[2]◆ 4271[2] 4631[2]

**Endlessly (IRE)** *Martyn Meade* 39
2 b g Nathaniel(IRE) What's Up Pussycat (IRE) (Danehill Dancer (IRE))
8560[11]

**Endless Summer (ITY)** *M Guarnieri* a94 98
4 ch m Pounced(USA) Arafura (IRE) (Barathea (IRE))
4679a[10]

**Endless Tangent (IRE)**
*Tom Dascombe* 72
2 br f Lawman(FR) Passion Planet (IRE) (Medicean)
5990[10] 7608[2] 8425[5]

**Endless Time (IRE)** *Charlie Appleby* a76 112
5 b m Sea The Stars(IRE) Mamonta (Fantastic Light (USA))
2803[4] 3996[10] (5569) 6981a[10]

**Enduring Power (IRE)** *Jo Hughes* a47 72
4 b g Approve(IRE) Our Dear Ruth (USA) (Baldski (USA))
5490a[9] 6302a[9]

**Energia Flavio (BRZ)** *Patrick Morris* a75 43
6 gr g Agnes Gold(JPN) Lira Da Guanabara (BRZ) (Pitu Da Guanabara (BRZ))
2140[10] 4728[2]◆ 6637[2] 8749[11] 9272[10]

**Energia Fox (BRZ)** *Richard Fahey* a85 88
6 ch m Agnes Gold(JPN) Super Eletric (BRZ) (Choctaw Ridge (USA))
269[5] (609) 2558[3] (3065) 3582[4] 4692[4] 5060[6] 5686[4] 6881[8] 7142[10]

**Energy Chop (FR)**
*Matthieu Palussiere* 62
2 b c Deportivo My Princess (FR) (Soave (GER))
5989a[8]

**Enfolding (IRE)** *James Fanshawe* a91 61
3 b g Fastnet Rock(AUS) Althea Rose (IRE) (Green Desert (USA))
498[2]◆ (1069) (1404) 9205[2]◆

**Enforcement (IRE)** *Martin Keighley* a30 54
2 b g Lawman(FR) Elodie (Dansili)
6967[6] 7906[8] 8309[8]

**Engaging Smile** *J Moon* a52 60
5 b m Exceed And Excel(AUS) Bronze Star (Mark Of Esteem (IRE))
1933a[3] 3957a[RR] 5628a[9]

**England Expects** *K R Burke* a55 67
3 b f Mount Nelson Fanny's Fancy (Groom Dancer (USA))
1471[5] 1705[6] 2495[4] 3431[8] 3913[2] 4473[5] 5838[3] 8386[2] 8515[2]◆ 8682[7]

**English Deer (IRE)** *A R Al Rayhi*
7 b g Shamardal(USA) Ya Hajar (Lycius (USA))
250a[16]

**English Hero** *John Mackie* a69 72
4 b g Royal Applause Merton Matriarch (Cadeaux Genereux)
1820[4]

**English Illusion (CAN)** Daniel J Vella a107 101
4 ch g English Channel(USA) Stormy Illusion (CAN) (Woodman (USA))
7178a[5]

**Englishman** Milton Bradley 90
7 b g Royal Applause Tesary (Danehill (USA))
1768[8] 2040[12] (2692) 3074[4] 3424[8] 3757[4] 4411[2] 4505[8] 5123[6] 6275[4] 6877[4] 7612[13] 8077[10]

**English Summer** Ian Williams a63 70
10 b g Montjeu(IRE) Hunt The Sun (Rainbow Quest (USA))
74[7] 325[2] 423[6] 958[7] 1330[6]

**Englishwoman** David Evans a80 77
4 b m Acclamation Tesary (Danehill (USA))
22[3]◆ (152) 312[4]◆ 416[2] 582[3]

**Enigmatic (IRE)** Jamie Osborne a79
3 b g Elnadim(USA) Meanwhile (IRE) (Haafhd)
(7322) (8841) 9100[2] 9236[4] 9464[8]

**Enjazaat** Owen Burrows 101
2 b c Acclamation Miliika (Green Desert (USA))
2779[13] (3437) 4812[6] (6521)◆ 7394[9]

**Enjoy Life (IRE)** Kevin Ryan a81 82
4 b m Acclamation Jeu De Plume (IRE) (Montjeu (IRE))
1105[4] 1346[4] 1833[5] 2684[6] 4209[5] 4629[2]

**Enjoy The Silence (FR)** C Boutin a80 73
4 b h Elusive City(USA) Cerita (IRE) (Wolfhound (USA))
(606a) 2696a[13]

**Enjoy Vijay (GER)** P Schiergen 111
3 b c Nathaniel(IRE) Enjoy The Life (Medicean)
2246a[2] 3115a[6] 4422a[2] 5464a[4] 6255a[4]

**Enki Girl (FR)** P Leblanc a70 58
4 b m Youmzain(IRE) Holly Girl (IRE) (Testa Rossa (AUS))
6125a[5]

**Enlighted (IRE)** F Head a69 103
3 b f Invincible Spirit(IRE) Flash Dance (IRE) (Zamindar (USA))
(5777a) 6054a[5] (7341a)

**Enmeshing** James Fanshawe a80 66
4 ch g Mastercraftsman(IRE) Yacht Club (USA) (Sea Hero (USA))
(353)

**Ennaadd** Roger Varian a114 116
4 b h King's Best(USA) Zayn Zen (Singspiel (IRE))
1773[4] 2290[2] 3924[15]

**Ennjaaz (IRE)** Saeed bin Suroor a91 78
3 b c Poet's Voice Hall Hee (IRE) (Invincible Spirit (IRE))
6277[2] 6851[2] (7542) 7949[2]

**Ennobled Friend (USA)**
A bin Harmash a100 80
7 b g Malibu Moon(USA) Seek To Soar (USA) (Seeking The Gold (USA))
695a[2] 1043a[9] 9361a[11]

**Enola (IRE)** Amy Murphy a62 60
3 b f Lawman(FR) Kelowna (IRE) (Pivotal)
(3248) 4348[6] 4761[9] 8883[7] 9026[6] 9317[6]

**Enriching (USA)** Robyn Brisland a66 69
9 ch g Lemon Drop Kid(USA) Popozinha (USA) (Rahy (USA))
7831[4]

**Enrolment** Richard Fahey a71 64
2 b f Equiano(FR) Enrol (Pivotal)
6559[5] 7269[9] 8212[3] (8586) 8817[4]

**Ensign** A P O'Brien 74
3 b c Invincible Spirit(IRE) Alta Moda (Sadler's Wells (USA))
5689a[12]

**En Souplesse (FR)** E Lellouche a68 75
4 b m Air Chief Marshal(IRE) Saroushka (FR) (Westerner)
7721a[5]

**Entangling (IRE)** Chris Wall a93 85
3 b g Fastnet Rock(AUS) Question Times (Shamardal (USA))
1083[6]◆ 1299[3] 1692[9] 5319[2]◆ (5853) 8143[2] (8893)

**Enterprising (USA)** Michael J Maker a101 112
6 b g Elusive Quality(USA) Indy Blaze (USA) (A.P. Indy (USA))
5977a[4] 8099a[7]

**Entertaining Ben** Amy Murphy a73 70
4 b g Equiano(FR) Fatal Attraction (Oasis Dream)
451[4] 886[9] 1031[3] 1200[5] 1805[2] 1981[2] 2858[2] 3659[5] 3812[4] 4352[4] 5748[4] 6157[5] 6615[5] 7494[9] (7767) (8816)◆ 9189[4] 9389[6]

**Enter The Red (IRE)**
Aidan Anthony Howard a51 87
8 b g Red Clubs(IRE) Inter Madera (IRE) (Toca Madera (IRE))
(4327a) 6971a[12] 7425a[3]

**Entihaa** Dai Burchell a61 62
9 b g Tiger Hill(IRE) Magic Tree (UAE) (Timber Country (USA))
3[4] 467[6] 746[6] 1153[10] 1405[3] 1798[9] 3494[5] 4158[3] 5251[5] 6344[8]

**Entsar (IRE)** William Haggas a92 108
4 b m Fastnet Rock(AUS) Starfish (IRE) (Galileo (IRE))
3219[3] 4308[4] (5381)

**Envisaging (IRE)** James Fanshawe a85 78
3 b g Zoffany(IRE) Star Of Stars (IRE) (Soviet Star (USA))
114[2] 504[4] 3781[2] 4508[4] 6068[3] 6637[4] 7321[7] (8592) 9339[2]◆

**Envoy** James Eustace 82
3 gr g Delegator La Gessa (Largesse)
(2930) 3504[11]

**Envy (IRE)** Robert Collet a50 64
2 b f Casamento(IRE) Rags (IRE) (Whipper (USA))
6542a[9]

**Enzemble (IRE)** David Elsworth 81
2 b c Zoffany(IRE) Fifer (IRE) (Soviet Star (USA))
5887[7] 6653[2]

**Enzo (IRE)** Ed Walker 74
2 b g Exceed And Excel(AUS) Zamhrear (Singspiel (IRE))
5531[7] (6279) 6859[6] (7915) 8595[6]

**Enzo's Lad (IRE)** K R Burke a73
2 b g Society Rock(IRE) Geht Fasteur (IRE) (Chineur (FR))
7513[6] 8189[3] 8587[4]

**Eolian** Andrew Balding 74
3 b g Poet's Voice Charlecote (IRE) (Caerleon (USA))
2711[3]◆ 2892[5] 3864[6] (5565) 6657[7] 7202[3]

**Epaulement (IRE)** Tom Dascombe 74
2 b g Epaulette(AUS) Little Whisper (IRE) (Be My Guest (USA))
7391[5]

**Epeius (IRE)** Ben Haslam a69 62
4 b g Arakan(USA) Gilda Lilly (USA) (War Chant (USA))
(1203) 1972[5] 2923[9] 4310[3] 5836[3] 6318[7] 8721[6]

**Epic Adventure (FR)** S Cerulis a90
2 ch c Shamalgan(FR) Larafale (FR) (Lion Heart (USA))
5952a[4] (6453a)

**Epic Fantasy** Charles Hills a77 77
2 b c Invincible Spirit(IRE) Impressionism (IRE) (Elusive Quality (USA))
7392[3] 8382[2] 9050[2] 9372[2]

**Epicharis (JPN)** Kiyoshi Hagiwara a114
3 bb c Gold Allure(JPN) Stapes Mitsuko (JPN) (Carnegie (IRE))
1375a[2]

**Epicurious (IRE)** Brian Meehan 56
3 ch g Makfi Indolente (IRE) (Diesis)
2039[7] 2576[7]

**Epileptic (FR)** Henk Grewe 77
3 b f Soldier Hollow Eva (GER) (Areion (GER))
8025a[3]

**Episcia (IRE)** Stuart Williams a69 64
2 b f Arcano(IRE) Violet Flame (IRE) (Kalanisi (IRE))
5717[4] 6719[2] (7482) 8349[14]

**Epitaph (IRE)** Michael Appleby a72 73
3 b g Henrythenavigator(USA) Chartres (IRE) (Danehill (USA))
5131[3] 5404[3] 5853[2] 6210[6] 7832[7] 7960[2] 8497[3] 8749[6] 8770[2] 8979[2] 9341[3]

**Eponina (IRE)** Ben Haslam a66 63
3 b f Zoffany(IRE) Dame Rochelle (IRE) (Danehill Dancer (IRE))
1199[5] 2470[2] 3296[4] 4303[6] 6568[3] 8256[3]

**Epsom Bounty** Pat Phelan a48 15
2 ch g Bahamian Bounty My Amalie (IRE) (Galileo (IRE))
4805[13] 8502[8]

**Epsom Day (IRE)** Laura Mongan a57 51
4 b g Teofilo(IRE) Dubai Flower (Manduro (GER))
290[6] 555[7]

**Epsom Icon** Mick Channon 99
4 b m Sixties Icon Hairspray (Bahamian Bounty)
542a[9] 698a[12] 1046a[8] 2392[5] 2605[4] 3319[8] 3843[7] 4308[7]

**Epsom Secret** Pat Phelan a60 61
3 ch f Sakhee's Secret My Amalie (IRE) (Galileo (IRE))
1596[3] 2017[2] 3250[6] 4006[2] (4971) 5298[7] 6557[7] 7879[4] 8507[2]

**Eqleem** David Evans a83 86
4 b g Acclamation Blessing (Dubai Millennium)
1606[16] 2528[10] 3471[2]◆ 4294[4]

**Eqtidaar (IRE)** Sir Michael Stoute a88 91
2 b c Invincible Spirit(IRE) Madany (IRE) (Acclamation)
(6146)◆ 6935[4]

**Eqtiraan (IRE)** Richard Hannon a97 108
3 b g Helmet(AUS) Miranda Frost (IRE) (Cape Cross (IRE))
1621[3] 2400[2]◆ 2831[9] (3867) 5423[5] 6198[8] 8044[6]

**Equally Fast** Peter Hiatt a70 86
5 b g Equiano(FR) Fabulously Fast (USA) (Deputy Minister (CAN))
94[6] 685[9] 989[7] 2608[16] 3424[10] 4629[10]

**Equal Rights** Eve Johnson Houghton a57 57
3 b g Equiano(FR) Australia Fair (Pivotal)
1790[4] 2018[4] 2507[10]◆ 3250[3] 7158[8] 7833[4]

**Equiano Springs** Tom Tate a84 75
3 b g Equiano(FR) Spring Clean (FR) (Danehill (USA))
3054[3] 3984[2] 4604[4] 5806[4] 6238[3] (6667) 7474[12] (8556) (9101)◆

**Equidae** James Tate a48 66
2 ch c Equiano(FR) Dularame (IRE) (Pivotal)
3930[2] 8987[11]

**Equijade** Robert Stephens a68 63
4 b m Equiano(FR) Royal Jade (Last Tycoon)
1429[7]

**Equilateral** Charles Hills 92
2 b c Equiano(FR) Tarentaise (Oasis Dream)
(6178)◆ 6969[6]

**Equilibrium** Ivan Furtado a34 64
2 b f Equiano(FR) Piste (Falbrav (IRE))
5026[8] 6719[7] 7250[3] 9370[9]

**Equimou** Robert Eddery a85 99
3 ch f Equiano(FR) Culture Queen (King's Best (USA))
1765[4] (2425) 3835[7] 4098[5] 4864[9] 6025[8] 6450[8] (7286) 7809[4] 8238[4] 8913[13]

**Equinette (IRE)** Amanda Perrett a73 47
4 b m Equiano(FR) Rougette (Red Ransom (USA))
327[9]

**Equipe** Richard Whitaker a17 40
3 b f Equiano(FR) Charlevoix (IRE) (King Charlemagne (USA))
2853[10] 6469[11] 7036[11]

**Equitant** Richard Fahey a69 77
2 ch c Equiano(FR) Intrusion (Indesatchel (IRE))
(6056)◆ 6689[3] 7482[3] 8010[6]

**Equitation** Roger Varian 88
3 b g Equiano(FR) Sakhee's Song (IRE) (Sakhee (USA))
5645[3] (6184) (7287)◆

**Equity** David Brown a58 57
3 ch g Equiano(FR) Trinny (Rainbow Quest (USA))
2181[12] 2897[13] 3831[10] 4161[3] 4448[4]

**Equo** Chris Wall 14
2 b g Equiano(FR) Catfish (IRE) (One Cool Cat (USA))
7280[11] 8118[5]

**Eraad (IRE)** Charles Hills a52
2 b c Dark Angel(IRE) Tickled Pink (IRE) (Invincible Spirit (IRE))
8308[5]

**Eragon (ARG)** Laura Wohlers a112 110
5 b h Offlee Wild(USA) Express Time (ARG) (Shy Tom (USA))
469a[12]

**Erasmus (GER)** Markus Klug
2 bb c Reliable Man Enora (GER) (Noverre (USA))
(8091a)

**Erastus** Mick Channon a41 55
2 b g Swiss Spirit Blakeshall Rose (Tobougg (IRE))
2577[6] 3025[6] 5063[7] 5785[4] 5933[9] 6154[7] 6585[12]

**Erato (GER)** Karin Suter-Weber
6 ch g Tertullian(USA) Eibe (IRE) (Black Sam Bellamy (IRE))
716a[6] 915a[5]

**Erdiska (FR)** F Seguin 30
2 b f Lilbourne Lad(IRE) Carmona (Rainbow Quest (USA))
5815a[10]

**Erdogan** John Gosden 81
3 b c Frankel Dar Re Mi (Singspiel (IRE))
6194[3]

**Erhaaf (USA)** Charlie Fellowes a91 85
5 b g Street Sense(USA) Saraama (USA) (Bahri (USA))
352[7]

**Eric (GER)** C Von Der Recke 106
6 ch h Tertullian(USA) Ericarrow (IRE) (Bollin Eric)
(714a)

**Erica (GER)**
Lennart Hammer-Hansen 100
4 b m Mamool(IRE) Ericarrow (IRE) (Bollin Eric)
6710a[3] 7673a[12]

**Erica Bing** Jo Hughes a25 93
3 b f Captain Gerrard(IRE) Monica Geller (Komaite (USA))
2523[7] 3612a[8] 4334[5]

**Erik The Red (FR)** Kevin Ryan a100 105
5 b g Kendargent(FR) Norwegian Princess (IRE) (Fairy King (USA))
1779[6] 2735[9] 4918[11] (5634) 6399[3] 7395[8]

**Erinyes (IRE)** Archie Watson a78 73
3 gr f Dalakhani(IRE) Endearing (Selkirk (USA))
(4497) 5658[11] 6628[4] 9208[6]

**Erissimus Maximus (FR)**
Chris Dwyer a85 93
3 b c Holy Roman Emperor(IRE) Tegan (IRE) (Cape Cross (IRE))
(41) 404[2] 877 1124[7] (1294) 1731[3] 2130[4] 3146[7] 5029[2] (5338) 6137[2] (6945) (7809) 8416[9]

**Ernestine (FR)** J-M Lefebvre a59 48
4 b m Jeremy(USA) Graten (IRE) (Zieten (USA))
837a[4] 6365a[7] 7069a[6]

**Ernesto (GER)** Markus Klug
2 ch c Reliable Man Enrica (Niniski (USA))
6986a[2] 8091a[8]

**Ernie (FR)** F Foresi 51
4 b g High Chaparral(IRE) The Living Room (FR) (Gold Away (IRE))
7069a[3]

**Ernststavroblofeld (USA)**
Martyn Meade a85 87
3 ch c Elusive Quality(USA) Minute Limit (IRE) (Pivotal)
1907[5] 2284[2] 2567[8] 6289[5] 6882[5]

**Erquy (FR)** Anthony Mullins 48
3 b g Sinndar(IRE) Eblouissante I (FR) (Cardoun (FR))
1389a[10]

**Ershaad (IRE)** Shaun Harris a54 49
5 b g Acclamation Emerald Peace (IRE) (Green Desert (USA))
26[11] 51[5] 167[9] 3550[9] 4323[6] 4682[7] 5511[4]

**Ertidaad (IRE)** Suzi Best a51 49
5 b g Kodiac Little Scotland (Acclamation)
282[7] 544[11] 614[9] 880[2] 1146[6] 1322[11] 1544[3] 1818[9] (9141) 9237[5]

**Ertijaal (AUS)** M F De Kock a58 102
5 ch h Hard Spun(USA) Alharir (AUS) (Jeune)
86a[5] 1046a[P]

**Ertijaal (IRE)** A R Al Rayhi a105 123
6 b g Oasis Dream Shabiba (USA) (Seeking The Gold (USA))
(84a) (773a) 1376a[3]

**Ertiyad** William Haggas 96
2 b f Dark Angel(IRE) Lily Again (American Post)
2563[2]◆ (3491) 4028[16]◆ 5941[4] 6418[6]

**Erupt (IRE)** H Graham Motion 117
5 b h Dubawi(IRE) Mare Nostrum (Caerleon (USA))
2249a[4] 4423a[9] 6461a[5] 8099a[5]

**Escalating** Michael Appleby a89 91
5 ch g Three Valleys(USA) Pure Joy (Zamindar (USA))
(851) 1185[2]◆ 1423[3] 3052[3] (3625) 4306[7] 7809[9] 8012[16] 8293[9]

**Escalator** Charlie Fellowes a71 71
2 b c Cape Cross(IRE) Sayyedati Symphony (USA) (Gone West (USA))
8136[5]◆ 8492[2]

**Escape Clause (IRE)** Grant Tuer a31 89
3 b g Lawman(FR) Discophilia (Teofilo (IRE))
8718[12] 9031[5]

**Escape The City** Hughie Morrison a80 83
2 b f Cityscape Jasmeno (Catcher In The Rye (IRE))
4806[4] 5216[4] 6100[2] (6433) 7814[4] 8424[10] 8871[3]◆ 9240[4]

**Escobar (IRE)** Hugo Palmer a98 107
3 b g Famous Name Saying Grace (IRE) (Brief Truce (USA))
3013[2] 3959[13] 5593[5] 6401[15] 7275[7] 8032[9]

**Escondida (IRE)** J S Bolger 82
4 br g Vocalised(USA) Maidin Moch (IRE) (High Chaparral (IRE))
4327a[12]

**Eshaan (IRE)** Georgios Alimpinisis a64 57
4 ch g Tamayuz Ebalista (IRE) (Selkirk (USA))
8251a[10]

**Es'hail (USA)** R Al Jehani 72
2 bb c Giant's Causeway(USA) Much Obliged (USA) (Kingmambo (USA))
9446a[4]

**Eskendash (USA)** Pam Sly a81 82
4 ch g Eskendereya(USA) Daffaash (USA) (Mr Greeley (USA))
(1420) 2477[2]◆ 2893[6] 6273[3] 6937[5] 7949[6]

**Eskimo Bay (IRE)** Clive Cox a27 64
3 b g Kodiac Magilini (IRE) (Bertolini (USA))
3157[5]◆ 4500[11]

**Eskimo Point (IRE)** Mario Hofer a70 102
5 ch g Lope De Vega(IRE) Diamond Star (IRE) (Daylami (IRE))
2643a[8] 3614a[9]

**Esloobaha (IRE)** N Caullery a39 58
3 ch f Intikhab(USA) Esloob (USA) (Diesis)
5910a[5]

**Esme Kate (IRE)** Michael Bell 29
2 b f Arch(USA) Francisca (USA) (Mizzen Mast (USA))
8006[12] 8323[11]

**Espadrille** Charlie Appleby a72 70
2 b f Dubawi(IRE) High Heeled (IRE) (High Chaparral (IRE))
8163[5] (8668)

**Espaldinha (FR)** Y Barberot a55 57
2 b f George Vancouver(USA) Bidart (FR) (Elusive City (USA))
1594a[11] 5585a[3]

**Esperitum (FR)** D & P Prod'Homme a70 66
3 b g Siyouni(FR) Nona Allegrina (FR) (Scribe I (IRE))
4783a[6] 8959a[4]

**Espoir Bere (FR)** D Prod'Homme a62 68
3 b g Hurricane Cat(USA) Triple Witching (USA) (Pulpit (USA))
584a[6] 847a[5]

**Espresso Freddo (IRE)**
Robert Stephens a83 58
3 b g Fast Company(IRE) Spring Bouquet (IRE) (King's Best (USA))
72[3] (221) (512) 1149[5] 1472[2] 1945[15] 8718[10] 9053[5] 9271[12] 9464[4]

**Espresso Martini** Brian Meehan a31 60
3 b g Royal Applause Sceilin (IRE) (Lil's Boy (USA))
1962[9] 2366[10] 2783[12]

**Esprit De Corps** Roger Charlton a82 87
3 b g Sepoy(AUS) Corps De Ballet (IRE) (Fasliyev (USA))
(1761) 2831[10] 3664[4] 4887[2] 5661[4] 6576[5] 7398[2] 7780[10]

**Esquisse** A Fabre a83 104
3 b f Dansili Legerete (USA) (Rahy (USA))
(5196a) 6054a[4] 7341a[2]

**Essaka (IRE)** Tony Carroll a53 62
5 b g Equiano(FR) Dream Vision (USA) (Distant View (USA))
1791[4] 2229[5] 2917[7] 3545[7] 4723[6] 5271[5] 5784[5] 5871[3] 6174[5] 6615[8] 7195[4] 7705[3] 7993[5]

**Essenaitch (IRE)** David Evans a76 79
4 b g Zoffany(IRE) Karlisse (IRE) (Celtic Swing)
(26) (67) 419[6] 850[9] 1007[6] 1687[7] 2785[2] 2909[2] 3409[3] 3616[6] 4699[7] 5427[7] 5518a[10] (6273) 6763[3] (7960) 8142[3] 8295[6]

**Essendon (FR)** Andrew Balding a28
2 gr g Aussie Rules(USA) Inhibition (Nayef (USA))
8643[13] 8794[12] 9155[8]

**Essential** George Scott a69 58
3 b g Pivotal Something Blue (Petong)
878[5]◆ 1287[3] 7247[2] 8216[12] 8874[7] 9243[6]

**Esspeegee** Alan Bailey a61 59
4 b g Paco Boy(IRE) Goldrenched (IRE) (Montjeu (IRE))
2281[9] 2972[5] 3389[5] 4756[3] 5142[2] 5923[8] 6530[3] (7215) (7918) (9261)

**Esteaming** Keith Dalgleish a84 61
7 b g Sir Percy Night Over Day (Most Welcome)
422[5] 526[3] 728[8] 1865[4]

**Estelle Ma Belle (FR)** T Castanheira a75 91
3 ch f Air Chief Marshal(IRE) Ozalid (FR) (Rudimentary (USA))
2665a[10] 4424a[7]

**Esther (IRE)** Amy Murphy 53
2 b f Kodiac Good For Her (Rock Of Gibraltar (IRE))
2173[8] 3023[8]

**Estibdaad (IRE)** Paddy Butler a69 52
7 b g Haatef(USA) Star Of Siligo (USA) (Saratoga Six (USA))
922[4] 1283[3] 1620[4] 2095[4] 5793[6] 6632[6] (7325) 9211[11] 9459[5]

**Estijlaa** F Head a77 80
2 gr f Tamayuz Yanabeeaa (USA) (Street Cry (IRE))
6803a[3] 7969a[3]

**Estrellada** Mick Channon 59
3 b f Oasis Dream Gallic Star (IRE) (Galileo (IRE))
3007[10] 3309[5] 4042[5] 4914[9]

**Estrella Eria (FR)** George Peckham a69 60
4 gr m Mastercraftsman(IRE) Madrid Beauty (FR) (Sendawar (IRE))
(1758) 3036[4] 5747[4] 6144[7] 7762[8] 8313[9]

**Etaad (USA)** Lucinda Egerton a74 37
6 b g Intidab(USA) Red's Lucky Lady (USA) (Lucky Lionel (USA))
214[10] (351) 922[2] 1683[12] 2914[14] 5023[10] 7478[11] 8206[10] 8909[12] 9077[5] 9178[5] 9258[8]

**Etatinka (FR)** J-M Beguigne a70 79
3 b f Vision D'Etat(FR) Latinka (Fantastic Light (USA))
3353a[5] 4232a[5]

**Etefaaq (IRE)** Richard Hannon 93
2 b c Kodiac Sheila Blige (Zamindar (USA))
3754[7] (4266) 4906[8] 5570[4] 6330[16] 8039[8]

**Eternal** Declan Carroll 92
5 ch g New Approach(IRE) Sharp Mode (USA) (Diesis)
1799[4] 2226[3] (2701) 3160[6] 3743[10]

**Eternal Army (FR)** *H-A Pantall* a84 89
4 ch h American Post Earth Affair (GER) (Acatenango (GER))
5979a[18]

**Eternal Dream** *William Knight* a45 63
3 ch g Dream Ahead(USA) Get Happy (IRE) (Zamindar (USA))
3394[4] 4347[8] 5031[10] 6067[8] 6846[8] 7122[13]

**Eternalist** *Jim Goldie* a65 64
4 ch m Equiano(FR) Eternal Instinct (Exceed And Excel (AUS))
1828[5] (3944) 4531[4] 6267[13] 8873[3] 9001[2] 9414[5]

**Eternally** *John Gosden* a75 109
4 b m Dutch Art Ardent (Pivotal)
5597[2] 7113[2] 7808[3]

**Etienne Gerard** *Nigel Tinkler* a71 66
5 b g Captain Gerrard(IRE) Alucica (Celtic Swing)
1972[9] 2821[11] 3401[10] 3949[6] 4509[14] 4695[6] 5543[2] 5836[5] 6046[7] 7540[8]

**Etijaah (USA)** *Doug Watson* a107 86
7 b g Daaher(CAN) Hasheema (IRE) (Darshaan)
319a[5] 650a[2] (891a) 1373a[7] (9360a)

**Etikaal** *Simon Crisford* a85 74
3 ch g Sepoy(AUS) Hezmah (Oasis Dream)
2072[6] (3000) 5245[8] 6686[9]

**Etisalat** *Owen Burrows* a79
2 gr c Lethal Force(IRE) Chalet Girl (Oasis Dream)
8028[3]◆ (8536)

**Etoile Du Ficheaux (FR)**
*J-P Gallorini* 60
2 b f Cokoriko(FR) Next Best (FR) (Alberto Giacometti (IRE))
7969a[11]

**Etta (FR)** *M Boutin* a45 61
3 bb f Hurricane Cat(USA) Centralienne (USA) (Dixie Union (USA))
838a[10]

**Ettie Hart (IRE)** *Mick Channon* a58 59
4 b m Bushranger(IRE) Miss Megs (IRE) (Croco Rouge (IRE))
2056[2] 2255[6] 2915[3] 3265[11] 3522[5] 3661[9]

**Ettihadi (IRE)** *Tim Vaughan* 76
3 b g Rip Van Winkle(IRE) Bright And Clear (Danehill (USA))
3291[11] 4966[6]

**Ettisaal** *F Head* 100
3 ch f Dubawi(IRE) Al Ishq (FR) (Nureyev (USA))
5196a[2] 6804a[3]

**Ettu** *S Wattel* a86 77
3 b f Excelebration(IRE) Tragic Moment (USA) (Pivotal)
236[6] (442) (5268a) 5910a[2] 8025a[6]

**Euchen Glen** *Jim Goldie* a76 95
4 b g Authorized(IRE) Jabbara (IRE) (Kingmambo (USA))
779[9] 1307[7] (2497) 3154[3] 3790[10] (4038) 4614[9] (5912) 6329[3] 8038[18] 8740[17]

**Eugenic** *Tracey Barfoot-Saunt* a57 52
6 br g Piccolo Craic Sa Ceili (IRE) (Danehill Dancer (IRE))
2042[9] 3028[5] 3575[4] 4734[2] 5787[3] 6305[7] 8261[2]

**Euginio (IRE)** *Richard Hannon* a89 109
3 b c Fastnet Rock(AUS) Starstone (Diktat)
1886[2] (4585) 5925[4] 6698[5] (7091)

**Eula Varner** *Henry Candy* 68
3 b f Showcasing Tremelo Pointe (IRE) (Trempolino (USA))
2171[3] 3217[3]

**Euqranian (USA)** *Jeremy Noseda* a74 79
3 b f Galileo(IRE) Anne Of Kiev (IRE) (Oasis Dream)
2908[2] 3329[5] 4409[2] 5611[4] (6577)

**Eurato (FR)** *Steve Gollings* a78 70
7 ch g Medicean Double Green (IRE) (Green Tune (USA))
162[2] 380[2] 619[2] 1073[3] (1291) 1548[3] 8511[9]

**Eureka Springs** *Lisa Williamson* a14
4 b m Mullionmileanhour(IRE) Shaymee's Girl (Wizard King)
5335[7] 6904[9]

**Euro Mac** *Neville Bycroft* a46 58
5 ch m Sir Percy Oomph (Shareef Dancer (USA))
5002[10] 5215[5] (6003) 6549[7] 7271[P]

**Euro Nightmare (IRE)**
*Keith Dalgleish* 98
3 b f Kodiac Kilakey (IRE) (Key Of Luck (USA))
(2376) 3335[3] (3981) 4431[3] 4886[5] 5095[4] (5470) 6357[6] 6671[6] 7816[9]

**Eurvad Pembo (FR)** *Y Gourraud* 28
3 ch f Honolulu(IRE) Miss Des Aigles (FR) (Alamo Bay (USA))
6566a[12]

**Eurystheus (IRE)** *Michael Appleby* a82 86
8 b g Acclamation Dust Flicker (Suave Dancer (USA))
359[11]

**Evabienchope (FR)** *P Sogorb* a66 75
2 b f Captain Chop(FR) Free Track (FR) (Solid Illusion (USA))
(1335a) 5090a[8]

**Eva Docc (IRE)** *Keith Dalgleish* a43 65
2 ch f Dandy Man(IRE) La Rochelle (IRE) (Salse (USA))
3237[2]◆ 6347[8] 8102[3] 8741[7] 8804[6]

**Evaguei (FR)** *W Menuet* 15
2 ch f Evasive Beauchamp Xiara (Compton Admiral)
1282a[5] 1594a[14] 1929a[10]

**Evalya Senora (FR)** *Y Barberot* a58 75
3 b f Youmzain(IRE) Nina Senora (FR) (My Risk (FR))
4455a[13] 4943a[5]

**Evanescent (IRE)** *Tony Carroll* a60 74
8 b g Elusive City(USA) Itsanothergirl (Reprimand)
50[9] 1071[11] 1427[2] 2961[10] 3572[3] 7691[6] 9219[11] 9457[9]

**Evasion Absolue (FR)** *E Lellouche* a70 67
3 gr f Rajsaman(FR) Aglaia (IRE) (Invincible Spirit (IRE))
4289a[7]

**Evening Attire** *William Stone* a86 87
6 b g Pastoral Pursuits Markova's Dance (Mark Of Esteem (IRE))
287[4] 760[5] 1606[2] 2618[7]

**Evening Hill** *Richard Hughes* a84 75
3 b c Harbour Watch(IRE) Al Hawa (USA) (Gulch (USA))
(2707) 3392[9] 4537[6] 5053[2] 5218[4] 6766[7] (7457)◆ (7769)

**Evening Starlight** *Ron Hodges* a70 67
4 gr m Kyllachy Night Haven (Night Shift (USA))
161[8] 4842[4] 4990[5] 5711[8] 5784[8] 6179[4] (7190) 7494[3]

**Ever Desdemone (FR)**
*T Castanheira* a61 70
4 b m Shakespearean(IRE) Ever Fair (FR) (Always Fair (USA))
391a[9]

**Everdina** *Ed Walker* a57 51
3 b f Pour Moi(IRE) Silent Music (IRE) (Peintre Celebre (USA))
236[7] 504[5] 881[7] 7199[5] 8152[7]

**Evergate** *Robert Cowell* a86 98
3 b g Exceed And Excel(AUS) Lion Forest (USA) (Forestry (USA))
1838[2] 2215[2]◆ 2570[2]◆ (3159)◆ 3861[5] 6450[3] 7144[15] 7809[2]

**Everkyllachy (IRE)** *J S Moore* a68 70
3 br f Kyllachy Superfonic (FR) (Zafonic (USA))
377[6] 2362[3] (2734) 3171[6] 3536[5] 5050[9] 6004[12] (6097) 6724[3] 7217[3]◆ (7692) 7912[9] 8512[9] 9183[6] 9414[3]

**Everlasting Sea** *Stuart Kittow* a58 57
3 b f Harbour Watch(IRE) Doliouchka (Saumarez)
3682[5] 4146[3] 5362[9] 6509[7] 7278[8] 8157[3]

**Evertogether (IRE)** *H-F Devin* 82
2 b f Kodiac Indian Belle (IRE) (Indian Ridge (IRE))
4595a[2] 6251a[4]

**Every Chance (IRE)** *Jamie Osborne* a97
4 b g Frozen Power(IRE) Runway Dancer (Dansili)
599[5] 809[2] 1240[3] (1628) 2165[4] 8315[10] 8892[8] 8956[3] 9306[2] 9458[4]

**Every Nice Girl (USA)** *Marco Botti* a57 57
3 gr f Mizzen Mast(USA) Joop (USA) (Zilzal (USA))
1685[11] 3261[7]

**Everything For You (IRE)**
*Kevin Ryan* a75 81
3 b g Pivotal Miss Delila (USA) (Malibu Moon (USA))
1259[2] (1830) 4376[11] 6468[3] 7162[4]

**Evident (IRE)** *Tony Carroll* a59 55
7 b g Excellent Art Vestavia (IRE) (Alhaarth (IRE))
51[10] 309[8]

**Evies Wish (IRE)** *John C McConnell* a74 54
3 b f Holy Roman Emperor(IRE) Sharapova (IRE) (Elusive Quality (USA))
3896[3] 6028[6] (8716)

**Evil Spell** *Robert Cowell* 98
5 b m Dutch Art Yajala (Fasliyev (USA))
1936[5] 2623[8] 3632a[11] 6979a[7] 7697a[12]

**Exacting** *Daniel Kubler* 48
3 b f Excelebration(IRE) Blue Azure (USA) (American Chance (USA))
2585[9]

**Exaggerated (USA)**
*Arnaud Delacour* 76
5 bb m Blame(USA) Miz United States (USA) (Valid Appeal (USA))
1813a[7]

**Examiner (IRE)** *Stuart Williams* a97 100
6 ch g Excellent Art Therry Girl (IRE) (Lahib (USA))
1148[4]◆ 1492[18] 3300[4] (4223) 5157[8] 5517a[14] 5914[6] 7619[6]

**Exceedingly Diva** *Marcus Tregoning* 79
2 b f Exceed And Excel(AUS) Anqooda (USA) (Oasis Dream)
4151[2] (6070)

**Exceeding Power** *Martin Bosley* a85 84
6 b g Exceed And Excel(AUS) Extreme Beauty (USA) (Rahy (USA))
36[3] 306[4] (769) 3750[4] (4912) 5788[8] 6134[4] 6700[2] 7452[2]

**Exceed The Limit** *Robert Cowell* a96 98
4 b g Exceed And Excel(AUS) Clinet (IRE) (Dockside (USA))
2262[2] 2780[9] 3321[11] 3967[7] 5354[8] 5811[4] (6794)

**Excel Again** *James Tate* a85 80
3 b c Exceed And Excel(AUS) Adonesque (IRE) (Sadler's Wells (USA))
503[3]◆ (777) 3040[3] 3700[4] (4304) 5484[5] 7569[3]

**Excellent Addition (IRE)**
*Lee James*
7 ch g Excellent Art Race The Wild Wind (USA) (Sunny's Halo (CAN))
4059[7] 7020[12]

**Excellent Aim** *George Margarson* a64 69
10 b g Exceed And Excel(AUS) Snugfit Annie (Midyan (USA))
64[7] 215[8] 602[4] 874[2] 1076[6] 1435[5] 9075[9]

**Excellent George** *Stuart Williams* a84 73
5 b g Exceed And Excel(AUS) Princess Georgina (Royal Applause)
857[6] 1370[2] 2038[7] 3231[2] 4566[4] 5587[5] 6430[7] (9280)

**Excellently Poised** *Bryan Smart* 81
2 b g Sepoy(AUS) Excelette (IRE) (Exceed And Excel (AUS))
(1803) 3556[6] 3929[10] 4866[4]

**Excellent Puck (IRE)** *Shaun Lycett* a80 75
7 b g Excellent Art Puck's Castle (Shirley Heights)
62[6] 422[6] 2270[5] 2752[5] 4095[3] 5810[2] 9270[4] 9408[3]

**Excellent Result (IRE)**
*Richard Spencer* a92 71
7 b g Shamardal(USA) Line Ahead (IRE) (Sadler's Wells (USA))
2788[4] 4073[15]

**Excellent Sounds** *Hughie Morrison* a80 89
4 b m Exceed And Excel(AUS) Siren Sound (Singspiel (IRE))
3334[7] (3869) (4617) 5422[6] 6234[6]

**Excellent Story** *John Davies* a48 58
3 b g Excelebration(IRE) Storyland (USA) (Menifee (USA))
4784[4] 5458[7] 5670[6] 6902[11]

**Excellent Sunset (IRE)**
*David Lanigan* a69 73
3 b f Exceed And Excel(AUS) Sunset Avenue (USA) (Street Cry (IRE))
1889[2] 2344[2] 3194[2] 4256[6]

**Excellent Times** *Tim Easterby* 78
2 b f Excelebration(IRE) Al Janadeirya (Oasis Dream)
3491[7] 4116[7] 5210[4] 6043[2] 7041[4] 7518[2] 7734[3] (8475) 8741[2]

**Excellent World (IRE)** *Tony Coyle* a54 48
4 b m Excellent Art Granny Kelly (USA) (Irish River (FR))
1977[6] 2472[4] 6046[6] 6785[4] 7020[10] 8259[4] 8428[4] 8490[11] 8774[2] 9103[5] 9181[4] 9344[4]

**Excellor (FR)** *Charley Rossi* a64 50
4 gr g Excellent Art Exgray (IRE) (Exceed And Excel (AUS))
6125a[13]

**Excessable** *Tim Easterby* a80 95
4 ch g Sakhee's Secret Kummel Excess (IRE) (Exceed And Excel (AUS))
1777[3] (2409)◆ (2899)◆ 3321[13] 3827[12] 4600[9] (4867) 6758[6]

**Exchequer (IRE)** *David O'Meara* a92 89
6 ch g Exceed And Excel(AUS) Tara's Force (IRE) (Acclamation)
8872[11] 9272[3]◆

**Exclusive Waters (IRE)**
*Tina Jackson* a70 71
7 b g Elusive City(USA) Pelican Waters (IRE) (Key Of Luck (USA))
(607) (4439) 4722[6] 8205[9] 8909[2]

**Exec Chef (IRE)** *David Simcock* a70
2 ch g Excelebration(IRE) Donnelly's Hollow (IRE) (Dockside (USA))
7488[3] 8501[2]

**Executive Force** *William Haggas* a96 99
3 b g Sepoy(AUS) Mazuna (IRE) (Cape Cross (IRE))
1797[2] 2560a[4] 3997[15] 4904[8] 5147[4] 5392[12] 5943[5] 6672[5] 8392[4]

**Exemplar (IRE)** *A P O'Brien* 110
3 ro c Galileo(IRE) Miarixa (FR) (Linamix (FR))
2766[8] 6957a[2]

**Exhort** *Richard Fahey* 81
2 ch f Dutch Art Entreat (Pivotal)
5056[2] (5874)◆ (6659) 7621[6]

**Exit Europe** *Sir Mark Prescott Bt* a72 58
5 ch g Bahamian Bounty Depressed (Most Welcome)
7881[5]◆ 8551[2] 8907[12]

**Exmouth** *Sir Michael Stoute* 88
3 b f Elusive Quality(USA) Havant (Halling (USA))
2400[9]

**Exotic Guest** *Ruth Carr* a59 72
7 ch g Bahamian Bounty Mamoura (IRE) (Lomond (USA))
2843[9] 3289[2] (3524) 3897[3] (4426) (Dead)

**Expecting** *Charles Hills* a83 78
2 b c Bated Breath Oasis Jade (Oasis Dream)
3668[5] 3917[4] 4972[3] 6304[2] (6950) (7787)

**Expediate** *Robert Cowell* 56
2 ch g Bahamian Bounty Welanga (Dansili)
3776[5] 4539[6] 5851[5]

**Expelled** *James Fanshawe* a69 62
2 b c Exceed And Excel(AUS) Pellinore (USA) (Giant's Causeway (USA))
4973[7] 5844[4]◆ 6826[4] 7706[5] 8702[7] 8996[3]

**Expensive Liaison (IRE)**
*Hugo Palmer* 74
2 b f Camelot Indigo Lady (Sir Percy)
7733[5]◆ 8419[2]

**Expert Eye** *Sir Michael Stoute* 116
2 b c Acclamation Exemplify (Dansili)
(3747) (5501) 8037[9]

**Explain** *Ruth Carr* a78 95
5 ch g Kyllachy Descriptive (IRE) (Desert King (IRE))
1346[5] 2081[6] (2592) 3095[12] 4037[2] (4294) 5059[7] 5669[9] 6414[10] 6879[2] (7108) 7626[12] 7886[10]

**Expressiy (FR)** *Charlie Appleby* a89 95
2 b f Siyouni(FR) Express American (FR) (American Post)
5349[3] (6385) 6731a[5] (7757) 8002[6] 8424[3]

**Express Lady (IRE)** *Hugo Palmer* a83 77
3 b f Helmet(AUS) Star Express (Sadler's Wells (USA))
(2581) 4351[5] 7241[2] (8636)

**Exprompt (FR)** *Hugo Palmer* a74 58
2 b c Choisir(AUS) Councilofconstance (IRE) (Footstepsinthesand)
5365[8] 6884[3] 7512[2] 7946[6]

**Exquisite Ruby** *Charles Hills* a63 63
3 b f Exceed And Excel(AUS) Ruby Rocket (IRE) (Indian Rocket)
75[5] 1626[3] 2121[6] 3331[5] 3806[3] 6339[2] 7494[4] 7951[5] 8824[6]

**Exspectation (IRE)**
*Michael Blanshard* a54 63
3 b g Excelebration(IRE) Emeralds Spirit (IRE) (Rock Of Gibraltar (IRE))
1686[11] 2395[11] 7769[9] 8346[U] 9211[8] 9457[5]

**Extinguish (FR)** *P Sobry* a93 77
4 b h Dansili Silver Fame (USA) (Quest For Fame)
7636a[16]

**Extortion** *Bryan Smart* a46 75
4 b g Kheleyf(USA) Virtuality (USA) (Elusive Quality (USA))
32[10]

**Extraction (USA)** *Martyn Meade* a70 47
2 b c More Than Ready(USA) Coppermine (USA) (Unbridled's Song (USA))
4094[6] 8155[4]

**Extra Elusive** *Roger Charlton* 82
2 ch c Mastercraftsman(IRE) Nessina (USA) (Hennessy (USA))
(8389)

**Extra Mile** *Saeed bin Suroor* a63 79
3 b f Frankel Marie De Medici (USA) (Medicean)
1581[4] 2227[2] 3866[4]

**Extrasolar** *Geoffrey Harker* a69 84
7 b g Exceed And Excel(AUS) Amicable Terms (Royal Applause)
783[10] 1110[7] 1475[10] 1833[8] 2550[3] 2990[2] 3183[5] 3974[7] 5481[11] 6546[10] 7018[6]

**Extremely Vintage (IRE)** *Endo Botti* 93
4 ch m Dylan Thomas(IRE) Birthday (IRE) (Singspiel (IRE))
8096a[7]

**Extremis (IRE)**
*Jassim Mohammed Ghazali* a80 107
5 b h Invincible Spirit(IRE) Fidelite (IRE) (In The Wings)
914a[5]

**Exultant (IRE)** *M Halford* 109
3 b g Teofilo(IRE) Contrary (IRE) (Mark Of Esteem (IRE))
3100a[3] 3994[5]

**Eye Burner** *J R Jenkins* a17
3 ch c Equiano(FR) Tilly's Dream (Arkadian Hero (USA))
7254[8] 7907[12] 8242[9] 9139[7] 9344[8]

**Eyecatcher (IRE)** *Simon Crisford* a69 66
2 b g Camelot For Joy (Singspiel (IRE))
6159[3] 6883[6] 7890[4]

**Eyecatsher (IRE)** *M Weiss*
9 gr g Intikhab(USA) Docklands Grace (USA) (Honour And Glory (USA))
915a[3]

**Eye In The Sky (IRE)**
*Niels Petersen* a84 97
6 gr h Sinndar(IRE) Saudade (GER) (Linamix (FR))
4825a[3] 5676a[2]

**Eye Of The Storm (IRE)**
*Amanda Perrett* a76 98
7 ch g Galileo(IRE) Mohican Princess (Shirley Heights)
5500[10] 6201[4] 6675[6] 7354[7] 7785[4] 8244[12]

**Eye On You (IRE)** *John Murray* a32
4 b m Tagula(IRE) Hollow Haze (USA) (Woodman (USA))
198[8]

**Eyes Designer** *M Delcher Sanchez* a64 56
3 b f Rock Of Gibraltar(IRE) Vizinga (FR) (Marju (IRE))
3353a[8]

**Eyesight** *Charlie Fellowes* a19
3 ch g Medicean Look So (Efisio)
1900[8]

**Eyes Of Fire** *Ollie Pears* 51
2 gr g Helmet(AUS) Lady Xara (IRE) (Xaar)
2029[8] 3399[5] 3791[10] 7518[15]

**Eyes On Asha (IRE)** *Kevin Ryan* a79
3 b f Redoute's Choice(AUS) Sunday Nectar (IRE) (Footstepsinthesand)
(1003) 6579[5]

**Eynhallow** *Roger Charlton* 100
3 b g Nathaniel(IRE) Ronaldsay (Kirkwall)
(3005) 3778[3] (5033)◆ 5330[2] 6474[4] 7252[3] 8005[2]

**Eyreborn (IRE)** *Keith Dalgleish* a34 67
3 b f Born To Sea(IRE) Eyrecourt (IRE) (Efisio)
5648[4] 6048[2] 6436[5] 6692[2] 7048[5] 7560[5] 7982[2] 8478[4] 8655[5] 8806[9]

**Ezanak (IRE)** *D K Weld* 92
4 b g Sea The Stars(IRE) Ebaza (IRE) (Sinndar (IRE))
5488a[17]

**Eziyra (IRE)** *D K Weld* 109
3 ch f Teofilo(IRE) Eytarna (IRE) (Dubai Destination (USA))
4928a[3] (5766a) (6957a)

**Ezz (IRE)** *Mrs Ilka Gansera-Leveque* a39
2 b c Intello(GER) Looby Loo (Kyllachy)
8149[13]

**Faadhel (GER)** *Roger Varian* 64
2 b c Maxios Firedance (GER) (Lomitas)
5631[6] 8136[7]

**Faay (IRE)** *Ed Dunlop* a51 66
2 gr f Dark Angel(IRE) Folga (Atraf)
6385[8] 7238[11] 7620[4]

**Fab (IRE)** *Jamie Osborne* a44 70
2 br f Society Rock(IRE) Dubai Princess (IRE) (Dubai Destination (USA))
3023[2] 4160[7] 4440[5] 6525[5] 7193[4] 8110[4]

**Fabella Bere (FR)** *K R Burke* a53 53
2 b f Peer Gynt(JPN) L'Ete (CHI) (Hussonet (USA))
3483[3]◆ 4528[7] 8213[7] 8783[9] 9175[4]

**Fabric** *Richard Hannon* a11 72
3 b f Acclamation Decorative (IRE) (Danehill Dancer (IRE))
1970[6] 2508[2] 3171[11] 4619[3]

**Fabricate** *Michael Bell* a107 115
5 b g Makfi Flight Of Fancy (Sadler's Wells (USA))
1068[3] 1779[4] 2519[4] 4614[6] (5500) (6441) 7393[5]

**Fabrino (IRE)** *M Weiss* 74
9 b h Elnadim(USA) Trullitti (IRE) (Bahri (USA))
716a[2]

**Fabuleuse Bere (FR)** *J Boisnard* 74
2 b f Pedro The Great(USA) Shadow Of The Day (FR) (Until Sundown (USA))
7415a[7]

**Fabulous Flyer** *Jeremy Gask* a53 51
4 b m Equiano(FR) Lucky Flyer (Lucky Story (USA))
(143) 622[2] 743[2] 1022[2] 1220[3] 1557[3] 3331[8] 4009[2] 4352[6]

**Fabulous One (NZ)** *W Y So* a111 104
5 b g Elusive City(USA) Beautiful Unicorn (NZ) (Faltaat (USA))
694a[9] 1044a[10]

**Fabulous Red** *Ed Dunlop* a79 77
2 b f Red Jazz(USA) Red Fantasy (IRE) (High Chaparral (IRE))
4296[2]◆ 4815[4] 5834[4] (6932)

**Face Like Thunder** *Andrew Balding* 70
2 b g Passing Glance Violet's Walk (Dr Fong (USA))
7391[8] 7929[3]

**Face Off (CAN)** *Charles O'Brien* 60
2 rg f Mizzen Mast(USA) Randyanna (USA) (Dynaformer (USA))
7423a[6]

**Face The Facts (IRE)** *John Gosden* 109
3 ch g Nathaniel(IRE) Aricia (IRE) (Nashwan (USA))
1607[2] (1963) 3081[4] 4032[8] 4811[6] 6930[2] (7547) 8011[10]

**Face Value** *Adrian McGuinness* a64 75
9 b g Tobougg(IRE) Zia (GER) (Grand Lodge (USA))
5689a[6]

**Facilitate** *D Smaga* 99
3 br f Bated Breath Emergency (Dr Fong (USA))
6979a[8]

**Faheem** *Lydia Richards* a39
6 b g Halling(USA) White Star (IRE) (Darshaan)
9455[8]

**Faience** *William Haggas* a68
3 b f Holy Roman Emperor(IRE) Delft (Dutch Art)
168[7] (758) 1029[5]

**Faintly (USA)** *Ruth Carr* a68 72
6 b g Kitten's Joy(USA) Tinge (USA) (Kingmambo (USA))
1365[4] 1717[10] 2064[6]◆ 2224[9] 2919[2] 3344[5] 4554[4] 5835[8] 6435[14]

**Fair Comment** *Michael Blanshard* a65 64
7 b m Tamayuz Cliche (IRE) (Diktat)
1699[P]

**Fair Cop** *Andrew Balding* a73 81
3 b f Exceed And Excel(AUS) Speed Cop (Cadeaux Genereux)
2112[2]◆ 2510[2] (3157)◆ 4154[5] 5029[3] 5574[2]

**Fair Eva** *Roger Charlton* 110
3 ch f Frankel African Rose (Observatory (USA))
2434[5]

**Fair Island** *Sarah Hollinshead* 29
2 b f Trans Island La Vie Est Belle (Makbul)
8380[14]

**Fair Loch** *Brian Ellison* a71 74
9 gr g Fair Mix(IRE) Ardentinny (Ardross)
1002[2] 1344[4]

**Fair Power (IRE)** *Sylvester Kirk* a82 86
3 b g Power Pitrizzia (Lando (GER))
2088[4] 3412[5] (4462) (4798) 5525[12] 7132[3] 7880[9]

**Fair Selene** *Heather Main* a60 68
3 b f Equiano(FR) Jane Jubilee (IRE) (Mister Baileys)
2309[6] 2911[2] 3751[3] 4714[2] 4846[3] (5359) 6102[7]

**Fair Trade (GER)** *Henk Grewe* 76
6 b h Tertullian(USA) Foreign Music (FR) (Tiger Hill (IRE))
7070a[2]

**Fairway To Heaven (IRE)**
*Lee Carter* a84 65
8 b g Jeremy(USA) Luggala (IRE) (Kahyasi (IRE))
219[4] 547[2] 783[7] 1087[2] 2230[9] 2608[15] 3454[12] 4251[12] 4752[10] 5333[5] 6586[4] 7320[5] 7951[3] 8495[2] 8743[9]

**Fairyland (USA)** *Wesley A Ward* a85 88
2 ch f Scat Daddy(USA) Dame Ursula (Elusive Quality (USA))
4028[12] 8602a[8]

**Fairy Lights** *Roger Varian* a73 38
3 b f Shamardal(USA) Suba (USA) (Seeking The Gold (USA))
1581[6] 2585[11] 6568[4]

**Fairy Lock (IRE)** *David Barron* a53 56
3 b f Sir Prancealot(IRE) Too Close (IRE) (Danehill Dancer (IRE))
73[5] 376[4] 2349[2] 2790[4] 3627[6] 3913[5]

**Fairy Mist (IRE)** *John Bridger* a54 30
10 b g Oratorio(IRE) Prealpina (IRE) (Indian Ridge (IRE))
1425[6] 1894[9] 2255[2] 2916[6] 3304[6] 4180[8] 5296[6] 5817[7] 9127[8] 9454[12]

**Faithful Creek (IRE)**
*Michael Appleby* a89 91
5 b g Bushranger(IRE) Open Verse (USA) (Black Minnaloushe (USA))
43[4] 163[5] (526) 991[3] 1608[2] 2086[11] 7284[3] 7880[8] 8289[4]

**Faithful Promise** *Mark Johnston* a54 80
2 b f Acclamation Devotion (IRE) (Dylan Thomas (IRE))
1627[6] 1909[2] (2373) 2801[10] 3482[4] (4739) 5659[2] 6330[12] 6778[6]

**Fajjaj (IRE)** *Hugo Palmer* 100
2 ch c Dawn Approach(IRE) Pleasantry (Johannesburg (USA))
(6916) 7546[4]

**Fake News** *David Barron* 75
2 b g Paco Boy(IRE) Day Creek (Daylami (IRE))
4503[11] (6545) 7814[9]

**Fakhoor (IRE)** *Owen Burrows* a78
2 b c Oasis Dream Darajaat (USA) (Elusive Quality (USA))
7513[2] 8809[2]◆

**Fakir Bere (FR)** *Y Barberot* a87
2 b c Pedro The Great(USA) Triple Witching (USA) (Pulpit (USA))
(5952a)

**Falabelle (IRE)** *Kevin Ryan* 80
2 ch f Choisir(AUS) Mooching Along (IRE) (Mujahid (USA))
4204[3] 5150[10] (5879) 6448[8]

**Falak (IRE)** *Roger Varian* a71 81
4 b g Teofilo(IRE) Family (USA) (Danzig (USA))
2167[3] 2997[6] 3698[3] (4630)

**Falbon** *Marco Botti* a81 69
3 b g Mayson Eleodora (Dubawi (IRE))
2260[2] 3000[2] 3715[8] 6068[8] 6792[3]

**Falcao (IRE)** *John Butler* a71 84
5 br g Majestic Missile(IRE) Cafe Lassere (USA) (Giant's Causeway (USA))
116[9] 528[6] 734[10]

**Falcao Negro** *M Delzangles* a69 73
4 b h Canford Cliffs(IRE) Really Lovely (IRE) (Galileo (IRE))
(1181a)

**Falcon Cliffs (IRE)** *William Muir* a73 79
3 b f Canford Cliffs(IRE) Circle (IRE) (Galileo (IRE))
(862)◆ 3006[6] 3457[11] 5932[2] 6477[5]

**Falconet (DEN)** *Bent Olsen* 102
7 b h Falco(USA) Seattle's Wood (USA) (Woodman (USA))
5676a[6]

**Falcon Eye (IRE)** *Charlie Appleby* a72 71
2 gr g Dubawi(IRE) Asi Siempre (USA) (El Prado (IRE))
4860[6] 7273[5] 7758[4] 8537[8]

**Falcon's Fire (IRE)** *Keith Dalgleish* a74 73
4 ch g Thewayyouare(USA) Matadora (IRE) (Kris)
1113[5] 1292[8] 1716[2] 1891[5] 2375[3] 3046[3] 3240[7] 3830[12] 4357[10] 4899[9] 5096[3] 5599[5] 5883[5] 7015[9] 7236[5] 7659[7] 7936[3] 8946[6] 9261[11] 9375[4]

**Falcon's Reign (FR)**
*Michael Appleby* a60 66
8 ch g Haafhd Al Badeya (IRE) (Pivotal)
390[12]

**Falcon's Vision** *David Simcock* a63 70
2 b f Iffraaj New Falcon (IRE) (New Approach (IRE))
3312[4] 4528[3] 5795[8] 7621[7]

**Falcon Wings** *N Clement* 109
3 b c Nathaniel(IRE) Cast In Gold (USA) (Elusive Quality (USA))
2250a[2] 2947a[4] 3879a[3] 4878a[5]

**Falling Wood (IRE)** *Marco Botti* a24
2 rg c Zebedee Wood Nymph (IRE) (Acclamation)
9335[10]

**Falmouth Light (FR)** *Mark Johnston* 78
2 b g Cape Cross(IRE) Wonderous Light (IRE) (Montjeu (IRE))
(3783)◆ 4183[4] 5179[4] 6330[14] 7106[7]

**False Id** *Daniel Steele* a67 55
4 b g Aqlaam Miss Dutee (Dubawi (IRE))
355[6]◆ 984[7] 1224[7] 1683[6] 1758[4] 3036[6] 3432[3] 4298[9] 5214[7] 5897[5] 6346[9] 6560[3] 6681[6] 7216[5] 7990[12]

**Family Fortunes** *Sylvester Kirk* a92 76
3 ch g Paco Boy(IRE) Barawin (IRE) (Hawk Wing (USA))
(920) (1601) 2334[3] 6397[4] 7156[5] 7456[3] 8344[10] 9025[10]

**Famous Dynasty (IRE)**
*Michael Blanshard* a67 67
3 b g Famous Name Daffodil Walk (IRE) (Captain Rio)
1550[7] 3024[3] 3412[7] 3864[4] 4348[4] 4914[2] 5275[6] 5867[6] 6866[3] 7216[6] 8031[9] 8550[7]

**Famous Kid (USA)**
*Saeed bin Suroor* a109 112
6 ch g Street Cry(IRE) Moyesii (USA) (Diesis)
268[2] 1042a[7] 1374a[10]

**Fanan** *Simon Crisford* a8 19
2 ch g Iffraaj Paradise Isle (Bahamian Bounty)
7105[5] 7765[12]

**Fanatic (NZ)**
*David A & B Hayes & Tom Dabern* 97
4 b m Shocking(AUS) Komplete Klass (NZ) (Groom Dancer (USA))
8056a[6]

**Fanciful Angel (IRE)** *Chad C Brown* a112 113
5 rg g Dark Angel(IRE) Fanciful Dancer (Groom Dancer (USA))
(205a) 538a[6] 774a[6] 1960[11] (2999) 4584[6] 5977a[2] 7633a[2] 8610a[11]

**Fanciful Miss** *Tom Dascombe* 34
2 b f New Approach(IRE) Fann (USA) (Diesis)
5107[13]

**Fancify** *F Caenepeel-Legrand* a33 35
4 b m Exceed And Excel(AUS) Shane (GER) (Kornado)
837a[10]

**Fancy Dresser (FR)**
*Matthieu Palussiere* 69
2 ch c Style Vendome(FR) Kenhoaden (FR) (Sunday Break (JPN))
1929a[3] 2881a[7] 3444a[4] 4166a[4] 4389a[6]

**Fanfair** *Richard Hannon* a48 69
3 b f Royal Applause Fugnina (Hurricane Run (IRE))
2911[3] 3661[4] (4493) (5023) 5782[3] 6006[2] 7917[6]

**Fanfare Lady (IRE)** *William Knight* a29 49
2 br f Society Rock(IRE) Silk Fan (IRE) (Unfuwain (USA))
7688[4] 8432[8]

**Fang** *William Jarvis* a84 86
4 b g Lawman(FR) Desert Tigress (USA) (Storm Cat (USA))
4099[8] 4566[9] 5513[9] 7214[6]

**Fankairos Ranger (USA)**
*Cedric Rossi* a78 81
3 b g US Ranger(USA) Dancin Up A Storm (USA) (Stormin Fever (USA))
427a[7] (748a)

**Fannaan (USA)** *M Al Mheiri* a87 105
5 ch g Speightstown(USA) Titian Time (USA) (Red Ransom (USA))
651a[8] 772a[5]

**Fanoulpifer** *Michael Attwater* a73 45
6 b g High Chaparral(IRE) Furbeseta (Danehill Dancer (IRE))
6514[5] 9186[9] 9467[6]

**Fanta Dielo (USA)** *Mme Pia Brandt* a49
3 b f Bernardini(USA) Hoh Buzzard (IRE) (Alhaarth (IRE))
4288a[10]

**Fantastic Love (FR)** *J-M Capitte* a75 72
8 b g Azamour(IRE) Pray For Sun (IRE) (Fantastic Light (USA))
691a[5]

**Fantastic Way (FR)**
*Mme C Barande-Barbe* a50 44
8 b g Way Of Light(USA) Fantastic Fire (GER) (Platini (GER))
515a[9]

**Fantasy Gladiator** *Michael Appleby* a68 83
11 b g Ishiguru(USA) Fancier Bit (Lion Cavern (USA))
47[5] 517[P] 641[10] 992[5] 1283[4] 1735[3] 2282[6] 3221[2] 3628[6] 5126[5] 5854[6] (6846) 7324[2] 7791[4]

**Fantasy Justifier (IRE)**
*Ronald Harris* a61 65
6 b g Arakan(USA) Grandel (Owington)
2709[9] 3573[9] 4467[9] 5657[3] 6041[2] 6179[5] 7190[5] 7693[5] 8496[2] 8772[12]

**Fantasy Keeper** *Michael Appleby* a68 79
3 b g Mayson Expressive (Falbrav (IRE))
638[3] (2927) 3584[3] 5122[2] 6686[8] 7287[7] 7737[2]◆ 8680[2]

**Fantasy King** *James Moffatt* a72 68
11 b g Acclamation Fantasy Ridge (Indian Ridge (IRE))
2609[6]

**Fantasy Queen**
*Eve Johnson Houghton* a64 73
4 b m Aqlaam Regal Curtsy (Royal Applause)
1603[3] 2285[5] (3772) 4468[3] (5049) 6340[5] 6866[4] 7769[7]

**Faraasah (IRE)** *Brian Meehan* a30 75
2 br g Arcano(IRE) Falsafa (Dansili)
3591[2]◆ 4826[6] 7090[12] 7536[12]

**Faradays Spark (IRE)**
*Richard Fahey* a59 61
2 br c Dragon Pulse(IRE) High Reserve (Dr Fong (USA))
2154[8] 2590[4]◆ 3237[6] 3791[9] (4054) 4504[3] 5279[3] 5742[4] (6127) 6940[6] 7519[13] 8371[7]

**Farage (IRE)** *John Patrick Shanahan* 16
3 b f High Chaparral(IRE) Advertising Space (IRE) (Galileo (IRE))
6194[12] 6782[4]

**Faraway Fields (USA)** *Charles Hills* 65
2 b c First Defence(USA) Faraway Flower (USA) (Distant View (USA))
8387[6]

**Far Dawn** *Simon Crisford* a69 62
2 ch g Helmet(AUS) Windlass (IRE) (Teofilo (IRE))
2786[9] 3930[5] 5144[3] 5756[9] 6613[3] 7239[2]◆ 7829[3] 8537[4] 8848[5] 9097[4]

**Fareeq** *Charlie Wallis* a77 75
3 gr g Dark Angel(IRE) Spate (IRE) (Danehill Dancer (IRE))
3588[5] 4313[9] 5606[5] 6197[11] 6888[6] 7881[10] 8874[10] 9142[10] 9469[6]

**Farhh Away** *Michael Dods* a67 58
2 ch g Farhh Bukhoor (IRE) (Danehill (USA))
6897[6]◆ 7520[5]

**Farleigh Mac** *Andrew Balding* a66 83
3 ch g Equiano(FR) Le Badie (IRE) (Spectrum (IRE))
2293[7] 3000[6] (3673) 4521[3] 5051[2] 5272[3] 6198[9] 6695[7] 7405[7]

**Farlow (IRE)** *Richard Fahey* a62 103
9 ch g Exceed And Excel(AUS) Emly Express (IRE) (High Estate)
3842[12] 4353[10] 5059[8] 5396[8]

**Farook (IRE)** *Charles Hills* a87 73
3 gr g Raven's Pass(USA) Wrong Answer (Verglas (IRE))
1488[2] 1837[2] (2727) 4100[6]

**Farquhar (IRE)** *Michael Appleby* a82 93
6 ch g Archipenko(USA) Pointed Arch (IRE) (Rock Of Gibraltar (IRE))
2136[6] 2797[3] 4002[8] 4614[16] 5609[6] 6202[5]

**Farrah's Choice** *James Grassick* a38 50
5 b m Equiano(FR) Esplanade (Danehill (USA))
334[9]

**Farrier (USA)** *S Seemar* a106 103
9 b g Tapit(USA) Wild Vision (USA) (Wild Again (USA))
429a[6] 1373a[6] 9360a[7]

**Farshad (GER)** *Henk Grewe* 108
3 rg c Kendargent(FR) Forever Midnight (IRE) (Night Shift (USA))
1660a[7] (5522a)

**Farz (USA)** *Kiaran McLaughlin* 105
5 bb h Smart Strike(CAN) Ocean Drive (USA) (Belong To Me (USA))
3553a[7]

**Fas (IRE)** *Mme Pia Brandt* 113
3 b c Fastnet Rock(AUS) Sotka (Dutch Art)
(1660a) 5690a[13] 6497a[7]

**Fascinator** *Ann Duffield* a68
2 ch f Helmet(AUS) Mary Read (Bahamian Bounty)
8926[2]

**Fashaak (IRE)** *John Butler* a71 87
4 b g Starspangledbanner(AUS) Szabo (IRE) (Anabaa (USA))
2317[2] 2730[6] 4587[6] 6143[4] 7246[2]

**Fashaar** *Anthony McCann* a76 68
4 b g Showcasing Avessia (Averti (IRE))
7331[10]

**Fashion Business** *Roger Charlton* a78 103
3 b g Frankel Icon Project (USA) (Empire Maker (USA))
236[2]◆ (437)◆

**Fashion Parade** *Charles Hills* a89 86
4 b m Fastnet Rock(AUS) Festivale (IRE) (Invincible Spirit (IRE))
4829[7]

**Fashion Queen** *David O'Meara* 109
3 b f Aqlaam Pizzarra (Shamardal (USA))
(2768) 3835[6] 6979a[3] 7670a[9]

**Fashion Sense (IRE)** *Clive Cox* 61
2 b f Clodovil(IRE) Speckled Hen (IRE) (Titus Livius (FR))
6868[3] 7688[6]

**Fashion Theory** *Charlie Appleby* 73
2 b f Dubawi(IRE) Lady's Purse (Doyen (IRE))
2131[5] 5022[4]

**Fas Le Fios (IRE)** *J S Moore* a57 66
2 b f Epaulette(AUS) Saffa Garden (IRE) (King's Best (USA))
1594a[7] 1776[4] (2073a)

**Fast Act (IRE)** *Kevin Ryan* a77 67
5 ch g Fast Company(IRE) Nullarbor (Green Desert (USA))
2899[11] 4787[6] 5204[6] 5920[8] 7055[15] 7538[9] 8106[5] 8745[2] 8853[7] 9244a[5]

**Fastalong (IRE)** *Tim Easterby* 59
2 b f Fastnet Rock(AUS) Nidina (IRE) (Hurricane Run (IRE))
3662[6] 4291[4] 5372[7] 6561[6] 7041[7] 7222[5]

**Fast And Accurate (USA)**
*Michael J Maker* a103
3 rg c Hansen(USA) It's Heidi's Dance (USA) (Green Dancer (USA))
2420a[17]

**Fast And Furious (IRE)**
*James Bethell* a86
4 b g Rock Of Gibraltar(IRE) Ocean Talent (USA) (Aptitude (USA))
730[13]

**Fast And Hot (IRE)** *Richard Hannon* a78 85
4 gr g Fastnet Rock(AUS) Hotelgenie Dot Com (Selkirk (USA))
286[8] 922[9] 1620[2] 1758[5] 2153[5] (2785) (2909) 3616[4]◆ 4147[2] (5218) 5475[3] 6189[3] 7132[9] 7452[6] 7959[2] 8295[9]

**Fastar (IRE)** *Brian Meehan* a69 95
3 ch g Fast Company(IRE) Asterism (Motivator)
1619[3] 2330[5] (5478) 5961[2] 6387[6] (7131) (7566)

**Fast Dancer (IRE)** *Joseph Tuite* a85 88
5 b g Fast Company(IRE) Tereed Elhawa (Cadeaux Genereux)
2054[4] 2528[6]◆ 3065[5] 3938[2] 4698[3] (5276) 5643[7] 6195[2] 6701[4] 7649[4]

**Fast Enough (IRE)** *Doug Watson* a76 76
4 b g Kodiac La Chicana (IRE) (Invincible Spirit (IRE))
8836a[4]

**Fastidious (FR)** *Louis Baudron* a80 96
2 b c Zanzibari(USA) Rapid Transaction (USA) (A.P. Indy (USA))
1919a[7] 5679a[3] 7011a[3] 8777a[2]

**Fastidious** *M D O'Callaghan* a71 63
8 b g Exceed And Excel(AUS) Felicitous (King's Best (USA))
6801a[3]

**Fast Kar (IRE)** *Barry John Murphy* a53 48
3 b f Fast Company(IRE) Karlinha (IRE) (Desert Style (IRE))
1127[4] 1367[6] 1564[10] 2656a[7] 9012[10]

**Fast Landing** *Saeed bin Suroor* a79
3 b g Raven's Pass(USA) Miss Lucifer (FR) (Noverre (USA))
331[2] (500)

**Fastnet Blast (IRE)** *Ed Walker* a73 71
4 b g Fastnet Rock(AUS) Bright Bank (IRE) (Sadler's Wells (USA))
29[2] 382[4]

**Fastnet Spin (IRE)** *David Evans* a54 80
3 b f Fastnet Rock(AUS) Lucky Spin (Pivotal)
2361[5] 2690[12] 3142[3] 3167[6] 4153[3] 4537[2] 4698[5] 5358[2] 6028[2] 6274[3] (7199) (7463) 8113[6] 8392[6]

**Fastnet Tempest (IRE)**
*William Haggas* a98 106
4 b g Fastnet Rock(AUS) Dame Blanche (IRE) (Be My Guest (USA))
1960[3]◆ (2606) (3064) 3963[9]◆ 5393[22] 6685[11] 8057a[8] (8750a)

**Fast 'N' Rocking (AUS)**
*David A & B Hayes & Tom Dabern* 113
6 b g Fastnet Rock(AUS) For The Good Times (AUS) (Hennessy (USA))
(8057a)

**Fast On (IRE)** *Seamus Fahey* a53 52
8 gr g Verglas(IRE) Dream State (IRE) (Machiavellian (USA))
1146[5]

**Fast Pepite (FR)** *C Plisson*
2 bb f Great Journey(JPN) Montana Moon (FR) (Hernando (FR))
1282a[10] 1929a[11]

**Fast Play (IRE)** *Conor Dore* a79 58
5 b m Fast Company(IRE) Akariyda (IRE) (Salse (USA))
(233) 497[3] (688) 786[7] 958[5] 1175[8] 2163[10] 2956[8] 3547[6] 5142[9] 5483[12] 6524[8]

**Fast Tack (IRE)** *John Quinn* a48
3 b g Fast Company(IRE) Green Vision (IRE) (Green Desert (USA))
244[5] 1004[7]

**Fast Track** *David Barron* a95 84
6 b g Rail Link Silca Boo (Efisio)
(219)◆ 818[4] 957[3] 1454[3] 1794[3] 2262[3] 3827[7] 8639[10] 8913[10] 9079[2] 9269[4]

**Fatale Bere (FR)** *Leonard Powell* 104
2 b f Pedro The Great(USA) Mofa Bere (FR) (Saumarez)
8575a[5]

**Fataliste (FR)** *Endo Botti* 89
3 b f Siyouni(FR) Minimal Chic (IRE) (King's Best (USA))
2244a[14]

**Fata Morgana** *Christine Dunnett* 28
2 b f Society Rock(IRE) Life's A Whirl (Machiavellian (USA))
8323[10]

**Fata Morgana (JPN)**
*Yoshiyuki Arakawa* 112
9 b g Deep Impact(JPN) Tanino Mirage (JPN) (Helissio (FR))
2203a[10]

**Father Ailbe (IRE)** *John Butler* a63
2 b g Excelebration(IRE) Ms Sophie Eleanor (USA) (Grand Slam (USA))
8794[7] 9137[4] 9417[3]◆

**Father Bertie** *Tim Easterby* a81 97
5 b g Firebreak Magical Music (Fraam)
1492[16] 2155[9] 6209[6] 6520[8] 7044[6] 7246[6] 7823[11]

**Father Frost (IRE)** *Josef Vana* a82 102
5 b g Rip Van Winkle(IRE) Yaria (IRE) (Danehill (USA))
3120a[2] [2] 8095a[5]

**Father McKenzie** *James Eustace* a75 77
3 b g Sixties Icon Queen Of Narnia (Hunting Lion (IRE))
1731[5]◆ 2122[8] 2579[2] 2927[3] 4500[2] 7287[4] 7738[7] 8158[5]

**Fatou (FR)** *F Chappet* a75 75
2 b f Penny's Picnic(IRE) Kensita (FR) (Soviet Star (USA))
6453a[4] 7637a[6]

**Fattsota** *David O'Meara* a93 97
9 b g Oasis Dream Gift Of The Night (USA) (Slewpy (USA))
779[5] 921[6] 1865[5]

**Fauguernon (FR)** *C Ferland* 99
3 b g Martaline I'm Right (USA) (Rahy (USA))
(4654a)

**Faulkner** *Doug Watson* a104
7 ch h Pivotal Fibou (USA) (Seeking The Gold (USA))
9360a[3]

**Faulkwood** *K R Burke* a21 67
3 gr g Hellvelyn Sleep Dance (Sleeping Indian)
6526[9] 7932[12] 8217[10]

**Fauneta (FR)** *P Sogorb* 59
2 bb f Anabaa Blue Sage Melody (FR) (Sageburg (IRE))
7470a[5]

**Fauvism (USA)** *R Bouresly* a68 95
8 b g Zamindar(USA) Chaffinch (USA) (Lear Fan (USA))
776a[8]

**Favorite Girl (GER)**
*Michael Appleby* a72 73
9 b m Shirocco(GER) Favorite (GER) (Montjeu (IRE))
99[4] (497) (789) 3699[2] 4344[4] 9054[10]

**Favoritisme (FR)** *C Ferland* a75 72
2 b f Dabirsim(FR) Faviva (USA) (Storm Cat (USA))
(9086a)

**Favourite Royal (IRE)**
*Eve Johnson Houghton* a84 83
3 b f Acclamation Affirmative (Pivotal)
1888[2]◆ 2151[4] (3189) 4209[7] 5242[7] (6555) 7094[10] 7815[8] 8546[9] (8947) 9089[5]

**Favourite Treat (USA)** *Ruth Carr* a74 75
7 b g Hard Spun(USA) Truart (USA) (Yes It's True (USA))
2119[9] 3402[17] 3816[3] 4039[3] 4293[6] (4724) 5481[5] 5948[3] 6464[5] 6663[4] 7553[9]

**Fawaareq (IRE)** *Owen Burrows* 97
4 b g Invincible Spirit(IRE) Ghandoorah (USA) (Forestry (USA))
2142[3]◆ 4854[3] 5393[15] 8104[7]

**Fawley (IRE)** *M Boutin* a87 59
5 b h Makfi The Wise Lady (FR) (Ganges (USA))
6300a[10]

**Fawree (USA)** *M F De Kock* a97
3 b c Candy Ride(ARG) Keeper Hill (USA) (Deputy Minister (CAN))
(201a) 1040a[U] 1375a[7]

**Fayez (IRE)** *David O'Meara* a99 85
3 b g Zoffany(IRE) Gems (Haafhd)
2106[5] 3199[3] 3862[5] 4610[5] 5376[2]◆ 5669[6] (6158) 6617[4] 7162[5] (7569) 8315[3] (8880)◆ 9053[12]

**Fayrouz** *Ismail Mohammed* 50
2 ch f Sepoy(AUS) Mango Mischief (IRE) (Desert King (IRE))
7021[9]

**Fayrouz Rose (IRE)** *Mick Channon* 76
2 b f Epaulette(AUS) Very Nice (Daylami (IRE))
(7733)◆

**Fazendera (IRE)** *D Guillemin* 88
3 br f Elusive City(USA) Apulia (USA) (Street Cry (IRE))
3103a[7]

**Fearless Fire (IRE)** *Andrew Balding* 98
3 b c Acclamation Pediment (Desert Prince (IRE))
2126[2] 2824[2] 3994[7]

**Fearless Lad (IRE)** *John Best* a41 64
7 b g Excellent Art Souffle (Zafonic (USA))
6258[5]◆ 7490[6]

**Fearsome** *Ralph Beckett* a76 74
3 b c Makfi Lixian (Linamix (FR))
328[3] 6277[3] 6775[3] 8151[3]

**Fear The Fury (USA)** *K R Burke* a76 45
3 ch g Elusive Quality(USA) O Beautiful (USA) (Unbridled's Song (USA))
(127) 788[5] 2145[3] 3040[10] 4313[10]

**Feathery** *J S Bolger* 79
3 b f Teofilo(IRE) Huma Bird (Invincible Spirit (IRE))
1389a[14]

**Federico** *Mlle C Nicot* a89 102
4 b g Acclamation Frangy (Sadler's Wells (USA))
9112a[7]

**Feebs** *Michael Easterby* 74
2 ch g Assertive Fujakka (IRE) (Vettori (IRE))
6231[7] 6567[3] (7562) 7891[6] 8741[6]

**Feeltherhythm (IRE)** *Chris Grant* a52 52
6 b m Yeats(IRE) Queen Althea (IRE) (Bach (IRE))
1197[6]

**Feel The Vibes** *Michael Blanshard* a60 54
3 b g Medicean Apple Dumpling (Haafhd)
2151[7] 3751[6] 4747[4] 5485[5] 6069[11]

**Feel The Wrath (IRE)** *Denis Quinn* a12 17
2 br g Arcano(IRE) Takaliya (IRE) (Darshaan)
7788[13] 8350[12] 8560[14]

**Feint** *William Haggas* a81 75
3 ch f Teofilo(IRE) Ruse (Diktat)
2144[3]◆ 2585[5] 4042[2] (7762)

**Feisty Girl** *Michael Mullineaux*
7 ch m Erhaab(USA) Dolly Duff (Alflora (IRE))
457[8]

**Feisty Katerina (IRE)**
*Brendan W Duke* 78
2 b f Vocalised(USA) Miss Ekaterina (IRE) (Teofilo (IRE))
6242a[8]

**Feisty One U R** *George Baker* a54
3 b f Monsieur Bond(IRE) Formidable Girl (USA) (Roman Ruler (USA))
283[10] 503[9]

**Felician (GER)** *Ferdinand J Leve* 106
9 b g Motivator Felicity (GER) (Inchinor)
6451a[8] 7672a[3]

**Felisa** *David Evans* a64 64
2 b f Multiplex Limegrove (Captain Gerrard (IRE))
1627[4] 2292[3] 2522[5] 3066[6] 3712[5] 5279[6] 5893[4] 6127[2] 6517[2] (7023) 7458[4] 8120[4] 8467[4] 9090[3]◆ 9439[2]

**Felix Leiter**
*Jassim Mohammed Ghazali* 106
5 ch g Monsieur Bond(IRE) Spiralling (Pivotal)
914a[13]

**Felix Mendelssohn (IRE)**
*Joseph Patrick O'Brien* a90 102
6 b g Galileo(IRE) Ice Queen (IRE) (Danehill Dancer (IRE))
5638[12] 7860a[21]

**Felstead Knight (IRE)** *Joseph Tuite* a26
2 b g Tough As Nails(IRE) Fine Day (Fantastic Light (USA))
8308[8]

**Felstead Queen** *Joseph Tuite* a39 56
3 ch f Bated Breath Today's The Day (Alhaarth (IRE))
3423[9]

**Fenagh (IRE)** *David Loughnane* a44 66
2 b f Dabirsim(FR) Book Of Manners (King's Best (USA))
3491[8] 5048[4]◆ 6064[11] 6860[11]

**Fen Caroline** *Robert Cowell* 22
2 gr f Sir Percy Half Moon Hotel (With Approval (CAN))
8163[14]

**Fencing (USA)** *R Bouresly* a74 62
8 ch g Street Cry(IRE) Latice (IRE) (Inchinor)
84a[16]

**Fendale** *Antony Brittain* 96
5 b g Exceed And Excel(AUS) Adorn (Kyllachy)
6205[18]

**Fengate** *Roger Charlton* a76 86
4 ch m Champs Elysees Allegro Viva (USA) (Distant View (USA))
3693[4] 5439[2] 6152[4] 7338[7]

**Fenisa's Hook** *Warren Greatrex* a72 64
2 ch g Lope De Vega(IRE) Islandia (USA) (Johar (USA))
8389[8] 8987[4]

**Fennaan (IRE)** *John Gosden* a71 88
2 br c Footstepsinthesand Sanadaat (Green Desert (USA))
6884[5] (7391)

**Fennann** *Natalie Lloyd-Beavis* a54
6 b g Dutch Art Embraced (Pursuit Of Love)
141[9] 721[8]

**Fenner Hill Neasa (IRE)** *Pat Phelan* a37 49
4 b m Alfred Nobel(IRE) A Woman In Love (Muhtarram (USA))
2295[8] 2914[9] 4177[9]

**Feragust** *Marco Botti* a64 30
2 b g Poet's Voice Faciascura (Oratorio (IRE))
6883[10] 8161[9] 8492[5]

**Feralia (FR)** *J-C Rouget* 101
2 b f Pedro The Great(USA) Centralienne (USA) (Dixie Union (USA))
6912a[2] 7637a[5]

**Fergall (IRE)** *Seamus Mullins* a87
10 br g Norwich Gaybrook Girl (IRE) (Alderbrook)
1502[11] 3458[4]

**Fergand (FR)** *F Sergeant* a64 68
8 b g Great Journey(JPN) Queen Elodie (FR) (Cardoun (FR))
1070a[5]

**Ferik (IRE)** *David Evans* 81
2 b g Arcano(IRE) Love And Laughter (IRE) (Theatrical (IRE))
3037[6] 3742[6] 4465[2] 5079[2]◆ 6008[2]

**Ferngrove (USA)** *Susan Corbett* a41 49
6 gr g Rockport Harbor(USA) Lucky Pipit (Key Of Luck (USA))
5831[9] 6129[3] 6898[10] 7885[8] 8219[10]

**Fern Owl** *Hughie Morrison* a89 77
5 ch g Nayef(USA) Snow Goose (Polar Falcon (USA))
(666) 1590[3]

**Ferocity (IRE)** *Robyn Brisland* a78 49
3 b g Poet's Voice Foreign Language (USA) (Distant View (USA))
643[5] 926[6] 7571[10] 8158[8] 8433[6]

**Feroe D'Illiat (FR)** *P Decouz* 60
2 b c Naaqoos Akasti (IRE) (Holy Roman Emperor (IRE))
5679a[12]

**Ferrier** *Sir Mark Prescott Bt* 47
2 b f Iffraaj Ratukidul (FR) (Danehill (USA))
5576[5] 6480[14] 7021[10]

**Ferro Sensation (GER)**
*C Von Der Recke* 107
11 b g Paolini(GER) Fit To Ski (Niniski (USA))
715a[4] 834a[6]

**Ferryview Place** *Ian Williams* a56 46
8 b g Compton Place Songsheet (Dominion)
46[10] 123[4] 239[10] 421[4] 690[5] 733[6]

**Festival Of Ages (USA)**
*Charlie Appleby* 91
3 b g Medaglia d'Oro(USA) November (USA) (A.P. Indy (USA))
3717[2] (5364)

**Festive (FR)** *Eric Saint-Martin* a77 76
3 gr f Literato(FR) Path Of Life (USA) (Vindication (USA))
2644a[17] 3881a[13]

**Fethiye Boy** *Ronald Harris* a71 82
3 br g Pastoral Pursuits Ocean Blaze (Polar Prince (IRE))
264[8] (638) (2235) 2720[3] 3411[4] (4200) (4581) 4732[4] 6072[8]

**Fever Few** *Chris Wall* a58 40
8 b m Pastoral Pursuits Prairie Oyster (Emperor Jones (USA))
2124[11] 5039[9] 6113[8] 6813[2] 7487[8]

**Fibonacci** *Hugo Palmer* a73 85
3 ch c Galileo(IRE) Tereschenko (USA) (Giant's Causeway (USA))
1584[3] 2314[2] 3860[5] (6852) 7927[4]

**Ficanas** *Marco Botti* 83
2 b f Sepoy(AUS) Windermere Island (Cadeaux Genereux)
8380[2]◆

**Fico Senza Spine (IRE)**
*Luigi Riccardi* a86 73
4 b h Zoffany(IRE) Milenka (USA) (Cape Cross (IRE))
2004a[5]

**Fidaawy** *Sir Michael Stoute* 110
4 ch g New Approach(IRE) Haymana (IRE) (Pivotal)
(2136)◆ 3300[10] 5353[7] (6399) 7395[2] 8041[9]

**Fidaslemei (IRE)** *M Ramadan* a58
4 ch g Kyllachy Furbeseta (Danehill Dancer (IRE))
8583a[7]

**Fidelma Moon (IRE)** *Tracy Waggott* a44 80
5 b m Dylan Thomas(IRE) Ridiforza (FR) (Starborough)
1879[9] 2285[8] 3151[3] 3488[5] 4451[5] 5497[6] 5650[9] 6435[18] 7225[11] 7523[6] 8650[8]

**Fidji D'Emra (FR)** *C Plisson* 54
2 ch f Kandidate Royalrique (FR) (Enrique)
1335a[14]

**Fidra Bay (IRE)** *Alan Swinbank* 70
4 b m Roderic O'Connor(IRE) Halicardia (Halling (USA))
2377[6] 2685[11]

**Field Of Courage (CAN)**
*Mark Casse* a100 110
5 bb g Marchfield(CAN) Miss Crissy (CAN) (Bold n'Flashy (CAN))
(8097a)

**Field Of Vision (IRE)** *John Flint* a69 79
4 b g Pastoral Pursuits Grand Design (Danzero (AUS))
3161[6] 3777[7] 4910[3] 5112[2] 5379[6] (5711) 6303[2] 6442[3] 7002[5] 8645[11] 8906[4] 9297[5]

**Fieldsman (USA)** *David O'Meara* a82 95
5 b g Hard Spun(USA) R Charlie's Angel (USA) (Indian Charlie (USA))
2348[6] 2838[10] 3199[4] 3388[5] 4887[7] 5379[8] 5948[2] 6297[2] 6663[3] 7321[6] 7789[5] 8240[7]

**Fields Of Athenry (IRE)**
*Flemming Velin* a65 97
5 b h Galileo(IRE) Last Love (IRE) (Danehill (USA))
2667a[16] 5676a[7] 7428a[7]

**Fields Of Fortune** *Alan King* a65 74
3 b g Champs Elysees Widescreen (USA) (Distant View (USA))
1685[5] 2394[5] 3088[3] 3531[7] 3779[6] 6291[5] 6580[4] 7744[2]

**Fiendish (USA)** *Mark Johnston* a76 75
3 ch f Street Cry(IRE) Evil (USA) (Hennessy (USA))
1003[3] 1581[2] 1756[3] 1939[5] 2496[2] 2894[9] 3828[10] 4121[4] 4748[6]

**Fierce Impact (JPN)** *David Simcock* a100 99
3 b c Deep Impact(JPN) Keiai Gerbera (JPN) (Smarty Jones (USA))
2128[5] 3032[2] 4032[13] 5095[6] 6514[3] 8244[4]

**Fiery Breath** *Robert Eddery* 60
2 br c Bated Breath Sunset Kitty (USA) (Gone West (USA))
4973[4] 5437[5] 6388[9]

**Fiery Spice (IRE)** *Robert Cowell* a76
3 ch g Dream Ahead(USA) High Spice (USA) (Songandaprayer (USA))
140[3] (415) (972) (1204) 1294[2]

**Fiftyshadesofgrey (IRE)**
*George Baker* a95 93
6 gr g Dark Angel(IRE) Wohaida (IRE) (Kheleyf (USA))
275[3]◆ 896[4] 2390[13] 3777[5]

**Fighting Irish (IRE)** *Harry Dunlop* 106
2 b c Camelot Quixotic (Pivotal)
3164[4] 4826[5] (5430) 6967[4] (7335) (8024a)

**Fighting Temeraire (IRE)**
*Dean Ivory* a78 86
4 b g Invincible Spirit(IRE) Hot Ticket (IRE) (Selkirk (USA))
6192[10] 6484[4] 7622[16] 9025[12] 9314[10]

**Fikhaar** *Kevin Ryan* a61 54
3 b f Oasis Dream Fawaayed (IRE) (Singspiel (IRE))
4309[9] 5670[7] 6150[7] 6903[4]◆ (7487) 7951[9] 9019[4] 9214[6]

**Filament Of Gold (USA)**
*Roy Brotherton* a61 60
6 b g Street Cry(IRE) Raw Silk (USA) (Malibu Moon (USA))
1067[3] 1403[9] (2272) 3805[2] 4967[8] 6953[8] 8249[3] 8661[10]

**Filatore (IRE)** *Bernard Llewellyn* a21 35
8 ch g Teofilo(IRE) Dragnet (IRE) (Rainbow Quest (USA))
2363[7]

**Filbert Street** *Robert Cowell* a59
2 ch c Poet's Voice Tinnarinka (Observatory (USA))
8809[4] 9123[6]

**Fileva (IRE)** *A Giorgi* a21
2 b f Society Rock(IRE) Russian Roubles (IRE) (Sadler's Wells (USA))
5585a[13]

**Fille De Reve** *Ed Walker* a76 74
2 b f Iffraaj Danehill Dreamer (USA) (Danehill (USA))
5795[2]◆ 6861[3] (8147)

**Fille Du Septembre (IRE)** *D K Weld* a78 85
2 b f Choisir(AUS) Rocking (Oasis Dream)
4418a[6] 7421a[6]

**Fille The Force** *Scott Dixon* 50
3 b f Sakhee's Secret Coup De Torchon (FR) (Namid)
2819[6] 4341[9] 4604[5]

**Fillydelphia (IRE)** *Patrick Holmes* a41 56
6 b m Strategic Prince Lady Fonic (Zafonic (USA))
2079[2] 2687[4]◆ 3043[8] 3405[8] 4018[8] 4244[3] 5017[6] 5284[8] 7885[9] 8241[11] 9262[8]

**Filly Mignon** *Brendan Powell* a15 21
2 b f Piccolo One Pixel (Primo Valentino (IRE))
4253[15] 6260[11] 6575[11]

**Filou (SWI)** *P Schaerer* 92
6 b h Lord Of England(GER) Fujairah (SWI) (Sri Pekan (USA))
(715a) 834a[3] 953a[3]

**Filrine (FR)** *Jean-Raymond Breton* 55
2 b f Orpen(USA) Filring (FR) (Bering)
5585a[6] 7415a[10] 8228a[U]

**Fils Anges (IRE)** *Ali Jan* a90 110
7 gr h Dark Angel(IRE) La Piaf (FR) (Fabulous Dancer (USA))
87a[12]

**Fils De L'Air (FR)** *S Cerulis* a89 79
3 ch c Areion(GER) Chica Loca (FR) (American Post)
2536a[9] 4289a[9] 6455a[6]

**Final** *Mark Johnston* a95 99
5 b g Arabian Gleam Caysue (Cayman Kai (IRE))
719[2] (817) 1178[2] (1307) 1502[9] 1704[2] 1779[U] 1911[2] 2431[5] 2735[7]◆ 3300[8]

**Finale** *Hughie Morrison* a68 85
3 b f Holy Roman Emperor(IRE) Sell Out (Act One)
168[6] 479[2] 849[3] (4276)◆ (5332) 5789[4] 7276[2] 8113[5]

**Final Frontier (IRE)** *Clive Cox* 89
4 b g Dream Ahead(USA) Polly Perkins (IRE) (Pivotal)
3294[7] 4622[8]

**Final Go** *Sally Haynes* 47
2 b g Equiano(FR) Ipsa Loquitur (Unfuwain (USA))
6311[6]

**Finalize (FR)** *T Lemer* a82 69
3 b f Vertigineux(FR) Fligane (FR) (Bering)
6455a[5]

**Final Rock** *Sir Mark Prescott Bt* a32 32
2 b g Rock Of Gibraltar(IRE) Up At Last (Cape Cross (IRE))
3754[11] 4213[9] 4520[9] 4792[7]

**Final Set (IRE)** *Sir Michael Stoute* a67 61
2 b f Dark Angel(IRE) Two Sets To Love (IRE) (Cadeaux Genereux)
5795[5]◆ 6862[6]

**Final Treat (IRE)** *William Haggas* a58 79
2 b f Acclamation Musical Treat (IRE) (Royal Academy (USA))
7351[4] 8006[3] 8796[8]

**Final Venture** *Paul Midgley* a109 114
5 b g Equiano(FR) Sharplaw Venture (Polar Falcon (USA))
(207a) 433a[3] (696a) 1044a[5] 1376a[8] 3079[4] (3539) 3926[9] 4354[5] 4920[2] 5595[7] 6402[7] 6668[2] 7051[4]

**Financial Crime (IRE)**
*Mick Channon* a55 40
2 b g Red Jazz(USA) Clodilla (IRE) (Clodovil (IRE))
8388[14] 8794[6] 8943[5]

**Finche** *A Fabre* 111
3 ch c Frankel Binche (USA) (Woodman (USA))
3680a[3] (4941a) 6980a[3]

**Fine Example** *Kevin Ryan* a70 76
4 b g Showcasing Belle Reine (King Of Kings (IRE))
1700[7] 2082[2] (2224) 2888[4] 4168[9] 4851[2] 5258[2] 6076[2] 7249[8] 7881[8] 8107[9] 8433[8]

**Finelcity (GER)** *Harry Dunlop* a92 78
4 b g Elusive City(USA) Finity (USA) (Diesis)
6289[8] 6936[4] 7456[10] 8393[7]

**Finest City (USA)** *Ian Kruljac* a117 105
5 ch m City Zip(USA) Be Envied (USA) (Lemon Drop Kid (USA))
8605a[8]

**Fingal's Cave (IRE)** *Philip Kirby* a85 96
5 ch g Fast Company(IRE) Indiannie Moon (Fraam)
32[9] (1007) (1718) 2081[3] 2457[3] 2884[10] (3565) 3842[7] 4377[13] 5434[2] 5926[7] 6676[7] 7140[5] 7612[12] 8486[9] 8736[12]

**Finisher (USA)** *Kevin Ryan* a64
2 br g Street Cry(IRE) Morena (PER) (Privately Held (USA))
7237[8]

**Finishing Touch** *Saeed bin Suroor* 83
3 b f Invincible Spirit(IRE) Dubai Smile (USA) (Pivotal)
(4378)◆ 4861[3] 5324[3] 8836a[10]

**Fink Hill (USA)** *Richard Guest* a68 68
2 b g The Factor(USA) Matroshka (IRE) (Red Ransom (USA))
2786[6] 4502[4] 6432[3]◆ 7363[4] 7787[3] 8120[11]

**Finley'sluckycharm (USA)**
*W Bret Calhoun* a110
4 bb m Twirling Candy(USA) Day Of Victory (USA) (Victory Gallop (CAN))
8605a[9]

**Finn Class (IRE)** *Michael Dods* a80 96
6 b g Exceed And Excel(AUS) Finnmark (Halling (USA))
1512[15] 2030[11] (2838) 3651[3] 4077[6] 4662[2] 5668[15] 7246[8] 7566[9] 7702[6]

**Finnion Fox** *Tim Easterby* 64
2 b g Foxwedge(AUS) Chushka (Pivotal)
5874[5] 6311[4] 7141[9] 7891[5]

**Finniston Farm** *Tom Dascombe* 97
2 b c Helmet(AUS) Logic (Slip Anchor)
(3037) 4906[6]

**Finn McCool (IRE)** *A P O'Brien* 101
3 b c Galileo(IRE) Mystical Lady (IRE) (Halling (USA))
2555[7] 3109a[3]

**Finsbury Park** *Robyn Brisland* a68 80
2 b g Finjaan Fonnie (IRE) (Barathea (IRE))
4452[5] (5030) 5501[8] 6140[3] 6425[3] 6934[7] 8343[5]

**Finsbury Square (IRE)** *F Chappet* a95 110
5 b g Siyouni(FR) Diamond Square (FR) (Dyhim Diamond (IRE))
1376a[12] 2643a[3] 3370a[2] 4071[5] 6497a[2] 7670a[7]

**Fintech (IRE)** *Philip Hide* a69 64
3 b g Dark Angel(IRE) Final Legacy (USA) (Boston Harbor (USA))
6633[5] 6817[7] 7254[4] 7932[11] 8429[7] 9128[2] 9236[5]

**Fintry Flyer** *Jim Goldie* a48 42
3 ch f Compton Place Primo Heights (Primo Valentino (IRE))
5006[7] 5619[8] 6184[9] 6596[8] 7164[10] 9019[3]◆ 9265[3]

**Firby (IRE)** *James Bethell* a58 62
2 b g Rock Of Gibraltar(IRE) Huffoof (IRE) (Dalakhani (IRE))
4956[4] 5631[5] 7266[5] 7938[4]

**Fire Brigade** *Michael Bell* a75 102
3 b g Firebreak Island Rhapsody (Bahamian Bounty)
2071[3] (2755) 3077[4] (3713) 4322[5] 5392[3] (5928) 6870[2] 7582[3] (8469)◆

**Fire Diamond** *Tom Dascombe* a77 44
4 b g Firebreak Diapason (IRE) (Mull Of Kintyre (USA))
(426) 570[4] 736[4] 896[10] 1728[5] 2369[6] 5258[7] 5917[13] 6288[12] 7034[12] 7723[8] (8401) (8749) 9126[6] 9410[2]

**Fire Empress** *James Unett* a41 35
4 b m Firebreak Tedsmore Dame (Indesatchel (IRE))
605[10] 3137[6] 4981[6] 6305[6]

**Fire Fighting (IRE)** *Mark Johnston* a111 116
6 b g Soldier Of Fortune(IRE) Savoie (FR) (Anabaa (USA))
1355a[2] 1500[5] 1757[7] 2158[3] 2604[8]

**Fire For Goga** *Gabor Maronka* 69
2 b f Vale Of York(IRE) Fire And Sparks (Shamardal (USA))
8461a[4]

**Firefright (IRE)** *Jeremy Noseda* 96
3 b g Dragon Pulse(IRE) Emsiyah (USA) (Bernardini (USA))
1862[3] (2135) 3303[7] 4634[3] (5059) 5612[5] 6484[2]

**Fireguard** *Emma Owen* a16
4 b g Firebreak Leaping Flame (USA) (Trempolino (USA))
9139[6] 9304[7] 9441[5]

**Fire In Babylon (IRE)** *Giles Bravery* a42 26
9 b g Montjeu(IRE) Three Owls (IRE) (Warning)
741[9] 988[11] 1188[5] 1864[6]

**Fire Jet (IRE)** *John Mackie* a88 94
4 ch m Ask Lightning Jet (Dutch Art)
1405[4] 2125[2] (2622)◆ 3840[3] 4301[4] 5108[9] (6391) 7507[6] (8166) 8548[8]

**Fire Leopard** *David O'Meara* a69 83
3 b f Lawman(FR) Catopuma (USA) (Elusive Quality (USA))
3542[5] 4055[3] 4720[5] 5617[3]◆ (6002)◆ 6210[7] 6573[2] 7032[8] (7524) 7925[4]

**Firenze Fire (USA)** *Jason Servis* a113
2 b c Poseidon's Warrior(USA) My Every Wish (USA) (Langfuhr (CAN))
8609a[7]

**Firenze Rosa (IRE)** *John Bridger* 77
2 b f Zebedee Our Nana Rose (IRE) (Viking Ruler (AUS))
2037[9] 2251[4] 3029[3] 3821[3] (4758) 5526[10] 5963[4] 6651[10]

**Fire Orchid** *Richard Hannon* a67 56
2 gr f Lethal Force(IRE) Ring Of Love (Magic Ring (IRE))
8147[5] 8593[7] 8840[4] 8996[2] (9090)

**Fire Palace** *Robert Eddery* a76 74
3 b f Royal Applause Inflammable (Montjeu (IRE))
1907[11] 2293[8] 4975[4] 5439[5] 6006[5] 7052[2] 7464[5] 7780[8] 7881[11] 8929[5] 9243[11]

**Firesnake (IRE)** *Lisa Williamson* a66 50
4 b g Dandy Man(IRE) La Bataille (USA) (Out Of Place (USA))
172[7] 303[5] 3265[12] 4509[8] 5282[4] (5748) 6046[8] 6850[5] 7487[3] 8490[9] 8816[3]◆ 9267[8]

**Firestorm (GER)** *Richard Ford* a47 76
6 b g Dylan Thomas(IRE) Fitness (IRE) (Monsun (GER))
233[3] 517[11] 893[6] 1191[10] 1695[4] 2095[9] 3449[6] 4034[6] 4627[6] (5320) 5701[11]

**Fire Tree (IRE)** *Charlie Fellowes* a75 85
4 b g Cacique(IRE) Monicalew (Refuse To Bend (IRE))
922[3] 1735[5] (2685)◆ (4832) 5643[9] 6700[10] 7582[16]

**Fire Whirl** *William Knight* a44
3 b g Sixties Icon Cyclone Connie (Dr Devious (IRE))
6851[7] 7514[8] 7768[9] 8346[12]

**Firey Speech (USA)** *D K Weld* 105
3 b c Street Cry(IRE) Firey Red (IRE) (Pivotal)
1633a[4]

**Firgrove Bridge (IRE)** *Kevin Frost* a39 58
5 ch g Dandy Man(IRE) Over Rating (Desert King (IRE))
51[11] 216[10]

**Firmament** *David O'Meara* a104 115
5 b g Cape Cross(IRE) Heaven Sent (Pivotal)
2290[3] 3089[2] 3765a[5] 4884[6] 5393[5] 6105[5] 6355[3] 6918[5] 7807[8] 8234[8]

**Firmdecisions (IRE)** *Dean Ivory* a95 95
7 b g Captain Rio Luna Crescente (IRE) (Danehill (USA))
66[2] 275[6] 459[3] 896[5] 2283[3] 3792[17] 5744[11] 6289[3]◆ 7622[17] 8600[14] 8706[13] 9020[5] 9272[9]

**Firnas** *Charlie Appleby* 97
4 b g Dubawi(IRE) Crystal Music (USA) (Nureyev (USA))
3597[9] 4316[4] 4916[9]

**First America (FR)**
*A Lamotte D'Argy*
3 b g American Post First Sandia (FR) (Sabiango (GER))
6256a[12]

**First Bombardment** *David O'Meara* a87 76
4 br g Pastoral Pursuits Magic Myth (IRE) (Revoque (IRE))
1777[5] 2123[7] 2409[6] 3052[7] 3183[7] 4379[4] 4600[6] 5211[5] 5930[11] 6089[10] 7939[13] 8557[3]◆ 8816[10] 9001[8]

**First Cat** *K Kukk* a9 35
10 b g One Cool Cat(USA) Zina La Belle (Mark Of Esteem (IRE))
(1931a) 2669a[7] 3957a[3] 4143a[4] 4656a[5] 5201a[3] 5985a[4]

**First Dance (IRE)** *James Tate* a84 81
3 b f Cape Cross(IRE) Happy Wedding (IRE) (Green Tune (USA))
1885[11] (6066) 7545[6] 8150[9]

**First Down (USA)** *A R Al Rayhi* a83 67
5 b h Street Sense(USA) Storm Lily (USA) (Storm Cat (USA))
8583a[4]

**First Drive** *Michael Bell* a61 76
2 b f Street Cry(IRE) Dawn Glory (Oasis Dream)
3697[2] 4212[7] (5120) 5659[7] 6481[5] 8702[9]

**First Eleven** *John Gosden* 73
2 b c Frankel Zenda (Zamindar (USA))
7273[9] 7955[6] 8389[2]

**First Excel** *Roy Bowring* a73 55
5 ch g First Trump Exceedingly Good (IRE) (Exceed And Excel (AUS))
(362) 1473[8] 2119[7] 3202[4] 3758[12] 8427[6] (8772) (9033) 9363[6]

**First Experience** *Lee Carter* a80 66
6 b m Tamayuz Lolla's Spirit (IRE) (Montjeu (IRE))
232[3] 677[2] 964[2] 996[2] 1261[6] 2028[4] 3455[4] 4010[3] 6439[5] 7130[7] 7493[4] 8646[12] 8886[9] 9093[5] 9316[7]

**First Flight (IRE)** *Heather Main* a90 99
6 b g Invincible Spirit(IRE) First Of Many (Darshaan)
3597[2] 5037[7] 6449[6] 6978a[8] 7395[16] 8414[4] 8672[4] 9053[4] 9205[9]

**First Mohican** *Alan King* a107 106
9 ch g Tobougg(IRE) Mohican Girl (Dancing Brave (USA))
858[3] (1360) 1770[7] 2525[11] 4073[7] 8038[29]

**First Moon** *Hugo Palmer* a72 67
3 b f Oasis Dream Flood Plain (Orpen (USA))
814[2]◆ 1151[4] 2019[4] 2900[6]

**First Name Terms**
*Matthieu Palussiere* 81
2 b c Havana Gold(IRE) Ares Choix (Choisir (AUS))
4596a[6]

**First Nation** *Charlie Appleby* a79 106
3 b g Dubawi(IRE) Moyesii (USA) (Diesis)
1518[2] 1886[10] 2132[2] 3998[2] 5525[4] 6920[5] 7400[2] (8005)

**First Of Never (IRE)** *Lynn Siddall* a44
11 b g Systematic Never Promise (FR) (Cadeaux Genereux)
176[8]

**First Pond (FR)** *Y Gourraud* a23 60
2 b f Sageburg(IRE) Flower War (USA) (War Chant (USA))
5585a[7] 6050a[9] 8228a[9]

**First Quest (USA)** *Ed Dunlop* a75 77
3 b g First Defence(USA) Dixie Quest (USA) (Coronado's Quest (USA))
3727[9] 5298[5] 5932[4] 7386[2]◆ 7924[4] 8326[2]

**First Rate** *Marjorie Fife* a25 34
4 b g Kyllachy Hooray (Invincible Spirit (IRE))
3238[6] 4607[7]

**First Selection (SPA)**
*Simon Crisford* a91 109
4 b g Diktat Villa Sonata (Mozart (IRE))
204a[5] 653a[5] 888a[10] 4072[18] 4916[5] 5594[16]

**First Sitting** *Chris Wall* 115
6 b g Dansili Aspiring Diva (USA) (Distant View (USA))
2127[7] (3069) 3856a[3] (6052a) 7638a[8] 8041[7]

**First Summer** *Shaun Harris* a69 63
5 b g Cockney Rebel(IRE) Silken Dalliance (Rambo Dancer (CAN))
122[7] 689[6] 2687[8] 3221[5] 6622[7]

**First Up (IRE)** *Oliver Greenall* a86 85
3 b g Rip Van Winkle(IRE) Doregan (IRE) (Bahhare (USA))
2126[8] 2567[13] 3077[6] 5066[2] 5484[6] 9419[3]

**First Voyage (IRE)** *Charlie Appleby* 87
4 ch g Dubawi(IRE) Concordia (Pivotal)
3716[3] 4763[U] 5060[4]

**First Wheat** *Michael Easterby* a60 76
4 b g Monsieur Bond(IRE) Ballet Fame (USA) (Quest For Fame)
1498[20] 1706[12] 2224[6]

**Fishergate** *Richard Rowe* a44 68
4 b g Pastoral Pursuits Miss Meggy (Pivotal)
278[11] 1181a[10] 1425[9] 2313[10] 2914[12] 4755[8]

**Fisherman's Blues (IRE)**
*Peter Niven* a63 57
4 b g Zebedee Southern Barfly (USA) (Southern Halo (USA))
1498[15] 2375[5] 3983[4] 4558[8]

**Fit For Function** *Joseph G Murphy* a87 90
4 b g Captain Gerrard(IRE) Victoria Peek (IRE) (Cape Cross (IRE))
4327a[11]

**Fit For The Job (IRE)** *Jonjo O'Neill* a54 82
5 b g Lawman(FR) Spesialta (Indian Ridge (IRE))
2708[10] 3920[3]◆ (4446)◆ 5559[3] 7083[13] 7999[10]

**Fityaan** *M Al Mheiri* a104 110
9 b g Haafhd Welsh Diva (Selkirk (USA))
84a[4] 207a[5] 433a[11] 543a[3] 696a[2]

**Fitzgerald (USA)** *A bin Harmash* a111
5 b g Elusive Quality(USA) Filarmonia (ARG) (Slew Gin Fizz (USA))
85a[9] 541a[6] 1373a[4] 9361a[6]

**Fitzrovia** *Ed de Giles* a49 29
2 br c Poet's Voice Pompey Girl (Rainbow Quest (USA))
5437[7] 8028[8] 8309[5]

**Fitzwilliam** *Mick Channon* a49 58
5 ch g Sixties Icon Canadian Capers (Ballacashtal (CAN))
2914[5] 3263[8] 3661[8] 3809[8]

**Fitzwilly** *Mick Channon* a77 73
7 b g Sixties Icon Canadian Capers (Ballacashtal (CAN))
2388[5] 2966[4] 3618[6] 4471[3] 4750[2] 5025[2] 5590[6] 6259[2] (6565) 6889[7] 7766[5] 8072[7] 8394[3] 9242[2]

**Fivehundredmiles (IRE)**
*John Patrick Shanahan* a58 84
4 b g The Carbon Unit(USA) There's A Light (IRE) (Fantastic Light (USA))
2430[4] (2773) 3451[2] 5072[4] 5650[6] (6139)

**Five Ice Cubes (FR)** *D Smaga* 82
2 ch c Rip Van Winkle(IRE) Victoria College (FR) (Rock Of Gibraltar (IRE))
5776a[4] 8196a[5]

**Five Star Frank**
*Eve Johnson Houghton* a77 58
3 b g Exceed And Excel(AUS) Anadolu (IRE) (Statue Of Liberty (USA))
2112[3] 3157[6] 4161[4]

**Fivetwoeight** *Peter Chapple-Hyam* a75 81
3 b c Kyllachy Super Midge (Royal Applause)
3814[3] 5156[5] 6442[4]◆ 7709[7]

**Fivos** *David Bridgwater* a44 50
3 ch g Piccolo Bold Diva (Bold Edge)
2393[6] 2957[11] 3407[3] 4458[15] 7692[5]◆ 7910[6] 8298[6] 8395[12] 8805[6] 8984[U] 9202[8] 9282[8]

**Flag Fen** *N Caulfery* a85 73
4 b g Oasis Dream Kid Gloves (In The Wings)
4653a[5] 5979a[16]

**Flag Festival** *Charlie Appleby* a57
2 gr g New Approach(IRE) Blue Bunting (USA) (Dynaformer (USA))
8703[7]

**Flag Of Honour (IRE)** *A P O'Brien* 101
2 b c Galileo(IRE) Hawala (IRE) (Warning)
8036[5] (8440a)

**Flamboyant (FR)** *Patrick Gallagher* a73 106
6 b g Peer Gynt(JPN) Relicia Bere (FR) (Until Sundown (USA))
8099a[3]

**Flameaway (CAN)** *Mark Casse* a98 107
2 ch c Scat Daddy(USA) Vulcan Rose (CAN) (Fusaichi Pegasus (USA))
8577a[8]

**Flamin Audi (GER)** *Lee Smyth* 61
2 b f Medicean Flames To Dust (GER) (Oasis Dream)
5990[9] 7855a[9]

**Flaming Fynn** *Paul Burgoyne*
4 ch g Paco Boy(IRE) La Polka (Carnival Dancer)
8152[12]

**Flaming Marvel (IRE)**
*James Fanshawe* a77 73
3 b g Redoute's Choice(AUS) Flame Of Hestia (IRE) (Giant's Causeway (USA))
2584[3]

**Flaming Sea (IRE)** *Conor O'Dwyer* 82
4 b m Sea The Stars(IRE) Lahaleeb (IRE) (Redback)
7261a[7]

**Flaming Spear (IRE)** *Kevin Ryan* a108 112
5 ch g Lope De Vega(IRE) Elshamms (Zafonic (USA))
(199) 5393[9] (6355) 6928[8] 7807[14]

**Flannery (IRE)** *Tim Vaughan* a11 34
6 b g Excellent Art Magic Sister (Cadeaux Genereux)
5362[5] 5787[6] 6509[9] 7233[7]

**Flash City (ITY)** *Ruth Carr* a60 78
9 b g Elusive City(USA) Furnish (Green Desert (USA))
1819[4] 2551[6] 3257[7] 3944[2] 4278[2] 5211[6] 5804[3] 6267[11] 7268[2] 7522[9]

**Flash Fire (IRE)** *Charlie Appleby* 114
5 b g Shamardal(USA) Flamelet (USA) (Theatrical (IRE))
(87a) 320a[2] 653a[2] 774a[7]

**Flash Flower (FR)** *H-A Pantall* 14
3 b f Never On Sunday(FR) Fleur Du Bonheur (FR) (Vaguely Pleasant (FR))
4943a[12]

**Flashing Light** *Tim Easterby* a57 58
3 b f Compton Place Heliograph (Ishiguru (USA))
1715[3] 2897[5] 3624[10]

**Flash Of Dreams (IRE)**
*Jean-Pierre Carvalho* a71 59
3 b f Shirocco(GER) Flashing Colour (GER) (Pivotal)
6496a[6]

**Flash Of White** *Bryan Smart* a52 72
3 b g Excelebration(IRE) Aberdovey (Mister Baileys)
2304[10] 4058[8]

**Flashy Snapper** *Simon Crisford* a88 83
3 ch g Raven's Pass(USA) Super Sleuth (IRE) (Selkirk (USA))
(1818) 2385[7] 2739[12] 5744[7] 6617[5]

**Flatlined (USA)** *Charles L Dickey* 113
5 b g Flatter(USA) Buttercup's Song (USA) (Unbridled's Song (USA))
7851a[9]

**Flavius Titus** *Roger Varian* a80 74
2 ch c Lethal Force(IRE) Furbelow (Pivotal)
3754[9] 8381[2] (8888)

**Flawed Diamond (FR)** *K R Burke* a53 53
3 gr f Tin Horse(IRE) Anaphora (IRE) (Goofalik (USA))
1297[6] 1726[7] 3275a[10] 4289a[8] 5286[4]

**Flawlessly (FR)** *Ms Sheila Lavery* a75 75
3 b f Exceed And Excel(AUS) Privalova (IRE) (Alhaarth (IRE))
1782[8] 2080[2] 2372[2] 3152[3] (4060) 9244a[3]

**Fleckerl (IRE)** *Conor Dore* a80 82
7 b g Danehill Dancer(IRE) Spinola (FR) (Spinning World (USA))
93[8] 516[8] 685[11] 844[3]◆ 1063[2]◆ 1140[8] 2161[8] 3177[5] 3666[3] 4495[9] 4979[6] 5535[5] 6157[5]

**Fledermaus (IRE)** *Tina Jackson* a20 45
7 br g Jeremy(USA) Khayrat (IRE) (Polar Falcon (USA))
4018[12] 5021[13] 5544[8] 6092[5] 6523[6] 7478[15]

**Fleetfoot Jack (IRE)** *David O'Meara* 73
3 b g Kyllachy Move (Observatory (USA))
2107[6] 3745[6] 5319[7] 5666[5] (6381) (6783)

**Fleeting Francesca** *Chris Gordon* a62 49
3 ch f Paco Boy(IRE) Fleeting Echo (Beat Hollow)
(1596) 2018[2] 3031[7]

**Fleeting Freedom** *Alan Bailey* a76 78
2 b f Equiano(FR) Fleeting Image (Sir Percy)
3491[6] 4902[5] 5372[3] 5939[3] 6875[4] 7764[2] 8796[3] 9336[2]

**Fleeting Glimpse** *Dai Burchell* a63 60
4 b m Passing Glance Perfect Act (Act One)
172[6] 293[9] (1557) 2053[4] 2969[6] 4011[9] 6106[10] 6156[5] 6888[5] 7190[2] 7494[7] 7692[8] 9084[12]

**Fleeting Motion** *Richard Hannon* 85
3 ch f Sepoy(AUS) Fleeting Image (Sir Percy)
2287[4] 2755[9] 4096[3] 4794[5] 5789[5]

**Fleeting Steps (IRE)**
*Sir Mark Prescott Bt* a53
2 b g Footstepsinthesand Breedj (IRE) (Acclamation)
7876[8] 8309[6] 8536[8]

**Fleeting Visit** *Eve Johnson Houghton* a89 89
4 b g Manduro(GER) Short Affair (Singspiel (IRE))
1964[5] 2603[6] 3458[2] 4206[2] 5164[2] 5912[4] 6323[3] 6779[4] 7412[6] 7880[3]

**Fleet Review (USA)** *A P O'Brien* 116
2 b c War Front(USA) A Star Is Born (IRE) (Galileo (IRE))
6326[9] 7618[2]

**Fleetwood Poppy** *Michael Attwater* a43 28
5 br m Kheleyf(USA) Steppin Out (First Trump)
39[9] 646[10] 1699[5] 5866[4] 6309[13]

**Flemish Duchesse (FR)**
*Andreas Suborics* 99
4 b m Duke Of Marmalade(IRE) Fabiana (Ashkalani (IRE))
2201a[7] 4518a[4] 7204a[2] 8089a[7] 8665a[8]

**Flere Imsaho (IRE)** *Tom Dascombe* 57
2 b c Kodiac Florida City (IRE) (Pennekamp (USA))
5665[12] 7141[3] 7953[11]

**Flers (GER)** *Ecurie Fievez* a60 55
8 gr g Verglas(IRE) Firedance (GER) (Lomitas)
(6543a) 7534a[2]

**Fleur Forsyte** *James Fanshawe* a60 105
3 b f Teofilo(IRE) Fleurissimo (Dr Fong (USA))
(2759)◆ 3749[8] 5658[3] (6357) 7577[4]

**Fleurtille** *Ray Craggs* a40 53
8 b m Tillerman Miss Fleurie (Alzao (USA))
2900[11]

**Flexible Flyer** *Chris Dwyer* a85 79
8 b g Exceed And Excel(AUS) Windermere Island (Cadeaux Genereux)
211[3] 551[2] 1606[9] 2582[4] 3518[3]

**Flicka's Boy** *P Monfort* a79 78
5 b g Paco Boy(IRE) Selkirk Sky (Selkirk (USA))
1965[5] 2034[5] 2424[3] 4233a[13] 4955a[13]

**Flight Of Fantasy** *Harry Dunlop* a89 82
3 b f Nathaniel(IRE) Luminda (IRE) (Danehill (USA))
504[2] 814[3] (1607) 2613[6] 4809[2] 5108[4] 5550[4] 8143[8] 8506[2]

**Flight Officer** *Michael Easterby* a75 99
6 b g New Approach(IRE) Danuta (USA) (Sunday Silence (USA))
4355[12]

**Flight Risk (IRE)** *J S Bolger* a78 112
6 ch g Teofilo(IRE) Raghida (IRE) (Nordico (USA))
(3765a) 4383a[4] 4935a[8] 6119a[7] 7424a[8] 7663a[4] 8438a[5]

**Flinty Fell (IRE)** *Keith Dalgleish* a73 73
4 b m Rock Of Gibraltar(IRE) Manoeuvre (IRE) (Galileo (IRE))
2377[4] 3241[5] 3833[4] 5258[5] 5922[7] 6591[11]

**Flirt (IRE)** *J P Murtagh* a80 93
4 ch m Duke Of Marmalade(IRE) Miss Intimate (USA) (War Chant (USA))
6080a[8]

**Flirtare (IRE)** *Amanda Perrett* a70
2 b f Oasis Dream Federation (Motivator)
2958[5]

**Flood Defence (IRE)** *Chris Wall* a66 73
3 b f Harbour Watch(IRE) Krynica (USA) (Danzig (USA))
2793[8] 3627[2] (4298)◆ 5359[3] 6766[4] (7278) 7902[9]

**Flooded** *Daniel Kubler*
3 ch g Archipenko(USA) Spate Rise (Speightstown (USA))
3720[14] 4347[9]

**Flood Warning** *Clive Cox* a84 102
3 ch f Pivotal Sabreon (Caerleon (USA))
(717) (1195) 1518[6] (2132) 2827[2] 7283[5] 8666a[2]

**Flora Sandes (USA)**
*Charlie Appleby* a83
2 b f War Front(USA) Aloof (IRE) (Galileo (IRE))
8373[6] (8796)◆

**Flora Tristan** *Marco Botti* a44
2 ch f Zoffany(IRE) Red Roxanne (Rock Of Gibraltar (IRE))
9239[5]

**Flor De Seda (FR)** *Jo Hughes* a49
2 b f George Vancouver(USA) Toile De Soie (FR) (Peintre Celebre (USA))
7453[7]

**Floreat Floreat (IRE)**
*Tom Dascombe* 35
2 b c Epaulette(AUS) Flying Flag (IRE) (Entrepreneur)
5136[6]

**Florencio** *Roger Fell* a90 75
4 b g Equiano(FR) Mary Pekan (IRE) (Sri Pekan (USA))
93[5] (857) 1302[8] 1778[11] 3288[8] 3492[5] 3847[12] 4264[2] 4556[6] 5415[5] 5948[9] 6637[3] (8257) 8319[4] 8872[7] 9016[6]

**Florenza** *Chris Fairhurst* 94
4 b m Haafhd Danzatrice (Tamure (IRE))
1512[6] 2138[2] 2805[2] (3314) 4375[6] 4794[3] (5668) 6145[3] 6520[9] 7283[10] 7609[7]

**Florida Times (IRE)** *David O'Meara* 92
3 b f Elzaam(AUS) Brooklands Time (IRE) (Danetime (IRE))
2823[3] 3632a[4] 4864[11]

**Flo's Melody** *Richard Fahey* a57 64
2 br f Swiss Spirit Ginger Cookie (Bold Edge)
1909[3] 2816[8] 3662[4] 4739[5] 5479[7] (5893) (6517) 6951[8] 7264[2]

**Floss The Hoss (IRE)** *David Evans* a18 63
2 b f Havana Gold(IRE) Paradise Way (Elusive Quality (USA))
1872[4]◆ 2251[3] 3066[7] 3712[8] 4335[3]◆ 7954[8] 8397[7]

**Flourishing** *Sir Michael Stoute* a84 79
3 b f Exceed And Excel(AUS) Mi Anna (GER) (Lake Coniston (IRE))
1948[7] 3931[2] (4332)◆ 5185[3] (6015)
**Flower Cup** *Chris Dwyer* a63 66
4 b m Acclamation Amber Queen (IRE) (Cadeaux Genereux)
1837[7] 2463[7] 2969[11] 3729[2] 4561[2] 5339[3] 5855[2] 6638[8]
**Flower Fashion (FR)** *N Clement* a72 103
3 b f Flower Alley(USA) Winter Fashion (FR) (Kendor (FR))
1270a[6] 3612a[7] 5196a[4]
**Flowers On Venus (IRE)**
*Tom Dascombe* a91 90
5 ch g Raven's Pass(USA) Chelsea Rose (IRE) (Desert King (IRE))
(551) (1087) (2331)
**Flowers Will Bloom (IRE)**
*David O'Meara* a54 57
3 b f Fastnet Rock(AUS) Natural Bloom (IRE) (Galileo (IRE))
3286[4] 3717[6] 4611[8] 5850[6]
**Flowing Clarets** *John Bridger* a62 68
4 ch m Pastoral Pursuits Flying Clarets (IRE) (Titus Livius (FR))
171[10] 468[7] 735[6] 2229[10] 2969[8] (3331)◆ 3659[4] 4256[11] 4352[3] 5295[3] 5723[2] 6072[6] 7000[3] 7099[4] 7509[2] 7912[2] (8298) 8823[8]
**Flutterbee** *Mrs A Malzard* a52 55
5 b m Equiano(FR) Dunya (Unfuwain (USA))
1932a[4] 2670a[3] 5986a[4]
**Fly At Dawn (USA)** *Charlie Appleby* a106 106
3 ch g Discreet Cat(USA) Emirates Girl (USA) (Unbridled's Song (USA))
(430a) 887a[2] 1375a[5] 9360a[6]
**Flyboy (IRE)** *Richard Fahey* 84
4 b g Zoffany(IRE) In Dubai (USA) (Giant's Causeway (USA))
1677[11] 2133[8] 2888[3] 3396[2] 4103[6] 5288[2] 6555[7] 7223[2] 8240[12]
**Flying Author (IRE)** *Phil McEntee* a48 50
6 b g Authorized(IRE) Fly Free (Halling (USA))
636[3] 880[11] 988[7] 1322[3] 1698[10] 3440[2] 3958a[2] 3916[5]
**Flying Ballerina (IRE)** *F Allonche* a62 63
3 b f Elzaam(AUS) Amorous Pursuits (Pursuit Of Love)
3446a[7] 4455a[11]
**Flying Bear (IRE)** *Jeremy Gask* a83 74
6 b g Kodiac Marinebird (IRE) (Bad As I Wanna Be (IRE))
2368[6]
**Flying Expectation (ITY)**
*Des Donovan* a45 24
3 gr g Zebedee Folcara (IRE) (Brief Truce (USA))
3260[6] 5252[9]
**Flying Fairies (IRE)** *John M Oxx* 102
4 b m Holy Roman Emperor(IRE) Bright Birdie (IRE) (Sadler's Wells (USA))
1387a[3] 1568a[4] 2637a[7] 3874a[4] 5766a[6] 6490a[8]
**Flying Fantasy** *Michael Appleby* a66 81
5 b g Oasis Dream Disco Volante (Sadler's Wells (USA))
287[10] 760[11] 1419[7] 1898[3] 2070[4]◆ 2318[2] 3396[3] 4185[5] 4728[10] 5245[5] (5857) 6111[10] 6947[8] 7249[P]
**Flying Foxy** *Michael Wigham* a68 71
3 b f Foxwedge(AUS) Fauran (IRE) (Shamardal (USA))
(4604) 5041[7] 6155[4]
**Flying Fynn (IRE)** *Jose Santos* a59
3 ch g Byron Can She Dance (IRE) (Danehill Dancer (IRE))
393[3] 615[3] 875[9] 1089[6]
**Flying Hope (IRE)** *Nigel Tinkler* a49 49
3 ch f Tagula(IRE) Unknowndestination (IRE) (Authorized (IRE))
179[7] 511[2] 787[8] 960[5] 1474[10] 1715[6] 1973[8]
**Flying North** *Richard Hannon* a75 88
3 b f Raven's Pass(USA) Round The Cape (Cape Cross (IRE))
2517[6] 3031[9] (4155) 4621[3] 5323[7] 5889[5] 6377[4] 7276[8]
**Flying Onsite (FR)** *Nigel Tinkler* a32 61
3 ro g Rajsaman(FR) Infinitely (Fantastic Light (USA))
1514[9] 2349[12] 2792[7] 4303[14] 5167[4] 5374[5]
**Flying Power** *John Norton* a58 51
9 b g Dubai Destination(USA) Rah Wa (USA) (Rahy (USA))
3400[4] 4087[4] 4630[5] 5080[8] 5850[3] 7360[8] 8430[5] 9077[10]
**Flying Pursuit** *Tim Easterby* a83 109
4 ch g Pastoral Pursuits Choisette (Choisir (AUS))
1515[19] 2113[5] 2736[5] 3463[6] (4037) 5094[8] (5435) 6206[5] (7626) 8044[3] 8383[2] 8738[8]
**Flying Raconteur** *Nigel Tinkler* a69 48
3 b g Bated Breath Abunai (Pivotal)
8479[5] 8781[2] 9030[2]
**Flying Sakhee** *John Bridger* a52 51
4 b m Sakhee's Secret Sister Moonshine (Averti (IRE))
2043[10] 2762[7] 2969[2] 3532[9] 3823[5] 5429[6] 5657[5] 6106[6] 6373[3] 7099[8] 7910[5] 8824[8] 8994[2] 9213[9]
**Flying Sparkle (IRE)** *Michael Bell* 87
2 b f Fast Company(IRE) Titian Saga (IRE) (Titus Livius (FR))
(4440)◆ 7334[2] 7821[2]
**Flying Tiger (IRE)** *Nick Williams* 105
4 bl g Soldier Of Fortune(IRE) Ma Preference (FR) (American Post)
7805[5]◆
**Flymetothestars**
*Sir Mark Prescott Bt* a106 111
4 b g Sea The Stars(IRE) Precious Gem (IRE) (Sadler's Wells (USA))
(2788) 4356[3] 6447[2]◆ 6984a[4]
**Fly True** *Suzzanne France* a72 40
4 b m Raven's Pass(USA) Have Faith (IRE) (Machiavellian (USA))
330[2] 573[7] 2967[8] 3281[8] 4011[6] 9308[10]

**Fog Of War** *Saeed bin Suroor* a41 100
6 b g Azamour(IRE) Cut Short (USA) (Diesis)
319a[10] 699a[12]
**Foie Gras** *Chris Dwyer* a71 56
7 b g Kyllachy Bint Zamayem (IRE) (Rainbow Quest (USA))
641[6] 968[2] 1334[9] (1449) 1893[5] 2464[5] 2996[3] 3966[3] 5747[6] 7601[9] 7759[6] 7791[10]
**Folega** *Stefano Botti* 105
3 b f Oasis Dream Rosa Del Dubai (IRE) (Dubai Destination (USA))
(3121a) 8096a[5] 8450a[7]
**Folie De Louise (FR)**
*Carmen Bocskai* 99
3 gr f Tin Horse(IRE) Folie Folie (GER) (Observatory (USA))
8088a[3]
**Folies Bergeres** *Jonathan Portman* a45 6
2 ch f Champs Elysees May Fox (Zilzal (USA))
7488[7] 8180[10]
**Folklore (GER)**
*Mrs Ilka Gansera-Leveque* 64
2 b f Lethal Force(IRE) Focal (Pivotal)
6494a[9]
**Folkswood** *Charlie Appleby* 114
4 b g Exceed And Excel(AUS) Magic Nymph (IRE) (Galileo (IRE))
322a[2] (654a) 1046a[2] 1882[2] 2553[3] 3320[5] (8100a) 8446a[3] 8753a[5]
**Folk Tale (IRE)** *Charlie Appleby* 99
2 ch g Dubawi(IRE) Causeway Lass (AUS) (Giant's Causeway (USA))
3002[4] (3591) 4386a[5]
**Following Breeze (IRE)** *Jim Boyle* 45
2 b f Kodiac Xaloc (IRE) (Shirocco (GER))
2691[7] 4696[8] 5865[6] 6609[2] 8110[8]
**Follow Me (IRE)** *Lee Carter* a55 51
3 b f Zoffany(IRE) Flower Of Kent (USA) (Diesis)
814[7] 1421[8] 2018[9] 7210[6] 7833[6] 8673[12]
**Followmeifucan (IRE)** *C Lerner* a85 90
3 b f Elusive City(USA) Russiana (IRE) (Red Ransom (USA))
(4288a)
**Follow The Feeling (USA)**
*Henry Spiller* a49 57
2 br f More Than Ready(USA) Crystal Lake Drive (USA) (Giant's Causeway (USA))
5749[4] 6433[5] 6844[7]
**Followthesteps (IRE)** *Ivan Furtado* a75 56
2 b g Footstepsinthesand Excellent Mariner (IRE) (Henrythenavigator (USA))
3390[6] (4160)◆
**Fond Du Coeur (IRE)**
*Mme Pia Brandt* a54
3 b f Fastnet Rock(AUS) Fill My Heart (IRE) (Peintre Celebre (USA))
8885a[12]
**Fondest** *James Fanshawe* a63
2 b f Mayson Fondled (Selkirk (USA))
8148[7] 8670[5]
**Fongani (FR)** *Simone Brogi* a87 85
3 b f Siyouni(FR) Maggi Fong (Dr Fong (USA))
2244a[10] (5521a) 6455a[3]
**Fons Salera (IRE)** *A Wohler* a75 84
3 gr f Clodovil(IRE) Mixora (USA) (Mizzen Mast (USA))
6254a[7]
**Font Vert (FR)** *Ralph Beckett* 62
2 b g Sinndar(IRE) Fontaine Margot (FR) (Ballingarry (IRE))
3783[7] 4520[7] 5063[6] 5756[5] 6613[4]
**Foolaad** *Roy Bowring* a93 89
6 ch g Exceed And Excel(AUS) Zayn Zen (Singspiel (IRE))
361[4] (971) (1472) (1971) 2381[3] 2840[3] (9443)
**Fool For You (IRE)** *Richard Fahey* 75
2 b f Lawman(FR) Bosphorus Queen (IRE) (Sri Pekan (USA))
6969[4] (7919)
**Fools And Kings** *Robyn Brisland* a71 89
3 bb g Sakhee(USA) Mookhlesa (Marju (IRE))
4347[5] (4981) 6094[3] (7231) 8011[2]◆
**Footbridge (USA)** *Charlie Appleby* a105
7 b g Street Cry(IRE) Thousand Islands (Dubai Millennium)
775a[4]
**Footlight** *Richard Fahey* a84 78
4 br m Showcasing Wood Fairy (Haafhd)
120[2] (524) 781[3] 1178[3] 1911[4] 2774[7] 3558[3] 4865[4] 5470[5] 6188[4]
**Footman (GER)** *Richard Hughes* a86 76
3 b g Cacique(IRE) Flames To Dust (GER) (Oasis Dream)
2475[9] 3457[2]◆ 4156[5] 5298[2] 6194[6] 7542[2] 7989[2]
**Footprintinthesand (IRE)** *M Weiss* a58
7 bb g Footstepsinthesand Cha Cha (IRE) (Charnwood Forest (IRE))
715a[2] 834a[2] (953a)
**Footsteps Forever (IRE)**
*Mark Johnston* a76 77
2 ch f Footstepsinthesand Ceoil An Aith (IRE) (Accordion)
3576[6] (4116) 5255[2] 6900[3]
**Footstepsintherain (IRE)**
*Daniel Steele* a55 49
7 b g Footstepsinthesand Champagne Toni (IRE) (Second Empire (IRE))
9207[5]
**For Ayman** *Joseph Tuite* a72 61
6 b g Bertolini(USA) Saharan Song (IRE) (Singspiel (IRE))
50[8] 303[8] 468[6] 815[9] (Dead)
**Forban Du Large (FR)**
*J-P Perruchot* a64
2 b c George Vancouver(USA) Gulf Stream Lady (IRE) (Cadeaux Genereux)
5952a[8]
**Forced Family Fun** *George Baker* a60 82
7 b g Refuse To Bend(IRE) Juniper Girl (IRE) (Revoque (IRE))
141[7]

**Forceful Appeal (USA)** *Simon Dow* a99 88
9 bb g Successful Appeal(USA) Kinetic Force (USA) (Holy Bull (USA))
148[3] 574[7] 817[5] 1148[2] 1446[6] (1769) (2291) 3014[11] 3298[4] 8843[8] 8999[11] 9210[13]
**Forecast** *Martin Keighley* a64 64
5 ch g Observatory(USA) New Orchid (USA) (Quest For Fame)
924[2]◆ 1303[10]
**Foresee (GER)** *Tony Carroll* a74 63
4 b g Sea The Stars(IRE) Four Roses (IRE) (Darshaan)
1517[15] 3213[8] 4336[7] 5166[5] 6880[12] 8000[11]
**Foreseeable Future (FR)**
*James Tate* 77
2 b c Harbour Watch(IRE) Russian Spirit (Falbrav (IRE))
7352[6] (8118)
**Foresight (FR)** *Kevin Ryan* a68 83
4 b g Dream Ahead(USA) Madhya (USA) (Gone West (USA))
660[8] 1202[8] 1972[8] 2428[6] 4529[10] 6591[9] 7042[10]
**Forest Angel (IRE)** *James Tate* a61 61
3 gr f Dark Angel(IRE) Fruit O'The Forest (IRE) (Shinko Forest (IRE))
882[4] 1123[7] 1817[6]
**Forest Dragon** *Hugo Palmer* a37 54
2 b f Teofilo(IRE) Lion Forest (USA) (Forestry (USA))
5114[9] 5371[9] 6386[6] 7920[4]◆ 8190[11]
**Forest Lakes (IRE)** *Paul D'Arcy* a74 57
4 b m Iffraaj Cala (FR) (Desert Prince (IRE))
222[6]
**Forest Ranger (IRE)** *Richard Fahey* a107 112
3 b c Lawman(FR) Alava (IRE) (Anabaa (USA))
(1780) 2766[6] 3927[5] 4817[2] 5559[3] 6444[2] 8041[8]
**Forestry** *Jonathan Portman* a39
3 b g Firebreak Oak Leaves (Mark Of Esteem (IRE))
1410[6] 2092[9]
**Forest Steps (IRE)** *J S Moore* a49
3 b f Footstepsinthesand Zeena (Unfuwain (USA))
149[8] 305[12] 637[7]
**For Ever (FR)** *Carina Fey* a93 95
6 gr h Literato(FR) Ever In Love (FR) (Neverneyev (USA))
3354a[7] 6540a[3] 8251a[5]
**Forever A Lady (IRE)**
*Keith Dalgleish* a68 79
4 b m Dark Angel(IRE) Unicamp (Royal Academy (USA))
1104[3] 1879[4] 2458[2] (2888) 3241[2] 3577[2] 3828[7] 4248[5] 4901[4] 5699[9] 5881[5] 6382[4] 6629[4] 7161[4] 7658[3]◆ 8108[7]
**Forever Excel (IRE)** *Charles Hills* 35
3 b f Excelebration(IRE) Never A Doubt (Night Shift (USA))
3075[5]
**Forever In Love** *Sir Michael Stoute* a68 70
2 ch f Dutch Art Ardent (Pivotal)
5026[5] 6010[2] 6876[2] 7335[4] 8131[4]
**Forever Song** *A bin Harmash* a72 50
3 b g Dubawi(IRE) Echoes In Eternity (IRE) (Spinning World (USA))
1967[9] 3720[5] 8710a[14]
**Forever Unbridled (USA)**
*Dallas Stewart* a121
5 b m Unbridled's Song(USA) Lemons Forever (USA) (Lemon Drop Kid (USA))
(8578a)
**Forever Yours (IRE)** *Dean Ivory* a69 64
4 b g Canford Cliffs(IRE) Gilded (IRE) (Redback)
734[9] 2962[5] 3468[2]◆ 3971[7] 4695[4] 5341[4] 9142[13] 9470[3]
**Forgino (GER)** *T Potters* a94 108
6 b g It's Gino(GER) Forlea (GER) (Lead On Time (USA))
4517a[7] 6495a[12]
**Forgivethenforget** *A bin Harmash* a57 70
3 br c Foxwedge(AUS) Search Party (Rainbow Quest (USA))
201a[6]
**Forgotten Hero (IRE)** *Kim Bailey* a85 76
8 b g High Chaparral(IRE) Sundown (Polish Precedent (USA))
8244[10]
**Forgotten Rules (IRE)** *D K Weld* 110
7 b g Nayef(USA) Utterly Heaven (IRE) (Danehill (USA))
4420a[7]
**Formative** *Noel Wilson*
4 ch g Champs Elysees Chasing Stars (Observatory (USA))
3465[8]
**Formidable Kitt** *Tom Dascombe* 86
2 b f Invincible Spirit(IRE) Ceiling Kitty (Red Clubs (IRE))
(1884) 3960[16] 4582[4] 6728a[7]
**Formiga (IRE)** *Jose Santos* a67
2 b f Worthadd(IRE) Hymn Of Love (IRE) (Barathea (IRE))
4595a[6] 5893[3] 6456a[2] 7033[5] 8482a[6]
**Forricherforpoorer (IRE)**
*William Knight* a54
2 gr g Casamento(IRE) Ghedi (IRE) (Aussie Rules (USA))
8387[16] 9313[12]
**Fort Bastion (IRE)** *Brian Ellison* a94 101
8 b g Lawman(FR) French Fern (IRE) (Royal Applause)
117[4] 199[2] 6186[10] 6520[4] 7523[2]
**For The Roses** *J P Murtagh* 68
3 b f Nathaniel(IRE) Ivory Rose (Green Desert (USA))
7224[3]
**Fortia** *Dean Ivory* a59 62
3 b f Nathaniel(IRE) Veenwouden (Desert Prince (IRE))
6623[5] 7253[3] 7790[8]
**Fortinbrass (IRE)** *John Balding* a67 61
7 b g Baltic King Greta D'Argent (IRE) (Great Commotion (USA))
21[6] (386) 663[5] 1076[3] 1209[3] 1431[6] 1593[6] (1823) 2469[9] 3758[5] 6531[10] 8772[6] 8980[5] 9307[6]

**Fortissimo (GER)** *R Rohne* 90
3 b c Lord Of England(GER) Francfurter (Legend Of France (USA))
2868a[9] [6]
**Fortitude (IRE)** *Hugo Palmer* a75 82
3 b f Oasis Dream Sweepstake (IRE) (Acclamation)
2619[4] (3313) 4078[11] 4752[6] 5473[3]◆ 6149[3] (7282)
**Fort Jefferson** *Andrew Balding* a43 72
4 br g Passing Glance Florida Heart (First Trump)
156[8] 4522[10] 5686[8] 6866[10] (7917)
**Fort Moville (FR)** *Ahmed Kobeissi* a90 103
5 ch h Le Havre(IRE) Fancy Dance (Rainbow Quest (USA))
934a[13]
**Fortuities (IRE)** *John James Feane* a59 65
3 b f Soldier Of Fortune(IRE) Inez (Dai Jin)
1471[3] 2921[6] 3461[4] 4432[6] 5467[12] 6550[8] 9376[9]
**Fortunate Vision** *David Brown* a68 71
2 b g Libranno How Fortunate (Haafhd)
4760[4] 5494[4] 6262[3] (7920)◆ 8288[2] 8586[3]
**Fortune And Glory (USA)**
*Joseph Tuite* a66 46
4 b g War Front(USA) Spain (USA) (Thunder Gulch (USA))
5937[5] 6009[8] 6526[2]◆
**Fortune's Pearl (IRE)**
*Andrew Balding* 99
2 ch c Harbour Watch(IRE) Princess Mood (GER) (Muhtarram (USA))
(4465) 5380[4] (6388) 7546[5]
**Forward Contract (USA)**
*Hughie Morrison* a57 24
3 ch g Exchange Rate(USA) Persistent Penny (USA) (A.P. Indy (USA))
1900[6] 2584[11]
**Forward Thinker** *David Simcock* 72
2 ch f Dream Ahead(USA) Avodale (IRE) (Lawman (FR))
8348[5]
**For You (FR)** *P Chevillard* 21
2 gr f Rajsaman(FR) D'Outremer (FR) (Choisir (AUS))
7415a[11]
**Forza Capitano (FR)** *H-A Pantall* a91 91
2 bl c Captain Marvelous(IRE) Fantasia (GER) (Monsun (GER))
(6170a) 8884a[7]
**Forza Libranno (FR)** *F Chappet* a68 83
4 b g Dick Turpin(IRE) Bella Vento (Shirocco (GER))
4233a[10]
**Fossa** *Mark Brisbourne* a56 44
7 b g Dubai Destination(USA) Gayanula (USA) (Yonaguska (USA))
51[3] 222[3] 455[5] 495[5] 784[3] 854[7] (1075) 1407[5] 4162[9] 4726[8] 5482[9] 5848[7] 6528[3]
**Fosun (GER)** *Markus Klug* 95
4 b m Soldier Hollow Flamingo Sky (USA) (Silver Hawk (USA))
6710a[7] 7673a[5] 8462a[3]
**Foundation (IRE)**
*David A & B Hayes & Tom Dabern* 111
4 ch g Zoffany(IRE) Roystonea (Polish Precedent (USA))
8857a[12]
**Foundry (IRE)** *Robert Hickmott* 102
7 b g Galileo(IRE) Sharp Lisa (USA) (Dixieland Band (USA))
8056a[10] 8633a[3]
**Fountain (IRE)** *J S Bolger* 88
4 b g Pour Moi(IRE) Teolane (IRE) (Teofilo (IRE))
5582a[16]
**Four Champs** *Tom Dascombe* a61
2 gr c Champs Elysees Lana Jolie (GER) (Whipper (USA))
8399[8]
**Four Dragons** *Tom Dascombe* a72 57
3 ch f Dragon Pulse(IRE) Mysterious Girl (IRE) (Teofilo (IRE))
6411[10] 6878[8] 7409[9] 8243[2]
**Four Fifty Three** *Mark H Tompkins* a57 58
2 b c Kheleyf(USA) Velvet Waters (Unfuwain (USA))
3390[14] 3965[10] 4725[4]◆ 5507[4] (6022) 6845[3]
**Fou Rire (IRE)** *F Chappet* a89 83
2 b f Iffraaj Dolled Up (IRE) (Whipper (USA))
6228a[7] 8884a[10]
**Four Kingdoms (IRE)** *K R Burke* a65 63
3 b g Lord Shanakill(USA) Four Poorer (IRE) (Oasis Dream)
1977[7] 3243[6] 6946[6] 7928[2] (8122) (8312) 8654[8] 8909[13]
**Four Mile Beach** *Malcolm Jefferson* a45 49
4 gr g Dalakhani(IRE) Rappel (Royal Applause)
8386[14]
**Fourstar Crook (USA)**
*Chad C Brown* 110
5 b m Freud(USA) Avril A Portugal (USA) (D'Accord (USA))
8098a[3]
**Fourth Way (IRE)** *Ralph Beckett* 94
4 b m Iffraaj Spiritual Air (Royal Applause)
3314[4] 4375[9]
**Four Wishes** *Tim Easterby* a68 67
3 b g Sepoy(AUS) Postage Stampe (Singspiel (IRE))
(2077) 2886[4] 3461[6] 3975[3] 5319[11] 6091[6] 7034[2]◆
**Foxangel** *Jose Santos* 38
2 ch f Foxwedge(AUS) Tech Zinne (Zinaad)
6132[11] 6747[8] 7392[13]
**Foxcatcher** *Clive Cox* 73
3 ch f Foxwedge(AUS) Copy-Cat (Lion Cavern (USA))
2757[8] 3692[7] 4530[6]
**Foxford** *Patrick Chamings* a43 58
6 b m Clodovil(IRE) Pulau Pinang (IRE) (Dolphin Street (FR))
1557[11] 2370[7] 2969[5] (3569) 7692[11]
**Foxinthehenhouse** *John Holt* a68 17
4 ch m Bahamian Bounty Pants (Pivotal)
1842[9]

**Fox King** *Ralph Beckett* a42 57
3 b g Foxwedge(AUS) King's Siren (IRE) (King's Best (USA))
***2090***[9]

**Fox Mint** *Karen George* 45
3 ch f Foxwedge(AUS) Unasuming (IRE) (Orpen (USA))
**6345**[11]

**Foxrush Take Time (FR)**
*Richard Guest* a60 63
2 b g Showcasing Stranded (Montjeu (IRE))
4374[4] 4919[10] 5127[9] **5562**[2]◆ 5875[3] 6366[3] 8467[11] *8658*[8] *8847*[3] *9014*[5]

**Fox Tin (FR)** *C Ferland* a79 96
3 gr g Tin Horse(IRE) Fox Force Five (IRE) (Araafa (IRE))
**1114a**[5]

**Foxtrix** *Michael Dods* 38
3 b f Foxwedge(AUS) Royal Pardon (Royal Applause)
**3150**[8]

**Foxtrot Charlie (USA)** *D K Weld* 101
4 ch h English Channel(USA) Flashy Four (USA) (Storm Cat (USA))
**4383a**[6] 6491a[26]

**Foxtrot Knight** *Ruth Carr* a75 86
5 b g Kyllachy Rustam (Dansili)
*1370*[7] **(1915)** 2123[5] 2683[7] 3183[3] 3741[4] 4249[7] 4686[2] 5098[6] 5580[4] 6062[4] 6574[4] 7055[4] 7625[8] 7825[8]

**Foxtrot Lady** *Andrew Balding* 81
2 ch f Foxwedge(AUS) Strictly Dancing (IRE) (Danehill Dancer (IRE))
5528[13] 6070[3] 6480[2] 7352[2] **7821**[3]◆

**Fox Trotter (IRE)** *Brian Meehan* a64 96
5 br g Bushranger(IRE) Miss Brief (IRE) (Brief Truce (USA))
2390[7] 2617[3] 3030[7]◆ 3572[2] 4524[6] 4854[6] **(5302)** 6419[6]◆ 6870[3] 7129[11] 7780[15]

**Foxxy Brown** *Richard Fahey* 40
2 b f Paco Boy(IRE) Odense (USA) (Medaglia d'Oro (USA))
2836[9] **3483**[5] 3791[12] 4054[4]

**Foxy Boy** *Michael Dods* a38 81
3 ch g Foxwedge(AUS) Suzy Wong (Auction House (USA))
2897[11] 3403[5] (4107)◆ (4174)◆ **(4531)** 4576[5] 5495[3] 5920[6] 6945[6] 7268[4] 7738[11] 7825[9]

**Foxy Forever (IRE)**
*Michael Wigham* a96 91
7 b g Kodiac Northern Tara (IRE) (Fayruz)
*79*[7] *358*[3] *443*[2]◆ *1222*[10] *(1370)* *1487*[7] 1863[11] 2835[8] 3834[3] 4816[5]◆ (5098) (6430) *7604*[2] *7994*[4] ***(8129)*** 8416[12]

**Foxy Lady** *Kevin Ryan* a63 57
2 b f Foxwedge(AUS) Catherine Palace (Grand Lodge (USA))
4503[6] 4995[4] 5702[7] 6626[4]◆ ***7030***[2] *7938*[6] 8213[4]

**Foxy Lass** *William Haggas* a64 48
3 b f Foxwedge(AUS) Domitia (Pivotal)
*1503*[6] ***2311***[10]

**Foxy Rebel** *Ruth Carr* 46
3 ch g Cockney Rebel(IRE) Foxholes Lodge (Nasheyt)
1830[8] **2185**[10] 2681[11] 3975[7] 4721[4] 5266[8]

**Foxy's Spirit** *Tim Easterby* 54
2 b f Foxwedge(AUS) Jessie's Spirit (IRE) (Clodovil (IRE))
2105[10] 3858[10] 4291[12] **6204**[4] 6940[10]

**Foylesideview (IRE)** *Harry Chisman* a47 47
5 b g Dark Angel(IRE) Showerproof (Peintre Celebre (USA))
***124***[6] *425*[10] *1260*[6] ***1620***[7]

**Framley Garth (IRE)** *Patrick Holmes* a67 79
5 b g Clodovil(IRE) Two Marks (USA) (Woodman (USA))
*992*[7] 1707[6] 2146[7] 3402[6] **3450**[2] **4609**[3] 5091[5] 5650[11]

**Franca Florio (IRE)** *Kevin Ryan* 72
3 b f Acclamation Lyca Ballerina (Marju (IRE))
**1975**[8] 4324[5]

**Francesco Bere (FR)** *D Guillemin* 100
2 b c Peer Gynt(JPN) Monatora (FR) (Hector Protector (USA))
**(6229a)** 7667a[6]

**Francisco** *Tony Carroll* a71 93
5 b g Paco Boy(IRE) Blue Goddess (IRE) (Blues Traveller (IRE))
**5304**[2] 6192[8] 6780[3] 7742[5] 8393[11]

**Francis Of Assisi (IRE)**
*Charlie Appleby* 109
7 b g Danehill Dancer(IRE) Queen Cleopatra (IRE) (Kingmambo (USA))
**5925**[8]

**Francis Xavier (IRE)** *Hugo Palmer* a82
3 b g High Chaparral(IRE) Missionary Hymn (USA) (Giant's Causeway (USA))
*7768*[3] ***8554***[2] *(8781)*

**Franco's Secret** *Peter Hedger* a94 59
6 b g Sakhee's Secret Veronica Franco (Darshaan)
*(349)* *(548)* *736*[2] *918*[9] ***1023***[2]

**Frangarry (IRE)** *Alan Bailey* a54 41
5 b g Lawman(FR) Divert (IRE) (Averti (IRE))
*1219*[7] *1372*[10] ***(2370)*** *3186*[5] 3385 [7] 4695[12] 5146[10] 6114[10] *6814*[5] *7605*[2] *7763*[9] *8538*[13] *8807*[6] *8985*[6]

**Frank Bridge** *Eve Johnson Houghton* a73 95
4 b g Avonbridge First Among Equals (Primo Valentino (IRE))
*2369*[5] (3144) 4210[13] 4523[2] (5064) **(5548)**◆ 5842[3] 6419[15] 7129[6]

**Frank Conversation (USA)**
*Doug O'Neill* a102 107
4 b h Quality Road(USA) Rushen Heat (USA) (Unusual Heat (USA))
**6461a**[7]

**Frank Cool** *Tony Carroll* a59 59
4 b g Royal Applause Queen Of Heaven (USA) (Mr Greeley (USA))
*1394* *1080*[3] *1407*[3] *(2024)* 3660[2] 4695[11] **6174**[2] **7190**[3] ***7951***[4]

**Frankie** *Jimmy Fox* a47 13
6 gr g Firebreak Winterbourne (Cadeaux Genereux)
***621***[3] *1082*[5] 2615[13]

**Frankki M** *Mrs A Corson* 12
7 b g Denounce Natacha Rostow (Pursuit Of Love)
1932a[8]

**Franko Folie (FR)** *Gay Kelleway* a46 51
4 bb m Kendargent(FR) Atlantic Festival (USA) (Theatrical (IRE))
*6125a*[12] **6365a**[4] 7069a[5]

**Frank's Legacy** *Ivan Furtado* a59
3 ch g Aqlaam Quite A Thing (Dutch Art)
*1*[7] *819*[9] *1004*[6] *(3260)* ***7481***[2] *7539*[4]

**Frankster (FR)** *Micky Hammond* a15 72
4 b g Equiano(FR) Milwaukee (FR) (Desert King (IRE))
2301[8] 3432[10] 4170[5] 7331[2] **(7896)**

**Frank The Barber (IRE)**
*Steph Hollinshead* a65 57
5 gr g Zebedee Red Rosanna (Bertolini (USA))
*215*[6] *723*[2] *742*[5] ***(1022)*** ***1340***[3] *1759*[3] 1965[3] 2216[3] *2995*[4] *7607*[3] *8168*[14] *8494*[3] *8816*[7] *9267*[2] *9374*[4]

**Frankuus (IRE)** *Mark Johnston* 112
3 gr c Frankel Dookus (IRE) (Linamix (FR))
2128[3]◆ 2614[4] 4029[8] 4584[4] 5095[2] **(5925)**◆ 6441[5] 7506[6]

**Frankyfourfingers (FR)**
*S bin Ghadayer* a109 101
7 b h Sunday Break(JPN) Texaloula (FR) (Kendor (FR))
*85a*[10] ***432a***[2]

**Franny Nisbet** *William Muir* a64 62
3 b f Mount Nelson Don't Stop Me Now (FR) (Zamindar (USA))
3145[7] 3770[7] 5780[3] 6376[5] ***(6820)*** 7232[3]

**Frantical** *Tony Carroll* a51 61
5 b g Observatory(USA) Quest For Freedom (Falbrav (IRE))
2762[3] 3221[3] 3771[5] 5053[4] **(5249)** 6370[6] *7495*[12]

**Franz Schubert** *A Fabre* 104
3 b g Dansili Measured Tempo (Sadler's Wells (USA))
**1658a**[3] 2560a[2]

**Frap** *Ian Williams* a50 63
4 b g Makfi Frizzante (Efisio)
*605*[13] ***689***[4] *1403*[10] *1560*[5] *2272*[8] *3192*[8] *3688*[9] 3940[3]

**Freddo Du Desert (FR)**
*Louis Baudron* 59
2 gr g Shakespearean(IRE) Styla Louva (FR) (Desert Style (IRE))
4389a[7] **5907a**[3]

**Freddy With A Y (IRE)** *J R Jenkins* a69 83
7 b g Amadeus Wolf Mataji (IRE) (Desert Prince (IRE))
*159*[7] *480*[7] ***812***[2]◆ *1086*[5] ***1285***[3] *1338*[4] *2465*[4] 4350[9] *5793*[5] *6528*[11] *7945*[8] *(8133)* *8307*[5]

**Frederic** *Keith Dalgleish* a88 95
6 b g Zamindar(USA) Frangy (Sadler's Wells (USA))
(2889)◆ **(3663)** 4120[4] 5524[6] 8038[22] *9082*[5]

**Fredricka** *Ivan Furtado* a84 66
6 ch m Assertive Vintage Steps (IRE) (Bahamian Bounty)
*45*[5] *194*[7] *358*[2] *443*[3] *1030*[2] *1140*[2] *(1326)* 1936[13] 2462[3] **3253**[2] 3617[8] 4566[3] 5564[4] 6943[6] 7055[11] *8320*[5] *8542*[4] ***(8798)*** *8907*[5] *9280*[5]

**Fred's Filly** *Nick Mitchell* a42 27
4 ch m Avonbridge Regal Quest (IRE) (Marju (IRE))
***9216***[9]

**Freebe Rocks (IRE)** *Michael Bell* a62 57
2 ch g Camacho Shamardyh (IRE) (Shamardal (USA))
**4885**[8] 5365[11] 5851[4] 6585[5]

**Free Bounty** *Philip McBride* a74 55
4 b g Dick Turpin(IRE) Native Ring (FR) (Bering)
*62*[4] ***(315)***◆ *477*[4] *1092*[4] *1412*[4]

**Free Code (IRE)**
*Eugene M O'Sullivan* a66 67
6 b g Kodiac Gerobies Girl (USA) (Deposit Ticket (USA))
***(581)*** *730*[6] *989*[6] *1202*[3] 1512[19] 5519a[15]

**Freediver** *John Berry* a55 51
3 ch f Bated Breath Grand Coral (Grand Lodge (USA))
***8869***[7] *9376*[10]

**Freedom Beel (IRE)** *Stefano Botti* 97
4 b h Pour Moi(IRE) Querida (Rainbow Quest (USA))
**2004a**[4]

**Freedom Chimes** *Edward Lynam* a53 57
3 b g Champs Elysees Ombre (Galileo (IRE))
**1389a**[11]

**Freedom Fighter (IRE)** *Tim Pinfield* a65 42
7 b g Danehill Dancer(IRE) Rose Of Petra (IRE) (Golan (IRE))
6031[5] ***6817***[6] *7600*[6]

**Freedom Square (IRE)**
*Mark Michael McNiff* a27 31
6 b g Lawman(FR) Manger Square (IRE) (Danehill (USA))
***6800a***[8]

**Free Drop Billy (USA)**
*Dale Romans* a116
2 ch c Union Rags(USA) Trensa (USA) (Giant's Causeway (USA))
***8609a***[9]

**Free Forum (IRE)** *David Simcock* a72 69
3 b g Holy Roman Emperor(IRE) Kentucky Warbler (IRE) (Spinning World (USA))
*1485*[8] *1692*[11] 2066[11] (5509) 5867[3] ***7063***[3] *7712*[6]

**Freemanip (ARG)** *Peter Jardby*
5 b h Manipulator(USA) Free Runner (ARG) (Freelancer (USA))
*2943a*[10]

**Freescape** *David Marnane* a88 73
2 ch g Cityscape Careless Freedom (Bertolini (USA))
6977a[27]

**Free Spirited** *Richard Fahey* 55
2 ch g Equiano(FR) Tagula Sunrise (IRE) (Tagula (IRE))
3165[8] **3826**[7] 4740[5] 7264[8]

**Free Talkin** *Michael Attwater* a51 33
2 b f Equiano(FR) Where's Broughton (Cadeaux Genereux)
5655[11] 6472[6] ***7875***[5] *9436*[6]

**Free To Roam (IRE)**
*Adrian McGuinness* a55 55
4 gr m Bushranger(IRE) Operissimo (Singspiel (IRE))
*761*[8] ***1084***[2] 1298[8] 2278[5] 3137[3] 3688[7] 5991[5] 6798a[3]

**Free Zone** *Claes Bjorling* a89 92
8 b g Kyllachy Aldora (Magic Ring (IRE))
***94***[3] *211*[2] *551*[4] *2943a*[9]

**Freight Train (IRE)** *Adrian Wintle* a49 56
5 b g Manduro(GER) Sigonella (IRE) (Priolo (USA))
***122***[9] *548*[9] *1085*[12] *1553*[9] *8307*[14]

**French** *Antony Brittain* a71 74
4 ch m Monsieur Bond(IRE) Guadaloup (Loup Sauvage (USA))
1721[6] 2124[2] (2843) **3216**[2] *3548*[2] 3666[5] *4310*[11] *4979*[7] *8717*[7] *9215*[3]

**French Bere (FR)** *N Clement* a82 77
2 b g Peer Gynt(JPN) Madame Beatrice (FR) (Hold That Tiger (USA))
**7012a**[8]

**French Cricket (FR)** *George Baker* a46
2 b g Sunday Break(JPN) Hambye (Distant Relative)
*9200*[12] ***9465***[9]

**French Encore** *Debbie Mountain* a82 90
4 b g Showcasing French Connexion (IRE) (Chineur (FR))
**932a**[10]

**French Flyer (IRE)** *Michael Dods* 74
2 b g Pour Moi(IRE) Leavingonajetplane (IRE) (Danehill (USA))
(4074)◆ 4956[3]◆ 5918[4] **6658**[2]

**French Heroine** *William Haggas* 58
2 b f Redoute's Choice(AUS) Hasaiyda (IRE) (Hector Protector (USA))
**7620**[7]

**French King** *H-A Pantall* 15
2 ch c French Fifteen(FR) Marina Piccola (IRE) (Halling (USA))
**2664a**[9]

**French Kiss (IRE)** *Hughie Morrison* 54
2 b g French Fifteen(FR) Ms Cordelia (USA) (Anabaa (USA))
7120[9] 7503[9] **8162**[7]

**French Mix (USA)**
*Joseph Patrick O'Brien* a75 58
3 bb f Dalakhani(IRE) Alharmina (Linamix (FR))
***8648***[4]

**French Pass** *E Jeanne* a40 18
3 gr f Aussie Rules(USA) Etroubles (FR) (Indian Ridge (IRE))
***317a***[11] *430a*[13]

**French Pegasus (FR)** *Y Barberot* 96
2 b c French Fifteen(FR) Etrangere (USA) (Fusaichi Pegasus (USA))
6247a[2] **7306a**[3] **8024a**[3]

**French Reflection (IRE)** *G Botti* a42 34
2 b f Declaration Of War(USA) Spira (IRE) (Sadler's Wells (USA))
***9086a***[10]

**French Resistance (IRE)**
*Roger Fell* 64
2 b g Elusive Pimpernel(USA) Ivy Batty (IRE) (King's Best (USA))
6380[6] 6854[6] **7654**[3] 8164[8] 8287[10]

**French Silk** *Chris Fairhurst* a51 46
2 b f Pour Moi(IRE) Green Silk (IRE) (Namid)
2836[10] 3662[11] 5537[13] 6567[6] ***7362***[4]

**French Silver (FR)** *Tony Carroll* a34 40
3 gr f Rajsaman(FR) Senanque (IRE) (Pivotal)
**4274**[9] 4754[9] 5405[8]

**French Sparkle** *Robert Cowell* a60
2 b f Swiss Spirit Chantilly Jewel (USA) (Century City (IRE))
8472[10] ***9022***[8] *9416*[7]

**Fresh Fox** *Jonathan Portman* 57
3 ch f Sakhee's Secret May Fox (Zilzal (USA))
**1944**[12]

**Fresh Terms** *Ralph Beckett* a62
2 b f New Approach(IRE) Best Terms (Exceed And Excel (AUS))
***9081***[6]

**Freud (FR)** *Ian Williams* a61 62
7 b g Dalakhani(IRE) Ailette (Second Set (IRE))
***719***[8] *958*[11] *1562*[8] *9408*[9]

**Friday Night Light (FR)** *David Pipe* a43 92
4 b g Air Chief Marshal(IRE) Peninsula (FR) (Dansili)
**8038**[26]

**Frightened Rabbit (USA)**
*Susan Corbett* a38 64
5 b g Hard Spun(USA) Champagne Ending (USA) (Precise End (USA))
*1101*[8] **5701**[10]

**Frisson Du Large (FR)** *M Narduzzi*
2 b c George Vancouver(USA) Sharp's Love (IRE) (Fasliyev (USA))
4131a[8]

**Frivolous Prince (IRE)** *K Kukk* a59 55
4 b g Baltic King Sweet Reflection (IRE) (Victory Note (USA))
*46*[2] *(121)* *281*[2] *820*[2] ***(839)*** 1930a[4] 2671a[5]

**Frizzanto (FR)** *Mario Hofer* 85
2 b c Dabirsim(FR) Fiere (FR) (Authorized (IRE))
**5461a**[8] 8524a[6]

**Frolic** *Sir Mark Prescott Bt* a58 74
2 b f Dutch Art Jamboretta (IRE) (Danehill (USA))
**5660**[3] 5990[8] **6666**[2] 7226[2] *7757*[6]

**From A Distance (IRE)**
*David Simcock* a49
3 b f Power Meek Appeal (USA) (Woodman (USA))
*983*[5] ***1286***[5] *1401*[10] *2018*[10]

**Front Contender (IRE)** *C Ferland* a90
3 b f Teofilo(IRE) Zeiting (IRE) (Zieten (USA))
***8986a***[15]

**Frontiersman** *Charlie Appleby* 119
4 br h Dubawi(IRE) Ouija Board (Cape Cross (IRE))
1516[4] (2431) **3299**[2] 4814[2] 6191[3] 6499a[6] (7581) 8421[6]

**Frontispiece** *Sir Michael Stoute* 93
3 b c Shamardal(USA) Free Verse (Danehill Dancer (IRE))
(3505) 4640[3] **5568**[2]◆ 6474[7]

**Frontline Phantom (IRE)** *K R Burke* a53 49
10 b g Noverre(USA) Daisy Hill (Indian Ridge (IRE))
*400*[9] *733*[11] ***865***[3]◆ 3760[4] 4034[10] 5254[11]

**Frostbite** *Eve Johnson Houghton* a41 64
2 gr g Lethal Force(IRE) Red Sovereign (Danzig Connection (USA))
3305[7] **3570**[2] *8308*[6]

**Frosting** *William Haggas* 83
3 ch f Kyllachy Ice Palace (Polar Falcon (USA))
2316[4] 4460[2] (5124) **5822**[3] 6369[5]

**Frosty Bay (FR)** *N Caulléry* a68 84
3 gr g Silver Frost(IRE) Grosgrain (USA) (Diesis)
***272a***[7] 2697a[2] 5909a[3]

**Frown** *Ralph Beckett* a70
3 b f Nathaniel(IRE) Scorn (USA) (Seeking The Gold (USA))
***8663***[3]◆

**Frozen Angel (IRE)** *Tom Dascombe* 108
2 gr c Dark Angel(IRE) Cut No Ice (IRE) (Verglas (IRE))
1858[9] (2286) 3010[2] 3993[4] **5195a**[2] 5973a[5] 6446[8] 7618[10]

**Frozen Lake (USA)** *John O'Shea* a73 65
5 b g Elusive Quality(USA) Creative Design (USA) (Stravinsky (USA))
***1224***[4]◆ 2133[6] *8958*[9] *9219*[8]

**Frozon** *Brian Ellison* a63 56
4 b g Kheleyf(USA) Crozon (Peintre Celebre (USA))
3977[5] 4439[5] *4980*[2] ***(5850)*** *6953*[10] ***(7413)*** *7936*[11]

**Fruit Salad** *James Bethell* a80 74
4 ch m Monsieur Bond(IRE) Miss Apricot (Indian Ridge (IRE))
2409[3] 3793[6] *4305*[2] 4787[5] 6267[14] *7939*[6]◆ ***(8320)*** *8717*[8]

**Frutireu (IRE)** *Stefano Botti* 80
2 ch c Casamento(IRE) Farthing (IRE) (Mujadil (USA))
**8620a**[4]

**Fuchias De Cerisy (FR)** *M Planard* a21 31
4 b g Confuchias(IRE) Nagha (FR) (Enrique)
***930a***[11]

**Fuel Injection** *Paul Midgley* a61 57
6 gr g Pastoral Pursuits Smart Hostess (Most Welcome)
***270***[4] *446*[6] *1759*[6] 2076[12]

**Fuenteesteis (FR)** *R Avial Lopez* a79 94
3 ch f Falco(USA) Fantasy Lady (USA) (Grand Slam (USA))
**2978a**[7] 4027a[8]

**Fujaira Bridge (IRE)** *Roger Varian* 90
3 b g Sea The Stars(IRE) Garanciere (FR) (Anabaa (USA))
(1914) 2569[7] 3700[3] 4491[6] 6001[2] **(6516)** 7650[2]

**Fujaira Prince (IRE)** *Roger Varian* 84
3 rg g Pivotal Zam Zoom (IRE) (Dalakhani (IRE))
**5220**[2]◆

**Fujin** *Shaun Harris* a91 81
6 b g Oasis Dream Phantom Wind (USA) (Storm Cat (USA))
*229* *(303)* *(468)* *480*[2] *663*[6] *783*[5] *(1140)* *(1586)* *1820*[7] ***2114***[3] *2462*[4]◆ 6062[2] 6411[4] (6720) 7192[5] 7923[U]

**Fulham (IRE)** *Robyn Brisland* a83 73
3 b g Sir Prancealot(IRE) Bond Deal (IRE) (Pivotal)
*642*[2]◆ *(925)* 6880[6] 7386[3] **7766**[2]◆

**Full Court Press (IRE)** *J P Murtagh* a59 89
4 b g Frozen Power(IRE) Share The Feeling (IRE) (Desert King (IRE))
**6344**[4]

**Full Drago (ITY)** *Stefano Botti* 114
4 b h Pounced(USA) Almata (IRE) (Almutawakel)
(2866a) (3884a) 4879a[5] (7205a) **(8275a)**

**Full Intention** *Tom Dascombe* a77 89
3 b g Showcasing My Delirium (Haafhd)
*(1453)* 1838[5] 2557[5] **3038**[2] 3584[4] 4616[11] 5708[3] 6662[10]

**Fullmoon In Paris (FR)** *J-C Rouget* a79 88
3 ch f Literato(FR) Isalou (FR) (Unfuwain (USA))
***(6124a)***

**Full Of Promise** *Richard Fahey* a63 71
4 b m Kyllachy Arculinge (Paris House)
2843[6] 3332[2] **(3899)** **4438**[2] 4999[9] 5829[4] 6549[11] *7364*[8]

**Fullon Clarets** *Laura Mongan* a60 66
5 ch g Equiano(FR) Palinisa (FR) (Night Shift (USA))
*7878*[12] 8296[7] ***8881***[8] *9094*[9] *9323*[9]

**Full Sentimentale (FR)** *C Plisson* 15
2 gr f Stormy River(FR) Full Success (IRE) (Acclamation)
**6409a**[7]

**Full Shilling (IRE)** *Mrs Ann Mooney* a62 47
9 b m Intikhab(USA) Full Cream (USA) (Hennessy (USA))
***6798a***[5]

**Full Tilt Lad (IRE)** *Tim Easterby* 40
3 b g Lilbourne Lad(IRE) Tiltili (IRE) (Spectrum (IRE))
**1701**[5] 2135[10] 2345[9] 3180[12]

**Fully Focussed (IRE)** *Ann Duffield* 46
3 br f Intense Focus(USA) Folcungi (IRE) (Mukaddamah (USA))
*77*[9]

**Fulminato (GER)** *Andreas Suborics* 99
3 b c Excelebration(IRE) Fulminante (GER) (Dashing Blade)
**2002a**[5] 2869a[6]

**Fumbo Jumbo (IRE)** *Michael Dods* a60 90
4 b m Zebedee Baraloti (IRE) (Barathea (IRE))
4379[2] 5281[3] 5602[3] 6412[4] 6593[4] 7055[5] 8012[11]

**Fundamental (USA)** *J Smart* 105
5 rg h Arch(USA) Halo's Verse (USA) (Unbridled's Song (USA))
934a[3]

**Funding Deficit (IRE)** *Jim Goldie* a74 81
7 ch g Rakti Bukat Timah (Inchinor)
4477[9] 4854[14] 5184[5] 5994[9] 6434[11] 7525[18]

**Funkadelic** *Ben Haslam* a59 64
2 ch c Dandy Man(IRE) Cape Elizabeth (IRE) (Invincible Spirit (IRE))
2134[6] 3149[6] 3430[6] 4488[3] 4866[9] (6011) 7385[4] 8588[6]

**Funky Footsteps (IRE)**
*Eve Johnson Houghton* 75
3 ch f Footstepsinthesand Felin Gruvy (IRE) (Tagula (IRE))
2754[6] 4372[3] 5332[3] 5718[2] 6075[3] 7902[13]

**Fun Mac (GER)** *Hughie Morrison* a83 107
6 ch g Shirocco(GER) Favorite (GER) (Montjeu (IRE))
2525[3] 4073[5] 4639[4] (5198a) 7116[9] 8038[28] 8740[9]

**Funny Oyster (IRE)** *Chris Gordon* a21 62
4 gr m Dark Angel(IRE) Carpet Lover (IRE) (Fayruz)
1544[9] 2914[6] 3519[6]

**Fun Raiser (IRE)** *Harry Dunlop* a56
3 ch f Dream Ahead(USA) Party Appeal (USA) (Mr Greeley (USA))
393[6] 624[4] 1083[11] 1418[5]

**Fun To Mas (FR)** *C Lerner* a65 73
2 bb c Intense Focus(USA) Croisiere (USA) (Capote (USA))
6170a[5]

**Furia Cruzada (CHI)** *S Kobayashi* a108 111
5 b m Newfoundland(USA) Nuestra Machi (CHI) (Hussonet (USA))
(541a) 1045a[3] 1380a[13] 3961[10] 5460a[7] 6248a[9] 7177a[4] 7635a[6] 8273a[8]

**Furious Des Aigles (FR)**
*Mme C Barande-Barbe* a74 74
5 b g Fuisse(FR) Folie Des Aigles (FR) (Ocean Of Wisdom (USA))
2696a[16]

**Furni Factors** *Ronald Thompson* a38 55
2 b g Captain Gerrard(IRE) Calgary (Pivotal)
1495[8] 1872[9] 3460[6] 6567[8] 7518[11] 8780[7]

**Furous (FR)** *J Albrecht* a68
3 b g Oasis Dream February Sun (Monsun (GER))
6256a[13]

**Fursa (AUS)** *M F De Kock* 91
3 b f Hard Spun(USA) Red Princess (AUS) (Red Ransom (USA))
652a[11]

**Furze Boy** *Michael Easterby* 45
2 b g Mazameer(IRE) Alustar (Emarati (USA))
2221[9] 2740[8]

**Furzig** *Richard Fahey* a78
2 b g Monsieur Bond(IRE) Princess Cocoa (IRE) (Desert Sun)
8587[3]◆ 8916[5] (9465)

**Fusion Central (IRE)**
*Richard Hannon* a58 65
2 ch f Bahamian Bounty Whatever You Do (IRE) (Barathea (IRE))
2910[8] 3210 [4] 5216[9] 5933[5] 6504[2] 7226[8] 7985[2]

**Futoon (IRE)** *Kevin Ryan* a86 99
4 b m Kodiac Vermilliann (IRE) (Mujadil (USA))
1936[2] 2623[2] 3080[3] 4078[4] 4864[7] 5435[6] 5828[7] 7697a[10]

**Future Score (IRE)**
*Saeed bin Suroor* a66
2 br g Cape Cross(IRE) Theola (IRE) (Kalanisi (IRE))
7726[10] 8904[4]

**Fuwairt (IRE)** *Gavin Cromwell* a93 93
5 b g Arcano(IRE) Safiya Song (IRE) (Intikhab (USA))
1492[7] 2568[4] 3064[3] 3743[4] 5517a[16] 8222a[2]

**Fyre Cay (IRE)** *Kevin Ryan* 77
2 b c Red Jazz(USA) Anklesocks (IRE) (Night Shift (USA))
4760[2] (5334) (6432)◆

**Fyrecracker (IRE)** *Grant Tuer* a52 76
6 ch g Kheleyf(USA) Spirit of Hope (IRE) (Danehill Dancer (IRE))
1971[8]

**Fyxenna** *Clive Cox* 61
2 ch f Foxwedge(AUS) Good Enough (FR) (Mukaddamah (USA))
8472[5] 9080[P]

**Gabr** *Sir Michael Stoute* 107
2 ch c Intello(GER) Spacious (Nayef (USA))
5608[2]◆ 6403[2] (7333) 8415[5]

**Gabrial (IRE)** *Richard Fahey* a109 111
8 b g Dark Angel(IRE) Guajira (FR) (Mtoto)
86a[9] 429a[5] 934a[11] 1494[4] 2129[2] 2553[4] 3320[2] 3843[4] 4884[4] 5456[3] 5925[5] 6444[5] 6676[11] 8234[5] 8843[3]

**Gabrials Centurion (IRE)**
*David O'Meara* 67
2 b g Society Rock(IRE) Flamanda (Niniski (USA))
6347[5] 6674[5] 7141[4]◆ 8467[6]

**Gabrial's Kaka (IRE)** *Richard Fahey* a74 101
7 b g Jeremy(USA) Love In May (IRE) (City On A Hill (USA))
1492[15] 2568[10] 3064[8] 3589[7] 4293[5] 5382[10] 5683[3] 6014[5] 6414[7] 7142[4] 7595[3]

**Gabrial's King (IRE)** *Richard Fahey* a91 96
8 b g Hurricane Run(IRE) Danella (IRE) (Platini (GER))
(1976) 2157[7] 2552[6] 3067[3] 3594[7] 4355[5] 4921[4] 5924[7] 6680[9] 7143[6] 7615[7]

**Gabrial's Star** *Richard Fahey* a89 82
8 b g Hernando(FR) Grain Only (Machiavellian (USA))
2574[8] (3190) 3580[4] 4338[4] 4921[8] 5468[4] 6151[10] 6680[6] 7143[5] 7599[4] 7983[3] 8394[4] (8771) 8876[4] 9082[9] (9367)

**Gabrial The Devil (IRE)**
*David O'Meara* a69 65
2 b g Epaulette(AUS) Grasshoppergreen (IRE) (Barathea (IRE))
3576[9] 4101[5] 4956[5] 5752[6] 6951[2]◆ 7106[4] 8190[2]

**Gabrial The Duke (IRE)**
*Patrick Morris* a52 60
7 ch g Duke Of Marmalade(IRE) Literacy (USA) (Diesis)
3564[3] 4338[6] 5021[9] 5403[14] 6632[4] 8246[9]

**Gabrial The Hero (USA)**
*Richard Fahey* a98 101
8 b g War Front(USA) Ball Gown (USA) (Silver Hawk (USA))
1802[10]

**Gabrial The Saint (IRE)**
*Richard Fahey* 78
2 ch g Society Rock(IRE) Green Briar (Compton Place)
7141[2] 7593[3]

**Gabrial The Terror (IRE)**
*Patrick Morris* a64 57
7 b g Kheleyf(USA) Simla Bibi (Indian Ridge (IRE))
6[8] 380[3] 603[2] 727[10] 5021[5] 6632[3] 8955[7] 9270[5]

**Gabrial The Thug (FR)** *Ian Williams* a69 61
7 b g Azamour(IRE) Baliyna (USA) (Woodman (USA))
7[7] (383) (684) 928[2] 954[3] 1334[7] (2276) 3304[3] 4088[4]

**Gabrial The Tiger (IRE)**
*Richard Fahey* a53 94
5 b g Kodiac Invincible (Slip Anchor)
1606[11] 1910[12] 2528[8] 3565[8] 4294[3] 5683[2] 5929[10] 6672[7] 7108[5] (7594) 8107[3]

**Gabrielle** *Dr Jon Scargill* a61 63
4 b m Paco Boy(IRE) Bounty Box (Bahamian Bounty)
575[10] 1066[7] 5369[7] 5857[5] 7158[7] 8125[9] 8328[2]

**Gabriel's Oboe (IRE)** *Mark Walford* 55
2 b g Rip Van Winkle(IRE) Tinaar (USA) (Giant's Causeway (USA))
6658[7]

**Gabster (IRE)** *K Kukk* a47 42
4 ch m Iffraaj Mozie Cat (IRE) (Mozart (IRE))
1932a[5] 2670a[6] 5986a[5]

**Gaea (FR)** *S Jesus* a62 55
4 b m Prince Arch(USA) Pale Captive (IRE) (Barathea (IRE))
6365a[6] 7069a[8]

**Gaea (GER)** *Jean-Pierre Carvalho* 67
3 bb f Holy Roman Emperor(IRE) Guantana (GER) (Dynaformer (USA))
4393a[7]

**Gaelic Silver (FR)** *Gary Moore* a55 73
11 b g Lando(GER) Galatza (FR) (Johann Quatz (FR))
648[5] 998[2] 1695[5] 2365[6] 3304[7] 3753[16]

**Gaelic Spirit (IRE)** *Joseph Tuite* a64 69
2 b f Fast Company(IRE) Mystic Dream (Oasis Dream)
2756[4] 3215[5] 3611a[10] 6682[3] 7126[6] 7491[5]

**Gaelic Tiger** *David O'Meara* a90 92
4 b g Teofilo(IRE) Green Swallow (FR) (Green Tune (USA))
1781[2]◆ 2109[2] 2770[9] (3240)◆ 3671[3] 4429[8] 5397[5] 6000[P] (Dead)

**Gaelic Wizard (IRE)** *Karen Tutty* a53 58
9 b g Fasliyev(USA) Fife (IRE) (Lomond (USA))
1593[4] 2034[9] 2633[7] 3256[9] 3704[7] 3979[5] 4509[6] 4789[4] (5542) 6046[4] 6271[7] 6437[8] 7165[7] 8480[5] 8590[6]

**Gaetano Donizetti (IRE)** *D Smaga* a98 82
4 b h Makfi Galipette (Green Desert (USA))
5979a[12]

**Gaia Princess (IRE)** *Gary Moore* a65 52
3 gr f Dark Angel(IRE) Mount Eliza (IRE) (Danehill (USA))
3162[10] 3695[7] 4458[3] 5297[5] 7487[7] 8185[9]

**Gaillon (FR)** *T de Vlaminck* 37
3 b c Henrythenavigator(USA) Norfolk Broads (IRE) (Noverre (USA))
6256a[9]

**Gailo Chop (FR)** *Darren Weir* a110 114
6 ch g Deportivo Grenoble (FR) (Marignan (USA))
(8058a) 8446a[5] 8753a[11]

**Gaining** *Mme C Head-Maarek* 104
3 b f American Post Acquisition (Dansili)
(8666a)

**Gainsay** *Jonathan Portman* 43
2 b f Sayif(IRE) Pesse (IRE) (Eagle Eyed (USA))
4806[13] 5717[8] 6824[10]

**Gakku** *Roger Varian* a93 87
3 ch f Pivotal Gakalina (IRE) (Galileo (IRE))
2316[2]◆ 3006[5] 6760[2] 7109[2] 8548[4] 8979[3]

**Gala Celebration (IRE)**
*John Gallagher* a71 66
3 b g Excelebration(IRE) Elusive Galaxy (IRE) (Elusive City (USA))
(1428)◆ 1554[3] 3000[7] 3621[3] 4290[9] 6345[10] 6753[4] 7122[15] 7414[7] 7916[3] 8299[4]

**Galactic (IRE)** *Richard Hannon* a62 66
2 b c Roderic O'Connor(IRE) Star Cluster (Observatory (USA))
4577[5] 4885[6] 5547[5] 6395[6] 7057[5] 7764[9] 8164[7] 8349[9] 8595[2]

**Galactic Prince** *Andrew Balding* a76 86
3 ch g Dubawi(IRE) Opera Gal (IRE) (Galileo (IRE))
2174[7] 2998[3] 3531[3] (3779) 4886[3] 5525[7] 6415[2] 7397[7]

**Galactic Spirit** *Marco Botti* a73
2 ch c Dutch Art Gino's Spirits (Perugino (USA))
9154[2]◆

**Galahad** *Richard Fahey* a67 67
3 ch g Sir Prancealot(IRE) Miss Mediator (USA) (Consolidator (USA))
401[5]

**Galantes Ivresses (FR)** *J-P Gauvin* a75 62
4 ch m Nombre Premier Loyal Lass (USA) (Cadeaux Genereux)
8251a[9]

**Galapiat** *Mark Johnston* a84 109
4 b h Galileo(IRE) Lady Jane Digby (Oasis Dream)
(1608)◆ (2085) 2398[4] 3072[4] 3637a[6] 5353[8] 6857[8]

**Galikeo** *F Head* a84 97
3 b c Dansili Galikova (FR) (Galileo (IRE))
5982a[6]

**Galilee Chapel (IRE)**
*Alistair Whillans* a72 47
8 b g Baltic King Triple Zero (IRE) (Raise A Grand (IRE))
4430[9] 5097[7] 5701[16] 7236[11] 7885[13] 8909[3]◆ 9262[11]

**Galileo Gold** *Hugo Palmer* 123
4 ch h Paco Boy(IRE) Galicuix (Galileo (IRE))
2825[5]

**Galinka (FR)** *J-C Rouget* a78 71
3 b f Soldier Hollow Syllable (Halling (USA))
(6455a)

**Galinthias** *Simon Dow* a73 70
5 b g Sixties Icon Tidie France (USA) (Cape Town (USA))
354[9] 2913[6] (3521) 4523[5] 5788[7] 6557[8] 7216[7] 8641[8]

**Galipad** *A Fabre* 104
3 b c Galileo(IRE) Never Green (IRE) (Halling (USA))
1826a[4] 3879a[5] 5982a[3] 6913a[4]

**Galiteo (FR)** *Mme Pia Brandt* 96
4 b h Teofilo(IRE) Queen Of Poland (Halling (USA))
5198a[7]

**Galizzi (USA)** *Tim Vaughan* 99
6 b g Dansili Dancing Abbie (USA) (Theatrical (IRE))
3928[18]

**Gallante (IRE)** *Robert Hickmott* 112
6 b g Montjeu(IRE) Crazy Volume (IRE) (Machiavellian (USA))
8667a[23]

**Gallarate (FR)** *N Caullery* a68 70
4 b g Whipper(USA) Grise Bomb (USA) (Mr Greeley (USA))
(6125a)

**Galles (USA)** *S bin Ghadayer* a99 75
3 br c Bernardini(USA) Gracefield (USA) (Storm Cat (USA))
(8836a)

**Gallic Chieftain (FR)** *Darren Weir* a90 103
4 ch h Tamayuz Katerini (FR) (Cacique (IRE))
8056a[3] 8751a[5]

**Gallifrey** *Lucy Wadham* a88 88
3 b f Sir Percy Crystal Gal (IRE) (Galileo (IRE))
3507[2] 4364[2] 5155[8] 5715[4] 7507[4] 8548[12] (9096)

**Gallipoli (IRE)** *Richard Fahey* a90 95
4 b g Compton Place Altadena Lady (IRE) (Imperial Ballet (IRE))
(1606)◆ 2384[2] 3294[9] 3842[15]

**Galloping Hogan (IRE)**
*Sylvester Kirk* a55 63
2 b g Most Improved(IRE) Rapparee (USA) (Red Ransom (USA))
3965[8] 4520[8] 5641[10] 7082[7] (8141)

**Galloway Hills** *David Elsworth* a78
2 b c Kyllachy Bonnie Brae (Mujahid (USA))
8945[3]◆

**Galuppi** *J R Jenkins* a59 47
6 b g Galileo(IRE) La Leuze (IRE) (Caerleon (USA))
278[5] 461[5] 645[5] 820[9] 1699[8] 5405[3] 6109[5] 8815[12]

**Galvanize (USA)** *Doug Watson* a97 89
4 b h Medaglia d'Oro(USA) Enthused (USA) (Seeking The Gold (USA))
537a[2]◆ (8714a)

**Gambia Bird (IRE)**
*Lennart Hammer-Hansen* 96
3 b f Rajsaman(FR) Gaggia (GER) (Monsun (GER))
8838a[4]

**Gambino (IRE)** *John David Riches* a62 70
7 b g Red Clubs(IRE) Temptation Island (IRE) (Spectrum (IRE))
1409[8] 1893[8] 6635[P] (Dead)

**Gambissara (FR)**
*Lennart Hammer-Hansen* 100
4 b m Adlerflug(GER) Gaggia (GER) (Monsun (GER))
1659a[11]

**Gambit** *Robert Cowell* a93 77
4 b g New Approach(IRE) Sospel (Kendor (FR))
1512[12] 1969[5] 2301[6] 4699[8] 5744[10] 6617[8] 7999[9]

**Gambol (FR)** *Ian Williams* a62 64
7 ch g New Approach(IRE) Guardia (GER) (Monsun (GER))
218[7] 333[6] 924[5] (3026) 3863[3] 4809[10]

**Game Player (IRE)** *Roger Varian* 77
2 gr c Dark Angel(IRE) Lucky Clio (IRE) (Key Of Luck (USA))
3037[7] 5420[4]

**Gamesome (FR)** *Paul Midgley* a77 102
6 b g Rock Of Gibraltar(IRE) Hot Coal (USA) (Red Ransom (USA))
1876[3] 2391[4] 3092[6] 3829[13] 5129[3] 5402[10] 5920[7] 6593[5] 7557[4] 7939[5] 8293[8]

**Game Starter (IRE)**
*Saeed bin Suroor* 112
3 b c Dubawi(IRE) Opera Cloak (IRE) (Cape Cross (IRE))
(4097) (5609)◆ (7150)

**Gamesters Icon** *Bryan Smart* 72
2 b f Sixties Icon Gamesters Lady (Almushtarak (IRE))
4528[5] 5371[8] 6659[2] 7160[2] 8287[4]

**Gamesters Lad** *Oliver Greenall* a39 15
5 b g Firebreak Gamesters Lady (Almushtarak (IRE))
733[9] 1072[6] 1322[9] 1563[6] 2313[8] 2679[8]

**Game Theory (IRE)** *N Clement* a86 105
5 b m Aussie Rules(USA) Atullia (GER) (Tertullian (USA))
(3883a) 6804a[2] 7305a[8] 8665a[9]

**Gamgoom** *Mario Hofer* a87 91
6 b g Exceed And Excel(AUS) Danidh Dubai (IRE) (Noverre (USA))
(81a)

**Gamrah (IRE)** *James Tate* a66
4 ch m Exceed And Excel(AUS) Fashionable (Nashwan (USA))
165[4] 394[6]

**Ganayem (IRE)** *Owen Burrows* 68
2 gr f Frankel Rose Of Summer (USA) (El Prado (IRE))
6480[4]

**Gangland** *Richard Fahey* a69 74
2 gr g Lethal Force(IRE) Miss Dutee (Dubawi (IRE))
2786[7] 3460[2] 4101[2] 5121[5] 6466[4] 6977a[17] 7362[2] (8325)◆ 8741[3]

**Gang Warfare** *Jamie Osborne* a107 100
6 b g Medicean Light Impact (IRE) (Fantastic Light (USA))
268[5] 746[11]

**Gannicus** *Brendan Powell* a69 73
6 b g Phoenix Reach(IRE) Rasmani (Medicean)
2511[5] 2913[8] 5555[5] 5968[10] 7216[9]

**Ganton Par** *Michael Easterby* 49
2 b g Frozen Power(IRE) Sheer Indulgence (FR) (Pivotal)
4862[5] 6403[17]

**Garam (IRE)** *Hugo Palmer* a77
3 b f Pivotal Coy (IRE) (Danehill (USA))
(76) 458[9]

**Garance (FR)** *J-C Rouget* a101 102
3 b f Teofilo(IRE) Germance (USA) (Silver Hawk (USA))
4027a[2] 8088a[2] 8986a[3]

**Garboesque (IRE)** *Shaun Harris* a29 19
3 b f Elzaam(AUS) Princess Nicole (IRE) (Alhaarth (IRE))
1[8]

**Garcon De Soleil** *Michael Blanshard* a51 46
4 b g Danehill Dancer(IRE) Darinza (FR) (Dalakhani (IRE))
3694[7] 4967[5] 5716[7] 6796[4]◆ 8135[6] 8846[7] 9158[9]

**Garden Oasis** *Sir Michael Stoute* 62
2 b c Excelebration(IRE) Queen Arabella (Medicean)
4367[6] 5655[4]

**Gardinia** *Tim Easterby* 26
2 b f Pivotal Garden Row (IRE) (Invincible Spirit (IRE))
5179[9] 5631[13]

**Garlingari (FR)**
*Mme C Barande-Barbe* a94 115
6 b g Linngari(IRE) Garlinote (FR) (Poliglote)
3856a[2] 5046a[2] 6052a[2] 6499a[5] (7177a) (7638a) 9171a[9]

**Garnetta** *Amanda Perrett* a45 41
3 b f Poet's Voice Petit A Petit (IRE) (Holy Roman Emperor (IRE))
1286[8] 1503[9] 2231[11]

**Garopaba (IRE)** *M Delzangles* 64
3 b f Pour Moi(IRE) Zigarra (Halling (USA))
8732a[4]

**Garrick** *John Gosden* a81 90
3 b c Galileo(IRE) Rimth (Oasis Dream)
(580)◆ 8111[7] 8561[2]

**Garsington** *Ed Dunlop* a37
2 b c Intello(GER) Ruse (Diktat)
8952[13] 9137[7] 9433[10]

**Garter (IRE)** *Richard Fahey* a66 58
4 b m Fastnet Rock(AUS) Princess Iris (IRE) (Desert Prince (IRE))
394[3] 505[3] 6964[18] 7571[6] 8108[6]

**Garth Rockett** *Brendan Powell* a62 62
3 b g Delegator Leelu (Largesse)
3024[12] 4150[9] 5076[4] (5512) 7005[10] 8031[7] (8551) 9093[4]

**Gasalto (FR)** *Y Barberot* a58 64
3 ch g Medicean Sainte Colombe (IRE) (Danehill Dancer (IRE))
3554a[4]

**Gas Monkey** *Julia Feilden* 55
2 b g Cityscape Bavarica (Dansili)
4291[11] 5507[9] 7913[4]

**Gasta (IRE)** *J S Bolger* 92
2 b f Vocalised(USA) Buille Cliste (IRE) (Smart Strike (CAN))
4418a[8] 6488a[6] 6974a[6] 7859a[5] 8265a[7]

**Gather** *Amanda Perrett* a74 61
2 b f Showcasing Acquisition (Dansili)
6861[7] 7453[2] 7997[3]

**Gatillo** *Julia Feilden* a55 58
4 gr g Showcasing Crystal Gale (IRE) (Verglas (IRE))
6[6] 986[8] 1498[9] 2762[11] 2974[6] 7465[10] 8124[4]◆ 8473[4] 8807[3] 8985[9] 9073[12]

**Gato Del Oro (USA)** *Richard Baltas* a100
3 b c Medaglia d'Oro(USA) Funny Feeling (USA) (Distorted Humor (USA))
8576a[7]

**Gattaia (USA)** *Ralph Beckett* a64
2 ch f Kitten's Joy(USA) Shaaraat (USA) (Distorted Humor (USA))
6575[7] 9313[5]

**Gaudi (IRE)** *John Gosden* a74
2 b c Invincible Spirit(IRE) Alava (IRE) (Anabaa (USA))
8642[5]◆ 8839[2]

**Gaval** *David Barron* a62 82
3 b g Major Cadeaux Bold Bidder (Indesatchel (IRE))
2924[3] 3403[6] (5291) (5535)◆ 5959[5]

**Gavarnie Encore** *Michael Blanshard* a55 42
5 b h Intikhab(USA) Greeley Bright (USA) (Mr Greeley (USA))
854[5] 1084[3] 1298[9] 1894[6] 3809[10]

**Gavlar** *William Knight* a98 97
6 b g Gentlewave(IRE) Shawhill (Dr Fong (USA))
746[4] (1309) 1770[8] 2157[4] 2788[7] 3534[6] 4356[10] 5351[6] 5912[6] 6793[5] 7412[3] 7785[5]

**Gavota** *Roger Charlton* 105
2 b f Bated Breath Ombre (Galileo (IRE))
(5885) (6583) 7578[3]◆ 8002[2]

**Gavroche (USA)** *Maria Ritchie* a80 79
6 ch g Distorted Humor(USA) Michita (USA) (Dynaformer (USA))
8836a[6]
**Gawdawpalin (IRE)** *Sylvester Kirk* a93 97
4 b g Holy Roman Emperor(IRE) Dirtybirdie (Diktat)
1341[2]◆ 1502[4] 2086[3] 3323[9] (5353) 5913[2] 6872[4] 7354[4] 7903[6] 8468[4] 8740[5]
**Gealach Ghorm (IRE)**
*Sarah Hollinshead* a73 53
3 b g Finsceal Fior(IRE) Saintly Wish (USA) (St Jovite (USA))
8497[8] 9159[7]
**Geesala Brave (IRE)** *John Quinn* a65 68
2 b c Arcano(IRE) Wong Again (Araafa (IRE))
4995[8] 5537[4] 6311[2] 7362[5] 8288[5]
**Gee Sixty Six** *Mark H Tompkins* a63 68
3 b g Mount Nelson Azure Mist (Bahamian Bounty)
4376 5525◆ 1226[2] 2264[5] 2998[5] 5034[3] 6023[6] 7060[7] 7992[10]
**Geetanjali (IRE)** *Michael Bell* a20
2 b f Roderic O'Connor(IRE) Scylla Cadeaux (IRE) (Cadeaux Genereux)
7757[12]
**Gembari** *Ivan Furtado* a62 62
2 b g Denounce Zagarock (Rock Of Gibraltar (IRE))
6108[6] 6654[9] 6897[10] 8120[8] 8371[11] 8848[2] (9238)
**Gemini** *Charles Hills* 40
2 b f Makfi Gaze (Galileo (IRE))
8347[7]
**Gemologist (IRE)** *Mark Johnston* a47 69
2 b f Sir Percy Tiffany Diamond (IRE) (Sadler's Wells (USA))
3965[9] 4340[3] 5154[8] 5756[6] 8676[9]
**Gen Chi (GER)** *P Vovcenko* 57
3 rg f Tai Chi(GER) Galla Placidia (GER) (Kaldounevees (FR))
4393a[9]
**Gendarme (IRE)** *Richard Hannon* 73
2 b c Lawman(FR) Gravitation (Galileo (IRE))
7120[11] 8162[3]
**General Alexander (IRE)**
*Brian Ellison* a57 81
4 gr g Zebedee Alexander Express (IRE) (Sri Pekan (USA))
1915[3] 5379[17] 5696[7] 6429[2] 6672[10] 7933[2]
**General Allenby** *Henry Tett* a55 58
3 b g Medicean Cat Hunter (One Cool Cat (USA))
2060[11] 2371[6] 3180[5] 3520[6] 4742[4] 5209[5] 5581[2] 6376[4] 6820[2] 7233[3] (7922) 9095[7]
**General Brook (IRE)** *John O'Shea* a57 65
7 b g Westerner Danse Grecque (IRE) (Sadler's Wells (USA))
421[6] 2178[6] 9092[13]
**General Gerrard** *Michael Madgwick* a34 50
3 b g Captain Gerrard(IRE) Dockside Strike (Docksider (USA))
2171[8] 2674[4] 3157[7] 4458[12] 5871[6] 6724[6] 8185[5]
**General Hazard (IRE)**
*Archie Watson* a91 77
4 gr g Cacique(IRE) In The Soup (USA) (Alphabet Soup (USA))
440[2] (992)◆ (1144) 1502[7] 4206[14] 4712[5] (8956) (9205)
**General Jack (IRE)**
*Eve Johnson Houghton* a67
2 br c Society Rock(IRE) City Dazzler (IRE) (Elusive City (USA))
9465[4]
**General Line (USA)** *Doug Watson* a70 39
3 ch f Sidney's Candy(USA) Greeley Appealing (USA) (Mr Greeley (USA))
649a[12]
**General Macarthur (USA)**
*David Simcock* a88 102
4 b h War Front(USA) Imagine (IRE) (Sadler's Wells (USA))
205a[9] 698a[7] 2310[5] 3837[4] 4410[4] 4916[10]
**General Marius (IRE)** *Roger Varian* 64
2 gr c Holy Roman Emperor(IRE) Megaspiel (Singspiel (IRE))
5144[6] 5786[6] 6147[5] 6749[3] 7914[10] 8120[5]
**General Marshall (USA)**
*M F De Kock* a52 47
5 b g War Front(USA) Julie From Dixie (USA) (Dixie Union (USA))
250a[13]
**General Tufto** *Charles Smith* a57 54
12 b g Fantastic Light(USA) Miss Pinkerton (Danehill (USA))
7[3] 68[3] 390[5] 482[2] 636[7] 1075[2] 1187[2] 1545[3] 1823[4] 1868[6] 3137[11] 9343[5]
**Generalyse** *Anabel K Murphy* a58 66
8 b g Cadeaux Genereux Dance To The Blues (IRE) (Danehill Dancer (IRE))
80[12] 2214[2] 2962[4] 3469[6] 4182[6] 5081[7]
**General Zoff** *William Muir* 71
2 b g Zoffany(IRE) Aunt Julia (In The Wings)
3165[10] 3668[6] 4909[3] 5366[7] 6395[9]
**Genereuse Lady (FR)**
*Mme C Barande-Barbe* a59 57
2 ch f Tigron(USA) Genereuse Gold (FR) (Gold Away (IRE))
8691a[9]
**Generous Times** *Chris Grant*
3 b f Bahri(USA) Gerardina (Generous (IRE))
1822[7]
**Genetics (FR)** *Andrew Balding* a81 85
3 b c Manduro(GER) Garmerita (FR) (Poliglote)
8111[8] 8423[9] 9206[5]
**Genres** *Sally Haynes* a73 73
5 b g Champs Elysees Musical Horizon (USA) (Distant View (USA))
(174)◆ 613[3] 727[P] (2427) 2920[7]
**Gentil J (IRE)** *H Rogers* 90
4 b m Jeremy(USA) Lady Pitrizza (IRE) (Night Shift (USA))
1388a[12] 3108a[8]
**Gentle Jaime (IRE)** *Leo Braem* a47
4 gr g Amadeus Wolf Lady Georgina (Linamix (FR))
1070a[8]

**Gentleman Giles (IRE)**
*Jamie Osborne* a62 39
3 b c Dutch Art Sularina (IRE) (Alhaarth (IRE))
(126) 264[6] 456[5]
**Gentlemen** *Phil McEntee* a101 66
6 ch g Ad Valorem(USA) Stoney Cove (IRE) (Needwood Blade)
33[8] 170[2] 326[9] 639[4] 795a[4] 957[7] 1152[8] 1454[4] 1622[8] 7455[4] 7828[12] 8129[7] 8540[10] 8872[9] 8905[U] 9206[6]
**Genuine Approval (IRE)**
*John Butler* a66 52
4 ch m Approve(IRE) Genuinely (IRE) (Entrepreneur)
36[8] 648[9] 1028[7] 1364[10] 2909[12] 4165[10] 4982[13] 9212[9]
**Geoff Potts (IRE)** *Richard Fahey* a78 76
4 ch g Zebedee Our Sheila (Bahamian Bounty)
355[3] 808[2] 2404[8] 3278[6] 4379[15] (5750) 6314[5] 7244[3] 7923[4] 8818[3] 8990[7]
**Geoffrey's Girl (FR)** *Richard Rowe* a64 75
4 b m Croco Rouge(IRE) Camas (FR) (Hamas (IRE))
5217[6]
**Geological (IRE)**
*Damian Joseph English* a88 102
5 b g Rock Of Gibraltar(IRE) Bean Uasal (IRE) (Oasis Dream)
1233a[6] 1385a[15] 5517a[18] 5688a[13] 6961a[10] 8222a[12] 8438a[14] 9247a[2]
**Geonpi (IRE)** *N Bellanger* a84 76
6 b g Footstepsinthesand Maria Gabriella (IRE) (Rock Of Gibraltar (IRE))
5979a[6] 6648a[16]
**Geophony (IRE)** *Mark Johnston* a71 76
3 b g Canford Cliffs(IRE) Dawn Chorus (IRE) (Mukaddamah (USA))
1678[4] 2107[9] 2703[9] 3243[7] 8108[10]
**Geordie George (IRE)**
*Rebecca Menzies* a62 66
5 b g Kodiac Trika (First Trump)
1868[3] 2919[6] (3487)◆ 4608[7] 5497[8] 6528[6]
**Geordielad** *Jamie Osborne* a43 9
3 ch g Geordieland(FR) Adees Dancer (Danehill Dancer (IRE))
2092[8] 2584[13] 2957[8] 3326[9] 7324[8]
**George (IRE)** *Sylvester Kirk* a82 83
2 b g Dragon Pulse(IRE) Before The Storm (Sadler's Wells (USA))
2779[3] 3164[5] 5504[9] 6065[2] 7647[2] 8180[2]
**George Bailey (IRE)**
*Suzzanne France* a53 46
5 b g Zebedee Zuzu (IRE) (Acclamation)
445[6] 1371[7] 1973[7] 3201[5] 4997[8] 6046[9] 8258[8] 8590[14]
**George Baker (IRE)** *George Baker* a65 66
10 b g Camacho Petite Maxine (Sharpo)
145[5] 426[6] 1086[7] 1603[13] 4713[4] 5985a[3]
**George Bowen (IRE)** *Richard Fahey* a86 97
5 gr g Dark Angel(IRE) Midnight Oasis (Oasis Dream)
1515[13] 2156[9] 2736[6] 3324[3] (3757) 4925a[7] 5435[10] 5637[6] 6206[6] 6971a[11] 7612[3] 8383[15]
**George Cinq** *George Scott* a99 99
7 b g Pastoral Pursuits Fairnilee (Selkirk (USA))
598[6] (1208)◆ 1494[21]
**George Dryden (IRE)** *Ann Duffield* a87 98
5 gr g Zebedee Key To Fortune (GER) (Big Shuffle (USA))
2611[5] 4072[17] 5616[7] 6206[17] 7828[9]
**George Of Hearts (FR)**
*Richard Hughes* 78
2 gr c Kendargent(FR) Bugie D'Amore (Rail Link)
7352[4] 8388[2]
**George Reme (IRE)** *John Quinn* a78 75
3 ch g Power My Sweet Georgia (IRE) (Royal Applause)
1878[4] 2376[5] 3317[8] 3934[3] 4557[5] 4999[6] 5666[11] 6067[11] 9017[6]
**George Villiers (IRE)** *John Gosden* a77 75
2 b c Dubawi(IRE) Comic (IRE) (Be My Chief (USA))
3783[3]◆ 8140[4] (8634)
**George William** *Richard Hannon* a95 105
4 b g Paco Boy(IRE) Basque Beauty (Nayef (USA))
(1734) 1960[4] 2606[2] 3963[22] 4636[10] 7356[3] (7901) 8234[16]
**Georgian Bay (IRE)** *K R Burke* a102 94
7 b g Oratorio(IRE) Jazzie (FR) (Zilzal (USA))
459[9] 2283[6] 2730[4] 2884[3] 4207[3] 4410[7] (5396) 6322[6] 6933[11] 8138[7] 8811[2]
**Georgian Manor (IRE)**
*Sir Michael Stoute* a73 57
2 br g Iffraaj Southern House (IRE) (Paris House)
5608[6] 7511[3]
**Georgiezar** *Brian Forsey* a16
4 ch m Winker Watson Quaker Parrot (Compton Place)
8995[9] 9304[6]
**Georgio (GER)** *Andrew Balding* a50 60
3 b g Approve(IRE) Gillenia (GER) (Greinton)
385[7] 895[11] 1107[11]
**Gepard (GER)** *C Zschache* 91
3 b c Soldier Hollow Golden Time (GER) (Surumu (GER))
4422a[11]
**Geraldine (GER)** *Stuart Williams* a65 52
3 b f Royal Applause Golden Whip (GER) (Seattle Dancer (USA))
160[3] 323[2]
**German Bight (IRE)** *Keith Dalgleish* a75
2 br f Makfi Saint Lucia (IRE) (Whipper (USA))
(8802)
**German Whip** *Gary Moore* a74 56
4 b g Zoffany(IRE) Tan Tan (King's Best (USA))
6263[5] 6753[7] 7769[8] 9094[7] 9431[9]
**Gerrard's Return** *Joeri Goossens* a41 54
3 ch c Captain Gerrard(IRE) Dawn Lightning (Dark Angel (IRE))
8305a[9]

**Gerry** *Matthew Salaman*
4 ch m Captain Gerrard(IRE) Bhima (Polar Falcon (USA))
600[10] 1064[8]
**Gerry The Glover (IRE)**
*Brian Ellison* a89 81
5 b g Approve(IRE) Umlani (IRE) (Great Commotion (USA))
2030[4]◆ 2291[6] 2701[3]◆ 4358[2] 4959[4] 7034[3]◆ 7570[3] 8315[4]
**Getback In Paris (IRE)**
*Richard Hughes* a92 99
4 ch g Galileo(IRE) Elusive Wave (IRE) (Elusive City (USA))
1079[2] 1502[5] 2233[2] 2959[4] 3160[2] (3534) 4828[2] 5638[3] 7614[7] 8038[5]
**Get Even** *Jo Hughes* a77 87
2 b f Multiplex Retaliator (Rudimentary (USA))
1335a[2] (1627) 2801[6]◆ 3611a[8] 5026[3] 5448a[5] 5978a[7] 7621[12]
**Getgo** *David Lanigan* a67 69
3 b g Excelebration(IRE) Hip (Pivotal)
2071[5] 2625[11] 4601[9] 5126[6] 5509[2] 6471[10] 7235[4] 7917[4]
**Get Knotted (IRE)** *Michael Dods* a101 106
5 ch g Windsor Knot(IRE) Genuinely (IRE) (Entrepreneur)
2384[6] 2767[5] 3089[3] 3842[9] 4353[4] 5094[5] (5434) 6186[4] 6922[3] 7611[5] 8104[6] 8737[8]
**Getna (USA)** *Richard Hannon* a75 70
3 b f Lonhro(AUS) Aquarius Star (IRE) (Danehill Dancer (IRE))
1503[3] 2564[5] 3472[2] 4145[2] 5656[3] 6340[8]
**Gettin' Lucky** *John Balding* a54 28
4 ch g Bertolini(USA) Loose Caboose (IRE) (Tagula (IRE))
271[4] 446[11] 852[2] 1371[6] 7763[10] 9071[3] 9344[3] 9444[6]
**G Eye Joe** *James Given* a60 59
2 ch c Lethal Force(IRE) Winifred Jo (Bahamian Bounty)
5350[7] 8982[4] 9177[13]
**G Force (IRE)** *Adrian Paul Keatley* a83 104
6 b g Tamayuz Flanders (IRE) (Common Grounds)
4072[20] 4925a[17] 7856a[4] 8738[7] 9247a[10]
**Ghaamer (USA)** *A R Al Rayhi* a66 111
7 b g Hard Spun(USA) Teeba (USA) (Seeking The Gold (USA))
87a[3] 892a[10] 1044a[16]
**Ghadaayer (IRE)** *Sir Michael Stoute* a82 88
3 b f Shamardal(USA) Eldalil (Singspiel (IRE))
(2078) 3189[2] (4096) 5506[4] 6358[14] 7484[9]
**Ghaiyyath (IRE)** *Charlie Appleby* 111
2 b c Dubawi(IRE) Nightime (IRE) (Galileo (IRE))
7117[3] (7543) (8036)
**Ghalib (IRE)** *Amy Murphy* a92 101
5 ch g Lope De Vega(IRE) Gorband (USA) (Woodman (USA))
2115[5] 2617[2] 3294[8] 5159[6] 6936[7] 7909[2] (8297)
**Ghanimah** *William Haggas* a75
2 b f Invincible Spirit(IRE) Gile Na Greine (IRE) (Galileo (IRE))
7995[4] 8544[4] (8998)
**Ghaseedah** *Simon Crisford* a76 70
3 b f Kyllachy Represent (IRE) (Exceed And Excel (AUS))
3595[8] 4568[3] 6265[9] 7793[3] (9071)◆
**Ghayadh** *Hugo Palmer* a73 80
2 b g Kyllachy Safe House (IRE) (Exceed And Excel (AUS))
(4598) 5151[4] 5531[4] 6330[10] 7536[4] 8343[4]
**Ghayyar (IRE)** *Richard Hannon* a82 85
3 b g Power Al Ihtithar (IRE) (Barathea (IRE))
933a[11] 2520[4] 3505[6] 6344[7]
**Ghazan (IRE)** *Clive Cox* 72
2 ch c Iffraaj Sweet Firebird (IRE) (Sadler's Wells (USA))
5709[7] 7026[5] 8161[3]
**Gheedaa (USA)** *William Haggas* a87 96
3 b f Tamayuz Soohaad (USA) (Hard Spun (USA))
3835[4] 4864[5] 6358[6]
**Ghepardo** *Richard Hannon* a74 73
2 b f Havana Gold(IRE) Clincher (Royal Applause)
2217[3]◆ 2502[14] 5480[2] 6375[8] (6719) 7482[2] 8746[3] 9023[2] 9188[2] 9415[3]
**Ghinia (IRE)** *Pam Sly* 89
6 b m Mastercraftsman(IRE) Jorghinia (FR) (Seattle Slew (USA))
1687[6] 2358[3] 3009[3] 3683[2] 4621[9] 5888[2] 7279[5] 8142[10]
**Ghor (FR)** *R Roels* a42 80
9 ch g Gold Away(IRE) Pragmatica (Inchinor)
5176a[14]
**Ghost** *John Quinn* 59
2 gr f Footstepsinthesand Action Platinum (IRE) (Act One)
5665[4] 6056[5] 6567[7]
**Ghost Hunter (USA)** *Jamie Ness* a101 105
7 b g Ghostzapper(USA) Hartfelt (USA) (Kafwain (USA))
5977a[11]
**Ghostly Arc (IRE)** *Noel Wilson* a48 67
5 b g Arcano(IRE) Cheyenne's Spirit (IRE) (Sadler's Wells (USA))
6551[5] 7659[9] 8314[9]
**Ghost Serge (IRE)** *Archie Watson* 97
2 gr c Zebedee Cornakill (USA) (Stormin Fever (USA))
(3244) (3895) 5395[5] 6396[6]
**Ghost Train (IRE)** *Tim McCarthy* a69 59
8 b g Holy Roman Emperor(IRE) Adrastea (IRE) (Monsun (GER))
768[RR] 1490[RR]
**Ghostwatch (IRE)** *Charlie Appleby* 76
2 b c Dubawi(IRE) Nature Spirits (FR) (Beat Hollow)
6142[3] 6854[3]
**Ghurfah** *J-C Rouget* 87
3 ch f Tamayuz Indian Ink (IRE) (Indian Ridge (IRE))
1657a[8]

**Giant Expectations (USA)**
*Peter Eurton* a116
4 ch h Frost Giant(USA) Sarahisittrue (USA) (Is It True (USA))
8576a[6]
**Giant Redwood (IRE)** *Ben Haslam* a71
5 b g Galileo(IRE) Gwynn (IRE) (Darshaan)
8771[P]
**Giant Sequoia (USA)** *Des Donovan* a47 17
13 ch g Giant's Causeway(USA) Beware Of The Cat (USA) (Caveat (USA))
645[6] 839[4]
**Giant Spark** *Paul Midgley* a87 97
5 b g Orientor Annie Gee (Primo Valentino (IRE))
1103[8] 1520a[8] 2736[14] 4037[4] 4505[7] 5123[5] 5457[14]
**Giantstepsahead (IRE)** *Alan Bailey* a82 86
8 br g Footstepsinthesand Salty Air (IRE) (Singspiel (IRE))
163[7] 507[10] 1289[5]
**Giant's Treasure (IRE)**
*Richard Hannon* a86
3 b c Shamardal(USA) Ballybacka Lady (IRE) (Hurricane Run (IRE))
(1244)
**Gianyar (FR)** *E Lellouche* a88 101
4 b h Le Havre(IRE) Chandi Dasa (IRE) (Sadler's Wells (USA))
6915a[5]
**Gibbs Hill (GER)** *Roger Varian* a109 98
4 gr g Mastercraftsman(IRE) Gold Charm (GER) (Key Of Luck (USA))
(2165)◆ 2804[3] (4498)◆
**Giennah (IRE)**
*Daniel Mark Loughnane* a58 58
3 b f Tamayuz Jamaayel (Shamardal (USA))
765[5] 2506[6] 3729[5]
**Gifted Heir (IRE)** *Ray Peacock*
13 b g Princely Heir(IRE) Inzar Lady (IRE) (Inzar (USA))
5895[11] 6345[15]
**Gifted Master (IRE)** *Hugo Palmer* a114 113
4 b g Kodiac Shobobb (Shamardal (USA))
774a[4] 1373a[9] 5149[7] (5633) (6428) 8003[8] (8845)◆
**Gift From God** *Hugo Froud* a54 57
4 b g Teofilo(IRE) Piffling (Pivotal)
9232[5]
**Gift In Time (IRE)** *James Given* a81 82
2 b g Society Rock(IRE) Gift Of Time (Cadeaux Genereux)
3490[2]◆ 3993[15] (4888)◆ 5596[3] 6330[13] 7318[8] 7919[4]
**Gift Of Hera** *Sylvester Kirk* 68
2 ch f Nathaniel(IRE) Premier Prize (Selkirk (USA))
6777[8]◆ 7399[5] 7898[5] 8354[5]
**Gift Of Loulins** *Tony Coyle* 42
2 b f Aussie Rules(USA) Gift Of Love (IRE) (Azamour (IRE))
4258[9] 5371[10] 5999[7]
**Giftorm (USA)** *Fredrik Reuterskiold* a101 96
7 b g War Pass(USA) High Cholesterol (USA) (Until Sundown (USA))
321a[P]
**Gigi (IRE)** *Charles Hills* a59 65
2 bb f Iffraaj Dubai Flower (Manduro (GER))
3174[5] 3815[9] 6037[6]
**Gilded Heaven** *Roger Varian* 59
2 ch f Medicean Heavenly (Pivotal)
5938[6]
**Gilded Hour (IRE)** *Ralph Beckett* a72 70
2 b f Bated Breath Mimisel (Selkirk (USA))
8130[2] 8735[3]
**Gilded Reflection** *Ralph Beckett* a80 77
4 b m Zoffany(IRE) Vanity (IRE) (Thatching)
2135[6] 2952[5]◆ 4698[4] 5549[4]
**Gilgamesh** *George Scott* a94 90
3 b g Foxwedge(AUS) Flaming Cliffs (USA) (Kingmambo (USA))
(902) (1149)◆ (2348)◆ 8812[4]◆
**Gilmer (IRE)** *James Ewart* a57 83
6 b g Exceed And Excel(AUS) Cherokee Rose (IRE) (Dancing Brave (USA))
3567[2] (4080) 5093[3] 5415[9] 5471[6] 7223[6] 7923[9] 8296[4]
**Ginbar (IRE)** *Tom Dascombe* 83
2 b c Kodiac Double Fantasy (GER) (Indian Ridge (IRE))
4888[2] 5262[2] 6231[3] (6853) (7596)◆ 8008[16]
**Ginger Charlie** *Ruth Carr* a35 50
4 ch g Haafhd Mandarin Lady (Timeless Times (USA))
1545[10] 2918[10] 3242[10]
**Ginger Jack** *Jo Hughes* a84 94
10 ch g Refuse To Bend(IRE) Coretta (IRE) (Caerleon (USA))
4057[2] 5032[4] 5668[11]
**Ginger Lady (IRE)** *Mark H Tompkins* a57 54
3 ch f Helmet(AUS) Theola (IRE) (Kalanisi (IRE))
3438[6] 9088[4] 9202[9]
**Ginger Love** *Bryan Smart* 53
3 ch g Kheleyf(USA) La Peinture (GER) (Peintre Celebre (USA))
1680[13] 3984[7] 6571[4]◆
**Ginger Truffle** *Brett Johnson* a51 51
3 ch f Sixties Icon Whassup (FR) (Midyan (USA))
288[9] 397[5] 3942[5] 4179[4] 4458[7] 5052[9]
**Gin In The Inn (IRE)** *Richard Fahey* a79 98
4 b g Alfred Nobel(IRE) Nose One's Way (IRE) (Revoque (IRE))
(1833)◆ (2303) 2528[2] 3593[12] 4925a[8] 5457[2] 5637[13] 6971a[6] 8393[10] 9074[8]
**Gino Severini (IRE)** *J A Stack* a75 90
3 b g Fastnet Rock(AUS) Green Castle (IRE) (Indian Ridge (IRE))
(1386a)
**Ginzan** *Malcolm Saunders* a82 85
9 b m Desert Style(IRE) Zyzania (Zafonic (USA))
3424[6] 3919[4] (4178) 4732[5]
**Gio Game (USA)** *Mark Casse* a79 96
2 b f Gio Ponti(USA) Game For More (USA) (More Than Ready (USA))
8603a[9]

**Giogiobbo** *Francesco Santella* a95 89
4 b h Bahamian Bounty Legnani (Fasliyev (USA))
(384a)

**Giovanni Dal Ponte** *J-C Rouget* 72
2 gr c Holy Roman Emperor(IRE) Cheriearch (USA) (Arch (USA))
5776a[3]

**Giovanni Medici** *Seamus Durack* a43 63
2 b c Medicean Hadeeya (Oratorio (IRE))
3783[8]◆ 4465[5] 5292[3] 6613[7] 7510[8] 8349[10]

**Gipoia (FR)** *M Delzangles* 103
3 ch f Medicean Really Lovely (IRE) (Galileo (IRE))
2978a[4] 4424a[10] 6914a[6]

**Girlofinkandstars (IRE)** *Rae Guest* a21 53
3 b f Power Gaselee (USA) (Toccet (USA))
637[9]

**Girl's Hope (IRE)** *F-H Graffard* a82 90
4 gr m Dark Angel(IRE) Allegrina (IRE) (Barathea (IRE))
798a[5] 3883a[7]

**Girl Squad** *William Jarvis* a58 51
3 b f Intikhab(USA) Foxtrot Alpha (IRE) (Desert Prince (IRE))
168[4] 5611[7] 6288[13]

**Girls Talk (IRE)** *Michael Bell* 67
2 b f Shamardal(USA) Tasha's Dream (USA) (Woodman (USA))
6385[5] 7733[7] 8322[9]

**Girvin (USA)** *Joe Sharp* a116 90
3 bb c Tale Of Ekati(USA) Catch The Moon (USA) (Malibu Moon (USA))
2420a[13] (5463a)

**Gisele's Angel** *Richard Guest* 72
2 b g f Dark Angel(IRE) Lovely Thought (Dubai Destination (USA))
(2029)◆

**Giuseppe Garibaldi (IRE)**
*A P O'Brien* 98
2 b c Galileo(IRE) Queenscliff (IRE) (Danehill Dancer (IRE))
8440a[2]

**Giuseppe Piazzi (IRE)**
*Flemming Velin* 98
5 b h Galileo(IRE) Belesta (Xaar)
(4825a) (5676a)

**Give And Take** *William Haggas* 87
2 b f Cityscape Grace And Glory (IRE) (Montjeu (IRE))
5349[2] 6292[2] (7153)◆

**Giveaway Glance** *Alan King* 85
4 br m Passing Glance Giving (Generous (IRE))
2478[5] (2893) 7908[6]

**Give Em A Clump (IRE)**
*David Evans* a67 65
2 br c Camacho Pixie's Blue (IRE) (Hawk Wing (USA))
1681[9] 1934[5] 3918[3] 4054[2] (4504) 6366[2]◆ 6613[5] 7057[6] (7196) 8475[6] 8804[2] 8887[10] 9345[9]

**Giveitsomeginger** *Jo Hughes* 45
3 ch f Stimulation(IRE) Glaze (Kyllachy)
5409[7] 7080[9] 7523[7] 7905[6]

**Give It Some Teddy** *Tim Easterby* 78
3 b g Bahamian Bounty Croeso Cariad (Most Welcome)
1514[5] 2185[4] (8217) 8600[2]

**Give Love (FR)** *J-Y Artu* a58 63
7 ro g Urgent Request(IRE) Donna Lorcy (FR) (Great Palm (USA))
8303a[8]

**Givemeaminit (USA)** *Dallas Stewart* a105
2 b c Star Guitar(USA) Powerful Nation (USA) (Turkoman (USA))
8609a[4]

**Give Us A Belle (IRE)**
*Christine Dunnett* a52 43
8 b g Kheleyf(USA) Bajan Belle (IRE) (Efisio)
622[7] 722[2] 901[9] 1184[8] 2069[5] 2621[12] 2967[11] 3544[9]

**Giving Glances** *Alan King* 68
2 b f Passing Glance Giving (Generous (IRE))
6037[5] 7504[3] 8322[10]

**G K Chesterton (IRE)**
*Charlie Appleby* 104
4 ch g Poet's Voice Neptune's Bride (USA) (Bering)
1734[2] (2799) (3298) 3963[19] 5594[17] 6355[11]

**Glaceon (IRE)** *Richard Hannon* a67 69
2 b f Zoffany(IRE) Ihtiraam (IRE) (Teofilo (IRE))
3502[3] 3782[3] 4212[5] 5150[8] 7123[5]

**Glacier (IRE)** *Richard Hannon* 42
2 b c Canford Cliffs(IRE) Ice Pie (Mount Nelson)
3747[9] 5106[9] 6142[10]

**Glacier Fox** *Tom Tate* a55 76
2 ch g Foxwedge(AUS) Beat Seven (Beat Hollow)
5180[2] 7929[4]◆ 8555[8]

**Glacier Point** *Clive Cox* 79
3 ch f Foxwedge(AUS) Ahwahnee (Compton Place)
1762[3] 2927[8] 4352[2] (4842) 5263[2] 6098[4] 8186[4] 8512[5]

**Glade** *C Ferland* 94
4 b m Bertolini(USA) Alpen Glen (Halling (USA))
2946a[8] 7673a[4]

**Gladys Cooper (IRE)** *Richard Fahey* a61 56
4 b m Arcano(IRE) Anthyllis (GER) (Lycius (USA))
444[8] 880[7]

**Glamorous Approach (IRE)**
*J S Bolger* 105
4 ch m New Approach(IRE) Maria Lee (IRE) (Rock Of Gibraltar (IRE))
1808a[3] 3874a[3] 5766a[4] 6080a[4] 6490a[6] 6957a[3] 7171a[6] 7837a[6]

**Glamorous Dream (IRE)**
*Ronald Harris* a64 41
2 b f Dark Angel(IRE) Glamorous Air (IRE) (Air Express (IRE))
7079[7] 7725[6] 8851[10]

**Glamorous Rocket (IRE)**
*Ronald Harris* a21 54
2 gr f Dark Angel(IRE) Glamorous Spirit (IRE) (Invincible Spirit (IRE))
3022[6] 4160[8] 4972[5] 5654[4]

**Glam'Selle** *Ronald Harris* a48 53
3 b f Elnadim(USA) Town And Gown (Oasis Dream)
554[5] 787[2] 960[6] 1363[4] 1688[12] 2362[13] 3141[4] 4731[11] 5252[7]

**Glance My Way (IRE)** *Tim Easterby* a30 56
4 ch g Rock Of Gibraltar(IRE) Glympse (IRE) (Spectrum (IRE))
2225[8] 2741[14] 3065[9] 3910[6] 6316[10] 7982[5]

**Glan Y Gors (IRE)** *David Simcock* a92 81
5 b g High Chaparral(IRE) Trading Places (Dansili)
759[8] 1223[3] 1505[2]

**Glaring** *Amanda Perrett* 104
6 b h Champs Elysees Brightest (Rainbow Quest (USA))
2176[6] 3073[9] 3534[9] 4222[8]

**Glasgon** *Ray Craggs* a63 41
7 gr g Verglas(IRE) Miss St Tropez (Danehill Dancer (IRE))
174[4]

**Glassalt** *Michael Bell* a64 67
3 b f Medaglia d'Oro(USA) Abergeldie (USA) (Street Cry (IRE))
2997[13] 6293[3]◆ 7537[2] 7879[10]

**Glass Office** *David Simcock* a95 101
7 gr h Verglas(IRE) Oval Office (Pursuit Of Love)
3867[4] 5595[8] 6428[6]

**Glassy Waters (USA)**
*Saeed bin Suroor* 87
3 ch c Distorted Humor(USA) Captivating Lass (USA) (A.P. Indy (USA))
1607[3] 2963[3] (6236)

**Glastonbury Song (IRE)**
*G M Lyons* a104 100
3 ch g Casamento(IRE) Nesmeh (USA) (More Than Ready (USA))
1633a[5] 3100a[4] 3959[20] 6961a[6] 8891[10]

**Gleaming Girl** *David Simcock* a83 76
5 b m Arabian Gleam Desert Liaison (Dansili)
(97)◆ 285[6] 499[4]

**Gleaming Sun** *Michael Easterby* 57
2 b g Arabian Gleam Cara's Delight (AUS) (Fusaichi Pegasus (USA))
7242[4] 7623[4] 7819[9]

**Glenalmond (IRE)** *Daniel Steele* a78 85
5 b g Iffraaj Balladonia (Primo Dominie)
47[4] 517[2] 928[3] 1549[4] 1788[7] 2257[4]

**Glenamoy Lad** *Michael Wigham* a102 89
3 b g Royal Applause Suzy Alexander (Red Ransom (USA))
4759[3] (5606) 5936[4] (7405) (9016)◆

**Glenbank King (IRE)** *Lee Smyth* a80 73
9 b g Desert King(IRE) Miss Glenbank (IRE) (Over The River (FR))
(4684)

**Glencadam Glory** *John Gosden* 109
3 b c Nathaniel(IRE) Lady Grace (IRE) (Orpen (USA))
2132[5] 2614[2] 3322[9] 4029[5]

**Glencadam Master** *John Gosden* a83 73
2 gr c Mastercraftsman(IRE) Coquet (Sir Percy)
8678[3]◆ 8987[2] (9312)

**Glendevon (USA)** *Richard Hughes* a95
2 ch c Scat Daddy(USA) Flip Flop (FR) (Zieten (USA))
6885[2] (7946)

**Glendun (USA)** *James Eustace* a83 80
3 b g First Defence(USA) La Mina (USA) (Mineshaft (USA))
2071[2]◆ 3000[3] 3700[2] 4632[2] (8341) 9025[6] 9236[3]

**Glengarry** *Keith Dalgleish* 91
4 b g Monsieur Bond(IRE) Lady McBeth (IRE) (Avonbridge)
2500[2] 3045[2] 4037[5] 4683[7]

**Glenn Coco** *Stuart Williams* a82 66
3 gr g Aussie Rules(USA) Las Hilanderas (USA) (El Prado (IRE))
4269[3] 5577[3] 6268[4] (7414) 8640[2] (9126) 9281[3]

**Glenrowan Rose (IRE)**
*Keith Dalgleish* a74 102
4 b m Bushranger(IRE) Choice House (USA) (Chester House (USA))
1800[7] 1936[9] 3539[7] 4078[9] 4435[7] (5093) (5281) (5647) 6234[P] 7611[8] 7887[3]

**Glen Shiel** *A Fabre* 106
3 ch g Pivotal Gonfilia (GER) (Big Shuffle (USA))
3680a[2] 5522a[6] 6172a[4] (7845a)

**Glens Wobbly** *Jonathan Geake* a62 79
9 ch g Kier Park(IRE) Wobbly (Atraf)
2357[4] 2512[2] 3574[3] (4041) 5140[4] 6139[5] 8426[10]

**Glen Valley (IRE)** *Keith Dalgleish* a7
2 ch f Society Rock(IRE) Glen Ginnie (IRE) (Red Clubs (IRE))
1588[4] 1873[12] 2343[7]

**Glenville Gardens (USA)** *Sid Attard* a88 110
5 bb g Street Cry(IRE) Navy Gardens (USA) (Storm Cat (USA))
7179a[9]

**Glenys The Menace (FR)**
*John Best* a88 89
3 b f American Post Elle S'Voyait Deja (USA) (Carson City (USA))
1685[4] 2395[3] 3178[4] 4012[2] (5113) (5404) 5841[2]◆ (5915) 6445[12] 6920[11] 8385[6] 8820[3] 9205[8]

**Glicourt (FR)** *M Boutin* 73
3 b g Rajsaman(FR) Fusee Francaise (FR) (Anabaa (USA))
3355a[6]

**Glimpse Of Dirhams** *Chris Gordon* 9
2 b f Passing Glance Jemiliah (Dubai Destination (USA))
1681[10]

**Glitterdust** *Sir Michael Stoute* 67
2 b f Intello(GER) Glitterball (IRE) (Smart Strike (CAN))
7620[10] 8323[3]

**Glitter Girl** *William Haggas* 102
3 b f Invincible Spirit(IRE) Glitterball (IRE) (Smart Strike (CAN))
1958[7] 2623[7] 3334[3]

**Glittering** *James Eustace* a6 57
4 ch m Firebreak Razzle (IRE) (Green Desert (USA))
4323[4]

**Glittering Jewel (USA)**
*Charlie Appleby* a91 91
3 b f Bernardini(USA) Bedazzle (USA) (Dixieland Band (USA))
1885[4] 2564[2] 3366a[6] (4729) 5745[5]

**Global Academy (IRE)**
*Gay Kelleway* a79 72
2 b g Zebedee Lady Meagan (IRE) (Val Royal (FR))
3149[4]◆ 5151[6] 5474[2] 5879[6] 8657[4] (9122)

**Global Alexander (IRE)** *Clive Cox* a74 65
3 br f Dark Angel(IRE) Taraeff (IRE) (Cape Cross (IRE))
1286[2] 1503[4] 1761[2] 2503[8]◆ 3536[6]

**Global Angel** *Ed Dunlop* a63 40
2 b c Dark Angel(IRE) Authoritarian (Authorized (IRE))
7026[9] 7273[11] 7758[7] 8371[5] 8870[7]

**Global Applause** *Ed Dunlop* 103
3 b c Mayson Crown (IRE) (Royal Applause)
5633[3] 7901[5] 8416[5]

**Global Art** *Ed Dunlop* 72
2 b c Dutch Art Constant Dream (Kheleyf (USA))
5350[5]

**Global Conqueror** *Simon Crisford* 85
2 b c Dubawi(IRE) Nargys (IRE) (Lawman (FR))
4859[6] 6057[3]◆ 6854[2] 7544[2]

**Global Empire (IRE)** *Simon Crisford* a51
3 b g New Approach(IRE) Lady Zonda (Lion Cavern (USA))
2164[9]

**Global Exceed** *Ed Dunlop* a62 74
2 b c Exceed And Excel(AUS) Blue Maiden (Medicean)
2052[5] 2926[3] 3187[5] 5121[4] 5933[2] 6063[6] (6825)◆ 7081[2] (8110) 8746[6]

**Global Excel** *Ed Walker* a62 58
2 b c Exceed And Excel(AUS) Seta (Pivotal)
6367[6] 7726[11] 8508[6]◆

**Global Giant** *Ed Dunlop* 89
2 b c Shamardal(USA) Aniseed (IRE) (Dalakhani (IRE))
4094[3] (4860)◆

**Global Humor (USA)** *Ed Dunlop* a76
2 b c Distorted Humor(USA) In Bloom (USA) (Discreet Cat (USA))
3254[3] (4452)

**Global Pass** *Ed Walker* a69
2 b g Exceed And Excel(AUS) Mary Boleyn (IRE) (King's Best (USA))
8989[4]

**Global Passion (FR)** *Charles Hills* a78 76
2 b g Penny's Picnic(IRE) Lili St Cyr (IRE) (Rock Of Gibraltar (IRE))
3782[2] 4782a[2] 6147[7] (6682) 7318[7]

**Global Revival (IRE)** *Ed Dunlop* a77 78
3 b g Kyllachy Soliza (IRE) (Intikhab (USA))
100[3]◆ 292[2] (647)◆ (1877) 2526[8]

**Global Roar** *John Weymes* a35 68
4 b g Arabian Gleam Kungfu Kerry (Celtic Swing)
3435[6] 6522[3] 6899[9]

**Global Rose (IRE)** *Gay Kelleway* a14 73
2 b f Dark Angel(IRE) Classic Falcon (IRE) (Dubawi (IRE))
4972[2]◆ 5327[3] 6806[4] 9416[8]

**Global Spirit** *Ed Dunlop* a67 54
2 b c Invincible Spirit(IRE) Centime (Royal Applause)
6424[8] 7580[9] 8308[3] 8658[2] 8817[7]

**Global Style (IRE)** *Ed Dunlop* 72
2 b c Nathaniel(IRE) Danaskaya (IRE) (Danehill (USA))
6142[8] 6553[3] 7128[7]

**Global Tango (IRE)** *Charles Hills* a80 80
2 gr g Zebedee Beautiful Dancer (IRE) (Danehill Dancer (IRE))
2286[4] 2769[6] 8112[2] (8587)

**Global Wealth** *Ed Dunlop* a59 66
2 b g Havana Gold(IRE) Inner Sea (USA) (Henrythenavigator (USA))
3591[5] 3930[3] 4560[7] 5366[5]

**Global Wonder (IRE)** *Ed Dunlop* a59 65
2 b c Kodiac Traveller's Tales (Cape Cross (IRE))
5036[6]◆ 5934[5] 8309[8] 8848[9] 9238[4]

**Globetrotter (IRE)** *James Tate* a71 82
3 ch g Helmet(AUS) Shimna (Mr Prospector (USA))
1347[2] 1906[8] (2408) 3665[5] 8188[10]

**Gloriosus (USA)** *Mark Johnston* 78
3 b c Lonhro(AUS) Sky Song (IRE) (Sadler's Wells (USA))
2338[6] 2704[5] (3206) 3780[8] 4438[6] 4736[6]

**Glorious Army** *Ed Walker* a73
2 ch c Declaration Of War(USA) Shibina (IRE) (Kalanisi (IRE))
8634[5]

**Glorious Artist (IRE)** *Charles Hills* a91 80
3 b g Zoffany(IRE) Queenie Keen (IRE) (Refuse To Bend (IRE))
1033[3] (1625) 1724[3] 2385[5] (5484)

**Glorious Asset** *Ivan Furtado* a66 63
5 b g Aqlaam Regal Asset (USA) (Regal Classic (CAN))
154[3] 421[7] 690[3] 1067[2] (1210) 1498[7]

**Glorious Forever** *Ed Walker* 96
3 ch g Archipenko(USA) Here To Eternity (USA) (Stormy Atlantic (USA))
2118[2] 2824[12] 3504[3] 4035[4] 5928[2] (6701)

**Glorious Journey** *Charlie Appleby* 108
2 b c Dubawi(IRE) Fallen For You (Dansili)
(3590) (6912a)

**Glorious Player (IRE)**
*Tom Dascombe* a61
2 b g Kyllachy Playwithmyheart (Diktat)
9050[5]

**Glorious Poet** *John Spearing* a77 82
4 ch g Poet's Voice Sky Wonder (Observatory (USA))
1105[7] 1606[7] 2960[3] 3396[8] 4501[2] 5221[6] 6273[6] 6811[5] (7158) 7474[10] 8297[3]

**Glorious Politics** *David Barron* a83 55
3 b g Delegator Pelican Key (IRE) (Mujadil (USA))
(27) 1311[6] 8014[19] 8640[11]

**Glorious Power (IRE)** *Charles Hills* a77 59
3 ch g Power Arpege (IRE) (Sadler's Wells (USA))
(1358) 2088[13] 2588[9] 2998[6]

**Glorious Rocket** *David Barron* a78 72
3 b g Bated Breath Up And About (Barathea (IRE))
1895[7] 3462[7] 3814[5] 5100[4] 8556[11] 9176[7]

**Gloriux** *Charles Hills* a49 78
3 b g Exceed And Excel(AUS) Najraan (Cadeaux Genereux)
2510[3] 3085[7] 4341[8] 5132[4]

**Glorvina (IRE)** *David O'Meara* a68 62
3 b f Dragon Pulse(IRE) Hawk Dance (IRE) (Hawk Wing (USA))
1829[5] 2110[2] 2588[7] 3175[3] 3649[3] (4540)

**Glory Awaits (IRE)** *David Simcock* a82 103
7 ch g Choisir(AUS) Sandbox Two (IRE) (Foxhound (USA))
2283[8] 2761[14] 3837[3] 4636[12] 5294[2] 6483[3] 6918[12]

**Glory Of Paris (IRE)** *Rod Millman* a81 78
3 b g Sir Prancealot(IRE) Paris Glory (USA) (Honour And Glory (USA))
(1554) 1945[12] 2757[2] 3504[6] 4215[5] 4810[8] 6073[5] 7084[5]

**Glyder** *John Holt* a53 58
3 b f Camacho Blades Princess (Needwood Blade)
2181[11] 2897[2]◆ (3285) 3812[6] 4576[6] 5134[9] 5736[4] 6339[4] 7014[7]

**Gm Hopkins** *John Gosden* 116
6 b g Dubawi(IRE) Varsity (Lomitas)
2606[17] 3963[7] 4636[2] 5594[13] 7619[10] 8234[2]

**Gnaad (IRE)** *Alan Bailey* a77 80
3 b g Invincible Spirit(IRE) Areyaam (USA) (Elusive Quality (USA))
554[2] 960[3] (1183) 1363[3] (1821) 2065[3] 5920[U] (6372) (6652) 6970[7] 8803[6] 9074[5] 9308[3]

**Gnily (IRE)** *C Lerner* a81 73
3 b f Arcano(IRE) Mary Spring Rice (IRE) (Saffron Walden (FR))
3554a[2] (6084a)

**Goadby** *John Holt* a49 47
6 gr m Kodiac Gone Sailing (Mizzen Mast (USA))
1593[11] 2589[12] 3468[3] 3728[4] 4619[8] 5282[2] 5738[9] 7763[6] 8496[10] 9420[5]

**Go Amber Go** *Rod Millman* a66 72
5 ch m Compton Place Lady Chef (Double Trigger (IRE))
(1723) (2043) 3021[6] 3278[8] 4149[2] 4993[4] 6507[6]

**Go Bananas** *Brian Meehan* a41 51
2 b f Bahamian Bounty Ribbon Royale (Royal Applause)
3277[4]◆ 3687[10] 3960[22] 5030[9] 6043[4] 6609[9]

**Gobi Desert** *G M Lyons* 102
2 b c Oasis Dream Household Name (Zamindar (USA))
7290a[2] (7855a)

**Go Charlie** *Lisa Williamson* a39 42
6 b g Myboycharlie(IRE) Branston Gem (So Factual (USA))
9102[9] 9268[5] 9471[8]

**God Given** *Luca Cumani* 105
3 b f Nathaniel(IRE) Ever Rigg (Dubai Destination (USA))
2834[2]◆ (3542) (5155) (5981a) 6981a[6]

**Gododdin** *Hugo Palmer* a65 63
2 b c Camelot Spritza (IRE) (Spectrum (IRE))
6683[4] 7543[8]◆

**God Willing** *Declan Carroll* a92 98
6 b g Arch(USA) Bourbon Ball (USA) (Peintre Celebre (USA))
1103[5] 1492[13] 1799[5] 2406[6] 2840[7] 3792[13] 4719[9] 5379[5] 5669[10] 6663[2] 6964[5] 7223[4] 8240[3]

**Go Far** *Alan Bailey* a104 103
7 b g Dutch Art Carranita (IRE) (Anita's Prince)
957[4] (1152) 1501[12] 1794[9] 2433[3] 3034[3] 3593[6] 4816[12] 5640[20] 6371[2] 7828[11] 8383[17]

**Go Fast (IRE)** *N Caullery* a60 102
3 b c Born To Sea(IRE) Juno Blackie (JPN) (Sunday Silence (USA))
1826a[7]

**Go Fox** *Tom Clover* a68 58
2 ch g Foxwedge(AUS) Bling Bling (IRE) (Indian Ridge (IRE))
7281[9] 8119[12] 8502[3]

**Gog Elles (IRE)** *J S Moore* a56 47
3 b f Helmet(AUS) Hear My Cry (USA) (Giant's Causeway (USA))
91[5] 149[4] 627[5] 766[4] 5910a[8] 6225a[9] 6496a[9] 6947[6] 8152[10] 8247[5] 8543[8]

**Go George Go (IRE)** *Sally Haynes* a76 78
4 gr g Zebedee La Bella Grande (IRE) (Giant's Causeway (USA))
(30)◆ 509[3] 1113[4] 1630[2] 1716[3] 2375[2] 4357[9]

**Going Native** *Ed Walker* a65 61
2 ch f Speightstown(USA) Latin Love (IRE) (Danehill Dancer (IRE))
6385[4] 7237[3] 7758[5] 8153[4]

**Going Up (IRE)** *Rae Guest* a85 85
4 ch g Duke Of Marmalade(IRE) Guilia (Galileo (IRE))
2431[9] 3086[3] 5799[7] 6849[P]

**Going Viral (IRE)** *G Botti* a73 56
4 b g Kodiac Dark Indian (IRE) (Indian Ridge (IRE))
(391a) 1078a[2]

**Go Kart (IRE)** *P J Prendergast* a91 96
4 b m Intense Focus(USA) Kartiste (IRE) (Kalanisi (IRE))
3873a[2] 4416a[7] 5308a[9]

**Gokena (FR)** *P Sogorb* 98
3 b f Kendargent(FR) Gooseley Chope (FR) (Indian Rocket)
1270a[4] 1690a[5] 2644a[9]

**Golconda Prince (IRE)**
*Richard Fahey* 71
3 b g Arcano(IRE) Mujarah (IRE) (Marju (IRE))
1678[3] 2854[4] 3484[2] 4276[3] 4721[2] 5604[2] 6091[3]◆ 6431[8]

**Gold Actor (JPN)** *Tadashige Nakagawa* 121
6 bb h Screen Hero(JPN) Heilong Xing (JPN) (Kyowa Alysheba (USA))
**2203a**[7]

**Goldakoya** *Daniel Mark Loughnane* a12
2 ch f Captain Gerrard(IRE) Just Lille (IRE) (Mull Of Kintyre (USA))
***5480***[7]

**Gold And Rock (IRE)** *Stefano Botti* 63
2 b c Fastnet Rock(AUS) Goldendale (IRE) (Ali-Royal (IRE))
**4131a**[6]

**Gold Award (IRE)** *Mick Channon* 72
3 gr g Bushranger(IRE) Sandtail (IRE) (Verglas (IRE))
**2361**[8] 2894[8]

**Gold Chain (IRE)** *Dianne Sayer* a41 65
7 b m Authorized(IRE) Mountain Chain (USA) (Royal Academy (USA))
1716[5] **5700**[5] 6628[3]

**Gold City (IRE)** *S Seemar* a109 97
8 b g Pivotal Storm Lily (USA) (Storm Cat (USA))
***85a***[4] *541a*[5] *891a*[7]

**Gold Class** *Olly Murphy* a46 45
6 ch g Firebreak Silken Dalliance (Rambo Dancer (CAN))
***5850***[4] 5866[2] *7992*[7]

**Gold Club** *Lee Carter* a82 62
6 b g Multiplex Oceana Blue (Reel Buddy (USA))
*94*[7] *1140*[3] ***1631***[2] 2320[4] 3074[6] 3941[6] *5481*[8] *6156*[3] *7058*[7] *9183*[2] *(9470)*

**Gold Dream (JPN)** *Osamu Hirata* a115
4 b h Gold Allure(JPN) Mon Vert (JPN) (French Deputy (USA))
***1380a***[14]

**Gold Dust** *Clive Cox* 63
3 b f Choisir(AUS) Afrodita (IRE) (Montjeu (IRE))
3329[4] 4409[5] **5712**[5] 7957[8]

**Gold Eagle** *Philip McBride* a65 62
2 b f Paco Boy(IRE) Fin (Groom Dancer (USA))
3697[7] 4815[11] 5534[4]◆ *6285*[9] *7510*[3] ***7829***[2]◆ 8354[7]

**Golden Amber (IRE)** *Dean Ivory* a98 102
6 b m Holy Roman Emperor(IRE) Time Of Gold (USA) (Banker's Gold (USA))
*170*[4] *617*[4] *810*[7] **1515**[5] *2113*[4] *2518*[8] 8077[11] 8736[13]

**Golden Apollo** *Tim Easterby* 103
3 ch g Pivotal Elan (Dansili)
2739[4]◆ 3434[3] (3664) (3844) 4813[4] 5423[9] **(5916)**◆ 7626[3] 8044[9]

**Golden Attitude (USA)** *F Head* a70 93
3 b f Redoute's Choice(AUS) Gold Round (IRE) (Caerleon (USA))
**2978a**[2]

**Golden Birthday (FR)** *Harry Fry* a87 96
6 b g Poliglote Gold Or Silver (FR) (Glint Of Gold)
(7462) *(7880)* **(8384)**◆

**Golden Bowl (FR)** *John Quinn*
7 b g Turtle Bowl(IRE) Maid Of Dawkins (IRE) (Kendor (FR))
7599[8] 8239[P]

**Golden Cannon** *Sheena West* a43 49
6 b m Winker Watson Kalmina (USA) (Rahy (USA))
1787[8] **2580**[5] 3329[7] 7212[14] 8185[11] *8994*[9] *9213*[8]

**Golden Cape** *Michael Mullineaux* a31 53
4 ch m Native Ruler Lake Sabina (Diktat)
*2063*[11] **3148**[7] 3575[16]

**Golden Deal (IRE)** *Richard Phillips* a59 48
2 b f Havana Gold(IRE) Lady Rockfield (IRE) (Rock Of Gibraltar (IRE))
5717[6] 6824[9] ***7725***[8] *8887*[8]

**Golden Doyen (GER)** *Philip Hobbs* 84
6 b g Doyen(IRE) Goldsamt (GER) (Rienzi (EG))
**5524**[9]

**Golden Dragon (USA)** *Mikhail Yanakov* a38 98
2 ch c Skipshot(USA) La Belle Marquet (USA) (Marquetry (USA))
***8609a***[11]

**Golden Easter (USA)** *Robert Cowell* a73 55
3 ch f Distorted Humor(USA) Easterette (USA) (Hard Spun (USA))
**2674**[3] 6009[7] *6526*[7]

**Golden Escape (FR)** *Mlle C Courtade* 63
2 ch f Evasive La Madonnina (FR) (Medaaly)
**5815a**[5]

**Golden Eye** *Sylvester Kirk* a65 66
3 ch g Kheleyf(USA) Gennie Bond (Pivotal)
1686[13] *2259*[9] **2911**[6] *4211*[11] 5410[12]

**Golden Footsteps (IRE)** *Ed Walker* a66 69
2 b f Footstepsinthesand Contemplate (Compton Place)
*3687*[4] **4533**[3] *6064*[9] 6860[10]

**Golden Frost (FR)** *H De Nicolay* a42
2 b f Silver Frost(IRE) Collina D'Oro (FR) (King's Best (USA))
***9086a***[11]

**Golden Gazelle (IRE)** *P Schiergen* 88
4 ch m Galileo(IRE) Grey Lilas (IRE) (Danehill (USA))
**8090a**[7]

**Golden Glimmer (IRE)** *Tom Dascombe* 85
4 b m Danehill Dancer(IRE) Gilded Vanity (IRE) (Indian Ridge (IRE))
**3541**[5]

**Golden Goal (IRE)** *Saeed bin Suroor* a95 78
3 gr c Dark Angel(IRE) Golden Rosie (IRE) (Exceed And Excel (AUS))
*(4562)* *(5245)* *6026*[6] ***(6617)***◆ 7781[9] *8812*[6]

**Goldenground (IRE)** *Henry Spiller* a66 46
2 b g Zebedee Bryana Gold (IRE) (Namid)
3244[6] ***3999***[2] *5240*[5]

**Golden Guest** *George Margarson* a76 72
3 ch g Bated Breath Si Belle (IRE) (Dalakhani (IRE))
1686[2] 2228[2] 2793[10] 3443[3] 3751[8] (4463) (5039) 5560[5] 6485[2] 6664[8] ***(7878)*** *8433*[9]

**Golden Guide** *K R Burke* a43 58
2 b f Havana Gold(IRE) Blonde (IRE) (Pivotal)
6658[4] **8380**[12] *8782*[5]

**Golden Harbour (FR)** *Alex Hales* a47 12
3 b g Harbour Watch(IRE) Make Up (Kyllachy)
***545***[12] 3695[9] *5239*[12] *6846*[7]

**Golden Image** *Jonathan Portman* a68 69
2 b f Havana Gold(IRE) Photographie (USA) (Trempolino (USA))
**6100**[3] 6824[8] *9371*[2]

**Golden Isles (IRE)** *Heather Main* a60 61
4 ch m Mastercraftsman(IRE) Aphorism (Halling (USA))
2915[6] 3771[6] **(4088)** 4538[6]

**Golden Jeffrey (SWI)** *Iain Jardine* 74
4 b g Soldier Hollow Ange Doree (FR) (Sinyar (IRE))
4611[7] 4738[4] 5003[4] **(5884)** **5923**[4] 7983[10]

**Golden Jubilee (USA)** *Nigel Twiston-Davies* a77 76
8 bb g Zavata(USA) Love Play (USA) (Friendly Lover (USA))
***173***[5] *1505*[5] 2357[10] *3213*[7]

**Golden Legend (FR)** *H-F Devin* a77 109
3 b f Doctor Dino(FR) Gold Harvest (FR) (Kaldounevees (FR))
(2978a) 4988a[2] (6732a) **(7305a)** 8273a[6]

**Golden Muscade (USA)** *Brian Barr* a53 57
4 b m Medaglia d'Oro(USA) Kinda Spicy (USA) (A.P. Indy (USA))
*549*[7] *747*[6] *1283*[7] **2219**[2] 3026[4] 3805[5] 4967[9]

**Golden Nectar** *Laura Mongan* a78 78
3 ch f Sakhee's Secret Mildoura (FR) (Sendawar (IRE))
3786[5]◆ **4699**[5]

**Golden Opportunity** *James Tate* a77
3 ch c Kheleyf(USA) Golden Waters (Dubai Destination (USA))
***(178)*** *356*[3] ***458***[3]

**Golden Orb (USA)** *Christophe Clement* 89
2 ch f Orb(USA) Day Of Victory (USA) (Victory Gallop (CAN))
**7206a**[6]

**Golden Pearl** *M Halford* a76 86
4 b m Oasis Dream Pearl Banks (Pivotal)
**4327a**[5] *9247a*[11]

**Golden Raven (IRE)** *Jamie Osborne* a81 73
5 bb g Raven's Pass(USA) Superfonic (FR) (Zafonic (USA))
*1598*[8] ***2960***[8] *3471*[11] 4105[7]

**Golden Sage (FR)** *J Phelippon* a39 65
3 bb f Sageburg(IRE) Golden Tale (FR) (Pivotal)
***427a***[9]

**Golden Salute (IRE)** *Andrew Balding* 80
2 b f Acclamation Golden Shadow (IRE) (Selkirk (USA))
4367[7] (4972) (5270) **6778**[2]

**Golden Set** *Eve Johnson Houghton* a66 68
3 b f Bated Breath Match Point (Unfuwain (USA))
5632[6] 6194[11] **6823**[3] 7560[9] *8204*[3] *9178*[9]

**Golden Spear** *A J Martin* 94
6 ch g Kyllachy Penmayne (Inchinor)
**2525**[14]

**Golden Spell** *J P Murtagh* 95
2 b f Al Kazeem Cross Pattee (IRE) (Oasis Dream)
5344a[4] 6488a[5] 7290a[3] **7855a**[2]

**Golden State (USA)** *Archie Watson* a67 77
3 b f Elusive Quality(USA) Bronze Route (USA) (Mud Route (USA))
*2311*[7]◆ **(2898)** 4027a[7]

**Golden Steps (FR)** *Jamie Osborne* a58 68
6 b g Footstepsinthesand Kocooning (IRE) (King's Best (USA))
***8906***[5]

**Golden Stunner (IRE)** *Ralph Beckett* a77 109
4 ch m Dream Ahead(USA) Pina Colada (Sabrehill (USA))
(3089) **3843**[2] 4512a[2] 5352[8] 7356[8]

**Golden Wedding (IRE)** *Eve Johnson Houghton* a88 88
5 b g Archipenko(USA) Peace Lily (Dansili)
*2026*[2] *2582*[2] *2960*[2] *3214*[6] **3750**[2] 4832[7] *6322*[2] 6700[4] ***6933***[3] *7456*[9] 8297[7] *9314*[9]

**Golden Wolf (IRE)** *Richard Hughes* a73 89
3 bb g Big Bad Bob(IRE) Jeunesse Doree (IRE) (Rock Of Gibraltar (IRE))
*1410*[2] *2092*[4] *4981*[2] 5686[2] (5931) 6657[3] **7651**[2]

**Golden Wood (FR)** *N Caullery* a79 107
7 ch g Gold Away(IRE) Twisting (FR) (Pivotal)
**(82a)**

**Goldfield (ARG)** *Ricardo Colombo* a89 86
3 b g Heliostatic(IRE) Heaven To Sally (ARG) (Honour And Glory (USA))
***1375a***[9]

**Gold Filigree (IRE)** *Richard Hughes* a76 74
2 gr f Dark Angel(IRE) Gold Lace (IRE) (Invincible Spirit (IRE))
2037[5] 2750[3] 3023[4] 5546[2] *6021*[2] *6844*[2] *8154*[2] ***(8850)***

**Gold Flash** *Richenda Ford* a82 64
5 b g Kheleyf(USA) My Golly (Mozart (IRE))
*(50)*◆ *(267)*◆ *760*[6] ***1065***[2] *1238*[4] *1696*[8] 2040[9] 2893[9] *9124*[14] *9280*[7]

**Goldfox Girl** *Michael Appleby* a50 43
2 b f Phenomena Baileys Honour (Mark Of Esteem (IRE))
8347[6] ***8802***[4]

**Gold Hunter (IRE)** *Adrian Wintle* a84 82
7 b g Invincible Spirit(IRE) Goldthroat (IRE) (Zafonic (USA))
3074[7] (3696) 4099[6] 4844[2] 5821[3] 6303[4] 7094[3] ***(7321)***◆ *7789*[14] *8640*[10] *9020*[11]

**Gold Luck (FR)** *F Head* 109
3 b f Redoute's Choice(AUS) Born Gold (USA) (Blushing Groom (FR))
(1657a) 2665a[5] 3367a[2] **4666a**[3] 5980a[6] 7640a[7]

**Goldmadchen (GER)** *James Given* a46 41
9 b m Ivan Denisovich(IRE) Goldkatze (GER) (Czaravich (USA))
***621***[9] *839*[8]

**Goldmember** *David Simcock* a98 106
4 ch g New Approach(IRE) Sister Act (Marju (IRE))
3090[8] 4639[6] 6427[8] ***8244***[2]

**Gold Merlion (IRE)** *Mark Johnston* a68 70
4 b m Alhaarth(IRE) Sea Of Time (USA) (Gilded Time (USA))
*769*[9] 3501[5] 4627[9] *(5296)* **5555**[2] 5872[9] 6556[7] 7015[8] *7413*[7] *7760*[2] *8261*[11]

**Gold Mount** *A S Cruz* a74 113
4 b g Excellent Art Dolcetto (IRE) (Danehill Dancer (IRE))
3129a[5] **9167a**[5]

**Goldream** *Robert Cowell* a102 114
8 br g Oasis Dream Clizia (IRE) (Machiavellian (USA))
2397[3] **3079**[2] 3926[10] 4635[3] 4920[6] 5116[3] 6402[9] 7396[12] 8139[4]

**Gold Return (IRE)** *John Ryan* a62
4 b m Gold Away(IRE) Ourika (IRE) (Danehill Dancer (IRE))
*116*[8] *304*[6] ***420***[4] *550*[4] *1175*[5]

**Goldrush (IRE)** *J S Bolger* a99 79
3 b f Frankel Alexander Goldrun (IRE) (Gold Away (IRE))
***(8407a)***

**Goldslinger (FR)** *Dean Ivory* a74 77
5 b g Gold Away(IRE) Singaporette (FR) (Sagacity (FR))
*2111*[6] 3694[4] 4573[6] **5362**[2] 6038[4] 6343[4] 7233[4] *7766*[8]

**Gold Spinner (IRE)** *G M Lyons* 99
3 ch c Pivotal Morinqua (IRE) (Cadeaux Genereux)
1389a[5] 5517a[15] **6491a**[6]

**Goldspun** *Ed Dunlop* 61
2 b f Nathaniel(IRE) Dream Day (Oasis Dream)
**8323**[7]

**Gold Star** *Saeed bin Suroor* a104 90
3 b c Nathaniel(IRE) Tanzania (USA) (Darshaan)
5364[3]◆ (6194)◆ ***(6952)***◆ 8011[13]

**Gold Stone** *Kevin Ryan* 73
2 b f Havana Gold(IRE) Slatey Hen (IRE) (Acclamation)
5210[2] **(6086)**

**Gold Town** *Charlie Appleby* a79 99
2 b g Street Cry(IRE) Pimpernel (IRE) (Invincible Spirit (IRE))
(1941)◆ *2786*[5] 3098a[5] 4068[7] 4858[3] **(5939)**

**Gold Trail (IRE)** *Charlie Appleby* a106 113
6 ch h Teofilo(IRE) Goldthroat (IRE) (Zafonic (USA))
**(428a)** 1400a[4] (Dead)

**Gold Vibe (IRE)** *P Bary* a95 113
4 ch g Dream Ahead(USA) Whisper Dance (USA) (Stravinsky (USA))
*5628a*[2] **6979a**[2] 7697a[2] 8526a[2]

**Goldy Espony (FR)** *Bob Baffert* a83 106
6 rg m Vespone(IRE) Goldy Honor (FR) (Highest Honor (FR))
**8601a**[14]

**Golfindia (FR)** *J-V Toux* 24
2 gr f Silver Frost(IRE) Grosgrain (USA) (Diesis)
**1335a**[16]

**Golly Miss Molly** *Martin Bosley* a72 60
6 b m Exceed And Excel(AUS) Amicable Terms (Royal Applause)
*677*[6] *1338*[9] *1620*[8] *2332*[3] *(3724)* ***(4217)*** 6889[U] *7766*[9] *8505*[5]

**Gondaro (GER)** *Frau C Barsig* a55
4 b g Sholokhov(IRE) Gondola (FR) (Lando (GER))
***691a***[6]

**Gondora (GER)** *R Dzubasz* 85
3 b f Soldier Hollow Gondola (FR) (Lando (GER))
**3371a**[6] 4393a[6] **5693a**[10]

**Gone To Sea (IRE)** *David Evans* 46
2 b f Born To Sea(IRE) Chaguaramas (IRE) (Mujadil (USA))
**3421**[9] 4054[6] 4620[5]

**Gone Viral (IRE)** *George Baker* a62 70
6 ch g Virtual Dorinda Gray (IRE) (Docksider (USA))
***92***[10] *382*[12]

**Gone With The Wind (GER)** *Rebecca Bastiman* a69 50
6 b g Dutch Art Gallivant (Danehill (USA))
**2501**[6] *9180*[11]

**Goninodaethat** *Jim Goldie* a38 64
9 b g Proclamation(IRE) Big Mystery (IRE) (Grand Lodge (USA))
1805[4] 2454[12] (2949) 3385[6] **3653**[3] 4080[7] 4682[6] 4958[4] **5203**[2] 5472[6] 5919[9] 5994[4] 6318[6] 6631[6] 7218[11] 7660[4] 7888[11]

**Go Now Go Now (IRE)** *Mark Johnston* 74
2 b g Kodiac Ms Mary C (IRE) (Dolphin Street (FR))
2452[4] 2698[7] 3495[2] 4101[4] (5279) **(6087)** **6762**[2] 7121[6] **7904**[4]

**Good Bond** *Linda Jewell* a34 39
5 b g Monsieur Bond(IRE) Seminole Sun (IRE) (Invincible Spirit (IRE))
*3456*[10] **3825**[3] *4562*[7] *5296*[P]

**Good Boy Jasper** *James Moffatt* 55
3 ch g Doncaster Rover(USA) Mitchelland (Namaqualand (USA))
**2455**[9] 5738[11] 6131[14]

**Good Business (IRE)** *Jeremy Noseda* a53 51
3 ch f Dutch Art Parakopi (IRE) (Green Desert (USA))
2798[10] 4409[4] 5611[9] 6751[4] ***7480***[4]

**Goodbye Lulu (IRE)** *George Baker* a51 51
2 b f Exceed And Excel(AUS) Guarantia (Selkirk (USA))
6438[8] **7351**[11] ***7724***[7]

**Goodby Inheritence** *Seamus Durack* a70 58
5 b g Medicean Chili Dip (Alhaarth (IRE))
*549*[8] *893*[5] *1283*[9] **2042**[5]

**Good Contact (USA)** *S Seemar*
5 b g Teofilo(IRE) Mayoress (Machiavellian (USA))
*9360a*[13]

**Good Impression** *Ali Stronge* a62 50
2 b g Showcasing Daintily Done (Cacique (IRE))
3305[9] 6070[8] 8466[7] ***9302***[2]◆

**Good King (GER)** *Carmen Bocskai*
3 b c Call Me Big(GER) Good Harmony (King's Best (USA))
3554a[3]

**Good Luck Charm** *Gary Moore* a65 82
8 b g Doyen(IRE) Lucky Dice (Perugino (USA))
1687[10] 3030[9] *3454*[7] 3938[4] 4176[2] 5119[10] (5870) 6378[5] **(7002)** 7653[8] 8184[8]

**Goodluck Joey** *Emmet Michael Butterly* a38
3 b g Sayif(IRE) Cozette (IRE) (Danehill Dancer (IRE))
*644*[RR]

**Good Magic (USA)** *Chad C Brown* a119
2 ch c Curlin(USA) Glinda The Good (USA) (Hard Spun (USA))
***(8609a)***

**Good Man (IRE)** *Karen McLintock* a48 38
4 ch g New Approach(IRE) Garden City (FR) (Majorien)
*4309*[13] 5458[5] 7331[6] 7885[3] 8241[10] ***8585***[6]

**Good Move (IRE)** *Brian Rothwell* 35
5 b m Aussie Rules(USA) Lady Lafitte (USA) (Stravinsky (USA))
2628[14]

**Goodnight Girl (IRE)** *Jonathan Portman* 79
2 ro f Clodovil(IRE) Leenavesta (USA) (Arch (USA))
5885[3] **6862**[2] 7226[5] 7621[5]

**Good Night Out (IRE)** *David Evans* a22
2 b f Fast Company(IRE) Titus Tina (IRE) (Titus Livius (FR))
***2277***[8]

**Good Omen** *David Simcock* a92 107
3 b g Holy Roman Emperor(IRE) Magic Nymph (IRE) (Galileo (IRE))
*430a*[12] 887a[8] (3316)◆ 3998[12] (5037) **(5568)**◆

**Good Run (FR)** *Saeed bin Suroor* a103 98
4 ch g Iffraaj Tadawul (USA) (Diesis)
***1309***[2] *1779*[11] 2157[6] *4356*[11]

**Good Samaritan (USA)** *William Mott* a112 110
3 b c Harlan's Holiday(USA) Pull Dancer (USA) (Pulpit (USA))
**4652a**[4]

**Goodthingstaketime (IRE)** *J A Stack* 99
2 b f Canford Cliffs(IRE) Addictedtoprogress (IRE) (Holy Roman Emperor (IRE))
**6241a**[2] 6977a[6]

**Good Time Ahead (IRE)** *Philip Kirby* a82 67
3 b g Iffraaj Good Time Sue (IRE) (Commander Collins (IRE))
*1493* *(378)* *766*[2] *967*[2] *1195*[5] 2854[8] 3489[6] 4016[4] 5005[5] *5831*[3] 6270[2] *6901*[3] *7568*[9] *(7936)* 8478[9] *8806*[3] *(8978)* ***(9178)***◆ *9341*[2]

**Good To Talk** *Y Barberot* a72 80
2 b c Camacho Talkative (Oasis Dream)
4196a[3] **(6409a)** **(6608a)** (8524a)

**Good Tradition (IRE)** *Donald McCain* 85
6 b g Pivotal Token Gesture (IRE) (Alzao (USA))
**2525**[15]

**Good Trip (IRE)** *A R Al Rayhi* a100 103
4 bl h Dansili Counterclaim (Pivotal)
**82a**[5] **208a**[2] 428a[6] 654a[10] 1042a[10]

**Good Way Off (USA)** *Luca Cumani* a84 87
4 b m Northern Afleet(USA) Out Of Reach I (Warning)
(6614) 7576[8] **8111**[4]

**Goodwood Crusader (IRE)** *Richard Hughes* a82 97
3 b g Sir Prancealot(IRE) Pale Orchid (IRE) (Invincible Spirit (IRE))
*324*[6] *813*[2] *1088*[2] *1328*[6] (1762) (1940) (3517) (3814)◆ **(4099)** 4813[7] 5637[14] 5916[7] *7455*[10] 8077[9]

**Goodwood Showman** *William Knight* a61 11
2 b g Showcasing Polly Floyer (Halling (USA))
8560[13] ***8840***[5]

**Goodyearforroses (IRE)** *Richard Baltas* a108 108
5 b m Azamour(IRE) Guilia (Galileo (IRE))
**8606a**[13]

**Go On Gal (IRE)** *Julia Feilden* a61 61
4 b m Approve(IRE) Jeritza (Rainbow Quest (USA))
*120*[6] *414*[2] *853*[3] ***1188***[2] *1548*[5] **2295**[3] 2964[8] 3439[4] 4545[5] 5787[5] ***(6524)*** *9445*[4]

**Go On Go On Go On** *Clive Cox* a72 100
4 b m Medicean Piranha (IRE) (Exceed And Excel (AUS))
3080[10] 6668[10] **7051**[3] 7396[16]

**Go On Mayson** *Christian Williams* 72
3 br g Mayson Red Tiara (USA) (Mr Prospector (USA))
1730[13] 3040[8] 3392[11] **4144**[5] 5249[7] 6342[9]

**Gopsies Daughter (IRE)** *Denis Gerard Hogan* a53 57
6 ch m Captain Rio Brief Journey (IRE) (Brief Truce (USA))
**(2656a)**

**Gorane (IRE)** *Henry De Bromhead* a82 104
3 b f Dream Ahead(USA) Holy Norma (Nashwan (USA))
2863a[4] 3873a[7] **(6640a)** 6973a[7]

**Gordon Lord Byron (IRE)** *T Hogan* a109 116
9 b g Byron Boa Estrela (IRE) (Intikhab (USA))
207a[9] 433a[9] *1353a*[2] 1653a[5] 2440a[4] (3099a) 3765a[4] 4935a[4] **5974a**[3] 6401[7] 7424a[6] 7663a[6] 8003[3] 8738[6]

**Gorgeous (FR)** *Tony Carroll* a61 37
4 b m Assertive Agent Kensington (Mujahid (USA))
***8873***[2]◆ *9214*[4]

**Gorgeous Kitten (USA)** *Michael J Maker* 98
3 b c Kitten's Joy(USA) Gorgelicious (USA) (More Than Ready (USA))
5953a[5]

**Gorgeous Noora (IRE)** *Luca Cumani* a91 61
3 b f Raven's Pass(USA) Aneedah (IRE) (Invincible Spirit (IRE))
7405[10] 8129[4] 8540[2] (8879)

**Gorham's Cave** *Roger Varian* a62 67
3 b g Rock Of Gibraltar(IRE) Moiava (FR) (Bering)
5315[5] 7930[5] 8342[3]

**Goring (GER)** *Eve Johnson Houghton* a100 90
5 b g Areion(GER) Globuli (GER) (Surako (GER))
2230[2] 2692[5] 3330[4] (3572) 4207[13] 5530[5] 5637[8] 6275[11] (7084) 7612[5] 8310[6] (9206)◆ (9468)

**Gormlaith (FR)** *P Monfort* a53 60
3 b f Whipper(USA) Decency (IRE) (Celtic Swing)
4943a[2]

**Gormley (USA)** *John Shirreffs* a116
3 b c Malibu Moon(USA) Race To Urga (USA) (Bernstein (USA))
2420a[9]

**Gorokai (IRE)** *David Simcock* a80 80
4 b g Kodiac Damask (IRE) (Red Clubs (IRE))
194[8]

**Go Roo** *Clive Cox* a73 66
2 br c Kyllachy Cross My Heart (Sakhee's Secret)
6304[3]◆ 7351[12] 7876[2]

**Gorse (IRE)** *Ann Duffield* a48 60
2 b g Zebedee Golden Flower (Royal Applause)
5834[10] 6432[5] 6755[4] 7920[3] 8475[12] 9098[6]

**Go Sandy** *Lisa Williamson* a46 48
2 ch f Captain Gerrard(IRE) Lily Jicaro (IRE) (Choisir (AUS))
4888[6] 5398[9] 5844[8] 6609[10]

**Gossip Column (IRE)** *Charles Hills* a63 71
2 b c Arcano(IRE) Monicalew (Refuse To Bend (IRE))
4696[4] 5608[4] 6353[13] 7106[5] 7489[4] 8349[8]

**Gossipe (FR)** *Y Gourraud* a36 64
2 bb f Deportivo Suricat Girl (IRE) (Antonius Pius (USA))
6171a[6]

**Gossiping** *Gary Moore* a92 98
5 b g Dubawi(IRE) Gossamer (Sadler's Wells (USA))
(166)◆ 382[5] (460) (1288)◆ 1422[3] (2390) (3003)◆ 4905[7] 5393[23] 5594[15] 6933[10] 7727[13]

**Gothic Empire (IRE)** *Richard Rowe* a89 79
5 b g Dark Angel(IRE) Box Of Frogs (IRE) (One Cool Cat (USA))
1622[7] 2283[5]◆ 3792[15] 5415[12] 6484[5] 7780[12] 8344[4] 8880[10] 9205[5]

**Got My Mojo** *Gary Sanderson*
7 b g Motivator Habla Me (IRE) (Fairy King (USA))
8256[9] 8479[11]

**Gotti (USA)** *Jeremy Noseda* a88 75
2 b c More Than Ready(USA) Soot Z (USA) (Empire Maker (USA))
3516[4] (3917) 4539[4]

**Gowanbuster** *Susan Corbett* a70
2 b g Bahri(USA) Aahgowangowan (IRE) (Tagula (IRE))
8316[5] (8915)◆

**Gowanless** *Michael Dods* a43 61
4 b g Monsieur Bond(IRE) Aahgowangowan (IRE) (Tagula (IRE))
1006[10] 1203[9]

**Gower Gold** *John Gallagher* a13
2 b f Mayson Mistressofthelake (IRE) (Mastercraftsman (IRE))
3174[9]

**Gowing Gowing Gone (IRE)** *Richard Spencer* a31 5
2 ch f Society Rock(IRE) Face The Storm (IRE) (Barathea (IRE))
6827[10] 7724[11] 8028[9]

**Gozo Girl** *Joseph Tuite* 15
2 b f Nayef(USA) Trust The Wind (Dansili)
7739[7]

**Graceful Act** *Ron Barr* a54 56
9 b m Royal Applause Minnina (IRE) (In The Wings)
1679[7] 2900[9] 4018[7] 4627[7] (5002) 5181[2] 5499[5] 5950[8] 6092[2] 6431[5] 7479[6] 8218[13]

**Graceful James (IRE)** *Jimmy Fox* a85 64
4 ch g Rock Of Gibraltar(IRE) Little Miss Gracie (Efisio)
3009[9] 4751[3] (5747)◆ 6848[4]◆ 7358[11] 7949[10] 9205[7]

**Graceful Lady** *Robert Eddery* a69 81
4 b m Sixties Icon Leitzu (IRE) (Barathea (IRE))
279[6] 645[3] 1082[2] 1556[4] 2281[2] (2972) (3863) (4000) 4630[2] (5438) 6968[4] 7402[5] 8394[5] 8565[7]

**Graceland (FR)** *Michael Bell* a94 96
5 gr m Mastercraftsman(IRE) Jeunesse Lulu (IRE) (Montjeu (IRE))
(2562) 2770[2] 3968[4] 4355[2] 5912[3] 6675[9] 6929[2] 7507[8]

**Grace Rafaela (IRE)** *M D O'Callaghan* a82 68
2 bb f Dragon Pulse(IRE) Emsiyah (USA) (Bernardini (USA))
7797a[5]

**Gracesome (IRE)** *Michael Blanshard* a66 38
6 b m Shirocco(GER) Simonda (Singspiel (IRE))
7711[10] 8993[9]

**Grace's Secret** *Ed Walker* a70 54
2 ro f Mastercraftsman(IRE) Silent Music (IRE) (Peintre Celebre (USA))
7021[8] 7454[8] 7995[6] 8817[3] 9097[10]

**Gracious Diana** *John Gosden* a83 93
3 ch f Foxwedge(AUS) Generous Diana (Generous (IRE))
(1944) 2827[4] 3995[10] 8739[7] 8986a[14]

**Gracious George (IRE)** *Jimmy Fox* a66 68
7 b g Oratorio(IRE) Little Miss Gracie (Efisio)
90[8] 812[5] 986[5] 3718[8] 8313[11] 8908[3] 9456[6]

**Gracious John (IRE)** *David Evans* a114 103
4 b g Baltic King Dorn Hill (Lujain (USA))
200[4] 572[4] 932a[4] 1772[2] 2397[10] 3926[14] 4635[8] 6039[6] 6325[11] 6677[6] 7027[3] 7286[5] (8139) 8679[5] (9187) (9373)

**Gracious Tom (IRE)** *David Evans* a82 63
3 b c Roderic O'Connor(IRE) Bigalo's Laura B (IRE) (Needwood Blade)
125[5] (155) 243[2] 291[3] 458[6]

**Graffiti Master** *John Gosden* a81 98
2 b c Dubawi(IRE) Independence (Selkirk (USA))
6654[4] (7451) 8035[3]

**Graffitista (IRE)** *George Scott* a53 62
2 b f Kodiac Noble Galileo (IRE) (Galileo (IRE))
4312[5] 5026[6] 6272[5] 7057[10]

**Grainne's Dream (IRE)** *W P Mullins* a62 72
4 b m Acclamation Cold Cold Woman (Machiavellian (USA))
5519a[8]

**Gramercy (IRE)** *Ian Williams* a78 78
10 b g Whipper(USA) Topiary (IRE) (Selkirk (USA))
304[4] 551[7] 783[9] 1365[3] 1674[4] 3581[10] 4091[4] 4810[7]

**Grams And Ounces** *Grace Harris* a55 65
10 b g Royal Applause Ashdown Princess (IRE) (King's Theatre (IRE))
924[7] (3575) (3805) 4494[4] 4804[7] (5362) 5968[5] 6509[6] 7336[8]

**Grand Acclaim (IRE)** *Harry Dunlop* a55 53
2 ch c Monsieur Bond(IRE) Endless Applause (Royal Applause)
3689[9] 4977[5] 5779[4] 6790[8]

**Grandad Chunk (IRE)** *Colin Teague* a40 47
6 gr g Acclamation Silverdreammachine (IRE) (Marju (IRE))
2342[8] 3185[8]

**Grandad's World (IRE)** *Richard Fahey* 93
5 b g Kodiac Nose One's Way (IRE) (Revoque (IRE))
1831[3] 2184[5] 3052[8] 3653[7] 6267[6] 6669[4] 7099[2] 7554[9]

**Grand Argentier (FR)** *Doug Watson* a102 86
5 b h Palace Episode(USA) Ashkadima (IRE) (Ashkalani (IRE))
319a[4] (537a)

**Grand Daddy** *P Bary* 67
2 b c Scat Daddy(USA) Long Face (USA) (Whywhywhy (USA))
5626a[5]

**Grandee (IRE)** *Mrs John Harrington* 105
3 b g Lope De Vega(IRE) Caravan Of Dreams (IRE) (Anabaa (USA))
1636a[6] 4387a[9] 5862a[6]

**Grand Facile** *Gary Moore* a59 36
5 b g Henrythenavigator(USA) Santolina (USA) (Boundary (USA))
35[2] 436[8] (646) 820[8] 4346[4] 4756[10]

**Grandfather Tom** *Robert Cowell* a66
2 b c Kheleyf(USA) Kassuta (Kyllachy)
9123[5]

**Grand Gala (FR)** *S Labate* a60 67
6 gr g Creachadoir(IRE) Natt Musik (FR) (Kendor (FR))
364a[2]

**Grand Inquisitor** *Ian Williams* a81 95
5 b g Dansili Dusty Answer (Zafonic (USA))
1622[9] 2115[12] 2828[6] 4294[9] 6134[3] 6700[3] 7131[4] 7959[4] (8048) 9407[8]

**Grand Jete** *Chad C Brown* a89 109
4 b m Dansili Modern Look (Zamindar (USA))
5954a[2] 8606a[9]

**Grand Koonta (IRE)** *Clive Cox* 97
2 gr c Dark Angel(IRE) Wrong Key (IRE) (Key Of Luck (USA))
2779[4] 3590[2] (4367) 4812[8] 7394[5]

**Grandma Tilly** *Steph Hollinshead* 52
2 b f Hellvelyn Sleep Dance (Sleeping Indian)
2502[8]

**Grand Meister** *John Quinn* a78 50
6 gr g Mastercraftsman(IRE) Wait It Out (USA) (Swain (IRE))
196[9] 958[6] 1257[5] 1716[12]

**Grand Myla (IRE)** *Gary Moore* a65 63
3 gr f Dark Angel(IRE) Selfara (Oasis Dream)
4990[4] 6106[8] 6581[7] 7494[2] 7767[8] 9471[3]

**Grand Partner (IRE)** *Thomas Mullins* 86
9 b g Millenary Bens Partner (IRE) (Beneficial)
7860a[7]

**Grandscape** *Ed Dunlop* 72
2 b c Lemon Drop Kid(USA) Unnatural (USA) (Proud Citizen (USA))
7281[4] 8381[4]

**Grand Vintage (FR)** *A Schutz* a76 102
8 b h Marchand De Sable(USA) Fifty Niner (FR) (Fijar Tango (FR))
7416a[3] 8089a[5]

**Granite City Doc** *Lucy Normile* 49
4 b g Arabian Gleam Hansomis (IRE) (Titus Livius (FR))
5997[7] 6690[2] 7703[9]

**Gran Maestro (USA)** *Peter Winks*
8 ch g Medicean Red Slippers (USA) (Nureyev (USA))
7893[10]

**Granny Anne (IRE)** *Natalie Lloyd-Beavis* a51 41
9 ch m Redback Krayyalei (IRE) (Krayyan)
1933a[2] 3575[7]

**Granny Roz** *David Barron* 73
3 b f Bahamian Bounty Hulcote Rose (IRE) (Rock Of Gibraltar (IRE))
2180[5] 2898[7] 3568[2] 4106[2] (5167) 5636[2] 5877[2] 7522[15]

**Gran Paradiso (IRE)** *Micky Hammond* 63
5 ch g Galileo(IRE) Looking Lovely (IRE) (Storm Cat (USA))
1703[6] 2032[5]

**Gran Pierino (ITY)** *Antonio Marcialis* a81 81
3 b c Montalegre(IRE) Universal Shade (ITY) (Pursuit Of Love)
5909a[7]

**Grantchester (IRE)** *James Eustace* a63
3 ch g Exceed And Excel(AUS) Emily Blake (IRE) (Lend A Hand)
5746[4] 6851[6]

**Grapevine (IRE)** *Charles Hills* 92
4 b g Lilbourne Lad(IRE) High Vintage (IRE) (High Chaparral (IRE))
1964[2] 2396[8] 3300[13] 4585[4] 5609[5] 6515[5] 7358[7] 8111[6]

**Graphite (FR)** *A Fabre* 107
3 gr g Shamardal(USA) Fairly Grey (FR) (Linamix (FR))
(1658a) 6498a[5]

**Graphite (IRE)** *David Simcock* a66 72
3 ro g Galileo(IRE) Simply Perfect (Danehill (USA))
4409[3] 5220[4] 5632[7] 7896[2] 8434[6]

**Graphite Girl (IRE)** *Tim Easterby* a40 48
2 gr f Kodiac My Girl Lisa (USA) (With Approval (CAN))
4888[7] 5665[9] 6312[8] 7243[5] 7518[7] 8588[7]

**Graphite Storm** *Clive Cox* 99
3 gr g Delegator Ice Haven (IRE) (Verglas (IRE))
1945[6] 2567[2] 3077[7] 5294[5] 6192[2] (7025)◆ 7784[6]

**Grasmere (IRE)** *Alan Bailey* a49 54
2 b f Society Rock(IRE) Silk Point (IRE) (Barathea (IRE))
6292[7] 6776[5] 7141[7] 8793[6]◆ 9230[7]

**Gravina** *Alan King* 36
2 b f Havana Gold(IRE) Dolcetto (IRE) (Danehill Dancer (IRE))
2779[11]

**Gravity Flow (IRE)** *William Haggas* a72 105
4 ch m Exceed And Excel(AUS) Landela (Alhaarth (IRE))
3080[8] 4864[10] 6025[11] 7811[12]

**Gravity Wave (IRE)** *Sylvester Kirk* a50 75
3 br g Rip Van Winkle(IRE) Phrase (Royal Anthem (USA))
1737[7] 2132[7] 3457[12] 3922[6] 4623[6]

**Graystorm (TUR)** *Mehmet Cucel* 94
4 gr h Luxor(TUR) Setryn (TUR) (Strike The Gold (USA))
320a[7]

**Great And Small** *Andrew Balding* a54 92
4 b m Galileo(IRE) Gryada (Shirley Heights)
2176[8]

**Great Aventura (IRE)** *Cristiano Davide Fais* 94
3 b f Clodovil(IRE) Gold Blended (IRE) (Goldmark (USA))
3121a[10]

**Great Beyond** *Roger Charlton* 66
2 b c Dansili Solar Pursuit (Galileo (IRE))
8678[8]

**Great Colaci** *Gillian Boanas* a50 59
4 b g Sulamani(IRE) Fairlie (Halling (USA))
(3831) 4744[9] 6112[12] 6902[7] 7165[6]

**Great Court (IRE)** *Roger Varian* a95 85
3 gr f Mastercraftsman(IRE) Neat Shilling (IRE) (Bob Back (USA))
2227[5] 5549[3] (6161) 6722[2] 7816[5] (8398)◆ 8992[7]

**Great Dora (FR)** *T Castanheira* a74 69
4 bl m Great Journey(JPN) Dora De Green (IRE) (Green Tune (USA))
515a[8]

**Great Expectations** *J R Jenkins* a57 70
9 b g Storming Home Fresh Fruit Daily (Reprimand)
88[3] 438[4] 1006[7] 1359[6] 2298[7] 2733[9] 2800[7] 4323[9]

**Great Fighter** *Jim Goldie* a66 89
7 b g Street Cry(IRE) Evil Empire (GER) (Acatenango (GER))
991[6] (3046)◆ (3830) 4921[5] 5882[2] 6929[5] 7402[16]

**Great Hall** *Mick Quinn* a106 108
7 b g Halling(USA) L'Affaire Monique (Machiavellian (USA))
1341[4] 1704[7] 2086[4] 2396[6] 3300[6] 3597[13] 4370[3] 5037[5] 5421[6] (5913) (6872) (7337) 7805[6]

**Great Minds (IRE)** *J A Stack* 70
7 ch g Bahamian Bounty Raja (IRE) (Pivotal)
1520a[5]

**Great Prospector (IRE)** *Richard Fahey* 103
2 b c Elzaam(AUS) Guana (IRE) (Dark Angel (IRE))
(3754)◆ 4906[3] 6353[2] 7090[4] 8037[6]

**Great Return** *Warren Greatrex* a64 59
4 b g New Approach(IRE) Under The Rainbow (Fantastic Light (USA))
2887[6] 3062[7] 3935[10] 4088[5] 9095[3] 9317[2]

**Great Roar (USA)** *Ronald Thompson* a13
9 b g Thunder Gulch(USA) Boasting (USA) (Kris S (USA))
29[6] 687[6]

**Great Shot Sam (USA)** *Andrew Balding* a70 52
2 ch f Shackleford(USA) Universal Peace (JPN) (Sunday Silence (USA))
6286[2] 7556[6] (8914)

**Great Soprano (USA)** *Hans-Inge Larsen* a72 78
8 bb g Arch(USA) Insan Mala (IRE) (Bahhare (USA))
2941a[7]

**Great Sound (IRE)** *John Gosden* 96
3 b c Galileo(IRE) Wanna (IRE) (Danehill Dancer (IRE))
(3427)◆ 4221[3] (6135) 6930[6] 8384[5]

**Great Uncle (IRE)** *Brendan W Duke* a53 58
3 ch g Intense Focus(USA) Abigail's Aunt (Efisio)
1389a[8]

**Great Vizier** *Eve Johnson Houghton* 70
2 b g Sir Percy Special Green (FR) (Sadler's Wells (USA))
5030[6]◆ 6093[2] 6777[9]

**Great White Shark (FR)** *James Fanshawe* 94
3 gr f Le Havre(IRE) Trip To Fame (FR) (Lordmare (FR))
3506[5] (4300) (5630) 6914a[8]

**Grecian Divine (IRE)** *Joseph Tuite* a70 83
3 b f Kodiac Grecian Glory (IRE) (Zafonic (USA))
877 1090[4] 1294[5] 1487[8] 1731[14] 3035[6] 7122[11]

**Grecian King** *David Barron* a46 30
4 b g Kheleyf(USA) Grecian Air (FR) (King's Best (USA))
1203[8] 2082[10] 2453[5]

**Grecian Light (IRE)** *Charlie Appleby* 103
3 b f Shamardal(USA) Akrivi (IRE) (Tobougg (IRE))
1270a[3] 3964[21]

**Grecian Spirit** *James Tate* a73
2 b c Teofilo(IRE) Ghar Shoop (IRE) (Dubai Destination (USA))
8492[3]◆ 8987[3]

**Greeleys Love (USA)** *Ecurie Fievez* a26 43
7 ch g Mr Greeley(USA) Aunt Winnie (IRE) (Deputy Minister (CAN))
6543a[2]

**Green Byron (FR)** *Mlle S Sine* a16 59
7 b g Green Tune(USA) Heritiere (AUS) (Anabaa (USA))
4457a[9]

**Green Door (IRE)** *Robert Cowell* a89 105
6 b g Camacho Inourhearts (IRE) (Pips Pride)
4881[11] 5505[3] 5911[7] 6039[3] 6640a[4] 6927[12] 7610[14] 8139[3] 8238[6] 8679[3] 8913[7]

**Greeneyedafghan** *William Muir* 69
2 b g Sepoy(AUS) Extremely Rare (IRE) (Mark Of Esteem (IRE))
(5561) 6761[6] 7197[5]

**Green Fortune** *William Haggas* a87 79
2 b c Sayif(IRE) Shyrl (Acclamation)
(3245) 4526[3] (5240)◆ 6330[17] 6935[2] 7821[13]

**Greengairs** *Keith Dalgleish* a34 63
3 b g Delegator Shore Light (USA) (Gulch (USA))
385[6] 3709[6] 4687[3] 5205[4] 5467[5]

**Green Howard** *Rebecca Bastiman* a81 78
9 ch g Bahamian Bounty Dash Of Lime (Bold Edge)
122[6] 363[10] 968[6] 1409[6] 1610[5] 2224[7] 3402[2] 3560[3] 3977[7] 5544[11] 5649[3] 6003[2] 6783[5] 7703[2] 7980[2] 8300[6] 8514[7]

**Green Light** *Brian Ellison* a74 97
6 b g Authorized(IRE) May Light (Midyan (USA))
1976[4] 2375[4] 3323[10] 4355[11] 5417[11]

**Green Or Black (IRE)** *Neil Mulholland* a67 84
5 gr m Zebedee Boucheron (Galileo (IRE))
353[5] 609[6] 6307[3]

**Green Power** *John Gallagher* 92
2 b c Kheleyf(USA) Hakuraa (IRE) (Elnadim (USA))
1966[7] (2926) 4526[2] 5570[5] 6521[6]

**Greenside** *Henry Candy* a81 105
6 b g Dubawi(IRE) Katrina (IRE) (Ela-Mana-Mou)
3014[2]◆ (3837) 4636[6] 5594[12] 7619[17] 8234[9]

**Greenview Paradise (IRE)** *Brian Barr* a54 62
3 gr f Exchange Rate(USA) Senza Rete (IRE) (Barathea (IRE))
1913[12] 2228[8] 2993[2] 3561[2] 3900[3] 4332[2] 4603[2] 5212[4] 6784[2] 7902[10] 8707[4] 8957[13]

**Greg Pass (IRE)** *Nicolo Simondi* 108
5 b g Raven's Pass(USA) Baranja (USA) (St Jovite (USA))
2663a[2] 3120a[3] 7442a[2] 8448a[5]

**Grendisar (IRE)** *Marco Botti* a115 55
7 b h Invincible Spirit(IRE) Remarkable Story (Mark Of Esteem (IRE))
574[4] 919[5] 1775[8]

**Greshnitsia (FR)** *V Luka Jr* a76 72
3 b f Redoute's Choice(AUS) Gadalka (USA) (Giant's Causeway (USA))
8976a[5]

**Greta (FR)** *Frau Erika Mader* 55
4 b m High Chaparral(IRE) Give Me Five (GER) (Monsun (GER))
7673a[9] 8090a[11]

**Greta G (ARG)** *John Gosden* 104
3 gr m Exchange Rate(USA) Gringa Nativa (ARG) (Orpen (USA))
3961[9] 4857[6] 6697[10]

**Grey Britain** *John Ryan* a90 104
3 gr g Arcano(IRE) Reaching Ahead (USA) (Mizzen Mast (USA))
649a[5]◆ 887a[6] 1026[4] 1801[2] 2402[4] (2829) 3994[10] 4817[5] 5568[4]

**Grey Caviar (FR)** *M Le Forestier* a86 61
4 bb g Air Chief Marshal(IRE) Trip To Fame (FR) (Lordmare (FR))
2696a[14]

**Grey Danube (IRE)** *D J Bunyan* a99 57
8 gr g Verglas(IRE) Redrightreturning (Diktat)
795a[9] 1769[14] 8222a[4]

**Grey Destiny** *Antony Brittain* a71 64
7 gr g Desideratum Mother Corrigan (IRE) (Paris House)
(1408) 1823[6] 2278[7] 2918[2] 3263[3] 3912[6] 4165[4] 4743[2] 5497[7] 5802[7] 6529[6] 6902[5]◆ 7240[7] 7573[3] 8210[9] 8402[2] (8659) (9219)

**Grey Diamond** *Denis Quinn* a52 62
3 gr g Shamardal(USA) Tiffany Diamond (IRE) (Sadler's Wells (USA))
4247[7] 4579[5] 5075[3] 5485[13] 5800[5] 6257[9] 9317[12]

**Greyfriarschorista** *David Evans* a64 52
10 ch g King's Best(USA) Misty Heights (Fasliyev (USA))
6[7] 287[11] 460[10] 663[9] 1086[4] 1109[4] 1186[3] 1449[8] 2465[2] 2763[4] 2916[8] 4970[8] 6342[8]

**Grey Gem (IRE)** *K Kukk* a49 30
6 gr g Danehill Dancer(IRE) Tiffany Diamond (IRE) (Sadler's Wells (USA))
1933a[7] 2672a[9] 5987a[4]

**Greyjoy (IRE)** *Sylvester Kirk* a60 47
3 gr g Mastercraftsman(IRE) American Jewel (USA) (Quiet American (USA))
236[8] 895[10] 1297[4] 1564[9] 1790[6] 2027[8] 2726[9] 3191[8] 3657[4] 3939[8] 4982[7] 5935[8] 6076[10] 6821[8] 7210[12]

**Grey Lion (IRE)** *Matt Cumani* a75 108
5 gr h Galileo(IRE) Grey Lilas (IRE) (Danehill (USA))
8100a[3] 8751a[2]

**Grey Magic (FR)** *N Caullery* a52 81
3 gr g Kendargent(FR) Magical Flower (Oasis Dream)
3446a[10]

**Grey Magic Night (FR)** *L Rovisse* a67 60
4 gr m Smadoun(FR) Red Valentine (IRE) (Bad As I Wanna Be (IRE))
**8338a**[5]

**Grey Mirage** *Gay Kelleway* a50 41
8 b g Oasis Dream Grey Way (USA) (Cozzene (USA))
*199*[8] *384a*[7]

**Grey Mist** *Tim Easterby* 66
3 gr g Mastercraftsman(IRE) Kekova (Montjeu (IRE))
**4569**[7] 5128[3] 5632[9] 6436[7] 7047[7] 7248[7] 8291[7]

**Grey Panel (FR)** *T Le Brocq* 46
9 gr g Largesse Minnie's Mystery (FR) (Highest Honor (FR))
1932a[6] 2672a[6] **4143a**[2] **4656a**[2] 5201a[5]

**Grey Spirit (IRE)**
*Sir Mark Prescott Bt* a55 61
2 gr g Dark Angel(IRE) Buttonhole (Montjeu (IRE))
**7079**[6] *7765*[9] *8149*[10]

**Grey Waters (IRE)**
*Joseph Patrick O'Brien* a68 67
3 gr f Mastercraftsman(IRE) Pelican Waters (IRE) (Key Of Luck (USA))
*(8647)*◆

**Greyway (FR)** *J-M Lefebvre* a95 95
3 gr c Myboycharlie(IRE) Aliyeska (IRE) (Fasliyev (USA))
**1824a**[6] 2561a[7]

**Grieg Hall** *John Gosden* a81 83
3 b g Halling(USA) Woven Lace (Hard Spun (USA))
**1906**[5]◆ *2521*[2] 3533[3]

**Grimeford Lane (IRE)**
*Michael Dods* a63 66
2 b g Zoffany(IRE) Bean Uasal (IRE) (Oasis Dream)
3895[9] 4597[7] **4956**[2] 5756[8] 7023[3] *(7827)* **8213**[2]

**Grinty (IRE)** *Michael Dods* 75
3 b c Elnadim(USA) Fire Line (Firebreak)
**(2345)** 3434[6] 4437[3] 5132[8] 5697[6] 6265[6] 7249[2] 8216[2] 8651[3]

**Gripper** *Ralph Beckett* a67
2 b g Thewayyouare(USA) Hold On Tight (IRE) (Hernando (FR))
*6636*[4]◆ *7489*[5]

**Gris D'Argent (FR)** *D De Watrigant* a85 88
3 bb c Silver Frost(IRE) Belle Lagune (Barathea (IRE))
*799a*[5]

**Grise Lightning (FR)** *Richard Fahey* a68 68
2 gr f Wootton Bassett Tenepia (FR) (Keltos (FR))
**6347**[2]◆ *7033*[4]

**Grizzel (IRE)** *Michael J Doyle* a97 103
3 b f Kodiac Milana (FR) (Mark Of Esteem (IRE))
**4650a**[5]

**Gronkowski (USA)** *Jeremy Noseda* a90 79
2 b c Lonhro(AUS) Four Sugars (USA) (Lookin At Lucky (USA))
7391[7] 7810[2]◆ *(8703)*◆

**Groor** *Mohamed Moubarak* a86 86
5 b h Archipenko(USA) Alta Moda (Sadler's Wells (USA))
*537a*[4] 3857[4] 4861[6] 5313[9] 6516[5]◆ 7098[U] *7493*[6]

**Groovejet** *Richard Spencer* a83 102
6 b m Cockney Rebel(IRE) Vino Veritas (USA) (Chief's Crown (USA))
5658[5] **6391**[3] 7089[10] 7817[10]

**Groovy Filly (FR)** *Y Gourraud* 83
3 b f Motivator Grigiamine (IRE) (Hawk Wing (USA))
**6566a**[3]

**Groundfrost (IRE)**
*John James Feane* a81 86
3 gr f Excelebration(IRE) Evening Time (IRE) (Keltos (FR))
4385a[4] **6334a**[5] *9316*[2] *9464*[7]

**Groundnut** *Jonathan Portman* 74
2 b g Rip Van Winkle(IRE) Hard Walnut (IRE) (Cape Cross (IRE))
3156[4]◆ 3690[2] 5030[7] **(7211)** 7913[3]

**Ground Rules (ITY)** *Stefano Botti* 97
3 bb c Aussie Rules(USA) Grivele (IRE) (El Prado (IRE))
**2868a**[6]

**Groundskeeperwilly** *Frank Sheridan* a28
3 ch g Camacho Hello Deauville (FR) (Alhaarth (IRE))
*600*[9] **785**[4] *956*[9] 4783a[12]

**Groundworker (IRE)** *Paul Midgley* a68 56
6 b g Tagula(IRE) Notepad (King's Best (USA))
*1200*[6] *1558*[4] 2034[7] 2628[7] 3944[6] 4559[5] 4896[5] 6631[4] **(7036)** *7366*[13] 7884[11] *8557*[10]

**Groupie** *Tom Tate* a64 86
3 b f Requinto(IRE) Amour Fou (IRE) (Piccolo)
2856[11] 3462[8] 3946[6] **(4529)** 5376[10] 5881[8] *7789*[9]

**Groveman** *Charles Hills* 72
2 b c Holy Roman Emperor(IRE) Raving Monsun (Monsun (GER))
4909[4] **5420**[6] 5786[5]

**Growl** *Richard Fahey* a79 117
5 b g Oasis Dream Desert Tigress (USA) (Storm Cat (USA))
2737[7] 3587[7] 4071[U] 4907[6] **5640**[4] 6206[9] 6926[7] 7611[10] 8044[11]

**Grumeti** *Alan King* a87 92
9 b g Sakhee(USA) Tetravella (IRE) (Groom Dancer (USA))
**(1405)** 2770[6] *4499*[4] 4998[3] 5944[4]

**Guanabara Bay (IRE)**
*Adrian McGuinness* a70 73
4 b g Clodovil(IRE) Sakaka (Tobougg (IRE))
*1233a*[7] **5518a**[5] *6797a*[4]

**Guanacaste (IRE)** *H-A Pantall* 83
3 gr g Whipper(USA) Divine Promesse (FR) (Verglas (IRE))
(8959a)

**Guardini (FR)** *Darren Weir* 111
6 rg h Dalakhani(IRE) Guantana (GER) (Dynaformer (USA))
**8100a**[12]

**Guard of Honour (IRE)**
*George Baker* a90 90
6 b g Galileo(IRE) Queen Of France (USA) (Danehill (USA))
*227a*[5] **1942**[4] 4073[6] 5524[8]

**Guerre (USA)** *Flemming Velin* a93 97
6 bb h War Front(USA) Golden Toast (USA) (Hennessy (USA))
**6500a**[4]

**Guessthebill (IRE)** *J P Murtagh* 99
2 b c Reckless Abandon Tussie Mussie (Royal Applause)
4926a[5] **8265a**[4]

**Guiding Passion (FR)** *K R Burke* 64
3 b f Iffraaj Right Ted (IRE) (Mujadil (USA))
**2345**[4]◆ 7388[5] 7896[7] 8959a[14]

**Guiding Star** *Patrick J McKenna* a40 62
3 b f Iffraaj Still I'm A Star (IRE) (Lawman (FR))
2455[8] 2949[3] **3525**[3] *8924*[5]

**Guignol (GER)** *Jean-Pierre Carvalho* 117
5 bb h Cape Cross(IRE) Guadalupe (GER) (Monsun (GER))
2249a[6] (3116a) 4392a[4] (6727a) **(8527a)** 8975a[9]

**Guiliana (FR)** *Waldemar Hickst* 90
3 b f Zoffany(IRE) Guiana (GER) (Tiger Hill (IRE))
**8088a**[10]

**Guiri (GER)** *Jean-Pierre Carvalho* 107
2 ch c Motivator Guardia (GER) (Monsun (GER))
**8621a**[2]

**Guishan** *Michael Appleby* a93 101
7 b m Ishiguru(USA) Fareham (Komaite (USA))
*4*[4] *639*[6] 5117[12] (5758) 6205[4] (6412) **(6787)**

**Guitar Pete (IRE)** *Nicky Richards* 65
7 gr g Dark Angel(IRE) Innishmore (IRE) (Lear Fan (USA))
**4684**[2]

**Gulf Of Poets** *Michael Easterby* a83 97
5 b g Oasis Dream Sandglass (Zafonic (USA))
(1707)◆ *(1892)* (3451) **(3744)** 4475[4] 5382[7] 6449[19] 7595[7] 8048[8] 8652[3]

**Gulland Rock** *Anthony Carson* a74 70
6 b g Exceed And Excel(AUS) Sacre Coeur (Compton Place)
***(1419)*** *1728*[3] 2120[3] 2731[5] *3454*[4] 4350[12] 4766[6]

**Gullane One (IRE)** *Tim Easterby* 60
2 ch g Dream Ahead(USA) Shamsalmaidan (IRE) (Fantastic Light (USA))
6939[8] **7562**[3] **8010**[7]

**Gulliver** *Hugo Palmer* a110 97
3 b g Sayif(IRE) Sweet Coincidence (Mujahid (USA))
1904[7] 2692[4] 3844[17] 5513[2] 5942[7] 6275[6] 6922[2] *(7828)* *(8547)* ***(8639)*** *8944*[7] *9409*[2]

**Gumriyah** *John Gosden* 80
2 b f Shamardal(USA) Yummy Mummy (Montjeu (IRE))
8006[7] **8380**[3]

**Gun Case** *Alistair Whillans* a70 65
5 b g Showcasing Bassinet (USA) (Stravinsky (USA))
*2923*[11] 3897[9] 4663[10] 5206[3] 5993[5] 6435[4] *7034*[10] *7573*[2] *8210*[4] ***(8590)*** ***8721***[2] ***8928***[3] *9101*[9]

**Gung Ho Jack** *John Best* a79 73
8 b g Moss Vale(IRE) Bijan (IRE) (Mukaddamah (USA))
*715a*[6] *834a*[5] *953a*[4] **2320**[8] 2608[8] **3758**[4]

**Gunmaker (IRE)** *David Simcock* a66 69
3 b g Canford Cliffs(IRE) Can Dance (Manduro (GER))
*1241*[4] *1488*[5] *1889*[4] 3088[8] 3621[10] **4542**[2] 5326[5] 5855[4] 7247[4]

**Gunmetal (IRE)** *Charles Hills* 101
4 gr g Clodovil(IRE) March Star (IRE) (Mac's Imp (USA))
1515[18] **(1880)** 2433[7]◆ 2780[6] 3593[11] 4854[14] 8383[20]

**Gunnar Julius (USA)** *Ed Walker* a44 36
2 b c Lonhro(AUS) Peinture Ancienne (USA) (Seeking The Gold (USA))
7079[8] ***8945***[6] *9404*[8]

**Gunner Lindley (IRE)**
*Stuart Coltherd* a34 48
10 ch g Medicean Lasso (Indian Ridge (IRE))
**3654**[5]

**Gunner Moyne** *Emma Owen* a64 40
5 b g Excellent Art Maramkova (IRE) (Danehill Dancer (IRE))
*2381*[0] *570*[6] ***(1544)*** *2095*[7] 2615[9] *5296*[3] *6524*[12] *7729*[11] *8675*[9] *9141*[7] *9343*[3]

**Gunnevera (USA)** *Antonio Sano* a119
3 ch c Dialed In(USA) Unbridled Rage (USA) (Unbridled (USA))
*2420a*[7] *2851a*[5] ***8611a***[5]

**Gun Runner (USA)**
*Steven Asmussen* a130
4 ch h Candy Ride(ARG) Quiet Giant (USA) (Giant's Causeway (USA))
*1380a*[2] ***(8611a)***

**Guns Drawn (IRE)** *Richard Hannon* a73
2 b f Dandy Man(IRE) Just Like Ivy (CAN) (Street Cry (IRE))
*7453*[4] *7725*[4] ***(8130)***

**Gunvald (USA)** *Fredrik Reuterskiold* a90
4 b h Proud Citizen(USA) Perfeck Connect (USA) (Yonaguska (USA))
*2942a*[3] ***4940a***[3]

**Gurkha Friend** *Karen McLintock* a78 98
5 b g Showcasing Parabola (Galileo (IRE))
1799[3] (2155) (2855) **3498**[3] 3842[8] 6520[6] 7886[8] 8469[10] 8737[15] *8910*[7]

**Gustav Klimt (IRE)** *A P O'Brien* 110
2 b c Galileo(IRE) Massarra (Danehill (USA))
**(4906)**

**Gustavo Fring (IRE)**
*Richard Spencer* a74
3 b g Kodiac Maleha (IRE) (Cape Cross (IRE))
***2090***[4] *8995*[2] *(9344)*

**Gustavus Vassa** *W P Mullins* 94
3 b g Equiano(FR) Poldhu (Cape Cross (IRE))
**7860a**[13]

**Guvenor's Choice (IRE)** *K R Burke* a84 73
2 ro g Intikhab(USA) Exempt (Exceed And Excel (AUS))
5030[4]◆ 5557[2]◆ *(8748)* *8951*[5] ***(9405)***

**Guzman (IRE)** *Richard Fahey* a75 79
2 b g Camacho Casablanca Jewel (IRE) (Kalanisi (IRE))
(2403) *(3339)* **4858**[5] 6353[11] 7050[4] *7536*[9] 8008[5] 8349[5]

**Gwendolyn (GER)** *Amy Murphy* a73 87
4 b m Invincible Spirit(IRE) Golden Whip (GER) (Seattle Dancer (USA))
*816*[9] ***1302***[7] 1915[6]

**Gworn** *R Mike Smith* a46 87
7 b g Aussie Rules(USA) Crochet (IRE) (Mark Of Esteem (IRE))
2458[4] (2953) (3197) **3651**[2] (4035)◆ 4658[6] 5207[2] 5470[3] 5996[4] 6383[11] 7701[7]

**Gymkhana** *Mrs John Harrington* 98
4 ch g Equiano(FR) Village Fete (Singspiel (IRE))
**(1385a)** 1520a[10] 8438a[12]

**Gymnaste (IRE)** *John Gosden* a93 100
3 b f Shamardal(USA) Galipette (Green Desert (USA))
(2572) *3211*[2]◆ 3964[15] **4903**[2] 5422[7] 8040[6]

**Gypsy Major** *John Weymes* a67 61
5 ch g Major Cadeaux Romany Gypsy (Indesatchel (IRE))
**5620**[4] 7245[11]

**Gypsy Rider** *Henry Tett* a42 52
8 b g Ishiguru(USA) Spaniola (IRE) (Desert King (IRE))
*1671*[0] *495*[6] 2053[5] **(2294)** 3823[4] *6813*[6]

**Haabis (USA)** *George Peckham* a52 18
4 bb g Super Saver(USA) Raise Fee (USA) (Menifee (USA))
***811***[7] *1146*[8] *1458*[9] ***1695***[3] 2729[10]

**Haader (FR)** *Owen Burrows* a70
2 ch c Sepoy(AUS) Idle Tears (Selkirk (USA))
***8149***[5]

**Haaf A Sixpence** *Ralph Beckett* a94 53
8 b g Haafhd Melody Maker (Diktat)
***918***[4]

**Haafdasee** *Tim Easterby*
2 b g Haafhd See Clearly (Bertolini (USA))
2698[11]

**Haaffa Sovereign** *Laura Morgan* a53 20
6 ch g Haafhd Royal Nashkova (Mujahid (USA))
***281***[8] *1629*[10]

**Haalick (IRE)** *D Selvaratnam* a76 103
4 ch g Roderic O'Connor(IRE) Lucky Pipit (Key Of Luck (USA))
**892a**[11]

**Habbad (FR)** *Richard Hannon* a75 75
3 ch c Choisir(AUS) Arikaria (IRE) (Sri Pekan (USA))
2361[7] 4537[8] 5139[6] 5560[3] **(6182)** *6792*[4] 7083[12]

**Hab Reeh** *Ruth Carr* a56 32
9 gr g Diktat Asian Love (Petong)
***1209***[7] *1407*[10] 1978[18] 2633[14] *3256*[13]

**Hackbridge** *Pat Phelan* a57
2 br g Archipenko(USA) Famcred (Inchinor)
*8501*[9] ***9201***[6]

**Hackney Road** *John Butler* a86 77
4 b m Aqlaam West Lorne (USA) (Gone West (USA))
*1899*[2] 3729[3] ***(4495)*** *4752*[2]◆ *6290*[3] *7709*[6] *8645*[8]

**Haddaf (IRE)** *James Tate* a89 97
2 b g Dawn Approach(IRE) Deveron (USA) (Cozzene (USA))
2148[2]◆ 2607[3] 3010[3] 3925[17] *(4359)* **5090a**[3] 5681[5] 6448[10]

**Haddaj (FR)** *A Fabre* 60
2 gr c New Approach(IRE) Mizdirection (USA) (Mizzen Mast (USA))
**8252a**[5]

**Haddeya** *Ed Walker* a37
3 b f Poet's Voice Sakhya (IRE) (Barathea (IRE))
***424***[7]

**Hadeeqa (IRE)** *Simon Crisford* a66 86
3 b f Cape Cross(IRE) Khulood (USA) (Storm Cat (USA))
1885[8] (3007) 4915[8] **5506**[3] 6369[3] 7959[9]

**Hadfield (IRE)** *Neil Mulholland* a58 80
5 b g Sea The Stars(IRE) Rezyana (AUS) (Redoute's Choice (AUS))
***8151***[8]

**Hadith (IRE)** *Charlie Appleby* 98
2 bb f New Approach(IRE) Discourse (USA) (Street Cry (IRE))
7399[3] (8163) **(8597)**

**Hadley** *Tracy Waggott* a54 65
4 b g Royal Applause Brush Strokes (Cadeaux Genereux)
*21*[2] *158*[7] *311*[3] *583*[3] *1006*[3] 1978[4] 2627[2] *3256*[3] 4847[2] 5004[3] *5419*[2] 5736[3] **(6045)** 6631[2]◆ *7366*[7]

**Haggle** *H-F Devin* 109
4 ch m Pivotal Barter (Daylami (IRE))
2946a[3] 6248a[7] **7177a**[3] **(8755a)**

**Hail Caesar (IRE)** *Bram Bruneel*
11 gr g Montjeu(IRE) Alabastrine (Green Desert (USA))
6543a[9]

**Hail Clodius (IRE)** *Roger Fell* a76 90
5 gr g Clodovil(IRE) Dhairkana (IRE) (Soviet Star (USA))
*24*[4] *7821*[0] *1105*[5] **1517**[2] 2593[7]

**Hail Cloud (IRE)** *Marco Botti* a56
3 b c Hail(IRE) Wasmi (IRE) (Exceed And Excel (AUS))
*9202*[10] ***9455***[7]

**Hailstone (IRE)** *P J Prendergast* a98 98
3 ch g Dream Ahead(USA) Candy Ride (IRE) (Pivotal)
**1386a**[2]

**Haines** *Andrew Balding* a98 93
6 ch g Shirocco(GER) Spring Dream (IRE) (Kalanisi (IRE))
***(746)*** *1068*[6] *1770*[9] *9157*[5]

**Hairdryer** *Andrew Balding* a84 72
4 b g Motivator Londonnetdotcom (IRE) (Night Shift (USA))
*599*[2] *809*[3] *1144*[3] *1583*[2] ***8886***[2]

**Hajaam (IRE)** *Charlie Fellowes* a96 92
3 b g Invincible Spirit(IRE) Doula (USA) (Gone West (USA))
*916*[6] *1083*[8] 6277[5] *7063*[4] (7567) *(7711)* (8142) (8326) *8506*[5] ***(9390)***

**Hajaj (IRE)** *Charlie Fellowes* a78 87
3 b g Dark Angel(IRE) And Again (USA) (In The Wings)
*626*[3] (2567) 3318[7] 3838[2] 4408[5] 4904[5] **(6110)**

**Hajjam** *David O'Meara* a71 87
3 b g Paco Boy(IRE) Amanda Carter (Tobougg (IRE))
*(1426)* *2334*[8] 3434[4] (4058) 4557[4] 5288[3] (5948) 7156[3] 7780[2] 8418[3] **8736**[2]

**Hakam (USA)** *Michael Appleby* a98 100
5 bb g War Front(USA) Lauren Byrd (USA) (Arch (USA))
*(66)* *(1501)* *1769*[9] 2433[14] *2943a*[4] **4830**[2] 7144[10] *7828*[6] *8944*[3] *9264*[6]

**Hakeem** *William Haggas* 79
3 b g Exceed And Excel(AUS) Khazeena (Oasis Dream)
**(2066)** 3700[7]

**Halawain (USA)** *John Quinn* a55 75
3 b g Congrats(USA) Screen Giant (USA) (Giant's Causeway (USA))
2304[3] **3784**[3]◆ 4122[4] 4741[5]

**Haldaw** *Mick Channon* a61 63
3 b f Halling(USA) Dawnus (IRE) (Night Shift (USA))
*2062*[2] *2515*[6] **2892**[6] 5142[4] 5406[8] *5846*[6] 7215[4] *7990*[2] *8249*[10] *8498*[5] *8800*[6] *9221*[11] *9278*[5]

**Halima Hatun (USA)**
*Ismail Mohammed* a80 59
2 ch f Algorithms(USA) Extravaganza (USA) (Elusive Quality (USA))
**6861**[9]

**Halinka (IRE)** *Roger Varian* a64 72
3 gr f Dark Angel(IRE) Mahaazen (IRE) (Cape Cross (IRE))
2993[6] **3870**[2] 4144[4] 5007[4] 5813[3] 6664[2] *7241*[10] *8156*[9]

**Hallingham** *Ken Cunningham-Brown* a61 67
7 b g Halling(USA) In Luck (In The Wings)
*1699*[2] 2219[3] **(4040)** 4494[3] 6280[5] *9459*[10]

**Hallings Comet** *Shaun Lycett* a66 87
8 ch g Halling(USA) Landinium (ITY) (Lando (GER))
***806***[4]

**Halling's Wish** *Gary Moore* a69 60
7 br g Halling(USA) Fair View (GER) (Dashing Blade)
*555*[3] **1284**[2] **2022**[3] **3208**[3] 4181[3] 4733[4] 5274[4] 5787[8] 6589[3]

**Hallstatt (IRE)** *John Mackie* a71 67
11 ch g Halling(USA) Last Resort (Lahib (USA))
*28*[4] *(423)* 2270[3] 3623[3] 3907[2] 4630[6] 6233[5] *(6898)* *8187*[3] ***8876***[2] *9158*[4]

**Hamba Kashe (IRE)** *Tim Easterby* 62
3 gr g Clodovil(IRE) Final Favour (IRE) (Unblest)
1913[14] **3525**[2]

**Hamba Moyo (IRE)** *Tim Easterby* 57
2 gr f Mastercraftsman(IRE) Back In The Frame (Dutch Art)
3398[11] 4167[7] **5180**[3] 6625[10] 6940[8] 8213[5]

**Hameem** *John Gosden* 65
2 br f Teofilo(IRE) Tres Ravi (GER) (Monsun (GER))
**8323**[5]◆

**Hamelin (IRE)** *George Scott* a102 99
7 b g Cape Cross(IRE) Love Divine (Diesis)
***(779)*** *1309*[5] *1779*[5] *2999*[12]

**Hamelin Pool** *Henry Candy* a7 43
3 b g High Chaparral(IRE) Presbyterian Nun (IRE) (Daylami (IRE))
2175[5] **2584**[9]

**Hamidans Girl (IRE)** *Keith Dalgleish* a69 79
3 ch f Bahamian Bounty Moynsha Lady (IRE) (Namid)
1688[4] 2372[3] *2924*[7] 3285[5] 4107[5]◆ 4428[3] 4788[4] 5167[3] 5645[2] 5919[4] 6351[4] (6469) **(6896)**◆ 7014[4] *8159*[6]

**Hamish McGonagain**
*David O'Meara* a77 69
4 b g Kyllachy Inya Lake (Whittingham (IRE))
*(217)* ***(327)*** *575*[4] *685*[5] *1631*[8] *1980*[3] 2608[11] *3177*[4] 3532[5] *4495*[4] 5930[3] (6148) 6298[5] *8211*[10] *8557*[4] *8874*[3] *(9001)* *9297*[2] *9437*[3]

**Hammer Gun (USA)** *Derek Shaw* a87 58
4 b g Smart Strike(CAN) Caraboss (Cape Cross (IRE))
*(1109)* *(1187)* *(1324)* ***(1433)*** *1598*[4] *2518*[9] 3589[11] *4001*[4]◆ *4261*[11] *4563*[7] *8257*[4] 8486[10] *8706*[4] *8812*[12] *9025*[11] ***(9179)*** *9305*[4]

**Hammurabi (IRE)** *S Seemar* a76
7 b g Exceed And Excel(AUS) Hashimiya (USA) (Gone West (USA))
***8583a***[8]

**Hamriyah** *Tim Easterby* 53
3 ch g Harbour Watch(IRE) Golden Dirham (Kheleyf (USA))
2887[10] **4604**[6] 5019[4] 5543[10] 6181[8] 6381[7] 7247[8]

**Hamster Jam (IRE)** *Mark Johnston* 73
3 ch f Dutch Art Hecuba (Hector Protector (USA))
2078[6] 2429[2] 3039[5] 3656[5] **4557**[2] 4800[3]

**Handazan (IRE)** *Ivan Furtado* a75 101
8 b g Nayef(USA) Handaza (IRE) (Be My Guest (USA))
***4499***[8]

**Handiwork** *Steve Gollings* a87 87
7 ch g Motivator Spinning Top (Alzao (USA))
**(2125)** 2562[8]

**Handsome Bob (IRE)**
*Keith Dalgleish* a72 63
2 b c Most Improved(IRE) Beautiful Dreamer (Red Ransom (USA))
6312[6] 7654[4] ***8493***[3] *8848*[3] *8925*[4]

**Handsome Dan (IRE)**
*Sarah Hollinshead* a71
11 b g Busy Flight Beautiful City (IRE) (Jurado (USA))
220[3] 422[7] 688[8] 1257[11] 5483[8]

**Handsome Dude** *David Barron* a93 92
5 b g Showcasing Dee Dee Girl (IRE) (Primo Dominie)
(783)◆ 1515[10] 1831[5] 2381[8] 2840[2]◆ (3585) 7612[11] 9016[13] 9305[3]

**Handytalk (IRE)** *Rod Millman* a82 92
4 b g Lilbourne Lad(IRE) Dancing With Stars (IRE) (Where Or When (IRE))
1606[6] 2369[2] 3030[3] 3919[6] (4489) 5064[2] 5720[5] 6554[2] 7604[4]

**Hang Man (IRE)** *Ed Vaughan* 77
3 ch g Windsor Knot(IRE) Halliard (Halling (USA))
6871[2]

**Hangman Jury** *Richard Hughes* a50
4 gr g Indian Haven Non Disclosure (IRE) (Clodovil (IRE))
68[7]

**Hannah Just Hannah**
*Matthew Salaman* a38 66
8 gr m Proclamation(IRE) Evaporate (Insan (USA))
457[5] 965[9]

**Hanningfield** *Michael Bell* a40 37
3 ch g Mayson Arch Of Colours (Monsun (GER))
3234[8] 3824[8] 4764[9] 5512[7]

**Hannington** *Michael Appleby* a63 65
6 ch g Firebreak Manderina (Mind Games)
49[10] 690[6] 841[8] 924[6] (1145) 1260[7] 1484[2] 1758[2] 2687[2] 3400[9] (4753) 5183[2] 6188[9] (6479) 6673[8] 7761[9] 8219[6] 8327[2]

**Hanseatic** *Michael Easterby* a62 82
8 b g Galileo(IRE) Insinuate (USA) (Mr Prospector (USA))
1517[7] 2133[4] 3049[2] 3845[6] 4210[12] 4339[5] 5698[4] 7958[8]

**Han Sense (USA)** *Maria Ritchie* a87 83
3 rg c Hansen(USA) Humble Retha (USA) (Siberian Pine (USA))
697a[5] 1040a[11]

**Han Solo Berger (IRE)**
*Keith Dalgleish* 80
2 b g Lord Shanakill(USA) Dreamaway (IRE) (Oasis Dream)
3895[3] (5092) 6545[4] (7883)

**Happily (IRE)** *A P O'Brien* 112
2 b f Galileo(IRE) You'resothrilling (USA) (Storm Cat (USA))
(5344a) 6242a[2] (6974a) (7667a) 8575a[14]

**Happy Approach (FR)** *M Nigge* a90 103
4 ch m New Approach(IRE) Eire (Medicean)
2201a[3] 7753a[3] 8273a[7]

**Happy Clapper (AUS)**
*Patrick Webster* 119
6 b g Teofilo(IRE) Busking (AUS) (Encosta De Lago (AUS))
8446a[6] 8753a[2]

**Happy Dream (ITY)** *J Parize* a84 85
3 b c Blu Air Force(IRE) Happy Sue (IRE) (City On A Hill (USA))
7308a[3] 8305a[6] 8960a[3]

**Happy Ending (IRE)**
*Seamus Mullins* a37 54
2 b f Big Bad Bob(IRE) Heroic Performer (IRE) (Royal Applause)
5710[8] 6747[9] 8147[9]

**Happy Escape** *Neil Mulholland* a71
3 ch f Delegator Saharan Song (IRE) (Singspiel (IRE))
1426[4] 1503[7] 2330[7] 4211[2] 9203[3]

**Happy Jack (IRE)** *Dai Burchell* a58 44
6 b g Elusive City(USA) Miss Pelling (IRE) (Danehill Dancer (IRE))
146[9] 865[12]

**Happy Like A Fool (USA)**
*Wesley A Ward* a93 99
2 ch f Distorted Humor(USA) Lastofthsummerwine (USA) (Sky Mesa (USA))
3960[2] 6354[6]

**Haraka (IRE)** *Ralph Beckett* a72 65
3 b f Fastnet Rock(AUS) Luna Wells (IRE) (Sadler's Wells (USA))
417[2] 718[4]

**Haraz (IRE)** *Jamie Osborne* a82 74
4 b g Acclamation Hanakiyya (IRE) (Danehill Dancer (IRE))
2064[4] 2586[4] 3204[2] 3976[4] 4332[5] 4887[4] 5379[9] 6181[3] 6799a[2] 7052[5] 8400[2] 8646[9] 8805[4] 9207[2] 9296[3] 9432[3] 9470[2]

**Harba (IRE)** *William Haggas* a79 87
3 ch f Frankel Kirinda (IRE) (Tiger Hill (IRE))
2316[3] (3931) (5031)◆ (5341) 6261[2] 7484[7] 8150[12]

**Harbour Belle** *Michael Dods* 52
3 b f Harbour Watch(IRE) Sans Reward (IRE) (Barathea (IRE))
2898[11] 3404[5] 4659[11]

**Harbour Breeze (IRE)**
*Lucy Wadham* a65
2 b c Le Havre(IRE) Retiens La Nuit (USA) (Grand Slam (USA))
8987[5]

**Harbour Force (FR)** *William Muir* 62
3 b g Harbour Watch(IRE) Dam Beautiful (Sleeping Indian)
2475[6] 2930[6] 3691[12] 5935[9]

**Harbour Grey (IRE)**
*Richard Hannon* a69 79
3 b f Zoffany(IRE) Caterina Di Cesi (Cape Town (IRE))
(2121) 2739[9] 3847[P] 4810[6] 5325[7]

**Harbouring** *Jonathan Portman* 38
3 ch f Harbour Watch(IRE) Juncea (Elnadim (USA))
2019[13] 2760[8]

**Harbour Law** *Laura Mongan* a80 116
4 b h Lawman(FR) Abunai (Pivotal)
2288[7] 3996[3]

**Harbour Lightning** *Noel Wilson* a67 65
3 ch f Harbour Watch(IRE) Divine Power (Kyllachy)
2080[7] 3047[8] 3384[5] 3915[6] 4997[9]

**Harbour Nights** *Hugo Palmer* a60
2 b g Harbour Watch(IRE) Irtahal (USA) (Swain (IRE))
7451[5] 8155[7] 8987[8]

**Harbour Patrol (IRE)**
*Rebecca Bastiman* a45 60
5 b g Acclamation Traou Mad (IRE) (Barathea (IRE))
1106[6] 1408[7] 1587[6] 2342[3] 3831[3] 4323[12] 4682[2] (5050) 5467[3] 5992[4] 6437[14] 7165[4] 7889[5]

**Harbour Pilot** *David Loughnane* a48
2 b c Harbour Watch(IRE) Bountiful Girl (Bahamian Bounty)
9372[8]

**Harbour Quay** *Jeremy Gask* a51
3 b c Foxwedge(AUS) Whatcameoverme (USA) (Aldebaran (USA))
1083[9]

**Harbour Rock** *David Simcock* a70 85
3 b c Harbour Watch(IRE) Rock Lily (Rock Of Gibraltar (IRE))
(3781) 4912[2] 5868[2] 6822[2] 7400[6] 8375[10]

**Harbour Rose** *Philip Kirby* 51
2 b f Harbour Watch(IRE) Serrenia (IRE) (High Chaparral (IRE))
3491[9] 3902[12] 4340[7] 5756[11] 7029[10]

**Harbour Seal** *Henry Spiller* a28 50
2 b f Archipenko(USA) River Naiad (Nayef (USA))
5534[7] 6747[7] 7141[6] 7996[10]

**Harbour Siren** *David Brown* a56
3 b f Harbour Watch(IRE) Dee Dee Girl (IRE) (Primo Dominie)
1102[3]

**Harbour Storm** *Laura Mongan* a52 49
2 b c Sayif(IRE) Minette (Bishop Of Cashel)
6262[5] 7482[8]

**Harbour Sunrise** *Shaun Harris* 22
2 b f Harbour Watch(IRE) Nairobi (FR) (Anabaa (USA))
8380[15]

**Harbour Town** *Harry Dunlop* a57 62
3 ch g Harbour Watch(IRE) Dress Code (IRE) (Barathea (IRE))
813[6] 3173[9] 3695[10] 5714[9] 7952[11] 8342[6]

**Harbour Vision** *David Brown* a74 69
2 gr c Harbour Watch(IRE) Holy Nola (USA) (Silver Deputy (CAN))
5507[3] 6042[6] (7535) 8715[3] 9021[4]

**Hard Aces (USA)** *John W Sadler* a110 86
7 b h Hard Spun(USA) All In With Aces (USA) (Quiet American (USA))
6252a[5]

**Hard Divorce (USA)** *M Al Balushi* a21 9
6 b g Hard Spun(USA) Divorce Settlement (USA) (Stormin Fever (USA))
319a[11]

**Hard Drink (USA)** *C Laffon-Parias* a61 69
3 bb c Lemon Drop Kid(USA) Toppisme (USA) (Saint Ballado (CAN))
3310a[3]

**Hard Graft** *David Brown* a75 74
2 rg g Lethal Force(IRE) Molly Brown (Rudimentary (USA))
3037[4] 3789[7] 4359[5] 6036[4] 7335[5] 7734[7] 8349[20] (9345)

**Hardham (AUS)** *David Brideoake* 112
3 b c Redoute's Choice(AUS) Nureyev's Girl (AUS) (Nureyev (USA))
8250a[10] 8446a[8]

**Hard Talk (FR)** *Y Barberot* 98
3 b c Redoute's Choice(AUS) Soft Ice (IRE) (Kingmambo (USA))
8464a[2]

**Hard Toffee (IRE)** *Louise Allan* a75 73
6 b g Teofilo(IRE) Speciale (USA) (War Chant (USA))
1602[8] 2728[4] 4755[5] 5888[5] 6144[4] 6479[2] 6781[5] 7601[4] 8386[5] 8813[4] 9027[4]

**Hard To Handel** *Mrs A Malzard* a69 92
5 b g Stimulation(IRE) Melody Maker (Diktat)
382[3] 507[11] 599[10] 928[6] 1065[6] 1334[3] 1498[13] 1932a[3] 2276[6] 2670a[2] 5201a[4] 5986a[7]

**Harebell (IRE)** *Ralph Beckett* a67 87
3 ch f Halling(USA) Prairie Flower (IRE) (Zieten (USA))
1944[13] (2929) 3693[3] 4571[3] (4701)◆ 5715[6] 7024[3]

**Hargeisa (USA)** *Mario Hofer* 102
3 ch f Speightstown(USA) Hasay (Lomitas)
1846a[3] 3882a[8] 6495a[7]

**Haripour (IRE)** *D K Weld* 88
3 b c Shamardal(USA) Hazariya (IRE) (Xaar)
4032[11]

**Harlem**
*David A & B Hayes & Tom Dabern* 112
5 b h Champs Elysees Casual (Nayef (USA))
1994a[6] 8250a[8] 8753a[7]

**Harlem Shake (IRE)**
*Marco Gasparini* 95
6 b g Moss Vale(IRE) Ladylishandra (IRE) (Mujadil (USA))
2867a[6]

**Harlequeen** *Mick Channon* 108
4 b m Canford Cliffs(IRE) Aurelia (Rainbow Quest (USA))
5569[9] 6191[5] 6440[5] 6675[3]◆ 7089[7] 7547[9]

**Harlequin Rock** *Mick Quinn* a65 65
4 bl g Rock Of Gibraltar(IRE) Berry Baby (IRE) (Rainbow Quest (USA))
1610[4] 2070[2] 2318[3] 2729[8] 3442[3] 4047[9] 5854[4] 6296[8] 6751[7] (8124) 8514[5]

**Harlequin Rose (IRE)**
*Patrick Chamings* a47 57
3 ch f Dutch Art Miss Chaussini (IRE) (Rossini (USA))
2362[8] 3810[2] 4458[2] 6174[12] 7487[10] 8948[12]

**Harlequin Storm (IRE)** *Dean Ivory* a71 60
3 gr g Clodovil(IRE) Convidada (IRE) (Trans Island)
600[3] 956[4] 1179[4]◆ 6009[3] (7320) 8311[8]

**Harlequin Striker (IRE)** *Dean Ivory* a84 84
5 b g Bahamian Bounty Air Maze (Dansili)
1288[8] 2960[4]◆ 3670[3] 4800[4] 5300[4] 6134[10] 7098[7] (7958) 8297[6] 8797[9] 9029[5] 9419[7]

**Harlow** *Hugo Palmer* a88 56
3 b g Harlan's Holiday(USA) Glowing (IRE) (Dansili)
(970)◆ 1582[3] 2437[8] 5153[7] 7941[4]

**Harlow Gold (NZ)**
*David A & B Hayes & Tom Dabern* 103
3 b f Tavistock(NZ) Belongs In Lights (AUS) (Belong To Me (USA))
8056a[7]

**Harmonica** *Sir Mark Prescott Bt* a73 73
2 b f Pivotal Affinity (Sadler's Wells (USA))
5575[4]◆ 5934[3] 6575[2]

**Harmonic Wave (IRE)**
*Rebecca Menzies* a66 43
4 b m Zebedee Pure Folly (IRE) (Machiavellian (USA))
80[4] 216[2] 362[12] 468[3]

**Harmonise** *Mick Channon* a42 78
3 b f Sakhee's Secret Composing (IRE) (Noverre (USA))
2266[6] (2754) 3592[12] 4096[6] 4845[6] 6818[12] 7464[3] 7735[4] 8390[7]

**Harome (IRE)** *Roger Fell* a52 84
3 ch g Bahamian Bounty Clytha (Mark Of Esteem (IRE))
3295[7] (3982) 4530[5] 4835[4] 5416[6] 5708[2] 6519[3] 6945[4]

**Haroon (IRE)** *Tony Coyle* 71
3 ch c Lope De Vega(IRE) Hazarista (IRE) (Barathea (IRE))
6350[2] 6548[2] 7225[10]

**Harper's Choice (AUS)**
*Gerald Ryan* 112
3 bk c Street Cry(IRE) Oxigenada (ARG) (Ibero (ARG))
6714a[7]

**Harpers Ruby** *Lynn Siddall* a59 44
7 b m Byron La Belle Katherine (USA) (Lyphard (USA))
523[9] 742[2] 3544[4] 3710[4] 4479[9] 4847[8]

**Harrison** *Mick Channon* a108 106
4 b g Sixties Icon Excellent Day (IRE) (Invincible Spirit (IRE))
(2519) 3090[4] 3996[11]

**Harrison Stickle** *John Gallagher* 66
5 gr g Hellvelyn Hollybell (Beveled (USA))
2514[2]◆ 3280[7] 4256[15] 5750[8] 6478[10] 7692[6]

**Harrogate (IRE)** *James Bethell* 76
2 br g Society Rock(IRE) Invincible Me (IRE) (Invincible Spirit (IRE))
5825[7] 6264[2] 6755[2] 7326[3] 8010[10]

**Harry Angel (IRE)** *Clive Cox* 128
3 b c Dark Angel(IRE) Beatrix Potter (IRE) (Cadeaux Genereux)
2289[2] (3078) 4030[2] (4907) (6926)◆ 8230[4]

**Harry Beau** *David Evans* a57 67
3 ch g Kheleyf(USA) Lovellian (Machiavellian (USA))
2393[3] 3088[5] 3531[8] 4492[5] 5111[8] 8124[2] 8328[5] 8473[11] 9153[8]

**Harry Callahan (IRE)**
*Tom Dascombe* 58
2 b g Dutch Art Sovana (IRE) (Desert King (IRE))
7392[9] 8382[7] 8677[12]

**Harry Holland** *Oliver Greenall* a82 45
5 b g Dutch Art Common Consent (IRE) (Common Grounds)
(293) 445[9] 734[11] 4293[11] 4728[12] 5261[10]

**Harry Hunt** *Graeme McPherson* a52 86
10 b g Bertolini(USA) Qasirah (IRE) (Machiavellian (USA))
3086[5] 8072[4]

**Harry Hurricane** *George Baker* a99 106
5 b g Kodiac Eolith (Pastoral Pursuits)
318a[2] 543a[14] 773a[7] 3092[4] 3829[2] 4072[14] 4881[7] 5505[9] 5640[19] 7144[19]

**Harry Speed (IRE)** *Garvan Donnelly* a57 68
4 b g Dark Angel(IRE) Starfly (IRE) (Invincible Spirit (IRE))
(5992)

**Hartnell** *James Cummings* 121
6 b g Authorized(IRE) Debonnaire (Anabaa (USA))
8058a[9] 8667a[20]

**Hartside (GER)** *Peter Winks* 65
8 b g Montjeu(IRE) Helvellyn (USA) (Gone West (USA))
1703[10]

**Hart Stopper** *Michael Bell* a74 87
3 b g Compton Place Angel Song (Dansili)
221[3] 1543[4] 1888[3] (2474)◆ 4268[2] (4616) (5035)◆ 5423[10] 6141[5] 6662[4]◆ 7405[8]

**Harvest Day** *Michael Easterby* a48 47
2 b f Harbour Watch(IRE) Miss Wells (IRE) (Sadler's Wells (USA))
3093[6] 3398[10] 3495[6] 8780[5]◆ 8902[4] 9302[7]

**Harvest Moon** *Richard Fahey* a48 64
3 b f Mayson Hamsat Elqamar (Nayef (USA))
3403[12] 4058[5] 4602[6]

**Harvest Ranger** *Michael Appleby* a44 36
3 b g Bushranger(IRE) Time Of Gold (USA) (Banker's Gold (USA))
667[4] 8255[5] 9232[6] 9365[8]

**Harvest Wind (IRE)** *Clive Cox* a78 80
3 b c Elzaam(AUS) Harvest Joy (IRE) (Daggers Drawn (USA))
5247[2] 5794[3] 6655[7]

**Harvey's Hope** *Paul Collins*
11 b g Sinndar(IRE) Ancara (Dancing Brave (USA))
7248[12]

**Harwood** *David O'Meara* 60
3 b g Dutch Art Amicable Terms (Royal Applause)
2383[6] 3054[5] 3313[5]

**Harwoods Star (IRE)** *John Butler* a79 64
7 br g Danehill Dancer(IRE) Showbiz (IRE) (Sadler's Wells (USA))
25[3] 528[5] 665[4] 850[11] 1109[5] 1431[9]

**Harwoods Volante (IRE)**
*David O'Meara* a95 94
6 ch g Kheleyf(USA) Semiquaver (IRE) (Mark Of Esteem (IRE))
2840[17] 3288[3] 3565[3] 4037[7] 4477[2] 5093[2] 5415[7] 5806[2] 6205[19] 6348[5] 6874[8]

**Has (TUR)** *Fehmi Dizdaroglu* 74
2 b c Country Reel(USA) Olive Lady (TUR) (Always A Classic (CAN))
6745a[5]

**Hasanoanda** *John Gosden* a78
2 b c Champs Elysees Indian Mystery (IRE) (Indian Ridge (IRE))
8903[4]◆ 9299[6]

**Hasanour (USA)** *M Halford* 106
7 b g Giant's Causeway(USA) Hasanka (IRE) (Kalanisi (IRE))
208a[8] 322a[11] 698a[8] 888a[4]

**Hasselnott** *J F Levins* a64 82
4 b g Hellvelyn Unwrapit (USA) (Tapit (USA))
5519a[3] 6491a[14]

**Hastenplace** *Rod Millman* a39 58
2 b f Compton Place Hasten (USA) (Lear Fan (USA))
2173[7] 2756[8] 3689[6] 4758[4] 4991[7] 7193[5] 7510[13] 8027[6]

**Hateel (IRE)** *William Haggas* 65
2 b f Kodiac Vee Gita (IRE) (Vettori (IRE))
8593[3]

**Hateya (IRE)** *Jim Boyle* 69
2 b f Footstepsinthesand Selfsame (USA) (Dansili)
2910[2] 3655[6] 6510[2] 7093[3] 7647[6]

**Hathal (USA)** *William Haggas* 115
5 ch h Speightstown(USA) Sleepytime (IRE) (Royal Academy (USA))
4884[3] 5436[3] 6420[3] 7640a[4]

**Hathfa (FR)** *Richard Hughes* a71 70
3 gr f Dark Angel(IRE) Nepali Princess (IRE) (Mr Greeley (USA))
75[2] (288) 623[5]◆

**Hatsaway (IRE)** *Pat Phelan* a66 76
6 b g Dubawi(IRE) Scotch Bonnet (IRE) (Montjeu (IRE))
2562[6] 3213[5] 4222[9] 7651[8] 8647[13] 8878[5]

**Hats Off To Larry** *Mick Channon* a61 79
3 b g Sixties Icon Highland Jig (Norse Dancer (IRE))
5220[3]◆ 5931[3] 6413[3] 6775[2] 7331[4] 7768[4]

**Haulani (USA)** *Philip Hide* a74 82
3 ch g Algorithms(USA) License To Speed (USA) (Thunder Gulch (USA))
2174[8] 2998[8] 3780[7] 4501[5] 5218[3] 7004[3] 7902[2] 8295[3]

**Hautot (FR)** *P Sogorb* 76
2 b c Zoffany(IRE) Super Hantem (IRE) (Royal Anthem (USA))
1919a[4] 2881a[4] 8101a[2]

**Havana Beat (IRE)** *Tony Carroll* a90 99
7 b g Teofilo(IRE) Sweet Home Alabama (IRE) (Desert Prince (IRE))
728[7] 1942[7] 3091[7] 7402[20]

**Havana Grey** *K R Burke* 111
2 gr c Havana Gold(IRE) Blanc De Chine (IRE) (Dark Angel (IRE))
1966[2]◆ (2452)◆ (3010) 3993[10] (4582) (5526) 6249a[2] 7114[2]

**Havana Heart** *Ismail Mohammed* a53 66
2 ch f Havana Gold(IRE) Glee Club (Kyllachy)
4503[9] 6262[2] 6747[5] 7986[5] 8471[5]

**Havana Mariposa** *K R Burke* a64 68
2 b f Havana Gold(IRE) Critical Path (IRE) (Noverre (USA))
5370[8] 6545[3] 7937[8] 8325[3] 8871[4]

**Havana Star (IRE)** *Kevin Ryan* 76
2 b g Havana Gold(IRE) Nagham (IRE) (Camacho)
(2222)◆ 3051[3] 5537[3] 6379[2] 7041[10] 8008[14]

**Have A Nice Day** *John James Feane* a94 95
7 b g Oratorio(IRE) Centrepiece (Pivotal)
4327a[6] 6961a[4] 8222a[6] 9247a[7]

**Havelock (IRE)** *Peter Fahey* a71 77
3 ch g Helmet(AUS) Pearl Grey (Gone West (USA))
500[4] 662[3] 863[2] 997[2] 1179[7] 1805[8] 2080[8] 9346[4]

**Haven's View** *Richard Hughes* a45 50
2 b g Reckless Abandon Haven's Wave (IRE) (Whipper (USA))
2473[6] 3782[8] 4367[8] 9002[9] 9230[6]

**Haveoneyerself (IRE)** *John Butler* a47 70
2 b c Requinto(IRE) Charismas Birthday (IRE) (Choisir (AUS))
2556[5] 3277[2] 3972[2] 4760[3] (5785) 7706[6] 8131[10] 8746[7]

**Haverland (IRE)** *Charlie Fellowes* a70 49
2 b g Big Bad Bob(IRE) Pivotal's Princess (IRE) (Pivotal)
8112[7] 9231[5]◆ 9335[5]

**Havre De Paix (FR)** *David Menuisier* a86 99
5 b m Le Havre(IRE) Bridge Of Peace (Anabaa (USA))
1960[20] 2767[13] 4883[2] 5393[7] 6919[2] 7808[12] (8665a)

**Hawaiian Freeze** *J Moon* a51 45
8 b m Avonbridge Autumn Affair (Lugana Beach)
820[4] 1930a[3] 2671a[3] 4656a[4] 5985a[2]

**Hawatif (IRE)** *Anthony Carson* a83 78
4 b m Royal Applause Excellerator (IRE) (Exceed And Excel (AUS))
235[6] 499[5] 810[9] 2254[6] 7285[3] 7710[3] 8947[6] 9337[7]

**Hawkbill (USA)** *Charlie Appleby* a94 121
4 ch h Kitten's Joy(USA) Trensa (USA) (Giant's Causeway (USA))
2249a[5] (2822) 3299[3] 4423a[6] (4814) 5983a[2] 7178a[2]

**Hawker Hurricane (IRE)**
*Luke McJannet* a42
3 gr g Dalakhani(IRE) Kitty Hawk (Danehill Dancer (IRE))
5794[12]

**Hawkerland (IRE)**
*Marcus Tregoning* a57 83
4 b g Sea The Stars(IRE) Zarara (USA) (Manila (USA))
1420[6] 2039[4] (3698) (4471)◆ 5524[10] 7402[10]

**Hawkesbury** *S Seemar* a101 106
5 gr g Shamardal(USA) Nahoodh (IRE) (Clodovil (IRE))
207a14

**Hawksmoor (IRE)** *Arnaud Delacour* a84 108
4 b m Azamour(IRE) Bridal Dance (IRE) (Danehill Dancer (IRE))
5954a7

**Haworth** *James Bethell* a71 72
3 b g Showcasing Some Diva (Dr Fong (USA))
28208 32965 35845 46943 51825 (5826) 63137 752210 75726

**Hawridge Flyer** *Stuart Kittow* 80
3 b g Sir Percy Strictly Lambada (Red Ransom (USA))
27832◆ 34263 (6031) 68808

**Hawridge Glory (IRE)** *Rod Millman* a74 76
3 b g Royal Applause Saint Lucia (IRE) (Whipper (USA))
31625 39223 (4804) 54272 58002 (6393) 70974 75414 81143 83866

**Haxby Juniors** *Antony Brittain* a18 37
2 ch f Monsieur Bond(IRE) Mozayada (USA) (Street Cry (IRE))
32836 858710 90499

**Haya Of Fortune (FR)** *N Leenders* a71 86
3 b f Soldier Of Fortune(IRE) Haya Samma (IRE) (Pivotal)
3881a12 4988a8

**Haylah (IRE)** *Richard Hannon* a49 69
2 b f Epaulette(AUS) Pearls Of Wisdom (Kyllachy)
73525 76882 88095

**Haymarket** *R Mike Smith* a53 66
8 b g Singspiel(IRE) Quickstyx (Night Shift (USA))
4007 32423◆ 36503 (4034) 46605 (5074) (5254) 59173 59979 64313 82197 858911

**Hayward Field (IRE)** *Noel Wilson* a76 70
4 b g Cape Blanco(IRE) Keepers Hill (IRE) (Danehill (USA))
24566 35016 (5005) 58327 64676 74138 80003◆ 890910

**Hazamar (IRE)** *Sophie Leech* a64 83
4 gr g Manduro(GER) Hazarafa (IRE) (Daylami (IRE))
11905 58944

**Hazapour (IRE)** *D K Weld* 93
2 ch c Shamardal(USA) Hazarafa (IRE) (Daylami (IRE))
8440a3

**Hazarfan** *Ed Dunlop* 70
2 b c Frankel Debonnaire (Anabaa (USA))
78106 82152

**Hazarfiya** *Sir Michael Stoute* 69
2 b f Fastnet Rock(AUS) Hazariya (IRE) (Xaar)
84193

**Hazariban (IRE)** *Seamus Fahey* a59 67
8 b g Kahyasi(IRE) Hazarista (IRE) (Barathea (IRE))
6165

**Hazell Berry (IRE)** *Karen George* a48
3 b f Big Bad Bob(IRE) Mudalalah (IRE) (Singspiel (IRE))
3762 4636 8486 9873 78267 824811

**Hazit (USA)** *Todd Pletcher* a94
2 b c War Front(USA) Rumor (USA) (Indian Charlie (USA))
8609a8

**Hazy Manor (IRE)** *Julia Brooke* 42
3 b f Tagula(IRE) Hazarama (IRE) (Kahyasi (IRE))
29038 37086 65946 721913

**Headline Act** *Archie Watson* a42 41
2 ch f Helmet(AUS) Accede (Acclamation)
3210 6 39029 52927 60225

**Head Space (IRE)** *Brian Barr* a53 42
9 b g Invincible Spirit(IRE) Danzelline (Danzero (AUS))
2429 3552 4682 5756 8155 8439 10874 12063 13394 188711 23316 589211 65823 71907 79008 82968 93406

**Heads Together** *S Kobayashi* a66 76
2 b f Kodiac Sand Grouse (Mr Greeley (USA))
5679a11 8271a3

**Heads You Win** *Jamie Osborne* a73 67
4 ch m Compton Place Miss Rimex (IRE) (Ezzoud (IRE))
(120) 5177

**Headway** *William Haggas* 107
2 b c Havana Gold(IRE) On Her Way (Medicean)
19412 (3066) 39252 55706 64463

**Headwear (IRE)** *David Brown* a48 43
2 ch f Helmet(AUS) Indian Dumaani (Indian Ridge (IRE))
38589 505615 553413

**Heartache** *Clive Cox* 110
2 b f Kyllachy Place In My Heart (Compton Place)
(3023)◆ (3960) 5195a3 (7114)◆

**Heart Angel (FR)** *C Scandella* a51 90
4 b g Whipper(USA) Berceuse (Mtoto)
6125a8

**Heartbeat (IRE)** *F Chappet* a70 74
4 b g Lope De Vega(IRE) Heart Of Ice (IRE) (Montjeu (IRE))
3274a3

**Heartbreak City (FR)** *A J Martin* a82 118
7 b g Lando(GER) Moscow Nights (FR) (Peintre Celebre (USA))
1374a11 (Dead)

**Heart Locket** *Michael Easterby* a75 54
5 b m Champs Elysees Zante (Zafonic (USA))
4405 6884 9582 11757

**Heart Of An Angel** *Henry Spiller* a40 59
4 ro m Dark Angel(IRE) How High The Sky (IRE) (Danehill Dancer (IRE))
4619 68413 7575

**Heart Of Gold** *William Muir* 68
3 b f Kyllachy Secret Era (Cape Cross (IRE))
35954◆ 42554 51262 57833

**Heartstone (IRE)** *David Evans* a75 77
4 b m Fastnet Rock(AUS) Eva's Request (IRE) (Soviet Star (USA))
992◆ 2132 4974 6097 7892 11512 12455 46218 (4845) 55913 57459

**Heart To Heart (CAN)**
*Brian A Lynch* a95 116
6 b h English Channel(USA) Ask The Question (USA) (Silver Deputy (CAN))
7851a2 8608a10

**Hearty (IRE)** *Richard Rowe* a65 68
4 b g Big Bad Bob(IRE) Ulanova (IRE) (Noverre (USA))
29093 47557

**Heather Lark (IRE)** *John Gosden* a75 72
2 b f Shamardal(USA) Heather Rose (GER) (Montjeu (IRE))
74033 77586 83222 86693

**Heatongrad (IRE)** *Richard Fahey* a63 89
3 b g Kodiac Best Mother (IRE) (King's Theatre (IRE))
21867 26255 (3461) 39755 565010 (7162) (7650)◆ 78924

**Heat Storm (IRE)** *James Unett* a45 47
6 b g Lawman(FR) Coconut Show (Linamix (FR))
32216

**Heatstroke (IRE)** *Charles Hills* a86 89
5 b g Galileo(IRE) Walklikeanegyptian (IRE) (Danehill (USA))
17348

**Heavenly Angel** *Ruth Carr* a41 73
3 gr f Dark Angel(IRE) Ballyalla (Mind Games)
191316 38698 53769 583510

**Heavenly Cry** *Phil McEntee* a62 45
3 b g Dick Turpin(IRE) Acclamatory (Royal Applause)
12 2126 6384 8197

**Heavenly Gait** *Jason Ward* a52
5 b m Revoque(IRE) Still Runs Deep (Karinga Bay)
9938 13088

**Heavenly Guest** *George Margarson* 53
2 ch g Havana Gold(IRE) Maid In Heaven (IRE) (Clodovil (IRE))
81124 83828

**Heavenly Love (USA)** *Mark Casse* a108 94
2 b f Malibu Moon(USA) Darling My Darling (USA) (Deputy Minister (CAN))
8603a11

**Heavenly Pulse (IRE)** *Ann Duffield* a28 47
2 ch g Dragon Pulse(IRE) Bogini (IRE) (Holy Roman Emperor (IRE))
17926 28828 33998 40146 48367 51617 52775 56135 60226 606311

**Heaven On Earth (FR)** *C Gourdain* a91 99
6 b g Archange D'Or(IRE) Between You And Me (FR) (Kendor (FR))
7943a4

**Heaven Scent** *Donald McCain* a20 59
4 ch m Phoenix Reach(IRE) Hel's Angel (IRE) (Pyrus (USA))
54936 72197

**Heaven's Door (FR)** *P Demercastel* a63 66
3 b g Elusive City(USA) European Style (FR) (Ezzoud (IRE))
1460a9

**Heavensfield** *Mark H Tompkins* a65 71
4 b m Motivator Astrodiva (Where Or When (IRE))
2337

**Heaven's Guest (IRE)**
*Richard Fahey* a91 94
7 b g Dark Angel(IRE) Bakewell Tart (IRE) (Tagula (IRE))
149420 17667 260613 384218 539326 69183 77814 81048 873710 92642

**Heaven's Rock (IRE)**
*Tom Dascombe* a68 76
3 b g Requinto(IRE) Rockfleet Castle (Rock Of Gibraltar (IRE))
62653 (6855) 77366 83928

**Heavy Metal** *S bin Ghadayer* a119 110
7 b g Exceed And Excel(AUS) Rock Opera (SAF) (Lecture (USA))
204a2 (432a) 695a4 (775a) (1043a) 1373a8

**Hebah (IRE)** *J-C Rouget* 104
3 b f Sea The Stars(IRE) Lia (IRE) (Desert King (IRE))
1657a3 2665a4 8755a6

**Hedging (IRE)**
*Eve Johnson Houghton* 75
3 rg g Mastercraftsman(IRE) Privet (IRE) (Cape Cross (IRE))
51114 57116◆ (6345) 68074 (7157) 77365 82996

**Hediddodinthe (IRE)** *Richard Guest* a58
3 gr g Kendargent(FR) Damoiselle (USA) (Sky Classic (CAN))
820510 88002 91289

**Hedonism (IRE)** *Hugo Palmer* 53
2 b f Excelebration(IRE) Knapton Hill (Zamindar (USA))
72425

**Hee Haw (IRE)** *Paul Midgley* 87
3 b g Sleeping Indian My American Beauty (Wolfhound (USA))
24952 37092 (3897) (4250) 50935 56466 62059 (6519)◆ 69705 75533

**Heeyaam** *Marco Botti* a74
2 b f Invincible Spirit(IRE) Shalwa (Galileo (IRE))
89972◆

**Heezararity** *Jonathan Geake* a54 52
9 b g Librettist(USA) Extremely Rare (IRE) (Mark Of Esteem (IRE))
547710 61756

**Heidi** *Richard Hannon* 53
2 b f Swiss Spirit Mysterious Girl (IRE) (Teofilo (IRE))
62726

**Heir Of Excitement (IRE)**
*Kevin Ryan* a72 82
3 b g Tagula(IRE) Gimli's Treasure (IRE) (King's Best (USA))
11496 16782 20352 (2885) 42903 47412 55414 63152 70162 7656P

**Heir To A Throne (FR)** *Leo Braem* a70 85
4 ch g Siyouni(FR) Boaka (FR) (Kahyasi (IRE))
16772 240612 28847 42942 49574 566817 64149 71409 801415 9309a4

**Helene Charisma (FR)** *John Moore* 106
4 b h Air Chief Marshal(IRE) Lidana (IRE) (King's Best (USA))
3129a4 9167a12

**Helene Paragon (FR)** *John Moore* 120
5 b h Polan(FR) High Zaff (High Chaparral (IRE))
2492a3 9170a3

**Helen Sherbet** *K R Burke* a68 64
2 br f Makfi Clifton Dancer (Fraam)
553411 68766 72656 86587 (8804) 93455

**Helf (IRE)** *Richard Hannon* a57 73
3 b c Helmet(AUS) Causeway Song (USA) (Giant's Causeway (USA))
38603 45696 51414 56524 60756 68127 78799

**Helfire** *Hughie Morrison* a79 82
4 b m Archipenko(USA) Relkida (Bertolini (USA))
17555 (2961)◆ 34542◆ (4010) 48833◆ 57883 66562

**Helis (FR)** *Michael Scudamore* a40 57
4 b g Footstepsinthesand Xaara (SWE) (Xaar)
94379

**Helium (FR)** *Alexandra Dunn* a50 56
12 b g Dream Well(FR) Sure Harbour (SWI) (Surumu (GER))
6466

**Hellarious** *Geoffrey Deacon* a42 33
4 gr g Hellvelyn Yarrita (Tragic Role (USA))
60211 17237 52508 58239

**Hellavashock** *Alistair Whillans* a52 54
4 gr g Hellvelyn Surprise Statement (Proclamation (IRE))
291811 34503 403413 56496 63529 67883 77044 79795 90174 92175

**Hello (IRE)** *A R Al Rayhi* a57
4 b g Teofilo(IRE) Creese (Halling (USA))
8711a7

**Hello Brigette (IRE)**
*M D O'Callaghan* a79 74
2 b f Kodiac Fern Tycoon (IRE) (College Chapel)
(9415)◆

**Hell Of A Band** *Richard Hughes*
2 b c Kyllachy Chilli Green (Desert Sun)
5504P (Dead)

**Hell Of A Lady** *Michael Attwater* a32 42
3 gr f Hellvelyn Lady Killer (IRE) (Daggers Drawn (USA))
172713 25814 32793 907110 926810

**Hello Girl** *Dean Ivory* a71 67
2 ch f Bated Breath Elysee (IRE) (Fantastic Light (USA))
29586 32102 39022 515015 (6012) 62626 69504

**Hello Humpfrey (IRE)** *Peter Casey* a53 40
8 b g Hurricane Run(IRE) Karamiyna (IRE) (Shernazar)
1014a10

**Hellomoto** *Kevin Ryan* a50 62
3 b g Firebreak Dayville (USA) (Dayjur (USA))
20772◆ 42764 47215 58804 65945 72704 79917 81226

**Hello My Love (FR)** *Carina Fey* a97 109
6 gr g Literato(FR) Ciao My Love (FR) (Touch Down (GER))
6454a2

**Hello My Sunshine**
*Karen McLintock* a66 71
2 ch c Captain Gerrard(IRE) Dalmunzie (IRE) (Choisir (AUS))
33397 42584 52553 85869 90987

**Hello Princess (FR)** *Louis Baudron* 80
2 b f Sageburg(IRE) Victoria Princess (FR) (Muhtathir)
(5988a) 8443a6

**Hellovaqueen** *Bill Turner* a52 54
2 gr f Hellvelyn Regal Quest (IRE) (Marju (IRE))
14964 16277

**Hells Babe** *Michael Appleby* a79 104
4 gr m Hellvelyn Blues In Cee (IRE) (Sinndar (IRE))
12613 13685 (2138) (2805) 33344 6605a6 78089 87376

**Helmsdale** *S Cerulis* a79 58
3 b f Nathaniel(IRE) Sky Boat (IRE) (Dansili)
8732a5

**Helovaplan (IRE)** *Bryan Smart* 86
3 b g Helmet(AUS) Watsdaplan (IRE) (Verglas (IRE))
18045 (2186) (3862) 42994 60014 71196

**Helvetian** *Mick Channon* 99
2 b c Swiss Spirit Lucky Dip (Tirol (IRE))
51519 (5586) 5973a8 65214 6977a10 709014 77414

**Hemingford (IRE)** *Charlie Fellowes* a63 68
2 ch c Famous Name Fantastic Anna (IRE) (Fantastic Light (USA))
31568 42586 48609 (5756) 72514 78907 82878

**Hemingway (IRE)** *Kevin Ryan* a78 81
3 ch g Dragon Pulse(IRE) Degree Of Honor (FR) (Highest Honor (FR))
11242 13118 17023 197511 48355 79428

**Hemp Hemp Hurray (CAN)**
*Wesley A Ward* 106
2 b c Artie Schiller(USA) Druidess (USA) (Malibu Moon (USA))
8577a14

**Hence (USA)** *Steven Asmussen* a118
3 ch c Street Boss(USA) Floating Island (USA) (A.P. Indy (USA))
2420a11 2851a9 5463a7

**Henley** *Tracy Waggott* a87 87
5 b g Royal Applause Making Waves (IRE) (Danehill (USA))
15472 20342 (2700) 28375 (3257) (3707) 437910 56476 76255 794011 82932

**Henpecked** *Alistair Whillans* a76 70
7 b m Footstepsinthesand Poule De Luxe (IRE) (Cadeaux Genereux)
303 13454 32522 42602 56485 62084 67892 70322◆ 848510 891211 90968

**Henrietta's Dream** *John Wainwright* a36 52
3 b f Henrythenavigator(USA) Timeless Dream (Oasis Dream)
12448 23728 26995 326010 36246 41065 43033 54195 56367 646912 66944 82172 865611

**Henriqua** *Denis Coakley* a10 27
3 b f Henrythenavigator(USA) Child Bride (USA) (Coronado's Quest (USA))
345613 49117 54098

**Henry Brulard (FR)** *C Boutin* a12
2 ch c Planteur(IRE) Agent Mimi (FR) (Medecis)
8482a12

**Henry Croft** *Tony Carroll* a72 48
4 b g Dubawi(IRE) Karen's Caper (USA) (War Chant (USA))
1954 7373 34277 47509

**Henry Did It (IRE)** *Tony Carroll* a59 51
3 b g Henrythenavigator(USA) The Fairies Did It (USA) (Elusive Quality (USA))
272610 36573 47546 57904 66116 82473

**Henry Grace (IRE)** *Jimmy Fox* a59 35
6 b g Oratorio(IRE) Little Miss Gracie (Efisio)
2823 (740) 8658 12846 20958 914112

**Henryhudsonbridge (USA)**
*John Flint* a57 68
5 b g Henrythenavigator(USA) Harlan Ash (USA) (Harlan (USA))
3338 27225 40415 44704 (4734)

**Henry Smith** *John Weymes* a58 90
5 b g Firebreak So Discreet (Tragic Role (USA))
51644 69444 76274 82393 84852

**He Or She (AUS)**
*David A & B Hayes & Tom Dabern* 112
6 ch g Kendel Star(AUS) Danessa (AUS) (West Point (AUS))
8059a13

**Hepplewhite** *William Muir* a71 73
4 b g Rail Link Millistar (Galileo (IRE))
24783 29663 34597 40892 47123 55562 65564 66104 (7712)

**Heptathlete (IRE)** *George Baker* a73
2 gr f Mount Nelson Jessica Ennis (USA) (English Channel (USA))
74544

**Heraldic (USA)** *S Seemar* a77 67
4 br g Discreet Cat(USA) Chilukki's Song (USA) (Elusive Quality (USA))
8711a9

**Herculean** *Roger Charlton* 88
2 ch c Frankel African Rose (Observatory (USA))
(6869)◆

**Hercullian Prince** *Conor Dore* a65 33
5 b g Royal Applause Thara'A (IRE) (Desert Prince (IRE))
1459 21411 69011 317210 35508 36886 41775

**Herdwick** *Sir Michael Stoute* 70
2 b c Makfi Bellwether (Three Valleys (USA))
72804◆ 81195

**Here And Now** *Ralph Beckett* a77 96
3 b g Dansili Look Here (Hernando (FR))
8552 (1239)◆ 17253 (2526)◆ 48914 56822 64453 800512

**Herecomesthesun (IRE)**
*Archie Watson* 93
2 b f Invincible Spirit(IRE) Intimacy (IRE) (Teofilo (IRE))
(6861) 80027◆ 85973

**Here Comes When (IRE)**
*Andrew Balding* a98 118
7 br g Danehill Dancer(IRE) Quad's Melody (IRE) (Spinning World (USA))
(2767) 43713 (5527) 82329

**Here For The Craic (IRE)**
*David Kenneth Budds* a78 83
10 br g Millenary Tongabezi (IRE) (Shernazar)
7860a12

**Here I Go Again (IRE)**
*Christine Dunnett*
3 b g Fast Company(IRE) Jaldini (IRE) (Darshaan)
440910 50757 59588

**Here In The Dark** *Keith Dalgleish* 68
2 b g Harbour Watch(IRE) Behest (Rainbow Quest (USA))
36483 42454 52554◆ 608710 66263 75194 76982

**Here's The Deal** *Lisa Williamson* 16
3 b f Sakhee's Secret Quite Something (Footstepsinthesand)
44459 53356

**Here's Two** *Ron Hodges* a72 79
4 b m Hellvelyn There's Two (IRE) (Ashkalani (IRE))
16875 18975 21777 27104◆ 34553 37722 47287 (5357) 63402 (6656) 759410

**Hergame** *F Head* 94
2 b f Motivator Kayaba (Anabaa (USA))
4391a4 5448a3

**Herm (IRE)** *David Evans* a58 60
3 b g Bushranger(IRE) School Holidays (USA) (Harlan's Holiday (USA))
24748 37517 42559 48437 65028 79118 (9052)

**Hermana Santa (IRE)** *David Barron* 67
2 b f Arabian Gleam La Zamora (Lujain (USA))
39439 45993 53704 60365 65472

**Hermann** *Richard Hannon* a85 89
4 b h Authorized(IRE) Alamanni (USA) (Elusive Quality (USA))
1632 24784 (2752)◆ 33152 36704

**Hermarna (IRE)** *Neil King* a61 59
4 br m Heliostatic(IRE) Louverissa (IRE) (Verglas (IRE))
29645 47562 63438 82462

**Hermeneutics (USA)** *Ed Walker* a55
3 b g Scat Daddy(USA) Rosangela (USA) (El Prado (IRE))
349 26510

**Herminio (FR)** *Gary Moore* a44 59
5 b g New Approach(IRE) Histoire Sainte (FR) (Kendor (FR))
794912

**Hermosa Vaquera (IRE)**
*Gary Moore* a59 64
7 b m High Chaparral(IRE) Sundown (Polish Precedent (USA))
(5405) (6589) (7151) 81833 909210

**Hermosita** *Roger Varian* 77
2 b f Exceed And Excel(AUS) Honorlina (FR) (Linamix (FR))
(3697)

**Hernandes (FR)** Ian Williams a71 74
3 gr g Clodovil(IRE) Gontcharova (IRE) (Zafonic (USA))
2820[4] 3412[2]◆ 4295[5] 5218[5] 6256a[3]
**Hernandoshideaway** Michael Dods a75 85
5 b g Hernando(FR) Alba Stella (Nashwan (USA))
3050[9] 3559[3] 4260[6]◆ 4722[3] 4959[6] (5539)
**Hernando Torres** Michael Easterby a73 75
9 b g Iffraaj Espana (Hernando (FR))
(757) 1007[8] 1189[4] 1498[14] 1969[11] 2301[7] 3344[6] 4165[3] 4690[2] (5091) 5359[2] 5950[10] 6564[2] 7571[8] 8209[7] 8773[8] 9029[7] 9307[9]
**Heroic Heart (FR)** W McCreery 62
4 b m Invincible Spirit(IRE) Because (IRE) (Sadler's Wells (USA))
1520a[9]
**Heron (USA)** Brett Johnson a66 71
3 b c Quality Road(USA) Dreamt (Oasis Dream)
4055[2] 4569[8] 7331[3] 9325[9]
**Hersigh** Saeed bin Suroor a80 80
3 ch f Poet's Voice Zayn Zen (Singspiel (IRE))
2894[3] 3700[5] 4501[3]
**Her Terms** Clive Cox a63 72
3 ch f Pivotal Best Terms (Exceed And Excel (AUS))
6478[3]◆ (6724) 7689[5]
**Hertford Dancer** John Gosden a75 104
3 ch f Foxwedge(AUS) Tebee (Selkirk (USA))
1404[3] 1736[2] (2613) 3995[3] 4613[4]
**He's A Dreamer (IRE)** F Sanchez a76 60
4 ch g Dream Ahead(USA) Illuminise (IRE) (Grand Lodge (USA))
606a[2]
**He's A Lad (IRE)** Andrew Balding a76 68
3 b g Lilbourne Lad(IRE) Make Amends (IRE) (Indian Ridge (IRE))
466[2] 662[5] (1111)
**He's Amazing (IRE)** Clive Cox 78
2 b g Fastnet Rock(AUS) Kahyasi Moll (IRE) (Brief Truce (USA))
5106[3]◆ 6133[2]
**He's A Toff (IRE)** Tim Easterby 63
3 br g Dandy Man(IRE) Prevarication (IRE) (In The Wings)
2107[3] 2702[9] 3431[7] 3913[3]
**Heshem (IRE)** C Ferland a112 120
4 b h Footstepsinthesand Doohulla (USA) (Stravinsky (USA))
1378a[2]
**He's Magic** Tim Fitzgerald a38 34
6 b g Court Masterpiece Lady Magician (Lord Bud)
98[6] 610[9] 990[5]
**He's My Boy (IRE)** James Fanshawe a74 74
6 gr g Dark Angel(IRE) Rose Of Battle (Averti (IRE))
3074[9] 4542[8] 6197[7]
**He's My Cracker** Clive Cox a80 85
4 ch g Captain Gerrard(IRE) Dalmunzie (IRE) (Choisir (AUS))
857[8] 1606[15] 2821[8]
**He's Our Rokkii (NZ)**
David A & B Hayes & Tom Dabern 111
4 b g Roc De Cambes(NZ) Clerihew (Lomitas)
8250a[16]
**He's Our Star (IRE)** Ali Stronge 68
2 b g Lord Shanakill(USA) Afilla (Dansili)
4805[3] 5586[5] 6260[6] 8467[9]
**Hessoesse (FR)** Pavel Tuma 83
3 b f Cima De Triomphe(IRE) Be In Motion (IRE) (Motivator)
2447a[8]
**Hestina (FR)** Dan Skelton 91
4 b m Soldier Of Fortune(IRE) Diagora (FR) (Highest Honor (FR))
5658[14]
**Heuristique (IRE)** F-H Graffard 107
3 b f Shamardal(USA) T'As D'Beaux Yeux (Red Ransom (USA))
1270a[2] 2644a[3] 3367a[5] 7305a[3] 7845a[4]
**Hewouldwouldnthe**
Jonathan Portman a67
3 b f Sixties Icon Gib (IRE) (Rock Of Gibraltar (IRE))
7492[8] 8770[4] 9159[3]
**Hey Gaman** James Tate 109
2 b c New Approach(IRE) Arsaadi (IRE) (Dubawi (IRE))
3164[2] 4068[9] (4539)◆ 4812[12] (5424)◆ (6190) 7146[2]
**Hey Jonesy (IRE)** Kevin Ryan 108
2 b c Excelebration(IRE) Fikrah (Medicean)
4834[2]◆ (5437) 6353[3]◆ 7618[4]◆
**Hibou** Iain Jardine a80 100
4 ch g Street Cry(IRE) Arlette (IRE) (King Of Kings (IRE))
2457[6] 3154[6] 3597[8] 4076[3] (4475) 5517a[2] 6491a[10] 7609[8] 8042[7]
**Hic Bibi** David Brown a61 52
2 b f Cityscape Real Me (Mark Of Esteem (IRE))
4526[12] 5136[5] 6312[7] (8500)◆ 8793[2]
**Hidden Affair** Henry Candy 76
2 b g Equiano(FR) Love Action (IRE) (Motivator)
5430[5]◆ 8734[3]
**Hidden Charms (IRE)**
David Simcock a75 51
3 b f Canford Cliffs(IRE) Gilded Vanity (IRE) (Indian Ridge (IRE))
(1333)◆ 3693[7] 5324[6] 6818[8] 7364[7]
**Hidden Cyclone (IRE)**
John Joseph Hanlon 90
12 b g Stowaway Hurricane Debbie (IRE) (Shahanndeh (IRE))
5488a[6]
**Hidden Depths (IRE)**
Sir Michael Stoute 25
2 b c Dark Angel(IRE) Liber Nauticus (IRE) (Azamour (IRE))
5887[12]
**Hidden Dream (IRE)**
Christine Dunnett a56 43
2 b f Casamento(IRE) Anything (IRE) (Rock Of Gibraltar (IRE))
6286[5] 7786[6] 8163[12]
**Hidden Gem** Stuart Williams a62 47
4 b m Shamardal(USA) Hidden Brief (Barathea (IRE))
620[2] 784[8] 1325[2] 2053[6]
**Hidden Oasis (IRE)** Jonjo O'Neill 82
6 b g Lawman(FR) Spesialta (Indian Ridge (IRE))
2893[8] 3540[7] 4256[14] 5248[3] 5578[6]
**Hidden Rebel** Alistair Whillans a84 87
5 b m Cockney Rebel(IRE) Medicea Sidera (Medicean)
1368[4] 1832[3] 2406[13] 2884[4] 3828[3] 4431[4] 5072[6] 7161[5]
**Hidden Stash** William Stone a63 46
3 b g Sakhee's Secret Marajuana (Robellino (USA))
1194[3] 1411[6] 1693[6] 2252[4] 2911[9] 3695[5] 4463[5] 6846[4] 7325[7] 7928[5] 8543[U] (8949) (9232)
**Hidden Steps** Andrew Balding a86 89
3 b f Footstepsinthesand Hidden Valley (Haafhd)
1796[6] 2523[5] 4618[5] (8113)◆ 8351[5] 8820[5]
**Hier Encore (FR)** David Menuisier a60 60
5 ch g Kentucky Dynamite(USA) Hierarchie (FR) (Sillery (USA))
1191[6] 1703[9]
**Higgy's Heartbeat** Dean Ivory a55 58
3 b g Acclamation Adorn (Kyllachy)
1551[8] 2231[10] 2727[3] 5748[9] 6502[4] 7157[11] 7540[10]
**High Acclaim (USA)** Roger Teal a86 91
3 b g Elusive Quality(USA) La Reine Lionne (USA) (Leroidesanimaux (BRZ))
1026[5] 1841[5] 2402[3] 2818[3] 4100[3] 4407[4] 6655[3] 7053[6] 7780[11] 8344[13]
**High Alpha (FR)** Mario Hofer 109
3 b g Fuisse(FR) Kikinda (FR) (Daliapour (IRE))
1658a[11]
**High Anxiety** John Weymes a43 11
3 ch f Bated Breath Odense (USA) (Medaglia d'Oro (USA))
3383[6] 6904[5] 7365[5]
**High Baroque (USA)** Richard Fahey a90 61
5 b g Lookin At Lucky(USA) Yesterday (IRE) (Sadler's Wells (USA))
173[7] 1258[6] 3905[6] 4358[8]
**Highbrow** David Simcock a81
2 b c Intello(GER) Wild Gardenia (Alhaarth (IRE))
8643[3]◆ (9201)◆
**Highcastle (IRE)** Ed Dunlop a55 35
2 b g High Chaparral(IRE) Green Castle (IRE) (Indian Ridge (IRE))
7543[15] 8353[9] 8840[8]
**High Command (IRE)** Roger Varian a94 76
4 b g High Chaparral(IRE) Plaza (USA) (Chester House (USA))
3086[6] 4355[3] 5799[3] 6323[10]
**High Draw (FR)** K R Burke a70 78
4 ch g Falco(USA) Augusta Lucilla (USA) (Mr Greeley (USA))
1700[12] 2893[10] (3274a) 5330[3] 5843[2] 6700[12] 7699[2] 8338a[2]
**High Dream Milena (FR)**
Mme C Head-Maarek 105
2 b f Dabirsim(FR) High Limits (IRE) (High Chaparral (IRE))
5195a[4] 6249a[5] 7754a[5]
**High End** Saeed bin Suroor a94 106
3 bb g Dubawi(IRE) Crystal Music (USA) (Nureyev (USA))
(5243)◆ (5849)◆ (6515)◆ 7252[2] 8005[14]
**Higher Court (USA)** Emma Owen a79 59
9 b g Shamardal(USA) Nawaiet (USA) (Zilzal (USA))
94[5] 808[3] 1140[9] 1290[4] 1450[3] 1728[2] 7409[8] (7882)◆ (8990)
**Higher Power** James Fanshawe a114 110
5 b g Rip Van Winkle(IRE) Lady Stardust (Spinning World (USA))
1798[2] 3011[2] (4356)◆ 5503[11] 6400[9] 7547[7]
**Highest Rank (IRE)** K R Burke 69
2 b c Epaulette(AUS) La Noe (Nayef (USA))
(6311) 6938[10] 8046[9]
**Highest Rockeur** P Bary a83 73
3 b c Lawman(FR) Rajastani (IRE) (Zamindar (USA))
5521a[2]
**High Expectations (FR)**
Gordon Elliott a40 71
6 b g High Rock(IRE) Tashifiya (FR) (Sendawar (IRE))
(3193)◆ 3449[3]
**Highfield Lass** Tracy Waggott a48 10
6 b m Cayman Kai(IRE) Jendorcet (Grey Ghost I)
3529[10] 5950[13] 8554[8]
**Highgarden** John Gosden 81
2 b f Nathaniel(IRE) Regalline (IRE) (Green Desert (USA))
(8425)
**High Hopes** David Simcock 99
4 b m Zamindar(USA) Dixielake (IRE) (Lake Coniston (IRE))
2817[2] (3558)◆ 5155[7] 6074[2] 7283[3] 8007[11]
**High Jinx (IRE)** Tim Easterby 112
9 b g High Chaparral(IRE) Leonara (GER) (Surumu (GER))
2803[3] 4917[5] 5503[12] 6400[5] 7116[5] 7639a[4] 8733a[12]
**Highland Acclaim (IRE)**
David O'Meara a96 95
6 b g Acclamation Emma's Star (ITY) (Darshaan)
4[9] 234[6] 547[11] 3946[2]◆ 4521[7] (4803) 5513[5] 6185[13] (6554) 7828[13] 8383[19] 8547[7] 8812[13] 8879[7] 9241[7]
**Highland Bobby** David O'Meara a58 66
2 b g Big Bad Bob(IRE) Eolith (Pastoral Pursuits)
2221[5] 2590[5] 3149[8] 3930[6] 6043[8] 6634[4] 7029[3]
**Highland Castle** Lucinda Egerton a73 94
9 b g Halling(USA) Reciprocal (IRE) (Night Shift (USA))
728[9] 4998[6] 6000[6] 6944[9]
**Highland Clearance (FR)**
Giles Bravery a48 3
3 b f Kyllachy Let My People Go (FR) (Country Reel (USA))
6324[11] 8255[8]
**Highland Colori (IRE)**
Andrew Balding a87 105
9 b g Le Vie Dei Colori Emma's Star (ITY) (Darshaan)
1494[18] 1860[4] 2232[4] 4475[6] 5157[7] 5966[5] 7044[4] 7622[4]◆ 8009[12] 8600[4]
**Highland Cradle** Sir Michael Stoute a80 64
3 b g Bated Breath Orford Ness (Selkirk (USA))
1485[2] 2689[13] 3500[5]
**Highland Fling (IRE)**
Gavin Cromwell a69 82
5 br g Country Reel(USA) High Fun (FR) (Kahyasi (IRE))
5689a[2]
**Highland Mary** Richard Hannon a39 70
2 b f Dark Angel(IRE) Albertine Rose (Namid)
2173[6] 4799[5] 5327[2] 5839[5] 6178[5] 6806[7] 7410[7] 7690[7]
**Highland Pass** Andrew Balding a71 77
3 bb f Passing Glance Lady Brora (Dashing Blade)
2572[2] (3062) 3786[6] 4617[5] 8392[5] 8797[8]
**Highland Reel (IRE)** A P O'Brien 124
5 b h Galileo(IRE) Hveger (AUS) (Danehill (USA))
1379a[7] (3299) (3962) 5394[4]◆ 8233[3] 8610a[3] (9167a)
**Highland Sky (IRE)** David Simcock a64 23
2 b c Camelot Healing Music (FR) (Bering)
6777[11] 8849[6]
**High Language (IRE)**
Joseph Patrick O'Brien 88
3 b f Lawman(FR) Benedicte (IRE) (Galileo (IRE))
8086a[7]
**Highlight Reel (IRE)** Michael Bell a80 80
2 b g Big Bad Bob(IRE) Dance Hall Girl (IRE) (Dansili)
3245[2] 4068[12] 5412[3] (6140)
**Highly Bay (FR)** H-A Pantall a57 59
3 gr f Literato(FR) High Limits (IRE) (High Chaparral (IRE))
3310a[7]
**Highly Focussed (IRE)** Ann Duffield a58 43
3 b g Intense Focus(USA) Mood Indigo (IRE) (Indian Ridge (IRE))
357[4] 415[7] 787[7]◆ 1204[5] 2792[2] 3387[6]
**Highly Sprung (IRE)** Mark Johnston a86 93
4 b g Zebedee Miss Donovan (Royal Applause)
1301[5] 1831[13] 2147[3] 2368[2] 2516[3] 3052[9] 3330[5] 3827[9] 4201[5] 4897[6] (5184) 5869[11] 6237[8] 7214[4] 7882[10] 8433[3]
**High One (FR)** P Demercastel a82 92
3 b g Spirit One(FR) Higha (FR) (Vettori (IRE))
5521a[7]
**High On Life** S bin Ghadayer a103 95
6 b g Invincible Spirit(IRE) Lovely Thought (Dubai Destination (USA))
84a[7] 318a[9] 1041a[9] 1377a[12]
**High On Light** David Barron a79 82
4 b m Makfi Estephe (IRE) (Sadler's Wells (USA))
497[2] 613[2] 781[5] 3933[2] 5414[3] (5873) 6880[7]
**High On Love (IRE)**
Charlie Fellowes a80 81
3 br f Requinto(IRE) Cant Hurry Love (Desert Prince (IRE))
3786[8] 4975[2] 6576[9] 7771[5] 8374[9]
**High Quality (IRE)** A Fabre a86 97
4 gr m Invincible Spirit(IRE) High Maintenance (FR) (Highest Honor (FR))
6804a[7] 7697a[9] 8251a[7]
**Highsalvia Cosmos** Mark Hoad a43 43
6 b g High Chaparral(IRE) Salvia (Pivotal)
2332[12] 2966[8]
**High Seas (IRE)** Hugo Palmer a67 73
2 b f Henrythenavigator(USA) High Days (IRE) (Hennessy (USA))
7238[6] 7898[4] 8347[2] 8817[11]
**High Secret (IRE)** Paul Nicholls a98 100
6 b g High Chaparral(IRE) Secret Question (USA) (Rahy (USA))
3073[2] 3928[9] 8539[3]
**High Shaw** Ann Duffield 42
3 b g Paco Boy(IRE) Mondovi (Kyllachy)
2110[6] 2632[9] 3151[10]
**Hightime Girl** Roger Fell a61 58
4 ch m Pivotal Hightime Heroine (IRE) (Danetime (IRE))
44[7]
**High Waves (IRE)** Saeed bin Suroor a76 79
3 br c Dream Ahead(USA) Lake Moon (Tiger Hill (IRE))
3583[7] 4691[6]
**Highwayman** David Thompson a59 59
4 b g Dick Turpin(IRE) Right Rave (IRE) (Soviet Star (USA))
509[5] 1122[5] 1469[8] 8218[10] 9077[8]
**Highway One (USA)** George Baker 73
3 b f Quality Road(USA) Kinda Wonderful (USA) (Silver Train (USA))
1947[4]◆ 2778[2] 3748[8] 5248[7] 6378[7] 7157[3] 8300[7]
**Highway Robber** Wilf Storey a56 58
4 b g Dick Turpin(IRE) Lawyers Choice (Namid)
176[2] 607[2] 3252[4] (3706) 5413[5] 5832[3] 6352[5] 6788[4] 7979[6] 8314[3]
**Highway Star (USA)** Rodrigo Ubillo a113 62
4 ch m Girolamo(USA) Stolen Star (USA) (Cat Thief (USA))
8605a[11]
**High Wells** Seamus Durack 73
3 b g High Chaparral(IRE) Valencha (Domedriver (IRE))
2359[7] 3506[11] 3839[7] 4492[2] 4914[4] 5780[7] (6611) 6892[2]
**Hi Ho Silver** Chris Wall a64 35
3 gr g Camacho Silver Spell (Aragon)
7930[3] 8504[5] 8995[4]
**Hijran (IRE)** Michael Appleby a68 67
4 ch m Mastercraftsman(IRE) Sunny Slope (Mujtahid (USA))
267[11] 2267[7] 2587[3] 3203[8] 4506[12] 5760[2]
**Hikmaa (IRE)** Ed Vaughan a80 104
2 b f Roderic O'Connor(IRE) Alice Liddel (IRE) (Dark Angel (IRE))
(5834) (6844)◆ 7578[4] 8002[5] (8424)
**Hilarant (FR)** C Laffon-Parias 62
3 b g Azamour(IRE) Comique (USA) (Distorted Humor (USA))
3554a[9]
**Hilario** Charles Hills a83 91
3 b g Sepoy(AUS) Persario (Bishop Of Cashel)
1901[8]
**Hilary J** Ann Duffield a86 89
4 b m Mount Nelson The Terrier (Foxhound (USA))
2899[5]◆ 3847[4] 4379[7] 5457[12] 6669[5] (8321) 8913[3]
**Hilborough** Mick Channon a62 65
2 b c Makfi Ambrix (IRE) (Xaar)
8162[5] 8560[6] 9137[5] 9300[4]
**Hillbilly Boy (IRE)** Tom Dascombe a95 107
7 b g Haafhd Erreur (IRE) (Desert King (IRE))
2568[9] 4890[9] (Dead)
**Hillhouse High (USA)**
Richard Baltas a82 104
6 b m Exchange Rate(USA) Pleasant Laughter (USA) (Coronado's Quest (USA))
8601a[10]
**Himalayan Queen** William Jarvis a73 69
4 b m Poet's Voice Annapurna (IRE) (Brief Truce (USA))
1140[4] 1326[6] 2043[7] 2969[9] (3702) 5482[2] 5857[7] 6439[3] 7770[5] 8374[10]
**Hi Milady (IRE)**
Dominic Ffrench Davis a49 65
3 b f Sir Prancealot(IRE) Hi Katriona (IRE) (Second Empire (IRE))
3246[13] 4971[10] 5250[7] 5713[6] 5958[5]
**Himself** Richard Hannon a76 77
3 b g High Chaparral(IRE) Self Centred (Medicean)
2151[8] 3621[9] 6442[2] 7882[6]
**Hindsight** Michael Appleby 72
3 b f Sayif(IRE) Classic Vision (Classic Cliche (IRE))
2344[3] 2682[2]◆ 3626[3] 4378[6] (6828) 7155[4] 7932[7]
**Hint Of Grey (IRE)** Don Cantillon a46 57
4 gr m Mastercraftsman(IRE) Anamarka (Mark Of Esteem (IRE))
462[7] 2281[3] 3575[6] 8122[4] 9334[6]
**Hiorne Tower (FR)** John Best a63 68
6 b g Poliglote Hierarchie (FR) (Sillery (USA))
(4756) (5407)
**Hipodamo De Mileto (FR)**
J Calderon 90
3 ch c Falco(USA) La Atalaya (Montjeu (IRE))
4654a[2]
**Hippeia (IRE)** Jedd O'Keeffe 71
2 b f Lilbourne Lad(IRE) Majestic Oasis (Oasis Dream)
5058[4] 5702[4] 6590[5] 7458[3]
**Hippocampus (IRE)**
Richard Hannon a62 47
3 b c Born To Sea(IRE) Tolzey (USA) (Rahy (USA))
1358[5] 1551[7] 1961[9] 2395[10] 3024[9] 4006[10]
**Hipster Boy** John Gosden a77 73
2 b c Dubawi(IRE) Mandellicht (IRE) (Be My Guest (USA))
8677[3] (8952)
**Hipz (IRE)** Ivan Furtado a67 70
6 br m Intense Focus(USA) Radha (Bishop Of Cashel)
620[7] 860[2] 1285[6] (1755) 1868[8] 2464[4] 3139[5]
**Hisar (IRE)** Michael Appleby a60 58
3 ch g Dragon Pulse(IRE) Delphie Queen (IRE) (Desert Sun)
1287[2] 1453[6] 1724[4] 2361[6] 2778[6] 3621[6] 4444[5] 5247[7] 5956[5] 6507[4] 7459[7] 8395[6] 8495[4] 8949[3] 9013[4] (9267)
**His Dream (IRE)** Jonjo O'Neill 76
4 b g Yeats(IRE) Rosa Muscosa (USA) (Dixie Union (USA))
4073[12]
**Historia (FR)** F Chappet a20 74
2 b f Siyouni(FR) Hieroglyph (Green Desert (USA))
(8252a)
**Historic Event (IRE)**
Saeed bin Suroor a75 80
3 gr f Invincible Spirit(IRE) Scenica (ARG) (Interprete (ARG))
1626[2] (2112) 2630[2]
**History Writer (IRE)**
David Menuisier 77
2 b c Canford Cliffs(IRE) Abhasana (IRE) (Hawk Wing (USA))
6653[3]
**Hitchcock** Kevin Ryan a69 71
3 b g Equiano(FR) George's Gift (Haafhd)
731[2] 2033[5] 2595[8] 4265[8] 4602[8] 5182[7] 6271[12] (7165) 8514[2] 8651[5]
**Hi There Silver (IRE)**
Michael Madgwick a48 59
3 gr g Clodovil(IRE) Elaborate (Sadler's Wells (USA))
434[9] 627[4] 1726[6] 2679[10] 8673[5] 9391[3]
**Hitman** Rebecca Bastiman 80
4 b g Canford Cliffs(IRE) Ballymore Celebre (IRE) (Peintre Celebre (USA))
3433[3] 3845[12] 4438[5] 5165[6] 5739[3]◆ 6181[11] 7052[9] 7474[6] 7888[6] (8216)
**Hit The Beat** Clive Cox a73
2 br f Fast Company(IRE) Dance Express (IRE) (Rail Link)
8130[4] (8945)
**Hit The Bid** D J Bunyan a109 109
3 b c Exceed And Excel(AUS) Selinka (Selkirk (USA))
1742a[6] 3370a[8] (3873a) 4416a[2] 4927a[4] 7396[13] 8225a[2]
**Hit The Jackpot (IRE)**
Caroline Fuchs a74 93
8 ch g Pivotal Token Gesture (IRE) (Alzao (USA))
798a[4]
**Hit The Lights (IRE)** Marjorie Fife a34 74
7 b g Lawman(FR) Dawn Chorus (IRE) (Mukaddamah (USA))
2994[5] 3979[7] 4682[8]

**Hit The Silk (IRE)** *P J F Murphy* 97
4 br g Majestic Missile(IRE) Queen Of Silk (IRE) (Brief Truce (USA))
**8438a**[7]

**Hochfeld (IRE)** *Mark Johnston* a79 106
3 b g Cape Cross(IRE) What A Charm (IRE) (Key Of Luck (USA))
647[4] 846[2] (4336)◆ (4891)◆ 5071[2] 5525[6] **(6427)**◆ 6930[9] 7783[3] 8005[5]

**Hocus Focus (IRE)** *Richard Guest* a39
2 b c Intense Focus(USA) Hedera (USA) (Woodman (USA))
**9015**[5] 9372[6]

**Hogar Seguro (IRE)**
*David Loughnane* a25 54
2 b f Casamento(IRE) Gemma's Pearl (IRE) (Marju (IRE))
**4116**[5] **4597**[5]

**Hogy (USA)** *Michael J Maker* a111 113
8 bb g Offlee Wild(USA) Floy (USA) (Petionville (USA))
**8604a**[11]

**Hoku (IRE)** *Bent Olsen* a48 90
6 b m Holy Roman Emperor(IRE) Scylla Cadeaux (IRE) (Cadeaux Genereux)
**6500a**[3]

**Holdenhurst** *Sylvester Kirk* 71
2 gr g Hellvelyn Michelle Shift (Night Shift (USA))
2706[5] **(2910)** 3297[6] **4175**[2] 4827[7] 5150[20]

**Hold Firm** *Mark H Tompkins* a65 59
5 b h Refuse To Bend(IRE) Four Miracles (Vettori (IRE))
383[4] 636[2] (966) (1139) 1225[6] 1409[5] 1484[6] 2257[3] **(2465)** 2996[5] 3731[3]

**Hold Hands** *Brendan Powell* a61 58
6 b m Lawman(FR) Tiponi (IRE) (Traditionally (USA))
**9406**[9]

**Holding Gold (USA)** *Mark Casse* a37 116
4 b g Lonhro(AUS) In The Gold (USA) (Golden Missile (USA))
**8604a**[7]

**Hold Me Tight (IRE)** *J S Moore* a56 56
3 b g Zoffany(IRE) All Embracing (IRE) (Night Shift (USA))
763[11] 897[3] 1107[5] 1428[3] 2726[7] 3162[7] 3819[3] **5523a**[7] **5909a**[6] 6084a[10]

**Hold On Magnolia** *Richard Fahey* a70 44
4 ch g Monsieur Bond(IRE) Mawjoodah (Cadeaux Genereux)
159[3] 480[3]

**Hold Sway (IRE)** *Charlie Appleby* a73 90
3 b g Dubawi(IRE) Annabelle's Charm (IRE) (Indian Ridge (IRE))
1083[2] 1497[3] 2300[2] **(2751)** **3505**[3] 5568[5] 5915[8]

**Holdthasigreen (FR)** *C Le Lay* a90 112
5 ch g Hold That Tiger(USA) Greentathir (FR) (Muhtathir)
2202a[9] (3637a) **6250a**[3] **6984a**[2] **8274a**[3]

**Hold Your Breath** *Tony Carroll* 47
2 b f Bated Breath Chittenden (USA) (Raven's Pass (USA))
4806[10] **6417**[8] 7126[9]

**Holidayend (IRE)** *M Weiss*
5 ch g Nayef(USA) I Hearyou Knocking (IRE) (Danehill Dancer (IRE))
715a[3] (834a) 953a[F]

**Holiday Girl (IRE)**
*Eve Johnson Houghton* a78 70
3 b f Acclamation Bikini Babe (IRE) (Montjeu (IRE))
**6614**[3] 7080[2] 7907[2] 8479[3]

**Holiday Magic (IRE)**
*Michael Easterby* a102 97
6 gr g Dark Angel(IRE) Win Cash (IRE) (Alhaarth (IRE))
**(5)** 199[4] **730**[2] 1148[3] 1492[14] 1769[7] 2606[6] 3324[6] 3585[5] 4905[15] 8257[9] 8812[10] 9125[7]

**Holistic Approach (IRE)** *J S Bolger* a89 82
3 b c New Approach(IRE) Sway Me Now (USA) (Speightstown (USA))
**1742a**[5]

**Hollander** *William Muir* 75
3 ch g Dutch Art Thrill (Pivotal)
2620[2] 3085[6] 4368[5] 4965[5] **(5723)**

**Hollie's Dream** *David Evans* 51
2 ch f Rip Van Winkle(IRE) In A Silent Way (IRE) (Desert Prince (IRE))
2904[5] 6272[10] **6583**[6] 7081[12] 7756[14]

**Holly Bush Henry (IRE)**
*Graeme McPherson* a62
6 b g Yeats(IRE) Maslam (IRE) (Robellino (USA))
**353**[6]

**Hollydaze (IRE)** *Richard Hughes* 80
2 b f Big Bad Bob(IRE) Fashionable (Nashwan (USA))
6584[3] **(7093)** 7608[5]

**Hollywood All Star (IRE)**
*Graeme McPherson* a41 42
8 b g Kheleyf(USA) Camassina (IRE) (Taufan (USA))
414[11]

**Hollywood Dream** *Neil Mulholland* a58 67
2 b f Delegator Royal Obsession (IRE) (Val Royal (FR))
4533[8] **5528**[4] **6480**[5] 7458[5] 8153[12] 9199[6] 9436[12]

**Hollywood Harry (IRE)**
*Keith Dalgleish* a57 62
3 ch g Dandy Man(IRE) Alifandango (IRE) (Alzao (USA))
1034[DSQ] 1123[2] 1564[6] 1835[8] **2455**[2] 3047[5] 3387[3] 3913[10] 4265[9] 4744[11]

**Hollywood Road (IRE)**
*Don Cantillon* a82 90
4 b g Kodiac Rinneen (IRE) (Bien Bien (USA))
(3670) 4254[3] 4976[2] 6059[2] **6513**[3] 7096[4]

**Hollywood Star (USA)**
*Dale Romans* a96
2 bb c Malibu Moon(USA) Hollywood Story (USA) (Wild Rush (USA))
**8609a**[6]

**Hollywood Style** *Brendan Powell* 44
3 b f Royal Applause Brazilian Style (Exit To Nowhere (USA))
**89**[11] 5511[RR]

**Holmeswood** *Michael Dods* a81 103
3 b g Mayson Anglezarke (IRE) (Acclamation)
2122[3] 2831[4] 3664[5] 4683[4] (5204) (5708) **(6450)** 6927[4]

**Holmfirst** *Paul Midgley* 48
2 b g Finjaan Forrest Star (Fraam)
2373[5] **3200**[5] 3791[16] 5603[8]

**Holte End** *Kevin Frost*
2 b f Stimulation(IRE) Ellway Queen (USA) (Bahri (USA))
8555[10]

**Holy Cat (IRE)** *M D O'Callaghan* a93 85
3 ch f Kitten's Joy(USA) Holy Freud (USA) (Freud (USA))
**2441a**[5] 6961a[16]

**Holy Heart (IRE)** *John Gosden* a68
2 b c Holy Roman Emperor(IRE) Heart Of Ice (IRE) (Montjeu (IRE))
**9154**[3]◆

**Holyroman Princess** *Daniel Kubler* a27 47
3 b f Holy Roman Emperor(IRE) Princess Ellen (Tirol (IRE))
1968[11] **2726**[5] 3087[8] 3657[13] 4494[7] 9073[5]

**Holy Shambles (IRE)** *Marco Botti* a67
2 b c Holy Roman Emperor(IRE) Shim Sham (IRE) (Danehill Dancer (IRE))
**9200**[5]

**Holy Tiber (IRE)** *George Scott* 77
2 b f Holy Roman Emperor(IRE) Quiet Waters (USA) (Quiet American (USA))
(2816) 3421[6] **(4273)** 5596[4] 6481[4] 7814[11]

**Hombre Casado (FR)** *Ed Walker* 58
2 b c Siyouni(FR) Storma (FR) (Starborough)
**8678**[11]◆

**Home Again** *Lee Carter* a57 66
4 b g Bahamian Bounty Celestial Welcome (Most Welcome)
761[2] 982[3] 1451[2] **1894**[3] 3001[7]

**Home Cummins (IRE)**
*Richard Fahey* a98 99
5 b m Rip Van Winkle(IRE) Alava (IRE) (Anabaa (USA))
1960[16] 2767[11] **3298**[3] 3837[6] 4377[7] 4718[4] 5382[2] **6520**[2] 8009[3] 8469[5]

**Home Of The Brave (IRE)**
*Hugo Palmer* a100 118
5 ch g Starspangledbanner(AUS) Blissful Beat (Beat Hollow)
**(2150)** **(4362)** 5502[2] 7145[3] 8608a[14]

**Homeopathic** *Sir Michael Stoute* a77
2 b f Dark Angel(IRE) Holistic (Pivotal)
**(7454)**

**Homerton** *Robyn Brisland* a65 71
2 b c Finjaan Canis Star (Wolfhound (USA))
4583[4] **6142**[4] 7273[8] 7929[5] 8207[3]

**Homesman (USA)** *A P O'Brien* a77 109
3 b c War Front(USA) My Annette (USA) (Red Ransom (USA))
(3109a) 3998[5] **4652a**[3]

**Homing Star** *Jonathan Portman* a57 25
2 b f Harbour Watch(IRE) Nightunderthestars (Observatory (USA))
8425[12] **8668**[8]

**Honcho (IRE)** *Mrs A Malzard* a62 49
5 gr g Dark Angel(IRE) Disco Lights (Spectrum (IRE))
1932a[7] **2669a**[6]

**Honey Badger** *Michael Herrington* a67 58
6 bb g Pastoral Pursuits Taminoula (IRE) (Tagula (IRE))
6296[2] 7240[2] **(7606)** 8376[8] **(8721)** 8930[3]

**Honey Blossom** *Denis Quinn* 32
2 b f Makfi Seasonal Blossom (IRE) (Fairy King (USA))
**3697**[9] 4709[8] 5886[6]

**Honey Gg** *Declan Carroll* 41
2 b f Mayson Local Fancy (Bahamian Bounty)
5210[11] 5801[7] **7264**[5] 8475[5]

**Honeymoon Honey (USA)**
*Katharina Stenefeldt* a63
6 ch g Curlin(USA) Chantel D (USA) (Holy Bull (USA))
**4940a**[10]

**Honeymoon Trip (FR)**
*L A Urbano-Grajales* 53
3 b f Myboycharlie(IRE) Helsinka (FR) (Pennekamp (USA))
**4027a**[10] 5196a[12]

**Honeysuckle Lil (IRE)** *Tim Easterby* a47 83
5 b m Alfred Nobel(IRE) Twinberry (IRE) (Tagula (IRE))
1910[4] 2592[4] 2856[5] **3452**[2] 3707[2] 4249[4] 4788[7] 5635[9] 6382[5] 7245[3] 7628[11]

**Hong Kong Joe** *Lydia Richards* a50 42
7 b g Oasis Dream Singed (Zamindar (USA))
**1081**[4] 1698[7] 3575[17] 4257[7] 5299[10] 8507[3] 8846[8] 9237[4]

**Honiara** *J-M Capitte* a73 88
4 b g Rock Of Gibraltar(IRE) Indian Maiden (IRE) (Indian Ridge (IRE))
287[3] 548[5] **896**[2] (3938) 4587[2] (5821) 6617[10] 7285[5] 8344[12] 9309a[3]

**Honorable Spirit (FR)** *F Chappet* a25
2 ch c Kendargent(FR) Seralia (Royal Academy (USA))
**5952a**[12]

**Honor Oak (IRE)** *T Hogan* a78 82
5 gr m Zebedee Ishimagic (Ishiguru (USA))
**4385a**[2] 5519a[14]

**Honourable Knight (IRE)**
*Mark Usher* a48 49
9 b g Celtic Swing Deemeh (IRE) (Brief Truce (USA))
2332[13] 2966[10] **3756**[4] 4756[9] 5267[6] 8135[3]

**Hoofalong** *Michael Easterby* a90 105
7 b g Pastoral Pursuits Baymist (Mind Games)
5435[11] 6206[12] **6325**[7]◆ 7086[7] 7610[13]

**Hoof It** *Michael Easterby* a89 105
10 b g Monsieur Bond(IRE) Forever Bond (Danetime (IRE))
5094[12] **5640**[6] 6325[6] 8044[12] 8383[4] 8679[4]

**Hoover Fever** *Carroll Gray* 53
3 b f Compton Place Aswaaq (IRE) (Peintre Celebre (USA))
5713[14] **6180**[10]

**Hope Against Hope (IRE)**
*Mark Johnston* a45 69
3 b f Dark Angel(IRE) Hope Of An Angel (IRE) (Intikhab (USA))
**(4184)**

**Hope And Glory (IRE)**
*Tom Dascombe* a53 52
2 ch f Dandy Man(IRE) Tashyra (IRE) (Tagula (IRE))
2502[7] 2987[8] 3502[5] 5143[3] 5933[7] **6634**[3] 7081[9] 7756[2] 8397[3]

**Hope Is High** *John Berry* a55 79
4 b m Sir Percy Altitude (Green Desert (USA))
2281[4]◆ 2964[4] (3726) 3916[2] 4733[3] 5508[2] (6109)◆ (6309) **(7336)**

**Hopeless (FR)**
*Mme C Barande-Barbe* 91
4 ch g Tigron(USA) Phalaee (FR) (Ski Chief (USA))
**8526a**[10]

**Hope Solo (IRE)** *Tim Easterby* 89
3 ch f Dutch Art In Safe Hands (IRE) (Intikhab (USA))
3793[9] 4435[4] 4889[5] 5828[8] **(6759)** 6970[4] 7329[3]

**Hoppertunity (USA)** *Bob Baffert* a118
6 b h Any Given Saturday(USA) Refugee (USA) (Unaccounted For (USA))
**1380a**[6]

**Hoquilebo (FR)** *T Castanheira* a65 53
2 b c Falco(USA) Honey Gem (FR) (Gold Away (IRE))
**6247a**[3] 8169a[11]

**Hornby** *Michael Attwater* a56 13
2 b g Equiano(FR) Kindia (IRE) (Cape Cross (IRE))
3002[10] 4213[10] **8819**[5] 9188[6]

**Horroob** *Roger Varian* a95 91
3 b c Showcasing Funny Enough (Dansili)
(1619)◆ (2334) 3071[4] 3997[24] **5415**[2] 6404[14]

**Hors De Combat** *Denis Coakley* a84 109
6 ch g Mount Nelson Maid For Winning (USA) (Gone West (USA))
205a[2] 654a[3] **1766**[2] 2606[9] 3963[13] 4636[4] 7275[2] 8234[15]

**Horseguardsparade**
*Nigel Twiston-Davies* a76 70
6 b g Montjeu(IRE) Honorlina (FR) (Linamix (FR))
**853**[6]

**Horse Of Fortune (SAF)** *A T Millard* 118
6 b g Stronghold Sweet Virginia (SAF) (Casey Tibbs (IRE))
**9170a**[6]

**Horseplay** *Andrew Balding* 100
3 b f Cape Cross(IRE) Mischief Making (USA) (Lemon Drop Kid (USA))
**(2436)** 3301[4] 4424a[4] 8231[8]

**Horsforth** *Richard Guest* a71 71
5 b m Kyllachy Lady McBeth (IRE) (Avonbridge)
**1031**[2] 1200[3] 2305[4] 2925[4] (3345) 3944[8] 4664[5]

**Horsili (FR)** *Mlle E Schmitt* a15
3 b g Tin Horse(IRE) Pausili (FR) (Dansili)
**8692a**[11]

**Horsted Keynes (FR)**
*David Simcock* a96 98
7 ch g Giant's Causeway(USA) Viking's Cove (USA) (Miswaki (USA))
199[10] 465[3] 730[3] 999[3] 1177[7] 2283[2] 3003[3] 4103[2] **(4321)** 5415[3] 5662[4] **6484**[3] 6949[3]

**Hot Beat (IRE)** *David Simcock* a100 74
5 b g Dylan Thomas(IRE) Hungry Heart (IRE) (Hawk Wing (USA))
(269)◆ **728**[3] 3594[10] 4356[18] 5803[4]

**Hotfill** *David Barron* a70 66
3 b g Showcasing Reel Cool (Reel Buddy (USA))
160[5] **401**[2] 578[6] 2186[9] 2886[5]

**Hot Gossip (IRE)** *Dianne Sayer* a41 41
3 b f Fast Company(IRE) On The Make (IRE) (Entrepreneur)
**1308**[10] 1514[11] 6048[9] **7220**[6]

**Hot Hannah** *Michael Dods* a53 70
3 gr f Hellvelyn Toy Top (USA) (Tactical Cat (USA))
2080[6] 2630[8] 3345[5] 3624[12] (5472) **6384**[2] 7014[8] 7522[19]

**Hot Lick** *Dan Skelton* a56 44
3 b g Phoenix Reach(IRE) Sweet Mandolin (Soviet Star (USA))
**627**[3] 881[9] 2711[9]

**Hot Mustard** *William Muir* a73 77
7 b g Pastoral Pursuits Lihou Island (Beveled (USA))
2511[2] **3028**[4] 3282[5] 4203[6] 5823[7] 6310[5] 7062[4] 7605[7] (8248) 8854[11]

**Hot Natured (IRE)** *K R Burke* a71
3 b f Canford Cliffs(IRE) Teddy Bears Picnic (Oasis Dream)
**658**[2] 1003[5] 1818[8]

**Hot Off The Press (IRE)**
*Michael Bell* a54 45
2 b f Camelot Jewel In The Sand (IRE) (Bluebird (USA))
8163[11] **8668**[10]

**Hot Rock (IRE)** *Bryan Smart* 64
2 ch g Society Rock(IRE) Red Roar (IRE) (Chineur (FR))
**1873**[4] **2221**[6] 2896[11]

**Hot Stuff** *James McAuley* a48 45
4 b g Assertive Even Hotter (Desert Style (IRE))
(554) **961**[3] 1340[6] 2025[5] 2995[3] 5052[10] 6114[6] 9244a[12]

**Hot Zone (USA)** *J-C Rouget* a67
2 b f War Front(USA) Storybook (UAE) (Halling (USA))
**4677a**[4]

**Houlanbator (FR)** *Mlle G Meijer* a23 47
2 b f Hurricane Cat(USA) Advenio (IRE) (Ad Valorem (USA))
**9087a**[16]

**Houlton** *Marco Botti* a49
2 ch c Declaration Of War(USA) Greek Goddess (IRE) (Galileo (IRE))
**8849**[10] 9312[12]

**Hourglass (IRE)** *Marco Botti* 62
2 b f Galileo(IRE) Helsinki (Machiavellian (USA))
**8323**[6]◆

**House Captain** *Georgios Alimpinisis* a56 56
6 ch h Captain Gerrard(IRE) Dalmunzie (IRE) (Choisir (AUS))
**9112a**[10]

**House Edge** *Michael Bell* 87
2 gr c Nathaniel(IRE) Bezique (Cape Cross (IRE))
7128[5]◆ **(7654)**

**House Of Commons (IRE)**
*Michael Appleby* a84 80
4 b g Sea The Stars(IRE) Reality (FR) (Slickly (FR))
**(6)** 306[5] 719[5] 1433[5] 1700[3] 1969[8] 2586[10] 4722[4] 5664[7] 6763[6] 7083[2] 7524[4] 8254[3]

**House Of Frauds (IRE)**
*Tony Newcombe* a35 19
9 b g Storming Home Bogus Penny (IRE) (Pennekamp (USA))
331[12] 1205[10] 3426[7] **7215**[7]

**Hout Bay (FR)** *Mario Hofer* a81 81
4 bb g Whipper(USA) Iocaste (GER) (Acatenango (GER))
**5490a**[7]

**Howardian Hills (IRE)**
*Victor Dartnall* a64 56
4 b g Vale Of York(IRE) Handsome Anna (IRE) (Bigstone (IRE))
4187[10] (4980) 6069[8] **6796**[2] 7085[9] 8507[7] 8955[5] 9317[8]

**Howbaar (USA)** *James Bethell* a58
2 b g Lonhro(AUS) Going Day (USA) (Daylami (IRE))
**8316**[8]

**How Bizarre** *Kevin Ryan* 63
2 ch g Society Rock(IRE) Amanda Carter (Tobougg (IRE))
**6890**[4] 7266[4] 7818[4]

**How's Lucy** *Jane Chapple-Hyam* a56 50
3 b f Approve(IRE) Murielle (Diktat)
1596[8] 2733[2] 4006[5] 8675[6] **9141**[3] 9282[3]

**Huda (FR)** *B Legros* a67 61
4 b m Equiano(FR) Leni Riefenstahl (IRE) (Mull Of Kintyre (USA))
4653a[6]

**Huddersfilly Town** *Ivan Furtado* a62
3 b f Major Cadeaux Mortitia (Dansili)
983[4] 1205[7] 2016[10]◆ 2790[5] 8249[6] 8673[6] (8799) 9127[4] **(9278)**

**Hug (IRE)** *F Chappet* 68
3 b f Dark Angel(IRE) Tender Is Thenight (IRE) (Barathea (IRE))
1459a[4]

**Huge Future** *Saeed bin Suroor* a89 103
4 b g Shamardal(USA) Time Honoured (Sadler's Wells (USA))
322a[5] **888a**[3]

**Hugging The Rails (IRE)**
*Tim Easterby* a44 62
3 b g Royal Applause Aqraan (In The Wings)
**2349**[4] 2703[5] 3041[7]

**Hugie Boy (IRE)** *Scott Dixon* a53 68
5 ch g Art Connoisseur(IRE) Piece Unique (Barathea (IRE))
8807[9] 9076[8] **9176**[3] 9347[6] 9444[7]

**Hugin (IRE)** *David Simcock* a86 94
3 b g Henrythenavigator(USA) Silver Star (Zafonic (USA))
(2791) 3713[3] 4618[4] **(5541)**◆ 6562[2] **7339**[2]

**Hugoigo** *Jim Goldie* a36 55
3 b g Sulamani(IRE) Gargoyle Girl (Be My Chief (USA))
2496[5] **2842**[5] 4657[5]

**Hugs And Pats** *Dean Ivory* 6
2 b g Big Bad Bob(IRE) Zambujeiro (Dutch Art)
**4044**[5]

**Hukamaa** *F Head* a66 96
3 b f Dansili Motmayza (Nayef (USA))
**8733a**[8]

**Hula Girl** *Charles Hills* 87
2 gr f Oasis Dream Tropical Paradise (IRE) (Verglas (IRE))
6138[4] 7021[5] **8562**[7]

**Human Nature (IRE)**
*Stuart Williams* a95 83
4 b g Kodiac Sundown (Polish Precedent (USA))
3330[6] 4099[5] (4746) 5064[4] 6289[9] 8344[2] 9020[2] (9241)

**Humbert (IRE)** *Hugo Palmer* a89 82
3 b g Kodiac Fee Eria (FR) (Always Fair (USA))
**(9202)**

**Humble Gratitude** *K R Burke* 86
2 ch g Foxwedge(AUS) Gilt Linked (Compton Place)
5099[4] **5825**[2]◆ (6689)◆ 7090[22]

**Humble Hero (IRE)** *William Haggas* a93 90
3 b g High Chaparral(IRE) Alamouna (IRE) (Indian Ridge (IRE))
2143[2] 2963[2] (3860) 4612[4] **(7031)** 8005[15]

**Humbolt Current** *William Haggas* 79
2 b c Fastnet Rock(AUS) Humdrum (Dr Fong (USA))
**8119**[2]◆

**Humidor (NZ)** *Darren Weir* 122
4 b g Teofilo(IRE) Zalika (NZ) (Zabeel (NZ))
8250a[5] **8446a**[2] 8667a[19]

**Humour (IRE)** *Christine Dunnett* a61 55
6 b g Invincible Spirit(IRE) Hucking Hot (Desert Prince (IRE))
**302**[6] 521[9] 724[12] 2069[7] 2733[6] 3001[3] 3728[7] 4766[7] 5239[8]

**Hunaina (IRE)** *M Halford* a99 93
3 b f Tamayuz Hanakiyya (IRE) (Danehill Dancer (IRE))
8407a10

**Hungarian Rhapsody**
*Jamie Osborne* a58 54
3 b g Exceed And Excel(AUS) Sharp Terms (Kris)
8075 11832 14322 49704 58925

**Hunni** *Tom Clover* a56 77
2 b f Captain Gerrard(IRE) Lady O Malley (IRE) (Oratorio (IRE))
295811 38215 44402 (5659) 782110

**Hunt (IRE)** *Philip D'Amato* a71 111
5 rg g Dark Angel(IRE) Mansiya (Vettori (IRE))
8610a13

**Hunter O'Riley (USA)**
*James J Toner* a76 111
4 b r Tiz Wonderful(USA) Oblige (USA) (Bernardini (USA))
3553a5 6461a4

**Hunters Creek (IRE)**
*S bin Ghadayer* a70 88
6 b g Cape Cross(IRE) Cinnamon Rose (USA) (Trempolino (USA))
203a3

**Hunting Ground (USA)**
*S bin Ghadayer* a105 82
7 b g Street Cry(IRE) Panty Raid (USA) (Include (USA))
83a2 (319a)

**Huntsmans Close** *Robert Cowell* a97 103
7 b g Elusive Quality(USA) Badminton (Zieten (USA))
36256 39678 48032 55133 65545 83938

**Hurricane Alert** *Mark Hoad* a52 59
5 b g Showcasing Raggle Taggle (IRE) (Tagula (IRE))
81910 8746 12202 13404 14904 17592 (2069) 22146 36592 40934 453210 58718 674810

**Hurricane Breizh (FR)** *W Walton* a32 56
2 b f Hurricane Cat(USA) Shinaway (FR) (Gold Away (IRE))
1929a4 2321a6

**Hurricane Hollow** *David Barron* a65 76
7 b g Beat Hollow Veenwouden (Desert Prince (IRE))
13085 19848 28413◆ 35012 47425 56675 58723◆ 75614 79832 84873 87715

**Hurricane Light (FR)** *S Wattel* a76
2 b g Orpen(USA) City Of Light (Singspiel (IRE))
8169a4

**Hurricane Lil (IRE)** *George Baker* a54 61
2 b f Big Bad Bob(IRE) Ladylishandra (IRE) (Mujadil (USA))
61387 64176 72269 78975 86448 89433 90907

**Hurricane Red (IRE)**
*Lennart Reuterskiold Jr* a102 106
7 ch h Hurricane Run(IRE) Bounce (FR) (Trempolino (USA))
2942a5 4825a2 5676a4 6501a4 7428a5

**Hurricane Rock** *Simon Dow* a56 66
4 ch g Rock Of Gibraltar(IRE) Seasonal Cross (Cape Cross (IRE))
8079 14279 35324 43508 54108 58489 (6635) 74872 83955

**Hurricane Volta (IRE)** *Peter Hedger* a68 71
6 ch g Hurricane Run(IRE) Haute Volta (FR) (Grape Tree Road)
40893

**Hurry (IRE)** *P Sogorb* a58
3 b f Arcano(IRE) Neutrina (IRE) (Hector Protector (USA))
8304a7

**Husani (IRE)** *C Lerner* a76 53
3 b g Elusive City(USA) Afra Tsitsi (FR) (Belong To Me (USA))
799a9 6084a15

**Hushood (IRE)** *Richard Hannon* 92
3 b c Champs Elysees Cochin (USA) (Swain (IRE))
(1764)◆

**Hussar Ballad (USA)**
*Antony Brittain* a72 65
8 b g Hard Spun(USA) Country Melody (USA) (Gone West (USA))
16304 18913 33433 35473 433610 54984 595012 (6953) 74134 79364 82056 (8396) 905411

**Hustle (IRE)** *Clare Hobson* a30 32
12 ch g Choisir(AUS) Granny Kelly (USA) (Irish River (FR))
148410 432313

**Hyanna** *Tim Easterby* 63
2 b f Champs Elysees Highly Spiced (Cadeaux Genereux)
72663 75564 80137 82875◆

**Hydeandseek (FR)** *John Best* 52
3 b f Mullionmileanhour(IRE) Retainage (USA) (Polish Numbers (USA))
40923 47595 54095

**Hyde Park** *John Gosden* 104
3 b g Oasis Dream Deliberate (King's Best (USA))
30713 39978 481316 (6484) 70535 76227 81383

**Hydrangea (IRE)** *A P O'Brien* 119
3 b f Galileo(IRE) Beauty Is Truth (IRE) (Pivotal)
(1634a) 243410 3110a3 40313 55714 (6958a) 7669a2 (8231)

**Hydrant** *Richard Guest* a67 67
11 b g Haafhd Spring (Sadler's Wells (USA))
2388 4626 6088 6365 7279 1146P

**Hydroxide** *Hugo Palmer* a73 84
3 b g Lope De Vega(IRE) Craighall (Dubawi (IRE))
18373 34345 39483

**Hygrove Katie** *J Reynier* a80 72
4 b m Monsieur Bond(IRE) Hygrove Gal (Auction House (USA))
4679a9

**Hyland Heather (IRE)**
*Richard Fahey* a73 74
4 b m Lilbourne Lad(IRE) Maidservant (USA) (Seeking The Gold (USA))
1515

**Hymn For The Dudes** *Lee Smyth* a54 54
4 br g Sakhee's Secret Hermione's Dream (Oasis Dream)
3838 6053 11457 43232◆

**Hyperfocus (IRE)** *Hugo Palmer* a50 104
3 bb g Intense Focus(USA) Jouel (FR) (Machiavellian (USA))
16016 21303 48304 54236 (6877) (7612) 838318

**Hyper Hyper** *Mario Hofer* a76 79
3 b g Fastnet Rock(AUS) Guerande (IRE) (Diesis)
1660a10

**Hyperlapse (IRE)** *G M Lyons* 79
2 ch g Casamento(IRE) Makheelah (Dansili)
4020a2

**Hyperlink (IRE)** *Clare Ellam* a66 50
8 b g Cape Cross(IRE) Surf The Web (IRE) (Ela-Mana-Mou)
7418

**Hyperloop** *William Haggas* a84 74
3 br c So You Think(NZ) Fabulous Speed (USA) (Silver Hawk (USA))
34563◆ 47002 52432 (7600)

**Hypnotic Dancer (IRE)**
*Keith Dalgleish* a52 48
2 b f Sir Prancealot(IRE) Red Trance (IRE) (Soviet Star (USA))
162710 21055 23734 61542 71596 819012

**I Am A Star (NZ)** *Shane Nichols* 109
3 b f I Am Invincible(AUS) Star Band (USA) (Dixieland Band (USA))
8059a18

**I Am Charlie (FR)** *J-P Gauvin* a99 82
4 bb m Great Journey(JPN) Freedom Sweet (FR) (Sicyos (USA))
6226a5

**I Am Dandy (IRE)** *James Ewart* a23 54
2 b c Dandy Man(IRE) Acushladear (IRE) (Tagula (IRE))
18035 278613 32835 45277 61548 66265

**I Am Not Here (IRE)** *Brian Ellison* a89 88
6 b g Amadeus Wolf Newgate Lodge (IRE) (Namid)
35896 42067 43558

**I Am What I Am (GER)**
*Lennart Hammer-Hansen* 36
2 ch f Adlerflug(GER) Intigra (GER) (Tiger Hill (IRE))
8269a9

**Iballisticvin** *Gary Moore* a75 69
4 b g Rail Link Guntakal (IRE) (Night Shift (USA))
32086 38203 47553 (5652) 74834 77112 (8313)

**Ibazz** *Ian Williams* a92 66
4 br m Kyllachy Quite Elusive (USA) (Elusive Quality (USA))
8108 9945 117810 34098 40857 469910 60142 62885 (7364) 83745

**Iberica Road (USA)** *Grant Tuer* a82 66
4 bb g Quality Road(USA) Field Of Clover (CAN) (Bluegrass Cat (USA))
3069 38136 41054 (4554) 52619 58355

**Ibiza (FR)** *N Clement* 105
3 b f Redoute's Choice(AUS) Olga Prekrasa (USA) (Kingmambo (USA))
(4665a) 6227a8

**Ibn Al Emarat (IRE)** *David Simcock* a84 84
2 b g Excelebration(IRE) Grace Of Dubai (FR) (Dubai Destination (USA))
45605 54122 57432 (6472)

**Ibn Malik (IRE)** *Charles Hills* a94 105
4 ch g Raven's Pass(USA) Moon's Whisper (USA) (Storm Cat (USA))
43624 51372 61936 668512 71545

**Ibraz** *Roger Varian* 73
2 b c Farhh Wadaa (USA) (Dynaformer (USA))
48605

**Ibreeq (IRE)** *Roger Fell* a50 50
4 b g Intikhab(USA) Cerulean Sky (IRE) (Darshaan)
7807 11226 16756 23407 32843 443910

**Ibsen (IRE)** *Gordon Elliott* a67 78
8 b g Dubawi(IRE) Really (IRE) (Entrepreneur)
7860a11

**I Can (IRE)** *Henry Candy* a69
2 b g So You Think(NZ) Walk On Water (Exceed And Excel (AUS))
88883◆

**I Can Fly** *A P O'Brien* a91 102
2 b f Fastnet Rock(AUS) Madonna Dell'Orto (Montjeu (IRE))
80023

**I Can't Stop** *Milton Bradley* a47
4 gr m Kyllachy Vellena (Lucky Story (USA))
1668 42611 5054 61410 7408 16038 21669 273210

**Icart Point** *Clive Cox* a68 42
2 br g Poet's Voice Maziona (Dansili)
739211 85013 88906

**Ice Age (IRE)**
*Eve Johnson Houghton* a78 106
4 b g Frozen Power(IRE) Incendio (Siberian Express (USA))
(2054) 23904 27802◆ 34103 44114 48167 (5720) (6275)◆ (6971a) 76113

**Ice Alert (IRE)** *John Ryan* a71 64
4 b g Frozen Power(IRE) Karenka (IRE) (Arakan (USA))
43118 47652

**Iceaxe** *John Holt* a57 46
4 b m Stimulation(IRE) Laser Crystal (IRE) (King's Theatre (IRE))
14895 222415 32656 37029 73908 79006 867511

**Iceberg (IRE)** *C Laffon-Parias* a61 72
5 b g Shamardal(USA) Soft Ice (IRE) (Kingmambo (USA))
8338a4

**Ice Breeze** *P Bary* 118
3 b c Nayef(USA) Winter Silence (Dansili)
2947a2 (3879a) 4878a4 6980a4 (7634a) (8274a)

**Icebuster** *Rod Millman* a79 86
9 ch g Iceman Radiate (Sadler's Wells (USA))
366 2408 4403 6193 10922 14056 17634 20592 23578

**Ice Canyon** *Mark Brisbourne* a84 69
3 b g Raven's Pass(USA) Picture Hat (USA) (El Prado (IRE))
90543◆

**Icecapada (IRE)** *Niels Petersen* a82 95
5 gr m Mastercraftsman(IRE) Bounce (FR) (Trempolino (USA))
2201a8 7428a4

**Ice Cold In Alex (IRE)** *K J Condon* a87 85
3 b c Olden Times Telesina (ITY) (Marju (IRE))
4327a13

**Ice Dancing (IRE)** *Michael Bell* a86 78
3 ch f Raven's Pass(USA) Dancing Abbie (USA) (Theatrical (IRE))
(1151)◆ 30949 40965 46324 (6160) 68482 78163 838617

**Icefall (IRE)** *Tim Easterby* a77 91
4 b g Frozen Power(IRE) Silvertine (IRE) (Alzao (USA))
46925 58035 694410 72348 804714 83849

**Ice Galley (IRE)** *Philip Kirby* a52 76
4 br g Galileo(IRE) Ice Queen (IRE) (Danehill Dancer (IRE))
14987 24562◆ 277013 33118 45726 53138 62339

**Ice Lord (IRE)** *Chris Wall* a59 99
5 gr g Verglas(IRE) Special Lady (FR) (Kaldoun (FR))
211513 28332◆ 32944 42707 56123 (6922) 76222

**Ice Royal (IRE)** *Jamie Osborne* a94 88
4 b g Frozen Power(IRE) Salford Princess (IRE) (Titus Livius (FR))
614 2403 5482 9183 11774 14464 17578 21167 778910 88215 (9025) 91405 93143

**Ice Slice (IRE)** *James Eustace* a81 98
6 b g Dark Angel(IRE) Ice Rock (IRE) (Rock Of Gibraltar (IRE))
173410 25683 30649 37435 52946 71406 80784

**Icespire** *John Gosden* 91
3 b f Frankel Quest To Peak (USA) (Distant View (USA))
22872 30067 66552

**Ickymasho** *Jonathan Portman* a103 44
5 b m Multiplex Icky Woo (Mark Of Esteem (IRE))
1734 6835 (1178) (1446) 22612 31607 (4002) 4679a3 66872 76025 79884 87055

**Iconic Belle** *Mick Channon* a70 76
3 ch f Sixties Icon Five Bells (IRE) (Rock Of Gibraltar (IRE))
35354 40423 64734

**Iconic Boy** *David Elsworth* a56 43
2 b c Cape Cross(IRE) Snoqualmie Girl (IRE) (Montjeu (IRE))
758013 883910

**Iconic Code** *Mick Channon* a63 69
2 ch f Sixties Icon Silca Key (Inchinor)
61594 65534 70436 (8287)

**Iconic Knight (IRE)** *Ed Walker* a74 75
2 b g Sir Prancealot(IRE) Teutonic (IRE) (Revoque (IRE))
39178 41753 46963 55968 68162 74502 (8294)

**Iconic Sunset** *James Tate* a74 74
2 ch c Farhh Manila Bay (IRE) (Halling (USA))
27505 40832 45972 57498 (6319) 84913◆

**Icons Image** *Alan Bailey* a22 19
4 ch g Sixties Icon Marrimeclaire (IRE) (Spartacus (IRE))
272911

**Idaho (IRE)** *A P O'Brien* 122
4 b h Galileo(IRE) Hveger (AUS) (Danehill (USA))
32996 (4070) 53943 6461a6 7668a8 8099a4 8975a5

**I Dare To Dream** *Lisa Williamson* a30 53
3 b f Mullionmileanhour(IRE) Shaymee's Girl (Wizard King)
218211 476410 53746 66307

**Ideal Candy (IRE)** *Karen Tutty* a68 49
2 b f Canford Cliffs(IRE) Forever More (IRE) (Galileo (IRE))
39086 85553 89142 90975 93713

**Ideal Spirit** *Karen Tutty* a52 49
2 b f Swiss Spirit Silver Sail (Daylami (IRE))
45559 50155 89167 92663 94404

**Ididitforyoooo (IRE)** *Brian Meehan* 68
3 b g Fast Company(IRE) Ann's Annie (IRE) (Alzao (USA))
33936 38395 55772 68523 74625 79055

**Idlers Dream (IRE)**
*Damian Joseph English* a34 57
4 b m Dandy Man(IRE) Smart Starprincess (IRE) (Soviet Star (USA))
2656a18

**Idle Talker (IRE)** *Nick Gifford* a52 29
5 b g Dandy Man(IRE) Special Pearl (IRE) (Alhaarth (IRE))
3155 271212

**Idol Deputy (FR)** *James Bennett* a77 32
11 gr g Silver Deputy(CAN) Runaway Venus (USA) (Runaway Groom (CAN))
4712 1223 3828 (928) 21639 548410 601411 61587 69489 840010 896412 91539

**I Don't Believe It** *Micky Hammond* a31 50
3 ch g Choisir(AUS) Special Destiny (Tobougg (IRE))
112311

**Idroscalo (GER)** *Antonio Marcialis* 54
3 b g Mamool(IRE) Intriguing (IRE) (Fasliyev (USA))
3310a11 4783a8

**Idyllic Acrylic** *W M Roper* a77 73
3 b f Art Connoisseur(IRE) Mother's Hope (IRE) (Idris (IRE))
4416a17

**Ifan (IRE)** *Tim Vaughan* a58 64
9 b g Ivan Denisovich(IRE) Montana Miss (IRE) (Earl Of Barking (IRE))
4218 69012

**If I Say So** *M Boutin* a73 71
3 b g Sayif(IRE) Glen Molly (IRE) (Danetime (IRE))
2536a2 3355a4 4783a10 7308a9 8960aDSQ

**Iframe (IRE)** *Il Cavallo In Testa* 79
2 b c Ramonti(FR) Irene Watts (Miswaki Tern (USA))
4131a4 8276a8

**Iftitah (IRE)** *George Peckham* a69 42
3 b g Harbour Watch(IRE) Solstice (Dubawi (IRE))
30008 362712 43505 60676 (6638) 705811 78819

**Ifubelieveindreams (IRE)**
*Ismail Mohammed* a82 75
3 b f Iffraaj Oratrix (IRE) (Oratorio (IRE))
16093 76002 81924◆ (8707)◆ 89472

**Ifwecan** *Martin Smith* a96 99
6 b g Exceed And Excel(AUS) Kirk (Selkirk (USA))
(2833) 43626 55308 762218

**If We Can Can** *Mark Johnston* 60
2 ch g Sepoy(AUS) Kirk (Selkirk (USA))
275013 34473 41675

**Ignacio Zuloaga (IRE)** *Jo Hughes* a52
3 ch g Lope De Vega(IRE) Indian Express (Indian Ridge (IRE))
89843 92025

**Ijmaaly (IRE)** *A R Al Rayhi* a60 95
5 ch g Makfi Wedding Gown (Dubai Destination (USA))
698a6◆

**Ikc Dragon Heart (USA)**
*Lennart Reuterskiold Jr* a92 69
7 b g Lion Heart(USA) Champaigne Amelia (USA) (Cure The Blues (USA))
2943a8 4940a2

**Iken Water (FR)** *H-A Pantall* a79
3 ch f Kyllachy Danny's Choice (Compton Place)
4288a3

**Ikerrin Road (IRE)** *Vito Armata* a104 96
4 b g Iffraaj Fantastic Spring (USA) (Fantastic Light (USA))
8097a4

**I Know How (IRE)** *Julie Camacho* 65
2 b g Epaulette(AUS) Blue Crystal (IRE) (Lure (USA))
79537 84746

**Iley Boy** *John Gallagher* a54 55
3 b g Delegator Menha (Dubawi (IRE))
296310 372013 55324 65094 70855 791811 86732 88156 (9221) 93916

**Illadore (FR)** *D Guillemin* 43
2 ch f Lope De Vega(IRE) Pestagua (IRE) (Lawman (FR))
6608a7

**Illaunmore (USA)** *Mme Pia Brandt* a99 53
3 bb f Shamardal(USA) Illaunglass (IRE) (Red Clubs (IRE))
17603 25173 32332 37227 8986a5

**I'll Be Good** *Alan Berry* a9 86
8 b g Red Clubs(IRE) Willisa (Polar Falcon (USA))
713 81055

**Illegally Blonde (IRE)**
*Jamie Osborne* a92 68
4 b m Lawman(FR) Kayak (Singspiel (IRE))
939 2116

**Illusional** *Mark Johnston* a67 70
2 b g Bernardini(USA) Illustrious Miss (USA) (Kingmambo (USA))
70012 87793 89156

**Illustrissime (USA)** *Tony Coyle* a77 94
4 b g Mizzen Mast(USA) Ghost Friendly (USA) (Ghostzapper (USA))
325512

**Ilovetoboogie (FR)** *P Monfort* a61 34
3 ch f Kendargent(FR) Mark Of Brazil (FR) (Mark Of Esteem (IRE))
838a7

**Il Piccolo Grande (IRE)** *G M Lyons* a70 79
4 ch g Iffraaj Soxy Doxy (IRE) (Hawk Wing (USA))
5518a12 6802a9

**Il Pittore (FR)** *G Botti* a77 73
6 b g Mr Greeley(USA) Spira (IRE) (Sadler's Wells (USA))
81a9

**Il Primo Sole** *John Gosden* a91 91
2 b c Raven's Pass(USA) Sweet Alabama (Johannesburg (USA))
(6108)◆ 72742 85453

**Il Sicario (IRE)** *Bill Turner* a72 77
3 b g Zebedee Starring (FR) (Ashkalani (IRE))
17903 (2228)◆ 25063 28855 35614 (3813) 93386

**I'm A Believer** *Mick Channon* 41
3 b f Sixties Icon Fascinatin Rhythm (Fantastic Light (USA))
62835

**Image** *Philip McBride* a65 68
2 b f Sepoy(AUS) The Terrier (Foxhound (USA))
64807 73346 79863◆ 834916 87023

**Image Seconde (FR)** *J-F Lelievre* a50 58
5 b m Literato(FR) Red Cattiva (Red Ransom (USA))
4233a4

**Imaginative (IRE)** *Roger Varian* 66
2 b c Camelot Just Wondering (IRE) (Danehill Dancer (IRE))
81624

**Imagine If (IRE)** *G M Lyons* 87
3 br g Dream Ahead(USA) Bogini (IRE) (Holy Roman Emperor (IRE))
1385a4 7425a10

**I'm A Star (IRE)** *Stuart Williams* a61 73
2 b g High Chaparral(IRE) Etoile De Lune (Zamindar (USA))
54205 65532 88498

**Imbucato** *Tony Carroll* a19 57
3 b g Paco Boy(IRE) L'Invitata (Dr Fong (USA))
160010 63412 937411

**Imdancinwithurwife (IRE)**
*Tom Dascombe* a69 41
3 b f Sir Prancealot(IRE) Bishop's Lake (Lake Coniston (IRE))
2433 4046

**Im Dapper Too** *John Davies* a62 75
6 b g Dapper Lonely One (Perryston View)
31819 (3530) (4608) (5802) 63162 70423 752411

**I'm Improving (IRE)** *Keith Dalgleish* 86
2 b c Most Improved(IRE) Shebelia (GER) (Black Sam Bellamy (IRE))
59183◆ 63803 (8476)◆

**Imjin River (IRE)** *William Stone* a54 43
10 b g Namid Lady Nasrana (FR) (Al Nasr (FR))
2719 3873 5238 11844

**Immediate** *H-F Devin* a79 99
5 b m Oasis Dream Emergency (Dr Fong (USA))
7697a[4] 8526a[6]

**Imminent Approach** *James Tate* a67
2 b f New Approach(IRE) Nashmiah (IRE) (Elusive City (USA))
6575[5] 8155[5]

**Immortalised** *K R Burke* 84
3 ch c Frankel Noahs Ark (IRE) (Charnwood Forest (IRE))
1497[9] 1967[4] 2857[6] 3528[2]◆ 4314[6]

**Immortal Romance (IRE)** *Michael Bell* 68
2 br g Society Rock(IRE) Sundown (Polish Precedent (USA))
3437[3] 6005[7] 6867[5] 8235[3]

**Impact Point (JPN)** *Andrew Balding* a83
3 b c Deep Impact(JPN) Rumba Boogie (Rainbow Quest (USA))
1624[2]◆ 5894[2]

**Impart** *David O'Meara* a80 75
3 b g Oasis Dream Disclose (Dansili)
2557[6] (3462) 3579[5] 3844[6] 4333[8] 5383[6] 5708[6] 6450[7] 6679[5] 7137[9] 7557[8] 8320[2] 8541[2]

**Imperial City (USA)** *Charles Hills* a61 65
3 ch f City Zip(USA) Imperial Pippin (USA) (Empire Maker (USA))
323[6]

**Imperial Focus (IRE)** *Simon Waugh* 80
4 b g Intense Focus(USA) Mrs Cee (IRE) (Orpen (USA))
1832[10] 3976[2]

**Imperial Hint (USA)** *Luis Carvajal Jr* a124
4 bb h Imperialism(USA) Royal Hint (USA) (Lahint (USA))
8607a[2]

**Imperial Legend (IRE)** *Alan Brown* a71 60
8 b g Mujadil(USA) Titian Saga (IRE) (Titus Livius (FR))
45[10] 4428[8] 5377[8] 5930[4] 6384[5] 7036[4]◆ 7575[9] 7825[7] 7926[3] 8484[4] 8559[6] 8776[8]

**Imperial Link** *John O'Shea* a50 63
5 b m Rail Link Imperia (GER) (Tertullian (USA))
123[11] 8651[3] 2178[8] 3142[7] 3422[10] 4626[3] 5290[6] 5713[8] 6342[3] 7199[10] 7463[5]

**Imperial Past** *Charlie Appleby* 73
2 b c Dubawi(IRE) Divorces (AUS) (Domesday (AUS))
(7280)

**Imperial Red (IRE)** *William Haggas* a56 65
2 ch g Zoffany(IRE) Scoville (GER) (Sholokhov (IRE))
8389[7] 9051[8] 9137[8]

**Imperial State** *George Scott* a85 87
4 b g Holy Roman Emperor(IRE) Seldemosa (Selkirk (USA))
2116[6] 2586[9] 2975[3] 3723[3] (4587) 5396[4]

**Imperial Tango (FR)** *Stefano Botti* a91 98
3 b f Sageburg(IRE) Driving Miswaki (USA) (Miswaki (USA))
8449a[3]

**Imphal** *Marcus Tregoning* a86 80
3 b g Nathaniel(IRE) Navajo Rainbow (Rainbow Quest (USA))
3276[2] (4045) (4994) (6376) (7766)

**Implausible** *Jonathan Portman* a69 37
3 b f Royal Applause Tease (IRE) (Green Desert (USA))
96[5] (393)

**Important Mission (USA)** *William Haggas* a95 94
3 b g More Than Ready(USA) Laura's Pleasure (USA) (Cactus Ridge (USA))
3691[9] (4309) 5242[4] (6026) 7053[4]

**Impressive Day (IRE)** *Gary Moore* a62 87
4 b m Cape Cross(IRE) Shieldmaiden (USA) (Smart Strike (CAN))
1299[9] 1687[11] 2028[6] (2913) 3658[2] 4089[6] (5822) (6722)

**Imprudent (IRE)** *J-M Beguigne* 52
3 gr c Literato(FR) Excelita (FR) (Lavirco (GER))
6256a[6]

**I'm Right On Time** *Dean Ivory* a61
3 ch g Dutch Art Euroceleb (IRE) (Peintre Celebre (USA))
2164[5] 3209[P] 9088[6] 9455[5]

**I'm Running Late** *Dean Ivory* a71 34
3 ch g Sepoy(AUS) Clinet (IRE) (Docksider (USA))
1420[7] 2164[6] (3175) 3721[10] 7744[11] 8160[5] 8883[3] 9026[11]

**Imshivalla (IRE)** *Richard Fahey* a58 97
6 b m Acclamation Subtle Affair (IRE) (Barathea (IRE))
1704[9] 2141[9] 2593[5] 2817[5] 3300[12] 3841[7]

**I'm So Fancy (IRE)** *Mrs John Harrington* 105
3 b f Rajj(IRE) Royal Jelly (King's Best (USA))
6080a[7] 6642a[4] 7171a[2] 7663a[8] 8083a[3]

**I'm Super Too (IRE)** *Karen Tutty* a60 51
10 b g Fasliyev(USA) Congress (IRE) (Dancing Brave (USA))
1544[2]◆ 2224[4]◆ 2687[6] 2919[10] 3203[3] 3708[11] 3935[9] 4554[3] 5002[4] 5214[9] 6092[6] 6470[10] 6673[6] 7478[7]

**Imtiyaaz (IRE)** *Roger Varian* a72 96
5 b m Starspangledbanner(AUS) Endure (IRE) (Green Desert (USA))
1936[3] 2623[12]

**Im Waiting (IRE)** *Anthony McCann* a62 62
4 b m Excellent Art Margot (Sadler's Wells (USA))
1955[5] 8187[4]◆

**I'mwaitingforyou** *Peter Bowen* a36 12
8 ch m Needwood Blade Elegant Lady (Selkirk (USA))
6031[7] 6368[10] 8152[8]

**I'm Yer Man** *Ann Duffield* a79 48
2 b g Foxwedge(AUS) Coffee Cup (IRE) (Royal Academy (USA))
8010[9] 8587[2]◆ 8926[4] 9098[3]◆ (9231)

**Inaam (IRE)** *Richard Fahey* a87 85
4 b g Camacho Duckmore Bay (IRE) (Titus Livius (FR))
32[5] (782)◆ (1202) 1778[2] 2457[4] 2922[4] 4304[5] 5415[10] 9220[2]

**Inca Gold (IRE)** *A P O'Brien* 83
3 b c Galileo(IRE) Queen Of France (USA) (Danehill (USA))
1389a[7]

**Incampo (FR)** *H-A Pantall* a91 103
3 b c Campanologist(USA) Indian Cat (IRE) (One Cool Cat (USA))
1824a[7] 3613a[3]

**Incandescent** *H Al Ramzani* a64 75
3 b f Pivotal Bedazzled (Authorized (IRE))
933a[13]

**Incentive** *Stuart Kittow* 67
3 b f Stimulation(IRE) Folly Drove (Bahri (USA))
1705[5] 2725[2] 3536[9] 5429[5] (6028) 7122[12]

**Inch Pincher** *Rae Guest* a58
2 b f Captain Gerrard(IRE) Elfine (IRE) (Invincible Spirit (IRE))
8794[11] 9081[10]

**Inch Wing (IRE)** *Mark Hoad*
9 b m Winged Love(IRE) Incharder (IRE) (Slip Anchor)
2476[13]

**Incitator (FR)** *Mme M Bollack-Badel* a80 65
4 b g Motivator Summer Wave (IRE) (King's Best (USA))
5269a[6]

**Included** *David Dennis* a78 72
5 b m Champs Elysees Cordoba (Oasis Dream)
38[10] 497[5] 856[5]

**Inconceivable (IRE)** *Ralph Beckett* a77 81
3 b f Galileo(IRE) Mohican Princess (Shirley Heights)
1944[3] 2515[2] 3770[3] 4809[3] 5432[3] 6723[2] 7202[2]

**Incredible Dream (IRE)** *Dean Ivory* a56 69
4 b g Vale Of York(IRE) Finnmark (Halling (USA))
504[7] 747[10] 2521[5] (3628) 4320[7] 5722[2] 6509[3] (7085) 7744[5] 8326[13]

**Incredible Red** *Ed Dunlop*
3 b f Invincible Spirit(IRE) Sweet Stream (ITY) (Shantou (USA))
4300[12]

**Incus** *Ed de Giles* a45 72
4 b g Bertolini(USA) Cloudchaser (IRE) (Red Ransom (USA))
2966[5] (3311) (3623) 4301[7] 5267[2] 5716[11] (6370) 6880[5] (8394)

**Independence Day (IRE)** *Robert Cowell* a70 74
4 b h Dansili Damson (IRE) (Entrepreneur)
1863[7]◆ 2262[7] 2839[7]

**India** *Michael Bell* a61 55
2 b f Poet's Voice Miss Brown To You (IRE) (Fasliyev (USA))
7403[6] 8029[6]

**India Jane (FR)** *Henry Spiller* a18
3 b f Zoffany(IRE) Irisijana (GER) (Diktat)
96[11]

**Indiana Dawn** *Robert Stephens* a57 54
4 b m Sleeping Indian Street Diva (USA) (Street Cry (IRE))
4969[6] 5357[5] 6296[3] 7210[4] 8182[3] 8662[3] 8869[8]

**Indian Admiral** *Mark Johnston* a49 55
2 ch c Sepoy(AUS) Love And Cherish (IRE) (Excellent Art)
5202[5] 8649[5] 9154[9]◆

**Indian Affair** *Milton Bradley* a73 70
7 b h Sleeping Indian Rare Fling (USA) (Kris S (USA))
242[2] 302[5] 734[6] 844[9] 1063[4] 1290[8] 1980[2] (2709) 3084[6] 3573[6] 3774[3] 4256[4] 4844[4] 5473[5] 5784[2] 6156[2] 6635[9] 8427[2] 8874[4] (9183)

**Indianapolis (USA)** *S Seemar* a80
6 br h Medaglia d'Oro(USA) Pretty N Smart (USA) (Beau Genius (CAN))
321a[7] 694a[5]

**Indian Blessing** *Ed Walker* a105 93
3 ch f Sepoy(AUS) Alpen Glen (Halling (USA))
1796[3] 3006[3] 3749[4] 4988a[4] 6074[9] 7815[9] (8986a)

**Indian Chief (IRE)** *Rebecca Bastiman* a41 90
7 b g Montjeu(IRE) Buck Aspen (USA) (Seeking The Gold (USA))
1549[7] 2225[6] 3050[6] 4608[4] 5097[3] (5499) 5648[2] 5824[2] (6789) 6965[3] 7555[6] 7735[2]◆ 7959[5] 8165[7]

**Indian Dandy (IRE)** *Marco Botti* a83 94
3 b g Dandy Man(IRE) Danealla (IRE) (Indian Danehill (IRE))
(115)◆ 577[2] (1176) 2284[DSQ]◆ 3077[2] 3997[4]◆

**Indian Giver** *John David Riches* a39 62
9 b m Indesatchel(IRE) Bint Baddi (FR) (Shareef Dancer (USA))
2430[6] 3242[9] 3978[8] 5074[8] 5254[5] 6316[8] 6690[10]

**Indian Mistress (IRE)** *S Wattel* 59
2 b f Dutch Art Rajastani (IRE) (Zamindar (USA))
1919a[8]

**Indian Pursuit (IRE)** *John Quinn* a69 71
4 b g Compton Place Church Melody (Oasis Dream)
602[2] (732) 1200[2] 1475[12] 1720[3] 1979[7] 4433[8] 5281[5] 5836[11] (6571) (7017) 8320[10]

**Indian Raj** *Stuart Williams* a82 80
3 b g Iffraaj Princess Georgina (Royal Applause)
4368[2] (5289) (5837)

**Indian Red** *Mark H Tompkins* a64 43
3 ch g Sir Percy Missouri (Charnwood Forest (IRE))
758[7] 1001[4] 1559[4] 3291[10] 7319[7] 7790[7] 8647[5]

**Indian Tinker** *Robert Cowell* a62 73
8 b g Sleeping Indian Breakfast Creek (Hallgate)
1819[2]

**Indian Vision (IRE)** *Micky Hammond* 51
3 ch g Iffraaj Sweet Fairnando (Hernando (FR))
1914[6] 5319[8] 6564[10] 8219[5]

**Indian Warrior** *Ed Dunlop* a74 74
2 b g Sepoy(AUS) Night Gypsy (Mind Games)
2279[4] 2691[3] 3917[2] 4349[3] 5865[3] 6951[10] 7362[3] 8702[5]

**Indicia** *Charles Hills* a66 79
2 b f Bated Breath Indication (Sadler's Wells (USA))
4815[2] 5349[4] 6010[4] 7123[6]

**Indigo Princess** *Michael Appleby* a70 70
4 b m Native Ruler Red To Violet (Spectrum (IRE))
232[7] 444[6] 1455[5] 2285[2] (2626) 3147[2] 3906[9] 5261[6] 9337[6]◆

**Indira** *John Berry* a81 95
6 ch m Sleeping Indian Forever Loved (Deploy)
3160[3]◆

**Indiscretion (IRE)** *Jonathan Portman* a71 34
2 b f Big Bad Bob(IRE) Fleeting Affair (USA) (Gone West (USA))
7153[12] (8029) 8890[U]

**Indomeneo** *Richard Fahey* a78 83
2 b c Piccolo Cherrycombe-Row (Classic Cliche (IRE))
2786[2]◆ (3908) 4452[2] (5144)◆ 6029[2] 6900[6] (7624) (7929)

**Indomitable Spirit** *Martin Smith* a33 19
5 b g Zebedee Gayala (IRE) (Iron Mask (USA))
4567[13]

**In Dreams** *Brian Meehan* a67 31
3 b c Sixties Icon Tidal Run (Hurricane Run (IRE))
5563[5] 6633[7]

**In Due Time (IRE)** *Alan Swinbank* 12
5 br g Big Bad Bob(IRE) Bravada (GER) (Dai Jin)
1829[12]

**Indulged** *James Fanshawe* a88 99
4 b m Teofilo(IRE) Fondled (Selkirk (USA))
(2817) 5529[3] 6152[2] 7283[4] 8739[5] 8992[9]

**Indulgent** *Mike Sowersby* a51 49
4 b g Makfi Santa Agata (FR) (Anabaa (USA))
853[8]

**Indus Valley (IRE)** *Lee Carter* a48 47
10 ch g Indian Ridge(IRE) Gloriously Bright (USA) (Nureyev (USA))
273[7] 966[5] 1427[6] 1557[9] 2053[7] 2255[11]

**Indy (IRE)** *John Quinn* 90
6 b g Indian Haven Maddie's Pearl (IRE) (Clodovil (IRE))
2893[5] 3497[4] (5166) (5830) 6383[6] 7627[2]

**Ineffable (IRE)** *Rodger Sweeney* a72 62
4 b g Fastnet Rock(AUS) Leonia (IRE) (Sadler's Wells (USA))
1014a[5]

**Inexes** *Marjorie Fife* a82 84
5 gr g Exceed And Excel(AUS) Likeable (Dalakhani (IRE))
2133[2] 2952[2] (3452) 3652[4] 4897[2] 5699[8] 6348[4] 6663[9] (7554) 8319[5] 8640[4] 8872[6] 9124[9]

**Infamous Lawman (IRE)** *David O'Meara* a71 70
3 b g Lawman(FR) Infamous Angel (Exceed And Excel (AUS))
2887[5] 4332[3]◆ 5003[3] 5540[6] 7476[5] 7984[4] 8205[4]

**Infanta Isabella** *George Baker* 59
3 b f Lope De Vega(IRE) Shemissa (IRE) (Fairy King (USA))
3770[5]

**Inference (AUS)** *Michael, Wayne & John Hawkes* 112
3 b c So You Think(NZ) Pontiana (AUS) (Redoute's Choice (AUS))
8058a[5] 8250a[15]

**Infernal Majesty (FR)** *S Wattel* a90 84
2 b c Siyouni(FR) Healing Dream (FR) (Montjeu (IRE))
7175a[2]

**Infinite Cheers (FR)** *J-C Rouget* 74
2 b f Acclamation Wadjet (IRE) (Shamardal (USA))
6171a[2]

**Infiniti (IRE)** *Barry Leavy* a61 53
4 b m Arcano(IRE) Seraphina (IRE) (Pips Pride)
1610[10] 2308[4] (3192) 4187[7] 4730[6]◆ 6270[7] 6953[6] 8396[10]

**In First Place** *Richard Fahey* 86
3 b g Bated Breath Carved Emerald (Pivotal)
1912[3] 2385[4] 3040[6] 3713[4] 4865[3] (5378) 6176[4] 6881[5] 8165[3]

**Inflexiball** *John Mackie* a62 67
5 b m Refuse To Bend(IRE) Sphere (IRE) (Daylami (IRE))
1560[2] 1864[4] 2308[7] 3053[6] 3761[5] (4344) (5290) 6060[3] 7028[3] 7567[6] 9270[8]

**Influent (IRE)** *James Tate* a83
3 b f Shamardal(USA) Kaabari (USA) (Seeking The Gold (USA))
(6287) 7710[9] 8636[4] 9271[3]

**In Focus (IRE)** *Dianne Sayer* a37 58
6 ch g Intense Focus(USA) Reine De Neige (Kris)
1312[12] 2082[4] 2501[5] 3402[12] 3899[11] 5599[2] 6269[8] 7047[2] 7922[2] 8487[8]

**Ingenuity** *Jedd O'Keeffe* a84 87
2 b c Slickly(FR) Onlyyouknowme (IRE) (Martino Alonso (IRE))
4205[3]◆ (4834) 5834[2]

**Ingleby Angel (IRE)** *David O'Meara* a74 62
8 br g Dark Angel(IRE) Mistress Twister (Pivotal)
3540[8] 3845[8] 4210[10] 4601[2]◆ 4960[3] 5091[4] 5578[7] 6673[12] 7573[4] 7703[3] 7979[10] 8514[3] 8854[2] 8957[5] 9017[3] 9406[5]

**Ingleby Erin** *Colin Teague*
4 b m Medicean Mistress Twister (Pivotal)
3404[8] 5831[14]

**Ingleby Hollow** *David O'Meara* a67 71
5 ch g Beat Hollow Mistress Twister (Pivotal)
3050[8] 3464[5] 3907[6] 5186[3] 5737[2] 6233[7] 6569[4] 7561[8] (8214) 8487[6] 8655[4] 9054[7]

**Ingleby Mackenzie** *Mick Channon* a69 69
3 b g Sixties Icon Natalie Jay (Ballacashtal (CAN))
3163[5] 3745[8] 4156[7] 4449[3] 4738[2] (5061) 5618[2] 5780[8] 6291[7] 6766[2]

**Ingleby Molly (IRE)** *David O'Meara* a47
2 ch f Choisir(AUS) Mistress Twister (Pivotal)
9049[4] 9415[4]

**Ingleby Spring (IRE)** *Richard Fahey* a63 61
5 br m Zebedee Jouel (FR) (Machiavellian (USA))
4722[8] 5214[4] 5544[5] 6092[9] 6690[7] 7042[8] 7704[7] (8219) 8515[6] 8985[2] 9212[4] (9445)

**Inglorious** *Keith Dalgleish* a61 73
3 gr g Kheleyf(USA) Impulsive Decision (IRE) (Nomination)
4663[2]◆ 4851[3] 5205[7] 5485[12] 5604[3] (5922) 6265[5] 6315[8] 6627[3] 6893[2] 7703[10] (8108) 8958[4]

**Iniciar (GER)** *David Pipe*
7 b g Galileo(IRE) Iota (GER) (Tiger Hill (IRE))
3928[17]

**Iniesta (IRE)** *Fergal O'Brien* a69 73
6 b g Galileo(IRE) Red Evie (IRE) (Intikhab (USA))
2909[5] 3574[2] 4750[4] 9367[3]

**Initiative (IRE)** *Henry Spiller* 79
2 b c Excelebration(IRE) Viking Fair (Zamindar (USA))
2750[2]◆ (3689)

**Injam (IRE)** *Jedd O'Keeffe* a19 94
4 b g Pour Moi(IRE) Sniffle (IRE) (Shernazar)
1309[8] (2770) 3527[5] (4301)

**Injun Sands** *Jane Chapple-Hyam* a87 84
6 b g Halling(USA) Serriera (FR) (Highest Honor (FR))
683[P]

**Inke (IRE)** *Jim Boyle* a81 80
5 br m Intikhab(USA) Chifney Rush (IRE) (Grand Lodge (USA))
1323[6] 2028[2] 2575[2] 5330[4] 6013[8] 7132[10] 7651[9] 8160[9]

**In Ken's Memory** *Michael Appleby* a69 79
4 b m Sakhee(USA) Suzi Spends (IRE) (Royal Applause)
(2676)◆ 2973[4] 5039[2] 5341[3] 5806[5]

**Inkerman (IRE)** *Leo Braem* a60 48
7 b g Duke Of Marmalade(IRE) Lady Taufan (IRE) (Taufan (USA))
1070a[4]

**Inlawed** *Ed Walker* a74 68
3 b g Bahamian Bounty Regent's Park (Green Desert (USA))
2474[3]◆ 3038[10] 4446[10] 5031[6] 5855[6] (6581) 7723[3] (8311) 8874[6]

**Inner Circle (IRE)** *Richard Hannon* a80 85
3 b c Choisir(AUS) Eternity Ring (Alzao (USA))
2117[3] 2567[10] 3040[2] 3862[4] 4887[13] 6203[2] 7398[12]

**Innevera (FR)** *C Laffon-Parias* 76
3 b f Motivator Loxandra (Last Tycoon)
8088a[9]

**Inniscastle Lad** *Donald McCain* a78 86
5 b g Kyllachy Glencal (Compton Place)
1178[8] 1583[6] 1788[2] 6416[8]

**Innish Man (IRE)** *John Mackie* a56 52
5 b g Fastnet Rock(AUS) Super Gift (IRE) (Darshaan)
7413[11] 7831[9] 8396[11]

**Innocent Touch (IRE)** *Richard Fahey* 99
6 bl g Intense Focus(USA) Guajira (FR) (Mtoto)
1704[3] 2086[7] 2735[6]◆ 3300[2] 3790[4] 5382[5] 6515[4] 6965[5]

**Innoko (FR)** *Robert Stephens* a69 68
7 gr g Carlotamix(FR) Chalana (Ashkalani (IRE))
806[6] 1101[7] 1560[4] 2295[2] 2964[2] 3428[6] (4733) 5274[2] 5590[3] 7336[2] 8505[2] 8778[5]

**Inns Of Court (IRE)** *A Fabre* a77 120
3 b c Invincible Spirit(IRE) Learned Friend (GER) (Seeking The Gold (USA))
2666a[6] (3354a) (4390a) 5980a[2]◆ 6982a[5]

**Innstigator** *Ralph J Smith* a59 44
3 b g Delegator Page (Elmaamul (USA))
3784[12] 4303[13] 5339[8] 6324[4] 8133[9]

**Inn The Bull (GER)** *Alan King* 74
4 ch g Lope De Vega(IRE) Ile Rousse (Danehill (USA))
3683[8] 4257[2] 4809[11]

**Insayshable (IRE)** *G M Lyons* 107
3 b g Rajj(IRE) Imitation (Darshaan)
2442a[4]

**Inscribe (USA)** *Sir Michael Stoute* a65 88
3 b g Harlan's Holiday(USA) Reflections (Sadler's Wells (USA))
1499[5]

**Inshaa** *Simon West* a70 56
5 b g Dansili Hidden Brief (Barathea (IRE))
843[5] 1203[3] 1419[9] 1887[3] 2161[3] 2923[7] 8721[5] 8930[6] 9032[7]

**Inshiraah (FR)** *George Peckham* a76 101
3 b f Holy Roman Emperor(IRE) Blessed Catch (USA) (Storm Cat (USA))
2704[3] 3188[3] (3472) 4313[3]◆ (4903) (5422)◆

**Insolenceofoffice (IRE)** *Richard Ford* a52 49
9 b g Kodiac Sharp Diversion (USA) (Diesis)
446[12] 583[8] 743[9] 981[8] 1407[8] 2306[2] 3468[7] 5695[3] 6688[8]

**Inspector (IRE)** *Hugo Palmer* a62 68
3 b c Lawman(FR) Helter Helter (USA) (Seeking The Gold (USA))
2842[4] 3717[7] 4623[10] 5209[12] 6023[4]

**Inspector Norse** *Tim Easterby* a43 57
6 b g Norse Dancer(IRE) Indiana Blues (Indian Ridge (IRE))
3740[6] 4034[4] 4439[6] 4627[8] 5002[7] 7220[4] 7478[2] 7885[2] 8241[3]

**Inspire** *Matthew Salaman*
5 gr m Hellvelyn Time Clash (Timeless Times (USA))
600[11]

**Instant Attraction (IRE)** *Jedd O'Keeffe* a78 106
6 b g Tagula(IRE) Coup De Coeur (IRE) (Kahyasi (IRE))
1494[11] 2767[7] 3255[9] 4377[10] 5382[8] 7044[2] 7140[3] 7566[5] 8014[9] 8510[7]

**Instant De Reve (FR)** *Mme C Barande-Barbe* a98 103
4 ch g Vision D'Etat(FR) Argomilla (FR) (Dansili)
1691a[5] 3104a[5] 8089a[4]

**Instant Karma (IRE)** *Michael Bell* a86 76
6 b g Peintre Celebre(USA) Kotdiji (Mtoto)
(1289) 1719[11] 4216[11]

**Instigator (GER)** *Jean-Pierre Carvalho* 110
3 b c Nayef(USA) Imagery (GER) (Monsun (GER))
3115a[7] 5983a[5]

**Instill** *Mandy Rowland* a64 2
5 ch g Pivotal Insijaam (USA) (Secretariat (USA))
382[7] 688[5] 1892[5] 2728[7]

**Institution (IRE)** *Charles Hills* 62
2 ch c Zoffany(IRE) Became (USA) (Giant's Causeway (USA))
7128[9] 7813[7]

**Insurgence** *James Fanshawe* a77 70
2 ch g Sepoy(AUS) Isis (USA) (Royal Academy (USA))
4859[10] 6071[6] 6827[7] (8817)◆

**Insurplus (IRE)** *Jim Goldie* a72 66
4 b g Bushranger(IRE) Emly Express (IRE) (High Estate)
2424[4] 2776[6] 3385 [5] 3704[10] 5203[3] 5467[7] 5919[2] 6182[3] (6435) 7249[5] 8552[3] 8721[3] (8930)

**Intellect (IRE)** *Sir Michael Stoute* a47 95
3 b c Nathaniel(IRE) Shesasmartlady (IRE) (Dolphin Street (FR))
1624[6] (4274) (5153)◆ 6445[19] 7252[4]

**Intelligence Cross (USA)**
*A P O'Brien* a100 114
3 b c War Front(USA) Good Vibes (USA) (Unbridled's Song (USA))
1742a[4] 4030[9] 4907[5] 5690a[12] 5974a[6] 8230[12]

**Intello Kiss** *Stefano Botti* 90
2 ch f Intello(GER) Just One Kiss (Cape Cross (IRE))
8094a[6]

**Intendantin (GER)** *Ferdinand J Leve* 94
4 b m Lando(GER) Incenza (GER) (Local Suitor (USA))
4518a[8] 6254a[10] 8089a[8]

**Intense Life (IRE)** *Endo Botti* 98
5 ch h Intense Focus(USA) Miswadah (IRE) (Machiavellian (USA))
8449a[6]

**Intense Romance (IRE)**
*Michael Dods* a81 97
3 b f Intense Focus(USA) Hedera (USA) (Woodman (USA))
(656) (1005) 1332[4] 1913[3] 2304[6] (2925) 3709[4] (4305) 4835[2] (5355) 5574[4] (6450) 7887[8]

**Intense Starlet (IRE)**
*Thomas P O'Connor* a48 52
6 ch m Intense Focus(USA) Glady Starlet (GER) (Big Shuffle (USA))
158[6] 362[9] 494[6] 8225a[10]

**Intense Style (IRE)** *Les Eyre* a92 97
5 ch g Intense Focus(USA) Style Queen (IRE) (Galileo (IRE))
1103[4] 1515[16] 2840[10] 3294[2] 3565[7] 4339[10] 5457[8] 5949[6] 6209[9] 7156[2] (7474) 8240[11] 8821[4]

**Intense Tango** *K R Burke* a96 103
6 b m Mastercraftsman(IRE) Cover Look (SAF) (Fort Wood (USA))
268[6] 858[4] 1779[12] 2157[8] 3594[12] 5924[11] 6391[5] 6880[9] 7614[8]

**Intensical (IRE)** *Ivan Furtado* a81 81
6 b g Intense Focus(USA) Christinas Letter (IRE) (Galileo (IRE))
984[2] 1224[3] 1323[4] 1867[6] 2684[3] 3140[6] 3857[DSQ] 4207[15] 5049[3] 5788[6] 7342a[3]

**Interchoice Star** *Ray Peacock* a41 18
12 b g Josr Algarhoud(IRE) Blakeshall Girl (Piccolo)
8258[5] 8772[13]

**Interconnection** *Ed Vaughan* a52 95
6 ch g Mount Nelson Lacework (Pivotal)
1734[9] 2796[2] 4763[2] 5643[4]

**Interlink (USA)** *Marjorie Fife* a78 73
4 b g Kitten's Joy(USA) Seattle Tac (USA) (Seattle Slew (USA))
3049[9] 4310[2] 4566[5] 5379[16] 6141[3] 6267[17] 6527[2] 7244[2] 8556[13]

**Intermodal** *Jamie Osborne* a67 72
3 b g Rail Link Rule Of Nature (Oasis Dream)
7452[5] 8111[11] 8814[6] 9017[5] 9138[3]

**Intern (IRE)** *David Simcock* a104 102
3 b g Rip Van Winkle(IRE) Uliana (USA) (Darshaan)
2128[2] 4029[11] 9091[3] 9388[4]

**International Law** *Brian Meehan* 75
3 gr g Exceed And Excel(AUS) Cruel Sea (USA) (Mizzen Mast (USA))
(1939) 2567[15] 3713[7] 4736[5] 5033[8] 5404[7] (8300)

**International Man** *Richard Fahey* 82
2 b g Epaulette(AUS) Right Answer (Lujain (USA))
(3846) 5492[4] 6057[2] 7090[16] 8008[15] 8379[8]

**Interpret (USA)** *M Al Mheiri* a108 79
9 b g Distorted Humor(USA) Quendom (ARG) (Interprete (ARG))
650a[10]

**Interweave** *Sir Michael Stoute* a77 77
3 ch f Dutch Art Interlace (Pivotal)
(1581) 3392[8]

**In The House (IRE)** *Lucinda Egerton* a29 65
5 b m Montjeu(IRE) O' Bella Ballerina (USA) (Fusaichi Pegasus (USA))
3724[11] 5183[7]

**In The Lope (IRE)** *Mme Pia Brandt* a104 76
3 b g Lope De Vega(IRE) Biswa (USA) (Kafwain (USA))
8844[4]

**In The Red (IRE)** *Martin Smith* a88 86
4 b g Elusive Pimpernel(USA) Roses From Ridey (IRE) (Petorius (IRE))
(277)◆ 1960[18] 2617[6] 3324[12] (3777) 4524[8] 4832[6] 5643[10] 5940[7] 6442[9] 6964[16] 8821[9]

**In The Spotlight (IRE)** *Henry Spiller* a73 86
3 b f Exceed And Excel(AUS) Naruko (USA) (Street Cry (IRE))
77[2] (456) 522[3] 2503[5]◆ (3729) 4198[5] 5965[5] (6113) 6392[6]

**Intibaah** *George Baker* a81 102
7 b g Elnadim(USA) Mawaared (Machiavellian (USA))
194[9] 3617[4] 4219[2] 5176a[6]

**Intimate Art (IRE)** *Andrew Balding* a88 72
3 ch g Dutch Art Intimacy (IRE) (Teofilo (IRE))
1945[10] 3232[3]◆ 3713[10] (4564) 5400[6] 9314[11]

**Intimately** *Jonathan Portman* a48 63
4 b g Intense Focus(USA) Midnight Fling (Groom Dancer (USA))
1427[8] 2319[6] (2762) 3397[5] 4047[5] 4459[3] 5285[9] 5857[4] 6076[12] (7006) 7465[11] 7899[10]

**Intimation** *Sir Michael Stoute* a91 110
5 b m Dubawi(IRE) Infallible (Pivotal)
2392[2] 6490a[2] 6697[5] 8041[6] (8273a)

**Intimidator (IRE)** *Miss Joey Ellis* a60 49
6 b g Intikhab(USA) Zither (Zafonic (USA))
3724[2] 4217[5] 6820[7] 7730[11]

**Intisaab** *David O'Meara* a114 112
6 b g Elnadim(USA) Katoom (IRE) (Soviet Star (USA))
(2156)◆ 2433[5] 2907[5] 4072[23] 4354[2] 4907[7] 5149[6] 5640[13] 6428[3] 7603[4] 7806[6] 8417[4] 8845[4] 8991[2] (9409)

**Intisha (IRE)** *Jonathan Portman* 66
3 b f Intikhab(USA) Shawaaty (IRE) (Monsun (GER))
1331[9] 1685[10]

**Intiwin (IRE)** *Linda Perratt* a64 62
5 b g Intikhab(USA) Muluk (IRE) (Rainbow Quest (USA))
2497[7] 3197[7] 4035[5] 4661[9] 6346[10] 7240[5] (7573) 8210[3] 8591[7]

**Into The Lane (IRE)** *Stefano Botti* 71
3 ch f Excelebration(IRE) Paint In Green (IRE) (Invincible Spirit (IRE))
2244a[13]

**Intoxikating** *Gay Kelleway* a54 23
3 b g Phoenix Reach(IRE) Chocolada (Namid)
3669[7] 7035[5] 7574[6]

**Intransigent** *Andrew Balding* a98 100
8 b g Trans Island Mara River (Efisio)
33[4] (275) 459[2] 680[2] 999[5] 1769[10] 2568[11] 6289[2] 6676[10] 8639[2]

**Intrepidly (USA)** *Jeremy Noseda* a94 98
3 b g Medaglia d'Oro(USA) Trepidation (USA) (Seeking The Gold (USA))
3838[4] (4443)◆ 7516[7] 8005[16] 9186[4]

**Intricately (IRE)**
*Joseph Patrick O'Brien* 113
3 b f Fastnet Rock(AUS) Inner Realm (IRE) (Galileo (IRE))
1634a[4] 2434[12] 3110a[4] 4419a[6] 4928a[7] 6119a[5] 6958a[8]

**Intrude** *Stuart Williams* a97 94
5 b g Intikhab(USA) Don't Tell Mum (IRE) (Dansili)
459[13] 918[6] 1258[4] 1757[2] 2261[5] 2730[2] (3441) 3743[11] 7549[10]

**Inuk (IRE)** *Richard Hughes* a59 50
2 b f Kodiac Elkmait (Trade Fair)
3174[4] 3421[8] 4349[5] 5079[6] 6063[4] 7196[4] (8027) 8882[3] (9182)

**Invermere** *Richard Fahey* 83
4 b m Kyllachy Kootenay (IRE) (Selkirk (USA))
1512[2] 1766[8] 2138[5] 3287[5] 4375[7] 4901[3] 5699[5] 6691[4] 7161[2] 7658[7] 8596[8]

**Investigation** *Shaun Harris* a65 57
3 gr g Rip Van Winkle(IRE) Syann (IRE) (Daylami (IRE))
1559[3] (2067)◆ 2807[9] 3457[13] 6202[8] 7744[14] 9391[11]

**Invictus (GER)** *David Loughnane* a68 90
5 b g Exceed And Excel(AUS) Ivowen (USA) (Theatrical (IRE))
1323[7] 2586[6] 2913[9] 3428[7] (4185) 4608[8] 5872[4] 6789[3] 7328[8]

**Invincible Army (IRE)** *James Tate* a109 111
2 b c Invincible Spirit(IRE) Rajeem (Diktat)
3002[2] (4049) 4812[4] 5526[2] 6446[2] (6935)◆ 7394[2]

**Invincible Man (IRE)** *James Tate* a71
3 b c Invincible Spirit(IRE) Elshabakiya (IRE) (Diktat)
127[5] 504[3] 785[2] 1205[2]

**Invincible Queen (FR)** *F Head* 97
3 b f Invincible Spirit(IRE) Rhythm Queen (IRE) (Danehill Dancer (IRE))
1270a[7]

**Invincible Ridge (IRE)** *Eric Alston* a81 83
9 b g Invincible Spirit(IRE) Dani Ridge (IRE) (Indian Ridge (IRE))
79[6] 886[2] 923[2] 1370[8] (1836) 2951[3] 3741[5] 4337[4] 4686[6] 6267[5] 6411[8] 6878[7] 8167[7] 8745[3] (8874) 9152[10]

**Inviolable Spirit (IRE)**
*Richard Fahey* 75
2 b g Zebedee Mediska (Medicean)
(1673) 2286[3] 3051[2] 5150[11] 5685[5] 6353[9] 7050[8] 7821[17]

**Iona Island** *Peter Hiatt* a67 69
4 b m Dutch Art Still Small Voice (Polish Precedent (USA))
738[3] (900) 1303[3] 2723[4] 4217[14] 6398[8]

**Ionization (IRE)**
*John Patrick Shanahan* a71 98
4 ch m The Carbon Unit(USA) The Mighty Atom (USA) (Sky Mesa (USA))
1799[9] 2500[3] 2772[2] 3589[2] 4475[3] 6192[4] 6642a[10] 7171a[11]

**Ipazia** *Mme A Fabre* a66
3 b f Shamardal(USA) Intarsia (GER) (Pentire)
3134a[10]

**Ipcress File** *Scott Dixon* a59 62
2 ch g Sixties Icon Solmorin (Fraam)
7211[3] 8502[6] 8802[5]

**Ipompieridiviggiu (ITY)**
*Il Cavallo In Testa* 98
2 b c Pastoral Pursuits Sabdala (Sakhee (USA))
(4131a) 5195a[5]

**Ipsilante** *Jonathan Portman* a40 41
2 b f Nayef(USA) Rosacara (Green Desert (USA))
7153[11] 7814[24] 8502[9]

**Iquitos (GER)** *H-J Groschel* 118
5 b h Adlerflug(GER) Irika (GER) (Areion (GER))
3116a[2] 4392a[2] (5464a) 6727a[2] 7668a[7] 8527a[2] 8975a[15]

**Iraklion (GER)** *Christian Sprengel* 102
5 ch h Areion(GER) Ircanda (GER) (Nebos (GER))
2667a[4] 4879a[10] 8090a[4]

**Irap (USA)** *Doug O'Neill* a115
3 b c Tiznow(USA) Silken Cat (CAN) (Storm Cat (USA))
2420a[18]

**Irish Hawke (IRE)** *Donald McCain* a36 83
5 b g Montjeu(IRE) Ahdaab (USA) (Rahy (USA))
3470[7]

**Irish Ilie (FR)** *Mlle G Gadbled*
4 b h Creachadoir(IRE) Irish Love (GER) (Perugino (USA))
4955a[16]

**Irish Rose (IRE)** *Carina Fey* a57
2 b f Iffraaj Irish Style (IRE) (Mujadil (USA))
8691a[10]

**Irish Sky (IRE)** *Henry Spiller* a39 53
3 b f Elnadim(USA) Royal Aly (USA) (Royal Academy (USA))
1286[7] 1605[3] 8842[8] 9103[3] 9340[10]

**Irish Times** *Henry Spiller* a27
2 b c Swiss Spirit Amouage Royale (IRE) (Mr Greeley (USA))
9335[9]

**Irish War Cry (USA)**
*H Graham Motion* a118
3 ch c Curlin(USA) Irish Sovereign (USA) (Polish Numbers (USA))
2420a[10] 5463a[4]

**Iron Born (FR)** *Mme G Rarick* a46
4 b g Iron Mask(USA) Turfani (IRE) (Danetime (IRE))
391a[12]

**Iron Fist (USA)** *Steven Asmussen* a111
5 rg h Tapit(USA) Successful Outlook (USA) (Orientate (USA))
8576a[5]

**Iron Islands** *K R Burke* 72
3 b g Dutch Art Night Premiere (IRE) (Night Shift (USA))
1678[8] 3310a[10] 4276[6]

**Iron Lady (IRE)** *William Muir* a60 59
3 b f Exceed And Excel(AUS) Kahlua Kiss (Mister Baileys)
2911[10]◆ (3543) 4046[2] 5040[6] 6724[8]

**Iron Sky** *Keith Dalgleish* a43
2 b g Showcasing Addiena (Golan (IRE))
8982[7]

**Iron Spirit (FR)**
*Mme M Bollack-Badel* a84 94
7 b g Turtle Bowl(IRE) Irish Vintage (FR) (Loup Solitaire (USA))
1920a[11] 5979a[3] 6648a[3]

**Irvine Lady (IRE)** *R Mike Smith* a46 49
4 ch m Footstepsinthesand Ascot Lady (IRE) (Spinning World (USA))
464[6] 722[7] 981[6] 4687[2] 5205[10] 5992[6] 6690[13] 6782[3] 7889[10] 7979[13]

**Isaac Bell (IRE)** *Alex Hales* a87
9 b g Fruits Of Love(USA) Oso Well (IRE) (Oscar (IRE))
(7708) 8672[2] 8893[6] 9204[5]

**Isabel De Urbina (IRE)**
*Ralph Beckett* 103
3 b f Lope De Vega(IRE) Roscoff (IRE) (Daylami (IRE))
2436[2] 3301[6] 5155[2] 5658[4] 7577[8]

**Isabella (IRE)** *David O'Meara* 93
3 ch f Galileo(IRE) Song Of My Heart (IRE) (Footstepsinthesand)
(5670) (6235) 6691[2]◆

**Isabella Mayson** *Stuart Kittow* 66
2 b f Mayson Sydney Star (Machiavellian (USA))
4252[6] 5534[2] 6824[6] 7458[6]

**Isabella Ruby** *Lisa Williamson* a37 50
2 b f Power Scarlet Rocks (IRE) (Chineur (FR))
7045[7] 7141[5] 7563[5] 8190[10]

**Isabel's On It** *William Haggas* a77 92
3 ch f Dubawi(IRE) Check The Label (USA) (Stormin Fever (USA))
1905[3]◆ 2463[2] (3329)◆ 4208[4] 4864[13]

**Iseemist (IRE)** *John Gallagher* a97 99
6 gr m Verglas(IRE) Krasivaya (IRE) (Soviet Star (USA))
1362[3]◆ 1936[6] 2623[6] 3307[2] 3861[10] 4411[12] 5828[6] 6720[2] 7461[3] 8077[3]

**Isharah (USA)** *Mark Johnston* a99 97
4 b g Kitten's Joy(USA) Menekineko (USA) (Kingmambo (USA))
(196) (389) 746[3] 1360[2] 1802[7] 2157[5] 2788[8] 5351[8] 6329[13] 7110[4] 8244[7]

**Ishebayorgrey (IRE)** *Patrick Martin* a92 88
5 gr g Clodovil(IRE) Superjet (IRE) (Soviet Star (USA))
1233a[3] 1479a[3]

**I Should Coco** *Karen George* a25
4 b m With The Flow(USA) Follow The Dream (Double Trigger (IRE))
8151[11] 8810[4] 9202[11]

**Isis Blue** *Rod Millman* a69 73
7 b g Cockney Rebel(IRE) Bramaputra (IRE) (Choisir (AUS))
1683[5] 2365[2]

**Is It Off (IRE)** *Gary Moore* a65 70
2 b c Clodovil(IRE) French Doll (IRE) (Titus Livius (FR))
8073[2]◆ 8388[7] 8890[10] 9199[8] 9466[5]

**Iskra** *D Ergin* 98
4 b m Mount Nelson Euro Empire (USA) (Bartok I (IRE))
6718a[5]

**Island Affair (IRE)**
*Adrian McGuinness* 68
2 b f Tagula(IRE) Subtle Affair (IRE) (Barathea (IRE))
4020a[5] 5990[6]

**Island Authority** *Eugene Stanford* a57 64
5 b m Authorized(IRE) Island Odyssey (Dansili)
6578[5] 7730[10]

**Island Brave (IRE)** *Heather Main* a84 74
3 b c Zebedee Tip the Scale (USA) (Valiant Nature (USA))
962[3] (1241) 1724[7] 5777a[10] 6124a[6] 6455a[14] 8111[9] (8497)◆ (9000) 9434[3]

**Island Cloud** *Heather Main* a67 74
3 b f Harbour Watch(IRE) Cloud Illusions (USA) (Smarty Jones (USA))
2503[3] 3517[5] 4157[3] 4990[2] 6106[2] (6373) 7508[7]

**Island Court (IRE)** *J S Moore* a71 64
2 b c Camelot First Breeze (USA) (Woodman (USA))
3305[6] 8839[9] 8951[3] 9336[5] 9405[6]

**Island Drive (IRE)** *William Haggas* a78 63
2 b f Kodiac Redstone Dancer (IRE) (Namid)
(4749)◆ 5576[4] 8043[10]

**Island Flame (IRE)** *Richard Fahey* a80 70
4 b m Kodiac Noble Flame (IRE) (Doyoun)
2741[9] 3341[5] 4056[3] 4571[7] 5417[4] 5830[6] 6467[5] 8204[6] 8429[8]

**Island In The Sky (IRE)** *R Le Gal* a75 68
3 b f Kodiac When Not Iff (IRE) (Iffraaj)
(2536a)

**Island Of Life (USA)**
*Saeed bin Suroor* 72
3 b f Dubawi(IRE) Pimpernel (IRE) (Invincible Spirit (IRE))
4911[3] 5670[3]

**Island Remede** *Henry De Bromhead* a69 97
6 b m Medicean Island Odyssey (Dansili)
1808a[2] 3586[7]

**Island Sound** *Heather Main* 81
2 gr c Havana Gold(IRE) Cloud Illusions (USA) (Smarty Jones (USA))
6132[9] 6505[4] 7146[6]

**Island Vision (IRE)** *David Simcock* a54 90
3 ch f Arcano(IRE) Boo Boo Bear (IRE) (Almutawakel)
317a[8] 649a[7] 887a[10] 4051[7] 4903[7]

**Isle Of Avalon (IRE)**
*Sir Mark Prescott Bt* a56 66
2 b f Camelot Adeste (Dansili)
7045[5] 7454[10] 7733[8]

**Isle Of Man** *Clive Cox* a39 39
2 b c Exceed And Excel(AUS) One So Marvellous (Nashwan (USA))
6654[11] 8245[10]

**Isntshesomething** *Richard Guest* a62 58
5 br m Assertive Princess Almora (Pivotal)
(1451) 1755[2] 2063[2] (2342) 3139[7] 6620[10] 6902[6] 7606[2] (7945) 8401[2] 8659[9]

**Isole Canarie (IRE)**
*Melania Cascione* 93
2 b f Rip Van Winkle(IRE) Hairicin (IRE) (Hurricane Run (IRE))
8094a[4]

**Isoletta** *Ed Walker* a64 65
2 b f Oasis Dream Miss Cap Estel (Hernando (FR))
2265[8] 3421[7] 4007[4] 5366[3] 9090[9] 9436[3]

**Isomer (USA)** *Andrew Balding* 99
3 ch g Cape Blanco(IRE) Nimue (USA) (Speightstown (USA))
4584[7] 6105[6] 7609[8]

**Ispolini** *Charlie Appleby* a79 74
2 b c Dubawi(IRE) Giants Play (USA) (Giant's Causeway (USA))
8509[4] (8987)

**Issauroma (FR)** *C Escuder* a67
4 b m Iron Mask(USA) Joha Fong (FR) (Dr Fong (USA))
606a[5]

**Isstoora (IRE)** *Archie Watson* a71
3 b f Fastnet Rock(AUS) Shegotloose (USA) (Dynaformer (USA))
6287[4]◆ 6899[7] 7485[5] 7878[6] 8374[2] (9030) 9295[6]

**Istanbul Pasha (IRE)** *David Evans* a58 51
2 b g Fast Company(IRE) Red Red Rose (Piccolo)
4218[10] 4841[5] 5474[4] 6063[13] 7082[5] 7518[3] 8475[2] 8783[6] 9002[10]

**Istanbul Sultan (IRE)**
*William Haggas* 76
2 gr g Zoffany(IRE) Far Away Eyes (IRE) (High Chaparral (IRE))
6133[5] 7333[2]◆ (8075)◆

**Istimraar (IRE)** *Alexandra Dunn* a66 65
6 b g Dansili Manayer (IRE) (Sadler's Wells (USA))
19[7]

**Italian Beauty (IRE)**
*John Wainwright* a72 76
5 b m Thewayyouare(USA) Edelfa (IRE) (Fasliyev (USA))
232[5] 677[7] 4554[9] 7598[10] 8650[5] 9032[8]

**Italian Heiress** *Clive Cox* 85
3 ch f Medicean Regal Heiress (Pivotal)
2908[3] 3615[3]◆ 4365[5]◆ 5533[2]◆ 5915[9] (7125) 7959[6]

**Italian Riviera** *Kenneth Slack* a81 68
8 b g Galileo(IRE) Miss Corniche (Hernando (FR))
5008[2] 5740[4] 6569[2]

**It Dont Come Easy (IRE)**
*Richard Fahey* a87 97
2 b g Kyllachy Eleganza (IRE) (Balmont (USA))
2740[4] (3333) 3993[5] 4812[10] 5526[6] 7596[2] 8043[2] 8317[3]

**Iteratif** *K Borgel* a73
3 b g Dunkerque(FR) Goritie (FR) (Anabaa (USA))
584a[10]

**Itlaaq** *Michael Easterby* a84 83
11 b g Alhaarth(IRE) Hathrah (IRE) (Linamix (FR))
1719[10] 2622[8] 3050[2] 3795[4] 4301[6] 5208[5] 5737[5] 6757[7] 8386[3] 8876[5]

**It Must Be Faith** *Michael Appleby* a75 78
7 b g Mount Nelson Purple Rain (IRE) (Celtic Swing)
240[5] 480[8] 844[2] 901[7] 1475[13] 2669a[4]

**Itorio (IRE)**
*Mohammed Jassim Ghazali* 102
5 b h Oratorio(IRE) Image Of (IRE) (Close Conflict (USA))
914a[10]

**Itsakindamagic** *Andrew Balding* a86 91
3 b g Mount Nelson Carsulae (IRE) (Marju (IRE))
(1448) 2117[4] 3578[5] 4507[2] 5300[3] 6422[6] 7595[4]◆

**Itsalonglongroad** *John C McConnell* 82
3 b c Lawman(FR) Alabelle (Galileo (IRE))
4657[2] 6129[5]

**Its A Sheila Thing** *Tony Carroll* a45 45
4 ch m Sir Percy Sefemm (Alhaarth (IRE))
2914$^{10}$ 3760$^9$ 4753$^2$ 5296$^7$

**It's A Wish** *Clive Cox* a60
2 b f Invincible Spirit(IRE) Sun Bittern (USA) (Seeking The Gold (USA))
8850$^3$ 9049$^7$

**It's How We Roll (IRE)**
*John Spearing* a60 68
3 b g Fastnet Rock(AUS) Clodora (FR) (Linamix (FR))
875$^4$ 1205$^3$ 3163$^4$ 3922$^4$ 4446$^9$ 5565$^2$ 6291$^6$ 7902$^7$ 8299$^5$

**Itsinthepost (FR)** *Jeff Mullins* a104 109
5 b g American Post Sakkara Star (IRE) (Mozart (IRE))
8610a$^7$

**Its My Story (FR)** *J Reynier* a63 65
5 b g Vatori(FR) Family Story (FR) (Gold Away (IRE))
6541a$^8$

**It's Not Unusual** *Roger Charlton* a63 62
2 b f Exceed And Excel(AUS) Welsh Anthem (Singspiel (IRE))
4496$^4$ 6424$^5$ 7513$^5$

**It's Somewhat (USA)**
*James Cummings* 114
6 b g Dynaformer(USA) Sometime (IRE) (Royal Academy (USA))
8753a$^3$

**Ivan Grozny (FR)** *W P Mullins* a88 100
7 b g Turtle Bowl(IRE) Behnesa (IRE) (Suave Dancer (USA))
6447$^{15}$

**Ivanhoe** *Michael Blanshard* a56 71
7 b g Haafhd Marysienka (Primo Dominie)
2388$^8$ 2781$^5$ 3311$^5$ 4630$^4$ 5432$^9$ 6309$^9$ 7232$^2$ 7730$^8$ 8157$^{11}$

**I'vegotthepower (IRE)**
*Brian Meehan* 93
3 b g Power Waterways (IRE) (Alhaarth (IRE))
1737$^4$ (2220) 2513$^2$ 2824$^{11}$ (3780) (4491)◆

**Ivirka (FR)** *C Laffon-Parias* 70
2 ch f Mastercraftsman(IRE) Akrivi (IRE) (Tobougg (IRE))
7637a$^{14}$

**Ivo (GER)** *P Vovcenko*
2 b g Areion(GER) Ivowen (USA) (Theatrical (IRE))
6986a$^9$

**Ivor's Fantasy (IRE)** *David Elsworth* a49 46
3 ch f Zebedee Fantasy Princess (USA) (Johannesburg (USA))
920$^4$ 1605$^6$

**Ivors Involvement (IRE)**
*Tina Jackson* a46 52
5 b g Amadeus Wolf Summer Spice (IRE) (Key Of Luck (USA))
2918$^9$ 3560$^{10}$ 3979$^6$ 4744$^7$ 5499$^3$ 6003$^{10}$ 6092$^7$ 6269$^3$ 6592$^4$ (6673) 7479$^8$ 7704$^6$

**Ivor's Magic (IRE)** *David Elsworth* a61 63
3 ch f Zebedee Rinneen (IRE) (Bien Bien (USA))
763$^{10}$ 1242$^4$ 2017$^9$ 2968$^8$

**Ivy Leaguer** *Brian Meehan* a49 67
2 b c Compton Place Brick Tops (Danehill Dancer (IRE))
3668$^8$ 3925$^{18}$ 4582$^7$ 4991$^3$ 6021$^8$ 6651$^3$ 8294$^7$

**Ivy Matilda** *Colin Teague* a39 16
4 b m Monsieur Bond(IRE) Ingleby Princess (Bold Edge)
510$^6$ 655$^7$ 2627$^6$ 3568$^6$

**I Was Only Joking (IRE)**
*Richard Fahey* a67 60
2 ch f Helmet(AUS) Lady Angele (FR) (Ski Chief (USA))
8235$^4$ 9416$^2$

**I Will Excel (IRE)** *John James Feane* a68 78
5 b g Exceed And Excel(AUS) Da's Wish (IRE) (Sadler's Wells (USA))
1014a$^9$

**I Wouldn't Bother** *Daniel Kubler* a61 45
3 b g Captain Gerrard(IRE) Dalmunzie (IRE) (Choisir (AUS))
3525$^9$ 3818$^8$

**Ixelles Diamond (IRE)** *Lee Carter* a61 42
6 br m Diamond Green(FR) Silk Point (IRE) (Barathea (IRE))
739$^3$ (1237) 1447$^4$ 1618$^4$ 2095$^2$ 3507$^{10}$ 4010$^7$ 7213$^8$ 8307$^3$ 9084$^3$ 9282$^5$

**Izzthatright (IRE)**
*Jassim Mohammed Ghazali* 107
5 b g Moss Vale(IRE) Miss Adelaide (IRE) (Alzao (USA))
(932a)

**Izzy Bizu (IRE)** *Mark Johnston* a73 95
2 br f Kodiac Dame Hester (IRE) (Diktat)
(2545)◆ 2801$^{11}$ (3483)◆ (3815)◆ 4434$^3$ (5448a) 6418$^7$ 6863$^{10}$ 8562$^2$ 9156$^6$

**Jaalboot** *Owen Burrows* a55 63
2 b g Invincible Spirit(IRE) Selinka (Selkirk (USA))
3187$^7$ 4709$^4$

**Jaameh (IRE)** *Mark Johnston* a89 103
4 b g Iffraaj Miss Gibraltar (Rock Of Gibraltar (IRE))
2609$^2$ (3067)◆ (3594) 4356$^{17}$ 5164$^5$ 5638$^5$ 6427$^3$ 6929$^3$ 7548$^3$

**Jaarih (IRE)** *George Scott* a81 81
5 ch g Starspangledbanner(AUS) Bridge Note (USA) (Stravinsky (USA))
1487$^9$

**Jabbaar** *Iain Jardine* a69 80
4 ch g Medicean Echelon (Danehill (USA))
1706$^8$ 2458$^5$ 3153$^2$ 3582$^3$ 3976$^6$ 6894$^7$ 7142$^3$◆ 7524$^{10}$ 7595$^3$ (8239) 8485$^5$

**Jabbarockie** *Eric Alston* a74 77
4 b g Showcasing Canina (Foxhound (USA))
3313$^2$ 5459$^{11}$ 5619$^3$ (6526) 7522$^6$ (8168) 8680$^3$

**Jacbequick** *David O'Meara* a90 88
6 b g Calcutta Toking N' Joken (IRE) (Mukaddamah (USA))
43$^7$ 2226$^4$ 2701$^7$ 3204$^6$ 3497$^3$ 3744$^4$ 4017$^3$ (4380) 4865$^8$ 5163$^2$ 5924$^9$ 6349$^{12}$ 6563$^3$ 6965$^{10}$ 7627$^3$ 8048$^{18}$

**Jack Bear** *Harry Whittington* a81 76
6 b g Joe Bear(IRE) Colins Lady (FR) (Colonel Collins (USA))
6889$^6$ 8072$^5$

**Jackblack** *Brett Johnson* a62
5 b g Crosspeace(IRE) Saharan Royal (Val Royal (FR))
738$^5$ 3724$^8$

**Jack Blane** *Keith Dalgleish* a63 63
3 br g Kheleyf(USA) Blane Water (USA) (Lomond (USA))
904$^4$ (1367) 1564$^5$ 2016$^5$ 3913$^4$ 4713$^5$ 5467$^2$ 5741$^4$ 5992$^2$ 6630$^3$ 6903$^2$ 7240$^{12}$ 7573$^9$ 7889$^4$ 8401$^9$ 8948$^2$ 9052$^5$ (9215)

**Jack Blue (IRE)**
*Mrs John Harrington* a55 55
5 b g Duke Of Marmalade(IRE) Key Secure (IRE) (Sadler's Wells (USA))
6799a$^6$

**Jack Crow** *Eve Johnson Houghton* a73 74
2 b c Bahamian Bounty Here To Eternity (USA) (Stormy Atlantic (USA))
6319$^2$ 7351$^2$

**Jack Dexter** *Jim Goldie* a91 106
8 bb g Orientor Glenhurich (IRE) (Sri Pekan (USA))
2611$^8$ 2839$^6$◆ 3829$^{12}$ 4306$^4$ 4686$^5$ 5094$^4$ (5354) 5393$^{13}$ 6205$^P$ (Dead)

**Jackfinbar (FR)** *Harry Dunlop* a77 72
2 b c Whipper(USA) Anna Simona (GER) (Slip Anchor)
7120$^5$ 7637a$^{11}$ (9299)

**Jack Flash (FR)** *Les Eyre* a85 84
3 gr g Dark Angel(IRE) Lexi The Princess (IRE) (Holy Roman Emperor (IRE))
(119) 578$^2$ (765) 1731$^{13}$ 1975$^3$ (2160) 2806$^{10}$ 3982$^2$ 4530$^3$

**Jackhammer (IRE)** *Dianne Sayer* a86 97
3 b g Thewayyouare(USA) Ask Annie (IRE) (Danehill (USA))
1725$^4$ 3778$^6$ 4322$^7$ 5323$^8$ 6397$^5$ 8386$^{16}$

**Jack Hobbs** *John Gosden* a116 123
5 br h Halling(USA) Swain's Gold (USA) (Swain (IRE))
(1379a) 3962$^8$ 5394$^9$

**Jackie Ellis (IRE)** *Paul W Flynn* a62 66
6 b m Excellent Art Dancing With Stars (IRE) (Where Or When (IRE))
(4901)

**Jack Luey** *Lawrence Mullaney* a70 82
10 b g Danbird(AUS) Icenaslice (IRE) (Fayruz)
2034$^3$ 2700$^8$ 3238$^2$ 3524$^4$ 5211$^4$ 5459$^{10}$ 5804$^{10}$ 7522$^{17}$ 7825$^{15}$

**Jackman** *Lee James* 45
3 gr g Aussie Rules(USA) Fit To Burst (Pastoral Pursuits)
2758$^5$ 7271$^8$

**Jack Nevison** *Michael Appleby* a65 63
4 b g Dick Turpin(IRE) Creative Mind (IRE) (Danehill Dancer (IRE))
2727$^7$ 3391$^2$ 4298$^8$ 4765$^3$ 6288$^{10}$ 7389$^7$ (7480) 8376$^5$

**Jack Of Diamonds (IRE)**
*Roger Teal* a86 76
8 b g Red Clubs(IRE) Sakkara Star (IRE) (Mozart (IRE))
240$^7$ 460$^{12}$ 1085$^7$ 1562$^4$ 2041$^2$ 2478$^6$ 3009$^6$ 3771$^4$ 4257$^4$◆ 4730$^{10}$ 5299$^8$ 6101$^2$ (6947) 7735$^{15}$ 8664$^2$ 8813$^2$ 9078$^3$ (9338)

**Jackontherocks** *Michael Dods* 72
2 b g Bated Breath Desert Kiss (Cape Cross (IRE))
2948$^8$ (3648) 4834$^6$ 6087$^8$ 6940$^{11}$ 7243$^9$

**Jackpot Royale** *Michael Appleby* a60 65
2 b g Sixties Icon Sofia Royale (Royal Applause)
7482$^5$ 7929$^6$ 8982$^6$

**Jack Regan** *Charles Hills* 73
2 b g Rock Of Gibraltar(IRE) Chelsey Jayne (IRE) (Galileo (IRE))
4363$^3$ 4880$^6$ 5380$^6$ 6867$^7$ 7624$^7$

**Jacksonfire** *Michael Mullineaux* a40 59
5 ch g Firebreak Fitolini (Bertolini (USA))
3185$^9$ 3704$^{11}$ 4149$^5$ 5285$^3$ 5535$^2$ 6099$^2$ 6345$^7$ 6786$^4$ 7218$^4$ 7597$^4$ 7934$^{12}$ 8495$^7$ 8743$^{10}$ 9267$^{10}$ 9347$^8$

**Jack's Revenge (IRE)**
*George Baker* a84 95
9 br g Footstepsinthesand Spirit Of Age (IRE) (Indian Ridge (IRE))
61$^5$ 240$^6$

**Jack Taylor (IRE)** *Richard Hughes* a76 58
2 b c Invincible Spirit(IRE) Glory Power (IRE) (Medicean)
8073$^6$ 8536$^2$ (9087a)

**Jack The Laird (IRE)** *Dean Ivory* a65 67
4 b g Acclamation Pretty Demanding (IRE) (Night Shift (USA))
172$^8$ 468$^4$ 602$^3$ 742$^7$ 901$^3$ 1325$^3$ 1603$^4$ 1755$^3$ 2043$^{12}$ 2732$^5$ 2968$^4$ 3660$^4$ 4179$^5$

**Jack The Truth (IRE)** *George Scott* a81
3 ch g Dandy Man(IRE) Friendly Heart (CAN) (Lion Heart (USA))
679$^4$ 904$^2$ (9304)

**Jacob Black** *Kenny Johnson* a67 61
6 b g Amadeus Wolf First Eclipse (IRE) (Fayruz)
3255$^{13}$ 3857$^7$ 4103$^9$ 4609$^5$ 5540$^9$ 5836$^{12}$ 7166$^6$ 7573$^{12}$

**Jacob Cats** *William Knight* a97 95
8 b g Dutch Art Ballet (Sharrood (USA))
(1504) (1555) 2959$^3$ 3671$^2$◆ 4370$^7$ 5913$^{10}$ 6201$^3$ 6779$^3$ 8076$^6$

**Jacob's Pillow** *Rebecca Bastiman* a70 83
6 b g Oasis Dream Enticing (IRE) (Pivotal)
312$^8$ 523$^4$ 732$^8$ (1184) 1547$^6$ 1869$^2$ 2469$^5$ (3201) 3667$^2$ 4433$^6$ 5459$^8$ (5646) 5994$^2$ 6964$^{17}$ 7268$^3$ 7738$^2$ 8106$^2$ 8488$^5$

**Jacquard (IRE)** *Mark Johnston* a87 86
3 b c Pivotal Camlet (Green Desert (USA))
6570$^{11}$ 6942$^5$ 7570$^{11}$ 8318$^4$

**Jacques** *John Balding*
4 b g Sixties Icon Laminka (Intikhab (USA))
1675$^8$

**Jacquinot Bay (AUS)**
*David A & B Hayes & Tom Dabern* 103
9 b g Galileo(IRE) La La Land (AUS) (Last Tycoon)
8059a$^9$ 8750a$^3$ 8857a$^3$

**Jacquotte Delahaye** *David Brown* a86 88
6 ch m Kyllachy Mary Read (Bahamian Bounty)
232$^6$ (505) (810)

**Jadala (FR)** *K Borgel* a65 68
4 b m Gentlewave(IRE) Jade Colour (IRE) (Peintre Celebre (USA))
691a$^9$

**J'Adore (FR)** *J-P Dubois* 64
2 b f Zanzibari(USA) Stadore (FR) (Kendor (FR))
5988a$^{11}$

**Jafetica** *James Fanshawe* a75 63
3 ch f New Approach(IRE) Fann (USA) (Diesis)
4729$^3$ 5721$^7$ 6817$^3$ 7492$^4$ 8192$^3$

**Jaffar** *Scott Dixon* a42 66
2 b g Mawatheeq(USA) Velvet Jaguar (Hurricane Run (IRE))
3399$^7$ 3742$^5$ 4167$^4$ 4963$^7$ 9177$^7$ 9345$^7$ 9439$^{11}$

**Jaganory (IRE)** *Christopher Mason* a67 67
5 b g Dylan Thomas(IRE) Jacquelin Jag (IRE) (Fayruz)
2709$^4$ 3280$^3$ 3569$^7$ (3811) 4256$^{12}$ 4731$^4$ 5271$^7$ (5778) (6179) 6615$^4$ 7195$^7$ 7691$^5$

**Jahaafel (FR)** *William Haggas* a61
2 gr c Style Vendome(FR) Irisijana (GER) (Diktat)
8794$^4$

**Jai Hanuman (IRE)** *Seamus Durack* a55
3 b g Requinto(IRE) Almost Blue (USA) (Mr Greeley (USA))
221$^6$ 415$^8$

**Jaimie's Joy** *Tony Coyle* 49
2 b g Sleeping Indian Mad Jazz (Sir Percy)
4502$^6$ 4996$^7$ 5945$^5$ 6517$^{10}$

**Jakeboy** *Sylvester Kirk* a45
3 ch g Equiano(FR) Teyateyaneng (IRE) (Hawk Wing (USA))
8842$^6$◆ 9273$^6$

**Jake's Hill** *Eve Johnson Houghton* a46 108
3 b c Mount Nelson Flower Market (Cadeaux Genereux)
2689$^2$ (3506) 4584$^3$ 5639$^4$

**Jalapeno (IRE)** *Agostino Affe'* 98
4 br h Windsor Knot(IRE) Danza Nera (IRE) (Dansili)
322a$^{14}$ 654a$^9$ 8448a$^4$

**Jalela** *Richard Hannon* a91 93
3 b f Canford Cliffs(IRE) Divine Grace (IRE) (Definite Article)
1857$^2$ 2311$^2$ (2753) 6026$^{11}$ (6882) 7276$^4$ 7815$^{13}$

**Jalingo (IRE)** *Ali Stronge* a67 67
6 b g Cape Cross(IRE) Just Special (Cadeaux Genereux)
9324$^6$

**Jallota** *Charles Hills* a87 115
6 b g Rock Of Gibraltar(IRE) Lady Lahar (Fraam)
2129$^3$ 3587$^2$ 3924$^{10}$ 4890$^3$ 5502$^8$ 6401$^4$ 6729a$^5$ 7579$^3$ (7822) 8417$^2$ 8599$^4$

**Jal Mahal** *John Gosden* a47
2 b f Sepoy(AUS) Eminently (Exceed And Excel (AUS))
8889$^{11}$

**Jamacho** *Brian Ellison* a68 78
3 ch g Camacho Obsessive Secret (IRE) (Grand Lodge (USA))
1977$^3$ 2376$^2$ 2703$^2$ 3485$^3$ 5207$^6$

**Jamaican Jill** *William Muir* a69
2 b f Teofilo(IRE) Kahlua Kiss (Mister Baileys)
8373$^3$ 8796$^6$

**Jameerah** *Bryan Smart* a87 53
4 b m Dansili Jira (Medicean)
2840$^{14}$ 5379$^{11}$ 8639$^5$ 8913$^{11}$ 9124$^{10}$

**James Garfield (IRE)** *George Scott* 113
2 b c Exceed And Excel(AUS) Whazzat (Daylami (IRE))
3165$^3$ 3929$^3$ (4792) 5501$^4$ 6326$^2$ (7394) 8577a$^{10}$

**Jamesie (IRE)** *David Marnane* a103 105
9 b g Kodiac Pretty Woman (IRE) (Night Shift (USA))
207a$^3$ 433a$^6$ 651a$^2$

**James Lane (USA)** *S bin Ghadayer* a64
4 b g Bernardini(USA) Brushed Gold (USA) (Touch Gold (USA))
8714a$^P$

**Jamih** *John Gosden* a60
2 ch c Intello(GER) Hannda (IRE) (Dr Devious (IRE))
8703$^6$ 8987$^9$

**Jamil (IRE)** *Roger Varian* 79
2 b c Dansili Havant (Halling (USA))
(7740)

**Jampower** *Stuart Williams* a48
2 b g Equiano(FR) Wiki Tiki (Dixie Union (USA))
8989$^7$ 9311$^{10}$

**Janabiya** *George Peckham* 65
2 b f Nathaniel(IRE) Date With Destiny (IRE) (George Washington (IRE))
4902$^{10}$

**Jan De Heem** *Tina Jackson* a55 65
7 ch g Dutch Art Shasta (Shareef Dancer (USA))
3155$^5$ 3559$^4$ 3795$^4$◆ 5186$^2$ 5454$^4$ 5951$^7$ 6431$^6$ (7248) 8241$^2$ 8654$^2$

**Jane Rose (IRE)** *Richard Hannon* a45 69
2 b f Acclamation Miss Champagne (FR) (Bering)
4296$^4$◆ 4749$^8$ 5107$^6$

**Jannia** *Eve Johnson Houghton* a51
3 b f Iffraaj Fairy Moss (IRE) (Amadeus Wolf)
34$^8$

**Jan's Joy** *Stuart Williams* a62 48
2 br f Kheleyf(USA) Overwing (IRE) (Fasliyev (USA))
3437$^4$ 4440$^{10}$ 5026$^4$ 6285$^5$

**Jan Smuts (IRE)** *Wilf Storey* a63 61
9 b g Johannesburg(USA) Choice House (USA) (Chester House (USA))
(28) 174$^{11}$ 399$^5$ 610$^2$ 990$^4$ 1344$^5$ 1716$^6$ 2125$^4$ 2594$^3$ 2889$^5$ 3340$^4$ 4790$^3$ 5008$^7$ 5259$^5$ 5740$^7$ 6565$^2$ 6898$^4$ 7922$^6$ 8187$^7$ 8487$^5$

**Janszoon** *Charlie Appleby* a90 90
3 gr g Dubawi(IRE) Adventure (USA) (Unbridled's Song (USA))
2039$^2$ (2576) 3081$^6$ 3998$^9$ 5328$^5$

**Jantine (FR)** *E Wianny* a44 55
3 b f Medecis Jabberwocky (Catcher In The Rye (IRE))
838a$^{11}$

**Jaqen H'Ghar (IRE)**
*Joseph Patrick O'Brien* a100 97
4 b h Fastnet Rock(AUS) Small Sacrifice (IRE) (Sadler's Wells (USA))
4822a$^{10}$

**Jashma (IRE)** *Richard Hughes* a63 81
3 b g Power Daganya (IRE) (Danehill Dancer (IRE))
819$^3$ 956$^5$ 2235$^4$ (2720) 3035$^3$ 3692$^4$ 4200$^2$ 5588$^2$ 6373$^2$ 6780$^2$ (7127) (7509)

**Jasi (IRE)** *David O'Meara* a68 74
2 b g Kodiac Late Night Movie (IRE) (Holy Roman Emperor (IRE))
(1588) 2299$^2$ 4888$^4$ 8431$^9$

**Jasmincita (IRE)** *George Baker* a50 59
3 b f Dark Angel(IRE) Jasmine Flower (Kyllachy)
1242$^9$ 1685$^{13}$ 2017$^{10}$ 6814$^6$ 7763$^8$ 8133$^4$

**Jasmine A La Plage (FR)**
*Matthieu Palussiere* a38 55
2 b f Palace Episode(USA) Diner En Ville (FR) (Barathea (IRE))
2642a$^7$ 3679a$^{11}$ 5907a$^8$

**Jasmiralda (FR)** *S Wattel* a90 80
4 b m Desert Style(IRE) Maid Of Dawkins (IRE) (Kendor (FR))
9003a$^{11}$

**Jasnin (FR)** *Waldemar Hickst* a91 100
5 gr g Palace Episode(USA) Jaillissante (FR) (Verglas (IRE))
(8127a) 8463a$^3$

**Javelin** *Richard Fahey* 62
2 ch f Lethal Force(IRE) Amitola (IRE) (Choisir (AUS))
3943$^5$◆

**Jawan** *Michael Bell* 54
2 b c Sepoy(AUS) Luluti (IRE) (Kheleyf (USA))
8119$^{10}$◆

**Jawwaal** *John Gosden* 78
2 ch c Bahamian Bounty Avenbury (Mount Nelson)
5420$^3$ 6133$^3$

**Jaycols Star** *Philip Kirby* 56
2 ch g Medicean A Lulu Ofa Menifee (USA) (Menifee (USA))
4291$^7$ 5179$^6$ 6939$^{10}$ 7519$^7$ 8141$^6$

**Jay Em Gee (IRE)** *Bryan Smart* 14
4 gr g Mastercraftsman(IRE) Pallas Athena (IRE) (Sadler's Wells (USA))
5538$^{12}$

**Jay Kay** *K R Burke* a26 84
8 b g Librettist(USA) Turn Back (Pivotal)
1867$^7$ 3199$^2$ 3388$^3$ 3652$^6$ 4663$^7$ 5333$^4$ 5993$^2$ 6549$^3$ 7042$^2$ (7702) (7981) 8254$^8$

**Jaywalker (IRE)** *Rebecca Bastiman* a97 95
6 b g Footstepsinthesand Nipping (IRE) (Night Shift (USA))
(1103) 1454$^8$ 1831$^4$ 2381$^2$ 5435$^{12}$ 5705$^3$ (7455)

**Jazaalah (USA)** *Owen Burrows* a73 56
3 ch f Hard Spun(USA) Teeba (USA) (Seeking The Gold (USA))
5712$^9$ 6287$^3$ 7826$^3$

**Jazeel (IRE)** *Mick Channon* a84 80
2 b c Roderic O'Connor(IRE) Simla Bibi (Indian Ridge (IRE))
4880$^3$◆ (5655) 6326$^8$ 6934$^2$ 8029$^2$

**Jazirat (IRE)** *Charlie Appleby* 71
2 b g Dark Angel(IRE) Layla Jamil (IRE) (Exceed And Excel (AUS))
4183$^3$◆ 4709$^2$

**Jazri** *Milton Bradley* a53 43
6 b g Myboycharlie(IRE) Read Federica (Fusaichi Pegasus (USA))
124$^7$ 621$^2$ 880$^4$ 1145$^3$ 1322$^7$ 3028$^8$ 6305$^8$ 6754$^3$ 7324$^9$ 7760$^{11}$

**Jazz Affair (IRE)** *Jamie Osborne* a49 44
2 b g Red Jazz(USA) Kiss And Don'Tell (USA) (Rahy (USA))
4367$^{10}$ 4805$^{10}$ 5030$^{13}$ 8500$^6$ 8847$^7$ 9002$^7$ 9182$^3$

**Jazz Legend (USA)** *Mandy Rowland* a54 55
4 b g Scat Daddy(USA) Champion Ride (USA) (Candy Ride (ARG))
1869$^9$ 2589$^{15}$ 3728$^5$ 4179$^6$ 4727$^5$◆ (5081) 5738$^5$ 5892$^6$ 6814$^{10}$ 7218$^7$ 7487$^{12}$

**Jazz Magic (IRE)** *Sally Haynes* 51
2 ch g Red Jazz(USA) Caerella (IRE) (Alzao (USA))
3093$^7$

**Jazz Melodie (FR)** *P De Chevigny* a89 88
3 b f Soul City(IRE) Quatz Melody (FR) (Johann Quatz (FR))
5777a$^3$

**Jazzy (IRE)** *Martin Keighley* a44 79
4 b g Roderic O'Connor(IRE) Lucayan Beauty (IRE) (Marju (IRE))
3409$^6$ 4000$^5$ (4755)

**Jazzy Girl (IRE)** *Brendan Powell* a48 45
2 br f Red Jazz(USA) Intimate Secret (IRE) (Invincible Spirit (IRE))
7352$^{13}$ 7725$^{10}$ 8294$^9$ 8793$^7$ 8887$^5$

**J Boys Echo (USA)** *Dale Romans* a113
3 b c Mineshaft(USA) Letgomyecho (USA) (Menifee (USA))
2420a$^{15}$

**Jeanie's Place** *Charlie Wallis* a66 55
4 ch m Compton Place Good Again (Dubai Destination (USA))
815$^8$ 1180$^{10}$ 1490$^6$ 2509$^7$ 2969$^{12}$ 3469$^7$

**Jeannajonh (FR)** *W Walton* a82 82
3 b f Deportivo Flower (Zamindar (USA))
272a$^3$ 2484a$^{12}$

**Jean Paget (IRE)** *Mick Channon* a49 57
2 b f Choisir(AUS) Betty Fontaine (IRE) (Mujadil (USA))
5107$^{12}$ 5408$^4$ 5613$^7$ 5893$^6$ 6285$^8$ 6517$^8$

**Jeany (IRE)** *Bryan Smart* a51 70
3 b f Kodiac Flower Bowl (IRE) (Noverre (USA))
4604$^2$ 6155$^6$ 6596$^2$

**Jebel Tara** *Alistair Whillans* a60 54
12 b g Diktat Chantilly (FR) (Sanglamore (USA))
5919[11] 6688[3] 7166[5] 7575[13]
**Jebulani** *Barry Murtagh* a34 46
7 b g Jelani(IRE) Susan's Dowry (Efisio)
1402[7] 2340[6] 3043[7] 3449[4] 4660[11] 5740[6]
**Jedi Master (IRE)** *Richard Fahey* 82
2 ch c Red Jazz(USA) Misrepresent (USA) (Distorted Humor (USA))
1604[6] 2148[4] 2816[2] (3399) (3430) 4922[5] 5572[4] 6699[6] 7090[10] 7821[20]
**Jedlitzka (IRE)** *Mick Channon* 17
2 b f Kodiac Jeritza (Rainbow Quest (USA))
4806[14] 5154[11]
**Jeeraan (USA)** *Doug Watson* a91 82
7 b g Distorted Humor(USA) Jaish (USA) (Seeking The Gold (USA))
83a[9]
**Jellmood** *Marco Botti* a92 87
2 b g Acclamation Emotif (ARG) (Giant's Causeway (USA))
2134[3] 2607[2] 4318[2] 5109[9] (9051) 9405[2]
**Jelly Monger (IRE)**
*Dominic Ffrench Davis* a92 92
5 b m Strategic Prince Royal Jelly (King's Best (USA))
2387[4] 3033[2] 3968[2] 4828[6] 5108[5] 5715[3] 6104[5] 7283[7] 7817[3] 8007[9] 8414[7]
**Jelmood (FR)** *Mme J Hendriks* 39
3 b g Lawman(FR) Secret Question (USA) (Rahy (USA))
6256a[8]
**Jenji (IRE)** *David Evans* a19 25
3 b f Pour Moi(IRE) Distant Symphony (FR) (Dalakhani (IRE))
2758[4]
**Jenniechild (IRE)** *Peter Fahey* a57 71
4 b m Tagula(IRE) Belle Child (IRE) (Bijou D'Inde)
2656a[16] 9244a[14]
**Jennies Gem** *Ollie Pears* a48 45
4 b g Mount Nelson Kaspirit (IRE) (Invincible Spirit (IRE))
2887[9] 3568[3] 4106[4] 4743[9] 5215[12] 6529[4]◆ 8784[4] 9072[5] 9368[12]
**Jeopardy John** *Michael Attwater* a67
2 b g Delegator Daysiwaay (IRE) (Daylami (IRE))
7512[6] 8028[4] 8545[7] 9199[3] 9465[3]
**Jeremiah** *Charlie Fellowes* a77 78
2 ch c Kheleyf(USA) Tessie (Tiger Hill (IRE))
7758[3] 8353[3]
**Jeremy's Jet (IRE)** *Tony Carroll* a41 61
6 b g Jeremy(USA) Double Vie (IRE) (Tagula (IRE))
1610[8] 2276[9] 3575[8] 4545[6] 6530[P] 7215[6]
**Jeremys Joy (IRE)**
*Keith Henry Clarke* a51 93
5 b m Jeremy(USA) Desert's Queen (IRE) (Desert Prince (IRE))
7066a[8] 7261a[8] 8086a[6]
**Jersey Breeze (IRE)** *Mick Channon* a60 85
4 gr m Dark Angel(IRE) Sixfields Flyer (IRE) (Desert Style (IRE))
2177[4] 2618[6] 2917[3] 3307[6] (3941) (4043) 4536[8] 5355[6] 5587[3] 5869[9] 6197[12] 6586[5] 8150[13]
**Jersey Bull (IRE)** *Michael Madgwick* a68 42
5 b g Clodovil(IRE) Chaguaramas (IRE) (Mujadil (USA))
169[9] 286[4] 806[5] 893[3] 1283[6] 4538[7] 5024[9] 6796[3] 7717[6] 8135[11]
**Jersey Jewel (FR)** *Peter Bowen* a74 66
5 b m Naaqoos Nikolenka (IRE) (Indian Ridge (IRE))
3325[4] 5320[9] 5968[7] 9295[9]
**Jess** *Kevin Ryan* a51 53
4 b m Equiano(FR) Poyle Meg (Dansili)
363[11] 732[11] 1030[6] 1200[9] 5282[3] 5543[12] 6045[12]
**Jesse Tree (IRE)** *John Flint* a39 44
4 ch m Approve(IRE) Dane Blue (IRE) (Danehill Dancer (IRE))
2255[12] 3280[14] 4011[3] 4735[11]
**Jessica Jo (IRE)** *Mark Johnston* a58 64
4 ch m Mastercraftsman(IRE) Naomh Geileis (USA) (Grand Slam (USA))
282[8] 525[7]
**Jessie Allan (IRE)** *Jim Goldie* a51 54
6 b m Bushranger(IRE) Ishimagic (Ishiguru (USA))
445[7] 579[9] 969[4] 1125[8] 1372[6] 2342[4] 2454[6] 3185[4] 3831[5] 4263[3] 4688[2] 5205[3] 5466[4] 5917[9] 5991[2] 7979[4] 8591[9] 8924[2] 9012[2] 9267[4] 9420[3]
**Jessinamillion** *James Bethell* a70 75
3 b g Mine(IRE) Miss Apricot (Indian Ridge (IRE))
2383[7] 3054[3] 4309[5] 5316[3] 5947[6] (6694) 7287[6]
**Je Suis Charlie** *Michael Bell* 88
3 b g High Chaparral(IRE) Fin (Groom Dancer (USA))
1886[9] 3291[2] 3520[3] 4295[2] 4580[7] 5589[5] (6573) 7387[2] 8011[5]
**Jethro (IRE)** *Brian Ellison* a39 49
6 b g Craigsteel Wee Mo (IRE) (Zaffaran (USA))
2467[4]
**Jetpac** *Laura Mongan* a20
2 b g Paco Boy(IRE) Emperor's Hope (IRE) (Holy Roman Emperor (IRE))
7512[12] 9319[9]
**Jet Setter (IRE)** *Tony Carroll* a64 59
3 ch g Fast Company(IRE) Raven One (IRE) (Titus Livius (FR))
2[4] 157[3] 813[4] 903[2] 1127[7] 1605[4] (3166) 3621[5] 4290[10] 5288[11] 6181[5] 6866[5] 7459[6] 7928[4] 8401[8]
**Jetstream (IRE)** *Charles Hills* 46
2 b c Galileo(IRE) Bewitched (IRE) (Dansili)
4860[11]
**Jet Streaming (IRE)**
*Adrian Paul Keatley* 101
3 ch f Born To Sea(IRE) Sateen (Barathea (IRE))
6978a[7] 7577[5] 8086a[11]
**Jeu Celebre (IRE)** *J-C Rouget* a61 71
3 b c Excelebration(IRE) Jeu De Vivre (IRE) (Montjeu (IRE))
6084a[7]
**Jewel House** *John Gosden* a57 88
3 b c Dubawi(IRE) Arizona Jewel (Dansili)
1513[3] (1862) 2565[8]
**Jimenez (IRE)** *Brian Meehan* a86 86
4 b h Acclamation Fritta Mista (IRE) (Linamix (FR))
(61)
**Jimmy Two Times (FR)** *A Fabre* 114
4 gr h Kendargent(FR) Steel Woman (IRE) (Anabaa (USA))
(1531a) (2248a)
**Jim Rockford** *Ralph Beckett* a62 81
2 ch g Showcasing Positivity (Monsieur Bond (IRE))
1941[6] 2382[4] 2756[5] 4527[2] 4922[7] 6525[2] (7193) (7690)
**Jinkie Pink (IRE)** *Ed Walker* 67
3 b f Teofilo(IRE) Hurricane Havoc (IRE) (Hurricane Run (IRE))
1947[5] 3571[3] 4145[4]
**Jinx (FR)** *J Boisnard* a57
2 bb c Siyouni(FR) Kestria (IRE) (Keltos (FR))
9087a[10]
**Jiro Boy** *Rebecca Bastiman* 28
2 b c Compton Place Foolish Lady (IRE) (Exceed And Excel (AUS))
7818[12] 8381[10]
**Jive Factor (USA)** *Ed Dunlop* a59 58
3 b g The Factor(USA) Jive Talk (USA) (Kingmambo (USA))
1445[6] 1817[4]
**Jive Lady (IRE)** *Mark Johnston* a75 77
2 b f Exceed And Excel(AUS) Fair Sailing (IRE) (Dockside (USA))
2771[7]◆ 3169[8] 3826[2] 4628[3] (5068) 5440[5] 6021[4] 6466[6]
**Jive Talking (IRE)** *Michael Bell* a80 81
3 ch f Zoffany(IRE) Inis Boffin (Danehill Dancer (IRE))
3759[2] (4603) 5217[2] 6104[4] 6722[9] 7338[4] 7817[6] 8886[3]
**Joaldo** *Antony Brittain* a47 36
5 b g Monsieur Bond(IRE) Labba (Tiger Hill (IRE))
1544[5] 3468[4] 4162[4] 4453[11]
**Joan Jet (FR)** *H-F Devin* a42 61
2 b f Equiano(FR) Amarinda (GER) (Tiger Hill (IRE))
5585a[2]
**Jock Talk (IRE)** *Gordon Elliott* a58 56
3 b g Famous Name Katdogawn (Bahhare (USA))
6342[4] 9072[10]
**Joe Cable (IRE)** *Nigel Tinkler* 31
2 b g Camacho Happy Talk (IRE) (Hamas (IRE))
7472[6] 7818[11] 8013[15] 8475[14]
**Joegogo (IRE)** *David Evans* a83 72
2 b g Approve(IRE) Joyfullness (USA) (Dixieland Band (USA))
2756[2] 3083[3] 3689[4] 5430[6] 6816[3] 7138[7] 7690[3] (8746) (8882) (8954) 9156[5] 9452[2]
**Joe Packet** *Jonathan Portman* a66 83
10 ch g Joe Bear(IRE) Costa Packet (IRE) (Hussonet (USA))
(3074) 3777[4] 6780[4]
**Joe's Spirit (IRE)** *Michael Bell* a84 74
2 b g Swiss Spirit Dimensional (Dansili)
2217[2] (3135) 3556[7] 4827[3] 5366[4] (5742)◆ 7536[10]
**Joe The Tinker (FR)** *C Boutin* a50 66
2 ch c George Vancouver(USA) Louve Rouge (FR) (Gold Away (IRE))
1919a[5]
**Joey's Destiny (IRE)** *Kevin Frost* a93 50
7 ch g Kheleyf(USA) Maid Of Ailsa (USA) (Pivotal)
275[2] 598[4] 896[11] 1718[3] 3471[8] (4451) 5245[11] 6949[6] 7409[10] 7932[9] 8557[13] 8875[7]
**Johann Bach (IRE)**
*Patrick G Harney* a99 89
8 b g Oratorio(IRE) Belleinga (IRE) (Orpen (USA))
6491a[16]
**Johannes Vermeer (IRE)**
*A P O'Brien* 117
4 b h Galileo(IRE) Inca Princess (IRE) (Holy Roman Emperor (IRE))
2240a[4] 3108a[5] 3962[7] (4417a) 5862a[2] 8058a[2] 8250a[3] 8667a[2]
**Johann Strauss** *M F De Kock* a72 93
6 br h High Chaparral(IRE) Inchmina (Cape Cross (IRE))
653a[7] 892a[12]
**John Caesar (IRE)**
*Rebecca Bastiman* a65 68
6 b g Bushranger(IRE) Polish Belle (Polish Precedent (USA))
239[4] 841[10] 1125[5] 1403[5] 4323[7] 4659[6] 5215[3] 5498[2] 5997[10] (7270) (7479) 7704[5] 7960[3] 8301[7]
**John Constable (IRE)**
*Evan Williams* 73
6 b g Montjeu(IRE) Dance Parade (USA) (Gone West (USA))
8038[21]
**Johni Boxit** *Gay Kelleway* 63
2 ch g Sakhee's Secret Pink Supreme (Night Shift (USA))
4539[3] 4995[2]◆ 5398[4] 8325[13]
**John Joiner** *Peter Hedger* a51 68
5 b g Captain Gerrard(IRE) Nigella (Band On The Run)
2621[10] 3170[6] 4352[8] 5429[3] 5723[3] 6652[2] 6810[4] 7509[3] 8298[9]
**John Kirkup** *Michael Dods* 92
2 ch g Assertive Bikini (Trans Island)
2948[7] (3523) (4204) 4922[2] (5615)◆ 6330[4] 7049[2] 7821[21]
**Johnny Barnes (IRE)** *John Gosden* 111
5 b h Acclamation Mahalia (IRE) (Danehill (USA))
2907[7] 4390a[4] 5147[3] 5393[4] (6419) 7611[6]◆ 7807[5]
**Johnny Bear (CAN)** *Ashlee Brnjas* 112
6 ch g English Channel(USA) In Return (USA) (Horse Chestnut (SAF))
(7178a) 8099a[10]
**Johnny Cavagin** *Ronald Thompson* a81 86
8 b g Superior Premium Beyond The Rainbow (Mind Games)
1512[14] 2303[2] 2592[3] 2821[2] 3463[7] 3757[5] 4339[2] 4897[5] 5457[3] 6186[6] 6570[5] 7553[2] 8319[6] 8718[8] 9241[8]
**John Reel (FR)** *David Evans* a101 103
8 b g Country Reel(USA) John Quatz (FR) (Johann Quatz (FR))
352[6] 720[7] 779[7] 1068[7] 1360[4] 1628[5] 1770[12]
**Jollify (IRE)** *A Fabre* 100
4 b m Manduro(GER) Jomana (IRE) (Darshaan)
6914a[9]
**Jolly Roger (IRE)** *Dai Burchell* a52 74
10 b g Oratorio(IRE) Chalice Wells (Sadler's Wells (USA))
861[6] (Dead)
**Jonathans Girl** *Christine Dunnett*
2 b f Equiano(FR) Jewelled (Fantastic Light (USA))
7875[11]
**Jonboy** *David Barron* 80
2 b c Delegator Cavallo Da Corsa (Galileo (IRE))
6347[6] (7326)◆
**Jonh Jonh (FR)** *Jane Soubagne* a87 89
6 b g Chineur(FR) Flower (Zamindar (USA))
6540a[8]
**Jon H The Lawman (IRE)**
*Ronald Thompson* a21 44
4 b g Lawman(FR) Lan Pham Ti (IRE) (Librettist (USA))
2312[10] 4105[12]
**Jonnie Skull (IRE)** *Phil McEntee* a38 49
11 b g Pyrus(USA) Sovereign Touch (IRE) (Pennine Walk)
2057[2] 2255[7] 3731[5]
**Jonny Delta** *Jim Goldie* 84
10 ch g Sulamani(IRE) Send Me An Angel (IRE) (Lycius (USA))
2340[2] (2456) 3193[3] 3338[3] 4684[7] 4849[6] (5257) 5884[3] 6592[2] 6895[6] (7659) 8109[4] (Dead)
**Jonnysimpson (IRE)**
*Brendan Powell* a70 60
2 gr f Zebedee Applauding (IRE) (Royal Applause)
1767[4] 3210 [3] 3821[12] 6609[3] 7695[2] (8145)
**Jon Snow (NZ)**
*Murray Baker & Andrew Forsman* 116
3 b c Iffraaj Orinda (NZ) (O'Reilly (NZ))
8058a[3] 8250a[9]
**Jordan James (IRE)** *Brian Ellison* a50 73
4 b g Equiano(FR) Deira (USA) (Green Desert (USA))
2430[7] 3181[7] 3487[3] 4304[9] 7042[11]
**Jordan Sport** *David Simcock* a99 101
4 b g Dubawi(IRE) Wonder Why (GER) (Tiger Hill (IRE))
(234) 842[4] 3410[4] 3967[4] 4830[3] (5890) 6922[4] 7822[4]
**Jordan's Tiger (FR)**
*Jolanda Van Wesel*
6 b g Tiger Hill(IRE) Nagaoka (GER) (Goofalik (USA))
1070a[3]
**Jordaura** *Alan Berry* 6
11 br g Primo Valentino(IRE) Christina's Dream (Spectrum (IRE))
123[8] 8218[12]
**Jorvik Prince** *Karen Tutty* a79 59
3 br g Kheleyf(USA) Wotatomboy (Captain Rio)
1715[4] 2372[4] 2897[3] 3624[9] 4107[10] 4559[8] 7575[12] 8395[2] 8490[4] 8924[12] 9268[2] (9374) (9420)
**Jo's Girl (IRE)** *Micky Hammond* a63 71
2 b f Zebedee Diamond Finesse (IRE) (Red Clubs (IRE))
3022[4] 3429[4] 4028[15] 4709[3] 5752[9] 7914[2] 8848[7] 9097[6]
**Joshlee (IRE)** *Emma Owen* a53 40
3 b f Dark Angel(IRE) Kay Es Jay (FR) (Xaar)
4006[6] 5410[9] 5792[7] 7705[4] 7993[8] 9129[11] 9344[6]
**Josh The Plod (IRE)**
*Andrew Balding* a67 61
3 b g Arcano(IRE) Dune Breeze (IRE) (Azamour (IRE))
3408[3] 4347[6] 4981[3] 5532[3] 6075[7]
**Joshua Reynolds** *John Gosden* a100 97
3 b g Nathaniel(IRE) Dash To The Front (Diktat)
1497[5] 3717[3] (4314) (5328)◆ 6930[7] 8011[12] (8539)
**Journey** *John Gosden* a70 120
5 b m Dubawi(IRE) Montare (IRE) (Montjeu (IRE))
3299[5] 4419a[10] 6981a[2] 8231[6]
**Journey Home (USA)**
*H Graham Motion* 99
3 bb f War Front(USA) Soul Search (USA) (A.P. Indy (USA))
4650a[8]
**Jousi** *Hugo Palmer* a85 82
2 ch f Dubawi(IRE) Soon (IRE) (Galileo (IRE))
4902[4] (5349) 5941[9] 6886[2] 8002[13]
**Joy** *Laura Mongan* a31 23
3 b f Equiano(FR) On Wings Of Love (IRE) (Hawk Wing (USA))
1600[6] 2090[11] 2366[8] 2911[14] 3819[11]
**Joycetick (FR)** *P Sogorb* a82
3 b c Myboycharlie(IRE) Joyce (GER) (Chato (USA))
272a[8]
**Joyful Dream (IRE)** *John Butler* a66 55
3 ch f Dream Ahead(USA) Tearsforjoy (USA) (Street Cry (IRE))
96[6] 435[4] 686[4] 897[5] 1605[8] 2331[5] 8498[3] 9217[7]
**Joyful Star** *Fred Watson* a45 53
7 b g Teofilo(IRE) Extreme Beauty (USA) (Rahy (USA))
2501[3] 3196[4] 3530[4] 4660[6] 5880[9]
**Joyful Trinity (IRE)** *John Moore* a93 120
5 b g Zanzibari(USA) Bargouzine (USA) (Stravinsky (USA))
9170a[9]
**Joyroo (IRE)** *Michael Easterby* a50
3 b g Tagula(IRE) Memphis Belle (Linamix (FR))
157[5] 415[6]
**Joys Delight** *Daniel Mark Loughnane* a64 63
3 b f Stimulation(IRE) Lambadora (Suave Dancer (USA))
221[10] 4164[3] 4759[2] 5485[10] 6016[4] 6638[4] 7035[2] 7934[10] 8659[6] 8957[3] 9085[2] 9406[6]
**Joysunny** *Jacqueline Coward* a44 51
3 b f Camacho Alustar (Emarati (USA))
1183[6] 1543[5] 1715[2] 3141[6] 3285[3] 4107[9] 4478[4] 4847[7] 4997[2] 5703[8] 6469[10]
**Juan Horsepower** *Richard Hannon* a80 85
3 b g Foxwedge(AUS) Elysee (IRE) (Fantastic Light (USA))
155[4] 623[2] 765[3] (1090) 1601[3] (2215) 2992[5]◆ 3146[9] 4521[8] 5051[8] 5473[6] 8158[4] 9020[8] 9234[7] 9437[2]◆
**Juanito Chico (IRE)** *William Jarvis* a77 96
3 br g Pour Moi(IRE) Miss Kittyhawk (IRE) (Hawk Wing (USA))
2126[5] 2567[3] (3303) 3592[4]◆ 4831[2] 5392[4]◆
**Jubilance (IRE)** *Bent Olsen* a85 96
8 b g Oratorio(IRE) Literacy (USA) (Diesis)
4825a[6] 5676a[3] 6501a[2] 7428a[3]
**Jubilee Brig** *Alan Swinbank* a75 73
7 b g Kheleyf(USA) Voile (IRE) (Barathea (IRE))
32[3]◆ 363[6] 513[3] 968[3] 1210[4] 1718[5]
**Judicial (IRE)** *Julie Camacho* a99 111
5 b g Iffraaj Marlinka (Marju (IRE))
842[7] 1152[6] 1501[5] (2031) (2573) (3932) 4920[4] 5684[2] 7396[6]
**Judicious** *Geoffrey Harker* a48 61
10 ch g Pivotal Virtuous (Exit To Nowhere (USA))
2183[12] 3935[6] 5215[11] 5831[7] 6673[11]
**Judy Woods (IRE)** *Bryan Smart* a59 65
3 b f Excelebration(IRE) Snowpalm (Halling (USA))
1835[2] 2181[6] 3184[9]
**Jufn** *John Butler* a84 82
4 b g Nayef(USA) Deyaar (USA) (Storm Cat (USA))
1288[6] 2233[7] 2893[4] (3771) 4522[5] 5643[15] 6848[3] 7728[11] 8398[6]
**Jugeotte (FR)** *Y Gourraud* a61 67
2 b f George Vancouver(USA) Margot Mine (IRE) (Choisir (AUS))
4166a[6] 5585a[4] 6050a[4]
**Jukebox Jive (FR)**
*Anthony Honeyball* a84 103
3 b g Jukebox Jury(IRE) Sweetheart (Sinndar (IRE))
(1559) 2526[3] (3503) 4612[9] (5110) 7547[4]
**Jule In The Crown** *Richard Hannon* 90
3 b f Harbour Watch(IRE) Jules (IRE) (Danehill (USA))
1702[2] 1945[14] 3167[8] 3822[5] (5325) 5758[3] 6429[3]
**Juliet Capulet (IRE)** *John Gosden* 110
2 b f Dark Angel(IRE) Capulet Monteque (IRE) (Camacho)
3312[7] 4253[4] 4902[3] (5372) 5941[2] (7578) 8575a[11]
**Juliet Foxtrot** *Charles Hills* 96
2 b f Dansili Kilo Alpha (King's Best (USA))
5938[5] (6776)◆ 7421a[5]
**Julietta (FR)** *Mario Hofer* a26
2 ch f Lingarri(IRE) La Julie (IRE) (Peintre Celebre (USA))
9086a[14]
**Julio (GER)** *Mario Hofer* 96
2 b c Exceed And Excel(AUS) Julissima (Beat Hollow)
6726a[3] 7754a[3]
**Jumbo Prado (USA)**
*Daniel Mark Loughnane* a72 49
8 rg g El Prado(IRE) Sant Elena (Efisio)
49[9] 641[4]◆ 928[8] 1065[8]
**Jumbo's Boy** *Peter Bowen* 43
3 b g Multiplex Silver Gyre (IRE) (Silver Hawk (USA))
6368[9] 6808[5] 7080[8]
**Jumira Bridge** *Roger Varian* 101
3 b g Invincible Spirit(IRE) Zykina (Pivotal)
(1785) (2130) 2768[3] 4098[2] 4816[10] 7286[2] 8139[8]
**Jumira Prince (IRE)** *Roger Varian* 79
3 ch g Exceed And Excel(AUS) Aoife Alainn (IRE) (Dr Fong (USA))
1862[6] 2171[4] (3627) 4084[5] 5139[2] 6134[5]
**Jump Around** *Ali Stronge* a36 37
3 b f Medicean Mountain Leap (IRE) (Sadler's Wells (USA))
1497[14] 2159[7] 2408[9] 4968[7] 5823[6] 6621[8] 7210[9] 7790[10]
**Jumping Around (IRE)** *Ian Williams* a70 69
3 b f Dark Angel(IRE) Box Of Frogs (IRE) (One Cool Cat (USA))
1838[8] 2407[5] 3588[9] 4084[7] 4741[7] 6015[3] 6681[2] 7414[8] 8158[9] 9414[6]
**Jumping Jack (IRE)** *Chris Gordon* a77 81
3 b g Sir Prancealot(IRE) She's A Character (Invincible Spirit (IRE))
625[2] 846[4] 1760[6] 2293[5] 2625[10] 3784[7]◆ (4176) 4446[2]◆ 4698[6] 9314[8]
**Junderstand** *Alan King* a64
2 ch f Champs Elysees Sienna Sunset (IRE) (Spectrum (IRE))
8147[3]
**June Dog** *Richard Hannon* 78
2 b c Helmet(AUS) Broadway Dancer (Fantastic Light (USA))
2134[11] (3165) 3929[21] 4527[4] 4991[10] 7596[7]
**Jungle Cat (IRE)** *Charlie Appleby* 116
5 b h Iffraaj Mike's Wildcat (USA) (Forest Wildcat (USA))
433a[2] 773a[2] (1044a) 1376a[4] 2737[9] 4362[2] 4890[2] (5137)◆ 5502[12] 6401[6]
**Jungle George** *Scott Dixon* a41 15
3 b g Kheleyf(USA) Amouage Royale (IRE) (Mr Greeley (USA))
212[7] 415[10] 4970[10] 6528[12] 7760[9] 8183[7] 8770[9]
**Jungle Queen (IRE)**
*Eve Johnson Houghton* 64
2 ch f Leroidesanimaux(BRZ) Elusive Gold (IRE) (Elusive City (USA))
2037[6] 2502[6] 3689[3]
**Jungle Room (USA)** *Kevin Ryan* 61
2 b g Violence(USA) Raised Right (USA) (Giant's Causeway (USA))
4567[7]◆ 5202[4]
**Junoesque** *John Gallagher* a62 62
3 b f Virtual Snake Skin (Golden Snake (USA))
2931[6] 3507[6] 5031[7] 5545[3] 7485[4] 7902[12] 8538[3] 8841[2] 9138[2]

**Jupiter** *Henry Candy* a68 79
2 b g Finjaan Medicea Sidera (Medicean)
4367[4] 5144[2] **6005**[2] **6827**[3] *7536*[8]
**Jupiter Ascending** *Michael Appleby*
3 b g Excelebration(IRE) Habita (IRE) (Montjeu (IRE))
3207[8] 3627[14] 4276[7]
**Jupiter Light** *John Gosden* a84 101
3 b g Lonhro(AUS) Fantasia (Sadler's Wells (USA))
*(1366)* 2126[10] 2567[12] *3262*[7] (3787)◆ 4640[5] 7277[2] **(8165)**
**Jurisprudance (FR)** *M Boutin* 65
2 b f Panis(USA) L'Aventura (FR) (Librettist (USA))
1335a[3] 1496[6] 2321a[2] 2642a[3] **3444a**[3] 4196a[6] 8253a[4]
**Jurz (IRE)** *Roger Varian* 67
2 ch c Exceed And Excel(AUS) Bahja (USA) (Seeking The Gold (USA))
**6108**[3]
**Jus Pires (USA)** *Jeremy Noseda* a83 90
3 bb g Scat Daddy(USA) Liza Lu (USA) (Menifee (USA))
2798[7] 4444[2]◆ *(5794)* **(8111)**
**Just A Formality (FR)** *C Escuder* a87 98
3 bb c Spirit One(FR) Formalite (FR) (Equerry (USA))
**1114a**[4]
**Just An Idea (IRE)** *Harry Dunlop* a81 88
3 b c Lilbourne Lad(IRE) Emreliya (IRE) (Danehill Dancer (IRE))
*(140)* *2914*[4] 2130[8] **2823**[4] 4412[3] 5396[14] *8310*[11] *8879*[10]
**Justanotherbottle (IRE)**
*Declan Carroll* 99
3 ch g Intense Focus(USA) Duchess K (IRE) (Bachelor Duke (USA))
(1731) 2806[9] 3159[3] 3844[3] (4342) 4813[12] 5402[9] 6450[4] 7144[3] **8012**[3]
**Just Be Lucky (IRE)** *Conor Dore* a47 84
5 ch g Intense Focus(USA) Anda (Selkirk (USA))
2119[12]
**Just Brilliant (IRE)**
*Peter Chapple-Hyam* 78
2 b c Lope De Vega(IRE) Mauresmo (IRE) (Marju (IRE))
**(7813)**
**Juste Pour Nous** *David Pipe* a69 46
4 b g Pour Moi(IRE) Steam Cuisine (Mark Of Esteem (IRE))
***1028***[6]
**Just Fab (IRE)** *Lee Carter* a57 57
4 b m Canford Cliffs(IRE) Unlock (IRE) (Key Of Luck (USA))
*273*[9] *740*[10] *1084*[9] *1325*[7] *(3137)* *3688*[11] **5714**[3] *6621*[2] *7323*[5] *8152*[4] *8800*[7] *8994*[12]
**Just For Fun** *Richard Fahey* a64 57
2 b f Showcasing Lady Le Quesne (IRE) (Alhaarth (IRE))
3902[4]◆ 4503[5] 5262[4]◆ 6043[5] *(6634)* *6951*[9] 7814[14] ***8191***[2]
**Just For Show (IRE)** *Shaun Lycett* a58 50
4 b m Poet's Voice Starchy (Cadeaux Genereux)
***421***[9]
**Just For The Craic (IRE)**
*Neil Mulholland* a39 68
2 b g Most Improved(IRE) Beziers (IRE) (Fasliyev (USA))
1673[7] 1872[3] 2403[5] 3200[4] 4204[9] (4740) 6609[12] 7081[5] **(7695)** *8795*[8]
**Just Fred (IRE)** *Neil Mulholland* a54 48
4 br g Excellent Art Consignia (IRE) (Definite Article)
*121*[11] *334*[6] *1322*[8] ***1629***[5] 2914[13] ***3470***[5] 3805[8] 4734[4] 6306[4] *7761*[7] *8846*[11] *9077*[4] *9368*[5]
**Just Glamorous (IRE)**
*Ronald Harris* a71 114
4 ch g Arcano(IRE) Glamorous Air (IRE) (Air Express (IRE))
2397[15] 2657a[9] 3926[17] 5354[13] 7396[14] (7804)◆ **8139**[2] 8416[7]
**Just Heather (IRE)** *John Wainwright* a32 32
3 gr f Zebedee Miss Sundance (IRE) (Desert Sun)
***681***[6] *3261*[8] 3627[13] 5632[10] 6413[7] 7109[8] 7597[6] 8653[7] *9030*[6]
**Just Hiss** *Tim Easterby* 97
4 b g Lawman(FR) Feather Boa (IRE) (Sri Pekan (USA))
2136[7] 3498[6] 3790[8] **(4377)** **4916**[4] 5634[6] 5926[5] 6209[8] 7149[6] **7609**[3] 8009[5] 8469[7]
**Justice (IRE)** *Jose Santos* a44 42
4 b m Lawman(FR) Sheboygan (IRE) (Grand Lodge (USA))
***398***[9]
**Justice Frederick (IRE)** *Paul D'Arcy* a63 79
3 br g Lawman(FR) Sheer Spirit (IRE) (Caerleon (USA))
***1411***[8] 1685[8] 3700[10] *4447*[10] 4633[5] 5336[8] *6023*[7]
**Justice Good (IRE)** *David Elsworth* a106 100
5 b g Acclamation Qui Moi (CAN) (Swain (IRE))
***200***[2] *572*[6] *1501*[9] 2764[12] (Dead)
**Justice Lady (IRE)** *David Elsworth* a64 89
4 br m Dream Ahead(USA) Celestial Dream (IRE) (Oasis Dream)
2835[3] 3865[5] 4272[3] (4574)◆ 5355[4] 6072[4] **(6695)** 7809[12]
**Justice Pleasing** *Roger Fell* a65 61
4 b g Kodiac Spangle (Galileo (IRE))
*67*[6] *400*[8] *445*[2] *579*[2] ***969***[2] *(1106)* 5835[12] *9012*[7]
**Justice Rock** *Phil McEntee* a55 55
4 b g Acclamation Fashion Rocks (IRE) (Rock Of Gibraltar (IRE))
*64*[6] *143*[6] *438*[2] *601*[4] *622*[3] *981*[2] *1247*[5] *1305*[2] *1452*[4] *1557*[7] *2091*[7] *3468*[5] *(3728)* 4656a[3] **4710**[2] 6114[3] 6298[3] 7212[6] *7480*[3] *7605*[6] ***(7763)*** 7993[6] **8329**[4] *8495*[9] *9183*[8] *9420*[6]
**Justice Well** *Luciano Vitabile* a104 98
5 b g Halling(USA) Porthcawl (Singspiel (IRE))
**3120a**[5] [4]
**Just In Time** *Alan King* a83 85
3 b g Excelebration(IRE) Flying Finish (FR) (Priolo (USA))
5753[2] (6423) *(7063)*◆ **(7927)**◆ *8638*[7]
**Just Marion (IRE)** *Clare Ellam* a29 26
5 b m Bushranger(IRE) Dolphin Stamp (IRE) (Dolphin Street (FR))
*269* ***6141***[3] 3661[U] (Dead)
**Just Over** *Robert Cowell* a55
4 b m Bahamian Bounty Kassuta (Kyllachy)
***75***[8] *455*[8] *722*[10] *1305*[8]
**Just Right** *John Flint* a37
2 ch f Medicean Rightside (High Chaparral (IRE))
*9080*[10]
**Just Surprise Me (IRE)**
*Mohamed Moubarak* a41 72
4 b g Makfi Bayalika (IRE) (Selkirk (USA))
3438[9] **5158**[3] 5611[11] *6527*[9] *8811*[4]
**Just That Lord** *Bill Turner* a91 90
4 ch g Avonbridge Lady Filly (Atraf)
*1793*[3] **2083**[2] 2391[10]
**Just Us Two (IRE)** *Robert Cowell* a89 87
5 b g Royal Applause Sarah's First (Cadeaux Genereux)
*816*[5] ***(995)*** *1222*[3] *1465*[3] *1793*[6] 2391[7] 3183[6] 3834[7] (4795) 5811[5] 6430[6] 6891[6]
**Just You And Me (FR)** *Henk Grewe* 62
4 b g Mr. Sidney(USA) Mermaids Quay (IRE) (Key Of Luck (USA))
**(7430a)**
**Kaaba Stone (IRE)** *David Simcock* 73
2 b f Society Rock(IRE) Wattrey (Royal Academy (USA))
6559[6] **6806**[3]
**Kaaber (USA)** *Michael Blake* a62 56
6 b g Daaher(CAN) Taseel (USA) (Danzig (USA))
*514* *332*[9] 2709[3]◆ 3774[12] 4149[12] (6041)◆ 7191[10] 7900[9] ***(8258)*** *8980*[13]
**Kaatskill Nap (FR)** *Venetia Williams* 88
4 ch g Rip Van Winkle(IRE) Last Cast (FR) (Marju (IRE))
**5913**[9]
**Kabir (GER)** *A Wohler* 81
2 b c Lord Of England(GER) Karena (GER) (Midyan (USA))
6726a[9] **7592a**[3]
**Kabrit (IRE)** *Andrew Balding* 53
2 ch c Mastercraftsman(IRE) Twinkling Ice (USA) (Elusive Quality (USA))
**7128**[12]
**Kachess** *David Loughnane* a66 54
3 b f Kyllachy Fibou (USA) (Seeking The Gold (USA))
**1828**[3] 2503[7]◆ *3257*[5] 4081[5] *4728*[8] 5134[7] *8243*[8] *8742*[8] *8930*[12] *9203*[8] *9456*[7]
**Kachumba** *Rae Guest* a61
2 b f Mayson Native Nickel (IRE) (Be My Native (USA))
*8809*[7] ***9198***[3] *9465*[6]
**Kachy** *Tom Dascombe* 113
4 b h Kyllachy Dubai Bounty (Dubai Destination (USA))
2397[4]◆ 3079[5] 4071[10] **4615**[2] 5595[10] 7027[2]
**Kadrizzi (FR)** *Dean Ivory* a101 96
4 ch g Hurricane Cat(USA) Kadiania (FR) (Indian Rocket)
*818*[6] *999*[9] ***1769***[5] *2114*[2] 2606[24] 3034[6] 4411[11] 4905[12] *5241*[4] *9016*[10] *9210*[8]
**Kaeso** *Nigel Tinkler* 77
3 b g Excelebration(IRE) Bahia Breeze (Mister Baileys)
1513[11] (2181) (3184)◆ (3496)◆ **(5316)**◆ 6519[4]
**Kafeel (USA)** *Gary Moore* a67 59
6 b g First Samurai(USA) Ishraak (USA) (Sahm (USA))
*67*[8] *332*[4] 2255[4] *3263*[6] *8134*[2] *(8307)* ***(9456)***
**Kafeine La Grange (FR)**
*Caroline Auvray* 12
5 b m Shaanmer(IRE) Romance (FR) (Dounba (FR))
**6018a**[12]
**Kafoo** *Michael Appleby* a66 50
4 b g Dansili Nidhaal (IRE) (Observatory (USA))
*2163*[6] 3906[8] 4459[7] 5991[9] *6946*[10] 8181[6] *8401*[4] ***8659***[2] *9012*[5] *9432*[5]
**Kafuji Take (JPN)** *Sachio Yukubo* a110
5 bb h Precise End(USA) Take The Cake (JPN) (Scan (USA))
***1373a***[5]
**Kahlo (IRE)** *Jonathan Portman* 29
2 b f Mastercraftsman(IRE) Sky Boat (IRE) (Dansili)
**6861**[10] *7453*[13]
**Kahouanne (FR)** *G Botti* a92 85
5 ch g Cockney Rebel(IRE) Bramaputra (IRE) (Choisir (AUS))
**1159a**[7] *6226a*[9]
**Kahrab (IRE)** *R Bouresly* a67 70
3 gr c Dark Angel(IRE) Dance Club (IRE) (Fasliyev (USA))
***430a***[8]
**Kaisan** *Bernard Llewellyn* a56 64
4 b g Rip Van Winkle(IRE) Orinoco (IRE) (Darshaan)
3574[6] **4966**[5] 5566[4] 6095[5] 6821[5] *7831*[10] *8135*[7] *8430*[2] *(8815)* *9095*[2] *9221*[4]
**Kai Tak And Back** *William Muir* a64 44
3 b g Exceed And Excel(AUS) Beldarian (IRE) (Last Tycoon)
6548[4] ***6851***[4] 7462[6]
**Kajaki (IRE)** *Kevin Ryan* a69 89
4 gr g Mastercraftsman(IRE) No Quest (IRE) (Rainbow Quest (USA))
(1716) 2770[8] 4336[2] 4898[2] 5403[2] 6427[2] **(7143)** 7599[5]
**Kalagia (IRE)** *Mark Johnston* 72
2 b f Kodiac Esuvia (IRE) (Whipper (USA))
3980[3] **(4427)** 5453[2] 6330[9]
**Kalakchee** *Amy Murphy* a51
2 b c Kyllachy Maysarah (IRE) (Green Desert (USA))
*5847*[5] *6286*[6] *7001*[6] *7996*[5] ***8306***[5]
**Kalamkan (USA)** *T G McCourt* a45 52
4 b g Kitten's Joy(USA) Kaloura (IRE) (Sinndar (IRE))
***8876***[8]
**Kalani Rose** *Ben De Haan* 52
3 b f Sixties Icon Dance To The Blues (IRE) (Danehill Dancer (IRE))
2908[9] **3309**[4] 4444[7] 6283[8]
**Kalann (IRE)** *Denis Gerard Hogan* a80 64
10 b g Barathea(IRE) Karkiyla (IRE) (Darshaan)
***7766***[11]
**Kalibur (GER)** *Mlle Y Vollmer* a57 50
5 ch g Astronomer Royal(USA) Kigoma (IRE) (Daylami (IRE))
**7430a**[5]
**Kalimantan (IRE)** *Tim Vaughan* a40 51
7 b g Azamour(IRE) Kalamba (IRE) (Green Dancer (USA))
**2972**[7] 4756[11] 7233[6]
**Kalk Bay (IRE)** *Michael Easterby* a87 91
10 b g Hawk Wing(USA) Politesse (USA) (Barathea (IRE))
1512[21] *1778*[3] **2184**[2]◆
**Kallikrates (FR)** *Y Barberot* a57 56
2 b f Planteur(IRE) Rebecca's Filly (FR) (Elusive City (USA))
**8252a**[7]
**Kamili (IRE)** *Joseph Patrick O'Brien* 83
3 b f Invincible Spirit(IRE) Shreyas (IRE) (Dalakhani (IRE))
6080a[13] **6490a**[13]
**Kamra (USA)** *Michael Herrington* a82 81
3 b g Stay Thirsty(USA) Milliondollarbill (USA) (Speightstown (USA))
*458*[2] *1124*[6] 2122[7] 3152[4] 4104[3] *4500*[6] 4892[4] ***5481***[2] 5869[7] 6679[3]
**Kanade (IRE)** *Emmet Mullins* a28 44
4 b m Poet's Voice Ra Hydee (USA) (Rahy (USA))
***1112***[5]
**Kanaf (IRE)** *M Al Mheiri* a94 102
10 b g Elnadim(USA) Catcher Applause (Royal Applause)
87a[11] **205a**[10]
**Kandy Kove (IRE)** *Robert Cowell* 62
2 b f Kodiac Kondakova (IRE) (Soviet Star (USA))
**4628**[6] 5575[7]
**Kanji (GER)** *Waldemar Hickst*
3 ch f Linngari(IRE) Key To Win (FR) (Halling (USA))
8088a[11]
**Kannapolis (IRE)** *Michael Easterby* 61
2 b g Makfi Alta Definizione (IRE) (Hawk Wing (USA))
**3399**[2]◆ **6403**[13] 7890[6]
**Kant Excell (FR)** *N Caullery* a58 60
5 bb g Excellent Art Eva Kant (Medicean)
***822a***[9]
**Kapstadt (FR)** *Ian Williams* a83 99
7 bb g Country Reel(USA) King's Parody (IRE) (King's Best (USA))
*798a*[2] 2558[2] 3065[2] **(3597)** 4614[7] 5913[6]
**Karaganda (IRE)** *D K Weld* 34
3 b f Cape Cross(IRE) Karawana (IRE) (King's Best (USA))
**1389a**[9]
**Karam Albaari (IRE)** *J R Jenkins* a74 64
9 b h King's Best(USA) Lilakiya (IRE) (Dr Fong (USA))
***(39)*** *154*[8] *619*[7] *1028*[5] *1364*[9] *2336*[4] *2971*[5] *3547*[7] *4217*[11] *5261*[8] *6069*[13] *8846*[6]◆ *9092*[4]
**Karapiro Boy** *Roger Fell*
3 b g Arabian Gleam Littlemiss (Cosmonaut)
3286[6]
**Karar** *F-H Graffard* 117
5 b g Invincible Spirit(IRE) In The Light (Inchinor)
2248a[8] 3354a[3] (6729a) 7671a[3] **8608a**[7] 9170a[13]
**Karawaan (IRE)** *Sir Michael Stoute* a85 83
3 b g Sea The Stars(IRE) Magic Sister (Cadeaux Genereux)
1963[2] 2576[3] ***(5746)*** 6474[6]
**Kareva** *Charles Hills* a61 78
2 b f Oasis Dream Kilasiki (IRE) (Pivotal)
4312[2] **4806**[3]◆ 5356[3] 6417[4] *7725*[7]
**Karijini (GER)** *Archie Watson* a76
3 b f Siyouni(FR) Kalahari Dancer (Dalakhani (IRE))
*2463*[3] *3188*[6] ***(9139)***◆
**Karisma (IRE)** *Roger Varian* a83 80
4 gr m Lawman(FR) Lucky Clio (IRE) (Key Of Luck (USA))
***1897***[2] *2138*[4] *3455*[2]
**Kasalla (GER)** *Markus Klug* 108
4 b m Soldier Hollow Kastila (GER) (Sternkoenig (IRE))
**2450a**[3] 7429a[6]
**Kasaqui (ARG)** *Ignacio Correas IV* a82 113
6 rg h Lasting Approval(USA) Kemosheba (USA) (Alysheba (USA))
**5977a**[9]
**Kasbaan** *Owen Burrows* 70
2 br c Dansili Aghareed (USA) (Kingmambo (USA))
**8389**[4]◆
**Kasbah (IRE)** *Amanda Perrett* a104 94
5 b g Acclamation Dance Hall Girl (IRE) (Dansili)
*234*[2] *(326)* ***818***[2] *1025*[4] *1501*[4] 2391[5] 3034[13] 4581[2] 5505[15] 6695[5] *8639*[8] *8911*[11] *9187*[6] *9453*[2]
**Kaser (IRE)** *Saeed bin Suroor* a78
2 b c Invincible Spirit(IRE) Lethal Quality (USA) (Elusive Quality (USA))
***9155***[2]
**Kashani (IRE)** *Frau C Barsig* a42 18
4 ch g Manduro(GER) Kastania (USA) (Gone West (USA))
*515a*[7] ***691a***[10]
**Kashgar** *Bernard Llewellyn* a69 71
8 b g Hernando(FR) Miss Katmandu (IRE) (Rainbow Quest (USA))
**(2364)** 3775[4]
**Kashmar (GER)** *Werner Glanz* 101
4 ch m Samum(GER) Kapitol (GER) (Winged Love (IRE))
2450a[6] **8090a**[6]
**Kashmiri Sunset** *Iain Jardine* 82
6 b g Tiger Hill(IRE) Sagamartha (Rainbow Quest (USA))
(5208) 5873[4] **6317**[2]◆ 6968[11]
**Kashtan** *J S Moore* a80 74
4 ch m Sakhee's Secret Gitane (FR) (Grand Lodge (USA))
***808***[8] *879*[4] *1078a*[7]
**Kasperenko** *David Lanigan* a100 98
3 b g Archipenko(USA) Jardin (Sinndar (IRE))
*2092*[2] *(2521)* 4035[2] (4796) 5915[6] *6887*[8] ***8244***[3]
**Kaspersky (IRE)**
*Jane Chapple-Hyam* 114
6 b h Footstepsinthesand Croanda (IRE) (Grand Lodge (USA))
2290[5] 3218[2] 3924[5] **4884**[2] 6193[7] **6928**[2] 8059a[16]
**Kassandra (IRE)** *Amy Murphy* a67 51
3 b f Dandy Man(IRE) Gala Style (IRE) (Elnadim (USA))
*1179*[3] ***1333***[4] 1686[10] 6101[12]
**Kassar (IRE)** *Roger Charlton* a77
2 b g Exceed And Excel(AUS) Inchiri (Sadler's Wells (USA))
***(7726)*** *8877*[6]
**Kassia (IRE)** *Mick Channon* 106
4 b m Acclamation Speedy Sonata (USA) (Stravinsky (USA))
1903[4] 4071[17] 6428[5] **6864**[2] 7811[5]
**Kassiani (IRE)** *X Thomas-Demeaulte* a21
3 b f Bated Breath Keisha (FR) (Green Tune (USA))
***2536a***[12]
**Kastano (GER)** *Markus Klug* 99
3 b c Nathaniel(IRE) Kastila (GER) (Sternkoenig (IRE))
**2246a**[3] **3115a**[3] **4422a**[8]
**Kastini** *Mme J Hendriks* a41 53
7 b g Halling(USA) Toucantini (Inchinor)
***7534a***[5]
**Katabatika** *Hughie Morrison* a64 60
3 b f Shirocco(GER) Landinium (ITY) (Lando (GER))
*4565*[6] 5250[5] 6032[3] 6812[4] *(7879)*◆ *8135*[5] ***8993***[3] *9391*[7]
**Katalan (GER)** *John Butler* a46
4 b g Adlerflug(GER) Kalla (Monsun (GER))
*279*[RR] *733*[4] ***893***[4] *9158*[13]
**Katebird (IRE)** *Mark Johnston* a41 79
3 gr f Dark Angel(IRE) She Basic (IRE) (Desert Prince (IRE))
2347[6] 2702[6] *3178*[8] 3981[3] (4171) 4761[8] 5212[3] 5579[4] **(6208)** 6416[4] 6692[5] **7598**[2] 7824[11] 8142[6]
**Katheefa (USA)** *Charles Hills* a59 73
3 gr g Street Cry(IRE) Wid (USA) (Elusive Quality (USA))
*1889*[8] 4793[4] 6184[4] **(6808)** 7398[9]
**Katherine Place** *Sylvester Kirk* 35
2 b f Showcasing Folly Drove (Bahri (USA))
**2502**[11]◆
**Kath's Boy (IRE)** *Tony Carroll* a46 59
3 b g Bushranger(IRE) Elayoon (USA) (Danzig (USA))
*3260*[8] 3624[8] ***4211***[4] 4969[5] 6004[4] 6341[8] 7693[10]
**Kath's Legacy** *Richard Hughes* a76 76
4 ch m Cockney Rebel(IRE) It's Dubai Dolly (Dubai Destination (USA))
***2028***[3] 5217[4] 5549[5] **6722**[3] *7762*[7] 8390[P] *8893*[8] *9325*[5]
**Kath's Legend** *Ben De Haan* a58 46
3 b f Dick Turpin(IRE) It's Dubai Dolly (Dubai Destination (USA))
6283[7] *7492*[9] **8300**[11]
**Kath's Lustre** *Richard Hughes* a65 49
2 b f Dick Turpin(IRE) It's Dubai Dolly (Dubai Destination (USA))
6272[7] ***9465***[2]
**Kathy** *Scott Dixon* 23
2 b f Bated Breath Lolita Lebron (IRE) (Royal Applause)
3066[9] **4335**[8] 5161[5]
**Kathy Dream (IRE)** *Luigi Biagetti* 107
5 ch m Arcano(IRE) Katy Guest (IRE) (Be My Guest (USA))
**2867a**[7]
**Katie Canford** *Mark Hoad* a45 34
4 b m Canford Cliffs(IRE) Serafina's Flight (Fantastic Light (USA))
5823[P] ***7480***[11]
**Katie Gale** *Michael Appleby* a78 76
7 b m Shirocco(GER) Karla June (Unfuwain (USA))
***666***[3] ***1073***[2] *1223*[5] *9028*[5] *9242*[11] *9442*[6]
**Katie Lee (IRE)** *Henry Candy* a64 64
2 b f Camacho Katherine Lee (IRE) (Azamour (IRE))
5779[3]◆ 6826[6] **8472**[4]◆ ***9320***[6]
**Katiymann (IRE)** *M Halford* a95 93
5 b g Shamardal(USA) Katiyra (IRE) (Peintre Celebre (USA))
5688a[9] 6491a[5] ***(8222a)***
**Katmandoo (USA)** *Tom Dascombe* 63
3 b c Kitten's Joy(USA) Granny Franny (USA) (Grand Slam (USA))
**1967**[5] 2527[8] 3180[8]
**Katrine (IRE)** *David O'Meara* a55 73
3 b f Kodiac Falcolnry (IRE) (Hawk Wing (USA))
1786[6] **3331**[7] 4188[7]
**Kauttio (IRE)** *A Wohler* a86 88
3 b c Excelebration(IRE) Pinacotheque (IRE) (In The Wings)
**2002a**[8]
**Kavora** *George Baker* a59
2 b f Havana Gold(IRE) Anadiya (FR) (Bahri (USA))
***7453***[5]
**Kawasir (USA)** *Roger Varian* a74
2 ch c Speightstown(USA) Bashful Bertie (USA) (Quiet American (USA))
***7946***[3]◆
**Kay Kay Boy (IRE)** *G E Mikhalides* 100
4 b h Kodiac Namibia (GER) (Galileo (IRE))
**5979a**[10]
**Kaylen's Mischief** *Philip Kirby* a26 59
4 ch g Doyen(IRE) Pusey Street Girl (Gildoran)
***6522***[4] *6904*[8] *7365*[8] 7980[14]
**Kay Sera** *Tony Newcombe* a64 52
9 b g Kayf Tara Inflation (Primo Dominie)
*333*[5] ***(762)*** *1256*[6] *2722*[6] *4733*[7] *9070*[7] *9346*[9]

**Kazanan (IRE)** *Michael Dods* a51 44
3 b f Tamayuz Bosphorus Queen (IRE) (Sri Pekan (USA))
1034[2] 1348[8] 2349[7] 2902[9]

**Kazaroza (FR)** *V Luka Jr* a54 58
3 b f Redoute's Choice(AUS) Katyusha (USA) (Kingmambo (USA))
7471a[8]

**Kazawi** *Roger Charlton* 81
3 ch g Dubawi(IRE) Kazeem (Darshaan)
1963[8] 2963[4] 3427[2] 5141[3]

**Kazeera** *Roger Charlton* 36
2 ch f Dubawi(IRE) Kazeem (Darshaan)
6385[9]

**Kazimiera** *Charlie Appleby* 91
3 b f Dubawi(IRE) Kailani (Monsun (GER))
1883[8] 2436[6]

**Kazoey** *Chris Fairhurst* a30 43
4 b m Stimulation(IRE) Dubawi's Spirit (IRE) (Dubawi (IRE))
2162[7] 3340[11] 9368[13]

**Keef D'Ouilly (FR)** *F Lenglart* a27 3
3 b g Maiguri(IRE) Eubea (FR) (Anabaa (USA))
6256a[11]

**Keem Bay** *Michael Mullineaux*
3 b f Multiplex Copsehill Girl (IRE) (Carroll House (IRE))
6852[5]

**Keene's Pointe** *Steph Hollinshead* a65 67
7 br g Avonbridge Belle's Edge (Danehill Dancer (IRE))
222[4] 332[3]◆ 724[6] 1285[4] 1325[9] 2589[9] 2961[7] 5285[11] 5482[8] 6546[9] 7693[4] 7934[13]

**Keen Ice (USA)** *Todd Pletcher* a116
5 b h Curlin(USA) Medomak (USA) (Awesome Again (CAN))
469a[4] 1380a[7]

**Keeper's Choice (IRE)**
*Denis Coakley* 76
3 ch f Intikhab(USA) Crossing (Cape Cross (IRE))
4152[5] 4737[2]◆ (5712) 6657[6] 7816[10]

**Keep It Dark** *William Knight* a60 71
8 b g Invincible Spirit(IRE) Tarneem (USA) (Zilzal (USA))
3008[9] 4011[7]

**Keepup Kevin** *Pam Sly* a70 75
3 b g Haafhd Black Salix (USA) (More Than Ready (USA))
(2793) 3412[6] 4050[5] 4999[3] 5961[3] 7894[5]

**Keiba (IRE)** *Murty McGrath* a69 53
4 gr g Dark Angel(IRE) True Magic (Magic Ring (IRE))
481[10]

**Kelpie Spirit (IRE)** *John Weymes* a38 46
3 b g Born To Sea(IRE) Lady Of Kildare (IRE) (Mujadil (USA))
1676[5] 2159[8] 2455[6] 3831[2] 3913[8] 5074[6] 5374[11] 6902[10]

**Kencharova (FR)** *F Vermeulen* 52
5 b m Kendargent(FR) Kirona (Robellino (USA))
7342a[7]

**Ken Colt (IRE)** *F Chappet* 98
2 b g Kendargent(FR) Velvet Revolver (IRE) (Mujahid (USA))
(4595a) 6051a[3]

**Kencumin (FR)** *Ralph Beckett* a79
3 ch c Kendargent(FR) Cumin (USA) (Fusaichi Pegasus (USA))
127[3] (662)◆

**Kendemai (FR)** *J-C Rouget* 75
6 gr g Carlotamix(FR) Kendorya (FR) (Kendor (FR))
8127a[4]

**Kendergarten Kop (IRE)**
*Tom Dascombe* a62 15
2 ch g Kendargent(FR) Elsa T (IRE) (Duke Of Marmalade (IRE))
7105[6] 7562[5] 7827[2]

**Kenmare River** *Jedd O'Keeffe* 33
2 gr g Kendargent(FR) Isabella Glyn (IRE) (Sadler's Wells (USA))
7221[7] 7819[10]

**Kenny George** *Mick Channon* 16
2 b g Mawatheeq(USA) One For Philip (Blushing Flame (USA))
8387[15]

**Kenny The Captain (IRE)**
*Tim Easterby* a93 86
6 ch g Captain Rio Kelso Magic (USA) (Distant View (USA))
1515[22] 1831[12] 2381[14] 2840[8] 3463[9] 3847[6] 4250[4] 4683[2] 4897[3] 5696[4] 5947[7] (6943) 7086[2] 7554[4] 8014[13] 8319[2] 9016[5]

**Ken Party (FR)** *B Delariviere* a58 56
3 b g Kendargent(FR) Summer Exhibition (Royal Academy (USA))
6256a[7]

**Kensai (FR)** *Simone Brogi* a74 102
3 gr c Jukebox Jury(IRE) Olive Danon (IRE) (Dylan Thomas (IRE))
1658a[4] 2868a[10]

**Kenshow (FR)** *P Sogorb* a72 81
2 ch f Kendargent(FR) Show Gorb (SPA) (Caradak (IRE))
5679a[9] 6229a[8]

**Kensington Palace (IRE)**
*Marjorie Fife* a51 59
4 b g Kodiac Anthyllis (IRE) (Night Shift (USA))
1818[4] 2135[9] 2819[5] 3185[2] 3704[4]◆ 3912[4] 4900[11] 5991[8] 7240[11] 8247[8] 8980[10] 9073[7]

**Kensington Star** *Keith Dalgleish* a91 91
4 b g Pivotal Wild Silk (Dansili)
(1676) 2426[2]◆ 2774[2] (3527)◆ 3830[2] 4355[4] 5164[6] 5882[5] 6383[7] 8384[3]

**Ken's Sam's (IRE)**
*Adrian Brendan Joyce* a56 60
4 b m Intense Focus(USA) Hannah's Smile (IRE) (Cape Cross (IRE))
732[7]

**Kenstone (FR)** *Adrian Wintle* a82 93
4 gr g Kendargent(FR) Little Stone (FR) (One Cool Cat (USA))
145[2] 641[2] (986) 1324[3] 2116[3] (3402) 4563[3] 5699[2] (6414) 7140[7] 8032[11] 8706[8]

**Kentish Waltz (IRE)** *E J O'Neill* 84
2 ch f Dandy Man(IRE) Imelda Mayhem (Byron) (1919a) 2801[7] 5090a[6] 7846a[11]

**Kentucky Blueblood (USA)**
*Richard Guest* a23 46
2 ch f Awesome Again(CAN) All Due Respect (USA) (Value Plus (USA))
3210 [8] 5507[6]

**Kentuckyconnection (USA)**
*Bryan Smart* a97 93
4 b g Include(USA) Youcanringmybell (USA) (Street Cry (IRE))
1974[5] 2735[19] 4077[5] 4261[2]◆ 6449[15] 7727[9] 9125[12]

**Kenya (IRE)** *A P O'Brien* 107
2 b c Galileo(IRE) Tender Morn (USA) (Dayjur (USA))
(8265a)

**Kenyan (FR)** *Seamus Durack* a45 25
3 b g Kendargent(FR) Landora (FR) (Lando (GER))
3326[5]

**Kerre (IRE)** *William Jarvis* a27
3 b f Pour Moi(IRE) Double Green (IRE) (Green Tune (USA))
7989[6]

**Kerrera** *Paul Webber* a71 70
4 ch m Champs Elysees Questa Nova (Rainbow Quest (USA))
2615[5]◆ (5607) 6578[3] 7319[8]

**Kerry Icon** *Iain Jardine* a50 52
4 b m Sixties Icon La Gifted (Fraam)
424[5] 608[2] 1101[2] (1679) 2378[3] 2687[5] 3343[5] 4900[9] 5254[2] 5831[4] 6523[3] 7936[13] 8249[5]

**Kerrymerry (IRE)**
*Dr Richard Newland* a73 73
5 b g Vale Of York(IRE) Reasonably Devout (CAN) (St Jovite (USA))
2111[3]◆ 2966[2]

**Kestrel Call (IRE)** *Michael Appleby* a50 80
4 b g Acclamation Winged Harriet (IRE) (Hawk Wing (USA))
1431[7] 1833[16] 3202[5] 3667[13] 4464[4]

**Kestrel Dot Com** *Chris Dwyer* a84 91
5 br g Oasis Dream Tanfidh (Marju (IRE))
1288[4]◆ 1598[6] 2317[4] (2730) 3212[7] (3750)

**Keswick** *John Gosden* a76
3 b c Dansili Marywell (Selkirk (USA))
65[3] (328)

**Kevlar** *Jonathan Portman* a27
2 b g Helmet(AUS) Madhaaq (IRE) (Medicean)
9200[13]

**Kew Gardens (IRE)** *A P O'Brien* 106
2 b c Galileo(IRE) Chelsea Rose (IRE) (Desert King (IRE))
6955a[2] 7426a[4] (8035)

**Key Bid** *Charlie Appleby* 92
3 ch g Dubawi(IRE) Silca Chiave (Pivotal)
1682[8] 2408[2] (2841) 5630[3] 6107[5] (6415) 7110[3] 8384[7]

**Key Master (IRE)** *R Biondi*
2 b f Mastercraftsman(IRE) Maggie Lou (IRE) (Red Ransom (USA))
8094a[5]

**Keynote (IRE)** *David C Griffiths* a23
2 b g Dragon Pulse(IRE) Taalluf (USA) (Hansel (USA))
4151[14] 9372[9]

**Key Player** *Eve Johnson Houghton* a75 62
2 ch g Kheleyf(USA) My Pretty Girl (Arakan (USA))
7765[2] 8180[5] 8877[2] 9050[6]

**Keyser Soze (IRE)** *Richard Spencer* a92 85
3 ch g Arcano(IRE) Causeway Queen (IRE) (Giant's Causeway (USA))
(1977) (3211) 3997[26]

**Keystroke** *Jeremy Noseda* a109 97
5 b h Pivotal Fondled (Selkirk (USA))
(459)◆ 1150[2] 1773[6] 8891[2]

**Key To My Heart (IRE)** *A P O'Brien* a83 101
3 b f Galileo(IRE) A Z Warrior (USA) (Bernardini (USA))
2637a[5] 3874a[7] 4650a[11] 5766a[5] 6490a[4] 7171a[4]

**Key Victory (IRE)** *Charlie Appleby* 91
2 b c Teofilo(IRE) Patroness (Dubawi (IRE))
(8350)

**K'Gari Spirit** *Jeremy Gask* a73 52
4 b m Major Cadeaux Ivory Silk (Diktat)
(64) 518[5] (1062) 1290[7] 1599[8] 1981[4] 2335[2] 3177[6] 4795[6]

**Khafoo Shememi (IRE)**
*Richard Hannon* a109 111
3 b c Dark Angel(IRE) Appleblossom Pearl (IRE) (Peintre Celebre (USA))
(1797)◆ 2565[5] (3013) 3843[9] (7275) 8891[4]

**Khairaat (IRE)** *Sir Michael Stoute* 110
4 b g Shamardal(USA) Mumayeza (Indian Ridge (IRE))
(2552)◆ 4069[13] 5500[3]◆ 6449[17]

**Khala (POL)** *Frau Marion Rotering*
5 b m Rhodesian Winner(GER) Koronea (POL) (Don Corleone)
1196a[3]

**Khaleefa Bay** *Martin Smith*
3 br f Kheleyf(USA) Langland Bay (Diktat)
681[7] (Dead)

**Khalidi** *John Gosden* 113
3 br c High Chaparral(IRE) Bezique (Cape Cross (IRE))
1518[3] (1861) 2401[3] (3032) 3322[14] 4029[2] 5639[2]

**Khamaary (IRE)** *Mark Johnston* a71 105
3 br f Tamayuz Nufoos (Zafonic (USA))
(2900) 3828[2] 4270[5] (5294) 5942[6] 6676[4]◆ (7823)◆ 8546[12]

**Khamry** *Owen Burrows* a77
4 b g Poet's Voice Poppets Sweetlove (Foxhound (USA))
8554[3]◆

**Khan (GER)** *Henk Grewe* 113
3 b c Santiago(GER) Kapitol (GER) (Winged Love (IRE))
3636a[8] 4422a[12] 7203a[3] 8527a[5]

**Kharbetation (IRE)** *David O'Meara* a60 95
4 b g Dream Ahead(USA) Anna's Rock (IRE) (Rock Of Gibraltar (IRE))
5382[6] 5744[13] 6520[10] 7328[3]◆ 7649[5] 8048[16]

**Khartoum (AUS)** *Pat Carey* 89
3 ch g Helenus(AUS) Katsumi (AUS) (Galileo (IRE))
8633a[5] 8857a[7]

**Khataaf (IRE)** *Roger Varian* 74
3 b g Shamardal(USA) Sana Abel (IRE) (Alhaarth (IRE))
3438[7] 3755[7]

**Khazaf** *Marcus Tregoning* 75
2 b c Dawn Approach(IRE) Winds Of Time (IRE) (Danehill (USA))
7355[6]

**Kheleyf's Girl** *David Evans* a62 59
2 br f Kheleyf(USA) Handsome Molly (Halling (USA))
1588[2]◆ 1776[7] 3187[4] 4836[5] 5886[4] 7196[2] 8658[11] 8983[2] 9300[6]

**Khelman (IRE)** *Richard Fahey* 89
7 b g Kheleyf(USA) Mandolin (IRE) (Sabrehill (USA))
1512[9] 2428[7] (2821) 3581[8] 4294[7] 5093[4] (5471) 7086[8] 7553[8] 8014[17] 8488[7] 8736[18]

**Kheskianto (IRE)** *Michael Chapman* 21
11 b m Kheleyf(USA) Gently (IRE) (Darshaan)
7478[12]

**Khitaamy (IRE)** *Ed Dunlop* a66 74
3 b g Approve(IRE) Halliwell House (Selkirk (USA))
2266[3] 3456[4] 3970[5] (5019)

**Khochenko (FR)** *Mme Pia Brandt* 65
2 ch g Pastoral Pursuits Flam (Singspiel (IRE))
5776a[8]

**Khudha (IRE)** *J P Murtagh* a63 80
3 b g Helmet(AUS) Seeking Dubai (Dubawi (IRE))
1389a[12]

**Khukri (IRE)** *Mrs John Harrington* 108
3 b g Sepoy(AUS) Fraulein (Acatenango (GER))
2863a[5] 5974a[10] 7424a[7]

**Khusoosy (USA)** *A R Al Rayhi* a97 98
5 b g Hard Spun(USA) Elmaleeha (Galileo (IRE))
428a[8] 542a[8] 776a[9] 9360a[12]

**Kibaar** *Ruth Carr* 93
5 b g Pastoral Pursuits Ashes (IRE) (General Monash (USA))
1876[13] 2409[8] 4337[11] 4850[5] 5379[15] 6062[10] 7522[13] 7825[12]

**Kick And Rush (GER)** *Mario Hofer* a90 93
3 b c Tertullian(USA) Kittiwake (Barathea (IRE))
799a[6] 6255a[5] 6987a[4]

**Kickass D'Aumone (FR)** *S Jesus* a87 71
2 gr c Redback Salut Simone (FR) (Simon Du Desert (FR))
3445a[9]

**Kickboxer (IRE)** *Michael Appleby* a93 64
6 gr g Clodovil(IRE) Ajig Dancer (Niniski (USA))
(2839)◆ 7611[16] 8044[20] 8238[12] 8383[21] 8812[7] 9125[8] 9366[2]◆

**Kicking The Can (IRE)** *Noel Wilson* a46 63
6 gr g Aussie Rules(USA) Silk Meadow (IRE) (Barathea (IRE))
42[5] 444[2] 841[3] 1312[11] (4059) 6893[7] 7541[11] 8205[13]

**Kick On Kick On** *Clive Cox* 89
2 b c Swiss Spirit Catmint (Piccolo)
(1604)◆ 3002[6] 6070[2] (7954)

**Kidd Malibu (USA)** *Maria Ritchie* a71 61
4 ch g Malibu Moon(USA) Kiddari (USA) (Smarty Jones (USA))
8583a[6]

**Kidmenever (IRE)** *Charlie Appleby* a86 109
4 b h Baltic King Pepys Tillergirl (IRE) (Tillerman)
699a[4] 888a[2] 4069[3] 4584[2] 8056a[8] 8857a[2]

**Ki Ki** *Bryan Smart* a68 69
5 ch m Kheleyf(USA) Peryllys (Warning)
583[4] (1030) 1203[5] 4605[6] (5375) 6546[12] 7332[10]

**Kikini Bamalaam (IRE)**
*Keith Dalgleish* a62 63
2 b f Society Rock(IRE) Crimson Sunrise (IRE) (Holy Roman Emperor (IRE))
1872[11] 2154[5] 2988[7] 4740[2] 5603[6] (5878) (6626) 6940[4] 8848[8] 8983[5]

**Kil Al Jamal (FR)** *J Albrecht* a64 37
4 b m Youmzain(IRE) Song Of Time (IRE) (Kheleyf (USA))
6365a[10]

**Kilbaha Lady (IRE)** *Nigel Tinkler* a67 68
3 b f Elnadim(USA) Sidney Girl (Azamour (IRE))
2228[10] 3561[6] 4058[3] 4721[3] 5001[9] 5666[4] 6664[4] (7240) 7792[9] (8125)

**Kilim** *John Berry* a59 64
4 b m Dansili Kibara (Sadler's Wells (USA))
461[6] 645[11] 924[4] 1256[5] 4040[6] 4971[6] 5362[8] (6280) 7215[2] 7918[2]

**Killay** *Eve Johnson Houghton* 85
3 b f Aqlaam Avessia (Averti (IRE))
4911[2] 5431[2] (6103) 7398[3] 8113[3]

**Killermont Street (IRE)**
*Mark Johnston* a71
3 b f Dream Ahead(USA) Leopard Creek (Weldnaas (USA))
178[4] 434[3] (659) 788[2] 846[3] 1243[4] 1434[5]

**Killing Joke (FR)** *M Boutin* a66 67
3 bl c Sageburg(IRE) Zanyeva (IRE) (Oasis Dream)
838a[3] 8305a[7]

**Kilmah** *Mark Johnston* 104
3 b f Sepoy(AUS) Perfect Star (Act One)
1883[6] 2434[11] 3319[9] 3964[11]

**Kilowatt** *Tim Easterby* 89
3 ch g Power Bogside Theatre (IRE) (Fruits Of Love (USA))
1497[8] 2159[2] 2842[2] 3465[2] (4016) 4691[2]

**Kimberella** *Richard Fahey* a114 114
7 b g Kyllachy Gleam Of Light (IRE) (Danehill (USA))
(1362) (1772) 2397[7] 3321[10] 3829[3] 4354[3] 4940a[15] (5684) 5974a[8] 6668[4] 6926[8] 9409[7]

**Kimene** *William Stone* a60
3 b f Aqlaam Aditi (Dansili)
2260[10] 2834[8] 4003[4] 4981[8]

**Kimifive (IRE)** *Joseph Tuite* 77
2 ch c Born To Sea(IRE) Appletreemagic (IRE) (Indian Danehill (IRE))
3690[4] 4220[4] 5048[2] 5685[2] 7647[4] 8073[3] 8741[4]

**Kinaesthesia** *Ralph Beckett* 72
2 b f Sea The Stars(IRE) Kinetica (Stormy Atlantic (USA))
(8678)

**Kind Act (USA)** *Charlie Appleby* a80 80
2 b g Distorted Humor(USA) Kind Words (USA) (A.P. Indy (USA))
6142[5] 6616[2] (7411) 8595[3]

**Kind Of Beauty (IRE)** *Hugo Palmer* 77
3 ch f Helmet(AUS) Extreme Beauty (USA) (Rahy (USA))
3693[5] 5217[5] 5667[9]

**Kinema (IRE)** *Chris Waller* a67 109
6 b g Galileo(IRE) Bon Nuit (IRE) (Night Shift (USA))
1994a[9]

**King And Empire (IRE)**
*Andrew Balding* a78
2 b c Intello(GER) Fraloga (IRE) (Grand Lodge (USA))
(8339)◆

**King Athelstan (IRE)** *John Best* a60 56
2 b g Mayson Ashtaroute (USA) (Holy Bull (USA))
6510[6] 7093[8] 7707[8]

**King Bolete (IRE)** *Roger Varian* 107
5 b g Cape Cross(IRE) Chanterelle (FR) (Trempolino (USA))
1042a[9] 3154[7] (4370) 5353[3] 6440[3] 7150[4]

**King Calypso** *Denis Coakley* a87 70
6 ch g Sir Percy Rosa De Mi Corazon (USA) (Cozzene (USA))
2021[2] (3213) 4499[2] 5799[5] 6793[3] 7412[5] 8505[6]

**King Christophe (IRE)**
*Miss Nicole McKenna* a64 73
5 b g Duke Of Marmalade(IRE) Mini Brush (USA) (Broad Brush (USA))
(1014a)

**King Crimson** *John Butler* a86 89
5 ch g Captain Gerrard(IRE) Elegant Lady (Selkirk (USA))
416[10] 886[10] 1071[9] 1819[7]

**King David (FR)** *M Boutin* a67 71
9 b g Iffraaj Azucar (IRE) (Desert Prince (IRE))
4955a[3] 5176a[8]

**Kingdomforakitten (USA)**
*David Lanigan* a53
3 b c Kitten's Joy(USA) Mayakoba (USA) (War Chant (USA))
5746[8]

**Kingfast (IRE)** *David Dennis* 56
2 b g Fast Company(IRE) Monarchy (IRE) (Common Grounds)
3908[5] 5964[5] 8112[9]

**Kingfisher (IRE)** *A P O'Brien* 103
6 b h Galileo(IRE) Mystical Lady (IRE) (Halling (USA))
1374a[14]

**Kingfisher Girl** *Michael Appleby* a39 46
4 gr m Hellvelyn Caribbean Star (Soviet Star (USA))
309[6] 2633[18] 3702[5] 4323[3] 5285[12] 7605[9] 8185[8]

**King Julien (IRE)** *John Ryan* a43 51
4 b g Canford Cliffs(IRE) Western Sky (Barathea (IRE))
425[12] 1402[3] 1458[4] 1585[4] 1834[11] 2162[4]

**King Kevin** *Ed Dunlop* a75 50
3 b g Holy Roman Emperor(IRE) Annalina (USA) (Cozzene (USA))
1967[10] 2689[14] 2997[12] 3657[6] 3819[5] 7270[7] 7760[3] 8123[3] (8800) (9056) 9262[2] (9406)

**Kinglami** *John O'Shea* a73 84
8 b g Kingsalsa(USA) Red Japonica (Daylami (IRE))
2229[8] (3453) (3573) 4426[3] 4844[6] (5360) (5564) 5646[4] 6098[2] 6371[6] 7610[11] 8990[6] 9124[12]

**King Malpic (FR)** *T Lemer* a103 95
4 gr g King's Best(USA) Sablonniere (FR) (Verglas (IRE))
8251a[2] 9274a[7]

**King Of Camelot (FR)** *A Fabre* 92
2 b c Camelot Miss Emma May (IRE) (Hawk Wing (USA))
5776a[7] 7847a[3]

**King Of Castilla** *Colin Teague* a39 35
3 br g Sayif(IRE) Thicket (Wolfhound (USA))
4107[15] 4246[7] 5004[7] 5374[12]

**King Of Country** *M Halford* a41 40
5 b g Dubawi(IRE) Country Star (USA) (Empire Maker (USA))
1014a[14]

**King Of Dreams** *David Simcock* a78 72
4 ch g Dream Ahead(USA) Complexion (Hurricane Run (IRE))
611[4] 876[2] 1085[3]◆ 1224[5] 1788[8] 3095[10] 5800[4] 6479[3]

**Kingofmerrows (IRE)**
*Jamie Osborne* a78 77
3 br g Kodiac Tamara Gervasoni (IRE) (Namid)
8931[2] 9139[2] 9273[3]

**King Of Naples** *James Fanshawe* a79 91
4 b g Excellent Art Avon Lady (Avonbridge)
1512[11] 2833[8] 4339[3]

**King Of Nepal** *Henry Candy* a79 63
3 b g Sepoy(AUS) Empress Anna (IRE) (Imperial Ballet (IRE))
2151[10] 9101[7] (9410)

**King Of Paradise (IRE)** *Eric Alston* a35 68
8 b g Hurricane Run(IRE) Silly Game (IRE) (Bigstone (IRE))
2183[15] 2688[9] 3242[7] 3740[4] 4575[8]

**King Of Paris** *Roger Varian* 76
3 b g Exceed And Excel(AUS) Dubai Queen (USA) (Kingmambo (USA))
**1787**[2] 2751[7] **4100**[4] 4793[6]

**King Of Rooks** *Henry Spiller* a71 102
4 b g Acclamation Slap Shot (IRE) (Lycius (USA))
**4816**[8]◆

**King Of Scotland (FR)**
*Hughie Morrison* a61 68
3 b g Rip Van Winkle(IRE) Water Fountain (Mark Of Esteem (IRE))
*48*[9] **(2892)** 4348[7] 7561[5] 7982[9]

**King Of Spades (FR)**
*Gianluca Bietolini* a72 79
3 b c Foxwedge(AUS) And I (Inchinor)
**1658a**[9] 7308a[4] (8025a)

**King Of Spin** *Richard Hughes* a70 87
4 b g Pivotal Regina (Green Desert (USA))
(2230)◆ 3161[4] **3919**[2]◆ 5264[5] 5720[8]

**King Of Swing** *Richard Hughes* a75 83
4 b g Dutch Art Mystic Spirit (IRE) (Invincible Spirit (IRE))
*79*[9] *219*[9] *547*[10] *682*[7] *1290*[11] 2038[8] 2709[6] *3177*[2] 3396[5] 5651[3] *(6681)* 7002[2] **7653**[2]

**King Of The Celts (IRE)**
*Tim Easterby* 71
9 b g Celtic Swing Flamands (IRE) (Sadler's Wells (USA))
2225[5] 3205[6] 3559[5] 3935[8] **5021**[2] 5284[6] 5499[2] 5701[14] 6858[8]

**King Of The Sand (IRE)**
*Gary Moore* 86
2 ch c Footstepsinthesand Lough Mewin (IRE) (Woodman (USA))
6279[3] 7093[2] **(8180)**◆

**Kingofthesingers**
*Sir Mark Prescott Bt* a59
2 b c Leroidesanimaux(BRZ) Songerie (Hernando (FR))
*7535*[7] ***7987***[8] *8372*[7]

**King Olav (UAE)** *Tony Carroll* a72 41
12 ch g Halling(USA) Karamzin (USA) (Nureyev (USA))
***(436)*** *1464*[3] 4346[3] *5244*[4]

**King Oswald (USA)** *James Unett* a70 67
4 b g Street Cry(IRE) Northern Melody (IRE) (Singspiel (IRE))
*164*[5] ***421***[2] *841*[5] *954*[5] *1312*[6] *1560*[6] 2140[3] (2974) 3282[3] 3730[5] 5276[5] 5510[5] *9153*[2]

**King Otto** *Phil McEntee* a49 32
3 b g Holy Roman Emperor(IRE) Que Puntual (ARG) (Contested Bid (USA))
***863***[6] *1083*[10] *2792*[10] 3661[10] 4180[10]

**King Platin (FR)**
*Mme C Barande-Barbe* a89 94
5 ch h Konig Shuffle(GER) Couture Platine (FR) (Top Waltz (FR))
**4454a**[7]

**King Robert** *Bryan Smart* a100 93
4 b g Royal Applause Generously Gifted (Sakhee (USA))
*639*[7] *(957)* ***1454***[2]◆ 1880[8] 2736[7] 4505[3] 5094[7] 6205[6] *7828*[7]

**Kings Academy** *Paul Cole* a75 72
3 ch g Mayson Intrusion (Indesatchel (IRE))
2506[7] 2757[7] 2970[4] 3166[6] 3692[6] 4368[3] (5962) 6768[4] ***7056***[3] 7459[2]

**Kings City (IRE)** *Luca Cumani* a58 64
3 b g Rock Of Gibraltar(IRE) Muluk (IRE) (Rainbow Quest (USA))
2476[10] *3209*[7] 3839[8] **5867**[2] 6281[4] *7879*[5] *8312*[9]

**King's Coinage (IRE)** *Ruth Carr* a65 75
3 b g Holy Roman Emperor(IRE) Seducing (IRE) (Galileo (IRE))
1968[2] **(3752)** 5667[6] **6210**[4] 6757[6] *7234*[12] *7832*[11] *8206*[9]

**Kings Full (IRE)** *Kevin Ryan* 71
2 b g Galileo(IRE) Half Queen (USA) (Deputy Minister (CAN))
**6854**[4]◆

**Kings Gift (IRE)** *Michael Dods* 104
3 ch g Casamento(IRE) Jawaaneb (USA) (Kingmambo (USA))
1959[4] 2666a[9] 3994[9] **4916**[3] 5568[12] **6404**[3] 7619[25]

**Kings Heart (IRE)** *Mark Usher* a68 68
3 b c Zoffany(IRE) Queens Flight (King's Best (USA))
1940[8] 2579[4] 2927[11] ***3260***[2] ***3543***[2] *3971*[5] *4500*[4] *5028*[6] 5411[4]

**King's Hollow (FR)** *Henk Grewe* 76
4 b g Soldier Hollow Konigin Shuffle (GER) (Big Shuffle (USA))
**7342a**[4]

**Kingsley Klarion (IRE)** *John Butler* a83 57
4 b g Arcano(IRE) May Day Queen (IRE) (Danetime (IRE))
*66*[9] *234*[8] *1778*[6] *2064*[10] 2500[7] ***3140***[2] *3471*[3]◆ 3567[8] *3969*[8] *4746*[2] *6637*[12] *7759*[12] *8818*[11] *9297*[10]

**Kings Of Luxor** *R P Burns* a47 35
4 b g Royal Applause Tut (IRE) (Intikhab (USA))
**3387**[10]

**Kingspan Ellie (IRE)** *G T Cuthbert*
5 b m Le Cadre Noir(IRE) Minnie Kc (IRE) (Toca Madera (IRE))
*6799a*[10]

**King's Pavilion (IRE)** *David Barron* 101
4 b g King's Best(USA) Embassy (Cadeaux Genereux)
1734[5]◆ 2457[5] 4207[2]◆ 4961[4] 5668[13] (7044) 7140[2] **7609**[4] 8469[9]

**King's Proctor (IRE)** *Mark Johnston* 83
2 b c Cape Cross(IRE) Alimony (IRE) (Groom Dancer (USA))
4083[5] **(8508)**

**King's Shadow (USA)** *S Seemar* a35 20
3 b g Distorted Humor(USA) Love Theway Youare (USA) (Arch (USA))
***8710a***[9]

**Kings Shield (USA)** *John Gosden* a87
2 b c Scat Daddy(USA) Gender Dance (USA) (Miesque's Son (USA))
***(8779)***◆

**Kingstar (FR)** *Mme Pia Brandt* 104
2 ch c Evasive King's Parody (IRE) (King's Best (USA))
**7847a**[2]

**Kingston Kurrajong**
*Michael Attwater* a91 93
4 b g Authorized(IRE) Kingston Acacia (King Of Roses (AUS))
***118***[4] *465*[6] *918*[8] *1208*[5] *1422*[4] 1766[11] 2232[5] *3212*[8] 3750[8] 4223[3] 4807[3] 5300[2] 6134[15] 6700[5]◆

**Kingston Mimosa** *Mark Gillard* a1 23
5 b g Kheleyf(USA) Derartu (AUS) (Last Tycoon)
**4257**[11]

**Kingston Tasmania** *Andrew Balding* a29 41
3 b g Kheleyf(USA) Derartu (AUS) (Last Tycoon)
*891*[2]

**Kingstreet Lady** *Richard Price* a51 54
4 b m Royal Applause Intellibet One (Compton Place)
*602*[5] *784*[6] *1180*[7] *1408*[3] **(2214)** 2725[4] 3280[8]◆ **3774**[4] 4043[4] 4969[7] 6028[3] 6372[3] 6810[3]

**Kings Will Dream (IRE)**
*Micky Hammond* 79
3 ch g Casamento(IRE) Road Harbour (USA) (Rodrigo De Triano (USA))
3500[3] 4693[3] **(5458)**

**Kingthistle** *Rebecca Menzies* a76 78
4 ch g Monsieur Bond(IRE) Chez Cherie (Wolfhound (USA))
*(47)* *517*[3] *(809)* 1707[3] 2146[6] **2225**[2] 3240[5] 4118[3] 4899[3] 5698[7]

**King Tut (USA)** *Roger Charlton* a66
2 b c Animal Kingdom(USA) St Malo's Gate (USA) (Dynaformer (USA))
*8339*[7] ***8849***[5]

**Kingwilliamstown** *Jose Santos* 50
3 gr g Hellvelyn Honesty Pays (Dr Fong (USA))
**5931**[8] 7215[8] *7879*[13]

**King Wood (TUR)** *F Foresi* a10 57
7 ch g Dilum(USA) DancinginthecloUds (IRE) (Rainbow Quest (USA))
***515a***[12]

**Kinloch Pride** *Noel Wilson* a69 73
5 ch m Kyllachy Pride Of Kinloch (Dr Devious (IRE))
*(1006)* (1722) 1828[2] (2076) (2628) 3847[8] *4305*[3] 4850[4] **(6593)**

**Kirbec (IRE)** *Keith Dalgleish* 71
2 b f Lord Shanakill(USA) Monsusu (IRE) (Montjeu (IRE))
1909[7] 3491[3] 4245[2] **5990**[2] 6347[3] 8236[6] **8467**[3] 8676[7]

**Kiribati** *Mark Johnston* a53 76
3 b g Poet's Voice Oasis Jade (Oasis Dream)
2252[8] 3047[6] **3975**[4] 4144[7] 4741[6] *5239*[6]

**Kiringa** *Robert Cowell* a67 60
4 ch m Kyllachy Good Health (Magic Ring (IRE))
***1981***[5] 2967[7] 3903[4] 5055[6]

**Kiri Sunrise (IRE)**
*Ivan Lopez Santiago* 55
4 b m Iffraaj Lucky Flirt (USA) (Gulch (USA))
**7307a**[8]

**Kirkby's Phantom** *Alan Berry* a33 25
3 gr f Sayif(IRE) Demolition Jo (Petong)
5538[13] 6268[13] 7388[6] *8559*[8] 8656[13] ***9103***[4]

**Kirkham** *Julie Camacho* a70 76
4 b g Pastoral Pursuits Royal Grace (Royal Applause)
2119[6] 2684[15] *3344*[2] 3949[2] 4506[2] 5288[4] 5948[6] (6663) **7474**[2]

**Kirkland Forever** *Brendan Powell* a62 64
3 ch f Sakhee(USA) Maystock (Magic Ring (IRE))
5022[8] **6194**[7] 6765[6] *7729*[4] 8114[7]

**Kirkman (IRE)** *Peter Hiatt* a50 6
6 ch g Virtual Validate (Alhaarth (IRE))
3775[7]

**Kiruna Peak (IRE)** *Mick Channon* 70
3 ch f Arcano(IRE) Kirunavaara (IRE) (Galileo (IRE))
1737[10] 2269[5] **2686**[3] 3276[6] 3909[5] 4494[5] **(4697)** 5217[3] **5275**[2]

**Kiseki (JPN)** *Katsuhiko Sumii* 118
3 b c Rulership(JPN) Blitz Finale (JPN) (Deep Impact (JPN))
**9167a**[9]

**Kismat** *Alan King* a58
2 b f Sepoy(AUS) Magic Destiny (Dubai Destination (USA))
***8148***[9]

**Kiss Me Daily (FR)** *Ralph Beckett* 56
2 b f Reliable Man Via Saleria (IRE) (Arazi (USA))
5655[9] **8419**[7] *8903*[10]

**Kissy Suzuki** *Hughie Morrison* a73 52
5 b m Sakhee's Secret Yonder (And Beyond (IRE))
***233***[6]

**Kisumu** *Micky Hammond* a45 51
5 b g High Chaparral(IRE) Arum Lily (USA) (Woodman (USA))
**2549**[6] 3566[7] *6898*[8] *8187*[10]

**Kitaabaat** *Owen Burrows* 85
2 b c Dansili Ausus (USA) (Invasor (ARG))
5710[4] 6374[2] **(7273)**

**Kitasan Black (JPN)**
*Hisashi Shimizu* 125
5 b h Black Tide(JPN) Sugar Heart (JPN) (Sakura Bakushin O (JPN))
(2203a) **8975a**[3]

**Kitesurf** *A Fabre* 106
3 b f Dubawi(IRE) Shimmering Surf (IRE) (Danehill Dancer (IRE))
2447a[2] (3366a) 3881a[10] 5691a[5] **7635a**[3] 8274a[5]

**Kit Marlowe** *Mark Johnston* a83 82
2 b g Poet's Voice La Nuit Rose (FR) (Rainbow Quest (USA))
2435[2]◆ 2826[5] 3754[3] *(4258)* ***5742***[2] 6683[3] 6900[4] ***8207***[2]

**Kitsey (IRE)** *Richard Hannon* 67
3 b f High Chaparral(IRE) Thistlestar (USA) (Lion Heart (USA))
1968[12] 3024[11] **3819**[6] 5142[6] 7210[8] 7820[9]

**Kitten's Johnstown (USA)**
*Kevin Ryan* a72 49
3 ch c Kitten's Joy(USA) Cellars Shiraz (USA) (Kissin Kris (USA))
1912[5] 4408[6] 5664[11] ***7999***[5] *8400*[8]

**Kitten's Roar (USA)**
*Michael J Maker* 111
5 bb m Kitten's Joy(USA) Bambolina (USA) (War Chant (USA))
5954a[5] **8098a**[2] (8601a)

**Kitty Boo** *Luca Cumani* a85 79
3 b f Invincible Spirit(IRE) Kitty Wells (Sadler's Wells (USA))
3626[2] 4300[4] 6143[2] 6722[8] *(7485)* 8113[7] ***8636***[3]

**Kiunguja (FR)** *M Boutin* a43
2 ch f Linda's Lad Nera Divine (FR) (Divine Light (JPN))
1282a[7]

**Kiwia (AUS)** *Darren Weir* 105
3 ch g Reset(AUS) Single View (AUS) (Danehill Dancer (IRE))
**8633a**[2] 8751a[7]

**Kiwi Bay** *Michael Dods* a78 72
12 b g Mujahid(USA) Bay Of Plenty (FR) (Octagonal (NZ))
*3591*[3] *611*[8] *(968)* *1125*[4] *1473*[3] 1706[4] 2458[7] **(2955)** 3402[4] 4439[2] 4833[4] **(5183)** 5698[6] 7894[7] 8651[10] *8930*[13]

**Kiwi Green Suite (BRZ)** *D Smaga* 106
3 gr h T. H. Approval(USA) Hypnose (BRZ) (Know Heights (IRE))
5269a[3] **8127a**[2]

**Klosters (IRE)** *Roger Charlton* a72 73
2 b f Kodiac Seminova (Cape Cross (IRE))
*2958*[3] **(3769)**

**Kloud Gate (FR)** *Gianluca Bietolini* 104
5 ch g Astronomer Royal(USA) Talkata (IRE) (Suave Dancer (USA))
2202a[8]

**Klungel (GER)** *Markus Klug*
2 b c Jukebox Jury(IRE) Konigstochter (GER) (Dai Jin)
6986a[4]

**Knight Commander** *Olly Murphy* a65 79
4 br g Sir Percy Jardin (Sinndar (IRE))
***7992***[3]◆

**Knight Destroyer (IRE)**
*Jonjo O'Neill* 83
3 b g Dark Angel(IRE) Do The Deal (IRE) (Halling (USA))
2711[2]◆ (3428) 5153[6] **7231**[2]

**Knighted (IRE)** *Kevin Ryan* 73
2 b g Sir Prancealot(IRE) Olympia Theatre (Galileo (IRE))
6853[2] **7953**[5] **8649**[2]

**Knight Errant (IRE)** *William Jarvis* a48
2 b c So You Think(NZ) Lamanka Lass (USA) (Woodman (USA))
***9240***[5]

**Knight In Armour (IRE)**
*Mark Johnston* 70
2 b g Camelot Madeira Mist (IRE) (Grand Lodge (USA))
**3742**[4] 4291[2] 5136[4] 7624[3] 7956[6]

**Knightly Spirit** *Roger Varian* 72
2 br c Dalakhani(IRE) Elysian (Galileo (IRE))
6142[7] **6777**[3]◆ **7503**[3]

**Knight Music** *Michael Attwater* a81 89
5 b g Sir Percy Lyric Art (USA) (Red Ransom (USA))
6202[4] ***7515***[7] 8326[4]◆

**Knight Of The Air** *Joseph Tuite* a67 57
5 b g Bushranger(IRE) Picolette (Piccolo)
***1219***[4] 2178[9] 3304[4] 3660[6] *4561*[12] 6475[4]◆ 6754[6] *7952*[12]

**Knight Owl** *James Fanshawe* a93 99
7 b g Rock Of Gibraltar(IRE) Miss Ivanhoe (IRE) (Selkirk (USA))
**2855**[3]◆ 5157[10] 5914[7] 7549[2]

**Knightsbridge Liam (IRE)**
*Michael Easterby* a59 60
3 b g Lilbourne Lad(IRE) Carmona (Rainbow Quest (USA))
*198*[6] *479*[6] *718*[2] *1331*[7] 3901[3] 4436[5] 5001[4] **6088**[2] 6892[5] *7236*[4]◆ *8206*[8]

**Knights Table** *James Tate* a78 106
4 b h Sir Percy Whole Grain (Polish Precedent (USA))
**(2158)** 2604[4]◆

**Knight To Behold (IRE)**
*Harry Dunlop* 95
2 b c Sea The Stars(IRE) Angel Of The Gwaun (IRE) (Sadler's Wells (USA))
**7355**[2] (8352)

**Knockamany Bends (IRE)**
*John Wainwright* a48 55
7 b g Majestic Missile(IRE) Sweet Compliance (Safawan)
3202[10] 3710[11] 5459[5] 5542[11] 5695[2] (6384) 6688[2] 7164[9] 7218[9] **(7884)** 8168[12]

**Knockmaole Boy (IRE)**
*Gordon Elliott* a56 79
5 b g Echo Of Light Kashmir Lady (FR) (Rock Of Gibraltar (IRE))
**(5519a)** 5582a[17] *6801a*[9]

**Knockout Blow** *Mark Johnston* a75 74
2 b g Lethal Force(IRE) Elidore (Danetime (IRE))
2740[7] 3066[2] 3846[4] 4335[6] ***(7450)*** *7876*[6]

**Knotty Jack (IRE)** *Chris Grant* a34 35
5 b g Zebedee Half-Hitch (USA) (Diesis)
**6667**[5] 7165[10]

**Knowing Glance (IRE)**
*Richard Fahey* a60 68
2 bl g Kodiac Shauna's Princess (IRE) (Soviet Star (USA))
3846[5] *4359*[4] **5179**[3]◆ 7106[3]

**Know The Truth** *Andrew Balding* a69 68
3 b f Lawman(FR) Snow Key (USA) (Cozzene (USA))
*2366*[6]◆ 2908[8] 3748[7] ***4214***[4] 4537[13] *5797*[11] *7058*[10] 7465[6] 7907[4] *8256*[4] *(8774)*

**Know Your Limit (IRE)** *Ed Walker* a67 84
3 ch g Tamayuz Rapid Ransom (USA) (Red Ransom (USA))
1685[3] 2145[2] 5478[2] 6075[2] **6657**[2] 8291[3]

**Know Your Name** *Donald McCain* a72 67
6 ch g Halling(USA) Lady Agnes (Singspiel (IRE))
*1983*[4] 3899[10] ***(4453)*** 4833[5] 5544[6] *6158*[5] *6638*[10] *6947*[3] 7111[11] *8429*[12] *8664*[5] *8854*[6]

**Kodiac Express (IRE)** *Mike Murphy* a68 72
2 b f Kodiac Excel Yourself (IRE) (Exceed And Excel (AUS))
*1792*[4] *2459*[3] 2904[3] 3516[6] 4199[2] 5107[8] *6021*[4] 6651[2] 6825[2] **(7732)**

**Kodiac Khan (IRE)** *Mark Johnston* a82 79
3 b c Kodiac Mirwara (IRE) (Darshaan)
**2106**[4] 3700[8] *4304*[6] 4658[8]

**Kodiac Lady (IRE)** *Simon West* a67 41
5 b m Kodiac Weeping Willow (IRE) (Kheleyf (USA))
*525*[5] ***425***[4]

**Kodiac Pearl (IRE)** *Robert Cowell* a31 39
3 b f Kodiac Valmirez (USA) (Smart Strike (CAN))
**2139**[5] *2924*[8] 5006[6] 6339[10] *7407*[8] 8185[6]

**Kodi Beach** *David Barron* 64
2 b g Kodiac Annie Beach (IRE) (Redback)
5665[10] **7732**[6]

**Kodicat (IRE)** *Kevin Ryan* a73 73
3 b f Kodiac Mimiteh (USA) (Maria's Mon (USA))
*1004*[3] **(2080)** 2630[12] 4342[4] 4745[4] 5375[3] 6768[2] ***8243***[3] *8557*[7]

**Kodiline (IRE)** *Clive Cox* a89 88
3 b c Kodiac Kris Spring (Kris S (USA))
3302[6] 3844[13] 6392[5] ***8129***[5] ***8879***[4]

**Kodimoor (IRE)** *Christopher Kellett* a57 64
4 b g Kodiac Victoria Lodge (IRE) (Grand Lodge (USA))
*153*[3] *722*[6] *2472*[2] (2994) 3563[6] (5069) 5605[4] 6130[9] *6531*[5] 7018[7] **7660**[2] 8681[9]

**Kodina** *Charles Hills* 64
2 b f Kodiac Quan Am (FR) (Invincible Spirit (IRE))
6138[8] **6806**[5]

**Koditime (IRE)** *Clive Cox* 89
2 b c Kodiac Eponastone (IRE) (Footstepsinthesand)
(2134) 2826[3]◆ **3993**[8] 5526[7]

**Kody Ridge (IRE)** *Roger Fell* a77 77
3 b g Kodiac Top Of The Ridge (IRE) (Celtic Swing)
2151[9] 2720[8] (3391) (4694) 4745[3] 5132[11] 5495[5] **6313**[2] *9308*[6]

**Koeman** *Mick Channon* a91 86
3 b c Dutch Art Angelic Note (IRE) (Excellent Art)
*1552*[4] 2174[3] 3068[2] 3520[4] 3779[3] 4221[5] (4913) *(5298)* 6423[3] *6937*[3] ***(7516)*** 8005[8] *8638*[8]

**Kohinoor Diamond (IRE)**
*Sir Mark Prescott Bt* a70 38
3 b f Excelebration(IRE) Gems Of Araby (Zafonic (USA))
*(7760)*◆ *7990*[6] ***8883***[2] *9208*[8] *9442*[8]

**Kohinur** *Hugo Palmer* a71 85
3 b f Dubawi(IRE) Vita Nova (IRE) (Galileo (IRE))
**5364**[2] *5796*[3] 7477[2]

**Koin** *Mark H Tompkins* 13
2 b f Kheleyf(USA) Tenpence (Bob Back (USA))
**3437**[8] 6480[16] 7023[8] *7985*[7]

**Kolokol (IRE)** *M Cesandri* a13 56
10 b g Statue Of Liberty(USA) Hecterine (IRE) (Hector Protector (USA))
**5176a**[9]

**Kolo Tamam** *Roger Charlton* a47
2 b c Al Kazeem Sensiz (IRE) (Marju (IRE))
***9155***[7]

**Kommander Kirkup**
*Michael Herrington* a71 68
6 ch g Assertive Bikini (Trans Island)
4277[10] 5132[3] 5318[10] 6237[10] 6669[9] 7249[7] *8194*[2]◆ *8552*[13] *(8980)* ***(9347)***

**Komodo (IRE)** *Jedd O'Keeffe* 94
3 ch g Dragon Pulse(IRE) Salydora (FR) (Peintre Celebre (USA))
1680[4]◆ 1977[2] (2682) 3862[2] (4658) **(5704)**◆

**Konig Dax (GER)** *Alistair Whillans* 80
7 b g Saddex Konigin Shuttle (GER) (Big Shuffle (USA))
1974[6] 3240[3] **4658**[4] 4959[5] 7225[12]

**Konig Hall** *Anthony McCann* a66 58
9 b g Halling(USA) Konigin Shuffle (GER) (Big Shuffle (USA))
***5483***[4]

**Kontrast (IRE)** *M Weiss*
4 ch h Intikhab(USA) Common Charisma (IRE) (Highest Honor (FR))
*714a*[3] *915a*[2]

**Kool And The Gang (IRE)**
*J Albrecht* a83 66
7 b g Elusive City(USA) Knightsbridge (BRZ) (Yagli (USA))
*6226a*[3] ***6454a***[5]

**Kool Kompany (IRE)**
*Richard Hannon* 112
5 br h Jeremy(USA) Absolutely Cool (IRE) (Indian Ridge (IRE))
**(1493)** 2129[8] 3320[4] 3924[12] 4890[6] 5527[7] 6746a[9] 7275[10]

**Kopassus (IRE)** *Lawrence Mullaney* a49 57
5 b g Holy Roman Emperor(IRE) Couverture (USA) (Lear Fan (USA))
***311***[5] *481*[11]

**Korak Boy (IRE)** *Joseph Tuite* 13
2 bz g Zebedee Facce Tarzan (IRE) (Exceed And Excel (AUS))
*3999*[7] 4488[5] **4841**[6]

**Korbous (IRE)** *Richard Brabazon* a80 84
8 ch g Choisir(AUS) Puppet Play (IRE) (Broken Hearted)
***6801a***[7] 7111[10]

**Korevsky (IRE)** *Simone Brogi* 91
2 b c Intello(GER) Voie De Printemps (FR) (Della Francesca (USA))
**7847a**[5]

**Koropick (IRE)** *Hugo Palmer* a113 110
3 b c Kodiac Kathoe (IRE) (Fayruz)
2823[7] 3302[5] 3835[2] ***(4354)*** 5149[8] 5974a[7] 7356[11]

**Koubba (IRE)** *Neil Mulholland* a45 40
4 b m Peintre Celebre(USA) Elyaadi (Singspiel (IRE))
5022[10] 5428[7] 5712[11] 6305[10] ***8815***[4]

**Kourkan (FR)** *J-M Beguigne* 113
4 bb g American Post Kourka (FR) (Keos (USA))
(1159a) 1531a[4] **2248a**[2] 3880a[7] 6915a[2] 7638a[4]

**Kowaiyess (IRE)**
*Mohamed Moubarak* a74 78
3 b g Exceed And Excel(AUS) Nidhaal (IRE) (Observatory (USA))
*1321*[2] 1762[5] **(7099)** *7882*[11]

**Kozier (GER)** *Alan King* a53 71
3 ch g Muhtathir Kasumi (GER) (Poliglote)
*4978*[5] 6376[2] **(7233)**

**Krafty One** *Michael Scudamore* a51 19
5 ch m Mastercraftsman(IRE) Wonderful Desert (Green Desert (USA))
***121***[8] 5782[P] 6306[9] 7215[11]

**Kraka (IRE)** *Tom Dascombe* a72 78
2 b g Dark Angel(IRE) Manuelita Rose (ITY) (Desert Style (IRE))
3742[7] *4452*[3] **5874**[2] 6997a[26]

**Krazy Paving** *Anabel K Murphy* a60 73
5 b g Kyllachy Critical Path (IRE) (Noverre (USA))
*88*[2] *(438)* *640*[2] ***(982)*** *1304*[6] *2091*[6] *7517*[10] *8824*[10] *9323*[3] *9469*[8]

**Kreb's Cycle (IRE)** *Ian Williams* a82 76
3 ch g Helmet(AUS) La Noe (Nayef (USA))
2557[8] 2831[6] 4634[10] 4868[4] 5664[4] 6387[7] *7942*[2] *8209*[10] ***8798***[2] *9272*[8]

**Kripke (IRE)** *David Barron* 74
2 b g Fast Company(IRE) Tranquil Sky (Intikhab (USA))
**8381**[3]◆

**Kristal Hart** *Neil Mulholland* a61 58
8 b m Lucky Story(USA) Moly (FR) (Anabaa (USA))
***238***[7]

**Kristjano (GER)** *Jimmy Frost* a27 73
5 b g Nayef(USA) Kalahari Dancer (Dalakhani (IRE))
**3494**[4]

**Kristoff (IRE)** *Jim Boyle* a50 39
4 b g Frozen Power(IRE) Easter Girl (Efisio)
*614*[3] *854*[8] *1139*[8] *1425*[5] ***2024***[2] 2057[6] 2675[4] *2961*[13] 5410[5] 5651[7]

**Kronprinz (GER)** *P Schiergen*
2 ch c Lord Of England(GER) Kaiserwiese (GER) (Sholokhov (IRE))
(6986a)

**Kroy** *Ollie Pears* a63 57
3 b g Sleeping Indian Valley Of The Moon (IRE) (Monashee Mountain (USA))
2181[5] 2853[8] 3403[3]◆ 5283[9] ***(8194)*** ***8591***[2] *8807*[7] *9019*[5]

**Krypton Factor** *Fawzi Abdulla Nass* a88 107
9 br g Kyllachy Cool Question (Polar Falcon (USA))
318a[11] **(651a)** 1044a[14] *9361a*[5]

**Kryptos** *John Berry* 106
3 b g Cacique(IRE) Posteritas (USA) (Lear Fan (USA))
4097[3] (4894) 6073[2] (6942) **(7149)**◆

**Krystallite** *Scott Dixon* a60 43
4 ch m Kheleyf(USA) Chrystal Venture (IRE) (Barathea (IRE))
*71*[7] ***(3466)*** 3944[10] *4305*[9] *5481*[13] *5845*[5] *6527*[6] *7486*[9] *8853*[6] *9001*[4] *9181*[6] *9414*[10]

**Kuiper Belt (USA)** *David Lanigan* a56 53
3 b g Elusive Quality(USA) Youre So Sweet (USA) (Storm Cat (USA))
2581[6] *4262*[9] ***4727***[6]◆

**Kulgri** *Kevin Ryan* 55
3 ch f Monsieur Bond(IRE) Jord (IRE) (Trans Island)
2121[9] 2897[14] 5019[3] 5741[5] **6381**[3] **7271**[2] 8123[8]

**Kullu (IRE)** *Charlie Fellowes* a93 84
4 b m Oasis Dream Mussoorie (FR) (Linamix (FR))
(2575) ***3341***[2]

**Kunani (USA)** *John Gosden* 59
3 br g Arch(USA) Sweet Sonnet (USA) (Seeking The Gold (USA))
**5611**[5]

**Kuraka** *K R Burke* 76
3 b g Cacique(IRE) Puzzling (Peintre Celebre (USA))
2376[6] 2991[4] 3489[7] **4575**[2]

**Kwikstep** *Andi Brown* a35
3 b f Nathaniel(IRE) Enchufla (Danehill Dancer (IRE))
*7059*[6] *7462*[7] ***9159***[9]

**Kyleque (IRE)** *Paul Midgley* 46
2 br g Equiano(FR) Dispol Kylie (IRE) (Kheleyf (USA))
**2154**[7] 2816[9] 3562[5]

**Kylie Rules** *Ann Duffield* a67 66
2 bl f Aussie Rules(USA) Africa's Star (IRE) (Johannesburg (USA))
3495[4] 4834[8] 5371[4] *5833*[3] ***7239***[6]

**Kylie Style** *Steph Hollinshead* a49 50
2 b f Aussie Rules(USA) Stilettoesinthemud (IRE) (Footstepsinthesand)
*6950*[9] **7326**[7] 7953[8] *8795*[7] *9002*[5] *9302*[14] *9436*[9]

**Kylla** *Alan Brown* a26 29
4 b m Kyllachy Mamounia (IRE) (Green Desert (USA))
3185[12] 4246[9] 4847[6] **5472**[8] 7247[6]

**Kyllach Me (IRE)** *Bryan Smart* a61 63
5 b g Kyllachy Good For Her (Rock Of Gibraltar (IRE))
*80*[9] *216*[3] *601*[2] *852*[12] 1720[10] (1978) **2633**[2] 3979[9] 7018[10] *8194*[9] *8924*[6] *9216*[5]

**Kyllachy Dragon (IRE)** *Iain Jardine* 81
2 b g Dragon Pulse(IRE) Lafayette (GER) (Artan (IRE))
5370[6] 6056[2] 7242[3] **8008**[2]◆

**Kyllachy Gala** *Marco Botti* a109 104
4 b g Kyllachy Tenuta Di Gala (IRE) (Nashwan (USA))
***396***[2] 654a[12] 888a[12] 2141[3] *2999*[6] *8032*[8] *8999*[4] *9186*[2] *9407*[3]

**Kyllachys Tale (IRE)** *Roger Teal* a71 87
3 b f Kyllachy Betray (King's Best (USA))
*210*[7] *502*[6] *(848)* 3088[6] (4255) 5332[2] **(6274)** 7276[11] 8297[8]

**Kyllang Rock (IRE)** *James Tate* 108
3 b g Kyllachy Megec Blis (IRE) (Soviet Star (USA))
(1732) 2768[2] 3539[2] 4920[11] 5595[6] **6039**[2] **6979a**[4] 7804[6]

**Kyllukey** *Milton Bradley* a83 76
4 b g Kyllachy Money Note (Librettist (USA))
2040[8] 2230[6] ***2516***[6] 3021[3] 3281[6] 3903[5] *4495*[7] *4979*[3] *5481*[12] 6303[7] *7320*[7] *7767*[3] *7951*[2] *8128*[2] *8743*[4] *8853*[2] *9001*[5] *9183*[7]

**Kyneton (IRE)** *John Gosden* a31
3 b c Fastnet Rock(AUS) Kahyasi Moll (IRE) (Brief Truce (USA))
***737***[9]

**Kynoch (USA)** *J Smart*
2 rg c
**9446a**[8]

**Kynren (IRE)** *David Barron* a76 98
3 b g Clodovil(IRE) Art Of Gold (Excellent Art)
*4309*[3] (4784) (6203) **(7246)**

**Kyshoni (IRE)** *Mike Murphy* a41 62
3 ch f Casamento(IRE) Curious Lashes (IRE) (Footstepsinthesand)
2707[7] **3438**[5] 4152[0] 4444[8] 5853[5] *6621*[10]

**Kytalpha's Sun (FR)**
*Mme A-C Trouve* a57 26
4 ch g Kitalpha(USA) Quail Landing (Mark Of Esteem (IRE))
**7069a**[10]

**Kyvon Des Aigles (FR)**
*Mme C Barande-Barbe* a60 67
2 gr g Style Vendome(FR) Kiva Des Aigles (FR) (Enrique)
**1335a**[7] 3679a[7]

**La Bacouetteuse (FR)** *Iain Jardine* a59 63
12 b g Miesque's Son(USA) Toryka (Vettori (IRE))
2889[8] 3663[11] 4852[5] *5413*[7] **5700**[4] 6595[3] 7700[3] 7922[7] 8109[2] 8487[10] 8654[7] *9258*[11]

**La Belle Mayson** *Richard Fahey* 64
2 ch f Mayson Excellent Show (Exceed And Excel (AUS))
3980[5] 6086[3] **7563**[4] 8110[5]

**Labhay (IRE)** *William Haggas* a82 65
3 b f New Approach(IRE) Sooraah (Dubawi (IRE))
3039[6] ***(4565)*** *8947*[9]

**Labradorite (JPN)** *Takashi Saito* 102
8 b g King Kamehameha(JPN) Tanzanite (JPN) (Sunday Silence (USA))
**2203a**[17]

**Labrega** *Hugo Palmer* a70
2 b f Cacique(IRE) Postale (Zamindar (USA))
***8634***[6]

**La Cabana** *Richard Fahey* a53 58
2 b f Havana Gold(IRE) Mania (IRE) (Danehill (USA))
*7238*[10] *8189*[7] ***8472***[6] *8954*[6] *9175*[13]

**Lacan (IRE)** *Brett Johnson* a88 71
6 b g New Approach(IRE) Invincible Isle (IRE) (Invincible Spirit (IRE))
***266***[7] *548*[6] *(1065)* *1422*[9] *1598*[9] 2291[9] 3030[11] 4699[9] 5555[6] *6068*[9] *7493*[9] *7878*[5]◆ *(8503)* *9314*[4]

**La Canche (FR)** *T Clout* 78
2 bb f Le Havre(IRE) L'Authie (FR) (Linamix (FR))
1919a[2] 2881a[2] 6171a[3] **6803a**[4]

**La Casa Tarifa (IRE)** *Mark Johnston* a80 85
3 b f Casamento(IRE) Cool Tarifa (IRE) (One Cool Cat (USA))
*(1489)* ***(1912)***◆ 2268[5] 5529[9] 6001[5] *6687*[RR] 7555[7] *(8315)*

**La Cataleya (FR)** *R Le Dren Doleuze* a63 64
2 b f Alianthus(GER) Zurserl (GER) (Neshad (USA))
6171a[11] **8228a**[5]

**Lacazar (GER)** *P Schiergen* 111
3 ch f Adlerflug(GER) Laey Diamond (GER) (Dai Jin)
(4393a) **(5693a)** 7669a[9]

**La Celebs Ville (IRE)**
*Tom Dascombe* a51 81
4 b m Sea The Stars(IRE) Bryanstown (IRE) (Galileo (IRE))
(2140) **(3540)** 4525[4] 5135[5] 6274[5] 7130[5] 8113[8]

**Lackaday** *Noel Wilson* a60 65
5 gr g Kyllachy Day Creek (Daylami (IRE))
*1126*[3] 1978[7] 2990[3] **(3563)** 4250[5] 4682[9] 5282[8] 6631[10] 7020[7] 7660[8] 8490[7] *9075*[7]

**Lac Leman (GER)** *Pauline Robson* a85 72
6 b g Doyen(IRE) Learned Lady (JPN) (Fuji Kiseki (JPN))
*399*[2] *(613)* ***991***[2] *1781*[3] 2741[6] 3486[4] *4357*[4] *5417*[6]

**La Coronel (USA)** *Mark Casse* a78 110
3 bb f Colonel John(USA) Listen (USA) (Chester House (USA))
4031[5] **(8071a)**

**La Cumparsita (FR)** *C Lerner* a53 59
3 ch f American Post Tenepia (FR) (Keltos (FR))
**3310a**[4]

**Ladakhi** *Rod Millman* a53 63
3 b f Compton Place Charpoy Cobra (Mark Of Esteem (IRE))
*7514*[10] **7907**[5] *8504*[7]

**La Dame En Rouge (FR)**
*J Phelippon* a63 59
3 b f Requinto(IRE) Philosophers Guest (IRE) (Desert Prince (IRE))
***838a***[2] 3310a[8] *8304a*[6]

**Ladies First** *Michael Easterby* a65
3 b f Monsieur Bond(IRE) Forever Bond (Danetime (IRE))
***8869***[3]◆ *9071*[2] *9304*[2] *9464*[9]

**La Diva** *Roger Varian* 76
2 b f Helmet(AUS) Craigmill (Slip Anchor)
**5154**[2] 6140[4] 7733[2] **8348**[3]

**Ladofash** *Chris Gordon* a65 71
3 b g Canford Cliffs(IRE) Curras Spirit (Invincible Spirit (IRE))
*329*[5] *659*[4] *967*[6] ***(1331)*** *1591*[4] *2273*[6] 3220[6] 6821[7]

**Ladurelli (IRE)** *Paul Cole* a83 85
5 b g Mastercraftsman(IRE) Chanter (Lomitas)
**4254**[5] 4522[9] 5276[6]

**Ladweb** *John Gallagher* a55 87
7 ch g Bertolini(USA) Adweb (Muhtarram (USA))
**2839**[2] 3617[7] 6137[5] 6923[7] 7214[3]◆

**Lady Alavesa** *Gay Kelleway* a66 66
2 b f Westlake Matilda Peace (Namaqualand (USA))
2563[10] **2890**[2] *3210*[5] *4977*[4] (5562) ***7239***[4] 7621[8]

**Lady Al Thumama** *Charlie Fellowes* a70 57
2 gr f Leroidesanimaux(BRZ) Mrs Micawber (Nayef (USA))
***7875***[3] 8347[4] *9310*[4]

**Lady Anjorica (IRE)** *Keith Dalgleish* 85
2 ch f Camacho Adaria (Sleeping Indian)
2545[5] 2987[2] 3611a[5] **3960**[12] 4689[2] 5150[12] 5702[6] 7596[4] 7821[12] 8045[8] (8236) 8413[3]

**Lady Aurelia (USA)** *Wesley A Ward* a98 124
3 b f Scat Daddy(USA) D'Wildcat Speed (USA) (Forest Wildcat (USA))
(1813a) **(3926)**◆ 6402[2] 8604a[10]

**Lady Bacchus** *Richard Guest* a60 46
4 b m Compton Place Beauty (IRE) (Alzao (USA))
***(270)*** *446*[10] *723*[4] *1006*[6] *1221*[3] *1371*[9]

**Lady Bayside** *Malcolm Saunders* a64 73
9 ch m Ishiguru(USA) Seldemosa (Selkirk (USA))
**3422**[13]

**Lady Bergamot (FR)**
*James Fanshawe* a78 85
3 gr f Mastercraftsman(IRE) Mahima (FR) (Linamix (FR))
2689[8] *(3342)* (4621)◆ 5439[3] **(6477)** **7401**[3]

**Lady Buttons** *Philip Kirby* 29
7 b m Beneficial Lady Chapp (IRE) (High Chaparral (IRE))
**7124**[6]

**Lady Camelot (IRE)** *Gavin Cromwell* 85
2 b f Camelot Queen Jock (USA) (Repent (USA))
**7859a**[7]

**Ladycammyofclare (IRE)**
*Mark Johnston* a46 43
2 b f Camacho County Clare (Barathea (IRE))
4199[5] 4689[7] 5278[9] 5878[7] 6625[4] *7030*[6] 7519[6] ***8306***[4] *8644*[7]

**Lady Carduros (IRE)**
*Neil Mulholland* a6
3 b f Byron Saranjo (IRE) (Carrowkeel (IRE))
*8504*[11] ***8805***[7] *8984*[8]

**Lady Cashmere (IRE)**
*Alistair Whillans* a21 32
2 b f Lord Shanakill(USA) Erreur (IRE) (Desert King (IRE))
**5202**[7] *5834*[13] 6380[8] *7029*[9]

**Lady Clitico (IRE)** *Rebecca Menzies* a66 67
6 b m Bushranger(IRE) Villa Nova (IRE) (Petardia)
*1312*[5] *1560*[8] 2079[5] **(2549)** 3338[4] *8778*[11] *9258*[9]

**Lady Cristal (IRE)** *K R Burke* a70 72
3 b f Footstepsinthesand Scarborough Lily (Dansili)
*404*[4] *(612)* *972*[3] *1203*[6] *1693*[2] 1940[4] **(2372)** 3152[7] *4305*[4] 4717[7] *7940*[12] *8321*[8] *8875*[2] *9315*[4]

**Lady Dancealot (IRE)**
*David Elsworth* a63 73
2 b f Sir Prancealot(IRE) Mayorstone (IRE) (Exceed And Excel (AUS))
**5107**[3] 5528[7] **6867**[2]◆ *7706*[4] **(8073)**

**Lady Eli (USA)** *Chad C Brown* 114
5 b m Divine Park(USA) Sacre Coeur (USA) (Saint Ballado (CAN))
**8606a**[7]

**Lady Emma** *Steph Hollinshead* a42 51
4 b m Mount Nelson Songbook (Singspiel (IRE))
*1754*[7] ***5896***[8]

**Lady Ensign** *Mark Brisbourne* a17 19
2 ch f Captain Gerrard(IRE) Ensign's Trick (Cayman Kai (IRE))
3791[17] **5398**[7] *5893*[8]

**Lady Frankel** *A Fabre* 114
3 b f Frankel Lady Vettori (Vettori (IRE))
1825a[3] 2665a[6] 3612a[3] (6054a) 6982a[7] **7669a**[3]

**Lady Freyja** *John Ryan* a49 84
3 b f Mayson Third Party (Terimon)
2066[3] **(3595)** 3964[16] 8351[11] 8600[13]

**Lady Godiva (IRE)** *Richard Hannon* 69
2 b f Camelot For Evva Silca (Piccolo)
5349[8] 5885[6] 6747[4] 7914[9] **8325**[4]

**Lady Grand** *Richard Fahey* 20
2 ch f Poet's Voice Lady Gorgeous (Compton Place)
**3943**[11] 5210[10] 5665[13]

**Lady Grigio (IRE)** *Iain Jardine* a44
2 gr f Casamento(IRE) Park Approach (IRE) (Indian Ridge (IRE))
***9099***[9]

**Lady Gwhinnyvere (IRE)**
*John Spearing* a17 43
3 b f Sir Prancealot(IRE) Johar Jamal (IRE) (Chevalier (IRE))
**4969**[3] 5783[9] 7212[12]

**Lady Hester (USA)** *John Gosden* a67
3 b f Bernardini(USA) Questing (Hard Spun (USA))
*8453* *1003*[4] ***1445***[2]

**Lady In Question (IRE)**
*Richard Fahey* a78 79
3 b f Elzaam(AUS) Black Meyeden (FR) (Black Minnaloushe (USA))
2820[5] 3588[4] 4268[3] 4741[4] 5400[5] 5922[2] 6265[2] (6550) *7241*[3] *7771*[3]◆ **8240**[2] 8736[4]

**Lady Isle** *Grant Tuer* 31
2 b f Monsieur Bond(IRE) Ailsa Craig (IRE) (Chevalier (IRE))
**5735**[7] 6057[11]

**Lady Jayne (IRE)** *Ian Williams* a43 36
2 b f Henrythenavigator(USA) Stellavera (FR) (Anabaa (USA))
3712[10] 6653[15] 8381[8] ***8783***[3] *9090*[5]

**Lady Joanna Vassa (IRE)**
*Richard Guest* a63 54
4 ch m Equiano(FR) Lady Natilda (First Trump)
1722[11] *3345*[7] **3563**[3] 3710[5] 3915[7] 4559[6] 4789[8] *5419*[6] 5567[2] **5736**[2] 5995[3] 6130[3] 6372[4] 6631[7] *7407*[7] (7660) 7692[3] 7926[2] *(7993)* *8494*[11] *8559*[4]

**Lady Kathleen (FR)** *N Caullery* 44
3 b f Kingsalsa(USA) Tikisol (FR) (Solid Illusion (USA))
**6225a**[10]

**Lady Kaviar (IRE)**
*George Margarson* a61 54
3 b f Lope De Vega(IRE) Maoin Dor (IRE) (Manduro (GER))
2794[7] 4320[8] 5867[7] ***(8152)*** *8345*[8]

**Lady Lintera (IRE)** *Ann Duffield* a51 51
2 b f Lilbourne Lad(IRE) Lintera (GER) (Night Shift (USA))
1673[8] 2105[7] **5162**[4] 6043[12] 6517[5] 7081[8] 7264[4] 7655[6] *8397*[2] *8780*[3] *9002*[4] *9302*[3]

**Lady Lunchalot (USA)** *Polly Gundry* a50 63
7 b m More Than Ready(USA) Betty Johanne (USA) (Johannesburg (USA))
*3208*[9] **3575**[2] (Dead)

**Lady Lydia (IRE)** *Hugo Froud* a83 67
6 b m Kheleyf(USA) Piece Unique (Barathea (IRE))
*2510* *285*[5] *499*[6] *879*[5] ***(1066)*** *1261*[9] *1771*[11] 2178[7] 7523[4] *7830*[9] 8126[6] *8374*[7] *8636*[8] *9020*[12] *9316*[8]

**Lady Macapa** *Clive Cox* a71 110
4 b m Equiano(FR) Brazilian Style (Exit To Nowhere (USA))
1946[3] 2623[13] 5149[3] **(6979a)**

**Lady Macha** *Marco Botti* a73
3 b f Mount Nelson Lady Francesca (Montjeu (IRE))
*4003*[8] *4497*[5] ***5796***[2] *6320*[5]

**Lady Makfi (IRE)** *Johnny Farrelly* a82 66
5 b m Makfi Dulcet Tones (IRE) (Singspiel (IRE))
*1405*[8] ***3190***[4] 5251[6] *5896*[2] *8548*[13]

**Lady Maldiva (IRE)** *Jose Santos* 6
2 b f Thewayyouare(USA) Rapid Review (IRE) (Observatory (USA))
**4090**[8] 5557[5] 6100[10]

**Lady Marigold (IRE)**
*Eve Johnson Houghton* 70
2 b f Intense Focus(USA) Peace Lily (Dansili)
3821[6] 5048[6] 6583[4] **(7688)**

**Lady Maritime (IRE)** *Brett Johnson* a48
3 b f Delegator No Song (Zamindar (USA))
*681*[8] ***1468***[3] *1900*[7]

**Lady Molly (IRE)** *Keith Dalgleish* a34 62
3 b f Kodiac Beth (Deportivo)
*1204*[6] **1828**[6] 2499[6] 3047[7] 3914[6] 4478[9] 5991[6] 6594[8] 7164[2] *7575*[11] 7660[6] 7884[10]

**Lady Momoka (IRE)** *Roger Varian* 70
2 b f Shamardal(USA) Juno Marlowe (IRE) (Danehill (USA))
**5349**[6]

**Lady Montdore (USA)** *A Fabre* 102
3 b f Medaglia d'Oro(USA) Hystericalady (USA) (Distorted Humor (USA))
**5981a**[3]

**Lady Morel (IRE)** *Joseph Tuite* a58 52
3 b f Arcano(IRE) Heart's Desire (IRE) (Royal Applause)
*987*[4] *1367*[8] *5239*[5] 5713[11] 5792[2] 6283[4] **(6748)** 7212[5] *8908*[15]

**Lady Nahema (IRE)** *Martin Bosley* a54 49
4 b m Zoffany(IRE) Jamary (IRE) (Grand Reward (USA))
2785[11] ***3172***[7] **5336**[9] *6621*[6]

**Lady Natasha (IRE)** *K R Burke* 65
4 b m Alfred Nobel(IRE) Hot To Rock (IRE) (Kalanisi (IRE))
**3311**[2] 3654[3] 4476[5] 5267[5] 5872[5] 7048[7]

**Lady Nayef** *John Butler* a86 69
4 b m Nayef(USA) Luck Will Come (IRE) (Desert Style (IRE))
*(22)* *(215)* *388*[4] ***664***[3] *851*[3] *1110*[5]

**Lady Noorah** *Richard Fahey* a72
2 ch f Nathaniel(IRE) Vital Statistics (Indian Ridge (IRE))
*8839*[6] ***9080***[2]

**Lady Of Aran (IRE)** *Charlie Fellowes* a82 73
2 b f Sir Prancealot(IRE) Tipperary Boutique (IRE) (Danehill Dancer (IRE))
6824[4] 7153[2] *(7707)* ***8671***[2]

**Lady Of Authority** *Murty McGrath* a65 22
2 b f Kheleyf(USA) Miss Authority (Authorized (IRE))
4151[12] *4749*[9] *5026*[7] ***9081***[3] *9436*[4]◆

**Lady Of Petra**
*Eve Johnson Houghton* a56 55
2 b f Compton Place Aqaba (Lake Coniston (IRE))
5321[3] ***5795***[10] 6584[5] *7756*[13]

**Lady Of Shalott** *David Simcock* 79
2 b f Camelot Silent Act (USA) (Theatrical (IRE))
**(8323)**◆

**Lady Of Steel** *John Butler* a52
3 b f Sir Percy Steel Free (IRE) (Danehill Dancer (IRE))
*6817*[11] *7322*[8] *7708*[9] ***8673***[7] *9092*[12]

**Lady Of The Court (IRE)** *J S Moore* 78
2 b f Camelot Caserta (Dansili)
5107[10] **5448a**[9] 5815a[6]

**Lady Of The Lamp (IRE)** *Rae Guest* a72 55
3 b f Invincible Spirit(IRE) Lady Angola (USA) (Lord At War (ARG))
6184[8] *6904*[2] *(7365)* ***(8552)*** *(8722)*

**Lady Of York** *Alan Bailey* a51 52
3 b f Sir Percy Parsonagehotelyork (IRE) (Danehill (USA))
2679[5] *3326*[3] **(4087)** 5215[4] *6069*[5]

**Lady Of Yue** *Eugene Stanford* a65 71
7 b m Manduro(GER) Desert Royalty (IRE) (Alhaarth (IRE))
*1416* **3148**[5] 7893[7]

**Lady Paname (FR)** *E Lellouche* 104
3 bl f Soldier Of Fortune(IRE) Business Class (FR) (Aussie Rules (USA))
2447a[3] 3366a[3] 5981a[5] **7634a**[4]

**Lady Parker (IRE)** *J S Moore* a48 4
3 gr f Zebedee Westering Home (IRE) (Mull Of Kintyre (USA))
***96***[9] *637*[8] *1424*[4]

**Lady Perignon** *Andrew Balding* a81 82
4 b m Poet's Voice Amalina (Green Desert (USA))
4410[9] 5529[8] 6700[11] **(7098)** 7815[4] *8257*[3] *8947*[4]

**Lady Petrus** *K Kukk* a23 24
12 b m Oasis Dream Odalisque (IRE) (Machiavellian (USA))
**2672a**[8] 3958a[6]

**Lady Prima** *Mike Murphy* a46 45
3 b f Sir Percy Alla Prima (IRE) (In The Wings)
*1727*[7] 5158[6] 5577[11] 6006[7] *6820*[12] *7537*[8]

**Lady Ramon (ITY)** *A Di Dio* 102
3 b f Ramonti(FR) Lady Praeneste (IRE) (One Cool Cat (USA))
**2244a**[2] 7441a[6]

**Lady Rocka** *Anabel K Murphy* a19 59
4 ch m Rock Of Gibraltar(IRE) Tap Dance Way (IRE) (Azamour (IRE))
*1629*[P] **1937**[7]

**Lady Rowena** *Mark Johnston* a43
3 ch f Sepoy(AUS) Miss Ivanhoe (IRE) (Selkirk (USA))
***305***[11]

**Lady Sandy (IRE)** *David Barron* a53 54
2 ch f Dandy Man(IRE) Surf's Up (IRE) (Encosta De Lago (AUS))
4296[8] **5210**[5] 6567[9] 7041[8] 7518[6] *8783*[10] *9302*[4]

**Lady Sophiebella** *Bryan Smart* a59 36
2 b f Monsieur Bond(IRE) Lady Paris (IRE) (Invincible Spirit (IRE))
8288[10] 8474[12] ***8851***[6] *9345*[3]

**Lady Sundew (IRE)** *Iain Jardine* a37
4 b m Roderic O'Connor(IRE) Dawaama (IRE) (Dansili)
*8554*[7] *8781*[8]

**Lady Turpin (IRE)** *Richard Fahey* a61 55
4 gr m Arakan(USA) Proficiency (El Prado (IRE))
*726*[3] ***(1188)*** *1330*[4] 3405[4]◆

**Lady Valdean** *Jose Santos* a76 74
3 ch f Helmet(AUS) Symphonic Dancer (USA) (Smart Strike (CAN))
3353a[2] 4232a[3] 5022[6] (6566a) 7505[9] 8390[9] 8732a[2] ***8976a***[6]

**Lady Volante (IRE)**
*Rebecca Menzies* a57 72
3 b f Teofilo(IRE) Empress Of Rome (IRE) (Holy Roman Emperor (IRE))
***48***[5] ***418***[6] *662*[7] *686*[2] *1123*[9] *1367*[5] *1564*[8] 1605[5] *2089*[3] **2338**[3] 6664[7] *7573*[10] 7820[6] 8122[12]

**Lady Willpower** *John Quinn* a75 75
2 b f Multiplex Gagajulu (Al Hareb (USA))
5702[9] 6146[4] 7022[5] 8236[2] **8471**[2] 8734[2] ***(9022)***

**Lady Wulfruna** *P Marion* a69 25
4 ch m Dutch Art My Girl Jode (Haafhd)
***391a***[15]

**Laem Sing (FR)** *Alain Couetil* a69 57
3 b f Myboycharlie(IRE) Miss Bio (FR) (River Mist (USA))
**6566a**[7]

**La Estrella (USA)** *Don Cantillon* a79 64
14 b g Theatrical(IRE) Princess Ellen (Tirol (IRE))
***666***[5] *1207*[6]

**La Farfallina** *Frank Sheridan* a62 65
2 ch f Compton Place La Fortunata (Lucky Story (USA))
4595a[4] ***8482a***[2]

**La Fibrossi (FR)** *H-A Pantall* a73 78
3 b f Myboycharlie(IRE) Tamada (Lucky Story (USA))
**2697a**[4] 3446a[5] 5910a[3]

**La Figlia (IRE)** *Jeremy Noseda* a67 101
3 ch f Frankel Finsceal Beo (IRE) (Mr Greeley (USA))
*6791*[2] **7576**[4]

**La Fortuna** *Charlie Wallis* a55
4 b m Zamindar(USA) Hyperspace (Dansili)
*5218* **5892**[9] *8395*[11] ***9129***[6] *9340*[5]

**La Fougasse (FR)** *R Kleparski* 29
9 b m Laury Royale(FR) Belle De La Baie (FR) (Winter Carnival (FR))
**4457a**[12]

**La Fritillaire** *James Given* a56 73
5 b m Champs Elysees Generous Diana (Generous (IRE))
2032[6] (2594) 2889[3] 4120[2] 4998[4] 6233[6] 6565[3] (7330) 7893[3] **8292**[3]

**Laganore (IRE)** *A J Martin* 111
5 b m Fastnet Rock(AUS) Lady Bones (IRE) (Royal Applause)
2637a[2] 4419a[5] 4934a[3] **(7171a)** **(8450a)**

**L'Age D'Or** *Robert Cowell* a54
2 b f Iffraaj Goleta (IRE) (Royal Applause)
***8851***[8]

**Lagenda** *Kristin Stubbs* a82 85
4 b g Dick Turpin(IRE) Whirly Dancer (Danehill Dancer (IRE))
1515[17] 2081[4] **2528**[3] 2952[6] 4207[12] 5610[6] 6570[2] 6964[4] 8014[18] *9025*[3] *9220*[3] *9281*[2]

**Lagertha (IRE)** *Hugo Palmer* 55
3 b f Oasis Dream Tafiya (Bahri (USA))
2834[6] **3866**[8] 4713[7]

**La Glorieuse (FR)** *T Castanheira* a55 53
2 gr f Rajsaman(FR) Cat Princess (IRE) (One Cool Cat (USA))
***6453a***[DSQ]

**La Gommeuse (IRE)**
*Mme C Head-Maarek* 98
3 gr f Zamindar(USA) Symba's Dream (USA) (Vindication (USA))
**3121a**[6] 6732a[7]

**Lagopus** *David Simcock* a50 39
4 b m Shirocco(GER) Pelagia (IRE) (Lycius (USA))
***1300***[5] 3542[10] *4003*[10] 4545[7]

**Lagostovegas (IRE)** *W P Mullins* 96
5 b m Footstepsinthesand Reine De Coeur (IRE) (Montjeu (IRE))
5488a[3] **8038**[3]◆

**La Goulue** *John Gallagher* a47 35
3 ch f Kheleyf(USA) Quotation (Medicean)
*1581*[5] 2266[8] 3309[8] *4164*[9] *8800*[11] *8956*[6] *9085*[4] ***9270***[10] *9430*[4]

**La Guapita** *Andrew Balding* a69 20
3 ch f Bahamian Bounty Somersault (Pivotal)
***34***[2] *625*[8] *1192*[4] 3571[4]

**Laharna (IRE)** *Noel Wilson*
2 b f Epaulette(AUS) Maughami (Manduro (GER))
5998[9] 8474[14] *8715*[9]

**La Haule Lady** *Paul Midgley* a34 63
3 ch f Helmet(AUS) Sea Of Leaves (USA) (Stormy Atlantic (USA))
*1123*[12] **1835**[4] 2372[5] 2897[10] 4479[7] 4997[5]◆ 6469[3] *7366*[12] 7926[9]

**La Havrese (FR)** *Lynn Siddall* a65 68
6 ch m Le Havre(IRE) La Buena (IRE) (Big Shuffle (USA))
3053[7] 3560[6] **4575**[5]◆ 5950[6] 6188[8] 6673[3]

**Lahayeb** *Michael Appleby* a46 72
5 b m High Chaparral(IRE) Tea Break (Daylami (IRE))
2817[7] **3558**[5] 3905[5] 4621[12]

**Lahdan (FR)** *F Rohaut* 73
2 ch c Style Vendome(FR) Home And Away (USA) (Skip Away (USA))
**5776a**[5]

**Lahore (USA)** *Roger Varian* 103
3 b c Elusive Quality(USA) Nayarra (IRE) (Cape Cross (IRE))
(2139)◆ (4407)◆ 6497a[5] **(7053)**◆ 7822[3]

**La Houblonniere (FR)** *J-C Rouget* a73 76
2 b f Le Havre(IRE) Mixed Intention (IRE) (Elusive City (USA))
**5815a**[2]

**La Houssay (FR)** *C Escuder* a76 76
5 b m Le Havre(IRE) Our Dream Queen (Oasis Dream)
***384a***[9]

**Laidback Romeo (IRE)** *Clive Cox* 104
5 b g Kodiac Belmora (USA) (Scrimshaw (USA))
(3014) **3837**[2] 6520[3] **7275**[5]

**Laieth** *Saeed bin Suroor* a79
2 b c Dubawi(IRE) First City (Diktat)
*7946*[4] ***(8492)***

**La Isla Bonita** *Richard Spencer* a66
3 b f Foxwedge(AUS) Excello (Exceed And Excel (AUS))
*1426*[6] *1727*[12] *(5848)* *6016*[3] *6846*[2] ***7540***[2] *8551*[11]

**Laith Alareen** *David O'Meara* a46 64
2 b g Invincible Spirit(IRE) Bewitchment (Pivotal)
2698[10] **3789**[5] 5162[9] *5479*[8]

**Lajatico** *Doug O'Neill* a50 91
4 b m Equiano(FR) Italian Connection (Cadeaux Genereux)
**1813a**[11]

**Lake Shore Drive (IRE)**
*Johnny Farrelly* a69 56
5 b g Thewayyouare(USA) Labrusca (Grand Lodge (USA))
5590[9] 7233[12] *(8878)* ***8955***[2]

**Lakeski** *Scott Dixon* a49 51
3 b f Sir Percy Floating (Oasis Dream)
*1293*[4] *1589*[6] 2227[6] **3913**[7] 4298[14] 4969[10]

**Lake Volta (IRE)** *Mark Johnston* a98 98
2 b g Raven's Pass(USA) Ghanaian (FR) (Shamardal (USA))
5504[7] (5865) **(6207)**◆ 6521[3] *6935*[3] ***7797a***[3] *8317*[6]

**La La Land (IRE)** *Jamie Osborne* a82 71
2 br c Dark Angel(IRE) Taraeff (IRE) (Cape Cross (IRE))
5547[3]◆ *6883*[5] 7503[5] *8491*[2] ***(8848)***◆

**Lalania** *Stuart Williams* 65
2 br f Kheleyf(USA) George's Gift (Haafhd)
**5851**[3]

**La Magique (GER)** *Henk Grewe* 78
2 b f Dabirsim(FR) La Miraculeuse (GER) (Samum (GER))
**6494a**[6]

**La Maquina** *George Baker* a81
2 b c Dutch Art Miss Meltemi (IRE) (Miswaki Tern (USA))
*8889*[4] ***9311***[2]

**Lamb Chop** *Rod Millman* a50 69
2 b f Havana Gold(IRE) Mutoon (IRE) (Erhaab (USA))
4806[9] 5216[10] **7226**[3] 7897[3] 8419[12] *9021*[8]

**Lambrini Legacy** *Lisa Williamson* 57
3 b f Captain Gerrard(IRE) Lambrini Lace (IRE) (Namid)
1785[4] 2280[2] **2674**[2] 3285[4] 3818[9] 4576[8] 4892[7] 5826[6] 6724[7]

**Lamchope (FR)** *Y Barberot* a86 73
2 b f Captain Chop(FR) Selam (GER) (Tertullian (USA))
(1282a) **(2642a)** 3515a[3] ***6452a***[2]

**La Mernancia (IRE)** *Jamie Osborne* a63
2 b f Kodiac Nashatara (USA) (Nashwan (USA))
***9081***[5] *9417*[5]

**La Michodiere (IRE)** *Henk Grewe* a81 88
3 gr f Power Lady Gray (IRE) (High Chaparral (IRE))
**(6650a)** 8959a[12]

**L'Ami De Rouge** *Ralph J Smith* a53 54
4 b m Excellent Art Coup De Torchon (FR) (Namid)
*2831*[2] *504*[8] *894*[4] *2272*[7] **3251**[4] *3724*[6] 4756[P] *8346*[11] *8846*[16]

**La Miss (FR)** *Y Gourraud* 70
2 b f Mount Nelson Glint Of Green (USA) (Jade Hunter (USA))
**6803a**[5]

**Lamloom (IRE)** *David O'Meara* 86
3 b g Cape Cross(IRE) Lulua (USA) (Bahri (USA))
1514[3] 1914[2] 2857[4] 3383[2] (4036) 4685[2] **5265**[2] 5664[6] 6468[5] 7327[7]

**Lamya (GER)** *Richard Hannon* 78
2 b f Choisir(AUS) Livia's Wake (IRE) (Galileo (IRE))
4815[6] (6438) **7357**[4]

**Lancaster Bomber (USA)**
*A P O'Brien* a110 119
3 b c War Front(USA) Sun Shower (IRE) (Indian Ridge (IRE))
*1375a*[4] 2399[4] 3100a[5] **3927**[2] 5527[6] 7179a[2] 8232[14] 8608a[2] 9170a[5]

**Lancelot Du Lac (ITY)** *Dean Ivory* a115 113
7 b g Shamardal(USA) Dodie Mae (USA) (Capote (USA))
***(63)*** *(572)* *917*[2] *1772*[4] 4072[10] (5640) 6966[5] 7144[12]

**Lanceur (FR)** *William Stone* a84 30
8 b g Rail Link Lanciana (IRE) (Acatenango (GER))
*744*[5] *1178*[9] ***1555***[5] 2752[10] *3459*[2]◆ *4499*[5] 5944[8]

**Landing Night (IRE)**
*Rebecca Menzies* a87 81
5 b g Kodiac Night Delight (IRE) (Night Shift (USA))
*4*[8] *219*[6] 2683[3] 3337[4] 3707[6] 4795[4] 5098[3] 5281[2] 6267[9] 6574[2] (6891) 7137[6] ***(7940)***◆ ***8660***[2] *8913*[5] *9079*[5]

**Land Of Mind** *M Delcher Sanchez* 69
2 b c Myboycharlie(IRE) Coco (USA) (Storm Bird (CAN))
**3679a**[5]

**Land's End (DEN)** *Francisco Castro* a96
5 b h Academy Award(IRE) Lois (SWE) (Fraam)
***(4940a)***

**Landshark** *Mrs John Harrington* 96
2 b c Bated Breath Tremelo Pointe (IRE) (Trempolino (USA))
**6488a**[2]

**Landsman (IRE)** *A J Martin* a61 90
4 b g Canford Cliffs(IRE) Mowaadah (IRE) (Alzao (USA))
6399[10] **6956a**[8]

**Landue** *Marcus Tregoning* a41 54
2 b c Champs Elysees Time Of Gold (USA) (Banker's Gold (USA))
4218[9] **4465**[9] *6816*[7]

**Landym (FR)** *H-A Pantall* a51 104
6 b h Lando(GER) Ymlaen (IRE) (Desert Prince (IRE))
1691a[7] **3104a**[7]

**Langham** *Michael Appleby* a70 59
4 b m Royal Applause Three Ducks (Diktat)
***501***[4]◆ *729*[5] 2993[8] 3729[8] *5482*[6] *6015*[8] 6296[9]

**Langlauf (USA)** *Rod Millman* a89 79
4 gr m Raven's Pass(USA) Emirates Girl (USA) (Unbridled's Song (USA))
*99*[8] *5073*◆ *(856)* 2387[5] *(3458)* ***(3968)*** 6865[5] 7401[8] 8166[8] *8893*[9] *9458*[11]

**Langley Vale** *Roger Teal* a70 66
8 b g Piccolo Running Glimpse (IRE) (Runnett)
*1979*[4] 3084[2] 3532[7] 4695[3] 5784[7] **(7191)** *8159*[8]

**Langtang (GER)** *A Wohler* 104
3 b c Campanologist(USA) La Vinchina (GER) (Oasis Dream)
2002a[2] **(3115a)**

**Langtree Lane** *Bryan Smart* 5
2 b f Equiano(FR) Saunta (Invincible Spirit (IRE))
**4834**[9]

**Lani (USA)** *Mikio Matsunaga* a114 90
4 rg h Tapit(USA) Heavenly Romance (JPN) (Sunday Silence (USA))
*1045a*[6] ***1380a***[8]

**Lanjano** *Kevin Ryan* a55 69
3 ch c Foxwedge(AUS) Hot Property (USA) (Thunder Gulch (USA))
2122[11] 5759[4] 6519[8] **8216**[5] *8958*[5]

**Lannister (FR)** *M Boutin*
2 b c Palace Episode(USA) Boulba D'Alben (FR) (Dark Angel (IRE))
1282a[11]

**Lansky (IRE)** *Jeremy Noseda* a81 100
2 b c Dark Angel(IRE) Goldthroat (IRE) (Zafonic (USA))
(6005)◆ **6326**[3] 7394[4] *(8028)*

**La Peregrina (FR)** *J-C Rouget* 74
2 bb f Excelebration(IRE) Private Eye (FR) (American Post)
**7415a**[2]

**La Perle Doloise (FR)** *A Bonin* a64 69
4 gr m Kingsalsa(USA) Claire Des Fieffes (FR) (Adieu Au Roi (IRE))
**4233a**[8]

**Lapilli** *William Haggas* a89 51
4 b g Bahamian Bounty Blue Lyric (Refuse To Bend (IRE))
**4867**[14]

**La Plusbelle** *Richard Fahey* a42 8
2 b f Champs Elysees Cat O' Nine Tails (Motivator)
4689[8] ***5412***[7] 6433[U]

**L'Apogee** *Richard Fahey* a61 62
4 ch g Rip Van Winkle(IRE) Pappas Ruby (USA) (Red Ransom (USA))
***147***[2]◆ *482*[9]

**La Poutanesca (IRE)** *D Smaga* 92
3 ch f Falco(USA) Victoria College (FR) (Rock Of Gibraltar (IRE))
3612a[6] 5777a[8] **7341a**[4] 8665a[4]

**Laqab (IRE)** *Roger Varian* a86 79
4 b g Teofilo(IRE) Ghaidaa (IRE) (Cape Cross (IRE))
**6482**[5] *6952*[7]

**Laraaib (IRE)** *Owen Burrows* 107
3 b c Pivotal Sahool (Unfuwain (USA))
(2359) (3042)◆ **(4882)**◆ 5925[3]

**La Rav (IRE)** *Luca Cumani* a100 95
3 b g Footstepsinthesand Swift Acclaim (IRE) (Acclamation)
2798[5] (3691) (4807)◆ ***5744***[3] 6404[10]

**Larch (IRE)** *Mrs A Malzard* 29
5 b m Acclamation Shady Nook (IRE) (Key Of Luck (USA))
5201a[9] **5985a**[5]

**Larchmont Lad (IRE)**
*David O'Meara* 109
3 b c Footstepsinthesand Fotini (IRE) (King's Best (USA))
1904[5] 2399[9] **2830**[2] 4817[4] 5925[11] 7275[3] **8438a**[2]

**Largent Du Bonheur (FR)**
*M Delzangles* 104
4 b g Kendargent(FR) La Joie (FR) (Montjeu (IRE))
2643a[6] **3370a**[4] 5450a[5] **6979a**[5] 7670a[8]

**Larno (FR)** *M Boutin* a76 85
3 gr g Milanais(FR) Honorable Sister (FR) (Highest Honor (FR))
3355a[2] 4783a[9] **8025a**[5]

**La Sardane (FR)** *B De Montzey* 108
3 b f Kingsalsa(USA) Foresta (FR) (Forestier (FR))
1270a[9] 1825a[2] **(3367a)**

**Laseen (IRE)** *James Cassidy* a89 100
6 b m Dylan Thomas(IRE) La Seine (USA) (Rahy (USA))
**8601a**[5]

**Lashabeeh (IRE)** *Roger Varian* a72
2 gr c Acclamation Do The Honours (IRE) (Highest Honor (FR))
***8988***[2]

**La Sioux (IRE)** *Richard Fahey* a39 69
3 ch f Casamento(IRE) Dakota Sioux (IRE) (College Chapel)
**(6568)**◆ *9464*[10]

**Lasqueti Spirit (AUS)** *Lee Curtis* 107
3 b f Beneteau(AUS) Supriym Story (AUS) (General Nediym (AUS))
1994a[12] **6714a**[12]

**Lassana Angel** *Roger Charlton* 70
3 b f High Chaparral(IRE) Diara Angel (IRE) (Hawk Wing (USA))
2231[6] 2760[5] **3425**[4]

**Last Chance Paddy (USA)**
*Alan Swinbank* a37 60
3 gr g Paddy O'Prado(USA) Mizzcan'tbewrong (USA) (Mizzen Mast (USA))
*1111*[4] **2429**[5] 2632[8]

**Last Enchantment (IRE)**
*Eve Johnson Houghton* a71 71
2 b f Camelot Illandrane (IRE) (Cape Cross (IRE))
***4496***[2] 5528[9] **6868**[2] 7621[9]

**Last Gift (IRE)** *M Narduzzi* 96
5 b m Starspangledbanner(AUS) Super Bobbina (IRE) (Daggers Drawn (USA))
**2867a**[9]

**Last Impact (JPN)** *Katsuhiko Sumii* a99 112
7 bb h Deep Impact(JPN) Superior Pearl (JPN) (Timber Country (USA))
**8975a**[14]

**Last Kingdom (USA)** *A Fabre* 110
3 b c Frankel Compelling (IRE) (Kingmambo (USA))
**(4235a)** 6053a[4]

**Lastmanlastround (IRE)** *Rae Guest* a87 86
4 b g Azamour(IRE) Lastroseofsummer (IRE) (Haafhd)
(2256)◆ ***3212***[2] *4001*[6] *6933*[7]

**Lastoneforthecraic (IRE)**
*David Evans* a23 47
2 b f Red Jazz(USA) Charming Vista (Josr Algarhoud (IRE))
3156[7] **3917**[10] 4440[14] *8793*[10]

**Last Page** *David Evans* 89
2 b g Pastoral Pursuits No Page (IRE) (Statue Of Liberty (USA))
1495[2] 1767[2] 2691[U] 3025[2] **3929**[5] 4582[6]

**Last Star Falling (IRE)** *Henry Spiller* a68 62
4 b m Acclamation Star Port (Observatory (USA))
***171***[5] *308*[6] *1490*[7] *1823*[9]

**Last Summer** *Grace Harris* a51 57
6 ch g New Approach(IRE) Evil Empire (GER) (Acatenango (GER))
*4141*[2] ***8591***[0]

**Last Voyage (USA)** *Charlie Appleby* a86 91
2 bb c Eskendereya(USA) Shipboard Romance (USA) (Pulpit (USA))
(2691) **7274**[3] *8149*[4]◆

**Last Word** *Joseph Tuite* a55 52
3 b f Bated Breath Intermission (IRE) (Royal Applause)
***8948***[8]

**Lastyouni (FR)** *Matthieu Palussiere* 16
2 ch f Siyouni(FR) Last Storm (Marju (IRE))
1335a[17] 1594a[12] 3444a[11] **6409a**[6]

**La Tanzania (GER)** *Eva Fabianova* 13
4 bb m Holy Roman Emperor(IRE) La Martina (GER) (Seattle Dancer (USA))
**7673a**[13]

**Late Change** *David Simcock* 58
2 b f Exceed And Excel(AUS) Khione (Dalakhani (IRE))
**5938**[7] 7399[6] 7620[9]

**La Testerine (FR)** *F Chappet* 45
3 b f Deportivo Mishkina (FR) (Vettori (IRE))
**1417a**[10]

**Latest Quest (IRE)** *Sylvester Kirk* a72 49
3 b g Zebedee Fancy Theory (USA) (Quest For Fame)
1685[7] 2056[3] 7005[7] **7212**[4] *7481*[3] *7540*[7] *8134*[10] *8543*[7] *9083*[9] *9268*[11]

**Lat Hawill (IRE)** *Keith Dalgleish* a100 96
6 b g Invincible Spirit(IRE) Arbella (Primo Dominie)
1492[10] **1799**[2] 2406[16] 2568[7] 3064[5] 4077[8] 4475[9] 8104[12] *8315*[8]

**Lathom** *Julie Camacho* a88 86
4 b g Compton Place Wigan Lane (Kheleyf (USA))
2083[8] ***2262***[5]◆ 2592[6] 2899[7] 4686[3] 5098[4]◆ 5602[4] 5929[7] 7625[4] 8167[5] 8680[4] *8927*[8]

**Laubali** *David O'Meara* a70 69
2 ch c Kyllachy Different (Bahamian Bounty)
6071[8] 6826[3] 7269[3] 8325[11] *8916*[4] ***9370***[3]

**Laugh Aloud** *John Gosden* a100 112
4 ch m Dubawi(IRE) Opera Comique (FR) (Singspiel (IRE))
*1795*[5] **(2392)** **(3319)**

**Laugh A Minute** *Roger Varian* 98
2 b c Mayson Funny Enough (Dansili)
4885[3]◆ 5380[2] 6403[3] **(7090)**

**Laughton** *Kevin Ryan* 87
4 b g Acclamation Peach Pearl (Invincible Spirit (IRE))
1831[7] **2123**[4] 2840[15] 4505[5] 5379[14] 6877[10] 8106[9] 8489[9]

**Launceston Place (FR)**
*Henry Spiller* a74 73
2 br c Le Havre(IRE) Last Song (Singspiel (IRE))
7281[8] 7819[3] ***8634***[3]

**Launched (IRE)** *P Bary* a92 111
5 b h Galileo(IRE) Apsara (FR) (Darshaan)
1871a[4] 2559a[7]
**La Undecima (FR)**
*M Delcher Sanchez* a61 74
3 b f Acclamation Nessa (FR) (Marchand De Sable (USA))
1417a[6]
**Laura Knight (IRE)** *Gary Moore* a64 56
2 gr f Dark Angel(IRE) Mauri Moon (Green Desert (USA))
3070[8] 3687[5] 4212[8] 4991[6] 6285[2] 6634[2] 7057[7] 7491[4]
**Laureate** *Mark Johnston* a69 72
3 b f Poet's Voice Step This Way (USA) (Giant's Causeway (USA))
1190[4] 2273[3] 2892[7] 3909[2] 5209[4]
**Laurens (FR)** *K R Burke* 113
2 b f Siyouni(FR) Recambe (IRE) (Cape Cross (IRE))
(5056) 6228a[2] (7088) **(8004)**
**Laureva Chope (FR)** *A Chopard* 64
2 b f Panis(USA) Gooseley Lane (Pyramus (USA))
5629a[9]
**Laur Net (USA)** *Robert B Hess Jr* 87
6 ch m Strong Hope(USA) Lady Lionel (USA) (Lucky Lionel (USA))
8601a[13]
**Lavetta** *Sally Haynes* a73 91
5 b m Peintre Celebre(USA) Card Games (First Trump)
1860[9] 3255[11] 4662[5] 5616[2] 6358[7] 8417[6]
**La Vie En Rose** *Mark Johnston* a78 73
3 b f Henrythenavigator(USA) Lady Jane Digby (Oasis Dream)
149[7] 305[2] 637[4] (2027)◆ (2991) 3261[2] 3933[3] 6013[2] 6680[4] 7568[2]
**La Volta Buona** *F Camici* 61
2 b c Royal Applause Ommadawn (IRE) (Montjeu (IRE))
8620a[8]
**Law And Order (IRE)** *James Tate* a107 109
3 b c Lawman(FR) Catbells (IRE) (Rakti)
(1621) 1861[3] 2399[10] 3013[4] 3592[10] 4322[4] 5037[4]◆ 6440[2] 6931[5] 7395[17] 7805[8] 8042[10]
**Lawfilly** *Richard Hughes* a59 57
3 b f Lawman(FR) Red Boots (IRE) (Verglas (IRE))
2362[5] 2733[3]◆ 3661[3] 3751[5] 4180[2] 4713[3] 5050[2] 5817[6] 6752[3]
**Lawless Louis** *David O'Meara* a73 79
3 ch g Equiano(FR) Peace And Love (IRE) (Fantastic Light (USA))
2104[3]◆ 2223[3] 2776[5] 3257[9] 4015[2] 4159[2] 4717[2]
**Lawless Secret** *Simon Crisford* a90 90
3 b f Lawman(FR) Lamentation (Singspiel (IRE))
(5721) 7119[2] 7908[3] 8414[2] 8838a[9]
**Lawmaking** *Henry Spiller* a80 93
4 b g Zamindar(USA) Canada Water (Dansili)
2692[8] 3919[8] 4556[7] (5363) 6145[5] 6422[2]◆ 7582[14] 8111[10] 8596[6]
**Lawman's Justice (IRE)**
*John Quinn* a45 14
4 b g Lawman(FR) Brazilian Bride (IRE) (Pivotal)
1758[9] 3450[6]
**Lawn Ranger** *Michael Attwater* a74
2 b g Cityscape Baylini (Bertolini (USA))
**(9385)**
**Laws Of Spin (IRE)** *W P Mullins* 101
4 b g Lawman(FR) Spinning Well (IRE) (Pivotal)
(6956a) 8038[32]
**Lawyer (IRE)** *David Barron* a84 85
6 b g Acclamation Charaig (Rainbow Quest (USA))
1202[4]
**Layali (FR)** *F Rohaut* 100
3 ch f Rip Van Winkle(IRE) Candicans (Dansili)
3366a[4] 8755a[7]
**Layali Al Andalus** *S Seemar* a71 83
10 b g Halling(USA) Lafite (Robellino (USA))
203a[13]
**Laydee Victoria (IRE)** *Ollie Pears* a51 51
2 b f Sir Prancealot(IRE) Damask (IRE) (Red Clubs (IRE))
2896[10] 3791[7] 4504[4] 5161[3] 8780[10] 9302[5]
**Layl (USA)** *Doug Watson* a102 71
7 br h Street Cry(IRE) Cymbal (IRE) (Singspiel (IRE))
650a[5] 891a[5]
**Layla's Hero (IRE)** *Roger Teal* a80 75
10 b g One Cool Cat(USA) Capua (USA) (Private Terms (USA))
267[10] 734[12]
**Laytown (IRE)** *Jamie Osborne* a64
2 ch f Footstepsinthesand Miss Mocca (Bahamian Bounty)
6636[7] 7535[3] 7875[4]
**Lazarus (IRE)** *Amy Murphy* a54 76
3 b g Zoffany(IRE) Knysna (IRE) (Rock Of Gibraltar (IRE))
5757[6] 6765[2] 7629[5] 8326[12] 8682[10] 9321[2]
**Lazio (IRE)** *Jamie Osborne* a61 61
4 b g Intikhab(USA) La Spezia (IRE) (Danehill Dancer (IRE))
4750[7] 5407[5]
**Lazizah** *Marcus Tregoning* 57
4 b m Medicean Atyaab (Green Desert (USA))
4461[9] 6846[9] 8183[10]
**Lbretha (FR)** *F-H Graffard* a89 97
4 b m Exceed And Excel(AUS) Actrice Francaise (USA) (Dynaformer (USA))
6697[7] 8089a[6]
**L C Saloon** *David C Griffiths* a70 78
4 ch g Equiano(FR) Aberdovey (Mister Baileys)
1542[5] 6267[19]
**Lead A Dance (IRE)** *John Butler* a51 14
3 b f Henrythenavigator(USA) Dancing Diva (FR) (Sadler's Wells (USA))
7080[10] 7542[5]
**Leaderofthepack** *Bryan Smart* a60 52
2 gr g Lethal Force(IRE) Spontaneity (IRE) (Holy Roman Emperor (IRE))
4599[8] 4996[5] 6012[3] 6951[6] 8190[5]
**Leader's Legacy (USA)**
*Saeed bin Suroor* 99
3 bb c War Front(USA) Bauble Queen (USA) (Arch (USA))
(2087) **(2612)** 3997[7]
**Leader Writer (FR)** *Henry Spiller* a73 104
5 b h Pivotal Miss Emma May (IRE) (Hawk Wing (USA))
5241[10] 5914[3] **(6873)** 7619[24]
**Leahcar** *James Ewart* a60
2 b f Delegator Certral (Iffraaj)
8316[11] 8914[7] 9099[4]◆
**Lean And Keen (IRE)** *Sean Byrne* a43 78
7 b g Antonius Pius(USA) Fury Dance (USA) (Cryptoclearance (USA))
1388a[13]
**Leanda J** *Ann Duffield* a14
2 ch f Equiano(FR) Wedding Dream (Oasis Dream)
5453[7] 8397[8]
**Lean On Pete (IRE)** *Ollie Pears* a67 49
8 b g Oasis Dream Superfonic (FR) (Zafonic (USA))
1864[3] 2687[11] 3205[5] 3935[4] (4169) 5002[8] 5483[10] 6088[4] 6524[2] 7479[14] 9077[2] (9346)
**Leapt** *Richard Hughes* a58 69
3 b g Nathaniel(IRE) Liel (Pivotal)
4347[7] 5034[5] 5406[2] 6370[4] 7232[4] 7560[4] 7879[8]◆
**Learn By Heart** *William Haggas* 97
2 b c Frankel Memory (IRE) (Danehill Dancer (IRE))
3037[3]◆ (4297)◆ 6190[4] 6925[2] 8290[4]
**Le Bernardin (USA)** *A R Al Rayhi* a112
8 br h Bernardini(USA) La Rosa (USA) (Wild Again (USA))
(85a) 541a[4] 1043a[8] 1373a[12]
**Le Brivido (FR)** *A Fabre* a80 118
3 b c Siyouni(FR) La Bugatty (IRE) (Dr Fong (USA))
2666a[2] (3959)◆
**Le Chat D'Or** *Michael Dods* 93
9 b g One Cool Cat(USA) Oh So Well (IRE) (Sadler's Wells (USA))
2155[13] 3651[6] **(4685)** 7566[10] 7981[2]
**Ledbury (IRE)** *Lee Carter* a69 11
5 b g Lawman(FR) Truly Magnificent (USA) (Elusive Quality (USA))
621[13] 865[5] 1402[9] 1698[6] 2332[11]
**Le Deluge (FR)** *Micky Hammond* a51 46
7 b g Oratorio(IRE) Princess Sofia (UAE) (Pennekamp (USA))
5539[3] 6901[12] 7235[11]
**Le Depute (FR)** *Ecurie Saint Simeon* a49 57
5 ch g Literato(FR) Hamida (USA) (Johannesburg (USA))
5269a[9]
**Ledham (IRE)** *Sir Michael Stoute* 69
2 b c Shamardal(USA) Pioneer Bride (USA) (Gone West (USA))
5547[4]
**Leeshaan (IRE)** *James Tate* a65 76
2 b c Bated Breath La Grande Elisa (IRE) (Ad Valorem (USA))
2222[3]◆ 3165[4]◆ **(3742)** 4465[6] 5875[7] 7363[6]
**Lefortovo (FR)** *Jo Hughes* a88 90
4 b g Arcano(IRE) Lorientaise (IRE) (Xaar)
1920a[3] 2696a[5] 4570[3] 4854[16]
**Left Alone** *Hugo Palmer* a79 77
2 b f Reckless Abandon Akhmatova (Cape Cross (IRE))
7334[3]◆ 7725[2] 8348[2]
**Left Hand** *C Laffon-Parias* 113
4 ch m Dubawi(IRE) Balladeuse (FR) (Singspiel (IRE))
2946a[6] 3369a[4] 4423a[5] 6248a[3] 6981a[3] 7669a[5] 8231[9]
**Legacy (GER)** *Jean-Pierre Carvalho*
2 b c Tertullian(USA) Lady Luck (GER) (Monsun (GER))
6986a[13]
**Legal History (IRE)** *Ed Walker* a66
2 b c Lawman(FR) Nina Celebre (IRE) (Peintre Celebre (USA))
9313[8]
**Legalized** *James Given* a47 48
3 br f Authorized(IRE) Laurena (GER) (Acatenango (GER))
5209[6] 6530[10] 7248[6] 7790[4] 8187[11]
**Legato (IRE)** *Tom Dascombe* 67
3 ch g Power Lisa Gherardini (IRE) (Barathea (IRE))
1730[6] 2110[4] 2527[7] 3489[3] 4623[8] 5753[8]
**Legendary Lunch (IRE)**
*Richard Hannon* 104
3 ch c Dragon Pulse(IRE) Taalluf (USA) (Hansel (USA))
2289[9] 4030[10]
**Legendoire (IRE)** *John Gallagher* a60 60
3 b g Fast Company(IRE) Last Shaambles (IRE) (Shaamit (IRE))
1421[7] 1787[3] 2362[9]
**Legend Status (IRE)**
*Adrian Paul Keatley* a58 48
3 b c Sir Prancealot(IRE) Baby Bunting (Wolfhound (USA))
3387[4]◆
**Le Gitan (FR)** *C Boutin* 71
2 ch c Dunkerque(FR) Voyageuse (FR) (Kentucky Dynamite (USA))
2073a[5] 3444a[6] 4389a[3]
**Legitimus (IRE)** *J S Bolger* 92
3 b f Lawman(FR) Imeall Na Speire (USA) (Galileo (IRE))
1387a[8] 1636a[8]
**Le Grand Voyage (FR)** *E Daure* a60 42
8 gr g Great Journey(JPN) Litlina (FR) (Linamix (FR))
364a[8]
**Le Gros Serpant (IRE)**
*Keith Dalgleish* a50 51
2 b c Zoffany(IRE) Fatwa (IRE) (Lahib (USA))
5068[5] 5278[8] 5665[11] 6022[4]
**Leigh's Law (IRE)** *Hugo Palmer* a43
2 b f Lawman(FR) Delira (IRE) (Namid)
8669[11]
**Leith Bridge** *Mark Usher* a47 39
5 b g Avonbridge Ishibee (IRE) (Ishiguru (USA))
622[8] 4969[8] 5410[11] 6004[9] 6174[6] 6529[12]
**Le Juge (IRE)** *A Fabre* a101 102
4 b h Dansili Mambo Light (USA) (Kingmambo (USA))
1691a[3] 4454a[3] 5269a[5] 6226a[2]
**Le Ken (ARG)** *Ignacio Correas IV* a104 107
3 b h Easing Along(USA) Le Yaca (CHI) (Hussonet (USA))
7851a[8]
**Le King (FR)** *J-M Capitte* 70
2 b c Alexandros Mermaids Quay (IRE) (Key Of Luck (USA))
5627a[3]
**Le Laitier (FR)** *Scott Dixon* a41 49
6 b g Milk It Mick La Brigitte (Tobougg (IRE))
3666[11] 3949[8] 5542[9] 6572[4] 8259[5] 8490[8] 8776[12] 9076[12]
**Le Manege Enchante (IRE)**
*Derek Shaw* a60 65
4 gr g Zebedee Beth (Deportivo)
80[8] 4509[3] 5318[4]◆ 5620[7] (6046) 6197[6] 7017[9] 8329[3]
**Lemon Drop** *Jim Boyle* a33 57
3 b f Paco Boy(IRE) Zia (GER) (Grand Lodge (USA))
1686[9] 2056[6] 2679[3] 5405[4] 5652[5] 6291[8] 7918[5]
**Lemon Thyme** *Mike Murphy* a63 45
4 b m Sakhee's Secret Limonia (GER) (Perugino (USA))
677[5]◆ 954[9] 1067[10] 1403[12]
**Lenin (IRE)** *J S Moore* a58
2 gr c Arakan(USA) Virginia Woolf (Daylami (IRE))
9231[7] 9385[6]
**Lenoire** *Michael Appleby* a54 58
3 b f Galileo(IRE) Latice (IRE) (Inchinor)
5319[6] 5591[7] 5997[3]
**Leodis (IRE)** *Tom Tate* a46 57
5 ch g Shirocco(GER) Leonica (Lion Cavern (USA))
4569[9] 8979[5]
**Leo Minor (USA)** *Robert Cowell* a93 88
3 b c War Front(USA) Kissed (IRE) (Galileo (IRE))
8991[12] 9453[6]
**Leonardo (GER)** *Shaun Lycett* a38 53
5 ch g Areion(GER) Lolli Pop (GER) (Cagliostro (GER))
2042[2] 2308[9] 2909[9] 4967[13] 7705[9] 9457[10]
**Leonard Thomas** *Rebecca Menzies* a61 49
7 b g Singspiel(IRE) Monawara (IRE) (Namaqualand (USA))
444[3] 841[7] 1028[3] 1312[7] 2082[6] 2687[10] 3529[4] 4260[7] 4744[5] 6003[6] 6470[6] 9261[10]
**Leonidas (IRE)** *Marcus Tregoning* a59 69
3 b g Dalakhani(IRE) Marque Royale (Royal Academy (USA))
3531[6] 8114[4]
**Leontes** *Andrew Balding* a87 76
3 ch g Paco Boy(IRE) Robema (Cadeaux Genereux)
1311[5] 3579[8] 6371[7] 6936[2]
**Leopard (IRE)** *Tony Coyle* a58 59
3 b g Iffraaj Appletreemagic (IRE) (Indian Danehill (IRE))
1552[9] 4602[4] 5485[6] 5880[8] 6549[9] 7220[3]◆ 7820[8] 8654[3]
**Le Pinchy (GER)** *Tom Dascombe* 13
3 ch g Adlerflug(GER) Lady Manners (USA) (Montbrook (USA))
7629[8]
**Le Professeur (FR)** *C Boutin* a43 55
2 b c Thewayyouare(USA) Litianinne (FR) (Invincible Spirit (IRE))
3445a[8] 8524a[7]
**Le Rebel (FR)** *K Borgel* a91 99
5 b h Linngari(IRE) Slitana (FR) (Dansili)
81a[7]
**Le Roi Du Temps (USA)** *Tom Tate* a63 45
4 ch g Leroidesanimaux(BRZ) Minute Limit (IRE) (Pivotal)
1606[18] 2684[14] 9100[9]
**Lesanti** *Ed de Giles* a48 55
3 b g Royal Applause Kammaan (Diktat)
2507[7]◆ 2792[4] 3823[2] 5067[5] 5545[6] 5792[3] 6324[5] 6751[8] 7480[8] 8248[8] 8800[10]
**Les Arceaux (IRE)** *J P Murtagh* a50 76
3 b g Arcano(IRE) Amoureux (USA) (Deputy Minister (CAN))
1596[5] **(7219)**
**Les Darcy** *Ken Cunningham-Brown* a34 38
6 b g Haatef(USA) Overcome (Belmez (USA))
739[8] 1075[9]
**L'Es Fremantle (FR)**
*Michael Chapman* a18 44
6 b g Orpen(USA) Grand Design (Danzero (AUS))
7479[7]
**Les Gar Gan (IRE)**
*Daniel Mark Loughnane* a65 61
6 b m Iffraaj Story (Observatory (USA))
461[1] 282[10] 605[12] 884[5]
**Leshlaa (USA)** *Saeed bin Suroor* a107 111
3 ch c Street Cry(IRE) Vine Street (IRE) (Singspiel (IRE))
1780[8] (2437) 2829[4] 3997[5] 4856[4]◆ 6024[9]◆ (6717a) 7395[6]
**Les Pecheurs (IRE)** *James Ewart* 57
3 b f Lilbourne Lad(IRE) Sweet Kristeen (USA) (Candy Stripes (USA))
2344[5] 3404[3] 3945[3] 4659[10] 5499[4] 5649[11] 6524[11]
**Lester Kris (IRE)** *Richard Hannon* a73 82
3 b g Fame And Glory Wood Sprite (Mister Baileys)
1877[4] 2807[2] 3286[3] 6763[2] 7063[7] 7462[2] 7744[3] 8464a[4]
**Letbygonesbeicons** *John Balding* a63 62
4 b g Sixties Icon Composing (IRE) (Noverre (USA))
20[4] 362[11]
**Lethal Angel** *Stuart Williams* a67 65
2 gr f Lethal Force(IRE) Heliograph (Ishiguru (USA))
8348[6] 8850[8] 9123[3]◆
**Lethal Impact (JPN)** *David Simcock* a78 76
3 b c Deep Impact(JPN) Musical Way (FR) (Gold Away (IRE))
1963[6] 2963[8] 3711[5] 6580[3] 7060[6]
**Lethal Lady** *Michael Dods* 19
2 ch f Lethal Force(IRE) Lady In The Bath (Forzando)
4689[9] 5180[6]
**Lethal Lunch** *Clive Cox* 83
2 gr c Lethal Force(IRE) Pin Cushion (Pivotal)
1681[7] 3406[3] **(4826)** 6699[4] 7353[7]
**Lethal Steps** *G M Lyons* a97 97
2 gr c Lethal Force(IRE) Tanda Tula (IRE) (Alhaarth (IRE))
6975a[5] 7797a[4]
**Le Tissier** *Michael Attwater* a61 66
4 ch g Sir Percy Incarnation (IRE) (Samum (GER))
395[2] 645[2] 859[8] 1486[4] 2042[7] 2332[7] 3756[12] 4756[6] 5787[9]
**Let It Go** *Tony Carroll* a29 14
5 b m Halling(USA) Kisses (Sakhee (USA))
274[13] 1246[8]
**Letmestopyouthere (IRE)**
*David Evans* a89 88
3 b g Sir Prancealot(IRE) Romanylei (IRE) (Blues Traveller (IRE))
(31)◆ 276[4] 626[5] 902[6] 1149[8] 1311[2] 1774[7] 2554[6] 3588[8] 4154[3] 5100[3] 5929[8] 6506[3] 7084[3] 7554[3]◆ 7612[2] 8077[7] 8736[6] 8881[6] 9305[5]
**Let Right Be Done** *Linda Perratt* a39 51
5 gr g Lawman(FR) Cheerfully (Sadler's Wells (USA))
44[14] 2378[5] 2955[12] 3048[3] 3196[9] 3831[6] 4039[5] 4659[7]◆ **(4687)** 5205[6] 5254[4] 5466[7] 5880[3] 5917[4] 5992[9] 6346[7] 6688[10] 7704[8] (7888) 7980[12] 8107[7] 8590[5]
**Le Tronquay (FR)** *P Sogorb* a56
2 b c Rajsaman(FR) Dasani (FR) (Dansili)
8482a[5]
**Letsbe Avenue (IRE)**
*Richard Hannon* a73 61
2 b c Lawman(FR) Aguilas Perla (IRE) (Indian Ridge (IRE))
4363[6]◆ 5105[7] 6140[6] **(7510)** 8349[17]
**Let's Be Happy (IRE)**
*Richard Hughes* a67 67
3 gr f Mastercraftsman(IRE) Corrozal (GER) (Cape Cross (IRE))
2259[6] 3326[2] **(3939)** 4462[2] 5722[3] 6556[5] 7712[3] 8312[4]
**Let's Go Donki (JPN)**
*Tomoyuki Umeda* 113
5 ch m King Kamehameha(JPN) Marutoku (JPN) (Marvelous Sunday (JPN))
9168a[6]
**Let's Sway** *Amy Murphy* a44 47
3 b f Authorized(IRE) Let's Dance (IRE) (Danehill Dancer (IRE))
2066[13] 2679[4] 3327[4] 3674[7] 4087[6]
**Let's Twist** *Kristin Stubbs* a80 64
5 ch g Piccolo Takes Two To Tango (Groom Dancer (USA))
1450[6] 2346[3] 6181[6] 6550[7] 7523[10]
**Le Vagabond (FR)** *E J O'Grady* a98 99
5 b g Footstepsinthesand Miryale (FR) (Anabaa (USA))
4822a[6] 6956a[5]
**Levante Player (IRE)**
*Tom Dascombe* a68 68
2 b g Kodiac Isolde's Return (Avonbridge)
2134[8] 3066[3] 4335[5] 6353[16] 7764[4] 8155[6]
**Leven (IRE)** *John Patrick Shanahan* 56
3 b g The Carbon Unit(USA) The Real Thing (IRE) (Traditionally (USA))
2496[4] 4476[6] 5074[5] 5648[9]
**Lever Du Soleil (FR)** *Tim Easterby* 50
2 b g Le Havre(IRE) Morning Dust (IRE) (Invincible Spirit (IRE))
2852[7] 3742[8] 7521[7]
**Lewinsky (IRE)** *Antony Brittain* a72 66
3 b f Famous Name Happy Flight (IRE) (Titus Livius (FR))
4003[2]◆ 4981[4] 6277[4] 7322[4] 8193[2] 8911[3] 9376[11]
**Lexington Abbey** *Kevin Ryan* a102 101
6 b g Sleeping Indian Silvereine (FR) (Bering)
1800[2] 4306[2] 4881[4]◆ 5911[3] 7144[4]
**Lexington Empire** *David Lanigan* a40
2 ch g Intello(GER) Emperice (USA) (Empire Maker (USA))
8643[11] 8952[10]
**Lexington Grace (IRE)**
*Richard Hannon* 79
2 bb f Sir Prancealot(IRE) Bronze Baby (USA) (Silver Charm (USA))
2265[6] 2583[2] 2987[3] (3902) 4252[5] 4739[4] 5150[23] (5886) (6552) 7914[3] **(8349)**
**Lexington Law (IRE)** *Alan King* a90 85
4 b g Lawman(FR) Tus Nua (IRE) (Galileo (IRE))
1457[2]◆ 2609[4] 3427[3] 5060[3] 5579[3] 6273[9] **(9458)**
**Lexington Place** *Ruth Carr* a67 92
7 ch g Compton Place Elidore (Danetime (IRE))
1876[6]◆ 2899[4] 3337[6] 3625[7] 4079[7] 4600[4] 5263[4] (5804) 6314[6] 6758[8] 7557[9]
**Lexington Sky (IRE)** *Roger Fell* a44 78
3 b f Iffraaj Hurricane Lily (IRE) (Ali-Royal (IRE))
1913[9] 5375[5] 5635[11] **(5759)** 5826[3] 6149[5] 6382[6] 6527[8] 7244[10] 8107[6] 8470[5]
**Lexington Times (IRE)** *Ruth Carr* a86 89
5 b g Paco Boy(IRE) Fuaigh Mor (IRE) (Dubai Destination (USA))
5[9] 2875[4]◆ 441[2] 506[2] 896[9] 2795[2] 3294[10] 3792[7] 4277[2] 4477[5] 5123[2] **(5379)** 5929[3] 6205[15] 6662[5] 7554[6] 8014[7]
**Lexi's Hero (IRE)** *Patrick Morris* a57 73
9 b g Invincible Spirit(IRE) Christel Flame (Darshaan)
2837[11] 4337[5]

**L'Explora (USA)** *Roger Charlton* a46
2 b f War Front(USA) Damson (IRE) (Entrepreneur)
7724[8]

**L Frank Baum (IRE)**
*Bernard Llewellyn* 23
10 b g Sinndar(IRE) Rainbow City (IRE) (Rainbow Quest (USA))
2364[8]

**Liamba** *David O'Meara* 39
2 b f Equiano(FR) Hisaronu (IRE) (Stravinsky (USA))
8483[5]

**Liberatum** *Ruth Carr* a77 78
3 b g Paco Boy(IRE) Fine Lady (Selkirk (USA))
4060[3] 5020[2] 5377[3] 5784[9] (6276) 6679[2] 6891[4] 7408[3] 7923[2] 8321[5]

**Liberty Belle (FR)** *E Lellouche* 71
2 b f Le Havre(IRE) Belle Lumiere (Fantastic Light (USA))
7969a[4]

**Liberty Lass (USA)** *Emmet Mullins* a37 65
2 b f Hat Trick(JPN) Libertaire (USA) (Highest Honor (FR))
7797a[7]

**Liberty Lynx** *William Haggas* a46
2 b f High Chaparral(IRE) Stella Point (IRE) (Pivotal)
9433[7]

**Libran (IRE)** *Chris Waller* 110
6 b g Lawman(FR) True Crystal (IRE) (Sadler's Wells (USA))
1994a[P] 6714a[6] 8667a[8]

**Librisa Breeze** *Dean Ivory* a104 121
5 gr g Mount Nelson Bruxcalina (FR) (Linamix (FR))
4071[4]◆ 5502[9] 6193[2] (8230)

**License To Thrill (USA)**
*Simon Dow* a63 17
3 b c Mizzen Mast(USA) Mystic Miracle (Dalakhani (IRE))
114[3] 210[5] 284[5]

**Licinius** *Charles Hills* a39
2 b g Rock Of Gibraltar(IRE) Vespasia (Medicean)
9433[9]

**Licinius (GER)** *Yasmin Almenrader* a72 87
4 b h Halling(USA) La Vinchina (GER) (Oasis Dream)
9003a[15]

**Lifeboat (IRE)** *Charles Hills* 77
2 b g Born To Sea(IRE) Mrs Seek (Unfuwain (USA))
3746[5] 4218[2] 7093[6] 7818[7]

**Lifeboat Lad (USA)** *Dean Ivory* 50
3 br g Exchange Rate(USA) Bema (USA) (Pulpit (USA))
2475[13] 2782[7] 4152[7]

**Life For Rent** *Tim Easterby* a61 68
2 b g Sleeping Indian Sea Flower (IRE) (Acclamation)
2882[4]◆ 5127[3] 5834[7] 6547[5] (6756) 7734[5]

**Life Happens** *Jonathan Portman* a53
3 b f Pastoral Pursuits Halfwaytoparadise (Observatory (USA))
552[6] 9127[11]

**Life Knowledge (IRE)**
*Patrick Holmes* a60 60
5 ch g Thewayyouare(USA) Rosa Bellini (IRE) (Rossini (USA))
(726) 2183[4] 2427[2] 7479[11] 8909[6] 9261[3]

**Life Less Ordinary (IRE)**
*Chris Waller* a89 101
5 b g Thewayyouare(USA) Dont Cross Tina (IRE) (Cape Cross (IRE))
6714a[5]

**Life Of Fame** *Rebecca Menzies* a62 58
4 b m Equiano(FR) Fame Is The Spur (Motivator)
44[10] 217[4] 386[7] 1721[9] 2063[9]

**Life Of Luxury** *Mark Brisbourne* a62 54
4 b g Shamardal(USA) Champagnelifestyle (Montjeu (IRE))
127[7] 2167[6] 3264[4] 4163[5] 4982[2] 5485[3] 6294[5] 6953[12] 7413[6] 8135[8] 8507[6] 9084[10]

**Life Won't Wait** *John Quinn* a60
3 b g Showcasing Manbaa (USA) (Jazil (USA))
27[2] 402[3] 766[6]

**Ligeti (IRE)** *Joseph Patrick O'Brien* a79 79
4 b g Rip Van Winkle(IRE) Dollar Chick (IRE) (Dansili)
1014a[2] 4898[5]

**Lightening Dance** *Amanda Perrett* 82
3 b f Nathaniel(IRE) Dance Lively (USA) (Kingmambo (USA))
2759[2] (3615) 4155[2] 5715[8] 8390[12]

**Lightening Fast** *G M Lyons* a70 97
3 b g Frankel Lightening Pearl (IRE) (Marju (IRE))
3997[23] 8222a[14]

**Lightening Quick** *G M Lyons* 92
2 b f Frankel Lightening Pearl (IRE) (Marju (IRE))
7578[8]

**Light From Mars** *Ronald Harris* a66 52
12 gr g Fantastic Light(USA) Hylandra (USA) (Bering)
745[3] 1085[11] 1419[2] 1728[8] 3084[8] 9083[5]

**Light Gunner (IRE)** *Henry Tett* a52 52
3 b g Lawman(FR) Neve Lieve (IRE) (Dubai Destination (USA))
1499[7] 2027[9] 3087[3]◆ 3674[8] 5780[6] 6821[4]

**Light Humor (USA)** *Jeremy Noseda*
3 bb f Distorted Humor(USA) Aldebaran Light (USA) (Seattle Slew (USA))
4444[9]

**Lightly Squeeze** *Philip Hide* a75 83
3 b g Poet's Voice Zuleika Dobson (Cadeaux Genereux)
(1840) 2690[6] 3392[6] 4632[6] (5319) 6189[7] 7277[4] 7927[6]

**Lightning Charlie** *Amanda Perrett* a91 94
5 b g Myboycharlie(IRE) Lighted Way (Kris)
1586[2] 2040[2] 2390[5] (4830) 5637[15] 6275[10] 7455[11]

**Lightning Mark (IRE)** *John Gosden* 45
3 b f Invincible Spirit(IRE) Maakrah (Dubai Destination (USA))
2753[5]

**Lightning Spear** *David Simcock* a93 122
6 ch h Pivotal Atlantic Destiny (IRE) (Royal Academy (USA))
2825[2] 3924[9] 4638[7] 5527[3] (6420) 6982a[6] 8232[6] 9170a[10]

**Light Of Air (FR)** *Gary Moore* a76 79
4 b g Youmzain(IRE) Height Of Vanity (IRE) (Erhaab (USA))
549[2] 965[3] 1289[4] 1683[4] 2055[3] (2678) 3308[2] 4519[3] 6258[2]

**Light Of Joy (USA)** *David Lanigan* a83 83
3 ch f Kitten's Joy(USA) Light Blow (USA) (Kingmambo (USA))
2311[8]◆ 3342[3] (4042)◆ 4621[2] 5822[4] 6307[4] 6848[9] 7762[3]

**Light Of The World (IRE)**
*Georgios Alimpinisis* a54 42
5 b m Fastnet Rock(AUS) Gassal (Oasis Dream)
8127a[5]

**Lightoller (IRE)** *P Monfort* a70 70
3 ch g Harbour Watch(IRE) April (IRE) (Rock Of Gibraltar (IRE))
1411[9] 1625[7] 1970[7] 2235[5] 2362[2] 2474[7] 2720[U] 3035[2] 3624[4] 3692[5] (4046) 4157[2] 4532[5] 4717[3] 5588[3] 5956[2] 6558[4] 7308a[2]

**Light Pillar (IRE)** *A Fabre* a69 100
3 b c Galileo(IRE) Burning Sunset (Caerleon (USA))
5982a[4] 6913a[5]

**Light Relief** *James Tate* a73 51
2 b f Medicean Tickle Me (GER) (Halling (USA))
6385[6] 8147[2] 8670[11]

**Lights** *Declan Carroll* a46 23
3 b f Delegator Sirenuse (IRE) (Exceed And Excel (AUS))
1715[11]

**Lightscameraction (IRE)**
*Gay Kelleway* a94 102
5 ch g Pastoral Pursuits Silca Boo (Efisio)
200[8] 388[10] 4333[11] 5116[6] 5402[13] 7604[10]

**Lightsome** *Harry Dunlop* a56 53
4 b m Makfi Aunty Mary (Common Grounds)
303[4] 495[3]

**Light The Lights (SAF)**
*M F De Kock* 112
5 b g Western Winter(USA) First Arrival (SAF) (Northern Guest (USA))
(86a) 429a[2] 774a[5] 1046a[6]

**Light Up Dubai** *Charlie Appleby* a64
2 b c Kodiac Tuscan Light (Medicean)
8703[4]

**Lightupthenight** *F-H Graffard* a80 98
3 b f Dutch Art Nuit Polaire (IRE) (Kheleyf (USA))
4666a[5]

**Like A Diamond (IRE)** *Brian Ellison* a85 48
7 b g Antonius Pius(USA) Silk Law (IRE) (Barathea (IRE))
359[14]

**Like A Star (IRE)** *A P O'Brien* 56
4 b m Galileo(IRE) Anna Karenina (IRE) (Green Desert (USA))
3874a[10]

**Like Lightning (IRE)** *J S Moore* 82
2 b c Fast Company(IRE) Sara Mana Mou (Medicean)
2779[7] (3444a) (4166a)

**Like Minds** *David Brown* a40 38
3 b f Royal Applause Creative Mind (IRE) (Danehill Dancer (IRE))
8242[6] 8395[9] 8707[7]

**Like No Other** *Les Eyre* a84 79
4 b g Approve(IRE) Blue Beacon (Fantastic Light (USA))
32[8] 581[11] 1778[9] 2684[2] 3433[9] 4556[9] 5739[9] 7157[12] 7474[13]

**Lilac Fairy (FR)** *F-H Graffard* 92
2 b f Redoute's Choice(AUS) Border Bloom (Selkirk (USA))
6171a[8] 7637a[2] (8443a)

**Lila Mahyana (FR)** *C Boutin* a41 47
4 b m Muhaymin(USA) Lila Rose (IRE) (Kendor (FR))
1078a[11]

**Lil Gem (IRE)** *Keith Dalgleish* 51
2 b f Sepoy(AUS) Cynthia Calhoun (Exceed And Excel (AUS))
2836[7] 3482[5] 5015[11] 5878[8] 7222[8] 7698[9]

**Lili Du Sud (FR)** *Y Gourraud* 79
2 gr f Lord Du Sud(FR) Lipari (FR) (Rock Of Gibraltar (IRE))
4596a[7] (5629a) 6228a[11]

**Lilly Ballerina (IRE)** *Lee James* 21
3 b f Lilbourne Lad(IRE) Entrechat (Green Desert (USA))
2362[10] 6047[13]

**Lilly Kafeine (FR)** *J C Napoli* a85 83
3 b f Myboycharlie(IRE) Hamida (USA) (Johannesburg (USA))
799a[4] 1270a[8]

**Lil Sophella (IRE)** *Patrick Holmes* a87 71
8 ch m Indian Haven Discotheque (USA) (Not For Love (USA))
2805[9] 3567[7] 3828[8] 5185[7] 6047[4] 6591[4]◆ 6893[5] 7476[15] 8206[7] 8429[10]

**Lily Ash (IRE)** *Mike Murphy* a59 42
4 b m Lilbourne Lad(IRE) Ashdali (IRE) (Grand Lodge (USA))
735[5] 983[2] 1325[6] 5855[7] 7605[4]

**Lily Cliff** *Paul D'Arcy* a32
3 b f Canford Cliffs(IRE) Night Lily (IRE) (Night Shift (USA))
311[8] 463[8]

**Lily Edge** *John Bridger* a54 49
8 b m Byron Flaming Spirt (Blushing Flame (USA))
35[4] 278[6]

**Lily Fontana (IRE)** *Richard Fahey* a37
3 b f Dandy Man(IRE) Lily's Dream (IRE) (Celtic Swing)
139[10] 1367[7]

**Limario (GER)** *Doug Watson* a96 101
7 br h Areion(GER) Limaga (Lagunas)
205a[11] 538a[5] 654a[7] 888a[5]

**Limato (IRE)** *Henry Candy* a100 126
5 b g Tagula(IRE) Come April (Singspiel (IRE))
1376a[10] 4071[3] 4907[2] 5502[4] (8003)

**Lime And Lemon (IRE)** *Clive Cox* a59 83
4 b m Makfi Nimboo (USA) (Lemon Drop Kid (USA))
1517[5] 2234[3] 3158[2] 8111[2] 8390[8]

**Li Mei (IRE)** *William Haggas* a50
3 b f Iffraaj Rose Of Battle (Averti (IRE))
8554[5]

**Limelite (IRE)** *Richard Hannon* 75
3 b f Dark Angel(IRE) Light It Up (IRE) (Elusive City (USA))
2503[10]◆ 3246[2] (3751) 5078[3] 6397[3] 7094[8]

**Lime Pickle** *John Davies* a44
2 b g Major Cadeaux Ocean Grove (IRE) (Fairy King (USA))
8587[8]

**Limerick Lord (IRE)** *Julia Feilden* a58 53
5 b g Lord Shanakill(USA) Hollow Green (IRE) (Beat Hollow)
7[5] 69[3] 481[8] 614[5] 761[4] 1075[5]◆ 1187[4] 1325[8] 5146[4] 5791[3] 6751[5] 7212[2] 9076[6] 9343[2]

**Limited Edition (FR)** *E Lellouche* a77 103
3 bl f Kendargent(FR) Apperella (Rainbow Quest (USA))
2945a[8] 5196a[3] 6054a[3] 7341a[6] 8665a[5]

**Limonata (IRE)** *Harry Whittington* a67 69
4 b m Bushranger(IRE) Come April (Singspiel (IRE))
147[9]

**Limoncino (IRE)** *Michael Dods* a67 30
3 b f Arcano(IRE) Come April (Singspiel (IRE))
8217[7] 8592[3]◆ 8931[3] 9304[4]

**Lina's Star (IRE)** *David O'Meara* a67 63
2 b f Lawman(FR) Readyandaway (USA) (More Than Ready (USA))
3447[4] 4895[3] 5494[2] 6547[3] (7363) 8954[7] 9345[6]

**Lincoln (IRE)** *Mick Channon* a72 100
6 b g Clodovil(IRE) Gilt Linked (Compton Place)
1515[12] 2736[3] 4411[7] 7809[3]◆

**Lincoln Rocks** *David O'Meara* a88 110
4 b m Rock Of Gibraltar(IRE) Redskin Dancer (IRE) (Namid)
2268[2] 2593[4] 2789[3] (3828) 4578[4] (4718) 5152[2] 5506[2]◆ 5927[2] (6358) 6697[9] 7576[5]

**Linda Doris (IRE)** *Gay Kelleway* a49 40
3 b f Art Connoisseur(IRE) Kai Mook (Littletown Boy (USA))
3595[9] 7907[9] 8342[4] 8784[8] 8994[5] 9237[7]

**Lindikova (FR)** *R Rohne*
3 ch f Linda's Lad Pivotal Answer (IRE) (Pivotal)
3134a[16]

**Lindo Amor (ARG)** *M F De Kock* a109 65
4 ch h Dynamix(USA) Linda Love (ARG) (Salt Lake (USA))
85a[3] 541a[7] 695a[3] 1043a[10]

**Lindsar** *M G Mintchev* a66 61
3 ch c Shamardal(USA) Lady Linda (USA) (Torrential (USA))
6124a[9]

**Line Des Ongrais (FR)**
*P Chemin & C Herpin* a72 91
6 b m Voix Du Nord(FR) Kitzmaid (GER) (Midyan (USA))
5198a[6]

**Line Drummer (FR)** *J Reynier* 92
7 b g Galileo(IRE) Miss Bio (FR) (River Mist (USA))
1691a[8] 2696a[10] 5490a[10]

**Line House** *K R Burke* a75
2 ch f Kheleyf(USA) Wood Fairy (Haafhd)
7453[3] 7757[4] (8208) 9177[2]

**Lineman** *Sarah Hollinshead* a54 61
7 b g Rail Link Shamana (USA) (Woodman (USA))
98[2] 721[5] 900[7] 1369[7] 1629[9] 3756[11]

**Line Of Beauty** *Simon Crisford* a74 69
3 b f Helmet(AUS) Bisou (Tiger Hill (IRE))
3866[7] 5124[5] 6027[2]◆ 6852[2] 7279[8] 8770[3] 9276[2] 9455[3]

**Lineofintelligence** *Richard Fahey* 59
2 b g Intello(GER) Linea (King's Best (USA))
5680[5] 7520[8]

**Line Of Reason (IRE)** *Paul Midgley* a108 106
7 br g Kheleyf(USA) Miss Party Line (USA) (Phone Trick (USA))
84a[5] 318a[4] 543a[6] 651a[5] 773a[8] 1800[3] 2031[4] 3092[7] 3321[9] (3829) (4306) 4635[7] 5505[8] 6668[8] 7144[21] 7396[7] 7475[2] 9409[8]

**L'Inganno Felice (FR)** *Iain Jardine* a90 81
7 br g Librettist(USA) Final Overture (FR) (Rossini (USA))
(42) (154) 389[2]◆ 991[9] 1307[5]

**Linguine (FR)** *Seamus Durack* a35 73
7 ch g Linngari(IRE) Amerissage (USA) (Rahy (USA))
5025[6] 6259[4] 6889[9]

**Linguistic (IRE)** *S bin Ghadayer* a106 107
4 b g Lope De Vega(IRE) Dazzle Dancer (IRE) (Montjeu (IRE))
1500[2] 7619[18] 8042[3] 8234[17] 9360a[11]

**Links Bar Marbella (IRE)**
*Eric Wheeler* 27
4 ch g Intense Focus(USA) Silesian (IRE) (Singspiel (IRE))
2581[7] 3440[6]

**Linngaria (FR)** *Mario Hofer* a59 7
2 b f Linngari(IRE) Syllable (Halling (USA))
8252a[9]

**L'Invincible (FR)** *J-P-J Dubois* a39 79
3 b f Invincible Spirit(IRE) Brasileira (Dubai Destination (USA))
3613a[6]

**Lionrockspirit (IRE)** *Marco Botti* a108 54
4 b g Fastnet Rock(AUS) Phillippa (IRE) (Galileo (IRE))
1757[4]

**Lions Charge (USA)**
*Seamus Mullins* a67 59
10 ch g Lion Heart(USA) Fellwaati (USA) (Alydar (USA))
279[12]

**Lions Hill (GER)** *J-Y Artu* a58
4 b g Tiger Hill(IRE) Laccata (Lomitas)
9112a[9] 9309a[12]

**Liquid (IRE)** *David Barron* a79 75
3 ch g Zoffany(IRE) Playful Promises (IRE) (Elnadim (USA))
2139[2] 2405[2] (5006) 5708[7] 6430[4]◆ 6891[9] 7939[2] 8320[3]

**Liquid Amber (USA)** *W McCreery* 107
2 ch f Kitten's Joy(USA) Pachattack (USA) (Pulpit (USA))
(6487a)

**Liquid Gold (IRE)** *Richard Fahey* 76
3 b f Nathaniel(IRE) Northern Mischief (USA) (Yankee Victor (USA))
2704[2]◆ 3500[2] 4036[2] 5454[6] (6060) 7598[4] 8295[7]

**Lisala (FR)** *Mlle M Henry* a53 60
4 b m Siyouni(FR) Lilac Charm (IRE) (Marju (IRE))
391a[10]

**Lisard Lady (IRE)** *Thomas Cooper* 74
2 b f Bated Breath Shirley Blake (IRE) (Acclamation)
8082a[7]

**Lisbon Legend** *Tony Carroll* 30
2 b c Kyllachy Expect (Invincible Spirit (IRE))
3516[9] 4620[6] 5408[6]

**Lisheen Castle (IRE)** *John Quinn* 94
2 b c Most Improved(IRE) Mafaaza (USA) (Jazil (USA))
(6380) 7648[4] 8290[2]

**Lisnamoyle Lady (IRE)**
*Martin Smith*
2 ch f Roderic O'Connor(IRE) Allegheny Dawn (IRE) (Teofilo (IRE))
8245[11]

**Lisnavagh (FR)** *Jane Soubagne* a70 60
5 ch m Doctor Dino(FR) Sweet Lady Jane (FR) (Kaldounevees (FR))
384a[6]

**Lisp (IRE)** *Charles Hills* 68
3 ch g Poet's Voice Hora (Hernando (FR))
2476[11]

**Listen Alexander (IRE)** *David Evans* 79
2 br f Kodiac Private Alexander (IRE) (Footstepsinthesand)
1909[4] 2904[2] 3611a[6] (4841) 5109[6] 6136[9] 6863[13]

**Listen In (IRE)** *F Head* 107
3 ch f Sea The Stars(IRE) Es Que (Inchinor)
2003a[2] 4424a[2] 5449a[2] 7635a[2] 8273a[3]

**Litaara (GER)** *P Schiergen* 95
3 b f Wiener Walzer(GER) Linton Bay (GER) (Funambule (USA))
3371a[3] 5693a[12] 6710a[10] 8462a[6]

**Little Aub** *Mark Usher* a58
2 b g Milk It Mick Makindi (Makbul)
8988[9] 9231[6]

**Little Belter (IRE)** *Keith Dalgleish* a52 60
5 gr g Dandy Man(IRE) On Thin Ice (IRE) (Verglas (IRE))
1006[13] 1126[8] 1372[3] 2342[9] 2949[11] 5203[8]

**Little Boy Blue** *Bill Turner* a81 80
2 gr g Hellvelyn Dusty Dazzler (IRE) (Titus Livius (FR))
5270[2] 7731[2]◆ (9188) 9404[3]

**Little Choosey** *Roy Bowring* a65 67
7 ch m Cadeaux Genereux Little Nymph (Emperor Fountain)
7[6] 69[2] 390[11] 1225[3] 1449[4] 2276[2] 2626[2] 3628[7] 6673[9] 7323[8] 8401[5]◆ 8591[4] 9056[11] 9343[7]

**Little Cupcake** *Denis Quinn* a49 37
6 b m Myboycharlie(IRE) Imco Cracking (IRE) (Piccolo)
2454[11] 3686[4] 4008[4] 4458[6] 4997[10]

**Little Ghetto Boy** *Tamara Richter* a74 47
4 b g Lawman(FR) Ahea (USA) (Giant's Causeway (USA))
1078a[3] 6302a[5]

**Little Indian** *J R Jenkins* a64 57
7 b g Sleeping Indian Once Removed (Distant Relative)
(167) 739[5] 1304[DSQ] 1557[4] 2732[8] 4727[9] 6112[11] 6814[7]

**Little Jo** *Brian Ellison* a56 49
3 b g Major Cadeaux Discoed (Distinctly North (USA))
5458[4] 6236[9] 6548[3] 7047[6] 7895[7] (8719)

**Little Kingdom (IRE)** *Tracy Waggott* a58 59
3 b f Royal Applause Hadba (IRE) (Cape Cross (IRE))
179[4] (511) 1835[13] 2853[2] 2925[7] 4107[8] 4694[7] 5741[6] 6437[12] 7166[4] 8591[13] 8924[11] 9019[9] 9265[6]

**Little Kipling** *Stuart Williams* a70 70
4 b m Royal Applause Victoria Sponge (IRE) (Marju (IRE))
883[4] 1237[2] 1618[3] 1789[4]

**Little Lady Katie (IRE)** *K R Burke* 91
5 b m Lord Shanakill(USA) Akarita (IRE) (Akarad (FR))
3589[8] 4366[4] 4662[4] 5317[5] 5926[9] 6691[5]

**Little Lizzie** *Paddy Butler* a21
4 ch m Sleeping Indian Quality Street (Fraam)
1785[6]

**Littlelordconford (IRE)**
*Richard Spencer* a50 34
2 b g Intikhab(USA) Anna Law (IRE) (Lawman (FR))
5654[5] 7731[9] 8028[7]

**Little Lotte (IRE)** *Tom Gretton* a1 34
4 b m Kodiac Dancing Steps (Zafonic (USA))
1329[7]

**Little Luna (IRE)** *John Geoghegan* 56
2 b f Epaulette(AUS) Lady Pitrizza (IRE) (Night Shift (USA))
6977a[20]

**Little Miss Daisy** *William Muir* a71 64
3 b f Arabian Gleam Desert Liaison (Dansili)
324[2] (623) 1474[2] 1786[7] 2235[13]◆ 4990[3] 5837[3] 6372[2] 7272[8] 7912[8] 8953[9]

**Little Miss Kodi (IRE)**
*Daniel Mark Loughnane* a78 81
4 b m Kodiac Sensasse (IRE) (Imperial Ballet (IRE))
*1890$^{8}$* **2888$^{2}$** 3287$^{6}$ 4887$^{12}$ *6015$^{10}$ 9316$^{5}$*

**Little Miss Lilly** *Clive Cox* a66 67
2 b f Lethal Force(IRE) Malilla (IRE) (Red Clubs (IRE))
2905$^{8}$ **3815$^{3}$** 4533$^{9}$ *8131$^{7}$ 9090$^{4}$*

**Little Miss Lola** *Lynn Siddall* a58 52
3 ch f Dandy Man(IRE) Purepleasureseeker (IRE) (Grand Lodge (USA))
**2630$^{5}$** 3171$^{9}$ 4122$^{5}$ 4509$^{7}$ *7575$^{6}$ (8558) 9019$^{6}$ 9265$^{2}$*◆

**Little Miss Tango** *Roger Teal* a15
3 ch f Steele Tango(USA) Many Welcomes (Young Ern)
4490$^{5}$ ***8869$^{10}$***

**Little Monkey** *Antony Brittain* a9 45
2 b f Monsieur Bond(IRE) Lujiana (Lujain (USA))
4555$^{11}$ 4740$^{9}$ **5945$^{2}$** 7518$^{13}$ *8191$^{11}$*

**Little Nosegay (IRE)** *David Evans*
3 gr f Clodovil(IRE) Bank On Black (IRE) (Big Bad Bob (IRE))
*77$^{4}$ 456$^{7}$ 787$^{10}$* **(960)** *1204$^{4}$ 1220$^{9}$*

**Little Orchid** *Julia Feilden* a55 56
4 b m Observatory(USA) Bushy Dell (IRE) (King Charlemagne (USA))
2281$^{7}$ **2972$^{4}$** 3756$^{10}$ 4181$^{6}$

**Little Palaver** *Clive Cox* a85 97
5 b g Showcasing Little Nymph (Emperor Fountain)
**(2040)** 2566$^{3}$ 3410$^{10}$ 4830$^{11}$ 5720$^{6}$

**Little Pippin** *Tony Coyle* a47 52
4 b m Sir Percy Lady Le Quesne (IRE) (Alhaarth (IRE))
*4262$^{10}$* 5215$^{9}$ 5649$^{4}$ 6346$^{5}$ 7270$^{5}$ **7979$^{3}$** 8477$^{3}$ 8653$^{4}$ *9342$^{10}$*

**Little Poem** *Marco Botti* a46 51
2 b f Holy Roman Emperor(IRE) Gerika (FR) (Galileo (IRE))
**5886$^{3}$** 7023$^{6}$ *7985$^{5}$*

**Little Red Berry (IRE)** *James Given* a48 33
2 b f Red Jazz(USA) Passi Di Danza (IRE) (Bertolini (USA))
6432$^{11}$ ***6897$^{9}$*** 7472$^{5}$

**Little Stampy (IRE)** *D Broad* a72 64
6 ch m Artan(IRE) Gold Stamp (Golden Act (USA))
***3190$^{2}$***

**Liva (IRE)** *David Evans* 69
2 ch g Champs Elysees Resistance Heroine (Dr Fong (USA))
2779$^{5}$ 4466$^{3}$◆ **(4963)** 6030$^{2}$

**Live Dangerously** *John Bridger* a55 64
7 b g Zamindar(USA) Desert Lynx (IRE) (Green Desert (USA))
1683$^{7}$ 2057$^{7}$ 2678$^{4}$ 2914$^{4}$◆ (3522) 3940$^{5}$ 4523$^{6}$ 5023$^{3}$ **5410$^{2}$** 5823$^{3}$ 6378$^{8}$ 7002$^{7}$ 7158$^{3}$ *7729$^{10}$ 7900$^{5}$ 8133$^{11}$*

**Livella Fella (IRE)** *Keith Dalgleish* a76 79
4 b m Strategic Prince Ardent Lady (Alhaarth (IRE))
*1104$^{4}$ 1679$^{6}$ 1879$^{6}$* 3053$^{2}$ (3292) **3537$^{2}$** 4292$^{4}$ 6208$^{5}$ 6628$^{5}$ 7524$^{6}$ *8206$^{14}$ 8773$^{10}$ 8813$^{3}$ 9027$^{9}$*

**Live Twice** *P D Deegan* a77 72
4 b m Monsieur Bond(IRE) Astrantia (Dansili)
***6799a$^{3}$***

**Livinginafantasy (FR)** *S Wattel* a88 88
4 ch m Monsun(GER) All Is Vanity (FR) (Gold Away (IRE))
**4454a$^{8}$**

**Living In The Now** *Charles Hills* 25
2 b f Elzaam(AUS) Jardin (Sinndar (IRE))
**6747$^{10}$**

**Living Leader** *Grace Harris* a57 53
8 b g Oasis Dream Royal Jade (Last Tycoon)
*124$^{9}$ (854)* ***(1425)***◆ 2178$^{2}$ *3688$^{10}$* 4203$^{5}$ 6393$^{7}$ *8307$^{8}$ 9084$^{6}$ 9218$^{3}$ 9457$^{2}$*

**Livingstones Quest (IRE)**
*Rod Millman* 71
2 b g Showcasing Maramba (Rainbow Quest (USA))
4218$^{12}$ **5430$^{2}$**◆ **(6029)** 6699$^{8}$ 7904$^{7}$

**Livrable** *C Ferland* a83 92
3 gr g Exchange Rate(USA) Medolina (USA) (Aragorn (IRE))
**(1337a)** 3103a$^{8}$ 6963a$^{9}$

**Livvys Dream (IRE)** *Charles Hills* 61
2 b f Declaration Of War(USA) Briolette (IRE) (Sadler's Wells (USA))
7153$^{7}$ **7620$^{5}$**

**Liwanu (FR)** *A Fabre* 105
3 b c Excelebration(IRE) Lausanne (IRE) (Lawman (FR))
**7845a$^{2}$**

**Liwa Palace** *Rod Collet* a95 95
4 b m Oasis Dream Ladeena (IRE) (Dubai Millennium)
***4679a$^{4}$*** 6254a$^{5}$ 7441a$^{3}$

**Lizzie L'Amour (NZ)**
*Murray Baker & Andrew Forsman* 106
4 b m Zabeel(NZ) Sabia (FR) (Sadler's Wells (USA))
**8100a$^{10}$**

**Lizzy's Dream** *Rebecca Bastiman* a49 59
9 ch g Choisir(AUS) Flyingit (USA) (Lear Fan (USA))
*1531$^{1}$ 622$^{5}$* ***723$^{5}$ 899$^{5}$*** *1246$^{3}$* ***1452$^{3}$*** 2076$^{7}$ 2337$^{2}$ 2949$^{4}$ 3915$^{4}$ 5472$^{9}$ 5605$^{3}$ 6114$^{9}$ 6896$^{4}$

**Llamrei** *Jo Hughes* a59 56
2 b f Multiplex Nalear (FR) (Lear Fan (USA))
2251$^{5}$ 3022$^{5}$ 4199$^{4}$ 4991$^{5}$ 5785$^{2}$ *6154$^{4}$ 6634$^{7}$* 7920$^{5}$ 8110$^{3}$ *8500$^{11}$* ***9188$^{4}$***

**Llewellyn** *Declan Carroll* a65 59
9 b g Shamardal(USA) Ffestiniog (IRE) (Efisio)
*663$^{10}$ 852$^{9}$* 1718$^{4}$ 2082$^{8}$ ***(2472)*** 2843$^{7}$ *3186$^{4}$ 8776$^{10}$ 8980$^{3}$*

**Lmntrix** *George Margarson* a62 32
5 b g Mount Nelson Big Mystery (IRE) (Grand Lodge (USA))
***26$^{7}$***

**Lobster Cocktail (IRE)** *Ed Walker* a63 59
4 b h Footstepsinthesand Sanpala (Sanglamore (USA))
***(278)***◆

**Loca Furiosa (IRE)** *C Lerner* a65 51
3 ch f Mastercraftsman(IRE) Miss Bex (IRE) (Dalakhani (IRE))
**6566a$^{9}$**

**Local Artist (IRE)** *John Quinn* a58 65
3 b f Requinto(IRE) A L'Aube (IRE) (Selkirk (USA))
***179$^{3}$*** *357$^{6}$ 511$^{8}$ 1247$^{6}$*

**Lockheed** *William Haggas* 88
3 gr c Exceed And Excel(AUS) Clinical (Motivator)
**2869a$^{2}$**

**Locommotion** *Matthew Salaman* a57 60
5 gr g Proclamation(IRE) Miss Madame (IRE) (Cape Cross (IRE))
*966$^{7}$ (1427) 1451$^{8}$ 2063$^{10}$* 2762$^{4}$ **2968$^{5}$** 3522$^{9}$ *6813$^{3}$* 7157$^{7}$ *7952$^{10}$ 8948$^{5}$ (9454)*

**Lodi (FR)** *N Caullery* a76 79
3 b c Whipper(USA) Grise Bomb (USA) (Mr Greeley (USA))
***6124a$^{4}$***

**Logi (IRE)** *Richard Guest* a78 74
3 b g Kodiac Feet Of Flame (USA) (Theatrical (IRE))
*(904)* 1913$^{7}$ 2160$^{3}$ 2499$^{3}$ 3184$^{2}$ 4122$^{6}$ ***7409$^{2}$*** *8541$^{3}$*

**Log Off (IRE)** *Karen George* a62 57
3 b f Sir Prancealot(IRE) Dolphin Stamp (IRE) (Dolphin Street (FR))
*73$^{3}$ (310) 502$^{5}$ 848$^{5}$ 1331$^{6}$ 1445$^{7}$ 1822$^{6}$* ***(2060)*** 2991$^{7}$ 3143$^{4}$ 3813$^{4}$ 4177$^{3}$ 4462$^{3}$ 4697$^{5}$ *8854$^{10}$ 9128$^{6}$*

**Log Out Island (IRE)**
*Charlie Appleby* a87 112
4 b g Dark Angel(IRE) White Daffodil (IRE) (Footstepsinthesand)
**696a$^{6}$**

**Lohit** *Luis Alberto Acuna* 103
6 ch h Dutch Art Lovina (ITY) (Love The Groom (USA))
**2867a$^{11}$**

**Lolita** *J R Jenkins* a74 63
5 ch m Sir Percy Miss Ippolita (Diktat)
***161$^{5}$***

**Lomu (IRE)** *Keith Dalgleish* a81 89
3 ch g Dandy Man(IRE) Miss Me (Marju (IRE))
**(4075)** 6235$^{4}$ 7656$^{9}$

**Londinium** *Mark Johnston* 99
3 b g New Approach(IRE) Historian (IRE) (Pennekamp (USA))
4016$^{2}$◆ 4295$^{3}$ (5525) **5598$^{2}$** 6399$^{5}$ 6920$^{4}$

**London (FR)** *Phil McEntee* a94 94
4 b g Galileo(IRE) Altana (USA) (Mountain Cat (USA))
*269$^{9}$ 876$^{6}$ 1074$^{6}$ 1324$^{2}$ (1450) 6617$^{9}$* 7285$^{2}$ (7653) 8138$^{9}$ **8600$^{3}$** 8737$^{17}$ *9125$^{5}$* ***9233$^{2}$*** *9468$^{9}$*

**London Glory** *David Thompson* a65 67
4 b g Archipenko(USA) Reflected Image (IRE) (Refuse To Bend (IRE))
*1007$^{7}$* 1610$^{9}$ 2146$^{3}$ **2629$^{3}$** *3252$^{5}$* 3566$^{4}$ 4102$^{3}$◆ *4357$^{6}$* 5186$^{6}$ *5413$^{10}$* **(6788)** 7659$^{2}$ 7983$^{9}$ *8261$^{13}$ 8909$^{4}$*

**London Grammar (IRE)**
*Ralph J Smith* a56 54
3 b f Sir Prancealot(IRE) Emmas Princess (IRE) (Bahhare (USA))
*502$^{12}$ 895$^{7}$* ***(1597)*** *2017$^{8}$* 3250$^{9}$ 5653$^{7}$ 7230$^{3}$ *7833$^{5}$ 8846$^{9}$ 9213$^{11}$*

**Londonia** *Graeme McPherson* a51 65
5 gr g Paco Boy(IRE) Snowdrops (Gulch (USA))
**4733$^{2}$** 4994$^{2}$

**London Master** *Chris Wall* a66 63
3 ch c Mastercraftsman(IRE) Reflected Image (IRE) (Refuse To Bend (IRE))
***(2060)*** 2711$^{5}$ 5061$^{5}$ 6144$^{8}$ *7235$^{6}$*

**London Prize** *Ian Williams* a97 105
6 b g Teofilo(IRE) Zibet (Kris)
*728$^{2}$* (3618)◆ *(4355)* **8038$^{2}$**◆ (Dead)

**London Protocol (FR)** *K R Burke* a98 101
4 ch g Muhtathir Troiecat (FR) (One Cool Cat (USA))
1492$^{8}$ 1960$^{14}$ 2833$^{4}$ 3743$^{9}$ 4454a$^{5}$ (5269a) 5979a$^{7}$ 6648a$^{4}$ *(7636a)* **8469$^{8}$** *8891$^{11}$*

**London Rebel (IRE)**
*Richard Spencer* a43
4 ch m Arcano(IRE) Piccadilly Filly (IRE) (Exceed And Excel (AUS))
***168$^{10}$*** *415$^{11}$ 761$^{14}$*

**London's Burning** *Ralph Beckett*
2 ch g Cityscape Even Hotter (Desert Style (IRE))
3868$^{8}$

**Lonely The Brave (IRE)**
*Mark Johnston* a83 79
3 b g Lawman(FR) Luckbealadytonight (IRE) (Mr Greeley (USA))
3578$^{9}$ **4290$^{7}$** 4609$^{4}$ 5280$^{6}$ *5797$^{9}$*

**Long Embrace** *Simon Crisford* a58 55
2 b f Poet's Voice Loveable (Oasis Dream)
***6010$^{5}$*** 6876$^{9}$ 7334$^{12}$ *7756$^{5}$ 8847$^{8}$*

**Longing (IRE)** *A P O'Brien* 81
3 b f Galileo(IRE) Like A Dame (Danehill (USA))
**8086a$^{9}$**

**Long Island Sound (USA)**
*A P O'Brien* a108 78
4 b h War Front(USA) Treasure Trail (USA) (Pulpit (USA))
**1378a$^{12}$** *7588a$^{11}$*

**Long John Silver (IRE)**
*Jamie Osborne* a86
3 b g Rip Van Winkle(IRE) Tropical Lady (IRE) (Sri Pekan (USA))
*681$^{2}$*◆ ***(1190)***◆

**Long On Value (USA)** *William Mott* a93 120
6 b h Value Plus(USA) Long Message (USA) (Orientate (USA))
**1376a$^{2}$**◆ 4071$^{12}$ 7179a$^{3}$

**Longray (FR)** *G Botti* a84 36
5 ch g Le Havre(IRE) Isanous (FR) (Zamindar (USA))
***(6300a)***

**Long River (USA)** *S bin Ghadayer* a112
7 ch h A.P. Indy(USA) Round Pond (USA) (Awesome Again (CAN))
*85a$^{2}$*◆ *541a$^{8}$* ***(1045a)*** *1380a$^{11}$*

**Longroom** *Noel Wilson* a54 87
5 b g Oasis Dream Phantom Wind (USA) (Storm Cat (USA))
(2337)◆ (2453) (3337) **4850$^{2}$**◆ 6412$^{10}$ 8238$^{11}$

**Longside** *James Eustace* a68 70
5 b g Oasis Dream Hypoteneuse (IRE) (Sadler's Wells (USA))
1519$^{8}$ **2282$^{2}$**◆ 2728$^{5}$ 4572$^{4}$ *7495$^{13}$*

**Long Socks** *Alan King* 63
3 ch g Notnowcato Sienna Sunset (IRE) (Spectrum (IRE))
2930$^{5}$ 3714$^{6}$ **5577$^{4}$**

**Long Water (USA)** *H Al Alawi* a88 80
6 b g Elusive Quality(USA) Round Pond (USA) (Awesome Again (CAN))
**86a$^{10}$** *316a$^{8}$ 8836a$^{3}$*

**Lookin At Lee (USA)**
*Steven Asmussen* a119
3 b c Lookin At Lucky(USA) Langara Lass (USA) (Langfuhr (CAN))
***2420a$^{2}$*** *2851a$^{4}$*

**Looking Good** *S Curling* 70
5 b m Makfi Primo Heights (Primo Valentino (IRE))
**5917$^{2}$**

**Lookintomyeyes**
*Mrs Ilka Gansera-Leveque* a32 14
3 b f Cockney Rebel(IRE) Wizby (Wizard King)
2066$^{14}$ 4911$^{8}$ ***7600$^{7}$***

**Look My Way** *Andrew Balding* a80 96
3 b g Pour Moi(IRE) Casual Glance (Sinndar (IRE))
*1623$^{3}$ (1822) 2264$^{2}$* 3335$^{5}$ 3788$^{2}$◆ 4612$^{3}$ 4891$^{2}$ 5944$^{3}$ 6445$^{9}$ **(7200)**

**Looks A Million** *Joseph Tuite* 88
2 b f Kyllachy Look Busy (IRE) (Danetime (IRE))
3306$^{2}$◆ (3502) 5109$^{7}$ 6136$^{5}$ 6448$^{9}$ **7846a$^{3}$** 8562$^{6}$

**Look Surprised** *Roger Teal* a69 70
4 ch m Kier Park(IRE) Cloridja (Indian Ridge (IRE))
4445$^{7}$ **(6009)** 6612$^{4}$ 7272$^{6}$ *8243$^{5}$ 8953$^{3}$ 9315$^{7}$*

**Lope De Loop (IRE)** *David Evans* 64
2 b f Lope De Vega(IRE) Patroller (USA) (Grand Slam (USA))
**5356$^{4}$** 5561$^{2}$

**Lopes Dancer (IRE)** *Sally Haynes* a83 81
5 b g Lope De Vega(IRE) Ballet Dancer (IRE) (Refuse To Bend (IRE))
*(1308) 1781$^{6}$* 3744$^{6}$ *4260$^{4}$* 5455$^{8}$ 6944$^{2}$ ***(7234)*** *8188$^{9}$*

**Lopito** *Andrew Balding* 59
2 b c Lope De Vega(IRE) Stellar Brilliant (USA) (Kris S (USA))
**8677$^{8}$**

**Lopito De Vega (IRE)**
*David C Griffiths* a30 69
5 ch g Lope De Vega(IRE) Athenian Way (IRE) (Barathea (IRE))
2108$^{10}$ **2815$^{4}$** 3432$^{6}$ 3740$^{8}$ 4659$^{4}$◆ 4802$^{4}$ 5135$^{7}$ 6470$^{7}$ 7015$^{11}$ *7729$^{12}$*

**Lord Caprio (IRE)** *Ben Haslam* a65 54
2 b g Lord Shanakill(USA) Azzurra Du Caprio (IRE) (Captain Rio)
5735$^{6}$ 6311$^{8}$ *6897$^{11}$* ***(8783)***◆ ***(8925)***

**Lord Clenaghcastle (IRE)**
*Gary Moore* a71 85
3 b g Big Bad Bob(IRE) Clenaghcastle Lady (IRE) (Acclamation)
*625$^{6}$* 4463$^{2}$ (5067) **(5788)** **6516$^{2}$** 7094$^{7}$ 7650$^{5}$

**Lord Commander** *Richard Fahey* a70 75
3 b g Nayef(USA) Kashoof (Green Desert (USA))
1675$^{4}$ **2266$^{2}$** 2807$^{11}$ 3336$^{6}$ *6014$^{10}$* 7095$^{6}$ 7957$^{4}$ *(8193)*

**Lord Cooper** *Jose Santos* a80 80
3 b g Sir Percy Zooming (IRE) (Indian Ridge (IRE))
*323$^{5}$ (813) (903)* ***(1332)*** 1959$^{9}$ 2579$^{5}$ **3355a$^{5}$** ***4783a$^{4}$*** *5416$^{7}$ 6455a$^{8}$* ***7408$^{2}$*** 7709$^{8}$ *8542$^{6}$* 8960a$^{7}$

**Lord Del Boy** *Bill Turner*
2 b g Delegator Lady Prodee (Proclamation (IRE))
3083$^{7}$

**Lord Divine (USA)**
*Cathrine Erichsen* 86
4 b g Divine Park(USA) Celtic Gift (USA) (Van Nistelrooy (USA))
**4825a$^{7}$**

**Lord Durante (AUS)**
*Simone Ferchie* 97
8 b g Lord Jim(ARG) Kalahanna (AUS) (Jeune)
**8857a$^{11}$**

**Lord E (IRE)** *Gary Moore* a54 56
3 b g Lord Shanakill(USA) Elouges (IRE) (Dalakhani (IRE))
*1241$^{5}$ 1426$^{7}$* 1862$^{9}$ 2679$^{6}$ **3247$^{3}$** 4087$^{3}$

**Lord Erskine (IRE)** *H Rogers* a65 87
4 b g Fast Company(IRE) Lindoras Grace (Galileo (IRE))
**(7860a)**

**Lord Fandango (GER)**
*Archie Alexander* a64 103
4 b h Lord Of England(GER) Fitness (IRE) (Monsun (GER))
**(8056a)** **8250a$^{4}$**

**Lord Franklin** *Eric Alston* a31 80
8 ch g Iceman Zell (IRE) (Lend A Hand)
2030$^{15}$ 2555$^{7}$ 2624$^{8}$ **3168$^{2}$** 3582$^{6}$ 4336$^{4}$ 4893$^{6}$ 5455$^{5}$ 5924$^{10}$ 7567$^{10}$ 7735$^{12}$ *8261$^{9}$*

**Lord George (IRE)**
*James Fanshawe* a103 103
4 gr g Sir Percy Mahima (FR) (Linamix (FR))
*1779$^{3}$* **2603$^{3}$** *4356$^{4}$*◆ 5198a$^{8}$ 7115$^{7}$ *8539$^{4}$ 8892$^{2}$ 9259$^{4}$*

**Lord Glitters (FR)** *David O'Meara* a93 113
4 gr g Whipper(USA) Lady Glitters (FR) (Homme De Loi (IRE))
*(1920a)* 7807$^{2}$◆ **(8234)** 8599$^{2}$

**Lord Huntingdon** *Alan King* a34 86
4 b g Lord Of England(GER) Marajuana (Robellino (USA))
**5432$^{6}$**

**Lord Kitten (USA)** *David Lanigan* a68 67
3 b g Kitten's Joy(USA) Iteration (USA) (Wild Again (USA))
2152$^{9}$ 3533$^{5}$ 4086$^{3}$ 4602$^{3}$ *5485$^{8}$* 6470$^{3}$ ***7236$^{3}$*** *7792$^{7}$*

**Lord Murphy (IRE)**
*Daniel Mark Loughnane* a64 54
4 b g Holy Roman Emperor(IRE) Tralanza (IRE) (Traditionally (USA))
*614$^{12}$ (1406) 1563$^{2}$ 1894$^{2}$* ***(2166)*** *3263$^{5}$ 4165$^{7}$ 5898$^{4}$ 6443$^{7}$ 8662$^{3}$ 8957$^{7}$ 9406$^{11}$*

**Lord Napier (IRE)** *John Ryan* a81 77
4 b g Galileo(IRE) Jacqueline (IND) (King Charlemagne (USA))
*457$^{2}$* ***921$^{4}$*** *1505$^{3}$* 2431$^{10}$

**Lord Of Persia (USA)** *Peter Jardby* a76 68
9 bb g Speightstown(USA) Norwoods (USA) (Deputy Minister (CAN))
*2941a$^{6}$*

**Lord Of The Glen** *Jim Goldie* a71 57
2 b g Orientor Glenlini (Bertolini (USA))
2134$^{12}$ 2452$^{6}$ 2771$^{5}$ 3648$^{7}$ 5603$^{5}$ 6379$^{8}$ 7159$^{4}$ 7518$^{12}$ *8190$^{6}$ 8588$^{2}$ (8780)* ***9098$^{2}$***

**Lord Of The Rock (IRE)**
*Michael Dods* a42 98
5 b g Rock Of Gibraltar(IRE) La Sylphide (Rudimentary (USA))
1492$^{19}$ **(5382)** 7609$^{13}$ 8737$^{19}$

**Lord Of The Storm** *Michael Attwater* a65 50
9 b g Avonbridge Just Run (IRE) (Runnett)
***164$^{4}$*** *641$^{11}$ 1225$^{5}$ 1484$^{9}$* 2257$^{7}$ 6847$^{4}$ *7761$^{8}$* 8183$^{8}$ *9127$^{10}$*

**Lord Reason** *John Butler* a75 82
5 b g Sixties Icon Luck Will Come (IRE) (Desert Style (IRE))
**(4523)** 5000$^{7}$ 6110$^{5}$

**Lord Riddiford (IRE)** *John Quinn* 77
2 gr g Zebedee Beacon Of Hope (IRE) (Barathea (IRE))
2029$^{2}$ **(2698)** 8294$^{4}$

**Lord Rob** *David Thompson* a50 49
6 b g Rob Roy(USA) First Grey (Environment Friend)
*176$^{3}$ 607$^{4}$* ***1312$^{3}$*** *1469$^{6}$ 2919$^{4}$ 3342$^{10}$*

**Lord Vetinari** *Andrew Balding* 71
2 br g Lethal Force(IRE) Princess Luna (GER) (Grand Lodge (USA))
**5350$^{6}$** 6071$^{5}$

**Lord Yeats** *Jedd O'Keeffe* 110
4 b g Yeats(IRE) Bogside Theatre (IRE) (Fruits Of Love (USA))
(2804) **(4360)** 5592$^{5}$ 6447$^{17}$ 6976a$^{5}$

**Lorelei** *William Muir* a64 59
5 b m Excellent Art Light Dreams (Fantastic Light (USA))
***436$^{7}$***

**Lorelina** *Andrew Balding* a56 90
4 b m Passing Glance Diktalina (Diktat)
2254$^{3}$ 2906$^{3}$ 3582$^{2}$ 6515$^{2}$◆ (7201) 7816$^{8}$ **8390$^{2}$**

**Lorenzetta (IRE)** *Riccardo Santini* 92
5 ch m Mastercraftsman(IRE) Louise Aron (IRE) (Intikhab (USA))
**7441a$^{5}$** 8096a$^{3}$

**Lorikeet (USA)** *Mark Johnston* a73 40
3 ch g Street Cry(IRE) Ishitaki (ARG) (Interprete (ARG))
***100$^{8}$***

**Los Altos (FR)** *E J O'Neill* 65
2 b g Rio De La Plata(USA) Tequila Heat (IRE) (Clodovil (IRE))
**8443a$^{7}$**

**Los Barbados (IRE)**
*Fawzi Abdulla Nass* a93 105
5 b g Galileo(IRE) Milanova (AUS) (Danehill (USA))
*319a$^{3}$* 540a$^{2}$ 699a$^{6}$ **890a$^{5}$** *9360a$^{4}$*

**Los Camachos (IRE)** *David Evans* a63
2 b c Camacho Illuminise (IRE) (Grand Lodge (USA))
***9266$^{2}$*** *9404$^{6}$*

**Los Cerritos (SWI)** *Oliver Greenall* a55 103
5 ch g Dr Fong(USA) La Coruna (SWI) (Arazi (USA))
***282$^{4}$*** *716a$^{3}$ 1196a$^{4}$*

**Losingmyreligion (FR)** *Marco Botti* a70 68
2 b g Planteur(IRE) Marie Dar (FR) (Sinndar (IRE))
5808$^{5}$◆ *7361$^{5}$* ***(8501)***

**Lost At Sea** *K R Burke* a47 86
3 b g Dutch Art Tahlia Ree (IRE) (Acclamation)
**4904$^{9}$** 5530$^{9}$ 8736$^{20}$

**Lostock** *Michael Dods* a51 59
3 b c Kodiac Green Silk (IRE) (Namid)
***904$^{3}$***◆ *1064$^{4}$*

**Lost The Moon** *Mark H Tompkins* a81 67
4 b m Authorized(IRE) Missouri (Charnwood Forest (IRE))
*(619)* ***1027$^{2}$***◆ *2461$^{P}$ 3138$^{4}$ 6849$^{6}$* 8047$^{13}$ 8565$^{6}$ *9082$^{8}$ 9324$^{2}$*

**Lotara** *Jim Goldie* a65 59
5 b m Monsieur Bond(IRE) Cheviot Heights (Intikhab (USA))
*4513$^{3}$* **3384$^{4}$** 3827$^{13}$ 4958$^{9}$ 5635$^{5}$ 5922$^{5}$ 6546$^{8}$ *7036$^{5}$ 8496$^{9}$ (9013) 9102$^{7}$*

**Lots Of Tea (FR)**
*Mme C Head-Maarek* 70
2 b f Lord Of England(GER) Lots Of Dreams (GER) (Dai Jin)
**7969a$^{5}$**

**Lots O' Lex (USA)**
*Gerald Russel Aschinger* 93
6 bb m Kitalpha(USA) Via Lactea (CAN) (Capote (USA))
**1813a$^{9}$**

**Lotus Garden (FR)** *F Chappet* a91 87
6 gr g Dark Angel(IRE) Lili St Cyr (IRE) (Rock Of Gibraltar (IRE))
**5490a$^{3}$** ***6300a$^{6}$***

**Loud And Clear** *Iain Jardine* a75
6 b g Dalakhani(IRE) Whispering Blues (IRE) (Sadler's Wells (USA))
***7935$^{5}$***

**Lough Salt (IRE)** *Richard Guest* 61
6 b g Brian Boru Castlehill Lady (IRE) (Supreme Leader)
**7629$^{3}$**

**Louis D'Or (IRE)** *T Castanheira* a86 95
2 ch c Intello(GER) Soudanaise (IRE) (Peintre Celebre (USA))
5626a[3] 7637a[3] (8195a) 8884a[2]

**Louis Vee (IRE)** *John O'Shea* a55 50
9 bb g Captain Rio Mrs Evans (IRE) (College Chapel)
309[7] 495[7] 981[5] 1247[9] 1721[8] 1896[3] 2509[3] 2732[7] 3569[2] 4149[8] 6850[11] 7605[11] 7693[7] 7910[2] 8259[9] 9129[8]

**Loujain (IRE)** *John Gosden* 76
3 ch g Dubawi(IRE) Eshaadeh (USA) (Storm Cat (USA))
1514[4] 2895[2]

**Loulin** *David O'Meara* 59
2 ch g Exceed And Excel(AUS) Wimple (USA) (Kingmambo (USA))
6231[5] 7269[6] 8483[6]

**Loumarin (IRE)** *Michael Appleby* a63 56
5 b m Bushranger(IRE) Masela (IRE) (Medicean)
151[7] 386[9] 601[3] 1063[3] 1328[3] 1413[3] 1759[8] 2589[3] 2994[3] 3391[6]

**Loup Des Steppes (FR)**
*J-C Rouget* 67
2 b c Sunday Break(JPN) Aster Nox (USA) (Elusive Quality (USA))
5989a[4] 8101a[4]

**Loures (IRE)** *Maria Ritchie* a75
4 ch h Shamardal(USA) Lura (USA) (Street Cry (IRE))
8710a[3]

**Louvain (FR)** *G Nicot* a80 76
8 b g Vatori(FR) Loupy Glitters (FR) (Loup Solitaire (USA))
6300a[7]

**Louversey** *P Sogorb* a99 104
3 b f Arcano(IRE) Albisola (IRE) (Montjeu (IRE))
7341a[10] 8755a[5] 8986a[4]

**Love And Be Loved** *John Flint* a58 75
3 b f Lawman(FR) Rightside (High Chaparral (IRE))
435[8] 1246[10] 1564[3] 2060[4] 3191[4] (3423) 3870[3] 4150[6] (5714)◆ (7464) (8299)

**Love And Peace (FR)**
*Mme Pia Brandt* 83
2 ch f Linngari(IRE) Indochine (BRZ) (Special Nash (IRE))
6542a[4]

**Loveatfirstsight** *Jane Chapple-Hyam* a67 14
4 b m Bertolini(USA) Starbeck (IRE) (Spectrum (IRE))
3139[6] 3758[11] 4162[3] 4726[2] 5482[3]◆ 6015[9] 8031[11] 8376[12] (8675) (8948) 9142[5] 9316[6]

**Love Candy (IRE)** *Sally Haynes* 55
3 b f Canford Cliffs(IRE) Love Thirty (Mister Baileys)
3404[9] 4117[3] 5707[6]

**Love Cape (USA)** *D Windrif* a59 44
4 bb g Cape Blanco(IRE) Inmyheartforever (USA) (Medaglia d'Oro (USA))
6125a[4]

**Love Conquers (JPN)**
*Ralph Beckett* a75 75
3 b f Deep Impact(JPN) Love And Bubbles (USA) (Loup Sauvage (USA))
2131[9] 3921[2]◆ 4808[2] 6443[2] 7762[6] (8585)

**Love Dreams (IRE)** *Mark Johnston* 106
3 b c Dream Ahead(USA) Kimola (IRE) (King's Theatre (IRE))
3836[5] 4813[6] (5159) 5662[3] 6401[10] 6676[6]

**Love In The Dark** *Nikki Evans* a27 53
4 b m Sleeping Indian Love In The Park (Pivotal)
167[14] 644[10] 1407[11]

**Love Is Enough (JPN)**
*John Gosden* a39
2 b f Deep Impact(JPN) Soinlovewithyou (USA) (Sadler's Wells (USA))
8997[11]

**Love Island** *Richard Whitaker* a89 91
8 b m Acclamation Sally Traffic (River Falls)
2856[10] 3063[4] (3253) 3757[2]

**Lovell** *Charlie Appleby* 96
4 b g Dubawi(IRE) Cosmodrome (USA) (Bahri (USA))
2735[20]

**Lovely Acclamation (IRE)**
*Ismail Mohammed* a60 67
3 b f Acclamation Titova (Halling (USA))
2898[6] 3970[6] 5007[9] 5536[4] 6016[7] 7540[6] 7916[7] 8329[14]

**Lovely Demon (FR)** *T Lemer* 40
2 gr f Rajsaman(FR) Ulivate (IRE) (Poliglote)
3444a[10]

**Lovely Story (IRE)** *Seamus Durack* a74 96
6 b m Cape Cross(IRE) Hush Money (CHI) (Hussonet (USA))
2041[6] 4809[14]

**Love Me Again** *Charlie Fellowes* a57 65
3 b f Kheleyf(USA) Midnight Allure (Aragon)
4764[6] 5577[5] 6439[7] 8328[13] 8635[6] 9127[9]

**Lovemenot (IRE)** *W McCreery* 84
3 b f Teofilo(IRE) Birthstone (Machiavellian (USA))
8086a[8]

**Love Money (FR)** *Y Barberot* a79 71
3 ch f Muhtathir Sapfo (FR) (Peintre Celebre (USA))
4232a[6] 8464a[5]

**Love Not War** *George Scott* 22
3 b f Sepoy(AUS) Jumeirah Palm (USA) (Distorted Humor (USA))
2171[7] (Dead)

**Love Oasis** *Mark Johnston* a73 81
3 b f Oasis Dream Pickle (Piccolo)
2776[3] 3239[2]◆ (3384) 3974[5] (4188) 4435[8] 4892[2] 5018[2] 5272[2] 5612[6] 6392[7] 6780[5] 7554[10] 7923[6] (8243) 8542[7] 8818[7]

**Love On The Rocks (IRE)**
*Charles Hills* a83 96
4 ch m Exceed And Excel(AUS) My Love Thomas (IRE) (Cadeaux Genereux)
(1768) 3092[14] 4581[9] (4974) 5505[12] 6512[2] 8225a[6]

**Love Potion (IRE)** *A P O'Brien* a94 93
4 b m Galileo(IRE) Potion (Pivotal)
1808a[6] 8086a[14] 8407a[5]

**Love Rat** *Scott Dixon* a74
2 b g Mawatheeq(USA) Watersilk (IRE) (Fasliyev (USA))
9177[5]

**Love Spirit** *Louis Baudron* a72 111
7 b g Elusive City(USA) Indian Maiden (IRE) (Indian Ridge (IRE))
2643a[7] 3370a[10] 4234a[6] 7697a[11]

**Love To Breeze** *Ed Vaughan* 48
2 b f Azamour(IRE) Burn The Breeze (IRE) (Beat Hollow)
8593[8]

**Love To Rock (IRE)**
*Adrian Paul Keatley* a53 50
4 b m Fastnet Rock(AUS) I'm In Love (USA) (Zafonic (USA))
4982[5] 5254[10]

**Loving** *William Haggas* a67 76
3 rg f Mayson Courting (Pursuit Of Love)
4342[6] 5338[4] 5845[4] 6511[5]

**Loving Your Work**
*Ken Cunningham-Brown* a61 62
6 b g Royal Applause Time Crystal (IRE) (Sadler's Wells (USA))
290[8] 2909[4] 3694[5] 4257[3]◆ 5653[4] 9092[13]

**Low Profile** *Roger Charlton* 66
2 ch c Galileo(IRE) Dynaforce (USA) (Dynaformer (USA))
7906[6]

**Lowrie** *John David Riches* a10 54
4 b m Assertive Miacarla (Forzando)
2453[7]

**Loxley (IRE)** *Charlie Appleby* 100
2 b c New Approach(IRE) Lady Marian (GER) (Nayef (USA))
(8075)◆ 8415[7]

**Loyalty** *Derek Shaw* a93 47
10 b g Medicean Ecoutila (USA) (Rahy (USA))
61[6] 349[4] 760[2]◆ (876) 1023[4] 1177[5] 2115[9] 2518[5] 2922[9] 8905[5] 9125[6] 9272[5]

**Lozah** *Roger Fell* a68 63
4 b m Lawman(FR) Princess Luna (GER) (Grand Lodge (USA))
361[6] 444[4] 609[5] 2919[5] 3181[4] 3911[7] 5181[3] 5831[8] 6003[9] 6471[2] 6549[6] 7240[8] 8314[6] 8719[3] 9084[7]

**Lualiwa** *Kevin Ryan* a75 98
3 b g Foxwedge(AUS) Sunpearl (Compton Place)
(1141) 1878[3] 2739[2] (4334) (4868) 5916[2] 6918[6] 8104[11]

**Luang Prabang (IRE)** *Chris Wall* a76 56
4 b m Invincible Spirit(IRE) Sauvage (FR) (Sri Pekan (USA))
2120[12] 5656[4] 6795[4] 7158[9] 7878[3] (8400) 8749[2] 8947[8]

**Luath** *Suzzanne France* a64 51
4 ch g Archipenko(USA) Delaware Dancer (IRE) (Danehill Dancer (IRE))
1125[7] (1868) 2179[6] 2918[3] 4298[12] 5835[6] 6528[4] 7240[6] 8210[10] 8801[3] 9032[2]

**Lubinka (IRE)** *Peter Chapple-Hyam* 99
2 ro f Mastercraftsman(IRE) Petite Nymphe (Golan (IRE))
6183[2] 6917[3] 8004[6]

**Lucata (IRE)** *Alan Berry* 49
3 b g Sir Prancealot(IRE) Toy Show (IRE) (Danehill (USA))
8217[11]

**Lucca (IRE)** *Jarlath P Fahey* a56 72
5 b g Echo Of Light San Michele (Vettori (IRE))
7860a[9]

**Lucent Dream (IRE)**
*John C McConnell* a67 79
6 b g Teofilo(IRE) Cheyenne Star (IRE) (Mujahid (USA))
(1249) 1409[2] 2955[6] (3898) 4658[2] (4959)

**Lucifers Shadow (IRE)**
*Mrs C Gilbert* a62 52
8 gr g Dark Angel(IRE) Marianne's Dancer (IRE) (Bold Fact (USA))
(1933a) 2672a[2] 3958a[5] (5985a)

**Lucifugous (IRE)** *Stuart Williams* 62
2 gr f Footstepsinthesand Krasotka (IRE) (Soviet Star (USA))
3697[6]◆ 4291[3] 5154[5] 6472[3] 7251[6]

**Lucky Beggar (IRE)**
*David C Griffiths* a76 92
7 gr g Verglas(IRE) Lucky Clio (IRE) (Key Of Luck (USA))
1475[6] 1833[2] 2104[4] 2341[3] (2683) 2837[2] (3288) 3324[8] 3581[4] 4333[2] 4867[7] 5129[5] 5637[7] 5929[12] 6412[8] 6677[9] 8012[18] 8260[10] 8489[4]

**Lucky Bubbles (AUS)** *K W Lui* 125
5 ch g Sebring(AUS) Bubble Below (AUS) (Hussonet (USA))
9168a[4]

**Lucky Clover** *Malcolm Saunders* a64 64
6 ch m Lucky Story(USA) Willisa (Polar Falcon (USA))
2214[11] 3466[10] 3811[5] 4532[7] (4731) 5052[2] 5778[4] 7951[7] (8128)

**Lucky Deal** *Mark Johnston* a83 72
2 ch c Mastercraftsman(IRE) Barter (Daylami (IRE))
8476[3] (8904)

**Lucky Di** *Peter Hedger* a51 40
7 br m Araafa(IRE) Lucky Date (IRE) (Halling (USA))
3686[2] 4162[8] 6373[8] 6748[13] 7911[5] 8133[3] 8948[6] 9207[6]

**Lucky Ellen (IRE)** *Jennie Candlish* a53 51
3 b f Elusive Pimpernel(USA) Dona Alba (IRE) (Peintre Celebre (USA))
7270[3] 8498[6] 9262[5] 9375[10]

**Lucky Esteem** *Neil Mulholland* a43 68
3 b f Yorgunnabelucky(USA) Dream Esteem (Mark Of Esteem (IRE))
5712[6] 6766[8] 7902[11] 8513[9]

**Lucky Gal** *Martin Hill* a58
7 b m Overbury(IRE) Lucky Arrow (Indian Ridge (IRE))
687[4]

**Lucky Hussler (AUS)** *Darren Weir* 114
7 b g Husson(ARG) Talaq Dancer (AUS) (Black Hawk)
8057a[11]

**Lucky Lodge** *Antony Brittain* a69 67
7 b g Lucky Story(USA) Melandre (Lujain (USA))
1637[3] 1890[2] 2119[4] 3344[4] 3758[3] 4509[4] 4744[6] 5318[5] 5738[10] (5836) 7525[10] 8722[9]

**Lucky Louie** *Roger Teal* a67 74
4 ch g Dutch Art Ardessie (Bahamian Bounty)
20[7] 214[2] 482[7] (860) 1729[2] 2119[3] 2763[2] 5326[2] 6034[2] 7158[2]

**Lucky Lucky Man (IRE)**
*Richard Fahey* a69 82
2 gr g Clodovil(IRE) Regrette Rien (IRE) (Chevalier (IRE))
4919[11] 5480[4] 6012[2] 6545[2] (7041)

**Lucky Lucrecia (IRE)**
*William Haggas* 76
3 b f Dansili Politesse (USA) (Barathea (IRE))
(4568)

**Lucky Mistake (IRE)** *J Reynier* a43 90
3 b g Fast Company(IRE) Torrmana (IRE) (Ela-Mana-Mou)
2536a[10]

**Lucky Reset** *David Evans* a50 35
2 ch f Yorgunnabelucky(USA) Reset City (Reset (AUS))
5056[12] 6064[10] 6575[10]

**Lucky Robin (IRE)** *W J Burke* 33
5 ch g Mister Fotis(USA) Bewilderment (IRE) (Loup Sauvage (USA))
6799a[8]

**Lucky Rock (FR)** *J Merienne* 37
2 ch f Rock Of Gibraltar(IRE) Licky Star (FR) (Key Of Luck (USA))
5585a[10]

**Lucky's Dream** *David Evans* 57
2 ch g Yorgunnabelucky(USA) Dream Esteem (Mark Of Esteem (IRE))
3746[10] 5106[7] 6029[4] 7519[17]

**Lucky Team (FR)** *J Boisnard* a100 86
5 gr h Namid Kestria (IRE) (Keltos (FR))
7636a[8] (8251a) 9274a[4]

**Lucky Violet (IRE)** *Iain Jardine* a57 72
5 b m Dandy Man(IRE) Rashida (King's Best (USA))
7658[8] 8108[5] 8318[5]

**Lucrezia** *Sir Michael Stoute* a67 48
3 b f Nathaniel(IRE) Nannina (Medicean)
144[7]

**Lucymai** *Dean Ivory* a90 71
4 b m Multiplex Miss Lesley (Needwood Blade)
90[12] 505[2] 641[3] (2464) 3139[2]◆ 8341[13] 8798[3] (8907)

**Lucy's Law (IRE)** *Tom Tate* a67 73
3 b f Lawman(FR) Lucy Limelites (Medicean)
1678[6] 2186[2]◆ 2854[2] 4056[4] 5950[3] 6208[3]

**Lucy The Painter (IRE)** *Ed de Giles* a93 102
5 b m Excellent Art Royal Bounty (IRE) (Generous (IRE))
1494[16] 1795[9] 2392[6] 3219[5] 3586[4] 4119[2] 4613[6] 5569[10] 6104[6] 6924[4] 7401[6] 8390[5] 8636[6]

**Ludorum (IRE)** *Richard Fahey* 74
3 ch g Lope De Vega(IRE) Savignano (Polish Precedent (USA))
5670[5] 6236[4] (6760) 7328[6]

**Luduamf (IRE)** *Richard Hannon* a63 58
3 ch c Tamayuz Aphorism (Halling (USA))
1367[3] 1564[4] 2018[6] 2309[8] 2758[8] 2968[7] 5145[7] 5410[6] 5958[3] 6342[5] 6587[2] 7540[9] 8948[10] 9232[4]

**Lugano** *Sir Mark Prescott Bt* a84 92
4 b g Galileo(IRE) Swiss Lake (USA) (Indian Ridge (IRE))
(3547) (3740) (3907) 4038[3] 5663[5]

**Luire (IRE)** *D De Watrigant* a65 98
3 gr f Dark Angel(IRE) Glitter Baby (IRE) (Danehill Dancer (IRE))
8444a[10]

**Luis Fernandez (USA)** *Kevin Ryan* 83
2 b c Gio Ponti(USA) Escape To Victory (Salse (USA))
2221[3]◆ (2896)◆ (4805) (5851)◆

**Luis Vaz De Torres (IRE)**
*Richard Fahey* a75 88
5 b g Tagula(IRE) Tekhania (IRE) (Dalakhani (IRE))
33[6] 403[7] 1103[7] 1238[5] (2081) (3045) 3565[6] 4957[3] 5530[6] 6672[4] 7108[2] 7594[11] 8014[6] 8736[9]

**Lukoutoldmakezebak**
*David Thompson* a49 40
4 b g Arabian Gleam Angelofthenorth (Tomba)
2179[10] 2792[5] 3488[7] 3912[11] 4743[6] 5539[4] 6316[9] 6571[7] 7389[8] 8258[9] 8591[3] 9013[3]

**Lulu Star (IRE)** *Richard Fahey* a59
2 b f Oasis Dream Jeanie Johnston (IRE) (One Cool Cat (USA))
7238[8]

**Lulu The Rocket** *John Butler* a57 37
3 b f Authorized(IRE) Sagina (Shernazar)
305[7] 5846[9] 6621[7] 7790[11] 8673[9]

**Luminate (IRE)** *F Head* 106
2 b f Lawman(FR) Kalandara (IRE) (Rainbow Quest (USA))
(7847a)

**Luminous** *Simon Crisford* a66 73
3 b f Champs Elysees Tamzin (Hernando (FR))
3549[3] 4173[2] 5131[10] 6899[6] 7278[2] 7762[13] 8852[2]

**Luminous Mind (USA)** *F-X Belvisi* a51 60
9 b g Lemon Drop Kid(USA) Nibbana (USA) (Giant's Causeway (USA))
9309a[16]

**Luna Bear** *Gary Moore* a48 78
3 b f Dick Turpin(IRE) Royal Tavira Girl (IRE) (Orpen (USA))
1727[9] 2092[7]◆ 2580[2] (4050) 4883[10]

**Luna Eclipse (IRE)** *Andrew Balding* 65
2 b c Bahamian Bounty Luna Forest (IRE) (Holy Roman Emperor (IRE))
2756[3] 3868[7]

**Luna Lady** *Ann Duffield* a12
2 ch f Paco Boy(IRE) Tamara Moon (IRE) (Acclamation)
8555[9]

**Luna Magic** *Lydia Pearce* a65 70
3 b f Mayson Dayia (IRE) (Act One)
1756[4] 4808[4] 5632[4] 6320[4] 7278[9] 8125[5] 8801[10] (9457)

**Luna Mare (IRE)** *Richard Fahey* a68 81
4 b m Galileo(IRE) Pale Moon Rising (IRE) (Kingmambo (USA))
2302[5] 2906[5]

**Lunar Corona** *Sir Michael Stoute* 63
2 br f Dansili Starscope (Selkirk (USA))
8380[8]

**Lunar Deity** *Stuart Williams* a92 78
8 b g Medicean Luminda (IRE) (Danehill (USA))
304[2] 680[5] 1598[5] 2319[3] (3731) (3940) 4541[4] 8126[4] 8706[11] 8881[9] 9206[11]

**Lunardo (SWI)** *J Stadelmann*
7 ch g Vespone(IRE) La Traviata (SWI) (Grand Lodge (USA))
834a[7]

**Luna Riska (FR)** *J-P Gallorini* 62
2 b f No Risk At All(FR) Lamaya (FR) (Azamour (IRE))
7969a[10]

**Lunar Jet** *John Mackie* a64 83
3 ch g Ask Lightning Jet (Dutch Art)
1497[11] 2145[4]◆ 2588[2] 3787[7] 4580[6] 6389[2] (7505) 8295[4]

**Lunar Maria** *Charlie Appleby* 68
2 b f Dubawi(IRE) Ama (USA) (Storm Cat (USA))
7153[3]

**Lunar Mist** *Ed Dunlop* a61
3 b f Bated Breath Time Will Show (FR) (Exit To Nowhere (USA))
8663[6] 8911[4] 9276[5]

**Lunastorta (USA)** *Agostino Affe'* 89
3 bb f Brilliant Speed(USA) Limerick (USA) (Black Minnaloushe (USA))
3121a[7]

**Lunch (IRE)** *Jamie Osborne* a71
3 br c Big Bad Bob(IRE) All Day (CHI) (Jaded Dancer (USA))
(642)◆

**Lungarno Palace (USA)**
*John Gallagher* a66 73
6 b g Henrythenavigator(USA) Good Time Sally (USA) (Forestry (USA))
9000[11] 9208[13]

**Lupie (IRE)**
*Mohammed Jassim Ghazali* a103 97
5 b h Lope De Vega(IRE) Valeriocia (IRE) (Invincible Spirit (IRE))
932a[7]

**Lupin (USA)** *Sir Michael Stoute* 58
3 b f Medaglia d'Oro(USA) Promising Lead (Danehill (USA))
2759[7] 3626[6]

**Luqyaa** *John Gosden* 72
3 b f Smart Strike(CAN) Maqaasid (Green Desert (USA))
3595[5]

**Lush Life (IRE)** *Jamie Osborne* a76
2 gr f Mastercraftsman(IRE) Break Of Day (USA) (Favorite Trick (USA))
(8670)◆

**Lustre (FR)** *H De Nicolay* a71 60
9 b h American Post Lunaska (FR) (Ashkalani (IRE))
6018a[6]

**Lustrous Light (IRE)** *Ralph Beckett* 104
4 ch h Galileo(IRE) Glinting Desert (IRE) (Desert Prince (IRE))
1654a[5] 1999a[4] 2735[13] 4033[7] 4863[3] 7124[3] 8414[6]

**Lutine Charlie (IRE)** *Emma Owen* a52 50
10 br g Kheleyf(USA) Silvery Halo (USA) (Silver Ghost (USA))
425[2] 544[6] 690[9] 854[4] 1145[6] 1406[3] 1587[8] 2057[3] 2255[8] 2916[10] 4180[7] 4453[8] (5817) 6752[4] 7213[2] 8134[9] 8185[3] 8994[4] 9141[10] 9232[8]

**Luv U Always** *Iain Jardine* a54 60
3 b f Captain Gerrard(IRE) Lady Suesanne (IRE) (Cape Cross (IRE))
415[2] 667[3] 5418[12] 5605[5] 6596[6] 7036[7] 7657[3] 7884[5]

**Luv U Whatever** *Marjorie Fife* a89 73
7 b g Needwood Blade Lady Suesanne (IRE) (Cape Cross (IRE))
3[3] 269[8] 389[3] 519[4] 759[7] (1108) (1464) 1628[4] 1865[2] 3580[7] 4158[2] 4572[2] 5320[5] 5701[6] 6269[7] 7234[10] 7452[9] 7728[6] 8315[9] 8638[6] 9028[2] 9070[2] 9208[10] 9295[3]

**Luxford** *John Best* a63 62
3 b f Mullionmileanhour(IRE) Dolly Parton (IRE) (Tagula (IRE))
1428[4] 1597[4] 2507[4] (4180) 4211[3]◆ (4713) 5545[7] 7005[6] (7761) 8549[4] 8813[9] 9212[5]

**Lyavenita (FR)** *J-V Toux* a73 73
5 b m Execute(FR) Yaven (FR) (Marchand De Sable (USA))
6648a[10]

**Lydia's Place** *Richard Guest* a78 84
4 ch m Equiano(FR) Peace And Love (IRE) (Fantastic Light (USA))
1475[3] 1805[5] (2104) 2899[9] (3183) 3904[5] 4574[7] 5811[3] 6072[3] 6276[2] 6593[8] 6695[6]◆ 7127[8] 7268[11] 7738[10]

**Lydiate Lady** *Eric Alston* a74 71
5 b m Piccolo Hiraeth (Petong)
5069[4] 5377[5] 5877[3] (6531) (7020) (7825) 8512[2] 8853[4] (8953)

**Lyfka** *Paul Cole* a68 69
5 ch m Kheleyf(USA) Tarkamara (IRE) (Medicean)
2054[6] 2912[3]

**Lyford (IRE)** *Sylvester Kirk* a28 51
2 ch g Intense Focus(USA) Nurture (IRE) (Bachelor Duke (USA))
3244[5] 4090[5] 4465[11] 6063[10]

**Lyin Eyes** *K J Condon* a48 67
3 b f Equiano(FR) Christmas Tart (IRE) (Danetime (IRE))
8774[4]

**Lynique (IRE)** *William Haggas* 50
3 ch f Dylan Thomas(IRE) Danse Grecque (IRE) (Sadler's Wells (USA))
4808[12]

**Lynn's Memory**
*Joseph Patrick O'Brien* 72
2 b f Acclamation Roxelana (IRE) (Oasis Dream)
3023[3] (3807) 5150[9]

**Lynwood Gold (IRE)**
*Mark Johnston* 96
2 ro c Mastercraftsman(IRE) Witch Of Fife (USA) (Lear Fan (USA))
(6553) 7026[6] 7654[2] 7978[2] (8354)

**Lypharty Ka (FR)** *Y Gourraud* a68 77
2 b f Dunkerque(FR) Sauzelle (FR) (Gold Away (IRE))
6542a[6] 7969a[2]

**Lyrical Pursuit** *Michael Easterby* a70 50
2 ch f Poet's Voice Crinklelini (Bertolini (USA))
3093[9] 4359[2] 4919[8]

**Lyrica's Lion (IRE)** *Michael Attwater* a63 62
3 b g Dragon Pulse(IRE) Shishangaan (IRE) (Mujadil (USA))
237[9] 1342[5] 4446[12] (4914) 5843[6] 6723[3] 7729[5] (8135)

**Lyric Harmony (IRE)** *Giles Bravery* 78
3 b f Teofilo(IRE) Musical Bar (IRE) (Barathea (IRE))
1905[7] 2898[5] (3404) 4096[7] 5478[3] 5829[2] 6369[7]

**Lytham St Annes (IRE)**
*Doug Watson* a88 74
4 b g Bahamian Bounty Kerrys Requiem (IRE) (King's Best (USA))
250a[10]

**Maakaasib** *Simon Crisford* a92 74
3 b g Equiano(FR) Majoune (FR) (Take Risks (FR))
2334[9] 3584[6] (4752) 5574[3] (6290)

**Maarek** *Miss Evanna McCutcheon* a47 106
10 b g Pivotal Ruby Rocket (IRE) (Indian Rocket)
1385a[3] 4416a[9] 4925a[12] 6206[8] 6971a[17] 7425a[4] 7856a[3] 8738[9]

**Maarit (IRE)** *Denis Coakley* a32
3 b f Harbour Watch(IRE) Atamana (IRE) (Lahib (USA))
545[11]

**Maariyah (FR)** *A Fabre* a74 75
3 b f Oasis Dream Ana Marie (FR) (Anabaa (USA))
4288a[6]

**Maaward (IRE)** *Richard Hannon* a75
2 b c Kodiac Caterina Di Cesi (Cape Town (IRE))
8340[2]◆

**Maazel (IRE)** *Roger Varian* a79 77
3 b g Elzaam(AUS) Laylati (IRE) (Green Desert (USA))
4104[4] 4715[2] 5837[6] 6276[6] 7882[2]

**Mable Lee (IRE)** *Iain Jardine* 70
2 ch f Zoffany(IRE) Mexican Milly (IRE) (Noverre (USA))
2988[5] 3482[2]◆ 4681[6] (5614)◆ 7138[2] 7564[4] 8741[9]

**Mabo** *Richard Fahey* 69
2 gr c Aussie Rules(USA) Crochet (IRE) (Mark Of Esteem (IRE))
2816[5] 3398[7] 4862[9] 5373[7] 5685[7] 6379[7] 7041[3] 8191[14]

**Mabrook** *Marco Botti* a71 76
3 b c Dubawi(IRE) Mahbooba (AUS) (Galileo (IRE))
2260[4]◆ 2783[5] 3438[2]

**Mabrouka** *Doug Watson* a3 2
3 b f Sir Prancealot(IRE) No Nightmare (USA) (Lion Heart (USA))
317a[6]

**Mabs Cross** *Michael Dods* a74 105
3 b f Dutch Art Miss Meggy (Pivotal)
1705[8]◆ 2180[3]◆ (2924)◆ (3672)◆ (4081)◆ (7887)◆

**Macaque** *Andrew Balding* 90
2 b g Rock Of Gibraltar(IRE) Spiliada (FR) (Falco (USA))
4218[7] 5030[2]◆ (5819) 6472[2] 7355[4]

**Ma Cherie** *A Fabre* 96
3 b f Galileo(IRE) Zaneton (FR) (Mtoto)
8273a[10] 8666a[6]

**Machiavelian Storm (IRE)**
*Richard Mitchell* a44 43
5 gr m Dark Angel(IRE) Terri's Charmer (USA) (Silver Charm (USA))
2255[10] 2294[5] 2915[4] 3519[8] 4040[5] 6102[11] 9073[10] 9218[11]

**Machine Learner** *Joseph Tuite* a76 93
4 b g Sir Percy My First Romance (Danehill (USA))
(3840) 4586[2] 6135[4] 6956a[2] 8076[7] 8740[13]

**Macho Guest (IRE)**
*George Margarson* 29
2 b g Camacho Alabama Grace (IRE) (Teofilo (IRE))
2926[7] 3437[7]

**Macho Mac** *Hughie Morrison* a79 62
4 ch g Pastoral Pursuits Clarice Orsini (Common Grounds)
25[9] 159[5] 419[11] 1109[6] 1238[6]

**Macho Mover (IRE)** *Mick Channon* a58 47
2 b g Camacho Fanciful Dancer (Groom Dancer (USA))
7391[15] 7788[7] 8387[13]

**Mach One** *Archie Watson* a80 64
3 b g Makfi Perfect Spirit (IRE) (Invincible Spirit (IRE))
2931[10] 6067[5] 7761[3] 8376[2] (8538) 8801[2] (9180) 9303[3] 9464[5]

**Machree (IRE)** *Declan Carroll* 72
2 b f Lord Shanakill(USA) Faleena (IRE) (Verglas (IRE))
6559[3] 8010[4]◆ (8483)

**Mackiri (IRE)** *Michael Appleby* a48 28
4 b g Makfi Inchiri (Sadler's Wells (USA))
7010[10]

**Macksville (IRE)** *James Eustace* a65 66
4 gr g Mastercraftsman(IRE) Fairest Of All (IRE) (Sadler's Wells (USA))
39[2] 218[5] 4573[3] 5267[3] 6343[5] 6820[6] (7319) 7490[5] 8326[7]

**Mac Mahon (ITY)** *Stefano Botti* 112
3 b c Ramonti(FR) Miss Sultin (IRE) (Celtic Swing)
(2868a) 4878a[8] 7205a[3] 8963a[2]

**Mac O'Polo (IRE)** *Tom Dascombe* a71 67
3 b g Henrythenavigator(USA) Topka (FR) (Kahyasi (IRE))
3062[6] 3493[5] 4164[5] 5139[3]◆ 9153[3] 9376[2]

**Mac's Kyllachy** *James Fanshawe* a62 54
3 ch g Kyllachy Folly Lodge (Grand Lodge (USA))
209[7] 502[2]

**Madakheel (USA)** *Simon West* a43 43
6 b m Mr Greeley(USA) Manaal (USA) (Bahri (USA))
9076[10] 9343[11]

**Madam Dancealot (IRE)**
*Richard Baltas* 105
3 ch f Sir Prancealot(IRE) Sisal (IRE) (Danehill (USA))
8071a[3]

**Madame Bounty (IRE)** *Ed Walker* a67 85
3 b f Bahamian Bounty Madame Boulangere (Royal Applause)
(3407) (4532) 4752[7] 6137[6] 7811[4] 8541[9]

**Madame Claud** *Mark Gillard* a23 62
4 ch m Champs Elysees Change Partners (IRE) (Hernando (FR))
8301[10]

**Madame Jo Jo** *Sarah Hollinshead* 59
2 ch f Havana Gold(IRE) Paradise Place (Compton Place)
4116[10] 5056[14] 6304[5] 7081[4] 7690[6]

**Madame Mime Artist**
*Natalie Lloyd-Beavis* a11
6 b m Dutch Art Silent Waters (Polish Precedent (USA))
9072[11]

**Madame Ritz (IRE)** *Richard Phillips* a48
2 b f Canford Cliffs(IRE) Sky Red (Night Shift (USA))
9049[3]

**Madame Stripes (ARG)**
*Neil Drysdale* a92 103
4 b m Equal Stripes(ARG) Courtisane (ARG) (Silver Finder (USA))
8601a[11]

**Madam Lilibet (IRE)** *Sharon Watt* 71
8 b m Authorized(IRE) Foxilla (IRE) (Foxhound (USA))
1703[5] 2032[2] 2712[9] 3340[12] 6233[4] 7330[5] (7893)

**Madam Mai Tai** *Rebecca Bastiman* 52
5 ch m Compton Place Dash Of Lime (Bold Edge)
1075[12]

**Madam Pomfrey** *Jonathan Portman* 16
2 b f Sayif(IRE) Miss Poppy (Averti (IRE))
2037[11] 8471[7]

**Madam Prancealot (IRE)**
*Karen George* a39 63
3 b f Sir Prancealot(IRE) Delia (IRE) (Darshaan)
210[9] 435[6] 686[5] 2089[4] 2758[2] 3327[10] 5536[5]

**Maddi** *Luke Dace*
2 b f Foxwedge(AUS) Sulis Minerva (IRE) (Arakan (USA))
6178[7]

**Maddys Dream** *Lydia Pearce* a44 61
4 b g Arabian Gleam Group Force (IRE) (Montjeu (IRE))
4766[5] 5511[6] 8137[7]

**Madeleine Bond** *Henry Candy* a63 86
3 ch f Monsieur Bond(IRE) Spin A Wish (Captain Rio)
2957[5] (3571) (4810) (5591) 6655[U] 7276[10]

**Madeline (IRE)** *Roger Varian* 105
2 b f Kodiac Madhulika (FR) (Marchand De Sable (USA))
2563[5] (3070) 4028[5] (5109) 6354[2] 7617[3] 8575a[13]

**Mademoiselle Marie (FR)** *K Borgel* 101
3 b f Evasive Tempera Noire (FR) (Miesque's Son (USA))
2003a[6] 2945a[5] 3881a[6] 5981a[9]

**Mad Endeavour** *Stuart Kittow* a71 71
6 b g Muhtathir Capefly (Cape Cross (IRE))
(2367) 3532[8] 4842[6] 5535[4] 6635[8] 7272[4] 7932[4]

**Made Of Honour (IRE)** *K R Burke* a74 77
3 ch f Casamento(IRE) Bonne (Namid)
1513[2] 2135[3]◆ (3194)◆ 6787[7] 7892[7] (8304a)

**Madiva (FR)** *C Lotoux* a86 97
5 gr m Aussie Rules(USA) Mahradeva (GER) (Medicean)
3883a[3]

**Madrasa (IRE)** *Ken Wingrove* a37 49
9 b g High Chaparral(IRE) Shir Dar (FR) (Lead On Time (USA))
6632[5] 8430[12]

**Madrinho (IRE)** *John Butler* a65 77
4 ch g Frozen Power(IRE) Perfectly Clear (USA) (Woodman (USA))
2838[6]◆ 3845[7] 4168[4] 4887[6] 7245[6] 8556[7] 8958[6] 9279[7]

**Madroos** *Michael Easterby* a81 83
4 ch g Teofilo(IRE) Hedaaya (IRE) (Indian Ridge (IRE))
2081[2] 3095[3] 3790[7] 4210[3] 5125[3] 6158[4] 7941[13] 8240[10]

**Mad Rose (IRE)** *Denis Quinn* a64 56
3 b f Royal Applause Na Zdorovie (Cockney Rebel (IRE))
2094[9] 2474[15] 3536[3] 4214[10] 4619[10] 8480[9] 8980[14] 9454[7]◆

**Maestro Mac (IRE)** *Tom Clover* a78 83
4 b g Roderic O'Connor(IRE) Union City Blues (IRE) (Encosta De Lago (AUS))
1602[7] 2388[13] 3813[3] 4257[6] (5809) 6781[2] (7601) 8326[10]

**Mafaaheem (IRE)** *Owen Burrows* a70 97
3 b c Shamardal(USA) Hammiya (IRE) (Darshaan)
1906[2] 3506[2] 4097[2] (5757) 6482[2]

**Mafdet** *Bryan Smart* a41 60
2 b f Rip Van Winkle(IRE) Fabulous Speed (USA) (Silver Hawk (USA))
5372[5] 8215[5] 8779[6]

**Ma Fee Heela (FR)** *M D O'Callaghan* a74 92
3 b g Siyouni(FR) Olympic Skater (IRE) (Loup Solitaire (USA))
4327a[3] 4925a[4] 5688a[12] 6971a[7]

**Mafeking** *Harry Dunlop* 60
2 b g Makfi Save Me The Waltz (FR) (Halling (USA))
2779[9] 3679a[12] 5246[6] 7120[6] 7637a[17]

**Maftool (USA)** *M Al Mheiri* a111 106
5 br g Hard Spun(USA) With Intention (USA) (Mr Greeley (USA))
86a[12] 208a[12]

**Magdalene Fox** *Ed Dunlop* a67
3 ch c Foxwedge(AUS) Malelane (IRE) (Prince Sabo)
(77) 264[2] 404[3]

**Magellan** *Roger Charlton* a80 76
3 b g Sea The Stars(IRE) Hector's Girl (Hector Protector (USA))
1962[6] 2783[9] 3506[6] (7935)

**Maggie Jonks** *Andrew Balding* 53
2 ch f Sixties Icon Lighted Way (Kris)
7504[7] 8348[9]

**Maggie Pink** *Michael Appleby* a83 51
8 b m Beat All(USA) Top Notch (Alderbrook)
97[4]◆ 285[7] 810[11] 4375[10] 5399[7] 7111[9] 8374[6] 8798[4] 8907[13] 9076[9]

**Maggies Angel (IRE)** *Richard Fahey* 93
2 b f Dark Angel(IRE) Last Bid (Vital Equine (IRE))
(1908)◆ 2801[4] 3557[2] 4361[2]◆ 5150[3]

**Maggie The Third M** *John Davies* a12
3 b f Haafhd Markila (FR) (Mark Of Esteem (IRE))
7935[9]

**Maggi May (IRE)** *David Brown* a52 52
3 b f Kodiac Virevolle (FR) (Kahyasi (IRE))
1432[3] 1821[2] 2065[2] 3544[2] 3818[3] 4478[10] 4997[4] 5419[12] 6298[6]

**Maghaweer (IRE)** *Richard Hannon* a69 81
2 ch c Dubawi(IRE) Indian Ink (IRE) (Indian Ridge (IRE))
7513[4] 8046[3] (8560)

**Maghfoor** *Saeed bin Suroor* a79 89
3 b g Cape Cross(IRE) Thaahira (USA) (Dynaformer (USA))
1584[2] (2143) 3005[9] 6090[4] 6849[7] 8188[7]

**Magical (IRE)** *A P O'Brien* 112
2 b f Galileo(IRE) Halfway To Heaven (IRE) (Pivotal)
(6242a) 6974a[2] 7666a[4] 8004[4]

**Magical Dreamer (IRE)**
*James Fanshawe* a75 89
3 b f Acclamation Double Fantasy (GER) (Indian Ridge (IRE))
2122[9] (3171) 4317[4] 5758[2] 6878[2] 7256[2]◆ 7811[2]

**Magical Effect (IRE)** *Ruth Carr* a76 92
5 ch g New Approach(IRE) Purple Glow (IRE) (Orientate (USA))
(1910) 2404[2] 3757[6] 4719[3] 5457[5] (5947) 6205[3] 6570[3]◆ 6894[5] 7626[5]

**Magical Forest (IRE)** *G Botti* a75 77
3 b f Casamento(IRE) Hurry Home Hydee (USA) (Came Home (USA))
201a[5] 889a[7] 1293[2] 3446a[4] 4455a[3]

**Magical Memory (IRE)**
*Charles Hills* 114
5 gr g Zebedee Marasem (Cadeaux Genereux)
2737[2] 4071[18] (4615) (5149) 5690a[4] 6926[11] 7806[3]

**Magical Molly Joe** *David Barron* a65 56
3 b f Arabian Gleam Magical Music (Fraam)
442[5] 612[2] 1348[9] 5375[7] 6181[7] 7628[8] 7980[3]

**Magical Peak** *John O'Shea* a34 35
5 gr m Hellvelyn Enjoy The Magic (Namaqualand (USA))
282[12] 1299[12] 1791[5]

**Magic Applause (IRE)**
*George Scott* a32 70
2 b f Zebedee Last Hooray (Royal Applause)
2502[4] 2988[2] (3328) 4252[10] 9440[7]

**Magic Approach** *David Simcock* a63 50
3 b f Piccolo Diane's Choice (Komaite (USA))
1003[6] (1192) 4536[6] 5295[5] 5845[3]

**Magic Beans** *Hughie Morrison* a56 61
3 br g Pastoral Pursuits Jasmeno (Catcher In The Rye (IRE))
1968[5] 3087[4] 5034[4] 5846[10] 6436[4] 7253[8] 7711[7]

**Magic Bear (IRE)** *Edward Lynam* a77 96
4 b m Kodiac Good To Follow (IRE) (Kyllachy)
6640a[6] 7425a[9] 7856a[7]

**Magic Buddy** *J R Jenkins* 22
2 ch f Captain Gerrard(IRE) Magic By Bell (Reel Buddy (USA))
6525[8] 8472[9]

**Magic Circle (IRE)** *Ralph Beckett* a102 106
5 b g Makfi Minkova (IRE) (Sadler's Wells (USA))
1798[5] 2525[5]◆ 3928[7] (6329) 6447[5] 8038[13]

**Magic City (IRE)** *Michael Easterby* a83 89
8 b g Elusive City(USA) Annmarie's Magic (IRE) (Flying Spur (AUS))
240[4] 516[3] 685[2] 984[8] (1201) 1583[5] 2030[6] 2586[3] (3433) (4017) 4692[6] 5643[5] 7566[6] 7959[8] 8048[13] 8510[3] 8652[8]

**Magicinthemaking (USA)**
*Mike Murphy* a32 51
3 br f Wildcat Heir(USA) Love In Bloom (USA) (More Than Ready (USA))
3970[8]

**Magic Jazz (IRE)** *Kevin Ryan* 82
2 b g Red Jazz(USA) Ishimagic (Ishiguru (USA))
1872[7] 2698[5] 4606[2] (5644) (6693)◆ 7090[21]

**Magic Journey (IRE)** *John Quinn* a56 62
3 gr g Zebedee Journey's End (IRE) (In The Wings)
73[8] 245[3] 1123[5] 1348[7] 3387[2] 3831[7] (4688) 5050[3] 5205[2] 5466[2] 5991[4]

**Magic Lily** *Charlie Appleby* 111
2 ch f New Approach(IRE) Dancing Rain (IRE) (Danehill Dancer (IRE))
(7403) 8004[3]

**Magic Mark** *K R Burke* a70 71
2 b g Helmet(AUS) Silken Aunt (Barathea (IRE))
2882[3] 3789[3] 4919[6] 6547[6] 9298[3]

**Magic Mc Henry (IRE)**
*Mme G Rarick* a48 54
4 gr g Zebedee Mata Bhani (IRE) (Mull Of Kintyre (USA))
713a[9]

**Magic Mirror** *Mark Rimell* a69 55
4 b m Dutch Art Balatoma (IRE) (Mr Greeley (USA))
(282) (1285) 1729[7] 2070[6] 2916[4] 3397[3] 3906[4] 4214[7] 6814[2] 7464[6] 7952[2] (8134) (8641) 9316[3]

**Magic Moments** *Alan King* a68 63
4 b m Kheleyf(USA) Magic Rhythm (Librettist (USA))
929[10] 1407[2] 2057[5] (2732)◆ 3397[5] 4529[5] (6157) 7409[4] 8243[6]

**Magic Pass** *Andrew Balding* a62 29
3 ch g Raven's Pass(USA) Magic America (USA) (High Yield (USA))
882[6] 1259[4] 1818[3] 2395[12]

**Magic Pulse (IRE)** *David C Griffiths* a71 54
2 b f Dragon Pulse(IRE) Invincible Magic (IRE) (Invincible Spirit (IRE))
4204[8] 4598[9] 7269[4] 8145[2]◆ (8795) 9122[5] 9440[2]

**Magic Ship (IRE)** *Ollie Pears* a37 53
2 b c Kodiac Baltic Belle (IRE) (Redback)
4995[7] 5665[8] 6231[6] 7518[16] 7938[9] 8191[9]

**Magistral** *Linda Perratt* a65 73
7 b g Manduro(GER) Tamalain (USA) (Royal Academy (USA))
509[2]◆ 992[10] 1257[4] 1716[7] 2456[3] 3652[2]◆ 4039[2] 4661[8] 5469[12] 7699[5] 8103[6] 8589[4] 9101[11] 9261[2]

**Magnapal (AUS)** *Daniel Bowman* 94
7 ch g Magnus(AUS) Luxapal (AUS) (Kenny's Best Pal (AUS))
8100a[11]

**Magnetic Boundary (USA)**
*George Scott* a75
2 ch c Union Rags(USA) Enthused (USA) (Seeking The Gold (USA))
8981[2] 9177[3]

**Magnificent** *Richard Hannon* 85
2 b c Zebedee Barathea Dancer (IRE) (Barathea (IRE))
3747[6] 4860[4]◆ 5710[2] 7392[2]

**Magnificent Madiba** *George Baker* 68
4 b g Mount Nelson Mrs Penny (AUS) (Planchet (AUS))
2257[9]

**Magnolia Ridge (IRE)** *Mark Walford* a51 46
7 b g Galileo(IRE) Treasure The Lady (IRE) (Indian Ridge (IRE))
5021[7]

**Magnolia Springs (IRE)**
*Eve Johnson Houghton* 90
2 b f Shamardal(USA) Rainbow City (IRE) (Rainbow Quest (USA))
(7357) 8424[6]

**Magnus (IRE)** *Tom Dascombe* 74
2 b c Makfi Royale Danehill (IRE) (Danehill (USA))
2154[9] 2896[6] (3429) 3929[18] 4527[3] 5079[4] 5685[6] 5875[8] 7106[2]◆ (Dead)

**Magnus Maximus** *Robyn Brisland* a110 95
6 b g Holy Roman Emperor(IRE) Chanrossa (IRE) (Galileo (IRE))
543a[8] 696a[7] 1044a[12] 2114[6] 6922[9] 7603[6]

**Magnus Romeo** *Johnny Farrelly* a48 27
6 b g Manduro(GER) Chili Dip (Alhaarth (IRE))
3026[9] 7490[7]

**Magojiro (USA)** *Jeremy Noseda* a48
2 b g Hat Trick(JPN) Rebuke (USA) (Carson City (USA))
8340[6]

**Magpie (FR)** *Gerard Martin* a57
3 ch c Shakespearean(IRE) Miss Gazduram (AUT) (Gazduram)
8692a[9]

**Mags Well (IRE)** *Geoffrey Deacon* a62 52
3 gr f Thewayyouare(USA) Sliabh Aniaran (IRE) (Oratorio (IRE))
3473[4] 4723[4] 7190[14] 7951[10] 9214[8]

**Mahaarat** *Sir Michael Stoute* a82 70
2 ch f Dubawi(IRE) Ashaaqah (IRE) (Dansili)
4253[9]◆ 5349[5] (6575)◆ 7552[9]

**Mahabba (IRE)** *Luca Cumani* a72 78
3 gr f Galileo(IRE) Bewitched (IRE) (Dansili)
3866[3] 5124[3] 7935[4] 8377[6]

**Maharad (FR)** *Ecurie Avant-Garde* a66 69
7 b g Meshaheer(USA) Danse Mecene (FR) (Dansili)
7307a[3]

**Mahati (FR)** *A Fabre* a75 97
4 b m Montjeu(IRE) Minaccia (GER) (Platini (GER))
6914a[4] 7753a[8] 8838a[5]

**Mahican (IRE)** *Jennie Candlish* a61 61
7 b g Cape Cross(IRE) Dark Indian (IRE) (Indian Ridge (IRE))
162[7] 395[4]

**Mahna Mahna (IRE)**
*David W Drinkwater* a55 30
3 b g Kodiac Namu (Mujahid (USA))
1244[6] 1426[5] 2167[8] 2507[9] 3260[5] 3810[6] 6324[12]

**Maid In Brittain** *Antony Brittain* a42 47
3 ch f Monsieur Bond(IRE) Guadaloup (Loup Sauvage (USA))
2078[7] 2585[14] 4309[12] 5007[11] 8248[12]

**Maid In India (IRE)** *Eric Alston* 84
3 br f Bated Breath Indian Maiden (IRE) (Indian Ridge (IRE))
(4793) (5635) 6149[2] 7737[5]

**Maid Of Rock (IRE)** *Mike Murphy* a34
3 b f Rock Of Gibraltar(IRE) Embark (Soviet Star (USA))
6287[10] 6817[14] 8635[9]

**Maid Of Tuscany (IRE)**
*Neil Mulholland* a52 31
6 b m Manduro(GER) Tuscania (USA) (Woodman (USA))
9317[11]

**Maid To Remember** *Ralph Beckett* 84
3 b f Redoute's Choice(AUS) Maid To Believe (Galileo (IRE))
(2585)◆ 4155[5]

**Maid Up** *Andrew Balding* a51 52
2 gr f Mastercraftsman(IRE) Complexion (Hurricane Run (IRE))
7997[8] 8425[10]

**Maifalki (FR)** *Jason Ward* a85 79
4 b g Falco(USA) Makila (IRE) (Entrepreneur)
1677[9] 1911[11] 6855[7] 7824[14] 8596[11] 9000[4] 9271[10]

**Mail Order** *Mark Johnston* a54 69
2 b f Nathaniel(IRE) Mail The Desert (IRE) (Desert Prince (IRE))
5246[5] 5743[4] 6666[3] 7160[3] 8461a[6]

**Mailshot (USA)** *Mark Johnston*
3 ch c Hard Spun(USA) Newsreel (IRE) (A.P. Indy (USA))
177[3] (350) 553[2] (1142) 1801[11] 2554[7] 3077[9]

**Maimara (FR)** *M Delzangles* 101
5 b m Makfi Hideaway Heroine (IRE) (Hernando (FR))
1531a[7] 8088a[6] 8665a[3]

**Main Desire (IRE)** *Michael Bell* 94
2 b f High Chaparral(IRE) Purple Glow (IRE) (Orientate (USA))
(2265) (2801)

**Maine D'Ange (IRE)** *P Sogorb* a44 42
2 b f Motivator Maine Rose (Red Ransom (USA))
6171a[10] 6456a[8]

**Main Fact (USA)** *Dianne Sayer* a53 63
4 b g Blame(USA) Reflections (Sadler's Wells (USA))
782[11] 1307[8] 1716[10] 7982[3]◆

**Main Stay (KOR)** *Kim Young Kwan* a98
4 b g Tale Of The Cat(USA) No Bull Baby (USA) (Indian Charlie (USA))
(321a) 694a[4]

**Mainstream** *Sir Michael Stoute* 107
4 b g Dansili Golden Stream (IRE) (Sadler's Wells (USA))
2431[3]◆ 4033[6] 4863[2] 5638[11]

**Main Street** *John Gosden* a85 57
2 b c Street Cry(IRE) My Special J'S (USA) (Harlan's Holiday (USA))
4094[5] (7987)◆

**Mai O'Higgins (IRE)** *Tracey Collins* a67 61
4 br m Strategic Prince Zaafran (Singspiel (IRE))
953a[6]

**Maison Brillet (IRE)** *Clive Drew* a57 48
10 b g Pyrus(USA) Stormchaser (IRE) (Titus Livius (FR))
2972[11]

**Maison D'Or (IRE)** *Robert Collet* a68 69
3 b g Galileo(IRE) Thai Haku (IRE) (Oasis Dream)
5523a[3] 6225a[4]

**Mais Si** *Gordon Elliott* a67 73
4 b m Montjeu(IRE) Magic America (USA) (High Yield (USA))
6858[5]

**Maitresse (IRE)** *Seamus Durack* 18
3 ch f Mastercraftsman(IRE) L'Amour Toujours (IRE) (Montjeu (IRE))
2359[8] 3770[8]

**Majboor (IRE)**
*Dominic Ffrench Davis* a76 81
3 ch g Dragon Pulse(IRE) City Vaults Girl (IRE) (Oratorio (IRE))
5431[3] 6103[2] 6808[3] 7358[5] 8117[2] 8663[2]

**Majdool (IRE)** *Noel Wilson* a80 47
4 b g Acclamation Maany (USA) (Mr Greeley (USA))
2922[8] 3388[7] 3946[9] 6943[7] 8209[4] 8556[LFT] 8929[6] 9101[14]

**Majeed** *David Simcock* a96 107
7 b g Mount Nelson Clever Millie (USA) (Cape Canaveral (USA))
208a[10] 428a[4] 699a[8] 3597[12] 4069[2] 4918[17] 5592[6] 9390[7]

**Majeste** *Richard Hannon* a76 102
3 b g Acclamation Winged Valkyrie (IRE) (Hawk Wing (USA))
1881[6] 2569[8] 5147[6] 5661[6] 6026[7] 6700[9] 7405[11]

**Majestic Dunhill (USA)**
*George Weaver* 86
2 bb c Majesticperfection(USA) Candy Fortune (USA) (Candy Ride (ARG))
8602a[10]

**Majestic Girl (IRE)** *Steve Flook* a45 53
4 b m Royal Applause Pretty Majestic (IRE) (Invincible Spirit (IRE))
2724[3] 3001[5] 3137[8] 3569[13] 4162[6] 5791[8] 5817[8] 8470[8]

**Majestic Heat (USA)**
*Richard E Mandella* 103
5 bb m Unusual Heat(USA) Chi Chi Nette (USA) (Ole (USA))
8601a[6]

**Majestic Hero (IRE)** *Ronald Harris* a75 90
5 b g Majestic Missile(IRE) Xena (IRE) (Mull Of Kintyre (USA))
1863[2] (2083) 2524[9] 3321[14] 4416a[18] 4974[3] 5219[7] 6177[5] 6512[3] 6695[10]◆ 7538[5] 7994[8]

**Majestic Man (IRE)**
*Ronald Thompson* a41
4 b g Majestic Missile(IRE) Windomen (IRE) (Forest Wind (USA))
8781[4]

**Majestic Moon (IRE)** *Julia Feilden* a93 89
7 b g Majestic Missile(IRE) Gala Style (IRE) (Elnadim (USA))
459[7] 2283[7] 2833[10] 3030[5] 3777[2] 4091[2] 4294[10] 4854[12] 5035[3] 5396[10] 7086[9] 7214[5] 8254[4] 9029[3]

**Majestic Mount** *S Seemar* a92 93
7 b h Exceed And Excel(AUS) Our Poppet (IRE) (Warning)
433a[10]

**Majestic Myles (IRE)** *Lee Carter* a86 58
9 b g Majestic Missile(IRE) Gala Style (IRE) (Elnadim (USA))
116[7] 860[9] 1086[9] 1896[5]

**Majestic Stone (IRE)**
*Julie Camacho* a49 60
3 b g Casamento(IRE) Pretty Majestic (IRE) (Invincible Spirit (IRE))
1244[7] 1474[8] 2182[2] 4303[2] 5291[5] 6313[8] 6437[16]

**Majik Charly (FR)** *T Castanheira* a60 63
5 ch g Soave(GER) Kapi Creek (FR) (Sicyos (USA))
713a[7] 930a[4] 5176a[10]

**Major Assault** *Matthew Salaman* a49 43
4 b h Kyllachy Night Premiere (IRE) (Night Shift (USA))
545[8] 2140[12] 2709[8] 8659[11]

**Major Ben** *Michael Blake* a70 8
4 ch g Major Cadeaux La Jwaab (Alhaarth (IRE))
290[2] 9421[8]

**Major Cornwallis (IRE)**
*Richard Fahey* a70 70
3 ch g Dandy Man(IRE) Macnas (USA) (Orientate (USA))
659[3] 1029[7] 1410[4] 1840[4] 2228[5] 2993[9] 3751[4] (5076) 5958[4]

**Major Crispies** *David O'Meara* a89 76
6 b g Pastoral Pursuits Nellie Melba (Hurricane Sky (AUS))
277[10] 857[10] 1301[6] 1606[17] (1896) 2331[2] 2923[10] 3136[3] 4506[3] 4999[2] 5258[4] 6237[3] 6620[8] 7056[9] 7332[6] 7572[2] (8211) 8722[4] 9152[5] 9411[4]

**Majorette** *Martin Smith* a56 61
3 ch f Major Cadeaux So Discreet (Tragic Role (USA))
1948[6] 6791[4] 7254[3]

**Major Franko** *Sarah-Jayne Davies* a47 41
5 ch g Major Cadeaux Royal Future (IRE) (Royal Academy (USA))
98[8]

**Majoris (IRE)** *Hugo Palmer* a86 95
3 b g Frankel Drops (IRE) (Kingmambo (USA))
1621[5] 2401[4] 3998[17]

**Major Jumbo** *Kevin Ryan* a91 100
3 gr g Zebedee Gone Sailing (Mizzen Mast (USA))
155[2] (404)◆ 657[2] (926)◆ 1732[2] 2806[3] 4412[2] 6450[9] (6970)

**Major Minus** *Tim Easterby* a35 24
3 b g Sir Percy Eminencia (Sadler's Wells (USA))
6268[12] 6522[6] 6899[8]

**Major Muscari (IRE)** *Shaun Harris* a62 42
9 ch g Exceed And Excel(AUS) Muscari (Indian Ridge (IRE))
80[3] 293[2] 398[3] 579[5] 860[7] 1076[8] 1359[3] 2063[6] 3201[10] 5848[5] 6271[10]

**Major Peirson (IRE)** *Jo Hughes* 85
2 b g Society Rock(IRE) Snowtime (IRE) (Galileo (IRE))
2706[6] 3390[4] (4534) 5109[5] 7112[6]

**Major Pusey** *John Gallagher* a68 92
5 ch g Major Cadeaux Pusey Street Lady (Averti (IRE))
1302[9] 2083[7] 2837[7] (3161) 3585[2] 4830[7] 5426[3] 5720[2] 5890[2] 6275[7] (6878) 7144[11] 7612[15]

**Major Rowan** *John Davies* a76 61
6 b g Captain Gerrard(IRE) Julie's Gift (Presidium)
613[4] 991[7] 1292[3] 1834[4] 3155[4] 3436[4] 4102[7] 5832[5] 6901[4] 7936[10]

**Major Tom** *Michael Appleby* a44
3 b g Native Ruler Top Level (IRE) (Fasliyev (USA))
265[9] 662[6] 1107[7]

**Major Valentine** *John O'Shea* a74 80
5 b g Major Cadeaux Under My Spell (Wizard King)
171[7] 844[4] (1290) (1720) (1965) 2621[3] (3281) 4532[4] (4965) 5580[3] 5967[2] 6098[3] 6506[2] 6586[3] 7408[11]

**Makaarim** *Hughie Morrison* a92 80
3 b g Tamayuz Dubawi Cheetah (IRE) (Dubawi (IRE))
626[2] 1142[6] 4254[8] 4564[2] 8392[10] (8872) 9210[5]

**Makahiki (JPN)** *Yasuo Tomomichi* 123
4 b h Deep Impact(JPN) Wikiwiki (JPN) (French Deputy (USA))
8975a[4]

**Makambe (IRE)** *Charles Hills* 65
2 gr g Dark Angel(IRE) Pink Diva (IRE) (Giant's Causeway (USA))
5504[13] 6071[7] 6438[4]

**Makanah** *Julie Camacho* a73 73
2 b c Mayson Diane's Choice (Komaite (USA))
2769[3] 3467[2] 4213[5] 8010[5]

**Makarios (USA)** *Nicholas Zito* 105
3 ch c Giant's Causeway(USA) Blissful (USA) (Mr Prospector (USA))
4652a[6]

**Make Good (IRE)** *David Brown* 79
2 b g Fast Company(IRE) Rectify (IRE) (Mujadil (USA))
4567[13] (5058) 5631[2] 6510[5] 7647[9]

**Make Music** *Andrew Balding* a95 94
4 b m Acclamation Come What May (Selkirk (USA))
142[7] (287) 617[7] 810[5] (1091) 1771[4] 2390[2] 9210[4]◆

**Make On Madam (IRE)** *Les Eyre* a64 76
5 b m Captain Rio Rye (IRE) (Charnwood Forest (IRE))
1106[3] (1879) 2224[3] 2685[8] 3203[2] 3934[5] 4168[2] 4525[6] 5000[6] 5496[4] 6049[8] 7476[6] 8192[8]

**Make Sail** *Tony Carroll* 24
3 b f Assertive Mabel's Song (Sakhee (USA))
3407[7] 4368[6] 6828[6]

**Make Time (IRE)** *David Menuisier* 109
3 ch c Makfi Poppet's Lovein (Lomitas)
1959[7] (5032) 5593[2] 6444[7]

**Makhfar (IRE)** *Mark Usher* a67 83
6 b g Bushranger(IRE) Let Me Shine (USA) (Dixie Union (USA))
1139[4] 1729[4] 2313[2] (3264) 4165[2] 4747[2] 6288[9] 8429[13] 9153[11]

**Makhzen (FR)** *M Boutin* a60 64
3 b g Motivator Hatikva (Hawk Wing (USA))
838a[5] 8960a[4]

**Makin (IRE)** *T de Vlaminck* a64 70
7 b g Shirocco(GER) Cuca Vela (USA) (Devil's Bag (USA))
1070a[12]

**Making Light (IRE)** *D K Weld* a62 104
3 b f Tamayuz Instant Sparkle (IRE) (Danehill (USA))
6080a[2] 6490a[7] 8083a[2] (8438a)

**Making Miracles** *Mark Johnston* a76 79
2 b g Pivotal Field Of Miracles (IRE) (Galileo (IRE))
7237[13] 7654[6] 7890[2] 8353[2] 8704[5]

**Making Trouble (GER)** *D Moser* a91 103
5 bb g Paco Boy(IRE) Making Hay (Dr Fong (USA))
6495a[5] 8845[9]

**Makin It** *William Knight* a57
2 b f North Light(IRE) Saltpetre (IRE) (Selkirk (USA))
8668[9]

**Makkaar (IRE)** *Mark Johnston* 84
3 b g Raven's Pass(USA) Beneventa (Most Welcome)
3199[7] 3713[8]

**Makkadangdang** *Andrew Balding* a72 69
3 ro g Mastercraftsman(IRE) Penny Cross (Efisio)
2296[2] 7277[8] 7766[13] 8114[8] 8313[5]

**Maklau (FR)** *J Boisnard* a61 66
3 gr f Air Chief Marshal(IRE) Mappa (FR) (Linamix (FR))
3134a[2] 4232a[7]

**Makofitwhatyouwill** *Nigel Tinkler* 43
2 b g Makfi Frequent (Three Valleys (USA))
3399[6] 4503[10] 6432[13] 7519[8]

**Maksab (IRE)** *Mick Channon* 86
2 bb c Makfi Azeema (IRE) (Averti (IRE))
3590[5] (4183) 4906[10] (6425) 7148[4] 7544[5] 8039[4]

**Maktava (FR)** *D Smaga* 66
2 b c Makfi Poltava (FR) (Victory Note (USA))
7012a[11]

**Makzeem** *Roger Charlton* a90 111
4 b g Makfi Kazeem (Darshaan)
2310[2] 3014[8] (4270)◆ 4854[2] 5393[6] (7622) 7807[4]◆

**Malak El Hawa (FR)** *P Lenogue* 51
7 b g Meshaheer(USA) Lune Du Rheu (FR) (Epistolaire (IRE))
5269a[10]

**Malalaika (FR)** *Mlle B Renk* 57
2 b f Siyouni(FR) Masaola (FR) (Anabaa Blue)
6251a[8]

**Malaspina (ITY)** *Ivan Furtado* a94 77
5 b m Pounced(USA) Modern Goddess (USA) (Gulch (USA))
6541a[3] (7342a) (8928) (9029)◆

**Malaysian Boleh** *Phil McEntee* a75 51
7 ch g Compton Place Orlena (USA) (Gone West (USA))
116[2] 745[2] 1062[4] (1147) (1327) 1487[5] 2319[9] 2675[6] 3201[6] 5340[6] 7692[7] 8329[13] 8541[8] 8816[6] 9184[5] 9432[7]

**Malcolm The Pug (IRE)**
*David Brown* a64 74
3 b c Acclamation La Zona (IRE) (Singspiel (IRE))
3234[5] 3673[5] 4092[2] 4500[8] 4843[4] 5271[6] 6148[5] (6582) 7016[7] 8115[13] 8427[11]

**Maldonado (FR)** *Michael Easterby* a41 69
3 ch g Rio De La Plata(USA) Spanish Winner (IRE) (Choisir (AUS))
3588[7] 4057[5] 4631[5] 5541[6] 5948[10] 7628[12] 7957[6] 8721[8] 9019[10]

**Maleficent Queen** *Keith Dalgleish* 108
5 b m Mount Nelson Manila Selection (USA) (Manila (USA))
1516[5] 1802[2] 2288[4] 2954[3] 3586[6] 4356[P] 4849[4] 6447[18]

**Malefique (FR)** *H-A Pantall* a60 10
3 b f Kendargent(FR) Magie Noire (IRE) (Marju (IRE))
3275a[11]

**Malibu Stacy (USA)** *George Weaver* a101 101
4 bb m Tizway(USA) Malibu Pier (USA) (Malibu Moon (USA))
8601a[4]

**Malik (FR)** *A De Mieulle* a62 77
4 ch h Equiano(FR) Queenly Bearing (Night Shift (USA))
932a[11]

**Maljaa** *M Al Mheiri* a56 104
5 ch g Paco Boy(IRE) Kerry's Dream (Tobougg (IRE))
318a[6] 543a[13]

**Mallory Heights (IRE)**
*Garvan Donnelly* a43 49
7 gr g Dalakhani(IRE) My Dark Rosaleen (Sadler's Wells (USA))
3193[9]

**Mallymkun** *David Loughnane* a69 67
5 b m Kheleyf(USA) Harriet's Girl (Choisir (AUS))
4467[4] 5205[11] 5750[7] 6345[14]

**Ma Lougie (FR)** *J-L Dehez* a50
2 bb f Cat Junior(USA) Stoa (IRE) (Peintre Celebre (USA))
9086a[9]

**Malt Teaser (FR)** *John Best* a68 65
3 ch g Muhtathir Abondante (USA) (Thunder Gulch (USA))
397[4]◆ 763[5]◆ 1550[8] 2394[7] 3327[2] 3721[5] 4798[5] 5843[4] 6812[6] 7760[6] 7879[2] 8160[7] 8993[2] 9391[4]

**Mama Africa (IRE)** *David Barron* a81 73
3 br f Big Bad Bob(IRE) Colourpoint (USA) (Forest Wildcat (USA))
356[4] 510[4] 1199[4] 2035[5] 2374[5] 2900[2] 3461[2] 3627[5] 4276[2] 4785[4] 5536[7] 5666[2] 6047[9] 7464[2] 7894[10] (8256) (9303)

**Mamba Noire (FR)** *K J Condon* 102
2 b f Wootton Bassett Baileys Applause (Royal Applause)
2861a[5] 3960[13] 4418a[3] 4855[3] 5941[7] 6354[3]

**Mambo Dancer** *Mark Johnston* a71 75
3 b g So You Think(NZ) Mambo Halo (USA) (Southern Halo (USA))
65[5] 5883[2] 6293[2] 6573[3] 7019[7] 7558[5] 7832[3] 7982[10] 8312[10]

**Mambo Spirit (IRE)**
*Tony Newcombe* a69 66
13 b g Invincible Spirit(IRE) Mambodorga (USA) (Kingmambo (USA))
330[10] 604[6] 1180[2] 1723[6] 2178[3] 2995[5] 4731[5]

**Mamdood (IRE)** *Susan Corbett* a64 77
3 gr g Clodovil(IRE) Fact (American Post)
4912[4] 7016[4] 7570[10] 7656[6] 8510[10]

**Mametz Wood (IRE)** *K R Burke* a73 72
2 b g Elzaam(AUS) Shaanbar (IRE) (Darshaan)
7520[2]◆ 8208[3] 8649[3]

**Mamillius** *George Baker* 89
4 b g Exceed And Excel(AUS) Laika Lane (USA) (Street Cry (IRE))
1606[4]◆ (3816) 4832[9] 6506[7]

**Mamnoon (IRE)** *Roy Brotherton* a63 63
4 b g Cape Cross(IRE) Masaafat (Act One)
457[4] 855[5] 1330[5] 1556[11] (3028) 3809[3] 4734[3] 6035[9] 8515[14] 8662[10] 8957[12] 9368[4]

**Mamoo** *Mike Murphy* a63 62
4 ch g Sir Percy Meredith (Medicean)
162[6] 555[5] 880[6]

**Mam'Selle (IRE)** *William Haggas* 93
3 b f Teofilo(IRE) Coquette Rouge (IRE) (Croco Rouge (IRE))
(2760) 3531[5] (5024) (6196) 6920[3] 8838a[8]

**Manaahil** *Charles Hills* a76 64
3 b f Dubawi(IRE) Mudaaraah (Cape Cross (IRE))
1503[2] 1905[5] 7600[5] 8707[3]

**Man About Town (IRE)** *K R Burke* a71 65
3 ch g Dandy Man(IRE) Zanida (IRE) (Mujadil (USA))
512[6] 813[11] (1127) (1348) 2630[11] 3814[7] 4310[14]

**Manahir (FR)** *H-A Pantall* 95
3 ch c Naaqoos Lerina (FR) (Priolo (USA))
6963a[4]

**Manangatang (IRE)** *Luca Cumani* a76 77
3 b g Fastnet Rock(AUS) Mona Lisa (Giant's Causeway (USA))
1875[3]◆ 2690[9] 3392[12] 7493[8] 7999[4]

**Manas Ata (FR)** *M Pimbonnet* a46 29
2 gr c Orpen(USA) Karalka (IRE) (Brief Truce (USA))
1594a[9]

**Manatee Bay** *Noel Wilson* a85 75
7 b g Royal Applause Dash Of Lime (Bold Edge)
2346[6] 3095[14] 3974[4]◆ 4477[4] 5016[3] (6546) 7245[8] 8211[9] 8722[7]

**Manchego** *Hugo Palmer* a86 70
3 b g Lope De Vega(IRE) Gooseberry Pie (Green Desert (USA))
(2167) 2784[10] 5157[12] 7909[9] 8398[11]

**Manchester City (GER)** *S Smrczek* 80
2 b c Approve(IRE) Maxima (GER) (Platini (GER))
7844a[3]

**Mancini** *Jonathan Portman* 77
3 ch g Nathaniel(IRE) Muscovado (USA) (Mr Greeley (USA))
2963[6] 3408[2] 4224[4] (5128) 6423[7]

**Manco Inca (IRE)** *Joseph Tuite* 46
2 b g Sir Prancealot(IRE) Night Delight (IRE) (Night Shift (USA))
1604[9] 1767[11] 5151[5] 5933[11]

**Mandalayan (IRE)**
*Jonathan Portman* 77
2 b g Arakan(USA) Danza Nera (IRE) (Dansili)
7739[2]

**Mandarin (GER)** *Marco Botti* a85 58
3 ch c Lope De Vega(IRE) Margarita (GER) (Lomitas)
2818[5] 3232[5] 8344[5]◆

**Mandarin Princess** *Philip McBride* a49 60
2 b f Vale Of York(IRE) Little China (Kyllachy)
6140[8] 6884[10] 7250[5] 8120[13]

**Mandatario** *J S Bolger* a95 99
6 br h Manduro(GER) Crystal Mountain (USA) (Monashee Mountain (USA))
227a[3]

**Mandrell (USA)** *Charlie Appleby*
4 b m Dubawi(IRE) Country Star (USA) (Empire Maker (USA))
1104[5]

**Mangaia (FR)** *S Wattel* a78 70
3 b f Orpen(USA) Mapiya (Green Tune (USA))
4288a[5] 6455a[2]

**Mangata (FR)** *Philip Kirby* a26
3 b g Cape Cross(IRE) Kong Moon (FR) (Hernando (FR))
9445[9]

**Mango Chutney** *John Davies* a60 77
4 b g Sleeping Indian Crimson Topaz (Hernando (FR))
2120[7] 3402[3] (3912) (4506) 5739[2] 6663[8]

**Mango Tango (FR)** *Ibrahim Al Malki* a76 106
4 b m Siyouni(FR) Alexandrina (GER) (Monsun (GER))
934a[7]

**Mangusto (FR)** *M Delcher Sanchez* a82 93
4 b h Roderic O'Connor(IRE) Mantadive (FR) (Okawango (USA))
5490a[2]

**Maniaco** *A Fabre* 112
4 b h Galileo(IRE) Plumania (Anabaa (USA))
1659a[3]

**Maningrey (GER)** *Waldemar Hickst* a83 101
8 b g Soldier Hollow Mandrella (GER) (Surumu (GER))
1920a[8]

**Manipur (GER)** *Markus Klug* 85
3 b c Lord Of England(GER) Manipura (GER) (Dansili)
2246a[7] 6084a[2]

**Manipura** *Derek Shaw* a64 54
4 gr m Sleeping Indian Ming Meng (IRE) (Intikhab (USA))
2124[10] 2589[7] *2925*[6] **3728**[3] 4053[6] 4619[4] 5340[4] 5535[3] 6041[10] *7487*[11]

**Manito (GER)** *Frau S Steinberg* 38
4 b g Soldier Hollow Mistic World (Monsun (GER))
**7430a**[7]

**Manjaam (IRE)** *Ed Dunlop* a102 98
4 ch g Tamayuz Priory Rock (IRE) (Rock Of Gibraltar (IRE))
***1361***[2] 3073[8] 4033[14] 5913[8] *6887*[12]

**Mankib** *F Head* 100
3 ch c Tamayuz Natagora (FR) (Divine Light (JPN))
2666a[8] **4942a**[6]

**Mankind (FR)** *George Scott* 76
2 b g Dabirsim(FR) Pastiches (Street Cry (IRE))
**4826**[4] 5365[10]

**Manners Maketh Man (IRE)**
*Ralph Beckett* a60 52
3 b c Lope De Vega(IRE) Dabawiyah (IRE) (Intikhab (USA))
6368[6] ***6817***[9] 7652[6]

**Manners Please** *Ralph Beckett* a72 75
3 b g Sixties Icon Humility (Polar Falcon (USA))
**4529**[2] 5248[6]

**Manny Owens (IRE)** *Jonjo O'Neill* a67 72
5 bb g Manduro(GER) Arabian Coral (IRE) (Intikhab (USA))
**5320**[4] 6858[3]

**Man Of His Word (AUS)**
*Bruce W Hill* 94
4 b g Lope De Vega(IRE) Mandalina (AUS) (Fasliyev (USA))
**8750a**[6]

**Man Of La Mancha (IRE)**
*Ben Haslam* a37 44
4 b g Zoffany(IRE) Sarella Loren (USA) (Theatrical (IRE))
*5441*[3]

**Man Of Verve (IRE)** *John Quinn* 78
3 b g Dandy Man(IRE) She's Our Rock (IRE) (Rock Of Gibraltar (IRE))
2630[DSQ] 3434[8]

**Manolito** *Hughie Morrison* a76 65
5 b g High Chaparral(IRE) Break Time (Dansili)
***24***[5]

**Manomine** *R K Watson* a62 62
8 b g Manduro(GER) Fascinating Hill (FR) (Danehill (USA))
**(4853)** ***9262***[3]

**Manorov** *T G McCourt* a69 52
7 b g Sholokhov(IRE) Mandel Set (GER) (Second Set (IRE))
***1014a***[8]

**Manor Park** *Alan King* 66
2 b g Medicean Jadeel (Green Desert (USA))
5547[6] **6674**[6] 7105[2]

**Manouka (FR)** *Mlle B Renk* a57 66
3 b f Sinndar(IRE) Masaola (FR) (Anabaa Blue)
1459a[7]

**Mansfield** *Michael Wigham* a80 61
4 b g Exceed And Excel(AUS) Jane Austen (IRE) (Galileo (IRE))
*1023*[10] ***1423***[6] 2155[11] 2838[12] 3589[12] 4017[8] 8295[8] *9094*[2] *9219*[2]

**Manshood (IRE)** *Paul Midgley* a83 90
4 b g Iffraaj Thawrah (IRE) (Green Desert (USA))
1804[4] 2821[6] *3257*[2] 3524[2] 4250[2] (4897) 5637[16] **(6348)** 6877[6]

**Manson** *Dominic Ffrench Davis* a101 98
4 ch g Equiano(FR) Swain's Gold (USA) (Swain (IRE))
**776a**[7] *1079*[3] **4636**[5] ***6024***[3] 7129[13] *7727*[14]

**Manthoor (IRE)** *Owen Burrows* a79 79
2 gr c Swiss Spirit Enchanting Way (Linamix (FR))
3754[6] 5851[2]◆ **6827**[2] ***7511***[2] *8587*[5]

**Manton Grange** *George Baker* a95 88
4 b g Siyouni(FR) Emulate (Alhaarth (IRE))
1939[2] 2267[3] (3396) 3920[2] ***(6289)***

**Man Whipp (FR)** *W Delalande* a40 21
4 b g Whipper(USA) Lady Ragazza (IRE) (Bering)
**1181a**[9]

**Many A Tale** *Ismail Mohammed* a75 73
3 br f Poet's Voice Rustam (Dansili)
4797[5] **5248**[4] *6015*[6] *6818*[13] *7771*[13]

**Many Dreams (IRE)** *Gary Moore* a61 74
4 b m Kodiac Deeday Bay (IRE) (Brave Act)
**(2763)** 3521[2] 4372[6] 5843[5] 6866[6] 7158[6] 8137[2]

**Many Waters (USA)**
*Andrew Balding* a77 80
3 b f Street Cry(IRE) Satulagi (USA) (Officer (USA))
*9164*◆ *1499*[2] 1944[6] 3425[2]◆ *4730*[4] **5331**[2]

**Maoi Chinn Tire (IRE)**
*Jennie Candlish* a73 79
10 b g Mull Of Kintyre(USA) Primrose And Rose (Primo Dominie)
**3046**[5] 3907[5]

**Maori Bob (IRE)** *Michael Bell* a64 87
3 b g Big Bad Bob(IRE) Tekhania (IRE) (Dalakhani (IRE))
*(864)* *967*[5] 3596[2]◆ 4314[2] 5581[4] (6061)◆ (6467) **(7024)**

**Ma Peek (USA)** *Brian Meehan* 53
4 bb h Arch(USA) Downtown Drifter (USA) (Devil His Due (USA))
**2357**[7]

**Ma Petite Toscane (FR)**
*T Castanheira* a55 73
2 ch f Evasive Rava (IRE) (Nayef (USA))
6803a[6] **8252a**[3]

**Maple Stirrup (IRE)** *Patrick Holmes* a61 60
5 b m Duke Of Marmalade(IRE) Street Shaana (FR) (Darshaan)
*28*[7] *1197*[8] **5186**[7] 5884[4] 6565[4] 7330[9]

**Mapped (USA)** *Charles Hills* 73
2 b c Mizzen Mast(USA) Geographic (USA) (Empire Maker (USA))
**8389**[3]

**Mappin Time (IRE)** *Tim Easterby* a97 81
9 b g Orientate(USA) Different Story (USA) (Stravinsky (USA))
***4***[3]◆

**Maraakib (IRE)** *David O'Meara* a72 68
5 b g Dark Angel(IRE) Mrs Cee (IRE) (Orpen (USA))
**1911**[8] 2136[8] 2741[8] 3497[5] 3651[8] 5455[6] 6059[5] 6557[2] *6948*[6] 7225[8] 7524[8] 7820[2] *8206*[2] 8386[7] 8682[3] *8814*[4] *9017*[2] *9153*[6] *9346*[5]

**Maratha (IRE)** *Stuart Williams* a85 86
3 gr g Cape Cross(IRE) Middle Persia (Dalakhani (IRE))
*2467*[2] 2930[2] 3465[5] **(4631)**◆ 6389[7] 7339[4] 7736[3] 8510[9] *9025*[4] *9206*[3] *(9419)*

**Marauder** *Henry Candy* a58
5 b g Thewayyouare(USA) Louise D'Arzens (Anabaa (USA))
*37*[5] ***289***[4] *894*[6] *2095*[11]

**Marble Bar** *Henry Candy* 69
2 b g Makfi Presbyterian Nun (IRE) (Daylami (IRE))
4909[6] 5709[5] 8350[8] **8676**[2]◆

**Marble Statue** *Ralph Beckett* 70
2 b f Makfi Czarna Roza (Polish Precedent (USA))
**6862**[5]

**Marbooh (IRE)** *Miss Joey Ellis* a77 66
4 b g Dark Angel(IRE) Muluk (IRE) (Rainbow Quest (USA))
2339[8] ***3140***[3] 3934[6] *4728*[6] 6182[8] 6263[6] *7792*[6] *8429*[11] *9142*[12]

**Marcano (IRE)** *Rod Millman* 81
5 b g Arcano(IRE) Aquatint (Dansili)
**1687**[2] 2133[11] *3325*[P]

**Marcella** *David C Griffiths*
2 b f Showcasing Cool In The Shade (Pastoral Pursuits)
7563[12] 8046[12]

**Marchingontogether** *Ivan Furtado* a62 73
2 ch f Havana Gold(IRE) Transvaal Sky (Avonbridge)
**(2502)** 3929[11] *7482*[6] 7883[5]

**March X Press (USA)** *Todd Pletcher* 97
2 bb f Shanghai Bobby(USA) Indian Rush (USA) (Indian Charlie (USA))
7206a[4] **8602a**[5]

**Marconi** *John Davies* 54
2 ch g Monsieur Bond(IRE) Tamara Bay (Selkirk (USA))
5370[10] 5801[5] **6264**[9] 7518[9]

**Marcoussis** *Y Barberot* a69 65
3 ch g Tamayuz Nightdance Sun (GER) (Monsun (GER))
2697a[11] ***6496a***[2]

**Marettimo (IRE)** *Charles Hills* a64 55
3 b g Harbour Watch(IRE) Renowned (IRE) (Darshaan)
***328***[7] 2039[8] *3178*[7] 4633[9] 4964[6]

**Margherita** *Roger Varian* a74 61
3 b f Mayson Phillipina (Medicean)
***2311***[3] *2957*[3] 3824[3]

**Margie's Music (FR)** *P Schiergen* 92
3 ch f Hurricane Run(IRE) Margie's World (GER) (Spinning World (USA))
3371a[5] **7673a**[6] 8462a[9]

**Margub** *Marcus Tregoning* 65
2 ch c Bated Breath Bahamian Babe (Bahamian Bounty)
**3305**[5]

**Mariah's Melody (IRE)**
*Lisa Williamson* 52
2 gr f Graydar(USA) In Seconds (USA) (Giant's Causeway (USA))
5398[8] 6410[4] **6678**[5] 7106[6]

**Maricruz (IRE)** *John C McConnell* a66
2 gr f Most Improved(IRE) Miss Fancy Pants (Act One)
***8715***[4]

**Marie De Medicis** *J-C Rouget* 88
2 b f Cape Cross(IRE) Caterina De Medici (FR) (Redoute's Choice (AUS))
**(6542a)**

**Mariee** *Mark Johnston* a85 84
4 b m Archipenko(USA) Maria Di Scozia (Selkirk (USA))
***460***[3] *611*[2] *781*[2] *1324*[5] 2225[3] 2504[5]

**Marie Josephe** *Richard Hughes* 86
3 b f Cape Cross(IRE) Maria Letizia (Galileo (IRE))
2476[4]◆ 2834[4] (3921) 4699[2] **5822**[2] 6722[7]

**Mariele (IRE)** *U Schwinn* a45 54
6 b m Shirocco(GER) Mureefa (USA) (Bahri (USA))
**7342a**[10]

**Marie Of Lyon** *Richard Fahey* 99
3 b f Royal Applause Virginia Hall (Medicean)
3964[13] 4903[4] 5422[3] 6382[9] (7214)◆ (7329)◆ 7811[14] **8040**[2]

**Marie Toulouse (IRE)** *K R Burke* a57
2 b f Oasis Dream Virginia Waters (USA) (Kingmambo (USA))
***8997***[8]

**Marilyn** *Chris Wall* a51 72
3 ch f Sixties Icon Donatia (Shamardal (USA))
**1907**[7] **2929**[6] 4761[7] *6067*[10] *7457*[6] 8124[6]

**Marilyn M (IRE)** *George Scott* a54 47
2 b f Red Jazz(USA) Jilly Choo (Bahamian Bounty)
3215[9] ***9320***[8]

**Marina Palace (FR)** *A Junk* a41 68
2 b f Palace Episode(USA) Mariners Doll (IRE) (King Charlemagne (USA))
**1335a**[11] *8482a*[9]

**Marine One** *David Simcock* a82 73
3 b g Frankel Marine Bleue (IRE) (Desert Prince (IRE))
2066[5] 2751[4] ***3720***[3] *4307*[2] *8377*[2]

**Marinka (FR)** *R Rohne* 44
2 b f Planteur(IRE) Marie Galante (Beat Hollow)
**8461a**[7]

**Mariobasset (FR)** *J Boisnard* a68
2 b g Wootton Bassett Maria Candela (Spectrum (IRE))
***9087a***[7]

**Marju's Quest (IRE)** *Adrian Wintle* a61 81
7 b g Marju(IRE) Queen's Quest (Rainbow Quest (USA))
***6819***[6] *8647*[14]

**Markazi (FR)** *J-C Rouget* a99 107
3 gr g Dark Angel(IRE) Marasima (IRE) (Barathea (IRE))
**1824a**[4] 3855a[6]

**Market Choice (IRE)** *Tracy Waggott* a58 69
4 b g Majestic Missile(IRE) Ron's Secret (Efisio)
**2184**[6] 3567[6] 4433[9] 4605[5] 5646[3] 6546[7] 6943[5] 7245[9] 7525[14] 7657[6] 8656[5] *9102*[8]

**Markhan (USA)** *David Marnane* a79 91
4 b g Birdstone(USA) Royal Flush (USA) (Smart Strike (CAN))
***8375***[12]

**Mark Hopkins** *David Elsworth* 95
5 b g Mount Nelson Halska (Unfuwain (USA))
2176[7] 2603[4] **(3086)**◆ 3794[5] 4828[8] 5351[3] 5944[7]

**Mark Of Approval (USA)**
*John Gosden* a91 86
3 ch g Lemon Drop Kid(USA) Agreeable Miss (USA) (Speightstown (USA))
1857[3]◆ ***(2467)***◆

**Mark Of Excellence (IRE)**
*Saeed bin Suroor* a67 52
3 ch g Sepoy(AUS) Cheyenne Star (IRE) (Mujahid (USA))
2895[6] 4409[6] **4693**[4] 5536[8]

**Marmajuke Bay** *Mark Usher* a89 95
4 b g Duke Of Marmalade(IRE) Shimoni (Mark Of Esteem (IRE))
*1555*[2] *2165*[2] 2741[12] (3716) 4828[4] 6151[7] **(6857)** 7548[5] 8468[7]

**Marmalad (IRE)** *Shaun Lycett* a73 42
5 b g Duke Of Marmalade(IRE) Primissima (GER) (Second Set (IRE))
*6891*[2] ***1338***[12]

**Marmelo** *Hughie Morrison* a85 115
4 b h Duke Of Marmalade(IRE) Capriolla (In The Wings)
(2202a) 2803[5] 4879a[2] **(6250a)** 8250a[6]◆ 8667a[9]

**Marmion** *Les Eyre* a54 77
5 b g Cape Cross(IRE) Margarula (IRE) (Doyoun)
*1248*[6] 1517[17] *2333*[9] **(3501)** 3983[5] 4476[7] 5163[7] 6858[6] 7267[3] *7936*[9] 8386[9] *8846*[10]

**Marnie James** *Iain Jardine* 81
2 b g Camacho Privy Garden (IRE) (Oasis Dream)
1673[5] 2771[2]◆ 3333[6] 3789[8] **(4866)** 6353[8] **(8102)**

**Maroc** *Nikki Evans* a64 77
4 b g Rock Of Gibraltar(IRE) Zietory (Zieten (USA))
*220*[5] 1684[3] 2785[4] 3537[3] **4755**[2] **5477**[2] 5968[4]

**Marqoom** *Mark Johnston* a58 73
3 ch c New Approach(IRE) Night Frolic (Night Shift (USA))
*1347*[6] **1701**[2] 2159[3] 3596[7] 4436[7]

**Marquee Club** *Jamie Osborne* a88 74
3 b c Sixties Icon Rose Cheval (USA) (Johannesburg (USA))
*178*[2] *(356)* ***(458)*** ***678***[2] *778*[4] *1026*[6] *1774*[9]

**Marseille (IRE)** *Julie Camacho* a75 76
3 b f Excelebration(IRE) Marlinka (Marju (IRE))
*(1782)* *2925*[2]◆ 4342[2] **5316**[2]◆ 6149[7]

**Marsha (IRE)** *Sir Mark Prescott Bt* a100 122
4 b m Acclamation Marlinka (Marju (IRE))
*(2397)*◆ 3926[3] 4927a[2] 5595[3] **(6402)** 7670a[2] 8604a[6]

**Marshal Dan (IRE)** *Heather Main* a59
2 b c Lawman(FR) Aunt Nicola (Reel Buddy (USA))
*9051*[9] ***9433***[6]

**Marshal Dan Troop (IRE)**
*Robyn Brisland* a63 73
4 b h Lawman(FR) Corrozal (GER) (Cape Cross (IRE))
*169*[6] ***233***[2] *423*[4]

**Marshall Aid (IRE)** *Mark Usher* a74 64
4 b g Lawman(FR) Dievotchkina (IRE) (Bluebird (USA))
*1628* *555*[2] *786*[2] ***1466***[3] *1697*[3] *2460*[3] 2966[9] 3623[4] 3916[4] *8878*[10] *9095*[10] *9375*[9]

**Marshall Jennings (IRE)**
*Mrs John Harrington* a98 105
5 b g Lawman(FR) Zuniga's Date (USA) (Diesis)
1388a[10] **1568a**[2] 3765a[6] 5517a[8] 6961a[11]

**Marshgate Lane (USA)**
*Neil Mulholland* a89 72
8 b g Medaglia d'Oro(USA) Louvain (IRE) (Sinndar (IRE))
***24***[2] ***117***[5] *304*[5] *719*[6] *884*[2]

**Marsh Harbour (FR)** *Mario Hofer* 75
2 b c Zafeen(FR) Moon Romance (FR) (Nayef (USA))
5989a[9] **7012a**[6]

**Marsh Pride** *K R Burke* a72 92
5 b m Stimulation(IRE) Peneia (USA) (Nureyev (USA))
**1734**[7] **2136**[4] 2906[4] 3580[3] 4364[6] *5414*[6] 7142[2]◆ (7598)

**Marsh Storm (IRE)** *K R Burke* a62 48
2 b f Choisir(AUS) Margaret's Dream (IRE) (Muhtarram (USA))
***1776***[3] 2299[5] 5371[7] *6634*[11] *7029*[4] *7239*[11] *7938*[10]

**Martha Jane (FR)** *B De Montzey* a72 75
2 b f Cockney Rebel(IRE) Artistic Light (Fantastic Light (USA))
**8228a**[6]

**Martinengo (IRE)**
*Peter Chapple-Hyam* 52
2 b c Elusive Pimpernel(USA) Albiatra (USA) (Dixieland Band (USA))
**8387**[10]

**Marvellous Night (FR)**
*H De Nicolay* a82 85
2 b f Captain Marvelous(IRE) Makaye (FR) (Kendor (FR))
2664a[7] 3445a[5] *4677a*[2] **6251a**[3]

**Marwa** *Ed Dunlop* a61 26
3 b f Exceed And Excel(AUS) La Cucina (IRE) (Last Tycoon)
***34***[5] *434*[7]

**Mary Anne Evans** *John Gosden* a53 75
3 b f Oasis Dream Gertrude Bell (Sinndar (IRE))
*1404*[6] 1737[5] **2613**[5]

**Mary Elise (IRE)** *Ed Walker* a60
2 b f Mastercraftsman(IRE) Je T'Adore (IRE) (Montjeu (IRE))
***8668***[7]

**Marylebone** *Ed Walker* a85 46
4 b g Shamardal(USA) Mary Boleyn (IRE) (King's Best (USA))
2133[DSQ] ***6936***[3] *7947*[11]

**Mary Le Bow** *Victor Dartnall* a68 47
6 b m Sir Percy Bermondsey Girl (Bertolini (USA))
***47***[6] *351*[5]

**Mary Tudor (IRE)** *W McCreery* 104
2 gr f Dawn Approach(IRE) Antiquities (Kaldounevees (FR))
**6242a**[3] 7421a[4]

**Marzouq (USA)** *Jeremy Noseda* a79 100
3 b c Spring At Last(USA) Smart 'n Special (USA) (Smart Strike (CAN))
*625*[3] *1029*[2] 1907[2] 3317[4] 3780[2] **(4856)**

**Masaarr (USA)** *Roger Varian* a84 84
2 ch c Distorted Humor(USA) Aryaamm (IRE) (Galileo (IRE))
**8350**[3] ***(8840)***◆

**Masamah (IRE)** *Ian Williams* a75 83
11 gr g Exceed And Excel(AUS) Bethesda (Distant Relative)
*93*[10] *355*[5] ***(501)*** *685*[12] *923*[6] *1189*[5]

**Masar (IRE)** *Charlie Appleby* 113
2 ch c New Approach(IRE) Khawlah (IRE) (Cape Cross (IRE))
(3002) 4068[3] (6696)◆ **7667a**[3] 8577a[6]

**Masarzain (IRE)** *Archie Watson* a86 88
4 br g Kodiac Cache Creek (IRE) (Marju (IRE))
*251*[1] *575*[11] *923*[7] *1310*[4] 1720[6] 2082[3] 5651[5] (6102) 6393[2] (6591)◆ **(6893)**◆ **7098**[2] *7456*[5]

**Mashaaref** *M Al Mheiri* a106 87
9 b g Cape Cross(IRE) Etizaaz (USA) (Diesis)
***321a***[2]

**Mashaheer** *William Haggas* 66
2 b g Dutch Art Faustinatheyounger (IRE) (Antonius Pius (USA))
3093[8] **6424**[6] 7250[6]

**Masham Star (IRE)** *Mark Johnston* a107 106
3 b g Lawman(FR) Croisiere (USA) (Capote (USA))
*430a*[11] 649a[6] 887a[4] *1780*[7] 2554[2] 2830[5] 3077[3] 3318[5] 3997[27] 4475[2] 4904[2] 5157[5] 5392[5]◆ 5594[6] *6024*[2] 6186[7] 6419[5] ***(6685)*** 6918[15] 8104[5]

**Masked Bandit** *Suzy Smith*
4 b g Dick Turpin(IRE) Plaisterer (Best Of The Bests (IRE))
*2092*[10]

**Masked Defender (USA)**
*Amanda Perrett* a73 71
2 b c First Defence(USA) Costume (Danehill (USA))
3002[9] 6653[5] *7765*[4] ***8309***[2]

**Mask Of Time (IRE)** *Hugo Palmer* a83 108
3 b c Holy Roman Emperor(IRE) Mission Secrete (IRE) (Galileo (IRE))
(1460a) (3103a) **3879a**[4] 5522a[5] 6053a[6] 8059a[4]

**Maskoon** *Philip Kirby* a71 71
6 ch g Aqlaam Tamazug (Machiavellian (USA))
1519[7] **2498**[6]

**Masonic (IRE)** *Robyn Brisland* a71 51
3 b g Intense Focus(USA) Green Tambourine (Green Desert (USA))
*642*[6] ***1760***[5] 2071[7] 2931[7] *5895*[7] *6946*[4] *8376*[13]

**Masons Belle** *Ronald Harris* a18 4
2 b f Piccolo Edge Of Gold (Choisir (AUS))
6367[8] 7739[10] ***8399***[10]

**Masquerade Bling (IRE)**
*Neil Mulholland* a64 60
3 b f Approve(IRE) Mataji (IRE) (Desert Prince (IRE))
*89*[7] *418*[4] *897*[2] *1242*[5] *1421*[4]◆ *1597*[2] *2017*[3] 5511[2] 6101[5] *(6902)* *7573*[5] *8985*[7] *9203*[4] ***9431***[2]

**Masqueraded (USA)**
*Frau R Weissmeier* a55 49
4 ch g Drosselmeyer(USA) Maudie May (USA) (Gilded Time (USA))
**1181a**[8]

**Massaat (IRE)** *Owen Burrows* 118
4 b h Teofilo(IRE) Madany (IRE) (Acclamation)
**(6193)** 6982a[3] 8003[2]

**Massif Central (IRE)**
*John Joseph Murphy* a86 102
3 b g Arcano(IRE) Melaaya (USA) (Aljabr (USA))
1386a[11] **6243a**[2]

**Massina (FR)** *S Wattel* a83 91
2 ch f Style Vendome(FR) Mapiya (Green Tune (USA))
*8195a*[4] **8525a**[6]

**Master Archer (IRE)**
*James Fanshawe* a82 83
3 gr g Mastercraftsman(IRE) Kinigi (IRE) (Verglas (IRE))
1682[4] 2118[4] *3720*[8] 4809[4] 5550[2] 6038[2] *7060*[2] **8511**[2]

**Master Billie (IRE)** *Roger Teal* a51 52
3 ro g Mastercraftsman(IRE) Billie Jean (Bertolini (USA))
***305***[6] *627*[10] *881*[10] *1107*[9]

**Master Carpenter (IRE)**
*Rod Millman* 111
6 ch h Mastercraftsman(IRE) Fringe (In The Wings)
1494[12] 1960[15] **(2735)** 4033[15] 4918[12] 6698[12] 7149[7] 7743[4] 8042[4] 8423[11]

**Master Dan** *S Dehez* a62 87
6 b g Mastercraftsman(IRE) Danella (IRE) (Platini (GER))
**(7070a)**

**Master Dancer** *Tim Vaughan* a71 75
6 gr g Mastercraftsman(IRE) Isabella Glyn (IRE) (Sadler's Wells (USA))
2363[3] *4000*[6] **(7232)**

**Masterfilly (IRE)** *Ed Walker* a56 50
3 gr f Mastercraftsman(IRE) Waldena (USA) (Storm Cat (USA))
***149***[5] *627*[9] 4967[3] 5761[8] 6611[8] *7833*[10]

**Masterful Act (USA)** *John Balding* a49 23
10 ch g Pleasantly Perfect(USA) Catnip (USA) (Flying Paster (USA))
885[8] 1344[6] 1781[8] 2787[8] 9070[6] 9445[11]

**Master Grey (IRE)** *Rod Millman* 61
2 gr g Mastercraftsman(IRE) Market Day (Tobougg (IRE))
2926[5] 4218[6] 5246[7]

**Master Me (IRE)** *K R Burke* a5 65
3 b f Masterofthehorse(IRE) Miss Starlight (Trade Fair)
3039[7] 3649[2] 4449[7]

**Mastermind (SAF)** *M F De Kock* 108
5 b g Var(USA) Model I.Q. (SAF) (Jallad (USA))
87a[8] 433a[5] 651a[10] 892a[13]

**Masterofdiscovery** *Clive Cox* a66 77
3 b c Henrythenavigator(USA) Wonderful Desert (Green Desert (USA))
(1685) 2088[10] 3780[5] 6310[3] 6792[5] 7452[14]

**Master Of Finance (IRE)**
*Malcolm Jefferson* a43 102
6 ch g Mastercraftsman(IRE) Cheal Rose (IRE) (Dr Devious (IRE))
6399[13]

**Master Of Heaven** *Jim Boyle* a55 58
4 b g Makfi Maid In Heaven (IRE) (Clodovil (IRE))
281[13] 636[6] 880[9] (1146) (2914) 3753[11] 4461[6] 5023[8] 5790[10] 6621[3] 6754[5] 7324[3] 7990[3] 8799[7] 8994[7] 9278[3]

**Master Of Irony (IRE)** *John Quinn* a63 96
5 b g Makfi Mother Of Pearl (IRE) (Sadler's Wells (USA))
1719[7] 2774[8] 7614[5]

**Master Of Song** *Roy Bowring* a44 40
10 ch g Ballet Master(USA) Ocean Song (Savahra Sound)
6622[8] 7324[12] 8258[3] 9445[3]

**Master Of War** *D Selvaratnam* a92 98
7 ch g Compton Place Mamma Morton (IRE) (Elnadim (USA))
84a[14] 318a[12]

**Master Of Wine (GER)**
*Andrew Balding* 77
2 b g Maxios Magma (GER) (Dubai Destination (USA))
3783[2] 4583[6]

**Masterpaver** *Richard Fahey* a94 90
6 gr g Mastercraftsman(IRE) Most-Saucy (Most Welcome)
197[2] 728[4] 921[5] 1240[2] 3841[4] (3947)

**Master Pekan** *Roy Brotherton* a47 41
4 b g Piccolo Lady Pekan (Sri Pekan (USA))
270[9] 415[9] 1147[8] 1452[10]

**Masterpiece (FR)** *A Fabre* 90
2 b c Mastercraftsman(IRE) Modern Eagle (GER) (Montjeu (IRE))
(5520a) 6229a[5]

**Master Plan (USA)** *Todd Pletcher* a111
3 b c Twirling Candy(USA) Sage Mist (USA) (Henny Hughes (USA))
1375a[3]

**Master Poet** *Robert Cowell* a31
2 b g Poet's Voice Lilli Marlane (Sri Pekan (USA))
7877[9]

**Master Reset (AUS)** *Matt Laurie* 102
5 b g Reset(AUS) Glowing Tribute (AUS) (Zeditave (AUS))
8750a[5]

**Masters Apprentice (IRE)**
*Sylvester Kirk* a65 56
2 ch g Mastercraftsman(IRE) Maghzaa (IRE) (Aqlaam)
5710[10] 6472[5] 7451[4] 8371[2] 8537[5]

**Master Singer (USA)** *John Gosden* a102 94
3 br c Giant's Causeway(USA) Ring Of Music (Sadler's Wells (USA))
1963[3] (2921)◆ 3998[11] 6445[16] 7785[9] (8244) 8910[5] 9259[5]

**Masterson (IRE)** *Mick Channon* a81 75
4 gr g Lawman(FR) Indian Dumaani (Indian Ridge (IRE))
(1486) (1585) (2275) 2622[5] 3190[3]

**Master Speaker (IRE)** *M J Tynan* a83 87
7 b g Danehill Dancer(IRE) First Breeze (USA) (Woodman (USA))
1520a[S] 4925a[14] 6978a[11]

**Master's Spirit (IRE)** *J Reynier* a95 106
6 gr h Mastercraftsman(IRE) Lavayssiere (FR) (Sicyos (USA))
3637a[3]

**Master The World (IRE)**
*David Elsworth* a110 113
6 gr g Mastercraftsman(IRE) Zadalla (Zaha (CAN))
208a[7] 542a[4] 776a[5] 3963[8] 5157[2] (5594) 6105[4] 6444[4] 7619[31] 8234[12] 8468[6] 8740[16] (8844) 8992[2] 9388[7]

**Masucci (IRE)** *G M Lyons* 82
2 b g Zoffany(IRE) Meeting In Paris (IRE) (Dutch Art)
6977a[15]

**Matar (FR)** *F-H Graffard* a82
2 b c Penny's Picnic(IRE) Miss Gazduram (AUT) (Gazduram)
5952a[2]

**Matauri Jewel (IRE)** *M Delzangles* 92
4 b m Authorized(IRE) Moonrise (GER) (Grand Lodge (USA))
5198a[4] (6123a)

**Match Maker (IRE)** *Simon Crisford* 81
2 b c Declaration Of War(USA) I'm In Love (USA) (Zafonic (USA))
3164[3]◆ 4068[10]

**Matchmaking (GER)**
*Sir Mark Prescott Bt* a49 51
2 ch g Mastercraftsman(IRE) Monami (GER) (Sholokhov (IRE))
7250[11] 7512[9] 7946[9]

**Match My Fire (IRE)** *Michael Dods* 71
4 ch g Makfi High Lite (Observatory (USA))
1498[11] 3193[10] 3708[2]◆ 8386[10]

**Matchwinner (GER)** *A Kleinkorres* 110
6 ch h Sternkoenig(IRE) Mahamuni (IRE) (Sadler's Wells (USA))
2485a[4] (4487a) 6451a[6] (7722a) 8270a[3]

**Materialist** *Roger Varian* 83
3 b c Dansili Mundana (IRE) (King's Best (USA))
2185[2] (2857) 3583[6] 4299[3]

**Materialistic** *Luca Cumani* a101 99
4 b m Oasis Dream Pongee (Barathea (IRE))
1795[2] 2392[7] 4308[6] 5352[7] 5927[5]

**Matewan (IRE)** *Ian Williams* 60
2 b g Epaulette(AUS) Cochin (USA) (Swain (IRE))
4583[9] 5710[7]◆ 7392[12]

**Mathix (FR)** *S Kobayashi* a66 83
3 b g Kendargent(FR) Matwan (FR) (Indian Rocket)
1692[2] 2857[3] 4508[2] 7471a[5]

**Mathonville (FR)** *J-C Rouget* a42 62
3 b f Rajsaman(FR) Tunis (FR) (Dubai Destination (USA))
427a[8]

**Maths Prize** *Roger Charlton* 99
3 b g Royal Applause Hypoteneuse (IRE) (Sadler's Wells (USA))
1943[5] 3997[29] 4904[3] 5548[4] 6870[4] 7784[8]

**Matilda Grace (IRE)**
*Lisa Williamson* a25
2 gr f Lilbourne Lad(IRE) New Deal (Rainbow Quest (USA))
8916[9] 9080[9] 9465[10]

**Matken (FR)** *D & P Prod'Homme* a75 70
5 gr g Kendargent(FR) Matwan (FR) (Indian Rocket)
6648a[7]

**Matorico (IRE)** *Jonjo O'Neill* 88
6 gr g Mastercraftsman(IRE) Hashbrown (GER) (Big Shuffle (USA))
4443[7]

**Matravers** *Mary Hambro* a75 71
6 b g Oasis Dream Maakrah (Dubai Destination (USA))
736[7] 1178[4] 2291[7] 3771[3] 4523[3] 5053[5]

**Mattmu** *Tim Easterby* 112
5 b h Indesatchel(IRE) Katie Boo (IRE) (Namid)
5633[4] (6206)

**Mattymolls Gaga (IRE)**
*Mrs John Harrington* 93
2 ch c Dragon Pulse(IRE) Clenaghcastle Lady (IRE) (Acclamation)
6955a[7]

**Maudlin Magdalen (IRE)**
*Donal Kinsella* a82 81
7 b m Dylan Thomas(IRE) Carolines Secret (Inchinor)
6978a[5]

**Maulesden May (IRE)**
*Keith Dalgleish* a78 80
4 b m Dark Angel(IRE) Jemima's Art (Fantastic Light (USA))
3197[3] 3898[2] (4056) 4344[6] (5207) (5921) 7032[6] 7824[8]

**Maureb (IRE)** *Tony Coyle* a71 79
5 br m Excellent Art Almost Blue (USA) (Mr Greeley (USA))
2119[5] 2428[4] 2888[8] 3063[7] 3287[2] 3526[4] 4059[6] (4788) 5211[9] 5881[3] 6570[10] (8427)

**Maverick Officer** *David Simcock* a77 61
2 b c Exceed And Excel(AUS) Gradara (Montjeu (IRE))
6108[7] 6367[5] (9433)

**Maverick Wave (USA)**
*John Gosden* a64 113
6 ch h Elusive Quality(USA) Misty Ocean (USA) (Stormy Atlantic (USA))
4069[4] 5394[8] 8233[8]

**Maverik** *Neil Mulholland* a70 62
9 ch g Iceman Nouvelle Lune (Fantastic Light (USA))
(238) 517[9] (Dead)

**Maveway (IRE)** *David Evans* a20 25
2 b f Sir Prancealot(IRE) Stef's Girl (IRE) (Petardia)
3156[10] 4725[10] 6005[10] 6585[15]

**Mavilla** *E Lyon* a65 52
4 b m Pour Moi(IRE) Syvilla (Nayef (USA))
6018a[4]

**Mawaany (IRE)** *G M Lyons* a75 98
4 gr g Teofilo(IRE) Middle Persia (Dalakhani (IRE))
6978a[2]

**Mawaqeet (USA)** *Michael Appleby* a60 79
8 b g Dynaformer(USA) Lady Ilsley (USA) (Trempolino (USA))
4921[9] 5873[5]

**Mawhub** *S Seemar* a100 72
8 b g Singspiel(IRE) Native Blue (Seeking The Gold (USA))
208a[11]

**Max Beddow (IRE)** *Geoffrey Deacon* a55 22
4 b g Tagula(IRE) Copper Harbour (IRE) (Foxhound (USA))
2915[8] 3809[12]

**Max Dynamite (FR)** *W P Mullins* a72 113
7 b g Great Journey(JPN) Mascara (GER) (Monsun (GER))
8667a[3] 9167a[6]

**Maximinus Thrax (FR)**
*David Simcock* a83
3 b c Holy Roman Emperor(IRE) Ziride (FR) (Valanour (IRE))
9202[2]◆

**Maximum Aurelius (FR)**
*F-H Graffard* 108
4 b g Showcasing Feld Marechale (FR) (Deputy Minister (CAN))
4653a[2] (7416a)

**Maximus Daia (IRE)** *J P Murtagh* a52 74
3 b g Holy Roman Emperor(IRE) Bayberry (UAE) (Bering)
1633a[7]

**Max Zorin (IRE)** *Andrew Balding* 103
3 b g Cape Cross(IRE) My (King's Best (USA))
1861[4] 2569[3]

**Mayalee** *Richard Fahey* 41
2 b f Iffraaj Moma Lee (Duke Of Marmalade (IRE))
8474[10]

**Maya Malibu (USA)**
*H Graham Motion* a106
2 b f Malibu Moon(USA) Island Sand (USA) (Tabasco Cat (USA))
8603a[12]

**Mayasa (IRE)** *John Flint* a83 32
4 ch m Iffraaj Lanzana (IRE) (Kalanisi (IRE))
6033[7] 6610[6] 7831[7] 8157[12] 8647[12]

**Mayaseen (FR)** *Hugo Palmer* a54
2 gr f Style Vendome(FR) Wing Stealth (IRE) (Hawk Wing (USA))
8668[11]

**Maybride** *Richard Fahey* 87
2 b f Mayson Wedding Party (Groom Dancer (USA))
3491[2] 3960[10] 4815[5] 7563[2] 7821[5] (8472)

**Mayer** *Luca Cumani* a44
2 b c Nathaniel(IRE) Paisley (Pivotal)
9200[14] 9417[10]

**Mayfair Lady** *Richard Fahey* 111
4 b m Holy Roman Emperor(IRE) Lady Luachmhar (IRE) (Galileo (IRE))
1903[5] 3080[7] 4078[7]

**Mayfield Boy** *Antony Brittain* a42 63
6 b g Authorized(IRE) Big Pink (IRE) (Bigstone (IRE))
1403[11] 2919[11] 5214[5] 5497[9]

**Mayflair** *Jonathan Portman* a67 60
3 b f Zamindar(USA) Madhaaq (IRE) (Medicean)
144[6] 283[3] 718[3] 4442[4]

**May Girl** *Robert Cowell* 92
2 b f Mayson Instructress (Diktat)
3725[4] 5015[2]◆ (5327) (6969) 7114[3] 7846a[9]

**Maygold** *Ed Walker* a68 63
2 b f Mayson Spanish Gold (Vettori (IRE))
5107[7] 5575[3]◆ 6338[4]◆ 7194[2] (7491)

**Mayhem Maybe (IRE)** *Gay Kelleway* 19
2 b f Art Connoisseur(IRE) Altalena (ITY) (Marju (IRE))
6824[13] 7551[8]

**Mayleaf Shine (IRE)** *Iain Jardine* 98
3 b f Mayson Let Me Shine (USA) (Dixie Union (USA))
3579[4] 4078[10] 5402[11] 5602[2] 6450[5] (6927) 7610[6] 8105[3]

**Mayleen (IRE)** *Ann Duffield* a27 40
3 br f Big Bad Bob(IRE) Miss Megs (IRE) (Croco Rouge (IRE))
2993[10] 7240[13]

**May Mist** *Trevor Wall* a62 37
5 b m Nayef(USA) Midnight Mist (IRE) (Green Desert (USA))
164[6] 954[8] 3529[9] 4469[9] 7028[14] 7826[6] 8249[13]

**Maypole** *Richard Hannon* a73 66
2 ch c Mayson Constitute (USA) (Gone West (USA))
8073[4]◆ 8350[6] 8701[2]

**May Remain** *Paul Cole* a81 84
2 b c Mayson Ultimate Best (King's Best (USA))
1681[5] 2706[2] (3029) 3776[2] 4841[2] (5262)◆ 5526[5] 8431[4]

**May Sky** *John Gosden* 72
3 b f Mayson Millinsky (USA) (Stravinsky (USA))
1947[2] 2619[4] 2970[5]

**Maysonri** *Mark Hoad* a28 50
3 b g Mayson Roshina (IRE) (Chevalier (IRE))
2315[9] 7210[10] 7918[13] 8181[8]

**Maysoor (AUS)** *S Seemar* 74
5 b g Fastnet Rock(AUS) Cinq Rouge (AUS) (Red Ransom (USA))
203a[10]

**May Spirit** *Michael Blanshard* a30 17
2 b f Mayson World Spirit (Agnes World (USA))
3689[8] 7211[7] 8819[8]

**Maytheorsebewithu (IRE)**
*Pat Phelan* a53
2 b f Shirocco(GER) Amoya (GER) (Royal Dragon (USA))
9385[7]

**Maytime (FR)** *C Ferland* a72 92
3 b f Henrythenavigator(USA) Timepecker (IRE) (Dansili)
4027a[4] 5196a[9]

**Mayyasah (USA)** *Richard Hannon* 91
2 b f More Than Ready(USA) Whipsaw City (FR) (Elusive City (USA))
(5107)◆ 5941[6] 6678[2]

**Mazaaher** *David Evans* a73 73
7 b g Elnadim(USA) Elutrah (Darshaan)
688[7] 928[12] (1312) 1469[2] 1891[2] 2357[2] 3036[8] 3574[5]

**Mazalto (IRE)** *Pat Phelan* a73 77
4 b m Teofilo(IRE) Mazaaya (USA) (Cozzene (USA))
1602[5] 2388[6] 3618[4] 5407[4]

**Mazeed (USA)** *M F De Kock* a81 52
3 ch g Street Cry(IRE) Speed Succeeds (USA) (Gone West (USA))
201a[3] 430a[10]

**Mazyoun** *Hugo Palmer* a93 95
3 br g Mayson Hypnotize (Machiavellian (USA))
1801[4] 2400[5] 2739[6] 3842[5] 4634[4] 5159[3] 5642[4] (6068) 6322[5] 6933[9] (7339) 8469[4]

**Mazzini** *James Fanshawe* a109 86
4 ch g Exceed And Excel(AUS) Firenze (Efisio)
2566[6] 3034[8]◆ 3969[2] 4353[6] (5241)◆ 6025[3] 6685[3] 7603[2] 8845[10] 8991[6]

**McCools Gold** *Alan King* a55 71
4 b g Yeats(IRE) Gold Reef (Double Trigger (IRE))
2111[7] 2928[2] 3685[6]

**McCraken (USA)** *Ian Wilkes* a116
3 b c Ghostzapper(USA) Ivory Empress (USA) (Seeking The Gold (USA))
2420a[8] 5463a[2]

**McDelta** *Geoffrey Deacon* a63 59
7 b g Delta Dancer Mcnairobi (Josr Algarhoud (IRE))
1284[3] 1556[5] 3753[9] 4747[9] 5427[3] 6101[4] 6393[3] 7062[11] 8346[4]◆ 8799[8]

**Mcelligott (IRE)** *Richard Price* a17 44
4 b g Dark Angel(IRE) Nina Blini (Bertolini (USA))
26[13] 239[11]

**McErin (USA)** *Wesley A Ward* a93 93
2 ch g Trappe Shot(USA) Erin Rose (USA) (Purge (USA))
3993[7] 8602a[12]

**Mcklaya (FR)** *D Zarroli* a38 62
2 b f Big Bad Bob(IRE) Wimple's Girl (IRE) (Cape Cross (IRE))
8482a[11]

**Mcmunigal (IRE)** *G M Lyons* 104
2 b g Epaulette(AUS) Picture Of Lily (Medicean)
8265a[2]

**Mc Queen (FR)** *Yasmin Almenrader* a83 104
5 gr g Silver Frost(IRE) Misdirect (Darshaan)
3105a[3] 4517a[4] 6495a[8] 8251a[3]

**Mcvicar** *John Davies* a59 66
8 b g Tobougg(IRE) Aries (GER) (Big Shuffle (USA))
525[5] 5008[3] 5403[6] 6233[3] 6898[9] 7219[8]

**Meadow Cross (IRE)**
*Denis Gerard Hogan* a70 47
5 b m Cape Cross(IRE) Hovering (IRE) (In The Wings)
3193[8]

**Meadway** *Bryan Smart* a96 100
6 b g Captain Gerrard(IRE) Tibesti (Machiavellian (USA))
4[2] 388[9] 664[5] 1876[11] 3827[14]

**Meandmyshadow** *Alan Brown* a77 73
9 ch m Tobougg(IRE) Queen Jean (Pivotal)
1971[5] 2124[3] 2550[6] 3216[7] 3666[13] 5379[7] 5836[2] 6435[10] 7017[2] 7525[2] 8552[4] 8742[10] 9033[3] 9347[3]

**Mearing** *Iain Jardine* a68 71
2 b g Aussie Rules(USA) Director's Dream (IRE) (Act One)
3430[2]◆ 4213[6] 8235[5]

**Mears (USA)** *A R Al Rayhi* a62 72
3 b g Street Cry(IRE) Indy Five Hundred (USA) (A.P. Indy (USA))
8711a[8]

**Me Before You (IRE)** *David O'Meara* 61
2 gr f Clodovil(IRE) Pinewoods Lily (IRE) (Indian Ridge (IRE))
4689[3] 5210[3] 6056[8] 7159[9]

**Meccabah (FR)** *Andrew Balding* a79 78
3 gr f Makfi Mintly Fresh (USA) (Rubiano (USA))
2019[2] 2527[3] 3533[2] 5721[5] 7824[4] 8635[4] 8869[2] 9209[8]

**Mecca's Minstrel (IRE)**
*Michael Dods* 42
2 b f Poet's Voice Hairy Rocket (Pivotal)
2836[8]

**Mecca's Spirit (IRE)** *Michael Dods* a41 61
2 gr f Dark Angel(IRE) Wiltshire Life (IRE) (Camacho)
3943[6] 4834[5] 5801[4] 7938[8]

**Medahim (IRE)** *Richard Hannon* a95 104
3 b g Kodiac Novel Fun (IRE) (Noverre (USA))
1841[2] 2126[13] 3071[2] 3997[14] (4904) 5642[3]◆ 6404[4]

**Medalla De Oro**
*Peter Chapple-Hyam* a68 85
3 b g Teofilo(IRE) Nyarhini (Fantastic Light (USA))
2347[8] 3596[5] 3752[3] 4048[7] (5722) (6006) 7024[2] 7267[6] 8005[6] 8561[6]

**Medal Of Honour**
*Joseph Patrick O'Brien* a82 94
2 ch c Lope De Vega(IRE) Rich Gift (Cadeaux Genereux)
6955a[6] 7090[18] 8634[2]

**Medburn Cutler** *Peter Hedger* a62 84
7 ch g Zafeen(FR) Tiegs (IRE) (Desert Prince (IRE))
2562[4] 3004[2] 3618[2] 4073[10] 6096[4] 6508[2] 7402[7] 8072[3] 8565[3]

**Medburn Dream** *Peter Hedger* a44 94
4 b h Showcasing Tiegs (IRE) (Desert Prince (IRE))
2232[3] 2390[6] 2828[5] 3030[4]◆ 3620[2] (4091) 4410[6] 5530[11] 5914[9] 7549[9] 8078[5] 8600[8]

**Media World (IRE)** *Julie Camacho* a49 43
4 ch g Medicean Panoptic (Dubawi (IRE))
3945[5] 5214[10] 6182[10] 7605[5] 8924[13]

**Medicean Ballet (IRE)** *Henry Candy* a77 73
3 b f Medicean Ballet Dancer (IRE) (Refuse To Bend (IRE))
3786[4]◆ 5324[2] 6274[6] 7083[8] 7710[2] 7958[4] 8341[11]

**Medicean El Diablo** *Jimmy Fox* a78 72
4 b g Medicean Al Joudha (FR) (Green Desert (USA))
4810[3] 6620[6] 7058[2] (8132) 8907[6] 9314[13]

**Medicean Man** *Jeremy Gask* a110 110
11 ch g Medicean Kalindi (Efisio)
(318a) 543a[2] 932a[8] 1376a[9] 3926[16]

**Medicean Queen (IRE)**
*Phil McEntee* a68 37
6 b m Medicean Qui Moi (CAN) (Swain (IRE))
39[8] 278[4] 436[5]

**Medici Banchiere** *K R Burke* a78 91
3 ch g Medicean Fairy Shoes (Kyllachy)
1901[7] 3844[11] 4868[3] 7118[6] 7784[4] 8418[7] 8879[9]

**Medici Moon** *Scott Dixon* a70 53
3 ch g Medicean Cockney Fire (Cockney Rebel (IRE))
175[9] 385[3] 848[2] 5761[7] 6760[3] 7792[4] (8255) 8498[2] (8773) 9180[10] 9303[8]

**Medicine Hat** *Marjorie Fife* a79 76
6 b g Multiplex Blushing Heart (Observatory (USA))
28[2] 509[4] 958[9] (1344) 1703[3]

**Medicine Jack** *G M Lyons* 107
3 ch g Equiano(FR) Agony Aunt (Formidable I (USA))
3078[5]

**Medici Oro** *David Brown* a64 60
2 ch g Medicean Anapola (GER) (Polish Precedent (USA))
3237[3] 4503[7] 4995[6] 6525[4] 8190[9] 8658[3] 9175[2] 9439[4]

**Medieval (IRE)** *Paul Cole* 100
3 b g Kodiac Quickstyx (Night Shift (USA))
2402[10] 3997[9] 4856[9] 5530[4] 6870[7] (7404)

**Medieval Bishop (IRE)** *Tony Forbes* a50 58
8 b g Bachelor Duke(USA) On The Backfoot (IRE) (Bob Back (USA))
4158[5] 4980[5] 5850[7] **8246[6]**

**Medina Sidonia (IRE)** *Tim Easterby* 78
5 b g Montjeu(IRE) Valdara (Darshaan)
2594[5] 2889[6] **3464[6] 3663[5]**

**Meerwind (GER)**
*L W J Van Der Meulen*
5 b g Areion(GER) Mouette (GER) (Tertullian (USA))
(1196a)

**Meet And Greet (AUS)**
*Chris Meagher* 87
3 bk g Champions Gallery She's Neat (NZ) (Kinjite (NZ))
**8633a[7]**

**Meetings Man (IRE)** *Ali Stronge* a69 65
10 gr g Footstepsinthesand Missella (IRE) (Danehill (USA))
5274[7] **6796[5]** 7490[13] 8878[8]

**Megalala (IRE)** *John Bridger* a46 52
16 b g Petardia Avionne (Derrylin)
2615[6] 2914[8] **3683[5]** 4087[10] 5405[6] 7006[8] 8301[12]

**Megan Lily (IRE)** *Richard Fahey* a73 92
3 b f Dragon Pulse(IRE) Nebraas (Green Desert (USA))
1975[5] 2570[3] 2806[2] **(3579)** 3835[9] 4333[9] 5574[7] **5916[3]** 6382[7] 7329[5]

**Megera (FR)** *A Wohler* 110
3 b f Motivator Mantissa (Oratorio (IRE))
4393a[8] **5693a[2]** 6710a[8]

**Megnaas (ARG)** *M F De Kock* a34 61
3 b g Asiatic Boy(ARG) Fennana (USA) (Fusaichi Pegasus (USA))
430a[14] **649a[11]**

**Mehdi (IRE)** *Patrick Morris* a81 58
8 b g Holy Roman Emperor(IRE) College Fund Girl (IRE) (Kahyasi (IRE))
267[2] (513) **685[3]** 6637[9]

**Meisho Felicity (FR)** *S Kobayashi* a76 89
3 b f So You Think(NZ) Reform Act (USA) (Lemon Drop Kid (USA))
**2447a[7]**

**Mekhtaal** *H Graham Motion* 116
4 ch h Sea The Stars(IRE) Aiglonne (USA) (Silver Hawk (USA))
1659a[2] **(3118a)** 3962[6] 5977a[10] 7633a[10]

**Mekong** *Sir Michael Stoute* a71 66
2 b c Frankel Ship's Biscuit (Tiger Hill (IRE))
7128[6] **8372[4]**

**Melabi (IRE)** *Richard Ford* a69 73
4 b g Oasis Dream Briolette (IRE) (Sadler's Wells (USA))
169[5] 7274[4]◆ 1707[4] **(2183)** 2678[2] 3537[6] 3740[10] 5686[6] 6270[9] 6723[4] 8909[14]

**Melaniemillie** *Ruth Carr* 60
3 gr f Hellvelyn Real Diamond (Bertolini (USA))
1913[17] 2699[8] 3525[7] 4058[4] 4687[7] 5007[2] 5374[2] (5738) 6571[2]◆ 6785[2] 7390[7] **7888[2]**

**Melanna (IRE)** *Richard Ford* a63 80
6 b m Camacho Colour's Red (IRE) (Red Ransom (USA))
**382[11]** 609[8] 992[9] 3311[9] 5607[4] 7220[5] 7918[10]

**Melburnian (FR)** *H-A Pantall* 65
2 ch f Zambezi Sun Moscow Nights (FR) (Peintre Celebre (USA))
**7415a[5]**

**Melcano** *Shaun Harris* a7 51
3 b f Arcano(IRE) Sablonne (USA) (Silver Hawk (USA))
**8807[10]** 9034[11] 9237[12]

**Melesina (IRE)** *Richard Fahey* a91 102
3 b f Dark Angel(IRE) Lastroseofsummer (IRE) (Haafhd)
652a[9] 889a[4] **(1270a)** 6732a[9] 7669a[12] 8546[8] 8739[3]

**Melgate Melody** *Michael Easterby* a61 55
4 b g Royal Applause Maeander (FR) (Nashwan (USA))
**1983[3]**

**Melinoe (FR)** *F-H Graffard* 27
2 b f Maxios Hecate (IRE) (Act One)
**2321a[7]**

**Melinoe** *Sir Mark Prescott Bt* a71 89
3 b f Sea The Stars(IRE) Persefona (IRE) (Montjeu (IRE))
2311[4] 2921[3] 4571[4]◆ 5108[3] (6038)◆ 6391[2] 7507[2]◆ **8166[3]**

**Meliora (IRE)** *N Clement* 101
5 b m Starspangledbanner(AUS) Messelina (Noverre (USA))
**(6665a)** **7753a[5]**

**Melissa Jane** *Y Barberot* a92 82
3 b f Foxwedge(AUS) Queensgate (Compton Place)
**(838a)** 2484a[14]

**Mellor Brook (IRE)** *Michael Dods* 75
3 b c Born To Sea(IRE) Prima (Primo Dominie)
1829[3] 2429[7] **3714[4]** 6315[9]

**Mellow** *Hughie Morrison* a53 11
3 ch f Bahamian Bounty Tarqua (IRE) (King Charlemagne (USA))
7487[9] **8134[8]** 8994[13]

**Melodic Motion (IRE)**
*Ralph Beckett* a96 107
3 b f Nathaniel(IRE) Quad's Melody (IRE) (Spinning World (USA))
(2302)◆ (3033)◆ (4364)◆ **5569[3]**◆ 7089[2]◆ 8548[2]

**Melodienne (USA)** *C Laffon-Parias* a61
2 ch f Kitten's Joy(USA) Melody Maiden (USA) (Saint Ballado (CAN))
**8691a[7]**

**Melodies** *Ed Dunlop* a70 81
2 ch f Iffraaj Singersongwriter (Raven's Pass (USA))
6862[4] **7357[2]** 7997[5]

**Melodine** *Sir Mark Prescott Bt* a63 63
3 ch f Archipenko(USA) Monda (USA) (Cozzene (USA))
**283[6]** 658[4] 1333[8] **3745[4]** 4462[5]

**Melodino (GER)** *K Demme* 88
2 b c Dabirsim(FR) Melody Fair (IRE) (Montjeu (IRE))
**8621a[3]**

**Melo Magic** *J R Jenkins* a44 9
3 b f Dick Turpin(IRE) Sakhacity (Sakhee (USA))
1111[7] **1293[5]** 1596[12]

**Melonade** *David Barron* a69 75
3 b f Mayson Cambridge Duchess (Singspiel (IRE))
(1349) **(4619)** 7127[10]

**Melrose Girl** *Bryan Smart* 60
3 b f Monsieur Bond(IRE) Keyaki (IRE) (Shinko Forest (IRE))
3150[4] 3984[5] 5006[4] **5543[3]** 6313[6] 7525[4] 7888[8]

**Melting Dew** *Sir Michael Stoute* a84 95
3 b c Cacique(IRE) Winter Sunrise (Pivotal)
(2998)◆ 3528[3] 4535[2] 4886[6] 6232[2] **6920[2]** 8005[10]

**Members Only (FR)** *H-A Pantall*
3 ch f Way Of Light(USA) Mes Bleus Yeux (FR) (Exit To Nowhere (USA))
6084a[17]

**Memorial Day (IRE)**
*Saeed bin Suroor* a67 110
6 b g Cape Cross(IRE) Reunite (IRE) (Kingmambo (USA))
891a[9] **1042a[6]**

**Memories Galore (IRE)** *Roger Fell* a95 91
5 b g Invincible Spirit(IRE) Persian Memories (IRE) (Indian Ridge (IRE))
**234[5]** 1501[11] 3585[13] 4379[18] 5920[5] (6267) 6878[4] 8012[2] 8238[2]◆ 8680[8] 8913[4]

**Menardais (FR)** *N Caullery* a69 74
8 b g Canyon Creek(IRE) Madeleine's Blush (USA) (Rahy (USA))
**7342a[2]**

**Mendacious Harpy (IRE)**
*Mrs A Malzard* a33 40
6 b m Dark Angel(IRE) Idesia (IRE) (Green Desert (USA))
1931a[8] 2670a[7] 5201a[7] **5985a[7]**

**Mendali** *David C Griffiths* 54
2 b g Multiplex Future Regime (IRE) (Xaar)
3149[11] **4996[4]**

**Mendelssohn (USA)** *A P O'Brien* 115
2 b c Scat Daddy(USA) Leslie's Lady (USA) (Tricky Creek (USA))
7146[7] **8037[2]**◆ **(8577a)**

**Menelik (IRE)** *Des Donovan* a85 40
8 b g Oasis Dream Chica Roca (USA) (Woodman (USA))
52[3] 123[6] 494[3] (640)◆ 860[2] (1180) (1429)◆ **3176[2]** 3969[4] 8540[3]

**Menuhin (ITY)** *Stefano Botti* 85
3 b c Mujahid(USA) Victorian Girl (GER) (Lomitas)
**2868a[8]**

**Men United (FR)** *Roy Bowring* a54 50
4 b g Acclamation Moore's Melody (IRE) (Marju (IRE))
215 153[8] 362[8] 4726[7] 5543[11] 6114[7] **6531[2]** 7926[13] 8428[8] 9181[7]◆ 9348[5]

**Meran (FR)** *M Nigge* a61 14
2 bb c Never On Sunday(FR) Baie Des Fleurs (FR) (Chelsea Manor)
2664a[10] **4678a[9]** 6409a[8]

**Mercers** *Paddy Butler* a62 63
3 b f Piccolo Ivory's Joy (Tina's Pet)
679[2] **(819)** 1088[3] 3035[4]◆ 4157[5] 5027[5] 5723[5] 5869[6] 6724[2] 7494[5] 8128[3] 8298[4] 8823[4] 9323[10] 9471[4]

**Mercers Row** *Martin Todhunter* a63 44
10 b g Bahamian Bounty Invincible (Slip Anchor)
2633[16] 3897[14] 4174[8] **4554[6] 5016[5]** 5282[5] 5418[11] 8591[11]

**Merchant Marine (IRE)**
*Ralph Beckett* 69
3 b g Epaulette(AUS) Chantilly Beauty (FR) (Josr Algarhoud (IRE))
2473[7] **3305[3]** 3769[3] 4858[12] 6860[13]

**Merchant Of Medici**
*Micky Hammond* a71 71
10 b g Medicean Regal Rose (Danehill (USA))
3537[5] **4018[5]**

**Mercury** *Adrian Brendan Joyce* a55 58
5 ch g Showcasing Miss Rimex (IRE) (Ezzoud (IRE))
**(9129)**

**Mercury Rising** *Andrew Balding* 40
2 b c Henrythenavigator(USA) Millistar (Galileo (IRE))
**7551[4]**

**Mercy Me** *John Ryan* a77 67
5 b m Mawatheeq(USA) Fantastic Santanyi (Fantastic Light (USA))
120[3] 306[6] **769[2]** 922[5] 1144[4] 1345[2] 1455[3]

**Merdon Castle (IRE)**
*Jane Chapple-Hyam* a88 72
5 b g Acclamation Siren's Gift (Cadeaux Genereux)
**32[4]**◆ 403[6] 581[8] 783[4]◆ 989[8] **(2883)** 3946[4] 4339[6] 4683[11] 5288[7] 5696[9] 6058[5] 6652[7] 7127[3] 7522[16] 8186[5] 9184[8]

**Mere Anarchy (IRE)**
*Robert Stephens* a75
6 b g Yeats(IRE) Maracana (IRE) (Glacial Storm (USA))
1002[6] **(6889)**

**Mer Et Jardin** *M Le Forestier* a52 64
5 b m Lord Shanakill(USA) Mirandola's Dream (FR) (Dalakhani (IRE))
**6018a[5]**

**Merikha** *A Fabre* a71 103
3 ch c Shamardal(USA) Only Green (IRE) (Green Desert (USA))
**2947a[5]**

**Merkava** *Robyn Brisland* a74 67
2 b c Sayif(IRE) Dubawi's Spirit (IRE) (Dubawi (IRE))
5334[3] 5834[5] 6636[2] 7535[2] **(7786)**

**Merlin** *Michael Bell* 99
3 b g Oasis Dream Momentary (Nayef (USA))
1830[2] (2620) (3715) 4100[2] (5100) **6198[3]** 7144[8] 7782[13]

**Merlin Magic** *David Elsworth* 86
2 b c Camelot Seattle Ribbon (USA) (Seattle Dancer (USA))
5350[3] 6132[2] 6869[5] **(7955)** 8415[9]

**Merriment** *Peter Niven* a68 58
4 ch m Makfi Trianon (Nayef (USA))
**28[6]** 315[9]

**Merry Banter** *Paul Midgley* a83 88
3 b f Bated Breath Merry Diva (Bahamian Bounty)
778[3] 1090[2] 1732[4] 2425[5] **2992[2]** 4078[8] 4530[2] 4867[8] 5708[5] 6679[10] 7538[10]

**Mesa Arch (FR)** *Mlle V Dissaux* a41
3 b g Dobby Road(FR) Emotional Rescue (FR) (Diableneyev (USA))
**748a[9]**

**Mesbaar** *Roger Varian* a75 63
3 b g Dalakhani(IRE) Wahylah (IRE) (Shamardal (USA))
3394[5] **6633[2]** 7331[7]

**Meshardal (GER)** *Ruth Carr* a71 83
7 b g Shamardal(USA) Melody Fair (IRE) (Montjeu (IRE))
971[3] 1296[3] 1542[2] 1833[10] 2550[2] (2990) (3401)◆ (3847) 4099[3] 4616[3] **(5018)** 5671[7] 6429[8] 6877[8] 7594[8]

**Meshaykh (IRE)** *Sir Michael Stoute* a68 79
3 b f Lope De Vega(IRE) French Lady (NZ) (Entrepreneur)
2019[5] **(3142)** 4153[4] 5533[6]

**Mesmeric Moment** *Shaun Harris* a57 36
3 b f Showcasing Shared Moment (IRE) (Tagula (IRE))
**313[4] 667[7]** 1204[7] 1821[5] 2309[10] 3141[9]

**Mesmerism (USA)**
*Christos Kouvaras* a83 61
5 b h Dubawi(IRE) Bedazzle (USA) (Dixieland Band (USA))
**6540a[5]**

**Mesophere** *Harry Fry* a65 70
3 ch g Exceed And Excel(AUS) Monturani (IRE) (Indian Ridge (IRE))
175[5] 1499[8] **7083[4]** 8313[10]

**Mesquite** *Ralph Beckett* a61
2 b f High Chaparral(IRE) Puff (IRE) (Camacho)
8373[9] **8634[8]**

**Messi (GER)** *H Graham Motion* 112
7 ch g New Approach(IRE) Messina (GER) (Dashing Blade)
**7178a[3]** 8099a[9]

**Mesti Boleh** *Michael Scudamore* a39 36
6 b g Cape Cross(IRE) Miss Meltemi (IRE) (Miswaki Tern (USA))
**2467[5]** 3575[10]

**Metatrons Cube (IRE)** *Charles Hills* a63 70
2 b g Artie Schiller(USA) Quiet Down (USA) (Quiet American (USA))
4363[4] **5106[4]** 6133[12] 7946[8]

**Met By Moonlight** *Ron Hodges* a70 68
3 b f Sakhee's Secret Starlight Walk (Galileo (IRE))
898[2] 1088[9] 1688[2] 2474[13]◆ 2720[5] 3423[6] 9184[6] **(9471)**

**Meteoric Riser (USA)**
*Richard Hughes* a65 62
3 b c More Than Ready(USA) Silimiss (Dansili)
1299[7] 1619[5] **2395[6]** 3024[10] 3721[9] 4144[8]

**Meteorite (FR)** *S Smrczek* a60 62
3 ch f Medecis Amber Two (Cadeaux Genereux)
**4455a[5]**

**Meteor Light (IRE)** *Ed Vaughan* 91
3 b g Clodovil(IRE) Nordkappe (GER) (High Chaparral (IRE))
(2266) **(3392)** 4376[9]

**Methag (FR)** *Alex Hales* a74 77
4 b m Pour Moi(IRE) Kyria (Grand Lodge (USA))
2336[5] **2781[2]** 3458[7] 4222[10] 8648[6]

**Metisian** *Jedd O'Keeffe* a61 73
3 b g Sleeping Indian Blushing Heart (Observatory (USA))
2924[4] **(4303)**◆ 5070[3] 5459[4] 6313[5] 7245[2]◆ 7933[3]

**Metkaif** *Richard Hannon* a72
2 b g Iffraaj Martagon Lily (Manduro (GER))
7726[6] 8149[6] **8545[4]**

**Me Too Nagasaki (IRE)**
*Jeremy Noseda* a85 94
3 b g Iffraaj Distinguish (IRE) (Refuse To Bend (IRE))
1582[4] (2818) 3262[4] 3504[2] 7505[3] **7892[2]**

**Metronomic (IRE)** *Peter Niven* a62 66
3 b g Roderic O'Connor(IRE) Meon Mix (Kayf Tara)
139[3] 376[3] 463[5] 1597[3] (2017) 2259[5] (2591) 3499[4] **(4172)** 5404[10] 6901[10] 7476[12] **(8653)**

**Metropol (IRE)** *F Vermeulen* a109 76
6 b h Holy Roman Emperor(IRE) Monetary (GER) (Winged Love (IRE))
**1775[6]** 6454a[7]

**Met Spectrum** *Stefano Botti* 98
2 b c Helmet(AUS) Mara Spectrum (IRE) (Spectrum (IRE))
**8276a[5]**

**Mette** *Mark Usher* a42 49
4 b m Virtual Regal Gallery (IRE) (Royal Academy (USA))
2095[12] 2909[10] 7514[12] **8949[7]** 9076[11]

**Mewtow** *George Scott* a76
2 b c Helmet(AUS) White Spirit (IRE) (Invincible Spirit (IRE))
9051[6] **(9319)**

**Meyandi** *Andrew Balding* a56 79
3 ch c Mount Nelson Susi Wong (IRE) (Selkirk (USA))
2468[2] 5320[2] **(6812)** 7085[4]

**Meyrick** *William Haggas* 64
3 b g Helmet(AUS) Esteemed Lady (IRE) (Mark Of Esteem (IRE))
3394[9] **3825[5]**

**Mezmaar** *Mark Usher* a84 68
8 b g Teofilo(IRE) Bay Tree (IRE) (Daylami (IRE))
**1301[8]** 1696[9] 2064[9] 3214[4] 3454[9] 4728[11] 6288[3] 7058[4] 7723[11]

**Mezyan (IRE)** *John Butler* a48 52
3 b f Acclamation Queen Of Carthage (USA) (Cape Cross (IRE))
**456[4]** 522[5]

**Mezzotint (IRE)** *Lee Carter* a86 70
8 b g Diamond Green(FR) Aquatint (Dansili)
2871[2] 349[6] 2762[10] **3140[5]** 3966[10] 4446[11]

**Mia Cara** *David Evans* a69 72
3 b f Camacho Vita Mia (Central Park (IRE))
(245) 417[3] (763) 1242[6] 1306[2] 1411[4] 4536[7] 5007[6] 5357[2] 5826[7] 6340[3] **7111[2]**

**Miami Sunset** *Philip McBride* a47 70
3 b f Archipenko(USA) Laraib (IRE) (Invincible Spirit (IRE))
615[2] **(6295)** 6888[8]

**Mia Tesoro (IRE)** *Charlie Fellowes* a99 82
4 b m Danehill Dancer(IRE) Souter's Sister (IRE) (Desert Style (IRE))
5745[6]◆ 6722[6] 7358[3] 8007[8] 8546[4] 8844[3] **9388[2]**

**Mia Wallace (IRE)** *David O'Meara* a49
3 b f Elzaam(AUS) Perfectly Clear (USA) (Woodman (USA))
**656[3]** 1192[7]

**Mica Mika (IRE)** *Richard Fahey* a88 91
9 ch g Needwood Blade Happy Talk (IRE) (Hamas (IRE))
117[3] **683[3]** 991[11] 3790[13]

**Mi Capricho (IRE)** *Keith Dalgleish* 72
2 b c Elzaam(AUS) Mavemacullen (IRE) (Ad Valorem (USA))
4848[5] 5465[5] **6590[2]** 6890[7]

**Michael's Mount** *Ed Dunlop* a60 89
4 ch g Mount Nelson Dumnoni (Titus Livius (FR))
2085[7] 2574[5] 3618[7] 4336[5] (5140) 6273[2] 6881[3] **(7627)** 8076[3]

**Michele Strogoff** *Tony Coyle* a94 93
4 b g Aqlaam Maschera D'Oro (Mtoto)
2568[5] **2884[2]** 3199[8] 4001[8] (4293) 5457[9] 5683[7] 6515[7] 6949[4] 8811[3] 8956[4] 9179[8]

**Michigan (USA)**
*Mohamed Moubarak* a64 59
3 ch c Galileo(IRE) I'm So Excited (USA) (Street Cry (IRE))
8663[7] **9208[12]** 9430[7]

**Mickey (IRE)** *Tom Dascombe* a83 96
4 b g Zoffany(IRE) Enchantment (Compton Place)
**9210[11]**

**Mickey Rich** *Hughie Morrison* a72 92
3 ch g Sepoy(AUS) Pivotal Drive (IRE) (Pivotal)
(2506) 3077[8] **(4861)**

**Mick The Poser (IRE)**
*Jennie Candlish* a36 54
3 b g Art Connoisseur(IRE) Naked Poser (IRE) (Night Shift (USA))
3191[11] **4611[6]** (6352) 7048[9]

**Micolys (FR)** *J-M Lefebvre* a68 73
3 b f Myboycharlie(IRE) Lady Sadowa (Nayef (USA))
4455a[12] 5523a[11] **(6225a)**

**Midas Maggie** *Charles Hills* a48 61
2 b f Archipenko(USA) Algarade (Green Desert (USA))
6776[6] 7535[5] **8380[9]**

**Middle Creek** *John Gosden* a60
3 b f Poet's Voice Mezzogiorno (Unfuwain (USA))
9018[5] **9301[4]**

**Middle East (IRE)** *J-C Rouget* a74 91
3 b f Frankel Rose Bonheur (Danehill Dancer (IRE))
**6254a[3]**

**Middle Kingdom (USA)**
*John Gosden* a99 96
3 b c War Front(USA) River Belle (Lahib (USA))
(1886) **8705[3]** 8880[4]

**Midge Hall (IRE)** *Bryan Smart* a39 38
3 ch f Helmet(AUS) Allegrissimo (IRE) (Redback)
**150[5]**

**Midhmaar** *Owen Burrows* a78 95
4 b g Iffraaj Merayaat (IRE) (Darshaan)
**1734[4]** 3014[4] 3808[3] 4578[3]

**Midi** *Sir Michael Stoute* 54
2 b c Frankel Midday (Oasis Dream)
**7543[13]**

**Midlander (IRE)** *S Seemar* a67 84
5 b g Shamardal(USA) Mille (Dubai Millennium)
**318a[8]**

**Midlight** *Ruth Carr* a57 61
5 b g Elusive City(USA) My Heart's Deelite (USA) (Afternoon Deelites (USA))
1868[14] 2688[10] **(3196)** 3560[5] 4019[4] 4690[7]

**Midnight Blue** *Sir Mark Prescott Bt* a36
2 gr f Pivotal Arabescatta (Monsun (GER))
4160[10] 4496[9] **4749[10]** 5844[10]

**Midnight Chica (USA)**
*D Selvaratnam*
3 b f Midnight Lute(USA) Anita Chica (USA) (Kitten's Joy (USA))
317a[9] **889a[2]** 1375a[16]

**Midnight Express (FR)**
*G E Mikhalides* a69 63
3 b f Myboycharlie(IRE) High Will (FR) (High Chaparral (IRE))
**6496a[8]**

**Midnight Fair (IRE)** *H-A Pantall* 76
3 ch f Raven's Pass(USA) Nightime (IRE) (Galileo (IRE))
**4654a[8]**

**Midnight Guest (IRE)**
*George Margarson* a58
2 b f Acclamation Midnight Martini (Night Shift (USA))
**8809[3]** 9023[6]

**Midnightly** *Rae Guest* a78 74
3 b f Acclamation Midnight Shift (IRE) (Night Shift (USA))
819[2]◆ (1321) 2235[3] 3035[5] 4324[4] 5041[2] **(6155)** 7994[9]

**Midnight Macchiato (IRE)**
*David Brown* a83 80
4 b g Dark Angel(IRE) Lathaat (Dubai Destination (USA))
2133[7] 2795[3] 3857[5] **8375[2]** 8706[14] 9179[9] 9443[7]

**Midnight Malibu (IRE)** *Tim Easterby* a96 93
4 b m Poet's Voice Midnight Martini (Night Shift (USA))
2407^2◆ 2899^8 3337^2 3904^6 4081^2 4379^16 5098^2 5355^3 (6512) 6927^10 7625^9 7887^4 8238^8 8660^3 (8803) 9187^5

**Midnight Man (FR)** *K R Burke* a60 40
3 ch g Evasive Moon Tree (FR) (Groom Dancer (USA))
1434^3 2902^5 3819^9 6783^8 7236^9

**Midnight Mood**
*Dominic Ffrench Davis* a54 56
4 b m Aqlaam Inflammable (Montjeu (IRE))
4913^7 5336^11 5790^6 7028^10 7215^3 7992^9 8346^5 8507^5

**Midnight Storm (USA)**
*Philip D'Amato* a116 116
6 bb h Pioneerof The Nile(USA) My Tina (USA) (Bertrando (USA))
8608a^12

**Midnight Vixen** *Sir Michael Stoute* a63 72
3 b f Foxwedge(AUS) Midnight Ransom (Red Ransom (USA))
2269^10 3786^7

**Midnight Warrior** *Ron Barr* a45 62
7 b g Teofilo(IRE) Mauri Moon (Green Desert (USA))
2079^7 2549^7 3155^2 4102^5 4558^2 (5186) 5599^3 5951^10 6126^4 7387^8 8214^9

**Midnight Whistler (USA)**
*Martyn Meade* a76 79
5 b g Henrythenavigator(USA) Ball Gown (USA) (Silver Hawk (USA))
(5062) 5363^5

**Midnight Wilde** *John Ryan* a72 88
2 br g Poet's Voice Si Belle (IRE) (Dalakhani (IRE))
4090^3 4919^2◆ (5507) 6425^6 6684^6 7251^2 7616^5

**Midnitemudcrabs (IRE)**
*John James Feane* a75 74
4 ch m Arcano(IRE) Ma Nikitia (IRE) (Camacho)
5519a^5 7161^3

**Midsummer Knight** *K R Burke* a74 75
2 b c Dream Ahead(USA) High Spice (USA) (Songandaprayer (USA))
3083^4 3406^2 6950^2◆ 7114^6 8010^2◆ 8432^2 8916^3 9049^2 9404^2

**Midtech Star (IRE)** *Ian Williams* a92 72
5 b g Kodiac Royal Rival (IRE) (Marju (IRE))
269^6 (519) 759^3 (1153) 1361^3 1628^2 (1763) (2386)

**Midterm** *Sir Michael Stoute* a105 117
4 b g Galileo(IRE) Midday (Oasis Dream)
1957^5 2822^3 4360^6 (6514) 6931^6 7805^4

**Mightaswellsmile** *Ron Barr* a46 68
3 b f Elnadim(USA) Intishaar (IRE) (Dubai Millennium)
2080^5 3152^11 4694^11

**Mightily** *A Fabre* a86 81
3 b c Dubawi(IRE) Mandellicht (IRE) (Be My Guest (USA))
8885a^3

**Mighty Bond** *Tracy Waggott* a41 52
5 b g Misu Bond(IRE) Mighty Flyer (IRE) (Mujtahid (USA))
3710^8 5167^6 5418^10 5543^4 6046^2 6437^17 7247^3 7660^9 8217^4 8479^7 8656^8 8784^13

**Mighty Lady** *Robyn Brisland* a76 67
4 ch m Mighty Spia (USA) (Diesis)
2906^8 4501^6 5140^5 6323^12 6948^3 7541^5 7762^5 8341^10

**Mighty Like (AUS)** *Mick Price* 96
7 ch g Host(CHI) Mighty Fine (AUS) (Keltrice (AUS))
8057a^10

**Mighty Mac (IRE)** *Ralph Beckett* 55
2 b g Dragon Pulse(IRE) Invincible Fire (IRE) (Invincible Spirit (IRE))
7126^8

**Mighty Missile (IRE)** *Brian Barr* a52 28
6 ch g Majestic Missile(IRE) Magdalene (FR) (College Chapel)
741^7 5716^12

**Mighty Zip (USA)** *Lisa Williamson* a66 68
5 ch g City Zip(USA) Incredulous (FR) (Indian Ridge (IRE))
302^8 602^9 742^8 (874) 982^2 1180^3 1220^DSQ (1490) 1759^4◆ 2263^5 (2621) 2858^3 (2995) 3812^3 4337^9 4531^10 9136^8

**Mignolino (IRE)** *R Roels* a56 68
5 b g Kodiac Caterina Di Cesi (Cape Town (IRE))
4955a^12

**Migwar (IRE)** *A De Mieulle* 115
5 b h Sea The Stars(IRE) Katyusha (USA) (Kingmambo (USA))
934a^5

**Migyaas (USA)** *Saeed bin Suroor* a20 16
3 b g Lonhro(AUS) Nasmatt (Danehill (USA))
1675^3 2164^3 3909^9 4632^7

**Mikey Ready (USA)** *Ed Walker* a67
3 b g Frankel Reaching (IRE) (Dansili)
354^4 718^6

**Mikmak** *William Muir* a89 92
4 b g Makfi Rakata (USA) (Quiet American (USA))
2310^6 2893^2 3235^5 4763^7 5330^5 5781^2 6189^8 6701^8 7358^12 7957^2 8297^9

**Milan Reef (IRE)** *David Loughnane* 62
2 br f Famous Name Jagapaw (IRE) (Manduro (GER))
3179^9 3712^9 5056^10 5752^2 6613^8 (7082) 7519^9 8287^2 8676^5

**Milburn Jack** *Clive Cox* a73 69
3 br g Foxwedge(AUS) Tintac (Intikhab (USA))
1619^4 2090^5 3784^10 4537^5 5031^9 5797^8

**Milchik** *Michael Attwater* a48 52
2 b f Lethal Force(IRE) Millsini (Rossini (USA))
2015^6 3029^9

**Mildenberger** *Mark Johnston* 106
2 b c Teofilo(IRE) Belle Josephine (Dubawi (IRE))
(4577)◆ (5105)◆ 5501^3 (6396) 7616^3

**Miles To Memphis (IRE)**
*Mrs Denise Foster* 87
8 b g Old Vic Phillis Hill (Karinga Bay)
5488a^5 7860a^4

**Military Hill (IRE)**
*Adrian McGuinness* a67 75
4 b g Majestic Missile(IRE) Grateful Thanks (FR) (Bering)
5518a^6 6802a^4

**Military Law** *John Gosden* 82
2 b c Dubawi(IRE) Marine Bleue (IRE) (Desert Prince (IRE))
7117^9 (8387)

**Military Madame (IRE)** *John Quinn* a56 27
2 b f Epaulette(AUS) Sweet Kristeen (USA) (Candy Stripes (USA))
7033^8 8236^11 8553^8

**Military Parade** *Saeed bin Suroor* a78
3 b g Dutch Art Bahia Emerald (IRE) (Bahamian Bounty)
5746^2◆ 6633^3 7935^7

**Militia** *Richard Fahey* a73 73
2 b c Equiano(FR) Sweet As Honey (Duke Of Marmalade (IRE))
6969^3 7326^4 8010^3 8657^3

**Milky Way (IRE)** *Gary Moore* a79 76
5 b g Galileo(IRE) Beauty Bright (IRE) (Danehill (USA))
3616^7 4804^2 6763^4

**Millady Percy** *Roy Brotherton* a36 27
4 b m Sir Percy Steady Rain (Zafonic (USA))
840^5

**Mille Et Mille** *C Lerner* a83 112
7 b g Muhtathir Quezon Sun (GER) (Monsun (GER))
(2559a) 4879a^7 6499a^7 7639a^2 8274a^8

**Mille Pieds (FR)** *J-C Rouget* 91
3 b c Zoffany(IRE) Providanza (FR) (Okawango (USA))
1337a^2

**Miller And Cook (IRE)**
*Mark Michael McNiff* 38
6 b g Oratorio(IRE) Canaan (IRE) (Alhaarth (IRE))
6352^6

**Mille Tank** *William Muir* a56 44
2 b f Mastercraftsman(IRE) Millevini (IRE) (Hawk Wing (USA))
8419^13 8997^7

**Millie May** *Jimmy Fox* 31
3 b f Sixties Icon Maydream (Sea Freedom)
3691^11 4409^8 5712^12

**Millie's Kiss** *Philip McBride* a76 72
3 b f Aussie Rules(USA) Aliena (IRE) (Grand Lodge (USA))
(997) 1343^4 2517^9 3700^6 4544^3 4761^3◆ 5334^DSQ 5718^4 6722^5 7279^3 7541^3 7830^6 8400^3 8813^8

**Millowitsch (GER)** *Markus Klug* 108
4 bb h Sehrezad(IRE) Muriel (IRE) (Fath (USA))
1661a^4 3105a^2 (4517a) 4939a^3 6495a^3 6987a^2 (7672a)

**Millybond** *David Brown* a5 26
3 b f Misu Bond(IRE) Noble Attitude (Best Of The Bests (IRE))
1107^10

**Milly May (FR)** *L Rovisse* 47
3 b f Youmzain(IRE) Clochette De Sou (FR) (Ajdayt (USA))
6566a^10

**Milord (GER)** *Kim Bailey* 76
8 br g Monsun(GER) Montserrat (GER) (Zilzal (USA))
3618^8

**Milrow (IRE)** *Dr Richard Newland* a77 69
4 b g Tamayuz Cannikin (IRE) (Lahib (USA))
2965^8

**Milton Road** *Mick Channon* a80 75
2 b c Mazameer(IRE) Blakeshall Girl (Piccolo)
1681^6 2052^2 2292^2 2556^3 2882^6 3245^6 (3619) 3791^5 (4620) (5121) 5546^6 (6021) 6330^8 6684^4 6951^3◆ 7536^5 8431^5

**Mime Dance** *John Butler* a70 78
6 b g Notnowcato Encore My Love (Royal Applause)
441^4 513^4 745^6 986^7 1285^9 1603^11 3971^11

**Mimic's Memory** *Ann Duffield* a67 60
3 b f Sayif(IRE) Blue Crest (FR) (Verglas (IRE))
72^4 442^3 1193^7 1835^5 2182^4 (2470) 2790^2 8107^10 8480^6 8656^12 8854^5◆ 9034^3 9243^5

**Mimram** *Dean Ivory* a47
2 b f Kheleyf(USA) Tobaranama (IRE) (Sadler's Wells (USA))
2459^4 3135^8 4496^7 7510^9

**Minding (IRE)** *A P O'Brien* 123
4 b m Galileo(IRE) Lillie Langtry (IRE) (Danehill Dancer (IRE))
(2240a)

**Mind Juggler (ITY)** *Simone Brogi* a62
3 b c Red Rocks(IRE) Gioconda (IRE) (Fasliyev (USA))
748a^5

**Mind Of Madness (IRE)**
*Ibrahim Al Malki* 50
5 gr h Azamour(IRE) Sioduil (IRE) (Oasis Dream)
914a^16

**Mind Your Biscuits (USA)**
*Chad Summers* a125
4 ch h Posse(USA) Jazzmane (USA) (Toccet (USA))
(1377a) 8607a^3

**Ming Dynasty (FR)** *Marco Botti* a97 94
5 b g King's Best(USA) Memoire (FR) (Sadler's Wells (USA))
6984a^5 9390^5

**Ming Jung (FR)** *Markus Klug* 98
3 b c Kallisto(GER) Muriel (IRE) (Fath (USA))
2002a^6 3115a^4 4422a^10 6255a^2

**Miniature Daffodil (IRE)**
*Christian Williams* 44
2 b g Thewayyouare(USA) Queen Of Stars (USA) (Green Desert (USA))
7079^11 8388^12

**Minimiss (FR)** *Mme S Adet* 48
3 bl f Spirit One(FR) Mama Mia (FR) (Linamix (FR))
4943a^6

**Mini Moruga** *Gary Moore* a12
3 b f Cockney Rebel(IRE) Artzola (IRE) (Alzao (USA))
6283^9 7514^13

**Mininggold** *Michael Dods* a48 82
4 b m Piccolo Rosein (Komaite (USA))
1828^10 2407^3 2858^7 3384^3 (4433) 5696^5 6574^3 (6669) 6923^3 7268^7 7738^3 8512^6

**Miningrocks (FR)** *Conor Dore* a52 78
5 b g Lawman(FR) Fashion School (Shamardal (USA))
1498^12 2953^4 (3221) (3559) (4279) 4575^3 5455^3 5667^7 6431^4 7225^5 7735^7 (7820) 8143^9 8477^2 8806^11 9029^8 9176^10

**Minminwin (IRE)** *Gay Kelleway* a59 71
4 ch m Art Connoisseur(IRE) Anne-Lise (Inchinor)
232^4 391a^14 713a^10 930a^9

**Minotaur (IRE)** *Jonjo O'Neill* a90 105
5 b g Azamour(IRE) Mycenae (Inchinor)
7931^4◆ 8292^4 8740^19

**Mint Julep (FR)** *J E Hammond* a90 105
4 gr m Mastercraftsman(IRE) Minted (USA) (Mineshaft (USA))
3883a^4 4679a^7 7753a^4 8444a^3

**Minty Jones** *Michael Mullineaux* a43 51
8 b g Primo Valentino(IRE) Reveur (Rossini (USA))
51^12 216^7 2076^8 2994^6 3201^7 3704^2 4479^2 5052^5 5360^5 7926^5

**Mio Ragazzo** *Marco Botti* a65 60
3 b g Mayson Mia Diletta (Selkirk (USA))
2791^5 3493^4 4562^9 8503^3 9153^7 9406^13

**Mi Raccomando** *Stefano Botti* 102
3 br f Poet's Voice Maschera D'Oro (Mtoto)
(2244a) 3121a^8

**Miracle Des Aigles (FR)**
*Mme C Barande-Barbe* a90 103
4 b g Siyouni(FR) Folie Des Aigles (FR) (Ocean Of Wisdom (USA))
7416a^2 7943a^3 9274a^12

**Miracle Garden** *Ian Williams* a82 66
5 ch g Exceed And Excel(AUS) Sharp Terms (Kris)
312^9 886^8 955^3 1370^10 2932^8 3811^4 4201^6 5481^3 6637^5 6795^3 (7408) 7789^3 8706^2 8797^5 9083^3

**Miracle Ninetynine (IRE)**
*Joeri Goossens* a74 50
5 b g Big Bad Bob(IRE) Scrumptious (Sakhee (USA))
66^3◆ 277^9 6018a^8

**Miracle Of Medinah** *Mark Usher* a92 93
6 ch g Milk It Mick Smart Ass (IRE) (Shinko Forest (IRE))
1974^4 2606^14 4854^7 (6540a) 8547^11

**Mirage Dancer** *Sir Michael Stoute* 113
3 b c Frankel Heat Haze (Green Desert (USA))
2569^4 3994^3 6327^3 7054^4

**Miramonte Dancer (IRE)**
*David C Griffiths* a4 62
4 b m Fast Company(IRE) Bonne (Namid)
139^12

**Mirdif** *M D O'Callaghan* 100
3 b g Kodiac Irina Princess (Selkirk (USA))
649a^10

**Mirek (IRE)** *Patrick Chamings* a50 36
2 gr g Zebedee My Trust (IRE) (Exceed And Excel (AUS))
1934^7 2277^6 2910^9 3918^6 7410^5 7914^11 8793^12

**Miriam Violet** *Paul Henderson* a36 20
3 b f Dick Turpin(IRE) Velvet Band (Verglas (IRE))
4914^8

**Mirimar (IRE)** *Ed Vaughan* a53 74
3 br g Kalanisi(IRE) Peratus (IRE) (Mujadil (USA))
310^4 3755^13 (5653) 6812^2 7558^2 7895^4

**Mirror Magic** *Geoffrey Deacon* 43
2 br f Nathaniel(IRE) Mirror Effect (IRE) (Shamardal (USA))
5292^6 6100^8 7913^6

**Mirror Mirror (IRE)**
*Peter Chapple-Hyam* 55
2 ch f Intello(GER) Nouvelle Lune (Fantastic Light (USA))
8006^10 8419^8

**Mirsaale** *Keith Dalgleish* a54 95
7 ch g Sir Percy String Quartet (IRE) (Sadler's Wells (USA))
8038^19 8740^18

**Mirza** *Rae Guest* a65 111
10 b g Oasis Dream Millyant (Primo Dominie)
3829^5 4635^2 5911^9 6668^5 7396^5 7804^4 8139^5

**Mirzam (IRE)** *Mick Channon* a64 78
3 gr f Mastercraftsman(IRE) Luxie (IRE) (Acclamation)
1944^8 2307^4 (2711)◆ 3087^2 3759^3 4307^6

**Mischief Managed (IRE)**
*Tim Easterby* 66
3 ch g Tagula(IRE) Cape Clear (Slip Anchor)
4341^4 5670^4 5946^4 6546^6 7390^4◆ 7979^9

**Mischievous Rock** *Michael Appleby* a66
2 b f Society Rock(IRE) Twilight Pearl (Pastoral Pursuits)
8802^6 9023^4 9310^7

**Mise En Rose (USA)**
*Charlie Appleby* a98 108
4 bb m War Front(USA) Buy The Barrel (USA) (E Dubai (USA))
617^3

**Mishaal (IRE)** *Michael Herrington* a76 79
7 ch g Kheleyf(USA) My Dubai (IRE) (Dubai Millennium)
957^12 1799^7 2592^7 2840^18 4013^2 4719^2 5132^7 5457^10 6238^4 6464^4 6888^2 7056^2 7572^4 7882^4 8433^12

**Mishari** *David Lanigan* a62 62
3 b c Oasis Dream Nessina (USA) (Hennessy (USA))
4269^5 4964^3 7414^4

**Mishko (IRE)** *Steve Gollings* a71 61
6 b g Amadeus Wolf Miss Shangri La (Rainbow Quest (USA))
(2460) 3311^6 3494^3 5244^P

**Miskin** *Robert Stephens* a44 61
8 b g Motivator Castellina (USA) (Danzig Connection (USA))
3575^3 4469^2 4853^8 5716^2 7233^5

**Miss Anticipation (IRE)**
*Roger Charlton* a58 71
3 b f Bated Breath Dusting (IRE) (Acclamation)
3296^12 4843^2 5797^10 7414^6

**Miss Ballygally (IRE)**
*Mark Michael McNiff* 67
7 b m Ramonti(FR) Miss Gally (IRE) (Galileo (IRE))
5518a^13

**Miss Bar Beach (IRE)**
*Keith Dalgleish* a88 97
2 b f Choisir(AUS) Whitegate Way (Greensmith)
2105^2 (3447) 4028^9 5057^5 (5833) 6418^3 7088^8 8424^4

**Miss Bates** *Ann Duffield* a55 65
3 b f Holy Roman Emperor(IRE) Jane Austen (IRE) (Galileo (IRE))
2036^4 2702^8 7476^14 8031^10 9012^3

**Miss Blondell** *Marcus Tregoning* a71 66
4 ch m Compton Place Where's Broughton (Cadeaux Genereux)
8156^6 8549^2

**Misscarlett (IRE)** *Sally Haynes* 73
3 b f Red Rocks(IRE) Coimbra (USA) (Trempolino (USA))
6044^3◆ (7331)◆ 8289^12

**Miss Condi** *Martin Keighley* a10 42
2 b f Most Improved(IRE) Mildenhall (Compton Place)
5246^8 6806^9 7079^10 8644^11 8887^11

**Miss Danby (IRE)** *Mark Johnston* a67 65
3 gr f Mastercraftsman(IRE) Dunbrody (FR) (Jeune Homme (USA))
2035^6 6060^7 6518^9 7895^10 8814^11

**Miss Dd (IRE)** *Tom Dascombe* a59 70
2 b f Dandy Man(IRE) Dynaperformer (IRE) (Dynaformer (USA))
3179^2 (3662) 4361^8 5057^7 5891^5

**Miss Dusky Diva (IRE)**
*David W Drinkwater* a62 55
5 gr m Verglas(IRE) Dispol Veleta (Makbul)
(35) (241) 721^7 8955^11 9158^8 9421^U

**Miss Fay (IRE)** *Michael Bell* a59 68
3 br f Sayif(IRE) Lough Mewin (IRE) (Woodman (USA))
4003^5 5367^5

**Miss Fuisse (FR)** *P Monfort* a59 55
4 b m Fuisse(FR) Pragmatica (Inchinor)
6365a^12

**Miss Germany (GER)** *P Schiergen* 78
3 ch f Lord Of England(GER) Mahamuni (IRE) (Sadler's Wells (USA))
8666a^8

**Miss Geronimo**
*Ken Cunningham-Brown* a37 32
5 b m Hellvelyn Churn Dat Butter (USA) (Unbridled (USA))
6106^9

**Miss Goldsmith (IRE)**
*Rebecca Menzies* a65 69
4 gr m Mastercraftsman(IRE) Golden Legacy (IRE) (Rossini (USA))
44^5 419^13 860^4 1066^8 1842^2 2464^3 3048^5 3833^9 4105^2 4474^6 (5466) (6047) 7111^5

**Missguided (IRE)** *Alex Hales* a61 63
4 b m Rip Van Winkle(IRE) Foolish Ambition (GER) (Danehill Dancer (IRE))
7028^8 7712^10 8641^10 8957^11

**Miss Icon** *Patrick Chamings* a69 72
3 b f Sixties Icon Pretty Miss (Averti (IRE))
2293^3 3000^9 3869^6 4198^3 5711^5 6753^2 7723^9 8818^9

**Miss Infinity (IRE)** *Mark Johnston* 103
3 b f Rock Of Gibraltar(IRE) Muravka (IRE) (High Chaparral (IRE))
1881^7 2436^4 2738^5 3964^22 4208^9 4903^8 6426^4

**Miss Inga Sock (IRE)**
*Eve Johnson Houghton* a60 71
5 ch m Tagula(IRE) Support Fund (IRE) (Intikhab (USA))
(2257) (2710) 3425^3 (3519) 4185^3 5299^6 (5555) 7151^4

**Mission Impassible (IRE)**
*J-C Rouget* 111
2 ch f Galileo(IRE) Margot Did (IRE) (Exceed And Excel (AUS))
5448a^4 7666a^3

**Miss Island Ruler** *Shaun Harris* a31 40
3 b f Elzaam(AUS) Kodiac Island (Kodiac)
4174^10 4540^5 5076^6

**Mississippi Miss** *Dr Jon Scargill* a68 55
3 ch f Equiano(FR) Junket (Medicean)
4313^8 6026^8 7058^13 7771^6

**Miss Julia Star (FR)** *B De Montzey* a88 102
3 rg f Never On Sunday(FR) My Juju (FR) (Blackdoun (FR))
(6963a)

**Miss Katie Mae (IRE)**
*H Graham Motion* 99
4 b m Dark Angel(IRE) Kate The Great (Xaar)
1813a^5

**Miss Laila (IRE)** *Tom Clover* a70 72
3 b f Dark Angel(IRE) Sister Red (IRE) (Diamond Green (FR))
2094^4 2754^5

**Miss Liguria** *Ed Walker* a72 74
3 b f Galileo(IRE) Miss Cap Ferrat (Darshaan)
1944^11 2834^5 4497^3◆ 5401^3 6578^8 9208^2 9408^7

**Miss M (IRE)** *William Muir* a61 53
3 b f Mastercraftsman(IRE) Tintern (Diktat)
624^6 1151^3 1333^6 1790^8 5591^8 6766^6 (7990) 9027^8

**Miss Macchiato (IRE)**
*Keith Dalgleish* a53 36
4 b m Holy Roman Emperor(IRE) Cafe Lassere (USA) (Giant's Causeway (USA))
70^2◆ 414^5 839^5

**Miss Mayson** *Karen Tutty* a59 48
3 b f Mayson High Class Girl (Royal Applause)
4559[12] **7926**[7] 8484[9] 8776[14]

**Miss Mazzie** *Michael Easterby* a47 47
2 b f Mazameer(IRE) Fizzy Lady (Efisio)
3460[8] 3791[15] 4740[6] **5277**[4] 6022[9] **7827**[5] 8213[8]

**Miss Melbourne (FR)**
*A De Watrigant* 104
3 b f Kentucky Dynamite(USA) Miss Alabama (FR) (Anabaa (USA))
**3353a**[3]

**Miss Milla B** *Ed Vaughan* a60
2 b f Sepoy(AUS) Dreamily (IRE) (New Approach (IRE))
**9239**[4]

**Miss Milliner** *Jo Hughes* 33
2 ch f Helmet(AUS) Elegant Pursuit (Pastoral Pursuits)
4196a[8] **5585a**[11]

**Miss Minding (IRE)** *Ed Dunlop* 56
2 b f Kodiac Lady Hawkfield (IRE) (Hawk Wing (USA))
**6480**[10] 7334[13] 7620[11]

**Miss Minuty** *Jeremy Scott* a77 64
5 gr m Verglas(IRE) Miss Provence (Hernando (FR))
4915[7] 6307[7] 6948[8] **(9212)**

**Miss Mirabeau** *Sir Mark Prescott Bt* a70 63
3 b f Oasis Dream Miss Corniche (Hernando (FR))
819[4]◆ 1024[3] 1488[6] 4463[3] 6681[5] 7541[10] 8376[3] 8538[5] 8814[5] 8957[2] **(9027)**

**Miss Mo Brown Bear (IRE)**
*Richard Hannon* a70 70
2 b f Kodiac Currentis (IRE) (Dylan Thomas (IRE))
**2958**[4] **3421**[5] **4212**[3] **5057**[3] 5322[4] 5537[2] 6057[7] 7123[7] 8981[7]

**Miss Mollie** *James Given* a33
2 b f Havana Gold(IRE) Erebis (Green Desert (USA))
**9415**[6]

**Miss Monro (IRE)** *Brian Ellison* a41 57
3 br f Intense Focus(USA) Runway Girl (IRE) (Dansili)
**2790**[8] 3142[11] **3813**[5]

**Miss Mumtaz (IRE)** *Tony Carroll* a69 64
2 ch f Lope De Vega(IRE) Ispanka (Invincible Spirit (IRE))
6159[2] 6403[10] **7411**[2]

**Miss Nouriya** *Marco Botti* 61
3 b f Galileo(IRE) Nouriya (Danehill Dancer (IRE))
**5124**[8]

**Miss Osier** *Rae Guest* a53 67
3 ch f Mastercraftsman(IRE) Lacy Sunday (USA) (King's Best (USA))
310[3] 2625[4] 3175[5] **(4625)** 5268a[8] 6102[5] 6656[3] 7539[9] 8125[4]

**Miss Pacific** *William Jarvis* a73 74
3 ch f Bated Breath Ocean View (USA) (Gone West (USA))
3234[7] 4097[5] 4764[5] **5367**[2] 5856[3] 7131[10] 8156[3] 8549[9]

**Miss Paris** *Charles Hills* 41
2 b f Champs Elysees Bantu (Cape Cross (IRE))
5573[6] **7153**[9]

**Miss Patience** *Peter Chapple-Hyam* a56 63
3 b f Excelebration(IRE) Connote (Oasis Dream)
1626[4] **3595**[3] **4619**[7] 5635[10]

**Miss Pepper (IRE)** *Paul Midgley* 41
3 b f Acclamation Somerset Falls (UAE) (Red Ransom (USA))
1715[9] 2181[13] 2897[9]◆ 3624[7] **4246**[3] 4997[12]

**Miss Perception** *Tom Dascombe* a46 58
2 b f Vision D'Etat(FR) Monster Munchie (JPN) (Deep Impact (JPN))
4116[8] 5056[11] **6875**[6] 7827[6]

**Miss Puddles (IRE)** *Richard Fahey* 84
2 b f Canford Cliffs(IRE) Puddles (FR) (Holy Roman Emperor (IRE))
4689[4] **(5398)**

**Miss Quick** *Ann Duffield* a40
3 b f Equiano(FR) Quixada (GER) (Konigstiger (GER))
2495[5]

**Miss Quoted** *Seamus Mullins*
5 b m Proclamation(IRE) Ambience Lady (Batshoof)
7227[8]

**Miss Ranger (IRE)** *Brian Ellison* a68 76
5 gr m Bushranger(IRE) Remiss (IRE) (Indian Ridge (IRE))
1879[7] 2587[6] 3292[2] **(3580)**

**Miss Recycled** *Michael Madgwick* 41
2 b f Royal Applause Steel Free (IRE) (Danehill Dancer (IRE))
6584[9] **7153**[10] 8179[5]

**Miss Rosina (IRE)**
*George Margarson* a64 62
3 ch f Choisir(AUS) Vera Lilley (IRE) (Verglas (IRE))
1688[8] **3260**[4] 4157[9] **4324**[2] 5041[4] 5871[9] 6298[2] 7494[6] 8146[4] 8428[5]

**Miss Sheridan (IRE)**
*Michael Easterby* a50 79
3 br f Lilbourne Lad(IRE) Sues Surprise (IRE) (Montjeu (IRE))
(1678) (2036)◆ 3094[6] (3900) **4525**[2] 5317[6] 6026[12] 7942[9] 8486[13]

**Miss Sienna** *H-F Devin* 89
2 b f Equiano(FR) Candycakes (IRE) (Cape Cross (IRE))
6251a[5] 7637a[9] **8170a**[6]

**Miss Steff (IRE)** *B Lefevre* a70 69
4 b m Dark Angel(IRE) Stefanella (IRE) (Alzao (USA))
**798a**[7]

**Miss Temple City (USA)**
*H Graham Motion* 112
5 bb m Temple City(USA) Glittering Tax (USA) (Artax (USA))
3924[13] **7851a**[6]

**Miss Tenacity** *Jane Chapple-Hyam*
4 b m Rail Link Desert Secrets (IRE) (Almutawakel)
9235[7]

**Miss Tiger Lily** *Harry Dunlop* a77 73
7 b m Tiger Hill(IRE) Waitingonacloud (In The Wings)
141[2] 280[3] 571[2] 1364[4] **1697**[2] 2388[12]

**Miss Tree** *John Quinn* a58 60
6 b m Literato(FR) Tunguska (Silver Patriarch (IRE))
70[5] 174[5] (3155) **4469**[3] 5021[4] 5700[7]

**Miss Uppity** *Ivan Furtado* a46 49
4 ch m Notnowcato Instructress (Diktat)
445[10] **6748**[2] 7020[9] 7763[5] 8543[3] 9267[11]

**Miss Van Gogh** *Richard Fahey* a68 94
5 b m Dutch Art Accede (Acclamation)
**2155**[5] 2855[6] 3433[6] 4248[7]

**Miss Van Winkle** *Mark Johnston* a2 52
2 b f Rip Van Winkle(IRE) Lasso (Indian Ridge (IRE))
**3179**[8] 3662[7] 8914[8] 9238[7]

**Miss Wolverine** *Michael Easterby* 58
2 b f Amadeus Wolf Mille Etoiles (USA) (Malibu Moon (USA))
**6085**[4] 7563[6] 7818[10]

**Missy Mischief (USA)**
*Jeremy Noseda* 88
2 b f Into Mischief(USA) Ring True (USA) (Is It True (USA))
3070[5] **3960**[9]

**Missy Wells** *Marjorie Fife*
7 b m Misu Bond(IRE) Aqua (Mister Baileys)
8241[12]

**Mister Anthony** *C Impelluso* 58
3 b c Sakhee's Secret Green And Bleue (Green Tune (USA))
**2245a**[9]

**Mister Art (IRE)** *Matthieu Palussiere* a83 72
3 b c Art Connoisseur(IRE) Miss Chaumiere (Selkirk (USA))
**7308a**[6]

**Mister Belvedere** *Michael Dods* a60 90
3 b g Archipenko(USA) Diablerette (Green Desert (USA))
2385[6] 3583[5] 4429[4] 4891[3] **5630**[2] 6920[12] 7328[7]

**Mister Blue Sky (IRE)**
*Sylvester Kirk* 88
3 gr g Royal Applause Mujdeya (Linamix (FR))
2126[7] (2625) 3318[6] (4408) 4886[7] 5915[7] **(6657)** 7277[3]

**Mister Bob (GER)** *James Bethell* a82 60
8 ch g Black Sam Bellamy(IRE) Mosquera (GER) (Acatenango (GER))
196[5] 1002[4] 1291[3] 5951[4] **(6618)** 7412[8]

**Mister Chow** *Gary Moore* a73 64
3 ch g Nathaniel(IRE) Skimmia (Mark Of Esteem (IRE))
1287[7] 1862[8] 2581[8] 2778[10] 4748[4]◆ 5565[3]◆ 8312[8] 8674[2] **(9026)**

**Mister Five Euros (FR)** *F Chappet* 93
2 bb c Diamond Green(FR) Vilavella (FR) (Shamardal (USA))
5090a[7] **6051a**[7]

**Mister Fizz** *Miss Imogen Pickard* a59 59
9 b g Sulamani(IRE) Court Champagne (Batshoof)
196[8] **603**[5] **8426**[7] 9054[9]

**Mister Flip Flop (IRE)** *Adam West* a25
4 b g Danehill Dancer(IRE) Heavenly Bay (USA) (Rahy (USA))
**1358**[8] 1695[6]

**Mister Freeze (IRE)**
*Patrick Chamings* a76 63
3 ch g Frozen Power(IRE) Beacon Of Hope (IRE) (Barathea (IRE))
244[4] **(418)**◆ 8184[6] 8646[10] 8990[11] 9184[2] 9469[7]

**Mister Impatience** *Michael Moroney* 95
7 b g Hernando(FR) Katy Nowaitee (Komaite (USA))
**1994a**[8]

**Mister Jo (IRE)** *J-C Rouget* 96
2 b c High Chaparral(IRE) Zanzibar Girl (USA) (Johannesburg (USA))
**5776a**[10]

**Mister Maestro** *Richard Hannon* a61 64
2 b g Showcasing Basque Beauty (Nayef (USA))
4826[8] **7079**[5] 8382[6] 8658[4]

**Mister Manduro (FR)**
*Mark Johnston* a82 96
3 ch g Manduro(GER) Semenova (FR) (Green Tune (USA))
1764[2] 2437[9] 3335[4] **4032**[7] 4612[10] **5351**[2] 5682[8] 6779[6] 7402[15] 7785[10]

**Mister Marcasite** *Antony Brittain* a40 56
7 gr g Verglas(IRE) No Rehearsal (FR) (Baillamont (USA))
**1402**[4]

**Mister Moosah (IRE)**
*Micky Hammond* 73
3 gr g Clodovil(IRE) Hendrina (IRE) (Daylami (IRE))
**2035**[4] 2186[6] 5617[9] 6518[7] 6892[8]

**Mister Music** *Tony Carroll* a84 87
8 b g Singspiel(IRE) Sierra (Dr Fong (USA))
548[4] 736[3] 1512[20] **1606**[3] 3144[7] 3620[4] 4215[4] 4746[5] 5300[5] 6378[4] 6882[8]

**Mister Musicmaster** *Ron Hodges* a64 76
8 b g Amadeus Wolf Misty Eyed (IRE) (Paris House)
1365[8] 1553[5] 2023[3] 2178[7] (2511) (3282) 3808[7] 4698[7] 5276[7] 5788[10] **(6310)** 6809[6]

**Mister Picnic (FR)** *D Guillemin* 97
2 b c Penny's Picnic(IRE) Mysterious Lina (FR) (Linamix (FR))
3611a[3] **5461a**[3] 6728a[6]

**Mister Raffles** *Mohamed Moubarak* a20
3 b g Cockney Rebel(IRE) Shrewd Decision (Motivator)
**221**[9] 807[12] 1069[7]

**Mister Saxman** *G M Lyons* 51
3 b g Piccolo Jane's Payoff (IRE) (Danetime (IRE))
1389a[20]

**Mister Showman** *Keith Dalgleish* a69 64
4 b g Showcasing Theatre Royal (Royal Applause)
(8261) 8806[5] **9346**[2]

**Mister Smart (FR)** *N Caullery* a77 75
7 b g Smadoun(FR) Miss Canon (FR) (Cadoudal (FR))
**7070a**[11]

**Mister Sunshine (IRE)** *Clive Cox* a32 79
3 ch g Fast Company(IRE) Second Omen (Rainbow Quest (USA))
**625**[7]

**Mister Trader** *D J Bunyan* 99
3 br c Hellvelyn Rehlaat (USA) (Swain (IRE))
**2863a**[7] 7804[8]

**Mistime (IRE)** *Mark Johnston* a74 73
3 b f Acclamation Out Of Time (IRE) (Anabaa (USA))
**5856**[4] 6382[8] 6759[4] 7771[12]

**Mistiness (IRE)** *Keith Henry Clarke* 67
6 b g Astronomer Royal(USA) Misty Daylight (USA) (Seeking Daylight (USA))
**(3449)** 5648[6]

**Mistiroc** *John Quinn* a103 104
6 br g Rocamadour Mistinguett (IRE) (Doyoun)
779[6] 1068[4]◆ 1779[2] 2552[3] 4033[9] **4918**[3]

**Mistress Of Venice** *James Given* 99
2 b f Bated Breath Rohlindi (Red Ransom (USA))
1872[5]◆ 2801[3]◆ 4028[4] **4855**[4] 5391[7] 6432[2]

**Mistress Quickly (IRE)**
*Ralph Beckett* 93
3 b f Mastercraftsman(IRE) In My Life (IRE) (Rainbow Quest (USA))
1682[2] 2227[3] 3291[5] (4267) 4612[5] **(5108)** 6930[8] 8733a[10]

**Mistress Viz (IRE)**
*Sarah Hollinshead* a55 51
3 gr f Mastercraftsman(IRE) Vizean (IRE) (Medicean)
**1737**[6] 2269[7] 6257[7] 7199[9] 7833[7] 8673[3] 9026[9]

**Mistry** *Mark Usher* a51
4 b m Mullionmileanhour(IRE) Smart Ass (IRE) (Shinko Forest (IRE))
88[5] 274[7] 455[2] **764**[2] 874[5] 8496[8] **(8824)**

**Misty Birnam (SAF)** *J A Stack* 100
3 gr g Toreador(IRE) In The Mist (SAF) (Verglas (IRE))
**3873a**[10] 4383a[9]

**Misty Breese (IRE)** *Paul D'Arcy* a40 36
2 b f Zebedee Geordie Iris (IRE) (Elusive City (USA))
2148[6] 3244[8] 3999[5] 7057[11] **8371**[9] 8870[11]

**Misty Spirit** *David Elsworth* a73 79
2 br f Swiss Spirit Irrational (Kyllachy)
4440[7] 5026[2] (5534) 6136[8] 6863[12] **7814**[3] 8308[4]

**Misu Mac** *Neville Bycroft* a49 57
7 b m Misu Bond(IRE) Umbrian Gold (IRE) (Perugino (USA))
**362**[13]

**Misu Moneypenny** *Scott Dixon* a63 50
4 b m Misu Bond(IRE) Watersilk (IRE) (Fasliyev (USA))
**215**[4] 416[7] 480[9] 1071[7] 1209[6] 1435[4] 2294[8] 3385[2] 3728[6] 4246[5] 5283[7] 5738[4] 6531[4]

**Misu Pete** *Mark Usher* a63 61
5 b g Misu Bond(IRE) Smart Ass (IRE) (Shinko Forest (IRE))
222[7] 494[4] 784[4] 1298[12] 2278[4] 3001[2] 3265[3] 3550[U] (3971) 4561[7] (4970) 5793[7] 7198[5] 7900[2] 8300[5] 8664[7] **9334**[2]

**Mitcd (IRE)** *George Bewley* a51 61
6 gr m Mastercraftsman(IRE) Halicardia (Halling (USA))
8187[6] **9261**[4]

**Mitchum** *Ron Barr* a58 76
8 b g Elnadim(USA) Maid To Matter (Pivotal)
**2858**[5] 3238[5] 3488[3] 4509[11] 4896[7] 5419[3] 5543[6] 6045[4] 6271[5] 6688[5] 7020[6] 7366[8] 7926[4] 8480[7]

**Mitchum Swagger** *David Lanigan* a97 114
5 b g Paco Boy(IRE) Dont Dili Dali (Dansili)
2129[5] 2825[7] **3587**[4] (5616) 6928[5] 7807[12]

**Mithqaal (USA)** *Michael Appleby* a97 85
4 ch g Speightstown(USA) Bestowal (USA) (Unbridled's Song (USA))
**(156)**◆

**Mitigate** *Jane Chapple-Hyam* a67 80
3 b f Lawman(FR) Marika (Marju (IRE))
288[3] (863)◆ 1859[6] 2177[6] 3031[10] 3722[9] **6562**[3] 7341a[9] 8299[7]

**Mittens** *Sir Michael Stoute* a76 100
3 b f New Approach(IRE) Warm Hands (Oasis Dream)
2302[3]◆ 3535[3] (4366)◆ **(4883)**◆ **5352**[5] 5927[6] 7576[6] (Dead)

**Mix And Mingle (IRE)** *Chris Wall* 111
4 ch m Exceed And Excel(AUS) Mango Lady (Dalakhani (IRE))
(1902) **(2616)** 3961[12] 6401[12] 8003[6]

**Mixboy (FR)** *Keith Dalgleish* a87 91
7 gr g Fragrant Mix(IRE) Leston Girl (FR) (Lesotho (USA))
(7629) 7983[5] **(8485)**◆ 9055[6]

**Mizaah (IRE)** *Kevin Prendergast* 102
4 b g Invincible Spirit(IRE) Miss Beabea (IRE) (Catrail (USA))
1385a[8] **5517a**[7] 6491a[18]

**Mizbah** *Doug Watson* a107 82
8 b g Dubai Destination(USA) Candice (IRE) (Caerleon (USA))
**(83a)** 650a[6] 1045a[8]

**Mizen Master (IRE)** *Olly Murphy* a55 67
4 b g Captain Rio Nilassiba (Daylami (IRE))
**7730**[7]

**Mizpah (IRE)** *Ken Wingrove* 35
5 b m Excellent Art Philosophers Guest (IRE) (Desert Prince (IRE))
**3143**[6]

**Mjjack (IRE)** *K R Burke* 103
3 gr c Elzaam(AUS) Docklands Grace (USA) (Honour And Glory (USA))
1702[7] (2820) (3588) 4383a[7] 5393[2] **6918**[2] 7807[6] 8438a[8]

**Moabit (GER)** *Paul Nicholls* a71 89
5 b g Azamour(IRE) Moonlight Danceuse (IRE) (Bering)
4471[5] (5432) 6033[2] **(7903)** 9341[6]

**Moakkad** *Mark Johnston* 65
2 b g Helmet(AUS) Generously Gifted (Sakhee (USA))
3164[9] 4014[8] **5120**[5]

**Moamar** *Ed Dunlop* a73
3 ch g Sepoy(AUS) Palitana (USA) (Giant's Causeway (USA))
(198) **498**[3]

**Moana** *Dr Jon Scargill* 12
4 b m Kheleyf(USA) Torver (Lake Coniston (IRE))
**8137**[8]

**Moans Cross (USA)** *Alan King* 51
3 ch g Spring At Last(USA) Playful Wink (USA) (Orientate (USA))
**3717**[8]

**Moayadd (USA)** *Neil Mulholland* a76 82
5 b g Street Cry(IRE) Aryaamm (IRE) (Galileo (IRE))
309[3]◆ (608) (733) (1283) 1430[2]◆ **(2357)**

**Mobbhij** *Saeed bin Suroor* a91
3 b g New Approach(IRE) Anaamil (IRE) (Darshaan)
(6623) 7359[4] 7880[11]◆ **(8778)**

**Mo Big Cat (CAN)** *Mark Casse* 83
2 bb f Uncle Mo(USA) Sweet Kitten (USA) (Kitten's Joy (USA))
**7206a**[7]

**Mobley Chaos** *John Flint* a46 28
7 b g Darnay Emmarander (Bob's Return (IRE))
**614**[11] 784[F] 2255[13] 2294[7] 3280[11] 4011[8] 4735[12]

**Mobsta (IRE)** *Mick Channon* 110
5 b h Bushranger(IRE) Sweet Nicole (Okawango (USA))
1491[11] 2737[4] **3099a**[5] 4071[16] 4615[5] 5435[9] 5640[25] 6966[3] 7626[13] 8383[13] 8737[12]

**Moccasin (FR)** *Geoffrey Harker* a43 53
8 b g Green Tune(USA) Museum Piece (Rainbow Quest (USA))
176[10] 2183[9] **2546**[5] 3284[4]

**Mocead Cappall** *John Holt* a33 60
2 b f Captain Gerrard(IRE) All Fur Coat (Multiplex)
1966[6] **2583**[3] 6012[6] 6265[5] 7385[5] 8145[9] 8945[7]

**Mochalov** *Jane Chapple-Hyam* a32
2 b g Denounce Awesome Asset (USA) (Awesome Again (CAN))
**9299**[11]

**Mod** *James Fanshawe* a67 75
3 b f Sixties Icon Panna (Polish Precedent (USA))
2681[8] **3542**[2] 4497[6]

**Model (FR)** *Richard Hannon* 94
2 gr f Mastercraftsman(IRE) Goddess Of Love (Galileo (IRE))
(4340) **5448a**[2] 6228a[8] 8424[11]

**Modernism** *Ian Williams* a84 84
8 b g Monsun(GER) La Nuit Rose (FR) (Rainbow Quest (USA))
62[8] **(381)** 599[6] 884[3] **2574**[3] 3580[6] 4893[8] 5403[11] 6416[5] 6858[4] 7925[6] 8955[12] 9262[9]

**Modern Love (IRE)**
*M D O'Callaghan* a78 84
2 gb f Dark Angel(IRE) The Hermitage (IRE) (Kheleyf (USA))
**7725**[3]

**Modern Tutor** *Miss Nicole McKenna* a61 47
8 b g Selkirk(USA) Magical Romance (IRE) (Barathea (IRE))
2454[10] 3529[3] **6800a**[5]

**Moggy (USA)** *Richard Hughes* a67 32
2 b f Kitten's Joy(USA) Day Glow (USA) (Dehere (USA))
3687[3] 4253[14] **6886**[4]

**Mohab** *Kevin Ryan* a84 91
4 b g Sir Percy Princess Aurora (USA) (Mr Greeley (USA))
1832[6] 2348[5] 2701[2] 4377[9] **(5072)** 6422[9] 7044[3] 8009[9]

**Mohatem (USA)** *Owen Burrows* a89 96
5 ch g Distorted Humor(USA) Soul Search (USA) (A.P. Indy (USA))
**(2068)**◆ 2603[7]

**Moheet (IRE)**
*Jassim Mohammed Ghazali* 101
5 b g High Chaparral(IRE) Abunai (Pivotal)
**914a**[7]

**Mo Henry** *Adrian Paul Keatley* a78 75
5 b g Monsieur Bond(IRE) Mo Mhuirnin (IRE) (Danetime (IRE))
3385[4] 5519a[13] **6797a**[6] **9244a**[8]

**Mohsen** *Marcus Tregoning* a58 77
3 b r Bated Breath Harryana (Efisio)
3984[5] 5158[4] 6184[2] 6791[6] **7229**[2] **7930**[2]

**Moi Aussie** *Michael Appleby* a59 67
4 gr m Aussie Rules(USA) Oceana Blue (Reel Buddy (USA))
1062[9] 1245[3] 1338[10] 1544[10] 2063[4] 2313[7] (2733) (2976) 3577[4] **4203**[3] **4766**[3] 5214[12] 5813[4] 7465[7] 9334[5]

**Moi Moi Moi (IRE)** *Ibrahim Al Malki* a73 87
3 b c Acclamation I'm Sensational (Selkirk (USA))
**933a**[7]

**Moisson Precoce** *F Rohaut* 96
2 b f Lawman(FR) Arch Of Colours (Monsun (GER))
**8525a**[3]

**Mojito (IRE)** *William Haggas* a80 107
3 b c Requinto(IRE) Narva (USA) (Grand Slam (USA))
3082[3]◆ 3317[3] (4634) (5661)◆ **(6404)** 7807[18]

**Mokaatil** *Owen Burrows* a67 101
2 br c Lethal Force(IRE) Moonlit Garden (IRE) (Exceed And Excel (AUS))
3083[2]◆ 3929[4] 5891[2] (6755) **8001**[3]

**Mokarris (USA)** *Simon Crisford* 107
3 b c More Than Ready(USA) Limonar (IRE) (Street Cry (IRE))
**2289**[8]

**Mokhalad** *Sir Michael Stoute* a76 65
4 ch g Dubawi(IRE) Model Queen (USA) (Kingmambo (USA))
2135[4]◆ 2547[2]

**Molans Mare (IRE)**
*Keith Henry Clarke* a46 51
7 ch m Shirocco(GER) Devious Diva (IRE) (Dr Devious (IRE))
2656a[9] 3453[3] 6802a[5]

**Molecule (IRE)**
*John Patrick Shanahan* 56
3 ch f The Carbon Unit(USA) The Mighty Atom (USA) (Sky Mesa (USA))
4426[6]

**Molliana** *Neil Mulholland* a29 4
2 b f Olden Times The Screamer (IRE) (Insan (USA))
7898[10] 8501[10] 8802[8]

**Molly Jones** *Matthew Salaman* a48 52
8 b m Three Valleys(USA) And Toto Too (Averti (IRE))
3277 7228 1022[7] 2360[4] 2969[4] 3280[10] 3811[11] 4043[6] 6478[13] 7993[7]

**Molly Kaye** *S M Duffy* a55 60
4 b m Multiplex Persian Lass (IRE) (Grand Lodge (USA))
8246[5]

**Molly Mayhem (IRE)** *Richard Fahey* a55 41
2 ch f Casamento(IRE) Inez (Dai Jin)
4258[7] 5180[4] 5743[6]

**Molten Lava (IRE)** *Philip Kirby* a68 55
5 b g Rock Of Gibraltar(IRE) Skehana (IRE) (Mukaddamah (USA))
2276[7] 2961[11] 3723[9] 4727[11] 5897[6] 7360[9] 8249[12]

**Momentarily** *Hugo Palmer* 75
2 b f Cityscape Firebelly (Nicolotte)
6292[3]◆

**Momentori** *Scott Dixon* 24
4 ch m Observatory(USA) True Melody (IRE) (Grand Lodge (USA))
1205[8]

**Moment To Dream** *Ken Wingrove* a57
5 b m Halling(USA) Pretty Majestic (IRE) (Invincible Spirit (IRE))
7[12]

**Mom Said (IRE)** *Ed Walker* a51 66
2 b g Lawman(FR) Istishaara (USA) (Kingmambo (USA))
7707[12] 8140[6] 8643[9]

**Monaadhil (IRE)** *Marcus Tregoning* 89
3 b g Dark Angel(IRE) Urban Daydream (IRE) (Oasis Dream)
(3394) 8126[2] (8510)◆

**Monaco Rose** *Richard Fahey* a64 79
4 b m Sir Percy Pallas (Statue Of Liberty (USA))
1679[4]◆ (2079) (2815) 3033[4] 3580[2] 4336[3] 5208[4] 5403[3] 6013[5] 6880[4] 7387[6] 7598[8]

**Monadee** *Roger Varian* a77 57
2 b g Showcasing Messelina (Noverre (USA))
8735[6] 8989[3] (9198)

**Mon Amie Chop (FR)** *F Vermeulen* a80 91
2 b f Captain Chop(FR) Bouboulina (Grand Lodge (USA))
3611a[9] 6453a[3] 8443a[2]

**Monarch Maid** *Peter Hiatt* a70 63
6 b m Captain Gerrard(IRE) Orange Lily (Royal Applause)
1599[5] 3008[8] 3216[5] 3774[11] 5081[4] 6004[5] 6485[7] 7517[9] 8496[4] 8743[8] 9267[12]

**Monarchs Glen** *John Gosden* a100 117
3 b g Frankel Mirabilis (USA) (Lear Fan (USA))
(1725) 2128[4] 3032[4] 6698[2]◆ (7506) (8041)◆

**Monargent (FR)** *F-H Graffard* 76
2 gr c Kendargent(FR) Monava (FR) (El Prado (IRE))
5520a[5]

**Monar Lad (IRE)** *Dai Burchell* 58
5 b g Mountain High(IRE) Cottage Lady (IRE) (Moscow Society (USA))
5141[5] 5428[6] 6031[4] 7085[6]

**Mon Beau Visage (IRE)**
*David O'Meara* a86 92
4 br g Footstepsinthesand Hurricane Lily (IRE) (Ali-Royal (IRE))
1778[5] 2226[4] 2685[4] (3049) 3857[3] 4085[3] 4556[3] 5000[3] (6266) (6434) 7582[11] 7823[5] 8009[17]

**Monday Club** *Dominic Ffrench Davis* a59 65
4 ch g Strategic Prince Support Fund (IRE) (Intikhab (USA))
8183[6] 8515[8]

**Mondelino (FR)**
*Mme C Head-Maarek* a55 64
4 b g Youmzain(IRE) Mishina (FR) (Highest Honor (FR))
837a[3]

**Mondialiste (IRE)** *David O'Meara* a80 118
7 b h Galileo(IRE) Occupandiste (IRE) (Kaldoun (FR))
1378a[11] 2290[6] 3012[4] 3843[6] 5436[2] 6444[6] 7179a[4] 7851a[5]

**Money For Luck (IRE)** *Brian Ellison* 41
2 br g Arakan(USA) Invincible Wings (IRE) (Invincible Spirit (IRE))
3430[8] 3972[6]

**Money In My Pocket (IRE)**
*Harry Dunlop* a45 70
3 b f Acclamation Azabara (Pivotal)
3134a[12] 3571[5]

**Money Multiplier (USA)**
*Chad C Brown* 112
5 bb r Lookin At Lucky(USA) Intensify (USA) (Unbridled's Song (USA))
6461a[2] 7633a[8]

**Moneyoryourlife** *Richard Hannon* a68 71
3 b c Dick Turpin(IRE) Truly Pink (Mr Greeley (USA))
763[2] 864[2] (1445) 1623[4] 2137[3] 2394[2] 3041[4] 9325[7]

**Money Sister** *Francesco Santella* a78 74
2 b f Harbour Watch(IRE) Broughtons Flight (IRE) (Hawk Wing (USA))
5629a[3] 8169a[3]

**Money Talks** *Michael Madgwick* a61 56
7 br g Motivator Movie Mogul (Sakhee (USA))
462[4] 859[4] 1303[4] 2964[6] 4217[7] 4756[5]

**Money Team (IRE)** *David Barron* a79 86
6 b g Kodiac Coral Dawn (IRE) (Trempolino (USA))
1346[6] 1777[4] 2821[9] 3847[14] 6943[8]

**Mongolian Saturday (USA)**
*Enebish Ganbat* a104 115
7 b g Any Given Saturday(USA) Miss Hot Salsa (USA) (Houston (USA))
8604a[12]

**Mongolian Wolf (AUS)** *Darren Weir* 107
3 br g Pluck(USA) Oomaroo (AUS) (Tale Of The Cat (USA))
8057a[13]

**Monika Jem (FR)** *S Jesus* a59 55
6 ch m Redback Beauty Jem (FR) (Red Ransom (USA))
364a[5] 822a[3]

**Monjeni** *Ian Williams* a75 84
4 b g Montjeu(IRE) Polly's Mark (IRE) (Mark Of Esteem (IRE))
(1191) (1412) 2426[3] (2609) 3794[3]

**Monkey Magic** *Nigel Tinkler* a36 55
2 b f Acclamation Happy (JPN) (Bago (FR))
2105[8] 2590[6] 3399[3] 4716[5] 5373[5] 6043[7] 7242[9] 8780[8]

**Monks Stand (USA)** *Tim Easterby* a81 83
3 b g More Than Ready(USA) Return The Jewel (USA) (Broken Vow (USA))
1702[9] 2106[6] 2739[14] 3982[3] 4342[3] 4892[11] 5929[9] 6519[5]

**Monna Valley** *Stuart Williams* a64 62
5 ch g Exceed And Excel(AUS) Monnavanna (IRE) (Machiavellian (USA))
1625 6908 1249[7] 1403[4] 2095[6]

**Monocle** *Georgios Alimpinisis* a34 79
4 gr g King's Best(USA) Spectacle (Dalakhani (IRE))
8251a[11]

**Monologue (IRE)** *Neil Mulholland* a57 48
4 ch g Manduro(GER) Homily (Singspiel (IRE))
(1298) 1456[4] 2022[5] 4980[8]

**Monoshka (IRE)** *James Given* a63 51
3 b g Kodiac Coastal Waters (Halling (USA))
78[7] 356[6] 1194[4]

**Monreal (IRE)** *Jean-Pierre Carvalho* 104
3 b c Peintre Celebre(USA) Montezuma (GER) (Monsun (GER))
2483a[4] 3636a[6] 4422a[6] 6913a[2] 7634a[7]

**Monroe Bay (IRE)** *P Bary* 104
3 b f Makfi Lune Rose (High Chaparral (IRE))
1657a[2] 2665a[11] 3881a[9] 4665a[2] 6054a[6]

**Monsieur Bay** *Ismail Mohammed* a70
3 b c Sir Percy Pilcomayo (IRE) (Rahy (USA))
8663[5] 9209[5]

**Monsieur Glory** *Tom Clover* a75 82
4 ch g Monsieur Bond(IRE) Chushka (Pivotal)
2282[3] 3205[4] 3820[2] (4538) 6188[6] (6610) 7234[7]

**Monsieur Jamie** *Clare Ellam* a25 19
9 b g Monsieur Bond(IRE) Primula Bairn (Bairn (USA))
8775[7] 9075[13]

**Monsieur Jimmy** *Declan Carroll* a73 61
5 ch g Monsieur Bond(IRE) Artistic License (IRE) (Chevalier (IRE))
528[7] 1076[2] 1431[5] 1593[7] 1868[4] 2469[3]◆ 2627[4] 3151[2] 4105[8] 4688[8] 5214[2] 5466[8] 6003[8] (6528) 7934[8] 8254[2]◆ (8801)

**Monsieur Joe (IRE)** *Paul Midgley* a83 113
10 b g Choisir(AUS) Pascali (Compton Place)
1800[5] 2657a[7] 3539[4] 3873a[5] 4816[13] 5116[2] 5354[11] 6039[5] 6695[9] 6927[5] 7425a[2] 8012[12]

**Monsieur Mel** *Antony Brittain* a50 33
3 b g Monsieur Bond(IRE) Melandre (Lujain (USA))
4164[7] 5019[7] 5946[8] 6437[18]

**Monsieur Paddy** *Tony Carroll* a65 52
4 ch g Monsieur Bond(IRE) Minnina (IRE) (In The Wings)
172[5] 7321[0] 1558[8] 3391[8] 4142a[2] 5252[4] 6174[13]

**Monsieur Renard** *Charlie Wallis*
2 ch g Monsieur Bond(IRE) Slightly Foxed (Royal Applause)
3230[5]

**Monsieur Rieussec**
*Jonathan Portman* a81 87
7 bl g Halling(USA) Muscovado (USA) (Mr Greeley (USA))
92[9] (306) 507[9]

**Monsieur Royale** *Clive Drew* a53 49
7 ch g Monsieur Bond(IRE) Bond Royale (Piccolo)
282[5] 739[6] 2976[4] 5511[3] 7606[11] 8949[5]

**Montague (IRE)** *Jamie Osborne* a80 74
2 b c Poet's Voice Silicon Star (FR) (Starborough)
3002[5] 3591[6] 6868[4]◆ 7489[6] (7985) 8213[3] (8493) 8817[5] 9345[2] 9452[3]◆

**Montaigne (FR)** *F-X Belvisi* a61 61
4 ch g Astronomer Royal(USA) Materialiste (IRE) (Zafonic (USA))
4457a[10]

**Montalban (FR)** *D De Waele* a52 42
10 b g Elusive City(USA) Realy Queen (USA) (Thunder Gulch (USA))
713a[5]

**Montaly** *Andrew Balding* a93 114
6 b g Yeats(IRE) Le Badie (IRE) (Spectrum (IRE))
(2525) 4639[2] (6400) 7116[6] 8274a[7]

**Montana Dawn (USA)** *Bryan Smart* a42
2 b f Jimmy Creed(USA) Page Dancer (USA) (Hennessy (USA))
7757[8]

**Montanna** *Jedd O'Keeffe* a80 75
3 ch g Notnowcato Asi (USA) (El Prado (IRE))
2408[5] 2857[5] 3286[2] (4307) 5706[4] 7359[6] 8214[6] 8778[2]

**Montataire (IRE)** *Mark Johnston* 100
3 b c Cape Cross(IRE) Chantilly Pearl (USA) (Smart Strike (CAN))
1861[7] 6404[15] 6671[4]

**Monteamiata (IRE)** *Ed Walker* a79 79
3 b f Dream Ahead(USA) Tiger Spice (Royal Applause)
(212) 2235[2]◆ 2725[3] 3331[2] 4500[5] (5295) 5711[4] 7000[2] 7771[4] 8158[6]

**Monte Cinq (IRE)** *Jason Ward* a88 66
3 b g Bushranger(IRE) Invincible Me (IRE) (Invincible Spirit (IRE))
291[2] 926[5] 1090[3] 5383[5] 6411[9] 7522[5] 7825[4] 8651[8] 9124[11] 9308[5]

**Montesquieu (FR)** *M Boutin* a43 74
7 b g Silvano(GER) Beiramar (IRE) (Monsun (GER))
7070a[5] 7721a[2]

**Monteverdi (FR)** *Jamie Osborne* a89 50
4 b g Kyllachy West Of Saturn (USA) (Gone West (USA))
3161[7] 3777[8] 4294[8] (6802a) 7947[2] 9179[3]◆

**Monticello (IRE)** *Mark Johnston* a66 96
3 b g Teofilo(IRE) Towards (USA) (Fusaichi Pegasus (USA))
31[5] 3316[3] 4048[2] 4316[2] 4856[10] 5568[13] 6563[7] 7400[7]

**Mont Kiara (FR)** *Kevin Ryan* a84 93
4 b g Kendargent(FR) Xaarienne (Xaar)
1501[8] 1880[4] 2764[11] 4379[12] 4816[14] (5612) 6923[4] 7405[2]◆ 9016[11]

**Mont Kinabalu (IRE)** *Kevin Ryan* 79
2 b g Society Rock(IRE) Startori (Vettori (IRE))
2948[4] 4792[4] 7013[2] 7473[3] (8046) 8413[7]

**Mont Ras (IRE)** *Roger Fell* a99 88
10 ch g Indian Ridge(IRE) Khayrat (IRE) (Polar Falcon (USA))
43[6]

**Mon Tresor (FR)** *G Botti* a69 70
3 ch f Kendargent(FR) Salamanque (FR) (Medicean)
2244a[15] 6124a[8]

**Mont Royal (FR)** *Ollie Pears* a47 73
3 gr g Naaqoos Take Blood (FR) (Take Risks (FR))
2304[4]◆ 3296[10] 3949[4] (5000)◆ 6091[10] 6518[6] 7457[10]

**Montycristo** *Philip Hide* a40 48
4 br g Motivator Water Gipsy (Piccolo)
576[5] 3506[13] 4177[4] 5405[7] 5866[3] 6259[8]

**Monumental Man** *Michael Attwater* a87 81
8 b g Vital Equine(IRE) Spark Up (Lahib (USA))
(211) 618[4] 816[2] 1025[6] 1222[4] (1465) 2083[9] 2368[8] 3581[11] 4178[3] 4803[8] 6278[2] 6764[2] 7127[5] 7538[6] 9234[5]

**Monzino (USA)** *Michael Chapman* a53 17
9 bb g More Than Ready(USA) Tasso's Magic Roo (USA) (Tasso (USA))
1108[3] 1207[7] 1436[6] 3564[4] 4047[10] 9342[4] 9445[8]

**Mood For Mischief** *Ed Walker* a25
2 b c Nathaniel(IRE) Tina's Spirit (IRE) (Invincible Spirit (IRE))
9336[9]

**Moojaned (IRE)** *John Flint* a59 61
6 b g Raven's Pass(USA) Mufradat (IRE) (Desert Prince (IRE))
169[7] 414[8] 1498[18] 1684[6] 3916[3] 4471[6] 4966[2] 5477[5] 5716[5] 6524[5] 7028[5] 7479[5] 7561[6] 8301[6] 8430[8]

**Moolazim** *Marco Botti* a95 90
3 b c Tamayuz Empire Rose (ARG) (Sunray Spirit (USA))
(1488) 1895[4]◆ (3700)◆ 4299[5] 6026[4] (7456)

**Mooltazem (IRE)** *John Gosden* a79 85
3 b c Elzaam(AUS) Whisper Dance (USA) (Stravinsky (USA))
2066[6] (4693) 5242[3] 7736[2]◆

**Moon Arrow (IRE)** *Michael Blake* a58 49
4 b g Authorized(IRE) Moon Sister (IRE) (Cadeaux Genereux)
2219[7] 7991[6] 8815[8]

**Moon Dash (USA)** *Michael Stidham* 93
2 b f Malibu Moon(USA) In The Slips (USA) (More Than Ready (USA))
8575a[10]

**Moondust (IRE)** *John Gosden* a68 64
3 b f Exceed And Excel(AUS) Lady Hawkfield (IRE) (Hawk Wing (USA))
418[2] 8751[0]

**Moondyne Joe (IRE)**
*Mark Pattinson* a20 84
4 b g Bushranger(IRE) Golden Shine (Royal Applause)
387[4] 2608[17]

**Moon Eclipse (FR)** *M Nigge* a77
3 b f Paco Boy(IRE) Cinta (Monsun (GER))
4288a[4]

**Moonlight Bay** *G M Lyons* 91
2 b f Pivotal Naadrah (Muhtathir)
2862a[4] 8424[9]

**Moonlight Blue (IRE)** *Michael Dods* a60 62
3 b g Approve(IRE) Nouvelle Reve (GER) (Acatenango (GER))
2921[2] 3901[6] 4838[4] 6091[12] 6436[9]

**Moonlight Dash** *S Seemar* a75 92
9 b g Monsun(GER) Kind Regards (IRE) (Unfuwain (USA))
322a[4] 654a[5]

**Moonlight Gambler (FR)**
*N Caullery* a75 81
8 b g Westerner Zuppa Inglese (FR) (Le Balafre (FR))
1920a[14] 2696a[8]

**Moonlight Magic** *J S Bolger* 115
4 b h Cape Cross(IRE) Melikah (IRE) (Lammtarra (USA))
2240a[2] 3108a[7] 4417a[3] (5087a) 6960a[4]

**Moonlightnavigator (USA)**
*John Quinn* a77 93
5 br g Henrythenavigator(USA) Victorica (USA) (Exbourne (USA))
2406[9] 2799[2] 3255[8] 3792[14] 4377[12] 4961[8] (5668)

**Moonlight Silver** *William Muir* a65 62
3 gr f Makfi Moon Empress (FR) (Rainbow Quest (USA))
2311[9] 2754[10] 3425[6] 5001[5] 5565[7] (6578) 7879[11]

**Moonlit Sands (IRE)** *Brian Ellison* 66
2 b f Footstepsinthesand Dusty Moon (Dr Fong (USA))
2987[5] 3557[5] 4555[3] 5057[4] 6036[10]

**Moonmeister (IRE)** *A J Martin* a86 90
6 b g Mastercraftsman(IRE) Moon Unit (IRE) (Intikhab (USA))
4614[12] 6399[11] 6956a[14]

**Moonovermanhattan (AUS)**
*Darren Weir* 85
5 gr g Manhattan Rain(AUS) Lunaspur (AUS) (Flying Spur (AUS))
8100a[7]

**Moon Over Mobay**
*Michael Blanshard* a60 61
4 b m Archipenko(USA) Slew The Moon (ARG) (Kitwood (USA))
1935[4] 2332[10] 3208[10] 4469[10]

**Moon Over Rio (IRE)** *Ben Haslam* 65
6 b m Captain Rio Moonchild (GER) (Acatenango (GER))
2183[11] 2891[2] 3978[5] 5493[5] 6352[11]

**Moonraker** *Mick Channon* a96 98
5 ch g Starspangledbanner(AUS) Licence To Thrill (Wolfhound (USA))
84a[10] 318a[7]◆ 543a[10] 1880[3] 2566[2] 3034[10] 3593[7] 4353[3] 4830[9] 5612[8] 6506[4] 7405[4] 7780[13] 8393[11]

**Moonrise Landing (IRE)**
*Ralph Beckett* a106 110
6 gr m Dalakhani(IRE) Celtic Slipper (IRE) (Anabaa (USA))
1733[3]

**Moonshine Dancer**
*Christian Williams* a70 64
3 b f Dark Angel(IRE) Raggle Taggle (IRE) (Tagula (IRE))
(75) 3063[9] 4188[6] 5031[4] 6076[3] 6393[8]

**Moonshine Memories (USA)**
*Simon Callaghan* a108
2 b f Malibu Moon(USA) Unenchantedevening (USA) (Unbridled's Song (USA))
8603a[7]

**Moonshiner (GER)**
*Jean-Pierre Carvalho* 111
4 ch h Adlerflug(GER) Montezuma (GER) (Monsun (GER))
2485a[6] 3884a[6] 4879a[4] 6250a[8] 7203a[2] 8090a[3]

**Moonshine Ridge (IRE)**
*Alan Swinbank* a76 62
6 b m Duke Of Marmalade(IRE) Dreams Come True (FR) (Zafonic (USA))
477[5]

**Moons Of Jupiter (USA)** *A Fabre* 84
2 b f War Front(USA) Daisy Devine (USA) (Kafwain (USA))
5448a[8]

**Moon Song** *Clive Cox* a74
2 gr f Lethal Force(IRE) West Of The Moon (Pivotal)
8544[5] 9022[2] 9310[6]

**Moonstone Rock** *Jim Boyle* a57 63
3 ch f Rock Of Gibraltar(IRE) Komena (Komaite (USA))
1685[6] 3246[9] 3656[6] (3937) 4714[4] 5067[7] 6102[6] 7216[11] 8031[5] 8156[12]

**Moon Trouble (IRE)** *E J O'Neill* a85 109
4 ch g Lope De Vega(IRE) Shake The Moon (GER) (Loup Solitaire (USA))
1920a[9] 5450a[8] 7697a[3]

**Moonwise (IRE)** *Ralph Beckett* a57 79
3 ch f Exceed And Excel(AUS) Moonstone Magic (Trade Fair)
2172[3] (2887) 3814[6] 4617[4] 6936[11]

**Moorea** *John Bridger* a21
3 ch g Medicean Priena (IRE) (Priolo (USA))
1241[6] 1420[10] 1624[7] 5409[9] 6767[8] 7902[14] 8342[7] 9088[10] 9212[11] 9321[5]

**Mooroverthebridge** *Grace Harris* a58 58
3 b f Avonbridge Spennymoor (IRE) (Exceed And Excel (AUS))
5247[5] 5969[4] 6577[3] 7899[6]

**Moorside** *Charles Hills* a82 98
4 b m Champs Elysees Marching West (USA) (Gone West (USA))
2389[5] 3928[15] 5088a[4] 5658[9] 6391[6]

**Moosir (USA)** *Doug Watson* a84 79
7 b g Daaher(CAN) Torrestrella (IRE) (Orpen (USA))
8711a[11]

**Mootaharer (IRE)** *Charles Hills* 81
4 b h Dubawi(IRE) Tahrir (IRE) (Linamix (FR))
2290[7] 3597[14] 4321[6]

**Mopotism (USA)** *Doug O'Neill* a107
3 b f Uncle Mo(USA) Peppy Rafaela (USA) (Bernardini (USA))
8578a[5]

**Mops Tango** *Michael Appleby* a25 50
2 b f Piccolo Tanning (Atraf)
2583[7] 2987[9] 4340[8] 9175[12]

**Moqarrab (USA)** *Saeed bin Suroor* a80 74
2 b c Speightstown(USA) Grosse Pointe Anne (USA) (Silver Deputy (CAN))
8560[4] (9050)

**Moqarrar (USA)** *Sir Michael Stoute* a84 75
2 bb c Exchange Rate(USA) Time To Enjoy (USA) (Distorted Humor (USA))
6424[3] 7946[2] (8316)

**Morache Music** *Patrick Chamings* a81 80
9 b g Sleeping Indian Enchanted Princess (Royal Applause)
2230[4]◆ 2618[3] 3074[2] 3518[4] (4441) 5051[3] 7653[7] 8296[3] 8881[7]

**Morando (FR)** *Roger Varian* 116
4 b g Kendargent(FR) Moranda (FR) (Indian Rocket)
(4371) 6119a[4] 6928[3] 7943a[2]

**Morawij** *D Selvaratnam* a115 111
7 ch g Exceed And Excel(AUS) Sister Moonshine (FR) (Piccolo)
(1041a) 1377a[3]

**Mordin (IRE)** *Simon Crisford* a83
3 b g Invincible Spirit(IRE) Bryanstown (IRE) (Galileo (IRE))
***(9088)***◆

**Mordoree (IRE)** *Clive Cox* a59 63
3 ch f Mayson Lisieux Orchid (IRE) (Sadler's Wells (USA))
2581[3] 3250[5] 4968[2] **(5266)** 5783[6] *7061*[8]

**More Beau (USA)** *Noel Wilson* a74 73
6 bb g More Than Ready(USA) Frontier Beauty (USA) (Gone West (USA))
***3257***[8] 4013[6]

**More Harry** *Neil Mulholland* a6
2 b g Aussie Rules(USA) Native Ring (FR) (Bering)
***8888***[13] *8982*[9]

**Morello (IRE)** *Henry Candy* a61 50
3 b f Medicean Mullein (Oasis Dream)
***2019***[7] 3162[11] 4302[6] 5145[8] 6041[5] *6324*[2] *6813*[5] 7122[8]

**More Mischief** *Jedd O'Keeffe* a105 105
5 b m Azamour(IRE) Mischief Making (USA) (Lemon Drop Kid (USA))
***(4308)*** 5155[3] **6357**[2]

**Moremoneymoreparty (IRE)**
*Richard Guest* a51 55
2 b f Epaulette(AUS) Three Times (Bahamian Bounty)
4472[9] 5334[6] **5561**[3] 8475[13] *8793*[4]

**More Than More (USA)**
*George Peckham* 40
2 b f More Than Ready(USA) Donamour (USA) (Langfuhr (CAN))
**6386**[7]

**Moretti (IRE)** *David O'Meara* a58 58
2 b f Requinto(IRE) Hassaya (IRE) (King's Best (USA))
**8471**[3] ***8851***[7]

**Morever (FR)** *Mme P Butel* a54 69
2 b f Penny's Picnic(IRE) Evermore (FR) (Ski Chief (USA))
**3515a**[4]

**Morga (IRE)** *Desmond McDonogh* a69 97
7 b m Whipper(USA) Langfuhrina (USA) (Langfuhr (CAN))
**1999a**[5]

**Morgan Le Faye** *A Fabre* 96
3 b f Shamardal(USA) Molly Malone (FR) (Lomitas)
**8733a**[2]

**Mori** *Sir Michael Stoute* 105
3 b f Frankel Midday (Oasis Dream)
1944[5] (2564)◆ (3006) **3995**[2] 6357[7] 7577[6]

**Morigane Forlonge (FR)** *A Giorgi* a83 89
3 b f American Post Wonderful Life (GER) (Tiger Hill (IRE))
**2244a**[8] *5521a*[4]

**Moritzburg** *M Halford* 89
3 ch c Dutch Art Providencia (Oasis Dream)
**3997**[22]

**Mori Yoshinari (IRE)**
*Richard Hannon* a52 53
3 b g Helmet(AUS) Malyana (Mtoto)
***(916)*** 1736[13] 2690[7] 3621[8]

**Morlock (IRE)** *Charlie Appleby* a83 80
2 b c Epaulette(AUS) Mon Bijou (IRE) (Green Desert (USA))
*(6884)* 7546[7] ***7987***[3]

**Morning Beauty** *Hugo Palmer* a66
2 ch f Dawn Approach(IRE) Extreme Beauty (USA) (Rahy (USA))
***8997***[5]

**Morning Chimes (IRE)**
*Mark Johnston* 73
3 b f Shamardal(USA) Maidin Maith (IRE) (Montjeu (IRE))
**6236**[3]◆

**Morning Has Broken (IRE)**
*David Elsworth* a81
2 ch f Dawn Approach(IRE) Romie's Kastett (GER) (Halling (USA))
***9201***[5]

**Morning Sequel** *Neil Mulholland* a34 22
4 b m Revoque(IRE) Silver Sequel (Silver Patriarch (IRE))
2359[9] 2721[9] ***3472***[11]

**Morning Suit (USA)** *Mark Johnston* a81 92
3 rg g Street Boss(USA) Blue Dress (USA) (Danzig (USA))
*(114)* (2677)◆ *2922*[7] 3336[4] 4223[2] **4763**[3] 5130[6] 5568[8] 5643[14] 6235[6] *6882*[10] 7246[P] (Dead)

**Mornington** *Marcus Tregoning* a71 93
4 b g Aussie Rules(USA) Giusina Mia (USA) (Diesis)
(1788) (2218)◆ **3658**[3]

**Morning Wonder (IRE)** *Kevin Ryan* 78
2 ch c Dawn Approach(IRE) Mount Elbrus (Barathea (IRE))
5492[2] **(7026)**

**Mor Spirit (USA)** *Bob Baffert* a125
4 bb r Eskendereya(USA) I'm A Dixie Girl (USA) (Dixie Union (USA))
***8576a***[8]

**Mosalim (IRE)** *William Haggas* 75
2 b g Arcano(IRE) Vision Of Peace (IRE) (Invincible Spirit (IRE))
**4318**[3] 5106[6]

**Moscow Eight (IRE)** *E J O'Neill* a46 56
11 b g Elusive City(USA) Hurricane Lily (IRE) (Ali-Royal (IRE))
**7307a**[7]

**Moseeb (IRE)** *Saeed bin Suroor* a75 76
2 b g Invincible Spirit(IRE) Boastful (IRE) (Clodovil (IRE))
**(4374)** 5162[6] *5891*[6] *7536*[3] 7914[6]

**Moses (FR)** *Mario Hofer* 80
2 b g Dabirsim(FR) Mon Zamin (IRE) (Zamindar (USA))
**8777a**[7]

**Mosman** *Paul W Flynn* a51 38
7 b g Haafhd Last Dream (IRE) (Alzao (USA))
***1403***[6]

**Mosseyb (IRE)** *William Haggas* a69
2 b g Epaulette(AUS) Allegrissimo (IRE) (Redback)
***8819***[3]

**Mossgo (IRE)** *John Best* a74 69
7 b g Moss Vale(IRE) Perovskia (USA) (Stravinsky (USA))
*5734* ***(961)*** *1429*[3] *2025*[4] *2368*[7] 4093[7] *8816*[9] *9189*[10] *9389*[5]

**Mossketeer** *John Best* a68 55
2 b g Moss Vale(IRE) Gracilia (FR) (Anabaa (USA))
3245[7] 3782[7] 4972[9] *8145*[5] ***(8793)*** 9021[3] *9452*[4]

**Moss Street** *Conor Dore* a45 60
7 b g Moss Vale(IRE) Street Style (IRE) (Rock Of Gibraltar (IRE))
***121***[7] *146*[11]

**Mossy's Lodge** *Anthony Carson* a68 29
4 b m Royal Applause Tee Cee (Lion Cavern (USA))
***812***[9] *1729*[12] *7255*[7] *7723*[12] *9052*[4] *9268*[3]

**Mostahel** *Richard Hannon* a94 95
3 b c Acclamation Entente Cordiale (IRE) (Ela-Mana-Mou)
1609[2] *(1837)* **2400**[3] 4813[17]

**Mostaneer (IRE)** *N Bachalard* 107
5 ch g Dutch Art King's Doll (IRE) (King's Best (USA))
**205a**[14]

**Mostashreqah** *Milton Bradley* a48 47
4 ch m Equiano(FR) China Cherub (Inchinor)
*2278*[8] *2724*[6] *3136*[4] ***3545***[3] 4148[3] 4731[7] 5052[6]

**Mostawfee (IRE)** *John James Feane* a51 58
4 b g Dandy Man(IRE) Grainne Mhaol (IRE) (Spectrum (IRE))
**4659**[9]

**Motabaary (IRE)** *Mme Pia Brandt* a83 56
7 b g Tamayuz Truly Yours (IRE) (Barathea (IRE))
***1920a***[5]

**Motabassim (IRE)** *Brian Meehan* a77 74
2 gr c Zebedee Coastal Waters (Halling (USA))
3746[8] 4526[8] 5557[3] 6395[2] ***(7764)***

**Motherland (IRE)**
*Joseph Patrick O'Brien* 104
4 ch h Galileo(IRE) Pipalong (IRE) (Pips Pride)
**3057a**[3] 4073[11]

**Mother Of Dragons (IRE)**
*Phil McEntee* a60 81
2 ch f Society Rock(IRE) Queen O'The Desert (IRE) (Green Desert (USA))
2037[2] 3029[2] **3960**[15] 5150[6] 5575[8] 6719[3] 7126[7] *8701*[7] *8902*[2] *9024*[2] *9122*[3] *9182*[2]

**Motley Crew** *Michael Easterby* a37
4 b g Mount Nelson Greensand (Green Desert (USA))
***9301***[6]

**Motown Mick (IRE)** *Richard Hannon* a89 81
2 ch g Intikhab(USA) Top Row (Observatory (USA))
1941[8] 5105[5] 6761[4] (7228) (7904) ***8343***[2] *8671*[3] ***(9322)***

**Motym (FR)** *H-A Pantall* 67
2 b c Motivator Ymlaen (IRE) (Desert Prince (IRE))
**8271a**[4]

**Mouchee (IRE)** *David Evans* a61 61
2 b c Zebedee Nashaat (Redoute's Choice (AUS))
5047[5] 5430[9] *5891*[7] **6585**[2] *6815*[7] *7829*[5] *8371*[8] ***(8870)***

**Mouille Point** *Richard Hannon* 82
3 b f Motivator Turning Leaf (IRE) (Last Tycoon)
1885[6]◆ (2269) 4155[3] 5033[7] **7083**[3] 7598[9]

**Mounirchop (FR)** *S Smrczek* a40 28
3 ch g Soave(GER) Moon Serenade (Key Of Luck (USA))
**6084a**[12]

**Mountain Angel (IRE)** *Roger Varian* a74 89
3 b g Dark Angel(IRE) Fanciful Dancer (Groom Dancer (USA))
*1272*[2]◆ *2135*[2]◆ (2704) **3317**[2] 4904[7] 6483[2] 6942[2] 7582[5]

**Mountain Approach (IRE)**
*Richard Fahey* 61
2 b c Shamardal(USA) River Mountain (Reset (AUS))
3037[9] 4956[6] **5735**[4] 6625[8] 7243[8]

**Mountain Bell** *Ralph Beckett* a100 103
4 b m Mount Nelson Shenir (Mark Of Esteem (IRE))
**8421**[4]◆ *8992*[4] *(9259)*

**Mountain Breath** *Chris Fairhurst* a72
2 b f Bated Breath Araminte (One Cool Cat (USA))
*7238*[3]◆ ***(8189)***

**Mountain Fox (IRE)** *F Oakes* a63 72
4 b g Fast Company(IRE) Opa Loca (Shirocco (GER))
**5518a**[7]

**Mountain Guard (IRE)** *Roger Varian* 81
2 b c Society Rock(IRE) Morinda (Selkirk (USA))
**6146**[2] 6827[4]

**Mountain Hunter (USA)**
*Saeed bin Suroor* a102 101
3 b g Lonhro(AUS) Tamarillo (Daylami (IRE))
(5611) (6422)◆ ***6887***[4]

**Mountain Meadow** *Richard Fahey* a42 49
2 ch f Dutch Art Romantic Settings (Mount Nelson)
**3312**[10] 3858[8] 4786[6] 5756[10] *7029*[6] 7698[5] 8467[13]

**Mountain Peak** *Ed Walker* a68 49
2 b g Swiss Spirit Nolas Lolly (IRE) (Lomitas)
4151[9] 5151[10] 5365[12] *(6063)* ***(6815)*** ***8131***[5]

**Mountain Rescue (IRE)** *Chris Wall* a92 96
5 b g High Chaparral(IRE) Amber Queen (IRE) (Cadeaux Genereux)
1960[10] 3014[7] 3743[7] *4261*[6] 5159[2] **(5610)** 6192[7] **7340**[2]

**Mount Cheiron (USA)** *Richard Ford* a56 53
6 b g Henrythenavigator(USA) Chalamont (IRE) (Kris)
*46*[9] ***239***[3] *400*[10] *608*[3] *1260*[5] *1406*[5] *1563*[8] *2312*[5] 3242[4] 3530[3] 4034[7] 4839[6] *5831*[12] 6092[12] 6523[5]

**Mount Cleshar** *John Butler* a43 32
3 b g Mount Nelson Resal (IRE) (Montjeu (IRE))
***681***[5] *959*[6] *1205*[9] 2705[12]

**Mount Hellvelyn** *Clive Mulhall* 57
2 b g Hellvelyn Sugar Mountain (IRE) (Lomitas)
1872[6] 2222[7] **2896**[8] 3398[5] 6043[10]

**Mount Logan (IRE)** *Roger Varian* 113
6 ch g New Approach(IRE) Vistaria (USA) (Distant View (USA))
3069[3] 4360[3] 5925[2] 6514[2] **(7054)**

**Mount Moriah** *Ralph Beckett* a73 113
3 b g Mount Nelson Rule Britannia (Night Shift (USA))
(2784) (4828)◆ 5639[3] 6976a[3] 7783[5] **8229**[4]

**Mount Rock** *Michael Easterby* a65 72
3 b g Mount Nelson Holamo (IRE) (Montjeu (IRE))
2185[5] 3465[6] **5378**[3] 6209[F] (Dead)

**Mount Tahan (IRE)** *Kevin Ryan* a100 96
5 b g Lope De Vega(IRE) Sorpresa (USA) (Pleasant Tap (USA))
1492[5]◆ 1974[3] *2518*[2] 5393[10] 5616[4] 6419[P] 7622[12] *8999*[2]◆ ***(9407)***

**Mount Vesuvius (IRE)**
*Paul Henderson* a50
9 b g Spartacus(IRE) Parker's Cove (USA) (Woodman (USA))
***37***[6]

**Mount Victoria (IRE)** *James Given* 71
2 b f Arakan(USA) Salingers Star (IRE) (Catcher In The Rye (IRE))
1908[2] **2801**[8] 3557[6]

**Mount Wellington (IRE)**
*Henry Spiller* a79 87
2 b g Invincible Spirit(IRE) Marvada (IRE) (Elusive City (USA))
**3098a**[7] ***(9372)***

**Movees (IRE)** *Stefano Botti* 84
3 b f Cape Cross(IRE) Katajan (Halling (USA))
2244a[12] **7441a**[7]

**Move In Time** *Paul Midgley* a83 108
9 ch g Monsieur Bond(IRE) Tibesti (Machiavellian (USA))
2764[10] 3321[15] 3829[17] **4867**[5] 5435[8] 6325[9] 7144[13] 7625[6] 8167[6]

**Move It Move It** *Keith Dalgleish* a79 74
2 gr c Lethal Force(IRE) Madam Valentine (Primo Valentino (IRE))
*2786*[3] 3523[3] *4259*[2] 4836[3]◆ 7821[19] ***8586***[2] ***9098***[4]

**Move Over** *Richard Hannon* a64 97
2 b c Acclamation Framed (Elnadim (USA))
3093[4] *4007*[7] *4560*[6] 5246[2] (5709) (6367) 6985a[4] 7648[2] **8276a**[4]

**Move Swiftly** *William Haggas* a79
2 b f Farhh Hurricane Harriet (Bertolini (USA))
***(9335)***◆

**Move To The Front (IRE)** *Clive Cox* 76
2 b g Lord Shanakill(USA) Dress Up (IRE) (Noverre (USA))
1496[11] 2910[4] 3655[4] 5752[5] (6860) **(7913)** 8349[15]

**Move Up** *Saeed bin Suroor* a106 116
4 b h Dubawi(IRE) Rosinka (IRE) (Soviet Star (USA))
***1045a***[4] *1380a*[10]

**Movie Magic** *Mark Hoad* a46 48
6 b m Multiplex Alucica (Celtic Swing)
*35*[10] *436*[4] *1081*[10] *1303*[9] ***1699***[3] *2332*[8] 2964[9]

**Moviesta (USA)** *Edward Lynam* a112 109
7 b g Hard Spun(USA) Miss Brickyard (USA) (A.P. Indy (USA))
*206a*[5] *539a*[6] 773a[9] **5974a**[4] 6325[13] *8225a*[4]

**Moving Robe (IRE)** *Conrad Allen* a54 45
4 b m Iffraaj Emma Dora (IRE) (Medaglia d'Oro (USA))
*309*[2] *614*[8] *761*[6] *1322*[5] *2729*[6] 3442[7] *3550*[3] 4323[5] 6296[7] *7991*[14] 8386[19] *8707*[6] ***(8984)*** *9342*[6]

**Mowafrost (FR)** *Mme P Butel* a62 63
3 b g Silver Frost(IRE) Mowaajaha (USA) (Invincible Spirit (IRE))
**6256a**[5] **6649a**[6]

**Mowhoob** *Brian Barr* a57 58
7 b g Medicean Pappas Ruby (USA) (Red Ransom (USA))
*274*[4] *425*[5] *(614)* *854*[11] *1139*[2] *1484*[2] *2465*[3] *3172*[2] **3809**[2] 4968[3] 5713[9] *8675*[7] *8994*[6] *9141*[11] *9334*[4]

**Moxy Mares** *Daniel Mark Loughnane* a55 71
2 ch g Motivator Privalova (IRE) (Alhaarth (IRE))
5631[3] *6636*[8] **8382**[3]

**Mr Adjudicator** *Joseph G Murphy* 86
3 b g Camacho Attlongglast (Groom Dancer (USA))
**1386a**[4] 5689a[10]

**Mr Andros** *Brendan Powell* a58 48
4 b g Phoenix Reach(IRE) Chocolada (Namid)
*1007*[9] 3820[8] 5248[8] 6076[7] *6528*[7] 7212[8] 7916[8] ***(8543)*** *8948*[11] *8985*[3] *9141*[9] *9334*[3]

**Mraseel (IRE)** *James Tate* a77 77
2 b f Sir Prancealot(IRE) Suffer Her (IRE) (Whipper (USA))
1884[8] 2265[4] *2958*[2] 3815[2] (4199) 4739[U] 5751[3] **6481**[2] *7536*[6] ***(8432)***

**Mr Bossy Boots (IRE)**
*Amanda Perrett* a101 77
6 b g Teofilo(IRE) Zelding (IRE) (Warning)
***235***[2] 5610[10] *6685*[13] 7129[9] *7727*[12] *8032*[5] *8547*[12]◆ *9125*[9] *9210*[9]

**Mr Boycie Quest** *Gary Moore* a57
3 gr c Air Quest Salt Kettle (Royal Applause)
***8151***[9] *8822*[8]

**Mr Brownstone** *Brendan Powell* a18
3 b g Sakhee(USA) Sweet Child O'Mine (Singspiel (IRE))
***9202***[13]

**Mr C (IRE)** *Ollie Pears* a59 59
3 b g Fast Company(IRE) Vanitycase (IRE) (Editor's Note (USA))
2857[9] 4172[3] **(5131)** 5761[4] 6471[7] ***7833***[3] *8206*[5]

**Mr Caffrey** *John Flint* a46 57
5 b g Duke Of Marmalade(IRE) Quest For Eternity (IRE) (Sadler's Wells (USA))
**2781**[10] 3428[9]

**Mr Carbonator** *Philip Kirby* a62 58
2 b g Bated Breath Diamond Lass (IRE) (Rock Of Gibraltar (IRE))
*3187*[8] 3791[13] 5277[2] 5756[2] 6087[3] 6940[9] 8141[7] 8475[3] *8783*[11] *9014*[2] ***(9175)*** *9439*[3]

**Mr Christopher (IRE)**
*Tom Dascombe* a82 51
5 b g Bahamian Bounty Embassy Pearl (IRE) (Invincible Spirit (IRE))
*2878* *1890*[10] *3471*[10] *8433*[7] ***9029***[2]◆ *9220*[7] *9410*[6]

**Mr Chuckles (IRE)** *Mme G Rarick* a57 56
4 b g Arcano(IRE) Caribbean Escape (Pivotal)
*217*[2] *455*[3] *495*[8] *899*[2] *1247*[3] *1371*[2] *1887*[4] *2091*[4] **2675**[2] *3469*[3] **3569**[2] 4955a[5]

**Mr Coco Bean (USA)** *David Barron* a74 66
3 b g Gio Ponti(USA) Ing Ing (FR) (Bering)
1680[6] 2374[8] 3561[7] 4789[12] *6902*[4] *7240*[9] ***9072***[2]

**Mr Conundrum** *Lynn Siddall* a54 46
4 b g Paco Boy(IRE) Folly Drove (Bahri (USA))
*362*[10] 3912[15] 4605[9] **4789**[6] *5482*[11] 5827[9] 6181[10] 6550[6] 6786[8]

**Mr Cool Cash** *Richard Guest* a64 73
5 b g Firebreak Cashleen (USA) (Lemon Drop Kid (USA))
*1842*[7] *2276*[5] *2466*[9] 3402[11] **(3560)** 3845[11] 4298[5] 5497[5] 6049[5] 6549[5] 6783[4] 7046[4] 7327[2] 7476[4] 7894[16]

**Mr Cripps** *Ralph Beckett* a80 85
5 b g Sir Percy Pella (Hector Protector (USA))
1608[8] **2770**[7]

**Mr Davies** *David Brown* a68 68
3 ch g Shirocco(GER) Pasithea (IRE) (Celtic Swing)
**1497**[7] 2137[4] 2892[8] 5096[7] 5509[7] 6293[7] *7537*[3] *7790*[2] *8187*[5]

**Mr Enthusiastic** *Noel Wilson* a45 53
3 b g Assertive Selkirk Rose (IRE) (Pips Pride)
2455[5] 3290[7] 3915[9] 4847[9] 5703[2] 6130[4] 6596[7] ***(7926)*** *8428*[6] *8776*[5] *9019*[12]

**Mr Everest (IRE)**
*Joseph Patrick O'Brien* 86
4 b g Cape Cross(IRE) Incitatus Girl (IRE) (Galileo (IRE))
**7860a**[14]

**Mr Fickle (IRE)** *Gary Moore* a68 67
8 b g Jeremy(USA) Mamara Reef (Salse (USA))
**8301**[8]

**Mr Frankie** *Adrian Wintle* a65 61
6 b g Sleeping Indian Shes Minnie (Bertolini (USA))
*806*[10] *1284*[4] 3519[2] 6095[7] ***7413***[2] 8327[9] *9375*[5] *9406*[7]

**Mr Garcia** *Richard Fahey* 101
4 b g Paco Boy(IRE) Birdie (Alhaarth (IRE))
**4918**[5]◆ 5500[7]

**Mr Gent (IRE)** *Ed Dunlop* a77 71
2 br c Society Rock(IRE) Furnival (USA) (Street Cry (IRE))
7280[6]◆ 7740[3] 8179[3] ***9199***[2] *9370*[7]

**Mr Globetrotter (USA)** *Iain Jardine* a69 81
4 b g Henrythenavigator(USA) Sunshine For Life (USA) (Giant's Causeway (USA))
*1197*[3] *(1369)* 1834[3] (3338) **(3566)** 3830[8] *5896*[9] 7386[7] 8214[7]

**Mr Greenlight** *Tim Easterby* 71
2 b g Bahamian Bounty Nos Da (Cape Cross (IRE))
4374[5] 5370[3] 5879[4] **6353**[12] 7138[6] 7472[3]

**Mr Khalid** *Roger Charlton* a74 79
4 b g Pour Moi(IRE) Island Dreams (USA) (Giant's Causeway (USA))
**(2041)** *2959*[5] 3534[10]

**Mr Lando** *Johnny Farrelly* a62 41
8 b g Shirocco(GER) Capitana (GER) (Lando (GER))
***3724***[5] 4733[6]

**Mr Large (IRE)** *Jamie Osborne* a66 66
2 b c Footstepsinthesand Oh Happy Days (IRE) (Galileo (IRE))
4465[7] 4885[9] **5655**[3] **6613**[6] *8537*[7] *8870*[5] ***8943***[2]

**Mr Little (IRE)** *Jamie Osborne* a31
2 b c Kodiac Shining Hour (USA) (Red Ransom (USA))
**3999**[6] 4466[P] (Dead)

**Mr Lupton (IRE)** *Richard Fahey* a93 116
4 ch g Elnadim(USA) Chiloe Wigeon (IRE) (Dockside (USA))
1765[2]◆ **(2433)**◆ 2907[3] 3867[8] 4907[9] 5633[2] 5974a[5] 6926[6] 7611[4] 8044[8]

**Mr Mac** *Peter Hedger* a64 24
3 b g Makfi Veronica Franco (Darshaan)
*502*[8] *2018*[3] *3327*[12] *8908*[13] ***(9203)*** *9456*[4]

**Mr Magill (FR)** *Karen George* a47
5 b g Hamairi(IRE) Marie Cuddy (IRE) (Galileo (IRE))
*1190*[6] ***1556***[9] *4217*[12]

**Mr Maximum (USA)** *F-H Graffard* a66 69
3 bb g Creative Cause(USA) Allegro Lady (USA) (Souvenir Copy (USA))
3554a[8] **6649a**[2]

**Mr Michael (IRE)**
*Adrian Brendan Joyce* a50 63
4 b g Big Bad Bob(IRE) Mastoora (IRE) (Acclamation)
***743***[4] *1246*[7] 8481[6]

**Mr Minerals** *Richard Hughes* a91 88
3 ch g Poet's Voice River Song (USA) (Siphon (BRZ))
3780[4] ***(4501)*** 4807[2]

**Mr Morse** *Brian Ellison* a66 67
4 ro g Hellvelyn Songsheet (Dominion)
*67*[10] ***514***[4] *971*[13]

**Mr Opulence** *T Le Brocq* a39 51
8 ch g Generous(IRE) Miss Opulence (IRE) (Kylian (USA))
1930a[5] **2671a**[4]

**Mr Orange (IRE)** *Paul Midgley* a64 78
4 b g Paco Boy(IRE) Shirley Blake (IRE) (Acclamation)
1717[9] 2303[4] 2883[4] 3666[2] (4605) **(5132)** 5806[3] 6238[5] 7554[7] *8211*[7]

**Mr Owen (USA)** *David Simcock* a108 102
5 b h Invincible Spirit(IRE) Mrs Lindsay (USA) (Theatrical (IRE))
429a[7] 892a[7] 8417[3] ***8891***[3] *(9274a)*

**Mr Pocket (IRE)** *Paul Cole* a77 84
3 b c Acclamation Midnight Martini (Night Shift (USA))
(1940) 3278[7] **3865**[2] **4178**[2] 4992[6] 5473[4]◆ *8310*[9] *8645*[6] *8950*[6] *9234*[2] *9389*[8]

**Mr Potter** *Richard Guest* a63 48
4 ch g Assertive Enclave (USA) (Woodman (USA))
360[4] 445[4] 640[5] (761) 1106[4] 1408[5] 6903[8] 7481[6] (7605) 8328[9] 8719[5] 8930[9] 9013[7] 9142[4] 9243[3]

**Mr Reckless (IRE)** *Jamie Osborne* a76
2 gr c Reckless Abandon Zarabaya (IRE) (Doyoun)
7488[5] 8951[DSQ]◆ (9154)◆

**Mr Red Clubs (IRE)** *Henry Tett* a78 82
8 b g Red Clubs(IRE) Queen Cobra (IRE) (Indian Rocket)
1065[4] 1224[2] (1329) 1562[2] (1982) 2796[3] 3235[6] 3546[3] 6158[6] (6475) 7111[3] 7505[8] 9295[11]

**Mr Right (IRE)** *J F Levins* a70 96
5 b g Echo Of Light Danetime Lily (IRE) (Danetime (IRE))
1388a[11]

**Mr Ritz** *Jeremy Noseda* a84
2 b c Oasis Dream Que Puntual (ARG) (Contested Bid (USA))
(9311)

**Mr. Roary (USA)**
*George Papaprodromou* a37 106
4 ch g Scat Daddy(USA) If Angels Sang (USA) (Seattle Slew (USA))
8608a[13]

**Mrs Benson (IRE)**
*Michael Blanshard* a68
2 ch f Rip Van Winkle(IRE) Ebble (Oasis Dream)
7875[6]◆ 8889[4]

**Mrs Biggs** *Declan Carroll* a61 69
5 ch m Paco Boy(IRE) Hoh Chi Min (Efisio)
2183[8] (2688) 3043[3] 3405[3] 4558[7]

**Mrs Burbidge** *Neil Mulholland* a54 46
7 b m Pasternak Twin Time (Syrtos)
6175[5]

**Mr Scaff (IRE)** *Paul Henderson* 64
3 br g Vocalised(USA) Nancy Rock (IRE) (Rock Of Gibraltar (IRE))
1686[8] 2394[11] 2892[3] 4348[5]

**Mr Scaramanga** *Simon Dow* a102 99
3 b c Sir Percy Lulla (Oasis Dream)
177[4] (933a) 1621[2] 1959[8] 3302[4] 3927[7] 4334[9] 6024[8] 6746a[6] 9091[4] 9468[8]

**Mr Scarlet** *Ms Sheila Lavery* 103
3 b g Dandy Man(IRE) Scarlet Buttons (IRE) (Marju (IRE))
2863a[3] 4030[5]◆ 5974a[9] 7424a[10]

**Mrs Danvers** *Jonathan Portman* 106
3 gr f Hellvelyn Rebecca De Winter (Kyllachy)
1660a[6]

**Mrs Gallagher** *William Jarvis* 90
2 b f Oasis Dream A Huge Dream (IRE) (Refuse To Bend (IRE))
(2563) 3960[11] (4628) 6136[3] 6863[7] 8001[9]

**Mrs Hitchcock (IRE)**
*Miss Katy Brown* a57
2 b f Requinto(IRE) Bells Of Ireland (UAE) (Machiavellian (USA))
8225a[11]

**Mr Skinnylegs** *Brian Ellison* a46 57
3 b g Dream Win Impeccable Guest (IRE) (Orpen (USA))
1513[10] 1973[2] 2897[4]◆ 4159[5]

**Mr Slicker (FR)** *Tom Dascombe* a56 56
3 b g Exceed And Excel(AUS) Glory Power (IRE) (Medicean)
5538[7] 6236[6] 7597[3] 8402[6]

**Mrs Loreen (SWE)**
*Lennart Reuterskiold Jr*
5 ch m Needwood Blade Irish Dolly (IRE) (Docksider (USA))
2942a[4]

**Mrs McDougal (USA)**
*Richard E Mandella* a85 107
5 b m Medaglia d'Oro(USA) Distorted Passion (USA) (Distorted Humor (USA))
8601a[9]

**Mr Sneaky (AUS)**
*Anthony Freedman* 105
3 bb g High Chaparral(IRE) Danesty (AUS) (Danehill (USA))
8059a[12]

**Mr Splendid (FR)** *G Doleuze* a64 76
8 gr g Zieten(USA) Salina Sea (FR) (Baryshnikov (AUS))
2696a[15]

**Mrs Sippy (USA)** *David Simcock* a71 86
2 b f Blame(USA) Qushchi (Encosta De Lago (AUS))
7997[4]◆ (8380)◆

**Mr Standfast** *Alan Phillips* a39 52
4 b g Mullionmileanhour(IRE) Phantom Ridge (IRE) (Indian Ridge (IRE))
457[6] 636[13] 2891[3] 3756[9] 5267[14] 6306[12]

**Mrs Teasdale** *Archie Watson* a68 70
2 ch f Harbour Watch(IRE) Ardessie (Bahamian Bounty)
3210[11] 3655[3] 4090[2] (4725)

**Mr Strutter (IRE)** *Ronald Thompson* a60 68
3 ch g Sir Prancealot(IRE) Khajool (IRE) (Haafhd)
126[2] 264[7] 578[4] 897[4] 1127[6] (2182) (2699) 2989[7] 4107[2] 4694[2] (6660) 7408[6] 8557[12] 8874[12] 9001[6]

**Mr Stunning (AUS)** *J Size* 125
4 b g Exceed And Excel(AUS) With Fervour (USA) (Dayjur (USA))
(9168a)

**Mr Sundowner (USA)** *Wilf Storey* a56 75
5 bb g Scat Daddy(USA) Bold Answer (USA) (Dynaformer (USA))
400[6] 1125[6] 1473[5] 2183[2] (2687) 3043[5] 3343[11] 4018[9] 4659[5] (5181) 5698[3] (6592) 7015[2] (7387) 8239[6] 8485[3]

**Mr Top Hat** *David Evans* 85
2 b c Helmet(AUS) Tut (IRE) (Intikhab (USA))
2779[10] 3668[2] 7351[3] (7741) 8420[2]

**Mr Turner** *Mark H Tompkins* a40 58
4 b g Nayef(USA) Seasonal Blossom (IRE) (Fairy King (USA))
614[7] 761[9] 1146[7]

**Mr Tyrrell (IRE)** *Richard Hannon* a80 81
3 b c Helmet(AUS) Rocking (Oasis Dream)
1241[3] 1619[2] 2580[3] 3062[2] 5077[2] 5559[4] 6134[12] 7398[5] 7768[2]

**Mr Wagyu (IRE)** *John Quinn* a28 77
2 ch g Choisir(AUS) Lake Louise (IRE) (Haatef (USA))
2154[6] 3398[2] (4014) (4922) 5373[6] 6951[11]

**Msaikah (IRE)** *Luca Cumani* a46
2 b f Galileo(IRE) Light Quest (USA) (Quest For Fame)
8903[6]

**Ms Arsenal** *Giles Bravery* a4 58
5 b m Mount Nelson Magical Dancer (IRE) (Magical Wonder (USA))
879[6] 1139[10]

**Msayyan (IRE)** *John Gosden* a76 75
2 b c Camelot Elusive Girl (IRE) (Elusive City (USA))
7726[2] (8161)

**Ms Gillard** *David Simcock* a72 72
4 b m Aussie Rules(USA) Oval Office (Pursuit Of Love)
29[3] 609[2] 747[2] 993[2] 1237[4] 1455[2] 1789[2] 2282[4] 3292[3] (3699)

**Ms Tilly** *David Brown* a15 4
2 b f Milk It Mick Clumber Pursuits (Pastoral Pursuits)
6147[9] 7326[12] 7757[13] 8493[6]

**Mt Augustus** *Henry Candy* 79
2 b g Champs Elysees In Secret (Dalakhani (IRE))
5840[4] 6777[6] 7503[2]

**Muarrab** *A R Al Rayhi* a116 85
8 b g Oasis Dream Licence To Thrill (Wolfhound (USA))
206a[2] 539a[2] 1041a[6] 1377a[14] (9361a)

**Muatadel** *Roger Fell* a82 86
4 b g Exceed And Excel(AUS) Rose Blossom (Pastoral Pursuits)
1290[5] 3524[3]◆ 4060[2] 4531[6] 4896[6] (5055) (5318) 5804[2] (6062) 6758[2] 7055[3] 7557[7] 7612[4] 7939[3] 8293[5]◆

**Mubaalegh** *J E Hammond* 99
3 b g Dark Angel(IRE) Poppet's Passion (Clodovil (IRE))
6979a[10]

**Mubajal** *A bin Harmash* a64 56
4 br g Dubawi(IRE) Jadhwah (Nayef (USA))
3065[8] 8714a[10]

**Mubakkir (AUS)**
*Bill Papazaharoudakis* 96
6 b g Commands(AUS) Albakoor (AUS) (Zabeel (NZ))
8057a[6]

**Mubtaahij (IRE)** *Bob Baffert* a118 78
5 b h Dubawi(IRE) Pennegale (IRE) (Pennekamp (USA))
891a[2] 1380a[4] 8611a[8]

**Mubtaghaa (IRE)** *M Al Mheiri* a16 80
5 b g Acclamation Mabalane (IRE) (Danehill (USA))
84a[12] 206a[7]

**Mubtasim (IRE)** *William Haggas* 109
3 b g Arcano(IRE) Start The Music (IRE) (King's Best (USA))
2289[3] 3078[3] 3959[3]◆ 4935a[7] 6401[11]

**Mudaarab (USA)** *Sir Michael Stoute* a70 91
3 b c Distorted Humor(USA) Middle Club (Fantastic Light (USA))
1485[4] (2300) (3778) 6671[9]

**Mudajaj (USA)** *Charles Hills* 72
3 bb g Arch(USA) Checkered Flag (USA) (A.P. Indy (USA))
2152[4] 2721[6] 3427[5]

**Mudallel (IRE)** *Ed Dunlop* a89 68
3 b g Invincible Spirit(IRE) Lixirova (FR) (Slickly (FR))
3293[5] 3669[4] 4332[4] 5797[4] (6067) (6576) 7456[7]

**Mufeed (USA)** *S Seemar* a74 86
3 ch g Gemologist(USA) Hannah's Dowery (USA) (Stephen Got Even (USA))
430a[9] 887a[7]

**Muffri'Ha (IRE)** *William Haggas* a111 112
5 b m Iffraaj Grecian Dancer (Dansili)
431a[3] 771a[3] 1046a[3] 1771[2] 2432[4] (7576) 7812[7] 8041[5] (8546)

**Muhajjal** *George Peckham* a71 52
3 b c Cape Cross(IRE) Muqantara (USA) (First Samurai (USA))
4269[7] 8375[11] 8646[7] 8907[9] 9094[6] (9431)

**Muharaaj (IRE)** *Frau Erika Mader* a70 99
6 b h Iffraaj Desert Sprite (IRE) (Tagula (IRE))
3105a[7]

**Muhtaram** *M Al Mheiri* a91 58
7 b g Shamardal(USA) Neshla (Singspiel (IRE))
316a[2]

**Muirin (IRE)** *Edward Lynam* 97
2 b f Born To Sea(IRE) Girouette (IRE) (Pivotal)
6974a[4] 8004[10]

**Muirsheen Durkin** *Neville Bycroft* a69 85
3 b g Fastnet Rock(AUS) Be My Queen (IRE) (Sadler's Wells (USA))
3262[8] 4210[2]◆ 5213[6] 5669[8] 6468[6]

**Mujassam** *David O'Meara* a90 90
5 ch g Kyllachy Naizak (Medicean)
6662[12] 7554[2]◆ 8014[16] 8486[6] 8803[8] (9074)◆ 9305[6]

**Mukalal** *Marcus Tregoning* a99 100
3 b g Mawatheeq(USA) Misdaqeya (Red Ransom (USA))
1862[5] (2330) (3262) 4563[2] 5744[4] 6419[4]◆ (7784)

**Mukhaater** *Charles Hills* 70
2 ch g Bahamian Bounty Dame Shirley (Haafhd)
8381[5]

**Mukhayyam** *Tim Easterby* a86 98
5 b g Dark Angel(IRE) Caster Sugar (USA) (Cozzene (USA))
1719[6] 1976[7] 2741[11] 3497[2]◆ 3841[2] 4206[13] (4863) (5164)◆ 5913[5] 6399[12] 6929[9] 7387[3] 8414[8]

**Mulhimatty** *Charles Hills* 86
3 b f Invincible Spirit(IRE) Raasekha (Pivotal)
(1947) 2802[5] 7130[8]

**Mullarkey** *John Best* a76 76
3 b g Mullionmileanhour(IRE) Hannah's Dream (IRE) (King's Best (USA))
647[2] 1000[3] (1736) 2784[5] 3787[5] 4865[7] 5820[5] 8000[7] 8814[3] (9236)

**Mulled Wine** *John Best* a56 45
4 b g Mullionmileanhour(IRE) Numanthia (IRE) (Barathea (IRE))
279[8] 740[2] 1338[8] 1894[5] 3137[10]

**Mulligatawny (IRE)** *Roger Fell* a91 95
4 b g Lope De Vega(IRE) Wild Whim (IRE) (Whipper (USA))
1911[6] 2528[4] 2838[3] 3255[10] 3790[6] 4017[2] 4658[5]◆ 4692[2] (5163) 5470[4] 6209[4] 6563[2] 7619[30]

**Mullionheir** *John Best* a86 87
5 b g Mullionmileanhour(IRE) Peyto Princess (Bold Arrangement)
93[4] 275[10] 3750[9] 4887[9] 6192[9] (6874)◆

**Mullion Star** *Michael Madgwick* 23
2 b g Mullionmileanhour(IRE) Leading Star (Motivator)
1681[11] 2473[10] 4909[11] 5408[7]

**Mulsanne Chase** *Brian Barr* a42 68
3 b g Sixties Icon Hot Pursuits (Pastoral Pursuits)
2778[9] 3691[3] 4097[7] 5326[6] 6791[9] 7457[11] 7899[5] 8181[5]

**Multellie** *Tim Easterby* 89
5 b g Multiplex Bollin Nellie (Rock Hopper)
3794[9] 4206[9] 4380[4] 8384[8]

**Multicolours** *Iacopo Bindi* 78
6 b g Multiplex Sopran Cross (ITY) (Cape Cross (IRE))
2866a[5]

**Multicultural (IRE)** *James Tate* a80 84
3 b f Fastnet Rock(AUS) Cochabamba (IRE) (Hurricane Run (IRE))
1471[2] 4579[3] (6111) 6297[3] 7398[4] 7947[6] 8600[5] 8947[5]◆ 9053[8]

**Multicurrency (USA)**
*David Simcock* a47
2 gr c Exchange Rate(USA) Istamara (Teofilo (IRE))
8642[7]

**Multi Facets (IRE)** *David Simcock* a79 93
3 b c Lope De Vega(IRE) Red Kyte (Hawk Wing (USA))
(48) 2567[4]◆ 3317[5]◆ (4322)

**Multigifted** *Michael Madgwick* a69 76
4 b m Multiplex Attlongglast (Groom Dancer (USA))
290[5] 2022[2] (2781) (3574) 4499[6] 5607[5] 7151[5]

**Multiplier (USA)** *Brendan P Walsh* a106
3 b c The Factor(USA) Trippi Street (USA) (Trippi (USA))
2851a[6]

**Multi Quest** *John E Long* a53 54
5 b m Multiplex Ryan's Quest (IRE) (Mukaddamah (USA))
(88) 273[6] 521[5] 852[7] 982[5] 1304[4] 1593[8] 2589[5] 2969[10] 3728[12] 5146[3] 5339[9] 6041[4] 7911[6] 8496[5] 8823[9]

**Multitask** *Gary Moore* a80 34
7 b g Multiplex Attlongglast (Groom Dancer (USA))
3214[10] 3723[10] 4501[10] 5300[7] 6288[14] 6947[12]

**Multiviz** *S M Duffy* a44 55
4 b m Multiplex Vizean (IRE) (Medicean)
8249[9]

**Mulwith (IRE)** *Scott Dixon* 64
3 b g Kodiac Crying Aloud (USA) (Street Cry (IRE))
3461[10] 3949[11] 4303[17] 4744[10]

**Mulzamm (IRE)** *James McAuley* a38 26
5 b g Cape Cross(IRE) Vine Street (IRE) (Singspiel (IRE))
1014a[12]

**Mulzim** *Ed Dunlop* a81 77
3 b c Exceed And Excel(AUS) Samaah (IRE) (Cape Cross (IRE))
1488[4] (1888) 3173[2] 5376[5] 6113[2] 6936[9] 7709[10]

**Mumgala (FR)** *F Vermeulen* a71 68
7 b m Samum(GER) Stamingala (IRE) (Alzao (USA))
7070a[8]

**Mums The Word** *Richard Fahey* a79 85
3 b f Mayson Tell Mum (Marju (IRE))
(424) 678[4] 902[3] 1176[3]

**Munaaser** *A R Al Rayhi* a98 95
6 b g New Approach(IRE) Safwa (IRE) (Green Desert (USA))
85a[7] 319a[7] 432a[8] 542a[10] 8714a[2]

**Munaashid (USA)** *Ed Dunlop* 89
4 bb g Lonhro(AUS) Freefourracing (USA) (French Deputy (USA))
3014[12] 3597[6] 4091[5]

**Munaawib** *Ray Peacock* a64 6
9 b g Haafhd Mouwadh (USA) (Nureyev (USA))
684[3] 4453[7] 5285[10]

**Munawer** *J Phelippon* a74 70
3 ch g Dutch Art Cantal (Pivotal)
1907[4] 2677[2]◆ 3310a[2]

**Munazan (FR)** *Jan Keppens* 42
9 ch g Munaafis(USA) Belle Alezan (GER) (Risk Me (FR))
4955a[10]

**Mundersfield** *David Simcock* a61
3 b f Nathaniel(IRE) Captain's Paradise (IRE) (Rock Of Gibraltar (IRE))
8869[4] 9209[6]

**Munfallet (IRE)** *David Brown* a77 96
6 b g Royal Applause Princess Mood (GER) (Muhtarram (USA))
1831[10] 2381[13] 2840[5] 3424[4] 4477[6] 5051[5] 6555[3] 7094[4] 7653[4] 8541[4]

**Mungo Madness** *Julia Feilden* a52 71
3 gr g Sir Percy Emma's Gift (IRE) (Aussie Rules (USA))
385[4] 848[12] 3701[6] 4540[4] 5532[8] 6524[3] 7537[11] 8122[3]

**Munsarim (IRE)** *Lee Carter* a61 53
10 b g Shamardal(USA) Etizaaz (USA) (Diesis)
738[10] 965[8] 1283[5] 1620[9] 2022[11]

**Munstead Gold** *Andrew Balding* a57 53
2 ch c Sir Percy Royal Patron (Royal Academy (USA))
7120[8] 8029[9] 8476[5]

**Munstead Star** *Andrew Balding* a82 76
3 ch f Sir Percy Royal Patron (Royal Academy (USA))
2515[3] 3145[2] 5153[4] 5401[6] (6320) (7060)

**Muntadab (IRE)** *Roger Fell* a89 105
5 b g Invincible Spirit(IRE) Chibola (ARG) (Roy (USA))
1515[2]◆ 2156[2] 2736[2] 4072[26] 5094[6] 5435[13] 6206[14] 6662[9] (6879) 7118[2] 7609[5] (8104)◆ 8737[18]

**Muntahaa (IRE)** *John Gosden* a97 116
4 gr g Dansili Qertaas (IRE) (Linamix (FR))
1516[3] (1957) 2803[7] 4070[9] 4814[6]

**Muntazah** *Owen Burrows* a103 108
4 b g Dubawi(IRE) Rumoush (USA) (Rahy (USA))
2127[5] 2604[7] 4069[8] 4636[3] 6024[7] 7149[10]

**Munthany (USA)** *Charles Hills* a67 75
3 b g Raven's Pass(USA) Safarjal (IRE) (Marju (IRE))
3839[4] 4808[5] 5707[3] 6851[3] 7896[4]

**Muqaatil (USA)** *A bin Harmash* a65 64
3 b g Lonhro(AUS) Lightning Lydia (USA) (Broad Brush (USA))
1141[2] 1404[4] 2145[5] 4275[4] 8711a[10] 9257a[6]

**Muqarred (USA)** *Roger Fell* a79 83
5 bb g Speightstown(USA) Bawaara (FR) (Quiet American (USA))
727[7] 841[6] (1186) 1292[4] 1433[2] 1700[14] 2466[2] 2920[8] 4260[14] 5698[10] (8254) 8315[14] 8718[13] 9029[11] 9180[2] 9303[2]

**Muraadef** *Ed Dunlop* 62
2 b g Kodiac Dominatrix (Whipper (USA))
4567[6]

**Murad Khan (FR)** *Hugo Palmer* a103 107
4 b g Raven's Pass(USA) Lady Elgar (IRE) (Sadler's Wells (USA))
2767[15] (4410) 5500[13] 6024[10] 7275[8] 7988[5]

**Murafej (IRE)** *F Rohaut* a90 98
5 ch g Halling(USA) Mokaraba (Unfuwain (USA))
2202a[6] 3637a[4]

**Murasaki** *Charlie Appleby* a53
2 b f Dubawi(IRE) Michita (USA) (Dynaformer (USA))
7453[6] 7997[7]

**Murchison River** *Henry Candy* 71
3 b g Medicean Free Offer (Generous (IRE))
2476[9] 2783[18] 5220[8] 5780[4] (6509) 7744[12]

**Murdanova (IRE)** *Denis Quinn* a78 73
4 gr g Zebedee Agnista (IRE) (Iffraaj)
(734) (929) 1189[6] 2676[2] 6620[3] 7409[6] 7998[5] 8434[3] 8646[13]

**Murgan** *Stuart Kittow* a84 82
5 b g Galileo(IRE) Approach (Darshaan)
3458[5] 5873[6] 6508[6] 7231[4] 7880[10]

**Mur Hiba (IRE)** *M D O'Callaghan* a71 93
3 b f Helmet(AUS) Miss Brief (IRE) (Brief Truce (USA))
5308a[8]

**Murillo (USA)** *A P O'Brien* 106
2 b c Scat Daddy(USA) Mostaqeleh (USA) (Rahy (USA))
3925[3] 4386a[3]

**Murraqib (USA)** *Brett Johnson* a43
4 ch g Summer Bird(USA) Golden Party (USA) (Seeking The Gold (USA))
436[10]

**Musaahim (USA)** *Roger Varian* a80 86
3 b g Distorted Humor(USA) Lear's Princess (USA) (Lear Fan (USA))
3839[2] 4569[2] 5364[7] 7708[3] 8377[4]

**Musa D'Oriente** *M Gonnelli* 97
6 b m Nayef(USA) Musa Golosa (Mujahid (USA))
7441a[2]

**Musawaah (USA)** *F Head* 101
3 b f Union Rags(USA) Mudreqah (USA) (Seeking The Gold (USA))
(2447a) 3366a[7]

**Musawaat** *Charles Hills* 93
3 b c Equiano(FR) Starry Sky (Oasis Dream)
2820[2] 3303[6] 5661[3] (6426) 6870[5]

**Musbaq (USA)** *Mark Johnston* 66
2 b c Union Rags(USA) Eraada (Medicean)
2852[5] 3783[5]

**Muscika** *David O'Meara* a74 87
3 b g Kyllachy Miss Villefranche (Danehill Dancer (IRE))
(2180) 2739[8] (3386) 4683[6] 5184[2] 6392[4] 6970[3]

**Mushaakis (IRE)** *A R Al Rayhi* a96 94
7 b g Shamardal(USA) Shamayel (Pivotal)
250a[6]

**Mushahadaat (IRE)** *Brian Meehan* a77 76
2 b f Invincible Spirit(IRE) Jamaayel (Shamardal (USA))
5107[2] 5528[12] 6806[6] (7724)

**Mushaireb** *Richard Fahey* a80 89
3 b g Invincible Spirit(IRE) Hidden Brief (Barathea (IRE))
1518[10] 6942[4] (7327)◆ 7892[3]◆

**Mushareefa (IRE)** *Ed Dunlop* a24 39
3 b f Makfi Winesong (IRE) (Giant's Causeway (USA))
1609[9] 2231[13] 2585[12] 3326[10]

**Musharrif** *Declan Carroll* a85 86
5 b g Arcano(IRE) Cefira (USA) (Distant View (USA))
1831[9] 2123[9] 2409[9] 3052[6] (5211) 5495[4] 6430[5] 7557[5] 7940[3] 8260[5] 8680[5] 8803[5] 9179[5]◆

**Mushibest (ITY)** *Stefano Botti* 87
3 b c Desert Prince(IRE) Mandoki (IRE) (Dalakhani (IRE))
7205a[5]

**Mushtaq (IRE)** *Richard Hannon* a81
2 b g Zoffany(IRE) Iamfine (IRE) (Whipper (USA))
8888[4] (9123)◆

**Musical Art (IRE)** *Paul Cole* 95
2 ch f Dutch Art Musical Bar (IRE) (Barathea (IRE))
(4533) 5391[3] 6228a[6] 8004[7] 8424[12]

**Musical Comedy** *Mike Murphy* a73 79
6 b g Royal Applause Spinning Top (Alzao (USA))
3834[10] 4272[5] 4974[6] 5473[2] 6113[7] 8600[11] 9029[14]

**Musical Dream** *Sylvester Kirk* a21
2 ch f Dream Ahead(USA) Gift Of Music (IRE) (Cadeaux Genereux)
4749[11]

**Musical Fire** *Peter Hedger* a40
3 b f Equiano(FR) Music In Exile (USA) (Diesis)
6066[6] 6828[7] 8504[8]

**Musical Moon** *Steve Flook* a33 40
7 b g Piccolo Lunasa (IRE) (Don't Forget Me)
900[8]
**Musical Taste** *Pat Phelan* a61 53
4 b m Makfi Blas Ceoil (USA) (Mr Greeley (USA))
505[5] 2229[9] 2916[5]
**Musical Terms** *William Haggas* a84 78
3 b g Shamardal(USA) Dysphonia (AUS) (Lonhro (AUS))
1962[2] 3062[3] 3438[4] (6522) (7759) 8375[5]
**Musical Theatre** *David Simcock* a70 55
2 b f Exceed And Excel(AUS) Wise Melody (Zamindar (USA))
6747[6] 7986[2] 8850[4]
**Music Box (IRE)** *A P O'Brien* a75 110
3 b f Invincible Spirit(IRE) Liscune (IRE) (King's Best (USA))
3632a[8] 4385a[8] 4512a[6] 5308a[2] 6119a[2] 6642a[3] (7113)
**Music Lesson** *Hughie Morrison* a74 75
3 ch f Dutch Art Triple Sharp (Selkirk (USA))
2585[4] 3075[2] 4351[4] 5242[2] 6067[9] 7097[2]◆ 7762[14]
**Music Lover (FR)** *A De Watrigant* a92 102
3 b f Palace Episode(USA) Lucky Game (FR) (Montjeu (IRE))
2003a[4]
**Music Major** *Michael Attwater* a74 51
4 br g Bertolini(USA) Music Maid (IRE) (Inzar (USA))
(922) 1144[5] 1553[6] 7131[14] 7878[9] 8503[8] (8946) 9211[2]
**Musico (IRE)** *Patrick Holmes* a34
3 b g Lilbourne Lad(IRE) Viola Da Gamba (IRE) (Alhaarth (IRE))
2185[13]
**Music Seeker (IRE)** *James Eustace* 89
3 b g Henrythenavigator(USA) Danehill Music (IRE) (Danehill Dancer (IRE))
(2798) 3317[6] 5323[3] 7277[6] 7736[7]
**Music Society (IRE)** *Sylvester Kirk* a97 67
2 b c Society Rock(IRE) Absolutely Cool (IRE) (Indian Ridge (IRE))
5047[2] (8794)◆ 9156[2]◆
**Musikel (IRE)** *Chris Gordon* a73 72
3 ch g Frankel Musical Treat (IRE) (Royal Academy (USA))
(1347) 1907[12] 2931[3] 3484[3]◆ 4295[6] 9208[15]
**Mustaaqeem (USA)** *Richard Fahey* a95 78
5 b g Dynaformer(USA) Wasseema (USA) (Danzig (USA))
5164[7] 9096[6]
**Mustajeer** *Owen Burrows* a101 101
4 b g Medicean Qelaan (USA) (Dynaformer (USA))
1779[9] 2431[11] 3716[4]
**Mustajjid** *Wido Neuroth* a70
6 b g Byron Skara Brae (Inchinor)
2941a[3]
**Mustallib (IRE)** *A R Al Rayhi* a106 92
4 b g Iffraaj Rocking (Oasis Dream)
1044a[6]
**Mustaqbal (IRE)** *Michael Dods* a49 79
5 b g Invincible Spirit(IRE) Alshamatry (USA) (Seeking The Gold (USA))
1677[13] 2458[6] 3487[2] 3899[4] 4439[7] 4833[7] 5699[7] 6049[3] 7052[8] 7476[3] (7703) 7984[5]
**Mustaqqil (IRE)** *Christos Kouvaras* a58 39
5 b g Invincible Spirit(IRE) Cast In Gold (USA) (Elusive Quality (USA))
6541a[9]
**Mustarrid (IRE)** *Richard Hannon* a93 98
3 b g Elzaam(AUS) Symbol Of Peace (IRE) (Desert Sun)
(1582)◆ 2385[2] 3077[5] 4299[2] 5392[8] 5926[8] 6933[12]
**Mustashry** *Sir Michael Stoute* a113 114
4 bb h Tamayuz Safwa (IRE) (Green Desert (USA))
5594[10] (6024)◆ (6444) 7579[7]
**Must Be Amazing** *Jeremy Gask* a51 51
3 b f Foxwedge(AUS) Be Amazing (IRE) (Refuse To Bend (IRE))
4092[6]
**Must Be Magic (IRE)**
*Andrew Balding* 74
2 b f Camelot Saturn Girl (IRE) (Danehill Dancer (IRE))
7399[4]
**Mustn't Grumble (IRE)**
*David Loughnane* a66 65
4 ch g Intense Focus(USA) Lough Mist (IRE) (Captain Rio)
26[3] 158[3] 386[10] 481[6]
**Mutaaqeb** *Owen Burrows* 99
2 b c Invincible Spirit(IRE) Mejala (IRE) (Red Ransom (USA))
(7250)◆ 8412[2]
**Mutabaahy (IRE)** *Ed Dunlop* 61
2 b g Oasis Dream Habaayib (Royal Applause)
3169[10] 6826[5] 7562[4] 8325[5]
**Mutadaffeq (IRE)** *David O'Meara* a77 93
4 b g New Approach(IRE) Saajidah (USA) (Dynaformer (USA))
(2629) (3050) 3716[2] 4038[5] 5397[9] (5803) 6232[6] 6872[7] 8048[15]
**Mutafarrid (IRE)** *Owen Burrows* a67 80
2 gr g Dark Angel(IRE) Margarita (IRE) (Marju (IRE))
3746[9] 4560[4] 5844[5] (8120)◆
**Mutahaady (IRE)** *K R Burke* a91 90
3 b g Elzaam(AUS) Midnight Oasis (Oasis Dream)
2565[9] 3592[13] (4057) 4507[3]
**Mutajawel (USA)** *Charles Hills* a47
2 bb c Lonhro(AUS) How Cheeky (USA) (Mr Greeley (USA))
7512[10]
**Mutakatif (IRE)** *Charles Hills* 84
2 b c Acclamation Gorband (USA) (Woodman (USA))
3037[2] 3747[2] 4567[3] (6674)
**Mutakayyef** *William Haggas* 122
6 ch g Sea The Stars(IRE) Infallible (Pivotal)
1378a[5] 3924[2] (4884)
**Mutamaded (IRE)** *Ruth Carr* 91
4 b g Arcano(IRE) Sahaayeb (IRE) (Indian Haven)
2610[7] 5996[8] (6563) 7595[9]
**Mutamarida (IRE)** *Rod Collet* a70 68
3 br f Teofilo(IRE) Penny Post (IRE) (Green Desert (USA))
8692a[3]
**Mutamid** *Ismail Mohammed* a88 75
5 b g Medicean Inchberry (Barathea (IRE))
1202[2]◆ 1778[8] 2462[6] 3214[2] 4215[6] 5125[7]
**Mutanaaseq (IRE)** *Richard Hannon* 86
2 ch c Red Jazz(USA) Indaba (IRE) (Indian Ridge (IRE))
(1934) (2382)◆ 5939[4]
**Mutanaqel** *Owen Burrows* a72 69
2 b c Havana Gold(IRE) Audaz (Oasis Dream)
7543[5] 8372[3]
**Mutarabby (IRE)** *Saeed bin Suroor* a102 92
3 ch c Tamayuz Shaarfa (USA) (Dynaformer (USA))
2152[2] 2751[3] 3714[2] (4563)◆ 5744[2]
**Mutarakez (IRE)** *Brian Meehan* a93 92
5 ch g Fast Company(IRE) Nightswimmer (IRE) (Noverre (USA))
1023[5] 1492[11] 1860[8]◆ 2406[8] 2828[3] 3298[8] 4001[3] 4585[3] 4882[10] 6698[11] 8165[6] 8423[6]
**Mutasayyid** *Doug Watson* a94 102
5 ch h Bahamian Bounty Clear Voice (USA) (Cryptoclearance (USA))
322a[7]
**Mutawakked (IRE)** *Brian Meehan* 84
3 b g Kodiac Your Opinion (IRE) (Xaar)
2215[3]◆ 2831[5] 3592[8] 4084[2] 4831[6] 5928[4]
**Mutawathea** *Simon Crisford* a106 106
6 b g Exceed And Excel(AUS) Esteemed Lady (IRE) (Mark Of Esteem (IRE))
87a[4] 432a[9] 892a[6] 3003[6] 3842[2] 4905[8] 7154[2] 7807[10] 8547[8] (9233) 9468[6]◆
**Mutawatheb (IRE)** *Richard Hannon* a97 102
3 gr c Dark Angel(IRE) Queen Myrine (IRE) (Oratorio (IRE))
1142[2]◆ (2554)
**Muthla (FR)** *J-M Beguigne* 93
3 b f Muhtathir Latinia (FR) (Barathea (IRE))
2447a[6]
**Muthmir (IRE)** *William Haggas* a112 116
7 b g Invincible Spirit(IRE) Fairy Of The Night (IRE) (Danehill (USA))
(1765) 2397[12] (3370a) 3926[4] 4635[4] 7396[3]
**Muthmira** *Simon Crisford* a75 85
3 ch f Arcano(IRE) Carding (USA) (Street Cry (IRE))
1895[P] (Dead)
**Muthraab Aldaar (IRE)** *Jim Boyle* a70 57
4 b g Baltic King Vertigo On Course (IRE) (Anabaa (USA))
734[2] 1427[5] (3263) 3718[4] 4523[8] 7878[13] 8299[11] 8797[6]
**Mutineer** *Daniel Kubler* a76 57
3 ch g Sepoy(AUS) Violet (IRE) (Mukaddamah (USA))
2220[6] 2886[6] 4350[6] 4747[5] 5485[2] (5793) (5898) 6101[13] 7541[6] 8341[7] 8841[3] 9138[5]
**Mutoondresdashorse** *Paul Cole* a64 77
3 ch g Harbour Watch(IRE) Mutoon (IRE) (Erhaab (USA))
(2782) 3211[8] 4268[6] 5111[P]
**Mutual Force (USA)** *A R Al Rayhi* a64 79
9 b h Arch(USA) Freeroll (USA) (Touch Gold (USA))
203a[9]
**Muwaary (AUS)** *M F De Kock* 89
4 b h O'Reilly(NZ) Silently (AUS) (Anabaa (USA))
433a[12] 538a[7] 698a[11]
**Muzaahim (IRE)** *Laura Morgan* a61 76
6 ch g Tamayuz Elizabeth Swann (Bahamian Bounty)
1146[2] 1338[11] 2276[3] 2918[6] 4453[12] 4627[14]
**Muzaawel** *Saeed bin Suroor* 47
2 ch c New Approach(IRE) Jilnaar (IRE) (Dansili)
7521[5]
**My Amigo** *K R Burke* a79 81
4 gr g Stimulation(IRE) Blue Crest (FR) (Verglas (IRE))
1515[21] 6879[5] 7566[4] 7780[7] 8718[7] 9101[3] 9410[7]
**My Angel** *Ollie Pears* 45
3 gr f Dark Angel(IRE) Tanda Tula (IRE) (Alhaarth (IRE))
4793[5] 5538[8] 6268[8] 7390[11]
**My Approach (IRE)** *Robert Collet* a63 66
7 b g New Approach(IRE) Zelding (IRE) (Warning)
713a[4]
**Mybee Davis (IRE)** *G Botti* a76 74
3 b c Myboycharlie(IRE) Majesty Davis (IRE) (Dansili)
6084a[3]
**My Billionaire (TUR)** *S Mutlu* a75
4 b h Victory Gallop(CAN) Vaselina (USA) (Giant's Causeway (USA))
6717a[7]
**Myboyhenry (IRE)** *K R Burke* 88
2 b g Footstepsinthesand Renaissance Rio (IRE) (Captain Rio)
2948[5] (5255) (5600) 6229a[7] 6721[2] 7546[8]
**My Boy Jack (USA)**
*J Keith Desormeaux* 108
3 b c Creative Cause(USA) Gold N Shaft (USA) (Mineshaft (USA))
8577a[7]
**My Boy Sepoy** *Stuart Williams* a58
2 ch c Sepoy(AUS) Emily Carr (IRE) (Teofilo (IRE))
9311[3]
**My Brother (IRE)** *Lee Smyth* 89
4 b g Roderic O'Connor(IRE) Victory Peak (Shirley Heights)
3240[2] 4429[6]
**Mybrotherjohnny** *Fergal O'Brien* a31 47
6 b g Tiger Hill(IRE) Montjeu's Melody (IRE) (Montjeu (IRE))
98[7] 279[11]
**My Brother Mike (IRE)** *Kevin Frost* a75 49
3 b g Bated Breath Coming Back (Fantastic Light (USA))
503[6] 864[5] 5617[7] 6160[2] 6611[5] (7235)◆ 7495[4] 8205[2] 8497[10] 9054[6] 9325[4]
**My Brunette (IRE)** *Geoffrey Deacon* a36 62
3 bb f Arcano(IRE) Holda (IRE) (Docksider (USA))
8117[4] 9085[7]
**My Catch (IRE)** *Doug Watson* a110 102
6 b g Camacho Catch The Sea (IRE) (Barathea (IRE))
1377a[10] 9361a[3]
**My Cherokee** *Michael Dods* 41
3 b f Sleeping Indian Another Paris (Paris House)
4793[7]
**My Cherry Blossom** *Tim Easterby* a19 62
3 b f Kyllachy Echo River (USA) (Irish River (FR))
2631[6] 3403[13]
**Mydadsared** *Tony Coyle*
2 b g Captain Gerrard(IRE) Hoppy's Flyer (FR) (Country Reel (USA))
5180[9] 6410[8]
**My Dad Syd (USA)** *Ian Williams* a80 82
5 bb g Acclamation Weekend Fling (USA) (Forest Wildcat (USA))
2404[5] 3847[3] 4887[2] 5610[11] 6663[10] 8211[8]
**Mydearlaura (FR)** *L Gadbin* a15 9
3 b f Myboycharlie(IRE) Aurore Boreale (IRE) (Zamindar (USA))
3275a[12]
**My Direction** *Miss Ellmarie Holden* a94 90
7 ch g Singspiel(IRE) Ejlaal (IRE) (Caerleon (USA))
4822a[12]
**My Distant Murphy**
*Jacqueline Coward* a35
3 b g Distant Peak(IRE) So Cannie (Sakhee (USA))
6129[7] 8781[5] 8979[9]
**My Dream Boat (IRE)** *Clive Cox* 122
5 b h Lord Shanakill(USA) Betty Burke (Choisir (AUS))
2127[3] 2822[2] 4423a[4] 5394[7] 6328[7] 7393[8]
**My Fantasea (IRE)** *David Evans* a81 65
4 b g Sea The Stars(IRE) Speed Song (Fasliyev (USA))
154[7] 5403[13] 6310[4] 6946[11] 7791[7]
**My Girl Jo (FR)** *John Balding* a12 47
5 b m Whipper(USA) Prairie Moon (Halling (USA))
9441[4]
**My Girl Maisie (IRE)** *Richard Guest* a63 69
3 b f Fast Company(IRE) Queen Al Andalous (IRE) (King's Best (USA))
2792[3] 3260[3] (3525) 4302[5] 5339[6] 6016[9] 6437[2]◆ (6630)◆ 7332[2] 7540[5] (7889) 8473[2] 8721[4]
**My Good Brother (IRE)**
*T G McCourt* a76 66
8 b g Elusive City(USA) Final Favour (IRE) (Unblest)
6797a[2] 9244a[9]
**My Guy (IRE)** *J S Moore* a40 41
2 b g Lilbourne Lad(IRE) Royale Life (FR) (Anabaa (USA))
1767[8] 2052[6] 4725[9] 6063[7] 6815[9]
**My Heart** *Ismail Mohammed* a28
2 b f Universal(IRE) Mazuna (IRE) (Cape Cross (IRE))
8888[12]
**My Hollow (FR)** *Frau Hella Sauer* a51 54
4 b m Soldier Hollow Maine (GER) (Big Shuffle (USA))
6125a[7]
**Myhorsewithnoname (IRE)**
*Mark Hoad* 5
3 gr g Lilbourne Lad(IRE) Colleville (Pharly (FR))
7230[7] 7790[12]
**My Illusionist** *Harry Dunlop* a70 31
3 b g Kheleyf(USA) Shimoni (Mark Of Esteem (IRE))
2330[6] 2957[4] 3456[8] 4164[2] 5332[5] 6792[9] 7514[3] 7948[2] 8744[4] 9208[9]
**My Lady Marie** *Amanda Perrett* a69
3 b f Bated Breath Poppo's Song (CAN) (Polish Navy (USA))
284[8]
**My Lea (IRE)** *V Fazio* 100
3 b f Dandy Man(IRE) Luvmedo (IRE) (One Cool Cat (USA))
(8449a)
**Mylenajonh (FR)** *Jane Soubagne* a78 75
4 ch m Namid Flower (Zamindar (USA))
6540a[6]
**Myllachy** *Tim Easterby* a37 53
3 b f Kyllachy Enchanted Princess (Royal Applause)
2181[9] 3831[11] 4303[10]
**My Lord** *Paddy Butler* a50 41
9 br g Ishiguru(USA) Lady Smith (Greensmith)
440[8] 648[10] 757[3] 893[7] 6754[7] 9095[11] 9325[10] 9430[6]
**My Lord And Master (IRE)**
*William Haggas* 89
2 ch c Mastercraftsman(IRE) Affability (IRE) (Dalakhani (IRE))
8161[6] (8677)
**My Lucille (IRE)** *Chris Wall* 81
4 b m Lawman(FR) Stroke Of Six (IRE) (Woodborough (USA))
1606[10] 2708[5] 3540[6] 4311[5]
**My Matador (IRE)** *Victor Dartnall* a72 59
6 b g Kandahar Run My Special (IRE) (Peintre Celebre (USA))
286[9] 655[8]
**My Meteor** *Natalie Lloyd-Beavis* a41 44
10 b g Bahamian Bounty Emerald Peace (IRE) (Green Desert (USA))
1931a[7] 2669a[8] 2724[8] 3466[6] 4148[4]
**My Mistress (IRE)** *Phil McEntee* a54 53
5 ch m Mastercraftsman(IRE) Majestic Eviction (IRE) (King's Theatre (IRE))
46[12] 123[10]
**My Mo (FR)** *David Dennis* a48 56
5 b g Silver Frost(IRE) Anna Ivanovna (FR) (Fasliyev (USA))
1758[10] 2712[2] 3756[5]
**My Name Is Jeff** *Julia Feilden* 56
3 b g Mount Nelson Vale Of Belvoir (IRE) (Mull Of Kintyre (USA))
3839[6] 5075[5] 6277[7] 8123[6]
**My Name Is Rio (IRE)**
*Michael Dods* a63 91
7 ch g Captain Rio Walk In My Shadow (IRE) (Orpen (USA))
1515[20] 2381[10] 2840[12] 3295[2] (3653) 4079[6] 4686[8] 5671[5] 6314[8] 8293[7]
**Myredbush (IRE)** *Simon Dow* a44 25
3 b f Bushranger(IRE) Damask (IRE) (Red Clubs (IRE))
1597[9]
**My Renaissance** *Sam England* a71 54
7 bb g Medicean Lebenstanz (Singspiel (IRE))
146[2] (414) (525) 853[5] 3400[6] 7478[5] 8261[7]
**My Reward** *Tim Easterby* a98 103
5 b g Rail Link Tarot Card (Fasliyev (USA))
1802[11] (2157) 4356[5] 5638[4] 6329[2] (6675) 7139[4] 7931[3]
**My Rock (IRE)** *David Dennis* 37
2 b g Rock Of Gibraltar(IRE) Laureldean Lady (IRE) (Statue Of Liberty (USA))
6093[7] 7953[10] 8189[11]
**My Rosie (IRE)** *John Gosden* a70
3 b f Redoute's Choice(AUS) My Branch (Distant Relative)
144[2] 718[7] 967[8]
**Mysaan (IRE)** *Brian Meehan* 65
2 ch c Havana Gold(IRE) Oblique (IRE) (Giant's Causeway (USA))
1941[7] 2750[11] 3769[7] 4805[12] 5562[3]
**My Silver Nails (IRE)**
*Michael Mulvany* a55 82
2 gr f Tough As Nails(IRE) The Silver Crown (IRE) (Verglas (IRE))
7290a[6]
**My Society (IRE)** *David Dennis* 49
2 b g Society Rock(IRE) Greek Easter (IRE) (Namid)
8734[9]
**My Soul** *Mme P Butel* a63 39
3 b f Elusive City(USA) Tia Kia (IRE) (Montjeu (IRE))
3275a[9]
**Mysterial** *Declan Carroll* a53 75
7 b g Invincible Spirit(IRE) Diamond Dilemma (IRE) (Sinndar (IRE))
1517[12] 2109[4] 2386[4] 2594[4] 3050[7] 3795[6] 4169[5] (4722) 5005[6] 5183[5] 5454[5] 5706[3] 6060[6] 6467[7] 6968[12] 7235[12]
**Mysterious Glance**
*Sarah Hollinshead* a70 44
4 b m Cacique(IRE) Largo (IRE) (Selkirk (USA))
4965[8] 6267[8] 8243[11] 8745[6] 8953[7] 9152[11]
**Mysterious Look** *Sarah Hollinshead* a77 63
4 ch m Sakhee's Secret Look Here's Carol (IRE) (Safawan)
416[3] 1110[8] 8167[14] 8745[5] 8953[11]
**Mystery Of War (IRE)** *George Scott* a48 48
3 b g Canford Cliffs(IRE) Mystiara (IRE) (Orpen (USA))
615[4] 3188[11] 4097[6] 4839[9] 5532[5]
**Mystery Sky (FR)** *Mme F Chenu* a35 57
3 b f Naaqoos Water Feature (Dansili)
8960a[8]
**Mystical Mac (IRE)** *Iain Jardine* a58 40
2 b c Clodovil(IRE) Long Lost Love (Langfuhr (CAN))
7326[8] 8189[5]
**Mystical Nelly** *Jonathan Portman* a49 55
3 b f Sakhee's Secret Dancing Nelly (Shareef Dancer (USA))
1424[3] 2711[12] 3250[4] 3939[7]
**Mystical Spirit (FR)** *Martyn Meade* a88 82
5 ch g Spirit One(FR) Miss Maguilove (FR) (Dyhim Diamond (IRE))
506[6]
**Mystic Dawn (IRE)** *David Simcock* 108
3 b f Oasis Dream Frivolity (Pivotal)
1958[6] 2623[10] 3080[5] (4864)
**Mystic Maeve (IRE)** *Roger Fell* a50 58
3 b f Tagula(IRE) Celtic Lynn (IRE) (Celtic Swing)
1751[0] 3180[11] 4436[8]
**Mystic Meg** *Hugo Palmer* 71
2 b f Camelot Hypnology (USA) (Gone West (USA))
7403[2]
**Mystikana** *Marcus Tregoning* a77 72
4 ch m Sir Percy Peintre D'Argent (IRE) (Peintre Celebre (USA))
92[7] 549[5] (893) 1175[2] 8326[11]
**Mystique** *Charles Hills* a53 42
2 b f Oasis Dream Hidden Brief (Barathea (IRE))
4533[15] 8670[9]
**Mystique Moon** *Charlie Appleby* a96
3 ch g Shamardal(USA) Celestial Girl (Dubai Destination (USA))
(331) (577) 2117[2] 9468[4]
**My Sweet Meera (FR)** *J-M Lefebvre* a69 65
4 b m Myboycharlie(IRE) Elodie Des Charmes (FR) (Diesis)
391a[7]
**My Target (IRE)** *Michael Wigham* a111 92
6 b g Cape Cross(IRE) Chercheuse (USA) (Seeking The Gold (USA))
(235) (680) (1023) 1150[6] 1773[7] 3064[7] 3963[29] 9468[10]
**Mythical Madness** *David O'Meara* a106 105
6 b g Dubawi(IRE) Miss Delila (USA) (Malibu Moon (USA))
148[2] (266)◆ 574[5] 744[2] 919[8] 1773[12] 2141[7] 2735[18] 3298[2] (3743) 4069[15] 4636[11] 5594[9] 6355[10] 8999[6]◆ 9233[5] 9407[5]
**Mythical Magic (IRE)**
*Charlie Appleby* 108
2 b c Iffraaj Mythie (FR) (Octagonal (NZ))
(5350) (5978a) 7146[3] 7667a[5] 8422[3]
**Mythical Spirit (IRE)** *James Tate* a63 48
3 b f Dragon Pulse(IRE) Call This Cat (IRE) (One Cool Cat (USA))
1401[5] 1727[4] 3971[6] 4723[3]
**Mythmaker** *Bryan Smart* a111 108
5 b g Major Cadeaux Mythicism (Oasis Dream)
200[6] 572[2] 1772[5] (2611) 3867[2] 6428[7] 8845[2] 9409[3]

**Mythological (IRE)** *Peter Chapple-Hyam* a28 52
2 gr c Galileo(IRE) Pembina (IRE) (Dalakhani (IRE))
**7906**[9] 8353[8] *9336*[8]

**My Time** *Michael Mullineaux* a13 13
8 b g Mind Games Tick Tock (Timeless Times (USA))
**3397**[9]

**My Valentino (IRE)** *Dianne Sayer* a42 60
4 ch g Duke Of Marmalade(IRE) Nadwah (USA) (Shadeed (USA))
***1312***[10] 5701[15]

**Mywayistheonlyway (IRE)** *Grant Tuer* a80 80
4 b g Tamayuz Soul Custody (CAN) (Perfect Soul (IRE))
1910[13] *3255*[6] 3652[7] 4556[5] **(4999)** 5739[6] 6964[15] ***7571***[3]

**Mzoon (IRE)** *Charlie Fellowes* a54 65
2 b f Dark Angel(IRE) Lethal Lena (IRE) (Thousand Words)
**6876**[5] *7877*[5]

**Mzuri (IRE)** *Adrian McGuinness* a74 77
5 b m Tagula(IRE) Meadow (Green Desert (USA))
***6800a***[3]

**Naab (FR)** *John Gosden* a77 72
3 ch c Siyouni(FR) Magdala (FR) (Hawk Wing (USA))
***500***[2]

**Naadheer (IRE)** *F Rohaut* a78
3 ch c Casamento(IRE) Precious Citizen (USA) (Proud Citizen (USA))
*584a*[2]

**Naadirr (IRE)** *Kevin Ryan* a95 99
6 b g Oasis Dream Beach Bunny (IRE) (High Chaparral (IRE))
207a[15] **651a**[6] 696a[5] *1150*[8] 2611[7] 4881[10] 6206[18] *7455*[8] 8383[3] *9247a*[6]

**Naaeebb (USA)** *Saeed bin Suroor* a80 74
3 b c Lonhro(AUS) My Dubai (IRE) (Dubai Millennium)
3714[5] 6268[3] *6899*[5] ***(8711a)***

**Nabbaash** *R Bouresly* a34 43
6 b h Aqlaam Poppo's Song (CAN) (Polish Navy (USA))
**320a**[8] *695a*[7]

**Nabhan** *Bernard Llewellyn* 80
5 b g Youmzain(IRE) Danidh Dubai (IRE) (Noverre (USA))
2574[9] 3067[6] 3574[4] (4966) **5251**[2] 6508[10] 7143[8]

**Nabunga (FR)** *Gianluca Bietolini* a76 93
5 b g Aussie Rules(USA) Grantsville (GER) (Trempolino (USA))
**8733a**[3]

**Nachi Falls** *Nigel Hawke* a69 72
4 ch g New Approach(IRE) Lakuta (IRE) (Pivotal)
*1984*[5] *2164*[4] *3340*[2] **3775**[2]

**Nacida (GER)** *Yasmin Almenrader* a58 83
3 bb f Wiener Walzer(GER) Nacella (GER) (Banyumanik (IRE))
5981a[10] **8462a**[5]

**Nadaitak** *Sir Michael Stoute* a90 91
3 b g Teofilo(IRE) Tanfidh (Marju (IRE))
2175[2] *3209*[3] (4611) **5328**[2]◆ 5682[7] *6580*[2] 7337[6]

**Nadeem Alward (FR)** *F Vermeulen* a72 64
4 b h Exceed And Excel(AUS) Dunes Queen (USA) (Elusive Quality (USA))
***391a***[2]

**Nadia Promise** *William Haggas* 65
3 ch f Galileo(IRE) Majestic Sakeena (IRE) (King's Best (USA))
**4737**[3]

**Nafaath (IRE)** *Donald McCain* a46 68
11 ch g Nayef(USA) Alshakr (Bahri (USA))
*19*[4] **1519**[2] 3193[5] 3494[6]

**Nafaayes (IRE)** *Charles Hills* 63
3 ch f Sea The Stars(IRE) Shamtari (IRE) (Alhaarth (IRE))
**1944**[10]

**Nagamaat (IRE)** *Nikki Evans* a41 52
3 b f Raven's Pass(USA) Shawka (Oasis Dream)
**4042**[6] *7708*[12] *8663*[10] *9217*[12]

**Nagano Gold** *V Luka Jr* a90
3 b c Sixties Icon Never Enough (GER) (Monsun (GER))
***(8976a)***

**Naggers (IRE)** *Paul Midgley* 104
6 ch g Excellent Art Trika (First Trump)
1515[4]◆ (2840)◆ **3324**[2]◆ 4416a[10] 5094[14] 7626[10] 8383[8]

**Nag's Wag (IRE)** *Conor Dore* a78 69
4 b m Approve(IRE) Street Kitty (IRE) (Tiger Hill (IRE))
*25*[12] *575*[7] *808*[7] ***1599***[2] *2335*[5] *(3686)* *(4008)* 4441[3] 4619[5] (5004) 5514[4] 6040[4] *6527*[10] *7320*[6] *8542*[9] *8873*[11]

**Nahuel** *M Delzangles* 81
3 b c Mr. Sidney(USA) Singing Machine (USA) (Rossini (USA))
1460a[4]

**Nailed On Nina (IRE)** *P M Mooney* a64 46
2 b f Tough As Nails(IRE) Anne-Lise (Inchinor)
**6977a**[7] 7593[8]

**Najashee (IRE)** *Owen Burrows* a77 78
3 gr g Invincible Spirit(IRE) Tonnara (IRE) (Linamix (FR))
1961[8] *2997*[3]◆ **(4086)** 6700[7]◆

**Najmah (IRE)** *Ismail Mohammed* a64
2 br f Dawn Approach(IRE) Dream Of The Hill (IRE) (Tiger Hill (IRE))
***5795***[6]

**Nakeeta** *Iain Jardine* a96 113
6 b g Sixties Icon Easy Red (IRE) (Hunting Lion (IRE))
2525[10] 3090[2] 3594[4] **(6447)** 8667a[5]

**Nalaini (IRE)** *Declan Carroll* a38
2 b f Holy Roman Emperor(IRE) Lanark Belle (Selkirk (USA))
***9416***[5]

**Nalout (USA)** *S Seemar* a57
3 br f Afleet Alex(USA) Glory Glory (USA) (Honour And Glory (USA))
***9257a***[8]

**Namar (IRE)** *C Laffon-Parias* a75 70
2 b f Intello(GER) Ballybacka Lady (IRE) (Hurricane Run (IRE))
**5907a**[2]

**Namara (GER)** *Waldemar Hickst*
2 ch f Lord Of England(GER) Nowosti (GER) (Lomitas)
8461a[8]

**Nameitwhatyoulike** *Bryan Smart* a78 111
8 b g Trade Fair Emma Peel (Emarati (USA))
**1491**[5] 2737[10] *4354*[9] 5435[14] 6206[19] **7626**[2] 8044[19]

**Name That Toon** *Derek Shaw* a42 18
4 b m Paco Boy(IRE) Saktoon (USA) (El Prado (IRE))
***64***[4] *852*[8] *1006*[8] *1221*[8]

**Namibie** *H-A Pantall* 77
2 gr f Dark Angel(IRE) Mambia (Aldebaran (USA))
(3679a) **5448a**[10]

**Namirah** *Michael Bell* a48
3 b f Sepoy(AUS) Fairy Efisio (Efisio)
***169***[9]

**Nampara** *Paul D'Arcy* a62 59
2 b f Kyllachy Nurai (Danehill Dancer (IRE))
2502[5] 2750[7] *7482*[4] 7814[16] ***8746***[2]

**Namran (FR)** *P Decouz*
3 b c Medicean Naan (IRE) (Indian Charlie (USA))
847a[8]

**Nanabad (IRE)** *Jarlath P Fahey* a69 93
4 b m Big Bad Bob(IRE) Tequise (IRE) (Victory Note (USA))
**1808a**[5]

**Nancy Hart** *Tom Dascombe* 71
3 b f Sepoy(AUS) Lucky Token (IRE) (Key Of Luck (USA))
**2144**[4] 2587[11] 4797[7] 5185[8]

**Nanny Makfi** *Keith Dalgleish* a15 57
4 b m Makfi Pan Galactic (USA) (Lear Fan (USA))
**2427**[6]

**Nanodes (SWE)** *Lennart Reuterskiold Jr*
4 ch g Helsinki(USA) Swedish Girl (SWE) (Swedish Shave (FR))
*2941a*[2]

**Naples Bay** *John Quinn* a47 64
3 b g Kodiac Trombe (FR) (Bering)
3386[5] 4250[8] **8106**[6]◆ *8722*[11] *8927*[9]

**Napoleon (IRE)** *Laura Mongan* a48
4 b h Jeremy(USA) Desert Drama (IRE) (Green Desert (USA))
***9088***[7] *9455*[11]

**Napoleon Solo** *David Barron* a69 68
5 b g Cockney Rebel(IRE) Trump Street (First Trump)
***426***[7] *583*[10] *1109*[8]

**Napping** *Anabel K Murphy* a60
4 b m Sleeping Indian Vax Rapide (Sharpo)
***1287***[5] *2024*[3] 4092[5] *8823*[3]◆ *9323*[5]

**Naqaawa (IRE)** *Owen Burrows* 74
2 b f Shamardal(USA) Hammiya (IRE) (Darshaan)
5528[6] 7357[7] **8163**[3]

**Naralsaif (IRE)** *Derek Shaw* a53 53
3 b f Arcano(IRE) Mejala (IRE) (Red Ransom (USA))
3626[9] *4003*[11] 4341[10] **5635**[3] 5956[6] 8298[11] *8558*[6]◆ ***9019***[2] *9340*[3]

**Narcos (IRE)** *Richard Fahey* 81
2 bl g Lethal Force(IRE) Western Eyes (IRE) (Rock Of Gibraltar (IRE))
**(5631)** 7613[6]

**Nardo (FR)** *F Foucher* a73 93
7 b g Aussie Rules(USA) Nannetta (IRE) (Mark Of Esteem (IRE))
**8733a**[4]

**Narella (IRE)** *Markus Klug* 103
2 gr f Reliable Man Naomia (GER) (Monsun (GER))
**(6726a)** 7666a[7]

**Narellan (FR)** *F Rohaut* a51
3 bb f Rio De La Plata(USA) Wivenhoe (UAE) (Timber Country (USA))
***427a***[6]

**Nargis Queen (FR)** *P Baudry* a56
4 gr m Slickly(FR) Quiet Queen (Sulamani (IRE))
7069a[11]

**Nargiza (USA)** *Chris Wall* a61 48
3 ch f Elusive Quality(USA) Any For Love (ARG) (Southern Halo (USA))
***5485***[11] 6281[7] *7240*[10]

**Narjes** *Laura Mongan* a80 64
3 b f Sepoy(AUS) Dubai Sea (USA) (Street Sense (USA))
*3188*[2] *4728*[9] *5797*[3] ***6818***[2] *7485*[3] *8150*[6] *9088*[2] *9276*[3]

**Narnia Dawn (IRE)** *F-H Graffard* a80 96
4 b m Roderic O'Connor(IRE) Nordkappe (GER) (High Chaparral (IRE))
**1531a**[9] 2616[7] *5628a*[7]

**Narodowa** *David Lanigan* 65
2 ch f Iffraaj Zacheta (Polish Precedent (USA))
6385[10] **6861**[5] 7399[8]

**Nasee** *Sir Michael Stoute* a51
2 b c Intello(GER) Mischief Making (USA) (Lemon Drop Kid (USA))
***7788***[10]

**Naseem (IRE)** *John Gosden* a91 95
3 br g Sea The Stars(IRE) Chiosina (IRE) (Danehill Dancer (IRE))
2132[4] **4322**[3]

**Nashmiah (KSA)** *N Bachalard* a96
3 b f Alnajim Althakeb(KSA) Qereerah (KSA) (Blue Burner (USA))
***(652a)***

**Nashville (IRE)** *Andrew Crook* a44 62
8 b g Galileo(IRE) Brown Eyes (Danehill (USA))
***3340***[10] 3566[6] 5700[11]

**Nasri** *Emma Owen* a60 42
11 b g Kyllachy Triple Sharp (Selkirk (USA))
*88*[6] *172*[2] *398*[8] *521*[2] *620*[4] *1180*[4] ***(1304)*** *1490*[3] *1723*[11] *2043*[9]

**Nassya** *John Gosden* 65
2 b f Dubawi(IRE) Gemstone (IRE) (Galileo (IRE))
**8380**[5]

**Nastenka** *N Caullery* a68 69
3 b f Aussie Rules(USA) Nezhenka (With Approval (CAN))
*(100)*◆ *439*[5] 2269[6] 2761[6] **(3656)** 7471a[6]

**Natajack** *Richard Fahey* a65 80
3 ch g Showcasing Douro (Manduro (GER))
1513[9] *3188*[7] 3862[7] **(4609)** 5265[4] 5802[6] 7095[5]

**Natalia** *Sarah Hollinshead* a47 44
8 ch m Dutch Art Pintle (Pivotal)
*1545*[9]

**Natalie Express (FR)** *Henry Spiller* a62 62
3 b f Excelebration(IRE) Miss Emma May (IRE) (Hawk Wing (USA))
***9315***[6]

**Natavia** *Roger Charlton* 101
3 ch f Nathaniel(IRE) Our Queen Of Kings (Arazi (USA))
1885[2] **(2827)** 3301[9] 8007[7] 8421[8]

**Natch** *John Gosden* a76
2 b c Nathaniel(IRE) Angara (Alzao (USA))
***9336***[4]◆

**Nathalie** *James Fanshawe* 83
3 b f Nathaniel(IRE) Deirdre (Dubawi (IRE))
2227[4] 3866[5] 5022[2] (6044) **7092**[5]

**Nathan** *Alan King* 98
3 b c Nathaniel(IRE) Maid To Treasure (IRE) (Rainbow Quest (USA))
1967[3]◆ 2783[8] 5075[2] (5589) (6189) **7107**[3]

**Nathania** *Richard Hughes* a68 88
3 ch f Nathaniel(IRE) Glen Rosie (IRE) (Mujtahid (USA))
*1624*[4] (2721)◆ 3535[2] 4364[3] 4829[3] **5715**[2] 6477[4] 7507[7]

**Nathan Mayer** *Sir Michael Stoute* a72 75
3 b g Nathaniel(IRE) Rosacara (Green Desert (USA))
2152[6] **(2588)** *3457*[6] 4156[4]

**Natheer (USA)** *Roger Varian* a75 52
3 rg f Exchange Rate(USA) Ishraak (USA) (Sahm (USA))
***6066***[2] 7227[3] *7826*[4]

**Nathr (USA)** *Doug Watson* a61 40
6 br h Dixie Union(USA) Sweet Rider (USA) (Seeking The Gold (USA))
***(316a)*** ***775a***[2] *1043a*[11]

**Nathra (IRE)** *John Gosden* 115
4 b m Iffraaj Rada (IRE) (Danehill (USA))
5352[6] 6193[3] 6697[2] 7145[2] 7812[3] **8232**[4]

**National Anthem** *John Butler* 68
2 ch c Intikhab(USA) Song Of Passion (IRE) (Orpen (USA))
**7732**[4]

**National Defense** *Mme C Head-Maarek* 119
3 b c Invincible Spirit(IRE) Angel Falls (Kingmambo (USA))
**1689a**[2] 2666a[13]

**National Service (USA)** *Clare Ellam* a48 51
6 b g War Chant(USA) Cotton Club Ballet (USA) (Street Cry (IRE))
*217*[8] *438*[6] *455*[7] ***899***[3] *982*[8] *1372*[4] *1407*[9] 1931a[2] 2454[9] 2669a[3] 4458[11] *4727*[10] 4970[9] (5200a) 5984a[2] (6544a) *7480*[9] 8185[12]

**National Velvet (FR)** *S Dehez* a56 67
3 ch f Sinndar(IRE) Neumark (GER) (High Chaparral (IRE))
**6649a**[7]

**Native Appeal (IRE)** *Charlie Appleby* a79
2 b c Exceed And Excel(AUS) Picture Hat (USA) (El Prado (IRE))
*9050*[3] ***(9313)***

**Native Falls (IRE)** *Alan Swinbank* a52 69
6 ch g Elnadim(USA) Sagrada (GER) (Primo Dominie)
**1721**[10]

**Native Prospect** *Andrew Balding* a82 91
3 ch c Bated Breath Jakarta Jade (IRE) (Royal Abjar (USA))
*(849)* 1518[8] 2088[2] 3005[4] 4800[2] 6094[2] 7107[2] **(7649)**

**Native Soldier (IRE)** *John Flint* a76 82
3 b g Sepoy(AUS) Electra Star (Shamardal (USA))
*2117*[6] 2755[8] 3784[11] **(4537)** 6195[4] 7083[10] 7781[10] *9314*[12]

**Natural (IRE)** *Richard Hannon* 96
2 b f Kodiac Catch The Sea (IRE) (Barathea (IRE))
(3312)◆ 4028[14] **5109**[2] 6354[7]

**Natural History** *Andrew Balding* 73
2 b c Nathaniel(IRE) Film Script (Unfuwain (USA))
**8136**[3]◆

**Naturalist (IRE)** *W McCreery* 84
3 b c Nathaniel(IRE) Vassiana (FR) (Anabaa (USA))
2442a[P]

**Naturally High (FR)** *P Bary* 80
2 b c Camelot Just Little (FR) (Grand Slam (USA))
**5776a**[9]

**Natural Scenery** *Saeed bin Suroor* a109 111
4 b m Dubawi(IRE) Argentina (IRE) (Sadler's Wells (USA))
*(197)*◆ *(728)* *1770*[6] *4356*[2] 5569[4] **6447**[3]◆ 7089[8]

**Nature Boy (IRE)** *Peter Chapple-Hyam* a75 69
3 ch c Intikhab(USA) Miss Latina (IRE) (Mozart (IRE))
**1680**[5]

**Naughty Or Nice (IRE)** *John M Oxx* 92
3 b f Fastnet Rock(AUS) Monty's Girl (IRE) (High Chaparral (IRE))
3995[12] **4928a**[10]

**Naupaka** *Brian Ellison* a68 45
3 b f Haafhd Lily Lenor (IRE) (Bertolini (USA))
*115*[9] *580*[3] ***659***[5] *1029*[6] *1411*[10] 1968[8] 2686[5] 3431[9] 4660[9] 4687[8] 5076[5] *8314*[4] *8720*[9] *9026*[10]

**Nautica (IRE)** *Jonathan Portman* a60
2 ch f Born To Sea(IRE) Moynsha Lady (IRE) (Namid)
***9080***[5]

**Nautical Haven** *Kevin Ryan* a88 45
3 b g Harbour Watch(IRE) Mania (IRE) (Danehill (USA))
***877***◆ 2831[7] ***9241***[2]◆

**Navajo Grey (IRE)** *Michael Appleby* a53 54
3 gr f Dark Angel(IRE) Spring View (Fantastic Light (USA))
*1471*[8] **1967**[8] *2307*[6] 2991[6] 4623[12]

**Navajo Squaw** *Ed Dunlop* 58
2 ch f Sir Percy Navajo Charm (Authorized (IRE))
**7733**[11] 8322[6]◆

**Navajo Star (IRE)** *Michael Appleby* a63 44
3 b f Mastercraftsman(IRE) Champagne Aerial (IRE) (Night Shift (USA))
*545*[10] *717*[4] *1143*[6] *1445*[8] 1968[10] 2705[10] 5142[7] *7537*[4] *(7992)* *(8187)* ***8246***[4] *8674*[4] *9317*[10]

**Navajo Storm (IRE)** *Michael Appleby* a49 57
4 gr m Dark Angel(IRE) Strike Lightly (Rainbow Quest (USA))
5336[5] 6035[5] **6294**[4] 7028[13] 7464[8]

**Navajo Thunder (IRE)** *Michael Appleby* a53 55
3 b f High Chaparral(IRE) Evening Dress (Medicean)
**3053**[5] 4761[6] 5181[P]

**Navajo War Dance** *K R Burke* a83 90
4 bb g Makfi Navajo Rainbow (Rainbow Quest (USA))
**1517**[4] 1964[8] *2787*[3] 3240[8] 4413[8]

**Naval Officer** *Nigel Tinkler* a62 32
2 b c Helmet(AUS) Ariyfa (IRE) (Cape Cross (IRE))
8649[7] ***8915***[4]◆

**Naval Warfare (IRE)** *Andrew Balding* 105
3 b c Born To Sea(IRE) Three Days In May (Cadeaux Genereux)
(2505) 4636[13] 5392[10] (5943) **7275**[4] 7619[14]

**Navaro Girl (IRE)** *P Schiergen* 103
3 b f Holy Roman Emperor(IRE) Neele (IRE) (Peintre Celebre (USA))
4393a[3] 5693a[7] 6710a[5] 7722a[2] **(8270a)** 8622a[6]

**Navarone (IRE)** *Richard Fahey* a72 80
3 b g Casamento(IRE) Flash And Dazzle (IRE) (Bertolini (USA))
1801[5] 2151[3] *2791*[3] (3555)◆ **4075**[2] 5213[4] 5683[8] 6879[7] 7474[5] *7942*[10]

**Navarra Princess (IRE)** *Don Cantillon* a48 46
2 b f Intense Focus(USA) Navarra Queen (Singspiel (IRE))
5162[8] 5665[7] 6055[5] 6609[11] *8783*[7] ***9302***[6]

**Nawassi** *John Gosden* 82
2 b f Dubawi(IRE) Maqaasid (Green Desert (USA))
5938[9] **(8593)**

**Nawwaar (USA)** *A R Al Rayhi* a64 72
8 ch h Distorted Humor(USA) Mostaqeleh (USA) (Rahy (USA))
***9361a***[7]

**Nayel (IRE)** *Richard Hannon* 95
5 b h Acclamation Soliza (IRE) (Intikhab (USA))
**(3905)** 4882[9] 6422[7] 8165[9]

**Nayyar** *Charles Hills* a87 86
3 ch c Exceed And Excel(AUS) Miss Queen (USA) (Miswaki (USA))
***1838***[3] 2130[9] 3672[5]

**Nazzaa (IRE)** *Steve Flook* a55 71
4 b g Shamardal(USA) Multicolour Wave (IRE) (Rainbow Quest (USA))
*2167*[7] 2721[8] *3209*[9] **(6035)**◆ 7567[7]

**Near England (IRE)** *Markus Klug* 107
4 br m Lord Of England(GER) Near Galante (GER) (Galileo (IRE))
**2667a**[6] 6710a[11] 7203a[8]

**Near Kettering** *Luca Cumani* 85
3 ch c Medicean Where's Broughton (Cadeaux Genereux)
2475[4] (3182) 4048[5] 5455[9] **6389**[4] 7024[6]

**Nearly Caught (IRE)** *Hughie Morrison* a103 115
7 b g New Approach(IRE) Katch Me Katie (Danehill (USA))
2288[3] 2667a[2] 3996[9] (4639) **6250a**[4] 6984a[6] 7547[2] 8229[8]

**Nebo (IRE)** *Charles Hills* 109
2 b c Kodiac Kindling (Dr Fong (USA))
(2779)◆ 3925[9] 4906[2] 5570[2] 6446[6] **7394**[3] 8024a[2] (8422)

**Nebuchadnezzar (FR)** *Alan King* 68
2 b g Planteur(IRE) Trexana (Kaldoun (FR))
5106[5] **6859**[4] **7503**[4]◆

**Nebulla** *James Leavy* 84
5 ch g Iffraaj Kelowna (IRE) (Pivotal)
**5582a**[5]

**Needless Shouting (IRE)** *Joanne Foster* a12 26
6 b g Footstepsinthesand Ring The Relatives (Bering)
**2032**[9]

**Need To Know (SAF)** *A R Al Rayhi* a104 95
8 b g Western Winter(USA) Promisefrommyheart (SAF) (Elliodor (FR))
**86a**[7] *204a*[6] *432a*[7]

**Neeraan (USA)** *Roger Varian* a74 76
2 gr c Mizzen Mast(USA) Ishraak (USA) (Sahm (USA))
5876[4] *7726*[5] **8353**[4]

**Neeran** *H-F Devin* 70
2 b f Style Vendome(FR) Bea Remembered (Doyen (IRE))
**3515a**[2]

**Nefetari** *Alan Brown* a52 47
4 b m Kodiac Town And Gown (Oasis Dream)
***357***[5] *899*[10] 3915[5] 4174[7] 4847[11] *5418*[9] 6046[10]

**Neguev (IRE)** *J-C Rouget* 105
3 b c So You Think(NZ) Lady Bering (Bering)
**4235a**[3] 6172a[5]

**Ne Jamais Renoncer (IRE)** *J-C Rouget* a66
2 b c Most Improved(IRE) Supreme Quest (Exceed And Excel (AUS))
***5952a***[7]

**Nellie Deen (IRE)** *Simon West* a46 47
4 b m Dream Ahead(USA) Dorothy Dene (Red Ransom (USA))
1237[5] 5007[10] 5283[6] 5620[5] 6045[6] 6437[11] 6528[5] 8259[10] 8591[10] 8719[10] 9031[4]

**Nellie's Dancer** *Scott Dixon* a63 59
3 b f Mount Nelson Xaphania (Sakhee (USA))
2470[8] 3387[8] 4303[9] 4766[2] 5741[7] 6112[3] 6850[2] 8256[2] 8656[2] 8774[3] 8807[12]

**Nelson (IRE)** *A P O'Brien* 110
2 b c Frankel Moonstone (Dalakhani (IRE))
(6955a) 7616[2]◆

**Nelson River** *Clive Cox* 61
2 b g Mount Nelson I Say (IRE) (Oratorio (IRE))
6869[8] 7543[10] 7955[7]

**Nelson's Bay** *Wilf Storey* a59 46
8 b g Needwood Blade In Good Faith (USA) (Dynaformer (USA))
44[8]◆ 969[12] (1125) 1473[12] 2082[11] 2378[6] 2918[8] 3402[16] 4262[7] 4690[10] 5181[6] 5254[7] 8590[13] 8720[5]

**Nelson's Hill** *William de Best-Turner* a28
7 b g Mount Nelson Regal Step (Royal Applause)
9435[8]

**Nelson's Touch** *Denis Coakley* a75 71
4 gr g Mount Nelson Lady Friend (Environment Friend)
5894[3] 6623[4] 7462[3] 8565[8]

**Neola** *Mick Channon* 92
2 b f Foxwedge(AUS) Effie B (Sixties Icon)
1966[5] (2583)◆ 2801[2] 3960[5] 5391[6] 5659[6] 6354[8] (6778) 7090[15] 8001[10] 8412[7] 8562[5]

**Neolithic (USA)** *Todd Pletcher* a114
4 bb h Harlan's Holiday(USA) Swingit (USA) (Victory Gallop (CAN))
469a[3] 1380a[3]

**Neorealism (JPN)** *Noriyuki Hori* 120
6 ch h Neo Universe(JPN) Tokio Reality (USA) (Meadowlake (USA))
9171a[3]

**Nepal (GER)** *Dr A Bolte* 105
4 b m Kallisto(GER) Nassau (GER) (Soldier Hollow)
2450a[5] 4392a[3]

**Nepeta (USA)** *Mark Johnston* a70 71
3 ch f Kitten's Joy(USA) La Coruna (USA) (Thunder Gulch (USA))
6091[8] 6551[4] 7032[5] 7992[11]

**Neptune Star** *Michael Easterby* a42 49
3 b f Born To Sea(IRE) Nimbus Star (Nayef (USA))
76[9] 288[8] 554[4] 2228[6] 2911[12]◆ 3423[7] 4971[9] 5215[7] 6048[7] 6470[4] 7325[8]

**Nerud (USA)** *A Wohler* 94
3 bb c Bernardini(USA) Night Lagoon (GER) (Lagunas)
2246a[6]

**Neshmeya** *Charles Hills* 92
3 b f Lawman(FR) High Heeled (IRE) (High Chaparral (IRE))
2131[7] (3866) 6152[3] (7816)◆ 8598[7]

**Ness Of Brodgar** *Mark H Tompkins* 30
2 b f Harbour Watch(IRE) Missouri (Charnwood Forest (IRE))
8593[9]

**Nest Love (FR)** *J-P Gallorini* 75
3 b f Sageburg(IRE) Nid D'Amour (FR) (Ultimately Lucky (IRE))
2978a[9]

**Neteb (FR)** *J-L Guillochon* 43
2 gr f Style Vendome(FR) Dalakiya (FR) (King's Best (USA))
7415a[9]

**Netley Abbey** *Karen George* a51 43
3 b g Myboycharlie(IRE) Ana Style (FR) (Anabaa Blue)
1726[5] 2027[6] 2679[9] 3326[7] 4978[6] 5846[3] 8815[14] 9221[12]

**Nevalyashka** *Marcus Tregoning* a66 53
3 b f Sir Percy Ninotchka (USA) (Nijinsky (CAN))
7652[5] 8151[6] 8663[4] 9027[10] 9235[5]

**Nevasca (IRE)** *Lydia Pearce* a22 10
3 gr g Invincible Spirit(IRE) Snowdrops (Gulch (USA))
2090[13] 2798[9] 5611[14]

**Neve (GER)** *Yasmin Almenrader* a19 60
5 b m Tertullian(USA) Navalde (GER) (Alkalde (GER))
7204a[10]

**Never A Word (USA)** *Oliver Greenall* a73 54
3 br g Lonhro(AUS) Janetstickettocats (USA) (Storm Cat (USA))
6236[8] 7476[10] 8209[9] 8497[4] 8814[7] 8993[8] 9270[6]

**Never Back Down (IRE)**
*Hugo Palmer* a100 88
2 b c Kodiac Steer By The Stars (IRE) (Pivotal)
1858[2] (2148) 7821[6] 8412[5] (9156)

**Neverbeen To Paris (IRE)**
*Michael Bell* a63 69
2 b g Champs Elysees Island Paradise (IRE) (Trans Island)
3965[7] 5749[2] 6093[3]

**Never Compromise (FR)**
*Henk Grewe* a55 86
4 b g Astronomer Royal(USA) Noor Forever (FR) (Highest Honor (FR))
4233a[3]

**Never Folding (IRE)**
*Seamus Durack* a61 55
3 b f Requinto(IRE) Sarella Loren (USA) (Theatrical (IRE))
96[4]◆ 962[2] 1333[11] 1550[5] 2726[13] 4754[4] 6069[10] 7323[6]◆ 7945[7] 8538[2]◆ 8799[2]

**Never Give In** *John Weymes* a22 50
4 b g Alfred Nobel(IRE) Mad Annie (USA) (Anabaa (USA))
3910[7] 4105[9] 4509[15]

**Never Say (IRE)** *Sam England* a39 48
4 b m Monsieur Bond(IRE) Wong Again (Araafa (IRE))
334[7] 607[5] 969[7] 2591[6] 3529[5] 3564[2] 4660[2] 4980[10] 9077[11] 9368[11]

**Never Surrender (IRE)**
*Charles Hills* 91
3 b g High Chaparral(IRE) Meiosis (USA) (Danzig (USA))
1497[2] 2084[5] (2527) 3998[7] 4612[7] 5525[9] 6474[9]

**Never To Be (USA)** *Nikki Evans* a67 70
6 b g Thewayyouare(USA) Kitty Foille (USA) (Black Minnaloushe (USA))
222[11] 1084[6] 1298[14]

**Neverushacon (IRE)**
*Mrs John Harrington* 80
6 b g Echo Of Light Lily Beth (IRE) (Desert King (IRE))
7860a[5]

**Never You Mind (IRE)** *Charles Hills* 52
3 b g Bated Breath Bimini (Sadler's Wells (USA))
1514[7] 1730[15] 1862[7] 4350[16]

**New Abbey Angel (IRE)**
*Keith Dalgleish* a56 60
4 gr g Dark Angel(IRE) Alinda (IRE) (Revoque (IRE))
1125[9] 2342[2] 2501[2] 3196[6] 3529[6] 3977[4] 4853[5] 5254[6] 5997[2] 6352[7] 6690[3] 8205[11] 8662[2] 9221[2]

**New Agenda** *Paul Webber* a86 90
5 b g New Approach(IRE) Prove (Danehill (USA))
1598[3] 6007[2] 6701[3]

**New Bidder** *David Barron* 99
6 bb g Auction House(USA) Noble Nova (Fraam)
3593[13] 4411[13]

**Newborough** *Charles Hills* a51 48
2 b g Farhh Comeraincomeshine (IRE) (Night Shift (USA))
6403[16] 7273[10] 8339[9]

**New Bresil (FR)** *S Wattel* a58
2 ch c Dylan Thomas(IRE) Miss Recif (IRE) (Exit To Nowhere (USA))
4678a[7]

**Newcomer** *E Leenders* a59
3 ch f New Approach(IRE) Khor Sheed (Dubawi (IRE))
8692a[6]

**New Decade** *Jim Goldie* a40 41
8 ch g Pivotal Irresistible (Cadeaux Genereux)
1978[10] 2454[15] 2949[5] 3196[11] 3387[7] 3704[8] 4687[4] 5206[8] 5467[10] 5991[7]

**New Delhi (IRE)** *Mark Johnston* a55 61
3 ch f Sepoy(AUS) Crossover (Cape Cross (IRE))
2898[3] 3259[5] 3931[3] 4473[6] 4687[9]

**New Empire** *Peter Chapple-Hyam* a68 78
2 b g Kodiac Quantum (IRE) (Alhaarth (IRE))
2769[7] 3782[4]◆ 3993[16] 4527[10] 5596[2] 7335[3] 8420[7] 8871[5]

**Newgate Duchess** *Tony Coyle* 22
3 b f Haafhd Arctic Queen (Linamix (FR))
6044[6] 7629[7] 8477[6] 8650[6]

**Newgate Sioux** *Tony Coyle* a33 48
3 b f Sleeping Indian Rio's Girl (Captain Rio)
2223[8] 2897[6] 3285[7] 4107[14] 6469[9] 8558[7]

**New Identity (IRE)** *W J Martin* a43 63
6 b g Rock Of Gibraltar(IRE) Zaafran (Singspiel (IRE))
(5567)

**Newmarket Warrior (IRE)**
*Iain Jardine* a77 73
6 b g Dalakhani(IRE) Heavens Peak (Pivotal)
44[4] 655[3] (1473) 1677[3] 3181[8] 4039[11] 4661[7] 7570[2] 7981[4] (8209) 8929[3] 9100[4]

**New Money Honey (USA)**
*Chad C Brown* a101 110
3 b f Medaglia d'Oro(USA) Weekend Whim (USA) (Distorted Humor (USA))
(4650a) 8071a[6]

**New Rich** *Eve Johnson Houghton* a66 53
7 b g Bahamian Bounty Bling Bling (IRE) (Indian Ridge (IRE))
171[2] 302[7] 815[4] 1080[8] 1723[9] 2091[3] 3084[5] 3660[5] 7952[4] 8675[4] 8949[4]

**New Road Side** *Richard Guest* a82 84
4 b m Paco Boy(IRE) Spring Green (Bahamian Bounty)
995[7] 1110[2] 1777[13] 3253[3] 3492[7] 3667[11] 4433[7] 4566[8] 4850[7]

**New Show (IRE)** *Kevin Ryan* 80
2 b c New Approach(IRE) Music Show (IRE) (Noverre (USA))
(5465)◆

**New Signal** *S bin Ghadayer* a22 23
4 b g New Approach(IRE) Davie's Lure (USA) (Lure (USA))
8711a[14]

**New Society (IRE)** *James Bethell* a79 74
3 b g Rock Of Gibraltar(IRE) Ajiaal (Cape Cross (IRE))
2408[6] (3180)◆ 3711[4] 4436[2] 5832[2] 7031[4]

**Newspeak (IRE)** *Fred Watson* a24 53
5 b g New Approach(IRE) Horatia (IRE) (Machiavellian (USA))
2496[7] 3945[2] 5466[12]

**Newstead Abbey**
*Michael Herrington* a74 48
7 b g Byron Oatcake (Selkirk (USA))
783[8] 989[3] 1346[7] 1890[6] 2464[6] 3897[13] 4616[10] (6156) 6635[2] (6850) 7408[4] 7881[7] 8434[10] 8874[8] (9176)

**New Strategy (IRE)** *E Charpy* a57 76
5 b g Lawman(FR) Kate The Great (Xaar)
203a[6]

**Newt** *Chris Wall* a63 73
3 b f Sixties Icon Froglet (Shaamit (IRE))
2686[7] (3276)◆ 4045[3] 4790[2] 8487[9] 9178[8]

**New Tale** *Olly Williams* a49 50
3 b g Harbour Watch(IRE) Perfect Story (IRE) (Desert Story (IRE))
1513[12] 1977[5] 2682[7] 3543[3] 4447[12] 8395[13] 9030[4] 9365[3]

**New Tarabela** *Tony Carroll* a60 48
6 ch g New Approach(IRE) Tarabela (CHI) (Hussonet (USA))
645[8] 1191[11]

**Newton Heath (IRE)**
*Daniel Mark Loughnane* a47
3 b g Casamento(IRE) Carpet Lover (IRE) (Fayruz)
48[8] 331[8] 662[9] 1564[7] 2060[12] 2507[13]◆

**New To Town (IRE)** *J S Bolger* 85
2 br f New Approach(IRE) Tiffed (USA) (Seattle Slew (USA))
7421a[8]

**Newtown Cross (IRE)** *Jimmy Fox* a57 48
7 ch g Kheleyf(USA) Sacred Pearl (IRE) (Daylami (IRE))
436[3] 859[5] 1303[8]

**New World Power (JPN)**
*David Simcock* a78 90
4 b h Deep Impact(JPN) Listen (IRE) (Sadler's Wells (USA))
2386[5] 3947[2] 4712[2] 5287[6] 6135[5] 6849[3]

**New Youmzain (FR)** *Lucy Normile* 69
8 b g Sinndar(IRE) Luna Sacra (FR) (Sadler's Wells (USA))
5468[7] 7047[3]◆ 7700[4] 7983[8]

**Newz Watch** *Mick Quinn* a53 55
3 ch f Harbour Watch(IRE) Angus Newz (Compton Place)
1605[9]

**Nexius (IRE)** *Emma Lavelle* a74 104
8 b g Catcher In The Rye(IRE) Nicolaia (GER) (Alkalde (GER))
467[9]

**Next Challenge (GER)**
*Saeed bin Suroor* a79 82
3 ch g Shamardal(USA) Next Holy (IRE) (Holy Roman Emperor (IRE))
2039[3]

**Next Edition (IRE)** *Philip Kirby* a66 67
9 b g Antonius Pius(USA) Starfish (IRE) (Galileo (IRE))
1197[7] 1834[9]

**Next Stage** *Saeed bin Suroor* a79 103
4 ch h Dubawi(IRE) Dash To The Front (Diktat)
(1860)◆ 2396[2] (Dead)

**Next Train's Gone** *James Eustace* a87 59
4 b g Rail Link Coh Sho No (Old Vic)
(2021) (3138)

**Nezar (IRE)** *Dean Ivory* a84 84
6 ch g Mastercraftsman(IRE) Teddy Bears Picnic (Oasis Dream)
808[12] 1062[6] 1290[2] (1631) 2608[4] 3518[2] 6794[4] 7508[2] 8319[11] 8645[2] 8881[2] 9124[5] 9339[5]

**Nezwaah** *Roger Varian* a108 115
4 b m Dubawi(IRE) Ferdoos (Dansili)
(2954)◆ (4419a) 6356[4] 8098a[5] 8606a[10]

**Nibiru (IRE)** *A J Martin* 86
2 b c Casamento(IRE) Cnocan Gold (IRE) (Danehill Dancer (IRE))
8440a[6]

**Niblawi (IRE)** *Neil Mulholland* a95 98
5 b g Vale Of York(IRE) Finnmark (Halling (USA))
4118[5] 5397[2]◆ 5913[4] 6857[5] 8740[11]

**Nibras Again** *Ismail Mohammed* a73 75
3 b g Kyllachy Regina (Green Desert (USA))
2072[5] 3038[5] 3673[4] 4624[2] 5132[12] 6067[7]

**Nibras Galaxy (IRE)**
*Ismail Mohammed* a70 67
2 b c Nathaniel(IRE) Galaxy Dancer (USA) (Kingmambo (USA))
8136[6] 8678[7] 8903[3]

**Nice Name (IRE)** *Marco Gasparini* 95
4 b h Royal Applause Grand Zafeen (Zafeen (FR))
7442a[4]

**Nice Shot (IRE)** *David Simcock* a81
2 b c Kodiac Emma Dora (IRE) (Medaglia d'Oro (USA))
7513[8] 8915[3] (9137)

**Nice To See You (FR)** *Robert Collet* a102 105
4 b h Siyouni(FR) Around Me (IRE) (Johannesburg (USA))
5979a[11] 6648a[12] 7636a[6] 9274a[5]

**Nice Vintage (IRE)** *Katie Scott*
5 bb m Big Bad Bob(IRE) High Vintage (IRE) (High Chaparral (IRE))
8929[8] 9100[12]

**Nicholas T** *Jim Goldie* a69 96
5 b g Rail Link Thorntoun Piccolo (Groom Dancer (USA))
782[9] 1677[8] (2133) 2457[2] 2772[3] (2952)◆ (4077) 4475[7] 4961[3]◆ 5393[14] 5914[2] 6449[9] 7619[26] 8009[7]

**Nicklaus** *William Haggas* a70 73
2 ch g Exceed And Excel(AUS) Nianga (GER) (Lomitas)
4266[6] 7511[5] (8212)

**Nick Vedder** *Michael Wigham* a77 55
3 b g Rip Van Winkle(IRE) Devotion (IRE) (Dylan Thomas (IRE))
198[3] (1470) 2118[8] 3317[12] 4304[3] 9464[3]

**Nicky Baby (IRE)** *Dean Ivory* a47 61
3 gr g Dark Angel(IRE) Moon Club (IRE) (Red Clubs (IRE))
160[6] 463[4] 875[5] 4006[11] 5339[4] 8329[15] 8659[10] 8949[9] 9128[7] 9391[9]

**Nidnod** *John Bridger* a65 51
4 b m Myboycharlie(IRE) Littlemisstutti (IRE) (Noverre (USA))
88[8] 143[10] 438[5] 739[7] 860[10]

**Niedziela (IRE)** *C Lerner* a91 94
3 b f Henrythenavigator(USA) Kartica (Rainbow Quest (USA))
3612a[5] 4027a[5] 8986a[9]

**Nietzsche** *Brian Ellison* a62 89
4 ch g Poet's Voice Ganga (IRE) (Generous (IRE))
7150[5] 7860a[15]

**Nifty Niece (IRE)** *Ann Duffield* a28 60
3 gr f Zebedee Hasty Harriet (IRE) (Choisir (AUS))
1715[5]◆ 2897[16] 3525[10] 6571[9] 8590[7] 9072[9]

**Nigh Or Never (IRE)**
*Rebecca Curtis* a40 63
3 b g Excelebration(IRE) Nigh (IRE) (Galileo (IRE))
1730[7] 2366[7] 2903[4] 3745[11] 6370[7]

**Night Air** *Derek Shaw*
2 b f Pastoral Pursuits Night Kiss (FR) (Night Shift (USA))
5534[14] 5891[9] 7732[9]

**Night Call (FR)** *A Spanu* a58 57
4 b m Silver Frost(IRE) Udina (Unfuwain (USA))
4233a[9]

**Night Circus (IRE)** *Charlie Appleby* 96
3 b g Invincible Spirit(IRE) Surrealism (Pivotal)
(1857)◆ 2401[5] 4507[4] 5943[2] 7053[3]◆ 7549[6]

**Nightdress (IRE)** *Tony Coyle* 43
3 b f Rip Van Winkle(IRE) Haute Volta (FR) (Grape Tree Road)
1676[6] 2841[9] 3206[5] 4602[9] 5374[9]

**Night Generation (GER)**
*Chris Gordon* a69 68
5 ch g Sholokhov(IRE) Night Woman (GER) (Monsun (GER))
141[5] 395[3] 859[2] (2332) 3685[2] 4000[3] 7490[8] 8072[8] 9324[7]

**Nightingale Valley** *Stuart Kittow* a83 82
4 ch m Compton Place Dancing Storm (Trans Island)
(1599) 3214[5] 4495[2] 5558[2] 6321[10]

**Night Law** *Barry John Murphy* a46 58
3 b f Lawman(FR) Night Carnation (Sleeping Indian)
3462[4] 3982[4] 4437[5] 5383[8] 5697[5] 9019[13]

**Night Myth (IRE)** *Richard Hannon*
2 b f Epaulette(AUS) Angel Nights (IRE) (Night Shift (USA))
6584[10] 7022[9]

**Night Of Glory** *Andrew Balding* a78 99
3 b g Sea The Stars(IRE) Kesara (Sadler's Wells (USA))
4032[10] 4863[7] 6445[14] 7615[2] 7931[5]

**Night Poetry (IRE)** *Charlie Appleby* a49
3 b f Sea The Stars(IRE) Aquila D'Oriente (ITY) (Dubawi (IRE))
424[3] 1143[8]

**Night Queen (GER)**
*Frau Erika Mader* 85
5 b m Areion(GER) Najinskaja (GER) (Tannenkonig (IRE))
8463a[5]

**Night Run (FR)** *Y Al Blooshi* 58
5 gr h Martaline Spring Morning (FR) (Ashkalani (IRE))
322a[13] 537a[9]

**Night Shadow** *Alan Brown* a63 48
3 ch g Haafhd Totally Trusted (Oasis Dream)
402[7] 731[4] 960[4] (1193) 3184[8] 8721[9] 8930[11] 9019[11] 9267[9]

**Night Spark (GER)** *Ralph Beckett* a49 39
2 b g Soldier Hollow Nocturna (GER) (Dai Jin)
6653[14] 9417[7]

**Nightswift** *James Evans* a56 46
5 b g Midnight Legend Sharbasia (IRE) (King's Best (USA))
5285[4] 5714[5] 6306[6]

**Nikita (IRE)** *Hughie Morrison* a47
2 b f Exceed And Excel(AUS) Rosinka (IRE) (Soviet Star (USA))
9198[6]

**Nimble Alpha (FR)** *R Roels* a27 25
6 bb g Authorized(IRE) Nouvelle Amie (GER) (Noverre (USA))
7534a[7]

**Nimr** *Richard Fahey* a107 87
4 b g Shamardal(USA) Riberac (Efisio)
199[6] (598) (1148)◆ 1492[20] 1773[2] 2150[4]

**Nine Below Zero** *Ralph Beckett* 90
2 b c Showcasing Finesse (Shamardal (USA))
(3083) (3406)◆ 3993[12] 4866[8] 7741[5]

**Ninedarter** *Antony Brittain* a19 37
3 b g Monsieur Bond(IRE) Caranbola (Lucky Story (USA))
3948[6] 4164[P] 8217[8] 8558[8]

**Nine Ou Four (IRE)** *V Luka Jr* a75 78
6 b h Medicean Neutrina (IRE) (Hector Protector (USA))
81a[5]

**Ninepin Bowler** *Michael Dods* a70 71
3 b g Rip Van Winkle(IRE) Smooth As Silk (IRE) (Danehill Dancer (IRE))
1347[3] 1829[4] 2185[6] 7568[8]

**Ninety Years Young** *David Elsworth* a67 64
3 b g Paco Boy(IRE) Lady Of Windsor (IRE) (Woods Of Windsor (USA))
178[3] 458[5]

**Ningara** *Mohammed Jassim Ghazali* a98 99
7 b g Singspiel(IRE) Garanciere (FR) (Anabaa (USA))
934a[16]

**Ninian Des Aigles (FR)**
*Mme C Barande-Barbe* a72 66
3 b g Le Houssais(FR) Boum Des Aigles (FR) (Slickly (FR))
3554a[7]

**Ninjago** *Paul Midgley* a94 90
7 b g Mount Nelson Fidelio's Miracle (USA) (Mountain Cat (USA))
957[5] 1454[9] 1515[3] 1831[6] 2736[11] 3324[5] 4037[8] 4353[8] 5671[8] 5947[5] (6429) 7405[3] 7737[3] 8645[7]

**Nip Down The Jug** *Michael Attwater* 50
3 b g Piccolo The City Kid (IRE) (Danetime (IRE))
3660[7] 4180[13] 4754[10]

**Niqnaaqpaadiwaaq** *Eric Alston* a62 70
5 b g Aqlaam Aswaaq (IRE) (Peintre Celebre (USA))
2120[11] 3666[15] 5827[8] 7046[6] 7980[8] 8956[8]

**Niron (GER)** *M Mayer* 70
8 b h Mamool(IRE) Ninon (GER) (Zinaad)
2667a[13]

**Niseko** *William Muir* 66
3 b g Cacique(IRE) Snow Crystal (IRE) (Kingmambo (USA))
2476[12] 3393[5] 3939[2] 4172[6] 4697[7]

**Nisham (IRE)** *J Phelippon* a84 81
5 b g Footstepsinthesand Jailamigraine (IRE) (King Charlemagne (USA))
2696a[9]

**Nitro** *Roy Brotherton* a10 15
3 b g Fight Club(GER) Come On Molly (Dreams End)
4964[7] 6808[6] 7230[5] 8117[9] 8774[7] 8995[10]

**Noah Amor (IRE)** *David O'Meara* a75 78
4 b g Kodiac Jumbo Romance (IRE) (Tagula (IRE))
330[9] 732[3] (1674) (1973) 2305[2] (2627) 3238[4] 4013[5] 5514[3] (6089) 6670[2] 6891[2] 7137[5] 7486[2] 7939[12] 8260[4]

**Noah From Goa (SAF)** *M F De Kock* 109
4 ch g Tiger Ridge(USA) Limerick (SAF) (Fort Wood (USA))
320a[3]◆ 774a[2]

**Nobelium (USA)** *R Bouresly* a92 97
3 br c Sky Mesa(USA) Striking Example (USA) (Empire Maker (USA))
649a[2] 887a[5] 1040a[4]

**Noble Act** *Phil McEntee* a73 65
4 b m Kyllachy Noble Desert (FR) (Green Desert (USA))
161[7] 984[4] 1326[5] 1755[8] 3265[4] 3971[9] 4566[10] 5239[11] 6156[6]

**Noble Agrippina (GER)** *E Lyon* a24 58
4 bb m Manduro(GER) Nouvelle Noblesse (GER) (Singspiel (IRE))
1181a[2]

**Noble Asset** *Milton Bradley* a71 78
6 ch g Compton Place Chance For Romance (Entrepreneur)
95[5] 330[4] 604[3] 1328[7] 1340[7]

**Noble Aussie (IRE)** *Miss Nicole McKenna* a43 46
6 gr g Aussie Rules(USA) Nobilissima (IRE) (Orpen (USA))
9261[9]

**Noble Ballad** *Ralph Beckett* a63 45
3 b g Royal Applause Melody Maker (Diktat)
210[8] 5545[8] (6529) 8328[10] 8801[5] 9307[7]

**Noble Behest** *Robert Stephens* a84 72
3 b g Sir Percy Lady Hestia (USA) (Belong To Me (USA))
1962[7] 3087[10] (6023) (6661) (7412) (9324)

**Noble Bird (USA)** *Mark Casse* a115
6 ch h Birdstone(USA) Anyhow (USA) (Tiznow (USA))
469a[6]

**Noble Conquest (FR)** *Sir Michael Stoute* a74 88
3 b g Siyouni(FR) Visualize (Medicean)
2475[3] 2997[5] 5670[2] 8344[14]

**Noble Deed** *Michael Attwater* a68 56
7 ch g Kyllachy Noble One (Primo Dominie)
116[5] 355[11] 815[3] 1080[6] 1427[4] 2091[2] 2367[2] 2962[6] 3522[8] 3941[3] 4179[7] 5791[12] 7957[8] 8551[12] 9470[6]

**Noble Expression** *Roger Varian* a79 53
2 b c Sir Percy Disposition (Selkirk (USA))
7929[8] 8643[6] (8903)◆

**Noble Gift** *William Knight* a104 104
7 ch g Cadeaux Genereux Noble Penny (Pennekamp (USA))
1502[6] (2261) 2999[2] 4316[3] 5353[10] 5500[5] 6698[10] 7602[4] 8468[3]

**Nobleman (GER)** *Hughie Morrison* a56 57
3 b g Lord Of England(GER) Naomia (GER) (Monsun (GER))
2027[7]◆ 2395[9] 3489[8] 4348[10]

**Noble Manners (IRE)** *Mark Johnston* 77
2 b f Myboycharlie(IRE) New Story (USA) (Dynaformer (USA))
1884[4] 2221[2]◆ 2948[6] 3712[3] 4716[4] (5366) 6561[5] 7251[5]

**Nobleman's Nest** *Simon Crisford* 93
2 br c Poet's Voice Tamzin (Hernando (FR))
4567[2]◆ (5365) 6446[10] (7050) 8039[7]

**Noble Masterpiece** *Sir Michael Stoute* a88 81
3 ch g Dutch Art Elysian (Galileo (IRE))
2580[10] 3970[3] 5431[4] (6485) 6792[2] 7340[5]

**Noble Peace** *Lydia Pearce* a91 93
4 b g Kyllachy Peace Concluded (Bertolini (USA))
2093[5] 2606[18] (3030) 3777[3] 4524[5] 5530[2] 6192[6] 6879[4] 7404[5] (8078) 9186[6]

**Noble Star (IRE)** *James Fanshawe* a80 84
4 b g Acclamation Wrong Answer (Verglas (IRE))
277[3] 7404[2]◆ 7947[4]

**Noble Sword** *Jedd O'Keeffe* a43 54
3 b g Sayif(IRE) Noble Nova (Fraam)
2033[6] 2595[7] 2924[6] 3403[F] 4107[13]

**Noble Thought (USA)** *Malcolm Pierce* 104
4 bb h Harlan's Holiday(USA) No Use Denying (USA) (Maria's Mon (USA))
7178a[6]

**Nobly Born** *John Gosden* 107
3 ch c Mayson Noble One (Primo Dominie)
4407[3] 5423[4]◆ 5916[4]◆ 6922[6] (7782)

**Nobody's Fault (USA)** *Neil Pessin* 94
4 b m Blame(USA) Appealing Storm (USA) (Valid Appeal (USA))
1813a[2]

**Nobrassnolass (IRE)** *Tom Dascombe* 58
2 b f Kodiac Hams (USA) (Dixie Union (USA))
1673[4] 1909[8] 2556[6] 3215[6] 6609[8]

**No Civil Justice** *David Thompson*
2 b g Milk It Mick Flashing Floozie (Muhtarram (USA))
8649[8]

**No Comment (DEN)** *Bent Olsen* a68 87
4 b h Naaqoos Vytinna (FR) (Victory Note (USA))
2943a[3] 4940a[8]

**Nocturn** *Ronald Harris* a54 80
8 b g Oasis Dream Pizzicato (Statoblest)
1080[11]

**No Damage (IRE)** *Michael Attwater*
3 ch f Roderic O'Connor(IRE) Flashing Blade (Inchinor)
6283[10] 7768[10]

**No Education** *John James Feane* 93
4 b g Showcasing Ceilidh Band (Celtic Swing)
8438a[11]

**Noguchi (IRE)** *Chris Dwyer* a73 69
12 ch g Pivotal Tuscania (USA) (Woodman (USA))
315[2] 440[10] 853[2] 1073[6] 1436[5] 1754[2] 2111[9] 4158[4]

**No I'm Easy (IRE)** *Tom Dascombe* 81
2 b c Zoffany(IRE) Caribbean Queen (IRE) (Celtic Swing)
5350[2] (6264) 7394[8]

**Noir Intense (FR)** *J-P Gauvin* a65
3 b g Silver Frost(IRE) Holiday Maker (Dubai Destination (USA))
6496a[3]

**Noivado (IRE)** *G M Lyons* a105 94
3 b g Casamento(IRE) Maybe I Will (IRE) (Hawk Wing (USA))
1742a[2] 6961a[17]

**No Joy (USA)** *C Ferland* 87
3 b c Kitten's Joy(USA) Underwater (USA) (Theatrical (IRE))
5982a[10]

**Nolohay (IRE)** *Doug Watson* a91 81
6 ch g Dubawi(IRE) Antiquia (Singspiel (IRE))
699a[13] 8714a[4]

**Nomadic (IRE)** *Miss B Deutrom* a35 36
4 ch h Raven's Pass(USA) Turkana Girl (Hernando (FR))
9257a[10]

**Nomorecalls (IRE)** *Robert Cowell* a75 65
2 b g Dawn Approach(IRE) Semayyel (IRE) (Green Desert (USA))
3460[3]

**No More Commisery (IRE)** *Mick Quinn* a61
2 b f Dandy Man(IRE) Lady Bracknell (IRE) (Definite Article)
7450[4] 8819[6] 9188[5]

**Nomorerichblondes (USA)** *A bin Harmash* a97
3 b f Hard Spun(USA) Miss Luann (USA) (Unbridled's Song (USA))
317a[7] 652a[2] (889a) 1375a[14]

**No More Thrills** *Richard Hannon* a62 60
2 ch f Dutch Art The Thrill Is Gone (Bahamian Bounty)
7724[3] 8388[6]

**Nonchalant** *Hugo Froud* a68 96
6 gr g Oasis Dream Comeback Queen (Nayef (USA))
(46) 214[6] 648[12]

**Noneedtotellme (IRE)** *James Unett* a48 44
4 gr m Fast Company(IRE) Gemma's Delight (IRE) (Clodovil (IRE))
5512[5] 6748[8] 8242[4] 9129[9] 9267[3] 9420[4]

**Nonios (IRE)** *David Simcock* a90 77
5 b g Oasis Dream Young And Daring (USA) (Woodman (USA))
885[3]◆ 7358[9] 8078[7] 9055[8] 9271[5]

**Nonnie And Norny** *Shaun Harris* 30
3 b f Frozen Power(IRE) Sophie'Jo (Agnes World (USA))
1259[6] 1471[10] 2180[9] 3701[9] 5040[8] 7213[11]

**Nonno Giulio (IRE)** *Conor Dore* a67 81
6 ch g Halling(USA) Contrary (IRE) (Mark Of Esteem (IRE))
2685[13] 3049[7] 4059[4] (4105) 4554[8] 5119[8] 5341[7] 5544[3] 5835[14] 6681[4] 7006[6] 7481[10] 7606[8]

**No No Cardinal (IRE)** *Mark Gillard* a46 51
8 ch g Touch Of Land(FR) Four Moons (IRE) (Cardinal Flower)
621[8] 739[4] 966[6]

**No Not Again (IRE)** *Richard Hannon* a66 71
3 b c Roderic O'Connor(IRE) Bella Bella (IRE) (Sri Pekan (USA))
209[3] 434[6] 987[2] 1421[3] 1580[2] 2293[4]

**Nonza (FR)** *H-F Devin* a88
3 b f Zanzibari(USA) Terra Alta (FR) (Kaldounevees (FR))
8885a[2]

**Noodles Blue Boy** *Ollie Pears* a57 77
11 b g Makbul Dee Dee Girl (IRE) (Primo Dominie)
1722[8] 2337[4]

**Noor Al Hawa (FR)** *A Wohler* 110
4 ch h Makfi Majestic Roi (USA) (Street Cry (IRE))
934a[2] 4130a[3] 5464a[5] 7640a[3]

**Nootka Sound (USA)** *Wesley A Ward* a86 50
2 bb f Lonhro(AUS) Miss Red Delicious (USA) (Empire Maker (USA))
3929[17]

**Norab (GER)** *Bernard Llewellyn* a74 80
6 b g Galileo(IRE) Night Woman (GER) (Monsun (GER))
5251[3] 6096[8] 6508[4] 7200[5] 7832[6]

**Nora Batt (IRE)** *John W Nicholson* a43 57
4 ch m Art Connoisseur(IRE) Mrs Batt (IRE) (Medecis)
159[9] 355[10] 468[11] 604[8] 1006[4] 1126[12] 7020[4]

**Nordenfelt (IRE)** *Natalie Lloyd-Beavis* a8 14
4 b g Lilbourne Lad(IRE) There With Me (USA) (Distant View (USA))
4700[7] 6306[11]

**Nordic Combined (IRE)** *Brian Ellison* 81
3 b g Haafhd Chilly Filly (IRE) (Montjeu (IRE))
2807[5] 3489[2] 4809[9] 6126[11] (6880) 7565[2] 8478[8]

**Nordic Dream (IRE)** *A Fabre* a90 106
4 b h Dream Ahead(USA) Nyramba (Night Shift (USA))
3880a[6] 6498a[4] 7416a[4]

**Nordico (GER)** *Mario Hofer* a68 101
6 ch h Medicean Norwegian Pride (FR) (Diktat)
1661a[6] 4939a[8]

**Noreena** *Paul D'Arcy* a48 14
3 b f Medicean Nurai (Danehill Dancer (IRE))
863[7] 1141[5] 1596[7]

**No Refund (IRE)** *Martin Smith* a52 29
6 b g Invincible Spirit(IRE) Evangeline (Sadler's Wells (USA))
398[10] 8473[13] 9213[10]

**Norilsk (FR)** *Y Barberot* a71 76
3 b c My Risk(FR) L'Aiglone (FR) (Lost World (IRE))
5523a[2]

**Normal Equilibrium** *Ivan Furtado* a79 94
7 b g Elnadim(USA) Acicula (IRE) (Night Shift (USA))
4[10] 443[7] 886[5] 1327[2] 1370[9] 2083[3] 2516[7] 3903[3] (4337) 5402[8] (6411) 7307a[9] 7538[7] 8012[17]

**Normandel (FR)** *Mme Pia Brandt* 105
3 b f Le Havre(IRE) Lidana (IRE) (King's Best (USA))
1690a[6] 4424a[8] 5449a[6] 6732a[3] 8273a[5]

**Normandie (GER)** *Mme Pia Brandt* 81
3 b f Redoute's Choice(AUS) Ninas Rainbow (Rainbow Quest (USA))
3881a[14]

**Normandie Attack (FR)** *Charlie Fellowes* a79 77
3 gr c Kendargent(FR) Agenda (IRE) (Sadler's Wells (USA))
4146[4] 4611[2] 5141[2] 5799[4] 6880[11]

**Normandie Lady** *Richard Fahey* a86 86
4 b m Kheleyf(USA) Normandie Art (Rainbow Quest (USA))
(2268) 3233[3] 3828[6] 4662[3] 5125[5] 7710[6]

**Normandy Barriere (IRE)** *Nigel Tinkler* 103
5 b g Rock Of Gibraltar(IRE) Ma Paloma (FR) (Highest Honor (FR))
1880[2] (2566) 4072[9] 4925a[16] 5662[5] 6186[5]

**Normandy Blue** *Richard Fahey* a58 67
2 ch g Le Havre(IRE) Ballerina Blue (IRE) (High Chaparral (IRE))
5631[12] 6159[6] 6410[2] 7624[6] 8287[3]

**Normandy Eagle (IRE)** *F Head* a79 105
3 b c New Approach(IRE) Secrete (FR) (Cape Cross (IRE))
1826a[3]

**Normandy Kitten (USA)** *Gianluca Bietolini* a79 79
4 ch h Kitten's Joy(USA) Keeping Watch (IRE) (Danehill (USA))
6302a[10]

**Norse Castle** *Martin Bosley* a62 5
4 b g Norse Dancer(IRE) Hursley Hope (IRE) (Barathea (IRE))
290[9]

**North America** *S Seemar* a115 84
5 b g Dubawi(IRE) Northern Mischief (USA) (Yankee Victor (USA))
(204a) (695a)◆ 1373a[10]

**North Angel (IRE)** *David Brown* 30
2 gr f Dark Angel(IRE) Woodcock Moon (Kyllachy)
6545[8]

**North Bay Sunrise (IRE)** *Ed Vaughan* a63
2 b f Kodiac Cat Fire (IRE) (One Cool Cat (USA))
7033[7] 7489[3] 8796[13]

**North Creek** *Chris Wall* a86 67
4 b g Iffraaj Maine Rose (Red Ransom (USA))
2116[5]◆ 2960[6] (3723) 4563[4] 5245[4] 6111[7] 6874[6] 7255[5] 8344[6]

**Northdown** *David Lanigan* a77 55
3 b g Paco Boy(IRE) Hazita (Singspiel (IRE))
2088[12] 2794[10] 4186[6] 4728[5] 5536[9] 6160[4] 6948[10]

**Northern Angel (IRE)** *John Quinn* 69
2 b f Dark Angel(IRE) Muzdaan (IRE) (Exceed And Excel (AUS))
5278[2] (6147)

**Northern Beam (IRE)** *H-A Pantall* a75
2 ch f Teofilo(IRE) Raaya (USA) (Giant's Causeway (USA))
8691a[2]

**Northern Force** *Roger Fell*
2 b g Lethal Force(IRE) Border Minstral (IRE) (Sri Pekan (USA))
6938[13]

**Northern Fox (GER)** *Yasmin Almenrader*
2 ch c Areion(GER) Nadischa (GER) (Protektor (GER))
6986a[6]

**Northern Hollow (GER)** *Markus Klug*
2 b c Soldier Hollow Narooma (GER) (Silver Hawk (USA))
6986a[10]

**Northern Law (IRE)** *John Quinn* 68
2 b g Lawman(FR) Polly Perkins (IRE) (Pivotal)
3093[5] 3973[5] 4848[4] 5752[3] 6087[9]

**Northern Surprise (IRE)** *Timothy Doyle* a90 73
6 b g Azamour(IRE) Surprise Treat (IRE) (Shalford (IRE))
795a[6] 1479a[4] 5519a[10]

**Northgate Lad (IRE)** *Brian Ellison* a99 95
5 gr g Dark Angel(IRE) Canosa (IRE) (Catrail (USA))
1515[6] 2031[3] 2736[4] 3585[10] 4353[2] (5415) 6355[12] 7118[4]

**North Road Revue** *Tim Easterby* a50 49
2 b f Dick Turpin(IRE) Revue Princess (IRE) (Mull Of Kintyre (USA))
4834[7] 5537[8] 5834[8]

**Northsea Star (GER)** *Markus Klug* 100
3 bb c Sea The Stars(IRE) North Queen (IRE) (Desert King (IRE))
2246a[4] 3636a[3] 4422a[17]

**Northwest Frontier (IRE)** *Richard Fahey* a79 86
3 b g Galileo(IRE) Francesca D'Gorgio (USA) (Proud Citizen (USA))
3465[3] (4055) 4898[3] 5667[2] 6445[8] 7701[4] 8239[10] 8893[7]

**Norville (IRE)** *Lee Smyth* a47 61
10 b g Elusive City(USA) Saraposa (IRE) (Ahonoora)
2501[7]

**Norwegian Highness (FR)** *H-A Pantall* a72 72
3 ch f Kendargent(FR) Norwegian Princess (IRE) (Fairy King (USA))
3171[10] 5606[6] 6650a[13] 8025a[2]

**Norwegian Lord (FR)** *M Boutin* a58 41
2 ch c Kendargent(FR) Norwegian Lady (FR) (Hold That Tiger (USA))
2073a[9] 3515a[6] 4196a[7] 8101a[6] 9086a[8]

**Nosongsosweet (IRE)** *M Delzangles* 72
3 b f Manduro(GER) Afaf (FR) (Spectrum (IRE))
4232a[2]

**Nostalgie** *James Tate* a85 43
3 gr f Archipenko(USA) Neige D'Antan (Aussie Rules (USA))
(2274) 2754[7] 3189[3] 4983[2] 6321[2] 7321[11]

**Nostromo (FR)** *M Boutin* a57 86
5 gr g Mastercraftsman(IRE) Louve De Saron (FR) (Loup Solitaire (USA))
822a[4]

**No Surrender (FR)** *Ferdy Murphy*
2 ch c Rock Of Gibraltar(IRE) Plantation (FR) (Singspiel (IRE))
8482a[14]

**Not A Bad Oul Day (IRE)** *John James Feane* a56 100
5 ch g Captain Rio Woodville (Deploy)
20[12] (2501) 5688a[10]

**Not After Hours (FR)** *F Rohaut* 96
3 b f Wiener Walzer(GER) Nota Bene (GER) (Slickly (FR))
4654a[4] 8838a[6]

**Not After Midnight (IRE)** *Daniel Kubler* a72 69
2 bb f Big Bad Bob(IRE) Zenella (Kyllachy)
2905[3] 3244[2] 6776[8] 8153[2] 8817[12] 9015[3]

**Not A Given (USA)** *A R Al Rayhi* a68
8 b g Any Given Saturday(USA) Any For Love (ARG) (Southern Halo (USA))
316a[11]

**Notalot (IRE)** *Tariq Issa* a70 72
3 b g Sir Prancealot(IRE) Hapipi (Bertolini (USA))
933a[3]

**Noteworthy (IRE)** *Richard Hughes* a60
2 b f Acclamation Church Melody (Oasis Dream)
8544[6]

**Nothing Compares** *Mark Johnston* a59 53
3 b f Harbour Watch(IRE) Endorsement (Warning)
91[4] 881[6] 1623[6] 2264[6] 2705[3] 3180[9] 5209[3] 5581[8] 5780[10]

**Nothing To Lose (IRE)** *John C McConnell* a49 83
3 b g Fast Company(IRE) Invincible Woman (IRE) (Invincible Spirit (IRE))
(4663)◆ (5248)

**Notice (IRE)** *David Simcock* a85 90
4 ch m New Approach(IRE) Classic Remark (IRE) (Dr Fong (USA))
3033[3] 3968[3] 5108[2] 6104[2] 6391[4] 7507[3]◆ 8121[7]

**Not Listenin'tome (AUS)** *John Moore* a102 121
6 b g Dylan Thomas(IRE) Flame Of Sydney (AUS) (Encosta De Lago (AUS))
1377a[7] 9168a[10]

**Notnowivorheadache** *Roger Ingram*
8 b m Notnowcato Inchcoonan (Emperor Jones (USA))
4497[14]

**Not Now Nadia (IRE)** *Michael Dods* a56 58
3 b f Footstepsinthesand Lake Wanaka (IRE) (Fasliyev (USA))
667[2] 787[5] 1127[8]

**Notnow Seamus** *Marjorie Fife* 49
6 b g Notnowcato Special Beat (Bustino)
3286[5]

**Not So Sleepy** *Hughie Morrison* a101 105
5 ch g Beat Hollow Papillon De Bronze (IRE) (Marju (IRE))
2735[8]◆ (3300) 8992[5] 9388[8]

**Notte D'Oro (IRE)** *Mme Pia Brandt* 95
5 b m Montjeu(IRE) Notting Hill (BRZ) (Jules (USA))
6123a[3]

**Notte Illuminata (IRE)** *K R Burke* a76 75
4 b m Acclamation Sogno Verde (IRE) (Green Desert (USA))
142[6]

**Nouvelle Ere** *Tony Carroll* a65 61
6 b g Archipenko(USA) Sinister Ruckus (USA) (Trippi (USA))
124[2] 636[8] (880) 1067[8] 1699[4] 2282[7] 3208[4] 3761[7] 4971[4] 5790[2] 6175[7] 6280[6] 7761[15] 8346[13]

**Nouvelli Dancer (IRE)** *David C Griffiths* a74 84
4 b m Lilbourne Lad(IRE) Kiralik (Efisio)
994[7] 1261[8] 1586[9] 2805[7]

**Novabridge** *Karen Tutty* a53 48
9 ch g Avonbridge Petrovna (IRE) (Petardia)
446[8] 732[4] 1126[5] 1435[2] 1547[5] 1869[8] 2628[9] 3345[6] 8559[7] 8776[2] 9075[10] 9265[4] 9374[7]

**N Over J** *William Knight* a64 75
2 b g Kodiac Risk A Look (Observatory (USA))
(7897) 8545[8] 8748[6]

**Novis Adventus (IRE)** *Jeremy Noseda* a96 100
5 b g New Approach(IRE) Tiffed (USA) (Seattle Slew (USA))
467[10]

**Novoman (IRE)** *William Haggas* 104
3 ch g Sir Prancealot(IRE) Rublevka Star (USA) (Elusive Quality (USA))
1801[10] 3592[9] 4322[6] (4865) (6474) 7619[28]

**No Win No Fee** *Barry Leavy* a41 50
7 b g Firebreak Millisecnt (Primo Dominie)
1982[4] 2624[9] 3036[9]

**Now Say Yes (IRE)** *David Lanigan* a57
2 b f Elusive Quality(USA) Say No Now (IRE) (Refuse To Bend (IRE))
9099[7] 9385[5]

**Now We Can** *N Clement* a110 111
8 b g Martillo(GER) Notre Dame (GER) (Acatenango (GER))
934a[8] 2202a[4] **3553a[3]** 5198a[9]

**Now You're Talking (IRE)**
*Joseph Patrick O'Brien* 104
2 b f Zoffany(IRE) Granadilla (Zafonic (USA))
3960[4] **7617[4]**◆ 8575a[8]

**Nozomi (AUS)** *Anthony Freedman* 94
5 b g Street Cry(IRE) Rose Of Danehill (AUS) (Danehill (USA))
**8100a[5]** 8857a[8]

**Nsnas Alward** *Kevin Ryan* a45 60
2 b f Poet's Voice Rosa Mundi (Alhaarth (IRE))
*1776[8]* **2545[3]** 3179[11]

**Nuala Tagula (IRE)** *John Quinn* a63 62
4 b m Tagula(IRE) Dangle (IRE) (Desert Style (IRE))
*161[4]* *446[9]* 1978[16] (2777) 3289[3] 3563[4] 3710[7] 4559[4] ***5418[2]*** 5605[2] 6130[8]

**Nucky Thompson** *Richard Spencer* a78 78
4 b g Cockney Rebel(IRE) Vino Veritas (USA) (Chief's Crown (USA))
3009[11] **4267[6]**

**Nudge** *Mrs A M O'Shea* 70
4 b m Dansili Take The Hint (Montjeu (IRE))
**3063[8]**

**Nuee Ardente (FR)** *K Borgel* a84 76
3 b f Soave(GER) Country Jane (FR) (Country Reel (USA))
3355a[3] **(4783a)**

**Nuits St Georges (IRE)**
*David Menuisier* a71 72
2 ch c Mount Nelson Twelfth Night (IRE) (Namid)
**5840[2]** 6859[9] *8029[3]*

**Nullemont (IRE)** *C Ferland* 93
3 gr f Rajsaman(FR) Nonsuch Way (IRE) (Verglas (IRE))
**4654a[7]**

**Numancia (FR)** *P Monfort* 17
2 b f Palace Episode(USA) Lady Nour (FR) (Valanour (IRE))
**1929a[8]**

**Numeration (FR)** *Alex Fracas* a61 57
3 b f Shakespearean(IRE) Addition (FR) (Numerous (USA))
***427a[4]*** 4943a[4] 5268a[2]

**Numerion (GER)** *S Smrczek*
2 b c Areion(GER) Numero Uno (GER) (Lavirco (GER))
6986a[11]

**Nuncio** *Daniel Kubler* a72 74
3 b g Authorized(IRE) Sweet Pilgrim (Talkin Man (CAN))
**2901[2]** **3824[2]** 4624[5] 5409[3] 6295[4] *7322[6]* *7769[6]* *8376[9]*

**Nunnery Lane** *Michael Easterby* 42
2 b g Mazameer(IRE) Prices Lane (Gentleman's Deal (IRE))
**5180[5]** 6057[10]

**Nuns Walk** *Tim Easterby* a73 70
3 ch f Sleeping Indian Dance Card (Cape Cross (IRE))
5619[2] 6184[7] 6568[2] *(6904)* (7525) 7825[5] *8552[2]* ***8717[2]***

**Nuova Scuola** *Jim Goldie* 43
4 b m Mount Nelson La Vecchia Scuola (IRE) (Mull Of Kintyre (USA))
**2496[6]** 2841[6] 3182[5] 4962[9] 5257[7] 5923[7]

**Nuptials (USA)**
*Eve Johnson Houghton* a32 51
3 b f Broken Vow(USA) European Union (USA) (Successful Appeal (USA))
***77[8]*** *456[8]*

**Nurse Nightingale** *Michael Bell* a77 74
3 b f Nathaniel(IRE) Whazzat (Daylami (IRE))
*144[3]* 2760[6] 3759[5] *7032[4]* ***7319[2]*** *7935[3]* 8485[4] *8822[2]* *9325[6]*

**Nutini (IRE)** *Malcolm Saunders* a73 68
4 b g Lope De Vega(IRE) My Eurydice (Exceed And Excel (AUS))
6310[8] 6807[9] 7083[7] 7693[2] **(7910)** ***8427[3]*** ***8743[3]***

**Nutzma** *Mike Murphy* a47 38
4 b m Multiplex Nut (IRE) (Fasliyev (USA))
*70[8]*

**Nuzha** *Tony Newcombe* a71 61
3 ch f Mayson Always On My Mind (Distant Relative)
*155[5]* *313[3]* ***4011[2]***◆ *4500[7]* 7122[14] 7689[3] 8298[10] *8742[7]*

**Nyala** *Daniel Kubler* 35
2 b f Vale Of York(IRE) Cio Cio San (IRE) (Dalakhani (IRE))
**6862[9]**

**Nyaleti (IRE)** *Mark Johnston* 110
2 ro f Arch(USA) America Nova (FR) (Verglas (IRE))
(3868)◆ 4068[2] 4855[2] **(5391)** 6249a[6] 7088[3] 7578[2] 8004[9]

**Nyx** *Richard Guest* 36
3 ch f Harbour Watch(IRE) Fantastic Santanyi (Fantastic Light (USA))
1715[10] 2897[15] **4058[6]**

**Oak Bluffs (IRE)** *Richard Fahey* a68 70
6 b g Royal Applause Key Stage (IRE) (King's Best (USA))
*332[8]* ***445[8]***

**Oak Brook (USA)** *Brian Williamson* a78 109
5 b g Giant's Causeway(USA) Crafty Oak (USA) (Crafty Prospector (USA))
**5977a[6]**

**Oakley Pride (IRE)** *Gay Kelleway* a61 64
3 b g Lilbourne Lad(IRE) There With Me (USA) (Distant View (USA))
*150[6]* *522[4]* ***(686)*** *895[8]* *1421[10]* 3151[7] 3391[3] *4726[3]* 5280[5] 5852[3] 7005[4] 7459[3] 8137[4] 8470[7]

**Oasis Charm** *Charlie Appleby* 96
3 b g Oasis Dream Albaraka (Selkirk (USA))
1906[2] (2152) 2437[6] 3998[13] **4856[2]**◆

**Oasis Fantasy (IRE)** *David Simcock* 109
6 br g Oasis Dream Cara Fantasy (IRE) (Sadler's Wells (USA))
322a[8] 542a[5] **2735[3]** 4033[18] 4863[4] 5500[6] 5913[3] 6698[9] 7649[6]

**Oasis Spear** *Chris Wall* a80 79
5 b g Oasis Dream Sunspear (IRE) (Montjeu (IRE))
2291[8] ***2920[4]*** 3670[7] 5664[5] 6110[7] *7452[13]*

**Obboorr** *James Given* a78 78
8 b g Cape Cross(IRE) Felawnah (USA) (Mr Prospector (USA))
*3[5]* ***380[5]*** *526[5]* *688[3]* *856[8]*

**Oberyn (IRE)** *Sylvester Kirk* a69 61
3 b f Holy Roman Emperor(IRE) Daraliya (IRE) (Kahyasi (IRE))
*(96)* *245[6]* ***(434)*** *647[6]* 2394[12] 3087[7] 3520[8]

**Obeya** *Roger Varian* 68
3 b f Oasis Dream Loulou (USA) (El Prado (IRE))
4568[5] **5118[4]** 5538[3]

**Obiwan (FR)** *C Boutin* a14 44
4 bb m American Post Decency (IRE) (Celtic Swing)
**1181a[5]**

**Obrigada** *Tom Clover* a58 57
2 b f Worthadd(IRE) Oblige (Robellino (USA))
***6064[8]*** 7153[6] *7724[5]* ***8658[5]*** ***8887[3]*** *9014[6]*

**Ocala** *Andrew Balding* a69 76
2 ch f Nathaniel(IRE) Night Carnation (Sleeping Indian)
**7953[2]**◆ *8634[3]*

**Occhiobello (FR)** *Robert Collet* a53 63
2 b f Zambezi Sun Shinabaa (FR) (Anabaa (USA))
**5629a[6]** 6050a[6]

**Occupy (USA)** *Ralph Beckett* a81
2 b c Declaration Of War(USA) Circumstances (IRE) (Galileo (IRE))
***(8642)***◆

**Ocean Air (FR)** *James Tate* a70 77
3 b c Rio De La Plata(USA) Silver Miss (FR) (Numerous (USA))
**(2151)** 2755[7] 8418[6]

**Ocean Bentley (IRE)** *Tony Carroll* a37 30
5 b g Amadeus Wolf Bentley's Bush (IRE) (Barathea (IRE))
**6589[8]**

**Ocean Crystal** *Mrs A Malzard* a29 34
5 b m Stimulation(IRE) Crystal Gale (IRE) (Verglas (IRE))
1933a[5] 2672a[5] 3958a[7] **5987a[3]**

**Ocean Drive (IRE)** *William Haggas* a77 75
3 b f Sea The Stars(IRE) Cap Coz (IRE) (Indian Ridge (IRE))
*(144)* ***439[2]*** 3759[4] 5932[5]

**Oceane (FR)** *Alan King* a92 97
5 b g Kentucky Dynamite(USA) Zahrana (FR) (Zamindar (USA))
*746[9]* *1361[5]* 1942[5] **2562[2]** 3928[10] **6329[7]** 7402[8] 8038[15]

**Ocean Eleven** *Martin Keighley* a80 33
4 b g Equiano(FR) Fittonia (FR) (Ashkalani (IRE))
***8956[7]***

**Ocean Fairy (IRE)** *Carina Fey* a66 56
3 gr f Mastercraftsman(IRE) Ocean Talent (USA) (Aptitude (USA))
**6566a[8]**

**Ocean Gale** *Richard Price* a52 55
4 b m Shirocco(GER) Ocean Transit (IRE) (Trans Island)
**3426[4]** 4187[3] 5054[4] (5716) 6370[3] 7048[4] *7730[3]* *8246[3]* *8647[11]*

**Ocean Legend (IRE)** *Tony Carroll* a75 65
12 b g Night Shift(USA) Rose Of Mooncoin (IRE) (Brief Truce (USA))
***171[6]***

**Ocean Of Love** *Saeed bin Suroor* a89
3 ch f Distorted Humor(USA) Michita (USA) (Dynaformer (USA))
*8377[3]* *8744[2]* *9159[2]* ***(9408)***

**Ocean Princess (IRE)**
*Michael Dods* a61 60
3 b f Acclamation Fathoming (USA) (Gulch (USA))
***1474[5]*** 3296[9]

**Ocean Promise (USA)**
*Richard Hughes* a65 64
3 b f Quality Road(USA) I'm From Dixie (USA) (Dixieland Band (USA))
***100[6]*** *284[6]* 2220[5] *4214[8]* 4445[4]

**Ocean Side** *Richard Hannon* 68
2 gr c Dark Angel(IRE) Mundus Novus (USA) (Unbridled's Song (USA))
4534[8] **6654[8]** 7128[8] 8074[4]

**Ocean Spray** *Richard Hannon* a9
2 ch f Showcasing Gibraltar Lass (USA) (Concerto (USA))
*8308[9]* *8670[12]* ***9022[10]***

**Ocean Tempest** *John Ryan* a65 93
8 gr g Act One Ipsa Loquitur (Unfuwain (USA))
***277[11]***

**Ocean Temptress** *John Ryan* a66 77
3 b f Equiano(FR) Ipsa Loquitur (Unfuwain (USA))
*2017[5]* 3413[3] 3701[2] 4313[5] 5038[6] 5852[2] (6283) (6586) *6681[7]* (7255) 7508[4] **(7932)** 8563[4]

**Oceanus (IRE)** *Julia Feilden* a48 75
3 b g Born To Sea(IRE) Alkhawarah (USA) (Intidab (USA))
*323[8]* 2315[3]◆ 2903[5] 6754[2]◆ **(7210)** 7917[10] **8327[3]** 8682[6]

**Ocean Voyage (IRE)** *Richard Fahey* a74 70
2 b f Most Improved(IRE) Minshar (Noverre (USA))
(7221) *8245[4]* ***8748[2]***

**Ocelot** *Robert Cowell* 87
3 b f Poet's Voice Desert Lynx (IRE) (Green Desert (USA))
(2280) 2631[5] (3812)◆ **(5029)**◆ 6177[6] 6923[8] 8167[4]

**Ochos Rios** *Neil Mulholland* a61 61
4 b g Shirocco(GER) Society Rose (Saddlers' Hall (IRE))
***(9368)***

**O'Connor (IRE)** *Rod Millman* 51
4 ch g Roderic O'Connor(IRE) Fly By Magic (IRE) (Indian Rocket)
**4911[6]**

**Ocotillo (IRE)** *Kevin Frost* a55 47
4 ch g Raven's Pass(USA) Meiosis (USA) (Danzig (USA))
*158[9]* *640[7]* ***899[4]***

**October Storm** *Mick Channon* a76 87
4 br g Shirocco(GER) Cyber Star (King's Best (USA))
(2388) 3004[3] **4073[8]** *4355[7]* 5524[12] *6323[8]* (8047)

**Octoking (FR)** *R Martens* 90
5 gr h Kingsalsa(USA) Marie Octobre (FR) (Daylami (IRE))
**6915a[7]**

**Oddsocks (IRE)** *Tony Carroll* a30 41
5 b m Tagula(IRE) Datura (Darshaan)
*554[6]* *640[12]* 5357[8] 5823[8] **6283[6]** *6635[10]* 7020[11]

**Odds On Oli** *Richard Fahey* a52 47
2 b g Camelot Red Blooded Woman (USA) (Red Ransom (USA))
*4259[6]* *4725[8]* 5262[7] *8676[6]* ***8847[4]***

**O Dee** *J Phelippon* a55 74
5 ch g Iffraaj Queen's Grace (Bahamian Bounty)
*3469[4]* **(4233a)** (4955a) 7307a[5]

**Odelouca (IRE)** *Brendan Powell* a68 46
3 b f Elusive City(USA) Church Road (IRE) (Danehill Dancer (IRE))
**2474[11]** *3722[8]* 4350[15]

**Oden** *Roger Varian* 88
3 ch g Lope De Vega(IRE) Dashing (IRE) (Sadler's Wells (USA))
4808[8] 5632[3] 6518[2] **(7004)**

**Odeon (NZ)**
*Mathew Ellerton & Simon Zahra* 107
3 bb g Zacinto Theatre Buff (USA) (Theatrical (IRE))
**8753a[8]**

**Ode To Autumn** *John Gosden* a75 77
2 br g Showcasing Turning Leaf (IRE) (Last Tycoon)
**5105[2]** **5709[2]** 6388[6] *9433[2]*

**Ode To Glory** *Rae Guest* a68 69
3 b f Poet's Voice Blue Lyric (Refuse To Bend (IRE))
2702[10] 4320[6] 4761[2] 5275[3] 5718[3] **6556[2]**◆ *7831[6]* *8883[4]* 9026[13] *9430[5]*

**Ode To Paris** *Ed Dunlop* a64 64
3 b g Poet's Voice Dream Belle (Oasis Dream)
***78[4]*** *209[8]* *401[7]*

**Odyssa (IRE)** *Richard Hughes* a79 81
2 b f Kodiac Deliziosa (IRE) (Iffraaj)
*6010[3]* ***(6868)*** *7454[2]*

**Oeil De Tigre (FR)** *Tony Carroll* a57 76
6 b g Footstepsinthesand Suerte (Halling (USA))
*93[7]* *745[7]* 2229[3] 3573[8] 4373[4] (4844) 5112[3] 6099[6] (6615) **7691[2]**

**Off Art** *Tim Easterby* a70 76
7 ch g Dutch Art Off Camera (Efisio)
**1706[5]** 2133[12] 2838[7] 5496[5] 6266[6] 6434[3] **(7052)** **7823[3]** 8510[6] *8928[5]* *9100[3]*

**Offering Plan (USA)** *Chad C Brown* 106
5 bb h Spring At Last(USA) Rosalie Road (USA) (Street Cry (IRE))
**7851a[7]**

**Officer In Command (USA)**
*Alan Bailey* a55 36
11 bb g Officer(USA) Luv To Stay N Chat (USA) (Candi's Gold (USA))
***333[11]***

**Off The Scale (IRE)**
*Rebecca Menzies* 77
5 b g Strategic Prince Vanilla Delight (IRE) (Orpen (USA))
1833[15] 2224[12] **3488[8]**

**Ogbourne Downs** *Ben Pauling* a67 74
7 b g Royal Applause Helen Sharp (Pivotal)
3920[4] **4976[4]** 7131[9] *7878[11]* *7998[9]*

**Oglum Berat (TUR)** *Mulayim Anat* 87
5 b h Victory Gallop(CAN) Halling Charge (Halling (USA))
**6744a[6]**

**Oglum Beratim (TUR)**
*Mulayim Anat*
3 b c Dai Jin Sly (GER) (Monsun (GER))
*6717a[8]*

**O'Goshi (FR)** *J Phelippon* a68
3 b c Kentucky Dynamite(USA) Hier Deja (FR) (Neverneyev (USA))
*584a[9]*

**Oh Geno** *Richard Spencer* a64 63
3 b g Paco Boy(IRE) Key Light (IRE) (Acclamation)
***264[4]***

**Oh Grace (IRE)** *J S Bolger* a88 93
3 b f Lawman(FR) Flea Cheoil (IRE) (Galileo (IRE))
**1386a[12]**

**Oh It's Saucepot** *Chris Wall* a58 84
3 b f Sir Percy Oh So Saucy (Imperial Ballet (IRE))
2794[3] (5367) (5854) **(6767)**

**Oh James** *Tim Easterby* 74
4 b g Monsieur Bond(IRE) Sea Flower (IRE) (Acclamation)
**2184[10]** 2821[14] 3401[11]

**Oh So Dandy (IRE)** *Derek Shaw* a58 52
3 ch g Dandy Man(IRE) Kelso Magic (USA) (Distant View (USA))
***41[5]*** 8329[12] *8980[12]* *9103[2]* *9214[7]*

**Oh So Sassy** *Chris Wall* a78 94
7 b m Pastoral Pursuits Almasi (IRE) (Petorius (IRE))
**1863[3]**◆ 2578[5] 3625[8] 4816[6] 5426[5] 6430[8] *7538[4]*◆ *7994[6]*

**Oh This Is Us (IRE)** *Richard Hannon* a104 115
4 b h Acclamation Shamwari Lodge (IRE) (Hawk Wing (USA))
653a[3] 892a[5] 1494[2] **(1766)** **2142[2]** **(2610)** 3320[3] 3924[8] 5502[11] 6420[4] 7154[3] 8234[7] 8599[5]

**Oi The Clubb Oi'S** *Ian Williams* a57
2 gr g Champs Elysees Red Boots (IRE) (Verglas (IRE))
*9201[10]* ***9417[6]***

**Ojala (IRE)** *Simon Dow* a79 76
2 b c Epaulette(AUS) Sonny Sunshine (Royal Applause)
3690[7] 6005[3] *6636[6]* (7121) ***(9466)***◆

**Ok By Me (IRE)** *David Evans* a54 66
3 ch f Arcano(IRE) Kindest (Cadeaux Genereux)
*967[9]* ***1401[7]*** *2274[11]* 3163[7]

**Okool (FR)** *Owen Burrows* 89
3 b g Cape Cross(IRE) Seschat (IRE) (Sinndar (IRE))
1967[2] (2584) 3068[4] 5033[3] **(6202)** 7397[4]

**Olala (GER)** *W Mongil* 96
4 b m Tertullian(USA) Ostdogin (GER) (Doyen (IRE))
**2201a[6]**

**Olaudah** *Henry Candy* a59 50
3 b g Equiano(FR) Bookiesindexdotnet (Piccolo)
5260[6] 5995[5] *9129[4]* ***9340[2]***◆

**Old China** *John Davies* a45 72
4 b g Archipenko(USA) Porcelain (IRE) (Peintre Celebre (USA))
3529[2] 4345[6] 4690[4] 5214[13] 6435[2]◆ **(7388)** *8209[11]*

**Old Fashioned (CHI)**
*Luke McJannet* a77 87
4 ch g Neko Bay(USA) Hebrides (CHI) (Schossberg (CAN))
*1152[9]* ***1362[7]*** 1863[10] *8913[9]* ***9079[7]***

**Old Fox (IRE)** *Stefano Botti* 98
2 b c Lord Shanakill(USA) Mia Madonna (Motivator)
**8620a[3]**

**Old Persian** *Charlie Appleby* a90 97
2 b c Dubawi(IRE) Indian Petal (Singspiel (IRE))
5887[3] *(6683)* **(7810)**◆ 8290[7]

**Old Time Waltz (USA)** *A P O'Brien* a73 88
3 b f War Front(USA) Together (IRE) (Galileo (IRE))
**5308a[10]** 8083a[14]

**Old Town Boy** *Philip McBride* a85 90
6 b g Myboycharlie(IRE) Native Ring (FR) (Bering)
***268[7]***

**Olimar (FR)** *Marjorie Fife*
3 gr f Kendargent(FR) Onega Lake (IRE) (Peintre Celebre (USA))
*8554[9]*

**Olive Mabel** *Dean Ivory* a56 32
2 b f Captain Gerrard(IRE) Shembara (FR) (Dylan Thomas (IRE))
***3135[6]*** 3502[6] *4496[8]*

**Oliver Reed (IRE)** *Richard Hannon* 80
2 b c Footstepsinthesand Montbretia (Montjeu (IRE))
4534[5] **5151[2]** 5504[5]

**Oliver's Betty** *Michael Appleby* 13
2 br f Dick Turpin(IRE) Luck Will Come (IRE) (Desert Style (IRE))
**5755[9]**

**Oliver's Gold** *Mark Walford* a39 52
9 b g Danehill Dancer(IRE) Gemini Gold (IRE) (King's Best (USA))
**5951[5]**

**Olivia Fallow (IRE)** *Paul Midgley* 94
5 b m Vale Of York(IRE) Spinning Maid (USA) (Forestry (USA))
1863[4]◆ 2407[7] **2899[3]** 3321[12] 3827[8] 4078[6] 4787[4] 5281[4] 6267[10] 6758[7] 7657[5]

**Olivia Pope (FR)** *E Lellouche* 72
4 b m Magadan(IRE) Mission Sauvage (FR) (Super Celebre (FR))
**7070a[4]**

**Olmedo (FR)** *J-C Rouget* 113
2 b c Declaration Of War(USA) Super Pie (USA) (Pivotal)
(5776a) 6730a[2] **7667a[2]**

**Olsztyn (FR)** *M Boutin* a81 46
4 b g Canford Cliffs(IRE) Kalahaag (IRE) (Iffraaj)
***1078a[5]***

**Olympic Duel (IRE)** *Peter Hiatt* a63 62
4 b g Acclamation Olympic Medal (Nayef (USA))
***(1603)*** 2082[7] *2961[12]* 5145[12] 6101[P] (Dead)

**Olympic Legend (IRE)**
*Martin Bosley* a68 54
3 ch g Choisir(AUS) Margaret's Dream (IRE) (Muhtarram (USA))
*292[4]* ***647[5]*** *846[5]* 3922[7] 4537[11] *8550[8]* *8846[4]* *9026[2]*

**Om (USA)** *Dan L Hendricks* a104 119
5 ch h Munnings(USA) Rare Cat (USA) (Tabasco Cat (USA))
**8608a[8]**

**Omaha Beach (IRE)**
*Mme Pia Brandt* 82
2 b f Epaulette(AUS) Hundredsnthousands (IRE) (Thousand Words)
**8884a[3]**

**Omei Sword (AUS)** *Chris Waller* 106
3 b f High Chaparral(IRE) Irish Lights (AUS) (Fastnet Rock (AUS))
**8059a[11]**

**Omeros** *Hugo Palmer* a88 84
3 ch g Poet's Voice Caribbean Pearl (USA) (Silver Hawk (USA))
3713[5] 4763[5] ***6617[3]***◆ 7246[7] *7941[14]*

**Omid** *Kenneth Slack* a52 58
9 b g Dubawi(IRE) Mille Couleurs (FR) (Spectrum (IRE))
**2889[7]** *3340[13]*

**Ominotago** *Michael Appleby* a73 70
5 ch m Aqlaam Sharp Dresser (USA) (Diesis)
*(23)* *162[4]* *1548[2]* 4319[2]◆ ***8978[2]***

**Omneeya** *Marco Botti* a63 71
3 b f Frankel Amanee (AUS) (Pivotal)
**1947[3]** *2463[4]* 3595[6] 4445[3] 5335[3]

**Omotesando** *Oliver Greenall* a74 72
7 b g Street Cry(IRE) Punctilious (Danehill (USA))
*3252[6]* 3898[4] 4082[4] 4608[3] *5483[3]* 5701[2] (5872) 6175[3] 7560[6] *7831[2]* 8239[9] *8497[5]* ***(8876)*** *9000[9]*

**Omran** *Marco Botti* a98 95
3 ch c Choisir(AUS) Ruff Shod (USA) (Storm Boot (USA))
1945[4]◆ ***(2922)***◆ 3592[6] 3997[17] 5147[8] *6685[15]* *7727[7]*

**On A Roll** *Richard Hannon* 59
2 b f Swiss Spirit Amary (IRE) (Acclamation)
**1884[6]**

**Once In A Moon (JPN)** *Makoto Saito* 111
4 b m Admire Moon(JPN) Two Days Notice (JPN) (Hector Protector (USA))
9168a[12]

**One And Only (JPN)** *Shinsuke Hashiguchi* 115
6 bb h Heart's Cry(JPN) Virtue (JPN) (Taiki Shuttle (USA))
2203a[11] 8975a[16]

**One Big Surprise** *Richard Hughes* a73 78
5 b m Kier Park(IRE) Cloridja (Indian Ridge (IRE))
(2058) 2676[4] 3696[6] 4093[5] 4711[2] 5078[5] 5869[3] 7771[7] 8875[13]

**One Boy (IRE)** *Paul Midgley* a76 80
6 ch g Captain Gerrard(IRE) Paris Song (IRE) (Peintre Celebre (USA))
443[5] 995[8] 1805[3] 2341[5] 2656a[12] 3653[6] 3903[6] 5211[3] 5459[9] 5930[9] (6351) 6891[7] (7268) 8106[10]

**One Deal (FR)** *J-L Dubord* a42 56
6 b g Nombre Premier Diluvienne (FR) (Kaldoun (FR))
515a[5]

**One Drunken Night** *Gay Kelleway* 26
2 ch g Sakhee's Secret Amandian (IRE) (Indian Ridge (IRE))
3619[5] 5277[7]

**Onefootinfront** *Daniel Mark Loughnane* a61 61
2 b c Sir Percy Anaya (Tobougg (IRE))
5876[5] 6159[5] 7026[7] 8164[4] 8870[10] 9014[8]

**One Foot In Heaven (IRE)** *A De Royer-Dupre* a85 117
5 b h Fastnet Rock(AUS) Pride (FR) (Peintre Celebre (USA))
1659a[7] 2398[2] 7177a[2] 7668a[11] 8087a[3]

**Onefootinparadise** *Philip McBride* a69 71
2 b f Footstepsinthesand Sancai (USA) (Elusive Quality (USA))
3169[5] 3725[3] 4220[2] 5150[17] 5659[9] 6651[6] 7363[2] 7814[13]

**One For Jodie (IRE)** *Michael Appleby* a61 28
6 ch g Majestic Missile(IRE) Tough Chic (IRE) (Indian Ridge (IRE))
747[5] 1225[8] 1409[4] 1593[3] 1978[19]

**One For June (IRE)** *William Haggas* a53 71
2 b f Arcano(IRE) Worthington (IRE) (Kodiac)
3215[8] 4252[4] (4757) 5150[22] 6200[9] 7985[3] (8213)

**Onehelluvatouch** *Philip Hide* a63 61
4 gr m Hellvelyn Soft Touch (IRE) (Petorius (IRE))
1789[8] 2055[8] 3820[6] 4442[7]

**One Last Hug** *Jim Goldie* 31
2 b g Orientor Gargoyle Girl (Be My Chief (USA))
1496[10]

**One Liner** *John O'Shea* a60 62
3 b g Delegator Quip (Green Desert (USA))
9219[10]

**One Man Army** *Julia Brooke* a55 45
5 b g Mount Nelson Hms Pinafore (IRE) (Singspiel (IRE))
419[12] 663[8]

**One Master** *William Haggas* 108
3 b f Fastnet Rock(AUS) Enticing (IRE) (Pivotal)
6184[3]◆ (7254) (7808)◆

**One Minute (IRE)** *William Haggas* 96
2 b f Kodiac Amwaj (IRE) (Dubawi (IRE))
(2577) 3725[2] (4862) 6136[10] 6863[4] 8002[14] 8562[8]

**One More Chance (IRE)** *David Brown* a75
2 b f Epaulette(AUS) Hi Katriona (IRE) (Second Empire (IRE))
9177[4]◆

**One More Dawn** *Mark Pattinson* a18
2 b f Kheleyf(USA) Jocasta Dawn (Kyllachy)
8889[13] 9310[11]

**Onenightidreamed (IRE)** *J A Stack* 104
6 ch g Footstepsinthesand Pivotalia (IRE) (Pivotal)
1388a[8] 1568a[3] 7663a[5]◆ 8438a[6]

**One One One (FR)** *H-A Pantall* a74 107
3 b c Le Havre(IRE) Acola (FR) (Acatenango (GER))
2250a[4]

**Oneoveryou (IRE)** *S J Mahon* a86 90
6 b m Tagula(IRE) Sun Slash (IRE) (Entrepreneur)
795a[3]

**One Pekan (IRE)** *Roger Varian* a91 79
7 b g Hard Spun(USA) Stormy Blessing (USA) (Storm Cat (USA))
61[8]

**One Pursuit (IRE)** *Charlie Mann* a34 61
9 br g Pastoral Pursuits Karinski (USA) (Palace Music (USA))
3004[8]

**Oneroa (IRE)** *Ivan Furtado* a61 23
2 b f Dandy Man(IRE) Alexander Express (IRE) (Sri Pekan (USA))
3902[11] 9023[5] 9372[4]

**Onesarnieshort (FR)** *Mme G Rarick* a30 63
2 b g Penny's Picnic(IRE) La Atomica (FR) (Silent Times (IRE))
4074[3] 4606[5] 5068[3] 7362[9] 8475[4] 9087a[15]

**One Second** *Mark Johnston* 70
2 b f Intello(GER) Albavilla (Spectrum (IRE))
3858[4] 4297[2] 4902[9]

**One Too Many (IRE)** *David Brown* a57 70
3 gr f Zebedee Speckled Hen (IRE) (Titus Livius (FR))
2900[7] 4303[4]◆ 5081[3]

**One Word More (IRE)** *Tim Easterby* a97 106
7 b g Thousand Words Somoushe (IRE) (Black Minnaloushe (USA))
3218[7] 4261[4] 4916[12] 5594[5] 6355[15] 6520[5] 7582[7] 7781[2] 8009[13]

**On Fire** *James Bethell* a82 82
4 b g Olden Times La Notte (Factual (USA))
286[2] 738[2] (993) 1307[2]◆ (2270) 2770[5] 3794[4] 5138[2] 6000[3] 6661[2] 7359[2] 8047[12]

**On Her Toes (IRE)** *William Haggas* 103
3 b f Kodiac Dancing Jest (IRE) (Averti (IRE))
2802[2] 3964[8] 4903[3] (5352) 7113[5] 7576[10]

**Onirique (IRE)** *M Boutin* a87 57
6 b m Teofilo(IRE) Blue Blue Sky (IRE) (Anabaa (USA))
713a[8]

**On Leave (USA)** *Claude McGaughey III* 106
4 rg m War Front(USA) Meghan's Joy (USA) (A.P. Indy (USA))
8601a[3]

**Only Bacan (CHI)** *Francisco Castro* a71
3 b g Astronomer Royal(USA) King's Folly (FR) (King's Best (USA))
2943a[5] 4940a[7]

**Onlyhuman (IRE)** *Edward Lynam* 86
4 b g Invincible Spirit(IRE) Liscune (IRE) (King's Best (USA))
6491a[20]

**Only Mine (IRE)** *Joseph G Murphy* 111
4 b m Pour Moi(IRE) Truly Mine (IRE) (Rock Of Gibraltar (IRE))
1520a[3] 3099a[2] 3632a[2] (5308a) 7424a[9]

**Only Orsenfoolsies** *Micky Hammond* 75
8 b g Trade Fair Desert Gold (IRE) (Desert Prince (IRE))
7924[6] 8239[2] 8487[4]

**Only Ten Per Cent (IRE)** *J R Jenkins* a69 40
9 b g Kheleyf(USA) Cory Everson (IRE) (Brief Truce (USA))
171[9] 734[8] 1080[5] 1184[7] 2069[8] 6114[8] 8776[7] 9340[9]

**Only William (IRE)** *Gordon Elliott* 64
2 b g Kyllachy Perino (IRE) (Speightstown (USA))
4020a[8]

**Onorina (IRE)** *Jim Boyle* a64 72
5 b m Arcano(IRE) Miss Honorine (IRE) (Highest Honor (FR))
1697[7] 2388[9] 3694[2] 4809[12] 7744[8] 8160[11]

**On The High Tops (IRE)** *Colin Teague* a4 30
9 b g Kheleyf(USA) Diplomats Daughter (Unfuwain (USA))
2076[11] 2453[3] 2994[9]

**Onthemoonagain (FR)** *J-C Rouget* 108
3 b f Cape Cross(IRE) Ma Preference (FR) (American Post)
3881a[F] 5449a[3] 6227a[2] 7669a[10]

**On The Warpath** *Sir Mark Prescott Bt* a92
2 ch c Declaration Of War(USA) Elusive Pearl (USA) (Medaglia d'Oro (USA))
7788[4] 8545[2] (8982)◆ (9177)◆

**On To Victory** *Eve Johnson Houghton* a74 108
3 b g Rock Of Gibraltar(IRE) Clouds Of Magellan (USA) (Dynaformer (USA))
1724[2] (2894)◆ 3505[2] (4221)◆ 4535[3] 5525[2] 6445[4] (7124)◆ 7783[4]

**Oona (FR)** *P Sogorb* 72
2 b f Declaration Of War(USA) Salorina (USA) (A.P. Indy (USA))
5629a[5] 6608a[4]

**Oor Jock (IRE)** *Adrian McGuinness* a62 52
9 ch g Shamardal(USA) Katdogawn (Bahhare (USA))
(52) 495[2] 1247[2]

**Ooty Hill** *Charlie Fellowes* 92
5 gr g Dubawi(IRE) Mussoorie (FR) (Linamix (FR))
7548[4] 8414[9]

**Opal Tiara (IRE)** *Mick Channon* a82 109
4 b m Thousand Words Zarafa (Fraam)
431a[2] (771a) 1378a[13] 2129[4] 3101a[2] 3961[13] 4857[7] 6420[6] 6697[4]

**Opening Time** *Richard Hannon* a55 61
3 b g Harbour Watch(IRE) Dozy (IRE) (Exceed And Excel (AUS))
2259[8] 2726[11] 3695[2] 4150[8]

**Open Wide (USA)** *Amanda Perrett* a88 90
3 bb g Invincible Spirit(IRE) Nunavik (IRE) (Indian Ridge (IRE))
2579[6] 3038[3] 3672[2] 4154[2] (4992) 6026[5] 6392[3]

**Opera Buffa (IRE)** *Steve Flook* 49
4 b m Exceed And Excel(AUS) Dubai Opera (USA) (Dubai Millennium)
4461[10] 5787[U] 6305[11]

**Opera Queen** *Andrew Balding* 52
3 b f Nathaniel(IRE) Opera Glass (Barathea (IRE))
3506[10] 3866[9] 4808[11]

**Operateur (IRE)** *Ben Haslam* a49 45
9 b g Oratorio(IRE) Kassariya (IRE) (Be My Guest (USA))
2272[11] 3449[5]

**Operative** *Ed de Giles* 83
4 ch g Pastoral Pursuits Gilt Linked (Compton Place)
4810[9] 5750[2] 6040[2] (6478) (7272) 7737[9]

**Opinionate** *Amanda Perrett* a79 93
3 b g Cacique(IRE) Comment (Sadler's Wells (USA))
(237) 5598[7] 6202[3] (6865) 7252[5]

**Opinion Maker (IRE)** *G Botti* a80 94
3 gr c Zoffany(IRE) Bella Estella (GER) (Sternkoenig (IRE))
8885a[7]

**Opposition** *Ed Dunlop* a90 90
4 gr g Dalakhani(IRE) Censored (Pivotal)
2752[6] 3409[2] (3795) 4908[7] 6865[4] 7412[2] 8047[4]

**Optical High** *Tony Forbes* 24
8 b g Rainbow High Forsweets (Forzando)
2891[6]

**Optima Petamus** *Patrick Holmes* a62 57
5 gr g Mastercraftsman(IRE) In A Silent Way (IRE) (Desert Prince (IRE))
727[8] 5096[8] 7015[7] 7659[13] 8219[11] 8799[5] 9127[6]

**Optimickstickhill** *Scott Dixon* a57 57
2 gr f Milk It Mick Stylistickhill (IRE) (Desert Style (IRE))
4296[7] 5278[4] 6085[7] 8804[4] 9302[9] 9439[7]

**Optimum Time (IRE)** *Eve Johnson Houghton* 79
2 b g Manduro(GER) Mypreciousblue (Peintre Celebre (USA))
(3156)◆ 4068[13] 4805[9] 6977a[22]

**Optionality** *D J Bunyan* a32
3 b f Bated Breath Celebrity (Pivotal)
8225a[13]

**Oracle Boy** *Michael Chapman* a13 13
6 b g Mount Nelson Snow Princess (IRE) (Ela-Mana-Mou)
3726[8] 4018[11] 6530[9] 7922[9]

**Orange Suit (IRE)** *Richard Hannon* 75
2 b c Declaration Of War(USA) Guantanamera (IRE) (Sadler's Wells (USA))
(7351)◆

**Orangey Red (IRE)** *W T Farrell* 95
4 b m Lawman(FR) Triple Try (IRE) (Sadler's Wells (USA))
4890[4] 6476[4] 7808[11]

**Oratorio's Joy (IRE)** *Daniel Mark Loughnane* a75 73
7 b m Oratorio(IRE) Seeking The Fun (USA) (Alhaarth (IRE))
(325) 497[6] 786[5] 1175[4] 1412[3] 2275[3]

**Oratory Davis (FR)** *V Luka Jr* a62 74
7 b g Oratorio(IRE) Panarea (FR) (Highest Honor (FR))
8303a[7]

**Orbolution (USA)** *Todd Pletcher* a63 105
2 bb f Orb(USA) My Rachel (USA) (Horse Chestnut (SAF))
8575a[9]

**Orchid Lily** *John Gosden* 70
2 b f Dansili Helleborine (Observatory (USA))
6292[4] 8322[4]

**Order Of Service** *K Kukk* a76 69
7 ch g Medicean Choir Gallery (Pivotal)
363[12] 745[5] 1210[2] 1433[3]◆ 1867[5] 3095[16] 3833[10] (5201a) 5984a[4]

**Order Of St George (IRE)** *A P O'Brien* 125
5 b h Galileo(IRE) Another Storm (USA) (Gone West (USA))
1999a[2] (3057a) 3996[2] (6214a) (6976a) 7668a[4] (8229)

**Orderofthegarter (IRE)** *A P O'Brien* 114
3 b c Galileo(IRE) Kitty Kiernan (Pivotal)
(1389a) (1633a) 2666a[5] 3368a[6]◆ 3994[2] 4878a[7]

**Oregon Gift** *Brian Ellison* a67 59
5 b g Major Cadeaux Dayville (USA) (Dayjur (USA))
6435[17] 7042[6] 8429[5]

**Oregon Point (USA)** *Tim Easterby* 69
3 b g Cape Blanco(IRE) Dream The Blues (IRE) (Oasis Dream)
1513[4] 1977[8] 2345[5] 3499[7] 4436[9]

**Oregon's Day (AUS)** *Mick Price* 104
3 br f Domesday(AUS) Oregon Seal (NZ) (Oregon (USA))
8057a[5]

**Orewa (IRE)** *Brian Ellison* 90
3 ch g Helmet(AUS) Lucky (IRE) (Sadler's Wells (USA))
2384[9] 2739[10]

**Oriental (JPN)** *C Laffon-Parias* a78 80
3 b c Smart Strike(CAN) Iron Lips (Iron Mask (USA))
1689a[7]

**Oriental Arrow (IRE)** *Stefano Botti* 91
3 b f Dark Angel(IRE) Samya (Invincible Spirit (IRE))
2244a[6]

**Oriental Eagle (GER)** *J Hirschberger* 107
3 bb c Campanologist(USA) Oriental Pearl (GER) (Big Shuffle (USA))
(7203a) 8274a[6]

**Oriental Fox (GER)** *Mark Johnston* a100 108
9 ch g Lomitas Oriental Pearl (GER) (Big Shuffle (USA))
2797[2] 3073[5] (4073) 4639[5] 5503[14] 6329[10] 7402[4]

**Oriental Ghost (GER)** *Dagmar Geissmann*
5 b g Tiger Hill(IRE) Oriental Pearl (GER) (Big Shuffle (USA))
714a[2]

**Oriental Khan (GER)** *R Dzubasz* 85
3 ch c Campanologist(USA) Oriental World (GER) (Platini (GER))
3636a[7] 4422a[15]

**Oriental Lilly** *Jim Goldie* a71 69
3 ch f Orientor Eternal Instinct (Exceed And Excel (AUS))
2121[8] 3194[3]◆ 3948[5] 5134[2] 5375[2] 5636[5] 6891[3] 7657[8] 8927[3]

**Oriental Power** *Jim Goldie* 39
2 b g Orientor Star In The East (Observatory (USA))
2771[9] 5202[8] 5879[5] 6626[9] 7159[12]

**Oriental Relation (IRE)** *James Given* a90 80
6 gr g Tagula(IRE) Rofan (USA) (Cozzene (USA))
4[11] 79[3] 219[2] 547[5] 618[3] 857[9] 1454[11] 1696[3] (2034) (2305) 2551[3] 3052[11] 3834[4] 4600[11] 5129[6] 6670[9] 8237[4]

**Oriental Song (IRE)** *Owen Burrows* 92
2 ch f Shamardal(USA) Oriental Melody (IRE) (Sakhee (USA))
3421[2] (4312) 6863[5]

**Oriental Splendour (IRE)** *Ruth Carr* a70 75
5 br g Strategic Prince Asian Lady (Kyllachy)
2034[8] 2700[10] 3345[2] (3667) 4015[6] 4433[4] 5055[4] 5459[3] 5930[10] 6574[7] 7557[3] 7738[6] 8320[9]

**Orient Class** *Paul Midgley* a82 93
6 ch g Orientor Killer Class (Kyllachy)
664[8] 851[8] 1475[2] 1777[6] 2409[2] 2764[4] 2839[5] (3827) 4333[4] 5402[4] 6185[9] 6593[3] 7286[6]

**Orientelle** *Richard Whitaker* a39 39
3 ch f Compton Place Oriental Girl (Dr Fong (USA))
2682[8] 3555[3] 3913[9] 5666[15] 5802[3] 7980[10] 8255[10] 8650[3] 8908[12]

**Orient Line (AUS)** *John Moloney* 97
5 b g Show A Heart(AUS) Zilzie (NZ) (Generous (IRE))
8057a[7]

**Orient Princess** *Paul Midgley* 45
2 ch f Orientor Killer Class (Kyllachy)
2403[8] 4599[6] 5398[6] 7159[11]

**Original Choice (IRE)** *William Haggas* a90 101
3 ch g Dragon Pulse(IRE) Belle Watling (IRE) (Street Cry (IRE))
(1841) 2565[6] 3713[2] (4507) 5400[2] 7609[2]

**Orin Swift (IRE)** *Jonathan Portman* 75
3 b g Dragon Pulse(IRE) Hollow Green (IRE) (Beat Hollow)
2039[14] 2689[4] 3248[3] 5810[3] 6293[6] 8114[2]

**Orion's Bow** *Tim Easterby* a111 111
6 ch g Pivotal Heavenly Ray (USA) (Rahy (USA))
2156[6] 2611[4] 3829[11]◆ 4306[3] 4881[5] 6325[15] 7611[14] 8044[18] 8238[7] 8416[14]

**Orithia (USA)** *Seamus Durack* a65 66
3 b f More Than Ready(USA) Tiz My Time (USA) (Sharp Humor (USA))
1790[5] 2259[2] 3721[4]◆ (3819) 4442[6] 4804[6] 7061[4] 8156[10] 8550[11]

**Orlando Rogue (IRE)** *Keith Dalgleish* a69 72
5 b g Bushranger(IRE) Boston Ivy (USA) (Mark Of Esteem (IRE))
44[2] (360) 1106[5]

**Ormering** *Roger Teal* a43 48
4 b m Kyllachy Lihou Island (Beveled (USA))
1112[8] 1563[11] 2056[7]

**Ormesher** *Donald McCain* 73
2 b g Sir Percy Marakabei (Hernando (FR))
6312[2]◆ 7043[5] 7551[3]

**Ormindo (USA)** *A bin Harmash* a88 60
7 ch g Discreet Cat(USA) Dearly (Rahy (USA))
537a[5]

**Ormixa (FR)** *F Vermeulen* 23
2 bb f Orpen(USA) Maximova (IRE) (Dylan Thomas (IRE))
1282a[4] 1594a[8]

**Ornamental** *Henry Candy* 79
2 b c Iffraaj Tulipe Rose (FR) (Shamardal (USA))
6070[5] 8735[2]

**Ornate** *Robert Cowell* a53 112
4 b g Bahamian Bounty Adorn (Kyllachy)
1903[2] 2397[6] 3539[6] 4354[10] 4920[5] (5116) (6039) 6428[4] 7027[4] 7475[3] 8105[2]

**Orrery (USA)** *P Bary* 77
3 b f Smart Strike(CAN) It's Midnight (USA) (Shamardal (USA))
2978a[5]

**Orsera (IRE)** *Peter Chapple-Hyam* 85
2 b f Clodovil(IRE) Lally Mut (ITY) (Muhtathir)
(7022) 8597[5]

**Orsino (IRE)** *Andrew Balding* a76 80
3 b c Galileo(IRE) Birmanie (USA) (Aldebaran (USA))
1984[2] 2314[3] 3209[6] 4586[4] 5328[3] (6107) 6930[5] 7565[3]

**Or So (USA)** *Derek Shaw* a34
5 ch g Rock Slide(USA) Miss Santa Anita (CAN) (Ide (USA))
158[11]

**Ortiz** *Henry Candy* a83 54
2 ch f Havana Gold(IRE) Almatinka (IRE) (Indian Ridge (IRE))
5216[5] (6816) 7875[2]

**Orvar (IRE)** *Robert Cowell* a96 97
4 b g Dandy Man(IRE) Roskeen (IRE) (Grand Lodge (USA))
2578[2] 4079[3] 4816[11] 6177[3] 6927[6] (7994)◆

**Oscar Nominated (USA)** *Michael J Maker* a100 110
4 ch r Kitten's Joy(USA) Devine Actress (USA) (Theatrical (IRE))
5977a[8] 8099a[2]

**Oscar Performance (USA)** *Brian A Lynch* 117
3 b r Kitten's Joy(USA) Devine Actress (USA) (Theatrical (IRE))
(4652a) (5953a) 7633a[3] 8610a[9]

**Oscar Ranger (IRE)** *Richard Fahey* 37
3 b g Bushranger(IRE) Bruno Maris (IRE) (Bachelor Duke (USA))
3984[6] 4341[12] 5286[5]

**Oscars Journey** *J R Jenkins* a71 71
7 ch g Dubai Destination(USA) Fruit Of Glory (Glory Of Dancer)
1112[3] 1184[6] 2069[3]

**Oskemen** *Clive Cox* a72 71
2 gr c Mastercraftsman(IRE) Ollie Olga (USA) (Stormy Atlantic (USA))
8389[9] 8678[4] 9319[2]

**Ospector (USA)** *F Alloncle* a71 63
3 b g Smart Strike(CAN) Stormica (USA) (Storm Cat (USA))
3554a[6]

**Ostaad (IRE)** *Doug Watson* a60 94
7 b g Marju(IRE) Almansoora (USA) (Bahri (USA))
203a[12]

**Ostana (GER)** *Daniel Paulick* 97
4 bb m Contat(GER) Oviva (GER) (Lomitas)
(7673a) (8462a)

**Ostatnia (IRE)** *W McCreery* a97 98
5 b m Amadeus Wolf Ostrusa (AUT) (Rustan (HUN))
1353a[4] 1936[11] 2657a[5] 3873a[6] 4416a[11] 6640a[7]

**Ostilio** *Simon Crisford* a82 79
2 ch c New Approach(IRE) Reem Three (Mark Of Esteem (IRE))
8140[2]◆ 8779[2]

**Oswald (IRE)** *Robyn Brisland* a73 72
2 gr c Mastercraftsman(IRE) Tough Chic (IRE) (Indian Ridge (IRE))
4725[2] 5292[8] 5847[2] 6890[3] 7482[7] 8349[2]

**Otomo** *Philip Hide* a71 74
3 b g Equiano(FR) Akhira (Emperor Jones (USA))
(2252)◆ 3517[4] 4093[6] 4178[6] 5711[3] 6282[4] 6888[7] 7881[6]

**Ottonian** *Charlie Appleby* 90
3 ch g Dubawi(IRE) Evil Empire (GER) (Acatenango (GER))
(2842) (3711)

**Oud Metha Bridge (IRE)** *Ed Dunlop* a81 71
3 ch g Helmet(AUS) Central Force (Pivotal)
916[2] (1198) 2088[14] 2894[7] 5363[4] 6265[7] 7569[8]

**Ouja** *John Gosden* a93 97
3 b f Sea The Stars(IRE) Royale Danehill (IRE) (Danehill (USA))
4808[6] 5364[4] (5796) 6357[4] 7283[11] 8007[6] 8548[5] 8986[8]

**Our Boy (IRE)** *David Evans* a79 74
3 ch g Raven's Pass(USA) Burren Rose (USA) (Storm Cat (USA))
1875[4] 3392[7] 4730[2] 5630[5] 6344[5] 6579[6] 7063[11]

**Our Boy Jack (IRE)** *Conor Dore* a44 87
8 b g Camacho Jina (IRE) (Petardia)
1606[12] 2133[16] 3172[11] 4298[13]

**Our Boy John (IRE)** *Richard Fahey* a53 62
3 b c Dandy Man(IRE) Jina (IRE) (Petardia)
149[11] 377[7]

**Our Century (IRE)** *Robert Hickmott* 104
6 b g Montjeu(IRE) Mixed Blessing (Lujain (USA))
8100a[4]

**Our Channel (USA)** *Jamie Osborne* a107 82
6 ch g English Channel(USA) Raw Gold (USA) (Rahy (USA))
148[4] 574[8] 1079[5] 1464[5]

**Our Charlie Brown** *Tim Easterby* a67 83
3 b g American Post Cordoba (Oasis Dream)
1878[5] 2107[5] 2885[2] (3047)◆ 4075[4] (4741) 5400[8] 5948[7] 6627[2] (7016) 7656[3] 7892[5] 8240[8] (8486)

**Our Cilla** *Julia Feilden* a35 63
3 gr f Sixties Icon Kinetix (Linamix (FR))
1468[4] 1822[5] 4117[4] (5142) 5581[3] (7152) 8241[8]

**Our Folly** *Stuart Kittow* a37 70
9 b g Sakhee(USA) Regent's Folly (IRE) (Touching Wood (USA))
1703[8]

**Our Greta (IRE)** *Michael Appleby* a69 68
3 gr f Exchange Rate(USA) Academicienne (CAN) (Royal Academy (USA))
3171[8] 4525[3] 5378[6] 6664[9] (8328) 8875[5] 9101[10]

**Our Kid (IRE)** *Richard Fahey* a64 63
2 b g Elnadim(USA) Red Shoe (Selkirk (USA))
(2277) 4205[6] 5537[6] 6036[9] 7057[9] 7655[8] 8804[3] 9002[3] 9345[4]

**Our Kim (IRE)** *John Butler* a50 51
3 b g Lawman(FR) Kayd Kodaun (IRE) (Traditionally (USA))
1514[8] 2033[7] 2997[11] 3674[5] 4320[9] 5653[8] 8673[10] 9034[9] 9278[2]

**Our Kylie (IRE)** *Brian Ellison* a61 68
5 b m Jeremy(USA) Prakara (IRE) (Indian Ridge (IRE))
2815[6] (4018) (4790)

**Our Little Pony** *Lawrence Mullaney* 67
2 b f Bated Breath Cracking Lass (IRE) (Whipper (USA))
2343[2]◆ (3200) 3791[3] 4555[2] 4866[3] 5453[5] 6085[3] 6466[5] 8008[13]

**Our Little Sister (IRE)**
*Hughie Morrison* a66
4 b m Big Bad Bob(IRE) Rehearsed (IRE) (In The Wings)
19[DSQ] 241[DSQ] 414[DSQ]

**Our Lois (IRE)** *Keith Dalgleish* a40 52
3 b f Bushranger(IRE) Atishoo (IRE) (Revoque (IRE))
848[10] 967[7] 1297[7]

**Our Lord** *Michael Attwater* a65 91
5 gr g Proclamation(IRE) Lady Filly (Atraf)
3281[4] 4148[2] 4532[2] (5429)◆ (5784) (6303) 6652[4] (7195) 7742[9]

**Our Man In Havana** *Richard Price* a78 73
2 b c Havana Gold(IRE) Auntie Kathryn (IRE) (Acclamation)
1694[4] 2816[6] 3187[2] 3895[4] (4527) 5127[2] 5685[9] 6977a[29] (7410) 8431[2] (8871) 9322[5]

**Our Max** *Georgios Pakidis* a49 58
7 gr g Intikhab(USA) Petula (Petong)
6800a[6]

**Ourmullion** *John Best* a84 59
3 b g Mullionmileanhour(IRE) Queen Ranavola (USA) (Medaglia d'Oro (USA))
209[2] (895) 1176[2] 4564[3] 5242[8] 5888[6] (6848) (7541) 8295[10] 9140[4] 9458[12]

**Our Oystercatcher** *Philip Hide* a60 73
3 b g Pastoral Pursuits The Dark Eider (Superlative)
(7907) 9411[10]

**Our Place In Loule** *Noel Wilson* a54 58
4 ch g Compton Place Show Off (Efisio)
1978[2] 2454[3] 2633[4] 3185[7] 3710[6] 5006[3] 5260[2] (5695) 6318[5] 7884[3] 8559[3] 8776[11]

**Our Power (IRE)** *Christian Williams* 47
2 b g Power Scripture (IRE) (Sadler's Wells (USA))
7197[4]

**Our Ruth** *Jimmy Fox* a23 14
4 ch m Assertive My Jeanie (IRE) (King Charlemagne (USA))
624[10] 2957[12] 5712[13] 6577[5] 7481[11] 8345[13]

**Our Tony** *Keith Dalgleish* a6
2 b f Rock Of Gibraltar(IRE) E'Cusson (Singspiel (IRE))
9049[11]

**Outback Blue** *David Evans* a69 82
4 gr g Aussie Rules(USA) Beautiful Lady (IRE) (Peintre Celebre (USA))
1683[15] 2558[4] 4468[4] 5135[2] 5686[3] 5888[3] 6273[4] 6416[7] 7142[6] 7905[3] 8497[9] 8653[3]

**Outback Guy (IRE)**
*Daniel Mark Loughnane* a52 23
4 b g Bushranger(IRE) Little Doll (Gulch (USA))
3575[11]

**Outback Traveller (IRE)**
*Robert Cowell* a85 100
6 b g Bushranger(IRE) Blue Holly (IRE) (Blues Traveller (IRE))
2606[11] 4072[12] 5640[26] 6922[10] 8044[5] 8383[22] 8991[8]

**Outcrop (IRE)** *Hughie Morrison* a62 77
3 b g Rock Of Gibraltar(IRE) Desert Sage (Selkirk (USA))
(1737)◆ 2784[3] 5218[10] 6579[7] 6821[2] (7230)

**Out Do** *David O'Meara* a105 109
8 ch g Exceed And Excel(AUS) Ludynosa (USA) (Cadeaux Genereux)
2156[3] 3092[17] 3593[4] (4072) 4920[8] 6206[15] 7950[5] 8845[3] 8991[5]

**Outer Space** *Jamie Osborne* a79 80
6 b g Acclamation Venoge (IRE) (Green Desert (USA))
275[8] 459[12] (760) 1208[2] 1295[2] 2115[5] 2518[7] 3593[9] 3969[7] 4293[7] 4887[11] 5245[6] 6297[6] 7094[9] 8344[8] 8706[5]◆ 8881[5] 9083[6] 9411[3]

**Outfox** *Bryan Smart* a66 41
3 b f Foxwedge(AUS) Spontaneity (IRE) (Holy Roman Emperor (IRE))
1913[15] 5019[5] 6016[2] 6435[19] 7241[4]

**Outlane** *Luca Cumani* a50
2 b f Camelot Batik (IRE) (Peintre Celebre (USA))
8877[9]

**Out Last** *Keith Dalgleish* a9 45
2 b f Lilbourne Lad(IRE) Ludynosa (USA) (Cadeaux Genereux)
5600[6] 5998[5] 6545[7] 8783[13]

**Outlaw Kate (IRE)**
*Michael Mullineaux* a20 40
5 b m Bushranger(IRE) Diosper (USA) (Diesis)
158[10] 386[13]

**Outlaw Torn (IRE)** *Richard Guest* a58 58
8 ch g Iffraaj Touch And Love (IRE) (Green Desert (USA))
(123) 176[5] 607[6] (689) 865[4] 1145[5] 1403[3] 1758[7] 2166[5] 2313[6] 2687[3] 3550[4] 3761[3] 5215[6] (5336) 5895[6] 6306[7] 6471[3] 6673[2] 7324[4] 7479[12] 7760[7] 7991[9] 8249[8] 8800[4] 9237[6]

**Out Of Money** *Jo Hughes*
2 b c Mazameer(IRE) Jane's Payoff (IRE) (Danetime (IRE))
1282a[8]

**Out Of Order (IRE)** *Tim Easterby* a65 45
3 b g Holy Roman Emperor(IRE) Barring Order (IRE) (Barathea (IRE))
401[4]◆ 659[2] 967[4]

**Out Of System** *F Chappet* a80 62
2 b c Makfi Smartest (IRE) (Exceed And Excel (AUS))
8302a[5]

**Out Of The Ashes**
*Mohamed Moubarak* a81 73
4 ch g Phoenix Reach(IRE) Shrewd Decision (Motivator)
66[6] 460[9] 1007[2] 1450[5] 2320[6] 2800[6] 3170[7] 3971[2] 8907[14] 9126[7]

**Out Of The Flames** *Richard Hannon* 99
2 ch f Showcasing Primo Lady (Lucky Story (USA))
2563[3] (2904) 3960[3] 4855[5] 6136[7] 6448[3] 8602a[3]

**Outofthequestion** *Alan King* 62
3 b g Delegator Why Dubai (USA) (Kris S (USA))
4274[5] 5220[7] 5931[6] 7097[7] 8114[5]

**Outrage** *Daniel Kubler* a100 87
5 ch g Exceed And Excel(AUS) Ludynosa (USA) (Cadeaux Genereux)
639[8]

**Overhaugh Street** *Ed de Giles* a67 70
4 b g Bahri(USA) Bom Chicka Wah Wah (USA) (Dynaformer (USA))
1473[4] 2708[9]◆ 3252[10] 3809[4] 4561[9] 4969[11] 5271[12] (5790) 6280[3] (6781) 7267[2]

**Over Reacted (FR)** *F Chappet* 99
2 b f Planteur(IRE) Ivory Style (Desert Style (IRE))
5461a[5] 6728a[3] 7846a[8]

**Overrider** *Shaun Lycett* a56 30
7 b g Cockney Rebel(IRE) Fustaan (IRE) (Royal Applause)
1260[11] 1402[11] 1563[9] 3440[8] 3550[7]

**Over The Ocean (USA)**
*Niels Petersen* a85 92
7 rg h Rockport Harbor(USA) Endless Sea (CAN) (Mt. Livermore (USA))
2943a[6] 4940a[5]

**Overtrumped** *Mike Murphy* a56
2 b f Champs Elysees Perfect Hand (Barathea (IRE))
8987[7] 9299[10]

**Owen The Law** *David Evans* a24 55
2 b c Equiano(FR) Ewenny (Warrshan (USA))
1941[10] 3165[6] 3570[4] 5121[6] 6634[12] (7081) 7695[5]

**Ower Fly** *Richard Hannon* a94 94
4 b g Pastoral Pursuits Contrary Mary (Mujadil (USA))
1515[7] 2115[3] 3003[10] 3572[4] 4339[12] 5369[3] 6068[2] (7156) 7622[10]

**Owners Day** *Neil Mulholland* a66 72
7 gr m Fair Mix(IRE) Charmeille (FR) (Exit To Nowhere (USA))
120[8]

**Oxford Blu** *Sir Mark Prescott Bt* a72 75
3 b g Aqlaam Blue Zealot (IRE) (Galileo (IRE))
3261[4] 3788[3] 5025[3] 5581[5] 6023[2] (6343)

**Oxford Don** *David Simcock* a71
3 b g Archipenko(USA) Oval Office (Pursuit Of Love)
882[7] 1190[2] 1840[3] 5298[8]

**Oxford Thinking (IRE)**
*John Gosden* a67 72
3 b g Holy Roman Emperor(IRE) Larceny (IRE) (Cape Cross (IRE))
40[4] 464[5]

**Oyster Card** *Michael Appleby* a49 48
4 b g Rail Link Perle D'Or (IRE) (Entrepreneur)
241[5] 508[5] 762[3] 1191[4] 1369[5] 1585[3] 1870[6] 2460[8] 8815[7]

**Oyster Pearl (IRE)** *Carroll Gray* a18 26
4 gr m Thousand Words Rectify (IRE) (Mujadil (USA))
4158[6] 4469[11]

**Ozeville (FR)** *D Guillemin* a70 95
4 ch m Le Havre(IRE) Racemate (Hurricane Run (IRE))
7753a[6]

**Ozz** *Frank Sheridan* 66
8 gr m Aussie Rules(USA) Spicey (Mizoram (USA))
1070a[11]

**Paca Punch** *John Flint* a25 31
4 b m Paco Boy(IRE) Plumage (Royal Applause)
3809[9] 4493[8]

**Pachadargent (FR)** *J-P Gauvin* a92 92
6 b g Kendargent(FR) Sabasha (FR) (Xaar)
4457a[2]

**Pacharana** *Luca Cumani* a91 98
4 b m Oasis Dream Cascata (IRE) (Montjeu (IRE))
2109[5] 3033[5] (3684) 4364[4] (4712) (5273)◆ 6104[3] 7092[2]◆ 8121[3] 8548[6] 8838a[12]

**Pachinko (USA)** *A Fabre* 74
3 rg f Tapit(USA) Hachita (USA) (Gone West (USA))
3353a[6]

**Pacific Fleet (USA)** *Archie Watson* 79
2 b c Elusive Quality(USA) Coronado Rose (USA) (Coronado's Quest (USA))
4101[3]◆ 5380[3]

**Pacific Salt (IRE)** *Pam Sly* a72 79
4 gr g Zebedee Villa Nova (IRE) (Petardia)
2267[6] 3396[6] 4047[2] 4541[3] (5126) (5760) 6143[3] 7098[6] 7957[3] 8596[9]

**Pacify** *Ralph Beckett* a66 101
5 b g Paco Boy(IRE) Supereva (IRE) (Sadler's Wells (USA))
1960[12] 4069[16] 4585[5] 5421[2] 6698[7]◆

**Pack It In (IRE)** *Alexandra Dunn* a32 74
4 br g Big Bad Bob(IRE) Evening Dress (Medicean)
2055[5] 2512[4] 3683[3] 4804[5] 5299[7] 6075[5] 6176[2] 9208[14]

**Paco Bleue** *Tim Easterby* 60
2 b f Paco Boy(IRE) Poulaine Bleue (Bertolini (USA))
3179[5]◆ 3662[5] 3902[10]

**Paco Dawn** *Philip Hide* a43
3 ch f Paco Boy(IRE) First Dawn (Dr Fong (USA))
376[11] 502[13]

**Paco Escostar** *Paul Midgley* 70
2 ch f Paco Boy(IRE) Shesastar (Bahamian Bounty)
6567[2]◆ 7269[10] 7919[2]

**Pacofilha** *Paul Cole* a72 71
3 b f Paco Boy(IRE) Seradim (Elnadim (USA))
2220[4] 2754[3] 5910a[6] 6281[3] 6578[4] 7230[2]

**Paco Filly** *Nikki Evans* a48
3 b f Paco Boy(IRE) Respectfilly (Mark Of Esteem (IRE))
7948[10] 8869[11]

**Paco Lady** *Ivan Furtado* a16 39
3 b f Paco Boy(IRE) Rosa Luxemburg (Needwood Blade)
1514[10] 2121[7] 7018[9] 8345[12]

**Pacolita (IRE)** *Sylvester Kirk* a80 79
5 ch m Paco Boy(IRE) Clara (IRE) (In The Wings)
677[3] 994[2] 1261[7]

**Pacommand** *David Barron* a70 40
4 b g Paco Boy(IRE) Indian Story (IRE) (Indian Ridge (IRE))
314[7] 968[10] 1473[7]

**Paco's Angel** *Richard Hughes* a84 100
3 b f Paco Boy(IRE) Papabile (USA) (Chief's Crown (USA))
1621[4] 3964[3] 4637[5]

**Paco's Prince** *Martin Smith* 58
2 b c Paco Boy(IRE) Equitissa (IRE) (Chevalier (IRE))
4151[8]

**Paco Style** *Michael Attwater* a24
2 b g Paco Boy(IRE) Al Aqabah (IRE) (Redback)
9311[13]

**Pact Of Steel** *Harry Dunlop* a54 63
2 ch c Declaration Of War(USA) She's My Dandy (IRE) (Holy Roman Emperor (IRE))
7391[9] 7765[8]

**Pactolus (IRE)** *Stuart Williams* a104 90
6 b g Footstepsinthesand Gold Marie (IRE) (Green Desert (USA))
199[11] (720) 1148[13] 1446[2] 1757[3] 2261[4] 3597[4]◆ 4636[8] 5744[9] 6024[4] 7602[3] 8705[2] (8999) 9233[4]

**Paddy A (IRE)** *Ian Williams* a74 75
3 b g Holy Roman Emperor(IRE) Lilting (IRE) (Montjeu (IRE))
1550[4] (2259) 2793[4] 3727[3] 4048[6] 4267[8] 8295[11] 8682[11] 9410[11]

**Paddyplex** *Keith Dalgleish* a91 83
4 b g Multiplex Turtle Bay (Dr Fong (USA))
(2496) (8912)

**Paddy Power (IRE)** *Richard Fahey* a78 90
4 ch g Pivotal Rag Top (IRE) (Barathea (IRE))
1777[2]◆ (2835)◆ 3324[10] 3827[U] 4379[17] 5256[5] 6205[14] 7086[3] (7557) (8115) 8416[8]

**Paddy's Rock (IRE)** *Lynn Siddall* a58 64
6 b g Whipper(USA) Hedera (USA) (Woodman (USA))
146[5] 414[3] 726[4] 1249[8] 3706[4] (4345) 4722[5] 5267[8] 5824[5] 6352[2] 6788[2] 7219[4] 7560[3]

**Paddys Runner** *Alan King* a76 77
5 gr g Sir Percy Frosty Welcome (USA) (With Approval (CAN))
688[2]

**Paddy The Chef (IRE)** *Ian Williams* a74
2 b g Dandy Man(IRE) The Reek (Tiger Hill (IRE))
8890[4] 9240[2]

**Padleyourowncanoe**
*Daniel Mark Loughnane* a65 60
3 b g Nayef(USA) Pooka's Daughter (IRE) (Eagle Eyed (USA))
(1107) 1822[4] 2060[5] 3261[3] 4978[2] 5846[5] 6524[U] 6901[2] 7360[2]

**Padrinho (IRE)** *John Best* a57 77
3 b g High Chaparral(IRE) Belanoiva (IRE) (Motivator)
1089[4] 1737[8] 2686[2]◆ (5034) 5550[3] 6107[6] 6849[8]

**Page Of Wands** *George Bewley* a20 27
4 b m Multiplex No Page (IRE) (Statue Of Liberty (USA))
29[4] 195[6] 7225[9] 7936[12]

**Pahente** *Tony Carroll*
9 bg g Silver Patriarch(IRE) Miss Tehente (FR) (Tehente (FR))
6530[7]

**Paiardina (IRE)** *Stefano Botti* 104
3 ch f Casamento(IRE) Sinful Pleasure (IRE) (Sinndar (IRE))
3121a[2] 8450a[9]

**Paint** *Richard Hannon* a70 76
2 b f Dutch Art Love Magic (Dansili)
4533[11] 5430[3] 5795[4] (6613) 7544[3] 7904[6]

**Pak Choi** *Andrew Balding* a31
2 ch c Paco Boy(IRE) Spring Green (Bahamian Bounty)
9310[10]

**Palace Ball** *Stuart Coltherd* 36
3 ch f Choisir(AUS) Catherine Palace (Grand Lodge (USA))
3044[4] 3896[5] 4247[11]

**Palace Moon** *Michael Attwater* a49 56
12 b g Fantastic Light(USA) Palace Street (USA) (Secreto (USA))
214[7] 740[6] 1425[10] 3172[8] 8994[8] 9456[10]

**Palace Prince (GER)**
*Jean-Pierre Carvalho* 113
5 bb h Areion(GER) Palace Princess (GER) (Tiger Hill (IRE))
1271a[5] 1659a[5] (3019a) 4130a[7] 5464a[10] (6451a) 6647a[2] 8270a[4]

**Paladin (IRE)** *Michael Blake* a74 75
8 b g Dubawi(IRE) Palwina (FR) (Unfuwain (USA))
(70) 286[11] (Dead)

**Palang (USA)** *Andreas Suborics* 100
5 bb g Hat Trick(JPN) Pavlova (USA) (Stravinsky (USA))
1661a[7] 5490a[4] (8338a)

**Palavicini Run (IRE)** *J F Levins* a78 79
4 ch m Palavicini(USA) Dawn's Sharp Shot (IRE) (Son Of Sharp Shot (IRE))
2656a[2] 9337[5]

**Palawan** *Jamie Osborne* a85 97
4 b g Mount Nelson Apple Sauce (Prince Sabo)
2232[8] 3212[9] 3808[2] 4091[7] 5369[6] 5821[4] 6801a[6] 8318[7]

**Palenville (IRE)** *Grant Tuer* a79 78
4 ch m Rip Van Winkle(IRE) Faithful Duchess (IRE) (Bachelor Duke (USA))
151[3] 514[2] 729[4] 3253[4]

**Palermo (IRE)** *Michael Wigham* a47
3 b g Intikhab(USA) La Spezia (IRE) (Danehill Dancer (IRE))
115[10]

**Palindrome (USA)** *Marjorie Fife* a65 49
4 b g Poet's Voice Hi Dubai (Rahy (USA))
28[9] 195[8] 527[5] 689[10] 988[8] 2313[3] 4900[10] 5649[5] 6058[4] 7479[3] 8314[7] 8719[2]

**Pallasator** *Sir Mark Prescott Bt* a86 116
8 b g Motivator Ela Athena (Ezzoud (IRE))
2288[5] 5503[6] 6250a[6] 7116[8]

**Palmer (IRE)** *Bryan Smart* 74
2 b g Acclamation Aneedah (IRE) (Invincible Spirit (IRE))
2029[6] 2740[3] 3826[3] 4427[2] 4888[3] 5615[3] 7269[2] 7919[7]

**Palmerston** *Michael Appleby* a63 86
4 b g Oasis Dream Marywell (Selkirk (USA))
1517[14] 1832[2] 2226[2] (3204) 3837[8] 5125[6] 5484[9] 6434[5] 7823[9] 8375[13]

**Palombe (IRE)** *A Fabre* 101
3 gr f Nathaniel(IRE) Grey Lily (IRE) (Boreal (GER))
2003a[5]

**Palya (FR)** *B Legros* a68 79
2 b f Panis(USA) Skalya (FR) (Sagacity (FR))
4166a[3] 4389a[5] (5585a) 6050a[5] 8169a[6] 8884a[5]

**Pammi** *Anthony Carson* a42 42
2 b f Poet's Voice Bright Girl (IRE) (Invincible Spirit (IRE))
5507[8] 5885[7] 6816[6] 9230[8]

**Pamplemousse (IRE)** *A Fabre* a82 103
3 b f Siyouni(FR) Acatama (USA) (Efisio)
1883[4]

**Pancake Day** *David C Griffiths* a63 63
5 b g Mullionmileanhour(IRE) Fangfoss Girls (Monsieur Bond (IRE))
20[3] (153) 273[5]

**Pandagreen (IRE)** *Gavin Cromwell* 82
3 ch f Casamento(IRE) Special Touch (IRE) (Spinning World (USA))
6491a[23]

**Pandana (FR)** *M Rosseel*
7 b m Desert Style(IRE) Pink And Red (USA) (Red Ransom (USA))
6543a[7]

**Pandinus Imperator (IRE)**
*Martin Smith* 48
4 b g Scorpion(IRE) Casiana (GER) (Acatenango (GER))
8291[6]

**Pando (IRE)** *N Caullery* a84 85
3 b c Born To Sea(IRE) Aguilas Perla (IRE) (Indian Ridge (IRE))
(3554a) 6124a[2]

**Pangania (GER)** *P Vovcenko* 59
3 b f Rio De La Plata(USA) Paragua (GER) (Nayef (USA))
6566a[4]

**Pangolin (FR)** *M Delzangles* 77
3 b f Panis(USA) Park Acclaim (IRE) (Clodovil (IRE))
(8464a)

**Panko (IRE)** *Ed de Giles* a82 86
4 b g Iffraaj Engraving (Sadler's Wells (USA))
2146[5]◆ 2624[3] (2965) 3795[2] 4206[6] 4908[5] 6344[6] 7651[11] 7880[6]

**Panophobia** *Richard Fahey* a66 64
2 br g Bated Breath Methayel (IRE) (Araafa (IRE))
2926[6] 4606[6] 5162[7] 5878[3] 6552[6] 7057[2] 7624[5] 8213[6]

**Panos (FR)** *Henk Grewe* a50 31
3 b g Panis(USA) Prairie Scilla (GER) (Dashing Blade)
2536a[11] 4943a[13]

**Panova** *Sir Michael Stoute* a80 94
3 b f Invincible Spirit(IRE) Safina (Pivotal)
3031[2] 4051[5] 4794[4] 5856[2] 6377[2] 7406[2] 7815[7]

**Panstarr** *J S Bolger* a76 96
3 b f Pivotal Halle Bop (Dubai Millennium)
(6978a) 8083a[4]

**Pantera** *David O'Meara* 44
3 b f Dutch Art Plethora (Sadler's Wells (USA))
5458[8] 6129[4]

**Pantera Negra (IRE)** *David Barron* 75
3 b f Champs Elysees Penchee (Grand Lodge (USA))
4602[2]◆ 5185[11] (5604) (6091) 6691[3]

**Panthelia (FR)** *P Sogorb* 103
3 gr f Gentlewave(IRE) Panthesilea (FR) (Kendor (FR))
2945a[2] 3881a[7] 6732a[8] 8666a[4]

**Panther In Pink (IRE)** *Ann Duffield* a40 49
3 gr f Zebedee Annus Iucundus (IRE) (Desert King (IRE))
377[8] 848[3] 1034[5] 1297[9] 2902[4] 3196[2] 3708[5] 4473[10] 5374[14] 5539[6] 8477[8]

**Panther Patrol (IRE)**
*Eve Johnson Houghton* a79 78
7 b g Tagula(IRE) Quivala (USA) (Thunder Gulch (USA))
682[5] 1062[5] 1290[9] 1791[3] 2229[4] 2762[8]

**Pantomime (IRE)** *Rebecca Menzies* a50 51
5 gr m Mastercraftsman(IRE) Dama'A (IRE) (Green Desert (USA))
8654[5] 9368[6]

**Papa Delta** *Tony Carroll* 45
3 b g Makfi Step Softly (Golan (IRE))
3407[5] 3818[7]

**Papagayo (IRE)** *Barry Murtagh* a24 31
5 b g Shirocco(GER) Jomana (IRE) (Darshaan)
7219[10]

**Papa Stour (USA)** *Andrew Balding* a86 57
2 b c Scat Daddy(USA) Illaunglass (IRE) (Red Clubs (IRE))
9097[7]

**Papa Winner (FR)** *S Jesus* a63 67
3 b g Salut Thomas(FR) Palea (GER) (Red Ransom (USA))
748a[6]

**Paper Faces (USA)** *Roger Varian* a68 65
4 ch m Lemon Drop Kid(USA) Liffey Dancer (IRE) (Sadler's Wells (USA))
23[2] 333[4] 421[3]

**Papou Tony** *George Baker* a79 61
4 b g Raven's Pass(USA) Lukrecia (IRE) (Exceed And Excel (AUS))
90[4] 501[10] (812) (1728)◆ 3454[3]◆ 4810[11] 6284[3] 7006[4] 7213[6] 7947[12]

**Paques Island (FR)** *J Phelippon* a62 70
4 b m Slickly Royal(FR) Isula Di Isula (IRE) (Anabaa (USA))
391a[4]

**Paquita Bailarina** *James Given* a50 54
3 ch f Paco Boy(IRE) Prima Ballerina (Pivotal)
1626[6] 2181[4] 2734[8] 3260[7] 3913[13] 5852[5]

**Parabak (FR)** *M Delzangles* 91
2 b c Maxios Parandeh (FR) (Kahyasi (IRE))
7847a[4]

**Parabellum (IRE)** *A Fabre* 108
3 b g Dubawi(IRE) Pacifique (IRE) (Montjeu (IRE))
4878a[6] 5692a[5]

**Paradise Cove** *Charlie Fellowes* a43 75
3 ch f Harbour Watch(IRE) Peace Signal (USA) (Time For A Change (USA))
2908[4] (3649) 5331[3] 6139[9] 7201[5] 7762[12]

**Paradise Found** *Emma Owen* a41 24
6 b m Pastoral Pursuits Crochet (IRE) (Mark Of Esteem (IRE))
3157[8] 3456[9]

**Paradise Lake (IRE)** *Ed Walker* a73 75
3 b g Siyouni(FR) Kalandara (IRE) (Rainbow Quest (USA))
2260[3]◆ 3005[6] 8116[2] 9435[2]

**Paradise Woods (USA)**
*Richard E Mandella* a119
3 b f Union Rags(USA) Wild Forest (USA) (Forest Wildcat (USA))
8578a[3]

**Paradwys (IRE)** *Archie Watson* a64 75
3 b f Exceed And Excel(AUS) First Of Many (Darshaan)
4305[8] (4964) 5965[4] 6485[4] 7058[8] 7770[8]

**Para Mio (IRE)** *Seamus Durack* 74
2 b c Pour Moi(IRE) Malaspina (IRE) (Whipper (USA))
6869[4]◆ 7543[9]

**Paramount Love** *Richard Fahey* 73
2 b f Pivotal Portraitofmylove (IRE) (Azamour (IRE))
3312[3] 3858[3] 4786[2] 5659[5] 6561[3] 7647[7]

**Parasail** *Mark Johnston* a2
3 ch f New Approach(IRE) West Wind (Machiavellian (USA))
2921[10]

**Parauari (FR)** *A De Royer-Dupre* a75 90
3 b g Lawman(FR) Parade Militaire (IRE) (Peintre Celebre (USA))
5777a[7]

**Par Coeur (GER)** *W Mongil* 96
3 bb Adlerflug(GER) Palucca (GER) (Big Shuffle (USA))
8090a[5]

**Parfait (IRE)** *John Gosden* a88 111
3 b g Invincible Spirit(IRE) Rakiza (IRE) (Elnadim (USA))
1841[3] 3146[5] (3592) 3959[4] (4854)

**Parin** *Henk Grewe* 63
3 b f Motivator La Bikina (Avonbridge)
4455a[6] 5268a[5] 8464a[7]

**Paris Bound** *Andrew Balding* a63
4 b g Champs Elysees Averami (Averti (IRE))
687[5] 894[5] 1108[2] 1436[2] 7730[2]

**Parish Boy** *David Loughnane* a90 87
5 gr g New Approach(IRE) Requesting (Rainbow Quest (USA))
1148[11] 2552[7] 3716[5] 4336[9] 5060[2] 5313[7] 6195[3] 6701[9] 6965[6] 7558[6] 8142[11]

**Parisian (IRE)** *Ralph Beckett* a46 58
2 ch g Champs Elysees La Persiana (Daylami (IRE))
4859[7] 8340[8] 8951[11]

**Parisian Chic (IRE)** *Lee Carter* a60 51
3 b f Kodiac Divine Design (IRE) (Barathea (IRE))
34[6] 434[8] 1000[7] 4211[12] 6004[8] 6813[10] 8543[9]

**Paris Magic** *Hugo Palmer* a81 85
4 b g Champs Elysees Belgooree (Haafhd)
519[6]

**Paris Protocol** *Richard Hannon* a87 93
4 b g Champs Elysees Island Vista (Montjeu (IRE))
2176[3] 3076[3] 3618[5] 4073[14] 6135[3] 7397[5] 7903[5] 8398[4]

**Paris Rooftops (IRE)** *Luca Cumani* a5 71
3 b f Galileo(IRE) Daneleta (IRE) (Danehill (USA))
3007[6] 3615[4] 4497[12] 5401[4]

**Parissa (IRE)** *Carina Fey* 61
3 b f Roderic O'Connor(IRE) Green Empire (IRE) (Second Empire (IRE))
427a[11]

**Parkori (FR)** *G Bertrand* a72 84
9 ch g Vatori(FR) Parkohio (FR) (Script Ohio (USA))
4457a[5]

**Parkour (IRE)** *Marco Botti* a85 46
4 b g Holy Roman Emperor(IRE) School Holidays (USA) (Harlan's Holiday (USA))
857[4] 1346[3] 2462[5]

**Park Paddocks (IRE)**
*William Haggas* a59 74
3 b g Sea The Stars(IRE) Dream Of The Hill (IRE) (Tiger Hill (IRE))
2152[5] 2721[4] 3720[9] 4202[2]

**Parkwarden (IRE)** *Chris Grant* a54 54
3 b g Bushranger(IRE) Honour And Obey (IRE) (Hurricane Run (IRE))
2349[13] 4839[3] 7248[11]

**Parlance (IRE)** *Sir Michael Stoute* a87 87
3 b f Invincible Spirit(IRE) Pleasantry (Johannesburg (USA))
3722[4] 4317[3]◆ 5078[4] 6321[7] 7545[2] 8150[7]

**Parliamentarian (IRE)**
*Charlie Appleby* a48 68
4 b g Dubawi(IRE) Forum Floozie (NZ) (Danasinga (AUS))
3076[5] 3534[4] 4828[7]

**Parmenter** *Alan King* a56 67
2 b f Dick Turpin(IRE) Triple Cee (IRE) (Cape Cross (IRE))
6862[7] 7226[4] 8399[7]

**Parnassian (IRE)** *Amanda Perrett* a90 92
3 b g Elzaam(AUS) Adaptation (Spectrum (IRE))
2739[13] 3664[2] (4154)◆ 4610[4] 6275[12] 7782[12] 8310[4] 8639[7]◆ 8821[6]

**Parole (IRE)** *Tim Easterby* a61 73
5 ch g Mastercraftsman(IRE) Leniency (IRE) (Cape Cross (IRE))
3315[7] 5166[7] (5698) 6855[3] 7225[4] 7735[6]

**Part Exchange** *Hugo Palmer* a91
3 b f Champs Elysees Market Forces (Lomitas)
(7492)◆ 8820[8]

**Par Three (IRE)** *Tony Carroll* a57 50
6 bb g Azamour(IRE) Little Whisper (IRE) (Be My Guest (USA))
35[7] 646[7] (988) 1256[2] 1486[6] 2332[6] 2972[6] 4756[4] 5787[P]

**Parti Pris** *Mlle S Verrier* 65
4 b m American Post Pirogue Bleue (IRE) (Peintre Celebre (USA))
6365a[8]

**Partitia** *Sir Michael Stoute* 92
3 br f Bated Breath Palmette (Oasis Dream)
2130[7] 2570[4] 3526[3]◆ 4435[2] 5117[6]

**Partry Flyer (IRE)** *Oliver Greenall* a40 30
2 b g Zoffany(IRE) Whitethorne Scent (Monsieur Bond (IRE))
3742[9] 6146[8] 6410[7] 7030[10] 8190[7] 8644[10] 8783[5]

**Partyday (IRE)** *V Luka Jr* a80 99
4 ch m Footstepsinthesand Jolie Clara (FR) (Kahyasi (IRE))
4518a[10]

**Party Fears Too (IRE)** *Jim Goldie* 44
2 b c Society Rock(IRE) Comedic Art (IRE) (Dansili)
6590[8]

**Party Royal** *Nick Gifford* a64 65
7 b g Royal Applause Voliere (Zafonic (USA))
90[11] 1028[4] 1556[3] 2042[3] (2964) 3753[5] 5320[7] 8301[5]

**Party Tiger** *Richard Fahey* a76 76
3 b g Excelebration(IRE) Poly Pomona (Green Desert (USA))
78[2] 498[5] 788[4] 1386a[10] 2820[6] 3388[4] 4310[7] 4694[9]

**Parviz (IRE)** *Waldemar Hickst* 106
3 b c Lope De Vega(IRE) Sur Choix (Galileo (IRE))
4422a[7] 5464a[11] 7429a[5]

**Parys Mountain (IRE)** *David Brown* 83
3 gr g Dark Angel(IRE) Muzdaan (IRE) (Exceed And Excel (AUS))
2072[7]◆ 3814[2] (3974) 4892[8] 5948[11] 6519[6]

**Parzival (IRE)** *G Botti* a62 56
5 b g Myboycharlie(IRE) Slyta (FR) (Slickly (FR))
4457a[11]

**Pascasha D'Or (FR)** *S Wattel* a88 93
3 ch c Mr. Sidney(USA) Reine Annicka (FR) (Lord Of Men)
8976a[3]

**Pas D'Action** *Mrs A Malzard* 54
9 ch g Noverre(USA) Bright Vision (Indian Ridge (IRE))
5201a[6] 5984a[6]

**Pas De Blanc** *Brian Barr* a57 45
2 b f Major Cadeaux Mancunian Way (Green Desert (USA))
8472[7] 8669[12] 8988[4] 9302[11]

**Pas De Deux (GER)**
*Yasmin Almenrader* a100 117
7 b g Saddex Palucca (GER) (Big Shuffle (USA))
4939a[5] (6647a)

**Pas De Secrets (IRE)** *Wido Neuroth* a96 93
4 b g High Chaparral(IRE) Quiet Waters (USA) (Quiet American (USA))
6501a[5] 7428a[6]

**Pas La Pas La Bas** *Gerard Martin* a16
4 b h Paco Boy(IRE) Pompey Girl (Rainbow Quest (USA))
391a[16]

**Passcode** *Andrew Balding* a68 70
3 b f Camacho Passata (FR) (Polar Falcon (USA))
(1866) 2794[5] 4372[5]

**Passing Clouds** *Michael Attwater* a68
2 b g Kheleyf(USA) Steppin Out (First Trump)
8340[3] 9312[7]

**Passing Star** *Daniel Kubler* a88 73
6 b g Royal Applause Passing Hour (USA) (Red Ransom (USA))
117[7] 1224[8] 1890[7] 2267[5] (3136) 3696[5] 4529[7] 5481[9] 6102[4] 6502[6] 7770[2] 8400[7] 9094[5]

**Passionatta (IRE)** *J P Murtagh* a40 63
3 b f Intense Focus(USA) Hasanat (Night Shift (USA))
(6339) (7218)

**Passion Nonantaise (FR)**
*J-P Gauvin* a82 82
3 b f Chichi Creasy(FR) Une Nonantaise (FR) (Kaldounevees (FR))
(8885a)

**Passior (FR)** *D De Waele* a55 44
8 b g Vatori(FR) Abedissa (FR) (Bishop Of Cashel)
930a[2]

**Pass Mark** *Mrs Ilka Gansera-Leveque* 54
2 b g Raven's Pass(USA) Examinee (GER) (Monsun (GER))
8119[9] 8634[10]

**Pass The Cristal (IRE)** *William Muir* a67 65
3 b g Raven's Pass(USA) Crystal Melody (Nureyev (USA))
2309[2] (2911) (3561) 3937[6] 5031[5] 5835[4] 6485[8] 6753[3] 7540[4] (7791) 9126[5] 9243[4]

**Pass The Time** *Neil Mulholland* a66 57
8 b m Passing Glance Twin Time (Syrtos)
610[3]

**Pastamakesufaster** *David Evans* a73 76
2 b f Multiplex Sopran Cross (ITY) (Cape Cross (IRE))
4466[6] 6272[4] 6584[6] (7504) 8196a[7] 9405[5]

**Pastfact** *Malcolm Saunders* 81
3 br g Pastoral Pursuits Matterofact (IRE) (Bold Fact (USA))
2252[7] 2720[4] (3810) (4198)◆ (6099) 6511[3] 7192[4] (7691)◆ 8115[4]

**Pastichop (FR)** *A Chopard* a81 91
3 b c Bertolini(USA) Perle De Star (FR) (Indian Rocket)
272a[6]

**Pastime** *Gay Kelleway* a92 92
3 b g Pastoral Pursuits Piddies Pride (IRE) (Indian Lodge (IRE))
2547[6] 2970[2] (3549) (4265)◆ 4831[3] 5369[2] 8418[2] 8736[3] 8905[10] 9264[3]

**Past Master** *Henry Candy* a69 75
4 gr g Mastercraftsman(IRE) Millestan (IRE) (Invincible Spirit (IRE))
9209[2]◆

**Pastoral Dreams** *Simon Dow* a53
2 b c Pastoral Pursuits Engaging (Oasis Dream)
9312[9]

**Pastoral Music** *Hughie Morrison* a80 78
4 b g Pastoral Pursuits Jasmeno (Catcher In The Rye (IRE))
3459[3] 4222[5] 4750[3] 5590[4] 6610[2] 7202[4] (8000) 8426[5]

**Pastoral Player** *Hughie Morrison* a52 94
10 b g Pastoral Pursuits Copy-Cat (Lion Cavern (USA))
2618[2] 3030[2] 3777[6] (4524) 7340[4] 7781[6] 8736[16]

**Patanjali (IRE)**
*Eve Johnson Houghton* a61 61
4 b m Poet's Voice Penang (IRE) (Xaar)
3028[7] 3688[3]◆ 4163[10]

**Patascoy (FR)** *X Thomas-Demeaulte* 96
2 b c Wootton Bassett Noble World (GER) (Winged Love (IRE))
5679a[4]

**Patch (USA)** *Todd Pletcher* a107
3 b c Union Rags(USA) Windyindy (USA) (A.P. Indy (USA))
2420a[14]

**Patching** *Giles Bravery* a66 72
3 b f Foxwedge(AUS) Crinolette (IRE) (Sadler's Wells (USA))
1333[9] 1968[4] 2269[9] 3217[4] (3701) 4144[2] 4883[8] 5510[2] 5813[2] 6203[5] 6485[3] 7052[10] 7710[11]

**Patchwork** *Richard Hughes* a65 86
3 ch g Paco Boy(IRE) Medley (Danehill Dancer (IRE))
1727[5] 2393[2] (2901) 4313[2] 4830[10] 6141[2] 7192[7] 8310[8]

**Patent** *Peter Niven* a43 69
4 b g Paco Boy(IRE) Film Script (Unfuwain (USA))
1101[6] 2471[6] 3760[7]◆ 5499[7] 6035[8] 7015[6] 7248[3] 7922[8] 8655[7]

**Pathfinder (GER)** *K Demme*
2 ch c Wiener Walzer(GER) Picobella (GER) (Big Shuffle (USA))
8091a[4]

**Patienceisavirtue** *Christine Dunnett* 34
2 b f Libranno Patience (Kyllachy)
8118[6] 8472[8]

**Patrick (IRE)** *Richard John O'Brien* a90 93
5 b g Acclamation Red Liason (IRE) (Selkirk (USA))
795a[8] 1353a[5] 1479a[7] 4416a[3]

**Patriot Hero (IRE)** *Endo Botti* 75
3 ch g Pivotal Noble Hero (IRE) (Daggers Drawn (USA))
2245a[2] 2868a[5]

**Patron Of Explores (USA)**
*Patrick Holmes* a52 27
6 b g Henrythenavigator(USA) India Halo (ARG) (Halo Sunshine (USA))
176[6] 400[12] 607[8] 739[9] 761[12]

**Pattie** *Mick Channon* a71 82
3 ch f Sixties Icon Excellent Day (IRE) (Invincible Spirit (IRE))
115[2] 2761[3] 3182[2] 3749[6] (4121) 4491[4] 4883[5] 5591[5] (6340)

**Patty Patch** *Richard Spencer* a43 61
2 b f Big Bad Bob(IRE) Cockney Dancer (Cockney Rebel (IRE))
3179[6] 3687[7] 4266[5]

**Patuano (IRE)** *W McCreery* a45 89
3 b f Choisir(AUS) Musical Rain (IRE) (Val Royal (FR))
4416a[5] 6971a[8]

**Paulaim (FR)** *E Lellouche* a66 62
4 ch h American Post Elanaaka (Lion Cavern (USA))
6018a[9]

**Paulamey** *David Evans* a2 32
2 gr f Piccolo Tryptonic (FR) (Baryshnikov (AUS))
2037[12] 2343[6] 6861[11] 7827[9]

**Paulassilverlining (USA)**
*Chad C Brown* a113
5 b m Ghostzapper(USA) Seeking The Silver (USA) (Grindstone (USA))
8605a[6]

**Paulina Dream (FR)**
*Edouard Thueux* a24
2 b f French Fifteen(FR) Pavlovna (FR) (Singspiel (IRE))
9086a[15]

**Paul's Saga (FR)** *J-P Gauvin* a72 78
3 gr f Martaline Humoriste (FR) (Saint Cyrien (FR))
8976a[7]

**Pauvre Moi (IRE)** *John Butler* a24
2 b f Pour Moi(IRE) Aitch (IRE) (Alhaarth (IRE))
7410[9] 7827[8]

**Pavarella Shoes** *Noel Wilson* 54
2 ch f Lethal Force(IRE) Shena's Dream (IRE) (Oasis Dream)
6056[9] 6624[3]

**Paved With Gold (IRE)**
*John Joseph Murphy* a67 57
4 b g Champs Elysees Luminous Gold (Fantastic Light (USA))
5518a[14] 7792[2]◆

**Pavel (USA)** *Doug O'Neill* a116
3 rg c Creative Cause(USA) Mons Venus (CAN) (Maria's Mon (USA))
8611a[10]

**Pavers Pride** *Noel Wilson* a57 65
3 ch g Bahamian Bounty Pride Of Kinloch (Dr Devious (IRE))
1782[9] 2897[8]◆ 3914[5] 4694[10] (5619) 6596[4] 7522[4] 7884[9]

**Pavillon** *Clive Cox* a87 90
3 b f Showcasing Park Law (IRE) (Fasliyev (USA))
(2517) 3262[3] 4637[6] 5152[3]

**Pavlenko (JPN)** *A P O'Brien* a90 91
3 b f Deep Impact(JPN) Maybe (IRE) (Galileo (IRE))
3874a[8] 6080a[10] 6490a[15] 7261a[4] 8083a[5] 8407a[8]

**Payroll (AUS)** *Richard Laming* 99
4 b m Not A Single Doubt(AUS) Workhard (AUS) (Red Ransom (USA))
(8857a)

**Pazeer (FR)** *Ibrahim Al Malki* 107
3 b c Siyouni(FR) Parandeh (FR) (Kahyasi (IRE))
933a[2]

**Pc Dixon** *Mick Channon* a64 73
4 ch g Sixties Icon Lakaam (Danzero (AUS))
351[10] 1409[9] 2762[9]

**Peace And Plenty** *William Muir* a83 47
3 ch c Exceed And Excel(AUS) Putois Peace (Pivotal)
1404[2] 1736[10] 6657[9] 7457[3]◆ 7769[3] 8497[2] (8886) 9140[8]

**Peace Dreamer (IRE)**
*Robert Cowell* a30 77
3 b f Sir Prancealot(IRE) See Nuala (IRE) (Kyllachy)
2727[2] (4106) 5606[7] 6511[4]

**Peace Envoy (FR)** *A P O'Brien* a78 112
3 b c Power Hoh My Darling (Dansili)
2666a[10] 3927[8] 4935a[9] 7145[8]

**Peaceful Passage (USA)**
*John Gosden* a77 60
3 b f War Front(USA) Flying Passage (USA) (A.P. Indy (USA))
(737)

**Peace In Motion (USA)**
*Waldemar Hickst* 100
3 bb f Hat Trick(JPN) Peace Royale (GER) (Sholokhov (IRE))
1846a[3] 2665a[8] 3882a[2]

**Peace Prevails** *Richard Fahey* a47 66
2 ch f Declaration Of War(USA) Miss Mediator (USA) (Consolidator (USA))
1776[6] 3662[3]◆ 4296[5] 5751[6] 6825[3] 7938[13]

**Peace Terms (IRE)** *Ralph Beckett* a72
3 b f Teofilo(IRE) Intapeace (IRE) (Intikhab (USA))
8504[3] 9273[2]

**Peace Trail** *Charlie Appleby* a85 83
2 b f Kyllachy Path Of Peace (Rock Of Gibraltar (IRE))
(5938) 6418[10] (7238)

**Peachey Carnehan**
*Michael Mullineaux* a74 65
3 ch g Foxwedge(AUS) Zubova (Dubawi (IRE))
(150) 435[3] 686[3] (1194) 1463[3] 1940[7] 3517[6] 4161[2] 4576[4] 4843[5] 5291[4] (5636) 5826[2]◆ (5956) 6308[5] 6679[7] 6878[6] 7933[9] 8489[6] 8875[9] 9176[6]

**Peach Melba** *Mark Johnston* a88 100
3 b f Dream Ahead(USA) Nellie Melba (Hurricane Sky (AUS))
2887[2] 3234[3] 3493[2] 4248[4] 4624[3] 5248[2] (5358)◆ (5754) (6261) 6629[2] 6919[8] 7658[2] (7815) (8463a) 8747[3]

**Peach Pavlova (IRE)** *Ann Duffield* 74
3 b f Elzaam(AUS) Zvezda (USA) (Nureyev (USA))
2886[7] 3979[8] 4559[13]

**Peak Hill** *Adrian Wintle* a62 65
4 ch g Bahamian Bounty River Naiad (Nayef (USA))
6811[8] 8031[3] 8402[3] 8662[8] 8957[4] 9084[11]

**Peak Princess (IRE)**
*Richard Hannon* a94 85
3 b f Foxwedge(AUS) Foot Of Pride (IRE) (Footstepsinthesand)
3816[2] 4271[4] 5317[2] (6321) 6686[5] 7545[8] 8150[2] 8407a[7]

**Peak Storm** *John O'Shea* a28 86
8 b g Sleeping Indian Jitterbug (IRE) (Marju (IRE))
3144[8] 3282[7] 3572[6] 4147[4] 4587[5] 4846[7] 5359[4] 7567[11] 8299[8] 9218[10]

**Pealer (GER)** *John Gosden* a88 102
3 b g Campanologist(USA) Praia (GER) (Big Shuffle (USA))
1559[2] 1906[4] (2468)◆ 3322[18] (4800) 5392[2]◆

**Pearl Acclaim (IRE)**
*David C Griffiths* a82 73
7 b g Acclamation With Colour (Rainbow Quest (USA))
2551[5] 2837[6] 3136[2] 3667[7] 4005[5] 4448[2] 5256[2] 5930[6] 6593[9] 8557[8] 8816[3] 9033[5] (9181) (9308) 9348[2]

**Pearl Castle (IRE)** *K R Burke* a84 84
7 b g Montjeu(IRE) Ghurra (USA) (War Chant (USA))
985[6] 8910[6]

**Pearl Dragon (FR)** *M Delzangles* a84 99
6 b g Nicobar La Marlia (FR) (Kaldounevees (FR))
6123a[5] 7639a[5]

**Pearl Nation (USA)**
*Michael Appleby* a92 68
8 b g Speightstown(USA) Happy Nation (USA) (Lear Fan (USA))
478[2] 720[8] 9031[2] 9305[7]

**Pearl Noir** *Scott Dixon* a57 67
7 b g Milk It Mick Cora Pearl (IRE) (Montjeu (IRE))
21[4] 523[3] 604[2] 743[6] 874[4] 1006[2] 1413[5] 1722[14] 2076[4] 2628[2] (2858) 3201[11] 3812[8] 4015[3] 4219[3] 4795[5] 6089[7] 6531[3] 7036[6] 7217[5]

**Pearl Of The West (IRE)** *P A Fahy* 91
3 b f Teofilo(IRE) Creese (Halling (USA))
7261a[9]

**Pearl River Star** *H-A Pantall* 48
2 b c Motivator Kong Moon (FR) (Hernando (FR))
7470a[7]

**Pearl's Calling (IRE)** *David Barron* a48 56
2 ch f Dandy Man(IRE) Celtic Heroine (IRE) (Hernando (FR))
4340[6] 4597[8] 5277[6] 8141[8] 8371[10]

**Pearl Spectre (USA)** *Phil McEntee* a93 81
6 ch g Street Cry(IRE) Dark Sky (USA) (Storm Cat (USA))
403[3] 506[4] 760[8] 876[3] (999) 1233a[4] 1353a[3] 1479a[6] 1794[7] 2115[7] 3324[9] 3777[9] 7456[11] 7789[4] 8257[2] (8706) 8812[5] 8905[7] 9210[3] 9241[4] 9453[5]

**Pearly Prince** *Martin Bosley* a75 49
5 b g Cockney Rebel(IRE) Princess Raya (Act One)
1364[5]◆ 2336[6]

**Pearly Queen** *Dean Ivory* a63 57
4 b m Dutch Art Surprise (IRE) (Anabaa Blue)
147[10]

**Pea Shooter** *Brian Ellison* a81 87
8 b g Piccolo Sparkling Eyes (Lujain (USA))
1820[8] 2123[11] 2409[7] 4015[4] 5018[5] 6062[5] 6267[16]

**Peas On Earth** *Derek Shaw* a49 16
2 ch f Showcasing Meditation (Inchinor)
3215[11] 3622[U] 4160[5] 6950[11] 9298[4]

**Pecheurs De Perles (IRE)**
*Iain Jardine* a69 80
3 b g Pour Moi(IRE) Annacloy Pearl (IRE) (Mull Of Kintyre (USA))
5376[8] 5928[3] 6855[11] 8596[10]

**Pedestal (IRE)** *A P O'Brien* 91
3 b c Invincible Spirit(IRE) Ashley Hall (USA) (Maria's Mon (USA))
2863a[6]

**Peggie Sue** *Adam West* a56 49
2 b f Captain Gerrard(IRE) Aunt Minnie (Night Shift (USA))
6583[7] 7093[10] 7391[14] 7915[7] 8500[3]

**Peggy's Angel** *Jo Hughes* 83
2 b f Captain Gerrard(IRE) Dora's Sister (IRE) (Dark Angel (IRE))
3491[5] (4696) (6678) 8043[11]

**Pegi Browne (IRE)** *Paul Midgley* a44 40
4 ch m Fast Company(IRE) Alta Petens (Mujadil (USA))
8133[10]

**Peking Flyer (IRE)** *Ed Walker* a43 47
3 b g Zoffany(IRE) Wing Diva (IRE) (Hawk Wing (USA))
1619[7] 3191[10] 3657[5] 4177[10]

**Pelagie (FR)** *H-A Pantall* 53
3 b f Kendargent(FR) Planete (IRE) (Danehill Dancer (IRE))
3134a[5]

**Pelice (IRE)** *Mark Johnston* 62
2 b f Epaulette(AUS) Almansa (IRE) (Dr Devious (IRE))
6890[6] 7266[7] 7608[4] 8164[10]

**Peloton** *Pat Phelan* 70
3 b f Mount Nelson Les Verguettes (IRE) (Iffraaj)
2088[8] 3163[2] 3507[5] 4347[3] 5067[4]

**Pemina (GER)** *J Hirschberger* 103
3 b f Soldier Hollow Princess Lala (GER) (Royal Dragon (USA))
3371a[7] 5693a[16] 8463a[7]

**Penalty (ITY)** *Stefano Botti* 95
3 b c Mujahid(USA) Fidate Correnti (IRE) (Noverre (USA))
2867a[3]

**Pendo** *John Best* a84 81
6 b g Denounce Abundant (Zafonic (USA))
61[3] 277[2] 460[7] (2116) 2730[7] 3670[5] 4563[10] 5788[2] 6617[6] 7505[7]

**Penelope Pitstop** *Lee Smyth* a47 51
5 b m Captain Gerrard(IRE) Obsessive Secret (IRE) (Grand Lodge (USA))
2955[4] 3242[8] 3708[4] 4323[11] 4660[7] 5997[8]

**Penglai Pavilion (USA)**
*Charlie Appleby* 104
7 bb g Monsun(GER) Maiden Tower (Groom Dancer (USA))
1994a[7] 6329[4] 7115[6]

**Peniaphobia (IRE)** *A S Cruz* 120
6 b g Dandy Man(IRE) Umlani (IRE) (Great Commotion (USA))
9168a[9]

**Pennerley** *Micky Hammond* a34 69
4 b m Aqlaam Penelewey (Groom Dancer (USA))
3405[6] 3983[6] 5017[8] 6270[6] 6569[6] 7360[7] 8241[9] 8477[9]

**Pennine Warrior** *Scott Dixon* a53 67
6 b g Lucky Story(USA) Discoed (Distinctly North (USA))
3203[10] 3702[4] 4250[7]

**Pennington** *Mark Johnston* a43 68
3 b g Poet's Voice Pryka (ARG) (Southern Halo (USA))
2036[8] 3024[13] 3431[10] 4900[12]

**Pennsylvania Dutch**
*William Haggas* 90
3 b g Dutch Art Map Of Heaven (Pivotal)
(3584) 4868[5] 5959[3] 6450[10] 6970[8]

**Penny Dreadful** *Scott Dixon* a76 78
5 b m Piccolo Trina's Pet (Efisio)
308[4] 735[3] 879[3] 1180[6] 1413[4] 1721[3] 1978[3] 2124[5] 2631[3] 3290[2] (3903) 4053[4] 4574[4] 4965[4] (6574) 7055[9] 7940[14] 8260[3] 8540[4] 8950[4] 9074[11] 9136[4] 9234[4] 9443[8]

**Penny Lane (GER)** *F-H Graffard* 101
3 b f Lord Of England(GER) Peace Time (GER) (Surumu (GER))
1657a[5] 2945a[3] 4665a[5] 6227a[6] 8088a[5]

**Penny Pepper (IRE)**
*Kevin Prendergast* a84 98
5 b m Fast Company(IRE) Evening Time (IRE) (Keltos (FR))
1520a[2] (3632a)

**Penny Poet (IRE)** *Neil Mulholland* a53 55
4 b m Intikhab(USA) Mneme (FR) (Ocean Of Wisdom (USA))
283[9] 504[6] 717[5] 1256[3] 6309[4]◆

**Penny Pot Lane** *Richard Whitaker* a75 82
4 b m Misu Bond(IRE) Velvet Band (Verglas (IRE))
2124[8] 2883[2] 5635[8] 6238[2] 6550[3] (7244) (7332) 7628[3] 8240[4] 8717[4]

**Penny Red** *Nikki Evans* a67 61
3 ch f Medicean Peintre D'Argent (IRE) (Peintre Celebre (USA))
1682[7] 3178[5] 3721[8] 4765[8] 5401[S] 6032[4]

**Pensax Boy** *Daniel Mark Loughnane* a92 87
5 b g Rail Link Cyclone Connie (Dr Devious (IRE))
(2884) 4207[6] 5634[5] (6014) 7129[12] 9053[9] 9271[8]

**Pensax Lady (IRE)**
*Daniel Mark Loughnane* a59 49
4 b m Fast Company(IRE) Aljafliyah (Halling (USA))
690[2] 1067[4] 2710[6] 3221[7] 3550[2] 4262[11] 8249[7] 8661[8] 8800[5] 9218[7]

**Pensierieparole** *Il Cavallo In Testa* a76 98
5 ch g Exceed And Excel(AUS) Pursuit Of Charge (Pursuit Of Love)
384a[2] 2867a[2]

**Pension Madness (IRE)**
*Mark Usher* a58 55
4 b g Vocalised(USA) Grinneas (IRE) (Barathea (IRE))
988[10]

**Pentathlon (NZ)** *John Wheeler* 103
5 ch g Pentire Pinders Prize (NZ) (Prized (USA))
1994a[13]

**Pentito Rap (USA)** *Rod Millman* a50 50
3 b g Smart Strike(CAN) Sing Like a Bird (USA) (Lawyer Ron (USA))
1597[6] 2371[5] 3024[7] 3819[10] 9073[3]

**Pentland Hills (IRE)** *Chris Wall* 54
2 b g Motivator Elle Galante (GER) (Galileo (IRE))
6854[8] 7543[14] 8352[5]

**Penwortham (IRE)** *Richard Fahey* a84 95
4 b g Dandy Man(IRE) Portofino Bay (IRE) (Montjeu (IRE))
1799[12] 2142[9] 3064[2] 3792[16] 4264[8] 5688a[8] 6414[5] (6676)◆ 7108[3] 7886[7] 8257[5]

**Peny Arcade** *Alistair Whillans* a57 53
3 b f Misu Bond(IRE) Bond Royale (Piccolo)
2455[7] 2790[6] 3832[6] 4263[14] 4688[6] 6131[6] 6903[9] 7889[3] 8248[3] 8591[12] 9013[10]

**Pepita (IRE)** *Richard Hannon* a88 86
3 ch f Sir Prancealot(IRE) Esterlina (IRE) (Highest Honor (FR))
466[3] (624) 2177[3] 2517[5] 3822[2] 4315[2] 4892[6] (5965) 6759[2] 7155[5] 8747[2]

**Pepper Street (IRE)** *Hugo Palmer* a59
2 b f Born To Sea(IRE) Mindy (IRE) (Zamindar (USA))
7488[6] 8030[4] 8890[11]

**Pepys** *Bryan Smart* a63 65
3 b g Aqlaam Generously Gifted (Sakhee (USA))
3047[4]◆ 4602[5] 5601[4] 8210[6]

**Pequeninha** *David Simcock* a72 66
3 b f Acclamation Choral (Oratorio (IRE))
3626[4] 5428[8] 6287[6] 6899[3]◆

**Perambulation** *Stuart Kittow* a31
2 ch f Stimulation(IRE) Love In The Park (Pivotal)
8819[7]

**Perceived** *Antony Brittain* a71 73
5 ch m Sir Percy New Light (Generous (IRE))
1345[5] 1549[6] 1892[4] 3559[2] 4260[11] 5212[6] 6060[4] 6470[8] 7236[2]◆ 7960[12] 9078[5]

**Percipio** *Alan King* a43 50
3 b f Indian Haven Perception (IRE) (Hawk Wing (USA))
3309[6] 3866[10] 5022[9] 7152[4]◆ 8674[5] 9026[8]

**Percy (IRE)** *G M Lyons* 99
3 gb g Kodiac Bysshe (Linamix (FR))
6956a[17]

**Percy B Shelley** *John Gosden* a62 74
3 ch g Archipenko(USA) Oshiponga (Barathea (IRE))
3921[4]◆ 4569[4]

**Percy Prosecco** *Noel Williams* a24 55
2 b c Sir Percy Grapes Hill (Kingsalsa (USA))
7511[11] 8140[9] 8388[10]

**Percys Princess** *Michael Appleby* a73 74
6 b m Sir Percy Enford Princess (Pivotal)
1458[3] (1630) 2061[5] (2546) 3148[3] (4572) 5290[7] (6270) 7925[5] 9070[3]

**Percy Street** *Nicky Henderson* 104
4 br g Sir Percy Star Of Gibraltar (Rock Of Gibraltar (IRE))
6857[7]

**Percy's Word** *Simon Crisford* a93 92
3 b g Sir Percy Laverre (IRE) (Noverre (USA))
2149[3] (6580)◆ 8011[6]◆

**Percy Thrower (IRE)** *Charles Hills* a66 60
3 ch g Sir Percy Dayrose (Daylami (IRE))
1591[3] 2394[8] 3087[5] 4978[9] 5780[2] 6180[3] 6820[5] 7152[6] 8312[5]

**Percy Toplis** *Christine Dunnett* a49 70
3 b g Kheleyf(USA) West Lorne (USA) (Gone West (USA))
1688[13] 2072[8] 2734[10] 3141[2] 3545[8] 4005[10] 4543[4] 5040[7] 5338[5] 6114[12] 7027[5] 7481[5] 7932[10]

**Percy Veer** *Sylvester Kirk* a90 91
5 ch g Sir Percy Fandangerina (Hernando (FR))
62[3] 422[3] 746[7] 6323[5] 7402[17]

**Percy Verence** *Tracy Waggott* a48 52
4 b g Sir Percy Bermondsey Girl (Bertolini (USA))
607[3] 880[3] 3155[6] 3343[9] 3530[5] 4102[2] 4558[4] 4853[9] 5008[9] 5951[11] 6088[5] 6560[5] 8585[7] 9261[5]

**Perego (ITY)** *Silvia Casati* 92
4 b h Mujahid(USA) Pietrasanta (Singspiel (IRE))
5

**Perfect Angel (IRE)** *Andrew Balding* 106
3 br f Dark Angel(IRE) The Hermitage (IRE) (Kheleyf (USA))
2823[5] 3844[9] 4813[10] 5149[2] 5597[10] 8738[13]

**Perfect Art** *Ralph Beckett* a46
3 b f Archipenko(USA) Bassinet (USA) (Stravinsky (USA))
6817[12] 8151[13]

**Perfect Blue (IRE)** *Mark Johnston* a69 51
2 b c Pour Moi(IRE) Prairie Runner (IRE) (Arazi (USA))
8075[6] 8399[3] 8849[12]

**Perfect Clarity** *Clive Cox* 79
2 b f Nathaniel(IRE) Clarietta (Shamardal (USA))
(6037)◆

**Perfect Cracker** *Clive Cox* a95 91
9 ch g Dubai Destination(USA) Perfect Story (IRE) (Desert Story (IRE))
266[3] 720[6] 1258[3] 9053[11] 9271[11]

**Perfect Hustler (USA)**
*Jeremy Noseda* a80 60
2 ch g Jimmy Creed(USA) Jacqui's Promise (USA) (Loup Sauvage (USA))
4367[5] 5631[7] 7877[2] (8308)

**Perfect In Pink** *Mick Channon* 78
3 ch f Raven's Pass(USA) Fashion Rocks (IRE) (Rock Of Gibraltar (IRE))
2039[6] 2576[4] (3145) 3711[6] 4571[6] 5957[4]

**Perfection** *John Gosden* a71
2 ch f Dutch Art Cantal (Pivotal)
8796[4] 9320[3]

**Perfect Lady** *Clive Cox* a52
3 b f Excelebration(IRE) Theladyinquestion (Dubawi (IRE))
9273[4]

**Perfectly Fair** *Georgios Alimpinisis* a54 69
4 bb m Invincible Spirit(IRE) She Storm (IRE) (Rainbow Quest (USA))
8665a[10]

**Perfect Madge (IRE)** *Kevin Ryan* a81 91
3 b f Acclamation Soul Mountain (IRE) (Rock Of Gibraltar (IRE))
1796[5] 2856[4] 4315[3] 5661[2]

**Perfect Pastime** *Jim Boyle* a47 71
9 ch g Pastoral Pursuits Puritanical (IRE) (Desert King (IRE))
1898[8] 2367[7] (2917) 3696[9] 4373[5] 5936[7] 6748[11] 7099[10] (7694)

**Perfect Pasture** *Michael Easterby* a90 113
7 b g Pastoral Pursuits Word Perfect (Diktat)
(2907) 4354[7] 5149[5] 5640[24] 6401[17] 7611[9] 8044[13] (8383) (8679) 8738[2]

**Perfect Quest** *Clive Cox* a73 83
4 br m Bushranger(IRE) Love Quest (Pursuit Of Love)
(1683) (2358) 2906[2] 3693[6] 7728[10] 8561[11]

**Perfect Sense** *Saeed bin Suroor* a76 75
3 b g Sepoy(AUS) Miss Chicane (Refuse To Bend (IRE))
5937[3] 6522[5] 7254[2] 7793[2] 8583a[3] 9257a[11]

**Perfect Soldier (IRE)**
*M D O'Callaghan* a81 86
3 b g Kodiac Independent Girl (IRE) (Bachelor Duke (USA))
9419[2]

**Perfect Spy** *Luca Cumani* a66 66
3 b f Nathaniel(IRE) Heavenly Whisper (IRE) (Halling (USA))
4052[3] 5746[3] 6633[4] 7151[6] 8429[9]

**Perfect Storm (IRE)**
*Ibrahim Al Malki* a62 71
3 b g Excelebration(IRE) Lady Miletrian (IRE) (Barathea (IRE))
933a[5]

**Perfect Summer (IRE)** *Ian Williams* a69 81
7 b m High Chaparral(IRE) Power Of Future (GER) (Definite Article)
2061[8] 2388[7] (3158) 3968[7] 4921[7] 7110[2] 7785[3]

**Perfect Symphony (IRE)**
*Sophie Leech* a77 76
3 b g Dandy Man(IRE) Fields Of Joy (GER) (Waky Nao)
2104[11] 4433[3] 5132[2]◆ 6265[11] 6874[7] 7245[5] 7572[5] 8211[4] 8958[8] 9297[9] 9410[12]

**Perfect Thought** *William Haggas* a76 78
2 ch f Dawn Approach(IRE) Masaya (Dansili)
4312[4] 5702[2] 6480[3] 7757[2] 8236[4] (8594)

**Perfect To Play (IRE)**
*Joseph G Murphy* 67
3 ch g Born To Sea(IRE) Centreofattention (AUS) (Danehill (USA))
3109a[2]

**Perfect Words (IRE)** *Marjorie Fife* a49 72
7 ch g Thousand Words Zilayah (USA) (Zilzal (USA))
2454[5] 2633[9] 3453[5] 4246[2] (4664) 5472[4] 5695[4] (5736) 6045[5] (6130) 6384[3] 7522[11] 7825[11] 8557[11]

**Performance Art (IRE)**
*Seamus Mullins* a42 34
3 b f Art Connoisseur(IRE) Heroic Performer (IRE) (Royal Applause)
2759[9] 3939[4] 4754[8] 6752[5] 7230[4] 7918[9]

**Pericles (IRE)** *Denis Quinn*
4 ch g Danehill Dancer(IRE) Althea Rose (IRE) (Green Desert (USA))
8137[10]

**Perla Blanca (USA)**
*Marcus Tregoning* a61 66
3 gr f Dalakhani(IRE) Trend Line (IRE) (Holy Roman Emperor (IRE))
1726[4] 4967[2] 5298[3] 6293[5] 7152[2] 7744[4] 8312[6]

**Perle De La Mer (IRE)** *W McCreery* 88
3 b f Born To Sea(IRE) Law Review (IRE) (Case Law)
2441a[4] 8083a[6] 8438a[13]

**Perle Et Or (FR)** *D & P Prod'Homme* 70
2 b f Harbour Watch(IRE) Pearl Princess (FR) (Astronomer Royal (USA))
5988a[6] 6542a[7]

**Permanent** *Eric Alston* a27 43
3 b g Invincible Spirit(IRE) Love Everlasting (Pursuit Of Love)
2903[6] 3250[2] 3701[8] 4971[5] 5831[13] 6257[8] 6560[6] 7926[12] 8395[10]

**Permian (IRE)** *Mark Johnston* a79 114
3 b c Teofilo(IRE) Tessa Reef (IRE) (Mark Of Esteem (IRE))
1764[3] 2084[2] (2401) (2766) 3322[10] (4029) 4878a[2] 5953a[6] (Dead)

**Permission** *James Fanshawe* 106
4 b m Authorized(IRE) Continua (USA) (Elusive Quality (USA))
2605[2]◆ 3219[4] 4718[5] 5757[6] 8007[2] (8598)

**Pernickety** *Lucy Wadham* a71 75
4 b m Sir Percy Nicola Bella (IRE) (Sadler's Wells (USA))
(1789) 2254[2] 3009[7] 3981[4] 4319[5] 5822[5] 7338[5] 7601[7]

**Perpetrator (IRE)** *Roger Charlton* a46
2 b c Shamardal(USA) Palmeraie (USA) (Lear Fan (USA))
8642[8]

**Persaverance** *Gary Moore* a34 65
4 b g Sir Percy Marliana (IRE) (Mtoto)
7905[7]

**Pershing** *Kevin Frost* a61 70
6 gr g Mount Nelson La Gandilie (FR) (Highest Honor (FR))
7085[7] 7832[5] 8346[7]

**Persian Steel (IRE)** *Brian Ellison* a76
5 ch g Lucarno(USA) Persian Walk (FR) (Persian Bold (IRE))
(195) 613[5] 1248[5]

**Persistence (IRE)** *Ralph Beckett* a74 77
3 b f Invincible Spirit(IRE) Lady Glinka (IRE) (Galileo (IRE))
283[4]◆ 3007[4] 5428[3] 7598[5] 8390[3] (8822)

**Perspicace** *David Pipe* a69 62
6 b g Sir Percy Cassique Lady (IRE) (Langfuhr (CAN))
380[7] 616[7]

**Persuasive (IRE)** *John Gosden* a98 121
4 gr m Dark Angel(IRE) Choose Me (IRE) (Choisir (AUS))
5460a[5]◆ 6958a[3] 7812[2] (8232)

**Persun** *Mick Channon* a88 89
5 ch m Sir Percy Sunley Shines (Komaite (USA))
269[4] (507)◆ 1002[5]

**Pertuis (IRE)** *Micky Hammond* a58 69
11 gr g Verglas(IRE) Lady Killeen (IRE) (Marju (IRE))
2183[7] 8314[13] 8654[11] (Dead)

**Per Un Dixir (IRE)** *P Bary* 100
4 b h Holy Roman Emperor(IRE) Cottonmouth (IRE) (Noverre (USA))
2663a[5] 6915a[6]

**Pescedora (IRE)** *Roger Charlton* a42 65
2 b f So You Think(NZ) Poisson D'Or (Cape Cross (IRE))
7733[15] 8163[7] 8425[13] 8817[13]

**Pesk Ebrel (FR)** *Y Gourraud* 64
3 b g Enrique River Flyer (FR) (River Majesty (USA))
5982a[9]

**Peterhof (FR)** *M Lehmann* a64 64
2 b g Sageburg(IRE) Peace Touch (FR) (Muhtathir)
6456a[3] 9086a[13]

**Peterhouse (USA)** *Jason Ward* a69 82
5 ch g Elusive Quality(USA) Dynaire (USA) (Dynaformer (USA))
2109[3] 2629[4] 3153[5] 3795[3] 4267[4] 5138[5] 6061[3] 7328[2] 8239[7]

**Peter Leonard** *Richard Fahey* 54
2 b g Kyllachy Nardin (Royal Applause)
3093[10] 3622[4] 4862[7] 7920[12]

**Peter Park** *Clive Cox* a63 75
4 b g Kheleyf(USA) Go Go Girl (Pivotal)
6874[3] 7691[4] 8158[7]

**Peterport** *John Gosden* a74 66
3 b c Nathaniel(IRE) Spinning Queen (Spinning World (USA))
2783[6] 3209[4]

**Peters Folly** *Peter Hiatt* a42
4 ch m Captain Gerrard(IRE) Lipica (IRE) (Night Shift (USA))
9085[5] 9202[6] 9435[7]

**Peter Stuyvesant (IRE)**
*Denis Coakley* a51 51
3 b g Elusive City(USA) Dream For Life (FR) (Oasis Dream)
6817[13] 7514[6] **8116**[7] **9056**[9] 9454[14]

**Pete So High (GER)**
*Richard Hannon* a75 83
3 b g High Chaparral(IRE) Paulaya (GER) (Peintre Celebre (USA))
(265) 2264[4] 3503[5] 4197[2] 4755[4] 4989[3] (5706) 6126[3] (6258) **(6723)**

**Peticoatgovernment (IRE)**
*W McCreery* a78 97
4 b m Holy Roman Emperor(IRE) Fotini (IRE) (King's Best (USA))
1479a[5] 3632a[6] **5308a**[5] 6234[5] 7856a[9]

**Petite Jack** *Archie Watson* a105 96
4 ch g Champs Elysees Pilcomayo (IRE) (Rahy (USA))
(38) 779[2] (1240) 1770[10] 4033[19] 5037[2] 5913[7] **(7602)** 8705[6] 8844[4] 9091[2] **(9388)**

**Petite Slickly (FR)** *S Labate* a36 87
4 gr m Slickly(FR) Highest Height (FR) (Highest Honor (FR))
**606a**[9]

**Petit Filous** *Giles Bravery* a64 59
3 b g Equiano(FR) Haiti Dancer (Josr Algarhoud (IRE))
**2259**[4] 2793[6] 4171[9] 5001[10] 8661[11]

**Petitioner (IRE)** *Roger Charlton* a85 89
3 b g Dansili Reflective (USA) (Seeking The Gold (USA))
1984[3] (3720) **5368**[2]

**Petit Palais** *John Gosden* 59
2 ch c Champs Elysees Galicuix (Galileo (IRE))
**8509**[6]

**Petit Poulain (FR)** *Mme D De Wulf* 23
3 b g Toylsome Timm's Diamant (HOL) (Platini (GER))
838a[14]

**Petra's Pony (IRE)** *Brian Meehan* 46
2 b g Big Bad Bob(IRE) Gabriellina Klon (IRE) (Ashkalani (IRE))
5301[7] **6140**[7]

**Petrify** *Bernard Llewellyn* a56 60
7 b g Rock Of Gibraltar(IRE) Frigid (Indian Ridge (IRE))
**(2219)** 3026[7] 3805[6] 4967[4] 5493[3] 5716[6] 7233[10]

**Petrology (AUS)**
*David A & B Hayes & Tom Dabern* 97
5 b g Fastnet Rock(AUS) Romantic River (USA) (Irish River (FR))
**8059a**[3]

**Petrosinella (FR)** *N Clement* a65 64
2 b f Worthadd(IRE) La Tour Rouge (Monsun (GER))
**7969a**[8]

**Petrucci (IRE)** *Derek Shaw* a67 47
5 b g Azamour(IRE) Spring Symphony (IRE) (Darshaan)
**164**[8] 4345[7]

**Petrus (FR)** *Cedric Rossi* 54
2 b g Sageburg(IRE) Peinture Rose (USA) (Storm Cat (USA))
**5626a**[6]

**Petrus (IRE)** *Brian Meehan* 102
2 b c Zoffany(IRE) Ambrosine (Nashwan (USA))
3747[4] (4583) **7616**[4] 8036[4]

**Petticoat** *M Halford* 91
3 b f Cape Cross(IRE) Minidress (Street Cry (IRE))
**8083a**[7]

**Pettochside** *John Bridger* a69 94
8 b g Refuse To Bend(IRE) Clear Impression (IRE) (Danehill (USA))
2040[5] 2608[7] 3074[3] 3617[2] (4219) 4803[4] 5219[3] 5354[2] 5505[6] 5637[11] 6275[9] (6923) 7809[13] (8077) **8393**[3] 8639[11]

**Peut Etre Ici (IRE)** *G Botti* a50 56
4 b h Holy Roman Emperor(IRE) Muccia (IRE) (Fasliyev (USA))
**6541a**[10]

**Peveril Point (IRE)** *Henry Tett* 11
2 b c Canford Cliffs(IRE) Galeaza (Galileo (IRE))
**5292**[10]

**Phalaborwa** *Ed Vaughan* a88 74
3 b f Poet's Voice Sigurwana (USA) (Arch (USA))
3167[7] 3869[5] (4983) **6321**[3] 6936[6] 9020[7]

**Phantasmic** *Sir Michael Stoute* a44
2 b f Frankel Diary (IRE) (Green Desert (USA))
**8796**[11]

**Pharoh Jake** *John Bridger* a67 55
9 ch g Piccolo Rose Amber (Double Trigger (IRE))
215[3] 327[4] **815**[2] 961[4] 1340[5] 2025[2] 2370[5] 2967[4] 4009[6] 5027[6] 9471[6]

**Phebes Dream (IRE)**
*John C McConnell* a49 55
4 b m Roderic O'Connor(IRE) Alexander Family (IRE) (Danetime (IRE))
**5250**[3]

**Pheidippides** *Tom Clover* 73
2 ch c Sepoy(AUS) Bounty Box (Bahamian Bounty)
4151[7] **5120**[3]

**Phelps Win (FR)** *H-A Pantall* 112
3 b c Muhtathir Take Grace (FR) (Take Risks (FR))
1658a[2] **(2448a)** 4941a[5]

**Phenix Bay (FR)** *Mlle A Voraz* a58 68
4 b g Slickly Royal(FR) Desmounia (FR) (Smadoun (FR))
**6125a**[10]

**Phijee** *William Muir* 96
3 gr c Sepoy(AUS) Likeable (Dalakhani (IRE))
**6476**[6]

**Philamundo (IRE)** *Richard Spencer* a63 63
2 b g Sir Prancealot(IRE) Rublevka Star (USA) (Elusive Quality (USA))
6424[9] **7352**[8] 7512[8]◆ 8308[7] **8996**[4]◆

**Philba** *David Lanigan* a98 57
5 b g Cockney Rebel(IRE) Hisaronu (IRE) (Stravinsky (USA))
**5**[3] 2283[9] 3030[12]

**Phillimore** *Richard Hannon* a10
2 b f Invincible Spirit(IRE) Chibola (ARG) (Roy (USA))
**3687**[12]

**Philosopher (IRE)** *S bin Ghadayer* a79 92
5 ch g Shamardal(USA) Philae (USA) (Seeking The Gold (USA))
**8714a**[7]

**Phoceen (FR)** *F Chappet* a102 103
3 b g Myboycharlie(IRE) Atlantic Slew (FR) (Helissio (FR))
272a[2] (799a) **1114a**[2] 1658a[7] 2448a[4]

**Phoenician Star (IRE)**
*Brian Meehan* 60
2 ch g Mastercraftsman(IRE) Place De L'Etoile (IRE) (Sadler's Wells (USA))
**8389**[12]

**Phoenix Dawn** *Brendan Powell* 72
3 b g Phoenix Reach(IRE) Comtesse Noire (CAN) (Woodman (USA))
1736[9] 3088[2] 4016[3] **6107**[2] 7024[7]

**Phoenix Lightning (IRE)**
*Rebecca Menzies* a66 72
2 b c Lawman(FR) Royal Fizz (IRE) (Royal Academy (USA))
3973[3]◆ 4834[3] **5600**[2] 6977a[19] 7647[8] 9370[6]

**Phoenix Rose (FR)** *N Clement* 72
2 ch f Siyouni(FR) Landing Site (FR) (Peintre Celebre (USA))
**7637a**[10]

**Phosphorescence (IRE)**
*George Scott* a82 79
7 b g Sakhee(USA) Eccentricity (USA) (Kingmambo (USA))
(2070) **3718**[2] 5510[7]

**Photographer** *John Gosden* a84
2 b c New Approach(IRE) Approach (Darshaan)
**(8704)**◆

**Photonics (IRE)** *Hugo Palmer* a69 51
2 b c Power Naval Affair (IRE) (Last Tycoon)
**7237**[2]◆ 8013[11] 8553[6] 9097[12]

**Phu Hai (FR)** *V Luka Jr* a84 43
8 b g Elusive City(USA) Piste Sauvage (IRE) (Brief Truce (USA))
**1920a**[7]

**Physical Power (IRE)**
*Richard Hannon* a70 44
2 b f Power Street Shaana (FR) (Darshaan)
8425[11] 8669[9] **8998**[3]

**Physicist (IRE)** *Paul Cole* a75 70
3 b g Galileo(IRE) Impressionist Art (USA) (Giant's Causeway (USA))
**1900**[2] 2164[10]

**Piaffe (USA)** *Jane Chapple-Hyam* a52
3 b f Successful Appeal(USA) Palisade (USA) (Gone West (USA))
**1756**[5] 2066[15]

**Piazon** *John Butler* a86 69
6 br g Striking Ambition Colonel's Daughter (Colonel Collins (USA))
22[2] (665) (1206) 7272[5] **(8260)** 8803[10] 9366[6] 9443[6]

**Piazzini (IRE)** *Gerard Keane* 78
4 b m Kyllachy Polite Reply (IRE) (Be My Guest (USA))
**2656a**[11]

**Picansort** *Peter Crate* a74 57
10 b g Piccolo Running Glimpse (IRE) (Runnett)
768[7] **961**[2] 1429[5] 2025[3]◆ 4008[2] 4710[3] 5297[4] 5871[2] 7767[7]

**Picc And Go** *Matthew Salaman* 54
4 b m Piccolo Just Down The Road (IRE) (Night Shift (USA))
3279[6] **3806**[4] 4445[8] 6810[7] 7190[8]

**Piccola Collina (IRE)**
*Charlie Appleby* 58
2 b f Dubawi(IRE) La Collina (IRE) (Strategic Prince)
**5056**[7]

**Piccola Poppy** *John Bridger* a31 40
4 br m Piccolo Waraqa (USA) (Red Ransom (USA))
2580[8] **2915**[7]

**Piccolino** *John David Riches* a34
3 b f Piccolo Miacarla (Forzando)
**2311**[11] 3385 [10]

**Piccoloro** *Jonathan Portman* a25
3 b g Piccolo Spanish Gold (Vettori (IRE))
**1414**[5] 1682[9] 2330[8]

**Pichola Dance (IRE)** *Roger Varian* a77 93
3 ch f Distorted Humor(USA) Liffey Dancer (IRE) (Sadler's Wells (USA))
1958[10] 2623[15] **4208**[6]

**Pick A Little** *Michael Blake* a72 70
9 b g Piccolo Little Caroline (IRE) (Great Commotion (USA))
3422[5] 4176[5] 4846[4] **5823**[2] 6101[7] 7916[2] (8182) 8641[6]

**Picket Line** *Geoffrey Deacon* a75 77
5 b g Multiplex Dockside Strike (Docksider (USA))
808[10] 1063[6] 1419[3] 1728[7] **(2229)** 2608[13] **3573**[4] 3919[9] 4495[6] 5271[3]◆ 6099[10] 6874[11]

**Pickett's Charge** *Richard Guest* a75 72
4 b g Clodovil(IRE) Chelsea Morning (USA) (Giant's Causeway (USA))
**(361)** 782[8] 968[8] 1706[10] 2267[8] 7571[12] 8125[6] 8209[5] 8514[4]

**Pick Of Any (IRE)** *David Loughnane* a58 67
4 b g Zoffany(IRE) Choice Pickings (IRE) (Among Men (USA))
274[3] (899) 1112[4] **1305**[4] **1372**[2] 2063[5] 2633[13] 3136[6]

**Picks Pinta** *John David Riches* a63 66
6 b g Piccolo Past 'N' Present (Cadeaux Genereux)
2428[5] 3239[7] **3912**[3] 4789[3] 5069[2] 5467[8] **6318**[4] 6688[7] 9297[4]

**Picture Dealer** *Lydia Pearce* a78 78
8 b g Royal Applause Tychy (Suave Dancer (USA))
219[7] 575[8] **(2320)** 3074[8] 5481[7] 6113[9] 7056[10] 8311[7]

**Picture No Sound (IRE)**
*Richard Fahey* 85
2 b c Dark Angel(IRE) Little Audio (IRE) (Shamardal (USA))
4567[4] 5120[4] 6312[4] 7819[5] **(8388)**

**Picture Painter (IRE)** *Jim Goldie* 73
4 gr g Zoffany(IRE) Sisceal (Dalakhani (IRE))
2498[5] 4476[3] **4853**[3] 5186[5] 5599[7]

**Piedi Bianchi (USA)** *Doug O'Neill* a107
2 rg f Overanalyze(USA) Adore You (USA) (Tactical Cat (USA))
**8603a**[5]

**Piedita (IRE)** *Sir Mark Prescott Bt* a86 82
3 b f Authorized(IRE) Archina (IRE) (Arch (USA))
4738[3] (5209) (6259) **6618**[2]

**Pier Cesar (FR)** *Antonio Marcialis* 78
2 b c Siyouni(FR) Crossed Fingers (IRE) (Cape Cross (IRE))
**6170a**[3]

**Pif D'Avril (FR)** *F-X De Chevigny* 28
2 bb f Vertigineux(FR) Poca (FR) (Carlotamix (FR))
**2881a**[8] 3445a[11] 4196a[9] 5585a[12]

**Pilaster** *Roger Varian* 63
2 b f Nathaniel(IRE) Portal (Hernando (FR))
**8380**[7]

**Pilgrim Soul** *Andrew Balding* a60
2 b f Yeats(IRE) Sabah (Nashwan (USA))
**8890**[5]

**Pilgrim's Treasure (USA)**
*Charlie Appleby* a87 90
3 b c Dubawi(IRE) La Pelegrina (USA) (Redoute's Choice (AUS))
1914[5] 2681[3] (3485) **4254**[2] 5323[6]

**Pilkington** *David O'Meara* a76 68
2 ch c Helmet(AUS) Aroundthebay (Diktat)
**(3254)** 3993[13] 4862[6] 7821[18]

**Pillar** *Adrian McGuinness* a63 64
4 b g Rock Of Gibraltar(IRE) Ceilidh House (Selkirk (USA))
494[8] 1246[2] 2656a[6] **5995**[2] 6797a[9]

**Pillard (FR)** *Jonjo O'Neill* a67 62
5 b g Muhaymin(USA) Ultime Moment (IRE) (Anabaa (USA))
**806**[3]

**Pillar Of Society (IRE)**
*Richard Hannon* a75 93
3 b g Roderic O'Connor(IRE) Specific (IRE) (Dubawi (IRE))
1907[6] 2330[2] (3412) 4491[2] **(5425)** 6655[5] 7053[8]

**Pimpinehorse (FR)** *R Chotard* a79 81
2 gr c Tin Horse(IRE) Pimpinella (FR) (Highest Honor (FR))
**3611a**[7] 5679a[10] 6452a[3]

**Pindaric** *Alan Lockwood* a41 56
3 ch g Poet's Voice Hunter's Fortune (USA) (Charismatic (USA))
2107[7] 2703[8] 3431[5] 5181[7] 5831[11] 7270[8] **8219**[2] 8985[8] 9445[10]

**Pink Paint (FR)** *M Delcher Sanchez* 97
3 b f Redoute's Choice(AUS) Peinture Rose (USA) (Storm Cat (USA))
**2945a**[6]

**Pink Phantom** *Paul Cole* a63 59
2 b f Oasis Dream Pink Symphony (Montjeu (IRE))
8425[7] **8668**[5]

**Pink Ribbon (IRE)** *Sylvester Kirk* a68 71
5 gr g Dark Angel(IRE) My Funny Valentine (IRE) (Mukaddamah (USA))
2785[8] **3304**[2] 3753[8] 5427[8] 5868[4] 6557[4] 7004[5] 7495[7] 8946[2] (9078) 9212[8] 9236[6] 9459[4]

**Pinnata (IRE)** *Stuart Williams* a83 72
3 b g Shamardal(USA) Lavande Violet (GER) (Hurricane Run (IRE))
642[4] 925[4] 2152[10] (4144) 5067[8] 7457[2]◆ (8797)◆ **9236**[2]

**Pinter** *E Charpy* a60 49
5 b g Exceed And Excel(AUS) Pickle (Piccolo)
**8711a**[12]

**Pinwood (IRE)** *Adam West* a78 80
4 b g Bushranger(IRE) Anne Bonney (Jade Robbery (USA))
(290)◆ 616[3] **965**[2] 1073[5] 1555[6]

**Pinzolo** *Ismail Mohammed* a110 109
6 b g Monsun(GER) Pongee (Barathea (IRE))
**(352)** 919[2] 1770[11] 2398[3]

**Pioneering (IRE)** *David O'Meara* 89
3 b g Shamardal(USA) Oregon Trail (USA) (Gone West (USA))
2185[9] 4186[4] 4601[6] 5073[2] 5666[14] (6471) (7476)◆ **(7894)**◆

**Pioneer Spirit** *John Gosden* 76
2 b f Galileo(IRE) Ladys First (Dutch Art)
**(7608)** 8597[11]

**Pioneertown (IRE)**
*Sir Mark Prescott Bt* a86 73
3 b g High Chaparral(IRE) Tempura (GER) (Cape Cross (IRE))
3234[6] 3456[7] 3755[3]◆ 5298[4] 6398[4] 6937[2] 7163[5] (7568) **(8188)**◆

**Pious Alexander (IRE)**
*Edward Lynam* a48 90
3 b f Acclamation Lady Alexander (IRE) (Night Shift (USA))
3873a[9] **5308a**[6] 6973a[11]

**Pipe Dreamer** *Kevin Ryan* a32 46
3 ch g Piccolo Card Games (First Trump)
2211[11] 2792[9] **5467**[4]◆ 5992[8] 7888[7]

**Pipers Note** *Ruth Carr* a101 106
7 ch g Piccolo Madam Valentine (Primo Valentino (IRE))
1491[3] 2156[8] 2839[3] 3092[10] (3463) **(3861)** 4615[3] 4881[3]◆ 5911[4] **6206**[2] 6668[9] 7144[5] 8044[17] 8139[7]

**Pipers Piping (IRE)** *Mandy Rowland* a57 43
11 b g Noverre(USA) Monarchy (IRE) (Common Grounds)
334[4] 1084[12] **1260**[3] 1406[7] 1563[5] 2313[9]

**Pipers Way** *Richard Fahey* 54
3 b c Piccolo Emmone (First Trump)
3150[7] 3568[7] **4784**[5]

**Pippin** *Hughie Morrison* 60
2 ch g Intello(GER) Golden Delicious (Cadeaux Genereux)
**6859**[7] 7543[11] 8161[8]

**Pique Sous (FR)** *W P Mullins* a98 98
10 gr g Martaline Six Fois Sept (FR) (Epervier Bleu)
**985**[3] 1355a[6]

**Pirate Look (IRE)** *Marco Botti* a77 82
3 b g Canford Cliffs(IRE) Gerika (FR) (Galileo (IRE))
2118[5] 2998[4] **3583**[2] 4580[3] **6822**[3] 8289[8]

**Pirate's Treasure** *Jennie Candlish* a73 49
4 b g Iffraaj Musical Sands (Green Desert (USA))
2586[11] 3471[7] **3966**[6]

**Pirouette** *Hughie Morrison* a92 106
4 ch m Pivotal Passiflora (Night Shift (USA))
2616[3] 3334[2] 3961[8] 4718[3] 5352[2] **(6254a)** 7113[6] 7808[5]◆ 8546[5]

**Pistol (SWE)** *Patrick Wahl* a85
4 ch h Eishin Dunkirk(USA) Love's Mirage (IRE) (Pivotal)
**204a**[4]◆

**Pitch High (IRE)** *Julia Feilden* a55 54
3 br g Requinto(IRE) Distant Skies (Tiger Hill (IRE))
1589[5] 2733[5] 3657[12] 5001[6] 5536[2] 6341[4] 7271[5] **(8784)** 9084[5] 9334[8]

**Pit Stop (IRE)** *S bin Ghadayer* a85 82
6 b g Iffraaj Journey's End (IRE) (In The Wings)
204a[10] 316a[12] **537a**[7]

**Pivoine (IRE)** *Sir Michael Stoute* a92 91
3 b g Redoute's Choice(AUS) Fleur De Cactus (IRE) (Montjeu (IRE))
1945[9] 3504[9] 5589[4] **(6579)** (7119)◆

**Pivotal Dream (IRE)**
*Mark Brisbourne* a52 52
4 br m Excellent Art Oasis Fire (IRE) (Oasis Dream)
124[4] 147[6] 383[3] **(425)** 605[11] 2313[5] 3137[9] 3550[5] 4180[6] 4982[10] 5897[2] 6296[4]

**Pivotal Flame (IRE)** *Pat Phelan* a66 55
4 b m Pivotal Saadiah (IRE) (Dubai Destination (USA))
286[10] 571[6] **806**[7] 2254[4] 6588[6]

**Pivot Bridge** *Adrian McGuinness* a79 69
9 ch g Pivotal Specifically (USA) (Sky Classic (CAN))
(74) **(218)**

**Pivotman** *Michael Easterby* a67 74
9 ch g Pivotal Grandalea (Grand Lodge (USA))
6[3] 267[3] **(382)** 517[4] 719[7] 992[13] (1610) 2140[11] 2685[15] 3204[7] 3845[10] 6014[12] 9236[8]

**Pixeleen** *Malcolm Saunders* a78 99
5 b m Pastoral Pursuits Ballyalla (Mind Games)
1765[5] 2083[4] 2623[4] 3867[3] (4201) 4889[7] 6864[5] 7195[3] (7811) **8040**[3]

**Pixie Cut (IRE)** *Alistair Whillans* a24 22
7 b m Chineur(FR) Fantastic Cee (IRE) (Noverre (USA))
**361**[9]

**Placebo Effect (IRE)** *Ollie Pears* 71
2 b g Lilbourne Lad(IRE) Hawaiian Dream (IRE) (Catcher In The Rye (IRE))
1873[8] 2343[3] 3791[8] 4740[3] (5161) (5277) 6043[3] (6625) 7050[3] **7243**[3]

**Place Des Vosges (IRE)**
*David Menuisier* a38
2 b f Rip Van Winkle(IRE) Red Blossom (USA) (Silver Hawk (USA))
**8691a**[13]

**Plage Depampelonne**
*James Bethell* a60 71
3 gr f Redoute's Choice(AUS) Arabescatta (Monsun (GER))
2307[2] 3220[2] 3909[6] 6013[7] **(6436)** 7060[8]

**Plain Talking (IRE)** *Gavin Cromwell* 58
5 b m Primary(USA) Assir (Daylami (IRE))
**5689a**[4]

**Planetaria (IRE)** *Julie Camacho* a84 62
4 b g Lilbourne Lad(IRE) Red Planet (Pivotal)
4210[9] 5165[7] 5469[11] 8718[11] **8928**[2] 9100[6]

**Planet Suite (FR)** *Jonathan Portman* a42
4 b m Astronomer Royal(USA) Happy Clapper (Royal Applause)
**23**[3]

**Plansina** *Tim Easterby* 49
2 b f Planteur(IRE) Sina (GER) (Trans Island)
2105[6] 2896[14] 4503[8] **5878**[6] **6517**[3] 7222[7] 7734[10]

**Plant Pot Power (IRE)**
*Richard Hannon* a86 87
3 b c Lawman(FR) Featherweight (IRE) (Fantastic Light (USA))
2520[8] 3303[5] 4564[8] **4894**[2] 5400[3] 6068[5] **6426**[2] 6936[5] 7229[4] 7780[17] 8392[3] 8596[5]

**Plata O Plomo** *David O'Meara* 86
3 ch g Paco Boy(IRE) Branston Gem (So Factual (USA))
**1732**[3] 1975[9] 2425[4] 6945[7] (Dead)

**Platitude** *Sir Michael Stoute* a74 110
4 b g Dansili Modesta (IRE) (Sadler's Wells (USA))
4360[5]◆ 4917[4] 5638[6] **6329**[5] 7547[5]

**Plato's Kode (IRE)** *Seamus Durack* a69 73
3 b g Kodiac Speedy Sonata (USA) (Stravinsky (USA))
1000[4] 2017[6] 2711[4] 3276[3] 4045[2] **(4494)** 4989[2] 7319[5]

**Playcity (FR)** *J-P Lopez* 43
2 ch c Soul City(IRE) Playland (Cape Cross (IRE))
1929a[6] **3679a**[13]

**Playful Dude (USA)** *Phil McEntee* a68 50
4 b g Drosselmeyer(USA) Choice Play (USA) (Vindication (USA))
7[2] (68) **390**[2] 482[4]

**Playful Sound** *Sir Michael Stoute* 104
4 b m Street Cry(IRE) Giants Play (USA) (Giant's Causeway (USA))
(2396) 3219[7] **5381**[3] 6074[6]

**Play The Blues (IRE)** *Roger Ingram* a34
10 gr m Refuse To Bend(IRE) Paldouna (IRE) (Kaldoun (FR))
5823[11] 6284[5]

**Playtothewhistle** *Michael Appleby* a67 68
6 b g Sakhee's Secret Prima Ballerina (Pivotal)
32[6] 527[3] 663[7] 1074[8] 1330[3] 1983[5] 2153[6] 3628[10]

**Play With Me** *Keith Dalgleish* a50 50
3 ch f Captain Gerrard(IRE) Plead (FR) (Bering)
845[5] 1198[4] 1626[5] 2455[3]

**Playwriter (IRE)** *Charlie Appleby* 78
3 b g New Approach(IRE) The Shrew (Dansili)
1830[3] 4052[2]

**Plead** *Archie Watson* a73 84
3 ch f Dutch Art Entreat (Pivotal)
1195[4] 1736[3] 2269[2] 2827[5] 3786[9] 4155[4] 4580[5] 6160[8] 8886[RR]

**Pleadings (USA)** *Charlie Wallis* a58 50
4 ch g Street Cry(IRE) Say No Now (IRE) (Refuse To Bend (IRE))
119[5] 438[3] 544[9] 768[9] 2214[9] 2727[6] 3728[8] 4011[4]

**Pleasant Surprise (IRE)**
*Luca Cumani* a73 106
3 b f Mastercraftsman(IRE) Ibiza Dream (Night Shift (USA))
1874[3]◆ (2307)◆ 3749[5] (4571) 5658[2] 6914a[2] 7577[2] 8273a[9]

**Please Be True (IRE)**
*Matthieu Palussiere* 57
2 ch c Camacho Semper Fi (Royal Applause)
5907a[6] 8101a[8]

**Pleaseletmewin (IRE)**
*Jassim Mohammed Ghazali* a66 82
3 b g Power Jacaranda Ridge (Indian Ridge (IRE))
933a[6]

**Pleasure Dome** *Jonjo O'Neill* a54 90
4 b m Makfi Nouvelle Lune (Fantastic Light (USA))
4222[7]

**Plucky Dip** *John Ryan* a89 78
6 b g Nayef(USA) Plucky (Kyllachy)
219[8] 459[8] 760[4] 857[3] 1202[6] 2113[6] (2462) 2975[7] 4091[6] 4524[7] 5035[7] 5610[9] 6113[4] 6290[5] 6795[7] 7321[8] 8640[9] 8907[3] 9020[9] 9297[8]

**Plumatic** *A Fabre* 114
3 b c Dubawi(IRE) Plumania (Anabaa (USA))
2448a[2] 3368a[12] 7176a[2] 7668a[13]

**Plundered (IRE)** *David Brown* a59 49
2 b g Camacho Jouel (FR) (Machiavellian (USA))
2148[5] 3339[5] 3973[4] 6043[13] 8191[13]

**Plunger** *Paul Cole* a70 84
2 ch c Helmet(AUS) Percolator (Kheleyf (USA))
(1792) 8560[2]

**Plusquemavie (IRE)** *V Fazio* 106
6 b h Kheleyf(USA) Kathy Pekan (IRE) (Sri Pekan (USA))
2867a[4] 3370a[3] 8449a[5]

**Plutocracy (IRE)** *Gary Moore* a95 95
7 b g Dansili Private Life (FR) (Bering)
269[2] 1068[P] 4370[5] 4908[4] 6952[3] 8076[5]

**Plutonian (IRE)** *Charles Hills* a96 91
3 b c Raven's Pass(USA) Ripalong (IRE) (Revoque (IRE))
3188[5] 3691[6] (4152) 5943[3] 8032[6] (8705)

**Ply** *Roger Charlton* a100 81
3 b g Dubawi(IRE) Polygon (USA) (Dynaformer (USA))
1551[2] 2039[5] 2783[13] 3457[5] 6389[3] (7452)◆ (7728) (8638)

**Plymouth Sound** *Bernard Llewellyn* a77 84
5 b g Fastnet Rock(AUS) Shardette (IRE) (Darshaan)
2176[4] 2218[2] 3086[4] 3459[6] (4089) 6176[7] 7143[4] 7599[2]

**Poana (FR)** *John Gosden* 48
3 ch f New Approach(IRE) Porlezza (FR) (Sicyos (USA))
1948[9]

**Pobbles** *George Scott* a69 50
3 b f Medicean Oystermouth (Averti (IRE))
284[2] 392[6] 2587[10] (3151) 4105[6]

**Pocketfullofdreams (FR)**
*A P O'Brien* a90 95
3 b f Invincible Spirit(IRE) Dubai Rose (Dubai Destination (USA))
1389a[4] 2613[2] 3301[7] 4419a[9] 4934a[5] 6080a[5] 6334a[7] 7171a[9] 8083a[10] 8407a[9]

**Pocket Warrior** *Martin Bosley* a63
6 b g Tobougg(IRE) Navene (IRE) (Desert Style (IRE))
916[7] 1024[6] 1287[6] 1723[8]

**Podemos (GER)** *Ralph Beckett* a78
2 b c Shamardal(USA) Pearls Or Passion (FR) (Monsun (GER))
8643[2]

**Poeta Diletto** *Marco Botti* a97 102
4 ch h Poet's Voice Mia Diletta (Selkirk (USA))
1500[7] 2141[6] 3218[6]

**Poetic Affair** *Mark Johnston* 47
2 ch g Poet's Voice Wendylina (IRE) (In The Wings)
7211[6]

**Poetic Charm** *Charlie Appleby* a88 96
2 b f Dubawi(IRE) Speirbhean (IRE) (Danehill (USA))
(4902) 5941[5] (6886)

**Poetic Choice** *Keith Henry Clarke* a81 79
6 b m Byron Ennobling (Mark Of Esteem (IRE))
3451[5]

**Poetic Dream (IRE)** *A Wohler* 109
3 b c Poet's Voice Zain Al Boldan (Poliglote)
(2869a) 4939a[7] 6647a[3]

**Poetic Force (IRE)** *Tony Carroll* a84 77
3 ch g Lope De Vega(IRE) Obligada (IRE) (Beat Hollow)
(292) (498) (927) 1142[3] 1764[7] 2567[9] 3780[6] 4290[4] 4831[5] 6111[8] 6866[2] 7653[5]

**Poetic Imagination** *John Gosden* a70 51
2 b f Exceed And Excel(AUS) Portrayal (USA) (Saint Ballado (CAN))
8594[8] 8840[2] 9081[4] 9370[5]

**Poetic Queen (IRE)** *Eric Alston* a66
4 b m Dylan Thomas(IRE) Jubilant Lady (USA) (Aptitude (USA))
600[2] (956) 1200[7]

**Poetic Steps (FR)** *Mark Johnston* 81
2 ch f Poet's Voice Step This Way (USA) (Giant's Causeway (USA))
(4472) (4786) 5572[12] 6693[8] 7087[5] 7814[26]

**Poetic Voice** *Eric Alston* 43
3 b g Poet's Voice Perfect Flight (Hawk Wing (USA))
2527[9]

**Poet's Beauty (IRE)**
*Ismail Mohammed* a79 51
4 ch g Poet's Voice Extreme Beauty (USA) (Rahy (USA))
7246[9] 7941[11] 8344[9]

**Poet's Charm (IRE)** *Martin Hill* a64 33
3 b g Poet's Voice Antillia (Red Ransom (USA))
210[6] 6094[5] 6503[10] 7712[14] 9375[11]

**Poet's Dawn** *Tim Easterby* a65 79
2 ch g Poet's Voice Dudley Queen (IRE) (Excellent Art)
1873[5] 2221[7] 2896[7] (4167) 4597[3] 5492[6] 6087[5] 6561[2] 6900[5] 7384[2] 7624[2] 7921[4]

**Poets Dream (IRE)**
*Mohammed Hussain Afroz* 81
2 b c Poet's Voice Sparkling Smile (IRE) (Cape Cross (IRE))
4318[4] 6260[4] (6938) 7818[2] 8290[8] 9446a[3]

**Poet's Pride** *David Barron* 68
2 b g Arcano(IRE) Amber Heights (Kyllachy)
6311[3]◆ 6689[4]

**Poet's Prince** *Mark Johnston* a67 75
2 b g Poet's Voice Palace Affair (Pursuit Of Love)
3538[2] 3973[2] (4956) 5572[13] 6693[9] 8586[5]

**Poet's Princess** *Hughie Morrison* 91
3 ch f Poet's Voice Palace Affair (Pursuit Of Love)
1958[11] 2831[2]◆ 3632a[9] 5117[11] 6358[13] 6864[9] 7742[3] 8077[4]

**Poet's Quest** *Michael Appleby* a17 44
3 b f Poet's Voice Quest For Freedom (Falbrav (IRE))
1083[12] 4764[11] 6150[9] 6847[8] 8908[16] 9073[8]

**Poet's Reward** *David Barron* a76 54
3 b g Hellvelyn Oceanico Dot Com (IRE) (Hernando (FR))
1004[2] 1782[2] 2495[3] 3152[9]

**Poet's Rock (FR)** *J-M Lefebvre* a82 81
4 b h Poet's Voice Tropical Glamour (IRE) (Rock Of Gibraltar (IRE))
4955a[8]

**Poet's Society** *Mark Johnston* a88 92
3 ch g Poet's Voice Rahiyah (USA) (Rahy (USA))
125[2] 2215[4] 2557[4] 2992[8] 3462[3] 3579[2] 3844[4] (4272) 4813[9] 5129[7] 5574[5] 6198[6] 6554[3] 6677[8] 6922[11] (7256) 7610[12] 7828[8] 8238[14]

**Poet's Time** *Tim Easterby* a42 46
3 ch f Poet's Voice Sandtime (IRE) (Green Desert (USA))
2595[5] 2898[10] 4576[3] 5069[5] 5418[6] 5703[3] 6572[6] 7574[5]

**Poet's Vanity** *Andrew Balding* 105
3 b f Poet's Voice Vanity (IRE) (Thatching)
1883[3]◆ 2434[7] 3078[4] 6193[8]

**Poet's Word (IRE)**
*Sir Michael Stoute* a113 120
4 b h Poet's Voice Whirly Bird (Nashwan (USA))
(1757) 2553[2] (5592)◆ 6960a[2] 8233[2] 9171a[6]

**Poignant** *Archie Watson* a60 65
2 ch c Sepoy(AUS) Brigh (IRE) (Galileo (IRE))
1604[7] 1966[3] 2459[2] 3648[8] 3936[3]

**Point Hope (IRE)** *Richard Hannon* a70 67
2 b f Kodiac Frosted (Dr Fong (USA))
3815[3]◆ (9081)

**Point In Time (IRE)** *Mark Usher* a66
2 b f Champs Elysees Creme Anglaise (Motivator)
8029[8] 8668[6] 8998[5]

**Point North (IRE)** *John Balding* a76 67
10 b g Danehill Dancer(IRE) Briolette (IRE) (Sadler's Wells (USA))
242[11] 1147[2] (3258) 4724[5] 8745[8] 9001[11] 9414[4]◆

**Point Of Discovery** *Marco Botti* a44
3 b c Exceed And Excel(AUS) Saggiatore (Galileo (IRE))
2921[7]

**Point Of Woods** *Tina Jackson* a73 78
4 b g Showcasing Romantic Myth (Mind Games)
2700[12] 3847[11] 4509[9] 5055[2] 5377[2] 5620[2] 6267[8] 6669[3] 7244[4] 7525[6] (7628) 8480[2] 8651[14]

**Polar Forest** *Richard Guest* a78 84
7 br g Kyllachy Woodbeck (Terimon)
42[4] 359[7] 460[8] 4260[13] 4608[6] (5498) 5809[3] 6551[6] 7225[3] 7524[5] 7735[9] 7960[9] 8218[7] 8327[8]

**Polarisation** *Charlie Appleby* a75 106
5 b g Echo Of Light Concordia (Pivotal)
(1994a)

**Polar Kite (IRE)** *Michael Attwater* a71 80
9 b g Marju(IRE) Irina (IRE) (Polar Falcon (USA))
214[4] (570) 1086[2] 1449[7] 1898[7]

**Polar Light** *David Elsworth* a62 67
2 b f Norse Dancer(IRE) Dimelight (Fantastic Light (USA))
3591[8] 4212[6] 5114[4] 6036[7]◆ 8164[6] 9021[9]

**Polar River (USA)** *Doug Watson* a112
4 b m Congrats(USA) Bayou Tortuga (USA) (Empire Maker (USA))
85a[8] 1043a[13]

**Polarstern (GER)** *U Schwinn* a30
5 ch g Tertullian(USA) Page Dans Ma Vie (FR) (Generous (IRE))
9309a[15]

**Poldina (FR)** *H-A Pantall* a47
2 b c Penny's Picnic(IRE) Rampoldina (Montjeu (IRE))
4678a[10]

**Poldi's Liebling (GER)** *A Wohler* 108
2 ch c Tai Chi(GER) Pinea (GER) (Platini (GER))
(8621a)

**Political Slot** *Derek Shaw* a39 44
2 ch f Helmet(AUS) Lady Elalmadol (IRE) (Shamardal (USA))
8324[6] 8594[9] 8997[10]

**Polkadot Princess (IRE)**
*Nikki Evans* 49
3 b f Sir Prancealot(IRE) Miriam's Song (Royal Applause)
4735[9] 6099[9] 9085[8]

**Polkarenix (FR)** *Brendan Powell* 58
5 b g Policy Maker(IRE) Arenix (FR) (Fragrant Mix (IRE))
6038[8] (Dead)

**Polly Douglas (IRE)** *Kieran P Cotter* a50 75
4 b m Le Cadre Noir(IRE) Isabella Rose (IRE) (City On A Hill (USA))
(2950) 7425a[6]

**Polly Glide (IRE)** *Luca Cumani* 74
3 ch f Nathaniel(IRE) Majestic Dancer (IRE) (Danehill Dancer (IRE))
1885[5] 3039[4]◆ 4042[4]

**Pollyissimo** *Richard Hughes* a46 40
2 ch f Nathaniel(IRE) Fleurissimo (Dr Fong (USA))
4749[7] 6138[10] 7226[10]

**Polly's Gold (IRE)** *Richard Hughes* 72
2 ch f Havana Gold(IRE) Keyta Bonita (IRE) (Denon (USA))
4440[4]◆ 4806[6] 5356[2] 5963[2] 6417[3] 7079[3]

**Polo (GER)** *Carina Fey* a55 73
7 ch g Sholokhov(IRE) Poule D'Essai (GER) (Dashing Blade)
(691a) 7430a[2]

**Polybius** *David Simcock* a108 109
6 b g Oasis Dream Freedonia (Selkirk (USA))
207a[4]◆ 543a[12] 696a[3] 4072[4] 4881[2]◆ 6428[8] 9409[5]

**Polydream (IRE)** *F Head* 112
2 b f Oasis Dream Polygreen (FR) (Green Tune (USA))
(6228a) 7666a[2]

**Polymnia** *Richard Hannon* a63 40
4 br m Poet's Voice Lucky Token (IRE) (Key Of Luck (USA))
(214)

**Pomme De Terre (IRE)**
*Michael Dods* a58 89
5 ch g Sakhee's Secret Suzie Quw (Bahamian Bounty)
2184[8] 3401[3] 4343[3] 5379[2] 5920[3] 6314[9] 6943[4] 7554[5] 8321[10] 8722[12]

**Pompey Chimes (IRE)** *Gary Moore* a78 76
2 b g Big Bad Bob(IRE) Zamarelle (Zamindar (USA))
6654[5] 7211[2] (8502)

**Pondering** *Eve Johnson Houghton* a60 74
3 br f So You Think(NZ) Lebenstanz (Singspiel (IRE))
2062[3] 2359[6] 2892[4] 3247[2] (4347) 4989[4] (5331) 6094[4] 7201[4]

**Ponfeigh (IRE)** *Debbie Mountain* 100
6 gr h Teofilo(IRE) Water Fountain (Mark Of Esteem (IRE))
934a[14]

**Pontecarlo Boy** *Richard Whitaker* a46 46
3 ch g Piccolo Dahshah (Mujtahid (USA))
2077[8] 2349[11] 3555[6] 4302[11] 6471[4] 7271[7] 8291[8] 8719[7]

**Pont Neuilly (FR)** *Yves de Nicolay* a73 72
7 ch h Medecis Panzella (FR) (Kahyasi (IRE))
1920a[13] 2696a[12]

**Pool House** *Mike Murphy* a75 45
6 b g Sakhee's Secret Gitane (FR) (Grand Lodge (USA))
49[2] 360[6] 745[9] 1065[7] 1186[2] 1329[3] 1484[7] 2465[5]

**Poorauldjosephine** *J R Jenkins* a41
2 ch f Piccolo Moment In The Sun (Dubai Destination (USA))
3993[17] 8130[8] 9023[8]

**Poor Duke (IRE)** *Michael Mullineaux* a53 61
7 b g Bachelor Duke(USA) Graze On Too (IRE) (Rainbow Quest (USA))
239[9] 1456[8] 2454[14] (3397) 4625[7] 5848[10] 6341[6] 7052[14] 7465[12]

**Popeswood (IRE)** *Lee Carter* a55 79
5 b g Haatef(USA) Binfield (IRE) (Officer (USA))
2676[5] 4747[10] 5145[13] 5656[6]

**Poppyinthepark** *Michael Mullineaux* a49 51
4 b m Bahri(USA) Lark In The Park (IRE) (Grand Lodge (USA))
4611[10] 6044[4] 6413[5] 6788[5] 8955[8]

**Poppy In The Wind** *Alan Brown* a81 78
5 b m Piccolo Vintage Steps (IRE) (Bahamian Bounty)
45[2]◆ (358) 582[2] 1030[3] 1475[7] 2104[6] 2631[2]◆ 3257[4] 3847[15] 8321[6] 8722[6] 8927[6] (9297)

**Poppy Jag (IRE)** *Kevin Frost* a49 23
2 b f Kodiac Jacquelin Jag (IRE) (Fayruz)
4502[12] 6950[8] 7450[5] 8027[7] 8500[8] 8780[6] 9002[6]

**Poppy Line** *Derek Shaw* 44
2 b f Equiano(FR) Ming Meng (IRE) (Intikhab (USA))
8324[5] 8735[9]

**Poppy May (IRE)** *James Given* a51 49
3 b f Zoffany(IRE) Lara Amelia (IRE) (Ishiguru (USA))
126[3] 377[10] 9072[8]

**Poppy Pivot (IRE)** *Michael Appleby* a19
3 b f Pivotal Havin' A Good Time (IRE) (Jeremy (USA))
264[10] 404[7]

**Poppy Time** *James Eustace* a10 68
4 b m Pour Moi(IRE) Shamandar (FR) (Exceed And Excel (AUS))
1735[10] 2615[2] 2729[4] 4761[4]

**Poppy Walton (IRE)** *Ollie Pears* 64
2 ch f Society Rock(IRE) Bellacoola (GER) (Lomitas)
3943[4] 4689[6] 6057[4] 6465[4] 7920[7]

**Popsi** *Marjorie Fife* a10 56
2 b f Captain Gerrard(IRE) Deslaya (IRE) (Green Desert (USA))
1335a[12] 1594a[5] 1929a[5] (2343) 3200[2] 3557[7] 6154[10]

**Popsicle (IRE)** *Richard Hannon* a61 62
2 b f Acclamation Katchy Lady (Kyllachy)
4367[2]◆ 8851[9] 9022[7]

**Popsies Joy (IRE)** *Tim Easterby* a63 74
5 b m Alfred Nobel(IRE) Senzate (Lujain (USA))
2301[9] 3203[5] 3488[6] 3833[6] 4168[5] 5497[12]

**Popsilca** *Mick Quinn* a56 41
3 b f Captain Gerrard(IRE) Silca Destination (Dubai Destination (USA))
(324) 546[2] 898[4] 1363[7] 2734[7] 4157[6] 4543[5] 7705[6] 7993[3]

**Porchy Party (IRE)** *Tom Dascombe* a71 81
2 ch g Dragon Pulse(IRE) Shawaaty (IRE) (Monsun (GER))
2221[4] 2698[2] 3390[3] 5121[7] 5479[2] (6547) 6756[5] (7138) 7564[5]

**Porrima (IRE)** *Ben Haslam* 62
2 gr f Kodiac El Morocco (USA) (El Prado (IRE))
3943[3]

**Porsenna (IRE)** *F Vermeulen* a87 100
7 b h Dylan Thomas(IRE) Miss Mariduff (USA) (Hussonet (USA))
5046a[4]

**Portamento (IRE)** *A R Al Rayhi* a63 76
5 gr h Shamardal(USA) Octave (USA) (Unbridled's Song (USA))
9361a[8]

**Porta Rosa (USA)**
*Mohamed Moubarak* a75 57
4 b m Street Cry(IRE) Sander Camillo (USA) (Dixie Union (USA))
3214[F] 3723[6] 3969[10]

**Porth Swtan (IRE)** *Charles Hills* 83
2 b c Invincible Spirit(IRE) Propaganda (IRE) (Sadler's Wells (USA))
4297[3] 5680[2] 6403[11] 7460[2] 8039[2] 8560[2]

**Port Isaac (IRE)** *Marcus Tregoning* a74 56
4 b g Sakhee's Secret Dombeya (IRE) (Danehill (USA))
3085[5] 8842[10]

**Port Lairge** *Michael Chapman* a62 43
7 b g Pastoral Pursuits Stylish Clare (IRE) (Desert Style (IRE))
70[7] 315[10] 853[9] 1545[6] 2255[5] 5499[8] 6035[11] 7006[3] 7210[7] 8182[4] 8985[13] 9077[9] 9368[10]

**Portland Street (IRE)** *Bryan Smart* a65 73
4 b g Dream Ahead(USA) Danaskaya (IRE) (Danehill (USA))
1833[9] 2428[2] 2776[2] 3897[10] 4897[7] 5836[9]

**Portledge (IRE)** *James Bethell* a80 77
3 b g Acclamation Off Chance (Olden Times)
577[3] 5541[3]◆ 6091[7] 6235[3] 6899[4] 7571[9] (7942)◆ 8640[3]

**Port Master** *Ann Duffield* a58 50
3 b g Harbour Watch(IRE) Gentle Guru (Ishiguru (USA))
27[3] 511[9] 3979[10] 4479[8] 6549[13]

**Port Moody (IRE)** *Patrick Tallis* 63
3 b g Bushranger(IRE) Hurricane Irene (IRE) (Green Desert (USA))
1389a[3]

**Port Of Call** *Amanda Perrett* a64 72
2 b g Harbour Watch(IRE) Valiantly (Anabaa (USA))
6654[6] 7093[7] 7512[4]

**Porto Ferro (IRE)** *Dr Jon Scargill* a83 64
3 b f Arcano(IRE) Sassari (IRE) (Darshaan)
307[5] (764) 1463[5] 2071[9] 3246[4] 4214[12] 5558[7] 6620[12]

**Port Paradise** *William Jarvis* a27 65
4 gr g Paco Boy(IRE) Yacht Woman (USA) (Mizzen Mast (USA))
1329[8] 4753[4]

**Portrush Storm** *Ray Peacock* a34 51
12 ch m Observatory(USA) Overcast (IRE) (Caerleon (USA))
494[9] 784[7] 5146[5] 8742[9]

**Port Soif** *David O'Meara* a31
3 b f Foxwedge(AUS) Positivity (Monsieur Bond (IRE))
7574[8] 8554[6] 8716[6]

**Poseidon (IRE)** *Ed Walker* a64 78
3 ch g Born To Sea(IRE) Maskaya (IRE) (Machiavellian (USA))
3727[6] 4267[5] 6767[2] (7902) 8295[5]◆

**Posh Bounty** *Paul Burgoyne* a43 79
6 ch m Bahamian Bounty Fission (Efisio)
3214[9] 3573[12] 4214[14] 5295[6] 5357[9] 5936[5] 6106[12] 6813[7] 7191[13]

**Possible Future** *Karl Thornton* a79 51
4 b g Compton Place Lalectra (King Charlemagne (USA))
6802a[6]

**Postponed (IRE)** *Roger Varian* 126
6 b h Dubawi(IRE) Ever Rigg (Dubai Destination (USA))
1042a[2] 1379a[3]

**Postulation (USA)** *Edward Graham* a93 103
5 b g Harlan's Holiday(USA) Supposition (Dansili)
8099a[8]

**Potemkin (GER)** *A Wohler* 114
6 bb g New Approach(IRE) Praia (GER) (Big Shuffle (USA))
2249a[7] 5464a[3] 6451a[3] 7722a[4]

**Potioka (FR)** *Matthieu Palussiere* a67 62
2 b c Deportivo Thaa Valley (Whipper (USA))
8482a[4]

**Poucor** *Mick Channon* 54
2 b g Pour Moi(IRE) Corinium (IRE) (Turtle Island (IRE))
6093[4] 6777[10]

**Poudreuse (FR)** *J-P Gauvin* a65 62
3 gr f Silver Frost(IRE) Ellipsis (Singspiel (IRE))
6649a[5]

**Pound Note** *Michael Mullineaux* 35
5 b g Top Line Dancer(IRE) Avondale Girl (IRE) (Case Law)
5315[7] 6184[12] 7694[10] 8259[11]

**Pour La Famille (IRE)**
*Christos Kouvaras* 70
2 b f Pour Moi(IRE) Wooded Glade (Oasis Dream)
6608a[3]

**Pour L'Amour (IRE)**
*Daniel Mark Loughnane* a70 68
4 b m Aqlaam Passion Fruit (Pursuit Of Love)
*164[3] 726[2] 954[4] 1257[8] 1458[2] 1560[3]* ***(2308)***
2781[11] *3547[4]* 4169[3] 5054[3] *5483[5] 9270[7]*

**Pour La Victoire (IRE)** *Tony Carroll* a73 73
7 b g Antonius Pius(USA) Lady Lucia (IRE) (Royal Applause)
2360[8] 2608[18] 3008[6] 4803[6] 5788[11] **5869**[2] 6373[7] 6478[11] 8184[7]

**Pourquoi Moi** *George Scott* a51
4 b m Multiplex Sweet Applause (IRE) (Acclamation)
***1300***[4]

**Pouvoir Magique (FR)**
*John Gosden* a93 94
3 b c Le Havre(IRE) Barmaid (FR) (Cape Cross (IRE))
**3506**[3] (4657) 5368[4] 8385[7] *(8718)*

**Powderhouse (IRE)** *Charlie Appleby* 76
3 b g Raven's Pass(USA) Monday Show (USA) (Maria's Mon (USA))
2681[6] 3394[3] **6150**[4]

**Powderonthebonnet (IRE)**
*Sam Thomas* a39 50
9 b g Definite Article Zuhal (Busted)
**2364**[3]

**Powerallied (IRE)** *Richard Fahey* 90
4 b g Camacho Kaplinsky (IRE) (Fath (USA))
1876[10] 3581[6] 4337[2]◆ 5129[2] 5402[7] 6412[7] **(6677)** 7610[8]

**Power And Peace (IRE)**
*David Simcock* a74 71
2 b f Arcano(IRE) Dubai Power (Cadeaux Genereux)
3245[4] 3908[2] ***7454***[3]

**Power Becqua (FR)** *P Van De Poele* 70
3 gr c Tin Horse(IRE) Khayriya (FR) (Valanour (IRE))
5909a[5] **6650a**[8]

**Power Blade (KOR)**
*Kim Young Kwan* a102
4 b h Menifee(USA) Cheonmachong (KOR) (Lost Mountain (USA))
*204a[3]* ***541a***[3] *1043a[5]*

**Powercell (IRE)** *Tim Easterby* 46
3 b f Power Celtic Heroine (IRE) (Hernando (FR))
**2682**[6] 3404[7] 3945[4] 4602[7]

**Powered (IRE)** *David Evans* a61 64
4 b g Frozen Power(IRE) Confirm (IRE) (In The Wings)
*7[4] 69[5] 390[8] 684[6] 865[7] 1067[5] 1081[2] 1188[4] 1403[2] 1698[4]* 2964[3] 3143[2] 3251[2] 3805[4] **(3916)** 4181[5] 4494[8] *5483[9]* 5968[2] *6069[3]* 6309[3] 6509[5] *6953[2]*

**Powerful (GER)** *B Recher* 41
2 b f Liquido(GER) Pierette (GER) (Local Suitor (USA))
**8228a**[10]

**Powerful Dream (IRE)**
*Ronald Harris* a74 76
4 b m Frozen Power(IRE) Noble View (USA) (Distant View (USA))
*604[4] (955) 1328[2] 1558[3] 1981[7]* 2216[U] (2514) 2725[6] **(3021)** 4043[2] 4795[7] 5587[4] 6612[8] *8853[3] 8953[6] 9189[6] 9315[5]*

**Powerful Love (IRE)** *Mark Johnston* a63 71
3 b g Clodovil(IRE) Ruby Ridge (IRE) (Acatenango (GER))
2854[5] 3499[8] **3901**[2] 4430[5] 4959[8] 5753[7]

**Powerful Rose** *Michael Blanshard* a33 17
2 b f Power Fenella Rose (Compton Place)
3690[9] 4757[5] ***8989***[8]

**Powerful Society (IRE)**
*Richard Fahey* a68 70
2 b f Power Society Gal (IRE) (Galileo (IRE))
5127[7] **5755**[4] 6510[3] **(7222)** 7956[5] *(8983)*

**Powerful Wind (IRE)** *Charlie Wallis* a70 82
8 ch g Titus Livius(FR) Queen Of Fools (IRE) (Xaar)
*221[2] 330[11]* ***1071***[4] *1429[2] 1869[3]* 2360[9] 2967[5] *4009[4]* 5514[5]

**Power Game** *David O'Meara* a96 90
5 ch g Shamardal(USA) Counterclaim (Pivotal)
3790[12] **4377**[8]

**Power Home (IRE)** *Denis Coakley* a64 62
3 ch f Power Ascendancy (Sadler's Wells (USA))
*2018[5]* 3327[3] 4012[6] *(8498)* **8661**[2] *8993[10]*

**Power Of Darkness**
*Marcus Tregoning* 79
2 b c Power Summer's Lease (Pivotal)
5641[6] **6388**[3]

**Power Of Ten (IRE)** *R P McNamara* a62 49
3 b g Power Stones Peak (IRE) (Rock Of Gibraltar (IRE))
***1353a***[8]

**Power Of The Cross** *Charley Rossi* a79 72
3 b f Cape Cross(IRE) Portmeirion (Polish Precedent (USA))
***4289a***[6]

**Power Power (IRE)** *Marco Botti* a71 58
3 ch g Power Charmingly (USA) (King Of Kings (IRE))
*1299[5] 1550[2]* ***2259***[3]

**Power Sail** *Tim Easterby* a55 59
2 gr g Frozen Power(IRE) Gone Sailing (Mizzen Mast (USA))
6939[12] 8013[8] **8215**[4] *8555[6] 8870[8]*

**Powersbomb (IRE)**
*Brian M McMahon* 88
7 ch g Trans Island Black Ouzel (IRE) (Taipan (IRE))
**5488a**[15]

**Power Surge (IRE)** *Ralph Beckett* a81
3 ch g Power Silver Skates (IRE) (Slip Anchor)
***(6633)***

**Powersville (IRE)** *Thomas Mullins* 80
2 b f Frozen Power(IRE) Spiritville (IRE) (Invincible Spirit (IRE))
**(7423a)** 8082a[5]

**Power Up** *Luke McJannet* a65
6 b m Rail Link Melpomene (Peintre Celebre (USA))
*517[P] 1284[10] 8799[11]*

**Pow Wow** *Martyn Meade* a88 84
3 b g Medicean Ship's Biscuit (Tiger Hill (IRE))
(3087) (3864) (4197) ***7515***[3]

**Poyle Charlotte** *Ralph Beckett* a69
2 b f Farhh Poyle Caitlin (IRE) (Bachir (IRE))
***7454***[5]

**Poyle Emily** *Michael Madgwick* a47 55
4 b m Compton Place Poyle Dee Dee (Oasis Dream)
**5712**[10] 6656[9] *7061[13]*

**Poyle Thomas** *Michael Madgwick* a80 90
8 b g Rail Link Lost In Lucca (Inchinor)
**6135**[8] 6872[6] 8038[33] *8505[4] 9204[8] 9434[6]*

**Poyle Vinnie** *Michael Appleby* a106 105
7 b g Piccolo Poyle Dee Dee (Oasis Dream)
*33[3]* ***(388)*** *818[5]* 1946[7] 2433[10] 2764[3] 3092[15] 4072[13] 5505[4] 5640[17] 6971a[21] 7610[9]

**Practical Joke (USA)**
*Chad C Brown* a117
3 b c Into Mischief(USA) Halo Humor (USA) (Distorted Humor (USA))
*2420a[5]* ***5463a***[3] *8576a[4]*

**Prado's Sweet Ride (USA)**
*Chris Block* a94 102
5 b m Fort Prado(USA) Excellent Idea (USA) (General Meeting (USA))
**5954a**[10]

**Praeceps (IRE)** *Sir Mark Prescott Bt* a54
2 b g Canford Cliffs(IRE) Sliding Scale (Sadler's Wells (USA))
*8029[10]* ***8340***[5] *8553[11] 8703[10]*

**Prairie Impulse** *Rebecca Menzies* a29 59
4 b m Major Cadeaux Prairie Sun (GER) (Law Society (USA))
***726***[5]

**Pranceabootthetoon (IRE)**
*John Ryan* a72 72
2 ch c Sir Prancealot(IRE) Cabopino (IRE) (Captain Rio)
**(4175)** ***5480***[6] 5865[4] 8118[3]

**Prancelina (IRE)** *Phil McEntee* a54 62
3 ch f Sir Prancealot(IRE) Fingal Nights (IRE) (Night Shift (USA))
*1088[7]* 1688[6] **1786**[3] 2508[3] *4161[7]* 4715[4]

**Prancing Oscar (IRE)** *Ben Haslam* a71 62
3 b g Sir Prancealot(IRE) Beguiler (Refuse To Bend (IRE))
*1198[2]* 1680[11] 3317[11] 4473[4] ***(5485)*** 6594[3]

**Praxedis** *James Fanshawe* a49
2 b f Dutch Art Angel Song (Dansili)
***8130***[7]

**Prayer For Relief (USA)**
*Dale Romans* a79 53
9 bb h Jump Start(USA) Sparklin Lil (USA) (Mr Sparkles (USA))
***469a***[10]

**Prazeres** *Les Eyre* a64 63
3 b g Sepoy(AUS) Sewards Folly (Rudimentary (USA))
*956[3] 1064[3] 1474[7]* **1913**[5] 2372[7] 3285[6] 4122[3] 4509[17] 5167[8] (6131) 6558[5] 7332[8] *8552[14]*

**Preacher Man (IRE)** *Jamie Osborne* 79
2 b c Lope De Vega(IRE) Daniysha (IRE) (Doyoun)
4218[4] **4880**[2]◆ 5641[5]

**Precieuse (IRE)** *F Chappet* 113
3 ch f Tamayuz Zut Alors (IRE) (Pivotal)
1660a[2] **(2644a)** 4031[7]

**Precious Angel (IRE)**
*Richard Hannon* a72 69
3 b f Excelebration(IRE) Evangeline (Sadler's Wells (USA))
2131[8] 2760[3] ***6067***[2]◆ 6657[5] 7278[4] *7878[10]*

**Precious Equity (FR)**
*David Menuisier* a40 9
3 b f Equiano(FR) Anasy (USA) (Gone West (USA))
*1192[8]*

**Precious Ramotswe** *John Gosden* a79 92
3 b f Nathaniel(IRE) Miss Pinkerton (Danehill (USA))
**(8390)** 8838a[11]

**Precious Rock (IRE)** *Jedd O'Keeffe* 51
3 b g Fastnet Rock(AUS) Attasliyah (IRE) (Marju (IRE))
**4247**[10] 5538[11] 6268[9]

**Precious Silk (IRE)** *Jose Santos* a66
2 ch f Harbour Watch(IRE) Fine Silk (USA) (Rahy (USA))
***9231***[3] *9465[5]*

**Precious Skye (IRE)**
*Ronald Thompson* 27
3 b f Born To Sea(IRE) Secret Flame (Machiavellian (USA))
1973[9] 2699[7] **6660**[7]

**Precision** *Sir Michael Stoute* 84
3 b c Galileo(IRE) Pearl Earrine (FR) (Kaldounevees (FR))
2039[10] 3506[7] 4720[3] **(5550)** **6151**[4]◆

**Precision Five** *Nick Lampard* a91 75
8 b m Proclamation(IRE) Sashay (Bishop Of Cashel)
*921[P]* ***1457***[7]

**Prediction (IRE)** *Kevin Ryan* 36
2 b g Dream Ahead(USA) Sho Girl (IRE) (Lawman (FR))
2299[8] **5380**[10]

**Preening** *James Fanshawe* a76 65
2 b f Dutch Art Striving (IRE) (Danehill Dancer (IRE))
7021[7] ***(7997)***

**Premier Currency (IRE)**
*Mike Murphy* a42 44
4 b g Elusive Pimpernel(USA) Zeena (Unfuwain (USA))
***8957***[10]

**Premier Division (FR)**
*Matthieu Palussiere* a68 68
2 b c Wootton Bassett Premier Acclaim (IRE) (Acclamation)
***4678a***[5]

**Premiere Gachette (IRE)**
*J-C Rouget* a79 79
3 b f Excelebration(IRE) Time Pressure (Montjeu (IRE))
**6650a**[2]

**Prendergast Hill (IRE)** *Ed de Giles* a85 90
5 b g Raven's Pass(USA) Daraliya (IRE) (Kahyasi (IRE))
***2020***[2] 2477[3] **3027**[2] 3785[3] **5313**[2] 5820[4]

**Preobrajenska** *William Jarvis* a72 69
3 b f Paco Boy(IRE) Unex Mona Lisa (Shamardal (USA))
*76[3]* ***(1286)*** *1554[6]*

**Prerogative (IRE)** *Tony Carroll* a79 75
3 b g Rock Of Gibraltar(IRE) Tedarshana (Darshaan)
*1692[5]* **2359**[2] 3921[3] 4224[2] 4913[5] 6258[3] 7004[2] 7905[2] *9235[2]*

**Presence Process** *Pat Phelan* a66 57
3 b g Dansili Loulwa (IRE) (Montjeu (IRE))
***209***[4] *3457[9] 4747[6]* 6006[6] *9391[8]*

**Presenting Julio (IRE)**
*Gordon Elliott* a69 54
9 b g Presenting Ouro Preto (Definite Article)
**4018**[10]

**Present Tense** *John Gosden* 93
3 b f Bated Breath Zenda (Zamindar (USA))
1609[7] (2316) **3395**[3] 3964[20]

**Presley (ITY)** *Stefano Botti* 106
4 b h Gladiatorus(USA) Pasionaria (IRE) (Celtic Swing)
**8963a**[3]

**Prestbury Park (USA)**
*Mark Johnston* a87 90
2 br g Shamardal(USA) Sutra (USA) (Meadowlake (USA))
4826[7] (5099) **(5681)** 8039[3]◆ 8420[4] *8671[4]*

**Prestige Vendome (FR)**
*Yannick Fouin* 104
6 gr g Orpen(USA) Place Vendome (FR) (Dr Fong (USA))
**1691a**[9]

**Presto Boy** *John Balding* a58 32
5 b g Compton Place Presto Levanter (Rock Of Gibraltar (IRE))
*143[8]* ***622***[4] *899[8] 2923[12]*

**Presumido (IRE)** *Simon Dow* a91 59
7 b g Iffraaj Miss Megs (IRE) (Croco Rouge (IRE))
*459[10] 680[4]* ***918***[5] *1288[7] 6322[8] 6933[7] 7456[12] 7998[10] 8640[7]*

**Pretend (IRE)** *Charlie Appleby* a113 99
6 b g Invincible Spirit(IRE) Fafinta (IRE) (Indian Ridge (IRE))
*(170)*◆ ***572***[5] *917[5] 1772[10]*

**Pretoria (FR)** *E Libaud* 64
3 b f Smadoun(FR) One Way I (FR) (Exit To Nowhere (USA))
**4232a**[10]

**Pretty Asset (IRE)** *Charlie Appleby* 89
3 b f Shamardal(USA) What A Picture (FR) (Peintre Celebre (USA))
(5118) **5506**[5]

**Pretty Baby (IRE)** *William Haggas* a82 77
2 b f Orpen(USA) Premiere Danseuse (Gold Away (IRE))
6969[2]◆ ***(7986)***

**Pretty Boy Floyd (IRE)**
*Sarah Dawson* a70 83
2 ch c Footstepsinthesand Hitra (USA) (Langfuhr (CAN))
**6977a**[2]

**Pretty Bubbles** *J R Jenkins* a89 87
8 b m Sleeping Indian Willmar (IRE) (Zafonic (USA))
*94[2]* ***660***[2] *1423[5]* 2040[3] 2230[5] 3063[6] 3919[7] 5325[3] 5965[6] 7000[5] 7282[6] *8374[4] 8818[2] 8990[6] 9185[5] 9315[2]*

**Pretty Jewel** *Kevin Frost* a60 66
4 b m Aqlaam Highland Jewel (IRE) (Azamour (IRE))
*1334[6]*◆ 2042[8] *3192[4]* 3753[7] 4804[8] (5427) 6153[4] **6549**[2]

**Pretty Lady (USA)** *Mark Casse* 89
2 bb f Scat Daddy(USA) Classic Strike (USA) (Smart Strike (CAN))
**7206a**[5]

**Pretty Obvious (FR)** *Jonjo O'Neill* 63
4 b g Montmartre(FR) Societe (FR) (Panis (USA))
**3921**[8] 4275[6] 4700[6] 5718[8]

**Pretty Passe** *William Haggas* a78 71
3 b f Exceed And Excel(AUS) Passe Passe (USA) (Lear Fan (USA))
4568[2]◆ 5038[4] *6161[2]* ***7492***[2] *7989[3]*

**Pretty Pearl** *Robert Eddery* a39 31
2 b f Canford Cliffs(IRE) Hijab (King's Best (USA))
***7786***[7] 8347[9] *9231[8]*

**Pretty Perfection (USA)**
*Kelly Breen* a94 81
5 b m Majesticperfection(USA) Suchaprettygirl (USA) (Mazel Trick (USA))
**1813a**[8]

**Pretty Risky** *Patrick Chamings* a17 54
2 b f Royal Applause Pretty Miss (Averti (IRE))
**6719**[5] *7450[9]*

**Prezzie** *William Muir* a57 45
2 b f Major Cadeaux Yearbook (Byron)
3244[4] 3821[9] ***6010***[6] *7510[11]*

**Priceless** *Clive Cox* 112
4 b m Exceed And Excel(AUS) Molly Brown (Rudimentary (USA))
(1936) 2397[5] **(3079)** 3926[12] 5595[9] 6402[5] 7396[8]

**Pride Of Angels** *Gary Moore* a69 67
4 gr m Dark Angel(IRE) Openness (Grand Lodge (USA))
2581[5] 3157[4] 3669[3]◆ 4368[4] 5429[7] 7912[3] ***(9469)***

**Primadonia** *Richard Hughes* a55 54
3 b f Bated Breath Pretty Primo (IRE) (Kyllachy)
*2366[4] 2620[6]* ***3191***[7] *3695[6] 4211[8]*

**Primanora** *Michael Appleby* 67
4 ch m First Trump Danzanora (Groom Dancer (USA))
2139[4] **2620**[4] **3216**[4] 5263[6] 8168[13] 8513[13]

**Prima Violetta (IRE)** *A Wohler* 92
3 b f Areion(GER) Power Penny (GER) (Galileo (IRE))
**5693a**[9]

**Prime Chief (IRE)** *George Baker* a57 52
2 b c Air Chief Marshal(IRE) La Dame De Fer (IRE) (Mr Greeley (USA))
3936[6] 7732[8] ***8028***[6] ***8658***[6]

**Prime Minister (IRE)** *Ed Vaughan* 71
2 b c Dream Ahead(USA) Logica (IRE) (Priolo (USA))
**7280**[2] 8140[5]

**Primero (FR)** *David O'Meara* a105 104
4 b g Cape Cross(IRE) Flamenba (USA) (Kingmambo (USA))
1271a[8] 3104a[2] *8999[5]*◆ ***9390***[2]◆

**Primogeniture (IRE)** *Mary Hambro* a85 93
6 b g Glory Of Dancer Jacqueline (IND) (King Charlemagne (USA))
1608[10] 2041[5] 2504[4] **4254**[4]

**Primo's Comet** *Jim Goldie* 49
2 b g Orientor Primo Heights (Primo Valentino (IRE))
1495[11] **2948**[10]

**Primo Uomo (IRE)** *Gerard O'Leary* a96 107
5 b g Strategic Prince Mooching Along (IRE) (Mujahid (USA))
**2657a**[8]

**Primrose Place** *David Evans* a32 65
3 ch f Compton Place Pretty Girl (IRE) (Polish Precedent (USA))
3250[11] **4846**[5] 5249[9]

**Prince Ahwahnee** *Clive Cox* 81
2 b c Harbour Watch(IRE) Ahwahnee (Compton Place)
3165[2] 3668[4] 4826[3] 6353[19] **7352**[3]

**Prince Alzain (USA)** *Doug Watson* a75 63
8 b h Street Sense(USA) Monaassabaat (USA) (Zilzal (USA))
***83a***[8]

**Prince Apache** *Andreas Suborics* a81 91
4 b h Royal Applause Park Melody (IRE) (Refuse To Bend (IRE))
**5269a**[2] 6648a[14]

**Prince Consort (IRE)** *Brian Meehan* a57 57
2 b g Most Improved(IRE) Fame And Fortune (IRE) (In The Wings)
6388[11] 6721[6] **7460**[6] 8013[9] 8349[13] *9238[5]*

**Prince Gris (FR)** *F Foresi* a37
12 gr g Slickly(FR) Princesse Baie (FR) (Highest Honor (FR))
***930a***[5]

**Prince Jai** *Ian Williams* a59 55
4 ch g Showcasing Play Around (IRE) (Niniski (USA))
5126[13] *5482[4] 5897[3] 7323[2]* ***(7481)*** *(7540) 7952[7]* ***9052***[2] *9243[7]*

**Princely** *Richard Hannon* 38
2 b c Compton Place Royal Award (Cadeaux Genereux)
**5504**[12]

**Prince Maurice (USA)**
*Jeremy Noseda* 49
2 gr c The Factor(USA) Ramblin Rosie (USA) (Roar (USA))
**6438**[7]

**Prince Of All** *A R Al Rayhi* a70 72
6 ch h Iffraaj Ya Hajar (Lycius (USA))
**205a**[16]

**Prince Of Arran** *Charlie Fellowes* a108 108
4 b g Shirocco(GER) Storming Sioux (Storming Home)
***1502***[3] *1770[5]* **2288**[2] **3996**[8] 5503[10] 6400[8] 7124[5]

**Prince Of Cardamom (IRE)**
*Jonathan Geake* a56 61
5 b g Nayef(USA) Tiger Spice (Royal Applause)
*2023[6]* **2095**[5] **5050**[5] 5145[6] 5714[8]

**Prince Of Clappers** *Tim Easterby* 57
3 b g Royal Applause Blodwen (USA) (Mister Baileys)
**4186**[7] 5182[14]

**Prince Of Cool** *H Aashoor* a80 80
3 b c Royal Applause Methayel (IRE) (Araafa (IRE))
**933a**[14]

**Prince Of The Dark** *Clive Cox* 102
2 gr c Lethal Force(IRE) Fanrouge (IRE) (Red Clubs (IRE))
(3025)◆ **3925**[6]

**Princeofthequeen (USA)**
*David O'Meara* a44 71
3 br c Lonhro(AUS) Catch The Queen (USA) (Miswaki (USA))
**3152**[10] 4509[16]

**Prince Of Time** *Richard Ford* a70 69
5 ch g Bahamian Bounty Touching (IRE) (Kheleyf (USA))
*52[2] 309[4] 544[2] 644[RR] 852[3] 969[3] 1408[2] (1587) 1868[2] (2063)* ***(2278)*** 3454[11] 6049[9] *7881[12] 8556[10]*

**Prince Rock (IRE)** *Simon Dow* a29
2 ch g Society Rock(IRE) She's A Queen (IRE) (Peintre Celebre (USA))
*7511[12]* ***7876***[10]

**Princess Asta (FR)** *Mario Hofer* a78 99
4 b m Canford Cliffs(IRE) Lune Rouge (IRE) (Unfuwain (USA))
4390a[5] **8526a**[7]

**Princess De Lune (IRE)**
*Roger Charlton* 90
3 gr f Shamardal(USA) Princess Serena (USA) (Unbridled's Song (USA))
**(1948)** 7356[9] **7808**[7]

**Princesse Hartwood (FR)**
*H De Nicolay* a64 56
3 b f Sageburg(IRE) Calyx (FR) (Irish River (FR))
**6084a**[11]

**Princess Gibraltar (FR)** *N Clement* a88 101
4 b m Rock Of Gibraltar(IRE) Princess Sofia (UAE) (Pennekamp (USA))
4653a[4]

**Princess Harley (IRE)** *Mick Quinn* 77
2 gr f Dark Angel(IRE) Tonle Sap (IRE) (Manduro (GER))
6747[3]◆ 7620[3]

**Princess Jessica (FR)**
*Richard Fahey* 35
2 gr f Style Vendome(FR) Scoutingaround (USA) (Deputy Minister (CAN))
4273[5] 5056[13] 5999[6]

**Princess Karen (USA)** *Jeff Bonde* a104
3 b f Stay Thirsty(USA) Chitka (USA) (Jade Hunter (USA))
8605a[5]

**Princess Keira (IRE)** *Mick Quinn* 77
2 b f Acclamation La Reine De Pearls (IRE) (Dubawi (IRE))
4628[2]◆ 5327[5] 6480[12] 7731[6]

**Princess Kodia (IRE)**
*Mrs A Malzard* a40 66
4 b m Kodiac Pixie's Blue (IRE) (Hawk Wing (USA))
1931a[6] 2670a[4] 4655a[4] 5200a[4] 5984a[5] 6544a[5]

**Princess Lyla (IRE)** *Richard Hughes* a65 64
2 ch f Arakan(USA) Hi Lyla (IRE) (Lahib (USA))
2258[3] 2910[5] 3328[5] (5933) (6154) 6749[6] 7228[6] 7827[4]

**Princess Nearco (IRE)**
*Patrick Holmes* 64
3 b f Elzaam(AUS) Royal Jubilee (IRE) (King's Theatre (IRE))
3206[4] 4432[5] 5073[4] 5618[4] 6048[5] 6551[3] 7248[5] 7477[4]

**Princess Nia (IRE)** *Brian Meehan* a77 81
4 b m Acclamation Shirley A Star (USA) (Cozzene (USA))
(1938) 2575[3]

**Princess Ophelia** *Michael Appleby* a57 59
3 b f Notnowcato Royal Bloom (IRE) (Royal Applause)
2572[6] 4275[5] 4729[4] 5485[9] 7323[15]

**Princess Peggy (USA)**
*Wesley A Ward* a84 80
2 b f Scat Daddy(USA) Peggy Jane (USA) (Kafwain (USA))
4028[10]

**Princess Raihana** *Marco Botti* a75 72
4 br m Cape Cross(IRE) Raihana (AUS) (Elusive Quality (USA))
213[5]

**Princess Roania (IRE)**
*Peter Bowen* a55 77
6 b m Dubai Destination(USA) Lady Roania (IRE) (Saddlers' Hall (IRE))
2270[6]

**Princess Warrior (USA)**
*Kenneth McPeek* a96
2 b f Midshipman(USA) Sessa (USA) (Consolidator (USA))
8603a[8]

**Princess Way (IRE)** *David Evans* a61 54
3 gr f Zebedee Stef's Girl (IRE) (Petardia)
78[5] 435[9] 686[7] 1123[10] 4163[3] 5817[5] 6324[6] 6345[4] 7910[4] 8137[3] 8395[4] 9268[7] (9365)

**Prince Suhail (IRE)** *E Charpy* a82 81
7 b g Marju(IRE) Larme (IRE) (Soviet Star (USA))
203a[8]

**Prinz Hlodowig (FR)** *M Delzangles* 106
3 b c Rajsaman(FR) Princess Cheri (GER) (Mondrian (GER))
1658a[8] 2560a[5]

**Priors Brook** *Andrew Balding* a81 83
6 b g Champs Elysees Dyanita (Singspiel (IRE))
38[4] 1113[2] 1555[7] 3409[5] (4147) 5747[3] 6811[4]

**Priscilla's Dream** *Philip McBride* a59 67
2 ch f Bated Breath Be Free (Selkirk (USA))
5885[4] 6844[3] 7814[10]◆

**Prisom (IRE)** *Gay Kelleway* a64 50
4 gr m Zebedee Crystal Theatre (IRE) (King's Theatre (IRE))
26[2] 222[2] 391a[13] 606a[8] 1618[6] 1868[11] 2285[6] 8259[6] 8784[12]

**Private Donald** *Robert Cowell* a62
4 ch g Sakhee's Secret Excello (Exceed And Excel (AUS))
1[3]

**Private Matter** *Richard Fahey* 100
3 b g Mayson Privacy Order (Azamour (IRE))
1881[4] 2823[8] 3844[10] 4813[11] 5423[7] 5916[8] 6970[9]

**Private School (IRE)** *D Smaga* a58 58
4 ch m Mastercraftsman(IRE) Poltava (FR) (Victory Note (USA))
6125a[15]

**Private View** *Sir Michael Stoute* a62
2 b f Exceed And Excel(AUS) Confidential Lady (Singspiel (IRE))
8147[4]

**Prize Diva** *David Elsworth* a63 71
3 b f Motivator Premier Prize (Selkirk (USA))
814[4] 2929[7] 3507[3] (3759)◆ 4319[4] 5367[8]

**Prize Money** *Saeed bin Suroor* 117
4 b g Authorized(IRE) Dresden Doll (USA) (Elusive Quality (USA))
428a[2] (699a)◆ (1042a) 1379a[4] 3299[9] 4070[11] 5464a[6] 6727a[6]

**Procedure** *Sir Michael Stoute* a73 72
2 gr f Invincible Spirit(IRE) Clinical (Motivator)
4116[2] 7725[5] 8308[2] 8702[4]

**Proctor** *Stuart Kittow* a70 87
4 b g Makfi Super Motiva (Motivator)
3785[8] 4498[5]

**Proctor's Ledge (USA)**
*Brendan P Walsh* 108
3 b f Ghostzapper(USA) Archstone (USA) (Arch (USA))
8071a[8]

**Procurator (IRE)** *Richard Hannon* a74 83
3 b c Canford Cliffs(IRE) Lulawin (Kyllachy)
2088[9] 2567[5] 3862[9] 4468[2] 4910[5] 7789[8] (8184) 8640[8]

**Professor** *Michael Attwater* a91 89
7 ch g Byron Jubilee (Selkirk (USA))
459[5] 1103[9] 1501[7] 2230[3] 3003[7] 3620[3] 4270[6] 4746[8] 5302[3] 5842[6] 6936[10]

**Profitable (IRE)** *Clive Cox* 120
5 b h Invincible Spirit(IRE) Dani Ridge (IRE) (Indian Ridge (IRE))
2643a[2] 3926[2] 5595[2] 6402[6] 7670a[3]

**Profound (IRE)** *Roger Varian* a77 69
2 b c Intello(GER) Bahama Spirit (IRE) (Invincible Spirit (IRE))
7906[7] 8387[5] 8952[2]

**Progressive Jazz (IRE)** *K R Burke* a54 50
2 b g Red Jazz(USA) Kind Regards (IRE) (Unfuwain (USA))
1872[12] 2403[9] 4597[9] 5752[8] 6940[7] 7519[3] 8120[3] 8306[2] 8870[2] 9238[3] 9439[5]

**Project Bluebook (FR)** *John Quinn* a72 87
4 bl g Sinndar(IRE) Apperella (Rainbow Quest (USA))
4742[2] 6096[2]

**Projection** *Roger Charlton* 113
4 b g Acclamation Spotlight (Dr Fong (USA))
2433[6] 4072[3] 5640[14] 7806[2]

**Proletariat (JPN)** *Shigeyuki Kojima* 106
6 b m Heart's Cry(JPN) Agartha (JPN) (King Kamehameha (JPN))
2203a[16]

**Prominna** *Tony Carroll* a61 62
7 ch g Proclamation(IRE) Minnina (IRE) (In The Wings)
2967[3]◆ 4532[6] 5253[3] 5567[4] 6179[3] 6478[6] 7195[8] (7494) 8128[4]

**Promise Of Peace (JPN)** *A Wohler* a92 105
3 ch c King Kamehameha(JPN) Peace Of World (JPN) (Sunday Silence (USA))
4422a[5] 8270a[5] 9003a[12]

**Promise To Be True (IRE)**
*A P O'Brien* 111
3 b f Galileo(IRE) Sumora (IRE) (Danehill (USA))
1634a[6]

**Promising (IRE)** *Richard Hannon* a60 99
3 b f Invincible Spirit(IRE) Lethal Quality (USA) (Elusive Quality (USA))
1958[3]

**Promising Run (USA)**
*Saeed bin Suroor* a93 108
4 b m Hard Spun(USA) Aviacion (BRZ) (Know Heights (IRE))
(429a) 776a[3] 1046a[7] 7506[4] 8546[3]

**Pronounced (IRE)**
*Joseph Patrick O'Brien* a63 57
3 b g Power Le Montrachet (Nashwan (USA))
4900[7]

**Prontamente** *F Chappet* 95
2 b f More Than Ready(USA) Specific Dream (Danehill Dancer (IRE))
8170a[3]

**Proper Discretion (USA)**
*Philip D'Amato* a103 73
4 b m Discreetly Mine(USA) Prizes (USA) (Prized (USA))
8605a[12]

**Proschema (IRE)** *Tom Dascombe* 79
2 ch c Declaration Of War(USA) Notable (Zafonic (USA))
7543[2] 8387[3]◆

**Prosecute (FR)** *Ali Stronge* a50 40
4 b g Lawman(FR) Dissitation (IRE) (Spectrum (IRE))
4538[8] 5333[7] 7711[11] 8132[12]

**Prosecution** *Hughie Morrison* a67 74
3 b c Lawman(FR) Convention (Encosta De Lago (AUS))
3392[4] 3922[2] 4623[3] 5578[2] 6281[2] 6767[4] 8000[8]

**Prosper** *Roger Varian* a89 90
3 gr f Exceed And Excel(AUS) Ela Athena (Ezzoud (IRE))
1760[2] (2287) 2827[6] 3964[14] 4915[6] 5745[4] 6687[5]

**Prost (GER)** *Ed Vaughan* a91 92
3 b g Tin Horse(IRE) Plebeya (IRE) (Dubawi (IRE))
1337a[4] 4634[7] 5719[2] 7404[6] (7941)◆ 9003a[16]

**Protected Guest** *George Margarson* a74 64
2 b g Helmet(AUS) Reem Star (Green Tune (USA))
4885[7] 7250[12] 7489[2]

**Proud Archi (IRE)** *Michael Dods* a53 83
3 b g Archipenko(USA) Baharah (USA) (Elusive Quality (USA))
(1878) 2374[3] 3040[5] 3862[10] 4556[4] 4894[3] 5376[7] (6265) 6672[9] 8240[13] 8486[7]

**Proud Kate** *Christine Dunnett* a26 41
3 b f Proud Citizen(USA) Oceans Apart (Desert Prince (IRE))
2071[11] 2727[9] 4543[2] 5040[10] 5855[9] 6526[6]

**Prove The Point (IRE)**
*Michael Mulvany* a69 72
4 b m Arakan(USA) Love City (IRE) (Spectrum (IRE))
5518a[8] 6797a[5]

**Provoking (USA)** *David Evans* a43 55
4 bb g Any Given Saturday(USA) Fair And Lively (USA) (Lively One (USA))
2255[3]◆ 2914[7] 4180[5] 4458[8] 4726[4] 5050[12]

**Prufrock (IRE)** *David Simcock* a62 66
3 ch f Roderic O'Connor(IRE) Indaba (IRE) (Indian Ridge (IRE))
76[5] 307[6] 496[6]

**Prussian Eagle (IRE)** *Evan Williams* a36 68
6 br g Jeremy(USA) Absolutely Cool (IRE) (Indian Ridge (IRE))
6034[4] 7202[5]

**Prying Pandora (FR)** *Richard Fahey* a86 85
4 b m Dark Angel(IRE) Leniency (IRE) (Cape Cross (IRE))
1606[5]◆ (2789) 3255[5] 3558[2] 3981[6] 5163[6] 5889[2] 7981[5] 8390[11] 8718[9]

**Psychedelic Funk** *G M Lyons* 110
3 ch c Choisir(AUS) Parabola (Galileo (IRE))
2863a[2] 3765a[3] 6334a[4] 6959a[3] (7663a)

**Psychology** *Kenny Johnson* a58 5
4 b g Shamardal(USA) Emotion Parade (ARG) (Parade Marshal (USA))
175[6] 580[7] 969[13] 1197[4] 1469[5] 1834[12] 3340[9] 3860[6]

**Psychotic** *David Menuisier* a76 66
4 b g Nayef(USA) Palatial (Green Desert (USA))
6103[5] 6775[5] (7514) 7998[11]

**Ptarmigan Ridge** *James Fanshawe* a69 82
3 b g Kyllachy Joshua's Princess (Danehill (USA))
2819[2] 4341[3] 5937[2] 6791[3] (7930)

**Puchita (IRE)** *Richard Hannon* a59 66
2 b f Acclamation Violet Ballerina (IRE) (Namid)
4533[6] 4880[7] 5528[8] 6008[3] 6699[2] 8153[6]

**Pucon** *Simon Dow* a13 79
8 b m Kyllachy The Fugative (Nicholas (USA))
5967[5]

**Pudding Chare (IRE)** *Richard Fahey* a68 40
3 b g Arcano(IRE) Rosy Dudley (IRE) (Grand Lodge (USA))
7574[3] 8479[8] 8931[5] 9219[4]

**Puds** *Charles Hills* a75 69
2 br f Bated Breath Missy Wassie Gal (USA) (High Chaparral (IRE))
4296[9] 8324[2] 8850[2]

**Pulitzer** *Hugo Palmer* 86
2 b f Kodiac Solola (GER) (Black Sam Bellamy (IRE))
4815[9] 5528[3] (6876) 8043[5] 8424[13]

**Pullman Brown (USA)** *Philip Kirby* a69 88
5 b g Big Brown(USA) Touch Too Much (USA) (Holy Bull (USA))
850[6]◆ 1677[5]◆ 2497[6] 5949[4]

**Pull The Pin (IRE)** *Mandy Rowland* a57 33
8 b g Kheleyf(USA) Inscribed (IRE) (Fasliyev (USA))
153[10] 311[12] 722[5] 899[11]

**Pulsating (IRE)** *Archie Watson* a74 66
3 b f Dragon Pulse(IRE) Safqa (Singspiel (IRE))
2[3] 157[2] 324[4] 458[7] 496[4] 813[5] (923) 1090[5] 1547[7] 1786[5] 2094[8] 2252[5] 2793[7] 7212[13] 7945[11] 8551[7] 9129[2] (9268) 9340[4]

**Pumaflor (IRE)** *Philip Kirby* a75 87
5 b g Aussie Rules(USA) Krasotka (IRE) (Soviet Star (USA))
1832[9] 2133[5] 2586[2] 2884[5] 5000[2]◆ 5559[2] 5849[8] 6516[P] 6855[10] 7595[8]

**Pumblechook** *Mark Johnston* a71 94
4 b g Dalakhani(IRE) Chiang Mai (IRE) (Sadler's Wells (USA))
3050[3] 3464[3] (3817) (4095) 4498[7] 5110[4] (5737) 6383[8] 6929[8] 7627[5]

**Pumpkin Rumble (USA)**
*Kevin Attard* 101
6 ch g English Channel(USA) Clarins (USA) (Storm Cat (USA))
7178a[7]

**Pump Pump Palace (FR)**
*J-P Gauvin* a92 103
4 b h King's Best(USA) Pump Pump Girl (FR) (Kendor (FR))
2559a[3] 3637a[5]

**Punkawallah** *Tom Dascombe* a62 81
3 b g Sepoy(AUS) Max One Two Three (IRE) (Princely Heir (IRE))
2366[9] (4575) (5824)

**Puppetshow (IRE)** *A P O'Brien* a78 86
3 b f Galileo(IRE) Lesson In Humility (IRE) (Mujadil (USA))
5766a[7] 6490a[11]

**Puramente** *Jo Hughes* a59 57
2 ch g Pastoral Pursuits Sahend (IRE) (Danehill Dancer (IRE))
3187[10] 5786[7] 6304[7] 7082[4] 7996[2] 8141[5] 8847[6]

**Purana** *Ms N M Hugo*
6 ch m Pastoral Pursuits Arruhan (IRE) (Mujtahid (USA))
3397[12]

**Pure Action (IRE)**
*John James Feane* a79 78
4 ch g Haatef(USA) Pure Jazz (IRE) (Marju (IRE))
8510[4]

**Pure Art** *Ralph Beckett* a77 101
4 b m Dutch Art Pure Song (Singspiel (IRE))
2954[4] 4119[4] 5381[9]

**Pure Pride (NZ)** *Murray Johnson* 96
4 b m Shocking(AUS) Mamasan (NZ) (Shinko King (IRE))
8857a[6]

**Pure Sensation (USA)**
*Christophe Clement* a94 118
6 rg g Zensational(USA) Pure Disco (USA) (Disco Rico (USA))
8604a[5]

**Pure Shores** *Ian Williams* a76 65
3 b f Dubawi(IRE) Polly's Mark (IRE) (Mark Of Esteem (IRE))
1756[2] 2131[6] 2754[13] 9202[3] (9301) 9418[6]

**Purley Queen (IRE)** *Mrs C Gilbert* a44 51
8 b m Piccolo Queenie (Indian Ridge (IRE))
(2669a) 4655a[3] 5200a[5] 5984a[3] 6544a[4]

**Purple Jazz (IRE)** *George Baker* a50
2 b g Red Jazz(USA) Breakmeheart (IRE) (Galileo (IRE))
8545[10] 8888[9] 9299[9]

**Purple Rock (IRE)** *Michael Easterby* a86 88
5 b g Fastnet Rock(AUS) Amethyst (IRE) (Sadler's Wells (USA))
2741[2] 3046[9] 3841[9] 4206[8] 4921[6] 5667[4] 8289[6] 8912[10] 9295[5]

**Purser (USA)** *John Gosden* a99 101
2 b c Mizzen Mast(USA) Solo Piano (USA) (Empire Maker (USA))
(6132)◆ 6696[4] (7765)◆ 8036[3]

**Pursuing Steed** *Hughie Morrison* a80 82
3 b g Pastoral Pursuits Emma Peel (Emarati (USA))
1727[8] (2507) (3296) (4251)◆ (5288) 6134[9] 7398[8] 7998[7]

**Pursuing The Dream (IRE)**
*Jamie Osborne* 100
2 b f Dream Ahead(USA) Crimson Lass (IRE) (Dubawi (IRE))
2502[9] 3029[4]◆ 3283[2] 3960[6] 4488[4] 5150[5] (6051a) 7114[4] 8001[8]

**Pushaq (IRE)** *Anthony McCann* a85 81
4 b g Roderic O'Connor(IRE) Et Dona Ferentes (Green Desert (USA))
(2163) 2920[2] 5484[2] 7327[10]

**Pushjockeypush** *Stuart Williams* a51 39
3 gr g Silver Frost(IRE) Daraiyna (FR) (Refuse To Bend (IRE))
1358[7] 1727[11] 3657[9] 5034[8] 5336[12]

**Pushkin Museum (IRE)**
*Patrick Morris* a72 72
6 gr g Soviet Star(USA) Chaste (Groom Dancer (USA))
80[7] 362[3] (495) (601) 843[3] 1063[5] 1887[2] 1979[2] 3257[3] 3941[2] 4337[3] 4724[3] 5827[4] 7607[5] 8743[5] 8853[5]

**Push N'Pull (IRE)** *Richard Fahey* a49 61
2 b c Epaulette(AUS) Zoudie (Ezzoud (IRE))
4919[9] 5437[4] 5844[9]

**Put The Boot In (IRE)** *Nikki Evans* a43 30
5 ch g Duke Of Marmalade(IRE) Mubkera (IRE) (Nashwan (USA))
1458[6] 1698[9] 5361[7]

**Pyjamarama** *Roger Varian* a68 66
3 b f Exceed And Excel(AUS) Dylanesque (Royal Applause)
2094[7] 2587[9] 3473[2]◆ 3751[2]

**Pyla (IRE)** *Luke Comer* a71 56
5 b m Footstepsinthesand Beautiful Hill (IRE) (Danehill (USA))
1014a[11]

**Pyramid First (FR)** *L Gadbin* a44 64
2 b f Evasive Pyramid Painter (IRE) (Peintre Celebre (USA))
7969a[9]

**Pyroclastic (IRE)** *Nick Kent* a45 40
5 b g Tagula(IRE) Gypsy Royal (IRE) (Desert Prince (IRE))
386[12] 1978[11] 3758[9] 3906[7] 4626[10]

**Pythius (IRE)** *Riccardo Santini* 94
4 b h Lord Shanakill(USA) Silicon Star (FR) (Starborough)
7442a[5]

**Python** *Andrew Crook* a40 35
5 b g Dansili Imbabala (Zafonic (USA))
3342[9] 3706[6] 5021[14] 5413[8] 5740[8] 6088[9]

**Qaaraat** *Ed Dunlop* a70 77
2 b g Acclamation Ladyship (Oasis Dream)
1941[4] 2435[3] 3025[3] 5480[3] 6338[3] 6756[2]◆

**Qaboos (FR)** *F Chappet* a65 9
4 b g Equiano(FR) Oui Dire (Oasis Dream)
713a[2]

**Qadiriyyah** *Mohamed Moubarak* a62 75
2 b g Harbour Watch(IRE) Quadri (Polish Precedent (USA))
8180[6] 8399[6]

**Qaffaal (USA)** *Michael Easterby* a96 86
6 b g Street Cry(IRE) Wasseema (USA) (Danzig (USA))
199[9] 817[2] (1177) 1446[3] 1757[6] 2999[3] 4261[3] 4916[11] 8652[9] 8905[3] 9264[4]◆

**Qafilah (IRE)** *Charles Hills* a59 67
2 ch f Arcano(IRE) Janina (Namid)
6583[3] 7238[7]

**Qaroun** *Sir Michael Stoute* 81
2 b c Dark Angel(IRE) Exotic Isle (Exceed And Excel (AUS))
5314[2]◆ (6133)

**Qasr** *Keith Dalgleish* a43
3 b c Excelebration(IRE) Blur (Oasis Dream)
8979[4]

**Qassem (IRE)** *Hugo Palmer* a105 105
4 b g Lope De Vega(IRE) Biswa (USA) (Kafwain (USA))
2735[5] (5744)◆ 6355[2] 7619[21] 8234[14]

**Qaswarah (IRE)** *Ed Dunlop* a57 59
2 b f Nayef(USA) Katoom (IRE) (Soviet Star (USA))
8380[10] 8796[9]

**Qatar Bolt** *F Head* 63
2 ch c French Fifteen(FR) Yellow And Green (Monsun (GER))
5776a[11]

**Qatar Divine (FR)** *H-A Pantall* a70 76
3 b f Myboycharlie(IRE) Accordia (USA) (Smart Strike (CAN))
8304a[2]

**Qatari Hunter (IRE)** *J S Bolger* a106 107
4 b h Footstepsinthesand Inis Boffin (Danehill Dancer (IRE))
6243a[4]

**Qatari Riyals (IRE)** *Richard Hannon* a79 73
3 b f Kodiac Mary Frith (Acclamation)
(1626) 2757[10] 4797[4] 5636[4] 6373[4] (7409)

**Qatar Light (IRE)** *Majed Seifeddine* a59 90
5 bb g Zebedee Belle Child (IRE) (Bijou D'Inde)
932a[12]

**Qatar Magic (FR)** *Yannick Fouin* a36
2 b f French Fifteen(FR) Shifting Sands (FR) (Hernando (FR))
9086a[12]

**Qatar Man (IRE)** *Marco Botti* a102
3 b g Archarcharch(USA) Dough On The Go (USA) (Bernardini (USA))
697a[4]◆ 1040a[2] 1375a[6]

**Qatar Sunshine** *H-A Pantall* a72 74
2 br f Kendargent(FR) Lykea (IRE) (Oasis Dream)
1335a[13] 8271a[5]

**Qaviy Cash** *Dan Skelton* a84 92
3 b g Oasis Dream Neartica (FR) (Sadler's Wells (USA))
2476[6]◆ 2783[7] 3720[2] (4430) 6445[15]

**Qawamees (IRE)** *Ed Dunlop* 77
2 b c Exceed And Excel(AUS) Jabhaat (USA) (Hard Spun (USA))
8678[2]◆

**Qayed (CAN)** *David Simcock* a72
2 b c Blame(USA) Endless Journey (USA) (A.P. Indy (USA))
9313[4]◆

**Qayes** *John Gosden* 63
2 b c Exceed And Excel(AUS) Time Control (Sadler's Wells (USA))
3590[9] 5321[2]

**Qaysar (FR)** *Richard Hannon* a85 85
2 b c Choisir(AUS) Coco Demure (IRE) (Titus Livius (FR))
8350[2] (8889)

**Qazyna (IRE)** *Roger Varian* 70
2 b f Frankel First (Highest Honor (FR))
**8322**[3]
**Q Cee** *Eugene Stanford* a66 66
4 b g Denounce Gibraltar Lass (USA) (Concerto (USA))
*808*[9] 2120[9] **5081**[5]◆ *7320*[11] 7693[6] *8345*[3]
**Qelmim (IRE)** *Richard Hannon*
3 gr f Dark Angel(IRE) Bun Penny (Bertolini (USA))
3748[12]
**Qemah (IRE)** *J-C Rouget* 117
4 b m Danehill Dancer(IRE) Kartica (Rainbow Quest (USA))
2616[2] **(3961)** 5460a[4] 6958a[5] 7812[6]
**Qewy (IRE)** *Charlie Appleby* 112
7 b g Street Cry(IRE) Princess Nada (Barathea (IRE))
4073[4]◆ 5503[13] **(8633a)** 8751a[6]
**Qeyaadah (IRE)** *Michael Appleby* 92
4 b g Acclamation Effervesce (IRE) (Galileo (IRE))
1902[6] 2381[6] 2730[5] 3498[5] **(4103)** 4524[3] 5159[4] 5610[4] 6186[2] 7025[3] 7622[8] 8014[10]
**Qianlong** *Roger Varian* a71 79
2 b c Dragon Pulse(IRE) Dream Day (FR) (Spectrum (IRE))
5755[2] 6272[3] **6939**[2] **8013**[2] *8316*[3]
**Qibtee (FR)** *Les Eyre* a45 61
7 b g Antonius Pius(USA) Embers Of Fame (IRE) (Sadler's Wells (USA))
*46*[7] *218*[8]
**Qool** *Markus Klug* 88
3 b f Soldier Hollow Quiza Quiza Quiza (Golden Snake (USA))
**1846a**[7]
**Qortaaj** *David Loughnane* a71 71
4 b g Kyllachy Cardrona (Selkirk (USA))
*92*[12] *1691*[10] *1285*[11] **2057**[4] 2626[7] 2916[12] 3397[7]
**Q Ten Girl (IRE)** *James Unett* a54 15
4 ch m Zebedee Regresa A Mi (IRE) (Spartacus (IRE))
*145*[8]
**Quadriga (IRE)** *Chris Grant* a48 41
7 b g Acclamation Turning Light (GER) (Fantastic Light (USA))
*7*[8] *414*[7] *661*[4] *1544*[4] ***1823***[3] *2166*[4] *2312*[6] 7523[8] *8259*[3] *8807*[8] *9368*[7]
**Quality Art (USA)** *Simon Hodgson* a71 64
9 b g Elusive Quality(USA) Katherine Seymour (Green Desert (USA))
*215*[5] ***(1452)*** *1759*[P] (Dead)
**Quality Seeker (USA)** *Ed Walker* a62
2 b c Quality Road(USA) Arravale (USA) (Arch (USA))
***8703***[5]
**Quandary Peak** *J S Moore* a63 88
3 b f Mount Nelson Sahariri (IRE) (Red Ransom (USA))
**2361**[4]
**Quantatmental (IRE)**
*Tom Dascombe* a65 66
2 ch c New Approach(IRE) Anayid (A.P. Indy (USA))
**7117**[7] 8136[9] *8399*[5]
**Quantum Dot (IRE)** *Ed de Giles* a72 68
6 ch g Exceed And Excel(AUS) Jeed (IRE) (Mujtahid (USA))
2360[5] 2967[10] 3281[7] **(4148)** 4842[3] 6278[3] 6810[6]
**Quargent (USA)** *Jeremy Noseda* a81 71
2 b f War Front(USA) Naples Bay (USA) (Giant's Causeway (USA))
4902[8] ***(6064)***
**Quarterback (GER)** *Rune Haugen* a105 108
5 b h American Post Quebra (GER) (Surumu (GER))
***1500***[6] 1957[8]
**Quartier Francais (USA)**
*A R Al Rayhi* a78
3 br c Street Cry(IRE) Divine Dixie (USA) (Dixieland Band (USA))
***8710a***[10]
**Quatrieme Ami** *Philip McBride* a92 87
4 b g Equiano(FR) Hundred Year Flood (USA) (Giant's Causeway (USA))
***234***[7] *639*[9] 1915[5] ***2331***[3] 2621[9] 7255[2]◆ **(7522)** 7737[12]
**Quay Point (IRE)** *Laura Mongan* a42 60
4 b m Royal Applause Merle (Selkirk (USA))
2564[8] 3145[5] *4497*[9] ***(5267)***◆ 5716[8] 6309[10]
**Quayside** *Richard Fahey* 75
2 ch c Harbour Watch(IRE) Fantacise (Pivotal)
3169[7] 3576[3] **(4245)** 5099[6] 5596[6] 6128[5] 6693[6]
**Quebec** *Roger Ingram* a68 74
6 b g Dansili Milford Sound (Barathea (IRE))
***9325***[8]
**Quechua (ARG)** *Ricardo Le Grange* 108
6 b g Pure Prize(USA) Queen Cabaret (BRZ) (Wild Event (USA))
**1374a**[12]
**Queen Adelaide** *John Ryan* a64 64
2 b f Helmet(AUS) Spunger (Fraam)
4363[5] **4902**[11] ***6286***[3] 7814[23]
**Queen Anne's Lace (USA)**
*D K Weld* 96
3 gr f Lonhro(AUS) Harpeth (USA) (Sadler's Wells (USA))
**1387a**[4]
**Queen Beatrice** *William Muir* 55
3 b f Iffraaj Skirrid (Halling (USA))
2908[12] 3615[8] 4409[7] **5250**[6] 5958[2] 7459[9]
**Queen Boudica** *A Fabre* 82
3 b f Dansili Satwa Queen (FR) (Muhtathir)
(3134a)
**Queen In Waiting (IRE)**
*Mark Johnston* a91 96
3 ch f Exceed And Excel(AUS) Princess Taise (USA) (Cozzene (USA))
*(1838)* 2130[2] 2400[4] 3034[4] 3793[5] **(4098)**◆ 4333[5] 4581[5] 4889[8] 5602[8] 6450[19]
**Queen Kindly** *Richard Fahey* 112
3 ch f Frankel Lady Of The Desert (USA) (Rahy (USA))
1958[5] 2434[9] 4078[3] **4864**[2] (6234) 6926[10] 7670a[5]◆ 8040[4]
**Queen Maureen (USA)**
*Hugo Palmer* a43 58
2 b f Elusive Quality(USA) Star Of Paris (USA) (Dayjur (USA))
*8147*[8] **8593**[6]
**Queen Moon (IRE)** *Andrew Balding* a45 57
3 bb f Lawman(FR) Movie Queen (Danehill (USA))
2707[5] **3691**[8] 4086[4] 6139[4] 6767[5] *8255*[3] *9073*[4]
**Queen Of Desire (IRE)**
*Roger Varian* a68
2 b f Dubawi(IRE) Beyond Desire (Invincible Spirit (IRE))
***9022***[5]
**Queen Of Dreams (IRE)**
*William Knight* a46 35
2 b f Epaulette(AUS) Celestial Dream (IRE) (Oasis Dream)
8347[8] *8850*[9] ***9023***[7]
**Queen Of Kalahari** *Charles Hills* a75 76
2 b f Lethal Force(IRE) Aromatherapy (Oasis Dream)
1884[5] 2502[3]◆ (2890) *3230*[2] (4252) 4827[6] 5751[5] **6749**[2] 7458[2] *8131*[2]
**Queen Of Time** *Henry Candy* 97
3 b f Harbour Watch(IRE) Black Belt Shopper (IRE) (Desert Prince (IRE))
(2393) (3031) 3964[4] **4637**[2]
**Queen Penn** *Richard Fahey* 78
2 gr f Dark Angel(IRE) The Manx Touch (IRE) (Petardia)
2265[7] 2832[2]◆ 4374[3] 5659[3] **(6347)**
**Queen Roselyn (USA)**
*A De Royer-Dupre* a67
2 bb f Savabeel(AUS) Senorita Lucy (NZ) (Senor Pete (USA))
***8691a***[4]
**Queensbrydge** *Robyn Brisland* a86 78
3 ch f Dutch Art Meydan Princess (IRE) (Choisir (AUS))
4617[6] 5506[12] *6068*[7] *6576*[4] *7484*[4] ***(7710)***◆
**Queens Care (IRE)** *A Wohler* 56
2 b f Born To Sea(IRE) Athlumney Dancer (Shareef Dancer (USA))
**8461a**[5]
**Queens Gallery** *Richard Hannon* a46 60
2 b c Dutch Art Raymi Coya (CAN) (Van Nistelrooy (USA))
**6005**[4] 6721[5] *7511*[9]
**Queen's Parade (USA)**
*D Selvaratnam* 96
6 ch m Giant's Causeway(USA) Queen Of Kills (USA) (Unbridled's Song (USA))
205a[13] **431a**[8] 888a[13]
**Queens Royale** *Michael Appleby* a75 59
3 b f Stimulation(IRE) Sofia Royale (Royal Applause)
*3719*[5] 4619[6] 5266[4] 5935[3] 6265[4] *(6814)* *8402*[11] *(8807)* *9142*[7] *(9307)* ***(9363)***
**Queen's Sargent (FR)** *Kevin Ryan* 86
2 gr g Kendargent(FR) Queen's Conquer (King's Best (USA))
2029[7] 3093[3] 4848[2] 5875[4] 6330[2] **7090**[8]
**Queen's Trust** *Sir Michael Stoute* a85 115
4 b m Dansili Queen's Best (King's Best (USA))
2765[4] **3962**[4] 5571[6] 6356[3] 7669a[8] 8606a[5]
**Quel Avantage (IRE)** *R Bouresly* 90
7 b h Galileo(IRE) Necklace (Darshaan)
**86a**[11]
**Quelindo (GER)** *Gabor Maronka* 102
5 rg h Aussie Rules(USA) Quintana (GER) (Fantastic Light (USA))
2866a[4] **3884a**[3]
**Quench Dolly** *John Gallagher* a71 104
3 gr f Hellvelyn Hollybell (Beveled (USA))
*1463*[6] 1731[8] (2503) (2579) 2831[3] 3835[8] 4407[2] 5117[4] **(5574)** 7610[7] 8040[9]
**Quest For More (IRE)**
*Roger Charlton* a85 117
7 b g Teofilo(IRE) No Quest (IRE) (Rainbow Quest (USA))
**1374a**[9] 3011[7] 3996[12]
**Question Of Faith** *Martin Todhunter* a56 74
6 b m Yeats(IRE) Anastasia Storm (Mozart (IRE))
1834[5] 3155[7] 3566[2] (4962) 5257[2] 5701[7] 5923[2] (6569) (7047) **(7700)**
**Questo** *Tracy Waggott* a60 73
5 ch g Monsieur Bond(IRE) Ex Gracia (Efisio)
1972[3] 3401[5] 3897[5] **(4509)** 5947[3]
**Quick Breath** *Jonathan Portman* 63
2 b g Bated Breath Shy Appeal (IRE) (Barathea (IRE))
5105[11] 6070[6] **7351**[7] 8120[7]
**Quick Look** *Michael Easterby* a70 91
4 b g Kheleyf(USA) Weqaar (USA) (Red Ransom (USA))
*1586*[8] 2303[7] 2837[4]◆ 6411[3] 6943[2] 6964[12] 7557[6] (8488) **(8680)**
**Quick Monet (IRE)** *Shaun Harris* a45 46
4 b g Excellent Art Clinging Vine (USA) (Fusaichi Pegasus (USA))
*4448*[5] **4604**[7] 5315[8] *7606*[6] *8259*[7] *8345*[5] *9072*[3] *9217*[11] *9342*[9]
**Quick N Quirky (IRE)** *Tim Easterby* 85
4 b m Lilbourne Lad(IRE) Beseech (IRE) (Danehill (USA))
2138[8] 2884[6] 3287[7] 3845[17] **4209**[2]◆ 4605[4]
**Quick Recovery** *Jim Boyle* 40
2 gr f Lethal Force(IRE) Lisiere (IRE) (Excellent Art)
**4799**[6] 6654[12] 7093[9]
**Quick Skips Lad (IRE)** *J S Moore* a64 62
2 b g Lilbourne Lad(IRE) Tallawalla (IRE) (Oratorio (IRE))
1496[7] 1594a[4] ***1792***[3] 2073a[6] 2642a[4] 3619[2] 3918[4] (4196a)
**Quids In (IRE)** *Oliver Greenall* a45 72
4 b g Pour Moi(IRE) Quixotic (Pivotal)
**7960**[6]
**Quidura** *H Graham Motion* 106
4 b m Dubawi(IRE) Quetena (GER) (Acatenango (GER))
**8098a**[6]
**Quiet Company** *Adrian Paul Keatley* a53 51
3 ch g Showcasing Kameruka (Auction House (USA))
**5206**[5] 5997[11]
**Quiet Moment (IRE)** *Keith Dalgleish* a54 57
3 b f Dandy Man(IRE) Easee On (IRE) (Hawk Wing (USA))
4745[7] 5375[6] 5703[5] 6630[6] 7165[2] 7888[3] **(7979)** *8255*[2] *8801*[13]
**Quiet Reflection** *K R Burke* 120
4 b m Showcasing My Delirium (Haafhd)
3079[10] **(7424a)** 8230[9]
**Quiet Warrior (IRE)**
*Michael Easterby* a57 63
6 b g Kodiac Pretty Woman (IRE) (Night Shift (USA))
***1325***[4] 2053[2] *4310*[13] 5070[6] 5377[9] *8401*[10]
**Quiet Weekend** *James Bethell* 28
3 b g Mawatheeq(USA) Maid Of Perth (Mark Of Esteem (IRE))
**5632**[11] *6901*[13]
**Quina Brook (IRE)**
*Daniel Mark Loughnane* a36 16
4 b m Peintre Celebre(USA) Barconey (IRE) (Danehill Dancer (IRE))
4967[11]
**Quindiana (FR)** *H-A Pantall* 87
3 ch f Linngari(IRE) Belle Suisse (FR) (Hamas (IRE))
**1337a**[6]
**Quinquereme** *Michael Bell* 55
3 b f Elusive Quality(USA) Finding Neverland (FR) (Green Desert (USA))
2753[6] **3293**[7] 3595[7]
**Quinteo (IRE)** *Jo Hughes* a78 74
3 b g Requinto(IRE) Haraplata (GER) (Platini (GER))
*3262*[11] ***4450***[3] 4891[5] *5523a*[10] *6160*[9] *7457*[9]
**Quintessential** *Richard Fahey* a23
3 b f Dick Turpin(IRE) Quiquillo (USA) (Cape Canaveral (USA))
***245***[8]
**Quintus Cerialis (IRE)**
*Karen George* a61 53
5 b g Vale Of York(IRE) Red Fox (IRE) (Spectrum (IRE))
***116***[4]◆ *398*[6]◆ *734*[4] *1285*[8] *1407*[6] 2178[4] 2763[10] 3823[9] 4441[4] 5081[2] 5535[7] *9129*[7]
**Quite A Story** *Archie Watson* a68 58
5 ch m Equiano(FR) Perfect Story (IRE) (Desert Story (IRE))
**2043**[3] 3008[4] 4149[6] *5482*[5] *6157*[7] *6850*[4] *8495*[8] *8824*[9]
**Quite Sharp** *Charlie Fellowes* 42
3 ch f New Approach(IRE) Balisada (Kris)
4300[8] **5364**[10]
**Quite Subunctious (IRE)**
*Keith Henry Clarke* a67 43
2 b f Rip Van Winkle(IRE) Beyond The Sea (IRE) (Fasliyev (USA))
**6487a**[7]
**Quivery (USA)** *Jeremy Noseda* 96
2 b f Violence(USA) Passion Du Coeur (USA) (Distorted Humor (USA))
(3858) (5114)◆ **6418**[4] 8004[11]
**Quixote (GER)** *Michael Easterby* a95 98
7 b h Pivotal Quebrada (IRE) (Devil's Bag (USA))
*275*[4]◆ *1546*[5] ***(2141)*** 6355[13] 7609[11] 8009[8]
**Quizical (IRE)** *Ms Sheila Lavery* 91
2 b c Roderic O'Connor(IRE) Twenty Questions (Kyllachy)
**8082a**[2] 8265a[6]
**Quloob** *Owen Burrows* a70 101
3 b c New Approach(IRE) Jadhwah (Nayef (USA))
(2513) (3520) (4908) **6151**[2]
**Quoteline Direct** *Micky Hammond* a69 66
4 ch g Sir Percy Queen's Pudding (IRE) (Royal Applause)
3181[11] 3910[3] 4439[11] 5540[2] 6316[4] 7219[6] 7960[5] (8515) ***9295***[2]
**Quothquan (FR)** *Michael Madgwick* a83 82
3 b g Myboycharlie(IRE) Lonestar Spirit (IRE) (Invincible Spirit (IRE))
*439*[3] 2088[6] 3005[7] *3721*[2] *6792*[10] 7097[5]◆ (7744) ***8506***[3]
**Qurbaan (USA)** *F Rohaut* a106 110
4 ch h Speightstown(USA) Flip Flop (FR) (Zieten (USA))
*1773*[5] **3104a**[4] 5046a[3] *6717a*[4] 7943a[5]
**Raafid** *A R Al Rayhi* a85 39
4 b g Shamardal(USA) Time Away (IRE) (Darshaan)
***772a***[6] *1041a*[8]
**Raaghib** *J-C Rouget* 84
3 ch c Dutch Art Safe House (IRE) (Exceed And Excel (AUS))
(847a)
**Raashdy (IRE)** *Peter Hiatt* a69 52
4 b g Intikhab(USA) Maghya (IRE) (Mujahid (USA))
*47*[7] *351*[8] *527*[6] 2708[6] 3537[8] 3761[8] *5897*[8] 6342[10] *7760*[8] *(7991)* *(8346)* *(8430)* *(8846)* ***8955***[3] *9270*[2] *9421*[3]
**Raawy** *Simon Crisford* 75
3 b g Dutch Art Age Of Chivalry (IRE) (Invincible Spirit (IRE))
**4269**[2] 5315[3] 6103[7]
**Racehorse** *Hughie Morrison* a62
2 ch f Equiano(FR) Lovely Dream (IRE) (Elnadim (USA))
***9231***[4]◆ *9371*[5]
**Racemaker** *Andrew Crook* a64 74
3 b g Stimulation(IRE) Sophies Heart (Hurricane Run (IRE))
2186[4] 2854[3] 3499[3] **(4690)** 5704[5] 6315[7] 6564[4] *7034*[7]
**Race Time (USA)** *Zoe Davison* a43
4 bb m Street Sense(USA) Well At The Top (IRE) (Sadler's Wells (USA))
*281*[11] ***839***[6] *1186*[10] 2964[P] *7990*[14]
**Rachael's Rocket (IRE)** *C Boutin* a58 71
2 ch f Sir Prancealot(IRE) Red Blanche (IRE) (Red Clubs (IRE))
5327[6]◆ 5629a[2] **5988a**[4] 6251a[10] *6452a*[5] 7592a[4] 8228a[2] 8524a[2]
**Racing Angel (IRE)** *Adrian Nicholls* a58 67
5 b m Dark Angel(IRE) Roclette (USA) (Rock Of Gibraltar (IRE))
*1899*[6] **2835**[4]◆ 3729[7] 4053[5] 5514[2] 5962[4] 7522[7] 7628[6] 8168[10] *8558*[4] *8924*[9] *9075*[5] *9444*[4]
**Racing Bay (FR)** *M Lelievre* a70 98
6 bl g Racinger(FR) Stiren Bay (FR) (Alamo Bay (USA))
**8444a**[4]
**Racing Country (IRE)**
*Saeed bin Suroor* a66 69
2 b c Dubawi(IRE) Movin' Out (AUS) (Encosta De Lago (AUS))
**8075**[5] *8642*[4]
**Racing History (IRE)**
*Saeed bin Suroor* 117
5 b h Pivotal Gonbarda (GER) (Lando (GER))
**5983a**[3]
**Racing Radio (IRE)** *David Barron* a45 54
2 b g Dandy Man(IRE) Vale Of Avoca (IRE) (Azamour (IRE))
5494[9] 5945[6] **6517**[4] *7030*[5] 7519[11] (Dead)
**Racing Spirit** *Dave Roberts* a33 41
5 ch g Sir Percy Suertuda (Domedriver (IRE))
**7232**[6]
**Racquet** *Ruth Carr* a61 79
4 br g Pastoral Pursuits Billie Jean (Bertolini (USA))
1971[9] 2303[3] 2821[10] 3288[6] 3666[14] *4310*[6] (4682) 5203[5] **(5919)** **6318**[3] 6786[7] 7244[11] 7825[10] 8168[6] 8484[2] 8656[10]
**Radio Source (IRE)**
*Sir Michael Stoute* 84
2 ch c Raven's Pass(USA) Roshanak (IRE) (Spinning World (USA))
5036[2]◆ **(6260)**◆
**Radjash** *Charlie Appleby* a77 77
3 b g Shamardal(USA) White Moonstone (USA) (Dynaformer (USA))
**1682**[4] 2677[4]
**Rafaaf (IRE)** *Peter Hiatt* a54 57
9 b g Royal Applause Sciunfona (IRE) (Danehill (USA))
*854*[3] *1298*[3] *1456*[5] **2762**[6] 3522[6] 7465[8] 7911[4] *8258*[7]
**Raffle King (IRE)** *Mick Channon* a69 74
3 b g Kodiac Tap The Dot (IRE) (Sharp Humor (USA))
*1600*[3] **2252**[2]◆ 2579[8] 3085[9] 4910[8] *7365*[2] *7767*[2] *8242*[3]
**Raghu (NZ)** *Jason Warren* 38
4 br h Showcasing Fantasy World (NZ) (Zabeel (NZ))
**8857a**[13]
**Ragstone Ridge (FR)**
*Richard Hughes* a55
2 ch g Choisir(AUS) Almogia (USA) (Gone West)
***8889***[10] *9200*[10]
**Ragstone Road (IRE)**
*Richard Hughes* 77
2 b g Kodiac Greenflash (Green Desert (USA))
6071[2]◆ **(6826)** 7274[4]
**Ragstone Sand (IRE)** *Gary Moore* a56 39
2 b g Footstepsinthesand Speedy Storm (IRE) (Invincible Spirit (IRE))
*6816*[10] 7897[7] ***9385***[8]
**Ragstone View (IRE)**
*Richard Hughes* a72 75
2 b g Requinto(IRE) Highland Miss (USA) (Theatrical (IRE))
**3868**[5] **4266**[4] 5048[3] (5408) *6065*[5] 7121[5]
**Ragtag Rascal (IRE)**
*Amanda Perrett* a64
3 b g Tagula(IRE) Trebles (IRE) (Kenmare (FR))
***1499***[6]
**Rag Tatter** *Kevin Ryan* a75 59
3 b g Kheleyf(USA) Golden Nun (Bishop Of Cashel)
*920*[2] ***1179***[2] 1913[13] 2682[5] 3166[5]
**Rahaaba (IRE)** *Owen Burrows* a57
2 b f Dubawi(IRE) Muthabara (IRE) (Red Ransom (USA))
***7454***[9] *8669*[10]
**Raheen House (IRE)** *Brian Meehan* 113
3 b c Sea The Stars(IRE) Jumooh (Monsun (GER))
1943[2] 3032[3] 4029[4] (4811) 7147[7] (7783)◆ **8421**[2]
**Rahmah (IRE)** *Geoffrey Deacon* a74 76
5 b g Vale Of York(IRE) Sweet Home Alabama (IRE) (Desert Prince (IRE))
*169*[4] 1519[5] 2781[6] 3428[2]◆ **(4470)** 5432[4] 6095[3]
**Raid (IRE)** *David Simcock* 85
2 b c Havana Gold(IRE) Remarkable Story (Mark Of Esteem (IRE))
**(8734)**
**Rail Dancer** *Richard Rowe* a78 57
5 b g Rail Link Mara Dancer (Shareef Dancer (USA))
*(281)* *461*[3] *738*[9] *1081*[3] *(1556)*◆ *(2022)*◆ ***(2956)*** 5556[6]
**Railport Dolly** *Michael Appleby* 68
2 b f Rail Link Polly Adler (Fantastic Light (USA))
6037[7] **7021**[6] 7520[6]
**Rainbow Chimes (IRE)**
*Ann Duffield* a44 55
3 b f Galileo(IRE) Chiming (IRE) (Danehill (USA))
***175***[7] 4172[8] 4789[13]
**Rainbow Dreamer** *Alan King* 98
4 b g Aqlaam Zamhrear (Singspiel (IRE))
1608[3]◆ (1942) **3928**[4]
**Rainbow Jazz (IRE)** *Mark Usher* a59 69
2 b g Red Jazz(USA) Let's Pretend (Rainbow Quest (USA))
3776[3] **4805**[4] 5292[11] **6552**[4] 6860[8] *7764*[11] 8074[3] **8467**[2] *8671*[5]
**Rainbow Lad (IRE)** *Michael Appleby* a62 66
4 b g Lilbourne Lad(IRE) Carmona (Rainbow Quest (USA))
*146*[3] *(1436)* (1930a) **2671a**[2]

**Rainbow Line (JPN)**
*Hidekazu Asami* 118
4 b h Stay Gold(JPN) Regenbogen (JPN) (French Deputy (USA))
2203a[12] 8975a[6]

**Rainbow Orse** *Robert Cowell* a56 83
5 b g Zebedee Khafayif (USA) (Swain (IRE))
(2932) (4278) 5580[8]

**Rainbow Rebel (IRE)**
*Mark Johnston* a92 94
4 b g Acclamation Imperial Quest (Rainbow Quest (USA))
2593[6] 2855[4] 3154[2] 3486[2] 3790[5] 4076[5] 8414[3] 8705[4] 8910[2] 8999[7] 9271[4] 9467[3]

**Rainbow Rising (FR)**
*David Menuisier* a75 75
3 b f Henrythenavigator(USA) Rainbow Goddess (Rainbow Quest (USA))
4808[7] 5124[7] 5931[2] 6578[2] 7151[3] 7948[3] 8692a[4]

**Rainford Glory (IRE)** *Tim Fitzgerald* a50 51
7 ch g Rock Of Gibraltar(IRE) My Dolly Madison (In The Wings)
839[9]

**Rain Goddess (IRE)** *A P O'Brien* 112
3 b f Galileo(IRE) Where (IRE) (Danehill Dancer (IRE))
1634a[7] 1958[4] 2644a[5] 3964[2] 4419a[2] 4928a[2] 5954a[8] (6490a) 6972a[3] 8098a[7]

**Rainha Da Bateria (USA)**
*Chad C Brown* a92 106
5 ch m Broken Vow(USA) Amelia (USA) (Dixieland Band (USA))
5954a[4] 8098a[4]

**Raining Stars** *James Fanshawe* a41 71
3 b g Sea The Stars(IRE) Sayyedati Symphony (USA) (Gone West (USA))
3209[11] 5220[11] 5757[2]

**Rain In The Face** *Karen Tutty* a75 3
4 b g Naaqoos Makaaseb (USA) (Pulpit (USA))
6[9]

**Rain Wind And Fire (USA)**
*Ronald Harris* a46
5 ch g Eskendereya(USA) Call Mariah (USA) (Dixie Union (USA))
1890[11] 3686[6]

**Raise A Little Joy** *J R Jenkins* 22
2 b f Pastoral Pursuits Ray Of Joy (Tobougg (IRE))
4440[16] 5534[12] 6480[15]

**Raise The Game (IRE)** *Bill Turner* a64
4 b g Bushranger(IRE) Fancy Feathers (IRE) (Redback)
127[11] 724[3] 860[8] 1249[11] 1823[7] 5817[P] (Dead)

**Raising Sand** *Jamie Osborne* a94 105
5 b g Oasis Dream Balalaika (Sadler's Wells (USA))
1492[P] 2828[15] 5157[6] (5914) 6918[4] 7807[3]◆

**Rajaam (IRE)** *Richard Hannon* a77
2 b c Invincible Spirit(IRE) Midnight Partner (IRE) (Marju (IRE))
(8877)

**Rajapur** *David Thompson* a37 53
4 rg g Dalakhani(IRE) A Beautiful Mind (GER) (Winged Love (IRE))
1469[7] 2162[8] 2501[8] 6565[10] (8655) 9070[4]

**Rajar** *Richard Fahey* a90 95
3 b f Archipenko(USA) Barnezet (GR) (Invincible Spirit (IRE))
317a[3] 652a[3] 889a[6] 6629[3]◆ 7108[6] 8563[2] 8747[4] 8905[8] 9269[2]

**Rajasinghe (IRE)** *Richard Spencer* a89 108
2 b c Choisir(AUS) Bunditten (IRE) (Soviet Star (USA))
(2786) (3925) 4812[3] 7618[11] 8577a[11]

**Raj Balaraaj (GER)** *George Baker* 74
3 b g Kyllachy Ragazza Mio (IRE) (Generous (IRE))
2220[2] 3412[9] 4255[8] 4804[3] (5718)

**Rajeline (FR)** *M Boutin* a69 67
3 gr f Rajsaman(FR) Tengeline (FR) (Cardoun (FR))
4289a[5] 8304a[3]

**Rakematiz** *Brett Johnson* a67 63
3 ch g Pivotal Regal Velvet (Halling (USA))
2507[12]◆ (3250) 4462[6] 8550[10] 9211[5] 9456[2]◆

**Rake's Progress** *Heather Main* a76 85
3 b g Sir Percy Cartoon (Danehill Dancer (IRE))
(2794) 3392[3] 4757[5] (5323) 5915[4] 6920[8]

**Rakhsh (FR)** *Carina Fey* a87 87
5 gr g Carlotamix(FR) Kendorya (FR) (Kendor (FR))
1531a[10] 2696a[3]

**Raktiman (IRE)** *Sam England* a64 63
10 ch g Rakti Wish List (IRE) (Mujadil (USA))
7893[4]

**Ralphy Boy (IRE)** *Alistair Whillans* a56 81
8 b g Acclamation Silcasue (Selkirk (USA))
1778[10] 2339[4] 2888[6] 3045[6] 3332[3] 3899[9] 4506[6] 5467[6] 5880[6]

**Ralphy Lad (IRE)** *Alan Swinbank* a82 57
6 b g Iffraaj Hawattef (IRE) (Mujtahid (USA))
174[8] 315[4] 661[2] 853[7]

**Rambling Queen (IRE)**
*Brian Rothwell* 27
4 gr m Mastercraftsman(IRE) Dos Lunas (IRE) (Galileo (IRE))
4055[9] 4568[9]

**Ramblow** *Michael Appleby* a63 52
4 b m Notnowcato Nsx (Roi Danzig (USA))
314[2] 482[10] 1072[7]

**Rampant Lion (IRE)** *Mark Johnston* 65
2 ch g Bahamian Bounty Mamma Morton (IRE) (Elnadim (USA))
3156[6] 3430[5]

**Rancheria (FR)** *S Wattel* a58 60
3 b f Acclamation Rosa Bonheur (USA) (Mr Greeley (USA))
8304a[10]

**Randall's Alannah (IRE)**
*Seamus Fahey* a52 45
7 b m High Chaparral(IRE) Randall's Diana (IRE) (Monashee Mountain (USA))
614[2] 1139[6]

**Randulina (FR)** *K Borgel* a71 79
4 b m Early March Rada Angel (IRE) (Le Vie Dei Colori)
606a[6]

**Rangali** *D Guillemin* 98
6 ch g Namid Tejaara (USA) (Kingmambo (USA))
2643a[5] 4234a[7]

**Range Of Knowledge (IRE)**
*E J O'Neill* a61 70
4 b g Bushranger(IRE) Pearls Of Wisdom (Kyllachy)
5176a[4]

**Rannan (FR)** *H-F Devin* a69 72
2 b c Style Vendome(FR) Footsteppy (IRE) (Footstepsinthesand)
5776a[6]

**Ransom The Moon (CAN)**
*Philip D'Amato* a117
5 b h Malibu Moon(USA) Count To Three (CAN) (Red Ransom (USA))
8607a[5]

**Rantan (IRE)** *David Barron* a66 87
4 b g Kodiac Peace Talks (Pivotal)
1910[9] 3492[2] 3757[9] 4277[5]

**Raphaelus (FR)** *P Khozian* a28 36
10 b g Whipper(USA) Eximius (Atticus (USA))
691a[11]

**Rapid Applause** *M D O'Callaghan* a85 91
5 b g Royal Applause Madam Ninette (Mark Of Esteem (IRE))
795a[7] 4925a[11] 6971a[16] 8222a[8]

**Rapid Ranger** *David O'Meara* a79 70
3 b g Kyllachy Director's Dream (IRE) (Act One)
4604[3] 5167[5] 5619[4] 6157[4] 6596[3] 7018[2]◆ 7525[3] (7933) 8247[12] (8875) (9152)◆ 9410[10]

**Rapid Rhythm (USA)**
*Michael Stidham* 96
5 b m Successful Appeal(USA) Patriot Miss (USA) (Quiet American (USA))
1813a[6]

**Rapid Rise (IRE)** *Milton Bradley* a51 40
3 b g Fast Company(IRE) French Doll (IRE) (Titus Livius (FR))
625[5] 1000[6] 2151[6] 2931[9] 6155[5] 6581[10] 7191[15] 7517[8] 8134[7] 8395[7] 8823[6] 8948[7] 9268[4] 9454[6]

**Rapier (USA)** *Sir Michael Stoute* a62
2 ch g Animal Kingdom(USA) Shadow Cast (USA) (Smart Strike (CAN))
7726[9]

**Rapper Dragon (AUS)** *John Moore* 115
4 ch g Street Boss(USA) Swing Dance (AUS) (Danehill Dancer (IRE))
2492a[P] (Dead)

**Raramauri (IRE)** *W McCreery* 88
2 b f Fast Company(IRE) Spinning Ruby (Pivotal)
6241a[4]

**Rare Groove (IRE)** *Jedd O'Keeffe* a73 76
2 ch c Lope De Vega(IRE) Ascot Lady (IRE) (Spinning World (USA))
7520[4] 8140[3] 8782[2]

**Rare Rhythm** *Charlie Appleby* 115
5 b g Dubawi(IRE) Demisemiquaver (Singspiel (IRE))
(4033) (4917)

**Rasasee (IRE)** *Tim Vaughan* a74 81
4 gr g Rip Van Winkle(IRE) Gleaming Silver (IRE) (Dalakhani (IRE))
780[6]

**Raseed** *F Head* a90 110
4 b h Dubawi(IRE) Sudoor (Fantastic Light (USA))
1659a[9] 5046a[6]

**Raselasad (IRE)** *Tracy Waggott* 93
3 b g Acclamation Wajaha (IRE) (Haafhd)
2887[3] (3948) 4610[2] 5541[5] 5948[5] (6627)◆ 7656[2]

**Rashaan (IRE)** *Colin Kidd* a82 89
5 ch g Manduro(GER) Rayyana (IRE) (Rainbow Quest (USA))
5488a[13] 7837a[5]

**Rashdan (FR)** *Hugo Palmer* 70
2 b c Big Bad Bob(IRE) On Fair Stage (IRE) (Sadler's Wells (USA))
7120[4]

**Rasheeq (IRE)** *Tim Easterby* a64 97
4 b g Vale Of York(IRE) Limber Up (IRE) (Dansili)
1876[8] 2156[12] 2764[2] 3092[2] 3827[5] 4306[9] 5129[8] 5435[3] 5637[12] 6205[13] 6878[3] 7610[2] 8012[7] 8416[11]

**Rashford's Double (IRE)**
*Richard Fahey* a87 84
3 b g Zoffany(IRE) Ardent Lady (Alhaarth (IRE))
1801[9] 2755[6] 5072[3] 5392[11] 5949[2] 6235[5] 6855[4] 7569[2] 7823[10] 7941[9] 8289[3]

**Rasima** *Roger Varian* a68 68
2 gr f Iffraaj Raushan (IRE) (Dalakhani (IRE))
6064[5]◆ 6776[3]

**Rasmee** *Roger Charlton* a87 52
4 b g Fastnet Rock(AUS) Reem (AUS) (Galileo (IRE))
7234[3]

**Raspberry Princess** *Phil McEntee* a27
3 b f Royal Applause Eraadaat (IRE) (Intikhab (USA))
126[9] 546[4] 878[8] 1580[7] 2016[13]

**Rastacap** *Mark Johnston* a79 78
2 ch f Helmet(AUS) Caribbean Dancer (USA) (Theatrical (IRE))
6559[4] (6897)◆ 7623[2] 7891[3] 8536[4]

**Rastrelli (FR)** *Charlie Appleby* 91
2 b g Siyouni(FR) Ponte Di Legno (FR) (Sinndar (IRE))
5887[5] 6374[4] (7001) (7544) 8035[4]

**Rat Catcher (IRE)** *Lisa Williamson* a41 44
7 b g One Cool Cat(USA) Molly Marie (IRE) (Fasliyev (USA))
723[8] 899[9] 1221[7] 1452[8] 2628[12] 3290[5] 3544[8] 3942[3] 4458[9] 4731[8] 5069[8] 6157[9] 6298[8]

**Rathealy (IRE)** *Christine Dunnett* a42 21
6 b g Baltic King Baltic Belle (IRE) (Redback)
1182[4] 7253[10]

**Rathmuck Native (IRE)** *Peter Fahey* a53 74
9 b m Definite Article Fern Fields (IRE) (Be My Native (USA))
227a[7]

**Ratiocination (IRE)** *P Bary* 102
3 b c Excelebration(IRE) Denebola (USA) (Storm Cat (USA))
2944a[3] 3855a[5]

**Rattle On** *Jim Boyle* a66 64
4 ch g Pivotal Sabreon (Caerleon (USA))
1729[3] (2023) 2615[4] 3172[4] 4165[8] 4587[4] 5062[5] 5651[2] 5823[4] 7158[10]

**Rattling Jewel** *Miss Nicole McKenna* a73 92
5 b g Royal Applause Mutoon (IRE) (Erhaab (USA))
2656a[10] 4416a[14] 4925a[5] 6971a[19] 7856a[12]

**Raucous** *William Haggas* a98 109
4 b g Dream Ahead(USA) Shyrl (Acclamation)
(2114) 2907[4] 4072[8] 5149[4] 5640[12] 6419[11] 6971a[10] 8044[16]

**Ravenhoe (IRE)** *Mark Johnston* a72 75
4 ch g Bahamian Bounty Breathless Kiss (USA) (Roman Ruler (USA))
122[2] 306[8] 611[7] 876[4] 1085[5] 1323[3] 1707[8] 1839[3] 2108[6] 2153[2] (2301) 2708[12] 2884[8] 3325[6] 3899[6] 4833[3] 5062[4] 5843[7] 6263[4] 6947[9] 7476[7] 7894[13] 8376[7] 9032[5] 9213[6]◆

**Ravenous** *Luke Dace* a74 83
6 b g Raven's Pass(USA) Supereva (IRE) (Sadler's Wells (USA))
2617[4] 3409[7] 4441[3] 5397[4] 6151[3] 6929[7] 7949[11] 8505[7]

**Raven's Girl** *Michael Madgwick* 38
2 b f Raven's Pass(USA) Ravenel (GER) (Touch Down (GER))
2910[10] 3570[5] 4090[7] 5216[12] 9090[11]

**Raven's Lady** *Marco Botti* a88 99
3 ch f Raven's Pass(USA) Pivotal Lady (Pivotal)
1796[2] 2605[5] 3722[3] (4315) (5117) 6234[3] 6619[4]

**Ravens Quest** *John Ryan* a78 84
4 ch g Raven's Pass(USA) Seradim (Elnadim (USA))
163[3] 286[7] 517[8] (958) 1153[4] 1457[3] 1504[7] 2165[5]

**Raven's Raft (IRE)** *Michael Appleby* a56 66
2 gr f Raven's Pass(USA) Sea Drift (FR) (Warning)
3902[3] 4503[3] 5576[6] 6285[6] 9177[9] 9439[10]

**Raven's Song (IRE)** *Harry Dunlop* 59
2 b f Raven's Pass(USA) Lyric Of Fife (IRE) (Strategic Prince)
4909[9] 5934[4] 6553[7]

**Ravenswood** *Patrick Chamings* a53 60
4 b g Lawman(FR) Whatami (Daylami (IRE))
2042[10] 5652[3] 6589[2] 7152[3] 7918[12] 8507[10]

**Raweeya** *Marco Botti* a57
3 b f Oasis Dream Raihana (AUS) (Elusive Quality (USA))
283[7]

**Raw Impulse** *Darren Weir* 100
5 b h Makfi Marika (Marju (IRE))
8750a[2] 8857a[4]

**Rayaa** *Michael Appleby* a76 72
4 b m Virtual Winsa (USA) (Riverman (USA))
1897[3] 3402[9] 3454[6] 4010[6] 4621[7] 5290[2] 5533[4] 7762[2] 8143[4] (8813)

**Raydiance** *K R Burke* 100
2 b c Mayson Iridescence (Dutch Art)
2926[2] (3538) (5395)

**Ray Donovan (IRE)** *David O'Meara* 65
3 b g Acclamation Always The Lady (Halling (USA))
2036[7] 2347[7] 2591[7] 3151[5]

**Raymonda (USA)** *D K Weld* 106
4 b m Lonhro(AUS) Daring Diva (Dansili)
2440a[2] 3101a[4] 4512a[3] 6642a[11]

**Rayna's World (IRE)** *Philip Kirby* 76
2 b f Poet's Voice Salmon Rose (IRE) (Iffraaj)
5056[6]◆ 5999[3] 6875[5] (7251)

**Rayon Vert (FR)** *H-A Pantall* a84 91
3 b c Harbour Watch(IRE) Mansoura (IRE) (Kalanisi (IRE))
7697a[8]

**Ray Purchase** *Keith Dalgleish* a49 49
2 b g Lethal Force(IRE) Raggle Taggle (IRE) (Tagula (IRE))
3895[11] 4472[7] 4895[8] 5878[4] 6625[2] 6815[3] 7518[10] 8191[12]

**Ray's The Money (IRE)**
*Michael Bell* a84 85
3 b g Dragon Pulse(IRE) Riymaisa (IRE) (Traditionally (USA))
(1033) 1760[4] 2284[5] 3040[4] (4084) 5160[2] 5568[6] 6189[9] 6563[5] 7516[5] 8239[11]

**Razin' Hell** *John Balding* a91 76
6 b g Byron Loose Caboose (IRE) (Tagula (IRE))
(4) 388[2] 664[11] 4531[2] 5098[7] 6794[7] 8803[4] 9074[9] 9366[2]

**Razzmatazz** *Clive Cox* a71 98
3 b f Monsieur Bond(IRE) Tibesti (Machiavellian (USA))
2620[3] 5969[5] (6791) 7051[2] 7804[7]

**Reachforthestars (IRE)**
*David O'Meara* 94
3 b f Sea The Stars(IRE) Behkiyra (IRE) (Entrepreneur)
2287[6] 2612[4] (3583) 3998[18] 5381[7] 5915[10]

**Reach High** *Saeed bin Suroor* a99 89
3 ch c Distorted Humor(USA) Silent Moment (USA) (Giant's Causeway (USA))
(8032)

**Ready (IRE)** *Mark Pattinson* a94 46
7 ch g Elnadim(USA) Fusili (IRE) (Silvano (GER))
117[6] 266[8] 1329[6] 3920[9] 7131[13] 8497[13] 9126[8]

**Ready To Impress (USA)**
*Mark Johnston* a73
2 b g More Than Ready(USA) Menekineko (USA) (Kingmambo (USA))
7987[7] 8245[3]

**Real Estate (IRE)** *James Tate* a63 41
2 b c Dansili Maskunah (IRE) (Sadler's Wells (USA))
4094[7] 6683[5] 8952[8]

**Real Gent** *Kevin Ryan* 76
2 gr c Kendargent(FR) Ebatana (IRE) (Rainbow Quest (USA))
6057[5]◆ (7613)

**Reality Show (IRE)** *Shaun Harris* a48 48
10 b g Cape Cross(IRE) Really (IRE) (Entrepreneur)
7729[7] 8135[12] 8346[10]

**Realize** *David Simcock* a107 96
7 b g Zafeen(FR) Relkida (Bertolini (USA))
118[2] 730[7] 1150[7] 1772[6] 2283[4] (2975) (3808) 5147[7]

**Really Special** *Saeed bin Suroor* a100 100
3 b f Shamardal(USA) Rumh (GER) (Monsun (GER))
(317a) 652a[5] 887a[3] 3964[23]

**Really Super** *Ralph Beckett* 81
3 b f Cacique(IRE) Sensationally (Montjeu (IRE))
1963[4] 2834[3] 3596[4] 3909[4] 5065[2] 5273[3] 6398[2]

**Realpolitik (IRE)** *Roger Varian* a70
2 b f So You Think(NZ) Mare Imbrium (USA) (Mr Greeley (USA))
8998[8] 9299[4]

**Realtra (IRE)** *Roger Varian* a107 109
5 gr m Dark Angel(IRE) Devious Diva (IRE) (Dr Devious (IRE))
431a[7] 771a[6] (1771) 2616[4] 3334[5] (4512a) 5460a[9] (6642a) 7671a[10]

**Real Value (FR)** *Mario Hofer* 103
3 b c Rip Van Winkle(IRE) Rosey De Megeve (Efisio)
1460a[5] 3115a[5] 3680a[6] (6255a) 7429a[7]

**Reason To Believe (FR)**
*David Bridgwater* a58 53
3 b f Rip Van Winkle(IRE) Showcall (USA) (Kingmambo (USA))
8307[7] 8784[11] 9278[4]

**Reaver (IRE)** *Eve Johnson Houghton* a87 89
4 b g Sabiango(GER) Mattinata (Tiger Hill (IRE))
(1969)◆ 2406[17] 3212[4] 3808[5] 4882[3] 6189[4] 6422[8] 6933[5] 7395[11] 7909[3]

**Rebecamille (FR)** *N Branchu* a58 54
4 b m Anabaa Blue Burgaudine (FR) (Marchand De Sable (USA))
837a[6]

**Rebecca (FR)** *C Lerner* a80 80
3 b f Myboycharlie(IRE) Jules J (USA) (Action This Day (USA))
2484a[9] 6650a[4] 8025a[7]

**Rebecca Rocks** *Henry Candy* 78
3 b f Exceed And Excel(AUS) Rebecca Rolfe (Pivotal)
2139[3] (3035)

**Rebel Assault (IRE)** *Mark Johnston* 96
2 b f Excelebration(IRE) Naomh Geileis (USA) (Grand Slam (USA))
(2988) 3333[2] 3557[4] (4369) 4582[8] 5391[5] 7846a[6] (8043) 8412[4]

**Rebel Cause (IRE)** *Richard Spencer* a71 87
4 b g Cockney Rebel(IRE) Happy Go Lily (In The Wings)
5849[9] 7119[5] 7999[7] 8386[8]

**Rebel De Lope** *Charles Hills* a87 86
3 b g Lope De Vega(IRE) Rivabella (FR) (Iron Mask (USA))
2126[11] 2554[10] 3592[5]◆ 4271[5] 4736[3]◆ 6397[2] 8344[7]

**Rebel Flame** *John Weymes* a40 24
3 b c Firebreak Spirit Of Dixie (Kheleyf (USA))
331[5] 7270[10] 7389[10]

**Rebel Heart** *Bill Turner* a52 58
3 b f Kyllachy Just Like A Woman (Observatory (USA))
2065[6] 2757[6] 3423[10] 3818[6] 5052[4] 5892[7] 6748[4] 7122[10] (8185)

**Rebel Lightning (IRE)** *P Monfort* a66 65
4 gr g Zebedee Bellechance (Acclamation)
50[3] 267[9] 501[2] 1189[2] 6541a[7]

**Rebello (FR)** *D & P Prod'Homme* 100
3 ro c Manduro(GER) Rafale Bere (FR) (Verglas (IRE))
3115a[2]

**Rebel State (IRE)** *Jedd O'Keeffe* a72 60
4 b g Zoffany(IRE) Stately Princess (Robellino (USA))
(37) 166[4] 516[11] 2458[3] 3402[10]◆ 4034[11] 5544[2] 5917[6] 6092[4] 7271[4] 8589[2]◆ 8773[9]

**Rebel Streak** *Andrew Balding* a74 93
2 b g Dark Angel(IRE) Siren's Gift (Cadeaux Genereux)
4213[4] 4826[2]◆ 5504[2] 6199[3] 7394[7]

**Rebel Surge (IRE)** *Richard Spencer* a89 93
4 b m Kodiac Face The Storm (IRE) (Barathea (IRE))
142[4] 285[3] 810[4] 1261[5] 1771[10] 2973[2] (3147) 3541[2] 4375[4] 5352[9] 6261[4] 7086[6] 7545[4] 8150[10]

**Rebel Woods (FR)** *Geoffrey Deacon* a29 44
4 br g Cockney Rebel(IRE) In The Woods (You And I (USA))
1081[13] 2056[4]

**Reboot (IRE)** *Matthieu Palussiere* 60
2 bb c Society Rock(IRE) Dream Applause (IRE) (Royal Applause)
2664a[6] 3444a[9] 4389a[8]

**Rebounded** *Mark Walford* 60
3 ch g Mayson Winter Dress (Haafhd)
1678[9]

**Reckless Endeavour (IRE)**
*Jamie Osborne* a105 58
4 b g Kodiac Red Fanfare (First Trump)
5688a[14] 6971a[20] 8991[3] 9264[5] 9453[3]

**Reckless Gold (IRE)**
*Joseph Patrick O'Brien* 106
4 ch h Pivotal Golden Shadow (IRE) (Selkirk (USA))
3108a[6] 6243a[5]

**Reckless Serenade (IRE)**
*Keith Dalgleish* a56 61
3 b f Bushranger(IRE) Tomintoul Singer (IRE) (Johannesburg (USA))
1294[4] 1805[6] 3239[6] 3384[6] 6785[6] 7884[8] 8484[8]

**Reckless Wave (IRE)** *Ed Walker* a69 73
4 b m Cape Cross(IRE) Fairybook (USA) (El Prado (IRE))
(2308) 2781[8] 3292[4] (4257)

**Reckless Woman (IRE)**
*Jeremy Noseda* a13 15
3 b f Helmet(AUS) Paint The Town (IRE) (Sadler's Wells (USA))
1286[9] 3438[12]

**Recks (IRE)** *K R Burke* 24
2 ch c Reckless Abandon Welsh Diva (Selkirk (USA))
7520[9]

**Recognition (IRE)** *Barry Murtagh* a6
4 gr g Rip Van Winkle(IRE) Bali Breeze (IRE) (Common Grounds)
2427[7] 5832[9]

**Recoletos (FR)** *C Laffon-Parias* a65 114
3 b c Whipper(USA) Highphar (FR) (Highest Honor (FR))
(2483a) 3368a[3] 6053a[7] (7176a) 8233[4]

**Recollect** *Luca Cumani* a80 67
2 b c Invincible Spirit(IRE) Forgotten Dreams (IRE) (Olden Times)
7580[5] 8149[2]

**Red Alert** *William Muir* a81 77
3 b g Sleeping Indian Red Sovereign (Danzig Connection (USA))
638[2]◆ (878) 2757[5] 3692[2] 4159[6] 6652[3] 7192[3] 7882[8] (8159)

**Red All Star (IRE)** *Gerard Keane* a56 47
7 b g Haatef(USA) Star Of Russia (IRE) (Soviet Star (USA))
(6798a)

**Red Alto (AUS)** *Brent Stanley* 87
4 b g High Chaparral(IRE) La Sangre (AUS) (Fastnet Rock (AUS))
8100a[8]

**Redarna** *Dianne Sayer* a56 66
3 ch g Aqlaam Curtains (Dubawi (IRE))
777[4] 1308[7] 4607[5] (5467) 5697[3] 6315[3]◆ 7046[3] 7223[3]

**Red Avenger (USA)**
*Damian Joseph English* a90 83
7 bb g War Front(USA) Emotional Rescue (USA) (Smart Strike (CAN))
1388a[17] 5517a[13] 6491a[17] 8222a[9]

**Red Baron (IRE)** *Eric Alston* a97 103
8 b g Moss Vale(IRE) Twinberry (IRE) (Tagula (IRE))
842[11] 1110[9] 1800[6]

**Red Bordeaux (FR)** *Tony Carroll* 42
3 ch g Myboycharlie(IRE) Blue Sail (USA) (Kingmambo (USA))
3755[14] 4275[7] 5076[7]

**Redbrook (IRE)** *Doug Watson* a57 87
6 b g Raven's Pass(USA) Nawal (FR) (Homme De Loi (IRE))
204a[15]

**Red Caravel (IRE)** *Richard Hughes* a70 58
3 b g Henrythenavigator(USA) Red Fantasy (IRE) (High Chaparral (IRE))
1300[2] 2273[5] 3220[5] 4348[8]

**Red Cardinal (IRE)** *A Wohler* a82 115
5 bb g Montjeu(IRE) Notable (Zafonic (USA))
(2667a) (3553a) 6250a[5] 8667a[11]

**Red Charmer (IRE)** *Ann Duffield* a58 75
7 b g Red Clubs(IRE) Golden Charm (IRE) (Common Grounds)
1700[10] 2224[13]

**Red Chois (IRE)** *E J O'Neill* a78
3 b f Choisir(AUS) Red Blossom (Green Desert (USA))
4288a[2]

**Redcold (FR)** *C Laffon-Parias* a79 95
4 b m Nayef(USA) Russiana (IRE) (Red Ransom (USA))
2946a[7]

**Red Cossack (CAN)** *Paul Webber* a75 75
6 ch g Rebellion Locata (USA) (Stravinsky (USA))
922[10] 1085[9] 1683[14] 2974[7] 8503[10]

**Red Cymbal** *William Haggas* a80 69
2 b c Pivotal Red Baton (Exceed And Excel (AUS))
8466[3] (8809)◆ 9123[4]

**Red Douglas** *Scott Dixon* a40 12
3 ch c Sakhee(USA) Chrystal Venture (IRE) (Barathea (IRE))
4968[13] 9034[7] 9072[6] 9365[6]

**Red Dragon (IRE)**
*Michael Blanshard* a50 58
7 b g Acclamation Delphie Queen (IRE) (Desert Sun)
3753[15] 5362[7] (5713) 6102[9] 7062[9]

**Red Duma (FR)** *H-A Pantall* 83
2 b f Air Chief Marshal(IRE) Red Shot (FR) (Gentlewave (IRE))
5988a[2]

**Redeeming** *Eric Alston* 18
3 b g Exceed And Excel(AUS) Quiet Elegance (Fantastic Light (USA))
5619[7] 6184[14]

**Red Emperor (IRE)** *Amanda Perrett* 62
3 b g Holy Roman Emperor(IRE) Rougette (Red Ransom (USA))
2475[5]◆ 2782[6] 3922[8] 4537[12]

**Red Ensign (IRE)** *Simon Crisford* a88 83
3 b g Dark Angel(IRE) Rayon Rouge (IRE) (Manduro (GER))
1797[4] 2520[6]

**Red Excitement (AUS)** *Gerald Ryan* 112
7 b g Excites(AUS) Red Obsession (AUS) (Red Ransom (USA))
6714a[2]

**Red Flute** *Michael Appleby* a56 23
5 ch g Piccolo Fee Faw Fum (IRE) (Great Commotion (USA))
215[9] 622[6] 961[6] 1022[3] 1184[3] 1206[2] 1435[6] 1452[6] 2472[7] 9181[9]

**Red Force One** *Tom Dascombe* 74
2 ro g Lethal Force(IRE) Dusty Red (Teofilo (IRE))
2769[2] 3538[4] 4526[4] 5680[4] 6395[5]

**Red For Danger**
*Eve Johnson Houghton* a47 49
2 b f Equiano(FR) Red Shareef (Marju (IRE))
3328[8] 3807[7] 4175[4] 6285[7] 6609[5] 7081[6] 7695[4] 8397[4] 8644[9]

**Red Forever** *Thomas Cuthbert* a37 49
6 ch g Major Cadeaux Spindara (IRE) (Spinning World (USA))
4664[2] 5695[9] 6631[3] 7164[3]◆ 7926[8]

**Red Galileo** *Saeed bin Suroor* a102 111
6 b g Dubawi(IRE) Ivory Gala (FR) (Galileo (IRE))
(202a) 540a[3] 890a[7] 4033[8] 5353[2] 6399[2] 7581[2]

**Red Ghost (GER)** *Waldemar Hickst* a49 66
8 ch g Dai Jin Ripley (GER) (Platini (GER))
7430a[6]

**Redgrave (IRE)** *Charles Hills* a66 85
3 b g Lope De Vega(IRE) Olympic Medal (Nayef (USA))
1485[5] (4311) 5059[3] 5842[2] 6203[7] 6809[2] 7229[5] 8392[2]

**Red Gunner** *David O'Meara* a78 70
3 b g Oasis Dream Blue Maiden (Medicean)
356[2] 2304[9] 3814[8] 4983[6] 5797[7] 6620[14] 7056[5] 7942[6]

**Red Hot Calypso (IRE)** *Dr A Bolte* 93
6 ch h Art Connoisseur(IRE) Nesaah's Princess (Sinndar (IRE))
716a[5]

**Red Hot Chilly (IRE)** *Dai Burchell* a74 72
4 ch g Frozen Power(IRE) She's Got The Look (Sulamani (IRE))
687[3]

**Redicean** *David O'Meara* a83 89
3 b g Medicean Red Halo (IRE) (Galileo (IRE))
(1675) 4221[6] 6187[4] 6445[11] 6757[3] 8188[6] (8478)

**Red Invader (IRE)** *John Butler* a71 48
7 b g Red Clubs(IRE) Tifariti (USA) (Elusive Quality (USA))
172[9] 468[10] 768[6]◆ 1071[8] (1340) 2700[13] (5297) 5723[7] 7486[8] 8311[9] 8853[10] 9189[7]

**Red Label (IRE)** *Marco Botti* 104
3 b c Dubawi(IRE) Born Something (IRE) (Caerleon (USA))
3109a[5] 8095a[3] 8963a[5]

**Red Line (FR)** *A De Watrigant* 92
2 b f Sageburg(IRE) Red Love (USA) (Gone West (USA))
5679a[2] (6803a)

**Red Master (IRE)** *Ed Dunlop* a53
3 ch c Mastercraftsman(IRE) Yaqootah (USA) (Gone West (USA))
2164[8] 2521[8] 2997[9] 3674[12] 4436[10]

**Red Miracle** *Rod Millman* 60
2 b f Dylan Thomas(IRE) Under Milk Wood (Montjeu (IRE))
6859[5] 7739[6] 8163[9]

**Red Mist** *Simon Crisford* 102
2 b c Frankel Red Dune (IRE) (Red Ransom (USA))
(5301)◆ 6190[2]◆ 7146[4]

**Red Mohican** *Phil McEntee* a54
3 ch f Harbour Watch(IRE) Magical Cliche (USA) (Affirmed (USA))
77[6]

**Red Ochre** *John Quinn*
4 b g Virtual Red Hibiscus (Manduro (GER))
2408[8]

**Red Onion** *C Lerner* a69 75
3 b c Fast Company(IRE) Capsicum (Holy Roman Emperor (IRE))
1689a[6]

**Red Persian (IRE)** *P J Prendergast* 88
2 ch g Haatef(USA) Wajaha (IRE) (Haafhd)
(4020a) 5345a[6] 8082a[3]

**Red Pike (IRE)** *Bryan Smart* a99 102
6 ch g Kheleyf(USA) Fancy Feathers (IRE) (Redback)
33[7] 2156[7] 3861[3] 5094[10] 5705[4] 6205[2] 6662[3] 7626[6] 8383[12]

**Red Rannagh (IRE)** *David Simcock* a92 89
4 b g Teofilo(IRE) Red Top (IRE) (Fasliyev (USA))
2741[7] 3249[3] 3905[3] 4413[4] 5524[14]

**Red Riverman** *Nigel Twiston-Davies* 59
9 b g Haafhd Mocca (IRE) (Sri Pekan (USA))
6370[5]

**Red Roman** *Charles Hills* 92
2 b c Holy Roman Emperor(IRE) Domitia (Pivotal)
2435[4]◆ (2750) 3925[16] 4858[7] (5596) 6330[5] 7353[2] 7821[4] 8412[8]

**Redrosezorro** *Eric Alston* 60
3 b g Foxwedge(AUS) Garter Star (Mark Of Esteem (IRE))
1715[12] 3243[9] 4529[8] 4741[3] 5182[13] 5741[2] 6549[8] 7390[3] (8490)

**Red Royalist** *Marcus Tregoning* 81
3 b g Royal Applause Scarlet Royal (Red Ransom (USA))
1961[3] 2682[4] 6390[3] (6775) 7358[6] 8078[3]

**Red Sabor** *Andrew Slattery* a84 94
3 ch g Bated Breath Really Ransom (Red Ransom (USA))
1386a[9] 4327a[9]

**Red Seeker** *Andrew Crook* 49
2 ch g Red Jazz(USA) Purepleasureseeker (IRE) (Grand Lodge (USA))
7819[8]

**Red Shadow** *Alistair Whillans* a50 45
8 b m Royal Applause Just A Glimmer (Bishop Of Cashel)
3385[8] 4246[6] 4687[5] 5466[3] 5992[10] 6346[4] 6690[6] 7165[9] 7703[8]

**Red Shanghai (IRE)** *Charles Smith* a41 43
3 ch f Tamayuz Rouge Noir (USA) (Saint Ballado (CAN))
667[6] 1107[8] 1297[11] 1605[10] 2078[8] 2470[4] 3260[11] 4332[8] 7597[5] 8256[8] 8481[8] 8774[5] 8984[7]

**Red Snapper** *William Stone* a50 52
2 b f Kheleyf(USA) Amistress (Kalanisi (IRE))
2292[6] 4312[6] 5114[8] 5886[2] 6585[14] 7023[7] 7756[11] 8795[6] 9387[2]

**Red Star Dancer (IRE)**
*David Barron* a42 53
3 b g Tamayuz Red Planet (Pivotal)
3383[5] 4247[8] 4657[3] 5073[6] 5921[6] 5997[13] 7220[8] 7982[4] 8241[6] 8314[8]

**Red Starlight** *Richard Hannon* 76
2 br f Pivotal Star Chart (IRE) (Dubawi (IRE))
7898[6] (8419)

**Red Stars (IRE)** *John M Oxx* 98
4 ch m Manduro(GER) Magen's Star (IRE) (Galileo (IRE))
1808a[4] 1999a[6] 3874a[9] 7261a[3] 7837a[3] (8086a)

**Red Striker (IRE)** *Sir Michael Stoute* a65
2 b c Sea The Stars(IRE) Coolree Marj (IRE) (Marju (IRE))
7987[6]

**Red Stripes (USA)** *Lisa Williamson* a78 66
5 b g Leroidesanimaux(BRZ) Kaleidoscopic (USA) (Fortunate Prospect (USA))
194[6] 330[6] 416[6] 955[8] 1071[6] 4333[12] 4803[5] 5098[5] 5695[6] 5930[2] 6156[4] 7099[7] 7486[7] (7607) 8159[5] 8816[5] 9001[3] 9136[3] 9280[6] 9308[2] 9443[3]

**Red Tea** *Peter Hiatt* a86 95
4 ch m Sakhee(USA) Maimoona (IRE) (Pivotal)
1562[5] (2030) 3589[9] 5130[2] 6145[4] 6483[6] 7619[12] 8566[3] 8880[9]

**Redtedd** *Tom Dascombe* a37 16
2 ch g Mazameer(IRE) Mermaid Melody (Machiavellian (USA))
5048[9] 5844[11] 6304[8]

**Red Tornado (FR)** *Dan Skelton* a82 97
5 ch g Dr Fong(USA) Encircle (USA) (Spinning World (USA))
1068[8]

**Red Touch (USA)** *Michael Appleby* a79 58
5 bb g Bluegrass Cat(USA) Touchnow (CAN) (Pleasant Tap (USA))
25[8] 441[5] 1074[5] 1296[2] 1867[4] 3433[8] 6637[6] 7789[13] 8400[6] 8773[2]◆ 9303[7]

**Red Trooper (FR)** *George Baker* a81 50
4 ch g Shamardal(USA) Solar Midnight (USA) (Lemon Drop Kid (USA))
506[5] 5958[6] 6582[2] (7056)

**Red Turtle (FR)** *Rune Haugen* a67 67
6 ch g Turtle Bowl(IRE) Morlane (IRE) (Entrepreneur)
269[9] 1504[6]

**Red Tycoon (IRE)**
*Ken Cunningham-Brown* a74 85
5 b g Acclamation Rugged Up (IRE) (Marju (IRE))
1302[6] 1696[5] 2608[2] 3581[7] 4343[13] 6141[9] 6555[2] 7571[11] 9124[3] 9339[7]

**Red Vancouver (FR)** *C Lerner* a62 72
2 b f George Vancouver(USA) Siro (GER) (Grand Lodge (USA))
9087a[9]

**Red Verdon (USA)** *Ed Dunlop* a110 109
4 ch h Lemon Drop Kid(USA) Porto Marmay (IRE) (Choisir (AUS))
2571[6] 3012[5] 3299[7] 4360[4] 7054[2] 7581[6] 7988[3] 8637[2] (8992)

**Redvers (IRE)** *Noel Wilson* a52 70
9 br g Ishiguru(USA) Cradle Brief (IRE) (Brief Truce (USA))
2684[16] 3949[10] 4661[10]

**Reedanjas (IRE)** *Gay Kelleway* a69 76
3 b f Sir Prancealot(IRE) Blue Holly (IRE) (Blues Traveller (IRE))
1732[7] 3729[4] 4043[3]◆ 4305[6] 5117[9] 5355[8] 6155[7] 7255[3] 8742[3] 9315[8]

**Reel Leisure (GR)** *Amanda Perrett* a53 35
4 ch m Reel Buddy(USA) Leisurely Way (Kris)
1420[5] 4497[11] 5220[13] 5787[11]

**Reel Mr Bond** *Kevin Ryan* 58
2 ch c Monsieur Bond(IRE) Reel Cool (Reel Buddy (USA))
2852[6] 4504[2]

**Reflation** *Patrick Holmes* a44 67
5 b g Stimulation(IRE) Miss Poppy (Averti (IRE))
2843[12] 3453[6] 4426[7] 4605[10] 5620[11] 5695[7] 6384[8] 6688[11] 6785[3] 7218[6] 7888[9]

**Reflect Alexander (IRE)**
*David Evans* 86
2 b f Kodiac Moon Club (IRE) (Red Clubs (IRE))
2905[4] 3421[3] 4361[4] 4739[3] (5015) 6051a[5] 6136[13] 6678[4] 6863[9]

**Reflektor (IRE)** *Tom Dascombe* a90 99
4 ch g Bahamian Bounty Baby Bunting (Wolfhound (USA))
2573[6] 3585[9] (4333) 5402[3] 6412[11] 6927[8] 9269[8]

**Refrain (IRE)** *Sir Michael Stoute* a49
2 b c Dubawi(IRE) Folk Opera (IRE) (Singspiel (IRE))
9051[10]

**Refuse Colette (IRE)**
*Adrian Nicholls* a62 66
8 ch m Refuse To Bend(IRE) Roclette (USA) (Rock Of Gibraltar (IRE))
1359[4] 2969[7] 3728[9] 5512[8] 7390[9]

**Refuseeveryoffer (FR)**
*Andreas Suborics* 23
2 ch c Evasive Rosie Thomas (IRE) (Dylan Thomas (IRE))
5776a[16]

**Refuse To Bobbin (IRE)**
*M Narduzzi* 98
7 ch g Refuse To Bend(IRE) Super Bobbina (IRE) (Daggers Drawn (USA))
2866a[2] 3884a[P]

**Regal Decree** *Jedd O'Keeffe* a45 60
3 b g Lawman(FR) Regal Riband (Fantastic Light (USA))
1835[3]◆ 2182[3] 4694[4] 5182[3] 6437[5] 6902[9] 7389[9]

**Regal Director (IRE)**
*Simon Crisford* 71
2 b c New Approach(IRE) Dubai Queen (USA) (Kingmambo (USA))
7026[4] 7955[5]

**Regal Gait (IRE)** *Harry Whittington* a71
4 b g Tagula(IRE) Babylonian (Shamardal (USA))
(1754)◆ 7319[13]

**Regal Mirage (IRE)** *Tim Easterby* 75
3 ch g Aqlaam Alzaroof (USA) (Kingmambo (USA))
1680[12] 2903[3] (3977) (4659)◆ (5096) (5454) 6061[5] 7560[8] 7824[6]

**Regal Miss** *Patrick Chamings* a66 57
5 b m Royal Applause Pretty Miss (Averti (IRE))
4009[5] 5297[2] 5871[10] 8494[10] 9471[5]

**Regal Reality** *Sir Michael Stoute* 76
2 b c Intello(GER) Regal Realm (Medicean)
(7281)◆

**Regarde Moi** *Marco Botti* a89 24
9 b g King's Best(USA) Life At Night (IRE) (Night Shift (USA))
24[3] 304[3] (478) 884[4] 1177[6] 2968[9]

**Reggae Traou Land (FR)** *G Derat* a51
2 ch c Milanais(FR) La Blue Hill (Tiger Hill (IRE))
6456a[9]

**Regicide (IRE)** *James Fanshawe* a90 80
4 b g Archipenko(USA) Armoise (Sadler's Wells (USA))
(2092) 2959[2] 4498[6] 7132[8] 7515[5]

**Regimented (IRE)** *Richard Hannon* 93
2 b c Epaulette(AUS) Colour Coordinated (IRE) (Spectrum (IRE))
(5292) 5964[3] (6505) 7148[2] 7648[6] 8379[2]

**Regular Income (IRE)** *Adam West* a63 77
2 b c Fast Company(IRE) Max Almabrouka (USA) (Hennessy (USA))
7105[3] 7512[5] 7739[3] 8354[4] (8676)

**Regulator (IRE)** *Richard Fahey* 87
2 b g Acclamation Rasana (Royal Academy (USA))
4598[2] (5202) 5681[2] 6521[5] 7821[7]

**Rehana (IRE)** *M Halford* 107
3 b f Dark Angel(IRE) Rayka (IRE) (Selkirk (USA))
1634a[3] (2241a) 3110a[6] 5308a[3] 8003[4]

**Reiffa (IRE)** *William Haggas* a73
2 b f Epaulette(AUS) Phi Phi (IRE) (Fasliyev (USA))
(9404)

**Reinas Queen (IRE)** *Sarah Dawson* a57 64
4 b m Tagula(IRE) Darling Smile (IRE) (Darshaan)
3650[2]

**Reinbeau Prince** *Richard Fahey* 68
2 br c Rip Van Winkle(IRE) Bridle Belle (Dansili)
2698[9] 3495[5] 3930[4] 5373[2] 6087[6] 7243[7] 8045[4] 8349[6]

**Reine Du Lukka (FR)** *Mme F Chenu*
2 b f Apsis Star Du Lukka (FR) (Limnos (JPN))
8524a[9]

**Reinforced** *Michael Dods* a49 71
4 ch g Equiano(FR) Fonnie (IRE) (Barathea (IRE))
2119[10] 2843[10] (3488) 4039[7] 4960[5] 5466[9] 6550[2] 7046[2] 7934[4]

**Reinstorm** *Richard Fahey* a44 65
3 b g Canford Cliffs(IRE) Bridle Belle (Dansili)
2036[5] (2703) 3499[9] 4430[4] 4899[7] 5455[7]

**Rekindling** *Joseph Patrick O'Brien* 121
3 b c High Chaparral(IRE) Sitara (Salse (USA))
(1636a) 2766[4] 3322[16] (4420a) 6214a[2] 7147[4] (8667a)

**Related** *Paul Midgley* a101 101
7 b g Kheleyf(USA) Balladonia (Primo Dominie)
170[5] 2381[11] 2736[16] 3792[19] 4103[8] (4629) (6141) 6205[17] 6662[7] 7086[4] 7405[5] (8310)

**Relevant (IRE)** *Stuart Williams* a64 68
3 b f So You Think(NZ) Germane (Distant Relative)
2842[3] 3542[4] 6027[4] 7224[2] 8218[5] 8585[2] 8883[8] 9338[3] 9455[2]

**Relief Quest (IRE)** *J-C Rouget* 72
3 b f Iffraaj Supreme Quest (Exceed And Excel (AUS))
5777a[5]

**Relight My Fire** *Tim Easterby* a70 76
7 ch g Firebreak Making Music (Makbul)
3203[13] 4506[10] 4999[10] 5214[3] 5497[2] (5880) 6092[3] 6591[3] 7474[3] 8216[6]

**Religify (AUS)** *Chris Waller* 108
6 ch g Choisir(AUS) Sacred Witness (AUS) (El Moxie (USA))
8057a[2]

**Rely On Me (IRE)** *Andrew Balding* a85 89
3 br f Kyllachy Life Rely (USA) (Maria's Mon (USA))
2517[4] 3167[2] 3715[6] 4788[2] 5433[5] (6392) 6864[3] 7811[11]

**Rema Al Kuwait (IRE)**
*David O'Meara* 53
2 b f Kodiac Relinquished (Royal Applause)
3980[6] 5015[4] 6085[6] 7518[17]

**Remarkable** *John Gosden* a82 116
4 b g Pivotal Irresistible (Cadeaux Genereux)
2606[10] 3298[12] 3963[6] 5147[2] 5393[11] (6918)

**Remarkable Lady (IRE)** *H Rogers* a44 96
4 b m Zoffany(IRE) Casual Remark (IRE) (Trans Island)
(5582a) 6491a[24] 6961a[14] 7171a[8] 7261a[2] 8086a[13]

**Rembrandt** *Rebecca Menzies* a64 70
5 b g Dutch Art Authoritative (Diktat)
1629[3] 1834[2] 2183[3] 2594[2]

**Rembrandt Van Rijn (IRE)**
*S bin Ghadayer* a65 110
6 b g Peintre Celebre(USA) Private Life (FR) (Bering)
202a[3] 428a[3] 699a[2] 1042a[4] 1374a[7]

**Remember Me** *Hughie Morrison* a77 70
4 b m Acclamation Forgotten Me (IRE) (Holy Roman Emperor (IRE))
232[2] (550) 996[3] 1455[4] 1897[6]

**Remember Nerja (IRE)** *Barry Leavy* a42 47
3 ch f Lord Shanakill(USA) Tequise (IRE) (Victory Note (USA))
8852[3] 9221[7]

**Remember Rocky** *Lucy Normile* a42 69
8 ch g Haafhd Flower Market (Cadeaux Genereux)
2498[9] 2955[3] 3530[6] 4659[3] 5206[2] (5917) 5993[8] 6591[6] 7042[9]

**Remember The Days (IRE)**
*Joseph Patrick O'Brien* a82 87
3 b c Kyllachy Pointed Arch (IRE) (Rock Of Gibraltar (IRE))
1012a[4]

**Remember The Man (IRE)**
*Ralph Beckett* a82 73
4 b g Dalakhani(IRE) Perfect Hedge (Unfuwain (USA))
74[3] 576[2] (861)◆

**Remnant (IRE)** *K R Burke* 45
2 b g Dawn Approach(IRE) Arbaah (USA) (Invasor (ARG))
4681[7]

**Rene Mathis (GER)** *Richard Fahey* a99 101
7 ch g Monsieur Bond(IRE) Remina (GER) (Erminius (GER))
87a[2] 653a[9] 1150[5] 1491[10] (1974) 7611[17] 8138[5] 9264[11]

**Renfrew Street** *Mark Johnston* a95 99
4 br m Iffraaj Malpas Missile (IRE) (Elusive City (USA))
1457[9] (2061) 2426[5] 5108[7] 6000[2] (6317)◆ 6849[2] 7092[6] (7507) (8090a)

**Renneti (FR)** *W P Mullins* 111
8 b g Irish Wells(FR) Caprice Meill (FR) (French Glory)
6214a[5] 6956a[13] (7422a) 8274a[4]

**Renny's Lady (IRE)** *David Evans* a66
2 ch f Excelebration(IRE) Moriches (IRE) (Alhaarth (IRE))
9320[4]◆ 9465[8]

**Renny Storm (CZE)**
*C Von Der Recke* a93 93
7 b g Stormy Jail(IRE) Renaissance (CZE) (High Extreme (IRE))
(835a)

**Renounce (FR)** *D De Waele* a60 60
6 b g Peer Gynt(JPN) Former Probe (USA) (Dynaformer (USA))
5176a[13] 7307a[4]

**Renown** *Elizabeth Voss* 102
6 ch g Champs Elysees Fame At Last (USA) (Quest For Fame)
3553a[12]

**Renton** *Tony Coyle* 29
2 ch g Dandy Man(IRE) Private Equity (IRE) (Haafhd)
3066[8] 3576[10] 4335[7] 8476[6]

**Repercussion** *Charlie Fellowes* a89 101
4 b g Manduro(GER) Summertime Legacy (Darshaan)
1860[6] 2735[16] 2999[7] 4882[6] 5966[2] 6483[4] (7549)

**Replenish (FR)** *S Cerulis* a101 80
4 ch g Le Havre(IRE) Brambleberry (Cape Cross (IRE))
2093[3]◆ 2799[6] 4261[8] 7727[11] 8032[10] 9003a[3]

**Repton (IRE)** *Richard Hannon* 103
3 b g Zebedee African Moonlight (UAE) (Halling (USA))
5916[6] 6419[17] 6922[8] 7782[10] 7901[3] 8393[4]

**Reputation (IRE)** *John Quinn* 98
4 b g Royal Applause Semaphore (Zamindar (USA))
1880[5] 2156[10] 2736[15] (3324) 3842[14] 4521[4] 5890[4] 6205[11] 6554[7]

**Requinto Dawn (IRE)**
*Richard Fahey* 83
2 br g Requinto(IRE) Till Dawn (IRE) (Kheleyf (USA))
(1496) 1803[2] 2522[7] 5150[19] 5440[6] 6466[2] 7090[11] 7472[2] 7821[9]

**Re Run (IRE)** *Richard Fahey* a74 70
3 b g Harbour Watch(IRE) Encore View (Oasis Dream)
512[4]

**Reshaan (IRE)** *Richard Hannon* a73 62
2 b c Dark Angel(IRE) Bluebell (IRE) (Mastercraftsman (IRE))
6884[4] 7391[11]

**Reshoun (FR)** *Ian Williams* a87 98
3 b g Shamardal(USA) Radiyya (IRE) (Sinndar (IRE))
5598[6] 6427[7] 7927[2]◆ 8188[3] (8414)

**Respectability** *David C Griffiths* a29 29
5 b m Echo Of Light Respectfilly (Mark Of Esteem (IRE))
289[6]

**Respectable** *Ralph Beckett* 79
2 b f Champs Elysees Dalandra (Montjeu (IRE))
6917[4]◆

**Restive (IRE)** *Iain Jardine* a84 70
4 b g Rip Van Winkle(IRE) I Hearyou Knocking (IRE) (Danehill Dancer (IRE))
156[7] 363[7] 727[2] 992[8] 2427[3] 2773[4] 2953[7] 3898[8] 7235[3] 7703[6] 7936[2] (8218) 8315[6] 8653[2] (9028)◆ (9070) 9341[7]

**Restless Rose** *Stuart Williams* a77 61
2 ch f Power Albany Rose (IRE) (Noverre (USA))
6867[6] (9023)

**Restorer** *William Muir* a105 106
5 gr g Mastercraftsman(IRE) Moon Empress (FR) (Rainbow Quest (USA))
1271a[9] 2127[8] 2604[3] 3072[5] 4069[7] 5148[5] 5925[10] 7150[3]◆ 7805[9] 8423[10]

**Retained (FR)** *John Best* a65 61
2 b f Kentucky Dynamite(USA) Retainage (USA) (Polish Numbers (USA))
3437[6] 4007[3] 4496[3] 6825[8] 6932[4] 8153[8]

**Retirement Beckons** *Linda Perratt* 45
2 b g Epaulette(AUS) Mystical Ayr (IRE) (Namid)
5092[5] 5918[6] 6347[7] 7698[6]

**Retribution** *David Lanigan* a52 69
3 b g Iffraaj The Giving Tree (IRE) (Rock Of Gibraltar (IRE))
5023[2] 5509[4] 6783[6]

**Retrieve (AUS)** *Johnny Farrelly* a97 67
9 b g Rahy(USA) Hold To Ransom (USA) (Red Ransom (USA))
478[5] 767[4] (884) 985[4] 1341[7] 2546[3] (2891) 3284[2] 3470[3] (3546) 4002[6] 4158[RR] 5643[12] 6176[6] 7744[13] 9242[7]

**Return Ace** *James Fanshawe* a86 97
5 b m Zamindar(USA) Match Point (Unfuwain (USA))
3586[5] 5155[11] 7422a[4] 8166[9]

**Returning Glory** *Saeed bin Suroor* a71
2 b c Exceed And Excel(AUS) Tanzania (USA) (Darshaan)
9201[2]◆

**Revalue** *Charles Hills* a76 81
2 b f Dansili Take The Hint (Montjeu (IRE))
7022[7] (8148) 8593[2]

**Revel** *Stuart Williams* a78 75
3 b g Makfi Cecily (Oasis Dream)
34[4] (284) 1411[3] 2894[6] 3784[4]◆ 4537[10]

**Reveleon** *Sir Michael Stoute* a52
2 ch c Exceed And Excel(AUS) Rosika (Sakhee (USA))
8339[10] 8643[10] 8839[11]

**Revenge** *Tim Easterby* a56 57
2 b g Arcano(IRE) Queens Revenge (Multiplex)
1803[6] 2154[4] 2890[8] 6634[5]◆ 7057[3] 7362[6] 7734[12]

**Reverberation** *Sylvester Kirk* 68
2 ch g Excelebration(IRE) Echo Ridge (IRE) (Oratorio (IRE))
2756[6] 5321[5] 5786[4] 6860[7] 7647[3]

**Reverend Jacobs** *William Haggas* 83
3 b g Nathaniel(IRE) Light Impact (IRE) (Fantastic Light (USA))
4579[2] 5404[2] 6194[2] (6871)

**Revived** *Michael Bell* 75
2 b f Dark Angel(IRE) Tan Tan (King's Best (USA))
5528[5]◆ (6559) 8562[10]

**Revolutionary Man (IRE)**
*Simon Crisford* a71 33
2 b c Exceed And Excel(AUS) Bint Almukhtar (IRE) (Halling (USA))
6388[10] 7987[5]◆ 8703[3]

**Revolutionary War (USA)**
*Jamie Osborne* a84
4 b h War Front(USA) My Annette (USA) (Red Ransom (USA))
165[2] (354) 460[5] 581[7]

**Rewaayat** *Charles Hills* 58
2 br c Pivotal Rufoof (Zamindar (USA))
7352[9]

**Rey De Oro (JPN)** *Kazuo Fujisawa* 122
3 b c King Kamehameha(JPN) La Dorada (JPN) (Symboli Kris S (USA))
8975a[2]

**Rey Loopy (IRE)** *Ben Haslam* a73 51
3 b g Lope De Vega(IRE) Al Basar (USA) (Sahm (USA))
1034[4] 1596[4] (2792) 4265[6] 5126[10] 5835[2] (8589)◆ 8929[2]

**Reynaldothewizard (USA)**
*S Seemar* a114
11 b g Speightstown(USA) Holiday Runner (USA) (Meadowlake (USA))
(206a) 1377a[8]

**Rezwaan** *Murty McGrath* a51 52
10 b g Alhaarth(IRE) Nasij (USA) (Elusive Quality (USA))
281[3] 733[3] 1082[4] 1322[6] 3251[6] 8815[10]

**Rhenius (FR)** *M Nigge* a82 75
3 ch g Soldier Of Fortune(IRE) Rhenania (IRE) (Shamardal (USA))
799a[7]

**Rhigolter Rose (IRE)**
*William Haggas* 56
2 ch f Leroidesanimaux(BRZ) Landela (Alhaarth (IRE))
8348[8]

**Rhode Island (IRE)** *John Gosden* a62 66
2 ch c Galileo(IRE) Native Force (IRE) (Indian Ridge (IRE))
8677[5] 8877[5]

**Rhodes House** *Paul Cole* 69
3 b c Frankel Intrigued (Darshaan)
1963[9]

**Rhododendron (IRE)** *A P O'Brien* 117
3 b f Galileo(IRE) Halfway To Heaven (IRE) (Pivotal)
2434[2] 3301[2] 3881a[P] 6958a[7] (7669a) 8606a[2]

**Rhosneigr (IRE)** *Charles Hills* 81
2 ch c Iffraaj Sadinga (IRE) (Sadler's Wells (USA))
3164[6] 4183[2] (5246) (5875) 7148[5] 7544[6]

**Rhythm Of Life (GER)** *G Bernaud* a58 60
8 b h Auenadler(GER) Rosomachia (GER) (Machiavellian (USA))
5176a[12]

**Rianna Star** *Gary Moore* a59 60
4 b m Haafhd Sayrianna (Sayaarr (USA))
278[7] 646[2] 4461[7] 6069[2] 6280[2] 6796[8] 7918[8]

**Ribbing (USA)** *David Simcock* a65 67
4 ch m Distorted Humor(USA) Contentious (USA) (Giant's Causeway (USA))
37[2] 353[4]

**Ribchester (IRE)** *Richard Fahey* 126
4 b h Iffraaj Mujarah (IRE) (Marju (IRE))
1378a[3] (2825)◆ (3924)◆ 5527[2] (6982a) 8232[2] 8608a[5]

**Rich Again (IRE)** *James Bethell* a93 77
8 b g Amadeus Wolf Fully Fashioned (IRE) (Brief Truce (USA))
(194) (443)◆ 957[10] 6185[7] 8012[20] 8660[9] 8913[6]◆ 9079[9]

**Rich And Famous (USA)**
*Mark Johnston* 93
3 b g Bernardini(USA) Enrichment (USA) (Ghostzapper (USA))
1901[2] (2122) 2570[7] 3092[18] 5094[9] 5423[11]

**Richard Pankhurst** *John Gosden* a76 110
5 ch h Raven's Pass(USA) Mainstay (Elmaamul (USA))
4362[8] 6420[5] 7275[9] 7603[7]

**Richard's Boy (USA)** *Peter Miller* a103 115
5 rg g Idiot Proof(USA) Marissa's Joy (USA) (Cee's Tizzy (USA))
1376a[5] 8604a[2]

**Richenza (FR)** *Ralph Beckett* 71
2 b f Holy Roman Emperor(IRE) Nantha (IRE) (King's Best (USA))
4253[8]◆ 5154[6] 6776[2]

**Rich Girl (FR)** *Edouard Thueux* 49
2 b f Penny's Picnic(IRE) Unborn Spring (IRE) (Whipper (USA))
5988a[12]

**Rich Identity** *Roger Varian* 75
2 gr c Dubawi(IRE) Rose Diamond (IRE) (Daylami (IRE))
7281[2]◆ 7818[3] 8509[2]

**Richie McCaw** *Ian Williams* a78 82
4 b g Zamindar(USA) Cochin (USA) (Swain (IRE))
3785[5]◆ 4380[5]

**Rich Legacy (IRE)** *Ralph Beckett* 103
3 b f Holy Roman Emperor(IRE) Borghesa (GER) (Galileo (IRE))
2523[4] 3995[4]◆ 4613[5] 5569[7] 7139[3]

**Richter Scale (IRE)** *Iain Jardine* a74 60
4 gr m Lilbourne Lad(IRE) Danamight (IRE) (Danetime (IRE))
22[4] 45[4]

**Rickyroadboy** *Mark Walford* 8
2 b g Mazameer(IRE) Black Baccara (Superior Premium)
3399[10] 3895[10]

**Ride Like The Wind (IRE)**
*Kevin Ryan* a92 106
5 b g Lope De Vega(IRE) Biswa (USA) (Kafwain (USA))
917[8] 1491[9] 2736[13]

**Ride The Lightning** *Archie Watson* a87 73
4 b g Dalakhani(IRE) Bright Halo (IRE) (Bigstone (IRE))
(163) 519[2]

**Rien Que Pour Toi (FR)**
*T Castanheira* a72 99
4 b m Orpen(USA) Ilinka (FR) (Gentlewave (IRE))
2616[9]

**Right About Now (IRE)**
*Chris Dwyer* a68 61
3 b c Famous Name Right Reason (IRE) (Manduro (GER))
2778[11] 3456[2] 4164[4] 5009[5] 5656[2]◆ 7083[11] 8813[10]

**Right Action** *Richard Fahey* a82 81
3 b g Dandy Man(IRE) Rockaby Baby (IRE) (Beckett (IRE))
(600) 877 1463[4] 1913[6] 2499[4] (2886) 3434[2] 4290[2] 4894[5] 5376[3] 5948[8] 6558[2] 8600[7] (9411)

**Right Flank (USA)** *Doug Watson* a70 57
3 b c War Front(USA) Principal Role (USA) (Empire Maker (USA))
8711a[5]

**Right Madam (IRE)**
*Sarah Hollinshead* a41 55
5 b m Jeremy(USA) Mawaared (Machiavellian (USA))
146[8]

**Right Rebel** *Alan Bailey* a76 70
5 b m Cockney Rebel(IRE) Right Rave (IRE) (Soviet Star (USA))
47[11]◆ 460[6] 1243[7] 2070[4]◆

**Right Touch** *Richard Fahey* a104 102
7 b g Royal Applause Amira (Efisio)
2156[5] 3089[5] 4264[6] 5434[6] 6206[7] 7108[7] 7626[4] 8104[2] 8737[4] 9016[9] 9210[2]◆

**Rightway (IRE)** *Tony Carroll* a73 72
6 b g Cockney Rebel(IRE) Caeribland (IRE) (Namaqualand (USA))
90[3] 524[6] 1553[8] 2956[5] 3616[12] 4747[8] 7061[11]

**Rigid Rock (IRE)**
*Adrian McGuinness* a51 51
10 b g Refuse To Bend(IRE) Delia (IRE) (Darshaan)
51[6]

**Rigoletto (SWI)** *Luca Cumani* 98
3 b c Zoffany(IRE) Rumina (FR) (Dashing Blade)
2778[5] (3438) (4271) 5115[4] 6073[3] (6809) 7549[7]

**Rigolleto (IRE)** *Anabel K Murphy* a77 72
9 b g Ad Valorem(USA) Jallaissine (IRE) (College Chapel)
172[4] 355[9] 768[10] 1080[12] 1723[4] 2367[8]

**Rimini (FR)** *C Ferland* 106
2 b c Elusive City(USA) Kelty In Love (FR) (Keltos (FR))
5090a[2] 6051a[10] (6728a) 7670a[6]

**Rinaria (IRE)** *K R Burke* a87 76
3 b f Tamayuz Riynaaz (IRE) (Cape Cross (IRE))
1333[2]◆ (2110) 2754[11] 3911[4] 4121[2] 5378[4] 6310[2] (6468) 7364[9] (7830) 8546[6]

**Ring Eye (IRE)** *John O'Shea* a43 64
9 b g Definite Article Erins Lass (IRE) (Erins Isle (IRE))
2357[6] 3026[10] 3575[9] 4469[5] 4840[5] 5361[9] 5787[7]

**Ringside Humour (IRE)** *J S Bolger* a95 94
5 b m Teofilo(IRE) Intriguing Humor (CAN) (Distorted Humor (USA))
5088a[8]

**Rioja Day (IRE)** *Jim Goldie* a43 59
7 b g Red Clubs(IRE) Dai E Dai (USA) (Seattle Dancer (USA))
2501[4] 2955[11] 3196[8] (3387) 3652[9] 4034[12] 5091[6] 5206[7] 5992[3] (6346) 6690[12] 7704[2] 7980[9]

**Rio Ronaldo (IRE)** *Mike Murphy* a80 92
5 b g Footstepsinthesand Flanders (IRE) (Common Grounds)
1606[8] 2040[6] 2608[10] 3161[3] (3834) 4272[4]

**Rio Santos** *Rod Millman* 48
2 ch g Casamento(IRE) Midnight Flower (IRE) (Haafhd)
2890[7] 3690[8] 4805[8] 5562[4] 6585[9] 7081[7] 7196[5]

**Rio's Cliffs** *Martyn Meade* a84 80
4 b m Canford Cliffs(IRE) What's Up Pussycat (IRE) (Danehill Dancer (IRE))
277[5]

**Rioticism (FR)** *Matthieu Palussiere* 98
2 b f Rio De La Plata(USA) Romanticism (IRE) (Cape Cross (IRE))
1335a[6] 3611a[4] 3960[18] (5090a) 6728a[4] 7846a[4] 8777a[8]

**Rio Tigre (IRE)** *S bin Ghadayer* a82 104
6 b h Teofilo(IRE) Braziliz (USA) (Kingmambo (USA))
82a[3] 322a[10] 540a[5] 890a[9]

**Ripley (IRE)** *Charles Hills* 84
2 b f Declaration Of War(USA) La Conquerante (Hurricane Run (IRE))
5573[2] 6190[6]◆

**Rip N Roar (IRE)** *Tom Clover*
5 b g Rip Van Winkle(IRE) Aine (IRE) (Danehill Dancer (IRE))
2580[9] 3465[P] (Dead)

**Ripoll (IRE)** *Sylvester Kirk* a88 82
4 b g Alfred Nobel(IRE) Lahu Lady (Red Ransom (USA))
1964[4] 2115[8] 2477[4] (3212) 3750[7] 4636[9] 4854[8] 5719[4] 6933[13]

**Riponian** *Susan Corbett* a6 62
7 ch g Trade Fair Dispol Katie (Komaite (USA))
2082[12] 3387[12] 4244[8] (5649) 6690[11] (7166) 8513[11]

**Ripped (IRE)** *Gavin Cromwell* a45 51
5 b g Rip Van Winkle(IRE) State Crystal (IRE) (High Estate)
3193[7]

**Ripper Street (IRE)**
*Christine Dunnett* a61 52
3 b g Big Bad Bob(IRE) Caster Sugar (USA) (Cozzene (USA))
2732[11] 3250[12] 3701[4] 4180[14] 4626[8] 5336[6] 5854[3] 6621[12] 6851[8] 8123[4] 8538[15] 8883[9]

**Riptide** *Michael Scudamore* 72
11 b g Val Royal(FR) Glittering Image (IRE) (Sadler's Wells (USA))
1703[7] 2032[3] 2363[2] 2889[4] 3663[9] 4471[7] 5361[3] 6343[2] 7893[6] 8394[9]

**Rip Van Go** *Sally Haynes* a14
3 b g Rip Van Winkle(IRE) Thousandkissesdeep (IRE) (Night Shift (USA))
2921[9]

**Rip Van Suzy (IRE)** *Jo Hughes* a42 45
4 b m Rip Van Winkle(IRE) Suzy Bliss (Spinning World (USA))
9309a[10]

**Rise Hit (FR)** *H-A Pantall* a63 66
3 b c American Post Rose The One (FR) (Meshaheer (USA))
4783a[7]

**Rising (IRE)** *Brian Meehan* a61 81
3 b g Rip Van Winkle(IRE) Cause Celebre (IRE) (Peintre Celebre (USA))
1906[7] 6150[2] 6657[4] 7908[8] 8151[7]

**Rising Sunshine (IRE)**
*Milton Bradley* a52 56
4 b g Dark Angel(IRE) Little Audio (IRE) (Shamardal (USA))
605[7] 724[10] 1084[5] 1298[5] 1408[4] 2278[11] 2733[10] 3137[4] 3809[6] 4982[9] 6503[9] 8134[13] 9456[8]

**Risk Adjusted (IRE)**
*Mohammed Hussain* a85 101
4 b h Bushranger(IRE) Silk Fan (IRE) (Unfuwain (USA))
932a[5]

**Risk Major (FR)** *V Luka Jr* a82 79
4 b h My Risk(FR) Major's Love (FR) (Majorien)
2696a[6]

**Risky Dory (FR)** *S Wattel* a60
2 b f Authorized(IRE) Southwold (FR) (Take Risks (FR))
8691a[8]

**Ristretto (USA)** *Ralph Beckett* 67
3 bb f Medaglia d'Oro(USA) Visit (Oasis Dream)
4911[5]

**Rita's Girl** *K R Burke* a45 56
3 b f Harbour Watch(IRE) Brazilian Breeze (IRE) (Invincible Spirit (IRE))
96[10] 463[7]

**Ritas Legacy** *Roy Brotherton*
3 b g Passing Glance Rita's Rock Ape (Mon Tresor)
7930[6] 8805[9]

**Rita's Man (IRE)** *Keith Dalgleish* a66 75
3 b c Lawman(FR) French Fern (IRE) (Royal Applause)
212[5] 1888[4] (2349) (2854) 3162[3] 4443[8] 5033[6] 6139[8] 6620[11] 6937[7] 7820[3] (7928) 8464a[3] 8978[8]

**Ritasun (FR)** *Harry Whittington* a41 35
4 bb g Monsun(GER) Baselga (GER) (Second Set (IRE))
6475[8] 7820[7]

**Rite To Reign** *Philip McBride* a85 73
6 b g Tiger Hill(IRE) Magical Cliche (USA) (Affirmed (USA))
6680[10] 7359[10] 7785[8] 8398[8] 8771[3] 8978[6] 9408[6]

**Ritha** *Richard Hannon* 61
2 b f Poet's Voice Danat Al Atheer (Shamardal (USA))
4533[16] 5349[9] 6133[11]

**Rivas Rob Roy** *John Gallagher* 70
2 ch g Archipenko(USA) Rivas Rhapsody (IRE) (Hawk Wing (USA))
3570[U] 3936[2]◆ 4583[8] 5063[5] 5865[5]

**Rivellino** *Adrian McGuinness* a85 85
7 b g Invincible Spirit(IRE) Brazilian Bride (IRE) (Pivotal)
4925a[6] (6801a) 9247a[4]

**Rivendicato** *Joseph Tuite* 46
2 b f Showcasing Carsulae (IRE) (Marju (IRE))
3668[P] 7732[7]

**Riven Light (IRE)** *W P Mullins* 105
5 b g Raven's Pass(USA) Vivacity (Trempolino (USA))
(5517a) 5688a[5] (7066a) 8058a[7]

**River Boyne (IRE)** *Gordon Elliott* a86 60
2 b c Dandy Man(IRE) Clytha (Mark Of Esteem (IRE))
8317a[2]

**River Cafe (IRE)** *Sylvester Kirk* a62 62
2 b f High Chaparral(IRE) Dingle View (IRE) (Mujadil (USA))
7153[4] 7898[7] 8998[7]

**River Cannes (FR)** *T Castanheira* a88 87
2 b f Orpen(USA) Cannes To Capri (IRE) (Galileo (IRE))
(6251a) 7306a[5] 7846a[5]

**River Dart (IRE)** *Tony Carroll* a83 80
5 ch g Dutch Art Sky Galaxy (USA) (Sky Classic (CAN))
38[8] 196[3] 571[3] 1466[6] 3308[9] 4801[6]

**River Icon** *Iain Jardine* 84
5 b m Sixties Icon River Alder (Alderbrook)
7109[3] (7477) 8047[10]

**River Of Gold (IRE)** *John Gosden* a43
2 ch c New Approach(IRE) Nahoodh (IRE) (Clodovil (IRE))
8849[11]

**River Roquette (IRE)** *J S Moore* 4
3 b f Fastnet Rock(AUS) On The Nile (IRE) (Sadler's Wells (USA))
**3426**[8]
**River Rule** *Stuart Williams* 45
2 b f Bated Breath Ocean Countess (IRE) (Storming Home)
**5476**[6] 6827[9] 8347[5]
**Riverside Bridge (IRE)**
*Brian Ellison* a38
5 gr g Rugby(USA) Sahara Gold (IRE) (Desert Prince (IRE))
*9441*[2]
**Riverside Walk** *Keith Dalgleish* a68
2 b f Showcasing Distant Waters (Lomitas)
*8189*[4]◆ **8555**[2]◆ *8914*[4]
**Rivers Of Asia** *Martin Smith* a76 43
4 ch g Medicean Aliena (IRE) (Grand Lodge (USA))
*5161*[0] 928[11] 1498[16] *7514*[5] 8376[10] **8551**[4]◆ *8908*[11]
**River Warrior** *Richard Fahey* a33 5
3 b c Majestic Warrior(USA) Triveni (FR) (Lando (GER))
*331*[10] *580*[9] *777*[7] **1297**[5] 2902[8]
**Rivet (IRE)** *William Haggas* 99
3 b c Fastnet Rock(AUS) Starship (IRE) (Galileo (IRE))
1904[2] **2666a**[3] 3368a[8] 3927[6]
**Riviera (FR)** *E J O'Neill* 48
2 ch f Rio De La Plata(USA) Portella (GER) (Protektor (GER))
**7415a**[8]
**Riviere Argentee (FR)** *K R Burke* a53 82
3 gr f Hurricane Cat(USA) River Trebor (USA) (Myrakalu (FR))
4580[8] 5533[7] 5630[6] 6225a[8] 6649a[8] 7019[6] **(7924)** 8464a[6]
**Riyazan (IRE)** *M Halford* a100 100
2 b c Iffraaj Riyaba (IRE) (Dalakhani (IRE))
6955a[4] **7426a**[5] ***(7797a)***
**Rizzle Dizzle** *K R Burke* a76 59
2 b f Foxwedge(AUS) Greensand (Green Desert (USA))
8288[4]◆ ***8851***[2] *9416*[4]
**Road To Dubai (IRE)** *George Scott* a63 91
3 ch c Aqlaam Fragrancy (IRE) (Singspiel (IRE))
*863*[4] 1736[5] (2394) 3291[3] (3531) 3779[2] 4365[4]◆ 5838[5] 6423[4] 7505[4]◆ (7824) **(8295)**
**Roar (IRE)** *Brian Ellison* a61 84
3 b g Pour Moi(IRE) Evening Rushour (IRE) (Mull Of Kintyre (USA))
3578[6] (4365) 5166[4] **6872**[3] 7548[6]
**Roaring Forties (IRE)**
*Rebecca Bastiman* a90 90
4 b g Invincible Spirit(IRE) Growling (IRE) (Celtic Swing)
2840[11] 3792[18] 4683[12] 5213[5] 5601[2] 6297[5] 6894[2]◆ 7594[6] **(8107)**◆ 8240[5] 8486[4] 8736[15]
**Roaring Lion (USA)** *John Gosden* a92 118
2 rg c Kitten's Joy(USA) Vionnet (USA) (Street Sense (USA))
(6142) *(6883)*◆ (7616)◆ **8415**[2]
**Roaring Rory** *Ollie Pears* a69 68
4 ch g Sakhee's Secret Barbieri (IRE) (Encosta De Lago (AUS))
*446*[4] **(743)** *901*[6] 1722[7] 1973[3] 2627[3] 3202[3] 3944[5] 4174[3] (4997) 6089[3] 6670[8] ***(8775)*** *8927*[7] *9308*[9]
**Robanne** *William Knight* a97 101
4 b m Paco Boy(IRE) Arctic Song (Charnwood Forest (IRE))
***1795***[4] 2616[11] 3003[9]
**Robben** *Alexandra Dunn* a64 52
5 b g Dutch Art Little Greenbird (Ardkinglass)
***35***[6]
**Robben Rainbow** *David Barron* 79
3 b g Delegator Sally Can Wait (Sakhee (USA))
3946[10] **4600**[10] **5018**[6] 5495[6]
**Robbian** *Charles Smith* a40 57
6 b g Bertolini(USA) Crathes (Zilzal (USA))
*21*[8] *153*[9] 3563[8] 5738[6] **6041**[3] 7017[5] 7255[4] 8329[7] 8490[3] 8656[6]
**Robbie Roo Roo**
*Mrs Ilka Gansera-Leveque* a69 60
4 br m Kheleyf(USA) Haiti Dancer (Josr Algarhoud (IRE))
2043[5] *2962*[3] 3728[2] *(4214)* 5119[3] *6638*[2] ***(6888)*** 7899[9] *8243*[9] *9142*[8]
**Robero** *Michael Easterby* a95 101
5 b g Piccolo Ceilidh Band (Celtic Swing)
*1867*[2] *2116*[2] (2608) *4353*[5] **(4719)** 4905[5] 6206[16] 7622[9] 8104[3] 8383[14] 8737[7]
**Robin Of Navan (FR)** *Harry Dunlop* a112 115
4 ch h American Post Cloghran (FR) (Muhtathir)
1659a[4] **3118a**[2] **(3856a)** 4423a[8] 6982a[4] 7638a[5] **8041**[2] 9171a[8]
**Robinson Crusoe (IRE)**
*Richard Hannon* 69
2 b c Footstepsinthesand Corrozal (GER) (Cape Cross (IRE))
4049[5] **6132**[6] 6916[6] 8467[5]◆
**Robin's Purse** *Charles Hills* a37 61
3 b f Sir Percy Morant Bay (IRE) (Montjeu (IRE))
*2016*[11] 2732[9] **4711**[5]
**Robin Weathers (USA)**
*William Haggas* a77 84
3 ch g Elusive Quality(USA) Sharnberry (Shamardal (USA))
**(4911)** 6655[6] 7404[7] 8418[9] 8600[17] *9020*[4]
**Robot Boy (IRE)** *David Barron* a106 97
7 ch g Shamardal(USA) Pivotal's Princess (IRE) (Pivotal)
*326*[7] *(842)* ***1025***[3] ***1793***[2] 2764[8] 3829[6] *4306*[5] 4881[17] 5354[7] 6325[12] 6923[2]
**Rob's Legacy** *Shaun Harris* a33 46
4 ch g Phoenix Reach(IRE) Clumber Pursuits (Pastoral Pursuits)
1834[8] 2364[6] 3698[5] 5267[9] *6530*[5]◆ 7233[8] **7982**[6]
**Roc Angel (FR)** *F Chappet* a86 105
3 ch c Rock Of Gibraltar(IRE) Forewarned (IRE) (Grand Lodge (USA))
(2484a) 3855a[3] **4235a**[4] 5522a[7]
**Roc Astrale (IRE)** *Amanda Perrett* a82
3 ch g Teofilo(IRE) Lumiere Astrale (FR) (Trempolino (USA))
***1624***[3]◆
**Roche Rose (IRE)** *E Lellouche* a84 92
4 gr m Rock Of Gibraltar(IRE) Roche Ambeau (FR) (Chichicastenango (FR))
**7753a**[7] 8838a[7]
**Rockabilly Riot (IRE)**
*Martin Todhunter* a62 65
7 br g Footstepsinthesand Zawariq (IRE) (Marju (IRE))
**4839**[8]
**Rock A Doodle Doo (IRE)**
*Sean Regan* a55 56
10 b g Oratorio(IRE) Nousaiyra (IRE) (Be My Guest (USA))
***30***[4] 5951[12] *6901*[8]
**Rockafilly (FR)** *J A Nash* 42
2 b f Dabirsim(FR) Barzas River (IRE) (Dalakhani (IRE))
**7423a**[12]
**Rockalater** *John Spearing*
3 b f Delegator Rock Candy (IRE) (Rock Of Gibraltar (IRE))
***96***[8] *244*[6] *644*[4] *897*[9] *1297*[8] 6097[8] 7907[13]
**Rock Chic** *Rod Millman* 29
2 ch f Pastoral Pursuits Glittering Prize (UAE) (Cadeaux Genereux)
6438[9] **7740**[6]
**Rockesbury** *Kevin Frost* a34 49
2 b g Foxwedge(AUS) Nellie Ellis (IRE) (Compton Place)
**1604**[8] 2029[9] *8657*[6]
**Rocket Man Dan (IRE)**
*Keith Dalgleish* a44 67
2 b g Dandy Man(IRE) Manalisa (IRE) (Manduro (GER))
1495[7] **2154**[2] 2740[6] 3333[3] 3826[8] 6547[8] 7159[8] 7655[5] *7938*[12] *8431*[7]
**Rocket Ronnie (IRE)** *Brian Barr* a59 78
7 b g Antonius Pius(USA) Ctesiphon (USA) (Arch (USA))
***239***[7] *390*[6] *740*[5] *1145*[4] 3809[7] *4453*[5] 4968[5] *5898*[3] 6101[6]
**Rock Hill (IRE)** *Paul Midgley* 67
2 br g Rock Of Gibraltar(IRE) Pascali (Compton Place)
4598[13] **5370**[5] 5665[6] 7564[6] 8475[9]
**Rock Icon** *J S Moore* a61 63
4 b g Sixties Icon Monashee Rock (IRE) (Monashee Mountain (USA))
**(6284)** 6588[3] *9213*[5]
**Rockies Spirit** *Denis Quinn* 85
2 br c Swiss Spirit Red Mischief (IRE) (Red Clubs (IRE))
4049[4] (4503) **6424**[2]
**Rockin Fella (IRE)** *H Al Ramzani* 61
2 b c Society Rock(IRE) Dearest Daisy (Forzando)
1673[3]◆ 1803[3] **2222**[2] 3523[7] 4427[4] 9446a[12]
**Rocking Lady (IRE)** *J-M Lefebvre* a73 86
4 b m Fastnet Rock(AUS) Hashbrown (GER) (Big Shuffle (USA))
***6540a***[7]
**Rocking Rudolph (USA)**
*Robert Cowell* a56 55
4 b m Discreetly Mine(USA) Empire Spring (USA) (Empire Maker (USA))
*416*[11] ***8953***[8]
**Rock In Peace (IRE)** *G M Lyons* a85 89
3 br g Kodiac Felina (IRE) (Lawman (FR))
***1012a***[2]
**Rock Island Line** *Mark Walford* a63 64
3 b g Haafhd Diablo Dancer (Zafeen (FR))
1513[6] 1829[8] 2185[12] 3499[6] **5950**[4] *7360*[6] 8218[6] *(8662)*
**Rockley Point** *Paul D'Arcy* a72 67
4 b g Canford Cliffs(IRE) Statua (IRE) (Statoblest)
*257* *575*[2] ***984***[3] *1365*[5] 2320[7] 2800[8] 3816[6] 4256[13] *5481*[6] *7408*[7] 8327[14] *8743*[2] *8875*[6] *9093*[8] *9142*[3]
**Rockliffe** *Micky Hammond* a34 65
4 b g Notnowcato Hope Island (IRE) (Titus Livius (FR))
**1700**[6] 3205[8] 3501[4] 3935[12] 4690[6] 5074[7] 5807[3] 6560[2]
**Rock My Love (GER)** *Markus Klug* 104
2 b f Holy Roman Emperor(IRE) Rondinay (FR) (Cadeaux Genereux)
**(8269a)**
**Rock'n Gold** *Adrian Wintle* a76 52
4 b g Fastnet Rock(AUS) La Concorde (FR) (Sadler's Wells (USA))
*1365*[10] *1598*[10] 5843[8] 7028[12] 7960[11] 8515[13]
***9092***[2]
**Rock N Rolla (IRE)** *Keith Dalgleish* a79 82
3 ch g Intikhab(USA) Fantastic Opinion (IRE) (Fantastic Light (USA))
3713[11] 4295[7] 4685[4] 5376[6] 5601[6] **7162**[2] *7570*[9] 7886[9] 7981[6] *8433*[5] *8749*[4]
**Rock N Roll Global (IRE)**
*Richard Hughes* a71 68
3 ch g Power Laughter (IRE) (Sadler's Wells (USA))
*236*[4] *545*[3] 1907[9] 2394[10] 3276[4] ***4748***[3] 6257[2]
**Rock Of America (USA)**
*David O'Meara* a89 79
3 b g Arch(USA) Elusive Noise (USA) (Elusive Quality (USA))
*(1004)* *1487*[2]◆ *1838*[4] 4104[5] 4530[4] 5256[4] ***7538***[2]
**Rock Of Estonia (IRE)** *Charles Hills* 82
2 ch c Society Rock(IRE) Estonia (Exceed And Excel (AUS))
**(1681)** **(2217)**
**Rock Of Monaco** *Antony Brittain* a46 26
4 b m Monsieur Bond(IRE) Melandre (Lujain (USA))
*1406*[12] *3265*[7] *4263*[9] ***4982***[6] 5215[15] *6528*[9]
**Rock Of Romance (IRE)** *A Wohler* a69 104
7 br h Rock Of Gibraltar(IRE) Romantic Venture (IRE) (Indian Ridge (IRE))
**2667a**[15]
**Rock Of Tiger (GER)** *T Potters*
5 b g Tiger Hill(IRE) Rosobolda (GER) (Never So Bold)
*1196a*[5]
**Rock On Baileys** *Chris Dwyer* a61 47
2 ch f Rock Of Gibraltar(IRE) Ring For Baileys (Kyllachy)
3697[11] 4349[4] *7986*[6] 8325[7] *8780*[2]◆ ***(8902)***
**Rock On Bertie (IRE)** *Nigel Tinkler* a56 56
2 b c Rock Of Gibraltar(IRE) Princess Banu (Oasis Dream)
1872[8] 2222[8] *2786*[10] 3398[8] 4014[5] 4297[7] 5121[2] **5933**[3] 6585[3] *7029*[5] 7518[5] *8783*[2] ***9014***[3] *9175*[7]
**Rock On Bollinski** *Brian Ellison* 77
7 b g Bollin Eric Bred For Pleasure (Niniski (USA))
2032[8] 2928[8] **3663**[6] 4120[11] 7893[5] 8487[11]
**Rock On Dandy (FR)** *Harry Dunlop* a76 66
3 gr g Rajsaman(FR) Minnie's Mystery (FR) (Highest Honor (FR))
4626[5] **4971**[2]◆ 6443[6] *7712*[9] 8123[2]
**Rock On Rosie (IRE)**
*Adrian Brendan Joyce* a68 58
8 b m Gamut(IRE) Macs Goose (Kayf Tara)
*1245*[4] ***1257***[6]
**Rock Palm (IRE)** *Laura Morgan*
4 b m Rock Of Gibraltar(IRE) Palm Pilot (IRE) (Oasis Dream)
4187[11]
**Rocksette** *Philip Hide* a40 57
3 b f Mount Nelson Native Nickel (IRE) (Be My Native (USA))
*624*[8] *962*[5] 1787[5] 5935[2] 6257[4]◆ *6622*[5] **7917**[2] 8183[2]
**Rockshine** *Richard Hannon* a52 49
3 b f Fastnet Rock(AUS) Shine Like A Star (Fantastic Light (USA))
7227[5] 8327[12] ***8664***[6]
**Rock Song** *John Mackie* a72 79
8 b g Rock Of Gibraltar(IRE) Jackie's Opera (FR) (Indian Ridge (IRE))
***1562***[6]
**Rock Steady (IRE)** *Roger Charlton* a105 90
4 ch g Intikhab(USA) Mannsara (IRE) (Royal Academy (USA))
***352***[2] *767*[5] 8468[8] *8892*[9]
**Rock Warbler (IRE)** *Oliver Greenall* a81 73
4 ch g Raven's Pass(USA) Rare Tern (IRE) (Pivotal)
*(44)*◆ *359*[2] *513*[2] 3095[18] 4529[6] 6143[7] *7034*[5] ***(7571)*** *7998*[6] *8556*[6] *8749*[3] *9100*[7] *9220*[4] *9411*[8]
**Rockwell Lloyd (IRE)**
*Mick Channon* 50
2 b c Fast Company(IRE) Lucy Liu (IRE) (Grand Lodge (USA))
5105[10] **5655**[7] 5886[5] 6472[8]
**Rockwood** *Karen McLintock* a78 82
6 b g Rock Of Gibraltar(IRE) Hannah Frank (IRE) (High Chaparral (IRE))
(1706) 2030[5] **(2772)** *3255*[4] 3845[5] *4358*[4] 4865[5] 5469[4] *9100*[10]
**Rocky Elsom (USA)** *Adrian Wintle* a46 57
10 b g Rock Of Gibraltar(IRE) Bowstring (IRE) (Sadler's Wells (USA))
***1092***[6] 2781[9] 6343[10] *8396*[12]
**Rockyl (IRE)** *D De Waele* a60 66
5 b g Rock Of Gibraltar(IRE) Kylayne (Kyllachy)
***384a***[5] 5490a[11]
**Rocky Shores (IRE)** *Mick Channon* 62
2 b c Canford Cliffs(IRE) Josphiel (IRE) (Okawango (USA))
**8389**[11] **8677**[6]
**Rocky Two (IRE)** *Philip Kirby* a22 45
7 ch g Rock Of Gibraltar(IRE) Toorah Laura La (USA) (Black Minnaloushe (USA))
*28*[8]
**Rococo** *John Gosden* 62
2 b f Dubawi(IRE) Intrigued (Darshaan)
**8593**[5]
**Rocus (IRE)** *Mark Usher* a13
2 br g Rock Of Gibraltar(IRE) Mythologie (FR) (Bering)
5292[13] ***5847***[7]
**Rodaini (USA)** *Simon Crisford* 104
3 ch g Exchange Rate(USA) Blessings Count (USA) (Pulpit (USA))
**1881**[2] 3013[5] 3994[11] (6562)
**Roddy (IRE)** *Tom Tate* 80
3 ch g Roderic O'Connor(IRE) Sweet Chilli (IRE) (Intikhab (USA))
4055[5] 4720[2] **5632**[2]
**Rod Of Iron** *Michael Madgwick* a41 46
4 br g Alkaased(USA) Leading Star (Motivator)
5405[5] 5866[5] **6589**[4]
**Rodyana (FR)** *P Monfort* a68 66
4 ch m Muhtathir Romanticism (IRE) (Cape Cross (IRE))
**7070a**[3] 7721a[6] ***8303a***[4]
**Roger Thorpe** *John Balding* a27 44
8 b g Firebreak Nunthorpe (Mystiko (USA))
**4626**[7] 6181[12] *6528*[8] *9075*[12] *9343*[8]
**Rogue** *Richard Hannon* 81
2 b g Epaulette(AUS) Miskin Diamond (IRE) (Diamond Green (FR))
**2826**[4]◆ 3746[4] 5641[4] (6071) **(7353)** 8413[4]
**Rogue Hero (IRE)** *Paul Cole* a65 54
2 b g Oasis Dream Pink Damsel (IRE) (Galileo (IRE))
7352[10] ***9051***[4] ***9154***[4]
**Roibeard (IRE)** *Eamonn O'Connell* 87
4 b g Big Bad Bob(IRE) Queen Myrine (IRE) (Oratorio (IRE))
5519a[11] **5582a**[9]
**Roicead (USA)** *D Selvaratnam* a107 108
10 b g Giant's Causeway(USA) Coachella (Danehill (USA))
207a[12] 433a[13] **651a**[9] 1044a[9]
**Roi De Vitesse (IRE)** *Ali Jan* a102 102
10 ch h Chineur(FR) Face The Storm (IRE) (Barathea (IRE))
84a[13] **207a**[8] 651a[7] 1046a[11]
**Rojina (IRE)** *Lisa Williamson* a50 48
4 ch m Intense Focus(USA) Hurricane Havoc (IRE) (Hurricane Run (IRE))
*64*[5] *143*[5] *743*[8] *1221*[9] *1452*[7] 1785[5] 2069[6] *2278*[6] 2633[17] **3062**[8]
**Roksaneh (FR)** *A Fabre* 77
2 ch f Kendargent(FR) Ramora (USA) (Monsun (GER))
**6171a**[4]
**Roland Rocks (IRE)** *John Ryan* 93
2 b c Red Jazz(USA) Toy Show (IRE) (Danehill (USA))
(3826) 4266[3] **4812**[7] 5501[7] 7114[5]
**Rolanna (IRE)** *W J Martin* a47 54
5 b m Strategic Prince Dalaika (CAN) (Rhythm (USA))
**5590**[7]
**Roller** *Michael Easterby* a82 92
4 b g Rail Link Buffering (Beat Hollow)
*322*[2]◆ *359*[6] (1832)◆ 1969[3]◆ **3498**[2]◆ 3743[6]
**Rolling Dice** *Dominic Ffrench Davis* a16 61
6 b g Rail Link Breathing Space (USA) (Expelled (USA))
*2471*[7] 2909[11] 6101[9] 7006[5] **7198**[3] 7900[4] 8182[5]
**Rolling Maul (IRE)** *Peter Bowen* 91
9 b g Oscar(IRE) Water Sports (IRE) (Marju (IRE))
(4202) (5566)◆ **(5944)** 7200[4] 8038[16]
**Roll On Rory** *Jason Ward* a84 88
4 b g Mullionmileanhour(IRE) Fangfoss Girls (Monsieur Bond (IRE))
1799[8] 2390[12] 2840[16] 3792[12] 4339[11] 4622[6] 5125[4] 5948[4] 6672[3] 6964[2]◆ *7570*[4] **(8596)** *8999*[12]
**Roly Poly (USA)** *A P O'Brien* 116
3 b f War Front(USA) Misty For Me (IRE) (Galileo (IRE))
1883[7] 2644a[6] 3110a[2] 4031[2] (4857) (5460a) 6958a[6] **(7812)**◆ 8608a[11] 9170a[14]
**Romaana** *Simon Crisford* 68
2 b f Iffraaj Baheeja (Dubawi (IRE))
**7022**[4]
**Roman Approval (USA)**
*David Cannizzo* 109
6 bb h Roman Ruler(USA) Highest Approval (USA) (High Fly (USA))
**3553a**[11]
**Romance Khaleesi (FR)**
*X Thomas-Demeaulte* 72
2 gr f Tin Horse(IRE) Romance Bere (FR) (Verglas (IRE))
**5815a**[3]
**Roman De Brut (IRE)** *Denis Quinn* a73 82
5 ch g Rock Of Gibraltar(IRE) Nesmeh (USA) (More Than Ready (USA))
*47*[3] *382*[2] *727*[5] *928*[5] *1334*[4] *1620*[3] *(1893)* **(2708)** 3144[3] *4304*[8] 5265[3] 7894[12] 8596[7]
**Roman Holiday (IRE)** *Ed Vaughan* a81 84
4 b m Holy Roman Emperor(IRE) Burn The Breeze (IRE) (Beat Hollow)
3216[3]◆ **(4051)** 4617[8] *7484*[6]
**Romanised (IRE)** *K J Condon* 105
2 b c Holy Roman Emperor(IRE) Romantic Venture (IRE) (Indian Ridge (IRE))
3925[7] **5973a**[6] 6696[2]
**Roman Legend (IRE)**
*Jassim Mohammed Ghazali* a70 110
6 b h Holy Roman Emperor(IRE) Taking Liberties (IRE) (Royal Academy (USA))
**914a**[3]
**Roman Legion (IRE)** *Dean Ivory* a42 59
3 b g Holy Roman Emperor(IRE) Kibini (Galileo (IRE))
*209*[9] **4714**[5] 6112[13]
**Romann Angel** *Michael Mullineaux*
8 b m Sir Harry Lewis(USA) Roman Gospel (Roi De Rome (USA))
5401[8]
**Roman Navigator (IRE)**
*Marco Botti* a75
3 b c Henrythenavigator(USA) Lollina Paulina (Holy Roman Emperor (IRE))
*1193* ***(307)***
**Romanor** *Ed Walker* a82 83
3 b g Holy Roman Emperor(IRE) Salinia (IRE) (Rainbow Quest (USA))
2087[2] 2689[5] 3787[4] 4691[5] 5559[5] **(6763)** *7728*[3] *8398*[7]
**Roman River** *Martin Smith* 71
2 b c Holy Roman Emperor(IRE) Inagh River (Fasliyev (USA))
**3622**[2] 4598[12]
**Roman Spectrum** *Il Cavallo In Testa* a78 91
4 b g Holy Roman Emperor(IRE) Mara Spectrum (IRE) (Spectrum (IRE))
***384a***[4]
**Roman Spinner** *Rae Guest* a72 65
2 ch f Intikhab(USA) Pompeia (Singspiel (IRE))
3390[8] 4757[4] 5507[5] *6154*[6] *(6790)* *7510*[2]◆ 7734[2] *(8887)*◆ ***9466***[3]
**Romantic (IRE)** *Noel C Kelly* a57 59
8 b g Holy Roman Emperor(IRE) Welsh Love (Ela-Mana-Mou)
***9056***[5]
**Romantic Story** *Robert Cowell* a22
3 ch f Poet's Voice Scallywag (IRE) (Raven's Pass (USA))
***9071***[8]
**Romantic Vision (USA)**
*George R Arnold II* a111
5 b m Lemon Drop Kid(USA) Perfect For You (USA) (Giant's Causeway (USA))
***8578a***[7]
**Roman Times (IRE)** *Alan Berry* a44 59
4 b m Holy Roman Emperor(IRE) Timeless Dream (Oasis Dream)
3289[7] 4174[14] 4479[6] 5016[9] ***5418***[5] 5919[8] 7660[10] *8558*[11]
**Roman Warrior** *Harry Dunlop* a66
2 b c Holy Roman Emperor(IRE) Meet Marhaba (IRE) (Marju (IRE))
***6884***[8] *7511*[8]

**Romasparita (IRE)** *Endo Botti* a60
4 b h Rip Van Winkle(IRE) Cromac (ITY) (Machiavellian (USA))
391a[8]

**Romina** *Richard Hughes* a80 77
3 b f Raven's Pass(USA) Dolores (Danehill (USA))
4911[4] 5721[4] (7059)

**Rominou (FR)** *C Lerner* a80 77
4 ch g Excellent Art La Romana (Bijou D'Inde)
6648a[9]

**Ronaldinho (IRE)** *Dianne Sayer* a45 54
7 b g Jeremy(USA) Spring Glory (Dr Fong (USA))
4034[9]

**Ronald R (IRE)** *Michael Bell* 107
3 ch g Nathaniel(IRE) Amazon Beauty (IRE) (Wolfhound (USA))
(2402)◆ 3997[2]◆ 4817[6] 6355[14]

**Ronchois** *E Lellouche* a72 74
4 b g Pour Moi(IRE) Freeing (Dansili)
4457a[7]

**Ronnie The Rooster** *David Barron* a69 71
3 b g Captain Gerrard(IRE) Piranha (IRE) (Exceed And Excel (AUS))
577[4] 1029[3] 2036[2] 2347[2] 2703[7]

**Ronni Layne** *Louise Allan* a63 52
3 b f Native Ruler Cindy Incidentally (Shinko Forest (IRE))
2316[9] 3250[8] 4006[9] 4754[2] 5266[5] 5761[3] 7005[9] 7539[3] 8133[5] 8538[7] 8948[4] 9276[4] 9365[2]

**Ron's Ballad** *K Kukk* a21 49
4 ch g Sakhee's Secret Nom De La Rosa (IRE) (Oratorio (IRE))
1933a[6] 2669a[5] 3957a[2] 4142a[3] 4655a[5] 5200a[3] 5985a[6] 6544a[3]

**Ronya (IRE)** *Tracy Waggott* a43 66
6 b m Bushranger(IRE) Beenablaw (IRE) (Alzao (USA))
1679[2]

**Roof Garden** *Mark H Tompkins* a58 57
2 ch c Cityscape Celebrity (Pivotal)
6844[8] 7281[10] 7786[5] 8306[7]

**Roossey (IRE)** *D Selvaratnam* a83 93
5 b g Acclamation Tatiana Romanova (USA) (Mr Greeley (USA))
250a[5]

**Roryslittlesister (IRE)** *S M Duffy* a43 38
7 ch m Captain Rio Teacher Preacher (IRE) (Taufan (USA))
3544[7]

**Rosabelle** *Alan Bailey* a74 90
3 b f Mayson Kirk (Selkirk (USA))
2570[6] 3579[6] 4315[4] 5513[8] (7155) 7811[13] 8680[9] 9185[7]

**Rosa Damascena (FR)** *Alan King* a79 78
4 b m Kalanisi(IRE) Rosewater (GER) (Winged Love (IRE))
(1143) 2965[3] 4222[4]

**Rosa Imperial (IRE)** *A Fabre* 110
4 b m Pivotal Rose Trail (USA) (Kingmambo (USA))
(3614a) (4234a) 5690a[9]

**Rosamaria (IRE)** *Julie Camacho* 72
4 gr m Rip Van Winkle(IRE) Rosa Grace (Lomitas)
1879[8] 2138[6] 2900[4] 3560[7]

**Rosamunde (FR)** *Andreas Suborics* 91
3 b f Nayef(USA) Rosie Thomas (IRE) (Dylan Thomas (IRE))
[2] 4393a[10]

**Rosarno (IRE)** *Charles Hills* a64 83
3 b c Fastnet Rock(AUS) Jouet (Reprimand)
2690[10] 3505[4] 4535[6] 6701[P] 7277[5] (7957) 8510[2]

**Rosealee (IRE)** *Jeremy Gask* a83 82
4 gr m Zebedee Why Now (Dansili)
79[10] 573[6] 1091[2]◆ 1370[4] 1768[3] 3176[4] 3278[4] 4093[2] 4337[8]

**Roseau City** *David Elsworth* a65 58
2 ch f Cityscape Dominica (Alhaarth (IRE))
5365[6] 5885[5] 7153[8] 8325[12] 8793[5] 9024[6] (9230) 9322[2]

**Rose Berry** *Chris Dwyer* a86 85
3 b f Archipenko(USA) Desert Berry (Green Desert (USA))
1838[6] (2407) 3063[3] (3904)◆ 4889[4] 5355[7] 6759[5] 7287[3] 7811[6] 8418[5] 8645[5] 8879[2]

**Rosecomb (IRE)** *Frank Sheridan* a3 24
4 b m Rip Van Winkle(IRE) Malyana (Mtoto)
7342a[11]

**Rosedale Topping (IRE)**
*Ed Vaughan* 62
2 b f Zebedee Callmeakhab (IRE) (Intikhab (USA))
5655[5] 7093[4] 8112[10] 8467[15]

**Rose De Pierre (IRE)** *D K Weld* 105
4 b m Dubawi(IRE) Profound Beauty (IRE) (Danehill (USA))
(1568a) 2241a[2]

**Rose Eclair** *Tim Easterby* a75 77
4 b m Major Cadeaux Katie Boo (IRE) (Namid)
1828[4] 2124[7] 2631[4] 3524[6] 4305[5] 4607[3] 5134[6] 5542[2] 5738[7] 6046[3] 6271[6] 6903[5] (7249) 7474[7] 7573[8] 8216[7]

**Rose Marmara** *Brian Rothwell* a66 83
4 ch m Exceed And Excel(AUS) Show Rainbow (Haafhd)
2184[3]◆ 2683[6] 2856[8] 3401[9] 4574[2] 5134[4] 6237[7] 6759[3]

**Rosemay (FR)** *Iain Jardine* a69 69
3 b f Mayson Maine Rose (Red Ransom (USA))
1003[7] 1348[3]◆ 1680[8] 2274[7] 3243[4] 4172[2] 4603[3] 5648[8] 5997[5] 6594[2] 6892[3] 7598[3] 8103[5]

**Rosenborg Rider (IRE)**
*Adrian McGuinness* a69 69
4 b g Kodiac Miss Sundance (IRE) (Desert Sun)
5518a[11] 5998a[4] 6798a[4] 9052[7]

**Rosenpurpur (GER)** *P Schiergen* 110
3 b g Pour Moi(IRE) Rosenreihe (IRE) (Catcher In The Rye (IRE))
4422a[3]

**Rosental** *Luca Cumani* a97 108
5 b m Pivotal Rose Trail (USA) (Kingmambo (USA))
2946a[4] 5381[5] 6074[3] 6972a[5] (7753a) 8755a[4]

**Rose Of Shiraz** *J S Moore* a36 47
2 b f Mazameer(IRE) Redeemed (Red Ransom (USA))
7126[10] 7688[5] 8253a[5] 8943[4] 9230[11]

**Roses In June (IRE)** *J S Moore* a42 47
2 ch f Society Rock(IRE) Majestic South (Bertolini (USA))
2904[7] 3467[6] 3791[11] 3918[2] 4620[4] 5293[3] 6063[8] 6790[4] 7081[15] 7996[6] 8306[9]

**Rose Tinted Spirit** *Ralph Beckett* a67 49
2 b c Swiss Spirit Woolfall Rose (Generous (IRE))
8388[11] 8701[5] 9372[3]

**Rosie Briar** *Andrew Balding* 94
3 ch f Mayson Lighted Way (Kris)
2289[10] 3539[3] 7396[15] 7806[9]

**Rosie Crowe (IRE)** *Shaun Harris* a53 55
5 b m Approve(IRE) Tolzey (USA) (Rahy (USA))
761[3] 1325[5] 2976[2] 3832[4] 4561[3] 5214[11] 5512[6] 6296[10] 7605[8] 9141[14]

**Rosie Hall (IRE)** *John Wainwright*
7 ch m Lion Heart(USA) Baltic Dip (IRE) (Benny The Dip (USA))
8719[11]

**Rosie Lea (FR)** *Stuart Kittow* a35
4 b m Manduro(GER) Saralea (FR) (Sillery (USA))
8151[10] 8822[6] 9159[8]

**Rosie Royale (IRE)** *Roger Teal* a58 76
5 gr m Verglas(IRE) Fearn Royal (IRE) (Ali-Royal (IRE))
2357[3] 2723[2] 3684[3]

**Rosina** *Ann Duffield* a92 86
4 b m Showcasing Mondovi (Kyllachy)
3183[9] 4867[12] (5920) 6593[10] 8660[8] 8913[8] (9234)

**Ross (IRE)** *P Schiergen* a112 92
5 b h Acclamation Ronja (USA) (El Corredor (USA))
432a[5] 772a[2] 1043a[2] 1373a[2] (5628a) 9274a[10]

**Rossall** *Michael Dods* 75
2 b c Mayson Medina (IRE) (Pennekamp (USA))
4599[5] 5202[3] 5665[2] 6547[4] 7326[5]

**Ross Castle (IRE)**
*Matthieu Palussiere* a88 92
4 b g Bushranger(IRE) Bulrushes (Byron)
5979a[8]

**Rossetti** *Neil Mulholland* a48 48
9 gr g Dansili Snowdrops (Gulch (USA))
7096[9]

**Ross Raith Rover** *Robert Eddery* a70 72
4 b g Oasis Dream Baqah (IRE) (Bahhare (USA))
(139) 570[7] 1610[3] 2070[3] (2731) 3730[6] 4446[3] 5610[3] 5664[8] 9243[2]

**Rostam (IRE)** *Daniel J Murphy* a57
3 ch c Helmet(AUS) Mythologie (FR) (Bering)
8710a[12]

**Rostam (USA)** *A Wohler* 93
3 bb c Hat Trick(JPN) Summer Cruise (USA) (Vicar (USA))
2246a[5] 2869a[9]

**Rostropovich (IRE)** *A P O'Brien* 106
2 b c Frankel Tyranny (Machiavellian (USA))
(6240a) 6975a[3]

**Rosvana (FR)** *A De Royer-Dupre* 100
4 b m Dansili Rosanara (FR) (Sinndar (IRE))
6665a[8]

**Rosy Ryan (IRE)** *Tina Jackson* a59 72
7 b m Tagula(IRE) Khaydariya (IRE) (Akarad (FR))
3912[2] 4298[2]◆ (5007) (5497) 6047[12] (6564) 8216[14]

**Rothenburg (USA)** *H Al Alawi* a93
3 br c Street Cry(IRE) Rcuandry (USA) (A.P. Indy (USA))
(8710a)

**Rotherhithe** *Robyn Brisland* a72 72
2 b f Finjaan Reeling N' Rocking (IRE) (Mr Greeley (USA))
6433[2]◆ 7707[2] 8179[2]◆

**Rotherwick (IRE)** *Paul Cole* a87 94
5 ch g Starspangledbanner(AUS) Pivotalia (IRE) (Pivotal)
2505[4] (3249) 3905[2] (4763) 5643[6] 6698[3]◆ 7284[2] 7582[8] 8165[10]

**Roubles (USA)** *Julie Camacho* a45 55
3 b f Speightstown(USA) Soviet Song (IRE) (Marju (IRE))
2121[5] 4793[8] 7365[6] 8494[8] 9374[6]

**Rouge Nuage (IRE)** *Conrad Allen* a82 72
7 ch g Indian Haven Nom Francais (First Trump)
4451[4] 5245[9] 6111[4] (6637) 7321[2] 7789[7] 8706[9] 8907[10] (9220)

**Rougeoyant (FR)** *Gerard Martin* a72 70
4 b g Air Chief Marshal(IRE) Red Vixen (IRE) (Agnes World (USA))
6302a[6]

**Roulette** *Michael Bell* 87
2 ch f Poet's Voice Unex Mona Lisa (Shamardal (USA))
4902[6] (5573) 7578[10]

**Roundabout Kitten (USA)**
*David Lanigan* a59
2 ch g Kitten's Joy(USA) Shining Jewel (USA) (Gulch (USA))
9155[6] 9417[4]

**Roundabout Magic (IRE)**
*Simon Dow* a69 67
3 ch c Zebedee Cayo Largo (IRE) (Captain Rio)
324[9] 379[3] 623[4] (898) (1088) 1786[4] 2235[9] 6478[4]◆ 7509[4] 7767[5] 8816[8] 9189[2] (9389)

**Roundabout Time (IRE)**
*Ann Duffield* a20 33
4 gr g Zebedee Brosna Time (IRE) (Danetime (IRE))
580[11]

**Roundhay Park** *Nigel Tinkler* 79
2 ch g Mayson Brave Mave (Daylami (IRE))
4205[8] 4599[2] (4996)◆ 6466[3] (7194)◆ 8008[10]

**Roundhead** *Richard Hannon* 65
2 ch c Helmet(AUS) Blue Mistral (IRE) (Spinning World (USA))
6916[7] 7740[5]

**Round The Island** *Richard Whitaker* a65 72
4 b g Royal Applause Luanshya (First Trump)
3401[2]◆ (3666) 3946[3] 4616[12] 6663[5] 7245[7] 7572[9] 8427[10] 8907[4]

**Round Two (IRE)** *J S Bolger* 101
4 b h Teofilo(IRE) Khazina (USA) (Kingmambo (USA))
1568a[5]

**Rousayan (IRE)** *David O'Meara* a86 97
6 b g Invincible Spirit(IRE) Rose Quartz (Lammtarra (USA))
2155[4] 2406[5] 2701[8] 4207[9] 5165[3] 5668[6] 6209[3] (6464) (6672) 7886[2]

**Roussel (IRE)** *Charlie Appleby* 100
2 b c Kodiac Sodashy (IRE) (Noverre (USA))
(3169) 3929[2] 4582[2] 5424[2]

**Rowlestone Lass** *Richard Price* a81 79
7 b m Hernando(FR) Charmante Femme (Bin Ajwaad (IRE))
381[8] 789[P] (1175) 1405[5] 2061[7] 2270[4] 3067[2]

**Rowlestonerendezvu** *Tony Carroll* a59 61
4 b m Rail Link Charmante Femme (Bin Ajwaad (IRE))
4187[5] (4967) 5607[2] 6307[6] 6811[6] 7711[4] 8327[13] 9056[7] 9221[5]

**Rownak (IRE)** *Brian Ellison* 51
4 ch g Rip Van Winkle(IRE) Apache Dream (IRE) (Indian Ridge (IRE))
5003[8]

**Royal Acclaim (IRE)**
*Rebecca Bastiman* a29 56
5 b g Acclamation Top Row (Observatory (USA))
124[10] 360[10]

**Royal Albert Hall** *Kristin Mulhall* a103 94
5 b g Royal Applause Victoria Sponge (IRE) (Marju (IRE))
934a[12] 6252a[6]

**Royal Artillery (USA)** *John Gosden* 117
4 bb h War Front(USA) Masseuse (USA) (Dynaformer (USA))
2127[4] 2553[6]

**Royal Associate** *Charlie Appleby* 99
3 b g Cape Cross(IRE) Queen Consort (USA) (Kingmambo (USA))
(4569) (5397)◆ 5982a[7] 7565[5]

**Royal Battalion** *Gary Moore* a61 43
6 b g Sea The Stars(IRE) Yummy Mummy (Montjeu (IRE))
7730[5]

**Royal Birth** *Stuart Williams* a109 77
6 b g Exceed And Excel(AUS) Princess Georgina (Royal Applause)
200[7] 842[3] (917) 1772[9] 2397[13] 3967[2] 4881[14] 6025[5] 6685[6] 8845[8] 9187[2]◆

**Royal Blessing** *Peter Fahey* a57 56
5 b g Royal Applause Zuleika Dobson (Cadeaux Genereux)
(334) 690[7]

**Royal Brave (IRE)**
*Rebecca Bastiman* a78 93
6 b g Acclamation Daqtora (Dr Devious (IRE))
995[4] 1475[7] (1805) (2341) (2951) 3337[3] 4686[4] 5204[3] (5256) 5637[4] 6185[4] 6593[2] 7625[7] 8012[6] 8293[6]

**Royal Caper** *Miss Joey Ellis* a56 56
7 b g Royal Applause Ukraine (IRE) (Cape Cross (IRE))
2961[3] 3823[14] 6814[4] 7606[10] 8133[6]

**Royal Celebration** *Bryan Smart* a59 52
3 b g Excelebration(IRE) Auntie Kathryn (IRE) (Acclamation)
41[4] (179) 511[3] 787[3] 2372[6]

**Royal Connoisseur (IRE)**
*Richard Fahey* a75 86
6 b g Art Connoisseur(IRE) Valferno (IRE) (Val Royal (FR))
1512[7] 1910[8] 2684[4] 3452[5] 4343[12] 5132[5] 5457[7] 5646[2] 6894[3] 7628[4] 8486[5]

**Royal Cosmic** *Richard Fahey* a57 64
3 b f Wootton Bassett Cosmic Case (Casteddu)
3243[3] 3901[5] 4436[6] 4962[7] 7479[2] (7885) (8103) 8515[3]

**Royal Crown (IRE)** *David O'Meara* a16 59
2 b f Kodiac Lear's Crown (USA) (Lear Fan (USA))
2105[3] 2545[6] 3328[6] 7159[13] 8793[11]

**Royal Diplomat (IRE)**
*Richard Fahey* a85 79
2 b c Zebedee Pretty Priceless (IRE) (Pearl Of Love (IRE))
5162[5] 5596[9] (6525)◆ 6950[7] 7564[7]

**Royal Dolois (FR)** *J-M Lefebvre* a86 104
5 gr h Silver Frost(IRE) Mixture (Linamix (FR))
7177a[5]

**Royal Duchess** *Lucy Normile* 77
7 b m Dutch Art Royal Citadel (IRE) (City On A Hill (USA))
2500[6] 3652[5] 4039[4] 4663[3] 5922[4] 7981[7]

**Royal Etiquette (IRE)** *Lawney Hill* a37 50
10 b g Royal Applause Alpine Gold (IRE) (Montjeu (IRE))
4181[4] 5968[9]

**Royal Flag** *Brian Ellison* a72 76
7 b g New Approach(IRE) Gonbarda (GER) (Lando (GER))
196[4] (399) 990[2] (1519) 2386[6] 3580[5] 4338[3] 5138[3] 5689a[7] 6090[3]

**Royal Flute** *Mark Walford* a51 8
3 b f Piccolo Princess Almora (Pivotal)
1471[9] 1830[10] 7235[13]

**Royal Goldie (IRE)** *Mick Channon* 68
2 b f Havana Gold(IRE) Dream Maker (IRE) (Bahamian Bounty)
7733[6]◆ 8180[3]

**Royal Hall (FR)** *Gary Moore* a60 12
5 b g Halling(USA) Royal Fantasy (IRE) (King's Best (USA))
5141[6] 5428[9] 5746[5] 6557[9] 7483[7]

**Royal Headley (IRE)** *David O'Meara* a62 64
3 b g Nathaniel(IRE) Fearless Flyer (IRE) (Brave Act)
1676[4] 2143[4] 6760[4] 7248[10] 7832[8]

**Royal History** *A Al Shamsi* a15
6 b g New Approach(IRE) Tessa Reef (IRE) (Mark Of Esteem (IRE))
8711a[13]

**Royal Holiday (IRE)** *Marjorie Fife* a68 42
10 ch g Captain Rio Sunny Slope (Mujtahid (USA))
419[2] 1210[3] 3402[13] 5002[11] 5698[9] 6529[10] 7478[6] 7979[8] 9076[13]

**Royal Household** *Richard Hannon* 77
2 b g Camacho Dusting (IRE) (Acclamation)
3093[2] (3776) 4919[4] 5572[8] 6375[4] 7335[2] 8074[5] 8420[6]

**Royalickly (FR)** *S Gouvaze* a77 102
3 bb c Slickly Royal(FR) Belle Americaine (FR) (American Post)
4654a[5] 8444a[2]

**Royal Icon** *Kevin Ryan* a63 65
3 b f Sixties Icon Gillstown Great (Royal Applause)
1680[3] 3189[6] 4432[7] 5206[9] 5897[10] 6435[9] 7220[2] 7885[5] 8204[7]

**Royalistic (IRE)** *John Gosden* a71
3 ch g New Approach(IRE) Do The Honours (IRE) (Highest Honor (FR))
681[3] 1226[0] (Dead)

**Royal Julius (IRE)** *J Reynier* a86 107
4 b h Royal Applause Hflah (IRE) (Dubawi (IRE))
(4653a) 6729a[8] 7640a[6] 8448a[2] 9003a[13]

**Royal Liberty** *Mark Johnston* a59 72
2 b c Acclamation Anadolu (IRE) (Statue Of Liberty (USA))
3328[4] (3655) 4074[4] 4758[7] 6932[6] 7814[25] 8467[10]

**Royal Line** *John Gosden* 103
3 ch c Dubawi(IRE) Melikah (IRE) (Lammtarra (USA))
(6765) (7615) 8391[3] 8740[7]

**Royal Marskell** *Gay Kelleway* a94 67
8 b g Multiplex Socialise (Groom Dancer (USA))
197[4] 389[5] 683[RR] 1027[3] (1361) 2085[8] 2562[10] 4355[9] 9204[9] 9341[RR]

**Royal Melody** *Heather Main* a62 59
3 b f Royal Applause Wannabe Free (Red Ransom (USA))
2726[4] 3695[8] 4162[5] 5050[8] (5935) 6342[2] 7463[3] 8498[10]

**Royal Mezyan (IRE)** *Henry Spiller* a84 85
6 b g Royal Applause Rice Mother (IRE) (Indian Ridge (IRE))
2835[7] 3834[2] 4489[6] 6411[6] 7538[3] 8167[12] 8260[7]

**Royal Normandy** *Grace Harris* a50 68
5 b g Royal Applause Border Minstral (IRE) (Sri Pekan (USA))
273[4] 398[11] 640[9] 854[12] 2724[9] 3084[7] 3774[10] 4148[7] 5252[3] 6004[7] 6345[13] 6507[8] 7694[7]

**Royal Opera House (IRE)**
*Jamie Osborne* a84
3 b c Royal Applause Jackie's Opera (FR) (Indian Ridge (IRE))
1124[10]

**Royal Parks** *James Tate* a80 82
2 b f Bated Breath Kensington Gardens (Oasis Dream)
3697[5] (4528) 5329[8] 6064[3]

**Royal Peace (IRE)** *Richard Hannon* a65 65
3 b f Royal Applause Trianon (Nayef (USA))
1448[2] 1889[6] 3173[4] 3536[4] 4150[3] 4714[7] 5239[9]

**Royal Prize** *Mme M Bollack-Badel* a73 62
7 ch g Nayef(USA) Spot Prize (USA) (Seattle Dancer (USA))
7342a[5]

**Royal Prospect (IRE)**
*Julie Camacho* a77 70
2 b g Thewayyouare(USA) Jillian (USA) (Royal Academy (USA))
7953[6] 8474[4] (8916)

**Royal Pursuit (USA)** *Kevin Ryan* a68
2 br c Lonhro(AUS) Catch The Queen (USA) (Miswaki (USA))
6897[5] 9404[7]

**Royal Regent** *Lucy Normile* a33 89
5 b g Urgent Request(IRE) Royal Citadel (IRE) (City On A Hill (USA))
2497[2] 2953[3] (3651) 4035[3] 4658[3] 5207[3] 5996[2] 7702[3]◆ 8048[6]

**Royal Request (IRE)** *James Tate* a71
3 b f Royal Applause Garbah (IRE) (Kodiac)
1192[2] 1349[4]

**Royal Reserve** *David O'Meara* a89 83
4 b g Duke Of Marmalade(IRE) Lady Hawkfield (IRE) (Hawk Wing (USA))
1422[11] 1969[10] 2133[15] 3036[10] (4730)◆ 5002[2]◆ 5417[3]◆ 5706[5] 6188[2] 6467[2] (6819) 7949[8] 8638[2] 8892[3]◆ 9096[9] (9434)

**Royal Residence** *James Tate* a75 64
2 b c Epaulette(AUS) Jubilant Queen (Kyllachy)
7351[6] 8189[2] 9311[4]

**Royal Rettie** *Paddy Butler* a52 51
5 b m Royal Applause Bended Knee (Refuse To Bend (IRE))
735[8] 1285[7] 1557[8] 8985[12] 9232[10]

**Royal Sentiment (IRE)** *Mark Usher* a49 31
3 b g So You Think(NZ) Rose Parade (Machiavellian (USA))
2679[12] 3087[11] 3327[11]

**Royal Shaheen (FR)**
*Alistair Whillans* 88
4 b g Myboycharlie(IRE) Viola Royale (IRE) (Royal Academy (USA))
2952[3]◆ 3651[5]◆ 4085[6] 4661[3] (4960) 5469[6] 5996[3] 6416[3] 6944[5] (7328) 7555[4] 8289[7] 8652[7]

**Royal Sunday (FR)** *Alan King* 68
3 gr g Never On Sunday(FR) Royale Malaisie (FR) (Villez (USA))
2783[16] 3426[6]

**Royal Symphony (AUS)**
*Tony McEvoy* 107
2 bb c Domesday(AUS) Naturalist (AUS) (Palace Music (USA))
8446a[4]

**Royal Wave** *William Knight* a40 29
2 b f Royal Applause Air Biscuit (IRE) (Galileo (IRE))
3815[10] 5528[14] 6100[9] 8793[8] 9436[5]

**Royal Youmzain (FR)** *A Wohler* 105
2 b c Youmzain(IRE) Spasha (Shamardal (USA))
6985a[2] (8276a)

**Royboy** *Bryan Smart* a42 9
4 b g Equiano(FR) Pretty Bonnie (Kyllachy)
5542[12]

**Roy H (USA)** *Peter Miller* a128
5 b g More Than Ready(USA) Elusive Diva (USA) (Elusive Quality (USA))
(8607a)

**Roy Rocket (FR)** *John Berry* a53 79
7 gr g Layman(USA) Minnie's Mystery (FR) (Highest Honor (FR))
(2055) 2913[5] 3658[5] 4257[10] 5299[5] 5555[3] 5868[5] 6513[5] 7744[7] 8394[6]

**Roys Dream** *Paul Collins* a69 73
3 b f Monsieur Bond(IRE) Velvet Jaguar (Hurricane Run (IRE))
2925[5] 3239[3] 3897[2] 5182[10] 6313[4] 7332[5] 8243[4] 8552[9]

**Roy's Legacy** *Shaun Harris* a70 71
8 b h Phoenix Reach(IRE) Chocolada (Namid)
271[3] 327[3] 523[5] 1022[4] 1340[2] (1435) (1759) 1965[2] 2263[2] (2360) 2858[4] 3453[4] 4005[9] 4664[3] 5055[7] 5580[6] 6040[7] 6531[11] 7407[5] 7926[14] 9075[6] (9214) 9265[7] 9348[7]

**Roystonia (IRE)** *Hugo Palmer* 56
2 b f Redoute's Choice(AUS) Waterlilly (IRE) (Galileo (IRE))
8380[13]

**Rozanne (IRE)** *P Monfort* a73 74
2 b f Canford Cliffs(IRE) Spinning Lucy (IRE) (Spinning World (USA))
5660[7] 6584[7] 7334[4] 7731[3] 9087a[2]

**Rozy Boys** *David Barron* a86 62
3 b g Kyllachy Responsive (Dutch Art)
5602[11] 6450[13]

**Rua Augusta (USA)** *Kevin Ryan* a78 78
2 b c Arch(USA) Wend (USA) (Pulpit (USA))
5876[2]◆ 6616[3] 7987[2]

**Rubens Dream** *Charles Hills* 78
3 ch c Dutch Art Apace (IRE) (Oasis Dream)
2135[8] (3493) 4153[5] 6143[9] 8596[12]

**Rubensian** *David Simcock* a86 78
4 ch g Medicean Hymnsheet (Pivotal)
2913[4] 3658[4] 5798[5] 6294[6] 6819[7]

**Rubheira** *Neil Mulholland* a14
5 ch m Arkadian Hero(USA) Devon Ruby (Zilzal (USA))
602[12] 815[10] 961[8] 1237[6] 7760[12] 8800[9] 9128[10]

**Rubis** *Richard Fahey* a63 67
4 ch m Monsieur Bond(IRE) Princess Cocoa (IRE) (Desert Sun)
3053[3] (3650) 4018[6] 4959[3] 5498[7] 7219[2] (7699) 8327[5] 8886[8]

**Ruby Flash (FR)** *A Lamotte D'Argy* a27 40
2 b c Sri Putra Miryea (FR) (Shining Steel)
5952a[13] 7470a[8]

**Ruby Gates (IRE)**
*Joseph Patrick O'Brien* a71 71
4 b m Avonbridge Wild Academy (IRE) (Royal Academy (USA))
5088a[7]

**Ruby Looker** *J R Jenkins* a7
6 b g Bertolini(USA) Ellcon (IRE) (Royal Applause)
22[14]

**Ruby Notion (USA)** *Wesley A Ward* a81 93
4 b m Great Notion(USA) Modena Bay (NZ) (Volksraad)
1813a[3]

**Ruby's Gem** *Philip McBride* a65 65
2 b f Havana Gold(IRE) News Desk (Cape Cross (IRE))
4363[7] 5114[4] 6140[5] 6824[12] 8491[6]

**Ruby Sound** *Steph Hollinshead* a40
2 b f Assertive Vermilion Creek (Makbul)
5047[9] 5893[7] 7410[6]

**Ruby Taylor** *Nick Lampard*
5 b m Passing Glance Bold Rose (Bold Edge)
2963[12] 3770[9]

**Ruby Wednesday** *John Best* a71 65
4 b m Mullionmileanhour(IRE) Cheap N Chic (Primo Valentino (IRE))
355[5] (549) 1620[6]

**Rude Awakening**
*Sir Mark Prescott Bt* a66 45
2 b g Rip Van Winkle(IRE) First Exhibit (Machiavellian (USA))
4007[5] 4560[8] 5047[6]

**Rue Cambon (IRE)**
*George Peckham* a18 38
2 ch f Exceed And Excel(AUS) Exciting Times (FR) (Jeune Homme (USA))
2904[8] 4160[9] 4599[7] 6285[10] 7996[11]

**Rue De Lille (FR)** *I Endaltsev* a47 15
2 b f Zanzibari(USA) Villa Molitor (FR) (Muhtathir)
4595a[5] 6251a[12]

**Rueing (USA)** *A Fabre* a83 93
3 ch f Street Cry(IRE) Wavering (IRE) (Refuse To Bend (IRE))
7341a[5]

**Ruffina (USA)** *John Gosden* a68
2 b f Street Cry(IRE) Rubina (IRE) (Invincible Spirit (IRE))
7995[9] 8668[2] 9099[3]

**Rufus King** *Mark Johnston* a74 102
2 ch g Iffraaj Mosqueras Romance (Rock Of Gibraltar (IRE))
2786[4] (3051) 3556[2]◆ 4020a[4] (4827) 5596[7] 6353[10] 6745a[5] 7596[6] (8039)

**Ruled By The Moon** *Ivan Furtado* a41 61
3 b g Mawatheeq(USA) Hallingdal (UAE) (Halling (USA))
2135[7] 2383[8] 3393[7] 8541[7]

**Rule Of Honour** *Ismail Mohammed* 79
2 ch c New Approach(IRE) Our Queen Of Kings (Arazi (USA))
7250[2]◆

**Ruler Of Course (IRE)**
*Niels Petersen* 101
4 b g Roderic O'Connor(IRE) Scarpe Rosse (IRE) (Sadler's Wells (USA))
6501a[7]

**Ruler Of The Nile** *Robert Stephens* a77 49
5 b g Exceed And Excel(AUS) Dinka Raja (USA) (Woodman (USA))
1223[4] 1561[2] 3685[8] 5896[6] 8771[4] 9082[4] 9242[4] 9442[2]

**R U Mine (IRE)** *Keith Dalgleish* a45
3 b f Elzaam(AUS) Imco Career (FR) (Barathea (IRE))
1003[8] 1102[5] 1198[6]

**Rumpole** *Hughie Morrison* a85 85
3 b g Lawman(FR) Complexion (Hurricane Run (IRE))
1961[4] (2475) 3317[7] 4153[2] 5568[11] 6387[3] 7358[4] 7949[5]

**Rum Ration** *Mark H Tompkins* a25
2 b g Mount Nelson Myriades D'Etoiles (IRE) (Green Tune (USA))
4725[11] 5292[14]

**Rum Runner** *Richard Hannon* 84
2 b c Havana Gold(IRE) Thermopylae (Tenby)
4805[11] 6133[4] (6653) 7050[7]

**Rumshak (IRE)** *Michael Dods* 81
2 ch g Arcano(IRE) Scarlet Rosefinch (Cockney Rebel (IRE))
3789[4] (4606) 5370[2] 5879[2] 6466[7] 7821[23]

**Rum Swizzle** *Harry Dunlop* a74 77
5 b m Mawatheeq(USA) Port Providence (Red Ransom (USA))
1630[3] (2028)◆ 2358[2] 4089[4] 4804[9] 7278[7] 8000[5] 8549[12] 9054[12]

**Runaiocht (IRE)** *Paul Burgoyne* a66 43
7 ch g Teofilo(IRE) Julie Girl (USA) (Jules (USA))
238[5] 351[3] 549[4] (690) 922[6] 1284[8] 1620[5] 2615[11] 2785[6] 3208[8] 3718[6] 8503[6] 8993[7] 9212[7] 9456[9]

**Run For Eva** *Olly Williams*
4 b m Westerner Glorybe (GER) (Monsun (GER))
8979[8]

**Running Cloud (IRE)**
*Eve Johnson Houghton* a82 76
2 b g Cacique(IRE) Nimbus Star (Nayef (USA))
(3467)◆ 4220[5] 4973[3] 7353[5]

**Runthatbymeagain (IRE)**
*David Evans* 40
2 bz f Sir Prancealot(IRE) Romanylei (IRE) (Blues Traveller (IRE))
1908[7] 3421[11] 3918[5]

**Run To The Hills (USA)**
*George Peckham* a88 88
4 b g Quality Road(USA) Masada (USA) (Pleasant Tap (USA))
2838[14] 6322[7] 6882[4]

**Run With Pride (IRE)** *Derek Shaw* a71 70
7 b g Invincible Spirit(IRE) Zibilene (Rainbow Quest (USA))
5318[9] (7951) 9297[7] 9414[2]

**Runyon Rattler (IRE)** *P J Rothwell* a48 54
7 b g Runyon(IRE) Lake Majestic (IRE) (Mister Majestic)
5689a[5]

**Rupert Boy (IRE)** *Scott Dixon* a50 21
4 ch g Frozen Power(IRE) Curious Lashes (IRE) (Footstepsinthesand)
1075[3] 1187[5] 1587[5] 6092[14] 8261[10]

**Rupertcambellblack (IRE)**
*Ronald Harris*
3 b g Canford Cliffs(IRE) Negotiate (Red Ransom (USA))
378[7]

**Rupert's Lass** *Michael Bell* 63
2 b f Myboycharlie(IRE) Elusive Flash (USA) (Freud (USA))
5717[10] 7334[7] 7913[5]

**Rural Celebration** *Kevin Ryan* a91 97
6 b m Pastoral Pursuits Queens Jubilee (Cayman Kai (IRE))
2623[9] 4078[2] 4686[9] (5602)

**Rushing Fall (USA)** *Chad C Brown* 110
2 b f More Than Ready(USA) Autumnal (USA) (Forestry (USA))
(8575a)

**Rusper (IRE)** *Jamie Osborne* a85
2 b g Holy Roman Emperor(IRE) Sweet Dreams Baby (IRE) (Montjeu (IRE))
7411[4] (8839) (9200)

**Russian Miner (USA)** *Doug Watson* a64
3 b g Discreetly Mine(USA) Barton Springs (USA) (Fusaichi Pegasus (USA))
8710a[5]

**Russian Radiance**
*Jonathan Portman* a89 71
5 ch m Paco Boy(IRE) Russian Ruby (FR) (Vettori (IRE))
61[7] 142[2] 285[4]

**Russian Ranger (IRE)**
*Jonathan Portman* a61 64
4 b g Bushranger(IRE) Pink Sovietstaia (FR) (Soviet Star (USA))
2276[4] 2996[9] 4165[9] 5296[4] 5898[5] 7210[11] 8031[8]

**Russian Realm** *Paul Midgley* a83 99
7 b g Dansili Russian Rhythm (USA) (Kingmambo (USA))
1799[10] 2142[6] 2384[5] 3199[10] 3581[2] 4327a[10] 4719[7] 5457[4] (5929) 6877[5] 7612[9]

**Russian Regard (IRE)**
*Jonathan Portman* a63 54
3 ch g Intense Focus(USA) Russian Rave (Danehill Dancer (IRE))
2371[4] 3087[9] 3819[8] 4971[7] 6032[6] 6473[7]

**Russian Reward (IRE)**
*Amanda Perrett* a79 82
5 b g Iffraaj Forever Times (So Factual (USA))
516[9] 769[6] (998) 1144[2] 1462[6] 2055[2] 2333[5] 4041[3] (4699)

**Russian Royale** *Micky Hammond* a55 79
7 b m Royal Applause Russian Ruby (FR) (Vettori (IRE))
1716[11] 2079[6] 3155[11] 5017[5] 6565[6] 6895[RR]

**Russian Soul (IRE)** *M Halford* a94 91
9 b g Invincible Spirit(IRE) Russian Hill (Indian Ridge (IRE))
598[2] 730[4] 957[6] 1152[4] (2528) 3030[6] 4524[4] 5241[7] 6141[10] 9247a[5]

**Rustang (FR)** *Richard Hughes* a71 62
2 b g Holy Roman Emperor(IRE) Oppamattox (FR) (Munir)
4973[5] 5641[8] 6133[10] 6762[4] 7510[4] (8371) 8537[2]

**Rustique** *Ed Walker* a64 68
5 ch m Pastoral Pursuits Nihal (IRE) (Singspiel (IRE))
812[8] 996[5] 1334[10] 2318[4] 2731[2] 3731[2] 4459[4]

**Rusty Blade (IRE)**
*Daniel Mark Loughnane* a18 49
2 ch g Zebedee Flashing Blade (Inchinor)
2556[7] 3277[6] 9404[9]

**Rusumaat (IRE)** *Mark Johnston* a94 111
3 b g Arcano(IRE) Queen Wasp (IRE) (Shamardal (USA))
1801[7] 2115[2] 2565[2] (3077) 3997[19] 4636[7]◆ (5147) 6401[16] 6928[7]

**Rutherford (IRE)** *Kevin Ryan* a69 85
3 ch f Dutch Art Carraigoona (IRE) (Rock Of Gibraltar (IRE))
845[2] (1102) 3167[4] 4610[3] (5399) 6382[2] 6787[4] 7822[8]

**Ruth Melody (IRE)** *Lee Smyth* a64 64
5 b m Intikhab(USA) Mermaid Melody (Machiavellian (USA))
3706[3]◆ 4962[10]

**Ruwasi** *Gary Moore* a38 97
6 b g Authorized(IRE) Circle Of Love (Sakhee (USA))
2085[9]

**Ruxleys Star (USA)** *Richard Hannon* 63
3 b f Artie Schiller(USA) Ladue (USA) (Demons Begone (USA))
1947[8]

**Rux Ruxx (IRE)** *Andrew Balding* a64 50
2 b f Dark Angel(IRE) Lady Duxyana (Most Welcome)
8474[7] 8889[7]

**Ruysch (IRE)** *Ed Dunlop* 74
2 b f Dutch Art Convention (Encosta De Lago (AUS))
4340[4] 5114[3] 5660[6] 6552[5]◆ 7265[5] (8164)

**Ruzeiz (USA)** *Peter Hedger* a59 37
8 b g Muhtathir Saraama (USA) (Bahri (USA))
39[3] 290[7] 3251[7]

**Ryan The Giant** *Keith Dalgleish* a55 58
4 b g Fastnet Rock(AUS) Comeraincomeshine (IRE) (Night Shift (USA))
121[12] 436[2] (610) 990[3] 1197[2] 1369[3]

**Rydan (IRE)** *Gary Moore* a98 91
6 ch g Intense Focus(USA) Lough Mewin (IRE) (Woodman (USA))
467[2] 921[3] 3534[2] 4828[5] 5663[4] 6135[7] 7903[3] 8511[5] 8672[5] 9204[2] 9434[2]

**Ryedale Encore** *Tim Easterby* 62
2 b f Canford Cliffs(IRE) Jackie's Opera (FR) (Indian Ridge (IRE))
4528[4] 5371[5] 5999[4] 6626[6] 7041[12]

**Ryedale Rio (IRE)** *Tim Easterby* a67 63
4 b g Captain Rio Hallucination (IRE) (Last Tycoon)
1071[5] 1328[5] 1720[9] 1869[6] 2628[6] 3185[5] 3831[8] 4453[10] 5167[9]

**Rythmique (IRE)** *J-C Rouget* a78 102
3 b f Casamento(IRE) Reclamation (IRE) (Red Ransom (USA))
2003a[3] 2945a[4] 4424a[9]

**Sa'ada (USA)** *George Peckham* a57 42
2 b f Bellamy Road(USA) Hey Seattle (USA) (Seattle Slew (USA))
6108[13] 6884[9]

**Saaheq** *Brian Meehan* a72 66
3 b g Invincible Spirit(IRE) Brevity (USA) (Street Cry (IRE))
1962[10]◆ 3234[4] 3691[4] 6203[3]

**Saayerr** *D Selvaratnam* a65 100
6 b g Acclamation Adorn (Kyllachy)
84a[6]◆ 318a[5] 651a[13]

**Sabador (FR)** *Ed Walker* a79 93
3 gr g Kendargent(FR) Sabadora (FR) (Anabaa (USA))
(1299) 2505[2]◆ (3199)◆ 3997[13]

**Sabato (IRE)** *Fergal O'Brien* a46 41
4 ch g Shamardal(USA) Mondalay (Monsun (GER))
2724[12] 3280[9] 3661[7] 4180[15]

**Sabawa (FR)** *R Rohne* a60 62
3 bb f Air Chief Marshal(IRE) Star Of Pompey (Hernando (FR))
4455a[8]

**Sabellum (IRE)** *Richard Fahey* 28
2 b f Iffraaj Startarette (USA) (Dixieland Band (USA))
5453[6] 6086[8] 6755[8]

**Sabha (IRE)** *K R Burke* a43 46
5 b m Thewayyouare(USA) Genipabu (IRE) (Danetime (IRE))
19[5]

**Sable Island (IRE)**
*Sir Michael Stoute* a79 83
3 b g New Approach(IRE) Ratukidul (FR) (Danehill (USA))
1874[2] 4450[4] 5368[3] 6107[3] (6413) 7231[3]

**Saborido (USA)** *Amanda Perrett* a84 26
11 gr g Dixie Union(USA) Alexine (ARG) (Runaway Groom (CAN))
280[5] 571[5]

**Sabree** *F-H Graffard* 67
3 ch g Kyllachy King's Doll (IRE) (King's Best (USA))
2697a[10]

**Sabre Squadron (IRE)** *Alan King* 82
4 b g Lope De Vega(IRE) Caravan Of Dreams (IRE) (Anabaa (USA))
6865[7]

**Sackeb** *Hugo Palmer* 50
2 b c Invincible Spirit(IRE) Qilaada (USA) (Bernardini (USA))
4709[9] 6142[9]

**Sacred Act** *Michael Bell* a106 103
6 b g Oasis Dream Stage Presence (IRE) (Selkirk (USA))
1492[9] 1860[3]◆ 6873[6] 8547[2]◆ 8843[2]

**Sacred Life (FR)** *S Wattel* 113
2 b c Siyouni(FR) Knyazhna (IRE) (Montjeu (IRE))
(7754a)

**Sacred Way** *Kevin Ryan* a70 69
3 b g Oasis Dream Heronetta (Halling (USA))
6268[2] 7542[4] 8117[3]

**Sacrifice My Soul (IRE)**
*Mme Pia Brandt* a86 97
5 b m Nayef(USA) Via Saleria (IRE) (Arazi (USA))
8548[11]

**Sadhbh (IRE)** *John Flint* a66
3 b f Lilbourne Lad(IRE) Stoney Cove (IRE) (Needwood Blade)
439[6] 9295[12]

**Sadieroseclifford (IRE)**
*Giles Bravery* a44 58
3 b f Poet's Voice Voltairine (Selkirk (USA))
2734[4] 3141[3] (3703) 4302[10] 4458[5] 5040[11] 5791[7] 6141[11]

**Sadler's Joy (USA)**
*Thomas Albertrani* 114
4 ch h Kitten's Joy(USA) Dynaire (USA) (Dynaformer (USA))
2641a[3] (6461a) 7633a[4] 8610a[4]

**Safarhi** *Alan King* a47 38
2 b g Farhh Swarm (IRE) (Hurricane Run (IRE))
7726[12] 8162[9] 8339[11]

**Safe Voyage (IRE)** *John Quinn* a90 93
4 b g Fast Company(IRE) Shishangaan (IRE) (Mujadil (USA))
(363) (441) 581[10] 989[2] 2772[4] (3388) 4264[4]

**Safe Waters** *Eve Johnson Houghton* 63
2 ch f Helmet(AUS) Golden Waters (Dubai Destination (USA))
2910[6] 3690[5] 4090[6]

**Saffah (USA)** *Charles Hills* a63
2 br f More Than Ready(USA) Elghayoor (USA) (Ghostzapper (USA))
7453[8] 7995[8]

**Safira Menina** *Martin Smith* a78 79
5 b m Paco Boy(IRE) Isla Azul (IRE) (Machiavellian (USA))
173[6] 856[3] 1289[2] 1684[2] 5113[3] 5556[4] 6513[4] 7744[9]

**Safrani (IRE)** *David O'Meara* 58
2 b g Lope De Vega(IRE) Wadjeka (USA) (Oasis Dream)
3648[4] 6403[15]

**Saga Sprint (IRE)** *J R Jenkins* a74 64
4 b m Excellent Art Queen Of Malta (IRE) (Exceed And Excel (AUS))
2333[7] 2710[7] 3439[3] 4279[3] 4545[4] 6153[8] 8122[11] 8346[6] 9077[7] 9278[6]

**Sagely (IRE)** *Ed Dunlop* a90 100
4 b m Frozen Power(IRE) Saga Celebre (FR) (Peintre Celebre (USA))
2605[7] 3558[4] 4002[3] 4915[3] 5745[7] 7401[9]

**Sageness (IRE)** *Ed Dunlop* 59
2 b f Most Improved(IRE) Saga Celebre (FR) (Peintre Celebre (USA))
7733[14] 8380[11]

**Saglawy (FR)** *N Clement* 101
3 b c Youmzain(IRE) Spasha (Shamardal (USA))
1114a[3] 1658a[5] 2448a[5]

**Sagres** *F-H Graffard* 84
2 b f Henrythenavigator(USA) Ascot Family (IRE) (Desert Style (IRE))
6051a[6] 7011a[8]

**Sahaafy (USA)** *M Al Mheiri* a94 57
5 br g Kitten's Joy(USA) Queen's Causeway (USA) (Giant's Causeway (USA))
653a[10] 772a[8]

**Sahalin** *John Flint* a53
4 b m Red Rocks(IRE) Tamathea (IRE) (Barathea (IRE))
9093[10]

**Saharan Star** *Patrick Chamings* a42 51
3 br f Winker Watson Saharan Royal (Val Royal (FR))
7514[11] 8116[4] 8635[7]

**Sahreej (IRE)** *Adrian Paul Keatley* a92 82
4 gr g Zebedee Petite Boulangere (IRE) (Namid)
1385a[11] 4327a[2] 5204[7] 5994[7] 6640a[8] 7425a[8]

**Saigon City** *Declan Carroll* a96 102
7 b g Mount Nelson Hoh Chi Min (Efisio)
1516[2] (2797) 5638[9] 6329[6]

**Sai Kung Star** *Nigel Tinkler* 33
3 ch f Harbour Watch(IRE) Warden Rose (Compton Place)
1914[10] 2903[9] 4055[11]

**Sailana (GER)** *Christina Bucher* 79
3 ch f Call Me Big(GER) Still Standing (FR) (Martillo (GER))
6605a[7]

**Sailing Home** *Michael Bell* 72
2 b f Shamardal(USA) Tidespring (IRE) (Monsun (GER))
7733[4] 8380[4]

**Sailor Malan** *Suzy Smith* a24 19
5 b g Mount Nelson Flying Hi (Kyllachy)
3192[9] 4165[12]

**Sailors Warn (IRE)** *Ian Williams* a61 61
10 b g Redback Coral Dawn (IRE) (Trempolino (USA))
3547[10] 8473[8]

**Sail With Sultana** *Mark Rimell* a43 56
6 ch m Black Sam Bellamy(IRE) Strathtay (Pivotal)
2363[6] 2928[5] 3464[8]

**Saimaa (IRE)** *H-F Devin* 99
4 b m Zoffany(IRE) Serisia (FR) (Exit To Nowhere (USA))
2946a[5]

**Saint Anthony** *Mark H Tompkins* a15 29
2 ch c Pastoral Pursuits Mega (IRE) (Petardia)
7280[10] 7788[12] 8642[14]

**Saint Contest (FR)** *Alan King* a80 64
4 b g Air Chief Marshal(IRE) Sainte Adresse (Elusive City (USA))
3308[11] 4413[7]

**Saint Cuthberts** *David Brown* 7
3 b g Shirocco(GER) Gladys' Gal (Tobougg (IRE))
3342[11]

**Sainted** *William Haggas* 104
4 ch m Dutch Art Blithe (Pivotal)
(4375) 5597[6] **(5828)**◆ 7611[12] 8738[10]

**Saint Equiano** *Keith Dalgleish* 87
3 b g Equiano(FR) St Athan (Authorized (IRE))
2775[5] 3388[8] **(4610)** 5213[2] 5669[4] 7044[9] 7656[8]

**Sainte Tempete (FR)**
*Heike Dorothea Altevogt* a37
4 b m Getaway(GER) Cool Storm (IRE) (Rainbow Quest (USA))
***798a***[9]

**Saint Ferdinand (IRE)** *P Favereaux* 77
3 b c Footstepsinthesand Alta Lena (FR) (Alzao (USA))
4783a[13] **6256a**[10]

**Saint Helena (IRE)** *Mark Gillard* a57 66
9 b m Holy Roman Emperor(IRE) Tafseer (IRE) (Grand Lodge (USA))
**2722**[4] 3282[6] 4041[6] 5782[2] 7210[5] 8183[9] *9092*[7]

**Saint Honore** *Pat Phelan* a74 72
5 b m Champs Elysees Gwyneth (Zafonic (USA))
***92***[6] ***861***[5]

**Saintmont (FR)** *Christian Williams*
3 b g Monitor Closely(IRE) Saintheze (FR) (Saint Des Saints (FR))
3426[9]

**Saint Nicolas (FR)** *C & Y Lerner* a67 68
2 gr c Dark Angel(IRE) Sierra Slew (Fantastic Light (USA))
1919a[9] **2881a**[6]

**Saint Pois (FR)** *J-P Sauvage* a72 79
6 b g Le Havre(IRE) Our Dream Queen (Oasis Dream)
**(6648a)**

**Saint Rhuys (FR)** *C Lotoux* a67
3 b g Fuisse(FR) La Bardane (FR) (Marignan (USA))
***6124a***[7]

**Saint Roch (FR)** *Mme Pia Brandt* a75 78
2 bl c Myboycharlie(IRE) Seelland (FR) (Linamix (FR))
6170a[4] ***8195a***[7]

**Saint Thomas (IRE)** *John Mackie* a59 64
10 b g Alhaarth(IRE) Aguilas Perla (IRE) (Indian Ridge (IRE))
***1630***[5]

**Saisons D'Or (IRE)** *Jedd O'Keeffe* a73 70
2 ro g Havana Gold(IRE) Deux Saisons (Chineur (FR))
5099[5] 6264[5] ***6897***[3] 8212[4]

**Sakhalin Star (IRE)** *Richard Guest* a61 71
6 ch g Footstepsinthesand Quela (GER) (Acatenango (GER))
*2312*[4] 2688[3] *3264*[2] 3708[8] *4263*[13] *4453*[6] 4660[3] (5250) 5499[6] *5831*[5] (6088) **6305**[2] 6592[5] 7220[7] 7478[F] 7885[4] 8515[15]

**Sakhee's Jem** *Gay Kelleway* a68 59
4 ch m Sakhee's Secret Amandian (IRE) (Indian Ridge (IRE))
2285[7] 2969[13] *3473*[10] 3702[10] 4543[3] **5340**[3] 6112[16] 6298[9] *7605*[3] 8329[11] *8675*[10]

**Sakhee's Return** *Tim Easterby* a75 90
5 b g Sakhee's Secret Sofia Royale (Royal Applause)
**2348**[3] 3565[9] 3792[10] 4103[5] 5059[4] 5669[11] (6570) 6894[4] *7321*[10] 7886[4]

**Sakhra** *Mark Brisbourne* a48 45
6 b g Nayef(USA) Noble Desert (FR) (Green Desert (USA))
*98*[5] ***241***[2]

**Sakurajima (IRE)** *Charles Hills* a47 68
3 ch g Helmet(AUS) Park Approach (IRE) (Indian Ridge (IRE))
1686[3] 2035[7] 3162[8] 4255[5] **4575**[4] 6293[9] 6812[9] *8160*[10]

**Salamah (IRE)** *Michael Bell* a83 64
3 b f Shamardal(USA) Spirit Of Dubai (IRE) (Cape Cross (IRE))
***2517***[2] 3964[24] 5324[5]

**Salateen** *David O'Meara* a109 111
5 ch h Dutch Art Amanda Carter (Tobougg (IRE))
87a[16] (653a) 892a[14] *(1150)* *1773*[3] 1902[4] 3842[3] 4890[5] **5662**[2] 6476[2] *9409*[6]

**Salazar (IRE)** *Kevin Ryan* 70
2 ch g Raven's Pass(USA) Queen Padme (IRE) (Halling (USA))
**(5918)** 8013[5]

**Saldier (FR)** *T Castanheira* a81 103
3 b c Soldier Hollow Salve Evita (Monsun (GER))
**1826a**[6] 2250a[6] 2483a[5]

**Saleh (IRE)** *Lee Carter* a80 57
4 b g Iffraaj Pellinore (USA) (Giant's Causeway (USA))
*(90)* *986*[3] *1085*[2] *(1301)* ***1462***[4] *3454*[5] *4746*[7] 5064[6] *6686*[6]

**Salient** *Michael Attwater* a44 42
13 b g Fasliyev(USA) Savannah Belle (Green Desert (USA))
*279*[9] ***555***[6] *820*[11]

**Salieri (FR)** *Alan King* a53 56
3 b g Paco Boy(IRE) Ticklestone (IRE) (Mark Of Esteem (IRE))
**3627**[9] 4255[11]

**Salire (IRE)** *Ann Duffield* a57 62
2 b f Intense Focus(USA) Gariepa (GER) (Black Sam Bellamy (IRE))
5702[11] **6938**[3] 7473[5] 8236[8] *8996*[5] *9175*[8] *9439*[8]

**Sallab (IRE)** *Richard Hannon* 86
2 b c Havana Gold(IRE) Waveband (Exceed And Excel (AUS))
3783[6] (4520) 5501[10] 6505[2] **7355**[3]

**Sallee** *Adrian Wintle* a42 32
3 b f Sakhee's Secret Rabshih (IRE) (Green Desert (USA))
*546*[5] ***987***[8] *1367*[10]

**Salmon Sushi** *Tim Easterby* a91 88
6 ch g Dalakhani(IRE) Salsa Steps (USA) (Giant's Causeway (USA))
3497[6] 4017[9] ***4358***[5] 4658[12]

**Salouen (IRE)** *Sylvester Kirk* 111
3 b c Canford Cliffs(IRE) Gali Gal (IRE) (Galileo (IRE))
1861[2] 3322[13] 4029[7] 4638[8] **6053a**[2] **7638a**[3]

**Salsabeel (IRE)** *Charlie Appleby* 104
3 b g Exceed And Excel(AUS) Tokyo Rose (UAE) (Jade Robbery (USA))
**1859**[2]◆ 2666a[12]

**Salsa Verde (IRE)** *Ed de Giles* 49
2 b g Canford Cliffs(IRE) Bridal Dance (IRE) (Danehill Dancer (IRE))
**4534**[7] 5151[8]

**Saltarin Dubai (ARG)** *M F De Kock* a114 72
4 ch g E Dubai(USA) Saltarina Fitz (ARG) (Fitzcarraldo (ARG))
***83a***[6] 542a[7] 699a[14]

**Salt Lake City (FR)** *Robert Collet* a90 91
2 b c Holy Roman Emperor(IRE) Fleur De Sel (Linamix (FR))
1919a[11] **5978a**[3] 7011a[6] *8195a*[5] 8884a[6]

**Saltonstall** *M Halford* 96
3 ch g Pivotal Macleya (GER) (Winged Love (IRE))
**1636a**[9]

**Salt Whistle Bay (IRE)** *Rae Guest* a60 86
3 b c Royal Applause Quantum (IRE) (Alhaarth (IRE))
*115*[4] *737*[5] 3700[9] 4626[4] (5411) (6143) 7229[3] **(7736)** **8566**[2]

**Salty Sugar** *Paul Cole* a55 49
2 b f Oasis Dream Shamandar (FR) (Exceed And Excel (AUS))
3070[7] 5371[11] *7724*[9] ***8500***[4] *8783*[14]

**Salute The Soldier (GER)**
*Clive Cox* a77 77
2 br c Sepoy(AUS) Street Fire (IRE) (Street Cry (IRE))
**8388**[3] ***8888***[2]

**Saluti (IRE)** *Amanda Perrett* a80 84
3 b g Acclamation Greek Easter (IRE) (Namid)
**(4269)** 4887[10] (5433) 5842[7] *6576*[8]

**Salvadori (IRE)** *R Bouresly* a83 89
6 b g Teofilo(IRE) Rachelle (IRE) (Mark Of Esteem (IRE))
**250a**[2]

**Salvatore Fury (IRE)**
*Keith Dalgleish* a88 66
7 b g Strategic Prince Nocturnal (FR) (Night Shift (USA))
*335* *358*[7] ***403***[4] *547*[6] *857*[7] *1091*[6]◆ ***1696***[2] 1910[10] 2424[6] 2608[20] 3897[7] 3974[6] 4249[6] 4428[6] 4789[10] 4896[8] 6571[8] *7572*[10]

**Salve Del Rio (IRE)**
*Jean-Pierre Carvalho*
2 b c Rio De La Plata(USA) Salve Aurora (GER) (King's Best (USA))
8091a[2]

**Samael (FR)** *W Walton*
2 b c Reply(IRE) Lady Chope (FR) (Sin Kiang (FR))
5816a[6]

**Samarmadi** *Hugo Palmer* a80 78
3 ch g Sepoy(AUS) Sweet Folly (IRE) (Singspiel (IRE))
(4341) ***4979***[2]◆ 5326[7] 6141[7] 7244[8] ***8211***[2] *8722*[5]

**Samba Bresilienne (FR)**
*Yannick Fouin* a57
3 ch f Muhtathir Fille Du Bresil (FR) (Smadoun (FR))
***8692a***[8]

**Sambuca Nera** *James Given* 49
3 b f Black Sam Bellamy(IRE) Bebe De Cham (Tragic Role (USA))
1701[7] 2841[5] **3542**[9] 5209[10] 6436[6]

**Same Jurisdiction (SAF)**
*Ed Dunlop* 102
5 b m Mambo In Seattle(USA) Diana De Carlo (SAF) (Captain Al (SAF))
**3395**[2] 3961[11] 5597[5] 6642a[12]

**Sam Gold (IRE)** *Roger Varian* 87
2 b c Iffraaj Samdaniya (Machiavellian (USA))
6653[7] **7391**[2] 7955[2]

**Samharry** *John Gosden* a74 81
3 b g Exceed And Excel(AUS) Ballymore Celebre (IRE) (Peintre Celebre (USA))
***9025***[9]

**Sam James (IRE)** *Iain Jardine* a64 50
2 b g Camacho Breathless Kiss (USA) (Roman Ruler (USA))
2452[7] 2948[9] ***3339***[4] 3648[9] 4836[6] 6517[9]

**Sam Missile (IRE)** *James Fanshawe* a96 67
4 b g Smart Strike(CAN) Kitty Matcham (IRE) (Rock Of Gibraltar (IRE))
2136[2] 2774[4] 3534[5] ***4356***[6] 6151[11] *6887*[9]

**Sammy's Choice** *J R Jenkins* a2
5 ch g Pastoral Pursuits Diane's Choice (Komaite (USA))
***9282***[10]

**Samovar** *Scott Dixon* a66
2 b g Finjaan Chrystal Venture (IRE) (Barathea (IRE))
*8432*[7] 8981[4] ***9177***[6]

**Samovare (AUS)**
*David A & B Hayes & Tom Dabern* 103
3 br f Savabeel(AUS) Sambar (AUS) (More Than Ready (USA))
**8753a**[12]

**Sampaquita (FR)** *J-M Lefebvre* 50
3 b f Poet's Voice Forest Fire (SWE) (Never So Bold)
3007[11] 3682[7] **6277**[6] 7215[5] 8959a[7]

**Samphire (FR)** *H-F Devin* 73
2 b f Rajsaman(FR) Lausanne (IRE) (Lawman (FR))
3679a[6] 6542a[5] **7637a**[7]

**Samphire Coast** *Derek Shaw* a71 63
4 b g Fastnet Rock(AUS) Faslen (USA) (Fasliyev (USA))
*26*[4] *(69)*◆ *390*[3] *524*[4] *812*[7] *1225*[7] *(1484)* 2731[4] *2996*[7] 7934[7] 8328[4] *8538*[4] *8773*[3] *8907*[2] *9126*[2] ***(9243)***

**Samson's Reach** *Richard Price* a33
4 b g Phoenix Reach(IRE) Court Wing (IRE) (Hawk Wing (USA))
***8744***[5]

**Sam The Rebel** *Mike Hammond*
3 b g Cockney Rebel(IRE) Casablanca Minx (IRE) (Desert Story (IRE))
7230[6]

**Samtu (IRE)** *Marjorie Fife* a87 62
6 b g Teofilo(IRE) Samdaniya (Machiavellian (USA))
*(1073)* ***(1182)*** 2741[15] 3841[8] 4120[9] 6467[8] *7880*[14] *8188*[13] *8778*[12] *9178*[3] *9367*[2]

**Sanaadh** *A Wohler* 92
4 ch h Exceed And Excel(AUS) Queen's Logic (IRE) (Grand Lodge (USA))
**4517a**[6]

**Sanam** *Ed Dunlop* a52
3 b c Oasis Dream Seta (Pivotal)
***8663***[8] *9088*[9] *9202*[7]

**Sanam (USA)** *Louis Baudron* a71 77
5 rg g More Than Ready(USA) Saliyna (FR) (Linamix (FR))
***6541a***[14]

**Sancerre (IRE)** *Sylvester Kirk* a57 70
2 b f Canford Cliffs(IRE) Kawaha (IRE) (Danehill Dancer (IRE))
*4977*[3] **(5779)**

**Sanches** *Dr Jeremy Naylor* a58
3 b g Delegator Flamenco Dancer (Mark Of Esteem (IRE))
*221*[8] *8842*[9] *9085*[6] ***(9391)***

**Sandacres** *Laura Mongan* a65 28
4 b g Frozen Power(IRE) Lady Golan (IRE) (Golan (IRE))
4350[10] ***5793***[12] 6303[8] *7487*[13] ***8152***[9]

**Sandama (IRE)** *Richard Fahey* a47 47
2 b f Footstepsinthesand Nurama (Daylami (IRE))
3662[8] 4472[6] 5127[10] **5613**[3] ***6011***[3] *7029*[7]

**Sandaryann (IRE)** *D K Weld* 66
2 b c Rip Van Winkle(IRE) Sanariya (IRE) (Darshaan)
**8440a**[8]

**Sandbetweenourtoes (IRE)**
*Mubarak Al Khayarin* a94 95
8 b g Footstepsinthesand Callanish (Inchinor)
**932a**[13]

**Sand Fox (FR)** *A Fabre* 98
3 b g Redoute's Choice(AUS) Sandy Girl (FR) (Footstepsinthesand)
**2250a**[5]

**Sandfrankskipsgo** *Peter Crate* a81 81
8 ch g Piccolo Alhufoof (USA) (Dayjur (USA))
*234*[10] ***618***[5] *816*[8] *1465*[2] 2083[6] **2253**[2] *3176*[3] 4178[4] 5818[4] 6276[4] 7217[8] *9189*[5] *9389*[9]

**Sandgate** *Kenny Johnson* a34 63
5 ch g Compton Place Jump Ship (Night Shift (USA))
*1469*[10] ***3252***[9] 3343[12] 3708[12]

**Sandie Gem** *Richard Fahey* a24 34
2 ch f Equiano(FR) Spirit Na Heireann (IRE) (Dubawi (IRE))
5015[10] *5891*[8] **6559**[11]

**Sandkissed (IRE)** *Amy Murphy* a22 36
2 b f Sir Prancealot(IRE) Hapipi (Bertolini (USA))
2583[8] **8324**[7] *8701*[8]

**Sandra's Secret (IRE)** *Les Eyre* a85 81
4 gr m Zebedee Good For Her (Rock Of Gibraltar (IRE))
*1370*[11] 1876[7] *(2335)* 2856[6] 3063[5] 3741[9] 4379[13] 5129[4] 5804[6] (6237) 6669[2] 7329[6] ***(7939)***

**Sandro Botticelli (IRE)** *John Ryan* a106 110
5 b g Galileo(IRE) Ask For The Moon (FR) (Dr Fong (USA))
***268***[4] *858*[5]

**Sands Chorus** *James Given* a88 100
5 b g Footstepsinthesand Wood Chorus (Singspiel (IRE))
*25*[4] *(240)* *548*[7] *876*[7] *1433*[4] 2030[2] (2593) 3065[6] (3497) 4017[4] (4692) 5130[5] 5517a[12] 6209[2] 6563[6] **7619**[2] 8598[5] *8844*[9] *8999*[13]

**Sands Of Mali (FR)** *Richard Fahey* 115
2 b c Panis(USA) Kadiania (FR) (Indian Rocket)
4919[7] (5576) **(6446)** 7618[12] 8577a[9]

**Sandstream** *Tracy Waggott* a54 61
4 ch g Paco Boy(IRE) Descriptive (IRE) (Desert King (IRE))
*198*[7] *445*[3] *969*[8] 1829[7] **2346**[5]◆ *3256*[11]

**Sandwood Bay** *Mark H Tompkins* a51 68
3 b f Footstepsinthesand Diverting (Nayef (USA))
**3142**[9] 4350[14]

**Sandy Cove** *James Eustace* a72
6 br g Oasis Dream Maganda (IRE) (Sadler's Wells (USA))
*286*[6] ***619***[4] *856*[6] 1519[13] 5508[RR]

**Sandy Shores** *Brian Meehan* a76 73
3 b f Sixties Icon Salim Toto (Mtoto)
*236*[5] *624*[3] *895*[5] 3922[9] 4625[2] 5067[2] 5545[4] (6439) 6766[5] **7769**[2] 8113[4]

**Sandytown (IRE)** *Kevin Ryan* 57
2 b g Tamayuz Wild Ways (Green Desert (USA))
1673[9] **4567**[8]

**Sanguine** *George Peckham* 48
3 ch f Tamayuz Dubai Media (CAN) (Songandaprayer (USA))
**3755**[10]

**Saniyaat** *George Peckham* a61 76
3 b f Galileo(IRE) Starlit Sands (Oasis Dream)
1885[9] 4300[5] **5124**[4] 6044[2] 6765[3] *7492*[6]

**Sankari Royale (IRE)** *J P Murtagh* 93
2 b f Epaulette(AUS) Amethystos (IRE) (Danehill Dancer (IRE))
**6136**[2] 6488a[4] 8001[11] 8412[9]

**San Quentin (IRE)**
*Dr Richard Newland* a78 63
6 gr g Lawman(FR) In The Soup (USA) (Alphabet Soup (USA))
**2546**[2] 3817[6] *5747*[5]

**San Remo (IRE)** *A P O'Brien* a88 94
3 b c Frankel Rosie's Posy (IRE) (Suave Dancer (USA))
**7860a**[16]

**San Salvador (GER)**
*Andreas Suborics* 108
4 ch g Lord Of England(GER) Saratina (IRE) (Monsun (GER))
**2667a**[3] 5198a[10]

**Sanshaawes (SAF)** *M F De Kock* a113 113
7 b g Ashaawes(USA) Vicario (SAF) (Northern Guest (USA))
86a[4] 208a[3] **(542a)** 776a[4] 1046a[4]

**Sans Souci Bay** *Scott Dixon* a77 84
3 b c Medicean Cumana Bay (Dansili)
*329*[6] *1149*[7] *1238*[2] *1554*[4] *(2089)* (2758) *3000*[5] 4524[9] **5433**[2] *6686*[7] 7156[8] (8137) 8470[2] 8736[14]

**Santa Anna (IRE)**
*Mrs Caroline McCaldin* a14
2 b f Canford Cliffs(IRE) Ardent Lady (Alhaarth (IRE))
***7937***[9]

**Santadelacruze** *Mark Hoad* a58 53
8 b g Pastoral Pursuits Jupiters Princess (Jupiter Island)
***461***[2] *646*[3] *820*[5] *1082*[3]

**Santafiora** *Julie Camacho* a63 53
3 b f Poet's Voice Acquifer (Oasis Dream)
2503[9]◆ ***3173***[5] 4845[5] *8427*[7] *9019*[8]

**Sant'Amanza (FR)**
*R Le Dren Doleuze* a94 94
6 bl m American Post Davia (IRE) (Marchand De Sable (USA))
**5979a**[2]

**Santa Monica** *Charles O'Brien* a98 99
4 b m Mastercraftsman(IRE) Zacchera (Zamindar (USA))
**(3874a)** 4419a[8] 5862a[5] 6972a[7] *7588a*[4] *8548*[9]

**Sante (IRE)** *Jean-Pierre Carvalho* 91
4 b m Dream Ahead(USA) Zeiting (IRE) (Zieten (USA))
3314[2]◆ 4085[2] **6605a**[3]

**Santiago Rock (IRE)** *Noel Williams* 29
2 b g Rock Of Gibraltar(IRE) Snowpalm (Halling (USA))
*7489*[9] 7739[9] **8678**[14]

**Santiburi Spring** *John Best* a74 69
4 b m Mullionmileanhour(IRE) Santiburi Girl (Casteddu)
***92***[2]

**Santorini Sun (IRE)** *Mick Channon* a70 82
2 b f Born To Sea(IRE) Trentini (IRE) (Singspiel (IRE))
(5839) **6418**[8] *6886*[5]

**Santo Spirito** *D & P Prod'Homme* a77 83
6 ch g Monsun(GER) San Sicharia (IRE) (Daggers Drawn (USA))
**4457a**[3]

**Santry (IRE)** *Declan Carroll* 106
2 b c Harbour Watch(IRE) Babylonian (Shamardal (USA))
(1495) (2740) **3993**[2]◆

**Sanus Per Aquam (IRE)** *J S Bolger* a94 97
4 b h Teofilo(IRE) Fainne (IRE) (Peintre Celebre (USA))
***1355a***[5]

**Saphil (IRE)** *John Ryan* 31
2 b g Holy Roman Emperor(IRE) Lafite (Robellino (USA))
**6868**[8]

**Saphirblue (FR)** *J Parize*
3 b c Slickly(FR) Saphira (FR) (Shirocco (GER))
847a[6]

**Saphir Chop (FR)** *Mme S Adet* 29
3 ch g Captain Chop(FR) Selam (GER) (Tertullian (USA))
**4943a**[9]

**Saphirrouge (FR)** *M Figge* 60
2 b f Manduro(GER) Saphira (FR) (Shirocco (GER))
**8252a**[8]

**Sapotille (FR)** *E Libaud* 43
3 b f Bated Breath Macotte (FR) (Nicolotte)
3134a[4] **4232a**[13]

**Sapper** *Ed Walker* a55 34
2 b c Sepoy(AUS) Green Poppy (Green Desert (USA))
6853[6] 7392[14] ***7707***[11] ***8306***[6]

**Sarabi** *Scott Dixon* a69 67
4 b m Rip Van Winkle(IRE) Xaphania (Sakhee (USA))
*22*[6] ***152***[2] *303*[9] 2858[6] 3170[8] 3384[7] 4559[2] 6130[6] *6527*[5] 7017[12] *8258*[4] 8484[6] *8772*[3] *9075*[8] *9176*[8]

**Saracen Knight (IRE)** *A P O'Brien* 89
2 b c Camelot Za'hara (IRE) (Raven's Pass (USA))
**8440a**[5]

**Saradani Bay** *Rae Guest* a60 55
3 b g Mawatheeq(USA) Sadaharu (FR) (Dansili)
5577[8] ***7322***[7] *8193*[P] (Dead)

**Sarakova (IRE)** *Kevin Frost* a53 45
4 b g Iffraaj Mary Pickford (USA) (Speightstown (USA))
***124***[8] *334*[5] *425*[7] **1406**[4] 1563[12] 2626[5] 3440[7] *4158*[6]

**Sarandia (GER)** *P Schiergen* 105
4 b m Dansili Salontasche (GER) (Dashing Blade)
**5954a**[6]

**Sarangoo** *Malcolm Saunders* a77 82
9 b m Piccolo Craic Sa Ceili (IRE) (Danehill Dancer (IRE))
2256[4] 2708[11] **3869**[3] 4251[9] *4746*[4] 5064[3] 6656[8] 7002[4] 7229[8]

**Sarasota (IRE)** *Jamie Osborne* a66
2 b f Zoffany(IRE) Saldenaera (GER) (Areion (GER))
***6064***[7]

**Sardenya (IRE)** *Roger Charlton* a78 73
3 b f Kodiac Pitrizza (IRE) (Machiavellian (USA))
3070[6] *3687*[2] 4296[3] *5742*[3] 6395[8] ***(8153)***

**Sargas (IRE)** *Jean-Pierre Carvalho* 98
3 b c Shirocco(GER) Servenya (GER) (Dashing Blade)
**4422a**[16]

**Saria** *Tony Carroll* a40 52
2 b f Stimulation(IRE) Dijarvo (Iceman)
2473[9] 3215[7] 3576[8] 6790[5] **7228**[2] 7734[6] *8027*[5]

**Sark (IRE)** *David Evans* a56 80
4 b g Zoffany(IRE) Breezeway (IRE) (Grand Lodge (USA))
2477[6] 2781[13] **4147**[3] 5362[6]

**Saroog** *Simon Crisford* 76
3 b g Nathaniel(IRE) Bahama Bay (GER) (Dansili)
**4808**[3] **5428**[4]

**Sarookh (USA)** *Roger Varian* a85
2 b c Speightstown(USA) Yaqeen (Green Desert (USA))
*6897*[4] ***(7513)*** *8317*[5]

**Sarrab (IRE)** *Conrad Allen* a49
3 b f Footstepsinthesand Credibility (Komaite (USA))
***520***[4]

**Sarrasin** *Chris Waller* 88
5 b h Monsun(GER) Sand River (IRE) (High Chaparral (IRE))
**6714a**[11]

**Sarshampla (IRE)** *David Simcock* 83
2 b f Elzaam(AUS) Red Riddle (IRE) (Verglas (IRE))
4533[7] (5654) **6136**[6]

**Sarstedt** *Henry Candy* 72
2 b g Sixties Icon Saluem (Salse (USA))
4466[5]◆ **5292**[2] 7001[4] 7647[10] 8466[5]

**Sary Arqa** *Roger Varian* 65
2 ch f Dubawi(IRE) Rock Salt (Selkirk (USA))
**8594**[5]

**Sasha Waltz (IRE)**
*Fredrik Reuterskiold* a83
3 b f Rip Van Winkle(IRE) Dowager (Groom Dancer (USA))
***317a***[4] *652a*[6]

**Sasini** *Charles Hills* 78
3 b f Fastnet Rock(AUS) Eva's Request (IRE) (Soviet Star (USA))
**2585**[2]◆ 3039[2] 3626[5]

**Sassie (IRE)** *Sylvester Kirk* a69 50
2 b f Rip Van Winkle(IRE) Star Of Gibraltar (Rock Of Gibraltar (IRE))
6504[4]◆ *7937*[3] ***8399***[2] *8748*[3]

**Sassy Little Lila (USA)** *Brad H Cox* 105
4 b m Artie Schiller(USA) Sharp Apple (USA) (Diesis)
**8601a**[12]

**Satanicjim (IRE)** *Alain Couetil* a93 107
8 ch h Pivotal Infinity (FR) (Bering)
6123a[8] **8444a**[7]

**Satchville Flyer** *David Evans* a60 81
6 ch g Compton Place Palinisa (FR) (Night Shift (USA))
*152*[7] *386*[6] *481*[3] *969*[9] *1126*[9] *1184*[5] 2040[11] 2708[4] (3424) 3573[5] **3773**[3] 4219[5] 4339[4] *4727*[3]◆ 4965[6] 5248[5] *5793*[2] *6288*[8] 6371[5] 7742[2] *7945*[4]◆ *9217*[3] *9342*[2] *9444*[5]

**Satellite Express (IRE)** *Tim Pinfield* a28 39
6 ch m Observatory(USA) Composition (Wolfhound (USA))
3811[13] **5871**[5] *6531*[9] *7606*[7]

**Satica** *P Schiergen* 6
3 b f Lope De Vega(IRE) Sorrenta (USA) (Bernstein (USA))
**6084a**[16]

**Satine (FR)** *N Clement* 95
3 ch f Motivator Honorable Love (Highest Honor (FR))
3366a[5] **4424a**[6]

**Satin Ribbon** *David Elsworth* a36
3 ch f Shamardal(USA) Seattle Ribbon (USA) (Seattle Dancer (USA))
***283***[14]

**Satisfy (IRE)** *K R Burke* 79
3 b f New Approach(IRE) Venturi (Danehill Dancer (IRE))
**(5957)** 6307[5] **7558**[3] 8166[7]

**Satish** *David O'Meara* a79 71
4 b g Dansili Maycocks Bay (Muhtarram (USA))
1716[9] ***2275***[4] 3036[5] 3795[8] *4260*[5] 5131[4] 5540[3] *5832*[6] 6350[3]

**Satis House** *Susan Corbett* a35
3 b f Bahri(USA) Ex Mill Lady (Bishop Of Cashel)
***2921***[8]

**Satono Aladdin (JPN)**
*Yasutoshi Ikee* 121
6 b h Deep Impact(JPN) Magic Storm (USA) (Storm Cat (USA))
**9170a**[11]

**Satono Crown (JPN)** *Noriyuki Hori* 124
5 bb h Marju(IRE) Jioconda (IRE) (Rossini (USA))
**8975a**[10]

**Satono Diamond (JPN)**
*Yasutoshi Ikee* 124
4 b h Deep Impact(JPN) Malpensa (ARG) (Orpen (USA))
**2203a**[3] 6983a[4] 7668a[15]

**Satono Noblesse (JPN)**
*Yasutoshi Ikee* 114
7 bb h Deep Impact(JPN) Cry With Joy (JPN) (Tony Bin (IRE))
**6983a**[6] **7668a**[16]

**Satpura** *Mick Channon* a45 71
3 b f Indian Haven Selinda (Piccolo)
*75*[9] ***434***[10]

**Sattar (IRE)** *Luke McJannet* a54
3 b g Zebedee Patroller (USA) (Grand Slam (USA))
***2366***[5] 2734[12]

**Sattelac** *Keith Dalgleish* a70 70
4 b m Kodiac Sattelight (Fraam)
*99*[7] *853*[3] ***1072***[2]

**Satwa Story** *S Seemar* a44 26
7 ch g Street Cry(IRE) Satwa Queen (FR) (Muhtathir)
*9361a*[10]

**Sauchiehall Street (IRE)**
*Sylvester Kirk* a56 36
2 b g Mastercraftsman(IRE) Top Trail (USA) (Exchange Rate (USA))
*4725*[5] 4963[5] *5847*[6] ***(8306) 8644***[4]◆ ***8870***[6]

**Saumur** *Denis Coakley* a75 76
5 b m Mawatheeq(USA) Sparkling Montjeu (IRE) (Montjeu (IRE))
*2061*[4] 2781[4] **3684**[2] 4442[5] *6819*[3] *7515*[6] 7817[4] 8390[4]

**Saunter (FR)** *Ian Williams* a87 104
4 gr g Myboycharlie(IRE) Marie Des Fleurs (FR) (Smart Strike (CAN))
1691a[6] 2735[10] 4882[7] 5353[4] 6151[8] 7548[2] **(8740)**

**Sausage Fingers** *Tom Dascombe* 61
2 b c Red Jazz(USA) Italian Affair (Fumo Di Londra (IRE))
3245[8] **4291**[5] 5120[6] 5293[5] 5945[7]

**Savaanah (IRE)** *Roger Varian* a74 62
2 b f Olden Times Tanouma (USA) (Mr Greeley (USA))
7022[6] 7504[2] ***8890***[2]

**Savalas (IRE)** *Kevin Ryan* 79
2 gr c Zebedee Tap The Dot (IRE) (Sharp Humor (USA))
2740[5] 4598[3] **(5370)** 6330[7] 6969[5] 8008[7]

**Savannah Beau** *Derek Shaw* a74 74
5 b m Major Cadeaux Mancunian Way (Green Desert (USA))
*161*[6] *514*[5] *4305*[7] 4574[3] 5134[8] **5355**[2] 5930[8] 7268[9] *7486*[4] *8320*[6] *8557*[9]

**Savannah Dusk (IRE)**
*Eve Johnson Houghton* a45
2 b f Dream Ahead(USA) First Class Favour (IRE) (Exceed And Excel (AUS))
***7453***[9]

**Savannah Moon (IRE)** *Kevin Ryan* a67 68
3 b f Canford Cliffs(IRE) Tennessee Moon (Darshaan)
2499[5] 3142[10] *4265*[2] **4785**[3] 5319[4] 5648[7] **(6316)** *7235*[8]

**Savannah's Dream** *David O'Meara* 86
3 b f Showcasing Grandmas Dream (Kyllachy)
(2405) **2806**[6] 3526[5] 5383[9] 5759[5]

**Savannah Slew** *James Given* 89
3 b f Kheleyf(USA) Saratoga Slew (IRE) (Footstepsinthesand)
1731[10] 2856[7] (3526) 4208[5] 5317[3] 6234[7] **6787**[3] 7329[4] 8040[12]

**Savannah's Show** *Richard Guest* a24 70
2 b f Showcasing Grandmas Dream (Kyllachy)
1673[11] 4895[5] 5262[5] *6154*[9] 7159[2] (7655) **8043**[8]

**Savannah Storm** *G M Lyons* 101
4 b g Dubawi(IRE) Savannah Belle (Green Desert (USA))
**7066a**[6]

**Saved By The Bell (IRE)**
*Lawrence Mullaney* a72 74
7 b g Teofilo(IRE) Eyrecourt (IRE) (Efisio)
1976[8] **2770**[10] 3527[7] 4120[7] 4762[2]◆ 5438[7] 6090[7] 7330[7] 8214[3] 8511[4] 8565[4] *8778*[7]

**Saved My Bacon (IRE)** *Chris Dwyer* a85 78
6 b m Camacho Sally Green (IRE) (Common Grounds)
*618*[7] *1110*[6] *1326*[4] *2516*[4] *3231*[3] *(4005)* ***(4566)*** *7604*[6] *7994*[7] *8540*[8]

**Save The Bees** *Declan Carroll* a83 90
9 b g Royal Applause Rock Concert (Bishop Of Cashel)
1517[10] 1832[7] 2225[7] 2701[6] 3153[3] 3744[5] 4170[2] 4893[5] (5540) 5704[2] (6059) 6449[10] **6965**[2] 7328[4] 8048[11] 8289[13]

**Save The Date (FR)** *T Castanheira* a73 71
2 b f Rio De La Plata(USA) Pink And Red (USA) (Red Ransom (USA))
**7969a**[6]

**Saveurs British (IRE)** *Y Durepaire* 44
2 ch f Raven's Pass(USA) Hidden Girl (IRE) (Tamayuz)
**5815a**[9]

**Savile Row (FR)** *Frau Erika Mader* a56 101
3 b g Ransom O'War(USA) Shikoku (Green Desert (USA))
1460a[6] 2002a[3] **2869a**[5] 3994[13] *8885a*[11]

**Saving Grace** *Luca Cumani* 65
2 b f Mastercraftsman(IRE) Lady Of Everest (IRE) (Montjeu (IRE))
**8163**[8]

**Saving Kenny (IRE)** *Roy Arne Kvisla* a54 93
7 b h Footstepsinthesand Cycle Of Life (USA) (Spinning World (USA))
*694a*[10] *4940a*[11] **6500a**[5]

**Savoir Vivre (IRE)**
*Jean-Pierre Carvalho* 114
4 ch h Adlerflug(GER) Soudaine (GER) (Monsun (GER))
5692a[6] 6499a[4] 7429a[4] **8275a**[2]

**Savoken (FR)** *Cedric Rossi* a105 105
6 b g Kentucky Dynamite(USA) Savoya (FR) (Anabaa (USA))
**1271a**[4]

**Sawlaat (IRE)** *Richard Hannon* a40
3 gr c Clodovil(IRE) Jaywick (UAE) (Jade Robbery (USA))
***1179***[8]

**Saxo Jack (FR)** *Sophie Leech* a50 78
7 b g King's Best(USA) Gamma (FR) (Sadler's Wells (USA))
2586[7] 3036[3] 3795[7] **5135**[3]

**Saxon Flames (GER)** *William Muir* a72
3 b c Shamardal(USA) Saphira's Fire (IRE) (Cape Cross (IRE))
***464***[2] *777*[U] (Dead)

**Saxon Gold (IRE)** *John Davies* a30 54
4 ch m Zoffany(IRE) Apple Brandy (USA) (Cox's Ridge (USA))
2179[12] ***4263***[12]

**Saxonroad Boy (USA)**
*Richard Fahey* a46 49
2 b g Mastercraftsman(IRE) Good Strike (USA) (Smart Strike (CAN))
*4977*[8] 5537[11] 5874[6] 6626[8] *7239*[9] **7698**[3]

**Saxon Rose** *A Fabre* 94
3 b f Manduro(GER) White Rose (GER) (Platini (GER))
**5981a**[7] 8666a[7]

**Saxon Warrior (JPN)** *A P O'Brien* 119
2 b c Deep Impact(JPN) Maybe (IRE) (Galileo (IRE))
(7426a) **(8415)**

**Saxony** *Matthew Salaman* a45 32
6 b m Bertolini(USA) Just Down The Road (IRE) (Night Shift (USA))
***311***[13] *601*[11] 3809[11] 7199[11]

**Say About It** *J S Moore* a57 46
2 b g Sayif(IRE) Manaaber (USA) (Medicean)
5776a[14] 6050a[10] *6456a*[7] ***8030***[7]

**Sayedaati Saadati (IRE)**
*John Butler* a64 39
4 b g Montjeu(IRE) Guessing (USA) (Kingmambo (USA))
*7*[9] ***278***[12] *988*[14]

**Sayem** *Ed Walker* a74 85
3 b f Sayif(IRE) Usem (Bahamian Bounty)
*2334*[7] 3167[5] 3729[6] (4372) **(4975)**◆ 5506[9] 7545[3] **8297**[4]

**Sayesse** *Mick Channon* a84 87
3 b g Sayif(IRE) Pesse (IRE) (Eagle Eyed (USA))
*1607*[4] **1940**[3] **2557**[3] 3146[8] 3844[14] 4154[6] 5272[5]

**Sayeuri** *Frank Sheridan* a43 53
5 b m Siyouni(FR) Nalear (FR) (Lear Fan (USA))
**5176a**[7]

**Say No More (IRE)** *Doug Watson* a78
4 b g Shamardal(USA) Nasheej (USA) (Swain (IRE))
*8583a*[12] ***8836a***[9]

**Sboog (USA)** *A bin Harmash* a48
3 b g The Factor(USA) Touch Of Joy (USA) (Crafty Prospector (USA))
***201a***[7]

**Sbraase** *J F Levins* a72 71
6 ch g Sir Percy Hermanita (Hernando (FR))
**5519a**[16]

**Scala Regia (FR)**
*Sir Mark Prescott Bt* a84 65
3 b f Kyllachy Caprarola (USA) (Rahy (USA))
*288*[6] *397*[3] *612*[3] *(1123)* *1348*[4] 3870[5] *(4748)* *5242*[6] *6160*[10] ***6818***[3]

**Scales Of Justice (IRE)**
*Charles Hills* a50 74
3 b g Galileo(IRE) Half Queen (USA) (Deputy Minister (CAN))
**2359**[3] *3209*[8]

**Scandaleuse (USA)**
*Sir Michael Stoute* a75
2 b f War Front(USA) Aruna (USA) (Mr Greeley (USA))
*2958*[10] *7724*[2] ***7995***[2] ***8544***[3]

**Scannermandango** *Jim Goldie* a51 28
4 b m Bahamian Bounty Regal Asset (USA) (Regal Classic (CAN))
*40*[9] ***402***[6] *655*[6] *1473*[10] 2498[10] 3196[10] 3650[5]

**Scapina (GER)** *Henk Grewe* 83
3 bb f Tai Chi(GER) Sunshine Story (IRE) (Desert Story (IRE))
**6254a**[8] 6605a[8] **7204a**[3]

**Scapusc** *Marco Botti* 60
2 b c Bated Breath Fularmada (Manduro (GER))
**7250**[10]

**Scarlet Dragon**
*Eve Johnson Houghton* a111 112
4 b g Sir Percy Welsh Angel (Dubai Destination (USA))
4069[6] 4918[10] **5592**[3] 6447[12] *6931*[2] 7393[11]

**Scarlett Chope (FR)** *R Le Gal* a53 54
2 b f Panis(USA) Ducie (Distant Relative)
2073a[7] **2321a**[4] 5585a[9]

**Scarlet Thrush (IRE)**
*Luke McJannet* a65 51
3 b f Kodiac Reveal The Star (USA) (Aptitude (USA))
***718***[5] *1195*[7] 4541[6] 5286[3] 7157[9] *7992*[6] *8673*[8]

**Scarlett Lady (FR)** *M Delzangles* 81
3 ch f Nathaniel(IRE) Grenade (FR) (Bering)
**3353a**[4]

**Scealtara (IRE)** *David O'Meara* a55
3 b f Holy Roman Emperor(IRE) Sceal Nua (IRE) (Iffraaj)
*442*[4] *554*[7] ***983***[3] *1367*[9] *1564*[11]

**Scenery** *Eve Johnson Houghton* 75
2 ch g Elnadim(USA) Widescreen (USA) (Distant View (USA))
6394[4] **6867**[3]◆ 7814[15]

**Scenic River** *Tim Easterby* 69
2 ch f Dutch Art Camp Riverside (USA) (Forest Camp (USA))
6876[8] 8288[6] **8474**[2] 8735[4]

**Scent Of Power** *Barry Leavy* a53 42
5 b m Authorized(IRE) Aromatherapy (Oasis Dream)
*2166*[8] 2687[7] **3143**[3] 3761[6] 4184[4] 4625[5] 7028[11] 8477[4] *8801*[11]

**Schang (GER)** *P Vovcenko* 106
4 b h Contat(GER) Shaheen (GER) (Tertullian (USA))
3105a[5] **4517a**[3] 5450a[7] 6495a[10]

**Schesaplana (GER)**
*C Von Der Recke* 84
2 b f Dabirsim(FR) See Me Well (IRE) (Common Grounds)
**6494a**[4]

**Schirkan (GER)** *R Werning*
5 ch g Hamond(GER) Sola Fide (GER) (Zampano (GER))
*1196a*[8]

**Schmooze (IRE)** *Linda Perratt* a48 58
8 b m One Cool Cat(USA) If Dubai (USA) (Stephen Got Even (USA))
**3338**[2] 3706[7] 3978[6] 4244[6] 4853[4] 4962[8] 5096[2] 5883[3] 5923[6] 6352[8] 6895[5] 7659[3] 7885[7]

**School Run (IRE)** *David O'Meara* a67
3 b f Invincible Spirit(IRE) By Invitation (USA) (Van Nistelrooy (USA))
*76*[4] *357*[2] ***(787)***

**Schottische** *Alan Bailey* a62 56
7 ch m Pastoral Pursuits Calligraphy (Kris)
*(482)* *605*[4] ***684***[5] *1067*[9] 4047[8] *4453*[4]◆ *5296*[10] 5917[14]

**Sciacchetra (JPN)** *Katsuhiko Sumii* 118
4 bb h Manhattan Cafe(JPN) Samaaha (Singspiel (IRE))
**2203a**[9] 8975a[11]

**Scofflaw** *Richard Fahey* 90
3 b g Foxwedge(AUS) Belle Des Airs (IRE) (Dr Fong (USA))
1913[4] (2630) 3146[10] 3861[6] **4616**[2] 5018[4] 5671[3] 5959[4] 6554[6] (7094) 7622[15] 8418[8]

**Scoones** *James Fanshawe* a77 48
3 ch g Sepoy(AUS) Hannda (IRE) (Dr Devious (IRE))
1830[7] *5243*[5] *6067*[4] ***(7495)*** 8142[12]

**Scorching Heat** *Andrew Balding* a65 93
3 b g Acclamation Pink Flames (IRE) (Redback)
(2757) 3146[2] 3593[2]◆ 4037[3] 5423[2]◆ **(5637)**

**Scotch Myst** *Richard Fahey* a59 59
3 gr g Sepoy(AUS) Shena's Dream (IRE) (Oasis Dream)
***(2)*** *264*[5] *903*[4] *1204*[2] 1835[10] **2181**[3] 2949[10] 8329[8] *9216*[4] *9444*[3]

**Scots Piper** *Mark Johnston* 69
3 b g Shamardal(USA) Miss Jean Brodie (USA) (Maria's Mon (USA))
2793[9] **3461**[5] 4633[6]

**Scots Snap (IRE)** *Marcus Tregoning* 36
2 b f Kyllachy Sensational Samba (IRE) (Exceed And Excel (AUS))
8466[9] **8734**[11]

**Scottish (IRE)** *Charlie Appleby* 116
5 b g Teofilo(IRE) Zeiting (IRE) (Zieten (USA))
**3962**[5]

**Scottish Glen** *Patrick Chamings* a94 93
11 ch g Kyllachy Dance For Fun (Anabaa (USA))
2833[7] 3620[6] **4622**[4] 5302[4] 7780[18] 8600[12] *8821*[8] *9206*[4]

**Scottish Jig (USA)** *John Gosden* a61
2 ch f Speightstown(USA) Light Jig (Danehill (USA))
***9313***[7]

**Scottish Summit (IRE)**
*Geoffrey Harker* a70 75
4 b g Shamardal(USA) Scottish Stage (IRE) (Selkirk (USA))
3050[11] **3910**[2] 5135[4] 5993[6] 7524[3]

**Scottish Sun (FR)** *C Boutin* a49 56
4 b m Zambezi Sun Scottish Diva (Selkirk (USA))
**6365a**[3]

**Scottsdale** *Brian Ellison* 43
4 b g Cape Cross(IRE) High Praise (USA) (Quest For Fame)
**6413**[6]

**Scrafton** *Tony Carroll* a70 69
6 b g Leporello(IRE) Some Diva (Dr Fong (USA))
*74*[5] *477*[3] *(741)* *900*[6] *1027*[7] ***(1870)*** *8549*[11] *8978*[9]

**Screaming Gemini (IRE)**
*Roger Varian* a68 69
3 b g Shamardal(USA) Littlefeather (IRE) (Indian Ridge (IRE))
4188[2]◆ **5870**[5] 6265[12]

**Scribbler** *Rae Guest* a50 59
3 b f Excelebration(IRE) Ja One (IRE) (Acclamation)
**3329**[3] 5611[8] *6287*[8]

**Scribner Creek (IRE)** *Denis Quinn* a73 68
4 b g Roderic O'Connor(IRE) Nebraska Lady (IRE) (Lujain (USA))
*166*[3]◆ *812*[6] *(1225)* 1735[2] ***(1983)*** 2267[4] *2996*[6] *7541*[8] *7878*[7] *8400*[5] *8641*[5]

**Scruffy McGuffy** *Ann Duffield* a51 67
4 b g Firebreak Eloquent Isle (IRE) (Mull Of Kintyre (USA))
***1983***[9] 2378[7] 2955[10] 3529[7] 6088[10]

**Scrutineer (IRE)** *Mick Channon* a98 106
4 br g Intense Focus(USA) Royal Esteem (Mark Of Esteem (IRE))
651a[12] **1491**[7] 2780[11] 3463[8]

**Scrutiny** *Kevin Ryan* a11 86
6 b g Aqlaam Aunty Mary (Common Grounds)
***9100***[11] *9346*[11]

**Scuzeme** *David Barron* a75 77
3 ch g Kheleyf(USA) Barbieri (IRE) (Encosta De Lago (AUS))
*(357)* **1731**[2]◆ 1975[6] 2992[7] *7940*[7]

**Seaborn (IRE)** *Tim Vaughan* a62 32
3 b g Born To Sea(IRE) Next To The Top (Hurricane Run (IRE))
*91*[7] ***(637)*** 7253[9]

**Seaborough (IRE)** *Alan King* a62 47
2 b g Born To Sea(IRE) Nobilissima (IRE) (Orpen (USA))
*7411*[6] ***8245***[9] 8509[10]

**Seaburge (AUS)**
*David A & B Hayes & Tom Dabern* 104
3 ch c Sebring(AUS) Polska (AUS) (Encosta De Lago (AUS))
**8059a**[5] 8446a[7]

**Sea Captain (IRE)** *Andrew Lee* a60 39
5 b g Captain Rio Kleinova (IRE) (Trans Island)
***6799a***[4]

**Sea Dweller** *Anthony Carson* a69
4 b m High Chaparral(IRE) Langoustine I (AUS) (Danehill (USA))
***717***[3] *747*[3] *7477*[5] *9236*[7]

**Seaella (IRE)** *F Vermeulen* a71 100
2 b f Canford Cliffs(IRE) Gems (Haafhd)
2545[4] 3179[7] (3791) 4786[3] 5279[4] *5833*[2] 6552[2] **8525a**[2]

**Sea Ess Seas (IRE)** *Jamie Osborne* a63
2 b c Swiss Spirit Rabshih (IRE) (Green Desert (USA))
*8988*[6] ***9310***[5] *9465*[7]

**Seafarer (IRE)** *Marcus Tregoning* 96
3 br g Henrythenavigator(USA) Rose Of Petra (IRE) (Golan (IRE))
3727[2] 4640[2] 5589[2] **(6344)**◆ 6920[13] 7397[6]

**Sea Fox (IRE)** *David Evans* 106
3 b g Kodiac City Maiden (USA) (Carson City (USA))
933a[4] 1959[6] 2402[6] 5616[6] **6671**[7] 7397[8] 7784[3]◆ 8423[5] 8737[14]

**Seahenge (USA)** *A P O'Brien* 110
2 b c Scat Daddy(USA) Fools In Love (USA) (Not For Love (USA))
5501[5] **(7146)** 8037[3]◆ 8415[8]

**Seamoor Secret** *Alex Hales* a44 49
5 b m Sakhee's Secret Labaqa (USA) (Rahy (USA))
274[8] 740[9]

**Seamour (IRE)** *Brian Ellison* a104 109
6 b g Azamour(IRE) Chifney Rush (IRE) (Grand Lodge (USA))
3090[3] 4356[12] 6447[10] 7115[4]

**Seamster** *David Loughnane* a87 78
10 ch g Pivotal Needles And Pins (IRE) (Fasliyev (USA))
664[7] 816[3]◆ 1091[3]◆ 1487[4] 1768[2] 2123[8] 2409[4] 2524[6] 2835[5] 3288[4] 3617[3] 3707[3] 3946[7] 4379[11] 4629[5] 4979[8] 5271[2] 5360[2] 5587[2] 5804[4] (5936) 6072[7] 6177[2] 6303[5] 7086[12] 7195[11] 7691[3] 7923[10] (8512) 8745[7]

**Sea My Diamond (IRE)** *Mark Hoad* 24
3 b f Born To Sea(IRE) She's My Rock (IRE) (Rock Of Gibraltar (IRE))
4445[11] 5027[7] 5935[10]

**Seanie (IRE)** *David Marnane* a83 70
8 b g Kodiac Cakestown Lady (IRE) (Petorius (IRE))
6801a[2]

**Sean O'Casey (IRE)**
*Michael Appleby* a66 85
4 b g Galileo(IRE) Lahinch (IRE) (Danehill Dancer (IRE))
(2728)◆ 3091[5] 3580[9] 4216[9] 6176[3] 7024[5]

**Sea Of Flames** *David Elsworth* a97
4 ch g Aqlaam Hidden Fire (Alhaarth (IRE))
204a[8] 650a[11] 1023[8]

**Sea Of Grace (IRE)** *William Haggas* 110
3 ch f Born To Sea(IRE) Lady Dettoria (FR) (Vettori (IRE))
1883[5]◆ 2644a[2] 4857[4]◆ (5927) 6972a[4] 8232[5]

**Sea Of Green** *Jim Goldie* a59 66
5 b m Iffraaj Sea Of Leaves (USA) (Stormy Atlantic (USA))
446[3] 583[5] 1006[5] (1126) 1978[14] 2454[2]◆ 2777[5] 2950[3] 3256[5] (3385 ) 3833[2] 4039[6] 4310[5] 4509[2] 4663[6] 4788[3] (4958) 5203[4] 5471[4] 5620[10] 5881[4]

**Sea Of Heaven (IRE)**
*Sir Mark Prescott Bt* a82 101
5 b g Sea The Stars(IRE) Maid Of Killeen (IRE) (Darshaan)
2525[17]

**Sea Of Hope (IRE)** *Henry Candy* a47 64
4 b m Rock Of Gibraltar(IRE) Labrusca (Grand Lodge (USA))
9431[8]

**Seaport** *Seamus Durack* a38 54
6 ch g Champs Elysees Cochin (USA) (Swain (IRE))
5353[11] 7402[19]

**Seaquinn** *John Best* a37 40
2 b f Equiano(FR) Marine Girl (Shamardal (USA))
6826[9] 7725[11]

**Searanger (USA)** *Rebecca Menzies* a70 65
4 b g US Ranger(USA) Baby Lets Cruise (USA) (Tale Of The Cat (USA))
1722[6] 2076[5] 2628[8] (2989) 3290[3] 3979[4] 4789[5] (5016) 5543[8] 6271[4] 6571[3] 8194[7] 8590[12] (8743)

**Sea's Aria (IRE)** *Mark Hoad* a56 67
6 b g Sea The Stars(IRE) Speed Song (Fasliyev (USA))
9317[7]

**Seasearch** *Andrew Balding* a50
2 b g Passing Glance Seaflower Reef (IRE) (Robellino (USA))
8642[13] 8840[11] 9154[8]

**Sea Shack** *William Knight* a82 79
3 b g Equiano(FR) Folly Bridge (Avonbridge)
1554[2] 2334[2] 3211[6] 3836[6] 4313[6] 6068[4] 7131[6]

**Seaside Dreamer** *Michael Bell* 33
3 b g Pivotal Striving (IRE) (Danehill Dancer (IRE))
3293[9] 5075[4]

**Sea Skimmer** *Saeed bin Suroor* a83 69
3 ch g Dubawi(IRE) Portmanteau (Barathea (IRE))
2476[8]

**Seasons Bloom (AUS)** *C S Shum* 115
4 br g Captain Sonador(AUS) Pyramisa's Lass (AUS) (Not A Single Doubt (AUS))
9170a[4]

**Sea Sovereign (IRE)** *Mark Pitman* 78
4 b g Sea The Stars(IRE) Lidakiya (IRE) (Kahyasi (IRE))
2476[3] 2963[5] 3860[4] 5218[8]

**Sea Swift (IRE)** *D K Weld* 103
4 b m High Chaparral(IRE) Agnetha (GER) (Big Shuffle (USA))
3874a[6] 4934a[7] 6080a[11] 6978a[13]

**Sea Tea Dea** *Anthony Carson* a68 47
3 b f Archipenko(USA) Half Sister (IRE) (Oratorio (IRE))
(323) 763[8] 5813[5] 6818[6] 7464[7] 9243[10] 9431[6]

**Sea The Lion (IRE)** *Jarlath P Fahey* 89
6 b g Sea The Stars(IRE) Ramona (Desert King (IRE))
6956a[16] 7860a[23]

**Sea The Spray (IRE)**
*Andrew Slattery* 32
2 gr g Kendargent(FR) Orikawa (FR) (Gold Away (IRE))
7423a[13]

**Sea The Sunrise** *David Menuisier* 60
2 ro f Sea The Stars(IRE) Tequila Sunrise (Dansili)
6861[8]

**Sea Tide** *Hugo Palmer* a75 87
3 b f Champs Elysees Change Course (Sadler's Wells (USA))
5124[2]◆ 5721[3] 6161[3] (6548) 7338[2]◆ 7816[7]

**Seaview** *David Brown* a70 71
3 b f Harbour Watch(IRE) Welanga (Dansili)
(73) 160[2] 1434[2] 1760[7] 2107[4] 2927[2] 3496[2] 7523[5] 7737[10] 8107[4] 8651[6] 9034[8] 9307[8]

**Sea Wolf (IRE)** *G M Lyons* 111
5 b g Amadeus Wolf Rose De France (IRE) (Diktat)
1388a[3] 4383a[2] 6119a[8]

**Sea Youmzain (IRE)** *Mark Johnston* 71
2 b f Sea The Stars(IRE) Chantilly Pearl (USA) (Smart Strike (CAN))
8136[2]◆ 8476[2]

**Sebastiano Ricci (IRE)**
*Joseph Patrick O'Brien* 82
2 b c Lope De Vega(IRE) Dear Dream (IRE) (Montjeu (IRE))
7090[13]

**Sebastian's Wish (IRE)**
*Keith Dalgleish* a59 87
4 b g Aqlaam Swish (GER) (Monsun (GER))
(333) (2340) (3043)◆ 3830[3] (5259) 5882[3] 7701[8]

**Secondo (FR)** *Joseph Tuite* a89 89
7 b g Sakhee's Secret Royal Jade (Last Tycoon)
4411[8] 5219[5] 6275[14] 6794[2] 8310[7]

**Second Page** *Richard Hannon* a77 67
3 b c Harbour Watch(IRE) Almunia (IRE) (Mujadil (USA))
1787[4] 3457[4] 3859[3] 4307[3] 5753[6] 6623[6] 7948[4] (8770)

**Second Step (IRE)** *Roger Charlton* 113
6 b g Dalakhani(IRE) My Dark Rosaleen (Sadler's Wells (USA))
1957[3] (3072) 4360[2] 5592[2] (6440)◆ 7393[2]

**Second Summer (USA)**
*Doug Watson* a113 92
5 ch g Summer Bird(USA) Greenstreet (USA) (Street Cry (IRE))
541a[2]◆ 1045a[7] (1373a) 9360a[8]

**Second Thought (IRE)**
*William Haggas* a109 108
3 b c Kodiac Bobby Jane (Diktat)
(276)◆ (1026)◆ (1774) 3078[2] 7356[6] 7806[5] (8891)

**Second Wave (IRE)** *Charlie Appleby* a109 112
5 b g New Approach(IRE) Tessa Reef (IRE) (Mark Of Esteem (IRE))
6201[5] (Dead)

**Secratario (FR)** *Richard Hughes* a63 49
2 ch g Kendargent(FR) Amoa (USA) (Ghostzapper (USA))
5030[12] 5292[5] 5819[2] 7996[4] 8306[3] (8644) 8887[6]

**Secret Advisor (FR)**
*Charlie Appleby* 106
3 b c Dubawi(IRE) Sub Rose (IRE) (Galileo (IRE))
(2185)◆ 2690[2]◆ 3005[2] 4032[3]◆ 5525[5] (6445)

**Secret Agent** *William Muir* a58 72
3 b g Equiano(FR) Varnish (Choisir (AUS))
2720[2]◆ (3692) 4198[2] 4993[2] 5588[5] 6308[4]

**Secret Ambition** *S Seemar* a94 73
4 b h Exceed And Excel(AUS) Inner Secret (USA) (Singspiel (IRE))
316a[5] 8714a[9]

**Secret Art (IRE)** *William Knight* a97 100
7 ch g Excellent Art Ivy Queen (IRE) (Green Desert (USA))
1860[13] (2232) 3014[10] 5157[13] 5744[5] 5966[3]◆ 6873[10] 7129[4] 7619[33] 8032[12]

**Secret Asset (IRE)** *Lisa Williamson* a72 86
12 gr g Clodovil(IRE) Skerray (Soviet Star (USA))
573[9] 995[9] 1327[6] 1487[6] 1836[5] 2573[8] 3021[4] 3834[9] 4559[10] 5252[10] 6041[7] 6652[8]

**Secret Bird (IRE)** *Dean Ivory* a64 48
5 br g Arcano(IRE) Asfurah (USA) (Dayjur (USA))
64[3] 303[2] 604[7]

**Secret Brief (IRE)** *Charlie Appleby* a73 109
5 b g Shamardal(USA) Discreet Brief (IRE) (Darshaan)
205a[4] 654a[4]

**Secret City (IRE)** *Rebecca Bastiman* 51
11 b g City On A Hill(USA) Secret Combe (IRE) (Mujadil (USA))
1674[5] 1978[8] 2454[4] 2950[4] 3832[2] 4688[10] 5050[7] 5543[9] 6783[7]

**Secret Clause** *Derek Shaw* a36 53
4 b g Sakhee's Secret Claws (Marju (IRE))
158[12] 1759[10] 1980[8]

**Secret Existence (IRE)**
*John James Feane* a87 87
4 b m Sakhee's Secret Mad Existence (IRE) (Val Royal (FR))
8083a[12]

**Secret Eye (IRE)** *Paul Cole* a62
2 ch f Street Cry(IRE) What A Treasure (IRE) (Cadeaux Genereux)
7997[11] 8670[6]

**Secretfact** *Malcolm Saunders* 79
4 br g Sakhee's Secret Matterofact (IRE) (Bold Fact (USA))
2038[6]◆ (2216)◆

**Secret Glance** *Adrian Wintle* a71 66
5 b g Sakhee's Secret Look Here's Dee (Dansili)
67[3] 481[2] 1718[6] 2466[3] 3718[10] 4747[11] 6947[11] 8801[12]

**Secret Icon** *Jamie Osborne* a37 44
3 b f Sixties Icon Stan's Smarty Girl (USA) (Smarty Jones (USA))
546[6]

**Secret Interlude (IRE)** *Roger Fell* a58 33
4 b m Clodovil(IRE) Elouges (IRE) (Dalakhani (IRE))
69[8]

**Secretjim (FR)** *Tim Devos* a54 87
4 b h Equiano(FR) Hometown (Storming Home)
7307a[6]

**Secret Lady** *Mme M Bollack-Badel* a82 82
3 b f Arcano(IRE) Lady McBeth (IRE) (Avonbridge)
8960a[5]

**Secret Lightning (FR)**
*Michael Appleby* a57 63
5 ch m Sakhee's Secret Dimelight (Fantastic Light (USA))
784[U] (1084) 1456[6] 1755[7] 8811[5] (9218) 9282[4]

**Secret Look** *Richard Phillips* a55 75
7 ch g Sakhee's Secret Look Here's Carol (IRE) (Safawan)
1285[10] 2043[13] 3468[10] 5653[10] 6342[11]

**Secret Memories (IRE)**
*Miss Katy Brown* a65 63
3 ch f Rip Van Winkle(IRE) Persian Memories (IRE) (Indian Ridge (IRE))
2726[2] (3913) 9052[6]

**Secret Millionaire (IRE)**
*Shaun Harris* a52 66
10 b g Kyllachy Mithl Al Hawa (Salse (USA))
80[11] 270[7]

**Secret Missile** *David C Griffiths* a74 73
7 b g Sakhee's Secret Malelane (IRE) (Prince Sabo)
1777[10] 2123[12] 2550[7] 2800[4] 2990[5] 3239[4]◆ 3332[5] 6943[11] 7052[12] 7571[13] 7933[10] 8216[15] 8402[10] 8551[9]

**Secret Number** *Saeed bin Suroor* a111 114
7 b g Raven's Pass(USA) Mysterial (USA) (Alleged (USA))
(6744a) 7393[3] 7805[3]

**Secret Poet (IRE)** *Jamie Osborne* a40
3 b f Poet's Voice Nawaashi (Green Desert (USA))
149[10]

**Secret Potion** *Ronald Harris* a40 74
3 b g Stimulation(IRE) Fiancee (IRE) (Pivotal)
3411[3] 3673[7] 4489[5]◆ (5272) 5588[4] 5784[3] 6099[3] 6308[2] 7192[6]

**Secret Return (IRE)** *Karen George* a68
4 ch m Roderic O'Connor(IRE) Quick Return (Polish Precedent (USA))
7826[2] 8995[3]

**Secret Salvage (IRE)**
*Jamie Osborne* a62
3 b f Roderic O'Connor(IRE) Violet Flame (IRE) (Kalanisi (IRE))
882[3] 1111[3] 1286[4]

**Secret Sands (IRE)** *Pat Phelan* a29
3 b f Cacique(IRE) Katy Nowaitee (Komaite (USA))
624[9] 855[7] 997[4]

**Secret Sharp (IRE)**
*Ermanno Covone* 85
3 ch f Arcano(IRE) Miss Frangipane (IRE) (Acclamation)
2244a[9]

**Secret Soul** *Ralph Beckett* a68 67
3 b f Street Cry(IRE) Shastye (IRE) (Danehill (USA))
1499[4] 2269[8] 3721[7] 4442[3] 4971[3] 7879[3]

**Secret Strategy (IRE)** *Julia Feilden* a70 74
3 b g Kodiac Shall We Tell (Intikhab (USA))
1453[2]◆ 1785[2] 2112[4] (2674) 3673[8] 4178[5] 5041[6] 6155[8] (6278)

**Secret Striker**
*Ken Cunningham-Brown* a39 36
5 ch m Sakhee's Secret Silver Purse (Interrex (CAN))
5431[6] 9348[10]

**Secret Weapon** *C H Yip* 118
7 b g Choisir(AUS) Just Devine (IRE) (Montjeu (IRE))
9171a[7]

**Secret Willow** *John E Long* a45 33
3 ch g Sakhee's Secret Willow Beauty (Val Royal (FR))
545[7] 1597[8] 2016[14] 4211[13] 5409[6] 8342[9]

**Secret Wizard (IRE)**
*Ms Sheila Lavery* a92 90
4 ch g Sakhee's Secret Truly Magic (Traditionally (USA))
5517a[17] 5688a[15] 6491a[25]

**Section D'Or** *David Menuisier* a69 61
3 ch g New Approach(IRE) Junia Tepzia (IRE) (Rock Of Gibraltar (IRE))
4808[9] 5243[6] 5794[7]

**Section Onesixsix (IRE)**
*Mick Channon* 66
2 b f Dandy Man(IRE) The Last Laugh (Kyllachy)
6719[6] 7126[5] 8073[7]

**Sedary (FR)** *H-F Devin* 79
2 ch f Style Vendome(FR) La Marisma (FR) (Sinndar (IRE))
2881a[3]

**Seduce Me** *K R Burke* 93
3 b f Dutch Art Deep Bleu (Kyllachy)
1702[4] 2374[4] 3217[2] 3900[5] (5324) (5559) 5889[3] 6919[4] 7815[6]

**See And Be Seen** *Sylvester Kirk* a69 69
7 b g Sakhee's Secret Anthea (Tobougg (IRE))
1561[3] 2021[5] 2275[5] 2562[5] 3213[4] 3459[9] 3775[3] 4000[2] 4217[2] 4750[8] 5025[4] 5896[4] 6343[7] 6820[9] 7490[11] 7730[14]

**Seebring (IRE)** *Brian Ellison* a58 49
3 b g Tagula(IRE) Sunlit Romance (IRE) (Hernando (FR))
3555[5] 4265[7] 5001[7] 6091[9] 6904[3] 7036[10] 7465[13] (8395)

**Seeing Things (IRE)** *Philip McBride* a55 26
3 b g Poet's Voice Sonning Rose (IRE) (Hawk Wing (USA))
354[7] 1554[7] 2060[9] 3191[12] 3442[6] 4177[6] 7991[11]

**Seeking Albert (CAN)**
*Michael P De Paulo* 106
3 bb c Einstein(BRZ) Purple Trillium (USA) (Seeking The Gold (USA))
7178a[4]

**Seeking Attention (USA)**
*George Scott* a54 44
3 b f Elusive Quality(USA) Love Of Dubai (USA) (More Than Ready (USA))
283[8] 1205[5] 1401[8] 1817[7] 2315[8] 3191[6]

**Seeking Magic** *Clive Cox* a96 96
9 b g Haafhd Atnab (USA) (Riverman (USA))
1863[5] 2433[9] 3034[12] 3757[3] 4581[8] (5123) 5720[4] 7455[2] 7828[5] 9269[7]

**Seek The Fair Land** *Daniel Steele* a70
11 b g Noverre(USA) Duchcov (Caerleon (USA))
551[6] 1238[10] 8641[11]

**Seek The Moon (USA)**
*David O'Meara* a36
2 b f Giant's Causeway(USA) Crescent Moon (USA) (Seeking The Gold (USA))
9022[9]

**Seen The Lyte (IRE)** *John Quinn* a66 67
2 b f Kodiac Highest Praise (Acclamation)
2403[3] 2987[7] 3523[4] 3980[2] 4866[6] 5479[4] 5603[2] 6128[3] 6756[6] (7264) 7655[4] 8588[5]

**See Of Rome** *Richard Hughes* 89
3 gr g Pour Moi(IRE) Balandra (Medicean)
2689[3] (4224) 4535[7] 5598[3] 6415[4] 7231[6]

**See The City (IRE)** *James Eustace* a68 77
3 b g Lawman(FR) Cedar Sea (IRE) (Persian Bold (IRE))
1737[9] 2588[4] 3727[8] 6657[8] 7063[9] 7895[5]

**See The Master (IRE)** *Clive Cox* 86
3 b c Dutch Art See Emily Play (IRE) (Galileo (IRE))
2171[2] 2778[8] 3412[4] (4468) (5125)◆ 5548[2] 6422[5] 7129[5]

**See The Rock (IRE)** *Jonjo O'Neill* 86
7 b g Shirocco(GER) Samara (IRE) (Polish Patriot (USA))
3249[2] 6189[5]

**See The Sea (IRE)** *Richard Hannon* a68 74
3 b f Born To Sea(IRE) Shahmina (IRE) (Danehill (USA))
2274[5] 2754[8] 3864[7] 4697[2] (5275) (5800)

**See The Sun** *Tim Easterby* a73 96
6 ch g Assertive Cocabana (Captain Rio)
1831[14] 2840[19] 3847[13] 4379[8] 5379[12] 5804[9] 7244[9] 7522[2]◆ 7657[2] 8321[3] 8489[7]

**See The Tar (IRE)** *Jo Hughes* a50 29
2 b g Born To Sea(IRE) Image Of Truce (IRE) (Brief Truce (USA))
4696[9] 7451[7] 8155[8] 8996[11]

**See Vermont** *Rebecca Bastiman* a64 62
9 b g Kyllachy Orange Lily (Royal Applause)
242[8] 446[5] 742[3] 1126[4] 1413[2] 1722[5] 2034[4] 2628[11] 4174[6] 4559[3] 4847[3] (5260) 5736[9] 6298[7] (6631) 7164[8] 7366[6] 7575[4]

**Seewolf (GER)** *S Smrczek* a66 86
7 b g Tertullian(USA) Seehexe (GER) (Greinton)
8463a[6]

**See You In Malta (IRE)**
*Jennie Candlish* a42 57
4 b g Holy Roman Emperor(IRE) Ice Box (IRE) (Pivotal)
3265[10] 3397[4] 4467[8]

**See You In Paris (IRE)**
*Gianluca Bietolini* 52
2 b f Worthadd(IRE) Credibility (Komaite (USA))
4196a[4] 6608a[5]

**See You Mush**
*Mrs Ilka Gansera-Leveque* a66 41
3 b g Archipenko(USA) Snow Shoes (Sri Pekan (USA))
(1580) 2181[7] 3971[4] 4447[5] 5748[2] 6581[2] 8210[2]

**See Your Starr (FR)** *P Lenogue* a78 66
4 b g Siyouni(FR) Bright Style (FR) (Fasliyev (USA))
1078a[6]

**See You Soon (FR)** *P Sobry* a73 73
6 b h Zafeen(FR) Summer Dance (FR) (Machiavellian (USA))
1920a[12] (6541a) (9309a)

**Segra (USA)** *P Bary* a61 95
3 b f Shamardal(USA) Sarah Lynx (IRE) (Montjeu (IRE))
8666a[3]

**Sehail (USA)** *George Peckham* a59 35
4 b g Giant's Causeway(USA) Persist (USA) (Tiznow (USA))
1420[4] 1984[7] 2282[8] 3343[4] 4217[9] 4558[9]

**Sehayli (IRE)** *Lee Carter* a56 80
4 b g Iffraaj Quaich (Danehill (USA))
172[10] 860[12]

**Seinesational** *William Knight* a29 31
2 b g Champs Elysees Kibara (Sadler's Wells (USA))
8353[10] 8642[10]

**Seinfeld** *David Simcock* a57 68
3 b g Medicean Despatch (Nayef (USA))
4460[4] 5220[14] 6194[8] 7561[7] 8674[6]

**Seirios (IRE)** *Jane Chapple-Hyam*
3 b g Frankel Drifting (IRE) (Sadler's Wells (USA))
5128[4] 8979[10]

**Seismos (IRE)** *Henk Grewe* a96 98
9 ch g Dalakhani(IRE) Sasuela (GER) (Dashing Blade)
2667a[12]

**Selati (IRE)** *N Clement* a55 65
3 gr f Mastercraftsman(IRE) Silent Secret (IRE) (Dubai Destination (USA))
1459a[5] 3275a[3]

**Selection (FR)** *William Haggas* a83 88
4 ch g Siyouni(FR) Perspective (FR) (Funambule (USA))
(1553)◆ 2291[3] 2796[5] (3730) 5032[2]

**Selena Rose** *Ronald Harris* a30 39
4 b m Stimulation(IRE) Dot Hill (Refuse To Bend (IRE))
457[7] 5866[6] 6305[4] 6509[10]

**Self Sense (AUS)** *David Brideoake* 95
6 br g Street Sense(USA) Be My Person (AUS) (Personal Flag (USA))
1400a[6]

**Sellingallthetime (IRE)**
*Michael Appleby* a67 85
6 ch g Tamayuz Anthyllis (GER) (Lycius (USA))
1719[2] 2218[3] 4380[3] 4796[3] 5060[5] 6126[2] 6757[5] 7387[4] 7924[2]

**Semana Santa** *David Barron* a78 77
4 b m Arabian Gleam La Zamora (Lujain (USA))
152[6] 514[DSQ] 1030[5] 1310[2] 1980[6] 5004[2] 5635[4] 6546[3] 7525[5]

**Semilla (FR)** *A Schaerer* 93
6 b m Dunkerque(FR) Rose Rose (USA) (Cozzene (USA))
915a[4]

**Semper Fortis (USA)** *Doug O'Neill* a108
4 bb h Distorted Humor(USA) Rebridled Dreams (USA) (Unbridled's Song (USA))
469a[7]

**Sempre Presto (IRE)** *Richard Fahey* 67
2 b f Nathaniel(IRE) Flandre (USA) (Elusive Quality (USA))
6659[4] 7265[4] 8046[8]

**Senatus (FR)** *Karen McLintock* a66 67
5 b g Early March Winter Brook (FR) (Al Nasr (FR))
1829[6] 2429[6] 2887[4]◆ 3432[7] 8909[5] 9258[4]

**Send Up (IRE)** *Sir Mark Prescott Bt* a71 67
3 b f Fastnet Rock(AUS) Briolette (IRE) (Sadler's Wells (USA))
6287[11] (7003) (7483) 7832[4] 9026[5]

**Seneca Chief** *Daniel Kubler* a65 61
3 b g Invincible Spirit(IRE) Albertine Rose (Namid)
638[5] 1064[5] 1453[5] 2792[11] (3141)◆ 3545[2] 4157[4]

**Senga (USA)** *P Bary* 112
3 b f Blame(USA) Beta Leo (USA) (A.P. Indy (USA))
(1825a) 2644a[11] 3367a[3] (3881a) 6227a[3] 7669a[11] 8606a[8]

**Senior Investment (USA)** *Kenneth McPeek* a108 88
3 ch c Discreetly Mine(USA) Plaid (USA) (Deputy Commander (USA))
2851a[3] 4652a[10]

**Seniority** *William Haggas* a95 90
3 ch g Dubawi(IRE) Anna Palariva (IRE) (Caerleon (USA))
2402[7] 4491[5] 6007[3] (7949)◆ 8638[3] 8999[8]

**Sennockian Song** *Mark Johnston* a70 67
4 ch g New Approach(IRE) Chorist (Pivotal)
174[6] 853[10]

**Sennockian Star** *Mark Johnston* a99 92
7 ch g Rock Of Gibraltar(IRE) Chorist (Pivotal)
(173) 352[3] (467) 720[4] 779[3] (921) 963[5] 1240[5] 1341[3] 1502[12] 2426[6] 2552[5] 3323[5] 4038[4] 4429[3] 5164[3] 5353[9] 5803[2] 6151[6] 6383[10] 6857[6] 7143[7] 7515[8] 7880[7] 8239[4] 8398[9]

**Senor George (IRE)** *Simon Hodgson* a70 62
10 b g Traditionally(USA) Mrs St George (IRE) (Orpen (USA))
146[4] 414[9] 839[7] 1084[7] 1629[2] 1985[3] 2272[2]

**Senoville (IRE)** *C Ferland* a77 79
2 br c Dabirsim(FR) Silver Face (FR) (Iron Mask (USA))
4678a[4] 5989a[3] 7592a[2] 8169a[2]

**Sens Des Affaires (FR)** *Y Barberot* 67
2 b c Whipper(USA) Sensuelle (Tiger Hill (IRE))
2881a[5] 3679a[10] 4166a[7]

**Sense Of Occasion (AUS)** *Kris Lees* 109
6 b g Street Sense(USA) Saywaan (AUS) (Zabeel (NZ))
6714a[8] 8753a[9]

**Sensory (IRE)** *John Gosden* a61 50
2 gr f Dream Ahead(USA) Dookus (IRE) (Linamix (FR))
2958[8] 3312[9] 3815[7]

**Sentimental Gent (FR)** *Kevin Ryan* 26
2 b g Kendargent(FR) Sentimental Union (USA) (Dixie Union (USA))
6264[12] 7221[6]

**Sentinel** *Charlie Fellowes* a70 69
3 b g Sepoy(AUS) Baralinka (IRE) (Barathea (IRE))
245[2] 6620[5] 7158[5] (8329) (8402)

**Senza Fine (FR)** *Mme Pia Brandt* a75
2 gr f Reliable Man Seltitude (IRE) (Fairy King (USA))
9087a[3]

**Seoul Bullet (KOR)** *Kim Young Kwan* a96
6 b g Peace Rules(USA) Wild Guess (USA) (Wild Rush (USA))
321a[4]◆

**Sepal (USA)** *Iain Jardine* a67 96
4 b m Afleet Alex(USA) Faraway Flower (USA) (Distant View (USA))
3911[6] 4248[6] 4962[11] 5648[3] (5997) (6269) (6383) (6929) 7614[2] 8166[6] 8740[22]

**Separationofpowers (USA)** *Chad C Brown* a108
2 b f Candy Ride(ARG) Shehadmefromhello (USA) (Empire Maker (USA))
8603a[4]

**Seprani** *Marco Botti* a78 78
3 b f Sepoy(AUS) King's Guest (IRE) (King's Best (USA))
323[3] 763[3] 4179[3] (5028) 5797[5]◆ (6511) 7709[3]

**September (IRE)** *A P O'Brien* 113
2 b f Deep Impact(JPN) Peeping Fawn (USA) (Danehill (USA))
(4068) 6242a[4] 6974a[3] 8004[2] 8575a[3]

**September Issue** *Gay Kelleway* a85 84
4 b g Dutch Art Alexander Ballet (Mind Games)
93[2] 194[4] 547[4] 1185[3] 4080[4] 4489[4] 4979[5] (5587)

**Seqania** *Mario Hofer* a73
2 b f Equiano(FR) Singuna (GER) (Black Sam Bellamy (IRE))
(8482a)

**Serabrina (IRE)** *David Menuisier* a55 41
2 b f Iffraaj Evening Frost (IRE) (Invincible Spirit (IRE))
7725[9] 8483[4] 9177[11]

**Serangoon** *Michael Appleby* a48 30
4 b m Authorized(IRE) Sharp Dresser (USA) (Diesis)
3292[6] 3726[10]

**Seraphima** *Lisa Williamson* a33 20
7 b m Fusaichi Pegasus(USA) Millestan (IRE) (Invincible Spirit (IRE))
9083[10] 9152[12] 9280[8]

**Serefeli (IRE)** *Peter Fahey* a71 74
5 b g Footstepsinthesand Seraya (FR) (Danehill (USA))
(5518a)

**Serenada** *Roger Varian* 98
3 b f Azamour(IRE) Serres (IRE) (Daylami (IRE))
(2131) 2738[3] 3995[9] 5155[10] 6074[5] 6357[5]

**Serenade The Stars (IRE)** *James Tate* a76 79
3 b g Sea The Stars(IRE) Silent Serenade (Bertolini (USA))
149[2] (305) (627) 1736[4]

**Serenity Now (IRE)** *Brian Ellison* a79 70
9 b g Key Of Luck(USA) Imdina (IRE) (Soviet Star (USA))
526[2]◆ 2471[2] 3663[8] 5186[8] 6126[9] 7267[4] 8261[4] (9442)

**Sergeant Pink (IRE)** *Dianne Sayer* a45 52
11 b g Fasliyev(USA) Ring Pink (USA) (Bering)
1519[14] 3193[6] 5701[12]

**Sergio Leone (IRE)** *Richard Hannon* a74 71
2 b c Acclamation Elizabelle (IRE) (Westerner)
5887[6] 6761[2] (7876)

**Serjeant Painter** *Marcus Tregoning* 70
2 b g Royal Applause Szabo's Art (Excellent Art)
4151[4]◆ 4880[5]

**Sermando (FR)** *J Phelippon* 76
3 ch g Fuisse(FR) Josephjuliusjodie (IRE) (Galileo (IRE))
6225a[3] (8732a)

**Servo (IRE)** *Lynn Siddall* a52 60
3 b g Power Parade Scene (USA) (Parade Ground (USA))
1470[5] 8651[12] 9018[3]

**Sestilio Jet (FR)** *Antonio Marcialis* 95
2 b c French Fifteen(FR) Hideaway Girl (Fasliyev (USA))
4131a[2] 6051a[8]

**Set In Stone (IRE)** *John Patrick Shanahan* 97
3 b f Famous Name Storminateacup (IRE) (Galileo (IRE))
2174[5] 2572[4] 3094[7] (4247) 4431[6] (5650) (6134) (7161) 7658[6]

**Setting Sail** *Charlie Appleby* 82
2 b c Dansili West Wind (Machiavellian (USA))
7026[2]◆ (7503)◆

**Settle For Red (IRE)** *David Marnane* a65 74
7 ch g Redback Balmy Choice (IRE) (Balla Cove)
1014a[3]

**Settle Petal** *Pat Phelan* a64 39
3 b f Peintre Celebre(USA) Shall We Dance (Rambo Dancer (CAN))
284[3] 4012[9] 4748[9] 5558[6]

**Settler's Son (IRE)** *J Michal* 105
6 b g Whipper(USA) Settler (Darshaan)
7721a[4]

**Settler's Stone (AUS)** *Troy Blacker* 97
5 b g Savoire Vivre Rock Chick (AUS) (Octagonal (NZ))
1400a[3]

**Set To Fire (IRE)** *John James Feane* a54 59
4 b m Big Bad Bob(IRE) Set Fire (IRE) (Bertolini (USA))
5689a[8]

**Seve** *Karen George* a55 55
5 ch g Exceed And Excel(AUS) Flamenco Dancer (Mark Of Esteem (IRE))
79[8] 664[9] 3231[6] 5304[U]

**Seven Clans (IRE)** *Neil Mulholland* a74 72
5 b g Cape Cross(IRE) Cherokee Rose (IRE) (Dancing Brave (USA))
(147) 351[2] 5509[3] (6144) 6811[3]

**Seven Heavens** *John Gosden* 107
3 b c Frankel Heaven Sent (Pivotal)
1881[3] 2289[7] 2830[3] 3302[2]

**Sevenleft (IRE)** *Ms Sheila Lavery* a98 98
4 br g Manduro(GER) Fleeting Affair (USA) (Gone West (USA))
3765a[7]

**Sevenna Star (IRE)** *John Gosden* 84
2 b c Redoute's Choice(AUS) Sevenna (FR) (Galileo (IRE))
7273[2]◆ 7955[3]

**Seventh Heaven (IRE)** *A P O'Brien* a94 121
4 b m Galileo(IRE) La Traviata (USA) (Johannesburg (USA))
1379a[2] (2398) 6972a[9] 7668a[14] 8610a[5]

**Seventii** *Robert Eddery* a21 65
3 b f Medicean Lowndes (Rail Link)
1497[15] 1906[9] 3823[7] 4765[7] 5787[4] 6622[9] (7253) 7918[3] 8301[2]◆

**Seven Treffles (FR)** *Y Barberot* 75
2 ch f Literato(FR) Don't Look Back (FR) (Slickly (FR))
8443a[5]

**Severus (GER)** *Des Donovan* a83 92
7 b g Shirocco(GER) Shikoku (Green Desert (USA))
5668[7]

**Sevilla** *Olly Murphy* a66 65
4 b m Duke Of Marmalade(IRE) Glittering Prize (UAE) (Cadeaux Genereux)
47[8] 2336[9] 2956[7] 4980[4] 5296[2] 6088[8] 6280[4]

**Sexton Blake (IRE)** *John Norton* a63 56
4 b g Rip Van Winkle(IRE) Soviet Treat (IRE) (Ashkalani (IRE))
1238[9] 1484[4] 2053[8] 5544[13]

**Sexy Juke (GER)** *P Schiergen* 48
3 b Jukebox Jury(IRE) Saldennahe (GER) (Next Desert (IRE))
8090a[8]

**Sexy Legs** *Rebecca Menzies* a65 88
5 b m Dutch Art Classic Lass (Dr Fong (USA))
2548[6] 5112[4] (7574) 8108[8] 8552[11] 8747[6]

**Sexy Secret** *Lydia Pearce* a52 60
6 b g Sakhee's Secret Orange Walk (IRE) (Alzao (USA))
238[9] 880[13] 2281[5] 2729[5] 3440[3] 5509[5] 7253[5] 7990[5] 8122[2]

**Seyaady** *Mark Johnston* a73 72
2 b c Exceed And Excel(AUS) Muwakaba (USA) (Elusive Quality (USA))
2888[2] 3490[3] 4598[6] (5479)◆

**Seyasah (IRE)** *Chris Wall* a67 72
3 b f Casamento(IRE) Defensive Boast (USA) (El Gran Senor (USA))
2071[8] 4619[2] 5635[2] 6295[2] 7282[8] 7723[4]

**Se You** *Tim Easterby* 75
2 b g Sepoy(AUS) Lady Hestia (USA) (Belong To Me (USA))
6545[5] 7551[2] 7814[28] 8215[6]

**Sfumato** *Iain Jardine* a73 83
3 br g Bated Breath Modern Look (Zamindar (USA))
2215[6] 3146[6] 4489[3] 6519[2]◆ 7398[6] 8319[9]

**S Grillo** *G Bernaud* a24 24
9 bl g Val Royal(FR) Santiago Blue (USA) (Relaunch (USA))
1070a[7] 9309a[17]

**Sgt Reckless** *Mick Channon* a86 90
10 b g Imperial Dancer Lakaam (Danzero (AUS))
1555[3] 2021[7] (3315) 3597[7]

**Shaaqaaf (IRE)** *John Gosden* a70 95
3 b f Sepoy(AUS) Burke's Rock (Cape Cross (IRE))
2753[2] (3309) 4366[2] 5399[2]◆ 6377[6]

**Shababy** *Owen Burrows* 107
2 br c Kyllachy On The Brink (Mind Games)
3868[3] (6199) (7049)◆ 8043[4]

**Shabbah (IRE)** *Sir Michael Stoute* a49 94
4 br g Sea The Stars(IRE) Alizaya (IRE) (Highest Honor (FR))
6482[4] 6698[8] 7395[14] 8076[2]

**Shabeeb (USA)** *Roger Varian* 103
4 b g Smart Strike(CAN) Sortita (GER) (Monsun (GER))
2735[15] 4033[11] 4828[3]

**Shabeeh (IRE)** *Mark Johnston* a71 76
3 b g Raven's Pass(USA) Mid Mon Lady (IRE) (Danetime (IRE))
78[3] 160[4] 402[2] 498[4]

**Shabra Emperor (IRE)** *Anthony McCann* a72 47
8 b g Holy Roman Emperor(IRE) Fearn Royal (IRE) (Ali-Royal (IRE))
6798a[10]

**Shackled N Drawn (USA)** *Peter Hedger* a79 78
5 b g Candy Ride(ARG) Cajun Flash (USA) (Bertrando (USA))
3865[3] 4732[6] 6276[7] 6764[5] 7486[5] 9001[10] 9189[3] 9389[2] 9471[2]

**Shackles** *Nicky Richards* a43 46
3 b g Equiano(FR) Silent Waters (Polish Precedent (USA))
9084[9]

**Shadad (IRE)** *P Sogorb* a75 53
4 b g Zamindar(USA) Tender Morn (USA) (Dayjur (USA))
(6226a)

**Shadele (IRE)** *Jeremy Noseda* a65 44
4 b m Rip Van Winkle(IRE) Zadalla (Zaha (CAN))
144[8]

**Shades Of Mist** *Tony Coyle* a66 56
2 b g Lilbourne Lad(IRE) Talqaa (Exceed And Excel (AUS))
4014[9] 4599[4] 5262[6] (9302)

**Shades Of Silver** *Ed de Giles* a90 47
7 b g Dansili Silver Pivotal (IRE) (Pivotal)
6793[6] 7200[6] 8505[9]

**Shadow Beauty** *Marco Botti* a63 63
3 b c Pivotal Rivara (Red Ransom (USA))
5794[8] 6587[4] 7061[12]

**Shadow Of Hercules (IRE)** *Michael Mullineaux* a43 39
3 ch g Roderic O'Connor(IRE) Baltic Princess (FR) (Peintre Celebre (USA))
385[10] 627[8] 5846[8]

**Shadow Sadness (GER)** *C Von Der Recke* 101
5 b h Soldier Hollow Shadow Queen (GER) (Lando (GER))
7203a[5] 8090a[9] 8733a[11]

**Shadow Seeker (IRE)** *Paul D'Arcy* a56 20
2 b f Arcano(IRE) New Atalanta (IRE) (Xaar)
4815[13] 6844[5] 7450[6] 8467[17] 8793[9] 8996[8] 9302[13]

**Shadow's Girl** *Bernard Llewellyn* a39
5 gr m Fair Mix(IRE) Special Beat (Bustino)
8635[8] 8852[5] 8995[7] 9217[8]

**Shadow Spirit** *Iain Jardine* a76 71
4 b m Makfi Highland Shot (Selkirk (USA))
497[8] 727[6] 954[6]

**Shadow Warrior** *Paul D'Arcy* a80 76
3 b g Born To Sea(IRE) Dolcetto (IRE) (Danehill Dancer (IRE))
1737[3] 2273[2] (3408) 4632[5] (9464)◆

**Shady McCoy (USA)** *Ian Williams* a107 106
7 b g English Channel(USA) Raw Gold (USA) (Rahy (USA))
1734[11] 2606[4] 3003[4]◆ 3842[17] 4270[4] 4854[9] 5393[8] 6419[10]◆ 6918[10] (7780)◆ (8014)◆ 8737[2] 8843[7] 8905[4]

**Shaella (IRE)** *Jane Chapple-Hyam* a59
3 ch f Casamento(IRE) Mouriyana (IRE) (Akarad (FR))
9235[4] 9455[9]

**Shaheen (IRE)** *John Quinn* a76 77
2 b g Society Rock(IRE) La Chicana (IRE) (Invincible Spirit (IRE))
2786[8] 3495[3] (4101) 5079[3]◆ 6065[3] (6466) 7318[4]

**Shaherezada (IRE)** *Clive Cox* a63 88
2 b f Dutch Art Shabyt (Sadler's Wells (USA))
5056[5] 5795[7] 6862[3] 7904[2] 8354[3] (8595)

**Shah Of Armaan (IRE)** *Kevin Ryan* a77 73
4 b g Fastnet Rock(AUS) Queen Of Tara (IRE) (Sadler's Wells (USA))
(165) 782[3] 1074[12] 1562[3] 2163[11] 2685[14] 5469[9] 6464[10]

**Shaishee (USA)** *M Al Mheiri* a91 85
7 br g Indian Charlie(USA) Hatpin (USA) (Smart Strike (CAN))
87a[15] 321a[3] 539a[5] 694a[3] 772a[4]

**Shaiyem (IRE)** *Richard Hannon* a80 97
4 b g Starspangledbanner(AUS) Shaanbar (IRE) (Darshaan)
1860[2]◆ 2116[10] (2617)

**Shakabula (IRE)** *Brian Ellison* a55 52
3 b g Kheleyf(USA) Tinaar (USA) (Giant's Causeway (USA))
2507[15] 5131[7] 5617[5]

**Shakeel (FR)** *A De Royer-Dupre* 114
3 b c Dalakhani(IRE) Shamiyra (FR) (Medicean)
2947a[3] 3879a[2] (4878a)

**Shakiah (IRE)** *Sharon Watt* 53
2 b f Farhh Dubai Sea (USA) (Street Sense (USA))
7045[6] 7563[8] 8212[5]

**Shakour (IRE)** *John Gosden* a70
2 b c Declaration Of War(USA) Another Storm (USA) (Gone West (USA))
8951[6] 9201[3]

**Shalailah (IRE)** *Joseph Patrick O'Brien* a83 92
2 b f Showcasing Perfect Venture (Bahamian Bounty)
5344a[2] 8597[9]

**Sha La La La Lee** *Tom Dascombe* 77
2 b c Helmet(AUS) Shamara (IRE) (Spectrum (IRE))
6403[6] 7117[2]

**Shalaman (IRE)** *Matthew J Smith* a95 94
8 b g Oratorio(IRE) Shalama (IRE) (Kahyasi (IRE))
1355a[7]

**Shalamzar (FR)** *Micky Hammond* a24 77
8 ch g Selkirk(USA) Shamalana (IRE) (Sinndar (IRE))
8654[9]

**Shalianzi (IRE)** *Chris Gordon* a64 69
7 b g Azamour(IRE) Shalama (IRE) (Kahyasi (IRE))
859[3] 1303[7]

**Shalimah (IRE)** *Clive Cox* a67 77
5 br g Dark Angel(IRE) Jemima's Art (Fantastic Light (USA))
141[4]

**Shamaal Nibras (USA)** *Doug Watson* a103 104
8 b g First Samurai(USA) Sashay Away (USA) (Farma Way (USA))
82a[9] 1043a[6]

**Shamaheart (IRE)** *Geoffrey Harker* a78 89
7 b g Shamardal(USA) Encouragement (Royal Applause)
581[12] 989[5] 1202[7] 1472[5] 1677[7] 2348[8] 3845[15] 4168[7] 5739[8]

**Shaman Ghost (CAN)** *James Jerkens* a118
5 b h Ghostzapper(USA) Getback Time (USA) (Gilded Time (USA))
469a[2]

**Shamar (FR)** *R K Watson* a53 68
9 br g Dr Fong(USA) Shamalana (IRE) (Sinndar (IRE))
4684[3] 5689a[P] 7015[5]

**Shamar Love (IRE)** *Carina Fey* a64 26
7 ch m Shamardal(USA) Quality Love (USA) (Elusive Quality (USA))
7342a[12]

**Shamash (IRE)** *John C McConnell* a77 5
5 b g Oasis Dream Shareen (IRE) (Bahri (USA))
(1257) 1412[2] (1457)

**Shambra (IRE)** *Roger Fell* a54 69
3 b f Clodovil(IRE) Shambodia (IRE) (Petardia)
1434[4] 1817[5] (2902) 5001[3] 5017[3] 5895[9] 6784[4] (7220)

**Shamlan (IRE)** *Kevin Frost* a61 51
5 br g Shamardal(USA) Atamana (IRE) (Lahib (USA))
841[11] 1334[12] 3001[10] 9084[2]◆

**Shamonix (IRE)** *Mark Usher* a40 39
3 b f Elusive Pimpernel(USA) Shamora (FR) (Oratorio (IRE))
2019[12] 2908[11] 3549[5] 4211[6] 4748[11] 5266[9] 5545[11] 6009[9] 6828[5] 7492[7]

**Shamreen (IRE)** *D K Weld* 111
4 b m Dubawi(IRE) Shareen (IRE) (Bahri (USA))
4417a[6] (6243a) (6972a) 7669a[13]

**Shamrock Emma (IRE)** *John Best* a55 36
2 ch f Mizzen Mast(USA) Lisselan Diva (IRE) (Barathea (IRE))
6816[4] 7450[7] 8294[11] 9024[7]

**Shamrokh (IRE)** *Michael Appleby* a87 85
3 b g Invincible Spirit(IRE) Alshakr (Bahri (USA))
(402) 927[2] 1142[4] 1907[10] 3838[6] 4831[7] 5397[6] 5924[12] 7892[6] 8596[2]◆ 8797[4] 9180[9]

**Shamsaya (IRE)** *Simon Crisford* a89 89
3 b f Shamardal(USA) Masaya (Dansili)
3793[7] 5123[3] 5828[4] 6970[6] 8879[5] 9185[2]

**Shamshad (FR)** *V di Napoli* 96
4 b g Sea The Stars(IRE) Shamakiya (IRE) (Intikhab (USA))
8963a[9]

**Shamshon (IRE)** *Stuart Williams* a102 95
6 b g Invincible Spirit(IRE) Greenisland (IRE) (Fasliyev (USA))
639[5]◆ 842[8] 1152[7] 2083[5] 2736[12] 4581[3] (4816) 5354[6] 6325[10] 6695[4] 6923[9] 7809[6] 8129[3] 9187[4] 9373[8]

**Shanakill Star (IRE)** *Miss Joey Ellis* 29
3 b f Lord Shanakill(USA) Lola Rosa (IRE) (Peintre Celebre (USA))
2316[7]

**Shanandoa** *Brian Barr* a18 60
6 b m Shamardal(USA) Divisa (GER) (Lomitas)
2759[6] 3615[7] 4497[10] 5023[9]

**Shanawest (FR)** *N Caullery* a81 69
5 b m Kingsalsa(USA) Anawest (IRE) (Anabaa (USA))
6648a[11]

**Shan Dun na nGall (IRE)** *Amy Murphy* a64 69
6 b g Shantou(USA) Omanah (USA) (Kayrawan (USA))
(395) 859[9] 8878[6] 9095[6] 9258[14]

**Shanghai Elastic** *David Barron* 52
2 b f Swiss Spirit Reveille (Sakhee's Secret)
2373[3]

**Shanghai Glory (IRE)** *Charles Hills* a72 108
4 ch g Exceed And Excel(AUS) Hecuba (Hector Protector (USA))
4072[27] 5640[5]◆ 6206[3]◆ 7611[11] 8383[9]

**Shanghai Shane (IRE)** *Brian Barr* a9
3 b g Lord Shanakill(USA) Lamassu (IRE) (Entrepreneur)
6633[10] 8117[0] 8504[13] 8852[6]

**Shania Says (IRE)** *Tony Carroll* a70 68
2 b f Red Jazz(USA) Vexatious (IRE) (Shamardal (USA))
2583[4] 3187[6] 4213[3] 5121[3] 5546[3] (6010) 6778[3] 7734[8]

**Shanjo (GER)** *Markus Klug* 108
3 bb c Soldier Hollow Shivara (GER) (Monsun (GER))
3636a[5] 4422a[4] 5983a[7]

**Shankara (IRE)** *David Simcock* a71 60
3 gr f Mastercraftsman(IRE) White And Red (IRE) (Orpen (USA))
717[2] 862[3] 4565[5] 5038[5] 5856[RR]

**Shannah Bint Eric** *Kevin Ryan* 33
3 ch f Poet's Voice Crystal Mountain (USA) (Monashee Mountain (USA))
2898[12]

**Shannon Soul (IRE)** *M Halford* a89 91
5 b g Shamardal(USA) Paimpolaise (IRE) (Priolo (USA))
*(1233a)*

**Shaolin (GER)** *P Schiergen*
2 b c Rock Of Gibraltar(IRE) Strela (GER) (Lomitas)
6986a[3]

**Shapes (IRE)** *G M Lyons* 84
2 b f So You Think(NZ) Maskaya (IRE) (Machiavellian (USA))
**2862a**[3]

**Shaqoos (FR)** *Jo Hughes* a38 22
3 ch f Naaqoos Shemrana (USA) (Woodman (USA))
73[6] 305[10]

**Shared Equity** *Jedd O'Keeffe* 103
6 b g Elnadim(USA) Pelican Key (IRE) (Mujadil (USA))
**2780**[7] 3463[10]

**Shargiah (IRE)** *Roger Varian* a94 104
4 ch g New Approach(IRE) Zacheta (Polish Precedent (USA))
2026[4] (2477) (2920) **(3785)**

**Sharja Bridge** *Roger Varian* 110
3 b c Oasis Dream Quetena (GER) (Acatenango (GER))
3714[3] 5458[2] (6150)◆ **7129**[2]

**Sharjah (IRE)** *Andrew Slattery* a80 80
7 b g Shamardal(USA) Lunar Lustre (IRE) (Desert Prince (IRE))
227a[4] **4041**[2]

**Sharja Silk** *Roger Varian* 68
2 b c Dubawi(IRE) So Silk (Rainbow Quest (USA))
**8389**[5]

**Sharliyna (IRE)** *D K Weld* 92
4 b m Pivotal Sharleez (IRE) (Marju (IRE))
1385a[18]

**Sharpalo (FR)** *A bin Harmash* a95 102
5 b g Shamardal(USA) Pony Girl (IRE) (Darshaan)
83a[5] 204a[12] **891a**[4]

**Sharp Azteca (USA)** *Jorge Navarro* a125
4 bb h Freud(USA) So Sharp (USA) (Saint Liam (USA))
1373a[3] **8576a**[2]

**Sharp Defence (USA)**
*John Patrick Shanahan* a103 99
3 br c First Defence(USA) Jazz Drummer (USA) (Dixieland Band (USA))
1804[2] (2171) 2554[5]◆ 2775[4] **(4477)** 5094[11] 6676[9]

**Sharp Operator** *Charlie Wallis* a53 43
4 ch g Medicean Helen Sharp (Pivotal)
9232[11]

**Sharp Reminder** *James Tate* a72
2 b f Kyllachy Sharp Relief (IRE) (Galileo (IRE))
6064[6] 7033[2]◆ 8669[4] **9097**[3]◆

**Shaslika (FR)** *D & P Prod'Homme* a51 70
7 gr m Slickly(FR) Green Shadow (FR) (Green Tune (USA))
**9309a**[7]

**Shawwal** *S Ibido* a72 71
2 b g Harbour Watch(IRE) Orton Park (IRE) (Moss Vale (IRE))
**3135**[5] 4520[2] 9446a[5]

**Shaya (IRE)** *Roger Fell* a55 82
2 b f Invincible Spirit(IRE) Nidhaal (IRE) (Observatory (USA))
4841[4] 6806[2] (7141) 7536[11] **7846a**[7] 8317[7]

**Shay C** *Declan Carroll* 65
2 b c Foxwedge(AUS) Sirenuse (IRE) (Exceed And Excel (AUS))
2134[10] **2452**[2] 2882[5] 3283[3] 4866[5] 5603[7] 7159[14]

**Shazain (FR)** *M Rolland* a48 43
3 b g Youmzain(IRE) Shadala (FR) (Dalakhani (IRE))
**5523a**[9]

**Shazzab (IRE)** *Richard Fahey* 78
2 b f Elzaam(AUS) Ceylon Round (FR) (Royal Applause)
2105[4] 2896[5]◆ (3390) 4836[4] 5875[6] 6762[3] **(7552)** 8045[7]

**Shearian** *Declan Carroll* a77 71
7 b g Royal Applause Regal Asset (USA) (Regal Classic (CAN))
(7) **(527)** 1074[9] 1700[4] 2030[14] 2466[6] 2996[8] 3560[9] 4626[2] 5126[8] 5497[11] 6266[11] 6673[7] 8254[6] 8773[5] (9032) 9180[6] 9364[3]

**Shearling** *Brian Ellison* 94
4 b m Rail Link Casual (Nayef (USA))
**4119**[3] 4849[5] 5401[2] 6357[9] 6968[2]

**She Believes (IRE)** *Sylvester Kirk* 95
2 ch f Arcano(IRE) African Moonlight (UAE) (Halling (USA))
2265[2] 3245[5] 4253[6] (5048) (5751) **(6375)** **7088**[6] 7814[7]

**Sheepscar Lad (IRE)** *Nigel Tinkler* a66 84
3 b g Arcano(IRE) Piccadilly Filly (IRE) (Exceed And Excel (AUS))
1349[2] 1543[3] 2033[4] 2223[5] 3403[2] 4122[2] (4717) 5383[4] 5759[3] (6670) **(6945)**

**Sheer Intensity (IRE)** *David Evans* a55 57
4 ch m Dutch Art Sheer Elegance (IRE) (Pivotal)
50[7] 239[8] 351[11] 420[9] 608[6] 690[10] 966[8] 1125[2] 1225[2] **1338**[2] 1406[8] 1447[3] 2063[3] 2626[4] (2915) 3550[10] 3772[4] 4010[8] 4493[5] 5250[4] 5653[6] 8799[4] 9218[2]

**Shee's Lucky** *Neil Mulholland* a67
3 b f Yorgunnabelucky(USA) She's The Lady (Unfuwain (USA))
718[8] **8503**[9]

**Shef Wedsneigh (IRE)** *Roger Fell* 43
2 ch f Choisir(AUS) Tullawadgeen (IRE) (Sinndar (IRE))
6042[9] **6433**[8] 7473[6]

**Sheikha Reika (FR)** *Roger Varian* 83
2 b f Shamardal(USA) Screen Star (IRE) (Tobougg (IRE))
**6917**[2] **7399**[2] 8163[2]

**Sheikhzayedroad** *David Simcock* 117
8 b g Dubawi(IRE) Royal Secrets (IRE) (Highest Honor (FR))
890a[3] **1374a**[3] 3996[6] 5503[7] 6400[4] 7116[3] 8229[7]

**Sheikspear** *Ed de Giles* a81 80
3 b c Bahamian Bounty Crinkle (IRE) (Distant Relative)
3673[9] (4843) 5111[3] **(5797)** 6378[2] 7947[5]

**Sheila Rose (IRE)** *Denis Coakley* a40
2 b f Rip Van Winkle(IRE) Al Ihsas (IRE) (Danehill (USA))
8888[11] **9311**[7]

**Sheila's Fancy (IRE)** *J S Moore* a63 66
3 ch g Casamento(IRE) Fancy Vivid (IRE) (Galileo (IRE))
1342[3]◆ **3427**[6] 4809[6] 5780[5] 8946[10] 9158[2] 9324[5]

**Sheila's Palace** *J S Moore* a60 66
3 ch f Sakhee's Secret Loreto Rose (Lahib (USA))
679[3] **1193**[3] 1428[6] 5845[P]

**Sheila's Return** *John Balding* a56 54
3 ch f Bated Breath Deora De (Night Shift (USA))
401[8] **667**[5] 960[9]

**Sheila's Rock (IRE)** *Denis Coakley* a71 67
3 b f Fastnet Rock(AUS) Crystal Curling (IRE) (Peintre Celebre (USA))
2231[3]◆ **8635**[3]

**She Is No Lady** *Ralph Beckett* a98 109
5 b m Lope De Vega(IRE) Capestar (IRE) (Cape Cross (IRE))
3011[3] **3996**[4] 5503[5] 7116[7]

**Shekiba (IRE)** *Joseph G Murphy* 95
2 ch f Arcano(IRE) Catbells (IRE) (Rakti)
**6242a**[5]

**Shelneverwalkalone** *Ivan Furtado* 54
3 b f Captain Gerrard(IRE) Rabarama (Xaar)
**2383**[5] 2819[4] 5567[6] 6114[4] 7912[7]

**Sheltered Waters**
*Eve Johnson Houghton* a46
3 b f Aqlaam Velvet Waters (Unfuwain (USA))
**1424**[5]

**Shemda (IRE)** *A De Royer-Dupre* a89 91
3 b f Dutch Art Shamooda (IRE) (Azamour (IRE))
**6732a**[6]

**Shenanigans (IRE)** *Roger Varian* a72 102
3 b f Arcano(IRE) Ladylishandra (IRE) (Mujadil (USA))
2820[3] 3722[6] 4794[2] (5506) (7406) **7815**[2]

**Shendini (IRE)** *F Caenepeel-Legrand* a58 59
5 b g Medicean Shehira (FR) (Sendawar (IRE))
**6543a**[4]

**Shenoya (FR)** *N Leenders* 91
2 ch f Zoffany(IRE) Shendama (FR) (Dr Fong (USA))
**8443a**[3]

**Shepherd Market (IRE)** *Clive Cox* 96
2 b f Reckless Abandon Shepherdia (IRE) (Pivotal)
5154[4]◆ (6093) 7021[2] **8424**[2]

**Shepherd's Purse** *David Loughnane* a94 84
5 b g Pastoral Pursuits Neyraan (Lujain (USA))
**795a**[2] 4925a[10] 6801a[4] 9272[2]

**Sherbert** *Richard Hannon* a61 33
3 b f Power Original (Caerleon (USA))
**1401**[4]

**Sheriff** *Michael Bell* a79 63
2 br g Lawman(FR) Chatline (IRE) (One Cool Cat (USA))
7281[6] 8119[13] **8545**[6]◆ 8794[5]

**Sheriff Garrett (IRE)** *Tim Easterby* a75 76
3 b g Lawman(FR) Few Are Chosen (IRE) (Sulamani (IRE))
2137[6] 2686[4] 3180[2] (4978) 5617[2] (5846) 6415[5] 7019[4] 7386[5] 7659[4] 8214[2] **8478**[2]

**Sheriff Of Nawton (IRE)** *Roger Fell* a63 75
6 b g Lawman(FR) Pivotal Role (Pivotal)
3050[12] 4899[8] 5005[4] **5313**[3]◆ 5701[5] **(6551)** 6944[6] 8876[6]

**Sherman McCoy** *Marjorie Fife* a57 71
11 ch g Reset(AUS) Naomi Wildman (USA) (Kingmambo (USA))
174[7] 3654[4] **5021**[6] 5284[10] 5701[13]

**Sherzy Boy** *Richard Hannon* 71
2 b c Champs Elysees Sherzam (Exceed And Excel (AUS))
6777[4]◆ 7117[6] **7543**[4] 8180[9]

**Shesaidyes (IRE)** *Henry Spiller* a30 62
2 bb f Kodiac Bluebell Park (USA) (Gulch (USA))
**6480**[8] 7033[11]

**She'sastorm (IRE)** *Henry Spiller* a19 53
2 b f Footstepsinthesand Snap Alam (IRE) (Alamshar (IRE))
**4815**[12] 5154[9]

**She's Different (IRE)** *Nigel Tinkler* 69
2 b f Epaulette(AUS) Quickstyx (Night Shift (USA))
4567[9] 5058[6] 5825[4] (6379) **7087**[3]

**Shesgotthelot** *J S Moore* a73 61
2 b f Finjaan Noble Nova (Fraam)
2015[3] 2277[3] 3174[3] 4389a[4] **4677a**[3] 5629a[7] 5907a[7] 6456a[5] 6608a[6] 7410[3] 7827[3]

**She's Pukka** *Iain Jardine* a63 71
3 ch f Makfi Chieftess (IRE) (Mr Greeley (USA))
**(7224)** 8192[6]

**Shes Ranger (IRE)** *H-F Devin* a87 94
3 b f Bushranger(IRE) Baraloti (IRE) (Barathea (IRE))
1387a[6] **2441a**[3] **5196a**[7]

**She's Rosanna** *Steph Hollinshead* 47
3 b f Poet's Voice She Storm (IRE) (Rainbow Quest (USA))
3166[7] **4149**[7] 4735[10] 5052[11]

**She's Royal** *Bryan Smart* a64 52
2 b f Delegator Sukuma (IRE) (Highest Honor (FR))
6938[7] 7937[6] **8553**[3] 8802[7] 8925[6]

**Shesthedream (IRE)** *David Barron* a53 71
4 b m Dream Ahead(USA) Tatiana Romanova (USA) (Mr Greeley (USA))
**(2124)** 7572[14] 8243[10] 8552[12]

**She's Zoff (IRE)** *John Quinn* a45 30
3 b f Zoffany(IRE) Vindication People (USA) (Vindication (USA))
3975[8] **5050**[4] 5374[4] 6437[13] 9012[9]

**Shevington Moor** *Bryan Smart* 47
3 b f Equiano(FR) Soapy Delight (Dansili)
**2345**[7]

**Shift Cross** *Marco Botti* a66
3 br f Cape Cross(IRE) Rose Shift (IRE) (Night Shift (USA))
**1333**[5]

**Shifting Star (IRE)** *John Bridger* a72 74
12 ch g Night Shift(USA) Ahshado (Bin Ajwaad (IRE))
1086[8] (1338) 1687[3] (2297) 2677[3] 3521[4] **(3920)** 4446[4] **4698**[2] 5221[5] 6516[3] 7098[8] 7770[6] 8300[9] 8549[6]

**Shift On Sheila** *Pam Sly* a60 54
4 b m Aussie Rules(USA) Black Salix (USA) (More Than Ready (USA))
**2688**[7] **3439**[5]

**Shikoba (IRE)** *Simon Crisford* 38
2 b f Kodiac Shoshoni Wind (Sleeping Indian)
**6862**[8]

**Shillbourne Lad (IRE)** *Bill Turner* a29
3 bz g Lilbourne Lad(IRE) Gemma's Delight (IRE) (Clodovil (IRE))
**3686**[5]

**Shillong** *H Al Alawi* a81
4 b h Dubawi(IRE) Rainfall (IRE) (Oasis Dream)
**(8583a)**

**Shilo (IRE)** *C Von Der Recke* 31
2 b f Most Improved(IRE) Sacre Fleur (IRE) (Acclamation)
**6494a**[11]

**Shiloh** *Simon Crisford* a51 20
3 b f Poet's Voice Loveable (Oasis Dream)
**34**[7] 502[14]

**Shimmering Light** *Michael Bell* a71 74
3 ch f Dubawi(IRE) Summertime Legacy (Darshaan)
3748[5]◆ 4300[9] 5118[6] 5721[9] **7279**[2] 7550[3] 8497[6] 9027[11]

**Shimmy Shoes (IRE)**
*Jamie Osborne* a33 39
2 b f Reckless Abandon Silver Shoon (IRE) (Fasliyev (USA))
**3070**[10] 9188[7]

**Shine Baby Shine** *Philip Kirby* a66 51
3 b f Aqlaam Rosewood Belle (USA) (Woodman (USA))
3542[8] 4474[7] 4784[6] 5319[9] 5831[6] (6530) **6898**[2]

**Shine Through (IRE)** *Hugo Palmer* a36
3 b f Poet's Voice She Wolf (Medicean)
737[10] **1143**[7]

**Shinghari (IRE)** *Denis Gerard Hogan* 83
5 br g Cape Cross(IRE) Sindiyma (IRE) (Kalanisi (IRE))
**5488a**[10]

**Shining Emerald** *A Wohler* 106
6 b g Clodovil(IRE) Janayen (USA) (Zafonic (USA))
**6495a**[4]

**Shining Romeo** *Denis Quinn* a67 72
5 b g Royal Applause Silver Pivotal (IRE) (Pivotal)
238[4] (461) 965[6] 1284[5] 2022[8] **(4187)** **(4545)**◆ 8682[9]

**Shinyanga (FR)** *C Boutin* 44
2 bl f Zanzibari(USA) She Say'S (Oasis Dream)
**8228a**[11]

**Shinzaro (GER)** *D Moser* 95
3 b c Invincible Spirit(IRE) Shimrana (IRE) (Daylami (IRE))
2002a[7] **2869a**[7]

**Ship Of The Fen** *Martyn Meade* 78
2 b c Champs Elysees Ruffled (Harlan's Holiday (USA))
5036[3]◆ 5840[5] 6777[2] **(7956)**◆ 8354[6]

**Shirataki (IRE)** *Peter Hiatt* a60 59
9 b g Cape Cross(IRE) Noodle Soup (USA) (Alphabet Soup (USA))
2281[11] **3148**[2] 3221[4] 3916[6] 4734[6]

**Shobrom (IRE)** *Richard Fahey* 73
2 b g Acclamation Strasbourg Place (Compton Place)
1858[6] **2373**[2] 3826[6] 4527[6]

**Shoofly (IRE)** *David Harry Kelly* a69 69
4 b m Azamour(IRE) Natural Flair (USA) (Giant's Causeway (USA))
**5483**[2] 8955[10]

**Shootingsta (IRE)** *Bryan Smart* a41 84
5 b g Fast Company(IRE) Kiva (Indian Ridge (IRE))
1105[8] **2377**[8] 2883[6]

**Shootingthe Breeze**
*Tom Dascombe* a59 62
2 b g Dutch Art Clinet (IRE) (Dockside (USA))
4577[4] **5058**[5] 5844[7] 6951[5] 7829[12]

**Short Call (IRE)** *Mick Channon* 80
2 b f Kodiac Wiwilia (Konigstiger (GER))
**(3306)**◆ 3807[3]

**Short Work** *David O'Meara* a75 87
4 ch g Kyllachy Agony Aunt (Formidable I (USA))
1778[12] 2377[5] 3095[6] 3540[5] 3845[19] 4605[3] 5739[4] (6238) 6964[3] (7245)◆ (7923) 8014[3] **(8489)** 8879[8]

**Shot In The Dark (FR)** *F Chappet* a100 102
4 b g Dark Angel(IRE) Velvet Revolver (IRE) (Mujahid (USA))
**3614a**[6]

**Shot In The Dark (IRE)**
*Jonathan Geake* a24 35
8 ch g Dr Fong(USA) Highland Shot (Selkirk (USA))
**5274**[6] 6309[12]

**Shouldertoshoulder** *Stuart Williams* a53 42
3 ch g Paco Boy(IRE) Miss Bond (IRE) (Danehill Dancer (IRE))
**1024**[5] 1600[9] 2911[11] 3703[5]

**Shouranour (IRE)** *Alan Brown* a52 90
7 b g Lawman(FR) Sharesha (IRE) (Ashkalani (IRE))
2155[3] 2838[9] 3565[2] 3792[6] 4207[14] **(5165)** 5669[3] 6209[7] 6570[7] 7140[10] 8014[11] 8486[8]

**Shovel It On (IRE)** *David Evans* a43 71
2 br c Elusive Pimpernel(USA) Fitrah (IRE) (Tamayuz)
1604[4]◆ 1767[5] 3467[7] 4527[5] 5277[3] **(5752)** (6036) **6860**[4] 6977a[9]

**Showboating (IRE)** *John Balding* a91 89
9 b g Shamardal(USA) Sadinga (IRE) (Sadler's Wells (USA))
5[6] 156[2] 359[12] **(1074)** **1208**[3] 3144[6] (3567) (4210) 5425[5] 5668[16] 7246[4] 7594[7] 8240[6] 8736[10]

**Showdaisy** *Keith Dalgleish* a94 94
4 ch m Showcasing Darling Daisy (Komaite (USA))
4[7] 388[6] 664[10] 3337[5] 3827[3] 4081[6] **(4686)**

**Showdance Kid** *Kevin Frost* a70 70
3 b g Showcasing Maid To Dance (Pyramus (USA))
2036[8] 3296[11] 3745[10] 4540[3] 6435[3] **7414**[2] **7934**[2] 8216[11] 9180[12]

**Showdancing** *James Tate* a55 46
2 b f Showcasing Lady Vermeer (Dutch Art)
1909[6] **8148**[10]

**Showing Off (IRE)** *Michael Wigham* a77 85
4 ch g Notnowcato Walk On Water (Exceed And Excel (AUS))
**25**[13] 419[14] 663[11] 850[13]

**Showmethedough** *Richard Fahey* a64 83
2 ch g Showcasing Silver Purse (Interrex (CAN))
5891[3] 6231[2] **(7623)**

**Showmethewayavrilo**
*Malcolm Saunders* a73 75
4 ch g Showcasing Avrilo (Piccolo)
1836[6] 2253[5] 2709[10] 3532[3] (3774) 4256[9] 4752[3] 5051[6] 5564[5] 5784[4] 6303[3] 6615[2] 6888[4] 7195[6] **(7508)** 7737[8] 7947[8]

**Show Of Force** *Jonathan Portman* a39 66
2 gr f Lethal Force(IRE) Craighall (Dubawi (IRE))
3210[7] 4252[7]◆ 4963[4] 5154[7] **5999**[2] **(6504)** 8164[5]

**Show Palace** *Jennie Candlish* a65 92
4 ch g Showcasing Palais Polaire (Polar Falcon (USA))
1965[11] 2843[2] 4005[4] (4607) 5263[3] (5580) (5930) 6314[7] (7137) **(7625)** 8012[15]

**Show Princess** *Michael Appleby* a49 62
2 b f Showcasing Irina Princess (Selkirk (USA))
3562[4] 5210[9] 6433[4] **7222**[3] 8164[9] 8804[5]

**Showroom (FR)** *Mark Johnston* 87
2 b c Motivator Lemon Twist (IRE) (Marju (IRE))
**(6777)**◆

**Show Stealer** *Rae Guest* a92 84
4 ch m Showcasing Winifred Jo (Bahamian Bounty)
2390[15] 4864[8] 6234[8] 6695[8] 7604[3]◆ 8310[2] 8905[6] **(9185)**

**Showtime Blues** *Jim Boyle* a66 15
5 b g Showcasing Night Symphonie (Cloudings (IRE))
**145**[3] 332[5] 8551[13]

**Shoyd** *Richard Hannon* a63 57
2 ch f Showcasing Yding (IRE) (Danehill (USA))
3421[10] 4252[8] 5107[9] **6063**[2] 6585[8] 6815[4]

**Shraaoh (IRE)** *Sir Michael Stoute* a97 99
4 b g Sea The Stars(IRE) Jumooh (Monsun (GER))
3323[4] **4614**[3] 5638[13] 6675[11]

**Shrewd** *Iain Jardine* a92 106
7 b g Street Sense(USA) Cala (FR) (Desert Prince (IRE))
**1802**[8] 3928[14] 6329[9] 7115[3] **7402**[3] 8038[24]

**Shrewd Approach (IRE)**
*Simon Crisford* a52 72
2 ch f Dawn Approach(IRE) Al Sharood (Shamardal (USA))
4496[5] 5246[3] (5735) 6200[6] **(7647)** 8884a[11]

**Shrill** *Robert Cowell* a49 92
4 b m Shamardal(USA) Wood Vine (USA) (Woodman (USA))
1936[10] **4078**[12]

**Shrubland** *Alexandra Dunn* a57 61
4 b g High Chaparral(IRE) Ratukidul (FR) (Danehill (USA))
1697[10]

**Shudbeme** *Neville Bycroft* a39 41
4 ch g Monsieur Bond(IRE) Oomph (Shareef Dancer (USA))
**3185**[6] 6673[13] 9013[5]

**Shuhood (IRE)** *Richard Hannon* 75
2 b g Tamayuz Walayef (USA) (Danzig (USA))
4792[10] **(7818)**

**Shujaha (AUS)** *Pat Murphy* 37
4 b m New Approach(IRE) Umoya (Nashwan (USA))
**2908**[13]

**Shulammite Man (IRE)**
*Sally Haynes* a48 45
4 ch g Arcano(IRE) Shulammite Woman (IRE) (Desert Sun)
525[6] **1197**[5] 9258[7]

**Shurooq** *Owen Burrows* a38 70
2 gr f Dubawi(IRE) Natagora (FR) (Divine Light (JPN))
7453[11] **8594**[4]

**Shutterbug (FR)** *M Figge* 107
5 ch h Soldier Of Fortune(IRE) Nazlia (FR) (Polish Precedent (USA))
**3856a**[4] 4942a[4] 6173a[3] 6915a[4]

**Shutter Speed** *John Gosden* 109
3 br f Dansili Photographic (Oasis Dream)
**(1943)**◆ (2738)◆ **3881a**[4] 6328[6]

**Shyamala** *E J O'Neill* 73
2 b f Sepoy(AUS) Poppet's Passion (Clodovil (IRE))
**3679a**[2]

**Shy Angel** *A Wohler* 92
3 b f Zamindar(USA) Shy Lady (FR) (Kaldoun (FR))
**3371a**[4] 5693a[15]

**Shyarch** *Christine Dunnett* a55 62
3 b g Archipenko(USA) Coconut Shy (Bahamian Bounty)
1857[12] 2727[4] 2970[6] 5040[4] 5339[2] **(5852)** 7480[6]

**Shyjack** *George Margarson* a47
2 ch g Archipenko(USA) Coconut Shy (Bahamian Bounty)
8794[9] **8981**[6] 9335[11]

**Shymkent** *David O'Meara* 94
4 b g Pivotal Shabyt (Sadler's Wells (USA))
(2681) 3032[5] **(3528)**◆ 3998[10] **5598**[4]

**Shypen** *Richard Fahey* a89 81
4 b m Archipenko(USA) Coconut Shy (Bahamian Bounty)
66[8] 581[3] 896[5] (1261) **1771**[5] 2805[8] 3793[8]

**Shyron** *George Margarson* a96 78
6 b g Byron Coconut Shy (Bahamian Bounty)
5[10] 199[7] 598[5] 896[7] **999**[2] 4622[3] 5610[8] 6111[3] 7404[10] 8547[3] 8812[8] 8905[9] (9210)

**Shy Witch (GER)** *H-J Groschel* 106
4 b m Areion(GER) Shyla (GER) (Monsagem (USA))
(4518a) 6605a[4]
**Sibilance** *Ralph Beckett* a94 96
3 gr f Bated Breath Santa Sophia (IRE) (Linamix (FR))
(1796) 2802[3] 3964[18] 7113[11] 7781[3] 9125[3]
**Sicario (IRE)** *Jamie Osborne* a62
2 b g Thewayyouare(USA) Blessed Beauty (IRE) (Alhaarth (IRE))
6286[4]
**Sichuan Dar (AUS)** *A T Millard* 111
5 b g Not A Single Doubt(AUS) Apocrypha (AUS) (Octagonal (NZ))
9170a[8]
**Sicilia (GER)** *H Blume* a26
3 b f Sinndar(IRE) Sisika (IRE) (King's Theatre (IRE))
8692a[10]
**Sidewinder (IRE)** *Tom Dascombe* a83 83
3 b g Majestic Missile(IRE) Ron's Secret (Efisio)
221[2] 356[5] 1149[3] 1411[2] (2145) (3040) 3713[9] 4084[4] 4290[5] 6266[8] 7998[3]
**Siege Of Boston (IRE)**
*David C Griffiths* a88 75
4 ch g Starspangledbanner(AUS) Milton Of Campsie (Medicean)
50[5] (620) 724[2] 3666[4]◆ 3949[3] (6620) (6795) 8344[3] 8737[16] 8872[4] 9241[6]
**Siempre Amigos (IRE)**
*Gavin Cromwell* a60 63
4 gr m Fast Company(IRE) Zamiyla (IRE) (Daylami (IRE))
9077[U]
**Siena Flyer (IRE)** *Jedd O'Keeffe* a32 39
2 b f Big Bad Bob(IRE) Raggiante (IRE) (Rock Of Gibraltar (IRE))
5210[12] 6086[7] 6755[6] 8588[9]
**Sienna Dream** *Alistair Whillans* a59 56
2 b f Swiss Spirit Angry Bark (USA) (Woodman (USA))
7654[5] 8208[4] 8587[9]
**Sienna Says** *Tony Carroll* a57 63
2 b f Bated Breath Broughtons Charm (IRE) (Invincible Spirit (IRE))
3169[6] 4252[3] 4806[5] 5785[3] 6634[6] 7920[9]
**Siglo De Oro (IRE)** *F Chappet* 66
2 b c Clodovil(IRE) Puerto Oro (IRE) (Entrepreneur)
7844a[5]
**Signature Piece (USA)** *D Smaga* 56
2 b f Lemon Drop Kid(USA) Aviate (Dansili)
6542a[12]
**Signe (IRE)** *Mrs John Harrington* a88 87
4 b m Sea The Stars(IRE) Green Room (USA) (Theatrical (IRE))
(658) (1345) (1964) 4119[7] 6490a[14] 7588a[9]
**Significant Form (USA)**
*Chad C Brown* 104
2 rg f Creative Cause(USA) Church By The Sea (USA) (Harlan's Holiday (USA))
8575a[4]
**Sign Of The Kodiac (IRE)**
*Tony Newcombe* a100 84
4 b h Kodiac Summer Magic (IRE) (Desert Sun)
234[3] 3261[0] 842[9] 917[6] (1353a) 1772[7] 2566[5] 3321[19] 5241[2] 6025[6] 6412[6] 7455[5] 7828[2] 9373[6]
**Signore Piccolo** *David Loughnane* 91
6 b g Piccolo Piccolo Cativo (Komaite (USA))
2821[4] 3170[2] 3492[4] (3741) 4337[6] 4600[2] 5402[6] 5929[4] 6185[8] 7084[6] 7809[10] 8167[3]
**Signs Of Blessing (IRE)** *F Rohaut* a109 123
6 b g Invincible Spirit(IRE) Sun Bittern (USA) (Seeking The Gold (USA))
(2643a) 3926[8] 5690a[5] (6497a) 7670a[12] 9168a[13]
**Sigrid Nansen** *George Scott* a66 66
2 b f Cityscape Hail Shower (IRE) (Red Clubs (IRE))
6292[6] 6666[4] 7620[8] 8006[8] 8676[10] 8870[4]
**Sigurd (GER)** *Jonjo O'Neill* 53
5 ch g Sholokhov(IRE) Sky News (GER) (Highest Honor (FR))
2364[5] 3756[3]
**Sikandar (IRE)** *Brian Ellison* a70 80
5 ch g Medicean Siniyya (IRE) (Grand Lodge (USA))
1517[19] 1976[9] 2629[8] 4260[10] 4960[6] 5417[2] 5698[5]
**Sikandarabad (IRE)** *D K Weld* 103
4 b g Dr Fong(USA) Sindiyma (IRE) (Kalanisi (IRE))
1388a[9]
**Silca Mistress** *Mick Channon* a39 72
2 ch f Dutch Art Strictly Silca (Danehill Dancer (IRE))
3070[4] 3312[5] (3943) 4361[12] 5057[2] 5373[9] 6065[6]
**Silca Star** *Alan King* a72 78
4 ch g Medicean Silca Chiave (Pivotal)
2039[9] 2728[3] 4216[7] 5287[9]
**Sileel (USA)** *Ed Dunlop* a78 76
3 b f War Front(USA) Gilt (USA) (Bernardini (USA))
2019[10] 3615[2] 4497[2] 5124[6] 5707[4] 6623[2] (7032)
**Silent Assassin (IRE)** *S Seemar* a41 47
3 b g Shamardal(USA) La Belle Dane (Danetime (IRE))
430a[6] 697a[9] 887a[11]
**Silent Attack** *Saeed bin Suroor* a88 105
4 b g Dream Ahead(USA) Chanterelle (FR) (Trempolino (USA))
86a[6] 205a[15] 698a[13]
**Silent Echo** *Roger Charlton* a88 94
3 b g Oasis Dream Quiet (Observatory (USA))
(2366) (3082)◆ 4868[6] 6198[4] 7782[2]
**Silently** *Daniel Kubler* a49 60
4 b m Zamindar(USA) Quiet Elegance (Fantastic Light (USA))
6009[2] 6295[5]
**Silent Romance (FR)** *J E Hammond* a49 70
4 b m Dream Ahead(USA) Silent Sunday (IRE) (Testa Rossa (AUS))
5176a[3]
**Silhuette (IRE)** *Colin Teague* a61 74
4 b m Canford Cliffs(IRE) Lisfannon (Bahamian Bounty)
514[7] 660[7] 1030[7] 1210[6] 1593[5] 1973[4] 2454[7] 3563[7] 3704[9]
**Silk Cravat** *G M Lyons* a79 78
4 ch g Kyllachy Polly Floyer (Halling (USA))
(6799a)
**Silken Dancer** *Charlie Appleby* 83
3 b g Dubawi(IRE) Silkwood (Singspiel (IRE))
(2476) 4908[6]
**Silken Moonlight** *Scott Dixon* 43
3 b f Aqlaam Silk (IRE) (Machiavellian (USA))
3555[7] 4764[8] 5670[8]
**Silk Mill Blue** *Richard Whitaker* a47 64
3 b g Piccolo Marysienka (Primo Dominie)
2595[4] 3897[6] 4726[9] 5182[8] 7270[9]
**Silk Of Rio (FR)** *P Van De Poele* a73 34
3 b f Rio De La Plata(USA) Silk Gallery (USA) (Kingmambo (USA))
6455a[9]
**Silk Trader (IRE)** *Sharon Watt* 31
3 b f Tagula(IRE) Silk Affair (IRE) (Barathea (IRE))
1675[7] 2300[4] 2681[9] 3243[8] 6898[11]
**Silva Eclipse** *Jedd O'Keeffe* a69 86
4 gr g Multiplex Linen Line (Double Eclipse (IRE))
1309[6] 2770[4] 3527[4] 4301[5] 5468[6]
**Silvanus (IRE)** *Paul Midgley* a90 97
12 b g Danehill Dancer(IRE) Mala Mala (IRE) (Brief Truce (USA))
79[4] 358[8] 618[6] 1222[7] 1768[6] 2341[2]◆ 2551[2] 3052[2] 3707[9] 4337[7] (4850) 5256[3] 6411[5] 6758[5] 7256[4]
**Silver Alliance** *Julia Feilden* a59 62
9 gr g Proclamation(IRE) Aimee Vibert (Zilzal (USA))
382[9] 806[8] 1707[10] 2282[5] 2729[9] 3325[7] 4461[4]◆ 5790[11]
**Silver Bid (USA)** *Karen Tutty* a75 40
5 gr g Exchange Rate(USA) Micaela's Moon (USA) (Malibu Moon (USA))
1431[8] 1869[5] 2627[5] 3256[8]
**Silverbook** *Charlie Appleby* a81
2 b c New Approach(IRE) Sahraah (USA) (Kingmambo (USA))
8704[2]
**Silver Bullet (IRE)** *Tom Dascombe* a56 58
2 gr f Camacho Sixfields Flyer (IRE) (Desert Style (IRE))
2265[5] 3687[9] 4440[6] 6285[4] 6634[8] 7510[10]
**Silver Cape (FR)** *T Clout* a75 101
3 b f Silver Frost(IRE) Cape Talks (IRE) (Cape Cross (IRE))
4665a[6] 5449a[9] 6804a[5] 7341a[7]
**Silver Casina (IRE)** *G Botti* a71 71
3 b c Casamento(IRE) Silvertine (IRE) (Alzao (USA))
6124a[5] 8959a[8]
**Silver Character (IRE)**
*Tom Dascombe* a67
2 gr c Camelot Convocate (USA) (Exchange Rate (USA))
8849[4]
**Silver Cloud (GER)** *S Smrczek* a75 86
3 b f Soldier Hollow Sassicaia (GER) (Doyen (IRE))
6254a[4]
**Silver Crescent** *Ralph Beckett* a64 62
2 b g Champs Elysees Winter Solstice (Unfuwain (USA))
6777[7] 7543[12] 8952[5]
**Silver Dixie (USA)** *Peter Hedger* a65 65
7 br g Dixie Union(USA) More Silver (USA) (Silver Hawk (USA))
3753[12] 4538[5] 5024[5] 6175[2]◆ 6588[2] 7495[5] 8386[12] 8549[3] 8946[5] 9092[P]
**Silver Duke (IRE)** *Jim Goldie* a48 67
6 gr g Papal Bull Dumaani's Dream (USA) (Dumaani (USA))
44[12] 3048[9] 4659[12] 5254[12]
**Silver Express (FR)**
*Mme Pia Brandt* a78 72
3 gr f Silver Frost(IRE) Surpressa (FR) (Take Risks (FR))
8885a[4]
**Silver Ghost (IRE)**
*Eve Johnson Houghton* a75 99
4 gr g Dark Angel(IRE) Aqualina (IRE) (King's Theatre (IRE))
2333[4] 3009[2] (3616) (4522) (5330) 6698[4] 7395[4] 7735[3]
**Silver Gleam (IRE)** *Chris Fairhurst* a30 59
3 gr f Zoffany(IRE) Gleaming Silver (IRE) (Dalakhani (IRE))
2705[6] 3180[7] 3489[9] 5017[4] 5617[6] 6270[4] 6565[7] 7248[4] 7629[4]
**Silverkode (IRE)** *Joseph G Murphy* 104
3 b g Kodiac Silver Tide (USA) (Silver Hawk (USA))
6961a[2] 7663a[9] 8438a[9]
**Silverlight (IRE)** *Philip Kirby* 47
2 gr f Fast Company(IRE) Rangooned (Bahamian Bounty)
5613[2] 5945[4] 6517[6]
**Silver Lining (IRE)** *Mark Hoad* a42 30
5 gr g Dark Angel(IRE) Out Of Woods (USA) (Woodman (USA))
123[9] 281[10] 621[11] 1402[10] 4177[8] 5296[9]
**Silver Link (IRE)** *Marcus Tregoning* a79 79
3 b f Arcano(IRE) Miss Bellbird (IRE) (Danehill (USA))
4449[2] 5273[2] 8166[4] 8478[6] (8744) 9082[8]
**Silver Look (ARG)** *S Kobayashi* a93 20
3 gr m Archipenko(USA) Silver Fortune (USA) (Labeeb)
9003a[14]
**Silver Meadow (IRE)** *F-H Graffard* a81 100
4 b m Teofilo(IRE) Silver Bark (Royal Applause)
3319[4] 6804a[4] 7672a[5]
**Silver Mist** *Sylvester Kirk* a22 37
3 gr f Kyllachy Mundus Novus (USA) (Unbridled's Song (USA))
1580[6] 5411[6] 5792[9] 6341[10]
**Silver Ocean (USA)** *Niels Petersen* a99 103
9 br g Silver Train(USA) Endless Sea (CAN) (Mt. Livermore (USA))
2942a[2]
**Silver Penny** *Jim Boyle* a50 50
3 gr f Hellvelyn Pennyspider (IRE) (Redback)
2235[12] 2725[7] 4011[5] 4500[9] 5295[6] 6324[7] 6581[6] 7191[7] 7692[4] 7993[2] 8298[3] 9075[3]◆ 9129[3]
**Silver Poker (FR)** *D Chenu* a62 60
3 b c Policy Maker(IRE) Silver Diane (FR) (Silver Rainbow)
1417a[8]
**Silver Quartz** *Hugo Palmer* 76
2 gr c Frankel Rosamixa (FR) (Linamix (FR))
7813[2]◆
**Silver Quay (IRE)** *Jimmy Frost* a92 89
5 gr g Dark Angel(IRE) She Runs (FR) (Sheyrann)
269[7] 467[4] 683[2] 759[5] 1153[7] 1590[2] 4801[3] 6508[7]
**Silverrica (IRE)** *Malcolm Saunders* 81
7 gr m Ad Valorem(USA) Allegorica (IRE) (Alzao (USA))
2360[2] 2621[10] 3021[2] 3281[5] 3865[7] 4489[7] 5587[6] 6303[6]
**Silver Ring (FR)**
*Mme C Head-Maarek* a61 70
3 b c Motivator Silver Fame (USA) (Quest For Fame)
6124a[10]
**Silver Saint (FR)** *F Foresi*
3 gr g Silver Frost(IRE) Sainte Glace (FR) (Grape Tree Road)
8959a[9]
**Silver Sea** *Seamus Mullins* a61 22
4 b g Sholokhov(IRE) Sword Roche (GER) (Laroche (GER))
4750[6] 5432[10]
**Silver Shuffle (IRE)** *Dianne Sayer* a57 66
10 ch g Big Shuffle(USA) Silvetta (Lando (GER))
1519[10]
**Silver Springs (IRE)** *Roger Ingram* a63 38
4 gr m Zebedee Charming Vista (Josr Algarhoud (IRE))
95[8] 468[12] 601[5] 860[14] 981[4] 2214[8] 2509[9] 3728[14] 4990[7] 7763[11] 9340[12]
**Silver Starlight** *Tim Easterby* 79
2 gr f Showcasing Pendulum (Pursuit Of Love)
2987[6] 3482[3] (3980) 4866[2] (5373) 5614[2] 6353[6] 7087[4] 7821[14]
**Silver Step (FR)** *Mme Pia Brandt* a81 107
4 gr m Silver Frost(IRE) Negra Del Oro (GER) (Danehill Dancer (IRE))
431a[4] 771a[4] 2432[6] 3319[6] 6804a[6]
**Silver Storm (FR)** *C Ferland* a77 101
3 gr f Kendargent(FR) Fantastic Filly (FR) (Myrakalu (FR))
1690a[3] 6054a[7]
**Silver Stripes (IRE)** *P Vovcenko* 71
2 gr f Red Jazz(USA) Pitullie (USA) (Rockport Harbor (USA))
8252a[2] 8777a[10]
**Silver Swift** *Andrew Balding* a41
2 b f Dutch Art Silver Kestrel (USA) (Silver Hawk (USA))
7724[10]
**Silver Treasure (FR)** *J-M Capitte* a49 94
6 gr g Clodovil(IRE) Ardesia Si (FR) (Treasure Kay)
930a[8]
**Silverturnstogold** *Neil Mulholland* a50
2 ch c Equiano(FR) Saharan Song (IRE) (Singspiel (IRE))
9198[8] 9311[6]
**Silverwave (FR)** *P Bary* a83 118
5 b h Silver Frost(IRE) Miss Bio (FR) (River Mist (USA))
2249a[3] (3369a) 4423a[2] 6983a[5] 7668a[18]
**Silver Wings (IRE)** *David Evans* a56 51
4 gr g Zebedee Daisy Hill (Indian Ridge (IRE))
2091[5] 2509[6]
**Silvery Moon (IRE)** *Tim Easterby* 95
10 gr g Verglas(IRE) Starry Night (Sheikh Albadou)
1911[5] 2155[10] 2406[11] 2855[8] 4207[4] 4377[6] 7246[5] 7566[2] 7823[7] 8048[7] (8289) 8652[4]
**Silvington** *Tony Carroll* a58 63
2 b c Firebreak Millinsky (USA) (Stravinsky (USA))
3244[3] 4273[3] 5561[5] 7707[10] 8658[9]
**Simmie (IRE)** *K R Burke* a77 92
3 b f Fast Company(IRE) Kathy Sun (IRE) (Intikhab (USA))
2823[2]◆ 3613a[5] 7806[8] 8526a[8]
**Simmo's Partytrick (IRE)**
*Geoffrey Harker* a47 50
4 b h Baltic King Goose Island (IRE) (Kahyasi (IRE))
4055[8] 4508[7] 4693[5] 6902[8]
**Simmy's Copshop** *Richard Fahey* 90
2 ch c Bahamian Bounty Conversational (IRE) (Thousand Words)
(1966)◆ 2861a[3] 3929[12] 4596a[2] 5109[4] 6207[2] 7138[3] 7564[3] 7821[16]
**Simple Thought (IRE)**
*Simon Crisford* 39
2 b f Teofilo(IRE) Punita (USA) (Distorted Humor (USA))
5938[8]
**Simple Verse (IRE)** *Ralph Beckett* a72 115
5 b m Duke Of Marmalade(IRE) Guantanamera (IRE) (Sadler's Wells (USA))
2803[2]◆ 3996[14]
**Simply Breathless** *Clive Cox* a71 71
2 b f Bated Breath Darling Grace (Nayef (USA))
2750[6] (3690) 5030[3] 6375[2] 7764[3]
**Simply Brilliant** *Richard Fahey* 88
3 ch g Frankel Red Bloom (Selkirk (USA))
2739[5]◆ 3997[6]
**Simply Clever** *David Brown* a60 60
4 ch m Stimulation(IRE) Well Of Echoes (Diktat)
605[2] 1260[2] 1545[2] 1893[7] 7760[10] 8122[8] 8498[8]
**Simply Genius (FR)** *F Chappet* a77 22
3 gr c Manduro(GER) Dinner Bell (FR) (Highest Honor (FR))
6084a[14]
**Simply Me** *Tom Dascombe* a85 62
4 b m New Approach(IRE) Ego (Green Desert (USA))
(394)◆ (677)◆ (996) 1066[3] 1368[6] (3548) 6321[5] 7484[8] 8546[11]
**Simply Sweet (FR)** *Louis Baudron* 76
3 b f Soldier Of Fortune(IRE) Super Nana (FR) (Anabaa (USA))
4232a[14]
**Simpson (IRE)** *Ed Walker* a65 89
2 ch g Dragon Pulse(IRE) Salydora (FR) (Peintre Celebre (USA))
3390[2] 3999[3] 4805[5] (6762) 7251[3] 7904[3] 8354[2]
**Sinaloa (IRE)** *Richard Fahey* a63 73
2 ch g Camacho Rose Of Battle (Averti (IRE))
2029[3] 2382[5] 5127[5] 5644[2] 6693[5] 7363[7] 8287[7]
**Sincerely Resdev** *Philip Kirby* 57
2 br g Rock Of Gibraltar(IRE) Sincerely (Singspiel (IRE))
6658[6] 7556[5] 7978[4]
**Sindarban (IRE)** *Keith Dalgleish* a80 94
6 ch g Teofilo(IRE) Sinndiya (IRE) (Pharly (FR))
1802[5] 2085[5] 3716[6] 9271[9]
**Sindarin** *Jim Goldie* 21
4 b g Sulamani(IRE) Aunt Rita (IRE) (Grand Lodge (USA))
2429[10] 2842[7]
**Sinfonietta (FR)** *David Menuisier* a91 97
5 b g Sinndar(IRE) Final Whistle (IRE) (Rossini (USA))
1492[2] 2828[7] 4882[4] 5530[10] 6491a[3] 7149[9] 7619[22] 8566[4] 9003a[10]
**Singapore Sling** *James Fanshawe* a78 80
4 b g Paco Boy(IRE) Buena Notte (IRE) (Halling (USA))
3441[3] 4019[3] 5140[2] 5663[7] 7601[3]
**Singer In The Sand (IRE)**
*Pat Phelan* a44
2 b f Footstepsinthesand Village Singer (USA) (Rahy (USA))
8987[12] 9200[11]
**Singeur (IRE)** *Rebecca Bastiman* a80 91
10 b g Chineur(FR) Singitta (Singspiel (IRE))
1876[9] 2409[5] 5671[4] 6205[5] 7055[7] 7940[5]
**Singing Sands (IRE)**
*Seamus Durack* a71 73
3 b f Harbour Watch(IRE) Elektra Marino (Mount Nelson)
1686[4] 2587[4]◆ 3142[6] 4184[10] 4810[10] 5275[7] 5748[6]
**Single Estate** *Simon Waugh* 54
3 b g Tamayuz Duo De Choc (IRE) (Manduro (GER))
2903[2] 3207[6] 3977[9] 6898[13] 7478[14]
**Single Gaze (AUS)** *Nick Olive* 111
4 ch m Not A Single Doubt(AUS) Redaluca's Gaze (AUS) (Intergaze (AUS))
8058a[4] 8250a[2] 8667a[17]
**Sing Out Loud (IRE)** *Gary Moore* a77 80
2 b g Vocalised(USA) Tus Maith (IRE) (Entrepreneur)
5641[9] (6262) 7513[3] 7913[2]◆ (8179)
**Singula** *Alan King* a51 45
3 b g Mayson Tagula Sunrise (IRE) (Tagula (IRE))
3784[13] 8242[7] 8742[12]
**Singular Quest**
*Daniel Mark Loughnane* a64 72
5 ch g Dalakhani(IRE) Singuliere (IRE) (Singspiel (IRE))
7413[3]◆ 7831[3] 8396[3]◆ 8955[4] 9421[6]
**Sing With Bess (IRE)** *M Weiss* 72
6 gr m Clodovil(IRE) Five Of Wands (Caerleon (USA))
716a[7]
**Singyoursong (IRE)** *David Simcock* a89 100
4 b m Aqlaam Dhan Dhana (IRE) (Dubawi (IRE))
(2254)◆ 2605[3] 3219[2] 5658[10] 9386[2]
**Sinour (IRE)** *Robert Stephens* a9 3
7 b g Observatory(USA) Siniyya (IRE) (Grand Lodge (USA))
19[6]
**Sinyor Samil (TUR)** *Ibrahim Cak* a92
3 b c Scarface(TUR) Figaro (TUR) (Senor Speedy (USA))
6717a[6]
**Sioux Frontier (IRE)** *Richard Fahey* a67 61
2 b g Excelebration(IRE) Sioux Rising (IRE) (Danetime (IRE))
7818[5] 8287[4]◆ 8715[2] 9097[8]
**Sioux Nation (USA)** *A P O'Brien* 115
2 b c Scat Daddy(USA) Dream The Blues (IRE) (Oasis Dream)
3098a[6] (3993) (5973a) 7618[6]
**Siouxperhero (IRE)** *William Muir* a67 61
8 b g Sleeping Indian Tintern (Diktat)
166[7] 420[2] 769[8] 954[2] (1067) 1334[11] 1839[5] 2055[4] 3519[5]
**Sir Billy Wright (IRE)** *David Evans* a91 92
6 b g High Chaparral(IRE) Lure Of The Moon (USA) (Lure (USA))
(664) 1110[3] 1295[4] 1515[14] 2528[11] 3161[8] 3424[2] (4505) 5123[4] 5705[5] 6371[3] 7612[6] 7742[4]
**Sir Chauvelin** *Jim Goldie* a102 102
5 b g Authorized(IRE) Jabbara (IRE) (Kingmambo (USA))
1802[6] 2157[2] 2525[7] (2774) 4356[6] 4849[2] 5638[7] 7619[20] 8740[23] (8910)
**Sir Commander (IRE)**
*William Haggas* a68
2 b c Lethal Force(IRE) Ronja (USA) (El Corredor (USA))
8988[3]
**Sir Compton** *Stuart Kittow* a63 56
4 b g Compton Place Dilys (Efisio)
1603[9] 4251[10] 4747[3] 5359[6] 5793[10]
**Sir Dancealot (IRE)** *David Elsworth* a97 114
3 b g Sir Prancealot(IRE) Majesty's Dancer (IRE) (Danehill Dancer (IRE))
1881[5] 2289[6] 3959[12] 4905[2] 5640[22] 6193[5] 7145[6]◆ 8138[2] (8417) 8738[5]
**Sir Derrick (IRE)** *Tim Easterby* 57
2 ch g Sir Prancealot(IRE) Alexander Confranc (IRE) (Magical Wonder (USA))
6056[6] 6432[12] 7013[6]

**Sir Domino (FR)** *Patrick Holmes* a46 80
5 b g Evasive Domino Queen I (IRE) (Primo Dominie)
2858[8] 3239[8] 4605[8] 5738[8] 6384[6] 6786[6] 7218[8] 7825[16]

**Sir Dudley (IRE)** *James Given* a84 74
4 b g Arcano(IRE) Rosy Dudley (IRE) (Grand Lodge (USA))
3903[2]

**Sir Dylan** *Polly Gundry* a55 46
8 b g Dylan Thomas(IRE) Monteleone (IRE) (Montjeu (IRE))
3192[2] 5716[10] 6309[8] 6589[6] 8430[6]

**Sir Ector (USA)**
*Miss Nicole McKenna* 90
10 br g Dynaformer(USA) Beyond The Waves (USA) (Ocean Crest (USA))
5488a[11] 7860a[20]

**Siren's Cove** *Kenneth Slack* a84 79
5 b m Sir Percy Siren Sound (Singspiel (IRE))
42[2]

**Sirens Rock (IRE)**
*Eve Johnson Houghton*
4 b m Fastnet Rock(AUS) Foolish Act (IRE) (Sadler's Wells (USA))
144[P]

**Sir Geoffrey (IRE)** *Scott Dixon* a66 56
11 b g Captain Rio Disarm (IRE) (Bahamian Bounty)
2076[6] (2298) 2472[3] 2994[2] (3289) 3563[5] 4695[8] 5282[7] 5736[7] 6130[2] 6531[8]

**Sir Gnet (IRE)** *Ed Dunlop* a70 70
3 b c Galileo(IRE) Ecoutila (USA) (Rahy (USA))
2167[5] 2783[17] 3293[6] 4255[2] 4541[2] 5131[5] 6160[3] 6948[2]◆ 7568[6] 7831[5] 8550[4] 9376[7]

**Sir Hamilton (IRE)** *Denis Quinn* a81 63
2 b c Canford Cliffs(IRE) Cawett (IRE) (Danehill Dancer (IRE))
8560[7] (9240)

**Sir Harry Collins (IRE)**
*Michael Appleby* a50 11
3 gr g Zebedee Unreal (Dansili)
1359[2] 1418[7] 2792[12] 3141[7] 3703[9] 8980[8] 9034[5] 9102[4] 9215[4] 9348[8]

**Sir Hector (IRE)** *Charlie Wallis* a59
2 ch g Sir Prancealot(IRE) Awwal Malika (USA) (Kingmambo (USA))
2577[7] 9123[8] 9198[5]

**Sirici (IRE)** *J A Stack* a85 97
2 ch f Choisir(AUS) Mironica (IRE) (Excellent Art)
2861a[6] 3960[14] 6241a[3]

**Sir Isaac Newton** *Robert Hickmott* a77 117
5 b g Galileo(IRE) Shastye (IRE) (Danehill (USA))
8250a[17]

**Sirius (GER)** *Andreas Suborics* 111
6 ch h Dashing Blade Saratina (IRE) (Monsun (GER))
2450a[2] 3119a[2] 4879a[3] 5983a[6] 6984a[8]

**Sir Jack** *Tony Carroll* a55 69
4 b g Sir Percy Play Bouzouki (Halling (USA))
278[3] 525[4] 1082[9] 1458[8] 2257[2] 2295[6] 2914[3] (3143) 3628[2] 3813[2] 5299[3] 5698[2]◆ 5820[2] 6188[5] 7028[7] 7735[11] 8135[10]

**Sirjack Thomas (IRE)**
*Madeleine Tylicki* 87
2 gr c Fast Company(IRE) Veliyka (IRE) (Linamix (FR))
6955a[9]

**Sir Jamie** *Tony Carroll* a53 41
4 ch g Monsieur Bond(IRE) First Dawn (Dr Fong (USA))
167[5] 425[3] 621[12] 1425[2] (1563) 2255[9] 3823[6] 4143a[5] 6846[5] 8994[10] 9218[8] 9454[10]

**Sir John Lavery (IRE)** *A P O'Brien* 112
3 b c Galileo(IRE) Race For The Stars (USA) (Fusaichi Pegasus (USA))
2614[6] 4029[9] 6959a[4] 7579[2] 8232[11]

**Sir Lancelott** *Adrian Nicholls* a66 40
5 b g Piccolo Selkirk Rose (IRE) (Pips Pride)
(239) 420[5] 689[8] 928[7] 1484[8] 5897[4] 6947[5] 7960[13] 8248[10] 9076[7] 9342[8]

**Sir Leonard Kitter (IRE)**
*Richard Hannon* a10 21
2 ro c Mastercraftsman(IRE) Trail Of Tears (IRE) (Exceed And Excel (AUS))
7740[7] 8155[9]

**Sirma Traou Land (FR)** *B Legros* a55 59
3 bl f Soul City(IRE) Peldrine (FR) (Pelder (IRE))
1417a[4] 2536a[3] 4289a[11]

**Sir Maximilian (IRE)** *Ian Williams* a96 105
8 b g Royal Applause Nebraska Lady (IRE) (Lujain (USA))
84a[8] 318a[2] 543a[11] 651a[3] 9187[7]

**Sir Ottoman (FR)** *Ivan Furtado* a86 54
4 b g Excellent Art Hali Layali (Green Desert (USA))
1078a[4] 1863[9] 3324[16] 7828[10] 8639[6] 9241[9]

**Sir Pass I Am** *Andrew Balding* a42 72
4 b g Passing Glance Orbital Orchid (Mujahid (USA))
2022[10] (2712)◆ 2966[7] 6096[6]

**Sir Plato (IRE)** *Rod Millman* a63 85
3 b g Sir Prancealot(IRE) Dessert Flower (IRE) (Intikhab (USA))
(1421) (1686) 1875[6] (3163) (4153) 5033[5] (5719)◆ 6516[7] 7131[7] 7909[6]

**Sir Reginald Brown** *Richard Fahey* 78
3 b g Archipenko(USA) Elusive Sue (USA) (Elusive Quality (USA))
(1680) 2739[7]◆ 3588[2] 4868[7] 6855[6] 8386[11]

**Sirrin (IRE)** *J-C Rouget* 103
3 b f Sea The Stars(IRE) Sindirana (IRE) (Kalanisi (IRE))
5981a[8]

**Sir Robert Cheval** *Robert Cowell* a102 108
6 b g Green Desert(USA) Aunt Ruby (USA) (Rubiano (USA))
(1946) 2657a[6] 3614a[7] 5911[2] 7804[2]

**Sir Roderic (IRE)** *Rod Millman* 101
4 b g Roderic O'Connor(IRE) Begin The Beguine (IRE) (Peintre Celebre (USA))
1492[12] 1960[19] 3014[3] 3837[11] 4223[5] 4916[8] 5393[18] 5594[14] 6192[3] 6676[8] 7129[10] 8297[10]

**Sir Runs A Lot** *David Barron* a59 58
5 b g Sir Percy Monjouet (IRE) (Montjeu (IRE))
2632[7] 3465[7] 3898[7] 4660[8] 5005[3] 5267[11] (6901) 7936[8]

**Sir Theodore (IRE)**
*Richard Spencer* a57 78
4 b g Arcano(IRE) Key Rose (IRE) (Key Of Luck (USA))
242[10] 518[9]

**Sir Titan** *Marcus Tregoning* a81 93
3 b g Aqlaam Femme De Fer (Hamas (IRE))
(4164)◆ (4698) 5642[2] 6289[11] 8736[17] 8880[7]

**Sir Valentine (GER)** *Alan King* a88 90
4 b g Cacique(IRE) Singuna (GER) (Black Sam Bellamy (IRE))
3067[5]

**Sir Walter (IRE)** *Eric Alston* 40
2 b g Camacho Damalis (IRE) (Mukaddamah (USA))
2522[10] 2948[11] 3490[6] 7518[20] 7919[9] 8475[10]

**Sisene (IRE)** *P Monfort* a77 99
4 b m Pivotal Atasari (IRE) (Whipper (USA))
3883a[8] 6914a[3]

**Sistah (IRE)** *Y Durepaire* 70
2 ch f Intello(GER) Sismix (IRE) (Diesis)
7415a[4]

**Sister Blandina (IRE)** *J P Murtagh* a53 95
4 rg m Mastercraftsman(IRE) Tara's Wells (IRE) (Sadler's Wells (USA))
8083a[8]

**Sister Celine (IRE)** *Roger Charlton* a43 54
2 b f Al Kazeem Quan Yin (IRE) (Sadler's Wells (USA))
6386[8] 7997[12] 8419[9]

**Sistercharlie (IRE)** *Chad C Brown* a75 110
3 b f Myboycharlie(IRE) Starlet's Sister (IRE) (Galileo (IRE))
(2003a) 3881a[2] 4650a[2]

**Sister Dude** *Jonathan Portman* 70
4 ch m Notnowcato Inaminute (IRE) (Spectrum (IRE))
2285[3] 3142[8] 3396[11] 4470[5] 5290[8]

**Sister Vic (FR)** *N Caullery* a57 62
3 gr f Tin Horse(IRE) Matsot (FR) (Maresca Sorrento (FR))
6496a[7] 6649a[3]

**Sisyphus** *Ollie Pears* a85 84
5 b g Halling(USA) Cape Dancer (IRE) (Cape Cross (IRE))
(1548)

**Sitar** *James Fanshawe* a63 76
3 b f Aqlaam Soundwave (Prince Sabo)
2072[9] 2725[5] (3624) 4324[3] (5263) 6040[6] 6877[7] 7282[5]

**Site Seeing (FR)** *N Clement* 92
3 ch f Muhtathir Landing Site (FR) (Peintre Celebre (USA))
2447a[5]

**Sitsi** *Bryan Smart* a25 49
2 ch f Captain Gerrard(IRE) Ayasha (Indesatchel (IRE))
5210[7] 5998[4] 6624[4] 8780[9]

**Situation** *Richard Guest* 66
2 ch g Lethal Force(IRE) Russian Dance (USA) (Nureyev (USA))
3051[4] 4503[4] 4895[9] 5279[5] 5366[8] 5752[4] 6625[9] 7519[19]

**Sivinsk (FR)** *Simone Brogi* a88 42
3 b c Siyouni(FR) Vinskaia (USA) (Vindication (USA))
4289a[3] 5521a[3] 6455a[4] 7308a[5]

**Six Of The Best** *Bryan Smart* a40 42
5 b m Monsieur Bond(IRE) Bond Casino (Kyllachy)
510[7] 956[8] 1349[5] 4478[6] 4997[6]◆ 6045[9] 6572[7] 8592[5]

**Six Silver Lane** *John James Feane* a75 69
9 gr g Aussie Rules(USA) Aurelia (Rainbow Quest (USA))
2498[4]

**Six Strings** *Richard Fahey* a83 91
3 b g Requinto(IRE) Island Music (IRE) (Mujahid (USA))
3592[2]◆ 5094[3] 5637[10] 6186[3] 7053[7]

**Sixth Of June** *Rod Millman* a39 54
3 b f Crosspeace(IRE) Eccentricity (Emarati (USA))
7900[7] 8345[6] 9237[13]

**Sixties Groove (IRE)**
*Jeremy Noseda* a102 102
4 b g Sixties Icon Gift Dancer (Imperial Dancer)
3298[7]◆ 4033[5] 4918[14]

**Sixties Habana** *Pat Phelan* a57 66
3 b g Sixties Icon Vilnius (Imperial Dancer)
323[7] 2016[6] 2911[8] 3660[3] 4211[7] 5028[3] 5411[3]

**Sixties Idol** *Sheena West* a46 54
4 b m Sixties Icon Fading Away (Fraam)
279[5] 462[5] 621[7] 1082[12]

**Sixties Secret** *Mick Channon* a49 49
2 b f Sixties Icon Jollyhockeysticks (Fantastic Light (USA))
4533[13] 4909[10] 5161[4] 5756[3] 6022[3] 6366[6]

**Sixties Song (ARG)**
*Alfredo F Gaitan Dassie* 112
3 b h Sixties Icon Blissful Song (USA) (Unbridled's Song (USA))
5394[10]

**Sixties Sue** *Luke Comer* a53 53
4 gr m Sixties Icon Rose Cheval (USA) (Johannesburg (USA))
1385a[13]

**Sixties Symphony** *John Flint*
3 b f Sixties Icon Moyoko (IRE) (Mozart (IRE))
2782[11] 3279[7] 3758[13]

**Sixty Sixty (FR)** *J-C Rouget* a95 97
3 b g Canford Cliffs(IRE) Spring Morning (FR) (Ashkalani (IRE))
(584a)

**Siyahamba (IRE)** *Bryan Smart* a41 53
3 ch g Helmet(AUS) Kalabunga (IRE) (Val Royal (FR))
3745[3] 4838[3] 5617[4] 6048[12] 7271[6] 7820[5] 8650[2] 9030[3] 9221[9]

**Siyougirl** *A Vetault* a63 61
2 ch f Siyouni(FR) Queen Of West (FR) (King Of Kings (IRE))
1929a[2] 7415a[6]

**Siyoushake (IRE)** *F Head* a74 115
5 b m Siyouni(FR) Shakeyourbody (USA) (Giant's Causeway (USA))
2248a[10] 3880a[3] 5460a[3] 6248a[2] 7812[10]

**Size Matters** *Mark Walford* a52 62
3 b g Captain Gerrard(IRE) Icky Woo (Mark Of Esteem (IRE))
2060[7] 2702[2] 3745[5] 4298[3]◆ 5126[4] 5666[3] (5991) 6529[5] 7934[5]

**Sizzling (IRE)** *A P O'Brien* 104
2 ch f Galileo(IRE) Weekend Strike (USA) (Smart Strike (CAN))
4902[2] 7088[4] 7421a[2] 7859a[4]

**Skalleto (FR)** *P Sogorb* a74 96
3 b g Kendargent(FR) Skallet (FR) (Muhaymin (USA))
6963a[6] 8089a[3]

**Skeaping** *Gordon Elliott* a74 83
4 b g Excellent Art Gale Green (Galileo (IRE))
2528[13]

**Skellig Michael** *Ben Haslam* a61 58
3 b g Arakan(USA) Ambonnay (Ashkalani (IRE))
178[5] (546) 1005[2] 2182[10]

**Sketch Book Venue (IRE)**
*Sally Haynes* 68
3 b g Rip Van Winkle(IRE) Parvenue (FR) (Ezzoud (IRE))
1676[2]◆ 5757[P] (Dead)

**Ski Blast** *Ivan Furtado* 80
6 ch g Three Valleys(USA) Chasing Stars (Observatory (USA))
2505[5] 3433[7] 4298[6] 5337[2] (6188)

**Skidby Mill (IRE)** *Laura Mongan* a78 69
7 b m Ramonti(FR) Glasnas Giant (Giant's Causeway (USA))
(232) 550[2] 677[4] 996[4] 1447[2] 1897[4] 2116[11] 6818[11] 7493[11] 8156[11] 8550[12]

**Skiddaw Valleys** *Sally Haynes* a56 78
5 ch g Three Valleys(USA) Skiddaw Wolf (Wolfhound (USA))
5706[6]

**Skiffle** *Charlie Appleby* 104
4 b m Dubawi(IRE) Princesse Dansante (IRE) (King's Best (USA))
2432[7] 5155[6] 5529[5] 6074[8]

**Skilful Lord (IRE)** *David Pipe* a45 47
3 ch g Lord Shanakill(USA) Monsusu (IRE) (Montjeu (IRE))
1597[7] 2060[6] 8673[11]

**Skilled** *Anabel K Murphy* a42 66
6 b g Mastercraftsman(IRE) Treacle (USA) (Seeking The Gold (USA))
74[9]

**Skiperia (FR)** *Y Barberot* a89 81
6 ch m Gold Away(IRE) Lerina (FR) (Priolo (USA))
5979a[9] 9003a[9]

**Skito Soldier** *K R Burke* a60 72
2 b g Sepoy(AUS) Kotsi (IRE) (Nayef (USA))
5874[3] 6465[3] 7613[7] 8316[7]

**Skulduggery (AUS)**
*Shawn Mathrick* 89
4 ch g Krupt(AUS) Aqua Modern (AUS) (Tiger Hill (IRE))
8633a[4]

**Sky Ballerina** *Simon Crisford* a74 66
3 b f Makfi Maid In Heaven (IRE) (Clodovil (IRE))
(160)◆ 392[2] 512[3]

**Sky Bandit** *Gary Moore* 54
2 gr f Dick Turpin(IRE) Aurora Sky (IRE) (Hawk Wing (USA))
7504[5]

**Sky Bolt (FR)** *H-A Pantall* a71 74
4 ch h Denon(USA) Suvretta Queen (IRE) (Polish Precedent (USA))
9112a[2]

**Sky Cape** *Heather Main* a71 51
5 b g Cape Cross(IRE) Green Swallow (FR) (Green Tune (USA))
809[5] 2796[4]

**Sky Eagle (IRE)** *Ed Walker* a71 62
3 ch c Lope De Vega(IRE) Penelope Star (GER) (Acatenango (GER))
5220[16] 6031[3]◆ 6852[4] 8312[2] (8993)

**Skye Diamonds (USA)** *Bill Spawr* a114
4 ch m First Dude(USA) Exonerated (USA) (Johannesburg (USA))
8605a[4]

**Sky Full Of Stars (GER)**
*Henk Grewe* 87
3 rg f Kendargent(FR) Sworn Mum (GER) (Samum (GER))
5693a[11] 8450a[6]

**Sky Gypsy** *David Brown* a27 69
3 gr f Dandy Man(IRE) Gypsy Style (Desert Style (IRE))
6526[5] 7522[14]

**Sky Jockey** *S Seemar* a74
6 ch g Dubawi(IRE) Danella (FR) (Highest Honor (FR))
8711a[4]

**Skylark Lady (IRE)** *Nikki Evans* a61 46
4 ch m Tamayuz Allegrissimo (IRE) (Redback)
39[5] 3026[8] 3775[5] 4733[8]

**Sky Marshal (IRE)** *Ed Walker* a62 54
3 b g Lawman(FR) Evensong (GER) (Waky Nao)
6103[12] 6817[10] 7080[4] 8299[9] 8854[9] (9092)

**Sky Rocket** *Sylvester Kirk* a71
2 b g Azamour(IRE) Roseum (Lahib (USA))
7120[14] 7786[3] 8502[2]

**Sky Ship** *Christos Kouvaras* a85 91
4 ch g Raven's Pass(USA) Angara (Alzao (USA))
6226a[4] 6454a[3] 7636a[2]

**Skyva** *Brian Ellison* a63 59
2 b g Dick Turpin(IRE) Skylla (Kyllachy)
2698[6] 3538[5] 6525[3] 7041[6] 7363[9] 8588[3] (9002)

**Slave To Freedom** *Ann Duffield* a50 9
3 b f Equiano(FR) Fontegiusta (IRE) (Desert Prince (IRE))
1474[11] 1718[8] 3151[8]

**Slaying The Dragon (IRE)**
*Martin Hill* a55 18
4 ch g Notnowcato Empress Charlotte (Holy Roman Emperor (IRE))
785[3] 993[6] 1680[15] 2179[11] 2591[4] 9421[5]

**Sleep Easy** *Neil Mulholland* a37 83
5 b g Rip Van Winkle(IRE) Strictly Lambada (Red Ransom (USA))
6096[5] 6865[8] 7728[12] 8394[7] 8771[6] 9178[7]

**Sleeping Giant (GER)** *P Schaerer* 79
7 gr g Dalakhani(IRE) Special Delivery (IRE) (Danehill (USA))
716a[8] 835a[3]

**Sleeping Lion (USA)**
*James Fanshawe* a70
2 ch c Teofilo(IRE) Flame Of Hestia (IRE) (Giant's Causeway (USA))
8643[4]

**Slemy (IRE)** *Ruth Carr* a41 85
6 b g Raven's Pass(USA) Wolf Cleugh (IRE) (Last Tycoon)
1472[11] 1717[12] 2348[9] 2684[13] 3652[10] 4168[10] 4851[7] 5205[9] 5836[14] 6182[9]

**Slewdra (FR)** *Remy Kennel* a36
2 ch f Alexandros Slew Bay (FR) (Beaudelaire (USA))
8691a[15]

**Sliceoflife** *Marco Botti* a71 32
3 b g Sayif(IRE) Cherrego (USA) (Borrego (USA))
210[2] 434[2]

**Slim Chance (IRE)** *Simon West* a62 63
8 b m Clodovil(IRE) Valluga (IRE) (Ashkalani (IRE))
153[6]

**Slingsby** *Michael Easterby* a78 80
6 b g Dutch Art Ballet Fame (USA) (Quest For Fame)
(660) 971[5] 2064[7] 2161[6] 3257[6]

**Slipalongtrevaskis** *J R Jenkins* a38
4 b g Kheleyf(USA) Tilly's Dream (Arkadian Hero (USA))
878[7] 1179[9] 1543[7] 2472[8] 8345[7] 8984[6]

**Slipper Satin (IRE)** *Simon West* a56 62
7 b m Excellent Art In The Ribbons (In The Wings)
5951[9]

**Slipstream (IRE)** *George Scott* 65
2 b c Invincible Spirit(IRE) Kiltubber (IRE) (Sadler's Wells (USA))
5420[8]

**Slon He** *E Dell'Ova* a55 41
5 b g Danehill Dancer(IRE) Key Figure (Beat Hollow)
364a[11]

**Slow To Hand** *William Jarvis* a62 67
3 ch g Sepoy(AUS) One Giant Leap (IRE) (Pivotal)
4269[6] 4562[4] 5611[12] (6112)◆ 6387[2] 7062[5] 7791[5] 8327[7]

**Slunovrat (FR)** *David Menuisier* a38 92
6 bb g Astronomer Royal(USA) Slewmamba (FR) (Kingsalsa (USA))
5303[2] 5944[6] 8047[15]

**Smart Call (SAF)** *Sir Michael Stoute* 112
5 b m Ideal World(USA) Good Judgement (USA) (Horse Chestnut (SAF))
2765[3] 3961[4] 4419a[7] 6248a[4] 6972a[6] 9167a[7]

**Smart Champion** *Simon Crisford* a68
2 b c Teofilo(IRE) Soryah (IRE) (Shamardal (USA))
8704[6]

**Smart Dart** *Ralph Beckett* a55
2 b f Mastercraftsman(IRE) Dark Missile (Night Shift (USA))
9080[6]

**Smart Dj** *Sarah Hollinshead* a60 51
6 ch g Major Cadeaux Katy-Q (IRE) (Taufan (USA))
216[11]

**Smart Layer (JPN)** *Ryuji Okubo* 113
7 gr m Deep Impact(JPN) Snow Style (JPN) (White Muzzle)
9171a[5]

**Smart Move (FR)** *F-H Graffard* 73
2 b c Style Vendome(FR) Ideechic (FR) (Chichicastenango (FR))
5776a[13] 7175a[4]

**Smart Mover (IRE)** *Nikki Evans* a58 57
4 b m Fast Company(IRE) Alltherightmoves (IRE) (Namid)
996[6] 2061[6] 2358[5] 2708[8] 3772[3] 5714[10] 6393[4] 9431[5]

**Smart Together (USA)**
*John Gosden* 87
3 b f Smart Strike(CAN) Forever Together (USA) (Belong To Me (USA))
(3039) 3749[3]

**Smart Whip (FR)** *C Lotoux* a89 112
6 b g Dylan Thomas(IRE) Green Girl (FR) (Lord Of Men)
3637a[2] (6173a) (8444a)

**Smash Williams (IRE)** *J S Bolger* 101
4 ch g Fracas(IRE) Take Flight (IRE) (Pivotal)
1653a[4]

**Smentana (GER)** *Waldemar Hickst* 61
3 rg f Mastercraftsman(IRE) Salona (GER) (Lord Of England (GER))
6225a[6]

**Smidgen (IRE)** *T Van Den Troost* a31 36
6 b g Bahamian Bounty Brazilian Style (Exit To Nowhere (USA))
7307a[11]

**Smiley Bagel (IRE)** *Ed Walker* a73 61
4 b g Kyllachy Epistoliere (IRE) (Alzao (USA))
146[6] (621) (820) (1082) (1560) 1891[6] 2815[8] 3683[7] 4730[8]

**Smiley Riley (IRE)** *Tony Coyle* 65
3 b g Fast Company(IRE) Betty Fontaine (IRE) (Mujadil (USA))
2470[7] 4473[11]

**Smokethatthunders (IRE)**
*James Unett* a78 75
7 gr g Elusive City(USA) Zinstar (IRE) (Sinndar (IRE))
267[8] 478[4] 9411[7]

**Smokey Lane (IRE)** *Christian Williams* a72 101
3 ch g Zebedee Masela (IRE) (Medicean)
1732[5] 2130[5] 2400[7] **(3146)** 3844[18] 4334[7] 5423[14] 5916[10] 6371[4] 7025[5] 7461[2] 7782[11] 8393[9]

**Smoky Hill (IRE)** *Tony Carroll* a60 68
8 gr g Galileo(IRE) Danaskaya (IRE) (Danehill (USA))
*1215* ***2794*** *1698[5]* 2281[8] 2972[9]

**Smooth Operator** *Mark Pitman* a40 67
5 b g Azamour(IRE) Teggiano (IRE) (Mujtahid (USA))
**4966**[4] 5556[5]

**Smooth Sailing** *Charles Hills* 48
2 b f Bated Breath Royal Confidence (Royal Applause)
4440[12] **6005**[8]

**Smoulder** *A P O'Brien* a87 94
3 b f Redoute's Choice(AUS) Yummy Mummy (Montjeu (IRE))
2644a[18] 3632a[12] 5308a[4] **6642a**[5] 7113[8] 8083a[13] *8407a*[11]

**Smugglers Creek (IRE)** *Iain Jardine* a75 65
3 b g Medicean Crystany (IRE) (Green Desert (USA))
***9411***[5]

**Smugglers Top** *Tom Dascombe* a59 65
2 ch g Kendargent(FR) Penny's Gift (Tobougg (IRE))
5058[8] 5537[10] **7079**[4] *7985*[4] 8349[18]

**Snaad** *F-H Graffard* a95 97
5 b g Invincible Spirit(IRE) Olivia Grace (Pivotal)
*1920a*[4] 5979a[13] ***7636a***[9] *8251a*[4] ***9274a***[8]

**Snaffled (IRE)** *David Brown* a66 51
2 b c Camacho Little Oz (IRE) (Red Ransom (USA))
1966[8] 6853[5] 7333[5] *8340*[11] ***8779***[4]

**Snapper Sinclair (USA)** *Steven Asmussen* a69 95
2 b c City Zip(USA) True Addiction (USA) (Yes It's True (USA))
**8577a**[12]

**Snappydresser** *Chris Grant* a35 55
4 b m Medicean Dand Nee (USA) (Kabool)
5181[11] ***5831***[10]

**Snap Shots (IRE)** *Tony Coyle* a91 98
5 b g Kodiac Refuse To Give Up (IRE) (Refuse To Bend (IRE))
2764[9] **3463**[2] 3585[3] **4925a**[2] 5435[7] 5705[RR] 6206[4] 6971a[13] 7626[RR]

**Snatty Dancer** *Hughie Morrison* a25 53
2 ch f Nathaniel(IRE) Spicy Dal (Dalakhani (IRE))
**8419**[11] *8796*[14]

**Snax** *Mark Johnston* a26 64
2 b f High Chaparral(IRE) Cosmodrome (USA) (Bahri (USA))
**6861**[6] *7361*[6]

**Snazzy Jazzy (IRE)** *Clive Cox* 98
2 b c Red Jazz(USA) Bulrushes (Byron)
(3305)◆ (6272) **(6977a)**

**Sniper Viper** *Daniel Kubler* 32
3 ch f Paco Boy(IRE) Brilliance (Cadeaux Genereux)
2405[4] **3309**[9] 4970[11]

**Snirvana (IRE)** *F Head* a80 78
3 b f Elusive Quality(USA) Snowgal (IRE) (Galileo (IRE))
***8885a***[5]

**Snitzson (AUS)** *David A & B Hayes & Tom Dabern* 106
3 b c Snitzel(AUS) Shock Pak (AUS) (Blackfriars (AUS))
**8059a**[14]

**Snoano** *Tim Easterby* a85 110
5 b g Nayef(USA) White Dress (IRE) (Pivotal)
(1704) 2553[5] 2855[7] **(4069)** 4918[15] 5592[4] 6449[16] 7395[9]

**Snobbery (IRE)** *Roger Charlton* a81
4 b g Duke Of Marmalade(IRE) Boast (Most Welcome)
*38*[11] ***381***[4]

**Snookered (IRE)** *Richard Fahey* a68 73
3 b g Born To Sea(IRE) Secret Quest (Pivotal)
1736[8] 2347[4] *3191*[3] 3431[2] 4432[3] **(5212)** 5921[7] 7097[3] 7895[6]

**Snooker Jim** *Steph Hollinshead* 75
2 b c Holy Roman Emperor(IRE) Lucia De Medici (Medicean)
4291[8] **4880**[4] 5680[3]

**Snoop** *David Loughnane* 21
2 b f Paco Boy(IRE) Carafe (Selkirk (USA))
**3037**[11] 3491[10]

**Snoozing Indian** *T J O'Mara* a74 78
5 ch g Sleeping Indian Balnaha (Lomond (USA))
**5582a**[15]

**Snoozy Sioux (IRE)** *Martin Smith* a63 63
3 b f Sleeping Indian Castalian Spring (IRE) (Oasis Dream)
*679*[6] ***(1363)*** 1688[11] 6339[8] *7494*[10] *8776*[4]◆

**Snoring** *John Davies* 28
3 b g Sleeping Indian Porcelain (IRE) (Peintre Celebre (USA))
3568[5] **4106**[6] 4693[7]

**Snow Blaze** *Michael Appleby*
3 b f Proclamation(IRE) Dancealot Lady (USA) (Theatrical (IRE))
3206[6]

**Snowdon** *Michael Dods* 30
2 b f Iffraaj Solva (Singspiel (IRE))
**6939**[9]

**Snow Excuse** *Bryan Smart* a52 41
3 gr g Hellvelyn Satin Doll (Diktat)
2033[8] 4793[9] 5619[6] *7763*[4] 8490[P] ***9215***[2] *9420*[7]

**Snow Falcon (IRE)** *Noel Meade* 104
7 b g Presenting Flocon De Neige (IRE) (Kahyasi (IRE))
6956a[15] **7860a**[2] 8038[14]

**Snowflake (FR)** *M Nigge* 76
2 b f Style Vendome(FR) Makisarde (FR) (Xaar)
**5988a**[3] 7415a[12]

**Snowflakes (IRE)** *A P O'Brien* 90
2 bg f Galileo(IRE) Laddies Poker Two (IRE) (Choisir (AUS))
**4028**[8]◆

**Snow Squaw** *David Elsworth* a75 77
3 ch f Excelebration(IRE) Snoqualmie Girl (IRE) (Montjeu (IRE))
*2124* (2172) 2754[12] **4372**[2] 5221[4]◆ 6274[4] 7130[3] *8150*[5]

**Snowstar (IRE)** *W McCreery* a59 102
3 b f Raven's Pass(USA) Central Line (USA) (Redoute's Choice (AUS))
**6640a**[2] 7856a[11]

**Snowy Dawn** *Steph Hollinshead* a75 73
7 gr g Notnowcato Tereyna (Terimon)
***(2111)*** 3067[9]

**Snowy Winter (USA)** *Archie Watson* a94 64
3 b f Elusive Quality(USA) Pamona Ball (USA) (Pleasantly Perfect (USA))
*4565*[7] (5073) 5604[4] 6153[3] 6611[2] 7152[8] *(7537)* *7790*[5] *(8204)* *(8648)* *8893*[5] ***(9341)***◆

**Snuggy (IRE)** *David Barron* a64 66
3 b f Elzaam(AUS) Mandhooma (Oasis Dream)
***179***[2] ***324***[3]

**Soaring Spirits (IRE)** *Dean Ivory* a67 73
7 ch g Tamayuz Follow My Lead (Night Shift (USA))
*1327*[5] 1687[12] 2058[7] 2917[4] **(3758)** **4176**[3] 5039[8] 5750[6] *6850*[6] *8158*[10] 8184[3] *8659*[4] *9142*[11] *9454*[2]

**So Beloved** *David O'Meara* a96 115
7 b g Dansili Valencia (Kenmare (FR))
2150[5] 2610[3] 3587[3] 4371[4] **4935a**[2] 5502[5] 6401[5] 6856[4] **7671a**[2] 8438a[4] *8891*[9]

**Sober Up** *Ivan Furtado* a64 61
5 b m Kheleyf(USA) Morning After (Emperor Jones (USA))
***309***[5] *1075*[8]

**Sobetsu** *Charlie Appleby* 113
3 b f Dubawi(IRE) Lake Toya (USA) (Darshaan)
(2665a) 3301[8] **5571**[3] **(6227a)**

**So Celebre (GER)** *Ian Williams* a77 79
4 ch g Peintre Celebre(USA) Saldennahe (GER) (Next Desert (IRE))
3744[11] 6195[7] 7132[6] *8000*[2] ***8160***[2] *8648*[7]

**Socialites Red** *Scott Dixon* a64 76
4 ch m Sakhee's Secret Tipsy Girl (Haafhd)
*22*[8] *216*[5] *302*[3] *601*[7] *742*[6] *1031*[5] *1200*[4] *1371*[3] 1720[4] 2058[5] (2589) 2700[3] 3063[2] (3216) **3904**[2] 4277[3] 4629[7]

**Society Lilly (IRE)** *Hugo Palmer* a13 40
2 b f Society Rock(IRE) Lilly Be (IRE) (Titus Livius (FR))
**6868**[6] *7724*[12]

**Society Power (IRE)** *William Haggas* a84 83
2 b c Society Rock(IRE) Yajala (Fasliyev (USA))
6272[2]◆ (6827)◆ ***(7788)***

**Society Prince (IRE)** *James Fanshawe* a68 68
2 br g Society Rock(IRE) Princess Atoosa (USA) (Gone West (USA))
**7250**[4] ***7876***[3] *8432*[5]

**Society Ranger (IRE)** *S M Duffy* a66 65
4 b g Bushranger(IRE) High Society Girl (IRE) (Key Of Luck (USA))
*(1456)* *(3550)* ***4982***[4]◆

**Society Red** *Richard Fahey* 87
3 ch g Arcano(IRE) Idonea (CAN) (Swain (IRE))
1801[6] 2437[3] 3077[11] 3583[4] 4376[2] 4886[9] 5568[10] 6187[7] **(6671)** 8048[10] **8385**[2]

**Society's Dream (IRE)** *K R Burke* a25 51
2 ch f Society Rock(IRE) Majestic Eviction (IRE) (King's Theatre (IRE))
1908[6] 2343[4] 3200[3] 5277[P] (5945) 6625[5] *7030*[9] **7518**[4] **7919**[8]

**Society Secret (IRE)** *Tom Dascombe* a49 33
2 ch c Society Rock(IRE) Bond Deal (IRE) (Pivotal)
*4977*[9] ***7411***[5] 8381[9]

**Socks And Shares (IRE)** *Derek Shaw* a59 33
4 b g Elnadim(USA) Al Andalyya (USA) (Kingmambo (USA))
*1889*[11] ***2112***[7] 2727[8]

**So Crafty** *Eve Johnson Houghton* 63
2 ch f Mastercraftsman(IRE) Mea Parvitas (IRE) (Oasis Dream)
**4253**[7]

**Socrates** *Daniel Kubler* a63 49
3 b g Dick Turpin(IRE) Lisathedaddy (Darnay)
3163[9] 3870[6] 4914[5] 5714[7] ***6324***[3] *7481*[8]

**Sod's Law** *Hughie Morrison* a75
2 b g Mayson Lawyers Choice (Namid)
***9200***[2]◆

**Soffia** *Edward Lynam* 74
2 br f Kyllachy Rime A Rien (Amadeus Wolf)
**7423a**[4]

**Sofia's Rock (FR)** *Mark Johnston* 106
3 b g Rock Of Gibraltar(IRE) Princess Sofia (UAE) (Pennekamp (USA))
1764[4] (2149) 2614[7] (3081) 3998[14] **4811**[3] 5525[14] 6201[2] 6445[18]

**Soft Sand** *Peter Crate* a32
2 b c Piccolo Ivory's Joy (Tina's Pet)
***6816***[8]

**Soghan (IRE)** *Richard Hughes* a83
3 br g Cape Cross(IRE) Quiet Dream (USA) (Seattle Slew (USA))
*7708*[4] *8151*[4] *8822*[3] ***(9159)***

**So Hi Society (IRE)** *Archie Watson* 100
2 b f Society Rock(IRE) Lilac Mist (Spectrum (IRE))
3022[3] (3421)◆ 4361[3]◆ 4855[6] 5329[4] **6354**[4] 7011a[4]

**So Hoity Toity** *Hughie Morrison* a51 76
3 ch f Harbour Watch(IRE) Dignify (IRE) (Rainbow Quest (USA))
**4050**[4] 4537[9] 5331[4]

**Soho Universe (FR)** *C Ferland* a60 78
3 ch g Exceed And Excel(AUS) Soho Star (Smarty Jones (USA))
**3355a**[7] *8305a*[5]

**Soie D'Leau** *Kristin Stubbs* a82 105
5 b g Monsieur Bond(IRE) Silky Silence (High Chaparral (IRE))
1946[4] 2764[7] 3092[5] 3539[5] 3932[2] *4306*[6] 4816[4] 5354[3] 6185[3] 6325[8] 6412[12] 6927[2]◆ (7461) 7610[5] 8139[10] **8416**[2]

**Soiesauvage (FR)** *Sophie Leech* a74 46
6 b m Lauro(GER) Taffetas (FR) (Nikos)
***1464***[4] 4073[16] *4730*[RR]

**So It's War (FR)** *Keith Dalgleish* a76 75
6 b g Orpen(USA) Impulsive Decision (IRE) (Nomination)
*6*[5] ***359***[5] *441*[6] *685*[8] *1201*[3] *1893*[3] 2224[8] 2430[3] 3198[5] 3899[2] 4690[11] 5214[8] 6673[5] 8107[2]

**Soizie (FR)** *N Bellanger* a54 59
2 b f Sandwaki(USA) Miss Balines (FR) (Grape Tree Road)
**5988a**[9]

**Sojourn (GER)** *Jean-Pierre Carvalho* 82
2 b f Iffraaj Songerie (GER) (Shirocco (GER))
**8461a**[3]

**Solajan (IRE)** *Ed Dunlop* a77 36
3 ch g Lope De Vega(IRE) Undercover Glamour (USA) (Kingmambo (USA))
*882*[2] ***(1089)*** *2520*[9] *3457*[10] 5218[9]

**Solamente Vos (ARG)** *Fredrik Reuterskiold* a68
3 b h Peer Gynt(JPN) Satarain (ARG) (Salt Lake (USA))
***4940a***[9]

**Solar Cross** *Roger Charlton* 88
3 b g Sea The Stars(IRE) Nantyglo (Mark Of Esteem (IRE))
2527[4] (3291) 4314[4] 6187[5] **(7908)**

**Solar Deity (IRE)** *Jane Chapple-Hyam* a111 95
8 b h Exceed And Excel(AUS) Dawn Raid (IRE) (Docksider (USA))
***574***[6] *919*[P] (Dead)

**Solar Flair** *William Knight* a108 106
5 b g Equiano(FR) Air Biscuit (IRE) (Galileo (IRE))
651a[11] 1044a[13] *1501*[2] ***(1794)*** *2114*[5] *4354*[6] 5640[8]

**Solar Wave (IRE)** *J S Bolger* 90
2 b f Vocalised(USA) Solar Outburst (IRE) (Galileo (IRE))
**7859a**[6]

**Soldier Blue (FR)** *Brian Ellison* a66 69
3 ch g Sepoy(AUS) Kocooning (IRE) (King's Best (USA))
2066[8] *4309*[6] **5458**[3] 7052[7] 7896[6]

**Soldier In Action (FR)** *Mark Johnston* a113 114
4 ch g Soldier Of Fortune(IRE) Ripley (GER) (Platini (GER))
1802[12] 2804[6] (3323) 4033[12] 4614[2] 4849[3] **(5638)** 6447[13] 7139[5] 7931[6] *8637*[4] *(8892)*

**Soldiers Bay (IRE)** *Brian Meehan* 73
2 b c Acclamation Viletta (GER) (Doyen (IRE))
6133[6]◆ 6916[5] **7813**[4]

**Soldier's Girl (IRE)** *Richard Hannon* a78 86
3 br f Sepoy(AUS) Crystal Bull (USA) (Holy Bull (USA))
**2287**[3] 4883[9] *5484*[8] 6377[7]

**Soldier's Minute** *Keith Dalgleish* 95
2 b c Raven's Pass(USA) Hadba (IRE) (Cape Cross (IRE))
6264[4] (6590)◆ **7112**[4]

**Soldier To Follow** *Andrew Balding* 78
2 b c Soldier Hollow Nota Bene (GER) (Slickly (FR))
5964[2] **7043**[2]

**Soleil Marin (IRE)** *A Fabre* a86 108
3 b c Kendargent(FR) Sousmarine (IRE) (Montjeu (IRE))
**(1826a)** 3368a[11] 6053a[8] 7634a[5] 8087a[4]

**Soleimana (FR)** *Freddy Grizon*
3 b f Vertigineux(FR) Sainte Foy (IRE) (Montjeu (IRE))
3134a[13]

**Solent Meads (IRE)** *Daniel Kubler* a73 64
3 ch g Intense Focus(USA) No Trimmings (IRE) (Medecis)
2588[11] 3041[6] 3422[7] 4347[4] 5722[4] 6257[6] ***6946***[2] *(7062)* *7457*[4] *8132*[6] *8400*[4]

**Sole Power** *Edward Lynam* a91 110
10 br g Kyllachy Demerger (USA) (Distant View (USA))
207a[7] **543a**[4]◆ 773a[6]

**Solid Justice (IRE)** *Mark Pattinson* a47 59
6 b g Rock Of Gibraltar(IRE) Burnin' Memories (USA) (Lit De Justice (USA))
4177[7] 4461[8] ***5296***[5] 6306[8]

**Solid Man (JPN)** *David Simcock* 54
2 b g Lord Kanaloa(JPN) Maruka Sawayaka (JPN) (Sunday Silence (USA))
2435[6] **3165**[5] 6070[9]

**Soliloquy** *Charlie Appleby* 84
2 b f Dubawi(IRE) Dysphonia (AUS) (Lonhro (AUS))
6386[2] **(6917)**

**Solitary Sister (IRE)** *Richard Spencer* a42 57
3 br f Cockney Rebel(IRE) Sweet Afton (IRE) (Mujadil (USA))
**3824**[6] *4565*[9] 6112[10] 6748[5] 7005[3] 7213[4] 7459[5] *7952*[6]

**Sollertia (IRE)** *Tracey Collins* 85
2 gr f Mastercraftsman(IRE) Royal Blue Star (IRE) (Dalakhani (IRE))
7290a[7] **8082a**[13]

**Solmen (FR)** *M Krebs* a54 62
9 b g Solon(GER) Amen (GER) (Dashing Blade)
***691a***[4]

**Solo Hunter** *Martyn Meade* a95 95
6 b g Sleeping Indian Night Owl (Night Shift (USA))
**(2233)** 3785[6] 7284[4]

**Solomini (USA)** *Bob Baffert* a109
2 ch c Curlin(USA) Surf Song (USA) (Storm Cat (USA))
***8609a***[2]

**Solo Mission** *William Haggas* a88 88
3 b g Sea The Stars(IRE) Lonely Ahead (USA) (Rahy (USA))
2315[2] (3901) 4913[4] (6210) ***6819***[2] **7163**[3]

**Solomon's Bay (IRE)** *Roger Varian* a109 110
3 ch g Exceed And Excel(AUS) Gentle On My Mind (IRE) (Sadler's Wells (USA))
1945[11] 2830[4] **(3302)** 3959[16] 5593[4] 6856[3] *(7950)*

**Solveig's Song** *Steve Woodman* a75 59
5 b m Norse Dancer(IRE) Ivory Lace (Atraf)
*1207* *2861*[2] *922*[8] ***1283***[2] 1789[6] 2055[6] 2257[6] 2615[7] *2956*[4] 3304[5] 3519[9] *8549*[10] *9211*[9]

**Somehow (IRE)** *A P O'Brien* 115
4 b m Fastnet Rock(AUS) Alexandrova (IRE) (Sadler's Wells (USA))
1387a[2] **(2432)** 2825[4] 3108a[2] (Dead)

**Some Nights (FR)** *Matthieu Palussiere* a58 51
2 b g Rio De La Plata(USA) Snow Lady (SWI) (Vision (USA))
1919a[14] **2642a**[5]

**Someone Exciting** *David Thompson* a42 62
4 b m Notnowcato Quite Something (Footstepsinthesand)
**1717**[4] 2140[8] 2633[10] 3487[4] 3899[3] 4209[6] 5185[4] 6131[3] 6437[3] (7390) 7980[4]◆ *8590*[11]

**Somepink (IRE)** *Daniel Mark Loughnane* a38
4 b m Lilbourne Lad(IRE) Cloonkeary (In The Wings)
***689***[11] *900*[9] *7761*[12] *8770*[8]

**Somerset House (USA)** *Charlie Appleby* a89
3 br g Hard Spun(USA) From Afar (USA) (Empire Maker (USA))
***1040a***[5]

**Somes Sound (IRE)** *Jane Chapple-Hyam* a43 47
3 b g Big Bad Bob(IRE) Zapping (IRE) (Lycius (USA))
*1299*[11] 1730[14] **2152**[8] 3207[7]

**Something Brewing (FR)** *Iain Jardine* 83
3 gr g Clodovil(IRE) Talwin (IRE) (Alhaarth (IRE))
3528[6] **4075**[5] 4377[14] 5400[10] 7699[7] 7894[8]

**Something Lucky (IRE)** *Michael Appleby* a55 64
5 gr g Clodovil(IRE) Lucky Leigh (Piccolo)
***45***[9] *682*[8] *808*[11] *1339*[9] 2800[5] *3545*[5] *6850*[12] 7217[7] *7517*[7] 7912[5] *9075*[2] *9214*[2] *9265*[5]

**Somethingthrilling** *David Elsworth* a95 88
5 b m Makfi Something Exciting (Halling (USA))
*97*[3] ***465***[8] 6919[7] 7283[9] 7576[13] *8546*[7]

**Sometimesadiamond (IRE)** *J S Bolger* 92
2 b f Vocalised(USA) Something Graceful (Galileo (IRE))
4418a[5] **6487a**[3] 7290a[4]

**Somewhere In Time (FR)** *M Pimbonnet* a76 89
3 b f Rio De La Plata(USA) Everlast (FR) (Anabaa (USA))
***(6496a)***

**Somewhere Secret** *Michael Mullineaux* 81
3 ch g Sakhee's Secret Lark In The Park (IRE) (Grand Lodge (USA))
4342[5] 4892[12] 5316[4] 5929[11] 6877[3] **(7055)** 7461[6] 8167[15] 8512[10]

**So Mi Dar** *John Gosden* 118
4 b m Dubawi(IRE) Dar Re Mi (Singspiel (IRE))
**5571**[5] 6248a[5]

**Somnambulist** *Keith Dalgleish* a75 73
3 b g Rip Van Winkle(IRE) Sister Moonshine (Averti (IRE))
1801[8] 2429[3] 4247[2] 4474[5] 5073[3] **5921**[3] 6210[5] 7163[6] *7568*[4] *8206*[13]

**So Much Fun (IRE)** *Ismail Mohammed* a70 73
4 b m Iffraaj Seminole Lass (USA) (Indian Charlie (USA))
***394***[2]

**So Much Water (FR)** *John Berry* 55
5 gr m Le Havre(IRE) Minnie's Mystery (FR) (Highest Honor (FR))
**1787**[6] 3921[10]

**Son Castello (IRE)** *Gary Moore* a24 44
3 b g Lilbourne Lad(IRE) Dancing Lauren (IRE) (Oratorio (IRE))
***376***[9] *637*[6]

**Son Cesio (FR)** *H-A Pantall* 112
6 b h Zafeen(FR) Slitana (FR) (Dansili)
2643a[4] 3370a[5] 4234a[2] 5450a[2] (6495a) 7670a[11] **8526a**[3]

**So Near So Farhh** *Mick Channon* 55
2 ch f Farhh Protectress (Hector Protector (USA))
6504[7] **7593**[5] 8013[14]

**Song Light** *Seamus Mullins* a59 86
7 b g Echo Of Light Blue Lullaby (IRE) (Fasliyev (USA))
**(8072)** *9204*[RR]

**Song Maker** *Charlie Appleby* a91 83
3 b f Oasis Dream Please Sing (Royal Applause)
5118[3] (7109) *7484*[3]◆ ***7830***[2] 8351[6]

**Song Of Life** *Mme M Bollack-Badel* a86 86
3 b f Poet's Voice Sign Of Life (Haafhd)
***6124a***[3]

**Song Of Love (IRE)** *Shaun Harris* a84 58
5 b g Fastnet Rock(AUS) Delicate Charm (IRE) (High Chaparral (IRE))
2804[8] 3795[9] 4801[4] *5798*[6] 6399[14] *8893*[11] ***9369***[4] *9442*[7]

**Song Of Namibia (IRE)** *G M Lyons* a73 97
6 br g Cape Cross(IRE) Spring Symphony (IRE) (Darshaan)
**6956a**[6]

**Song Of Norway** *D De Watrigant* a93 92
6 b m Halling(USA) Amarullah (FR) (Daylami (IRE))
***4679a***[5]

**Song Of Shadows** *Michael Wigham* a76 70
4 b g Invincible Spirit(IRE) Lyrique (IRE) (Iffraaj)
**2975**[5] *3969*[9]

**Song Of Summer** *Archie Watson* a62 69
2 ch f Choisir(AUS) Height Of Summer (IRE) (Alhaarth (IRE))
*2958[9]* 3712[6] 4296[6] (5057) **5751[2]** 6825[6] *8153[3]*

**Sonic Boom (USA)** *Ian Wilkes* 102
3 ch c More Than Ready(USA) Silent Circle (USA) (Indian Charlie (USA))
**5953a[4]**

**Sonjeu (FR)** *C Ferland* 95
2 b f Intello(GER) Wait And See (FR) (Montjeu (IRE))
5679a[5] **(7011a)** 7754a[7]

**Son Macia (GER)** *Andreas Suborics* 108
4 b m Soldier Hollow Sinaada (GER) (Zinaad)
2667a[7] 6710a[6] 7429a[2] **8273a[2]** 8755a[2]

**Sonneteer (USA)**
*J Keith Desormeaux* a108
3 bb c Midnight Lute(USA) Ours (USA) (Half Ours (USA))
***2420a[16]***

**Sonnetist** *David Evans* a78 74
3 b g Poet's Voice Society Rose (Saddlers' Hall (IRE))
2707[4] 3248[4] 3506[4] 4224[6] ***7728[5]*** 8142[9] 8682[4] *9159[6] (9369)*

**Sonnet Rose (IRE)** *Conrad Allen* a60 40
3 ch f Poet's Voice Arabian Pearl (IRE) (Refuse To Bend (IRE))
*4497[7]* 5364[11] *7059[3] 7761[13]* 8123[7] *8307[6] 8994[3]* ***(9073)◆*** *9180[8]*

**Son Of Africa** *Henry Candy* a54 103
5 b g Equiano(FR) Generously Gifted (Sakhee (USA))
3861[7] 4079[5] 4881[8] **5637[3]**

**Son Of Rest** *J A Stack* 114
3 b c Pivotal Hightime Heroine (IRE) (Danetime (IRE))
6640a[5] **6973a[3]** 7856a[2]

**Son Of The Stars** *Richard Hannon* a90 99
3 b g Delegator Michelle Shift (Night Shift (USA))
*(1760)◆* **2402[2]◆** 3997[11]

**Sooda (USA)** *Roger Varian* a60
2 b f Street Cry(IRE) Nayarra (IRE) (Cape Cross (IRE))
***8851[5]***

**Sooqaan** *Antony Brittain* a65 53
6 bl g Naaqoos Dream Day (FR) (Spectrum (IRE))
*1868[12]* ***3264[3]*** *3546[4] 4262[5]* 4601[4] 5181[5] 5807[5] 6092[13] 7476[13] *8249[4] 8662[13] (9217)*

**Sophie Gray (IRE)** *John Gosden* a54
2 b f Dansili Susan Stroman (Monsun (GER))
***9319[7]***

**Sophie P** *R Mike Smith* 108
4 b m Bushranger(IRE) Fountains Abbey (USA) (Giant's Causeway (USA))
(2457) 2954[2] 4077[2] 4961[7] 5381[8] 6924[7] (7658) **(7886)**

**Sophisticated Heir (IRE)**
*Kevin Frost* a86 67
7 b g New Approach(IRE) My Girl Sophie (USA) (Danzig (USA))
*219[5]* ***312[2]*** *551[3] 1423[7]* 2683[8] 4105[5] *4451[2]* 5288[10] 6181[9] *6637[11]* 7332[4] *7881[13] 8427[9] 8742[11]*

**So Pleasing (FR)** *G Collet* a68 66
3 bb g Naaqoos Midnight Flash (IRE) (Anabaa Blue)
**6256a[2]**

**Sopran Anny (ITY)** *Frank Sheridan* a52 88
4 b m Johnny Red Kerr(USA) Salamanna (ITY) (Dubawi (IRE))
***9309a[14]***

**Sopran Roccia (ITY)**
*Il Cavallo In Testa* 102
2 b c Red Rocks(IRE) Salamanna (ITY) (Dubawi (IRE))
**8276a[2]**

**Sopran Verne (IRE)**
*Il Cavallo In Testa* 98
3 b f Approve(IRE) Vermicelli (IRE) (Mujadil (USA))
**2244a[4]**

**Soqrat** *Ed Dunlop*
3 b g Paco Boy(IRE) Tamara Moon (IRE) (Acclamation)
3393[9]

**Sorina (GER)** *Henk Grewe* 26
2 bb f Tai Chi(GER) Sun Of Dubai (GER) (Dubai Destination (USA))
**2642a[8]** 4196a[10] 6494a[13]

**Sorority** *Mark Johnston* a43 67
2 ch f Exceed And Excel(AUS) Belonging (Raven's Pass (USA))
*3174[8]* 4014[3] 4799[3] **5878[2]** 6128[6] 7243[10] *8343[6]*

**Sors (IRE)** *Andrew Slattery* a89 100
5 b g Acclamation Maid Of Ailsa (USA) (Pivotal)
1520a[6] 4416a[16] **4925a[9]**

**So Sensible (IRE)** *Tracey Collins* a74 74
6 b g Tagula(IRE) Sensible Lady (Tobougg (IRE))
***1014a[7]*** 5518a[17]

**So She Thinks (IRE)** *J S Moore* 69
2 b f So You Think(NZ) Spice It Up (Authorized (IRE))
**8228a[3]**

**Sosian** *Richard Fahey* a70 72
2 b f Showcasing Leonica (Lion Cavern (USA))
*3254[2]* **3789[2]◆** 5453[4] *7362[7]*

**So Si Bon (AUS)** *Robbie Laing* 106
3 bk c So You Think(NZ) Black Minx (NZ) (Lonhro (AUS))
**8753a[10]**

**So Sleek** *Luca Cumani* a71 89
3 b f Lawman(FR) So Silk (Rainbow Quest (USA))
2131[3] 3145[3] 3770[2] (5022) (5715)◆ **(7338)◆**

**So Sora (FR)** *M Boutin* a57 73
2 b f Desert Blanc So Oder So (FR) (Areion (GER))
**(1594a)** **2073a[2]** 2642a[2] 3444a[2] 8524a[4]

**Sotomayor** *Richard Hannon* a63 63
2 b c Havana Gold(IRE) No Frills (IRE) (Darshaan)
4880[8] **5301[5]◆** 5840[7] 6860[9] *7829[7]* ***8644[2]*** *8887[7]*

**Soul Silver (IRE)** *David Simcock* a90 95
3 ch f Dragon Pulse(IRE) Free Lance (IRE) (Grand Lodge (USA))
4637[7] **(5152)** 5506[6] 6919[9] **7406[4]** 7815[11] *9418[4]*

**Souls In The Wind (IRE)**
*John Patrick Shanahan* a40 74
3 b f Fastnet Rock(AUS) Enchanted Evening (IRE) (High Chaparral (IRE))
649a[4] **887a[9]** (3448) 4248[8] 5646[5] 6442[10] (6786)

**Soul Stirring (JPN)** *Kazuo Fujisawa* 112
3 bb f Frankel Stacelita (FR) (Monsun (GER))
**8975a[7]**

**Sound Advice** *Keith Dalgleish* a100 108
8 b g Echo Of Light Flylowflylong (IRE) (Danetime (IRE))
2406[7] **(2568)** 3064[10] 4890[8] 5616[5] 6676[12]

**Sound And Silence** *Charlie Appleby* a97 110
2 b c Exceed And Excel(AUS) Veil Of Silence (IRE) (Elusive Quality (USA))
(1858)◆ 3010[4] (3929) 4812[11] (6448) 6728a[2] **(7306a)** 8001[2] 8602a[2] *9156[4]*

**Sound Bar** *Ralph Beckett* 82
3 b g Oasis Dream Milford Sound (Barathea (IRE))
3317[9] **4118[2]** 4865[6] 5404[4] 6515[8]

**Soundbyte** *John Gallagher* a48 48
12 b g Beat All(USA) Gloaming (Celtic Swing)
*8207[7]* ***988[4]*** *1585[5]*

**Sound Check (GER)** *P Schiergen* 101
4 bb h Lando(GER) Sky Dancing (IRE) (Exit To Nowhere (USA))
**7203a[4]** 8622a[4]

**Sounds Of Earth (JPN)**
*Kenichi Fujioka* 118
6 bb h Neo Universe(JPN) First Violin (USA) (Dixieland Band (USA))
1379a[6] **8975a[12]**

**Soundtrack (IRE)** *P Schaerer* a72 83
6 br g Excellent Art Umthoulah (IRE) (Unfuwain (USA))
*(716a)*

**Souriyan (FR)** *Peter Bowen* a11 35
6 b g Alhaarth(IRE) Serasana (Red Ransom (USA))
**6033[6]**

**Soustraction (IRE)** *C Laffon-Parias* 104
2 ch f Lope De Vega(IRE) Mathematicienne (IRE) (Galileo (IRE))
**(6731a)** 7666a[6]

**South Coast (GER)** *Henk Grewe* 71
2 bb f Areion(GER) South Bay (GER) (With Approval (CAN))
**6726a[7]**

**Southdown Lad (IRE)**
*William Knight* a91 98
4 b g Lilbourne Lad(IRE) Elizabelle (IRE) (Westerner)
*1502[10]* **2804[4]** 3594[6]

**Southern Belle (IRE)** *Robert Cowell* a90 99
4 b m Aqlaam Areyaam (USA) (Elusive Quality (USA))
*1793[4]* 2407[4] (2856) 3307[4]◆ 3793[2] 4889[5]◆ 5828[3] **6787[2]** 7329[7]

**Southern States** *Lydia Richards* a67 61
4 b g Medaglia d'Oro(USA) Little Belle (USA) (A.P. Indy (USA))
***1697[5]*** *3459[4] 4000[4] 4217[4] 4750[5]* 5407[3] 7744[10] *8647[9]*

**Southpark** *Richard Fahey* 66
2 b g Epaulette(AUS) Spirit Of Success (Invincible Spirit (IRE))
6890[8] 7221[3] **7883[2]**

**South Sea Belle (IRE)**
*David Menuisier* a62 69
3 ch f New Approach(IRE) South Atlantic (USA) (Stormy Atlantic (USA))
1905[4] **4568[4]** 6106[11] *6818[10] 7878[8]* 8114[10]

**South Seas (IRE)** *Andrew Balding* a91 108
3 ch g Lope De Vega(IRE) Let It Be Me (USA) (Mizzen Mast (USA))
***1780[5]*** 2666a[11]

**Southview Lady** *Sean Regan* a38 31
5 b m Misu Bond(IRE) Salalah (Lion Cavern (USA))
***176[7]*** 5126[12] 5544[9] 8218[11]

**Sovereign Bounty** *Jedd O'Keeffe* a74 85
5 ch g Bahamian Bounty Sovereign Abbey (IRE) (Royal Academy (USA))
2030[10] 2701[5] **(3857)** 4085[5] **5213[3]** 5668[9] 6266[7] 6464[7]

**Sovereign Debt (IRE)** *Ruth Carr* a112 117
8 gr g Dark Angel(IRE) Kelsey Rose (Most Welcome)
(914a) *1500[3] (1773)* (2129) **(3320)** 4884[5] 6444[3] 6928[4] 7579[4] 8041[4]

**Sovereign Duke (GER)**
*Henry Candy* a63
2 b c Jukebox Jury(IRE) Shadow Queen (GER) (Lando (GER))
***9200[7]***

**Sovereign Katie (IRE)** *Ollie Pears* 36
2 b f Society Rock(IRE) Dane Thyme (IRE) (Danetime (IRE))
3943[10] **4740[8]** 8235[7]

**Sovereign Nation (AUS)**
*David A & B Hayes & Tom Dabern* 101
4 b g Encosta De Lago(AUS) Sovereign Duchess (AUS) (Last Tycoon)
**8059a[2]**

**Sovereign State** *Robert Cowell* 64
2 b g Compton Place One Night In May (IRE) (Choisir (AUS))
3725[5] **5839[3]** 7326[9] 8294[5]

**Sovrano Dolce (IRE)** *Mike Murphy* a50 65
4 b m Roderic O'Connor(IRE) Tartufo Dolce (IRE) (Key Of Luck (USA))
***6066[5]*** *6846[6]*

**Sowgay (FR)** *C Plisson* a67 65
3 ch g Air Chief Marshal(IRE) Kitty Yield (FR) (High Yield (USA))
**(6649a)**

**So You Thought (USA)** *D K Weld* 89
3 bb c So You Think(NZ) Lady Of Akita (USA) (Fantastic Light (USA))
**6491a[4]**

**Space Artist (IRE)** *Nigel Tinkler* a43 66
7 b g Captain Marvelous(IRE) Dame Laura (IRE) (Royal Academy (USA))
**2104[12]**

**Space Cowboy (GER)** *Markus Klug* 100
5 ch g Adlerflug(GER) St Aye (USA) (Nureyev (USA))
4392a[5] **6451a[4]** 7722a[8]

**Space War** *Michael Easterby* a73 69
10 b g Elusive City(USA) Princess Luna (GER) (Grand Lodge (USA))
*1598 4198 655[5] (815) 1219[3] 1450[4] 1755[4]* ***(1887)*** 2305[3] 3288[5] 3897[12] 4433[12] 4833[8] 5695[5] *7320[4]*

**Spaday (IRE)** *C Laffon-Parias* 93
2 b f Exceed And Excel(AUS) Beautifix (GER) (Bering)
**8525a[4]**

**Spain Burg (FR)** *N Clement* 107
3 bb f Sageburg(IRE) Spain Blues (FR) (Anabaa Blue)
**6234[11]**

**Spangled** *Roger Varian* 111
5 ch m Starspangledbanner(AUS) Zykina (Pivotal)
6401[13] **7812[12]**

**Spanish Beauty** *Ollie Pears* a45 47
3 b f Paco Boy(IRE) Basque Beauty (Nayef (USA))
**4171[5]◆ 4603[5]** 5618[8]

**Spanish Bounty** *Mrs A Malzard* a36 47
12 b g Bahamian Bounty Spanish Gold (Vettori (IRE))
2669a[9] **(4142a)** 4656a[6]

**Spanish City** *Roger Varian* a90 83
4 ch g Exceed And Excel(AUS) Annabelle's Charm (IRE) (Indian Ridge (IRE))
**4099[4]**

**Spanish Fly (IRE)**
*M Delcher Sanchez* 86
3 b f Iffraaj Hundredsnthousands (IRE) (Thousand Words)
1660a[3] **2561a[5]** 7471a[4]

**Spanish History (USA)**
*Seamus Durack* 76
3 b g Street Cry(IRE) Infanta (IRE) (Cape Cross (IRE))
6368[2] **(8116)**

**Spanish Mane (IRE)** *Richard Fahey* a54 47
2 b f Havana Gold(IRE) Kiva (Indian Ridge (IRE))
8474[8] ***8850[6]*** *9049[6]*

**Spanish Moon (RUS)** *Doug Watson* a52
3 ch f Axeos(USA) Spanish Kid (USA) (Lemon Drop Kid (USA))
*317a[12]* ***652a[8]***

**Spanish Reef (AUS)** *Ken Keys* 99
3 b f Lope De Vega(IRE) Lemon Reef (USA) (Lemon Drop Kid (USA))
**8100a[9]**

**Spanish Star (IRE)**
*Patrick Chamings* a68 67
2 b g Requinto(IRE) Rancho Star (IRE) (Soviet Star (USA))
3776[4] 4757[2] 5586[3] 7193[3] ***7491[3]***

**Spanish Steps (IRE)** *A P O'Brien* 108
3 b c Galileo(IRE) Turbulent Descent (USA) (Congrats (USA))
4878a[9] **(5862a)** 6327[5] 6957a[5]

**Spanish Tenor (IRE)** *Timothy Doyle* 104
3 ch c Lope De Vega(IRE) Devious Soprano (IRE) (Orpen (USA))
1633a[6] 7663a[3] **8438a[3]**

**Spare Parts (IRE)** *Phil McEntee* a62 51
3 b g Choisir(AUS) Grandel (Owington)
*807[7] 1287[9] 1600[8]* 2362[4] 3496[4] 3823[12] 4458[4] 4969[2] 5051[10] 5792[4] 6101[8] ***9456[3]***

**Sparkalot** *Simon Dow* a85 71
3 b g Bated Breath Three Wrens (IRE) (Second Empire (IRE))
*1287[4] (1600)* 2692[6] ***(3719)***

**Sparkle** *Ed Dunlop* a72 69
3 b f Oasis Dream Gemstone (IRE) (Galileo (IRE))
**3822[7]** *4214[13]* 4711[4]

**Sparkling Cossack** *Jeremy Gask* a46 48
3 ch f Famous Name Eleanor Eloise (USA) (Minardi (USA))
*764[3] 1024[4] 1247[8] 2016[9]* **2580[4]** *2792[8] 4163[6]*

**Spark Of War (IRE)** *Keith Dalgleish* a60 65
2 b c Declaration Of War(USA) Acts Of Grace (USA) (Bahri (USA))
7613[4] **7978[3]** *8316[6]*

**Spark Plug (IRE)** *Brian Meehan* 115
6 b g Dylan Thomas(IRE) Kournikova (SAF) (Sportsworld (USA))
1882[3] **3069[2]** 3843[5] (4584) **6441[2]** 8041[3] 8598[6]

**Sparte Quercus (IRE)** *Ed Dunlop* a82 87
4 b g Canford Cliffs(IRE) Khaizarana (Alhaarth (IRE))
2689[9] *3342[5]* 3921[5] (4573) 5403[7] 6344[3] (6811) 7132[2] 7649[2] **8111[3]** *8398[5]*

**Spatial** *Sir Michael Stoute* a89 86
3 b f New Approach(IRE) Spacious (Nayef (USA))
***3233[5]***

**Speak In Colours** *Marco Botti* 101
2 gr c Excelebration(IRE) Maglietta Fina (IRE) (Verglas (IRE))
5755[3]◆ (6867) **(8412)**

**Special Boy (IRE)** *M Al Mheiri* a75 85
8 b g Invincible Spirit(IRE) Ezilla (IRE) (Darshaan)
**250a[9]**

**Special Code (IRE)** *Paddy Butler* a29 26
5 b g Iffraaj Najmati (Green Desert (USA))
5657[9] ***7705[10]*** 8298[13]

**Special Fighter (IRE)** *Maria Ritchie* a115 86
6 ch h Teofilo(IRE) Susu (Machiavellian (USA))
***1045a[2]*** *1380a[12]*

**Specialist (IRE)** *Mark Johnston* a73 70
3 b g Mastercraftsman(IRE) My Lass (Elmaamul (USA))
*758[5]* ***925[2]*** *1069[2] (1226)* 2437[7] 3665[3]

**Speciality (FR)** *Ralph Beckett* a72 70
3 b f Lawman(FR) Pride (FR) (Peintre Celebre (USA))
8682[5] ***8978[3]***

**Special Mission**
*Sir Mark Prescott Bt* a63
2 b f Declaration Of War(USA) Soft Morning (Pivotal)
***2958[7]◆***

**Special Purpose (IRE)**
*William Haggas* 100
2 b f Scat Daddy(USA) Pussycat Lips (IRE) (Holy Roman Emperor (IRE))
(4349)◆ (5210) **6354[5]** 6863[3] 8002[10]

**Special Relation (IRE)**
*Hughie Morrison* a74 84
3 b g Casamento(IRE) Sindiyma (IRE) (Kalanisi (IRE))
*48[2] 237[2]* **(3665)◆**

**Special Request (FR)** *N Caullery* a69 80
10 gr g Kaldounevees(FR) Radio Mesnil (FR) (Nashamaa)
*515a[3] 691a[2]* ***822a[5]***

**Special Season** *Jamie Osborne* a100 93
4 ch g Lope De Vega(IRE) Keep Dancing (IRE) (Distant Music (USA))
***465[7]*** *953a[2] 1208[4] 1422[5]*

**Specialv (IRE)** *Brian Ellison* a60 80
4 br m Big Bad Bob(IRE) Montbretia (Montjeu (IRE))
*1542[7]* 1972[4] 2684[12] 3203[11] 4629[8] 4683[3] 4958[5] 5471[3] **(5827)** 6149[6] 7223[7] 7737[13]

**Specific Gravity (FR)**
*Adrian McGuinness* a88 73
9 b g Dansili Colza (USA) (Alleged (USA))
**1388a[16]**

**Spectre (FR)** *M Munch* 116
4 ch m Siyouni(FR) Inez (Dai Jin)
2248a[9] 3354a[4] **3924[4]**

**Speculative Bid (IRE)**
*David Elsworth* a99 113
6 b g Excellent Art Barzah (IRE) (Darshaan)
7807[7] 8234[10] **(8737)** *9274a[6]*

**Speculator** *John Butler* a74 27
5 gr g Bahamian Bounty Swift Dispersal (Shareef Dancer (USA))
*169[14] 527[8]* ***1067[12]*** *3192[10]*

**Speed As (FR)** *A De Royer-Dupre* a86 103
3 b f Evasive As Speed (FR) (Keltos (FR))
1690a[4] **3367a[4]** 8665a[6] *8986a[13]*

**Speed Company (IRE)** *John Quinn* a56 103
4 b g Fast Company(IRE) Trentini (IRE) (Singspiel (IRE))
2086[5] 2735[11] 3300[11] **(4076) 4822a[5]** 5500[15] **6449[5]** 8042[12]

**Speed Craft** *James Eustace* a52 30
2 ch f Mastercraftsman(IRE) Exorcet (FR) (Selkirk (USA))
***6575[8]*** 7403[9] *7757[11] 8371[12]*

**Speed Freak** *Ralph Beckett* a70 71
3 b f Fastnet Rock(AUS) The Thrill Is Gone (Bahamian Bounty)
***212[2]*** *415[4]*

**Speed Hawk (USA)** *D Selvaratnam* a56 103
6 br g Henny Hughes(USA) Cosmic Wing (USA) (Halo (USA))
207a[6]◆ **(543a)** 773a[4] 1044a[8]

**Speedo Boy (FR)** *Ian Williams* a87 104
3 ch g Vision D'Etat(FR) Shamardanse (IRE) (Shamardal (USA))
*(65) 799a[2]* **(1114a)** 2401[2] 3994[6] 4856[7] 6399[7] 6920[7]

**Speed Of Thought (FR)** *J-V Toux* a77 83
7 b g Slickly(FR) Dynamic Dream (USA) (Dynaformer (USA))
***798a[3]***

**Speightowns Kid (USA)**
*Ann Stokell* a73 33
9 rg g Speightstown(USA) Seize The Wind (USA) (Maria's Mon (USA))
*21[P]*

**Spellmaker** *Tony Newcombe* a64 57
8 b g Kheleyf(USA) Midnight Spell (Night Shift (USA))
*95[9]* **1723[3]** 2589[14] 3280[4] 4149[9]

**Spenny's Lass** *John Ryan* 63
2 br f Bated Breath Midnight Hush (FR) (Anabaa (USA))
7732[5] 8112[3] **8324[3]**

**Spes Nostra** *Iain Jardine* a81 69
9 b g Ad Valorem(USA) Millagros (IRE) (Pennekamp (USA))
*381[7] 719[4] 958[8] 992[3] 2163[3]* 2497[8] ***(2787)*** 2953[10] 3651[9] 4430[8] 4658[11] 4959[7] 6789[7] 7984[7] *8398[10]*

**Spey Secret (IRE)** *Tom Dascombe* a47 13
4 br g Kyllachy Chiarezza (AUS) (Fantastic Light (USA))
***127[8]*** *479[7]*

**Spice Boat** *Paddy Butler* a28 19
5 ch g Shamardal(USA) Frizzante (Efisio)
*1425[12]*

**Spice Fair** *Mark Usher* a72 84
10 ch g Trade Fair Focosa (ITY) (In The Wings)
5251[4] **5566[3]** *6889[11]* 8072[11]

**Spice Mill (IRE)** *Michael Appleby* a69 62
4 b g Dream Ahead(USA) High Spice (USA) (Songandaprayer (USA))
*145[7] 923[5]* ***1076[5]*** *1187[8]*

**Spice War** *Brian Meehan* a52 58
2 b g Declaration Of War(USA) Blast Furnace (IRE) (Sadler's Wells (USA))
**7128[11]** *7451[6]*

**Spike (IRE)** *Donald McCain* a53 66
4 b g Lilbourne Lad(IRE) Vintage Allure (IRE) (Barathea (IRE))
***1979[6]*** 2305[7] 2989[4] 3914[7] 5016[4] 5282[9] *6156[7]* 6660[6]

**Spike's Princess (IRE)** *Brian Barr* a41 44
3 b f Bushranger(IRE) Deportment (Barathea (IRE))
*442[7] 656[4]* **5946[6]** *8707[5] 9237[8]*

**Spinart** *Pam Sly* a69 74
4 ch g Dutch Art Spinneret (Pivotal)
1683[13] 2909[7] 3628[3]◆ 4627[3] 5002[6] **5802[2]** *6288[6]* 7327[6] *8400[11]*

**Spin Doctor** *Richard Fahey* a84 75
3 gr f Mayson Doctor's Glory (USA) (Elmaamul (USA))
3526[6] **4435[6]**

**Spinnaka (IRE)** *Luca Cumani* a80 81
3 b f Invincible Spirit(IRE) Spinning Well (IRE) (Pivotal)
**1905**[2] *2311*[5] 2898[2] 3748[2] 4378[2] 5003[2] 6103[3] **(7227)** 8184[5] *8434*[2] *8646*[6]

**Spinnaker Bay (IRE)** *William Jarvis* a70 72
3 b f Lawman(FR) Wizz Kid (IRE) (Whipper (USA))
*27*[6] **5855**[5]

**Spinners Ball (IRE)** *Sylvester Kirk* a85 82
4 b g Excellent Art Meek Appeal (USA) (Woodman (USA))
2041[3] (2478) 3323[8] ***(4216)*** 5397[11] 5820[9]

**Spinning Melody (USA)**
*Simon Crisford* a84
3 b f Hard Spun(USA) Say No Now (IRE) (Refuse To Bend (IRE))
*(7989)* ***9000***[3] *9341*[4]

**Spin Point (IRE)** *Ian Williams* a69 53
5 b g Pivotal Daneleta (IRE) (Danehill (USA))
***92***[8] *1839*[6] 6556[6] *7936*[6] *9158*[5]

**Spin Top** *William Muir* a65 62
3 b g Acclamation Miss Work Of Art (Dutch Art)
*324*[5] *511*[4] *813*[10] ***8542***[3] *8816*[2] *9001*[7]

**Spinwheel** *John Davies*
3 ch f Pivotal Angel's Tears (Seeking The Gold (USA))
*75*[4]◆ *237*[4] *(401)*◆ ***(729)***◆ *927*[3] *1149*[9] *9101*[13]

**Spiorad Saoirse** *Andrew Slattery* 85
2 b g Iffraaj Alsalwa (IRE) (Nayef (USA))
**7423a**[8] 8082a[15]

**Spiraea** *Ivan Furtado* a73 72
7 ch m Bahamian Bounty Salvia (Pivotal)
*152*[10] *523*[2] ***732***[2] ***735***[2] *1063*[7] *1542*[6] 2043[4]

**Spirit Be With You (IRE)**
*Lee Smyth* a19 60
4 b m Dandy Man(IRE) Mar Sin De (IRE) (Danetime (IRE))
5991[10]

**Spirit De Cerisy (FR)**
*Matthieu Palussiere* a74 92
3 ch c Tagula(IRE) Child Bride (Invincible Spirit (IRE))
***5521a***[10] 5909a[9]

**Spirited Boss** *David Evans* a44
2 b g Swiss Spirit Bossy Kitty (Avonbridge)
***4160***[4]

**Spiritfix** *A Fabre* a97 105
4 b m Invincible Spirit(IRE) Beautifix (GER) (Bering)
3614a[3] 5450a[4] **6497a**[3] (7697a) 8526a[4]

**Spirit Mission (USA)** *J-C Rouget* a67
2 b c Scat Daddy(USA) Louve Royale (IRE) (Peintre Celebre (USA))
***5952a***[6]

**Spirit Of Appin** *Brian Meehan* 76
2 b f Champs Elysees Oshiponga (Barathea (IRE))
**8425**[2]

**Spirit Of Belle** *Paul Cole* a81 70
3 b g Sir Percy Yensi (Doyen (IRE))
*1559*[5] 3422[2]◆ 3745[9] 5009[2] 5139[7] 6034[3] 7083[9] (7459) ***(8646)***

**Spiritofedinburgh (IRE)**
*Brendan Powell* a70 70
3 b g Lilbourne Lad(IRE) Xema (Danehill (USA))
***1426***[3] 2220[7] 3163[10] 3391[7] 4350[13] *7056*[11] *7879*[6] *8346*[3]◆ *8673*[4]

**Spirit Of Gondree (IRE)**
*Milton Bradley* a47 46
9 b g Invincible Spirit(IRE) Kristal's Paradise (IRE) (Bluebird (USA))
*166*[5] ***332***[2] *426*[4] *739*[10] *1139*[7] *1305*[5] *2166*[7] *2961*[8] *3469*[8] *4451*[6] *8133*[7] *9457*[7]

**Spiritofhayton (IRE)** *David Barron* a71 64
3 br g Big Bad Bob(IRE) Teodelight (IRE) (Teofilo (IRE))
***40***[2]◆ *777*[3] *970*[4] 5650[8] 5950[9] 6692[6]

**Spirit Of Ishy** *Stuart Kittow* a24 33
2 b f Hellvelyn Our Piccadilly (IRE) (Piccolo)
*5026*[9] **7351**[14] 8112[11]

**Spirit Of Nayef (FR)** *F Vermeulen* a69 64
4 b g Nayef(USA) Spirit Of Pearl (IRE) (Invincible Spirit (IRE))
***9309a***[5]

**Spirit Of Rome (IRE)** *James Bethell* a60 59
3 ch f Mastercraftsman(IRE) Zagreb Flyer (Old Vic)
***881***[3] *1331*[3] 1877[5] 2705[7] 3405[5] *4978*[13] 6048[10]

**Spirit Of Rosanna**
*Steph Hollinshead* a46 68
5 gr m Hellvelyn Tharwa (IRE) (Last Tycoon)
2124[9] 2709[2] 3573[2] 5360[3] 5635[6] 5877[5] (7689) **(8186)**

**Spirit Of Sarwan (IRE)** *Julia Feilden* a77 78
3 b g Elzaam(AUS) Hidden Heart (USA) (Kingmambo (USA))
*(553)* *902*[5] *1343*[2] **2293**[2] 2625[7] 3836[7] 5115[6] 5821[6] *9093*[2] *9464*[6]

**Spirit Of The Law (IRE)**
*James McAuley* a50 34
8 b g Lawman(FR) Passion Bleue (In The Wings)
***1014a***[13]

**Spirit Of The Vale (IRE)**
*Oliver Greenall* a61 60
4 b m Royal Applause Nesmeh (USA) (More Than Ready (USA))
*1216* *(176)* *281*[4] *(1101)* *1312*[2] 1679[5] 1937[4] 2678[5] ***5831***[2] 6306[5] 6470[2] *6901*[11] *7236*[6] *7729*[RR]

**Spiritoftomintoul** *Tony Carroll* a72 70
8 gr g Authorized(IRE) Diamond Line (FR) (Linamix (FR))
*74*[4] ***399***[4] *786*[6] *1073*[7] 1519[4] 2388[10] 3311[3]◆ 3623[2] 4244[7] 5590[5] *6889*[5] 7336[5] 8394[8] *9317*[3]

**Spirit Of Valor (USA)** *A P O'Brien* a89 117
3 bb c War Front(USA) Stone Hope (USA) (Grindstone (USA))
*1375a*[8] 2399[8] 3100a[6] 3959[2] **(4935a)** 5502[10] 7145[4]

**Spirit Of Wedza (IRE)**
*Julie Camacho* a73 73
5 b g Footstepsinthesand Sampers (IRE) (Exceed And Excel (AUS))
*45*[6] *302*[2] *583*[6] ***(844)*** 1062[2] **(2424)** 4433[5] *5481*[4] 6669[6]

**Spirit Of Zebedee (IRE)**
*John Quinn* a71 69
4 gr g Zebedee Sampers (IRE) (Exceed And Excel (AUS))
*362*[2] *(583)* *(768)* ***1203***[2] ***1467***[3] *1980*[7] 4015[7] 4531[7] 4997[11] 6045[2] (6572) 7018[3] 7525[16] 8489[3]

**Spiritous (USA)** *E Charpy* 61
3 b g Invincible Spirit(IRE) Andina (IRE) (Singspiel (IRE))
*8714a*[11]

**Spirit Power** *Joseph Patrick O'Brien* a81 76
2 b c Swiss Spirit Verasina (USA) (Woodman (USA))
**4895**[6]

**Spirit Quartz (IRE)**
*Barry John Murphy* a93 112
9 b g Invincible Spirit(IRE) Crystal Gaze (IRE) (Rainbow Quest (USA))
84a[11] 207a[10] *321a*[6] 1520a[7] 2657a[4] **4416a**[4] 4927a[5] 6973a[9] 7425a[12]

**Spirits Minoru (JPN)** *Masaru Honda* 109
5 ch h Deep Sky(JPN) Basel Clover (JPN) (Lammtarra (USA))
**2203a**[14]

**Spirit Tango (FR)** *G Botti* a68 69
2 b c Captain Marvelous(IRE) Tech Opera (FR) (Orpen (USA))
***4678a***[6]

**Spiritual Lady** *Philip McBride* a86 103
3 b f Pastoral Pursuits Rouge Dancer (Elusive City (USA))
6966[7] 8040[8] **8679**[5]

**Spiritual Star (IRE)** *Lee Carter* a77 84
8 b g Soviet Star(USA) Million Spirits (IRE) (Invincible Spirit (IRE))
*90*[9] *641*[7] *1086*[3]◆ *(1409)* ***1553***[2] *1893*[2] *1982*[2] *3718*[P] 6101[10] *7493*[3] *8749*[10] *9094*[10]

**Spitfire Limited** *George Baker* a52 49
3 b f Excelebration(IRE) First Bloom (USA) (Fusaichi Pegasus (USA))
5431[7] 6009[6] 7907[10] *8428*[2] ***8824***[4] *9129*[5]

**Spix's Macaw** *Bill Turner* a45 38
2 ch f Footstepsinthesand Featherweight (IRE) (Fantastic Light (USA))
4440[15] ***5893***[5] 6583[8] 8179[6]

**Splash Around** *Sir Michael Stoute* a80 84
3 ch c Nathaniel(IRE) Splashdown (Falbrav (IRE))
2152[3] **2784**[2] **3503**[3] *4004*[4]

**Split Step** *C Boutin* a67 56
6 b g Bahamian Bounty Nellie Gwyn (King's Best (USA))
***(930a)***

**Split The Atom (IRE)**
*David Marnane* a87 82
5 ch g The Carbon Unit(USA) The Mighty Atom (USA) (Sky Mesa (USA))
*795a*[5] *1233a*[2] ***(1479a)***

**Spoken Words** *John David Riches* a16 49
8 b m Fruits Of Love(USA) Jerre Jo Glanville (USA) (Skywalker (USA))
2454[13] 2949[6] **3915**[2] 4789[14] 5260[5] *9420*[10]

**Spokesperson (USA)** *Fred Watson*
9 b g Henny Hughes(USA) Verbal (USA) (Kingmambo (USA))
*1469*[12] 5257[8]

**Spoof** *Charles Hills* 100
2 b g Poet's Voice Filona (IRE) (Motivator)
1941[5] 2473[2] 2698[3] 3516[7] 5546[5] (6338) (6651) 7114[7] **8001**[5]

**Sporting Bill (IRE)** *James Fanshawe* a58 70
2 br c Society Rock(IRE) Pandoras Secret (IRE) (Monashee Mountain (USA))
*7877*[7] **8466**[2]

**Sporting Times** *Ed Dunlop* a86 88
3 ch g Sir Percy Queen Of Iceni (Erhaab (USA))
2930[4] (3682) 4254[6] **4908**[3] 6427[6] *7515*[2] 7927[5]

**Sporty Doll (ITY)** *Silvia Casati* 93
5 b m Pounced(USA) Tell Me (ITY) (Machiavellian (USA))
**7441a**[4]

**Sporty Yankee (USA)**
*Martin Keighley* a51 80
4 gr g Paddy O'Prado(USA) I Insist (USA) (Green Dancer (USA))
**5251**[8] *6323*[11]

**Spotify (FR)** *C Ferland* a83 109
3 b c Redoute's Choice(AUS) Gwenseb (FR) (Green Tune (USA))
**1824a**[3] 2666a[4] **4235a**[2]

**Spotlight Dream (IRE)**
*Louis Baudron* a85 84
3 b g Holy Roman Emperor(IRE) Jeu De Plume (IRE) (Montjeu (IRE))
***272a***[5]

**Spot Lite** *Rod Millman* 51
2 b g Compton Place High Class Girl (Royal Applause)
3689[7] **4696**[6] 5430[7] 5933[8]

**Spowarticus** *Scott Dixon* a57 54
8 ch g Shamardal(USA) Helen Bradley (IRE) (Indian Ridge (IRE))
***20***[6] ***158***[4] *386*[8] *528*[8] *1076*[9] *1112*[2] *1209*[5] *1372*[8] 2298[8]

**Spray The Sea (IRE)** *Bryan Smart* a70 71
2 b g Intikhab(USA) Ramamara (IRE) (Trans Island)
*4259*[5] 4792[3] **6890**[2] 7221[5]

**Spring Ability (IRE)** *Laura Mongan* a66
2 b g Oasis Dream Because (IRE) (Sadler's Wells (USA))
*7488*[10] ***8502***[4] *8877*[11]

**Spring Beauty** *John Weymes* a37 35
3 b f Equiano(FR) Spring Goddess (IRE) (Daggers Drawn (USA))
5946[7] 7247[5] ***7574***[4] *9217*[10]

**Spring Cosmos (IRE)**
*Charlie Appleby* a57 91
2 b f Acclamation Sister Red (IRE) (Diamond Green (FR))
(4815) 5391[4] **6228a**[5] *8130*[6]

**Spring Dixie (IRE)** *Mrs A Malzard* a23 40
5 gr m Zebedee Dixie Jazz (Mtoto)
**1930a**[2] 2671a[6]

**Spring Eternal** *Charles Hills* 22
3 b f Oasis Dream Short Dance (USA) (Hennessy (USA))
**4092**[4]

**Spring Fling** *Henry Candy* a101 101
6 b m Assertive Twilight Mistress (Bin Ajwaad (IRE))
2623[16] 3080[4] 3867[6] **(4078)**◆ 4635[10]

**Springforth** *Richard Fahey* 64
3 ch g Mayson Spirit Na Heireann (IRE) (Dubawi (IRE))
2304[2] **2775**[2] 3496[8] 4188[3] 4745[5] 5374[8]

**Spring Loaded (IRE)** *Paul D'Arcy* a110 106
5 gr g Zebedee Nisriyna (IRE) (Intikhab (USA))
*170*[3] 2524[4] 3593[10] 4974[2] 6275[5] 6677[3]◆ **(7144)** **8044**[2] 8416[10] *8845*[6]

**Spring Offensive (IRE)**
*Richard Fahey* 98
5 b g Iffraaj Night Sphere (IRE) (Night Shift (USA))
1388a[5] **2406**[3] 3298[6] **4077**[4] 5130[3] 5643[8] 6449[11] 7566[7]

**Spring Praise (IRE)** *Marco Botti* a27 50
2 b c Oasis Dream Applauded (IRE) (Royal Applause)
8119[14] **8382**[9] *8952*[12]

**Spring Romance (IRE)** *Dean Ivory* 27
2 bb g Zebedee Love And Devotion (Shamardal (USA))
2473[8] **4973**[8] 5474[5]

**Spring Waterfall (IRE)**
*Saeed bin Suroor* a72
2 b f Exceed And Excel(AUS) Forest Pearl (USA) (Woodman (USA))
*8373*[10] ***8998***[2]

**Spritzig** *Chris Wall* a40
2 ch f Exceed And Excel(AUS) Generous Lady (Generous (IRE))
***7453***[10] *7997*[13]

**Spruce Lodge** *David Barron* a28 66
3 b g Compton Place Beautiful Lady (IRE) (Peintre Celebre (USA))
***7365***[7]

**Spruce Meadows (IRE)**
*John James Feane* a95 95
4 b g Intikhab(USA) Taziria (SWI) (Zilzal Zamaan (USA))
5582a[7] **6978a**[3]

**Spryt (IRE)** *John Butler* a70 55
5 b g Invincible Spirit(IRE) Out Of Thanks (IRE) (Sadler's Wells (USA))
*69*[9] *1146*[4] *1587*[9] ***(3688)***

**Spud (IRE)** *Tom Dascombe* 95
2 b c Fast Company(IRE) Nightswimmer (IRE) (Noverre (USA))
6674[2]◆ **(7105)**◆

**Spun Gold** *Charlie Fellowes* a68 67
3 ch g Exceed And Excel(AUS) Victoire Celebre (USA) (Stravinsky (USA))
*1692*[8] 2506[8]◆ 7157[2]◆ *8132*[9] *8503*[5] *8930*[8] *9027*[6] ***(9364)***

**Spunky Heart (IRE)** *Mlle L Kneip* a58 58
3 ch f Iffraaj Own Gift (Rahy (USA))
**6084a**[9]

**Sputnik Planum (USA)**
*David Lanigan* a76 70
3 b g Quality Road(USA) Shiva (JPN) (Hector Protector (USA))
2584[10] 3506[9] 4224[5] 5065[5] *6291*[4] ***7063***[2] *7319*[4] *7766*[6]

**Spykes Bay (USA)** *Vanja Sandrup* a89 89
8 ch g Speightstown(USA) She's A Rich Girl (USA) (Affirmed (USA))
*(2943a)* ***4940a***[4]

**Squats (IRE)** *William Haggas* a106 109
5 b g Dandy Man(IRE) Light Sea (IRE) (King's Best (USA))
2606[23] 4072[15] 4881[13] 5393[17] **(6192)** ***6685***[8] 6918[11]

**Squiggley** *Henry Candy* a37 79
4 b m Sir Percy Oat Cuisine (Mujahid (USA))
3771[2] 4621[6] 5218[2] 5715[7] **7098**[3]◆ 8143[6]

**Squire** *Michael Attwater* a81 79
6 b g Teofilo(IRE) Most Charming (FR) (Darshaan)
***61***[2] *277*[4] *516*[7] 4523[4] 5788[9] 6557[6] *7878*[14] *9212*[2]

**Squirrelheed** *Richard Guest* 32
2 b g Finjaan Valjarv (IRE) (Bluebird (USA))
4074[6] 4792[9] **5127**[11] *9097*[14]

**Sri Prada (FR)** *G Doleuze* a66 79
3 gr f Air Chief Marshal(IRE) Fenella's Link (Linamix (FR))
1459a[3]

**Sruthan (IRE)** *P D Deegan* a79 111
7 b g Arakan(USA) Giveupyeraulsins (IRE) (Mark Of Esteem (IRE))
**1568a**[6] 7663a[10]

**Ss Vega** *Jim Goldie* 54
4 b m Kheleyf(USA) Annie Gee (Primo Valentino (IRE))
2337[5] **2949**[2]◆ 3198[3]◆ 3387[5] **4682**[3] 5466[10] 5919[5] 6271[9]

**Staffa (IRE)** *Denis Coakley* a64 62
4 b m Rock Of Gibraltar(IRE) Gabriellina Klon (IRE) (Ashkalani (IRE))
*1557*[5]◆ *2367*[4] 3331[3] *(4009)* 4731[10] *5297*[6] 5778[2] 6174[10] ***(7407)*** 7607[4] *8128*[5] 8298[5]

**Staff College (FR)** *Henry Spiller* 76
3 b g Slickly(FR) School Of Music (FR) (Green Tune (USA))
1460a[7] **5931**[4] 7142[11]

**Stage Magic (IRE)** *Charlie Appleby* 106
2 b c Dark Angel(IRE) Witnessed (Authorized (IRE))
3742[2] (5106)◆ 6229a[2] **(6730a)** 7847a[6]

**Stage Name** *Hugo Palmer* 77
3 ch f Famous Name Striking Choice (USA) (Smart Strike (CAN))
**6390**[2]

**Stag Party (IRE)** *Julia Brooke* a50 57
3 b g Thewayyouare(USA) Betrothed (IRE) (Oratorio (IRE))
*73*[4] ***310***[6] *848*[4] *2060*[8] 2705[8] 4439[12]

**Stainless (USA)** *Todd Pletcher* a78 100
2 rg f Flatter(USA) Spring Storm (USA) (Unbridled's Song (USA))
***8603a***[10]

**Staintondale Lass (IRE)**
*Ed Vaughan* a87 98
4 b m Bushranger(IRE) Siphon Melody (USA) (Siphon (BRZ))
*8101*[2] *1091*[8] *1261*[2] *1771*[8] (2912) **(4536)** 5117[5] 6234[10]

**Stake Acclaim (IRE)** *Dean Ivory* a84 110
5 b g Acclamation Golden Legacy (IRE) (Rossini (USA))
2038[3] 2123[6] 2835[2] (3410)◆ 3625[2] 4411[6] 5640[15] (5911) 6275[3] 7144[16] **7611**[2] 8044[15] 8738[14]

**Stallwalkin' Dude (USA)**
*David Jacobson* a115 115
7 b g City Place(USA) Chelle Spendabuck (USA) (Dare And Go (USA))
***1377a***[6]

**Stamford Raffles**
*Jane Chapple-Hyam* a84 92
4 b g Champs Elysees Romantic Retreat (Rainbow Quest (USA))
4365[2]◆ **(5138)** **5663**[2] 6151[12] 7203a[10]

**Stamp Collecting (IRE)** *R Biondi* 95
3 b f Casamento(IRE) Almatlaie (USA) (Elusive Quality (USA))
**2244a**[3] 3121a[4] 7441a[8]

**Stamp Duty (IRE)** *Suzzanne France* a52 59
9 b g Ad Valorem(USA) Lothian Lass (IRE) (Daylami (IRE))
*608*[4] *2166*[2] *8247*[2] ***9217***[2]

**Stamp Hill (IRE)** *Richard Fahey* 102
4 b g Zoffany(IRE) Edelfa (IRE) (Fasliyev (USA))
2142[8] 2606[22] 3498[8] 4854[18] **(5393)** 7822[7]

**Stanarley Pic** *Sally Haynes* a59 70
6 b g Piccolo Harlestone Lady (Shaamit (IRE))
1834[7] 2270[7] *3340*[3] 3756[7] *5413*[4] (5951) **7248**[2] 7659[6] 8214[8]

**Stander (IRE)** *John C McConnell* a43 49
3 b c Famous Name Coill Cri (IRE) (Shinko Forest (IRE))
**6032**[2] *6530*[4]

**Stand Guard** *John Butler* a66 40
13 b g Danehill(USA) Protectress (Hector Protector (USA))
***(462)*** *7387* *8261*[14] *8846*[12] *9092*[15]

**Standing Rock (IRE)** *John Gosden* 97
3 b f Fastnet Rock(AUS) Great Hope (IRE) (Halling (USA))
(3748) (4915)◆ **5981a**[6]

**St Andrews (IRE)** *Ian Williams* a58 58
4 ch g Rip Van Winkle(IRE) Stellavera (FR) (Anabaa (USA))
*419*[9] *6851*[0] *1603*[12] 3028[2] 3698[4] **5054**[2] 5722[5] 6509[8] *7490*[2] ***(7730)***

**Stanghow** *Antony Brittain* a89 92
5 b g Monsieur Bond(IRE) Melandre (Lujain (USA))
*1777*[9] 2123[10] 3052[4] 3288[2] 3827[4] 4333[3] **(4600)** **4867**[4] *5241*[9] 6205[10] 6412[5] 6758[4] *7604*[7] *8660*[7]

**Stanhope** *Mick Quinn* 90
3 b g Equiano(FR) Nicoise (IRE) (Lear Spear (USA))
2072[4]◆ 2620[5] (4268) 5156[7] 5959[2] 6392[2] **7287**[2]

**Stanley** *Richard Hughes* a81 79
4 ch g Sea The Stars(IRE) Deirdre (Dubawi (IRE))
*6623*[3] ***7708***[2] *(8151)*

**Stanley (GER)** *Jonjo O'Neill* 81
6 bl g Pivotal Sky Dancing (IRE) (Exit To Nowhere (USA))
1700[9] 2301[4]◆ 3433[4] **5221**[2] 5805[2] 6475[3]

**Stanlow** *Michael Mullineaux* a46 54
7 b g Invincible Spirit(IRE) Ghazal (USA) (Gone West (USA))
***176***[13] *425*[11] 4626[9] 6092[16]

**Staphanos (JPN)** *Hideaki Fujiwara* 121
6 b h Deep Impact(JPN) Kokoshnik (JPN) (Kurofune (USA))
**9171a**[4]

**Staplehurst (IRE)** *Geoffrey Deacon* a58 45
4 b m Beat Hollow Kelpie (IRE) (Kahyasi (IRE))
***(279)***◆ *461*[8] 3694[6] 4187[6] 4469[8]

**Stararchitecture (IRE)**
*William Haggas* a63 76
3 b c Mastercraftsman(IRE) City Of Cities (IRE) (In The Wings)
*1448*[3] **2930**[3] 3485[4] 4537[4]

**Star Ascending (IRE)**
*Jennie Candlish* a64 53
5 ch g Thousand Words Sakaka (Tobougg (IRE))
*68*[5] *1249*[3]◆ *1545*[7] ***(1985)*** *2308*[3] 3043[6] 4187[4] 5080[9] *5483*[6] *6524*[4] *6953*[5] *8261*[5] *8430*[4] *(9077)* *9368*[2] *9445*[2]

**Star Attraction (FR)**
*David Menuisier* 54
2 b f Orpen(USA) Heaven (Reel Buddy (USA))
**8471**[4]

**Starboard** *David Simcock* a91 86
8 b g Zamindar(USA) Summer Shower (Sadler's Wells (USA))
*277*[6] ***(516)*** *648*[2]

**Starboard Watch** *James Given* a55 58
3 b f Harbour Watch(IRE) Makhsusah (IRE) (Darshaan)
2078[9] 2930[8] 3435[8] **5946**[2]◆ 6435[13] *7035*[3] *7514*[4] 8123[9]

**Starboy (IRE)** *George Scott* a68 69
2 br g Camacho New Magic (IRE) (Statue Of Liberty (USA))
2473[5]◆ *3135*[10] 3590[8] 5143[5] *7239*[5] **(7914)**

**Starcaster** *Hughie Morrison* 76
2 b c Dansili Shirocco Star (Shirocco (GER))
7026[3]◆ **8075**[3]◆

**Star Catch** *Charles Hills* a71 75
3 b f Cacique(IRE) Jolie Etoile (USA) (Diesis)
2033[9] ***3970***[4]

**Star Citizen** *Fred Watson* 68
5 b g New Approach(IRE) Faslen (USA) (Fasliyev (USA))
2821[12] 3667[6] **4249**[3]

**Star Cracker (IRE)** *Jim Goldie* a65 64
5 ch g Starspangledbanner(AUS) Champagne Cracker (Up And At 'Em)
1805[7] 2341[6] 2843[11] 4664[6] 5069[6] 5472[3] (5995) 6351[6] 7660[7] 7884[6] 8480[8] (9102)

**Stardrifter** *Linda Perratt* a53 51
5 b g Rock Of Gibraltar(IRE) Alchemilla (Dubai Destination (USA))
2430[11] 2953[11] 3450[5] 3977[10] 4039[8] 4660[10] 4900[6] 5074[3] 5097[4] 5467[9] 5917[5] 5997[4] 6352[10] 6690[5] 7703[5] 7979[12] 8590[2]◆ 8784[2]◆

**Starfall** *Christopher Wilson* 48
4 b g Misu Bond(IRE) Davana (Primo Valentino (IRE))
2547[9] 3448[4] 4106[7]

**Starfield** *Mandy Rowland* a73 64
8 b g Marju(IRE) Sister Moonshine (FR) (Piccolo)
6[12] 1186[6] 1449[10]

**Star General** *Marco Botti* a55
3 b c Galileo(IRE) Sweet Cecily (IRE) (Kodiac)
65[6]

**Star Glitter (FR)** *David O'Meara* a59 68
4 ch g Sea The Stars(IRE) Gadalka (USA) (Giant's Causeway (USA))
2079[4] 2427[4] 2456[4] 3547[9] 3813[7]

**Star Guide** *Sylvester Kirk* a71 71
3 b f Henrythenavigator(USA) Exorcet (FR) (Selkirk (USA))
5931[5] 6320[2] (6823) 7507[9]

**Star Gypsy (FR)** *Luca Cumani* a77 81
3 br g Myboycharlie(IRE) Melandia (IRE) (One Cool Cat (USA))
2689[10] 2997[4] (3435) 4544[5]

**Staring At The Sea (IRE)**
*Wido Neuroth* a19
6 b h Footstepsinthesand Prealpina (IRE) (Indian Ridge (IRE))
4940a[14]

**Stark Reality (IRE)** *Nigel Tinkler* a33 44
2 b f Arcano(IRE) Eliza Doolittle (Royal Applause)
5058[7] 6055[6] 6432[14] 7030[7]

**Starlight Circus (IRE)** *Marco Botti* a58 66
3 b f High Chaparral(IRE) Mountain Law (USA) (Mountain Cat (USA))
3507[9] 4319[3] 4761[5] 5853[4] 6436[3] 7712[12]

**Starlight Mystery (IRE)**
*Mark Johnston* 85
2 bb f Iffraaj Electra Star (Shamardal (USA))
1873[3] (2251) (2590) 2826[2]◆ 4028[13]◆ 4858[8] 5572[6] 6726a[6] 7814[19]

**Starlight Romance (IRE)**
*Richard Fahey* 95
3 b f Excelebration(IRE) Takizada (IRE) (Sendawar (IRE))
(2106) 2739[3] (3578) 4334[2] 5434[7] 6404[11] 8566[7]

**Star Links (USA)** *John Butler* a51 26
11 b g Bernstein(USA) Startarette (USA) (Dixieland Band (USA))
3137[12] 4453[2] 4982[12] 5296[8] 6796[9]

**Starlit Cantata**
*Eve Johnson Houghton* a86 82
6 b m Oratorio(IRE) Starlit Sky (Galileo (IRE))
36[5]

**Starlite Sienna (IRE)** *Richard Fahey* a57 61
3 b f Elusive Pimpernel(USA) Devious Diva (IRE) (Dr Devious (IRE))
2107[8] 2702[7] 4171[4]

**Star Maker** *Sylvester Kirk* a76 81
3 ch g Mastercraftsman(IRE) Snoqualmie Star (Galileo (IRE))
2088[3] 2395[7] 2892[2] 3178[3]◆ 3752[7] (4348) 5153[5] (5932) 6423[8] 7063[8] 7651[10]

**Star Max (GER)** *Markus Klug* 35
2 b c Maxios Startissima (Green Tune (USA))
8621a[6]

**Star Of Assisi (USA)** *John Ryan* 39
2 b f Arch(USA) Charming Tale (USA) (Kingmambo (USA))
8006[11]

**Star Of Bristol (USA)**
*Richard Hughes* a70 51
3 ch f Speightstown(USA) Starlight Dreams (USA) (Black Tie Affair)
1503[5] 2274[3] 2900[10] 4012[10]

**Star Of Doha** *Ralph Beckett* a68 64
3 b f Lawman(FR) Smart Step (Montjeu (IRE))
2759[4] 3425[5] 5607[8]

**Star Of Lombardy (IRE)**
*Mark Johnston* a82 76
4 b m Cape Cross(IRE) Million Waves (IRE) (Mull Of Kintyre (USA))
1345[3] (1455)◆ (1549) 1938[2] 2028[5] 2387[2] 2723[3] 3046[4] 3341[8] 3983[3] (4519) 5065[3] 5414[7] 5820[6] 6061[4] 6513[8] 7386[4] (7831) (8160)

**Star Of Paris (IRE)** *F-X Belvisi* a60 47
4 b g Alfred Nobel(IRE) Cealtra Star (IRE) (Mujadil (USA))
391a[6]

**Star Of Rory (IRE)** *Tom Dascombe* 98
3 b g Born To Sea(IRE) Dame Alicia (IRE) (Sadler's Wells (USA))
2569[6] 3042[4] 4376[10] 5841[3] 6881[2] 7555[8] 8048[17]

**Star Of Siena** *John Ryan* 68
2 ch f Exceed And Excel(AUS) Blagueuse (IRE) (Statue Of Liberty (USA))
3502[7] 8323[8] 8563[3]

**Star Of Spring (IRE)** *Iain Jardine* a73 75
5 b m Iffraaj Gift Of Spring (USA) (Gilded Time (USA))
360[3] 444[5]

**Star Of The East (IRE)**
*Mark Johnston* 91
3 b g Cape Cross(IRE) Serenity Star (Monsun (GER))
5598[11] 6202[2] 6344[2] 6872[5] 7163[4] 7337[4] (7614) 8011[4]

**Star Of The Stage** *John Butler* a75 40
5 b g Invincible Spirit(IRE) Enact (Kyllachy)
116[10] 570[9] 1285[12] 1868[13]

**Star Of Vendome (FR)**
*Harry Dunlop* a57 73
2 gr f Style Vendome(FR) Celestina Agostino (USA) (Street Cry (IRE))
3174[6] 4007[8] 5988a[7] 6251a[7] 6542a[3] 7415a[3] 7969a[12]

**Star Of Zaam (IRE)** *K R Burke* a75 75
2 br g Elzaam(AUS) Golconda (IRE) (Lahib (USA))
2590[3] 3149[5] 4205[2] 4836[2] (5278) 5644[3] 6636[3] 6900[8] 7384[3] 7921[3]

**Star On Sunday (FR)** *A Lopez* a54
3 b c Never On Sunday(FR) Septieme Etoile (FR) (Septieme Ciel (USA))
748a[8]

**Starplex** *Keith Dalgleish* 83
7 b g Multiplex Turtle Bay (Dr Fong (USA))
4036[4] (4474) 5166[3] 5830[2]

**Star Quality** *David Loughnane* a80 35
3 b f Champs Elysees Starfan (USA) (Lear Fan (USA))
3353a[10] (9273) 9418[2]◆

**Star Rider** *Hughie Morrison* a72 103
5 gr m Cape Cross(IRE) Starfala (Galileo (IRE))
1942[6] 3928[6] 5524[11] 6329[14] 8038[23]

**Star Rock** *Hughie Morrison* a67 103
3 b f Fastnet Rock(AUS) Starfala (Galileo (IRE))
1944[2] (2834) (7401) 8011[3] (8739)

**Starshell (IRE)** *Sir Mark Prescott Bt* a71 62
3 b g Sea The Stars(IRE) Aquarelle Bleue (Sadler's Wells (USA))
2371[2]◆ 3178[2] 6812[3] 7047[4] 7537[6] 7992[5]

**Starsovertheriver (IRE)**
*Ismail Mohammed* 68
3 b f Kodiac River Style (IRE) (Desert Style (IRE))
(4445)

**Stars Over The Sea (USA)**
*Henry De Bromhead* 109
6 b g Sea The Stars(IRE) Exciting Times (FR) (Jeune Homme (USA))
3057a[4] 7422a[2] 8229[12]

**Star Storm (IRE)** *James Fanshawe* a111 108
5 b h Sea The Stars(IRE) Sayyedati Storm (USA) (Storm Cat (USA))
2604[2] 4033[3] 6447[P]

**Star Story** *Ralph Beckett* a80 76
3 b f Sea The Stars(IRE) Stylish One (IRE) (Invincible Spirit (IRE))
5428[2]◆ 7652[4] 8564[3] 9000[2] 9260[3]

**Start Right** *S Seemar* a92 98
10 b g Footstepsinthesand Time Crystal (IRE) (Sadler's Wells (USA))
654a[11] 888a[9]

**Start Seven** *Jamie Osborne* a93 64
5 br g Dilum(USA) Dancingintheclouds (IRE) (Rainbow Quest (USA))
(162)◆ (380)◆ (477) 666[2] 1361[4] 5330[8] 5820[8] 6398[6] 8244[5] 9082[3] 9341[5]

**Start Time (IRE)** *Paul Midgley* a68 74
4 b g Invincible Spirit(IRE) Silca's Sister (Inchinor)
5434[10] 5669[12] 6205[12] 7554[8] 8319[13] 8512[3] 8722[8]

**Star Victory (FR)** *J-L Dubord* a88 108
6 b h Tot Ou Tard(IRE) Tadrou (FR) (Kadrou (FR))
1271a[2] 1659a[10]

**Statehood (IRE)** *Charlie Appleby* a82
2 b c Kodiac Analysis (Dubai Destination (USA))
(8545)◆ 9312[4]

**State Of Honor (CAN)** *Mark Casse* a105
3 b c To Honor And Serve(USA) State Cup (USA) (Elusive Quality (USA))
2420a[19]

**State Residence (IRE)**
*David O'Meara* a61 60
3 b g Arcano(IRE) Sugar Blossom (IRE) (Marju (IRE))
115[8] 221[4] 479[4] 895[6] 1297[10] 2349[10] 2790[9] 3151[4] 4263[5] 5848[3] (6437)◆ 6572[5] 6903[3] 7166[3] 7487[4]◆

**State Sovereignty**
*Michael Scudamore* a67 81
5 b m Authorized(IRE) Sovereign's Honour (USA) (Kingmambo (USA))
4497[4] 5707[2]◆ (6129) 6789[4] 7651[7]

**Statuario** *Eve Johnson Houghton* 79
2 b g Helmet(AUS) Cat Hunter (One Cool Cat (USA))
(7079) 7546[9] 7929[7]

**Staunch (USA)** *Jeremy Noseda* a72 72
2 b g Union Rags(USA) Stylish Storm (USA) (Storm Bird (CAN))
6260[2]◆ 7411[3]

**Staxton** *Tim Easterby* 101
2 b c Equiano(FR) Snake's Head (Golden Snake (USA))
(4526) 5437[2] (5825) 6446[5] 7394[6] 8043[3] 8412[3]

**St Brelades Bay (IRE)**
*Mrs John Harrington* a95 95
5 b g Camacho Tides (Bahamian Bounty)
1385a[12] 4327a[8] 8222a[13]

**St Dunstan (IRE)** *John Quinn* 59
4 b g Zoffany(IRE) Box Of Frogs (IRE) (One Cool Cat (USA))
(3760) 4470[7] 5215[14]

**Steady (IRE)** *Dan Skelton* a4
3 b f Tagula(IRE) First Rains (Green Desert (USA))
5577[13] 6287[12] 6577[6] 7912[10]

**Steady Major (IRE)**
*Mark Brisbourne* a61 14
5 b g Invincible Spirit(IRE) Combust (USA) (Aptitude (USA))
49[8] 333[10] 684[9] 865[9] 1629[7] 2272[4] 3546[6] 4158[10] 5850[12] 6305[9]

**Steady Pace** *Saeed bin Suroor* a112 113
4 b g Dark Angel(IRE) Cool Kitten (IRE) (One Cool Cat (USA))
207a[2] 433a[4] 696a[4] 892a[4] 4072[2] 4905[3] 6428[2] 6966[4] (7603)

**Stealth** *John Gosden* a53
2 b c Kodiac White Dress (IRE) (Pivotal)
9311[5]

**Steal The Scene (IRE)** *Kevin Frost* a89 68
5 b g Lord Shanakill(USA) Namoos (USA) (Sahm (USA))
1606[14] 2684[8] 3203[12] 3702[3] 3912[9] 7321[12] 7947[10] 8434[8] 9411[2]

**Steaming (IRE)** *Ralph Beckett* a77 80
3 ch g Rail Link Dazzling Day (Hernando (FR))
2164[2] 2841[2] 3408[4] 5556[3] 6765[5] (8377) 9082[7]

**Steccando (IRE)** *Sally Haynes* a63 65
4 b g Lawman(FR) Second Act (Sadler's Wells (USA))
1717[13] 2183[6] 3400[3] 5454[7] 5883[4] 6269[2] 7015[3] 7936[7] 8206[6]

**Steel Helmet (IRE)** *Brian Ellison* a63 63
3 ch g Helmet(AUS) Marine City (JPN) (Carnegie (IRE))
1875[5] 2903[7] 2991[8] 4263[2] 5417[9] 6902[12] 8477[5]

**Steelriver (IRE)** *David Barron* a83 68
7 b g Iffraaj Numerus Clausus (FR) (Numerous (USA))
79[2] 93[8] 857[5] 957[9] 1423[2] 1833[7] 2621[6] 3974[3]

**Steel Train (FR)** *David O'Meara* a104 102
6 b g Zafeen(FR) Silent Sunday (IRE) (Testa Rossa (AUS))
199[13] 730[10] 1148[12] 1494[7] 1773[10] 2384[8] 2606[21] 8009[16] 8737[13] (8905) 9233[7]

**Stella Di Camelot (IRE)**
*Gianluca Bietolini* 91
2 b f Camelot Star Force (ITY) (Blu Air Force (IRE))
5448a[11] 8525a[5]

**Stella D'Oroux (FR)** *Y Fertillet* a4 31
6 ch m Monos(GER) Stella Di Quattro (Best Of The Bests (IRE))
515a[13]

**Stellar Mass (IRE)** *J S Bolger* 114
4 b h Sea The Stars(IRE) Juno Marlowe (IRE) (Danehill (USA))
1654a[4] 4070[10] 4420a[4] 5862a[3]

**Stellar Surprise** *Stuart Williams* a90 86
3 b f Notnowcato Crystal Etoile (Dansili)
3786[3]◆ 4366[3]◆ 5591[6] (5856) 6919[5] 7204a[9] 7545[5] 8820[2] (9418)

**Stellarta** *Michael Blanshard* a100 97
6 b m Sakhee's Secret Torgau (IRE) (Zieten (USA))
1501[3]◆ 1794[2] 3034[5] 3593[5] 3867[9] 4411[3] 4830[8] 5637[5] 6412[9] 6864[7] 7455[3] 8077[8] 8991[7] 9453[9]

**Stellar Wind (USA)** *John W Sadler* a119
5 ch m Curlin(USA) Evening Star (USA) (Malibu Moon (USA))
8578a[8]

**Stellekaya (IRE)** *Mark H Tompkins*
3 gr f Mastercraftsman(IRE) Delitme (IRE) (Val Royal (FR))
3408[7] 6044[7]

**Stemster** *Ecurie Avant-Garde* a34 45
6 rg g Invincible Spirit(IRE) Mariyara (FR) (Daylami (IRE))
7342a[8]

**Stenographer (USA)** *J S Bolger* 94
4 ch g Distorted Humor(USA) Sadler's Secretary (IRE) (Sadler's Wells (USA))
1388a[14] 5688a[6] 6491a[9]

**Stephensons Rocket (IRE)**
*Ed Walker* 82
2 gr c Teofilo(IRE) Tipperary Honor (FR) (Highest Honor (FR))
7128[2] (8215)◆

**Stepney** *Robyn Brisland* a74 68
3 b f Mount Nelson Fancy Rose (USA) (Joyeux Danseur (USA))
1424[2] (2062) 4730[5] 6013[3] 6144[5] 7832[2] 8160[3] 8204[5]

**Stepper Point** *William Muir* a97 102
8 b g Kyllachy Sacre Coeur (Compton Place)
1222[2]◆ 1465[4] (2038) 2391[8] 2578[4] (3231) 3829[9] 4881[15] 4974[7]

**Sterling Lines** *P Monfort* a61 61
4 b g Equiano(FR) Owdbetts (IRE) (High Estate)
391a[11]

**Sterling Silva (IRE)** *Richard Hannon* a77 82
3 ch g Sakhee's Secret Silicon Star (FR) (Starborough)
2122[10] 2755[5] 5115[2] 5433[4] 5548[3] 5928[6] 6576[7] 8341[4]

**Sternkranz (GER)** *Markus Klug* 86
3 bb c Kamsin(GER) Sternstunde (GER) (Sir Warren (IRE))
4422a[14]

**Sternrubin (GER)** *Philip Hobbs* 99
6 b g Authorized(IRE) Sworn Mum (GER) (Samum (GER))
(2234) 3618[3] 4222[2]◆ 4586[3] (6033) 7402[12]

**Steve Prescott** *Patrick Morris* a70 97
5 gr g Dutch Art Toy Top (USA) (Tactical Cat (USA))
1454[10]

**Steve Rogers (IRE)** *Roger Varian* a108 101
6 b g Montjeu(IRE) Three Owls (IRE) (Warning)
268[3] 1770[3]

**Stevie Brown** *David Brown* a63 64
3 b g Bushranger(IRE) Oriental Romance (IRE) (Elusive City (USA))
1589[3] 2186[10] 3166[9]

**Stewardess (IRE)**
*John James Feane* a68 69
2 gr f Dandy Man(IRE) Smart Hostess (Most Welcome)
7423a[7]

**St Gallen (IRE)** *John Joseph Murphy* a84 86
4 b g Majestic Missile(IRE) Fly With Me (IRE) (Montjeu (IRE))
6334a[8]

**St Helens Gate (IRE)**
*Rebecca Menzies* 21
2 b f Lilbourne Lad(IRE) Lyca Ballerina (Marju (IRE))
1908[8] 2222[9] 5161[8]

**Stickleback** *Micky Hammond* 15
8 ch m Manduro(GER) The Stick (Singspiel (IRE))
3436[8]

**Still Believing (IRE)** *Evan Williams* 35
9 ch m Blueprint(IRE) Im A Believer (IRE) (Erins Isle (IRE))
6031[6]

**Still Got It** *Daniel Mark Loughnane* a61 57
2 b f Captain Gerrard(IRE) Petaluma (Teofilo (IRE))
6138[6] 6583[5] 6776[4] 7023[2] 8491[7] 8996[10] 9302[8]

**Still On Top** *Tim Easterby* 83
4 b g Royal Applause Poulaine Bleue (Bertolini (USA))
1910[5] 2303[6] 3540[9]

**Still Waiting** *William Jarvis* a63 69
3 b g Kheleyf(USA) First Approval (Royal Applause)
89[2] 210[3] 2794[6] 3937[2] 4463[7] 5341[2] 5870[2] 6485[6] 8328[6]

**Stimulator** *Andi Brown* a19 5
4 b g Motivator Fleeting Echo (Beat Hollow)
461[10]

**Stipulate** *Brian Ellison* 101
8 b g Dansili Indication (Sadler's Wells (USA))
1802[13] 2406[3] 3298[9] 3790[11] 5517a[11] 5688a[16]

**Stirling Value** *David Simcock* a60
2 b c Pour Moi(IRE) Celebre Vadala (FR) (Peintre Celebre (USA))
9299[8]

**St James's Park (IRE)**
*Luke McJannet* a60 7
4 br g Invincible Spirit(IRE) Rakiza (IRE) (Elnadim (USA))
3456[5] 4562[5] 5243[7] 7061[9] 7495[8] 8514[11]

**St. Joe Bay (USA)** *Peter Miller* a114 90
5 bb g Saint Anddan(USA) Dream Ride (USA) (Honor Glide (USA))
1377a[4]

**St Lawrence Gap (IRE)** *Eoin Doyle* a81 84
5 ch g Tagula(IRE) Kannon (Kyllachy)
5488a[9]

**St Malo (USA)** *Roger Varian* a91 77
4 b g Street Cry(IRE) Arkadina (IRE) (Danehill (USA))
3091[6] 4751[2]◆ 5421[10] 7880[2]

**St Mary's** *Andrew Balding* a92 91
4 b m Siyouni(FR) Once Over (Sakhee (USA))
(2574) 3580[8] 5108[6] 5566[2] (6680) 7143[2] 7507[5] 8166[2] (8511)◆ 8733a[6] 8892[4]

**St Michel** *Sir Mark Prescott Bt* a112 113
4 b h Sea The Stars(IRE) Miss Provence (Hernando (FR))
2519[2] 3553a[2] 6400[3]

**Stockhill Diva** *Brendan Powell* a53 97
7 ch m Haafhd April Stock (Beveled (USA))
2234[4] (3671)◆ 4370[6] 5273[5]

**Stock Hill Fair** *Brendan Powell*
9 b g Sakhee(USA) April Stock (Beveled (USA))
3086[8] 6865[9]

**Stockhill Star** *Brendan Powell* a6 25
3 b f Aqlaam April Stock (Beveled (USA))
7227[7] 8504[10]

**Stockings Lane (IRE)**
*Steph Hollinshead* 47
2 ch c Excelebration(IRE) Mubkera (IRE) (Nashwan (USA))
3769[8] 5547[7]

**Stockton (IRE)** *David Simcock* a22 41
3 b g Galileo(IRE) Walklikeanegyptian (IRE) (Danehill (USA))
2314[7] 2963[11] 3209[12]

**Stoic Boy** *Henry Candy* a56 18
5 ch g Paco Boy(IRE) Dramatic Turn (Pivotal)
9469[3]

**Stolen Angel (IRE)** *Antony Brittain* a45 56
3 b g Dark Angel(IRE) Tamarisk (GER) (Selkirk (USA))
5003[5] 5538[9] 6150[10] 7235[10] 7523[12]

**Stomachion (IRE)** *John Butler*
7 b g Duke Of Marmalade(IRE) Insight (FR) (Sadler's Wells (USA))
1108[5]

**Ston (IRE)** *Simone Brogi* a50 49
5 rg g Lope De Vega(IRE) Lady Raj (USA) (El Prado (IRE))
691a[7]

**Stoneboat Bill** *Declan Carroll* a69 68
5 ch g Virtual Applauding (IRE) (Royal Applause)
1735[7] 2153[3] 2498[2] 2955[2] 3400[2]◆ 3628[5] 5008[5] 6035[7] 7028[4] 7567[2] 9364[8]

**Stonecoldsoba** *Denis Quinn* a66 63
4 b g Aqlaam Aswaaq (IRE) (Peintre Celebre (USA))
70[3] 218[3] 461[4] 661[3] 924[3] 1256[7] 1985[9] 6953[11]

**Stoneham** *Iain Jardine* a76 75
6 b m Sixties Icon Cibenze (Owington)
(990) 1344[2] 3389[3] 3830[4] 4852[3] 5259[4] 6895[4] 7359[11]

**Stone Of Folca** *Lucinda Egerton*
9 b g Kodiac Soyalang (FR) (Alydeed (CAN))
5184[6]

**Stone The Crows** *Roger Charlton* a90 89
3 b g Cape Cross(IRE) Stars In Your Eyes (Galileo (IRE))
(2175) 3081[2] 4221[2] 6202[6] 7516[6]

**Stoney Broke** *James Fanshawe* a90 89
4 b m Dansili Alvee (IRE) (Key Of Luck (USA))
2728[2] (3341) 4829[5] 5414[2] 7092[3] 8166[5]

**Stoneyford Lane (IRE)**
*Steph Hollinshead* 84
3 b g Bushranger(IRE) Peace Talks (Pivotal)
2806[5] 3584[9] (4530) 4867[13] 5304[3] (5588) 5959[6]

**Stop And Stare (FR)**
*X Thomas-Demeaulte* 52
2 ch f Shamalgan(FR) Saryshnikova (FR) (Baryshnikov (AUS))
5815a[7]

**Stopdworldnletmeof** *David Flood* a46 42
3 b g Piccolo Dili Dancer (Dansili)
1183[4] 1543[6] 2853[6] 3569[3] 5792[6] 5935[4] 6339[9]

**Stopwatch** *Karen McLintock* a40 48
2 b g Harbour Watch(IRE) Almond Branches (Dutch Art)
3523[6] 3705[5] 5370[11] 5878[10] 7938[7]

**Storm Again** *Philip Hide* a53
2 ch c Nathaniel(IRE) Triveni (FR) (Lando (GER))
9200[9]

**Storm Ahead (IRE)**
*Marcus Tregoning* a80 95
4 b g Iffraaj Loose Julie (IRE) (Cape Cross (IRE))
1960[8] 2799[4] 4410[5] 5643[17] 6873[2] 7781[7]

**Stormardal (IRE)** *Ismail Mohammed* a106 100
6 b g Shamardal(USA) Dievotchkina (IRE) (Bluebird (USA))
1043a[4] 1373a[U]

**Storm Belt (USA)** *Doug Watson* a106 93
8 b h More Than Ready(USA) Mari's Thunder (USA) (Thunder Gulch (USA))
83a[7] 541a[9] 891a[6] 9360a[5]

**Stormberg (IRE)** *N Caullery* a54 29
3 b g Invincible Spirit(IRE) Toolentidhaar (USA) (Swain (IRE))
748a[2]

**Stormbound (IRE)** *Paul Cole* a67 71
8 b g Galileo(IRE) A Footstep Away (USA) (Giant's Causeway (USA))
1086[10] 1409[6] (2057) 2297[2] 4203[4] 6541a[5] 6946[8]

**Stormbringer** *Kevin Ryan* 96
2 b c Dutch Art Riva Royale (Royal Applause)
4681[3] (5537) 6446[7]

**Storm Cry** *Mark Johnston* a78 87
3 b f Poet's Voice Street Fire (IRE) (Street Cry (IRE))
1901[5] 2517[7] 3045[4] 3526[2] 3715[3] 4317[2] 4521[2] 4788[6] 5264[6] 6290[4] (7000) 7653[3] 7886[5] 8393[13]

**Storm Doris (IRE)** *James Unett* a53 39
2 br f Lilbourne Lad(IRE) Big Sylv (IRE) (Clodovil (IRE))
1934[6] 2277[2] 2522[8] 4977[7] 6585[11]

**Stormflower** *John Bridger* a73 73
4 gr m Arcano(IRE) Someone's Angel (USA) (Runaway Groom (CAN))
2038[5] 2368[5]

**Storm Hawk (IRE)** *Emma Owen* a44
10 b g Hawk Wing(USA) Stormy Larissa (IRE) (Royal Applause)
6820[13]

**Storming Ambition** *Conrad Allen* a45 26
4 b g Captain Gerrard(IRE) Lady Roxanne (Cyrano De Bergerac)
281[12] 455[6] 1305[7] 1593[10] 1823[8] 2280[5]

**Storming Harry** *Robin Dickin* a50 45
5 ch g Assertive Miss Pebbles (IRE) (Lake Coniston (IRE))
4217[8] 5361[10] 6069[7] 8246[11]

**Stormin Tom (IRE)** *Tim Easterby* a76 77
5 b g Dylan Thomas(IRE) She Storm (IRE) (Rainbow Quest (USA))
2386[9] 3046[8] 3464[4] 3830[11] 4791[2] 5259[2] 5700[6] (6000) 6661[3] 7627[7] 8047[6] 8511[3] 8778[4]◆

**Storm Jazz (IRE)** *Ed Dunlop* a54 66
2 b f Red Jazz(USA) Singitta (Singspiel (IRE))
5963[3] 6584[4] 7513[9]◆ 8467[14]

**Storm King** *David C Griffiths* a87 96
8 b g Shamardal(USA) Tarandot (IRE) (Singspiel (IRE))
42[6] 524[2] 683[4] 992[6] (1113) 1182[3] 1549[2] (2558) 3300[9] 3790[9] 4522[8] (4893) (5643) 6449[14] 8740[4] 9186[8] 9390[8]

**Storm Lightning** *Mark Brisbourne* a62 53
8 b g Exceed And Excel(AUS) All For Laura (Cadeaux Genereux)
7517[6] 8496[7] 8873[9] 9268[9] 9374[3] 9420[8]

**Storm Melody** *Jonjo O'Neill* 81
4 b g Royal Applause Plume (Pastoral Pursuits)
2608[5] 3847[7] 4629[4] 5271[4] 5656[5] 7195[2] 7932[8]

**Storm Over (IRE)** *Robert Cowell* a72 97
3 b c Elnadim(USA) Stormy View (USA) (Cozzene (USA))
(3152)◆ 6137[3] 6945[5] (8238)◆

**Storm Ranger (IRE)** *Patrick J Flynn* a75 78
5 b g Bushranger(IRE) Zanida (IRE) (Mujadil (USA))
5518a[16]

**Storm Rock** *Harry Dunlop* a90 85
5 b g Rock Of Gibraltar(IRE) Seasonal Cross (Cape Cross (IRE))
1502[13] 2959[6] 4223[4] 5421[8] 5781[4] 6881[9] 7743[3] 7959[3] 8423[8] 9205[12]

**Storm Runner (IRE)**
*George Margarson* a52 40
9 b g Rakti Saibhreas (IRE) (Last Tycoon)
4461[5] 8346[9]

**Storm Trooper (IRE)** *Adam West* a58 34
6 b g Acclamation Maid To Order (IRE) (Zafonic (USA))
80[5] 743[3] 1971[10] 2628[4] 3544[3] 4174[12] 4847[10] 9265[11] 9420[11]

**Stormy (FR)** *S Cerulis* a80 68
3 ch g Stormy River(FR) Compulsive Quality (USA) (Elusive Quality (USA))
2536a[4] 3355a[8]

**Stormy Antarctic** *Ed Walker* a109 115
4 ch g Stormy Atlantic(USA) Bea Remembered (Doyen (IRE))
1493[2] 2492a[5] 4371[2] 4935a[3] 5502[13] (8089a) 8891[6]

**Stormy Belle (IRE)** *P A Fahy* a72 92
3 ch f Dandy Man(IRE) Herrera (IRE) (High Chaparral (IRE))
1634a[10] 6491a[22] 6961a[13] 8083a[9] 8407a[14]

**Stormy Blues** *Charlie Appleby* 81
3 b g Sepoy(AUS) Miss Brown To You (IRE) (Fasliyev (USA))
2066[12] 4274[2] 5220[15]

**Stormy Liberal (USA)** *Peter Miller* 116
5 b g Stormy Atlantic(USA) Vassar (USA) (Royal Academy (USA))
(8604a) 9168a[11]

**Stormy Sand (IRE)** *Marco Botti* a64 66
2 br g Footstepsinthesand Think Again (Dubawi (IRE))
4560[10] 5365[5] 6147[4] 6825[7] 7764[6] 8120[12]

**Stormy Tale (IRE)** *Michael Mulvany* a47 55
2 gr f Stormy River(FR) Tell The Tale (FR) (Elnadim (USA))
4020a[7] 6977a[11]

**Story Begins (FR)** *A Spanu* a53 68
2 ch f Never On Sunday(FR) Groovin High (USA) (Elusive Quality (USA))
6050a[7]

**Story Minister (IRE)**
*Tom Dascombe* a60 73
2 ch g Camacho Hartstown House (IRE) (Primo Dominie)
2382[3] 2771[4] 4160[3] 5322[3] 6036[6] 7787[5] (8397)

**Stosur (IRE)** *Gay Kelleway* a83 78
6 b m Mount Nelson Jules (IRE) (Danehill (USA))
97[2] 285[8] 2268[3] 2973[3] 3548[3] 4010[2] 5062[3] 5591[2] 6111[5] 6294[2] 7484[2] 7830[7] 9029[12] 9337[4]

**St Patrick's Day (IRE)** *J R Jenkins* a67 55
5 b g Fastnet Rock(AUS) Race For The Stars (USA) (Fusaichi Pegasus (USA))
90[6] 164[7] 7062[13] 7792[10] 9077[6] 9342[3]

**Stracciatella (IRE)** *P Nador* a45 47
7 b m Stormy River(FR) Zuppa Inglese (FR) (Le Balafre (FR))
364a[7]

**Strada Di Carsoli** *Henry Spiller* a77
4 br g Showcasing Carsulae (IRE) (Marju (IRE))
1346[8]

**Stradivarius (IRE)** *John Gosden* a80 119
3 ch c Sea The Stars(IRE) Private Life (FR) (Bering)
(1875)◆ 2526[2] (4032)◆ (5503) 7147[3] 8229[3]

**Straffan (IRE)** *David O'Meara* a44 53
2 b f Clodovil(IRE) Laureldean Spirit (IRE) (Whipper (USA))
4598[7] 9049[5] 9266[5]

**Stragar** *Michael Appleby* a41 52
3 br g Delegator Roccabella (FR) (Rock Of Gibraltar (IRE))
1111[6] 1366[4] 2152[7] 3220[7] 6622[12] 7952[8] 8345[9] 9030[5]

**Straight Ash (IRE)** *Richard Hannon* a64 71
2 gr c Zebedee Blackangelheart (IRE) (Danehill Dancer (IRE))
1604[5] 2691[4] (3570) 8131[8] 8349[7] 8817[6]

**Straight Away** *Andrew Balding* a62 69
3 b f Dubawi(IRE) Ihsas (USA) (Rahy (USA))
(8479) 8773[6] 8990[9]

**Straightothepoint** *Bryan Smart* a66 90
5 b g Kyllachy Choisette (Choisir (AUS))
1910[2] 2592[2] 2951[6] 3827[6] 4600[3] 5018[3] 7940[9] 8293[10] 8680[6]◆

**Straight Right (FR)** *Andrew Balding* a103 103
3 b c Siyouni(FR) Sailor Moon (IRE) (Tiger Hill (IRE))
1689a[4] 2561a[3] 4030[7] 5147[5] 6419[3]◆ 7807[9]◆ 8991[4]

**Strait Of Zanzibar (USA)**
*K J Condon* a86 84
8 b g Arch(USA) Royal Opportunity (USA) (Kingmambo (USA))
1479a[8]

**Strange Society (IRE)** *Hugo Palmer* a76
2 br c Society Rock(IRE) Strange Magic (IRE) (Diamond Green (FR))
8794[3] (9015)

**Strategic (IRE)** *Richard Hannon* a52 70
2 b g Kodiac Run To Jane (IRE) (Doyoun)
4151[11] 4909[5] 5786[3] 6395[7] 8467[8] 9021[5]

**Strategic Force (IRE)**
*Gerard O'Leary* a80 75
6 b g Strategic Prince Mooching Along (IRE) (Mujahid (USA))
2656a[14]

**Strategic Heights (IRE)**
*Jamie Osborne* a71 69
8 b g Strategic Prince Shot Of Redemption (Shirley Heights)
6798a[7] 8775[2] 8874[5] 9176[9] 9469[2]

**Strategist (IRE)** *William Haggas* 77
2 ch g Shamardal(USA) Snow Powder (IRE) (Raven's Pass (USA))
5350[4] 6070[4]

**Strathspey** *A Fabre* 107
3 b f New Approach(IRE) Perfect Note (Shamardal (USA))
(4424a) 6227a[4] 6981a[5]

**Strawberryandcream**
*James Bethell* a65
2 ch f Cityscape Miss Apricot (Indian Ridge (IRE))
8208[5] 8914[3]

**Strawberry Thief** *F-H Graffard* 55
3 b f Rip Van Winkle(IRE) Squander (Dr Fong (USA))
3134a[9]

**Stream Song** *John Gosden* 84
2 gr f Mastercraftsman(IRE) Montare (IRE) (Montjeu (IRE))
5349[7] 6183[4] (7399)

**Street Art (IRE)** *Mike Murphy* a56 59
5 ch g Excellent Art Via Aurelia (IRE) (Antonius Pius (USA))
278[8] 733[2] 1082[8] (1322) (2729) 3440[5] 4279[5] 5023[6] 5790[12] 6622[10]

**Street Jazz** *James Given* a71 70
3 b f Acclamation Wake Up Call (Noverre (USA))
243[4] 379[2] 898[5]

**Street Jester** *Robert Stephens* a41
3 b g Avonbridge Street Diva (USA) (Street Cry (IRE))
331[7] 464[8] 6611[7] 7790[9]

**Street Marie (USA)** *John Gosden* 60
3 b f Street Cry(IRE) Real Sense (IRE) (Galileo (IRE))
2585[10] 3007[8] 4444[3] 5367[7]

**Street Of Dreams** *Doug Watson* a80 69
4 b h Shamardal(USA) Express Way (ARG) (Ahmad (ARG))
8710a[2]

**Street Poet (IRE)**
*Michael Herrington* a62 45
4 b g Poet's Voice Street Star (USA) (Street Cry (IRE))
2163[12] 2815[7] 4358[7] 5135[6] 8720[2] 9364[5]

**Street Sensation (IRE)**
*Richard Fahey* a29
2 b c Street Cry(IRE) Sweet Hope (USA) (Lemon Drop Kid (USA))
9266[8] 9440[6]

**Streets Of Joy** *Henry Spiller* a28
2 b f Champs Elysees Nellie Gwyn (King's Best (USA))
9099[10]

**Streets Of Rio (FR)** *H-A Pantall* a77 82
3 b c Rio De La Plata(USA) Snow Lady (SWI) (Vision (USA))
2484a[11] 6650a[6]

**Stretewise (IRE)** *Jason Ward* a64 21
3 b f Tagula(IRE) Leglen Wood (IRE) (High Chaparral (IRE))
658[5] 970[7] 1348[2] 1589[4] 2349[16]

**Strictly Art (IRE)** *Alan Bailey* a67 67
4 b g Excellent Art Sadinga (IRE) (Sadler's Wells (USA))
757[2] 865[6] 1225[9] (3304) 3519[3] 4018[2] 4181[2] 5508[4] 5968[6] (6523) 7729[2] 8396[2]◆ (9095) 9258[2]

**Strictly Carter** *Alan Bailey* a62 51
4 b g Multiplex Compolina (Compton Place)
(602) 1371[4] 2069[2] 2306[3] 3469[2] (4179) 5119[9] 5892[10] 6748[7] 8329[10] 9183[3] 9323[2]

**Strikemaster (IRE)** *Lee James* a32 50
11 b g Xaar Mas A Fuera (IRE) (Alzao (USA))
610[7] 1197[10] 5493[8] 6565[11]

**Striker (IRE)** *Tom Dascombe* 48
3 b g Nathaniel(IRE) Walk On Bye (IRE) (Danehill Dancer (IRE))
2143[5] 3427[8]

**Striking For Gold** *Sarah Hollinshead* a48 28
3 b g Equiano(FR) Crossbow (Mount Nelson)
150[4] 662[8] 3549[6] 4633[11] 5783[8] 6507[10] 7191[14]

**Stringybark Creek** *Daniel Steele* a60 47
3 b g Bushranger(IRE) Money Note (Librettist (USA))
1463[7] 1688[10] 1970[2] 2223[6] 2757[9] 3403[14] 5122[3] 5620[6] 5759[2] 6097[7] 6174[4] 6660[5] 7217[6] 7952[5] 8300[10] (9213) 9365[7]

**Stripey** *Richard Fahey* 51
2 ch f Sepoy(AUS) Birthday Suit (IRE) (Daylami (IRE))
5372[10] 6666[7]

**Stromboli (FR)** *T Lemer* 68
2 gr c Pedro The Great(USA) Sadaliya (FR) (Xaar)
6608a[2]

**Strongarm Chaser (IRE)**
*Richard Hannon* 60
2 b c Footstepsinthesand Sarawati (IRE) (Haafhd)
8161[7] 8353[7]

**Strong Belief (IRE)** *Charlie Appleby* 93
3 b g Cape Cross(IRE) Opinionated (IRE) (Dubai Destination (USA))
(3465) (Dead)

**Strong Challenge (IRE)**
*Saeed bin Suroor* a58 63
4 ch g Exceed And Excel(AUS) Miss Brief (IRE) (Brief Truce (USA))
66[4] 287[13]

**Strong Chemistry** *K Al Neyadi* a78 89
5 b g Oasis Dream Mambo Light (USA) (Kingmambo (USA))
8836a[7]

**Stronger Than Me (IRE)** *W T Farrell* a100 102
9 b g Marju(IRE) Easter Song (USA) (Rubiano (USA))
1355a[4] 1568a[8] 6978a[12]

**Strong Steps** *Jim Goldie* a82 90
5 br g Aqlaam Wunders Dream (IRE) (Averti (IRE))
1492[6] 1860[11] 2767[17] 2855[9] 3546[2] 3589[5] 4207[10] 4293[2] 4957[2] 5415[8] (5469) 5949[4] 6349[11] 7702[7]

**Struck By The Moon** *Charles Hills* a55 60
3 b f Fastnet Rock(AUS) Ho Hi The Moon (IRE) (Be My Guest (USA))
5721[8] 6413[4] 7032[9] 8662[12]

**Strummer (IRE)** *Kevin Ryan* a66 70
4 b g Frozen Power(IRE) Question (USA) (Coronado's Quest (USA))
1312[4] 2108[2] 2498[8] 2953[12] 4260[3] 5212[2] 5824[4]

**St Stephens Green (IRE)**
*Emmet Mullins* a65 86
6 b g Diamond Green(FR) Lily Shing Shang (Spectrum (IRE))
6956a[10] 7860a[18]

**Stubytuesday** *Michael Easterby* a72 71
3 b g Dick Turpin(IRE) Just Dreams (Salse (USA))
(1835) 2223[2]◆ 2630[6] 3403[9] 4694[6] (5741) 6016[5] 6664[5] 8216[4] 8651[7]

**Stuhna (FR)** *V Luka Jr* a33
3 ch f Kentucky Dynamite(USA) Stunning (USA) (Nureyev (USA))
8304a[11]

**Stun Gun** *Derek Shaw* a72 56
7 b g Medicean Tapas En Bal (FR) (Mille Balles (FR))
6[4] 419[3] 527[4] 850[10] 1186[7] 2318[6] 2465[7] 2729[3] 3439[6] 3760[5] 4169[8] 7236[10] 7573[11]

**Stunned** *Doug Watson* a103 86
6 b g Shamardal(USA) Amazed (Clantime)
432a[4] 539a[4] (772a) 1043a[7]

**Stunning Spirit** *F Head* a87 109
3 b c Invincible Spirit(IRE) Stunning View (USA) (Dynaformer (USA))
1824a[2] 2448a[3] 3855a[2] 6497a[4] 7697a[7]

**Sturdy Dawn** *Michael Mullineaux* 11
7 br m Striking Ambition Lucky Find (IRE) (Key Of Luck (USA))
5401[7] (Dead)

**Stylehunter** *John Gosden* a73 15
2 ch c Raven's Pass(USA) Sunday Bess (JPN) (Deep Impact (JPN))
8350[14] 9200[3]

**Style Icon (FR)** *H-F Devin* 102
3 b f Doctor Dino(FR) La Turbale (FR) (Ange Gabriel (FR))
(3353a) 6914a[7] 8755a[8]

**Stylish Dancer** *Luca Cumani* a73 69
3 b f Nathaniel(IRE) Hazy Dancer (Oasis Dream)
2564[6] 3720[7] 7629[2] 8157[2]◆ 8744[3] 9242[8]

**Stylish Grace (FR)** *J S Moore* 44
2 gr f Style Vendome(FR) Conciliatory (Medicean)
7126[12] 7352[12]

**Suada (GER)** *Markus Klug* 102
2 b f Maxios Shiramiyna (IRE) (Invincible Spirit (IRE))
8269a[2]

**Suanas (IRE)** *Richard Fahey* 7
2 br f Society Rock(IRE) Penny Serenade (IRE) (Lawman (FR))
2105[9] 2545[7]

**Subatomic** *Ralph Beckett* a60 76
3 b f Makfi Miss Universe (IRE) (Warning)
2894[4] 3578[7]

**Subcontinent (IRE)**
*Venetia Williams* a44 53
5 b g Dubawi(IRE) Saree (Barathea (IRE))
2574[10]

**Subhaan** *Roger Varian* a84 62
3 ch g Dutch Art Mamma Morton (IRE) (Elnadim (USA))
4562[2] 5243[4] 6103[4] 6899[2] (8318)

**Subjective** *David Simcock* a74 73
3 ch g Equiano(FR) Hope Island (IRE) (Titus Livius (FR))
3085[12] 3806[2] 4106[3]

**Subjectivity (USA)** *Michael Appleby* a52
3 ch g Girolamo(USA) Always Loyal (USA) (Zilzal (USA))
8256[5]

**Sublimation (IRE)** *Steve Gollings* a64 68
7 ch g Manduro(GER) Meon Mix (Kayf Tara)
684[11] 1146[3] 1406[2] 1983[2]

**Sublime** *Rod Millman* a44 50
3 b f Exceed And Excel(AUS) Singuliere (IRE) (Singspiel (IRE))
283[11] 503[10] 848[8] 2513[4] 3024[2] 3657[11] 4493[2]

**Sublissimo (FR)** *J Phelippon* a77 77
3 b g Bertolini(USA) Katie Arden (IRE) (Barathea (IRE))
2697a[8] 3446a[8]

**Subotal (IRE)** *Richard Guest* a45 16
4 ch g Pivotal Suba (USA) (Seeking The Gold (USA))
1830[11] 7247[7] 7793[4] 8248[4] 8498[9] 8538[11] 8720[8] 8799[12]

**Subway Dancer (IRE)** *Z Koplik* a101 113
5 b g Shamardal(USA) Sub Rose (IRE) (Galileo (IRE))
1271a[6] 5046a[5] 6052a[4] 7177a[6] 7638a[2] 9003a[6]

**Success Days (IRE)** *K J Condon* 116
5 gr h Jeremy(USA) Malaica (FR) (Roi Gironde (IRE))
1654a[2] 3108a[4] 4417a[2] (5436) 6960a[10] 8233[10]

**Sudden Wish (IRE)** *Gary Moore* a57 41
8 b m Jeremy(USA) Fun Time (Fraam)
645[9]

**Sudona** *Hugo Palmer* 58
2 b f Zoffany(IRE) Vickers Vimy (Montjeu (IRE))
8425[8]

**Suedois (FR)** *David O'Meara* a104 117
6 b g Le Havre(IRE) Cup Cake (IRE) (Singspiel (IRE))
2737[8] 3099a[3] 4071[7] 5502[3] 6401[3] (6959a) (7851a) 8608a[4]

**Suegioo (FR)** *Richard Fahey* a97 105
8 ch g Manduro(GER) Mantesera (IRE) (In The Wings)
1802[9] 2525[9] 3076[2] 3928[5] 4356[15] 5524[7] 6329[12] 7110[5] 7614[3] 8292[2] 8892[7]

**Sue's Angel (IRE)** *Richard Fahey* 68
3 gr f Dark Angel(IRE) La Chassotte (FR) (Until Sundown (USA))
1730[16] 2078[5] 2807[3]◆

**Suffragette City (IRE)**
*Richard Hannon* a71 71
3 b f Dragon Pulse(IRE) Queen Of Stars (USA) (Green Desert (USA))
160[7] 418[3]

**Sufi** *Ken Cunningham-Brown* a76 61
3 ch g Pivotal Basanti (USA) (Galileo (IRE))
1259[3] 1607[4] 2721[3] 3596[8] 4267[7] 8886[4] 9208[7]

**Sugar Bay** *C Ferland* a63 71
3 b f Makfi Jalousie (IRE) (Barathea (IRE))
2484a[10]

**Sugar Beach (FR)** *Ann Duffield* a57 62
3 b f Canford Cliffs(IRE) Aktia (IRE) (Danehill Dancer (IRE))
1705[4] 2304[8] 7390[10] 8206[11] 8591[8] 8908[4] 9084[4]

**Sugar Coating** *Richard Fahey* a67
2 b f Dutch Art Muscovado (USA) (Mr Greeley (USA))
9415[2]◆

**Sugardrop** *Amanda Perrett* a70 78
3 br f Cacique(IRE) Tates Creek (USA) (Rahy (USA))
3007[3] 4300[7] 6027[3] 6750[2] 8810[2]

**Sugar Free (GER)** *D Moser* 97
4 b m Exceed And Excel(AUS) Sugar Baby Love (GER) (Second Empire (IRE))
3080[6] 4864[12] 6605a[5]

**Sugarloaf Mountain (IRE)**
*Brian Ellison* a75 43
4 b g Fastnet Rock(AUS) Cherry Hinton (Green Desert (USA))
175[3] 780[4] 1122[2] 1870[2] 9028[3] 9260[4]

**Sugar Plum Fairy** *Tony Carroll* 45
2 ch f Halling(USA) Atyaab (Green Desert (USA))
6417[9] 7392[10]

**Sugar Town** *Peter Niven* a62 58
7 b m Elusive City(USA) Sweetsformysweet (USA) (Forest Wildcat (USA))
446[2] 582[4] 844[8]

**Suhayl Moon (IRE)** *Charlie Appleby* a68
2 b f Invincible Spirit(IRE) Sander Camillo (USA) (Dixie Union (USA))
9320[5]

**Suitcase 'N' Taxi** *Tim Easterby* 80
3 br g Major Cadeaux Finalize (Firebreak)
1913[2] (2304) 3038[9] 3462[6] 4122[8] (5697) 6519[7] 7553[5] 7923[8]

**Suited** *Tim Easterby* a61 12
3 b f Paco Boy(IRE) Birthday Suit (IRE) (Daylami (IRE))
1705[10] 2180[10] 2791[6]

**Suit Of Lights (IRE)** *Henry Tett* 53
3 b g Approve(IRE) Lindoras Grace (Galileo (IRE))
5431[5] 6103[9]

**Suitor** *Brian Ellison* a84 75
5 ch g Dutch Art Entreat (Pivotal)
1517[16] 2030[13] 3432[4] 3740[2] 4357[3]◆ 4893[10]

**Suitsus** *Geoffrey Deacon* a69 68
6 b g Virtual Point Perfect (Dansili)
238[3]◆ 689[3] 1067[11] 1729[9] (2916) (4203) 6102[3]
8641[2]◆ 8946[13]

**Sukhovey (USA)** *Michael Attwater* 64
2 b f Lookin At Lucky(USA) Allencat (USA) (Storm Cat (USA))
4253[5] 4902[14] 6374[7]

**Sukoot (IRE)** *Ed Dunlop* a62 62
3 ch g Sir Prancealot(IRE) Yandina (IRE) (Danehill (USA))
3755[5] 4309[8]

**Sulafaat (IRE)** *Mark Johnston* a70 59
2 ch f Haatef(USA) Elraabeya (CAN) (Seeking The Gold (USA))
3429[5] 5702[5] 6347[4] (7029) 8153[7]

**Sulafah (IRE)** *Simon West* a68 72
3 b f Mawatheeq(USA) Maany (USA) (Mr Greeley (USA))
1003[2] 1199[3] 1471[7] 6313[9] 8210[11]

**Sula Island** *Alan King* a63 72
3 ch f Sulamani(IRE) Cosmea (Compton Place)
5022[5] 5721[6] 6823[2] 8000[10] 9159[5]

**Sully (FR)** *Rod Collet* 99
2 gr f Siyouni(FR) Shaama Rose (FR) (Verglas (IRE))
5448a[6] 6229a[3]

**Sultanaa** *Ismail Mohammed* a39 74
2 gr f Acclamation Pink Opaque (Nayef (USA))
2832[4] 4340[2] 5056[3] 6200[7]

**Sultan Baybars** *Roger Varian* a90 95
3 b g Invincible Spirit(IRE) Rock Salt (Selkirk (USA))
3232[7] 3997[21] 4634[2] 5302[2] 6484[6] 7727[8] 8385[9]

**Sumbal (IRE)** *David Simcock* 107
5 gr h Danehill Dancer(IRE) Alix Road (FR) (Linamix (FR))
7054[3]◆ 7931[7]

**Summer Chorus** *Andrew Balding* a93 91
4 b m Exceed And Excel(AUS) Soviet Terms (Soviet Star (USA))
3410[8] 4099[11] 5117[3] 5610[2] 6686[2] 7545[7]

**Summer Collection (IRE)**
*K R Burke* a68 70
4 b m Teofilo(IRE) Towards (USA) (Fusaichi Pegasus (USA))
195[7]

**Summer Dove (USA)**
*George Peckham* a54 44
4 gr m Super Saver(USA) No Foul Play (CAN) (Great Gladiator (USA))
1144[6]

**Summer Dress** *Louis Baudron* a61 63
2 b f Bated Breath Winter Dress (Haafhd)
8482a[3]

**Summer Falls (IRE)** *Rae Guest* a64
4 b m Iffraaj Encouragement (Royal Applause)
283[5] 3472[4]

**Summerghand (IRE)** *David O'Meara* a83 80
3 b g Lope De Vega(IRE) Kate The Great (Xaar)
2383[4] (3970) 4616[5] 5316[7] (5814) 6511[2] 7244[5]
7709[2]◆ 8319[7]

**Summer Icon** *Mick Channon* a98 93
4 b m Sixties Icon Summer Cry (USA) (Street Cry (IRE))
(142) 499[3] 810[3] 1150[9] 1795[7] 2241a[3] 2616[6]
3334[6] 3961[14] 4375[5] 4718[7] 6918[13] 7154[4] 7781[5]
7901[4] 8706[3]◆ 9020[3] 9089[4] 9386[3]

**Summerinthecity (IRE)**
*Patrick Morris* a75 54
10 ch g Indian Ridge(IRE) Miss Assertive (Zafonic (USA))
923[3] 1147[7]

**Summerling (IRE)** *Rae Guest* a32 6
6 br m Excellent Art Sun Seasons (IRE) (Salse (USA))
9278[7]

**Summer Name (IRE)**
*Rebecca Curtis* a78
5 b g Duke Of Marmalade(IRE) Summer's Eve (Singspiel (IRE))
(8979)

**Summerseat Mist (IRE)**
*M D O'Callaghan* a77 76
2 ch f Dandy Man(IRE) Angel Bright (IRE) (Dark Angel (IRE))
6977a[16]

**Summer Shamal (FR)** *F-H Graffard* 91
2 b f Wootton Bassett Chinook Wind (IRE) (Encosta De Lago (AUS))
4028[19]

**Summershine (IRE)**
*Frau Anna Schleusner-Fruhriep* 99
6 ch m Three Valleys(USA) Sulamith (GER) (Acatenango (GER))
2667a[5] 7203a[9]

**Summer Thunder (USA)** *Paul Cole* a58 41
2 b f Street Cry(IRE) Satulagi (USA) (Officer (USA))
3070[9] 4496[6] 4972[10]

**Sumner Beach** *Brian Ellison* a76 79
3 ch g Aqlaam Cosmic Song (Cosmonaut)
3038[13] 3146[4] 3434[7] 7939[9] 8319[14] 8929[4] 9100[8]
9303[5] 9419[6]

**Sumou (IRE)** *Milton Bradley* 82
4 b g Arcano(IRE) Three Times (Bahamian Bounty)
1761[3] 2147[7] 2837[8] 3161[10] 3278[3] 3773[5] (Dead)

**Sun And Shadow** *Ed Walker* a61
2 b c Royal Applause Sonko (IRE) (Red Clubs (IRE))
4007[9]

**Sun Angel (IRE)** *Henry Candy* a40 77
3 ch f Sir Prancealot(IRE) Fuerta Ventura (IRE) (Desert Sun)
314[3]

**Sunblazer (IRE)** *Kim Bailey* a98 94
7 gr g Dark Angel(IRE) Damask Rose (IRE) (Dr Devious (IRE))
2176[2] 3067[8] 4498[4] 5524[15] 7397[10] 7949[3] (8565)
8893[3] (9204)

**Sunbreak (IRE)** *Mark Johnston* a74 65
2 b g Dawn Approach(IRE) Carry On Katie (USA) (Fasliyev (USA))
3025[5] 5278[3] 5608[5] (6845) (7057) 8045[9] 9097[11]

**Sunchisetagioo** *Marco Botti* a88 79
3 b f Exceed And Excel(AUS) Sunsemperchi (Montjeu (IRE))
5889[4] 6261[5] 7830[3]

**Sundance Boy** *Giuseppe Fierro* a23
8 gr g Proclamation(IRE) Just Beth (Carlingford Castle (IRE))
5894[8]

**Sunday Best** *Jonathan Portman* a49 53
2 ch f Nathaniel(IRE) Lacy Sunday (USA) (King's Best (USA))
4253[10] 5795[11] 6776[7]

**Sunday Prospect (FR)** *K R Burke* 70
3 ch g Sunday Break(JPN) Green Shadow (FR) (Green Tune (USA))
5315[2]

**Sunday Smart (IRE)**
*P J Prendergast* 88
2 b f Dandy Man(IRE) Sharp And Smart (IRE) (Dark Angel (IRE))
7423a[2] 8424[8]

**Sund City (FR)** *Harry Dunlop* a55 61
4 b m Turtle Bowl(IRE) Calithea (IRE) (Marju (IRE))
121[3]

**Sunderia (FR)** *Mme S Allouche* a45 70
3 b f Hannouma(IRE) Aldoussa (FR) (Numerous (USA))
8304a[9]

**Sun Devil (ITY)** *Stefano Botti* 99
3 b c Desert Prince(IRE) Dondup (IRE) (Hurricane Run (IRE))
2245a[5]

**Sunglider (IRE)** *David O'Meara* a82 85
4 br g High Chaparral(IRE) Desert Ease (IRE) (Green Desert (USA))
(2225) 2624[5] 3153[7] 3845[18] (4170) 4692[3] 6059[4]
6848[12]

**Sun Hat (IRE)** *Simon Crisford* a59
2 ch f Helmet(AUS) Bright Water (Refuse To Bend (IRE))
9051[5]

**Sunhill Lad (IRE)** *Ann Duffield* a65 62
2 gr g Lilbourne Lad(IRE) Gris Ladera (IRE) (Verglas (IRE))
7361[3] 7556[2] 9015[4] 9263[6] 9439[6]

**Suni Dancer** *Tony Carroll* a56 53
6 b m Captain Gerrard(IRE) Sunisa (IRE) (Daggers Drawn (USA))
521[7] 640[8] 5357[4] 5792[5] 7213[9] 8994[11]

**Sunlit Waters** *Tony Carroll* a51 49
4 ch m New Approach(IRE) Faraway Waters (Pharly (FR))
1729[6] 2281[6] 4493[6] 4967[6]

**Sun Lover** *Roger Varian* a86 96
4 b g Oasis Dream Come Touch The Sun (IRE) (Fusaichi Pegasus (USA))
3792[2]◆ 4570[2] 6414[2] 7549[11]

**Sun Maiden** *Sir Michael Stoute* a61
2 b f Frankel Midsummer (Kingmambo (USA))
9080[4]

**Sunnua (IRE)** *Richard Fahey* a79 83
4 gr m Dark Angel(IRE) Island Sunset (IRE) (Trans Island)
1700[5] 2030[9] 2900[8] 3402[8] 4431[5] 5258[6] 6049[4]
7249[4] 8210[12] (8513) 8773[12]

**Sunny Belle (IRE)** *P Schiergen* 92
3 b f Exceed And Excel(AUS) Survey (GER) (Big Shuffle (USA))
3105a[6] 4518a[9] 6605a[2] 7204a[7]

**Sunny Future (IRE)**
*Malcolm Saunders* a73 81
11 b g Masterful(USA) Be Magic (Persian Bold (IRE))
2218[4] 3086[7] 4966[8] 5590[10]

**Sunny Lane (IRE)** *J S Moore* 22
2 b f Arakan(USA) Four Kicks (IRE) (Pyrus (USA))
7120[13]

**Sunnyside Bob (IRE)**
*Neville Bycroft* a57 55
4 b g Big Bad Bob(IRE) Jinxy Jill (Royal Applause)
5836[13] 6631[8] 7366[11] 8247[7] 9052[8]

**Sun Or Shade (IRE)** *John Gosden* a27
3 b c Galileo(IRE) Desert Classic (Green Desert (USA))
855[8]

**Sunovarebel** *Alan Bailey* a62
3 b g Cockney Rebel(IRE) Atacama Sunrise (Desert Sun)
875[7] 1111[5]

**Sunrise Dance** *Kenny Johnson* a23 46
8 ch m Monsieur Bond(IRE) Wachiwi (IRE) (Namid)
3345[8] 3704[12] 4246[10]

**Sunrize (IRE)** *David O'Meara* 63
3 b c Azamour(IRE) Valmari (IRE) (Kalanisi (IRE))
1874[5] 2408[3] 2842[6]

**Sunset Bounty** *Julia Feilden* a30 44
3 b f Bahamian Bounty Sunset Kitty (USA) (Gone West (USA))
2316[8] 8117[7] 8504[9] 9218[12]

**Sunset Flyer** *Amy Murphy* 22
2 b f Arabian Gleam King's Guest (IRE) (King's Best (USA))
2904[9] 4199[6] 4504[7] 8306[P]

**Sunshada (FR)** *P Fleurie* a52 57
3 b f Sunday Break(JPN) Miss Oratorio (IRE) (Oratorio (IRE))
4232a[12]

**Sunshineandbubbles**
*Jennie Candlish* a61 52
4 b m Multiplex Dockside Strike (Docksider (USA))
238[6] 351[6] 482[5] 865[2] 5336[7] 6479[5] 6946[3] 8661[4]
9056[4] 9218[6] (9343)

**Sunstorm** *David Brown* a43 70
2 ch c Medicean Crimson Cloud (Kyllachy)
4567[10] 6260[7] 7521[2] 8046[11] 8553[10] 8915[7]

**Super Florence (IRE)**
*Eve Johnson Houghton* a64 62
2 gr f Zebedee Top Of The Ridge (IRE) (Celtic Swing)
2251[2]◆ 2706[7] 3655[7] 6063[3] 6585[4] 6815[6] 8027[2]

**Supergirl (FR)** *Mario Hofer* a79 56
2 ch f Sri Putra Sienna Bella (Anabaa (USA))
(8169a)

**Superioritycomplex (IRE)**
*Sir Michael Stoute* a77 82
3 ch f Hard Spun(USA) Justlookdontouch (IRE) (Galileo (IRE))
1947[9] 3866[2]◆ 4300[2] 5721[2] (6027)

**Super Julius** *Eve Johnson Houghton* a86 88
3 ch g Bated Breath Paradise Isle (Bahamian Bounty)
1940[5] 2130[10] 3865[4] (4159)◆ (4464) 4974[5]
6695[2] 8540[9] 8879[6]

**Super Major (IRE)** *Michael Dods* 71
2 b g Sir Prancealot(IRE) Majestic Alexander (IRE) (Bushranger (IRE))
2403[6] 3149[10] 4503[2] 6128[4] 7243[6]

**Supermoss** *Heather Main* a48 19
2 b f Cacique(IRE) Fairy Moss (IRE) (Amadeus Wolf)
7226[11] 8670[10] 9081[11]

**Supernova** *David Simcock* a77 73
2 b c Intello(GER) Carding (USA) (Street Cry (IRE))
7813[5]◆ 8704[3]

**Super Ridge (FR)** *J D Hillis* a48 67
4 b h Linngari(IRE) Superstition (FR) (Kutub (IRE))
8090a[10]

**Super Ruby** *K R Burke* a43 49
3 b f Equiano(FR) Danehill Dazzler (IRE) (Danehill Dancer (IRE))
2704[6] 3404[6] 3493[6] 5666[12] 7833[9] 8255[6]

**Supersta** *Michael Appleby* a105 92
6 ch g Pivotal Resort (Oasis Dream)
235[5] 266[2] 730[8] 1148[6] (1295) 1773[8] 2942a[8]
4270[2] 4861[4] 5396[7] 6024[11] 6685[14] 8257[7]

**Supersymmetry (IRE)**
*Tom Dascombe* a49 69
2 br f Kyllachy Duniatty (Green Desert (USA))
3491[4] 5528[15] 6678[8] 8153[10]

**Suprematism (USA)** *Marco Botti* a53
2 b c More Than Ready(USA) Exotic Behavior (USA) (Giant's Causeway (USA))
9137[6]

**Supreme Power (IRE)**
*Tracy Waggott* a62 65
3 b g Power Supreme Spirit (IRE) (Invincible Spirit (IRE))
5076[2] 5538[10] 5835[3] 6315[6] 6549[4] 7162[10] 8589[10]
8720[3] 9018[6]

**Suqoor** *Chris Dwyer* a96 86
4 b g Equiano(FR) Ukraine (IRE) (Cape Cross (IRE))
598[9] 818[3] 999[4] 1622[3] 1880[6] 2404[4] 2975[4]
3730[3] 4091[3]

**Suraat (IRE)** *Robert Cowell* a49 22
3 b f Kodiac Baltic Belle (IRE) (Redback)
6184[11] 7036[12]

**Sure To Explore (IRE)** *William Muir* a77 76
3 b f Henrythenavigator(USA) Shibina (IRE) (Kalanisi (IRE))
3145[4] (3770) 5273[4] 6013[6] 7060[4] 7766[12]

**Surewecan** *F Rossi* a74 56
5 b g Royal Applause Edge Of Light (Xaar)
384a[3]

**Sureyoutoldme (IRE)** *Ruth Carr* a73 61
3 ch g Tamayuz Place De Moscou (IRE) (Rock Of Gibraltar (IRE))
5538[4]

**Surfa Rosa** *Richard Hannon* a67 66
2 b c Delegator Beechnut (IRE) (Mujadil (USA))
5048[5] 5749[7] 6394[5] 8325[6] (8658)

**Surfer (USA)** *S Seemar* a103 12
8 ch g Distorted Humor(USA) Surf Club (USA) (Ocean Crest (USA))
695a[6]

**Surfside** *Mick Channon* a55
3 b f Sixties Icon Altona (IRE) (Redback)
115[7] 354[8] 552[7]

**Surrender** *Tim Easterby* 54
2 b g Sixties Icon Mango Music (Distant Music (USA))
4597[10] 5680[7] 6042[7] 7519[16]

**Surrey Blaze (IRE)** *Joseph Tuite* a55 42
2 b g Thewayyouare(USA) Catadalya (IRE) (One Cool Cat (USA))
5547[8] 6132[12] 6260[10]

**Surrey Hope (USA)** *Joseph Tuite* a84 97
3 b c Lemon Drop Kid(USA) She Be Classy (USA) (Toccet (USA))
(1083) (3504) 4271[3] (6073)

**Surrounding (IRE)** *M Halford* a95 93
4 b m Lilbourne Lad(IRE) Roundabout Girl (IRE) (Doubletour (USA))
6491a[2] 8407a[4]

**Surround Sound** *Tim Easterby* a66 66
7 b g Multiplex Tintera (IRE) (King's Theatre (IRE))
174[3]◆ 1191[2]◆ 1330[2] (1458) 1716[4] 2111[4]
3043[2] 3400[7] 4102[4] 4572[3] 5080[6] 5599[4] 6270[8]
6901[5] 8396[8]

**Suspect Package (USA)**
*James Fanshawe* a69 78
3 b g Lonhro(AUS) Pretty Meadow (USA) (Meadowlake (USA))
2625[3] 3412[3] 4082[3] 4632[3]

**Suspicious Mind (DEN)**
*Niels Petersen* 87
4 b g Appel Au Maitre(FR) Fleur En Fleur (FR) (Hernando (FR))
5676a[5]

**Sussex Girl** *John Berry* a51 68
3 ch f Compton Place Palinisa (FR) (Night Shift (USA))
2280[4] 3075[4] 5783[7] 6664[6] 7324[7] 7917[3] (8183)
(8327)

**Sussex Ranger (USA)** *Gary Moore* a79 80
3 b g Hat Trick(JPN) Purple (USA) (Royal Academy (USA))
3457[8] 4156[3] 5034[2] (5406) 6376[3] 7060[3]

**Sutoor (IRE)** *Mark Brisbourne* a40
3 b g Cape Cross(IRE) Yanabeeaa (USA) (Street Cry (IRE))
9159[10] 9301[5]

**Sutter County** *Mark Johnston* a107 78
3 b c Invincible Spirit(IRE) Rio Osa (AUS) (Canny Lad (AUS))
276[2] 643[2] (778) 1026[2] 1774[5] 2425[3] (3071)
3302[7] 3959[17] 4615[4] 4905[18] 6024[4] 6419[18] 6685[2]

**Suwaan (IRE)** *Ruth Carr* a73 79
3 ch g Exceed And Excel(AUS) Janina (Namid)
(1474) 1970[3] 3152[8] 3653[5]◆ 5204[5] 5837[2] 6155[3]
(6596) 7055[2]◆ 7268[10] 7939[7]

**Suyoof (AUS)** *M F De Kock* 106
4 ch g Magic Albert(AUS) Magic Harmony (AUS) (Danehill Dancer (IRE))
698a[2]◆ (892a)

**Suzi Icon** *Michael Appleby* a52 69
5 ch m Sixties Icon Suzi Spends (IRE) (Royal Applause)
2679[7] (3001) 3550[6] 4458[13]

**Suzi's Connoisseur** *Stuart Williams* a104 93
6 b g Art Connoisseur(IRE) Suzi Spends (IRE) (Royal Applause)
199[5] (730) 1769[6] 2390[14] 3324[13] 4854[17] 5942[3]
6419[16] 6685[7] 7622[14] 9269[3]

**Swaffham Bulbeck (IRE)**
*Ed Vaughan* a53 72
3 b g Jeremy(USA) Ballygologue (IRE) (Montjeu (IRE))
3755[6] 4981[5] (5577) 7097[6] 7902[6]

**Swag (IRE)** *Michael Easterby* a66 72
3 b g Bahamian Bounty Tahtheeb (IRE) (Muhtarram (USA))
3000[4] 3496[5] 4629[12]

**Swaheen** *Julie Camacho* a70 89
5 b g Lawman(FR) Whole Grain (Polish Precedent (USA))
1976[6] 2893[7] (3486) 4206[12] 5287[5] 5924[4] 6944[3]
7615[4] 8511[8]

**Swallow Dancer** *Harry Dunlop* a52
3 b f Danehill Dancer(IRE) Bay Swallow (IRE) (Daylami (IRE))
737[7] 959[5] 1069[6] 2137[9] 3327[8]

**Swallow Street (IRE)** *M Bebbu* a38 40
3 ch c Sir Prancealot(IRE) Fey Rouge (IRE) (Fayruz)
2867a[10]

**Swamp Fox (IRE)** *Joseph G Murphy* 94
5 br g Windsor Knot(IRE) Brogella (IRE) (King's Theatre (IRE))
5488a[2] 8038[6]

**Swanning Around (IRE)**
*Matthieu Palussiere* a75 77
3 ch f Dragon Pulse(IRE) Swan Sea (USA) (Sea Hero (USA))
5521a[6] 6455a[11]

**Swansea Beach (FR)** *Y Barberot* a69
2 b f George Vancouver(USA) Ma Legionnaire (FR) (Rail Link)
9086a[4]

**Swan Serenade** *Jonathan Portman* a41 58
3 b f Paco Boy(IRE) Accede (Acclamation)
1596[10] 3810[5] 4969[9]

**Swansway** *Michael Easterby* a70 73
4 ch g Showcasing Spring Stroll (USA) (Skywalker (USA))
360[2] 1473[2] 1893[4] 2466[8] 3343[6] 4018[3] 4627[2]
(5021) 5284[7] 6126[7]

**Swanton Blue (IRE)** *Ed de Giles* a69 77
4 b g Kodiac Cabopino (IRE) (Captain Rio)
(3084) 3696[3] 4256[2] 4532[9] 4910[6] 6238[6] 6615[6]
7058[12] 8158[3] 8742[6]

**Swashbuckle** *Andrew Balding* a87 96
4 b g Dashing Blade Inhibition (Nayef (USA))
1309[3]◆ 1942[3] 2562[3] 3076[7] (4222) 5912[9] 7547[6]
8038[25]

**Sweeping Rock (IRE)**
*John Spearing* a48 52
7 b g Rock Of Gibraltar(IRE) Sweeping Story (USA) (End Sweep (USA))
146[7] 645[4] 8391[2]

**Sweet Amazement** *Mark Usher* a36 41
3 ch f Kheleyf(USA) Sweetest Revenge (IRE) (Daggers Drawn (USA))
1626[8] 1837[6] 3141[5] 3818[10]

**Sweet And Dandy (IRE)** *Jimmy Fox* a52
2 b f Dandy Man(IRE) Translator (IRE) (Choisir (AUS))
8988[7]

**Sweetasever (IRE)**
*Joseph Patrick O'Brien* a73 73
3 br f Power In My Dreams (IRE) (Sadler's Wells (USA))
4901[2]

**Sweet Bay (FR)** *N Leenders* a56 54
3 ch f Falco(USA) Sweetner (FR) (Stravinsky (USA))
5523a[4]

**Sweet Charity** *Denis Coakley* a63
2 b f Mount Nelson Fanny May (Nayef (USA))
8877[3] 9319[3]

**Sweet Company (IRE)** *A J Martin* 84
6 b g Kalanisi(IRE) Almost Twilight (USA) (Silver Hawk (USA))
5488a[7]

**Sweetest Taboo (IRE)** *W McCreery* a63 71
6 b m Camacho Princess Clara (Dr Fong (USA))
2656a[8]

**Sweet Gentle Kiss (IRE)**
*Stefano Botti* 94
2 b f Henrythenavigator(USA) Cronsa (GER) (Martino Alonso (IRE))
(8094a)

**Sweeticon** *Antonio Marcialis* a78 77
3 b f Sixties Icon Dolce Nera (Dansili)
4783a[2] (7308a) 8304a[4]

**Sweet Lady Rose (IRE)**
*Andrew Balding* a57
2 ch f Shamardal(USA) Sweet Rose (New Approach (IRE))
8669[6]

**Sweet Piccolo** *Paddy Butler*
7 ch g Piccolo Quality Street (Fraam)
9232[12]

**Sweet Pursuit** *Rod Millman* a54 68
3 b f Pastoral Pursuits Sugar Beet (Beat Hollow)
2016[3] 2911[4]◆ 3536[2] 4467[3] (5146) (5657) 6106[3]◆ 6807[7] 7910[7]

**Sweet Selection** *Hughie Morrison* a73 107
5 b m Stimulation(IRE) Sweet Coincidence (Mujahid (USA))
(2288) 3996[7] 4879a[6] 5503[9] 7089[9]

**Sweet Sienna** *Dean Ivory* a46 31
3 ch f Harbour Watch(IRE) Look Busy (IRE) (Danetime (IRE))
5040[9] 6339[11] 6748[12]

**Sweet Symphony** *Marco Botti* a67
2 ch f Helmet(AUS) Solfilia (Teofilo (IRE))
8373[5]

**Sweet Vixen** *Tom Clover* a15 69
2 b f Foxwedge(AUS) Sugar Beet (Beat Hollow)
2258[6] 4273[2]◆ 5216[3] 7814[22]

**Sweety Dream (FR)** *P Bary* 100
2 ch f Dream Ahead(USA) Excellent Girl (Exceed And Excel (AUS))
7637a[13] (8525a)

**Sweet Zain (IRE)** *John Butler* a44 70
3 b f Requinto(IRE) Pillars Of Society (IRE) (Caerleon (USA))
(4053)

**Swendab (IRE)** *John O'Shea* a71 70
9 b g Trans Island Lavish Spirit (USA) (Southern Halo (USA))
153[7] 271[8] 494[2] (622) 722[9] 1221[4] 1246[5] (1305) 1723[5] 2216[2] 2360[6] 2514[3] 3278[2] 3544[5] (4093) 4182[4] 4842[7] 4965[7] 5360[6] 6097[5] 6372[5] 6612[3] 7407[3] 7607[2] 8146[5] (8494) (8873) 9136[2] (9414)

**Swift Approval (IRE)**
*Stuart Williams* a98 99
5 ch g Approve(IRE) Tiltili (IRE) (Spectrum (IRE))
1150[11] 1491[13] 2433[12] 4854[4] 5393[21] (5662) 6024[6] 6419[13] 6685[10] 8843[11] 8905[2] 9264[9]

**Swift Cedar (IRE)** *David Evans* a76 71
7 ch g Excellent Art Ravish (Efisio)
7111[6] 7558[7] 8143[3] 8978[5] 9369[2]

**Swiftee (IRE)** *Ivan Furtado* a63 43
4 ch g Camacho Algaira (USA) (Irish River (FR))
68[2] 482[8] 607[7] 1735[11] 2119[11] 3049[8] 4262[4] 5206[11] 6112[5] 7888[5] 8307[10]

**Swift Emperor (IRE)** *David Barron* a95 96
5 b g Holy Roman Emperor(IRE) Big Swifty (IRE) (Intikhab (USA))
782[4] (1032)◆ 1492[4] 2593[3] 3154[8] 3498[7] 4261[10] 8048[2] 8652[5] 9053[10] (9271)

**Swift Fox** *Gary Moore* a44 51
2 b g Foxwedge(AUS) Amontillado (IRE) (Pastoral Pursuits)
3782[9] 6133[9] 7001[5] 7756[10] 8027[4] 8795[4]

**Swiftsure (IRE)** *Sir Michael Stoute* 93
3 b g Dubawi(IRE) La Sylphide (SWI) (Barathea (IRE))
2039[12] 2807[7] (4118) 4365[3] 5598[9] (7284)

**Swilly Bay (IRE)** *Charles Hills* a54
3 gr g Mastercraftsman(IRE) Eastern Appeal (IRE) (Shinko Forest (IRE))
545[6] 863[5] 1226[3]

**Swilly Sunset** *Anthony Carson* a48 91
4 b g Kyllachy Spanish Springs (IRE) (Xaar)
1109[7] 1449[9] 2319[2]◆ 2733[4] 2976[3] (3442) (4459) (4846) (5888) 6701[2] 7119[7]

**Swinford Lass** *Tony Carroll* a38
5 b m Dutch Art Tidal (Bin Ajwaad (IRE))
283[13] 1322[12]

**Swing Glaz (FR)** *C Lotoux* a62 61
4 ch g Vatori(FR) Blue Sally (FR) (Della Francesca (USA))
6365a[2]

**Swing Out Sister (IRE)** *Clive Cox* a73 76
2 b f Kodiac Dance Club (IRE) (Fasliyev (USA))
4628[5] 5586[2] 6178[2] (7126) 8431[3] 8702[6]

**Swing Time (IRE)** *Eric Alston* a33 18
3 b g Choisir(AUS) Damalis (IRE) (Mukaddamah (USA))
5289[4] 6184[13] 6904[7] 8479[12]

**Swirral Edge** *David Brown* a76 83
4 b m Hellvelyn Pizzarra (Shamardal (USA))
1475[5] 1828[7] 2837[9]

**Swish (IRE)** *John James Feane* a81 88
3 gr f Lilbourne Lad(IRE) Maidservant (USA) (Seeking The Gold (USA))
1936[7] 6971a[5] 8407a[13]

**Swissal (IRE)** *David Dennis* a72 65
2 b c Swiss Spirit Al Gharrafa (Dutch Art)
4151[6] 5048[7] 6272[8] 7228[7] 8190[4] 8500[2] (9024) 9370[2]

**Swiss Bank (IRE)**
*Matthieu Palussiere* a52 76
2 b c Swiss Spirit Support Fund (IRE) (Intikhab (USA))
3679a[4]

**Swiss Chocolate (IRE)**
*William Haggas* a57 58
2 b f Swiss Spirit Aqua Vitae (IRE) (Camacho)
5891[4] 7238[13] 7919[6] 8475[11] (Dead)

**Swiss Cottage** *Joseph G Murphy* 95
2 b g Swiss Spirit Cheeky Girl (College Chapel)
6240a[5] 7423a[10]

**Swiss Cross** *Phil McEntee* a85 78
10 b g Cape Cross(IRE) Swiss Lake (USA) (Indian Ridge (IRE))
32[7] 287[6] 598[7] 999[8] 1091[7] 1302[4] 1423[4] 1696[7] 2054[3] 2253[3] (3957a) 3941[4] 4176[4] (4655a) 5612[9] 6555[5] 6797a[8]

**Swissie** *Ivan Furtado* 17
2 br g Swiss Spirit Princess Pivotal (Pivotal)
8474[13] 8779[10]

**Swiss Knight** *Charlie Appleby* a81
2 b c Oasis Dream Swiss Diva (Pivotal)
9051[2]

**Swiss Lait** *Patrick Holmes* a56 61
6 b m Milk It Mick Matilda Peace (Namaqualand (USA))
174[9] 608[5] 733[10] 757[6] 4601[8] 5215[8] 5649[8] 5698[11] 6346[8] 6788[8] 7478[10] 7703[7]

**Swiss Man (IRE)** *M Boutin* a73 73
6 b h Saddex Irish Flower (IRE) (Zieten (USA))
8338a[3]

**Swiss Marlin** *John Quinn* a51 39
2 b f Swiss Spirit Piranha (IRE) (Exceed And Excel (AUS))
6897[8] 7383[6] 8715[8]

**Swiss Psalm** *Mark Gillard* a32
2 b f Swiss Spirit Athwaab (Cadeaux Genereux)
1694[6] 6859[11] 7512[11] 8945[8] 9182[4]

**Swiss Storm** *David Elsworth* 86
3 b c Frankel Swiss Lake (USA) (Indian Ridge (IRE))
2766[9] 7650[3] 8566[8]

**Swiss Vinnare** *Phil McEntee* a74
3 b g Arabian Gleam Matilda Peace (Namaqualand (USA))
7322[2] 7600[4] 8770[5] 9209[3] (9435)

**Sword Exceed (GER)** *Ivan Furtado* a88 78
3 b g Exceed And Excel(AUS) Sword Roche (GER) (Laroche (GER))
(1463)◆ 1895[3]◆ 2692[7] 3814[4] 4616[4] (8818) 9272[11]

**Sword Peinture (GER)** *A Wohler* 45
2 ch f Peintre Celebre(USA) Swordhalf (Haafhd)
8269a[8]

**Swordshire (GER)** *Werner Glanz* 95
6 b h Shirocco(GER) Sword Roche (GER) (Laroche (GER))
6123a[6]

**Swot** *Roger Teal* a64 62
5 b g Exceed And Excel(AUS) House Point (Pivotal)
811[4] 6393[5] 7198[4] 7899[3] 8659[3] 9032[3]

**Symbol** *James Fanshawe* a78 76
3 ch f Nathaniel(IRE) Succinct (Hector Protector (USA))
2131[4]◆ 7059[2] 7708[6]

**Symbolic Star (IRE)** *Barry Murtagh* a72 50
5 b g New Approach(IRE) Epitome (IRE) (Nashwan (USA))
(969) 1408[6] 2179[5] (2918) 3708[7] (4262) 5254[8] 5835[7]

**Symbol In The Sand (NOR)**
*Rune Haugen* a28
3 b f Giant Sandman(IRE) Symbol Of Arch (USA) (Arch (USA))
2090[10]

**Symbolization (IRE)**
*Charlie Appleby* a91 87
2 b c Cape Cross(IRE) Yorkshire Lass (IRE) (Pivotal)
5887[2]◆ (6885)

**Symphonic** *Ann Duffield* a29 42
2 b f Mayson Musical Moonlight (Observatory (USA))
8236[12] 8474[9] 8915[8]

**Syncopate** *Pam Sly* a76 85
8 b g Oratorio(IRE) Millistar (Galileo (IRE))
1719[5] 2478[7]

**Syndex (IRE)** *Johnny Farrelly* a65
4 b m Frozen Power(IRE) Zankara (FR) (Linamix (FR))
8798[12]

**Syndicate** *Ralph Beckett* a79 69
3 b f Dansili Indication (Sadler's Wells (USA))
3031[6] 3722[10]

**Syndromos (FR)**
*J Bertran De Balanda* a66 81
5 b g Muhtathir Dexandra (GR) (Evippos (GR))
798a[6]

**Synodic (USA)** *Seamus Durack* a79 46
5 br g Henrythenavigator(USA) Seven Moons (JPN) (Sunday Silence (USA))
46[5] 147[3] (865) (1028) (1364) 1602[3] 2333[3]

**Syphax (USA)** *Kevin Ryan* a101 109
3 bb c Arch(USA) Much Obliged (USA) (Kingmambo (USA))
1780[2] 2766[7] 4817[8] 6404[7] 8042[2] 8740[15]

**Syrian Pearl** *Chris Wall* a77 92
6 gr m Clodovil(IRE) Syrian Queen (Slip Anchor)
2381[9] 3757[7] 5035[6] 5513[6] 6197[5]◆ 6429[4]◆ (7737)

**Syrita (FR)** *M Nigge* a102 94
4 ch m Siyouni(FR) Garmerita (FR) (Poliglote)
1920a[6] (4679a) 6248a[8] 7305a[9] 9003a[2]

**Szolnok (USA)** *S Cerulis* a90 92
3 bb f Elusive Quality(USA) Surf Song (USA) (Storm Cat (USA))
1657a[7] 2447a[4] 3366a[9]

**Taajub (IRE)** *Peter Crate* a73 79
10 b g Exceed And Excel(AUS) Purple Tiger (IRE) (Rainbow Quest (USA))
573[5] 1429[6] 2058[6] (2680) 2967[2] 3834[5] 4521[6] 6278[4] 7127[2] 7272[3] 7912[4]

**Taamol (IRE)** *Sir Michael Stoute* a96 105
3 b g Helmet(AUS) Supreme Seductress (IRE) (Montjeu (IRE))
1780[4] (2830) 3959[14] 5642[7]

**Taareef (USA)** *J-C Rouget* a95 121
4 ch h Kitten's Joy(USA) Sacred Feather (USA) (Carson City (USA))
(3880a) (4942a) 5980a[5] 6982a[2] (7640a)

**Tabarka (FR)** *J Boisnard*
3 b f Myboycharlie(IRE) Madhya (USA) (Gone West (USA))
3275a[14]

**Tabarrak (IRE)** *Richard Hannon* 114
4 b g Acclamation Bahati (IRE) (Intikhab (USA))
1902[2] (2290) 3963[5] 4905[9] 6105[2] (7356)◆

**Tabdeed** *Owen Burrows* 92
2 ch c Havana Gold(IRE) Puzzled (IRE) (Peintre Celebre (USA))
(5531)◆

**Tabernas (IRE)** *Charlie Appleby* a68
2 ch c Dawn Approach(IRE) Simonetta (IRE) (Lil's Boy (USA))
6883[9] 7237[4]

**Tabikat Elle (IRE)** *Ollie Pears* a39 72
4 ch m Showcasing Mansiya (Vettori (IRE))
1200[8]

**Tabla** *Lee Carter* a69 22
5 b m Rail Link Questa Nova (Rainbow Quest (USA))
116[6] 550[3] 677[8]

**Table Manners** *Wilf Storey* a68 46
5 b m Dutch Art Nine Red (Royal Applause)
(579) 968[5] 1203[7] (2919) 4608[9] 7034[13] 7364[2] 8589[6]

**Tadaany (IRE)** *Ruth Carr* a84 68
5 b g Acclamation Park Haven (IRE) (Marju (IRE))
2081[9] 2838[11] 5288[9] 5739[5] 7249[3] 7957[7] 8375[3] 8706[7] 8956[5] 9138[4]

**Tadaawol** *Roger Fell* a74 83
4 b g Kyllachy Bright Edge (Danehill Dancer (IRE))
843[8] 971[4] 1202[5] 1472[3] 1717[2] 2119[2] 2377[2] 2685[9] 3402[14] 4105[3] 4999[5] 5280[4] 5497[4] (5739) 6570[4] 6964[9] 7140[4] 7223[5]

**Tadbir (IRE)** *Brian Meehan* 56
2 b g Kodiac Queen Wasp (IRE) (Shamardal (USA))
2577[5]

**Tadeem (IRE)** *J E Hammond* 77
2 b c Poet's Voice Salhooda (IRE) (Nayef (USA))
4782a[3] 5989a[5] 7470a[6]

**Tadleel** *Ed Dunlop* a86 83
2 b c Dark Angel(IRE) Quelle Affaire (Bahamian Bounty)
2779[8] (4363) 5786[2] 6425[2] (6934)◆ 7544[7]

**Tadween (IRE)** *Richard Hannon* a54 59
3 b g Tagula(IRE) Stained Glass (Dansili)
1727[6] 2090[3] 2798[2] 3549[4] 4313[7]

**Tael O' Gold** *R Mike Smith* a57 33
3 ch f Zoffany(IRE) Wedding Dream (Oasis Dream)
2790[12] 3525[8] 3831[9] 4688[9] 5206[10] 5472[10]

**Taexali (IRE)** *John Patrick Shanahan* a82 97
4 ch g Raven's Pass(USA) Enchanted Evening (IRE) (High Chaparral (IRE))
84a[9] 543a[7] 1800[4] 2524[2] 2573[7] 3092[11] 3585[6] 5647[4] 6677[5] 8139[6]

**Tafaakhor (IRE)** *Richard Hannon* a83 88
3 gr g Dark Angel(IRE) Tellelle (IRE) (Trans Island)
1149[2] 1366[2] (1787) 2334[5] 3211[5] 3780[3] 4564[5] (5115) 5943[6]

**Tafteesh (IRE)** *Michael Easterby* a71 61
4 b g Kodiac Mudalalah (IRE) (Singspiel (IRE))
1631[4] 1890[5] 2224[14] 2843[4]◆ 3289[4] 7034[11] 8108[9] 8210[7] 8402[8] 8480[4]

**Taghee** *Marco Botti* a68 71
2 b c Acclamation Umneeyatee (AUS) (Encosta De Lago (AUS))
7280[3] 8381[7] 9050[9] 9300[5]

**Taghleeb (USA)** *Michael J Maker* 111
6 ch h Hard Spun(USA) Judhoor (Alhaarth (IRE))
2641a[2] 3553a[9]

**Taglioni** *A Fabre* a88 78
2 b c Cape Cross(IRE) La Sylphide (SWI) (Barathea (IRE))
8195a[3]

**Tagur (IRE)** *Kevin Ryan* a68 68
3 ch g Tagula(IRE) Westcote (USA) (Gone West (USA))
1348[6] 2625[8] 2886[3] 4302[8] 5167[7] 5741[8] 6630[2] (7046) 8108[4] 8556[9] 9347[4]

**Tahanee (ARG)** *M F De Kock* a80 105
4 ch m Stormy Atlantic(USA) Tawafeej (AUS) (Danehill Dancer (IRE))
205a[7] 431a[5] 653a[4] 892a[3] 1044a[11]

**Tahiti One** *Tony Carroll* a57 58
4 b m Bertolini(USA) Club Tahiti (Hernando (FR))
52[6] 640[11]

**Tahoo (IRE)** *K R Burke* 92
3 b f Zebedee Suffer Her (IRE) (Whipper (USA))
1660a[8] 1975[4] 2992[4] 3672[3] (4412) 5029[4] 6450[12] (8167)

**Tahreek** *Sir Michael Stoute* 67
2 b c Dansili Rifqah (USA) (Elusive Quality (USA))
7580[5]

**Taifbalady (IRE)** *Mark Johnston* 54
2 b c Dark Angel(IRE) Tartiflette (Dr Fong (USA))
2769[8] 4526[10] 6938[11]

**Tai Hang Dragon (IRE)**
*Richard Hannon* a87 93
3 b f Tamayuz Give A Whistle (IRE) (Mujadil (USA))
119[4] 331[3] (625) (2094) 2503[4] 3517[2] 3869[4] (4351) 4637[4] 5196a[10] 8351[8] 8636[5]

**Tailor's Row (USA)** *Mark Johnston* a73 79
3 ch c Street Cry(IRE) Raw Silk (USA) (Malibu Moon (USA))
329[2] 512[2] 626[6] 902[2] 2348[4] 3388[6] 4501[9] 4894[7] 5213[8] 5541[2] 5870[4] 6289[6] 7034[8] 7457[12] 8132[7] (8429)

**Tailwind** *Richard Hannon* a81 78
4 b g Dubawi(IRE) Time Saved (Green Desert (USA))
45[11] 2230[7] (3176)◆ 4093[3]

**Tai Sing Yeh (IRE)** *Charles Hills* a74 82
3 b g Exceed And Excel(AUS) Cherry Orchard (IRE) (King's Best (USA))
2348[2]◆ 3082[5] 3620[8] 4634[8] 7016[3]◆ 7947[9] 8706[12]

**Tajaanus (IRE)** *Richard Hannon* 102
2 b f Arcano(IRE) Rayaheen (Nayef (USA))
(2832)◆ 4361[6]◆ (5329) (5941)◆ 7088[7]

**Tajarrob (IRE)** *Ed Dunlop* a59
2 b f Intikhab(USA) Maany (USA) (Mr Greeley (USA))
8544[7]

**Takaful (USA)** *Kiaran McLaughlin* a118
3 bb c Bernardini(USA) Sablah (USA) (Distorted Humor (USA))
8607a[10]

**Takatul (USA)** *Charles Hills* a92 90
4 b g Smart Strike(CAN) Torrestrella (IRE) (Orpen (USA))
1622[4] (2093) 2799[5] 4570[4] 6483[5]

**Takbeer (IRE)** *Nikki Evans* a78 79
5 b g Aqlaam Precious Secret (IRE) (Fusaichi Pegasus (USA))
599[9] 1248[2] 2965[6] 3308[7] (4809) 5873[2] 6880[10] 9082[6]

**Take A Drop (IRE)** *Seamus Mullins* 50
4 b m Bushranger(IRE) Brogan's Well (IRE) (Caerleon (USA))
3940[2] 5714[11] 6341[11] 6748[15]

**Take A Guess (FR)** *Claudia Erni* 70
5 b g Palace Episode(USA) Somewhere (FR) (Noverre (USA))
835a[2]

**Take A Note** *Patrick Chamings* a64 81
8 b g Singspiel(IRE) Ela Paparouna (Vettori (IRE))
3136[5]

**Take A Turn (IRE)** *David Lanigan* a59 71
3 b g Henrythenavigator(USA) Satwa Pearl (Rock Of Gibraltar (IRE))
3327[7] 3819[4] (4660) 5618[6] (6257) 6594[4] 7902[5]

**Take Cover** *David C Griffiths* a109 115
10 b g Singspiel(IRE) Enchanted (Magic Ring (IRE))
3079[7] 3926[5] (4920) 5595[4] 6402[11] (6668) (7396) (8225a)

**Take Me Home (FR)** *H-A Pantall* a77 40
3 b c Henrythenavigator(USA) Trully Belle (IRE) (Bahri (USA))
1460a[3] (4289a)

**Take Me With You (USA)**
*Jeremy Noseda* 96
2 b f Scat Daddy(USA) Me And Miss Jones (USA) (Smarty Jones (USA))
3590[3]◆ 4028[3] (6761)

**Takeonefortheteam**
*Daniel Mark Loughnane* a59 59
2 b g Bahamian Bounty Miss Bond (IRE) (Danehill Dancer (IRE))
8466[4] 8915[5] 9440[5]

**Take Shelter** *James Tate* 76
2 b f Harbour Watch(IRE) Secret Night (Dansili)
1884[2] 2173[2] 2832[6] 3821[4] 5334[2] 5998[7]

**Take The Helm** *Brian Meehan* a97 89
4 ch g Monsieur Bond(IRE) Oasis Breeze (Oasis Dream)
66[7] 287[2] (896) 1177[2] (1622) 1769[4] 2093[2]

**Take The High Road**
*Keith Dalgleish* a33 80
3 b g Kyllachy China Tea (USA) (High Chaparral (IRE))
8805[5]

**Take This Waltz** *Bill Turner* a30 41
3 b f Royal Applause Constant Craving (Pastoral Pursuits)
8255[9] 9071[6]

**Take Two** *Alex Hales* a84 81
8 b g Act One Lac Marmot (FR) (Marju (IRE))
173[3] 440[6] 856[4] 992[4] 1498[4] 2020[4] 2785[3] 5320[3] (5968) (6858) 7908[4] 8426[2] 8648[2] 9000[5] (9208)

**Takiah** *Brian Meehan* 52
2 b f Arcano(IRE) Elmaam (Nayef (USA))
6386[5]

**Talaaqy (IRE)** *William Haggas* 74
2 b f Dansili Shabiba (USA) (Seeking The Gold (USA))
(8324)◆

**Talaayeb** *Owen Burrows* 111
3 b f Dansili Rumoush (USA) (Rahy (USA))
2434[4] 3749[7] (6401) 7113[4]

**Talas (IRE)** *Roger Varian* a74 64
2 b c Dansili Tamarind (IRE) (Sadler's Wells (USA))
8352[4] 8849[3] 9313[3]

**Talent Scout (IRE)** *Karen Tutty* a56 78
11 b g Exceed And Excel(AUS) Taalluf (USA) (Hansel (USA))
2224[10] 3049[6] (3203) 3845[9] (4168) (4601) 4999[4] 5213[9] (6058) 6464[9] 7474[8]

**Tale Of Tails (IRE)** *Brian Ellison* a65 82
2 b g Rip Van Winkle(IRE) Salute To Seville (IRE) (Duke Of Marmalade (IRE))
3754[2]◆ 4258[5]

**Talismana (IRE)** *E Lellouche* a51 63
4 b m Pour Moi(IRE) Acqua Verde (King's Best (USA))
3274a[6]

**Talismanic** *A Fabre* 118
4 bb h Medaglia d'Oro(USA) Magic Mission (Machiavellian (USA))
(1871a) 2485a[2] 3369a[2] (4879a) 6983a[3] (8610a) 9167a[2]

**Talksalot (IRE)** *Mark Bradstock* a65 61
6 b g Thousand Words Lady Piste (IRE) (Ali-Royal (IRE))
734[3]◆ 1603[6]

**Tallinski (IRE)** *Brian Ellison* a75 81
3 ch g Mayson Estonia (Exceed And Excel (AUS))
(1970) 3579[7] 4892[5] 5416[5] 6430[3] 6670[3] 7940[10]

**Tallow (IRE)** *William Haggas* a81 79
2 b f Kodiac Flames (Blushing Flame (USA))
8474[5] (8735) (8981)

**Tallulah Fleur** *David Loughnane* a30 47
4 b m Royal Applause Topflightcoolracer (Lujain (USA))
854[10] 1075[11]

**Tallulah Rose** *K R Burke* 91
3 b f Exceed And Excel(AUS) Blinking (Marju (IRE))
1883[9] 3793[10]

**Tallulah's Quest (IRE)** *Julia Feilden* a58 64
3 b f Tagula(IRE) Sarin Dubhe (IRE) (Catcher In The Rye (IRE))
1857[11] 2798[8] 3394[8] 4970[2] 5410[10] 6112[2] 6345[5] 7480[5]

**Tally (AUS)** *J O'Shea* 111
4 b g Street Cry(IRE) Itemise (USA) (Kris S (USA))
(1400a) 1994a[10]

**Tally's Son** *Grace Harris* 50
3 b g Assertive Talamahana (Kyllachy)
2895[4] 3423[8] 4969[4] 5714[6] 6341[5] 7198[8] 8513[8]

**Tally's Song** *Grace Harris* a51 45
4 b m Piccolo Talamahana (Kyllachy)
3569[8] 3811[10] 4149[4] 4735[4] 5052[8] 5567[5] 5778[5] 6099[7] 6502[10] 6615[7] 7191[12] 7693[8] 8496[3] 9216[3]

**Tamamo Best Play (JPN)**
*Katsumi Minai* 112
7 ch h Fuji Kiseki(JPN) Hot Play (JPN) (Northern Taste (CAN))
**2203a**[13]

**Tamarama (FR)** *D Smaga* a67 75
3 b f Vale Of York(IRE) Happy Way (FR) (Kingsalsa (USA))
***8304a***[5]

**Tamarin** *Lisa Williamson* a12 10
5 ch m Paco Boy(IRE) Les Hurlants (IRE) (Barathea (IRE))
2626[10] 3062[9] *3468*[11] 3717[9] **3940**[6] 4293[10]

**Tamayef (IRE)** *Hugo Palmer* a87 79
3 b g Sir Prancealot(IRE) Miss Glitters (IRE) (Chevalier (IRE))
2690[4] 3727[4] 4544[2]◆ 5404[9] 6195[5] *(6792)* ***7759***[3]◆ 8392[11]

**Tamayuz Magic (IRE)**
*Michael Easterby* a62 87
6 b g Tamayuz Anne Tudor (IRE) (Anabaa (USA))
1517[9] 3050[10] 4206[10] **5166**[2] 5667[3] 6757[10] 8239[5]

**Tambour** *Keith Dalgleish* a44 58
4 b g Notnowcato Tamso (USA) (Seeking The Gold (USA))
***91***[6] *993*[7] 1804[6] 2378[4] 3242[6] 3650[4] 6352[3] 6592[3]

**Tamboureen (IRE)**
*Mohammed Jassim Ghazali* 79
2 ch c Red Jazz(USA) Fritillary (Vettori (IRE))
**9446a**[11]

**Tamelly** *A Fabre* 104
4 ch h New Approach(IRE) Perfect Hand (Barathea (IRE))
**5692a**[3]

**Tamih (IRE)** *Roger Varian* a80 83
3 b c Dark Angel(IRE) Mairead Anne (USA) (Elusive Quality (USA))
*3188*[4]◆ *4309*[2] *6817*[2] **(7597)**

**Tamkeen** *Owen Burrows* 80
2 ch c Kyllachy Regatta (USA) (Giant's Causeway (USA))
7280[5] 7819[2] **8508**[2]

**Tamleek (USA)** *Saeed bin Suroor* 104
3 bb c Hard Spun(USA) Tafaneen (USA) (Dynaformer (USA))
(1906) **2555**[4] 3994[8] 4811[4] 5525[13]

**Tan** *Tony Coyle* a68 65
3 b g Aqlaam Sunburnt (Haafhd)
**4783a**[3] 5697[7] 6512[6] 6574[10] 7268[12] 7825[6]◆ 8106[7] 8484[7] *8552*[10] *8775*[4] *9013*[9]

**Tan Arabiq** *Michael Appleby* a74 68
4 b g Arabian Gleam Tanning (Atraf)
***(122)*** 4541[5] 6143[5] *6848*[5] *7601*[5] 8124[8] ***(9054)*** *9408*[2]

**Tanasoq (IRE)** *Owen Burrows* a69 83
4 b g Acclamation Alexander Youth (IRE) (Exceed And Excel (AUS))
**2147**[2] 3330[3] 6506[6]

**Tanawar (IRE)** *Ruth Carr* a66 70
7 b g Elusive City(USA) Parakopi (IRE) (Green Desert (USA))
(2082) 2342[5] 3198[4] **(3949)** 4506[9] 4999[11]◆ 5466[6] 6049[6] 6549[10] 7018[4] 7389[2] *7573*[13] 7889[6] 8480[10]

**Tanaya** *Richard Fahey* 56
2 b c Kodiac Serena's Pride (Danbird (AUS))
**3483**[4] 4472[8]

**Tandem** *D K Weld* a88 106
8 b g Dansili Light Ballet (Sadler's Wells (USA))
**(4822a)** 5517a[9]

**Tangled (IRE)** *Richard Hannon* a79 106
2 b c Society Rock(IRE) Open Verse (USA) (Black Minnaloushe (USA))
2286[5] *3135*[2] 3591[4]◆ (4858)◆ (6353) 7090[9] 7546[3] **8422**[2]

**Tango Fire (USA)** *Richard Hannon* a30 56
3 b c Frankel Latin Love (IRE) (Danehill Dancer (IRE))
**1730**[11] 1962[8] *7768*[8]

**Tango Sky (IRE)** *Paul Midgley* a65 58
8 b g Namid Sky Galaxy (USA) (Sky Classic (CAN))
***172***[3] *583*[7] 2843[8] *3256*[4] 3704[5] 5542[3] 6041[8] *6902*[13]

**Tangramm** *Dean Ivory* a85 20
5 bb g Sakhee's Secret Tripti (IRE) (Sesaro (USA))
***163***[4] *381*[5] ***599***[3] *1289*[8] *4751*[8] *6937*[4] *7452*[7] 8295[14] *9000*[7] *(9140)*◆

**Tanis (FR)** *R Martens* a23
3 b f Kentucky Dynamite(USA) Atlantic Festival (USA) (Theatrical (IRE))
***427a***[10]

**Tanksalot (IRE)** *Harry Dunlop* a48 50
3 b f Sir Prancealot(IRE) Pearly Brooks (Efisio)
***126***[5] *376*[7] *456*[6]

**Tannaaf (IRE)** *R Bouresly* a15 79
5 b h High Chaparral(IRE) Wanna (IRE) (Danehill Dancer (IRE))
**322a**[12]◆ *9360a*[10]

**Tanseeq** *William Haggas* a83 67
2 b c Havana Gold(IRE) Roslea Lady (IRE) (Alhaarth (IRE))
6108[2] *6885*[3] ***(8890)***

**Tansheet (IRE)** *William Haggas* a81 50
2 ch c Shamardal(USA) Sharedah (IRE) (Pivotal)
6132[10] *(7237)*◆ ***7726***[4]

**Tansholpan** *Roger Varian* 94
3 b f Dansili Tamarind (IRE) (Sadler's Wells (USA))
**2523**[3] 5982a[8]

**Tantheem** *F Head* a90 105
2 b f Teofilo(IRE) Riqa (Dubawi (IRE))
*(4677a)* **(5461a)** 6249a[7]

**Tanzeel (IRE)** *Charles Hills* 96
6 b g Elusive City(USA) Royal Fizz (IRE) (Royal Academy (USA))
**3842**[13]

**Taoiseach** *Hugo Palmer* a65
2 b c Roderic O'Connor(IRE) Munaa's Dream (Oasis Dream)
***8536***[5]

**Taopix** *Karen McLintock* a74 57
5 b g Rip Van Winkle(IRE) Sinister Ruckus (USA) (Trippi (USA))
***(509)*** ***727***[3]

**Tapdanceallthetway** *Amanda Perrett* a66 68
3 b f Nathaniel(IRE) Tap Dance Way (IRE) (Azamour (IRE))
*1468*[2] *1900*[4] *2963*[9] **5607**[3] *6578*[7] *7766*[10]

**Taper Tantrum (IRE)** *Michael Bell* a87 87
5 b g Azamour(IRE) Maramba (USA) (Hussonet (USA))
*1323*[5] *2787*[7] *3138*[2] **3840**[2] **6090**[2] *6618*[3] 8072[2]

**Tap For Me (ARG)** *Peter Jardby*
4 b h Dancing For Me(ARG) Tap On Quality (USA) (Elusive Quality (USA))
*2942a*[7]

**Tapis Libre** *Jacqueline Coward* a71 88
9 b g Librettist(USA) Stella Manuela (FR) (Galileo (IRE))
2741[3]◆ 3153[6] **(3841)** **(4801)** 5924[6] 6317[3] 6757[8] 7267[7]

**Tap On The Bar** *John Wainwright* 6
3 b g Sayif(IRE) Peneia (USA) (Nureyev (USA))
**4106**[8]

**Tap Tap Boom** *Mme P Butel* a69 90
3 ro g Foxwedge(AUS) Exclusive Approval (USA) (With Approval (CAN))
1417a[5] (2697a) **(3446a)** 5909a[10] 6650a[9]

**Tapwrit (USA)** *Todd Pletcher* a119
3 rg c Tapit(USA) Appealing Zophie (USA) (Successful Appeal (USA))
***2420a***[6]

**Tara Celeb** *Mick Channon* 81
3 b f Excelebration(IRE) Tara Moon (Pivotal)
**2567**[11]

**Tara Dylan (IRE)** *Thomas Mullins* a82 87
5 b m Dylan Thomas(IRE) Tara's Wells (IRE) (Sadler's Wells (USA))
5088a[6] 6956a[9] **7261a**[5] 7860a[19] 8086a[10]

**Taraja (GER)** *Henk Grewe* a49
2 b f High Chaparral(IRE) Taita (GER) (Big Shuffle (USA))
***8691a***[11]

**Tarakkom (FR)** *Peter Hiatt* a59 64
5 ch g Naaqoos Sahabah (USA) (Swain (IRE))
***859***[7] *1082*[14] 2712[11] 3311[10] *3724*[9] 7232[10]

**Tara River (FR)** *Brian Barr* a77 109
8 b g Stormy River(FR) Tarabela (FR) (Johann Quatz (FR))
***2165***[6]

**Tarboosh** *Paul Midgley* a76 101
4 b g Bahamian Bounty Mullein (Oasis Dream)
*660*[6] *995*[6] *1836*[8] 2104[7] (4015) 4600[7] (5495) 5804[5] (6314)◆ (6758) **7610**[3]

**Tarnemah (IRE)** *George Peckham* a47 39
2 b f Lope De Vega(IRE) Ice Rock (IRE) (Rock Of Gibraltar (IRE))
4792[5]◆ 5660[11] 6140[9] 6585[7] ***6815***[5]

**Tarnhelm** *Mark Johnston* a63 73
2 b f Helmet(AUS) Anosti (Act One)
**6417**[2] *6682*[4] *7472*[4] *8586*[7] *8804*[U] *8954*[4]

**Taroum (IRE)** *John Flint* a26 53
10 b g Refuse To Bend(IRE) Taraza (IRE) (Darshaan)
2364[7] **3428**[4] 3805[7]

**Tarseekh** *Chris Gordon* a70 65
4 b g Kyllachy Constitute (USA) (Gone West (USA))
**1687**[8] 2297[5] 3304[8] 3920[7] 4446[13] *8152*[2] *8307*[12] *8799*[6] *9213*[4]

**Tartan Bute** *Mark Johnston* a89 81
4 b g Azamour(IRE) On A Soapbox (USA) (Mi Cielo (USA))
*(603)* *(1027)* *1153*[3] ***(1466)***

**Tartaros (FR)** *M Rulec* a43
4 b g Lord Of England(GER) Tryphosa (IRE) (Be My Guest (USA))
***515a***[6]

**Tarte Tropezienne (IRE)**
*William Haggas* 89
3 b f Nathaniel(IRE) High Heel Sneakers (Dansili)
3615[5]◆ 5022[3] (5707)◆ **6307**[2] 7401[5]

**Tartini (USA)** *John Gosden* 97
3 ch c Giant's Causeway(USA) Vignette (USA) (Diesis)
2084[4] **2614**[3] **3318**[4] 3998[16] 8076[4]

**Tartufo Classico** *Derek Shaw* a36 27
4 b g Paco Boy(IRE) Tartatartufata (Tagula (IRE))
*1321*[6] *1543*[8] *2139*[6] ***2472***[6] *8428*[9]

**Tasaaboq** *Phil McEntee* a53 52
6 b g Aqlaam Seldemosa (Selkirk (USA))
*67*[12] *303*[7] *640*[6] *982*[4] *1075*[4] *(1246)* *(1372)* *1451*[4] ***1490***[2] *1759*[5] *1887*[7] *2319*[8] *7407*[2] *7487*[5] *7606*[5] *8259*[2] *8496*[6] *8772*[4] *8908*[6] *8980*[6] *9232*[3] *9279*[6] *9420*[2]

**Tashaaboh (IRE)** *Owen Burrows* a74 47
2 gr c Lethal Force(IRE) Rush (Compton Place)
7623[6] ***(8309)***

**Tashweeq (IRE)** *John Gosden* 114
4 b g Big Bad Bob(IRE) Dance Hall Girl (IRE) (Dansili)
2129[9] **3963**[3] 4905[16] 5456[4]

**Taskeen (IRE)** *Roger Fell* a22 76
4 b g Lilbourne Lad(IRE) Lola Rosa (IRE) (Peintre Celebre (USA))
1910[7] **2404**[3]◆ 2592[5] 3396[9] 3949[7] 4168[11] 7332[11] 8651[13] *9013*[8]

**Tasleet** *William Haggas* a109 119
4 b h Showcasing Bird Key (Cadeaux Genereux)
2150[2] (2737) **4071**[2] 4907[10] 6926[2] 8230[2]

**Taste The Wine (IRE)**
*Bernard Llewellyn* a47 58
11 gr g Verglas(IRE) Azia (IRE) (Desert Story (IRE))
**2363**[4] 2712[5] 5493[4] 5716[9] 7232[8]

**Tasty Ginger (IRE)** *J R Jenkins* a66 64
4 ch g Tamayuz Secret Fashion (King's Best (USA))
*462*[3] ***616***[2] *738*[4] *1072*[4] ***1303***[2] ***1486***[3]

**Tatawu (IRE)** *Peter Hiatt* a68 70
5 b g Mawatheeq(USA) Mooteeah (IRE) (Sakhee (USA))
2626[9] *2956*[9] 5477[8] **6589**[5] 7152[7]

**Tathmeen (IRE)** *Richard Hannon* 83
2 b c Exceed And Excel(AUS) Deyaar (USA) (Storm Cat (USA))
3002[7] 4049[3] **(5321)** 6330[15] **8420**[3] 8741[11]

**Tatlisu (IRE)** *Richard Fahey* a94 92
7 b g Red Clubs(IRE) Zwadi (IRE) (Dockside (USA))
***(33)***◆ *194*[3] *730*[11] ***1103***[3]◆ 1385a[17] 2381[12] 3386[2] (4013) 4683[10] 5471[2] 5890[3] 6464[6] *6949*[2] 8486[11] *8906*[3] *(9083)*

**Tatting** *Lawrence Mullaney* a86 72
8 ch g Street Cry(IRE) Needlecraft (IRE) (Mark Of Esteem (IRE))
*(3)* *389*[7] ***(1292)*** ***(1865)*** 2770[11]

**Tatvan Incisi (TUR)**
*Ibrahim Bekirogullari* 100
5 b m Scarface(TUR) Hanimkiz (TUR) (Always A Classic (CAN))
**6718a**[4]

**Taurean Dancer (IRE)** *Michael Bell* 69
2 b c Intello(GER) Traou Mad (IRE) (Barathea (IRE))
4860[7] **5808**[4] 6653[12]

**Taurean Gold** *John Bridger* a33 33
3 b g Piccolo Elsie's Orphan (Pastoral Pursuits)
*962*[6] *1299*[13] *1600*[7] **2235**[10] 2911[15] 3035[7] *9183*[10] *9469*[9]

**Taurean Star (IRE)** *Michael Bell* 96
4 b g Elnadim(USA) Marhaba (Nayef (USA))
**(2283)**◆ 2606[16] 3837[9] 7025[6] 7781[8]

**Taurian** *Ian Williams* a72 71
6 b m Central Park(IRE) Emma-Lyne (Emarati (USA))
*648*[11] ***789***[3]

**Tavener** *David C Griffiths* a80 82
5 b g Exceed And Excel(AUS) Sea Chorus (Singspiel (IRE))
*21*[3] *158*[5] *481*[9] *620*[3] *768*[4] *929*[2] *1338*[5] *(1407)* 1717[7] *1842*[3] *(1898)*◆ *2064*[3] (2377) *2464*[2] 2582[5] 3199[5] *3471*[5] 3581[3] 3833[5] **4524**[2]◆ 4803[7] 7086[13] *7572*[11] *7789*[12] 8106[8] *8433*[2]

**Tawaafoq** *Mick Quinn* a71 69
3 b g Showcasing Gilt Linked (Compton Place)
***1693***[4] 2293[9] 3085[4] 5289[3] 5855[3] 6724[5] 7254[7]

**Tawahid** *E J O'Neill* a91 76
2 b c Delegator Show Flower (Shamardal (USA))
**(8271a)**

**Tawaret (FR)** *Mme M-C Naim* a68 61
3 b f Mr. Sidney(USA) Divinatrice (FR) (Numerous (USA))
**1417a**[9]

**Tawdeea** *David O'Meara* a106 109
5 b g Intikhab(USA) Sharedah (IRE) (Pivotal)
1516[6] ***1779***[7] 2158[2] 2559a[4] 3594[14] 4614[5] 5353[6] 6857[3] 7150[6] 7615[5] 8038[30]

**Tawfeer** *Phil McEntee* a53 51
3 b g Lawman(FR) Wild Gardenia (Alhaarth (IRE))
*1889*[10] *2467*[7] ***3259***[6] 3703[8] *4982*[8] *5897*[11] *7325*[9] 8125[7] 8182[2] 8470[4] *8908*[14]

**Tawny Port** *James Given* a63 85
3 ch g Arcano(IRE) Tawaasul (Haafhd)
**2739**[11]

**Taws** *Rod Millman* a76 95
6 b m Hernando(FR) Reaf (In The Wings)
*4499*[7] 5524[4] (6096) **(6508)** 7402[6] 8038[11]

**Tawseef (IRE)** *Donald McCain* a66 72
9 b g Monsun(GER) Sahool (Unfuwain (USA))
5021[10] (5700) **(8109)**◆ 8426[4]

**Tax Exile (IRE)** *Matthieu Palussiere* 81
2 b g Kodiac Gutter Press (IRE) (Raise A Grand (IRE))
**5679a**[8] 6726a[4]

**Taxman (USA)** *H-F Devin* a71
2 b g Congrats(USA) Make A Dance (USA) (Empire Maker (USA))
*8302a*[4] ***9087a***[4]

**Taxmeifyoucan (IRE)**
*Keith Dalgleish* a76 93
3 b g Beat Hollow Accounting (Sillery (USA))
*(1591)* 2807[10] 3335[9] *4307*[5] (5648) (6692)◆ **(6930)** 7565[6]

**Tayaar (IRE)** *John Ryan* a62 42
4 b g High Chaparral(IRE) Ursula Minor (IRE) (Footstepsinthesand)
1519[12] ***5244***[5] 5810[4] 6293[11] *8815*[13]

**Tayara** *Rod Collet* 58
3 b f Lawman(FR) Break Time (Dansili)
**6566a**[6]

**Tazmania (IRE)** *Clive Cox* a53 50
3 b f Helmet(AUS) Red Fuschia (Polish Precedent (USA))
**7227**[4] *8031*[14]

**Tea El Tee (IRE)** *Gay Kelleway* a53 60
3 b g Holy Roman Emperor(IRE) Mayenne (USA) (Nureyev (USA))
*1418*[3] 1688[7] *2470*[5] 2734[6] 5040[5] **5289**[2] **(5812)** 6174[8] *7036*[8] 7692[9] *9075*[11] *9340*[8]

**Teak (IRE)** *Ian Williams* a69 66
10 b g Barathea(IRE) Szabo (IRE) (Anabaa (USA))
*1630*[6] *1891*[9] *2308*[6] **2889**[2] *3138*[3] 3663[4] 4120[8] *9258*[13]

**Team Meeting (USA)**
*Saeed bin Suroor* a63 43
3 br g Exceed And Excel(AUS) Sylvan Song (USA) (Street Cry (IRE))
*1693*[3] 2235[7] ***(3173)*** *3719*[6]

**Team Showme** *Michael Dods* a49
2 b f Harbour Watch(IRE) Straitjacket (Refuse To Bend (IRE))
***9177***[8]

**Tea Rattle** *Scott Dixon* a37 42
2 b f Finjaan Scrooby Baby (Mind Games)
**4440**[8] 4740[10] 6755[7] *8983*[4] *9175*[10] *9302*[12]

**Teaser** *James Fanshawe* a53
2 b c Dansili Tottie (Fantastic Light (USA))
***9201***[8]

**Teatro (IRE)** *James Given* 40
2 b c Shamardal(USA) Airline Hostess (IRE) (Sadler's Wells (USA))
8215[8] **8508**[9]

**Tebay (IRE)** *Michael Dods* 68
2 b g Elzaam(AUS) Maid Of Ale (IRE) (Barathea (IRE))
4205[5] 5179[5] **5801**[3]

**Technological** *George Margarson* 71
2 gr c Universal(IRE) Qeethaara (USA) (Aljabr (USA))
4792[6] 6653[10] **8381**[6]◆

**Teckwin (FR)** *J-V Toux* a83 79
2 ch c French Fifteen(FR) Ammia (IRE) (Medicean)
**6051a**[9]

**Tectonic (IRE)** *Keith Dalgleish* a70 69
8 b g Dylan Thomas(IRE) Pine Chip (USA) (Nureyev (USA))
**3197**[4] 3451[7] 4210[14] 4899[10] 5257[3] 5884[2] 5923[3] 6595[2] 6895[7] 8109[7] *8909*[9]

**Teddy Edward** *J Bossert* a54 56
3 ch g Medicean Pinkai (IRE) (Caerleon (USA))
**3310a**[9]

**Ted's Brother (IRE)** *Laura Morgan* a61 53
9 b g Fath(USA) Estertide (IRE) (Tagula (IRE))
*839*[3] *1081*[5] *1402*[2] *1754*[3] *3340*[8] 3449[2] 4034[2] 4627[5] *8430*[11] ***(9237)*** *9375*[3]

**Ted Veale (IRE)** *A J Martin* 99
10 b g Revoque(IRE) Rose Tanner (IRE) (Roselier (FR))
**7860a**[3]

**Tee It Up Tommo (IRE)**
*Daniel Steele* a79 68
8 gr g Clodovil(IRE) Lamh Eile (IRE) (Lend A Hand)
*460*[4] *(811)* *986*[2]◆ *1553*[3] 2070[7] *2116*[4] ***(2996)*** *3235*[4] *7999*[8] *8886*[7] *9206*[10]

**Teenage Gal (IRE)** *Ed Dunlop* a50 71
2 b f Acclamation Bobbie Soxer (IRE) (Pivotal)
*7454*[11] **7898**[2]

**Teepee Time** *Michael Mullineaux* a54 64
4 b m Compton Place Deora De (Night Shift (USA))
*270*[2] *455*[9] *(723)* *1452*[5] 2076[3] 2453[6] 3569[10] *4448*[3] (5134) **(5877)** 8168[5] *8494*[7] *8873*[10] *9374*[8]

**Tegara** *David Simcock* a82 72
4 ch m Hard Spun(USA) Damaniyat Girl (USA) (Elusive Quality (USA))
*(1897)* 2605[9] *3233*[4] ***(3455)*** *4308*[5]

**Tekedici (FR)** *Antonio Marcialis* 11
2 ch c Showcasing Aljafliyah (Halling (USA))
**6608a**[8]

**Te Koop** *David Simcock* a68
2 ch g Mastercraftsman(IRE) Miss You Too (Montjeu (IRE))
***7361***[2] *8502*[5]

**Tell A Story** *David Simcock* a64
4 b m Dutch Art Ghenwah (FR) (Selkirk (USA))
*37*[3] ***308***[3] *394*[5]

**Tell Me (IRE)** *Simon Crisford* a63 63
2 b f Kodiac Fearn Royal (IRE) (Ali-Royal (IRE))
3697[8] **5372**[4] ***5795***[9]

**Tellovoi (IRE)** *Richard Guest* a79 65
9 b g Indian Haven Kloonlara (IRE) (Green Desert (USA))
1832[5] *2116*[8] **2301**[2] 2684[5] 2888[9] 3095[7] 3567[4] 3934[4] 4506[8] 5126[7] 5341[5] 5544[RR] 6435[16] 7390[6] 7888[10] 8329[9] 8490[5] *8930*[2] *9032*[6] *9142*[6]◆ *9279*[3]

**Telltale** *Mick Channon* 42
2 ch g Monsieur Bond(IRE) Yarn (Dutch Art)
**8388**[13]

**Tell Your Mama (USA)**
*Robert B Hess Jr* a73
2 b f Blame(USA) Taletobetold (USA) (Tale Of The Cat (USA))
***8603a***[13]

**Temasek Star (IRE)**
*Anthony McCann* a72 64
6 b g Soviet Star(USA) Crazy About You (IRE) (Montjeu (IRE))
*174*[2] ***(2162)***

**Tember** *David Barron* 67
2 b g Sayif(IRE) Tranquil Flight (Oasis Dream)
**1673**[2]◆ 4204[6] 4995[3] 7814[20] 8325[8]

**Temeraire (FR)** *Hugo Palmer* a79 47
3 gr f Mount Nelson Tadorne (FR) (Inchinor)
*(8842)*◆ ***9089***[2]

**Temir Kazyk** *David Simcock* a65 46
3 b g Oasis Dream Tingling (USA) (Storm Cat (USA))
*970*[5] ***1239***[3] 1420[3] 5061[6] 5532[7]

**Tempel (FR)** *A Fabre* 78
2 bb f Deep Impact(JPN) Iron Lips (Iron Mask (USA))
**(7969a)**

**Tempera** *D K Weld* 89
3 b f Dansili Portodora (USA) (Kingmambo (USA))
6642a[6] **6961a**[9]

**Temple Church (IRE)**
*Hughie Morrison* 100
3 b g Lawman(FR) All Hallows (IRE) (Dalakhani (IRE))
1943[4] **2560a**[3] 3680a[5] **4376**[4] 5157[4] 7354[5]

**Templemary Boy (IRE)**
*Paul W Flynn* a49 43
4 b g Vocalised(USA) Marino Lil (IRE) (Lil's Boy (USA))
**4900**[4]

**Temple Road (IRE)** *Milton Bradley* a73 59
9 b g Street Cry(IRE) Sugarhoneybaby (IRE) (Docksider (USA))
***95***[2] *215*[2] *330*[5] *886*[4] *955*[4] *1327*[3] *1429*[4] *1558*[7] *1981*[8] *8853*[9] ***(9189)*** *9389*[3]

**Tempuran** *David Bridgwater* a73 72
8 b g Unbridled's Song(USA) Tenderly (IRE) (Danehill (USA))
*169*[8] *440*[7] *861*[3] *1073*[4] *1369*[9] 2678[3] **(4181)** 4791[7]

**Tempus Temporis (USA)**
*A R Al Rayhi* a44 43
5 b g Dynaformer(USA) Tempus Fugit (USA) (Alphabet Soup (USA))
**82a**[11]

**Temur Khan** *Hugo Palmer* a60
2 br c Dansili Slink (Selkirk (USA))
***8839***[8]

**Tenby Two** *Mick Channon* 62
3 gr f Rip Van Winkle(IRE) Ayla (IRE) (Daylami (IRE))
1948[5] 2393[4] 2759[5] 3180[10] 3770[6] 4045[4] 4493[3] 4994[4] 5286[2] 5532[2]

**Tenedos** *Hugo Palmer* a80
2 b c High Chaparral(IRE) Garanciere (FR) (Anabaa (USA))
(8340)

**Tenerezza (IRE)** *Iain Jardine* a73 59
4 b m Shamardal(USA) Geminiani (IRE) (King Of Kings (IRE))
609[4] 841[2] (883) 1014a[3]

**Tenerife Song** *Jamie Osborne* a50
4 b m Fastnet Rock(AUS) Dancinginthteclouds (IRE) (Rainbow Quest (USA))
8992[10]

**Tenger (IRE)** *M G Mintchev*
2 b c Galileo(IRE) Temida (IRE) (Oratorio (IRE))
8091a[6]

**Tenhoo** *Richard Ford* a48 60
11 b g Reset(AUS) Bella Bambina (Turtle Island (IRE))
176[4] 414[6] 645[7]

**Ten In The Hat (IRE)** *Tom Gretton* a28 21
3 b g Sir Prancealot(IRE) Vampire Queen (IRE) (General Monash (USA))
3708[10] 4473[8] 8255[11]

**Tennessee Belle** *James Tate* a61
3 b f Teofilo(IRE) Dixie Belle (Diktat)
6287[7] 7485[7]

**Tennessee Rose (IRE)**
*Luke McJannet* a61 62
3 b f Tagula(IRE) Bonny Rose (Zaha (CAN))
2732[2] 3162[4]◆ 3473[6] 4350[2]

**Tennessee Wildcat (IRE)**
*G M Lyons* a100 105
7 b g Kheleyf(USA) Windbeneathmywings (IRE) (In The Wings)
4822a[3] 5087a[3] 7588a[5]

**Tenorio (FR)** *Mlle V Dissaux* a43 53
4 b h Dobby Road(FR) Surtsey (FR) (Anabaa Blue)
930a[12] 5176a[11]

**Tenzing Norgay**
*Sir Mark Prescott Bt* a88 87
4 gr g Aussie Rules(USA) Miss Katmandu (IRE) (Rainbow Quest (USA))
4742[3]◆ 5303[3]◆ 5737[4]

**Teodoro (IRE)** *Tom Dascombe* a61 99
3 ch g Teofilo(IRE) Altesse Imperiale (IRE) (Rock Of Gibraltar (IRE))
1244[5] (2347) 2526[4] 3291[9] (4082) (4580)◆ (6482) 7395[18]

**Teofonic (IRE)** *Mark Johnston* a80 103
3 b f Teofilo(IRE) Dusty Answer (Zafonic (USA))
2436[5] 4376[8] 7817[2] (8076)◆ 8444a[5]

**Teomaria** *K R Burke* a56 69
3 b f Teofilo(IRE) Sylvestris (IRE) (Arch (USA))
5538[5] 6236[5] 6941[3] 7710[13] 8216[8] (8514) 8928[8]

**Teppal (FR)** *David Simcock* a90 85
2 b f Camacho Jummana (FR) (Cadeaux Genereux)
(6584) (7453)◆

**Teqany (IRE)** *Owen Burrows* a70 72
3 gr g Dark Angel(IRE) Capulet Monteque (IRE) (Camacho)
1609[6] 2293[6] 3784[6]◆ 4276[5]

**Term Of Art (USA)** *Doug O'Neill* a103
3 b c Tiznow(USA) Miles Of Style (USA) (Storm Cat (USA))
2851a[10]

**Termsnconditions (IRE)**
*Tim Vaughan* a63 56
3 b g Kodiac Sweet'n Sassy (IRE) (Grand Lodge (USA))
(1359) (2091)◆ 2853[5] 5919[7] 7191[8] 8194[5] 8824[2] 9432[6]

**Terrakova (IRE)** *F Head* a90 110
3 b f Galileo(IRE) Goldikova (IRE) (Anabaa (USA))
(2945a) 3881a[3]

**Terre (FR)** *F Head* 96
3 b f Motivator Trevise (FR) (Anabaa (USA))
2945a[7] 8088a[7]

**Terrific Feeling (IRE)**
*Dominic Ffrench Davis* a40 77
3 b g Sir Prancealot(IRE) Easy Feeling (IRE) (Night Shift (USA))
5338[6]

**Terri Rules (IRE)** *Julia Feilden* a55 55
2 b f Camacho Hawaiian Storm (Jeremy (USA))
2502[12] 2750[8] 3328[3] 3655[5] 4758[2] 5479[5] 5785[5] 6154[3] 6634[13] 7458[7] 7695[6]

**Tertian (SWE)** *Niels Petersen* a53
5 b g Tertullian(USA) Sweet Chili (SWE) (Diaghlyphard (USA))
4940a[12]

**Teruntum Star (FR)** *Kevin Ryan* a74 109
5 ch g Dutch Art Serailia (Royal Academy (USA))
4353[13] 5435[4] (6205) (8044)◆ 8738[4]

**Tesko Fella (IRE)** *Ruth Carr* a65 69
3 b g Myboycharlie(IRE) Foundation Filly (Lando (GER))
3085[10] 3824[4] 4152[4] 4562[3] 5206[6] 5666[8] 6091[2] 6381[2]

**Tesorina (IRE)** *William Knight* 62
2 b f Lilbourne Lad(IRE) Insieme (IRE) (Barathea (IRE))
6824[5]◆ 7211[4]

**Tess Graham** *Sarah Hollinshead* a31 39
3 b f Pastoral Pursuits Zartwyda (IRE) (Mozart (IRE))
2699[4] 3260[12] 3818[5] 4174[11] 4731[6] 6469[8]

**Testa Rossa (IRE)** *Jim Goldie* a86 86
7 b g Oratorio(IRE) Red Rita (IRE) (Kefaah (USA))
(43) 359[4] 581[5] 730[12] 1032[3] 1472[9] (2458) 2773[6] 3255[7] 4035[6] 4076[2] 4358[3] 4961[6] 5207[4] 5417[8] 5996[6] 6434[2] 7941[6] 8718[3] 8912[5]

**Testbourne (IRE)** *K R Burke* a62 72
3 b g Big Bad Bob(IRE) Magnificent Bell (IRE) (Octagonal (NZ))
1293[3] 1675[2] 2067[2] 3787[8] 4474[8] 5332[4]

**Tetradrachm** *David Simcock* a85 68
4 b g Holy Roman Emperor(IRE) Dahlia's Krissy (USA) (Kris S (USA))
519[3]◆ 1002[7] 1248[3] 3213[6] 4355[6] 6849[9] 7359[9] 8505[3]

**Tewafeedj** *Kevin Ryan* a61 65
3 b g Mawatheeq(USA) It's The War (USA) (Consolidator (USA))
849[4] 1122[4] 1968[7] 2703[6] 4171[3] (5618) 6002[4] 7537[13]

**Texas Ranger (FR)** *H-A Pantall* a66 70
4 b h Bushranger(IRE) Singapore Fairy (FR) (Sagacity (FR))
3274a[10]

**Texas Rock (IRE)** *M C Grassick* a85 110
6 b g Rock Of Gibraltar(IRE) Vestavia (IRE) (Alhaarth (IRE))
4383a[5] 6961a[5] (7856a) 8438a[15]

**Texas Wedge** *William Muir* a32 44
3 b g Foxwedge(AUS) Sacre Coeur (Compton Place)
3157[9] 3313[6] 3806[5] 4447[9] 5028[7] 5567[9]

**Textured (IRE)** *Sir Michael Stoute* a81 79
3 b f Dark Angel(IRE) Timbre (Dubai Destination (USA))
2517[8] 4100[5]

**T For Tango (IRE)** *J A Nash* a73 88
2 b g Zoffany(IRE) Diminish (IRE) (Raven's Pass (USA))
2861a[4] 3929[14]

**Thaaqib** *Charles Hills* a78 78
3 gr g Invincible Spirit(IRE) Light Shine (Dansili)
1895[6] 3040[7] 3784[5]

**Thackeray** *Chris Fairhurst* a50 50
10 b g Fasliyev(USA) Chinon (IRE) (Entrepreneur)
19[3] 315[3] 610[8] 1207[4] 1436[3] 3155[10] 3654[2] 4962[12] 5700[10]

**Thafeera (USA)** *Charles Hills* a77 102
3 b f War Front(USA) Aqsaam (USA) (Dynaformer (USA))
2019[3] 2798[3] 4565[4] (5335) (6149) (6864) 8040[11]

**Thahab Ifraj (IRE)** *Alexandra Dunn* a73 71
4 ch g Frozen Power(IRE) Penny Rouge (IRE) (Pennekamp (USA))
169[2] 286[3] 5968[3]

**Tha'ir (IRE)** *Michael Appleby* a80 78
7 b g New Approach(IRE) Flashing Green (Green Desert (USA))
5500[16] 7619[27] 8009[20] 8315[5] 8705[7] 8956[2] 9140[6]

**Thais (FR)** *P Bary* 107
3 bb f Rio De La Plata(USA) Tianshan (FR) (Lahint (USA))
1690a[2] 2644a[10] (3612a)

**Thama** *Mrs Ilka Gansera-Leveque* a49
2 b f Finjaan It's The War (USA) (Consolidator (USA))
9312[8]

**Thames Knight** *Marcus Tregoning* a64 88
5 b g Sir Percy Bermondsey Girl (Bertolini (USA))
2085[6] 2741[16] (3308)◆ 3616[2] 6513[2]

**Thammin** *Owen Burrows* a93 81
3 gr c Dark Angel(IRE) Gimme Some Lovin (IRE) (Desert Style (IRE))
2579[7] 7994[2]

**Thane Of Cawdor (IRE)**
*Joseph Tuite* a66 55
8 b g Danehill Dancer(IRE) Holy Nola (USA) (Silver Deputy (CAN))
46[8] 169[11]

**Thank You Bye Bye (FR)**
*J-P Gauvin* a94 103
5 b m Zanzibari(USA) Puritanical (IRE) (Desert King (IRE))
2201a[5] 6665a[2] 8088a[4]

**Thankyou Stars** *Jonathan Portman* a27 46
4 b m Exceed And Excel(AUS) Magic Music (IRE) (Magic Ring (IRE))
6759[6] 7408[12]

**Thankyou Very Much**
*James Bethell* a59 61
7 b m Lucky Story(USA) Maid Of Perth (Mark Of Esteem (IRE))
8187[2]◆ 8647[7]

**Thanx For Nothing (FR)** *P Decouz* a83 98
3 b f Myboycharlie(IRE) Zongoraora (FR) (Bering)
[3] 7441a[9]

**Thaqaffa (IRE)** *Amy Murphy* a86 85
4 b g Kodiac Incense (Unfuwain (USA))
760[10] 1288[5] 1706[6]◆ (2267) 3441[5] 5610[7] 6555[6] 7327[9] 7957[5] 8433[10] 8798[7] 9027[3] 9338[5]

**Thatcherite (IRE)** *Tony Coyle* a68 68
9 gr g Verglas(IRE) Damiana (IRE) (Thatching)
2104[10] 2700[5] 3201[8] (3905) 4174[5] 5211[14]

**That Is The Spirit** *David O'Meara* a104 103
6 b g Invincible Spirit(IRE) Fraulein (Acatenango (GER))
(2115) 2518[3] 3587[6] 4264[5] 5137[3] 5616[3] 5942[5] 6685[9] 7622[6]◆ 7886[3]

**That's A Surprise (IRE)** *Tony Coyle* 72
2 ch c Zoffany(IRE) Sweet Surprise (IRE) (Danetime (IRE))
(4599) 6264[7] 6446[9]

**That's My Girl (IRE)**
*Richard Hannon* a59 63
2 b f Mastercraftsman(IRE) Caribbean Ace (IRE) (Red Clubs (IRE))
3769[5] 4440[11] 4749[5] (5322) 6200[5] 6845[5] 7510[5] 8644[5] 9090[8]

**That's So Cool (IRE)**
*David Simcock* a75
2 b g Born To Sea(IRE) Bibury (Royal Applause)
9299[5]◆

**Thatsthewaytodoit (IRE)**
*Daniel Mark Loughnane* a56 27
4 ch m Lord Shanakill(USA) Van De Cappelle (IRE) (Pivotal)
176[9] 3137[5] 3530[8] 4163[7]

**That Which Is Not (USA)**
*F-H Graffard* a93 105
4 bb m Elusive Quality(USA) Shiva (JPN) (Hector Protector (USA))
2201a[4] 2946a[2] 3856a[5] 6248a[6]

**The Absent Mare**
*Sarah-Jayne Davies* a36 9
9 gr m Fair Mix(IRE) Precious Lucy (FR) (Kadrou (FR))
5896[10]

**The Amber Fort (USA)**
*David O'Meara* a80 74
3 b g Elusive Quality(USA) Unreachable (USA) (Giant's Causeway (USA))
2557[9] 3038[7] 3578[8] 4447[2] 4892[3] 4983[3] 6237[2] 7408[5] 8211[6] 8434[5] 9347[2]

**Theanswermyfriend (AUS)**
*Robert Smerdon* 101
3 b g High Chaparral(IRE) Blowin In The Wind (IRE) (Danehill (USA))
8059a[17]

**The Anvil (IRE)** *A P O'Brien* a84 108
3 b c Galileo(IRE) Brightest (Rainbow Quest (USA))
2555[3] 3322[17] 4387a[8] 7147[11]

**The Armed Man** *Chris Fairhurst* a75 82
4 b g Misu Bond(IRE) Accamelia (Shinko Forest (IRE))
1722[4] 2076[2] (2633) (2923) 3201[2] (3946) 4616[6] (5671) 6205[7] 6662[8]

**Theatre Royale** *Brian Barr*
5 ch m Sulamani(IRE) Theatre Belle (King's Theatre (IRE))
6320[7]

**The Auld Hoose (IRE)**
*Richard Fahey* a42 57
2 gr c Zebedee Merry Moon (IRE) (Night Shift (USA))
5278[7] 5834[11] 6567[5] 7041[13] 7385[6]

**The Bard's Advice** *Keith Dalgleish* a64 42
3 ch f Poet's Voice Flylowflylong (IRE) (Danetime (IRE))
402[4] 510[5] 1127[5] 2374[8] 5074[9]

**The Batham Boy (IRE)**
*Daniel Mark Loughnane* a35 45
3 b g Thewayyouare(USA) Margaux Dancer (IRE) (Danehill Dancer (IRE))
4981[7] 5850[10] 6180[8]

**The Bear Can Fly** *David Menuisier* a31 66
3 b f Pastoral Pursuits Torrecilla (General Monash (USA))
4759[4] 5409[2] 6283[3] 7199[3] 8376[11]

**The Bearfighter (IRE)**
*Charlie Fellowes* a60
2 b c Society Rock(IRE) Absolute Fun (IRE) (Lawman (FR))
8952[7]

**The Big Day (IRE)** *Nigel Tinkler* a23 55
4 gr m Le Cadre Noir(IRE) Grey Galava (Generous (IRE))
176[11]

**The Big Lad** *Richard Hughes* a80 81
5 ch g Kheleyf(USA) Cultured Pride (IRE) (King's Best (USA))
(71) 518[6] 1110[4] 1836[2] 2368[3] 2680[2] 3281[2] 3834[6] 5219[6] 5818[3] 6527[7] 7056[7] 8296[2] 8775[3]

**The Big Short** *Charles Hills* a61 73
3 ch g Bahamian Bounty Royal Punch (Royal Applause)
1970[5] 2306[8] (3818) 4352[5] 6148[3]◆ 6478[2] 7217[2] 7509[5] 8320[8]

**The Black Princess (FR)**
*John Gosden* a73 109
4 b m Iffraaj Larceny (IRE) (Cape Cross (IRE))
(2201a) 2765[2] (4613) 6981a[8] 7669a[7] 8231[5]

**The Blue Bomber** *Mick Channon* a60
5 b g Stimulation(IRE) Mar Blue (FR) (Marju (IRE))
894[3]

**The Blue Eye**
*Jassim Mohammed Ghazali* 109
5 b h Dubawi(IRE) Soneva (USA) (Cherokee Run (USA))
934a[9]

**The Blues Master (IRE)**
*Mark Johnston* a76 78
3 gr g Mastercraftsman(IRE) Catch The Blues (IRE) (Bluebird (USA))
(91) 1877[2]◆ 2526[7] 3335[8] 3711[3] 4004[3] 4307[7] 4998[5] 5799[6] 6210[3]

**The British Lion (IRE)**
*Mark Johnston* a76 43
2 b c Power Mala Mala (IRE) (Brief Truce (USA))
8735[7] 8916[2]◆ 9335[3]

**The Broghie Man**
*Adrian Paul Keatley* 91
2 ch g Cityscape Suelita (Dutch Art)
6977a[4] 7423a[4] 8082a[6] 8777a[3]

**The Burnham Mare (IRE)**
*Barry John Murphy* a70 59
4 b m Kodiac Courte Paille (IRE) (Common Grounds)
1126[10]

**The Cashel Man (IRE)**
*David Simcock* a92 97
5 b g High Chaparral(IRE) Hadarama (IRE) (Sinndar (IRE))
2525[16] 3073[3]

**Thechampagnesonice**
*Malcolm Saunders* a39 49
4 b m Compton Place Extremely Rare (IRE) (Mark Of Esteem (IRE))
5247[8] 6808[4] 7080[5] 7945[9] 8869[12]

**Thechildren'strust (IRE)**
*Gary Moore* 82
2 br g Society Rock(IRE) Estemaala (IRE) (Cape Cross (IRE))
(5504) 7741[3]

**The Cliff Horse (IRE)**
*Donald McCain* 63
2 b f Canford Cliffs(IRE) Ballet School (IRE) (Sadler's Wells (USA))
6433[6] 7045[2] 7819[7]

**The Commendatore** *David Barron* a81 90
4 b g Starspangledbanner(AUS) Donna Giovanna (Mozart (IRE))
(2381) 4353[11] 5671[6] 6429[9] 8014[4]

**Thecornishbarron (IRE)** *John Ryan* a71 68
5 b g Bushranger(IRE) Tripudium (IRE) (Night Shift (USA))
1201[4] 1553[7] 1687[13] 5854[5] 6294[3] 7061[10] 8327[10]

**The Daley Express (IRE)**
*Ronald Harris* a70 90
3 b c Elzaam(AUS) Seraphina (IRE) (Pips Pride)
4159[4] 4965[2] (5253) 5564[6] (6780)◆ 7084[4] 7742[6] 8167[9]

**The Dancing Lord** *Adam West* a44 42
8 br g Imperial Dancer Miss Brookie (The West (USA))
2336[8] 3172[9] 3546[5] 3823[8] 9211[10] 9430[P] (Dead)

**The Detainee** *Neil Mulholland* a61 66
4 b g Aqlaam Jakarta Jade (IRE) (Royal Abjar (USA))
820[3] 1283[8] 1698[2] 2340[5] 2781[14] (4469) (5508) 6095[2]

**The Dukkerer (IRE)** *James Given* a63 66
6 bb m Footstepsinthesand Saffron Crocus (Shareef Dancer (USA))
7[10] 239[6] 390[10] 636[4] 880[8] 1456[2] (2313) 2688[6] 3263[2] 3761[2] 4184[3] 4601[7] 5181[4] 5898[6] 6621[5] 7990[10]

**The Eagle's Nest (IRE)** *Rae Guest* a79 71
3 ch g Lope De Vega(IRE) Follow My Lead (Night Shift (USA))
500[3] 1389a[13] 2547[3] 3336[2] 3862[11] 5009[4] 7894[4]◆ (8206) (9281)

**The Emperor Within (FR)**
*Martin Smith* a58 53
2 b c Holy Roman Emperor(IRE) Watchful (IRE) (Galileo (IRE))
5887[9] 8339[8]

**The Feathered Nest (IRE)**
*Richard Fahey* a87 92
3 b f Dragon Pulse(IRE) Jorum (Dansili)
2122[4] 2856[2]◆ 3793[3] 4435[3] (5423) 7782[9] 9272[7]

**The Fettler (IRE)** *Kevin Frost* 58
2 ch g Rock Of Gibraltar(IRE) Green Empire (IRE) (Second Empire (IRE))
4297[6] 5314[5] 5960[7] 7829[13]

**The Fiddler** *Chris Wall* 60
2 b g Big Bad Bob(IRE) Strings (Unfuwain (USA))
7026[8] 7556[7] 8180[8]

**The Firm (IRE)** *J R Jenkins* a52 70
8 b g Acclamation Aspen Falls (IRE) (Elnadim (USA))
1755[9] 2464[8] 3264[7] 3971[10] 4047[7] 5857[3] 6296[6] 7006[7]

**The Foozler** *Peter Niven* a59
4 ch g Haafhd Blades Baby (Bertolini (USA))
6129[6] 6760[5] 7331[8] 9260[6]

**The Full Swipe (IRE)**
*Tom Dascombe* 60
2 b c Art Connoisseur(IRE) Mar Sin De (IRE) (Danetime (IRE))
1594a[2]

**The Gates Of Dawn (FR)** *F Head* a75 64
2 ch c Iffraaj Cheap Thrills (Bertolini (USA))
5952a[DSQ] 7175a[6] 8302a[2]

**The Gay Cavalier** *John Ryan* a64 72
6 b g Henrythenavigator(USA) Dear Daughter (Polish Precedent (USA))
36[7] 440[9] 958[4] 998[4] 1457[8] 1583[4] 1683[10] 2068[5] 2785[9] (3325) 3966[4] 4047[3] 4365[7] 4522[7] 5119[6] 5299[2] 5555[4] 5888[4] 6475[5] 6557[3] 6848[7] 7052[6] 7541[7] 7735[13] 8386[13] 8550[6] 8846[3] 9027[7] 9078[6] 9211[7] 9406[10]

**The Ginger Berry** *Dr Jon Scargill* a70 47
7 ch g First Trump Dolly Coughdrop (IRE) (Titus Livius (FR))
549[6] 893[2] 1758[8] 3208[7] 3726[6] (6796)

**The Gingerbreadman**
*Chris Fairhurst* a41 42
2 b g Misu Bond(IRE) Accamelia (Shinko Forest (IRE))
4101[7] 5834[12] 6939[7] 7518[19]

**Theglasgowwarrior** *Jim Goldie* a66 69
3 b g Sir Percy Sweet Cando (IRE) (Royal Applause)
1497[10] 1967[7] 2689[12] 3864[2] 4267[2]◆ 5024[3] 6002[2] 6565[9] 8103[4] 8478[5] (9262)

**The Golden Cue** *Steph Hollinshead* 70
2 ch g Zebedee Khafayif (USA) (Swain (IRE))
2522[6] 2890[4] 3406[5] 5262[3] (5546) 6651[8] 7954[7]

**The Graduate (IRE)** *A J Martin* 96
4 gr g Mastercraftsman(IRE) Ballyvarra (IRE) (Sadler's Wells (USA))
7402[9]

**The Grand Visir** *William Haggas* 98
3 b c Frankel Piping (IRE) (Montjeu (IRE))
(2314)◆ 3032[6] 4535[4] (5368) 6445[5] 8011[8]

**The Grape Escape (IRE)**
*Richard Hannon* 110
3 b c Arakan(USA) Bessichka (Exceed And Excel (AUS))
2126[3] 2612[2] 3997[20] (7129) (7892)◆ 8234[20]

**Thegreatcollection (USA)**
*Doug Watson* a105
3 b g Saint Anddan(USA) Cactus Cadillac (USA) (Cactus Ridge (USA))
1040a[9] 8714a[3]

**The Great Dandini (IRE)**
*Seamus Durack* 75
2 b c Dandy Man(IRE) Monivea (IRE) (Fasliyev (USA))
5504[10] 6071[3] 7013[4]

**The Great Wall (USA)**
*Michael Appleby* a88 77
3 b g Bernardini(USA) Music Room (USA) (Unbridled's Song (USA))
(9441)

**The Greedy Boy** *Steve Flook* a48 48
4 b g Atlantic Sport(USA) Indian Girl (Erhaab (USA))
1249[4] 1456[11] 2313[4] 2891[4] 3575[14] 4158[9]

**The Grey Gatsby (IRE)** *D K Weld* 105
6 gr h Mastercraftsman(IRE) Marie Vison (IRE) (Entrepreneur)
4417a[4] 5087a[5] 5862a[4] 6960a[9] 7633a[9]

**The Grey Hobbit** *Ed de Giles* a32
4 gr m Shirocco(GER) Princess Pivotal (Pivotal)
**23[4]**

**The Grey Warrior (IRE)** *Kevin Ryan* a59 73
3 gr g Mastercraftsman(IRE) Cranky Spanky (IRE) (Spectrum (IRE))
1198[3] **1676[3]** 2408[4]

**The Groove** *Fergal O'Brien* a69 70
4 b g Azamour(IRE) Dance East (Shamardal (USA))
4700[5] 5220[9] 5757[4] (6866) **7198[2]** **7465[2]** 7932[3] 8132[5]

**The Happy Hammer (IRE)**
*Eugene Stanford* a71 51
11 b g Acclamation Emma's Star (ITY) (Darshaan)
9849 2976[5] 3702[2] 5512[4] 6681[8] 7323[14] **7770[7]**

**The Happy Prince (IRE)**
*James Moore* a110 114
5 b h Rip Van Winkle(IRE) Maid To Dream (Oasis Dream)
**84a[2]** 206a[6] 696a[9] 773a[11]

**The Hooded Claw (IRE)**
*Patrick Morris* a56 59
6 ch g Dandy Man(IRE) Changari (USA) (Gulch (USA))
9711[0] **3567[5]** 4605[7] **5930[5]** 7910[8] 8742[5] 8873[8] 9267[5]

**The Hoppings** *John Davies* a52
2 b f Kyllachy Rosa Bud (Cape Cross (IRE))
7623[8] **8189[6]**

**The Iron Factor (USA)**
*Phil McEntee* a57
3 b c The Factor(USA) I Am Iron Woman (USA) (Any Given Saturday (USA))
3839[10] 5364[12] **5746[6]**

**The Jean Genie** *Clive Cox* 79
3 bb f Lawman(FR) Miracle Seeker (Rainbow Quest (USA))
1944[9] **3866[6]** 4621[11]

**The Juggler** *William Knight* a60 56
4 b g Archipenko(USA) Oblige (Robellino (USA))
1754[4] 2460[4] 3208[5] 3575[15] 5080[5] 5850[2] **(6621)** **7991[2]** 8346[8]

**The Juliet Rose (FR)** *N Clement* 113
4 bb m Monsun(GER) Dubai Rose (Dubai Destination (USA))
5691a[4] **(7635a)** 8231[4]

**The Jungle VIP** *Mark Johnston* a74
2 b c Leroidesanimaux(BRZ) Alakananda (Hernando (FR))
**8802[2]** 9336[7]

**The Kiddie Kid** *Mick Channon* 35
2 b c Mazameer(IRE) Hi Hoh (IRE) (Fayruz)
**3244[7]** 3655[8] 3918[8]

**The King's Steed** *Shaun Lycett* a54 52
4 b g Equiano(FR) King's Siren (IRE) (King's Best (USA))
2918[12] 3402[15] 3906[6] 5074[4] 7479[9] (7980) **8248[2]** 9237[3]

**The Knot Is Tied (IRE)**
*Tim Easterby* 55
2 b g Casamento(IRE) Really Polish (USA) (Polish Numbers (USA))
**6658[8]** 6967[5] 7556[8]

**The Lacemaker** *Ed Dunlop* a75 57
3 b f Dutch Art Sospel (Kendor (FR))
**2094[3]** 2625[12] 4624[4] 5325[5] 7241[8]

**The Lady Rules**
*Mrs Ilka Gansera-Leveque* a44 50
3 ch f Native Ruler Lady Author (Authorized (IRE))
**5577[9]** 7059[4] 7492[11]

**The Lamplighter (FR)**
*George Baker* a74 78
2 b g Elusive City(USA) Plume Rouge (Pivotal)
5641[11] **7012a[3]** 8302a[3] 8443a[8]

**The Lampo Genie** *Johnny Farrelly* a59 62
5 b g Champs Elysees Samar Qand (Selkirk (USA))
1191[8] **1585[2]** 2712[10]

**The Last Debutante** *Mark Johnston* a65 70
3 b f Henrythenavigator(USA) Lady Eclair (IRE) (Danehill Dancer (IRE))
100[5] 378[2] 627[2] 1331[5] **(2137)**◆

**The Last Emperor** *Roger Varian* 81
2 b c Azamour(IRE) Raskutani (Dansili)
(5036)◆ **5808[2]** 6396[5]

**The Last Melon** *James Bennett* a58 25
5 ch g Sir Percy Step Fast (USA) (Giant's Causeway (USA))
3921[9] 5563[6] **5894[5]** 6953[3] 7730[9] 8246[12] 8396[6] 8815[11]

**The Lincoln Lawyer** *Mark Johnston* a70 72
2 b g Lawman(FR) Adventure Seeker (FR) (Bering)
**8509[3]** 8782[3] 8951[4]

**Thello** *Jim Goldie* a81 70
5 b g Arcano(IRE) Silca Destination (Dubai Destination (USA))
(727) 4082[2] 4538[4] 5417[5] 7570[6] 8209[2] 8928[6] **(9100)**

**The Lock Master (IRE)**
*Michael Appleby* a77 64
10 b g Key Of Luck(USA) Pitrizza (IRE) (Machiavellian (USA))
1546 524[3] 688[6] (853) 1113[3] 1292[6] 1549[3] 2183[5] **(2471)** 3148[6] 3760[6] 4187[8] 8122[9] 8806[10] 9028[6] 9346[7] 9445[6]

**The Love Doctor (IRE)** *David Evans* a58 72
2 b c Elnadim(USA) Street Kitty (IRE) (Tiger Hill (IRE))
1496[2]◆ **1858[4]** 2473[3] 2826[6] 3791[2] 4716[2] 5322[5] 5742[5] 6762[6] 7410[2]

**The Lynch Man** *John Quinn* a69 71
4 b g Sakhee's Secret Diliza (Dilum (USA))
**2773[7]**

**The Magic Pencil (IRE)** *Kevin Ryan* a67 61
4 b g Dream Ahead(USA) Kylemore (IRE) (Sadler's Wells (USA))
1661[0] **360[5]** 1007[5] 1674[2] **1979[3]** 4250[9]

**The Major** *Michael Bell* a69 79
4 b g Major Cadeaux Ballerina Suprema (IRE) (Sadler's Wells (USA))
3009[4] (3537) **(3753)**

**The Mcgregornator (IRE)**
*Adrian Paul Keatley* 81
3 bz g Bushranger(IRE) Bridal Path (Groom Dancer (USA))
**3195[2]** 3386[4]

**The Moore Factor (IRE)** *A J Martin* 87
4 b g Baltic King Belleinga (IRE) (Orpen (USA))
**4822a[7]**

**The Mouse Doctor (IRE)** *A J Martin* a89 89
4 b g Lord Shanakill(USA) Afilla (Dansili)
**6978a[9]**

**The Mums** *John Gosden* a82 76
2 b f Holy Roman Emperor(IRE) Ballyalla (Mind Games)
4253[13] 4902[7] (6138) 7087[6] 8343[7] 9022[3] **9322[3]**

**The Name's Paver** *Noel Wilson* a51 69
4 ch g Monsieur Bond(IRE) Pride Of Kinloch (Dr Devious (IRE))
1680[7] (2179) 2918[7] **3198[2]** 3912[8] 4506[7] 5205[5]

**The Naughty Step (IRE)** *Jim Boyle* 32
2 b g Camacho Echad (IRE) (Kris Kin (USA))
4520[10] 5292[9] **6510[8]** 7273[12]

**The Navigator** *Richard Fahey* 68
2 gr g Mastercraftsman(IRE) Blessing (USA) (Pulpit (USA))
**8215[3]**◆

**The Nazca Lines (IRE)** *John Quinn* a74 80
3 ch g Fast Company(IRE) Princess Banu (Oasis Dream)
2992[3] 3664[7] 4104[2]◆ 4576[2] **(4835)** 5211[8] 5837[5] 6308[3] 6670[5] 7572[8]

**The New Master** *David Elsworth* a73 24
4 br g New Approach(IRE) Maziona (Dansili)
**2152[12]** 4267[9]

**The New Pharaoh (IRE)** *Chris Wall* a70 81
6 b g Montjeu(IRE) Out West (USA) (Gone West (USA))
2020[6] 2622[7] 4345[2] **(5313)** 5830[5] 7024[4] 7924[3] 8394[2]

**The Night Before** *Robert Cowell* 60
3 b g Equiano(FR) Morning After (Emperor Jones (USA))
4964[5] 5636[6] 6469[2]◆ **6896[2]**

**The Night King** *Mick Channon* a50 66
2 b g Arcano(IRE) Semplicita (IRE) (In The Wings)
6367[7] **6505[5]** 6859[8] 7829[11]

**Theo (GER)** *Waldemar Hickst*
2 bb c Manduro(GER) Tickle Me Pink I (Groom Dancer (USA))
6986a[8] 8091a[7]

**Theobald (IRE)** *J S Bolger* a93 102
2 ch c Teofilo(IRE) Sanaara (USA) (Anabaa (USA))
**4926a[2]** 5345a[2] 6955a[8] 8037[7] 8415[12]

**Theodorico (IRE)** *David Loughnane* a42 95
4 b g Teofilo(IRE) Yes Oh Yes (USA) (Gone West (USA))
1224[9] 2146[8] (2684) **(3095)** 3842[11] 4103[4] 4578[7] 5396[6] (5669) 6192[5] 6879[6] 7340[3] 7622[11] 8104[4]

**Theos Lolly (IRE)** *Richard Fahey* a78 85
4 b g Kodiac Aluana (IRE) (Alzao (USA))
1707[5] 2333[8] 2787[2] (3983) 4357[12] **4893[2]** 5403[5] 6232[5] 6757[4]

**The Otmoor Poet** *Alex Hales* a78 83
4 b g Yeats(IRE) Kristalette (IRE) (Leporello (IRE))
**2478[2]** 3067[10] 4216[5]

**The Pantry (IRE)** *A Giorgi* 88
2 gr f Zebedee Break Bread (IRE) (Big Bad Bob (IRE))
**(8253a)**

**The Pentagon (IRE)** *A P O'Brien* 112
2 b c Galileo(IRE) Vadawina (IRE) (Unfuwain (USA))
(5345a) **8415[3]**

**The Perfect Show** *Milton Bradley* a45 60
4 ch g Showcasing Nizhoni (USA) (Mineshaft (USA))
2675[7] **2962[7]** 3186[10] 3468[8] 4149[10] 5050[14] 5429[9] 8137[9]

**The Pizza Man (USA)**
*Roger Brueggemann* 113
8 b g English Channel(USA) I Can Fan Fan (USA) (Lear Fan (USA))
**5977a[12]**

**The Quarterjack** *Ron Hodges* a55 61
8 b g Haafhd Caressed (Medicean)
1369[8] **1697[6]** 2219[4] 2712[7] 3026[6]

**The Raven Master (IRE)**
*Michael Bell* a69 61
3 b g Raven's Pass(USA) Rainbow Desert (USA) (Dynaformer (USA))
1083[5] 1358[6] 1551[9] **2371[3]** 2703[3]

**The Reel Way (GR)**
*Patrick Chamings* a34 49
6 br m Reel Buddy(USA) Nephetriti Way (IRE) (Docksider (USA))
**274[9]** 640[10]

**The Resdev Way** *Philip Kirby* a83 56
4 b g Multiplex Lady Duxyana (Most Welcome)
1976[10] 5417[12] 6061[6] **7925[7]**

**The Revenant** *Hugo Palmer* 93
2 ch c Dubawi(IRE) Hazel Lavery (IRE) (Excellent Art)
(6854)◆ **7648[3]**◆

**The Right Choice (IRE)**
*Richard Fahey* 69
2 ch g Choisir(AUS) Expedience (USA) (With Approval (CAN))
2698[4]◆ **3538[3]** 4526[9] **4922[3]**◆

**The Right Man** *D Guillemin* 120
5 br g Lope De Vega(IRE) Three Owls (IRE) (Warning)
1044a[3]◆ **(1376a)** 4071[11] 5690a[7] **(8526a)** 9168a[8]

**Therthaar** *Ismail Mohammed* a83 76
4 b g Kyllachy Red Tiara (USA) (Mr Prospector (USA))
1839[2] 2267[2] 3036[2] (4260) 5820[7] **(6937)**◆

**The Salmon Man** *Brendan Powell* a77 68
5 b g Showcasing Donna Vita (Vettori (IRE))
3920[6] **4519[5]** 6293[12] 6610[5] 8813[P]

**The Secrets Out** *Luke Dace* a63 61
3 bl g Sakhee's Secret Brooksby (Diktat)
1550[11] 2016[12] 2732[6] (3674) 4087[2] 4156[2] 5406[4] **6180[2]** 6443[4]

**The Sky Is Blazing (IRE)**
*William Haggas* a83 94
3 b f Sea The Stars(IRE) Mamonta (Fantastic Light (USA))
(1471) 2613[3]◆ 3094[4] **3995[8]**

**Thesme** *Nigel Tinkler* 109
5 b m Exceed And Excel(AUS) Final Dynasty (Komaite (USA))
2397[14] 3079[12] 3932[3] **6325[3]** 7051[5] 7396[11] 7887[9]

**The Special One (IRE)** *Ali Stronge* a63 61
4 br m Cape Cross(IRE) Capote West (USA) (Capote (USA))
684[8] 1139[3] 1425[8] 2294[4] 2976[6] (4969) (5792) 6751[6] (7213) 7916[4] **9094[3]** 9431[3]

**The Stalking Moon (IRE)**
*John Quinn* a50 80
3 b f Arcano(IRE) Cornakill (USA) (Stormin Fever (USA))
2503[2] 3171[4] 3561[3] 4209[4] (4744) 5007[7] **(5601)** 5881[6] 6627[4] 7474[11] 8192[9]

**The Statesman** *Ian Williams* a75 99
3 b g Zoffany(IRE) Chelsey Jayne (IRE) (Galileo (IRE))
3293[3] (3838) 4376[7] 4904[6] 6187[3] 6671[2]◆ (7277) **(7400)**

**The Tabulator (USA)** *Larry Rivelli* a100
2 bb c Dialed In(USA) Fly To The Stars (USA) (Giant's Causeway (USA))
**8609a[5]**

**The Taj (USA)** *Doug Watson* a90 88
7 ch g Street Cry(IRE) India (USA) (Hennessy (USA))
**321a[5]**

**The Taj Mahal (IRE)** *A P O'Brien* a90 114
3 b c Galileo(IRE) You'resothrilling (USA) (Storm Cat (USA))
1633a[2] 3368a[4] 3994[4] 4387a[6] 4638[9] 5953a[2] **6960a[5]** 8058a[10] 8753a[4]

**The Tartan Spartan (IRE)**
*John Patrick Shanahan* 105
4 ch h The Carbon Unit(USA) The Real Thing (IRE) (Traditionally (USA))
1802[3] (2176) 3090[5] 6191[7] **6675[7]** 6976a[7]

**The Throstles** *Kevin Frost* a71 67
2 b g Poet's Voice Stylish Dream (USA) (Elusive Quality (USA))
4452[4] 5437[3] (5847) 7106[8] **8245[6]**

**The Tichborne (IRE)** *Patrick Morris* a75 75
9 b g Shinko Forest(IRE) Brunswick (Warning)
**363[8]**

**The Tin Man** *James Fanshawe* 120
5 b g Equiano(FR) Persario (Bishop Of Cashel)
2737[5] **(4071)** 4907[8] 6926[3] 8230[5]

**Thetrioandme (IRE)** *John Best* a66 43
3 b g Tagula(IRE) Peninsula Girl (IRE) (Cape Cross (IRE))
**464[4]**

**The Twisler** *Neil Mulholland* a59 100
5 b g Motivator Panna (Polish Precedent (USA))
38[9] 519[8] 5166[6] **6038[3]** 6398[3]

**The Wagon Wheel (IRE)**
*Richard Fahey* 102
3 b f Acclamation Bahati (IRE) (Intikhab (USA))
2400[6] 3071[9] 3844[2] **(4889)** 5637[9] 6234[12] 6668[3] 7887[6] 8040[9]

**The Warrior (IRE)** *Amanda Perrett* a95 97
5 b g Exceed And Excel(AUS) Aymara (Darshaan)
896[3] 1288[2] (1422) 1766[4] 2026[5]◆ 2390[3] 2606[8] 3003[2] 3620[5] 3837[10] 5530[7] 5942[4] 6322[4]◆ 6933[2] 7549[4] **8032[2]**

**The Way You Dance (IRE)**
*Neil Mulholland* a67 63
5 b g Thewayyouare(USA) Beautiful Dancer (IRE) (Danehill Dancer (IRE))
**1364[8]** 6781[3] 7413[10] 7730[12] 7992[4]

**The Wee Chief (IRE)** *Jimmy Fox* a49 59
11 ch g King Charlemagne(USA) La Belle Clare (IRE) (Paris House)
**1022[6]**

**Thewestwalian (USA)** *Peter Hiatt* a50 58
9 bb g Stormy Atlantic(USA) Skies Of Blue (USA) (Ogygian (USA))
3084[10] **3280[2]** 3696[11] 3811[7]

**The Wire Flyer** *Amy Murphy* a11
2 b g Champs Elysees Good Morning Star (IRE) (Shirocco (GER))
**9299[12]**

**Thewizardofoz (AUS)** *J Size* 121
5 b g Redoute's Choice(AUS) Princess Coup (AUS) (Encosta De Lago (AUS))
**9168a[7]**

**The Yank** *David Bridgwater* a70 52
8 b g Trade Fair Silver Gyre (IRE) (Silver Hawk (USA))
**1519[11]**

**Theydon Girls** *Peter Charalambous* a43 58
4 b m Poet's Voice Match Point (Unfuwain (USA))
2515[7] **(3440)** 3699[3] 5080[12]

**Theydon Grey** *William Haggas* a90 98
4 gr g Champs Elysees Cheerfully (Sadler's Wells (USA))
2068[4] 2741[4] (3091) (3794) **(4921)** 6427[5] 7337[8]

**The Yellow Bus** *Daniel Steele* a79 76
4 b m Zoffany(IRE) Caribbean Queen (IRE) (Celtic Swing)
1066[5] 1419[5] 2285[4] **(4728)** 5510[4] 6818[5] 7710[7] 8295[13] 8886[6] 9093[9] 9364[10]

**Thikriyaat (IRE)** *Sir Michael Stoute* a78 112
4 b g Azamour(IRE) Malaspina (IRE) (Whipper (USA))
2767[10] **3843[3]** 4362[7] 5148[4]

**Things Happen** *David Evans* a71 62
3 ch g Captain Gerrard(IRE) Aquasulis (IRE) (Titus Livius (FR))
2[2] 72[2] 221[5] 578[5] **(718)** 1343[5] 1686[12]

**Think Fashion (IRE)** *Brian Meehan* 88
3 b f So You Think(NZ) Passionforfashion (IRE) (Fasliyev (USA))
**1958[9]** 2619[3] 3157[3] (3669) 5325[8] 6098[5]

**Think So (IRE)** *Mark Johnston* 48
3 b g So You Think(NZ) Mabalane (IRE) (Danehill (USA))
**3248[7]** 3657[10] 4967[12]

**Third Order (IRE)**
*Jassim Mohammed Ghazali* a70 80
3 b c Hat Trick(JPN) Fifth Commandment (IRE) (Holy Roman Emperor (IRE))
**933a[12]**

**Third Time Lucky (IRE)**
*Richard Fahey* a106 93
5 gr g Clodovil(IRE) Speckled Hen (IRE) (Titus Livius (FR))
2354 (744) **1023[3]** 1494[17] 1775[5] 8843[9] 8999[9] 9468[3]◆

**This Girl** *Tom Dascombe* 84
2 b f Nathaniel(IRE) Fibou (USA) (Seeking The Gold (USA))
**(7563)**◆

**Thistimelastyear** *Philip Hide* a55
2 b f Cacique(IRE) Despatch (Nayef (USA))
8147[6] **9081[9]** 9318[3]

**Thistimenextyear** *Richard Spencer* a74 81
3 gr g New Approach(IRE) Scarlet Empire (IRE) (Red Ransom (USA))
2159[4] 3209[13] **(5141)** 6033[4]◆ 9000[10]

**Thomas Blossom (IRE)** *Ali Stronge* a70 66
7 b g Dylan Thomas(IRE) Woman Secret (IRE) (Sadler's Wells (USA))
290[3] **508[2]** 2364[4] 2972[10]

**Thomas Cranmer (USA)**
*Mark Johnston* a79 93
3 b g Hard Spun(USA) House Of Grace (USA) (Limehouse (USA))
1546[3] (2374) 3045[5] **(3336)** 3592[11] 3997[25] 4507[6] 5302[5] 5744[12] 6426[6] 6894[6] 7229[6] 7941[8] 8418[10]

**Thomas Crown (IRE)** *Roger Fell* 44
3 b g Helmet(AUS) Picture Of Lily (Medicean)
2110[5] **2345[6]**◆ 3461[8] 3913[12] 4172[5] 4839[7] 5209[8] 5493[7] 5618[7] 6565[5]

**Thomas Hobson** *W P Mullins* a68 115
7 b g Halling(USA) La Spezia (IRE) (Danehill Dancer (IRE))
**(3928)** 4073[2] 6400[7] 7116[2] 8667a[6]

**Thornaby Nash** *Karen Tutty* a61 61
6 br g Kheleyf(USA) Mistress Twister (Pivotal)
2918[5] **3181[2]** 3560[4] 4690[8] 5214[6] 5544[7] 6182[5] (6549) 7042[4] 7240[4] 8589[9] 8719[4]

**Thornaby Princess** *Colin Teague* a46 48
6 b m Camacho Ingleby Princess (Bold Edge)
2337[3] 2628[5] 2994[7] **3944[4]** 4559[11] 6631[9] 6896[3] 7366[4] 7575[8]

**Thornton** *Michael Dods* a63 74
3 b g Mayson Cardrona (Selkirk (USA))
**3435[2]** 4309[7] 5139[5] 5666[13]

**Thornton Frank** *Brian Rothwell*
3 b g Misu Bond(IRE) Byton (Byron)
8781[7] 9304[8]

**Thornton Mary** *Brian Rothwell* a42 38
3 b f Mawatheeq(USA) Bezant (IRE) (Zamindar (USA))
**2345[8]** 2902[7] 4603[7] 5182[12] 5617[8] 6048[11]

**Thorntoun Care** *Iain Jardine* a65 75
6 b g Rail Link Thorntoun Piccolo (Groom Dancer (USA))
509[6] 726[6] 990[6] 1257[1] 1458[7] (1629) 1985[4] 2340[4] 3043[9] 3193[4] 3978[2] (4839) 5454[2] 5701[4] (5883) 6551[2] **6858[2]** 7560[7]

**Thorntoun Lady (USA)** *Jim Goldie* a66 58
7 b m Henrythenavigator(USA) Valery Lady (ARG) (Roy (USA))
45[7] 362[5] 582[5] 732[9] **6437[4]**◆ 6896[6] 7889[11] 8402[7] **(8495)**

**Thousand Grands (GER)** *G Botti* 75
2 ch c French Fifteen(FR) Tintagel (Oasis Dream)
**(8101a)**

**Thousand Oaks (FR)** *B De Montzey*
2 b f Penny's Picnic(IRE) Brise Oceanne (FR) (Kendor (FR))
1282a[2]

**Thou Swell (IRE)** *Shaun Harris* a60 50
5 b g Tiznow(USA) Kamarinskaya (USA) (Storm Cat (USA))
315[7] 395[6] **(661)** 1188[3] 1629[6] 1864[7] 2312[7] 2815[9] 3726[9] 6035[13] 6524[10]

**Thrave** *Henry Candy* 89
2 b c Sir Percy Feis Ceoil (IRE) (Key Of Luck (USA))
6388[2]◆ **(7580)**

**Threading (IRE)** *Mark Johnston* 110
2 b f Exceed And Excel(AUS) Chaquiras (USA) (Seeking The Gold (USA))
(5528) **(6354)** 7617[7]

**Threat Assessed (IRE)** *Clive Cox* 90
4 b g Holy Roman Emperor(IRE) High Reserve (Dr Fong (USA))
7395[15] **8165[11]**

**Threeandfourpence (USA)**
*A P O'Brien* 108
2 b c War Front(USA) Liscanna (IRE) (Sadler's Wells (USA))
**8037[4]**

**Threebagsue (IRE)** *J S Moore* a82 72
4 ch m Lord Shanakill(USA) Feet Of Flame (USA) (Theatrical (IRE))
97[5] (304) **810[2]**

**Three Colours Red (IRE)**
*Robert Stephens* a68 65
5 b g Camacho Colour's Red (IRE) (Red Ransom (USA))
1436[4] **(2059)** 4791[3]

**Three C's (IRE)** *David Dennis* a59 78
3 b g Kodiac Ms Mary C (IRE) (Dolphin Street (FR))
1321[4] 1761[P] 2474[14] **3543[5]** **3810[3]** 4302[9] 4731[12] 5418[8] 5703[6] 6271[11]

**Threediamondrings** *Mark Usher* a69 47
4 ch g Geordieland(FR) Five Gold Rings (IRE) (Captain Rio)
163[9] 2111[10] 6196[8] 6588[7] **8313[7]** 8662[9]

**Three Duchesses** *Michael Bell* a64 89
3 b f Dutch Art Three Ducks (Diktat)
*2274[10] 2929[4] 3859[4]* (4761)◆ (5017)◆ 5529[6]
**6477[3]** 7119[3]◆

**Three Little Birds** *Sylvester Kirk* a73 73
2 b f Dandy Man(IRE) Oilinda (Nayef (USA))
*2258[2] 2545[2] 3230[3]* **3821[2]** 4220[3] 5150[7] 5575[6]
6719[4] *7491[2]* ***(8154)***

**Three Loves (IRE)** *Stuart Williams* a56 55
4 b m Duke Of Marmalade(IRE) Three Moons (IRE) (Montjeu (IRE))
**3726[4]** 4469[6] 5508[6]

**Three Majors (IRE)**
*Anthony McCann* a58 56
4 b g Lilbourne Lad(IRE) Saricana (IRE) (Invincible Spirit (IRE))
***2166[6]*** *2919[7]*

**Three's A Crowd (IRE)** *Ed de Giles* a50 33
3 br g Vocalised(USA) Tense (IRE) (Invincible Spirit (IRE))
*1727[10]* 2930[7] ***4164[8]*** *7323[13] 9073[9] 9268[6] 9454[13]*

**Three Saints Bay (IRE)**
*David O'Meara* a84 77
2 b g Kodiac Fiuise (IRE) (Montjeu (IRE))
5735[2] 6590[4] 7383[2] (7819) ***8317[4]***

**Three Star General** *David Pipe* 78
4 b g Montjeu(IRE) Honorlina (FR) (Linamix (FR))
**2388[11]**

**Three Weeks (USA)**
*William Haggas* a78
2 rg c Tapit(USA) Midnight Thoughts (USA) (Henrythenavigator (USA))
*8888[8]* ***(9318)***

**Thresholdofadream (IRE)**
*Amanda Perrett* 53
2 b f Camelot Signella (Selkirk (USA))
**8419[10]**

**Thrifty** *Tim Easterby* a63 55
2 b f Harbour Watch(IRE) Isobel Rose (IRE) (Royal Applause)
***1776[2]*** 2222[4] 2988[6] 4527[11]

**Throckley** *Conor Dore* a87 83
6 b g Passing Glance Porcelain (IRE) (Peintre Celebre (USA))
2629[2] **3845[2]** 4658[7] 5668[10] 6434[10] 7142[5] 7824[9]
***(8806)*** *9000[12]* ***(9306)***

**Thrones Game (FR)**
*A De Royer-Dupre* a78 100
4 b m Soldier Of Fortune(IRE) Sirenita (IRE) (Mull Of Kintyre (USA))
**5691a[6]**

**Thrtypointstothree (IRE)**
*Nikki Evans* a44 47
6 b g Kodiac Miss Taken (IRE) (Dubai Destination (USA))
***998[6]*** *1075[10]*

**Thrust Home (IRE)** *Y Durepaire* a68 97
3 b f Fastnet Rock(AUS) Garden City (FR) (Majorien)
**5196a[5]**

**Thunderbell** *Scott Dixon* a52
3 ch f Haafhd Trustthunder (Selkirk (USA))
***9071[7]***

**Thunderbolt Rocks** *Hugo Palmer* a76 47
2 b c Farhh Coquette Noire (IRE) (Holy Roman Emperor (IRE))
8387[12] ***(8951)***

**Thundercloud** *Scott Dixon* a37 58
2 gr f Aussie Rules(USA) Trustthunder (Selkirk (USA))
3312[12] **3858[6]** 4567[12] *8982[8] 9175[5] 9439[12]*

**Thunderhooves** *John Ryan* 61
2 ro c Raven's Pass(USA) Regrette Rien (USA) (Unbridled's Song (USA))
**7117[8]** 7580[15]

**Thundering Blue (USA)**
*David Menuisier* a78 96
4 gr g Exchange Rate(USA) Relampago Azul (USA) (Forestry (USA))
*1462[3]* 1969[13] *2369[3]*◆ 4522[3] (5066)◆ (5940)◆
**(6698) 7619[7]**

**Thundering Sky (USA)**
*George Weaver* 104
4 bb m Sky Mesa(USA) Uninhibited Song (USA) (Unbridled's Song (USA))
**8601a[2]**

**Thunder North (IRE)** *David Lanigan* a60 58
2 b c Dansili Maidin Maith (IRE) (Montjeu (IRE))
4049[7] 6108[11] ***7237[10]***

**Thunder Snow (IRE)**
*Saeed bin Suroor* a115 119
3 b c Helmet(AUS) Eastern Joy (Dubai Destination (USA))
*(697a) (1375a) 2420a[P]* **3100a[2]** 3927[3] **(4666a)**
**5980a[3]** 8232[15]

**Thurgovia (IRE)** *D Smaga* a84 85
4 b m Fastnet Rock(AUS) T'As D'Beaux Yeux (Red Ransom (USA))
**2559a[5]**

**Tia Maria (GER)** *A Wohler*
2 b f Maxios Trimurti (USA) (Harlan's Holiday (USA))
8461a[9]

**Tiara Gold** *Rae Guest* 60
2 ch f Poet's Voice Dress Code (IRE) (Barathea (IRE))
**7265[3]**

**Tiar Na Nog (IRE)** *Denis Coakley* a64
5 b m Ask Carmencita (Rock Of Gibraltar (IRE))
***6320[3]*** *7948[8] 9235[3]*◆

**Tiberian (FR)** *Alain Couetil* 115
5 b h Tiberius Caesar(FR) Toamasina (FR) (Marju (IRE))
(2485a) 4423a[7] (5692a) **(6499a)** 8667a[7] 9167a[11]

**Tiberio (SPA)** *F-X Belvisi* a55 64
7 ch g Panis(USA) Peinture D'Or (IRE) (Peintre Celebre (USA))
***713a[6]***

**Tibibit** *Henry Tett* a70 65
4 b m Kyllachy Cat Hunter (One Cool Cat (USA))
*168[5] 503[2]* ***624[2]*** *811[8]* 5118[5] *6795[8]*

**Ticks The Boxes (IRE)**
*John Wainwright* a82 72
5 ch g Fast Company(IRE) Swan Sea (USA) (Sea Hero (USA))
*1524* ***363[2]*** *551[8] 850[12] 971[6] 1007[4] (1310) 1592[2]*
2104[5] 2700[6] *2923[8]* 3666[6] 4506[5] 5620[3]◆ 5696[3]
6049[2] 6964[14] 7332[7] 8480[3] *8772[5] 9307[10]*

**Ticonderoga (USA)** *Chad C Brown* 103
3 b c Tapit(USA) Keertana (USA) (Johar (USA))
**4652a[9]**

**Tidal's Baby** *Adrian Brendan Joyce* a62 49
8 b g Dutch Art Tidal (Bin Ajwaad (IRE))
*273[2] 768[2] 1603[2]* 2294[2] **3397[2]** 5429[2] 5817[3]
*6800a[4] 8494[2]*

**Tidal Watch (IRE)** *Jonjo O'Neill* 72
3 b g Harbour Watch(IRE) Najmati (Green Desert (USA))
2475[10] **2782[3]** 3435[4] 4537[7]

**Tie Em Up Tel (IRE)** *David Evans* 64
2 b c Sir Prancealot(IRE) Cinarosa (IRE) (Kodiac)
*1694[7]* 2343[5] 3619[3] **(3918)** 4740[4] 5293[4] (5613)

**Tiepolo (IRE)** *Gary Moore* a68 74
2 gr g Dark Angel(IRE) Trempjane (Lujain (USA))
4151[13] **5865[2]** 6438[3] 6721[3] 7914[7] *8131[6]*

**Tiercel** *Roger Varian* a91 93
4 b h Olden Times Sharp Mode (USA) (Diesis)
*7941[7]* ***8821[3]***

**Tiffin Top** *John Gosden* 72
2 gr c Oasis Dream Mussoorie (FR) (Linamix (FR))
**7117[4]** 7543[7]

**Tifl** *Heather Main* a66 56
4 ch g Approve(IRE) Isobel Rose (IRE) (Royal Applause)
***354[5]*** *727[11] 986[9]* 5111[9] *5793[11]* (6507) 7212[3]◆
*7517[12] 8134[12]* 8470[3] *(8720)*

**Tigerfilly** *John Ryan* 56
2 ch f Equiano(FR) Bestfootforward (Motivator)
**7504[6]** 8118[4]

**Tigerfish (IRE)** *William Stone* a52 62
3 b f Lilbourne Lad(IRE) Nisriyna (IRE) (Intikhab (USA))
*210[4] 377[5] 463[3] (644) (897) 1451[5]* 2507[5]◆ 3246[7]
(3661) (4714) **5512[2]** *5848[6]* 7212[10] *8948[9] 9454[4]*

**Tiger Jim** *Jim Goldie* a82 92
7 b g Tiger Hill(IRE) Quintrell (Royal Applause)
1512[18] **1831[2]**

**Tiger Khan** *Harry Dunlop* 45
3 b g Zamindar(USA) Waitingonacloud (In The Wings)
2689[15] **3247[4]**

**Tiger Lyon (USA)** *John Butler* a65 29
2 b c Kitten's Joy(USA) Hold It (USA) (Discreet Cat (USA))
4862[10] *8149[8] 8703[11] 9024[3]* ***(9298)***◆

**Tigershark (IRE)** *Bryan Smart* 57
2 gr c Lethal Force(IRE) Fearless Flyer (IRE) (Brave Act)
**7818[6]**

**Tigerwolf (IRE)**
*Daniel Mark Loughnane* a73 75
4 br g Dream Ahead(USA) Singing Field (IRE) (Singspiel (IRE))
2054[5] 4719[10] 5842[5] **6378[6]** 6555[4] 7157[6] *7881[4]*
*8341[6] 9078[8] 9303[6]*

**Tight Lines** *Mark Johnston* 83
2 b f Fastnet Rock(AUS) Dusty Answer (Zafonic (USA))
4681[5] **(5180)**

**Tigre Du Terre (FR)**
*Richard Hannon* 100
2 b c Le Havre(IRE) Allmia (FR) (Johann Quatz (FR))
(4885)◆ 5395[4] 6396[3] **7112[2]**

**Tigserin (IRE)** *Giles Bravery* a73 63
4 ch m Approve(IRE) Mairead Anne (USA) (Elusive Quality (USA))
*1326[7]* **2124[4]** 2900[5] ***3139[3]*** 3702[8] *4561[6]* 5813[6]
*7517[5]*

**Tig Tog (IRE)** *Richard Hannon* a75 74
2 b f Dark Angel(IRE) Deira Dubai (Green Desert (USA))
3858[5] 4253[2]◆ 5056[4] 5659[8] 6375[3] ***6932[3]***

**Tihana** *John Murray* a50 55
4 b m Lawman(FR) La Bocca (USA) (Latent Heat (USA))
***95[4]***◆ *216[9]*

**Tikiouine (FR)** *Carmen Bocskai* a78 91
5 gr m Mastercraftsman(IRE) Mislix (FR) (Linamix (FR))
6451a[7] **6665a[7]**

**Tikitiki (FR)** *Mlle J Soudan* a77 93
3 b f Fastnet Rock(AUS) Green Diamond Lady (USA) (Johannesburg (USA))
**5196a[6]** 7845a[6]

**Tilly Devine** *Scott Dixon* a55 28
3 gr f Aussie Rules(USA) Cora Pearl (IRE) (Montjeu (IRE))
4302[7] 5542[13] *7761[14] 8538[10] 8801[14]* ***(9034)***
*9342[5] 9365[5]*

**Tilly's Bridge** *Steve Woodman* a49 3
4 b m Avonbridge Ivory Lace (Atraf)
***464[7]*** *863[8] 1287[8] 1894[10]* 2294[10] 4695[13]

**Tilly's Chilli (IRE)**
*Mrs John Harrington* a55 91
3 b f Excelebration(IRE) Scotch Bonnet (IRE) (Montjeu (IRE))
**5088a[3]** 5766a[8] 6956a[18] **8086a[2]**

**Tilly Tinker** *Michael Easterby* a14 60
3 ch f Doncaster Rover(USA) Lawless Bridget (Alnasr Alwasheek)
1680[10] 2185[14] 3054[6] **3448[3]** 4209[8] *8210[13]*

**Tilly Trotter (IRE)** *Declan Carroll* a92 82
3 b f Kodiac Inourthoughts (IRE) (Desert Style (IRE))
4435[5] 5117[10] 7055[8] 7553[6] *7939[4] (8717) 9016[7]*
*9079[2]* ***(9366)***

**Tilo (IRE)** *Simone Brogi*
3 ch c Sepoy(AUS) Wendy House (USA) (Medaglia d'Oro (USA))
*584a[4]*

**Tilsworth Lukey** *J R Jenkins* a37 48
4 b g Sixties Icon Chara (Deploy)
*1141[7] 1488[10]* 3438[11] 5285[8] **7254[6]** *9139[5] 9304[5]*

**Tilsworth Micky** *J R Jenkins* a64 56
5 br g Kheleyf(USA) Tilsworth Charlie (Dansili)
*209* ***(273)*** *601[P] 1180[8] 1490[P]* 3442[10] 4149[P]

**Time Change** *Ralph Beckett* 76
2 ch f Dutch Art Time Honoured (Sadler's Wells (USA))
3312[2]◆ (4253) **6396[4]** 7621[10]

**Time Chant** *Stefano Botti* 103
5 b g War Chant(USA) Snowfield (USA) (Tale Of The Cat (USA))
**2866a[3]** 3884a[7]

**Time Chaser** *Roger Charlton* a80 96
3 b f Dubawi(IRE) Passage Of Time (Dansili)
*(2019)* (3786) **(5841)**◆ 6924[3] 8739[8]

**Time Constraints (USA)**
*Anthony Carson* a77 33
3 b g Gio Ponti(USA) Escape To Victory (Salse (USA))
**7287[8]**

**Time Continuum** *Eric Alston* 23
5 b m Monsieur Bond(IRE) Primum Tempus (Primo Dominie)
**4604[8]** 5736[8] *6528[14]*

**Time Exposed (IRE)** *K R Burke* 15
2 b f High Chaparral(IRE) Palace Of Winds (IRE) (Monsun (GER))
**5537[12]**

**Time Flies** *S bin Ghadayer* a94 89
5 b g Exceed And Excel(AUS) Simply Times (USA) (Dodge (USA))
**250a[4]**

**Time For Treacle** *Ben Haslam* a13 60
2 b f Sayif(IRE) Fiancee (IRE) (Pivotal)
*1776[9]* **2890[3]** 3447[2] 4054[3] 5613[6] 7518[18]

**Time For Wine (IRE)** *David Evans* 73
2 b f Equiano(FR) Steam Cuisine (Mark Of Esteem (IRE))
3917[6] 5048[8] **5476[2] 5839[2] 6338[2]** 7126[3] 7688[3]

**Timeless Art (IRE)** *K R Burke* a92 91
4 b g Medicean Bellona (IRE) (Bering)
1512[3] 1860[7] 3014[5] 3651[4]◆ 4685[3] 5664[9] ***(6322)***
*6933[15] 7941[10]*

**Timeless Gift (IRE)**
*Matthieu Palussiere* a18 62
2 b f Camacho Thats Your Opinion (Last Tycoon)
*6452a[8]* **8253a[6]** *8482a[16]*

**Timeline (USA)** *Chad C Brown* a111
3 ch c Hard Spun(USA) Azorina (USA) (Empire Maker (USA))
***5463a[5]***

**Timely Arrival** *Amanda Perrett* a71 11
3 b c Cacique(IRE) Winter Bloom (USA) (Aptitude (USA))
5611[13] ***7542[3]***

**Time Medicean** *Tony Carroll* a47 66
11 gr g Medicean Ribbons And Bows (IRE) (Dr Devious (IRE))
3811[8] 5146[2] 5817[4] 6197[10] 6748[3] **7191[2]** 7692[2]
7911[7]

**Time Of My Life (GER)**
*Patrick Holmes* a88 88
6 ch g Nayef(USA) Tamaja (GER) (Tiger Hill (IRE))
*7285* ***991[4]***

**Time's Arrow (IRE)** *P Sogorb* a88 78
3 b c Redoute's Choice(AUS) Gilt Edge Girl (Monsieur Bond (IRE))
*1488[8] 2090[2]* ***2366[2]*** 3206[2] (3945) 5115[8] 6963a[7]

**Time Shanakill (IRE)** *G Botti* a97 90
4 b g Lord Shanakill(USA) Cherry Creek (IRE) (Montjeu (IRE))
***9003a[5]***

**Times In Anatefka (IRE)**
*Adrian Brendan Joyce* a66 29
7 b m Pyrus(USA) Brooklands Time (IRE) (Danetime (IRE))
*(722)* ***(742)***◆ 2656a[17]

**Time To Blossom** *Simon Crisford* a77 86
4 b m Cape Cross(IRE) Time Over (Mark Of Esteem (IRE))
**(6431)** 7231[9]

**Time To Choose** *Stefano Botti* 109
4 b h Manduro(GER) Penfection (IRE) (Orpen (USA))
**(2663a)** 3884a[4] 7442a[3] **(8448a)** 8963a[4]

**Time To Exceed (IRE)** *Henry Candy* 88
4 b m Exceed And Excel(AUS) In Your Time (Dalakhani (IRE))
(2147) **2692[2]** 3620[9]

**Time To Perfection (IRE)**
*Sylvester Kirk* a63
2 gr f Mastercraftsman(IRE) Time Ahead (Spectrum (IRE))
*7937[7]* ***8399[4]*** *8849[7]*

**Time To Reason (IRE)** *J P Murtagh* a87 83
4 b g Kyllachy Danehurst (Danehill (USA))
***8222a[7]***

**Timetosaygoodbye (TUR)** *S Bilgic* 67
2 b f Raven's Pass(USA) Enhance (Entrepreneur)
**6745a[7]**

**Time To Sea (IRE)** *John Butler* a69 70
3 b g Born To Sea(IRE) Eastern Glow (Cape Cross (IRE))
*1818[7]* 2231[7] 2931[5] **3627[4]** 4320[5] 5536[3] 6144[3]
6767[3] *7712[4]*

**Time To Study (FR)** *Mark Johnston* a85 108
3 ch c Motivator Dissertation (FR) (Sillery (USA))
2824[3] (3335) 4032[5] 6930[3] **(7115)** 8038[17] (8391)

**Time Trail** *Michael Dods* 76
2 b f Swiss Spirit Starbeck (IRE) (Spectrum (IRE))
(2221) **(2987)** 5150[21] 5614[5] 7954[4] 8102[RR]

**Time Warp** *A S Cruz* a79 119
4 ch g Archipenko(USA) Here To Eternity (USA) (Stormy Atlantic (USA))
**(9171a)**

**Time Zone** *Peter Chapple-Hyam* 83
3 b g Kheleyf(USA) Be Joyful (IRE) (Teofilo (IRE))
**1859[5]** 4861[7] 5548[5]

**Timia** *Keith Henry Clarke* a80 69
4 b m Cape Cross(IRE) Cinerama (IRE) (Machiavellian (USA))
**5650[4]**

**Timoshenko** *Sir Mark Prescott Bt* a27 51
2 ch g Archipenko(USA) Nezhenka (With Approval (CAN))
7280[9] *7726[13]* **8119[11]** *8399[9]*

**Timpani (IRE)** *John Gosden* a58 77
2 ch f Raven's Pass(USA) Fanny Cerrito (USA) (Gulch (USA))
*7454[7] 7997[6]* **(8348)**

**Tim Rocco (GER)** *Frau C Barsig* 89
5 ch h Doyen(IRE) Timbalada (GER) (Big Shuffle (USA))
**4931a[4]**

**Tina Teaspoon** *Derek Shaw*
3 b f Kheleyf(USA) Button Moon (IRE) (Compton Place)
5289[5]

**Tindaro (FR)** *Paul Webber* a77 82
10 gr g Kingsalsa(USA) Star's Mixa (FR) (Linamix (FR))
**8426[8]**

**Tinder (IRE)** *Mrs John Harrington* 96
3 gr f Fast Company(IRE) Platinum Darling (IRE) (Iffraaj)
**1634a[9]** 4385a[13]

**Tingo In The Tale (IRE)**
*Tony Forbes* a50 61
8 b g Oratorio(IRE) Sunlit Skies (Selkirk (USA))
*147[11] 383[7] 741[3] 900[2] 1191[3] 1556[7] 2059[3]* 2712[8]
4627[4] 5267[7] **(6153)** *6953[9]* 8515[7]

**Tink** *Mark Brisbourne* a51
3 ch f Captain Gerrard(IRE) Ensign's Trick (Cayman Kai (IRE))
***75[7]*** *244[8] 456[9] 1193[6]* ***1367[2]*** *1564[12] 2309[9] 3260[9]*
*4161[6] 8133[13] 9267[7] 9365[11]*

**Tinker Tailor (IRE)** *Denis Quinn* 74
4 ch m Intikhab(USA) Luanas Pearl (IRE) (Bahri (USA))
2632[3] **5364[5]** 5658[12] 6258[6]

**Tinnitus (IRE)** *Niels Petersen* a75 100
4 gr g Clodovil(IRE) Star Now (Librettist (USA))
*4940a[6]* **(6500a)**

**Tinos (GER)** *Ed Walker* 68
3 b g Soldier Hollow Ticinella (GER) (Hernando (FR))
**1961[6]**

**Tin Pan Alley** *David C Griffiths* a50 57
9 b g Singspiel(IRE) Tazmeen (Darshaan)
**2225[4]** 3205[9] **3935[11]** 4558[10] 6088[11]

**Tinsill** *Nigel Tinkler* a34 55
6 ch g Firebreak Concentration (IRE) (Mind Games)
1978[17] 2700[11] 3201[9] **3453[2]** 3710[9] 4174[9] 4479[4]
4997[3] 5377[7] *5419[10]* 5695[12] 6089[8] 6384[9] 7825[13]

**Tinted (IRE)** *John Gosden* a38
3 b f Galileo(IRE) Regal Rose (Danehill (USA))
***7708[10]***

**Tiny Tempest (IRE)**
*Eve Johnson Houghton* a69 65
2 b f Rip Van Winkle(IRE) Mahaazen (IRE) (Cape Cross (IRE))
4520[4] 5534[5] 6279[5] 6860[5] ***(7829)***

**Tioga Pass** *Paul Cole* a80 102
6 b m High Chaparral(IRE) Seren Devious (Dr Devious (IRE))
**4119[6]**

**Tioman (FR)** *Mlle B Renk* a56 47
3 gr g Rajsaman(FR) Cabulera (PER) (Prospector's Cap (CAN))
1460a[8]

**Tipi** *Charlie Wallis* a25
2 b g Sleeping Indian Jazan (IRE) (Danehill (USA))
*6636[P]* ***6816[9]*** *7482[10]*

**Tip Two Win** *Roger Teal* 105
2 gr c Dark Angel(IRE) Freddie's Girl (USA) (More Than Ready (USA))
(4973) 5476[3] 6521[2] **(7112) 7546[2]** (9446a)

**Tirage Au Sort (FR)** *J-P Dubois* 27
2 b g Sageburg(IRE) Severina (Darshaan)
**5776a[15]**

**Tirania** *William Haggas* 96
3 b f Pivotal Tiriana (Common Grounds)
1948[3] (2908) 3786[2] 4883[4] (6629)◆ 7329[2] **8040[5]**

**Tisa River (IRE)** *Milton Bradley* a48 42
3 b f Equiano(FR) Senta's Dream (Danehill (USA))
*1626[7]* 1762[7] ***3472[8]*** *4447[8]* 6004[11] 7190[4]

**Tisbutadream (IRE)** *David Elsworth* a87 105
3 ch f Dream Ahead(USA) Choose Me (IRE) (Choisir (AUS))
*(209) (392) (626) 1026[8]* (2605) 3319[3] 3964[9]
(4637) 5352[3] **6054a[2]** 6697[3] **7576[3]**

**Tishka (FR)** *C Ferland* a58
2 bb f Kendargent(FR) Tishkara (FR) (Xaar)
***9087a[13]***

**Tis Marvellous** *Clive Cox* 111
3 b g Harbour Watch(IRE) Mythicism (Oasis Dream)
**2289[4]** 4030[6] 4635[5] 6973a[8]

**Tis Wonderful (IRE)** *Carroll Gray* a63 60
3 b g Casamento(IRE) Cosenza (Bahri (USA))
**3423[4]**◆ 3870[4] *8641[7] 8993[4] 9375[2]*

**Titan** *Ed Dunlop* 63
3 b g Lawman(FR) Dragonera (Doyen (IRE))
1857[8] **4274[4]** 4569[11] 5142[5] *6291[10]*

**Titan Goddess** *Mike Murphy* a82 71
5 b m Equiano(FR) Phoebe Woodstock (IRE) (Grand Lodge (USA))
4887[5] 5369[8] 6134[11] 6725[3] 8125[2] *(8376)* 8596[3]
*8797[10] (9138)* ***9337[2]***

**Titchy Digits** *Michael Attwater* 71
2 ch f Helmet(AUS) Sarah Park (IRE) (Redback)
4806[8] **5573[5]** 6100[4] 6778[7] **(7458)** 7814[27]

**Titfortat Succes (FR)** *Miss V Haigh* a54 38
4 b m Zanzibari(USA) Verisca (IRE) (Common Grounds)
***837a[8]***

**Tithonus (IRE)** *Denis Gerard Hogan* a85 99
6 b g Glory Of Dancer Aurora Aurealis (IND) (Indictment (IND))
1388a[15] (4416a) **(4925a)** 5688a[11] **6325[5]**◆
6971a[4] 7425a[5]

**Titi Makfi** *Mark Johnston* a106 107
3 b f Makfi Titivation (Montjeu (IRE))
(3241)◆ (3507) (3976)◆ (4292) 4856[5]◆ 5529[2] (5889)◆ 6449[2] 7283[6] 7673a[3] (8637)
**Titus Bolt (IRE)** *Jim Goldie* a46 59
8 b g Titus Livius(FR) Megan's Bay (Muhtarram (USA))
7885[11] 8314[10]
**Titus Secret** *Malcolm Saunders* a71 76
5 ch g Sakhee's Secret Crimson Fern (IRE) (Titus Livius (FR))
2043[2] 2589[6] 3084[3] (3468) 4467[2]
**Tivoli (IRE)** *John Gosden* a83 83
2 b f Dark Angel(IRE) Fluvial (IRE) (Exceed And Excel (AUS))
5660[4] 6385[2]◆ 7021[3] (7725)
**Tizme (IRE)**
*Miss Denise Marie O'Shea*
5 b m Stowaway Isityourself (IRE) (Milan)
6799a[9]
**To Arms (USA)** *John Gosden* a70 56
2 b c War Front(USA) Moon Safari (USA) (Mr Prospector (USA))
6108[12] 6616[4]
**Toast Of London** *Antony Brittain* a49 49
4 ch m Haafhd First Harmony (First Trump)
1866[5] 2841[4] 4449[5] 5413[5] 6530[11]
**Toast Of New York (USA)**
*Jamie Osborne* a106 84
6 b h Thewayyouare(USA) Claire Soleil (USA) (Syncline (USA))
(9091)
**Tobacco Bay (IRE)** *J P Murtagh* a56 90
3 b f Dark Angel(IRE) Glamorous Air (IRE) (Air Express (IRE))
4385a[5] 4925a[15] 7663a[7] 8083a[11]
**Tobacco Road (IRE)** *David Pipe* a83 79
7 b g Westerner Virginias Best (King's Best (USA))
1608[7] 2574[6] 3235[2] 3582[5] 4216[10] 4809[8]
**To Be Wild (IRE)** *Hugo Palmer* a103 112
4 br g Big Bad Bob(IRE) Fire Up (Motivator)
1779[8] 2822[4]
**Toboggan's Fire** *Ann Duffield* a84 85
4 b m Firebreak Toboggan Lady (Tobougg (IRE))
(1368) 2789[4] 3497[7] 5699[4] 6349[10] 7225[6] 7924[8] 8315[11]
**Toboggan's Gift** *Ann Duffield* a55 52
5 b m Major Cadeaux Toboggan Lady (Tobougg (IRE))
1188[8] 1436[10]
**Tobouggaloo** *Stuart Kittow* a57 79
6 ch m Tobougg(IRE) Let Alone (Warning)
2388[14] 3428[5] (4840) (5054) 6095[U] 6610[3]
**Tobrave (IRE)** *Roger Varian* a80 20
3 b g Invincible Spirit(IRE) Qasirah (IRE) (Machiavellian (USA))
5797[2] 7321[9]
**To Dibba** *Roger Varian* 100
3 gr c Dubawi(IRE) Rose Diamond (IRE) (Daylami (IRE))
1514[2] (2895) 4322[2] 5425[3] 6349[2] 6920[9]
**To Eternity** *John Gosden* a77 108
4 b m Galileo(IRE) All's Forgotten (USA) (Darshaan)
(5658)◆ 6191[8] 7577[3]
**Toga Tiger (IRE)**
*Daniel Mark Loughnane* a84 78
10 b g Antonius Pius(USA) Minerwa (GER) (Protektor (GER))
719[3] 885[4] 4170[4] 5484[3] 5849[3] 7759[2] 9419[5]
**Together Again** *Stefano Botti* 99
3 ch c Pivotal Regal Aura (Teofilo (IRE))
2245a[8] 8095a[4]
**Togetherness (IRE)**
*Patrick Chamings* 81
4 b g Pour Moi(IRE) Madeira Mist (IRE) (Grand Lodge (USA))
1763[6] 2609[7] 3027[3] 8426[3]
**Togetherwecan (IRE)** *Iain Jardine* 61
5 b m Danehill Dancer(IRE) Crystal Bull (USA) (Holy Bull (USA))
7885[14]
**Togoville (IRE)** *Anthony McCann* a98 84
7 gr g Verglas(IRE) Road Harbour (USA) (Rodrigo De Triano (USA))
(795a) 1353a[6] (9247a)
**Tojosimbre** *Richard Hughes* a53 54
3 gr g Dark Angel(IRE) Shes Heavy Lifting (USA) (Broken Vow (USA))
807[6] 1287[10] 1787[7] 3657[7] 4087[9] (5787) 6180[7] 6821[6] 7210[3] 7490[4]◆
**Tolosane (FR)** *B De Montzey* 25
2 b f Rajsaman(FR) Trice (FR) (Highest Honor (FR))
5816a[5]
**Tomahawk Kid** *Ian Williams* 88
4 b g Major Cadeaux Say A Prayer (Indesatchel (IRE))
2133[14] 2624[2] 3160[5] 3750[13] 4832[5] 6007[7] 7735[5] (8386) 8561[9]
**Tom Dooley (IRE)**
*Richard John O'Brien* a67 65
6 b g Dylan Thomas(IRE) Shizao (IRE) (Alzao (USA))
(6800a)
**Tomily (IRE)** *Richard Hannon* a100 100
3 b g Canford Cliffs(IRE) Cake (IRE) (Acclamation)
276[3] (643) 1311[3] 1774[3] 2570[5] 3159[5] 3844[8] 4412[4] 4581[4] 4992[5] 6275[15] (8416) 8679[8] 8991[10] 9373[2]
**Tom Melbourne (IRE)** *Chris Waller* a79 109
6 b g Dylan Thomas(IRE) Roshanak (IRE) (Spinning World (USA))
8059a[6]
**Tommy Boy** *Ian Williams* a14 46
2 ch c Camacho Jacaranda Ridge (Indian Ridge (IRE))
6388[13] 7580[11] 9404[10]
**Tommy Docc (IRE)** *Keith Dalgleish* a90 89
5 b g Thewayyouare(USA) Liturgy (IRE) (Catcher In The Rye (IRE))
389[6]

**Tommy G** *Jim Goldie* a81 84
4 ch g Makfi Primo Heights (Primo Valentino (IRE))
1833[4] (2500) 2951[4]◆ 3827[10] 4037[6] 4079[4] 4683[5] 4854[10] 5396[3] 5637[2] 5947[10] 6348[7] 8319[8] 9101[5]
**Tommy Hallinan (IRE)** *W McCreery* 83
3 b g Intense Focus(USA) Bowstring (IRE) (Sadler's Wells (USA))
1389a[2]
**Tommys Geal** *Michael Madgwick* a63 62
5 b m Halling(USA) Steel Free (IRE) (Danehill Dancer (IRE))
120[5] 922[7] (1284) 1789[3] 2295[5] 2914[2] 3208[2] 8183[11] 8846[13] 9092[8] 9317[DSQ]
**Tommy Shelby (FR)** *Richard Fahey* a53 66
2 b g Dabirsim(FR) Interior (USA) (Fusaichi Pegasus (USA))
3648[5] 6636[9] 7237[12] 7883[3]
**Tommy's Secret**
*Jane Chapple-Hyam* a70 56
7 gr g Sakhee's Secret La Gessa (Largesse)
2731[6] 3442[4] 3731[4] 5285[6] 6112[8] 6622[2] 7325[3] 7990[4]
**Tommy Taylor (USA)** *Kevin Ryan* 108
3 b c Mizzen Mast(USA) Sharp Apple (USA) (Diesis)
1901[3] 4813[2] 5423[13] 6198[7] (6966) 7806[7]
**Tomorrow Mystery** *Jamie Osborne* a88 89
3 b f Nathaniel(IRE) Retake (Reset (AUS))
144[5] 328[2] 737[2] 5331[5] (6013) 6291[2] 6865[2]
**Tom's Anna (IRE)** *Sean Regan* a40 52
7 b m Antonius Pius(USA) Vanilla Delight (IRE) (Orpen (USA))
579[7] 1407[7] 2626[3] 3906[2] 4744[3] 5126[9] 6003[5] 9012[8]
**Tom's Rock (IRE)** *John Butler* a88 79
4 gr g Rock Of Gibraltar(IRE) Asheyana (IRE) (Soviet Star (USA))
1683[8] (2333) 2920[3] 4216[2] 4751[6] 5663[6] 7456[4] 7949[7]
**Tomyris** *Roger Varian* a70 106
3 b f Invincible Spirit(IRE) Totally Devoted (USA) (Seeking The Gold (USA))
(1905)◆ (2802) 4031[6] 5597[3] 7113[3] 7812[11]
**Tonahutu (IRE)** *Ed Vaughan* a71 80
3 b f Sir Prancealot(IRE) Really Polish (USA) (Polish Numbers (USA))
(3246)
**Toni's A Star** *Tony Carroll* a67 69
5 b m Avonbridge Canina (Foxhound (USA))
22[10] 743[7] 1413[6] 2472[5] 2962[8] 4531[3] (5052) 5695[11] 7407[9] 7689[2] 7910[3]
**Tonkolili (IRE)** *William Muir* a55 69
2 b f Kodiac Heart's Desire (IRE) (Royal Applause)
3807[2] 4369[2] 6559[7] 7194[5] 8110[6] 8746[5] 8902[7] 9387[3]
**Tonto's Spirit** *Kenneth Slack* a63 82
5 b g Authorized(IRE) Desert Royalty (IRE) (Alhaarth (IRE))
(3400) (3654)◆ 3978[3] 5021[3] 5701[9] 6126[8] (8241) (8487) 8778[13]
**Tony Curtis** *Richard Hannon* a92 110
4 b g Rock Of Gibraltar(IRE) Strawberry Lolly (Lomitas)
3069[7] 4905[4] 5594[2]
**Tony Soprano (IRE)** *Martyn Meade* a47 62
2 b g Lethal Force(IRE) Zarkalia (IRE) (Red Ransom (USA))
1941[9] 3187[9] 3437[5] 5756[4] 7082[3] 7510[7]
**Tony The Gent (IRE)** *G M Lyons* 101
4 b g Kodiac Becuille (IRE) (Redback)
5517a[10]
**Too Familiar (IRE)** *J P Murtagh* 93
2 gr f Clodovil(IRE) Amazon Beauty (IRE) (Wolfhound (USA))
4418a[4]
**Toofi (FR)** *John Butler* 101
6 b g Henrythenavigator(USA) Silver Bark (Royal Applause)
1515[15] 2736[9] 3034[11]◆ 3585[4] 4570[6] 5159[7] 5929[6] 6877[2] 7612[7] 8077[5]
**Toohottotouch** *Michael Dods* 43
2 b g Hellvelyn Soft Touch (IRE) (Petorius (IRE))
3908[7] 4956[7]
**Tookiedoo (IRE)** *J C Hayden* 73
3 b f Art Connoisseur(IRE) Eur Elusive (IRE) (Elusive City (USA))
4327a[7]
**Toola Boola** *Jedd O'Keeffe* a57 55
7 b m Tobougg(IRE) Forsythia (Most Welcome)
1469[3]◆ 7220[11] 8314[11]
**Toolain (IRE)** *S Seemar* a73 70
9 br g Diktat Qasirah (IRE) (Machiavellian (USA))
319a[9] 650a[8]
**Toolatetodelegate** *Brian Barr* a62 38
3 b f Delegator Little Caroline (IRE) (Great Commotion (USA))
717[6] 962[4] 1141[3] 1596[9] 2726[12] 3819[12] 4970[6] 6341[9] 7826[5] 8342[2] (8428) 8742[13] 8953[2] 9214[3] 9315[3]
**Too Many Shots** *John Best* a61 61
3 b g Mullionmileanhour(IRE) Neissa (USA) (Three Wonders (USA))
89[4] 502[4] 848[7] 1623[2] 2027[2] 2705[5] 3326[4] 4348[3] 7483[3] 8135[2] 8312[13] 9026[7]
**Toomer** *Richard Hannon* a61 71
2 ch f Iffraaj Harlem Dancer (Dr Devious (IRE))
4815[8] 5528[10] 6183[5] 6778[4] 7050[5] 8148[8]
**Tooty Fruitti** *Jo Hughes* a68 59
3 b f Captain Gerrard(IRE) Littlemisstutti (IRE) (Noverre (USA))
1192[6] 1321[3] 1543[2] 2065[4] 2720[7] 3810[4] 4046[4] (4448) 4723[2] 5027[3] 5845[2] 6635[5]
**Topaling** *Mark H Tompkins* a70 55
6 ch m Halling(USA) Topatori (IRE) (Topanoora (IRE))
218[RR]
**Topalova** *Mark H Tompkins* a53 51
4 ch m Champs Elysees Topatori (IRE) (Topanoora (IRE))
762[4] 988[3] 1191[7] 1486[2] 2332[5] 5244[3] 6259[7] 6820[11]

**Topamichi** *Michael Appleby* a77 70
7 b g Beat Hollow Topatori (IRE) (Topanoora (IRE))
7225[7] 7601[6] 8261[3] (8682) 8806[2] 9369[3]
**Topapinion** *Mark H Tompkins* a69 45
2 b c So You Think(NZ) Topatoo (Bahamian Bounty)
5887[11] 6683[6] 7788[3]
**Top Beak (IRE)** *Michael Attwater* a85 68
4 b g Lawman(FR) Tree Tops (Grand Lodge (USA))
1964[3] 2828[12] 3300[7] 3785[9] 4498[3] 6195[6] 6701[11] 7131[11] 7770[4] 9208[4]◆ 9458[6]
**Top Boy** *Derek Shaw* a91 87
7 b g Exceed And Excel(AUS) Injaaz (Sheikh Albadou)
63[6] 388[7] (618) 1222[8] 2262[6] 2516[5] 3969[5] 4343[6] 4816[2] 5354[5] 6878[9] 8012[14] 8540[5] 9079[6]
**Top Clearance (USA)**
*G Selvaratnam* a26
5 b g Majestic Warrior(USA) Sweet Beat (USA) (Tiznow (USA))
83a[3] 319a[8] 650a[7] 9360a[9]
**Top Cop** *Ronald Harris* a61 45
8 b g Acclamation Speed Cop (Cadeaux Genereux)
216[8]
**Top Diktat** *Gary Moore* a71 51
9 b g Diktat Top Romance (IRE) (Entrepreneur)
5838[6] 6475[9] 7495[11] 8515[10] 9321[3]
**Topmeup** *Gay Kelleway* a63 64
3 ch f Mayson Ambrix (IRE) (Xaar)
1107[3] 1297[3] 1428[2] 3423[3]◆ 3695[3] 4006[3] 4150[4] 4463[4] 5713[4] (6341) (7198) 7899[2] 8156[5] (8470) 8841[4] 9034[6] 9213[2] 9406[4]
**Top Mission** *Saeed bin Suroor* a92 83
3 b g Dubawi(IRE) Ever Love (BRZ) (Nedawi)
1862[2] 2778[3] (3234) 8821[2]
**Top Notch Tonto (IRE)**
*Brian Ellison* a101 108
7 ch g Thousand Words Elite Hope (USA) (Moment Of Hope (USA))
1148[10] 1494[14] 2141[4] 2767[12] 3597[11] 4261[7]
**Top Offer** *Patrick Morris* a71 76
8 b g Dansili Zante (Zafonic (USA))
426[3] 745[8] 929[5] 1842[6] 3265[9] 4453[3]◆ 5898[2] 6725[5] 6947[7] 8247[4] (8664) 8854[7] 9406[8]
**Top Of The Bank** *Kristin Stubbs* a77 73
4 b g Piccolo America Lontana (FR) (King's Theatre (IRE))
(216) 1031[7] (1339) (1467) 1631[5] 1972[10] 2424[2] 2990[6] 3177[3] 3833[8] 4629[9] 5070[5] 5869[8] 6635[3] 7320[9] 7767[10] 8743[6] 8875[8]
**Top Of The Glas (IRE)** *Brian Ellison* a84 87
6 gr g Verglas(IRE) Fury Dance (USA) (Cryptoclearance (USA))
197[3] 1517[13] 1976[5] 2629[6] 2920[6] 3486[3]
**Topology** *Joseph Tuite* a79 76
4 br g Passing Glance Bold Byzantium (Bold Arrangement)
2586[8] 3009[10] 4251[11] 5221[7] 6076[6] 7099[5] 7900[3] 8031[4]
**Top Score** *Saeed bin Suroor* a107 111
3 b g Hard Spun(USA) Windsor County (USA) (Elusive Quality (USA))
430a[3] (649a) (887a) 1375a[11] 2399[7] 3071[6] 3959[19] 5393[27] 6918[16] 7950[4]
**Topsoil** *Ronald Harris* a58 53
4 b g Kheleyf(USA) Edge Of Gold (Choisir (AUS))
64[2] (271) 742[9] 874[8]
**Toptempo** *Ralph J Smith* a25 53
8 ch m Halling(USA) Topatoo (Bahamian Bounty)
4217[13] 4756[7] 5407[2] 6530[13]
**Top Tug (IRE)** *Alan King* a103 110
6 ch g Halling(USA) Top Romance (IRE) (Entrepreneur)
2431[2] (3073) 4033[4] 6447[14] 8468[2] 8740[12]
**Top Ville Ben (IRE)** *Philip Kirby* 100
5 b g Beneficial Great Decision (IRE) (Simply Great (FR))
7124[4]
**Tor** *Iain Jardine* a65 93
3 ch g Orientor Dance In The Sun (Halling (USA))
1149[11] 1411[7] 1888[8] 2273[4] 3261[6] 3665[2] 3909[3] 4691[3] (5071) 5468[2] (5682) 6445[13] (7163) 7565[4]
**Torcedor (IRE)** *Mrs John Harrington* a92 116
5 b g Fastnet Rock(AUS) Magnolia Lane (IRE) (Sadler's Wells (USA))
(1999a) 3996[5] 6976a[2] 8229[2]
**Torcello (IRE)** *Conrad Allen* 99
3 ch c Born To Sea(IRE) Islandagore (IRE) (Indian Ridge (IRE))
3485[2]◆ 4474[3] (5428) (6389)◆ 6920[6] (7548) 8005[9]
**Torch** *John Butler* a80 44
4 b g Paco Boy(IRE) Singed (Zamindar (USA))
516[13] 7691[0] 1210[7] 2919[9] 4165[11]
**Torchlighter (IRE)** *S bin Ghadayer* a96 102
6 ch g Shamardal(USA) Ever Love (BRZ) (Nedawi)
208a[9]
**Torero** *Alan Phillips* a21 33
8 b g Hernando(FR) After You (Pursuit Of Love)
5361[8]
**Toretto (IRE)** *Jan Coomer* a28 28
9 ch g Peintre Celebre(USA) Petite-D-Argent (Noalto)
4143a[6]
**Toriano** *Nick Littmoden* a79 73
4 ch g Equiano(FR) Ticki Tori (IRE) (Vettori (IRE))
3214[8] 8821[12] 9206[7]
**Torment** *Charlie Wallis* a60 52
4 gr g Dark Angel(IRE) Selkirk Sky (Selkirk (USA))
2771[2] 1898[5] 2464[9] 2675[5] 3177[8] 5340[7] 5657[6] 5723[6] 6296[11]
**Tornequeta May** *Adam West* a21
2 b f Style Vendome(FR) Alabastrine (Green Desert (USA))
9320[11]
**Toronto Sound** *Sir Mark Prescott Bt* a47 58
3 b g Aussie Rules(USA) Caribana (Hernando (FR))
2521[6] 2997[10] 3342[8] 4320[3]

**Torremar (FR)** *Kevin Ryan* a68 77
4 br g Excellent Art Sabela (IRE) (Sinndar (IRE))
1292[7] 3050[4] 4170[3] 4684[9] 5873[8] 7659[12]
**Torrid** *Michael Easterby* a87 85
6 ch g Three Valleys(USA) Western Appeal (USA) (Gone West (USA))
(1677) 3255[2] 5165[5] 5668[12] 7569[7]
**Toscanini (IRE)** *Richard Fahey* a96 115
5 b g Shamardal(USA) Tuzla (FR) (Panoramic)
1493[4] 2248a[5] 2825[8] 3924[14] 5527[5] 6401[2] 7671a[8] 8232[13]
**Tosen Basil (JPN)** *Hideaki Fujiwara* 115
5 bb h Harbinger Careless Whisper (JPN) (Fuji Kiseki (JPN))
2203a[8] 9167a[3]
**Tosen Gift (IRE)** *S Kobayashi* 90
2 b f Lope De Vega(IRE) Miracolia (IRE) (Montjeu (IRE))
3679a[3] 8170a[5]
**Tosen Hardi** *S Kobayashi* 72
2 ch f Compton Place Penang Cry (Barathea (IRE))
5988a[10] 6542a[11] (8228a)
**Tosen Stardom (JPN)** *Darren Weir* 113
6 bb h Deep Impact(JPN) Admire Kirameki (JPN) (End Sweep (USA))
(8059a) (8753a)
**Total Demolition (IRE)** *J Larkin* a55 82
5 ch g Thewayyouare(USA) Margaux Dancer (IRE) (Danehill Dancer (IRE))
5582a[14]
**Totally Magic (IRE)**
*Richard Whitaker* a71 71
5 b m Captain Rio Hypocrisy (Bertolini (USA))
2685[12] 3287[3] 3911[2] 4797[2] 5007[3]◆ 5185[2] 6047[2] 6564[7] 7034[4] 7241[5] 7894[9]
**Total Power** *Brian Ellison* a43 69
4 b g Sleeping Indian House Of Frills (Paris House)
2700[7] 3186[7] 3666[12] 4682[10]
**Total Star** *Luca Cumani* a93 89
3 gr c Pivotal Millennium Star (IRE) (High Chaparral (IRE))
2520[3] 3042[5] 7516[9]
**Touched By Love (USA)**
*Ismail Mohammed* a60 45
4 b g Street Sense(USA) Love Of Dubai (USA) (More Than Ready (USA))
3028[10]
**Touching The Sky (IRE)**
*Alex Fracas* a87 92
3 b f Rip Van Winkle(IRE) Kyniska (IRE) (Choisir (AUS))
2484a[2]
**Touch Me (IRE)** *K R Burke* a68
3 b f Masterofthehorse(IRE) User Name (USA) (Mr Greeley (USA))
392[8] 1000[2] 1306[3] 2094[5] 2503[11]
**Touch Of Color** *Richard Fahey* a51 55
4 b m Sixties Icon Shesells Seashells (Tiger Hill (IRE))
7213[7] 7539[8] 8551[8] 9073[11]
**Touch Of Faith (IRE)**
*Michael Appleby* a26
3 ch g Zoffany(IRE) Jusoor (USA) (El Prado (IRE))
615[6] 849[6] 925[5]
**Touch Of Paradise (IRE)**
*Richard Fahey* a63
3 ch f Frankel Ramruma (USA) (Diesis)
40[3]◆ 580[10]
**Touch The Clouds** *William Stone* a50 47
6 b g Sleeping Indian Aptina (USA) (Aptitude (USA))
665[5] 3761[4] 4765[4] 5080[4] 5261[5] 5850[8] 6847[2] 7480[2] 8543[11] 8908[7] 9282[2]
**Touch The Wolf (TUR)** *A Sivgin* 105
4 b h Kurtiniadis(IRE) Acoustic (TUR) (Namid)
6746a[4]
**Tough Lass (IRE)** *George Peckham* a48
2 b f Kodiac Sagemacca (IRE) (Danehill Dancer (IRE))
9320[10]
**Tough Remedy (IRE)**
*Keith Dalgleish* 74
2 b g Tough As Nails(IRE) Remediate (USA) (Miswaki (USA))
3429[2] 3705[3]◆ 4204[5] 5202[2]
**Toulifaut (IRE)** *J-C Rouget* a87 104
3 b f Frankel Cassydora (Darshaan)
1825a[4] 2644a[14]
**Toulson** *Eve Johnson Houghton* a80 94
4 b g Champs Elysees Flower Market (Cadeaux Genereux)
(2624) (3160) 4614[14] 5421[4] 6007[5] 8165[4]
**Tour** *M Nigge* a62 41
4 b g Avonbridge Spennymoor (IRE) (Exceed And Excel (AUS))
6125a[3] 9112a[5]
**Tour De Paris (IRE)**
*Eve Johnson Houghton* a68 14
2 b g Champs Elysees Disco Lights (Spectrum (IRE))
7392[15] 7739[8] 8501[4]
**Toursoun (IRE)** *D K Weld* 50
3 b c Sea The Stars(IRE) Tarakala (IRE) (Dr Fong (USA))
1389a[6]
**Touwari (IRE)** *John Gosden* a70 73
3 b c Teofilo(IRE) Luminaria (IRE) (Danehill (USA))
1900[5] 2314[4] 3839[3] 4202[4] 4730[7]◆
**To Wafij (IRE)** *Roger Varian* 103
2 b c Kodiac Rajmahal (UAE) (Indian Ridge (IRE))
(2279) 2577[2] 4582[3] 5526[3] 6448[6] 8001[6]
**Towelrads Boy (IRE)** *Paul Cole* a78 55
2 b c Red Jazz(USA) Mystery Hill (USA) (Danehill (USA))
8466[6] (8657)
**Towerlands Park (IRE)**
*Michael Bell* a97 96
4 b g Danehill Dancer(IRE) Strategy (Machiavellian (USA))
8423[3] 8740[21] 9053[3]

**Tower Of Texas (CAN)**
*Roger L Attfield* a97 117
6 b g Street Sense(USA) Rare Opportunity (USA) (Danzig Connection (USA))
7179a[8]

**Tower Power** *Phil McEntee* a66 69
6 b g Nayef(USA) Voile (IRE) (Barathea (IRE))
6075[8] 7960[4] 9208[11]

**Towie (IRE)** *Hughie Morrison* 74
3 br c Sea The Stars(IRE) Epping (Charnwood Forest (IRE))
6194[9] 6765[4] 7462[4]

**Town Charter (USA)** *Tony Coyle* a67 88
3 gr c Lonhro(AUS) Summer Fete (IRE) (Pivotal)
3071[8] 3592[3]◆ 4057[4] 4334[4] 4662[6] 5165[4] 5415[6] 5949[8] 7824[10] 8928[9]

**Town's History (USA)** *S Seemar* a86 92
4 ch g Hard Spun(USA) Smooth Charmer (USA) (Easy Goer (USA))
(203a)

**Toy Theatre** *Michael Appleby* a84 84
3 b f Lonhro(AUS) Puppet Queen (USA) (Kingmambo (USA))
(522) 875[2]◆ (1243) 1582[5] 1625[2] 4564[7] 5242[5] 5400[4] 6620[9] (7545) (8418) 8747[5] 9179[6]

**Track Star (FR)** *Gerard Martin* a64 71
5 b h Monsun(GER) Turfquelle (IRE) (Shaadi (USA))
4457a[8] 7721a[10]

**Tractive Effort** *Michael Attwater* a51 37
4 b g Rail Link Anastasia Venture (Lion Cavern (USA))
278[10] (738) 3724[10]

**Trade Route (IRE)** *David Elsworth* a70 52
3 gr g Mastercraftsman(IRE) Shanghai Visit (IRE) (Peintre Celebre (USA))
237[5] 503[5] 916[3] 2625[13] 4050[7] 4720[6]

**Trading Point (FR)** *John Quinn* 72
3 b c Siyouni(FR) Zita Blues (IRE) (Zieten (USA))
6965[8] 8392[12]

**Trading Punches (IRE)**
*David Brown* 89
3 b g Elzaam(AUS) Kiralik (Efisio)
2755[2] 3505[5] 7277[7] 7736[8] 8392[9]

**Traditional Dancer (IRE)**
*Iain Jardine* a57 58
5 b g Danehill Dancer(IRE) Cote Quest (USA) (Green Desert (USA))
4036[8] 4853[2] 5257[6] 6898[3] 7659[5] 8187[9] 9258[5]

**Traffic Jam (IRE)** *N Clement* 110
4 b m Duke Of Marmalade(IRE) Place De L'Etoile (IRE) (Sadler's Wells (USA))
5691a[2] 6981a[4] (8087a)

**Trais Fluors** *A Fabre* 117
3 b c Dansili Trois Lunes (FR) (Manduro (GER))
(2944a) (3855a) 4666a[2] 5980a[4]◆

**Tranquil Daze (IRE)** *David Brown* a73 58
3 ch g Sir Prancealot(IRE) Endless Peace (IRE) (Russian Revival (USA))
77[3] (667) 813[3] 1005[4] 1306[4] 2927[12] 4107[11]

**Tranquil Soul** *David Lanigan* a65 41
2 b f Farhh Peaceful Soul (USA) (Dynaformer (USA))
3902[6] 4977[2]◆ 5847[3] 6366[5] 7057[8] 7786[4] 8371[3]◆

**Tranquil Star (IRE)** *Jeremy Noseda* a82 80
3 b f Galileo(IRE) We Can Say It Now (AUS) (Starcraft (NZ))
1885[7] 2564[3] 7125[3] 7708[5] 8291[2] (8911)

**Tranquil Tracy** *John Norton* a46 42
3 b f Stimulation(IRE) Tranquil Flight (Oasis Dream)
245[4] 376[6] 1123[6] 2016[7] 3472[9] 4262[6] 5761[6] 6381[6] 7523[11] 8247[11]

**Transmitting** *Ed Vaughan* a71 69
4 b g Cacique(IRE) Shuttle Mission (Sadler's Wells (USA))
2956[6] 3519[4] 4802[2] 5261[3] (6588) 7712[8]

**Transpennine Star** *Michael Dods* 80
4 ch g Mount Nelson Brave Mave (Daylami (IRE))
2629[9] 3794[7] 4684[4] 4790[4] 5700[2] 6968[3] 7330[2] 7893[8]

**Trapped (FR)** *F Belmont* a46 59
3 bb f Spirit One(FR) Fontcia (FR) (Enrique)
2536a[8] 3275a[8]

**Traumatised** *Michael Appleby* a22
2 b f Kheleyf(USA) Reveal The Light (Fantastic Light (USA))
9177[10]

**Trautmann (IRE)**
*Daniel Mark Loughnane* a53 56
3 ch g Casamento(IRE) Klang (IRE) (Night Shift (USA))
236[10] 545[5] 4171[7] 5061[3] 6032[5] 6611[4]

**Travelcard (USA)** *Mark Johnston* a74 78
2 b f Iffraaj Central Line (USA) (Redoute's Choice (AUS))
4749[3]◆ (5026) 6199[2] 6939[3] 7123[3] 8074[2]

**Traveller (FR)** *Charles Hills* a82 79
3 b g Henrythenavigator(USA) Nantes (GER) (Night Shift (USA))
115[5] 758[3] (962) 2151[2] 4807[4] 5754[4] 6558[3] 7095[2] 7999[2] 8341[9]

**Travellers Joy** *Richard Hughes* 13
2 b f Equiano(FR) Travelling (Dubai Destination (USA))
4465[12]

**Travel Lightly** *Tim Easterby* 41
2 b f Showcasing Upton Seas (Josr Algarhoud (IRE))
4116[9] 4502[9] 5372[11]

**Travelling Man** *F Head* 109
4 b g Oasis Dream Montare (IRE) (Montjeu (IRE))
2202a[3] 3119a[3] 5198a[3] 6499a[3]

**Traveltalk (IRE)** *Brian Ellison* a61 63
3 b g Fast Company(IRE) Laheen (IRE) (Bluebird (USA))
4310[9] 4999[12] 5411[5] 7017[10] 7459[8] 7928[3] 8206[3] (8477) 8909[8]

**Travertine (IRE)** *Niall Madden* a78 104
7 b g Danehill Dancer(IRE) Mer De Corail (IRE) (Sadler's Wells (USA))
7860a[22]

**Treacherous** *Ed de Giles* a70 44
3 b g Paco Boy(IRE) Black Baroness (Ishiguru (USA))
6103[10] 6368[8] 6791[7] (7517) 7723[7] 8646[4]

**Tread Lightly** *Tim Easterby* 72
3 b g Canford Cliffs(IRE) Step Lightly (IRE) (Danehill Dancer (IRE))
1914[7] 2185[11] 2902[2] 3243[2] 3745[7] 4247[3] 4891[6] 6518[10] 7895[9] 8514[9]

**Treagus** *Anthony Carson* a59 55
3 b g Mayson Danceatdusk (Desert Prince (IRE))
2470[3] 3431[4] 4172[4] 4697[6] 6529[9] 7945[2] 8185[2] 8395[3]

**Treasure The Ridge (IRE)**
*Martin Hill* a79 47
8 b g Galileo(IRE) Treasure The Lady (IRE) (Indian Ridge (IRE))
746[10] 2021[4] 7903[7]

**Treasuring** *Simon Callaghan* a70 101
2 ch f Havana Gold(IRE) You Look So Good (Excellent Art)
3960[8] (6241a) 7617[9] 8602a[7]

**Treaty Of Rome (USA)** *Derek Shaw* a80 61
5 bb g War Front(USA) Blading Gold Ring (USA) (During (USA))
20[2] 158[2]◆ 386[4] (523) 1071[2] (1431) (1820) 2462[7] 3625[9] 4343[10] 6527[3] 7572[12] 8260[2] 8803[7] 9074[3]

**Treble Strike (USA)**
*David C Griffiths* a68 39
4 bb g Hat Trick(JPN) Lady Simpson (Yankee Victor (USA))
289[2] 576[6] 737[6] 1092[3] 1303[6] 3459[8] 6898[5] 7330[8] 7730[13] 8261[8]

**Tred Softly (IRE)** *John Quinn* a62 62
4 b g Yeats(IRE) Elayoon (USA) (Danzig (USA))
(146) 278[9] 900[4] 1469[4] 2079[3] 3043[4] 4169[2] 6901[9] 8487[12] 9368[8]

**Tremendous (IRE)** *Richard Hannon* a56 55
3 b f Kodiac Clockwise (Pivotal)
2019[9] 2619[6] 4351[3]

**Tremont (FR)** *S Wattel* a81 72
2 b c Most Improved(IRE) Sheema (Teofilo (IRE))
6050a[2]

**Trenchard (USA)** *John Gosden* a78
3 b c Elusive Quality(USA) Temporada (USA) (Summer Squall (USA))
662[4] 970[2] 1244[2] 1485[6] (1724)

**Trending (IRE)** *Jeremy Gask* a73 66
8 gr g Dark Angel(IRE) Call Later (USA) (Gone West (USA))
(164) 333[2] 517[5] 928[10] 1257[3]

**Trendsetter (IRE)** *Micky Hammond* a67 67
6 b g Mastercraftsman(IRE) Fashion Trade (Dansili)
266[5] 6965[9] 7615[6] 8048[12] 8289[9] 8485[11]

**Tres Belle (IRE)** *N Clement* a88 92
3 b f Holy Roman Emperor(IRE) Mirabile Dictu (IRE) (King's Best (USA))
8462a[10]

**Tresor (IRE)** *Y Barberot* a69 76
3 b c Henrythenavigator(USA) Sapphire Pendant (IRE) (Danehill Dancer (IRE))
2484a[6] 5909a[8] 6084a[13]

**Tresorier** *Mme C Head-Maarek* 98
3 b c Dunkerque(FR) Treasure (FR) (Anabaa (USA))
1660a[5] 5777a[6]

**Tres Rock Glory (IRE)** *F Head* 98
4 b m Fastnet Rock(AUS) Tres Ravi (GER) (Monsun (GER))
1871a[5] 2450a[4] 4879a[9]

**Tres Rush (IRE)** *F Head* 80
3 b g Rip Van Winkle(IRE) Tres Ravi (GER) (Monsun (GER))
8732a[3]

**Trevithick** *Bryan Smart* a81 54
2 b c Champs Elysees New Choice (IRE) (Barathea (IRE))
8509[8] (8782)◆ 9263[2]

**Triangulate** *Micky Hammond* 69
5 b g Zamindar(USA) Heart Of Hearts (Oasis Dream)
1830[4] 2632[6]

**Tribal Beat (IRE)** *J S Bolger* 114
4 b h Street Cry(IRE) Tashelka (FR) (Mujahid (USA))
2440a[5]

**Tribal Conquest (IRE)**
*Charlie Appleby* 91
3 b g Shamardal(USA) Assabiyya (IRE) (Cape Cross (IRE))
2632[2]◆ 4508[3] (5632) 6474[8]

**Tribal Path (IRE)**
*Damian Joseph English* a90 92
7 b g Giant's Causeway(USA) Navajo Moon (IRE) (Danehill (USA))
1388a[4] 1479a[2] 2568[6] 5582a[3] 6491a[21] 8222a[11]

**Tribal Quest (USA)** *Charlie Appleby* 89
2 b g War Front(USA) Haka (USA) (Dynaformer (USA))
4049[2]◆ 4860[2] 5504[8]

**Tribal Warrior** *James Tate* a72
2 b c New Approach(IRE) Lunda (IRE) (Soviet Star (USA))
8889[6] 9200[8]

**Tribesman** *Marjorie Fife* a56 67
4 ch g Equiano(FR) Millsini (Rossini (USA))
270[3] 495[4] 3710[10]

**Tribute Act** *James Fanshawe* a87 94
3 b f Exceed And Excel(AUS) Sister Act (Marju (IRE))
2754[4]◆ (3722)◆ (4794)◆ 5506[13] 7784[2]

**Tricked Up (USA)**
*Naipaul Chatterpaul* 100
4 ch h Distorted Humor(USA) Satans Quick Chick (USA) (Sky Mesa (USA))
7633a[7]

**Trick Of The Light (IRE)**
*Roger Varian* a83 86
3 ch g Dragon Pulse(IRE) Galistic (IRE) (Galileo (IRE))
2072[3]◆ 2579[3] (3278) 4732[2] 5416[3] 6072[2] 6450[15]

**Trick Of The Lyte (IRE)** *John Quinn* a45 67
3 b c Kodiac Alpine River (IRE) (Redback)
578[7] 1005[6] 1913[11] 2630[10] 3496[7] 4745[6] 5282[6] 6630[4] 7018[5] 7366[10]

**Trick Shot Jenny** *Jamie Osborne* a56
2 b f Acclamation Chincoteague (IRE) (Daylami (IRE))
7535[6] 8502[7] 8748[9] (9014) 9238[6] 9300[7]

**Tricksy Spirit** *Mick Channon* 78
2 b f Lethal Force(IRE) Spritzeria (Bigstone (IRE))
4902[13] 5154[10] (6417)◆ 6863[11]

**Tricky Dicky** *Olly Williams* a89 80
4 b g Holy Roman Emperor(IRE) Tricky Situation (Mark Of Esteem (IRE))
1833[12] (2469) 2990[7] 3847[2] 4343[11] 5156[4] 5947[2] (6527)◆ 7737[7] 8319[3] 8489[5] 9074[2] 9305[2]

**Tricorn (IRE)** *John Gosden* a102 107
3 b g Helmet(AUS) Special Dancer (Shareef Dancer (USA))
545[2]◆ (785) (1029)◆ (1907) 3232[2] 3997[3] 4817[7]

**Tried And True (USA)**
*Doug Watson* a93 96
5 b g Medaglia d'Oro(USA) Dearly (Rahy (USA))
203a[4]◆

**Trigger Flash (FR)** *F Cheyer* a44 57
6 b m Librettist(USA) Trigger Shot (IRE) (High Chaparral (IRE))
7070a[7] 7721a[9]

**Trilliant (IRE)** *Ed Walker* 88
3 b f Dansili Priceless Jewel (Selkirk (USA))
1905[6] 2759[3] 3615[6] (4525) 6855[2]◆

**Trinity Force (IRE)** *A R Al Rayhi* a95 87
6 ch g Iffraaj Nasharaat (IRE) (Green Desert (USA))
83a[4] 650a[9]

**Trinity Star (IRE)** *Michael Dods* a70 84
6 gr g Kheleyf(USA) Zamiyla (IRE) (Daylami (IRE))
1032[5] 1201[6] 1472[10] 1700[8] 2301[5] 2953[2] 3197[5] 3910[5] 4438[3] 6471[6] 7327[4] 7894[2]

**Tripartite (IRE)** *Jeremy Gask* a79 78
4 b g Zebedee Baltic Belle (IRE) (Redback)
(685) 984[5] 1606[13] 2120[8] 2708[2]◆ 3422[3]◆ (3820) 4522[4]

**Triple Chelsea (USA)**
*Anthony Granitz* 89
4 bb m Hat Trick(JPN) Oceane Music (FR) (Ocean Of Wisdom (USA))
1813a[4]

**Triple Dream** *Milton Bradley* a72 61
12 ch g Vision Of Night Triple Joy (Most Welcome)
171[3] 4710[5] 6157[2] 6635[7] 7190[13] 7517[3] 8495[5]◆

**Triple First** *Seamus Mullins* a30 60
3 b f Dick Turpin(IRE) Orphina (IRE) (Orpen (USA))
6614[6] 7708[11]

**Triple Nine (KOR)** *Kim Young Kwan* a108
5 ch h Ecton Park(USA) A Little Poke (USA) (Pleasant Tap (USA))
319a[2] 650a[4] 1045a[5] 1373a[11]

**Trip To Paris (IRE)** *Ed Dunlop* a87 108
6 b g Champs Elysees La Grande Zoa (IRE) (Fantastic Light (USA))
1374a[13] 1733[4] 3996[13]

**Trip To Rhodos (FR)** *Pavel Tuma* 111
8 b g Rail Link Tropical Mark (Mark Of Esteem (IRE))
2202a[5] 6984a[3] 7639a[3]

**Tristram** *John Mackie* a74 66
3 b g Sinndar(IRE) Treasured Dream (Oasis Dream)
1358[3] 1900[3] 2359[4] 3520[7] 4197[4] 7895[8] 8806[13]

**Troarn (FR)** *J-C Rouget* a76 99
3 b f Wootton Bassett Darkova (USA) (Maria's Mon (USA))
3103a[2] 5449a[7]

**Trogon (IRE)** *Mick Channon* a67 68
2 ch g Leroidesanimaux(BRZ) Savanna Days (IRE) (Danehill Dancer (IRE))
4583[3] 5641[7] 6279[2] 6860[6] 7451[3] 7764[5] 8164[3]

**Trois Bon Amis (IRE)**
*Mark Campion* a46 63
3 gr g Lilbourne Lad(IRE) Vanozza (FR) (Dylan Thomas (IRE))
2182[9] 2790[7] 7331[9] 8193[6] 9073[2]

**Trois Points (FR)** *Gay Kelleway* a51 62
5 b g Motivator Trading (FR) (Anabaa (USA))
364a[16] 515a[15]

**Troop** *Ann Duffield* a53 51
2 gr g Lethal Force(IRE) Bendis (GER) (Danehill (USA))
5492[8] 6042[8] 6465[6] 7239[8]

**Trooper's Gold** *Kevin Ryan* a67 77
3 ch g Sepoy(AUS) Samira Gold (FR) (Gold Away (IRE))
2304[7] 2820[7]

**Tropical Bachelor (IRE)** *Ruth Carr* a38 48
11 b g Bachelor Duke(USA) Tropical Coral (IRE) (Pennekamp (USA))
4345[4] 4853[7] 6126[10]

**Tropical Rock** *Ralph Beckett* a87 84
3 b f Fastnet Rock(AUS) Tropical Treat (Bahamian Bounty)
2623[14] 4903[5] 8310[3] 8706[10]

**Tropical Waters (IRE)**
*Robert Cowell* 48
2 b f Acclamation Hurricane Havoc (IRE) (Hurricane Run (IRE))
8324[4]

**Tropics (USA)** *Dean Ivory* a98 96
9 ch g Speightstown(USA) Taj Aire (USA) (Taj Alriyadh (USA))
2907[6] 3867[10] 5116[4] 5911[8] 7118[7] 7455[7] 8639[4] 9016[2]◆ (9269) 9453[4]

**Trotter** *Stuart Kittow* a76 41
3 b g Piccolo Vintage Steps (IRE) (Bahamian Bounty)
600[6] 956[2] 1064[2] 1761[4] 7408[8] 8311[2] 8842[2] 9152[3]

**Trouble And Strife (IRE)**
*Sir Mark Prescott Bt* a54 51
2 br f Declaration Of War(USA) Rare Tern (IRE) (Pivotal)
7875[7] 8322[8] 8501[5]

**Trouble Of Course (FR)**
*Niels Petersen* 97
3 gr c Rajsaman(FR) Sister Trouble (FR) (Spectrum (IRE))
933a[8] (6501a)

**Troy Boy** *Rebecca Bastiman* a50 52
7 b g Choisir(AUS) Love Thing (Phountzi (USA))
176[14]

**True Blue Moon (IRE)**
*Joseph Patrick O'Brien* a82 98
2 gr c Holy Roman Emperor(IRE) Fancy Intense (Peintre Celebre (USA))
(2861a) 3993[6]◆ 4386a[6] 6935[6]

**True Colors** *Richard Fahey* a67 62
3 b g Sir Percy Shesells Seashells (Tiger Hill (IRE))
4784[3] 5577[6] 6236[7] 7062[3] 7541[9] 8218[9] 8801[8] 9034[10]

**True Companion (IRE)**
*Adrian Brendan Joyce* a51 67
4 b g Fast Company(IRE) Panglossian (IRE) (Barathea (IRE))
8473[5]

**True Destiny** *Roger Charlton* a40 47
2 ch g Mastercraftsman(IRE) Holy Dazzle (Sunday Break (JPN))
8677[11] 8840[10]

**True Gentleman** *Sylvester Kirk*
3 b g Bahamian Bounty Kampai (Sakhee (USA))
2090[14] 2957[13]

**True North (IRE)**
*Sir Mark Prescott Bt* a29 64
2 b g Henrythenavigator(USA) Cosmic Fire (FR) (Dalakhani (IRE))
5834[14] 6525[7] 6897[13] 7250[7]

**True Romance (FR)** *F-H Graffard* 95
2 b c George Vancouver(USA) Hallen (FR) (Midyan (USA))
5626a[2] (7012a)

**True Romance (IRE)** *James Given* a70 77
3 gr g Mastercraftsman(IRE) Full Of Love (IRE) (Hawk Wing (USA))
2186[5] 2702[3] (3261) 3665[4] 4838[2] 5540[4] 6187[6]

**True Valour (IRE)** *J P Murtagh* 110
3 b c Kodiac Sutton Veny (IRE) (Acclamation)
3302[3] 3959[8] (4383a) 6119a[9] 6959a[2] 8003[7]

**Truffles (IRE)** *Ms Sheila Lavery* a43 84
4 b m Canford Cliffs(IRE) Parlour (Dansili)
4385a[12] 5688a[7]

**Trulee Scrumptious**
*Peter Charalambous* a60 74
8 b m Strategic Prince Morning Rise (GER) (Acatenango (GER))
(4047) 4311[2] 5113[6]

**Trulove** *John David Riches* a23 31
4 b m Piccolo Snow Dancer (IRE) (Desert Style (IRE))
2312[11] 2950[6] 3977[11] 5069[7] 5472[11]

**Truly** *Paul Collins* a38 67
6 b m Archipenko(USA) Sincerely (Singspiel (IRE))
5835[13] 6131[11]

**Trump Alexander (IRE)**
*Richard Hannon* 76
2 b f Iffraaj Obama Rule (IRE) (Danehill Dancer (IRE))
6917[5] 7403[8]

**Trumps Up** *Mick Channon* 76
2 b c Cape Blanco(IRE) Zeva (Zamindar (USA))
(5749) (6658) 7624[4]

**Trusting Friend (USA)** *Kevin Ryan* a36 78
2 b c The Factor(USA) She's Justa Friend (USA) (Hussonet (USA))
2403[2] 3187[11] (4502)

**Trust In You (FR)** *Alex Fracas* 65
2 b f Pour Moi(IRE) Too Marvelous (FR) (Dansili)
6542a[10] 8228a[7]

**Trust Me Boy** *John E Long* a57 39
9 gr g Avonbridge Eastern Lyric (Petong)
390[9] 481[4] 1587[2] 1868[5] 6529[8] 9076[14]

**Trust The Indian** *Bill Turner* a45 46
3 ch g Sleeping Indian Trust Fund Babe (IRE) (Captain Rio)
126[7] 245[5] 377[9] 3166[8]

**Trust The Man (IRE)** *Adam West* a3 7
4 br g Manduro(GER) Saree (Barathea (IRE))
141[8] 7215[9] 7948[11]

**Trust You** *Endo Botti* 102
5 ch g Kheleyf(USA) Evening Guest (FR) (Be My Guest (USA))
(2867a) 8449a[4]

**Truth Or Dare** *James Bethell* a89 96
6 b g Invincible Spirit(IRE) Unreachable Star (Halling (USA))
2384[4]◆ 2799[3] 3294[6] 3565[4] 4103[3]◆ 4377[2] 4961[2] (5530) 6419[7] 6873[5] 8009[19]

**Try Again (IRE)** *Paul W Flynn* a74 74
4 b g Dubai Destination(USA) Diamond Katie (IRE) (Night Shift (USA))
(2430)

**Tryst (GER)** *Henk Grewe* a69 79
3 b c Kamsin(GER) Tamaja (GER) (Tiger Hill (IRE))
6496a[5]

**Tsarglas** *Christopher Wilson* a38 18
6 gr g Verglas(IRE) Russian Empress (IRE) (Trans Island)
361[5]

**Tsundoku (IRE)** *Alexandra Dunn* a49 56
6 ch m Medicean Toberanthawn (IRE) (Danehill Dancer (IRE))
1086[11] 1283[10] 1556[8] 3575[12] (5361) 7232[9]

**Ttmab** *Mark H Tompkins* a60 27
2 b c Mawatheeq(USA) Astrodiva (Where Or When (IRE))
8352[7] 9336[6]

**Tuamhain** *Kevin Prendergast* a40 60
2 b f Mayson Gandini (Night Shift (USA))
7423a[5]

**Tuff Love (IRE)** *G M Lyons* a84 83
3 b g Casamento(IRE) Hams (USA) (Dixie Union (USA))
1012a[3]

**Tuff Rock (USA)** *Ed Walker* a90 91
3 b g Fastnet Rock(AUS) Wonder Of Wonders (USA) (Kingmambo (USA))
2783[4] (3533) 5598[12] *6579*[2] **8289**[2]

**Tukhoom (IRE)** *Michael Herrington* 85
4 b g Acclamation Carioca (IRE) (Rakti)
3095[15] **4339**[7] 5059[5] 5664[10]

**Tulane (IRE)** *Richard Phillips* 67
2 br g Arcano(IRE) Jeunesse Doree (IRE) (Rock Of Gibraltar (IRE))
5047[7] **5749**[3] 7120[10] 8467[12]

**Tulipa Rosa (IRE)** *J Boisnard* a71
3 b f Excelebration(IRE) Tulipe Rose (FR) (Shamardal (USA))
***799a***[10]

**Tulip Dress** *Anthony Carson* a65 68
4 ch m Dutch Art White Dress (IRE) (Pivotal)
*689*[2] *806*[9] **(2053)** 2587[8] *3139*[4] 3521[3] 4047[6] 5119[7] 5367[4] **6345**[2] 6753[5] *7539*[6] *9279*[5]

**Tulip Fever** *William Haggas* 81
2 ch f Dutch Art Cara Gina (Bahamian Bounty)
3215[3]◆ (3789) 4199[3] (5143) 5614[3] **(6481)** 8008[9]

**Tullinahoo (IRE)** *Denis Coakley* a61 58
3 b g Elzaam(AUS) Pitullie (USA) (Rockport Harbor (USA))
*4983*[11]

**Tullius (IRE)** *Andrew Balding* a103 113
9 ch g Le Vie Dei Colori Whipped Queen (USA) (Kingmambo (USA))
**1493**[5] 3069[4]

**Tullyallen (IRE)** *Richard Hannon* a70 57
2 b c Arcano(IRE) Come April (Singspiel (IRE))
6199[4] *8030*[5] ***8339***[3]

**Tumbaga (USA)** *Saeed bin Suroor* a94 98
6 bb g E Dubai(USA) Brushed Gold (USA) (Touch Gold (USA))
*432a*[6] 698a[10] **4069**[10] 4918[20] *5744*[8]

**Tumblewind** *Richard Whitaker* 98
7 ch m Captain Rio African Breeze (Atraf)
2764[6] 2856[3] (3052) **(3295)** 3625[5]

**Tum Tum** *Martyn Meade* a79 72
2 ch c Dawn Approach(IRE) Lalectra (King Charlemagne (USA))
8560[5] *9200*[4] ***9312***[2]

**Tundra** *Roger Varian* a69 92
3 b f Bated Breath Tanouma (USA) (Mr Greeley (USA))
(3825) **5597**[9] 6234[13] 7811[7]

**Tunes (AUS)** *Grant Young* 83
8 br g Viscount(AUS) Tin Pan (AUS) (Commands (AUS))
**8751a**[10]

**Tunes Of Glory** *Sir Mark Prescott Bt* a77 78
2 b c Lope De Vega(IRE) Bay Tree (IRE) (Daylami (IRE))
*(4007)* *4452*[6] *5240*[3] **6367**[2] *6932*[5] 7384[6]

**Tuolumne Meadows**
*Tony Newcombe* a79 58
4 b m High Chaparral(IRE) Seren Devious (Dr Devious (IRE))
**1938**[4] *2515*[5] 3684[5] 4089[5] 4346[2] *6069*[4] *6796*[7] *8846*[15] *9077*[13]

**Tupi (IRE)** *Richard Hannon* 114
5 b g Tamayuz Carioca (IRE) (Rakti)
698a[9] 914a[15] 1044a[4] **(1491)** 2737[6] 4071[6] 5149[10] 5690a[3] 6428[9] 7356[7]

**Turaathy (IRE)** *Tony Newcombe* a56 41
4 b m Lilbourne Lad(IRE) Key Girl (IRE) (Key Of Luck (USA))
*7617*[10] ***1260***[9] 5713[13] 6752[8]

**Turanga Leela** *Ian Williams* a79 84
3 ch f Paco Boy(IRE) Sunday Bess (JPN) (Deep Impact (JPN))
2557[10] **(3063)** **3793**[4] **4889**[3] 6923[6] 7811[8] 8488[4] *9089*[7] *9269*[6] *9453*[10]

**Turbine (IRE)** *Denis Gerard Hogan* a82 92
4 b g Cape Cross(IRE) Chiquita Linda (IRE) (Mujadil (USA))
*1353a*[7] ***5517a***[4] 6491a[12] 6961a[12]

**Turf Express (AUS)**
*Christophe Mosse* a57 41
10 ch g Danehill Dancer(IRE) Newscaster (AUS) (Marscay (AUS))
*515a*[14]

**Turflady (GER)** *Frau C Barsig* a37 61
4 ch m Areion(GER) Turfblume (GER) (Lando (GER))
***384a***[10]

**Turf Laurel (IRE)** *S Kobayashi* a89 109
3 ch f Footstepsinthesand Dame D'Honneur (IRE) (Teofilo (IRE))
**3881a**[5] 4666a[4] 5449a[5] *8986a*[10]

**Turin Redstar** *Ralph Beckett* a80 86
3 b g Kyllachy Meddle (Diktat)
*276*[5] *(678)* **2557**[2] 3844[7]

**Turnbury** *Nikki Evans* a61 68
6 b g Azamour(IRE) Scottish Heights (IRE) (Selkirk (USA))
*333*[9] *648*[8] *1067*[6] ***1249***[5] *1698*[3] 4801[DSQ] 5249[4] 7085[3] 8301[4] 8682[8]

**Turning Gold** *Sir Mark Prescott Bt* a62 83
3 ch g Pivotal Illusion (Anabaa (USA))
2347[9] *2790*[3] 4050[2] (4541)◆ **(4765)**◆ 5115[7] 7119[8] 7550[2]

**Turning The Table (IRE)**
*David Simcock* 92
4 gr m Mastercraftsman(IRE) Duchess Dee (IRE) (Bachelor Duke (USA))
2387[3] **(2906)** 3158[4] 4915[5] 5529[7]

**Turnitaround (AUS)**
*Matthew Williams* 109
6 b g Hard Spun(USA) Devon Dancer (AUS) (Royal Academy (USA))
**8059a**[8]

**Turnpike Trip** *Henry Candy* a79 86
3 b g Champs Elysees Neqaawi (Alhaarth (IRE))
*328*[4] 2175[4] *3209*[2] 4221[4] 5364[6] (6277) **(6822)** 7505[5]

**Turquoise Bay (USA)** *Chris Dwyer* 62
2 b c Lonhro(AUS) Torre Di Pisa (USA) (Tiznow (USA))
**6108**[5] 7250[9]◆

**Turret Rocks (IRE)** *J S Bolger* 106
4 b m Fastnet Rock(AUS) Beyond Compare (IRE) (Galileo (IRE))
**(2637a)** 3101a[3] **3961**[6] **4419a**[3] 4934a[4]

**Tuscan Gold** *Micky Hammond* a71 69
10 ch g Medicean Louella (USA) (El Gran Senor (USA))
1703[2] **(2032)** 3663[7] 4120[5] 6233[8] 7330[4] 7893[2] 8292[5]

**Tuscan Pearl** *William Knight* 60
2 b f Medicean Western Pearl (High Chaparral (IRE))
**8425**[6]

**Tuscany (IRE)** *Paul Cole* a76 64
3 ch g Poet's Voice Avril Rose (IRE) (Xaar)
3691[5] 5458[10] *7063*[10] *(7723)* ***(8958)***

**Tusked Wings (IRE)**
*Jean-Pierre Carvalho* 105
3 ch f Adlerflug(GER) Tucana (GER) (Acatenango (GER))
(3371a) 5693a[4] 6710a[4] **8527a**[7]

**Tu Te Calmes (FR)** *F Chappet* a49 33
3 ch g American Post You Rock My World (IRE) (Red Ransom (USA))
***838a***[9] 1417a[11]

**Tuvalu** *J-M Osorio* 95
5 b h Shirocco(GER) Light Impact (IRE) (Fantastic Light (USA))
**5198a**[5]

**Twaddle** *Rae Guest* 25
3 b f Paco Boy(IRE) Blue Dream (IRE) (Cadeaux Genereux)
3657[14]

**Tweetheart** *Ron Barr* a52 52
4 ch m Dutch Art Strictly (USA) (Fusaichi Pegasus (USA))
**2898**[9] 3185[10]

**Tweeting** *John Quinn* 29
2 ch f Sleeping Indian Lady Sledmere (IRE) (Barathea (IRE))
3179[12] **4054**[5]

**Twelve A** *David O'Meara* 39
2 ch c Piccolo Nihal (IRE) (Singspiel (IRE))
**6311**[7] 7326[10]

**Twentysvnthlancers** *Paul Midgley* a52 74
4 b g Hellvelyn Subtle Move (USA) (Known Fact (USA))
1805[9] 2034[11] **2700**[4] 3202[9] 3667[3] 4015[9] 4795[8] 6660[3] 7164[4] 7660[5] 8168[8]

**Twenty Times (IRE)**
*Richard Hughes* 91
3 b f Dream Ahead(USA) Mad Existence (IRE) (Val Royal (FR))
2172[5] (3425)◆ 3779[5] 5113[2] 5682[5] **(6369)**◆ 7816[4]

**Twentytwowontdo (IRE)**
*David O'Meara* 69
2 ch f Dandy Man(IRE) Balladiene (IRE) (Noverre (USA))
2836[4] 3430[3] **(3562)**

**Twickenham (IRE)**
*John Joseph Murphy* a48 44
2 b c Champs Elysees Morinqua (IRE) (Cadeaux Genereux)
***8372***[8]

**Twiggy** *Iain Jardine* a48 64
3 b f Sixties Icon Queen's Pudding (IRE) (Royal Applause)
2293[10] **3142**[2] 5604[7] 5880[7] 6470[9] *6946*[9] 7704[3] 8479[4] *9334*[9]

**Twilight Angel** *Emma Owen* a52 45
9 ch m Compton Place Leaping Flame (USA) (Trempolino (USA))
*1671*[11] *315*[6] *436*[9] ***747***[7]

**Twilight Payment (IRE)** *J S Bolger* 112
4 b g Teofilo(IRE) Dream On Buddy (IRE) (Oasis Dream)
1999a[3] **3057a**[2] 6214a[3] 6976a[6]

**Twilight Spirit** *Tony Carroll* 66
3 b f Assertive Twilight Mistress (Bin Ajwaad (IRE))
3171[7] 4303[8] 5167[2] 5826[4] 6656[4] **(7122)** 8328[8]

**Twin Appeal (IRE)** *David Barron* a94 95
6 b g Oratorio(IRE) Velvet Appeal (IRE) (Petorius (IRE))
*1105*[3] *1295*[3] **(1799)** 2142[5] 2384[7] *2922*[6] 3842[6] 4270[3] 4622[2] 4916[7] 5434[4] 5668[8] 6414[6] 6879[8] 8014[8] 8736[5] *8872*[2] *(9272)*

**Twin Point** *Charlie Fellowes* a87 82
6 br g Invincible Spirit(IRE) Gemini Joan (Montjeu (IRE))
***(506)*** *896*[8] 2528[5] ***3723***[2]

**Twin Star (IRE)** *Andrew Balding* 97
3 ch g Tagula(IRE) Chronicle (Observatory (USA))
**3109a**[4] 3998[15] 5095[5] 6474[5]

**Twisted Logic (IRE)** *Keith Dalgleish* 49
2 b c Shamardal(USA) Myrine (IRE) (Sadler's Wells (USA))
**6854**[10] 7955[9]

**Twister (IRE)** *Sir Mark Prescott Bt* a63 49
2 ch g Hurricane Run(IRE) Arizona Sun (IRE) (Spinning World (USA))
7281[11] ***8245***[8] 8508[8]

**Twist Of Magic (IRE)**
*John James Feane* a72 73
3 b f Arcano(IRE) Walayef (USA) (Danzig (USA))
**8512**[8]

**Twiston Shout (IRE)**
*Richard Spencer* a47
3 b g Lawman(FR) Minkova (IRE) (Sadler's Wells (USA))
***1822***[3]

**Twistsandturns (IRE)**
*Declan Carroll* a58 44
6 b g Acclamation Shesthebiscuit (Diktat)
4575[10] 5181[10] *5848*[11] **6437**[7] *8134*[4]

**Twizzell** *K R Burke* a82 82
3 b f Equiano(FR) Greensand (Green Desert (USA))
1731[9] (2223) 2806[4] 3579[3] 3741[10] **4835**[3] 5383[3] **6314**[4] *7939*[8]

**Two Dollars (IRE)** *William Jarvis* a64 67
3 ch g Casamento(IRE) Two Marks (USA) (Woodman (USA))
*2921*[4] **3506**[8] 3909[7] 5061[4] 5406[6] 6293[8] *8377*[5]

**Two For Two (IRE)** *Roger Fell* a83 99
9 b g Danehill Dancer(IRE) D'Articleshore (IRE) (Definite Article)
1734[6]◆ 2155[2] 2406[2] 2735[14] 3498[9] **(4662)** 5382[9] 5668[4] 5926[3] 6209[8] 6520[7] 8009[15]

**Two In The Pink (IRE)**
*Ralph J Smith* a70 62
7 rg m Clodovil(IRE) Secret Circle (Magic Ring (IRE))
*120*[9] *482*[12] ***865***[10]

**Two Seas** *George Peckham* 60
2 b g Sepoy(AUS) Fifty (IRE) (Fasliyev (USA))
4151[10] 4598[8] **6146**[7]

**Two Weeks** *Clive Cox* a78 63
2 ch f Mayson Laurena (GER) (Acatenango (GER))
6138[5] ***(8851)***

**Ty Cobb (IRE)** *F Foresi* a64 55
6 b g Dandy Man(IRE) Mrs Moonlight (Ajdal (USA))
***822a***[8]

**Tyler U (USA)** *Troy S Wismer* a52 98
3 b g Into Mischief(USA) Vodianova (USA) (Tapit (USA))
**7851a**[13]

**Tylery Wonder (IRE)** *Paul Midgley* a80 92
7 ch g Choisir(AUS) Over The Tylery (IRE) (Swallow Flight (IRE))
*1777*[7] 2123[3] 2683[2] 2951[5] 3295[4] 3827[11] (4379) 4867[10] 5602[7] 6185[10] 7055[10] **(7425a)** 8012[4] 8238[9] *8540*[6]

**Tynecastle Park** *Robert Eddery* a59 67
4 b g Sea The Stars(IRE) So Silk (Rainbow Quest (USA))
*314*[6] *508*[7] *6530*[2] ***9242***[5]

**Tyrell (IRE)** *Micky Hammond* a77 77
4 b g Teofilo(IRE) Sleeveless (USA) (Fusaichi Pegasus (USA))
***3213***[3] 3907[3] **4471**[4] 5590[2] 7330[10]

**Ty Rock Brandy (IRE)** *Lee Smyth* a62 68
2 b f Dandy Man(IRE) Britain's Pride (Royal Applause)
3237[5] 3705[4] ***(9266)***

**Tyrolean** *Seamus Durack* a33 68
4 b g Raven's Pass(USA) Alessandria (Sunday Silence (USA))
*3456*[11] 3682[6] 5432[7] 6370[2] **7048**[3] *8396*[13]

**Tyrsal (IRE)** *Clifford Lines* a62 69
6 b g Jeremy(USA) Blanchelande (IRE) (Subotica (FR))
*169*[3] *461*[7] *636*[10] 2070[8] 2729[2]◆ 2971[2] 3726[5] 4185[4] (5080) 5336[2] 5421[9] **5809**[2] 6109[8] 7582[6] 8143[10] 8326[6] *8993*[6]

**UAE King** *Roger Varian* 104
3 b c Frankel Zomaradah (Deploy)
1963[5] 2576[2] (3717) (4586) (5351) 6421[3] **7547**[3]

**UAE Prince (IRE)** *Roger Varian* 104
4 b g Sea The Stars(IRE) By Request (Giant's Causeway (USA))
(1911) 2604[5] 4918[4] **5500**[4]◆ 6449[12]

**UAE Queen** *Roger Varian* 86
3 b f Oasis Dream Pongee (Barathea (IRE))
2898[3] 3626[7] (5038) 6274[2] **(7276)** 8007[13]

**UAE Soldier (USA)** *Roger Varian* 29
2 b g Dansili Time On (Sadler's Wells (USA))
**8508**[10]

**Uber Cool (IRE)**
*Jane Chapple-Hyam* 88
3 b g Born To Sea(IRE) My Uptown Girl (Dubai Destination (USA))
2681[5] 3717[5] (4738) (5667) **6865**[3] (7565)

**Ubla (IRE)** *Gay Kelleway* a67 61
4 ch g Arcano(IRE) Manuelita Rose (ITY) (Desert Style (IRE))
*6*[10] *570*[8] 5039[7] 5363[3] 5857[6] *6288*[7] *6795*[2] *7723*[6] 8328[3] ***9032***[4] *9219*[3] *9307*[5] ***(9432)***

**Ucel (IRE)** *F Chappet* a83 46
3 b g Kyllachy Umthoulah (IRE) (Unfuwain (USA))
2484a[15] ***4289a***[4] *5521a*[8] *6455a*[10]

**Uchronique (FR)** *M Boutin* 70
2 b f Palace Episode(USA) Arakawa (FR) (Indian Rocket)
1335a[5] 2642a[6] 3444a[5] **(4389a)** 6050a[3] 7592a[6]

**Uczitelka Tanca (POL)**
*M Borkowski*
6 b m Cloword(IRE) Ukajali (POL) (Royal Court (IRE))
*715a*[7] *953a*[5]

**Udogo** *Brendan Powell* a86 72
6 b g Lucky Story(USA) Welanga (Dansili)
3920[8] 4443[6] **4976**[5] 5477[9] 6139[6] *8641*[9] *9270*[9] *9459*[9]

**Udontdodou** *Richard Guest* a108 84
4 b g Fastnet Rock(AUS) Forever Times (So Factual (USA))
*(2113)*◆ 2736[8] 3410[7] *(3969)* *5241*[3] ***(7604)***◆

**Udzungwa Forest** *Henry Candy* 60
3 ch f Power Uvinza (Bertolini (USA))
**5124**[9]

**Uele River** *Henry Candy* a71 101
5 b m Refuse To Bend(IRE) Baddi Heights (FR) (Shirley Heights)
2392[9] 4915[4] 6074[7] 6440[4] **(6915a)** 7581[7]

**Ulshaw Bridge (IRE)** *James Bethell* a72 90
2 b c High Chaparral(IRE) Sharaarah (IRE) (Oasis Dream)
*4259*[4]◆ (4919)◆ **5681**[3] 6326[10] 8412[6]

**Ulster (IRE)** *Saeed bin Suroor* a76
2 rg c Intello(GER) Ronaldsay (Kirkwall)
***8704***[4]

**Ultima D (USA)** *Wesley A Ward* a80 99
2 ch f Scat Daddy(USA) La Violette (USA) (Coronado's Quest (USA))
**8575a**[12]

**Ultimate Avenue (IRE)** *Ed Walker* a89 105
3 b g Excelebration(IRE) Dance Avenue (IRE) (Sadler's Wells (USA))
*1797*[3] **4813**[3] 6419[9] 7782[6]

**Ultimate Dream (IRE)** *G M Lyons* 59
3 ch g Arcano(IRE) Miss Azeza (Dutch Art)
**1386a**[5]

**Ultra (IRE)** *A Fabre* 112
4 ch h Manduro(GER) Epitome (IRE) (Nashwan (USA))
**(1691a)**

**Ulysses (GER)** *Ralph Beckett* a71 68
3 b g Sinndar(IRE) Ungarin (GER) (Goofalik (USA))
***1001***[2] *1342*[2] 2039[13] 3788[6] 5025[5] 5581[6]

**Ulysses (IRE)** *Sir Michael Stoute* 127
4 ch h Galileo(IRE) Light Shift (USA) (Kingmambo (USA))
(2127) 3962[3] (4638) 5394[2] **(6328)** 7668a[3]

**Umaimah (USA)** *William Haggas* a26 60
2 b f Speightstown(USA) Soohaad (USA) (Hard Spun (USA))
**7620**[6] *8373*[12]

**Unabated (IRE)** *Marco Botti* a109 103
3 b c Bated Breath Elhareer (IRE) (Selkirk (USA))
*(1311)*◆ ***(4353)***◆ 4813[14] 5684[3]

**Unblinking** *Nigel Twiston-Davies* a60 56
4 b g Cacique(IRE) Deliberate (King's Best (USA))
2841[8] 7960[8] ***9317***[5]◆

**Unbridled Spirit** *Andrew Balding* 64
2 b g Passing Glance Sweet Mandolin (Soviet Star (USA))
**7273**[7] 7915[5] 8389[10]

**Unchaining Melody** *Marco Botti* 68
2 b f Excelebration(IRE) Sky To Sky (USA) (Sky Classic (CAN))
**6583**[2]

**Uncle Bernie (IRE)**
*Sarah Hollinshead* a76 77
7 gr g Aussie Rules(USA) Alwiyda (USA) (Trempolino (USA))
*74*[2] *380*[4] *1153*[6] **(1703)**◆ *2788*[6] 3663[10] 4120[6]

**Uncle Charlie (IRE)** *Ann Duffield* a56 69
3 b g Vale Of York(IRE) Velvet Kiss (IRE) (Danehill Dancer (IRE))
2885[8] (3403) 3897[11] 4303[7] **6313**[3] 7017[4] 7525[7] 8481[4]

**Uncovered** *Tom Dascombe* a47 16
2 b g Helmet(AUS) Caritas (Generous (IRE))
***4725***[6] 5292[12] 5749[9] *6790*[6]

**Under Approval** *Karen Tutty* a41 57
6 b g Captain Gerrard(IRE) Dockside Strike (Docksider (USA))
*1435*[3] 1722[13] 2076[10] 2337[6] 2628[13] **2994**[4] 3710[12] 3914[8]

**Under Attack (IRE)** *Ruth Carr* a78 83
4 b g Dubawi(IRE) Ship's Biscuit (Tiger Hill (IRE))
**1964**[6] 2965[7] 3947[5] 4796[7] 5265[5]

**Under Control (IRE)**
*William Haggas* a83 56
3 b g Power High Figurine (IRE) (High Chaparral (IRE))
***6576***[3]◆ 7162[9] ***7999***[3]

**Undercover Brother** *David O'Meara* a38 73
2 ch g Captain Gerrard(IRE) Socceroo (Choisir (AUS))
3562[3] (3972) **4895**[2] 5440[7] 6055[3] 6756[4] 7385[2] *7706*[8]

**Under Offer (IRE)** *James Tate* 68
2 ch f Bated Breath Bailonguera (ARG) (Southern Halo (USA))
**1908**[3] 2583[5]

**Under Siege (IRE)** *Stuart Williams* a88 88
5 b g Invincible Spirit(IRE) Interpose (Indian Ridge (IRE))
*547*[7] ***857***[2] *1302*[3] 2040[7]

**Understory (USA)** *Tim McCarthy* a55 53
10 b g Forestry(USA) Sha Tha (USA) (Mr Prospector (USA))
*621*[10] *820*[10] *1322*[4] *6621*[4] **7990**[7] *9237*[9]

**Under The Covers** *Ronald Harris* a66 96
4 b m Stimulation(IRE) Sakha (Wolfhound (USA))
*1889*[5] 2510[4] *3139*[8] (3279) 4201[2]◆ 5869[10] (6137) **(6371)** 6864[6] 7144[18] 7811[9]

**Undisclosed Desire (IRE)**
*Agostino Affe'* 75
2 b c Casamento(IRE) So Sweet (IRE) (Cape Cross (IRE))
**8620a**[5]

**Undiscovered Angel (FR)**
*K R Burke* a33 49
3 b f Wootton Bassett Angel Voices (IRE) (Tagula (IRE))
2033[3] **3044**[3] 3555[4] *4288a*[9] 5268a[4] 5910a[7] 7052[11] 7459[4] *8716*[5] 8960a[6]

**Unforgetable Filly** *Hugo Palmer* 106
3 b f Sepoy(AUS) Beautiful Filly (Oasis Dream)
**1883**[2] 2434[6] **(3334)** (3882a) 7113[13] 8071a[10]

**Unforgiving Minute** *John Butler* a92 66
6 b g Cape Cross(IRE) Ada River (Dansili)
*3212*[10] *4563*[9] ***(6949)*** *(8881)* ***9083***[2]

**Unfortunately (IRE)** *K R Burke* 115
2 b c Society Rock(IRE) Unfortunate (Komaite (USA))
1858[5] (2771) 3611a[2] 4434[2]◆ (5195a) **(6249a)** 7618[9]

**Unfurl (NZ)** *Darren Weir* 90
5 b m Raise The Flag Emerald Fire (NZ) (Honor Grades (USA))
**1400a**[9]

**Uni** *Chad C Brown* a93 106
3 ch f More Than Ready(USA) Unaided (Dansili)
1657a[6] (2560a) **4650a**[3] 8071a[4]

**Unified** *Clive Cox* a2 75
3 b f Oasis Dream Ensemble (FR) (Iron Mask (USA))
3329[2]◆ 3748[4] 4444[4] **(4737)** *7493*[12]

**Union Rose** *Ronald Harris* a88 92
5 b g Stimulation(IRE) Dot Hill (Refuse To Bend (IRE))
2578[6] 2764[5] 3092[8] 3321[17] 3741[7] **(4732)** 5219[4] 5505[7] 6137[4] 7461[5] 7809[7] 8167[10] *(9079)* *9234*[6]

**Unique Bella (USA)**
*Jerry Hollendorfer* a115
3 rg f Tapit(USA) Unrivaled Belle (USA) (Unbridled's Song (USA))
***8605a***[7]

**Unison (IRE)** *Jeremy Scott* a67 83
7 b g Jeremy(USA) Easter Song (USA) (Rubiano (USA))
4254[11] 5838[4] 6701[12] 7083[6]
**United Color (USA)** *D Selvaratnam* a104 94
8 b h Ghostzapper(USA) Silk Candy (CAN) (Langfuhr (CAN))
321a[9]
**United Kingdom** *Paul Cole* a63 44
2 b g Equiano(FR) Lucky Legs (IRE) (Danehill Dancer (IRE))
6868[7] 8028[5]
**Unite The Clans (IRE)**
*John Patrick Shanahan* 77
3 b g Danehill Dancer(IRE) Janna's Jewel (IRE) (Traditionally (USA))
2175[3] 2527[5] 4247[5] 4474[9] (6443)
**Unit Of Assessment (IRE)**
*William Knight* a70 74
3 b g Dragon Pulse(IRE) Before The Storm (Sadler's Wells (USA))
1857[10] 2783[11] 3393[2] 4764[3] 5589[6] 6310[9] 7095[3] 7902[4] 8549[8] 9211[3] 9459[2]
**Universal Command**
*Roger Charlton* a70 61
2 b g Delegator Telescopic (Galileo (IRE))
5106[10] 6132[8] 8029[4]
**Unnoticed** *Ollie Pears* a70 72
5 b g Observatory(USA) Celestial Empire (USA) (Empire Maker (USA))
67[2] 426[5] 663[2] 850[7] 8772[8] 9307[4]
**Unonothinjonsnow** *Richard Guest* a32 51
3 b g Arakan(USA) Kleio (Sadler's Wells (USA))
5536[6] 6529[7] 7219[3] 7325[10] 8513[12] 8654[6] 9026[12]
**Unsuspected Girl (IRE)**
*Milton Bradley* a58 57
4 b m Rip Van Winkle(IRE) Sweet Sioux (Halling (USA))
5024[8] 7319[10] (7905) 8313[12] 8661[7] 8957[8]
**Untamed Domain (USA)**
*H Graham Motion* 113
2 b c Animal Kingdom(USA) Ciao (USA) (Lear Fan (USA))
8577a[2]
**Until Midnight (IRE)**
*Eugene Stanford* a85 77
7 b g Moss Vale(IRE) Emma's Star (ITY) (Darshaan)
760[3] 1301[2]◆ 1622[5] 2320[2] 2975[6] 3723[5] 4887[8] 5245[2]
**Untold Secret** *S bin Ghadayer* a72 77
5 b g Shamardal(USA) Confidential Lady (Singspiel (IRE))
203a[7]
**Untrapped (USA)** *Steven Asmussen* a110
3 bb c Trappe Shot(USA) Exit Three (USA) (Giant's Causeway (USA))
2420a[12]
**Unveiling** *Jonathan Portman* a71
2 b f Mayson Silkenveil (IRE) (Indian Ridge (IRE))
(9371)
**Unwritten** *K R Burke* 85
2 b g Poet's Voice Passata (FR) (Polar Falcon (USA))
6380[4] (7556)◆ 8290[5]
**Unzipped** *Stuart Edmunds* a33 66
3 ch f Captain Gerrard(IRE) Justazippy (Where Or When (IRE))
1685[9] 1968[15] 2507[14]
**Upavon** *Stuart Williams* a98 79
7 b g Avonbridge Blaina (Compton Place)
63[3] 326[8] 957[2] 1152[2] 1222[9] 4272[6] 5241[8] (5818) 5869[4] 6720[3] 8660[5] 9079[8] 9339[3]
**Upended** *Chris Wall* a56 60
3 b g Paco Boy(IRE) Upskittled (Diktat)
2475[12] 2798[6] 3394[7] 5275[5] 5761[2] 6946[5]
**Upendi (FR)** *Robert Collet* a77 90
3 b f Siyouni(FR) Courchevel (IRE) (Whipper (USA))
1660a[9]
**Upgrade** *K R Burke* a75 74
3 gr c Excelebration(IRE) Pinch Of Posh (IRE) (Pivotal)
65[4] (417)
**Uphold** *Gay Kelleway* a67 57
10 b g Oasis Dream Allegro Viva (USA) (Distant View (USA))
364a[10] 691a[3] 822a[11] 1257[9] 2272[3] 4158[7]
**Upper Lambourn (IRE)**
*Denis Quinn* a44 11
9 b g Exceed And Excel(AUS) In The Fashion (IRE) (In The Wings)
386[5] 640[3]◆ 761[5] 6850[8] 7606[9]
**Upstaging** *Paul Cole* a100 107
5 b g Mount Nelson Corndavon (USA) (Sheikh Albadou)
3034[9]◆ 3410[2] (4411) 5640[3] 6275[2] 8044[7]
**Up Sticks And Go** *Keith Dalgleish* 79
2 gr c Equiano(FR) Reaching Ahead (USA) (Mizzen Mast (USA))
4074[2] 4472[4] 6689[2]◆ 7564[2] (8649)
**Up Ten Down Two (IRE)**
*Michael Easterby* a72 64
8 b g Hurricane Run(IRE) Darabela (IRE) (Desert King (IRE))
(1197) (1469) 3740[7] 5872[7] 6757[9] 7386[6] 7924[7] 8806[8] 9346[3]
**Uptown Funk (IRE)** *Keith Dalgleish* a74 73
3 b g Galileo(IRE) All's Forgotten (USA) (Darshaan)
2584[5] 3720[6] 4623[2] 6871[5] 7319[3] 8114[6] 9258[3]◆
**Uptown Girl** *Lydia Pearce* a20
3 b f Doncaster Rover(USA) Mon Petit Diamant (Hector Protector (USA))
9435[9]
**Urban Fox** *James Tate* a81 101
3 b f Foxwedge(AUS) Lomapamar (Nashwan (USA))
1958[2] 2434[8] 3319[7] 5352[4] 6697[8] 7356[4] 7808[4]
**Urban Poete (FR)** *M Delzangles* 69
2 b f Poet's Voice Turtle Bow (FR) (Turtle Island (IRE))
7637a[12]
**Urban Soul (IRE)** *James Bethell* a68 68
2 b g Worthadd(IRE) Capsaicin (IRE) (Invincible Spirit (IRE))
4577[7] 5380[7] 6042[3] 8586[8] 8848[4] 9238[2]
**Urban Space** *John Flint* a67 73
11 ch g Sulamani(IRE) Rasmalai (Sadler's Wells (USA))
1763[5] 2363[5] 3775[6]
**Urban Spirit (IRE)** *Roger Fell* a48 50
3 b g Born To Sea(IRE) Rose Of Mooncoin (IRE) (Brief Truce (USA))
2077[5] 2853[4] 3151[6] 6786[10] 7331[5] 7820[4] 8720[7] 9018[4]
**Urbino** *Sir Michael Stoute* a56
2 b c Dansili Novellara (Sadler's Wells (USA))
8340[4]◆
**Uriah Heep (FR)** *R Mike Smith* a50 61
8 b g Danehill Dancer(IRE) Canasita (Zafonic (USA))
3978[4] 4659[8] 4684[8]
**Ursus Belle (IRE)** *Richard Hannon* 57
2 b f Kodiac Switcher (IRE) (Whipper (USA))
3277[3] 3936[4]
**Usa (IRE)** *S J Mahon* a62 71
10 b g Bertolini(USA) Varnay (Machiavellian (USA))
5518a[2] 6801a[10]
**US Army Ranger (IRE)**
*Joseph Patrick O'Brien* 122
4 b h Galileo(IRE) Moonstone (Dalakhani (IRE))
1654a[3] 2571[2] 3299[10] 4073[3] 5503[8] 6957a[6] 8667a[18]
**Used To Be** *K R Burke* a59 75
3 ch g Kyllachy Polly Floyer (Halling (USA))
2071[10] 3715[7] 4247[6] 5358[3] 6562[4] 7942[5] 8328[7]
**Usher** *Roger Charlton* 29
2 b g Oasis Dream Nimble Thimble (USA) (Mizzen Mast (USA))
5476[7] 6260[13]
**Usherette (IRE)** *A Fabre* a102 119
5 b m Shamardal(USA) Monday Show (USA) (Maria's Mon (USA))
2248a[3] 3118a[3]◆ 3961[3]◆ 5460a[6] (6804a) 7812[4]
**U S Navy Flag (USA)** *A P O'Brien* a53 122
2 b c War Front(USA) Misty For Me (IRE) (Galileo (IRE))
3098a[3] 3925[14] 4812[2] 5973a[4] (6488a) (7618) (8037) 8609a[10]
**U S S Missouri (USA)** *Ed Walker* a79
2 b g War Front(USA) I'm So Excited (USA) (Street Cry (IRE))
7511[4]◆ 8149[3] 8642[3]
**Ustinov** *David O'Meara* a89 85
5 b g Exceed And Excel(AUS) Tamzin (Hernando (FR))
9016[8]
**Utah (IRE)** *A P O'Brien* 98
3 b c Galileo(IRE) Healing Music (FR) (Bering)
3109a[6] 3998[6] 6956a[11]
**Uther Pendragon (IRE)** *J S Moore* a79 89
2 b g Dragon Pulse(IRE) Unreal (Dansili)
1767[6] 1934[4] 3965[3] 4678a[3] 4858[2] 5520a[2] 5816a[2] 6017a[2] 6229a[6] 6453a[5] 8195a[6] 8443a[4]
**Utmost (USA)** *John Gosden* a104 87
3 ch c Giant's Causeway(USA) Fugitive Angel (USA) (Alphabet Soup (USA))
1780[3] 8843[4]◆ 9003a[8] 9388[3]
**Utopian Dream** *John Gosden* a85
3 b f High Chaparral(IRE) You Too (Monsun (GER))
144[4]◆ 862[4] 1414[2] (2515)
**Utterly Charming (IRE)** *Clive Cox* 74
2 b f Dandy Man(IRE) Dream Date (IRE) (Oasis Dream)
3502[4] (3821)
**Va Bank (IRE)** *M Janikowski* 113
5 b h Archipenko(USA) Vinales (IRE) (Dilshaan)
3116a[6]
**Vadsariya (FR)** *A De Royer-Dupre* 96
3 b f Exceed And Excel(AUS) Valasyra (FR) (Sinndar (IRE))
5777a[4]
**Valantino Oyster (IRE)** *Ali Stronge* a25 42
10 b g Pearl Of Love(IRE) Mishor (Slip Anchor)
169[13] 6891[3] 11458
**Valbchek (IRE)** *Jane Chapple-Hyam* a98 85
8 b g Acclamation Spectacular Show (IRE) (Spectrum (IRE))
275[4] 459[4] 896[12]
**Valcartier (IRE)** *John Gosden* 94
3 b g Redoute's Choice(AUS) Vadawina (IRE) (Unfuwain (USA))
(1730) 4408[2] 5160[3]
**Valdaye (FR)** *C Gourdain* 51
2 b f Gentlewave(IRE) Vadlaviria (IRE) (Bering)
5815a[8]
**Valdelino (FR)** *H-A Pantall* a67 73
3 b c Myboycharlie(IRE) Vallee Celebre (SWI) (Peintre Celebre (USA))
6256a[4]
**Val De Marne** *A Fabre* a88 95
3 b f Invincible Spirit(IRE) Vallericca (USA) (Dynaformer (USA))
6732a[4] 8548[7]
**Valdolobo (IRE)** *K R Burke* 78
2 b g Lope De Vega(IRE) Eucharist (IRE) (Acclamation)
5876[3] 7521[4]
**Valentana (IRE)** *W McCreery* a67 90
5 b m Haatef(USA) Miss Latina (IRE) (Mozart (IRE))
4385a[10] 6080a[12]
**Valentino Boy (IRE)** *Brian Ellison* a78 76
3 b g Bated Breath Capistrano Day (USA) (Diesis)
1975[10] 2338[2] 3555[2] (4290) 4894[4] 5604[5] 7571[2]
**Valentino Dancer** *David O'Meara* a59
2 ch c Mastercraftsman(IRE) Bertie's Best (King's Best (USA))
7765[5] 9050[8]
**Vale Of Flight (IRE)** *Luke McJannet* a64 54
4 b m Vale Of York(IRE) Barbera (GER) (Night Shift (USA))
844[5] 1080[10] 1558[2] 1981[6] 2370[3] 3466[5] 4005[2] 4352[7]
**Valeria** *Fabio Marchi* 59
2 ch f Kheleyf(USA) Rosy Alexander (Spartacus (IRE))
8620a[7]
**Valerie's Memory** *Philip Hide* 14
2 b f Sixties Icon Nadinska (Doyen (IRE))
6260[12]
**Valhala (FR)** *T Castanheira* a69 71
2 gr c Literato(FR) Burghelarab (IRE) (Dubai Destination (USA))
5907a[9] (6456a) 8169a[9] 8482a[8] 9086a[5]
**Validator** *William Haggas* 84
2 b f Kodiac Enact (Kyllachy)
2279[3]◆ (2836) 3502[2] 5440[2] 6136[11] 7123[2]
**Vallante (GER)** *J Hirschberger* 91
4 b m Soldier Hollow Vive La Reine (GER) (Big Shuffle (USA))
7204a[8] 7673a[14]
**Vallarta (IRE)** *Ruth Carr* a80 79
7 b g Footstepsinthesand Mexican Miss (IRE) (Tagula (IRE))
1185[6] 1431[3] 1586[3] 2377[3] (2550) 3195[4] 3652[3] 4080[5] 4663[8] 7572[7] 7923[5] 8321[9] 8722[10] 8875[10]
**Valle Inclan (IRE)** *Ana Imaz Ceca* 81
2 b c Elusive Pimpernel(USA) Sally Is The Boss (IRE) (Orpen (USA))
(7592a)
**Vallesa (IRE)** *David Brown* 40
2 b f Elzaam(AUS) Rousing Applause (USA) (Candy Ride (ARG))
3390[11] 3902[7] 4504[5]
**Valley Lodge** *Julia Feilden* a40 61
3 ch c Mayson Beat As One (Medicean)
376[8] 686[6] 897[6]
**Valley Of Fire** *Les Eyre* a91 94
5 b g Firebreak Charlie Girl (Puissance)
1185[9]
**Valley Of Light** *Saeed bin Suroor* a70
3 b f Dubawi(IRE) Elusive Sparkle (USA) (Elusive Quality (USA))
7492[3] 7989[5] 9018[2]
**Valley Of Rocks (IRE)**
*Mark Johnston* a74 74
3 b g Big Bad Bob(IRE) Arctic Hunt (IRE) (Bering)
2707[2] 3150[5] 3443[5] 3816[4] 4186[3] (4626) 5000[8] 5496[7] 6110[6] 8206[12]
**Val Nanda (IRE)** *Cristiana Signorelli* 100
3 b f Fast Company(IRE) Kristal Xenia (IRE) (Xaar)
3614a[2]
**Val's Magic Touch** *John O'Shea*
3 b f Captain Gerrard(IRE) Under My Spell (Wizard King)
6009[10] 6791[12] 7907[11]
**Valyrian** *Luca Cumani* a65
2 b c Dansili Victoire Finale (Peintre Celebre (USA))
9312[5]◆
**Van Der Decken** *Charlie Appleby* a105 91
3 b g Dutch Art Celeste (Green Desert (USA))
430a[5]
**Van Gerwen** *Les Eyre* a82 85
4 ch g Bahamian Bounty Disco Ball (Fantastic Light (USA))
1370[3] 1777[11] 2821[13] 6877[11] 7268[5] 7557[2] (8293) 8680[10]
**Van Huysen (IRE)**
*Dominic Ffrench Davis* a95 67
5 br g Excellent Art Tara Too (IRE) (Danetime (IRE))
117[2] 396[4] 817[3] 963[3] 1775[7] 2086[10] 2999[10] 8821[11] 9186[7]
**Vanisia (FR)** *C Lotoux* a54 54
3 b f Vision D'Etat(FR) Diversite (FR) (War Chant (USA))
4943a[3]
**Vanity Queen** *Luca Cumani* a78 78
3 b f Fastnet Rock(AUS) Victoire Finale (Peintre Celebre (USA))
2118[6] 2761[7] 6134[8] 7364[3] 8126[5]
**Vantage Point (IRE)** *Gary Moore* a85 80
3 b c Galileo(IRE) Adoration (USA) (Honor Grades (USA))
175[4] (479) (1434) 2088[5] 2690[8] 3262[2] 3504[10] 4215[9]
**Vantasy** *Chris Wall* a20 32
2 b g Rip Van Winkle(IRE) Tesary (Danehill (USA))
8119[15] 8642[11]
**Vanturi (IRE)** *J-V Toux* 31
2 gr g Rip Van Winkle(IRE) Ventura Ice (IRE) (Oratorio (IRE))
1919a[12] 2664a[8] 6409a[9]
**Van Velde (IRE)** *John Quinn* a63 68
3 ch g Dutch Art Woodcock Moon (Kyllachy)
442[2] 6667[2] (7247) 8216[13]
**Varing (FR)** *M Cesandri* a62 59
7 b g Vadasin(IRE) Noverings (Noverre (USA))
(364a) 822a[10]
**Varius (FR)** *M Nigge* 76
2 b c Myboycharlie(IRE) Rhenania (IRE) (Shamardal (USA))
4782a[4] 5520a[6]
**Varsovian** *Dean Ivory* a83 63
7 ch g Refuse To Bend(IRE) Queen Of Poland (Halling (USA))
(575) 1091[4] 1301[4] 1696[4] 2331[4] 3140[4]◆ 4495[8] 5481[10] 6068[12] (9093) 9437[4]
**Varun's Bride (IRE)** *Richard Hannon* a62 55
3 b f Lawman(FR) Belgique (IRE) (Compton Place)
2016[4] 2679[11] 3191[2] (4006) 4453[13]
**Vastly (USA)** *Sophie Leech* a76 69
8 rg g Mizzen Mast(USA) Valentine Band (USA) (Dixieland Band (USA))
6948[11] 7409[11]
**Vatican Hill (IRE)** *P Monfort* a68 90
3 b c Canford Cliffs(IRE) Empress Ella (IRE) (Holy Roman Emperor (IRE))
(329) 512[5] 1149[10] 1841[8] 2089[2] (3310a) 4654a[3]
**Vaudieu** *Dean Ivory* a53 31
3 ch f Bated Breath Gretna (Groom Dancer (USA))
1552[8] 2307[5] 2515[4] 7003[5]
**Vaulted** *Richard Fahey* 71
3 b f Kyllachy Palatial (Green Desert (USA))
3047[2]◆ 3715[4] (4557) 5185[5] 5666[7] 6266[5] 6691[6]
**Vaux (IRE)** *Ben Haslam* a59 43
3 b g Sir Prancealot(IRE) Greenflash (Green Desert (USA))
903[3] 1193[9] 1835[9] 2181[8] 2699[3] 4060[4] 5419[9] 6437[15]
**Vazirabad (FR)** *A De Royer-Dupre* 120
5 bb g Manduro(GER) Visorama (IRE) (Linamix (FR))
890a[2] (1374a) (3119a) (6984a) (7639a) 8274a[2]
**Vecellio (IRE)** *G Botti* a83 77
3 ch c Dragon Pulse(IRE) Gold Strike (IRE) (Rainbow Quest (USA))
2697a[3] (5523a)
**Vecheka (IRE)** *Kenny Johnson* a46 43
6 b g Lawman(FR) Lidanski (IRE) (Soviet Star (USA))
3256[2] 5419[7] 6045[10] 6902[14] 7164[5] 7660[12] 7926[6] 8559[2] 8924[7] 9013[6] 9265[9]
**Vedani (IRE)** *Tony Carroll* a57 60
8 b g Dalakhani(IRE) Velandia (IRE) (Sadler's Wells (USA))
508[3] 988[9]
**Vedeux (IRE)** *C Lerner* a79 70
6 b h Elusive City(USA) Qahatika (FR) (Polish Precedent (USA))
7636a[11]
**Veejay (IRE)** *Mick Channon* 88
2 b c Approve(IRE) Regresa A Mi (IRE) (Spartacus (IRE))
(4220) (5136) 5572[10] 5875[2] (6561) 6925[7] 7648[7] 8045[3] 8290[6]
**Veena (FR)** *David Simcock* a84 57
4 b m Elusive City(USA) Kensita (FR) (Soviet Star (USA))
151[4] (582) (879) 1030[4] 3080[9] 8717[5] 9089[8] (9316)
**Veeraya** *Julia Feilden* a68 66
7 b g Rail Link Follow Flanders (Pursuit Of Love)
685[6] 1186[8] 2582[7]
**Vegas Boy (IRE)** *Jamie Osborne* a76 47
2 ch c Society Rock(IRE) Consensus (IRE) (Common Grounds)
2292[5] 3467[5] 4367[9] 6285[3] 6585[6] 6790[2]◆ (7756) (8702) 8954[3]
**Veiled Secret (IRE)**
*Sir Mark Prescott Bt* a79 79
3 b g Teofilo(IRE) Seven Veils (IRE) (Danehill Dancer (IRE))
2991[5] 3503[2] 5034[6] (5810)◆ 6033[3] 6376[6] 7060[5] 7766[3]
**Velvet Charm** *Rae Guest* 53
3 b f Excelebration(IRE) Velvet Star (IRE) (Galileo (IRE))
2753[4] 3626[8] 4568[7] 5266[7] 5935[7]
**Velvet Revolution** *Marco Botti* a93 85
4 ch g Pivotal Gino's Spirits (Perugino (USA))
1798[4] 2461[2] 3076[8] 4355[10] (6323) 6793[2] (9157)
**Velvet Voice** *Mark H Tompkins* a60 65
3 b f Azamour(IRE) Battery Power (Royal Applause)
4623[9] 5653[2] 6048[8] 6851[5]
**Venetian Proposal (IRE)**
*Zoe Davison* a58 59
3 b f Fast Company(IRE) Ide Say (IRE) (Grand Lodge (USA))
78[6] 2016[8] 2911[13] 3246[3] 4184[7] (4754) 5331[8] 5653[3] 6257[3] 9127[3]
**Veneto (GER)** *Andreas Suborics* 110
4 b h New Approach(IRE) Venia Legendi (GER) (Zinaad)
(8622a)
**Venexiana (FR)** *G Collet* a25
3 b f Panis(USA) Speedy Amber (FR) (Desert Style (IRE))
838a[13]
**Venezia (IRE)** *M Halford* a78 84
6 gr g Galileo(IRE) St Roch (IRE) (Danehill (USA))
227a[2]
**Veneziano (FR)** *Robert Collet* a54 53
8 ch g Peintre Celebre(USA) Venetian Beauty (USA) (Lear Fan (USA))
364a[6]
**Vengeur Masque (IRE)**
*Michael Moroney* 106
5 b g Monsun(GER) Venetian Beauty (USA) (Lear Fan (USA))
1400a[2] (8751a)
**Venice Beach (IRE)** *A P O'Brien* 113
3 b c Galileo(IRE) Danedrop (IRE) (Danehill (USA))
(2555) 3322[12] 4878a[3] 6327[2] 7147[8]
**Ventdanslesarbres** *George Baker* 33
3 b f Aqlaam Velma Kelly (Vettori (IRE))
4759[7]
**Vent De Force** *Hughie Morrison* a58 102
6 b g Hurricane Run(IRE) Capriolla (In The Wings)
3011[4] 5198a[2] 6984a[7]
**Ventura Blues (IRE)**
*Richard Hannon* a94 83
3 bb f Bated Breath Salmon Rose (IRE) (Iffraaj)
1601[5] 3171[3] 3722[2] 4385a[9] 5156[6] 5591[4] 6576[2] (6818) 6933[4] 7456[2] 7737[11]
**Ventura Crest (IRE)** *Tim Easterby* 56
2 b g Elzaam(AUS) Ms Cromby (IRE) (Arakan (USA))
2299[6] 2852[4] 3895[6] 4527[8] 6087[11] 7519[2] 8287[9]
**Ventura Dragon (IRE)**
*Richard Fahey* 78
2 ch g Dragon Pulse(IRE) Dancing Duchess (IRE) (Danehill Dancer (IRE))
2299[3]◆ (2882) 3297[5] 5079[5] (6030) 6353[17] 7148[6] 7956[3]
**Ventura Gold (IRE)** *Richard Fahey* 67
2 b g Red Jazz(USA) Desert Shine (IRE) (Green Desert (USA))
1673[6]◆ 2222[6] 4427[5] 5143[4] 6626[2] 6977a[12] 8120[6]
**Ventura Jazz** *Richard Fahey* a47
3 b f Dandy Man(IRE) Aljafliyah (Halling (USA))
27[5] 323[9]

**Ventura Knight (IRE)**
*Mark Johnston* a76 95
2 b c Casamento(IRE) Alltherightmoves (IRE) (Namid)
1588[3] 2029[4] 3245[3] (3930) **(4836)**◆ (5079)◆ 5395[7] 6684[5] 7148[3] 7921[5] **(8379)**
**Ventura Magic** *Richard Hannon* a60
2 b c Mount Nelson Elle Desert (GER) (Next Desert (IRE))
**8839**[7] 9319[8]
**Ventura Royal (IRE)** *David O'Meara* 68
2 ch f Teofilo(IRE) Ermine And Velvet (Nayef (USA))
5372[9] 5990[5]◆ 6659[3] **(7521)**
**Ventura Secret (IRE)** *Tim Easterby* a67 77
3 ch g Roderic O'Connor(IRE) Bajan Belle (IRE) (Efisio)
2080[4] 3152[6] 3709[5] 4122[7] (4785) 5376[4] (5807) 5949[7] 6564[3] **(7042)** **7823**[4] 8318[8]
**Ventura Storm (IRE)**
*David A & B Hayes & Tom Dabern* 115
4 b h Zoffany(IRE) Sarawati (IRE) (Haafhd)
**8250a**[13] 8667a[21]
**Venture Capital (FR)** *U Schwinn* a80 49
5 b g Siyouni(FR) Babola (IRE) (Grand Lodge (USA))
1196a[9]
**Venturous (IRE)** *David Barron* 101
4 ch g Raven's Pass(USA) Bold Desire (Cadeaux Genereux)
**2156**[11] 2566[7] 3092[16] 6185[6] 7055[6]◆ 7625[3]◆ 8012[5]
**Venussio (FR)** *J-L Delaplace* a67 16
2 b c Maiguri(IRE) Vinskaia (USA) (Vindication (USA))
1929a[7] **9087a**[8]
**Venutius** *Charles Hills* a38 65
10 b g Doyen(IRE) Boadicea's Chariot (Commanche Run)
2795[5] 3920[5] **4699**[11] 6564[11] 9295[10]
**Veracious** *Sir Michael Stoute* 94
2 b f Frankel Infallible (Pivotal)
7357[3] **(8006)**◆
**Vera Drake (FR)** *Richard Fahey* a64 69
2 ch f Footstepsinthesand Venetian Beauty (USA) (Lear Fan (USA))
6042[4]◆ **6824**[2] **7266**[2] 7937[4]
**Veranda (FR)** *A Fabre* 94
3 bb c Canford Cliffs(IRE) Visinada (IRE) (Sinndar (IRE))
**2944a**[4]
**Verandah** *John Gosden* a84 95
2 b f Medicean Palatial (Green Desert (USA))
(5795)◆ **6418**[5]
**Verbal Dexterity (IRE)** *J S Bolger* 119
2 b c Vocalised(USA) Lonrach (IRE) (Holy Roman Emperor (IRE))
4386a[2] **(6975a)** 8415[4]
**Verbitude (IRE)** *J S Bolger* a59 67
2 b c Vocalised(USA) Bring Back Matron (IRE) (Rock Of Gibraltar (IRE))
**6955a**[10]
**Vercingetorix (IRE)** *Iain Jardine* a79 77
6 b g Dylan Thomas(IRE) Great Artist (FR) (Desert Prince (IRE))
154[4] 325[3] 2471[5] 2546[4] **(3389)** (5008) 5438[6] 9442[5]
**Verdi (IRE)** *John Ryan* a50 51
3 b g Invincible Spirit(IRE) Leopard Hunt (USA) (Diesis)
1600[5] **3832**[5] 4157[8] 4710[6] 5855[10] 6114[11] 6582[5] 7014[9]
**Verhoyen** *M C Grassick* 92
2 b c Piccolo Memory Lane (With Approval (CAN))
**2861a**[2] 3972[3] 6977a[13] 7855a[6] 8082a[12]
**Verity** *Sir Michael Stoute* a81 63
3 b f Redoute's Choice(AUS) Virtuous (Exit To Nowhere (USA))
3393[4] **4565**[2]
**Vernatti** *Pam Sly* a62 83
4 b m Teofilo(IRE) Speciosa (IRE) (Danehill Dancer (IRE))
1818[2] (2282)◆ **(3168)** 5060[7] 6701[7] **7338**[3] 8239[8]
**Verne Castle** *Andrew Balding* a102 79
4 ch g Sakhee's Secret Lochangel (Night Shift (USA))
79[5] (573) (816) **917**[3] 1362[6] 1772[11] 5354[10] 6025[4] 6677[10] 7950[6]
**Veronica's Napkin (IRE)** *J Moon* 16
5 b m Yeats(IRE) Adjisa (IRE) (Doyoun)
**8127a**[6]
**Verstappen (IRE)** *Marco Botti* a69 66
2 bz c Dark Angel(IRE) Hugs 'n Kisses (IRE) (Noverre (USA))
5036[7] 5960[4] **6883**[4]
**Vert Diamond (FR)** *T De Lauriere* 96
3 gr g Diamond Green(FR) Valprime (FR) (Nombre Premier)
**3103a**[4]
**Verti Chop (FR)** *C Boutin* a76 81
4 bb g Namid Very Astair (FR) (Astair (FR))
**6302a**[7]
**Verve (IRE)** *Hugo Palmer* 75
2 bb f Epaulette(AUS) Onomatomania (USA) (Mr Greeley (USA))
**7022**[2]◆
**Very Dashing** *Ralph Beckett* a103 102
4 br m Dansili Dash To The Top (Montjeu (IRE))
1500[4] 3219[6] **4308**[3] 5381[4]
**Very First Blade** *Michael Mullineaux* a61 50
8 b g Needwood Blade Dispol Verity (Averti (IRE))
**153**[2] 494[5] 852[11] 1184[9] 2777[4] 3710[3] 4148[8] 4478[7] 5695[8] 6130[7] 6271[8] 8258[12] 9181[3] 9348[9]
**Very Honest (IRE)** *Brett Johnson* a77 77
4 b m Poet's Voice Cercle D'Amour (USA) (Storm Cat (USA))
94[8] 547[9] 1467[7] **1899**[3] 2608[19] 3834[8] **4464**[3] 5558[4] 6652[5] 7882[5] 8645[3] 8990[3] 9185[3] 9437[5]
**Very Special (IRE)**
*Saeed bin Suroor* a103 113
5 ch m Lope De Vega(IRE) Danielli (IRE) (Danehill (USA))
**(431a)** 771a[5] 1378a[10]

**Vesper (GER)** *J-M Lefebvre* a64 51
7 b m Sholokhov(IRE) Vera Longa (GER) (Lando (GER))
**515a**[11] 691a[F]
**Vettori Kin (BRZ)** *Kenneth McPeek* a81 110
3 b h Vettori(IRE) Miss Kin (BRZ) (Laramie (ARG))
**1375a**[10]
**Vettori Rules** *Gay Kelleway* a103 87
4 gr g Aussie Rules(USA) Vettori Loose (IRE) (Vettori (IRE))
720[5] **858**[2] 1360[3] 1770[13] 2158[4] 4076[7] 4882[8] 5287[7] 6482[7] 7142[7] 7558[8] 8880[11] 9204[3]
**Vexillum (IRE)** *Neil Mulholland* a47 50
8 br g Mujadil(USA) Common Cause (Polish Patriot (USA))
3026[11] **3805**[3] 4040[4] 6309[5] 6796[6] 7336[11] 8135[9]
**Via Appia (FR)** *Matthieu Palussiere* a56 11
2 b f Amico Fritz(GER) Via Carolina (FR) (Xaar)
**8228a**[13]
**Via Cassia** *Gianluca Bietolini* a41 55
4 b g Elusive City(USA) Pingus (Polish Precedent (USA))
1531a[11]
**Via Egnatia (USA)** *John Gosden* 97
3 b c Distorted Humor(USA) Honest Lady (USA) (Seattle Slew (USA))
1859[3] **2554**[4]
**Via Firenze (IRE)** *Mme Pia Brandt* a100 108
4 b m Dansili Via Medici (IRE) (Medicean)
431a[6] **771a**[2] 3883a[6] 7305a[2] 8755a[3]
**Via Ravenna (IRE)** *A Fabre* a77 114
3 b f Raven's Pass(USA) Via Milano (FR) (Singspiel (IRE))
(1690a) 2644a[7] 4234a[4] **5460a**[2]
**Via Serendipity** *Stuart Williams* a90 93
3 b g Invincible Spirit(IRE) Mambo Light (USA) (Kingmambo (USA))
1959[5] 2402[8] 3997[12] 4563[6] 6026[3] 7549[5] **(8566)**
**Via Via (IRE)** *James Tate* a100 106
5 b h Lope De Vega(IRE) Atalina (FR) (Linamix (FR))
(1105) 8138[4]◆ **8599**[3] 8891[7]
**Vibes (IRE)** *Jamie Osborne* a65 79
3 ch g Helmet(AUS) Smoken Rosa (USA) (Smoke Glacken (USA))
3163[8] 5411[2] **(5656)** 5961[5] 8470[6]
**Vibrant Chords** *Henry Candy* a89 103
4 b g Poet's Voice Lovely Thought (Dubai Destination (USA))
1863[6]◆ (2391) 3034[2] 5505[11] **6185**[2] 7144[2] 8139[9]
**Vice Marshal (IRE)** *Charlie Fellowes* a61 33
2 b c Wootton Bassett Celsius Degre (IRE) (Verglas (IRE))
3164[10] 3783[9] **9313**[9]
**Viceroy Mac** *David Loughnane* a52 71
2 b g Sepoy(AUS) Tebee's Oasis (Oasis Dream)
4502[7] **5099**[3] 5531[5] **6552**[3]◆ 7764[12]
**Vice Versa** *Sir Michael Stoute* a78 70
3 b f Oasis Dream Mascarene (USA) (Empire Maker (USA))
1885[10] **(2311)** 3217[5] 5399[5]
**Vicky Park** *George Margarson* a43 34
3 b f Compton Place Sonko (IRE) (Red Clubs (IRE))
**1321**[5] 1821[4]
**Victoire De Lyphar (IRE)** *Ruth Carr* a7 85
10 b g Bertolini(USA) Victory Peak (Shirley Heights)
**1718**[2]
**Victoria Pollard** *Andrew Balding* a82 85
5 b m Sir Percy Victoria Montoya (High Chaparral (IRE))
**609**[3] 781[4] **1027**[4]
**Victoria's Angel (IRE)** *H-F Devin* a82 75
2 b f Dark Angel(IRE) Miss Spinamix (IRE) (Verglas (IRE))
**3445a**[2] 4677a[5]
**Victoriously** *Andi Brown* a64 70
5 b g Azamour(IRE) Ambria (GER) (Monsun (GER))
**(2095)** 9128[8] 9406[2]
**Victor Kalejs (USA)** *Roy Arne Kvisla* a69 89
3 ch c Spring At Last(USA) Make A Promise (USA) (Mr Greeley (USA))
430a[7] **697a**[7] 1040a[7]
**Victor's Bet (SPA)** *Ralph J Smith* a73 68
8 b g Leadership Marmaria (SPA) (Limpid)
1067[7] 1249[2] (1698) 2257[5] **(3208)** 3547[8] 5838[7] 6475[7] 7711[9] 8157[10] 8647[8] 8878[7] 9095[8]
**Victory Angel (IRE)** *Roger Varian* 104
3 b c Acclamation Golden Shadow (IRE) (Selkirk (USA))
(1901)◆ 2400[8] 4030[11] 4813[15] **(5513)** 7782[8]
**Victory Bond** *William Haggas* a110 108
4 b g Medicean Antebellum (FR) (Anabaa (USA))
2767[3] 4918[7]◆ 5436[4] 6355[8] 6928[9] **(7988)** 8844[2]
**Victory Chime (IRE)** *Ralph Beckett* a47 68
2 b g Campanologist(USA) Patuca (Teofilo (IRE))
**8161**[5] 8677[4] 8890[9]
**Victory Is Ours (TUR)**
*Aydin Kucukaksoy* 107
4 ch h Victory Gallop(CAN) Lovely Doyoun (TUR) (Doyoun)
**6744a**[3]
**Victory Laurel (IRE)**
*Ibrahim Al Malki* a97 97
7 b g Holy Roman Emperor(IRE) Special Cause (IRE) (Fasliyev (USA))
**932a**[9]
**Vida Loca (FR)** *M Boutin* a55 57
2 bb f Spirit One(FR) Vassileva (FR) (Lomitas)
1282a[3] 1594a[6] 4196a[5] 5585a[8] **5907a**[4] **6456a**[4] **9086a**[6]
**Vienna Woods (FR)** *Y Barberot* a77 95
3 bb f Cacique(IRE) Vienna View (Dalakhani (IRE))
8838a[10] **8976a**[4]
**Viennoise (FR)** *Mme V Botte* a51
7 b m Urbinol Danoise (BEL) (Yuushun (BEL))
1070a[9]
**Viento Sur (IRE)** *J A Remolina Diez* a60 63
2 b c Poet's Voice Kashoof (Green Desert (USA))
**6452a**[7]

**Vieux Moulin (FR)** *F Chappet* 70
3 b c Excelebration(IRE) Indiana Wells (FR) (Sadler's Wells (USA))
**(5909a)**
**Viewpoint (IRE)** *Harriet Bethell* a82 79
8 b g Exceed And Excel(AUS) Lady's View (USA) (Distant View (USA))
14575◆ (1695) **2261**[3] 2941a[4] (3284) 3470[2] **(4158)** 4796[5]
**Vigee Le Brun (IRE)** *Olly Williams* a67 74
3 gr f Dark Angel(IRE) Wonderful Town (USA) (Bernstein (USA))
2366[3] 3031[5] 3507[7] **4633**[2] 9369[5]
**Viking Hoard (IRE)** *Harry Dunlop* a58 79
3 b g Vale Of York(IRE) Tibouchina (IRE) (Daylami (IRE))
2174[4] 3505[7] 4468[5] **(6075)** 6657[10] 7880[13]
**Viking Way (IRE)** *Olly Williams* 47
2 ch g Society Rock(IRE) Patrimony (Cadeaux Genereux)
4273[6] 5631[9] **6432**[9]
**Vik The Billy** *Sergio Dettori* 86
2 b f Bated Breath Epiphany (Zafonic (USA))
**4391a**[6]
**Viktoriya Taraban (IRE)**
*Joseph Tuite* 46
2 b f Lilbourne Lad(IRE) Fritta Mista (IRE) (Linamix (FR))
**6100**[5] 6504[6]
**Vila Gracinda (FR)** *H-A Pantall*
3 gr f Never On Sunday(FR) Massaba (FR) (Tobougg (IRE))
3134a[6]
**Vilaro (FR)** *D Smaga* a88 102
4 b g Whipper(USA) Envoutement (FR) (Vettori (IRE))
**5979a**[14]
**Villa Maria** *K R Burke* a33
2 b f Makfi An Ghalanta (IRE) (Holy Roman Emperor (IRE))
**8877**[10]
**Villa Savina (IRE)** *Clive Cox* a70 69
2 b f Elusive Pimpernel(USA) Swan Sea (USA) (Sea Hero (USA))
(5216) 6977a[28] **7877**[3]
**Villa Tora** *Mark Johnston* a59 73
2 ch f Excelebration(IRE) Tatora (Selkirk (USA))
2222[4] **2832**[3] (3237) **3562**[2] 3972[5] 4895[4] 5615[4] 6379[6] 6977a[25] 8746[4]
**Villette (IRE)** *Dean Ivory* a81 85
3 b f Sixties Icon Spinning Lucy (IRE) (Spinning World (USA))
(1300) 1725[6] 2998[7] **(8143)** 8820[6] 9000[8]
**Vimy Ridge** *Alan Bailey* a80 89
5 ch g American Post Fairy Shoes (Kyllachy)
573[2] 808[5] 995[3] 1586[4] 2368[9] 2700[2] (4182) 5035[4] (5967) **(6764)** 7086[10] 7809[5] 8639[8]
**Vinaccia (IRE)** *C Lerner* a67
2 b f Poet's Voice Chicane (Motivator)
**8691a**[6]
**Vincent's Forever** *David Pipe* a87 36
4 b g Pour Moi(IRE) Glen Rosie (IRE) (Mujtahid (USA))
**4751**[9]
**Vincentti (IRE)** *Ronald Harris* a55 82
7 b g Invincible Spirit(IRE) Bint Al Balad (IRE) (Ahonoora)
2514[5] 3136[7] 3424[9] **3573**[7] 3774[7] 4441[2] 5051[9] 5711[10]
**Vincenzo Coccotti (USA)**
*Ken Cunningham-Brown* a76 70
5 rg g Speightstown(USA) Ocean Colors (USA) (Orientate (USA))
2763[6] 3401[6] 4256[3] **6197**[3] 6663[7]
**Vindicator (IRE)** *Michael Dods* a72 86
3 b g Delegator Monroe (Tomba)
2159[6] 3342[4] 4036[6] 4962[4] (5617)◆ 5951[2] **(7019)** **7701**[2]
**Vintage Dream (IRE)** *Noel Wilson* a50 65
3 b g Dream Ahead(USA) Stella Del Mattino (USA) (Golden Gear (USA))
1678[10] 2927[9] 3387[13] 3496[3] 4303[12] 4428[2] 4745[2] 5459[12] 6694[2] **7014**[2] 7657[4] 8194[11] 8479[6]
**Vintage Folly** *Hugo Palmer* a101 101
3 b f Makfi Katimont (IRE) (Montjeu (IRE))
2738[2]◆ 4424a[11] **7283**[2] **8739**[2] **8986a**[2]
**Vintager** *David Menuisier* 99
2 ro c Mastercraftsman(IRE) White And Red (IRE) (Orpen (USA))
(5887) 6696[5]◆ **8422**[5]
**Viola Da Terra (FR)** *F-H Graffard* a81 92
3 b f Requinto(IRE) Khandaar (IRE) (Xaar)
2978a[3] **4988a**[5]
**Viola Park** *Ronald Harris* a62 56
3 b g Aqlaam Violette (Observatory (USA))
89[8] 377[4] (875) 1107[4] 1367[4] 1564[2] 2309[5] 2362[11] 2726[3] 3423[5] **(4162)** 4726[5] 4968[8] 5783[5] 7539[2] 8401[6] 9142[2] 9203[2]
**Violate (AUS)** *Brent Stanley* 102
3 ch c Sebring(AUS) Shantha's Girl (AUS) (Redoute's Choice (AUS))
**8751a**[4]
**Violet Beauregarde** *Harry Dunlop* a50 24
2 b f Captain Gerrard(IRE) Style Award (Acclamation)
5327[9] **6950**[5] 7410[10]
**Violet Blue (USA)** *James J Toner* 95
3 bb f Americain(USA) Strike The Light (USA) (Smart Strike (CAN))
**4650a**[9]
**Violet Mist (IRE)** *Ben Haslam* a48 28
3 gr f Clodovil(IRE) Vision Of Peace (IRE) (Invincible Spirit (IRE))
**1004**[5] 1474[9] 1715[6] 1973[5]
**Violet's Lads (IRE)** *Brett Johnson* a65 61
3 b f Myboycharlie(IRE) Cape Violet (IRE) (Cape Cross (IRE))
3329[8] 4152[2] 5409[4] 6656[6] 7122[3] **8551**[3] 9203[9] 9431[4]
**Viren's Army (IRE)** *Charlie Appleby* a83 109
4 b g Twirling Candy(USA) Blue Angel (IRE) (Oratorio (IRE))
699a[11] **(888a)** 1882[5]

**Virginie (FR)** *T Clout* a86 91
4 b m Silver Frost(IRE) Hallen (FR) (Midyan (USA))
**4454a**[4]
**Virile (IRE)** *Sylvester Kirk* a59 70
6 ch g Exceed And Excel(AUS) Winding (USA) (Irish River (FR))
171[8] 426[10] 601[6] 981[3] 1247[4] 1557[2] 1898[2] 2053[3] **2298**[2] 2589[11] 2763[7] 3008[5] 6076[11]
**Virnon** *Alan Swinbank* a78 71
6 b g Virtual Freedom Song (Singspiel (IRE))
666[4] 1207[3] **(1590)** 1870[3]
**Visandi (FR)** *Jonjo O'Neill* 63
5 b g Azamour(IRE) Vadaza (FR) (Zafonic (USA))
**4586**[6] 5287[8]
**Viscount Barfield** *Andrew Balding* a96 109
4 b g Raven's Pass(USA) Madonna Dell'Orto (Montjeu (IRE))
1622[6] 2115[4] 2518[4] 3064[6] (3842) **(4890)** 5393[19] 6476[3] 7145[7]
**Viscount Loftus (IRE)**
*Mark Johnston* 86
2 b c Clodovil(IRE) Melpomene (Peintre Celebre (USA))
(3725) 3993[14] **(6231)** 7138[4] 7954[9]
**Visionary (IRE)** *Robert Cowell* a100 95
3 b g Dream Ahead(USA) Avodale (IRE) (Lawman (FR))
(125)◆ 643[3] (1012a) **1774**[2] (2823) 4030[8] 5149[9] 7806[10]
**Vision Clear (GER)** *Ed Dunlop* a65 51
2 b g Soldier Hollow Vive Madame (GER) (Big Shuffle (USA))
6883[11] **7237**[6] 7580[10]
**Vision Of Beauty (FR)**
*Keith Dalgleish* a62
4 b m Vision D'Etat(FR) Belle Dame (GER) (Pilsudski (IRE))
23[5] **420**[3] 689[9]
**Vision Rebelle (FR)** *Mme S Adet*
3 b f Monitor Closely(IRE) Opportunity Girl (FR) (Ballingarry (IRE))
3134a[3]
**Visitant** *David Thompson* a68 89
4 ch g Pivotal Invitee (Medicean)
(2498) 3153[4]◆ (3845) **4865**[2] 5609[3] 6965[7]
**Visor** *James Fanshawe* a57
2 b g Helmet(AUS) Entitlement (Authorized (IRE))
**8877**[8]
**Vitalized (IRE)**
*Damian Joseph English* a39 50
5 b m Vocalised(USA) Astralai (IRE) (Galileo (IRE))
6802a[8]
**Vitally Important (IRE)**
*Majed Seifeddine* a80 102
7 ch h Pivotal Kirkinola (Selkirk (USA))
**934a**[4]
**Vitamin (IRE)** *Richard Hannon* 84
2 b f Camelot True Verdict (IRE) (Danehill Dancer (IRE))
5938[3] **(6386)**
**Viva La Flora (GER)** *P Schiergen* 91
3 bb f Liang Kay(GER) Valiani (GER) (Big Shuffle (USA))
**1846a**[6] 3882a[9] 6254a[11]
**Vivardia (IRE)** *Ben Haslam* a48 56
3 ch f Rip Van Winkle(IRE) Raggiante (IRE) (Rock Of Gibraltar (IRE))
**2180**[8]
**Vivat Rex (IRE)** *Conor Dore* a83 66
6 b g Fastnet Rock(AUS) Strawberry Roan (IRE) (Sadler's Wells (USA))
**(24)** **156**[3] 306[10] 478[3] 9306[4]
**Viva Verglas (IRE)**
*Daniel Mark Loughnane* a74 75
6 gr g Verglas(IRE) Yellow Trumpet (Petong)
923[8] (1076) (1209) 1431[4] 1980[4] **2229**[2] 2469[7] 7099[6]◆ 7738[5] 8433[11] 8646[8] 9033[7] 9216[2] 9347[5]
**Vive La Difference (IRE)**
*Tim Easterby* 73
3 b g Holy Roman Emperor(IRE) Galaxie Sud (USA) (El Prado (IRE))
7388[2]◆ 8217[3] **8479**[2] 8651[4]
**Vive Marie (GER)** *J Hirschberger* 98
3 b f Jukebox Jury(IRE) Vive La Reine (GER) (Big Shuffle (USA))
4518a[7] 6647a[5] **8463a**[2]
**Vivernus (USA)** *M Al Mheiri* a74 71
4 br h Street Cry(IRE) Lady Pegasus (USA) (Fusaichi Pegasus (USA))
**537a**[3]
**Vivian Ward** *John Gosden* a47
3 b f Kyllachy Al Joudha (FR) (Green Desert (USA))
**397**[6]
**Vivlos (JPN)** *Yasuo Tomomichi* 116
4 bl m Deep Impact(JPN) Halwa Sweet (JPN) (Machiavellian (USA))
**(1378a)**
**Vivre La Reve** *James Unett* a60 40
5 b m Assertive Noor El Houdah (IRE) (Fayruz)
158[8] 784[2] 852[6] **(1260)** 1406[8] 2166[3] 5898[7] 8498[7]
**Vixen (IRE)** *Eve Johnson Houghton* a57 63
3 b f Kodiac Radio Wave (Dalakhani (IRE))
2171[5] 2782[5] 3749[3] 6106[4] 7122[2] **(7899)** 9203[6]
**Vizier** *David O'Meara* a67 79
4 b g Pivotal Rare Ransom (Oasis Dream)
2339[6] 3168[5] **3966**[8] 4430[6]
**Vj Day (USA)** *Kevin Ryan* 69
2 br g War Front(USA) Sassy Image (USA) (Broken Vow (USA))
2769[5] **4526**[6] 6590[3]
**Vlatka (IRE)** *Mme Pia Brandt* 68
2 ch f Dawn Approach(IRE) Sotka (Dutch Art)
**6251a**[11]
**Vocalisation (IRE)** *John Weymes* a47 47
3 ch f Poet's Voice Mi Rubina (IRE) (Rock Of Gibraltar (IRE))
77[5] **126**[4] 511[7] 960[7] 1193[4] 1372[9] 1715[8]

**Vocal Music (IRE)** *J S Bolger* 75
2 b c Vocalised(USA) Christinas Letter (IRE) (Galileo (IRE))
8082a[9]

**Vociferous Marina (IRE)** *J S Bolger* 100
3 b f Vocalised(USA) Marina Of Venice (IRE) (Galileo (IRE))
1386a[8] 2738[4] 3109a[9]

**Vodka Double (FR)** *C Lotoux* a74 72
4 ch m Peintre Celebre(USA) Volga Volga (USA) (Speightstown (USA))
6125a[9]

**Vodka Pigeon** *Adam West* a43 71
2 ch f Sepoy(AUS) Hanging On (Spinning World (USA))
3712[2] 4312[3] 5056[8] 9416[3]

**Vodka Wells (FR)** *Rebecca Menzies* a22 49
7 b g Irish Wells(FR) Kahipiroska (FR) (Mansonnien (FR))
5131[8]

**Vogueatti (USA)** *Marco Botti* a84 26
4 b m Arch(USA) Not Here (USA) (Gone West (USA))
99[3] (781)◆ 2817[6] 3341[4] 5745[2]◆ 6687[4] 8893[10] 9140[11]

**Voguela (IRE)** *Tim Easterby* 28
2 b f Arcano(IRE) Trading Places (Dansili)
7563[11] 8010[11] 8288[9]

**Voi** *Conrad Allen* a78 78
3 b f Holy Roman Emperor(IRE) Bride Unbridled (IRE) (Hurricane Run (IRE))
510[3] 3395[5] 4003[7] (4544) 5331[6] 6110[2] 7816[6] 8561[3] 8820[4]

**Voicemail** *James Tate* a73 75
2 b f Poet's Voice Dame Helen (Royal Applause)
5371[3] (5999) 6575[3] 8848[11]

**Voice Of A Leader (IRE)**
*Andi Brown* a72 94
6 b g Danehill Dancer(IRE) Thewaytosanjose (IRE) (Fasliyev (USA))
(1403)

**Voice Of Love (IRE)** *Stefano Botti* 107
4 ch h Poet's Voice Snowfield (USA) (Tale Of The Cat (USA))
(2004a) 2663a[3] ( ) 8095a[2] 8963a[8]

**Voice Of The North** *Mark Johnston* 68
2 b c Mount Nelson Darakshaana (IRE) (Barathea (IRE))
6510[4]◆ 7043[4] 7503[7] 8287[12]

**Voice Of The North (USA)**
*S Seemar* a65
3 b g Biondetti(USA) Rebooted (USA) (Mr Greeley (USA))
8710a[13]

**Voice Of Truth (IRE)**
*Saeed bin Suroor* a76 79
3 ch f Dubawi(IRE) Express Way (ARG) (Ahmad (ARG))
317a[10] 652a[10]

**Voladora (IRE)** *A Fabre* a78
2 b f Medaglia d'Oro(USA) Aviacion (BRZ) (Know Heights (IRE))
(8691a)

**Volatile** *James Tate* a96 91
3 b g Poet's Voice Neshla (Singspiel (IRE))
1026[3] 1780[6] 3071[7] 4154[4] 5032[5] 6026[10]

**Volcanic Jack (IRE)**
*Michael Chapman* a24 28
9 b g Kodiac Rosaria Panatta (IRE) (Mujtahid (USA))
5021[12]

**Volevo Lui** *Marco Botti* a75 29
2 b c Farhh Veronica Franco (ITY) (Lomitas)
7333[6] 8987[6]

**Volfango (IRE)** *F Head* 107
3 b c Dutch Art Celebre Vadala (FR) (Peintre Celebre (USA))
4941a[4] 6172a[3] 7176a[5]

**Volpone Jelois (FR)** *Paul Nicholls* a77 80
4 gr g Vol De Nuit Jenne Jelois (FR) (My Risk (FR))
1498[3]◆ 3086[2] 9208[3] 9324[3]

**Volturnus** *Jamie Osborne* a57 37
3 b g Azamour(IRE) Daffydowndilly (Oasis Dream)
2584[12] 4274[11] 5141[7] 5846[4] 6180[9] 7537[10] (8674) 8815[3] 9026[4] 9158[11]

**Voluminous** *James Fanshawe* 52
2 b f Nathaniel(IRE) Capacious (Nayef (USA))
8163[10]

**Volunteer Point (IRE)**
*Mick Channon* a104 100
5 b m Footstepsinthesand Piffling (Pivotal)
199[12] 617[2] 994[6] 1771[9]

**Volzapone (FR)** *Y Fertillet* a70 74
7 ch g Vespone(IRE) Liberte De Penser (FR) (Pennekamp (USA))
(822a)

**Vona (IRE)** *Richard Fahey* a11 92
3 b f Dark Angel(IRE) Trading Places (Dansili)
1859[4] 3578[2] 4334[3]

**Von Blucher (IRE)**
*Rebecca Menzies* a103 102
4 ch g Zoffany(IRE) Tropical Lady (IRE) (Sri Pekan (USA))
2610[5] 3963[25] 4905[6]◆ 5434[3] 6918[14] 7822[2] 8104[9] 8737[11]

**Von Tunzelman (NZ)** *Roger James* 104
4 gr g Zabeel(NZ) J'Adane (NZ) (Danehill (USA))
8857a[5]

**Voski (USA)** *Mark Johnston* a78 78
3 b c Medaglia d'Oro(USA) Say You Will (IRE) (A.P. Indy (USA))
(1342)◆ 3068[3] 3528[5] 4450[6] 5798[8] 6573[5] 7031[5] 7831[11] 8313[13]

**Vosne Romanee**
*Dr Richard Newland* a78 67
6 ch g Arakan(USA) Vento Del Oreno (FR) (Lando (GER))
(786)

**Vote** *James Eustace* a67 54
3 b f Aqlaam Bidding Time (Rock Of Gibraltar (IRE))
5635[7] 6581[3]

**Voting Control (USA)**
*Chad C Brown* 112
2 b c Kitten's Joy(USA) Manda Bay (USA) (Empire Maker (USA))
8577a[3]

**Voyager Blue** *Jamie Osborne* a76
2 br c Footstepsinthesand Bristol Fashion (Dansili)
8952[3]◆ 9299[2]

**Vrika Bay** *Robert Eddery* a60 41
3 b f Mastercraftsman(IRE) Fascination Street (IRE) (Mujadil (USA))
65[7] 502[11] 987[7]

**Vroom (IRE)** *Gay Kelleway* a83 70
4 ch g Poet's Voice Shivaree (Rahy (USA))
152[3] (528) 850[2] 1185[4] (1592) 1820[2] 3471[9] 5754[5] 6302a[8] 6541a[13] 8296[6] 8541[5] 8775[5] 9033[6] (9216) 9347[7]

**Vue Fantastique (FR)** *F Chappet* 105
3 bb f Motivator Exit The Straight (IRE) (Exit To Nowhere (USA))
1657a[4] 2665a[2] 3881a[11] (5449a) 6227a[7]

**Vuela** *Luca Cumani* a76 88
4 ch m Duke Of Marmalade(IRE) Victoire Finale (Peintre Celebre (USA))
(2387) 3840[4] 5957[2] 7401[7]

**Waady (IRE)** *John Gosden* 113
5 b g Approve(IRE) Anne Bonney (Jade Robbery (USA))
2611[6] 3079[9] (7027)◆ 7396[4] 7804[3]

**Waarif (IRE)** *David O'Meara* a87 75
4 b g Arcano(IRE) Indian Belle (IRE) (Indian Ridge (IRE))
7941[2]◆ 8718[5] 8912[3] 9025[5] 9140[7]◆ 9419[4]

**Wadigor** *Roger Varian* a108 100
4 b h Champs Elysees Haven's Wave (IRE) (Whipper (USA))
(2959)◆ 4033[16]

**Wadilsafa** *Owen Burrows* 84
2 b c Frankel Rumoush (USA) (Rahy (USA))
6869[2]◆

**Wadood (IRE)** *Robert Cowell* a35 80
3 b c Kodiac Cakestown Lady (IRE) (Petorius (IRE))
2160[5] (4324) 5020[4] 7939[14]

**Wafeer (IRE)** *Richard Hannon* 78
2 b c Equiano(FR) Star Approval (IRE) (Hawk Wing (USA))
4526[5] 5314[4] 7126[2] 7953[4]

**Wafy (IRE)** *Charles Hills* 92
2 br c Dubawi(IRE) Ghanaati (USA) (Giant's Causeway (USA))
5887[10] (7274) 8036[7]

**Waggle (IRE)** *Michael Wigham* a41 28
4 b g Acclamation Week End (Selkirk (USA))
807[11] 3137[7] 3940[4]

**Wahaab (IRE)** *Sophie Leech* a66 79
6 ch g Tamayuz Indian Ink (IRE) (Indian Ridge (IRE))
44[9] 363[4] 5482[10] 6097[4]◆ 6502[3] (6807) 7083[5] (7934) 8184[4] 8798[9] 9083[7]

**Wahash (IRE)** *Richard Hannon* a85 100
3 gr c Dark Angel(IRE) Delira (IRE) (Namid)
1886[4] 2437[5] 2818[2] 3303[2] 3844[16] 4334[8] 6404[9]

**Wahiba (GER)** *Marco Botti* a67 73
4 b m Poet's Voice Walayta (GER) (Oasis Dream)
169[12] 986[6] (2285) 3216[6] 5039[4] 7241[6]

**Wahoo** *Michael Dods* 77
2 b g Stimulation(IRE) Shohrah (IRE) (Giant's Causeway (USA))
1873[2]◆ 3149[3] 5127[4]◆ (6042) 7814[6]

**Wai Key Star (GER)** *A Wohler* 109
4 b h Soldier Hollow Wakytara (GER) (Danehill (USA))
3116a[3] 4487a[2]

**Waikita (GER)** *Markus Klug* 93
3 b f Kallisto(GER) Zaynaat (Unfuwain (USA))
4

**Waitaki (IRE)** *D K Weld* a76 77
4 b m Invincible Spirit(IRE) Bluebell Park (USA) (Gulch (USA))
4385a[6]

**Wait Forever (IRE)** *Stefano Botti* 102
2 b c Camelot Mount McLeod (IRE) (Holy Roman Emperor (IRE))
8620a[2]

**Waiting A Lot (IRE)** *David O'Meara* a63 58
3 b f Iffraaj Love Intrigue (IRE) (Marju (IRE))
3931[4] 4474[10] 6633[6]◆ 8664[P] (Dead)

**Waitingforachance** *Mick Channon* 22
3 b f Sayif(IRE) Alice's Girl (Galileo (IRE))
2778[12]

**Waiting For Richie** *Tom Tate* a77 77
4 b g Rail Link Heart Of Hearts (Oasis Dream)
2386[3] 3311[7] 3794[2] 4791[5] 5832[4] (7359) 8565[2] 8778[3]

**Waiting Room** *James Tate* a34
2 ch c Bated Breath Lily In Pink (Sakhee (USA))
8502[11]

**Waitomo** *Charles Hills*
3 b f Equiano(FR) Lucky Legs (IRE) (Danehill Dancer (IRE))
2344[6] 6295[9]

**Wajaaha (IRE)** *Saeed bin Suroor* a66
2 b c New Approach(IRE) Thaahira (USA) (Dynaformer (USA))
7765[3]

**Wajnah (FR)** *F Rohaut* 107
3 bb f Redoute's Choice(AUS) Benzolina (IRE) (Second Empire (IRE))
2644a[4] 4665a[7] 5449a[8]

**Wake Forest (GER)** *Chad C Brown* 114
7 b h Sir Percy Wurfspiel (GER) (Lomitas)
2641a[5]

**Waki Delight (FR)** *F Alloncle* a54 56
4 b m Sandwaki(USA) Green House (FR) (Houston (FR))
837a[7]

**Walatah (GER)** *Markus Klug* 53
3 b f Soldier Hollow Wakytara (GER) (Danehill (USA))
3371a[8]

**Waldenon (FR)** *S Jesus* a60 54
4 b g Denon(USA) Waldouma (FR) (Ajdayt (USA))
6365a[11] (7069a)

**Waldgeist** *A Fabre* 117
3 ch c Galileo(IRE) Waldlerche (Monsun (GER))
2483a[2] 3368a[2]◆ 4387a[4] 7805[2]◆ 8527a[4]

**Walec** *P Sogorb* a96 102
5 b g Shamardal(USA) Sail (IRE) (Sadler's Wells (USA))
3354a[8] 5628a[3] 6540a[4]

**Walkabout (IRE)** *Gordon Elliott* a57 44
5 b g Papal Bull Dainty Steps (IRE) (Xaar)
333[7]

**Walking In Rhythm (IRE)**
*Barry Leavy* a52 49
4 b m Lord Shanakill(USA) So Sweet (IRE) (Cape Cross (IRE))
1735[9] 1983[8] 2626[6] 4980[9]

**Walk On Walter (IRE)**
*David Simcock* a74 62
2 b g Footstepsinthesand Hajmah (IRE) (Singspiel (IRE))
6921[6] 7876[4]◆ 8432[4]

**Wallflower (IRE)** *Rae Guest* a31
2 b f Thewayyouare(USA) Gaselee (USA) (Toccet (USA))
9080[8]

**Wall Of Fire (IRE)** *Hugo Palmer* a87 114
4 b h Canford Cliffs(IRE) Bright Sapphire (IRE) (Galileo (IRE))
1374a[6] 1733[2] 2571[4] 3553a[8] 6191[2] 8056a[2] 8667a[16]

**Walsingham (GER)**
*Waldemar Hickst* 103
3 b c Campanologist(USA) Winterkonigin (GER) (Sternkoenig (IRE))
2250a[3] 2947a[6] 6980a[5]

**Walsingham Grange (USA)**
*Pam Sly* 76
4 b g Paddy O'Prado(USA) Mambo Queen (USA) (Kingmambo (USA))
7558[4]◆ 8426[6]

**Walton Street** *Charlie Appleby* 102
3 b g Cape Cross(IRE) Brom Felinity (AUS) (Encosta De Lago (AUS))
(4720) (5598) 6421[4]

**Waltz Key (FR)** *J-C Rouget* a97 94
3 ro f Henrythenavigator(USA) Lia Waltz (FR) (Linamix (FR))
6963a[8] 8986a[11]

**Waneen (IRE)** *John Butler* a80 59
4 b g Approve(IRE) Million All Day (IRE) (Daylami (IRE))
416[8] 682[4] 886[11] 1071[9] 1290[12] 1819[8] 2962[11] 8873[7]

**Wannabe Friends** *Richard Hughes* a73 85
4 ch g Dubawi(IRE) Wannabe Posh (IRE) (Grand Lodge (USA))
1969[2] 2624[4] 4254[10] 4912[3] 5315[4] (6378) 6882[9] 7404[3] 8078[6]

**Wannabe Like You** *Archie Watson* a65 64
3 b g Sepoy(AUS) Wannabe Posh (IRE) (Grand Lodge (USA))
4097[4] 5611[10] 8504[4] 8810[3] 9088[5] 9364[12]

**Want The Fairytale** *Alan King* a64 48
4 b m Mount Nelson Tattercoats (FR) (Whywhywhy (USA))
2162[5]

**Wapping (USA)** *David Lanigan* a58 93
4 b g Smart Strike(CAN) Exciting Times (FR) (Jeune Homme (USA))
2068[3]◆ 2504[2] (3027) (3658)

**Waqaas** *Charles Hills* 94
3 b g Showcasing Red Mischief (IRE) (Red Clubs (IRE))
5423[12] 5890[5] 7782[3]◆

**Waqt (IRE)** *Marcus Tregoning* a69 66
3 b g Acclamation Needles And Pins (IRE) (Fasliyev (USA))
4964[2] 6103[8] 6807[8] 7254[5] 7723[2] 8132[10] 9432[8]

**War Again (FR)** *C Martinon* a55 49
4 b m Whipper(USA) Fee Du Nord (Inchinor)
837a[5] 1181a[3]

**War At Sea (IRE)** *David Simcock* a78 80
3 gr g Mastercraftsman(IRE) Swirling (IRE) (Galileo (IRE))
580[2]◆ 840[2] 3779[8] 4408[4] 5066[3] 6110[3]◆ 6823[4] 8151[5]

**Warba (IRE)** *Mohamed Moubarak* a58 33
3 ch f Intense Focus(USA) Have A Heart (IRE) (Daggers Drawn (USA))
245[7] 813[9] 1220[7] 8345[2] 8675[3] 8949[2] 9268[7]

**War Brigade (FR)** *David Simcock* 74
3 b g Manduro(GER) Adjudicate (Dansili)
3717[P] 5632[8] 6031[2] 6871[4] 8291[4]

**War Chief** *Alan King* a71 86
3 ch g Aqlaam My Colleen (USA) (Discreet Cat (USA))
2361[2]◆ 3005[3] 3838[7]

**War Decree (USA)** *A P O'Brien* a114 113
3 b c War Front(USA) Royal Decree (USA) (Street Cry (IRE))
1904[6] 3368a[5] (7588a) 8611a[9] 9171a[10]

**War Department (IRE)**
*Keith Dalgleish* a99 96
4 b g Frozen Power(IRE) On My Kness (FR) (Fasliyev (USA))
25[2] 275[7] 581[4] (989) 1105[2] 1295[6] 3792[4] 4077[3] (4264) 5091[3] 6024[12] 8257[8]

**War Drums** *Luca Cumani* 72
3 b g Authorized(IRE) Crystal Swan (IRE) (Dalakhani (IRE))
2963[7]

**Wardy (IRE)** *Peter Chapple-Hyam* a59 63
3 b c Dandy Man(IRE) Why Now (Dansili)
4341[5] 4759[6] 8504[6] 8801[9]

**War Envoy (USA)** *Mick Ruis* a80 83
5 b h War Front(USA) La Conseillante (USA) (Elusive Quality (USA))
469a[11]

**Warfare** *Tim Fitzgerald* a79 80
8 b g Soviet Star(USA) Fluffy (Efisio)
359[3] 648[6] 782[7] 1201[2] 2466[4] 2787[6] 3537[7] 5498[5] 6316[5] 6901[7] 7236[7] 7479[10]

**War Flag (USA)**
*Claude McGaughey III* a102 108
4 b m War Front(USA) Black Speck (USA) (Arch (USA))
8606a[6]

**War Glory (IRE)** *Richard Hannon* a98 97
4 b g Canford Cliffs(IRE) Attracted To You (IRE) (Hurricane Run (IRE))
1622[2]◆ 1769[2]◆ 2141[5] 3089[4] 4854[5] 5530[3] 5942[2] 6676[2] 7025[4] 8138[8]

**Warleggan (FR)** *Linda Perratt* a44 30
3 gr g Rajsaman(FR) Nostalchia (FR) (Genereux Genie)
2455[11] 2949[8] 3196[12] 3385 [9] 4246[8] 4479[5] 4682[12] 5203[7] 5645[4]

**Warm Love** *David O'Meara* 73
3 ch f Dutch Art Irish Song (FR) (Singspiel (IRE))
2300[3] 2854[7] 3499[5]

**Warm Oasis** *James Fanshawe* a79
3 gr g Oasis Dream Warling (IRE) (Montjeu (IRE))
5075[6] 8151[2] 8822[4] (9260)

**Warm Order** *Tony Carroll* a50 44
6 b m Assertive Even Hotter (Desert Style (IRE))
271[7] 723[7] 1221[5]

**Warm The Voice (IRE)**
*Brendan W Duke* 105
2 b g Vocalised(USA) Heir Today (IRE) (Princely Heir (IRE))
7426a[3]

**Warm Words** *Ralph Beckett* a71 64
3 b f Poet's Voice Limber Up (IRE) (Dansili)
314[4] 479[3]

**Warofindependence (USA)**
*John O'Shea* a70 63
5 bb g War Front(USA) My Dear Annie (USA) (Smart Strike (CAN))
6368[5]

**War Of Succession**
*Tony Newcombe* a89 77
3 b g Casamento(IRE) Rohlindi (Red Ransom (USA))
1804[3] 3435[5] (4173) 6322[11] 7277[9] 7998[12] 9093[6] 9376[8]

**Warp Factor (IRE)**
*John Patrick Shanahan* 90
4 b g The Carbon Unit(USA) Storminateacup (IRE) (Galileo (IRE))
2497[3] 2574[2] 3091[3] 4429[5] 5071[3] 6189[6] 6680[8]

**Warren (FR)** *Y Barberot* 78
2 b c Elusive City(USA) Danlepordamsterdam (IRE) (War Front (USA))
(2664a) 4596a[8]

**Warrigal (IRE)** *Leo Braem* a55 57
7 ch g Mount Nelson Waldblume (GER) (Halling (USA))
6018a[2]

**Warring States (JPN)** *A Wohler* 104
3 ch c Victoire Pisa(JPN) Ciliege (JPN) (Sakura Bakushin O (JPN))
(2246a) 3636a[4] 4422a[18]

**Warrior Of Light (IRE)**
*Brendan Powell* a87 97
6 b g High Chaparral(IRE) Strawberry Fledge (USA) (Kingmambo (USA))
202a[4] 540a[6] 1942[8] 2431[12] 4370[8] 5303[6]

**Warrior Prince** *Ed Dunlop* a73 69
4 ch g Sakhee(USA) Queen Of Iceni (Erhaab (USA))
3966[5] 5313[10] 6763[5] 7319[12]

**Warrior's Spirit (IRE)**
*Richard Hannon* a67 79
3 b g Requinto(IRE) Sandbox Two (IRE) (Foxhound (USA))
1945[7]◆ 2755[4] 3588[6] 6397[7] 6792[6] 7493[10]

**Warrior's Valley** *David C Griffiths* a33 28
2 b c Mayson Sand And Deliver (Royal Applause)
7242[10] 8483[8] 8657[7]

**Warsaan** *Owen Burrows* a70 73
2 b c Oasis Dream Tanfidh (Marju (IRE))
4534[2] 5608[3] 6884[6] 7914[5]

**Warsaw Road (IRE)** *Luca Cumani* 90
3 b g Zebedee Warda (Pivotal)
2798[4] 3293[8] (3824) 5288[8] (6297)◆ (7398)

**War Secretary (USA)** *A P O'Brien* a106 48
3 b c War Front(USA) Upperline (USA) (Maria's Mon (USA))
(1742a) 1959[10]

**War Story (USA)** *Jorge Navarro* a122
5 ch g Northern Afleet(USA) Belle Watling (USA) (Pulpit (USA))
469a[5] 8611a[4]

**War Whisper (IRE)** *Richard Hannon* a70 84
4 b h Royal Applause Featherweight (IRE) (Fantastic Light (USA))
2608[3] 3030[8] 3757[8] 6442[8] 7709[9]

**Wasatch Range** *John Gosden* 88
3 b c High Chaparral(IRE) Pearl City (IRE) (Zamindar (USA))
1497[4] (2039) 2784[8] 4701[3]

**Waseem Faris (IRE)**
*Ken Cunningham-Brown* a83 91
8 b g Exceed And Excel(AUS) Kissing Time (Lugana Beach)
2038[2] 2391[6] 3617[6] 3865[6] 4219[4] 5587[7] (6072) 6764[4] 8115[9]

**Washeek (IRE)** *Mark Johnston* 56
2 b c Kodiac Starring (FR) (Ashkalani (IRE))
1803[4] (Dead)

**Washington Blue** *Clive Cox* a72 72
3 b f Rip Van Winkle(IRE) Powder Blue (Daylami (IRE))
392[7]

**Washington DC (IRE)** *A P O'Brien* a110 114
4 b h Zoffany(IRE) How's She Cuttin' (IRE) (Shinko Forest (IRE))
1376a[7] 2397[2] 3079[6] 3926[15] 5595[5] (5974a) 6402[10] 8230[7] 8604a[8]

**Wasim (IRE)** *Ismail Mohammed* a89 85
2 b c Acclamation Quiet Protest (USA) (Kingmambo (USA))
(4567) 5136^3 5631^8 6867^4

**Wasm** *Roger Fell* a71 78
3 ch g Exceed And Excel(AUS) Finchley (Machiavellian (USA))
1730^9◆ 2584^7 (5315) 5760^4 6855^8 7699^3 8209^6 8510^8

**Wassail** *Ed de Giles* a41 54
4 b m Shamardal(USA) Gower Song (Singspiel (IRE))
3026^3 (3756) 4733^5 6309^2 6796^10 7336^9 7992^8

**Wasseem (IRE)** *Simon Crisford* a66 67
4 ch g Approve(IRE) Vintage Escape (IRE) (Cyrano De Bergerac)
139^5

**Wasted Sunsets (FR)** *John Berry* a40
3 b f Myboycharlie(IRE) Freezing (USA) (Bering)
6577^4 7542^6

**Watar Day** *Linda Jewell*
3 b f Watar(IRE) Hopeshedoes (USA) (Johannesburg (USA))
997^5 2330^9 9088^11

**Watchable** *David O'Meara* a109 101
7 ch g Pivotal Irresistible (Cadeaux Genereux)
207a^13 433a^7 651a^4 773a^5 1044a^15 1362^4 1793^5 2566^4 3092^3 3324^4 3969^6 6325^14 7828^4

**Watching Spirits** *Michael Appleby* a56 40
2 br g Harbour Watch(IRE) Naayla (IRE) (Invincible Spirit (IRE))
1873^9 7551^5 8212^7 8432^3 8793^3

**Watch Tan** *George Baker* a52 41
2 gr f Harbour Watch(IRE) High Tan (High Chaparral (IRE))
3687^8 4440^13 5408^5 5893^2 6790^7 7023^4

**Waterclock (IRE)** *Micky Hammond* a54 78
8 ch g Notnowcato Waterfall One (Nashwan (USA))
2032^4 4998^P

**Watersmeet** *Mark Johnston* a110 104
6 gr g Dansili Under The Rainbow (Fantastic Light (USA))
1973^3 (767) (985) 1770^2 2525^6 8038^31 8539^2 9259^3

**Waterville Dancer (IRE)**
*Richard Hughes* a79 85
3 b g Nathaniel(IRE) Tobiano (USA) (Mt. Livermore (USA))
840^3 1089^2 1607^5 4730^3◆ 5432^2 5563^2 6580^5 7903^4

**Watheeqa (USA)** *Roger Varian* a68
2 b f More Than Ready(USA) Tafaneen (USA) (Dynaformer (USA))
8148^5

**Watheer** *Marcus Tregoning* a75 75
2 ch g Leroidesanimaux(BRZ) Sunset Shore (Oasis Dream)
3868^4 (4560) 6396^7

**Wattaboutsteve** *Ralph J Smith* a52 21
6 b g Araafa(IRE) Angel Kate (IRE) (Invincible Spirit (IRE))
143^7 1305^3 2370^10

**Waves (IRE)** *Eve Johnson Houghton* a43 72
3 b f Born To Sea(IRE) Johannesburg Cat (USA) (Johannesburg (USA))
1432^5 (2726) 3142^5 3759^6 5276^8 7199^3 7464^4

**Wax And Wane** *K R Burke* 86
2 b c Maxios Moonavvara (IRE) (Sadler's Wells (USA))
5301^6◆ (7043) (7978)

**Way Of Wisdom** *Charlie Appleby* a78 83
2 b g Lonhro(AUS) La Pelegrina (USA) (Redoute's Choice (AUS))
(2435) 2852^2 5109^8 5844^2

**Wayside Magic** *Neville Bycroft* a26 55
4 b g Thewayyouare(USA) Poppy's Rose (Diktat)
607^9 1188^7 2549^8

**Way To Paris** *Antonio Marcialis* 106
4 gr h Champs Elysees Grey Way (USA) (Cozzene (USA))
2485a^3 3884a^2 6250a^7 7205a^2 8275a^3

**Way Up High** *Steve Flook* a39
5 b m Getaway(GER) High Life (Kayf Tara)
331^9 479^8 747^8 964^4 1260^8 1425^11

**Wazin** *Simon Crisford* a70
2 b f Dutch Art Azameera (IRE) (Azamour (IRE))
8536^3 8851^4

**Wealth Tax** *Ed Dunlop* a78 85
4 gr g Canford Cliffs(IRE) Firoza (FR) (King's Best (USA))
2020^5 2785^7 3344^3 (4001) 4563^11 (5578) (5843) 6349^6 7285^6 7582^9 8297^5

**Weapon Of Choice (IRE)**
*Dianne Sayer* a66 72
9 b g Iffraaj Tullawadgeen (IRE) (Sinndar (IRE))
5698^8

**Weardiditallgorong** *Des Donovan* a59 62
5 b m Fast Company(IRE) Little Oz (IRE) (Red Ransom (USA))
121^4 1789^7 2615^3 5250^2 6035^10 9056^3

**We Are The World** *Archie Watson* a75 77
2 b g Sir Percy Emerald Sea (Green Desert (USA))
2896^3◆ 4068^8 4963^3 (6286) 6934^6

**Wear It Well** *Henry Candy* 74
2 b f Kodiac Choosey Girl (IRE) (Choisir (AUS))
4533^10 5476^4 (6747) 7954^5

**Weather Front (USA)**
*Karen McLintock* a77 64
4 ch g Stormy Atlantic(USA) Kiswahili (Selkirk (USA))
611^6 7524^7 8209^12 8589^13

**Wedding Breakfast (IRE)**
*Richard Ford* a67 22
3 ch f Casamento(IRE) Fair Countenance (IRE) (Almutawakel)
424^2◆ 862^5 1840^2 2274^9 6047^10

**Wedding Photo (USA)**
*Saeed bin Suroor* a61
3 b f Lonhro(AUS) Well At The Top (IRE) (Sadler's Wells (USA))
7485^6

**Wedding Song (IRE)**
*M Delcher Sanchez* a67 53
3 ch g Casamento(IRE) Flaming Song (IRE) (Darshaan)
838a^6

**Wedgewood Estates** *Tony Carroll* a55 60
6 ch m Assertive Heaven (Reel Buddy (USA))
273^3 601^8 981^P 1557^6 2298^4 2969^3 3811^3 4735^2 6112^14 8185^7 8949^8

**Wedgewood Wonder** *Tony Carroll* 26
3 b f Medicean Katya Kabanova (Sadler's Wells (USA))
3279^5

**Wee Bogus** *Alistair Whillans* a45 54
4 b g Multiplex Silver Gyre (IRE) (Silver Hawk (USA))
4247^9 4657^4 5539^5 6592^7 6898^6 7659^11 8314^5

**Wee Jock (IRE)**
*John Patrick Shanahan* 60
3 b c Pour Moi(IRE) Wee Mad Snout (IRE) (Soviet Star (USA))
(4246) (4479) 5429^10

**Weekender** *John Gosden* a78 106
3 b c Frankel Very Good News (USA) (Empire Maker (USA))
(1584) 3042^3 (4048) 7397^2 7783^2◆

**Weekend Offender (FR)**
*Kevin Ryan* 102
4 ch g Lope De Vega(IRE) Huroof (IRE) (Pivotal)
1734^3◆ 4475^P 4916^6 5470^2 (5996)◆ 6449^20 7619^23 8042^11 8423^7

**Weekfair (FR)** *J Phelippon* a66 97
3 gr f Stormy River(FR) Lady Time (FR) (Orpen (USA))
1417a^2

**Weellan** *John Quinn* a76 73
2 ch g Mayson Regal Salute (Medicean)
2852^3 3648^2◆ 4258^2 4858^10 5492^3 5918^2 6900^2 7473^4 8207^4

**Weetamoo (FR)** *J-Y Artu* a43
2 b f Authorized(IRE) Absent Minded (Medicean)
8691a^12

**Weeton (IRE)** *Julie Camacho* a62 77
2 br c Society Rock(IRE) Petite Boulangere (IRE) (Namid)
4204^2◆ 4606^7 6056^4 6844^4 (7472)

**Wefait (IRE)** *Richard Hannon* a79 83
3 br c Harbour Watch(IRE) Night Club (Mozart (IRE))
1308^2 (1499) 2149^2 3081^3 3503^4 (4156) 5153^3 5630^4 6196^4 6849^4

**Weinberg** *Donald McCain* 54
2 b g Cityscape Willmar (IRE) (Zafonic (USA))
6658^9 7105^4

**We Know (IRE)** *Simon Crisford* 71
2 b c Teofilo(IRE) Yellow Rosebud (IRE) (Jeremy (USA))
6553^6 8075^4 8476^4

**Weld Al Emarat** *Michael Easterby* a61 92
5 b g Dubawi(IRE) Spirit Of Dubai (IRE) (Cape Cross (IRE))
8485^9 8736^8

**Weld Arab (IRE)** *Michael Blake* a73 51
6 b g Shamardal(USA) Itqaan (USA) (Danzig (USA))
2022^6

**Welease Bwian (IRE)**
*Stuart Williams* a82 73
8 b g Kheleyf(USA) Urbanize (USA) (Chester House (USA))
219^10 518^7

**Well Acquainted (IRE)**
*Ismail Mohammed* a64 76
7 b h Orientate(USA) Stunning Rose (IRE) (Sadler's Wells (USA))
250a^8

**Well Fleeced** *Carina Fey* a75 75
5 b g Excellent Art Diksie Dancer (Diktat)
6541a^4 9309a^2

**Welliesinthewater (IRE)**
*Derek Shaw* a92 84
7 b g Footstepsinthesand Shadow Ash (IRE) (Ashkalani (IRE))
760^9 (984) (1224) 2116^9 (2518) 3294^12 4264^3 4622^5 5415^11 8600^10 8812^9 9020^6

**Well Painted (IRE)** *Daniel Steele* a40
8 ch g Excellent Art Aoife (IRE) (Thatching)
806^12

**Wells Farhh Go (IRE)** *Tim Easterby* 110
2 b c Farhh Mowazana (IRE) (Galileo (IRE))
(5380) (6326)

**We'll Shake Hands (FR)** *K R Burke* a30 70
6 b g Excellent Art Amou Daria (FR) (Kendor (FR))
1498^17 1707^7

**Well Spoken (GER)** *Markus Klug* 103
3 b f Soldier Hollow Well American (USA) (Bertrando (USA))
3371a^2 4393a^5 5693a^13 7722a^7

**Well Suited (IRE)** *Simon Crisford* 77
2 ch c Dandy Man(IRE) Dame D'Honneur (IRE) (Teofilo (IRE))
4696^2◆

**Well Tried** *Vanja Sandrup* 85
7 b g Three Valleys(USA) Diamond Reef (Alzao (USA))
(2941a)

**Weloof (FR)** *John Butler* a80 64
3 b g Redoute's Choice(AUS) Peinted Song (USA) (Unbridled's Song (USA))
(1259) 3262^10 3862^12 5849^6 6387^9 6792^8 8958^11 9142^9 9469^4

**Welsh Inlet (IRE)** *John Bridger* a57 63
9 br m Kheleyf(USA) Ervedya (IRE) (Doyoun)
167^8 398^4 (544) 644^2 860^11 1237^3 1425^4 1618^5 3661^2 4176^6 4459^6 5651^4 6076^8 6814^9 7916^6 8307^11

**Welsh Lord** *Saeed bin Suroor* a75
2 gr c Dark Angel(IRE) Welsh Angel (Dubai Destination (USA))
7987^4◆

**Welsh Rose** *Archie Watson* a76 51
4 b m Exceed And Excel(AUS) Nantyglo (Mark Of Esteem (IRE))
2335^3 4043^5 6015^7 6850^10

**Weltstar (GER)** *Markus Klug* 77
2 bb c Soldier Hollow Wellenspiel (GER) (Sternkoenig (IRE))
8621a^4

**Wemyss Point** *Philip Kirby* a44 15
5 b g Champs Elysees Wemyss Bay (Sadler's Wells (USA))
1984^9 2496^8

**Wensara Dream** *Andrew Balding* a39 54
4 b m Lilbourne Lad(IRE) Emerald Fire (Pivotal)
52^9

**Wensley** *James Bethell* 76
2 b c Poet's Voice Keladora (USA) (Crafty Prospector (USA))
4472^5 4996^2◆ (5453) 6056^3 6693^4 7814^17 8413^5

**Wentwell Yesterday (IRE)**
*Jamie Osborne* a72 57
3 b c Kodiac Roisin's Star (IRE) (Accordion)
160^8 496^2

**Wentworth Falls** *Geoffrey Harker* a70 100
5 gr g Dansili Strawberry Morn (CAN) (Travelling Victor (CAN))
851^7 (1515)◆ (1831) 2736^10 3861^4 4505^9 5705^8

**We Ride The World (IRE)**
*Louis Baudron* a59 75
2 b g Orpen(USA) Meulles (FR) (Scat Daddy (USA))
2664a^3 3445a^6

**Werther (NZ)** *John Moore* 120
5 b g Tavistock(NZ) Bagalollies (AUS) (Zabeel (NZ))
(3129a) 9171a^2

**Westadora (IRE)** *J Reynier* a84 95
4 b m Le Havre(IRE) Stranded (Montjeu (IRE))
4679a^8 6665a^5

**Westbrook Bertie** *Mick Channon* 70
2 b c Sixties Icon Evanesce (Lujain (USA))
6653^9 7120^3 7915^F 8508^4

**West Coast (USA)** *Bob Baffert* a123
3 b c Flatter(USA) Caressing (USA) (Honour And Glory (USA))
8611a^3

**West Drive (IRE)** *Roger Varian* 92
4 ch g Sea The Stars(IRE) Fair Sailing (IRE) (Docksider (USA))
2965^4 (3409) 4206^5 (5303)◆ 6000^5 7143^9

**Westerland** *John Gosden* a89 94
2 b c Frankel Arabesque (Zafonic (USA))
2779^2◆ (3164) 4068^11 5547^2 6684^2 (7148) 8035^5

**Western Boy (IRE)** *P A Fahy* 89
8 b g Antonius Pius(USA) Skala (IRE) (Hernando (FR))
7860a^17

**Western Duke (IRE)** *Ralph Beckett* a95 91
3 b g High Chaparral(IRE) Witch Of Fife (USA) (Lear Fan (USA))
1518^7 1886^8 2690^3 5475^4 (6887) 8638^5

**Western Dynamisme (FR)**
*Harry Dunlop*
2 b f Manduro(GER) Western Hope (IRE) (High Chaparral (IRE))
5586^8 6504^8 7410^11

**Western Express (AUS)** *J Size* 117
4 ch g Encosta De Lago(AUS) Alsatia (AUS) (Marauding (NZ))
9170a^2

**Western Hymn** *John Gosden* a112 112
6 b g High Chaparral(IRE) Blue Rhapsody (Cape Cross (IRE))
(2571)◆ 4070^7 4814^4 6976a^10 8421^10 8637^5 8992^8

**Western Presence** *Richard Fahey* a65 62
3 ch c Sleeping Indian Mawjoodah (Cadeaux Genereux)
(157) 418^7

**Western Prince** *Michael Appleby* a83 74
4 b g Cape Cross(IRE) Vigee Le Brun (USA) (Pulpit (USA))
62^5 389^4 3050^5 3794^8 4586^5

**Western Safari (IRE)**
*Richard Hannon* a64 59
3 b f High Chaparral(IRE) Shamwari Lodge (IRE) (Hawk Wing (USA))
1286^3◆ 2144^5 6287^9 7157^8 7539^10

**Western Way (IRE)** *Don Cantillon* a65 75
8 b g Westerner Faucon (Polar Falcon (USA))
9013^2 9261^8

**Westfalica (GER)**
*Jean-Pierre Carvalho* 95
3 b f Areion(GER) Walburga (GER) (One Cool Cat (USA))
6495a^9

**Westfield Wonder**
*Ronald Thompson* a53 53
2 b c Captain Gerrard(IRE) Flying Highest (Spectrum (IRE))
3460^9 3754^10 4895^10 5453^3 6043^11 8996^6 9230^5

**Westit** *C Laffon-Parias* a93 93
3 rg f Tapit(USA) West Ocean (USA) (Elusive Quality (USA))
1270a^10 4027a^3 5196a^11 7471a^2

**West Leake (IRE)** *Paul Burgoyne* a63 41
11 b g Acclamation Kilshanny (Groom Dancer (USA))
282^6 544^3 740^4 1298^10 1425^3 1563^4

**West Palm Beach (IRE)**
*John Gosden* a81
2 br f Scat Daddy(USA) Shelley Beach (IRE) (Danehill Dancer (IRE))
5795^3◆ 7757^5 (8544) (8997)

**Westward Ho (IRE)** *James Bethell* a81 72
4 b g Fastnet Rock(AUS) Thought Is Free (Cadeaux Genereux)
2030^8 2624^6

**We Win** *J R Jenkins*
3 b f Hellvelyn Pink Champagne (Cosmonaut)
8842^11

**W G Grace (IRE)** *Mark Johnston* a64 65
2 b c Exceed And Excel(AUS) Ownwan (USA) (Kingmambo (USA))
3283^4 3622^5 4888^5 (6285) 6825^4 7228^3 7734^9 7920^8 8191^7 8475^8

**Whaleweigh Station** *J R Jenkins* a66 65
6 b g Zamindar(USA) Looby Loo (Kyllachy)
(274) (455) 521^3 620^6 815^6 1076^10 1305^6 2091^8 3001^14 6813^11 7763^7 7952^3 8134^6 9129^10

**Whaling Story (GER)** *M Rulec* 79
2 ch f Lord Of England(GER) Wanna Be (GER) (Nayef (USA))
6494a^5

**What About Carlo (FR)**
*Eve Johnson Houghton* a79 113
6 b g Creachadoir(IRE) Boccatenera (GER) (Artan (IRE))
2999^9 3300^3 4370^2 (5148) 5500^12 7393^9 7506^2 8421^5

**What A Home (IRE)** *William Haggas* 89
3 b f Lope De Vega(IRE) Inchmahome (Galileo (IRE))
3748^3◆ 4300^3◆ (5401)◆ (7092)◆

**Whatalove** *Martin Keighley* a49 52
3 ch f Arcano(IRE) Secret Happiness (Cape Cross (IRE))
875^3 987^5 1421^2 1596^6 2911^7 3423^2 4150^2 4754^7 7911^3

**What A Scorcher** *Nikki Evans* 76
6 b m Authorized(IRE) Street Fire (IRE) (Street Cry (IRE))
2357^5 3770^4 4840^2 6095^4

**What A Surprise (IRE)**
*Ibrahim Al Malki* a80 89
3 b g Rip Van Winkle(IRE) Superstitious (USA) (Kingmambo (USA))
933a^9

**What A Welcome** *Patrick Chamings* a78 24
3 ch g Nathaniel(IRE) Hometime (Dubai Destination (USA))
5428^12 6277^10 7768^5 (8549) (8883)

**Whatdoesthefoxsay (NOR)**
*Dina Danekilde*
5 ch m Royal Experiment(USA) Antarktis (Dubai Destination (USA))
2941a^5

**What Do You Think (IRE)**
*Michael Dods* a52 51
2 b f Excelebration(IRE) Dama'A (IRE) (Green Desert (USA))
4116^8 5015^6 5537^7 7030^3

**Whatelseaboutyou (IRE)**
*Richard Fahey* a60 59
3 b f Canford Cliffs(IRE) Brigids Cross (IRE) (Sadler's Wells (USA))
305^5 864^4 967^3

**Whatsthemessage (IRE)**
*Keith Dalgleish* a63 94
3 b f Bushranger(IRE) Fatwa (IRE) (Lahib (USA))
31^6 417^4 846^6 1124^5 3900^4 (4209) 4785^2 5258^3 (5666) (5881) (6349) (6691)◆ 7113^12 7658^4

**Whats The Plot (IRE)** *A L T Moore* a57 68
5 b g Alfred Nobel(IRE) Hazarama (IRE) (Kahyasi (IRE))
5689a^9

**What's The Story** *Keith Dalgleish* 97
3 b c Harbour Watch(IRE) Spring Fashion (IRE) (Galileo (IRE))
(1804) (8736)◆

**What's Up Walter** *Philip Kirby* a37 23
3 ch g Stimulation(IRE) Pose (IRE) (Acclamation)
40^10 150^7 378^6 3708^9 5617^11

**What Usain** *Michael Appleby* a74 66
5 b g Misu Bond(IRE) Bond Shakira (Daggers Drawn (USA))
166^2◆ 419^5 525^3 (806) 928^4 1210^5 1257^2 (1602) 1892^3 2471^8 2971^6

**What Wonders Weave (IRE)**
*John Patrick Shanahan* a76 79
3 b f Famous Name Jagapaw (IRE) (Manduro (GER))
(2429) 4430^3 5432^8 6196^5 (6784) 7162^3 8142^4

**Whatwouldyouknow (IRE)**
*Richard Guest* a35 46
2 b g Lope De Vega(IRE) Holamo (IRE) (Montjeu (IRE))
8474^11 8779^8

**Wheal Leisure (AUS)**
*Archie Alexander* 103
3 b f Artie Schiller(USA) Sadiya (AUS) (Encosta De Lago (AUS))
8751a^3

**Wherearainbowsend (IRE)**
*Bryan Smart* a60
2 br f Roderic O'Connor(IRE) Mikes Baby (IRE) (Key Of Luck (USA))
8914^5◆ 9371^6

**Where's Jeff** *Michael Easterby* a51 62
2 b g Haafhd Piece Of Magic (Alflora (IRE))
3791^6 4359^6 4862^8 6043^9 7655^2 8996^9

**Where's Stewart** *Nigel Tinkler* 30
3 ch g Firebreak Sukuma (IRE) (Highest Honor (FR))
2349^15 2989^8

**Whigwham** *Gary Sanderson* a36 66
3 ch f Sleeping Indian Normandy Maid (American Post)
2223^7 2699^2◆ 2989^5 6089^9

**Whinging Willie (IRE)** *Gary Moore* a87 88
8 b g Cape Cross(IRE) Pacific Grove (Persian Bold (IRE))
2085^2 3323^6 4801^2 5798^2 6196^6 6513^7 (7651) 8511^6

**Whinmoor** *Nigel Tinkler* 48
2 gr g Havana Gold(IRE) Makhsusah (IRE) (Darshaan)
7623^7 8010^8

**Whipcrackaway (IRE)** *Peter Hedger* a37 58
8 b g Whipper(USA) Former Drama (USA) (Dynaformer (USA))
5362^3 5722^6 6069^9

**Whip My Love (FR)** *Y Barberot* a76 74
3 bb f Whipper(USA) Arabian Beauty (FR) (Dubawi (IRE))
272a[9]

**Whip Nae Nae (IRE)**
*Richard Hannon* a79 86
3 ch c Dragon Pulse(IRE) Love In May (IRE) (City On A Hill (USA))
2118[3] 2526[6] 2784[6] 3317[10] 6073[4] (6387) 7909[7]

**Whipper Snapper (FR)** *J-V Toux* a45 64
7 b g Whipper(USA) Margot Mine (IRE) (Choisir (AUS))
(5176a)

**Whipphound** *Ruth Carr* a43 56
9 b g Whipper(USA) Golden Symbol (Wolfhound (USA))
80[10] 2633[8] 2950[5]◆ 3704[3]◆ 4789[11] 5283[3] 5543[7] 5738[3] 6045[7] (6271) 6688[4] 7020[8] 7218[10] 7926[11] 8490[10]

**Whip Up A Frenzy (IRE)**
*David O'Meara* a45 47
5 b g Vale Of York(IRE) Answer Do (Groom Dancer (USA))
281[6] 621[6] 880[10] 6131[10] 7165[8] 7820[10] 8248[5] 8800[8]

**Whirl Me Round** *George Peckham* a70 84
3 ch g Piccolo Give Her A Whirl (Pursuit Of Love)
8872[10] 9124[13] 9437[7]

**Whirlwind Romance (IRE)**
*Hugo Palmer* a49
3 b f Canford Cliffs(IRE) Tencarola (IRE) (Night Shift (USA))
48[7] 328[8] 504[9]

**Whiskey Sour (IRE)** *W P Mullins* a82 105
4 b g Jeremy(USA) Swizzle Stick (IRE) (Sadler's Wells (USA))
(5488a)

**Whisky Baron (AUS)** *B Crawford* 112
4 b g Manhattan Rain(AUS) Tazkara (FR) (Sinndar (IRE))
7579[6]

**Whisper A Word (IRE)**
*Tim Easterby* 45
3 ch f Bated Breath Affability (IRE) (Dalakhani (IRE))
2180[7] 3832[11] 4172[7] 4623[11]

**Whispered Kiss** *Mike Murphy* a67 91
4 b m Medicean Desert Kiss (Cape Cross (IRE))
(1894) 2312[2] (3172) 4446[14] (5119) (5664) (5813) 6358[9] 6919[3]

**Whispering Bell (IRE)** *John Gosden* 90
3 b f Galileo(IRE) Red Avis (Exceed And Excel (AUS))
(4409) 5352[10]

**Whispering Soul (IRE)** *Brian Baugh* a56 51
4 b m Majestic Missile(IRE) Belle Of The Blues (IRE) (Blues Traveller (IRE))
95[7] 271[5] 899[7] 9267[6] 9374[10]

**Whispering Wolf** *Suzzanne France* a47 51
4 b m Amadeus Wolf Ashover Amber (Green Desert (USA))
271[6] 446[7] 723[6] 1126[11] 1973[6] 3202[8] 4997[13] 6045[11]

**Whistle Stop (SAF)** *M F De Kock* 103
6 b g Silvano(GER) Gap Year (SAF) (Rich Man's Gold (USA))
87a[9] 208a[6] 322a[9] 654a[8]

**Whitchurch** *Iain Jardine* a37 58
5 b g Mawatheeq(USA) Silvereine (FR) (Bering)
1312[9] 2166[10] 2891[5] 3650[6] 4034[8] 4659[14]

**Whiteandgold** *Bryan Smart* 72
3 b f Major Cadeaux Irrational (Kyllachy)
4717[5] 5211[15] 6596[5]

**White Chocolate (IRE)**
*David Simcock* a70 92
3 gr f Mastercraftsman(IRE) Coco Demure (IRE) (Titus Livius (FR))
(2761) (3535) 4292[2] 5529[4] 6477[2] 6722[4] 7817[7]

**Whitecliff Park (IRE)** *Brian Ellison* a76 55
4 b g Canford Cliffs(IRE) Venetian Rhapsody (IRE) (Galileo (IRE))
1519[6] 1839[4] 2183[13] 2688[4] 3192[6] (3340) 4684[10] 5267[13] (5896)◆ 6323[4] 6889[4] 7359[8]

**Whitecliffsofdover (USA)**
*A P O'Brien* 113
3 b c War Front(USA) Orate (USA) (A.P. Indy (USA))
(1881) 3959[15] 4652a[7] 6959a[5] 7579[7]

**Whitecrest** *John Spearing* a73 78
9 ch m Ishiguru(USA) Risky Valentine (Risk Me (FR))
1965[9] (2306) (2675) (2969) 3177[7] 3919[5] 4277[4] 4495[5] 4910[2]◆ 5295[4] 5711[2] 5936[2] 6373[5] 6586[2] 7000[4] 7214[2] 7409[5] 7933[6] 8243[7] 8311[3]

**White Desert (IRE)** *Charlie Appleby* 77
3 ch g Teofilo(IRE) Artisia (IRE) (Peintre Celebre (USA))
(4808) 6423[5]

**White Dog (IRE)** *Sarah Humphrey* a52 43
5 b g Le Cadre Noir(IRE) Little Annie (Compton Place)
281[9]

**White Feather** *Jo Hughes* 72
2 ch g Bated Breath Just Wood (FR) (Highest Honor (FR))
1919a[3] 2664a[2] 3515a[5] 5270[3] 7906[5]

**White Flag (USA)**
*Christophe Clement* 102
3 b c War Front(USA) Shared Hope (USA) (Gone West (USA))
8097a[3]

**Whitefountainfairy (IRE)**
*Andrew Balding* 99
2 ch f Casamento(IRE) Groupetime (USA) (Gilded Time (USA))
4028[17] 5329[5]◆ 6418[2]

**White Guard** *Sir Mark Prescott Bt* 65
2 b c Frankel Arbella (Primo Dominie)
7460[3]◆

**Whitehall** *Sir Michael Stoute* 64
2 b g Dansili Majestic Roi (USA) (Street Cry (IRE))
6108[9] 7460[4] 8136[8]

**White Lake** *Roger Varian* 105
5 b g Pivotal White Palace (Shirley Heights)
2767[9] 8234[6]

**Whiteley (IRE)** *Mick Channon* a50 61
3 b f Dark Angel(IRE) Carallia (IRE) (Common Grounds)
1686[5] 2625[6] 3142[4] 3656[4] 3937[5] 4447[6] 4715[3] 5340[5] (5791) 6339[3] 6724[4] 7191[9] 7517[4] 8146[7]

**White Light (FR)** *J-M Capitte* a48 46
6 b m Peintre Celebre(USA) Lovely Sea (FR) (Bering)
364a[13]

**White Mocha (USA)** *Hugo Palmer* 98
2 ch c Lope De Vega(IRE) Lastroseofsummer (IRE) (Haafhd)
(5876) 6859[2] (7355)

**White Nile (IRE)** *Laura Young* a49 42
8 b h Galileo(IRE) Super Gift (IRE) (Darshaan)
4380[8] 5781[5]

**White Rosa (IRE)** *Hugo Palmer* a57 73
3 b f Galileo(IRE) Dhanyata (IRE) (Danetime (IRE))
3404[2]◆ 4378[3] (6350) 7673a[10] 8986a[16]

**White Royale (USA)** *Kevin Ryan* a76 46
3 b f Speightstown(USA) Sweet Hope (USA) (Lemon Drop Kid (USA))
41[3] 313[2] 458[8]

**White Tower (IRE)** *Mark Johnston* 91
3 b g Cape Cross(IRE) Star Blossom (USA) (Good Reward (USA))
1912[4] 4223[6] 5066[4] 5425[6] 5760[6]

**Whitkirk** *Jedd O'Keeffe* a69 75
4 b g Iffraaj Bedouin Bride (USA) (Chester House (USA))
2140[2] 3049[4] (3906) 6266[3] 6564[5] 7571[7] 8216[9] 8589[12]

**Whitlock** *John Gosden* a54
2 ch c Dutch Art Barynya (Pivotal)
8703[8]

**Whitmel** *Michael Appleby* a25
4 b g Sulamani(IRE) My Valentina (Royal Academy (USA))
9235[6]

**Whitmore (USA)** *Ronald Moquett* a117
4 ch g Pleasantly Perfect(USA) Melody's Spirit (USA) (Scat Daddy (USA))
8607a[8]

**Whitstable Pearl (IRE)**
*Sophie Leech* a56 42
4 b m Kodiac Amber's Bluff (Mind Games)
3028[9] 3772[5] 4982[11]

**Who Dares Wins (IRE)** *Alan King* a81 103
5 b g Jeremy(USA) Savignano (Polish Precedent (USA))
2525[4] 3928[3] 6675[10] (7402)◆ 8038[10]

**Who Shot Thebarman (NZ)**
*Chris Waller* 115
8 b g Yamanin Vital(NZ) Ears Carol (NZ) (Carolingian (AUS))
1994a[2] 6714a[9]

**Who's Shirl** *Chris Fairhurst* a59 61
11 b m Shinko Forest(IRE) Shirl (Shirley Heights)
361[10]

**Whosyourhousemate** *Ed Vaughan* a86 83
3 ch g Bahamian Bounty Starlit Sky (Galileo (IRE))
236[3] (1293) 5664[3] 6110[4] 7339[3]◆ (8375)

**Who Told Jo Jo (IRE)** *Joseph Tuite* a68 72
3 b g Bushranger(IRE) Shenkara (IRE) (Night Shift (USA))
623[6] 898[3] 1332[7] (1688) 2235[6]◆ 3719[4] 4576[9] 5429[11] 5956[4] 6581[5] 7517[11]

**Why Me** *Gavin Cromwell* a47 56
7 b g Dubai Destination(USA) My Golly (Mozart (IRE))
9076[2] 9343[4]

**Why We Dream (IRE)**
*Mick Channon* 58
2 b f Al Kazeem Sandreamer (IRE) (Oasis Dream)
8388[8]

**Wicker** *Jane Chapple-Hyam* a74 70
3 b f Myboycharlie(IRE) Lady Berta (Bertolini (USA))
2266[7] 2908[7] 3438[3] 8646[2] 9126[3] (9276)

**Wicklow Brave** *W P Mullins* 115
8 b g Beat Hollow Moraine (Rainbow Quest (USA))
3553a[4] 4420a[2] 5503[4] 6214a[4] 6976a[4] 8250a[12] 8667a[10]

**Wick Powell** *David Barron* a96 84
3 b g Sakhee's Secret London Welsh (Cape Cross (IRE))
155[3] (1124) 1311[4] 1774[4] 2831[8]

**Widnes** *Alan Bailey* a72 69
3 b g Showcasing Largo (IRE) (Selkirk (USA))
1242[2]◆ 1625[4] 2071[4]◆ 2895[7] 5039[6] 6620[4] 7062[10] 7791[8] 8327[4] 8883[5] 9092[6] 9391[2]

**Wiesenbach** *Il Cavallo In Testa* 102
2 gr c Jukebox Jury(IRE) Wurfscheibe (GER) (Tiger Hill (IRE))
(8620a)

**Wiff Waff** *Stuart Williams* a58 61
2 b g Poet's Voice Eraadaat (IRE) (Intikhab (USA))
3135[9] 3782[5] 4792[8] 6021[7] 8431[6] 8588[4]◆

**Wigan Warrior** *David Brown* a80 80
3 b g Doncaster Rover(USA) Rattleyurjewellery (Royal Applause)
2957[2] (3332) 4084[6] (5139)◆ 5928[5] 6855[12] 7759[4] 8126[7] 8375[14]

**Wikita (FR)** *T Lemer* a82 81
6 b m Desert Style(IRE) Vagabonde (FR) (Valanour (IRE))
81a[2]

**Wilamina (IRE)** *Martyn Meade* 102
4 b m Zoffany(IRE) Tropical Lake (IRE) (Lomond (USA))
(3219) 4934a[2] 6248a[10] 7171a[3] 8007[5]

**Wild Acclaim (IRE)** *Michael Appleby* a53 71
3 b g Acclamation Anam Allta (IRE) (Invincible Spirit (IRE))
2033[2] 2595[3] 3524[7] 8798[8] 9203[10] 9376[12]

**Wild Approach (GER)** *D Moser* 102
4 ch m New Approach(IRE) Wildfahrte (GER) (Mark Of Esteem (IRE))
4518a[2] 5597[4] 6254a[2] 7204a[6]

**Wild Approach (IRE)** *Robert Cowell* a75 74
3 b g Approve(IRE) Mike's Wildcat (USA) (Forest Wildcat (USA))
(313)◆ (657) 926[4] 4159[3] 5041[3] 5338[3] 6155[2] 6574[U] (Dead)

**Wild As The Wind (IRE)**
*W McCreery* 93
4 ch m Approve(IRE) Money Penny (ITY) (Montjeu (IRE))
1387a[5] 1568a[7]

**Wild Bud (USA)** *H-A Pantall* a80 100
3 ch f Dubawi(IRE) Wild Wind (GER) (Danehill Dancer (IRE))
8449a[7]

**Wildcat Red (USA)** *Doug Watson* a104
6 b h D'Wildcat(USA) Racene (USA) (Miner's Mark (USA))
204a[11] 432a[10]

**Wild Chief (GER)** *J Hirschberger* 107
6 ch h Doyen(IRE) Wild Angel (IRE) (Acatenango (GER))
(4130a) 5464a[7] 7638a[7] 8527a[9]

**Wild Comet (GER)** *J Hirschberger* 78
4 b m Soldier Hollow Wild Angel (IRE) (Acatenango (GER))
7673a[8]

**Wild Dancer** *Patrick Chamings* a67 79
4 b m Mawatheeq(USA) Pretty Miss (Averti (IRE))
2335[4] 3278[10] 5711[7] 7771[11]

**Wild Dude (USA)** *M Halford* a100
7 br h Wildcat Heir(USA) Courtly Choice (USA) (Doneraile Court (USA))
206a[3] 539a[3] 772a[7] 1041a[5] 1377a[13]

**Wilde Extravagance (IRE)**
*Julie Camacho* a54 65
4 ch g Dandy Man(IRE) Castanetta (IRE) (Dancing Dissident (USA))
1972[6] 2404[6] 3345[4] 3667[9] 4509[12] 5543[5] 8481[7] 8924[10]

**Wilde Inspiration (IRE)**
*Julie Camacho* a82 97
6 ch g Dandy Man(IRE) Wishing Chair (USA) (Giant's Causeway (USA))
2155[7] 2838[5]

**Wilderness Now (IRE)** *F Chappet* a81 79
2 b g Kendargent(FR) Full Snow Moon (USA) (Vindication (USA))
5952a[3] 7012a[4]

**Wild Flower (IRE)** *Jimmy Fox* a61 63
5 b m Approve(IRE) Midsummernitedream (GER) (Thatching)
1451[6] 4179[2] (4710) 5748[3] (6004) 6373[6] 7190[6] 8495[3] (8823) 9183[4] 9470[4]

**Wild Hacked (USA)** *Marco Botti* a110 102
4 b h Lemon Drop Kid(USA) Dance Pass (IRE) (Sadler's Wells (USA))
1502[2]◆ (1779) 2604[6] 3884a[5] 6447[9] 6931[3] 7354[3] 8740[8]

**Wild Illusion** *Charlie Appleby* 115
2 b f Dubawi(IRE) Rumh (GER) (Monsun (GER))
(6292)◆ 6731a[3] (7666a)

**Wild Impala (FR)** *John Gosden* 84
2 b f Monsieur Bond(IRE) Dilag (IRE) (Almutawakel)
4815[7] 6480[9] 8006[5] (8347) 8597[6]

**Wild Irish Rose (IRE)** *A P O'Brien* 104
3 b f Galileo(IRE) Sea Picture (IRE) (Royal Academy (USA))
(5088a) 5569[5] 5766a[3] 7089[5] 7422a[3] 8231[10]

**Wild Max (GER)** *A Wohler*
2 bb c Maxios Wildfahrte (GER) (Mark Of Esteem (IRE))
8091a[3]

**Wildnightinvegas (IRE)**
*Richard Hannon* a59 73
2 b g Kodiac Wild Whim (IRE) (Whipper (USA))
2691[5] 3467[3] (4709)

**Wildpark (GER)** *D Moser* 103
6 b g Shamardal(USA) Wildfahrte (GER) (Mark Of Esteem (IRE))
6987a[6]

**Wild State (IRE)** *J S Moore* 62
2 ch c Reckless Abandon Be Glad (Selkirk (USA))
3029[7]

**Wild West Hero** *Sir Michael Stoute* a60 44
2 b c Exceed And Excel(AUS) Hi Calypso (IRE) (In The Wings)
8352[6] 8703[9] 8951[8]

**Wiley Post** *Tony Carroll* 83
4 b g Kyllachy Orange Pip (Bold Edge)
3161[9] 4278[3] 5219[2] 5967[3] 6764[3]

**Wilfred Owen** *John Gosden* a44 40
2 br c Poet's Voice Mini Mosa (Indian Ridge (IRE))
7810[8] 8162[8] 8794[10] 9230[4]

**Willbeme** *Simon West* a68 69
9 b m Kyllachy Befriend (USA) (Allied Forces (USA))
443[6] 1475[11] 1972[2] 2550[4] 3541[3] 3897[4] 4426[5] 5318[8] 6572[3] 7166[7] 7575[5] 8194[6] 8590[8] 8924[8] 9033[10]

**William Booth (IRE)** *Ivan Furtado* a65 71
3 b g Born To Sea(IRE) Chaguaramas (IRE) (Mujadil (USA))
2584[4] 4173[3] 4633[7] 7958[3] 8300[4] 8814[9] 9376[3]

**William Hunter** *Alan King* a87 92
5 b g Mawatheeq(USA) Cosmea (Compton Place)
1502[8] 2085[4] 2603[5] 5287[3] 5924[3] 7337[3]◆

**William Of Wykeham (IRE)**
*Sir Michael Stoute* a43
2 ch c Arcano(IRE) Highland Gift (IRE) (Generous (IRE))
6885[9]

**William Sayle** *John Gosden* a79 67
3 ch g Bahamian Bounty Incarnation (IRE) (Samum (GER))
503[8] (1410) 7959[10] 8797[12] 9100[5]

**Willie John** *William Haggas* 83
2 b c Dansili Izzi Top (Pivotal)
(8119)◆

**Willie's Anne (IRE)**
*Daniel Mark Loughnane* a53 48
3 b f Lilbourne Lad(IRE) Cape Sydney (IRE) (Cape Cross (IRE))
149[6] 881[5]

**Willingforshilling (IRE)**
*Harry Dunlop* 51
2 br f Dabirsim(FR) Anavera (GER) (Acatenango (GER))
8348[10]

**Willow Spring** *Denis Quinn* a51 55
5 b m Compton Place Upstream (Prince Sabo)
143[3] 622[10] 1022[9] 1304[7] 4053[9] 4543[6] 6114[14]

**Willow Tiger Lily** *J R Jenkins* 27
3 ch f Sakhee's Secret Tinkerbell Will (Where Or When (IRE))
2121[10] 2619[7] 4445[10]

**Willpower (TUR)**
*Ibrahim Bekirogullari* 107
7 b m Victory Gallop(CAN) Free Trade (TUR) (Shareef Dancer (USA))
6718a[3]

**Willsy** *Karen Tutty* a73 76
4 b g Sakhee's Secret Blakeshall Rose (Tobougg (IRE))
1717[11] 2120[5] 3049[10] 3181[6] 3402[7] 4789[2] 5318[3] 5696[2] 6181[4] 6435[12] 6546[11] 7525[13] 8210[5] 8513[5]

**Willwams (IRE)** *Richard Hannon* a69
3 b g Duke Of Marmalade(IRE) Aweebounce (IRE) (Dubawi (IRE))
237[8] 882[5] (1238) 2365[4]

**Willyegolassiego** *Neil Mulholland* a74 65
4 br m Kheleyf(USA) Kryena (Kris)
(645)◆ 762[2] (1699) 3026[2] (9421)

**Willytheconqueror (IRE)**
*William Muir* a89 107
4 b g Kodiac Jazzie (FR) (Zilzal (USA))
1765[3] 2657a[3] 3370a[7] 3926[13] 4635[6] 5116[7] 5911[5] 6677[11] 7461[4] 7809[11]

**Wilson (IRE)** *Luca Cumani* 82
2 b c Born To Sea(IRE) Alkhawarah (USA) (Intidab (USA))
5420[7] (6721) 8180[4]

**Wilspa's Magic (IRE)** *Ron Hodges* 60
4 gr m Zebedee Triple Zero (IRE) (Raise A Grand (IRE))
2214[10] 2724[13] 3422[11] 5052[12] 5791[5] 6507[5]

**Wiltons (FR)** *Harry Dunlop* a54
2 b c Thewayyouare(USA) Pink Sapphire (IRE) (Danehill Dancer (IRE))
4805[14] 5144[7] 5847[4]

**Wily Rumpus (IRE)** *Ed Walker* a65 65
3 b g Intense Focus(USA) Supercat (IRE) (Indian Rocket)
209[5] 434[5] 1242[3] 1790[7]

**Wimboldsley** *Scott Dixon* a54 52
6 ch g Milk It Mick Chrystal Venture (IRE) (Barathea (IRE))
20[5] (311) 386[3] 3256[12] 3812[9] 5892[3] 6531[6] 8772[11]

**Wimpole Hall** *William Jarvis* a83 79
4 b g Canford Cliffs(IRE) Sparkling Eyes (Lujain (USA))
8297[12] 8821[7] 9140[3]◆

**Wind Chimes** *A Fabre* a85 100
2 b f Mastercraftsman(IRE) Militante (IRE) (Johannesburg (USA))
(8884a)

**Windfast (IRE)** *Brian Meehan* 111
6 b g Exceed And Excel(AUS) Fair Sailing (IRE) (Docksider (USA))
1903[3] 4071[15] 6428[11]

**Windforpower (IRE)** *Tracy Waggott* a66 61
7 b g Red Clubs(IRE) Dubai Princess (IRE) (Dubai Destination (USA))
362[7] (446) 732[6] 1031[4] 1126[2] (1200) 1721[2] 2104[9] 2550[5] 2990[8] 3345[3] 3944[3] 4607[6] 5495[2] 5736[5] 6089[6] 6130[5] 6571[5] 6903[7] 7164[7] 7366[2] 8558[3] (9265)

**Wind In My Sails** *Ed de Giles* a84 91
5 b g Footstepsinthesand Dylanesque (Royal Applause)
2232[7] 2960[9] 3750[3] 6014[9] 6422[11] 7456[6]

**Windjammer (GER)** *A Wohler* 71
3 ch f Campanologist(USA) Warrior Czarina (USA) (Pleasantly Perfect (USA))
3121a[9]

**Wind Law (FR)** *J Schiestel Fils* a22 17
10 b g Classic Law Wind Of Grace (FR) (Exit To Nowhere (USA))
7070a[10]

**Wind Place And Sho**
*James Eustace* a80 95
5 b g Shirocco(GER) Coh Sho No (Old Vic)
5944[5] 6323[9] 6968[10] 8072[6]

**Winds Of Fire (USA)**
*Charlie Appleby* a78
2 b g Kitten's Joy(USA) Laureldean Gale (USA) (Grand Slam (USA))
9154[7] 9336[3]◆

**Windsor Beach (IRE)** *J P Murtagh* a84 100
5 ch g Starspangledbanner(AUS) Highindi (Montjeu (IRE))
4822a[4] 5517a[5] 6491a[27]

**Windsor Cross (IRE)** *Richard Fahey* a77
2 gr g Camacho Lizzy's Township (USA) (Delaware Township (USA))
8316[4] 8553[5] (8926) 9263[3] 9405[4]

**Windsorlot (IRE)** *Tony Carroll* a63 61
4 ch g Windsor Knot(IRE) Majestic Jenny (IRE) (Zamindar (USA))
3573[11] 4047[4] 4626[6] 5714[4]◆ (6306) 7712[5] 8661[6] 8957[6] 9056[2] 9406[3]

**Windsor Whirlybird (IRE)**
*Ali Stronge* 10
2 ch f Harbour Watch(IRE) Charaig (Rainbow Quest (USA))
5717[11] 8471[8]

**Windstoss (GER)** *Markus Klug* 118
3 bb c Shirocco(GER) Wellenspiel (GER) (Sternkoenig (IRE))
3636a[2] (4422a) 6727a[4] (7429a)

**Windsun Laujac (FR)** *J Parize* a21
3 b g Sunday Break(JPN) Wind Merchant (FR) (Marchand De Sable (USA))
6124a[11]

**Wind Turbine (IRE)** *Tim Easterby* a34 13
3 b g Power First Breeze (USA) (Woodman (USA))
8217[9] 8479[10] 8781[6] 9261[12]

**Wine List** *Andrew Balding* a75 71
3 ch g Champs Elysees Masandra (IRE) (Desert Prince (IRE))
5563[4] 7652[3] (7948)

**Winged Spur (IRE)** *Mark Johnston* a64
2 ch f Motivator Mark Of An Angel (IRE) (Mark Of Esteem (IRE))
8840[3] 9263[4] 9385[3]

**Wingingit (IRE)** *Andrew Balding* a71 103
3 ch f Helmet(AUS) Chirkova (USA) (Sadler's Wells (USA))
5088a[2] 7393[6] 8121[8]

**Wings of Desire** *John Gosden* a79 119
4 ch h Pivotal Gull Wing (IRE) (In The Wings)
4070[5] 4814[5]

**Wings Of Eagles (FR)** *A P O'Brien* 121
3 b c Pour Moi(IRE) Ysoldina (FR) (Kendor (FR))
2555[2] (3322) 4387a[3]

**Wings Of Esteem (IRE)**
*Luke McJannet* a72 72
4 b m Sir Percy Wings Of Fame (IRE) (Namid)
2317[3] 2974[3] 3723[4] 4311[3]

**Wings Of Gold (IRE)**
*Saeed bin Suroor* 57
2 ch c Raven's Pass(USA) Rosa Clara (IRE) (Peintre Celebre (USA))
5105[8]

**Wings Of The Rock (IRE)**
*Scott Dixon* a60 83
2 ch f Rock Of Gibraltar(IRE) Bless You (Bahamian Bounty)
2583[6] (3215)◆ 3960[20] 5526[4] 6136[12] 7114[9] 8431[8]

**Winklemann (IRE)** *John Flint* a76 82
5 br g Rip Van Winkle(IRE) Kykuit (IRE) (Green Desert (USA))
1766[10] 2232[6] 2960[7] 3572[8]

**Wink Oliver** *Jo Hughes* a86 82
5 b g Winker Watson Nadinska (Doyen (IRE))
145[4] 293[4] 398[2] 620[5] 724[5] (784) 929[4] (1086) 1462[2] 1553[4] 2064[2] 2297[3] (3181) 3203[7] (3471) 3792[9] 3808[6] 6300a[2] 6676[5] 7456[13]

**Win Lose Draw (IRE)**
*Michael Appleby* a67 42
5 b g Dark Angel(IRE) Caherassdotcom (Compton Place)
363[5] 501[8] 2465[6] 2976[8] 4163[9] 6131[9] 8800[3] 8985[4]

**Winners Follow Me (GER)**
*James Tate* a75 63
4 ch g Lope De Vega(IRE) Aglow (Spinning World (USA))
548[3]◆ (885)◆ (1258) 1911[7]

**Winning Story** *Saeed bin Suroor* a111 109
4 b g New Approach(IRE) Tanzania (USA) (Darshaan)
985[2] (1770) 2571[5] 4073[13] 6447[7] 7547[P] (Dead)

**Winning Ways (IRE)**
*Jeremy Noseda* a79 98
3 b g Lope De Vega(IRE) Sahara Sky (IRE) (Danehill (USA))
(397) 643[4] 1945[3]◆ (2565) 3959[11] 4362[5]

**Winslow (USA)** *Doug Watson* a97 72
5 b g Distorted Humor(USA) Justwhistledixie (USA) (Dixie Union (USA))
537a[6]

**Winston C (IRE)** *Michael Bell* a88 93
3 b g Rip Van Winkle(IRE) Pitrizza (IRE) (Machiavellian (USA))
3457[3] 4048[3] (4450)◆ 5525[3] 6445[6] 6930[4] 8005[13]

**Winter (IRE)** *A P O'Brien* a82 119
3 gr f Galileo(IRE) Laddies Poker Two (IRE) (Choisir (AUS))
1634a[2] (2434) (3110a) (4031) (5571)◆ 6958a[2] 7668a[9]

**Winter Lightning (IRE)**
*Saeed bin Suroor* 83
2 b f Shamardal(USA) Eastern Joy (Dubai Destination (USA))
8006[2]

**Winter Lion (IRE)** *Matthew J Smith* a91 67
7 ch g Galileo(IRE) Hill Of Snow (Reference Point)
(227a) 5488a[20]

**Winterlude (IRE)** *Jennie Candlish* a110 83
7 b g Street Cry(IRE) New Morning (IRE) (Sadler's Wells (USA))
197[6] (396) 720[2] (858) 1068[2] 1360[5] 1770[14] 4356[16]

**Winter Spice (IRE)** *Sam Thomas* a81 75
6 gr g Verglas(IRE) Summer Spice (IRE) (Key Of Luck (USA))
280[6] 1223[6]

**Win The Space (USA)**
*George Papaprodromou* a115 91
5 rg h Pulpit(USA) Teamgeist (ARG) (Mutakddim (USA))
8611a[11]

**Wintour Leap** *Robert Stephens* a61 57
6 b m Nayef(USA) Mountain Leap (IRE) (Sadler's Wells (USA))
2966[6] 3724[3] 5244[7] 7232[7] 7730[3] 8878[3] 9158[12] 9317[13]

**Winwhip (FR)** *P Adda* 41
3 b f Whipper(USA) Laureldean Desert (Green Desert (USA))
5268a[7]

**Winx (AUS)** *Chris Waller* 130
5 b m Street Cry(IRE) Vegas Showgirl (NZ) (Al Akbar (AUS))
(6714a) (8446a)

**Wireless (FR)** *V Luka Jr* a73 108
6 ch h Kentucky Dynamite(USA) Sachet (USA) (Royal Academy (USA))
1691a[2] 4942a[5] 6498a[2] 7640a[5] 8963a[6]

**Wirral Girl (IRE)** *Richard Fahey* 74
2 b f Kodiac Ursula (IRE) (Namid)
3482[6] (4555)◆ 6136[15] 6678[7] 7919[3]

**Wisconsin (JPN)** *A P O'Brien* 106
3 b g Deep Impact(JPN) Peeping Fawn (USA) (Danehill (USA))
4032[12] 4420a[5] 4811[8]

**Wise Wishes (FR)** *Robert Collet* 40
2 b g Whipper(USA) Nunez (FR) (Zieten (USA))
6050a[11]

**Wishful Thinking (FR)** *J-V Toux* a63 63
3 b f Naaqoos Libera (Turtle Island (IRE))
838a[15]

**Wishing Time (IRE)** *David O'Meara* a55 66
3 b f Frankel Beyond Desire (Invincible Spirit (IRE))
1004[4] 1453[3] (1715)

**Wishing Tree** *Brian Ellison* a54 50
4 ch m Haafhd Ananda Kanda (USA) (Hero's Tribute (USA))
3473[8] 4262[12]

**Wishing Well** *Micky Hammond* a74 74
5 b m Bahri(USA) Amourallis (IRE) (Dushyantor (USA))
1719[8] 2594[6] (3464) 9096[7]

**Wissahickon (USA)** *John Gosden* a83
2 ch c Tapit(USA) No Matter What (USA) (Nureyev (USA))
(8245)◆ 8904[2]

**Witchcraft (FR)** *J-M Beguigne* a78 78
4 b g Elusive City(USA) Latinia (FR) (Barathea (IRE))
3274a[2]

**With Approval (IRE)** *Laura Mongan* a70 63
5 b g Approve(IRE) Kelsey Rose (Most Welcome)
90[7] 214[5] 922[11] 998[3] 1338[6] 1449[6] 2095[3] 2916[2] 3522[2] 4176[7] 6284[4] (6752) 7216[3] 7916[14] 8182[5] 8908[9] 9456[5]

**Withernsea (IRE)** *Richard Fahey* 103
6 b g Dark Angel(IRE) Charlene Lacy (IRE) (Pips Pride)
1494[9] 2606[12] (2828) 3963[12] 4905[10] 5393[3] 5594[4] 6961a[3] 7611[7] 7807[11] 8234[19]

**With Hindsight (IRE)** *Steve Gollings* a64 64
9 b g Ad Valorem(USA) Lady From Limerick (IRE) (Rainbows For Life (CAN))
381[9] 666[7] 958[10] 1291[4] 2162[2] 2972[3] 3436[2] 4102[8]

**Withhold** *Roger Charlton* a86 102
4 b g Champs Elysees Coming Back (Fantastic Light (USA))
7397[3] (8038)◆

**With Intent** *Ollie Pears* a5 24
3 gr g Monsieur Bond(IRE) Dim Ofan (Petong)
2887[11]

**Without Parole** *John Gosden* a92
2 b c Frankel Without You Babe (USA) (Lemon Drop Kid (USA))
(9263)◆

**With Pleasure** *John Flint* a63 75
4 b g Poet's Voice With Fascination (USA) (Dayjur (USA))
494 648[7] 4538[3] 5276[3] (5590) 6196[2] 7336[4] 7785[7]

**With You** *F Head* 103
2 b f Dansili In Clover (Inchinor)
(8170a)

**Woggle (IRE)** *Geoffrey Deacon* a59
2 ch f Camacho Radio Wave (Dalakhani (IRE))
9310[9]

**Wolfcatcher (IRE)** *Ian Williams* a52 86
5 b g King's Best(USA) Miss Particular (IRE) (Sadler's Wells (USA))
3928[11] 5351[5] 5912[7] 6508[9]

**Wolfcatcherjack (IRE)**
*Sir Mark Prescott Bt* a82 83
3 b g Lawman(FR) Alleluia (Caerleon (USA))
3188[9] 3456[12] 3755[11] (6069)◆ (6291) (6632) 7019[2]

**Wolf Country** *Charlie Appleby* 104
3 b g Dubawi(IRE) Goathemala (GER) (Black Sam Bellamy (IRE))
(2250a) 2766[5] 4811[5] 5525[11]

**Wolf Heart (IRE)** *Lucy Normile* a45 22
9 b g Dalakhani(IRE) Lisieux Orchid (IRE) (Sadler's Wells (USA))
4034[14] 4660[12] 5917[12] 6592[6] 7219[12]

**Wolfofbaggotstreet (IRE)**
*J P Murtagh* 94
2 b g Equiano(FR) Blue Dune (Invincible Spirit (IRE))
6241a[6] 6977a[18]

**Wonderfillo (IRE)** *David O'Meara* a74 75
3 b g Teofilo(IRE) Wonderfilly (FR) (Invincible Spirit (IRE))
1083[4] 1299[2] 3394[2] 4490[2] 9301[2]

**Wonderful Gorl (GER)**
*Gerald Geisler* 95
2 b f Areion(GER) Wonderful Filly (GER) (Lomitas)
6494a[12] 8461a[2]

**Wonderful Life (IRE)**
*Richard Spencer* a63 69
4 b m Canford Cliffs(IRE) Feeling Wonderful (IRE) (Fruits Of Love (USA))
151[6] 314[8] 520[5]

**Wonder Gadot (CAN)** *Mark Casse* a108 98
2 bb f Medaglia d'Oro(USA) Loving Vindication (USA) (Vindication (USA))
7206a[3] 8603a[6]

**Wonder Laish** *C Byrnes* 100
5 b g Halling(USA) Wonder Why (GER) (Tiger Hill (IRE))
5488a[14] 7860a[6]

**Wonder Of Dubai (IRE)**
*Michael Bell* a52 74
3 b g So You Think(NZ) Ruby Suesday (Refuse To Bend (IRE))
1426[2] 2345[2]◆ 2793[2] 3443[4] 4624[6]

**Wonder Of Qatar (IRE)** *R Bouresly* 81
5 b h Exceed And Excel(AUS) Imperial Quest (Rainbow Quest (USA))
318a[10] 543a[9]

**Wonnemond (GER)** *S Smrczek* 112
4 b g Areion(GER) Windaja (GER) (Surako (GER))
(1661a) 3019a[3] 4130a[6] 4939a[2] (6746a) 7640a[9]

**Woodacre** *Richard Whitaker* a72 74
10 b g Pyrus(USA) Fairy Ring (IRE) (Fairy King (USA))
30[DSQ] 509[U] (Dead)

**Wood Avens (FR)** *H-A Pantall* 51
3 b f Redoute's Choice(AUS) Border Bloom (Selkirk (USA))
5268a[6]

**Woodmax (GER)** *N Clement* 109
2 br c Maxios Waldtraut (GER) (Oasis Dream)
7667a[4]

**Woody Bay** *Mark Walford* a40 76
7 b g New Approach(IRE) Dublino (USA) (Lear Fan (USA))
3845[14] 4609[6] 6049[7] 7246[3] 7823[8]

**Woofie (IRE)** *Laura Mongan* a73 71
5 b g Duke Of Marmalade(IRE) Violet Ballerina (IRE) (Namid)
2020[7] 2909[8] 3143[5] 4217[3] (5244) 7319[11] 8647[10]

**Wooldix (FR)** *C Escuder* a72 70
2 ch c Evasive In Love Kelty (FR) (Green Tune (USA))
3444a[7] (5627a)

**Wootalove (FR)** *Mme Pia Brandt* a67 77
3 bb f Wootton Bassett Latakia (GER) (Tertullian (USA))
2697a[7] (3275a) 4455a[4]

**Wootton (FR)** *H-A Pantall* 105
2 b c Wootton Bassett American Nizzy (FR) (American Post)
(8196a)

**Wootyhoot (FR)** *James Fanshawe* a65 48
3 b g Wootton Bassett Orlena (USA) (Gone West (USA))
2475[11]◆ 3755[12] 4211[9] 7761[2] 8538[12] 9128[5] 9391[10]

**Wordiness** *David Evans* a76 75
9 br g Dansili Verbose (USA) (Storm Bird (CAN))
28[10] 196[7] 280[4] 571[4] 1763[3] 1935[3] 2460[5] 2622[4] 3863[2] 4471[2] (4791) 5138[4] 5896[5] (6233) 6508[5] 7412[4] 8157[9] 8778[6] 8876[7] 9158[3] 9442[4]

**Wordismybond** *Amanda Perrett* a62 76
8 b g Monsieur Bond(IRE) La Gessa (Largesse)
3753[6] 4804[11] 5427[6] 6393[6] (7916) 8181[4] 8473[3]

**Wordsearch (USA)** *Hugo Palmer* a73 64
3 b g Pleasantly Perfect(USA) Jibe (USA) (Danzig (USA))
2092[5] 4476[8]

**Work (IRE)** *David Pipe* a44 57
4 b m Mastercraftsman(IRE) Abbeyleix Lady (IRE) (Montjeu (IRE))
2712[4] 3724[7] 7233[11]

**Working Class** *Peter Chapple-Hyam* 78
3 b g Bahri(USA) Louise D'Arzens (Anabaa (USA))
4224[3] 4764[2] (5409) 6387[5] 7339[4] 7894[14] 8600[9]

**Working Together** *Antony Brittain* a52
2 b f Monsieur Bond(IRE) Melandre (Lujain (USA))
4258[8] 8189[10]

**Wor Lass** *Donald Whillans* a78 85
9 br m And Beyond(IRE) Patience Please (King Of Spain)
3341[3] 3527[6] 3830[7] 4357[11] 5259[3] 5468[3] 6317[5] 6628[2]◆ 7032[7] 7359[12] 7700[2] 8109[5]

**World Approval (USA)** *Mark Casse* 123
5 rg g Northern Afleet(USA) Win Approval (USA) (With Approval (CAN))
(7179a) (8608a)

**World Breaker (ITY)** *Marco Botti* a54
2 b c Helmet(AUS) Serata Di Gala (FR) (Footstepsinthesand)
8643[8]

**World Of Good** *Anabel K Murphy* a73 62
4 ch m Danehill Dancer(IRE) Edaraat (USA) (Rahy (USA))
986[4] 1243[3] 1618[7] 1898[6] 8132[13] 9153[10]

**World Power (IRE)** *F Vermeulen* a72 80
3 ch f Power Izzy Lou (IRE) (Spinning World (USA))
1947[7] 2180[2]◆ 3259[2] 3896[2] (5111) 5521a[9] 5910a[4] 6650a[11]

**World Record (IRE)** *Mick Quinn* a51 65
7 b g Choisir(AUS) Dancing Debut (Polar Falcon (USA))
2915[2] 4765[9] 6263[2] 7006[2] 8181[3] 8513[6]

**Worlds His Oyster** *John Quinn* a91 88
4 b g Pivotal Regal Salute (Medicean)
(611) 782[6] 1766[5] 2155[8] 2406[14] 3065[3] 3905[4] 4207[7] 5000[4] 5699[3] 6266[10] 6672[2] 7594[3] 8486[3]

**Worship (IRE)** *David Simcock* a73
2 b f Havana Gold(IRE) Up In Time (Noverre (USA))
(9310)

**Worth Waiting** *David Lanigan* 76
2 b f Bated Breath Salutare (IRE) (Sadler's Wells (USA))
8594[2]

**Worthy Spirit (GER)** *Adrian Wintle* a42
6 b g Shirocco(GER) Wakytara (GER) (Danehill (USA))
289[5] 503[U]

**Wotabond** *Richard Whitaker* a28 37
4 ch g Monsieur Bond(IRE) Wotatomboy (Captain Rio)
1112[7] 1187[6] 1587[7]

**Wotabreeze (IRE)** *John Quinn* 86
4 ch g Excellent Art Sparkling Crystal (IRE) (Danehill Dancer (IRE))
1719[13] 2629[10] 3315[9] 4519[2] 4840[3] 5403[8] 6126[5] 6467[9] (7015) 7387[7]

**Wotadoll** *Dean Ivory* a52 67
3 b f Harbour Watch(IRE) Rhapsilian (Dansili)
2734[2] 3703[3] 4211[5] (5340) 5812[4] 7122[4] (7912) 8168[3] 8743[7]

**Wotamadam** *Dean Ivory* a29 51
2 gr f Lethal Force(IRE) Rhapsilian (Dansili)
4749[12] 6147[6] 7334[10] 7756[12]

**Would Be King (IRE)** *G M Lyons* 100
2 b c Lethal Force(IRE) Smart Coco (USA) (Smarty Jones (USA))
3098a[2] 5345a[3]

**Would You Believe (IRE)**
*G M Lyons* 81
2 b g Dream Ahead(USA) Queen Grace (IRE) (Choisir (AUS))
7423a[P]

**Wowcha (IRE)** *John Quinn* a78 84
4 b m Zoffany(IRE) Muravka (IRE) (High Chaparral (IRE))
3632a[7] 4653a[P]

**Wowsham (IRE)** *Keith Dalgleish* a55 38
2 b c Elzaam(AUS) Shams Wa Matar (Polish Precedent (USA))
7654[7] 8316[10] 8748[7]

**Wrap Star (IRE)** *Anthony McCann* a70 70
6 bb g Cape Cross(IRE) Twinkling (NZ) (Star Way)
196[6]

**Wrenthorpe** *Bryan Smart* 72
2 b g Hellvelyn Milly-M (Cadeaux Genereux)
7562[2] 8212[2] 8474[3]

**Wright Patterson (IRE)** *John Quinn* a45 44
4 b g Dream Ahead(USA) Anam Allta (IRE) (Invincible Spirit (IRE))
608[7]

**Wuheida** *Charlie Appleby* 115
3 ch f Dubawi(IRE) Hibaayeb (Singspiel (IRE))
4857[2]◆ 5693a[3] 6598a[4] 7669a[4] (8606a)

**Wurood** *William Haggas* a74 71
3 gr f Dark Angel(IRE) Key Rose (IRE) (Key Of Luck (USA))
(1401) 2071[6] 3171[5]

**Wyndspelle (NZ)** *Michael Kent* 100
3 b c Iffraaj Western Star (NZ) (High Chaparral (IRE))
8059a[10]

**Wynfaul The Wizard (USA)**
*Richard Guest* a58 43
2 b c Bodemeister(USA) Red Dot (USA) (Diesis)
7883[6] 8555[7] 8782[6] 9097[13]

**Wynford (IRE)** *David Loughnane* a74 79
4 ch g Dylan Thomas(IRE) Wishing Chair (USA) (Giant's Causeway (USA))
1092[5]

**Xaarino (FR)** *A Fabre* 102
3 gr c Kendargent(FR) Xaarienne (Xaar)
1824a[5]

**Xaar Island** *David Evans* a40
2 b f Trans Island Nihil Petere (IRE) (Xaar)
2277[7] 3467[10]

**Xarco (IRE)** *Christos Kouvaras* a74 66
4 br g Kheleyf(USA) Xeralda (IRE) (Xaar)
6541a[2]

**Xclusive** *Ronald Harris* a34 37
7 b g Pivotal Dance A Daydream (Daylami (IRE))
1084[11]

**Xedra** *H De Nicolay* a60 52
5 ch m Naaqoos Xstase (SWE) (Trempolino (USA))
6541a[11] 7342a[6]

**Xenobia (IRE)** *W T Farrell* 93
3 ch f Falco(USA) Acago (USA) (Royal Academy (USA))
7808[8]

**Xenophanes (IRE)** *M Boutin* a63 57
7 b g Shamardal(USA) Nipping (IRE) (Night Shift (USA))
4955a[7] 5176a[2]

**Xotic (FR)** *D & P Prod'Homme* a80 85
8 b g Holy Roman Emperor(IRE) Xstase (SWE) (Trempolino (USA))
6648a[4]

**X Rated (IRE)** *Mark Johnston* a79 82
3 gr g Exceed And Excel(AUS) Screen Star (IRE) (Tobougg (IRE))
2284[4] 2612[6] 3727[7] (4492) 5072[5] 5475[2] 5686[5] 6848[6] 7516[10] 8638[4] 8912[7] 9096[3] 9295[4]

**Xylophone** *Archie Watson* a57 14
3 ch f Medicean Piano (Azamour (IRE))
3435[10] 4003[6] 4729[7] 6069[14]

**Yaafour** *Richard Hannon* a74 85
2 br c Poet's Voice Whatizzit (Galileo (IRE))
4213[8] 4859[3] 5365[3] (5934) 6859[3] 7814[5] 8245[5]

**Yaarmen (USA)** *William Haggas* a74 79
3 b g Nayef(USA) Haamaat (IRE) (Shamardal (USA))
3549[2]◆ (4052) 4580[4]

**Yabass (IRE)** *Archie Watson* a81 84
2 ch c Lope De Vega(IRE) Fresh Mint (IRE) (Sadler's Wells (USA))
(5964) 6925[6] 8155[2]

**Yabrave** *Roger Varian* a74 91
3 b g Bahamian Bounty Dare To Dream (Exceed And Excel (AUS))
1727[3] (5431) 6936[8]

**Yafta** *Richard Hannon* a89 83
2 gr c Dark Angel(IRE) Swiss Dream (Oasis Dream)
3066[4]◆ 4094[2] 5531[2] (6304)◆ (7536)

**Yair Hill (IRE)** *Thomas Cuthbert* a46 54
9 b g Selkirk(USA) Conspiracy (Rudimentary (USA))
5696[10] 5917[10] 6092[15] 7046[8]

**Ya Jammeel** *Mick Channon* 86
4 b g Dubawi(IRE) Silver Touch (IRE) (Dansili)
3540[3] 3820[4] (4470) (5065) (5556) 6680[7] 7231[8]

**Yajooll** *William Haggas* 57
2 b c Invincible Spirit(IRE) Tafiya (Bahri (USA))
8734[7]

**Yalawin (IRE)** *Roger Varian* a80 93
3 b c Lawman(FR) Urgele (FR) (Zafonic (USA))
(2595) 3159[2]◆ 4992[4]

**Yalta (IRE)** *S bin Ghadayer* a102 41
3 b c Exceed And Excel(AUS) Lacily (USA) (Elusive Quality (USA))
2289[5] 4030[12] 6025[10] 9361a[4]

**Yamakatsu Ace (JPN)**
*Kaneo Ikezoe* 120
5 ch h King Kamehameha(JPN) Yamakatsu Marilyn (JPN) (Grass Wonder (USA))
8975a[8]

**Yamakatsu Raiden (JPN)**
*Kaneo Ikezoe* 110
5 bb h Symboli Kris S(USA) Yamakatsu Orchid (JPN) (Dance In The Dark (JPN))
**2203a**[15]

**Yamarhaba Malayeen (IRE)**
*Michael Bell* a83 82
3 ch c Rip Van Winkle(IRE) Obama Rule (IRE) (Danehill Dancer (IRE))
*(1727)*◆ 2567[6] 3336[3] *8506*[4] ***8893***[4]

**Yamuna River** *James Tate* a70 58
2 b f Foxwedge(AUS) Harryana To (Compton Place)
5372[6] *8715*[6] ***8997***[3] *9299*[7]

**Yanling (FR)** *Matthieu Palussiere* 70
3 ch f Rio De La Plata(USA) Hijaziyah (Testa Rossa (AUS))
3134a[7]

**Yaraki** *William Haggas* a74 80
3 b f Frankel Superstar Leo (IRE) (College Chapel)
**(2619)** *3722*[5]

**Yarmouk (FR)** *Richard Fahey* a73 60
3 ch g Siyouni(FR) Tassara (FR) (Sendawar (IRE))
2304[5] 2885[7] ***(4310)***

**Yasir (USA)** *Conor Dore* a59 66
9 b g Dynaformer(USA) Khazayin (USA) (Bahri (USA))
***(98)*** *241*[4] *508*[8] ***786***[3] *990*[9] *2163*[5] *2460*[6] *3547*[5] *4165*[6] *4980*[3] *5483*[7] 5951[8] *6530*[6] *6953*[4] *7761*[10] *8246*[7]

**Yasood (IRE)** *Phil McEntee* a64 66
4 b g Acclamation Lucina (Machiavellian (USA))
*124*[3] *(400)* ***516***[4]

**Yattwee (USA)** *Saeed bin Suroor* a90 109
4 b g Hard Spun(USA) Alzerra (UAE) (Pivotal)
**6856**[2] 7822[5]

**Yayajonh (FR)** *Jane Soubagne* 97
2 ch c Muhaymin(USA) Flower (Zamindar (USA))
5679a[6] **7011a**[5]

**Yeah Baby Yeah (IRE)**
*Gay Kelleway* a90 88
4 b m Art Connoisseur(IRE) Royal Interlude (IRE) (King's Theatre (IRE))
2268[4] 3314[3] 4051[6] 4375[3] 4883[6] 5422[5] ***5628a***[4] *6226a*[8] *6454a*[4] 6787[6] *9089*[3]

**Yeeoow (IRE)** *K R Burke* a76 80
8 b g Holy Roman Emperor(IRE) Taraya (IRE) (Doyoun)
*211*[4] *1592*[4] 2303[5] 2883[5] **3195**[3] 4277[7] 5132[10] *7056*[4] *8881*[10] (Dead)

**Yele (TUR)** *Fehmi Dizdaroglu* 80
2 gr f Divine Light(JPN) Yamis (TUR) (Distant Relative)
**6745a**[3]

**Yellowhammer** *Roger Charlton* a86 90
3 b f Raven's Pass(USA) Magical Romance (IRE) (Barathea (IRE))
(5369) *(8150)* **(8600)**

**Yellow Storm (FR)** *Alain Couetil* 92
3 b f Tiberius Caesar(FR) Yellow Queen (FR) (Slickly (FR))
**3881a**[8]

**Yemnaak (FR)** *George Peckham* a38 43
3 b g Medicean Aujiang (GER) (Royal Dragon (USA))
*1226*[4] **1497**[13] *1692*[12] 4346[7]

**Yensir** *Grant Tuer* a69 73
4 ch g Sir Percy Yensi (Doyen (IRE))
*3252*[3] **3706**[2]◆ 4210[5] 4690[9] 5284[4] **5950**[2] 6060[2] 6789[5] *7034*[9]

**Yes Daddy (IRE)** *Robert Stephens* a75 75
9 b g Golan(IRE) Hollygrove Samba (IRE) (Accordion)
**4852**[2] 6508[8] *7766*[7]

**Yes You (IRE)** *Iain Jardine* 72
3 ch f Choisir(AUS) Mexican Milly (IRE) (Noverre (USA))
4302[2]◆ 4688[3] (5070) (5543) 5991[3] (6313) 6546[5] 7218[5] **(8480)** 8738[12]

**Y Fyn Duw A Fydd** *John Gallagher* 30
2 b f Nathaniel(IRE) Dignify (IRE) (Rainbow Quest (USA))
**8677**[13]

**Yildirimbey (TUR)** *Adil Yilmaz* 105
6 b h Sabirli(TUR) Dicos (TUR) (Sun Music (IRE))
**6746a**[3]

**Yisty** *Derek Shaw* a49 29
4 ch m Compton Place Meditation (Inchinor)
*64*[8] ***874***[7] *1006*[11] *1220*[8]

**Yogi's Girl (IRE)** *David Evans* a52 86
2 ch f Harbour Watch(IRE) Ayr Missile (Cadeaux Genereux)
*1627*[9] (2037) (2522) **6136**[4] **6678**[3] 7114[8] *8317*[8] *9156*[7] *9387*[4]

**Yogiyogiyogi (IRE)** *Denis Coakley* a64
3 ch f Finsceal Fior(IRE) Zelloof (IRE) (Kheleyf (USA))
*2330*[4] *7322*[3] *7768*[6] ***8946***[3] *9212*[6]

**Yolo Star (IRE)** *J P Murtagh* 97
2 br f Society Rock(IRE) Pearly Brooks (Efisio)
**8001**[4]

**Yorbelucky** *David Evans* 74
2 b g Yorgunnabelucky(USA) Circle Of Angels (Royal Applause)
4151[5] 5710[9] 6367[3] **(7197)**

**Yori (IRE)** *P Vovcenko* 85
2 b f Kodiac Yashila (IRE) (Indian Haven)
**4391a**[7] 7011a[7]

**Yorkee Mo Sabee (IRE)**
*Stuart Williams* a55 79
4 ch g Teofilo(IRE) Pivotal's Princess (IRE) (Pivotal)
2226[9] 2701[4]◆ 2888[7] **3934**[2] 4168[3] 4438[4] 7405[12] *9136*[6]

**Yorkidding** *Mark Johnston* a100 104
5 b m Dalakhani(IRE) Claxon (Caerleon (USA))
2157[3] 2525[2] 2774[3] **(3076)** 3928[8] 4119[5] *4356*[13] **(5882)** 6329[8]

**Yorkshiredebut (IRE)** *Paul Midgley* 80
3 ch f Sir Prancealot(IRE) Yasmeena (USA) (Mr Greeley (USA))
1786[2] 2160[4] (2631) 3152[5] 3904[3] 4574[6] **(5020)** 5574[6] 6450[16] 6679[4] 6945[3] 7625[10]

**Yorkshireman (IRE)** *Lynn Siddall* a54 47
7 b g Red Clubs(IRE) Ossiana (IRE) (Polish Precedent (USA))
*610*[4] ***721***[6]

**Yorkshire Monarch (IRE)**
*Sarah Hollinshead* a20 54
6 b g Montjeu(IRE) Inkling (USA) (Seeking The Gold (USA))
***6632***[7]

**Yorkshire Pudding** *Tim Easterby* 63
3 b f Sleeping Indian Cadeau Speciale (Cadeaux Genereux)
1977[4] 2547[5] **3150**[2] 3984[3] 4619[9] 5007[5] 5375[4] 5666[6] 6047[6]

**Yorkshire Rover** *David Brown* a56 62
3 b g Doncaster Rover(USA) Mother Jones (Sleeping Indian)
2405[3] *2924*[5] 3568[4] *4447*[4] *4723*[5] **(5040)**

**Yorkshire Star (IRE)** *Bill Turner* a36 42
3 ch g Fast Company(IRE) March Star (IRE) (Mac's Imp (USA))
5791[9] **6342**[6] *6622*[11]

**Yorkton (CAN)** *Stuart C Simon* 76
3 b c Speightstown(USA) Sunday Affair (USA) (A.P. Indy (USA))
**8097a**[7]

**Yosemite** *J Reynier* a63 77
4 gr m Makfi Dansa Queen (Dansili)
***606a***[7]

**Yoshida (JPN)** *William Mott* 105
3 b c Heart's Cry(JPN) Hilda's Passion (USA) (Canadian Frontier (USA))
**4652a**[5]

**Youareiffraaj (IRE)**
*John James Feane* 72
2 b c Iffraaj Katajan (Halling (USA))
**6488a**[7] 6977a[23]

**You Bank (IRE)** *Kieran P Cotter*
3 b g Dandy Man(IRE) Faithfulbond (IRE) (Elbio)
1389a[16]

**Youkan (IRE)** *Stuart Kittow* 76
2 b g Choisir(AUS) Ellikan (IRE) (Exceed And Excel (AUS))
**(2756)**

**Youl Dash For Cash (AUS)**
*Peter Gelagotis* 88
5 br g Dash For Cash(AUS) Hill Part (AUS) (Danehill Dancer (IRE))
**1400a**[10]

**You Look Different** *Antony Brittain* a41 40
3 ch f Sleeping Indian First Harmony (First Trump)
**4173**[5] *4978*[12]

**You Make Me Smile (FR)**
*N Clement* 58
2 ch f Soave(GER) Nova Spirit (IRE) (Invincible Spirit (IRE))
**3444a**[8] 5907a[5]

**Youmkin (USA)** *Saeed bin Suroor* 84
3 ch g Street Cry(IRE) Aryaamm (IRE) (Galileo (IRE))
**2084**[6] 3316[4]

**Youmsovain (FR)** *N Clement* 69
3 b f Youmzain(IRE) Height Of Vanity (IRE) (Erhaab (USA))
**4232a**[8]

**Young John (IRE)** *Mike Murphy* a84 89
4 b g Acclamation Carpet Lady (IRE) (Night Shift (USA))
***5***[4] *275*[11] *581*[9] *2922*[5] 3567[3] 5610[12] 6134[16]

**Young Officer (IRE)** *Brian Meehan* a49 50
3 b g Fast Company(IRE) Sara Mana Mou (Medicean)
*245*[9] ***502***[10] *864*[6]

**Young Rascal (FR)** *William Haggas* 74
2 b c Intello(GER) Rock My Soul (IRE) (Clodovil (IRE))
**8677**[2]◆

**Young Tiger** *Tom Tate* a67 57
4 b g Captain Gerrard(IRE) Blades Princess (Needwood Blade)
1978[6] 2633[6] 3202[7] 3944[7] 4559[14] *5419*[11] *7036*[2] *(7366)* ***(8559)***◆ *8927*[12]

**Young Tom** *Sue Smith* a65 56
4 b g Sir Percy Enford Princess (Pivotal)
***1864***[2] 2729[7] 3501[3] 8806[12]

**Yourartisonfire** *Lisa Williamson* a77 86
7 ch g Dutch Art Queens Jubilee (Cayman Kai (IRE))
*6*[11]

**Your Choice** *Laura Mongan* a69 80
2 ch f Foxwedge(AUS) Mildoura (FR) (Sendawar (IRE))
**4533**[2] 5528[2] **6418**[9] *8148*[4] 8472[2]

**You're Cool** *John Balding* a84 74
5 b g Exceed And Excel(AUS) Ja One (IRE) (Acclamation)
*225* *(330)* *518*[2] *(886)* *1475*[9] *1981*[3] 3295[6] 4795[2] 6089[4] *(7486)* ***(8540)*** *9234*[3]

**You're Fired (IRE)** *K R Burke* a108 110
6 b g Firebreak My Sweet Georgia (IRE) (Royal Applause)
*118*[6] *919*[7] **1494**[10] **7149**[3] 7619[9]

**You're Hired** *Amanda Perrett* 95
4 b g Dalakhani(IRE) Heaven Sent (Pivotal)
**5643**[16] 7397[11]

**Your Gifted (IRE)** *Lisa Williamson* a53 52
10 b m Trans Island Dame Laura (IRE) (Royal Academy (USA))
*3186*[8] *3466*[9] 4559[9] (5252) 5877[6] ***8494***[5] *9214*[5] *9374*[2] *9414*[7]

**Yourholidayisover (IRE)**
*Tom Gretton* a46 48
10 ch g Sulamani(IRE) Whitehaven (Top Ville)
**4469**[4]

**Your Just Desserts (IRE)**
*Micky Hammond* 38
2 b f Requinto(IRE) Whats For Pudding (IRE) (Kheleyf (USA))
2836[11] 3460[7] **5015**[8] *7029*[11]

**Your Ladyship (IRE)** *Ralph Beckett* 67
3 b f Lawman(FR) Bufera (IRE) (King's Best (USA))
3506[12] **4700**[3]◆ 5712[7]

**Ypres** *Jason Ward* a51 66
8 b g Byron Esligier (IRE) (Sabrehill (USA))
*3256*[10] 3915[3] 4013[4] **(4789)** 5132[9] 6045[3] **6546**[4]◆ 7525[9] *8784*[6] *8980*[11]

**Yucatan (IRE)** *A P O'Brien* 112
3 b c Galileo(IRE) Six Perfections (FR) (Celtic Swing)
**1636a**[3] **2442a**[2]

**Yufften** *Roger Charlton* a108 111
6 b g Invincible Spirit(IRE) Majestic Sakeena (IRE) (King's Best (USA))
***1150***[3]◆ 1494[13] 3963[23] 5393[16] 6856[5]

**Yul Finegold (IRE)** *Conor Dore* a54 54
7 b g Invincible Spirit(IRE) Mascara (Mtoto)
***39***[6] *218*[9] *436*[6] *661*[6] *3192*[5] 3436[5] 4187[2] 5080[11]

**Yulong Baobei (IRE)** *M Halford* a69 103
3 ch f Choisir(AUS) Bless You (Bahamian Bounty)
**3873a**[8] 4416a[19]

**Yulong Gold Fairy** *D K Weld* 102
2 b f Mount Nelson Quite A Thing (Dutch Art)
**(8082a)**

**Yulong Xiongba (IRE)**
*Julie Camacho* a69 72
5 b g Kodiac Moon Legend (USA) (Gulch (USA))
***968***[11]

**Yuman (FR)** *H-A Pantall* a74 105
3 gr g Literato(FR) Dianaba (FR) (Diktat)
**3855a**[4] 7471a[3]

**Yume (FR)** *S Cerulis* a83 82
6 b h Dr Fong(USA) Lily Bolero (King's Best (USA))
**2696a**[4] 5490a[6] *6300a*[3] 6648a[8]

**Zaad (FR)** *Robert Collet* a16
2 b f Zizany(IRE) Freedom At Last (IRE) (Alhaarth (IRE))
***8691a***[16]

**Zaajer** *Owen Burrows* a68 78
2 b c Shamardal(USA) Zahoo (IRE) (Nayef (USA))
**6654**[3] 7128[4] *7788*[5]

**Zaaki** *Mohamed Moubarak* 99
2 b c Leroidesanimaux(BRZ) Kesara (Sadler's Wells (USA))
3437[2] **4906**[5] **6326**[4] 7112[5]

**Zaatar (IRE)** *Mick Channon* a37 57
3 b f Fast Company(IRE) Amazing Win (IRE) (Marju (IRE))
***77*** *3761*[0]

**Zabaletaswansong (GER)**
*Richard Hannon* a71 72
2 b c Maxios Zavaala (IRE) (Rock Of Gibraltar (IRE))
2607[5] **2816**[3] 3156[2] *3965*[4] 5292[4] 6986a[5] 7593[7] **8325**[2] *8982*[5] *9452*[5]

**Zabdi** *Lee Carter* a69 53
4 b h Zebedee Musical Moonlight (Observatory (USA))
*139*[2] *293*[3] *398*[5] ***(739)*** *1729*[10] *2023*[4] 2229[5] *2961*[4] *3971*[3]

**Zabeel Prince (IRE)** *Roger Varian* 109
4 ch g Lope De Vega(IRE) Princess Serena (USA) (Unbridled's Song (USA))
(4275)◆ (7285) **(8009)**◆ 8234[11]

**Zabeel Star (IRE)** *Karen McLintock* a79 80
5 ch g Arcano(IRE) Deep Winter (Pivotal)
*220*[2] ***507***[4] *769*[3] *992*[11] *1598*[7] *(1891)* *8315*[7] *8718*[6] *8912*[4] ***9096***[2]

**Zabriskie (IRE)** *A P O'Brien* 91
2 b c Frankel Moonlight's Box (USA) (Nureyev (USA))
**8036**[8]

**Zac Brown (IRE)** *Charlie Wallis* a103 88
6 b g Kodiac Mildmay (USA) (Elusive Quality (USA))
*(79)* *326*[3] *639*[2] *(818)* *1025*[2] *1362*[5] 1768[9] ***2113***[2] *(2262)* 2621[4] (3617) 3827[2] 4581[6] 5426[6] *6025*[12] *9187*[8] *9453*[7]

**Zacchetto (USA)** *Mark Johnston* a47 53
3 b g Bernardini(USA) Minister's Melody (USA) (Deputy Minister (CAN))
*1198*[5] **4055**[7] 4659[13] 5215[13]

**Zack Mayo** *Philip McBride* a76 96
3 b g Air Chief Marshal(IRE) White Wedding (IRE) (Green Desert (USA))
1857[9] *2521*[3] 3248[2] *(4449)* 5706[2] (6757) **(7252)**

**Zaeem** *Ivan Furtado* a87 77
8 b g Echo Of Light Across (ARG) (Roy (USA))
*5*[7] *736*[8] 5059[6] **5788**[5] 6111[9] *8773*[4] *8958*[3] *(9031)*

**Zafaranah (USA)** *Pam Sly* a73 43
3 ch f Raven's Pass(USA) Jiwen (CAN) (Singspiel (IRE))
***4565***[3] 5721[10] *6287*[5] *7492*[5] ***8156***[2] *8797*[7]

**Zafayan (IRE)** *D K Weld* 96
6 b g Acclamation Zafayra (IRE) (Nayef (USA))
**5488a**[19]

**Zafeeno (FR)** *H-A Pantall* a60 38
2 b c Zafeen(FR) Rocky Mixa (FR) (Rock Of Gibraltar (IRE))
**7012a**[10]

**Zafiro (FR)** *J-C Rouget* a105 110
5 b g Sageburg(IRE) La Romagne (FR) (Art Francais (USA))
6052a[3] 7416a[6] **(7943a)**

**Zafora (IRE)** *S Labate* a40
9 b m Lando(GER) Zalafira (FR) (Nashwan (USA))
***364a***[12]

**Zahiria (FR)** *P Adda* a57 41
3 b f Bertolini(USA) Remember Mix (FR) (Desert Style (IRE))
***838a***[12]

**Zahraa** *Robyn Brisland* a66 68
2 b f Finjaan Alzahra (Exceed And Excel (AUS))
7504[4] *7995*[5] **8236**[3]

**Zaidiyn (FR)** *Brian Ellison* a80 84
7 b g Zamindar(USA) Zainta (IRE) (Kahyasi (IRE))
5397[10] **8384**[2] *8778*[9]

**Zain Arion (IRE)** *John Butler* a77 87
4 b m Danehill Dancer(IRE) Shaanara (IRE) (Darshaan)
*(213)* 2146[2] **(2741)** 3586[8] 6357[10] *6793*[7] 8390[10]

**Zain Eagle** *Doug Watson* a85 86
7 b h Dylan Thomas(IRE) Pearl City (USA) (Carson City (USA))
**82a**[10]

**Zain Emperor (IRE)** *John Butler* a82 82
4 b g Holy Roman Emperor(IRE) Love Thirty (Mister Baileys)
*3591*[0] ***460***[2] ***(1462)***

**Zain Flash** *David Evans* a52 66
2 b c Royal Applause Jade (Cadeaux Genereux)
**1604**[2] 2926[4] 3769[6] 6825[9] *7491*[8] *8191*[5]

**Zain Hana** *Jeremy Noseda* 80
2 b f Shamardal(USA) Lavender And Lace (Barathea (IRE))
**(6480)**

**Zainhom (USA)** *Sir Michael Stoute* 106
3 ch g Street Cry(IRE) Kaseema (USA) (Storm Cat (USA))
1959[3] **3013**[3] 5593[6]

**Zain Smarts (IRE)** *David Evans* a61 70
2 b f Kodiac Indian Navy (IRE) (Elusive City (USA))
2173[10] 2987[4] 3570[3] 3917[7] *5479*[3] **(6609)** 7194[6] *7706*[7] 8110[7]

**Zain Star (IRE)** *John Butler* a82 64
3 b c Shamardal(USA) Astrologie (FR) (Polish Precedent (USA))
2066[9] ***5794***[2] *6817*[4] 7781[11]

**Zakatal** *Rebecca Menzies* a91 86
11 gr g Kalanisi(IRE) Zankara (FR) (Linamix (FR))
*196*[2] *422*[2] *728*[6] ***(1002)*** *2788*[5] *3190*[5]

**Zalamea (IRE)** *Carina Fey* a95 113
4 b h Lope De Vega(IRE) Tanzania (IRE) (Alzao (USA))
*606a*[3] *(1078a)* 2248a[6] 3880a[5] 4884[7] 5690a[8] 6729a[4] **7671a**[5] 8526a[5] *9274a*[9]

**Zalshah** *Richard Hannon* a83 74
2 ch c Mayson Regal Velvet (Halling (USA))
1767[7] 3917[3]◆ 4349[2] 4758[3] 5150[13] 5654[2] *6021*[6] 6651[9] 7121[2] 7647[5]◆ 8387[8] *8817*[2] *(9021)* ***9433***[3]

**Zalzilah** *S Seemar* a74 69
6 br g Kheleyf(USA) Tarneem (USA) (Zilzal (USA))
**250a**[15]

**Zamaam** *E Charpy* a69 110
7 br h Muhtathir Nasheed (USA) (Riverman (USA))
82a[4] (540a) 890a[6] **1374a**[5]

**Zamadance** *Ed Dunlop* a62 64
3 ch g Zamindar(USA) Opera Dancer (Norse Dancer (IRE))
1968[6] 2991[3] 3489[4] **3939**[3] 4623[7] 5336[10] *6069*[6]

**Zamalight** *Amanda Perrett* a76 74
3 ch g Zamindar(USA) Mountain Chain (USA) (Royal Academy (USA))
*1552*[5] ***2092***[3] *3787*[6]◆ 4460[3] 4912[DSQ] *7768*[7] 8111[12]

**Zaman** *Charlie Appleby* 104
2 b c Dutch Art Wake Up Call (Noverre (USA))
(3093) 3925[13] (4434)◆ 4906[4] **5501**[2]

**Zamandas (IRE)** *Roger Varian* 62
2 b c Pivotal Zimira (IRE) (Invincible Spirit (IRE))
**8678**[10]

**Zambeasy** *Philip Hide* a78 85
6 b g Zamindar(USA) Hanella (IRE) (Galileo (IRE))
*3458*[8] **4413**[2] 5397[7] 6701[5] 7908[7] *8648*[3] *9028*[7] *9325*[3]

**Zambezi Queen (IRE)** *Paul Cole* a62 70
3 gr f Helmet(AUS) Lesotho (IRE) (Excellent Art)
**(2362)** **4046**[3] 4843[3] 6028[5] *7767*[6]

**Zambucca (SAF)** *S Seemar* a90 91
8 ch h Lundy's Liability(BRZ) Jazz Champion (SAF) (Dancing Champ (USA))
**82a**[8]

**Zamfir** *Charlie Appleby* 84
3 b g New Approach(IRE) Antara (GER) (Platini (GER))
**(1609)**◆ 2614[P] 7908[9]

**Zamira (FR)** *S Wattel* a72 64
3 gr f Poet's Voice Zarafsha (IRE) (Alzao (USA))
**3275a**[5]

**Zamira (IRE)** *W McCreery* a60 85
4 b m New Approach(IRE) Zanara (IRE) (Kahyasi (IRE))
**5088a**[5]

**Zamjar** *Ed Dunlop* a83 83
3 b g Exceed And Excel(AUS) Cloud's End (Dubawi (IRE))
*877* *1124*[3] *1311*[7] **1945**[5] (2557) 3303[9] 4099[9] 5612[7] 5869[5] 6282[3] *6882*[6] *7570*[5] *7942*[4]

**Zamperini (IRE)** *Mike Murphy* a88 82
5 ch g Fast Company(IRE) Lucky Date (IRE) (Halling (USA))
*3067* ***1240***[6] 1608[6] 2752[7] 3785[7] 7132[4] 7505[2]◆ 7908[2] 8142[2]◆ 8561[8]

**Zamuja** *M Rosseel* a65 82
6 b h Mujahid(USA) Mazaya (IRE) (Sadler's Wells (USA))
*1070a*[13]

**Zanati (IRE)** *Hedi Ghabri* 40
3 b g Frozen Power(IRE) Madame Claude (IRE) (Paris House)
3446a[9]

**Zandradee (IRE)** *David Barron* a61
3 br f Zebedee Annie Beach (IRE) (Redback)
***(1)*** *511*[6] *787*[9] *1204*[3]

**Zanetto** *John Quinn* a64 99
7 b g Medicean Play Bouzouki (Halling (USA))
**(2184)**◆ 3861[11] 4505[10] 5018[7] 8238[13]

**Zanjabeel** *Gordon Elliott* a81 75
4 b g Aussie Rules(USA) Grain Only (Machiavellian (USA))
***6802a***[3]

**Zanzi Win (FR)** *J-P Dubois* a84 84
2 b g Zanzibari(USA) Go To Win (FR) (Coroner (IRE))
*(4678a)* **5520a**[3]

**Zap** *Richard Fahey* 91
2 b g Mayson Moonglow (Nayef (USA))
(2769) 3297[2] 4434[4] 6330[6] **7090**[5] 7596[5] 8008[6] 8413[2]

**Zapateado** *Richard Hughes* a60 57
2 b f Zoffany(IRE) Ziggy Zaggy (Diktat)
5216[7] 5779[2] *6012*[4] 7081[10] 7695[3] *8145*[4] *8500*[5] ***(8847)*** *8996*[7] ***9300***[2]◆

**Zapel** *Stefano Botti* 103
4 b h Kyllachy Viadeigiardini (Dubai Destination (USA))
2867a[8] **8449a**[2]

**Zaphiras Adventure** *S Richter*
6 b m Poseidon Adventure(IRE) Zaphiras Eyes (GER) (Laroche (GER))
*1196a*[6]

**Zappa** *Mick Channon*
2 b g Sixties Icon Vilnius (Imperial Dancer)
6472[7]

**Zapper Cass (FR)** *Tony Coyle* a85 86
4 bb g Elusive City(USA) Moonlight Cass (IRE) (Danehill Dancer (IRE))
2528[9] 3195[7] **(4277)** 4477[7] 5184[4] 5288[6] 5671[9] *6637*[8] 8105[4] *8803*[9] *9074*[7] *9152*[8]

**Zappeuse (FR)** *Y Barberot* a67 68
4 b m Zamindar(USA) Sans Chichi (FR) (Chichicastenango (FR))
**6018a**[3]

**Zarak (FR)** *A De Royer-Dupre* 119
4 b h Dubawi(IRE) Zarkava (IRE) (Zamindar (USA))
(776a) 1378a[4] **2249a**[2] 3118a[5] **(4423a)** 7668a[10]

**Zargun (GER)** *A Wohler*
2 b c Rock Of Gibraltar(IRE) Zenaat (Galileo (IRE))
8091a[9]

**Zaria** *Richard Price* a42 67
6 b m Tomba Princess Zara (Reprimand)
2708[7] 3422[9] 4184[5] 4845[3] 5261[4] 5713[12] 6341[3] **7028**[2] (7463) 8125[8]

**Zariyano (FR)** *Carina Fey* a78 79
5 ch g Linngari(IRE) Zariyana (IRE) (Desert Prince (IRE))
***(9112a)***

**Zarkavon** *John Wainwright* a17 14
3 b f Avonbridge Zarkavean (Medicean)
2704[7] 4302[13] 5182[15] 5946[9] **6268**[11] 7109[7] *8805*[8] *8979*[7]

**Zarliman (IRE)** *Roger Ingram* a37 27
7 ch g Zamindar(USA) Zarlana (IRE) (Darshaan)
*6796*[11] ***8135***[13] *9421*[9]

**Zarose (FR)** *H-A Pantall* a88 91
4 b h Zafeen(FR) Rose The One (FR) (Meshaheer (USA))
**5979a**[5] *7636a*[10]

**Zarras (GER)** *P Schaerer* a86 57
8 b g Big Shuffle(USA) Zanana (Zafonic (USA))
*715a*[5] *834a*[4] *953a*[F]

**Zaryio (FR)** *H-A Pantall* 78
3 ch g Rio De La Plata(USA) Zariyana (IRE) (Desert Prince (IRE))
**5909a**[11]

**Zatorius (GER)** *Andrew Balding* 79
2 b g Pastorius(GER) Zarah Top (GER) (Big Shuffle (USA))
**7593**[2] 8013[4]

**Zattera (IRE)** *Marco Gasparini* 86
4 b m Rail Link Zolletta (IRE) (Brief Truce (USA))
**8096a**[4]

**Zavikon** *Richard Hughes* a68 70
3 b c Compton Place Hakuraa (IRE) (Elnadim (USA))
*904*[5] *2306*[5] 2734[3]◆ (4157) *5028*[5] 5657[2] **6097**[3] 6753[6] 7912[6] *8427*[4]◆

**Zawadi (GER)** *Frau V Henkenjohann* 49
4 b m Kallisto(GER) Zandra (GER) (Lagunas)
**7430a**[4]

**Zawraq (IRE)** *D K Weld* 101
5 b h Shamardal(USA) Sundus (USA) (Sadler's Wells (USA))
**7066a**[2] 7837a[7]

**Zaytoon (IRE)** *Micky Hammond* 44
4 b g Cape Cross(IRE) Megec Blis (IRE) (Soviet Star (USA))
1829[11] **2547**[7] 3289[6] 3906[10] 5016[8]

**Zealous (IRE)** *Sally Haynes* a58 86
4 br g Intense Focus(USA) Velvet Kiss (IRE) (Danehill Dancer (IRE))
1512[8] 1677[12] 3743[8] *4304*[7] 4959[2] 5540[5] **7119**[4]◆ 7524[12]

**Zebedee's Girl (IRE)** *David Evans* a64 44
4 gr m Zebedee Rafelite (Fraam)
*982*[6] ***1084***[4] *1322*[13] *1406*[9]

**Zebedee's Son (IRE)** *Roger Ingram* a44 51
4 gr g Zebedee Lady Ginevra (IRE) (Touch Of The Blues (FR))
***1084***[8] *1298*[11] 2915[9]

**Zebedee Star** *Karen Tutty* 43
3 b f Zebedee Sonna Star (IRE) (Red Clubs (IRE))
**1835**[7] 2181[10] 2989[9] 4554[5] 5374[3] 6058[7] *6529*[13]

**Zebelini (IRE)** *Roy Bowring* a53 57
5 gr m Zebedee Ma Nikitia (IRE) (Camacho)
*20*[8] *153*[12] *311*[7] *1220*[4] *1451*[7] 1978[13] *2278*[3] ***(4163)*** *4727*[8] *7481*[9] *8784*[5] *9342*[7]

**Zebs Lad (IRE)** *Nikki Evans* a39 65
5 ro g Zebedee Dubai Princess (IRE) (Dubai Destination (USA))
5473[7] 6393[9] **7198**[10] 7465[14]

**Zebstar (IRE)** *Gay Kelleway* 78
4 b g Zebedee Zinstar (IRE) (Sinndar (IRE))
**3330**[7] 3834[P]

**Zebulon (IRE)** *Richard Hannon* a70 82
3 gr g Zebedee Novelina (IRE) (Fusaichi Pegasus (USA))
2151[5] (2510) 3673[6] 4537[3] 5478[4] 5961[6] 6197[2] **(6768)** 7508[6]

**Zed Candy Girl**
*Daniel Mark Loughnane* a64 58
7 ch m Sakhee's Secret Musical Twist (USA) (Woodman (USA))
***51***[8] *425*[8]

**Zeebullet (IRE)** *M Delcher Sanchez* 18
2 gr f Zebedee Windy Lane (Dubai Destination (USA))
**3515a**[7]

**Zeelander** *Roger Varian* 77
3 b c Dubawi(IRE) Zeeba (IRE) (Barathea (IRE))
5757[3] 6194[5] **(8114)**◆

**Zefferino** *Roger Charlton* a71 83
3 ch g Frankel Turama (Pivotal)
(2580) **3713**[6] 4634[9] *6068*[11]

**Zehrah (IRE)** *Simon Crisford* a72 73
3 b f Raven's Pass(USA) Ahla Wasahl (Dubai Destination (USA))
*424*[6] *1143*[2] 1944[7] 2588[6] **4633**[3] 5378[8]

**Zelaniya (IRE)** *D K Weld* 88
3 b f Lawman(FR) Zalanga (IRE) (Azamour (IRE))
**1386a**[3]

**Zelzal (FR)** *J-C Rouget* a108 122
4 b h Sea The Stars(IRE) Olga Prekrasa (USA) (Kingmambo (USA))
3880a[2] 5527[4] 7671a[6]◆ **8608a**[6]

**Zemindari (FR)** *H-F Devin* a91 101
5 b g Zanzibari(USA) Villa Joyeuse (FR) (Kahyasi (IRE))
*(798a)* **1871a**[2] 2559a[6]

**Zenafire** *Sarah Hollinshead* a60 78
8 b g Firebreak Zen Garden (Alzao (USA))
2609[3] (3494) 3740[3] **(4338)** 5138[6] 5403[4] 6680[5] 6968[8]

**Zenon (IRE)** *John Gosden* 101
3 b c Galileo(IRE) Jacqueline (IND) (King Charlemagne (USA))
2751[2] (3426)◆ (4612) 5682[3] 6421[5] **7337**[2] 7783[6]

**Zenovia (IRE)** *Archie Watson* a64
3 b f Invincible Spirit(IRE) Zallerina (Zamindar (USA))
*814*[6] *1445*[9] *7539*[5] *8210*[8] *(8496)*◆ *8742*[4] ***8823***[5] *8980*[7] ***9215***[5] *9323*[8]

**Zephyros (GER)** *David Bridgwater* a68 69
6 br g Areion(GER) Zandra (GER) (Lagunas)
*92*[11] *648*[4] *769*[5] *1284*[9] *3325*[3]◆ **3753**[2] 5140[3] 6092[11] 6807[6] *9459*[3]◆

**Zerafino (BEL)** *Jimmy Fox* a42 9
4 b g Piccolo Semiramis (BEL) (Zeami (IRE))
*464*[10] *807*[10] ***1287***[11] *3137*[16] 4695[14] 4971[13]

**Zermatta (CAN)** *J Baudron* 55
4 ch m Philanthropist(USA) Creekside Cafe (CAN) (Trajectory (USA))
**5269a**[8]

**Zeshov (IRE)** *Rebecca Bastiman* a72 82
6 b g Acclamation Fathoming (USA) (Gulch (USA))
1706[7] (2339) 4210[8] 4685[7] 5469[3] 6434[6] *7570*[8] **7823**[2] 8126[3] 8510[5]

**Zest (IRE)** *James Fanshawe* a100 89
4 b m Duke Of Marmalade(IRE) Affinity (Sadler's Wells (USA))
***1795***[3] 2392[8] 3101a[5] 5152[4] *6619*[3] *8546*[2] *(9386)*

**Zeteah** *Tony Carroll* a38 52
7 b m Passing Glance Ajeebah (IRE) (Mujtahid (USA))
*69*[6] *282*[9] *733*[7] ***1081***[9] *1256*[8]

**Zhui Feng (IRE)** *Amanda Perrett* a108 110
4 b h Invincible Spirit(IRE) Es Que (Inchinor)
*919*[4] 1494[8] 1960[13] 2606[3] **(3963)** 5594[7]

**Zhukova (IRE)** *D K Weld* 117
5 b m Fastnet Rock(AUS) Nightime (IRE) (Galileo (IRE))
(1808a) **(2641a)** 4419a[4] 6960a[8]

**Zia Melody (FR)** *J Boisnard* a59 59
4 b m Namid Zia Sofi (FR) (Le Balafre (FR))
**4233a**[2]

**Ziarah (IRE)** *James Tate* 79
2 b f Iffraaj Ashtown Girl (IRE) (Exceed And Excel (AUS))
1884[3] 2563[6] 6386[3] 7021[4] **7621**[4]

**Zie De Ket (FR)** *M Boutin* 49
2 b g Evasive Hatikva (Hawk Wing (USA))
**1335a**[15]

**Ziggy Lee** *Lawrence Mullaney* a86 61
11 b g Lujain(USA) Mary O'Grady (USA) (Swain (IRE))
***8913***[12]

**Zig Zag Girl** *John Butler* a12 40
3 b f Sixties Icon Mistic Magic (IRE) (Orpen (USA))
*41*[6] **4053**[7]

**Zihaam** *Roger Fell* 63
3 ch g Dutch Art Hymnsheet (Pivotal)
5458[9] 6316[6] **6573**[4] 6812[8] 7048[6]

**Zilara (IRE)** *Ralph Beckett* 74
2 bb f Big Bad Bob(IRE) Celtic Slipper (IRE) (Anabaa (USA))
**5573**[4] 6403[14]

**Zillion (IRE)** *John Gosden* a61
3 b g Zebedee Redelusion (IRE) (Hernando (FR))
***1448***[4]◆ *1889*[7]

**Zillion Dollar Cup (FR)** *F Cheyer* a57 68
9 ch g Anabaa Blue State Of Mind (FR) (Priolo (USA))
**7721a**[7]

**Zillione Sun (FR)**
*Mme P Butel & J-L Beaunez* a68 70
2 ch f Zambezi Sun Zillione Beauty (FR) (Ocean Of Wisdom (USA))
**7969a**[7]

**Zilza (IRE)** *Conrad Allen* a66 66
3 b f Paco Boy(IRE) Helen Glaz (IRE) (Giant's Causeway (USA))
*307*[4]◆ ***520***[2] *1489*[4] ***3473***[5] *4214*[5] **5038**[3] 5367[6] 5558[5] ***6581***[4]◆ ***7414***[3] **7907**[3] *8242*[5] ***(8342)***

**Zimri (FR)** *Mme M Bollack-Badel* a32 67
13 b g Take Risks(FR) Zayine (IRE) (Polish Patriot (USA))
**6018a**[11]

**Zing (FR)** *C Boutin* a2 68
3 ch g Zizany(IRE) Volhynie (FR) (Volochine (IRE))
**3310a**[12]

**Zinia Dei Grif (ITY)**
*Antonio Marcialis* a74 53
2 b f Red Rocks(IRE) Pesach (IRE) (Indian Danehill (IRE))
**8777a**[9]

**Zip Along (IRE)** *Richard Fahey* a66 67
2 b f Iffraaj Wizz Up (IRE) (Whipper (USA))
**6085**[2] *7238*[5]

**Zipedee** *John Ryan* a41 48
3 rg f Zebedee White Shift (IRE) (Night Shift (USA))
***1596***[11] *2027*[10] 2067[3]

**Zipedeedodah (IRE)** *Joseph Tuite* a85 74
5 gr g Zebedee Beverley Macca (Piccolo)
*(518)* *816*[6] *1370*[5] ***1487***[3] 1768[4] (2967) 3659[2] 4182[7] *4566*[7] 4965[3] 5723[4] 5967[4] 6478[5] 6810[2] 7127[6] 7217[4] *8950*[5] *9136*[5] *9437*[8]

**Zipessa (USA)** *Michael Stidham* 111
5 ch m City Zip(USA) Precious Princess (USA) (Horse Chestnut (SAF))
**5954a**[9] **8606a**[11]

**Zippy** *J F Levins* a66 71
4 b m Hellvelyn Ziggy Zaggy (Diktat)
**5518a**[3]

**Zizum** *George Scott* 65
2 ch c Showcasing Proud Duchess (IRE) (Duke Of Marmalade (IRE))
7250[8]◆ **7920**[2] 8325[9]

**Zlatan (IRE)** *Ed de Giles* a79 83
4 b g Dark Angel(IRE) Guard Hill (USA) (Rahy (USA))
1969[7] **(2586)** 2828[9] 3433[5] 4210[4] 4832[4] 5276[2] 5683[4]

**Zman Awal (IRE)** *H Al Ramzani* a84 89
6 ch m Dubawi(IRE) Pivotal Lady (Pivotal)
**914a**[12]

**Zodiakos (IRE)** *Roger Fell* a88 89
4 b g Kodiac Zonic (Zafonic (USA))
2030[3] 2684[10] 2952[4] 3204[4] 3845[13] (4661) (5496) 5668[5] **(5949)** 7044[8] 7823[6] 8009[18]

**Zoffalee (FR)** *Tom Dascombe* 81
2 ch c Zoffany(IRE) Senderlea (IRE) (Giant's Causeway (USA))
4083[6] **(5680)** 7112[7]

**Zoffanist (IRE)** *Amanda Perrett* a51 66
3 ch g Zoffany(IRE) Frynia (USA) (Cat Thief (USA))
**3864**[5] 4197[3] 4913[6] 5867[4] *6291*[9] 6473[3] 6587[3] 7005[8] 8183[4]

**Zoffany Bay (IRE)** *George Peckham* a68 70
3 b g Zoffany(IRE) Trois Graces (USA) (Alysheba (USA))
*1485*[7] **1730**[4] 2084[8] 3162[12] 4050[8] *7061*[7] *7457*[7] 7917[12] *8550*[5] *9027*[5] *(9128)* *9376*[5] *9459*[8]

**Zoffinia (IRE)** *Richard Fahey* 60
2 b f Zoffany(IRE) Princess Nala (IRE) (In The Wings)
4340[5] 5371[6] **6183**[6] 6940[5] 7519[10]

**Zomara (FR)** *F Head* 75
2 b f Dubawi(IRE) Merville (FR) (Montjeu (IRE))
**6542a**[2]

**Zonderland** *Clive Cox* a91 116
4 ch h Dutch Art Barynya (Pivotal)
**6420**[2] 8232[8]

**Zone In** *David C Griffiths* 60
3 b g Equiano(FR) Donna Giovanna (Mozart (IRE))
2185[8] 2595[6] **2704**[4] 3525[5] 4302[12] *4723*[9] 6091[11]

**Zone Regard (IRE)**
*M Delcher Sanchez* a77 76
2 b f Acclamation Lafleur (IRE) (Grand Lodge (USA))
1919a[6] 2664a[5] **(3445a)** *8169a*[5]

**Zonza (FR)** *D Guillemin* 107
2 b f Alex The Winner(USA) Zanyeva (IRE) (Oasis Dream)
(4391a) **6249a**[4] 7666a[5]

**Zophilly (IRE)** *Jeremy Gask* a62 53
4 b m Zoffany(IRE) Extreme Pleasure (IRE) (High Chaparral (IRE))
*88*[9] 2214[7] 2509[8] **(2724)** 3280[12]

**Zoravan (USA)** *Keith Dalgleish* a85 86
4 ch g More Than Ready(USA) Zaralanta (IRE) (Danehill Dancer (IRE))
*(314)* *419*[7] *1074*[2] **(1512)** 2142[7] 2457[7] 3199[6] 3582[8] 4207[16] 4475[10] *9101*[12]

**Zoraya (FR)** *Paul Cole* a69 81
2 b f Zoffany(IRE) Aztec Queen (Holy Roman Emperor (IRE))
*3174*[7] *4212*[4] 6542a[8] (7226) **(8074)**◆

**Zorba The Greek** *Ed Vaughan* a75 77
5 b g Invincible Spirit(IRE) Mistress Greeley (USA) (Mr Greeley (USA))
***516***[2] *641*[5] 1683[11] 4267[3] **5024**[2] *5747*[2] 6479[6] 7158[4]

**Zorion** *J S Bolger* 92
3 b c Smart Strike(CAN) Zofzig (USA) (Danzig (USA))
**1633a**[3]

**Zorlu (IRE)** *John O'Shea* a40 57
4 b g Invincible Spirit(IRE) Special Assignment (USA) (Lemon Drop Kid (USA))
***332***[7] 3280[13] 4969[12]

**Zouch** *J S Moore* a35 70
2 b g Sakhee's Secret Sabrina Brown (Polar Falcon (USA))
7731[5] **8252a**[4] *8945*[9]

**Zouk (FR)** *P Adda* a72 101
3 b f Delegator Singapore Belle (FR) (Sagacity (FR))
(1417a) **8838a**[2]

**Zryw (POL)** *Robert Swiatek*
5 b g Indy Champ(USA) Zgoda (POL) (Alywar (USA))
*714a*[8]

**Zubaidah** *Jane Chapple-Hyam* a57 62
5 b m Exceed And Excel(AUS) Bedouin Bride (USA) (Chester House (USA))
*1563*[10] (2281) (3251) **3726**[2]

**Zubayr (IRE)** *Paul Nicholls* a96 92
5 b g Authorized(IRE) Zaziyra (IRE) (Dalakhani (IRE))
*(3209)* *4498*[2] 5924[2] ***9458***[2]

**Zuckerprinz (FR)** *Frau Erika Mader* a48
4 b g Yeats(IRE) Zuckerpuppe (GER) (Seattle Dancer (USA))
***837a***[9]

**Zulu** *Rod Millman* a37 64
3 b g Cockney Rebel(IRE) Pantita (Polish Precedent (USA))
2172[4] **2707**[3] *9243*[9] *9459*[12]

**Zumran** *Philip McBride* a73 81
3 b f Rock Of Gibraltar(IRE) Maid For Winning (USA) (Gone West (USA))
*3970*[2] (4302) **(5122)**◆ 5325[4]

**Zumurud (IRE)** *Charles Hills* 74
2 gr g Zebedee Thaisy (USA) (Tabasco Cat (USA))
5270[5] **(8466)**

**Zumurudee (USA)** *Marco Botti* a97 80
3 b c Stormy Atlantic(USA) Voting Right (FR) (High Chaparral (IRE))
*1040a*[10] ***2520***[2] 2829[5] 8165[12]

**Zwayyan** *William Haggas* 101
4 ch g Pivotal Mail The Desert (IRE) (Desert Prince (IRE))
2390[11] (3589) 5157[3] 5634[4] 6881[4] (7781)◆ **8009**[4]

**Zylan (IRE)** *Roger Fell* a81 89
5 ch g Kyllachy Belgique (IRE) (Compton Place)
*(1547)* 1722[3] *(1819)* 1971[2] **(2428)**◆ 2840[13] 3463[11] 3946[5] 5471[8] 6663[6] 6943[10]

**Zymyran** *David Simcock* a88 88
3 b g Henrythenavigator(USA) Zimira (IRE) (Invincible Spirit (IRE))
2284[3] 2824[9] 3778[5] **(6145)** 6404[6] 6809[4] ***7941***[3]

**Zyrjann (IRE)** *Meret Kaderli* a40 87
5 ch g Rock Of Gibraltar(IRE) Zariziyna (IRE) (Dalakhani (IRE))
*714a*[4]

**Zyzzyva (FR)** *Robyn Brisland* 105
2 b c Siyouni(FR) Zanatiya (FR) (Sinndar (IRE))
4973[2]◆ (5989a) **6730a**[3]

**Zzoro (IRE)** *Amanda Perrett* a88 91
4 br g Manduro(GER) Krynica (USA) (Danzig (USA))
2233[5] **(2796)** *4002*[4] 4316[5] 7132[5] 7505[6] 8165[13]

# Season Statistics Trainers - GB Flat 2017 (Jan 1-Dec 31)

| NAME | WINS–RUNS | % | 2ND | 3RD 4TH | WIN PRIZE | TOTAL PRIZE | £1 STAKE |
|---|---|---|---|---|---|---|---|
| A P O'Brien | 32-165 | 19% | 24 | 1426-75 | £5,563,606 | £8,335,028 | +7.12 |
| John Gosden | 138-690 | 20% | 91 | 102103-225 | £4,558,364 | £6,185,144 | -81.86 |
| Richard Fahey | 200-1748 | 11% | 220 | 219142-298 | £2,467,394 | £4,239,127 | -506.07 |
| Sir Michael Stoute | 82-438 | 19% | 68 | 4757-135 | £2,370,249 | £3,855,061 | -58.90 |
| Mark Johnston | 215-1379 | 16% | 187 | 166116-217 | £2,409,999 | £3,555,120 | -223.79 |
| Richard Hannon | 194-1354 | 14% | 177 | 165136-268 | £1,850,403 | £3,000,248 | -79.49 |
| William Haggas | 158-590 | 27% | 78 | 77107-160 | £1,591,289 | £2,702,578 | +44.10 |
| Andrew Balding | 93-677 | 14% | 100 | 7367-160 | £1,702,066 | £2,565,905 | -67.39 |
| Charlie Appleby | 106-378 | 28% | 63 | 4880-140 | £1,274,325 | £2,161,034 | +45.18 |
| Roger Varian | 109-558 | 20% | 113 | 9075-162 | £1,217,848 | £1,913,490 | -117.57 |
| David O'Meara | 109-1078 | 10% | 125 | 13269-174 | £1,010,206 | £1,692,653 | -247.14 |
| David Simcock | 64-515 | 12% | 63 | 8247-129 | £798,073 | £1,544,347 | -110.69 |
| Clive Cox | 60-380 | 16% | 54 | 5344-103 | £943,050 | £1,496,548 | -10.16 |
| Roger Charlton | 65-321 | 20% | 38 | 2843-90 | £747,921 | £1,246,913 | +2.75 |
| Tim Easterby | 86-930 | 9% | 91 | 8852-146 | £800,913 | £1,232,495 | -238.55 |
| Saeed bin Suroor | 65-280 | 23% | 51 | 3644-94 | £683,146 | £1,230,927 | -60.77 |
| Charles Hills | 70-590 | 12% | 69 | 6749-143 | £719,128 | £1,206,220 | -161.41 |
| Kevin Ryan | 76-660 | 12% | 94 | 7357-124 | £647,994 | £1,146,221 | -215.46 |
| Ralph Beckett | 66-464 | 14% | 60 | 6949-136 | £581,520 | £1,089,252 | -103.21 |
| Hugo Palmer | 77-493 | 16% | 69 | 5157-134 | £573,734 | £1,066,185 | -127.21 |
| K R Burke | 74-617 | 12% | 63 | 8349-129 | £784,106 | £1,053,097 | +0.68 |
| Michael Bell | 53-346 | 15% | 61 | 4032-76 | £617,457 | £998,597 | -73.34 |
| James Fanshawe | 34-273 | 12% | 49 | 4227-66 | £656,267 | £958,713 | -103.61 |
| Dean Ivory | 38-386 | 10% | 39 | 3424-54 | £696,796 | £903,291 | -22.89 |
| Keith Dalgleish | 86-815 | 11% | 99 | 8947-129 | £504,280 | £799,402 | -259.17 |
| Michael Appleby | 91-853 | 11% | 84 | 10255-145 | £482,720 | £740,431 | -269.29 |
| Sir Mark Prescott Bt | 48-282 | 17% | 32 | 3825-60 | £422,677 | £687,484 | -64.47 |
| Eve Johnson Houghton | 53-375 | 14% | 47 | 4630-74 | £430,351 | £667,032 | +38.39 |
| Marco Botti | 40-325 | 12% | 43 | 4830-98 | £407,785 | £649,805 | -23.98 |
| Iain Jardine | 52-430 | 12% | 49 | 4630-70 | £502,567 | £639,020 | -90.69 |
| David Evans | 81-883 | 9% | 114 | 10549-112 | £357,598 | £629,912 | -331.37 |
| Ian Williams | 51-388 | 13% | 47 | 3833-69 | £389,352 | £617,338 | -61.58 |
| Henry Candy | 31-201 | 15% | 34 | 2124-55 | £265,894 | £586,573 | -47.46 |
| Tom Dascombe | 59-506 | 12% | 59 | 5137-109 | £371,215 | £576,550 | -158.52 |
| Ruth Carr | 49-480 | 10% | 48 | 5131-52 | £394,809 | £567,022 | -35.00 |
| David Elsworth | 24-184 | 13% | 20 | 2418-39 | £323,282 | £559,958 | -22.99 |
| Robert Cowell | 43-294 | 15% | 33 | 3726-70 | £317,658 | £549,431 | -27.26 |
| Brian Meehan | 28-247 | 11% | 27 | 2919-57 | £364,154 | £532,144 | -81.86 |
| Michael Dods | 62-432 | 14% | 51 | 5234-74 | £328,163 | £527,519 | -48.69 |
| David Barron | 50-430 | 12% | 60 | 5337-78 | £349,850 | £525,887 | -91.98 |
| Mick Channon | 59-588 | 10% | 49 | 7441-108 | £296,771 | £510,387 | -133.23 |
| Owen Burrows | 27-151 | 18% | 27 | 2319-53 | £319,587 | £490,538 | -28.12 |
| Paul Midgley | 34-363 | 9% | 27 | 3221-46 | £347,554 | £485,194 | -29.75 |
| Hughie Morrison | 43-331 | 13% | 39 | 3527-71 | £288,458 | £482,644 | -70.66 |
| James Tate | 34-241 | 14% | 39 | 3626-54 | £221,064 | £472,714 | -118.13 |
| John Quinn | 55-451 | 12% | 64 | 5538-76 | £281,734 | £471,701 | -61.80 |
| Ed Dunlop | 52-477 | 11% | 58 | 5436-105 | £250,303 | £470,160 | -214.95 |
| Archie Watson | 56-274 | 20% | 31 | 3930-48 | £268,872 | £458,985 | -1.17 |
| Martyn Meade | 13-81 | 16% | 9 | 911-27 | £277,292 | £452,494 | +35.37 |

# Season Statistics Jockeys - GB Flat 2017 (Jan 1-Dec 31)

| NAME | WINS–RUNS | % | 2ND | 3RD | 4TH | WIN PRIZE | TOTAL PRIZE | £1 STAKE |
|---|---|---|---|---|---|---|---|---|
| Silvestre De Sousa | 206-1081 | 19% | 157 | 148 | 97 | £1,635,387 | £2,318,940 | -195.92 |
| Luke Morris | 177-1510 | 12% | 157 | 192 | 180 | £1,019,189 | £1,752,680 | -291.81 |
| Jim Crowley | 161-855 | 19% | 119 | 83 | 105 | £3,174,200 | £5,243,361 | -82.45 |
| Adam Kirby | 146-905 | 16% | 128 | 102 | 99 | £1,386,885 | £2,107,292 | -212.35 |
| Joe Fanning | 140-849 | 16% | 112 | 100 | 89 | £1,010,036 | £1,429,390 | -23.23 |
| Ryan Moore | 137-572 | 24% | 82 | 48 | 72 | £5,746,724 | £8,147,097 | -54.00 |
| P J McDonald | 128-887 | 14% | 119 | 100 | 100 | £1,414,386 | £1,853,510 | -28.56 |
| Oisin Murphy | 127-854 | 15% | 121 | 112 | 82 | £1,270,921 | £2,555,292 | -113.98 |
| Daniel Tudhope | 122-735 | 17% | 103 | 89 | 78 | £1,062,423 | £1,612,101 | +8.65 |
| James Doyle | 110-501 | 22% | 69 | 72 | 52 | £1,848,921 | £3,337,313 | -98.93 |
| Josephine Gordon | 106-914 | 12% | 121 | 99 | 91 | £772,432 | £1,288,710 | -189.29 |
| Richard Kingscote | 100-682 | 15% | 82 | 71 | 70 | £694,901 | £1,094,807 | -169.77 |
| Andrea Atzeni | 95-504 | 19% | 70 | 79 | 49 | £1,866,595 | £3,177,648 | -50.98 |
| David Probert | 94-855 | 11% | 85 | 89 | 108 | £566,413 | £1,009,241 | -255.56 |
| Paul Hanagan | 92-711 | 13% | 91 | 95 | 75 | £890,308 | £1,520,528 | -191.48 |
| Jamie Spencer | 89-566 | 16% | 81 | 88 | 62 | £785,981 | £1,310,788 | -121.01 |
| Paul Mulrennan | 86-759 | 11% | 70 | 86 | 100 | £447,601 | £786,752 | -185.72 |
| Tom Marquand | 86-829 | 10% | 89 | 84 | 94 | £548,834 | £879,709 | -85.01 |
| Franny Norton | 83-683 | 12% | 80 | 79 | 82 | £693,138 | £1,068,023 | -89.38 |
| William Buick | 81-368 | 22% | 56 | 39 | 31 | £1,829,630 | £3,008,220 | +49.71 |
| Graham Lee | 80-756 | 11% | 52 | 80 | 80 | £452,597 | £737,454 | -148.98 |
| Ben Curtis | 79-685 | 12% | 79 | 73 | 53 | £375,037 | £583,182 | -90.44 |
| Phillip Makin | 75-598 | 13% | 68 | 79 | 74 | £449,981 | £716,472 | -126.99 |
| Sean Levey | 73-568 | 13% | 63 | 68 | 71 | £712,943 | £1,202,033 | -84.38 |
| Martin Harley | 71-565 | 13% | 79 | 66 | 72 | £436,539 | £916,742 | -169.85 |
| Tony Hamilton | 71-705 | 10% | 78 | 79 | 97 | £436,604 | £757,084 | -179.42 |
| Andrew Mullen | 68-806 | 8% | 66 | 94 | 106 | £299,300 | £556,370 | -285.98 |
| Tom Eaves | 68-852 | 8% | 94 | 87 | 80 | £451,059 | £791,755 | -218.84 |
| Pat Cosgrave | 67-471 | 14% | 83 | 65 | 49 | £445,578 | £900,701 | -154.93 |
| Robert Winston | 67-585 | 11% | 71 | 63 | 63 | £829,489 | £1,122,126 | -146.12 |
| Fran Berry | 66-708 | 9% | 75 | 84 | 88 | £456,004 | £836,752 | -279.06 |
| Shane Kelly | 66-750 | 9% | 87 | 78 | 104 | £299,696 | £536,152 | -374.85 |
| Kieran Shoemark | 65-530 | 12% | 56 | 70 | 61 | £454,619 | £708,806 | -109.18 |
| Frankie Dettori | 63-257 | 25% | 38 | 36 | 30 | £3,727,924 | £4,872,579 | +45.55 |
| David Allan | 63-528 | 12% | 59 | 51 | 53 | £616,600 | £908,907 | -17.70 |
| Dane O'Neill | 61-388 | 16% | 63 | 45 | 53 | £430,501 | £634,668 | -3.44 |
| Kevin Stott | 61-420 | 15% | 45 | 55 | 52 | £392,234 | £621,642 | +1.01 |
| David Egan | 61-512 | 12% | 68 | 73 | 66 | £317,689 | £617,934 | -86.80 |
| Jason Hart | 61-559 | 11% | 67 | 58 | 45 | £293,378 | £477,143 | -126.69 |
| Harry Bentley | 60-403 | 15% | 58 | 36 | 46 | £582,707 | £1,026,769 | -41.44 |
| J F Egan | 60-552 | 11% | 53 | 57 | 62 | £336,970 | £567,391 | -91.45 |
| Hollie Doyle | 59-516 | 11% | 62 | 57 | 60 | £311,670 | £541,298 | -50.83 |
| Dougie Costello | 57-650 | 9% | 52 | 63 | 66 | £239,922 | £407,477 | -95.23 |
| James Sullivan | 55-628 | 9% | 62 | 70 | 73 | £602,181 | £849,110 | -80.25 |
| Liam Keniry | 54-716 | 8% | 58 | 82 | 68 | £195,437 | £331,362 | -330.87 |
| Lewis Edmunds | 51-370 | 14% | 42 | 48 | 35 | £240,026 | £356,182 | -16.98 |
| Connor Beasley | 51-550 | 9% | 55 | 66 | 67 | £254,475 | £453,443 | -201.42 |
| George Wood | 49-395 | 12% | 44 | 59 | 25 | £400,533 | £597,301 | -15.76 |
| Martin Lane | 46-332 | 14% | 39 | 30 | 29 | £242,843 | £356,953 | -22.77 |

# Season Statistics Owners - GB Flat 2017 (Jan 1-Dec 31)

| NAME | WINS–RUNS | % | 2ND | 3RD | 4TH | WIN PRIZE | TOTAL PRIZE |
|---|---|---|---|---|---|---|---|
| Godolphin | 192-768 | 25% | 133 | 100 | 71 | £6,282,119 | -42.10 |
| D Smith & Mrs J Magnier & M Tabor | 10-42 | 24% | 5 | 7 | 6 | £3,576,241 | 38.32 |
| Hamdan Al Maktoum | 138-734 | 19% | 112 | 87 | 104 | £2,813,836 | -64.05 |
| K Abdullah | 58-287 | 20% | 37 | 34 | 29 | £2,086,640 | -46.4 |
| M Tabor & D Smith & Mrs J Magnier | 11-36 | 31% | 3 | 3 | 4 | £1,800,136 | 17.81 |
| Mrs J Magnier & M Tabor & D Smith | 6-49 | 12% | 10 | 3 | 4 | £1,774,530 | -29.61 |
| Cheveley Park Stud | 55-325 | 17% | 58 | 32 | 33 | £1,570,916 | -43.61 |
| Skh Hamdan bin M Al Maktoum | 60-363 | 17% | 41 | 44 | 37 | £1,397,666 | -51.77 |
| Flaxman Stables Ireland Ltd | 7-44 | 16% | 10 | 6 | 4 | £1,252,827 | -11.57 |
| A E Oppenheimer | 10-39 | 26% | 6 | 4 | 3 | £1,098,492 | -4.84 |
| Al Shaqab Racing | 56-306 | 18% | 42 | 41 | 49 | £1,081,620 | -10.51 |
| Qatar Racing Limited | 37-252 | 15% | 44 | 43 | 25 | £1,078,451 | -84.01 |
| Skh Mohmd Obaid Al Maktoum | 40-170 | 24% | 40 | 25 | 12 | £861,446 | -19.56 |
| Mrs Fitri Hay | 11-154 | 7% | 11 | 20 | 21 | £780,548 | -23.75 |
| Saeed Suhail | 14-62 | 23% | 6 | 5 | 8 | £772,688 | 23.31 |
| Tony Bloom | 7-34 | 21% | 2 | 2 | 2 | £676,157 | 20 |
| Saleh Al Homaizi & Imad Al Sagar | 25-165 | 15% | 22 | 18 | 16 | £571,783 | -48.57 |
| W J and T C O Gredley | 11-67 | 16% | 7 | 13 | 5 | £564,634 | -9.73 |
| B E Nielsen | 7-31 | 23% | 6 | 4 | 4 | £548,059 | 2.65 |
| John Dance | 17-162 | 10% | 25 | 22 | 25 | £529,234 | -62.12 |
| Elite Racing Club | 13-49 | 27% | 10 | 5 | 5 | £452,480 | 6.74 |
| Abdulla Al Mansoori | 25-134 | 19% | 15 | 14 | 20 | £450,408 | -24.25 |
| The Queen | 21-110 | 19% | 15 | 16 | 15 | £449,794 | -10.01 |
| Mrs Magnier/M Tabor/D Smith/M Jooste | 0-4 | 0% | 1 | 0 | 2 | £429,775 | -4 |
| The Cool Silk Partnership | 20-143 | 14% | 19 | 14 | 17 | £425,628 | -16.17 |
| Fred Archer Racing - Ormonde | 1-5 | 20% | 0 | 1 | 0 | £387,739 | 0.5 |
| Abdullah Saeed Al Naboodah | 15-95 | 16% | 11 | 9 | 15 | £385,406 | -34.82 |
| Geoff & Sandra Turnbull | 11-82 | 13% | 9 | 7 | 15 | £351,365 | -6.93 |
| M Tabor/D Smith/Mrs Magnier/L J Williams | 1-2 | 50% | 1 | 0 | 0 | £349,418 | -0.2 |
| Saeed Manana | 25-212 | 12% | 34 | 27 | 26 | £346,382 | -112.23 |
| Sir Evelyn De Rothschild | 6-32 | 19% | 4 | 3 | 2 | £344,598 | -3.75 |
| A D Spence | 17-79 | 22% | 9 | 8 | 5 | £338,985 | 10.07 |
| Denford Stud | 7-30 | 23% | 3 | 5 | 1 | £333,612 | 6.45 |
| Taylor's Bloodstock Ltd | 17-120 | 14% | 11 | 9 | 13 | £315,653 | 43.25 |
| Robert Ng | 9-54 | 17% | 6 | 9 | 3 | £308,492 | -17.78 |
| Sheikh J Dalmook Al Maktoum | 25-138 | 18% | 18 | 16 | 14 | £303,254 | -44.73 |
| Dr Marwan Koukash | 24-312 | 8% | 29 | 40 | 35 | £292,358 | -145.34 |
| Paul G Jacobs | 4-17 | 24% | 5 | 1 | 1 | £291,289 | -4.49 |
| King Power Racing Co Ltd | 8-48 | 17% | 4 | 6 | 7 | £281,934 | -7.38 |
| Paul & Clare Rooney | 25-153 | 16% | 23 | 16 | 16 | £266,484 | -17.58 |
| Al Asayl Bloodstock Ltd | 6-63 | 10% | 8 | 8 | 7 | £253,000 | -15.43 |
| Sheikh Ahmed Al Maktoum | 17-72 | 24% | 11 | 12 | 7 | £240,644 | -17.3 |
| John Cook | 1-19 | 5% | 1 | 4 | 1 | £233,050 | 32 |
| Stonestreet Stables/G Bolton/P Leidel | 1-1 | 100% | 0 | 0 | 0 | £226,840 | 3.5 |
| Martin Hughes & Nick Robinson | 2-8 | 25% | 2 | 1 | 1 | £220,658 | 8 |
| Michael & Heather Yarrow | 3-26 | 12% | 1 | 4 | 6 | £214,583 | 10.25 |
| Farleigh Racing | 4-18 | 22% | 3 | 3 | 1 | £207,760 | 28 |
| T A Rahman | 13-79 | 16% | 12 | 10 | 10 | £206,382 | 3.38 |
| M J Macleod | 8-67 | 12% | 9 | 7 | 6 | £203,331 | -5.5 |

# Season Statistics Sires - GB & Ire 2017 (Jan 1-Dec 31)

| | WINNERS–RUNNERS | % | WINS | RUNS | WIN PRIZE | TOTAL PRIZE |
|---|---|---|---|---|---|---|
| Galileo | 92-276 | 33% | 134 | 856 | £8,108,469 | £11,696,889 |
| Dark Angel | 112-380 | 29% | 149 | 1379 | £2,665,136 | £3,819,452 |
| Dubawi | 105-230 | 46% | 136 | 657 | £1,885,035 | £3,329,964 |
| Frankel | 43-102 | 42% | 59 | 261 | £1,651,863 | £2,756,683 |
| Kodiac | 136-408 | 33% | 192 | 1540 | £1,507,446 | £2,540,162 |
| Acclamation | 92-315 | 29% | 123 | 1252 | £1,318,082 | £2,172,435 |
| Iffraaj | 61-209 | 29% | 82 | 732 | £1,174,984 | £2,141,986 |
| Sea The Stars | 43-116 | 37% | 61 | 336 | £1,085,303 | £2,004,922 |
| Nathaniel | 36-131 | 27% | 51 | 343 | £1,689,966 | £1,930,970 |
| Invincible Spirit | 87-282 | 31% | 111 | 1032 | £971,110 | £1,830,987 |
| Exceed And Excel | 100-318 | 31% | 130 | 1096 | £1,134,255 | £1,747,716 |
| Teofilo | 67-194 | 35% | 95 | 655 | £1,083,917 | £1,700,001 |
| Fastnet Rock | 50-173 | 29% | 73 | 596 | £905,908 | £1,649,827 |
| Pivotal | 61-168 | 36% | 95 | 664 | £927,694 | £1,642,108 |
| War Front | 30-80 | 38% | 43 | 234 | £1,106,340 | £1,638,396 |
| Scat Daddy | 18-35 | 51% | 28 | 101 | £1,035,088 | £1,435,946 |
| Dansili | 44-147 | 30% | 59 | 472 | £948,314 | £1,355,218 |
| Shamardal | 64-193 | 33% | 84 | 588 | £853,119 | £1,331,291 |
| Pour Moi | 17-55 | 31% | 20 | 163 | £1,090,618 | £1,330,356 |
| Kyllachy | 83-254 | 33% | 126 | 1045 | £807,780 | £1,176,250 |
| New Approach | 51-184 | 28% | 76 | 524 | £755,632 | £1,170,680 |
| Lawman | 50-240 | 21% | 77 | 858 | £617,717 | £1,153,925 |
| Poet´s Voice | 57-223 | 26% | 73 | 723 | £424,486 | £1,153,548 |
| Mount Nelson | 23-108 | 21% | 29 | 366 | £640,496 | £1,098,456 |
| Equiano | 54-244 | 22% | 76 | 846 | £726,723 | £1,083,084 |
| Oasis Dream | 68-213 | 32% | 102 | 744 | £615,545 | £1,058,336 |
| Excelebration | 31-113 | 27% | 47 | 351 | £539,097 | £1,056,600 |
| Dutch Art | 68-232 | 29% | 93 | 796 | £601,515 | £1,046,466 |
| Lope De Vega | 62-153 | 41% | 79 | 495 | £640,836 | £1,046,055 |
| Cape Cross | 60-178 | 34% | 86 | 592 | £615,932 | £1,040,146 |
| Mastercraftsman | 64-251 | 25% | 82 | 791 | £656,209 | £1,034,108 |
| Zoffany | 55-178 | 31% | 74 | 647 | £679,170 | £1,018,194 |
| Champs Elysees | 41-162 | 25% | 58 | 457 | £673,626 | £985,408 |
| Arcano | 53-196 | 27% | 77 | 722 | £603,219 | £975,178 |
| Showcasing | 52-165 | 32% | 65 | 597 | £413,407 | £940,015 |
| Dream Ahead | 38-134 | 28% | 57 | 472 | £564,475 | £928,002 |
| Danehill Dancer | 15-60 | 25% | 17 | 216 | £814,593 | £922,416 |
| Fast Company | 51-158 | 32% | 69 | 638 | £537,689 | £879,724 |
| High Chaparral | 39-148 | 26% | 53 | 422 | £507,634 | £859,692 |
| Holy Roman Emperor | 59-201 | 29% | 82 | 719 | £551,729 | £849,669 |
| Rock Of Gibraltar | 39-154 | 25% | 57 | 643 | £472,126 | £832,381 |
| Footstepsinthesand | 43-157 | 27% | 62 | 573 | £373,588 | £831,477 |
| Zebedee | 61-220 | 28% | 84 | 865 | £515,422 | £803,159 |
| Bated Breath | 44-149 | 30% | 58 | 462 | £451,410 | £774,805 |
| Tamayuz | 26-86 | 30% | 35 | 316 | £404,704 | £761,075 |
| Bahamian Bounty | 41-163 | 25% | 62 | 640 | £446,707 | £721,560 |
| Raven´s Pass | 42-133 | 32% | 60 | 407 | £477,552 | £677,786 |
| Siyouni | 18-50 | 36% | 24 | 141 | £525,169 | £663,150 |
| Rip Van Winkle | 37-163 | 23% | 49 | 524 | £408,060 | £647,125 |

# Raceform Ratings - Flat 2017

## Two-Year-Olds

| | | |
|---|---|---|
| 122 | U S Navy Flag | A P O'Brien |
| 119 | Saxon Warrior | A P O'Brien |
| 119 | Verbal Dexterity | J S Bolger |
| 118 | Roaring Lion | John Gosden |
| 116 | Expert Eye | Sir Michael Stoute |
| 116 | Fleet Review | A P O'Brien |
| 115 | Mendelssohn | A P O'Brien |
| 115 | Sands Of Mali | Richard Fahey |
| 115 | Sioux Nation | A P O'Brien |
| 115 | Unfortunately | K R Burke |
| 115 | Wild Illusion | Charlie Appleby |
| 114 | Clemmie | A P O'Brien |
| 113 | Beckford | Gordon Elliott |
| 113 | James Garfield | George Scott |
| 113 | Laurens | K R Burke |
| 113 | Masar | Charlie Appleby |
| 113 | Olmedo | J-C Rouget |
| 113 | Sacred Life | S Wattel |
| 113 | September | A P O'Brien |
| 113 | Untamed Domain | H Graham Motion |

## All-Weather/Dirt

| | | |
|---|---|---|
| 130 | Gun Runner | Steven Asmussen |
| 130 | Arrogate | Bob Baffert |
| 128 | Roy H | Peter Miller |
| 126 | Collected | Bob Baffert |
| 126 | Drefong | Bob Baffert |
| 125 | Mor Spirit | Bob Baffert |
| 125 | Sharp Azteca | Jorge Navarro |
| 125 | Mind Your Biscuits | Chad Summers |
| 124 | Always Dreaming | Todd Pletcher |
| 124 | Roy H | Peter Miller |
| 124 | Imperial Hint | Luis Carvajal Jr |
| 123 | West Coast | Bob Baffert |
| 123 | Songbird | Jerry Hollendorfer |
| 123 | Mind Your Biscuits | Chad Summers |
| 122 | War Story | Jorge Navarro |
| 122 | Sharp Azteca | Jorge Navarro |
| 122 | Battle Of Midway | Jerry Hollendorfer |

## Three-Year-Olds

| | | |
|---|---|---|
| 129 | Almanzor | J-C Rouget |
| 131 | Cracksman | John Gosden |
| 129 | Enable | John Gosden |
| 128 | Battaash | Charles Hills |
| 128 | Harry Angel | Clive Cox |
| 125 | Churchill | A P O'Brien |
| 124 | Barney Roy | Richard Hannon |
| 124 | Caravaggio | A P O'Brien |
| 124 | Lady Aurelia | Wesley A Ward |
| 123 | Beat The Bank | Andrew Balding |
| 122 | Rey De Oro | Kazuo Fujisawa |
| 121 | Brametot | J-C Rouget |
| 121 | Capri | A P O'Brien |
| 121 | Suave Richard | Yasushi Shono |
| 121 | Wings Of Eagles | A P O'Brien |
| 120 | Al Wukair | A Fabre |
| 120 | Crystal Ocean | Sir Michael Stoute |
| 120 | Inns Of Court | A Fabre |

## Older Horses

| | | |
|---|---|---|
| 130 | Winx | Chris Waller |
| 127 | Ulysses | Sir Michael Stoute |
| 126 | Cloth Of Stars | A Fabre |
| 126 | Redzel | Peter & Paul Snowden |
| 126 | Ribchester | Richard Fahey |
| 125 | Beauty Only | A S Cruz |
| 125 | Kitasan Black | Hisashi Shimizu |
| 125 | Mr Stunning | J Size |
| 125 | Order Of St George | A P O'Brien |
| 124 | Satono Crown | Noriyuki Hori |
| 124 | Satono Diamond | Yasutoshi Ikee |
| 124 | Vega Magic | D & B Hayes & T Dabernig |
| 123 | Brave Smash | Michihiro Ogasa |
| 123 | Cheval Grand | Yasuo Tomomichi |
| 123 | Ertijaal | A R Al Rayhi |
| 123 | Highland Reel | A P O'Brien |
| 123 | Jack Hobbs | John Gosden |
| 123 | Limato | Henry Candy |
| 123 | Lucky Bubbles | K W Lui |
| 123 | Signs Of Blessing | F Rohaut |
| 123 | Terravista | Joseph Pride |
| 123 | World Approval | Mark Casse |

# Raceform Flat Record Times

## ASCOT

| Distance | Time | Age | Weight | Going | Horse | Date |
|---|---|---|---|---|---|---|
| 5f | 58.80 | 2 | 9-1 | Good To Firm | No Nay Never | Jun 20 2013 |
| 5f | 57.44 | 6 | 9-1 | Good To Firm | Miss Andretti (AUS) | Jun 19 2007 |
| 6f | 1m 12.39 | 2 | 9-1 | Good To Firm | Rajasinghe (IRE) | Jun 20 2017 |
| 6f | 1m 11.05 | 3 | 9-1 | Good To Firm | Blue Point (IRE) | May 3 2017 |
| 7f | 1m 26.55 | 2 | 9-0 | Good To Firm | Malabar | Jly 25 2014 |
| 7f | 1m 24.28 | 4 | 8-11 | Good To Firm | Galician | Jly 27 2013 |
| 7f 213y | 1m 39.55 | 2 | 8-12 | Good | Joshua Tree (IRE) | Sep 26 2009 |
| 7f 213y | 1m 37.22 | 3 | 9-0 | Good To Firm | Barney Roy | Jun 20 2017 |
| 1m | 1m 36.60 | 4 | 9-0 | Good To Firm | Ribchester (IRE) | Jun 20 2017 |
| 1m 1f 212y | 2m 1.90 | 5 | 8-11 | Good To Firm | The Fugue | Jun 18 2014 |
| 1m 3f 211y | 2m 24.60 | 4 | 9-7 | Good To Firm | Novellist | Jly 27 2013 |
| 1m 7f 209y | 3m 24.12 | 4 | 8-12 | Good To Firm | Mizzou | Apr 29 2015 |
| 2m 3f 210y | 4m 16.92 | 6 | 9-2 | Good To Firm | Rite of Passage | Jun 17 2010 |
| 2m 5f 143y | 4m 45.67 | 7 | 9-2 | Good To Firm | Oriental Fox | Jun 20 2015 |

## AYR

| Distance | Time | Age | Weight | Going | Horse | Date |
|---|---|---|---|---|---|---|
| 5f | 56.98 | 2 | 8-11 | Good | Boogie Street | Sep 18 2003 |
| 5f | 55.68 | 3 | 8-11 | Good To Firm | Look Busy (IRE) | Jun 21 2008 |
| 6f | 1m 9.73 | 2 | 7-10 | Firm | Sir Bert | Sep 17 1969 |
| 6f | 1m 8.37 | 5 | 8-6 | Good To Firm | Maison Dieu | Jun 21 2008 |
| 7f 50y | 1m 28.99 | 2 | 9-0 | Good | Tafaahum (USA) | Sep 19 2003 |
| 7f 50y | 1m 26.54 | 3 | 9-3 | Good | Sabador | May 31 2017 |
| 1m | 1m 39.18 | 2 | 9-7 | Good | Moonlightnavigator | Sep 18 2014 |
| 1m | 1m 36.00 | 4 | 7-13 | Firm | Sufi I | Sep 16 1959 |
| 1m 1f 20y | 1m 50.30 | 4 | 9-3 | Good | Retirement | Sep 19 2003 |
| 1m 2f | 2m 4.02 | 4 | 9-9 | Good To Firm | Endless Hall | Jly 17 2000 |
| 1m 5f 26y | 2m 45.81 | 4 | 9-7 | Good To Firm | Eden's Close | Sep 18 1993 |
| 1m 7f | 3m 13.16 | 3 | 9-4 | Good | Romany Rye | Sep 19 1991 |
| 2m 1f 105y | 3m 45.20 | 4 | 6-13 | Firm | Curry | Sep 16 1955 |

## BATH

| Distance | Time | Age | Weight | Going | Horse | Date |
|---|---|---|---|---|---|---|
| 5f 10y | 59.50 | 2 | 9-2 | Firm | Amour Propre | Jly 24 2008 |
| 5f 10y | 58.75 | 3 | 8-12 | Firm | Enticing (IRE) | May 1 2007 |
| 5f 160y | 1m 8.70 | 2 | 8-12 | Firm | Qalahari (IRE) | Jly 24 2008 |
| 5f 160y | 1m 8.10 | 6 | 9-0 | Firm | Madraco | May 22 1989 |
| 1m 5y | 1m 39.51 | 2 | 9-2 | Firm | Natural Charm (IRE) | Sep 14 2014 |
| 1m 5y | 1m 37.20 | 5 | 8-12 | Good To Firm | Adobe | Jun 17 2000 |
| 1m 5y | 1m 37.20 | 3 | 8-7 | Firm | Alasha (IRE) | Aug 18 2002 |
| 1m 2f 37y | 2m 5.80 | 3 | 9-0 | Good To Firm | Connoisseur Bay (USA) | May 29 1998 |
| 1m 3f 137y | 2m 25.74 | 3 | 9-0 | Hard | Top The Charts | Sep 8 2005 |
| 1m 5f 11y | 2m 47.20 | 4 | 10-0 | Firm | Flown | Aug 13 1991 |
| 2m 1f 24y | 3m 43.41 | 6 | 7-9 | Firm | Yaheska (IRE) | Jun 14 2003 |

## BEVERLEY

| Distance | Time | Age | Weight | Going | Horse | Date |
|---|---|---|---|---|---|---|
| 5f | 1m 0.89 | 2 | 8-12 | Good To Firm | Langavat | Jun 8 2013 |
| 5f | 59.77 | 5 | 9-3 | Good To Firm | Judicial (IRE) | Jun 20 2017 |
| 7f 96y | 1m 31.10 | 2 | 9-7 | Good To Firm | Champagne Prince | Aug 10 1995 |
| 7f 96y | 1m 31.10 | 2 | 9-0 | Firm | Majal (IRE) | Jly 30 1991 |
| 7f 96y | 1m 29.50 | 3 | 7-8 | Firm | Who's Tef | Jly 30 1991 |
| 1m 100y | 1m 43.30 | 2 | 9-0 | Firm | Arden | Sep 24 1986 |
| 1m 100y | 1m 42.20 | 3 | 8-4 | Firm | Legal Case | Jun 14 1989 |
| 1m 1f 207y | 2m 1.00 | 3 | 9-7 | Good To Firm | Eastern Aria | Aug 29 2009 |
| 1m 4f 23y | 2m 33.35 | 5 | 9-2 | Good To Firm | Two Jabs | Apr 23 2015 |
| 2m 32y | 3m 28.62 | 4 | 9-11 | Good To Firm | Corpus Chorister (FR) | Jly 18 2017 |

## BRIGHTON

| Distance | Time | Age | Weight | Going | Horse | Date |
|---|---|---|---|---|---|---|
| 5f 60y | 1m 0.10 | 2 | 9-0 | Firm | Bid for Blue | May 6 1993 |
| 5f 60y | 59.30 | 3 | 8-9 | Firm | Play Hever Golf | May 26 1993 |
| 5f 215y | 1m 8.10 | 2 | 8-9 | Firm | Song Mist (IRE) | Jly 16 1996 |
| 5f 215y | 1m 7.30 | 5 | 9-1 | Good To Firm | Blundell Lane | May 4 2000 |
| 5f 215y | 1m 7.30 | 3 | 8-9 | Firm | Third Party | Jun 3 1997 |
| 6f 210y | 1m 19.90 | 2 | 8-11 | Hard | Rain Burst | Sep 15 1988 |
| 6f 210y | 1m 19.40 | 4 | 9-3 | Good To Firm | Sawaki | Sep 3 1991 |
| 7f 211y | 1m 32.80 | 2 | 9-7 | Firm | Asian Pete | Oct 3 1989 |
| 7f 211y | 1m 30.50 | 5 | 8-11 | Firm | Mystic Ridge | May 27 1999 |
| 1m 1f 207y | 2m 4.70 | 2 | 9-0 | Good To Soft | Esteemed Master | Nov 2 2001 |
| 1m 1f 207y | 1m 57.20 | 3 | 9-0 | Firm | Get The Message | Apr 30 1984 |
| 1m 3f 198y | 2m 25.80 | 4 | 8-2 | Firm | New Zealand | Jly 4 1985 |

## CARLISLE

| Distance | Time | Age | Weight | Going | Horse | Date |
|---|---|---|---|---|---|---|
| 5f | 1m 0.10 | 2 | 8-5 | Firm | La Tortuga | Aug 2 1999 |
| 5f | 58.80 | 3 | 9-8 | Good To Firm | Esatto | Aug 21 2002 |
| 5f 193y | 1m 12.30 | 2 | 9-2 | Good To Firm | Burrishoole Abbey | Jun 22 2016 |
| 5f 193y | 1m 10.83 | 4 | 9-0 | Good To Firm | Bo McGinty (IRE) | Sep 11 2005 |
| 6f 195y | 1m 24.30 | 3 | 8-9 | Good To Firm | Marjurita (IRE) | Aug 21 2002 |
| 7f 173y | 1m 37.02 | 4 | 9-5 | Good To Firm | Edgar Balthazar | Jun 22 2016 |
| 1m 1f | 1m 53.84 | 3 | 9-0 | Firm | Little Jimbob | Jun 14 2004 |
| 1m 3f 39y | 2m 20.83 | 5 | 9-10 | Good To Firm | Sindarban | Jun 22 2016 |
| 1m 6f 32y | 3m 2.20 | 6 | 8-10 | Firm | Explosive Speed | May 26 1994 |
| 2m 1f 47y | 3m 46.20 | 3 | 7-10 | Good To Firm | Warring Kingdom | Aug 25 1999 |

## CATTERICK

| Distance | Time | Age | Weight | Going | Horse | Date |
|---|---|---|---|---|---|---|
| 5f | 57.60 | 2 | 9-0 | Firm | H Harrison | Oct 8 2002 |
| 5f | 57.10 | 4 | 8-7 | Firm | Kabcast | Jly 6 1989 |
| 5f 212y | 1m 11.40 | 2 | 9-4 | Firm | Captain Nick | Jly 11 1978 |
| 5f 212y | 1m 9.86 | 9 | 8-13 | Good To Firm | Sharp Hat | May 30 2003 |
| 7f 6y | 1m 24.10 | 2 | 8-11 | Firm | Linda's Fantasy | Sep 18 1982 |
| 7f 6y | 1m 22.56 | 6 | 8-7 | Firm | Differential (USA) | May 31 2003 |
| 1m 4f 13y | 2m 30.50 | 3 | 8-8 | Good To Firm | Rahaf | May 30 2003 |
| 1m 5f 192y | 2m 54.80 | 3 | 8-5 | Firm | Geryon | May 31 1984 |
| 1m 7f 189y | 3m 20.80 | 4 | 7-11 | Firm | Bean Boy I | Jly 8 1982 |

## CHELMSFORD (A.W)

| Distance | Time | Age | Weight | Going | Horse | Date |
|---|---|---|---|---|---|---|
| 5f | 58.72 | 2 | 9-7 | Standard | Sun'Aq | Nov 19 2015 |
| 5f | 57.30 | 7 | 8-13 | Standard | Brother Tiger | Feb 7 2016 |
| 6f | 1m 11.19 | 2 | 8-13 | Standard | Florencio | Oct 15 2015 |
| 6f | 1m 10.00 | 4 | 9-2 | Standard | Raucous | Apr 27 2017 |
| 7f | 1m 23.23 | 4 | 9-0 | Standard | Volunteer Point | Jan 16 2016 |
| 1m | 1m 37.15 | 2 | 9-3 | Standard | Dragon Mall | Sep 26 2015 |
| 1m | 1m 35.46 | 4 | 9-7 | Standard | Mindurownbusiness | Nov 23 2015 |
| 1m 2f | 2m 2.33 | 8 | 9-7 | Standard | Bancnuanaheireann | Nov 5 2015 |
| 1m 5f 66y | 2m 47.00 | 4 | 8-7 | Standard | Coorg | Jan 6 2016 |
| 1m 6f | 2m 55.65 | 4 | 10-0 | Standard | Castle Combe | Sep 3 2015 |
| 2m | 3m 22.37 | 5 | 9-3 | Standard | Notarised | Mar 3 2016 |

## CHEPSTOW

| Distance | Time | Age | Weight | Going | Horse | Date |
|---|---|---|---|---|---|---|
| 5f 16y | 57.60 | 2 | 8-11 | Firm | Micro Love | Jly 8 1986 |
| 5f 16y | 56.80 | 3 | 8-4 | Firm | Torbay Express | Sep 15 1979 |
| 6f 16y | 1m 8.50 | 2 | 9-2 | Firm | Ninjago | Jly 27 2012 |
| 6f 16y | 1m 8.10 | 3 | 9-7 | Firm | America Calling (USA) | Sep 18 2001 |
| 7f 16y | 1m 20.80 | 2 | 9-0 | Good To Firm | Royal Amaretto (IRE) | Sep 12 1996 |
| 7f 16y | 1m 19.30 | 3 | 9-0 | Firm | Taranaki | Sep 18 2001 |
| 1m 14y | 1m 33.10 | 2 | 8-11 | Good To Firm | Ski Academy (IRE) | Aug 28 1995 |
| 1m 14y | 1m 31.60 | 3 | 8-13 | Firm | Stoli (IRE) | Sep 18 2001 |
| 1m 2f 36y | 2m 4.10 | 3 | 8-5 | Good To Firm | Ela Athena | Jly 23 1999 |
| 1m 2f 36y | 2m 4.10 | 5 | 7-8 | Good To Firm | It's Varadan | Sep 9 1989 |
| 1m 2f 36y | 2m 4.10 | 5 | 8-9 | Hard | Leonidas | Jly 5 1983 |
| 1m 4f 23y | 2m 31.00 | 3 | 8-9 | Good To Firm | Spritsail | Jly 13 1989 |
| 1m 4f 23y | 2m 31.00 | 5 | 8-11 | Hard | The Friend | Aug 29 1983 |
| 2m 49y | 3m 27.70 | 4 | 9-0 | Good To Firm | Wizzard Artist | Jly 1 1989 |
| 2m 2f | 3m 56.40 | 5 | 8-7 | Good To Firm | Laffah | Jly 8 2000 |

## CHESTER

| Distance | Time | Age | Weight | Going | Horse | Date |
|---|---|---|---|---|---|---|
| 5f 15y | 59.94 | 2 | 9-2 | Good To Firm | Leiba Leiba | Jun 26 2010 |
| 5f 15y | 58.88 | 3 | 8-7 | Good To Firm | Peterkin | Jly 11 2014 |
| 5f 110y | 1m 6.39 | 2 | 8-7 | Good To Soft | Kinematic | Sep 27 2014 |
| 5f 110y | 1m 5.02 | 6 | 8-9 | Good | Ballesteros | Aug 22 2015 |
| 6f 17y | 1m 12.85 | 2 | 8-10 | Good To Firm | Flying Express | Aug 31 2002 |
| 6f 17y | 1m 12.02 | 5 | 9-5 | Good To Firm | Deauville Prince | Jun 13 2015 |
| 7f 1y | 1m 25.29 | 2 | 9-0 | Good To Firm | Due Respect (IRE) | Sep 25 2002 |
| 7f 1y | 1m 23.75 | 5 | 8-13 | Good To Firm | Three Graces (GER) | Jly 9 2005 |
| 7f 127y | 1m 32.29 | 2 | 9-0 | Good To Firm | Big Bad Bob (IRE) | Sep 25 2002 |
| 7f 127y | 1m 30.91 | 3 | 8-12 | Good To Firm | Cupid's Glory | Aug 18 2005 |
| 1m 2f 70y | 2m 7.15 | 3 | 8-8 | Good To Firm | Stotsfold | Sep 23 2006 |
| 1m 3f 75y | 2m 22.17 | 3 | 8-12 | Good To Firm | Perfect Truth (IRE) | May 6 2009 |
| 1m 4f 63y | 2m 33.70 | 3 | 8-10 | Good To Firm | Fight Your Corner | May 7 2002 |
| 1m 5f 84y | 2m 45.43 | 5 | 8-11 | Firm | Rakaposhi King | May 7 1987 |
| 1m 7f 196y | 3m 20.33 | 4 | 9-0 | Good To Firm | Grand Fromage (IRE) | Jly 13 2002 |
| 2m 2f 140y | 3m 58.89 | 7 | 9-2 | Good To Firm | Greenwich Meantime | May 9 2007 |

## DONCASTER

| Distance | Time | Age | Weight | Going | Horse | Date |
|---|---|---|---|---|---|---|
| 5f 3y | 58.04 | 2 | 9-1 | Good | Gutaifan (IRE) | Sep 11 2015 |
| 5f 3y | 57.31 | 7 | 9-10 | Good | Tabaret | Aug 14 2010 |
| 5f 143y | 1m 5.38 | 4 | 9-7 | Good | Muthmir | Sep 13 2014 |
| 6f 2y | 1m 10.65 | 2 | 9-7 | Good To Firm | Blossomtime | Jly 16 2015 |
| 6f 2y | 1m 9.56 | 3 | 8-10 | Good To Firm | Proclaim | May 30 2009 |
| 6f 111y | 1m 17.19 | 2 | 8-9 | Good | Mr Lupton | Sep 10 2015 |
| 7f 6y | 1m 22.78 | 2 | 9-5 | Good | Basateen | Jly 24 2014 |
| 7f 6y | 1m 21.81 | 6 | 8-7 | Good To Firm | Signor Peltro | May 30 2009 |
| 7f 213y | 1m 38.37 | 2 | 8-6 | Good To Soft | Antoniola (IRE) | Oct 23 2009 |
| 7f 213y | 1m 34.46 | 4 | 8-12 | Good To Firm | Staying On | Apr 18 2009 |
| 1m | 1m 36.72 | 2 | 8-12 | Good | Dance Of Fire | Sep 13 2014 |
| 1m | 1m 34.95 | 6 | 8-9 | Firm | Quick Wit | Jly 18 2013 |
| 1m 2f 43y | 2m 4.81 | 4 | 8-13 | Good To Firm | Red Gala | Sep 12 2007 |
| 1m 3f 197y | 2m 27.48 | 3 | 8-4 | Good To Firm | Swift Alhaarth | Sep 10 2011 |
| 1m 6f 115y | 3m 0.44 | 3 | 9-0 | Good To Firm | Masked Marvel | Sep 10 2011 |
| 2m 109y | 3m 34.52 | 7 | 9-0 | Good To Firm | Inchnadamph | Nov 10 2007 |
| 2m 1f 197y | 3m 48.41 | 4 | 9-4 | Good To Firm | Septimus (IRE) | Sep 14 2007 |

## EPSOM

| Distance | Time | Age | Weight | Going | Horse | Date |
|---|---|---|---|---|---|---|
| 5f | 55.02 | 2 | 8-9 | Good To Firm | Prince Aslia | Jun 9 1995 |
| 5f | 53.60 | 4 | 9-5 | Firm | Indigenous | Jun 2 1960 |
| 6f 3y | 1m 7.85 | 2 | 8-11 | Good To Firm | Showbrook | Jun 5 1991 |
| 6f 3y | 1m 7.21 | 5 | 9-13 | Good To Firm | Mac Gille Eoin | Jly 2 2009 |
| 7f 3y | 1m 21.30 | 2 | 8-9 | Good To Firm | Red Peony | Jly 29 2004 |
| 7f 3y | 1m 20.15 | 4 | 8-7 | Firm | Capistrano I | Jun 7 1972 |
| 1m 113y | 1m 42.80 | 2 | 8-5 | Good To Firm | Nightstalker | Aug 30 1988 |
| 1m 113y | 1m 40.75 | 3 | 8-6 | Good To Firm | Sylva Honda | Jun 5 1991 |
| 1m 2f 17y | 2m 3.50 | 5 | 7-11 | Firm | Crossbow I | Jun 7 1967 |
| 1m 4f 6y | 2m 31.33 | 3 | 9-0 | Good To Firm | Workforce | Jun 5 2010 |

## FFOS LAS

| Distance | Time | Age | Weight | Going | Horse | Date |
|---|---|---|---|---|---|---|
| 5f | 57.06 | 2 | 9-3 | Good To Firm | Mr Majeika (IRE) | May 5 2011 |
| 5f | 56.35 | 5 | 8-8 | Good | Haajes | Sep 12 2009 |
| 6f | 1m 9.00 | 2 | 9-5 | Good To Firm | Wonder Of Qatar | Sep 14 2014 |
| 6f | 1m 7.80 | 8 | 8-4 | Good To Firm | The Jailer | May 5 2011 |
| 1m | 1m 39.36 | 2 | 9-2 | Good To Firm | Hala Hala | Sep 2 2013 |
| 1m | 1m 37.12 | 5 | 9-0 | Good To Firm | Zebrano | May 5 2011 |
| 1m 2f | 2m 4.85 | 8 | 8-12 | Good To Firm | Pelham Crescent (IRE) | May 5 2011 |
| 1m 3f 209y | 2m 31.58 | 4 | 8-9 | Good To Firm | Men Don't Cry | Jly 23 2013 |
| 1m 6f | 2m 58.61 | 4 | 9-7 | Good To Firm | Lady Eclair | Jly 12 2010 |
| 2m | 3m 29.58 | 4 | 8-9 | Good To Firm | Annaluna | Jly 1 2013 |

## GOODWOOD

| Distance | Time | Age | Weight | Going | Horse | Date |
|---|---|---|---|---|---|---|
| 5f | 57.14 | 2 | 9-1 | Good | Yalta | Jly 27 2016 |
| 5f | 56.01 | 5 | 9-0 | Good To Firm | Rudi's Pet | Jly 27 1999 |
| 6f | 1m 9.81 | 2 | 8-11 | Good To Firm | Bachir (IRE) | Jly 28 1999 |
| 6f | 1m 9.10 | 6 | 9-0 | Good To Firm | Tamagin | Sep 12 2009 |
| 7f | 1m 24.99 | 2 | 8-11 | Good To Firm | Ekraar | Jly 29 1999 |
| 7f | 1m 23.88 | 3 | 8-7 | Firm | Brief Glimpse (IRE) | Jly 25 1995 |
| 1m | 1m 37.21 | 2 | 9-0 | Good | Caldra (IRE) | Sep 9 2006 |
| 1m | 1m 35.61 | 4 | 8-9 | Good To Firm | Spectait | Aug 4 2006 |
| 1m 1f 11y | 1m 56.27 | 2 | 9-3 | Good To Firm | Dordogne (IRE) | Sep 22 2010 |
| 1m 1f 11y | 1m 52.81 | 3 | 9-6 | Good | Vena (IRE) | Jly 27 1995 |
| 1m 1f 197y | 2m 2.81 | 3 | 9-3 | Good To Firm | Road To Love (IRE) | Aug 3 2006 |
| 1m 3f 44y | 2m 22.77 | 3 | 9-3 | Good | Khalidi | May 26 2017 |
| 1m 3f 218y | 2m 31.57 | 3 | 8-10 | Firm | Presenting | Jly 25 1995 |
| 1m 6f | 2m 57.61 | 4 | 9-6 | Good To Firm | Meeznah (USA) | Jly 28 2011 |
| 2m | 3m 21.55 | 5 | 9-10 | Good To Firm | Yeats (IRE) | Aug 3 2006 |

## HAMILTON

| Distance | Time | Age | Weight | Going | Horse | Date |
|---|---|---|---|---|---|---|
| 5f 7y | 57.95 | 2 | 8-8 | Good To Firm | Rose Blossom | May 29 2009 |
| 5f 7y | 57.95 | 2 | 8-8 | Good To Firm | Rose Blossom | May 29 2009 |
| 6f 6y | 1m 10.00 | 2 | 8-12 | Good To Firm | Break The Code | Aug 24 1999 |
| 6f 6y | 1m 9.30 | 4 | 8-7 | Firm | Marcus Game | Jly 11 1974 |
| 1m 68y | 1m 45.46 | 2 | 9-5 | Good To Firm | Laafiraaq | Sep 20 2015 |
| 1m 68y | 1m 42.70 | 6 | 7-7 | Firm | Cranley | Sep 25 1972 |
| 1m 1f 35y | 1m 53.60 | 5 | 9-6 | Good To Firm | Regent's Secret (USA) | Aug 10 2005 |
| 1m 3f 15y | 2m 18.66 | 3 | 9-3 | Good To Firm | Postponed (IRE) | Jly 18 2014 |
| 1m 4f 15y | 2m 30.52 | 5 | 9-10 | Good To Firm | Record Breaker | Jun 10 2009 |
| 1m 5f 16y | 2m 45.10 | 6 | 9-6 | Firm | Mentalasanythin | Jun 14 1995 |

## HAYDOCK

| Distance | Time | Age | Weight | Going | Horse | Date |
|---|---|---|---|---|---|---|
| 5f | 58.51 | 2 | 9-1 | Good | Four Dragons | Oct 14 2016 |
| 5f | 58.56 | 2 | 8-2 | Good To Firm | Barracuda Boy | Aug 11 2012 |
| 5f | 57.38 | 7 | 9-12 | Good To Firm | Foxy Forever (IRE) | Jly 21 2017 |
| 5f | 56.39 | 5 | 9-4 | Firm | Bated Breath | May 26 2012 |
| 6f | 1m 10.58 | 2 | 9-2 | Good To Firm | Prestbury Park | Jly 21 2017 |
| 6f | 1m 10.98 | 4 | 9-9 | Good To Firm | Wolfhound (USA) | Sep 4 1993 |
| 6f | 1m 9.40 | 7 | 9-3 | Good To Firm | Markab | Sep 4 2010 |
| 6f | 1m 8.56 | 3 | 9-0 | Firm | Harry Angel | May 27 2017 |
| 6f 212y | 1m 27.51 | 2 | 9-0 | Good To Firm | Royal Parks | Jly 6 2017 |
| 6f 212y | 1m 25.86 | 5 | 9-9 | Good | Jungle Cat | Jly 22 2017 |
| 7f 37y | 1m 27.57 | 2 | 9-2 | Good To Firm | Contrast | Aug 5 2016 |
| 7f 37y | 1m 25.50 | 3 | 8-11 | Good | Forge | Sep 1 2016 |
| 7f 212y | 1m 37.80 | 3 | 9-4 | Good To Firm | Sidewinder | May 26 2017 |
| 1m 37y | 1m 38.50 | 4 | 8-11 | Good To Firm | Express Himself | Jun 10 2015 |
| 1m 2f 42y | 2m 7.25 | 3 | 8-9 | Good To Firm | Laraaib | May 26 2017 |
| 1m 2f 100y | 2m 7.71 | 3 | 8-8 | Good To Firm | Royal Artillery | Aug 6 2016 |
| 1m 3f 140y | 2m 30.37 | 4 | 9-12 | Good | Lugano | Jun 15 2017 |
| 1m 3f 175y | 2m 25.53 | 4 | 8-12 | Good To Firm | Number Theory | May 24 2012 |
| 1m 6f | 2m 55.20 | 5 | 9-9 | Good To Firm | Huff And Puff | Sep 7 2012 |
| 2m 45y | 3m 26.98 | 5 | 8-13 | Good To Firm | De Rigueur | Jun 8 2013 |

## KEMPTON (A.W)

| Distance | Time | Age | Weight | Going | Horse | Date |
|---|---|---|---|---|---|---|
| 5f | 58.96 | 2 | 8-6 | Standard | Glamorous Spirit (IRE) | Nov 28 2008 |
| 5f | 58.26 | 7 | 9-5 | Standard To Slow | Foxy Forever | Oct 17 2017 |
| 6f | 1m 11.02 | 2 | 9-1 | Standard To Slow | Invincible Army | Sep 9 2017 |
| 6f | 1m 9.79 | 4 | 8-11 | Standard | Trinityelitedotcom | Mar 29 2014 |
| 7f | 1m 23.79 | 2 | 8-0 | Standard | Elsaakb (USA) | Nov 8 2017 |
| 7f | 1m 23.10 | 6 | 9-9 | Standard | Sirius Prospect | Nov 20 2014 |
| 1m | 1m 37.26 | 2 | 9-0 | Standard | Cecchini (IRE) | Nov 8 2017 |
| 1m | 1m 35.73 | 3 | 8-9 | Standard | Western Aristocrat | Sep 15 2011 |
| 1m 1f 219y | 2m 2.93 | 3 | 8-11 | Standard To Slow | Ply | Sep 25 2017 |
| 1m 2f 219y | 2m 16.09 | 4 | 8-7 | Standard | Salutation | Mar 29 2014 |
| 1m 3f 219y | 2m 28.99 | 6 | 9-3 | Standard | Spring Of Fame (USA) | Nov 7 2012 |
| 1m 7f 218y | 3m 21.50 | 4 | 8-12 | Standard | Colour Vision (FR) | May 2 2012 |

## LEICESTER

| Distance | Time | Age | Weight | Going | Horse | Date |
|---|---|---|---|---|---|---|
| 1m 53y | 1m 44.05 | 2 | 8-11 | Good To Firm | Congressional (IRE) | Sep 6 2005 |
| 1m 53y | 1m 41.89 | 5 | 9-7 | Good To Firm | Vainglory | Jun 18 2009 |
| 1m 1f 216y | 2m 5.30 | 2 | 9-1 | Good To Firm | Windsor Castle | Oct 14 1996 |
| 1m 1f 216y | 2m 2.40 | 3 | 8-11 | Firm | Effigy I | Nov 4 1985 |
| 1m 1f 216y | 2m 2.40 | 4 | 9-6 | Good To Firm | Lady Angharad (IRE) | Jun 18 2000 |
| 1m 3f 179y | 2m 27.10 | 5 | 8-12 | Good To Firm | Murghem (IRE) | Jun 18 2000 |

## LINGFIELD

| Distance | Time | Age | Weight | Going | Horse | Date |
|---|---|---|---|---|---|---|
| 4f 217y | 57.07 | 2 | 9-0 | Good To Firm | Quite A Thing | Jun 11 2011 |
| 4f 217y | 56.09 | 3 | 9-4 | Good To Firm | Whitecrest | Sep 16 2011 |
| 6f | 1m 8.36 | 2 | 8-12 | Good To Firm | Folly Bridge | Sep 8 2009 |
| 6f | 1m 8.13 | 6 | 9-8 | Firm | Clear Praise | Aug 10 2013 |
| 7f | 1m 20.55 | 2 | 8-11 | Good To Firm | Hiking | Aug 17 2013 |
| 7f | 1m 20.05 | 3 | 8-5 | Good To Firm | Perfect Tribute | May 7 2011 |
| 7f 135y | 1m 29.32 | 2 | 9-3 | Good To Firm | Dundonnell (USA) | Aug 4 2012 |
| 7f 135y | 1m 26.73 | 3 | 8-6 | Good To Firm | Hiaam | Jly 11 1987 |
| 1m 1f | 1m 52.40 | 4 | 9-2 | Good To Firm | Quandary (USA) | Jly 15 1995 |
| 1m 2f | 2m 4.61 | 3 | 9-3 | Firm | Usran | Jly 15 1989 |
| 1m 3f 133y | 2m 23.95 | 3 | 8-5 | Firm | Night-Shirt | Jly 14 1990 |
| 1m 6f | 2m 59.10 | 5 | 9-5 | Firm | Ibn Bey | Jly 1 1989 |
| 2m 68y | 3m 23.71 | 3 | 9-5 | Good To Firm | Lauries Crusador | Aug 13 1988 |

## LINGFIELD (A.W)

| Distance | Time | Age | Weight | Going | Horse | Date |
|---|---|---|---|---|---|---|
| 5f 6y | 58.11 | 2 | 9-5 | Standard | Ivors Rebel | Sep 23 2014 |
| 5f 6y | 56.67 | 5 | 8-12 | Standard | Ladies Are Forever | Mar 16 2013 |
| 6f 1y | 1m 9.99 | 2 | 8-12 | Standard | Swiss Diva | Nov 19 2008 |
| 6f 1y | 1m 8.75 | 7 | 9-2 | Standard | Tarooq | Dec 18 2013 |
| 7f 1y | 1m 22.67 | 2 | 9-3 | Standard | Complicit | Nov 23 2013 |
| 7f 1y | 1m 21.92 | 5 | 9-6 | Standard | Grey Mirage | Feb 22 2014 |
| 1m 1y | 1m 35.84 | 2 | 9-5 | Standard | Brave Hero | Nov 25 2015 |
| 1m 1y | 1m 34.34 | 5 | 8-13 | Standard | My Target (IRE) | Dec 31 2016 |
| 1m 2f | 2m 0.99 | 4 | 9-0 | Standard | Farraaj (IRE) | Mar 16 2013 |
| 1m 4f | 2m 26.99 | 6 | 9-11 | Standard | Pinzolo | Jan 21 2017 |
| 1m 5f | 2m 39.70 | 3 | 8-10 | Standard | Hidden Gold | Oct 30 2014 |
| 1m 7f 169y | 3m 15.18 | 4 | 9-1 | Standard | Winning Story | Apr 14 2017 |

## MUSSELBURGH

| Distance | Time | Age | Weight | Going | Horse | Date |
|---|---|---|---|---|---|---|
| 5f 1y | 57.66 | 2 | 9-2 | Good To Firm | It Dont Come Easy | Jun 3 2017 |
| 5f 1y | 57.10 | 6 | 8-6 | Good To Firm | Red Baron | Jun 13 2015 |
| 7f 33y | 1m 27.46 | 2 | 8-8 | Good | Durham Reflection | Sep 14 2009 |
| 7f 33y | 1m 25.00 | 9 | 8-8 | Good To Firm | Kalk Bay | Jun 4 2016 |
| 1m 2y | 1m 40.34 | 2 | 8-12 | Good To Firm | Succession | Sep 26 2004 |
| 1m 2y | 1m 36.83 | 3 | 9-5 | Good To Firm | Ginger Jack | Jly 13 2010 |
| 1m 208y | 1m 50.42 | 8 | 8-11 | Good To Firm | Dhaular Dhar | Sep 3 2010 |
| 1m 4f 104y | 2m 36.80 | 3 | 8-3 | Good To Firm | Harris Tweed | Jun 5 2010 |
| 1m 5f | 2m 46.41 | 3 | 9-5 | Good To Firm | Alcaeus | Sep 29 2013 |
| 1m 5f 216y | 2m 57.98 | 7 | 8-5 | Good To Firm | Jonny Delta | Apr 18 2014 |
| 1m 7f 217y | 3m 25.62 | 4 | 8-3 | Good To Firm | Aldreth | Jun 13 2015 |

## NEWBURY

| Distance | Tine | Age | Weight | Going | Horse | Date |
|---|---|---|---|---|---|---|
| 5f 34y | 5[illegible].19 | 2 | 8-6 | Good To Firm | Superstar Leo | Jly 22 2000 |
| 5f 34y | 5[illegible]44 | 5 | 9-1 | Good To Firm | Robot Boy (IRE) | Apr 17 2015 |
| 6f 8y | 1m 11.07 | 2 | 8-4 | Good To Firm | Bahati (IRE) | May 30 2009 |
| 6f 8y | 1m 9.42 | 3 | 8-11 | Good To Firm | Nota Bene | May 13 2005 |
| 6f 110y | 1m 18.06 | 2 | 9-5 | Good To Firm | Twin Sails | Jun 11 2015 |
| 7f | 1m 23.04 | 2 | 8-11 | Good To Firm | Haafhd | Aug 15 2003 |
| 7f | 1m 20.80 | 3 | 9-0 | Good To Firm | Muhaarar | Apr 18 2015 |
| 1m | 1m 37.50 | 2 | 9-1 | Good To Firm | Winged Cupid (IRE) | Sep 16 2005 |
| 1m | 1m 33.59 | 6 | 9-0 | Firm | Rakti | May 14 2005 |
| 1m 7y | 1m 37.29 | 2 | 9-0 | Good | Master Willie | Oct 1 1979 |
| 1m 7y | 1m [illegible]4.90 | 3 | 8-9 | Good To Firm | Philidor | May 16 1992 |
| 1m 1f | 1m [illegible]9.65 | 3 | 8-0 | Good To Firm | Holtye | May 21 1995 |
| 1m 2f | 2m [illegible].29 | 3 | 8-7 | Good To Firm | Wall Street II | Jly 20 1996 |
| 1m 3f 5y | 2m 6.54 | 3 | 8-9 | Good To Firm | Grandera (IRE) | Sep 22 2001 |
| 1m 4f 5y | 2m 8.26 | 4 | 9-7 | Good To Firm | Azamour (IRE) | Jly 23 2005 |
| 1m 5f 61y | 2m 4.90 | 5 | 10-0 | Good To Firm | Mystic Hill | Jly 20 1996 |
| 2m | 3m 5.42 | 8 | 9-12 | Good To Firm | Moonlight Quest | Jly 19 1996 |

## NEWCASTLE (A.W)

| Distance | Time | Age | Weight | Going | Horse | Date |
|---|---|---|---|---|---|---|
| 5f | 57.[illegible] | 3 | 9-4 | Standard | First Bombardment | Oct 7 2016 |
| 6f | 1m [illegible]86 | 3 | 9-2 | Standard | Unabated | Mar 22 2017 |
| 7f 14y | 1m [illegible]48 | 4 | 9-7 | Standard | Alice Thornton | Oct 14 2016 |
| 1m 5y | 1m [illegible]28 | 5 | 9-10 | Standard | Auspicion | Sep 12 2017 |
| 1m 2f 42y | 2m [illegible]48 | 3 | 8-6 | Standard | Palisade | Oct 16 2016 |
| 1m 4f 98y | 2m [illegible]76 | 3 | 8-7 | Standard | Ajman Prince | Oct 14 2016 |
| 2m 56y | 3m [illegible]87 | 4 | 9-8 | Standard | Dannyday | Jun 25 2016 |

## NEWMARKET

| Distance | Time | Age | Weight | Going | Horse | Date |
|---|---|---|---|---|---|---|
| 5f | 58.6[illegible] | 2 | 8-12 | Good To Firm | Mrs Danvers | Oct 7 2016 |
| 5f | 56.81 | 6 | 9-2 | Good To Firm | Lochsong | Apr 30 1994 |
| 6f | 1m 9.[illegible] | 2 | 8-12 | Good To Firm | Bushranger | Oct 3 2008 |
| 6f | 1m 9.[illegible] | 3 | 9-1 | Good To Firm | Captain Colby | May 16 2015 |
| 7f | 1m 2[illegible] | 2 | 9-1 | Good | U S Navy Flag | Oct 14 2017 |
| 7f | 1m 2[illegible] | 3 | 9-0 | Good To Firm | Tupi | May 16 2015 |
| 1m | 1m 3[illegible] | 2 | 8-12 | Good | Steeler (IRE) | Sep 29 2012 |
| 1m | 1m 3[illegible] | 4 | 9-0 | Good To Firm | Eagle Mountain | Oct 3 2008 |
| 1m 1f | 1m 4[illegible] | 5 | 8-12 | Good To Firm | Manduro (GER) | Apr 19 2007 |
| 1m 2f | 2m 2.[illegible] | 2 | 9-2 | Good | Kew Gardens | Oct 14 2017 |
| 1m 2f | 2m 0.[illegible] | 3 | 8-12 | Good | New Approach (IRE) | Oct 18 2008 |
| 1m 4f | 2m 26 | 3 | 8-9 | Good To Firm | Mohedian Lady (IRE) | Sep 22 2011 |
| 1m 6f | 2m 51[illegible] | 3 | 8-7 | Good | Art Eyes (USA) | Sep 29 2005 |
| 2m | 3m 18.[illegible] | 5 | 9-6 | Good To Firm | Times Up | Sep 22 2011 |
| 2m 2f | 3m 47.[illegible] | 3 | 7-12 | Hard | Whiteway | Oct 15 1947 |
| 2m 2f | 3m 45.[illegible] | 4 | 8-8 | Good | Withhold | Oct 14 2017 |

## NEWMARKET (JULY)

| Distance | Time | Age | Weight | Going | Horse | Date |
|---|---|---|---|---|---|---|
| 5f | 58.52 | 2 | 8-10 | Good | Seductress | Jly 10 1990 |
| 5f | 56.09 | 6 | 9-11 | Good | Borderlescott | Aug 22 2008 |
| 6f | 1m 10.[illegible] | 2 | 8-11 | Good | Elnawin | Aug 22 2008 |
| 6f | 1m 9.1[illegible] | 4 | 9-5 | Good To Firm | Lethal Force | Jly 13 2013 |
| 7f | 1m 23.[illegible] | 2 | 9-1 | Good To Firm | Birchwood | Jly 11 2015 |
| 7f | 1m 22.[illegible] | 3 | 9-7 | Firm | Ho Leng (IRE) | Jly 9 1998 |
| 1m | 1m 37.[illegible] | 2 | 8-13 | Good | Whippers Love | Aug 28 2009 |
| 1m | 1m 34.[illegible] | 3 | 8-12 | Good To Firm | Alice Springs | Jly 8 2016 |
| 1m 2f | 2m 0.91 | 3 | 9-5 | Good To Firm | Maputo | Jly 11 2013 |
| 1m 4f | 2m 25.1 | 3 | 8-11 | Good | Lush Lashes | Aug 22 2008 |
| 1m 5f | 2m 40.7 | 5 | 9-10 | Good | Wadi Al Hattawi | Aug 29 2015 |
| 2m 24y | 3m 20.2 | 7 | 9-10 | Good | Yorkshire I | Jly 11 2001 |

## NOTTINGHAM

| Distance | Time | Age | Weight | Going | Horse | Date |
|---|---|---|---|---|---|---|
| 5f 8y | 59.05 | 2 | 9-0 | Good To Firm | Main Desire | May 2 2017 |
| 5f 8y | 57.90 | 2 | 8-9 | Firm | Hoh Magic | May 13 1994 |
| 5f 8y | 57.40 | 3 | 9-6 | Good To Firm | Carlton Frankie | May 2 2017 |
| 5f 8y | 57.58 | 5 | 7-11 | Good To Firm | Penny Dreadful | Jun 19 2017 |
| 6f 18y | 1m 11.40 | 2 | 8-11 | Firm | Jameelapi | Aug 8 1983 |
| 6f 18y | 1m 10.00 | 4 | 9-2 | Firm | Ajanac | Aug 8 1988 |
| 1m 72y | 1m 45.14 | 2 | 9-6 | Good | Rashford's Double | Nov 2 2016 |
| 1m 72y | 1m 43.22 | 4 | 9-7 | Good To Firm | Reaver (IRE) | Apr 22 2017 |
| 1m 75y | 1m 45.23 | 2 | 9-0 | Good To Firm | Tactfully | Sep 28 2011 |
| 1m 75y | 1m 42.25 | 5 | 9-1 | Good To Firm | Rio De La Plata | Jun 2 2010 |
| 1m 2f 50y | 2m 7.13 | 5 | 9-8 | Good To Firm | Vasily | Jly 19 2013 |
| 1m 2f 52y | 2m 16.66 | 2 | 9-3 | Soft | Lethal Glaze (IRE) | Oct 1 2008 |
| 1m 2f 52y | 2m 9.40 | 3 | 9-5 | Good | Centurius | Apr 20 2013 |
| 1m 6f | 2m 57.80 | 3 | 8-10 | Firm | Buster Jo | Oct 1 1985 |
| 2m | 3m 25.25 | 3 | 9-5 | Good | Bulwark (IRE) | Sep 27 2005 |

## PONTEFRACT

| Distance | Time | Age | Weight | Going | Horse | Date |
|---|---|---|---|---|---|---|
| 5f 3y | 1m 1.10 | 2 | 9-0 | Firm | Golden Bounty | Sep 20 2001 |
| 5f 3y | 1m 0.49 | 5 | 9-5 | Good To Firm | Judicial | Apr 24 2017 |
| 6f | 1m 14.00 | 2 | 9-3 | Firm | Fawzi | Sep 6 1983 |
| 6f | 1m 12.60 | 3 | 7-13 | Firm | Merry One | Aug 29 1970 |
| 1m 6y | 1m 42.80 | 2 | 9-0 | Firm | Alasil (USA) | Sep 26 2002 |
| 1m 6y | 1m 42.80 | 2 | 9-13 | Firm | Star Spray | Sep 6 1983 |
| 1m 6y | 1m 40.60 | 4 | 9-10 | Good To Firm | Island Light | Apr 13 2002 |
| 1m 2f 5y | 2m 10.10 | 2 | 9-0 | Firm | Shanty Star (IRE) | Oct 7 2002 |
| 1m 2f 5y | 2m 8.20 | 4 | 7-8 | Hard | Happy Hector | Jly 9 1979 |
| 1m 2f 5y | 2m 8.20 | 3 | 7-13 | Hard | Tom Noddy | Aug 21 1972 |
| 1m 4f 5y | 2m 33.72 | 3 | 8-7 | Firm | Ajaan | Aug 8 2007 |
| 2m 1f 27y | 3m 40.67 | 4 | 8-7 | Good To Firm | Paradise Flight | Jun 6 2005 |
| 2m 2f 2y | 3m 51.10 | 3 | 8-8 | Good To Firm | Kudz | Sep 9 1986 |
| 2m 5f 139y | 4m 47.80 | 4 | 8-4 | Firm | Physical | May 14 1984 |

## REDCAR

| Distance | Time | Age | Weight | Going | Horse | Date |
|---|---|---|---|---|---|---|
| 5f | 56.88 | 2 | 9-7 | Good To Soft | Wolfofwallstreet | Oct 27 2014 |
| 5f | 56.01 | 10 | 9-3 | Firm | Henry Hall | Sep 20 2006 |
| 5f 217y | 1m 8.84 | 2 | 8-3 | Good To Firm | Obe Gold | Oct 2 2004 |
| 5f 217y | 1m 8.60 | 3 | 9-2 | Good To Firm | Sizzling Saga | Jun 21 1991 |
| 7f | 1m 21.28 | 2 | 9-3 | Firm | Karoo Blue | Sep 20 2006 |
| 7f | 1m 21.00 | 3 | 9-1 | Firm | Empty Quarter | Oct 3 1995 |
| 7f 219y | 1m 34.37 | 2 | 9-0 | Firm | Mastership | Sep 20 2006 |
| 7f 219y | 1m 32.42 | 4 | 10-0 | Firm | Nanton | Sep 20 2006 |
| 1m 1f | 1m 52.44 | 2 | 9-0 | Firm | Spear (IRE) | Sep 13 2004 |
| 1m 1f | 1m 48.50 | 5 | 8-12 | Firm | Mellottie | Jly 25 1990 |
| 1m 2f 1y | 2m 10.10 | 2 | 8-11 | Good | Adding | Nov 10 1989 |
| 1m 2f 1y | 2m 1.40 | 5 | 9-2 | Firm | Eradicate | May 28 1990 |
| 1m 5f 218y | 2m 59.81 | 4 | 9-1 | Good To Firm | Esprit de Corps I | Sep 11 2006 |
| 1m 7f 217y | 3m 24.90 | 3 | 9-3 | Good To Firm | Subsonic | Oct 8 1991 |

## RIPON

| Distance | Time | Age | Weight | Going | Horse | Date |
|---|---|---|---|---|---|---|
| 5f | 57.80 | 2 | 8-8 | Firm | Super Rocky | Aug 5 1991 |
| 5f | 57.28 | 5 | 8-12 | Good | Desert Ace | Sep 24 2016 |
| 6f | 1m 10.40 | 2 | 9-2 | Good | Cumbrian Venture | Aug 17 2002 |
| 6f | 1m 9.43 | 6 | 9-10 | Good | Kimberella | Sep 24 2016 |
| 1m | 1m 38.77 | 2 | 9-4 | Good | Greed Is Good | Sep 28 2013 |
| 1m | 1m 36.62 | 4 | 8-11 | Good To Firm | Granston (IRE) | Aug 29 2005 |
| 1m 1f | 1m 49.97 | 6 | 9-3 | Good To Firm | Ginger Jack | Jun 20 2013 |
| 1m 1f 170y | 1m 59.12 | 5 | 8-9 | Good To Firm | Wahoo Sam (USA) | Aug 30 2005 |
| 1m 4f 10y | 2m 31.40 | 4 | 8-8 | Good To Firm | Dandino | Apr 16 2011 |
| 2m | 3m 27.07 | 5 | 9-12 | Good To Firm | Greenwich Meantime | Aug 30 2005 |

## SALISBURY

| Distance | Time | Age | Weight | Going | Horse | Date |
|---|---|---|---|---|---|---|
| 5f | 59.30 | 2 | 9-0 | Good To Firm | Ajigolo | May 12 2005 |
| 5f | 59.18 | 7 | 8-10 | Good To Firm | Edged Out | Jun 18 2017 |
| 6f | 1m 12.10 | 2 | 8-0 | Good To Firm | Parisian Lady (IRE) | Jun 10 1997 |
| 6f | 1m 11.09 | 3 | 9-0 | Firm | L'Ami Louis | May 1 2011 |
| 6f 213y | 1m 25.97 | 2 | 9-0 | Firm | More Royal (USA) | Jun 29 1995 |
| 6f 213y | 1m 24.91 | 3 | 9-4 | Firm | Chilworth Lad | May 1 2011 |
| 1m | 1m 40.48 | 2 | 8-13 | Firm | Choir Master (USA) | Sep 17 2002 |
| 1m | 1m 38.29 | 3 | 8-7 | Good To Firm | Layman (USA) | Aug 11 2005 |
| 1m 1f 198y | 2m 4.00 | 4 | 9-2 | Good To Firm | Chain Of Daisies | Aug 10 2016 |
| 1m 4f 5y | 2m 31.69 | 3 | 9-5 | Good To Firm | Arrive | Jun 27 2001 |
| 1m 6f 44y | 3m 0.48 | 7 | 9-2 | Good To Firm | Highland Castle | May 23 2015 |

## SANDOWN

| Distance | Time | Age | Weight | Going | Horse | Date |
|---|---|---|---|---|---|---|
| 5f 10y | 59.48 | 2 | 9-3 | Firm | Times Time | Jly 22 1982 |
| 5f 10y | 58.57 | 3 | 8-12 | Good To Firm | Battaash (IRE) | Jly 8 2017 |
| 7f | 1m 26.56 | 2 | 9-0 | Good To Firm | Raven's Pass (USA) | Sep 1 2007 |
| 7f | 1m 26.36 | 3 | 9-0 | Firm | Mawsuff | Jun 14 1986 |
| 1m 14y | 1m 41.14 | 2 | 8-11 | Good To Firm | Reference Point | Sep 23 1986 |
| 1m 14y | 1m 38.87 | 7 | 9-10 | Good To Firm | Prince Of Johanne | Jly 6 2013 |
| 1m 1f | 1m 54.63 | 2 | 8-8 | Good To Firm | French Pretender | Sep 20 1988 |
| 1m 1f | 1m 52.40 | 7 | 9-3 | Good To Firm | Bourgainville | Aug 11 2005 |
| 1m 1f 209y | 2m 2.14 | 4 | 8-11 | Good | Kalaglow | May 31 1982 |
| 1m 6f | 2m 56.90 | 4 | 8-7 | Good To Firm | Lady Rosanna | Jly 19 1989 |
| 2m 50y | 3m 29.38 | 6 | 9-0 | Good To Firm | Caucus | Jly 6 2013 |

## SOUTHWELL (A.W)

| Distance | Time | Age | Weight | Going | Horse | Date |
|---|---|---|---|---|---|---|
| 4f 214y | 57.85 | 2 | 9-3 | Standard | Arctic Feeling | Mar 31 2010 |
| 4f 214y | 56.80 | 5 | 9-7 | Standard | Ghostwing | Jan 3 2012 |
| 6f 16y | 1m 14.00 | 2 | 8-5 | Standard | Panalo | Nov 8 1989 |
| 6f 16y | 1m 13.50 | 4 | 10-0 | Standard | Saladan Knight | Dec 30 1989 |
| 7f 14y | 1m 26.82 | 2 | 8-12 | Standard | Winged Icarus | Aug 28 2012 |
| 7f 14y | 1m 26.38 | 4 | 8-6 | Standard | Moon River | Mar 30 2016 |
| 1m 13y | 1m 38.00 | 2 | 8-9 | Standard | Alpha Rascal | Nov 13 1990 |
| 1m 13y | 1m 38.00 | 2 | 8-10 | Standard | Andrew's First | Dec 30 1989 |
| 1m 13y | 1m 37.25 | 3 | 8-6 | Standard | Valira | Nov 3 1990 |
| 1m 3f 23y | 2m 21.50 | 4 | 9-7 | Standard | Tempering | Dec 5 1990 |
| 1m 4f 14y | 2m 33.90 | 4 | 9-12 | Standard | Fast Chick | Nov 8 1989 |
| 1m 6f 21y | 3m 1.60 | 3 | 7-8 | Standard | Erevnon | Dec 29 1990 |
| 2m 102y | 3m 37.60 | 9 | 8-12 | Standard | Old Hubert | Dec 5 1990 |

## THIRSK

| Distance | Time | Age | Weight | Going | Horse | Date |
|---|---|---|---|---|---|---|
| 5f | 57.20 | 2 | 9-7 | Good To Firm | Proud Boast | Aug 5 2000 |
| 5f | 56.92 | 5 | 9-6 | Firm | Charlie Parkes | Apr 11 2003 |
| 6f | 1m 9.20 | 2 | 9-6 | Good To Firm | Westcourt Magic | Aug 25 1995 |
| 6f | 1m 8.80 | 6 | 9-4 | Firm | Johayro | Jly 23 1999 |
| 7f | 1m 23.70 | 2 | 8-9 | Firm | Courting | Jly 23 1999 |
| 7f | 1m 22.80 | 4 | 8-5 | Firm | Silver Haze I | May 21 1988 |
| 7f 218y | 1m 37.97 | 2 | 9-0 | Firm | Sunday Symphony | Sep 4 2004 |
| 7f 218y | 1m 34.80 | 4 | 8-13 | Firm | Yearsley I | May 5 1990 |
| 1m 4f 8y | 2m 29.90 | 5 | 9-12 | Firm | Gallery God | Jun 4 2001 |
| 2m 13y | 3m 22.30 | 3 | 9-0 | Firm | Tomaschek | Jly 17 1981 |

## WETHERBY

| Distance | Time | Age | Weight | Going | Horse | Date |
|---|---|---|---|---|---|---|
| 5f 110y | 1m 4.25 | 3 | 9-1 | Good To Firm | Dapper Man (IRE) | Jun 19 2017 |
| 7f | 1m 24.72 | 4 | 9-2 | Good | Slemy | Jly 21 2015 |
| 1m | 1m 38.82 | 3 | 8-13 | Good To Firm | Al Nafoorah | Jun 19 2017 |
| 1m 2f | 2m 5.13 | 5 | 9-5 | Good | First Sargeant | Jly 21 2015 |
| 1m 6f | 3m 0.41 | 3 | 9-7 | Good To Firm | Davy's Dilemma | Jun 19 2017 |

## WINDSOR

| Distance | Time | Age | Weight | Going | Horse | Date |
|---|---|---|---|---|---|---|
| 5f 21y | 58.69 | 2 | 9-0 | Good To Firm | Charles The Great | May 23 2011 |
| 5f 21y | 58.08 | 5 | 8-13 | Good To Firm | Taurus Twins | Apr 4 2011 |
| 6f 12y | 1m 10.50 | 2 | 9-5 | Good To Firm | Cubism I | Aug 17 1998 |
| 6f 12y | 1m 9.58 | 7 | 9-0 | Good To Firm | Tropics | Jun 1 2015 |
| 1m 31y | 1m 41.73 | 2 | 9-5 | Good To Firm | Salouen | Aug 7 2016 |
| 1m 31y | 1m 39.81 | 5 | 9-7 | Good | French Navy | Jun 29 2013 |
| 1m 1f 194y | 2m 1.62 | 6 | 9-1 | Good | Al Kazeem | Aug 23 2014 |
| 1m 3f 99y | 2m 21.50 | 3 | 9-2 | Firm | Double Florin | May 19 1980 |

## WOLVERHAMPTON (A.W)

| Distance | Time | Age | Weight | Going | Horse | Date |
|---|---|---|---|---|---|---|
| 5f 21y | 59.75 | 2 | 9-6 | Standard | Quatrieme Ami | Nov 13 2015 |
| 5f 21y | 59.39 | 5 | 9-8 | Standard | Boom The Groom | Feb 22 2016 |
| 6f 20y | 1m 12.67 | 2 | 9-6 | Standard | Parkour (IRE) | Nov 14 2015 |
| 6f 20y | 1m 11.84 | 3 | 8-6 | Standard | Pretend | Dec 19 2014 |
| 7f 36y | 1m 27.53 | 2 | 9-5 | Standard | Always Welcome | Dec 22 2015 |
| 7f 36y | 1m 25.35 | 4 | 9-3 | Standard | Mister Universe | Mar 12 2016 |
| 1m 142y | 1m 47.38 | 2 | 9-5 | Standard | Jack Hobbs | Dec 27 2014 |
| 1m 142y | 1m 45.43 | 4 | 9-4 | Standard | Keystroke | Nov 26 2016 |
| 1m 1f 104y | 1m 56.64 | 8 | 8-13 | Standard | Perfect Cracker | Mar 19 2016 |
| 1m 4f 51y | 2m 33.92 | 3 | 8-13 | Standard | Natural Scenery | Oct 21 2016 |
| 1m 5f 194y | 2m 58.68 | 3 | 9-2 | Standard | Instrumentalist | Oct 9 2012 |
| 1m 5f 194y | 2m 57.55 | 6 | 9-7 | Standard | Entihaa | Dec 6 2014 |
| 2m 120y | 3m 33.34 | 4 | 9-0 | Standard | Moonrise Landing | Dec 12 2015 |

## YARMOUTH

| Distance | Time | Age | Weight | Going | Horse | Date |
|---|---|---|---|---|---|---|
| 5f 42y | 1m 0.40 | 2 | 8-6 | Good To Firm | Ebba | Jly 26 1999 |
| 5f 42y | 59.80 | 4 | 8-13 | Good To Firm | Roxanne Mill | Aug 25 2002 |
| 6f 3y | 1m 10.40 | 2 | 9-0 | Firm | Lanchester (USA) | Sep 15 1988 |
| 6f 3y | 1m 9.14 | 3 | 9-0 | Good To Firm | Cartographer | May 24 2017 |
| 7f 3y | 1m 22.20 | 2 | 9-0 | Good To Firm | Warrshan | Sep 14 1988 |
| 7f 3y | 1m 22.12 | 4 | 9-4 | Good To Firm | Glenbuck (IRE) | Apr 26 2007 |
| 1m 3y | 1m 36.30 | 2 | 8-2 | Firm | Out Run | Sep 15 1988 |
| 1m 3y | 1m 33.90 | 3 | 8-8 | Firm | Bonne Etoile | Jun 27 1995 |
| 1m 1f 21y | 1m 52.00 | 3 | 9-5 | Good To Firm | Touch Gold | Jly 5 2012 |
| 1m 2f 23y | 2m 2.83 | 3 | 8-8 | Firm | Reunite | Jly 18 2006 |
| 1m 3f 104y | 2m 23.10 | 3 | 8-9 | Firm | Rahil I | Jly 1 1993 |
| 1m 6f 17y | 2m 57.80 | 3 | 8-2 | Good To Firm | Barakat | Jly 24 1990 |
| 2m | 3m 26.70 | 4 | 8-2 | Good To Firm | Alhesn (USA) | Jly 26 1999 |

## YORK

| Distance | Time | Age | Weight | Going | Horse | Date |
|---|---|---|---|---|---|---|
| 5f | 57.11 | 2 | 9-0 | Good | Big Time Baby | Aug 20 2016 |
| 5f | 56.16 | 3 | 9-3 | Good To Firm | Dayjur | Aug 23 1990 |
| 5f 89y | 1m 3.20 | 2 | 9-3 | Good To Firm | The Art Of Racing | Sep 9 2012 |
| 5f 89y | 1m 1.72 | 4 | 9-7 | Good To Firm | Bogart | Aug 21 2013 |
| 6f | 1m 8.90 | 2 | 9-0 | Good | Tiggy Wiggy | Aug 21 2014 |
| 6f | 1m 8.23 | 3 | 8-11 | Good To Firm | Mince | Sep 9 2012 |
| 7f | 1m 22.32 | 2 | 9-1 | Good To Firm | Dutch Connection | Aug 20 2014 |
| 7f | 1m 21.83 | 4 | 9-8 | Good To Firm | Dimension | Jly 28 2012 |
| 7f 192y | 1m 36.92 | 2 | 9-5 | Good | Awesometank | Oct 14 2017 |
| 7f 192y | 1m 35.10 | 4 | 8-12 | Good | Home Cummins | Jly 9 2016 |
| 1m 177y | 1m 46.76 | 5 | 9-8 | Good To Firm | Echo Of Light | Sep 5 2007 |
| 1m 2f 56y | 2m 5.29 | 3 | 8-11 | Good To Firm | Sea The Stars (IR) | Aug 18 2009 |
| 1m 3f 188y | 2m 26.28 | 6 | 8-9 | Firm | Bandari (IRE) | Jun 18 2005 |
| 1m 5f 188y | 2m 54.96 | 4 | 9-0 | Good To Firm | Tactic | May 22 2010 |
| 2m 56y | 3m 28.97 | 5 | 9-5 | Good To Firm | Gabrial's King | Jly 12 2014 |

# SPLIT SECOND SPEED RATINGS

The following lists the fastest performances of 3yo+ and 2yo horses which have recorded a speed figure of 105 or over during the 2017 season. Additional information in the parentheses following the speed figure shows the distance of the race in furlongs, course, state of going and the date on which the figure was achieved.

## THREE YEAR-OLDS PLUS
### Turf

**A Momentofmadness 116** *(5f,Goo,G,Aug 1)*
**Abareeq 108** *(10f,Eps,G,Apr 26)*
**Abdon 110** *(10f,Nby,S,Oct 28)*
**Abingdon 114** *(12f,Pon,GF,Jun 25)*
**Above The Rest 111** *(7f,Nmk,GF,Jly 15)*
**Absolute Blast 111** *(8½f,Eps,G,Jun 3)*
**Absolutely So 114** *(7f,Hay,G,May 13)*
**Abstraction 105** *(5f,Cur,GF,Jly 29)*
**Abushamah 113** *(8f,Hay,G,Jun 15)*
**Acapulco 117** *(5f,Cur,G,May 14)*
**Accalia 105** *(5f,Cur,G,Jly 2)*
**Accidental Agent 110** *(7f,Nby,G,Sep 22)*
**Acclaim The Nation 109** *(5f,Don,GF,Apr 28)*
**Aclaim 115** *(7f,Cha,S,Oct 1)*
**Across Dubai 109** *(10½f,Hay,GF,Jly 8)*
**Across The Stars 108** *(12f,Asc,GF,Jun 24)*
**Acrux 106** *(7f,Don,G,Aug 19)*
**Addeybb 121** *(10f,Goo,S,Aug 3)*
**Addicted To You 108** *(16f,Nmk,GS,Aug 12)*
**Adjective 106** *(12f,Nmk,S,Jly 22)*
**Aeolus 112** *(6f,Don,GS,Oct 27)*
**Afaak 108** *(8f,Don,S,Jun 3)*
**Afjaan 116** *(7f,Hay,GF,Apr 29)*
**Age Of Elegance 109** *(10½f,Chs,G,Jly 15)*
**Agent Murphy 105** *(13f,Nby,S,Aug 19)*
**Aim To Please 106** *(9f,Nmk,GF,May 7)*
**Air Pilot 114** *(10f,Nmk,GS,Nov 4)*
**Airton 107** *(12f,Pon,G,Aug 20)*
**Ajman Princess 114** *(10f,Dea,G,Aug 20)*
**Al Destoor 106** *(12f,Don,S,Nov 11)*
**Al Jazi 109** *(6f,Asc,GF,Jun 24)*
**Al Nafoorah 110** *(8½f,Not,GS,Jly 25)*
**Al Neksh 116** *(10f,Yor,S,May 17)*
**Al Qahwa 114** *(6f,Yor,S,May 17)*
**Al Wukair 111** *(8f,Nmk,GF,May 6)*
**Alaadel 112** *(6f,Nby,S,Oct 27)*
**Alabaster 105** *(14f,Mus,GF,Jun 3)*
**Alejandro 106** *(8f,Pon,GF,Apr 24)*
**Alemaratalyoum 105** *(8f,Chp,S,Sep 14)*
**Alexander M 106** *(10f,Bev,GF,Aug 16)*
**Alexios Komnenos 112** *(8f,Leo,G,Sep 9)*
**Alfarris 105** *(12f,Asc,G,Jly 15)*
**Alfred Hutchinson 105** *(8f,Hay,GF,Apr 29)*
**Alfredo Arcano 105** *(6f,Cur,G,May 13)*
**Algaith 110** *(8½f,Not,G,May 31)*
**Algometer 110** *(10f,San,GF,May 25)*
**Aljazzi 111** *(8f,San,G,Sep 2)*
**Aljezeera 106** *(12f,Yor,GS,Aug 24)*
**Aljuljalah 109** *(7f,Hay,GF,Jly 8)*
**Alkhor 107** *(6f,Wdr,G,May 15)*
**Allez Henri 108** *(10f,Asc,GF,Jun 24)*
**Alluringly 109** *(8f,Nmk,G,Oct 7)*
**Alnasl 106** *(8½f,Eps,G,Sep 14)*
**Alpha Delphini 111** *(5f,Bev,S,Sep 26)*
**Alphabet 119** *(5f,Cur,SH,Sep 10)*
**Alphabetical Order 105** *(12f,Bev,GF,Aug 16)*
**Alpine Dream 106** *(7½f,Chs,GS,Jun 10)*
**Alqalsar 105** *(8½f,Not,GF,Jun 15)*
**Alqamar 107** *(12f,Yor,S,May 19)*
**Altaayil 106** *(16f,Asc,GS,Oct 6)*
**Altharoos 111** *(8½f,Bev,GF,May 31)*
**Alwahsh 112** *(8½f,Not,GF,Jun 15)*
**Always Thankful 107** *(8f,Hay,GS,Aug 10)*
**Alyssa 109** *(16f,San,GF,Jly 8)*
**Amazour 109** *(6½f,Don,GS,Sep 15)*
**American Hope 108** *(8f,Mey,G,Feb 2)*
**Amlad 107** *(12f,Pon,G,Aug 20)*
**Amy Blair 112** *(8f,Ham,GF,May 19)*
**An Saighdiur 108** *(7f,Cur,YS,Aug 19)*
**Anaerobio 108** *(7f,Mey,G,Jan 19)*
**Anahita 108** *(8f,Mey,G,Jan 26)*
**Ancient Longing 107** *(10f,Sal,S,Jly 29)*
**Angel Down 109** *(8f,Wdr,G,Aug 13)*
**Angel Gabrial 110** *(16f,Bev,GF,Jly 18)*
**Angel Of Darkness 106** *(7f,Yor,GS,Aug 24)*
**Angel's Quest 108** *(8f,Nmk,GF,Jun 24)*
**Angelical 110** *(10f,Lin,GF,Jun 24)*
**Annie Salts 108** *(5f,Yar,GF,Aug 1)*
**Another Eclipse 107** *(10f,Don,G,Aug 5)*
**Another Touch 115** *(8½f,Not,G,May 31)*
**Anythingtoday 113** *(10f,Goo,G,Aug 27)*
**Apparition 106** *(12f,Cur,GF,Jly 29)*
**Appeared 108** *(12f,Asc,GF,Jun 23)*
**Apphia 111** *(12f,Nmk,S,Jly 22)*
**Appointed 107** *(10f,Yor,GS,Jly 29)*
**Aprovado 106** *(5f,Crl,GF,Jly 13)*
**Arabian Hope 111** *(8f,Yor,GF,Jun 17)*
**Arcadian Sea 110** *(14f,Lin,S,Jly 29)*
**Arcanada 108** *(8f,Yor,G,Jly 15)*
**Archetype 115** *(10f,Goo,S,Aug 3)*
**Archi's Affaire 108** *(11f,Ham,GS,Jly 15)*
**Archie 105** *(8f,Nby,S,Aug 18)*
**Archimedes 106** *(5f,Don,GF,Jly 13)*
**Archipeligo 107** *(9f,Ham,G,Jun 1)*
**Archippos 106** *(10f,Don,G,Apr 2)*
**Architecture 107** *(11f,Nby,G,Sep 23)*
**Ardhoomey 116** *(5f,Cur,G,May 14)*
**Areen Heart 109** *(8f,Hay,GF,Jly 7)*
**Ariena 105** *(7f,Nmk,GF,Aug 26)*
**Arsenio Lupin 107** *(8½f,Not,G,May 13)*
**Art Collection 115** *(6f,Don,GF,May 6)*
**Art Echo 105** *(7f,Nmk,G,Aug 4)*
**Art Obsession 106** *(6f,Thi,GF,May 6)*
**Art Wave 106** *(8f,Mey,G,Jan 12)*
**Artful Rogue 105** *(10f,San,GF,Jun 16)*
**Arthenus 109** *(12f,Asc,GS,Oct 7)*
**Arthur Mc Bride 110** *(20½f,Goo,GS,Aug 2)*
**Artigiano 110** *(10f,Mey,G,Jan 19)*
**Artscape 108** *(6f,Goo,GS,Jun 9)*
**Arty Campbell 106** *(16f,Chp,GS,Aug 17)*
**Arzaak 113** *(5f,Not,GF,May 2)*
**Asaas 105** *(9f,Lin,GF,Jun 13)*
**Ashadihan 105** *(7f,Lin,G,May 13)*
**Ashiana 114** *(10f,Cha,S,Oct 1)*
**Ashpan Sam 105** *(6f,Nby,S,May 19)*
**Ask The Guru 107** *(5f,Bat,GF,Jly 12)*
**Asking 110** *(7f,Cur,GY,Jly 1)*
**Atkinson Grimshaw 105** *(10f,Nmk,GS,Aug 12)*
**Atlas 107** *(8f,Leo,G,Aug 17)*
**Atletico 113** *(5f,Goo,G,Aug 1)*
**Attain 106** *(10f,Bat,F,Jun 23)*
**Attendu 108** *(7f,Cha,S,Oct 1)*
**Attention Seaker 106** *(16f,Bev,G,Aug 17)*
**Atteq 109** *(7f,Ayr,G,Jun 24)*
**Atty Persse 108** *(12f,Asc,GF,Jun 22)*
**Auntie Barber 105** *(8f,Nmk,GF,Jun 24)*
**Aurora Butterfly 108** *(12f,Cur,GF,Jly 15)*
**Aurora Gray 111** *(20½f,Goo,GS,Aug 2)*
**Aussie Valentine 107** *(8f,Cur,G,Jly 1)*
**Autocratic 111** *(10f,San,GF,May 25)*
**Aventinus 107** *(7f,Goo,G,Jun 11)*
**Avilius 116** *(10f,Cha,S,Sep 30)*
**Awake My Soul 114** *(10f,Yor,S,May 17)*
**Ayr Of Elegance 105** *(16f,Nmk,GF,Nov 3)*
**Ayrad 115** *(10f,San,GF,Jly 7)*
**Azaly 107** *(8f,Nmk,S,Aug 5)*
**Azari 111** *(10f,Yor,G,Oct 14)*

**Baashiq 111** *(10f,Nby,S,Jly 27)*
**Babyfact 108** *(6f,Bat,G,Jly 26)*
**Baccarat 111** *(6f,Mey,G,Jan 26)*
**Bacchus 108** *(6f,Asc,GS,Oct 6)*
**Badenscoth 105** *(8½f,Not,GS,Jun 11)*
**Bahamadam 105** *(7f,Lei,GS,May 30)*
**Bahamian Dollar 111** *(6f,Wdr,GS,May 29)*
**Bahamian Sunrise 105** *(5f,San,S,Jly 26)*
**Bainne 110** *(7f,Leo,S,Apr 5)*
**Balashakh 108** *(12f,Sal,GF,Jly 15)*
**Ballard Down 115** *(8f,Nmk,S,Jly 22)*
**Ballesteros 107** *(6f,Wdr,S,Oct 23)*
**Ballet Concerto 112** *(8f,Hay,HY,Sep 9)*
**Balmoral Castle 105** *(10f,Nby,G,Sep 22)*
**Banditry 112** *(10f,Eps,G,Apr 26)*
**Banish 105** *(10f,San,GF,Jly 7)*
**Banksea 115** *(8f,Nby,GF,Apr 22)*
**Baraweez 107** *(8f,Yor,GS,Aug 24)*
**Barney Roy 116** *(7f,Nby,GF,Apr 22)*
**Baron Bolt 111** *(6f,Nby,S,Oct 27)*
**Baroot 108** *(9f,Mey,G,Jan 28)*
**Barrington 109** *(6f,Yar,GF,Aug 1)*
**Barsanti 114** *(12f,Asc,GF,Jun 24)*
**Barwell 106** *(12f,Thi,S,Sep 9)*
**Basateen 109** *(14f,Mey,G,Feb 23)*
**Bashiba 108** *(5f,Don,GF,Apr 28)*
**Basil Berry 106** *(10f,Yar,G,Jly 19)*
**Bateel 117** *(12f,Cha,S,Sep 10)*
**Battaash 121** *(5f,Goo,S,Aug 4)*
**Batten The Hatches 110** *(5f,Not,GF,May 2)*
**Battered 110** *(7f,Goo,S,Aug 5)*
**Battle Of Marathon 106** *(9f,Nmk,GS,Sep 30)*
**Bay Of Poets 105** *(10½f,Chs,GF,May 12)*
**Bay Of Skaill 111** *(7f,Leo,GF,Jly 13)*
**Baydar 106** *(12f,Hay,GF,Jly 8)*
**Bazwind 105** *(8½f,Not,GS,Jun 11)*
**Be Bold 106** *(6f,Cat,S,Jly 26)*
**Be Kool 109** *(8f,Ham,GF,May 7)*
**Be Perfect 107** *(12f,Cat,GF,Apr 12)*
**Beach Break 107** *(12f,Cat,GF,Jun 2)*
**Beaming 106** *(7f,Leo,GF,Jly 13)*
**Bean Feasa 108** *(8f,Leo,GF,May 7)*
**Bear Valley 106** *(12f,Asc,GS,Aug 12)*
**Beardwood 111** *(10f,Nmk,G,Jun 10)*
**Beat The Bank 115** *(8f,Goo,S,Aug 4)*
**Beatbybeatbybeat 107** *(8½f,Not,GS,Oct 11)*
**Beautiful Morning 111** *(10f,Yar,S,Sep 20)*
**Beautiful Romance 114** *(16f,Mey,Y,Mar 25)*
**Beauty Energy 107** *(8f,Nmk,GF,May 6)*
**Becca Campbell 110** *(10f,Lin,GF,Jun 13)*
**Bedouin 111** *(10f,Nby,S,Jly 27)*
**Beechmount Whisper 113** *(7f,Leo,S,Apr 5)*
**Belgian Bill 109** *(10f,Mey,G,Feb 2)*
**Belgravia 110** *(12f,Leo,GF,May 7)*
**Belledesert 105** *(6f,Bat,F,Jun 28)*
**Bellevarde 107** *(6f,Hay,S,Jun 10)*
**Benbatl 115** *(12f,Asc,GS,Jly 29)*
**Bengal Lancer 107** *(7f,Sal,G,Aug 25)*
**Berghain 106** *(16f,San,GF,May 25)*
**Berkshire 107** *(10f,Nmk,G,Jun 10)*
**Berkshire Boy 106** *(7f,Chp,GS,Sep 19)*
**Bernie's Boy 106** *(7f,Cat,S,Jly 26)*
**Berrahri 105** *(14½f,Don,GS,Oct 27)*
**Bertiewhittle 111** *(7f,Asc,GS,Sep 9)*
**Best Fouad 111** *(10f,Cha,G,Apr 9)*
**Best Of Days 112** *(12f,Nmk,GS,Sep 29)*
**Best Solution 113** *(12f,Nby,S,Oct 28)*
**Betsalottie 110** *(10f,Lin,GF,Jun 24)*
**Betty Loch 106** *(7f,Cur,GY,Jly 1)*
**Beverley Bullet 105** *(7f,Crl,HY,Sep 18)*
**Bianca Minola 106** *(12f,Ffo,HY,Aug 15)*
**Big Baz 111** *(8f,Nby,GF,Apr 22)*
**Big Country 113** *(10f,Yor,G,Oct 14)*
**Big Orange 114** *(16f,Goo,G,Aug 1)*
**Big Time 108** *(6f,Don,GS,Oct 27)*
**Big Tour 113** *(10f,Nby,S,Jly 27)*
**Billesdon Bess 109** *(10f,Sal,GF,Aug 16)*
**Billy Bond 110** *(8f,Ham,GF,May 19)*
**Billy Roberts 105** *(8f,Pon,G,Apr 11)*
**Bin Battuta 113** *(10f,Don,G,Apr 2)*
**Bint Arcano 108** *(7f,Hay,GF,Jly 8)*
**Birchwood 112** *(7f,Asc,GS,Sep 9)*
**Black Bess 113** *(7f,San,S,Aug 10)*
**Black Caesar 106** *(7f,Bri,G,Sep 4)*
**Black Dave 109** *(7½f,Lin,G,May 24)*
**Black Ruby 105** *(10f,Cur,G,May 14)*
**Blaine 118** *(6f,Nby,S,May 19)*
**Blair House 110** *(8f,Asc,GF,Jun 21)*
**Blairmayne 107** *(6f,Cur,S,Sep 10)*
**Blakeney Point 110** *(12f,Nby,G,Sep 22)*
**Blazed 106** *(6f,Don,G,Aug 19)*
**Bless Him 107** *(8f,Asc,GF,Jun 22)*
**Bletchley 107** *(7f,Lei,GS,Jun 5)*
**Blithe Spirit 106** *(5f,Chs,GS,Jly 29)*
**Blond Me 117** *(10f,Goo,S,Aug 3)*
**Blue Bayou 109** *(6f,Don,GS,Apr 1)*
**Blue Point 122** *(6f,Asc,GF,May 3)*
**Bogart 105** *(5f,Yor,G,Oct 13)*
**Bolder Bob 105** *(12f,Bev,S,Sep 20)*
**Bonnie Arlene 105** *(10f,Pon,G,May 26)*
**Boom The Groom 106** *(5f,Eps,G,Jun 3)*
**Boomshackerlacker 108** *(8f,Goo,S,Aug 4)*
**Boots And Spurs 108** *(9f,Goo,S,Aug 5)*
**Born To Be Alive 110** *(9f,Goo,S,Aug 5)*
**Born To Boom 107** *(8f,Crl,GS,Aug 23)*
**Born To Please 105** *(8f,San,GS,Aug 2)*
**Bossipop 109** *(6f,Pon,S,Jly 30)*
**Bossy Guest 113** *(8f,Nby,GF,Apr 22)*
**Bounce 110** *(5f,Yor,G,Jly 15)*
**Bound For Nowhere 105** *(6f,Asc,GF,Jun 23)*
**Boundsy 110** *(5f,Don,GS,Oct 28)*
**Bowson Fred 109** *(5f,Nby,GF,Apr 21)*
**Boy In The Bar 115** *(6f,Nby,S,May 19)*
**Boy Royal 106** *(15f,Cha,GS,Sep 30)*
**Boycie 111** *(10f,San,GF,May 25)*
**Boynton 113** *(10f,Nmk,GS,Nov 4)*
**Braes Of Lochalsh 105** *(13f,Ayr,G,Jun 23)*
**Brametot 115** *(12f,Cha,S,Oct 1)*
**Brando 112** *(6f,Asc,S,Oct 21)*
**Brandon Castle 109** *(14f,Cat,GS,Sep 23)*
**Bravery 111** *(8f,Don,GS,Apr 1)*
**Bravo Zolo 110** *(7f,Mey,G,Feb 23)*
**Break The Silence 106** *(7f,Red,S,Nov 7)*
**Breakable 111** *(7f,Asc,GS,Sep 9)*
**Breanski 115** *(9f,Yor,G,Jly 28)*
**Breathe Easy 106** *(12f,Cur,GF,Jly 15)*
**Breden 109** *(10f,Nby,G,Sep 22)*
**Brendan Brackan 112** *(8f,Leo,YS,Jun 8)*
**Breton Rock 112** *(8f,Nby,S,May 20)*
**Brian The Snail 109** *(6f,Pon,G,Apr 11)*
**Briardale 112** *(10f,Red,G,May 29)*
**Brigliadoro 108** *(8f,Nby,S,May 20)*
**Brilliant Vanguard 109** *(8f,Rip,G,Aug 28)*
**Brimham Rocks 109** *(12f,Hay,S,Jun 8)*
**Brogan 113** *(7f,Hay,GS,Jun 14)*
**Bronze Angel 107** *(8f,Lei,GS,Oct 30)*
**Brorocco 113** *(10f,Nby,G,Sep 23)*
**Bryght Boy 107** *(7f,Lei,GS,Jun 5)*
**Bubbly Bellini 107** *(7f,Leo,S,Apr 5)*
**Buccaneers Vault 107** *(6f,Thi,GS,Jun 5)*
**Bumbasina 105** *(8f,Cur,GF,Jly 16)*
**Bumptious 107** *(7½f,Ffo,GS,Jly 25)*
**Burguillos 111** *(12f,Yor,S,May 19)*
**Burnt Sugar 114** *(6f,Don,GF,May 6)*
**Burrishoole Abbey 105** *(6f,Ayr,GF,May 9)*
**Bush House 108** *(10f,Don,G,Apr 2)*
**Busker 106** *(12f,Mey,G,Jan 26)*
**Busy Street 109** *(13f,Ham,GF,May 7)*
**Buthela 107** *(8f,Cha,S,Sep 30)*
**Butterflies 105** *(10f,Cur,G,May 13)*
**Buxted Dream 105** *(6f,Bri,GS,Aug 22)*
**Buyer Beware 106** *(14f,Mus,GF,May 26)*
**Buying Trouble 107** *(6f,Don,GS,Apr 1)*
**Buzz 106** *(10f,San,G,Jly 19)*
**Buzz Lightyere 105** *(10f,Lin,GS,Jly 19)*

**C'Est No Mour 113** *(10f,Lin,GF,Jun 13)*
**Cachao 107** *(8f,Mey,G,Jan 28)*
**Cadeaux Boxer 105** *(8f,Nby,S,Aug 18)*
**Cafe Royal 111** *(10f,Cha,G,Apr 9)*
**Calder Prince 114** *(8f,Hay,G,Jun 15)*
**Calderon 109** *(10f,San,GF,May 25)*
**Call To Mind 114** *(15f,Cha,GS,Sep 30)*
**Camerone 106** *(12f,Don,S,Sep 14)*
**Canary Row 108** *(7f,Cur,YS,Aug 19)*
**Canberra Cliffs 106** *(10f,Red,S,Nov 7)*
**Candelisa 110** *(8f,Don,GS,Apr 1)*
**Cannonball 112** *(12f,Leo,GY,Sep 9)*
**Cap Verite 108** *(15f,Cha,GS,Sep 30)*
**Cape Coast 107** *(12f,Asc,G,Jly 15)*
**Caponova 108** *(10f,Hay,GF,Apr 29)*
**Capri 117** *(14½f,Don,GS,Sep 16)*
**Capricious Cantor 111** *(12f,Nmk,S,Jly 22)*
**Captain Colby 109** *(6f,Don,GS,Apr 1)*
**Captain Courageous 105** *(8f,Hay,GF,Jun 24)*
**Captain Cullen 105** *(8f,Cur,G,Aug 7)*
**Captain Dion 111** *(6f,Pon,HY,Sep 28)*
**Captain Hawk 110** *(7f,Hay,GS,Jun 14)*
**Captain Revelation 109** *(8f,Hay,S,Jun 9)*
**Captain Ryan 105** *(5f,Bat,GF,Jly 12)*
**Captain Scooby 109** *(5f,Ffo,HY,Aug 3)*
**Capton 107** *(10f,San,G,Sep 15)*
**Caravaggio 121** *(5f,Cur,SH,Sep 10)*
**Carbon Dating 109** *(16f,Mey,G,Feb 2)*
**Card High 108** *(14f,Crl,S,Jun 9)*
**Carigrad 108** *(10½f,Hay,GF,Jly 8)*
**Carlton Frankie 116** *(5f,Not,GF,May 2)*
**Carnageo 107** *(8f,Crl,GS,Jun 28)*
**Carntop 106** *(12f,Hay,GF,Jly 8)*
**Carry On Deryck 109** *(9f,Nmk,GS,Sep 30)*
**Cartographer 106** *(6f,Yar,GF,May 24)*
**Case Key 107** *(6f,Yar,G,Jly 19)*
**Casement 111** *(8f,Goo,S,Oct 15)*
**Casla 106** *(8f,Cur,G,Jun 30)*
**Caspian Prince 116** *(5f,Cur,SH,Sep 10)*
**Cassells Rock 107** *(15f,Leo,G,Aug 10)*
**Casterton 110** *(15f,Cha,GS,Sep 30)*
**Catastrophe 105** *(9f,Ham,GS,Aug 5)*
**Catcher On The Go 107** *(12f,Ffo,HY,Aug 3)*
**Celebration 109** *(5f,Cur,G,Jly 2)*
**Celestial Spheres 106** *(10f,Nmk,GF,Nov 3)*
**Cenotaph 106** *(7f,Cur,GF,Jly 15)*
**Central Square 109** *(10f,Asc,GF,Jun 24)*
**Century Dream 111** *(10f,Nby,S,Oct 28)*
**Ceol Na Nog 108** *(10f,Leo,GF,Jly 13)*
**Certificate 112** *(7f,Hay,G,May 13)*
**Chain Of Daisies 110** *(10f,Nmk,G,Oct 13)*
**Champagne Champ 105** *(14f,Not,GS,Aug 18)*
**Championship 116** *(7f,Mey,G,Jan 19)*
**Chaplin Bay 106** *(7f,Ayr,G,Aug 12)*
**Charles Molson 107** *(7f,Goo,GF,May 6)*
**Chatez 107** *(8f,Lei,GS,Oct 30)*
**Chebsey Beau 105** *(14f,Mus,GF,Sep 8)*
**Cheerfilly 108** *(7f,Lei,GF,Jly 8)*
**Chelsea Lad 113** *(10f,Yor,G,Oct 14)*
**Chelwood Gate 108** *(7½f,Lin,G,May 24)*
**Chemical Charge 114** *(12f,Nby,GF,Apr 22)*
**Chessman 108** *(7f,Hay,F,May 27)*
**Cheval Blanche 108** *(7f,Sal,F,Apr 30)*
**Chickenfortea 106** *(6f,Cat,GS,Jly 12)*
**Chiefofchiefs 109** *(8f,Yor,G,Jly 15)*
**Chipping 108** *(6f,Ayr,G,Jun 24)*
**Chocolate Box 105** *(12f,Nby,G,Jun 15)*
**Chosen Character 113** *(8f,Hay,S,Jun 9)*
**Churchill 116** *(10f,Leo,G,Sep 9)*
**Ciaoadiosimdone 107** *(8f,Nmk,GS,Sep 29)*
**Circuitous 110** *(7f,Ayr,G,Jun 23)*
**Classic Collection 109** *(9f,Mey,G,Jan 28)*
**Classic Pursuit 105** *(5f,Not,G,Aug 15)*
**Classic Seniority 115** *(6f,Don,GF,May 6)*
**Classical Times 105** *(6f,Red,GF,May 4)*
**Clear Spring 111** *(6f,Nby,S,May 19)*
**Clem Fandango 111** *(5f,Mus,GS,Oct 9)*
**Clever Cookie 117** *(18f,Don,GS,Sep 15)*
**Cliff Bay 105** *(8f,Ham,GF,Jun 21)*
**Cliffs Of Moher 116** *(10f,Leo,G,Sep 9)*
**Cline 105** *(8f,Ham,GS,Jly 15)*
**Clon Coulis 108** *(6f,Nmk,G,Jly 21)*
**Clongowes 109** *(12f,Leo,GF,May 7)*
**Cloth Of Stars 118** *(12f,Cha,S,Oct 1)*
**Club Wexford 112** *(7f,Leo,S,Apr 5)*
**Coastal Cyclone 105** *(6f,Sal,GS,May 18)*
**Coconut Creme 107** *(10f,Sal,GF,Aug 16)*
**Codeshare 107** *(14f,Mus,GF,Aug 11)*
**Coeur De Lion 111** *(18f,Nmk,G,Sep 23)*
**Cohesion 105** *(12f,Don,S,Nov 11)*
**Colibri 106** *(8f,San,G,Apr 28)*
**Colonel Frank 108** *(8f,Nby,S,Oct 27)*
**Colonial Classic 106** *(12f,Nmk,GS,Sep 29)*
**Comhghairdeas 106** *(6f,Cur,G,Aug 7)*
**Comicas 109** *(6f,Yor,S,May 17)*
**Company Asset 108** *(10½f,Hay,HY,Sep 9)*
**Compas Scoobie 113** *(6f,Lin,GF,Jun 3)*
**Comprise 105** *(6f,Yar,GS,Sep 20)*
**Compton Mill 107** *(10f,Not,GS,Oct 4)*
**Computable 106** *(5f,Thi,GF,Apr 22)*
**Con Te Partiro 106** *(8f,Asc,GF,Jun 21)*
**Confessional 109** *(5f,Cat,S,Oct 21)*
**Connecticut 105** *(12f,Nmk,GS,Sep 29)*
**Conqueress 108** *(8f,Wdr,GF,Aug 26)*
**Contango 106** *(12f,Asc,GS,Aug 12)*
**Contrapposto 107** *(8f,Nmk,GF,Apr 20)*
**Contrast 105** *(8f,San,G,Apr 28)*
**Cool Sky 112** *(20½f,Goo,GS,Aug 2)*
**Coolfitch 106** *(5f,Yor,GF,Jly 14)*
**Copper Knight 112** *(5f,Yor,G,May 27)*
**Coral Sea 105** *(7f,Eps,GS,Aug 3)*
**Cordite 105** *(11f,Goo,G,Jun 11)*
**Cornborough 107** *(10½f,Chs,G,Jly 15)*
**Cornwallville 105** *(8f,Mey,G,Jan 12)*
**Coronation Cottage 105** *(5f,Bat,GF,Aug 31)*
**Coronation Day 108** *(6f,Bri,GF,Aug 11)*
**Coronet 115** *(14½f,Don,GS,Sep 16)*
**Corporal Maddox 106** *(7½f,Lin,G,May 24)*
**Corpus Chorister 112** *(16f,Bev,GF,Jly 18)*
**Corton Lad 112** *(13f,Ham,GF,May 7)*
**Cosmic Chatter 107** *(6f,Hay,S,Jun 10)*
**Cosmic Tigress 109** *(14f,Mus,GF,May 26)*
**Cosmopolitan Girl 105** *(5f,Mus,GS,Oct 9)*
**Cosy Club 107** *(7f,Ayr,G,Jly 24)*
**Cotai Glory 116** *(5f,Yor,G,Jly 15)*
**Cote D'Azur 112** *(8f,Thi,GF,May 6)*
**Cotton Club 107** *(12f,Sal,GF,Jly 15)*
**Cougar Mountain 108** *(8f,San,G,Apr 28)*
**Count Montecristo 106** *(10f,Rip,GF,Apr 20)*
**Count Octave 114** *(14½f,Don,GS,Sep 16)*
**Count Simon 106** *(12f,Pon,GF,Jly 21)*
**Courier 111** *(7f,Hay,S,Jun 9)*
**Covetous 109** *(8f,Cur,GF,Jly 16)*
**Cracksman 120** *(10f,Asc,S,Oct 21)*
**Cranesbill 107** *(12f,Leo,GF,May 7)*
**Cray 106** *(14f,Wet,G,May 15)*
**Crazy Horse 105** *(8f,Don,GS,Apr 1)*
**Crazy Tornado 113** *(8f,Ayr,G,Jly 24)*
**Creggs Pipes 111** *(8f,Cur,Y,May 27)*
**Cricklewood Green 106** *(8f,Nby,S,Aug 18)*
**Crimean Tatar 113** *(12f,Nby,GF,Apr 22)*
**Croquembouche 108** *(12f,Pon,G,Aug 20)*
**Cross Grain 105** *(7f,Mey,G,Jan 28)*
**Crowned Eagle 105** *(10f,Nmk,G,Sep 23)*
**Crowning Glory 111** *(8f,Pon,GF,Jly 21)*
**Crystal Ocean 116** *(14½f,Don,GS,Sep 16)*
**Crystal Secret 105** *(11½f,Lin,GF,Jun 24)*
**Cullingworth 106** *(8f,Asc,GS,Jly 29)*
**Culloden 107** *(5f,Cat,S,Jun 10)*
**Culturati 107** *(6f,Nmk,G,Jun 10)*
**Cunco 105** *(12f,Chs,G,May 11)*
**Curious Fox 107** *(6f,Goo,GS,Jun 9)*
**Curlew River 106** *(10f,Nby,G,Sep 23)*
**Custom Cut 114** *(8f,Pon,S,Jly 30)*
**Cymric 112** *(8f,Mey,G,Feb 16)*
**Cymro 109** *(12f,Yor,S,May 19)*

**D'bai 112** *(8f,Nmk,G,Jly 13)*
**Daban 113** *(8f,Nmk,GF,May 7)*
**Dabulena 106** *(10f,Cur,G,May 14)*
**Dabyah 108** *(7f,Nby,GF,Apr 22)*
**Daisy Boy 111** *(10f,Lin,GF,Jun 13)*
**Dakota Gold 110** *(5f,Thi,GF,Apr 22)*
**Dal Harraild 112** *(12f,Asc,GF,Jun 24)*
**Dame Du Roi 113** *(7f,Cha,S,Oct 1)*
**Dan Troop 111** *(7½f,Chs,GS,Jly 29)*
**Dance King 107** *(10f,Yor,G,Oct 14)*
**Dance The Dream 110** *(12f,Lei,GS,Oct 30)*
**Dancing Breeze 105** *(8f,San,G,Sep 2)*
**Dancing Star 112** *(6f,Wdr,G,May 22)*
**Dandy Flame 106** *(6f,Sal,GS,May 18)*
**Danecase 106** *(6f,Goo,G,May 25)*
**Danehill Kodiac 113** *(12f,Asc,GS,Oct 7)*
**Danglydontask 105** *(17f,Bat,F,Apr 21)*
**Danielsflyer 106** *(6f,Nmk,GF,May 6)*
**Danzeno 112** *(5f,Asc,G,Jly 15)*
**Daphne 108** *(12f,Nby,G,Sep 23)*
**Dapper Man 105** *(5½f,Wet,GF,Jun 19)*

**Daqeeq 105** *(7f,Mey,G,Feb 9)*
**Darbuzan 114** *(15f,Cha,GS,Sep 30)*
**Daring Guest 105** *(7f,Yar,G,Jly 12)*
**Dark Crystal 116** *(7f,Ayr,S,Jun 12)*
**Dark Defender 108** *(6f,Ayr,G,Jun 24)*
**Dark Devil 111** *(7½f,Chs,G,Aug 26)*
**Dark Emerald 105** *(6f,Sal,GF,Jun 18)*
**Dark Intention 105** *(9f,Yor,GF,Jun 17)*
**Dark Pearl 105** *(12f,Chp,GF,Jun 26)*
**Dark Power 108** *(6f,Lei,GS,Aug 13)*
**Dark Profit 119** *(7f,Ayr,G,Jun 23)*
**Dark Red 116** *(10f,Yor,G,Oct 14)*
**Dark Shot 108** *(5f,Eps,G,Jun 3)*
**Dartmouth 112** *(12f,Asc,GF,Jun 24)*
**Dashing Poet 110** *(5f,Not,GF,May 2)*
**Dawaaleeb 108** *(8f,Nmk,G,Aug 4)*
**Dawn Of Hope 113** *(8f,Don,GS,Apr 1)*
**Deauville 114** *(10½f,Cur,Y,May 28)*
**Declamation 111** *(7f,Ayr,G,Jun 23)*
**Decorated Knight 120** *(10f,Leo,G,Sep 9)*
**Deer Song 105** *(6f,Goo,G,May 25)*
**Defoe 115** *(11f,Ham,G,Jly 21)*
**Deinonychus 106** *(10f,Not,HY,Aug 3)*
**Delagate This Lord 106** *(5f,Bat,GS,Sep 17)*
**Delaire 106** *(9f,Leo,G,Aug 10)*
**Delectation 108** *(8f,Nmk,GF,Jly 14)*
**Delfie Lane 105** *(6f,Wdr,GF,May 8)*
**Denmead 108** *(20½f,Goo,GS,Aug 2)*
**Desert Ace 107** *(5f,Ayr,G,Jly 24)*
**Desert Dream 105** *(8f,Wdr,G,May 1)*
**Desert Encounter 113** *(10f,San,GF,Jly 8)*
**Desert Frost 106** *(6f,Don,GF,May 6)*
**Desert God 106** *(11½f,Wdr,GS,Oct 9)*
**Desert Haze 110** *(8f,Goo,GF,May 6)*
**Desert Law 112** *(5f,Mus,GF,Apr 15)*
**Desert Skyline 118** *(18f,Don,GS,Sep 15)*
**Destination Aim 112** *(7f,Ayr,G,Jly 9)*
**Destroyer 106** *(8f,Pon,GF,Jly 21)*
**Detailed 107** *(12f,Cur,YS,Aug 20)*
**Diamond Fields 107** *(8f,Leo,G,Sep 9)*
**Diamond Lady 114** *(6f,Lin,GF,Jun 3)*
**Diferent Dimension 108** *(8f,Mey,G,Feb 11)*
**Dinkum Diamond 105** *(7f,Leo,GF,May 7)*
**Diodorus 108** *(12f,Leo,GF,May 7)*
**Dirchill 107** *(6f,Wdr,GF,Jun 5)*
**Discreet Hero 105** *(5f,Bat,GF,Jly 12)*
**Distant Past 105** *(6f,Ham,GS,Aug 24)*
**Doctor Bartolo 107** *(10f,Nby,S,Aug 19)*
**Doha Dream 114** *(12f,Cha,S,Oct 1)*
**Dolphin Vista 113** *(9f,Nmk,GS,Sep 30)*
**Dominannie 106** *(8f,Ayr,G,Jly 17)*
**Dominating 108** *(16f,Mus,G,Jly 14)*
**Don Valentino 105** *(6f,Rip,G,Jun 21)*
**Don't Give Up 107** *(8f,Nmk,GS,Jly 29)*
**Don't Touch 110** *(7f,Leo,G,Jun 15)*
**Donjuan Triumphant 111** *(6f,Hay,HY,Sep 30)*
**Donncha 113** *(8f,Nby,GF,Apr 22)*
**Doodle Dandy 106** *(8f,Wdr,GF,Aug 26)*
**Dougan 108** *(6½f,Don,GS,Sep 15)*
**Douglas Macarthur 111** *(12f,Cur,G,Jly 1)*
**Dovils Date 113** *(14f,Lin,G,May 24)*
**Downforce 106** *(6f,Yor,GS,Sep 10)*
**Dr Julius No 105** *(8f,Mus,GF,Apr 15)*
**Dragon Falls 108** *(7f,Mey,G,Jan 28)*
**Dragon Fei 107** *(10f,Cur,S,Jun 11)*
**Dragon Mall 110** *(8½f,Not,G,May 31)*
**Dragons Voice 112** *(8f,Wdr,GS,Oct 9)*
**Dream Castle 113** *(7f,Nby,GF,Apr 22)*
**Dream Of Dreams 111** *(6f,Don,S,Nov 11)*
**Dream Serenade 108** *(14f,Yar,GF,May 24)*
**Dreaming Of Gold 106** *(7f,Leo,GF,Jly 13)*
**Drochaid 110** *(10f,Eps,G,Jun 3)*
**Drumochter 106** *(10f,Nby,S,Oct 27)*
**Dschingis Secret 115** *(12f,Cha,S,Oct 1)*
**Dubai Horizon 109** *(10f,Nmk,GF,May 7)*
**Dubai Sand 106** *(12f,Cur,G,Jly 1)*
**Dubai Thunder 109** *(12f,Eps,G,Jun 3)*
**Dubara 107** *(8f,Goo,G,Aug 25)*
**Dubawi Fifty 108** *(14f,Not,GS,Aug 18)*
**Duchess Of France 108** *(7f,Cur,GY,Jly 1)*
**Ducky Mallon 106** *(6f,Cur,G,Aug 7)*
**Duke Of Bronte 108** *(12f,Asc,S,Sep 9)*
**Duke Of Diamonds 105** *(12f,Lei,GS,Apr 7)*
**Duke Of Firenze 109** *(5f,Yor,S,May 18)*
**Duretto 111** *(16f,Asc,S,Oct 21)*
**Dutch Connection 116** *(7f,Goo,G,Aug 27)*
**Dutch Uncle 109** *(10f,Eps,G,Apr 26)*
**Dylan Mouth 111** *(12f,Hay,GF,Jly 8)*
**Dyllan 105** *(7f,Cat,S,Jly 26)*

**Eagle Creek 105** *(8f,Pon,G,Aug 20)*
**Early Morning 109** *(8f,Hay,GF,Apr 29)*
**Earnshaw 113** *(12f,Mey,Y,Mar 25)*
**Eartha Kitt 109** *(6f,Nmk,G,Oct 7)*
**East Coast Lady 105** *(7f,Lei,HY,Sep 25)*
**East Street Revue 114** *(5f,Yor,G,Oct 13)*
**Eastern Impact 110** *(6f,Nmk,GF,May 7)*
**Easy Tiger 106** *(7f,Lei,GS,Sep 12)*
**Ebbesbourne 110** *(10f,Nby,G,Jun 15)*
**Ebitda 107** *(5f,Cat,S,Oct 31)*
**Eccleston 108** *(6f,Hay,S,Jun 10)*
**Echo Of Lightning 105** *(8f,Pon,S,Aug 9)*
**Eddystone Rock 113** *(10f,Yor,G,Aug 26)*
**Edgar Allan Poe 105** *(7f,Red,S,Nov 7)*
**Edged Out 105** *(5f,Sal,GF,Jun 18)*
**Edward Lewis 111** *(5f,Pon,GF,Apr 24)*
**Ejaaby 113** *(6f,Lei,GS,May 29)*
**Ekhtiyaar 113** *(6f,Nmk,GS,May 20)*
**El Astronaute 117** *(5f,Goo,G,Aug 1)*
**El Cap 108** *(8f,Hay,GS,Aug 12)*
**El Hayem 113** *(8f,Nby,GF,Apr 22)*
**El Hombre 107** *(6f,Thi,GF,Sep 1)*
**El Principe 105** *(8f,Crl,GS,Aug 7)*
**El Torito 105** *(7f,Bri,GF,May 3)*
**El Vip 108** *(8f,Bat,F,Apr 14)*
**Elas Ruby 113** *(10f,Nby,G,Jun 15)*
**Elbereth 111** *(12f,Eps,G,Jun 2)*
**Elegant Pose 106** *(8f,Cur,G,May 13)*
**Elidor 118** *(14f,Cur,G,Jly 2)*
**Elite Excalibur 110** *(9f,Mey,G,Jan 26)*
**Elizabeth Browning 112** *(9f,Cur,GF,Jly 16)*
**Eljaddaaf 111** *(6f,Nby,S,May 19)*
**Elleval 106** *(10f,Leo,GF,Jly 13)*
**Eltezam 109** *(7f,Goo,GF,May 6)*
**Elusive Beauty 107** *(7f,Crl,GS,Jun 28)*
**Elusive Heights 108** *(8f,Leo,YS,Jun 8)*
**Elusive Time 107** *(8f,Cur,Y,Aug 27)*
**Elysian Fields 105** *(12f,Goo,GF,May 6)*
**Elysian Flyer 106** *(5f,Thi,S,May 20)*
**Emenem 113** *(10f,Goo,G,Aug 27)*
**Eminent 118** *(10f,Leo,G,Sep 9)*
**Emmaus 110** *(7f,Lei,GS,Oct 17)*
**Empire Of The Star 111** *(7f,Cha,S,Sep 3)*
**Enable 123** *(12f,Asc,GS,Jly 29)*
**Encipher 105** *(8f,Mey,G,Jan 12)*
**Encore D'Or 112** *(5f,Yor,G,Jly 15)*
**Endless Acres 106** *(20f,Asc,GF,Jun 20)*
**Endless Gold 109** *(8½f,Not,G,Jly 8)*
**Endless Time 110** *(14f,Yor,S,May 19)*
**Energia Fox 109** *(10½f,Chs,GF,May 27)*
**Englishman 109** *(6f,Wdr,G,May 15)*
**Enter The Red 107** *(6f,Cur,G,Jun 30)*
**Entsar 111** *(10f,Yor,GS,Jly 28)*
**Epsom Icon 108** *(8f,Goo,GF,May 6)*
**Eqtiraan 111** *(6f,Sal,GF,Jun 18)*
**Equimou 109** *(5f,Yar,GS,Sep 20)*
**Equitation 110** *(6f,Don,G,Aug 19)*
**Erik The Red 111** *(10f,Yor,S,May 17)*
**Erissimus Maximus 108** *(6f,Lei,GS,May 29)*
**Ertijaal 117** *(5f,Mey,G,Feb 16)*
**Escobar 109** *(8f,Goo,S,Aug 4)*
**Esspeegee 107** *(14f,Yar,GF,May 24)*
**Eternal 108** *(8f,Hay,G,Jun 15)*
**Eternalist 106** *(5f,Thi,GF,Jun 20)*
**Eternally 107** *(7f,Don,GS,Sep 15)*
**Euchen Glen 107** *(12f,Hay,GF,Jly 8)*
**Euginio 110** *(10½f,Hay,GS,Aug 12)*
**Euqranian 105** *(8f,Nmk,G,Aug 4)*
**Euro Nightmare 107** *(11f,Ham,G,Jly 21)*
**Evening Attire 105** *(7f,Lei,G,Apr 7)*
**Evergate 107** *(5f,Asc,GS,Oct 7)*
**Everkyllachy 106** *(5f,Bat,S,Oct 2)*
**Examiner 110** *(9f,Nmk,GS,Sep 30)*
**Exceeding Power 106** *(8f,Nby,S,Aug 18)*
**Excel Again 105** *(8f,Hay,GF,May 26)*
**Excellent Sounds 110** *(7f,Hay,GF,Jly 8)*
**Excessable 113** *(5f,Thi,GF,May 6)*
**Executive Force 106** *(8f,Nby,S,Oct 27)*
**Exemplar 112** *(12f,Leo,GY,Sep 9)*
**Explain 107** *(7f,Chs,HY,Sep 15)*
**Exultant 113** *(8f,Cur,G,May 14)*
**Eye Of The Storm 105** *(12f,Nby,G,Sep 22)*
**Eynhallow 111** *(10f,Goo,G,Aug 27)*
**Eziyra 113** *(12f,Leo,GY,Sep 9)*

**Fabricate 111** *(10f,Wdr,GF,Aug 26)*
**Face The Facts 119** *(16f,Nmk,GS,Sep 28)*
**Fair Cop 108** *(6f,Goo,S,Aug 3)*
**Fair Eva 110** *(8f,Nmk,GF,May 7)*
**Fairy Lock 107** *(8½f,Not,GS,Jun 11)*
**Faithful Creek 106** *(12f,Lei,GS,Apr 7)*
**Falbon 106** *(7f,Lin,GS,Jun 14)*
**Falcon's Fire 109** *(14f,Mus,GF,May 26)*
**Famous Kid 105** *(16f,Mey,Y,Mar 25)*
**Fanciful Angel 115** *(10f,San,GF,Jly 7)*
**Fanfair 108** *(10f,Lin,GS,Jly 19)*
**Fannaan 105** *(6f,Mey,G,Feb 9)*
**Fantasy Keeper 107** *(6f,Hay,S,Jun 10)*
**Farrier 108** *(9f,Mey,G,Jan 26)*
**Fas 110** *(6f,Cha,G,Apr 9)*
**Fashion Queen 110** *(5f,Cha,S,Sep 10)*
**Fast And Hot 107** *(10f,Nby,S,Aug 19)*
**Fast Dancer 106** *(9f,Goo,S,Aug 5)*
**Fastar 106** *(8f,Hay,HY,Sep 29)*
**Fastnet Spin 105** *(8f,Lei,G,May 29)*
**Fastnet Tempest 114** *(7½f,Chs,GF,May 27)*
**Father McKenzie 106** *(6f,Yar,GS,Sep 20)*
**Favorite Girl 107** *(10f,Yar,GF,Jun 13)*
**Favourite Royal 105** *(7f,Eps,GF,Aug 29)*
**Favourite Treat 115** *(7f,Ayr,G,Jun 23)*
**Fawaareq 113** *(7f,Hay,GF,Apr 29)*
**Fayez 106** *(7f,Ayr,G,May 31)*
**Fearless Fire 111** *(10f,Nby,S,May 20)*
**Felix Mendelssohn 107** *(12f,Cur,Y,May 27)*
**Fengate 106** *(10f,Yor,GS,Jly 29)*
**Festival Of Ages 107** *(12f,Nmk,GS,Jly 28)*
**Fethiye Boy 106** *(5f,Bat,G,May 17)*
**Fidaawy 112** *(10f,Nby,G,Sep 23)*
**Fields Of Fortune 108** *(14f,Sal,HY,Oct 4)*
**Fieldsman 112** *(7f,Red,GS,Aug 12)*
**Fierce Impact 107** *(10f,Eps,G,Aug 28)*
**Figure Of Speech 106** *(7f,Mey,G,Jan 28)*
**Final 113** *(10f,Yor,S,May 17)*
**Final Venture 117** *(5f,Yor,G,Jly 15)*
**Fingal's Cave 110** *(7f,Cat,S,Jun 10)*
**Finn Class 106** *(8f,Ayr,G,Jun 24)*
**Finn McCool 106** *(12f,Leo,YS,Jun 8)*
**Finsbury Square 111** *(6f,Asc,GF,Jun 24)*
**Fior Cliste 114** *(7f,Leo,GF,Jly 13)*
**Fire Brigade 109** *(8f,Asc,GS,Jly 29)*
**Fire Tree 105** *(8f,Wet,G,May 15)*
**Firmament 118** *(7f,Yor,GF,May 27)*
**Firnas 106** *(10f,Nmk,G,Jun 10)*
**First Bombardment 105** *(5f,Don,GF,Apr 28)*
**First Flight 113** *(10f,Nmk,G,Jun 10)*
**First Nation 112** *(10f,Don,G,Apr 2)*
**First Selection 109** *(7f,Mey,G,Feb 9)*
**First Sitting 113** *(10f,Cha,S,Sep 30)*
**Fit For Function 106** *(7f,Cur,GF,Jly 15)*
**Fityaan 110** *(6f,Mey,G,Feb 11)*
**Fitzwilly 111** *(14f,Lin,G,May 24)*
**Fivehundredmiles 113** *(8f,Ham,GF,May 19)*
**Flaming Spear 111** *(8f,Yor,GS,Aug 24)*
**Flash City 105** *(5f,Thi,GF,Jun 20)*
**Flash Fire 112** *(7f,Mey,G,Jan 19)*
**Flawlessly 107** *(5f,Red,G,Jun 23)*
**Fleeting Motion 105** *(8f,Nmk,GF,Jun 24)*
**Fleeting Visit 105** *(12f,Rip,S,Jly 22)*
**Fleur Forsyte 109** *(12f,Yor,GS,Aug 24)*
**Flight Of Fantasy 105** *(13f,Nby,GS,Jly 21)*
**Flight Risk 113** *(7f,Leo,G,Jun 15)*
**Flirt 106** *(10f,Cur,S,Jun 11)*
**Flood Defence 110** *(8½f,Not,GS,Jun 11)*
**Flood Warning 108** *(10f,San,G,Apr 28)*
**Florencio 105** *(7f,Red,GS,Aug 12)*
**Florenza 106** *(8f,Thi,G,Aug 5)*
**Flowing Clarets 105** *(5f,Goo,S,Sep 27)*
**Fly At Dawn 107** *(7f,Mey,G,Feb 23)*
**Flyboy 111** *(7f,Lei,GS,Jun 5)*
**Flying Fairies 106** *(8f,Leo,S,Apr 5)*
**Flying Fantasy 109** *(7f,Lei,GS,Jun 5)*
**Flying North 107** *(10f,Nby,S,Jly 27)*
**Flying Power 107** *(11½f,Lin,GF,Jun 24)*
**Flying Pursuit 113** *(6f,Don,GS,Oct 27)*
**Flying Tiger 109** *(12f,Asc,GS,Oct 7)*
**Flymetothestars 112** *(15f,Cha,S,Sep 10)*
**Folkswood 108** *(10f,Mey,G,Jan 19)*
**Foolaad 115** *(6f,Don,GF,May 6)*
**Forest Ranger 113** *(8f,Nmk,G,Jly 13)*
**Forever A Lady 105** *(7½f,Chs,GS,Jun 10)*
**Fortitude 109** *(5f,Don,S,Jun 3)*
**Fountain 106** *(8f,Leo,GY,Apr 8)*
**Fox Trotter 111** *(7f,San,GS,Jly 26)*
**Foxford 110** *(5f,Chp,S,Jun 10)*
**Foxtrot Knight 106** *(5f,Ayr,GS,Jly 10)*
**Foxy Boy 105** *(5f,Bev,G,Jun 27)*
**Foxy Forever 106** *(5f,Nmk,G,Jly 13)*
**Francis Of Assisi 106** *(10½f,Hay,GS,Aug 12)*
**Frank Bridge 113** *(8f,San,GS,Aug 2)*
**Frankuus 116** *(10f,San,GF,Jly 7)*
**Frederic 111** *(17f,Crl,GF,May 22)*
**Frontiersman 114** *(12f,Eps,G,Jun 2)*
**Frontispiece 123** *(10f,Goo,S,Aug 3)*
**Fruit Salad 109** *(5f,Thi,GF,May 6)*
**Fujin 107** *(6f,Bri,GF,Sep 3)*
**Full Intention 106** *(6f,Hay,S,Jun 10)*
**Fumbo Jumbo 106** *(5f,Mus,S,Aug 4)*
**Fun Mac 107** *(16f,San,GF,Jly 8)*
**Furia Cruzada 105** *(10f,Dea,G,Aug 20)*
**Fuwairt 113** *(8f,Hay,G,Jun 15)*

**G K Chesterton 108** *(8½f,Not,GF,Apr 12)*
**Gabrial 112** *(8f,San,G,Apr 28)*
**Gabrial The Tiger 107** *(7f,Chs,HY,Sep 30)*
**Gabrial's Kaka 108** *(7½f,Chs,GF,May 27)*
**Galactic Prince 106** *(12f,Asc,G,Jly 15)*
**Galapiat 110** *(12f,Lei,GS,Apr 7)*
**Galileo Gold 109** *(8f,Nby,S,May 20)*
**Gallifrey 107** *(12f,Nmk,S,Jly 22)*
**Gallipoli 106** *(7f,Lei,G,Apr 7)*
**Game Starter 106** *(10f,Nmk,G,Aug 4)*
**Gamesome 107** *(5f,Yor,G,May 27)*
**Garlingari 121** *(10f,Cha,S,Sep 30)*
**Garrick 105** *(10f,Nmk,GF,Nov 3)*
**Gaval 105** *(12f,Lei,GS,Aug 13)*
**Gawdawpalin 112** *(10f,Eps,G,Apr 26)*
**General Macarthur 105** *(8f,Mey,G,Feb 11)*
**Gentil J 108** *(10½f,Cur,Y,May 28)*
**Geological 109** *(7f,Leo,GF,May 7)*
**George Bowen 111** *(6f,Not,GF,Jun 15)*
**George William 114** *(8f,Nby,GF,Apr 22)*
**Georgian Bay 106** *(8f,Crl,GS,Jun 28)*
**Gerry The Glover 110** *(8f,Pon,GF,Apr 24)*
**Get Knotted 117** *(7f,Yor,GF,May 27)*
**Ghadaayer 109** *(8f,Nmk,GF,Jun 24)*
**Ghalib 110** *(8f,Wdr,GS,Oct 9)*
**Ghinia 112** *(10f,Lin,GF,Jun 13)*
**Gibbs Hill 110** *(12f,Yor,S,May 19)*
**Gifted Master 115** *(6f,Nmk,GF,Aug 26)*
**Gilgamesh 107** *(7f,Red,GF,May 4)*
**Gilmer 110** *(6f,Ayr,G,Jun 24)*
**Gin In The Inn 106** *(6f,Pon,S,Jly 30)*
**Ginzan 105** *(5f,Bri,GF,Jun 27)*
**Giveaway Glance 105** *(10f,Lei,S,May 22)*
**Glamorous Approach 112** *(12f,Leo,GY,Sep 9)*
**Glass Office 110** *(6f,Nmk,GF,Aug 26)*
**Glassy Waters 106** *(8f,Pon,G,Aug 20)*
**Glencadam Glory 111** *(12f,Asc,GF,Jun 23)*
**Glengarry 105** *(7f,Mus,GF,May 26)*
**Glenrowan Rose 111** *(5f,Mus,GS,Oct 9)*
**Glens Wobbly 108** *(10f,Bat,F,Jun 23)*
**Glenys The Menace 107** *(12f,Asc,GS,Aug 12)*
**Glitter Girl 107** *(7f,Mus,GF,Jun 3)*
**Global Applause 109** *(5f,Don,GS,Oct 28)*
**Glorious Forever 107** *(10f,San,G,Sep 2)*
**Glorious Poet 105** *(7½f,Lin,GS,Sep 16)*
**Glory Awaits 109** *(7½f,Lin,S,Jly 26)*
**Glory Of Paris 107** *(6f,Sal,GS,May 18)*
**Gm Hopkins 108** *(9f,Nmk,GS,Sep 30)*
**Go Far 110** *(6f,Goo,G,May 26)*
**Go Kart 108** *(5f,Cur,G,Jly 2)*
**God Given 115** *(12f,Nmk,S,Jly 22)*
**God Willing 107** *(8f,Thi,GF,May 6)*
**Gold Luck 105** *(8f,Cha,S,Sep 30)*
**Gold Star 105** *(12f,Nmk,GS,Jly 28)*
**Gold Trail 109** *(12f,Mey,G,Jan 26)*
**Gold Vibe 110** *(5f,Cha,S,Sep 10)*
**Golden Amber 105** *(6f,Don,G,Apr 2)*
**Golden Apollo 107** *(6f,Pon,G,Jun 12)*
**Golden Birthday 109** *(14½f,Don,GS,Oct 27)*
**Golden Isles 111** *(10f,Lin,GF,Jun 24)*
**Golden Stunner 121** *(7f,Yor,GF,May 27)*
**Goldream 112** *(5f,Yor,G,Jly 15)*
**Goninodaethat 105** *(5f,Ayr,S,Jun 12)*
**Good Luck Charm 105** *(7f,Bri,GS,Sep 11)*
**Good Omen 124** *(10f,Goo,S,Aug 3)*
**Good Trip 105** *(12f,Mey,G,Jan 26)*
**Goodwood Crusader 106** *(6f,Nmk,GF,Jun 24)*
**Gorane 110** *(5f,Cur,SH,Sep 10)*
**Gordon Lord Byron 109** *(7f,Yor,G,Aug 25)*
**Goring 106** *(6f,Lin,GF,Jun 3)*
**Gossiping 113** *(7f,Goo,GF,May 6)*
**Graceful Lady 109** *(14f,Yar,GF,May 24)*
**Gracious Diana 105** *(10f,Nby,GF,Apr 21)*
**Gracious John 107** *(5f,Yar,GS,Sep 20)*
**Grand Inquisitor 113** *(10f,Yor,G,Oct 14)*
**Grand Partner 106** *(15f,Leo,G,Aug 10)*
**Grandad's World 106** *(6f,Red,G,Apr 17)*
**Grandee 108** *(12f,Leo,YS,Jun 8)*
**Grapevine 107** *(10f,Nby,G,Sep 22)*
**Graphite Storm 108** *(7f,Lei,GS,Sep 12)*
**Great Fighter 112** *(14f,Mus,GF,May 26)*
**Great Hall 111** *(10f,Eps,G,Apr 26)*
**Great Sound 105** *(14½f,Don,GS,Oct 27)*
**Green Door 115** *(5f,Goo,G,Aug 1)*
**Greenside 106** *(8f,Goo,S,Aug 4)*
**Greta G 106** *(8f,Nmk,GF,Jly 14)*
**Grey Britain 121** *(10f,Goo,S,Aug 3)*
**Groundfrost 109** *(7f,Leo,YS,Jun 8)*
**Growl 110** *(6f,Goo,S,Aug 5)*
**Grumeti 110** *(16f,Bev,GF,Jly 18)*
**Guishan 110** *(6f,Ham,S,Sep 5)*
**Gulf Of Poets 106** *(9f,Ham,S,Jun 7)*
**Gulliver 114** *(6f,Yar,GF,Aug 1)*
**Gun Case 107** *(8f,Ayr,G,Jly 24)*
**Gunmetal 109** *(6f,Nmk,GF,Apr 19)*
**Gurkha Friend 107** *(8f,Rip,G,Apr 29)*
**Gworn 106** *(10f,Ayr,G,May 24)*
**Gymnaste 108** *(7f,Nmk,GF,Jly 15)*

**Habbad 107** *(7f,Don,G,Aug 19)*
**Hadeeqa 106** *(8f,Goo,G,Aug 1)*
**Haggle 107** *(10f,Dea,G,Aug 20)*
**Hail Clodius 105** *(10f,Don,G,Apr 2)*
**Hajaj 105** *(10f,Eps,G,Jun 3)*
**Hajjam 113** *(7f,Red,GS,Aug 12)*
**Hakam 112** *(6f,Asc,G,Jly 14)*
**Hamidans Girl 105** *(6f,Crl,GF,Jly 13)*
**Handsome Dude 112** *(6f,Hay,S,Jun 10)*
**Hang Man 105** *(12f,Asc,S,Sep 8)*
**Haraz 112** *(8½f,Bev,GF,May 31)*
**Harbour Grey 105** *(6f,Don,GF,Apr 28)*
**Harbour Law 107** *(20f,Asc,GF,Jun 22)*
**Harlequeen 106** *(13f,Nby,S,Aug 19)*
**Harlequin Striker 108** *(8½f,Not,GS,Oct 11)*
**Harmonise 105** *(10f,Nby,S,Oct 27)*
**Harry Angel 120** *(6f,Asc,GF,May 3)*
**Harry Hurricane 109** *(5f,Goo,G,Aug 1)*
**Hart Stopper 108** *(6f,Yar,G,Jly 19)*
**Harvest Wind 106** *(7½f,Ffo,GS,Jly 25)*
**Hasanour 105** *(8f,Mey,G,Feb 11)*
**Hathal 110** *(10f,Yor,GS,Jly 29)*
**Have A Nice Day 107** *(7f,Cur,GF,Jly 15)*
**Havre De Paix 105** *(7f,Asc,GS,Jly 29)*
**Hawkbill 112** *(12f,Eps,G,Jun 2)*
**Haymarket 105** *(9f,Mus,GF,Jly 25)*
**Heatongrad 107** *(8½f,Eps,HY,Oct 1)*
**Heaven's Guest 113** *(7f,Asc,GS,Sep 9)*
**Heaven's Rock 106** *(8f,Hay,GS,Sep 7)*
**Hee Haw 105** *(6f,Rip,G,Aug 19)*
**Heir Of Excitement 106** *(8f,Crl,GS,Aug 23)*
**Heir To A Throne 105** *(7f,Ayr,G,Jly 17)*
**Hells Babe 107** *(7f,Mus,GF,Jun 3)*
**Hemingway 106** *(6f,Pon,G,Apr 11)*
**Henley 105** *(5f,Ham,G,Jun 14)*
**Hepplewhite 112** *(14f,Lin,G,May 24)*
**Here And Now 106** *(12f,Chs,G,May 10)*
**Here Comes When 115** *(8f,Yor,GS,May 18)*
**Here For The Craic 106** *(12f,Cur,Y,May 27)*
**Hernando Torres 105** *(8f,Rip,G,Jly 10)*
**Hertford Dancer 106** *(12f,Asc,GF,Jun 22)*
**Heshem 111** *(9f,Mey,Y,Mar 25)*
**Hibou 112** *(10f,Yor,G,Oct 14)*
**Hidden Oasis 108** *(7½f,Ffo,GS,Jly 25)*
**High Acclaim 105** *(8f,Nmk,GF,May 6)*
**High End 107** *(10f,Eps,G,Aug 28)*
**High Haven 107** *(12f,Cur,S,Jun 11)*
**High Hopes 110** *(12f,Nmk,S,Jly 22)*
**High Jinx 113** *(18f,Don,GS,Sep 15)*
**Higher Power 110** *(16f,San,GF,May 25)*
**Highland Acclaim 109** *(6f,Thi,GF,Jun 20)*
**Highland Colori 107** *(8f,Wdr,G,May 1)*
**Highland Pass 106** *(7f,Hay,GF,Jly 8)*
**Highland Reel 117** *(10f,Asc,GF,Jun 21)*
**Highly Sprung 105** *(6f,Red,GF,Jly 23)*
**Highsalvia Cosmos 107** *(14f,Lin,G,May 24)*
**Himalayan Queen 108** *(8f,Wdr,GF,Aug 26)*
**Hit The Bid 110** *(5f,Cur,G,Jly 2)*
**Hochfeld 111** *(13f,Ham,G,Jly 20)*
**Hold Sway 119** *(10f,Goo,S,Aug 3)*
**Holdthasigreen 117** *(15f,Cha,S,Sep 10)*
**Holiday Girl 107** *(6f,Wdr,GS,Oct 9)*
**Holiday Magic 109** *(6f,Hay,S,Jun 10)*
**Hollywood Road 106** *(10f,Bev,GF,Aug 16)*
**Holmeswood 109** *(5f,Ayr,G,Jly 24)*
**Home Cummins 107** *(8f,Yor,G,Oct 13)*
**Home Of The Brave 115** *(7f,Lei,GF,Apr 29)*
**Homesman 108** *(8f,Cur,G,May 14)*
**Honiara 106** *(7f,Bri,GF,Jun 20)*
**Honor Oak 109** *(7f,Cur,GY,Jly 1)*
**Hoof It 112** *(6f,Don,GS,Oct 27)*
**Hope Solo 105** *(6f,Yor,GS,Sep 10)*
**Hors De Combat 109** *(8f,Mey,G,Jan 12)*
**Horseplay 106** *(10f,Nmk,GF,May 7)*
**Hugin 105** *(8f,Hay,GS,Jun 14)*
**Hunaina 106** *(7f,Cur,YS,Aug 19)*
**Huntsmans Close 110** *(6f,Yar,GF,Aug 1)*
**Hushood 110** *(11½f,Bat,F,Apr 14)*
**Hyde Park 108** *(7f,Lei,GS,Oct 17)*
**Hydrangea 117** *(8f,Leo,G,Sep 9)*
**Hyperfocus 108** *(6f,Asc,G,Jly 14)*

**Ibn Malik 108** *(7f,Hay,G,Jly 22)*
**Ice Age 116** *(6f,Nby,S,May 19)*
**Ice Alert 110** *(8f,Yar,G,Jly 12)*
**Ice Breeze 115** *(15f,Cha,GS,Sep 30)*
**Ice Cold In Alex 108** *(5f,Cur,GF,Jly 29)*
**Ice Lord 108** *(6f,Asc,S,Sep 9)*
**Ice Slice 112** *(8f,Hay,G,Jun 15)*
**Icespire 105** *(8f,Asc,GF,May 3)*
**Idaho 119** *(12f,Asc,GS,Jly 29)*
**Ifwecan 108** *(7f,Nmk,GS,May 20)*
**Ijmaaly 106** *(8f,Mey,G,Feb 11)*
**Im Dapper Too 107** *(9f,Crl,GS,Jly 8)*
**Imagine If 110** *(7f,Leo,YS,Jun 8)*
**Imphal 109** *(13f,Bat,F,Jly 18)*
**Impressive Day 107** *(10f,Bri,GF,Aug 10)*
**In First Place 117** *(9f,Yor,G,Jly 28)*
**In Ken's Memory 105** *(7f,Bri,G,May 15)*
**In The Spotlight 105** *(6f,Yar,GF,Aug 17)*
**Incredible Dream 110** *(10f,Not,GS,Jun 11)*
**Incus 109** *(14f,Lin,G,May 24)*
**Indian Blessing 109** *(10f,Nby,G,Jun 15)*
**Indian Chief 108** *(12f,Pon,G,May 26)*
**Indian Dandy 106** *(8f,Hay,F,May 27)*
**Indigo Princess 105** *(8½f,Not,G,May 13)*
**Indulged 106** *(10f,Yar,S,Sep 20)*
**Indy 105** *(12f,Rip,S,Jly 22)*
**Inexes 110** *(7f,Ayr,S,Jun 12)*
**Ingleby Angel 106** *(8f,Ayr,G,Jly 17)*
**Ingleby Mackenzie 105** *(12f,Cat,GS,Jly 12)*
**Inglorious 115** *(7f,Ayr,G,Jly 9)*
**Injam 105** *(14f,Crl,S,Jun 9)*
**Inlawed 105** *(6f,Wdr,GF,May 8)*
**Inner Circle 106** *(8f,Hay,GF,May 26)*
**Innocent Touch 113** *(10f,Yor,S,May 17)*
**Inns Of Court 105** *(8f,Cha,S,Sep 10)*
**Insayshable 107** *(10f,Leo,S,Apr 5)*
**Inshiraah 110** *(7f,Nmk,GS,Jly 29)*
**Instant Attraction 107** *(8f,Yor,GS,May 18)*
**Insurplus 106** *(7f,Don,G,Aug 19)*
**Intelligence Cross 106** *(6f,Nmk,GF,Jly 15)*
**Intense Romance 109** *(5f,Yor,G,Aug 26)*
**Intense Style 105** *(7½f,Bev,S,Sep 26)*

**Interconnection 109** *(10f,Nmk,S,May 19)*
**Interlink 105** *(6f,Red,S,Sep 19)*
**Intern 108** *(12f,Asc,GF,Jun 23)*
**Intimation 111** *(8f,Goo,GF,May 6)*
**Intisaab 114** *(6f,Nmk,GF,Aug 26)*
**Intricately 111** *(8f,Cur,Y,May 28)*
**Intrude 108** *(8f,Yar,GS,Jun 6)*
**Invermere 106** *(8f,Mus,S,Sep 16)*
**Iquitos 115** *(12f,Cha,S,Oct 1)*
**Isabel De Urbina 114** *(12f,Nmk,S,Jly 22)*
**Isabel's On It 105** *(7f,Crl,GS,Jun 28)*
**Isabella 107** *(8f,Pon,G,Aug 20)*
**Iseemist 106** *(6f,Bri,GF,Sep 3)*
**Isharah 105** *(14f,Mus,GF,Apr 15)*
**Ishebayorgrey 105** *(7f,Leo,GF,May 7)*
**Isomer 107** *(10f,San,GF,Jly 7)*
**Itlaaq 114** *(12f,Pon,G,May 26)*

**Jaameh 105** *(13½f,Chs,GF,May 27)*
**Jabbaar 105** *(12f,Cat,S,Oct 21)*
**Jabbarockie 105** *(5f,Don,S,Jun 3)*
**Jacbequick 107** *(9f,Rip,G,Jun 22)*
**Jack Dexter 111** *(5f,Asc,GS,Jly 28)*
**Jack Flash 109** *(5f,Rip,G,Apr 29)*
**Jack Hobbs 118** *(12f,Mey,Y,Mar 25)*
**Jack Nevison 105** *(8f,Yar,G,Jly 12)*
**Jackhammer 105** *(10f,Nby,S,Jly 27)*
**Jake's Hill 117** *(10f,San,GF,Jly 7)*
**Jallota 111** *(7f,Yor,G,Aug 25)*
**Jamesie 109** *(6f,Mey,G,Jan 12)*
**Jashma 110** *(5f,Bat,G,May 17)*
**Jay Kay 109** *(7f,Ayr,S,Jun 12)*
**Jaywalker 117** *(6f,Don,GF,May 6)*
**Jazzy 106** *(11½f,Lin,GS,Jly 12)*
**Jelly Monger 105** *(10f,Yar,S,Sep 20)*
**Jessie Allan 107** *(7f,Ayr,G,Aug 14)*
**Jet Streaming 107** *(12f,Nmk,GS,Sep 29)*
**Jive Talking 105** *(10f,Not,GF,Jun 15)*
**Joe Packet 109** *(6f,Goo,G,May 27)*
**Johannes Vermeer 114** *(12f,Leo,G,Aug 10)*
**John Joiner 105** *(5f,Goo,S,Sep 27)*
**Johnny Barnes 112** *(7f,Goo,G,Aug 26)*
**Johnny Cavagin 109** *(6f,Pon,HY,Sep 28)*
**Jordan Sport 111** *(6f,Asc,G,Jly 14)*
**Journey 115** *(12f,Cha,S,Sep 10)*
**Juan Horsepower 106** *(6f,Lei,GS,May 29)*
**Juanito Chico 109** *(8f,Asc,GS,Jly 29)*
**Judicial 114** *(5f,Pon,GF,Apr 24)*
**Jukebox Jive 116** *(16f,Nmk,GS,Sep 28)*
**Jule In The Crown 106** *(6f,Pon,G,Apr 11)*
**Jumira Bridge 108** *(5f,Yar,GS,Sep 20)*
**Jumira Prince 111** *(8½f,Not,GS,Jun 11)*
**Jungle Cat 114** *(7f,Hay,G,Jly 22)*
**Jupiter Light 106** *(10f,San,G,Sep 20)*
**Just Glamorous 108** *(5f,Cur,G,May 14)*
**Just Hiss 108** *(8f,Yor,G,Jly 15)*
**Just That Lord 105** *(5f,Eps,G,Apr 26)*
**Just Us Two 107** *(5f,Don,GF,Jly 13)*
**Justanotherbottle 111** *(5f,Yor,G,Oct 13)*
**Justice Lady 107** *(5f,San,G,Sep 2)*

**Kachy 110** *(6f,Hay,GF,Jly 8)*
**Kadrizzi 107** *(6f,Goo,G,May 26)*
**Kailee 107** *(8f,Cur,GF,Jly 16)*
**Kamili 112** *(8f,Cur,GF,Jly 16)*
**Kapstadt 114** *(10f,Nmk,G,Jun 10)*
**Karar 114** *(7f,Cha,S,Oct 1)*
**Karawaan 108** *(10f,Goo,G,Aug 27)*
**Kasbah 105** *(5f,San,GF,Jly 7)*
**Kasperenko 106** *(12f,Don,GF,Jly 13)*
**Kaspersky 112** *(8½f,Not,G,May 31)*
**Kassia 110** *(6f,Nmk,GF,Aug 26)*
**Katheefa 107** *(6f,Don,G,Aug 19)*
**Katiymann 108** *(8f,Leo,GY,Apr 8)*
**Kenny The Captain 111** *(6f,Thi,S,Sep 9)*
**Kensington Star 111** *(13f,Ham,GF,May 7)*
**Kenstone 115** *(7½f,Chs,G,Aug 26)*
**Kentuckyconnection 106** *(8f,Ayr,G,Jun 24)*
**Kerrymerry 112** *(14f,Lin,G,May 24)*
**Kestrel Dot Com 108** *(8f,Yar,G,May 17)*
**Key To My Heart 107** *(10f,Cur,G,May 13)*
**Khafoo Shememi 105** *(8f,San,G,Sep 20)*
**Khairaat 108** *(10f,Asc,GF,Jun 24)*
**Khalidi 113** *(12f,Asc,GF,Jun 23)*
**Khamaary 113** *(7½f,Lin,S,Jly 26)*
**Khelman 105** *(6f,Ayr,GS,Jly 31)*
**Kickboxer 105** *(5f,Thi,S,May 20)*
**Kidmenever 117** *(10f,San,GF,Jly 7)*
**Killay 106** *(7f,Sal,G,Aug 17)*
**Kilmah 106** *(8½f,Eps,G,Jun 3)*
**Kimberella 110** *(6f,Chs,GS,Aug 6)*
**King Bolete 107** *(12f,Asc,GS,Jly 28)*
**King Of Paris 105** *(7f,Bri,GF,Apr 15)*
**King Of Scotland 106** *(12f,Lei,S,May 22)*
**King Of Spin 107** *(6f,Wdr,GS,May 29)*
**King Of Swing 106** *(7f,Lei,GS,Jun 5)*
**King Robert 109** *(6f,Yor,S,May 17)*
**King's Coinage 106** *(12f,Nby,G,Jun 15)*
**King's Pavilion 108** *(7½f,Chs,HY,Sep 16)*
**Kings Gift 108** *(7f,Nby,GF,Apr 22)*
**Kinloch Pride 107** *(5f,Mus,GF,Aug 30)*
**Kirkham 109** *(7f,Red,GS,Aug 12)*
**Kitty Boo 105** *(8f,Nmk,GS,Aug 18)*
**Knights Table 109** *(12f,Rip,G,Apr 29)*
**Know The Truth 106** *(6f,Wdr,GS,Oct 9)*
**Koeman 110** *(12f,Sal,GF,Jly 15)*
**Kohinur 106** *(12f,Nmk,GS,Jly 28)*
**Kool Kompany 114** *(8f,Don,GS,Apr 1)*
**Korbous 108** *(7f,Leo,S,Apr 5)*
**Koropick 105** *(5f,San,GF,Jun 17)*
**Kourkan 119** *(10f,Cha,S,Sep 30)*
**Kozier 106** *(16f,Chp,GS,Sep 19)*
**Kroy 105** *(6f,Thi,GS,Jun 5)*
**Krypton Factor 110** *(6f,Mey,G,Feb 9)*
**Kryptos 110** *(8f,Don,GS,Sep 16)*
**Kullu 105** *(10f,Lin,GS,May 12)*
**Kyllachy Gala 108** *(8f,Hay,GF,Apr 29)*
**Kyllang Rock 111** *(5f,Goo,S,Aug 4)*
**Kynren 106** *(7f,Nmk,S,Aug 19)*

**La Celebs Ville 114** *(8f,Hay,S,Jun 9)*
**La Coronel 106** *(8f,Asc,GF,Jun 23)*
**La Figlia 111** *(8f,Nmk,GS,Sep 29)*
**La Fritillaire 108** *(16f,Bev,GF,Jly 18)*
**Lacazar 113** *(10f,Cha,S,Oct 1)*
**Lackaday 108** *(5f,Cat,S,Jun 10)*
**Ladakhi 105** *(6f,Wdr,GS,Oct 9)*
**Lady Aurelia 116** *(5f,Yor,G,Aug 25)*
**Lady Bergamot 106** *(10f,Lei,GF,Jly 8)*
**Lady Frankel 116** *(10f,Cha,S,Oct 1)*
**Lady In Question 107** *(7f,Ayr,G,Aug 12)*
**Lady Joanna Vassa 110** *(5f,Ffo,HY,Aug 3)*
**Lady Macapa 111** *(5f,Cha,S,Sep 10)*
**Lady Of York 111** *(11½f,Lin,GF,Jun 24)*
**Lady Paname 114** *(15f,Cha,GS,Sep 30)*
**Lady Perignon 105** *(8½f,Eps,G,Sep 14)*
**Laganore 110** *(10f,Cur,G,May 13)*
**Lagenda 105** *(7f,Cat,G,Aug 30)*
**Lahore 108** *(7f,Don,S,Sep 13)*
**Lamloom 108** *(8½f,Not,GS,Jly 25)*
**Lancaster Bomber 111** *(8f,Asc,GF,Jun 20)*
**Lancelot Du Lac 112** *(6f,Goo,S,Aug 5)*
**Landing Night 105** *(5f,Mus,GF,Sep 8)*
**Laraaib 110** *(10½f,Hay,GS,Aug 12)*
**Larchmont Lad 109** *(7f,Nmk,GS,May 20)*
**Largent Du Bonheur 106** *(5f,Cha,S,Sep 10)*
**Lassana Angel 105** *(10f,Chp,S,Jun 6)*
**Lat Hawill 111** *(7½f,Chs,GF,May 27)*
**Lathom 105** *(5f,Ayr,GS,Jly 10)*
**Laugh Aloud 116** *(8½f,Eps,G,Jun 3)*
**Laughton 107** *(5f,Don,GF,Apr 28)*
**Law And Order 109** *(10f,Yor,G,Oct 14)*
**Lawless Secret 107** *(11½f,Wdr,GS,Oct 9)*
**Lawmaking 106** *(8f,Nmk,GS,Jly 28)*
**Le Brivido 111** *(7f,Asc,GF,Jun 21)*
**Le Vagabond 107** *(10f,Leo,GF,Jly 13)*
**Leader Writer 106** *(8f,Asc,GS,Aug 12)*
**Leader's Legacy 107** *(8f,Hay,G,May 13)*
**Leapt 115** *(14f,Lin,S,Jly 29)*
**Lefortovo 106** *(7f,Don,GF,Jly 7)*
**Left Hand 116** *(10f,Cha,S,Oct 1)*
**Leshlaa 110** *(10f,Nmk,GF,May 7)*
**Lester Kris 105** *(12f,Lei,HY,Sep 25)*
**Let Right Be Done 112** *(7f,Ayr,G,Jun 23)*
**Letmestopyouthere 105** *(6f,Chp,G,Aug 28)*
**Lexington Abbey 108** *(5f,Asc,G,Jly 15)*
**Lexington Place 105** *(5f,Red,GF,May 22)*
**Lexington Times 107** *(6f,Yor,G,Jly 28)*
**Liberatum 105** *(5f,Red,G,Jun 23)*
**Librisa Breeze 119** *(6f,Asc,S,Oct 21)*
**Light Of Joy 105** *(10f,Lei,GF,Jly 8)*
**Light That 105** *(12f,Cur,GF,Jly 29)*
**Light The Lights 112** *(9f,Mey,G,Jan 26)*
**Lightening Dance 105** *(10f,Sal,GS,May 18)*
**Lightening Fast 105** *(8f,Leo,GF,Jly 13)*
**Lightning Charlie 113** *(6f,Asc,G,Jly 14)*
**Lightning Spear 115** *(8f,Nby,S,May 20)*
**Limario 106** *(8f,Mey,G,Feb 2)*
**Limato 114** *(6f,Asc,GF,Jun 24)*
**Lime And Lemon 105** *(10f,Nby,S,Oct 27)*
**Lincoln 111** *(6f,Yor,S,May 17)*
**Lincoln Rocks 109** *(7f,Yor,GS,Aug 24)*
**Line Of Reason 111** *(5f,Goo,G,Aug 1)*
**Linguistic 113** *(10f,Yor,G,Oct 14)*
**Liquid 105** *(5f,Don,GF,Apr 29)*
**Little Clarinet 105** *(6f,Cur,G,May 13)*
**Little Orchid 107** *(14f,Yar,GF,May 24)*
**Little Palaver 106** *(6f,Wdr,GF,Apr 24)*
**Live Dangerously 105** *(10f,Lin,GS,Jly 19)*
**Lomu 111** *(7f,Ayr,G,Jun 24)*
**Londinium 115** *(12f,Goo,S,Aug 2)*
**London Prize 106** *(18f,Nmk,G,Oct 14)*
**London Protocol 110** *(8f,Hay,G,Jun 15)*
**Londonia 106** *(13f,Bat,F,Jly 18)*
**Long On Value 109** *(6f,Mey,Y,Mar 25)*
**Longroom 105** *(5f,Mus,G,Jly 14)*
**Longside 106** *(10f,Yar,GF,May 2)*
**Look My Way 116** *(16f,Ffo,HY,Sep 17)*
**Lord Clenaghcastle 107** *(8½f,Eps,GS,Jly 20)*
**Lord Commander 105** *(8½f,Not,GS,Oct 11)*
**Lord E 109** *(11½f,Lin,GF,Jun 24)*
**Lord Franklin 105** *(10½f,Chs,G,Jly 15)*
**Lord Glitters 109** *(8f,Asc,S,Oct 21)*
**Lord Of The Rock 107** *(8f,Yor,GS,Jly 28)*
**Lord Yeats 115** *(12f,Yor,S,May 19)*
**Lorelina 112** *(10f,Nby,S,Oct 27)*
**Los Barbados 110** *(16f,Mey,G,Feb 2)*
**Love Dreams 106** *(7f,Nmk,S,Jly 22)*
**Love Island 105** *(6f,Not,GF,Jun 15)*
**Love Oasis 105** *(6f,Lei,G,Jun 27)*
**Love On The Rocks 106** *(5f,Goo,G,Aug 1)*
**Lualiwa 112** *(7f,Asc,GS,Sep 9)*
**Lucent Dream 108** *(10f,Ayr,G,Jly 17)*
**Lucky Beggar 105** *(6f,Cat,GF,Jun 2)*
**Lucky Clover 110** *(5f,Bat,GF,Jly 12)*
**Lucy The Painter 107** *(12f,Pon,GF,Jun 25)*
**Luis Vaz De Torres 107** *(7f,Ayr,G,Jly 17)*
**Lunar Jet 106** *(10f,Goo,S,Sep 27)*
**Lustrous Light 107** *(12f,Asc,GF,Jun 23)*
**Lyric Harmony 106** *(8f,Hay,GS,Aug 10)*

**Ma Fee Heela 112** *(7f,Leo,YS,Jun 8)*
**Maarek 106** *(5f,Cur,G,Jly 2)*
**Mabs Cross 113** *(5f,Mus,GS,Oct 9)*
**Machine Learner 106** *(12f,Don,S,Nov 11)*
**Madame Bounty 109** *(6f,Wdr,GF,Jun 5)*
**Mafaaheem 105** *(10f,San,G,Jun 8)*
**Magic City 108** *(9f,Rip,G,Jun 22)*
**Magic Journey 106** *(7f,Ayr,G,Jly 24)*
**Magical Dreamer 109** *(6f,Nmk,G,Oct 7)*
**Magical Effect 109** *(6f,Red,GS,Aug 12)*
**Magical Memory 113** *(6f,Nby,S,Jly 22)*
**Magistral 116** *(7f,Ayr,G,Jun 23)*
**Magnus Maximus 105** *(5f,Mey,G,Feb 2)*
**Mainicin 110** *(10f,Leo,G,Aug 17)*
**Mainstream 107** *(12f,Yor,GF,Jly 14)*
**Majboor 107** *(10f,Nby,G,Sep 22)*
**Majeed 112** *(10f,Asc,GF,Jun 24)*
**Majestic Hero 107** *(5f,Eps,G,Apr 26)*
**Majestic Moon 105** *(6f,Yar,G,Jly 19)*
**Major Jumbo 110** *(6f,Yor,GS,Sep 10)*
**Major Pusey 114** *(6f,Wdr,GS,May 29)*
**Major Valentine 106** *(5f,Wdr,G,Aug 13)*
**Make Music 112** *(7f,Goo,GF,May 6)*
**Make On Madam 105** *(8½f,Bev,GF,Apr 19)*
**Make Time 112** *(8f,Goo,S,Aug 4)*
**Making Light 108** *(8f,Leo,YS,Jun 8)*
**Makzeem 109** *(7f,Nmk,GS,Sep 30)*
**Malcolm The Pug 106** *(6f,Lin,GF,Aug 30)*
**Maleficent Queen 107** *(14f,Mus,GF,Apr 15)*
**Maljaa 106** *(5f,Mey,G,Jan 19)*
**Mam'Selle 106** *(12f,Asc,S,Sep 9)*
**Mama Africa 109** *(8½f,Not,GS,Jun 11)*
**Mamillius 105** *(7f,Lei,GF,Jun 17)*
**Mancini 107** *(12f,Pon,GF,Jly 21)*
**Maniaco 113** *(10f,Cha,G,Apr 9)*
**Manshood 106** *(6f,Ham,GS,Aug 24)*
**Manson 105** *(8f,San,GF,Jly 8)*
**Manton Grange 113** *(7f,Lei,GS,Jun 5)*
**Many A Tale 107** *(7½f,Ffo,GS,Jly 25)*
**Many Waters 106** *(10f,Chp,S,Jun 6)*
**Maoi Chinn Tire 107** *(14f,Mus,GF,May 26)*
**Maori Bob 107** *(12f,Bev,GF,Aug 16)*
**Maratha 111** *(8½f,Not,G,Jly 8)*
**Marie Josephe 106** *(10f,Bri,GF,Aug 10)*
**Marie Of Lyon 108** *(6f,Pon,S,Sep 21)*
**Mark Hopkins 110** *(14f,Sal,GF,May 27)*
**Markazi 106** *(8f,Sai,S,Mar 19)*
**Marmelo 115** *(15f,Dea,G,Aug 20)*
**Maroc 105** *(11½f,Lin,GS,Jly 12)*
**Marsh Pride 105** *(8½f,Not,GF,Apr 12)*
**Marsha 117** *(5f,Yor,G,Aug 25)*
**Marshall Aid 106** *(14f,Lin,G,May 24)*
**Marshall Jennings 109** *(8f,Leo,S,Apr 5)*
**Marzouq 106** *(10f,Nmk,GF,Jly 14)*
**Masarzain 107** *(8f,Mus,GF,Aug 30)*
**Masham Star 108** *(7f,Mus,S,Oct 16)*
**Massaat 110** *(7f,Nby,S,Aug 19)*
**Master Carpenter 120** *(10f,Yor,S,May 17)*
**Master Dancer 105** *(16f,Chp,GS,Sep 19)*
**Master The World 112** *(8f,Goo,S,Aug 4)*
**Mastermind 107** *(6f,Mey,G,Jan 26)*
**Materialistic 107** *(8f,Goo,GF,May 6)*
**Maureb 107** *(6f,Crl,GF,Jly 13)*
**Maverick Wave 111** *(10f,Asc,GF,Jun 24)*
**Mawaany 107** *(10f,Cur,G,May 14)*
**Max Zorin 105** *(10½f,Chs,GF,May 12)*
**Mayleaf Shine 109** *(5f,Hay,HY,Sep 9)*
**Mazyoun 106** *(7f,Yor,GF,Jun 17)*
**Mazzini 106** *(6f,Goo,G,May 26)*
**Me Too Nagasaki 106** *(8f,Pon,S,Oct 9)*
**Medahim 107** *(8f,Nmk,GF,Jly 15)*
**Medburn Cutler 107** *(18f,Nmk,G,Sep 23)*
**Medburn Dream 111** *(7½f,Lin,GF,Jun 24)*
**Medicean Man 110** *(5f,Mey,G,Jan 19)*
**Medieval 105** *(7f,Nmk,G,Sep 23)*
**Megalala 111** *(10f,Lin,GF,Jun 13)*
**Megan Lily 107** *(5f,Chs,S,Jun 10)*
**Mekhtaal 114** *(10f,Asc,GF,Jun 21)*
**Melesina 105** *(10f,Cha,S,Oct 1)*
**Melinoe 108** *(14f,Goo,S,Sep 27)*
**Melting Dew 107** *(12f,Asc,S,Sep 9)*
**Memories Galore 112** *(5f,Yor,G,Oct 13)*
**Merlin 114** *(7f,Hay,GS,Jun 14)*
**Meshardal 111** *(6f,Thi,GS,Jun 5)*
**Meshaykh 108** *(8f,Lei,G,May 29)*
**Metronomic 106** *(10f,Red,S,Nov 7)*
**Mia Tesoro 108** *(10f,Nby,G,Sep 22)*
**Michael's Mount 106** *(10f,Hay,S,Sep 8)*
**Michele Strogoff 105** *(8f,Crl,GF,May 22)*
**Mickey Rich 108** *(7f,Lei,GF,May 9)*
**Middle Kingdom 108** *(10f,Nmk,GF,Apr 19)*
**Midhmaar 109** *(8f,Hay,GF,Jly 7)*
**Midnight Malibu 108** *(5f,Eps,G,Aug 28)*
**Midtech Star 106** *(14½f,Don,GF,May 6)*
**Midterm 113** *(12f,Nby,GF,Apr 22)*
**Mikmak 105** *(8½f,Not,GS,Oct 11)*
**Miles To Memphis 107** *(12f,Cur,GF,Jly 15)*
**Ming Dynasty 110** *(15f,Cha,S,Sep 10)*
**Miningrocks 105** *(10f,Bev,GS,Jun 10)*
**Mirage Dancer 113** *(10f,Asc,GF,Jun 22)*
**Mirimar 107** *(10f,Lin,S,Aug 5)*
**Mirza 110** *(5f,Nby,G,Sep 23)*
**Miss Inga Sock 105** *(10f,Chp,S,Jun 6)*
**Miss Osier 105** *(8½f,Not,G,May 13)*
**Miss Power 106** *(5f,Cur,GF,Jly 29)*
**Miss Sheridan 105** *(8f,Pon,GF,Apr 24)*
**Mister Blue Sky 108** *(8½f,Not,G,May 13)*
**Mister Manduro 109** *(11½f,Bat,F,Apr 14)*
**Mister Music 105** *(7f,Lei,G,Apr 7)*
**Mistiness 109** *(13f,Ham,S,Jun 7)*
**Mistiroc 110** *(10f,Yor,G,Jly 15)*
**Mistress Quickly 108** *(13f,Nby,GS,Jly 21)*
**Misty Mountain 105** *(10f,Leo,G,Aug 17)*
**Mitchum Swagger 110** *(7f,Hay,S,Jun 10)*
**Mittens 108** *(8f,Nmk,GS,Sep 29)*
**Mix And Mingle 112** *(7f,Lin,G,May 13)*
**Mixboy 106** *(12f,Cat,S,Oct 31)*
**Mizaah 108** *(8f,Cur,G,Jly 1)*
**Mjjack 114** *(7f,Asc,GS,Sep 9)*
**Moabit 108** *(14f,Sal,S,Oct 9)*
**Moayadd 105** *(12f,Chp,GF,May 5)*
**Mobsta 107** *(6f,Yor,S,May 17)*
**Mohab 105** *(8½f,Bev,G,May 16)*
**Mohsen 108** *(6f,Don,G,Aug 19)*
**Mojito 109** *(8f,Yor,G,Aug 25)*
**Mokarris 106** *(6f,Asc,GF,May 3)*
**Mon Beau Visage 105** *(8f,Thi,G,Aug 21)*
**Monaadhil 107** *(8½f,Not,G,Nov 1)*
**Monarchs Glen 111** *(10f,Goo,S,Sep 27)*
**Mondialiste 111** *(10f,Yor,GS,Jly 29)*
**Monjeni 110** *(13f,Ham,GF,May 7)*
**Monreal 108** *(15f,Cha,GS,Sep 30)*
**Monsieur Glory 105** *(10f,Yar,GF,May 2)*
**Monsieur Joe 109** *(5f,Cur,G,May 14)*
**Mont Kiara 107** *(6f,Nmk,G,Aug 4)*
**Montaly 112** *(18f,Don,GS,Sep 15)*
**Mooltazem 105** *(8½f,Not,GS,Oct 4)*
**Moonlight Magic 117** *(10f,Leo,G,Sep 9)*
**Moonlightnavigator 106** *(8f,Thi,GF,May 6)*
**Moonmeister 105** *(12f,Hay,GF,Jly 8)*
**Moonraker 105** *(6f,Goo,G,May 26)*
**Moonshiner 108** *(15f,Dea,G,Aug 20)*
**Moonwise 108** *(7f,Hay,GF,Jly 8)*
**Morache Music 108** *(6f,Goo,G,May 27)*
**Morando 111** *(8f,Wdr,GS,Jly 1)*
**More Mischief 113** *(12f,Nmk,S,Jly 22)*
**Mori 106** *(12f,Asc,GF,Jun 22)*
**Morning Suit 115** *(10f,Goo,S,Aug 3)*
**Mornington 105** *(11½f,Bat,F,May 1)*
**Motherland 108** *(14f,Leo,GF,May 26)*
**Mount Logan 114** *(10½f,Hay,GS,Aug 12)*
**Mount Moriah 113** *(16f,Asc,S,Oct 21)*
**Mount Rock 113** *(9f,Yor,G,Jly 28)*
**Mount Tahan 107** *(8f,Don,GS,Apr 1)*
**Mountain Angel 107** *(8f,Don,S,Jun 3)*
**Mountain Bell 110** *(12f,Nby,S,Oct 28)*
**Mountain Hunter 110** *(8f,Nmk,G,Aug 4)*
**Mountain Rescue 113** *(7f,Nmk,G,Aug 4)*
**Mr Chuckles 108** *(5f,Chp,S,Jun 10)*
**Mr Cool Cash 107** *(8f,Pon,S,Sep 21)*
**Mr Everest 106** *(12f,Cur,S,Jun 11)*
**Mr Garcia 109** *(10f,Yor,G,Jly 15)*
**Mr Lupton 112** *(6f,Nmk,GF,May 7)*
**Mr Owen 107** *(9f,Mey,G,Jan 26)*
**Mr Right 106** *(7f,Leo,GF,May 7)*
**Ms Gillard 108** *(10f,Yar,GF,Jun 13)*
**Muatadel 106** *(5f,Red,G,Jun 23)*
**Mubtasim 118** *(6f,Asc,GF,May 3)*
**Muffri'Ha 115** *(8f,Mey,G,Jan 26)*
**Muirsheen Durkin 106** *(8f,Crl,GS,Jun 28)*
**Mukalal 107** *(7f,Goo,G,Aug 26)*
**Mukhayyam 109** *(12f,Yor,GF,Jly 14)*
**Mulligatawny 107** *(9f,Rip,G,Jun 22)*
**Mullionheir 105** *(6f,Asc,S,Sep 8)*
**Multi Facets 105** *(8f,Don,S,Jun 3)*
**Munaashid 106** *(10f,Nmk,G,Jun 10)*
**Munfallet 105** *(6f,Don,GF,May 6)*
**Muniza 111** *(8f,Cur,GF,Jly 16)*
**Muntadab 115** *(7f,Mus,S,Oct 16)*
**Muntahaa 115** *(12f,Nby,GF,Apr 22)*
**Muntazah 110** *(10f,Asc,GF,Jun 24)*
**Musawaat 107** *(7f,Nmk,GF,Aug 26)*
**Muscika 105** *(6f,Ayr,G,Jun 5)*
**Mushaireb 109** *(8f,Pon,S,Sep 21)*
**Music Box 109** *(7f,Don,GS,Sep 15)*
**Music Seeker 111** *(10f,Nby,S,Jly 27)*
**Mustashry 111** *(9f,Yor,G,Aug 26)*
**Mutadaffeq 115** *(12f,Pon,G,May 26)*
**Mutakayyef 115** *(8f,Asc,G,Jly 15)*
**Mutamaded 107** *(10f,Rip,G,Aug 29)*
**Mutarabby 106** *(8f,Hay,GS,Jun 14)*
**Mutarakez 107** *(10f,San,GF,Jly 7)*
**Mutasayyid 106** *(9f,Mey,G,Jan 28)*
**Mutawathea 108** *(7f,Yor,GF,Jun 17)*
**Muthmir 111** *(5f,Nby,G,Sep 23)*
**My Dream Boat 111** *(12f,Asc,GS,Jly 29)*
**My Girl Maisie 105** *(6f,Crl,S,Jun 9)*
**My Lucille 106** *(8f,Hay,S,Jun 9)*
**My Name Is Rio 109** *(6f,Don,GF,May 6)*
**My Reward 105** *(16f,Rip,G,Apr 29)*
**My Target 108** *(7½f,Chs,GF,May 27)*
**Mysterial 108** *(12f,Pon,G,May 26)*
**Mystic Dawn 108** *(6f,Yor,GF,Jly 14)*
**Mythical Madness 116** *(8f,Hay,G,Jun 15)*
**Mythmaker 110** *(6f,Sal,GF,Jun 18)*
**Mywayistheonlyway 108** *(7f,Ayr,S,Jun 12)*

**Naadirr 113** *(6f,Don,GS,Oct 27)*
**Naggers 108** *(6f,Thi,S,May 20)*
**Nameitwhatyoulike 108** *(6f,Rip,S,Sep 30)*
**Naseem 105** *(10f,San,G,Apr 28)*
**Natavia 106** *(12f,Nby,S,Oct 28)*
**Nathalie 105** *(12f,Don,S,Sep 14)*
**Nathan 109** *(10f,Nby,S,Aug 19)*
**Nathra 112** *(8f,Nmk,G,Oct 7)*
**Native Prospect 106** *(8½f,Eps,G,Jly 13)*
**Naturalist 106** *(10f,Leo,S,Apr 5)*
**Naval Warfare 108** *(8f,Nmk,GS,Aug 12)*
**Navarone 110** *(7f,Ayr,G,Jun 24)*
**Nearly Caught 118** *(16f,Nmk,GS,Sep 28)*
**New Direction 110** *(10f,Leo,GF,Jun 22)*
**New Identity 111** *(5f,Ffo,HY,Aug 3)*
**New Terms 107** *(8f,Cur,GF,Jly 16)*
**New World Power 105** *(14½f,Don,GF,May 6)*
**Newmarket Warrior 109** *(7f,Ayr,G,Jun 23)*
**Nezwaah 114** *(10f,Cur,G,Jly 2)*
**Niblawi 106** *(12f,Don,S,Nov 11)*
**Nicholas T 109** *(8f,Ayr,G,Jun 24)*
**Night Circus 105** *(8f,Nmk,GS,Aug 12)*
**Night Of Glory 108** *(10f,Cur,G,May 13)*
**Ninjago 107** *(6f,Don,G,Apr 2)*
**Noah Amor 105** *(5f,Bev,GF,Sep 2)*
**Noah From Goa 112** *(8f,Mey,G,Feb 16)*
**Nobelium 107** *(7f,Mey,G,Feb 9)*
**Noble Gift 107** *(12f,Lei,GS,Oct 30)*
**Noble Peace 114** *(8f,Goo,S,Oct 15)*
**Nobly Born 111** *(6f,Asc,GS,Oct 6)*
**Noor Al Hawa 107** *(8f,Cha,S,Sep 30)*
**Normal Equilibrium 109** *(5f,Chs,G,Aug 26)*
**Normandie Lady 108** *(8½f,Not,GF,May 2)*
**Normandy Barriere 105** *(7f,Don,G,Aug 19)*
**Northgate Lad 111** *(6f,Yor,S,May 17)*
**Northwest Frontier 107** *(12f,Thi,G,Aug 5)*
**Not A Whisper 107** *(8f,Cur,G,May 14)*
**Not So Sleepy 112** *(10f,Yor,S,May 17)*
**Nothing To Lose 117** *(7f,Ayr,G,Jly 9)*
**Notice 108** *(14f,Goo,S,Sep 27)*
**Novoman 114** *(10f,Goo,G,Aug 27)*
**Nutini 106** *(7f,Leo,S,Apr 5)*

**Oasis Charm 105** *(10f,Nmk,GF,Jly 14)*
**Oasis Fantasy 114** *(10f,Yor,S,May 17)*
**Ocean Temptress 108** *(7f,Bri,GS,Aug 22)*
**Oceane 106** *(18f,Nmk,G,Sep 23)*
**Oh Grace 112** *(7f,Leo,YS,Jun 8)*
**Oh So Sassy 105** *(5f,Nmk,G,Jly 13)*
**Oh This Is Us 115** *(7f,Hay,G,May 13)*
**Olivia Fallow 107** *(5f,Red,GF,May 22)*
**Omotesando 105** *(9f,Crl,GS,Jly 8)*
**On Her Toes 107** *(8f,Asc,GS,Jly 28)*
**On The Go Again 105** *(10f,Leo,G,Aug 17)*
**On To Victory 114** *(12f,Goo,S,Aug 2)*
**One Foot In Heaven 114** *(12f,Cha,S,Oct 1)*
**One Master 108** *(6f,Don,G,Aug 19)*
**One Word More 109** *(8f,Goo,S,Aug 4)*
**Onenightidreamed 108** *(8f,Leo,S,Apr 5)*
**Only Mine 106** *(6f,Cur,YS,May 27)*
**Onthemoonagain 112** *(10f,Cha,S,Oct 1)*
**Opal Tiara 115** *(8f,Mey,G,Jan 26)*
**Open Wide 106** *(5f,Wdr,GF,Jun 12)*
**Opinionate 106** *(12f,Sal,G,Sep 7)*
**Orangey Red 108** *(7f,Goo,G,Aug 27)*
**Order Of St George 117** *(14f,Cur,Y,Aug 19)*
**Orderofthegarter 113** *(10f,Asc,GF,Jun 22)*
**Orient Class 111** *(5f,Thi,GF,May 6)*
**Oriental Fox 109** *(18f,Nmk,G,Sep 23)*
**Oriental Lilly 106** *(5f,Hay,G,Jly 22)*
**Oriental Relation 107** *(5f,Pon,GF,Apr 24)*
**Original Choice 106** *(8f,Hay,GS,Jun 14)*
**Orion's Bow 105** *(5f,Asc,G,Jly 15)*
**Ornate 112** *(6f,Nmk,GF,Aug 26)*
**Orsino 105** *(14f,Sal,G,Aug 17)*
**Ostatnia 113** *(5f,Cur,G,May 14)*

**Ouja 105** *(12f,Yor,GS,Aug 24)*
**Our Charlie Brown 108** *(7f,Red,GS,Aug 12)*
**Our Cilla 106** *(14f,Lin,S,Jly 22)*
**Our Lord 105** *(5f,Sal,S,Jly 29)*
**Our Oystercatcher 108** *(6f,Wdr,GS,Oct 9)*
**Out Do 111** *(5f,Yor,G,Jly 15)*
**Ower Fly 106** *(7f,Lin,GS,Sep 16)*
**Oxford Blu 106** *(18f,Chp,GS,Aug 24)*

**Pacharana 108** *(11½f,Bat,G,Jly 26)*
**Pacific Salt 105** *(8½f,Not,GS,Oct 11)*
**Pacify 109** *(8f,Nby,GF,Apr 22)*
**Pack It In 111** *(10f,Lin,GF,Jun 13)*
**Pactolus 110** *(10f,Nmk,G,Jun 10)*
**Paddy Power 105** *(5f,Don,GS,Oct 28)*
**Padrinho 105** *(14f,Wet,G,May 15)*
**Palace Prince 111** *(10f,Cha,G,Apr 9)*
**Pallasator 111** *(15f,Dea,G,Aug 20)*
**Palmerston 113** *(8½f,Bev,GF,May 31)*
**Panova 106** *(8f,Goo,G,Aug 25)*
**Par Three 105** *(14f,Yar,GF,May 24)*
**Parfait 111** *(6f,Lei,GS,May 29)*
**Parole 105** *(8f,Hay,GS,Sep 7)*
**Pastfact 105** *(6f,Chp,GS,Aug 17)*
**Pastoral Player 105** *(7f,Lin,G,May 13)*
**Patrick 110** *(5f,Cur,G,Jly 2)*
**Pattie 107** *(10f,Nby,G,Jun 15)*
**Patuano 109** *(5f,Cur,G,Jly 2)*
**Pavlenko 105** *(7f,Cur,GF,Jly 29)*
**Peace Dreamer 106** *(6f,Red,GF,Jun 24)*
**Peach Melba 110** *(7½f,Ffo,GS,Jly 25)*
**Pealer 111** *(8f,Asc,GS,Jly 29)*
**Pennsylvania Dutch 108** *(6f,Hay,S,Jun 10)*
**Penny Dreadful 105** *(5f,Cat,G,Aug 30)*
**Penny Pot Lane 106** *(6f,Red,S,Sep 19)*
**Pensax Boy 106** *(8f,Crl,GF,May 22)*
**Penwortham 113** *(7½f,Chs,GF,May 27)*
**Percy 106** *(12f,Leo,YS,Jun 8)*
**Perfect Angel 111** *(6f,Nby,S,Jly 22)*
**Perfect In Pink 105** *(12f,Lei,GS,May 29)*
**Perfect Pasture 114** *(6f,Don,GS,Oct 27)*
**Perfect Summer 105** *(11½f,Wdr,GS,May 29)*
**Perla Blanca 106** *(12f,Ffo,G,Jly 17)*
**Permian 116** *(10f,Yor,GS,May 18)*
**Permission 115** *(10f,Nmk,GS,Nov 4)*
**Persistence 109** *(10f,Sal,S,Jly 29)*
**Persuasive 116** *(8f,Leo,G,Sep 9)*
**Peticoatgovernment 109** *(6f,Cur,YS,May 27)*
**Petite Jack 108** *(10f,Yar,G,Jly 19)*
**Pettochside 113** *(5f,Goo,G,Aug 1)*
**Philosopher 107** *(9f,Mey,G,Jan 28)*
**Pictograph 108** *(8f,Mey,G,Jan 28)*
**Pilgrim's Treasure 109** *(10f,Nby,S,Jly 27)*
**Pillar Of Society 108** *(8f,Nmk,GS,Jly 29)*
**Pioneering 110** *(8f,Pon,S,Oct 9)*
**Pipers Note 109** *(6f,Don,GS,Apr 1)*
**Pirouette 108** *(7f,Mus,GF,Jun 3)*
**Pivoine 106** *(10f,Don,GS,Sep 15)*
**Pixeleen 110** *(5f,Nmk,G,Oct 7)*
**Plant Pot Power 106** *(8f,Nby,S,Oct 27)*
**Platitude 112** *(16f,Nmk,GS,Sep 28)*
**Playful Sound 109** *(10f,Yor,GS,Jly 28)*
**Pleasant Surprise 109** *(12f,Nmk,GS,Sep 29)*
**Plough Boy 107** *(7f,Cur,GF,Jly 15)*
**Plumatic 113** *(12f,Cha,S,Oct 1)*
**Plutonian 107** *(8f,Wdr,GF,Jun 26)*
**Plymouth Sound 113** *(11½f,Lin,GF,Jun 24)*
**Pocketfullofdreams 105** *(10f,Cur,G,Jly 2)*
**Poet's Princess 112** *(6f,Nmk,GS,May 20)*
**Poet's Society 106** *(5f,Chs,S,Jun 10)*
**Poet's Word 119** *(10f,Leo,G,Sep 9)*
**Poeta Diletto 106** *(8f,Hay,GF,Apr 29)*
**Poetic Choice 105** *(7f,Leo,S,Apr 5)*
**Political Policy 105** *(12f,Cur,GF,Jly 29)*
**Polybius 110** *(5f,Asc,G,Jly 15)*
**Pomme De Terre 109** *(6f,Thi,GS,Jun 5)*
**Poor Duke 105** *(7f,Lei,GS,Jun 5)*
**Postponed 115** *(12f,Mey,Y,Mar 25)*
**Pour La Victoire 106** *(6f,Bri,GF,Aug 11)*
**Pouvoir Magique 105** *(10f,San,G,Jun 8)*
**Poyle Vinnie 114** *(5f,Goo,G,Aug 1)*
**Precieuse 105** *(6f,Cha,G,Apr 9)*
**Precious Ramotswe 113** *(10f,Nby,S,Oct 27)*
**Precision 106** *(14f,Not,GS,Aug 18)*
**Prerogative 107** *(10f,Chp,GF,May 5)*
**Priceless 108** *(5f,Yor,G,Aug 25)*
**Primo Uomo 108** *(5f,Cur,G,May 14)*
**Prince Of Arran 107** *(16f,Goo,G,Aug 1)*
**Princess De Lune 105** *(7f,Nby,G,Sep 22)*
**Prize Diva 108** *(10f,Not,GF,Jun 15)*
**Prize Money 115** *(12f,Mey,Y,Mar 25)*
**Procurator 105** *(7f,Bri,S,Oct 19)*
**Professor 106** *(7f,San,GS,Jly 26)*
**Profitable 117** *(5f,Goo,S,Aug 4)*
**Project Bluebook 107** *(16f,Chp,GS,Aug 17)*
**Projection 113** *(6f,Asc,GS,Oct 7)*
**Prominna 108** *(5f,Ffo,HY,Aug 3)*
**Promise To Be True 106** *(7f,Leo,GY,Apr 8)*
**Promising 105** *(7f,Nby,GF,Apr 22)*
**Promising Run 113** *(9f,Mey,G,Jan 26)*
**Prosper 106** *(8f,Asc,GF,May 3)*
**Prying Pandora 106** *(8f,Nmk,S,Aug 11)*
**Psychedelic Funk 114** *(8f,Leo,G,Sep 9)*
**Ptarmigan Ridge 107** *(6f,Don,HY,May 20)*
**Pumblechook 105** *(12f,Pon,G,May 26)*
**Punkawallah 105** *(10f,Hay,GS,Aug 10)*
**Pupil 109** *(7f,Mey,G,Jan 28)*
**Pure Art 105** *(12f,Pon,GF,Jun 25)*
**Pursuing Steed 108** *(7f,Lei,S,Jly 26)*

**Qassem 113** *(10f,Yor,S,May 17)*
**Qemah 112** *(8f,Leo,G,Sep 9)*
**Qeyaadah 114** *(6f,Don,GF,May 6)*
**Quarterback 108** *(12f,Nby,GF,Apr 22)*
**Queen In Waiting 109** *(6f,Goo,G,May 26)*
**Queen Kindly 108** *(5f,Cha,S,Oct 1)*
**Queen Of Time 105** *(8f,Not,GS,Aug 18)*
**Queen's Parade 110** *(8f,Mey,G,Jan 26)*
**Queen's Trust 115** *(10f,Goo,S,Aug 3)*
**Quench Dolly 113** *(5f,Goo,S,Aug 3)*
**Quest For More 107** *(16f,Mey,Y,Mar 25)*
**Questo 105** *(6f,Red,GS,Aug 12)*
**Quick Look 107** *(6f,Thi,S,Sep 9)*
**Quiet Reflection 110** *(6f,Asc,S,Oct 21)*
**Quixote 113** *(8f,Hay,GF,Apr 29)*
**Quloob 107** *(14f,Not,GS,Aug 18)*
**Quothquan 109** *(14f,Sal,HY,Oct 4)*

**Racemaker 106** *(8f,Rip,G,Jly 10)*
**Racing Angel 105** *(5f,Yar,GF,Aug 1)*
**Raheen House 112** *(12f,Asc,GF,Jun 23)*
**Rain Goddess 112** *(12f,Cur,GF,Jly 15)*
**Rainbow Dreamer 105** *(12f,Lei,GS,Apr 7)*
**Rainbow Rebel 107** *(10f,Red,G,May 29)*
**Raising Sand 112** *(7f,Asc,GS,Sep 9)*
**Rake's Progress 116** *(10f,Nby,S,Jly 27)*
**Rapid Applause 106** *(6f,Cur,YS,May 27)*
**Rare Rhythm 110** *(12f,Asc,GF,Jun 23)*
**Raseed 107** *(10f,Cha,G,Apr 9)*
**Raselasad 110** *(7f,Red,GS,Aug 12)*
**Rasheeq 110** *(5f,Yor,G,May 27)*
**Rattling Jewel 110** *(6f,Cur,YS,May 27)*
**Raucous 110** *(6f,Wdr,G,May 22)*
**Raven's Lady 109** *(6f,Nmk,G,Jly 21)*
**Ravenhoe 105** *(8f,Pon,GF,May 3)*
**Ravenous 107** *(14f,Not,GS,Aug 18)*
**Ray's The Money 118** *(10f,Goo,S,Aug 3)*
**Really Special 107** *(7f,Mey,G,Feb 23)*
**Realtra 111** *(8f,Mey,G,Jan 26)*
**Reaver 109** *(8f,Wdr,GS,Oct 9)*
**Rebecca Rocks 105** *(5f,Don,GF,Apr 29)*
**Rebel Surge 110** *(7f,Hay,S,Jun 9)*
**Reckless Gold 112** *(10½f,Cur,Y,May 28)*
**Recoletos 113** *(10f,Asc,S,Oct 21)*
**Red Cardinal 111** *(15f,Dea,G,Aug 20)*
**Red Galileo 112** *(12f,Nmk,GS,Sep 29)*
**Red Pike 113** *(8f,Rip,G,Aug 19)*
**Red Royalist 107** *(10f,Nby,G,Sep 22)*
**Red Tea 114** *(8f,Pon,GF,Apr 24)*
**Red Verdon 110** *(12f,Eps,G,Jun 2)*
**Redarna 106** *(8f,Crl,GS,Aug 23)*
**Redgrave 111** *(7f,San,S,Aug 10)*
**Reflektor 106** *(6f,Hay,S,Jun 10)*
**Regal Mirage 106** *(11f,Ham,G,Jly 21)*
**Rehana 109** *(7f,Leo,GY,Apr 8)*
**Reinforced 112** *(7f,Ayr,G,Jun 23)*
**Rekindling 119** *(14f,Cur,G,Jly 2)*
**Related 109** *(6f,Don,GF,May 6)*
**Relight My Fire 105** *(8f,Mus,GF,Aug 11)*
**Rely On Me 109** *(7f,Hay,GS,Jun 14)*
**Remarkable 115** *(7f,Asc,GS,Sep 9)*
**Rembrandt Van Rijn 109** *(16f,Mey,Y,Mar 25)*
**Remember Rocky 112** *(8f,Ayr,G,Jly 24)*
**Rene Mathis 105** *(7f,Lei,GS,Oct 17)*
**Renfrew Street 109** *(14f,Goo,S,Sep 27)*
**Renneti 109** *(14f,Cur,Y,Aug 19)*
**Repercussion 107** *(8f,Nmk,GS,Sep 28)*
**Repton 105** *(6f,Nby,S,Oct 27)*
**Reputation 105** *(6f,Eps,G,Jun 3)*
**Reshoun 109** *(12f,Don,GS,Oct 28)*
**Restive 110** *(8f,Ham,GF,May 19)*
**Restorer 110** *(10f,Asc,GF,Jun 24)*
**Retribution 107** *(10f,Lin,GS,Jly 19)*
**Return Ace 105** *(12f,Nmk,S,Jly 22)*
**Reverend Jacobs 106** *(12f,Asc,S,Sep 8)*
**Rhododendron 117** *(10f,Cha,S,Oct 1)*
**Ribchester 119** *(8f,Nby,S,May 20)*
**Rich And Famous 107** *(6f,Don,GF,Apr 28)*
**Rich Legacy 105** *(12f,Asc,GF,Jun 22)*
**Richard's Boy 106** *(6f,Mey,Y,Mar 25)*
**Ride Like The Wind 105** *(6f,Don,GS,Apr 1)*
**Right Action 108** *(7f,Red,GS,Aug 12)*
**Right Touch 114** *(7f,Yor,GF,May 27)*
**Rigoletto 107** *(8f,Sal,GF,Aug 16)*
**Rinaria 106** *(8f,Pon,GF,Jun 25)*
**Rio Ronaldo 108** *(6f,Wdr,GS,May 29)*
**Riponian 107** *(9f,Ham,GS,Aug 5)*
**Riptide 105** *(18f,Chp,GS,Aug 24)*
**Rivet 110** *(8f,Nmk,GF,Apr 20)*
**Roachdale House 108** *(7f,Leo,S,Apr 5)*
**Roar 106** *(12f,Asc,S,Sep 8)*
**Robero 111** *(7f,Mus,S,Oct 16)*
**Robin Of Navan 119** *(10f,Cha,S,Sep 30)*
**Rock Icon 105** *(8f,Bri,GS,Aug 22)*
**Rock N Roll Global 106** *(10f,Lin,GS,Aug 21)*
**Rock N Rolla 105** *(9f,Mus,S,Sep 16)*
**Rockwood 109** *(8f,Pon,GF,Apr 24)*
**Rodaini 107** *(8f,Rip,G,Aug 29)*
**Roi De Vitesse 105** *(6f,Mey,G,Feb 9)*
**Roll On Rory 111** *(7f,Red,GS,Aug 12)*
**Roller 112** *(8f,Hay,G,Jun 15)*
**Rolling Maul 109** *(16f,Nmk,GS,Aug 12)*
**Roly Poly 115** *(8f,Nmk,G,Oct 7)*
**Roman De Brut 107** *(8½f,Not,GS,Jly 25)*
**Ronald R 108** *(8f,Nmk,GF,May 6)*
**Rosabelle 105** *(6f,Lin,GS,Sep 16)*
**Rosarno 106** *(8½f,Not,GS,Oct 11)*
**Rose Berry 107** *(6f,Yar,GS,Sep 20)*
**Rose De Pierre 110** *(8f,Leo,S,Apr 5)*
**Rose Marmara 105** *(5f,Don,GF,Jly 7)*
**Rosental 107** *(10f,Sal,GF,Aug 16)*
**Rosina 107** *(5f,Ayr,G,Aug 12)*
**Ross Raith Rover 108** *(7f,Nmk,G,Aug 4)*
**Rotherwick 108** *(10f,San,G,Sep 2)*
**Round The Island 110** *(6f,Thi,GS,Jun 5)*
**Rousayan 109** *(8f,Thi,GF,May 6)*
**Rowlestonerendezvu 107** *(12f,Ffo,G,Jly 17)*
**Royal Brave 108** *(5f,Yor,G,Oct 13)*
**Royal Duchess 113** *(7f,Ayr,G,Jun 23)*
**Royal Flag 106** *(12f,Don,G,Apr 2)*
**Royal Julius 105** *(8f,Cha,S,Sep 30)*
**Royal Line 108** *(12f,Hay,HY,Sep 30)*
**Royal Regent 105** *(10f,Ayr,G,May 24)*
**Royal Shaheen 109** *(8f,Ayr,G,Jly 17)*
**Rubens Dream 105** *(7f,Hay,S,Jun 8)*
**Rumpole 110** *(10f,Goo,S,Aug 3)*
**Rural Celebration 107** *(5f,Mus,S,Aug 4)*
**Russian Realm 106** *(7f,Hay,GF,Apr 29)*
**Russian Reward 106** *(10f,Bat,F,Jun 23)*
**Rusumaat 111** *(7f,Nby,S,Jly 22)*
**Rutherford 107** *(7½f,Chs,GS,Aug 19)*
**Rydan 105** *(14f,Sal,S,Oct 9)*

**Saayerr 106** *(5f,Mey,G,Jan 19)*
**Sabador 112** *(7f,Ayr,G,May 31)*
**Sacred Act 106** *(8f,Don,GS,Apr 1)*
**Sagely 105** *(12f,Sal,GF,Jly 15)*
**Sahreej 106** *(6f,Cur,G,Jun 30)*
**Saigon City 107** *(14f,Nmk,S,May 19)*
**Saint Equiano 105** *(7f,Crl,GS,Jly 8)*
**Sakhee's Return 106** *(7f,Cat,G,Aug 30)*
**Salateen 113** *(7f,Goo,G,Aug 27)*
**Salouen 119** *(10f,Cha,S,Sep 30)*
**Salsabeel 105** *(7f,Nmk,GF,Apr 18)*
**Salt Whistle Bay 106** *(8½f,Not,GS,Oct 4)*
**Same Jurisdiction 105** *(7f,Lei,GS,Jun 5)*
**Sands Chorus 111** *(9f,Nmk,GS,Sep 30)*
**Sandstorming 106** *(12f,Cur,GF,Jly 15)*
**Sandy Shores 111** *(8f,Wdr,GF,Aug 26)*
**Sans Souci Bay 108** *(7f,Sal,GS,May 18)*
**Sanshaawes 111** *(10f,Mey,G,Feb 2)*
**Santa Monica 110** *(12f,Leo,G,Aug 10)*
**Saroog 108** *(10f,Sal,S,Jly 29)*
**Satono Diamond 112** *(12f,Cha,S,Oct 1)*
**Satono Noblesse 112** *(12f,Cha,S,Oct 1)*
**Saumur 108** *(10f,Nby,S,Oct 27)*
**Saunter 111** *(12f,Don,S,Nov 11)*
**Savannah Beau 105** *(5f,Don,GF,Jly 7)*
**Savannah Slew 107** *(6f,Ham,S,Sep 5)*
**Save The Bees 107** *(10f,Bev,GF,Aug 16)*
**Saved By The Bell 106** *(16f,Nmk,GF,Nov 3)*
**Savoken 106** *(10f,Sai,S,Mar 19)*
**Sayem 107** *(8f,Wdr,GF,Jly 17)*
**Sayesse 106** *(6f,Lei,GS,May 29)*
**Scarlet Dragon 111** *(10f,Asc,GF,Jun 24)*
**Scofflaw 106** *(6f,Hay,GF,Jly 8)*
**Scorching Heat 114** *(6f,Lei,GS,May 29)*
**Scottish 114** *(10f,Asc,GF,Jun 21)*
**Scrutineer 106** *(6f,Don,GS,Apr 1)*
**Sea Fox 105** *(7f,Asc,GS,Oct 6)*
**Sea Of Grace 109** *(8f,Nmk,GF,Jly 14)*
**Sea Of Green 112** *(7f,Ayr,G,Jun 23)*
**Sea Wolf 108** *(8f,Cur,G,Jly 1)*
**Seamster 107** *(5f,Thi,GF,May 6)*
**Sebastian's Wish 108** *(14f,Mus,GF,Aug 11)*
**Second Step 113** *(12f,Nby,GF,Apr 22)*
**Second Thought 108** *(6f,Hay,F,May 27)*
**Secret Advisor 109** *(12f,Goo,S,Aug 2)*
**Secret Agent 106** *(5f,Bat,G,May 17)*
**Secret Art 109** *(8f,Wdr,G,May 1)*
**Secret Brief 107** *(8f,Mey,G,Jan 12)*
**Secret Number 111** *(12f,Asc,GS,Oct 7)*
**Securities 105** *(8f,Mey,G,Jan 28)*
**Seduce Me 107** *(8½f,Eps,GS,Aug 3)*
**See The Master 108** *(8f,San,GS,Aug 2)*
**Seeking Magic 107** *(6f,Not,GS,Jly 21)*
**Sellingallthetime 106** *(12f,Cat,GF,Apr 12)*
**Senga 108** *(10f,Cha,S,Oct 1)*
**Sennockian Star 108** *(13f,Ham,GF,May 7)*
**Sepal 109** *(12f,Thi,G,Aug 21)*
**September Issue 108** *(5f,Bat,GS,Aug 4)*
**Serenada 106** *(12f,Nmk,S,Jly 22)*
**Set In Stone 109** *(8f,Nby,S,Aug 18)*
**Seven Heavens 113** *(8f,Asc,GF,May 3)*
**Sevenleft 106** *(8f,Leo,YS,Jun 8)*
**Seventh Heaven 116** *(12f,Mey,Y,Mar 25)*
**Severus 108** *(7f,Cur,GF,Jly 15)*
**Sfumato 109** *(6f,Lei,GS,May 29)*
**Sgt Reckless 106** *(10f,Nmk,G,Jun 10)*
**Shaaqaaf 107** *(8f,Goo,G,Jun 2)*
**Shabbah 106** *(10f,Nby,G,Sep 23)*
**Shabeeb 105** *(12f,Asc,GF,Jun 23)*
**Shady McCoy 110** *(7f,Asc,GS,Sep 9)*
**Shaiyem 107** *(7½f,Lin,G,May 13)*
**Shamrokh 107** *(8f,Nmk,GS,Nov 4)*
**Shamsaya 105** *(6f,Not,GS,Jly 21)*
**Shamshon 109** *(5f,Nmk,G,Jly 13)*
**Shanghai Glory 109** *(6f,Goo,S,Aug 5)*
**Shared Equity 105** *(6f,Nby,S,May 19)*
**Shargiah 107** *(10f,San,GF,Jun 16)*
**Sharja Bridge 107** *(8½f,Not,GS,Aug 18)*
**Sharjah 107** *(10f,Bat,F,Jun 23)*
**Sharp Defence 105** *(6f,Ham,S,Jly 4)*
**Shawaahid 107** *(7f,Mey,G,Jan 28)*
**Shawami 105** *(9f,Leo,G,Aug 10)*
**She Is No Lady 110** *(18f,Don,GS,Sep 15)*
**Shearling 106** *(12f,Pon,GF,Jun 25)*
**Sheepscar Lad 106** *(6f,Thi,GS,Jun 5)*
**Sheikhzayedroad 117** *(18f,Don,GS,Sep 15)*
**Shenanigans 108** *(8f,Goo,G,Aug 1)*
**Shifting Star 105** *(8f,Wdr,GF,Jun 19)*
**Short Work 109** *(8f,Hay,S,Jun 9)*
**Shouranour 108** *(7f,Cat,S,Jun 10)*
**Show Palace 107** *(5f,Rip,S,Sep 30)*
**Showboating 108** *(8f,Crl,GS,Jun 28)*
**Showdaisy 107** *(5f,Ayr,GS,Jly 10)*
**Shraaoh 108** *(12f,Hay,GF,Jly 8)*
**Shrewd 110** *(18f,Nmk,G,Sep 23)*
**Shutter Speed 107** *(10f,Nby,GF,Apr 21)*
**Shymkent 110** *(10f,Wet,G,May 15)*
**Sidewinder 107** *(8f,Hay,GF,May 26)*
**Siege Of Boston 105** *(7f,Thi,GF,Jun 20)*
**Silent Echo 109** *(7f,Hay,F,May 27)*
**Silken Dancer 105** *(10f,Wdr,GF,May 8)*
**Silva Eclipse 106** *(14f,Crl,S,Jun 9)*
**Silvanus 106** *(5f,Mus,G,Jly 14)*
**Silver Ghost 111** *(10f,Nby,G,Sep 23)*
**Silver Meadow 110** *(8½f,Eps,G,Jun 3)*
**Silver Step 114** *(8f,Mey,G,Jan 26)*
**Silverkode 107** *(7f,Cur,G,Jly 2)*
**Silvery Moon 105** *(10f,Red,S,Nov 7)*
**Simple Verse 110** *(14f,Yor,S,May 19)*
**Sindarban 106** *(14f,Mus,GF,Apr 15)*
**Sinfonietta 111** *(8f,Don,GS,Apr 1)*
**Singeur 108** *(6f,Rip,G,Aug 19)*
**Singyoursong 108** *(10f,Not,G,May 31)*
**Sir Billy Wright 107** *(6f,Thi,G,Jly 5)*
**Sir Chauvelin 105** *(14f,Mus,GF,Apr 15)*
**Sir Dancealot 114** *(6f,Asc,GF,May 3)*
**Sir Ector 105** *(16f,Cur,YS,Jun 10)*
**Sir Jack 109** *(10f,Not,GS,Jun 11)*
**Sir John Lavery 114** *(8f,Leo,G,Sep 9)*
**Sir Maximilian 107** *(6f,Mey,G,Feb 9)*
**Sir Pass I Am 107** *(14f,Lin,G,May 24)*
**Sir Plato 105** *(8f,Wdr,GS,Oct 9)*
**Sir Robert Cheval 111** *(5f,Cur,G,May 14)*
**Sir Roderic 106** *(8f,Yor,G,Jly 15)*
**Sir Titan 109** *(7f,Goo,S,Aug 5)*
**Six Strings 108** *(7f,Don,G,Aug 19)*
**Sixties Groove 107** *(12f,Asc,GF,Jun 23)*
**Siyoushake 113** *(10f,Dea,G,Aug 20)*
**Size Matters 109** *(7f,Ayr,G,Aug 14)*
**Skiffle 111** *(12f,Nmk,S,Jly 22)*
**Slow To Hand 106** *(7f,Yar,GF,Aug 17)*
**Slunovrat 105** *(14f,San,GS,Jly 26)*
**Smart Call 112** *(10f,Dea,G,Aug 20)*
**Smart Together 109** *(10f,Nby,G,Jun 15)*
**Smiley Bagel 107** *(10f,Lin,GF,Jun 13)*
**Smokey Lane 118** *(6f,Lei,GS,May 29)*
**Snap Shots 111** *(6f,Hay,S,Jun 10)*
**Snoano 113** *(10f,Asc,GF,Jun 24)*
**Snookered 105** *(10f,Bev,GS,Jly 24)*
**Snowstar 107** *(5f,Cur,GF,Jly 29)*
**So Beloved 114** *(7f,Cha,S,Oct 1)*
**So It's War 108** *(8f,Ham,GF,May 7)*
**So Mi Dar 116** *(10f,Goo,S,Aug 3)*
**So Sensible 106** *(8f,Cur,G,May 14)*
**So Sleek 105** *(11½f,Lin,G,Jly 19)*
**Sobetsu 117** *(10f,Goo,S,Aug 3)*
**Society Red 111** *(10f,Goo,S,Aug 3)*
**Sofia's Rock 110** *(12f,Lei,GF,Apr 29)*
**Soie D'Leau 111** *(5f,Don,GS,Oct 28)*
**Solar Cross 109** *(11½f,Wdr,GS,Oct 9)*
**Solar Flair 108** *(6f,Goo,S,Aug 5)*
**Solar Halo 106** *(6f,Cur,G,May 13)*
**Soldier In Action 109** *(12f,Hay,GF,Jly 8)*
**Sole Power 109** *(5f,Mey,G,Feb 2)*
**Soleil Marin 113** *(15f,Cha,GS,Sep 30)*
**Solomon's Bay 110** *(8f,Goo,G,Aug 4)*
**Somehow 116** *(10½f,Cur,Y,May 28)*
**Something Brewing 105** *(7f,Ayr,G,Jun 24)*
**Somewhere Secret 106** *(5f,Don,S,Sep 13)*
**Son Of Rest 117** *(5f,Cur,SH,Sep 10)*
**Song Of Namibia 108** *(10f,Leo,GF,Jun 22)*
**Sophie P 108** *(8f,Ayr,G,Jun 24)*
**Sound Advice 106** *(7½f,Chs,GF,May 12)*
**Sounds Of Earth 111** *(12f,Mey,Y,Mar 25)*
**Southdown Lad 109** *(12f,Yor,S,May 19)*
**Southern Belle 109** *(6f,Ham,S,Sep 5)*
**Sovereign Debt 113** *(8f,San,G,Apr 28)*
**Spanish Steps 115** *(12f,Leo,G,Aug 10)*
**Spanish Tenor 114** *(7f,Leo,YS,Jun 8)*
**Spark Plug 119** *(10f,San,GF,Jly 7)*
**Sparte Quercus 105** *(10f,San,G,Sep 15)*
**Special Relation 105** *(12f,Pon,G,Jun 12)*
**Spectre 108** *(8f,Asc,GF,Jun 20)*
**Speed Company 111** *(10f,Yor,S,May 17)*
**Speed Hawk 111** *(5f,Mey,G,Feb 2)*
**Speedo Boy 108** *(10f,Asc,GF,Jun 22)*
**Spinart 108** *(10f,Not,GS,Jun 11)*
**Spirit Of Belle 105** *(7f,Lei,HY,Sep 25)*
**Spirit Of Valor 110** *(7f,Asc,GF,Jun 21)*
**Spirit Quartz 113** *(5f,Cur,G,May 14)*
**Sporting Times 107** *(9f,Lin,GF,Jun 13)*
**Spring Fling 107** *(5f,Ayr,G,Jun 24)*
**Spring Loaded 113** *(6f,Don,GS,Sep 16)*
**Spring Offensive 109** *(8f,Thi,GF,May 6)*
**Spruce Meadows 107** *(12f,Cur,Y,May 27)*
**Squats 107** *(7f,Asc,GS,Sep 9)*
**St Brelades Bay 107** *(6f,Cur,Y,Aug 27)*
**St Lawrence Gap 105** *(13f,Leo,GF,May 26)*
**St Mary's 106** *(14f,Goo,S,Sep 27)*
**St Michel 107** *(16f,Yor,G,Aug 25)*
**Staintondale Lass 105** *(6f,Hay,GF,Jly 6)*
**Stake Acclaim 110** *(6f,Hay,HY,Sep 30)*
**Stamp Hill 110** *(7f,Asc,GS,Jly 29)*
**Standing Rock 106** *(10f,Sal,GF,Jly 15)*
**Stanghow 105** *(6f,Rip,G,Aug 19)*
**Stanhope 109** *(6f,Yar,GS,Sep 20)*
**Star Maker 105** *(12f,Lei,S,May 22)*
**Star Of Lombardy 107** *(14f,Mus,GF,May 26)*
**Star Of Rory 107** *(10f,Hay,S,Sep 8)*
**Star Of The East 106** *(14f,Yar,GS,Sep 21)*
**Star Rock 107** *(10f,Don,S,Nov 11)*
**Star Storm 107** *(12f,Asc,GF,Jun 23)*
**Star Story 110** *(10f,Sal,S,Jly 29)*
**Star Victory 112** *(7f,Sai,S,Mar 19)*
**Stardrifter 112** *(7f,Ayr,G,Jun 23)*
**Starlight Romance 106** *(7½f,Chs,S,Jun 10)*
**Stars Over The Sea 108** *(14f,Leo,GF,May 26)*
**Steady Pace 114** *(6f,Nmk,GF,Aug 26)*
**Steel Train 108** *(8f,Don,GS,Apr 1)*
**Stellar Mass 117** *(14f,Cur,G,Jly 2)*
**Stellarta 108** *(6f,Goo,G,May 26)*
**Stepper Point 109** *(5f,Wdr,GF,Apr 24)*
**Sternrubin 107** *(14f,Sal,GS,Jun 28)*
**Stipulate 109** *(8f,Thi,GF,May 6)*
**Stoneboat Bill 105** *(10f,Not,GS,Jun 11)*
**Stoneham 105** *(16f,Mus,GF,Jun 17)*
**Stoney Broke 106** *(12f,Don,S,Sep 14)*
**Stopdworldnletmeof 106** *(5f,Chp,S,Jun 10)*
**Storm Ahead 112** *(8f,Nby,GF,Apr 22)*
**Storm Cry 112** *(7f,Hay,GS,Jun 14)*
**Storm King 111** *(9f,Goo,S,Aug 5)*
**Storm Over 112** *(5f,Cat,S,Oct 21)*
**Stormin Tom 106** *(14f,Mus,GF,May 26)*
**Stormy Antarctic 113** *(8f,Don,GS,Apr 1)*
**Stormy Belle 107** *(8f,Cur,GF,Jly 16)*
**Stradivarius 116** *(14½f,Don,GS,Sep 16)*
**Straight Right 108** *(7f,Goo,G,Aug 26)*
**Strathspey 112** *(12f,Cha,S,Sep 10)*
**Strictly Carter 106** *(6f,Bri,GF,Jun 27)*
**Strong Belief 107** *(10f,Rip,GS,Jun 7)*
**Strong Steps 107** *(7f,Ayr,G,Jly 17)*
**Stronger Than Me 107** *(12f,Cur,Y,May 27)*
**Subway Dancer 120** *(10f,Cha,S,Sep 30)*
**Success Days 113** *(10½f,Cur,Y,May 28)*
**Suedois 115** *(8f,Leo,G,Sep 9)*
**Sultan Baybars 110** *(7f,San,GS,Jly 26)*
**Sumbal 109** *(10f,Don,S,Sep 13)*
**Summer Chorus 110** *(7f,Nmk,G,Aug 4)*
**Sumner Beach 113** *(6f,Lei,GS,May 29)*
**Sun Lover 111** *(7½f,Chs,G,Aug 26)*
**Sunblazer 108** *(16f,Nmk,GF,Nov 3)*
**Sunnua 106** *(8½f,Not,G,Nov 1)*
**Super Julius 105** *(5f,San,G,Sep 2)*
**Surrey Hope 109** *(8f,Sal,GF,Aug 16)*
**Surrounding 108** *(8f,Cur,GF,Jly 16)*
**Suspect Package 107** *(8½f,Not,G,May 13)*
**Sussex Ranger 116** *(14f,Lin,S,Jly 29)*
**Sutter County 107** *(7f,Goo,GF,May 27)*
**Suwaan 105** *(5f,Don,S,Sep 13)*
**Suyoof 111** *(7f,Mey,G,Feb 23)*
**Swashbuckle 109** *(16f,Nmk,GS,Sep 28)*
**Sweet Selection 107** *(16f,Goo,G,Aug 1)*
**Swift Approval 107** *(7f,Nmk,S,Aug 5)*
**Swift Emperor 109** *(10f,Yor,G,Oct 14)*
**Swiftsure 109** *(10f,Pon,GF,Jun 25)*
**Swilly Sunset 106** *(10f,San,G,Sep 2)*
**Syphax 114** *(10f,Yor,G,Oct 14)*
**Syrian Pearl 111** *(6f,Don,GF,May 6)*
**Syrita 106** *(10f,Dea,G,Aug 20)*

**Taamol 110** *(7f,Nmk,GS,May 20)*

Taareef 109 (8f,Cha,S,Sep 10)
Tabarrak 111 (7f,Nby,G,Sep 22)
Tadaawol 105 (7½f,Chs,HY,Sep 16)
Taexali 109 (6f,Hay,S,Jun 10)
Tafaakhor 106 (7f,Bri,GF,Apr 15)
Tahanee 113 (8f,Mey,G,Jan 26)
Tahoo 105 (5f,Not,GS,Oct 18)
Tai Sing Yeh 106 (7f,Red,GF,May 4)
Takatul 105 (7f,Don,GF,Jly 7)
Take A Turn 107 (10f,Lin,GS,Aug 21)
Take Cover 118 (5f,Yor,G,Jly 15)
Take Two 107 (11½f,Wdr,GS,Oct 9)
Talaayeb 113 (7f,Yor,G,Aug 25)
Talismanic 105 (12f,Cha,S,Sep 10)
Tally's Song 107 (5f,Ffo,HY,Aug 3)
Tamayuz Magic 106 (12f,Thi,G,Aug 5)
Tamih 106 (7½f,Chs,HY,Sep 30)
Tamleek 107 (12f,Chs,G,May 11)
Tanasoq 110 (6f,Lin,GF,Jun 3)
Tanawar 106 (7f,Thi,GF,Jun 20)
Tandem 109 (10f,Leo,GF,Jly 13)
Tarboosh 108 (5f,Hay,HY,Sep 30)
Tarte Tropezienne 105 (11½f,Bat,G,Aug 23)
Tartini 107 (10f,Eps,G,Jun 3)
Tashweeq 110 (8f,Asc,GF,Jun 21)
Tasleet 117 (6f,Asc,S,Oct 21)
Tatlisu 106 (6f,Don,GF,May 6)
Tavener 105 (7f,Ayr,G,May 31)
Tawdeea 108 (12f,Hay,GF,Jly 8)
Taws 108 (20½f,Goo,GS,Aug 2)
Taxmeifyoucan 109 (14f,Hay,HY,Sep 9)
Teak 108 (17f,Crl,GF,May 22)
Teepee Time 107 (5f,Hay,G,Jly 22)
Temple Church 108 (8f,Nmk,S,Jly 22)
Tennessee Wildcat 108 (10f,Leo,GF,Jly 13)
Teodoro 107 (10f,Yar,GF,Aug 27)
Teofonic 107 (12f,Goo,S,Oct 15)
Teruntum Star 114 (6f,Rip,G,Aug 19)
Testa Rossa 105 (8f,Ham,GF,May 19)
Texas Rock 109 (7f,Cur,YS,Aug 19)
Thafeera 109 (6f,Sal,G,Sep 7)
Thames Knight 106 (11f,Goo,G,Jun 11)
That Is The Spirit 108 (7f,Hay,S,Jun 10)
That Which Is Not 108 (10f,Dea,G,Aug 20)
The Anvil 108 (12f,Chs,G,May 11)
The Armed Man 110 (6f,Thi,GF,Jun 20)
The Black Princess 113 (10f,Cha,S,Oct 1)
The Blues Master 106 (16f,Bev,GF,Jly 18)
The Commendatore 118 (6f,Don,GF,May 6)
The Eagle's Nest 106 (8f,Mus,GF,Jun 3)
The Feathered Nest 106 (6f,Yor,GF,Jun 16)
The Grape Escape 109 (8f,Pon,S,Oct 9)
The Great Wall 105 (6f,Cur,G,Aug 7)
The Grey Gatsby 113 (10f,Leo,G,Sep 9)
The Major 106 (10f,San,GF,May 25)
The Moore Factor 106 (10f,Leo,GF,Jly 13)
The Mouse Doctor 106 (8f,Cur,G,May 14)
The New Pharaoh 105 (12f,Don,S,Jly 27)
The Right Man 110 (6f,Mey,Y,Mar 25)
The Secrets Out 110 (11½f,Lin,GF,Jun 24)
The Statesman 108 (10f,Nmk,G,Sep 23)
The Taj Mahal 117 (10f,Leo,G,Sep 9)
The Tartan Spartan 106 (14f,Mus,GF,Apr 15)
The Tin Man 116 (6f,Asc,GF,Jun 18)
The Wagon Wheel 108 (5f,Bev,GF,Sep 2)
The Warrior 112 (7f,Goo,GF,May 6)
Theodorico 109 (7f,Yor,G,May 27)
Theos Lolly 110 (10½f,Chs,G,Jly 15)
Thesme 107 (5½f,Yor,GS,Aug 23)
Theydon Girls 105 (10f,Yar,GS,Jun 6)
Theydon Grey 105 (12f,Yor,GF,May 27)
Thikriyaat 110 (8f,Yor,GF,Jun 17)
Thomas Cranmer 108 (8f,Mus,GF,Jun 3)
Thomas Hobson 117 (18f,Don,GS,Sep 15)
Throckley 105 (9f,Yor,GF,Jun 17)
Thunder Snow 111 (8f,Cur,Y,May 27)
Thundering Blue 110 (10f,San,G,Sep 2)
Tiger Jim 107 (6f,Red,G,Apr 17)
Tigris River 108 (16f,Cur,YS,Jun 10)
Time Chaser 107 (10f,San,S,Aug 10)
Time For Mabel 105 (12f,Cur,GF,Jly 29)
Time To Exceed 108 (6f,Wdr,G,May 15)
Time To Sea 109 (8½f,Not,GS,Jun 11)
Time To Study 108 (14f,Hay,HY,Sep 9)
Tirania 105 (6f,Pon,S,Sep 21)
Tis Marvellous 117 (6f,Asc,GF,May 3)
Tisbutadream 111 (8½f,Eps,G,Jun 3)
Titan Goddess 105 (8f,Nmk,GS,Nov 4)
Tithonus 111 (5f,Cur,G,Jly 2)
Titi Makfi 112 (10f,Yor,G,Aug 26)
To Be Wild 108 (12f,Nby,S,May 20)
To Choose 106 (12f,Cur,Y,May 27)
To Dibba 107 (7f,Lei,S,May 22)
To Eternity 108 (12f,Nmk,GS,Sep 29)
Tobacco Bay 107 (7f,Cur,GY,Jly 1)
Tobougaloo 105 (12f,Chp,G,Jly 20)
Tomahawk Kid 107 (10f,Not,G,May 13)
Tomily 112 (5f,Don,GS,Oct 28)
Tommy G 106 (7f,Ayr,GF,May 9)
Tommy Taylor 108 (6f,Nmk,G,Jly 13)
Tomyris 107 (7f,Don,GS,Sep 15)
Tony Curtis 111 (8f,Goo,S,Aug 4)
Tony The Gent 109 (8f,Cur,G,Jly 1)
Toofi 109 (6f,Hay,S,Jun 10)
Top Beak 106 (10f,Eps,G,Jun 2)
Top Boy 108 (5f,Nmk,G,Jly 13)
Top Notch Tonto 108 (8f,Hay,GF,Apr 29)
Top Score 109 (8f,Nmk,GF,May 6)
Top Tug 109 (12f,Lei,GS,Oct 30)
Tor 112 (13f,Ham,G,Jly 20)
Torcedor 114 (16f,Asc,S,Oct 21)
Torcello 111 (10f,Sal,S,Jly 29)
Torremar 110 (12f,Pon,G,May 26)
Toscanini 112 (7f,Yor,G,Aug 25)
Total Demolition 106 (10f,Leo,GF,Jun 22)
Toulson 109 (10f,Not,G,May 13)
Towerlands Park 109 (10f,Nby,S,Oct 28)
Town's History 105 (10f,Mey,G,Jan 12)
Traffic Jam 113 (12f,Cha,S,Sep 10)
Treaty Of Vienna 105 (6f,Cur,G,May 13)
Trevanna 105 (7f,Leo,YS,Jun 8)
Tribute Act 105 (7f,Asc,GS,Oct 6)
Trick Of The Light 105 (5f,Bat,GF,Jly 12)
Tricky Dicky 106 (6f,Red,GS,Aug 12)
Tricorn 108 (8f,Nmk,G,Jly 13)
Trilliant 105 (8f,Hay,GS,Sep 7)
Trinity Star 108 (8f,Pon,S,Oct 9)
Trip To Rhodos 113 (15f,Cha,S,Sep 10)
Tropics 105 (6f,Wdr,G,May 22)
True Valour 114 (8f,Leo,G,Sep 9)
Trulee Scrumptious 106 (8f,Nmk,GF,Jun 23)
Truth Or Dare 108 (7f,Goo,S,Aug 2)
Try Again 110 (8f,Ham,GF,May 7)
Tullius 111 (8f,Don,GS,Apr 1)
Tumbaga 109 (10f,Asc,GF,Jun 24)
Tumblewind 108 (5f,Don,S,Jun 2)
Tupi 115 (6f,Don,GS,Apr 1)
Turanga Leela 105 (6f,Yor,GF,Jun 16)
Turning Gold 118 (8f,Yar,G,Jly 12)
Turning The Table 108 (11½f,Wdr,G,May 22)
Turret Rocks 111 (10f,Cur,G,May 13)
Twenty Times 109 (10f,Chp,S,Jun 6)
Twiggy 107 (8f,Lei,G,May 29)
Twilight Payment 112 (14f,Cur,Y,Aug 19)
Twin Appeal 109 (7½f,Chs,G,Aug 26)
Twin Star 108 (10f,Goo,G,Aug 27)
Twizzell 105 (5f,Chs,S,Jun 10)
Two For Two 111 (8f,Thi,GF,May 6)
Tylery Wonder 109 (5f,Yor,G,Oct 13)

UAE King 117 (16f,Nmk,GS,Sep 28)
UAE Prince 110 (10f,Yor,G,Jly 15)
US Army Ranger 109 (16f,Goo,G,Aug 1)
Uber Cool 108 (12f,Thi,G,Aug 5)
Udontdodou 108 (6f,Yor,S,May 17)
Uele River 105 (10f,Sal,GF,Aug 16)
Ultimate Avenue 108 (6f,Nmk,G,Jly 13)
Ulysses 120 (12f,Asc,GS,Jly 29)
Unabated 105 (6f,Chs,GS,Aug 6)
Uncle Charlie 107 (6f,Thi,GS,Jun 5)
Under The Covers 107 (6f,Ffo,GS,Aug 25)
Unforgetable Filly 110 (7f,Mus,GF,Jun 3)
Union Rose 111 (5f,Goo,G,Aug 1)
Upstaging 110 (6f,Goo,S,Aug 5)
Urban Fox 109 (7f,Nby,G,Sep 22)
Used To Be 107 (7f,Hay,GS,Jun 14)
Usherette 112 (8f,Nmk,G,Oct 7)

Valentana 106 (8f,Leo,YS,Jun 8)
Vallarta 111 (7f,Ayr,S,Jun 12)
Vaulted 111 (7f,Hay,GS,Jun 14)
Vazirabad 118 (15f,Cha,S,Sep 10)
Velvet Voice 106 (10f,Lin,S,Aug 5)
Venetian Proposal 105 (10f,Lin,S,Aug 5)
Venice Beach 109 (12f,Chs,G,May 11)
Vent De Force 107 (15f,Cha,S,Sep 10)
Ventura Blues 105 (7f,Cur,GY,Jly 1)
Venturous 109 (5f,Yor,G,Oct 13)
Vernatti 108 (10f,Yar,GF,May 2)
Very Dashing 108 (10f,Yor,GS,Jly 28)
Very Special 116 (8f,Mey,G,Jan 26)
Via Firenze 112 (8f,Mey,G,Jan 26)
Via Serendipity 110 (7f,Nby,GF,Apr 22)
Via Via 107 (7f,Lei,GS,Oct 17)
Vibrant Chords 110 (6f,Goo,G,May 26)
Victory Angel 118 (6f,Yar,GF,Aug 1)
Victory Bond 112 (8f,Yor,GS,May 18)
Vimy Ridge 108 (5f,Wdr,G,Apr 24)
Vintage Folly 109 (10f,Yar,S,Sep 20)
Viren's Army 107 (10f,Mey,G,Feb 23)
Viscount Barfield 112 (7f,Goo,G,Aug 27)
Visitant 107 (9f,Yor,GF,Jun 17)
Vivlos 112 (9f,Mey,Y,Mar 25)
Voi 105 (10f,Nmk,GF,Nov 3)
Volpone Jelois 108 (14f,Sal,GF,May 27)
Von Blucher 110 (7f,Hay,G,May 13)
Vona 105 (7½f,Chs,S,Jun 10)

Waady 111 (5f,Nby,G,Sep 23)
Wahash 105 (7f,Eps,G,Jun 2)
Waitaki 107 (7f,Cur,GY,Jly 1)
Waiting For Richie 107 (16f,Nmk,GF,Nov 3)
Waldgeist 112 (12f,Asc,GS,Oct 7)
Wall Of Fire 111 (13f,Nby,S,Aug 19)
Walton Street 107 (11f,Goo,S,Aug 4)
Wannabe Friends 107 (8½f,Not,GF,Apr 22)
Waqaas 108 (6f,Asc,GS,Oct 6)
War Decree 105 (8f,Nmk,GF,Apr 20)
War Department 108 (8f,Ayr,G,Jun 24)
War Glory 116 (7f,Yor,GF,May 27)
Warp Factor 107 (13f,Ham,G,Jly 20)
Waseem Faris 108 (5f,Wdr,GF,Apr 24)
Washington DC 113 (5f,Goo,S,Aug 4)
Watchable 108 (5f,Yor,G,May 27)
Waterville Dancer 106 (12f,Ffo,HY,Aug 3)
Waves 105 (8f,Lei,G,May 29)
Way To Paris 110 (15f,Dea,G,Aug 20)
Website 107 (8f,Mey,G,Jan 28)
Weekend Offender 107 (8½f,Not,GF,Apr 12)
Weekender 107 (12f,Nby,G,Sep 23)
Wefait 107 (11½f,Wdr,GF,Jun 26)
Wentworth Falls 108 (6f,Red,G,Apr 17)
West Drive 106 (14f,San,GS,Jly 26)
Western Hymn 109 (12f,Asc,GF,Jun 24)
Western Prince 108 (12f,Pon,G,May 26)
Westward Ho 106 (8f,Pon,GF,Apr 24)
What A Home 108 (12f,Don,S,Sep 14)
What About Carlo 111 (10f,Nby,S,Jly 22)
What Wonders Weave 105 (9f,Mus,S,Sep 16)
Whatsthemessage 107 (9f,Ham,GS,Aug 24)
Whip Nae Nae 107 (8f,Sal,GF,Aug 16)
Whispered Kiss 112 (8f,Nmk,S,Aug 5)
White Lake 106 (8f,Yor,GS,May 18)
Whitecliffsofdover 113 (8f,Leo,G,Sep 9)
Whiteley 105 (8f,Lei,G,May 29)
Who Dares Wins 112 (18f,Nmk,G,Sep 23)
Whosyourhousemate 106 (8f,Nmk,S,Aug 5)
Wicklow Brave 118 (14f,Cur,G,Jly 2)
Wilamina 110 (9f,Cur,GF,Jly 16)
Wild Chief 116 (10f,Cha,S,Sep 30)
Wild Flower 105 (6f,Bri,GF,Jun 27)
Wild Hacked 108 (12f,Don,S,Nov 11)
Wild Irish Rose 107 (14f,Leo,GY,Jly 20)
Wiley Post 106 (5f,Wdr,GS,Jly 24)
Willbeme 107 (7f,Hay,S,Jun 9)
William Hunter 107 (14f,Yar,GS,Sep 21)
Willytheconqueror 115 (5f,Cur,G,May 14)
Windsor Beach 107 (10f,Leo,GF,Jly 13)
Wingingit 106 (14f,Leo,GY,Jly 20)
Wings Of Eagles 115 (12f,Eps,G,Jun 3)
Wings of Desire 112 (12f,Asc,GF,Jun 24)
Winning Ways 105 (7f,Asc,GF,May 12)
Winston C 113 (12f,Goo,S,Aug 2)
Winter 119 (10f,Goo,S,Aug 3)
Wintour Leap 109 (14f,Lin,G,May 24)
Wireless 105 (8f,Cha,S,Sep 9)
Wisconsin 116 (14f,Cur,G,Jly 2)
With Hindsight 108 (14f,Yar,GF,May 24)
Withernsea 110 (8f,Goo,S,Aug 4)
Withhold 108 (18f,Nmk,G,Oct 14)
Wolf Country 112 (10f,Yor,GS,May 18)
Worlds His Oyster 107 (10½f,Chs,GF,May 27)
Wuheida 116 (10f,Cha,S,Oct 1)

Xenobia 110 (7f,Cur,YS,Aug 19)

Ya Jammeel 111 (8f,Hay,S,Jun 9)
Yabrave 105 (6f,Sal,S,Jly 29)
Yalta 116 (6f,Asc,GF,May 3)
Yamarhaba Malayeen 105 (8f,Mus,GF,Jun 3)
Yard Line 107 (9f,Mey,G,Jan 28)
Yattwee 109 (7f,Hay,GS,Sep 7)
Yes Daddy 107 (16f,Mus,G,Jly 14)
Yes You 107 (7f,Ayr,G,Aug 14)
Yorkidding 109 (14f,Mus,GF,Aug 11)
Yorkshiredebut 106 (5f,Cat,GF,Jly 19)
You're Cool 106 (5f,Don,GF,Jly 13)
You're Fired 108 (9f,Nmk,GS,Sep 30)
Yucatan 106 (10f,Leo,GY,Apr 8)
Yuften 105 (8f,Don,GS,Apr 1)

Zabeel Prince 111 (8f,Yor,G,Oct 13)
Zac Brown 106 (5f,Goo,GS,Jun 11)
Zack Mayo 107 (11½f,Yar,S,Sep 19)
Zafayan 106 (16f,Cur,YS,Jun 10)
Zaidiyn 107 (14½f,Don,GS,Oct 27)
Zain Arion 105 (10f,Hay,GF,Apr 29)
Zainhom 109 (7f,Nby,GF,Apr 22)
Zalamea 113 (7f,Cha,S,Oct 1)
Zamaam 111 (16f,Mey,G,Feb 2)
Zambezi Queen 108 (6f,Chp,GF,May 5)
Zamperini 108 (11½f,Wdr,GS,Oct 9)
Zarak 114 (12f,Cha,S,Oct 1)
Zealous 110 (8f,Hay,G,Jun 15)
Zebulon 105 (6f,Bat,F,May 10)
Zeelander 105 (11½f,Wdr,G,Oct 16)
Zeftan 105 (12f,Cur,G,Jun 30)
Zelzal 113 (7f,Cha,S,Oct 1)
Zenon 108 (14f,Yar,GS,Sep 21)
Zest 106 (8f,Goo,GF,May 6)
Zhui Feng 111 (8f,Asc,GF,Jun 21)
Zhukova 116 (10f,Leo,G,Sep 9)
Zilza 107 (6f,Wdr,GS,Oct 9)
Zlatan 105 (8½f,Not,G,May 12)
Zodiakos 111 (8f,Pon,GF,Apr 24)
Zonderland 109 (8f,Goo,G,Aug 26)
Zoravan 105 (7f,Hay,GF,Apr 29)
Zwayyan 108 (8f,Nmk,S,Jly 22)
Zylan 106 (6f,Thi,GF,Apr 22)
Zymyran 107 (8f,Nmk,GS,Aug 18)
Zzoro 111 (10f,Nmk,S,May 19)

## THREE YEAR-OLDS PLUS AW

A L'Anglaise 106 (9½f,Wol,SD,Feb 6)
A Momentofmadness 111 (5f,Kem,SD,Apr 15)
Abareeq 113 (10f,Kem,SS,Mar 8)
Abdon 112 (10f,Cfd,SD,Sep 30)
Abingdon 110 (11f,Dun,SD,Sep 29)
Abjar 105 (12f,Wol,SD,Sep 9)
Able Jack 105 (7f,Ncs,SD,Dec 6)
About Glory 111 (14f,Wol,SD,Oct 27)
Abraj Dubai 105 (7f,Sth,SD,Nov 16)
Absolute Blast 111 (11f,Dun,SD,Sep 29)
Absolutely So 106 (6f,Cfd,SD,Apr 27)
Abstraction 105 (5f,Dun,SD,Jly 12)
Accidental Agent 106 (7f,Kem,SS,Sep 9)
Addicted To You 107 (12f,Lin,SD,Mar 3)
Admodum 105 (8f,Dun,SD,Oct 13)
Aeolus 107 (6f,Ncs,SD,Jly 1)
Afonso De Sousa 115 (12f,Lin,SD,Jan 28)
After Toniight 110 (12½f,Ncs,SD,Jan 12)
Age Of Wisdom 111 (16f,Kem,SS,Sep 8)
Aggression 105 (5f,Dun,SD,Nov 17)
Aguerooo 106 (6f,Ncs,SD,Mar 9)
Airton 107 (12½f,Ncs,SD,Jly 1)
Al Galayel 108 (8f,Lin,SD,Nov 17)
Al Hamdany 110 (11f,Kem,SS,Sep 8)
Al Zaman 111 (12f,Wol,SD,Apr 22)
Alabaster 111 (10f,Mey,FT,Feb 9)
Alareef 108 (6f,Mey,FT,Jan 28)
Alcatraz 111 (11f,Kem,SD,Feb 1)
Aldeburgh 106 (11f,Kem,SD,Apr 1)
Aleef 112 (6f,Cfd,SD,Dec 21)
Alejandro 109 (7f,Lin,SD,Dec 13)
Alexandrakollontai 105 (8f,Ncs,SD,Nov 10)
Alfarris 105 (11f,Kem,SS,Sep 27)
Alfred Hutchinson 113 (8f,Lin,SD,Dec 31)
Alfredo Arcano 106 (5f,Dun,SD,Nov 17)
Alinstante 105 (12f,Wol,SD,Jan 16)
Aljazzi 108 (8f,Kem,SD,Apr 15)
Aljuljalah 106 (7f,Cfd,SD,Sep 30)
Alkhor 105 (6f,Lin,SD,Apr 11)
All For The Best 106 (16½f,Wol,SD,Mar 27)
All The Mollies 105 (8f,Dun,SD,Oct 6)
Allee Bleue 111 (16f,Kem,SS,Sep 8)
Allez Henri 110 (10f,Lin,SD,Apr 14)
Allography 107 (8f,Dun,SD,Mar 10)
Allumage 106 (10f,Kem,SS,Mar 8)
Almoreb 107 (8f,Cfd,SD,Aug 31)
Alnaas 107 (7f,Cfd,SD,May 8)
Alnasl 106 (9½f,Wol,SD,Aug 11)
Alpha Tauri 106 (8f,Sth,SD,Jan 26)
Alsvinder 109 (5f,Lin,SD,Dec 12)
Alternate Route 105 (16½f,Wol,SD,Nov 20)
Amanto 108 (16f,Lin,SD,Mar 31)
Amazour 108 (7f,Wol,SD,Mar 11)
Ambitious Icarus 110 (5f,Ncs,SD,Mar 4)
Amlad 106 (10f,Kem,SD,Apr 1)
Among Angels 105 (6f,Ncs,SD,Feb 10)
Andok 110 (10f,Ncs,SD,Nov 23)
Andrassy Avenue 105 (11f,Kem,SD,Apr 12)
Aneen 108 (11f,Dun,SD,Sep 29)
Angelic Lord 105 (7f,Lin,SD,Mar 3)
Annie Salts 108 (5f,Wol,SD,Apr 22)
Anonymous John 108 (6f,Kem,SD,Feb 18)
Ansaab 105 (10f,Lin,SD,Feb 9)
Antiquarium 114 (16½f,Wol,SD,Jan 16)
Any Time 106 (12f,Dun,SD,Feb 10)
Apalis 108 (16f,Ncs,SD,Dec 16)
Apollo Kentucky 105 (10f,Mey,MY,Mar 25)
Aprovado 118 (6f,Ncs,SD,Mar 24)
Aqua Libre 105 (7f,Lin,SD,Mar 17)
Arab Moon 111 (11f,Kem,SS,Sep 8)
Arab Spring 116 (10f,Lin,SD,Feb 4)
Arbourfield 108 (7f,Dun,SD,Mar 24)
Arcadian Sea 106 (10f,Cfd,SD,Sep 21)
Arcanada 113 (8f,Lin,SD,Nov 18)
Archangel Raphael 108 (12f,Lin,SD,Jan 28)
Archetype 107 (8f,Kem,SS,Nov 22)
Archie Stevens 105 (5f,Wol,SD,Feb 23)
Archimedes 110 (5f,Sth,SD,Jan 26)
Archipeligo 106 (12½f,Ncs,SD,Sep 19)
Arctic Sea 105 (11f,Kem,SS,Jun 7)
Ardamir 107 (14f,Wol,SD,Mar 11)
Arnarson 108 (6f,Cfd,SD,Dec 17)
Arrogate 122 (10f,Mey,MY,Mar 25)
Arrowzone 106 (10f,Cfd,SD,Mar 13)
Art Collection 110 (5f,Ncs,SD,Apr 14)
Art Obsession 107 (6f,Ncs,SD,Mar 1)
Artful Rogue 105 (11f,Kem,SS,Oct 4)
Artistic Melody 108 (8f,Dun,SD,Nov 1)
Artscape 105 (6f,Kem,SD,Mar 22)
Asaas 107 (10f,Kem,SS,Sep 25)
Ascot Day 107 (5f,Lin,SD,Jan 18)
Ashadihan 112 (7f,Cfd,SD,Feb 8)
Asking 108 (8f,Dun,SD,Mar 31)
Assertive Agent 107 (6f,Kem,SD,Feb 15)
Astronomy's Choice 109 (12f,Kem,SD,Nov 29)
Atalante 106 (6f,Cfd,SD,Mar 23)
Athassel 108 (6f,Kem,SD,Mar 20)
Athletic 105 (7f,Wol,SD,Jan 26)
Athollblair Boy 107 (6f,Ncs,SD,Sep 29)
Atlas 110 (8f,Dun,SD,Oct 13)
Atletico 107 (5f,Ncs,SD,Nov 23)
Attain 107 (12f,Lin,SD,Jan 27)
Auntie Barber 106 (9f,Wol,SD,Mar 25)
Auspicion 108 (8f,Ncs,SD,Sep 12)
Aussie Valentine 105 (8f,Dun,SD,Feb 24)
Author's Dream 108 (16½f,Wol,SD,Dec 9)
Aventinus 106 (7f,Cfd,SD,Aug 15)
Aviator 105 (16f,Kem,SS,Sep 8)
Awardee 113 (10f,Mey,MY,Mar 25)
Ayr Of Elegance 106 (16f,Lin,SD,Dec 20)
Ayrad 107 (10f,Lin,SD,Nov 18)
Azam 112 (12f,Wol,SD,Nov 29)
Azari 107 (12f,Wol,SD,Jun 7)

Badenscoth 106 (8f,Cfd,SD,Jly 25)
Bahaarah 107 (7f,Cfd,SD,Feb 8)
Bahamian Dollar 107 (6f,Ncs,SD,Feb 17)
Bahamian Heights 109 (6f,Cfd,SD,Dec 17)
Bahango 110 (5f,Ncs,SD,Jan 4)
Ballard Down 107 (9f,Wol,SD,May 3)
Ballesteros 105 (5f,Wol,SD,Mar 25)
Ballymore Castle 105 (7f,Wol,SD,Dec 13)
Ballynanty 106 (12f,Lin,SD,Mar 24)
Bamako Du Chatelet 110 (14f,Wol,SD,Dec 27)
Banditry 111 (10f,Cfd,SD,Jun 22)
Banish 109 (11f,Kem,SS,Sep 8)
Bank Bonus 106 (12½f,Ncs,SD,Mar 2)
Baratti 109 (11f,Mey,FT,Jan 28)
Baraweez 108 (7f,Cfd,SD,Sep 2)
Barracuda Boy 106 (6f,Wol,SD,Oct 7)
Barye 115 (12½f,Ncs,SD,Jan 12)
Battalion 115 (10f,Lin,SD,Feb 4)
Battle Of Marathon 107 (9½f,Wol,SD,Nov 29)
Bayston Hill 107 (10f,Lin,SD,Dec 13)
Beach Bar 109 (7f,Dun,SD,Dec 22)
Beardwood 108 (10f,Cfd,SD,Jun 22)
Beau Mistral 108 (6f,Cfd,SD,Feb 23)
Beau Satchel 108 (8f,Dun,SD,Oct 6)
Belabour 106 (12f,Wol,SD,Dec 2)
Belgian Bill 109 (8f,Lin,SD,Nov 18)
Believe It 108 (7f,Kem,SS,Jun 7)
Belle Boyd 105 (8f,Dun,SD,Oct 27)
Berlusca 106 (10f,Cfd,SD,Jan 19)
Berrahri 107 (10f,Cfd,SD,Mar 13)
Bertiewhittle 110 (6f,Ncs,SD,Nov 30)
Best Example 105 (12f,Wol,SD,Dec 2)
Best Solution 105 (7f,Mey,FT,Jan 26)
Big Baz 105 (8f,Kem,SS,Oct 4)
Big Challenge 108 (11f,Kem,SD,Apr 12)
Big Country 113 (11f,Kem,SD,Apr 1)
Big Lachie 106 (5f,Ncs,SD,Nov 3)
Big Time 108 (6f,Lin,SD,Jan 20)
Big Tour 109 (7f,Cfd,SD,Sep 2)
Bint Dandy 105 (9f,Wol,SD,Mar 25)
Bishops Cannings 106 (12f,Lin,SD,Mar 3)
Black Caesar 108 (7f,Lin,SD,Jan 18)
Black Dave 106 (11f,Kem,SD,Feb 1)
Black Hambleton 106 (7f,Ncs,SD,Jan 27)
Blaze Of Glory 107 (8f,Lin,SD,Jan 14)
Blaze Of Hearts 107 (8f,Lin,SD,Dec 13)
Bless Him 105 (8f,Cfd,SD,Apr 1)
Blind Faith 105 (10f,Cfd,SD,Aug 8)
Blue De Vega 106 (6f,Kem,SS,Oct 11)
Blue On Blue 111 (7f,Cfd,SD,Oct 6)
Blue Surf 113 (12f,Lin,SD,Jan 21)
Bluff Crag 105 (8f,Kem,SD,Dec 20)
Blushing Rose 107 (10f,Cfd,SD,Aug 8)
Bobby Wheeler 106 (7f,Lin,SD,Dec 13)
Bochart 105 (7f,Mey,FT,Feb 16)
Bogsnog 107 (6f,Wol,SD,Mar 25)
Bold Prediction 105 (8f,Cfd,SD,Jly 7)
Bookmaker 106 (7f,Lin,SD,Jan 25)
Boom The Groom 112 (5f,Lin,SD,Feb 25)
Boomerang Bob 109 (6f,Cfd,SD,Feb 9)
Boost 105 (6f,Wol,SD,Jan 14)
Boots And Spurs 109 (7f,Sth,SD,Jan 1)
Border Prince 106 (8f,Dun,SD,Sep 22)
Born To Finish 112 (6f,Kem,SD,Feb 3)
Bosham 106 (6f,Lin,SD,Jan 20)
Bottleofsmoke 107 (12f,Wol,SD,Mar 27)
Bouclier 110 (6f,Kem,SD,Mar 22)
Boundsy 105 (6f,Ncs,SD,Jly 29)
Bounty Pursuit 106 (7f,Wol,SD,Feb 13)
Bowson Fred 114 (5f,Lin,SD,Mar 25)
Boxer Dunford 108 (8f,Dun,SD,Sep 22)
Boy In The Bar 108 (7f,Cfd,SD,Nov 17)
Boychick 107 (10f,Cfd,SD,Feb 2)
Boynton 112 (10f,Lin,SD,Nov 18)

**Bracken Brae 105** *(16½f,Wol,SD,Apr 5)*
**Brandon Castle 112** *(14f,Wol,SD,Dec 9)*
**Breathoffreshair 111** *(6f,Ncs,SD,Nov 30)*
**Breden 110** *(11f,Kem,SS,Sep 8)*
**Brex Drago 108** *(8f,Lin,SD,Dec 31)*
**Briardale 107** *(10f,Ncs,SD,Apr 14)*
**Bridge Builder 107** *(6f,Kem,SS,Jan 6)*
**Brigadoon 107** *(11f,Sth,SD,Apr 18)*
**Brigliadoro 108** *(8f,Kem,SS,Oct 4)*
**Brilliant Vanguard 111** *(8f,Kem,SS,Sep 9)*
**British Art 108** *(12½f,Ncs,SD,Nov 23)*
**Broadhaven Honey 106** *(5f,Sth,SD,Nov 13)*
**Brokopondo 106** *(16f,Dun,SD,Feb 10)*
**Brother Tiger 106** *(5f,Sth,SD,Dec 29)*
**Broughtons Knight 108** *(7f,Cfd,SD,Dec 17)*
**Bumptious 108** *(8f,Cfd,SD,Sep 26)*
**Bunbury 108** *(10f,Cfd,SD,May 2)*
**Burcan 109** *(10f,Ncs,SD,Oct 24)*
**Burn The Boats 109** *(7f,Dun,SD,Mar 24)*
**Burning Thread 105** *(5f,Ncs,SD,Jan 12)*
**Burnside 108** *(13f,Lin,SD,Feb 3)*
**Burtonwood 117** *(6f,Ncs,SD,Mar 24)*
**Bush House 111** *(11f,Kem,SS,Sep 8)*
**Busy Street 106** *(12f,Sth,SD,Mar 14)*
**Buxted Dream 106** *(7f,Cfd,SD,Jun 1)*
**Buying Trouble 109** *(5f,Lin,SD,Feb 25)*
**Bybrook 111** *(12½f,Ncs,SD,Jly 29)*
**Byres Road 109** *(9f,Wol,SD,Jan 14)*
**Byron Flyer 114** *(16f,Ncs,SD,Mar 22)*

**Cadeau Magnifique 109** *(10f,Ncs,SD,Mar 2)*
**Cainhoe Star 105** *(7f,Kem,SS,Oct 11)*
**Call Out Loud 105** *(7f,Sth,SD,Apr 4)*
**Calvinist 109** *(16½f,Wol,SD,Feb 15)*
**Camakasi 110** *(11f,Kem,SS,Jan 11)*
**Canford Bay 107** *(5f,Ncs,SD,Oct 24)*
**Cape Cova 112** *(16f,Ncs,SD,Dec 16)*
**Cape Peninsular 113** *(12½f,Ncs,SD,Jly 29)*
**Cape To Cuba 105** *(8f,Kem,SD,Nov 6)*
**Capolavoro 109** *(7f,Cfd,SD,Mar 30)*
**Cappananty Con 106** *(6f,Cfd,SD,Dec 7)*
**Capricious Cantor 110** *(10f,Cfd,SD,May 25)*
**Captain Bob 105** *(6f,Sth,SD,Mar 29)*
**Captain Cat 109** *(10f,Kem,SS,Mar 8)*
**Captain Cullen 105** *(8f,Dun,SD,Dec 8)*
**Captain Dion 111** *(7f,Wol,SD,Feb 6)*
**Captain Joy 110** *(8f,Dun,SD,Dec 8)*
**Captain Lars 107** *(6f,Cfd,SD,Nov 23)*
**Captain Navarre 110** *(16½f,Wol,SD,Dec 5)*
**Captain Peacock 106** *(12f,Kem,SS,Jun 7)*
**Captain Power 107** *(6f,Dun,SD,Aug 18)*
**Captain Revelation 106** *(7f,Sth,SD,Jan 1)*
**Captain Swift 110** *(14f,Wol,SD,Oct 27)*
**Cascavelle 108** *(8f,Dun,SD,Nov 10)*
**Caspian Prince 108** *(6f,Lin,SD,Nov 18)*
**Casterbridge 109** *(5f,Ncs,SD,Oct 24)*
**Castilo Del Diablo 114** *(12½f,Ncs,SD,Jan 12)*
**Castlelyons 109** *(12f,Kem,SD,Nov 8)*
**Celebration Day 108** *(10f,Cfd,SD,Jun 1)*
**Celestial Spheres 105** *(12f,Lin,SD,Dec 31)*
**Certificate 108** *(7f,Cfd,SD,Sep 30)*
**Ceyhan 106** *(12f,Wol,SD,Feb 11)*
**Chain Of Daisies 111** *(10f,Ncs,SD,Jun 30)*
**Champagne Champ 108** *(16f,Ncs,SD,Jly 1)*
**Chant 108** *(12½f,Ncs,SD,Aug 10)*
**Charles Molson 109** *(8f,Lin,SD,Nov 18)*
**Chelwood Gate 105** *(8f,Lin,SD,May 5)*
**Chester Street 106** *(8f,Kem,SS,Oct 14)*
**Chestnut Fire 107** *(8f,Kem,SD,Dec 20)*
**Chiclet 105** *(5f,Ncs,SD,Jan 12)*
**Chiswick Bey 105** *(8f,Ncs,SD,Feb 10)*
**Chocolate Box 110** *(14f,Cfd,SD,Sep 7)*
**Choral Clan 105** *(12f,Kem,SS,Jan 18)*
**Cinque Port 106** *(6f,Cfd,SD,Mar 13)*
**City Of Joy 109** *(8f,Cfd,SD,Jun 1)*
**Claim The Roses 108** *(8f,Ncs,SD,Jun 29)*
**Clever Cookie 110** *(16f,Ncs,SD,Jly 1)*
**Cliffs Of Capri 110** *(8f,Lin,SD,Dec 31)*
**Cloudy Miss 106** *(8f,Dun,SD,Nov 1)*
**Clovelly Bay 106** *(12f,Wol,SD,Jan 23)*
**Clowance One 108** *(12f,Kem,SS,Jun 7)*
**Cocoa Beach 105** *(7f,Dun,SD,Jan 6)*
**Codeshare 117** *(12½f,Ncs,SD,Mar 2)*
**Cohesion 118** *(16f,Lin,SD,Apr 14)*
**Coillte Cailin 108** *(10f,Lin,SD,Jan 7)*
**Comicas 111** *(6f,Mey,FT,Feb 11)*
**Commanche 108** *(6f,Ncs,SD,Feb 4)*
**Commodity 108** *(8f,Kem,SS,Sep 9)*
**Compas Scoobie 105** *(6f,Wol,SD,Apr 29)*
**Compatriot 106** *(8f,Dun,SD,Sep 22)*
**Compton Prince 105** *(6f,Kem,SS,Jan 11)*
**Compton River 105** *(5f,Ncs,SD,Mar 4)*
**Confrontational 106** *(6f,Dun,SD,Nov 3)*
**Constantino 110** *(8f,Ncs,SD,Jun 29)*
**Convey 112** *(10f,Lin,SD,Apr 14)*
**Cool Cowboy 106** *(6f,Mey,FT,Feb 2)*
**Cool Music 107** *(12f,Wol,SD,May 30)*
**Cool Team 107** *(8f,Ncs,SD,Sep 29)*
**Coronation Day 105** *(6f,Kem,SS,Oct 11)*
**Corpus Chorister 107** *(16f,Lin,SD,Mar 31)*
**Corton Lad 107** *(12½f,Ncs,SD,Oct 19)*
**Cosmelli 112** *(14f,Wol,SD,Dec 9)*
**Cosmo Charlie 113** *(7f,Mey,FT,Jan 26)*
**Costa Percy 111** *(14f,Wol,SD,Oct 27)*
**Count Montecristo 109** *(9½f,Wol,SD,Feb 6)*
**Count Octave 107** *(12f,Wol,SD,Mar 28)*
**Courier 107** *(6f,Cfd,SD,Dec 17)*
**Craftsmanship 107** *(10f,Cfd,SD,Mar 13)*
**Craggaknock 110** *(12½f,Ncs,SD,Mar 2)*
**Cray 105** *(14f,Cfd,SD,Jun 22)*
**Cribbs Causeway 109** *(12f,Lin,SD,Jun 22)*
**Cricklewood Green 107** *(8f,Lin,SD,Dec 13)*
**Crimson Rosette 109** *(10f,Lin,SD,Nov 17)*
**Cristy's Call 106** *(12f,Dun,SD,Feb 10)*
**Crosse Fire 105** *(6f,Sth,SD,Apr 4)*
**Crowned Eagle 105** *(12f,Wol,SD,Dec 2)*
**Cultured Knight 109** *(6f,Kem,SD,Mar 22)*
**Curious Fox 105** *(6f,Lin,SD,May 30)*
**Curzon Line 107** *(7f,Cfd,SD,Feb 16)*
**Custard The Dragon 110** *(7f,Sth,SD,Apr 18)*

**Daily Trader 106** *(8f,Sth,SD,Jan 24)*
**Daisy Bere 106** *(10f,Ncs,SD,Nov 23)*
**Daisy Boy 109** *(11f,Kem,SD,Feb 1)*
**Dakota City 110** *(11f,Kem,SD,Feb 1)*
**Dance Teacher 108** *(8f,Kem,SD,Dec 20)*
**Danz Gift 111** *(5f,Dun,SD,Jan 27)*
**Daphne 112** *(12f,Kem,SD,Nov 29)*
**Darebin 107** *(12f,Lin,SD,Feb 4)*
**Dark Alliance 106** *(8f,Dun,SD,Feb 24)*
**Dark Destroyer 105** *(6f,Lin,SD,Jan 7)*
**Dark Red 110** *(10f,Cfd,SD,May 25)*
**Dark Side Dream 113** *(6f,Cfd,SD,Jun 21)*
**Dark Titan 105** *(9½f,Wol,SD,Mar 14)*
**Dashing Poet 105** *(5f,Cfd,SD,Mar 16)*
**Dashing Star 105** *(12f,Lin,SD,Mar 24)*
**Dazacam 105** *(5f,Wol,SD,Jan 7)*
**De Coronado 112** *(11f,Dun,SD,Sep 22)*
**De La Vega 105** *(8f,Dun,SD,Sep 22)*
**Deansgate 108** *(7f,Ncs,SD,Dec 6)*
**Decorated Knight 117** *(10f,Lin,SD,Feb 4)*
**Deeley's Double 106** *(12f,Wol,SD,Dec 2)*
**Denmead 108** *(16½f,Wol,SD,May 2)*
**Desert Ruler 107** *(11f,Kem,SS,Oct 4)*
**Dhahmaan 107** *(6f,Lin,SD,Jan 20)*
**Diagnostic 106** *(7f,Cfd,SD,Oct 26)*
**Diamond Bear 106** *(10f,Kem,SS,Sep 25)*
**Diamond Lady 107** *(6f,Cfd,SD,Dec 21)*
**Dilmun 107** *(8f,Dun,SD,Jly 12)*
**Doc Sportello 114** *(5f,Ncs,SD,Jan 12)*
**Doctor Bartolo 106** *(10f,Ncs,SD,Jan 11)*
**Doctor Sardonicus 111** *(5f,Cfd,SD,Aug 15)*
**Dollar Reward 110** *(8f,Lin,SD,Jan 7)*
**Dolphin Village 105** *(12f,Lin,SD,Jan 4)*
**Dolphin Vista 109** *(10f,Lin,SD,Dec 23)*
**Domitilla 105** *(7f,Lin,SD,Dec 6)*
**Don't Give Up 105** *(8f,Kem,SS,Oct 4)*
**Donnachies Girl 115** *(12½f,Ncs,SD,Jly 29)*
**Double Up 108** *(6f,Wol,SD,Dec 26)*
**Dougan 111** *(5f,Ncs,SD,Jan 12)*
**Dr Julius No 105** *(7f,Lin,SD,Mar 4)*
**Draw Swords 105** *(10f,Cfd,SD,Jan 5)*
**Dream Ally 106** *(6f,Ncs,SD,Jun 1)*
**Dream Factory 106** *(12f,Wol,SD,Jan 23)*
**Dream Farr 109** *(6f,Kem,SD,Feb 18)*
**Dream Free 105** *(9f,Wol,SD,Nov 7)*
**Dream Magic 107** *(12f,Wol,SD,Dec 22)*
**Dream Serenade 109** *(14f,Wol,SD,Oct 27)*
**Drochaid 111** *(10f,Cfd,SD,May 10)*
**Dubai Horizon 105** *(10f,Lin,SD,Apr 8)*
**Dubai One 109** *(6f,Lin,SD,Dec 30)*
**Dubaitwentytwenty 106** *(8f,Sth,SD,Dec 22)*
**Ducky Mallon 105** *(7f,Dun,SD,Mar 16)*
**Duncan Of Scotland 106** *(6f,Dun,SD,May 12)*
**Dundonnell 109** *(6f,Mey,FT,Feb 11)*
**Dundunah 105** *(5f,Ncs,SD,Nov 24)*
**Dungannon 105** *(5f,Sth,SD,Mar 9)*
**Dutch Art Dealer 105** *(7f,Ncs,SD,Jan 3)*
**Dutch Golden Age 116** *(6f,Kem,SD,Feb 3)*
**Dutch Uncle 108** *(10f,Lin,SD,Feb 28)*
**Dutiful Son 108** *(6f,Kem,SD,Mar 29)*
**Dylan Mouth 105** *(12f,Kem,SD,Nov 6)*
**Dynamo Walt 108** *(5f,Lin,SD,Mar 4)*

**Eagle Creek 107** *(8f,Kem,SS,Oct 4)*
**Early Morning 106** *(7f,Lin,SD,Nov 25)*
**Earthly 105** *(12f,Lin,SD,May 30)*
**East Coast Lady 106** *(7f,Cfd,SD,May 29)*
**Eastern Impact 105** *(6f,Wol,SD,Mar 11)*
**Easy Tiger 110** *(7f,Cfd,SD,Oct 6)*
**Easy Wind 110** *(14f,Wol,SD,Aug 10)*
**Ebbisham 105** *(7f,Wol,SD,Dec 26)*
**Ebtkaar 105** *(7f,Cfd,SD,Dec 17)*
**Eccleston 111** *(6f,Ncs,SD,Nov 30)*
**Einstein 105** *(9f,Wol,SD,Jun 26)*
**El Astronaute 108** *(5f,Cfd,SD,Aug 15)*
**El Principe 105** *(6f,Kem,SS,Mar 8)*
**El Vip 105** *(8f,Kem,SS,Jun 1)*
**Elbereth 110** *(11f,Dun,SD,Mar 24)*
**Eldritch 109** *(12½f,Ncs,SD,Oct 19)*
**Election Day 105** *(8f,Cfd,SD,Jun 1)*
**Elegantly Bound 105** *(7f,Sth,SD,Feb 10)*
**Elishpour 106** *(16f,Dun,SD,Feb 10)*
**Eljaddaaf 116** *(6f,Kem,SS,Jan 6)*
**Elleval 111** *(8f,Dun,SD,Dec 8)*
**Eltezam 106** *(8f,Kem,SD,Dec 20)*
**Elucidation 105** *(10f,Cfd,SD,May 10)*
**Elusive Heights 106** *(11f,Dun,SD,Sep 29)*
**Elusive In Paris 108** *(7f,Dun,SD,Mar 24)*
**Elysian Fields 106** *(12f,Lin,SD,Dec 30)*
**Elysian Flyer 106** *(6f,Ncs,SD,Feb 10)*
**Elysian Prince 107** *(10f,Lin,SD,Jan 4)*
**Emenem 105** *(9½f,Wol,SD,Dec 2)*
**Emotionless 110** *(10f,Mey,FT,Feb 9)*
**Encapsulated 105** *(6f,Kem,SD,Mar 22)*
**Encipher 108** *(7f,Mey,FT,Feb 16)*
**Encore D'Or 116** *(5f,Lin,SD,Mar 4)*
**Endless Acres 106** *(16f,Ncs,SD,May 19)*
**Energia Flavio 105** *(7f,Wol,SD,Aug 31)*
**Enfolding 105** *(11f,Kem,SD,Dec 13)*
**Englishwoman 106** *(5f,Sth,SD,Jan 26)*
**Enjoy Life 115** *(6f,Ncs,SD,Mar 24)*
**Ennjaaz 106** *(11f,Kem,SS,Oct 11)*
**Ennobled Friend 110** *(8f,Mey,FT,Feb 11)*
**Entertaining Ben 108** *(5f,Ncs,SD,Mar 4)*
**Entihaa 108** *(16½f,Wol,SD,Feb 15)*
**Envisaging 111** *(6f,Cfd,SD,Dec 21)*
**Epeius 105** *(6f,Ncs,SD,Aug 10)*
**Epicharis 109** *(9½f,Mey,MY,Mar 25)*
**Epitaph 111** *(12f,Sth,SD,Dec 21)*
**Eqtiraan 109** *(8f,Lin,SD,Apr 8)*
**Equally Fast 106** *(6f,Kem,SS,Jan 6)*
**Equiano Springs 109** *(7f,Ncs,SD,Dec 6)*
**Escalating 107** *(5f,Sth,SD,Feb 21)*
**Eskendash 105** *(11f,Kem,SS,Oct 11)*
**Espresso Freddo 105** *(7f,Ncs,SD,Feb 1)*
**Etijaah 113** *(10f,Mey,FT,Feb 23)*
**Etikaal 109** *(7f,Cfd,SD,May 25)*
**Eugenic 105** *(12f,Sth,SD,Oct 22)*
**Evening Attire 111** *(7f,Lin,SD,Jan 18)*
**Every Chance 108** *(14f,Wol,SD,Apr 8)*
**Evies Wish 107** *(6f,Ncs,SD,Nov 10)*
**Examiner 105** *(9f,Wol,SD,Mar 11)*
**Exceeding Power 107** *(10f,Kem,SS,Sep 25)*
**Excellent George 111** *(6f,Cfd,SD,Dec 17)*
**Exclusive Waters 107** *(10f,Ncs,SD,Feb 7)*
**Executive Force 111** *(8f,Kem,SD,Apr 15)*
**Explain 114** *(6f,Ncs,SD,Mar 24)*
**Express Lady 106** *(8f,Kem,SD,Nov 6)*

**Fabricate 114** *(12f,Wol,SD,Mar 6)*
**Fairway To Heaven 112** *(6f,Kem,SD,Feb 3)*
**Faithful Creek 115** *(12½f,Ncs,SD,Mar 2)*
**Falbon 106** *(7f,Cfd,SD,May 25)*
**Family Fortunes 105** *(5f,Lin,SD,Feb 25)*
**Famous Kid 113** *(16½f,Wol,SD,Jan 16)*
**Fanciful Angel 114** *(10f,Cfd,SD,May 25)*
**Fantasy Gladiator 106** *(10f,Ncs,SD,Mar 2)*
**Fashion Business 105** *(8f,Lin,SD,Jan 14)*
**Fast Play 107** *(12f,Wol,SD,Jan 31)*
**Fast Track 109** *(6f,Wol,SD,Jan 13)*
**Favorite Girl 108** *(12f,Wol,SD,Jan 31)*
**Fayez 106** *(10f,Lin,SD,Nov 21)*
**Fergall 107** *(12f,Kem,SS,Jun 7)*
**Fern Owl 106** *(16½f,Sth,SD,Feb 10)*
**Fieldsman 106** *(7f,Cfd,SD,Oct 6)*
**Fiery Spice 105** *(5f,Sth,SD,Mar 15)*
**Fikhaar 106** *(6f,Ncs,SD,Nov 30)*
**Final 110** *(10f,Cfd,SD,Mar 13)*
**Financial Conduct 105** *(12f,Dun,SD,Dec 6)*
**Fintry Flyer 108** *(6f,Ncs,SD,Nov 30)*
**Fire Diamond 108** *(7f,Wol,SD,Jan 26)*
**Fire Fighting 109** *(11f,Dun,SD,Mar 24)*
**Fire Jet 106** *(16½f,Wol,SD,Mar 27)*
**First Flight 105** *(12f,Kem,SD,Nov 8)*
**First Mohican 118** *(16f,Lin,SD,Mar 25)*
**Fitzgerald 106** *(8f,Mey,MY,Mar 25)*
**Fitzwilly 107** *(16f,Kem,SS,Sep 8)*
**Fizzy Friday 105** *(7f,Dun,SD,Feb 10)*
**Fleckerl 108** *(6f,Wol,SD,Feb 20)*
**Fleeting Visit 109** *(12f,Kem,SS,Jun 7)*
**Flood Warning 106** *(9½f,Wol,SD,Mar 14)*
**Florencio 112** *(6f,Kem,SD,Feb 25)*
**Fly At Dawn 115** *(7f,Mey,FT,Jan 26)*
**Flying Fantasy 106** *(7f,Lin,SD,Jan 18)*
**Flymetothestars 111** *(16f,Ncs,SD,Jly 1)*
**Foie Gras 105** *(8f,Cfd,SD,Mar 30)*
**Foolaad 110** *(6f,Ncs,SD,Mar 1)*
**Footlight 109** *(10f,Ncs,SD,Feb 17)*
**Footman 108** *(11f,Kem,SS,Jun 7)*
**Forceful Appeal 108** *(10f,Lin,SD,Feb 4)*
**Forest Ranger 108** *(8f,Ncs,SD,Apr 14)*
**Fort Bastion 106** *(10f,Lin,SD,Jan 7)*
**Four Wishes 106** *(8f,Ncs,SD,Sep 12)*
**Foxy Forever 110** *(5f,Kem,SS,Oct 17)*
**Franco's Secret 109** *(8f,Lin,SD,Mar 4)*
**Frank The Barber 106** *(5f,Lin,SD,Mar 4)*
**Frankyfourfingers 108** *(8f,Mey,FT,Jan 26)*
**Frederic 107** *(16½f,Wol,SD,Dec 5)*
**Fredricka 107** *(5f,Ncs,SD,Jan 27)*
**Free State 105** *(12f,Dun,SD,Mar 10)*
**Free Zone 109** *(6f,Kem,SS,Jan 6)*
**Fujin 108** *(6f,Cfd,SD,Apr 6)*
**Fulham 107** *(16f,Lin,SS,Oct 5)*
**Furia Cruzada 105** *(9½f,Mey,FT,Feb 2)*

**Gabrial 111** *(8f,Lin,SD,Nov 18)*
**Gabrial's Star 107** *(16½f,Sth,SD,Nov 13)*
**Gakku 105** *(13f,Lin,SD,Nov 2)*
**Galilee Chapel 105** *(12½f,Ncs,SD,Nov 23)*
**Gallifrey 105** *(12½f,Ncs,SD,Dec 6)*
**Galvanize 106** *(9½f,Mey,FT,Feb 2)*
**Gang Warfare 106** *(16½f,Wol,SD,Jan 16)*
**Gavlar 117** *(16f,Ncs,SD,Mar 22)*
**Gawdawpalin 110** *(12f,Lin,SD,Mar 24)*
**General Hazard 110** *(10f,Ncs,SD,Mar 2)*
**Genetics 108** *(8f,Lin,SD,Dec 13)*
**Gentlemen 108** *(6f,Dun,SD,Feb 17)*
**Geoff Potts 108** *(6f,Kem,SD,Feb 18)*
**Geological 109** *(6f,Dun,SD,Sep 29)*
**George Cinq 110** *(7f,Sth,SD,Mar 15)*
**Georgian Bay 105** *(8f,Kem,SS,Sep 9)*
**Gerry The Glover 106** *(10f,Ncs,SD,Jly 1)*
**Get Knotted 107** *(6f,Ncs,SD,Jly 1)*
**Getback In Paris 111** *(10f,Kem,SS,Mar 8)*
**Ghaseedah 105** *(6f,Sth,SD,Dec 4)*
**Ghayyar 106** *(10f,Cfd,SD,May 10)*
**Giantstepsahead 105** *(11f,Kem,SD,Feb 1)*
**Gibbs Hill 106** *(12f,Wol,SD,Apr 29)*
**Gifted Master 112** *(6f,Lin,SD,Nov 18)*
**Gilgamesh 105** *(7f,Cfd,SD,Nov 17)*
**Glastonbury Song 111** *(8f,Dun,SD,Dec 8)*
**Glenamoy Lad 116** *(6f,Ncs,SD,Nov 30)*
**Glenys The Menace 109** *(10f,Lin,SD,Nov 17)*
**Glorious Artist 107** *(9f,Wol,SD,Jly 31)*
**Glory Of Paris 106** *(7f,Kem,SD,Apr 5)*
**Go Far 108** *(6f,Wol,SD,Mar 11)*
**Go Kart 110** *(5f,Dun,SD,Jan 27)*
**God Willing 108** *(6f,Ncs,SD,Mar 9)*
**Gold Flash 108** *(7f,Cfd,SD,Feb 16)*
**Gold Star 108** *(12f,Wol,SD,Sep 9)*
**Golden Amber 108** *(7f,Cfd,SD,Feb 8)*
**Golden Goal 109** *(7f,Cfd,SD,Jly 25)*
**Golden Wedding 110** *(8f,Kem,SS,Sep 9)*
**Goldmember 105** *(12f,Wol,SD,Oct 21)*
**Goldrush 106** *(8f,Dun,SD,Oct 27)*
**Good Run 116** *(16f,Ncs,SD,Mar 22)*
**Good Time Ahead 112** *(12f,Sth,SD,Dec 21)*
**Gordon Lord Byron 110** *(8f,Dun,SD,Dec 8)*
**Gorgeous Noora 106** *(6f,Lin,SD,Nov 21)*
**Goring 115** *(8f,Lin,SD,Dec 31)*
**Gossiping 109** *(8f,Kem,SD,Mar 20)*
**Gracious John 112** *(5f,Lin,SD,Dec 12)*
**Gracious Tom 106** *(5f,Sth,SD,Jan 10)*
**Grand Argentier 108** *(9½f,Mey,FT,Feb 2)*
**Grand Facile 107** *(16f,Lin,SD,Jan 4)*
**Great Court 109** *(12f,Kem,SD,Nov 29)*
**Great Fighter 110** *(12½f,Ncs,SD,Mar 2)*
**Great Hall 109** *(12f,Lin,SD,Mar 24)*
**Grendisar 115** *(10f,Lin,SD,Feb 4)*
**Grey Britain 108** *(7f,Lin,SD,Mar 4)*
**Grey Danube 107** *(8f,Dun,SD,Dec 8)*
**Groundfrost 106** *(8f,Dun,SD,Nov 1)*
**Grumeti 107** *(16½f,Wol,SD,Mar 27)*
**Guishan 105** *(5f,Sth,SD,Jan 1)*
**Gulland Rock 105** *(7f,Kem,SS,Jun 7)*
**Gulliver 110** *(6f,Kem,SD,Nov 6)*
**Gun Runner 120** *(10f,Mey,MY,Mar 25)*

**Hadley 107** *(6f,Ncs,SD,Feb 4)*
**Haines 115** *(16f,Lin,SD,Apr 14)*
**Hairdryer 107** *(9½f,Wol,SD,Feb 6)*
**Hajaam 108** *(12f,Lin,SD,Dec 23)*
**Hakam 110** *(6f,Kem,SD,Apr 1)*
**Halling's Wish 105** *(13f,Lin,SD,Feb 3)*
**Hallstatt 107** *(16½f,Wol,SD,Nov 20)*
**Hamelin 110** *(16f,Ncs,SD,Mar 22)*
**Hamish McGonagain 105** *(6f,Wol,SD,Apr 22)*
**Hammer Gun 110** *(8f,Cfd,SD,Mar 23)*
**Handsome Dude 110** *(6f,Ncs,SD,Feb 17)*
**Handytalk 105** *(8f,Lin,SD,May 5)*
**Harrison 106** *(14f,Cfd,SD,May 10)*
**Harwoods Star 107** *(7f,Sth,SD,Jan 2)*
**Have A Nice Day 108** *(6f,Dun,SD,Sep 29)*
**He's My Cracker 105** *(6f,Kem,SD,Feb 22)*
**Heart Locket 106** *(12f,Wol,SD,Feb 27)*
**Heartful 107** *(8f,Dun,SD,Feb 10)*
**Heartstone 106** *(9½f,Wol,SD,Jan 6)*
**Heavy Metal 110** *(8f,Mey,FT,Jan 26)*
**Helfire 106** *(7f,Kem,SS,Jun 7)*
**Henley 111** *(5f,Ncs,SD,Jun 1)*
**Henry Croft 106** *(12½f,Ncs,SD,Jan 12)*
**Here And Now 106** *(11f,Kem,SD,Apr 12)*
**Hermann 106** *(12f,Wol,SD,Jan 10)*
**Hes Our Music 105** *(7f,Dun,SD,Mar 24)*
**Hidden Steps 106** *(10f,Lin,SD,Nov 17)*
**High Acclaim 107** *(7f,Lin,SD,Mar 4)*
**High Altitude 107** *(8f,Dun,SD,Oct 13)*
**High On Light 114** *(12½f,Ncs,SD,Jly 29)*
**Higher Court 108** *(7f,Cfd,SD,Mar 30)*
**Higher Power 112** *(16f,Ncs,SD,Jly 1)*
**Hilary J 112** *(5f,Ncs,SD,Oct 24)*
**Holiday Magic 113** *(7f,Sth,SD,Jan 1)*
**Home Again 105** *(7f,Cfd,SD,Feb 16)*
**Honiara 112** *(7f,Lin,SD,Jan 18)*
**Hoppertunity 113** *(10f,Mey,MY,Mar 25)*
**Horsforth 109** *(5f,Ncs,SD,Mar 4)*
**Horsted Keynes 107** *(7f,Lin,SD,Mar 3)*
**Hot Beat 107** *(12f,Wol,SD,Jan 16)*
**House Of Commons 105** *(10f,Cfd,SD,Jan 19)*
**Howardian Hills 105** *(14f,Wol,SD,Nov 25)*
**Hugin 107** *(7f,Ncs,SD,May 19)*
**Human Nature 109** *(6f,Cfd,SD,Dec 15)*
**Humble Hero 106** *(12½f,Ncs,SD,Sep 12)*
**Hunting Ground 110** *(10f,Mey,FT,Jan 19)*
**Hussar Ballad 113** *(14f,Wol,SD,Oct 27)*

**Ice Canyon 106** *(12f,Wol,SD,Dec 2)*
**Ice Dancing 107** *(9½f,Wol,SD,Aug 18)*
**Ice Royal 109** *(9f,Wol,SD,Jan 14)*
**Icebuster 105** *(16½f,Wol,SD,Mar 27)*
**Ickymasho 112** *(10f,Cfd,SD,Mar 13)*
**Iconic Figure 105** *(8f,Dun,SD,Sep 22)*
**Iftitah 106** *(7f,Wol,SD,Aug 31)*
**Im Waiting 106** *(12½f,Ncs,SD,Jan 12)*
**Imphal 108** *(16f,Lin,SS,Oct 5)*
**Important Mission 110** *(7f,Cfd,SD,Aug 15)*
**In The Lope 116** *(10f,Lin,SD,Nov 18)*
**In The Red 111** *(8f,Kem,SS,Jan 17)*
**Inaam 110** *(7f,Wol,SD,Dec 13)*
**Included 105** *(12f,Wol,SD,Jan 31)*
**Indian Affair 106** *(6f,Wol,SD,Apr 22)*
**Indian Blessing 105** *(8f,Kem,SD,Apr 15)*
**Indian Dandy 105** *(8f,Lin,SD,Jan 7)*
**Indian Pursuit 105** *(5f,Ncs,SD,Feb 14)*
**Infiniti 109** *(12f,Wol,SD,May 30)*
**Influent 107** *(9½f,Wol,SD,Dec 16)*
**Ingleby Spring 105** *(11f,Sth,SD,Dec 29)*
**Inniscastle Lad 106** *(10f,Cfd,SD,Mar 13)*
**Innish Man 105** *(14f,Wol,SD,Oct 27)*
**Innoko 105** *(16f,Kem,SS,Nov 1)*
**Intense Style 108** *(6f,Ncs,SD,Mar 9)*
**Intensical 105** *(7f,Cfd,SD,Mar 2)*
**Intermodal 105** *(10f,Kem,SS,Sep 25)*
**Intern 110** *(10f,Lin,SD,Dec 23)*
**Intimate Art 108** *(8f,Cfd,SD,Jun 1)*
**Intisaab 110** *(6f,Ncs,SD,Jly 1)*
**Intransigent 109** *(6f,Kem,SD,Nov 6)*
**Invincible Ridge 106** *(5f,Wol,SD,Feb 23)*
**Isaac Bell 108** *(12f,Kem,SD,Nov 8)*
**Isabel's On It 105** *(7f,Cfd,SD,May 8)*
**Iseemist 113** *(5f,Lin,SD,Mar 25)*
**Isharah 117** *(16f,Lin,SD,Mar 25)*
**Ishebayorgrey 108** *(8f,Dun,SD,Nov 1)*
**Island Brave 114** *(12f,Wol,SD,Nov 29)*
**It Must Be Faith 109** *(6f,Wol,SD,Feb 20)*

**Jaameh 105** *(16f,Ncs,SD,Jly 1)*
**Jack Bear 107** *(16f,Kem,SS,Sep 8)*
**Jack Dexter 107** *(5f,Ncs,SD,Jun 30)*
**Jack Flash 106** *(6f,Lin,SD,Jan 7)*
**Jack Of Diamonds 107** *(9f,Wol,SD,Nov 7)*
**Jackhammer 105** *(11f,Kem,SD,Apr 12)*
**Jacob Cats 108** *(11f,Kem,SD,Apr 1)*
**Jacquotte Delahaye 107** *(7f,Kem,SD,Feb 18)*
**Jameerah 106** *(6f,Kem,SD,Nov 6)*
**Jaqen H'Ghar 110** *(11f,Dun,SD,Sep 22)*
**Jaywalker 111** *(6f,Ncs,SD,Mar 9)*
**Jimenez 105** *(8f,Cfd,SD,Jan 5)*
**Jive Talking 105** *(10f,Kem,SS,Nov 22)*
**Joey's Destiny 109** *(7f,Wol,SD,Feb 6)*
**John Reel 116** *(16f,Lin,SD,Mar 25)*
**Jolly Roger 105** *(16f,Lin,SD,Feb 22)*
**Jon Ess 109** *(8f,Dun,SD,Oct 13)*
**Jordan Sport 110** *(5f,Wol,SD,Feb 20)*
**Joshua Reynolds 105** *(14f,Cfd,SD,Nov 2)*
**Judicial 107** *(5f,Wol,SD,Feb 20)*
**Jukebox Jive 105** *(12f,Wol,SD,Apr 5)*
**Just That Lord 109** *(5f,Kem,SD,Apr 15)*
**Just Us Two 108** *(5f,Ncs,SD,Mar 2)*
**Justice Good 113** *(5f,Ncs,SD,Jan 12)*

**Kadrizzi 108** *(7f,Lin,SD,Dec 13)*
**Kafuji Take 105** *(8f,Mey,MY,Mar 25)*
**Karijini 108** *(6f,Cfd,SD,Dec 8)*
**Kasbah 110** *(6f,Lin,SD,Jan 20)*
**Kasperenko 109** *(11f,Kem,SS,Sep 8)*
**Katiymann 113** *(8f,Dun,SD,Dec 8)*
**Keen Ice 112** *(10f,Mey,MY,Mar 25)*
**Kencumin 106** *(7f,Sth,SD,Feb 10)*
**Kenny The Captain 110** *(5f,Ncs,SD,Nov 30)*
**Kenstone 107** *(8f,Cfd,SD,Jly 7)*
**Kentuckyconnection 108** *(8f,Ncs,SD,Jun 29)*
**Keyser Soze 106** *(7f,Kem,SS,May 31)*
**Keystroke 109** *(7f,Wol,SD,Mar 11)*
**Khabaray 106** *(8f,Dun,SD,Mar 3)*
**Khafoo Shememi 115** *(8f,Kem,SD,Apr 15)*
**Ki Ki 107** *(6f,Ncs,SD,Feb 4)*
**Kimberella 116** *(5f,Lin,SD,Mar 25)*
**King Calypso 107** *(6f,Kem,SS,Jly 5)*
**King Christophe 107** *(12f,Dun,SD,Feb 10)*
**King Cole 110** *(7f,Mey,FT,Feb 16)*
**King Of Nepal 107** *(7f,Wol,SD,Dec 26)*
**King Olav 106** *(16f,Lin,SD,Jan 27)*

King Robert 107 (6f,Wol,SD,Feb 27)
Kingofmerrows 105 (6f,Cfd,SD,Dec 8)
Kingsley Klarion 108 (6f,Cfd,SD,Jun 21)
Kingston Kurrajong 110 (8f,Lin,SD,Jan 7)
Kitty Boo 105 (8f,Kem,SD,Nov 6)
Kodiline 106 (5f,Kem,SS,Oct 17)
Koeman 107 (11f,Kem,SS,Sep 27)
Konig Hall 107 (12f,Wol,SD,Jly 31)
Koropick 111 (6f,Ncs,SD,Jly 1)
Kroy 106 (6f,Ncs,SD,Nov 30)
Kullu 107 (12½f,Ncs,SD,Jun 3)
Kyllachy Gala 109 (10f,Cfd,SD,May 25)

L'Inganno Felice 109 (12f,Sth,SD,Jan 10)
La Casa Tarifa 110 (10f,Ncs,SD,Oct 24)
La Vie En Rose 105 (12f,Lin,SD,Apr 24)
Lac Leman 116 (12½f,Ncs,SD,Mar 2)
Lacan 106 (8f,Kem,SS,Nov 1)
Lady Bergamot 105 (10f,Ncs,SD,Jun 3)
Lady Of The Lamp 105 (6f,Ncs,SD,Nov 3)
Lady Perignon 106 (7f,Sth,SD,Oct 22)
Lagenda 107 (7f,Wol,SD,Dec 13)
Lake Shore Drive 107 (14f,Wol,SD,Nov 25)
Lancaster Bomber 108 (9½f,Mey,MY,Mar 25)
Lancelot Du Lac 113 (5f,Lin,SD,Feb 25)
Lanceur 105 (16f,Kem,SS,Jly 5)
Landing Night 106 (5f,Ncs,SD,Oct 10)
Langlauf 110 (12f,Kem,SS,Jun 7)
Lani 109 (10f,Mey,MY,Mar 25)
Lastmanlastround 107 (8f,Kem,SS,Sep 9)
Latchet 106 (8f,Dun,SD,Nov 1)
Law And Order 111 (8f,Lin,SD,Apr 8)
Layl 108 (10f,Mey,FT,Feb 9)
Leo Minor 105 (6f,Lin,SD,Dec 30)
Lethal Impact 105 (16f,Kem,SD,Aug 30)
Letmestopyouthere 109 (6f,Ncs,SD,Mar 22)
Lexington Abbey 109 (5f,Ncs,SD,Jun 30)
Lexington Law 111 (12f,Lin,SD,Dec 30)
Lexington Times 111 (7f,Lin,SD,Jan 18)
Liberatum 107 (5f,Ncs,SD,Oct 24)
Life Knowledge 111 (12½f,Ncs,SD,Feb 14)
Lightning Charlie 105 (6f,Cfd,SD,Apr 6)
Lightscameraction 107 (5f,Ncs,SD,Jan 12)
Lindo Amor 106 (8f,Mey,FT,Feb 11)
Line Of Reason 110 (5f,Ncs,SD,Jun 30)
Linguistic 108 (10f,Kem,SD,Apr 1)
Locus Standi 108 (11f,Dun,SD,Apr 7)
London 110 (7f,Cfd,SD,Mar 30)
London Glory 105 (12½f,Ncs,SD,Nov 23)
Lopes Dancer 109 (12½f,Ncs,SD,Sep 19)
Lord George 111 (16f,Ncs,SD,Dec 16)
Los Barbados 107 (10f,Mey,FT,Jan 19)
Lost The Moon 109 (16½f,Wol,SD,Dec 5)
Loyalty 114 (7f,Cfd,SD,Feb 16)
Luang Prabang 105 (9f,Wol,SD,Oct 27)
Lucent Dream 105 (9½f,Wol,SD,Mar 17)
Lucky Gal 105 (12f,Wol,SD,Feb 11)
Lucky Lodge 107 (6f,Ncs,SD,Aug 10)
Lucymai 109 (7f,Cfd,SD,Nov 23)
Luis Vaz De Torres 105 (7f,Lin,SD,Mar 17)
Lunch 108 (10f,Lin,SD,Feb 9)
Luv U Whatever 108 (12f,Sth,SD,Dec 4)
Lydia's Place 105 (5f,Ncs,SD,Mar 31)

Macksville 107 (14f,Cfd,SD,Sep 21)
Maghfoor 105 (12½f,Ncs,SD,Oct 19)
Magic City 108 (9f,Wol,SD,Jan 14)
Magwadiri 105 (8f,Dun,SD,Oct 6)
Maifalki 112 (12f,Wol,SD,Nov 29)
Mailshot 106 (8f,Cfd,SD,Mar 11)
Main Stay 109 (6f,Mey,FT,Jan 19)
Mainicin 106 (11f,Dun,SD,Jan 20)
Major Crispies 106 (6f,Ncs,SD,Sep 29)
Major Jumbo 112 (5f,Ncs,SD,Feb 10)
Major Muscari 105 (7f,Lin,SD,Jan 25)
Major Rowan 108 (12½f,Ncs,SD,Mar 2)
Major Valentine 110 (6f,Kem,SD,Mar 20)
Majoris 105 (8f,Lin,SD,Apr 8)
Makaarim 109 (7f,Lin,SD,Dec 13)
Make Music 113 (7f,Lin,SD,Jan 18)
Malaspina 108 (7f,Sth,SD,Dec 1)
Mama Africa 105 (8f,Sth,SD,Dec 19)
Manjaam 105 (11f,Kem,SS,Sep 8)
Manshood 110 (5f,Ncs,SD,Jun 1)
Manson 109 (10f,Kem,SS,Mar 8)
Manton Grange 106 (7f,Kem,SS,Aug 22)
Many Waters 107 (10f,Kem,SD,Apr 1)
Mappin Time 106 (5f,Sth,SD,Jan 1)
Maratha 109 (8f,Lin,SD,Dec 13)
Mariee 109 (10f,Ncs,SD,Feb 17)
Mark Of Approval 107 (8f,Sth,SD,May 8)
Markhan 105 (8f,Dun,SD,Oct 13)
Marquee Club 106 (7f,Lin,SD,Mar 4)
Marsh Pride 107 (12½f,Ncs,SD,Jly 29)
Marshall Aid 108 (16f,Lin,SD,Mar 31)
Marshgate Lane 105 (10f,Lin,SD,Jan 7)
Mashaaref 105 (6f,Mey,FT,Jan 19)
Masham Star 110 (7f,Cfd,SD,Sep 2)
Massif Central 109 (8f,Dun,SD,Oct 20)
Master Plan 108 (9½f,Mey,MY,Mar 25)
Master Singer 116 (10f,Ncs,SD,May 23)
Master Speaker 105 (6f,Dun,SD,Sep 29)
Master The World 119 (10f,Lin,SD,Nov 18)
Masterpaver 118 (12½f,Ncs,SD,Jan 12)
Masterson 108 (16½f,Wol,SD,May 2)
Materialistic 106 (8f,Kem,SD,Apr 15)
Mathematics 106 (7f,Mey,FT,Feb 16)
Matravers 108 (10f,Cfd,SD,Mar 13)
Mazaaher 106 (12f,Wol,SD,Apr 19)
Mazyoun 107 (7f,Kem,SS,Aug 16)
Mazzini 115 (6f,Cfd,SD,Jun 21)
Mcguigan 107 (8f,Dun,SD,Jan 27)
Meadway 106 (5f,Sth,SD,Jan 1)
Meandmyshadow 106 (6f,Ncs,SD,Aug 10)
Melodic Motion 107 (13f,Lin,SD,Nov 2)
Menelik 112 (6f,Cfd,SD,Jun 21)
Mere Anarchy 112 (16f,Kem,SS,Sep 8)
Meshardal 107 (6f,Ncs,SD,Mar 1)
Metropol 107 (10f,Lin,SD,Apr 14)
Mia Tesoro 117 (10f,Lin,SD,Nov 18)
Mica Mika 108 (12f,Lin,SD,Feb 11)
Mickey 106 (7f,Lin,SD,Dec 13)
Middle Kingdom 105 (10f,Cfd,SD,Nov 9)
Midnight Malibu 108 (5f,Lin,SD,Dec 12)
Midnightly 105 (5f,Wol,SD,Aug 18)
Midtech Star 108 (14f,Wol,SD,Mar 11)
Mighty Zip 105 (6f,Cfd,SD,Apr 1)
Milton 108 (8f,Mey,FT,Jan 28)
Mind Your Biscuits 113 (6f,Mey,MY,Mar 25)
Miracle Garden 109 (7f,Cfd,SD,Oct 6)
Mise En Rose 109 (7f,Cfd,SD,Feb 8)
Mishaal 107 (6f,Kem,SS,Sep 13)
Miss Dusky Diva 109 (16f,Lin,SD,Jan 4)
Miss Liguria 105 (12f,Lin,SD,Dec 13)
Mister Music 106 (8f,Kem,SD,Feb 3)
Mister Showman 106 (12f,Sth,SD,Oct 22)
Mistiroc 114 (12f,Wol,SD,Mar 6)
Misu Pete 105 (7f,Cfd,SD,Jun 21)
Mithqaal 107 (8f,Sth,SD,Jan 10)
Mo Henry 105 (5f,Dun,SD,Sep 22)
Moabit 106 (12f,Sth,SD,Dec 21)
Moayadd 105 (10f,Ncs,SD,Feb 7)
Mobbhij 105 (16f,Ncs,SD,Nov 15)
Modernism 107 (12f,Wol,SD,Jan 23)
Monarchs Glen 109 (11f,Kem,SD,Apr 12)
Money Team 114 (6f,Ncs,SD,Mar 24)
Moneyoryourlife 107 (10f,Cfd,SD,Mar 30)
Monjeni 106 (14f,Wol,SD,Mar 28)
Monsieur Rieussec 109 (10f,Cfd,SD,Jan 19)
Monte Cinq 105 (5f,Lin,SD,Jan 18)
Monteverdi 105 (7f,Sth,SD,Dec 11)
Monumental Man 107 (5f,Lin,SD,Mar 31)
Moolazim 105 (7f,Cfd,SD,Aug 15)
Moonraker 107 (6f,Ncs,SD,Jly 1)
Morawij 108 (6f,Mey,MY,Mar 25)
More Mischief 112 (10f,Ncs,SD,Jun 30)
Mostahel 109 (6f,Wol,SD,Apr 17)
Mostawfee 107 (8f,Dun,SD,Sep 22)
Mount Tahan 107 (7f,Cfd,SD,May 10)
Mountain Bell 113 (16f,Ncs,SD,Dec 16)
Mountain Hunter 111 (11f,Kem,SS,Sep 8)
Mountain Rescue 105 (8f,Ncs,SD,Jun 29)
Moviesta 111 (5f,Dun,SD,Jly 12)
Mr Bossy Boots 107 (7f,Lin,SD,Dec 13)
Mr Christopher 109 (7f,Lin,SD,Jan 18)
Mr Chuckles 106 (6f,Wol,SD,Mar 25)
Mr Globetrotter 107 (16½f,Wol,SD,Mar 25)
Mr Ormsby 107 (8f,Dun,SD,Nov 1)
Mr Owen 109 (8f,Kem,SS,Nov 22)
Mr Potter 106 (7f,Cfd,SD,Feb 16)
Mr Red Clubs 108 (9½f,Wol,SD,Jun 9)
Mr Scaramanga 110 (8f,Lin,SD,Apr 8)
Muarrab 106 (6f,Mey,FT,Jan 12)
Muatadel 106 (6f,Kem,SD,Mar 20)
Mubtaahij 114 (10f,Mey,MY,Mar 25)
Mudallel 106 (8f,Kem,SS,Aug 16)
Muffri'Ha 107 (8f,Lin,SD,Nov 2)
Muhtaram 105 (8f,Mey,FT,Jan 19)
Mukalal 109 (8f,Cfd,SD,Jly 7)
Multiviz 105 (12f,Dun,SD,Feb 10)
Muntazah 106 (8f,Cfd,SD,Aug 15)
Murdanova 105 (7f,Kem,SD,Feb 15)
Murgan 106 (12f,Kem,SS,Jun 7)
Music Box 106 (8f,Dun,SD,Mar 31)
Music Major 105 (10f,Lin,SD,Dec 13)
Mustashry 110 (8f,Cfd,SD,Aug 15)
Mutahaddith 107 (6f,Mey,FT,Jan 28)
Mutarabby 110 (8f,Cfd,SD,Jly 7)
Mutarakez 106 (8f,Lin,SD,Mar 4)
Mutawathea 109 (8f,Lin,SD,Dec 31)
Mutineer 107 (8f,Kem,SS,Aug 9)
My Amigo 105 (7f,Ncs,SD,Dec 6)
My Brother Mike 105 (9½f,Wol,SD,Aug 18)
My Direction 106 (12f,Dun,SD,Sep 29)
My Good Brother 107 (5f,Dun,SD,Sep 22)
My Reward 111 (16f,Ncs,SD,Jly 1)
My Target 110 (8f,Lin,SD,Mar 4)
Mysterious Look 105 (5f,Sth,SD,Jan 26)
Mystique Moon 110 (8f,Lin,SD,Dec 31)
Mythical Madness 114 (10f,Lin,SD,Feb 4)
Mythmaker 110 (6f,Lin,SD,Nov 18)

Naadirr 105 (7f,Wol,SD,Mar 11)
Nadaitak 107 (16f,Kem,SD,Aug 30)
Naralsaif 110 (6f,Ncs,SD,Nov 30)
Narjes 107 (8f,Kem,SS,Sep 6)
Nasri 106 (6f,Kem,SD,Mar 22)
Nathan Mayer 106 (11f,Kem,SS,Jun 7)
Nathr 109 (8f,Mey,FT,Jan 19)
Native Prospect 105 (8f,Sth,SD,Feb 21)
Natural Scenery 119 (12½f,Ncs,SD,Jan 12)
Nautical Haven 107 (6f,Cfd,SD,Dec 15)
Neolithic 116 (10f,Mey,MY,Mar 25)
Netley Abbey 110 (14f,Wol,SD,Aug 10)
New Society 107 (12½f,Ncs,SD,Aug 10)
Newmarket Warrior 106 (8f,Ncs,SD,Sep 29)
Newstead Abbey 112 (6f,Ncs,SD,Mar 24)
Next Train's Gone 105 (16f,Cfd,SD,May 29)
Nezar 109 (6f,Kem,SD,Mar 20)
Nimr 113 (7f,Wol,SD,Feb 6)
Ninjago 105 (6f,Wol,SD,Feb 27)
Nivvo 106 (8f,Dun,SD,Mar 3)
Noble Behest 108 (16f,Lin,SD,Dec 20)
Noble Gift 113 (10f,Cfd,SD,May 25)
Noble Masterpiece 106 (8f,Kem,SS,Sep 5)
Noble Star 107 (8f,Kem,SS,Jan 17)
Noivado 105 (7f,Dun,SD,Apr 12)
Nonios 106 (9½f,Wol,SD,Dec 16)
North America 117 (8f,Mey,FT,Feb 11)
North Creek 107 (8f,Cfd,SD,Jly 7)
Northern Surprise 105 (6f,Dun,SD,Feb 17)
Northgate Lad 109 (6f,Ncs,SD,Jly 1)
Nostalgie 105 (7f,Wol,SD,Jly 17)
Not So Sleepy 110 (12f,Kem,SD,Nov 29)
Nuns Walk 105 (6f,Ncs,SD,Nov 10)
Nurse Nightingale 106 (14f,Cfd,SD,Sep 21)

Ocean Of Love 111 (14f,Wol,SD,Nov 11)
Oceane 107 (16½f,Wol,SD,Feb 15)
Ominotago 105 (12f,Sth,SD,Nov 28)
Omotesando 109 (12f,Wol,SD,Nov 29)
Omran 105 (7f,Ncs,SD,May 23)
One Boy 105 (5f,Ncs,SD,Jan 27)
One Word More 108 (8f,Ncs,SD,Jun 29)
Oneoveryou 110 (6f,Dun,SD,Feb 17)
Oor Jock 107 (7f,Dun,SD,Mar 24)
Oratorio's Joy 106 (16½f,Wol,SD,May 2)
Orient Class 106 (5f,Ncs,SD,Mar 31)
Oriental Lilly 105 (5f,Ncs,SD,Nov 24)
Oriental Relation 111 (6f,Kem,SD,Feb 3)
Orion's Bow 108 (5f,Ncs,SD,Jun 30)
Orsino 109 (12f,Wol,SD,Apr 22)
Orvar 107 (5f,Kem,SS,Oct 13)
Ostatnia 107 (6f,Dun,SD,Mar 24)
Ouja 105 (13f,Lin,SD,Nov 2)
Our Channel 107 (10f,Kem,SS,Mar 8)
Ourmullion 105 (10f,Cfd,SD,Sep 7)
Out Do 109 (6f,Lin,SD,Nov 18)
Outer Space 115 (7f,Cfd,SD,Feb 16)
Ower Fly 106 (7f,Kem,SS,Aug 16)

Paco's Angel 106 (8f,Lin,SD,Apr 8)
Pactolus 112 (10f,Cfd,SD,Sep 30)
Paddyplex 111 (10f,Ncs,SD,Nov 23)
Padleyourowncanoe 109 (14f,Wol,SD,Aug 10)
Panstarr 106 (8f,Dun,SD,Mar 31)
Papou Tony 105 (7f,Kem,SS,Jun 7)
Paris Protocol 105 (12f,Wol,SD,Oct 27)
Parkour 116 (6f,Ncs,SD,Mar 24)
Parnassian 106 (6f,Kem,SS,Oct 24)
Part Exchange 109 (10f,Lin,SD,Sep 26)
Patrick 107 (6f,Dun,SD,Feb 3)
Peace And Plenty 108 (10f,Kem,SS,Nov 22)
Peace Officer 105 (8f,Dun,SD,Sep 22)
Peaceful Passage 111 (12f,Kem,SD,Feb 15)
Peak Princess 105 (7f,Cfd,SD,Sep 2)
Pealer 108 (11f,Sth,SD,May 8)
Pearl Spectre 110 (7f,Lin,SD,Dec 13)
Pendo 108 (8f,Kem,SS,Jan 17)
Pennsylvania 106 (8f,Dun,SD,Oct 20)
Percy Veer 107 (16½f,Wol,SD,Feb 15)
Percy's Word 108 (16f,Kem,SD,Aug 30)
Percys Princess 107 (12f,Sth,SD,Dec 4)
Persian Steel 112 (12½f,Ncs,SD,Jan 12)
Persun 112 (11f,Kem,SD,Feb 1)
Petite Jack 116 (10f,Lin,SD,Nov 18)
Phalaborwa 107 (7f,Wol,SD,Jly 17)
Philba 109 (7f,Sth,SD,Jan 1)
Piazon 105 (5f,Sth,SD,Oct 22)
Pinwood 106 (13f,Lin,SD,Jan 18)
Pinzolo 115 (12f,Lin,SD,Jan 21)
Pioneertown 110 (12½f,Ncs,SD,Oct 19)
Pipes Of Peace 107 (8f,Dun,SD,Oct 20)
Pivot Bridge 112 (14f,Wol,SD,Jan 5)
Plato's Kode 105 (14f,Cfd,SD,Sep 21)
Plucky Dip 110 (7f,Cfd,SD,Feb 16)
Plutocracy 106 (12f,Wol,SD,Jan 16)
Plutonian 106 (10f,Cfd,SD,Nov 9)
Ply 111 (10f,Kem,SS,Sep 25)
Poet's Society 105 (5f,Wol,SD,Jan 7)
Poet's Word 106 (10f,Cfd,SD,Apr 13)
Poeta Diletto 105 (10f,Kem,SD,Apr 1)
Poetic Choice 105 (8f,Dun,SD,Feb 24)
Poitin 108 (11f,Dun,SD,Sep 22)
Polar Kite 106 (8f,Lin,SD,Mar 8)
Political Policy 106 (16f,Dun,SD,Feb 10)
Polybius 108 (6f,Wol,SD,Dec 26)
Polymnia 106 (8f,Lin,SS,Jan 13)
Poppy In The Wind 109 (5f,Ncs,SD,Jan 4)
Pour L'Amour 108 (12½f,Ncs,SD,Feb 14)
Pouvoir Magique 106 (8f,Ncs,SD,Nov 10)
Power Home 106 (9½f,Wol,SD,Oct 31)
Poyle Vinnie 107 (6f,Lin,SD,Feb 18)
Presumido 107 (8f,Kem,SS,Sep 9)
Pretend 111 (5f,Lin,SD,Feb 25)
Pretty Bubbles 110 (6f,Kem,SS,Jan 6)
Pretty Jewel 105 (12f,Wol,SD,May 30)
Primero 107 (12f,Lin,SD,Dec 23)
Primo Uomo 109 (5f,Dun,SD,Mar 3)
Prince Of Arran 117 (16f,Lin,SD,Apr 14)
Professor 105 (6f,Kem,SD,Apr 1)
Promising Run 105 (8f,Lin,SD,Nov 2)
Prosper 105 (10f,Cfd,SD,Aug 8)
Pure Action 108 (8f,Dun,SD,Sep 22)
Pushaq 108 (8f,Dun,SD,Nov 1)

Qaffaal 113 (10f,Cfd,SD,May 25)
Quarterback 106 (10f,Kem,SD,Apr 1)
Queen In Waiting 107 (5f,Wol,SD,Apr 17)
Queensbrydge 106 (8f,Kem,SS,Oct 3)
Quiet Company 107 (8f,Dun,SD,Sep 22)

Raashdy 108 (14f,Wol,SD,Dec 27)
Rahmah 105 (11f,Kem,SS,Jan 11)
Rainbow Rebel 107 (9½f,Wol,SD,Dec 16)
Rapid Applause 105 (6f,Dun,SD,Feb 17)
Rashaan 107 (16f,Dun,SD,Feb 10)
Rasmee 107 (12½f,Ncs,SD,Sep 19)
Rattle On 105 (8f,Lin,SD,Apr 24)
Raucous 109 (6f,Cfd,SD,Apr 27)
Raven's Corner 112 (7f,Mey,FT,Feb 16)
Raven's Lady 105 (8f,Kem,SD,Apr 15)
Ravens Quest 108 (12f,Wol,SD,Feb 27)
Ray's The Money 105 (11f,Kem,SS,Sep 27)
Rayaa 105 (10f,Cfd,SD,Nov 17)
Razin' Hell 107 (5f,Sth,SD,Jan 1)
Razzmatazz 105 (6f,Kem,SS,Sep 5)
Reach High 108 (8f,Kem,SS,Oct 14)
Realize 111 (8f,Lin,SD,Jan 7)
Really Special 105 (7f,Mey,FT,Jan 19)
Reaver 108 (8f,Kem,SS,Sep 9)
Rebel Surge 105 (7f,Kem,SD,Feb 18)
Reckless Endeavour 112 (6f,Dun,SD,Sep 29)
Reckless Lad 107 (8f,Dun,SD,Jan 27)
Reckless Wave 105 (12f,Wol,SD,May 3)
Red Avenger 109 (8f,Dun,SD,Nov 1)
Red Ensign 108 (8f,Kem,SD,Apr 15)
Red Hot Chilly 106 (12f,Wol,SD,Feb 11)
Red Stripes 105 (5f,Sth,SD,Dec 29)
Red Tornado 108 (12f,Wol,SD,Mar 6)
Red Trooper 108 (6f,Kem,SS,Sep 13)
Red Tycoon 105 (6f,Kem,SD,Mar 22)
Red Verdon 113 (12f,Kem,SD,Nov 29)
Redicean 107 (12½f,Ncs,SD,Oct 19)
Related 109 (6f,Kem,SS,Oct 24)
Remember The Man 111 (16f,Lin,SD,Feb 22)
Rene Mathis 106 (7f,Wol,SD,Mar 11)
Renfrew Street 109 (14f,Cfd,SD,Sep 7)
Repercussion 108 (10f,Cfd,SD,May 25)
Reshoun 108 (12½f,Ncs,SD,Oct 19)
Restive 111 (12f,Sth,SD,Dec 4)
Retrieve 109 (9½f,Wol,SD,Jun 9)
Reynaldothewizard 107 (6f,Mey,FT,Jan 12)
Rich Again 110 (5f,Ncs,SD,Jan 27)
Richter Scale 108 (5f,Ncs,SD,Jan 4)
Ride Like The Wind 108 (5f,Lin,SD,Feb 25)
Ride The Lightning 107 (12f,Wol,SD,Jan 10)
Right Touch 111 (7f,Lin,SD,Dec 13)
Rinaria 109 (9f,Wol,SD,Oct 7)
Rio's Cliffs 106 (8f,Kem,SS,Jan 17)
Robanne 105 (8f,Kem,SD,Apr 15)
Robbie Roo Roo 106 (6f,Kem,SS,Sep 8)
Robe Of Honour 107 (8f,Dun,SD,Mar 3)
Robero 109 (7f,Sth,SD,Apr 18)
Robot Boy 116 (5f,Wol,SD,Feb 20)
Rock Steady 114 (12f,Lin,SD,Jan 21)
Rock Warbler 107 (7f,Wol,SD,Dec 13)
Roll On Rory 105 (8f,Ncs,SD,Sep 29)
Roman De Brut 106 (9f,Wol,SD,Apr 19)
Romanor 106 (11f,Kem,SS,Oct 4)
Room To Roam 107 (8f,Dun,SD,Oct 13)
Rose Berry 105 (6f,Lin,SD,Nov 21)
Rosealee 107 (5f,Wol,SD,Mar 25)
Rosie Crowe 105 (7f,Cfd,SD,Feb 16)
Rosina 106 (5f,Cfd,SD,Dec 14)
Ross 111 (8f,Mey,MY,Mar 25)
Rouge Nuage 111 (7f,Wol,SD,Dec 13)
Roundabout Magic 107 (5f,Lin,SD,Dec 23)
Rowlestone Lass 105 (16½f,Wol,SD,Mar 27)
Royal Birth 114 (5f,Lin,SD,Feb 25)
Royal Brave 105 (5f,Ncs,SD,Mar 2)
Royal Marskell 117 (12½f,Ncs,SD,Jan 12)
Ruby Gates 105 (11f,Dun,SD,Jan 27)
Ruler Of The Nile 107 (16½f,Wol,SD,Dec 5)
Rummaging 107 (8f,Dun,SD,Nov 1)
Rumpole 105 (11f,Kem,SS,Oct 11)
Runaiocht 105 (9½f,Wol,SD,Feb 11)
Russian Soul 112 (7f,Wol,SD,Feb 6)
Ryan The Giant 105 (16½f,Wol,SD,Mar 25)
Rydan 115 (12f,Lin,SD,Jan 28)

Saafarr 108 (8f,Dun,SD,Apr 7)
Sacred Act 112 (8f,Lin,SD,Nov 18)
Sagely 108 (10f,Cfd,SD,Jun 22)
Saint Honore 106 (16f,Lin,SD,Feb 22)
Salateen 110 (7f,Wol,SD,Mar 11)
Saleh 106 (7f,Kem,SD,Mar 22)
Salvatore Fury 110 (6f,Kem,SD,Feb 3)
Sam Missile 110 (16f,Ncs,SD,Jly 1)
Samtu 107 (12f,Sth,SD,Mar 14)
Sandfrankskipsgo 106 (5f,Lin,SD,Mar 31)
Sandro Botticelli 110 (16½f,Wol,SD,Jan 16)
Sands Chorus 110 (9f,Wol,SD,Jan 14)
Sans Souci Bay 105 (7f,Lin,SD,Mar 17)
Santa Monica 109 (11f,Dun,SD,Sep 29)
Sanus Per Aquam 110 (11f,Dun,SD,Sep 22)
Satchville Flyer 105 (8f,Kem,SS,Aug 9)
Scala Regia 106 (8f,Kem,SS,Sep 6)
Scottish Glen 108 (8f,Lin,SD,Dec 13)
Scrafton 105 (14f,Wol,SD,Jan 5)
Scuzeme 106 (5f,Ncs,SD,Jan 21)
Sea Of Blue 105 (11f,Dun,SD,Apr 7)
Sea Of Green 105 (6f,Ncs,SD,Feb 4)
Seamour 109 (16f,Ncs,SD,Jly 1)
Seamster 105 (5f,Lin,SD,Feb 18)
Seanie 105 (8f,Dun,SD,Jly 12)
Second Page 107 (11f,Kem,SS,Jun 7)
Second Summer 112 (8f,Mey,MY,Mar 25)
Second Thought 115 (7f,Lin,SD,Mar 4)
Secret Ambition 107 (8f,Mey,FT,Jan 28)
Secret Wizard 111 (8f,Dun,SD,Dec 8)
See The Sun 108 (5f,Ncs,SD,Oct 24)
Seeking Magic 106 (6f,Kem,SS,Sep 25)
Senatus 106 (16f,Ncs,SD,Dec 16)
Seniority 107 (11f,Kem,SS,Oct 11)
Sennockian Star 116 (12f,Lin,SD,Jan 28)
Seprani 106 (6f,Kem,SS,Oct 3)
September Issue 111 (6f,Kem,SD,Feb 3)
Serefeli 106 (11f,Dun,SD,Jan 27)
Settle For Bay 107 (8f,Dun,SD,Nov 1)
Settle For Red 108 (11f,Dun,SD,Apr 7)
Seven Clans 108 (9½f,Wol,SD,Jan 9)
Shackled N Drawn 105 (5f,Lin,SD,Dec 23)
Shady McCoy 108 (8f,Lin,SD,Nov 18)
Shaishee 107 (7f,Mey,FT,Feb 16)
Shamash 105 (12f,Dun,SD,Feb 10)
Shamsaya 105 (6f,Lin,SD,Dec 12)
Shamshon 109 (5f,Lin,SD,Dec 12)
Shannon Soul 109 (8f,Dun,SD,Feb 24)
Sharjah 112 (11f,Dun,SD,Apr 7)
Sharp Azteca 110 (8f,Mey,MY,Mar 25)
Sharp Defence 108 (6f,Dun,SD,Aug 18)
Sharpalo 105 (10f,Mey,FT,Feb 23)
Sheila's Fancy 106 (16f,Lin,SD,Dec 20)
Sheisdiesel 105 (8f,Dun,SD,Nov 1)
Shelbe 106 (8f,Dun,SD,Sep 22)
Shepherd's Purse 111 (6f,Dun,SD,Feb 17)
Sheriff Garrett 113 (14f,Wol,SD,Aug 10)
Shoofly 108 (12f,Wol,SD,Jly 31)
Show Stealer 108 (6f,Kem,SS,Oct 24)
Showboating 108 (7f,Sth,SD,Mar 15)
Shukhov 105 (11f,Dun,SD,Apr 7)
Shyron 112 (7f,Lin,SD,Dec 13)
Sibilance 108 (8f,Kem,SD,Apr 15)
Sign Of The Kodiac 110 (6f,Dun,SD,Mar 24)
Signe 105 (11f,Dun,SD,Sep 29)
Silva Eclipse 108 (16f,Ncs,SD,Mar 22)
Silvanus 105 (5f,Wol,SD,Jan 5)
Silver Link 115 (14f,Wol,SD,Nov 11)
Silver Quay 109 (12f,Lin,SD,Jan 28)
Singular Quest 111 (14f,Wol,SD,Oct 27)
Sir Billy Wright 106 (5f,Sth,SD,Feb 10)
Sir Chauvelin 110 (16f,Ncs,SD,Jly 1)
Sir Danilo 107 (8f,Dun,SD,Mar 31)
Sir Dylan 108 (12f,Wol,SD,May 30)
Sir Gnet 105 (9½f,Wol,SD,Aug 18)
Sir Ottoman 106 (6f,Kem,SD,Nov 6)
Six Silver Lane 108 (8f,Dun,SD,Jly 12)
Skygazer 106 (11f,Mey,FT,Jan 28)
Slingsby 109 (6f,Ncs,SD,Feb 10)
Smugglers Creek 107 (8f,Dun,SD,Sep 22)
Snobbery 105 (12f,Wol,SD,Jan 23)
Snowy Winter 115 (12f,Sth,SD,Dec 21)
Socialites Red 106 (5f,Ncs,SD,Mar 4)
Solar Deity 114 (10f,Lin,SD,Feb 4)
Solar Flair 111 (6f,Kem,SD,Apr 15)
Solomon's Bay 107 (6f,Kem,SS,Oct 11)
Song Maker 108 (9f,Wol,SD,Oct 7)
Song Of Love 105 (11f,Dun,SD,Jan 20)
Sonnetist 105 (11f,Kem,SS,Oct 4)
Sophisticated Heir 107 (6f,Wol,SD,Jan 13)
Southdown Lad 106 (11f,Kem,SD,Apr 1)
Southern Belle 107 (5f,Kem,SD,Apr 15)
Sovereign Debt 108 (10f,Kem,SD,Apr 1)

**Space War 107** *(7f,Cfd,SD,Mar 30)*
**Sparkalot 105** *(6f,Kem,SD,Apr 7)*
**Special Season 106** *(7f,Sth,SD,Mar 15)*
**Specialist 108** *(10f,Cfd,SD,Mar 16)*
**Specific Gravity 105** *(11f,Dun,SD,Jan 20)*
**Speedo Boy 106** *(10f,Cfd,SD,Jan 5)*
**Spes Nostra 108** *(10f,Ncs,SD,Mar 2)*
**Spinners Ball 109** *(11f,Kem,SS,Jun 28)*
**Spinning Melody 112** *(12f,Wol,SD,Nov 29)*
**Spiraea 106** *(6f,Kem,SD,Feb 15)*
**Spirit Of Wedza 110** *(6f,Wol,SD,Feb 20)*
**Spirit Of Zebedee 109** *(6f,Ncs,SD,Feb 4)*
**Spiritoftomintoul 107** *(16f,Kem,SS,Sep 8)*
**Spiritual Star 106** *(8f,Lin,SD,Mar 8)*
**Split The Atom 108** *(7f,Dun,SD,Mar 31)*
**Spring Loaded 108** *(6f,Lin,SD,Nov 18)*
**Spruce Meadows 110** *(11f,Dun,SD,Sep 22)*
**Spun Gold 108** *(8f,Sth,SD,Dec 22)*
**Sputnik Planum 105** *(14f,Cfd,SD,Sep 21)*
**Squats 105** *(7f,Cfd,SD,Sep 2)*
**Squire 106** *(8f,Kem,SS,Jan 17)*
**St Brelades Bay 107** *(6f,Dun,SD,Nov 3)*
**St Gallen 109** *(11f,Dun,SD,Sep 22)*
**St. Joe Bay 108** *(6f,Mey,MY,Mar 25)*
**Stallwalkin' Dude 105** *(6f,Mey,MY,Mar 25)*
**Star Catch 105** *(6f,Cfd,SD,Jun 21)*
**Star Of Lombardy 106** *(11f,Sth,SD,Apr 4)*
**Star Story 113** *(12f,Wol,SD,Nov 29)*
**Starboard 105** *(8f,Kem,SS,Jan 17)*
**Starshell 106** *(12f,Lin,SD,May 5)*
**Start Seven 109** *(16½f,Wol,SD,Dec 5)*
**Steady Pace 112** *(7f,Cfd,SD,Sep 30)*
**Steel Train 109** *(7f,Cfd,SD,Nov 23)*
**Steelriver 108** *(5f,Wol,SD,Jan 5)*
**Stellar Surprise 110** *(10f,Lin,SD,Nov 17)*
**Stellarta 110** *(6f,Kem,SD,Apr 15)*
**Stepper Point 107** *(5f,Cfd,SD,Mar 16)*
**Steve Rogers 119** *(16f,Lin,SD,Apr 14)*
**Stone The Crows 105** *(11f,Kem,SS,Sep 27)*
**Stoneham 105** *(16f,Ncs,SD,Mar 2)*
**Stoney Broke 114** *(12½f,Ncs,SD,Jly 29)*
**Storm King 107** *(12f,Lin,SD,Feb 11)*
**Stormy Antarctic 107** *(8f,Kem,SS,Nov 22)*
**Stosur 107** *(8f,Cfd,SD,Sep 26)*
**Strada Di Carsoli 111** *(6f,Ncs,SD,Mar 24)*
**Strategic Force 110** *(5f,Dun,SD,Jan 27)*
**Strategic Heights 105** *(6f,Dun,SD,May 12)*
**Strictly Art 112** *(14f,Wol,SD,Oct 27)*
**Strong Steps 108** *(9½f,Wol,SD,Jun 9)*
**Stronger Than Me 108** *(11f,Dun,SD,Mar 24)*
**Stunned 111** *(7f,Mey,FT,Feb 16)*
**Stylish Dancer 110** *(14f,Wol,SD,Nov 11)*
**Suegioo 107** *(16f,Ncs,SD,Jly 1)*
**Suitor 106** *(12½f,Ncs,SD,Jly 1)*
**Summer Chorus 108** *(7f,Cfd,SD,Sep 2)*
**Summer Icon 106** *(7f,Kem,SD,Feb 18)*
**Summerghand 107** *(6f,Kem,SS,Oct 3)*
**Sunblazer 105** *(11f,Kem,SS,Oct 11)*
**Sunchisetagioo 107** *(9f,Wol,SD,Oct 7)*
**Supersta 110** *(7f,Sth,SD,Mar 21)*
**Suqoor 109** *(6f,Lin,SD,Feb 18)*
**Surround Sound 109** *(14f,Wol,SD,Oct 27)*
**Surrounding 105** *(8f,Dun,SD,Oct 27)*
**Sutter County 114** *(7f,Lin,SD,Mar 4)*
**Suzi's Connoisseur 106** *(7f,Cfd,SD,Sep 2)*
**Swashbuckle 114** *(16f,Ncs,SD,Mar 22)*
**Swift Approval 107** *(7f,Cfd,SD,Nov 23)*
**Swift Emperor 110** *(9½f,Wol,SD,Dec 16)*
**Swiss Cross 110** *(7f,Lin,SD,Jan 18)*
**Syphax 105** *(8f,Ncs,SD,Apr 14)*

**Tadaawol 107** *(6f,Ncs,SD,Mar 1)*
**Takbeer 107** *(16½f,Wol,SD,Dec 5)*
**Take The Helm 112** *(7f,Lin,SD,Jan 18)*
**Take Two 112** *(12f,Wol,SD,Nov 29)*
**Tamayef 107** *(8f,Kem,SS,Sep 5)*
**Tan Arabiq 107** *(12f,Wol,SD,Dec 2)*
**Tangramm 111** *(12f,Wol,SD,Nov 29)*
**Tartan Bute 110** *(16f,Lin,SD,Mar 31)*
**Tatlisu 109** *(6f,Ncs,SD,Mar 9)*
**Tatting 108** *(11f,Sth,SD,Apr 18)*
**Tee It Up Tommo 105** *(8f,Lin,SD,Dec 13)*
**Temasek Star 107** *(11f,Dun,SD,Apr 7)*
**Temple Road 105** *(5f,Lin,SD,Dec 23)*
**Templemary Boy 106** *(8f,Dun,SD,Oct 6)*
**Tempuran 107** *(16f,Lin,SD,Feb 22)*
**Tennessee Wildcat 109** *(11f,Dun,SD,Sep 29)*
**Testa Rossa 109** *(10f,Ncs,SD,Nov 23)*
**Thahab Ifraj 107** *(11f,Kem,SS,Jan 11)*
**Thammin 106** *(5f,Kem,SS,Oct 13)*
**That Is The Spirit 106** *(7f,Cfd,SD,May 10)*
**The Big Lad 105** *(5f,Sth,SD,Jan 5)*
**The Invisible Dog 106** *(8f,Dun,SD,Mar 3)*
**The Last Melon 110** *(14f,Wol,SD,Oct 27)*
**The Mouse Doctor 108** *(8f,Dun,SD,Jan 13)*
**The Otmoor Poet 106** *(11f,Kem,SS,Jun 28)*
**The Raven Master 106** *(12f,Lin,SD,May 5)*
**The Warrior 110** *(8f,Kem,SS,Sep 9)*
**Third Time Lucky 112** *(8f,Lin,SD,Dec 31)*
**Thistimenextyear 108** *(12f,Wol,SD,Nov 29)*
**Thorntoun Lady 105** *(5f,Ncs,SD,Jan 4)*
**Three Jacks 106** *(11f,Dun,SD,Sep 22)*
**Threebagsue 106** *(7f,Kem,SD,Feb 18)*
**Throckley 108** *(12f,Sth,SD,Nov 16)*
**Thunder Snow 110** *(9½f,Mey,MY,Mar 25)*
**Tiercel 106** *(8f,Lin,SD,Nov 17)*
**Tilly Trotter 107** *(6f,Ncs,SD,Nov 30)*
**Tilsworth Micky 105** *(6f,Kem,SS,Jan 17)*
**Time Chaser 105** *(8f,Kem,SD,Apr 24)*
**Time Of My Life 115** *(12½f,Ncs,SD,Mar 2)*
**Timeless Art 106** *(8f,Kem,SS,Aug 23)*
**Timia 106** *(8f,Dun,SD,Sep 22)*
**Tisbutadream 105** *(7f,Lin,SD,Mar 4)*
**Titi Makfi 106** *(12f,Kem,SD,Nov 6)*
**Toast Of New York 108** *(10f,Lin,SD,Dec 6)*
**Tobacco Road 107** *(10f,Cfd,SD,Jun 1)*
**Toboggan's Fire 107** *(9f,Wol,SD,Mar 25)*
**Togoville 113** *(6f,Dun,SD,Feb 17)*
**Tom Dooley 105** *(8f,Dun,SD,Sep 22)*
**Tom's Rock 108** *(11f,Kem,SS,Jun 28)*
**Tomily 107** *(6f,Ncs,SD,Mar 22)*
**Tommys Geal 106** *(11f,Kem,SD,Mar 20)*
**Tomorrow Mystery 109** *(12f,Wol,SD,Aug 14)*
**Tonkinese 109** *(8f,Dun,SD,Nov 1)*
**Top Beak 106** *(12f,Lin,SD,Dec 30)*
**Top Boy 110** *(6f,Cfd,SD,Jun 21)*
**Top Mission 107** *(7f,Cfd,SD,Jun 1)*
**Top Of The Glas 114** *(12½f,Ncs,SD,Jan 12)*
**Top Offer 108** *(9f,Wol,SD,Nov 7)*
**Top Score 106** *(7f,Mey,FT,Jan 26)*
**Topamichi 106** *(12f,Sth,SD,Nov 16)*
**Toriano 107** *(8f,Lin,SD,Dec 13)*
**Total Star 107** *(10f,Cfd,SD,May 10)*
**Totally Magic 105** *(8f,Ncs,SD,Sep 12)*
**Towerlands Park 105** *(9½f,Wol,SD,Dec 2)*
**Traditional Dancer 105** *(16f,Ncs,SD,Dec 16)*
**Treaty Of Rome 106** *(6f,Sth,SD,Mar 29)*
**Tred Softly 105** *(12f,Wol,SD,Jan 9)*
**Tribal Path 107** *(7f,Dun,SD,Mar 31)*
**Tricorn 108** *(8f,Cfd,SD,Jun 1)*
**Triple Nine 109** *(10f,Mey,FT,Jan 19)*
**Tropic Thunder 106** *(11f,Dun,SD,Dec 1)*
**Tropical Rock 107** *(6f,Kem,SS,Oct 24)*
**Tropics 112** *(6f,Ncs,SD,Nov 30)*
**Try Again 105** *(8f,Dun,SD,Mar 10)*
**Turnpike Trip 106** *(12f,Kem,SS,May 31)*
**Twin Appeal 110** *(7f,Ncs,SD,Mar 9)*
**Tyrsal 105** *(11f,Kem,SS,Jan 11)*

**Udontdodou 118** *(6f,Cfd,SD,Jun 21)*
**Ultimate Avenue 108** *(8f,Kem,SD,Apr 15)*
**Ulysses 106** *(12f,Lin,SD,Mar 3)*
**Unabated 110** *(6f,Ncs,SD,Mar 22)*
**Uncle Bernie 108** *(14f,Wol,SD,Jan 5)*
**Under Siege 111** *(6f,Kem,SD,Feb 22)*
**Until Midnight 110** *(7f,Cfd,SD,Feb 16)*
**Upavon 110** *(6f,Cfd,SD,Dec 21)*
**Uptown Funk 107** *(16f,Ncs,SD,Dec 16)*
**Ustinov 107** *(6f,Ncs,SD,Nov 30)*
**Utmost 111** *(8f,Lin,SD,Nov 18)*
**Utopian Dream 105** *(12f,Wol,SD,Mar 28)*

**Vale Of Flight 105** *(6f,Wol,SD,Feb 20)*
**Vallarta 105** *(6f,Cfd,SD,Apr 6)*
**Van Gerwen 108** *(5f,Wol,SD,Mar 25)*
**Van Huysen 107** *(10f,Lin,SD,Jan 7)*
**Vecheka 105** *(6f,Ncs,SD,Jun 1)*
**Veena 109** *(6f,Cfd,SD,Feb 23)*
**Veiled Secret 107** *(16f,Lin,SS,Oct 5)*
**Velvet Revolution 117** *(14f,Wol,SD,Dec 9)*
**Ventura Blues 109** *(8f,Kem,SS,Sep 9)*
**Verne Castle 112** *(5f,Lin,SD,Feb 25)*
**Very Dashing 111** *(10f,Ncs,SD,Jun 30)*
**Vettori Rules 116** *(16f,Lin,SD,Mar 25)*
**Via Serendipity 106** *(8f,Cfd,SD,Jly 7)*
**Via Via 111** *(7f,Ncs,SD,Mar 9)*
**Victoria Pollard 109** *(10f,Ncs,SD,Feb 17)*
**Victoriously 105** *(10f,Lin,SD,Apr 26)*
**Victory Bond 117** *(10f,Lin,SD,Nov 18)*
**Viewpoint 106** *(10f,Cfd,SD,May 2)*
**Villette 111** *(12f,Wol,SD,Nov 29)*
**Vimy Ridge 107** *(6f,Kem,SD,Feb 18)*
**Vincy 105** *(8f,Dun,SD,Mar 16)*
**Viscount Barfield 106** *(7f,Cfd,SD,May 10)*
**Visionary 107** *(5f,Wol,SD,Jan 7)*
**Vivernus 105** *(9½f,Mey,FT,Feb 2)*
**Vogueatti 111** *(10f,Ncs,SD,Feb 17)*
**Voi 108** *(10f,Lin,SD,Nov 17)*
**Volatile 111** *(7f,Lin,SD,Mar 4)*
**Volpone Jelois 107** *(16f,Lin,SD,Dec 20)*
**Volturnus 109** *(14f,Wol,SD,Aug 10)*
**Volunteer Point 110** *(7f,Cfd,SD,Feb 8)*

**Waarif 109** *(10f,Ncs,SD,Nov 23)*
**War Decree 113** *(11f,Dun,SD,Sep 29)*
**War Department 110** *(7f,Ncs,SD,Mar 9)*
**War Goddess 108** *(12f,Dun,SD,Feb 10)*
**War Secretary 106** *(7f,Dun,SD,Apr 12)*
**Watchable 112** *(5f,Lin,SD,Mar 25)*
**Watersmeet 120** *(16f,Lin,SD,Apr 14)*
**Wefait 108** *(10f,Kem,SD,Apr 1)*
**Welliesinthewater 108** *(7f,Cfd,SD,May 10)*
**Western Duke 112** *(11f,Kem,SS,Sep 8)*
**Western Hymn 106** *(12f,Kem,SD,Nov 29)*
**What A Welcome 105** *(10f,Lin,SD,Nov 2)*
**Whitecliff Park 110** *(16f,Kem,SS,Sep 8)*
**Wick Powell 108** *(6f,Ncs,SD,Mar 10)*
**Wild Approach 113** *(5f,Ncs,SD,Feb 10)*
**Wild Hacked 111** *(11f,Kem,SD,Apr 1)*
**William Hunter 107** *(11f,Kem,SD,Apr 1)*
**Willwams 106** *(7f,Lin,SD,Mar 17)*
**Willyegolassiego 111** *(14f,Wol,SD,Dec 27)*
**Windforpower 106** *(5f,Ncs,SD,Mar 4)*
**Wine List 106** *(11f,Kem,SS,Oct 11)*
**Wink Oliver 107** *(8f,Lin,SD,Mar 8)*
**Winners Follow Me 107** *(9½f,Wol,SD,Feb 23)*
**Winning Story 121** *(16f,Lin,SD,Apr 14)*
**Winston C 108** *(11f,Kem,SS,Jun 7)*
**Winter Lion 105** *(16f,Dun,SD,Jan 13)*
**Winterlude 115** *(12f,Wol,SD,Mar 6)*
**Wolfcatcherjack 105** *(12f,Kem,SS,Aug 22)*
**World Tax War 110** *(11f,Dun,SD,Sep 22)*
**Worlds His Oyster 106** *(8f,Ncs,SD,Feb 7)*

**X Rated 105** *(10f,Ncs,SD,Nov 23)*

**Yorkidding 109** *(16f,Ncs,SD,Jly 1)*
**You're Cool 107** *(5f,Wol,SD,Feb 23)*
**You're Fired 108** *(8f,Lin,SD,Jan 7)*
**Young John 108** *(7f,Sth,SD,Jan 1)*
**Young Tiger 106** *(5f,Ncs,SD,Sep 22)*
**Yuften 109** *(7f,Wol,SD,Mar 11)*
**Yul Finegold 105** *(12f,Wol,SD,May 30)*

**Zabeel Star 110** *(11f,Kem,SD,Feb 1)*
**Zac Brown 115** *(5f,Lin,SD,Mar 4)*
**Zack Mayo 107** *(12f,Wol,SD,Jly 3)*
**Zest 106** *(8f,Kem,SD,Apr 15)*
**Zipedeedodah 106** *(5f,Wol,SD,Mar 25)*
**Zubayr 110** *(12f,Lin,SD,Dec 30)*
**Zumran 105** *(6f,Cfd,SD,Jun 21)*
**Zumurudee 110** *(10f,Cfd,SD,May 10)*
**Zylan 105** *(5f,Sth,SD,Apr 16)*
**Zzoro 108** *(10f,Cfd,SD,Jun 22)*

## TWO YEAR-OLDS - Turf

**Aim Of Artemis 106** *(7f,Lei,GS,Sep 12)*
**Alwasmiya 107** *(6f,Nmk,GF,Nov 3)*
**Another Batt 107** *(6f,Cur,G,May 13)*
**Autumn Leaves 106** *(6f,Nby,G,Jly 13)*
**Awesome 107** *(5f,Chp,GS,Sep 6)*
**Awesometank 110** *(8f,Yor,G,Oct 14)*
**Ayutthaya 107** *(7f,Chs,HY,Sep 30)*

**Baroness 105** *(8f,Nmk,GS,Nov 4)*
**Beatbox Rhythm 106** *(6f,Yor,G,Oct 13)*
**Beckford 108** *(6f,Cur,G,May 13)*
**Bengali Boys 111** *(5f,Nby,S,Jly 22)*
**Beshaayir 108** *(6f,Nby,G,Sep 22)*
**Billesdon Brook 107** *(7f,Goo,G,Aug 26)*
**Black Sails 109** *(6f,Cur,G,May 13)*
**Buckstopper Kit 106** *(8f,Yor,G,Oct 14)*

**Camelback 107** *(7f,Leo,GF,May 26)*
**Cardsharp 109** *(6f,Nmk,G,Jly 13)*
**Che Bella 105** *(7f,Cat,GS,Oct 10)*
**Clemmie 112** *(6f,Nmk,GS,Sep 30)*
**Coat Of Arms 105** *(7f,Cur,YS,Aug 20)*
**Connect 113** *(7f,San,GS,Aug 2)*
**Cuban Heel 105** *(7f,Lei,S,Oct 10)*

**Dance Diva 110** *(6f,Asc,GS,Jly 29)*
**Dark Liberty 109** *(8f,Yor,G,Oct 14)*
**Darkanna 109** *(6f,Red,GS,Oct 7)*
**Dee Ex Bee 107** *(7f,Goo,S,Aug 5)*
**Different League 109** *(6f,Nmk,GS,Sep 30)*
**Dream Of Delphi 105** *(7f,Lin,G,Aug 30)*
**Dream Today 105** *(8f,Nmk,G,Oct 14)*

**El Chapo 106** *(7f,Cat,GS,Oct 10)*
**Elarqam 107** *(7f,Nmk,GS,Sep 28)*
**Electric Landlady 107** *(6f,Nby,G,Jly 13)*
**Enjazaat 107** *(6f,Yar,G,Jun 6)*
**Expert Eye 107** *(7f,Goo,G,Aug 1)*

**Face Like Thunder 105** *(7f,Lei,S,Oct 10)*
**Fighting Irish 107** *(6f,Yar,GS,Sep 21)*
**Fleet Review 108** *(6f,Nmk,GS,Sep 30)*
**Flying Sparkle 108** *(6f,Red,GS,Oct 7)*
**Foxrush Take Time 111** *(7f,Hay,GS,Aug 11)*
**Foxtrot Lady 106** *(6f,Red,GS,Oct 7)*

**Ghaiyyath 107** *(8f,Nmk,G,Oct 14)*
**Give And Take 107** *(7½f,Lin,GS,Sep 16)*
**Go Now Go Now 105** *(8f,Wdr,GS,Sep 4)*
**Golden Salute 105** *(6f,Goo,S,Sep 5)*
**Great Prospector 106** *(6f,Yor,GS,Aug 24)*
**Gustav Klimt 105** *(7f,Cur,G,Jly 2)*

**Hadith 107** *(8f,Nmk,GS,Nov 4)*
**Happily 112** *(7f,Cur,SH,Sep 10)*
**Havana Grey 115** *(5f,Goo,S,Aug 2)*
**Heartache 114** *(5f,Don,GS,Sep 15)*
**Herecomesthesun 105** *(8f,Nmk,GS,Nov 4)*
**Hey Gaman 107** *(6f,Nmk,GS,Jly 29)*
**Hey Jonesy 106** *(6f,Crl,GF,Jly 14)*
**Holy Tiber 106** *(5f,Don,S,May 20)*

**Iconic Code 105** *(8f,Pon,S,Oct 23)*
**Indomeneo 107** *(7f,Lei,S,Oct 10)*
**Ingenuity 107** *(6f,Crl,GF,Jly 14)*
**Invincible Army 112** *(5f,Goo,S,Aug 2)*

**James Garfield 109** *(6f,Nby,G,Sep 23)*
**Jazirat 106** *(7f,Lei,GF,Jun 27)*
**Jedi Master 105** *(5f,Don,S,May 20)*
**Juliet Capulet 105** *(7f,Nmk,GS,Sep 29)*

**Kareva 105** *(6f,Nby,G,Jly 13)*
**Kew Gardens 106** *(10f,Nmk,G,Oct 14)*
**King's Proctor 105** *(8½f,Not,G,Nov 1)*
**Kyllachy Dragon 105** *(6f,Yor,G,Oct 13)*

**Lake Volta 110** *(6f,Bri,GF,Aug 11)*
**Laugh A Minute 105** *(6½f,Don,GS,Sep 14)*
**Laurens 107** *(8f,Nmk,G,Oct 13)*
**Liquid Amber 108** *(8f,Cur,Y,Aug 27)*
**Lisheen Castle 107** *(8f,Ham,S,Aug 25)*

**Madeline 109** *(6f,Nby,GS,Jly 21)*
**Magic Jazz 105** *(6f,Ham,GS,Sep 2)*
**Magic Lily 106** *(8f,Nmk,G,Oct 13)*
**Magical 113** *(8f,Cha,S,Oct 1)*
**Magnus 109** *(7f,Hay,GS,Aug 11)*
**Maksab 110** *(7f,Lei,GF,Jun 27)*
**Mamba Noire 105** *(6f,Nmk,GF,Jly 14)*
**Marnie James 107** *(5f,Yor,GF,Jly 14)*
**Masar 108** *(8f,Cha,S,Oct 1)*
**May Girl 106** *(5f,Don,GS,Sep 15)*
**Mendelssohn 108** *(7f,Nmk,G,Oct 14)*
**Miss Bar Beach 105** *(7f,Goo,G,Aug 26)*
**Mission Impassible 113** *(8f,Cha,S,Oct 1)*
**Mr Top Hat 105** *(6f,Sal,HY,Oct 4)*
**Muirin 105** *(7f,Cur,SH,Sep 10)*
**Musical Art 108** *(6f,Asc,GS,Jly 29)*
**Mutaaqeb 107** *(6f,Don,GS,Oct 28)*

**Narella 107** *(8f,Cha,S,Oct 1)*
**Natural 106** *(6f,Nby,GS,Jly 21)*
**Nebo 107** *(6f,Nby,G,Sep 23)*
**Nelson 105** *(8f,Nmk,GS,Sep 30)*
**Neola 106** *(6f,Goo,S,Sep 5)*
**New To Town 106** *(7f,Leo,GF,May 26)*
**Nine Below Zero 107** *(5f,Wdr,GF,Jun 5)*
**Now You're Talking 107** *(6f,Nmk,GS,Sep 30)*
**Nyaleti 117** *(6f,Asc,GS,Jly 29)*

**Old Persian 105** *(8f,Nmk,G,Oct 7)*
**Olmedo 108** *(8f,Cha,S,Oct 1)*

**Poets Dream 105** *(7f,Thi,S,Sep 9)*
**Polydream 113** *(8f,Cha,S,Oct 1)*
**Pursuing The Dream 105** *(5f,Don,GS,Sep 15)*

**Queen's Sargent 110** *(7f,Hay,GS,Aug 11)*

**Rajasinghe 105** *(6f,Nmk,G,Jly 13)*
**Rebel Assault 107** *(6f,Asc,GS,Jly 29)*
**Red Persian 105** *(6f,Cur,G,May 13)*
**Red Roman 105** *(6f,Red,GS,Oct 7)*
**Reinbeau Prince 107** *(8f,Yor,G,Oct 14)*
**Rhosneigr 113** *(7f,Hay,GS,Aug 11)*
**Rimini 108** *(5f,Cha,S,Oct 1)*
**Roaring Lion 106** *(8f,Don,GS,Oct 28)*
**Rostropovich 106** *(7f,Cur,YS,Aug 20)*

**Sands Of Mali 109** *(6f,Yor,G,Aug 26)*
**Saxon Warrior 107** *(8f,Don,GS,Oct 28)*
**Seahenge 105** *(7f,Nmk,G,Oct 14)*
**September 107** *(7f,Cur,SH,Sep 10)*
**Shabaaby 109** *(6f,Don,S,Sep 13)*
**Shaya 106** *(5f,Chp,GS,Sep 6)*
**Shazzab 105** *(8f,Pon,HY,Sep 28)*
**Shepherd Market 105** *(7f,Lei,GS,Sep 12)*
**Showroom 107** *(8f,Goo,GS,Sep 5)*
**Shrewd Approach 106** *(7f,Eps,HY,Oct 1)*
**Simpson 106** *(8f,Wdr,GS,Sep 4)*
**Society Power 105** *(6f,Lin,GS,Sep 6)*
**Sound And Silence 105** *(5f,Yor,G,Aug 26)*
**Soustraction 107** *(8f,Cha,S,Oct 1)*
**Speak In Colours 108** *(6f,Don,GS,Oct 28)*
**Spring Cosmos 107** *(6f,Asc,GS,Jly 29)*
**Spud 109** *(7½f,Chs,S,Sep 15)*
**Staxton 106** *(6f,Don,GS,Oct 28)*
**Sweet Vixen 105** *(6f,Wdr,GS,Jly 24)*

**Take Me With You 111** *(6f,Wdr,GS,Sep 4)*
**Tangled 107** *(6f,Yor,GS,Aug 24)*
**Tathmeen 109** *(6f,Nby,S,Jly 27)*
**The Pentagon 108** *(7f,Leo,G,Jly 27)*
**Theobald 106** *(7f,Leo,G,Jly 27)*
**Threading 106** *(6f,Yor,GS,Aug 24)*
**Threeandfourpence 105** *(7f,Nmk,G,Oct 14)*
**Tivoli 105** *(7f,Lei,GS,Sep 12)*
**To Wafij 112** *(5f,Goo,S,Aug 2)*

**U S Navy Flag 111** *(7f,Nmk,G,Oct 14)*
**Unfortunately 108** *(6f,Dea,G,Aug 20)*

**Veejay 112** *(7f,Hay,GS,Aug 11)*
**Verbal Dexterity 110** *(7f,Cur,S,Jun 10)*
**Villa Savina 106** *(6f,Wdr,GS,Jly 24)*

**Wells Farhh Go 105** *(7f,Yor,GS,Aug 23)*
**Westerland 106** *(7f,San,GS,Aug 2)*
**Whitefountainfairy 106** *(7f,Goo,G,Aug 26)*
**Wild Illusion 115** *(8f,Cha,S,Oct 1)*
**Woodmax 106** *(8f,Cha,S,Oct 1)*
**Would Be King 105** *(7f,Leo,G,Jly 27)*

**Zonza 109** *(8f,Cha,S,Oct 1)*

## TWO YEAR-OLDS -AW

**Amazing Alice 105** *(6f,Cfd,SD,Jun 22)*

**Bow Street 106** *(8f,Kem,SD,Nov 7)*

**Cecchini 105** *(8f,Kem,SD,Nov 8)*
**Chilean 105** *(8f,Cfd,SD,Aug 31)*
**Corinthia Knight 111** *(6f,Kem,SS,Sep 9)*
**Craving 107** *(9½f,Wol,SD,Dec 18)*
**Cuppacoco 107** *(5f,Ncs,SD,Nov 4)*

**Di Fede 105** *(7f,Kem,SS,Oct 25)*

**Elizabeth Bennet 109** *(6f,Lin,SS,Jun 13)*
**Elsaakb 105** *(7f,Kem,SD,Nov 8)*

**Fenisa's Hook 105** *(10f,Kem,SD,Nov 29)*

**Glencadam Master 106** *(10f,Kem,SD,Nov 29)*
**Grecian Spirit 105** *(10f,Kem,SD,Nov 29)*

**Hasanoanda 106** *(9½f,Wol,SD,Dec 18)*

**Indomeneo 105** *(6f,Ncs,SD,May 19)*
**Invincible Army 113** *(6f,Kem,SS,Sep 9)*
**Ispolini 108** *(10f,Kem,SD,Nov 29)*

**Jackfinbar 108** *(9½f,Wol,SD,Dec 18)*

**Lake Volta 106** *(6f,Kem,SS,Sep 9)*
**Lord Of The Glen 106** *(5f,Ncs,SD,Nov 4)*

**Maverick Officer 106** *(7f,Lin,SD,Dec 28)*
**Move It Move It 105** *(6f,Ncs,SD,May 19)*

**Never Back Down 105** *(6f,Wol,SD,Dec 9)*

**Occupy 105** *(8f,Kem,SD,Nov 7)*
**Ode To Autumn 105** *(7f,Lin,SD,Dec 28)*
**On The Warpath 106** *(7f,Sth,SD,Dec 11)*

**Purser 106** *(7f,Lin,SS,Oct 5)*

**Rajasinghe 111** *(6f,Ncs,SD,May 19)*
**Realpolitik 107** *(9½f,Wol,SD,Dec 18)*
**Reiffa 105** *(5f,Wol,SD,Dec 26)*
**Royal Diplomat 106** *(5f,Sth,SD,Aug 28)*

**That's So Cool 107** *(9½f,Wol,SD,Dec 18)*
**Towelrads Boy 106** *(5f,Wol,SD,Nov 7)*

**Voyager Blue 107** *(9½f,Wol,SD,Dec 18)*

**Yamuna River 105** *(9½f,Wol,SD,Dec 18)*